DICTIONARY OF INTERNATIONAL BIOGRAPHY

DICTIONARY OF INTERNATIONAL BIOGRAPHY

PATRONS
Heads of State and Government

FIRST PRESIDENT
JEAN COCTEAU
de l'Académie Française

HON GENERAL EDITOR
Ernest Kay
Author of Biographical and Other Works
Editor and Publisher (London)

PUBLISHER
Nicholas S Law

EDITORIAL/PRODUCTION MANAGER
Jocelyn Timothy

EDITORIAL ASSISTANTS
Sheryl Rigby
Rebecca Thompson
Brenda White

All communications to: International Biographical Centre,
Cambridge CB2 3QP, England

DICTIONARY OF
INTERNATIONAL BIOGRAPHY

A BIOGRAPHICAL RECORD OF CONTEMPORARY ACHIEVEMENT

TWENTY SECOND EDITION

1993/94

International Biographical Centre
Cambridge, England

Volume One	1963
Volume Two	1965
Volume Three	1966
Volume Four	1967
Volume Five	1968
Volume Six	1969
Volume Seven	1971
Volume Eight	1972
Volume Nine	1973
Volume Ten	1974
Volume Eleven	1975
Volume Twelve	1976
Volume Thirteen	1977
Volume Fourteen	1978
Volume Fifteen	1979
Volume Sixteen	1980
Volume Seventeen	1982
Volume Eighteen	1984
Reprinted April	1984
Volume Nineteen	1986
Twentieth Edition	1987
Twenty First Edition	1990
Twenty Second Edition	1993

 **ISBN 0 948875 90 9**

Printed and bound in the UK by: The Bath Press
Lower Bristol Road, Bath BA2 3BL

FOREWORD BY THE HON GENERAL EDITOR

I am pleased to offer the Twenty Second Edition of the *Dictionary of International Biography* to its many readers or 'users' throughout the world. I was personally involved with the publication of the very First Edition in 1963 and this is the nineteenth volume to have been published since I was appointed Hon General Editor. This is one of the Who's Who reference works of which the International Biographical Centre is most proud.

The *Dictionary of International Biography* attempts to reflect contemporary achievement in every profession and field of interest within as many countries as possible. It is an ever-growing reference source since only a few biographical entries are repeated from edition to edition, and this when they have been updated with important new material, In this way each new Edition adds thousands of new biographies to those already published in the series; to date some 170,000 biographies have been presented from information supplied and checked by those individuals who are featured. The Dictionary's coding system permits further reference to other leading directories and Who's Whos.

As with previous editions of the Dictionary, the Twenty Second had been Dedicated to a number of individuals who have been chosen by our editorial board to represent the thousands whose lives and work have received notice in this title over the years. These are, in alphabetical order:

Dr Katsutoshi Ayano LFIBA

Mrs Georgia Mae Zeigler Beasley DDG

Mr Yun Cai

Dr Jianhua Chen

Dr Frederick Foo Chien

Mr Daryl Theodore Dodson

Mr Ole Kristian Ersgaard FIBA

Mr Wilhelm Flöttmann LPIBA DDG IOM

Professor Naoyoshi Fukuzumi IOM

Professor Hongxun Gao

Mr Ian Bennett Gibson

Professor Jean Roger Gontier MD LFIBA

Ms Nancy L Thompson Gunnoe

Professor Dr Kazuyosi Ikeda
  LPIBA LFWLA DDG

Dr Ernst Kohl

Dr Vernette Landers LPIBA LFWLA DDG

Ms Diana St Leger Lindbergh

Ms Iris Jean MacLeod

Dr Alan G McHughen

Dr Akio Miyake

Mr Werner N W Schramm LPIBA IOM

Dr Isadore Shapiro DDG IOM

Professor Arkady N Shevchenko

Mr Ah-Tee Sim

Dr Zahari Staikov

Dr Linda Marianne Taylor IOM

Professor Frans Joseph Uyttenbroeck

Mr Steven A Vladem
  PhD FUWAI LFIBA DDG IOM

Dr Wing Keung Wong

Professor Ichiro Yamashita DDG IOM

I would like to offer my personal congratulations to them and also to the other 5000 who appear in this Volume. Many of our Biographees are added to the *Dictionary of International Biography* Honours List all of whom are named in the Honours List which follows the biographical listings.

I am often asked how we select individuals for inclusion in the *Dictionary of International Biography* and for that matter other titles published by the IBC. Readers and researchers should know that we publish only information which has been provided by those listed and in every case we have had their permission to publish it. Selection is made on the grounds of achievement and contribution on a professional, occupational, national or international level, as well as interest to the reader. An additional intention is to provide librarians of major libraries with a cumulative reference work consisting of Volumes published annually.

It cannot be emphasized too strongly that there is no charge of fee of any kind for inclusion in the *Dictionary*. Every entrant was sent a typescript for approval before publication in order to eliminate errors and to ensure accuracy and relevance. While great care has been taken by our editors it is always possible that in a work of this size a few errors may have been made. If this is the case, my apologies in advance.

I would be also be grateful to hear from readers and researchers who feel that particular individuals should appear in future Volumes of the *Dictionary of International Biography* or any other relevant IBC reference work. Such recommendations may be sent to the IBC's Research Department. Since our researchers have great difficulty in contacting some important figures it is always helpful to us to have addresses.

Ernest Kay

International Biographical Centre,
Cambridge, CB2 3QP, England

INTERNATIONAL BIOGRAPHICAL CENTRE
RANGE OF REFERENCE TITLES

From one of the widest ranges of contemporary biographical reference works published under any one imprint, some IBC titles date back to the 1930's. Each edition is compiled from information supplied by those listed, who include leading personalities of particular countries or profession. Information offered usually includes date and place of birth; family details; qualifications; career histories; awards and honours received; books published or other creative work; other relevant information including postal address. Naturally there is no charge or fee for inclusion.

New editions are freshly compiled and contain on average 80-90% new information. New titles are regularly added to the IBC reference library.

Titles include:

Dictionary of International Biography

Who's Who in Australasia and the Far East

Who's Who in Western Europe

Dictionary of Scandinavian Biography

Dictionary of Latin American and Caribbean Biography

International Who's Who in Art and Antiques

International Authors and Writers Who's Who

International Leaders in Achievement

International Who's Who in Community Service

International Who's Who in Education

International Who's Who in Engineering

International Who's Who in Medicine

International Who's Who in Music and Musicians' Directory

International Who's Who of Professional and Business Women

Men of Achievement

The World Who's Who of Women

The World Who's Who of Women in Education

International Youth of Achievement

Foremost Women of the Twentieth Century

International Who's Who in Poetry and Poets' Encyclopaedia

Enquiries to:

International Biographical Centre

Cambridge, CB2 3QP

England

Numbering of the reference books mentioned in Dictionary of International Biography.

The numbers at the end of the majority of entries denote other reference books in which the subject is listed. The following is a 'key' to this information.

DEPUTY DIRECTORS GENERAL OF THE IBC

Prof Frank A Abban, West Africa
His Excellency S R Absy, Bahrain
Dr Mustafa A Abu-Lisan, Kuwait
Chief Adenrele Adejumo, Nigeria
Dr Richard J Alperin, USA
Dr M A Al-Thonayyan,
    Saudi Arabia
Dr Rowland Iwu Amadi, West Africa
Mr Jacob Oladele Amao, Nigeria
Rev Dr D L Amerasinghe, Sri Lanka
Prof B Angelopoulos, Greece
Prof Dr Joseph S Annan, Ghana
Mr M A Aranda-Gomez, Mexico
Dr Y Ashihara, Japan
Mr Roderick Honeyman Aya, USA
Mrs Katarina E Bader-Molnar,
    Switzerland
Dr Charles E Bagg, England
Ms Elisabeth Barker, USA
Mr Abdul R Batal, Syria
Prof Charles P Beardsley, USA
Ms Georgia Zeigler Beasley, USA
Mr Roger Benebig, New Caledonia
Mr Ismail Bhamjee, Botswana
Mr Franco Bircher, Switzerland
Mr Gerald Jude Boarman, USA
Mr Makhaola D P Bolofo, England
Ms Shauna D Boulton, USA
Dr Geoffrey H Bourne, USA
Ms Birgit Bramsaeck, Sweden
Ms Patricia H Breen, USA
Captain F W Brown, USN, USA
Mr Hubert A Buchanan, USA
Dr Theodor Caba, Romania
Ms Sondra L Campian, USA
Dr Birger Carlqvist, Sweden
Ms Phillita Toyia Carney, USA
Mrs Gertrude Esther Carper, USA
HRSH Leonard Carr, USA
Prof Marion E Carter, USA
Mr Manfredo Castro, Philippines
Mr Scott Clay Chaney, USA
Prof Yi-Feng Chen, China
Mr Michael Kuo-hsing Ch'in, China
Ms Chiao-Liang Juliiana Ching,
    Hong Kong
Dr Li Choy Chong, Singapore
Prof Liu Chung Chu, China
Mr Lowell Koon Wa Chun, USA
Mr J R Ciancia Y Muller, Spain
Dr J Civasaqui, Japan
Prof Charles W Cline, USA
Mr J H Cockcroft, England
Mr Irwin Cohen, USA
Ms Iris Colvin, USA
Dr George Corder, USA
Mrs A Crafton-Masterson, USA
Ms E A Crobaugh, USA
Dr Stefan E Csordas, Australia

Dr Jean-Pierre L Daem, Canada
Mr Alhaji M Danmadami, Nigeria
Dr Edward L Darden, USA
Dr Manfred A Dauses, Luxembourg
Dr M Davey-Hayford, West Africa
Prof Blanche Davis, USA
Mrs L De Backer, Belgium
Mrs E Z De Brault, Mexico
Ms Helen G Deer, USA
Dr Claude R DeLauter Jr, USA
Prof Ziji Deng, China
Mr Abdoulaye Diawara, West Africa
Dr C C Dickinson, III, USA
Sir Bayard Dill, CBE, JP, Bermuda
Dr Alfons F Doodoh, Indonesia
Dr M Dupont-Petersen, Denmark
Mr Karl Eickmann, Japan
Mr Arthur Eikenberry, USA
Mr Elhamy Mostafa El Zayat, Egypt
Ms Ester Erholm, Finland
Dr Alexei M Ermolaev, England
Dr Sonia Udechuku Ewo, Nigeria
Prof Gong-Xiu Fan, China
Mr Jacob Feldman, Australia
Mr Shun-Hua Feng, China
Prof Victor Fenigstein, Luxembourg
Prof Franja Ferenci, Yugoslavia
Mrs Betty Jean Fessler, USA
Dr David E Flinchbaugh, USA
Dr Jean D Floresco, France
Mr Wilhelm Flöttman, Germany
Mrs Vivian E S Fox, USA
Miss Charlotte A Frick, USA
Mr Hunter John H Fry, Australia
Mr Stanley Gavac, USA
Mr Sylvestre Kwadzo Gbewonyo,
    Kenya
Dr Curtis A Gibson, USA
Prof Makram Girgis, Australia
Mrs Maurine G Goldston-Morris,
    Australia
Mr Isaac Thomas Goodine, Canada
Ms Jo Ann Lavina Greene, USA
Prof S S Grozdanic, Yugoslavia
Mrs Padmin Gunaratnam, Singapore
Mrs Mildred Gunn, Canada
Prof Guillermo T Gutierrez,
    Philippines
Ms Mary Dolores Cruz Gwinn, USA
Prince A A Haastrup, Nigeria
Prof G Haddad, Iraq
Dr Gerardo W Hahn, Argentina
Mr Tran Quang Hai, France
Dr Thomas J Hammons, England
Miss L Harris, USA
Dr Kazuyuki Hatada, Japan
Prof Simon John Haynes, Canada
Mr Peter J Heine, Germany
Dr Leonard W Henderson, England

Mr Robert A Hendrickson, USA
Prof Hamed S Hillmi Abbas,
    Saudi Arabia
Mr Shung Pun Ho, Hong Kong
Dr R G L Holland, Canada
Mr Franz Holler, Luxembourg
Prof Dr F Hollwich, Germany
Dr Branton K Holmberg, USA
Mrs Margaret Horswell-Chambers,
    USA
Prof Zuey-Shin Hsu, China
Ms Catherine Harding Hudgins, USA
Dr Norman Huff, USA
Mr Charles Orvis Hunter, USA
Dr Alhaji Idris Ibrahim, Nigeria
Prof Dr Kazuyosi Ikeda, Japan
Dr John C G Isoba, Uganda
Rev Anath E Jackson, USA
Dr Jørgen Jensen, Denmark
Ms Margaret H Johnson, USA
Prof Simone Kadi, France
Dr Mirja A Kalliopuska, Finland
Dr George A Kanzaki, USA
Dr Richard W Kanzler, South Africa
Ms Marlene M Katchur, USA
Dr Shriniwas K Katti, USA
HSH Prince Dr George King
    de Santorini, USA
Mr J Jerone King, USA
Dr Algee Golden Kirby, USA
Dr Samson B M Kisekka, East Africa
Prof Dr Hisatoki Komaki, Japan
Dr Marvin Z Kurlan, USA
Mr Kisho Kurokawa, Japan
Mrs Tuulikki Kyllönen-Heikel, Finland
Mr TuMr Billy Lam, Hong Kong
Dr V Landers, USA
Ms M E Landsberg, Israel
Dr Harry C Layton, USA
Dr Joseph G Le Jeune, France
Dr William A Leavell, USA
Dr Charles L Leavitt, USA
Dr Irene Lee, USA
Dr Lee Kam-to, Macau
Prof Liang Dan-Fong, China
Dr Phillip K T Lim, USA
Dr Chin-Ching Lin, China
Prof Chung-Sheng Lin, China
Prof Jong-Teh Lin, China
Prof Ping-Wha Lin, USA
Ms June McKee Lindsay, USA
Mrs Julia M LoTempio, USA
Mr Alan Leonard Lovell, Australia
Dr Frederick W Lundell, Canada
Ms Joan Mahaffey, USA
Dr Virendra B Mahesh, USA
Mr Umaru-Sanda Maigida, Nigeria
Dr C O Majekodunmi, Nigeria
Dr Clarkson Majomi, England

Dr Howard Malin, USA
Ms Nellie J Marshal, USA
Mrs Deborah L M Martin, USA
The Hon John Ross Matheson, Canada
Mr Yoshihiko Matsui, Japan
Mrs Josephine W Mellichamp, USA
Mrs Pearl D Michaels, USA
Mr T E Miller, USA
Ms Carol Ann Mills, USA
Dr Tsutomu Mimura, Japan
Dr Victoria I Mojekwu, Zambia
Mr B Mollenhauer, USA
Mr Ralph E Montijo, USA
Mr E A Mordi, Nigeria
Prof Mineo Moritani, Japan
Prof E R Moses, USA
Dr Muhammad M Mukram Sheikh, Botswana
Dr Edwin Muniz, Jr, USA
Mr George K Mwai, Kenya
Mr Jack Charles Myers, USA
Mrs Yong-Gyun Nah, Korea
Dr Shrinivas H Naidu, USA
Sir Saburo Nakagawa, Japan
Dr Shigehisa Nakamura, Japan
Mr Kadaba V Narain, Japan
Mr Shiv Sahai Naraine, India
Mr Frederick L Neff, USA
Ms Elizabeth Nelson, USA
Prof Thu The Nguyen, USA
Dr Hiroshi Niimura, Japan
Dr Rev R N Nnamdi, Germany
Mr Oswald Stevens Nock, England
Mrs Bessie Wherry Noe, USA
Dr Khalida I Noor, Saudi Arabia
Senator Cyrus N Nunieh, Nigeria
Ms Mary Devon O'Brien, USA
Ms Rosa Margot Ochoa, Mexico
Dr Wilson R Ogg, USA
Prof U Okeke, Nigeria
Mr Pritam S Panesar, Kenya
Dr Lucy T Parker, USA
Ms Eugenia Pasternak, Canada
Dr Howard John Peak, Australia
Ms Lou Peel, USA
Lt Col Ralph M Persell, USA
Mr Gavin Alexander Pitt, USA
Alderman D R Plaister, Australia
Ms Dorothea Porter, USA

Dr M L Porter, USA
Mr Malcolm Frederick Potter, Australia
Dr Svein D Prydz, Norway
Dr Jerzy Z Przybojewski, South Africa
Mrs Lois Kathryn Pullig, USA
Mr Robert Pwee Kong Joo, Singapore
Ms Sherry L S Raatz, USA
Dr Srinivasa S Rajan, India
Mr A Guinn Rasbury, USA
Mr Orlando M Recinos Arguello, El Salvador
Dr Lonnie Royce Rex, USA
Mr Eugene E Rhemann, USA
Ms C L Richards, USA
Mr A Robertson-Pearce, Sweden
Dr Ralph R Robinson, USA
Ms Trudy Langsjoen Rodine, USA
Ms Irene B S Rodman, USA
Dr M H Rosen, USA
Prof Julius L Rothman, USA
Dr P A Rubio, MD, PhD, USA
Mr R P Sabaratnam, Hong Kong
Prof Eduardo Sanguinetti, Argentina
Ms Geraldine Savari-Ogden, USA
Ms Ragnhild Schioldborg, Norway
Prof Judith T Scholl, USA
Mrs Marjorie M Schuck, USA
Dr H E Schulz, Germany
Mr Ainsworth D Scott, Jamaica
Mr Dennis Screpetis, USA
Mr Roderick E Seeley, USA
Mr Jukka Tapani Seppinen, Finland
Dr Shirish Shah, USA
Dr Isadore Shapiro, USA
Mr Ralph Albert Sheetz, USA
Prof Koki Shimoji, Japan
Mrs Edwina Christine F Snow, USA
Miss Callie J Spady, USA
Mr Francis M J Spencer, USA
Ms Linda Spencer, USA
Mrs Joan E Starr, Australia
Mr Rupert St John Stephens, England
Mrs E V Stewart, USA
Ms M Strandell Thamm, USA
Mrs Bridie Sutton, England
Dr Srikanta M N Swamy, Canada

Prof Emeric Szegho, USA
Dr Emmanuel H Tadross, Canada
Mrs Neva B Talley-Morris, USA
Mr Walter H Taylor, Australia
Dr V A Thomas, Malaysia
Mr Francis M C Thomas, Sri Lanka
Mr Gary L Tipton, USA
Prof J H Tisch, Australia
Ms Mary J Thornton, USA
Dr Ljerka Tiska-Rudman, Yugoslavia
Mr Criton P Tomazos, England
Dr Orville W Trosper, USA
Mr Rudolf Vagner, Canada
Prof Arbo Valdma, Yugoslavia
Mr Constantin K Vereketi, Greece
Ms Morwenna A Vincent, Australia
Mr Steven A Vladem, USA
Prof R F Vliegen, Japan
Mt Rev Dr Robert A Voice, Canada
Dr Mary L S Wainwright, USA
Ms Annita C Walker, USA
Dr W W Walley, USA
Mr Chang Wan-hsi (Mo jen), China
Mr Rollin M Warner Jr, USA
Dr Letha Lloyd-Wayne, USA
Mr Norman Sidney Weiser, USA
Dr William W Wendtland, USA
Dr Don B Wethasinghe, Sri Lanka
Mr M R Wiemann, USA
Miss Annie John Williams, USA
Dr Joseph Roberts Williams, USA
Mrs Jeanne P Wilson, Jamaica
Mr Emmanuel A Winful, West Africa
Dr Abund Ottokar Wist, USA
Dr Sophie Mae Wolanin, USA
Dr Azi Wolfenson, Switzerland
Mr Wong Chin Wah, Singapore
Mr Vincent W S Wong, Malaysia
Prof Ichiro Yamashita, Japan
Mr Yan Yi, China
Prof Chen-Chung Yang, China
Mr Chi-Tung Yeh, China
Mr Yew Mui Leong, Hong Kong
Prof Dr K Yoshihara, Japan
Mrs Florence S Young, USA
Mr Zhongguang Zhang, China
Mr Jamil Gad Zilkha, Israel

RESEARCH ASSOCIATES OF THE IBC

Mr Peter Biliski, USA

Mr Rano Silidum Bofill, USA

Ms Esther M Campbell, USA

Dr Paula L Chen, USA

Prof Maria Ester Cobe de Celis
   Argentina

Dr Philippe Collery, France

Revd Mgr G M Coriaty, Canada

Ms Zaijun Deng, China

Donnelle Ianthe Eargle, USA

Ms Evelyn B Estabrook, USA

Mr Frederick Drummond Ferguson
   Canada

Mr T Funahashi, Japan

Mrs Mildred Gunn, Canada

Dr Herbert-Jean Huon, France

Ms Barbara Leslie Jordan, USA

Chief Charles Adebowale Joshua
   USA

Ms Lisa Fiaux-Kruse, Switzerland

Dr Lisa Lekis, USA

Mr Shraga Sinder Lidor, Israel

Dr Virendra B Mahesh, USA

Mr Patrick Matsikenyiri, USA

Mr William Douthitt McKinney
   USA

Ms Lois I D McNair, USA

Ms Jenna V Ownbey, USA

Dr Barbara B Peterson, USA

Dr Svein D Prydz, Norway

Ms Sherry L Raatz, USA

Mr Harry Charles Reinl
   USA

Dr Richard Liewelyn Rhodes
   USA

Ms Elizabeth Saarinen, USA

Ms Roswitha Sperber-Beck
   Germany

Mrs Lydia Steadman, USA

Prof Teng Chuan Kai, Taiwan

Dr Leevy h Vaughn, USA

Prof Hugo Walter, USA

Prof En-Hui Wu, China

Dr Yang Tian-En, China

RESEARCH FELLOWS OF THE IBC

Prof Antoine Abondo, Cameroun
Dr Anna J Allen, USA
Dr Rowland Iwu Amadi, West Africa
Professor Ba En-Xu, China
Margaret Baender, USA
Dr Isabel R Baumann, Switzerland
Ms Sheila Bellamy, Australia
Dr Guy Boillat, France
Captain F W Brown, USA
Mrs Gertrude Esther Carper, USA
Professor Chung-Yi Chen, Taiwan
Mr Michael Kuo-Hsing Chin, Taiwan
Mr James Dzu-Biao Chon, Hong Kong
Dr Frederick Foo Chien, China
Professor Kyu-bok Chung, South Korea
Mr Leonc jusz Ciuciura, Poland
Ms Iris Colvin, USA
Ms Panayote Elias Dimitras, Greece
Mr Eric Dixon-Cave Hiscock, Canada
Mr Robert Charles Dorion
   Central America
Prof Hermann W Eichstaedt, Germany
Mr Ole Kristian Ersgaard, Denmark
Professor Litian Feng, China
Dr Marianne B Fleck, USA
Mr Wilhelm Flottmann, Germany
Mrs Vivian E S Fos, USA
Professor Gao Hongxun, China
Dr Erwin E Girod, USA
Dr Rhoda Grant, USA
Mr Isaac Thoman Goodine, Philippines
Mrs Padmin Gunaratnam, Singapore
Ms Nancy L Thompson Gunnoe, USA
Ms Darlene Midori Hayashi, USA
Professor Mahmoud Hessaby, Iran
Mr Virapong Hongyok, South Thailand
Professor Dr Sadao Hoshimo, Japan
Professor Zuey-Shin Hsu, Taiwan
Mr Louis Lim Kim Huat
   Dar es Salaam
Ms Mildred F Hutchins, USA
Professor Dr Kazuyosi Ikeda, Japan
Dr Mirja A Kalliopuska, Finland
Ms Marlene H Katchur, USA
Dr Jerry Alvin Kirk, USA
Dr Samsom B H Kisokka, Uganda
Dr Philip Lai, Hong Kong
Professor Li Ji-Ren, China
Professor Li Yiyi, China
Professor Li Yonming, China
Dr Joanne L Linn, USA
Mr Edward James MacGilfrey, USA

Dr Francisca Martin-Molero, Spain
Mr Henri Martokoesoemo, Indonesia
Professor Masaie Matsumura
   Japan
Mr Joseph M Mayo, USA
Professor Ebden Lizo Mazwai
   South Africa
Dr Isutomu Mimura, Japan
Prof Iwao Miyachi, Japan
Ms Martha A Moore, USA
Ms Karen Wigley-Morrison, USA
Prof Dr Emil Mosonyi, Germany
Dr John Edward Mulvihill, USA
Prof Henry Ian A Nowik, USA
Ms Helen Mary Odamtten, Ghana
Professor Hidemichi Ota, Japan
Ms Ellis Ovesen, USA
Dr Danny Shiu-Lam Paau, Hong Kong
Dr Eugenia Pasternak, Canada
Ms Gwendolyn Brown Shepley
   Peacher, USA
Prof Tadeusz Popiela, Poland
Mr Nader E Rastegar, USA
Mr Robert John Richardson
   Canada
Dr Ralph R Robinson, USA
Ms Donna Jo Rolland, USA
Dr Jim R Ropchan, USA
Professor Julius L Rothman, USA
Mr Clayton Winfield Scott, USA
Dr Isadore Shapiro, USA
Ms Anna Pearl Sherrick, USA
Mr Ah-Tee Sim, Singapore
Mr Haji Soemario, Indonesia
Ms Carlene Stinnette, USA
Dr Helen Chien-fan Su, USA
Dr Masuichi Takino, Japan
Prof Giulio Filippo Tarro, Italy
Prof R F Vliegen, Japan
Mr Vincent W S Wong
   West Malaysia
Mrs Linda Wu Liu, China
Dr William L S Wu, USA
Ms Patricia Anne Yallop, Egypt
Prof Ichiro Yamashita, Japan
Prof Fuqing Yang, China
Mr Mui Leong Yew, Hong Kong
Prof Dr K Yoshihara, Japan
Professor Zhang Shi-ding, China
Mr Zheng Dun Xun, China
Mr Yu Zhixue, China
Ms Situ Zhiwen, China

CONTENTS

TABLE OF ABBREVIATIONS

The following abbreviations are frequently used in the compilation of biographical sketches

AA	Associate of Arts	Aux	Auxiliary
AAAS	American Association for the Advancement of Science	Ave	Avenue
		AZ	Arizona
AAUP	American Association of University Professors	b	born
AAUW	American Association of University Women	BA	Bachelor of Arts
		Bach	Bachelor
AB	Bachelor of Arts	BAgric	Bachelor of Agriculture
ABC	American Broadcasting Corporation	Balt	Baltimore
Acad	Academy, Academic	Bapt	Baptist
Acct	Accountant	BArch	Bachelor of Architecture
Acctcy	Accountancy	BAS	Bachelor of Agricultural Science
Acctng	Accounting	BBA	Bachelor of Business Administration
ACP	American College of Physicians	BBC	British Broadcasting Corporation
ACS	American College of Surgeons	BC	British Columbia
ACT	Australian Capital Territory	BCE	Bachelor of Civil Engineering
Adj	Adjunct	BChir	Bachelor of Surgery
Admin	Administration	BCL	Bachelor of Civil Law
Admnstr	Administrator	BCS	Bachelor of Commercial Science
Admnstv	Administrative	Bd	Board
Adv	Advance, Advanced	BD	Bachelor of Divinity
Advsr	Advisor	BE	Bachelor of Education
Advsry	Advisory	Beds	Bedfordshire
Advt	Advertisement, Advertising	BEE	Bachelor of Electrical Engineering
AFB	Air Force Base	Berks	Berkshire
AFD	Doctor of Fine Arts	BFA	Bachelor of Fine Arts
Agcy	Agency	Bibliog	Bibliography
Agric	Agriculture	Biog	Biography, Biographical
Agricl	Agricultural	BJ	Bachelor of Journalism
Agt	Agent	Bklyn	Brooklyn
AIA	American Institute of Architects	BL	Bachelor of Letters
AIM	American Institute of Management	Bldg	Building
AK	Alaska	BLS	Bachelor of Library Science
AL	Alabama	Blvd	Boulevard
ALA	American Library Association	BMus	Bachelor of Music
Alta	Alberta	BMusEd	Bachelor of Music Education
Am	American, America	Bot	Botany
AM	Master of Arts	Boton	Botanical, Botanist
AMA	American Medical Association	Br	Branch
Amb	Ambassador	Brig Gen	Brigadier General
Appt	Appointment	Brit	Britain, British
Apr	April	BS	Bachelor of Science
Apt	Apartment	BSA	Bachelor of Agricultural Science
AR	Arkansas	BSc	Bachelor of Science
Arch	Architecture	BST	Bachelor of Sacred Theology
Arch	Architect	BTh	Bachelor of Theology
Archtl	Architectural	Bucks	Buckinghamshire
Arts D	Doctor of Arts	Bur	Bureau
ASCAP	American Society of Composers, Authors & Publishers	Bus	Business
Assn	Association	CA	California
Assoc	Associate, Associated	Cambs	Cambridgeshire
Asst	Assistant	Can	Canada, Canadian
Astron	Astronomy	Cand	Candidate
Attng	Attending	Cantab	Cantabrigian (Cambridge University Degrees)
Atty	Attorney		
Aug	August	Capt	Captain
AUS	Army of the United States	Cath	Catholic
Aust	Australia, Australian	CB	Companion of the Bath
Auth	Authority	CBC	Canadian Broadcasting Corporation

CBE	Commander, Order of the British Empire	DC	District of Columbia
CBS	Columbia Broadcasting System	DCL	Doctor of Civil Law
CCNY	City College of New York	DCM	Distinguished Conduct Medal
Cert	Certificate, Certified	DCS	Doctor of Commercial Science
Ch	Church	DD	Doctor of Divinity
Chap	Chaplain	DDS	Doctor of Dental Surgery
Chapt	Chapter	DE	Delaware
ChD	Doctor of Chemistry	Dec	December
Chem	Chemist, Chemistry, Chemical	dec	Deceased
Chgo	Chicago	Def	Defence, Defense
Chmbr of		Deleg	Delegate
Comm	Chamber of Commerce	Dem	Democratic, Democrat
Chmn	Chairman	DEng	Doctor of Engineering
CIA	Central Intelligence Agency	Dept	Department
Cinn	Cincinnati	Derbys	Derbyshire
Civ	Civil, Civilian	Dev	Development
Clin	Clinic, Clinical	DFC	Distinguished Flying Cross
CM	Master of Surgery	DFM	Distinguished Flying Medal
Cmdng	Commanding	DHL	Doctor of Humane Letters
Cmdr	Commander	Dip	Diploma
Cmdt	Commandant	Dipl	Diplomate
Cnslr	Counsellor	Dir	Director
Co	County, Company	Dist	District
CO	Commanding Officer, Colorado	Distbn	Distribution
C of E	Church of England	Distbr	Distributor
Col	Colonel	Disting	Distinguished
Coll	College	Div	Division
Collect	Collection	div	Divorced
Comm	Committee	DLit	Doctor of Letters
Commn	Commission	DLitt	Doctor of Literature
Commng	Commissioning	DMD	Doctor of Dental Medicine
Commnr	Commissioner	DMS	Doctor of Medical Science
Comp	Comparative	DMus	Doctor of Music
Conf	Conference	Doct	Doctorate, Doctoral
Confedn	Confederation	DPh	Doctor of Philosophy
Congl	Congregational	Dpty	Deputy
Cons	Consultant, Consulting	Dr	Doctor, Drive
Conserv	Conservative, Conservation	DrPH	Doctor of Public Health, Doctor of
Const	Constitution		Public Hygiene
Constl	Constitutional	DSc	Doctor of Science
Constrn	Construction	DSC	Distinguished Service Cross
Contbn	Contribution	DSM	Distinguished Service Medal
Contbr	Contributor	DSO	Distinguished Service Order
Conven	Convention	DST	Doctor of Sacred Theology
Coop	Cooperative, Cooperation	DTh	Doctor of Theology
Coord	Coordinator, Coordinating	DVM	Doctor of Veterinary Medicine
Corp	Corporation	DVS	Doctor of Veterinary Science
Corres	Correspondent, Corresponding		
Coun	Council	E	East
CPA	Certified Public Accountant	Econ(s)	Economic(s)
Cres	Crescent	Ed	Editor, Edition, Editorial
Ct	Court	ED	Doctor of Engineering
CT	Connecticut	EdB	Bachelor of Education
Ctr	Centre, Center	EdD	Doctor of Education
Ctrl	Central	EdM	Master of Education
CUNY	City University of New York	Educ	Education
Curric	Curriculum	Educl	Educational
C'wlth	Commonwealth	EEC	European Economic Community
Czech	Czechoslovakia	Elec	Electric, Electrical
		Electn	Electrician
d	Daughter	Elem	Elementary
DAgric	Doctor of Agriculture	Ency	Encyclopedia
DAR	Daughters of the American Revolution	Engl	English
DBE	Dame Commander, Order of the	Engr	Engineer
	British Empire	Engrng	Engineering

ENT	Ear, Nose & Throat	**German**	
Episc	Episcopal, Episcopalian	**Dem Rep**	East Germany
Esp	Especially	**German**	
Estab	Established, Establishment	**Fed Rep**	West Germany
E Sussex	East Sussex	Glos	Gloucestershire
Etc	Et cetera	GM	George Medal
Exam	Examination	Gov	Governor
Exec	Executive	Govng	Governing
Exhib	Exhibit, Exhibition	Govt	Government
Exhibnr	Exhibitioner	Govtl	Governmental
Exped	Expedition	Grp	Group
Expmtl	Experimental	Gt	Great
Ext	Extension	Gtr	Greater
		Gtr Manc	Greater Manchester
Fac	Faculty		
FAO	Food and Agriculture Organization	Hants	Hampshire
FCA	Fellow, Institute of Chartered	Hd	Head
	Accountants	**Hereford &**	
FCII	Fellow, Chartered Insurance Institute	Worcs	Hereford & Worcester
FCIS	Fellow, Chartered Institute of	Herts	Hertfordshire
	Secretaries	HEW	Department of Health, Education and
Feb	February		Welfare
Fed	Federal	HHD	Doctor of Humanities
Fedn	Federation	HI	Hawaii
FGS	Fellow, Geological Society	Hist	History
FIB	Fellow, Institute of Bankers	Histl	Historical
Fin	Finance, Financial	Histn	Historian
FL	Florida	Hlth	Health
Fndn	Foundation	Hon	Honorary, Honour
Fndng	Founding	Ho of Dels	House of Delegates
Fndr	Founder	Ho of Rep	House of Representatives
For	Foreign	Hort	Horticulture, Horticultural
FPS	Fellow, Pharmaceutical Society	Hosp	Hospital
FRAM	Fellow, Royal Academy of Music	HQ	Headquarters
FRCP	Fellow, Royal College of Physicians	HS	High School
FRCS	Fellow, Royal College of Surgeons	Hwy	Highway
FRGS	Fellow, Royal Geographical Society		
FRIBA	Fellow, Royal Institute of British	IA	Iowa
	Architects	IBA	Independent Broadcasting Authority
FRIC	Fellow, Royal Institute of Chemistry	ibid	in the same place
FRICS	Fellow, Royal Institute of Chartered	IBM	International Business Machines
	Surveyors		Corporation
FRS	Fellow, Royal Society	i/c	in charge
FRSA	Fellow, Royal Society of Arts	ICA	Institute of Contemporary Arts
FRSL	Fellow, Royal Society of Literature	ID	Idaho
FSA	Fellow, Society of Antiquaries,	IEEE	Institute of Electrical and Electronics
	Society of Arts		Engineers
FSE	Fellow, Society of Engineers	IL	Illinois
Ft	Fort	ILO	International Labour Organization
FZS	Fellow, Zoological Society	IN	Indiana
		Inc	Incorporated
GA	Georgia	Incl	Include
Gall	Gallery	Inclng	Including
GB	Great Britain	Ind	Industry
GBE	Knight (or Dame), Grand Cross Order	Indep	Independent
	of the British Empire	Indl	Industrial
GC	George Cross	Indpls	Indianapolis
GCB	Knight, Grand Cross of the Bath	Info	Information
Gdns	Gardens	Ins	Insurance
Gen	General	Insp	Inspector, Inspection
Geog	Geography, Geographer	Inst	Institute
Geogl	Geographical	Instn	Institution
Geo Wash		Instr	Instructor
Univ	George Washington University	Instrn	Instruction
		Int	International

Jan	January	**MEd**	Master of Education
JB	Jurum Baccalaureus	**MEE**	Master of Electrical Engineering
JD	Doctor of Jurisprudence	**Mem**	Memorial
JP	Justice of the Peace	**Metall**	Metallurgy, Metallurgical
Jr	Junior	**Meth**	Methodist
Jrnl	Journal	**Metrop**	Metropolitan
Jrnlsm	Journalism	**MFA**	Master of Fine Arts
Jrnlst	Journalist	**Mfg**	Manufacturing
JSD	Doctor of Juristic Science	**Mfr**	Manufacturer
Jt	Joint	**Mgmt**	Management
		Mgr	Manager
KBE	Knight Commander, Order of the British Empire	**MI**	Michigan
		Mid Glam	Mid Glamorgan
KCB	Knight Commander of the Bath	**Mil**	Military
KS	Kansas	**Min**	Minister, Ministry
Kt	Knight	**Misc**	Miscellaneous
KY	Kentucky	**MIT**	Massachusetts Institute of Technology
LA	Louisiana	**Mkt**	Market
Lab	Laboratory	**Mktng**	Marketing
Lancs	Lancashire	**ML**	Master of Laws
Lang	Language	**MLA**	Modern Language Association
Ldr	Leader	**MLit**	Master of Literature
Lectr	Lecturer	**MLitt**	Master of Letters
Legis	Legislation, Legislative	**MLS**	Master of Library Science
Leics	Leicestershire	**MM**	Military Medal
LHD	Doctor of Humane Letters	**MME**	Master of Mechanical Engineering
LI	Long Island	**MMus**	Master of Music
Lib	Library	**MN**	Minnesota
Libn	Librarian	**Mng**	Managing
Lic	License, Licentiate	**MO**	Missouri
Lincs	Lincolnshire	**Mod**	Modern
Lit	Literature, Literary	**MP**	Member of Parliament
LittB	Bachelor of Letters	**Mpls**	Minneapolis
LittD	Doctor of Letters	**MS**	Manuscript, Master of Science, Mississippi
LLB	Bachelor of Laws		
LLD	Doctor of Laws	**MSc**	Master of Science
LLM	Master of Laws	**MSS**	Manuscripts
Lt	Lieutenant	**MST**	Master of Sacred Theology
Ltd	Limited	**MT**	Montana
Luth	Lutheran	**Mt**	Mount
		Mtn	Mountain
m	Married	**Mus**	Museum
MA	Master of Arts, Massachusetts	**MusB**	Bachelor of Music
Mag	Magazine	**MusD**	Doctor of Music
MAgric	Master of Agriculture	**MusM**	Master of Music
Maj	Major		
Man	Manitoba	**N**	North
Mar	March	**NAACP**	National Association for the Advancement of Coloured People
MArch	Master of Architecture		
MAT	Master of Arts in Teaching	**Nat**	National
Math	Mathematical	**NATO**	North Atlantic Treaty Organization
Mathn	Mathematician	**NB**	New Brunswick
Maths	Mathematics	**NBC**	National Broadcasting Corporation
MB	Bachelor of Medicine	**NC**	North Carolina
MBA	Master of Business Administration	**ND**	North Dakota
MBE	Member, Order of the British Empire	**NE**	Nebraska
Mbr	Member	**NEA**	National Education Association
Mbrship	Membership	**Nfld**	Newfoundland
MCE	Master of Civil Engineering	**NH**	New Hampshire
MCS	Master of Commercial Science	**NJ**	New Jersey
MD	Doctor of Medicine, Maryland	**NM**	New Mexico
ME	Maine	**Northants**	Northamptonshire
Mech	Mechanics, Mechanical	**Notts**	Nottinghamshire
Med	Medicine, Medical	**Nov**	November

NS	Nova Scotia	Prin	Principal
NSC	National Security Council	Prod	Producer, Production
NSF	National Science Foundation	Prof	Professor
NSW	New South Wales	Profl	Professional
NT	Northern Territory	Profn	Profession
Num	Numerous	Prog	Program, Programme
NV	Nevada	Psych	Psychiatrist, Psychiatric, Psychiatry
NY	New York	PTA	Parent-Teacher Association
NYC	New York City	Ptnr	Partner
N Yorks	North Yorkshire	Pt-time	Part-time
NY Univ	New York University	Pub	Public
NZ	New Zealand	Publng	Publishing
		Publr	Publisher
OBE	Officer, Order of the British Empire	Publs	Publications
Observ	Observatory	Pvte	Private
Obst	Obstetrics		
Obstrn	Obstetrician	QC	Queen's Counsel
Oct	October	Qld	Queensland
OECD	Organization of European Cooperation and Development	QM	Quartermaster
		QMG	Quartermaster General
OEEC	Organization of European Economic Cooperation	RAAF	Royal Australian Air Force
Off	Officer, Office	RAF	Royal Air Force
OH	Ohio	RC	Roman Catholic
OK	Oklahoma	RCAF	Royal Canadian Air Force
OM	Order of Merit	RCN	Royal Canadian Navy
Ont	Ontario	Rd	Road
Op	Operation	Rdr	Reader
OR	Oregon	Recip	Recipient
Orch	Orchestra	Ref	Reference
Orchl	Orchestral	Reg	Region, Regional
Org	Organization	Regt	Regiment
Oxon	Oxfordshire	Rehab	Rehabilitation
		Relig	Religion, Religious
PA	Pennsylvania	Rels	Relations
Parl	Parliament	Rep	Representative
Parly	Parliamentary	Repub	Republic, Republican
PC	Privy Councillor	Res	Resident, Residence
PEI	Prince Edward Island	Ret'd	Retired
PEN	Poets, Playwrights, Editors, Essayists and Novelists	Rev	Reverend
		RI	Rhode Island
Perf	Performance, Performer	RN	Royal Navy
Pharm	Pharmacy, Pharmaceutical	Rsch	Research
PharmD	Doctor of Pharmacy	Rte	Route
PharmM	Master of Pharmacy	Rt Hon	Right Honourable
PhB	Bachelor of Philosophy	Rt Rev	Right Reverend
PhD	Doctor of Philosophy		
Phil	Philharmonic	S	South
Phila	Philadelphia	s	son
Philos	Philosophy, Philosopher	SA	Société Anonyme, South Australia
Philosl	Philosophical	San Fran	San Francisco
Phys	Physical, Physics	SAR	Sons of the American Revolution
Physn	Physician	Sask	Saskatchewan
Pitts	Pittsburgh	SB	Bachelor of Science
Pk	Park	SC	South Carolina
Pkg	Packaging	ScB	Bachelor of Science
Pkwy	Parkway	SCD	Doctor of Commercial Science
Pl	Place	SD	South Dakota
Pol	Politics, Political	SEATO	Southeast Asia Treaty Organization
Postgrad	Postgraduate	Sec	Secretary
PQ	Quebec Province	Second	Secondary
PR	Public Relations, Puerto Rico	Sect	Section
Prac	Practice	Sem	Seminary
Pres	President	Sen	Senator
Presby	Presbyterian	Sept	September

Serv	Service	UN	United Nations
Sev	Several	Undergrad	Undergraduate
S Glam	South Glamorgan	UNESCO	United Nations Educational, Scientific
Sgt	Sergeant		and Cultural Organization
SHAEF	Supreme Headquarters, Allied	UNICEF	United Nations International
	Expeditionary Forces		Children's Emergency Fund
SHAPE	Supreme Headquarters, Allied	Univ	University
	Powers in Europe	USA	United States of America
SJD	Doctor of Juristic Science	USAAF	United States Army Air Force
SM	Master of Science	USAF	United States Air Force
Soc	Society	USDA	United States Department of
Sr	Senior		Agriculture
St	Street	USN	United States Navy
Staffs	Staffordshire	USNR	United States Naval Reserve
Statn	Statistician	USSR	Union of Soviet Socialist Republics
Stats	Statistics	UT	Utah
STB	Bachelor of Sacred Theology		
STD	Doctor of Sacred Theology	VA	Veterans' Administration, Virginia
STM	Master of Sacred Theology	Var	Various
Stn	Station	Vet	Veterinary
Sub	Subsidiary	VFW	Veterans of Foreign Wars
SUNY	State University of New York	VI	Virgin Islands
Supt	Superintendent	Vic	Victoria
Suptng	Superintending	Vis	Visiting, Visitor
Supvsr	Supervisor	Voc	Vocational
Surg	Surgeon, Surgical, Surgery	Vol	Volunteer, Voluntary, Volume
Switz	Switzerland	VP	Vice President
Symph	Symphony	VT	Vermont
S Yorks	South Yorkshire		
		W	West
Tas	Tasmania	w	with
Tchr	Teacher	WA	Western Australia, Washington
Tchng	Teaching	Warwicks	Warwickshire
TD	Teachers Training Diploma	Wash DC	Washington DC
Tech	Technical	W Glam	West Glamorgan
Techn	Technician	WHO	World Health Organization
ThD	Doctor of Theology	WI	Wisconsin
ThM	Master of Theology	Wilts	Wiltshire
TN	Tennessee	Wk	Week
Transl	Translation, Translator	Wm &	
Transp	Transport, Transportation	Mary Coll	William and Mary College
Treas	Treasurer	W Mids	West Midlands
Trng	Training	W Sussex	West Sussex
TTD	Teachers Training Diploma	WV	West Virginia
TV	Television	WWI	World War I
TVA	Tennessee Valley Authority	WWII	World War II
TX	Texas	WY	Wyoming
Ty	Territory	W Yorks	West Yorkshire
UAR	United Arab Republic	YMCA	Young Men's Christian Association
UCLA	University of California at Los	Yr	Year
	Angeles	YWCA	Young Women's Christian
UK	United Kingdom		Association

Dedications

Dr Katsutoshi Ayano LFIBA

For an Outstanding Contribution to Quality Management Education

DR KATSUTOSHI AYANO LFIBA

As a Quality Management Educator, with background education in computer and environmental science, Dr Katsutoshi Ayano is pursuing educational vocation to advance any human endeavour for the betterment of human environment quality, natural or man-made.

He is Associate Professor at Tokai University, Japan, since 1986 and Editorial Member of "Hinshitsu" (Quality), "Hinshitsu Kanri" (Total Quality Control) and "QC Circle" 1990 to the present.

Katsutoshi Ayano was born on 3 March 1949 in Hitoyoshi, Kumamoto, Japan and his university education was at University of Electro-Communications (BA, Management Engineering), Tsukuba University (MA, Economics), State University of New York and Syracuse University, United States of America (PhD, 1982).

Dr Ayano was a Telephone Operator and Supervisor at Kokusai Denshin Denwa Company Limited, 1970-78; Lecturer and Instructor, Union of Japanese Scientists and Engineers, 1975-79 and 1982-84; Member of Specialist Committee for Research on Waste Treatment Improvement by Recycle and Reuse, Japanese Government, Department of Health and Welfare, 1983-84; Counsellor, Union of Japanese Scientists and Engineers, 1984-86; a regular invited discussant at the semi-annual Quality Symposium sponsored by the Union of Japanese Scientists and Engineers and a regular Chairman at their semi-annual Quality Conference.

He is the author of the book: "Current Waste Problems" 1985, papers presented to learned societies and articles in professional journals.

Dr Ayano is a member of the Japanese and American Societies for Quality Control, Japanese Society for Operations Research, Society for Logistics Engineers, American Management Association, Senior Member of Society for Environmental Science, World Future Society, Society for Strategic Planning, International Associate Club and American Biographical Institute Research Association.

He married on 25 January 1976 and has three sons and a daughter.

A biography of Dr Katsutoshi Ayano appears in the main section of this Edition.

Georgia Mae Zeigler Beasley

For an Outstanding Contribution as a Counselor

GEORGIA MAE ZEIGLER BEASLEY

Georgia Mae Zeigler Beasley has been a Counsellor at Lamar University in Orange, Texas, USA, since 1987. Since the beginning of her working life she has held various positions such as Stenographer at Prairie View A&M University, 1970-71; Secretary at Texas Southern University, 1971-73; Substitute Teacher, West Orange, 1975-84 and Teacher at Lamar University in Orange, 1984-87.

Born on 14 May 1948 in Orange, Texas, USA, she holds a BS degree from Prairie View A&M Univesity, 1971, and MEd from McNeese State University in 1987.

Mrs Beasley is a memeber of the American Association for Counseling and Development; Texas Association for Counseling and Development; Texas Association for Collegiate Testing Personnel; Sabine Neches Association for Counseling and Development and the International Platform Association.

Her biography is listed in the National Distinguished Service Registry for Counseling and Development, 1989-90 and Who's Who in the South and Southwest, 1991-92.

She married Edward Beasley Jr on 5 June 1971 and they have two sons and a daughter.

Her main interest is planning activities for youth.

A biography of Georgia Mae Zeigler Beasley appears in the main section of this Edition.

Cai Yun

For an Outstanding Contribution to Chinese Fine Arts

CAI YUN

Mr Cai Yun was born in Beijing in 1942 and discovered his love of painting at an early age. He graduated from the Beijing School of Handicrafts and Fine Arts in 1961. In 1963 he began studying with the famous painter, Mr Xi Linlu, who taught him freehand brushwork for bird-and-flower paintings. Cai Yun's painting skills were now firmly in place. In 1976, Cai Yun sought further instruction from a famous professor at the Central Academy of Fine Arts, the specialist in fine brushwork and figure painting, Mr Huang Jun. Under his tutelage Cai Yun studied traditional techniques of painting classical Chinese beauties.

Cai Yun's paintings tend to keep the essentials taught him by his mentors. His human figures, exquisitely executed, are lively and graceful; his artistic conceptions are elegantly expressed within the boundaries of classical conventions. Although his use of colours is characterized by deep shades, these are used with discretion to give the effect of the clarity and delicacy one finds in nature. Although Cai Yun's works carry on the classical traditions of Chinese painting techniques and style, he is not confined by the teachings of former painters; he seeks after the new and continues to strive to perfect a unique style of his own. For instance, he has taken the thousands of images of classical beauties and combined them with a more contemporary look -- with stunning results. Likewise, he can depict with great accuracy and confidence the inner world and personality of a figure, using the brush to convey the spirit.

Cai Yun takes great pains with the colour washes and arrangement of the backgrounds in his paintings. In addition to paintings of human figures, Cai Yun's repertoire includes bird-and-flower paintings as well as landscapes executed in innovative styles. Mr Cai Yun is well versed in a numbher of disciplines, including history, literature, ancient costume and architecture and these interests further enrich and enhance the synthesis of his paintings.

In the last twenty or more years he has created a number of works whose themes derive from Chinese folk legends and stories. Examples of these include: "The Strange Story of Liu Yi" "Zhang Yu Crosses the Ocean" "Scarlet Thread Steal Box" "Robber Spirit Grass" "Chang E Goes to The Moon" "Two Courtesans of Puxiang" "Xi Shi The Beauty Washes by the River" "Li Bo" "Li Shizhen" and many others.

Cai Yun's paintings are now treasured by their owners in more than thirty countries including the United States, Japan, Canada, Singapore, Malaysia, England, France and Australia. They have been reproduced in calendars and others have been included in various published albums. Mr Cai Yun's paintings have also been on display in Beijing at the Great Hall of the People, the General Office of Central Military Commission, on the rostrum of Tiananmen, and many other highly prominent locations. They have also appeared in more than twenty newspapers.

Mr Cai Yun is currently a member of the Beijing Branch of the China Association of Artists, the China Society for the Study of Painting and the Beijing Fine Brushwork and Deep Colour Painting Society.

His works have been commented upon by Li Ruoshen, Wang Xuetao and Pu Songchuang.

For the past thirty years, he has lovingly studied painting and calligraphy and created mnay human figure paintings that are examples of exquisite brushwork, elegant colour composition and that give a real feeling for cultural styles and periods of history.

A biography of Mr Cai Yun appears in the main section of this edition.

Dr Jianhua Chen

For an Outstanding Contribution to Chinese Studies

DR JIANHUA CHEN

Dr Jianhua Chen is a Poet and Scholar of Chinese Literature and Culture who gained his MA degree in Chinese Literature from Fudan University in Shanghai, China and was awarded his PhD in May 1988.

From 1982-85 he was a Teacher at the College of Liberal Arts, Shanghai University and from 1988-90 Lecturer at Chinese Classics Research Institute, Fudan University and during the same period Academic Consultant at Chinese Great Dictionary Publishing House in Shanghai. From 1988-91 he was a Visiting Scholar in the Department of Comparative Literature and Centre for Chinese Studies at the University of California in Berkeley, United States of America. Currently he is a Research Associate at Center for Modern China, New York, USA.

An accomplished writer, Dr Chen has written numerous poems and articles imbued with pro-democratic spirit and published in newspapers and magazines in the United States, Taiwan and Hong Kong. They have included "Social Consciousness in Chinese Literature - Jiangsu and Zhejiang Literature From the Fourteenth to Seventeenth Century", Xue Lin Publishing House, Shanghai, 1992. Creative writings include: "Elegy for June 4th Massacre" in 'Chung -Wai Literary Monthly' 1991 and "A Shapeless Net" Square No.2, Indiana, USA. Creative writings include: "The 17th Building of F University" 1989; "Black Cave" 1989; and "White Pigeon" 1989.

He is a member American Association of Chinese Comparative Literature; Classical Drama Association of China; American Association for Asian Studies; Classical Literature Association of China, Shanghai Branch; International Center for Asian Studies, Hong Kong

In 1987 Dr Chen was awarded the Academic Award from Fudan University, Shanghai; The Zhao Jingshen Chinese Classics Award, Shanghai in 1988 and the Liang Shih-Ch'iu Literary Award, Taipei in 1990.

Jianhua Chen was born on 16 July 1947 in Shanghai, The People's Republic of China.

On 26 April 1981 he married Wei-Xing Wang and they have a son.

Apart from his profession Dr Chen is interested in Chinese Calligraphy, collecting stamps and reading.

A biography of Dr Jianhua Chen appears in the main section of this Edition.

Dr Fredrick F Chien

For an Outstanding Contribution to Foreign Affairs

DR FREDRICK F CHIEN

Dr Fredrick F Chien has been Minister of Foreign Affairs in the Republic of China since 1990.

Previous appointments he has held include: Secretary to the Premier, Executive Yuan; Visiting Associate Professor at National Chengchi University; Specialist, Section Chief in Department of North American Affairs, Ministry of Foreign Affairs; Director, Department of North American Affairs, Ministry of Foreign Affairs; Visiting Professor at National Taiwan University; Director-General, Government Information Office; Administrative Vice Minister, Ministry of Foreign Affairs; Political Vice Minister, Ministry of Foreign Affairs; Representative, CCNAA Office in USA; Minister of State, Chairman, Council for Economic Planning and Development, Executive Yuan and Member of Central Standing Committee KMT.

Fredrick F Chien was born on 17 February 1935 in China. He earned his BA degree from National Taiwan University in 1956; PhD from Yale University, USA in 1962; attended National War College and received an honorary LLD from Sung Kyun Kwan University.

Dr Chien is the author of "The Opening of Korea: A Study of Chinese Diplomacy, 1876-85"; "Speaking as a Friend; Faith and Resilience: The Republic of China Forges Ahead".

The many honours and awards Dr Chien has received include: The Order of Diplomatic Service Merit of the Republic of Korea, 1972; The Kim Khanh Medal of the Republic of Vietnam, 1973; Order of Brilliant Star with Grand Cordon of the Republic of China, 1975; Orden National Del Merito en el Grado Del Gran Cruz de la Republica del Paraguay, 1975; El Grado de Gran Cruz Placa de Plata, la Condecoracion de la Orden del Merito de Duarte, Sanchez y Mella de la Republica Dominicana, 1978; Gran Cruz De Plata de la Orden de Jose Cecilio Del Valle de la Republica de Honduras, 1979; Orden National Jose Matias Delgado en el Grado de Gran Cruz Placa de Plata de la Republica de El Salvador, 1979; L'ordre National Honneur et Merite Grand Officier de la Republique D'Haiti, 1979; Order of Good Hope in the Grand Cross Class of the Republic of South Africa, 1979 and Orden Merito en el Grado de Gran Cruz Extraordinario de la Republica del Paraguay, 1990; Royal Order of Sobhuza II Chief Counsellor of the Kingdom of Swaziland, 1991; Orden de Morazan Gran Cruz Placa de Plata de la Republica de Honduras, 1991.

In his leisure time Dr Chien enjoys reading and playing golf.

He married Julie Tien on 22 September 1962 and they have a son and a daughter.

A biography of Dr Fredrick F Chien appears in the main section of this Edition.

Daryl Theodore Dodson

For an Outstanding Contribution to the Theatrical Arts

DARYL THEODORE DODSON

Daryl Theodore Dodson is a Theatrical Manager, Arts Consultant and Artists' Representative in the United States of America.

He was in the United States Army from 1957-59; Assistant Director of "The Mikado" New York City Opera, 1959; Regisseur, Chicago Opera Ballet, 1960; Assistant Stage Manager, American Ballet Theatre, European and Russian Tour, 1960; Stage Manager, American Ballet Theatre, United States Tour, 1960; Production Stage Manager, American Ballet Theatre, 1961; Production Manager, American Ballet Theatre, 1963; General Manager, American Ballet Theatre, 1968- 77; Manager, American Tour, First Cultural Exchange between the People's Republic of Chin and the United States, 1978; Manager, National Ballet of Cuba United States Tour, 1979; Manager, Royal Ballet of England United States and Canadian Tour, 1981; President, Pine Cone Enterprises and Proprietor Pine Cone Inn, Haverhill, New Hampshire, 1977-81; Manager, Opera House, Kennedy Center, Washington, DC, 1981; Manager, United States and Canadian Tour "Sweeney Todd" 1982; Manager, United States Tour "Amadeus" 1982-83; Manager., United States Tour and Broadway Season "The Wiz" 1983-84; Manager, New York Engagement "The Golden Land" 1985; General Manager, John Curry Skating Company, 1985; Manager United States Tour "Porgy and Bess" 1986-87; Manager, United States Tour "La Cage aux Folles" 1987; Manager, New York Engagement and United States Tour, Paris Opera Ballet, 1987 and Manager, United States Tour "Les Miserables".

Daryl Theodore Dodson was born on 9 October 1934 in Warrensburg, Missouri in the United States of America.

He attended Central Missouri State University, receiving his BSc degree in 1956.

He was a member of Governor of South Carolina Council on the Arts, 1974 and Member of the Advisory Panel, Vermont Council on the Arts, 1978. He is also a member of Theta Chi and Theta Alpha Phi.

Mr Dodson collects antiques and enjoys travelling.

A biography of Daryl Theodore Dodson appears in the main section of this Edition.

Ole Kristian Ersgaard FIBA

For an Outstanding Contribution to Business Development

OLE KRISTIAN ERSGAARD FIBA

Ole Kristian Ersgaard is an International Development Consultant and Management Consultant in Denmark.

Since 1990 he is Development Consultant for various company owners his latest task being a retail project "First Danish" the first shop being opened in London on 2 September 1991. From 1984-85 he was with Illums Bolighus A/S, Centre of Modern Design in Copenhagen where he reported directly to the owner of the company and together they introduced the concept "Investment Account to the Consumer". It was a huge success and he had the entire overall responsibility of national and international marketing. The company was sold in 1985. From 1985-86 he was with Bramin Mobler A/S (Bramin Furniture Limited) where he was responsible for national and international marketing and sales in Scandinavia. From 1986-89 he was Chief Executive Officer and General Manager of ANVA-Esbjerg A/S, Department Store.

Ole Kristian Ersgaard was born on 9 September 1948 in Copenhagen, Denmark. He was awarded a Diploma in Public Relations from NKI, Stockholm in 1971; Diploma in Marketing, Danish Commercial Colleges, Copenhagen, 1975 and his postgraduate training was at Danish College of Commerce, London, 1979, London School of Foreign Trade, 1981, London Polytechnic, 1982 and DMC/INSEAD, France, 1988-89. He holds the Danish Professional Business Qualification Erhvervsoekonom MDM, and is a full Member of the Institute of Director, London among others. He is a recipient of the International Cultural Diploma (Hon).

He is a member of the Political Party Centrum Demokraterne (since 1989); member of The Think Tank (1990) and Adviser for the Council of The Danish Mercantile Association. He is Lifetime Deputy Governor (seat of representation, Board of Governors) and International Adviser of American Biographical Institute and was nominated "Man of the Year 1991" an American Biographical Institute Award.

He lives with Liselotte Larsen, his secretary and they have a dog, a Schnauzer, named Aston.

A biography of Ole Kristian Ersgaard appears in the main section of this Edition.

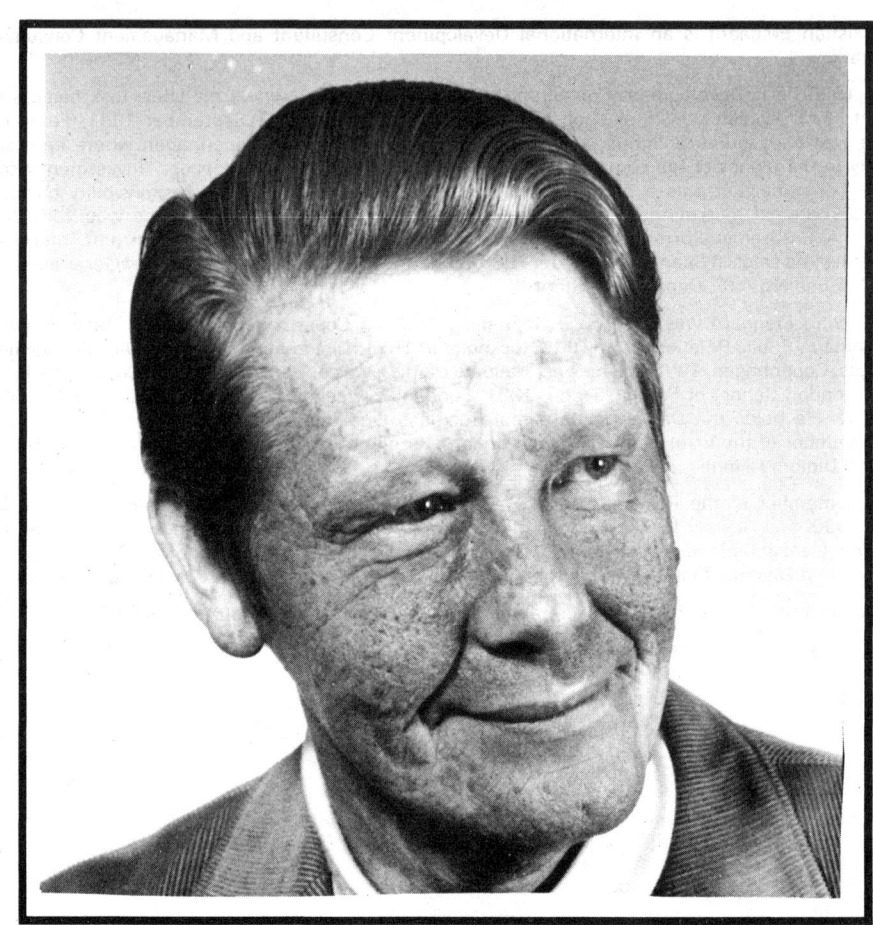

Wilhelm Flöttmann LPIBA IOM DDG

For an Outstanding Contribution to Research and Teaching

WILHELM FLÖTTMANN LPIBA IOM DDG

Wilhelm Flöttmann, German Pharmaceutical Chemist and Specialist Translator, has translated and adapted medical papers, philosophical essays and books and has contributed articles on medico-linguistic problems to various professional journals. He also serves as an "into-English" specialist for a number of university professors, consultants and freelance scientists. He has been an assessor of translation work in pharmacology and associated subjects submitted by candidates for the Translator's Diploma Examination of the London Institute of Linguists since 1967. He was also responsible for the revision of the Medical Dictionary of the English and German languages published by Wissenschaftliche Verlagsgesellschaft in 1982 and between 1970 and 1985 was Director of Studies of his own Language School in Gutersloh, Germany.

The list of books, scientific films and abstracts translated or written by Mr Flöttmann is long and includes: "Illuminating Love" 1943; "Essays on Faith and Morals" 1948; "Recovery of Faith" 1950; "Official Handbook of the German Health Resorts Association" 1953; "Biochemica Boehringer" 1955; "Cyclophosphamide in Chemotherapy of Cancer" 15 volumes (2,500 abstracts), 1958-79 and many other translations from German, French, Italian, Russian and Spanish into English. His translations of scientific film scripts include: "Rheological properties of cervical mucus"; "Applications of micro-NMR"; "Haemostasis"; "Urinary Tract Infections and Artificial Kidney"; "Ca- Antagonists" and "The Sleep-Wakefulness Cycle".

Wilhelm Flöttmann was born on 26 February 1921 in Gütersloh, Germany. He received his secondary school education in Gütersloh before attending the Chemistry School of Professor Fresenius in Wiesbaden where he gained his state examination in 1939; his studies also included biochemistry, biometry, pharmacology, oncology and related subjects.

Between 1941 and 1945 he served as an Assistant at Bayer Leverkusen and during the same period attended translators' courses, passing his final translators' examinations in Berlin and Danzig. After the war, he served as a Medical Translator with Boehringer and Soehne in Mannheim from 1946 to 1955 and since then has undertaken freelance translation work for several European drug manufacturers and scientific institutes.

He is a member of the Society of German Scientists and Physicians and the Association of German Translators and also belongs to the Institute of Linguists (London, England), Società Dantesca (Florence, Italy) and the World Federation of Scientific Workers (London).

Wilhelm Flöttmann married Inge Tinzmann in 1943 and they have two daughters, Berit and Mareile and five sons, Geribert, Holger, Hendrik, Till and Torsten.

In his leisure time Mr Flöttmann enjoys gardening, hiking and studying philosophy, literature and art.

He attributes his success in scientific writing and translation to the fact that he invariably aims at meeting the needs of his readers by employing a clear and concise style and by never mixing categories. He hopes that, through his work and enthusiastic optimism, he has contributed to scientific understanding. As Director of Studies, he tried to occupy his students both professionally and socially so as to ensure their holistic growth and progress enabling them to achieve their full potential. When he was young he fought the disease of cancer and as a teacher he fought the sickness of society. He believes that every individual has an obligation towards the enrichment of human society through the contribution of his natural talents.

A biography of Wilhelm Flöttmann appears in the main section of this Edition.

Professor Naoyoshi Fukuzumi

For an Outstanding Contribution to Medicine (Psych, Hosps, Dentists)

DR NAOYOSHI FUKUZUMI

Dr Naoyoshi Fukuzumi is Emeritus Professor of Pathology at Kyorin University College of Medicine in Tokyo, Japan. Her was Professor at Pathology at the same University from 1979 to 1991. From 1964 to 1972 he was Professor of Pathology at National Taiwan University and Consultant in Pathology, United States of American Naval Research Unit from 1964 to 1972.

His paper, ''Experimental Kernicterus'' was published in the 'American Journal of Pathology', 1966 and ''Human Cholera'' in 'Virch Arch', 1971.

This eminent Professor has received recognition for his work. In 1967 he was awarded the Prize for the advances in culture (Section of Medical Science) by the Government of China in Taiwan; Prize from the Taiwan Medical Association, President Tu in 1967; Prize from the Japanes Association of Medicine, President Kobayashi in 1971 and the Yomiuri Prize for the E B Virus Study Group in 1978.

Dr Fukuzumi is a member of the American Association for the Advancement of Science (USA); New York Academy of Science (USA); Japanese Cancer Association; Japanese Society for Cancer Therapy; Japanese Pathology Society and International College of Surgeons.

Naoyoshi Fukuzumi was born on 7 August 1924 in Taipei, Taiwan. He attended National Taiwan University, MD, 1947; and Chiba University, PhD, 1955. From 1972-78 he was a Research Fellow at the Institute for Research in Medical Science at Tokyo University.

Dr Fukuzumi is an avid reader and enjoys sports.

On 15 November 1960 he married Noriko and they have two daughters.

A biography of Dr Naoyoshi Fukuzumi appears in the main section of this Edition.

Professor Hong-Xun Gao

For an Outstanding Contribution to Nankai University

PROFESSOR HONG-XUN GAO

Hong-Xun Gao is Professor of Mathematics at Nankai University in The People's Republic of China (since 1981). Previously he was Assistant of Math at Beiyang University, Tianjin (1948-52) and Lecturer, Associate Professor (1952-80).

He is the author of many mathematical papers such as "The Algebraic Properties of Non-negative Matrix and Solved Certain Linking Open Problems in Algebra as Well as Topology"; "The Structure Theory and Algorithems in the Theory of M- sequence" (de Bruijn sequence). He proposed a new conception, Impredictability or equivalently Unpredictability, for examining the difficult problems of complexities.

Hong-Xun Gao was born in August 1924 in He Bei Province in The People's Republic of China.

He earned his BSc Degree from the Department of Math and Physics at China University, Beijing in 1948.

In 1984 Professor Gao was awarded a Certificate and Plaque for teaching for more than thirty years at Tianjin and in the same year Citation for Excellent Member of Tianjin Science and Technology Federation. In December 1990 Professor Hong-Xun Gao was presented with a Certificate and a Golden Galloping Horse Award mounted in a marble stand, for teaching for more than forty years, by the State Education Commission of China.

He is President of Operations Research Society, Tianjin, China;; Member of the Council of Math Society, Tianjin; Member of Combinatorial Math Council of China Math Society; Vice-Chairman of Information Security Society of China Computer Federation.

On 15 July 1950 he married Lu Yunshu and they have two daughters.

A biography of Hong-Xun Gao appears in the main section of this Edition.

Ian Bennett Gibson

For an Outstanding Contribution to International Shipping

IAN BENNETT GIBSON

Ian Bennett Gibson was born on 10 June 1936 in Leeds, England and from 1945 to 1952 attended Leeds Modern School.

After leaving school he was a Navigating Officer in the Merchant Navy Worldwide from 1952 to 1965; Ships Master, United Baltic Corporation, 1965; Sales Director, Carron Co, Falkirk, 1965-69; General Manager, Tractors, British Leyland (UK), 1969-74 and Consultant, 1974-78 until his present appointment as Managing Director, United Baltic Corporation (GmbH), Kiel Canal, Germany since 1978. Since 1988 he has been Honorary British Consul in Kiel, Germany.

He was a member of Agricultural Engineers Association, London from 1971-74 and member of General Council. He is a Life Member of The Farmers Club, London.

Married to Jane Macvean Graham-Pole on 3 June 1961, they have two sons.

Mr Gibson's hobbies are playing golf and bridge. He is a member of Glenbervie Golf Club, St Mellion Golf Club, Golf-Club Altenhof amd Golf-Club Lohersand.

A biography of Ian Bennett Gibson appears in the main section of this Edition.

Professor Jean Roger Gontier MD LFIBA

For an Outstanding Contribution as a Professor of Physiology

PROFESSOR JEAN ROGER GONTIER MD LFIBA

Jean Roger Gontier, MD, is not only a practician but he is also a Man of Science, a Physiologist. Moreover, he is not only a Professor in Medicine, but also a scientific writer and author of twenty-two books of Physiology to date.

He was born in Lens, mining town of Pas de Calais, Northern France, on the 8 March 1927, as son of Paul Maurice Gontier, an engineer working as a specialist consultant in reinforced concrete, and Marie-Jeanne Gontier, born Tricoche, housewife. Thus he spent his childhood surrounded by the special environment of coal mines and hardworking men. At school, Jean liked both the scientific and the literary subjects and was appreciated by his teachers as a very skilled student. A long illness, when he was thirteen years old stimulated him to become in the future a practician. After special study at Arras College, Jean graduated as honour student with a BA in 1943 and continued his formal education at Etampes College, receiving a BS in 1945. At the same time, Jean founded the Etampes College's Play Group and became the President of the Group.

Always interested in the phenomena of life and living beings, he studied first for Biology and he graduated with a MS in 1947 from the School of Sciences, Paris University. Afterwards, he entered School of Medicine, Paris University and graduated as Laureat with a MD in 1965. The Professors of the School of Medicine awarded to him the First Prize for his thesis "Rene Leriche" and he was awarded with the Silver Medal of Paris University as the best graduate of the year 1965. After graduating Professor Jean R Gontier began a crusade for International Red Cross, as National Instructor, teaching emergency cares.

Always interested in scientific education of students, Jean Gontier was appointed Professor of Physiology at UGSEL, Paris University from 1965-68 and Instructor in Medicine at the School of Medicine from 1966-68. In 1968 he was appointed Chief of the Laboratory of Physiology, School of Medicine, Reims University. The same year, he was appointed Attending Physician at University Hospital of Paris. His first scientific paper, "The Pulmonary Surfactant" was highly praised in North America. At about the same time, he published his first scientific monograph, "Hormones, Nervous System and Digestion". This book was followed by many others in the field of Human Physiology.

In 1969 Professor Jean R Gontier moved from Paris to Montreal, Canada, thus joining the staff of the Department of Physiology, School of Medicine, University of Montreal. Here he was Professor of Physiology from 1969-78. In 1979 he went back to Paris where he is now living. In 1984 he taught Physiology as Visiting Professor at St George's University, School of Medicine, Barbados.

His research interests are Physiology of Respiration and Circulation in Man and Cardiovascular and Respiratory adaptations to submersion in water in human subjects.

Today Professor Gontier is a Consultant in Internal Medicine and a Consultant Editor in the field of Scientific Books and especially in the field of Human Physiology.

Professor Gontier has presented many papers at various International Conferences and has written many influential books in his field, including: Respiration, Physiological Basis of Human Functions, Neurophysiological Basis of Nervous System's Functions, Laboratory Manual of General Physiology and Digestion. He has translated many books of Physiology in French including: "Textbook of Endocrinology"; "Textbook of Human Physiology" "Physiology and Biophysics of Circulation" "Physiology of the Digestive Tract" Physiology of Respiration ", "Human Physiology" and many others.

For his outstanding contribution to the teaching of medicine, Professor Gontier was awarded the Distinguished Leadership Award, The Certificate of Merit for Distinguished Service in the Field of Medicine, the Key Award for Medical Excellence, the 1992 International Cultural Diploma of Honor, the 1992 Silver Shield of Valor. Bestowed upon him were the titles of Grand Ambassador of Achievement, Man of the Year 1991, Personality of the Year 1991, International Man of the Year and Most Admired Man of the Decade.

His activities in various organisations are as follows: American Physiological Society, Respiratory Section, Teaching Physiology Section, APS History Section; Canadian Physiological Society; Association of Physiologists; New York Academy of Sciences; American Association for the Advancement of Sciences; International Biographical Association, Life Patron; American Biographical Institute, Research Association Life Fellow, Lieutenant Governor, Board of Advisors Honorary Advisor; International

Biographical Centre, Research Fellow, Honorary Member of Advisory Committee.

His biography is listed in numerous reference books.

On 9 December 1968 he married Sylviane Prevost, a daughter of Andre Prevost, an Engineer Specialist in Railway Traffic and Andree Prevost, born Vincent, a housewife. Their four children, Sylviane, Yannick, Jean-Yves and Yann are students.

Professor Gontier's future plans are to publish new books of Medicine and Physiology and to pursue his career as Educator in Medicine.

A biography of Professor Jean Roger Gontier appears in the main section of this Edition.

MS BETTY GOUR

Betty Gour began dancing at the age of six and now at 75 years old, she is still teaching. She says it was a chore to graduate from High School in 1932, as she was already in the Chicago Civic Opera Ballet, but she thanks God that she did, for after thirty-five years in the theatre, she has been able to teach at Butler University for a further twenty-two years. Many of her students are successful on stage while others are good teachers. Dancing has been her whole life, and, given the chance, she would do the same again.

Having had an extremely successful career with many varied appointments she went on to become a successful choreograper, her productions have included over thirty ballets for the Butler Ballet between 1964 to 1986, also making all her own costumes. She studied the piano for ten years, which has contributed greatly to her success as a choreographer.

Betty Gour believes that if you are dedicated and determined to make the grade you can do it.

Ms Nancy Lavenia Thompson Gunnoe

For an Outstanding Contribution to Art and Industry

NANCY LAVENIA THOMPSON GUNNOE

Nancy Lavenia Thompson Gunnoe is Secretary Treasurer of R G Gunnoe Farms Incorporated in West Virginia, United States of America.

Born on 7 January 1921 in Southside, Tennessee, United States of America, she graduated from Southside High School in 1938 before attending Austin Peay College in 1939 and University of Charleston in 1973 and 1987.

She married Raymond Glen Gunnoe on 6 December 1941 and they have a son and two daughters.

Mrs Gunnoe held a one-man Art Show in West Virginia Cultural Center in 1979, at University of Charleston in 1980, at Chequers in 1986. She held Miniature Show at Sunrise, 1974-80 and Jackson, Tennessee Pen Women.

She is a member of Charleston Historical and Preservation Society; Woman Builders of University of Charleston; Charleston Woman's Club; Sunrise Museum; Republican Presidential Task Force; Allied Artists of West Virginia; National League of American Pen Women and Hospice.

The honours Mrs Gunnoe has received include: Best of Show, 1977, Honourable Mention, 1984 and 90, First Place, 1984, Second Place, 1981 and 82 at Rhododendron Festival; Honourable Mention on a Watercolour, Parkersburg Art Center International Show.

Mrs Gunnoe, in her leisure time, enjoys sculpting, water aerobics, porcelain painting, personal shopper, oil and watercolour painting and fabric painting.

A biography of Nancy Lavenia Thompson Gunnoe appears in the main section of this Edition.

Professor Dr Kazuyosi Ikeda
LPIBA DDG IOM LFWLA
For an Outstanding Contribution as a Scientist and Poet

PROFESSOR DR KAZUYOSI IKEDA LPIBA DDG IOM LFWLA

Kazuyosi Ikeda is not only Professor of Theoretical Physics at Osaka University, Japan, but is also a Poet.

His papers on the statistical-mechanical theory of the condensation phenomena of gases and the phase transitions in substances, with the full use of his unique original rigorous mathematical method, have been widely noticed and highly evaluated in the international academic world. His interest also extends to the celestial mechanics of comets and he has theoretically investigated the orbit and motion of the comet whose appearance in 634 and 635 AD was recorded in Japanese history.

His poems on all creation, in seven-and-five-syllable metre, containing both lyric emotion and scientific lucidity, based on his sincere love for all things in nature, have gained many ardent and admiring readers.

Born on 15 July 1928 in Fukuoka, Japan, Kazuyosi Ikeda graduated from the local high school in 1948 and became a student at Kyushu University, in the Department of Physics, Faculty of Science. After graduating in 1951, he continued postgraduate studies until 1956. In 1954 he received an award from the Yukawa Scholarship Fund. Gaining a DSc degree in 1957, he was appointed Assistant in the Department of Physics in 1956, becoming Associate Professor in 1960. In 1965 he accepted a post at Osaka University, as Associate Professor in the Department of Applied Physics, Faculty of Engineering, and in 1968 was promoted to full Professor; in 1989 he transferred to Department of Mathematical Sciences.

Professor Ikeda is active in several organizations: Committee Member, 1970-, Physical Society of Japan; Director, Kansai Branch, Professors World Peace Academy, 1988-; Chairman, Osaka Branch, National Coalition for the Unification of North East West South, 1988-; Chairman, Osaka University Branch, Professors-Students Coalition for the Unification of North East West South, 1987-; Deputy Director General, International Biographical Centre, 1989-; Deputy Governor, American Biographical Institute Research Association, 1989-; Life Patron, International Biographical Association, 1990-; Life Fellow, World Literary Academy, 1991-.

He is the author of many books including: "Statistical Thermodynamics" 1975; "Mechanics without Use of Mathematical Formulae -- from a moving stone to Halley's comet" 1980; "Invitation to Mechanics -- from the fundamentals of calculus to the motion of a comet" with Appendix on a comet in ancient times, 1987; "Basic Thermodynamics - from entropy to osmotic pressure", 1991; "Bansyô Hyakusi" Collection of Poems, 1986. He translated ter Haar's "Thermostatistics" 1960, contributed "Statistical Thermodynamics of Imperfect Gases and Condensation Phenomena" to the book "Modern Developments in Thermodynamics" 1974 and authored over one hundred papers and monographs including: "On the Theory of Condensation" 1953, 56; "Generalized Theory of Condensing Systems" 1961, 65; "On the Yang-Lee Distribution of Zeros for a Gas Obeying van der Waals' Equation of State III -- Calculations for low temperatures" 1974 and "Statistical-Mechanical Theory of One-Dimensional Gases with Short-Range and Long-Range Intermolecular Forces II -- Phase transitions at the absolute zero" 1985.

On 20 November 1956 Kazuyosi Ikeda married Mieko Akiyama and they have a son and a daughter.

A biography of Dr Kazuyosi Ikeda appears in the main section of this Edition.

Dr Ernst Kohl

For an Outstanding Contribution to Library Service in the Community

DR ERNST KOHL

Dr Ernst Kohl is Chairman of the Section of Parliamentary Libraries in the International Federation of Library Associations and Institutions (IFLA).

Born in Elbing, East Prussia, Germany, and educated at the Luther Grammar School in Hanover and at the University of Kiel from which he graduated with a PhD, History, in 1964 he has been a professional librarian since 1966.

Libraries being the repositories of the recorded knowledge of mankind, the library service is under an obligation to mediate to the community information and ideas as a public good. In various positions during his professional career Dr Kohl has endeavoured to comply with this mission of the librarian. As a means he has been engaged in improving the quality of library service both by applying new library techniques and through standardizing rules and procedures both nationally and internationally. In the late 1960s he was instrumental in introducing data processing as a new medium in librarianship to the Bavarian State Library, at the time the largest library in the Federal Republic of Germany. Subsequently he served as Secretary to the Working Group which elaborated the exchange format for bibliographic informations in machine-readable form, MAB1, for the Federal Republic of Germany in 1972-73, and was Consultant to the International Working Group which devised the corresponding international exchange format UNIMARC in 1974-75. From 1973-81 he was also Chairman of the MAB1 Maintenance Agency. Another contribution he made concerned unifying cataloguing rules in the libraries of all German-speaking countries. As a member of the Working Group on Cataloguing of the Federal Republic of Germany he participated actively in the international negotiations which resulted in the publication of the Regeln fuer die alphabetische Katalogisierung, RAK, in 1976-77. For the first time in the history of German librarianship, a single set of rules was adopted for all libraries. Uniform rules as against a multiplicity of different rules certainly facilitate the consultation of library catalogues and, therefore, constitute an improvement for library users.

Dr Kohl has likewise been active in both the German Standards Institute DIN and in the International Organization for Standardization ISO, and has ten DIN Standards and four International Standards to his credit, the most significant ones being the International Standard ISO 7154-1983, Bibliographic Filing Principles and the ISO Technical Report 8393-1985, International Standard Bibliographic Filing Rules, containing a uniform set of filing rules, which, if they are widely applied by publishers, will make searches in dictionaries, directories, bibliographies and encyclopaedias easier for readers.

After joining, in 1980, the Administration of the German Bundestag, the Federal Parliament, in Bonn, Dr Kohl became involved in the activities of the International Section of Parliamentary Libraries which he served as Secretary from 1987-89 and as Chairman since 1989. Also in 1989 he was elected Vice-Chairman of the Libraries Working Group of the European Centre for Parliamentary Research and Documentation (ECPRD), an institution which is jointly directed by the Parliamentary Assembly of the Council of Europe and the European Parliament. During this time of office Dr Kohl very much concentrated his activities -- both as speaker at numerous international meetings and through publications -- on ascertaining the role of information for the operational success of democratic parliaments. After the dramatic political changes in Eastern Europe and the Soviet Union he used his position urging parliamentary libraries in Western Europe and North America to accept their obligation towards the newly established or re-established parliamentary libraries, thus furthering the cause of assistance and international cooperation among parliamentary libraries to the benefit of their parliaments and peoples.

Dr Kohl is author of a number of books and of well over a hundred articles on all aspects of library service, acquisition, cataloguing, indexing, thesaurus work, bibliographic information and the application of data processing in libraries. He is Editor of the "World Directory of National Parliamentary Libraries" and of the "World Directory of Parliamentary Libraries of Federated States and Autonomous Territories". For two years he was reader in library science at the Bavarian Civil Servants College in Munich.

He is a member of many professional organizations and is listed in a number of reference books. As a private man Dr Kohl, together with his wife, has engaged himself in diverse citizens' action groups dedicated to environmental issues. In his leisure time he is an eager reader, but also loves playing tennis or sailing.

A biography of Dr Ernst Kohl appears in the main section of this Edition.

Dr Vernette Trosper Landers LPIBA LFWLA DDG

For an Outstanding Contribution to Education and the Community

DR VERNETTE TROSPER LANDERS LPIBA LFWLA DDG

Vernette Trosper Landers was born in Lawton, Oklahoma, United States of America on 3 May 1912, the daughter of LaVerne Stevens and Fred Trosper. In 1918 she moved with her family to California whre she went to school. She graduated from the University of California, Los Angeles, with an AB (Honours) degree in Spanish and French (1933); MA (1935) and EdD (1953) with a total of nine honours. She also earned four credentials from the State of California, two of which are life diplomas.

Her first husband, Major Paul A Lum, MD, died in 1959 leaving her with a son, William Tappan. She then married Newlin J Landers, who died in June 1990, and they have two children, Lawrence and Marlin.

Dr Landers served in the public schools of California for thirty-seven years. In addition to teaching in secondary schools, she was an Assistant Professor at Los Angeles State College, where she taught methods and supervised student teachers in the Los Angeles City schools. She was also a Professor at Long Beach City College; Dean of Girls at the Twentynine Palm High School and District Counsellor for elementary schools and Coordinator of Adult Education; Director of a Title V Guidance Project in the Morongo United School District. As a side line, she served as clerk-in-charge of Landers Post Office from 1962-82.

Dr Landers has contributed articles to educational magazines and government publications for many years. She has written books in verse for children. Her first, "Impy" was published in 1974; "Impy's Children" and "Talkie" in 1975; "Nineteen O Four" and "Little Brown Bat" in 1976; "Slo-Go" in 1979 and "The Kit Fox and the Walking Stick" in 1980. Her verse can also be found in "New Voices in American Poetry" 1974, 75 and "An Anthology of World Peace and Brotherhood" 1981.

She was Soroptimist of the Year in 1967; received a Creativity Recognition Award from the International Personnel Research Association in 1972 and was named Poet Laureate for February 1981 by the Centre of International Studies and Exchanges.

She is a Life Fellow of the International Academy of Poets and member of National League of American Penwomen; Phi Beta Kappa and American Personnel and Guidance Association and many other memberships in civic and professional organizations.

Dr Landers has received numerous awards and honours for her civic work and writing.

She is a pioneer in the Hi-Desert of California and her hobby is raising bobcats and hybrids.

A biography of Dr Vernette Trosper Landers appears in the main section of this Edition.

Diana St Leger Lindbergh

For an Outstanding Contribution to Humanity

DIANA ST LEGER LINDBERGH

Diana St Leger Lindbergh is Marketing Director of Lindbergh Lodge (formerly Lindbergh Safaris) in Wolmaransstad, South Africa (since 1988). In 1978 she was Translator and News Reader at Italian Television Station in Florence, Italy; from 1978-79 General Office Worker for Gibb Hawkins & Partners, Consulting Engineers in Johannesburg and from 1984-85 Senior Bursar in Hebrew Studies Department, University of Witwatersrand and in 1986 Language Laboratory Monitor in the same Department.

She was born on 7 February 1957 in Johannesburg, South Africa and attended Roedean School in Johannesburg and Herschel School in Cape Town before going to University. In 1974 she attended Clos des beilles, Chateau d'Oex a Finishing School in Switzerland; in 1975 Birnam Business College in Johannesburg; 1975-76 Universite Paul Valery, Institut des Etudiants Etrangers in Montpellier, France; 1976-77 Centro Liguistico Dante Alighieri in Florence, Italy (Diploma di Conoscenza della Lingua Italiana); 1979-81 Hebrew University of Jerusalem; 1982-85 University of Witwatersrand (BA, 1984; BA Honours (with distinction); 1986-87 Hebrew University of Jerusalem; 1988-89 University of South Africa, Pretoria; 1991-present The Writing School, Howick, South Africa and College of Public Administration of Southern Africa, Cape Town.

Diana writes all the brochures and advertising copy for Lindbergh Lodge and is currently writing her first novel. She is hoping to complete a book on teaching foreign languages.

She is a member of South Africa Foundation; South African Institute of International Affairs; South African Institute of Race Relations; Associate of Institute for Multiparty Democracy; Life Member of Women for Peace; Member of Democratic Party; Institute for American Studies; Inanda Club and Johannesburg Country Club.

Diana St Leger Lindbergh has received many honours and awards. In 1973 she represented her school in the National Mathematics and Science Olympiad Examinations; Awarded a Certificate of Merit for Hebrew Studies Louis Landau Hebrew Bursary, 1983; Certificate of Merit for Hebrew Studies, Haymann-Gordon Scholarship, University Senior Bursary, Department of Portuguese Prize, 1984; Certificate of Merit for Hebrew Studies, University Senior Bursary, National Postgraduate Scholarship, 1985; Ben Tsion Scholarship of the Hebrew University of Jerusalem, 1986; Lindbergh Safaris was awarded the Silver Cup for the Best Stand in its category at the Great Safari and Holiday Show in Johannesburg, South Africa, 1990; The Travel Mix Laurel for the best personalised service in the hotel industry was awarded to Lindbergh Lodge, 1991.

She is well versed in English, French, Italian and Afrikaans. Conversant in Spanish and understands Portuguese, Russian and Arabic.

A sportswoman she enjoys riding, tennis, jogging, skiing, swimming, playing squash and golf. She also enjoys flying, ballooning and plans to sky dive. She plays the piano and guitar and is learning to play the violin.

A biography of Diana St Leger Lindbergh appears in the main section of this Edition.

Iris Jean MacLeod FIBA IOM

For an Outstanding Contribution as a Renaissance Gentlewoman of the Twentieth Century

IRIS JEAN MACLEOD FIBA IOM

Now resident in the United States of America, Iris Jean MacLeod was born in 1927 in Calgary, Alberta, Canada, the first child of Munroe and Ruth (Williams) MacLeod. Her parents met while students at the University of Alberta and married after their graduation. Iris' childhood was spent in Canmore, Vermilion, Strathmore and Calgary and while concluding her matriculation at high school, she studied Business at Mount Royal College for a year, before embarking on her career.

She has worked in various fields as diverse as the construction industry and university extension fine arts development. In the United States of America she has been involved in the electronics and music industries and has correlated research for space projects, first as a secretary and then as a technical writer.

In addition to her business career, Iris MacLeod has found success as a composer and writer. Her poetry has been published in various magazines and anthologies, and both her music and poetry have been the subject of TV productions, workshop readings and radio programmes. A fair amount of her time is spent in composition and in personal taping of her music, poetry and technical articles and she is also recording her father's autobiography as a pioneer in Cape Breton, Nova Scotia and subsequently as Superintendent of Schools in Alberta.

An untiring student, Ms MacLeod holds a BA in English with Philosophy gained in 1961 and a BA in Music awarded in 1982. For credit she attended the universities of Alberta, British Columbia and Washington, the University of California Extension, San Jose State University and California State University, as well as the Colleges of Notre Dame and San Mateo, Canada College and Foothill College. In addition she has studied at the University of Toronto, the University of Fribourg and the Peninsula Art Association. She explored the art of self-analysis, including the use of poetry as therapy, through private work with an individual psychiatrist, as well as in groups, partially funded by her employers. She has studied French, some German and a little Russian and Greek, and has an International Order of Merit, Music.

A current member of the World Poetry Society, Intercontinental and the Astronomy Society of the Pacific, Iris MacLeod is a Fellow of the International Biographical Association and also belongs to Clan MacLeod USA, California State University Alumni Association and other organisations.

The recipient of a Koerner Foundation Scholarship and Grant for Poetry from the University of British Columbia and poetry prizes from Friends of the Library, San Jose, Ms MacLeod was also awarded a San Mateo Arts Council Grant for the TV workshop reading of her "Alexander" based on the life of Alexander the Great. She has also received commendations for oil painting.

Twice married, Iris is currently divorced and has two sons, Barry David Cotterill, who is currently teaching and counselling at a community college in Oregon, and Roger Glenn Strassner, a stockbroker in the New York area. She has three grandchildren, Ben, Clay and Holly Cotterill.

A biography of Iris Jean MacLeod appears in the main section of this Edition.

Dr Alan G McHughen

For an Outstanding Contribution to the Body of Research in his field

DR ALAN G MCHUGHEN

Research Scientist and Educator Dr Alan G McHughen was Lecturer at Yale University in the United States of America from 1979-82 and Research Scientist at the University of Saskatchewan in Canada from 1982-91.

Dr McHughen is the author of over seventy-five scientific works published and presented and a United States Patent. He is the co-developer of crop cultivar "Andro" flax.

Alan G McHughen was born on 13 April 1954 in Ottawa, Canada. He attended Dalhousie University, BSc (Hons), 1976; Oxford University (Magdalen College), DPhil, 1979 and also holds the degrees of MIBiol, 1981 and CBiol, 1985.

He is a member of the Institute of Biology; Genetics Society of Canada; Canadian Society for Plant Molecular Biology; International Society for Plant Molecular Biology and International Association for Plant Tissue Culture.

He has been awarded the following honours: Research Fellow, Royal Commission for the Exhibition of 1851, 1979; NATO Research Fellow, 1981 and Robert B Anderson Fellow in Biochemistry, 1982.

On 12 July 1980 he married P Jane Billinghurst and they have two daughters.

Dr McHughen's interests include Genetic Engineering/biotechnology and environmental/regulatory issues and application of Genetic Engineering to Crop Improvement.

A biography of Dr Alan G McHughen appears in the main section of this Edition.

Dr Akio Miyake

For an Outstanding Contribution to Biology

DR AKIO MIYAKE

Akio Miyake is a Biology Professor of the University of Camerino. The second son of Yoshikazu and Yukie (Yamazaki) Miyake, he was born in Kyoto, Japan on 29 June 1931.

A graduate of Zoology Department of Kyoto University in 1953, he began his life work on sexual reproduction in microorganisms when he was an Assistant in Osaka City University (1953-63).

His first main academic achievement was chemical induction of conjugation in the ciliate Paramecium (a unicellular animal) (J. Inst. Polytech. Osaka City Univ. D9 251, 1958). When this technique is used, conjugation, which usually requires two complementary mating types, can be artificially induced in only one mating type. The discovery opened a new research field in the study of conjugation. Presenting a thesis on this subject, he obtained the degree of Doctor of Science from Kyoto University in 1959. During 1959-61 he was a Visiting Scholar in Indiana University, USA, invited by Professor T M Sonneborn (discoverer of mating types) to continue the research on chemical induction of conjugation (J.Exp.Zool. 167, 359, 1968). Returning to Japan, he taught genetics and physiology in Kyoto University as a Lecturer (1963-70). While he was teaching he also investigated the mechanism of conjugation (Science 146, 1583, 1964; Proc. Japan Acad. 44, 837, 1968).

He married Sadako Harada in 1965. Daughter Akiko and son Toshio were born in 1966 and 1969, respectively.

During 1970-74 he led an independent research group (SAG) in Max-Planck Institute for Molecular Genetics, West Berlin. With collaborators in Germany and Japan, he succeeded in isolating and identifying gamones (molecular signals in mating interaction) in the ciliate Blepharisma (Science 176, 400, 1973; 185, 621, 1974). Gamone of mating type I was a glycoprotein, while gamone of mating type II was a tryptophan derivative. These were first gamones isolated in ciliates. He also investigated how gamones induce conjugation (Exp. Cell Res. 76, 15, 1973; 100, 31, 1976; Nature 257, 678, 1975; Dev. Biol. 52, 221, 1976).

During 1975-77 he was a Visiting Scholar in the University of Pisa, Italy. He began investigating the mechanism of meiosis (reduction division occurring prior to gamete formation) in ciliate conjugation (Science 189, 53, 1975; Exp. Cell Res. 108, 245, 1977). Although his main interest was experimental biology, he was also deeply impressed by the warmth and beauty of people, arts and nature in the area of Toscany.

During 1978-83 he was a Visiting Scholar in the University of Münster, Germany. He challenged an ambitious project to isolate a signal molecule which initiates meiosis in ciliate conjugation. The project is still unifinished. He also continued the study of meiosis he started in Pisa (Protistol. 15, 473, 1979; Exp. Cell Res. 145, 105, 1983). For these and earlier works, he was awarded Zoological Society of Japan Prize in 1981.

These experimental researches led him to formulate a unifying theory of conjugation in ciliates. The theory, which conists of the gamone-receptor hypothesis and a few additionmal hypotheses, explains how complementary mating types interact, unite in pairs, and begin meiosis and other nuclear processes of sexual reproduction (Biochemistry and Physiology of Protozoa, 2nd Edc. Vol. 4 125, 1981, Academic Press; Biochemistry of Differentiation and Morphogenesis. 211, 1982, Springer Verlag).

Since 1983 he has been a Professor of the University of Camerino, Italy. There he discovered the hemisexual conjugation, a new reproductive process half sexual and half asexual (Eur. J Protistol. 27, 178, 1991).

In 1986 Sadako died of cancer inflicting him a deep mental trauma. He tried in vain to obtain a spirituial force to cope with it. He had long been fostering an idea that scientific understanding of the world can provide humans with a kind of spiritual force which can bring peace to their mind even in an extreme adversity, just as religions can do. According to this view, if one properly integrates what biology has so far achieved into a general concept, it can bring not only delight but also peace to one's mind. Sadako, who had Christian belief, was interested in the idea and used to encourage him to carry out this project. Belated realization that such a project is indeed highly required made him more serious in pursuing the general concept.

In 1988 he married Terue Harumoto, a biologist. Collaborating with her, he extended his research field to epigenetic determination of mating types (Exp. Cell Res. 190, 65, 1990) and cell recognition in predator-prey interaction in ciliates. In the latter field they established the defensive function of extrusomes (extruding cell organs), such as trichocysts in Paramecium and pigment granules in Blepharisma (Eur. J Protistol. 25, 310, 1990; J. Exp. Zool. 260, 84, 1991). Daughter Yuka was born in 1989.

He holds membership in American Association for the Advancement of Science, the Society of Protozoologists, the Zoological Society of Japan, the Genetics Society of Japan, Italian Zoology Union, Italian Society of Protozoologists, and The Planetary Society.

Dr Miyake's avocations include the origin and evolution of life and Italian opera music.

A biography of Dr Akio Miyake appears in the main section of this Edition.

MR FILIPPO NIBBI

Writer, Filippo Nibbi, attributes his success to his work on what he defines as 'Fantastica' a new work he invented meaning 'the art of inventing what is possible and of making it real through dream creativity and pleasure'. The first principle of 'Fantastica' concerns poetry and can be defined as follows: 'Every object is poetry in itself; if someone finds the words, who can define it, say it tell it....'

The son of Italo and Giuseppina Nibbi, Filippo was born in Cortona, Tuscany on 1 Fberuary 1935. He gained a Bachelor's degree in Mathematics and Physics from University Degli Studi, Bologna, Italy in 1962.

A successful author, Nr Nibbi's publications include: "Antifascists ad Arezzo", 1974; "Guida Storica di Arezzo", 1982 and the books of poetry entitled "Parlando di mio Nonno Polifemo", 1973; "Oleizzo di Poeta", 1983 and "Dopo la Polonia", 1985. He was co-author of "Esercizi di Fantasia", 1981 and editor of "All'insegna dell'A-Zteco"; founder of Titus Quaderni di Poesia, 1984.

A Roman Catholic, Filippo Nibbi married Paola Vaccari in November 1969, and the couple have two children, Pietro and Nicola.

Mr Nibbi is a Member of the National Syndicate of Writers.

Werner Schramm LPIBA IOM

For an Outstanding Contribution to Excellence in Literature and the Arts

WERNER SCHRAMM LPIBA IOM

Werner Schramm was born on 28 April 1926 in Hohenlockstedt, in the northern part of Germany. His father, Walter Schramm, was a "fremdsprachlicher Korrespondent". In 1927 his parents moved to Itzehoe, where he spent his school days.

After leaving school with O Levels in 1942, he began his education as a teacher at Lunden, a college of education in the province of Schleswig-Holstein. During his stay in Lunden, he was proposed as a candidate for the Langemarck study, an elite school which only accepted a few students. The students there were given a free special education, and Werner Schramm went there for some time.

For a better understanding of Mr Schramm's mental development and the making of his personality, it must be noted that the decisive years of his life were determined by war and the Hitler dictatorship. Nobody in Germany could escape the maelstrom of political events. An exclusively intellectual education did not exist, the lives of young people were subject to many outside coercions, and students were forced to participate in military matters as well. At the age of fifteen, Werner Schramm wore the Wehrmacht uniform for the first time, and at sixteen he was the leader of a group operating a searchlight. At seventeen he was in the Reichsarbeitsdienst, but then suffered a critical injury to the central nervous system.

Regarding his career, Werner Schramm writes: "I was wounded during World War II, and was then offered an admission to the Cultural Doctorate of the World University Round Table. But due to illness and pressure of work, I have not responded up to the present. My life was diverted from its anticipated course by a serious injury which I suffered in the war, but I made virtue of necessity. I went through my own self-instruction, and concentrated most of my interest on literature in its broadest sense. The essays I have written are concerned with historical, psychological and philosophical themes, for I regard Nietzsche, Schopenhauer, Stefan Zweig and Lee van Dovski as my spiritual fathers. However, my view of the world has also been molded by English and French philosophers. While it is my constant endeavour to make the best of any situation, when I reflect on the state of the world today, my view tends towards pessimism."

Friendship with a number of important personalities helped shape Mr Schramm's development. In his youth he belonged to Gustav Frenssen's circle of friends, and in the postwar period he had contact with Friderike Maria Zweig, the wife of Stefan Zweig, the most translated author of the 1930s. This relationship encouraged his own literary activity, and he has written the works "Stefan Zweig", "Im Maelstrom der Zeit" the essays, "Die Bacchantinnen", "Der Clown Gottes", and numerous other works. His writer-friend Lee van Dovski dedicated "Genie und Eros" to Werner Schramm.

Mr Schramm is listed in the "International Who's Who of Intellectuals"; "Men of Achievement"; "International Leaders of Achievement"; "The Dictionary of International Biography"; "The First Five Hundred" and the "German Calendar of Literature".

He has received several literary awards and recognition.

Werner Schramm relaxes by painting portraits and landscapes in oil.

A biography of Werner Schramm appears in the main section of this Edition.

Dr Isadore Shapiro DDG IOM

For an Outstanding Contribution to Material Science Technology

DR ISADORE SHAPIRO DDG IOM

Listed in many biographical books in the United States of America and the United Kingdom, Dr Isadore Shapiro is a Materials Scientist.

He was born on 18 April 1916 in Minneapolis, Minnesota, United States of America, the son of Jacob and Bessie (Goldman) Shapiro.

In 1938 he married Mae Hirsch and has two sons.

In 1938 also, Dr Shapiro received his Bachelor of Chemical Engineering degree with "High Distinction" and followed it with a PhD in 1944 -- both from the University of Minnesota, where he remained on a postdoctoral research fellowship for a further year.

He has been employed as a Research Chemist with E I DuPont de Nemours Company, Philadelphia (1946); as Head of the Chemical Laboratory at the United States Naval Ordnance Test Station in Pasadena, California (1947-52); Director of the Research Laboratory at Olin-Mathieson Chemical Corporation, Pasadena (1952- 59); Head of Chemistry for Hughes Tool Company's Aircraft Division, Culver City, California (1959-62); President of Universal Chemical Systems Incorporated, Los Angeles (1962-) and Aerospace Chemical Systems (1964-66); Director of Contract Research with HITCO, Gardena (1966-67); Principal Scientist for McDonnell-Douglas Astro Company (1967-79); Head of Materials and Processes woth AiResearch Manufacturing Company, Torrance (1971-82) and is now working as a Consultant.

Dr Shapiro enjoys all aspects of scientific research, as evidenced by his accomplishments in a wide scope and range of disciplines, viz, he is the discoverer of the Carborane Series of Chemical Compounds (and coined the term "carborane"), leader in the field of composites (resin and fibres), developer of an equation for compaction of powders (coordinating disciplines in chemistry, ceramics and powder metallurgy).

He has presented over fifty papers at scientific meetings, published over a hundred papers in scientific journals and holds twenty patents, both USA and European.

A Fellow of the American Institute of Chemists and Associate Fellow of the American Institute of Aeronautics and Astronautics, he is also Deputy Governor of the American Biographical Institute Research Association and Deputy Director General of the International Biographical Centre, England. He belongs to numerous professional and honorary societies including Sigma Xi, Tau Beta Pi and Phi Lambda Upsilon.

His personal statement reads: "Whatever your field of endeavour or discipline, you first must be honest with yourself, and this inner self-esteem will eventually permeate to your friends, associates and peers to yield proper recognition".

A biography of Dr Isadore Shapiro appears in the main section of this Edition.

Dr Arkady N Shevchenko

For an Outstanding Contribution to Freedom

DR ARKADY N SHEVCHENKO

Arkady N Shevchenko, the highest ranking Soviet official to defect to the West, is now a scholar, writer and lecturer on Soviet affairs. Dr Shevchenko is Adjunct Professor at the School of International Service, American University, and regular lecturer at the John F Kennedy School of Government, Harvard University. Since 1984 he has been President of A & E Associates Incorporated, a private copnsulting firm.

Dr Shevchenko became a United States citizen in 1986.

He is the author of the best-selling memoir "Breaking with Moscow" published by Alfred A Knopf Incorporated in 1985. It was also published in 1985-86 in Great Britain, Germany, France, Italy, Spain, Canada, Australia, Japan, Argentina, Brazil, as well as other countries. Mr Shevchenko is currently writing a new book on the Soviet foreign policy establishment under contract with Alfred A Knopf Incorporated. In addition he has recently written several articles. Among them: "The Soviet Union Under Gorbachev" (Encyclopaedia Britannica" 1986, Book of the Year),"Gorbachev or Not, Reform Will Stay" ("The New York Times" 10 July 1987). "A Lesson of the Yurchenko Affair" ("The New York Times". 12 November 1985), "Behind the Reagan-Gromyko Meeting" ("The New York Times" 23 September 1984), "The Old Order Hangs On -- But Watch Gorbachev" ("The New York Times" 21 February 1984).

Since the early 1980s, Dr Shevchenko has been an active lecturer and seminar participant in many forums. Within the United States Government community, some of these include: The Department of State, Arms Control and Disarmament Agency, The Foreign Service Institute, National Defense University, NSC, CIA, DIA, FBI, Lawrence Livermore Laboratory and Los Alamos National Laboratory. Among many academic institutions are included: Harvard, Yale, Chicago, Cornell, Indiana, Kent State, Tulane, Carnegie Mellon, Washington State, Duke, Florida, Trinity and Brigham Young Universities, the Fletcher School of Law and Diplomacy, University of California at Los Angeles, Hoover Institution, University of Texas, Sweet Briar College and the School of Advanced International Studies of the Johns Hopkins University. Among the corporations and business associations which he has addressed are: Institutional Investors, Business Week, Chief Executives and Young Presidents Organisations, VISA, National Committee for Monetary Reform, American Express, American Trucking Association, Massachusetts Mutual Life Insurance Company, Pfizer Corporation, Academy of Electrical Contractors, California Bankers Association and McDonald's Corporation.

He is the author of several books and many articles on international affairs, disarmament, law and various political subjects published in the Soviet Union. He was a part-time Senior Research Fellow at the Institute in the United States and Canada of the USSR Academy of Science (1970-73). He also conducted seminars at the Higher Diplomatic School in Moscow.

Arkady N Shevchenko was born on 11 October 1930 in Gorlovka, Ukraine, USSR, into a physician's family. He graduated from Moscow State Institute of International Relations in 1954 and later obtained from there the degree of PhD in State and International Law. He speaks Russian, English and French.

He is married to Natalia, a Russian citizen. His daughter and son from his first marriage live in Russia.

A biography of Dr Arkady N Shevchenko appears in the main section of this Edition.

Ah-Tee Sim

For an Outstanding Contribution to Industrial Coatings Lead Soldering Technology

AH-TEE SIM

Ah-Tee Sim, living in Singapore, is Company Director of Sun Industrial Coatings Pte Ltd. Previously he was Supervisor at General Insulation anmd Manager of Sun Yew Engineering Works.

Born on 6 July 1944 in Singapore he is the eldest son of Sim Hiang Meng. He has two brothers and a sister.

Mr Sim is the Inventor, Patentee of: Drag Solder Plating; DIL Carrier; Drag Solder Dip; Quad Pad Carrier and SOIC Carrier.

He is a member of Singapore Manufacturers Association (Committee); Association of Electronic Industries of Sinmgapore and Semiconductor Equipment and Materials International.

Mr Sim has no political or religious beliefs but believes one should always seek the truth and be fair and sincere to others.

On 26 June 1965 he married Alice-Elizabeth, Baptist, and they have two sons and a daughter.

His hobby is keeping tropical fish.

A biography of Ah-Tee Sim appears in the main section of this Edition.

Dr Zahari Staikov

For an Outstanding Contribution as a Sociologist

DR ZAHARI STAIKOV

Dr Zahari Staikov, Sociologist, is Professor and Head of Department at the Institute of Sociology in Sofia, Bulgaria (since 1977). He began his career as a Secondary School Teacher and then Editor, Bulgarian News Agency. From 1953- 66 he was Assistant Professor at the Higher Institute of Sports; Associate Professor at the Institute of Labour from 1966-73 and Director, Research Institute for Trade Union Studies from 1974-76.

He is the author of more than a hundred scientific works including: "The Modelling and Forecasting of Working and Leisure Time" (in Bulgarian), 1976; "The Deductive Approach to Time Budget Modelling" National Centre for Labour and Social Work Problems (in Bulgarian), 1976; "Time Budget of the Population in Yambol District" (in Bulgarian), 1978; "Global Issues" (in Bulgarian), 1986; "Time Budget Studies" Bulgarian Academy of Sciences (in Bulgarian), 1989; "It's About Time" Editor, Bulgaria 1980 and Sweden, 1978; "Authority Reward in Organizations" University of Michigan, USA, 1986 and "Time Use Studies Worldwide" Editor and Author of chapters, Sofia, Socioconsult Ltd, 1991.

Dr Staikov is a member of the International Association of Time Research; Research Committee on Leisure, International Sociological Association; and he is on the Editorial Board, International Play Journal, 1992.

Zahari Staikov was born on 19 December 1927 in Peshtera, Bulgaria. He holds a university degree in Economics, 1948-53; PhD, 1960 and Dr.Habil, 1978.

On 28 February 1953 he married Vasila Savova and they have three sons. In 1986 he married Lilia Petrova

In his leisure time the Professor enjoys travelling and playing bridge.

A biography of Dr Zahari Staikov appears in the main section of this Edition.

Dr Linda Marianne Taylor IOM

For an Outstanding Contribution to Education

DR LINDA MARIANNE TAYLOR IOM

Dr Linda Marianne Taylor has always been involved in education and at present holds the appointment in the Chair of the English Department at Tri-County Technical College in South Carolina in the United States of America, since 1988. She is also an Educational Consultant. She began her career as a Teacher in Woodruff, South Carolina; Instructor in English and Drama at North Greenville College and then Instructor in English and Speech at Tri-County Technical College from 1974-88 before her present appointment.

She is Founder and Co-Director of Dean Howard Drama Society; Founder and Adviser, Tri-County Technical College Oral Interp Troupe; Founder and Co-ordinator of Tri-County Annual Writing Contest and author of "Implementing Writing Across the Curriculum" 1985.

Dr Taylor is a member of Phi Delta Kappa; Delta Kappa Gamma; South Carolina Speech Communication Association; South Carolina Technical Education Association; National Council of Teachers of English; National Council of Instructional Administrators; Southeastern Conference on English in Two-year Colleges and Phi Theta Kappa.

She was awarded Presidential Medallion for Instructional Excellence in 1986; Fulbright Fellowship, 1986; Educator of the Year, 1986; Master Teacher/Advisor, 1987; Kentucky Colonel, 1986; Outstanding Tri-County Teaching Woman, chosen by Anderson County Womans Club, 1989.

Linda Marianne Taylor was born on 13 March 1948 in Woodruff, South Carolina, United States of America. Her mother was a school teacher and her father an overseer in a textile plant and the owner of Taylor Specialty Shop, a supplier of reed hooks for textile process. She has one brother who is Chief Financial Officer and Controller of a hospital.

She earned a BA degree in English (magna cum laude) from Limestone College in 1969; MA in English from Clemson University in 1975 and EdD in Technical- Vocational Education from Clemson University in 1986.

Her faith in God and courage to try have been, and still are, the cornerstones of her life. These cornerstones are the result of the love, care anmd beliefs her parents surrounded her with. Her parents taught her to love God and believe in herself. They also taught her that, while she might not always succeed, she could always gain from every experience, therefore she should always try.

Dr Taylor would like to do more consulting and also to begin writing fiction and to do more volunteer work.

She is listed in "Who's Who in American Education" "Who's Who in the South and Southwest" "Who's Who in the World" and "Personalities of America".

In her leisure time she enjoys reading, acting and travelling. She has a dog, Rags and a cat, Skeeter, and loves and babies them both.

A biography of Dr Linda Marianne Taylor appears in the main section of this Edition.

Professor Frans Joseph Uyttenbroeck

For an Outstanding Contribution to Gynaecology, Mammary Cancerology and Surgery

PROFESSOR DR FRANS JOSEPH UYTTENBROECK

Professor Dr Frans Joseph Uyttenbroeck is Professor and Chairman Emeritus, Department of Obstetrics and Gynaecology, University of Antwerp, Belgium; Chairman Emeritus of the Department of Obstetrics and Gynaecology of St Camille and St Augustin Clinics of Antwerp, University of Antwerp and Consultant for Gynaecological Oncology, University of Antwerp, St Camille Clinic, Antwerp.

He has had eighteen books published, sixteen concerning cancer and more than fifty other publications. He has presented seventeen lectures at Belgian, French and Dutch Academies and more than fifty lectures in many countries about cancer problems.

His fields of interest are comparative study of ovarian tumours in human beings and in animals; precancerous lesions of the genital tract and breast: early detection and treatment; gynaecological oncology; gynaecological surgery: prevention of complications and injury in gynaecological surgery.

Professor Uyttenbroeck is a member of the American Fertility Society; European Society of Mastology; European Society of Gynaecological Oncology and Honorary Member; International Society of Studies of Vulvar Disease; American Association for the Advancement of Science; Society of Pelvic Surgeons; Foreign Member of the Society of Gynaecologic Oncologists; Founding Member of the International Gynaecologic Cancer Society; New York Academy of Sciences; Foreign Member of the Academy of Surgery of Paris; Foreign Member of the National Academy of Medecine, Paris; Member of the Academia Europaea; Academy of Medecine of Belgium; Vice-President of the Royal Academy of Medecine of Belgium (Dutch speaking section), 1986; President of the Royal Academy of Medecine of Belgium (Dutch speaking section), 1987; Former President of the Royal Belgian Society of Gynaecology and Obstetrics; Member of ten other Societies of Gynaecology and Obstetrics; Honorary member of the French and Austrian Societies of Gynaecology.

He has been Decorated Commander Order of Leopold; Grand Officer Crown Order and Grand Officer Order of Leopold.

Frans Joseph Uyttenbroeck was born on 11 July 1921 in Lier, Belgium. He attended University of Louvain, MD, 1946 and University of Amsterdam, PhD, 1952.

On 24 October 1946 he married Elisabeth Switters and they have five daughters.

Professor Uyttenbroeck enjoys travelling to other countries.

A biography of Professor Frans Joseph Uyttenbroeck appears in the main section of this Edition.

Steven A Vladem PhD FUWAI LFIBA DDG IOM

For an Outstanding Contribution to in the Field of Computer Assisted Instruction

STEVEN ALLEN VLADEM PhD FUWAI LFIBA DDG IOM

Steven Allen Vladem, Educator and Computer Specialist, is Coordinator of Alternative 'School Without Walls' Programme, Chicago Public High School for Metropolitan Studies, 1982 to the present; Coordinator of Computer Assisted Instruction, Chicago Public High School of Metropolitan Studies, 1987 to the present.

He received the American Legion Gold Medal Essay Award in 1965 and was honoured as John W Rogers Educator of the Year presented by Junior Achievement at the Future Unlimited Banquet at Chicago Hilton and Towers Hotel on 26 April 1990.

He was chosen to serve as an ambassador for the laureates inducted in the Chicago Business Hall of Fame by the Chicago Association for Commerce and Industry. Dr Vladem has received the 'Key of Success' Award, the Silver Shield of Valor, and the Golden Academy Award for Lifetime Achievement from the American Biographical Institute. He was awarded the 'One in a Million' Medal and Testimonial and 'International Man of the Year 1991-92' from the International Biographical Centre. Dr Vladem received the International Order of Merit in 1991 and numerous awards for his work in the field of computer assisted instruction. In 1992, Dr Vladem received the Congress Star of Distinction at the International Congress on Arts and Communications at St John's College, Cambridge University, England.

Dr Vladem is a member of the International Platform Association; United Writers Association (Life Fellow); International Council for Computers in Education; Technology in Curriculum; National Council of Teachers of Mathematics; Illinois Council of Teachers of Mathematics; Junior Achievement; Illinois Council for Economic Education; MECC; ProComm; CompuServe; Theatre Historical Society of America; He is Deputy Director General of the IBC and Deputy Governor of the ABI Research Association. He serves on the Editorial Advisory Board of the American Biographical Institute.

Steven Allen Vladem was born on 24 July 1949 in Chicago, Illinois, United States of America. He holds a BA degree from University of Illinois with Honours and Distinction; Masters degree in Mathematics from Northeastern Illinois University; MA in Educational Administration and Supervision from Roosevelt University; and PhD in Computer Education from International University. He has taken additional coursework at Loyola University and Northwestern University.

Dr Vladem's accomplishments have been documented in many biographical reference volumes including: International Leaders in Achievement; International Who's Who of Intellectuals; International Register of Profiles; Dictionary of International Biography; Men and Women of Distinction; Community Leaders of America; Personalities of America; Five Thousand Personalities of the World; Two Thousand Notable American Men; International Directory of Distinguished Leadership; Five Hundred Leaders of Influence; Grand Ambassadors of Achievement International; and World Biographical Hall of Fame.

He is a computer enthusiast; plays backgammon and chess; an avid reader; world traveller; history and architecture buff; enjoys visiting the cinema and musical theatre; drama; performing arts; classical music; opera; symphony; stamp and coin collecting.

A biography of Dr Steven Allen Vladem appears in the main section of this Edition.

Dr Wing Keung Wong

For an Outstanding Contribution in the Field of Medicine and Business

DR WING KEUNG WONG

Wing Keung Wong is a Doctor of Medicine in Private Practice in Hong Kong, since 1979. He is Chairman of the Board of Directors of Computime Limited, an electronic company manufacturing electronic products, since 1979. He is also a Director, and later an Executive Director of Cheung Tai Hong Limited, Hong Kong, a trading company, since 1974. From 1955-69 he was a Medical Doctor at the First Hospital of Beijing Medical College, also involved in teaching medical students and doing research work at the Research Laboratory of Viruses and the Research Laboratory of Antibiotics. In 1969 he was sent by the Government to a commune clinic in Kanshu Province.

Dr Wong is the author of two essays published in 1965 and presented to the Third Scientific Conference of Antibiotics in China. "The Primary Observation of the Relationship between Antibiotic Resistance, Phage Typing and Other Biological Properties of Staphylococcus Aureus" and "The Laboratory Study of Antibiotic Combinations against Staphylococcus Aureus".

Dr Wong is a member of the Hong Kong Medical Association.

Wing Keung Wong was born on 5 January 1933 in Hong Kong. After finishing middle school in Hong Kong and Canton, China, he attended Beijing Medical College in Beijing, China and received MB BS in 1955. He moved back to Hong Kong in 1974 and was rewarded LMCHK in 1979.

On 28 May 1957 he married Ban Cho and they have two daughters, Hoi Ling and Hoi Yin.

In his leisure time Dr Wong enjoys travelling, photography, music and diving.

A biography of Dr Wing Keung Wong appears in the main section of this Edition.

Professor Ichiro Yamashita IOM DDG

*For an Outstanding Contribution to Philosophy of Medical
Treatment*

PROFESSOR ICHIRO YAMASHITA IOM DDG

Ichiro Yamashita is Professor, Faculty of Medicine, Department of Oral Surgery, University of Tokyo, Japan.

He was born on 15 July 1934 in Tokyo, Japan. After graduating from Tokyo Medical and Dental University in 1960 he studied at the University of Tokyo, gaining his Doctor of Medical Science degree in 1964.

His first appointment between 1964 and 1966 was as Chief of Stomatology at the National Cancer Centre. He then joined the staff of the Faculty of Medicine at the University of Tokyo, serving as a Lecturer from 1966-70 and Associate Professor, 1970-75 until his present appointment as Chief of the Department of Oral Surgery.

Dr Yamashita is the author of: "The status quo and the future of Dentistry and Orofacial Surgery in Japan" in "The Journal of Japan Stom. Society" 1976; "Principles of Oral Surgery" 1980 and "Theory of Oral Surgical Operation" 1980.

He is ex-President of Japan Stomatological Society, former Trustee of Japan Society of Cancer Therapy and former Delegate of Japanese Association of Medical Science.

A black belt in Taido, he serves as Trustee-General of the World Taido Federation.

Married to Tomoko on 9 May 1961, they have a son and two daughters.

A biography of Dr Ichiro Yamashita appears in the main section of this Edition.

A

AARLI Johan Arild, b. 1 May 1936, Kvinesdal, Norway. Prof of Neurology. m. Gullborg, 9 June 1962, 2 s, 3 d. *Education:* Univ of Bergen. *Appointments:* Prof of Neurology, 1977; Hd of Dept of Neurology, Univ Hosp, Bergen, 1977-. *Publications:* 180 Scientific Papers; 2 Books. *Memberships:* Norwegian Neurological Assn; American Acad of Neurology; American Neurological Assnl Scandinavian Soc of Immunology. *Honours:* Monrad Krohns Proze for Neurological Research; Ragnes Forbergs Prize. *Hobby:* History. *Address:* Dept Neurology, Haukeland Sykehus, 5021 Bergen, Norway.

AARON Raymond Leonard, b. 18 Sept 1944, Toronto, Canada. Lectr; Author; Investor. m. Isobel, 27 Aug 1981, 1 d. 2 step daughters. *Education:* BSc (hon) 1966, Univ Toronto. *Appointments:* Pres, Raymond Aaron Gp 1981-. *Publications:* You Can Make a Million in Canadian Real Estate, 1987; Vast Profits for the 1990s, 1990; Springboard to Success, 1991. *Membership:* Life mem, Canadian Natural Hygiene Soc. *Honours:* Maurice Hutton Alumni Scholarship 1962; Finalist, Intl Entrepreneur of the Year Awd 1988. *Hobbies:* Taekwondo; Walking; Reading. *Address:* 482 Queen Street, Newmarket, Ontario, Canada L3Y 2HY. 88.

ABADI-NAGY Zoltan, b. 16 Nov 1940, Abadszalok. m. Katalin Katona, 12 Dec 1964, 1 d. *Education:* L Kossuth Univ, 1960-65; Univ of Leeds, 1967-68; Kossuth Univ, Doctorate, 1968; Duke Univ, 1972-73; Hungarian Acad of Arts & Sci, 1979. *Appointments:* Kossuth Univ, English Dept, North American Dept, 1965-; Fulbright Prof, Univ of Minnesota, 1987-90; Chmn of Kossuth Univ, 1990-92; Dean, Faculty of Arts & Humanities, 1992-. *Publications include:* Books; 30 Critical Essays; Interviews; 60 Articles; Revies; Translations. *Memberships:* HUSSE; ESSE; HAAS; MFT. *Hobbies:* Music; Photography. *Address:* Inst of English & American Studies, Kossuth University, PO Box 73, H-4010, Debrecent, Hungary.

ABAZA Mohamed Maher, b. 12 Mar 1930, Sharkia, Egypt. Min of Electricity & Energy, ARE. m. Ezdehar Abo Eela, 14 Apr 1955, 1 s. 1 d. *Education:* BSc Elect Power Engrg 1951, Cairo Univ; Study in W Germany 1953, 1954; Study in Sweden 1955, 1956. *Appointments:* Engr, Min Public Works, 1951-64; Dir 1964-72, Insp 1973-74, G Elec Authority; 1st Undersecy of State 1975-80; Min of Electricity & Energy 1980-. *Memberships:* Nat Com of IEC; Nat Com of CIGRE; Nat Com of WEC; Inst Elec & Electronic Eng; Thomas Alva Edison Foun. *Honours:* 15 Awds incl: Order of the Republic (1st Class) Egypt; Royal Order of Polar Star (Grand Cross) Sweden; Grand Cross of Order of Merit FRG; Order of the Republic (1st Class) France; Grand Cross of Order of Merit Italy. *Hobbies:* Collecting stamps; Swimming; Reading; Photography. *Address:* 8 Taha Hussein Street, El-Zamalek, Cairo, Egypt.

ABBASI Tanveer, b. 7 Dec 1934, Sobhodero. Writer; Poet. m. Qamar, 14 Apr 1964, 1 s. 3 d. *Education:* MB, BS 1960. *Publications:* Ragoon Thiyoon Rabab, poetry; Shair, poetry; Sij Tirec Hethan, poetry; Hea Dharti, poetry; Shah Latey Ji Shairi, 3 vol, criticism; Dorey Dorey Deh, travelog; Moonh Tinee Mashal, sketches. *Memberships:* Bd Govs, Pakistan Acad Letters; Adv Com, Sindhi Lang Authority; Adv Com, Inst Sindhology; Advr Sachal Chair, SAL Univ; Selection Bd, SAL Univ. *Honours:* Best Poetry Awd, Inst Sindhology 1976, 1984; Sachal Sarmast Gold Medal 1987; Sindh Grad Assn Gold Medal 1989; Shah Abdul Lataf Acad Gold Medal 1989. *Hobbies:* read and write Poetry; Research work; Billiards. *Address:* Sarmad House, Khairpur Sindh, Pakistan.

ABBOTT Mary Elaine, b. 23 Apr 1922, LaGrange, Illinois, USA. Photographer; Lectr; Documentary Photographer. m. 8 Oct 1949, 1 s. 1 d. *Education:* Eng, Psychol 1944, Univ Iowa. *Appointments:* Child Welfare; Montgomery Co Children's Home, Dayton, Ohio; Mich Children's Inst, Ann Arbor, Mich; Dependent and Neglected Children, Adoption, Foster Home Approval placement, 1944-49. *Creative Works:* Documentary slide lectures, 13 years; Commissioned Documentary Photography incl retarded and closed-head injury dances; Ongoing commissions: Ella Sharp Museum; Jackson Symphony Orchestra; Carnegie Lib; St Paul's Episcopal Ch; Many juried and one- person shows; Photographs in many pvt, bus and public collections; Extensive Reschr. *Memberships include:* ssa 00Kappa Alpha Theta; Jr League; St Paul's Episcopal Ch; Intl Platform Assn; Advr, Jackson Co Historic District Comm; Nat Museum of Women in Arts; Nat Trust for Historic Preservation. *Hobbies include:* Music & chorale; Reading and res; Walking; Swimming; Yoga; Documentary photography and research; Sculpture; Cemeteries; Creative process; Architecture. *Address:* 721 Oakridge Drive, Jackson, MI 49203, USA. 8, 5, 52, 152.

ABBOTT William Thomas, b. 6 Jan 1938, Guthrie, Oklahoma, USA. Claim Spec. m. Jerri Evelyn Stacy, 20, Apr 1974. *Education:* BSc 1960, Central State Univ, Edmond, Okla; Assoc in Claims Designation 1990, Am Inst for Property & Liability Underwriters. *Appointments:* US Marine Corps 1960-64; Claim Adjuster, Crawford & Co Insurance Adjusters, 1964-67 in Lubbock, Tex, 1967-70 in Tulsa, Okla; State Farm Insurance Cos 1970-. *Memberships:* Tulsa Claims Assn, Pres 1981; Okla Claims Assn; Okla Arson Adv Coun; Intl Assn of Arson Investigators, Okla Chapt Pres 1991; Order of Blue Goose. *Honour:* Claimsman of the Year 1979, Tulsa Claims Assn. *Hobbies:* Informal writing; Bicycling; Regional history. *Address:* 3815 S St Louis Avenue, Tulsa, OK 74105, USA. 7.

ABDELA Lesley Julia, b. 17 Nov 1945, London, England. Journalist; Broadcaster. div, 1 s. *Education:* Schs, Eng and Switzerland; Hammersmith Col of Art & Bldg, London; London Col of Printing. *Appointments include:* Advtg exec, Royds Advertising, London; Derek Forsyth Design Partnership; Reschr, Liberal Whip's Office, House of Commons; Parliamentary Candidate (Liberal Party), East Hertfordshire, 1979; Freelance Journalist and Broadcaster, 1980-; Presented BBC TV prog, Great Expectations, on women in Brit politics 1991; Oversaw res for Unilever-sponsored video on Women making the break-through at work, 1991. *Creative work includes:* Books: Women in Politics, 1989; Women with X Appeal, 1990; Breaking Through the Glass Ceilings, 1991; Paintings (acrylics), The Gambia. *Memberships:* Travel Specialists Gp, Inst Journalists; Fellow, Royal Geographical Soc; Fdr, All-party 300 Gp (women in politics); Women in Mgmt; Fawcett Soc; Network; Friends of the Earth; Greenpeace; Amnesty Intl; Survival Intl; Electoral Reform Soc; Soc of Women Journalists; European Women's Mgmt Devel Network; Josephine Butler Soc. *Honours include:* MBE 1990; Leadership Grant, US Govt 1983; Fellowship, Royal Soc Arts. *Hobbies:* Travel; Politics; Painting; Desert Agriculture; Third World Development. *Address:* La Boursaie, 14140 Tortisambert, France.

ABDULKADIR Jemal, b. 25 Jan 1935, Gore, Ilubabor. Internal Med. m. Fatima Ibrahim, 5 May 1963, 2 s. *Education:* MD CM 1959; DCMT 1964; MRCP (Edin) 1966; FRCP (Edin) 1981. *Appointments:* Asst Prof 1966-72, Assoc Prof 1972-88, Prof 1988-, Fac Med, Addis Ababa Univ. *Creative Works:* Landscape painting in water colour. *Memberships:* Past-pres, mem Ethiopian Med Assn; Royal Col Physicians of Edinburgh. *Honour:* Haile Sellassie I Prize Trust Fellowship 1964. *Hobbies:* Painting; Gardening; Reading. *Address:* P O Box 1176, Faculty of Medicine, Addis Ababa University, Addis Ababa, Ethiopia.

ABDULKADIR Jimada Muhammad, b. Feb 1965, Minna. Mining Engr. m. Aishetu Sani, 9 Aug 1991. *Education:* Kaduna Polytech: WAEC City & Guilds in

Motor Mechanics 1982; Nat Dipl in Mining Engrg 1986; Higher Nat Dipl in Mining Engrg 1989. *Appointments:* Geol Survey Dept 1985; Nigerian Mining Corp 1991. *Membership:* Nigerian Soc Mining Engrs. *Hobbies:* Reading; Travelling. *Address:* SW 345d, Kongila Ward, Minna, Niger State, Nigeria.

ABER John Irwin, b. 15 Apr 1951, Newark, Ohio, USA. Assoc Prof of Eng; Creative Writer; Composition Scholar. *Education:* BA 1973, Otterbein Col; MA 1981, PhD 1986, Ohio State Univ. *Appointments:* Eng Tchr, Washington CH, OH Schs 1976-81; Asst Prof 1985-91, Assoc Prof 1991-, Col of Mount St Joseph. *Publications:* Var short stories in lit mags, latest Mounds, in Ambergris 1991; Var scholarly arts in composition studies in profl jours. *Memberships:* MLA; NCTE; CCCC; Cincinnati Writers' Project. *Honours:* Elected to Phi Kappa Phi 1983; Awd'd Fiction Writing Grant by Col of Mount St Joseph 1991. *Address:* Department of Humanities, College of Mount St Joseph, 5701 Delhi Road, Cincinnati, OH 45233, USA. 8.

ABHISHEKI Jitendra, b. 21 Sept 1929, Mangeshi, Goa. Profl Indian Classical Vocalist. m. Smt Vidya Godsay, 22 Jan 1969, 1 s. 1 d. *Education:* BA in Sanskrit Lang 1952; Tng in Classical Music under sev great musicians. *Career:* Music Dir, All India Radio, 1952-62; Profl Indian Classical Vocalist & Mus Dir 1962-. *Creative Works:* Music Dir for 25 Indian Musicals (in Marathi); Trend Setter in Marathi Musical and Choir Orchestra; Over 100 classical compositions and semi-classical compositions. *Memberships:* Exec Com, Goa Kala Acad; Ex-mem Sangeet Natak Acad; Former Chmn, Goa Hindu Assn; Judge for Tansen Awd 1990. *Honours:* Padmashree & Sangeet Natak Acad Awd from Govt of India; Homi Bhabha Fellowship for Res in Folk Mus; L N Gupta Awd for Contribution in Classical Mus; State Govt Felicitation Awd 1990; Rep India in Festival of India in USSR. *Hobbies:* Reading; Writing; Travelling; Cooking Goan Recipes; Gardening. *Address:* Maangirish Survey No 60/18, Sthairya Cooperative Housing Society, Hingane, Pune-411 052, Maharashtra State, India.

ABILDGAARD Paul, b. 30 Jan 1930, Denmark. CEO and Chmn of Bd. m. 7 Dec 1952, 3 s. 3 d. *Appointments:* Fdr, Chmn, CEO, Nanton Spring Water Co 1980-; Fdr: Nanton Soft Drink, Nanton Food, Appaloosa Beer, Nanton Interbrew; Owner, Crown A Ranches; FDR, CEO, Albert, Alberta Investment and Poll Co Inc, Linen House Inc and Lady Godiva Oats, Pellets and Cubes Ltd and Alberta Investments Ltd. *Hobby:* Horse breeding. *Address:* P O Box 656, Nanton, Alberta, Canada T0L IR0. 88.

ABLONCZY Laszlo, b. 14 Oct 1945, Bodrogkalasz. Dir Hungarian Nat Theatre. m. Magda Szabo, 4 Mar 1972, 2 s. 1 d. *Education:* Hungarian Lit and Grammar, Folk Ed, 1975-80, Debrecen; Journalists' Sch, 1970-71, Budapest. *Appointments:* Journalist at Magyar Hirlap newspaper 1971-75; Press Chf, Hungarian Film Distribution Co 1975-78; Journalist at Film, Szinhaz, Muzsika 1978-91; Edit, Tiszataj 1989-. *Publications:* Author: The Sight of Latinovits Zoltan 1987; Hard Dream-the Life of Andras Suto; Edit: 8 books of Transylvanian Writer Andras Suto 1981-91; Dramas of Zoltan Jekely 1984; Dramas of Aron Tamasi 1987-88; Essays and interviews about the Nat Theatre. *Memberships:* World Fedn Hungarians; Mem Presidency, Budapest. *Hobbies:* East-Central European theatrical life and Hungarian theatres beyond the frontier; French theatre. *Address:* Hevesi Sandor ter 4, Budapest 1077, Hungary.

ABPLANALP Delloy Orval, b. 28 Nov 1931, Salt Lake City, Utah, USA. Owner, Holistic Health Integrated. m. Kathleen Thurman, 21 Aug 1959, 2 s. 1 d. *Education:* BS, Elem & Sec Ed 1959, Brigham Young Univ, Provo, Utah. *Appointments:* Mission for the Church of Jesus Christ of Latter Day Saints, 1951-53; US Army Signal Corps 1953-55; Tchr: Jr HS, Utah 1959-60; Elem Sch, Utah 1960-61; Acct, Los Angeles Fire Dept and Water

and Power Dept 1961-74; Fdr, Holistic Health Bus 1974-; Sales Mgr, Los Angeles Herald Examiner Circulation Dept 1983-88. *Publications:* Dial an Herb Wheel, 1976; Holistic Health, 1977. *Memberships:* Regl Mgr, Natures Sunshine Products; Mgr, Enrich Intl; Million Dollar Club 1979-91; Delta Phi Frat 1955- 59; LDS Sociables 1965-70; Nat Fealth Fedn 1970-. *Honours:* Dist'd Leadership Awd, ABI; Co Chmn, Democratic Party, Uintah Co, Utah, 1959; Outstanding Sales Achm't, Natures Sunshine Products 1989-90; Devel Awd, Natures Sunshine Products 1990. *Hobbies:* Coaching and refereeing AYSO Soccer and little league Baseball. *Address:* 4917 Baldwin Avenue, Temple City, CA 91780, USA. 59.

ABRAHAMS Anne, b. 15 Apr 1951, Malta. Conslt Psychi. m. Andrew Leonard Abrahams, 24 May 1986, 3 d. *Education:* Convent of Sacred Heart, Malta; Royal Univ Malta. *Appointments:* Regist, Bethlem Roy & Maudsley Hosp, 1977-81; Sr Regist, St Thomas' Hosp, 1981-82; Lectr, Charing Cross Hosp Med Sch, 1982-85; Conslt Psychi, Wexham Park Hosp, 1985-. *Publications:* Papers on alcohol misuse and other psychi topics; Chapt on addiction in Essential Psychiatry. *Memberships:* Royal Col Psychis; Soc Study of Addiction; Med Coun on Alcoholism. *Honour:* On Call Awd for Res & Innovation 1980. *Hobbies:* Reading; Bridge; Travelling. *Address:* Department of Psychiatry, Wexham Park Hospital, Slough, Berks, England. 170, 146, 99.

ABRAMOV Alexandre A, b. 14 Feb 1926, Moscow. Mathematician. m. Nina I Abramova, 14 Mar 1945, 3 s. *Education:* Moscow State Univ 1942- 46; Postgrad 1946-49; PhD Thesis 1950; Doctorate Thesis 1975; Professor 1976. *Appointments:* Jr then Sr Reschr, Inst Precise Mechs, Acad Sci, 1949- 55; Chf of Dept of Numerical Methods, Main Reschr, Computing Centre of Acad Sci of USSR, 1955-. *Publications:* Over 100 arts and monographs on maths in gen and partic on numerical. *Honour:* Red Banner Order. *Hobbies:* Classical music; Literature; Theatre; Chess. *Address:* Computing Centre Academy of Science, Vavilova Street 40, GSP1, Moscow 117967, Russia.

ABRAMOV Sergei, b. 11 Apr 1946, Moscow. Mathematician; Professor. div. 1 s. *Education:* Moscow State Univ 1964-69; PhD in Computer Algebra 1972; Doctor degree in Computer Algebra and Programme Analysis 1983. *Appointments:* Investigator 1972-81, Major Investigator 1981-86, Leading Investigator 1986-91, Computing Centre Acad Sci of USSR; Professor, 1992-. *Publications:* Remark on the method of intermediat assertions, 1981; Exercises on Programming, 1988; Fast algorithms to search for the rational solutions of linear differential equations, 1991. *Membership:* Russian work gp on computer algebra. *Hobby:* Classical music. *Address:* Computing Centre of the Russian Academy of Science, Vavilova 40, Moscow, Russia.

ACAR Salih, b. 1927, Bulgaria. Painter. m. 1971, div 1980. *Education:* Grad Fresco Sec in Acad of Fine Arts, Sofia 1950; Grad Acad Fine Arts, Istanbul (Sculpture & gen degree) 1955. *Career:* Painter for 30 years. *Creative Works:* 30 personal exhibitions in Europe; Migrating Birds 1951; The Bald Ibis 1975; The Animals of the Wilderness 1976; Butterflies, Insects and Fish 1978; The Beautiful and the Ugly 1979; The Worlds of Birds of Prey 1980. *Memberships:* Co-Fdr, Turkish Br World Wildlife Fund; Co-Fdr, Soc for Protection of Wildlife in Turkey. *Hobbies:* Natural life; Birds. *Address:* Ihlamurdere Cad, Misirlibahce Sok, No 108, C Blok, Daire 4, Besiktas, Istanbul, Turkey.

ACCOMANDO Annette Marie Le Febvre, b. 15 Mar 1958, New Orleans, Louisiana, USA. Instr. m. Gerard Joseph Accomando, 25 July 1981, 2 d. *Education:* BEd 1981, MEd 1985, UNO. *Appointments:* Eng Instr, Chalmette High Sch 1981-88; ESL at Andrew Jackson High Sch 1988-89; Eng & Journalism, St Bernard Parish Community Col 1990-91. *Creative Work:* Presentation: Louisiana's Latent Leaders, at Mid-South Ednl Res Assn

Convention, New Orleans. *Memberships:* Intl Reading Assn, local chapt Pres; Delta Kappa Gamma, local Coun Secy; Phi Delta Kappa; Mid-South Ednl Res Assn; LA Tchrs of Eng to Speakers of Other Langs. *Hobbies:* Reading; Needlework. *Address:* 5 Gibbs Drive, Chalmette, LA 70043, USA. 15.

ACHEROY Marc Pierre Jules, b. 9 June 1948, Uccle. Prof. m. Francoise Gram, 24 Dec 1970, 3 d. *Education:* Engr in Mechs 1971, Royal Milit Acad, Brussels; Engr in Automatic Control 1978, PhD Applied Scis 1983, ULB. *Appointments:* Ofcr in a maintenance company 1971-73; Asst in Elect Engrg 1973-77; Engr in milit material 1978-84; Prof, Royal Milit Acad, Brussels 1985-. *Creative Works:* Devel of methods for the restoration of images; Method for automatic object recognition. *Memberships:* IEEE; SPIE; AIA; SRBE (Adm). *Honour:* Triennal Prize of the AIA. *Hobbies:* Music esp jazz and classical; Walking in mountains. *Address:* Royal Military Academy, Chaire d'Electricite, Av de la Renaissance 30, B 1040 Brussels, Belgium.

ACKAH Christian Abraham, b. 2 June 1908, Cape Coast, Ghana. Retd Hd of Univ. m. Georgina Ackah, Feb 1958, 1 s. 2 d. *Education:* Pvt Study, BA (Hons) in Philosophy 1934, MA in Sociol 1938, Univ of London; PhD Sociol 1959, LSE. *Appointments:* Tchr, St Nicholas Grammar Sch (now Adisadel Col), Cape Coast 1926-36; Acct, Civil Service 1937-51; Headmaster, Ghana Nat Col, Cape Coast 1953-56; Supvr of Ghana Students in UK and Ireland 1956-59; Sr Res Fellow, Univ of Ghana 1960-62; Principal, Univ Col (now Univ) of Cape Coast 1962-64, 1966-68; Mbr of Cncl of State in Ghanas 3rd Repub, 1979-81. *Publications include:* West Africa-A General Certificate Geography; Akan Ethics; Social Stratification in Ghana; Some Fundamentals in the Political Scene. *Memberships:* Fdr Fellow, Ghana Acad of Arts and Scis; Life Fellow, Royal Geographical Soc; Life Mem, Royal Inst of Philosophy; Brit Sociol Assn; LSE Club, London. *Honour:* Hon DLit, Univ Cape Coast, 1978. *Hobbies:* Music; Walking; Travel. *Address:* Baffoa Lodge, P O Box 264, Cape Coast, Ghana. 135, 3.

ADAMIK Josef, b. 29 June 1947, Kremacov, CSFR. Tchr of Mus; Composer. *Education:* Conservatory, piano and composition, Brno, 1965- 69; Janacek Acad of Arts, composition, 1969-74. *Appointments:* Tchr, Elem Mus Sch, Valasske Klobouky 1974-87; Tchr, Conservatory of Kromeriz 1987- 89; Tchr, Elem Mus Sch at Val Klobouky 1989-. *Creative Works:* Compositions include: The Pastures of Heaven, 16 string instruments, 1971-72, to the memory of John Steinbeck; Shading I, flute, 2 or 4 violins and piano, 1975; I Stop Somewhere Waiting for You, 6 male voices, 1981; 3 collections of children's songs on Czech texts by Jan Vodnansky 1979, 1981, 1984. *Membership:* Assn of Mus Artists and Scists. *Hobbies:* Literature; Tourism; Cacti. *Address:* Lucni 901, 766 01 Valasske Klobouky, CSFR.

ADAMS Freddy Camiel Valentin, b. 10 July 1938, Lede, Belgium. Rector. m. Denise Van den Bergh, 23 Sept 1963, 2 d. *Education:* Licentiate in Chem 1960, Doctor in Exact Scis 1963, State Univ Ghent. *Appointments:* Res Assoc, Interuniv Inst for Nuclear Scis (IIKW) 1960- 65; Tchg Asst, State Univ Ghent, Inst Nuclear Scis 1965-72; Res in analytical chem and radiochem 1960-72; Res at Cyclotron Inst, Texas A&M Univ, Col Station, Tex 1970-71; Prof of Chem, Univ Antwerp, tchg duties in analytical chem and radiochem 1972-; Rector, Universitaire Instelling Antwerpen 1983-. *Publications:* Co-author 2 books and over 250 pubs in intl sci lit. *Memberships include:* As Rector of UIA mem of number of couns and steering coms; Nat Coun of Sci Res (NRWB); Flemish Coun Sci Res; Pres, Special Comm for Res at Univs of the NRWB; Comm No 4 (Organic and inorganic chem) 1975-; Mem, Academia Europaea, 1989-; comm for radiochem 1987-, Nat Fund for Sci Res (NFWO); Mem Bd Flemish Chemical Soc; Pres Analytical Sect 1977-82; Am Soc for Mass Spectrometry and the Am Chem Soc; Mem var Edit Bds. *Honours:* Prize of European Res Assocs 1960; Prize

Stas-Spring, Royal Acad Scis 1964; Recip Travel Awd of Belgian Govt 1966-67; NATO Res Travel Grant 1969-70; Louis Gordon Mem Awd 1979; Castaing Awd for Best Student Paper 1984. *Hobbies:* Music; Literature. *Address:* Universitaire Instelling Antwerpen, Universiteitsplein 1, B-2610 Antwerpen, Belgium.

ADAMS (William) James, Sir, b. 30 Apr 1932. Retired Diplomat; Consultant. m. Donatella, 1961, 2 s. 1 d. *Education:* Queen's Col, Oxford. *Appointments:* Royal Artillery, Middle East Land Forces 1950-51; Foreign Office 1954; MECAS 1955; 3rd Secy, Bahrain 1956; Asst Polit Agent, Trucial States 1957; FO 1958; 2nd Secy Bahrain 1959; Manila 1960; 1st Secy and Pvt Secy to Min of State, FO 1963; 1st Secy (Info), Paris 1965-69; FCO 1969; Counsellor 1971; Hd of European Integration Dept (2), FCO 1971-72; seconded to Ec Comm for Africa, Addis Ababa 1972-73; Counsellor (Devel Countries), UK Permanent Rep to EEC 1973-77; Hd of Chancery and Counsellor (Ec), Rome 1977- 80; Asst Under-Secy of State (Pub Depts then Energy), FCO 1980-84; Amb to Tunisia 1984-87; Amb to Egypt, 1987-92. *Honours:* CMG 1976; KCMG 1991; Order of the Star of Honour (Hon), Ethiopia 1965; Order of the Two Niles (Hon), Sudan 1965. *Address:* 13 Kensington Court Place, London W8 5BJ, England.

ADAMS (Elie) Maynard, b. 29 Dec 1919, Clarkton, Virginia, USA. Retd Philosopher; Edr; Writer (still writing and lecturing). m. Phyllis Stevenson, 22 Dec 1942, 1 s. 1 d. *Education:* BA 1941, MA 1944, Univ Richmond; BD 1944, Colgate-Rochester Divinity Sch; MA 1947, PhD 1948, Harvard Univ. *Appointments:* Asst Prof Phil, Ohio Univ, 1947-48; Asst Prof Phil 1948-53, Assoc Prof Phil 1953-58, Prof Phil 1958-71, Kenan Prof Phil 1971-90, Kenan Prof Phil Emeritus 1991-, Univ NC at Chapel Hill. *Publications:* Fundamentals of General Logic, 1954; Logic Problems, 1954; Ethical Naturalism and the Modern World View, 1960; The Idea of America, 1977; Philosophy and the Modern Mind, 1975; The Metaphysics of Self and World, 1991; Religion and Cultural Freedom, forthcoming. *Memberships:* Am Phil Assn, Exec Com, Prog Chair; Srn Soc for Phil and Psych, Exec Coun, Prog Chair & Pres; NC Phil Soc, Pres; NC Humanities Coun, Vice Chair, Chair. *Honours:* Doctor of Humane Letters, Wake Forest Univ 1989; Doctor of Humanities, Univ of Richard, 1992; Alpha Mu Omicron Honour Soc; Golden Fleece Honour Soc; Dialectic Lit Soc, Hon mem; Francis Wayland Ayer Travelling Fellow, Colgate-Rochester Divinity Sch; James H Woods Fellow, Harvard Univ; Thomas Jefferson Awd; Outstanding Edr of Am Awd; NC Adult Ed Assn Special Awd for 1988. *Hobbies include:* Writing newspaper columns; Reading; Travelling; Construction projects; Yard work. *Address:* 813 Old Mill Road, Chapel Hill, NC 27514, USA. 2.

ADAMS Randall David, b. 12 Mar 1958, Oklahoma City. Financial Advr. m. Rebecca Ann Garner, 29 Dec 1979, 1 s. 2 d. *Education:* BS 1979, Southwestern State Univ; MBA 1981, Central State Univ; CFP 1987, Col for Financial Planing, Denver, Colorado. *Appointments:* Personnel Mgr, State Office of Personnel Mgmt 1979-84; CFP, Waddell & Reed 1984-. *Creative Works:* Seminars: Money the Users Manual, 1987; The Guide to Retirement Planning, 1988. *Memberships:* OK 4-H Key Club, Pres; edmond C of C, Ambassador; Nat Geol Soc; OK Jaycees, ChP, VP; OK City Personnel Assn; Young Democrats of OK; Okla Public Employees Assn. *Honours:* Lobbyist Okla Legislature; 5 million Table United Investors Life E Awd in Debate, EOSC; Awd for Excellence in Financial Planning, Waddell & Reed. *Hobbies:* Hiking; Writing; Spelunking. *Address:* 1009 Apollo Circle, Edmond, OK 73034, USA. 125, 46.

ADANIS Segum Bashik Adebayo, b. 11 Aug 1966, Maiduguri, Nigeria. Stockbroker. *Education:* Nigeria Ogun State Univ, 1985-89; Stockbroking Exams, 1992. *Appointments:* Samurabi Ltd, 1990-91; Nig Solihat Inv Fin & Trust Co, Lagos Nig, 1991-. *Publications:* peoms for Mature Minds; So Like the Thunderbolt; Just A Cry; The West Connections; Analogy of Historical Facts of our Time; The Vicissitude; The Array of Stars. *Memberships:* The Globmate Foundation; Young Stars Club; Inst of Writers; The Exec Club. *Honours:* The Globmate Award; Basic Studies Prize. *Hobbies:* Travel; Meeting People of High Repute; Poetry; Novelist; Swimming; Athlete. *Address:* 26 Opeifa Crescent, Anthony Village, Lagos, Nigeria.

ADDAI Joseph Akwasi, b. 10 Aug 1944, Boma, Ghana. Pastor; Social Wkr. m. Susana, 9 Aug 1975, 2 s. 2 d. *Education:* RSA (III) 1970, Ghana; BA 1974, Nigeria; MDiv 1982, Mich, USA; CPE 1988, In, USA; D Min 1988, Mich, USA. *Appointments:* Acct, SDA Ch, Ghana 1974-75; Acct, Book & Bible House, Ghana 1975-77; Pastor, Bantama SDA Ch, Ghana 1974-77; Chaplain, SDA Sec Sch, Ghana 1977-79; Supvr, Residential Sers of SW Mich 1983-; Chaplain, Mem Hosp of South Bend, Ind 1988-89. *Publication:* Causes of Apostasy and Inactivity in the SDA Church In Ghana, 1988. *Memberships:* Pres, West African Club, 1982; VP, Pan African Club 1983-84; Habitat for Humanity Intl. *Hobbies:* Gardening; Music; Helping others. *Address:* 306 South Bluff Street, Berrien Springs, MI 49103, USA.

ADEDOKUN Rizqat Adenike, b. 10 Jan 1971, Lagos. Secy. *Education:* OND in Secy Admin 1991, Lagos State Poly. *Appointments:* Secy, Metalum Ltd, 1991-. *Creative Work:* Feasibility Study for Mass Usage, done for the sch to tch others and to help start their own businesses. *Hobbies:* Reading; Walking; Meeting interesting people & visiting interesting places. *Address:* 9 Adedokun Close off Alimoso Road, Alimoso Local Government, Lagos State, Nigeria.

ADENIS Jacques Andre Marie, b. 29 Nov 1926, Paris, France. Intl Civil Servant; Linguist. m. Marruska de Ambrogi, 18 Apr 1973. *Education:* Dipl Inst d'Etudes Politiques, Paris 1948; Licence es Lettres, Univ de la Sorbonne, Paris 1968. *Appointments:* Commercial Attache, Trefileries et Laminoirs du Havre, Paris 1950-51; Chf Edit, Union Routiere de France et La Prevention Routiere, Paris 1952-60; Edit Translator UN Specialized Agencies, Geneva 1961-65; Official Relats Exec Ofcr, Intl Labour Org, Geneva 1966-88; With French army (Infanterie de Marine) 1949-50, 1958-59, Lt Col IRAT (Reserve Army Interpreters) 1960-. *Honours:* Medaille Commemorative Afrique du Nord 1958; Brevet de Langue Anglaise de L'Etat-Major des Forces Armees 1960; Chevalier de l'Ordre National du Merite 1980; Croix du Combattant 1982; Medaille d'Argent des Serv Militaires Volontaires 1986. *Hobbies:* Reading; Writing; Genealogy; Music; Tennis; Travelling. *Address:* 27 Route de Florissant, 1206 Geneva, Switzerland. 52.

ADEY Lionel, b. 4 Jan 1925, Wednesbury. Prof Emerit of Eng. m. Muriel Compton Race, 25 July 1953, 2 s. 1 d. *Education:* BA, Eng 1949, MA 1953, Birmingham; Cert in Ed 1955, London; PhD 1964, Leicester. *Appointments:* Eng Master, King Edward VII Sch, Sheffield 1950-52; Nicholas Chamberlaine Sch, Bedworth 1952-55; Gateway Sch, Leicester 1956-63; Sr Eng, Longslade Sch, Birstall 1964-67; Asst, Assoc and Prof, Univ of Victoria 1967-90, Emeritus 1990-. *Publications:* Books: C S Lewis's Great War, with Owen Barfield, 1978; Hymns and the Christian 'Myth' 1986; Class and Idol in the English Hymn, 1988; Affirmations, poems part author, 1989. *Memberships:* Leicester Poetry Soc, Secy and VP; Assn Cdn Univ Tchrs of Eng; Victorian Studies Assn of W Canada; Intl Hopkins Assn; Hymn Soc of GB; Hymn Soc of Am. *Honours:* 1st class Hons in Eng, Birmingham 1949; Grant-Robertson Res Scholarship 1949-50; Tibbatts Prize 1949; Clyde Kilby Res Fellowship, Wheaton Col 1985. *Hobbies:* Choral singing; Gardening; Music. *Address:* 3921 Cherrilee Crescent, Victoria, BC, Canada V8N 1R7. 13.

ADHIKARI Santosh Kumar, b. 24 Nov 1923, West Bengal. Retd Banker. m. Sadhona, 18 Mar 1948, 1 s. 2 d. *Education:* Grad Univ Calcutta 1943; Cert'd Assoc of Indian Inst Bankers 1948; Var mgmt courses. *Appointments:* Regl Mgr, Calcutta; Suptd, Small Bus Fin, Intl Banking; Principal, United Bank of India Staff Col, Calcutta 1979-83. *Publications:* Author 22 titles incl 5 books poems, 4 works of fiction and num essays and biographies; Currently working on Bengal Renaissance, India's Freedom Mvmt. *Memberships:* Fdr & former Secy, Vidyasagar Res Centre; PEN, West Bengal; Asiatic Soc, Calcutta. *Honours:* Vidyasagar Lectures, of Univ Calcutta 1979; Awd'd title Bharat Bhasha Bhushan, by Akhil Bhartiya Bhasha Sahitya Sammelarn Bhopal; PRASAD Awd for Poetry 1986; Delivered talk at Chicago Univ in 1990. *Hobbies:* Reading; Travelling. *Address:* 81 Raja Basanta Roy Road, Calcutta 700 029, India. 3.

ADIBE Ernest Chukwuemeka, b. 22 Dec 1950, Inyi, Nigeria. Sr Univ Lectr; Dean of Fac of Environ Sci. m. Mercy Ogoegbunam, 30 Sept 1978, 2 d. *Education:* BSc Geograpgy 1976; Postgrad Dipl 1979; MSc 1984; Fellow Royal Meteorological Soc of England; PhD 1986. *Appointments:* Asst Lectr 1076-78; Lectr I 1978-80; Sr Lectr & Hd Dept; Dean Fac Environ Scis. *Publications:* Man in Environmental Setting, textbook, 1978; Drive Towards Rural Developing, bk chapt, 1987; The Effects of Global Climate Variability on Water Resources and Agriculture, 1990. *Memberships:* Population Assn of Nigeria; Nigerian Geographical Assn; Nigerian Meteorological Soc; Fellow Royal Meteorological Soc of England; World Climate Change Soc. *Honours:* Best graduating student in master's degree 1984; Fellowship Awd of Royal Meteorological Soc of England 1986. *Hobbies:* Football; Travelling; Lawn tennis; Music. *Address:* Department of Geography and Meteorology, Faculty of Environmental Sciences, Anambra State University of Technology, PMB 01660, Enugu, Nigeria.

ADIELE Moses Nkwachukwu, b. 22 June 1951, Nigeria. Physician. m. Vickie I Eseonu, 7 July 1984, 1 s. 1 d. *Education:* BSHS 1976, Ga Inst Tech; MD 1980, Howard Univ; MPH 1981, Johns Hopkins Univ. *Appointments:* Public Health Clinician 1980-81; Med House Ofcr 1981-84; Dir of Public Health 1984-90; Dir of Med Quality Assurance Prog 1990-. *Creative Works:* Sci Res: Sickle Cell Triat and Sports, 1978; Brain Tumour: What the Primary Physician Needs to Know, 1983. *Memberships:* Active Profl Mem, Am and Va Assn Family Physicians 1982-; US Milit Reserve Ofcrs Assn 1988-; Assn African Physicians in North Am, Pres 1981-84, mem Bd of Dirs 1984-. *Honours:* Who Most Exemplifies a Family Physician Awd 1982; Mead-Johnson Sci Presentation Awd 1983; Physician Recognition Awd 1984, 1990; Community Ser Awd 1984, 1985, 1986, 1989. *Hobbies:* Reading; Writing; Gardening. *Address:* PO Box 24826, Richmond, VA 23224, USA. 2.

ADIGWE Hypolite, b. 30 Aug 1938, Ihiala, Nigeria. Rector All Hallows Seminary; Catholic Priest. *Education:* All Hallows Seminary, Onitsha 1954-58; Bigard Memorial Seminary, Enngu 1959-61; MA DD, Univ Vienna, Austria, 1961-69; PGDE, Univ Ibadan, 1974-75. *Appointments:* Ordained Catholic Priest 1965; Asst Priest, Vienna 1965-69, Orsumoghu 1969-71; Parish Priest, Okija 1970-72; Prof Dogmatic Theol, Ibadan 1972-75; Chancellor and Secy to Archbishop of Onitsha 1975-87; Rector, All Hallows Seminary, Onitsha 1987-. *Publications:* Stations of the Cross, 1974; Women Justice and Evangelisation, co-ed, 1980; Philosophical Motivations, 1982; Prayer Book for Politicians, 1984; Nigeria Joins Organisation of Islamic Conference, 1986; Christian Witness, 1985; Sharia, Canon, Common and Customary Law Courts, 1988; Jubilee Thoughts on Church and Society, 1990. *Memberships:* Constituent Assembly 1988-89; Ed Review Com, Anambra State; Spiritual Dir, CWO Nigeria 1965-87; Nat Chaplain, YCS, Nigeria 1989-. *Honours:* Ife NSO I of Ihiala 1980; Papal Chamberlain with title of Very Rev Monsignor 1984. *Hobbies:* Tennis; Reading; Chess; Photography. *Address:* All Hallows Seminary, PMB 1717, Onitsha, Anambra State, Nigeria. 139, 152.

ADKINS Harvey John, b. 22 Apr 1948, Oklahoma City, USA. Naval Ofcr; Microbiologist. m. Paula Gail North, 6 Jan 1973, 1 s. 1 d. *Education:* BS Microbiol 1971, MS Microbiol 1978, PhD Microbiol 1982, Univ Okla. *Appointments:* Line Ofcr, US Navy, 1971-75; Hd, Microbiol Dept, Naval Hosp, Oakland, 1982-83; Hd, Bacteriol Dept, Naval Med Res Unit No 2, Manila, 1983-86; Hd Microbiol Br, Naval Hosp, Bethesda, Md 1986-89; Asst Course Dir, Naval Sch of Health Scis Detachment, San Juan, PR 1989-. *Publications:* 7 pub sci arts. *Memberships:* Am Soc for Microbiol; Assn Milit Surgeons of the US; Phi Sigma Biol Res Hon Soc. *Honours:* Milit: Raytheon Awd for Outstanding Grad of ASW Sch, Newport, RI 1973; Nat Defense Ser Medal 1970; Pistol Expert Medal 1974; Overseas Ser Ribbon 1986, 6 awds; Humanitarian Ser Medal 1991; Civil: Selection to Phi Sigma 1977; Univ Okla Discretionary Res Aid Awd 1979. *Hobbies:* Playing tennis; Watching other sports; Astronomy & physics; Travel. *Address:* Naval School of Health Sciences Bethesda Detachment, Veterans Administration Medical Centre, One Veterans Plaza, San Juan, PR 00927, USA. 7.

ADRIAN (Warne) John Adrian Marie Edward, b. 29 Jan 1938, London, England. Admr. *Education:* Dulwich Col, London; Salesian Col, Burwash, Sussex. *Appointments:* RAF, served in Cyprus 1955-58; Singer and Dancer 1959-72; Performed at London Palladium, Moulin Rouge Paris, Carre Theatre Amsterdam; Theatre Mgr: Nat Youth Theatre, London; Stoll Theatres, London; St George's Theatre, London; Garrick Theatre, London; Royal Cultural Centre, Amman, Jordan; Theatre Royal, Windsor 1972-86; Secy & Administrator, Grand Order of Water Rats 1986-. *Memberships:* Brit Actors Equity; Soc for Theatre Res; Green Room Club. *Hobbies:* Theatre research; AIDS counselling; Swimming; Cycling. *Address:* Grand Order of Water Rats, 328 Gray's Inn Road, London WC1X 8BZ, England.

AEBERHARD John Peter, b. 6 Mar 1937, London, England. PR Conslt. m. Penelope Jane Rankin, 5 Sept 1964, 3 s. *Education:* MA Oxon Modern History 1961, Corpus Christi Col, Oxford. *Appointments:* Press Ofcr, Michelin Tyre Co Ltd 1962-66; Press Ofcr, ICL/Eng Elect Computers Ltd 1966-69; Conslt, Carl Byoir & Assocs 1969-75; Dir, PR, Honeywell UK 1975-78; Dir, PR, Advtg, Honeywell Info Systems, US 1978-80; Mng Dir, A Plus Gp Ltd, 1981-. *Publications:* Num arts on PR. *Memberships:* Inst Dirs; PR Conslts Assn. *Hobbies:* Travel; Walking; Running; History; Architecture; Rowing. *Address:* Millstones, Egypt Lane, Farnham Common, Buckinghamshire SL2 3LF, England.

AFZELIUS Bjorn Arvid, b. 30 June 1925, Stockholm. Prof. m. Ulla Elisabeth Fogelberg, 24 May 1957, 2 d. *Education:* PhD 1957, Stockholm Univ. *Appointments:* Prof, Biol Ultrastructure Res, Stockholm Univ. *Publications:* Anatomy of the Cell, 1964; The Biology of the Sperm Cell, 1976. *Memberships:* Nordic Soc Cell Biol; Scandinavian Soc Electron Microscopy. *Honours:* MD h c, Karolinska Inst, 1981; PhD h c, Univ Siena, 1986. *Hobbies:* Reading; Writing; Nature. *Address:* Department of Ultrastructure Research, Stockholm University, S-106 91 Stockholm, Sweden. 50.

AGARDI Peter, b. 15 Apr 1946, Budapest. Lit Historian; Critic. m. Zsuzsanna Malek, 11 Feb 1977, 2 d. *Education:* Eotvos Lorand Univ Budapest, Fac Arts, 1965-70; Doctorate in Hungarian Lit & Librarianship 1982; Candidate in Lit 1983. *Appointments:* Inst of Lit of Hung Acad of Sci 1970-75; Cultural Dept of the Hung Leading Party 1975-85; VP Hung Radio 1985- 90; Sr Mem Lukacs Gyorgy Archiv of Hung Acad Sci 1991-. *Publications:* About the Hungarian Baroque in 17 century, 1972; Fr. Fejtö's Literary work over the 1930's, 1982; Literary and Critical Essays, 1985; Ille's Mónus, the Social-democrate politician and writer, 1992. *Membership:* Assn of Hung Lit History. *Honours:* Sub Auspiciis Rei Publicae Popularis 1973; Prize Jozsef Attila 1987. *Address:* Bebo Karoly u 5, Budapest H-1038, Hungary.

AGGISS Liz, b. 28 May 1953, Essex, England. Dancer; Choreographer. *Education:* Madeley Col; Nikolais/Louis Dance Theatre Lab, NY. *Career:* Choreographer, Performer, Artistic Dir, in collaboration with Billy Cowie, of & with: The Wild Wigglers, formed 1982 touring world wide; With Divas Dance Co, formed 1985; Incl Torei En Veran Veta Arnold 1986-87; Eleven Execution 1988; Dorothy & Klaus 1989-91; Die Orchidee im Plastik Karton 1989-91; Drool and Drivel They Care 1990-91; La Petite Soupe 1990-91; La Chanson Bien Douce 1991; Solo performances incl: Grotesque Dancer 1986-89; Stations of the Angry 1989; Tell Tale Heart 1989; El Punal Entra En El Corazon 1991; Cafeteria for A Sit Down Meal, 1992; Commissions incl: Dead Steps/Die Toten Scritte 1988-89; For Extemporary Dance Theatre, Banda Banda, and La Soupe for Carousel 1989-90. *Honours:* Colorado Col Summer Scholarship, study Hanya Holm, 1980; Zap Awd for Dance, for Divas 1989 and La Soupe 1990; Alliance & Leicester Awd for La Soupe 1990; Time Out/Dance Umbrella Awd for Banda Banda 1990; BBC/Arts Council Dance for Camera Award, 1992. *Hobbies:* Cinema; Music. *Address:* 92, Centurion Road, Brighton, E. Sussex, BN1 3LN, England. 138.

AGHENTA Joseph Amiokhe, b. 24 Aug 1941, Emu, Bendel, Nigeria. Prof Ednl Planning. m. 4 Mar 1972, 4 s. 2 d. *Education:* BEd Hons 1968; MEd 1972; PhD 1979. *Appointments:* Non grad Sec Sch Tchr 1961-64; Grad Tchr 1968-74; Vice Principal 1974-75; Lectr 1975-79; Sr Lectr 1979-82; Ass Prof 1982-84; Prof 1984-; Dean of Ed 1985-89; Commr for Ed in Bendel State of Nigeria. *Publications:* Towards Efficiency in School Management, ed, 1980; Middle Level Manpower Training, ed, 1983; Educational Planning, 1991; 58 arts & chapts in books. *Memberships:* Nigerian Ednl Res Assn, Edit Advr; Ed Studies Assn; Nigerian Assn for Ednl Admin and Planning, Pres; Mem, C'Wealth Coun for Ednl Admin; Pres, Nigerian Assoc of Ed Admin and Planning; Nigerian Acad of Ed, Nat Assn Secy; Soc for Res into Higher Ed. *Honours:* Bendel State Scholar 1970; Fed Govt Scholar 1971-72; Univ Benin NASA Decoration 1989; C'Wealth Fellowship 1988-89. *Hobbies:* Reading; Analysing current and world affairs; Mysticism and religion; Little gardening. *Address:* Faculty of Education, University of Benin, Benin City, Nigeria.

AGNAIEFF Michel, b. 16 Sept 1939, Cairo, Egypt. Union Exec. m. Normande Villeneuve, 30 Dec 1985, 3 s. 1 d. *Education:* Col de la Salle Cairo Bacc francais 2eme partie 1958; Centre pedagogique La Sallien Cairo Cert d'aptitude pedagogique 1959Min Edn Que Brevet A 1967; Univ Montreal, studies in French Lit & Linguistics 1967-69; Laval Univ, postgrad studies in Policy Analysis 1981-83. *Appointments:* Tchr 1959-63; Mem film ind 1963-66 Cairo; Sec Sch Tchr and Hd French Dept Can 1966-70; Union Ofcr and Exec mem Alliance des Professeurs de Montreal 1968-71; Secy, CEQ 1971-72; Dir Communications 1972-76; Dir-Gen Centrale de l'Enseignement du Quebec (CEQ) 1976-. *Memberships:* Past Assoc Pres NDP Can; Vice Pres, Candn Comm for UNESCO, 1992-; General Secretary Comite' syndical francophone de l'education et de la formation, 1989-. *Address:* 1037 J J Joubert, Duvernay, Laval, Quebec, Canada H7G 4J5.

AGNIHOTRI Prabhu Dayalu, b. 20 July 1914, Shahjahanpur, UP. Prof. m. Sharda, 20 June 1941, 1 s. 1 d. *Education:* Sahitya Ratna (Hindi) 1937; Vyakaranacharya 1938; MA in Sanskrit 1950; PhD in Indalogy 1960. *Appointments:* Principal, Vidya Mandir, Akala 1942-54; Lectr, Jabalpur Univ 1954-60; Prof of Sanskrit, Gwaliar Univ 1960-69; Dir, Granth Acad 1969-72; Vice Chancellor, Jabalpur Univ 1973-76. *Publications:* Patanjali Kalina Bharat; Vedic Devala Darphan; Abhinav Manovignanam; Sanskrit Sahitya Chintan; Agnigarbha, collection of poems. *Memberships:* Pres, Hindi Sahilya Sammelan, MP; Pres, MP Historical Soc; Pres, Vedic Section of AIOC; VP, All India Oriental Conf; Res Degree ComSelection Bd; Bd of Studies in over 12 univs. *Honours:* Special hon and awd by Sanskrit Acad, UP; H C conferred by All India Hindi Sahitya, 1984; Cert of Hon by Pres of India Sammelan; Freedom Fighter's Cert, Copper Plate and Pension by Govt of India. *Hobbies:* Sightseeing; Travelling; Visiting mountains and sea coasts, beaches & archaeological places; Listening to classical Indian music and watching classical dance; Reading books. *Address:* E2/73 Mahavir Nagar, Bhopal (MP) 462016, India.

AGRAWAL Surendra Prasad, b. 23 May 1929, Gowan, India. Conslt Info Sci. *Education:* BSc 1949, BA 1952, Agra Univ; Cert in Lib Sci 1952, MA (Eng Prev) 1954, Aligarth Muslim Univ; French Course, Sch of For Langs, Govt of India, New Delhi 1966. *Appointments:* Sci Tchr & Tchr ic Library, District Bd Higher Sec Sch, Gabhana 1951-52; Lectr in Lib Sci (Hony), Aligarth Muslim Univ 1952; Librarian in var Libraries in New Delhi 1954-70; Documentation Ofcr, UNESCO Div, Min Ed, New Delhi 1970-72; Dep Dir, Documentation, ICSSR, New Delhi 1972-77; Coord, Study Centre, and Counsellor, Lib & Info Sci, Andhra Pradesh Open Univ, Northern Regl Centre 1985-86; Hon Conslt, Indira Gandhi Nat Open Univ, New Delhi, 1986-88; Divl Hd, Documentation, Indian Coun of Social Sci Res (ICSSR), New Delhi 1977-79; Dir, Nat Social Sci Documentation Centre, ICSSR, New Delhi 1979-88; Mem Secy, Indian Assn of Social Sci Insts, New Delhi 1988-89; Currently: Mem Hindi Adv Com, Min of Coal, Govt of India, New Delhi; Mem Bd of Studies of Sch of Archival Studies, Nat Archives of India, Govt of India. *Publications:* 35 books and monographs; 67 mimeographed pubs. *Memberships include:* Fellow: United Writers Assn, Mylapore, India; World Lit Acad; Life Mem: Acad of Info Sci; Acad Lib & Info Sers; Assn Gvt Librarians and Info Scists; Assn Writers Illustrators for Children; Authors Guild of India; 13 others; Also mem of 12 academic & profl assns and 5 social ser orgs. *Honours:* PhD in Ed hc by Intl Univ Foun 1988; D R Kalia Award for NASSDOC, Assn of Govt Librarians & Info Scists; Freedom Fighters Samman Pension. *Address:* B5/73 Azad Apartments, Sri Aurobindo Marg, New Delhi-110016, India. 3, 52, 93, 152.

AGUS Ayke, b. 30 Dec 1949, Indonesia. Concert Pianist; Chamber Mus Collaborator; Violinist. m. Michael Palotai, 1 Aug 1976, 1 d. *Education:* Studied as Violinist with Jascha Heifetz at USC; Bachelor's degree 1974; Master's degree in Performance on Piano with highest hons 1976. *Career:* Violinist, Buffalo Philharmonic 1969; Pianist in Master Classes of Jascha Heifetz 1972, and was his accompanist till his death in 1987; Served on USC Piano Fac 1974-82. *Creative Works:* Transcriptions: for violin & piano completed Jascha Heifetz' unfinished work on Gershwin's An American in Paris; Arranged Haydn's quartet for violin & piano; Mozart's Oboe Qrt for piano, violin, sopr, saxophone; Recorded piano solos, and as Collaborator for Protone label; Manuscript in progress: Accompanying Heifetz-my life for 15 years, a personal view. *Honours:* 1st Prize winner in piano compt at Rosary Hill Col, 1969; 2nd Prize winner in violin compt for the Young Musician Foun in Buffalo, NY 1970. *Hobbies:* Reading; Walking; Hiking; Nature; Cooking; Writing. *Address:* 1493 S Stearns Drive, Los Angeles, CA 90035, USA.

AHMAD Naeem, b. 15 Mar 1946, Lahore, Pakistan. Univ Tchr. m. Nasreen Ara, 14 Apr 1978, 3 s. *Education:* FA 1963, Islamia Col, Lahore; BA 1965, MA 1967, PhD 1988, Univ of the Punjab, Lahore. *Appointments:* Res Asst, Inst Edn & Res, PU 1968; Lectr Dept Phil 1967-83, Asst Prof 1983-, U Panjab Lahore; Lectr Dept Religious Studies and Phil, Kampala, Uganda 1978-80. *Publications:* History of Greek Philosophy, 1972; History of Modern Philosophy, 1983; Bergson's Philosophy, 1988; Iqbal's Concept of Immortality, 1989; Author 40 res arts. *Memberships:* Pakistan Philosophical Cong; Allama Iqba Intl Cong, organising com; Acad Staff Assn, Univ Panjab; Thinkers Alliance, Lahore, Pres 1986-88; Wilson Ctr Assocs, Boulder, Colorado, Secy-Treas, Mashal, Pakistan; Pres Alumni Assn, Dept Phil, Univ

Panjab 1988-. *Hobbies:* Literature; Photography. *Address:* E-48 Staff Colony, New Campus, Lahore 54590, Pakistan.

AHMAD Toheed, b. 15 Oct 1947, Lahore. Diplomat. m. Nausheen Ahmad, 22 Dec 1983, 2 s. *Education:* MA, Univ Punjab, Lahore. *Appointments:* Third Secy: Pakistan Emb, Paris 1973; Tunis 1973-76; 2nd Secy, Pakistan Emb, Hanoi 1976-79; Dir, M/O Foreign Affairs, Islamabad 1979- 83; Counsellor, Damascus, Pakistan Emb 1984-87; Min, Brussels, Pakistan Emb 1987-91. *Memberships:* Soc for South Asian Studies, London; Fdr mem, Iqbal Foun Europe, Brussels. *Honours:* Best Grad, FC Col, Lahore 1969; Gold Medal for first class hons in MA Eng, Univ of Punjab 1969. *Hobbies:* Reading; Languages; Computers; Cricket. *Address:* Director General, Ministry of Foreign Affairs, Islamabad, Pakistan.

AHMED Bolakale Ally Sardauna, b. 20 Oct 1967, Ilorin. Counselling Psycho. *Education:* Lafiagi F C 1978-83; Univ of Ilorin 1985-89. *Appointments:* Kwara Ed Mgmt Bd 1990-. *Creative Works:* Factors Influencing Students Performance in Geography in Ilorin LGA. *Membership:* Counselling Assn of Nigeria. *Honour:* Univ of Ilorin Postgrad Scholarship 1991. *Hobbies:* Reading; Travelling; Photography; Tennis. *Address:* 3 Pakata Road, Isaleoja Daudin's Compound, Ilorin, Kinara State, Nigeria.

AHMED Hasan Shareef, b. 19 Mar 1954, Comilla, Bangladesh. Publication Ofcr; Assoc Edit. m. Syeda Sajeda Hasan, 22 Feb 1981, 1 s. 1 d. *Education:* B Com Hons in Mgmt 1975; M Com in Mgmt 1976; LLB 1981; Tng in communication, editing and publication 1985, 1986. *Appointments:* Mng Edit, The Daily Millat 1977; Exec Dir, Book Promotion Ltd 1978-79; Publication Ofcr, Intl Centre for Diarrhoeal Disease Res, Bangaldesh (ICDDR,B) 1980-; Assoc Edit, Glimpse, ICDDR,B 1986- . *Publications:* Directory of Asian Diarrhoeal Disease Scientists and Practitioners, Co-compiler, 1985; Rice-based Oral Rehydration, 1987; Islamic Stories for Children, 1989. *Memberships:* VP and Fdr Life Mem, Editing and Publication Assn of Bangladesh 1987; Life Mem, Bangladesh Population Assn 1984; Bangladesh Ec Assn 1989; Progs Com, Mgmt Professionals Assn, Madras, India 1985-. *Honours:* Champion in Chess Compt of Fac of Commerce, Univ of Dhaka, 1975; IDRC Grant 1985 (India); IRRI Scholarship 1986 (Philippines). *Hobbies:* Reading; Gardening; Travelling. *Address:* 29 Purana Paltan, Dhaka 1000, Bangladesh.

AHOOJA-PATEL Krishna, b. 15 Mar 1929, Amritsar, India. Res Scholar. m. Prof Surendra J Patel, Sept 1950, 3 s. *Education:* BA in Polit Sci; Bar-at-Law, Inner Temple; MA in Ec of Industrialization; PhD in Intl Relats. *Appointments:* Foreign Correspondent, Economic & Political Weekly, Bombay 1965-67; Intl Labour Org, 1968-86; Dep Dir, UN/INSTRAW 1986-89; Nancy Rowell Jacjman Chair in Women's Studies, Mount Saint Vincent Univ, Halifax, Nova Scotia 1990, 1991. *Publications:* Edit, Women Studies & Development; Co-Edit, World Economy in Transition, 1986; Edit, Women in Economic Activity, ILO/INSTRAW, 1985. *Memberships:* Soc for Intl Devel; Cndn Assn for Studies in Intl Devel; Assn for Women in Devel; Cndn Women's Studies Assn. *Honour:* Italian Silver Medal 1989 for Intl Work on Women & Devel. *Hobbies:* Painting; Reading; Travelling. *Address:* Institute for the Study of Women, Mount Saint Vincent University, 166 Bedford Highway, Halifax, Nova Scotia, Canada B3M 2J6.

AHRENS Michael Heinz, b. 18 Dec 1949, Helmstedt. Trade Assn Admr. m. Christiane von Roden, 30 Mar 1972, 2 d. *Education:* MS in Chem 1974 (Dipl); Dr Ing 1979. *Appointments:* Sci Collaborator, Tech Univ Clausthal-Zellerfeld 1975-79; Sci Secy, Univ Georgia Augusta, Goettingen 1979- 85; Innovation Conslt, Chamber of Ind & Commerce, Oldenburg 1986-90; Dep Mgr, Chamber of Ind & Commerce, Oldenburg 1990- . *Memberships:* Fac Dept of Physics, Univ Goettingen

1981-85; Fdr Mem, Union for Cooperation between Sci & Ind, Goettingen 1985. *Hobby:* Member of the German Philatelic Soc. *Address:* Margarete-Gramberg-Strasse 16, D-W-2900 Oldenburg (Oldb), Germany.

AHRONOVITCH Yuri, b. 13 May 1933, Leningrad, USSR. Conductor. m. Tamar Sakson, 20 May 1973. *Education:* Grad Leningrad Conservatory of Music 1954; Prof Mus 1958-. *Career:* Principal Conductor and Mus Dir: Moscow Radio Symphony Orch 1964-72; Cologne Philharmonic Orch 1975-86; Stockholm Philharmonic Orch 1982-87; Guest Conductor of var orchestras world wide incl London Symphony Orch, Berlin, Hamburg, Frankfurt, Paris, Zurich, Rome, and Munich Radio Symphony Orchs, The Israel Phil Orchestra and NY Philharmonic Orch; Also Opera Guest Conductor with Bolshoi Theatre Moscow, Royal Opera House Covent Garden, Lyric Opera House Chicago, Main Italian Opera Houses, Munich's State Opera House and others. *Creative Works:* Recordings for Deutsche Grammophon, RCA, Melodia, BIS with London Symphony Orch, Vienna Symphony Orch, Stockholm Philharmonic and Moscow Radio Symphony Orch. *Honours:* Prize for Best Opera Productions, German Music Journal 1977, 1988; Elected mem of Royal Swedish Acad of Mus 1984; Royal Order of the Polar Star by King of Sweden 1987; Israeli Etinger Prize for the Arts 1988. *Address:* c/o Astrid Schoerke, Monckebergalle 41, 3000 Hannover 91, Germany. 21.

AHTIALA Kaarlo Pekka, b. 12 June 1935, Helsinki, Finland. Prof Ec. m. Anna-Maija Komsi, 24 Sept 1960, 1 s. 2 d. *Education:* BBA 1956, MBA 1958, Helsinki Sch of Ec; PhD 1964, Harvard Univ. *Appointments:* Tchg Fellow in Ec 1961-63, Instr in Ec 1964, Harvard Univ; Prof Ec 1965, Dean, Fac of Ec & Admin 1969-71, Univ Tampere, Finland; Min of Ec Affairs, Govt of Finland 1975; Vstg Prof Northwestern, Princeton Univs, Consultant, IMF, World Bank, sev central banks and govts, incl US Fedl Reserves System. *Publications:* Index-linked Debts, 1967; A Monetary Theory of the International Economy, 1967; Monetary Policy in National and International Economics, in International Monetary Fund, International Reserves: Needs and Availability, 1970; A General Equilibrium Model of the Balance of Payments; Arts in profl jours. *Memberships include:* Finland Jr C of C, Secy Gen 1957-59; Special Study Gp of the IMF on Intl Reserve Problems; Nobel Prize Com in Ec, Nomination Col; Finnish Coop Banks' Central Bank, Dir; Coop Bank of Tampere, Chm of Bd; Univ of Tampere, Trustee 1975-76, 1983-85, Chm of the Bd of Trustees 1979-80; Finnish Inst of Mgmt, Trustee 1971-76; Ec Coun of Finland, Vice Chm 1975, Alternate Mem 1976; Finnish Acad of Scis and Letters 1986-. *Honours:* Var Milit Medals for Finno-Russia War 1941-44; Blue Cross of Finland; Earhart Prize; Jaycees Intl, Senator (hon mem) 1974-; Omicron Delta Epsilon, Hon Mem, 1976; Knight Commander, Order of the Lion of Finland 1976; World Culture Prize, Centro Studi e Richerche Delle Nazioni, Italy 1985. *Address:* Liutunkuja 3, 36240 Kangasala, Finland. 6, 43, 52, 90, 130, 134, 139, 152.

AHUJA Hira Nand, b. 15 Mar 1929, Bannu, India. Profl Engrng Educ Provider; Prof. m. Mrs Kamal Ahuja, 14 Oct 1951, 1 s. 2 d. *Education:* Cert in Civil Engrg 1946, Brit India Tech Col; BA 1952, Panjab Univ; MASc 1969, Univ of Waterloo. *Appointments:* Resident Engr, K C Thapar & Bros Ltd 1952-66; Prof, Civil Engrg, Memorial Univ of Newfoundland 1969-84; Prof & Dir, Continuing Ed Div, Tech Univ of Nova Scotia, Halifax 1984-92; Adjunct Prof, Dept of Civil Engrg, Univ of Toronto, 1992-. *Publications:* Author of 4 books in the field of civil engrg and project mgmt; Co-Author, Successful Methods in Cost Engineering, 1983; Construction Estimating, 1987; Author & Co-Author 30 papers in tech jours and conf proceddings; Developer, Orgr and Supvr over 1200 Tech Advancement Seminars & Short Courses; Presenter, technical papers & keynote speaker. *Memberships include:* Fellow, Canadian Soc for Civil Engrg, Tech Prog Chmn ATL Reg 1988-92; Assn Profl

Engrs of Nova Scotia; Intl Assn Continuing Engrg Ed; Canadian Construction Res Bd 1983-87; Chmn, Construction Cost Mgmt Com, Am Assn Cost Engrs 1982-86. *Hobby:* Reading. *Address:* President, Engineering Program Innovations Centre, PO Box 9051, Station A, Halifax, Nova Scotia, Canada. 88.

AINE Veli Valo, b. 17 Feb 1919, Tornio, Finland. Counsellor of Commerce. m. Eila Rantanen, 23 June 1942, 1 s. 3 d. *Education:* Commercial Col of Bus, Helsinki. *Appointments:* Mng Dir & Owner, Bd Chm, Pres, Aine Oy, Tornio-Oulu-Rovaniemi-Kemi. *Creative Works:* Fdr, Aine Art Museum, Tornio, Finland, collection over 1400 pieces; Fdr: Aine Picture Foun, Lappi Picture Foun, Pohjois-Pohjanmaa Picture Foun. *Memberships:* Finnish Central C of C; Lappi C of C; Cultural Founs, Finland & Lappi; Automobile Assn, Finland; Hotel Assn of Finland; North Finland Fiar; Finland-Am Assn. *Honours:* Councillor of Commerce, 1969; Commander, Cross of Lion of Finland, 1975; Cross of Liberty, 3rd & 4th class, with Oak Leaf 1941, with Sword 1944; Knight Commander, Cross of Order of Lazarus; Chevalier Art et Lettres, France. *Hobbies:* Collecting pictures & old books; Rotary; Masons. *Address:* Uusikatu 1, SF-95 400 Tornio, Finland.

AIZINBUD Eliezer, b. 23 Feb 1921, Kirsanov, USSR. Retd Prof. m. Masha, May 1945, dec, 1 s. 1 d. *Education:* Lithuanian Vet Acad & Troick Vet Inst 1939-43; PhD in Animal Physiol 1940, Inst Exp Vet, Moscow; DSc in Animal Physiol 1959, Pavlov Inst of Physiol, Leningrad. *Appointments:* Lectr 1946, Asst Prof 1951-, Full Prof, Hd Dept of Animal Physiol 1959-72, Lithuanian Vet Akad, Kaunas; Sr Reschr, Inst Anim Sci, Agri Res Org, Bet Dagan, Israel 1973-88; Retd. *Publications:* The Initiator of the Studies of Electrical Impedance of Female Genitalia During the Ovulatory Cyclus, first publication, 1962; Pathological Physiology of Farm Animals, book, 1963. *Memberships:* Israel Vet Med Assn; Israel Soc for Med & Biol Engrg. *Honours:* Honoured Scist of the Republic, Vilnius, Lithuania 1971; Kimron Awd on Vet Med, Israel 1987. *Hobby:* Reading. *Address:* Kerem Haseitim 3, POB 3366, Savyon-56540, Israel.

AKAGU Christian Chukwudi, b. 10 Oct 1949, Awka. Univ Lectr; Arch. m. Ifeoma Chidinma, 11 Oct 1980, 2 s. 1 d. *Education:* BES (Hons) 1975, MED (Archt) 1977, Univ Lagos; Regd Arch by ARCON 1981. *Appointments:* Arch, Ella, Waziri Assocs 1977-78; Resident Arch, Fry, Drew Atkinson, Maiduguri 1978-83; Principal Ptnr, Starlite Des Conslts 1983-88; Lectr 1988-90, Sr Lectr 1990, Hd Dept of Arch & Bldg 1989-91, Anambra State Univ of Tech, Enugu; Hd, Dept of Arch, Nnamdi Azikiwe Univ, Awka, 1992-. *Creative Works:* 14 important commissions incl High Rise Office Block and Warehouse, Kano 1977; Book House, Onitsha, 1985; Market, Rivers State 1991; Students' Centre & Hostel, Enugu 1991; Over 60 Residential Houses; Author 6 books incl Effective Maintenance of Buildings and Infrastructure: Attitudes and Cost Implications, 1991. *Memberships:* Nigerian Inst of Archs; Assn Archl Edrs in Nigeria; Assoc Mem, Nigerian Inst Mgmt. *Hobbies:* Farming; Reading; Squash; Tennis; Classical music. *Address:* Department of Architecture, Nnamdi Azikiiwe University, Awka, Nigeria.

AKANDE Adewale Olalere, b. 2 Apr 1952, Ogbomosho, Nigeria. Univ Tchr. m. Taiwo Theresa, 12 Dec 1981, 3 d. *Education:* BSc in Botany 1972, Unibadan; MSc in Ecol & Bryol 1980; PhD in Bryol 1985; Specialist in Eco-physiol & Pollution Monitoring. *Appointments:* Sec Sch Tchr 1977- 79; Univ Tchr, Ogun State Univ 1983-85, Ondo State Univ 1985-; Sr Lectr 1989; Acting Chair of Botany 1991-92. *Publications:* 10 jour arts; 1 sec sch book; Initiated 2 res works of nat interest. *Memberships:* Fellow, Linnean Soc of London; Bot Soc Nigeria; Ecol Soc Nigeria; Sci Assn Nigeria; Intl Soc for Tropical Ecol. *Honour:* Ibadan Univ Scholar 1979-84. *Hobbies:* Photography; Travelling; Gardening. *Address:*

Dept of Botany, Ondo State University, Ado-Ekiti, Nigeria.

AKAY Erdil K, b. 22 Oct 1936, Athens. Career Diplomat; Amb. m. H Nukhet Selen, 18 Feb 1977, 1 s. 1 d. *Education:* Polit Scis Fac, Univ Ankara 1959. *Appointments:* Candidate Career Ofcr, Dept Intl Ec Affairs and Pvt Ofc Min, Turkish For Min (MOFA) 1959-60; Milit Ser 1960-61; 3rd Secy at NATO Dept, MOFA 1962-63; Second then 1st Secy, Turkish Emb, Wash, USA 1963- 66; 1st Secy, Turkish Emb, New Delhi, India 1966-68; Hd of Sect, Dept Mutual Security Affairs, MOFA 1968-70; Polit Advr, Intl Staff, NATO HQ, Brussels 1970-72; Dep Chf of Mission, Turkish Del to Coun of Europe, Strasbourg, 1973- 75; Acting Hd, Dept Defence Planning Dept, MOFA 1975-76; Dir Cabinet of Pres of the Repub, Ankara 1976-80; Turkish Amb to repub Korea, Seoul 1980-82; Amb at Large, Ankara 1982; Special Polit Advr to Pres of Republic, Ankara 1982-84; Mem Policy Planning Bd, MOFA 1984-85; Amb to Algeria, Algiers 1985- 89; Amb to Swden 1989-91. *Memberships:* Assn of Grads from Galatasaray, Ankara; Anadolu Klubu, Ankara; Intl Inst for Strategic Studies, London. *Honours:* Medallion of the Pres of the Repub for Meritorious Sers, Turkey 1980; Order of Diplomatic Ser Merit, Heung-in Medal, Korea 1982; Nat Security Coun Shield for Outstanding Sers, Turkey 1982. *Hobbies:* Turkish history; Intl strategic issues; Art; Tennis; Photography. 12.

AKERSTROM-HOUGEN Gunilla Ingrid Elisabeth, b. 6 Feb 1933, Uppsala, Sweden. Asst Prof; Lectr. m. Frithjof W Hougen, 1 Mar 1956. *Education:* Studies in Gothenburg and Greece; PhD 1974; Mem Bd of Comm for Sweden's Nat Museums 1981-87. *Appointments:* Asst Prof 1974, Lecturer 1976-, Univ Gothenburg. *Publications:* The Calendar and Hunting Mosaics of the Villa of the Falconer in Argos, 2 vols, 1974; Falconry as a Motif in Early Swedish Art, 1981. *Memberships:* Brit Assn of Art Historians; Swedish Inst in Athens; Swedish Inst in Rome. *Hobbies:* Falconry; Music; Travel. *Address:* University of Gothenburg, Department of Art History, Dicksonsgatan 2, S-412 56 Gothenburg, Sweden.

AKHTAR S Sultan, b. 3 Apr 1933, Bettiah, India. Tchg Prof of Psycho. m. Nafees Fatima, 27 Dec 1966, 2 s. 1 d. *Education:* MSc in Psycho 1957; PhD in Psycho 1963. *Appointments:* Lectr 1962-75; Reader 1975-85; Prof 1985-. *Publications:* 45 res papers in nat and intl jours of psycho. *Memberships:* Indian Psycho Assn, Exec Com Mem; Indian Acad of Applied Psycho, Life mem 1983-, Regl Pres 1985-89, Pres 1990-; Sports Psycho Assn of India, Exec Com Mem 1984-87, VP 1989-. *Honours:* Best Tchr Awd 1989, Lions Club Aligarh; Var posts and positions both academic and in the field of sport, AMU 1976-. *Hobbies:* Games and sport esp soccer, awd'd Colours by AMU Aligarh 1953-54, one time profl footballer. *Address:* Director of Career Planning Centre, AMU Aligarh 202002, (UP), India.

AKIMA Minoru, b. 3 Feb 1928, Tokyo. Director Prof. m. Emmi Krüger, 22 Dec 1956, 2 d. *Education:* Study of Western Phil, Univ Tokyo 1948-51; Advanced study there with State Scholarship 1951-54; Dipl for Phil. *Appointments:* Lectr then Assoc Prof, Univ Hokkaido 1954-68; Assoc Prof then Prof, Tokyo Metropolitan Univ 1968-91; Currently Prof Emeritus, Tomin Col (Tokyo Citizens Col). *Publications:* Author: Contemporary Sciences and Materialism, 1971; Essays in Philosophy of Science, 1974; Formation of Contemporary Physical Science and its Logic, 1979; An Introduction to Philosophy, 1981; Translator: F Engels, Ludwig Feuerbach, 1983; K Löwith, Nazism and My Life, 1990. *Memberships:* The Philosophical Assn of Japan, mem Directorate 1977-91; Japan Soc for Studies in Materialism, Pres 1984-86, 1988-90. *Hobbies:* Reading; Listening to music esp classic symphonies & concertos; Visiting art galleries & museums; Interest: Feminist movement & researches. *Address:* 2-21-23 Kotsubo, Zushi-shi, Kanagawa-ken, Japan.

AKIN Hikmet, b. 11 Nov 1948, Bozuyuk, Turkey. Pres Uranerz Exploation & Mining Ltd. m. Eva Maria Zang, 5 May 1978, 1 s. 2 d. *Education:* MSc Geol 1971, PhD Engrg (Mining Geol) 1974, Venia Legendi in Mining Geol & Mineral Ec 1978, Tech Univ of Berlin, Germany. *Appointments:* Asst Prof 1974-78, Lectr & Assoc Prof 1978-85, Prof 1985-, Tech Univ Berlin; Concurrently: Var positions with Uranerzbergbau-GmbH, Bonn 1978-88; Gen Mgr & VP Mining, Uranerz USA Inc, Denver 1988-90; Exec VP, Uranerz Exploration & Mining Ltd (Canada) and Uranerz USA Inc 1990-91; Pres & Chf Operating Ofcr, Uranerz Exploration & Mining Ltd (Canada) and Uranerz USA Inc 1991-. *Publications:* Praktische Geostatistik, co-Author textbook, 1988; Over 15 sci papers. *Memberships:* 10 assns incl: Mining & Metallurgical Assn; Canadian Inst of Mining, Metallurgy & Petroleum; Soc of Mining Engrs, USA; Intl Assn of Mathematical Geol; Supporters of Mining & Metallurgy at TU Berlin; Frat of Miners and Metallurgists. *Honour:* Robart-Scheibe Prize 1971, Tech Univ Berlin. *Hobbies:* Sporting activities; Fishing. *Address:* Uranerz Exploration & Mining Limited, 1300 Saskatoon Square, 410-22nd Street East, Saskatoon, Saskatchewan, Canada S7K 5T6.52.

AKINS Thomas, b. 15 Oct 1951, Atlanta, Georgia. Dir. m. Linda Ann Melton, 24 Aug 1974, 2 s. *Education:* Bachelor Industrial Engrg 1974 (Coop Plan), Ga Inst Tech; MBA 1977, Ga State Univ. *Appointments:* Mgmt Engr, First Nat Bank of Atlanta 1974-76; Ga Inst Tech, Coop Div 1976-. *Memberships:* Coop Ed Div of Am Soc for Engrg Ed, Nat Chmn, Secy- Treas; Ga Consortium for Intl Coop Ed, Co-Fdr & Pres; Conslt, Southeast Tng Centre for Coop Ed; Boy Scouts of Am, Pack Chmn. *Honours:* ASEE/CED, Chmn's Awd 1986; Best Prog Session 1990. *Hobbies:* Sports-running, basketball, softball; Boy Scouts of America; Church activities. *Address:* Cooperative Division, Georgia Institute of Technology, Atlanta, GA 30332, USA.

AKINYELE Alexander Opeyemi, Chief, b. 24 Apr 1938, Ondo. Min of Info, Nigeria. m. 18 Oct 1967, 4 s. 2 d. *Education:* BA (Hons) Eng 1966, Univ Ife (now OAU). *Appointments:* Tchr, Gboluji Grammar Sch 1961-63; Vice Principal, Olofin Grammar Sch 1966-67; Career in Dept of Custome & Excise, retd as Asst Controller, 1967-78; Industrialist & PR Conslt 1980-90; Min of Info, Fed Repub Nigeria 1990-. *Memberships:* Secy Gen, Nigerian Inst of PR 1977-80; Intl PR Assn; Inst PR, London; Pres of Ondo, Ondo State Chambers of Commerce, Industries, Mines & Agric; Fed Govt Nominee to the Const Assembly 1988-. *Honours:* Knighted with the Medal of the Order of St Augustine 1982; Tradl Titles of Lisa Jigan of Ondo Land 1982, Bobagunwa of Ikale-Land 1983, Jagunmolu of Ipetu-Ijesha 1985, Bagbimo of Ijebu-Ife 1986, Sasere of Efon Alaye, Toyen of Badagry 1990. *Hobbies:* Lawn tennis; Table tennis; Participating actively in debates and seminars; Writing; Reading; Swimming; Gardening; Horse riding. *Address:* Federal Ministry of Information, 15 Awolowo Road, Ikoyi, Lagos, Nigeria.

AKOBUNDU Enoch Nwankwo T, b. 28 Dec 1948, Umuigu, Oboro. Univ Tchr. m. Comfort N Kanu, 3 July 1972, 3 s. 2 d. *Education:* BSc 1975, Cornell Univ, NY; MSc, PhD 1976-80, LA State Univ, Baton Rouge, LA. *Appointments:* Sr Lectr & Ag Hd, Fed Poly, Akure, Nigeria 1981-83; Sr Lectr & Hd, Fed Univ of Tech, Owerri, Nigeria 1983-91. *Publications:* Author & Co-Author sev sci papers in reputable jours. *Memberships:* Inst Foof Technologist, USA, 1973-89, Profl mem 1989-91; Nigerian Inst Food Sci & Tech; Nutrition Soc of Nigeria. *Honour:* Gerber Foods Prize, USA 1972. *Hobbies:* Gardening; Tennis. *Address:* Department of Food Science and Technology, Federal University of Technology, PMB 1526, Owerri, Nigeria.

AKPALABA Charles Ohaka, b. 22 Sept 1951, Mbaise. Sec Sch Principal. m. Rebecca, 2 Oct 1988, 1 d. *Education:* HSC 1972; BSc 1977; MSc 1985; PGDE 1988; Area of specialisation in biochem & biophysics.

Appointments: Sci Master at Sec Sch Level 1972-73; Grad Asst 1982-85; School Principal, Sci Tchr 1985- . *Publications:* Vegetable tuber lipid analyses: BSc thesis; Biochemical Biophysical investigations of retinal pholic insult: MSc thesis; Biochemical research in ocular chemistry, 1986. *Memberships:* Biochem Assn Nigeria; LGA level Environ Protection Coordinator; Nigerian Union of Tchrs; Supreme Librarian, Eziudo Lib Project; Sci Tchrs Assn Nigeria; LGA Chmn; Community Ecologist. *Honours:* Best grad students prize: in biol 1970, 1972, in biochem 1977, in biophysics 1985; Local Govt Prize for environ devel 1990-91. *Hobbies:* Photography; Amateur geologist/archaeologist; Indefatigable bibliophile; Book collector; Ecological hazards monitor; Creative writing and newspaper columnist in science research; Lecturer. *Address:* Box 129, Obizi Post Office, Ezinihitte Mbaise LGA, Owerri, Imo State, Nigeria.

AL MAQALEH Abdul-Aziz Saleh, b. 1937, Al-Shi'r, Ibb, Yemen. Prof Modern Arabic Lit. m. 1956, 1 s. 4 d. *Education:* BA in Arabic 1971; MA in Arabic 1974; PhD in Arabic Lit 1977. *Appointments:* Dir, Yemen Studies & Res Centre 1978-; Pres, Sanaa Univ 1983- . *Publications:* La Bud Min Sanaa, 1971; Marib Yatakallam, in collaboration with Amb Abdo Othman, 1972; Risala Ila Saif Bin Thgi Yazen, 1973; Hawamish Yamaniyya Alka TaGHREEBAT Ibn Zuraiq Al Baghdadi, 1974; Audat Wadhdhah Al-Yaman, 1976; Al-kitabah bisaif Al-thair Ali Ibn Al-Fadl, 1978; Popular Yemeni Poetry, 1978; Modern Poetry in Yemen, 1978; Al-khurug Min Dawair Al-Saia Al-Suleimaniyya, 1981; Geniuses at the Turn of the Century, 1981; Voices from the New Age - The Dilemma of the Modern Arabic Poem, 1981; Poets From Yemen, 1983; From the verse to the Poem, Kasida, 1983; The Southern Beginnings, 1986; Auraq Al-Gasad Al-aid, 1986; The Meeting of the Edges, 1987; From the Depths of the Hidden to the Revealion, 1991; The Shock of Stone, 1992. *Honour:* Lotus Prize. *Hobbies:* Music; Painting. *Address:* University of Sanaa, P O Box 1247, Sanaa, Yemen.

AL-FISHAWI Sabet Girgis, b. 27 Oct 1930, Cairo, Egypt. m. Zaizef Selim Al-Fishawi, 3 Sept 1961. *Education:* BCom, Heliopolice, Univ of Cairo, 1953; PhD, Petroleum Econ(s), 1986. *Appointments:* Cons Advsr, Coun of Min of Kuwait, -1986; currently working in offs of Cairo & Canada. *Publications include:* International Supervision of Oil Trade. *Memberships:* Int Advt Assn; Int Consultative Bur; Pub Utilities Bur; YMCA; Nat Assn of Acct; Egyptian Shooting Club; Egyptian Rouring Club; Scout Master. *Address:* 68 Abol Maati Street, E'laan Agouza (12311), Cairo, Egypt.

AL-JALLAL Ibrahim A, b. 1952, Saudi Arabia. Saudi Aramco Official. m. Badriyah, 1977, 1 s. 2 d. *Education:* BSc in Geol & Chem, Riyadh Univ; MSc in Geol, Western Mich Univ, USA; PhD in Petroleum Geol, Imperial Col London. *Appointments:* Saudi Aramco Official working in reservoir description of oil & rocks. *Publications:* PhD thesis: Detail Description of the Permian Rocks in Saudi Arabia, its depositional environments, comparsonto recent; Many papers on the subject. *Memberships:* Am Assn Petroleum Geologists; Dhahran Geol Soc; Soc of Petrol Engrs, SA Sect; Soc Ec, Palaeontology & Mineralogy. *Honour:* Cert of Recog for Org a SPE/DGS Symposium. *Hobbies:* Reading; Swimming; Walking. *Address:* PO Box 8066, Saudi Aramco, Dhahran 31311, Saudi Arabia.

AL-KABBANI Samir, b. 4 Nov 1954, Damascus, Syria. MD; Neurologist; Neurosonologist. m. Carmen Irene Kabbani, 7 June 1982. *Education:* MD 1979, Sch Med Univ Damascus; Fellow Neurosonology 1981- 82, Thomas Jefferson Univ; MD Internship & Residency, St Louis Univ, Md 1983- 85; Resident & Chf Resident, Bowman Gray Sch of Med 1985-87. *Appointments:* Rauda Surgical Hosp 1978-80; Jersey Shore Neurology 1987-88; East Tenn Neurology Clinic pc, Knoxville, Tenn 1988-. *Publication:* Res paper at Thomas Jefferson Univ

Med Centre on Neurosonology, Phildelphia 1981-82. *Memberships:* AMA; AAN; AAAS; ASN; Alum AACP; AHA Stroke Coun; SMA; NYAS; SNIVT; NHF; NANJ; AMNJ; AMEEGA; AAEM; AACNP; TMA; TNA; ASCH; ASCNR; ACRM; IMPACT, Legislative Affairs Com. *Honour:* Caritas Krankenhaus Scholarship, Germany 1977. *Hobbies:* Swimming; Boating; Hiking; Walking; Travelling; Foreign Language; Other cultures. *Address:* East Tennessee Neurology Clinic, pc, Baptist Professional Building, Suite 501, Knoxville, TN 37920, USA. 2, 7.

AL-SAMARRAI Asal Yousif Izzidien, b. 27 May 1945, Bacuba. Prof Paediatric Surgery. m. 3 s. 2 d. *Education:* MBChB 1968; FRCS Edinburgh 1976; FACS USA 1989. *Appointments:* Pre-registration year, Cairo Univ Tchg Hosp 1968-69; Tng in Gen and Paediatric Surgery in UK as SHO, Registrar, Sr Registrar, Locum Conslt 1969-76; Lectr 1976-80, Asst Prof 1980-82, Conslt Paediatric Surgeon, Dept Surgery, Med Sch, Mosul, Iraq, Mosul Univ Tchg Hosps, Mosul Univ Children's Hosp; Assoc Prof, Conslt Paediatric Surgeon 1982-85, Prof of Paediatric Surgery and Neonatal Surgery 1985-, Dept Surgery Col Med & King Khalid Univ Hosp; Also Clinical Tchr, Lectr & Tutor. *Publications:* Author or co-Author of 52 publications in the field of paediatrics and neonatal surgery, incl 'Eventration of the diaphragm' 1991; Autotransplantation of Lingual thyroid into the Neck 1988; Circular myotomy for oesophageal stricture 1988; Spontaneous oesophageal perforation in a neonate; Surgery in Infant and Childhood 1989; Cystic hygroma in Arab children 1990; Congenital naso-pharyngeal teratoma 1990; Cryosurgery for Haemangiomatous in infancy and childhood 1989; Webbed penis in Arab children 1990; Midline cervical cleft 1991; Horseshoe lung differential diagnosis 1990; Eventration of the diaphragm 1991; Ambigous genitalia: medical, sociocultural and religious, factors affecting management in Saudi Arabia 1991; 18 papers read in meetings. *Membership:* Brit Assn Paediatric Surgery. *Hobby:* Computer technology. *Address:* Department of Surgery, PO Box 2925, Riyadh 11461, Saudi Arabia.

ALANEN Antti Arvi Tapani, b. 10 Apr 1955, Helsinki. Film Programmer. *Education:* Army Service, Vekaranjarvi 1973-74; MSc in Social Scis 1979, Tampere Univ; Freie Univ, Berlin 1982-86. *Appointments:* Res Asst, Tampere Univ 1974-80; Film Critic & Author of film books 1975-; Translator of books 1984-89; Film Programmer, Finnish Film Archive 1985- . *Publications:* Books: Marilyn: naked mask, 1982; Dark Mirror, 1986; Electric Dreams, 1992; Over 200 arts and essays on the cinema. *Address:* Eerikinkatu 43 C 56, 00180 Helsinki, Finland.

ALBEVERIO Sergio Angelo Ernesto, b. 17 Jan 1939, Lugano, Switzerland. Prof Maths. m. Solvejg Manzoni, 7 Feb 1970, 1 d. *Education:* Dipl thesis 1962, Dr rer nat (PhD) 1966, Maths & Physics, ETH, Zurich; Befahigungsausw, F d Hohere Lehramt, 1966. *Appointments include:* Tchg/Res positions: ETH, Zurich 1962-67; Imperial Col, London, UK 1967-68; Princeton Univ, USA 1969-72; Univ Oslo, Norway 1972-73, 1974-77; Univ Naples, Italy 1973-74; Univ Maiseille Luminy, 1977-78; Univ Bielefeld 1977-79; Full Prof, Ruhr Univ, Bochum 1979-; Co-Dir, Bibos Res Centre (Bielefeld-Bochum Stochastics) 1984-, Res Centre, CERFIM (Locarno), 1985-; Res Appts: var prestigious centres, West Germany, Switzerland, Italy, Japan, France, Norway, USSR, UK, China. *Publications include:* Mathematical Theory of Feynman Path Integrals, co-author, 1976; Non Standard Methods in Stochastic Analysis & Mathematical Physics, co-author, 1986; Solvable Models in Quantum Mechanics, co-author, 1988; Edit, Co-Edit 5 further books; Num sci arts, papers; Editl bds sev sci jours. *Memberships include:* Maths & res establishments, couns & coms, Germany & Switzerland. *Address:* auf dem Aspei 55, D-4630 Bochum 1, Germany.

ALBEVERIO-MANZONI Solvejg Giovanna-Maria, b. 6 Nov 1939, Arogno, Switzerland. Painter; Writer. m. Sergio, 7 Feb 1970, 1 d. *Education:* Textile Designer 1957-60; Courses Kunstgewerbeschule Zurich 1969; Statens Kunstindustriskole, Oslo 1975-77. *Career:* Textile Designer; Collaborations with Radio Svizzera Italiana (RSI) 1967-73; Many individual & group exhibs in several countries. *Creative Works:* Da stanze chiuse, poetry, drawings 1987; Il peusatore con il mantello come meteora, novel, 1990; Controcanto al chiuso, drawings with Bianca Maria Frabotta, poetry, 1991. *Memberships:* Assn of Swiss Painters, Sculptors, Architects; Assn of Women Painter Sculptors; PEN Club. *Honour:* Prize Ascona 1987 for unpub novel Il pensatore con il mantello come meteora. *Address:* auf dem Aspei 55, D-4630 Bochum 1, Germany. 3.

ALBREKTSEN Helge Normann, b. 8 Jan 1950, Bergen, Norway. Lawyer; Author. m. Marie J Albrektsen, 7 July 1973, 2 d. *Education:* Law degree (cand jur), Univ Oslo 1973; Postgrad Studies in Intl Ec, Columbia Univ Grad Sch of Bus, NY 1980. *Appointments:* Legal Mgr, Sovereign Marine Lines Inc; Contracts, Legal Mgr, Sea-Troll A/S, Stavanger; Counsel A/S Kristian Jebsens Rederi, Bergen; Lawyer in Bergen 1983-. *Publications:* Long Island Expressway, collection of short stories, 1979; Harlem Hotel, novel, 1982; Arethusa, novel, 1987; Weekly Columnist of newspaper Morgenbladet, Oslo. *Memberships:* Chmn of Bd Trustees, Intl Sch of Bergen, Norway; Norwegian Bar Assn; Intl Bar Assn; Chmn, Centura Foun 1990; Nat Vice Chmn Norwegian Progress Party 1984-85. *Honour:* Trygve de Lange Memorial Grant for the Promotion of Ec Freedom and Freedom of Expression. *Hobby:* Tennis. *Address:* Kalfarlien 7, 5018 Bergen, Norway.

ALDERDICE John Thomas, b. 28 Mar 1955, Lurgan, N Ireland. Psychi; Polit. m. 30 July 1977, 2 s. 1 d. *Education:* MB, B Ch, BAO, Queens Univ of Belfast 1973-78; MRCPsych 1983. *Appointments:* Jr House Ofcr, Lagan Valley Hosp 1978-79; Sr House Ofcr, Belfast City Hosp 1979-80; Registrar, Holywell Hosp 1980-81; Registrar, Shaftesbury Sq Hosp 1981-82; Registrar, Lissue & Belfast City Hosps 1982-83; Sr Tutor, Registrar, Queens Univ & Belfast City Hospital 1983-87; Conslt Psycho, Eastern Health & Soc Sers Bd 1988-; Concurrently Hon Lectr, Queen's Univ of Belfast 1990-; Polit career: Exec Com, Alliance Party 1984, Chmn Policy Com 1985, Vice Chmn 1987, Party Leader 1987-; Mem Exec Com, Federation of European Lib, Democratic & Reform Parties 1987-; Mem Belfast City Coun 1989-; Candidate for Northern Ireland in 1989 European Election. *Memberships:* Brit Med Assn; Royal Col Psychi; Ulster Med Soc; Soc of Clin Psychi; Assn for Psychoanalytic Psychotherapy; Dir of N Ireland Inst Human Relats 1990-. *Honour:* Galloway Medal, Nat Schizophrenia Fellowship, NI 1987. *Hobbies:* Music; Reading. *Address:* 55 Knock Road, Belfast BT5 6LB, Northern Ireland. 52.

ALDISS Thomas Edward, b. 8 Aug 1943, Wymondham, Norfolk, England. Chartered Acct. m. Barbara Helen Mitchell, 26 July 1969, 1 s. 1 d. *Education:* Reading Col of Tech; Univ Bath. *Appointments:* Thornton, Baker & Co, Horsham & Worthing 1971-78; Honey Barrett & Co, Lewes 1978-80; Principal, Aldiss & Co, Chartered Accts, Worthing 1981-. *Memberships:* Life mem, Guild of Freemen of the City of London; Inst Chartered Accts of Eng & Wales, FCA 1972; Rotary Club of Worthing Steyne, Pres 1991-92. *Hobbies:* Travel; Family; House & garden; Wine; Food; Veteran cycles. *Address:* Beechcroft, Offington Avenue, Worthing, West Sussex BN14 9PR, England.

ALE RUIZ Rafael, b. 4 Aug 1960, Utrera, Sevilla, Spain. Telecommunications Engr; Conslt. *Education:* MBA Inst de Empresa, Madrid; Cert Theoretical Physicists; PhD Sevilla Univ. *Appointments:* Prof Digital Electr u Extremadura, 1985; Telecom Engr, Telefonica, 1986; Mng Dir, Young Consulting, 1988; Principal Advr, Ahciet, 1989. *Publications:* Programacion 8088, 1987;

Teleinformatics, 1988; Comunicacion de Datos, 1988; Unix System U Bible, 1989. *Memberships:* Scuba diving club; Wine tasters club; Parachute club. *Hobbies:* Scuba diving; Motorcycling; Flying; Skiing; Gastronomy; Classical music; Medieval literature. *Address:* Vitrubio 7, Madrid 28006, Spain. 52.

ALEMANN Eduardo, b. 12 Jan 1922, Buenos Aires. Composer; Journalist. m. Leonor Forsthuber, 3 s. *Education:* Music with J Montes, piano, W Gratzer & H Veerhoff, composition, Martorelle Y Spatola, clarinet, J Florine, flute, H Zeoli, organ, G Houle, Stanford Univ, baroque music. *Career:* Edit, local German paper, Argentinisches Tageblatt; Composer of symphonic and chamber music; Performer, clarinet, piano, recorder, flute. *Creative Works:* Over 100 mus works, sev published by profl companies. *Memberships:* Fdr, Compositores Unidos de la Argentina; Assn Argentina de Compositores; Fdr & Conductor sev consorts & groups. *Honours:* Winner, ARS Composition Contest with Spectra for recorder Consort, 1971; Winner Comp Cont Fondo Nacional de las Artes with clarinet concerto Encuentro, 1973, and Kaleidoscopia, 1974; Prizes, Barry for Nostalgias Brasilenas 1977 & Enigmusic 1977, Breyer for 3 piezas 1977, Amigos de la Musica & Sadaic for Duo 1988 and others. *Address:* M T de Alvear 1199, (1058) Buenos Aires, Argentina.

ALESSANDRESCU Mihail Dan, b. 5 June 1913, Pitesti, Romania. Doctor. *Education:* MD 1941, Univ Med C Davilla, Bucharest; Internship 1938-42; Residency 1942-46; Chf Dept Ob Gyn 1947; PhD 1953. *Appointments:* Asst Prof 1948; Chf Dept Ob Gyn 1948-56, Brincovenesc Hosp, Giulesti Hosp, Central Hosp, Polizu Hosp; Chf Dept post-graduated Ob Gyn 1953; Univ Lectr 1957; Full Prof 1960; Chf Dept, Inst Health 1956-71. *Publications:* The Practice of Ob G emergencies, 1956; Textbook of Ob Gyn, 1959; Atlas of Colposcopy, 1965; The Biology of Human Reproduction, 1976; Colposcopy, 1984; Over 500 original texts and technics of ob gyn pub in Romania and abroad. *Memberships:* Rom Acad Med; Pres, Rom Soc Ob Gyn 1956-73, 1985-; Chf Edit, Rom Review of Ob Gyn 1973-85; German Soc Ob Gyn and French Soc Ob Gyn; Figo Mem Ofcr 1983-85; WHO's Expert for ob gyn; EAGO. *Honours:* Zemmelweis Prize of Hungarian Soc Ob Gyn; Hon Mem Hungarian, Bulgarian Soc Ob Gyn; Hon Mem, Redactional Com of Zeitscht ob gyn of Germany 1975-. *Hobbies:* Classical music; Painting. *Address:* 17th Stirbei Voda Str, Bucharest 1st, 70731 Romania.

ALEXANDER Jon, b. 2 Jan 1940, Carbondale, Illinois, USA. Edr. 2 s. 2d. *Education:* BA 1961, MA 1962 Southern Ill Univ; PhD 1966, Univ Kansas; Postdoctoral 1966, Centre for the Study of Democratic Insts. *Appointments:* Vstg Asst Prof, Emory Univ 1966; Vstg Asst Prof, Columbia Univ 1967; Asst Prof 1967, Assoc Prof 1983, Carleton Univ. *Publications:* Science for What, 1974; Data Capture, 1988; Science, Technology & Politics Yearbook, 1990; Evaluation des Politiques Scientific et Technologique: Experiences Nationales, 1990. *Memberships:* APSA Sci & Tech Studies Gp, Steering Com 1985-; Caucus for a New Polit Sci Steering Com 1974; Intl Sociol Assn; Sociotechnics Res Com Steering Com 1988-89. *Honours:* NATO, Technology Advanced Seminar Fellowship 1990; Social Scis & Humanities Res Coun Res Grant 1991; Phi Sigma Alpha. *Hobbies:* Sailing; Dancing; Skiing; Reading; Charitable fund raising. *Address:* Political Science Department, Carleton University, Ottawa, Ontario, Canada K1S 5B6. 30, 6, 129.

ALEXANDRU Nicolae Dumitru, b. 28 Nov 1947, Bucharest, Romania. Univ Prof; Elect Engr. m. Maria-Liliana Ioanitescu, 14 Feb 1976. *Education:* BSc 1970, PhD 1981, Poly Inst of Iasi, Romania. *Appointments:* Instr 1970; Asst Prof 1976; Assoc Prof 1990; All at Poly Inst of Iasi, Romania. *Publications:* General Electrotechnics, 1974; Telegraphy and Data Transmission, Modern Communication Techniques,

1989; Irotaprint, Iasil. *Memberships:* IEEE; IEEE Communications Soc; Romanian Scists Assn. *Honour:* Fulbright Scholar 1991. *Hobbies:* Foreign Languages; Mountaineering; Books; Art-painting. *Address:* Polytechnic Institute of Iasi, Department of Electronic Engineering, Bd Copou No 11, 6600 Iasi, Romania.

ALEXY Robert Werner, b. 9 Sept 1945, Oldenburg, Lower Saxony. Prof Pub Law & Legal Philosophy. m. Edith Alexy, 28 May 1971, 1 s. 1 d. *Education:* Studied Law & Philosophy, Georg-August-University, Gottingen 1968-73; LLD Gottingen 1976; Asst, Law Fac, Gottingen 1977-84; Habilitation 1984. *Appointments:* Docent, Univ Regensburg 1984-85; Prof, Christian-Albrechts-Univ, Kiel 1985-. *Publications:* Theorie der juristischen Argumentation, 1978, 2nd ed 1991, translated into Eng: A Theory of Legal Argumentation, 1989; Theorie der Grundrechte, Nomos 1985, repr Suhrkamp 1986; Begriff und Geltung des Rechts, Alber 1992. *Membership:* VP German Sect, Intl Assn for Philosophy of Law & Social Philosophy; Joachim Jungius-Gesellschaft der Wissenschaften, Hamburg. *Honour:* Prize of Acad of Scis in Gottingen 1982. *Hobbies:* Gardening; Reading. *Address:* Klausbrooker Weg 122, D-2300 Kiel, Germany.

ALEY Charles R, b. 3 Apr 1956, Beaver Falls, Pennsylvania, USA. Atty. m. Harriet M Baker, 21 June 1986. *Education:* BA Ec, BSBA Acctg, Data Processing, Bus Admin; BS Info Systems 1978, Geneva Col; JD 1981, Univ Pittsburgh Sch Law; LLD, Hon, London Inst of Applied Res, 1990. *Appointments:* Tax Atty, Arthur Young & Co, Pittsburgh, Pa 1981-82; Tax Atty, Edward J DeBartolo Corp, Youngstown, Ohio 1982-86; Tax Atty, Alcan Aluminium Corp, Warren, Ohio 1986-. *Memberships:* Am Bar Assn; PA Bar Assn; Allegheny County Bar Assn; Beaver County Bar Assn; Fed Circuit Bar Assn; Trumbull County Bar Assn; Assn Trial Lawyers of Am; Phi Alpha Delta Law Fraternity; Intl Platform Assn; International Parliament for Safety & Peace. *Honours:* WA Bliss Ec Awd, Geneva Col, 1978; Dist'd Ser Awd, Geneva Col, 1991. *Hobby:* Pipe organ restoration. *Address:* 1212 Sixth Avenue, Beaver Falls, PA 15010, USA. 2, 52, 130, 139, 152, 155, 162, 163.

ALI Ahmad Mohamad, b. 1932, Medina City, Saudi Arabia. Banker; Former Edr & Public Official. m. Ghada Mahmood Masri, 1 s. 3 d. *Education:* BA 1957, Cairo Univ; MA 1962, Univ Mich, USA; Doctorate Pub Adm 1967, State Univ NY, Albany. *Appointments:* Dir, Sci & Islamic Inst, Aden 1958-59; Deputy Rector, King Abdul Aziz Univ, Jeddah 1967-72; Dep Min Ed for Tech Affairs 1972-75; Pres, Islamic Devel Bank 1975-. *Publications:* Num arts & working papers, Islamic ec, banking, ed. *Memberships:* Councils: King Abdul Aziz Univ, King Saud Univ (Riyadh), Oil & Minerals Univ (Dhaharan), Islamic Univ (Medina), Imam Mohamad Ben Saud Univ (Riyadh); Adm Bds: Saudi Credit Bank, Saudi Fund for Devel. *Hobbies:* Cycling; Walking. *Address:* Islamic Development Bank, POB 5925, Jeddah 21432, Saudi Arabia.

ALIA Ramiz, b. 18 Oct 1925, Shkodra. Pres Albania. 1 s. 2 d. *Education:* Grad Polit Scis. *Appointments:* Mem anti-fascist youth org; Joined partisan units and fought for liberation of the country in Second World War, performing polit and milit functions, and Hd of Youth Org; Min Ed 1955-58; From 2nd Legislation (1950) was elected Deputy to People's Assembly; Also var party functions; Hd, Party of Labour of Albania 1985-91; Elected Chmn of Presidium of People's Assembly 1982; Elected Pres Republic of Albania 1991. *Publications:* Books, studies and a great number works in field of publicity, sociol & polit scis. *Hobby:* Reading. *Address:* Office of the President, Tirana, Albania.

ALIULIS Vaclovas, b. 14 Mar 1921, Lithuania. Roman Catholic Priest; Press Worker. *Education:* Licence of Theology 1945, Priest's Seminary, Theology Dept, Kaunas, Lithuania. *Appointments:* Pastor in sec churches 1945-78; Pres Liturgical Comm of Lithuanian Dioceses 1979-90; Edit of a catholic fortnightly 1989-91; Dir of a cath publishing house 1990-. *Publications:* Edit, Lithuanian New Testament translation 1972 and 1988 and the Salms translation 1973; Edit, Roman Missal translation 1982 and 1988 and Ritual 1966-67. *Memberships:* Lithuanian Catholic Acad of Sci 1990-; Leading Coun, Lithuanian Nat Movement Sajudis 1988-92; Pres, Lith Bible Soc 1992-; Assoc Pres, Lith Journalist Soc 1992-. *Hobby:* Literature. *Address:* Arkikatedra Bazilika, Vilnius 2001, Lithuania.

ALLAN John, b. 25 Nov 1991, Glasgow, Scotland. Sales Exec. *Education:* Natal Col, 1983-85. *Appointments:* Lt, South African Defence Force 1986-87; Computer Programmer, Beacon Sweets, SA 1988-90; Sales Exec, Save & Prosper 1991-. *Honour:* Natal 1st XV, SADF, Scotland, Rugby. *Hobbies:* Rugby; Cricket; Football; Athletics; All sports; Reading; Relaxing in front of tv. *Address:* 120 Rose Street, South Lane, Edinburgh, Scotland EH2 4BB, Scotland.

ALLAN Rosemary Elizabeth, b. 2 Oct 1911, Bromley, Kent. Painter; Draughtsman. m. Allan Gwynne-Jones, 22 Mar 1937, 1 d. *Education:* Central Sch of Art 1929; Slade Sch of Art 1930-34; DFA, London Univ. *Career:* Commissioned by War Artists Adv Com 1943; Pictures bought by Contemporary Art Soc, Nuffield Trust, Soc of Dilettanti. *Creative Works:* National Trust; HRH the Prince of Wales; Imperial War Museum; St John's Col, Cambridge. *Hobby:* Market shopping. *Address:* Eastleach, nr Cirencester, Glos GL7 3NQ, England. 19.

ALLARDT Erik Anders, b. 9 Aug 1925, Helsinki. Chancellor of Abo Akademi Univ. m. Sagi Nylander, 1947, 1 s. 2 d. *Education:* MA 1947, PhD in Sociol 1952, Univ Helsinki. *Appointments:* Prof in Sociol 1958-85, Dean of Fac of Social Scis 1969-70, Univ Helsinki; Vstg Prof num countries & univs; Fellow, Woodrow Wilson Intl Centre for Scholars 1978-79; Pres, Acad of Finland 1986-1991. *Publications:* Mass Politics, Studies in Political Sociology, 1970; Implications of the Ethnic Revival in Modern Industrialized Society, 1979; Sociologin i Sverige, vetenskap, miljo och organisation, 1988. *Memberships:* Finnish Soc of Scis & Letters 1961-, Hon mem 1988-, Chmn 1985-86; Norwegian Acad Sci & Letters 1982-; European Sci Foun, Ecex Coun 1987-, VP 1990-; Academia Europaea, Fdr mem 1988-; The Royal Swedish Acad of Letters, Hist and Antiquities, 1992-. *Honours:* Hon doctor's degree: Univ Stockholm 1978; Abo Akademi Univ 1978; Univ Uppsala 1984. *Hobbies:* Comparative sociology; Political sociology; Sociology of science and research policy. *Address:* Unionsgatan 45 B 40, SF-00170 Helsingfors, Finland. 52, 34, 139.

ALLEN Anthony Campbell, b. 6 May 1925, Weybridge, Surrey, England. Composer. 1 s. 2 d. *Education:* RADA; Studied pvtly with Bertie Scott & Lizi Pisk. *Appointments:* Voice Tchr, RADA 1955-56; Producer, Racine's Phedre, London, 1957; Lectr, Bristol Univ, 1959-61; Producer, Festpieltreffen Bayreuth 1962-63; Produced James's The Outcry, London 1968. *Creative Works:* Opera: The Wandering Planet; The Hallwyl- Kantate; 7 Concertos, 3 alphorn, 2 violin, 1 flute; Much Chamber music. *Memberships:* SUISA; Composers' Guild of Great Britain. *Hobby:* Earning enough money to pay for the music. *Address:* Die Schweizerische Campbell Allen-Gesellschaft, Postfach 4214, 8022 Zurich, Switzerland. 4, 191.

ALLEN Judith Christina, b. 8 July 1941, Wiltshire, England. Writer. *Education:* Pvtly. *Career:* Publishing to 1972; First book published 1973; Freelance Edit to 1980; Full time Writer 1980-. *Publications include:* Adult Fiction: December Flower, 1982, televised 1985, and read on radio; Bag and Baggage, 1988, tv rights bought in 1991 and read on radio; Jr Fiction: 12 including: Something Rare and Special, 1985, 1989; Travelling Hopefully, 1987, 1989; Awaiting Developments, 1988, 1989; Between The Moon and the Rock, 1992; 8 books of non-fiction for children; 3 books of non-fiction for adults; 9 Guidebooks; 4 plays for BBC Radio 4; Dramatisation of the Secret Garden by Frances Hodgson-Burnett for Radio 5, 1991. *Membership:* Soc of Authors. *Honours:* Winner, Children's Section of Whitbread, 1988; Winner, Friends of the Earth "Earthworm" Awd, 1989. *Hobbies:* Reading; Walking. *Address:* c/o Laurence Fitch Ltd, 483 Southbank House, Black Prince Road, Albert Embankment, London SE1 7SJ, England.

ALLENDER Peter John, b. 15 Sept 1921, Somerset, England, Freechurch Bishop; Theol Prof. m. Marjorie Edith Tomkins, 6 Nov 1955. *Education:* London BSc 1940, PhD 1947; Reading MA 1960, Open BA 1975; Oxford B Th 1987; Canterbury DD 1989. *Appointments:* Res Asst, BSA 1948-55; Res Engr, James Booth 1955-58; Materials Engr, 1958-84; Minister 1984-87; Dean 1987-89; Bishop 1989-. *Publications:* Monographs: Railway Engineering; Systems Engineering; Num sci arts; Sec short stories; Edit Bus & Trade Newsletters; Contbr to radio & TV Broadcast Programmes. *Memberships:* Fellow: Inst Company Accts; Order of St Luke; Order of St Andrew; Prior, Order of Bedfont Scholars; Mem var disabled orgs; Inst Journalists; Soc of Authors; Writers' Guild of GB. *Honours:* Fellow of Wessex Col (Bath) 1989; Knight Bachelor 1990. *Hobbies:* Reading; Writing; Motoring; Keen interest in social welfare of disabled since becoming severely disabled in 1985. *Address:* 9 Jeremy Grove, Solihull B92 8JH, England. 139, 161, 149.

ALLINDER Fumiko. Japanese Flower Arranger. *Education:* Studied with Sogetsu Sch of Ikebana Fdr and Master, Sofu Teshigahara. *Career:* Dir, Sogetsu Sch ikebana, USA; Taught & Demonstrated this ancient art form widely in Japan and USA for 20 years; Given Lectr-Demonstrations for many cultural and ednl orgs all over USA and Canada incl Columbia Univ and Metropolitan Museum of Art; In NY her work has appeared at Carnegie Hall, Alice Tully Hall, Lincoln Centre, United Nations, Japan House, NY Hilton and on TV; Participated in special promotions at Gimbel's & Macy's; Presently freelance Artist in NYC; Taught in Tokyo, Va, NJ, Penn and Japan-Am Inst, NYC; Currently giving classes at Nippon Club in bankei (miniature landscape) and ikebana. *Address:* 201 W 70th Street, New York, New York 10023, USA. 152.

ALLISON Stephen Galender, b. 11 Dec 1952, Springfield, Mo, USA. Radio Station Exec. m. (1)Linda Katharine Lavelle, 6 Apr 1978 (div 1983), 2 d. (2)Tara Rae Foster, 20 Aug 1986. *Appointments:* Cert Radio Mktg Cons Personality, Sta WSBB, New Smyrna, Fla 1971-72, Sta WMFJ-AM-FM, Daytona Beach, Fla 1972-75, Sta KADI-FM, St Louis 1975-76, Sta KAUM-FM, Houston 1976-79, Sta WKYS-FM, Wash 1979-81; Gen Mgr, Sta KSTM-FM, Phoenix 1981-85; Pres, Allison Broadcasting Co Inc, Phoenix 1985-, Allison Broadcast Group Inc, Dallas, Tx, Del Mar, Calif 1987-; Owner, Stas KGRX-FM/KIKO, Phoenix 1986-, Sta KDGE-FM, Dallas 1989-; Mktg Conslt, St Louis Post-Dispatch 1975-76, Houston Chronicle 1976-79, Wash Star 1980-81; Advtg Conslt, Celebrity Theatre, Phoenix 1985-86; Bd Dirs, Desert-Mt Foothills Assn, Scottsdale, Ariz 1981-; Alwun House Cultural Centre, Phoenix 1982-; Film in Ariz, Phoenix 1985-; Ariz Comm on the Arts, Phoenix 1986-. *Memberships:* Nat Rep Congl Com 1988-; No Tex Comm; Nat Assn Broadcasters; Ariz Broadcasters Assn; Tex Assn Broadcasters; Phoenix Active 20-30 Club; Intl Platform Assn; Am Mgmt Assn; AWRT; Las Colinas Sports Club. *Hobbies:* Collecting classic cars; Travelling; Reacquetball; Golfing. *Address:* 1809 Crockett Circle, Irving, TX 75038, USA. 52, 2, 7, 132.

ALLWELL-BROWN Senibo, b. 10 Mar 1935, Finima, Bonny, Nigeria. Chartered Acct. m. Helen Marguerita, 12 Oct 1963, 1 s. 4 d. *Education:* Llandaff Tech Col, Univ Wales; H C Hopkin & Co. *Appointments:* Shell BP Petrol Devel Co Ltd 1966-71; Akintola Williams & Co 1971-74; Fdr Ptnr, Allwell Brown & Co 1974-.

Memberships: Inst Chartered Accts in Eng & Wales; Inst Chartered Accts of Nigeria. *Hobbies:* Jazz music; Football; Lawn tennis; Table tennis. *Address:* 21 Obagi Road, PO Box 242, Port Harcourt, Rivers State, Nigeria.

ALMEDA Boris Raoul, b. 14 Oct 1936, Gibraltar. Businessman. m. Leta Ferguson Nunn, 5 June 1972. *Education:* Dipl 1953, Admiralty Tech Col, Gibraltar; Served with Gibraltar Regiment 1958-59. *Appointments:* Shipwright 1953-58, Fireman 1959-64, Admiralty Dockyard, Gib; Guitar Soloist, performing world wide 1964-80; Mng Dir, High Chaparral Holdings Ltd 1980-; Conslt, High Chaparral Conslts 1985-; Mgr, Gib-Office Mgmt 1985-; Dir, Bodel Ltd & Telesis Ltd 1987-. *Creative Works:* Introducing Photovoltaics, 1985; LP: Ole! Que Magnifico, 1977. *Memberships:* Assn Energy Engrs; Assn Trust & Co Mgmt; Gibraltar C of C; Gibraltar Red Cross; Assn for Advancement of Civil Rights. *Honours:* Contest Winner on TV Talent Prog, Opportunity Knocks, London 1971; Speaker at Inauguration Ceremony of the World's First Solar Breeder, Frederick, Md, USA 1982. *Hobbies:* History; Physics; Metaphysics; Archaeology; Cosmological Research; Music; Cats. *Address:* PO Box 486, 8 Morello's Ramp, Gibraltar.

ALONSO-FERNANDEZ Jose Ramon, b. 16 Mar 1946, Ourense, Spain. Clinical Chemist. *Education:* Chem grad 1971, Univ Santiago de Compostela. *Appointments:* Asst Lectr in Analytical Chemistry 1972-76, in Physical Chem 1977-78, in Paediatrics 1978-86; Assoc Prof of Paediatrics, Univ Santiago de Compostela 1986-; Hd Metabolopathy Section, Galicia Gen Hosp 1979-; Coord, Metabolopathy Screening Lab, Galicia Directorate Gen of Public Health 1989. *Publications:* 70 profl papers; Inventions: Procedure for preparing starch based lyophilized analytical reagents, 1976; Appts for plane chromatography with pressure and/or vacuum, 1990. *Memberships:* Galician Col of Chem; Spanish Soc of Clin Chem; Am Chem Soc; Chromatographic Soc; Soc for Study of Inborn Errors of the Metabolism; Intl Soc for Neonatal Screening; and others. *Address:* Quimico, Rua do Franco 52-2, 15702 Santiago de Compostela, Spain. 52.

ALSHECH Joseph, b. 14 Jan 1936, Tel Aviv. Economist. m. Varda, 21 Aug 1981, 1 s. 1 d. *Education:* Ec, Tel Aviv Sch of Ec 1959; MA Ec 1963, NY New Sch of Social Res. *Appointments:* Ec Counsellor, Israe Manufacturers Assn 1964-78; VP, First Intl Bank 1978-80; SVP, El Al Israel Air Lines 1981-83; Dir Gen, Fiat, Israel 1984-86; Teva Phamr Indust, Fin Dir of Overseas Subsidiaries, 1988-. *Memberships:* Israel Mgmt Assn; Finance Club of Tel- Aviv Univ; Bd Dirs: Klal Inds; First Intl Bank; Five J Gold Inds. *Hobbies:* Music; Tennis; Reading. *Address:* 15 Haim Hazaz Street, Tel-Aviv, Israel.

ALSTEAD Francis Allan Littlejohns, b. 19 June 1935, Glasgow, Scotland. Chf Exec, Scottish Sports Coun. m. 4 Apr 1964, 2 s. *Education:* Glasgow Acad 1948-54; Royal Milit Acad, Sandhurst 1954-55; Royal Naval Staff Col 1966; Joint Sers Staff Col 1971; NATO Res Fellow 1987-88; MPhil 1989, Univ Wales, Aberystwyth. *Appointments:* Commissioned into KOSB 1955; Lt Col, Commanding 1 KOSB 1974-76; MA to Quarter Master General 1976-79; GSO1, Staff Col, Camberley 1979-81; Col, Asst Chf of Staff, HQ BAOR 1981-84; Brigadier, Commander, 51 Highland Brigade 1984-87; NATO Reinforcement Coord 1988-90. *Publication:* Ten in Ten, NATO Res Thesis. *Memberships:* FBIM 1984; FIPM 1988; FCIT 1989; F Inst AM 1990, FRSA 1991; Regimental Trustee KOSB 1982; Royal Company Archers, Queen's Bodyguard in Scotland 1985; Deputy Hon Col, Edinburgh & Heriot-Watt Univ OTC 1990; Governor, Moray House Coll, 1991; Pres, Edinburgh and Lothians SSAFA, 1991. *Honours:* CBE 1984; Mention in Despatches 1976. *Hobbies:* Skiing; Running; Classical music. *Address:* Scottish Sports Council, Caledonia House, South Gyle, Edinburgh EH12 9DQ, Scotland.

ALTON David Patrick Paul, b. 15 Mar 1951, London, England. MP. m. Elizabeth Bell, 23 July 1988, 2 s. 1 d. *Education:* Christ Col, Liverpool 1969-72. *Appointments:* Tchr 1972-74; Tchr of children with special needs 1974-79; Liverpool City Councillor 1972-80; MP 1979-; Columnist, Universe newspaper. *Publications:* What Kind of Country, 1988; Whose Choice Anyway, 1989; Faith in Britain, 1991. *Memberships:* Nat VP, Life; Pres, Liverpool Old People's Hostels Assn; Trustee, Crisis (at Christmas). *Hobbies:* Walking; Gardening; Reading; Travel. *Address:* Laund House, 25 North Mossley Hill Road, Liverpool L18 8BL, England. 1.

ALUCHNA-EMELIANOW Marta Aniela, b. 29 Mar 1906, Koralowka, nr Chetm. Retd Tchr. m. (1) 1925, (2)1939, 1 d. *Education:* Stefan Butory's Univ, Wilno 1923-36 (with breaks). *Appointments:* Work at Elementary Sch 1923-39; Tchr of Polish; Tchr 1946-70. *Publications:* From under arcades, 1929; Looking for shape, 1962; Windmills 1962-66; Ash & Dust 1964; I Know and I don't Know, 1968; The day is dawning, 1975; Choice of the poems, 1978. *Memberships:* Zagary 1929; Meduza 1958-59; Polish Writers Assn 1962-. *Honours:* Awds in Koszalin, 1958, 1959, 1961, 1963; Awd from People's Provincial Coun 1968; Gold Cross of Merit 1969; Awd of Office Provincial 1970; Order of Cross of Regenerate Poland 1976. *Hobbies:* Literature; Animals. *Address:* ul Zamkowa 3/3, 76-200 Stupsk, Poland.

AMADOR Zeneida, b. 7 Feb 1933, Philippines. Theatre Dir; Actress. *Education:* Bach of Arts, Univ of Santo Tomas, 1953; Master of Arts, 1955; Doctoral Units; Post Grauade, American Acad of Dramatic Arts. *Appointments:* St Josephs Coll, Quezon City Univ, South Dakota Repertory Philippines Foundation. *Publications:* Exits & Entrances. *Memberships:* Zonta Club of Makati; TOWNS. *Honours:* Ten Oustanding Women of the New Soc, Towns; Aliw Award for Best Stage Dir; Outstanding Alumna St Jospehs Coll; 8th Brown Visiting Fellow, Trinity Coll; Josephine Achievement Award. *Hobby:* Reading. *Address:* Repertory Philippines Foundation Inc, 5th Level, Shangri la Plaza, EDSA Corner, Shaw Boulevard, Mandaluyong, Metro Manila, Philippines.

AMADUCCI Luigi A, b. 11 July 1932, Verona, Italy. Prof Neurol. m. Maria Pia Pasetto, 28 Apr 1963, 1 s. 2 d. *Education:* MD 1957, Univ Padua; Assoc Prof Neurol 1966, Full Prof Neurol 1975, Univ Florence. *Appointments:* Full Prof Neurol 1975-; Chmn Dept Neurol & Psychi 1979- 83; Dir Coord Centre WHO-PRA Age Associated Dementia 1988-; Dir Targeted Project "Aging" CNR-NRC 1991-96; Nat Del, European Com Biomed Res & Health 1991-94. *Publications:* The Early Story of AD; Alzheimer's First Case Rediscovered; Over 300 sci papers dealing with MS, dementia, clinical & experimental neurosci. *Honours:* Fullbright Scholar in Neuropathology, Harvard Med Sch 1958-60; Vstg Scist, Fogarty Intl Centre, Nat Insts Health 1983-84. *Hobbies:* Mountain climbing; History; Music; Ancient children's books collection. *Address:* Department of Neurology & Psychiatry, University of Florence, Viale Morgagni 85, 50134 Florence, Italy.

AMBROSI CARRARO Jose, b. 5 Dec 1905, Mexico DF. Civil Engr. *Education:* Escuela Nacional de Ingenieros con Titulo. *Appointments:* Nat Comm for Irrigation; Nat Comm for Public Ways and Public Works; Compania de Bienes Raices. *Publications:* Autobiog; Palacio Romano; La Espona Que Yo Ri. *Memberships:* Engineers Assn; Mexican Red Cross Assn; Milit Sch Assn. *Honours:* Plaque & Dipl, 50 years as an Engr, Mexican Arch & Engrs Assn; Awd from Pres Sandro Portini, Italy; Awd from Cuerpo de Defensores de la Republica. *Hobby:* Antique collecting. *Address:* Paseo de la Reforma 560, Col Lomas de Chapultepec, CP 11000, Mexico D F.

AMR Asad T, b. 21 Sept 1941, Lebanon. Consltg Environ Engr. m. Thea Brodsky Amr, 4 July 1965, 3 s. *Education:* BS in Civ Engr 1965, MS in Civ Engr 1966, Tehran Univ; MS Envir Engr 1973, PhD Envir Engr 1975, Drexel Univ. *Appointments:* Site Engr, Min Public Works 1969; Envir Engr, Gen Pub Utility 1969-75; Proj Engr, Exxon Chemical 1975-76; Dept Staff, Mitre Corp 1976-80; Prog Mgr, Amartech Ltd 1980-87; System Scist, Mitre Corp 1987-. *Publications:* Book: Energy Systems, 1981; Art: Energy & Environment, 1976. *Memberships:* Am Soc Civil Engrs; Profl Engr, NJ; Licensed Profl Engr, VA. *Honour:* Full Scholarship at Univ Tehran 1960-66. *Hobbies:* Soccer coaching; Coin collecting; Tennis; Travel. *Address:* 3612 N Woodstock Street, Arlington, VA 22207, USA. 2.

AN Sanyuan, b. 19 Feb 1929, Sanyuan County, Shaanxi Prov. Prof Geol. m. Ye Jian, 19 July 1952, 2 s. 3 d. *Education:* Grad Dept Geol, Northwest Univ 1952; Studied Petrology, Peking Col Geol 1954-55; Learned Russian, Peking Col Russian Lang 1958. *Appointments:* Asst 1952, Lectr 1956, Assoc Prof 1979, Dept Geol, Northwest Univ; Assoc Prof 1980, Prof 1986-, Hd Dept Geol 1983-86, Xi'an Col Geol. *Publications:* The tens papers about Petrology & Regl Geol; The Geology of Eastern Qinling; The Constituate and Evolution of North Qinling; The Research on Ultramafic and MaficRocks of North Qinling Orogenic Belt. *Memberships:* Dir, Chinese Soc Mineralogy, Petrology & Geochem 1988-; Mem Com Metamorphic Petrology, Chinese Soc Mineralogy, Petrology & Geochem 1989; VP Shaanxi Mineralogy, Petrology & Geochem Soc 1983-. *Honours:* Encouraged for achmt in sci & tech by Min of Geol & Mineral Resources, PRC 1986, for researches on ultramafic rocks in Northern Qinling Orogenic Belt; Id 1989 for researches on Geol in the Eastern Qinling. *Hobbies:* Historicalgeography; Chinese ancient poetry. *Address:* Xi'an College of Geology, Xi'an, China. 139.

AN Shi-chi (Xi-ji), b. 10 Jan 1916, Honan Province, China. Prof. m. 18 June 1950, 2 s. 1 d. *Education:* BS Agri Ec 1940, Northwestern Agri Univ, Sian, China; Sr Vstg Scholar, Univ Wash, Seattle, USA 1948-49. *Appointments:* Assoc Reschr, Ec Inst of China, Shanghai 1945-47; Prof, Northwestern Agri Univ 1950-53; Prof, Beijing Agri Univ 1953-. *Publications:* Agricultural Economics and Management, textbook for col & grad; Agricultural Production Economics, for grad schs; About 40 reports and arts 1978-. *Memberships:* VP, Assn Agri Ec of China 1979-; Pres, Soc Agri Practices Economy of China 1983-; Intl Assn Agri Econiomists and Rep of China. *Honours:* 2nd Prize on research work for vegetable marketing by Beijing Municipal Govt; Co-Ptnr on PhD tng: and res work with Hohenheim Univ, Germany 1985-90, with Univ of Brisbane, Australia 1988-90, with Iowa State Univ 1991-. *Hobby:* Swimming. *Address:* No 1 Small Building, Beijing Agricultural University, Beijing 100094, China.

AN Yuzong, b. 21 July 1928, Qingdao. Mech Sr Engr; Prof. m. Yuan Tongjian, 2 Jan 1954, 1 s. 1 d. *Education:* Grad, Mech Engrg Dept, Tsingtao Industry Col, 1949. *Appointments:* Engr, PRC Emb in Czechoslovakia 1956; Lab Chf 1971, VP 1978, Res & Des Inst of Rubber Ind; Chmn & Pres of CNCCC, Dir CITIC 1983. *Publication:* Tyre Performance Testing, 1982 in Rubber Industry. *Memberships:* Exec Vice Chmn CCPIT, Sub-Coun of Chemical Ind; Exec Vice Chmn CCOIC Chemical Industry C of C; Com of Rubber Ind, Chemical Ind & Engrg Soc China; Exec Dir, China Rubber Ind Assn; Edit Com, China Chem Ind Publication. *Honour:* 1st Prize Winner for Sci & Tech Progress of the MCI 1987. *Hobbies:* Classical Chinese poems and songs. *Address:* CNCCC Building No 16, Qiqu, Hepingli, Beijing 100013, China.

ANAGNOSTOPOULOY-CABOT Maria, b. 12 Mar 1942, Pyrgos, Ilias, Greece. Psychotherapist; Res Psycho. m. Robert Cabot, 15 June 1968, 1 s. *Education:* Arch, Technische Hochschule of Graz 1959-64; Arch, Acad of Florecne 1964-66; MA in Sch Planning 1967, Stanford Univ; Master in Psychology 1986, Boston Univ. *Appointments:* Psychotherapist & Res Psycho 1986-; Co-Fdr, Intl Assn Psycho & Heart; Volunteer

Psychotherapist, Harvard IndoChinese Psychi Clinic for Refugees, Boston 1984-86. *Creative Works:* Preparing for pub series of studies on Psycho aspects revealed by letters of Aldo Moro, Italian Statesman assasinated by the Red Brigade in 1978; Also res on the psycho aspects of cardiopathic illness. *Memberships:* Pres, Assn Intl di Psycologia e Cuore, Rome; Stanford Assn, Greece; Exec Com, Acad of Decorative Arts of Rome. *Hobbies:* Interior decorating of island home with collection of Greek traditional folk art; Guardian of piece of land in Cycladic Islands to preserve the Mediterranean Vegetation there; Playing flute. *Address:* Via del Tempio 4, Roma 00186, Italy.

ANAN Gabriel Jay Jaja, b. 6 July 1948, Nsawam, Ghana. Fin; Marine & Property Conslt. *Education:* PhD; MSc; Postgrad Dipl & Cert; Univ London; Univ Salford; City of London Poly; BA in Theol in progress. *Appointments:* Sales Exec; Shipping Mgr; Mng Dir J & H Services Ltf 1984-; Asst, Academic Adviser of Crown Coll of Theology, London, 1991; Adjunct Faculty Mem and Prof of Theology and Economics, 1992, by Int Correspondent Inst, American Recognised Bible Coll. *Publication:* Insight of a Spiritual Church, 1990. *Memberships include:* Fellow: Inst Sales & Mktg Mgmt; Inst Commerce; Property Conslt Soc; Member: Inst Export; MMem, Intellecutals Acad, MIDI: Maison Internationale Des Intellectuals, Paris, 1907; MCIT, Mem Chartered Inst of Transport; Inst Chartered Shipbrokers; Inst Admin Mgmt. *Honours:* Treas, Zebra Project in Tower Hamlet Churches in Community 1988-; Hon Gen Sec, East London Parish, Celestial Ch of Christ 1987; Hon Gen Sec, Bameke Parish, London, Celestial Ch of Christ/Celestial Evangelical World Crusaders; Shepherd in Charge (Minister), Holy Ch of Christ, The Temple of Divine Power, Walthamstowe, London. *Hobbies:* Football; Boxing; Reading; Church work; Cooking; Dancing. *Address:* 46 Stewart Road, Stratford, London E15 2BB, England.

ANANE-DARKO Daniel, b. 15 Sept 1943, Akurudwa, Ghana. Nurse Tutor. m. Elizabeth Nkwabeng, 4 Apr 1972, 6 s. *Education:* Nursing Training, 1964-67; Nursing Educ Diploma, 1969-71. *Appointments:* Reg Nurse, 1967-71; Nurse Tutor, 1971-78; Principal Nurse Tutor, 1978-92. *Memberships:* Ghana Nurses Assn; Intl Council on Alcohol & Addiction. *Hobbies:* Gardening; Evangelization. *Address:* Nurses Training College, PO Box 110, Kumasi, Ashanti Region, Ghana.

ANCIZAR-SORDO Jorge, b. 17 Sept 1908, Bogota, Colombia. Chem Conslt. m. Lucia Duque, 3 Aug 1933, 1 s. 2 d. *Education:* Inst Grunau, Berne, Switzerland 1925; PhD 1930, Univ Fribourg, Switzerland. *Appointments:* Chem then Dir, Lab Quimico Nacional, Bogota 1931-57; Prof Chem, Fac Pharmacy, Bogota; Prof Chem, Fac Med, Nat Univ Colombia, Bogota; Mem Bd, Nat Univ Columbia 1938-40; Mem Nat Coun of Ed and UNESCO Comm for Colombia 1948-52; Intl Comm for Uniform Methods of Sugar Analysis (ICUMSA) 1949, later VP of the Comm 1954; Mem Bureau Intl Union of Pure & Applied Chem (IUPAC) 1951-55; Mem Bd, Fulbright Comm for Colombia 1957-87; Gen Mgr, Productos Roche SA, Bogota 1957-66. *Publication:* Manuel Ancizar, 1985, biog of her grandfather. *Memberships:* Soc Suisse de Chimie; Soc Chimique de France; Deutsche Ges fur che Apparatewesen; Am Chem Soc; Am Assn for Advancement of Sci (AAAS); Gesellschaft Deutcher Chemiker; NY Acad Sci. *Honour:* AAAS Fellow with Rosette. *Hobbies:* Farming; Riding. *Address:* Apartado aereo 8623, Bogota, Colombia.

ANDEL Michal, b. 2 June 1946, Prague, Czechoslovakia. Hd of 2nd Dept of Internal Medicine; 3rd Medical Faculty, Charles Univ, Prague. m. Katerina Neuwirtova, 26 July 1985, 2 d. *Education:* Faculty of Medicine, Charles Univ, 1972; Inst for Clinical & Experimental Medicine, PhD, 1978. *Appointments:* Physician, Regional Hosp Kralupy, 1972-74; Postgrad Student, Research Worker, Inst for Clinical & Exptl Medicine, Prague, 1974-90. *Publications:* Books.

Glucagon, Physiology, Pathophysiology & Clinics; Texkbooks; 120 Original Papers. *Memberships:* Czech Diabetes Soc; European Soc for Study of Diabetes; Group of European Nutritionists; Council of Nutrition of the Czech Ministry of Health. *Honours:* Award of Czech Diabetes Soc; Award of Czech Literary Foundation; Assoc Prof of Internal Medicine. *Hobbies:* Tennis; Travel; Music. *Address:* IInd Medical Clinic, 3rd Medical Faculty, Charles Univ, Srobarova 50, 100 34 Prague 10, Czechoslovakia.

ANDERSEN Klaus Ejner, b. 21 June 1946. Prof. m. Anne Marie Gjedde, June 1973, 2 s. 1 d. *Education:* Cand med 1972, Doctorate of Med 1986, Univ Copenhagen; Specialist in Dermatovenerology 1980. *Appointments:* Dept of Dermatol, Gentofte Hosp, Copenhagen 1976-78 & 1979-84; Fellow, Univ Calif, San Francisco Dept of Dermatol 1978-79; Pvt Practice, Roskilde, Denmark 1984-88; Prof Dermatology & Venerology, Odense Univ Hosp, Denmark 1989-. *Publication:* Co-Author, Contact Allergy Predictive Tests in Guinea Pigs, 1985. *Memberships:* European Envir and Contact Dermatitis Res Gp 1984-. *Address:* Department of Dermatology, University Hospital, DK-5000 Odense, Denmark.

ANDERSEN Linda Matthews, b. 18 Aug 1943, Hollywood, Calif, USA. Elem Sch Principal; Violinist. m. Michael Andersen, 22 Aug 1964, 1 s. 3 d. *Education:* MusB 1966, USC; Standard Life Tchg Credential (CSUN) 1972; Grad Work in Pvt Sch Admin, CLU. *Appointments:* Pasadena Symphony 1963- 65; Principal Violinist, Westside Symphony 1964; Mitzelfelt Chorale Orchestra 1961, 1974; Conejo Symphony 1975-; Tchr 1967-71, Principal, St Mark's Episcopal Day Sch; Principal, St Patrick's Episcopal Day Sch 1979-85; Principal, Pinecrest Sch, Thousand Oaks 1987-. *Creative Works:* Composition: Film music for Tell Me in the Sunlight, with M Amdersen, BMI; Herbstag, for viola and soprano, for Mu Phi Epsilon Nat Composition Contest 1986; Book: WASC School District Evaluation, K-8 Division. *Memberships:* Mu Phi Epsilon, Pres 1964-65; Music Educators' Nat Conf, viola/string- section preparer for Jr High Orch, Long Beach 1970; Nat Episcopal Schs of Am, Com mem 1973; Western Assn of Schs and Cols (WASC), Com mem and Evaluator 1985. *Honours:* Scholarship, USC Sch of Mus 1961, Mus Ed Dept; Hon Mention, Mu Phi Epsilon Composition Contest 1963; WASC 6 year Certification for St Patrick's Day Sch 1984 (longest awd'd to schs). *Hobbies:* Reading; Spending time with his daughter and son, and friends; Plays; Musicals; Museums; Travel; Playing chamber music. *Address:* 6739 Pheasant Lane, Agoura, CA 91301, USA.

ANDERSEN Mogens, b. 8 Aug 1916, Copenhagen. Painter; Author. m. Inger Therkildsen, 28 Nov 1947, 1 s. 1 d. *Education:* Art Master P Rostrup Boyesen. *Appointments:* Vstg Prof, Royal Acad 1970-72; Pres, Danish State Art Foun 1977-80. *Creative Works:* Paintings in museums in Scandinavia and Yugoslavia, Poland, Japan, USA and Germany; Author of art books and autobiography. *Honours:* Eckersberg Medaille 1949; Thorvaldsen Medaille 1984; Knight of Dannebrog 1984; (Knight) Chevalier de la Legion d'Honneur 1984; Officier des Arts et Lettres 1984. *Address:* Strandagervej 28, DK 2900 Copenhagen, Denmark. 19, 43, 34, 139.

ANDERSEN Per Oskar, b. 12 Jan 1930, Oslo. Prof. m. Kari Sletten, 5 July 1955, 1 s. 3 d. *Education:* MD 1954, PhD 1960, Oslo Univ. *Appointments:* Asst Prof 1958-62, Assoc Prof 1962-72, Prof 1972-, Univ Oslo; Vstg Fellow, Oxford Univ 1970-71. *Publications:* Co-Author: Physiological Basis of Alpha Rhythm, 1968; Excitatory Synaptic Mechanism, 1970. *Memberships:* European Neurosci Assn, Councillor 1978-88, Pres 1989-90; Physiol Soc, UK 1986-; Scand Physiol Soc 1972-; Neurosci Res Prog 1986-; Soc for Neurosci, USA 1988-; Acad Euopaea 1987-. *Honours:* Anders Jahres Prize for Young Researchers 1967; Fridtjof Nansens Prize 1968; Hon Doctor, Univ Zurich 1988; Philip Bard Lecture, Johns Hopkins Univ 1988; Graham Goddard

Memorial Lecture, Dallousie 1989. *Hobbies:* Sailing; Skiing; Carpentry. *Address:* Institute of Neurophysiology, Postbox 1104 Blindern, N-0317 Oslo 3, Norway.

ANDERSON Carolyn Pollock, b. 7 Feb 1942, Sacramento, Calif, USA. Co Dir of Global Family. m. 1 s, 1 d. *Education:* BA, Stanford Univ, 1963; MA, San Jose State Univ, 1978. *Appointments:* Self Employed Conslt, 1978-85; Seminar Leader, 1985-86; Co Founder, Dir, Global Family, 1986-. *Publications:* Numerous Articles. *Honours:* Center for Soviet American Dialogue Award in Moscow; Star Alliance Award. *Hobbies:* Travel; Dancing; Reading; Being in Nature. *Address:* 112 Jordan Avenue, San Anselmo, CA 94960, USA.

ANDERSON Danny J, b. 8 Aug 1958, Houston, Texas, USA. Prof Spanish Am Lit. *Education:* BA Lib Arts 1980, Austin Col, Texas; MA Spanish & Portuguese 1982, PhD Spanish & Portuguese 1985, Univ Kansas. *Appointments:* Prof Spanish Am Lit, Univ Tex at Austin 1985-88; Prof Spanish Am Lit, Assoc Chair of Dept Spanish & Portuguese, Univ Kansas, Lawrence, Kansas 1988-. *Publication:* Vicente Lenero: The Novelist as Critic, book, 1989. *Memberships:* Modern Lang Assn; Midwest Modern Lang Assn; Latin Am Studies Assn; Am Assn Tchrs of Spanish & Portuguese. *Honours:* Robinson Valedictory Medal, Austin Col 1980; BA with Honours; Inducted into hon socs: Sigma Delta Pi (Spanish), Phi Sigma Iota (Romance Langs), Alpha Chi (Scholarship), 1980; ITT Intl Fellowship, Univ Veracruzana, Mexico 1982-83. *Hobbies:* Contemporary popular culture, music, tv, film; Mexican history & culture; History of publishing industry in Latin America. *Address:* Department of Spanish & Portuguese, University of Kansas, 3062 Wescoe, Lawrence, KS 66045, USA.

ANDERSON Elsie Jean Miners, b. 4 July 1931, Salisbury, Rhodesia. Assoc Prof Maths. m. Larry Vance Anderson, 22 Dec 1961, 2 d. *Education:* BS 1951, UED 1952, Rhodes Univ, Grahamstown, S Africa; MS in LS 1966, East Tex State Univ, Commerce, Tex. *Appointments:* Geography & Maths Tchr, Govt of Central African Fdn 1953-61; Exchange Geography Tchr, Mill Hill, London, England 1957; Math Tchr, Desdemona, Tex 1962-64; Head Librarian, Holding Inst, Laredo, Tex 1971-72; Assoc Prof of Math, Western Tex Col, Snyder, Tex 1973-. *Memberships:* Tex Jr Col Tchrs' Assn; Am Math Assn of Two-year Cols; Tex Math Assn of Two-year Cols; Math Assn Am; Western Tex Col Fac Assn, Acad Affairs Com mem, Chairperson 1980-81, 1985-86; Girl Guides 1940-53; Girl Scouts of Am 1972-. *Hobbies:* Stamp collecting; Swimming; Racquet ball; Travel. *Address:* 600 29th Street, Snyder, TX 79549, USA. 7, 15.

ANDERSON Eric George, b. 7 June 1940, Alyth, Perthshire. Conslt Orthopaedic & Traumatic Surgeon. m. Elizabeth Clare Cracknell, 26 Mar 1966, 1 s. 2 d. *Education:* MB ChB 1964, Univ St Andrews; MSc in Med Eng 1974, Univ Salford; Fellow Royal Col Surgeons Edinburgh 1971. *Appointments:* Sr Registrar, Robert Jones & Agnes Hunt Orthopaedic Hosp, Oswestry & Birmingham Accident Hosp 1973-78; Conslt Orthopaedic & Traumatic Surgeon, & Hon Clin Lectr, Western Infirmary, Glasgow 1978-. *Contributions to:* Common Foot Disorders, 1989; The Foot and its Disorders, 1991. *Memberships:* Brit Orthopaedic Assn; Hon Treas; Brit Ortho Foot Surgery Soc; Deputy Editor, Injury; Mem Editorial Bd, The Foot; Fellow, Royal Soc Med; Fellow, Brit Assn Clin Anatomists; Brit Assn Sport & Med; Hon Med Advr, Scot Amat Swimming Assn; Clin Assoc, Nat Centre for Tng & Ed in Prosthetics & Orthotics, Univ Strathclyde. *Hobbies:* Music; Modelling buses & trams. *Address:* University Department of Orthopaedic Surgery, Western Infirmary, Glasgow G11 6NT, Scotland.

ANDERSON Isabel Beatrice, b. 28 May 1939, Unity, SK, Canada. Prof Ec. m. Frederick Frazer Langford, 24

Apr 1982, 3 d. *Education:* BA Maths 1960, BA (Hons) Ec 1961, MA Ec 1963, Univ Saskatchewan; Horace Rackham Sch Grad Studies, Univ Michigan 1963-64; PhD (ABD) 1972, Queen's Univ, Kingston, Ontario; Centre Univ d'Etudes Francais, Univ Domaine, Grenoble, France 1981-82. *Appointments:* Reschr, Ec Coun of Canada, Ottawa 1964- 66; Prof Ec, Univ Saskatchewan 1968-; Vstg Asst, Prof Ec, Univ Victoria, BC 1972-73; Canadian NGO Del, UN Conf on Trade & Devel, Nairobi, Kenya 1976; Canadian Del, UN Conf on Sci & Tech, Vienna, Austria 1979; Trade Commr, Public Hearings, Province of Saskatchewan, Canada-US Bilateral Trade Negotiations 1986; Chairperson, Intl Studies Prog, Col of Arts & Sci, Univ Saskatchewan 1990-91; Bd Dirs, Potash Corp of Saskatchewan Inc 1989-. *Creative Works:* Regular Commentator, Editorialist, radio & tv, on nat & intl ec policy issues; Internal Migration in Canada, 1966; An Overview of Canada's Economy, 1988; An Overview of the Development of a National Resource Based economy, 1991. *Memberships:* Cndn Ec Assn; Western Ec Assn. *Hobbies:* Reading; Sailing; Skiing; Travelling. *Address:* 1212 Colony Street, Saskatoon, Canada S7N 0S6.

ANDERSSON Leif Per Roland, b. 18 May 1923, Gothenburg, Sweden. Inventor; Tech Designer. m. (1)Anna Stina Johansson, div 1968, 1 d. (2)Naemi Gunilla Strom, 1 s. 1 d. *Education:* Student in Bldg Engrg, NKI Corr Inst, Sweden; Self-taught during rest of life parallel with work; Lic pilot 1955-65. *Appointments:* Mng Dir & Owner,Johan Andersen Bleck & Platslageri, Gothenburg, Sweden 1950-70; Tech Dir, Flexi System, Vargarda, Sweden 1981-87; PPP Constrn AB, Gothenburg, Sweden 1987-. *Creative Work:* Patentee transp and bldg systems and hangar and terminal systems; Conslt, Skanska, Malmae, Sweden. *Membership:* Swedish Aeroclub, Gothenburg 1955-65. *Hobbies:* Photography; Film; Aviation; Travelling; Problem solving; His life and work is his hobby. *Address:* Bogatan 39A, 41272 Gothenburg, Sweden. 52.

ANDORKA Rudolf, b. 30 Apr 1931, Budapest, Hungary. Prof of Sociology; Univ Rector. m. 14 Mar 1970, 1 s. 3 d. *Education:* Univ Dipl 1963, Fac Law, Eotvos Lorand Univ of Budapest; PhD Sociol 1979, H Acad Sci. *Appointments:* Manual Worker 1949-60; Translator 1960-62; Reschr, Demographic Res, Inst of Centr Stat Off 1963-69, Reschr, Centr Stat Off 1970-83; Prof Sociol 1984-91, Rector 1991-, Budapest Univ Ec Scis. *Publications:* Author and Co-Author 13 books, Edit or Co-Edit 3 books, Author or Co-Author 35 jour arts and chapts in books; Determinants of fertility in advanced societies, 1978; Modernization in Hungary in the long and short run measured by social indicators, co-author, 1988. *Memberships:* Corresponding mem, Hung Acad of Scis 1990-; Exec Com, Intl Sociol Assn; Intl Union for Sci Study of Population and of the Regional Sci Assn. *Hobbies:* Hiking; Sailing; Skiing. *Address:* Ady Endre 9/B, H- 1024 Budapest, Hungary.

ANDREANSZKY Gabor L St, b. 7 May 1942, Budapest, Hungary. Mng Dir. m. Charlotte Elisabeth Ageman, 19 Mar 1988, 1 d. *Education:* Elect Engr 1972, Stockholm Tech Sch; MBA 1986, Univ Stockholm. *Appointments:* Design Engr, Component Mktg, Ericsson Gp 1965-80; Acct Mgr, Fairchild Semiconductor 1980-85; Area Sales Mgr Scandinavia, LSI Logic 1985-87; Mktg Mgr, Fujitsu Microelectronic GmbH 1987-88; Mng Dir, Pannonia Affarskonsult AB 1988-. *Memberships:* Profl Ec Soc, Stockholm; Swedish-Brit Soc, Stockholm; Golf Club, Bjorkliden; Yacht Club, Stockholm. *Hobbies:* Opera; Books; Theatre; Sailing; Skiing; Windsurfing. *Address:* Pannonia Affarskonsult AB, PO Box 20139, 104 60 Stockholm, Sweden.

ANDREIAN CAZACU Cabiria, b. 18 Feb 1928, Iasi, Iassy, Romania. Mathematician; Prof. m. Mircea Dimitrie Cazacu, 22 Sept 1954. *Education:* Licentiate in Maths 1949, Univ Bucharest; PhD Math 1955, Stipendium Ist Naz Alta Math 1963, Math Inst Romanian Acad; Second step in doctorship 1967, Univ Buch. *Appointments:* Asst

1949, Lectr 1950, Assoc Prof 1955, Prof 1968, Head Chair Analysis 1973-75, Dean Fac Math 1976-84, Univ Buch, Fac Math; Res Wkr 1951-69, Hon Res Wkr 1969-, Inst Math Rom Acad. *Publications:* Over 70 papers on Riemann and Klein Surfaces, Nevanlinna's Theory, Quasiconformality, Differential Rings; 5 books in Romanian. *Memberships:* Math Soc of Romania; Soc Romanian Mathematicians. *Honours:* Prize of Min of Ed 1964; Stoilow Prize of Rom Acad 1968; Vstg Prof Freie Univ, Berlin 1974, 1976, 1977; Organizer of 6 Rom-Finnish Seminars; Mem Intl Organizing Com of Complex Analysis, Polish Acad Sci. *Hobbies:* Ballet; Walking in mountains; Literature; Music. *Address:* University of Bucharest, Faculty of Mathematics, Str Academiei 14, 70109 Bucharest 1, Romania.

ANDRESIER Rose, b. 14 June 1942, London, England. Classical guitarist. m. Michael Daniels, 28 Dec 1962, 1 d. *Education:* LLCM 1963- 66 (London Col Mus). *Career:* Freelance Musician; Debut Wigmore Hall 1972. *Publications:* Arts in Classical Guitar; Edit for Berben & Cramer, Mornington Music, Music Publishers and Own Publishing Company, Andresier Editions; Pres, Lauderdale Guitar Soc. *Memberships:* Royal Soc Musicians 1984; Elected Fellow Royal Soc Arts 1991. *Honour:* Silver Medal, LLCM 1964. *Hobbies:* Collecting junk; Reading. *Address:* c/o DCM, 15 Victoria Avenue, London N3 1BD, England. 4.

ANDREW Kenneth, b. 21 Dec 1944, Darlington, England. Co. Dir;. m. Elisabeth Honora, 21 July 1967, 2 s. *Education:* B Eng (1st) 1968; MSc, DIC 1969; M Phil (Hon) 1984; D Phil 1990. *Appointments:* Var mgmt positions 1969-84, Natwest; GR. DIR, Good Relate, 1984-85; Dir of Consumer Mktg for Europe, Chase Manhattan Bank 1985-87; Mng Dir, N & P Financial Services 1989-90; GR DIR, N & P Building Soc 1987-90; Bus Conslt, all aspects of strategic & mktg 1990-91; Chairman & CEO, Aetna, F.M.I.L. *Publications:* The Bank Marketing Handbook, 1986; The Financial Public Relations Handbook, 1990; Bank Marketing in a Changing World 1991. *Memberships:* Inst Financial Planning, Intl Mgmt Centres, Brit Coun Aid for Refugees Homes; Fellow, Royal Soc of Arts; Fellow Inst Directors; Inst Bankers; Inst Mgmt; Inst Sci Bus; Bus Grad Assn; Mktg Gp of GB; Mktg Soc. *Honours:* Awd'd Bursary Nat Provincial Bank 1968-69; Twice Awd'd Best Engrg Student at Univ Wales, Cardiff; Hon M Phil for Contribution to Mktg, IMC 1985; Industrial Prof of Financial Services Mgmt, IMC 1990. *Hobbies:* Travel; 19th century literature, particularly European; Swimming; Political thought. *Address:* Aetna UK, Aetna House, 2-12 Pentonville Road, London N1 9XG, England.

ANDREWS Graham Eric, b. 9 May 1932, Newark-on-Trent, England. Conslt; Politician. m. (1)Muriel Dorothy Adams, dec, 11 Dec 1955, 2 d. (2)Margaret Eileen Alker, 21 Dec 1985. *Education:* Oxford Sch Cert 1948. *Appointments:* Retail Mgmt 1948-83; Conslt Retail Mgmt 1983-. *Publication:* The Councillor's Role, 1974. *Memberships include:* Combe Martin Parish Coun 1967-, Chmn 4 terms; Barnstaple Rural District Coun 1970-74; North Devon District Coun 1973-76, 1979-, Chmn 1984-86; Devon County Coun 1985-89; Berrynarbor Parish Coun 1987-; Chmn, 1991-92; Devon Assn of Parish Couns 1970-, Chmn 1978-; Dept Chmn, Northern Devon Health Care Trust 1991; N Devon Health Authority 1986-89; N Devon Community Health Coun 1974-80, Chmn 1976-79; ADC; ACC; NALC; var other sporting orgs. *Honours:* MRSH 1976; Maistre de Ordre de Anysetiers France 1987. *Hobbies:* National Health Service; Sport; Environment; Consumer affairs. *Address:* Treetops, Old Coast Road, Berrynarbor, North Devon EX34 9RZ, England.

ANDREWS Janice (Jan) Margaret, b. 6 June 1942, England. Writer; Storyteller; Arts Admr. m. Christopher John Andrews, 10 Aug 1963 (separated), 1 s. 1 d. *Education:* BA (Hons) 1963, Univ Reading; MA 1969, Univ Saskatchewan. *Appointments:* Dept of Secy of

State, Govt of Canada 1972-76; Writer, Arts Admr, Progs for Expo 86, Nat Gallery, Nat Library 1976-; Co-Fdr, Andrews- Cavley Enter 1987; Co-Fdr, The Chance to Give, Arts Ed with a Multicultural Focus, 1989 (now known as MASC). *Publications:* Children's books: Fresh Fish and Chips, 1972; Ella an Elephant, un Elephant, 1973; The Dancing Sun, Edit, 1981; Very Last First Time, 1985; Pumpkin Time, 1990; The Auction, 1990. *Memberships:* The Writer's Union of Canada; Canadian Soc of Children's Authors, Illustrators & Performers; Toronto Sch of Storytellers. *Honours:* Shortlisted: Canada Coun Children's Literature Awd, 1986; Governor General's Prize for Children's Literature, 1990. *Hobbies:* Wilderness canoeing; Kayaking; Hiking; Camping; Cross Country Skiing; Gardening. *Address:* 501 Edison Avenue, Ottawa, Ontario, Canada K2A 1V3. 88.

ANDROUTSELLIS Paul Theotokis, b. 27 Feb 1939, Corfu, Greece. Civil Engr; Conslt. m. Carla Cerruti, 1 Oct 1968, 2 s. *Education:* Drs Degree E Engrng, Turin Polytech, 1957-61, 1964-67; Post Grad, Seminar Road Constr, 1967; Technecon Formation Techn, Chamber Gr, 1972; Hotel Engrng, Cornell Univ, 1973. *Appointments:* Bridge Calc, Euroconsult, Turin It, 1967; Planning Nat Scale Min of Coorination, 1968-69; Chief Enge, Edok Eter, Vice pres, Georevna, 1969-78;Pres, Exte Tourist Development, 1979-82; Inv Conslt General Ins Co & Others, 1978-. *Memberships:* Greek Tech Chamber; Corfu Reading Soc; Athens Tennis Club; Athens Ski Club; Phoenix Philosophical Soc. *Honours:* Inst Spirotechnique Francais. *Hobbies:* Tennis; Sailing; Skiing; Classical Music; History. *Address:* 4 Charitos Str, 10675 Athens, Greece. 52.

ANG Ke Bing, b. 29 Mar 1950, China. Company Exec. *Education:* Chung Hwa Correspondence Sch 1964; BSEE, Adamson Univ 1974. *Appointments:* Salesman, Far Eastern Plimbing Co 1974-76; Asst Mgr, Ang Bros Merchandising Co 1976-78; Gen Mgr, ACG Builders Centre Inc 1978-; VP, ACG Realty Co; Dir, A E & W Realty Co. *Memberships:* St Stephen's Alumni Assn; Adamson Univ Alumni Assn; Inst Integrated Elect Engrs of the Phil (IIEE); Am Mgmt Assn; Inter Department of Transportation & Com Centre; Boy Scouts of China in the Phils, Scouts Master. *Honours:* Cert from Boy Scouts of Phils 1968; Cert from Malacanatu Palace 1968. (Big earthquake in Manila 1968). *Hobbies:* Travel; Mountain climbing; Swimming; Table tennis; Chinese karate. *Address:* 437 Calbayog Street, Mandaluyong, Metro Manila, 1501 Philippines.

ANGELIDIS Angel, b. 28 Oct 1946, Alexandroupolis, Greece. Directorate European Parliament. m. Gilberte Maryse Elisabeth, 18 Nov 1972, 3 s. 1 d. *Education:* MSc 1970, Athens Sch of High Agri Studies; PhD (Doctor Ingeniero Agronomo) 1974, Poly Univ Madrid; PhD (Docteur d'Etat es Sciences Economique) 1975, Univ Montpellier. *Appointments:* Hd Directorate Agriculture, Min of Coordination, Greece 1975-79; Principal Admr, European Comm, DG VIII 1985-87, DG VI 1979-85; Hd Div for Agri, Fisheries & Rural Devel, DG IV, European Parliament 1988-. *Publications:* Author num reports and documents within European Institutions, Reform of CAP, EEC AgriMonetary System, Common Forestry Policy, BSE and others. *Membership:* VP, Agri Ec Soc Greece 1978-79. *Honour:* Encomienda de la Orden Civil de Merito Agricola de Espana 1984. *Address:* European Parliament, Directorate General for Research, Division for Agriculture, Fisheries and Rural Development, Schuman Building, Office 6/16, L-2929 Luxembourg. 1.

ANGELL Dorothy Mae, b. 22 Oct 1921, Jackson, Miss, USA. Artist. m. 31 Jan 1942, 2 s, 3 d. *Education:* Hillman, Mississippi Baptist Coll, 1940-41, 1946; Southwestern Baptist Thed Seminary, 1952-54; Univ of Kansas, 1963; Kansas City Art Inst, 1965-68; Garden City Comm Coll, 1975; Univ of Colorado, 1984. *Appointments:* Homemaker, Wife, Mother, 1942-; US Civil Service, 1941-55; Full Time Dedicated Ministers Wife, 1950-

84; Special Ed Public Sch Tchr, 1961-62; Free Lance Profl Artist, Gallery Mgr, Painting Instr, 1975-. *Creative Works:* Book Illustratings; Story, Childrens Stories, Home Life Mag; Drawings; Poems; Childrens Books; Paintings. *Memberships:* Amer Bapt Miss Soc; Ks Baptist Miss Soc; High Country Art Assn; Colo Sps Poetry Fellowship; Hillman Coll Fr; Natl League of Amer Penwomen & Artists. *Honours include:* Mrs Mesehkes Cherry Tree Oil Cash Award; NLAPA Award for Sales Yearly; Paintings in Private Collections; Local & State Juried Art Schows. *Hobbies:* Sketching; Painting; Intl Travel; Photography; Family & Friends; Gormet Cooking. *Address:* 395 Buckeye Drive, Colorado Springs, CO 80919, USA.

ANGUS I R (Sandy), b. 24 Mar 1945, Ootacamund. Exhibition Organiser. m. Jane Elizabeth Scouler Buchanan, 27 Sept 1982, 2 s. 3 d. *Appointments:* Travelled extensively 1966-67; Specialised Exhibition 1968-70; Joined Andry Montgomery 1970, Dir Main Bd 1976-, Dir 1981-. Section Mgr and Conf Organiser 1970-73, Exhibition Mgr 1973-75, Exhibition Dir 1975-79, Interbuild (formerly Building Trades Exhibition); Dir, Building Trades Ltd 1973-; Dir, Scottish Industrial Trade Exhibitions Ltd 1974-; Assigned to UN Project 1975; Tech Com, Union des Foires Intl 1978-; Dir, Overseas Exhibition Services Ltd 1980-; Mem Nat Assn Exposition Mgrs 1982-; Chmn, Assn Exhibition Orgs 1985-87; Instigator & Fdr, Dept Chmn Exhibition Ind Federation 1986-88; Dir, Exhibition Audience Audits 1987-. *Hobbies:* Running; Skiing; Tennis. *Address:* 11 Manchester Square, London W1M 5AB, England.

ANGUS Robin John, b. 15 Sept 1952, Forres, Moray, Scotland. Stockbroker; Investment Trust Dir. m. Lorna Christine Campbell, 20 Aug 1977. *Education:* First Class Hons in Medieval and Modern History,Univ St Andrews 1970-74; Peterhouse, Univ Cambridge 1974-77. *Appointments:* Investment Mgr, Baume, Gifford & Co 1977-81; Investment Trust Analyst, Wood Mackenzie & Co 1981-; Dir, County NatWest Securities 1988-; Dir, Personal Assets Trust plc 1984-. *Publications:* Books: Independence: The Option for Growth, 1989; Independence and the Business Spirit, 1991; Dictionary of Scottish Church History & Theology, contbr, 1991; Many pub arts and light verse. *Memberships:* Auditor, Diocese of Moray, Ross & Caithness, Scottish Episcopal Ch; Trustee and Com mem, Scottish Centre for Ec & Social Res; Mem Adv Coun, Inst Investment Mgmt. *Hobbies:* Church work; Politics-Scottish Nationalist; History; Music; Reading; Writing verse. *Address:* County NatWest Securities Ltd incorporating Wood Mackenzie & Co Ltd, Kintore House, 74-77 Queen Street, Edinburgh EH2 4NS, Scotland.

ANISMAN Philip, b. 12 Sept 1941, Toronto, Canada. Barrister; Solicitor. *Education:* BA 1964; LLB 1967, Univ Toronto, Canada; LLM 1971; JSD 1974, Univ Calif at Berkeley. *Appointments:* Asst Prof, Fac Law, Univ Western Ontario, Canada 1968-71; Res Ofcr, Law Reform Comm of Canada 1971-73; Dir, Corporate Res Br, Dept of Consumer and Corporate Affairs, Canada 1973-78; Prof of Law, Osgoode Hall Law Sch, York Univ, Toronto 1978-85; Vstg Prof, Monash Univ, Mel, 1983; Conslt, Nat Companies and Securities Comm, Australia 1983-86; Special Counsel on Corp, Securities and Constitutional Law, Goodman & Carr, Toronto 1985-87; Sole Practice 1987-. *Publications include:* Author of 6 books incl, Takeover Bid Legislation in Canada: A Comparative Analysis, 1974; The Media, The Courts and the Charter, co-editor, 1986; Author of arts; Book Reviews; Notes; Comments for profl jours. *Memberships:* Law Soc of Upper Canada; Assoc Mem, Am Bar Assn. *Honours:* Walter Perry Johnson Fellowship, Univ Calif at Berkeley 1967-68; Lady Reading Prize in Criminal Law, Univ Toronto 1965. *Address:* 80 Richmond Street West, Suite 1905, Toronto, Ontario, Canada M5H 2A4.

ANNAN William George Taylor, b. 22 Feb 1931, Kumasi, Ghana. Conslt Physician. m. Patricia Ann Capenhurst, 29 July 1967, 3 d. *Education:* Univ Col Hosp, Ibadan, Nigeria 1955-60; MB, BS 1960, London; DTM&H 1964, Liverpool; MRCP 1972, FRCP 1988, Royal Col Physicians, UK. *Appointments:* SHO, Chest & Gen Med, City Gen Hosp, Stoke-on-Trent 1963; SHO Geriatric Med, St Edmunds Hosp, Northampton 1965-66; SHO Chest Med 1966-68, Registrar Gen Med 1969-73, Victoria Hosp, Blackpool; Registrar Chest Med, Monsall Hosp, Manchester 1968-69; Sr Registrar, Geriatric Med with weekly sessions in Neurol, Crumpsall Hosp, Manchester 1973-74; Sr Registrar Gen Med with weekly sessions in Neurol, Manchester Royal Infirmary 1974; Conslt Physician Geriatric Med, Blackpool Wyre & Fylde Health Authority 1974-. *Memberships:* Brit Med Assn; Royal Col Physicians, London; Fellow, Brit Geriatric Soc. *Hobbies:* Bridge; Gardening; Walking; Table tennis. *Address:* 3 Carleton Gardens, Poulton-le-Fylde, Blackpool, Lancs FY6 7PB, England.

ANWAR Tariq Rafiq, b. 21 Sept 1945, N Delhi, India. Film Edit. m. Shirley Natalie Hills, 29 Sept 1966, 1 s. 1 d. *Education:* Sir John Cass Col, London 1964-66. *Career:* Films include as Asst Film Edit: Corruption, 1968; Mackennas Gold, 1969; Cromwell, 1970; Loot, 1970; Jerusalem Fire, 1971; As BBC Film Edit 1972-90 include: Oppenheimer; Caught on a Train; Knockback; Beloved Enemy; Tenser is the Night; Breaking Up; Monocled Mutineer; Fortunes of War; The Mountain and the Molehill; One Way Out; Summers Lease; The March; 1990- Freelance, films include: The Orchid House; Galahad of Everest. *Membership:* ACTT. *Honours:* BAFTA Awd, Best Edit, Caught on a Train 1980; BAFTA Nomination Best Edit: Monocled Mutineer 1986, Fortunes of War 1987, Summers Lease 1989; ACE Nomination Best Edit, Tender is the Night 1985. *Hobbies:* Reading; Writing; Tennis; DIY; Motor cars. *Address:* c/o PTA, 21A Noel Street, London W1, England.

AOKI Masamitsu, b. 19 Dec 1945, Yamaguchi, Japan. Chem Engr. m. 19 Apr 1980, 2 s. 1 d. *Education:* BA Chem 1968, Kyushu Inst Tech. *Appointments:* Chem Engr, Toshiba Corp 1968-74; Gp Ldr 1974-76, Dep Tech Mgr 1977-82, Tech Mgr 1982-87, Sr Specialist 1987-91, Mgr 1991-, Toshiba Chem Corp. *Publications:* Electronic Packaging Technology, 1985; Advanced Technology for PCB, 1987; PCB Technical Handbook, 1987; Electronic Engineering, 1989; SMT Handbook, Polyimide Resin, 1991. *Memberships:* Inst for Interconnecting and Packaging Electronic Circuits (IPC); Japan Inst Printed Circuit; Japan Thermosetting Plastics Ind Assn; Japan Printed Circuit Assn. *Hobbies:* Skiing; Swimming; Travel. *Address:* Maeda Heights 1141, 511-2 Maedacho, Totsukaku, Yokohama 244, Japan. 52.

APETREI Eduard, b. 11 Oct 1937, Blagesti, Romania. Cardiol. m. 18 Oct 1975, 1 s. 1 d. *Education:* Med Fac Iasi, 1956-60; Postgrad Ed in Cardiology, Bucharest 1963-65; Tng in Cardiol in Helsinki, Paris, Bruxel 1972. *Appointments:* General Practice 1960-63; Post graded 1963-65; Tchg 1965-. *Publications:* Books: Fonocardiography, 1977; Peripheral Vascular Disease, 1979; Ischemic Heart Disease, 1981; Eschocardiography, 1990; 144 med arts. *Membership:* European Soc Cardiol. *Hobbies:* Tennis; Theatre; Reading. *Address:* Cardiology Department, Fundeni Hospital, Romania.

APPLEBY Robert Houston, b. 16 Dec 1931, Visalia, California, USA. Mgr Bldgs & Grounds; Statistics Conslt. m. Barbara Louise Verhalen, 16 June 1956, 3 s. 1 d. *Education:* BS Math 1954, Wash Col; MS Stat 1960, Va Poly Inst. *Appointments:* E I Pmt de Nemours & Co 1960-90; Immaculate Conception Parish 1990-. *Publication:* SASA-A sequential multiviable test of means. *Memberships:* ACM, Chapt Chair; ASM, District Dir; NCGA, State Dir; WFS, State Coord; ISA; IEEE; NCGOP, Precinct Chair. *Hobbies:* Evangelisation; Racquet sports; Bicycling. *Address:* 207 Watts Street, Durham, NC 27701, USA. 7, 46, 50.

ARAI Motosuke, b. 28 Aug 1932, Osaka, Japan. Prof Eng. m. Matsumoto Momoe, 18 Aug 1958, 1 s. 1 d. *Education:* BA 1962, Nihon Univ; MA 1964, Kansai Univ; Doctorate Programme, Kyoto Univ 1965-66; St Edmund's Col, Univ Cambridge 1984-85. *Appointments:* Asst Prof Eng 1964, Prof Eng 1971-, Chmn Eng Dept 1973-, Naniwa Col. *Publications:* Edited: Oscar Wilde's Short Stories, 1965; Mark Twain's Short Stories, 1968; Nathaniel Hawthorne's Short Stories, 1974; Edit, The Naniwa Library Review 1987-. *Memberships:* Eng Lit Soc Japan; Am Lit Soc Japan; Japan- Am Soc of Osaka; Dir, Centre for Intl Relats, Osaka Univ Arts. *Honours:* Hon Grad Prize, Nihon Univ 1962; Most Outstanding Scholar Awd for 1985, Matsumura and Kohe Foun 1985; Cert Merit from Min Ed, Japan 1990. *Hobbies:* Reading; Painting. *Address:* 5-194-2 Gakuen, Daiwacho Nara, Japan 631.

ARAI Thomas Yoshitami, b. 5 May 1931, Chiba, Japan. Chmn. m. Choko, 16 Jan 1963, 2 s. *Education:* Dipl 1953, Pitman's Col, London; AMP 1969, Harvard Bus Sch. *Appointments:* Rep, Japan Productivity Centre, USA 1956-59; Asst Gen Mgr, Sony Corp of Am, 1960-62; Mng Dir, Blue Chip Corp 1963-70; Chmn, Systems Intl Inc 1970-; Pres, Tokyu Hotels Intl 1977- 89. *Publications:* Sev books on mgmt in Japanese. *Memberships include:* Pacific Basin Ec Coun, Steering Com; Harvard Bus Sch Alumni Coun; Japan-Am Soc, Coun mem; Intl Al Foun, Coun mem; Tokyu Scholarship Foun for Foreign Students, Coun mem; Foun for Intl Bus Communication, Coun mem. *Honours:* Hon Citizen of State Alabama 1987; Los Meritos por Servicios Distinguidos, Republic of Peru 1990. *Hobbies:* Travel; Golf; Fishing; Study of origin of Japanese language. *Address:* 3-26-18 Kamikitazawa, Setagaya-ku, Tokyo, Japan 156.

ARBATOVA Maria, b. 17 July 1957, Russia. Playwright. m. Miroshnik Alexandra, 28 Aug 1976, 2 s. *Education:* Moscow Univ, Faculty of Philosophy; Inst of Literature. *Appointments:* Self Employed. *Creative Works:* Plays for Reading; Script Writing; Film. Not to Forget, Not to Forgive; Author of 10 Plays reformed in Russia. *Memberships:* Union of Soviet Writers; Intl Club of Feminists; The Club of New Style playwriters. *Hobbies:* Ecology; Protection of Fauna & Flora. *Address:* 25-6 Usacheva St, Moscow 119048, Russia.

ARBUTHNOT James Norwich, Esq, b. 4 Aug 1952, Deal, UK. MP; Barrister. m. Emma Louise Broadbent, 6 Sept 1984, 1 s. 2 d. *Education:* Wellesley House, Broadstairs 1960-65; Eton 1965-70; MA Law 1974, Trinity Col, Cambridge. *Appointments:* Called to Bar 1975; Practising Barrister 1977-; Elected as Conservative MP for Wanstead & Woodford 1987; PPS to Archie Hamilton 1988-90 & to Peter Lillie 1990-1992; Asst Govt Whip, 1992-. *Hobbies:* Skiing; Music; Theatre. *Address:* House of Commons, London SW1A 0AA, England. 1.

ARCHDEACON Antony, b. 25 Jan 1925, Forest Gate, England. Solicitor. m. (1) Elizabeth Ball, 3 Dec 1956, 1 s, dis 1965, (2) Ursula Mentze, 24 Aug 1992. *Education:* Assoc, Inst Linguists, French, German, Spanish, Italian 1943; LLB 1979, Buckingham Univ. *Appointments:* Town Clerk, Buckingham 1951-71; Dir, Skim Milk Supplies Ltd 1967-; Dir, Business Mortgages Trust plc 1969-86; Chmn, The Forum of St Albans plc 1985-. *Memberships:* Feltmakers Co, Freeman 1972; Rotary Club of Buckingham, Pres 1968; Northamptonshire Anglo-German Club, Pres, Secy 1988-; St Stephens, Constitutional Club. *Hobbies:* Languages; Walking. *Address:* Trolly Hall, Castle Street, Buckingham MK18 1PT, England.

ARCHIBALD Edward Hunter Holmes, b. 24 Jan 1927, Belfast. Rtd Marine Art Conslt. *Education:* MA, FRSA, Trinity Col, Cambridge 1945- 48. *Appointments:* Springfield Dying & Finishing Works, Belfast 1948- 52; Curator of Oil Paintings, Nat Maritime Museum, Greenwich 1952-84; Conslt on marine paintings to Christie's and Sotheby's 1984-. *Publications:* The Wooden Fighting Ship in the Royal Navy AD 897-1860, 1968; The Metal Fighting Ship in the Royal Navy 1860-1970, 1972; Combined and updated edition The Fighting Ship in the Royal Navy 897-1984, 1984, reprinted 1987; Dictionary of Marine Artists, 1981, enlarged edition 1989. *Memberships:* Soc Nautical Res; Greenwich Soc. *Honour:* FRSA 1984. *Hobbies:* Tropical fish; Birds; Dogs; Formerly yacht racing; Skiing; Cresta run; Bob sleigh; Collect paintings, glass, armour, books and ceramics; Cooking & entertaining. *Address:* 10 Park Vista, Greenwich, London SE10 9LZ, England.

ARCISZ Sabina Barbara, b. 13 Dec 1964, Zabrze, Poland. Scientist; Univ Tchr Asst. *Education:* Master of Library & Information Sci, 1998; Master of Philosophy, Inst of Philosophy Jagiellonian Univ, 1991. *Appointments:* Asst, Dept of Library & Information Sci, Jagiellonian Univ, Cracow, Poland, 1990-. *Publications:* Philosophical Aspects of Information Sci; Who is Who in Polish Libraries and Libranianship. *Memberships:* Polish Bibliological Soc. *Hobbies:* Information Sci; Philosophy of Sci; Artificial Intelligence in Information Sci; Information Sources & Processes in the Field of Business & Econimcs. *Address:* Dept of Library & Information Science, Jagiellonian Univ, ul Gotebia 16, 31 007 Krakow, Poland.

ARCULUS Robert Albert, b. 24 Nov 1924, Earlswood, Warwickshire, UK. Rtd Principal. m. Pauline Wall Browne, 14 July 1954, 1 s. *Education:* ONC 1943, HNC 1945, BSc 1949, Col of Tech, Birmingham; C Eng 1968; FIMechE 1972; BSc (1st class hons) Eng (London) 1949; FCGI 1991 (Fellowship of City & Guilds of London Inst). *Appointments:* Engrg Apprentice to Asst Works Mgr 1941-51; Lectr 1951-54, Col Tech, Birmingham; Dudley TC 1954-58; Wednesbury TC 1958-62; Principal, Coventry TC 1962-84; CBI Mem (p-time), Industrial Tribunals 1977-. *Publications:* Coventry CSE Document, 1965, Vocational Preparation Document (BACIE), 1975; Training for Skills (BACIE), 1979; Adult Retraining (BACIE), 1982; The Role of the College Principal, 1983. *Memberships:* UK Tech Del, Intl Youth Skill Olympics 1984-90; Coventry Community Relats Coun, CH Employment Panel 1969-82; Inst Mech Engrs, Fellow; Royal Soc Arts, Fellow; Magistrates Assn; JP 1970-; City & Guilds of London Inst, Mem of Coun 1970-90, Chmn Examination Bd 1974-88; Brit Accreditation Coun for Independent Further & Higher Ed 1986-91; Rotary Club of Coventry, Pres 1975-76; Guildhall Operatic Soc, Coventry, Pres 1962-. *Honours:* FRSA 1982-; Assn Principals of Cols, mem 1963-, Pres 1982, Hon Mem 1983-; Intl Youth Skill Olympics, Awd'd Hon Membership of Intl Org 1990; City & Guilds of London Inst, apptd Hon Mem 1972; Intl Youth Skill Olympics awd'd Hon Membership of Intl Vocational Tng Org in Amsterdam 1991. *Hobbies:* Rotary Club; Amateur operatics; Astronomy; Lawn tennis; Iqbal Academy, Fdr Trustee 1972; Survey of summer snow beds in the Scottish mountains 1955-88; Boy Scout movement. *Address:* 8 Asthill Grove, Coventry CV3 6HP, England. 1.

ARESTIS Philip, b. 24 Oct 1941, Famagusta, Cyprus. Prof Ec. m. Maro Motis, 30 Dec 1974, 1 s. 1 d. *Education:* BA 1965, Athens Sch of Ec & Bus Studies, Greece; MSc 1969, London Sch Ec, UK; PhD 1976, Univ Surrey, UK. *Appointments:* Lectr, p-time, Kingston Poly 1968-69; Lectr to Hd, Ec Div, Thames Poly 1969-87; P-time Lectr, Dept Extra-Mural Studies, Univ Cambridge and Dept Ec, Univ Surrey 1970-80; Prof Ec & Hd, Dept Applied Ec, Poly of East London; Univ of East London, 1988-. *Publications include:* Over 100 books and arts, latest includes: Post-Keynesian Approach to Economics: Alternative Analysis of Economic Theory & Policy. *Memberships:* Royal Ec Soc; Assn for Evolutionary Ec; European Assn for Evolutionary Polit Ec; Ec Bd, Res Degrees Com, panel of special advrs, Coun for Nat Acad Awds; Co-Chair, ESRC- financed Post-Keynesian Ec Study Gp. *Honours include:* Sev monetary awds for studies. *Hobbies:* Opera; Theatre; Cinema; Concerts;

Reading novels; Political material; Sports esp soccer. *Address:* 52 Albert Road, London NW4 2SD, England.

AREVSHATIAN Sen, b. 7 Jan 1928, Yerevan, Armenia. History of Phil Textologist; Translator. m. Ter-Davtian Knarik, 26 Mar 1950, 1 d. *Education:* Yerevan State Univ 1951; Post Graduate Courses 1954; D Phil 1971. *Appointments:* Chf Scist, Inst Philosophy 1954-59; Chf of Research & Publication of Mss of Matenadaran 1959-82, Dir of Matenadaran 1982-, Inst Ancient Manuscripts of Armenia. *Publications:* Philosoph views of G Tatevatsi, 1957; Definition of Philosophy of David the Invincible, 1960; Formation of philosophy science in Ancient Armenia, 1973; Works of David the Invincible, 1975, 1980; History of some philosoph schools of Medieval Armenia, 1980. *Memberships:* Corresponding Mem of Acad of Scis of Armenian Republic 1982-; Soc European Culture, Venice 1985-; Pres, Armenian Fund of Culture, Yerevan 1986-88. *Honours:* Armenian State Prize for Sci 1978; Order of the Red Banner of Labour 1986. *Hobbies:* Reading; Listening to music. *Address:* 111 Mashtots Avenue, Matenadaran, 375009 Yerevan, Armenia.

ARISS Herbert Joshua, b. 29 Sept 1916, Guelph, Ontario, Canada. Artist; Tchr. m. Margot Joan Phillips, 5 July 1950, 2 s. *Education:* Vocational Art, Ontario Col of Ed 1947. *Appointments:* Designer, Vibra-Lite, Toronto; Book Illustrator, Copp-Clarke and others; Tchr & Lectr; Hd Art Dept, H B Beal, London, Ontario. *Creative Works:* Works in public collections include: The Nat Gallery of Canada, The Art Gallery of Ontario, Vancouver, Calgary, Winnipeg, Sarna, Guelph and London Regl Art Galleries. *Memberships:* Royal Canadian Art Soc; Ontario Soc of Artists; Canadian Gp of Painters; VP, Canadian Soc of Painters in Water Colour; Pres, Western Art League; Canadian Soc of Graphical Arts. *Honours:* Canada Coun Fellowship 1960; Purchase Awd Winnipeg Biennial 1964; Hon Awd Canadian Soc Painters in Water Colour 1963; Mayor of London, Ontario Hon Awd for the Arts 1980. *Hobbies:* Reading; Photography. *Address:* 770 Leroy Crescent, London, Ontario, Canada N5Y 4G7. 88.

ARIYARATNE Ahangamage Tudor, b. 5 Nov 1931, Sri Lanka. Corporate Pres. m. Neetha Dhammachari, 25 July 1960. *Education:* BA, Vidyodaya Univ Sri Lanka. *Appointments:* Tchr, Bouna Vista Sr Sch, Galle 1954-56; Tchr, Govt Tchrs' Tng Col, Maharagama 1956-57; Tchr, Grade I Special Post, Nalanda Col, Colombo 1958-72; Fulltime Worker in Sarvodaya Shramadana Sangamaya Inc 1972-, presently Pres; Fdr Sarvodaya Movement in Sri Lanka 1958. *Publications:* Over 50 arts in nat & intl jours, most recent: The Need for a Holistic Vision in the Global Struggle Peace Through Development, 1989; Professionals and NGOs as Partners in National Development in a Participatory Democracy, 1989; Present Social Conflict in Sri Lanka, 1989. *Memberships include:* Pres, Lanka Jathika Sarvodaya Shramadana Sangamaya Inc; Chmn, Bd Trustees, Asian Inst of Rural Devel, Bangalore, India; VP, Liaison Com for Food Corps Progs Intl CILCA; Nat Ednl Coun, Sri Lanka; Chmn, APPROTECH ASIA, Philippines; Chmn, ASPBAE, Sri Lanka. *Honours:* 10 awds for his services to the Community incl: Jamnalal Bajaj Intl Awd for Promoting Gandhian Values outside India, 1990; August Forel Awd by Intl Org of Good Templars, 1990; Niwano Peace Awd, Niwano Peace Foun, 1992. *Hobbies:* Social service partic in helping individuals towards awakening themselves in all spheres. *Address:* Lanka Jathika Sarvodaya Shramadana Sangamaya Inc, 98 Rawatawatte Road, Moratuwa, Sri Lanka.

ARIZE Kanayo Austen, b. 12 Nov 1960, Awka, Nigeria. Publishing; Mass Communication. m. Ada Appolonia Nnaka, 30 Dec 1990. *Education:* Ord Nat Dipl 1984, Higher Nat Dipl 1987, Inst Mgmt & Tech, Enugu. *Appointments:* Sr Eng & Lit-in-Eng Tchr, Community Sec Sch, Udi 1980- 82; Producer, Hello Young People, and Hospital Requests, Radio Nigeria, Enugu 1984; PR,

Media Mgr, Max Publicity Ltd 1984-85; Correspondent, Daily Star newspaper 1986-87; Sub-Edit, Investigative Reporter, Today newspaper, Kaduna 1987-88; Sales Exec, Sr Sales Exec, Sales Coord, Northern Business Machines Ltd, Kaduna 1988-91; Pres, CEO, Zenith Marketing Communications Ltd, Kaduna, Publisher, Mng Edit, The International Tradelink. *Publications:* Over 150 news stories, news features, radio news commentaries and arts in newspapers, magazines and radio in Nigeria 1984-91. *Memberships include:* Nigeria Inst Mgmt; Nigeria Inst Mktg; IMT Alumni Assn, Asst Secy, Kaduna, Dir of Socials, Nthn Nigeria; Intl Assn of LEO Clubs, young wing of Lions Club Intl, Charter Pres, Enugu (IMT), Coord, Kaduna; Nat Assn Awka Students; Assn Mass Communications Students. *Hobbies:* Reading; Travelling; Indoor games partic scrabble; Making friends; Visiting friends; Devotion to God, Politics and Pursuit of Excellence. *Address:* AD10, Lagos Street, Kano Road, Kaduna, Nigeria.

ARJIA Losang Thubten, b. 21 Aug 1950, Haiyan County, Qinghai Province, China. Abbot of Kumbum Monastery; Pres, Qinghai Buddhist Assoc. *Education:* Xigatse Monastery, 1962-64; Tibetan Research Student, 1964-81; minorities Univ, 1987-88. *Appointment:* Monk. *Publications:* Kumbum Monastery; Tibetan Buddhist Art. *Honours:* Chinese Best Book of the Year; Assoc Research Fellow at Chinese Buddhism Coll. *Hobbies:* Ancient & Classical Arch Design. *Address:* Qinghai Buddhist Association, Qinghai Province, China.

ARKELL Kenneth Frederick, b. 6 Dec 1930, Calgary, Alberta. Supreme Court Justice. m. Olivia Tofteland, 23 July 1960, 2 s. 2 d. *Education:* Clinton (Ont) Col Inst; BA 1956, Univ W Ont; LLB 1959, Univ BC. *Appointments:* Served with RCMP 1950-52; Profl Footballer, BC Lions 1956-59; Called to Bar of BC 1960, Alta 1970; Ptnr, Lewin, Arkell & Callinson, City Solr & Prosecutor City of Dawson Creek 1960-69; Dist Judge, Prov Court of BC 1970-72; Dep Chief Judge 1972-75; Assoc Chief Judge 1975-76; Co Court Judge & Local Judge Supreme Court of BC 1976-90; Justice, Supreme Court of BC 1990-. *Memberships:* Mem & Vice Chmn Judicial Council BC 1970-76; Vice Chmn and Trustee St Joseph's Hosp Bd 1962-71; Vernon Jubilee Hosp Bd 1971-72; Dir, John Howard Soc 1971-73; Judicial Court Study & Report on Role & Salaries Prov Court Judges; Drafted Prov Court Act 1975; Hon Mem, Royal Candn Legion; Pres Dawson Creek C of C 1966-67; Pres, Cariboo Bar Assn 1968; Candn Bar Assn, Coun BC Sect 1968-70; Candn Inst Adm Justice; Candn Judges Conf; Kappa Alpha. *Honours:* 4 Scholarships 1953-55; Gold Medal, Vocal Solo, Ontario 1945. *Hobbies:* Golf; Skiing. *Address:* Law Courts, 3001-27th Street, Vernon BC, Canada V1T 4W5. 88.

ARLINGHAUS Sandra Judith Lach, b. 18 Apr 1943, Elmira, NY, USA. Mathematical Geographer. m. William C Arlinghaus, 3 Sept 1966, 1 s. *Education:* Grad Study in Math, Univ Chicago, 1964-66; AB, Vassar Coll, 1964; Univ of Toronto, 1966-67; Wayne State Univ, MA, 1976; PhD, Univ of Michigan, 1977. *Appointments:* Vis Asst Prof, Ohio State Univ, 1977-79; Asst Prof, Loyola Chicago, 1981-82; Lectr, Univ Mich, 1982-83; Rounding Dir, Inst of Mathematical Geography, 1985-. *Publications include:* Essays on Mathematical Geography; An Atlas of Steiner Networks; Down the Mail Tubes: The Pressured Postal Era; Over 50 Articles. *Memberships:* Amer Geographical Soc; Amer Mathematical Soc; Assoc of Amer Geographers; Mathematical Assn of Amer AAAS; NY AZcad of Sci; Engrng Soc of Detroit; Amer Soc of Photogrammetry & Remote Sensing. *Honours:* Honorary Member, Advisory Bd Intl Birmingham Centre; Univ Fellowship, Univ Michigan. *Hobbies:* Community Service; Swimming; Cooking. *Address:* 2790 Briarcliff, Ann Arbor, MI 48105, USA. 5, 8, 15, 138, 152.

ARLINGHAUS William Charles, b. 17 July 1944, Detroit, Michigan, USA. Prof; Dept Chmn. m. Sandra Judith Lach, 3 Sept 1966, 1 s. *Education:* BS 1964,

Univ Detroit; Univ Chicago, Math, 1965-66; Univ Toronto, Math, 1966-67; PhD Maths 1979, Wayne State Univ. *Appointments:* Extensive indl employment; Prof Math 4 locations 1977-82; Dept Chair, Math & Computer Sci, Lawrence Tech 1990-; Full Prof of Math, Lawrence Tech Univ 1991. *Publications:* 11 publications incl The Classification of Minimal Graphs with Given Abelian Automorphism Group, book in Memoirs series. *Memberships include:* Inst Math Geog, Bus Mgr; Am Math Soc; Assn Amer Geog; NY Acad Scis; Am Contract Bridge League; St Thomas' Pastoral Coun, past VP. *Honours:* Nat Sci Foun Math pre-doc, 1965, 1970; Tchg Asst Math, Wayne State Univ 1975-76; Putnan Exam 109th in USA 1964; Michigan Math Prize Compt, 2nd in State 1959-60, 1960-61; Num undergrad hons. *Hobbies:* Tournament duplicate bridge; Golf; Community service. *Address:* Department of Mathematics and Computer Science, Lawrence Technological University, 21000 W Ten Mile Road, Southfield, MI 48075, USA.

ARMINAS Anicetas, b. 9 Feb 1931, Lazdijai, Lithuania. Prof; Hd Mus Dept; Conductor of Choirs. m. 25 Nov 1961, 1 s. 1 d. *Education:* Student 1951-55, Postgrad Course 1955-58, Lithuanian Conservatoire; Study of Arts, Doctors degree 1969; Docent 1979; Prof 1990. *Appointments:* Ldr & Conductor of Orchestra of Lithuanian Theatre of Opera & Ballet, Concurrently studying in Lithuanian Conservatoire 1952-55; Lectr 1958-70, Hd Dept Choir Conducting 1964-70, Lithuanian Conservatoire; Chf Conductor of Choir of Lithianian Theatre of Opera & Ballet 1983-88; Hd Dept of Mus, Lithuanian Inst Culture 1989-; Chf Conductor of Winner of Intl Compt Male Voice Choir, Varpas, 1974-. *Publications:* 4 books: Plots and traits of evolution of Lithuanian Literature of Choirs, 1984; Sources of Lithuanian Choirs, 1988; Some problems of Lithuanian choirs, 1989; Some of leadership and conducting of choirs, 1991; 130 arts and reviews in books, mags and other pubs; Lectures in confs in Estonia and Ukraine; 5 lectures in Lithuanian confs; Art pub by APN agency (Moscow) in 60 langs; Conslt of editorship of Lithuanian Ency. *Memberships:* Mem Presidium, Hd Sci Com, Lithuanian Choirs Union; Sr Conductor, all Lithuania Songs Days; Mem Repertoire Comm of all Lithuanian Songs Days 1993-94. *Honours:* Honoured Art Wkr of Lithuania 1975; Dipl for taking part in intl festival of choirs in Estonia 1975. *Hobby:* His profession. *Address:* Taikos str 12-3, 4043 Vilnius-Bukiskis, Lithuania.

ARNDT Angelica, b. 19 Aug 1937, Santiago, Chile. Journalist. m. Georges De Bourguignon, 21 June 1958, 2 s. *Education:* BA 1954, Dunalastair Sch; Degree in Indl Des 1957, Univ Catolica; Degree in Journalism 1983, Col de Periodestas de Chile. *Appointments:* Editorialist, jour El Mercurio, de Santiago 1974-76; Columnist on intl affairs jour, La Tercera, 1976-77; Analytical Reporter world affairs, Ercilla magazine 1977-80; Paula magazine 1980-81 and Negocius 1980-82; Political Interviewer for Cosas magazine 1982-90. *Creative Works:* Producer, Edit of Political Cultural Progs for Chilean Natl TV Channel 7 and 11, based upon personal interviews to Presidents and Political Leaders as well as insights on diff subjects like think tanks and current affairs. *Memberships:* Assn de Mujeres Periodistas and Colegio Periodistas de Chile. *Honours:* Guest Speaker, Annual Meet of Am Women for Intl Understanding 1983; Multiple Prizes & Awds at sch, univ & sports compts. *Hobbies:* Skiing; Travel; Fashion; Reading; Writing; Swimming. *Address:* Casilla 19039, Correo 19, Lo Castillo, Santiago, Chile. 52.

ARNOTT Eric John, b. 23 June 1929, Sunningdale, Berks, UK. Conslt Ophthalmologist. m. Veronica Mary Langue, 19 Nov 1960, 2 s. 1 d. *Education:* Harrow Sch, Middx 1942-46; Trinity Col, Dublin 1949-53. *Appointments:* Sr Registrar, Univ Col Hosp 1961-63; Conslt Ophthalmologist: Royal Eye Hosp 1965-74; Royal Masonic Hosp 1971-; Charing Cross Hosp 1971-. *Creative Works:* Developer and Inventor of totally encircling loop intraocular lens for implantation into the capsular bag of the eye after surgery; Owner 3 worldwide patents. *Contributions to:* 4 book chapts and

co-Author, Intraocular Lens Implantation, textbook of cataract surgery, 1987. *Memberships:* Pres, European Phaco & Laser Soc; Tchr, Univ London; Tchr, Royal Col Ophthalmologists; Mem, Order St John; Fellow, Am Acad Ophthal; Royal Soc Med; OP Ophthalmic Surgery Soc. *Honour:* Trinity Surgery Prize, Trinity Col, Dublin 1952. *Hobbies:* Swimming-conqueror of Alcatraz Channel; Golf; Travel. *Address:* 11/12 Milford House, 7 Queen Anne Street, London W1M 9FD, England. 52.

ARP Halton Christian, b. 21 Mar 1927, NYC, USA. Astronomer. m. Marie-Helene Demoulin, 19 Jan 1984, 4 d. *Education:* AB cum laude 1949, Harvard Col; PhD cum laude 1953, Calif Inst Tech. *Appointments:* Carnegie Inst of Wash 1957-84; Max-Planck-Institut fur Astrophysik 1985-. *Publications:* Atlas of Peculiar Galaxies, 1966; A Catalogue of Peculiar Southern Galaxies and Associations, 1987; Quasars, Redshifts and Controversies, 1987. *Memberships:* Intl Astronomical Union; Am Astronomical Soc, Councillor 1973-76; Astronomical Soc of the Pacific, Pres 1980-83. *Honours:* Helen Warner Prize, Am Astr Soc 1960; Newcomb Cleveland Awd, Am Ass Adv Sci 1961; Alexander Humboldt Sr Scist Awd 1984-85. *Address:* Max-Planck-Institut fur Astrophysik, 8046 Garching Bei Munchen, Germany. 143.

ARREOLA Mona Jean, b. 4 Oct 1940, Brooklyn, NY, USA. Univ Admr. m. 12 May 1973, 2 s. 2 s. *Education:* BA 1961, Univ Fla; MS 1972, PhD 1979, Fla State Univ. *Appointments:* Asst Prof, Memphis State Univ 1979-82; Educ Curriculum Specialist 1982-85; Creativision Inc, Daytona Beach, Fla; Asst Dir 1985-89, Assoc Dir 1989-, Univ Tenn, Memphis Cancer Centre. *Memberships:* Nat Assn Female Execs; Intl Reading Assn; Am Assn Cancer Insts; Cancer Centre Admrs Forum; Am Mensa. *Honours:* Grad Summa Cum Laude 1961 (BA); Phi Beta Kappa 1961; Phi Kappa Phi 1961; Phi Delta Kappa 1972. *Hobbies:* Gardening; Reading; English history. *Address:* 5930 Grosvenor Avenue, Memphis, TN 38119, USA.

ARRINGTON Melvin Slay Jr, b. 26 July 1949, Jackson, Mississippi, USA. Univ Prof. m. Teresa Anne Ross, 10 Aug 1973, 2 d. *Education:* BA with distinction 1971, Miss Col; MALS 1972, MA 1974, PhD 1979, Univ Kentucky. *Appointments:* Actg Hd Librarian, Northside Library, Jackson 1972-73; Instr, Lenoir-Rhyne Col 1978; Instr, Asst Prof, Univ Tenn, Knoxville 1979-80, 1981-82; Asst Prof, Western Carolina Univ 1980-81; Asst Prof, Assoc Prof, Univ Miss 1982-. *Publications:* Author essays in ref vols on Latin American Lit as well as arts and reviews in profl jours. *Memberships:* Am Assn Tchrs Spanish & Portuguese; Assn de Columbianistas Norteamericanos; Inst Intl de Lit Iberoamericana; Latin Am Studies Assn; Miss Foreign Lang Assn; Modern Langs Assn of Am; South Central Modern Lang Assn; South Eastern Coun on Latin Am Studies. *Honours:* Sigma Delta Pi Spanish Honorary 1973; Fulbright Summer Seminar, Brazil 1983; Rotary Gp Exchange Awd, Argentina 1985; NEH Summer Seminar, Yale Univ 1985; Mellon Seminar, Vanderbilt Univ 1986; NEH Summer Inst, Univ Tex 1989; Miss Col Dist'd Foreign Language Alumnus of 1990. *Hobbies:* Reading; Sports. *Address:* Department of Modern Languages, University of Mississippi, University, MS 38677, USA. 7, 15.

ARRINGTON Teresa Ross, b. 2 July 1949, Detroit, Michigan. Univ Prof. m. Melvin Slay Arrington Jr, 10 Aug 1973, 2 d. *Education:* AB Summa cum laude with honours 1971, Univ Detroit; MA 1973, PhD 1977, Univ Kentucky. *Appointments:* Asst Prof, Lenoir-Rhyne Col, NC 1977-78; Asst Prof, Univ Tenn 1978-82; Instr, Asst Prof, Univ Miss 1982-. *Publications:* Author essays in ref vols on Feminist and Latin Am Lit as well as arts and reviews in profl jours. *Memberships:* Am Assn Tchrs Span & Port; Feminists Unidas; Miss Foreign Lang Assn, Exec Secy, Treas 1988-; Mod Lang Assn Am; South Central Mod Lang Assn; South Eastern Coun on Lat Am Studies. *Honours:* Ford Motor Co Fund Scholarship 1967; Outstg Span Student 1971; Natl Defense Ed Act

Fellowship 1971; Pi Mu Epsilon Math Honorary 1971; Sigma Delta Pi Span Honorary 1972; Haggin Grad Fellowship 1974; Mellon Grant 1981; NEH Summer Seminar 1982; Pi Delta Phi French Honorary 1986. *Hobbies:* Reading; Creative writing. *Address:* Department of Modern Languages, 312 Bishop Hall, The University of Mississippi, University, MS 38677, USA. 145.

ARRIZURIETA Jorge L. Govt Service. *Education:* Jr in academic standing pursuing double major in Finance and Public Adm, Sch of Bus, Sch Public Affairs. *Appointments:* Senator to Col of Bus at Fla Intl Univ 1985; Staff Asst to US Senator Paula Hawkins in S Fla 1985-86; Finance Dir to Tom Gallagher 1986; S Fla Fin Dir to Gov Bob Martinez 1986; Substitute Tchr, Msgr Edward Pace HS 1987; Host to Spanish Talk Show, La Voz de la Juventud 1987; Asst to Alec P Courtelis 1987-89; Dep State Dir to US Senator Connie Mack 1989-. *Memberships:* Co-Chmn, Gov Bob Martinez Re-election Campaign, 1990; Special Asst, Congresswoman Ileana Ros-Lehtinen Campaign 1989; Del to polit study tour of Argentina and Uruguay by Am Coun of Young Political Ldrs 1990; Bd Dirs, Tower Forum, Leadership Gp, Broward Co; Msgr Edward Pace HS's Endowment Fund Com; Fdr & Pres, Hialeah Young Repubs; Co-Chmn, Youth for Reagan-Bush Campaign 1984; Selected as Mentor for Mentor/Mentee Sibley Programme, Greater Miami C of C. *Honours:* Cert Appreciation, Pres Bush and VP Dan Quayle, Presidential Transition 1988-89; Cert Appreciation, Cuban Am Bar Assn 1989; Youth for Reagan-Bush '84, Excellence & Dedication Cert; Alumni of Year Awd, Msgr Edward Pace Sch 1988. *Address:* 1300 West 84th Street, Hialeah, FL 33014, USA. 117, 165.

ARTHURSDOTTER Karin Emilia, b. 19 Apr 1926, Rebbelberga, Scania. Translator. *Education:* Fil Kand 1969, Lund, Sweden; MA 1975, Leeds. *Appointments:* Var secretarial posts 1946-64; Asst Univ Tchr, Univ Newcastle-Upon-Tyne 1968-69, 1970-72; Asst Univ Tchr, Univ Lund 1969-70; HS Tchr, Toftaskolen, Engelholm, Sweden 1980-84; Tchr, Extramural Dept Lund Univ, Helsingborg 1984-85; Translator & Mgr, WORDS, Engelholm 1985-, at present translating parts of EEC Acquis Communautaire for Swdish Govt. *Publications include:* Translator of: Luigi Barzini: The Impossible Europeans, 1984; Walter Laqueur: Germany Today, 1987; Fernando Huici: Klimt, 1991; Massimo Gemin: Van Gogh, 1991. *Memberships:* Swedish Assn Authorized Translators; Swedish Writers' Union. *Honour:* Postgrad Res Scholarship, Swedish Govt 1976-80. *Hobbies:* Classical ballet; Literature; Dobermann called Rusty. *Address:* WORDS, Violgatan 4, S- 26262 Engelholm, Sweden. 52.

ARYE Avgust Genrihovich, b. 8 Aug 1938, Moscow. Ldg Sci Collaborator; Oil Geol; Hydrogeol; Specialist in underground fluids. m. V Isaenko, 11 May 1963. *Education:* MGRI, Moscow Geol Prosp Inst, 1963; PhD 1969; Doctor of geol-miner Scien 1987. *Appointments:* MGRI till 1965I VSEGINGEO, 1965-87; VNIGNI, 1987-; Physical bases of moving of underground waters 1984; Res of process of moving fluids in porous media 1982. *Publications:* 50 artsl 7 books-monographs; 5 patents. *Memberships:* Sci-Tech Oil & Gas Soc of USSR; Sci Coun VNIGNI. *Honours:* 2 Prizes for 2 fields discoveries. *Hobbies:* Reading; Music; Mechanics. *Address:* Novolesnaya 3, cor 2, kv 35, Moscow, Russia.

ARZOIU Ruxandra, b. 7 June 1961, Bucarest. Broadcasting Editor; Producer. m. Ion Arzoiu, 25 Sept 1982, 1 d. *Education:* Music Acad, Bucarest, 9814. *Appointments:* Music & Piano Tchr, 1984-88; Music Library, State Theatre of Operetta, 1988-90; Editor, Producer, Broadcasting, 1990-. *Creative Works:* Studies & Articles About Contemporary Music; Study about Repetor of Romanian Musicall; Monography, Michail Andrica. *Membership:* Rumanian Union of Courposer & Musicolrgist. *Hobbies:* Contemporary Arts. *Address:* Bd Dacia 20, Apt 9, Sector 1, Bucurest, Romania.

ASAZUMA Fumiki, b. 23 Aug 1931, Tokyo. Viola Edr; Orch Conductor; Viola d'amore Player. m. Michiko Nagamatsu, 19 June 1957, 1 s. 2 d. *Education:* Mus Br, Tokyo Nat Univ of Fine Arts and Music 1956; Viola and Viola d'amore studies, Vienna Acad 1966-67. *Appointments:* Prof Viola, Tokyo Nat Univ Fine Arts and Mus 1962-; Dir & Conductor, Tokio Akad Kommerorchester 1968-. *Publication:* Translator: The Interpretation of the Music of the XVII and XVIII Centuries by Arnold Dolmetsch, 1966. *Memberships:* Pres, Japan Viola Res Soc 1961-; Japan Musicology Soc; Nippon Conductors Assn; Rotary Club. *Hobbies:* Painting; Going for drive. *Address:* 13-17 Hachiyama-cho, Shibuya-ku, Tokyo 150, Japan.

ASCHENGREEN PIACENTI Kirsten, b. 29 Mar 1929, Madras. Museum Dir. m. Franco Piacenti, 19 Dec 1953, 1 s. *Education:* MA 1953, London Univ, Courtauld Inst; Dr 1966, Univ Florence. *Appointment:* Dir, Museo Degli Argenti, Florence 1971-. *Publications:* Il Museo Degli Argenti, 1967; Goldboxes at Waddesdon, 1975; Curiosita di una Reggia, 1979; Catalogues of the Costume Gallery and of the Museo D A, Edit. *Memberships:* Soroptimist Intl, Florence; Soc of Jewellery Historians; Italian Assn Textile Historians (CISST). *Honour:* Ufficiale al Merito Della Repubblica Italian 1988. *Hobby:* Gardening. *Address:* Costa San Giorgio 79, 50125 Florence, Italy. 95.

ASH Eric Albert Sir, b. 31 Jan 1928, Berlin. Rector. m. Clare Babb, 30 May 1954, 5 d. *Education:* Univ Col Sch 1945-52; Imperial Col: BSc 1948, DIC 1950, PhD 1952, DSc 1972. *Appointments:* Res Fellow, Stanford Univ, USA 1952-54; Res Asst, Queen Mary Col 1954-55; Res Engr, Standard Telecomms Col 1955-63; Sr Lectr & Reader 1963-67, Prof & Hd Dept Elec Engrg 1967-85, Rector 1985-, Imperial Col Sci, Tech & Med, London. *Creative Works:* Holds Patents, Published papers on topics in phys elect in engrg & physics jours. *Memberships:* Secy, Royal Inst 1984; Coun of Fellowship of Engrg 1981-84; Pres, IEE 1987-88; Acad Europaea 1989; FIEE; FIEEE; FInstPhys; FCGI. *Honours:* FRS 1977; FEng 1978; Faraday Medal, IEE 1980; CBE 1983; 10th Marioni Intl Fellowship 1984; Royal Medal of Royal Soc 1986; KT 1990; Hon Doctorates: Univ Leicester, INPG Grenoble, Univ Aston, Univ Edinburgh, Poly Univ NY. *Hobbies:* Music; Skiing; Swimming. *Address:* Imperial College of Science, Technology & Medicine, London SW7 2AZ, England. 1, 139.

ASHDOWN Paul George, b. 26 July 1944, New York, New York. Prof Journalism. m. Barbara Ann Green, 18 Apr 1975, 1 s. *Education:* BSJ 1966, MAJC 1969, Univ Fla; PhD 1975, Bowling Green State Univ. *Appointments:* United Press Intl 1969-70; Instr of Journalism, Univ Toledo 1971-75; Asst Prof Journalism, Western Kentucky Univ 1975-77; Prof Journalism, Assoc Dean, Communications, Univ Tenn 1977-. *Publication:* Edit, James Agee: Selected Journalism, 1985. *Membership:* Assn for Ed in Journalism and Mass Communication. *Honours:* Outstg Fac Awd 1983, 1992; Col of Communications Res Awd 1986; UT Outstg Teaching Awd, 1991. *Hobbies:* Theology; History; Opera; Baseball. *Address:* School of Journalism, University of Tennessee, Knoxville, TN 37996, USA. 30, 154.

ASHER Mukul G, b. 17 Dec 1943, Bombay, India. Univ Ec. m. Pragnya, 25 Aug 1969, 1 d. *Education:* BA Hons 1963, Bombay Univ; MA 1968, PhD 1972, Wash State Univ. *Appointments:* Staff Economist, Planning Office, Jersey City, NJ, USA 1973-75; Lectr 1975-77, Sr Lectr 1978- 89, Assoc Prof 1990-, Dept Ec & Stats, Nat Univ of Singapore. *Publications:* Co-Author, Indirect Taxation in ASEAN, 1983; Co-Author, ASEAW-South Asia Economic Relations, 1985; Edit, Fiscal Systems & Practices in ASEAW Countries, 1989. *Memberships:* Life Member: Am Ec Assn; Indian Ec Assn; Ec Soc Singapore; Hon Treas 1981-83, Hon Secy 1983-85, Ec Soc of Singapore; Intl Inst Public Fin. *Hobby:* Cricket. *Address:* Department of Economics & Statistics,

National University of Singapore, Clementi Road, Singapore 0511, Republic of Singapore. 52.

ASHIHARA Yoshinobu, b. 1918, Tokyo, Japan. Architect; Univ Prof. *Education:* BArch 1942, DArch 1962, Univ Tokyo; MArch 1953, Harvard Univ. *Appointments:* Marcel Breuer's 1953; Owner, Y Ashihara Architect & Assoc 1955-; Prof Arch: Musashino Art Univ 1965-89, Univ Tokyo 1970-79. *Publications:* Exterior Design in Architecture, 1970; The Aesthetic Townscape, 1983; The Hidden Order-Tokyo through the 21st Century, 1990. *Memberships:* Pres, Japan Arch Assn 1980-82; Arch Inst Japan 1985-87; Nat Art Acad; Rotarian. *Honours:* Hon Prof: Univ Tokyo, Musashino Art Univ; Hon Mem: Am Inst Archs, Royal Australian Inst Archs; NSID Golden Triangle Awd, USA 1970; Italian Order of Commendatore, 1970; Japan Acad Arts Awd, 1984; Order of Commander of the Lion of Finland, 1985. *Address:* Y Ashihara Architect & Associates, Sumitomo Seimei Building, 31-15 Sakuragaoka- cho, Shibuya-ku, Tokyo 150, Japan.

ASHRAF Syed Javed, b. 22 Feb 1940, Agra, India. Prof; Dir Computer Sci Inst. m. Farhat Afaza, 28 July 1981, 1 s. 2 d. *Education:* BS with hons 1960, MS in Maths 1961, Dipl in Stats 1961, Aligarth Univ, India; MS Stats 1969, Aberdeen Univ, Scotland; MS Computer Sci 1970, Queen's Univ, Belfast. *Appointments:* Lectr, Sind Univ, Jamshoro, Pakistan 1962-68; Programmer, Queen's Univ, Belfast 1970; Programmer, Anal, Karachi (Pak) Gas Co 1971-74; Mgr Comp, Pak Nat Oil Co, Karachi 1974-75; Asst Prof, Fac Sci, Garyounis Univ, Benghazi, Libya 1975-85; Prof, Dir, Inst Comp Sci, BCCI-Foun for Adv of Sci & Tech, Kar 1985-. *Publications:* Over 24 res pubs in field of Relational Databases, Automated Translation, Applied Artificial Intelligence and Applied Linguistics. *Memberships:* Fellow, Royal Stat Soc, London; Brit Computer Soc, London; IEEE, USA; People to People Intl, USA. *Honours:* First position in Hons of BS degree; Enlisted as Computer Conslt in Directory of the Brit Comp Soc. *Hobbies:* Reading; Computer logics; Educating people. *Address:* Director, Institute of Computer Science, BCCI-FAST, 22/E-6, PECHS 75400, Pakistan.

ASHTON William Michael Allingham, b. 6 Dec 1936, Blackpool, Lancs. Mus Dir. m. Kay Carol Watkins, 22 Oct 1966, 2 s. 1 d. *Education:* BA Hons Modern Langs, St Peter's Col, Oxford; Dip in Ed. *Appointments:* RAF Nat Service 1955-57; French Tchr 1963-73; Dir, Nat Youth Jazz Orch 1973-. *Creative Works:* Edit magazine, News from NYJO; Num press arts; 26 songs and 7 instrumental compositions incl: Songs: Don't Go To Her; When I'm With You; Looking Forward; Give Up; Why Don't They Write Songs Like This Anymore?; Instrumentals: Blood Orange; Getting Down To It; Pushover; Blue- Veined Gorganzola. *Memberships:* Com, Intl Year of the Child, 1979; Com, Assn Brit Jazz Musicians 1988-; Musicians' Union. *Honours:* MBE 1978; Winner of record awds for, They Don't Write Songs Like This Anymore, 1984 and Big Band Christmas, 1990; Winner, BP, ABSA Awd, for best us of Sponsorship Money, 1991. *Hobbies:* Song writing; Swimming; Reading. *Address:* 11 Victor Road, Harrow, Middlesex HA2 6PT, England.

ASHWORTH Graham William, b. 14 July 1935, Plymouth, England. Dir Gen, Tidy Brit Gp. m. Gwyneth Mai, 2 Apr 1960, 3 d. *Education:* BArch, MCD (Master Civic Design), Univ Liverpool. *Appointments:* London Co Coun 1959-61; Conslt, Graeme Shankland 1961-64; Arch 1964-65, Dir 1965-73, Civic Trust NW; Prof, Univ Salford 1973-; Dir Gen, The Tidy Brit Gp. *Publications:* An Encyclopaedia of Planning; International Journal of Environmental Education & Information; Britain in Bloom; Role of Local Government Environmental Protection. *Memberships:* RIBA; PPRTPI, Pres 1973; F Inst Env Sci, Ch of Coun; FBIM. *Honours:* CBE 1980; Deputy Lt County of Lancashire. *Hobbies:* Gardening; Painting; Church and welfare activities. *Address:* Manor

Court Farm, Preston New Road, Samlesbury, Preston PR5 0UP, England. 1.

ASIWAJU Anthony Ijaola, b. 27 Apr 1939, Imeko. Prof History; Commr Intl Boundaries. m. Victoria Abeke Fatuyi, 10 May 1970, 1 s. 3 d. *Education:* BA (Hons) History 1966, PhD 1971, Univ Ibadan. *Appointments:* Hd Dept Hist, Univ Lagos 1979-82; Dean Fac Arts 1983-85; Mem Appointment & Promotion Bd 1979-81; Mem Court of Governors, Col Med 1981- 83; Edit-in-Chf, Journal of Hist Soc Nigeria 1982-87; Commr Intl Boundaries, Nat Boundary Comm Nigeria 1988-. *Publications:* Over 50 publications; Bks include: Western Yoruba Land Under European Rule 1889-1945: A Comparative Analysis of French & British Colonialism, Longman, 1976; Artificial Boundaries, 1984; Partitioned Africans, 1985; Over 20 Intl Confs. *Memberships:* Adv Editorial Bd, Journal of African Hist, 1985-89; Intl Bd Edits, Journal of Borderland Studies, US Assn Borderlands Scholars, 1986-90; Adv Edit Com, Journal Intl Boundaries Studies, IBRU Dept Geo, Univ Durham 1989; Coord, UNRCPDA, Lome (Togo) Comm on Border Issues 1987. *Honours:* Three tradl Chieftaincy titles incl Bobagunwa of Adv Ods, Ogun State, Nigeria 1983; Fulbright Scholar, Hoover Inst, Stanford Univ 1979; First MacArthur Sr Scholar, Prog on Intl Coop in Africa, Northwestern Univ, Evanston, Ill 1989-90; US Assn Borderlands Scholars Award for Outstanding International Scholarship and Service, 1992. *Hobbies:* Travelling; Meeting people. *Address:* Department of History, University of Lagos, Lagos, Nigeria.

ASKER Gunnar Carl Fredrik, b. 3 Feb 1913, Stockholm, Sweden. Naval Arch; Marine Engr. m. (1)26 Apr 1938, dec 1973, 1 s. 1 d. (2)Feb 1983. *Education:* Grad, Naval Arch & Marine Engr, Royal Inst Tech 1936; Grad, Naval Engr, Royal Swedish Navy, 1936; Postgrad Studies, George Wash Univ, Wash DC 1946-47. *Appointments:* Lt 1937, Commander 1945; Engrg Duty, Royal Swedish Navy; Asst Naval Attache, Embassy of Sweden, Wash DC 1945-47; Engr to Chmn and Pres, Desomatic Products Inc, Falls Church, VA 1948-62; Engr to Chmn and Pres, Subsidiary of Atlantic Res Corp 1959-62; Chmn & Pres, Air Economy Corp. *Contributions to:* Tech Pubs on: Adsorption Dehumidification and Industrial and Marine Air Curtain Systems; also on Wind Assist Systems for Ship Propulsion; 22 patents on the above subjects incl: Submarine (Nuclear) Air Purification. *Memberships include:* Soc Naval Arch & Marine Engrs; Life mem, Am Soc Heating, Refrigerating & Airconditioning Engrs; Past mem, Nominating Com, Past Chmn, Nat Capitol Chapt, Wash DC; Am Soc Swedish Engrs, mem Bd; Gothenburg Royal Sailing Assn; Nat Arts Club, NYC; KTH Alumni Assn, Royal Inst Tech Alumni; Naval Ofcrs Club, Skeppsholmen. *Honours:* Selected Citizen Amb by People to People Intl Org for Marine Tech Exchange between USA and the Marine Scists of China, 1983 at conf in Peking, Dalian, Wuhan, Wuxi and Shanghai; Hon Cultural Doctorate in Environ Scis from the World Univ, Benson, Tex 1989. *Hobbies:* Photography; Sailing; Motor sailing; International travel. *Address:* 138 East 36th Street, Apartment 6C, New York, NY 10016, USA. 26, 153.

ASLAMAZOV Alexander, b. 29 Mar 1945, Vladikavckaz. Cl Composer. 1 d. *Education:* Grad, St Petersburg Conservatory, Composition Dept 1969. *Appointments:* Army Service 1969-70; Edit, St Petersburg TV 1970-71; Sr Edit, Pub House Muzyka 1971-92. *Creative Works:* 2 string quartettes 1967, 1969; Sonata for flute & piano 1968; Great Sonata for piano 1980; 3 vocal cycles 1975-83; 3 sonatas for clarinet solo 1985-86; Concerto for violin & symphony orchestra 1970; 2 symphonies 1972, 1985; Music for films; and others. *Membership:* Composer Union St Petersburg 1972-. *Hobbies:* Picture collecting; Reading; Jogging. *Address:* 5 Krasnogo Kursanta Street, ap 15, 197198 St Petersburg, Russia.

ASSA Gredi Haim, b. 29 Jan 1954, Pleven. Artist. m. Janna Borissova Damjanova, 17 Sept 1982, 1 d.

Education: Profl Sch for Furniture Design 1968-72; Army Service 1972-74; Col for Dental Mechanics 1974-77; Grad, St Cyril & Methodius Univ in Veliko Tarnova, Fac on Monum & Dec Art. *Career:* Freelance Artist; One Man Exhibitions: Sofia 1983, 1986, 1989, 1990, 1991; Moscow, Budapest, Hambourg 1989; Vienna 1990; Sweden, Galeria Flamingo 1991; The Chameleon, Actions with the City Gp 1990. *Creative Works:* Time & Limits, 1987; Utopic Map, 1989; and many other paintings. *Memberships:* Bulgarian Artists' Union 1984; The City Gp. *Honours:* South Spring Awd for Painting 1986; Bulgarian Artists' Union Awd for Drawing 1987. *Hobbies:* Reading; Cinema; Swimming; African Music; Architecture; Design. *Address:* No 1, Neofit Rilski Street, Sofia 1000, Bulgaria.

ASSIS Andre Koch Torres, b. 11 Aug 1962, Brazil. Physicist. m. Hsu Su Chiao, 15 Feb 1986, 1 s. 1 d. *Education:* Bachelor in Physics 1983; PhD in Physics 1987; Postdoctoral position at Culham Lab, UKAEA, England. *Appointments:* Prof, Physics Inst, State Univ of Campinas, Unicamp, Brazil 1989-. *Publications:* On Mach's Principle, 1989; Can a Steady Current Generate an Electric Field?, 1991. *Memberships:* Brazilian Soc Physics; Brazilian Soc for History of Sci. *Hobbies:* Reading; Swimming; Tennis. *Address:* Institute of Physics, DRCC, State University of Campinas-Unicamp, CP 6165, 13081 Campinas-SP, Brazil.

ATANASIU Michaela, b. 14 July 1944, Bucharest, Romania. Choreographer. *Education:* Sch of Coreographer, Bucharest, 1966; Belgium Maurice Bejart, 1967; USA G Balanchine A Ailey, 1971. *Appointments:* Ballerina, The Jassy Opera, Romania, 1963-73; Ballet Master, 1963-73; Coreographer, Opereta Theatre, Bucharest, 1968-90. *Creative Works:* Debussy Eine Kleine Nachimusik, Mozart; Esmerdalda Pugni; Night Dream. *Memberships:* Intl Theatre Inst; Assn of Theatre People. *Honours include:* Natl Art Festival for Life the Love of Man; Prize for Choreographic Work, Assn of Theatre People. *Hobbies:* Music; Litterature; Shakespeare; Writing Poems; Cinema. *Address:* Str Verigei nr 6, Bl 2, Sc 4, Apt 179, 75322 Bucharest sector 5, Romania.

ATCHISON John Francis, b. 29 Dec 1939, Sydney, NSW. Academic Historian; Toponymist. m. Margaret Jean Macdonald, 29 Dec 1971, 3 s. 1 d. *Education:* BA Hons 1969, Univ New Eng; PhD in Australian History 1974, Australian Nat Univ. *Appointments:* Res Fellow in Toponymy, UNE 1972- 74; Lectr 1975, Sr Lectr 1986, Armidale CAE; Univ New Eng 1989-. *Publications include:* Place Names of Northern New South Wales, 1979; Guidelines for Research in Australian Place Names, 1982; Naming Outback Australia, 1990; Australia and Toponymy, 1990. *Memberships:* Australian Historical Assn; Assn for Canadian Studies Aust & NZ; Chair, Com for Geographical Names in Australia; Aust Correspondent Intl Com for Onomastic Scis and Intl Migration; AUSTRALEX; Invited Corresponding Mem, Aust Nat Dictionary Centre. *Honours:* C'Wealth Univ Scholarship 1966; C'Wealth Postgrad Scholarship 1969; NSW Cultural Grant 1979, 1983; Candn Studies Fac Enrichment Awd 1987; J P Thomson Oration 1990. *Hobbies:* Bushwalking; Swimming; Gardening. *Address:* 5 Catherine Street, Armidale, NSW 2350, Australia.

ATEWOLOGUN Oladele Kayode, b. 25 Nov 1939, Ilogbo-Ekiti, Nigeria. Industrialist. m. 18 Aug 1962, 6 s. *Education:* Ekiti Parapo Col, WASC II 1960; Wandsworth Tech Col, London 1963-66; AIB; AMIEX; AIFF. *Appointments:* Brit Bank of (WA) Ltd, Ibadan 1962-63; Barclays Bank, London 1967-70; United Bank for Africa, Lagos 1970-71; Nat Bank of Nig, Lagos 1971-75; Chmn, Mng Dir, Liz-Olofin and Co PLC 1975-. *Memberships:* Fellow, Chartered Inst Bankers; Assoc, Inst Freight Forwarders, UK; Assoc, Inst Exports, UK; Island Club, Lagos; Former Pres, Hoteliers Assn Nig; Charter Mem, Eko Lions Club; Lagos C of C; Nig-Brit C of C; Nig-Brazil C of C; Nigerian-Asian C of C. *Hobbies:*

Table tennis; Film watching; Reading health books and biographies. *Address:* 13, Mosuro Street, Abule-Oja, Yaba, Lagos, Nigeria.

ATHINAIOS Andreas, b. 17 Feb 1949, Athens, Greece. Univ Prof; State Govr; Polit. *Education:* AAS in Ec & Polit 1968; BA in Law & Ec 1971; Master of City Planning (MCP) 1973; MA 1976; PhD (Academic Hons) 1978; Post Doctoral Scholar in Organizational Behaviour 1978-79; Vstg Scholar summer 1983 & 1984 in Quantitative methods of Social Res. *Appointments:* CCP 1973-76; St Joseph's Univ 1974-75; Penn State 1975; Dyke Col 1978-79; CWRU 1978-79; Villanova Univ 1983-91; Franklin & Marshal Col 1990-91; Penn State 1990-91; Concurrently: State Govr 1980-82; Rethymno Crete & Thesprotia Ipiros, Greece; Candidate for the Greek Parliament 1989; Mem Nat Assenmbly of Democratic Coalition 1990; Res Interests: Polit Behaviour; Polit Ec; Regl Devel Imbalances; Power Ec; Power Market; Equitable Capitalism. *Publications:* Substantial number arts & res papers; 7 Invention Patents; Books: The Individual in the Abstract and Systematic Models of Contemporary Soc, 1972; 7 Hellenic Issues, 1976; Social & Political Concepts of Regional Development in Greece: A case study of Thessaloniki, 1978; Regional Imbalances and Electoral Behaviour, 1983. *Memberships:* Am Assn Univ Profs; Nat Coun for Higher Ed; Am Planning Assn; Am Ec Assn; Intl Fed for Housing & Planning, Hague; Hellenic Ec Assn; Athens C of C; Greek Assn Journalists and Writers; FIJET; Inst Arts & Scis, Athens, Greece, Trustee. *Hobbies:* Philosophy; Plato; Aristotle; Values; Ideals; Freedom in Love. *Address:* 2142 Coventry Road, Lancaster, PA 17601, USA.

ATIA Abdel Kader Mohamed, b. 8 Mar 1938, Cairo. Prof Geol. m. 14 Oct 1973, 1 s. 1 d. *Education:* BSc 1958, Ain Shams Univ; MA 1962, PhD 1964, Columbia Univ. *Appointments:* Res Asst, NCR, Cairo 1958-60; Reschr, NRC, Cairo 1964-73; Conslt, Min Agri & Water, Riyadh, Saudi Arabia 1973-78; Prof Geol, NRC, CMRDI 1978-. *Memberships:* Soc of Sigma Xi; Number of Intl Sci Socs. *Address:* National Research Centre (CMRDI), Tahreer Street, Dokki, Cairo, Egypt. 52.

ATKINS Brenda Lee Stone, b. 17 Jan 1947, Sumter, South Carolina. Tchr. m. Sidney B Atkins, 2 s. 1 d. *Education:* BS 1968, MEd 1979, Livingston Univ; Addtl Studies, Univ Alabama 1989 and 1990. *Appointments:* Tchr Eng 21.5 years; At Sweet Water HS, Marengo Co, Alabama 1981-. *Publication:* Art in Alabama ed mag 1991. *Membership:* Delta Kappa Gamma Hon Tchrs Org. *Honours:* Advanced Placement Cert Eng Instr; On Bio-prep Steering Com for Eng Prog thru Univ of Ala. *Hobbies:* Reading; Watching sports. *Address:* Rt 2, Box 349, Sweet Water, AL 36782, USA.

ATKINS Frederick John, b. 24 Mar 1932, Lambeth, London, England. Train Crew Supvr, BR. m. 29 Jan 1962, 1 s. 2 d. *Appointments:* Railway Steam Engine Cleaner 1948; Steam Engine Fireman 1950-57; Steam Engine Driver 1957-62; Electric Train Driver 1962-70; Railway Traffic Insp 1970-87; Train Crew Supvr 1987-. *Membership:* Licentiate Mem, Chartered Inst Transport 1975-. *Honours:* Commended for Courage & Resource 1957 for saving a major rail disaster at Herne Hill Station, London, when faced with the prospect of imminent collision, stayed on foot plate and started his engine away from an oncoming boat train thus reducing the force of impact; Freeman of the City of London. *Hobbies:* Model engineering-boats; Gardening-water; DIY; Reading. *Address:* 472 Green Wrythe Lane, Carshalton, Surrey SM5 1JP, England.

ATKINS Sidney Bee, b. 6 Nov 1944, Columbus, Mississippi. High Sch Principal. m. 1 Sept 1968, 2 s. 1 d. *Education:* BS 1970, Livingston Univ; MA 1975, Univ N Alabama; Cert in Drivers' Ed 1977, Univ S Alabama. *Appointments:* Coached 1968-78; Principal 14 years, Sweet Water HS, Marengo Co, Ala 1981-. *Memberships:* Ala Assn Secondary Sch Principals; Bd

Dirs, Ala Coalition of Citizens for Excellence in Small Schs; Area Coord, Ala HS Athletic Assn; Scholarship Com, Bd Dirs, Sweet Water Little League; Marengo Co Umpires Assn. *Honours:* Appointed to Co Juvenile Justice Coord Coun; Little League and Babe Ruth Coach; Selected to attend Bioprep Seminar in NY in 1988; Sunday Sch Supt. *Hobby:* All sports. *Address: ssa 00Rt 2, Box 349, Sweet Water, AL 36782, USA.*

ATTENBOROUGH Michael John, b. 13 Feb 1950, London, England. Theatre Dir; Producer. m. Karen Lewis, 14 Apr 1984, 1 s. *Education:* BA Hons in Eng, Univ Sussex. *Appointments:* Assoc Dir, Mercury Theatre, Colchester 1972-74; Assoc Dir, Leeds Playhouse 1974-79; Assoc Dir, Young Vic 1979-80; Artistic Dir, Palace Theatre, Watford 1980-84; Artistic Dir, Hampstead Theatre 1984-89; Artistic Dir, Turnstyle Gp 1988-90; Exec Producer, Deputy Artistic Dir, Royal Shakespeare Company 1990-. *Memberships:* Mem Coun, Royal Acad Dramatic Art; Equity; Dirs Guild of GB. *Honours:* Time Out Theatre Awd as Best Dir 1987; London Fringe Awd as Dir of Hampstead Theatre for Outstg Achmt 1987. *Hobbies:* Music; Football; Reading. *Address:* c/o Royal Shakespeare Company, Barbican Theatre, Barbican, London EC2Y 8BQ, England.

ATU Ubandu Godson, b. 3 Mar 1943, Olokoro, Umuahia. Univ Lectr. m. Dorothy N Atu, 3 May 1974, 1 s. 7 d. *Education:* OND Gen Agri 1943; HND Gen Agri 1947; BSc Agri Biol 1978; MSc Pest Mgmt 1979; PhD Crop Sc, Nematology 1982. *Appointments:* Asst Chf Sci Ofcr, Nat Root Crops Res Inst, Umuahia, 1983; Sr Lectr, Fedl Univ Tech 1987; Assoc Prof, Univ of Tech Owerri 1989-. *Publications:* 41 pubs in jours & proceedings on pest mgmt, pesticides & environ. *Memberships:* Nig Soc for Plant Protection, VP; Agri Soc of Nig, Life Mem; Nig Environ Assn, Treas; Nig Environ Soc, Chmn Admission Com. *Honours:* Commendation for Organising Erosion Seminar, Participation in Draft Legislation for Nigeria on Pesticides. *Hobbies:* Gardening; Tennis; Jokes. *Address:* Crop Production Dept, Federal University of Technology, Owerri, Nigeria.

ATWAL Avtar Singh, b. 15 June 1927, Khanewal, British India. Prof; Mem Punjab State Planning Bd. m. Dr Sarjit Kaur Siddoo-Atwal, 25 June 1964, 1 d. *Education:* BSc Agri 1947, Punjab Univ, Lahore; PhD 1954, Univ Adelaide, Australia; Postdoctoral Res Fellow, NRC, Canada 1955-57. *Appointments:* Lectr, Col of Agri, Ludhiana 1947-55; Asst Prof, Punjab Univ 1957-58; Asst Prof, Col Agri, Ludhiana 1958-60; State Entomologist & Locust Control Ofcr 1960-62; Prof & Hd Ento Dept, Punjab Agri Univ, Ludhiana 1962-66; Dean of Agri Col, PAU 1966-73; Vice Chancellor & Agri Advr, Jammu & Kashmir Govt 1973-75; Dean Agri, Dean Postgrad Studies, PAU 1975-83; Dir Ecology & Dean PGS 1983-86; Mem Punjab State Planning Bd 1986-. *Publications:* 13 books incl: New Concepts in Ags Production, and monographs; Edit, Status of Wild Life in Punjab; 140 res papers; 26 sci reviews; 30 on agri ed; 30 arts in newspapers. *Memberships:* Fellow, VP, Ento Soc of India 1967-70; Fdr Pres, Indian Ecol Soc 1973-; Brit Bec Res Assn; Intl Assn Ecol; Soc Invertebrate Pathol. *Honours:* Gold Medallist at Grad level 1947; Two Best Book Awds, Punjab Agri Univ 1974, 1976; FICCI Awd 1979. *Hobbies:* Landscaping; Painting, oil & pastels; Western classical music. *Address:* 51, Sector 4, Chandigarh UT-160001, India.

AUBERT Maurice Jacques Gilbert, b. 26 Dec 1924, Geneva, Switzerland. Attorney-at-Law; Ptnr Law Firm; VP Intl Red Cross Com. m. Suzanne Boissier, 1 Apr 1950, 2 s. 3 d. *Education:* Dr in Law 1951, Univ Geneva, Fac Law; London Sch Ec 1949; Trainee, Brown Bros Harriman Bankers, NY 1953-54. *Appointments:* Mgr Legal Dept and Ptnr Bank Hentsch & Cie 1956-83; VP, Intl Com Red Cross 1984-; Attorney-at-Law and Ptnr Law Firm Schellenberg & Haissly, 1990-. *Publications:* Le Secret Bancaire Suisse, 1982; Arts on legal matters-intl humanitarian laws, intl exchange of info on criminal

matters and so on. *Memberships:* Mem & Pres, Geneva Municipal Coun 1957-68; Mem & Pres, Parliament of Canton of Geneva 1968-80; Pres, Foun Inst Univ d'Etudes du Devel 1974-; Intl Com of Red Cross 1979-; Intl Acad Estate & Trust Law 1980-; Cercle de la Terrasse. *Hobbies:* Jogging; Cross country skiing. *Address:* Etude Schellenberg & Haissly, 4 Place Neuve, 1204 Geneva, Switzerland.

AUDAER Clifford Harold, b. 3 Feb 1928, York, England. m. Janet Monro Hoggard, 11 Aug 1951, 1 s. 1 d. *Education:* BA 1949, Dip Ed 1950, Univ Leeds. *Appointments:* RAF 1950-78, appts incl: ADC to COS HQ AFCENT, Fontainebleau 1956-59; Chf Linguistic Sers, HQ AF South, Naples 1966-69; Gp Dir, Officers Command Sch 1976-78; Secy, Inst Orthopaedics, Univ Col London 1978-1991. *Memberships:* FFA 1978; FBIM 1978; Chmn ARISE, the Scoliosis Res Trust; MCC; Royal Air Force Club. *Hobbies:* Opera and classical music; Theatre; Cricket; Golf. *Address:* Thistledown, 54 Bois Lane, Chesham Bois, Bucks HP6 6BX, England.

AUER Benedict (LeRoy), b. 4 Nov 1939, Chicago, Illinois. Roman Catholic Priest; Teacher. *Education:* BS 1962, Loyola Univ; MA 1964, Creighton Univ; MDiv 1980, St Meinrad Sch Theology. *Appointments include:* Chmn of Humanities, Univ Sch, Milwaukee 1967-71; Tchr, St Viator HS 1972-76; Ordained, Order of St Benedict (OSB), 1980; Chmn Eng Dept, Marmion Acad, Aurora, Ill 1980-87; Dir of Campus Ministry, St Martin's College, Lacey, Wash 1987-. *Publications:* Touching Fingers With God, 1986; From Chicago to Canterbury: Poetic Journal, 1990; Godspeak, 1991; Poems in over 150 mags; Var jour arts incl homilies, Pastoral Life mag. *Memberships:* Campus Ministry Assn; Pi Gamma Mu (Social Studies); Phi Alpha Theta (History). *Honour:* Poem of Year, Jubilee Press, 1987. *Hobbies:* Writing poetry & short stories; Reading; Cycling. *Address:* St Martin's College, Lacey, WA 98503, USA. 139, 155.

AULOTTE Robert Desire Reneld, b. 15 Apr 1920, F Cerfontaine. Prof de Litterature. m. Legay Jeanine, 26 July 1941, 1 s, 1 d. *Education:* Licence es Letters, 1940; Agregation de Grammar, 1951; State Doctorate, 1965; Hon Officer, French Army Reserve. *Appointments:* Asst Fac of Letters, 1961; Prof, Univ of Nancy, 1969; Prof, 1987; Prof of Emeritus, Univ of Paris, 1987. *Publications:* Amyor et Plutarque; Mathurin Regnier, Satyres; Comedie Francaise de la Renaissance; Rousard, Amours; Montaigne, Essais. *Memberships:* Soc Francaise des Seiziemistes; V L Saulniez, Research centre; Intl Soc of Friends of Montaigne. *Honours:* Doctor H C Univ of Lodz, Poland. *Hobbies:* Reading; Sports; Travel.

AULT Thomas Jefferson III, b. 23 June 1911, Portland, Indiana, USA. Mfg Co Exec. m. Mary Carr, 30 June 1938, 1 s. *Education:* ABS 1932, Univ Calif, Berkeley; Cert 1933, Los Angeles Stock Exchange Inst; BA 1934, Univ Calif, Los Angeles; Num courses. *Appointments include:* US Army Reserve 1934-47; Borg-Warner Corp, Chicago 1935-58, incl Pres & Gen Mgr Detroit Gear Div 1954-57, Long Mfg Co Ltd, Canada 1956-58 and others; Saco-Lowell Shops (Intl), Boston 1958-60; Budd Co, Detroit 1960-64; McCord Corp, Detroit 1965-68; Avis Indl Corp, Madison Heights 1968-70; Flyer Inds Ltd, Canada 1970-73; Wash Heat Transfer Inc, 1976-79; Duffy Tool & Stamping Inc, Muncie 1979-80; Lectr, Ball State Univ Col of Bus 1979-84; Currently Pres, Chmn, Dir, T J Ault Company 1987-; Dir, Hattemon Villias Assn Inc, Muncie 1984-86, 1990-; Chmn, CEO Res & Devel Corp, Muncie 1990-. *Publications:* Arts, Chapts etc on material control, long-range planning & mgmt, robotics, inventory & quality control, intl & multinat mgmt. *Memberships include:* Num profl orgs; Offices, var civic & community orgs. *Honours include:* Num awds, certs, recognitions. *Address:* 4501 North Wheeling Avenue, apt 3-102, Muncie, IN 47304, USA. 52, 132.

AUNIN Martin, b. 17 May 1971, Tartu, Estonia. Student of Arch. *Education:* Art Biased High Sch, 1986-89; Tallinn Art Univ, 1989-. *Appointments:* Student of Arch, Private Arch Bureau, Luup & Masso, Tallinn, 1991-. *Creative Works:* Projects for Architectural Comp; Intl Comp of Single Family House; Memorial Park in Tallinn; Art Sch in Tartu, Estonia. *Memberships:* Soc of Students of Art & Arch in Tallinn. *Honours:* Silver Medal for Art High Sch; Tallinn Municipal Annual Award to Promising Young Arch. *Hobbies:* Drawing; Painting; History of Arts & Architecture; Sports; Volleyball; Tennis; Badminton; Skiing; Theatre. *Address:* Sole 13-52, EE 0006 Tallinn, Estonia.

AUSTIN David Brian, b. 27 Feb 1961, Donville, Kentucky, USA. Prof of Philosophy. m. Sandra Weldon, 24 May 1982, 1 s. *Education:* BA, Samford Univ, 1982; M Div, Southern Baptist Theological Seminary, 1985; PhD, Southern Baptist Theological Seminary, 1989. *Appointments:* Instr of Philosophy, 1987-88; Lectr, Univ of Louisville, 1987-91; Asst Prof, Cumberland Coll, 1990-. *Publications:* Regularity & Randomnes as Elements of Theodicy; Great Thinkers of the Western World. *Memberships:* American philosophical Assn; Kentucky Philosophical Assn. *Hobbies:* Classical Guitar; Woodworking. *Address:* Dept of Philosophy & Religion, Cumberland College, Williamsburg, KY 40769, USA.

AUSTRIACO Lilia Robles, b. 28 Dec 1940, Philippines. Civil- Structural Engr; Info Scist. m. Dr Nicanor C Austriaco, 24 June 1967, 2 s. 1 d. *Education:* BS Civil Engrg cum laude 1962; Master of Engrg (Structural Engrg) 1965; Dipl in Bus Eng with Distinction 1982; Dipl in Advanced Bus Eng with Distinction 1983. *Appointments:* Assoc Prof, Mapua Inst of Tech, 1965-73; Lectr, Univ sains Malaysia 1975-79; Sr Info Scist, Assoc Edit, IFIC, Asian Inst Tech 1980-85; Sr Info Scist II, Edit IFIC/AGE, Asian Inst Tech 1985-. *Publications:* 68 Tech Papers, 3 Conf Proceddings, papers in: Concrete Technology & Design Series, Do It Yourself Series & Slide Presentation Series, International Directory of Ferrocement Organizations and Experts 1982-84, and 7 Reports & Thesis, 3 monographs, all in the field of civil structural engrg, partic Ferrocement. *Memberships:* Philippine Inst Civil Engrs; Inst Info Scists; Fdr & Advr, Info Mgmt Profl Assn; Intl Coord, Ferrocement Info Network; European Assn of Sci Edits; Secy, Intl Coord Com on Ferrocement; Steering Com, Intl Ferrocement Soc; Fdr Mem, AIT Women Study Circle. *Honours:* Presidential Gold Medal for Acad Excellence, Mapua Inst Tech; Cert of Merit for Outstg Achmts in the Bd Exams, Mapua Inst Tech; SEATO Scholarship; Outstg Citizen Awd, Calabanga Integrated Barrio Municipal and Pastoral Councils, Philippines. *Hobbies:* Piano playing; Reading; Jogging; Cooking. *Address:* International Ferrocement Information Centre, Asian Geotechnical Engineering Information Centre, Asian Institute of Technology, GPO Box 2754, Bangkok 10501, Thailand. 23, 138.

AVGERINOU-GIANNOUDI Vivian, b. 22 Jan 1942, Crete, Greece. m. Themos Avgerinos, 25 Oct 1970, 1 s, 1 d. *Education:* Lyceum Dance & Theatre Workshops, 1961; Sec & Public Relations Coll, 1962-66; Fine Art & Restoration, 1970. *Appointments:* Government Employee, Ministry of the Presidency of the Government, 1966-. *Publications:* Poetic Selections. *Contributions to:* Numerous Literary Mag & Newspapers; Essays; Novels. *Memberships:* Panhellenic Assn of Authors; Panhellenic Union for Letters & Arts; Soc for Intellectual Quest & Study; Cultural Soc, Talos; Cretan Home. *Honours:* 1st Prize for Poetry; 1st & 2nd Prize for Short Stories; 3 Awards for Poetry; Honorary Award for Poetry; Award for the best Publication; 2 Honorary Awards for Contribution to Greek Literature. *Hobbies:* Dance; Music; Theatre; Reading; Painting; Decorations; Collecting Works of Art, Rare Editions. *Address:* Rega Feraiou 28, Neo Psychiko 15451, Greece.

AVIS Kenneth Edward, b. 3 June 1918, Elmer, New Jersey, USA. Emer Prof. m. Irma Jeanette Hildreth Avis,

19 Feb 1943, 1 s. 2 d. *Education:* BS 1942, MS 1947, DSc 1956, Philadelphia Col of Pharmacy & Sci. *Appointments:* Assoc Prof, Phil Col Pharm & Sci, 1948-61; Assoc Prof 1961-67, Prof 1967-83, Chmn Pharmaceutics Dept 1983-88, Emer Prof 1988-, Univ TN. *Publications:* Edit, 2 vol book, Pharmaceutical Dosage Forms: Parenteral Medications, 1984, 1986; 3 vol textbook, Pharmaceutical Dosage Forms: Parenteral Medications, 2nd Ed, 1991-. *Memberships:* Parenteral Drug Assn, Pres 1968-70; Am Assn Pharm Sci, Fellow, 1986; Am Soc Hosp Pharm; Am Pharm Assn; Acad Pharmaceutical Scis. *Honours:* Fac Recip, Parent Drug Assn Res Awd 1978; Recip, Res Achmt Awd from PDA, 1979; Alumni Public Ser Awd, UT Nat Alumni Assn, 1980; Commrs Spec Citation, FDA, Dept Health & Human Serv, 1987; Gen Counsel's Cert of Appreciation, Gen Counsel, FDA, 1988. *Hobby:* Flower gardening. *Address:* University of Tennessee at Memphis, Department of Pharmaceutical Sciences. 874 Union Avenue, Room 3P, Memphis, TN 38163, USA. 7, 125, 139, 140, 143, 155.

AVNI Tzvi, Jacob, b. 2 Sept 1927, Saarbrucken, Israel. Prof of Music Theory & Composition; Hd of Electrong Music Studio. m. Hanna Yaddor Avni, 26 Aug 1979, 1 s, 1 d. *Education:* Israel Music Acad, 1958; Columbia Univ, NY, 1963-64; Summer Course, 1963. *Appointments:* Music Tchr, Elem Schs, 1953-58; Lod Music Conserv, 1958-61; Dir, Amli Central Mus Libr, 1961-76; Lectr, Jerus Mus Acad, 1971-; Full Prof, 1976-. *Creative Works:* Several Works for Symph Orch; Two string Quarts; Various Works for Chamb Combinations; Choral Works; Solo Piano; Works for Ballet; Art Films; Radio. *Honours:* Acom Prize for Meditations on a Drama; Telavin City Prize for Holiday Metaphors; Lieberson Prize for Str Quart; Acum Prize for Life Achievements; Kustermeyer Prize. *Hobbies:* Contemp Visual Arts; Poetry; Literature; Wood Carving; Painting. *Address:* 54 Bourla str, Tel Aviv 69364, Israel.

AWFORD Ian Charles, b. 15 Apr 1941, London, England. Solicitor. m. (1)24 July 1965 (dis 1983), Claire Sylvia, 3 s. (2)Leonora Maureen, 2 Sept 1989. *Appointments:* Admitted Slr 1967; Ptnr with Barlow, Lyde & Gilbert 1973-; Admitted Slr Hong Kong 1988. *Publications:* Developments in Aviation Products Liability, 1985; Num arts on aviation law and the law relating to outer space. *Memberships:* Chmn, Outer Space Com, Intl Bar Assn 1986; Aerospace Law Com, Inter Pacific Bar Assn 1990-; Inter Pacific Aerospace Law Assn 1990-; Aerospace Law Com, Asia Pacific Lawyers Assn 1987- 90; Conf Com Asia Pacific Insurance Conf 1991-. *Hobbies:* Music; Opera; Ballet; Painting; Flying; Golf; Skiing. *Address:* 6 Keepier Wharf, 12 Narrow Street, Limehouse, London E14 8DH, England.

AXIONOV Vladimir, b. 26 Oct 1950. Musicologist; Hd Musicology Dept Acad of Sciences. m. Tsirkunova Svettana, 11 Jan 1975, 1 d. *Education:* Conservatoire Moscow, 1969-74; Postgard Course, 1974-77; Cand of Sci, 1979. *Appointments:* Snr Lectr, Dept of History of music, State Inst of Arts, 1977-83; Acting Asst Prof, 1983-84; Acting Asst Prof, Dept of History of Music, Moldaviou State Conserv, 1984-85; Snr Researcher, West European Symphones, Moscow, 1978; The Symphony 1120th Century Music, 1980. *Creative Works:* Co Author. The Moldovian Symbphony, Historical Evolution. *Membership:* Composers Union of Moldova. *Honour:* Acad Degree, Candidate of Sci, Acad Rank, Snr Researcher. *Hobbies:* ssa 00Jogging; Cooking. *Address:* Jon Neculce Street, 12/1 Apt 9, Kishinev, Moldova, Russia.

AYANO Katsutoshi, b. 3 Mar 1949, Hitoyoshi, Japan. Assoc Prof; Mgmt Edr. m. Chieko Yoshimitsu, 25 Jan 1976, 3 s. 1 d. *Education:* Bach Mgmt Engrg 1974, Univ Electrocommunications, Japan; Master in Ec 1978, Univ Tsukuba, Japan; PhD 1982, State Univ NY and Syracuse Univ. *Appointments:* Instr 1975-79, Counsellor 1982-86, Union of Japanese Scists & Engrs,

Tokyo; Assoc Prof, Tokai Univ, Hiratsuka, Japan. *Publications:* Current Waste Problems, 1985; Contbr to profl mags. *Memberships:* Japanese Soc for Quality Control; Am Soc for Quality Control; Inst for Environ Sci, Sr; World Future Soc; Am Mgmt Assn; Intl Soc for Strategic Mgmt & Planning; Japanese Soc for Operations Res. *Honours:* Edit: Hinshitsu Jour of Japanese Soc for Quality Control 1990-; QC Circle, Union of Japanese Scists & Engrs 1991-; Hinshitsu Kanri, Union of Japanese Scists & Engrs 1990-; HQ Advr to QC Circle Activity in Japan. *Address:* 2985-13 Honmachida, Machida, Tokyo 194, Japan.

AYE Maung Tin, b. 9 Aug 1941, Burma. Med Dir; Hd Haematol Sec. m. Barbara-Ann Egan, 19 July 1968, 1 s. 1 d. *Education:* BA 1963, Cambridge Univ; MB 1966, Cambridge Univ & St Thomas Hosp; PhD 1974, Univ Toronto; FRCP (C) 1982. *Appointments:* Nat Dir Blood Servs, Cdn Red Cross Soc, 1991-; Hd Haematol, Ott Gen Hosp 1988-91; Hd Haematol, Univ Ottawa 1988-91; Med Dir, Ottawa Centre, Candn Red Cross BTS 1989-91. *Publications:* Author, Word Wand/L'Editexte, French/Eng word proc prog for IBM personal computer, 1982; Other sci pubs. *Memberships:* Investigator, Univ Ottawa 1974; Panel Mem & Sci Ofcr, MRC Peer Review Panel on Cancer 1982-87; Chmn, Human Exp Com, OGH 1975-86; Univ Ottawa AIDS Study Gp 1988; Project Dir & Co-Author, Royal Soc of Candn study on Impact of AIDS in Canada 1988; Pres & Fdr, Tanda Software Inc 1982-86. *Honours:* Queen's Col (Cambridge) book prize 1966; MRC Fellow 1970-74; MRC Scholar 1976-81; Centennial Medal, Royal Soc of Canada 1988. *Hobbies:* Swimming; Computer programming. *Address:* 1800 Alta Vista Dr, Ottawa, Ontario, Canada K1G 4J5. 88.

AYER Anne, b. 23 June 1917, Topsfield, MA, USA. Writer. m. Edward F MacNichol Jr, 7 Sept 1940, 1 s. *Education:* Liberal Arts Dipl 1935, Spence Sch, NY. *Career:* Concert Singer; Recording Artist; Profl Singer for 30 years, toured USA, Europe, South Am, Middle East. *Publications:* Retrospect: Poems by Anne Ayer, 1989; Poems pub in var anthologies incl: New World Unlimited, American Poetry Assn Anthologies. *Honours:* Cert of Poetic Achmt, Awd of Merit, Amherst Soc; Golden Poet Awd, World of Poetry 1989, 1990; Cert of Poetic Achmt, Am Poetry Assn 1989; Nat Soc of Lit and the Arts, as singer. *Address:* 120 Racing Avenue, Falmouth, MA 02540, USA.

AYGUESPARSE Albert, b. Apr 1900, Ier. Writer. m. Rachel Tielemans, 27 Dec 1924, 1 d. *Education:* Free Studies, Free Unif of Brussels. *Appointments:* Sec, Natl Literature Funds, 1956-. *Publications include:* Various Novels. *Memberships:* PEN Club; Asoc of Belgian Huttors Committee; European Soc of Culture; Intl Assn of Literary Critics; Charles Plisnier Foundation; Intl House of Poetry. *Honours:* Royal Acad of French Language & Literate, Member; Grand Officer, Order of the Crown; Grand Officer, Order of Leopold; Victor Rossel Prize; Grand Prix Triennal, For Novel; Grand Prix du Mont Michel; Albert Mockel Grand Prix for Poetry. *Hobbies:* Reading; Music; Cinema; Walking. *Address:* Rue Marconi 118, B 1180 Brussels, Belgium.

AZARA Nancy J, b. 13 Oct 1939, NYC, USA. Sculptor. 1 s. 1 d. *Education:* AAS 1959, Finch Col, NY; Lester Polakov Studio of Stage Design, NYC 1960-62; Art Students League of NY, Sculpture with John Hovannes, Painting & Drawing with Edwin Dickinson 1964-67; BS 1974, Empire State Col. *Career:* 21 One Woman Exhibitions 1969-91, incl Borgo Pinti, Rosso, Italy 1969, SOHO 20 Gallery, NYC 1984, 1987, Lannon Gallery, Chicago 1990, James Chapel, Union Seminary, NYC 1991; Almost 100 Gp Exhibitions, latest being: Impulse 1991, Pyramid Atlantic, Astrae Bookstore, Wash DC 1991; Arts as a Healing Force, Bolinas Museum, Calif 1991; The Awakened Goddess, MUSE Gallery, Philadelphia 1991. *Publications:* Many Reviews and Acknowledgements 1971-90, latest one: The Art of Healing, Judith Bell, Taxi Magazine 1990; Guest Lectr

& Guest Instr 1972-; Women and Art, 1972; Ms Magazine, 1973; Contemporary Artists at Work: Sculptors, Sound Filmstrip, 1978. *Honour:* Adolph & Esther Gottlieb Foun Grant 1985. *Address:* 91 Franklin Street, New York City, NY 10013, USA. 6.

AZHER Muhammad ud-Din, b. 26 Apr 1938, Sundarpur, Bangladesh. Tchr. m. 5 June 1964, 3 s. *Education:* BA, 1958; MA, 1960; PhD, 1975. *Appointments:* Lectr, Rajshahi Coll, 1961-64; Snr Lectr, 1964-75; Assoc Prof, Raj Univ, 1975-83; Prof, 1983-; Registrar, 1981-82. *Publications:* 12 Research Papers; 6 Research Reports; 1 Book. *Memberships:* Bangladesh Economic Assn; Family planning Raj Bangladesh; Acad Council, Syndicate & Senate of the Univ. *Honours:* Several Prizes & Awards on Acad Proficiency in the Whole Life. *Hobbies:* Reading; Gardening. *Address:* Dean Social Science, Rajshahi University, Rajshahi 6205, Bangladesh.

AZIZ Abdul, b. 6 Jan 1939, Gujranwala. Design Engr (Elect Power). m. Kishwer Sultana, 25 Dec 1963, 2 s. 3 d. *Education:* FSc (Non-med) 1956, Islamia Col, Lahore; BSc in Engrg (Elec) 1959, Govt Col of Engrg & Tech, Lahore (Punjab Univ); 8 short courses. *Appointments:* Asst Divl Engrg, T/L Construction 1959-62, Divl Engrg, T/L Construction 1962-65, Construction Engrg Project, Incharge Design & Construction of T/L 1965-70, Dep Chf Engr 1971-74, Chf Design & Contract Engr 1974-76, The Imperial Electric Co Ltd, Lahore; Gen Mgr, Tubewell Project & Pile Foun, Impercon Ltd 1976-78; Chf Designer, Design & Constructs 1978-84, Dir Tech, Incharge of Design Office 1985-. *Publications:* 13 Tech Pubs incl: Transmission Lines Design Practice in USSR; Some Aspects of Mechanical Design of Towers & Conductors in USSR; Design of Grounding of Transmission Lines. *Memberships:* Fellow: Inst Engrs Pakistan; Inst Elect Engrs Pakistan; Mem, Pakistan Engrg Coun; Pakistan Inst Mgmt; Central Coun IEEP; Chmn Lib Com IEEP; Hon Secy, Chmn, Lahore Local Centre, IEEP; Assignments in Drafting Safety Regulation in the use of electricity in Pakistan, and Computer courses under IEEP. *Honour:* IEEP Shield by IEEP for Contributions towards Computer Ed. *Hobbies:* Computer-software; Foreign TV reception; Photomicrography. *Address:* Gosha-E-Aziz, 36 Tariq Block, New Garden Town, Lahore 54600, Pakistan.

AZIZ Alia, b. 19 Aug 1966, Sukkur. Lectr in Urdu. *Education:* MA in Urdu Lang 1989, Govt Col, Lahore. *Appointments:* Lectr in Urdu, Govt Col for Women, 1990-. *Publication:* Thesis: Professor Usman B-Taur Iqbal Shinas. *Honours:* Gold Medal, Punjab Univ 1989; Gold Medal, Govt Col 1990. *Hobbies:* Writing poetry in Urdu; Reading literary works. *Address:* Gosha-E-Aziz, 36 Tariq Block, New Garden Town, Lahore 54600, Pakistan.

AZIZ Qutubuddin, b. 29 Mar 1929, Lucknow, India. Journalist. m. Abida Mushtaq, 24 Nov 1957, 1 s. 3 d. *Education:* Studied in Intl Relats, London Sch Ec 1948-49; BA (Hons) 1948, MA, Univ Madras, India. *Appointments:* Weekly Columnist, Daily Hyderabad Bulletin, Hyderabad Deccan, India on intl affairs, esp WWII events 1944-46; Mng Edit, United Press of Pakistan News Service 1950-77; Spl Correspodent, Pakistan, US Daily Chritian Science Monitor, 1965-77; Min, Emb of Pakistan, London 1978-86; Chmn, Semi-Govt, Nat Press Trust, Islamabad 1986-88. *Publications:* Books: Mission to Washington, 1972; Blood & Tears, 1974; and many others incl most recently Am Ed of The Prophet and the Islamic State, 1992. *Memberships:* Dir, Population Communications Intl Inc, USA; Royal Overseas League, London; Inst Journalists, London; Royal C'Wealth Soc and C'Wealth Trust, London; Karachi Boat Club. *Honours:* Cert Appreciation, Govt of West Pakistan for social services, 1968, with gift of a Prize Revolver with licence; Tamgha-e-Pakistan Awd from Govt Pakistan, 1971; Cert Appreciation, Inst Journalists, London 1985. *Hobbies:* Intl affairs, social work, comparative religions, population welfare, family

planning, socio-economic development in 3rd World
Countries; Travel, Music, Rowing, Books, Talks on radio
& tv; Writing for newspapers in Pakistan & abroad;
Authoring books; Lecturing to professional bodies.
Address: Aziz Lodge, 6/8/D, Block 4, Nazimabad,
Karachi-18, Pakistan.

B

BABIUC Victor, b. 3 Apr 1938, Rachiti, Botosani, Romania. Min Interior. m. Lucia, 23 Dec 1978, 1 d. *Education:* Grad Law Fac, Bucharest 1958; Postgrad courses Maritime Law, Ec Sci Acad, Bucharest 1979; Doctor of Laws 1979. *Appointments:* Arbitral Conslt, State Arbitration in Brasov 1958-63; Legal Advr, within Tractorul enterprise, Brasov 1963-65, 1966-68; Judge, People's Court, Brasov City 1965-66; Conslt then Arbitral Advr, Central State Arbitration 1968-71; Legal Advr & Chf Legal Advr, Min For Trade 1971-77; Main Reschr II then I, World Ec Inst 1970-90; Assoc Prof, Acad for Social-Polit Studies & at Ec Sci Acad 1980-87; Temporary Advr at Legislative Coun 1985-89; Expert, Constitutional Comm of Provisional Coun of Nat Union 1990; Min of Justice 1990-91; Arbitrator 1976-, VP 1989-, Court of Intl Commercial Arbitration of Romanian C of C and Ind; Mem Arbitrators' panel of Am Arbitration Assn 1991-; Min Interior 1991-. *Publications:* Over 100 works mainly in the field of ec legislation and intl trade law, incl: Contractual Risks in International Commercial Purchase, 1982; Juridical Regime of Economic Contracts, co-Author, 1981; Institutions of International Commercial Law, 2nd vol, co-Author, 1985; Juridical Dictionary of Foreign Trade, co-Author, 1986; International Purchase of Goods Among Parties Within Member Countries of Mutual Economic Assistance Council, 1990. *Hobbies:* Reading; Theatre; Museums. *Address:* Str Libertatii 20, Bloc 103, Scara 3, Etaj 4, Ap 44, Bucharest, Romania.

BACON Jennifer Helen, b. 16 Apr 1945, Birmingham, England, Civil Servant. *Education:* BA Hons Cantab 1st class 1967, New Hall, Cambridge Univ. *Appointments:* Asst Principal, Min Labour 1967; Pvt Secy to Min 1971-72, Health & Safety at Work Act 1972-74, Ind Relats Legislation 1974-76, Principal Pvt Secy to Secy of State 1977-78, Dept Employment; Asst Secy, Manpower Sers Comm 1978-80; Sabbatical-Latin Am 1980-81; Civil Service Dept 1981-82; Dir Adult Tng, Under Secy, Manpower Sers Comm 1982-86; Dept Ed 1986- 89; Principal Fin Ofcr 1989-91, Grade 2, Dir Resources & Strategy 1991-92, Dept Employment; Grade 2, Dpty Dir-Gen, Hlth and Sfty Exec, 1992-. *Membership:* Vstg Fellow, Nuffield Col, Oxford 1989-. *Hobbies:* Travel; Walking; Classical music esp opera. *Address:* Health and Safety Executive, Baynards House, Chepstow Place, Westbourne Grove, London W2 4TF, England. 1.

BÁCS Miklós, b. 27 Sept 1964, Bucuresti. Actor. *Education:* Dramatic Art Acad 1984-88. *Career:* Hungarian Theatre, Cluj 1988; Collaboration with RTV-Romanian Broadcasting 1988-91. *Creative Works:* Over 35 parts incl: Mozart in Amadeus by Peter Schaffer 1988; Paolino in Man, Beast & Virtue by L Pirandello, The King in Escorial by M Ghelderode 1990. *Honour:* First Prize of ATM (Roumanian Actors Assn) for performance of In The Station by Cao Hsing Cien, 1989. *Hobbies:* Jazz; Reading; Collecting stamps. *Address:* Bd Dinicu Golescu Nr 31 Bl 1 Sc III Et 5 Ap 87, Bucharest, Romania.

BADEN HELLARD Ronald, b. 30 Jan 1927, London, England. Mgmt Conslt; Arbitrator. m. Kathleen Peggy Fiddes, 16 Dec 1950, 2 d. *Education:* Dipl in Arch 1952, Poly Regent Street; Fellow, Loughborough Univ. *Appointments:* Founding Ptnr, Polycon Gp 1955; Currently CEO of Polycon Gp (Building Ind Conslts), Polycon Aims Ltd & Pecas Ltd. *Publications:* Management in Architectural Practice, 1964; A Management Action Plan, 1971; Training for Change, 1972; Managing Construction Conflict, 1988; Principal Edit, Metripack; Editor-in-Chf: The Quality Coordinators Guide; The Construction Quality Auditors Manual, 1991. *Memberships:* FRIBA, Pres London Soc Archs; FBIM, Chmn S London Br, Chmn S Eastern Region; FCI Arb, mem Counc 1971-87. *Hobbies:* Tennis; Travel; Cinephotography. *Address:* Vanbrugh Park, Blackheath, London SE3 7AL, England.

BADENOCH (Ian) James Forster, b. 24 July 1945, Oxford, England. Queen's Counsel. m. Marie-Therese Victoria Cabourn-Smith, 5 Jan 1979, 2 s. 1 d. *Education:* Rugby Sch; MA, Magdalen Col, Oxford. *Appointments:* Called to Bar 1968; Mem Lincoln's Inn and Inner Temple; A Recorder of the Crown Court 1987-; Queen's Counsel 1989. *Contributor to:* Medical Negligence, 1990. *Memberships:* London Common Law Bar Assn; Profl Negligence Bar Assn. *Honour:* Classical Demyship of Magdalen Col, Oxford 1964. *Hobbies:* Family; Tennis; Garden; Travel. *Address:* 1 Crown Office Row, Temple, London EC4Y 7HH, England. 1.

BAER-KAUPERT Friedrich Wilhelm Ernst, b. 1 Oct 1930, Berlin, Germany. Polit Scist; Legal Edr. m. Barbara Haver, 13 Sept 1985, 2 s. 4 d. *Education:* Student, Univs Gottingen 1952, Berlin 1954, Saarbrucken 1956; Asst, Berlin 1955; 1st jur examen, Celle 1956; 2nd jur examen, Assessor 1958; Dr iur utr, Saarbrucken 1967. *Appointments:* Asst, Univ Saarbrucken 1956-65; Bd Dirs, developing company, Saarbrucken/St Ingbert 1965-74; Legal Advr, Assn of Communities with Problems Caused by Coal Mining 1963-74; Asst Prof, European Law, Univ Saarbrucken 1969-74; Vstg Prof, var univs, USA 1968; Prof Public Law & Polit Sci, Univ Berlin 1974; Dir Gen, Europrofession GmbH 1990-. *Publications include:* Num books & arts, law & security policy problems. *Memberships include:* Bd, Inst fur Europaische Politik; Europaische Akad Otzenhausen/ Saarland; and others. *Address:* Giesebrechstrasse 8, D-1000 Berlin 12, Germany. 52, 92, 154.

BAEV Georgi Dimitrov, b. 9 Nov 1924, Burgas. Painter. m. Evgenia Panaiotova Baeva, 5 Feb 1957, 2 s, 2 d. *Education:* Acad of Fine Arts, 1949. *Appointments:* Profl Football Player, 1951-54; Painter Cinematography, 1954-56; Puppet Theatre, 1956-58; Tchr Painting in Pedagogical High Sch, Burgas, 1958-65; Free Practice, 1965-. *Creative Works include:* Self Supported Exhib, Shows. *Memberships:* Union of Bulgarian Artists; Australian Union of Artists; Japanese Assn of Artists. *Honours:* Silver Medal in Natl Exhib of Young Bulgarian Artists; First Natl Prize for Landscape; Painting Award Vladimir Dimitrov Maistora; Gottfried Von Herder Award. *Hobbies:* Football; Reading; Sports. *Address:* Compl, Lazur, Bl5 , Ch 2, Et 9, Burgas 8000, Bulgaria.

BAGG Charles Ernest, b. 7 May 1920, London, England. Rtd Conslt Psychi. m. Diana Patricia Phoebe Ovenden, 24 Sept 1955, 2 d. *Education:* Cambridge Univ; Westminster Hosp, London; MA 1946; MRCS, LRCP 1946; DPM 1951; MRCPsych 1971; FRCPsych 1983; DSc (Hon Causea), MGS International University Foundation, 1987. *Appointments:* Gen Med & Psychiat appts 1946-51; Conslt Psychi, St John's Hosp, Aylesbury 1961-82, Oxford Reg Hlth Auth; Clin Dir, Amersham Child & Family Guidance Clinic 1975-82; Cons, Pre Psy, Bucks Co Coun, 1966-82. *Publications:* Handbook of Psychiatry for Social Workers and Health Visitors; Palmar Digital Sweating in Women Suffering from Depression; Responses of Neonates to Noise in Relation to Personalities of their Parents; Senile Dementia and Psychiatric Problems of the Aged; Rare Pre-senile Dementia Associated with Cortical Blindness; Arts in Samaritans Publications; Series of Psychi arts in Brit Med; Book Reviews. *Memberships:* Brit Med Assn; Fellow IBA; Fellow, World Lit Acad. *Honours:* Silver Medal IBA 1985; Gold Medal ABI 1987; Bronze Medal, Albert Einstein Intl Acad 1988. *Hobbies:* Music; Walking; Writing light verses. *Address:* 20A Westgate, Chichester, West Sussex, England. 52, 3, 149, 156, 158.

BAGGALEY Norman Reginald, b. 23 Jan 1937, Stoke-on-Trent, England, Dean, Sch of Art. m. Jean Frost, 26 Jan 1956. *Education:* Nat Dipl in Design-Painting 1957, UK; Art Tchrs Dipl 1958, Univ Liverpool; MSc in Ed 1975, S Ill Univ, USA. *Appointments:* Art Tchr, London 1960-65; Art Tchr, Sydney 1965-69; Hd, Div Creative & Fine Arts, Salisbury, CAE 1969-78; Dean, Sch of the Arts, Ballarat, CAE 1978-80; Dean, Sch Art & Design, Prahan, CAE 1980-81; Dean, Prahian Fac of Art &

Design, Victoria Col 1981-91. *Creative Works:* 18 solo exhibitions of paintings in Australia & USA; Sev major representative gp exhibitions in Australia, USA & SE Asia. *Memberships:* Chmn, Intercol Com of Art & Design, Victoria 1981-91; Dep Chmn, Nat Coun of Hds of Art & Design Schs, Australia 1989-90. *Honours:* Mem Hon Soc of Phi Kappa Phi 1974-91; Personal Chair, Prof of Visual Arts, Victoria Col, Melbourne 1991. *Hobbies:* Squash; Cricket. *Address:* 4 Leila Street, Prahran 3181, Victoria, Australia. 149, 139, 19.

BAGLOW John Sutton, b. 10 Dec 1946, Lambeth, England, Labour Unionist; Writer; Public Sector Wkr. *Education:* BA 1st class hons 1969, MA 1970, Carleton Univ; PhD 1973, Glasgow. *Appointments:* Research Grants Ofcr 1974-, Humanities & Social Scis Br, Canada Coun 1974- 78; Social Scis & Humanities Res Coun of Canada 1978-. *Publications:* Emergency Measures, poetry, 1976; Hugh MacDiarmid: The Poetry of Self, criticism, 1987; Entries in Grey Matters: The Peace Arts Anthology, poetry, 1985; Num arts & poems in magazines & newspapers. *Memberships:* Public Service Alliance of Canada, Nat Dir, Nat Capital Region; Ottawa and District Labour Coun, VP; Ontario and District Labour Coun, VP; Ottawa Labour Community Services, Mem Bd; Ottawa Labour Studies Inst, Mem Bd. *Honours:* Canada Coun Doctoral Fellowship 1971-72, 1972-73; Univ Glasgow Doctoral Fellowship 1970-71, 1971-72, 1972-73; Canada Coun Res Grant 1973-74. *Hobbies:* Writing; Music; Politics; Reading; Current events; Scuba diving; Fighting the neo-conservative agenda. *Address:* 53 Simcoe Street, Ottawa, Ontario, Canada K1S 1A3. 142.

BAHR Carman Eddythe Bloedow, b. 24 Mar 1931, Middletown, Ohio, USA. Physician; Assoc Prof Med. m. Walter Julien Bahr, 28 Aug 1968. *Education:* BA 1952, Miami Univ, Ohio; MD 1956, Ohio State Med Sch; Internship, St Lukes Hosp, Chicago 1956-57; Residency, Intl Med, UNOKIA 1957- 60; Diplomate, Am Bd Intl Med 1963; Fellow Am Col Physicians 1986; Cert Diabetes Edr 1986; Recertified Diabetes Edr, 1991. *Appointments:* Okla City, VA Med Centre 1960-; Clin Asst 1960-62; Instr Med 1962-66; Asst Prof Med 1966-71; Assoc Prof Med 1971-. *Memberships:* Phi Beta Kappa; AMA; Am Diabetes Assn 1973-; Am Med Women's Assn; Am Assn Diabetes Edrs. *Honours:* Robert K Endres Awd for Contributions in Diabetes 1985; Cert Appreciation for Contributions to Diabetic Care at VA Hosp 1987. *Hobbies:* Computer; Photography; Dog obedience; Gardening. *Address:* 5609 N Everest, Oklahoma City, Ok 73111, USA.

BAI Donglu, b. 8 Feb 1936, Zhejiang, China. Prof Org & Med Chem. m. Zhifang Ni, 20 Aug 1968, 1 d. *Education:* Sch Pharmaceutical Sci, Shanghai First Med Col 1953-57; PhD, Inst Biochem & Org Chem, Czechoslovak Acad Scis 1964-67; Postdoctoral Res Fellow, Univ Calif at Berkeley 1981-83. *Appointments:* Res Asst, Res Assoc, Assoc Prof, Shanghai Inst Materia Medica 1957-81; Vstg Prof, Nagoya Univ, Japan 1983-84; Assoc Prof, Prof, Dep Dir, Dir, Shanghai Inst Materia Medica, Chinese Acad Scis 1984-. *Publications:* 50 res papers and review arts. *Memberships:* Chinese Pharmaceutical Soc; Chinese Chemical Soc. *Honour:* Chinese Nat Natural Sci Prize 1989. *Hobby:* Stamp collecting. *Address:* Shanghai Institute of Materia Medica, Chinese Academy of Sciences, 319 Yue Yang Road, Shanghai, China 200031.

BAI Jing-wen, b. 12 Nov 1932, Tianjin, China. Prof Pathology; Chf Librarian Tianjin Med Col. m. Lu Jun-xin, 28 Dec 1960, 3 s. *Education:* Grad Tianjin Med Col 1956; Res Fellow, Patterson & Holt Radium Inst, Manchester Univ, England 1979-82. *Appointments:* Asst Pathologist 1956; Instr Pathol 1978; Asst Prof 1983; Prof Pathol and Ultrastructural Pathol 1987, Hd Dept Ultrastructural Pathol; Chf Librarian, Tianjin Med Col. *Publications:* Studies on the morphological aspect of IUD-induced uterine bleeding and New Concept about its pathogenesis, 1986; Discovery of microtunnel system

in mineralized matrix of cortical bone in human and vertebrae, 1991. *Memberships:* Dir, Tianjin Electron Microscope Assn; AAABI of ABI Res Assn. *Honour:* Discovery of the local DIC is the major reason in IUD induced uterine bleeding won the All China Sci & Tech Prize 1986. *Hobbies:* Foreign languages-English, French, German, Russian, Japanese, Italian, Spanish, Portuguese, Romanian, Polish, Latin; Literature; Painting; Collecting antiques. *Address:* Tianjin Medical College, Qi Xiang Tai Road, Heping District, Tianjin, China. 152, 158, 139.

BAILEY (Thomas) Alan, b. 28 Oct 1928, Sunderland, England. Mktg Conslt; Co-Dir; Writer; Cartoonist. m. Mary Jeer Baldock, 7 Aug 1950, 1 s. *Education:* Capt Intelligence Corp: NS 1946-49, TA 1949-64; Dipl in PR, Cam Foun. *Appointments:* Asst Clerk, Brentwood UDC 1950-62; Under Secy, Royal Institution of Chartered Surveyors 1962-69; Chf Exec, World of Property Housing Trust 1969-79; Chf Exec, Andrews Gp of Companies 1979-84; Chmn & Mng Dir, ABS Gp 1984-. *Publications:* Arts and 1000s cartoons in leading newspapers and magazines; Books: How to be a Property Developer, 1988; How to be an Estate Agent, 1991; Effective Communication, 1992. *Memberships:* Grad Mem, Communications, Advert & Mktg Foun; Chartered Inst Mktg; Inst PR; Soc Authors; Fdr Mem & Chmn, Placemakers Luncheon Club. *Hobbies:* Walking; Animals; Reading; Writing; Drawing. *Address:* The Bridge House, Queen Street, Sible Hedingham, Essex CO9 3RH, England.

BAILEY Anthony Charles, b. 14 July 1933, Kensington, London, England. Assoc prof; Hd Academic Dept. m. Georgiana Elmira Clifton-Brown, 7 Sept 1962, 1 s. 2 d. *Education:* MA, LLM, Trinity Hall, Cambridge 1954-58; Lincolns Inn 1956-59; Grad Dipl, Acctg & Fin, Chisholm Inst Tech, Australia 1976-78. *Appointments:* Chancery Barrister, Chambers of Rt Hon Sir Denys Buckley 1959-60; Helbert Wagg & Company Ltd, merchant bankers 1960-62; J Henry Schroder Wagg & Company Ltd 1962-72; Schroder, Darling & Company Ltd, Australia 1972-83; Hd Dept Accountancy, Royal Melbourne Inst of Tech 1983-. *Publications:* Var arts in merchant banking, accounting & bus jours; Also arts on heraldry & architecture. *Memberships:* Barrister & Solicitor, Supreme Court of Victoria; FCPA; FCIS; FCIM; FAIM; FIBA; MCT; Pres, Heraldry Soc Australia. *Honours:* Tancred Studentship, common law, Lincolns Inn 1956-59. *Hobbies:* Heraldry; Collecting antiques; Music. *Address:* 2 Coleridge Street, Elwood, Victoria 3184, Australia. 23, 157.

BAILEY John Robert, b. 19 Apr 1958, Cheverly, Md. Musician; Edr. *Education:* BS Music, Math 1980, Ind Univ; MusM 1981, MusD 1987, Northwestern Univ. *Appointments:* Assoc Prof Flute, Univ Neb 1986-; Prin Flute, Lincoln (Neb) Symphony Orch 1986-; Neb Chamber Orch, Lincoln 1986-. *Contributions:* program booklets to Am Inst Mus Studies 1982-; Arts to Flute Talk 1982, 1988, The Flutist Quarterly 1990; Programme Annotator, Orlando (Fla) Opera 1986-90. *Memberships:* Nat Flute Assn; Col Mus Soc; Mus Tchrs Nat Assn; Pi Kappa Lambda; Pres, Great Plains Chapter, Coll Music Soc, 1991-93. *Honour:* Recip 1st Place Awd, Young Artists Compt, Chgo Flute Soc 1984. *Address:* School of Music, University of Nebraska-Lincoln, Lincoln, NE 68588, USA.

BAILEY Mary Beatrice, b. 24 Dec 1933, Piittsburgh, Pennsylvania, USA. Nsg Admin. *Education:* Nursing Dipl 1956, Allegheny Gen Hosp, Pittsburgh; BSNE 1956, Chatham Col, Pittsburgh; MSN 1967, Duke Univ, Durham, NC. *Appointments:* Staff Nurse Med-Surg 1956-60, Paediatric Hd Nurse & Supvr 1960-62, Allegheny Gen Hosp; Asst Instr Paediatrics, Duke Univ Sch Nsg 1962-64; Instr Med-Surg Leadership, Community Health, Rex Hosp Sch Nsg 1966- 70; Supvr Pt Care Coord Med-Surg 1970-86, Clin Dir Med Surg 1986-87, Dir Nsg Info Systems 1987-92, Rex Hosp, Raleigh. *Memberships:* NC Bd Nsg 1991- 93; ANA; Nat

League for Nsg; Zonta Club of Raleigh; NCUERA; NCNOW; NCCWO; NC Coalition for Choice; The Great 100 Fundraising Com. *Honours:* ANA Cert in Nsg Admin 1981-86, Advanced 1987-91, 1992-; Named One of the Great 100, 1992. *Hobbies:* Reading; Gardening; Bicycling; Collecting; Music; Sports. *Address:* 311 Furches Street, Raleigh, NC 27607, USA. 5, 162, 156, 138.

BAILEY Sharon Lynette, b. 14 Aug 1960, Alexandria, Louisiana, USA. Reg Nurse. *Education:* Univ Southwestern LA 1978-81; BA Gen Studies, BS Gen Studies, Northwestern State Univ 1981-83; BSN 1984, Northwestern State Univ. *Appointments:* RN, Charge Nurse of ICU, St Francis Cabrini Hosp 1981-86; Profl Nsg Services, Travelling ICU RN 1986-88; Abbeville Gen Charge Nurse, Lafayette Gen Hosp 1990-. *Publication:* Poem, I am a Woman. *Membership:* Am Assn Critical Care Nurses. *Honour:* Apptd as an Am Red Cross Nurse 1985. *Hobbies:* Poetry; Reading contemporary and autobiographical novels; Latch hooking; Shopping. *Address:* 105 Westwood Drive, Apt 182, Lafayette, LA 70506, USA.

BAILEY Wilbert M, b. 23 Apr 1930, Flint, Michigan, USA. Clerk, Prosecuting Attorney's Diversion Prog. div 1972, 1 d. *Education:* US Women's Army Corps 1948-51; BS 1956, Mich State Univ; AGS 1988, Lansing Community Col; MS 1991, PhD 1991, Am Holistic Col Nutrition. *Appointments:* Departmental Exec, Mich Dept of Secy of State 1967-69; Acct, Mich Dept of Treasury 1969-77; Fin Analyst, Mich Dept Public Health 1977-84; Clerk, Ingham County Prosecuting Attorney's Diversion Programme. *Memberships:* Lansing Alumnae Chapt; Delta Sigma Theta Sorority Inc, Charter Mem; Intl Masons & Order of the Eastern Star, Eleanor Roosevelt Chapt, Worthy Matron 1977-79; Nat Assn Female Execs Inc; Mich State Univ Alumni Assn; Am Bus Women's Assn. *Honour:*Federal Civilian Employee Outstg Performance Awd 1988, 1989. *Hobbies:* Travel; Sight-seeing; Hiking; Reading; Concerts; Collecting gourmet recipes. *Address:* 900 Long Boulevard, Apartment 637, Lansing, MI 48911, USA.

BAILLIE STRONG Stuart, b. 25 Aug 1943, Alexandria, Egypt. Mgr Strategic Sourcing. m. Patricia Marjoribanks, 15 Sept 1970, 2 s. 1 d, dec. *Education:* BSc Chem Engrg 1st class Hons 1965, Edinburgh Univ, Scotland; Licence in Applied Ec 1970, Univ Louvain, Belgium; MBA 1973, Univ Chicago, USA. *Appointments:* Chem Engr in Res & Devel, Amoco Corp, Whiting, Indiana 1965-69; Systems Analyst Electronic Data Processing Dept, ICI Holland BV, Rozenburg, Netherlands 1970-73; Project Mgr in Systems Tech Dept, ICI Europa Ltd, Brussels 1973-78; Sr Sales Rep in ICD for Nrn & Ern Europe 1978-81, Product Mgr in ICD for Europe, Middle East & Africa 1981-85, Ethyl SA, Brussels; Phosphazene Devel Mgr in Corporate R&D 1985-86, Product Mgr in ICD for Latin Am & Far East 1986-87, Ethyl Corporation, Baton Rouge, LA; Mkt Devel Mgr in ICD 1987-89, Regl Sales Mgr for Srn & Ern Europe for ICD and Performance Products Divs 1989-90, Dir of Sales for Europe for ICD & PPD 1990- 91, Strategic Sourcing Mgr, Ethyl Europe 1991-, Ethyl SA, Brussels. *Publications:* Arts in jours of the Am Petroleum Inst, Am Soc of Lubrication Engrs and The Nat Lubricating & Grease Inst. *Memberships:* Cercle Gaulois, Brussels; Univ Chicago Alumni Assn, Chmn Belgium Chapt 1981-83; St Andrews Church, Brussels. *Honours:* 1st class Hons BSc 1965, Univ Edinburgh; Licence avec grand Distinction 1970, Univ Louvain; Dean's Honour Role, Univ Chcgo MBA Course, 1969. *Hobbies:* Skiing; Tennis; Geneology; Investment Management. *Address:* Veeweidestraat 29, B-3040 Huldenberg, Belgium. 52.

BAIQIU Sun, b. 12 Sept 1940, Jilin City, China. Gynaecologist. m. Yang Jing, 1966, 2 d. *Education:* Grad Med Dept, Harbin Med Univ, 1963. *Appointments:* Gynaecologist 1963-85; Assoc Prof Gynaecol & Obstetrics, No 1 Hosp affiliated to Harbin Med Univ, 1985; Dir, Clin Res Dept Beijing Gynaecology & Obstetrics Hosp & Beijing Family Planning Tech Guidance Inst, 1986. *Publications:* Over 30 papers pub in field of family planning; Handbook of Family Planning, 1983; Clinical Handbook of Family Planning, 1986; Prevention and Treatment of Complications after Sterilisation Operation, 1987; Life and Health of the Aged People, 1988; 4 other books. *Memberships:* Mem Standing Com, Revolutionary Com of Guomintang; Chinese People's Polit Consultative Conf; Exec Com, All-China Women's Federation; Bd Mem, China Coun for Promotion of Peaceful Nat Reunification; VP, Red Cross Soc China. *Honours:* Sev awds presented by Min of Pub Health and Provincial Com of Sci & Tech; First Prize of Achvmt of Sci Res for her res in birth control effect of Gansui, a Chinese Herbal Medicine; Sci & Tech Progress Prize of China Nat Family Planning Com for work in extended time of placement of metal IU device in womb. *Address:* 53 Ganmian Hutong, Beijing 100010, China.

BAKA Istvan, b. 25 July 1948, Szekszard. Journalist; Poet; Translator. m. 1 Feb 1969, 1 s. 1 d. *Education:* Univ Arts, Szeged, Tchr, 1967-72. *Appointments:* Secondary Nursery Sch 1972-74; Edit, Kincskereso, 1974-. *Publications:* Poems: Magdolna-Zápor, 1975; Tüzbe Vetett Evangèlium, 1981; Dòbling 4, 1985; Ègtajak Cèlkeresztjèn, 1990; Short stories, dramas: Szekszàrdi mise, 1984; A kisfiú es a vámpirok, 1984; Beavatàsok, 1991. *Memberships:* Assn Hungarian Journalists; Secy, Writers of Srn Hungary. *Honours:* Graves Prize, 1985; Jòzsef Attila Prize, 1989. *Hobbies:* Collecting records; Listening to classical music. *Address:* 4 Molnar Street, Szeged, Hungary.

BAKER Brian James, b. Uppingham, Rutland. Head Chef. *Appointments:* Head Chef, Hambleton Hall Hotel & Two Stages with Roux Bros 1982-; Tour of San Francisco & Fla 1990. *Publications:* My Favourite Place to Eat, Independant; Arts for Vogue, House & Gardens and other prestigious magazines. *Honours:* Michelin Star 1986; Badoij Restaurant of the Year 1987. *Hobbies:* Sailing; Tennis; Swimming; Horse riding; Old cookery books. *Address:* 3 Thistleton Road, Market Overton, Oakham, Rutland, England.

BAKER Earl Russel II, b. 30 Sept 1950, Phoenix, Arizona. Exec Search Firm Exec. m. Vicki Rose Skulley, 3 Dec 1977, 1 d. *Education:* BS in BA 1973, David Lipscomb Col, Nashville; MBA 1975, Univ W Fla, Pensacola, Fla. *Appointments:* Bus Mgr, Santa Rosa Co Mental Health Centre 1975; Ops Supvr 1976-77, Terminal Ops Mgr 1976-77, Roadway Express Inc, Nashville 1976-77; Terminal Mgr, Roadway Express Inc, Florence, Alabama 1979- 80; Corp Transportation Analyst 1980, Asst Corp Distribution Mgr 1980-81, Corp Distribution Mgr 1982, Gulf & Western Natural Resources Gp, Nashville; Dir Transportation Sers Eastern Div, Gulf Atlantic Distribution Sers Inc, Forest Park, Ga 1982-83; Dir Ops 1983-84, VP Ops 1985-86, Har-Bet Inc, Ga; Exec Recruiter, Dotson Benefield & Assocs Inc, Atlanta 1986-87; Owner, Distribution Recruiters, Atlanta 1987-. *Memberships:* Forest Park Church of Christ, Deacon 1990-; Republican Party; Intl Platform Assn; US Track Athletic Cong. *Honour:* Nat Employee of Month, Gulf Atlantic News 1982. *Hobbies:* Stamp collecting; Weightlifting; Competitive track & field athletics. *Address:* 2256 Fellowship Road, Suite 160, Atlanta, GA 30084, USA. 7.

BAKER Gary R, b. 26 May 1944, Beloit, Kansas, USA. Exec Dir. m. (1)Ena Patterson Fordham, 29 July 1966, div 1984, (2)Judith Anne Kaminer, 30 Aug 1985, 1 s. 2 stepsons, 1 d. 1 stepdaughter. *Education:* BS in Bus Admin, The Citadel, Charleston; MBA, Univ SC, Columbia. *Appointments:* US Army Capt in Field Artillery, served in Korea & Ft Jackson, SC 1966-69; US Textile Corporation, Columbia 1969; Dir Admissions, Palmer Col, Columbia 1970-72; Personnel Ofcr, Governor's Office, Columbia 1972-76; Exec Dir, South Carolina State Ethics Comm 1976-. *Publication:* Author: Cadets in Gray, 1990. *Memberships:* Steering Com,

Coun on Governmental Ethics Laws; Pres, SC Civil War Roundtable, Leadership South Carolina, 1988 Grad Mason; Commander, Am Legion; Assn Citadel Men; St Alban's Episcopal Church. *Hobbies:* Civil War and genealogical research and writing; Reading; Fishing. *Address:* 1249 Counts Ferry Road, Lexington, SC 29072, USA. 7.

BAKER George William, b. 7 July 1917, Devonport, England. Rtd Diplomat. m. Audrey Martha Elizabeth Day, 17 Oct 1942, 2 d. *Education:* Hertford Col, Oxford Univ 1948-49. *Appointments:* Royal Navy 1939- 46; RNVR to Lt Commander, now Chmn Exeter Flotilla; District Commr, HM Colonial Service, Tanganyika 1946-62, incl UK Delegation, UN Trusteeship Coun, Wash DC 1957, & Hd, Tanganyika Govt Info Dept 1959-62; C'Wealth Relats Ser, later HM Diplomatic Ser, 1962-77, up to Brit High Commr, Papua New Guinea 1975-77. *Publications:* Num official booklets, reports; Currently Edit, Clockmaker's Times; Num photographic exhibitions; Innumerable speeches. *Memberships include:* Past Chmn, E Sussex Com, Voluntary Service Overseas; VP, Royal African Soc; Com, Oxford Soc, Devon Br; Exec, Operation Drake; Conslt, Operations Raleigh; Liveryman, Worshipful Company of Clockmakers; Freeman, City of London; Hon Mem, Sci Exploration Soc; Chmn, E Devon Luncheon Club. *Honours:* Officer 1971, Commander 1977, OBE, Volunteer Reserve Decoration 1952, Clasp 1979. *Hobbies:* Photography; Horology; Cabinet-making; Writing; Public Speaking. *Address:* Crosswinds, Coreway, Sidford, Sidmouth, Devon EX10 9SD, England. 1.

BAKER Jack Sherman, b. 8 Aug 1920, Champaign, Illinois, USA. Edr; Practising Arch; Design Arch; Design Conslt. *Education:* Gold Medal, Prix d'Emulation Soc des Arch par le Govt Francais 1942; Cert, Beaux Art Inst of Design, NYC 1943; BArch with Hons 1943, Univ of Ill, Urbana-Champaign; MSc in Arch 1949, Univ Ill. *Appointments:* Aeronautical Engr, Designer, Boeing Aircraft Co, Seattle 1943-45; Topographical Engr, Designer, Allied Forces HQ Caserta, Italy, US Army ETO 1945-46; Fac Univ Ill 1947-50; Prof Arch 1950-; Assoc, Atkins, Barrow, Lasswith Arch 1947-50; Pvt Practice 1947-. *Publications:* Author of a broad spectrum of bldg types, preservation & adaptive reuse 1947-; Work pub in num profl jours and papers in US & abroad, Nat, Regl & Local Exhibitions of his Arch. *Memberships:* Hon Dir, Gerhart Music Festival; Hon Dir, Stravinsky Awds. *Honours:* Recip num awds and hons for ed and design excellence; IL/AIA Medal and Awd for Excellence in Education for Tchg, Practice & Public Service, 1989. *Hobbies:* Music; Theatre; Dance; Art; Biking; Hiking; Jogging. *Address:* School of Architecture, 608 East Larado Taft Drive, Champaign, IL 61820, USA. 15, 152, 139, 155.

BAKER John Harry Edmund, b. 8 Jan 1949. Conslt in spinal injuries; Rehab Med. *Education:* Epsom Col; Middlesex Hosp Med Sch; Univ Edinburgh; BSc 1970; MB BS Hon 1973; MRCP 1976; Fellow NY Acad Sci, USA 1988. *Appointments:* Lectr, Univ Nottingham Med Sch 1976-77; Registrar, Nat Hosp Nervous Disease, Queens Square 1977-80; Sr Registrar, Nat Spinal Injuries Centre, Stoke Mandeville 1980-83; Midland Spinal Injuries Centre, Oswestry 1983-85; Conslt Spinal Injuries & Rehab Med, S Glamorgan Health Authority & Welsh Health Common Services Authority 1985-. *Publications:* Arts in Med Jours in Immediate Care & Handling of Spinal Cord Injuries, Mgmt of Spinal Injury at accident site, Accident & Disaster Med; Author Chapts in ABC of Major Trauma, 1981, ABC of Spinal Injuries, 1989 and Management of Mass Casualties, 1984. *Memberships:* Advr in Rehab, Dept Social Security, Wales; Dep Chmn Med Exec, St John Ambulance; Med Bd, St John Ambulance; Vice Chmn & Mem Exec Bd, Br Assn of Soc of Immediate Care, Mem Med Bd St John Ambulance, Wales; Conslt Advr, Conjoint Com of Voluntary Aid Socs; Conslt Advr to Nat Rescue Tng Coun and Royal Lifesaying Soc UK, Mem Health; Care Gp Nat Coun for Vocational Qualifications; Advr, Med

Equestrian Assn RAC Nat Health Service Tng Authority. *Address:* Rookwood Hospital, Fairwater Road, Llandaff, Cardiff CF5 2YN, Wales.

BAKER Joseph Thomas, b. 19 June 1932, Warwick, Queensland. Res Dir. m. 5 Feb 1955, 2 s. 2 d. *Publications:* 2 books on Biologically Active Compounds from Marine Organisms; Num pubs in sci lit and many addresses to sci socs. *Memberships:* Fellow, Royal Australian Chemical Inst, Former Secy & Chmn North Queensland Section; Sigmasi; Fellow, Royal Australian Chem Inst; Former Chmn Australian Heritage Comm; Former Chmn Sci Com World Wildlife Fund Australia; Currently Chmn, Nat Com for Environ of Australian Acad Sci; Mem Heads of Marine Agencies Com, Australian Mem Intl Seaweed Assn, Mem Exec; UNESCO COMAR Com. *Honours:* Order Brit Empire 1981; Fellow, Acad Technological Scis 1989. *Hobbies:* Swimming; Scuba diving; Squash; Tennis; Theatre; Rugby league. *Address:* c/o House 1, Australian Institute of Marine, PMB 3, MC, Townsville 4810, Qld, Australia. 52, 23, 149.

BAKER Rebecca Louise (Flaten), b. 12 Apr 1951, Covina, Calif. Pianist; Recording Artist; Music Edr; Conslt. m. Jerry Wayne Baker, 22 Dec 1972, 1 s. 2 d. *Education:* Grad 1968, Walsh County Agri & Tng Sch; Attended Trinity Bible Inst, Jamestown, North Dakota 1968-69. *Career:* Pianist, Organist, Singer with Paul Clark Singers & Vic Coburn Evangelistic Assn 1969-72; Musician with Restoration Ministries 1972-79; Fdr, Psalmist Sch of Mus, Tyler, Tex 1983; Began Psalmist Recording Studio 1985; Started House of Levite Publ House 1990; Organist-Choir Dir, St Francis Episcopal, Tyler 1984-87; Pianist, Calvary Baptist Ch, Tyler 1987- ; Play professionally, Ramada Hotel, Willowbrook Country Club, var social functions 1985-; Pianist, Tyler Area Children's Chorale 1987-89; Entertainer Kiwanis, Am Assn Univ Women. *Creative Works:* Written many songs (Songwriter & Publisher-BMI); 4 Piano/Vocal Solo Albums out: Portrait of Praise; Christmas Piano with Rebecca Baker at the Concert Grand; It's a Wonderful Feeling (with Jerry Baker); Worship Piano; Producer & Arranger under Psalmist label of many songs & albums. *Membership:* Fdr & Pres of Christian Mus Tchrs Assn 1991-. *Honour:* Psalmist Sch of Mus Awd for Outstanding Piano Artistry (trophy) 1988. *Hobbies:* Travel; Music (jazz); Interior decorating; Gardening; His cats. *Address:* c/o Psalmist Productions, P O Box 961, Whitehouse, TX 75791, USA. 15.

BAKER Robert James, b. 9 Dec 1947, USA. Deputy Managing Director. m. Beverley Joan Lansford, 5 June 1974, 2 d. *Education:* Fairlawn Cambridge; Cambridge Col of Art & Tech; Univ E Anglia. *Appointments:* Deputy Managing Director, Hobson's Publishing plc, Cambridge 1973-. *Publications:* Pubr 28 books and directories in the careers field. *Memberships:* Reform Club; Race Horse Owners Assoc. *Hobbies:* Art; Racing; Walking. *Address:* Porters Farm, Over, Cambridge CB4 5NS, England.

BAKER Terry George, b. 27 May 1936, Brighton, Sussex, England. Biologist; Pathologist; Edr. m. Pauline Archer, 23 Aug 1958, 3 s. *Education:* BSc Hons in Zoology 1958, Univ Wales; PhD 1964, Birmingham Univ; DSc 1975, Edinburgh Univ; FRCPath; FIMLS; FIBiol; FRSA; FRSE. *Appointments include:* Lectr, anatomy, Birmingham Univ 1961-68; Lectr, Sr Lectr, Obstetrics & Gynaecology, Edinburgh Univ 1968-79; Prof Biomed Scis, Univ Bradford 1980-; Pro-Vice Chancellor 1986-89; Also: Mem, Bradford Health Authority 1982-86; Govr, Huddersfield Poly 1986-89. *Publications include:* Chapts, Effects of Ionising Radiations on the Ovary Devel of the Ovary in book The Ovary, 1976; Num books & sci arts on reproduction, radiation biology. *Memberships:* Fellow: Inst Biol, Inst Med Lab Scis, Royal Soc Arts, Royal Soc (Edinburgh); Royal Col Pathologists; Mem, Soc for Study of Fertility; Soc for Study of Reproduction; Brit Soc for Developmental Biol; Anatomical Soc of GB & Ireland; Am Assn for Advancement of Sci; Bradford Medico-Chirurgical Soc,

Pres 1990-91; Vice-Chair, Res Cttee of Yorkshire Health. Honour: FRSA. Hobbies: Sculpture; Music; Photography; Educating medical laboratory scientists. Address: Dept of Biomedical Sciences, University of Bradford, Bradford, West Yorkshire BD7 1DP, England. 149, 158, 161.

BAKHSH Qadir, b. 5 Jan 1944, Peshawar, Pakistan. Hd Race Relats Unit. m. Rukhsana Bakhsh, 4 Jan 1970, 2 d. Education: BA Eng 1963, MA Urdu 1965, MA Psycho, Peshawar Univ; MSc Social Psycho 1975, London Sch Ec, London Univ, Eng. Appointments: Sub-Edit, Daily Khyber Mail, Peshawar 1961-65; Res Psycho, Univ Peshawar 1967-68; Statistical Analyst, William Warne & Co, Barking, Essex, Eng 1972-74; Personnel Mgmt, L W Oldfield Ltd, London 1972-74; Community Relats Ofcr, Gravesend and District Community Relats Coun, Gravesend, Kent 1976-86; Mng Edit, Cheetah Books, Ajaib & QRB Pubrs 1981-; Race Relats Advr, Hd of Unit, Gravesham Borough Coun, Kent 1986-87; Hd Race Relats Unit, London Borough of Waltham Forest 1987-. Publications: Discussion papers, policy documents, review reports in field of politic socialisation of ethnic minorities; Res reports incl: Unrealised Potential 1980; Asian Youth and their unmet needs, 1984; Discrimination and Urban Deprivation in Kent, 1984; Teaching the Bilingual Child, 1985; Multi-faith Britain, 1985; Monitoring Equal Opportunity in Employment, 1986; Race and Housing, 1986; Education for Racial Equality, 1987; Provision for Ethnic Minority Elderly, 1987. Memberships: Chair, Interdepartment Working Party on Racial Harassment, mem Coun, Panel of Inquiry into Racial Harassment, Waltham Forest 1988-89; Series Edit, Waltham Forest Race Relats Res & Pubs 1990-; Exec Mem, Barking Muslim Assn; Trustee of Barking Mosque; Former Gov, Barking Col Tech, 2 Gravesend schs; Former Mem, Brit Psycho Soc; Inst Personnel Mgmt; Gen Arts Panel, South East Arts Assn; Barking Coun for Racial Equality. Honour: 1st Prize, Essay Compt, Iqbal Acad 1964; Community Services Award by Hand in Hand, UK, 1992. Hobbies: Cooking; Reading Urdu poetry and Iqbaliat; Listening to old Urdu/Hindi songs. Address: 14 Canterbury Avenue, Ilford, Essex 1G1 3NA, England.

BAKKER Paul-Jan, b. 1957, Vlaardingen, Netherlands. Cricket Player. Education: HAVO Dipl 1976; Pvt Pilot's Cert 1977; Ski Instructor 1980. Career: Cricketplayer, Hampshire CCC 1985-1992; Ski Instructor & Guide in Switzerland 1989-. Memberships: Quick HV & CC, The Hague, Holland; Hampshire CCC, Southampton; Marylebone CC, London. Honours: First Dutchman to play Professional County Cricket; J & B Whisky Player of the Month 3 X, Hampshire Press, Player of the Year once; Number of Dutch cricket prizes and honours; ICC Medals second place 2 X. Hobbies: Skiing; Golf; Beaches; Formula One motorracing; Sport events like Olympics; Papers. Address: Mozartlaan 79, 2555 3D The Hague, Netherlands.

BAKLAJA Radmila, b. 3 Aug 1931, Beograd. MD spec transfusiology. Education: Med Fac, Bgd Univ 1958; spec transf 1965; primarius 1971. Appointments: Blood Transfusion Inst of Srbija 1959, Hd of Centre for Med Care of Haemophiliacs and Dept Haemostasis and Haematology. Publications: 109 sci arts; Books: Haemostatic Disorders, 2 editions; Chapts on Haemostasis in Operative Surgery and Anaesthesia, WHO, 1972. Memberships: ISBT; ISHT; Mediterranean League for Thromboembolic Diseases, Pres; WFH, Sci Adv Com 1969-86; Throm Res, Edit 1972-76; Yu Transf & Haemat Bul, Edit. Honours: Serbian Physician Soc Awd; Yugoslav Soc Haemostasis and Thrombosis Awd; Yugoslav Assn Haematology & Transfusiology Awd-Hon Mem. Hobbies: Reading; Theatre; Films; Skiing. Address: Ustanicka 120, 11 000 Beograd, Yugoslavia.

BAKOSS Stephen L, b. 7 Mar 1938, Hungary. m. Eleonora, 10 Feb 1962, 1 s, 1 d. Education: BE, Univ Sydney, 1961; M Eng Sc, Univ of NSKI, 1969; MS, Univ of Calif, 1975; PhD, Univ of NSW, 1985. Appointments: Constr Engr, 1961-65; Structural Design Engr, 1965-

69; Acad Staff of NSW, Inst of Tech, 1969-; Prof of Civil Engr, Univ of Tech, Sydney, 1988-. Publications: Numerous. Memberships: Inst of Engrs; American Soc of Civil Engrs; Intl Assn of Bridge & Structural Engrs. Hobbies: Tennis; Theatre; Wine; Travel. Address: School of Civil Engineering, Univ of Technology, PO Box 123, Broadway, Sydney, NSW 2007, Australia.

BALAREVA Agapia, b. 28 Mar 1929, Rousse, Bulgaria. Musicologist. m. Velichko Gatev, 3 Aug 1958, div 1970, 1 d. Education: BA 1952, State Acad Mus, Sofia; MA 1969, PhD 1987, Prof, Inst Art Studies 1988, Bulgarian Acad Scis. Appointments: Inst Musicology 1954-88, when transformed into Inst Art Studies; Sci Secy, Inst Musicology and Inst Art Studies 1968-. Publications: Books: Bulgarian a cappella choral music, 1968; Bulgarian Musicians and the question of a national musical style, 1968; The Composer G Dimitrov, 1976; Cantata oratorio genre in Bulgarian music, 1979; Choral culture in Bulgaria (19c-WW2), 1992; Studies on the Bulgarian music culture in the 19th c. Membership: Union of Bulgarian Composers. Honours: Awds from Union of Bulgarian Composers for 2 books, 1976 & 1979, and for studies about the Bulgarian musical culture in the period of Bulgarian national revival, 1983; Order, 1300 Years of Bulgaria. Hobbies: Reading; Knitting. Address: 20 Dobromir Hriz st, 1124 Sofia, Bulgaria.

BALECH Enrique, b. 17 Aug 1912, Telen, Argentina. Marine Biologist; Planktologist. m. Electra Megias, 13 June 1939. Education: Prof on Natural Scis 1937. Appointments: Hd Lab of Protistology, Argent Mus Nat Scis (AMNC), Sr Planktologist, Inst Mar Biol 1961-62; Hd, Dir, Hydrobiol Stations at Quequen and Hd Div Hydrobiol, AMNC 1959-68; Mem of the carrier on Sci Res, CONICET, Emer Direct Hydr St 1968-. Publications: 4 books and over 120 sci contbrs, the latest being, The Genus Alexandrium, 1991. Memberships: Argentine Soc of Nat Sci, Secy 1939-41; Intl Com for the Study of Medit Sea, Plankton; Intl Phycological Soc; Arg Com of Oceanography. Honours: E L Holmberg Prize of Nat Acad Scis, Arg 1944; Hon Mem of Arg Com of Oceanography, 1973; Correspondong Mem, Nat (Arg) Acad Exact Physical & Nat Scis in Buenos Aires 1987; Awd'd for pioneering work at the 3rd Intl Conf on Toxic Dinoflagellates 1985. Hobbies: The international language, Esperanto; The conservation of natural environments. Address: Casilla de Correo 64, 7630 Necochea, Argentina. 50.

BALEY Geneve, b. 29 Oct 1923, Chicago, Illinois. Fdr US Horizontal Socio-Ec Sci. m. Jean-Claude Baley, 7 Dec 1951, 1 d. Education: AA, Wright Jr Col, Chgo; MM (2), Am Conservatory Mus; Painting and Drawing, Art Inst, Tanglewood; Berkshire Mus Centre, Composition; Mlle Nadia Boulanger, Paris, France 1951-52; Hunter Col, NY, Polit Sci 1967-69. Career: Poet; Composer; Artist; Mediator Pol Conslt, for UN, US Govt, Ford Motor Co; Glasnost/Perestroika resulted from creative negotiation, 1962 Cuban Missile Treaty, 1988 Missile Destruction Treaties, 1989 Berlin Wall end; Papal visit by Gorbachov. Creative Works: Books: Economic Critique; A New American Economics: Exerpts; Deed to the Future: A US Horizontal Socio-Economic Science; Art: Saugatuck Studio; Music: Bozo and the Bear; Tone Poems: The Circus; The Raven. Membership: DO music sorority. Honours: Music: Gold Medal Composition; Chamber work performed on WNYC radio; Scholarship chosen by Aaron Copland; Published poetry: Trophies, Certs; Grant. Hobbies: Nature; Sports; Travel; Meaningful social events. Address: 33-54 99th Street, Corona, NY 11368, USA. 155, 156, 151.

BALI Brigitta, b. 20 May 1948, Budapest, Hungary. m. Wally Keeler, 20 Sept 1986, 1 s. Education: Eotvos Lorand Univ of Law, Hungary; Faculty of Literature/Philosophy, Elte Univ; Faculty of Library & Information Sci, Univ of Toronto. Appointments: Post Grad Legal Apprenticeship, Central Court of Justice, 1973-74;

Jurist, Borough Council of Budapest, 1974-76; Consellor, District Presbitary Budapest, 1976-83; Researcher, Szecheny Natl Library, 1983-86; Conslt, Ministry of Community & Social Serv, Toronto, 1990-. *Publications:* Mischievous Miracle; On The Edge of Dreams; The Book of Revelations; Poems. *Address:* 37 Eden Place, Apt 208, Toronto, Ontario, Canada M5T 2V6.

BALIOZOV Roumen Dimitrov, b. 6 Sept 1949, Sofia, Bulgaria. Violoncello Player. *Education:* Mus Sec Sch, Sofia 1964-68; Mus Acad, Sofia: Violoncello Class 1968-72, Composing Class 1971-75. *Career:* Violoncello Player, Symphonic Orch of Bulgarian Radio 1974-. *Creative Works:* Scenical, symphonic, chamber, film, theatre and children's music; About 50 pubs on musical theory & critics. *Memberships:* Union of Bulgarian Composers 1977-; Soc for Contemporary Mus in Bulgaria 1990-. *Honours:* 3 Awds of Union of Bulgarian Composers 1977, 1982, 1987; 1 Awd of Bulgarian Cultural Com 1981. *Hobbies:* Literature; Theatre; Films; Art exhibitions. *Address:* 42 Ivan Vasov Str, 1000 Sofia, Bulgaria.

BALL Jonathan Macartney, b. 4 June 1947, Bude, Cornwall, England. Chartered Arch. m. Victoria Mary Ogilvie Blood, 29 June 1974, 2 d. *Education:* The Architectural Assn, London 1965-72; Chartered Arch 1972; Chartered Arbitrator 1978; Fellow Royal Soc Arts. *Appointments:* Principal, The Jonathan Ball Practice, Chartered Archs, Bude, Cornwall 1974-. *Memberships:* RIBA Coun 1981-; Chmn RIBA Parliamentary Affairs 1982-87; RIBA VP 1983-85; RIBA Hon Secy 1988-91; RIBA VP-Membership 1991; Trustee Brit Archl Library; Freeman City of London; Liveryman & Mem Court of Assistants, Worshipful Company of Chartered Archs. *Honours:* Jonathan Ball Practice, Design Awds; RIBA Awd for Arch (Commendation); Two Concrete Soc Awds (Special Mention); CLA/CPRE Henley Awd; OBE, 1992. *Hobbies:* Assessor for RIBA and Brick Development Assn Architecture Awds; Occasional Lecturer, Conference Speaker and Contbr to Architectural periodicals; RNLI Bude Lifeboat-crew member since 1966, now Sr Helmsman; President, Cornwall Region Surf Life Saving Association of Great Britain. *Address:* The Jonathan Ball Practice, 5 Belle Vue, Bude, Cornwall EX23 8JJ, England.

BALLA Zsófia, b. 15 Jan 1949, Cluj, Kolozsvár, Romania. Poet; Journalist; Translator. m. div. *Education:* Music Sch, speciality violin 1956-68; Acad Mus Cluj, speciality choir-dirigent and mus tchr 1968-72. *Appointments:* Reporter, Edit for music and literature, Hungarian section of Romanian Broadcasting Corp, Studio Cluj 1972-85; Journalist at daily newspaper Elöre 1985-90; Journalist, ldr of cultural department of monthly Családi Tukor-Family Mirror 1990-92; Journalist at weekly A HÉT, 1992. *Publications:* The Memory of Things, poems, 1968; Apocryphal Song, poems, 1971; Waterflame, poems, 1975; Second Person, poems, 1980; Danses of Cluj, poems, 1983; The Little Seal, children's poems, 1985; The Traces of Armour, poems, 1991; Selected poems, 1991; Many anthologies; Over 1000 radio programmes, interviews, reports, musical recordings. *Memberships:* Union of Writers in Romania, 1975, Leading Coun; Directory of Writers Assn of Cluj; Mem Hon, Union of Writers in Hungary, Budapest 1990-. *Honours:* Several prizes for poetry. *Hobbies:* Reading; Music; Travelling; Literary discussions. *Address:* 40, Piata Mihai Viteazul II/9, 3400 Cluj-Kolozsvár, Romania.

BALLARD Thomas William, b. 20 Nov 1950, Albuquerque. Hosp Exec. m. Sarah Emmalou Poynor, 25 June 1977, 2 d. *Education:* BS with Distinction 1972, Stanford Univ; MD 1976, Vanderbilt Univ; MBA 1989, Univ Western Fla, 1989; Diplomate Am Bd Family Practice. *Appointments:* Commd Capt USAF, 1976 advancing through grades to Col 1992; Resident Family Practice, Malcolm Grow USAF Med Ctr, Andrews AFB, Md 1976-79; Chief, Primary Care Svcs and Family

Physician USAF Hosp Misawa, Misawa AB, Japan 1979-82; Family Practice Staff Physician, USAF Clinic Ramstein, Ramstein AB, Germany 1982-85; Chief of Staff USAF Clinic Ramstein 1983-85; Asst Prof Family Practice, F Edward Hebert Sch Med Uniformed Svcs Univ Health Scis, Bethesda, Md 1986-89; Family Practice Residency Staff AFSC Regl Hosp, Eglin AFB, Fla 1985-88; Asst Prog Dir, Family Practice Residency AFSC Regl Hosp, Eglin AFB, 1986-88, Dir Med Edn 1987-88, Chf of Staff 1988-90; Resident in Radiology, Wilford Hall USAF Med Ctr, San Antonio 1990-; Cons in Family Practice Region VII, US Dept Defense 1989; Div Chief Judge, Northwest Fla Sci Fair, Ft Walton Beach 1988. *Memberships:* Uniformed Svcs Acad of Family Physicians; Am Acad Family Physicians; Assn Milit Surgeons of US; Christian Med Dental Soc; Radiol Soc N Am; Am Roentgen Ray Soc; Tex Radiol Soc. *Honours:* Recip Fellowship Reader's Digest Foun, Med Asst Prog, 1976, Medical Missionary, Nepal, 1976. *Hobbies:* Hiking; Skiing; Scuba; Stamp collecting. *Address:* 8402 Timberfair, San Antonio, TX 78250, USA. 7.

BALLESTEROS Carlos E, b. 30 Mar 1953, Madrid, Spain. Mgr. m. 10 Nov 1979, 1 s. 1 d. *Education:* Engr in Telecommunications; MBA, Inst de Empresa; Sales & Mktg degree. *Appointments:* Mixdorf Computer 1977-89; Data General 1989; Entel/Eritel 1989-91. *Creative Works:* Tchr sev courses: Local Area Network; Smart Buildings; Advanced Communications; Teleprocessing. *Memberships:* Colegio de Ingenieros Tec de Telecomunicacion. *Honours:* First Awd in Amateur Theatre 1973; First Awd in Nat Concourse of Chorus (Work Univ) 1974; Second Prize of Tennis (Nixdorf Com) 1979; Second Prize of Ping-pong (Nixdorf) 1979. *Hobbies:* Sports-Golf; Skiing; Squash; Tennis; Music; Movies; Books. *Address:* Plaza Andres Manjon 5-4o-B, 28.020 Madrid, Spain.

BALLINGALL Patrick Chandler Gordon, b. 5 Dec 1926, Devonport, Devon. Solicitor. m. Mary Hamilton Mackie, 10 May 1951, 1 s. 1 d. *Education:* Army Course, Edinburgh Univ 1944; MA 1950, Emmanuel Col, Cambridge; Qualified as Solicitor 1953. *Appointments:* Articled 1950- 53, Asst Solicitor 1954, Reynolds Gorst & Porter, London; Asst Solicitor, R V Stokes & Metcalfe, Portsmouth 1955-58; Asst Solicitor, Barwell & Blakiston, Seaford, East Sussex 1958; Ptnr 1959-89, Conslt 1990-, Barwell Blakiston & Ballingall, Solicitors, Seaford. *Memberships:* Pres, Sussex Law Soc 1974-75; Chmn, Lewes Constituency Conservative Assn 1978-81; Fin Ofcr, East Sussex European Constituency Coun 1981-85; Chmn of same 1985-89. *Honour:* MBE, 1984. *Address:* 4 Chyngton Gardens, Seaford, East Sussex BN25 3RP, England.

BALOGUN Taju Adedokun Akanni, b. 6 Jan 1935, Lagos, Nigeria. Prof Ed. m. Abisola Akintayo, 26 Apr 1968, 1 s. 1 d. *Education:* BSc 1963, MSc 1973, Univ London; MEd 1974, Univ Birmingham; MA 1975, EdD 1976, Columbia Univ, NY; Postgrad Dipl in Ed, Univ Ibadan; Dipl in Ednl Tech 1967, Univ Birmingham. *Appointments:* Sch Tchr 1963-67; Assoc Res Fellow 1967-68, UI; Curriculum Secy, Nigeria Ednl Res Coun 1969, Lectr & later Prof Ed, Univ Ibadan 1969-. *Publications:* Author or Co-Author of over 140 books, jour arts, conf/seminar papers on sci & tech ed, ednl tech and ed in gen. *Memberships:* Nigerian Acad Ed; Sci Tchrs Assn of Nigeria; Nigeria Assn for Ednl Media & Tech; Intl Org for Sci & Tech; The Gender and Sci & Tech Assn. *Honours:* Elected mem of Kappa Chapter of Kappa Delta Pi 1974; Admitted into Membership of Nigerian Acad of Ed 1985; Elected Fellow of Sci Tchrs Assn Nigeria 1989; Elected Luminary of Profl Edrs in Nigeria 1990. *Hobbies:* Environmental management and conservation; World watching especially through shortwave radio; Music; Occasional games. *Address:* Faculty of Education, University of Ibadan, Ibadan, Nigeria.

BALTAYAN Aroussiak Caro, b. 18 May 1971, Plovdiv, Bulgaria. Student; Music Performance Major At Univ of Central Arkausas, USA. *Education:* Plovdiv, Bulgaria, 1990. *Honours:* Presidential Scholar for the Oustanding Achievement of Having Complied the highest Possible Grades; Plovdiv Youth Newspapers Annual Award; Outstanding Student Award; The Absolute Winner Award; Aram Khachaturian Music Award; Mid American Violin Comp Award; Northeast Srkansas Symphony Young Artist Comp. *Hobby:* Piano. *Address:* 2400 Bruce Str, Apt 123, Conway, AR 72032, USA.

BAMFORD Colin, b. 28 Aug 1950, Blackburn, Lancashire. Solicitor. m. Nirmala Rajah, 31 Jan 1975, 2 s. 1 d. *Education:* BA 1971, MA 1973, Trinity Hall, Cambridge. *Appointments:* Articled Clerk 1972-74, Asst Solicitor 1974-77, Ptnr 1977-88, Herbert Oppenheimer Nathan & Vandyk; Ptnr, Richards Butler 1988-. *Memberships:* Intl Bar Assn; Union Intl des Avocats. *Hobbies:* Weight training; Collecting oriental textiles; Poetry. *Address:* Beaufort House, 15 St Botolph Street, London EC3A 7EE, England.

BANERJEE Arup Kumar, b. 28 Nov 1935, Calcutta, India. Conclt Physician in Elderly Med. m. Dr Aleya Banerjee, 23 Mar 1959, 3 s. *Education:* MB, BS Univ Calcutta Med Col. *Appointments:* Var jr hosp appts in India and UK 1958-67; Sr Registrar in Med, Southend Gen Hosp 1967-68; Lectr in Med, Univ Malaya Med Sch, Kuala Lumour 1968-71; Sr Registrar in Elderly Med, Portsmouth and Southampton Univ Hosps 1971-73; Conslt Physician in Elderly Med, Bolton Gen Hosp 1973; Hon Lectr in Geriatric Med, Univ of Manchester 1975; Conslt to Nat Health Advisory Service. *Publications:* Chapts in: Haematological Aspects of Systematic Disease, 1976; The Principles & Practice of Geriatric Medicine, 1985, 1991. *Memberships:* JP, Bolton Bench, Gtr Manchester; Nat Coun & Exec, Brit Geriatrics Soc; Central Conslts & Specialists Com, BMA; Geriatrics Com RCP London; Non-Exec Mem, NW Regl Health Authority; Panel of Experts for Nat Regd Homes Tribunal; Chmn, Bolton Med Exec Com. *Honours:* FRCP Glasgow 1979 (MRCP Glasgow 1965); FRCP Edin 1980 (MRCP Edin 1967); FRCP London 1982 (MRCP London 1967); Hon Fellow, Bolton Inst of High Educ. *Hobbies:* Travel; Music; Literature. *Address:* 2 Pilling Field, Egerton, Bolton, Greater Manchester BL7 9UD, England.

BANERJI Sara Ann, b. 6 June 1932, Stoke Poges, Bucks, England. Novelist. m. 4 Mar 1957, 3 d. *Education:* Var schs in Eng and S Rhodesia; Var art schs in Brit & Austria. *Publications:* 5 novels: Cobwebwalking; The Wedding of Jayanthi Mandel; The Tea Planter's Daughter; Shining Agnes; Absolute Hush; Writing on Skin. *Hobbies:* Trancendental meditation; Gardening; Painting; Family. *Address:* 7 London Place, Oxford OX4 1BD, England. 146.

BANKA Joseph, b. 27 Feb 1934, Nieszkow. Prof & Dir Inst Phil. m. Daniela Skrzypczak, 24 Jan 1967, 1 s. *Education:* MA Phil 1962, Catholic Univ Lublin; PhD Phil 1965, Adam Mickiewicz Univ, Poznan. *Appointments:* Asst & Assoc Prof, Adam Mickiewicz Univ in Poznan 1962- 74; Prof & Dir, Inst Phil, Silesian Univ in Katowice 1974-. *Publications:* 11 pubs incl: Philosophical & Social Views of Michal Wiszniewski, 1967; An Open Ontology, 1989; Epistemology as the Discovery of the Current Moment of Truth, 1990. *Membership:* Polish Philosophical Soc. *Honours:* Min of Ed Awds 1967, 1975, 1983. *Hobbies:* Chess; Theatre. *Address:* 40-057 Katowice ul, PCK 8/7 Poland.

BANKS Desmond Anderson Harvie, Lord, b. 23 Oct 1918, Ascot, Berkshire, England. Insurance Broker; Legislator. m. Barbara Wells, 12 June 1948, 2 s. *Education:* Univ Col Sch, Hampstead 1932-36. *Appointments:* Canada Life Assurance Company 1951-55; Life Assn of Scotland 1951-58; Insurance Broker 1959; Jago, Tweddle, 2 other Life & Pensions Broker 1960-82; Mng Dir, Lincoln Conslts Ltd, 1982-89. *Publications:* Clyde Steamers, Albyn Park, Edinburgh; Num pamphlets and booklets on polit subjects. *Memberships:* Pres, Liberal Party 1968-69; Chmn,

Liberal Party Exec 1961-63 & 1969-70; Hon Secy, Liberal Candidates Assn 1947-52; Dep Liberal Whip, House of Lords, 1977-82; Parliamentary Candidate, Harrow East 1950, St Ives, Cornwall 1955, South West Herts 1959; Pres, European Movement (Brit Coun) 1981-; Pres, Liberal European Action Group 1972-87. *Honours:* Commander of the Order of the British Empire 1972; Created Life Peer 1975. *Hobbies:* Clyde River Steamer; Gilbert & Sullivan Opera. *Address:* Lincoln House, The Lincolns, Little Kingshill, Great Missenden, Bucks HP16, OEH, England. 1, 34, 43.

BANKS William Allen, b. 9 June 1954, Bloomfield, Mo, USA. Physician Scist. m. 19 May 1979. *Education:* BA Biol 1975; MD 1979. *Appointments:* Veteran Affairs Med Ctr & Tulane Univ Sch Med 1985-. *Publications:* Author over 100 Sci Pubs. *Memberships:* Pres, Greater New Orleans Chapt Soc for Neurosci; Am Acad Advancement of Sci; NY Acad Sci. *Honours:* Career Devel Awd, Vets Admin 1982-85; Musser-Burch Soc; Am Med Assn Physician's Recog Awd 1990-93; Magnum cum laude (BA 1975). *Hobbies:* Music; Reading; Travel; Gardening. *Address:* 1701 Lake Superior, Harvey, LA 70058, USA.

BÄR Peter Rudolf, b. 8 Apr 1950, Makassar. Res Lab Hd. m. Jane Elizabeth Carrington Sykes, 10 Oct 1986. *Education:* Univ 1976; Doctor 1982. *Appointments:* Res Asst 1977-81; Dept Hd Neurol Lab 1981-83; Hd Res Lab Neurol 1983-; Assoc Prof Neurol 1989-. *Publications:* Sci arts in intl jours; Thesis: Membrane Phosphorylation and Nerve Cell Function, 1982. *Memberships:* Intl Soc Neurochem; Eur Soc Neurochem; Eur Neurosci Assn; Eur Soc Clinic Invest; Dutch-Belgian Soc for Exp & Clin Neurochem, Pres 1990-; Am Coll Sports Med; NY Acad Scis. *Honours:* Hon Mem, Royal Utr Stud Theatre 1972; Past Pres, Dutch Round Table 1, 1986. *Hobbies:* Photography; Music; Walking. *Address:* Research Lab of Neurology, AZU-Room 603.228, Heidelberglaan 100, 3584 CX Utrecht, Netherlands. 52, 100.

BARABANOV Victor Grigorievich, b. 25 Jan 1951, Kiev, Ukraine. Principal Viola Player. m. 8 Aug 1979, 2 d. *Education:* Special Music Sch numberLissenko 1959-69; Kiev Conservatoire (violin) 1969-74; Postgrad Student, Kiev Conservatoire 1981-84. *Career:* Violinist of Symphonic Orch of Ukrainian Radio and Television, and State Acad Symphonic Orch of Ukraine 1974-77; Solo Violinist of Mus Ensemble of Ukrainian Concert, Concertmaster of State Ukrainian Variety & Symphonic Orch 1977-79; Violinist of M Leontovych String Quartet based in Kiev, Ukrainian Kiev Philharmony, Touring Soviet Union, Far East, Ern Europe, NY, NJ and Connecticut 1979-89; Tchg position in Kiev Conservatory (Viola, quartet) 1982-89; Violist, Asst Principal of Symphonic Orch of Xalapa, Mexico 1990-91; Principal Violist of Orch Ensemble Kanazawa, Japan 1991-. *Honours:* Hon Artist of Ukrainian Repub; Laureate of 1st Ukrainian Chamber Contest 1983; Laureate of Lissenko Prize. *Hobbies:* Reading; Astronomy. *Address:* Kiev-86 str, Bakinskaya 37, fl 321, Ukraine.

BARABANOVA Natalia Orestovna, b. 6 Aug 1950, Lviv, Ukraine. Pianist. m. 8 Aug 1979, 2 d. *Education:* Musical Col, Donetsk, Ukraine 1966-69; Kiev Conservatoire, 1969-74. *Career:* Concertmaster of the Kiev Conservatoire 1974-79; Worked in Class of the Fdr of Flut's Sch of Ukraine Protsenko AF. *Creative Works:* Exhibitions of Paintings: Ukraine, Kiev 1974, 1979; Mexico, Merida 1990; Japan, Kanazawa 1991. *Honour:* Laureate of the 1st Ukrainian Chamber Contest 1983. *Hobbies:* Reading; Poetry; Painting. *Address:* Kiev-152, Seraphimovicha Str, 15/1, fl 92, Ukraine.

BARANOWSKI Tom, b. 3 Dec 1946, Brooklyn, NY, USA. Prof Health Behaviour in Paediatrics. m. Janice Carlson Henske, 2 June 1990, 1 s. 1 d. from prev marriage. *Education:* AB Polit 1968, Princeton Univ, New Jersey; MA Social Psycho 1970, PhD Social Psycho

1974, Univ Kansas, Lawrence, Kansas. *Appointments include:* Res Assoc, Div Consumer & Continuing Ed 1976-78, Asst Prof, Coord Div Consumer Ed, Clin Asst Prof Dept Behavioural Med & Psychi 1978-80, Dept Community Med, West Virginia Med Ctr-Charleston Div, West Virginia; Asst Prof, Depts Paediatrics (Div Sch Health & Community Paediatrics) and of Preventive Med and Community Health (Div Sociomed Scis), Univ Tex Med Br, Galveston, Tex 1980-84; Assoc Prof (with tenure), Dept Preventive Med & Community Health, Divs of Sociomed Scis & of Nutrition, Assoc Prof, Dept Paediatrics, Div Sch Health & Community Paediatrics, Univ Tex Med Br; Adj Assoc Prof, Dept Psycho, Univ Houston, Tex; Fac Assoc, Ctr for Health Promotion Res & Devel, Univ Tex, Health Sci Ctr, Houston, Tex 1984-990. *Publications:* Author or Co-Author 36 arts in non-refereed jours, 75 abstracts, 55 publ arts in peer-reviewed jours and 24 submitted, 10 books and chapts. *Memberships include:* With var posts & positions: Am Heart Assn; Am Psycho Assn; Am Pub Health Assn; Am Sch Health Assn; Assn on Hypertension in Black Populations; Assn for Study of Food and Soc; Assn of Tchrs of Preventive Med; N Am Soc of Paediatric Exercise Med; Soc Behavioural Med; Southwestern Soc for Res in Human Devel. *Honours:* NY State Regents Scholarship Awd 1964; Academic Scholarship, Princeton Univ 1964- 68; Dean's List 1967; USPHS Fellowship, Univ Kansas 1969-71; Citation, Am Diabetes Assn 1980; Recip, Anne Mooney Sch Health Awd, UTMB, Ann Tex Sch Health Conf 1990. *Address:* Professor and Director, Division of Behavioral Science and Health Education. Emory Univ, School of Public Health, 1599 Clifton Rd, NE, Atlanta, GA 30329, USA. 139, 125, 7, 2.

BARBER Lloyd Ingram, b. 8 Mar 1932, Regina, Sask, Canada. Univ Pres Emeritus. m. Muriel Pauline (Duna) MacBean, 12 May 1956, 3 s. 3 d. *Education:* BA Ec 1953; B Comm Admin 1954; MBA Mktg 1955; PhD 1964. *Appointments:* Instr in Commerce 1955, Asst Prof in Commerce 1957, Assoc Prof in Commerce 1964, Dean of Commerce 1965, VP 1968-74 (resigned), Prof of Commerce 1974-76, Univ Saskatchewan; Apptd as one of 3 Commrs to Saskatchewan Royal Comm on Govt Admin 1964, report completed 1965; Indian Claims Commr 1969-77; Special Inquirer for Elder Indian Testimony 1977-81; Pres, Univ regina, Regina 1976-90; Chmn, Barber Comm on Sask Energy, Report completed 1989. *Creative Works:* Co-Author, Report of the Royal Commission on Government Administration, Prov of Sask, 1965; Co-Author, Youth in Our Time, 1966. *Contributions:* Conslt & Speaker on Mgmt, Mktg, Ec, Admin & Candn Indian Peoples. *Memberships:* Current Mem 18 Boards or Directorships incl: Dir, Canadian Pacific Ltd, 1983-; Dir, Molson Companies 1978-; Dir, Inst for Sask Enterprise 1988-; Dir, STV 1990-; Coun of Advrs, Arms Control Centre 1990-; Member-at-Large, Candn Red Cross Soc 1990-; Dir, North West Company Inc 1991-. *Hobbies:* Hunting; Fishing; Sailing; Swimming; Travel; Reading; Gardening. *Address:* Box 510, Regina Beach, Saskatchewan, Canada SOG 4CO. 88, 2, 32.

BARBER Robert Russell, b. 7 June 1926, Brandon, Man. Rtd Milit; Writer. m. Shirley Maxine Bearance, 19 July 1949. *Education:* Milit Tng incl Gunners Tng 1944; Radar Tech Tng, Clinton, Ont 1946; Radio Navigator Course 1948 and Sr Navigators Course 1952, Summerside PEI; Aerospace Systems Course 1956, Winnipeg Man; RCAF Staff Col Course 1963, Toronto. *Appointments:* Enlisted RCAF 1943 as Boy Airman; Grad as Sergeant Air Gunner, served overseas; Returned to Canada 1945 as part of Pacific Volunteer Force; Rec'd King's Commission in RCAF 1948; Rtd Candn Armed Forces 1979, from Active Res Ser 1991. *Memberships:* Very active in community assns incl: Dir, Social Credit Assn, Cowichan, Malahat 1981; Dir, Agapeland Christian Nursery Sch, Duncan BC 1983; Chmn Fundraising, Candn Cancer Soc, Cowichan Unit 1984. *Hobbies:* Writing; Computers; Politics-Federal & Provincial; Community affairs; Canadian Cancer Society

volunteer work. *Address:* 1432 Kingsview Road, RR 5, Duncan BC, Canada V9L 4T6. 142.

BARBER Stephen Douglas, b. 18 Jan 1955, London, England. Investment Mgr. m. Kimiko, Apr 1983, 1 s. *Education:* MA in Maths & Philosophy, St Johns Col, Oxford. *Appointments:* Samuel Montagu & Co Ltd 1977-85; MIM Ltd, 1985-90, Dir INVESCO MIM Ltd 1991-; Pres, Investment Trust Mgmt Co Ltd. *Publications:* Book reviews, arts etc for var pubs incl Vogue, International Investor. *Memberships:* The Liszt Soc, London; Asiatic Soc, Tokyo; Vincents, Oxford; Oriental Club, London; Guild of Rahere, London. *Honour:* Japan Min of For Affairs, Essay Prize 1981. *Hobbies:* Antiquarian books; Japanese pen & ink drawing. *Address:* 3-20-2 EBISU, Shibuya-ku, Tokyo 150, Japan.

BARBOSA Ana Mae, b. 17 July 1936, Rio de Janeiro. Dir; Prof. 1 s. 1 d. *Education:* Bacharel Ciencias Juridicas, Univ Fed Pernambuco 1960; Mestrado Arte Educacao, Srn Connecticut State Col, USA 1974; Doutroado em Educacao Humanistica, Boston Univ 1979; Livre Docencia em Artes, Escola Comunicacoes e Artes, Univ Sao Paulo. *Appointments:* Asst Prof Doutora da Escola de Comunicacoes e Artes da Univ de Sao Paulo desde 1974; Dir Tecnica do Museu de Arte Contemporanea da Univ de Sao Paulo desde 1986; Assoc Prof da Escola Comunicacoes e Artes, Univ Sao Paulo desde 1990. *Publications:* Teoria e Practica da Educacao Artistica, 1986; Arte Educacao no Brasil, 1985; Recorte e Colagem: A Influencia de John Dewey no Ensino da Arte no Brasil, 1989; Arte Educacao: Conflitos/acertos, 1987. *Memberships:* AESP, Pres 1982-85; INSEA, Intl Soc of Ed through Art; Mem World Coun 1984-90, Pres 1991-93. *Honour:* Great Prize of Criticism, 1989, Assn Critics of S Paulo. *Address:* Museu de Arte Contemporanea, Parque Ibirapuera, Caixa Postal 22031, 01499 Sao Paulo-SP, Brasil.

BARBOUR Billy Michael, b. 28 Nov 1953, Williamson, WV, USA. Nsg Admin. m. Alice Ruth Rose, 14 Feb 1977, 1 s. 1 d. *Education:* AD Nsg 1977, Ashland Community Col; BSN 1989, Master's Prog 1991, Bellarmine Col, Kentucky. *Appointments:* Var nsg appts 1977-82; Sophomore Paediatric Clin Instr, Ashland Community Col 1990-91; Relief Nsg Supvr, Paediatric Staff Nse 1982-83, Nsg Dir-Paediatrics 1983-85, Dir-Rehab & Wellness Sers 1985-87, Nsg Dir Care Unit (Substance Abuse) 1987-90, Asst VP, Nsg Admin 1990-91, Our Lady of Bellefonte Hosp, Ashland, Ky. *Memberships include:* Notary Public Commr, State Ky 1990-94; C of C, Boyd/Greenup Counties 1990-91; Sigma Theta Tau, Lambda Psi Chapter, Bellarmine Col 1990-91; Ky Nurses' Assn, Dist 4 1990-91; Am Nurses' Assn 1990-91; Nat Nurses' Soc on Addictions 1990-91; Ky Coun of Middle Mgmt Affiliates 1988-91; Var committees. *Honours:* Nsg Preceptor, Undergrad, Bellarmine Col, Nsg Outreach Prog 1989-91; Nsg Excellence Awd, Ky Nurses' Assn 1989; Best Actor Awd, Ashland Community Col 1989; Honour Soc, Bellarmine Col 1989-91; Nsg Preceptor-Undergrad, Ohio State Univ Srn Campus, Ironton 1990; Nominee: Jaycee's Outstanding Young Man of the Year 1990. *Hobbies:* Theatre; Singing; Tennis. *Address:* 1506 Jonathan Street, Flatwoods, KY 41139, USA. 7.

BARCELO Caroline, b. 8 Oct 1946, Detroit, Michigan. USA. Prof; Mktng Conslt. m. 24 Mar 1984, 1 s, 1 d. *Education:* Public Admin, Goveneros State Univ, Illinois; Bach of Sci, Western Michigan Univ; Intl Business, Hankuk Univ of Foreign Studies. *Appointments include:* First Investors Copr, Detroit, 1969-74; Merlin Karlock US Congressional Cand, Illinois, Campaign Scheduler & Coordinator, 1976; Nexus Intl Inc, pres, 1979- 82; Kagins Numismatic Inc, Regional Rep, 1982-84; Electro Heat Resources Inc, Pres, 1984-92; Intl Fine Arts Coll, Prof, 1991-92. *Memberships include:* Womens Political Caucus, Miami; Natl Inst of Applied Scis; Intl Assn of Financial Planners; Intl Acad of Business Educ. *Hobbies:* Politics; Environmental Issues; Education; Swimming;

Sailing; Tennis. *Address:* 2447 Pinetree Drive, Miami Beach, FL 33140, USA. 138, 152.

BARCLAY Neil, b. 18 Apr 1917, Chelmsford, Essex. Milit Historian; Voluntary Wkr. m. Mary Emma (Mollie) Scott-Shurmer, 27 Sept 1941, 1 s. 3 d. *Education:* Pvtly home & abroad. *Appointments:* Writer & Journalist latterly Times, Telegraph, Morning Post 1933-39; 1933-39; Served RHA TA 1939-72; Served RA in Gibraltar Malta Cyprus, Egypt, Palestine, at sea with RN (HMS London in Bismark battle), West Africa, Northwest Europe (Airborne Forces), India, transferred RAOC 1951 served Libya, Egypt, Persia, Germany, East Africa, South Arabia and Persian Gulf; Lt Col 1958, Col 1964, Brig 1968; Sr Principal DOE (sen appeals inspector) 1972-92; Commander, St John Ambulance, Shropshire. *Publications:* Part author mil histories. *Memberships:* Mem County SSAFA; Vice Chmn ABF; Pres ACF League; Pres, RA Assn Br; VP RAOC Assn Br; FASMC 1962; FBIM 1968; FCIArb 1973. *Honours:* Deputy Lt for County of Shropshire 1984; Knight Order of St John of Jerusalem (KStJ) 1986. *Hobbies:* Travelling; Good companions; Gardening. *Address:* Strinebrook House, The Hincks, Lilleshall, Newport, Shropshire TF10 9HT, England.

BARCLAY WHITE Egon Oram, b. 27 June 1927, London, England. Dental Surgeon; Co Dir. m. (1) Sheila Meredith, 1951, 2 s, 2 d. (2) Catherine Mary, 1979, 1 s, 1 d. *Education:* Royal Dental Hosp, Californ State, 1985; Army Service. *Appointments:* Royal Dental Hosp; St Georges Hosp, Snr Reg; St peters Hosp, Chertsey; Weybridge Practice; Dentistry in all London Prisons, Santa Panla California. *Creative Works:* Active Founder Capital Radio Plc. *Membership:* Naval Military Club. *Hobby:* Worrying. *Address:* Warren Cottage, Camp End Road, Weybridge, Surrey KT8 0NR, England.

BARES Ludek, b. 5 July 1929, Mlada Boleslav. Sr Res Scist. m. Dr Edith Kurz, 4 Dec 1954, 2 s. *Education:* MD 1953, Charles Univ Sch Med; State Dipl in Clin Neurology with hons 1957; State Dipl in Neurology-superior degree 1968; PhDCSc 1984. *Appointments:* Demonstrator and Scist, Dept Biochem, Charles Univ Prague 1950; Vice Hd, Dept Neurology, Region Hosp Karlovy Vary, Carlsbad 1957; Hd, Dept Neurol, Hosp Rumburk, Postgrad Edr 1958- 64; Hd, Dept Neurol, Hosp Prague East, Sworn Export of High Court of Justice in Prague 1965-89; Sen Res Scist, CS Acad of Scis 1989. *Creative Works:* 2 med films; 2 books; 50 sci papers in Eng, German, French; 107 lectures in sci soc meetings, congs & postgrad ed; Instrument design co-author: EOG. *Memberships:* Am Acad of Neurol, Assoc Clin Mem; NY Acad of Scis, Active Mem 1987. *Honour:* Am Acad of Neurol, Hon Corresp member 1981. *Hobbies:* Art: partic baroque sculpture and architecture; Music, esp organ and cembalo; Middle Ages bibliography. *Address:* Stara Boleslav, Vestecka 1037, CS 250 01, Czechoslovakia.

BARKER David Faubert, b. 18 Feb 1922, London, England. Res Neurobiologist. m. (1)Kathleen Frances Pocock, 16 June 1945, 3 s. 2 d. (2)Patricia Margaret Drake, 29 Jan 1978, 1 s. 1 d. *Education:* Magdalen Col, Oxford 1941-43; BA 1st class Hons Zoology 1943, Oxford; D Phil Oxford 1948; MA Oxford 1954; DSc Oxford 1972. *Appointments:* Demonstrator in Zoology, Oxford 1947-50; Prof Zoology, Univ Hong Kong 1950-62; Prof Zoology 1962-87, Emeritus Prof Zoology 1987-, Univ Durham. *Publications:* Over 100 papers in learned jours on nerve & muscle; Edit & Fdr, Hong Univ Fisheries Journal 1954-58; Edit, Symposium on Muscle Receptors, 1962. *Memberships:* Physiol Soc; Anatomical Soc. *Honours:* Rolleston Memorial Prize 1948; Sr Demyship, Magdalen Col, 1946; Emeritus Fellowship, Leverhulme Trust 1989-90, 1991-92; Sir Derman Christopherson Fellowship, Durham Univ Res Foun 1984-85. *Hobbies:* Gardening; Reading. *Address:* Department of Biological Sciences, South Road, University of Durham, Durham DH1 3LE, England. 1.

BARKER Dennis (Malcolm), b. 21 June 1929, Lowestoft, GB. Journalist; Author. m. Sarah Katherine Alwyn, 1 d. *Education:* Reporter, Sub-Edit, Suffolk Chronicle & Mercury, Ipswich 1947-48; Reporter, Feature Writer, Theatre & Film Critic, East Anglian Daily Times 1948-58; Estates & Property Edit, Feature Writer, Theatre Critic, Radio Critic, Columnist, Express & Star, Wolverhampton 1958-63; Midlands Correspondent 1963-67, Reporter, Feature Writer, Media Correspondent, Columnist, Obituarist 1967-, The Guardian. *Publications:* Novels: Candidate of Promise, 1969; The Scandalisers, 1974; Winston Three Three Three, 1987; Non-fiction: The People of the Forces Trilogy-Soldiering On, 1981, Ruling the Waves, 1986, Guarding the Skies, 1989; One Man's Estate, 1983; Parian Ware, 1985; Fresh Start, 1990. *Memberships:* Nat Union Journalists, Secy Suffolk Br 1953-58, Chmn 1958; Chmn, Home Counties District Coun 1956-57; Writers Guild of GB; Broadcasting Press Guild; Soc of Authors; Life mem, Newspaper Press Fund. *Hobbies:* Painting; Music; Reading; Cinema; Sailing. *Address:* 67 Speldhurst Road, London W4 1BY, England. 3.

BARKER Godfrey Raymond, b. 14 Apr 1945, Gt Crosby. Arts & Polit Columnist. m. Ann Botsford Calender, 17 Feb 1974, 1 s. *Education:* Cambridge, Oxford & Cornell Univs 1963-69; MA; DPhil. *Appointments:* ITN 1969-72; HM Diplomatic Ser, 1972 (2nd Secy, UN Dept); Daily Telegraph 1972-92. *Publications:* Leader Writer and Parliamentary Sketchwriter 1981-92; Arts Edit 1986-87. *Membership:* Beefsteak Club. *Hobbies:* Schubert; Cricket; Campaigning for the National Heritage. *Address:* 26 Charles Street, Berkeley Square, London W1, England.

BARKER Joanna Mary, b. 20 Jan 1942, Napier, New Zealand. Prof. m. (2)David John Waddell, 20 July 1991, 1 s. from previous marriage. *Education:* Dipl in Occ Therapy (NZ) 1963; Grad Dipl in Health Scis (Wait) 1978; Masters in Applied Sci Wait 1980; PhD (Murdoch) 1988. *Appointments:* OT, NZ 1963-67; OT, Fremantle Hosp 1969-71; Sr OT, Claremont Hosp 1971-72; Principal OT, Mental Health Sers, WA 1973-79; Hd Sch OT of Curtis Univ 1979-; Awd'd Professorial Chair, Curtis Univ 1988. *Publications:* 20 pub arts in ref jours; Reviewer; 39 presentations at state, nat & intl confs. *Memberships:* WA OT Assn 1970-, On Exec 1971-; Held posts of Fedl Del, VP & Pres; Australian Del to World Fed of OT, On Exec 1980-, Pres 1986-90; Chair W A Branch Australian Hosp Assn; Chair of Sir Charles Gairdner Hosp Board; Mem 12 external coms. *Honours:* Awd'd Sylvia Docker Lectureship 1983-84; Awd'd Pioneer Awd 1987; Awd'd Candn C'Wealth Fellowship, Univ Western Ontario, 1988; Awd'd Hon Fellowship, W.FOT, 1992. *Hobbies:* Golf; Travel; Good food & wine; Music; Theatre. *Address:* 19 Bedford Avenue, Subiaco, Perth, WA, Australia. 138.

BARKER John Alfred, b. 2 Dec 1929, Shoreditch, London, England. Rtd Probation Service. m. Margaret Coutts Smith, 22 Sept 1962. *Education:* Neale's Math Sch; City of London Col. *Appointments:* Stock Exchange 1950-64; Inner London Probation Service 1965-90. *Memberships:* Corporation of London Common Councilman Cripplegate Without 1981-; Bethlem Royal Hosp and Maudsley Hosp Special Health Authority Mem 1983-; Bd Mgmt Barbican YMCA 1986-, Chmn; City Parochial Foun 1989-. *Hobbies:* Travel; Hill & mountain walking; Clubman. *Address:* 319 Willoughby House, Barbican, London EC2Y 8BL, England.

BARKER Nicholas John (Nick) Capt, b. 19 May 1933. Conslt; Chmn Sea Safety Centre. m. (1)Elizabeth Venetia Redman, 10 Aug 1957, dis 1989, 2 s. 2 d. (2)Jennifer Jane, 4 Mar 1989, 2 stepdaughters. *Education:* Canford, Naval Cols and Staff Col, Churchill Col Cambridge (Defence Fellow). *Appointments:* RN; 8 seagoing cmds incl: HMS Arrow 1975-77, HMS Endurance (Falklands) 1980-82, Fishery Protection Sqdn 1984-86, HMS Sheffield 1987-88; MOD Naval Sec Dept 1977-79; Chmn Sea Safety Centre Ltd; Dir, Glowsafe Ltd, Marr Tech Servs; Ptnr, Nicholas Barker Consultancy.

Publications: Books: The Falklands, a Common Denominator, 1984; Novels incl: Red Ice, 1987; Rig, 1990. *Memberships:* Nat Chm Royal Nat Mission to Deep Sea Fishermen; Mem Nat Cncl, Br Maritime League; SW Atlantic Gp, Jubilee Tst, patron local com; Younger Bro Trinity London 1967. *Honours:* CBE 1982; Hon Col Royal Marines RMR Tyne 1990; Freeman City of London, Liveryman Worshipful Co of Fishmongers 1986; FBIM 1977; MNI 1979; FRGS 1982; Royal Order of Merit Class IV Norway 1988. *Hobbies:* Shooting; Fishing; Golf; Spectator sports; Reading current affairs. *Address:* The Sea Safety Centre, South Dock, Sunderland, England.

BARKER Patricia Margaret, b. 8 May 1943, Thornaby, England. Novelist. m. David Faubert Barker, 29 Jan 1978, 1 s. 1 d. *Education:* BSc Ec 1965, LSE; Dip Ed 1966, Durham Univ. *Publications:* Union Street, 1982; Blow Your House Down, 1984; The Century's Daughter, 1986; The Man Who Wasn't There, 1989; Regeneration, 1991. *Memberships:* The Soc of Authors; Intl PEN. *Honour:* Fawcett Prize, 1982. *Hobbies:* Walking; Swimming; Reading. *Address:* c/o Anne McDermid, Curtis Brown & John Farquharson, 162-168 Regent Street, London W1R 5TB, England.

BARKER Simon, b. 4 Nov 1964, Farnworth, Lancs, England. Profl Footballer. m. Theresa Rean Knowles, 14 June 1987. *Education:* W R Tuson Col of Further Ed, Preston. *Career:* Blackburn Rovers 1982-88, debut v Swansea City 1983, appearances 221, goals 42; Queens Park Rangers, 1988-, debut v Manchester United, 1988, appearances 152, goals 16. *Honours:* 4 England U-21 Caps 1985-86; Full Members Cup Winners, Blackburn Rovers v Charlton 1987, Awd'd Man of the Match. *Hobbies:* Golf; Cricket; Fine wines; Autobiographies. *Address:* Queens Park Rangers, Rangers Stadium, South Africa Road, Shepherds Bush, London W12 7PA, England.

BARLEV Haim, b. 16 Nov 1924, Vienna. Mem Knesset (Parliament). m. Tamar Manarshak, 11 Apr 1949, 1 s. 1 d. *Education:* MBA 1963, Columbia Sch of Bus. *Appointments:* Palmach-Under Ground Mobilized Force 1942- 48; Served in Israel Defence Forces (IDF) 1948-72; Chf Gen Staff IDF 1968-72; Min of Trade & Industry 1972-77; Secy Gen Israel Labour Party 1977-84; Min Police 1987-90; March MP 1980. *Publications:* Sev arts on Defence & Ec. *Membership:* Chmn of Israel Arabian Horse Soc. *Honours:* Paratrooper's Wings 1951; Air Force Wings 1954. *Hobby:* Arabian horses. *Address:* 18 Hagefen Street, Neve Magen 47254, Israel.

BARLI Sasmitawinata, b. 18 Mar 1921, Bandung, Indonesia. Painter; Lectr. m. Atikah Basari, 1946, 1 s, 1 d. *Education:* Art Educ, Bandung, 1935-38; Acad Grande de la Chaumiere, Paris, 1950-51; Ryksacademie van Beeldenkunsten, Amsterdam, 1951-56. *Appointments:* Founding the Rangga Gempol Art Educ Studio, 1950-; Lectr, Bandung Inst of Tech, 1957-58; Snr Lecyr, Pajajaran Univ, 1957-68. *Membership:* Indonesian Artists Assn. *Honours:* Jaarmarkt Prize Surabaya, Indonesia; Keimin Bunka Shidoso, Jakarta; Barisan Propaganda, Jawa Barat; Culturele Stichting Samenwerking Nederland. *Hobbies:* Painting; Reading; Acting. *Address:* Museum Barli, Jl Prof Ir Sutami No, Bandung, Indonesia.

BARLINSKA Izabela, b. 10 Sept 1955, Gdansk, Poland. Exec Secy. *Education:* MA Eng Philology 1978, Warsaw Univ. *Appointments:* Polish Acad of Scis, Inst of Philosophy and Sociology 1978-80; Intl Sociological Assn. *Membership:* Exec Secy, Intl Sociological Assn. *Address:* International Sociological Association, Facultad de C. C. Politicas y Sociologia, Universidad Complutense, Campus de Somosaguas, 28223 Madrid, Spain. 52.

BARLOW Curtis Leonard, b. 2 May 1947, Canada. Diplomat; Lawyer; Cultural Exec. *Education:* BSc 1968;

LLB 1972; Bar Admission, Ontario 1974; LLM 1976. *Appointments:* Articled with Thomson, Rogers, Toronto 1972-73; Solicitor, Ont Min of Treasury, Ec & Intergovernmental Affairs 1974- 75; Exec Dir, Profl Assn of Canada Theatres 1977-86; Pres, Candn Conf of the Arts 1984-86; Pres, Candn Centre of the Intl Theatre Inst, Eng Lang 1981-86; Mem Exec Com, Intl Theatre Inst 1983-86; Pres World Encyclopaedia of Contemporary Theatre (Canada) 1984-86; Co-Pres, XXIst World Cong of the Intl Theatre Inst, 1985; Dir, Canada House Cultural Centre and Couns, Cultural Affairs, Candn High Commn, London, Eng 1986-90; Counsellor, Cultural Affairs, Candn Embassy, Wash DC 1990-. *Publication:* Co-Edit, Playwrights Guide to Canadian non-profit, professional theatres, PACT, 1984. *Memberships:* Intl Theatre Inst, Candn Pres 1981-86; ITI, Intl Exec Com 1983-86; Candn Conf of the Arts, Pres 1984-86; Soc West End Theatres Olivier Awds Theatre Panel, London 1988; PR Com, Duke of Edinburgh's Awd, Intl Secretariat, London 1987-90; Counc, Br Centre of Intl Theatre Inst 1989-90; Law Soc Upper Canada; Assn Cultural Execs. *Hobbies:* Travel; Literature; Languages. *Address:* Canadian Embassy, 501 Pennsylvania Avenue NW, Washington DC 20001, USA. 142.

BARLOW Harry James, b. 7 Apr 1951, England, Dir Issue Communications. m. Lucy Cuodon, 16 Apr 1987, 1 s. *Education:* Dane Court Tech High Sch; London Sch Ec 1970-79; BSc Hons; PhD. *Appointments:* Consultation Ofcr, Southwark Coun 1979-84; Publicity Mgr, GLC, Anti-Abolition Campaign 1984-86; Dir, Issue Communications 1986-. *Memberships:* Fellow, Royal Geographical Soc; Com Mem London Activities Com; LSE; LSE Club; Fabian Soc. *Hobbies:* Political advertising; Reading; Music. *Address:* 3 Hanson Street, London W1, England.

BARNABAS Seng Chi, b. 15 Aug 1948, Macau. Higher Ed Admin. m. Rebekah L M Iu, 31 Dec 1978, 1 s. 1 d. *Education:* Dipl Sociol 1975, HK Baptist Col; MBA 1988, Pacific SU, Calif; Grad Mem 1988, Can Inst Certify Adm Mgr; Bus Adm Fellow, Can Sch Mgmt 1989. *Appointments:* Higher Ed Admin Ofcr, Hong Kong Baptist Col; Music Min, A C Ch 1980-. *Creative Works:* The Rythm of Music (vol 1-3), Teachers' Music Handbook. *Memberships:* President, H.K. Church Music Service Ltd, Min of Ed, Coun Mem, HK Assn Culture, Ed & Communications; Secy & Bd Mem, World Chinese Ch Mus Assn; VP, Kowloon Tong & MTW Area Com, HK Govt apptd; Fight Crime Com (KC), HK Govt apptd. *Hobbies:* Music; Photography; Drama. *Address:* H K B C (SAO), 224 Waterloo Road, Kowloon Tong, Hong Kong.

BARNARD Michael John, b. 4 May 1944, Ipswich, England, Publisher. m. 24 June 1984, 1 s. *Education:* Licensed Victuallers Sch; Pitman Col. *Appointments:* Journalist, Associated Kent Newspapers 1961-67; Journalist, Thomson Intl 1967-70; Mng Edit, First Features Ltd 1970-72; Prod Mgr, Macmillan Ltd 1974-1980; Dir, Macmillan Ltd, 1980-; Dir, Gill & Macmillan, 1990-. *Publications:* Magazine and Journal Production, 1986; Introduction to Print Buying, 1987; Inside Magazines, 1989; Introduction to Printing Processes, 1991. *Memberships:* Non-Exec Dir, Periodical Assn Ltd 1988-90; Chmn Printing Div Printing Industs Res Assn; MAIE 1988; FRSA 1991. *Hobbies:* Music; Literature; Sailing; Swimming; Gardening. *Address:* Macmillan Ltd, 4 Little Essex Street, London WC2R 3LF, England.

BARNES Christopher John, b. 10 Mar 1942, Sheffield, England. Univ Prof. m. Alexa Hilla Dey, 26 July 1975, 2 d. *Education:* BA, MA 1967, PhD 1970, Cambridge Univ; Moscow Univ 1963-64; Cambridge Univ 1964-67. *Appointments:* Lectr in Russian, St Andrews Univ, Scotland 1967-89; Prof & Chmn of Dept of Slavic Langs & Lits, Univ Toronto, Canada 1989-. *Publications:* Boris Pasternok, Selected Prose, Ed, 1977; Studies in Twentieth Century Russian Literature, 1976; Boris Pasternak, The Voice of Prose, 2 vols, translated & edited, 1986-90; Boris Pasternak: A Literary Biography,

Vol I, 1989. *Memberships:* BASEES; Brit Univs Assn Slavists, Com Mem 1986-89; Royal Musical Assn; Am Assn for Advancement of Slavic Studies; Assn Tchrs of Slavic and East Euro Langs; Assn Tchrs of Russian; Candn Assn Slavists. *Hobbies:* Languages; Literature; Reading; Music (piano); Musicology. *Address:* Dept of Slavic Languages and Literatures, University of Toronto, 21 Sussex Avenue, Toronto, Canada M5S 1A1.

BARNES Colin Greenhill, b. 4 July 1936, Woodford, England. Conslt Physician (Rheumatol). m. Marian Nora Sampson, 22 Sept 1962, 2 s. *Education:* BSc (Hons) Anatomy 1958, MB BS 1961, London Hosp Med Col, Univ London; MRCP 1965; FRCP 1978. *Appointments:* Conslt Physician Rheumatol, Royal London Hosp 1968-; Hon Conslt Rheumatologist, St Luke's Hosp for Clergy; Rheumatologist, London Independent Hosp. *Publications:* Co- Edit: Behcet's Syndrome 1979; Behcet's Disease 1986. *Contributions:* book chapts: Clinical Rheumatology; Copeman's Textbook of Rheumatology; The Foot. *Memberships:* Brit Soc for Rheumatology; Hon Mem, Swiss Soc for Rheumatol; Hon Mem, Australian Rheumatol Assn; Pres, European League Against Rheumatism; Past Pres, Brit League Against Rheumatism; Fellow, Royal Soc Med; Brit Med Assn; Chmn, Exec & Fin Com, Arthritis and Rheumatism Coun for Res. *Hobbies:* Classical music & opera, Gardening; Travel. *Address:* 96 Harley Street, London W1N 1AF, England. 170.

BARNES Melver Raymond, b. 15 Nov 1917, nr Salisbury, NC, USA. Pvt Sci Res. *Education:* AB Chem 1947, UNC, Chapel Hill; Addl courses in physics, maths and chem while working, at Johns Hopkins Univ, Univ Utah & Brigham Young Univ. *Appointments:* Chemist, Pittsburgh Testing Labs, Greensboro' NC 1948-49; Chemist, NC State Highway & Public Works Comm, Raleigh 1949-51; Chemist, Dept of Army USA, Edgewood Arsenal 1951-61; Res Chem, Dept Army, Dugway Proving Ground 1961-70; Pvt sci res for pvt correspondence, Linwood, NC 1970-. *Publications:* Res reports in closed US Govt lit; Sci reports for pvt correspondence. *Memberships:* Am Chem Soc; Am Physical Soc; Am Assn for Advancement of Sci; Am Math Soc; Soc for Industrial & Appl Maths; NY Acad Scis; IBA of IBC; ABI Res Assn. *Honours:* 3 Hon Doctorates; Albert Einstein Bronze Medal Awd, by Albert Einstein Intl Assn Foun 1988; Intl Order of Merit by Intl Biog Inst 1991; World Decoration of Excellence Awd by ABI 1989. *Hobby:* Hiking. *Address:* Route 1, Box 646, Linwood, NC 27299, USA. 7, 9, 28, 125, 151, 152, 155, 156, 178.

BARNES Michael, b. 26 Sept 1934. Writer. *Education:* BA 1964, Univ Western Ontario; MEd 1971, Univ Toronto. *Appointments:* Edr: Tchr-Headmaster-Principal 1955-88; Writer 1968-. *Publications:* Num newspaper and magazine arts, short stories, books incl: Gold Camp Pioneer, 1973; Jake Englehart, 1973; Cobalt Adventure, 1973; The Thunder Bay Threat, 1977; A Souvenir of Kirkland Lake, 1981; Gateway City, 1982; Polar Bear Express Country, 1988; Timmins-The Porcupine Country, 1991; Temagami, 1992; The Gift, 1992; and many more. *Membership:* The Writers' Union of Canada. *Honour:* Hon Inspector in The Ontario Provincial Police 1991. *Hobbies:* Maintaining a property in bush at Round Lake; Reading. *Address:* Box 243, Kirkland Lake, Ontario, Canada P2N 2G0.

BARNES Rosemary Susan (Rosie), b. 16 May 1946, Nottingham, England. MP. m. Graham Barnes, 1967, 2 s. 1 d. *Education:* Hons degree in Social Sers and History spec in Brit History, Ec History, Polit Sci & Sociol 1967, Birmingham Univ. *Appointments:* Mgmt Trainee, Unilever spec in Mkt Res 1967-69; Mktg Exec, Yardley of London Ltd 1969-72; Primary Tchr 1973; Freelance Qualitative Reschr 1973-87; Elected MP for Greenwich 1987; Re-elected at Gen Election 1987; Social Democrat Spokesperson on Health & Ed plus cross the board responsibilities. *Address:* House of Commons, London SW1A 0AA, England.

BARNETT Eric Oliver, b. 13 Feb 1929, Johannesburg, SA. m. (1)Louise Francesca Lindenburg, 13 Feb 1950, dec 1984, (2)Vivienne Goodwin, 13 Mar 1986. *Education:* St Johns Col, Johannesburg; Witwatersrand Col Art 1945-47; Univ Cape Town 1950-52; Univ S Africa 1950-54; Univ Natal 1955-57; Univ Col, London 1957-63. *Appointments:* Lectr in Psych, Univ Natal 1956; Hon Vice-Chmn & Res Dir 1963-, Hon Chmn 1971-, Arthur Barnett Foun, a family charitable foun also involved in var res and welfare projects. *Publications:* Var arts & papers. *Memberships:* Intl Human Sexuality Survey, Hon Dir; Rural Ecology & Resources Com, Southern Africa, Hon Chmn 1978-; Var other philanthropic & charitable committees etc. *Hobbies:* Human Ethology; History of science; Music; Painting; Salmon fishing. *Address:* Kirkhill Castle, Colmonell, Ayeshire, KA26 0SB, Scotland.

BARNETT Marguerite Ross, b. 21 May 1942. Univ Pres. *Education:* AB Polit Sci 1964; AM Polit Sci 1966; PhD Polit Sci 1972. *Appointments:* Prof, Polit & Ed, Tchrs Col, Columbia Univ 1980-83; Vice Chancellor for Academic Affairs, CUNY 1983-86; Chancellor, Univ Missouri-St Louis 1986-90; Pres, Univ Houston 1990-. *Publications:* The Politics of Cultural Nationalism in South India, 1976; Public Policy for the Black Community: Strategies and Perspectives, Co-Edit, 1976; Teachings on Equal Education, vol 7, Co-Edit. *Memberships:* Mem Bd Dirs and Coun, Nat Conf of Black Polit Scists 1973-79; Am Polit Sci Assn 1979-; Mem Adv Bd, Rabinowitz Foun 1972-77; Conslt, United Negro Col Fund; Project on United Negro Col Fund Study on Career Patterns 1973-74. *Honours:* Excellence in Ed Awd 1990; Woman Who Has Made a Difference Awd, Women's Intl Leadership Forum 1990; Andersen Medal of Am Coun on Ed awd'd to Univ Missouri-St Louis' Partnerships for Progress Prog 1991. *Hobby:* Golf. *Address:* University of Houston, 4800 Calhoun, Houston, TX 77204, USA.

BARR John Wilmer Browning, b. 7 Dec 1916, Lanark, Canada. Rtd Milit Physician. m. Marion Sarah Crawford, 10 May 1945. *Education:* MD CM 1940, Queen's Univ; Dip Hosp Adm 1958, Univ Toronto; NDC 1965, Nat Def Col. *Appointments:* Med Ofcr, Cdn Army (WWII) 1939-45; Med Ofcr, Cdn Forces (Peace) 1946-70; Surgeon Gen, Cdn Forces 1970-73; Registrar, Med Coun of Canada 1974-81. *Publications:* 9 arts on The Medical Council of Canada, Can Med Assn J, 1974; A Story of the Canadian Forces Medical Services, 1983; Canadian Forces Medical Services: 25 Years of Unified Services. *Memberships:* Order of St John in Canada, CMO 1976-80; Defence Medical Assn of Canada, Hon VP 1974-; Med Br, Candn Forces, Col Commandant 1976-. *Honours:* Normal WWII Stars and Medals; Candn Centennial Medal; Queen's Jubilee Medal; Candn Forces Decoration, 3 clasps; Commander, Order of Milit Merit (Canada); Knight of Grace, Order of St John; Queen's Hon Physician 1965- 74, 1976-; Robert Wood Johnson Prize, 1959. *Hobbies:* Gardening; Stamp collecting; Military history. *Address:* 429 Huron Avenue South, Ottawa, Canada K1Y 0X3. 142.

BARRACLOUGH Robert James, b. 17 Apr 1942, Bradford, England. Chartered Accountant; Ptnr. m. Jill Mary Fennell, 8 Sept 1973, 4 s. *Appointments:* Ptnr in Yorkshire, Robson Rhodes 1971-90; Ptnr heading up Forensic Acctg & Litigation Support Unit, Haines Watts 1990-. *Memberships:* FCA (Inst Chartered Accts); MBAE (Brit Acad Experts); Bradford Club; Yorkshire Numismatic Soc, Pres 1973. *Hobbies:* Fell walking; Theatre; Travel; Numismatics. *Address:* Shipley, West Yorkshire BD18 4HP, England.

BARRASFORD Thomas Ian George, b. 20 July 1947, Colwyn Bay, England, Chf du Dept Tourisme; Secretariat of HM The Aga Khan. m. Sheelagh Mary O'Hagan, 5 Oct 1968, 2 s. 1 d. *Education:* Nat Dipl in Hotelkeeping & Catering 1968, Llandrillo Tech Col, Colwyn Bay. *Appointments:* Grand Metropolitan Hotels, London 1968-70; Trust House Forte Hotels 1970-82; Proprietor,

The Bryn Cregin Garden Hotel, Deganwy 1983- 86; Chf Exec, Serena Lodges and Hotels, Kenya 1986-90; Chf de Dept Tourisme, Secretariat of HM The Agha Khan 1991-. *Membership:* Fellow, The Hotel & Catering Institutional Mgmt Assn. *Honours:* Master Innholder 1985; Freeman City of London 1985. *Hobbies:* Golf; Windsurfing; Dinghy sailing. *Address:* Aiglemont, 60270 Gouvieux, France. 35.

BARRETT Nicholas Vincent John, b. 6 June 1956, London. Dentist. m. Gaynor Susan Duffett, 12 Sept 1991. *Education:* Haileybury & ISC 1969-74; BDS 1979, Guys Hospital; MS 1984, Univ Tex, San Antonio; Cert in Maxillofacial Prosthodontics 1985, M D Anderson Hospital. *Appointments:* House Surgn, Dept Maxillofacial Surgery 1980, House Ofcr, Dept Prosthetic Dent 1980-81, Guys Hosp; Assoc in Gen Dental Practice 1981; Dental Practice, London 1985-, Guys Hosp 1986- , Westminster Hosp 1985-90. *Publication:* Colour Atlas of Occlusion and Malocclusion, 1991. *Memberships:* Am Col Prosthodontics 1983; M D Anderson Hosp Assocs 1985; Am Dental Soc of London 1986, Hon Secy 1990-; Intl Col Prosthodontics 1987; Am Dental Soc Europe 1987; Intl Soc for Dental Ceramics 1990. *Honours:* Newland Pedley Travelling Scholar 1981; Am Dental Soc Awd 1981. *Hobbies:* Tennis; Theatre. *Address:* 38 Devonshire Street, London W1N 1LD, England.

BARRIE Dinah, b. 23 May 1936, London, England. Conslt Microbiol. m. Dr Herbert Barrie, Aug 1963, 1 s. 1 d. *Education:* MB, BS 1959, St Thomas's Hosp Med Sch; MRCPath 1972; FRCPath 1984. *Appointments:* Med Registrar: Worthing Gen Hosp 1960-61; Edgware Gen Hosp 1961-63; Asst Lectr then Lectr, St Thomas's Hosp 1963-67; Currently Conslt Microbiol, Charing Cross Hosp, Sr Reg 1970-72. *Publications:* Articles principally on Microbiol in med jours. *Memberships:* Hospital Infection Soc; Brit Soc of Antimicrobial Chemotherapy. *Hobbies:* Reading; Gardening. *Address:* 3 Burghley Avenue, Coombe Hill, Surrey KT3 4SW, England. 170.

BARRINGTON Donal Patrick Michael, b. 28 Feb 1928, Dublin. Judge. m. Eileen O'Donovan, 5 Sept 1959, 2 s. 2 d. *Education:* Belvedere Col Dublin 1939-46; BA 1949, LLB 1951, MA 1952, Univ Col Dublin; King's Inns Dublin 1947-51; Admitted Degee Barrister-at-Law 1951. *Appointments:* Called to Bar 1951; Admitted Inner Bar 1968; Appointed Judge of High Court 1979; Appointed Judge of Court of First Instance, European Communities 1989. *Publications:* Occasional arts on law & politics. *Memberships:* Chmn, Gen Coun, Bar of Ireland 1977-79; Bencher, King's Inns 1978; Pres, Irish Assn for Cultural Ec, Social Relats 1976-78. *Honours:* Chmn Comm on Safety at Work; Chmn, Stardust Victims Compensation Tribunal. *Hobbies:* Gardening; Music; Reading; Cooking. *Address:* Court of First Instance, European Communities, Luxembourg.

BARRINGTON-WARD Frank, b. 8 Apr 1928, Birmingham, England. District Judge. m. Heather Beatrice Warmington, 11 Aug 1951, 3 s, 1 dec. *Education:* MA, St Catherine's Col, Oxford. *Appointments:* Army 1946-48; RAEC HQ Berlin 1947; Overseas Magistrate, Fiji 1971-74; High Ct Distr Registrar, Birmingham 1974-80; High Ct Dist Registrar and Co Ct Registrar, Oxford 1980-91; District Judge, Oxford 1991-. *Memberships:* Rotary Club, Oxford; Oxfordshire CC 1958-67; The Law Soc 1956. *Hobbies:* Rowing; Skiing. *Address:* District Registry of High Court of Justice, Crown Court, County Court, Oxford Combined Court Centre, St Aldates, Oxford OX1 1TL, England.

BARRON Randall Franklin, b. 16 May 1936, Many, Louisiana, USA. Univ Prof. m. Shirley McDuffie Barron, 14 Mar 1958, 3 s. 1 d. *Education:* BS 1958, La Tech Univ; MS 1961, PhD 1964, Ohio State Univ, Columbus. *Appointments:* Instr, Mech Engrg, Ohio State Univ, 1958-65, promoted to Asst Prof 1965; Assoc Prof Mech Engrg 1965-, Professor 1970, Louisiana Tech Univ.

Publication: Book, Cryogenic Systems, 1985, translated into Russian 1989. *Memberships:* Am Soc Mech Engrs; Am Soc Engrg Ed; Am Assn for Advancement of Sci; La State Bd Registration for Profl Engrs & Land Surveyors 1988-94. *Honours:* Pi Tau Sigma Gold Medal Achmt Awd 1968; La Tech Alumni Foun Professorship Awd 1979; Engr & Sci Coun Profl Achmt Awd 1981; F J Taylor Outstanding Tchg Awd 1990; Dist'd Professorship Awd 1990. *Hobbies:* Golf; Music; Sci-Fi. *Address:* Mechanical Engineering Department, Louisiana Technical University, Ruston, LA 71272, USA. 139.

BARTH Markus K, b. 6 Oct 1915, Safenwil, Switzerland. Emeritus Prof of New Testament. m. 15 May 1940, 2 s. 3 d. *Education:* Theology Study, Bern 1934-35, Basel 1935-37, Berlin 1937, Edinburgh (Sc) 1938-39; Dr theol in Goettingen, Germany 1947. *Appointments:* Min, Evang Reformed Ch in Bubendorf, Switzerland 1940-53; Vstg Prof, Dubuque, Iowa 1953-55; Assoc Prof, Univ Chicago 1956-63; Prof of New Testament, Pittsburgh 1963-72; Prof of NT, Univ Basel 1973-85. *Publications:* Der Augenzeuge, 1946; Die Taufe- Ein Sakrament, 1951; Was Christ's Death a Sacrifice?, 1961; Conversation with the Bible, 1969; Ephesians, 2 vols, 1974; Das Mahl Des Herrn, 1987; and others. *Address:* Inzlinger-Str 275, 4125 Riehen BS, Switzerland. 2, 145.

BARTLETT Elizabeth Roberta, b. 20 July 1921, NYC, USA. m. Paul Alexander Bartlett, 19 Apr 1943, 1 s. *Education:* New York Tchr Coll, 19-40; Graduate Studies at Columbia Univ, 1940-42. *Appointments:* Poetry Editor, ETC, 1963-76; Poetry Editor, Crosscurrents, 1983-88; Editor of Intl Anthology, Literary Olmpians, 1984, 1988, 1992; Pres Literary Olympics inc. Acadamic; Prof Creative Writing, San Diego State Univ; Assoc Prof Eng Univ of California, Santa Barbara; Asst Prof, Eng San Jose State Univ; Instr, Speech and Theatre, Southern Methodist Univ. *Publications:* 17 books of poetry inc. It Takes Practise Not To Die, 1964; Threads, 1968; Address in Time, 1979; Memory is No Stranger, 1981; Candles, 1987; Around The Clock, 1989; Poems in many anthologies, magazines in the USA, Canada, England and France. *Memberships:* PSA; IWWG; PEN International, Authors Guild. *Honours:* Writing Fellowships; Huntingdon Hartford Foundation, 1959, 1960; Montalvo Assoc 1960, 1961; Yaddo, 1970, McDowell, 1970; Dorland Mt Colony, 1979; Ragdale Foundation, 1980; NEA Poetry, 1970; PEN Syndicated Fiction, 1983, 1985; Travel Grant LM Steele Trust, 1985; NEA Poetry, 1988. *Hobbies:* Art; Mustic. *Address:* 2875 Cowley Way, 1302, San Diego, CA 92110, USA.

BARTON-STEIN Paula Jean, b. 29 July 1929, Chicago, Illinois, USA. Hotel Brokerage and Investment Mgmt. m. Marshall Lowen Stein, 29 May 1954, 2 s. *Education:* AA 1949; BA 1951; 3 yrs Postgrad. *Appointments:* Reformer for Pres of USA 1951; Employers Assn, R&D & TV; Co-Fdr, Univ Chapt of World Federalists; Conslt, Natl Div Sers Inc, Bay Shore Inc, Pres Spindrift; Steinest Inc 1979-. *Publications:* Natl Anthology of Col Poetry 1951-; Oil Painting Prizes & Commissioned to Judge Art Socs; Fine Arts, Palm Beach, Fla; Everybody's Village, poem; Arrests of the Desert. *Memberships:* Alliance Francaise, Affairs Chmn; Union of Concerned Scists, profl mem; World Wildlife Soc; Edgar Royce Soc; Historical Prevention Soc; Greenpeace; World Future Soc, profl member. *Honours:* Natl Anthology of Poetry 1950; Everybody's Village, Awd for oil painting; Awd for fundraising, Fine Arts Soc, Palm Beach, Fla; Work accepted as profl member; Artists of Desert, work selected for exhibit in Germany. *Hobbies:* Oil painting; poetry; Natural health; Politics; Grand parenting; Future prognostigations; Ethics & religions. *Address:* 680 N Lake Shore Drive, Suite 1219, Chicago, IL 60611, USA. 8, 138.

BARTULIS Vidmantas, b. 3 Apr 1954, Lithuania, Kaunas. Composer. m. Sukyte Rima, 14 Nov 1975, 2 s. *Education:* Dipls Lithuanian Conservatoire 1972-80.

Appointments: Prof Mus, Juozas Gruodis High Sch 1980-83; Mus Ldr, Kaunas Drama Theatre 1983-. *Creative Works:* Music for Films & Theatre; 22 compositions incl: Two Questions to a Wild Plum-Tree, 1980; Songs of the Last, 1980; Herald, 1984; The Vision of 18 July 1750, 1984; Symphony, The Blue Angel, 1986; Lazarus's Songs, 1987; De Profundis, 1988; Mass, 1988; Requiem, 1989; Auge der Zeit, 1991. *Membership:* Lithuanian Composers Union 1980-. *Honours:* Awds of Am Lithuanian Foun Inc 1988; Balys Dvarionas Premium, 1988; V Svedas Premium, 1990. *Hobby:* Cooking. *Address:* Kaunas Drama Theatre, Laisvesal, 71, Kaunas, 233000 Lithuania.

BARY Etieme Roger Brice, b. 20 Nov 1962, St Avold, France. Painter Artist; Layout Designer. m. Shayda Keliddarzadeh, 4 Aug 1990. *Education:* Beaux Arts de Paris. *Appointments:* Layout Deisgner, Femne, Pratique, 1988; Vogue Decoration, Creation, 1989; Clamour, 1990. *Creative Works:* Paintings Exhib in Group Shows; Gilbert Brownstone Gallery; Marie Madeleine Cariou. *Hobbies:* Trumpet Collector; Books. *Address:* 21 Rue Beccaria, 75012 Paris, France. 43, 47, 50, 06, 1, 52.

BASALYGA Vladimir Samojlavich, b. 1 Apr 1940, Slutsk, Byelorussia. Graphic Artist; Reader of Byelorussian. m. Valentina Mikhaylovna, 26 Apr 1969, 2 s. 1 d. *Education:* Painter-Masters of Textiles Dipl 1960, Minsk Arts Sch; Painter of Decorative and Applied Arts Dipl 1967, The Byelorussian State Inst of Arts & Theatre. *Career:* Painter-dessinator, Minsk Worsted Works 1960-64; Chf Painter of People's Crafts of Byelorussia 1964-71; Chf Painter of Byelorussia Painters Union 1971-80; Creative Work 1980-89; Graphic Arts Dept Reader of Byelorussian Acad of Art 1989-91. *Creative Works:* 5 Series of graphic arts sheets; Diptih, 1941 and 1975 Indian ink, pen (2 sheets); Graphic sheet, Festival Minsk, coloured author's lithography; Artistic arrangement and illustration of publications for children, collections of poems by Byelorussian poets, photoalbums and other pubs (over 100 pubs); Miniature graphic arts-exLibrises-over 30 names. *Memberships:* Byelorussian Painters Union; Mgmt Bd of Byelorussian Painters Union; Presidium of Byelorussian Painters Union; Chmn Graphic Arts Section, Byelorussian Painters Union; Presidium of Byelorussian Bulgarian Soc of Friendship; Acad Bd of Byelorussian Acad of Arts. *Honours:* Many honours and awds for his achmts in arts incl the highest awds in field of book artistic arrangements, the Dipl & Medal of Frantsysk Skaryna. *Hobbies:* Investigation of People's Arts of the Byelorussian Development Ways and its collecting. *Address:* Surganova Street 42, apartment 12, Minsk, Russia.

BASDEN Paul, b. 6 Nov 1955, Dallas, Texas. Univ Minister. m. Denise Basden, 16 Dec 1977. *Education:* Baylor Univ 1974-77; M Div, S Western BTS 1978-81; PhD SWBTS 1981-86. *Appointments:* Assoc Pastor, 1st Bapt Benbrook, Tex 1979-83; Pastor, 1st Bapt, Clifton, Tex 1983-86; Pastor, Valley Ranch Bapt, Irving, TX 1986-90; Univ Minister, Samford Univ 1990-. *Publication:* Edit, The People of God; Ed, Has Our Theology Changed, forthcoming. *Contributions:* The Disciple's Study Bible, and Baptist Theologians; Co-author, Basden, Johnson; Spiritual Gifts Inventory. *Honours:* Outstanding Young Men in Am 1981, 1982, 1983. *Hobbies:* Racquetball; Reading; Fishing. *Address:* Minister to the University, Samford University, Birmingham, AL 35229, USA.

BASDEO Sahadeo Hon, b. 10 Sept 1945, Trinidad. Lecturer. m. Beverley Shirleen Young, 14 Aug 1971, 3 s. *Education:* Advanced GCE, 1964; BA in History & Polit Sci 1970; MA in Caribbean Labour & Brit Imperial History 1972; PhD in Caribbean Labour History 1975. *Publications:* Labour Organization and Labour Reform in Trinidad, 1919-1939. *Memberships:* Lions Club of Trinidad Central; St Andrew's Golf Club; Exec Com, Trinidad & Tobago Br, C'Wealth Parliamentary Assn; Chmn of Standing Com of Caricom Foreign Ministers;

Chmn Standing Com, Caricom Coun of Ministers (Trade) 1989-90. *Hobbies:* Golf; Cricket; Swimming. *Address:* Ministry of External Affairs and International Trade, Knowsley, Queen's Park West, Port of Spain, Trinidad, West Indies. 52.

BASSON Jacob Daniel DuPlessis, b. 25 July 1918, Paarl, South Africa. Rtd. m. Clare Strauss, 20 Sept 1947, 2 d. *Education:* BA (Law) 1939, Univ Stellenbosch. *Appointments:* Polit Journalist and Mem Parliamentary Press Gallery, Cape Town 1939-42; Polit Secy-Organiser, Pro-War Govt Party 1942-47; Settled in Namibia 1947; Elected MP for Namib 1950; Remained MP 1950-80; Broke with ruling NP over its apartheid policies, forming the Nat Union which later merged with the Opposition United Party (UP); MP for Namib 1950-61; MP for Bezuidenhout, Johannesburg 1961-80; Opposition UP Ldr in Transvaal 1975 and 1976, helped establish Progressive Fedl Party (PFP) as a broadened Opposition in 1977; Apptd to Pres's Coun as mem of Constitutional Com 1981; Mem Pres Coun 1981-84, 1986-89, preparing way for a Democratic Constitution for SA. *Publication:* Part 1, (The Road to Politics) of Parliamentary Memoirs under title, Advocate for South Africa, 1990. *Hobbies:* Reading; Writing; Gardening. *Address:* P O Box 1445, Cape Town 8000, South Africa.

BASTIANSEN Peter Ivan, b. 20 Sept 1912, Vadsoe, Norway. Industrialist; Businessman. m. Helga, 19 July 1969, 2 d. *Education:* Grad 1932, Drammen, Norway; Philosophy 1932, Law 1936, Univ Oslo, Norway; Special courses, Univ London, Eng 1943-45. *Appointments:* Law Office, Oslo 1939-43, 1945-48; Secy, Min Health and Lbour, Norwegian Admin, London 1943-45; Gen Dir & Pres, CA Indsutrias Savoy, Venezuela 1950-78; Own Office, 1975-. *Memberships include:* Dir, Camara Industrial de Caracus; Dir & Hon Pres, Asociacion Venezolana de Ex portacion; Dir, Assn Pro-Venezuela. *Honours:* Order, Francisco de Miranda 3rd Class 1963, 1st Class 1977; Order of Merit en el Trabajo, 1st Class 1974; Order of El Libertador 1976; Royal Order of Merit granted by His Majesty King Olav V, Norway 1986. *Hobby:* Agriculture. *Address:* Edificio Colonial Palace Apartameto 3, Corniza de Altamira, Caracas, Venezuela.

BATES Christopher, b. 10 Oct 1962, Leicester, England. Company Dir. *Education:* Carlton-le-Willows Sch, Gedling, Nottingham. *Appointments:* Speciality Lubrication 1980-; Partner in Family Bus. *Memberships:* Mem Nat Squad, Amateur Rowing Assn; Nottinghamshire County Rowing Assn; Nottingham Boat Club; GB Rowing Squad. *Honours:* Rowing: 45 GB & England Caps; World Champion 1991, 1992; World Championship Medals: 2 Gold, 3 Silver, 2 Bronzes; Commonwealth Games: Gold 1986; European Championship Medals: 2 Gold, 2 Silver, 1 Bronze; Nat Championship Medals: 7 Gold, 2 Silver; Henley Royal Regatta, 6 Gold Medals; Other Intl Regattas: 13 Gold, 2 Silver; World & Commonwealth Record Holder in Lightweight Coxless 4; Nat Record Holder in Lightweight & Heavyweight 8. *Hobbies:* Classic cars; Motor boats. *Address:* 2 St Ervan Road, Wilford, Nottingham NG11 7BU, England.

BATES Peter Francis, b. Aug 1934. Conslt Gen Surgeon, rtd. *Education:* Cambridge Univ; St Mary's Hosp, Paddington; Qualified as Doctor 1960; BA 1956; MA 1960; MBBChir 1961 (Cantab). *Appointments:* Jr House Surgeon, SHO, West Middx Hosp, Isleworth 1961-65; Surg Reg, Hillingdon 1965-68; Lectr Sen Reg, St Mary's Hosp 1968-71; Locum Cons Surgeon, Mount Vernon Hosp and Thames Gp 1971-73; Conslt Surg, Dartford & Gravesham Health Authority 1974-91. *Memberships include:* Livery Com of Apothecaries; Loriner Chmn Lunchtime Connent Club; Warden St Paul's Covent Garden, (Actors) Church; Fellow, RSM; Fellow, Brit Assn Surgs of GB & Ireland; Surgical Oncology Inter Col Surgeons; European Soc Surg Oncology & European Soc Gastroenterologists; World Med Assn; Brit Assn Gastro-Intestinal Surgery; City Livery Club; Guild Freeman Aldersgate Wards Club;

United Wards Club; Bassishaw Ward Club. *Hobbies:* Rugby; The arts; West End & fringe theatre; Building-up small Library; Collection of pictures and small sculptures; Skiing. *Address:* 1 River Court, 82 St George's Square, London SW1V 3QX, England. 146.

BATES Thomas St John Neville, b. 9 Jan 1944, London, England. Clerk of Tynwald; Prof of Law. m. 5 July 1985, 1 s. 1 d. *Education:* Pvtly & Christ's Col, Cambridge; BA 1967, LLM 1968, MA 1971, Cantab. *Appointments:* Res Fellow, Inst for Study of Intl Org, Univ Sussex 1968-69, Vstg Fellow 1969-71; Lectr 1969-83, Sr Lectr 1983-85, Fac Law, Univ Edinburgh; Vstg Prof, Univ Oklahoma 1972, 1974; John Millar Prof of Law and Hd Dept of Public Law, Univ Glasgow 1985-87; Dep Edit 1986-90, Edit 1990-, Statute Law Review; Clerk of Tynwald, Secy House of Keys and Counsel to the Speaker 1987-; Prof Law, Univ Luncaster, UK 1987-; Vstg Prof, Univ Strathclyde, UK, 1992-; Fellow, Wolfson Col, Cambridge 1990-1992. *Contributions:* to num books on public law, and Author of arts to jours in same area. *Membership:* FSA (Scot) 1975-. *Hobbies:* His family; Writing. *Address:* Office of the Clerk of Tynwald, Legislative Buildings, Douglas, Isle of Man, British Isles.

BATESON Frank Maine, b. 31 Oct 1909, Wellington, New Zealand. Astronomer. m. Doris McGoldrick dec, 4 Apr 1931, 2 d. *Education:* Scots Col, Sydney, NSW 1924-26; Royal NZ Navy 1940-45. *Appointments:* Acct var NZ firms 1927-38; Acct, Whangarei Harbour Bd 1939-40; Mng Dir, Cook Islands Trading Co KTD, Rarotonga 1945-59; Leader, Astronomical Site Survey of NZ 1960-63; Leader of Intl Solar Eclipse Expedition to South Pacific 1965; Dir, Mt John Univ Observatory 1963-69; Mng Dir, Astronomical Res Ltd 1969-; Dir, Variable Star Section, Royal Astronomical Soc of NZ 1927-. *Publications:* 1st Memoir, Variable Star Section, Royal Ast Soc NZ, 1944; The Observation of Variable Stars, 4 editions, 1958, 1973, 1978, 1984; Final Report of the Astronomical Site Selection Survey of NZ, 1964; Charts for Southern Variables, Series 1 to 22, 1960-91; Changing Trends in Variable Star Research, Proceedings of IAU, 1978; Paradise Beckons, autobiography, 1989; Over 600 sci papers in var sci jours 1927-. *Memberships:* Fellow, Royal Astr Soc, UK; Fellow, Royal Astr Soc, NZ; Mem Comms 27 & 42 of IAU; Australian Astr Soc; Am Astr Soc; Astronomical Soc Pacific; Hon Mem: Brit Astr Assn, NSW; Victorian Astr Soc; Queensland Astr Soc & sev NZ Astr Socs; Mem Explorers Club, NY; Gate PA Lodge; Order of St John. *Honours:* Donovan Trust Prize 1927, 1934; Murray Geddes Memorial Prize 1950; Hannah-Jackson Gwilt Medal, RAS, London 1960; Donovan Trust Lectr in NZ 1965; Mechaelis Memorial Prize & Gold Medal, Univ Otago 1968; OBE 1970; Hon D Univ Waikato 1978. *Address:* 20 Pooles Road, Greerton, Tauranga, New Zealand. 38.

BATHAM Cyril Ernest Kila Northwood, b. 29 June 1909, Sutton Coldfield. Company Director. m. Alys Gillian Drinkwater, 8 Aug 1931, 1 d. *Education:* Bishop Vesey's Sch, Sutton Coldfield. *Appointments:* Mgr, Bristol Br 1946-57, Manchester Br 1957-63, Liason Ofcr, Paris Br 1963-67, Hd Office Underwriter, London 1967-72; Yorkshire Insurance Co Ltd; Insurance Broker, Mann Rutter & Collins Ltd 1972-76; Company Director, QC Correspondence Circle Ltd 1976-. *Publications:* Num mag arts & reviews in Eng, USA, Cda & France. *Membership:* Assoc, Chartered Insurance Inst 1928. *Honours:* ACII, by examination, 1928; Freeman, City of London 1972; Worshipful Company of Gold & Silver Wyre Drawers 1972; Order of St John 1980; Prestonian Lectr 1981; Philethes Society Lectr, 1992; Order of Masonic Merit (Finland) 1992. *Hobbies:* Theatre-Chmn Bristol Old Vic Theatre Club 1955, Asst, Summer Sch for Tchrs of Eng, Stratford-upon-Avon 1948-71; Lectr-freemasonry, theatre, insurance, worldwide; Classical music. *Address:* 17 Romeland, Waltham Abbey, Essex EN9 1QZ, England.

BATLLE Alcira M Del C, b. Buenos Aires, Argentina. Prof of Biochem. m. 3 s. *Education:* Chem Degrees 1958, 2 Degrees BS Biological Chem and Technological Chem 1959, PhD Chem 1962, Univ Buenos Aires; PhD Sciences, Univ of London, England, 1965. *Appointments:* Tchr, Univ Buenos Aires, 1960-, Chair of Biochem, 1974; Hd, Dept Biochem, Schl of Sciences, Univ of Buenos Aires; Scientific Advsr, Chairperson of Rsch Insts in Chem, CONICET; Exec Dir, Nat Prog of Biotechnology at Sec of Science and Technology of the Presidence; Supvsr of PhD Thesis and postdoct work; Vis Prof at Univ Coll, London, England. *Publications:* 240 original papers in specialized jrnls, articles and transls of books; sev chapts in textbooks on Biochem and Clin Therapy; 310 lectures and 45 courses on her subject; Organizer of First Int Argentine Mtg on Porphyrins and Porphyrais in Buenos Aires in 1979, Nat Mtg of Lead Poisoning in Buenos Aires in 1984 and Int Symposium on New Frontiers in Biotechnology in Buenos Aires in 1991. *Memberships:* Brit Biochem Soc; Argentine Chem Soc; Argentine Biochem Soc; PAABS; AAAS; Tetrapyrrole Grp, UK; Argentine Assn of Dermatology; Spanish-Argentine Assn of Med and Related Sciences; Argentine and Latinamerican Assn of Toxicology; Argentine and American Assn of Protozoology; Mbr sev Ed Bds. *Honours:* She has received many prizes and awards. Prize Asociacion Argentina de Dermatologia, 1987; Annual Prize for Clinical Research Quinquela Martin; Prize Dr M Belascuain 1988; Annual Xavier Vilanova Prize by Argentine Society of Dermatology, 1990. *Hobbies:* Writing, Drawing, Painting, Gardening, Home Duties.

BATRA Ranjit, b. 18 Mar 1943, Bombay, India. Co Dir. m. Neelam Batra, 2 May 1974, 1 s, 2 d. *Education:* Graduate Sydenham Coll of Commerce and Econs, 1966. *Appointment:* Dir, Ratan Batra Pvt Ltd. *Memberships:* Former Sec-Treas, Int Advertising Assn, India Chapt; Jt Sec-Treas, Advertising Club, Bombay; Treas, Advertising Agencies Assn of India; Sec, The Sydenhamites Assn, The Commerce Graduates Assn; Mgmt Comm Mbr, The Indo-American Soc, Bombay; Save Bombay Comm; Citizens Comm for Shivaji Park. *Honours:* At School: Represented Maharashtra State Team twice at the National Schools Acquatic (Swimming) Championship 1959 held in Bombay, 1960 at Indore. At College: Represented and Captained the Sydenham College Swimming Team at the Inter Collegiate Meets; Active Member College Students Union; On Committee and Secretary of the College Gymkhana; Represented MGMO Swimming Pool in Water Polo and other events. *Hobbies:* Swimming; Hiking. *Address:* Starsway Co-operative Housing Society, Flat Nos. 6 & 7, Building No 2, Juhu Tara Road, Bombay 400 049, India.

BATTEI Antonio, b. 15 May 1949, Parma, Italy. Publisher. m. Anna Masseroni, 11 Mar 1973, 2 s. *Education:* Inst Tec Commerciale 1965-70; Facolta di Giurisprudenza 1970-74; Istituto d'Arte 1979-84. *Appointments:* Pubr 1970-, following family tradition, Pub House founded in 1872; Owner 4 Libraries. *Publications:* Pubr of many books. *Membership:* Lions, Secy & MC. *Honours:* Sov Milit Order of Malta; Recip Gold Medal Camera di Commercio Industria and Agriculture 1976; Decorated Mil Order Cross of Merit 1987 and Devotion of First Class 1989; Knight of Merit, Pres Italian Repub 1989. *Hobbies:* Classical music; Lyrical theatre. *Address:* Casa Editrice Battei, borgo Santa Brigida 1, 43100 Parma, Italy. 52.

BATTERBURY Paul Tracy Shepherd, b. 25 Jan 1934, London, England. Circuit Judge. m. Sheila Margaret Watson, 11 Apr 1962, 1 s. 1 d. *Education:* LLB, Univ Bristol. *Appointments:* Practising Barrister 1959-83; Recorder 1979-83; Circuit Judge 1983-. *Memberships:* Fdr Chmn, Gallipoli Meml Lectures 1985; Rep DL, London Borough of Havering 1989-. *Honours:* TD 1972, 2 bars 1978 & 1984; DL (Greater London) 1986. *Hobbies:* Walking; Caravanning. *Address:* Coutts & Co, Adelaide Branch, 440 Strand, London WC2R 0QS, England. 1.

BAUER Raymond Gale, b. 19 June 1934, Merchantville, New Jersey, USA. Mfgrs Rep. m. Jayne Whitehead, 15 Feb 1955, 1 d. *Education:* AA 1955, Monmouth Col, West Long Branch, NJ; BBA 1958, Univ Miami. *Appointments:* US Air Force Reserve 1959-64; Divisional Mgr, R J Reynolds Tobacco Co, Winston-Salem, NC 1959-68; Middle Atlantic Mgr, US Envelope Company, Springfield, Massachusetts 1968-74; Divisional Sales Mgr, Eastern Tablet Corporation, Albany, NY 1974-75; Owner, Ray Bauer Associates, Haddonfield, NJ 1975-. *Memberships:* Intl Platform Assn; US Senatorial Club; Smithsonian Associates; Am Mgmt Assn; Ofcr, US Air Force Auxiliary; Air Force Assn; Am Security Coun; Am Conservative Union; Nat Philatelic Soc; Haddonfield Republican Club; Haddonfield Civic Assn; Nat Audubon Soc; Friends of Haddonfield, Library. *Honours:* Honour Socs; Alumni Assns. *Hobbies:* Swimming; Tennis; Sports. *Address:* 132 Maple Avenue, Haddonfield, NJ 08033, USA. 6, 52, 132, 139, 155, 179.

BAUER Steven Michael, b. 8 Nov 1949, Hemet, Calif, USA. Cost Containment Engr. m. Myung-hee Min, 10 Sept 1983, 2 d. *Education:* BA Physics 1971; BS Physics 1984. *Appointments:* Nuclear Engr, SCE 1976- 88; Conslt, Res Dept, J L Ptts Hosp 1975-78; Engr, Cost Containment, S C Edison 1988-; Conslt, Alumni Relations, CSU San Bernardino 1988-89. *Publications:* Compiled letters 1978-91. *Memberships:* Americans for Energy Independence, Steering Com, Membership Chair; Los Angeles County Museum of Art; Knights of Columbus, Secy; Pro Life Chmn; Assn Computing Machinery; Am Nuclear Soc; Sierra Club. *Honours:* Exceptional Volunteer Service Awd, ARC 1990; Man of the Year 1990; One-in-a-Million Awd 1991. *Hobbies:* Aerobic exercise; Gardening; Hiking; 300; Reading. *Address:* 131 West Monroe Court, San Bernardino, CA 92408, USA. 9, 132, 155.

BAUER Yehuda, b. 6 Apr 1926, Prague. Univ Prof. m. Shula White, 21 Dec 1955, 2 d. *Education:* BA Hons (1st Class) 1950, Cardiff; PhD 1960, Jerusalem Hebrew Univ. *Appointments:* Lectr, Inst Contemporary Jewry, Hebrew Univ 1961; Assoc Prof, Hebrew Univ 1973; Full Prof 1977; Chmn, Dept Holocaust Studies at Inst 1964-; Acad Chmn of Inst 1979-; Chmn, Vidal Sassoon Intl Centre for the Study of Antisemitism. *Publications:* 10 books in Eng incl: History of the Holocaust, 1982; American Jewry and the Holocaust, 1981; The Holocaust in Historical Perspective, 1978; Out of the Ashes, 1989; and about 90 arts. *Memberships:* Edit, J of Holocaust & Genocide Studies; Chair, Intl Fed of Secular Humanistic Jews; Mem Executive, Yad Vashem. *Honour:* Hon PhD, Hebrew Union Col, NY 1984. *Hobbies:* Folk singing; Hiking. *Address:* Kibbutz Shoval, D N Negev 85320, Israel.

BAUM Carl Edward, b. 6 Feb 1940, Binghamton, NY, USA. Electromagnetical Theorist. *Education:* BS Hons 1962, MS 1963, PhD Elect Engrg 1969, California Inst Tech. *Appointments include:* 2nd Lt to Capt, US Air Force 1962-71; Sr Scist, Electromagnetics (civil servant), Air Force Weapons Lab 1971-; Advr, var Army, Air Force & Naval agencies. *Creative Works:* Author, 7 Bk Chapts, num papers in profl pubs; Co- Author, Transient Lens Synthesis: Differential Geometry in Electromagnetic Theory, 1991; Composer, 13 sacred works for choir, organ, piano & orchestra. *Memberships include:* Commissions A, B & E, US Nat Com, Del to sev gen assemblies, Intl Union of Radio Sci; Co-Chmn, Joint Tech Com on Nuclear Electromagnetic Pulse, Antennas & Propagation Soc; Electromagnetic Compatability Soc; Past Chmn, Albuquerque Joint Chapt, Antennas & Propagation Microwave Theory & Techniques, & Electromagnetic Compatability Socs; Fellow, IEEE. *Honours:* Num recogs & awds, most recent include: Richard E Stoddart Awd, Electromagnetic Compatability Soc, IEEE; Harry Diamond Memorial Awd 1987; Bd Dirs 1987, IEEE. *Address:* 5116 Eastern SE, Unit D, Albuquerque, NM 87108, USA. 2, 9, 22, 26, 52, 129, 130, 139, 151, 152, 162, 164, 179.

BAUTISTA Liberato C, b. 8 Oct 1959, Philippines. Coord, Prog Unit on Human Rights. m. Adora E Angeles, 19 Sept 1983, 1 s. 1 d. *Education:* AB Social Scis 1982, Master in Intl Studies 1989, Univ Philippines. *Appointments:* Coord, Prog Unit on Human Rights, Nat Coun of Churches in the Philippines 1983-; Fac, St Andrew's Theological Seminary 1989-90. *Publications:* Co-Edit, Witnessing and Hoping amid Struggle: Towards a Theology and Spirituality of Struggle, 1991; Edit or Co-Edit: Resistance, essays in Militarism and Militarization, 1992; Human Rights Reader for Filipinos, 1991; And She Said No: Human Rights, Womens Identities & Struggles, 1990; Religion and Society Towards a Theology of Struggle, 1988; Human Rights: Biblical and Theological Readings, 1988; Assoc Edit, Tugoni Ecumenical Journal 1983-. *Memberships:* Intl Affairs, Christian Conf of Asia 1990-95; Gen Comm, Christian Conf of Asia 1985-90; World Methodist Coun 1980-81; Vice Chmn, Phil Alliance of Human Rights Advocates 1986-90; Intl Peace Res Assn, USA 1991-. *Honour:* Recip for Office of the George Fritze Awd for Human Rights, Cologne, Germany 1990. *Hobbies:* Writing; Editing; Reading; Travelling. *Address:* National Council of Churches in the Philippines, 879 Epifanio de Los Santos Avenue, Quezon City, Philippines. 52, 145.

BAYES Paul E, b. 5 Oct 1944, Baltimore, Maryland. Col Prof. m. Emily Starkey, 12 Aug 1967. *Education:* BS 1965, Univ Ky; MS 1968, Ind State Univ; DBA 1983, Univ Kentucky. *Appointments:* Acctg Clerk, Western Electric 1965-66; Instr, Morehead State Univ 1967-69; Asst Prof, Clinch Valley Col 1969-73; Asst Prof, Belea Col 1973-75; Asst Prof, Eastern Ky Univ 1975-84; Assoc Prof, Eastern Tenn State Univ 1984-. *Publications:* Cases in Accounting Systems; Num profl pubs and presentations. *Memberships:* Am Acctg Assn, membership chair of Intl Section; Southwest Decision Scis Inst; Nat Assn of Accts. *Honours:* Outstg Jaycee 1970, Spark Plug 1971, Norton Wise Jaycees; Spark Plug of the Year, Va Jaycees 1971; Col of Bus Outstg Tchr, ETSU 1989. *Hobbies:* Reading; Fishing. *Address:* 702 Rambling Road, Johnson City, TN 37604, USA. 117.

BAYEV Alexander, b. 10 Jan 1904, Chita, Russia. Scist; Biologist. m. Ekaterina Kosyakina Yankovskaya, 27 Aug 1945, 1 s. 1 d. *Education:* Med Fac Kazan Univ 1927; Dr biol scis 1967; Prof 1971. *Appointments:* Postgrad Asst Prof Chair in Biochem, Kazan Univ 1930-35; Scist, Inst Biochem, USSR Ac Sci 1935-37, 1954-59; Country Physician 1937; Imprisonment during Stallin's time 1937-54; Scist, Hd Lab, Counsillor Inst Mol Biol, Russian Ac Sci 1959-; Academician Secy 1971-88, Councillor of Russian Ac Sci Presidium 1988-. *Publications:* 340 papers in biochem, molecular biol, molecular genetics, genetic engrg, biotech and gen problems of science. *Memberships:* Corresponding Mem 1968, Academician 1970, Russian Ac of Sci; Academician of USSR Agri Ac; Biotech Ac 1991; Emeritus Mem, Acad Europeae 1991; Ac Naturforscher Leopoldina 1973; Ak der Wissenschaft zu Berlin 1974; Ac Hungary 1975; Poland 1977, Bulgaria 1986; Ass mem, Eur Mol Biol Org; Hon mem, Am Soc for Biochem and Mol Biol; Mem Com, Gen Exp 1976; Human Genome Org 1989; Int Union Biochem, Pres, Past Pres 1976-82; Univ Greifswald, doctor h c; Edit Bds Gene, Bioscience. *Honours:* USSR State Prize 1964; Gold Medal for Service in Sci & Humanity 1977; Mendel Gold Medal 1988. *Hobbies:* Reading history; Memoirs. *Address:* Institute of Molecular Biology, Russian Academy of Sciences, 32 Vavilov Street, Moscow B-334, Russia 117984.

BAYTOK Taner, b. 20 Apr 1936, Manisa. Amb; Dir Gen Relats with European Communities; Advr to Dep PM. m. Sengun Baytok, 1960, 1 s. 1 d. *Education:* Grad 1958, Fac Law, Univ Ankara; London Sch Ec 1963-64; Naval Sch Mgmt, Monterey, USA 1970. *Appointments:* Joined Turkish Min of For Affairs (MFA) 1960; 3rd Secy, NATO Dept, MFA 1960-61; 3rd & 2nd Secy, Turkish Emb, New Delhi, India 1961-62; Vice Consul and Consul, Turkish Consulate Gen, London, UK 1962-65; Hd Section, Middle East Dept, MFA 1965-

67; Counsellor, Turkish Deleg to NATO, Brussels 1967-71; Hd NATO Dept, MFA 1971- 73; Turkish Rep to MBFR, Vienna 1973-79; Dir Gen for Policy Planning, Disarmament and Strategic Studies, MFA 1979-82; Turkish Amb to United Arab Emirates, Abu Dhabi 1982-86; Turkish Amb to Denmark, Copenhagen 1986-88; Polit Advr to Min of Defence, Ankara 1988-89; Mem Consultative Com for Foreign Policy, MFA 1989-91; Dir Gen for European Communities Affairs, MFA 1991; Advr to Dep PM 1991. *Publications:* Turkish Compensation Law, 1960; Turkish Independence War from British Resources, 1969; The World Communist Parties, 1967; Var arts in different newspapers and periodicals. *Hobbies:* Music; Theatre; Ballet. *Address:* Disisleri Bakanligi, A-kati, 103 nolu oda Balgat, Ankara, Turkey.

BEAL Leonie Alison, b. 18 Nov 1937, Perth, Western Australia. Amateur Musician (Composer). *Education:* Dip Chiropractic, The Chiropractic Coll of Aust, 1969; Cert, Chiropractic Clin Science, 1981. *Appointment:* Practicing Chiropractor, 1980-86. *Publication:* Poem in The Best of John Reids Poets Corner, 1986. *Membership:* Aust Chiropractors Assn. *Hobbies:* Pipe Organ, Violin, Piano, Choir Singing, Musical Compositions, Writing Prose and Poetry, Fine Art painting and sketching, Reading, Herb Gardening. *Address:* 16 Kelvin Grove, East Prahran 3181, Melbourne, Victoria, Australia. 86.

BEAMON Teresa Kristine Nkenge Z, b. 11 Apr 1954, Detroit, Michigan, USA. Radio Producer-Writer. 1 d. *Education:* Courses at Wayne State Univ, Univ Mich; Project BAIT Media Collective. *Appointments:* Host of Nkenge Zo! (jazz) Pgm, 1982-85, Host, Nkenge Zo! (music, readings, poetry, arts interviews) Pgm 1985-90, Producer-Host, Nkenge Zo! (local news anchor) Pgm 1990-, WDET-FM. *Publications:* All Things Considered, Co-edit; The Awakening, newsletter of NOAR; Co-edit, Loving Them to Life: Three Stories of Hope from Detroit. *Memberships:* Creative Community, Forum Coord 1990-; Rebirth Inc, Jazz Org 1985-; Creative Arts Collective; Nat Assn Black Journalists 1991; Women's Justic Centre, Bd Mem, 1990-; WINDS (Women for Independence and Democracy in El Salvador); Justice for Cuba Coalition. *Honours:* Recip, Jazz Host Awd, from Success Acad 1985; Subject, Spiritual Warrior Tribute, 1990; Host of Jazz Master's: Keepers of the Flame winner of var cable & video awds incl USA Home Video Awd 1991. *Hobbies:* Personal and Community transformation; Linguistics; Literature; Audio production; Arts; Matters of Spirit. *Address:* 91E Philadelphia, Detroit, MI 48202, USA.

BEASLEY Georgia Mae Zeigler, b. 14 May 1948, Orange, Texas, USA. Counsellor. m. Edward Beasley Jr, 5 June 1971, 2 s. 1 d. *Education:* BS 1971, Prairie View A&M Univ; MEd 1987, McNeese State Univ. *Appointments:* Stenographer, Prairie View A&M Univ; Secy, Texas Southern Univ 1971-73; Sub Tchr, West Orange, Cove CISD 1975-84; Tchr 1984-87, Counsellor 1987-, Lamar Univ, Orange. *Memberships:* Am Assn for Counselling & Devel; Tex Assn for Counselling & Devel; Tex Assn for Collegiate Testing Personnel; Sabine Neches Assn for Counselling & Devel; Intl Platform Assn. *Hobby:* Planning activities for youth. *Address:* 4309 Memorial Drive, Orange, TX 77630, USA. 7.

BEASLEY-MURRAY Paul, b. 14 Mar 1944, London, England. Baptist Minister. m. Caroline Wynne Griffiths, 3 s. 1 d. *Education:* BA 1966, MA 1969, Jesus Col, Cambridge; PhD 1970, Northern Baptist Col & Manchester Univ; Zurich Univ & Intl Baptist Theol Seminary. *Appointments:* Prof of New Testament, Nat Univ Zaire 1970-72; Minister, Altrincham Baptist Ch 1973- 86; Principal, Spurgeon's Col, London 1986-92; Senior Minister, Baptist Church, Chelmsford. *Publications:* Turning the Tide, 1981; Pastors Under Pressure, 1989; Dynamic Leadership, 1990; Faith & Festivity, 1991; Radical Believers, 1992. *Memberships:* Studiorum Novi Testamenti Societas; Tyndale Fellowship for Biblical Res; Brit Ch Growth Assn.

Hobbies: Music; Walking. *Address:* The Baptist Church, Victoria Road South, Chelmsford, Essex, England. 1.

BEAUCHAMP Linsey, b. 3 Mar 1960, Canada. Actress. *Education:* Am Sch in London 1970-76; TASIS 1977; Arts Edl Sch 1977-79; St Hilda's Col, Oxford 1989-92. *Career:* Anna in Anna of the Five Towns, BBCTV, 1985; Constance in Sophia & Constance, BBCTV, 1988; Ophelia in Hamlet, Salisbury Playhouse, 1989. *Membership:* Equity. *Honours:* TASIS, Valedictorian, 1977; St Hilda's Col, Bielley Scholar 1990-92. *Hobbies:* Badminton; Bowling; Needlecraft. *Address:* c/o Janet Welch, 486 Chiswick High Road, London W4 5TT, England.

BEAUDET Alain, b. 21 Sept 1947, Montreal, Quebec. Prof Neurol & Neurosurg. m. Natalia Diakiw, 24 July 1976, 1 s. *Education:* BA Humanities 1966; BA Biology 1967; MD Medicine 1971; PhD Neurological Scis 1977. *Appointments:* Asst Prof 1980-86; Assoc Prof 1986-89; Prof 1989-; Assoc Dir of Research 1985-; Coord, Neurobiol Gp 1988-. *Publications:* Over 80 original arts in learned jours and more than 25 chapts in books, pertaining to anatomical substrate of chemical neurotransmission. *Honours:* Scholarship, Med Res Coun of Canada, Awd 1980-85; Scist, Med Res Coun of Canada, Awd 1985-90; Murray L Barr Jr Scist Awd 1987. *Hobbies:* Gardening; Swimming; Reading. *Address:* Laboratory of Neuroanatomy, Room 896, Montreal Neurological Institute, 3801 University Street, Montreal, Quebec, Canada H3A 2B4.

BEAUMONT Mary Rose, b. 6 June 1932, Petersfield, Art Historian; Writer. b. Timothy Wentworth Beaumont (Baron Beaumont of Whitley), 13 June 1955, 2 s. 2 d. *Education:* BA History of Art 1978, Courtauld Inst Art, London Univ. *Appointments:* Founded The Centre for the Study of Modern Art, Inst of Contemporary Arts 1972; Self Employed as Writer on Art, Lectr, Exhibition Org 1978-91. *Memberships:* Contemporary Art Soc, Com & Exec, Com Mem. *Hobbies:* Music esp Opera; 19th & 20th Century Novels. *Address:* 40 Elms Road, London SW4 9EX, England.

BEAUWENS Renaud, b. 9 Feb 1944, Brussels, Belgium. MD; Prof Physiol. m. Claudine Deijaert dec, 30 May 1974, 2 s. *Education:* MD 1969, Univ Brussels, Belgium; Agnege de l'Enseignemon Superieur 1984, Univ Louvain, Belgium. *Appointments:* Fellow, Univ Geneva 1970; Fellow, Mass Gen Hosp 1972; Fellow, Univ Iowa, USA 1973; Asst, Univ Louvain 1976; Prof Physiol, Univ Brussels 1981. *Publications:* Sci papers in refereed jours. *Memberships:* Am Physiol Soc; NY Acad Scis; Intl Soc Physiology. *Honours:* Fellow, Nat Kidney Foun, USA 1974; Fellow, Alexandre Humbold Foun, Germany 1978; Prix Spa, The Original Spa Water, 1988. *Hobbies:* Membrane physiology; Transport of ions and water; Cellular mechanisms of hormonal action. *Address:* Rue LaVau 67, B 1420 Braine-L'Alleud, Belgium.

BEAVER Maxie Eugene, b. 1 July 1936, Kannapolis, North Carolina, USA. Col Prof; Musician; Edr. m. Elsie Lawrence, 16 May 1957, 2 s. *Education:* BA 1964, Wake Forest Univ; MAT 1964, Univ NC at Chapel Hill; EdD 1973, Univ NC at Greensboro. *Appointments:* Woodwind Tchr, Univ NC at Greensboro 1968-70; Dir of Bands, Myers Park HS 1970-71; Dir of FA, Charleston County Schs 1971-73; Music Prof, Western Carolina Univ 1973-. *Creative Works:* Das Liebesurbot, Overture, R Wagner, for Symphonic Band, Transcription; Num works for concert band and woodwind ensembles; Profl Performer on Clarinet, Oboe, Saxophone and Bassoon; Sev periodical arts. *Memberships:* NC Music Edrs Assn, Exec Secy 1968-71; Edit, NC Music Educator, 1976-81; SC Band Dirs Assn, Pres 1967-68; Col Mus Soc; Western Carolina Univ, Mus Dept Chair 1985-87, Secy of Fac 1991-, Secy Arts & Scis 1990-. *Hobbies:* Sailing; Motorcycles. *Address:* Department of Music, Western Carolina University, Cullowhee, NC 28723, USA.

BEAZLEY Malcolm Robert, b. 19 Feb 1944, Canberra, ACT, Australia. Ed Conslt; Lectr. *Education:* BA 1972, New England; MEd 1979, Sydney. *Appointments:* Tchr, NSW Dept Ed 1964; P-time Lectr, NSW Conservatorium of Music 1979; Ed Conslt to Australian Bicentennial Authority 1987; Ed Conslt to Australian Govt 1990-; Vstg Lectr, Univ Sydney 1989-91. *Publications:* The Development of Language/Writing Abilities in Children of English Speaking Backgrounds, 1983; Reflections Upon Recollections, 1986. *Memberships:* Chmn, Hds of Eng Depts of North Shore, Sydney; Life VP, Australian Opera Auditions, NSW; Fdr & Intl Pres, Computer Pals Across the World Inc. *Honours:* Fulbright Ednl Devel Grant, 1982; Fellow, Australian Col of Ed, 1987; Member of the Order of Australia, Queen's Birthday Honours, 1991. *Hobbies:* Community service; Music; Literature; Travel; Twenty years voluntary service to Life Line-telephone counselling. *Address:* PO Box 280, Manly, 2095, Australia.

BECHTHOLD Kim, b. 22 Sept 1938, Grand Junction, Colorado, USA. Venture Capital. m. Thomas Joe Lilly, 28 Dec 1960, div 1965, 1 s. *Education:* BSc 1967, Univ Colorado, Boulder. *Appointments:* Instr, Midland Col, Midland, Tex 1973-74; Dir, Office of Public Info, Midland, Tex 1973-75; Conslt, Embarcadero Properties, San Francisco, Calif 1980-85; Pres, BCI Inc, San Francisco 1985-88; Pres, BioCapital Corp, Toronto, Ontario 1988-; Chmn, CEO, Genmark Corp, San Francisco 1988-. *Memberships:* Commonwealth Club, San Francisco; California/Canada C of C. *Honours:* Photographer, Awd'd 1st place for photograph Surrender in 1974; Producer, Awd'd 1st place for a video presentation in the media category by Planned Parenthood in 1976. *Hobbies:* Photography; Producer; Skier; Writer. *Address:* Genmark Corporation, One Sansome Street, Suite 2100, San Francisco, CA 94104, USA.

BECK Charles Theodore Heathfield, b. 3 Apr 1954, England, Stockbroker. *Education:* Winchester Col 1967-72; MA 1975, Jesus Col, Cambridge. *Appointments:* Bank of England 1975-79; J M Finn & Co 1979-, Ptnr 1984, Fin Ptnr 1988-91. *Creative Works:* Co-Devel of Computer Software for Securities Industry Applications with E B Systems Analysis. *Membership:* AMSIA 1980. *Honour:* Scholar, Jesus Col, Cambridge 1975. *Hobbies:* Fencing; Japanese fencing; Archaeology. *Address:* c/o J M Finn & Co, Salisbury House, London Wall, London EC2M 5TA, England.

BECK Norman Wood, b. 8 July 1901, Cottage Grove, Oregon, USA. Rtd Edr. m. Evelyn Virginia Eastman, 15 Aug 1931, 1 s. *Education:* AB 1923, PhD 1941, Univ Chgo; Tchrs Col, Columbia Univ 1952, 1954. *Appointments:* Univ Mo 1929-30; Yale Univ 1931-32; Dartmouth Col 1932-38; Hunter Col 1939-43, 1950-51; Brooklyn Col 1941-42; NY Univ 1941-42; Smith Col 1943-44; Wilson Col, 1944-47; Jersey City State Col 1947-72; Emeritus of Pol Sci 1974-. *Publications:* New Jersey, The Encyclopaedia Britannica, 1952; A New Frontier for Civic Education, 1961; Report on the Year-'round College, 1965; Toward Understanding Power and Its Use: Machiavelli, Jesus, I-Thou, 1987. *Honours:* Phi Beta Kappa 1922; Univ Chgo Pol Sci Departmental Honours Fellow 1926; Trustee, Friends World Col, Huntington, NY 1971-74; Dist'd Service Awd, NJ Pol Sci Assn 1977; Dist'd Community Service Awd, Mendham Borough, NJ 1982. *Address:* 40 Morris Lake Road, Sparta, NJ 07871, USA. 6, 15, 129, 140.

BECK Walter, b. 19 Sept 1929, Mannheim. Regisseur. *Education:* DEFA Studio fur Regie Studium 1948-51. *Career:* Filme (Auswahl): Claudia 1958; Konig Drosselbart 1965; Käuzchenkuhle, 1968; Dornröschen 1970; Stülpner-Legende 7 Teile 1971-73; Trini 1976; Das Raubtier 1977; Des Henkers Bruder 1978; Der Prinz hinter den sieben Meeren 1982; Biberspur 1983; Der Bärenhäuter 1985; Froschkönig 1987; Der Streit um des Esels Schatten 1989; Viele Theatre Inst UVAM. *Creative Works:* Theorien zum Kinder-Film, UAM.

Honours: Goldener Spatz 1979, GERA; Silberner Greif 1983, Giffoni; Hauptpreis 1987, Mar del Plata; Goldener Spatz 1989, GERA. *Address:* 1636 Blankenfelde, Erich Klausener Str 135, Germany.

BECKER Carl Bradley, b. 27 Apr 1951. Chicago, Illinois, USA. For'n Instr in Philosophy. *Education:* BA (valedictorian) in Philosophy & Religion 1971, Principia Col, Illinois; Dipl in French Lang 1972, McGill Univ, Quebec; MA (valedictorian) in Asian Phil & Religion 1973, East-West Centre, Univ Hawaii; Sev courses in Japanese Lang & Religion 1974-79; PhD (Phi Kappa Phi in Asian Phil & Religion 1981, East-West Centre, Univ Hawaii. *Appointments:* Lectr & Reschr, Philosophy Dept & Ednl Affairs, Principia Col, Illinois 1971-72; Guest Columnist, p-time, Japan Times' Student Times, Tokyo 1974-78, 1984-87; Instr of Am Thought, p-time, Bukkyo Univ, Kyoto 1978-79; Reschr, East-West Centre Communication Inst, Hawaii 1979-80; Asst Prof Phil, Southern Ill Univ 1981-83; Fulbright Prof, Osaka Univ Bungakubu Eibun Gakka, Osaka 1983-85; Lectr, Osaka Univ Bungakubu Nihon Gakka, Osaka 1985-86; Assoc Prof Ei/Shukyo, Tenri Univ Bungakubu Tenri, Nara-ken 1985-86; Asst Prof Asian/Ethics, Curriculum Res & Devel, Univ Hawaii 1986-88; For'n Instr Philosophy, Tsukubu Univ JinBun Gakurui, Ibaraki-ken 1988-. *Publications:* 8 books incl: Christianity: History and Thought, 1984; Japan: My Teacher, My Love, 1983; Over 30 arts on religion & philosophy; 3 Book Reviews; 5 Translations; 7 arts on intercultural communication; 8 arts on Japanese politics and society. *Memberships:* Japan Eng Forensics Assn, VP 1978-85; SIETAR; IANDS; SRPR. *Honours:* Awd for Outstg Art of 1985-86, SIETAR; Awd for Best Article of 1985, NDE's and the Book of the Dead, IANDS; Robert Ashby Prize for Best Essay of the Year, SRPR. *Address:* 305 Ibaraki-ken, Tsukuba-shi, Amakubo 2-1-1-303, Gaikokujin, Kyoushi, Shukusha, Japan. 139, 152, 154.

BECKER Laurence Edward, b. 1943, Edmonton, Alberta. Prof Pathology & Paediatrics; Neuropathologist. m. Edna Jean Whitmore, 7 Aug 1971, 3 d. *Education:* MD 1967, Univ Alberta; Postgrad studies: McGill 1968; Univ Toronto 1969-72; Johns Hopkins Univ 1972-74; Fellow, Royal Col Physicians & Surgeons 1972. *Appointments:* Prof Pathology & Paediatrics, Univ Toronto 1974-; Neuropathologist, Hosp for Sick Children 1974-; Project Dir, Res Inst 1974-; Conslt, Toronto Hosp and Women's Col Hosp 1974. *Publications:* Active res in mental retardation (Downs Syndrome), sudden infant death syndrome, brain tumours in children; Over 200 pubs in med lit. *Memberships:* Candn Assn Neuropathologists; Am Assn Neuropathologists; Soc for Paediatric Pathology; Intl Acad of Pathology. *Honour:* Alpha Omega Alpha Hon Med Soc 1966. *Hobbies:* Squash; Swimming; Skiing. *Address:* 555 University Avenue, Toronto, Ontario, Canada M5G 1X8. 142.

BECKMAN Henry H G, b. 26 Nov 1921, Halifax, NS, Canada. Writer; Actor; Dir TV & Films; Producer. m. Cheryl Maxwell, 25 Nov 1955, 2 s. *Education:* Intelligence Courses 1941, Royal Milit Col, Kingston, Ontario; BA equiv, Am Acad Dramatic Arts, NYC. *Career:* 100s TV shows incl featured roles on Peyton Place, Here Come the Brides, McHale's Navy. *Publications:* How to 'Sell' Your Film Project, 1979; Writer, Producer, Director, Juvenile Court, tv series, 1991. *Memberships include:* Actor's Equity, US & Cda; Screen Actor's Guild; Writer's Guild, US & Cda; Am Fedn TV & Radio Artists; Alliance Candn TV & Radio Artists; Am Acad TV Arts & Scis, Blue Ribbon Emmy Panel; Brotherhood Rally All Veteran's Org, Bd Mem. *Honours:* Dubbed Sir Henry Beckman; Order of St John of Jerusalem; Knights of Malta-2nd oldest Order of Knighthood; Twice Awd'd Canada's Genie Awd, Best Actor in a Supporting Role 1976, 1979; Golden Halo, 1986, 1989, So Cal Mot Pic Soc LA. *Hobbies:* Fulfilling obligations to humankind as a Hospitaller Order of St John, Knights of Malta; Definitive Auteur Project 1993; Going for Doctorate in Cinema and Guiness Book of Records. *Address:* 3906 Nelson Road, Deming, WA 98244, USA.

BECSY Tamas, b. 28 Aug 1928, Budapest. Prof. m. Hajna Futaky, 21 May 1955, 1 d. *Education:* Univ Szeged, Fac Fine Arts. *Appointments:* Elem Sch Tchr 1954-60; Grammar Sch Tchr 1960-72; Prof, Univ Budapest 1978-; Tchr, Tchr Tng Col 1972-78. *Publications:* 11 books in theory of drama incl: On the Ontology of Drama; The Aesthetics of Drama; The Modells of Drama and the Contemporary Drama. *Membership:* Intl Comparative Lit Assn. *Honour:* Jozsef Attila Awd 1986. *Hobby:* Gardening. *Address:* Osszehasonlito es Vilagirodalmi Tanszek, Pesti B ul, Budapest 1052, Hungary.

BEDFORD Anthony John, b. 15 July 1943, Australia. Chf, Optoelectronics Div, DSTO. m. Margaret Elizabeth Mumme, 6 Jan 1966, 1 s. 2 d. *Education:* B App Sci (Hons), PhD 1971, Univ Adelaide. *Appointments:* Tech Asst, Dept Defence 1961-63; Cadet Defence Sci 1963-67; Postgrad Student 1967-70; Res Scist, Sr Res Scist, DSTO 1971-76, Principal Res Scist 1976-86; Counsellor Defence Sci, Wash DC 1986-89; Chf Explosives, DSTO/MRL 1989-1991; Chf Optoelectronics, DSTO 1991-. *Contributions:* arts & reports to sci jours. *Memberships:* Fellow, Inst Engrs Australia (FIEAust); Chartered Profl Engr (CPEng). *Hobbies:* Sailing; Golf; Tennis; Swimming; Computer. *Address:* P O Box 1500, Salisbury, SA 5108, Australia. 52.

BEDNARKIEWICZ Maciej Jozef, b. 22 Feb 1940, Warsaw. Lawyer; Attorney. m. 7 June 1969, 1 s. *Education:* Law degree 1963, Warsaw Univ. *Appointments:* Advocates Coop Soc, the Polish Bar Assn 1969-; Polish Bar Assn Coun 1983; Pres, Polish Bar Assn 1989-; Mem Parliament representing Solidarity Group 1989-. *Memberships:* Human Rights Intl Org; Intl Bar Assn; Fellow membership, Polish Club of Inteligensia. *Hobbies:* Cinema; Walking in the countryside; Human rights; Religion. *Address:* 13 Kozietulskiego, 01-571 Warsaw, Poland.

BEDNARSKA-RUSZAJ Krystyna Maria, b. 14 Oct 1945, Biecz. Reschr; Lib Sci. m. Adam Ruszaj, 15 Sept 1971, 1 s. *Education:* MSc 1968, PhD 1980, Jagiellonian Univ; Habilitation 1991, Univ Wroclaw. *Appointments:* Librarian 1968-74, Lectr 1974-80, Asst Prof 1980-, Jagiellonian Univ. *Publications:* Science & Scientist in the Monitor 1765-1785, 1983; The Model of erudite in Polish enlightenment literature, 1984; The Nationalsocialist library policy in Poland during the second world war, 1989; From Homer up to Jean Jacques Rousseau In the circle of reading of cracow professors during the Enlightenment period, 1991. *Memberships:* Polish Bibliological Soc; The Soc of Authors & Pubrs, UNIVERSITAS. *Honours:* Rector's Awd for achmts in didactics 1981; Minister's Awd for a book, co- author, 1987; Rector's Awd for res and didactics achmts 1990; Golden Service Cross for 20 years of res and didactics achmts at Jagiellonian Univ. *Hobbies:* Classical music; Hiking; Swimming. *Address:* Uniwersytet Jagiellonski, Instytut Filologii Polskiej, Katedra Bibliotekoznawstwa, ul Golebia 16, 31-007 Krakow, Poland. 138.

BEEDHAM Trevor, b. 30 July 1942, Nottingham, England. Conslt Ob & Gynaecologist. m. Anne Darnborough-Cameron, 21 May 1966, 2 s. 1 d. *Education:* London Univ. *Appointments:* Conslt Ob & Gynae, Royal London Hosp, London 1981-. *Publications:* Treatment and Prognosis in Obstetrics and Gynaecology, joint Author, 1989; The Examination of Women in Hutchinsons Clinical Methods, 1990. *Memberships:* Fellow, Royal Soc of Med; Liveryman, Worshipful Soc of Apothecaries, 1988; Freeman City of London, 1984. *Honours:* MB BS (Hons) 1972; FRCOG 1989. *Hobbies:* Swimming; Skiing. *Address:* 127 Harley Street, London W1M 1DJ, England.

BEER Lionel Edwin, b. 5 Feb 1940, Paignton. Antique Dealer. *Education:* South Devon Tech Col. *Appointments:* Bookseller, Distributor, 1967-. *Publications:* Pubr, Spacelink magazine (UFO news & reports) 1967-71. *Contributions:* var books on paranormal; Author, The Moving Statue of Ballinspittle and Related Phenomena, 1986. *Memberships include:* Fdr & VP, Brit UFO Res Assn; Life Mem: Assn for Sci Study of Anomalous Phenomena; Assn Railway Preservation Socs; English Heritage; National Trust; Founder, Travel & Earth Mysteries Society (TEMS), 1992. *Honours:* Appear in BBC/TV Rock & Roll Years 1979; Interviewed on radio & TV in connection with UFO interest. *Hobbies:* Antiques; Books; Earth mysteries; Steam railways; Travel; UFOlogy. *Address:* 115 Hollybush Lane, Hampton, Middlesex TW12 2QY, England.

BEERMAN Burton, b. 12 June 1943, Atlanta, Georgia, USA. Composer; Clarinetist; Video Artist; Tchr. m. 3 Aug 1961, 1 s. *Education:* MusB in Composition 1966, Fla State Univ; MusM in Composition 1968, Doctor Musical Arts in Composition 1971, Univ Michigan. *Appointments:* Prof Mus Composition & History, Bowling Green State Univ 1970-; Vstg Prof Music, Univ Utah 1975-76. *Creative Works:* Masks, for electric clarinet; Shades Of, for electric clarinet; Night Visions, for electric clarinet, dancer, synthesiazer, and virtual reality videographics. *Memberships:* Broadcast Music Inc; Am Composers Alliance; Soc Composers Inc; Soc of Electro-Acoustic Music for the United States. *Honours:* 1st prize, Martha K Cooper Orch Prize; 1st prize, Intl Brass Soc; 2nd Prize, Louisville Brass Quintet competitions. *Hobbies:* Running; Weightraining. *Address:* 713 Champagne Avenue, Bowling Green, OH 43403, USA. 4.

BEETHAM Stanley Williams, b. 2 Nov 1933, Montpelier, Idaho, USA. Int Mgmt Conslt. m. (2)Barbara Burnham Barnard, 20 June 1987, 1 s. 2 d. *Education:* BA 1956, Wesleyan Univ; MA 1957, Univ Amsterdam; Postgrad, Harvard Univ 1958-59. *Appointments include:* Intl Mkt Mgr, US Rubber/Uniroyal, NY & London 1960-63; Corporate Mktg Conslt, General Electric Company 1963-65; Assoc Dir, Benton & Bowles Inc 1965-67; Dir Corporate Planning, Esmark 1967-72; VP, Consolidated Packaging 1972-74; Sr Conslt, Booz, Allen, Hamilton & Hay Assocs 1975-80; Sr VP, US Tobacco Company 1981-87; Pres, S W Beetham & Assocs 1987-; Candidate, US Cong 1972-74. *Publications:* Arts on planning, mktg, intl & urban devel. *Memberships include:* Programme Dir, North Am Soc for Planning & Strategic Mgmt; Nat Assn of Bus Economists; Coun for Urban Ec Devel. *Honours:* Fulbright Scholar 1956-57; Marshall Scholar 1957; Woodrow Wilson Fellow 1958-59; Phi Beta Kappa 1955; Graduated highest hons, distinction in Govt 1956. *Hobbies:* Opera; Different cultures; Politics; World affairs. *Address:* PO Box N, Brinnon, WA 98320, USA. 2, 6, 9, 52, 132, 139.

BEHL Pran Nath, b. 1 Jan 1925, Delhi, India. Dermatologist. m. 29 Sept 1951, 1 s. 1 d. *Education:* MBBS 1946, Punjab Univ; MRCP (equiv MD Diplomate) with Dermatology as special subject 1951 (Edin), Lahore Univ; FRCP (Edin) 1964. *Appointments:* Ex Prof & Hd Skin Dept, Maulana Azad Med Col, New Delhi; Ex Lectr in Dermatol, Lady Hardinge Med Col, New Delhi; Ex Lectr, Jawahar Lal Nehru Inst of Physio-Occup Therapy; Ex Lectr, Col Nsg, New Delhi. *Publications:* Author of 12 books incl: Practice of Dermatology; Skin Irritant & Sensitising Plants found in India; Good Health; Health & Happiness; Herbs Useful in Dermatological Therapy; Practice of Dermal Histopathology. *Memberships:* Past VP, Intl Soc of Tropical Dermatology, Phil; Asian Dermatol Assn, Hong Kong 1990-93; Past Pres, Dermatol Soc, India; Hon Fellow, Intl Soc for Dermatologic Surgery, NY. *Honour:* Rotary Shield for Best Service Awd. *Hobbies:* Farming; Social Service; Rural development programmes. *Address:* Skin Institute & School of Dermatology, 'N' Block, Greater Kailash-1, New Delhi 110048, India. 2, 93.

BEHREND Manfred, b. 9 Apr 1930, Berlin, Germany. Histn. m. Hanna Behrend, 10 Sept 1962, 2 d. *Education:* Apprenticeship as Metal Worker, 1946-49; Var

Journalistic Activities, 1949-51; Student of Hist, 1951-57; Dip, 1957; Dr.Phil, 1971. *Appointments:* Ed work for GDR Broadcasting Corp, 1957-61; Rdr at Rutten & Loening Publrs, 1962; Acad Staff of Inst for Int Pols and Econs, 1962-90. *Publications:* Var publs on Contemporary problems of Federal Repub of Germany, German Conservatism, Franz Josef Strauss and CDU/CSU, Right Wing Extremism, Neofascism in the GDR, German Working Class Movement. *Hobby:* Reading. *Address:* 91 Artur-Becker-Strasse, O- 1055 Berlin, Germany.

BEKEN Alfred Keith, b. 16 Feb 1914, Cowes, I.O.W. Marine Photographer. 2 s. *Education:* Chemist MPS; Photographer FRPS. *Appointments:* Qualified Chemist in family's business 1937; Profl Marine Photographer 1946; Granted Fellowship, Royal Photographic Soc 1959. *Publications:* 15 books incl: Beauty of Sail, 1937; Glory of Sail, 1959; Batsford Book of Yachts, 1960; Beken of Cowes, vol 1, 1966, vol 2, 1968; A Hundred Years of Sail, 1981; A Century of Tall Ships, 1985; The New Ocean Thoroughbreds, 1988; The Americas Cup, 1990; Video, The Beauty of Sail, 1991. *Honours:* Royal Appointment granted by HRH The Duke of Edinburgh, Marine Photographers, 1971; Video, The Beauty of Sail, attained Gold Awd at Houston, Tex Film Festival 1991. *Hobbies:* Sailing; The sea in general. *Address:* Beken of Cowes, 16 Birmingham Road, Cowes, Isle of Wight, PO31 7BH, England.

BELCHEVA Diana, b. 8 Apr 1962, Pazardgik, Bulgaria. Curator Art Gallery. m. Ferdov Plamen, 28 July 1990, 1 d. *Education:* Eng Lang Sch, Sofia 1976-80; History of Art, Univ Budapest, Hungary 1980-86. *Appointments:* Curator Graphic Department, Art Gallery of S S Cyril & Methodius Foun 1986-; Postgrad Student, Budapest Univ, Dept History of Art 1988-92. *Publications:* Many arts in Bulgarian newspapers & magazines incl: The Drawings of Durer; Contemporary Portuguese grafic art; Contemporary Hungarian and Slovenian art; Arts at the Serbian Nat Museum Annuals, a catalogue of Bulgarian painter Peter Marinov. *Hobbies:* Collecting paintings, sculptures, graphics & decorative art objects; Contemporary theatre & cinema; Gardening; Culinary; Horse racing. *Address:* 12 Marin Drinov Street, Sofia 1504, Bulgaria.

BELCOURT Herbert Clifford, b. 6 July 1931, Lac St Anne, Alberta. Bus Exec. m. Lesley Marianne Fouthrop Tarrant, 30 June 1973, 2 s. *Education:* Univ Alberta. *Appointments:* Fdr & Pres, Herb's Upholstery Ltd 1957; Fdr & Pres, Mutual Telephone Service 1960; Fdr & Pres, Belcourt Construction Ltd 1965-80; Fdr & Pres, Canative Housing Corp 1971-87; Pres, News Building Syndicate 1980; Self employed as Pres & Fdr, Herbel Holdings 1980-; Fdr & Pres, Sword & Shield, a 4-plex movie theatre 1983-; Fdr & Pres, Bell & Court Pub & Restaurant 1986-89; Treasurer, Carnative Housing Corp 1987-; Secy-Treas, Tara Bel Inc, Australia 1987-; Fdr & Pres, Tara Bel Inc, Canada 1988-. *Memberships include:* Bdmem, Sr Citizens' Home, Gunn, Alberta 1986; Bdmem, Strathcona Women's Shelter 1982-83; One of 'Bishop's Men' 1981, and other ch activities; Lions Edmonton Breakfast Club 1972-83; Edmonton C of C; Sherwood Park C of C; Chmn Parks Com for Edmonton C of C; Alberta Trade Mission to Peru 1982; Northern Alberta Pres, Motion Picture Assn Alberta; Pres, Nat Urban Native Housing Assn; Chairperson of the Edmonton Unemployment Bd of Referees; Adv Coun CESO 1986-88; BdMem, Native Venture Capital Corp 1983-86; Cice Chmn & Exec, Alberta Arts Foun; Chmn, Bus Assistance for Native Albertans 1981-84. *Honour:* Queen's Silver Jubilee Medal for Community Service 1977. *Hobbies:* Gardening; Politics; Dog walking; Theatre. *Address:* 406 Evergreen Street, Sherwood Park, Alberta, Canada T8A 1K3. 142.

BELL Alexander Fulton, b. 20 Jan 1937, Glasgow, Scotland. Company Dir. m. (1)Sophia Lilian Elizabeth Morgan Elles, 4 Jan 1969, dec, 2 s. (2)Alison Mary Compton, 23 Apr 1984. *Education:* RMA Sandhurst

1955- 57; Dundee Col Tech 1970-73; Dundee Col Commerce 1974; CBA (Edin) 1973; Dipl in Mktg 1974. *Appointments:* Commissioned in the Argyll & Sutherland Highlanders 1957; Capt, H M Royal Guard, Balmoral 1963; Adjutant, 1st Bn Borneo/Malaya 1964-65; ADC to GOC, 51 Highland Div 1966; Rtd 1969; Major, 1/51 Highland Vols, TAVR 1972-74; Home Service Force 1982-83; Assoc Brit Maltsters 1969-87; Parent Company, Dalgety; Pauls Malt, Dir Mktg 1987-90; Sales Dir, Simpsons Malt 1990-. *Memberships:* Chmn, Pres Inst Mktg (Tayside) 1975-77; Adv Coun Mem, Dundee Col Commerce 1976-78; MCIM; MBIM; MIBrew; MIOD; Former Gov, Ardvreck Sch, Crieff. *Hobbies:* Golf; Fishing; Shooting; Skiing; Walking; Member Highland Brigade Club. *Address:* Drumclune, By Forfar, Angus DD8 3TS, Scotland.

BELL Andrew Richard, b. 23 July 1960, Stockport. Stockbroker. m. Elizabeth Jane Grant, 10 Feb 1990. *Education:* MA 1981, Mansfield Col, Oxford. *Appointments:* Asst Dir, E B Savory, Milln & Co 1981-86; Assoc Dir, Wood MacKenzie & Co 1986-88; Dir, Kleinwort Benson Securities 1988-. *Membership:* Intl Stock Exchange Soc of Investment Analysts. *Hobbies:* Skiing; Horse riding; Running; Tennis; Football; Travel. *Address:* Kleinwort Benson Securities, 20 Fenchurch Street, London EC3P 3DB, England. 53.

BELL James Bacon, b. 3 Aug 1952, Tellico Plains, Tennessee, USA. Environmental Profl. m. Camille Marie Carter, 17 June 1978. *Education:* AA Agricl Econs, Hiawassee Coll, TN, 1972; BSc, Biology, TN Technological Univ, 1975. *Appointments:* Owner, Bell Nursery Co and Jim Bell Landscaping Co, Lenoir City, TN, 1973-75; Count Agt, Univ TN Agricl Ext Serv, 1975-78; Pres, Bell-Bacon Farms Inc, Nevada, MO, 1979-; Pres, Midwestern Pecan Co Inc, Nevada, MO, 1980-; MO Petroleum Tank Servs Inc, 1979-; Co-owner, Possum Pete's R V Park, Nevada, MO, 1989-; Co-owner, SE Environmental, 1991-; Co-owner, American Boom and Barrier Corp, 1990-; Co-owner, Gen Mgr, Cape Canaveral Marine Servs, 1991-. *Memberships:* Hazard Materials Control Rsch Inst; Nat Environmental Hlth Assn; Nat Assn of Environmental Profls; FL Assn of Environmental Profls; Nat Asbestos Coun; Int Assn of Environmental Mgrs; City of Nevada Solid Waste Task Force, 1990; Small Bus Advsry Coun; Chmbr of Comm; Univ of MO Ext Coun, Bd Mbr, 1986-88; Boy Scouts of America. *Honours:* Nevada-Vernon Co Chmbr of Comm Pacesetter Award for Midwestern Pecan Co Inc, 1985; Outstanding Young Man of America, 1986, 87; Agricl Bus of The Year Award by Gov John Ashcroft to Midwestern Pecan Co Inc, 1988; Nevada-Vernon Co Chmbr of Comm Pacesetter Award for Midwestern Pecan Co Inc, 1988. *Hobbies:* Hunting, Fishing, Cooking, Reading, Travelling. *Address:* 427 Brightwaters Drive, Cocoa Beach, FL 32931, USA. 8, 52, 139.

BELL Marja-Liisa, b. 5 July 1930, Helsinki. Artmuseum Dir. m. 1962-74, 1 d. *Education:* MPhil 1959, Univ Helsinki; Postgrad 1961-62, NYU. *Appointments:* Asst to Dir, Ateneumin Taidemuseo, Helsinki 1953- 56; PR Dir, Villayhtyma Oy, Helsinki 1959-61; Curator, Gallen-Kallelan Museo, Espoo, Finland 1962-63; Lectr, Inst f Am Univ, Aix-en-Provence, France 1963- 64; Fine Arts Acad of Finland, Helsinki 1965-71; Exec Secy for Cult Affairs, City Chancellery of Helsinki 1966-78; Artmuseumdir, Helsingin kaupungin taidemuseo, Helsinki 1979-. *Memberships:* Bd mem, Fine Arts Comm, Helsinki Festival 1969-75, Chmn 1976-86; Nordic Art Assn, Secy Finnish Section 1959-63; Scandinavian Museum Assn 1969-, bm Finnish section 1979-; European Cultural Foun, mb Trustees of Finnish sect 1991-; Intl Coun for Museums (ICOM); ICOM Coun for Modern Arts Museums 1974-, mb 1977-, mem Exec Bd 1986-89; mb Trustees Foun, Naissance d'Europe, Paris 1991-. *Honours:* Ch, Order of the White Rose of Finland; Officier, Order of Arts et Lettres of France; Ch, Order of San Agatha of San Marino; Medal of Sculptors Assn Finland. *Address:* Helsingin kaupungin taidemuseo, Punavuorenkatu 6, 00120 Helsinki, Finland. 52.

BELL Quentin Ross, b. 24 June 1944, Reading, Berks. PR Conslt. m. Hilary Sian Jones, 14 July 1972, 2 d. *Education:* Presentation Col. *Appointments:* Reading Standard Newspaper 1961; Thomson Newspapers 1964; Mktg Dir, Safari Holidays 1966; Formed Bell Capper Assocs Ltd 1970; Formed The Quentin Bell Organisation plc 1973. *Publication:* The PR Business- An Insiders Guide to Real Life Public Relations. *Memberships:* Chmn, Devel Com, The PR Conslts Assn; MCIM; MIPR; IOD; RAC. *Hobbies:* Collecting: Cars; Wine; Clocks; Antiques; Houses; Parrots. *Address:* Rydal Mount, Heath Road, Weybridge, Surrey KT13 8SX, England.

BELL Ronnie Steven, b. 13 Aug 1943, Jackson, Tennessee, USA. Company Pres. m. Sandra Ellen Cook, 16 Oct 1964, 1 s. 2 d. *Education:* San Jacinto Col. *Appointments:* Gen Mgr, Pasadena Colonial Inc 1960- 61; Reg Sales Mgr, J B Williams Co 1967-70; Sales Mgr, Gen Dynamics Comm Inc 1970-75; VP, Telecommunication Inc 1975-80; Pres, Am Bus Tele Systems 1980-85; Sr VP, Bell South Communication 1985-88; Pres, Altus Technologies Inc 1988-. *Memberships:* Dir, Christian Review Magazine; Active var charitable orgs; Am Hotel Assn; North Am telephone Assn; Fdr Mem, Telepros Assn; Republican Nat Com; 1992 Presidential Trust; Charter mem, Republican Campaign Coun; Intl Platform Assn. *Honours:* Harry S Newton Awd, Teleconnect Mag 1987; Ofcr of the Year, Bell South Communication 1987. *Hobbies:* Music; Travel; Woodworking; Motorcycles; Sprots. *Address:* 2432 Corby, Plano, TX 75025, USA. 7, 132.

BELLA Istvan, b. 7 Sept 1940, Szekesfehervar. Poet; Journalist; Translator. m. Zayzon Marta, 4 Oct 1974, 2 s. 1 d. *Education:* Eotvos Lorand Univ, Hungarian- librari spec 1959-64; Assn Hungarian Journalists, Journalist Sch 1973. *Appointments:* Cantor 1949-53, Feller 1958, Erdert Wood Factory; Mechanic, Budapest Waterworks 1958-59; Adult Edr, Power Station Investor Factory 1961-62; Librarian, Eotvos Lorand Univ Fac of Law 1964; Librarian, Ganz-Mavag Metal Factory 1964- 70; Journalist, Hungarian Paper, bi-weekly of Hungarian Paper Works 1971-78; Lit Edit, Contbr at Elet es Irodalom, weekly, 1978-91. *Publications:* 11 pubs incl poems and arts, the latest being: I Request My Face Back, 1988; Sarkeresztur Song, 1989; Facing the Earth, 1991; Also 2 collective works; Translations from Polish, Russian, Vogul-Ostyak, Hebrew, Serbian & Rumanian poetry. *Memberships:* Assn Hungarian Writers, mem Presidency, Secy poet section; Hungarian PEN Club; Berzsenyi Daniel Lit Assn; REguly Antal Assn of Linguistics. *Honours:* Prize of the Communist Youth Org 1969; Jozsef Attila Prize 1970, 1986; Dery Tibor Prize 1988; Book of the Year 1989. *Hobbies:* Chess; Music; Playing the piano. *Address:* Landler Jeno u 12.I.10, Budapest 1078, Hungary.

BELLAMY Sheila, b. 5 Jan 1940, Kendal, Cumbria, England. Univ Lectr in Accountancy. m. Henry Noel Bellamy, 21 Apr 1962, 1 s. *Education:* MBA 1983, BEd 1984, Monash Univ; MEc 1985, Univ New England; BA 1986, MCom 1990, Univ Melbourne. *Appointments:* Bus Mgr, Col Nsg, Australia 1969- 70; Bursar, Firbank Girls Grammar Sch 1970-72; Statistics Ofcr, Chisholm Inst 1973-74; Dep Dir, Australian Soc CPAs, Victoria 1974-78; Tutor, Monash Univ 1980-83; Principal Lectr, RMIT, Univ 1983-. *Publication:* Accounting for Lawyers, 1988. *Memberships:* Fellow, Australian Soc CPAs; Sr Assoc, Australian Bankers' Inst; Australian Soc Corporate Treasurers; Assoc, Inst Corporate Mgrs, Secys & Admrs; Australian Inst Mgmt; Ec Soc Australia. *Honours:* C'Wealth Postgrad Course Awd, Monash Univ 1979; A G Whitlam Scholarship, Univ Melbourne 1989. *Hobby:* Reading. *Address:* 128 Brighton Road, Elsternwick, Victoria 3185, Australia.

BELLE Pamela Dorothy Alice, b. 16 June 1952, Ipswich, Suffolk, England. Author. m. Stephen Thomas, 6 Aug 1990, 1 s. *Education:* BA (Hons) Hist, Univ of Sussex, 1975; PGL.Ed, Coventry Coll of Educ, 1975-

76. *Appointments:* Class Tchr, St Mary's First Schl, Berkhamsted, Herts, 1978-85; Full-time Author, 1985- . *Publications:* Novels: The Moon in the Water, 1983; The Chains of Fate, 1984, Alathea, 1985; The Lodestar, 1987; Wintercombe, 1988; Herald of Joy, 1989; A Falling Star, 1990; Treason's Gift, 1992. *Membership:* Soc of Authors. *Hobbies:* Reading, Gardening, Photography, Drawing and Painting, Pottery, Films, Walking, Burmese Cats and Labrador Dogs, Archaeology and Old Houses. *Address:* c/o Vivienne Schuster, Curtis Brown John Farquharson, 162-168 Regent Street, London W 1, England.

BELLEZZA Maurizio Davide, b. 2 Dec 1957, Milan, Italt. Ballet Dancer. *Education:* Teatro Alla Scala Ballet Sch 1968-74; Dipl 1976, Moscow Ballet Sch (Bolshoi). *Career:* Teatro Alla Scala 1976-81; London Festival Ballet 1981-86; Bayerische Staatsoper Munich 1986- 89; English National Ballet 1990-. *Honours:* Bordighera's Prize, Italy 1980; Positano's Prize, Italy 1985; Quadrivio's Prize, Italy 1988. *Hobbies:* Reading; Collecting pen nibs; Antiques. *Address:* 56, St George Square, London SW1, England.

BELLOS David Michael, b. 25 June 1945, Rochford, England. Prof French Studies. 1 s. 2 d. *Education:* BA Hons 1967, MA 1970, D Phil 1971, Oxford Univ. *Appointments:* Lectr, Univ Edinburgh 1972-82; Prof, Univ Southampton 1982-85; Prof, Univ Manchester 1986-. *Publications:* Balzac Criticism in France, 1976; George's Perec, Life A User's Manual, translation, 1987; Old Goriot, 1987; George Perec, A Life in Words, 1993. *Honours:* IBM Translation Prize of French-Am Foun 1988; Chevalier de l'Ordre des Palmes Academiques, 1988. *Hobby:* Bicycles. *Address:* Department of French Studies, University of Manchester, Oxford Road, Manchester M13 9PL, England. 52.

BELSEVICA Vizma, b. 30 May 1931, Latvia, Riga. Writer; Translator. m. Zigurds Elsbergs, 16 May 1968, 1 s. *Education:* Gorkii Inst of World Lit, Moscow. *Appointments:* Newspaper, Pionieris, 1948- 50; Writer & Translator 1950-. *Publications:* Books in Latvian: 9 books poetry; 3 books Short Stories; 2 Children's books; In Swedish: 3 books of Poetry; In German: 1 book of Short Stories; 6 books have been pub'd in Russian translation, one in Armenian, one in Belorussian; In Danish: book of Poetry, 1992; Translated & pub'd in 40 langs; Translated into Latvian works by Shakespeare, A A Miln, T S Eliot, H Lofting, E Hemingway, Mark Twain and many others. *Memberships:* Latvian Writers Union; Intl PEN Latvian Centre; Hon Mem, Latvian Acad Scis. *Honours:* A Uptts Prize 1982; O Vacietis Prize 1988; Pastarins Prize 1989; J & E Forseth Prize 1992. *Hobbies:* Reading; Gardening. *Address:* Kr Valdemara 145/I-8, Riga, Latvia, LV-1013.

BELTRAMI Joseph, b. 15 May 1932, Rutherglen, Glasgow, Scotland. Solicitor; Notary. m. Delia Fallon, 14 Jan 1958, 3 s. *Education:* LLB, Glasgow Univ. *Appointments:* Sr Ptnr, Beltrami and Company, Solicitors, Glasgow. *Publications:* The Defender, 1980; Glasgow-A Celebration, 1984; Tales of the Suspected, 1988; The Meehan File, 1989. *Memberships:* Past Pres, Bothwell Bowling Club; Chmn, Testimonials for Soccer Stars, Jimmy Johnstone and Bobby Lennox 1976, Danny McGrain 1980; Solicitor Acting in cases of the only 2 Royal Pardons in Scotland this century, M Swanson 1975, P Meehan 1976; Instructed in more than 500 murder trials. *Hobbies:* Bowling; Snooker; Watching boxing. *Address:* Blenio, 5 St Andrew's Avenue, Bothwell, Scotland, G71 8DN. 184.

BELTRAMI Marco Edward, b. 7 Oct 1966, Huntington, NY. Composer. *Education:* BA in Urban Studies 1988, Brown Univ, Providence, RI; MM in Composition 1991, Yale Univ Sch Mus. *Career:* Commissions: Norfolk Chamber Mus Festival 1990; The Denver Brass and St John's Cathedral 1990; Bacchanalia Chamber Mus Festival 1991; Le Nouvel Ensemble Moderne 1991; Oakland Symphony Orch 1992; Am Dance Festival

1992. *Creative Works:* Iskios, City of Shadows, chamber orch, 1991; Short Pieces for 2 Pianos, 1992; Suite for Violin and Cello, 1991; La Citta Decadente, orch, 1991; String Quartet 1, 1990; Water's Edge, film score, 1991. *Memberships:* ASCAP; NACUSA; AMC. *Honours:* Woods-Chandler Prize for violin/cello suite, 1990; John Day Jackson Prize, for string quartet, 1991; National Winner Chgo Civic Orch Compt, 1991; US Winner of Forum 91 intl compt sponsored by UNESCO and the Univ of Montreal 1991. *Hobbies:* Skiing; Windsurfing; Tree pruning; Cooking; Reading. *Address:* 9 Southgate Road, Setauket, NY 11733, USA.

BENCIC Zvonko, b. 23 Apr 1940, Senj. Elect, Power Elect. m. Dubravka Cvitesic, 8 Apr 1967, 1 d. *Education:* Elect BEE 1963, MSc in Solid State Physics 1969, Univ Zagreb, Croatia, Fac Elect Engrg & Elect, Fac Natural Scis & Maths respectively; PhD 1988, Tech Scis-Elect Engrg & Electronics. *Appointments:* Assoc in Mercury Arc Rectifier Devel Unit 1962-70, Hd Dept Power Elect 1970-90, Dep Dir Elect 1991-, Rade Koncar Company, Inst Elect Engrg, Zagreb, Croatia, p-time Lectr in Semiconductor Devices at Rade Koncar Poly 1973-80; Asst Prof, 1976-91, Assoc Prof, 1991-, in Power Elect, undergrad & postgrad levels, Univ Zagreb, Croatia, Fac Elect Engrg & Elect. *Publications:* Author, univ textbook, Power Electronics I-Semiconductor devices, 1978; Author over 50 profl & sci papers. *Memberships:* Union Electrotech Engrs & Technicians of Croatia (SITH); Senior Mem, IEEE; Chmn TC22 (Power Elect) of Yugoslav Nat Com for Elect Engrg & Elect, 1982-91. *Honours:* Rade Koncar Company annual prize 1977; Cert of Merit from Yugoslav Nat Com for Elect Engrg & Elect 1983; Rade Koncar Inst of Elect Engrg annual prize 1984. *Hobby:* Mountaineering. *Address:* Faculty of Electrical Engineering and Electronics, Unska 3, 41000 Zagreb, Croatia.

BENCINI Edward, b. 29 Dec 1945, Malta. Arch; Civil Engr. m. Nathalie Formosa, 9 Sept 1973, 2 s. 1 d. *Education:* B Arch; A & CE, Dipl Arch & Civil Engr. *Appointments:* Joined I Raniolo, Archs & Civil Engrs 1971; Firm became Raniolo & Bencini, Archs & Civil Engrs 1975-. *Creative Works:* Var architectural & Engrg projects in Malta & Saudi Arabia. *Memberships:* Chamber of Archs & Civil Engrs, Malta, Pres 1977- 80, 1985-87; Fed Profl Bodies, Malta, Pres 1978-80; Chmn, Housing Authority, Malta 1987-90; Malta Students Rep Coun, Pres 1969-71. *Honours:* Univ Malta Sports Colours 1969-70. *Hobbies:* Yachting; Tennis. *Address:* Tamarisk, Triq Is-Sidra, Swieqi, Malta. 99.

BENDRUPE Mirdza, b. 23 Oct 1910, Livberze, Latvia. Poet. m. Dmitry Kostecky, 1 Mar 1978. *Publications:* Prose: His Majesty and the Monkey, 1938; The Whirlwinds of God, 1942; The Most Beautiful Garden, 1960; The Scandal arounds Valentin, 1965; Poetry: The Life, 1937; At the Sea, 1939; The Voice Insatiate, 1967; The Eye of the Typhoo, 1969; A Jug Full of Moonlight, 1974; The Words of Witchery, 1979; On the Way, 1970; All is Now Here, 1980; The Lamplighter, 1984; The Consciousness of the Heart, 1991; Translated into Latvian, Bhagavadgita, the sacred book of India, and many Russian poets. *Membership:* Writers Union of Latvia. *Hobby:* Philosophy of Yoga. *Address:* Varaviksnes gatre 16-34, Riga-80, Latvia, LV1080.

BENESOVA Olga, b. 25 Feb 1922, Prague, Czechoslovakia. Prof of Pharmacology; Rsch Scientist in Psychopharmacology. m. Vaicenbacher Vladimir Benes, 1 Apr 1952, 2 s. *Education:* MD, Schl of Med, Charles Univ, Prague, 1948; PhD 1958, ScD 1969, Czechoslovak Acad of Science, Prague. *Appointments:* Chief, Dept Biology Control of Drugs, Pharmaceutical Rsch Inst, Prague, 1948-55; Chmn, Prof, Dept Pharmacology, Med Schl, Charles Univ, Prague, 1955- 84; Chief, Dept of Pharmacology, State Inst for Drug Control, Prague, 1965-72; Chief, Dept of Brain Pathophysiology, Psychiatric Ctr, Prague, 1985-; Vis Scientist, Dept Pharmacology, Med Acad, Moscow, 1958, Laboratoire de Physiologie Comparee, Faculte des

Sciences, Paris, 1964. *Publications:* Over 300 scientific papers in med jrnls; Books: Psychotropic Drugs: Mechanism of Action, 1970; Perinatal Distress and Brain Development, 1980, 81; Brain Maldevelopment and Drugs, 1984; Nootropic Drugs, 1991; Ed, Embryotoxicity, Mutagenicity and Carcinogenicity in New Drugs, 1979. *Memberships:* Czechoslovak Purkinje Med Soc, var comms; IUPHAR, Toxicological Comm, 1981-87; IUTOX, Exec Comm, 1976-83; EUROTOX; Pres, two Int Symposia on Drug Toxicity, Prague 1971, 76; CINP; CIANS; Societe Francaise de Pharmacologie Clinique et de Therapeutique; ECNP; ISSWX; Ed Bd, Jrnl Perinatal and Prenatal Studies. *Honours:* Purkinje Medical Society Award for Best Puvblication, 1974, 80; Silver Medal for Merits, Charles University, Prague, 1990. *Hobbies:* Sport (canoe, swimming, skiing), Gardening, Travelling, Lit. *Address:* Psychiatric Center Prague, Ustavni 91, 181 03 Prague 8, Czechoslovakia.

BENHAM David Hamilton, b. 7 Jan 1942, Wales. Solicitor of Supreme Court. m. 14 Sept 1968, 1 s. 1 d. *Education:* Public Sch; BA (Hons) Southampton Univ. *Appointments:* Solicitor, Brit Oxygen Co Ltd 1970-72; Solicitor, British Petroleum Co Ltd 1972-74; Ptnr, Bischoff & Co 1974-. *Memberships:* Law Soc; City Solicitors Livery Co; Freeman, City of London; Royal Southampton Yacht Club; Lambs Club; Colets Club. *Honour:* BA (Hons). *Hobbies:* Squash; Photography; Collecting antiques; Power boating. *Address:* Epworth House, 25 City Road, London EC1, England.

BENITEZ John Griswold, b. 1 July 1957, St Louis, Missouri. Physician. m. Linda G Allison, 2 May 1982. *Education:* BA Chem 1978, MD 1981, Southern Ill Univ; Hyperbaric Med Fellowship 1988; Clin Toxicology Fellowship, Vanderbilt Univ 1989-91; Med Ed Fellowship, Univ Tex 1990-91. *Appointments:* Hillsboro Hosp 1982; Saran Bush Lincoln Med Ctr 1983; St John's Hosp 1984-88; Bromenn Healthcare 1988-89; Vanderbilt Univ Med Centre 1989-91; Univ Pittsburgh 1991-. *Publications:* 1 refereed art; 2 published abstracts; 2 book chapts: Acetaminophen Toxicity, and Vanadium, Titanium and Molybdenum Toxicology. *Memberships:* Am Col Emergency Physicians, Chmn 1988 Ill Chapt, EMS Com; Am Col of Sports Med; Soc for Academic Emergency Med; Undersea & Hyperbaric Med Soc; Am Acad of Clin Toxicology; Wilderness Med Soc. *Honours:* Dean's Col, Southern Ill Univ 1974-78; Undergrad Res Participant, Nat Sci Foun 1976; Fellow, Am Col Emergency Physicians 1989; Res Awd, Am Acad Clin Toxicology 1990. *Hobbies:* Sailing; Mountaineering; Backpacking; Astronomy; Photography; Bicycling. *Address:* Emergency Medical Centre, Montefiore University Hospital, 3459 Fifth Avenue, Pittsburgh, PA 15213, USA. 7, 8, 52.

BENJAMIN Don C Jr, b. 14 Mar 1942, Barksdale, Louisiana, USA. Univ Prof. *Education:* BA, St Bonaventure Univ, NY, 1964; MA Semitic Langs, Cath Univ of America, Wash DC, 1969; PhD Relig and Old Testament, Claremont Grad Schl, Claremont, CA, 1981. *Appointments:* Lectr, Rice Univ, Houston, TX, 1978-91; Vis Schlr, St Mary's Seminary and Grad Schl of Theology, Univ of St Thomas, Houston, 1980-83; Vis Scholar, Univ of Houston, TX, 1986, 88; Scholar in Res, Rice Univ, Houston, TX, 1991-93. *Publications:* The Prince and the Virgin, The Prophet, The Elder in The Bible Today; Bethel, Isaac, Jacob, Joseph, Sarah, Sodom and Gomorrah in Pastoral Dictionary of Biblical Theology; Dictionary of Biblical Theology, Ed C Stuhlmueller, D Bergant et al, forthcoming; The Adam and Eve Stories in Festschrift for Rolf P Knierim, in preparation. Cultural Anthropology and the Old Testament World w V H Matthews in preparation; Old Testament Story: An Introduction, in preparation; An Anthropology of Prophecy, 1991; Interview: The Middle East A Crossroads w J Elswick, 1991; The Divine Assembly w V H Matthews, 1991; The Stubborn Fool w V H Matthews, 1991; Old Testament Parallels: Laws and Storioes from the Ancient Near East w V H Matthews, 1991. *Memberships:* Soc of Biblical Lit; American Schls of Oriental Rsch; Cath Biblical Assn;

Archaeological Inst of America. *Hobbies:* Marathon Running, Carpentry, Gardening, Camping, Travelling. *Address:* 7637 Moline Street, Houston, TX 77087, USA.

BENNETT David Anthony, b. 4 Oct 1948, England. Mng Dir. *Education:* BSc Economics (Hons) 1972, London Univ; Dipl Intl Relats, Johns Hopkins Univ, SAIS 1973. *Appointments:* European Comm 1973-74; European Report 1975-76; British Gas 1977-84; Eurofi 1984-87; Powerhouse Europe 1988-. *Publications:* The European Economy in 1975; Towards an SDP Energy Policy. *Memberships:* Mem Inst Public Relats; Chmn Liberal Democrats European Gp. *Honours:* Scholarship, Johns Hopkins Univ 1972- 73; Stagiare, European Comm 1973; Alternate mem, European Ec & Social Cmmt 1981-83; Brit Parliamentary Candidate, SDP/ Alliance 1983, 87; European Parliamentary Candidate 1984. *Hobbies:* Tennis; Skiing; Walking; Travel; Theatre. *Address:* 1 The Vat House, 27 Regents Bridge Gardens, London SW8 1HD, England.

BENNETT Margaret Jane Larsen (Johnson), b. 3 Mar 1939, Tucson, Arizona, USA. Acct Exec; Reg'd Stockbroker; Insurance Broker. m. (1)1 s. 1 d. (2)Robert Charles Bennett, 18 Nov 1989, 2 stepsons. *Education:* Stockbroker, Series 7, Arizona, Calif, Colorado, 1986; State Stockbroker, Series 63, Arizona, California, 1986; Insurance License, Life, Health, Accident, Disability and Variable Annuity, 1986. *Appointments:* Securities Operations Mgr, Admin Asst, The Advisors, Phoenix, Arizona 1983-87; Stockbroker, MAI Securities, Phoenix 1986; Stockbroker, Value Equities Corporation, San Diego, Calif 1986-87; Securities Librarian, Nationwide Res Lib, Am Network Securities, Sun City, Az 1987-88; Stockbroker, Sun Am Securities, Dallas, Texas 1988-; Reg'd and Licensed Exec Sales Asst, Shearson Lehman Hutton, Peoria, Az 1988-89; Secy III Office of Admissions, Univ Az, Phoenix 1989; Investment and Estate Planning, Fin Discovery, Phoenix 1989-. *Memberships:* Paradise Valley Special Ed Parent Adv Gp, Phoenix, VP, Secy 1975; Dir, Ch Sch, Reorganised LDS Ch, Phoenix; Asst Coach, Coach, Paradise Valley Little League Girls' Softball, Phoenix 1976. *Honours:* Calif Scholarship Fed, 1957; 2 Plaques for assisting with Limited Partnerships, MAI Securities Corporation 1986, 1987; Hon Mention on completing Series 7, 63, Life Health and Accident/Variable Annuity Licences and Outstanding Service as Securities Operations Mgr, The Advisors, 1986. *Hobbies:* Music; Photography; Sports; Fishing; Volunteer work; Public service. *Address:* 3028 East Dahlia Drive, Phoenix, AZ 85032, USA. 5, 9.

BENNETT Patrick H, b. 4 Feb 1931, Paducah, Tex. Writer; Assoc Prof Eng. m. Charlene (Shay) White, 14 June 1958, 2 s. *Education:* BA in Eng 1958, Tex Tech Univ; MA in Eng 1969, Hardin-Simmons Univ. *Appointments:* The Paducah Post, 1950, 1953, 1955; US Army 1951-52; The Lorenzo Tribune 1954; The Chillicothe Valley News 1954; The Crosbyton Review 1958-63; The Abilene Reporter-News 1963-69; PR Dir 1969-80, Assoc Prof Eng 1980-, McMurray Univ. *Publications:* Books: Talking with Texas Writers: Twelve Interviews, 1980; Rough and Rowdy Ways: The Life and Hard Times of Edward Anderson, 1988; At Macon Sumerlin Wordsuite, co-Ed, 1982; Plus stories, poems, reviews etc in periodicals. *Memberships:* Western Lit Assn; West Tex Historical Assn; Tex Folklore Soc; The Episcopal Ch, US. *Hobbies:* Reading; Chess. *Address:* Box 636, McMurray University, Abilene, TX 79697, USA. 7, 30.

BENSON Betty B, b. Lafayette, Alabama, USA. Tchr, Cnslr, Lectr, Author. m Clifford Benson, 9 Sept 1972, 2 s. *Education:* Studies in Psychology, Metaphysics, Relig, Econs, Bus; Credentials in Relig studies and Metaphysics. *Appointments:* Med Asst, Sec, Schl Sec, Pres of non-profit org; Countless hours of work for humanitarian causes. *Publications:* Articles; Creator of Honey Hugger, Doll for unconditional love and world peace; currently working on book. *Memberships:* Assn of Unity Chs; Nat Assn for Female Execs; Global Family;

Sweet Adelines; Int Rsch Bd of Advsrs of ABI. *Honours:* Num awards, certificates, honours and medals and medals for winning regional and international competitions with chorus of Sweet Adelines Int. The other honours are for achievements and service. *Hobbies:* Singing, Gardening, Travelling, Reading, Writing, Creative Crafts. *Address:* 4083 Teale Avenue, San Jose, CA 95117, USA. 138.

BENYON Margaret, b. 29 Apr 1940. Artist; Holographer. m. Dr William Rodwell, 16 Mar 1974, 1 s. 1 d. *Education:* Dip FA Painting and Postgrad Year, Slade Sch Fine Art, Univ Col, London 1961-66. *Career:* Pioneered art holography in 1968; First solo holographic art show 1969; Profl Holographer for 23 years; 13 solo exhibitions and shown in 59 gp shows worldwide; Works in 15 pub collections incl: Victoria & Albert Mus, London; Australian Nat Gallery; Held arts fellowships in 3 univs, one Artist-in- Residence; Lectured in number countries. *Creative Works:* Published in 32 pubs, reviewed in 62 pubs; Interviewed on a number of world-service media progs; Holograms incl: Hot Air, 1970; Bird in Box, 1973; Solar Markers, 1979; White Rainbow, 1980; Tiresias, 1981; Conjugal Series, 1983; Tigirl, 1985; Cosmetic Series, 1986-91. *Memberships:* Fellow & Former Chair of Holography Gp, Royal Photographic Soc, UK; Mem Steering Com, First Intl Cong on Art in Holography; Edit Bd, First Holography Issue, Leonardo jour. *Honours:* Audrey Mellon Prize, 1964; Carnegie Trust Awd, 1972; Kodak Photographic Bursary, 1982; Calouste Gulbenkian Holography Awd, 1982; Agfa USA Best of Exhibition Awd, 1985; Shearwater Foun Holography Awd, USA for Artists who have provided the standard of excellence for the entire field, 1987. *Address:* Holography Studio, 40 Springdale Avenue, Broadstone, Dorset BH18 9EU, England. 171.

BENYON William, b. 17 Jan 1930, London, England. MP. m. Elisabeth Hallifax, 24 Aug 1957, 2 s. 3 d. *Education:* RNC Dartmouth. *Appointments:* Royal Navy 1947-57; Courtauld Ltd 1957-64; Self Employed 1964-; MP, 1970-1992. *Memberships:* Timber Growers UK, Adv Bo; Royal Agri Soc, Coun; Peabody Trust, Gov; Country Landowners Assn, Exec; Dominion Students Hall Trust, Gov; Reading Univ, Coun; Bradford Col, Gov; Order of Christian Unity, Treas. *Honour:* DL. *Hobbies:* Gardening; Historic houses & gardens. *Address:* Englefield House, Englefield, Berkshire RG7 5EN, England. 1.

BERENYI Denes, b. 26 Dec 1928, Debrecen. Res Prof; Physicist. m. Dr Elvira Bodor, 12 June 1956, 1 s. 1 d. *Education:* Dipl Physics 1953, PhD 1959, L Kossuth Univ, Debrecen; Cand Phys Sci 1963, Dr Sci 1971, Hung Acad of Sci, Budapest. *Appointments:* Doctoral Fellow, Inst for Exp Phys, Kossuth Univ, Debrecen 1952-54; Res Fellow 1952-63, Department Hd, Div Nucl Spectroscopy 1963-, Inst of Nucl Spectroscopy (ATOMKI); Dep Dir, same inst 1974-, Dir 1976-90, Res Prof 1991-. *Publications:* Over 250 pubs mainly in intl jours, additionally compiled works, ednl and popularizing papers and books. *Memberships:* Corresp mem 1973, Ord mem 1985, VP, Comm mem of Phys Comm of HAS, Hung Acad Sci; Div Mem, Hung UNESCO Comm; Mem Coun, Roland Eotvos Phys Soc, Hungary; Corresp mem, Ettore Majorana Centre, Erice, Italy; Pres, Intl Sci Comm on X-ray and Inner Shell Proc Conf 1990-93; VP IRPS. *Honours:* Acad Awds, HAS 1963, 1969; Selenyi Awd 1965; Medal of Roland Eotvos Phys Soc 1981; Govt Hons 1964, 1980; State Awd 1988. *Hobbies:* Literature; History. *Address:* Institute of Nuclear Research of Hungarian Academy of Sciences, ATOMKI, Debrecen, P O Box 51, H-4001 Hungary.

BERGHOLM Ernst Tauno Herman, b. 21 Mar 1935, Helsinki. Baron of Amida; Arch; Company Dir; Author. m. (1)Kerstin Sanden, 25 Mar 1955, 2 d. (2)Ulla-Maija Kanerva, 14 Mar 1975, 2 d. (3)Alli Anneli Hartikka, 22 Jan 1982. *Education:* Grad Arch, also advanced dipl, Can 1957. *Appointments:* Arch Sweden, 1953-54, 1960-64, Can 1956-59; Owner, Pres Bergholm & Co,

Helsinki 1964-; Works incl hosps, sch, chs, residential bldgs in sev countries. *Publications:* Anor till Sofia Fleming friherrinna af Liebelitz, 1971; Suomesta saksittua, 1976; Prinkkalan moniste eli Suomen kansan historia, 1976; Kasikirjaperhetalouden eri aloilta, 1985. *Contributions:* arts to var pubs; Writer TV and radio progs; Chmn or Bd Dirs sev cos, Finland, Liechtenstein. *Honours:* Decorated Knight Comdr, Order Holy Sepulchre; Recip Grand Medal, Order Cultural Merit, Grand Cross, Order of Sports Merit, Highest Medal of Honour VACRS, 1st class Social Svc Order, Repub of China; Grand Cross Tunghai Order Friendship, Knight of Merit, Order Cross of Constantin the Gt, Imperial House Order of Merit of Angelo- Comneno Dynasty, Plaque of Merit Finnish Anti-Aircraft Sch 1955; Citation, Tunghai Univ; Key to City of Taipei 1983; Silver Medal of Merit Cen Ch Commerce 1985. *Memberships:* Humanist Soc Finland, Fdr Bd Dirs 1969-70; Finland-Liechtenstein Soc, Fdr Pres 1977-85, Hon Pres 1985-; Geneal Soc Finland, Life; Also Bd Dirs sev Finnish Assns & Socs. *Hobbies:* Genealogy; Music; Writing. *Address:* P O Box 159, SF-00141 Helsinki, Finland. 43.

BERGMAN Howard, b. 3 Nov 1945, Montreal. Doctor. m. 5 Jan 1976, 1 s.1 d. *Education:* BSc 1967, MDCM 1969, McGill Univ; Cert 1986, Col Family Physicians of Canada; Specialist Cert in Geriatric Med 1987, Corporation Profl des Medecins du Quebec. *Appointments include:* Asst Prof, Depts Family Med & Med, McGill Centre for Studies on Ageing, McGill Univ 1986; Dir Community Geriatric Assessment Unit 1988, Dir, Div Geriatric Medicine 1991, Sir Mortimer B Davis-Jewish Gen Hosp, Montreal, 1992-acting co-dir, Division of Geriatric Medicine, Dept of Med, McGill Univ. *Publications:* 13 peer-reviewed papers; 3 chapts in books; 16 abstracts; 4 manuscripts submitted; 7 reviews; 7 other pubs. *Memberships:* Corp Profl des Medecins du Quebec; Fed des Medecins Specialistes du Quebec; Col of Family Physicians of Canada; Soc Quebecoise de Geriatrie; Am Geriatrics Soc; Candn Assn on Gerontology; Assn Quebecoise de Gerontologie; Candn Soc Geriatric Med; Mem many coms and bd dirs. *Honours:* Scarlet Key Hon Soc, McGill Univ 1968; Edit Bd Candn J of Geriatrics 1991. *Hobbies:* Sports; Literature; Quebecoise culture. *Address:* Division of Geriatric Medicine, Sir Mortimer B Davis-Jewish General Hospital, 3755 Cote Ste Catherine, Montreal, Quebec, Canada H3T 1E2.

BERGNER Heinz, b. 30 Apr 1936, Berlin. Chair Eng Lang & Medieval Lit. m. Ilse Schneider, 4 Aug 1964, 1 s. *Education:* Stud of Eng & Romance Philology, Univ Erlangen, Sheffield 1956-61; Tchrs' Tng Col, Bamberg 1961-63. *Appointments:* Asst of Eng Philology, Univ Erlangen, Mannheim 1964-74; Chair, Univ Giessen 1974-. *Publications:* Books and arts on Brit drama and fiction, on medieval Eng dramatic, narrative and lyric art, on the linguistic structure of Eng texts. *Memberships:* Arthurian Soc; Intl Courtly Lit Soc; Intl Assn Prof of Eng; Soc Linguistica Europaea. *Hobbies:* Art history; Archaeology; Music. *Address:* Fohnbachstr 52, D-6301 Wettenberg 1, Germany. 52, 154.

BERGQUIST Nils Robert, b. 7 Apr 1939, Uppsala, Sweden. Med Ofcr WHO. m. Annita Margith Elofsson, 27 May 1966, 1 s. 1 d. *Education:* MD 1967, PhD 1974, Cert Clin Immunology 1979, Karolinska Inst, Stockholm. *Appointments:* Lab Physician, Natl Bact Lab, Stockholm 1967-71, 1972- 74; Res Asst Prof Microbiol, State Univ NY at Buffalo 1971-72; Acting Prof & Chmn Dept Immunology, Karolinska Inst, Stockholm 1974-75; Dir, Armaur Hansen Res Inst, Addis Abbaba, Ethiopia 1975-76; Sr Lab Phys, NBL 1976-85; Sr Civil Servant, WHO 1985-; Swedish Navy Reserve Corps 1973-. *Contributions:* over 100 arts to intl sci jours, mainly on microbiol topics, spec Schistosomiasis, tropical med. *Memberships:* Swedish Soc Med; NY Acad Scis; Am Soc Tropical Med & Hygiene. *Hobbies:* Orchid growing; Gastronomy; Motor yachting; Reading-novels & science. *Address:* Division of Control of Tropical Diseases (CTD), World Health Organisation, 1211 Geneva 27, Switzerland.

BERINSKI Sergei, b. 14 Apr 1946, Novie Kaushany, Moldova. Composer. m. Ella Berinskaja, 22 July 1966, 2 d. *Education:* Grad from Gnesin Inst, Fac Composing 1975. *Creative Works:* Requiem, cannonic text, 1979; Symphony, To Orpheus, 1982; 14 Concertos for different instruments, 1980-92; Compositions for different chamber ensembles; Chamber music for voices, with poetry of Russian and Western poets; Music for films and theatrical productions. *Memberships:* Union of Composers of USSR, 1979-; ECC (European Culture Club), Moscow. *Hobbies:* Music journalism; Literature. *Address:* Studencheskaja str 44/28 flat 120, 121165 Moscow, Russia.

BERINSKY Lev, b. 6 Apr 1939, Kaushani, Bessarabia. Poet. m. Marina Antipova, 22 May 1965, 1 s, 2 d. *Education:* BA, Lit Inst Gorky, Moscow, 1965-70; High Course of Yiddish and Yiddish Lit, Lit Inst, Moscow, 1981-83. *Appointment:* Profl Man of Lit working at home according to contracts, 1974-. *Publications:* Yiddish: A Book of Poems, Der Zuniker Weltboi (The sun building world); transl to Russian from Yiddish; Verses and Prose by Mark Shagal; Isaac Bashevis Singer -- Stories; Haim Nachman Byalik, poems; Dora Teitelboem, poems. *Honour:* Literature Prize of Hersh Segal by Association of Yiddish Writers in Israel. *Hobby:* Kindererziehung. *Address:* Association of Yiddish Writers for Berinsky Lev, Str Dov Hos 30, Tel Aviv, Israel.

BERKOV Valery Pavlovich, b. 11 Aug 1929, Leningrad. Prof; Lexicographer; Translator. m. Mariya Frolova, 5 Nov 1953, 2 d. *Education:* Dr Philol 1971, Univ Leningrad. *Appointments:* Asst Prof 1951, Lectr 1959, Prof 1973, Hd of Scand Studies Depart 1978, Univ Leningrad. *Publications:* 8 books incl: Russian-English Dictionary of Winged Words, 1984, 1988; Russian-Norwegian Dictionary, 1987; Modern Germanic Languages 9, 1991; About 100 arts on Norwegian and Icelandic linguistics, general linguistics; Translations of Norwegian and Icelandic belles-lettres into Russian. *Membership:* The Norwegian Acad Sci & Letters 1988. *Honour:* 1st Prize of Soviet Union Ed Dept for Best Sci Paper, 1988. *Hobbies:* Sports-previously mountaineering, now jogging & skiing. *Address:* B Okhtinsky Pr 6-196, 195027 St Petersburg, Russia.

BERLANDT Herman. Editor; Pubr; Poet; Tchr; Producer; Filmmaker; Lectr; Dir; Admin. *Career:* Edit & Pubr: Three Penny Poets, newsletter, 1961-65; Anthology of Underground Poetry, Poets' Commune Publications 1969-71; SF Poetry Marathon, 4 anthologies 1981-84; Peace or Perish-A Crisis Anthology, 1984; Poetry: San Francisco, renamed Poetry: USA, 1987, a quarterly for bold and compassionate poetry, 1985-90; Soviet Poetry since Glasnost, tabloid anthology of younger Soviet poets 1985-90, 1990; Mozart: Contemporary Tributes, 1991; Teacher: Conducted 24 workshops of Word Magic and the Power of Language, 1985-91; Producer: Intl Poetry Festival, III Tchrs' Col in Chcgo, 1965; TheUnderground Poetry Festival, Museum of Modern Art, Berkeley, 1971; 26 other Festivals and Marathons 1975-90; Coord of Poetry Programs for San Francisco Arts Comm Civic Centre Fair and San Francisco City & County Fairs, 1981-85; Initiated annual 10 day National Poetry Week festival 1987-91; Produced the literary component of San Francisco's Mozart And His Time celebration, 1991; Filmmaker: Produced 27 poetry-films; Featured Filmmaker and Poet at 60th Annual Poet's Dinner in Berkeley, CA before 300 poets, 1986; Lectr: Conducted lecture & demonstration tours of poetry-films at 15 Calif cols and in Canada, 1980-82; Lectr'd on poetry-films with demonstrations at 2nd Convention of the World of Poetry in Orlando, Fla, 1986; Hosted over 500 live progs at Fort Mason covering a wide range of poetry themes, 1979-90; Repeated the Uniting the World Through Poetry series 1991; Established the Poetry-Film Festival Workshop 1979-86; Fdr, Chmn of Bd Dirs, National Poetry Assn Inc 1987-91. *Publications:* 6 books of poetry incl: Yu-Me Love Songs, 1988; A Musical Offering, 1990. *Address:* National Poetry Association, 2nd Flr Bldg D Fort Mason Centre, San Francisco, CA 94123, USA.

BERMAN Marcelo Samuel, b. 10 Apr 1945, Buenos Aires. Univ Prof; Physicist; Cosmologist. m. Geni Lima Berman, 21 June 1986, 1 s. 1 d. *Education:* EE-ITA, Brazil; MSc in Physics 1981, ITA, Brazil; Dr Sc in Physics 1988, UFRJ, Brazil. *Appointments:* Mng Ptnr, Plati-Tact 1974- 79; Ptnr, Constr Gustavo Berman 1980-88; Furj-Prof of Maths 1986-90, CNPQ Scholar, Univ of Florida, Dept of Astronomy, 1989-90, Adj Asst Prof 1991, Univ Alabama. *Publications:* 3 books, 40 Sci Arts and 45 papers in refereed internaitonal journals. *Memberships:* Int Astn Union; IEEE, Sr mem; NYAS, Active mem; AAS; APS; AAPT; AAAS; Brazilian Physical Soc. *Hobby:* Physics. *Address:* Rua Candidoo Hartman, 575 - ap 17, 80730, Cunitiba PR, Brazil. 52.

BERMAN Marlene Oscar, b. 21 Nov 1939, Philadelphia, PA. Prof Neurol & Psychi; Res Psycho. m. div, 1 s. *Education:* MA 1964, Bryn Mawr Col; PhD 1968, Univ Connecticut; Post-doc, Harvard Univ 1968-70. *Appointments:* Instr Psycho, Harvard Univ Ext Sch, Cambridge 1970-76; Res Psycho, Boston VA Med Ctr, Boston 1970-; Affil Prof Psycho, Clark Univ, Worcester 1973-; Prof Neurol & Psychi, BU Sch Med, Boston 1981-. *Publications:* Author 3 book chapts; Approx 70 jour arts. *Memberships:* Acad Aphasia; Fellow, Mass Psycho Assn; Fellow, Am Psycho Assn; NY Acad Scis; Soc for Neurosci; Mem & Nat Lectr, Soc for Sigma Xi. *Honours:* Grant recip, US Dept Veterans Affairs, 1970-; Clin Investigator Awd, US Vet Administration; Res Career Devel Awd, US Pub Health Serv NINCDS 1976-81; Natl Lectr, Sigma Xi Hon Soc 1980, 1981; Res Scist Devel Awd, US Pub Health Ser NIAAA, 1981-86; Awd Recip, Fulbright Foun Sr Scholar Awd (Australia), 1991. *Hobbies:* Jogging; Bicycling; Travel; Photography. *Address:* B U Medical Centre & Boston VA Medical Centre, 85 E Newton St, M-902, Boston, MA 02118, USA. 2, 5, 6.

BERNARDI Paola, b. 21 May 1930, Vicenza. Harpsichordist; Musicologist; Tchr. m. 4 July 1959, 1 s. 1 d. *Education:* Piano Dipl 1946, Milan Conservatory; Choir Music & Direction Dipl 1957, Harpsichord Dipl 1961, Rome Conservatory. *Appointments:* Chair of Harpsichord, Bologna Conservatory 1965-80; Chair of Harpsichord, Rome Sta Cecilia Conservatory 1980-; Many harpsichord concerts & recordings 1961-; Prof a contratto, Univ dell'Aquila 1989. *Creative Works:* Critical editions of harpsichord music of Alessandro Felici, Giovanni Battista Martini, Pietro Alessandro Guglielmi (Quartets & Sonatas); Critical edition of Damenico Corri's Treatise. *Memberships:* Assn Claricembalistica Bolognese, Pres 1972-; Edit Dir 1985- ; Intl Musicological Soc; IASA; IRTEM, Counsellor. *Address:* Via Montecristo 10, 00141 Roma, Italy.

BERNDT Jane Ann, b. 24 May 1954, Portsmouth, Ohio. Instr. 1 s. *Education:* BS 1977, MEd 1985, Ohio Univ; ABD (Doctoral Candidate) 1989, West Va Univ; Doctoral Student, The George Wash Univ. *Appointments:* Tchr, Friendship Elem Sch, OH 1977-79; Physical Sci & Math Tchr, Griswold HS, Cleveland 1982-83; Tchr, Andrew Jackson Middle Sch, Md 1985-86; Grad Asst, Curriculum & Instruction, Ohio Univ 1983-84; Grad Tchg Asst, Supvr Student Sci Tchrs, West Va Univ 1986-89; Fifth Grade Tchr, Takoma (open space) Sch, Wash DC 1989-90; Instr, Profl/Ed courses, Ohio Univ Br Campus 1991. *Publications:* ERIC Submitted Documents; Moral & Spiritual Development in the Adolescent; Interdisciplinary Science; Creativity, Inspiration & Reality. *Memberships:* Assn for Supervision & Curriculum Devel; NY Acad Scis; Centre for Study of Presidencies; NY Acad Politic Sci. *Honour:* Phi Kappa Phi, 1988. *Hobbies:* Hiking; Walking; Reading; Swimming; Canoeing; Travelling; Nature lore. *Address:* 1718 Franklin Avenue, Portsmouth, OH 45662, USA. 15.

BERNHEIM Alain, b. 23 May 1931, Paris XVII. Historian. *Education:* Bach es lettres 1947, Lycee Janson de Paris; 1st Prize for Piano 1953, Conservatoire Nat de Musique de Paris; Artist's Dipl 1953, New England Conservatory of Music, Boston. *Career:* 2000 concerts and piano recitals 1951-81. *Publications:* Over 50 papers publ in masonic historical pubs 1967-; Edit, Masonica, GRA. *Memberships:* or Corresp mem following masonic lodges (or gps) of res: Villard de Honnecourt, Paris; Quatuor Coronati Nr 808, Bayreuth; Freimaurerische Vereinigung Frederik, Flensburg; Quatuor Coronati 2076, London; Lodge No CC, Dublin; Groupe de Recherche Alpina (GRA), Lausanne. *Honour:* Norman B Spencer Awd 1986 from Quatuor Coronati odge No 2976, London. *Hobby:* Bridge. *Address:* Stemmerstrasse 91, CH-8238 Busingen, Switzerland.

BERNIER Bernard, b. 15 July 1942, Levis, QC, Canada. Prof Anthropology. m. Chantal Kirsch, 21 Oct 1975, 1 s. *Education:* BA 1962, MA studies 1962-64, Univ Laval; MA studies 1964-65, Univ Brit Columbia; Doctoral studies in Anthropology 1965-70, PhD in Anthropology 1970, Cornell Univ. *Appointments:* Asst Prof 1970-75; Assoc Prof, Univ Montreal 1975- 80; Dir d'Etudes, EHESS, Paris 1983-84; Dir, Cen for East Asian Studies 1984- 85, Prof Anthropology 1980-, Univ Montreal. *Publications:* Books: Capitalisme, societe et culture au Japon, 1988; Breaking the Cosmic Circle, Folk Religion in Japan, 1975; Edit, Le Japon face a l'Internationalisation, 1988; Edit, Le Japon Culture de l'Economie de la Culture, 1990. *Membership:* Am Anthropological Assn; Assn for Asian Studies; Candn Asian Studies Assn; Candn Anthropology Soc; Candn Assn for Japanese Studies. *Honours:* Bobbs-Merrill Awd in Anthropology, 1967; Canada-Japan Book Awd, 1989. *Hobbies:* Reading; Gardening; Tennis; Painting. *Address:* Department of Anthropology, Universite de Montreal, CP 6128, Succursale A, Montreal, Quebec, Canada H4C 3J7. 142.

BERRY Donald Kent, b. 29 Apr 1953, Gary, Indiana. Assoc Prof Religion. m. Sally Ann Howard, 11 Aug 1972, 2 s. *Education:* BA 1975, Kentucky Wesleyan Col; M Div 1978, PhD 1990, Srn Baptist Theol Seminary. *Appointments:* Pastor, Zion Baptist Ch, Reynolds Station, Kentucky, 1978-83; Assoc Prof Religion, Mobile Col 1987-. *Publications:* Diss: The Psalms and Their Readers: Interpretive Strategies for Psalm 18, 1992; Introduction to Wisdom and Poetry, 1993. *Memberships:* Soc Biblical Lit; Nat Assn Baptist Profs of Religion; Am Assn Univ Profs; Christus Inst, Chair Worship Comm, Mem Adv Bd. *Honours:* Robertson Religion Awd for combined ch related and acad achmt, Ky Wesleyan Col 1974, 1975. *Hobbies:* Wilderness sports & recreation; Basketball; The Fine Arts. *Address:* University of Mobile, PO Box 13220, Mobile, AL 36663, USA. 7.

BERRY Lemuel Jr, b. 11 Oct 1946, Oneonta, NY. Dean. 2 s. *Education:* BA Mus Ed 1969, Livingstone Col; MA Mus Ed 1970, PhD Mus Ed 1973, Univ Iowa. *Appointments:* Fayetteville St Univ 1973-76; Langston Univ 1976-83; Alabama St Univ 1983-86; Mercy Col 1986-88; Memphis St Univ 1988-90; Dean, Sch of Humanities & Social Scis, Va St Univ 1990-. *Publications:* Book: Biographical Dictionary of Black Musicians and Black Music Educators, 1981; Perspectives in Jazz, 1990; Essays on Popular Music, 1990. *Memberships:* Popular Culture Assn; Fulbright Adv Bd, Southern Conf on Afro-Am Studies; Assn of Intl Ed Administrators; Coun for Res in Music Ed; Natl Assn of Col Wind & Percussion Instructors; Am Anthropological Assn; Virginia Council of Colleges of Arts and Sciences, the Atlantic Council of the United States, National Association for African American Studies. *Honour:* German Academic Res Scholar 1980. *Hobby:* Collecting baseball cards. *Address:* P O Box 2247, Petersburg, VA 23803, USA. 2, 4, 7, 15, 117, 154.

BERRY OTTAWAY Peter, b. 17 Feb 1942, Derby, England. Intl Conslt in Food Sci & Tech; Company Dir. m. Andrea Sampson, 21 Dec 1963, 2 s. 2 d. *Education:* London Univ, Univ Col of Rhodesia & Nyasaland 1961-63; BSc (London); Chartered Biologist (C.Biol); Mem Inst Biol. *Appointments:* Res Biol, WHO/Zambian Govt,

Zambia 1963-65; Res Mgmt Food Ind, Unilever & Gen Foods, Europe 1965-74; Intl Conslt, Food Sci, Tech & Nutrition 1974-. *Publications:* Books, Food for Sport, 1985; Nutrition in Sport, co- Author, 1986; Preservatives in Food, 1988; Nutritional Enhancement of Food, co-author, 1989; Vitamins in Food, 1992; Num papers & arts. *Memberships:* Fellow, Inst Food Sci & Tech; Fellow, Royal Soc Health; Royal Inst Pub Health and Hygiene; Sports Nutrition Foun, Coun mem & Treas. *Honour:* C'Wealth Scholarship 1964. *Hobbies:* Light aviation; Art; Hill walking. *Address:* Nesscliffe House, Plough Lane, Hereford HR4 OEL, Egland.

BERRYMAN Treva Ann Griffith, b. 19 July 1952, Martin, Tennessee. Dietitian; Nutritionist. m. Hugh E Berryman, 14 Aug 1971, 1 s. 1 d. *Education:* BS in Home Ec Ed, minor in Nutrition 1974; MS in Food Systems Admin, minor in Home Ec Ed 1975, Univ Tenn; P-time Student in Doctoral Prog, Memphis State Univ in Higher Ed 1989-. *Appointments:* Area Supvr, Tng Dir, Shoney's 1975-79; Admin Asst, Col Home Ec, UT Knoxville 1979-80; Asst Dir Food & Nutrition Ser 1981-82, Dir 1983-86, Bowld Hosp, UT Memphis; Dir Auxiliary Admin, UT Memphis 1986-88; Res Nutritionist, Staff Asst, UT Memphis Med Sch 1988-. *Publications:* Nutrition: You and Baby Too, rapmusic video for nutrition ed during pregnancy; Nutrition for Building Better Babies, video for ed during pregnancy; Ednl pamphlets. *Memberships:* Bd Dietitian/Nutritionist Examiners, State Licensure; TN Dietetic Assn, Chair elect, Coun on Practice 1989, Chair, Coun on Practice, 1989, State Meeting Chair, 1988; Memphis District Assn, Pres elect 1984, Pres 1985, Chair elect, Coun on Practice 1990, Chair 1991; Am Bus Women's Assn, local chapt, Pres 1982, Secy 1988; Memphis Area Nutrition Coun, Program Chair 1990. *Honours:* Am Bus Women's Assn, local chapt, Woman of the Year 1986; Memphis District Dietetic Assn, Outstanding Dietition of the Year 1990. *Hobbies:* Baking bread; Collecting Victorian glass and antiques; White water rafting; 4-H activities and scout events with her children. *Address:* 853 Jefferson, E-100 Crump, Memphis, TN 38103, USA.

BERTHOLD Werner Horst Erich, b. 15 Sept 1923, Leipzig. Emeritus Prof; Historian. m. Regina Lebe, 6 Sept 1960, 2 s. *Education:* Apprenticeship as Lithographer 1938-40; Workers' and Farmers' Fac 1948-50; Study of History and Philosophy 1950-54; Res Asst 1956-59; PhD 1960; Habilitation 1967; Prof 1969; DSc 1971. *Appointments:* Lithographer, Painter 1938-41; Trad, Wehimacht, 194-44, Prisoner-of-War 1947-48; Lectr Evening Classes 1954-56; Aspirant 1956-59; Asst Sr Lectr and Lectr 1960-69; Prof, Chair Leader, Prodecan (Dean), Team Leader History of Social Scis 1978-89, Prof Emeritus 1989-, all at Univ Leipzig. *Publications:* Author books incl: Zur Entstehung und politischen Funktion der Geschichtsideologie, 1960; Marxistisches Geschichtsbild, 1970; Zur Geschichte der Geschichtswissenschaft vom Altertum, 1989; Co-Author, Co-Edit: Kritik der bürgerlichen Geschichtsschreibung, 1970; Zur Geschichte der Marxistischen Geschichtswissenschaft, 1986. *Contributions:* over 200 arts to profl jours. *Memberships:* Mem Comm for History of Historiography by Intl Com of Historical Scis; Mem, Karl.Lamprecht-Gesellschaft. *Honour:* Nat Prize State Coun, German Dem Repub 1979. *Hobbies:* Mushrooming; Cycling tours; Painting. *Address:* Str des 18 Oktober 8a/13, 0-7010 Leipzig, Germany. 52.

BERTIN Charles, b. 5 Oct 1919, Mons, Belgium. Poet; Novelist; Playwright. m. Colette Leblois, 9 June 1947, 1 s. 1 d. *Education:* Docteur en droit, Univ Bruxelles, 1942. *Appointments:* Barrister- at-Law 1942-47; Consltg Barrister 1947-52. *Publications:* Psaumes sans la Grace, poems, 1947; Don Juan, Theatre, 1947; Christophe Colomb, theatre, 1953; Le Roi Bonheur, theatre, 1966; Journal D'Un Crime, novel, 1961; Le Bel Age, novel, 1963; Les Jardins du Desert, novel, 1981; Le Voyage d'Hiver, novel, 1989. *Memberships:* Royal Acad 1967-; Pres, Belgian Com of the Societe des Auteurs; Officier de la Legion d'Honneur; Grand Officier

de l'Ordre de la Couronne. *Honours:* Prix triennal de Litt dramatique 1948; Prix Italia 1953; Prix Rossel 1963; Grand Prix du Roman de la Soc des Gens de Lettres 1982; Prix Montaigne de la Fondation Schiller de Hamburg 1989. *Hobbies:* History of art; Travelling; Bridge. *Address:* 9 Avenue des Erables, 1640 Rhode-Saint-Genese, Belgium.

BERTINI Gary, b. 1 May 1927, Russia. Conductor. m. Rosette Berengole, 26 Nov 1956, 2 d. *Education:* Conservatorio G Verdi, Milan, 1947; Dip, Music Educ Coll, Tel Aviv, 1949; Conservatoire Nat Superieur de Musique, Paris, 1951-54; Jacques Chailley Dip, Institut de Musicologie, Sorbonne, Paris, 1954; Ecole Normale de Musique, Paris, 1955. *Appointments:* Music Dir, Israel Chmbr Orch, Israel Chmbr Opera, 1965- 75; Music Dir, Rinat, Israel Chmbr Choir, 1955-73; Prin Guest Conductor, Jerusalem Symph Orch, 1977-86; Music Advsr, Detroit Symph Orch, 1981-83; Artistic Dir, Israel Festival, 1976-83; Gen Dir and Music Dir, Frankfurt Opera, 1987-90; Chief Conductor, Cologne Radio Symph Orch, 1983-91; Artistic Advsr, New Israeli Opera, 1988-; Music Dir, Bat Sheva Dance Co, 1964-69; Prof, Tel Aviv Univ, 1978; Artistic Dir, New Israeli Opera, 1994-; Guest Conductor orchs worldwide. *Creative Works:* Chmbr Music, Symphonic Music, 50 scores for theatre plays, recordings. *Memberships:* Israel State Council of Culture; Bd Dirs, Israeli Music Inst; Bd Dirs, Israel Broadcasting Auth. *Honours:* Israel State Prize for Music, 1978; The ACUM Prize for Interpretation of Israeli Music (twice); Officer of the Order of Merit, Italy; Officer of the Order of Art and Letters, France. *Hobbies:* Dogs, Photography. *Address:* c/o Concerto Winderstein, Leopold Strasse No. 25, Munich 40, Germany. 52.

BERZINS Boriss, b. 7 Oct 1930, Riga, Latvia. Prof of Painting. m. Rasma Bruzite, 18 Apr 1972. *Education:* Riga Art Sch 1947-52; Latvian Acad Arts 1952-59, Prof 1987-. Mem Acad Arts of USSR 1989-. *Appointments:* Participant in exhibitions in Latvia, USSR, France, Germany, USA, Belgium and others 1956-; Tchr Painting, Latvian Acad Arts 1964-. *Creative Works:* Oil paintings: Still Life, 1970; Coffee Pot, 1976; Revellers, 1978; Sunday, 1980; Autumn, 1983; Artist and model, 1985; Sitting Woman, 1988. *Membership:* Artists' Union of Latvia. *Honours:* 2nd Prize at Intl Drawing Biennale in Eng, 1979, 3rd Prize 1983; People's Artist of Latvia, 1985. *Hobby:* Gardening. *Address:* 7a Jaunsaules str, apt 59, 226083 Riga, Latvia, Russia.

BEST Keith Lander, b. 10 June 1949, Brighton. Dir Prisoners Abroad; Barrister. m. Elizabeth Margaret Gibson, 28 July 1990. *Education:* Brighton Col; Keble Col, Oxford; BA (Hons); Jurisprudence; MA. *Appointments:* Barrister-at-Law 1971-87; MP 1979-87; Parliamentary Pvt Secy to Secy State for Wales 1981-84. *Publications:* Write Your Own Will, 1978; The Right Way to Prove a Will, 1980, revised 1991; Num polit arts. *Memberships:* Fellow, Royal Soc Arts; Chmn, Conservative Action for Electoral Reform; Chmn Exec Coms, World Federalist Movement and Assn World Federalists. *Honour:* Territorial Decoration 1982. *Hobbies:* Politics; Skiing; Walking; Cycling; Being useful. *Address:* 15 St Stephen's Terrace, London SW8 1DJ, England. 1.

BEST Roger Norman, b. 16 Apr 1949, Los Angeles, California. Real Estate Investment Mgmt; Mgmt Conslt. m. Sheri Lyn Kruyer, 16 Oct 1982. *Education:* BA in Mktg, Intl Bus & Bus Law 1971, Univ Wash, Seattle; Calif licensed real estate broker 1985-. *Appointments:* Musician & Entertainer 1963-69; Pres, Best Enterprises, Los Angeles 1969-; Hd Electronic Media Sers for Cedars-Sinai Med Ctr, Los Angeles 1971-73; Pres, Tazio Productions, Los Angeles 1973-76; VP, Video Disco & Assocs, joint venture with Tazio Prods, Los Angeles 1975-76; VP, DSL Construction Corp, Los Angeles 1977- 85; VP and Chf Operating Ofcr, Scott Properties Inc, founded by DSL Construction Corp, Los Angeles 1978-85; Pres & CEO, Tazio Properties Inc, Los Angeles

1980-. *Creative Works:* Invented correctable typewriter ribbon, 1970; Created original music video concept with Visual Music, 1974; Featured Columnist, Apartment Age magazine 1989-; Over 20 arts in profl pubs. *Membership:* Mem Van Nuys Airport Adv Coun, Calif 1987-. *Honours:* Citations of Appreciation from City of Los Angeles for Community Service 1988, 1989; Hon appt to Res Bd of Advs of ABI Inc 1990. *Hobbies:* Boating; Skiing; Flying; Camping; Target shooting. *Address:* Tazio Properties Inc, 3580 Wilshire Boulevard, Seventeenth Floor, Los Angeles, CA 90010, USA. 9, 52, 59, 132, 139.

BETHEL Robert George Hankin, b. 7 June 1948, London, England. MD. *Education:* Pembroke Col, Cambridge Univ 1966-69; St Mary's Hosp Med Sch, London 1969-72; BA (Hons) 1969; MB, B Chir 1972; MA (Cantab) 1973; MRCGP 1979. *Appointments:* Registrar, West Middx Univ Hosp, 1974-76; Part-time Rheumatologist 1976-92; Principal in GP 1977-; Hosp Practitioner, Geriatrics 1977-91; Course Tutor, The Open Univ 1979-80; Approved Tnr in GP, Oxford Region 1984-; Adv Edit, Horizons 1988-91; Assoc Tchr (GP), St Mary's Hosp Med Sch 1989-; Medical Mem, Independent Tribunal Service, 1992-. *Publications;* Clin & sci papers in var med jours, esp on Rheumatology and GP Topics. *Memberships:* Fellow, Royal Soc Med, mem Coun of GP Sect; Fellow, Royal Soc of Health; Mem Fac Bd, Southwest Thames, Royal Col of GPs; Mem, Executive Council, The Cambridge Soc, 1991-; Chmn, Cambridge Soc, Surrey; Freeman of City of London; Liveryman (Apothecaries); Mem Guild of Freemen and the United Wards' Club of City of London; Wandsman of St Paul's Cathedral; Vice-Chmn of Old Windsor Day Centre. *Honours:* Royal Col of GPs Astra Res Prize 1980; OLJ 1989; CLJ 1990. *Hobbies:* Genealogy; Books; Medical journalism. *Address:* Newton Court Medical Centre, Burfield Road, Old Windsor, Windsor, Berkshire SL4 2QF, England. 170.

BETHIN Christina Y, b. 12 Aug 1950, Rochester, NY. Assoc Prof of Slavic Linguistics. *Education:* BA 1972, Univ Rochester; MA 1974, PhD 1978, Univ Ill at Urbana-Champaign. *Appointments:* Lectr, Univ Va 1978- 79; Asst Prof 1979-85, Assoc Prof 1985-, SUNY at Stony Brook. *Publications:* Co-Author, Reading Polish I, 1985; Polish Syllables: the Role of Prosody in Phonology and Morphology, 1992; Arts in profl jours incl: Phonological rules in the Serbo-Croatian Genitive Plural, 1983; Polish Nasal Vowels, 1991; Syllable Final Laxing in Ukrainian, 1987; Syllable Structure and the Polish Imperative Desinence, 1987; The Syllable in Slavic: Evidence From Liquid Diphthongs, 1992. *Memberships:* Linguistic Soc of Am; Am Assn for Advancement of Slavic Studies; Am Assn of Tchrs of Slavic and East European Langs; Ukrainian Acad of Arts & Scis in the US; Phi Beta Kappa; Am Assn for Ukrainian Studies; Early Slavic Studies Assn. *Honours:* Intl Res & Exchanges Bd Grants 1977, 1990; SUNY Chancellor's Awd for Excellence in Tchg 1983; Endowment for the Humanities Sr Fellowship 1988-89. *Hobbies:* Reading; Oriental carpets. *Address:* Department of Germanic & Slavic Languages & Literatures, State University of New York at Stony Brook, Stony Brook, NY 11794, USA.

BETTER Fred Cyprian, b. 16 Sept 1920, Cieszyn, Poland. Med Practitioner. m. Irene, 7 Aug 1948, 1 d. *Education:* MD Phys & Rehab Med 1944, First Med Inst, Moscow, USSR; B Phys Ed 1946, Acad for Phys Ed & Sport, Warsaw, Poland. *Appointments:* Med Ofcr, Polish Army, USSR, Poland 1944-50; Lectr, Acad of Physical Ed & Sport, Warsaw 1950-55; Dept Physical & Rehab Med, First Surgical Clinic, Vienna, Austria 1956; Remedial Gymnast 1957-70, Hon Rehab Med Ofcr 1957-85, Hampton Hosp, Hampton, Victoria, Australia; Hon Rehab Med Ofcr, Prince Henry's Hosp, Melbourne, Australia 1970- 87; Med Dir 1984-87, Exec mem 1987, Pres 1979-80, Hon Secy, Nat Coun mem 1981- 86, Nat Secy 1986-88, Pres Elect 1989-90, Australian Sports Med Fed, Victorian Br, City Baths Sports Med Centre, Melbourne; Dir, Jr Sport Subcom and Bd mem, Victorian Sports Fed, Vicsport, 1984-89;

Mem Sports Coun of Victoria 1988; Dir of Rehab Sers, Florence Nightingdale Hosp, Brighton, Victoria 1987-1992; Pres, Australian Sports Med Fed 1991. *Publication:* A Simple Method for the Determination of Serum Heptoglobulins, Co-Author, 1960. *Memberships:* Australian Med Assn 1970; Australian Coun for Health, Physical Ed & Recreation 1957; Royal Australian Col of Gen Practitioners 1971; Australian Sports Med Fed 1957; Australian Assn of Physical and Rehab Med 1957-78. *Honours:* WWII: Polish Cross of Valor 1944-45; Silver Cross of Merit 1944-46, for participation in battles from Stalingrad to Warsaw; OAM 1985 for services to Australian Sports Med. *Address:* 7 Yuille Street, Brighton, Victoria 3186, Australia.

BETTISON Paul David, b. 18 Apr 1953, Preston, England, Mng Dir. m. Jean Margaret Bradshaw, 15 May 1976, 2 d. *Education:* Dipl in Bus Mgmt, Guildford Col. *Appointments:* Mem Mgmt, Rockwell Graphic Systems 1978-87; Mng Dir, Graphic Systems Intl Ltd 1987-; Dir, Factistel Ltd 1988-; Dir, Tolerans Ingol (UK) Ltd 1990-; Dir, Topefa Ltd 1990-. *Membership:* F Inst SMM 1979. *Hobbies:* Travel; Cars; Wine; Flying. *Address:* Longdown House, Mickle Hill, Little Sandhurst, Camberley, Surrey GU17 8QL, England.

BETZER Peter Robin, b. 14 May 1942, Delavan, Wisconsin. Chmn; Prof Marine Sci. m. Dr Susan Beers Betzer, 18 June 1965, 2 d. *Education:* BA Geol 1964, Lawrence Univ; PhD Oceanography 1971, Univ RI. *Appointments:* Lab Instr, Univ RI 1970-71; Asst Prof 1971-75, Assoc Prof 1975-79, Prof 1979-83, Chair & Prof 1983-, Univ S Fla, Dept Marine Sci. *Publications include:* Book Chapt, Seasonal patterns in suspended calcium carbonate concentrations during the dry and wet seasons in the eastern Caribbean, co-author, 1977; Arts in sci jours incl (Co-Author): The oceanic carbonate system: a reassessment of biogenic controls, 1984; Acantharian fluxes and strontium to chlorinity ratios in the north Pacific Ocean, 1987; Long range transport of giant mineral aerosol particles, 1988; In-situ holographic imaging of settling particles: applications for individual particle dynamics and oceanic flux measurements, 1989. *Memberships:* Am Assn for Advancement of Sci; Am Geophys Union; Am Inst Chems; Fla Inst of Oceanography Adv Bd; Res Consortium of St Petersburg; St Petersburg C of C; UNOLS Coastal Vessel Sub-Com. *Honours include:* Invited Speaker at sev conf & meetings; Recip Dist'd Authorship Awd for Factors influencing the degree of saturation of the surface and intermediate waters of the North Pacific Ocean with respect to aragonite, US Dept Commerce, NOAA, 1985; Elected Fellow, Am Inst Chemists, 1986; Guest Edit, J of Geophys Res, for special volume dealing with the physical/biol production in the equatorial Pacific, 1991; Selected as one of ten most influential people in Tampa Bay Area by Maddux Report, 1991. *Hobbies:* Master's League swimming; Music; Playing the piano. *Address:* University of South Florida, Department of Marine Science, 140 Seventh Avenue South, St Petersburg, FL 33701, USA 143.

BEVAN Richard Justin William, b. 21 Apr 1922, St Harmon, Radnorshire. The Rev Canon. m. Sheila Rosemary Barrow, 4 Sept 1949, 4 sons (1 dec). 1 d. *Education:* St Augustine's Col, Canterbury 1939; Univ of Durham 1945; PhD 1980, Columbia Pacific Univ; PhD 1989, Greenwich Univ, USA. *Appointments:* Asst Curate, Stoke-on-Trent 1945-49; Chaplain, Aberlour, Scotland 1949-51; Asst Master, Burnley Tech HS 1951-60; Chaplain to Durham Univ, Rector of St Mary le Bow, Vicar of St Oswald's, Durham 1961-74; Rector of Grasmere 1974-82; Canon of Carlisle Cathedral 1982-89, Treas & Librarian 1982-89, Vice-Dean 1986-89; Chaplain to HM The Queen 1986-. *Publications:* Steps to Christian Understanding, Ed, 1958; The Churches and Christian Unity, Ed, 1964; Unfurl the Flame, poems, 1978; A Twig of Evidence: Does Belief in God Make Sense?, 1986. *Memberships:* Victory Services' Club, London 1988-; Pres, Fdr Mem, Grasmere Village Soc 1976; Gov, St Chad's Col, Durham 1969-89; VP, Friends of St Chad's Col 1990-; Convenor of Chaplains, Durham

Univ 1966-74; Mem local com, Dove Cottage, 1974-82. *Honours:* Univ Durham: Bishop Robertson Divinity Prize, 1945; Capel Cure Prize, 1945. *Hobbies:* Poetry reading; Train travel; Classics; The Philosophers. *Address:* Beck Cottage, Burgh-by-Sands, Carlisle CA5 6BT, Cumbria. 1.

BEVAN-THOMAS Philip Morgan, b. 2 Dec 1934, Hove, Sussex, England. Solicitor. m. Janet Mary Ward, 18 June 1962, 2 s. *Education:* Cheltenham Col 1948-53; St Edmund Hall, Oxford 1955-58. *Appointments:* Qualified Barrister 1960; Qualified Solicitor 1963; Herbert Smith Co 1963; Francis & Parkes 1963-86; Field Seymour Parkes 1987-. *Memberships:* Law Soc; Pres, Berks, Bucks, Oxon Law Soc 1982-83; Dir, Solicitors Benevolent Assn; Chmn, No 3 area Legal Aid Bd; Chmn, Shiplake Parish Coun 1985. *Hobbies:* Golf; Sailing; Member Leander Club; Sea View Yacht Club; Huntercombe Golf Club; Phyllis Court Club. *Address:* The Moorings, Wharfe Lane, Henley-on-Thames RG9 2LL, England.

BEWES Richard Thomas, b. 1 Dec 1934, Nairobi, Kenya. Min of Religion. m. Elisabeth Ingrid Jaques, 18 Apr 1964, 2 s. 1 d. *Education:* MA 1961, Emmanuel Col, Cambridge; Ridley Hall Theol Col, Cambridge 1957-59. *Appointments:* Asst Curate, Christ Church, Beckenham 1959-65; Vicar, St Peter's, Harold Wood, Essex 1965-74; Vicar, Emmanuel Ch, Northwood, Middx 1974-83; Rector, All Souls, Langham Place, London 1983-. *Publications:* God in Ward 12, 1973; Advantage Mr Christian, 1975; Talking About Prayer, 1979; The Pocket Handbook of Christian Truth, 1981; John Wesley's England, 1981; The Church Reaches Out, 1981; The Church Overcomes, 1983; On the Way, 1984; Quest for Life, 1985; Quest for Truth, 1985; The Church Marches On, 1986; When God Surprises, 1986; The Resurrection-Fact or Fiction?, 1989; A New Beginning, 1989. *Memberships:* Guild of Brit Songwriters, 1975; UK Chmn, African Enterprise; Chmn, The Church of England Evangelical Council, 1992-. *Honours:* Freedom of the City of Charlotte, NC, USA 1984; Prebendary of St Paul's Cathedral, London 1988. *Hobbies:* Tennis; Broadcasting; Reading; Writing. *Address:* All Souls Church, 2 All Souls Place, London W1N 3DB, England. 1.

BHARADWAJ Tapobroto, b. 1 Mar 1935, Tripura, Bengal. Nuclear Power Engr. m. Jharna Chowdhury, 5 Aug 1962, 2 s. 1 d. *Education:* Grad Engr in Mech Engrg 1956, Bengal Engrg Col, Shibpur, Univ Calcutta. *Appointments:* Trainee Engr, Chittaranjan Locomotive Works, West Bengal 1956-57; Res Fellow, Bengal Engrg Col, Calcutta 1957-58; Design Engr, Kuljian Corp, Calcutta 1958-60, Phila 1960-62; Project Engr, Develop Cons Pvt Ltd, Calcutta 1962-, Kuljian Corp, San Jose, Calif 1965-66; Chf Engr, Develop Cons Pvt Ltd, Bombay 1968-75, Puerto-Ordaz Venezuela 1975-78; Exec Dir, Develop Cons Ltd Calcutta, current. *Memberships:* Active in Salt Lake EC Block Assn, Calcutta; AAAS; Confed of Engrg Ind (C of C), Calcutta; Indian Nuclear Soc. *Hobbies:* Travel; Religion. *Address:* Development Consultants Limited, 24-B Park Street, Calcutta 700 016, India. 52.

BHARGAVA Ashok, b. 1 July 1943, Agra, India. Prof of Econs. m. Deviyani J Bhatt, 11 June 1970, 2 s, 1 d. *Education:* BA (Hons) Econs 1963, MA Econs 1965, Univ of Delhi; MS 1969, PhD 1975, Univ of WI, USA. *Appointments:* Siri Ram Coll of Commerce, Delhi, 1965-66; Prof 1980, Chmn 1981-87, Dir, Ctr for Bus & Mgmt Servs 1989-91, Univ of WI, Whitewater. *Publications:* Ed, Studies in the Indian Economy, 1984; Ed, Indian Economic Studies, 1985. *Memberships:* Chairperson, Assn of Indian Econ Studies, 1989-91, Sec-Treas 1981-89; Sec, Assn of Managerial Econs; Assn of Asian Studies; Eastern Econ Assn; Acad of Int Bus; American Econ Assn. *Honours:* Best Undergraduate Student in Economics, University of Delhi, 1963; 1st Prize Poverty Eradication Foundation, 1987 (with Dr Rashmi Luthra); University Service Award, University of Wisconsin-

Whitewater, 1992. *Hobbies:* Dir at Large, India Dev Serv, 1978-; Treas, Combat Blindness Fndn, Madison, WI; Sec, Gov's Coun on Asian Affairs; Mbr, Minority Bus Dev Fin Bd, WI; Squash, Volunteer Work. *Address:* 4806 Waukesha Street, Madison, WI 53705, USA. 2, 8, 132.

BHARGAVA Pushpa Mittra, b. Ajmer, Rajasthan. CSIR Dist'd Fellow. m. Edith Manorama Patrick, 1958, 2 d. *Education:* Theosophical and Queen's Cols, Varanasi; Lucknow Univ, Lucknow; BSc with Physics, Chem & Maths 1944; MSc in Org Chem 1946; PhD in Synthetic Organic Chem 1949. *Appointments:* 1949-58: Lectr in Chem, Lucknow Univ, Osmania Univ, Hyderabad; Res Fellow, Central Labs for Sci & Indl Res, Hyderabad; Project Assoc, McArdle Memorial Lab for Cancer Res, Univ Wisconsin, Madison, USA; Special Wellcome Res Fellow, Natl Inst Med Res, London, England; 1958-77: On staff, Regl Res Lab, Hyderabad; Apptd Scist B in 1958 then Scist C; Subsequent promotions to Scist E (Asst Dir) 1964, Scist F (Dep Dir) 1972, Dist'd Scist (Dir) 1975; Scist-in-Charge of Biochem Div, 1958-77; Worked 15 months 1971-72, Inst du Radium, Paris, France, as Eleanor Roosevelt Intl Cancer Res Fellow; 1977-: Scist-in-Charge then Dir, CCMB, Hyderabad to 1990; Max-Planck Inst fur Biophys Chemie, Goettingen, West Germany; Vstg Fellow, Clare Hall, Cambridge 1986; CSIR Dist'd Fellow, CCMB, Hyderabad 1990-. *Publications:* Over 120 major res pubs in sci jours & books; Edit, Nucleic Acids-Structure, Biosynthesis and Function, 1965; Co-author national text-book for integrated sci course, 1977, reprinted every year to 1987; Co-Author 496 page book on Proteins of Seminal Plasma and Secretions of the Male Reproductive Tract, 1989. *Memberships include:* Biochem Soc, UK; Soc for Study of Reproduction, USA; Am Assn for Advancement of Sci; Am Assn for Cancer Res; Am Fertility Soc; NY Acad Scis; Former mem Sigma Xi, USA, Chem Soc, UK, Swiss Chem Soc; Soc of Biol Chems, India; Indian Soc for Study of Reproduction and Endocrinology, Fdr mem; Guha Res Conf, India, Fdr; Indian Immunol Soc; Indian Assn Cancer Res; Mem many Coms and Couns. *Honours:* Very many honours and awds for achmts in his field, and many Fellowships. *Address:* Centre for Cellular and Molecular Biology, Hyderabad 500 007, India. 52, 93, 129.

BHAT Nama Vishnu, b. 13 Nov 1928, Bombay, India. Rehab of Disabled. m. 4 Sept 1977. *Education:* BA, 1952; LLB, 1955; Cert in Rehab of the Blind, 1957; Dip in Educ of the Blind, UK, 1963. *Appointments:* Prin, Dadar Schl for the Blind, 1956-72; Exec Sec and Dir, NASEOH; Gen of NASEOH's Nat Ctr for Handicapped. *Contributions:* papers at the Nat and Int Confs. *Memberships:* Lioness Club of Byculla; Nat Assn for the Blind, Hon Sec till 1979; Rehab Coordination India. *Honours:* Award from Government of Maharashtra as Friend of the Poor; Award from National Association for the Blind as Outstanding Professional Worker; Award from National Association of Instructors for the Blind as Outstanding Educationist. *Hobbies:* Classical Indian Music, Classical Indian Dancing, Reading. *Address:* 56 Patrakar Housing Society, Bandra East, Bombay 400 051, India.

BHATT Suzata, b. 6 May 1956, Ahmedabad, India. Writer; Translator. m. Michael Augustin, 5 Sept 1988, 1 d. *Education:* BA 1980, Goucher Col; MFA 1986, Univ Iowa. *Career:* Writer-in-Residence, Vstg Prof, Univ Victoria, BC, Canada 1992. *Publications:* Brunizem, poems, 1988; Monkey Shadows, poems, 1991. *Membership:* Verband Deutscher Schriftsteller (German Writers Guild) 1991. *Honours:* Alice Hunt Bartlett Prize 1988; C'Wealth Poetry Prize (Asia) 1989; Cholmondeley Awd 1991; Poetry Book Soc Recommendation. *Hobby:* Running. *Address:* Mozartstrasse 18, D-2800 Bremen, Germany.

BHATTACHARYA Amiya Kumar, b. 11 May 1926, Baroda. Med Practitioner. m. Manasi Devi, 22 Feb 1954, 1 d. *Education:* DMS 1949, Calcutta, India. *Appointments:* Pvt Med Practice 1949-. *Publications:*

Magnet & Magnetic Fields; Power in a Magnet to Heal; Eclectic Medicine or Simple Healing Methods; Septenate Mixtures in Homeopathy. *Memberships:* Pres, World Teletherapy Assn; Pres, Homoeo Devel Soc; Liga Medicorum Homoeopathica Intls. *Honours:* Hon Membership, Nat Acupuncture Assn of South Africa, 1976; DSc Medicina Alternativa, Colombo, Sri Lanka, 1986; Hon Fellowship Pax Mundi, 1986. *Hobbies:* Outdoor and indoor games; Astrology; Palmistry; Photograph Occult Sciences; Neumorology; Torot. *Address:* Shastri Villa, Naihati 743165, West Bengal, India.

BHATTACHARYYA Dhires Chandra, b. 17 May 1919, Mymensingh. Tchg & Research. m. Usha, 3 Mar 1951, 2 s. *Education:* AM, 1946. *Appointments:* Lecturer in Econ, 1947; Asst Prof in Econ, 1951; Sen Lecturer, Victoria Univ, Wellington, 1965-68; Head of Economics Dept, Calcutta Univ, 1974. *Publications:* Understanding India's Economy; A Concise History of the Indian Economy; Knowledge, Values & Economic Development; India's Five Year Plans; An Economic Analysis. *Memberships:* Pres Bengal Econ Assoc; Pres Socio-Econ Res Inst, Calcutta; Assis Sec RKM Inst of Culture, Calcutta. *Honours:* Eminent Tchr Award, Calcutta Univ; A G Sen Memorial Prize. *Hobbies:* Poetry; Philosophy; Music. *Address:* Y-12, Sivanath Bhavan, Calcutta 700 029, India.

BHATTACHARYA Purnendu Prasad, b. 10 Oct 1920, Mymensing, Gowripur (now Bangladesh). Edit; Freedom Fighters' Pension. m. Kabita, 10 July 1954, 2 s. 1 d. *Education:* BA 1942, MA 1957, Calcutta Univ; Statistical Dipl 1952, Indian Stats Inst. *Appointments:* Tchr, Cossipore Inst, Sub-Edit Lok Sevak, Secy to Edit of daily newspaper, Basumati, Calcutta 1949-50; Inspector, Nat Sample Survey Scheme, mem Edit Bd House Jour, Section Ofcr in Linguistic Unit & Personnel Unit, Indian Statistical Inst 1951-80; Prof, Value Oriented Tchrs' Tng Ctr, Bangavani-Nabadwip (Govt Subsidised) 1985-86. *Publications:* Pub'd quarterly jour, Nabanna 1957-66' Pub'd & Edit'd, quarterly jour, Sahitya Mela 1965-; 4 poetry collections; Collection of one acts in verse, Mancher Janya, 1965; Collection short stories, Jayantar Dinalipi, 1980, Bachhai Kabita, 1985; 2 collections devotional songs; Rethinking on Jaydev and his age: Jaydeber Ajaynade Charya Pader Dheu, 1980; Jaydeb o Tnar git gobinda, 1991; Seminar papers & lectures, Review,1985. *Memberships include:* Exec com, Bangiya Sahitya Parisat, Calcutta in 1960s, Assoc'd Writer of its pub, Bharat Kosh; Mem Governing Body, Nikhilbhart Banga Sahitya Sammelan, Delhi 1975; Exec Com, World Union Intl Ctr 1977-, Vice-Chmn 1982-88; Pondicherry Sri Awiobindo Ashram; VP, Akhil Bharatiya Bhasa Sahitya Sammelan, Bhopal 1977-, Working Pres 1983-. *Honours:* Nat Hon Cert, Bharat Bhasa Bhusan, 1987; Tamra Patra by Govt India for Freedom Fighters. *Hobbies:* Music; Vstg historical places. *Address:* Purnendu Prasad Bhattacharya, 28/1 Manna Para Road, Calcutta 700 090, India.

BHATTI Surindera Singh, b. 24 June 1983, Amritsar. Prin. Chndigarh College of Arch. m. Rita, 6 Dec 1968, 3 d. *Education:* B Arch Bombay Univ, 1961; M Arch, Univ of Qld, Australia, 1982. *Appointments:* Lect, 1961-64; Assoc Prof, 1964-76; Prof 1976-82; Prin, 1982-. *Publications:* More than 400 articles on Art, Architecture, and Allied Subjects; Author of 8 books in English and Urdu on Poetry, Art, Architecture and Criticism; Poems included in American Poetry Anthology 1988, 1990; Poems in English and Urdu. *Memberships:* FIIA; AIID; MCA. *Honours:* Chandigarh Admin for the conception and design of Republic Day Tabeaux; Artist of the Year Award by Art India 1989; Several prizes for drawing & painting. *Hobbies:* Drawing; Painting; Graphics; Sculpture; Vocal Music; Numerology; Palmistry; Journalism; Book Reviews. *Address:* Bougain-Villa, 5001, Punjab Engineering College Campus, Sector 12, Chandigarh 160 012, India. 93, 139.

BI Fuzhi, b. 28 Nov 1930, Shangzhi, Heilongjiang Prov Prof. m. Yuan Youshen, 28 Apr 1959, 1 s, 1 d. *Education:* B Sc Changchun Coll of Geology; Dept of Hydrogeology and Engineering Geology, 1953-1958. *Appointments:* Gold Digging & Chemical Ind of Heilongjiang Province, 1948-51; Assis Lect Assoc Prof, Peking Univ, Dept of Geology, 1958-86; Assoc Prof, Prof State Seismological Bureau, Inst. of Crustal Dynamics & North China Coll of Water Conservanct & Hydro Electricity, 1986-. *Publications:* 32 professional paper including: Cycle of Holocene Sea Level Changes in China and Future Sea-Level Changes in the World; Beachrocks and Paleoclimate in China Over Past 5000 yrs; Period of Coastal Elevation and Subsidence along SE Coast of China in the past 5000 yrs; The Latest NWW-Ward neatectonic zones and its background of big earthquake in Fujian-Guangdong-Taiwan costal area; The Periodic laws of several geological hazards in historical times; Beach Gravel Layer and Big Fossils in High Beachrocks at Putian; Fujian Province, and their Important Scientificance. *Memberships:* Geological Society of China; Seismological Society of China; Oceangraphical Seciety of China; Research Council Of Mosaic Structure. *Hobbies:* Ball Games; Swimming. *Address:* Inst of Crustal Dynamics, State Seismological Bureau, PO Box 2855, Beijing 100085, China. 152.

BI Ruchang, b. 4 Aug 1940, Hebei China, Protein Crystallographer, m. Chen Bicheng, 29 June 1969, 1 s. *Education:* Peking Inst of Foreign Language, 1959-60; Grauated Leningrad Univ USSR, 1960-65. *Appointments:* Peking Insulin Structure Research Group, 1970-74; Univ of York, 1980- 82; Inst of Biophysics, Academia Sinica, 1966-69, 1975-80, 1983-. *Publications:* Articles on Insulin Structure; Protein Crystallography and Protein Engineering. *Memberships:* Dir of Dept of Protein Crystallography; Inst. of Biolphysics; Academia Sinica. *Honour:* National prize, Peking Insulin Structure Research Group for the Determination of Pig Insulin Structure, 1982. *Hobbies:* Reading; Table Tennis. *Address:* Inst of Biophysics, Academia Sinica. Beijing 100101, China.

BIČÁK Jiři, b. 7 Jan 1942, Prague, Theoretical Physicist, m. Jana Bicakova Nee Kudrnova, 23 June 1964, 2 d. *Education:* Graduated Physicist at Charles Univ, Prague, 1964; PhD, 1968; Assoc Prof, 1982; D.Sc, 1983; Full Prof, 1991. *Appointments:* Dept of Theoretical Physics, Charles Univ, Prague, 1965; Visiting Appt, European Countries, USA, Israel, Canada, Australia, Japan. *Publications:* Over 150 original and review papers; Essays, on Relativity, Gravitation, Relativistic Astrophysics, Book, Einstein and Prague. *Memberships:* Internat Committee on General Relativity and Gravitation, 1980-89; Commission on Astrophysics of Intern Union of Pure and Appl Physics 1990-; Editorial Boards of General Rel and Gravitation, European J. of Physics. *Honours:* Copernicus medal 1973; Honorable Mention of Gravity Research Foundation, USA, 1977; Medal of the Union of Czechoslovak Mathematicians and Physicists 1988, Prize for Popularization of Science of Czech Academy 1991. *Hobbies:* Music; Art; The Work and Life of Czech Poet, O Březina; Hiking; Swimming. *Address:* Dept of Theoretical Physics, Faculty of Mathematics and Physics, Charles Univ, V Holesovickach 2, 18000 Prague 8, Czecheslovakia.

BIASCA Rodolfo Eduardo, b. 10 Oct 1944, Argentina, Management Consultant; Author; Prof. m. Alicia Elena Yesari, 11 July 1969, 2 s, 1 d. *Education:* Nat U 1967; Postgrad U Calif; Berkeley, 1980. *Appointments:* Mfg dir s cons CPMC, Chile, 1968-69; Systems engr, Siemens, Argentina, W Ger, 1969-71; mrg indsl project and product engring div Gillette Co, Argentina, 1971-76; Engring and Logistics mgr Bagley SA Argentina 1977; Co-owner dir Roces, Biasca & Assosc Mgmt. Cons, Buenos Aires 1977-83; Direct Asst to Ministry Industry and Mining, Argentina Central Govt 1981-; Prof Buenos Aires Nat U 1981-84; Ass Gen mgr Autotrol SA, Buenos Aires, Argentina, 1983-84; gen mgr, Intermetra Corp NYC USA, 1985-86; Vice-Dean Belgrano U Sch Tech, Buenos Aires, 1986-87; dir Via

Valrossa, Buenos Aires 1987-90; Chief Exec Officer Cia De Seguros La Franco Argentina Sa 1990-. *Publications:* Productivity 1984; An Industrial Policy for Argentina 1983; Strategic Management 1983; Downsizing 1989. *Contributions:* Articles to profl. jours. Humbert H Humphrey fellow 1980. *Memberships:* Argentine Mfg Mgmt Assn; M Inst. Indsl. Engrs, Argentina Council for Profl Endsl Engrs. *Address:* RB & Assocs, Vuelta De Obligado 2728, 1428 2P Buenos Aires, Argentina. 52, 132.

BICKNELL Julian, b. 23 Feb 1945, Cambridge, England, Architect, m. Treld Pelkey, 18 Nov 1967, 1 s, 1 d. *Education:* Winchester Coll, 1958-1963; Kings Coll, Cambridge 1963-1969; Ma Dip Arch 1969, RIBA 1971. *Appointments:* Edward Cullinan, 1967-1972; Royal Coll of Art, 1973-1980; Arup Assoc 1980-1983; Julian Bicknell Assoc 1983; Trustee of Prince of Wales, Institute of Architecture, 1990-. *Creative Works:* The Old Gaol Abingdon; Garden Hall & Library, Castle Howard; Bedford School Hall; Henbury Hall, Upton Viva, High Corner, Nagara Country Club. *Memberships:* RIBA; FFB; FRSA. *Honours:* RIBA Award 1979; Carpenters Award 1983. *Hobbies:* Music; Travel; The Countryside. *Address:* 29 Lancaster Park, Richmond, Surrey, TW10 6AB, England.

BIELAWIEC Michael, b. 20 Apr 1927, Penskie, Poland. Physn. m. Maria Zofia Mazgajska, 28 Jan 1951, 1 s. *Education:* Med Fac, Warsaw Univ, Poland, 1945-50; PhD 1962, DSc 1967, Prof of Med 1976, Med Schl, Bialystok, Poland. *Appointments:* Asst and Sr Asst 1954-62, Asst Prof and Assoc Prof 1962-70, Chmn, Dept of Haematology 1970-, Med Schl, Bialystok. *Publications:* About 250 scientific publs in med jrnls on haemostasis, vascular diseases, microcirculation. *Memberships:* Polish Med Assn, Bd Mbr; Polish Soc of Internal Med, Pres of Bialystok Chapt; Polish Soc of Haematology, Pres Bialystok Chapt; European Soc on Microcirculation; Int Soc of Haematology; Int Union of Angiology. *Honours:* Certificate awarded by Polish Minister of Health and Welfare for Outstanding Scientific Achievement, four times; Certificate awarded by President of Medical School, Bialystok, Poland, for Outstanding Scientific Achievement, many times. *Hobbies:* Travelling, Walking with Grandson. *Address:* Department of Haematology, Medical School, M Sklodowskiej-Curie 24, 15-276 Bialystok, Poland.

BIELECKI Janusz Tadeusz, b. 8 June 1924, Sosnowiec. Composer, Pianist, Tchr. m. Krystyna Szczygiet, 15 Jan 1956, 2 s. *Education:* State Academy of Music, 1945-51; Two Diplomas, Secondary in Zabrize, Higher in Katowice; Piano and Composition; Secondary Music School, 1945-1981. *Appointments:* Acknowledged by state as Composer and Concerting Musician. *Creative Works:* 5 Piano, 3 Vocal, 2 Ballet Recitals. *Memberships:* Assoc of Authors, 2AIKS; Assoc of Polish Artists and Musicians, SPAM. *Honours:* Awards from the Wojwodship Council in Katowice. *Hobbies:* History; Music; Concerts. *Address:* ul Damrota, 44-100 Gliwice, Poland.

BIENIASZ Bogumil, b. 12 June 1940, Gkuchow, Academic Tchr, m. Ewa Haduch, 11 Apr 1964, 1 s, 1 d. *Education:* Tech Univ of Krakow 1961; Inst. of Nuclear Research 1977; Silesian Tech Univ 1980. *Appointments:* Zelmer Rzeszow, Technology-Technician 1961; Wytwornia Sprzetu Komunikacyjnego, 1962-1963; Designer at the Engine Research Dept, Technical Univ of Rzeszow, 1963; Academic Tchr, Thermodynamics & Aircraft Engines Dept. *Publications:* Fluid Mechanics Lab 1974; Heat Lab 1979; Thermodynamics Lab 1983; Heat & Mass Transfer Lab 1987; Habilitation Work, Use of Electrolysis and Heat Mass Transfer Analogy for Designing Elements of Heat Exchangers with Forced Convection 1980. *Membership:* Thermodynamics and Combustion Committee of Polish Academy Of Sciences. *Honours:* Individual Award of Minister Of Science; Higher Education and Technique.

Hobbies: Mountain Walking; Skiing; Chamber Music. *Address:* Ul Ossolinskich 47, 35 328 Rzeszow, Poland.

BIENKOWSKI Wieslaw Jozef, b. 7 July 1926, Cracow, Poland, Historian, Bibliographer, Author, m. Barbara Klimala, 3 Aug 1966, 2 s. *Education:* Master of Phil, Hist 1951; Sociology 1952; PhD Hist, 1962; Postdoctoral Studies, Habilitacja, Poland 1970; Promoted Prof Polish Council of State 1981. *Appointments:* Librarian, The Gdansk Municipal Library, Biblioteka Miejska, Polish 1951-1953; Historical Inst, Cracow 1953; Prof Jagellonian Univ, Cracow 1975; Chair of Librarianshipand Information Science. *Publications:* Krzysztof Celestyn Mrongowiuss 1764-1855, 1964, 2nd Ed. 1983; Bibliography of Polish History 3 parts 1965-1978; Bibliography of Polish History Science 1975. *Honour:* Golden Cross of Merit 1972. *Hobbies:* Bibliophilism; Touring. *Address:* Jagellonian Univ, Golebia 16, 31 007 Krakow, Cracow, Poland. 152.

BIESELE John Julius, b. 24 Mar 1918, Waco, Texas. USA Prof. Emeritus of Zoology, Univ of Texas, m. (1) Marguerite Califee McAfee. 29 July 1943, 3 d, (2) Esther Aline Eakin, 1992. *Education:* BA with highest honors 1939; Ph.D. Zoology 1942, University of Texas. *Appointments:* Fellow International Cancer Research Foundation 1942-44; Temporary Reasearch Assoc. Dept of Genetics, Carnegie Inst of Washington, New York 1944-46; Asst. 1946-47; Research Fellow 1947; Assoc Member 1947-55; Head Cell Growth Section, Division of Experimental Chemotherapy 1947-58; Member 1955-58; Assoc. Scientist 1959-78; Sloan- Kettering Inst. for Cancer Research NYC; Prof. Emeritus of Zoology 1978, Univ of Texas at Austin. *Publications:* Mitotic Poisons and the Cancer Problem; About 160 Scientific Journal Articles and Book Chapters. *Memberships Include:* American Assoc. for Cancer Research; American Assoc. for Advancement of Science; American Society for Cell Biology; American Inst of Biological Sciences. *Honours:* Valedictorian, Austin High School;, Phi Eta Sigma; Phi Beta Kappa; Society of the Sigma Xi; Phi Kappa Phi. *Hobbies:* Nature Study and Conservation; Travel; History; Linguistics. *Address:* 2500 Great Oaks Parkway, Austin, TX 78756, USA. 2, 7, 15, 28, 30, 51, 51, 125, 129, 143, 152, 156.

BILLING Gert Due, b. 8 Apr 1946, Copenhagen. Prof of Chemistry. m. Inge Lise, 25 Apr 1970, 2 s, 1 d. *Education:* Univ of Copenhage, M Sc. 1970; PhD. 1973; Dr Scient, 1978. *Appointments:* Assoc Prof, 1975; Full Prof, 1989. *Publication:* Doctoreal Thesis, 1978. *Memberships:* Danish Chemical Society; European Physical Society; Danish Natural Science Acadamy; Royal Danish Acadamy of Sciences and Letters.*Hobbies:* Classical Music; Chess. *Address:* Clausholm Vei 35, 2720 Vanlose, Denmark. 139.

BILLINGE Roy, b. 21 Dec 1937, Buxton, England. Physicist, Computing Dir. m. Rosemary Fallows, 2 Apr 1960, 1 s, 1 d. *Education:* Buxton Coll, 1949-56; County Mayor Exhibition, Kings Coll, Univ of London, 1956-59. *Appointments:* Scientist at Rutherford Lab, 1959-67; Section Head, Femilab, USA 1968-71; Group Leader, CERN CH, 1971-75; Division Ldr, CERN 1981-90. *Publications:* Numerous Scientific. *Memberships:* Fellow of American Physical Soc, Fellow of Inst of Physics. *Hobbies:* Music; Singing; Skiing; Mountain Walking; Tennis; Gardening; Informatics. *Address:* Chemin Des Alpes, 1261 Trelex, Switzerland. 43, 50, 52.

BINET Luc Desiré René, b. 30 July 1951, Brussels, Marketing Consultant. *Education:* BS in Math and Latin, Athenée Royal, Belgium, 1969; Degree in Pharmacy, Brussels Univ, 1974. *Appointments:* Pharmacist, Pub Hosps, Brussels, 1974-78; Quality Control Manager Hypo Lab Sa, Switzerland, 1980-82; Product Manager Serono Ch, 1982-87; Mktg Manager, Baxter Dade, 1987-90. *Contributions to:* Profl Jours. *Memberships:* Order of Belgium Pharmacists; AACC; Swiss Assn Mktg Mgrs; CLAS. *Hobbies:* Writing Satyrical Assays.

Address: La Renardiere, En Chanta Merloz, CH-1137 YENS, Switzerland. 52.

BINNEY Caroline Thorn, b. 4 Sept, Newport, Rhode Island, Ballet Dancer and Choreographer. *Education:* Mary C Wheeler School, Diploma; Assoc in Arts Degree, Endicott Coll. *Appointments:* American Festical Ballet; NY Dance Ensemble; NY City Opera; Metropolitan Opera Company; NY Folk Ballet. *Creative Works:* Choreographed Dances, Carmen Gypsy Dance; La Traviata Gypsy Dance; Le Cid Spanish Ballet. *Membership:* AGMA. *Honours:* Wheeler School for Excelling in all Sports. *Hobbies:* Photography; Making Costumes; Singing; Bicycle Riding; Running; Folk Dancing; Swimming; Drawing; Music; Seeing Movies; Ballets; Operas; Concerts; Aerobics. *Address:* 314 West 58th Street, Apt 3B, NYC, NY 10019, USA. 138, 156.

BIRCH Clive Francis William, b. 22 Dec 1931, Edgware, Middx. Publisher, Author, m. Carolyn Rose, 16 Apr 1983, 3 s, 3 d. *Education:* Uppingham School, 1945-49; Royal Air Force, 1950-52. *Appointments:* Journalist, Kemsley Newspapers, 1952-58; Marketing, General Motors, Metro Cammell Weymann, Product Devlop Manger; Media Management, Modern Transport Publishing Co, Thompson Organisation, Northwood Publications, Textile Trade Publications, Mercury House Publications, 1965-74; Publishing Director, Barracuda Books, 1974-1992; Sporting and Leisure Press, 1976-; Quotes, 1985- ; SAGA, 1987-; Governor, Royal Latin School, 1989- ; Principal, Radmore Birch Associates, 1991-. *Publications inc:* Book of Chesham, 1974; 2nd ed 1975; 3rd ed 1988; Book of Aylesbury, 1975; paperback, 1984; Book of Amersham, 1976; 2nd ed 1979; Book of Beaconsfield, 1976; 2nd ed 1982; Chalfont St Giles In Camera 1985; 2nd ed 1989; Missendens In Camera 1986, 2nd edition 1988; Around Chesham In Camera, 1986; Buckingham in Camera, 1986, 2nd ed 1989; Around Milton Keynes in Camera, 1987; Chenies & Chorleywood In Camera, 1988, 2nd ed 1989; Chiltern Thames in Camera, 1990; Yesterdays Town: Amersham, 1991; The Vale of Aylesbury In Camera, 1991; Old Milton Keynes In Camera, 1992. *Memberships:* Freeman, City of London; Chmn, Buckingham Heritage Trust, 1985-; Ancient Monuments Society; Indep Publishers Guild; Founder-Chmn, Buckingham Chamber of Trade, Commerce and Indus, 1979-1983, Hon Vice-Pres, 1983-92; Master, Worshipful Company of Carmen, 1984-85; Past Master, 1985-. *Honours:* FRSA 1980; FSA 1981; Inst of the Royal Corps of Trans, 1985; Chiltern Car Club, 1956; Chevalier du Confrerie des Chevaliers du Trou Normand, 1991. *Hobbies:* Writing; Shooting; France. *Address.* Radclive Hall, Buckingham & Les Autels St Bazile, France.

BIRCHAK James Robert, b. 20 Mar 1939, Latrobe, PA, USA. Physicist. m. Beatrice Christiana Brennan, 29 June 1963, 2 s. *Education:* Carnegie Mellon U, Pittsburgh, PA, BS, Physics, 1961; Rice U, Houston TX, MA Physics, 1964; Rice U, Houston TX, PhD Physics, 1966; Wayne State Univ, Detroit MI, MBA 1971. *Appointments:* General Motors Res Labs, 1966-71; Southwest Res Labs, 1971-76; Babcock and Wilcox Res Labs, 1976-79; NL Ind MWD Labs, 1979-85; Reliability Inc, 1986-1991; Halliburton Logging Serv, 1991-. *Publications:* 8 Patents, 15 Scientific Jour Articles. *Memberships:* SIGMA XI; American Soc for Nondestructive Testing; American Physical Soc; IEEE. *Honours:* National Merit Scholarship, 1957-61; Rice Asst, Fellowship, 1961-1966. *Hobbies:* Guitar; Hiking; Solar Energy Res. *Address:* 3902 Cypressdale, Spring, TX 77388, USA. 7, 14.

BIRD Florence, the Honorable, b. 5 Jan 1908, Philadelphia, Penna, USA. Author, Broadcaster; Senator. m. John 1928 dec. *Appointments include:* Executive Central Volunteer Bureau, Winnipeg, 1939-40; Chairman, Editoral Board Welfare Magazine, 1947-1953; Canadian Delegation to UNESCO conf, New Delhi, India, 1956; Chairman, Royal Commission on the Status of Women in Canada, 1967-1970; CIDA conslt to the Govt of Jamaica, 1975, Barbados 1976; Refugees Advisory Com, Dept of Immigration, 1983-1985. *Publications:* Anne Francis, an Autobiography, 1974; Holiday in the Woods, 1976. *Memberships include:* National Liberal Party of Canada; United Nations Assoc; The Inst of Cultural Affairs; MATCH; Canadian Writers Foundation; Canadian Inst of Intl Affairs; Mem of The Senate of Canada, 1978-1983. *Honours include:* Companion of the order of Canada, 1971; D.Hum. Mount St Vincent Univ, 1973; LL.D Carleton Univ, 1975; The Governor General's Persons Award, 1983; Distinguished Canadian, Univ of Regina, 1989; B.Hum L. Univ of Windsor, 1990. *Hobbies:* Swimming; Walking; Reading; Writing; Classical Music; Ballet. *Address:* Apt 201-333 Chapel Street, Ottawa, Ontario, Canada KIN 8YB.

BIRD Harold Dennis (Dickie), b. 19 Apr 1933, Barnsley, Yorkshire, England. Prof Cricket Test Umpire. *Education:* Raley School, Barnsley. *Career:* County Cricket Player for Yorkshire County Cricket Club and Leicestershire County Cricket Club; Umpire, The Test and County Cricket Board, Lords Cricket Ground London; Umpired 132 Intl matches; Cup Quarter Finals and Semi Finals in England; World Cup Panel of Umpires; 3 Test Matches v India, 2 Test Matches v New Zealand; Umpired 50 Test Matches, World Record Holder; Umpired, One-Day Int Matches in Shayah & Sri Lanka; Umpired 3 World Cup Finals, West Indies v Australia, 1975, West Indies v England, 1979, West Indies v India, 1983; Umpired, World Cup, India, 1986-87; Umpired, Major Cup Finals in England. *Publications:* Not Out; Thats Out; From The Pavilion End. *Memberships:* Lords Taverners; Patron Wombwell Cricket Lovers Soc; . *Honours:* Yorkshire Personality of the Year 1977; MBE; Birthday Honours List 1986. *Hobbies:* Watching Football; Listening to Diana Ross and Barbara Streisand records. *Address:* White Rose Cottage, 40 Paddock Road, Staincross, Barnsley, Yorkshire, S75 6LE, England.

BIRGUS Vladimír, b. 5 May 1954, Frydek-Místek CS. Dir of the Inst of Creative Photography, Silesian Univ, Opava, Tutor, Film and TV Academy, FAMU, Prague. m. Darina Tauskova, 1 Feb 1986, 1 s. *Education:* History of Arts, Palacky Univ, Olomouc, CS, 1973-78; PhD, 1980; Photography, FAMU, Prague, extraordinary, 1974-78. *Appointments:* Asst Tutor and Tutor, Dept of Photography, FAMU, Prague, 1978-; Dir of the Inst of Creative Photography, Silesian Univ, 1990. *Publications:* M Bilek, 1982; M Borovicka, 1984; Mesto, (Town), 1984; Informatorium 2, 1984; F Drtikol, 1988, 1989 (with A Brany); Tschechoslowakische Fotografie de Gegenwart, 1990; Personal Photographic Exhibitions, inc. Olomouc 1971-72, 1974, 1976,1979, 1985; Amsterdam NL, 1985; Munich D, 1986; Warsaw PL, 1988; Tours F, 1990; Eisenach, Siegen D, 1991; Curatorship of Exhibitions, inc. Czechoslovak Photography of the 1980s, Amsterdam, 1989; Contemporary Czechoslovak Photography, Cologue, 1990. *Memberships:* Assoc of Czech Phtographers, Union Of Czech Fine Artists. *Hobbies:* Film; Fine Art; Literature: Tourism. *Address:* Na Poříčním Právu 4, CS 128 00 Praha 2, Czechoslovakia.

BIRTS Peter William, b. 9 Feb 1946, Brighton, Queens Counsel. m. Penelope Ann Eyre, 24 Apr 1971, 1 s, 2 d. *Education:* Lancing College, Sussex; St Johns College, Cambridge. *Appointments:* Called to Bar, Grays Inn, 1968; Appointed QC, 1990; Appointed Recorder, 1989. *Publications:* Trespass, 1987; Remedies for Trespass, 1990. *Membership:* Elected to General Council of Bar, 1990; Judicial Studies Board, 1991. *Honours:* Choral scholarship to St Johns Coll, Cambridge, 1963; BA, Cambridge, 1967; MA, 1990. *Hobbies:* Music; Shooting. *Address:* Farrars Building, Temple, London, EC4Y 8BD, England. 1.

BIRYLLO Mikalay, b. 10 Sept 1923, Philologist, Academician. m. Likhadziyeyskaya Yemiliya, 7 July 1947, 1 s. *Education:* Minsk State Pedagogical Inst, 1940, 1945-47; Candidate of Phil Sci, 1956; Dr of Phil

Sci, 1969; Prof, 1971; Corresponding Member of Byelourussian Academy of Sci, 1972; Academician of Byel Acadamy, 1977. *Appointments include:* Jnr Sci worker of the Inst of Language, Literature, Art, 1947-53; Prof of the Dept of the Byelourussian philology, 1956-58; Head of the Sci Worker, 1963-1965; Academician Secr of the Humantities Dept, 1977-. *Publications include:* Byelourussian Antroponimy. Minsk v1, 1966, v2, 1969, v3, 1982; Dic of stress in Byelourussian, 1991; Typology and Geography of Slavonic names, 1988. *Memberships:* Intl OLA Commission member; Slavonic onomastic Commission member; Internationa Soc of Byelorussists. *Honours:* The Badge of Honour, 1976; Scientist of Byelorussia, 1978; Order of the Red Banner of Labour, 1983. *Hobby:* Philately. *Address:* 15 Kul'man Ave, Apt 250, 220100 Byelorus, Minsk, Russia.

BISE William Lloyd Lafitte van, b. 3 June 1931, Slidell, Louisiana, USA. Inventor, Med Devices. m. Sallye Stilwell, 9 Feb 1950, div 1966, 3 d. *Education:* Elkins Inst Radio; Delgado Tech Inst; EE, Tulane Univ, 1957-62; MD (Hon), Univ of OR Hlth Sciences Schl of Med, 1975-79. *Appointments:* Radiation Sect, OR State Hlth Div; Cons, Instr Cal and Repair, 1973-76; Fndr Chair Rsch Scientist, Pacific NW Ctr for Study of Non- Ionizing Radiation, 1976-79; Clinical Inst Environmental Med, UOHSC Schl of Med, 1976-79; Chief, Biomed Rsch, Tecnic Rsch Labs, SL CA, 1984-88; Pres, Magtek Labs, 1988-. *Publications:* 56 tech papers, 1 book; Phil of Objective Measurement, 1988; 3 U S patents, 1988, 89. *Memberships:* Fndr 1976, Treas 1988, Pacific Northwest Ctr; Pres, Magtek Labs, 1988-; ICWA, 1984. *Honours:* Clinical Instructor of Environmental Medicine, Oregon Health Sciences, University School of Medicine, 1976-79; Invited Paper and Comment, Radiation Health and Safety Hearings before the Committee on Commerce, Science and Transportation, 95th Congress, U S Senate, 1977; Guest Lecturer, Learned Society Conference, Ottawa, Canada, 1980; Guest Lecturer, Staff Kaiser Permanente Hospital, Portland, Oregon, 1981. *Hobbies:* Photography, Environmental Medicine, Philosophy, Music, History. *Address:* Magtek Laboratories, 7685 Hughes Drive, Reno, NV 89506, USA. 59.

BISHOP Barney Tipton, b. 24 Dec 1951, Panama City Fl, USA. Assoc Executive. m. Shelby Lynn Stinson, 4 Feb 1989. *Education:* Miami Dade Community Coll, 1969-71; Emerson Coll, Boston, 1971-73; Bachelor of Sci Degree in Speech, 1973; post Graduate Study, Italy, 1973. *Appointments include:* Legal Aid Soc, Staff Investigator, 1973-74; Alliance Invest Agency, 1976-78; Florida Dept of Insurance, 1983-87; Academy of Florida Trial Lawyers, 1987-90; Florida Lawyers Action Group, 1990. *Memberships:* Florida Assoc of Private Invest, 1976-83; Orange County Young Democrats, 1978-82; American Soc of Assic Executives, 1989; Emerson Coll Alumi Assoc, 1990; Intl Platform Assoc, 1991. *Honours include:* National Serv Fraternity, 1970; New England Debate Tournament, 1973; Outstanding Young Democrat of the year, 1982-83; Apprec form the Academy of Florida Trial Lawyers, 1988. *Hobbies:* Gardening; Golf; Racquetball. *Address:* 10976 Luna Point Road, Tallahassee, FL 32312, USA. 7.

BISHOP Olga Bernice, b. 24 June 1911, Dover, New Brunswick, Canada. Prof Emeritus. *Education:* BA 1938, MA 1951, Mount Allison Univ; BPA, Carleton Univ, 1946; AMLS 1952, PhD 1962, MI Univ. *Appointments:* Asst Libn 1946-48, Acting Libn 1948-53, Mount Allison Univ; Gen Libn 1953-54, Med Libn 1954-65, Pt-time Lectr 1953-60, Univ of Western Ont; Assoc Prof 1965-70, Prof 1970-76, Pt-time Prof 1976-77, Prof Emeritus 1977-, Univ of Toronto. *Creative Works:* Slide/Tape with B L Anderson, The Growth of the Primary Literature of Science and Technology from the 16th to the 20th Century; Sev workshops; 9 books; Chapts in books; Sev Reviews, Articles and Editorships. *Memberships:* Assn of American Lib Schls; Assn of Coll and Rsch Libs; Assn Internationale des Documentalistes; Geoscience Info Soc; Ont Hist Soc; Assn for Can Studies; Var offs

Bibliographical Soc of Can; Beta Phi Mu. *Honours:* Doctor of Laws, Mount Allison University, 1971; Marie Thelmaine Medal, Canadian Bibliography, 1981; Canadian Association of Special Libraries Information Service Award for Special Librarianship in Canada, 1981. *Hobbies:* Crafts, Sewing, Knitting, Chocolate-making, Candle-making, Crocheting. *Address:* 62 Thornton Avenue, London, Ontario, Canada N5Y 2Y3. 142.

BITSKEY Istvan, b. 26 Mar 1941, Egar, Hungary. Univ Prof, Head of Dept. m. Domboroczki Katalin, 18 Aug 1973, 2 s. *Education:* Literature, History, German 1962-67; Candidates Degree, 1976; DSC, 1991. *Appointments:* Tchr in Eger, 1968-72; Research fellow MTA, 1972-75; Assoc Prof in Debrecen, 1975-80; Head of Dept on Univ KLTE, 1980-. *Publications:* Fire of Faith - Deboattkes, 1978; Humanists Erudition and Baroque, World Concept, 1979; Life of Gàbor Bethlen, 1984; Pazmany Peter, 1986. *Membership:* Intl Soc of Hungarian Studies. *Hobby:* Swimming. *Address:* Fay u 51, H-4027 Debrecen, Hungary.

BJARUP Jes, b. 17 Feb 1940, Aarhus, Denmark, Sen Lecturer in Jurisprudence. m. Bodil Hoegh, 31 May 1984. *Education:* Law School, 1964-1970; Doc of Philosophy, 1982. *Appointments:* Shippingman, 1958-64; Lctr, Aarhus Univ, 1970; Tutor in Jurisprudence, Univ of Edinburgh, 1976-78; Jean Manned Fellow, European Univ Inst, Florence, 1989-90. *Publications include:* Introduktion Sil alm retslaere; Skandinavischer Realismus, 1978; Reason, Emotion and the Law, Studies in the Philosophy of Axel Hägersträm, 1982; Intl Assoc for Philosophy of Law and Social Philosophy; Current Legal Theory; European Academy of Legal Theory. *Memberships:* Mind Assoc; British Soc for the History of Philosophy. *Hobbies:* Classical Music; Reading; Golf. *Address:* Oddervej 26, DK-8660 Skanderborg, Denmark.

BLACK Ann Dora, b. 2 July 1932, London, England, Conslt Child and Adol Psychiatrist. m. J Black, 4 Dec 1955, 2 s, 1 d. *Education:* U Birmingham, MB, ChB, 1950-55; U London, DPM, 1958; Royal Coll Psychiatrists, MRC, 1971; FRC, 1979. *Appointments:* Conslt C and A Psychiatrist, 1961- 68; Edgware General Hospital, 1968-84; Royal Free Hospital, 1984-. *Publications:* Child Psychiatry and the Law; numerous chapters and articles on childhood bereavement and trauma, family therapy, child psychiatry. *Memberships:* Past Chairman, Inst Family Therapy; Vice chairman, cruse bereavement care; Chairman, North east child and adolescent psychiatrist advisory com. *Hobbies:* Theatre; Music; Reading; Travel. *Address:* Royal Free Hospital, London NW3 2QG, England.

BLACK Anthony Edward Norman, b. 20 Jan 1938. Chief Exec Commissioner, The Scout Assoc. m. Susan Frances Copeland, 1 Oct 1963, 2 s. *Education:* Brighton Coll; RMA Sandhurst; Army Staff Coll, Camberley. *Appointments:* Comm into RE, 1957; Ghana, Armed Forces Staff Coll, 1976-78; Co 36 Engr Regt, 1978-80; Comdt AA Coll Chepstow, 1983-86; Chief Exec Comm The Scout Assoc, 1987. *Membership:* FBIM, 1981. *Honour:* OBE, 1981. *Hobbies:* Dinghy Sailing; Walking; Gardening; Bird Watching. *Address:* The Scout Assoc, Baden Powell House, Queens Gate, London, SW7 5JS, England. 1.

BLACKBURN George Richard (Dick), b. 19 Feb 1917, Leeds, Barrister. m. Duloie May Garrod, 6 Mar 1947, 1 s, 1 d. *Education:* Sherborne, Dorset, 1931-35; Christs Coll, Cambridge, (MA) 1935-38; Inner Temple, 1939; Barrister, 1948; London Academy Music and Dramatic Art, 1951 (ALAM). *Appointments inc:* War Service, LT (A) RNVR, (Pilot), Fleet Air Arm, 1940-46; Reserve. Flt LT RAFVR, 1949- 52; LT CDR RNVR, 1952-58; LT CDR RNR, 1958-72; Practice Barrister, 1949-56; Legal adviser with Shell Mex and BP Ltd, 1956-63; Dir, Airfield Company, 1963-67; Manager Legal Dept, HCITB, 1967-71; Group Legal Officer, Calor Gas Ltd, 1971-81. *Honours:* VRD, 1958. *Hobbies:* Family; Law; Languages;

Flying; Theatre; Church; Freemasonary; Social Work; Business; Walking; Swimming; Tennis. *Address:* 26 Pearl Court, Cornfield Terrace, Eastbourne, East Sussex, BH21 4AA, England.

BLAKER George, b. 30 Sept 1912, Simla, India. m. Richenda Dorothy Buxton, 1 June 1938, 1 d. *Education:* BA, Trinity Coll, Cambridge Univ, 1932-35; Ecole des Sciences Politiques, Paris, France. *Appointments:* Civil Service, 1938-71 inc; Middle East 1941-43; Cabinet Office, 1943-45; Cabinet Delegation to India, 1946; Sec Trade Mission to China, 1946; Treasury, 1948-63; Diplomatic work of Minister in India, Burma and Ceylon, 1957-63. *Creative Works:* Est and running a 12 hectare Nature Reserve in Surrey, 1964-87; Co-founding the Scientific and Medical Network, 1973. *Memberships:* Royal Society for Protection of Birds; British Ornithologists Union; Royal Geographical Society; The Scientific and Medical Netowrk; Surrey Trust for Nature Conservation, 1969-80. *Honours:* CMG, 1963; Gold Medal, Royal Society for the protection of Birds, 1934; Countryside Award, 1970. *Hobbies:* The Universe and the role of the Human Race within it; The Spiritual world view; Conservation of Wildlife; Ecology; Geography; India and the Himalayan Region; Tibet. *Address:* Lake House, Ockley, Dorking, Surrey RH5 5NS, England. 1.

BLANCHETTE James Edward, b. 28 Aug 1924, Syracuse, New York, USA, Phychiatrist. *Education:* BA, Syracuse Univ, 1950; MD, State Univ of New York, Syracuse Medical School, 1953. *Appointments:* Intern St Vinvents Hospital, New York City, 1953-57; State Hospital, Norwalk, 1957-59; Private Practice, psychiatry, Redlands, 1959-; Chief Professional education, Patton State Hospital, 1960-64; Tchr Conslt, 1964-; Staff, San Bernardino Community Hospital, St Bernadine Hospital. *Memberships:* Diplomate; American Board of Medical Examiners; American Medical Society of Vienna; American Psychiatric Assoc; Royal Society of Health, UK: American and California Medical Assoc; American Board, Psychiatry and Neurology. *Address:* 236 Cajon Street, Redlands, CA 93273, USA. 9, 17, 22, 57, 130.

BLAND John Hannam, b. 1 Dec 1930, Silsden, Yorkshire, UK. Journalist. m. Olive Mary Hirst, 17 Mar 1954, 2 s, 1d. *Education:* Giggleswick Grammar, 1940-47; Ermysted Grammar, 1947-49; Univ of Manchester, 1949-53; BA Double Honours, Modern Languages, 1953. *Appointments:* The Yorkshire Post Leeds, 1955-59; Reuters News Agency, 1959-72; Daily Telegraph Magazine, 1973-74; World Health Organization, Geneva, 1974-90; Conslt with WHO, 1991. *Membership:* European Assoc Of Science Editors. *Hobbies:* Books; Shakespeare; Classical Music; Travel; Skiing; Swimming; Arthurian Romance. *Address:* Côte de Mourex, Mourex, 01220 Grilly, France. 1.

BLANKE Mogens, b. 6 Oct 1947, Copenhagen, Professor. 1 s, 1 d. *Education:* MScEE for DTH, 1974; PhD Servolaboratory, DTH, 1982; Perspective in Management, Paris, 1989. *Appointments include:* Graduate Student, DTH, 1974-77; Asst Prof, DTH, 1978-81; General Manager for Marine Div, 1985-90; Prof, Univ of Aalborg, 1990- *Publications include:* Papers in Intl Sci Journals; Papers in Proceedings of International Conferences; Papers in International Journals. *Memberships:* Board of Directors, Danish Automation Society; Chairman IFAC; Working group on Control Applications in Marine Systems; Vice Chairman IFAC Applications commette; IFAC Committee on Theory. *Hobbies:* Classical Music; Opera; Play Piano; Amateur Singer. *Address:* Skorlykke 9, DK-9210 Aalborg, Denmark.

BLANTON John Arthur, b. 1 Jan 1928, Houston, Texas, USA, Architect. m. Marietta Newton, 10 Apr 1954, dec 1967, 3 d. *Education:* BA, 1948; BS Arch, 1949; Rice Univ. *Appointments:* Richard J Neuta, FAIA, 1950-64; Tchr, Univ of California at Los Angeles Extension and Harbor Coll, 1964-. *Publications include:* Bicentennial edition, AIA Journal; 6 buildings in Guide to Architecture

of Los Angeles and Southern California. *Memberships:* American Inst of Arch. *Honours include:* Red Cedar Shingle, AIA national merit award, 1979; Participant, CCAIA design conference, 1981; Monograph on work, Los Angeles Arch Magazine, 1982; 15 page monograph, L'architettura (Italy), 1988. *Address:* 1456 12th Manhatton Beach, CA 90266, USA. 9, 59, 120, 130, 39.

BLASZKOWSKI Janusz Andrzej, b. 8 Feb 1954, Zelistrzewo. Academic Tchr. m. Magdalena, 25 Dec 1984, 2 s. *Education:* Technical School for Agri, 1970-75; Academy of Agri, 1975-80. *Appointments:* Academy of Argi, Dept plant pathology, 1980-91. *Publications:* 32 Scientific papers. *Memberships:* Mycological Society of America; Polish Phytopathological Soc; Polish Botanical Soc. *Hobby:* Piano Music. *Address:* Dept of Plant Pathology, Academy of Agriculture, Slowackiego 17, PL 71434 Szczecin, Poland.

BLAU Joseph Norman, b. 5 Oct 1928, Conslt Physician, Neurologist. m. Jill Elise Seligman, 19 Dec 1968, 2 s, 1 d. *Education:* St Bartholomews Hospital, Medical Coll, 1947-52; MBBS, 1952; MRCP, 1955; MD, 1968; FRCP, 1968; FRC Path, 1973. *Appointments:* National Service RAMC, 1953-55; Registar Neurology, London and Maida Vale Hospitals, 1957-61; Conslt Neurologist, National Hospital, 1962-; Royal National Throat, Nose and Ear Hospital, 1965-; Northwick Park Hospital, 1972-; Migraine Clinic, 1980-. *Publications:* Headache and Migraine Handbook, 1986; Migraine - Clinical, Therapeutic, Conceptual and Research Aspects, 1987; Understanding Headaches and Migraine, 1991. *Memberships include:* Fellow Royal Soc Mcd; Ass British Neurologist; Advisor Migraine Trust and Brit Migraine Assoc; London Jewish Med Soc; Writers Group, Soc of Authors; London Medical Orchestra; Brit Soc Music Therapy. *Honours:* Open Science Scholarship, 1947-52; Nuffield Medical Research Fellowship, Boston, USA, 1962; Lect in Pathology, 1970-88. *Hobby:* Play Cello. *Address:* National Hospital Neurology, Queen Square, London, WC1N 3BG, England. 170.

BLAUG Mark, b. 3 Apr 1927, The Hague, Netherlands, Univ Economist. m. Ruth M Towse, 29 Mar 1969, 2 s. *Education:* Queens Coll NY BA, 1950; Columbia Univ NY MA, 1952; Columbia Univ NY PhD, 1955. *Appointments:* Asst Prof, Yale Univ, 1954-62; Sr Lect, Reader, Prof, Univ of London Inst of Education, 1963-84; Consult Prof Economics, Univ of Buckingham, 1984-92; Visiting Prof, Econ, Univ of Exeter, 1989-. *Publications:* Ricardian Econmics, 1958; Econmic Theory in Retrospect, 1962, 4th ed, 1985; The Causes of Graduate Unemployment in India, 1969; Intrduction to the Economics of Education, 1970; Education and the Employment Problem in Developing Countries, 1973; The Practice of Manpower Forecasting, 1973; The Cambridge Revolutions? 1974; The Methodology of Economics, 1980; Who's who in Economics, 1983, 2nd ed 1986; Great Econmists since Keynes, 1984; Great Economists Before Keynes, 1985; Economic History and the History of Economics, 1986; The Economics of Education and the Education of an Economist, 1987; Economic Theories, True or False?, 1990; John Maynard Keynes, Life, Ideas, Legacy, 1990; Appraising Economic Theories, 1991; FBA, 1992. *Hobbies:* Talking; Walking; Sailing. *Address:* Langsford Barn, Peter Tavy, Tavistock, Devon PL19 9LY, England. 1.

BLEISCH Carl Xaver, b. 8 June 1929, St Gall, Switzerland, Enterpreneur and Univ Prof. m. Rosalinda, 27 July 1986, 1 s, 2 d, (1 adopted). *Education:* PhD in Psi, 1971; JD, 1987; MD hc, 1988; Centre Yamauchi Hospital, Oita, 1970-80; Univ of Oxford, England, 1988. *Appointments include:* GLOBUS Enterprises, St Gallon, 1951-64; Patent Attorney, Zuerich, 1965-; Manufacturer of Bio Cosmetics, 1979-80; Tutor, Seminar leader, Univ's in England, USA, Switzerland; Partnerships in 12 considerable Philippine Corp; Pres of Great Pacific Islands Dev Corp. *Creative Works:* Further dev of Albert Einsteins Kaltemaschine mass

Production of Interferon and Biogene Stimulators; Senator SUZ and Advisory Conlt, Oxford; Author of The New Philippine Constiution; Guides for Univ Studies; Hochschulen de Schweiz; How to Establish a company in Switzerland. *Honours:* Guiness World Champion in cryobiolog; Appli under minus 180 centograndes; Adopted son of Urdaneta; RC Urdeneta North, Phil; MDhc; ABi Citation 1991; Man of The Year. *Hobbies:* Academic Traveling; Expeditions; Sports; Flying; Research; Metaphysical Studies; Collection of Asiatica; Numismatics; Minerals. *Address:* Strussistr 91, CH-8057 Zurich, Switzerland. 92, 152.

BLINDT SEGRAVES Kathleen A, b. 25 Aug 1947, Chicago, Illinois, Asst Prof of Psychiatry. *Education:* BA, Illinois Benedictine Coll, 1977; MA, Univ of Chicago, 1980; PhD, Univ of Chicago, 1984. *Appointments include:* Michael Reese Hospital, Chicago, 1979-80; Asst Prof, Case Western Reserve Univ, 1987; School of Medicine, Dept of Psychiatry, 1982-85. *Publications include:* Whatever Happened to Conversation?, 1982; Journal of Psychosomatic Research, 1986; Medical Aspects of Human Sexuality, 1989; Modern Medicin, 1990. *Memberships include:* Illinois Biofeedback Society; Assoc for Applied Psychophysiology and Biofeedback; National Assoc of Social Workers; American Soc for Psychosomatic Obstetrics and Gynecology; Society for Menstrual Cycle Research; Assoc for Behavioral Social Work. *Honours:* Advisory Comm of World Assoc of Sexology; Academic Scholarship, Univ of Chicago; Illinois Benedictine Coll Summa Cum Laude. *Address:* Metro Health Medical Centre, Dept of Psychiatry, 2500 Metro Health Drive, Cleveland, OH 44109, USA.

BLONDIN Carmen Joseph, b. 13 May 1930, Paterson, NJ, Deputy Asst Sec for Internation Interest, National Oceanic and Atmospheric Admin, Dept of Commerce. m. Barbara Barker, 26 May 1955, 2 s, 4 d. *Education:* US Coast Guard Academy, BS, 1955; Geo Wash Univ, Law School, JD, 1962. *Appointments inc:* US Navy Submarine Serv, 1948-51; US Coast Guard, 1955-73; Cheif Law Enforcement Div NMFS/NOAA, 1973-74; Internat'l Affairs NMFS/NOAA, 1974-82; Administrator for Resource Mgmt, 1982-88; Special Assoc for Trade, NMFS?NOAA, 1988; Sec for Internation Interest of Commerce, 1998-. *Publications:* Law Review, 1961-62; Fisheries Management, 1966; Maritime Law and Law Enforcement, 1971; Safety of Life at Sea Convention, 1972; Law of the Sea Negotations, 1973; Intl Fisheries Commissions, 1981; Habitat Concerns in the US, 1985. *Memberships:* Boy Scouts of America, Commissioner and Dist Chairman; American Legion. *Honours:* DOC silver Medal, 1982,1985; Meritorious Service Medal, 1973; USCG Commendation Medal, 1969,1970. *Hobbies:* Sailing; Golf. *Address:* 301 Rexburg Avenue, Ft Washington, MD 20744, USA.

BLOWFIELD Ian Stuart, b. 23 Jan 1947, Harrow, England, Fine Artist Auctioneer, Valuer. m. Jacueline, div Oct 1986, 2 s. *Education:* Assoc of Incorporated Soc Valuers and Auctioneers since 1978; Ass Gemmplogral Assoc of GB, 1964; Student Gemological Inst of America, 1986. *Appointments:* Jewel Buyer, 1963-70; Valuer and Catalguer, 1970-76; Auctioneering, Hereford, Manchester, 1976-78, 1978-80; European Director, Geneva, 1980-87; Senior Director, Geneva, 1987-91. *Creative Works:* Joint Founder of Phillips Fine Art Course, 1984; Intl Lectures and Seminars of Jewellary in America, UK, Europe, Sth Africa, 1984-90. *Honours:* Gemmological Assoc, GB, 1965; ISVA, 1978; Gemmological Inst of America, 1988. *Hobbies:* Fund Raising; Geneva English School; Golf; Skiing; Squash; Music; Theatre; Jewel Lectures; Travel; Museums, Galleries; Historial Locations. *Address:* Malagnou 32, CP 407, 1211 Geneva 17, Switzerland. 1.

BNINSKI Kazimierz Andrzej, b. 28 Feb 1939, Gdynia, Poland, Doc of Medicine, General Practice. m. Teresa Maria de Gallen Bisping, 2 July 1988, 1 s. *Education:* Univ of Gdansk, MD, Poland, 1964. *Appointments:*

House Officer, Nelson Hospital, London, 1967-68; St Mary Abbots Hospital, London, 1969-71; Reg in Med, St Marys Hospital, 1972-76; Physician V11 US Army, Germany, 1977-80; Jnr Partner General Practice, 1981-87; Dir ic Polish Clinic, London, 1988-. *Address:* 131 Harley Street, London W1, England.

BOBER Ireneusz Adam, b. 6 Apr 1957, Opatow, Scientist, Philosophy and Tchr. m. Elzbieta Moskwa, 14 July 1979, 1 s, 1 d. *Education:* Faculty of Philosophy, 1976-80; MA, Philosopht, 1980; Doctors Degree, 1989. *Appointments:* Pedagogical Univ, Kielce, Inst of Social Sciences. *Publications:* Izydora Damskas Philosophy of Culture, 1991; Concept of the Rule of Science in Izydora Damskas Philosophy; Some Disputes About the Philosophy in Poland between the Wars; Witwicki and Dambska; On some Izydora Dambskas Opinions Concerning Epistemology and Theory of Sciences. *Hobbies:* History of Polish Philosophy; Metaphilosophy; Epistemology; Philosophy of Culture. *Address:* os J Krasickiego 1 m. 35, 28 100 Busko Zdroj, Poland.

BOBYLIOV Leonid Borisovitch, b. 15 Oct 1949, Tula, USSR, Composer, Pianist, Musicologist. m. Poletaineva Ludmila, 27 Oct 1973, 1 d. *Education:* Moscow State Chaikovsky Conservatory, 1973. *Appointments:* Prof of Musical Coll, Tula, 1973-76; Moscow State Chaikovsky Conservatory 1976-. *Compositions:* 2 Operas; 6 Concerts, Symphony; 2 Concerti Grossi; Chamber Music for Solo Instruments; Music for Theatres, Motion Pictures. *Memberships:* Soviet Composers Union. *Hobbies:* Reading; Foreign Languages. *Address:* 109172 Gonchovcnaia Naberezhnaia 3, Apt 123, Moscow, Russia.

BOCIAN Miroslaw, b. 11 April 1952, Karpacz, Poland. Photographer. 2 s, 2 d. *Education:* State High School of Movie, TV and Theatre, Poland 1973-77. *Appointments:* Camerman in TV, 1977-78; News Reporter and Correspondent, 1979-81; Photographer, 1982-. *Creative Works:* Individual Photo Exhibitions. Nude and Portrait, 1981, 84, 92; Theatre, 1987; Bach Street of Cracow, 1988; Portrait, 1990. *Memberships:* Candiate of Assoc of Polish Artists, Photographers. *Honours:* 3rd Intl Biennale of Art photography. *Hobbies:* Music; Theatre; Rebirthing, unconventional methods of Healing. *Address:* ul Wyspianskiego 49/4, 64 920 Pila, Poland.

BOCKSTAELE Paul Pieter, b. 7 Feb 1920, Melle, Prof of Mathematics, retired. *Education:* Theology, Roman Catholic Seminary, 1940-44; Mathematics, Univ of Leuven, PhD, 1951. *Appointments:* Mathematics Tchr, St Vincentius Coll, Eeklo, 1947-53; Tchrs Coll, Sint Niklaas, 1953-62; Assoc Prof, 1963; Prof, 1967; Emeritus Prof, 1985, Univ of Leuven. *Publications:* Papers on History of Mathematics in Professional Journals. *Memberships:* Intl Academy of the History of Science; Koninklyke Academie voor Wetenschuppen von België. *Address:* Graetboslaan 9, B-3050 Oud Heverlee, Belgium. 1.

BOCSAN Nicolae, b. 24 Sept 1947, Bocsa, Romania. Assoc Prof. m. Malvina, 31 Aug 1974, 1 s. *Education:* Univ of Cluj, 1970; Doc in History, Univ of Cluj, 1985. *Appointments:* Bibliographer, Univ Library, CLuj, 1970-78; Asst in History, 1978-82; Lect, 1982-90; Assoc Prof, 1990; Dept Dean, 1991. *Publications include:* From The Enlightened Consciousness to the National Consciousness, 1978; Romainas Independence on the Belgian Opinion, 1980; Contributions to the History of Romanian Enlightenment, 1986; The Guide of the History Student; The OAS County, Biblography, 1983; Culture and Society in the Modern Age, 1990. *Memberships:* Historiography of the intl Committee of History; Intl Relations; Scientific Sec of the Inst of Central European Studies; Historians Assoc from Transylvania and Banat. *Honours:* Prize of the Romanian Academy, 1986. *Hobbies:* Reading; Football; History of Ideas; History of Mentalities. *Address:* STR Donath, no. 44 bl P4, sc3, et4, ap29, 3400 Cluj Napoca, Romania.

BODENHEIMER Henriette Hannah, b. 21 July 1898, Cologne, Germany. Writer; Biographer; Retired Tchr. *Education:* Matricultion, Friedrick Wilhelm, Univ Bonn, 1921; Tchrs Cert, Agri and Domestic Science, Coll of Agri Sciences, 1931; Cert, vocational Tchr, Tech Schools, 1932. *Appointments include:* Founder Manager, Jewish Womens Union, Munich, 1926-32; Pioneer work, Palestine, 1933; Res, Central Zionist Archives, Jerusalem, 1940. *Publications:* Numerous studies; Biographies; Zionism and related Subjects, Hebrew, German, English; Toldoth Tochnith Basel, 1947; Max Bodenheimer; So Wurde Israel, 1958, 82; Statutes of the Keren Kayemeth, 1964- 65; Bershit Hatnuah, 1965; Three Delegates Conf of German Zionists, 1971. *Hobbies:* Travel; Gardening; History of Art and Literature. *Address:* Sadja Gaon Street 8, Jerusalem, Israel. 151, 152.

BODIWALA Gautam Govindlal, b. 11 Oct 1943, Ahmedabad, India. Med Dr. m. Gita Thanawalam 28 Dec 1969, 1 s, 1 d. *Education:* MBBS, 1965; MS, 1969; FICS, 1979; FICA, 1981. *Appointments:* Lectr in Surg, Civ Hosp and B J Med Coll, 1969-70; Cons in Accident and Emergency, Derbyshire Royal Infirmary, Derby, 1976; Hd of Accident and Emergency Servs, Leicester Royal Infirmary, Leicester, 1977-. *Publications:* Num articles in profl jrnls. *Memberships:* Casualty Surgs Assn, Hon Treas, Trustee, Exec Mbr; BMA; Royal Soc of Med, Fndr Mbr and Coun Mbr, Accident and Emergency Sect; American Coll of Emergency Physns; Rotary Int. *Honours:* Fellow, International College of Surgeons, 1981; Fellow, International College of Angiology, 1979; Justice of the Peace, 1984. *Hobbies:* Reading, Music. *Address:* Lykkebo, 7 Blackthorn Lane, Oadby, Leicester LE2 4FA, England.

BODOR Adam, b. 22 Feb 1936, Cluj, Transilvania. Ed. m. Aniko, 14 Apr 1977. 2 d. *Education:* Protestant Theology. *Appointments:* Freelance Writer, 1965-; Ed, Magveto Publg House, Budapest, 1984-. *Publications:* 7 books, short stories; The Euphrates at Babylon, 1991. *Memberships:* Hungarian Writers Assn; Hungarian PEN Club. *Honours:*)Jozsef Attila Prize, 1986; Artisjus Prize, 1986; Dery Tibor Prize, 1989; Krudy Prize, 1991. *Hobbies:* Hiking, Mountaineering, Skiing. *Address:* VI Bajcsy-Zsilinszky 39, H-1065 Budapest, Hungary.

BODUNRIN Peter Oluwambe, b. 4 Dec 1936, Osi Ekiti, Vice Chancellor. m. V.O. Bodunrin, 3 s, 1 d. *Education:* St Josephs Catherlic School, 1943-49; Univ of Ibadan, Nigeria, 1962-66; Univ of Minnesocta, USA, PhD, 1967-71. *Appointments:* Vice Chancellor Ondo State Univ, Nigeria, 1990-; Visiting Prof of Philosophy, Indiana Univ of Pennsylvania, 1985-1986; Dean, Faculty of Arts, Univ of Ibadan, 1983-85. *Publications:* The Question of African Philosophy, Philosophy, 1981. *Memberships:* Nigerian Classical Assoc; Nigerian Philosophical Assoc; Aristotelian Soc of Great Britain; Inter African Council of Philosophy; Executive American Philosophical Assoc; Royal Inst of Philosophy, London. *Honours:* Dept prize in Classics, 1963; Irving and Bonnar, Univ of Ibadan, 1964; Nigerian Federal Government postgraduate Scholarship, 1965-66; Ford Foundation Grant for Research in Philosophy, 1972-74. *Address:* Vice Chancellors Office, Ondo State Univ, PMB 5363, Ado Ekiti, Ondo State, Nigeria, West Africa.

BOECHER Otto (Hermann Konrad), b. 12 Mar 1935, Worms, Univ Prof. m. Ortrud Eleonore nee Bauscher, 10 Dec 1962, 3 s, 1 d. *Education:* Matriculation Exam, Classical Second School, 1954; Dr Phil, Univ Mainz, 1958; Dr Theol, Univ Mainz, 1963; Dr Theol Habil, Univ Mainz, 1968. *Appointments:* Curate Evan, Church, Wiesbaden, 1960-61; Parson Evang, Church, Selzen, 1962-64; Asst Prof Univ, Mainz, 1963-68; Univ Lect, Univ Mainz, 1968-71; Prof Theol, Univ Mainz, 1971-75; Prof Theol, Univ Saarbrucken, 1975- 78; Prof Theol, Univ Mainz 1978-. *Publications include:* Die Alte Synagoge zu Worms, 1960; Christus Exorcista, 1972; Kirche in Zeit und Endzeit, 1983; Der Wein und die Bibel, 1989. *Memberships:* Deutscher Hochschulverband; Kommission fur die Geschiche der Juden in Hessen; Der Herold; Humboldt Gesellschaft; Order of St John; Wingolf. *Honours:* Chamber of the German Physicians, 1976; German Bishops Conference, 1978; Order of St John, Bonn, 1981. *Hobbies:* Genealogy; Heraldry. *Address:* Johannes Gutenberg Univ, Fachbereich 02, Seminar fuer Neues Testament, Postfach 3980, D 6500 Mainz, Germany. 1, 145.

BOELHOUWER Ton, b. 12 Aug 1960, The Hague, Artist. *Education:* Reitveldacademy Amsterdam, 1979-82; Croydon Coll of Art, London, 1982-83; Jan Van Eyckacademic Maastricht, 1983-85. *Exhibitions:* Museum Die Neue Galerie, Aken, BRD, 1986; Museum Van Bommel van Dam, Venio, 1987; KunstRAI, Amsterdam, 1987; Galerie van Krimpen, Amsterdam, 1990-91. *Honours:* ABC Prize, 1987; Royal Prize for Painting, 1991. *Hobbies:* History; Reading; Squash. *Address:* Mariabastion 11, 6217 NB Maastricht, The Netherlands.

BOETTCHER Diane Ruth, b. 19 Sept 1957, Syracuse NY, USA, Soccer Coach. *Education:* Bachelor of Sci, Univ of Vermont, 1979; Master of Education, East Stroudsburg Uni, 1985. *Appointments:* Saint Micheals Coll, Asst Basketball, Soccer Coach, 1978-80; Bates Coll, Asst Prof, Head Soccer Coach, 1980-89; Davidson Coll, Head Coach of Soccer, 1989-. *Memberships:* New England Womens Intercollegiate Soccer Assn; Lewiston Auburn Branch of the American Assn of Univ Women; National Soccer Coaches Assn of America; Coach of the Year, 1986; National Collegiate Athletic Assn; Maine Youth Soccer Assn. *Honours:* Outstanding Achievement in Physical Education; North Carolina Business and Professional Womens Club; NCAA 111, Womens Soccer Coach of the Year, 1986. *Hobbies:* Coaching Youth Soccer; Mentoring Young Professionals. *Address:* PO Box 1750, Davidson NC, 28036, USA.

BOETTCHER Winfried, b. 11 Mar 1936, Morbach, Univ Prof. m. Dr Ingrid Boettcher, 1 Aug 1963, 1 d. *Education:* Mechanical Engineering, 1957-63; History, Educational Sci, political Sci, 1963-67; State Exam, 1963- 65; Dr phil, 1970. *Appointments:* Prof for Political Sci, 1973- . *Publications:* The German Image in Great Britain, 1970; The European Ideas in Great Britain, 1969-73; Peace Politics, 1973; The Political System of the FRG, 1975; Social Europe 1993 - an Illusion, 1990. *Memberships:* Germany-British Society; German Soc for political Sci. *Address:* Gut Bau, Senserbachweg 219, 5100 Aachen, Germany. 92.

BOFILL Rano Solidum, b. Philippines, Physician. m. Judy Libo-On, 27 May 1972, 1 s, 2 d. *Education:* Pre Medical Grad, 1960; Medical Grad, Doc of Medicine Diploma, 1966. *Appointments:* Chief Radiologist, Appalachian Regional Hos, 1984-90; Radiologist, Memorial Hos, 1990-. *Publications:* Sing a long in Nursing Homes;Pmawr Newsletter; WV Acip; The Man Connection; UST '66 Newsletter; Assoc Editor, Philippine American Medical Bulletin. *Memberships:* Philippine Medical Assoc of WV; WV AM Coll Intl Physicians; AM Coll Intl Physicians; ARH Medical Staff; Logan Medical County Soc; Tri State Fil AA Assoc. *Honours:* Army Achmt and Commendation, 1983; American Red Cross, 1983; Assoc of Philipiine physicians of America, 1990; Multiple Civic and Medical Awards; Phila police Award; American Police Hall of Fame; Knight of St Michael; Intern of the Year; Logan County WV Award. *Hobbies:* Sing a long Nursing Home Entertainment; Leader Medical Missions to the Philippines; Editors in Newsletters, Yearbooks; Singin The National Anthem; Travelling. *Address:* 309 W Avis Avenue, Man, WV 25635, USA. 2.

BOGDANOV Ivan, b. 3 May 1910, Velico Turnovo. Wife dec, 1 s, 1 d. *Education:* Univ of Sofia, 1936. *Appointments:* Lawyers Practice; Public activity, Economic; Research into Hist, Lit. *Publications include:* A Short History of the Bulgarin Literature, 1969, 1970;

Bulgarian Periodics of Literature, 1972; Unforgetable Centuries of Bulgarian Literature, 1983; Literatary Critics, 1985; A Dictionary of Bulgarian Pen names, 1961, 1989; The Life Flame of Words; Names of the Bulgarian Chans. *Memberships:* Union of Bulgarian Sci; Soc for Hist and Theory of Sci at the Bulgarian Academy of Sci; Union of the Indep Bulgarian Writers. *Address:* 84 Tzar Boris 1 Str, Sofia 1000, Bulgaria.

BOGUCKI Dariusz Michał, b. 19 Dec 1927, Warsaw, Poland. Shipbuilding Eng. m. Irena Kuran-Bogucka, 19 Dec 1948, 2 d. *Education:* Techn Univ of Gdansk, M.Sc. Naval Arch, 1952; Phil Doc, 1968. *Appointments:* Fishing Vessels Shipyard, 1947-49; Tech Univ of Gdansk, 1952-57; Gdensk Shipyard Design Office, 1957-71; Ship Res Centre, 1971-87; Polarex Ltd, 1987-. *Publications:* Iceland Voyage, 1970; To The Greenland Coasts, 1973; Yacht Sailing on Polar Waters, 1980; Beyond Both Polar Circles, 1980; Before We Return, 1983; Geometry of Hull Shape, 1983. *Memberships:* Polish Soc of Eng; Explorers Club; Polish Polar Soc; Cape - Horners' Brotherhood; Brotherhood of the Coast. *Honours:* Silver Sextant for th Greatest Yacht Voyage of the Year; 3 x Conrad Award; 2 x Teliga Literary Reward; Golden Cross of Merit; Main Exhibitions: 2 x Labrador Sea; 3 x Iceland; 3 x Greenland; Spitsbergen; 2 x Jan Mayen; North - West Passage; 3 x Antarctic Coasts. *Hobby:* Polar Yachting. *Address:* Grunwaldzka 7, 80 236 Gdansk, Poland.

BOGUSŁAWSKI Andrzej, b. 1 Dec 1931, Warsaw, Prof of Linguistics. m. Maria Gillert, 30 Oct 1954, 1 d. *Education:* Univ of Warsaw, 1949-53; Slavistics PhD in Linguistics, 1960; Habilitation in Linguistics, 1966. *Appointments:* Faculty of philology , Univ of Warsaw, Asst Prof, 1967; Assoc Prof, 1977; Prof, 1989. *Publications:* Problems of the Thematic Rhematic Structure of Sentences, 1977; Semantic and Pragmatic Aspects of Reference, 1982. *Memberships:* Intl Assoc for Semiotic Studies; Intl Pragmatics Assoc; Conslt Board; Polish Linguistic Soc. *Address:* ul Opaczawska 25 m 33, 02-372 Warsaw, Poland.

BOHM Aleksander, b. 25 Nov 1943, Cracow, Poland, Architect. m. Mariola Mickowska, 29 June 1972, 1 s, 1 d. *Education:* Tech univ of Cracow, Dept of Arch, 1961-67; Diploma in Master of Sci, 1967; Univ of New Brunswick, 1971-72; Fundazione Romana, Italy, 1979; Doctorate Dissertation, 1972-74; Doc of Tech Sci, 1974. *Appointments:* Tech Univ of Cracow, Dept of Arch, Assoc Prof, 1967-; Voytec Szymanski Design Office, Designer, 1972; Univ of Bagdad, Sen Lectr, 1976-77; Fachhockschule Munster, Germany, Visiting Prof, 1989; The Municipality, Cracow, Arch, 1991. *Publications:* Structure and Synergy of Urban Interiors, 1981; Scientific publications; Arch and Urban Design and Research. *Memberships:* Polish Arch Assoc; Intl Fed of Landscape Arch; Commission of Town Planning; Arch of Polish Academy of Sciences; Group of Specialists on Heritage Landscape and Sites. *Honours:* Urban Design of Czyzyny Housing Est for 40,000 Inhabitants, 1967; Urban Design for the Development of the City Centre at Biala, 1971; Ministry of Foreign Affairs Building in Warsaw, 1973; Urban Plan of the Warsaw Centre of Learning, 1974; ministry of Educ in Poland, Structure and Synergy of Urban Interior, 1983. *Hobbies:* Fishing; Mountaineering; Symphonic Music; Graphic Art. *Address:* 7 Dziedzica Str, 31 416 Cracow, Poland.

BOIAJIEV Bozhidar, b. 15 Feb 1956, Sofia, Tchr in Painting, Academy of Art, Sofia. *Education:* Academy of Fine Art, Sofia. *Appointments:* Tchr, Academy of Fine Art, Sofia. *Cretive Works:* One Man Shows: Autumn Exhibitions, Municipal Galleries, Plovdiv, 1983; Shipka, 6 Gallery, Sofia, 1986; Rousky, 6 Gallery, Sofia, 1987; Municipal Gallery, Botevgrad, 1990; Hemus, Gallery, Sofia, 1992; ATA-RAI, Sheraton Gallery, Sofia, 1992. *Memberships:* Union of Bulgarian Artists, 1985-. *Honours:* Union of Bulgarian Artists, 1982; Youth Org of Bulgaria, 1983; 3 International Competition of Young Artists, Sofia, 1985; Haidubösörmeny Pleinair, Hungary,

1985; 21 Festival Intl de la Peinture Cagnes sur Mer, France, 1989; Intl Competition of Young Artists, Sofia, 1989. *Hobby:* Aircraft Model Making; Taekwon-Do. *Address:* 13 Hadjy Dimiter, Str. Sofia 1000, Bulgaria.

BOILLAT Guy Maurice Georges, b. 18 May 1937. Pontarlier, France. Mathematical Physicist. *Education:* Licence es Sciences, Univ Besancon, 1959; Docteur es Sciences, Mathematiques, Sorbonne, 1964; Studied Inst Henri-Poincase, Paris, Inst for Theor Phys, Copenhagen and Trondheim. *Appointments:* Univ of Clermont, 1966-. *Publications:* 80 Research articles, published in 20 different Intl Sci journals; Theme: Nonlinear fields, waves, shocks. *Hobbies:* Art; Bibliophilism; Horology. *Address:* 16 rue Ronchaux, F-25000 Besancon, France. 139, 151, 152, 156, 162.

BOJANOWSKI Grzegorz Seweryn, b. 23 May 1946, Lodz. Artistic Photographer. m. Ryszarda Śliwińska, 24 May 1969, 1 s. *Education:* Secondary Tech School of Chemistry, Lodz, 1965; Self taught in the field of Photography. *Appointments:* Man made Fibres prod, 1965-74; Leather Ind Inst, 1974; The Lodz Photographic Soc, 1975-76; State Higher School of Fine Arts, 1976-. *Creative Wroks:* Photographs, Lodz 1979; Photographs 11, Lodz, 1983; To Be .., Lodz, 1986; Photographed by G Bojanowski, 1962-, Lodz, 1987; Hommage a G. Eastman, 1989, Torun, 1990, Wroclaw. *Memberships:* Lodz Photographic Soc, 1969; Assoc of Polish Artistic Photographers, 1980. *Honours:* Medals and Awards for Photographic Art, 1965-1991; 150 Years of Photography Medal, 1989. *Hobbies:* Poetry; Contemplative Perception of Lanscapes; photography. *Address:* ul Stefana 4 m. 7, 91 463 Lodz, Poland.

BOJTAR Endre, b. 26 May 1940, Budapest. Historian of Literature. m. Anna, 15 Dec 1962, 2 s. *Education:* BA Czech and Russian Lit,Eotvos Lorand Univ, 1963; MA Theory of Lit, Hungarian Academy of Sci, 1975. *Appointments:* Inst for Literary Studies of the Hungariran Academy of Sci, 1963-; Head of Dept, Central and East European Lit, 1986-. *Publications:* East Uropean Avant-garde Literature, 1977; Slavic Structuralism, 1978; A companion to Lithuanias Cultural History, 1989; The Rape of Europe, 1990. *Memberships:* Intl Comparative Lit Assoc; Assoc for the Advancement of Baltic Studies. *Hobbies:* Football; Gardening. *Address:* Lonyay u 17, H-1093 Budapest, Hungary.

BOKO Haris, b. 13 Aug 1960, Zagreb, Clinical Engineer. *Education:* Matematics, Informatics Colleague, Zagreb, 1979; BSc, MSc, Faculty of Elec Eng; DSc, Univ of Zagreb. *Appointments:* Research Fellow, World Health Organisation Collaborating Ultrasonic Inst; Research Collaborator, Zagreb Univ Dir, Interuniversity Centre. *Publications:* 36 Scientific and Professional papers, Worldwide. *Memberships:* Pres Univ of Zagreb, Intl Centre for Culture and Education; American, Croatian Soc. *Honours:* Extraordinary Support of Intl Sci cooperation, MSKP, 1987. *Hobbies:* Tennis; Skiing. *Address:* Univ Hospital, Dept of Radiology, Zajceve 19, YU-41000 Zagreb, Croatia.

BOLTON Richard Andrew E, b. 16 Oct 1939, Montreal, Physicist. m. Sandra Cassidy, 2 s, 1 d. *Education:* B SC McGill, 1960; M Sc McGill, 1963; PhD Univ Montreal, 1966. *Appointments:* Asst Prof Dept of Physics, Univ Montreal, 1966-1968; Research Assoc UK Atomic Energy, 1968-73; Sen Researcher Hydro Quebec, 1973-82; Mngr, Fusion Res, 1982-87; Dir General Canadian Center for Magnetic Fusion, 1987-. *Publications:* 30 Scientific Articles. *Memberships:* Canadian Assoc of Physicist; Canadian Nuclear Soc; Sci Council of Canada, 1987-92; Governor Lower Canada Coll, 1986-92. *Honour:* NRC Scholarship, 1961-64. *Hobbies:* Tennis; Skiing; Carpentry. *Address:* 507 Argyle Avenue, Westmount Quebec, Canada, H3Y 3B6. 14, 88.

BONAR L George, b. 1 June 1934, Lodz, Poland. Business Executive. m. Stephanie Leonard, 1 June 1963, 1 s, 1 d. *Education:* BA Sc, Metakurgical Eng, Univ of Toronto, 1958; MS, Metallurgy, Univ of California, 1959; PhD, Metallurgy, Cambridge Univ, 1962. *Appointments incl:* Various Positions, Falconbridge Ltd, Tronto, 1962-70; Vice President, Amax Nickel, New York, 1972-80; Pres, Cabot Mineral Resources, New York, 1980-81; Chairman and Chief Exec, Eldorado Nuclear Offawer, 1987-88; Chairman Pres and Chief Executive, Intl UNP Holdings, Toronto, 1989-; Chmn Supervisory Board, IBIS Ltd, BIAWAR Ltd. *Honours:* Athlone Fellowship, 1959-61; Nat Research Council of Canada, 1961-62. *Address:* 96 Glen Road, Toronto, Canada, M4W 2V6. 88.

BOND Bronwell Christina, b. 22 Dec 1941, Chalotte, N.C. Instrumental Music Tchr and Flutist. m. Robert Augustine Bond, 9 June 1962, 1 s, 1 d. *Education:* Lamar Stringfield, 1955-58; Hamline Univ, St Paul, MN, 1960-63; B. of Arts with major in music, Milton College, 1970. *Appointments:* Milton Area Schools, 1971-81; Univ of Wisconsin Rock Campus, 1970; Beloit College, 1977-81; Craw Central School District, 1986-; Allegheny College, Meadville, PA 1987-. *Creative Works:* Principle Flutist, Beloit Sym, 1968-81; Allegheny Summer Music Festival Orch, 1982-90; Allegheny Woodwind Quintet, 1988-. *Memberships:* Wisconsin Educ Assoc; Nat Ed Assoc; Pennsylvnia Ed Assoc; Meadville Council on the Arts Board, 1983-85, 1988-90; Pres of MCA Board, 1988-89. *Honours:* Presser Scholar, Hamline Univ, 1961. *Hobbies:* Woodworking; Reading. *Address:* 686 Susquehanna Road, Meadville, PA 16335, USA.

BOND Martyn Arthur, b. 10 Oct 1942, Isle of Wight, Head of European Parliament Office. m. Dinah Macfarlane, 10 July 1965, 2 s, 1 d. *Education:* Winchester, 1956-61; Queens Coll, Cambridge, 1961-64; Univ of Sussex and Hamburg, 1964-66; MA DPhil, 1971. *Appointments:* BBC, 1966-70; Lectr, New Univ of Ulster, 1970-73; Press Officer, EC Council of Ministers, 1974-81; BBC Rep in Berlin, 1981-83; Sen Admin, EC Council of Ministers, 1983-88; Head of European Parliament, UK Office, 1989. *Publication:* A Tale of Two Germanys, 1990. *Memberships:* Intl Advisory Council of Salzburg Seminar; Fellow of the Royal Soc of Arts; Quaker Council for European Affairs. *Hobbies:* Travel; Classical Music; Theatre. *Address:* European Parliament UK Office, 2 Queen Annes Gate, London SW1H 9AA, England.

BONDI Enrico, b. 17 Jan 1933, Budrio. Steel Plants Proj Engr. m. Bettina Grassani, 18 April 1960, 1 s, 2 d. *Education:* Dr Mech, Engr, Univ Bologna, 1958; State Dert, 1959. *Appointments:* Steel Shop Asst, 1959-60; Rolling Mills Chief, 1960-68; Rolling Mills proj Manager, 1968-. *Creative Works:* Rolling Mills Patents; Collaborative meeting Univ Tech Articles. *Memberships:* Assoc Italiana di Metzllurgia. *Honours:* Gold Medal Assoc Italiana dei Cavalieri del Lavoro. *Hobby:* Photography. *Address:* Navielio Pavese, 46 20143 - Milano, Italy.

BONE John Bolam, b. 20 Mar 1913, West Hartlepool, Arch. m. Eleanor Patterson, 28 Aug 1943. *Education:* School of Arch, Newcastle upon Tyne, ARIBA 1946; FRIBA 1970. *Appointments:* Divisional Arch, Newcastle Upon Tyne Reg Hospital Board, 1948-52; NBC Senior Arch, 1952-60; Senior Arch Manchester Regional Board, 1960-67; WW Reg Hospital Board, 1969-73; Consulting Arch to Home Office, 1973-89. *Creative Works:* Hospital Works, Teeside, Manchester, NW London; Reconstruction Works, Coal Ind in Co Durham. *Memberships incl:* Doric Club; Village Soc. *Hobbies:* Water Colours; Music; Conservation. *Address:* 2 Thimbleby Cottages, Church Lane, Hampsthwaite, Harrogate, North Yorkshire, HG3 2HB, England.

BONTCHEV Panayot Rankov, b. 31 Dec 1933, Burges, Bulgaria. Univ Prof of Analytical and Coordination Chem. m. Hubinka Veltcheva, 4 Dec 1957, 1 s, 1 d. *Education:* M Sci, Sofi Univ, 1956; PhD, Sofia Univ, 1964; D Sci, Bulgarian Academy of Sci, 1975. *Appointments:* Asst and Assoc Prof, Sofi Univ, 1956-79; Full Prof, 1979; Vice Dean, Chem Faculty, 1975-79; Vice Rector, 1989-91; Head of Analytical Chem Dept, 1991-. *Publications:* Mechanisms of Inorg. Reactions, 1969; Chem Bond, 1971; Coordination and Catalytic Activity, 1972, 1975; Analytic Chem, 1974,79,83; Scientific Papers. *Memberships:* Intl Committee for Intl Conf Coordination Chem; Nat Commission for Ecolog Education; Intl Journal Talanta Adv Board; Europ Assoc for Intl Education; American, East Uropean Alliance Univ for Democracy; Bulg Chem Soc. *Honours:* StSt Cyril and Methodius Order; National award in Chemistry; Medal of Honor of the Slovak Tech Univ; Kliment Okridski medal. *Hobbies:* Tourism; Old Books of Science. *Address:* Univ of Sofia, Faculty of Chemistry, 1 J Bourchier Str, 1126 Sofia, Bulgaria. 139.

BOOMER Walter Fred, b. 10 Jan 1936, Frankfurt, Director General. m. Julia Pilkington, 11 Aug 1956, 2 s, 1 d. *Education:* Cambridge Univ, BA, 1956; Cambridge Univ, PhD, 1959. *Appointments:* Prof Dept of Genetics, Stanford, 1968-70; Prof of Genetics, Oxford, 1970-79; Dir General, Imperial Cancer, 1991; Dir of Research, Imperial Cancer, 1979-91. *Publications:* The Genetics of Human populations; Genetics Evolution and Man and our Future; Inheritance Choice or Chance. *Memberships include:* BBC Gen Adv Council, 1981; Union Against Cancer, 1982; Adv Bd for Res Coucils, 1983-88; Assoc for Science Educ, 1989-90; British Vice Pres, Red Defence Soc, 1990; Vice Pres, Parliamentary and Scientific Committe, 1990; Hon D Univ of Surrey, 1990. *Honours include:* American Academy of Arts and Sciences, 1972; Royal Statistical Soc, 1984-85; Hon Fellow Royal Coll of Surgeons of England, 1986; Hon DSc Iniv of Bath, 1988; American philosophical Soc, 1989; Hon DSc Univ of Hull, 1990; Hon Vice Pres, Research Defence Society,1990. *Hobbies:* Piano; Horse Riding; Swimming; Snorkelling; Scuba Diving. *Address:* Imperial Cancer Research Fund, PO Box 123, Lincolns Inn Fields, London WC2A 3PX, England. 2, 3, 30, 50, 69, 139, 161, 162.

BOOSS Dierk Helmuth, b. 11 Dec 1938, Berlin. Legal Advisor, Commission of the European Communities. 1 s, 2 d. *Education:* Law Univ, 1957-61; Asst of Law Faculty, 1962-66; Dr. Jur, 1965; Second State Law Exam, 1966. *Appointments:* Civil Servant, Fisheries Dept, Fed min for Agri, 1967- 77; Chairman Intl Commission, North West Atlanic Fisheries, 1976-78; Head of Div, Fisheries of the European Com, 1978-84. *Publications:* Articles on Intl and European Fisheries Law, European Agri Law. *Hobbies:* Gardening; Reading; 20th Century Operas. *Address:* CCE rue de la Loi 200, B-1049 Brussels, Belgium.

BORDE Damodhar S, b. 28 June 1939. Scientist, Engr. *Education:* BSc, Osmania Univ, India, 1959; BSEE, International Univ, Miss, USA. *Appointments:* Techn Staff position, ILEA, London 7 yrs; Mgmt, Personnel, Spencer Int Press, incl, Hollywood, Calif, USA. *Memberships:* Chmn, Int Students Club, Wichita, Kan; Comm, Crypt Club, Hampstead, UK; Debating Soc, Wichita Univ. *Honours:* Citetion, 2 US Pres, Kennedy and Eisenhower, 1962; Command & Control, Met Police, London SE1, 2 Years. *Address:* 33 G Rowley Way, Abbey Road, London NW8, England.

BORISLAVOV Ivan, b. 30 Mar 1946, Varna. Poet, Translater, Publicist. m. Rantcheva Pavlina, 9 July 1967, 1 s, 1 d. *Education:* Philology Graduate, Sofia Univ, 1970. *Appointments:* National Bulgarian Radio, Editor at Youth Dept, 1970-76; Managing Dir, Arts Dept, 1976-91. *Publications:* Growing to Manhood; Solar Avalanche; If You Come Tomorrow; Talk with Infinity; Instants with Paris; Laterna Magica; Verse and Shades, 1987; Essays on West European Twentieth Century Poetry and Painting; Books Translated from French, Selected Poetry by P Eluard, Aime, Cesaire, B Cendracs; To Say Everything; Sons of the Lightening; The Shadow of the

Days. *Memberships:* Bulgarian Writers Union; Bulgarian Translators Union; Bulgarian Journals Union; Managing Committee to Bulgarian Translators Union. *Honours:* Annual Award for Translation of Poetry; Gold Badge, Honorary Diploma, Skilful Translators Activity; National Bulgarian Radio. *Hobbies:* Reading; Travelling; Fine Arts. *Address:* Block 91, Eutrav V Ap 42, Dr Ludovic Zamenhof Str, 1517 Sofia, Bulgaria.

BORISSOVA Anna-Maria, b. 7 Jan 1950, Bjala Slatina, Bulgaria. Dr. m. Stephen Krivoshiev, 30 Sept 1973, 1 s. *Education:* Med, Sofia Univ, 1968-74; Postgrad specialization: Internal Diseases, 1980; Endocrinology, 1982; PhD, 1987. *Appointments:* Asst, 1980; Hd Asst, 1985-. *Publications:* Co-author, Clinical Endocrinology, 1992; Articles in profl jrnls. *Membership:* European Assn for Study of Diabetes. *Honour:* The Best Scientific Works of Diabetes in Bulgaria for 1988. *Hobbies:* Reading, Travelling. *Address:* Christo Michailov str 6, Sofia 1303, Bulgaria.

BOROS Janos, b. 23 Feb 1954, Pecs, Hungary. Prof of Philosophy. m. Orban Jolan, 25 May 1987. *Education:* Univ Veszprem, 1973-78; Dipl Chemical Engr, 1978; Rom Cath Academy of Theology, Budapest, 1979-82; Univ de Fribourg, Switzerland, 1982-87; Dr Phil, 1987. *Appointments:* Chem Engr in Pecs, 1978-79; Tchr, Switzerland, 1984-89; Rechercheur, Coll de France, 1989; Research Fellow, Boston Coll, USA, 1990; Chairman of the Dept of History of Phil, Janus Pannonius Univ, Pecs, 1991-. *Publications:* Die ungarische Wissenschaftstheorie; Marxistische and Nichtmarxistische Ansatze; Articles in Phil. *Memberships:* Hung Assoc of Phil of Religion, Budapest; Hung Assoc of phil, Budapest. *Hobbies:* Philosophy; Sports; Jogging; Alpinism; Skiing; Swimming; Reading; Theory of Literatur; Classical Music; Travel. *Address:* Univ Janus Pannonius, Ifjusag u 6, H-7624 Pecs, Hungary.

BORRELLI Mario Alfredo, b. 19 Sept 1922, Naples. m. Jilyan West, 19 Sept 1971, 1 d. *Education incl:* Naples Faculty of Theology, 1965; Sociology, Tufts Univ, 1967-68; London Sch of Econ, 1970. *Appointments incl:* Taught Religion, Sanazzari Liceo, 1947-50; Study Grouo, Community Dev, Ambit Europena Soc Dev , Oxford, 1973; Prof Sociology, Maryland Univ, 1973-76; Euro Assoc Development Int Conference, Milan, 1978; Intl Symposium on Street Youth, New York, 1983; Intl Conference of IPRA, Suusex Univ, 1987. *Publications incl:* La Filosofia di Tommaso d'Aquino, 1961; Le Costituzioni dell'Oratorio Napoletano, 1968; Il Cardinale Baronio ed i Fratolli Vosmeer, 1984; Human Rights and a Methonology for Peace, 1983; Approach to the political Dimension of Disarmament Educ, 1984. *Memberships incl:* Assoc Italiana della Stampa, 1952; La Federation Europeene Aide a Toute Detresse, 1974; Italian Peace Research Inst, 1977. *Honours incl:* Hon Member Kinderschutzbund, Lane Bryant Intern, 1963. *Address:* c/o Centro Comunitario Materdei, Casella Postale 378, Naples, Italy. 3, 52, 139.

BOSCHETTI Roger Phillip, b. 13 July 1921, Rome, Italy. Labour Union Executive, Telephone and Radio Producer, Personality. m. Racquel Ramon, Apr 1960, 1 s, 2 d. *Education:* Univ of San Francisco. *Appointments incl:* Military Officer US Merchant Marine, Honorably discharged from US Merchant Marine and US Coast Guard, World War 11, S Pacific; Organizer Marine Cooks and Steward Union, ALF C10; Business Agent Neg, Field Organizer, Asst Sec Treasurer, Port Agent, Hawaii; Delegate, California State Fed of Labour; Delegate, Merchant Ships inc Passenger Ships for MC&S; Business Agent, Seafarers Intl Union Of North America, ALF C10; Pres and Founder Unico National, San Fransico Chapter; Founder and Pres, Ital Inst. *Creative Works:* Editor Italian, American Family Scene. *Memberships incl:* Navy League; SF Italian AC; Sons of Italy; North Beach Lions; Irish Isreali Italian Soc; Godfathers Club; Republican Task Force; United States Senatorial Club. *Honours incl:* Gold Medal, City of Lucca,

Italy, 1977; Knighted, Republic of Italy, The Cavaliere Gold Cross. *Hobbies:* Soccer; Boxing; Golf. *Address:* 20 Carnelian Way, San Fransico, CA 94131, USA. 59.

BOSCHI Srdjan, b. 17 Feb 1927, Split. Medical Dr, Educator, Scientist. m. Prof Fani Rendic-Miocevic, 23 Jan 1960, 2 s. *Education:* Zegreb Univ, School of Med, 1957; MD Spec of Radiology, Zagreb Univ, 1962; PhD, 1970; Nephrologyst, 1985. *Appointments:* Prof of Radiology, Post Doctoral Studies, Zagreb Univ, 1975; Cheif Dept of Radiology, Clinical Centre Split, 1963; Chief Inst of Radiology, 1977; Chair Univ School of Medicine, Zagreb, 1983-. *Publications:* Articles to Scientific Journals; Establishment of the new Contrast Method in Examinations, Urinary Tract, 1968; Book of Radiology, 1991. *Memberships:* Croation Assoc for Radiology; Croatian Assoc for Nephrology, Croatian Medical Academy; American Assoc for the Advancement of Science; New York Academy of Sci; Planetary Soc. *Honours:* Dipl Croatians Medical Academy, 1979; Dipl Development of Sci, Clinical Center, Split, 1984; Zagreb Univ School of Medicine, 1981,85,87. *Hobbies:* Motonautica; Fishing; Protection Of Animals. *Address:* Aljinoviceva 26 B, 58000 Split, Croatia. 1.

BOSCHKOVA Nelly, b. 25 May 1949, Tolbuhin Bg. Opera Singer. 1 s. *Education:* High School of Music, Sofia, 1968-73. *Appointments:* Sofia Opera, 1973-78; Komische Oper-Beclin, 1978-82; opera, Theatre, Bremen, 1982-90; Volks ans Staats Opera, Wienna, 1990-. *Honours:* Silver Medal, T Maria Callas Comp, Thens, 1974; Bronze Medal, VI Tchaykovski Comp, Mosco, 1978. *Hobbies:* Piano; Reading; Cooking. *Address:* Bosendorferstz 6/16, A-1010 Wien, Austria.

BOSE Animesh, b. 8 Apr 1953, Calcutta, India. Materials Rsch Scientist. m. Prarthana, 24 Feb 1986. *Education:* B.Tech, Metall Engrng 1977, PhD Engrng (Powder Metall) 1982, Rsch Assoc 1985, Indian Inst of Technology, Kharagpur. *Appointments:* Vis Rsch Assoc, Rensselaer Polytechnic Inst, Troy, NY, USA, sponsored by CRT, NASA, Def Adv Rsch Project Agcy (DARPA) and US Army, 1985-89; Sr Rsch Engr, Southwest Rsch Inst, San Antonio, TX, 1989-. *Publications:* Over 50 tech papers in area of powder metall; Co-inventor 3 US patents granted to RPI; Retained by Butterworth Heinemann to write a tech book on Advanced Particulate Materials; Cons. *Memberships:* Powder Metall Assn, India, Life Mbr; American Powder Metall Inst; Materials Rsch Soc; The Minerals, Metals, Materials Soc. *Honour:* Best pair in intra-district round robin pairs bridge tournament. *Hobbies:* Stamp Collecting; Travelling, Cooking, Card Games. *Address:* 7655 Autumn Park, San Antonio, TX 78249, USA. 7.

BOSLER Nancy Delio, b. 24 Jan 1935, Strathfield, New South Wales. Community Dev Off. m. Wilfred Bosler, 16 Apri 1955, 1 s, 2 d. *Education:* Assoc Diploma, Adult Educ, 1988; Assoc Diploma Commun Org, 1989; Grad Diploma, Local and Applied History, 1990; Bach of Educ, 1992; Advisor Univ of Tech, Sydney, Assoc Diploma Adult Educ. *Appointments:* Commonwealth Bank, 1950-57; Creative Leisure Movements, 1971-; Educ Dept, 1979-84; Warringah Shire Council, 1979-92; Pittwater Municipal Council, 1992-; Freelance Journalist, 1973-. *Publications:* Australian Macrame Animals And Flowers; Christmas Decorations in Australia; Australian Patchwork & Applique; Anzac, Something to be Proud Of; Banners for the Handicapped; Manly Warringah Historic Reflections; Easter; Narrabeen, Memories of its School and Community. *Memberships:* Dir, Local History Resource Unit; Deputy Chairman, Creative Leisure Movement; Pres, Northern Beaches Interchange; Pres, Cubby House Toy Library; Australian Toy Library Assoc; Diversional Therapy Assoc of Australia; Manly Warringah Community Coll, Soc of Australian Authors. *Honours incl:* Australian Religious Press Assoc, 1975; Oustanding Citizen, Warringah Shire Council, 1975; Frank McAskill Trophy; Anzac of the Year, 1984;

Advance Australia Award, 1987; New South Wales Government Community Service Awd, 1990; Fellowship of the Fellowship of Australian Writers, 1990; Kiwanis Club, Distinguished Service Awd, 1992; Medal of the Order of Australia, 1992; Children's Week Awd, 1992. *Hobbies:* Writing; Photography; Crafts; People. *Address:* Narrabeen Community Learning Centre, Pittwater Road, North Narrabeen, NSW 2101, Australia.

BOSQUET Jean Paul Emile, b. 25 Mar 1907, Ixelles, Brussels, Belgium. Prof Emeritus. m. Denyse de Thoran 2 Apr 1932, 3 s. *Education:* Civ Engr, Mech-Elec, ULB, 1930; Heinrich Hertz Institut fur Schwingingsforschung, Berlin, 1931-32; Dr Mechanics, 1934; Agrege, ULB, 1935. *Appointments:* Rschr, Fonds Tasel, U, 1930-32; Asst, ULB, 1932-36; Prof, Ecole Techniques des Travaux Publics, Brussels, 1932-47; Asst Lectr, Acoustics and Electroacoustics, ULB, 1936; Active Participant, 1st Int Conf of Subcomm, Vocabulary, ISA Comm 43 Acoustics, Paris, 1 and 2 July 1937; Engr, John Cockerill Naval Shipyard, Hoboken, 1937; Engr, Union Chimie Belge (UCB since 1961), then successively Asst Mgr, 1946, Hd of Dept, 1950; Dir, Div of Enterprises and Constrn, 1961; Dpty Dir subsidiary co Enterprises et Constructions a l'Etranger, 1963; Pres, Dir UCB subsidiaries: Contracts in Pakistan, USSR, Romania, Bulgaria; Prof Extraordinary, Acoustics, Electroacoustics, 1948-77; Sec, Fondation Emile Tassel, ULB, 1956-69; Pres, ASBL La Maison d'Art, 1962; Hd, new course Elements of Physical and Physiological Acoustics, ULB, 1965-77. *Publications:* 77 publs on calculus of variations, gen acoustics, acoustics of halls, non-linear acoustics, small movements, engine silencers, musical acoustics, launching of large vessels, electrodynamic theory, coke furnace technics, chem engrng, hydrodynamics, pure and applied maths, modelling of mono-auditory fcunction, biogs. *Memberships:* VP then Pres, Association Belge des Acousticiens, Hon Pres, Dir, 1974; Pres, Orchestre des Jeunes de Belgique, 1972-86; Int Commn of Acoustics; Int Union of Pure and Applies Physics; Hon Pres, ABAV, 1977. *Honours:* Silver Medal, Groupement des Acousticiens de Langue Francaise, GALF, Paris, 1977; Adolphe Wetrems Prize, Mathematical and Physical Science, awarded by Science Section of Royal Academy of Belgium, 1982; Civic Medal, 1940-45; Chevalier, Officer, Order of Leopold; Commander Order of the Crown; Civic Medal 1st Class 1957; Grand Officer, Order of Leopold II, 1968. (F)Hobbies: Playing organ and harpsichord, Tennis, Hist, Musicology, Arch, Arts.

BOTEK Josef Mahatma, b. 9 June 1958, Hodenin. Housekeeper. m. Jana Propiova, 17 Aug 1990, 1 s. *Education:* Inst of Art, Photography, Slezian Univ, 1990-. *Appointments:* Librarian, 1979-80; Stoker, Housekeeper, 1981. *Creative Works:* Collection lyreiks, When you've got Talent You Can't Help it; When Nothing Shines In Your Head, Then Switch Off The Light In The Cellar; Oil Paintings; Photography. *Memberships:* Art Group, Nimble Mutation; ER atelier. *Honours:* Several awards for Photography; Literature. *Hobby:* Herpetology. *Address:* Konrimgka 16, 130 00 Praha 3, Czechoslovakia.

BOTTING Dale W, b. 1953, Saskatchewan. Dir, Prairie Region, Canadian Federation of Independent Business. m. Gerry, 1975, 2 s, 1 d. *Education:* Bach Sci, Biology, Bach Of Sci, Geography, Univ of Saskatchewan, 1975; Master Of Sci Studies (incomplete), 1975- 76; Bach of Educ Advanced, 1977; Cert in Socio economic Impact Assessmt, 1979; Exec Training by Government of Saskatchewan, 1982-84; Cert Techniques of Public Participation, 1982; Media Relations, Public Affairs, 1985-. *Appointments incl:* Water Quality Tech, 1971; Panning Conslt, 1975; Research Officer, 1978-80; Senior policy Analyst, 1981-84; Exec Dir Government Research, Sci and Technol Div, 1984-85; CFIB Dir of Provincial Affairs for Saskatchewan and Manitoba, 1985-. *Honours incl:* Canadian Assoc of Geographers, Most Distinguished Graduating Geographer, 1975; most Distinguished Intern, Faculty of Educ, 1977. *Hobbies:* Camping; Hiking; Canoeing; Naturalist Studies;

Photography; Coaching Kids Sports. *Address:* 1512 Lee Grayson Court North, Regina, Saskatchewan, Canada S4X 3Z6. 1.

BOUCHIER HAYES Thomas Anthony Ivan, b. 10 June 1937, Dublin. Prof of Army General Practice. m. 16 Sept 1964, 1 s, 1 d. *Education:* St Conleths, 1944-52; Clongowes Wood Coll, 1952-56; Royal Coll of Surgeons, Dublin, 1957-64. *Appointment:* Ministry of Defence. *Creative Works:* MRCGP Exam; MRCGP Study Book; PLAB, Emergencies in General Practice; Beechams Manual of General Practice; MCQ Tutor. *Memberships:* Pres Elect of GP Section of the Royal Soc of Medicine; Royal Coll of General Practice; London Medical Soc. *Honours:* Knott Medal, General Practice; Monfidori Medal for Surgery. *Hobbies:* Watching Rugby; Tennis; Bridge; Writing; Reading. *Address:* 9 Coldstream Gardens, Wandsworth, London SW18, England. 170.

BOUKAMEL Bassam Rafic, b. 2 June 1948, Beirut, Lebanon. Dir of RAAB, Boukamel Galleries. *Education:* BA Econ, American Univ of Beirut, 1970; MA Econ, Fordham Univ New York, 1973; Doctoral Work and Research in Economics, Fordham Univ, 1977. *Appointments:* Economist Career, 1977-86; Promoter of New Art and Publisher of Art Books. *Hobbies:* Visual Arts; Sports.

BOULDING Elise, b. 6 July 1920, Norway. Retired Prof of Sociology. m. 31 Aug 1941, 4 s, 1 d. *Education:* BA English, Douglas Coll; MS in Sociology, Iowa State Univ; PhD, Univ of Michigan. *Appointments:* Prof Emerita, Dartmouth Coll; Senior Fellow Dickey Endowment; Dept of Sociology, Inst of Behavioral Sci, Univ of Colorado, 1967- 78; Sec General, Intl Peace Research Assoc, 1988-91. *Publications incl:* The Underside of History, A View of Women Through Time; Handbook of Intl Data on Women; Childrens Rights and the Wheel of Life; Women and Social Cost of Development; One Small Plot of Heaven. *Memberships incl:* Intl Jury of the UNESCO, 1981-87; National Academy of Peace and Conflict Resolution; Int Peace Res Inst Foundation. *Address:* 624 Pearl St, Boulder, CO 80302, USA.

BOULDING Rachel Margaret, b. 13 Dec 1964, Chislehurst, Kent. Commissioning Editor of Religious Books. m. Martin Brooke, 24 Sept 1987. *Education:* BA, English Language and Literature, Pembroke Coll, Oxford, 1983-86. *Appointments:* Triangle Books, SPCK, 1987-; Liturgical Editor, SPCK, 1989-. *Hobbies:* Theatre; Films; Reading; Early Music. *Address:* c/o 5 St Johns Hill, Wareham, Dorset, BH20 4NA, England.

BOULIS Zoser, b. 1 Jan 1944, Khartoum North. Conslt Radiologist. m. Afaf Hanna Ayoub, 1 s, 1 d. *Education:* MB BS, Univ of Khartoum, 1965; MRCS, LRCP, Royal Coll of Surgeons, Physisions, 1975; FRCS, Royal Coll of Surgeons, England, 1973; FRCS, Edinborough, 1973; FRCS, Glasgow, 1975; DMRD, Royal Coll of Radiologist, 1980; FRCR, Royal Coll of Radiologist, 1982. *Appointments:* Sen House Officer, 1973; Registrar, General Surgery, Essex, 1974; Registrar and Senior Registrar, 1976; Conslt Radiologist, 1983. *Publications:* Head Injuries in Children, 1978; Mediastinal Fibrosis, 1983. *Memberships:* British Medical Assoc, Div of Radiology; Hospitals Medical Advisory Committee; Clinical Dir of Div of Radiology. *Hobbies:* Travelling Abroad; Reading; Music. *Address:* 24 Hayes Road, Bromley, Kent, BR2 9AA. England. 170.

BOUMANS Etienne Jean Emile, b. 26 May 1953, Antwerpen. European Civil Servant. m. Huguette Vanhecke, 1 Dec 1979, 1 s. *Education:* Law, Criminology, European Lae, VUB Brussels, 1971-77; European Admin, Coll of Europe Bruges, 1977-78; Common Law, Cambridge, 1978. *Appointments:* Adviser Various Ministers, 1979-84; Adviser to K Van Miert MEP, 1979-84; Admin European Parliament, 1984-. *Publications:* Europa in Vogelvlucht, 1984; The European Parliament and Human Rights, 1989.

Memberships: Intl Humanist and Ethical Union; European Humanist Federation Board; Humanistisch Verbond Belgium; Amnesty Intl. *Hobbies:* Reading; Walking; Music; Fine Arts. *Address:* 4 Rue Jean Engling, L-1466 Luxemburg. 1.

BOURGUIGNON Philippe E, b. 11 Jan 1948, France. President, Eurodisney. m. Martine Lemardeley, 25 June 1977, 1 s, 1 d. *Education:* Licence Sciences Economiques, France, 1971; MBA, IAE PAris, 1974. *Appointments:* Accor SA, 1973-87; Novotel Sieh, 1973-78; Novotel inc, Exec VP, 1978-82; Accor North America, Exec VP, 1982-84; Accor Asia Pacific, Pres, 1984-87; Eurodisney, Senior VP, 1988-. *Memberships:* YPO, 1990; ULI, USA; FNPC, France. *Hobbies:* Sailing; Skiing; Squash; Reading. *Address:* 4 Rue Thouin, 75005 Paris, France. 52, 26.

BOURNE Robert Charles Munroe, b. 5 Nov 1946, Montreal, Canada. Physician. m. Denise Holman, 11 June 1971, 1 s, 3 d. *Education:* B Sc, McGill Univ, Montreal, 1967; MDCM, McGill Univ, 1972; Intern, Montreal Gen Hosp, 1973; Family Practice Residency, McMaster Univ, Hamilton, Canada, 1973-75. *Appointments:* Caroline Med GP, Burlington ONT, 1975-77; Univ of Ca, Los Angeles, Asst Prof of Family Practice, 1977-79; Mid Valley Med Centre, 1979-80; Community Family Med Group, 1980-88; Beaver, Medical Clinic, San Bernadino, Ca, 1988-. *Memberships:* California Academy of Family Physicians; Soc of Tchr of Family Medicine; American Medical Assoc; Coll of Family Physician of Canada; San Bernadino Community Hospital, Redlands Community Hospital. *Honours incl:* Fellow, American Academy of Family Physicians, 1980; College of Family Physician of Canada; American Board of Family Practice. *Hobbies:* Gardening; Fly Fishing; Swimming; Church Choir. *Address:* 2 West Fen Avenue, Redlands, CA 92373, USA.

BOWE David Robert, b. 19 July 1955, Gateshead. Member of European Parliament. m. 1 s, 1 d. *Education:* Sunderland Polytechnic; Bath Univ, BSc. *Appointments:* Sci Tchr; Member of European Parliament. *Memberships:* Middlesbrough Borough Council; N Regl Sec; Socialist Educnl Assoc; NUPE. *Address:* 10 Harris Street, Middleborough, Cleveland TS1 5EF, England.

BOWEN Jewell Ray, b. 9 Jan 1934, Mississippi, USA. Dean of Engrng; Prof of Chem Engrng. m. Priscilla Joan Spooner, 4 Feb 1956, 1 s, 2 d. *Education:* SBChE 1956, SMChE 1957, MIT; PhD ChE, Univ of CA, Berkeley, 1963. *Appointments:* Asst Prof 1963, Assoc Prof 1967, Prof 1970, Chair of Chem Engrng 1971-73, 1978-81, Assoc V-Chancellor 1972-76, Univ of WI, Madison; Dean of Engrng 1981-, Prof, Chem Engrng 1981-, Univ of WA, Seattle. *Publications:* Ed, Progress in Astronautics and Aeronautics, Vol. 75, 76, 87, 88, 94, 95, 105, 106, 113, 114; Tech publs on reactive gas dynamics. *Memberships:* American Inst of Astronautics and Aeronautics; American Inst of Chem Engrs; American Phys Soc; American Soc for Engrng Educ; Chair, Engrng Dean's Coun, 1989-91, Pres 1992-93; Combustion Inst, Inst for Dybnamics of Reactive Systems, Pres 1988-. *Honours:* NATO-NSF Postdoctoral Fellow in Science, Cambridge University, 1962-63; NATO-NSF Senior Postdoctoral Fellow in Science, Imperial University, London, 1968; Richard Merton Visiting Professor (DFG), TH Karlsruhe, 1976-77. *Hobbies:* Hiking, Photography, Gardening, Birdwatching. *Address:* College of Engineering, University of Washington, 369 Loew Hall, FH 10, Seattle, WA 98195, USA. 2.

BOWEN John Hulan, b. 26 Dec 1928, Westminster, SC, USA. Conslt Landscape Arch. m. Thelma Joyce McGee, 16 Sept 1961, 1 s, 1 d. *Education:* Clemson Univ, BS Horticulture, 1950; Univ of Georgia, Master of Landscape Arch, 1957. *Appointments:* 1st Lt US Army, Korea, 1952-54; Landscape Arch, John V Townsend and Assoc, 1957; US Army Corps of Engrs, 1957-62; Pub Bldgs Svc, GSA, Washington, 1962-65;

Fed Hwy Admin, Washington, 1965-67; Asst Prof Miss State U, Starkville, 1967-69; US Army Corps of Engrs, 1969-89; Conslt Landscape Arch, 1989-. *Memberships:* American Soc of Landscape Arch; Alabama Chapter of American Soc of Landscape Arch; Southe Alabama Botanical and Horticultural Soc; Republican Party; Presbyterian Church USA. *Honours:* Recipient Cert of Appreciation bt Governor of Alabama, 1988; US Army Corps Engr, Superior Performance Award, 1977; Master of Landscape Arch Degree; Deacon, Presbyterian Church USA. *Hobbies:* Gardening; Geneology; Travel. *Address:* 2200 Freemont Drive, Mobile, AL 36609, USA. 7.

BOWEN Kenneth John, b. 3 Aug 1932, Llanelli. Prof of Singing, Royal Academy of Music, London. m. Angela Mary Evenden, 31 Mar 1959, 2 s. *Education:* Univ Coll of Wales; St Johns Coll, Cambridge; Inst of Educ, Univ Of London; MA Mns B Hon RAM FRSA ARCM. *Appointments:* Education Officer, RAF, 1958-80; Tenor Singer, 1960-86. *Creative Works:* Apperances in Europe, USA, Canada, Far East; Conductor, London Welsh Chorale. *Memberships:* RAM Club; AOTOS; Council Member, British Youth Opera; ISM AESS; Gorsedd Beirdd Ynys Prydain. *Honours:* Munich Intl Comp; Queens Prize. *Hobbies:* Golf; Cinema; Theatre; Wine; Fell Walking. *Address:* 12 Steeles Road, London, NW3 4SE, England. 4.

BOWEN Lynne Elizabeth, b. 22 Aug 1940, Saskatchewan. Freelance Historian. m. Richard Allen, 25 Aug 1962, 2 s, 1 d. *Education:* RN, 1962; B SC, 1963; MA, 1980. *Appointments:* Freelance Writing, Lectr, Video Writing, Archival Accessioning, 1980-91. *Publications:* Boss Whistle; Three Dollar Dreams; Muddling Through. *Memberships:* The Writers Union of Canada; Canadian Historical Assoc; Canadian Oral History Assoc; PEN. *Honours:* Eatons British Columbia Book Award; Canadian Historical Assoc Regional Cert; Lieutenant-Governors Medal for Writing History. *Hobbies:* Cooking; Sailing; Bicyling; Skiing; Gardening; Reading. *Address:* 4982 Fillinger Crescent, Nanaimo, BC, Canada V9V.1J1. 88.

BOWKER Robin Marsland, b. 15 Feb 1920, Kersal, Manchester. Retired. m. Mary Dora Elizabeth, 11 Jan 1956, 2 s, 2 d. *Education:* Charterhouse, 1933-38. *Appointments:* RAF AC2 to Corporal, 1940- 45; Joint MD, Burnes Shipyard Ltd, Bosham Yacht Yard, 1947-52; MD Bowker And Budd Ltd, 1952-73; MD Bowker and Bertram, 1975-87. *Publications:* Make Your Own Sails, 1957-84; A Boat of your Own; The Channel Handbook, Vols 1,11,111; Historical postscript to The Riddle Of The Sands; Mutiny Aboard H M Transpirt Bounty; Over 100 Articles in the Sailing Press of 15 countries. *Memberships:* The Society of Authors; Royal Ocean Racing Club; Island Sailing Club; Old Carthusian Yacht Club; Lloyds of London. *Hobbies:* Sailing; DIY. *Address:* Whitewalls, Harbour Way, Old Bosham, Chichester, PO18 8QH, England. 3, 43, 45, 52.

BOWMAN Clement Willis, b. 7 Jan 1930, Toronto, Canada. Technology Conslt. m. Marjorie Elizabeth, 21 Aug 1954, 1 s, 1 d. *Education:* BASc, Univ Of Toronto, 1952; MASc, 1958; PhD, 1961. *Appointments incl:* CIL/ DuPont of Canada, Plant and Research Engr, 1952-57; Syncrude Canada Ltd, Research Manager, 1963-69; Imperial Oil Enterprices, Petroleum Research Manager, 1971-75; Esso Petroleum Canada, Vice Pres, Research Dept, 1984-86; Alberta Research Council, Pres, 1987-91. *Creative Works:* Jours, Conf Presentations; holder 13 US and Can patents. *Memberships incl:* Canadian Soc for Chemical Engr; Chemical Inst of Canada; Canadian Research Management Assoc; Canadian Academy of Engr. *Honours:* Meritorious Service Medal, 1977; Queens 25 yr Jubilee Medal, 1977; KA Clark Distinguished Service Award, 1989; Centennial APEGGA Award, 1989; Alberta Achmt Award, 1991; Canadian Research Management Assoc R&D Management Award, 1991; ALberta Science and Technology AS Tech Award, 1991. *Hobbies:* Jogging;

Skiing; Golf. *Address:* 2112 Huron Shores Drive RR5, Sarnia, Ontario, Canada N7T 7H6. 1, 88.

BOYD Michael Manford, b. 15 Aug 1951, London, Ontario CDA. Investment Banker. m. Shelagh D Donovan, 7 Jan 1989, 1 s. 2 d. *Education:* BA, Univ of Western Ontario, 1974; Master of Business Admin, 1976. *Appointments:* Citibank Canada, Vice Pres, 1980-83; BG Acorn Management Ltd, Pres, 1983-89; Junior Ind Finance Corp, Pres, 1990-91; Senior Vice Pres, Marleau Lemire Inc, 1992-. *Memberships:* Eglinton and Caledon Hunt Club. *Hobbies:* Riding; Pigeon Fancier; Orchids. *Address:* RR1, Terra Cotta, Ontario, Canada L0P 1NO. 32, 88.

BOYD CARPENTER John Archibald, b. 2 June 1908, Harrogate. Dir of Companies, Peer of the Realm. m. Margaret Mary Hall, 25 June 1927, 1 s, 2 d. *Education:* Balliol Coll, Oxford, BA History, 1927-31; Diploma Economic, 1931. *Appointments:* Barrister at Law, 1934-39; Army Officer, 1939-45; MP 1945-72; Minister of the Crown, 1951-64; Company Chairman and Dir, 1964-91. *Publications:* Way Of Life, 1984. *Memberships incl:* Carlton Club, Chairman, 1983-89. *Honours:* Privy Councillor, 1954; Peer of the Realm, 1972; Deputy Lieutenant, Greater London, 1984. *Hobbies:* Swimming; Tennis; Gardening. *Address:* 12 Eaton Terrace, London SW1, England.

BOYTHA Gyorgy, b. 5 Oct 1929, Budapest. Ambassador; Assoc Prof Law Faculty, Budapest. m. (1)Eniko Varrok, 2 Feb, 1957, div, (2)Eva Fuzessery, 10 Aug 1979, 1 s, 2 d. *Education:* Univ Edtvus Lorand Law Faculty, Budapest, 1949-52; Doctor of Law, 1957; Private Intl Law Seminar, The Hague, 1964; Assoc Prof of Law, 1977. *Appointments:* Imprisoned under the Communist Regime, Political Reasons, 1952-56; Export Exec Tungsram Ltd, 1957-61; Dir of Division, World Intell Propert, 1977-85; Dir Gen, Bureau for Authors Rights, 1985-92; Permanent Rep of the Hungarian Repub, United Nations Organisations in Geneva, 1993-. *Publications:* Books in Hungarian, English, German on Authors Rights; Wipo Glossary, 1979; 90 Articles in the Field of Private Intl Law and Copyright. *Memberships:* Assoc President Hungarian Assoc for Ind Property; Pres, Intl Private Law Section; CISAC, Paris; VFITA, Munich; DAT, Buenos Aires. *Hobbies:* History of Modern Ages; Evolution; Dev of Human Perception of the Universe; Swimming; Cross country; Skiing. *Address:* XII Racz Aladar ut 7 11, H 1121 Budapest, Hungary.

BOZHILOV Georgi, b. 13 June 1935, Plovdiv, Bulgaria. Painter. 1 d. *Education:* Painting, Illustrations, Stageographics, Monumental Painting, Arts Acad, Sofia. *Creative works:* Solo exhibs: Paris, Vienna, Prague, W.Berlin, Autumn Salon in Paris, 1979; Young Painters Biannual Exhib, 1959-65; Gp Exhibs: France, Germany, Poland, USSR, India, SPain, Italy; Paintings in private collections in France, Switzerland, USA, Mexico, Belgium, Holland, Germany, Peru. *Membership:* Bulgarian Artists Assn. *Honours:* Nat Awards; Balkan Biennial Awd, Bucharest, 1981. *Hobbies:* Literature; Music; History. *Address:* 1 Tzar Ivailo Street, 4000 Plovdiv, Bulgaria.

BRACHMAN Malcolm K, b. 9 Dec 1926, Ft Worth, Texas. m. Minda Fay Delugach, 4 Sept 1951, 1 s, 2 d. *Education:* BA, Yale Unic, 1945; MA, Harvard Univ, 1947; PhD, Harvard Univ, 1949. *Appointments:* Asst Prof, Methodist Univ, Dallas, 1949-50; Assoc Physicist Argonne Nat Lab, Chicargo, 1950-53; Research Staff, Texas Instruments Inc, Dallas, 1953-54; VP Pioneer American Ins Co., Forth Worth, 1954-61; Pres, NW Oil Co, Dallas, 1956-; Dir, Farrar Straus and Giroux NYC, Capt USAAF 1950-57; Pres Pioneer American Ins Co., 1961-73; Chairman Bd CEO, 1973-79. *Memberships:* American Physicist Soc; Soc Of Petroleum Engrs; AM Mathematical Soc; IEEE; Soc of Exploration and Geophysics. *Hobbies:* Bridge; Riding. *Address:* 10036 Hollow Way Road, Dallas, TX 75229, USA. 1.

BRADEAN Traian, b. 4 July 1927, Comlaus, Romania. Painter, Lect at the Inst of Fine Arts. m. Angela Popa, 10 Mar 1957, 1 d. *Education:* Apprentice Painter, 1942; School of Fine Arts, 1946; Inst of Fine Arts, 1950; BA, Painting Diploma, 1956. *Appointments:* Asst at the Pedagogical Inst of Fine Arts, 1961; Dir Inst of Fine Arts, 1970. *Creative Works:* Paintings in Museums, Romania and Abroad; Book Illustrations; Frescoes and Mural mosaics. *Memberships:* Fine Arts Union, 1956. *Honours:* Best Illustrated Book, Germany 1967; Order of Merit, 1968; Romanian Academy, 1970; Fine Arts Union, 1973. *Hobbies:* Travel; Fishing. *Address:* Str Brezoianu 10 Sc C apt 61, 70624 Bucurest, Romania.

BRADLEY Kieran Saint Clair Moyse, b. 1 Oct 1957, Fintona, North Irl. Official of the European Parliament, Legal Serv. m. Anita Olga Pisano, 21 Dec 1989, 1 s. *Education:* BA, Trinity Coll, Dublin, 1975-79; Cert of Advanced European Studies, Law, Belgium, 1979-80; LLB, Queens Coll, Cambridge, 1980-81. *Appointments:* Part Time Research Asst, Sen Mary Robinson, Trinity Coll, Dublin, 1978-79. *Publications:* Numerous Articles, Contributions in Specialist Publications On European Community Law. *Honours:* Entrance Exhbn, Dublin, 1975; Padraig Pearse Scholarship, 1979; Harmsworth Scholarship, 1981; Robert Schuman Scholarship, 1981; Salzburg Seminar, American Studies, 1988. *Hobbies:* Anglo, Irish Litr; European Fiction; Snooker. *Address:* Office 324, Montoyer Building, European Parliament, B-1047 Brussels, Belgium. 1.

BRADLEY Patrick James, b. 10 May 1949, Thurles, Eire. Conslt Otdlaryngologist. m. Sheena Kelly, 17 May 1974, 3 s, 2 d. *Education:* Glenstal Abbey Sch, 1961-67; Univ Coll, Dublin, 1967-73; MB B Ch BAO, 1973; DCH, 1975; Royal Coll Surgeons, Ireland, 1977; Royal Coll Surgeons, Edinburgh, 1979. *Appointments:* Dublin Health Auth, 1973-77; Mersey Reg Health Auth, 1977-82; Nottingham Area Health Auth, 1982-. *Publications:* papers on Head and Neck Onlology; ENT MCQ; Books and Articles on Otolaryngology. *Memberships:* Soc of Head & Neck Onlologist of Gt Britain; Royal Soc of Medicine; Oncology Soc. *Honours:* Traveling Scholarship. *Hobbies:* Skiing; Squash; Golf. *Address:* 32A The Ropewalk, Nottingham, NG1 5EH, England.

BRAENDLI Heinrich, b. 18 Apr 1938, Wald, Zurich. Prof. m. Waldvogel Hanna, 15 Mar 1985, 2 s. *Education:* Swiss Fed Inst of Technology, Diploma 1961. *Appointments:* Private Engr Office, 1962-63; Public Transport City of Zurich, 1963-75; Prof Swiss Federal Inst of Technology, 1975-. *Publications:* Various seperate publications, text books. *Memberships include:* Assoc of Swiss Transport Engr; Swiss Soc of Engr and Arch; Various National public Transport Org; Intl Union Of Public Transport. *Honours:* Dr Friedrich Lehner Medal, German Federal Republic. *Address:* Erlenstrasse 63, CH-8154 Oberglatt, Switzerland.

BRAHAM Philip, b. 8 Apr 1959, Glasgow. Artist. m. Barbara Campbell, 21 June 1980, 1 d. *Education:* Duncan Fordanstone Coll Of Art, Dundee, 1976-80; Royal Academy of Fine Art, The Hague, 1980-81; Univ of California, LA, 1981-82. *Appointements:* One Man Exhibitions, Main Fine Art, Glasgow, 1984; Scottish Gallery, Edinburgh, 1985,87; RAAB Gallery, London, 1989; Group Exhibitions, UK, Europe, USA. *Creative Works:* A Risher Soil, 1985-86; Battleground Pinkie, 1986-88; Monuments to Caledonia, 1989-. *Memberships:* Soc of Scottish Artists. *Honours:* British Council Scholarship, 1980; Greenshields Award, 1981; Educ Inst of Scotland Award, 1985; Scottish Art Council Award, 1989. *Hobbies:* Music; Fitness Training; Photography; Philosophy. *Address:* c/o RAAB Gallery at Millbank, 6 Vauxhall Bridge Road, London, SW1V 2SD, England.

BRAHMA Rupendra Kumar, b. 18 May 1938, Calcutta. Conslt Psychiatrist. m. Mary Edwards, 28 Aug 1971. *Education:* MB BS, 1959; DPM, 1967; MRCP, 1968; MRCP sych, 1972; FRCP, 1986; FRCPsych, 1986.

Appointments: Sen Registrar, London Hospital, Claybury Hospital, 1969-72; Conslt i/c, Dept of Psychological Medicine, Whipps Cross Hospital; Consult Psychiatrist, Claybury Hospital. *Memberships incl:* Chair, North East Thames Reg Council, BMA; Vice-chair RCSC; RHA Medical Manpower Comm; RCPsych Manpower Comm; Counsel and Care for the Elderly. *Honours:* Class Asst in Medicine, Univ of Calcutta, 1957-59; Gold Medal in Medicine, 1958; First Cert of Honours in Medicine, 1959. *Hobbies:* Travel; Photography; Gardening. *Address:* Whipps Cross Hospital, Leytonstone, London E11 1NR, England.

BRAIMBRIDGE-BAXTER Nerissa Eusebia, b. 5 Mar 1943, Kingston, Jamacia, West Indies. Pres Dir, 4 d. *Education:* Shields Computer and Business Ch, 1962; Hotel and Motel Manag, Skyline Hotel, Jamacia, 1969. *Appointements:* Intl High Fashion Model; Intl Maniquins; Pres, Promtact Intl Inc; Pres, Intl Beautiful People Unlimited Inc; Dir, Intl Promotions, Intl Eseorts; model and Talen Agency; Public Relation Serv; Business Intermediary and Tourist Guide Serv. *Publications:* Appearances on, National TV, CBS, NBC, ABC; Radio inc. WOR, w NYC, WHBi; Magazines and Newspapers inc. The Stock Magazinge, Cue, Marketing Times, Bottom Line, Cosmopolitan, Visitors East, Herald News. *Memberships:* Nat Assoc for Female Exec. *Honours:* Woman of the Year, Multi Accupational Soc of NY, 1975. *Hobbies:* Worlwide Adventure Travel; Art Apprec; Backgammon; Spectator Sports; Dancing; Reading. *Address:* c/o Promtact Intl, 1841 Broadway, Suite 1000, New York, NY 10023, USA.

BRAIMOH Adeshina Dele, b. 24 Feb 1947, Ipoti, Ekiti. Tchr, Univ Lctr. m. Margaret Foluke, 2 Sept 1975, 1 s, 3 d. *Educaion:* Univ of Lefos, Akoka, Yaba Lapos, Nigeria, 1977-80, BSc, Hons, Mess Communs; Univ of Ibadam, Nigera, 1981-86. *Appointments:* Grad Asst, 1981-84; Asst Lectr, 1985-86; Lectr Grade II, 1986-88; Lectr Grade I, 1989-. *Publications:* English Language Fundamentals; CY English for Senior Secondary; Articles in Daily Newspapers, Reputable Academic Journals. *Memberships:* Nigerias Nat Council for Adult Educ; Nigerias Ind Relations Assoc; British Soc of Commerce; Commwealths Assoc for the Educ and Training for Adults; African Assoc for Literacy and Adult Education. *Hobbies:* Writing; Gardening; Travelling. *Address:* Dept of Adult Education, Univ of Ibadan, Ibdan, Oyo State, Nigeria.

BRAITHWAITE Leonard Austin, b. 23 Oct 1923, Toronto, Ontario. Barrister, Solicitor. 2 s. *Education:* Univ Toronto, Bach of Commerce, 1952; Harvard Business Sch, MBA, 1952; Osgoode Hall Law Sch,Bach of Laws, 1958. *Appointments:* General Cable Corp, USA, 1952-53; Univ of Toronto, 1953-54; Phillips Canada Ltd, 1954; City of Etobicoke, Board of Educ, 1960-62; City of Etobicoke, City Council, 1962-64; Province Ontario, MPP, 1963-75; Municipality Metropolitan Toronto, 1982-88; City Etobicoke, Board of Council, 1982-88; Leonard A Braithwaite QC, 1958-. *Memberships incl:* Harvard Business Sch Club, Toronto; Thistletown Lions Club; Board of Gov, Etobicoke Gen Hosp; Black Business and Prof Assoc; Criminal Lawyers Assoc; Advocates Soc; Canadian Bar Assoc; CORE. *Honours:* Special Veterans Proficiency Prize, Univ of Toronto, 1950; Gold Key Winner, 1958. *Address:* 1500 Royal York Road, Suite E, Etobicoke, Ontario, Canada M9P 3B6. 142.

BRAKONIECKI Kazimierz, b. 12 Dec 1952, Barczewo. Poet, Critic, Editor, Exhibitor. m. Hanna Wasik, 19 Aug 1977, 2 s. *Education:* Univ of Warsaw, Master of Arts, 1971-76; Univ of Warsaw, Post Grad Studies, 1986-88. *Publications:* Adhesions; Lifes; Bodily poems; Ideas; Identity. *Memberships:* Assoc of Polish Writers, Warsaw. *Honours:* Poetic Award, Literary Magazine; Olsztyn Voivode Award. *Hobbies:* Philosophy; History; Walking; Sight Seeing. *Address:* ul Jana Hanowskiego 3 m 10, 10 687 Olsztyn, Poland.

BRAME Marilyn, b. 17 Sept 1928, Indianapolis, Indiana, USA. Technical Publications Manager; Designer; Hypnotherapist. 1 s, 1 d. *Education:* PhD, Hypnotherapy, American Inst of Hypnotherapy, 1989; Various Courses: Meinzinger Art School, Detroit, Michigan; Univ of New Mexico, Albuquerque; Orlando Junior Coll, Orlando, Florida; El Camino Coll, Torrance, California. *Appointments:* Owner, Signs by Marilyn, Albuquerque, New Mexico, 1952-53; Electromechanical Designer Lead Man for Design Group, Martin Orlando, Orlando, Florida, 1957-65; Owner, The Arts, Art School and Graphic Design, Winter Park, Florida, 1964-66; Supervisor, Technical Publications, General Instrument Corporation, Hawthorne, California, 1967-76; Pres, Camart Design Advertising Agency, Westminister, California, 1977-86; Pres, Visual Arts, El Toro, California, 1978-; Instructor, Orange Coast Coll, Costa Mesa, California, 1986-; Hypnotherapist, El Toro, 1986-. *Creative Works:* Author: Folkdancing is for Everybody; 23 Israeli Dances textbooks; Dance notation system; Art shows: Indianapolis, Indiana, Orlando and Miami, Florida, Albuquerque, New Mexico, Orange County, California; Ed, Soc for Techinical Communication Newsletter, 1987. *Memberships:* Newsletter Ed, Prod Ed, 1st Vice-Pres, Soc for Techinical Communication. *Honours:* Excellence for Newsletter, 1986, Achievement for Newsletter, 1987, Distinguished Chapter Awd, 1989, Soc for Technical Communication. *Hobbies:* Folkdancing; Rock collecting. *Address:* 25422 Trabuco Road, No 105, El Toro, CA 92630, USA. 9.

BRAND Terence Edwin, b. 18 Oct 1924, London, England. Company Director, m. 6 Nov 1949, dis 1983, 2 s. *Education:* State. *Appointments:* WW11 RAF. Flt Lt Navigator, 1943-47; Pilot British Airways, 1947-79; Vice-Pres, Opas, 1983-; Dir Collins Wilde Plc, 1984-. *Creative Works:* Involved TV and Advertising BA Image; Public Speaker Occupational Pensions; Presentations; Three Films. *Memberships:* Trustee BALPA, Benevolent CTEE; Trustee Guild Of Air Pilots, Benevolent CTEE; Gov Crossnays Trust; ABAC; MCC, RAF and City Livery Club. *Honours:* Queens Commendation for Valuable Service in the Air; Freeman City of London; Liveryman Guild of Air Pilots and Air Navigators; British Airline Pilots Silver Medal. *Hobbies:* Squash; Bridge; People. *Address:* 126 The Avenue, Sunbury On Thames, Middlesex, TW16 5EA, England.

BRANDOW Judith Michael, b. Hamilton, Canada. Journalist. *Education:* Grantham High Sch, St Catharines, Ontario. *Appointments:* Reporter, St Catherines Standard, 1965-68; Reporter, Womens Editor, Toronto Telegram, 1968-71; Womens Editor, Hamilton Spectator, 1971-73; Jour Instr, Ryerson Polytechinical Inst, 1973-74; Copy Editor, Womens Editor, Toronto Star, 1974-77; Editor In Chief, Canadian Living Mag, 1977-88; Conslt, Canadian Gardening and Good Times, 1988-89; Features Editor, Toronto Sun, 1989-90; Proj Dir of Participaction, 1990-91; Columnist, Toronto Sun, 1991-. *Hobbies:* Sailing; Skiing; Gardening; Antiques. *Address:* 227 Lakeshore Drive, Toronto, Ontario, Canada M8V 2A7.

BRANDT Diana Ruth, b. 31 Jan 1952, Winkler, Manitoba. Writer. m. 28 Aug 1971, div June 1991, 2 d. *Education:* PhD, Univ of Manitoba, 1993; BA, Univ Of Manitoba, 1975; MA, Univ of Toronto, 1976. *Appointments:* Dept of English Lit, Univ of Winnipeg, 1985-; Artist in the School, Manitoba, 1987-; Poetry Editor, Pralrie Fire, 1989-92. *Publications:* Questions I Asked My Mother, 1987; Agnes In The Sky, 1990; Mother, Not Mother, 1992. *Memberships:* League of Canadian Poets; The Writers union Of Canada; PEN; Manitoba Writers Guild. *Honours:* McNally Robinson Award for Manitoba Book Of The Year; Gerald Lampert Award; Nom. for Govenor Generals Award for Poetry; Nom. Dillons Commonwealth Poetry Prize. *Hobbies:* Walking. *Address:* 932 Jessie Avenue, Winnipeg, Manitoba, Canada, R3M 1A9. 142.

BRANDT Roger D, b. 20 Aug 1939, Greenley, Colo, USA. President. m. Susan O Sidell, 1 Jan 1961, 2 s. *Education:* Univ of Nebraska, 1958; BS Bio Sci, Colorado State univ, 1959-62; Baylor Coll Medicine, 1972. *Appointments:* Dir Comm Dev, Warner Lambert, 1978-79; Vice Pres, Baylor Lab, 1979-81; Pres, Allerderm Inc, 1981-. *Creative Works:* Lectr Series, Vet; Dermatology, Brisban, Melbourn, Sidney, Australia. *Memberships:* Am Acad Vet Dermatology; Acad of Vet Allergy; Am Marketing Assoc; Am Foundation for Pharmaceutical Educ. *Honours:* Certif Merit, Continuing Educ for Family Physician. *Hobbies:* Antique Automabiles; Antique Boats; Reading; Gardening; Pulchritude Appreciation. *Address:* PO Drawer 277, Hurst, TX 76053, USA. 7.

BRANSKI Vladimir Pavlovich, b. 14 Jan 1930, Sverdlovsk, USSR. Philosopher, Physicist. m. Kustova Natali, 5 July 1958, 1 d. *Education:* Faculty Philosophy and physics, Leningrad State Univ, 1948-53; Post Grad Philosophy, 1953-57; Doc of Philosophy, 1957; Full Doc of Philosophy, 1973. *Appointments:* Lectr, Faculty of Philosophy, Leningrad State Univ, 1957-63; Asst Prof, 1963-75; Prof, 1975-. *Publications:* Philosophical Significance of Picturebility in Modern Physics; Philosophical Foundations of Synthesis of Relativistic and Quantum Priniciples; Theory of Elementary Particles as a Matter of Methodological Research. *Memberships:* Pres of Russian Inter Univ Centre for Philosophy of Sci. *Hobbies:* Mountaineering; Tourism; Collecting Postcards with Classic, Modern paintings; Artistic Photography; Skiing; Cycling; Swimming; Canoe Paddling; Philosopy of Art; History of Fine Art. *Address:* Dept of Philosophy, St Petersburg State Univ, Mendeleevskaya Line 5, 199034, St Petersburg, Russia.

BRAUNSCHWEIG Philippe Georges, b. 24 Aug 1928, Chaux de Fonds, Switzerland. Physicist, Businessman. m. Elvira Kremis, 3 April 1952, 1 s, 1 d. *Education:* Polytechnical Sch, Grad Physicist, 1952. *Appointments:* Pres, Intl Portescap Group, 1964; Chairman, 1974; Pres, Prix de Lausanne; Honorary Pres, Bejart Ballet, Lausanne. *Creative Works:* Prix de Lausanne, Intl Comp Young Dancers, 1973; Co Founder, Swiss Assoc for Prof Dancers, 1976; Co Founder, Swiss Prof Ballet Scj, 1986; Transfer of Maurice Bejart and Co from Bruxelles to Lausanne, 1987. *Memberships:* Inst Neuchatelois; Swiss Academy of Tech Sci. *Honours:* Knight of the Legion d'Honneur, 1978; Officer of the Order de Merite, 1990. *Hobbies:* Jogging; Visual Arts. *Address:* Residence Beauregard, Chemin Bellerive 8, CH-1007 Lausanne, Switzerland.

BRAVERMAN Doreen, b. 22 Jan 1932, Vancouver, Canada. Business Executive. m. Jack, 20 Aug 1965, 2 s, 2 d. *Education:* Matriculation, Richmond HS, 1949; Bach ED, Univ of BC, 1964; Master of Business Admin, Canadian Sch of Mgmt, 1984. *Appointments:* Tchr, Vancouver Sch, 1962-68; Man Dir, J BR Averman Inc, 1974-; Pres, The Van Flag Shop Inc, 1975-; Pres, Atlas Textile Print Ltd, 1983-. *Publications:* Govt Aid and Small Business, 1983; Editor, The Flag Banner. *Memberships:* Dir, Can, Labour Market Productivity Board; Can, Manuf Assoc; Can, Flag Assoc. *Honours:* Small Business Person Of The Year, 1988. *Hobbies:* Charities; Politics; Vexillology. *Address:* 1755 W 4 Avenue, Vancouver, BC Canada V6J 1M2. 32, 142.

BRAZAUSKAS Algirdas Mykolas, b. 22 Sept 1932, Rokishkis, Lithuania. Deputy of the Supreme Council, Lithuania, Chaiman of the Democratic Labour Party, Lithuania. m. Julija Styraite, 19 April 1958, 2 d. *Education:* Politechnic, Kaunas, Grad Hydrotechnical Eng, 1956; MA Economics, 1974. *Appointments:* Construction of Hydro Electric power Station, 1956-65; Minister, LSSR Building Materials Ind, 1965-67; Vice Chairman, LSSR Planning Committee, 1967-77; Deputy, Supreme Council, Lithuania, 1967-; Sec CC CPL, 1977-88; First Sec, 1988-90; Chairman, Democratic Labour Party, 1990-; Chairman, Presidium Supreme Council, Lithuania, 1990; Depury Prime Minister, Republic lithuania, 1990-91. *Honour:*

Distinguished Eng, 1982. *Hobby:* Yachting. *Address:* .Council of DLPL, B Radvilaites 1, 23200 Vilnius, Lithuania. 12, 52.

BREAM Julian, b. England. Musician (Guitarist, Lutanist). *Appointments:* Formed a Broken Consort in 1960s and was again reformed in 1976, touring Mexico for a month in 1979. Recitals w Sir Peter Pears and has performed w many of the most distinguished string quartets. Participated in Georg Malcolm's 70th birthday concert with Dame Janet Baker and Sir Yehudi Menuhin at Wigmore Hall, 1987; Recital at Wigmore Hall to celebrate the centenary of the birth of Villa-Lobos. Worked w Julian Bream Consort and Robert Tear in concerts at the Aldeburgh and Sevenoaks Festivals and filming for TVS. In Sept 1987 the Julian Bream Consort appeared at BBC Promenade Concerts and recorded for RCA. Made film of Elizabethan music and poetry w the late Dame Peggy Ashcroft for BBC TV in celebration of her eightieth birthday, 1987. The 1987-88 season included solo tours of the USA, the UK, Germany, Switz, Scandinavia and Spain. In autumn 1988 the Julian Bream Consort w Robert Tear made a world tour. Tour of Italy giving solo recitals in Bologna and Naples and perf of the Leo Brouwer Concerto elegiaco in Milan, autumn 1988. Numerous recital tours in 1989-90. 1990-91 performned w Scottish Chmbr Orch and toured Italy and UK, also USA and Europe. In summer 1993 Julian Bream celebrates his 60th birthday with a special concert at Wigmore Hall and a number of recitals at summer ferstivals. *Creative works:* Recordings with RCA and EMI Classics. *Honours:* International Awards including six from National Academy of Recording Arts and Sciences in USA, two Edison awards and var prizes from Gramophone Magazine. In 1979 RCA presented him with a platinum disc to mark record sales of half a million in the UK alone. Awarded the OBE for his services to Music in 1964; Villa-Lobos Gold Medal, 1976; Awarded the CBE in 1984. *Address:* c/o Harold Holt Ltd, 31 Sinclair Road, London W14 ONS, England.

BREDENKEMP Jurgen, b. 29 Mar 1939, Haburg. Prof. m. Kerin Spies, 9 Aug 1968, 2 d. *Education:* Diploma Psychology, 1963; Phd, 1964; Habilitation, 1972. *Appointments:* Asst Prof, Univ Heidelberg, 1964- 79; Prof, Univ Benn, 1972; Univ Jottinjen, 1972-80; Univ Trier, 1980-84; Univ Benn, 1984-. *Publications:* The Test of Significance in Psyhcal Research, 1972; Learning and Memory, 1977; Imergerg and Learning, 1979; Theory and Design of psychal Experiments, 1980. *Memberships:* German Psychal Soc. *Honours:* German Research Council, 1988-92; Pres, German Psychal Soc, 1990-92. *Hobby:* Music. *Address:* Bonner Logsweg 65, 5300 Bonn, Germany. 52, 154.

BREIDING G Sutton, b. 17 Aug 1950, West Virginia, USA. Warehouse Man. *Education:* High Sch Diploma. *Appointments:* Numerous. *Publications:* Autumn Roses; Necklace of Blood; Journal of an Astronaut. *Honours:* Rhysling Award. *Hobby:* Astral Poetics. *Address:* PO Box 248, Morgan Town, WV 26507, USA.

BREMNER Eric, b. 9 July 1958, Edinburgh. Fashion Designer. m. Jane Catherine Mary Scott, 1 Sept 1979, 1 s, 1 d. *Education:* MA, 1984; Diploma Fashion Design, 1982. *Appointments:* Designer Maxmara Sportmax, 1984-; Designer Marina Rinaldi Marina Sport, 1986- ; Designer Prisma, 1987-. *Honours:* Janey Ironside Memorial Prize, 1983; Mansfield Cache D'or Award, 1984. *Hobbies:* Music; Cooking. *Address:* The Old School, Garford, Oxfordshire, OX13 5PG, England.

BRERETON Donald, b. 18 July 1945, Plympton, Devon. Civil Servant. m. Mary Frances Turley, 12 April 1969, 1 s, 2 d. *Education:* Plymouth and Mannamead Coll, 1956-63; Plymouth Tech Coll, 1964-65; Univ Newcastle Upon Tyne, BA Hons, Politics and Soc Admin. *Appointments:* VSO, Malaysia, 1986-64; Ministry of Health, Asst principal, 1968; Asst private Sec, Sec of the State for Social Services, 1971; Private Sec, Perm Sec, DHSS, 1972; Private Sec, Sec of State for Social

Serv, 1979-82; Asst Sec, Head of Policy unit, 1982-83; Sec Housing Benefit Review Team, 1984; Head of Housing Benefit Branch, 1985-89; Under Sec, Head of Effiency unit. *Hobbies:* Squash; Tennis; Reading; Music; Bridge; Holidays; Gardening. *Address:* Cabinet office, 70 Whitehall, London SW1A 2AS, England. 1.

BREWER Arthur Bruce, b. 18 Oct 1951, Pasadena, Texas. Coll Admin, Adjunct Asst Prof and Conslt. m. Patricia Anne Lumley, 12 Mar 1977, 2 stepsons, 1 d. *Education:* AB, American Studies, 1974; MA, Counceling and Guidance, 1975; PhD, Educ Leadership, 1988; OD Inst, 1990, 1991, 1992. *Appointments:* Asst Dir Admissions, 1976-79; Auburn Univ, Coord of Car Dev Ctr, 1979-81; West Ga Col, Dir of Plac, Co-op Ed, Adj Asst Prof of Psych, 1981-. *Creative Works:* Presenter, Career placement and Cooperative Educ. *Memberships incl:* SEASCUS, 1990-91; Ga Consort for Intl Co-op Ed, 1991; Ga Sm Col Consort for Cars; Comm on Res and plan; Univ Sys Comm on Plac and Co-op. *Honours:* Distinguished Service to SCPA; Outstanding Leadership and Signicant Contribution to SEASCUS; Kappa Delta Pi Educ Honour Soc; Dept of US Educ Grants; District Award of Merit; Boy Scouts of America. *Hobbies:* Scouting; Camping; Gardening; Home Repairs; Chess; Music; Stamps. *Address:* 70 plantation Avenue, Carrollton, GA 30117, USA. 7.

BREWSTER Martyn Robert, b. 24 Jan 1952, Oxford. Artist, Painter. m. Hilary Carter, 2 Mar 1988, 1 d. *Education:* BA Fine Art, 1974; Post Grad Diploma, Printmaking, 1975; Art Tchr Cert, 1978. *Appointments:* Lectr in Art, East Herts Coll, 1980-89; Visiting lectr, Winchester Sch of Art; Visiting Lectr, Bournmouth Coll of Arts, 1988-. *Creative Works:* One Man Exhbn inc. Peterborough City Museum, Art Gallery, 1983; Winchester Gall, 1986; Warwick Arts Trust, London; Woodlands Art Gall, London, 1987; Bede Gall, Jarrow, 1988; Thumb Gall, London, 1988-90. *Honours:* Eastern Arts Award, 1977; British Council Travel Grant, 1991. *Hobbies:* Music; Reading; Walking. *Address:* c/o Jill George Galley, 38 Lexington Street, Soho, London W1R 3HR, England.

BRIELE Luc Van Den, b. 8 May 1930, Ieper, Belgium. Writer. m. Elsa Goris, 2 June 1955, 1 d. *Education:* Graduate, Bibliography and Lib Science, Lib Schl, Brussels. *Appointments:* Started as Hd of Documentation Lib Hoste Eds, Brussels, later Freelance Writer. Ed Boek en Bibliotheek (Book and Lib) and Graphia (Exlibris Art Review). *Creative works:* 26 Plays for Theatre and Radio; 5 books about exlibris-art; Articles in bookplate-reviews and yearbooks in Belgium, Denmark, Germany, Italy, Portugal and Spain; Book reviews about lit, hist and graphic art. *Memberships:*)Flemish Assn of Dramatists; Bd of Exlibris Mus in Sint-Niklaas, Belgium; Bd Mbr, Graphia, Assn of Bookplate Collectors. *Honours:* 8 Literary prizes in Belgium for Plays. *Hobby:* Collection of Bookplates. *Address:* Bleekstraat 6-309-92, B-2800 Mechelen, Belgium.

BRIGHAM Deirdre Helen Davis, b. 10 Oct 1934, Orlando, Florida. Dir Getting Well Program. m. Dr Robert Cyril, 22 June 1957. *Education:* AB Wellesley Coll, 1956; MS Florida Tech Univ, 1975; MPH Univ of South Florida; MA Univ of Central Florida. *Appointments:* Orlando Reg Medical Centre, 1975-87; Founder and Dir Getting Well, 1987-. *Publications:* The Use of Imagery in a Multimodal Psychoneuro Immunology Program, 1991. *Memberships:* Soc of Behaverial Medicine; Assn for the Study of Mental Imagery; Inst for the Clinical Appl of Behaveral Medicine. *Hobbies:* Reading; Painting. *Address:* 700 Euclid Avenue, Orlando, FL 32801, USA. 5, 138.

BRIGHAM Judith, b. 17 Nov 1915, Canada. American Citizenship, Cleveland, Ohio. Educator and Analyst in Intercutlural Relations. m. Burnett Magruder, 28 Dec 1939. *Education:* Univ of Toronto, BA English, History, 1938; Yale Univ, 1938-40; Columbia Univ MA, 1942; PhD, Philosophy, Religion, Educ, 1951. *Appointments:*

YWCA, Nat Student Council Wartime Program Staff, 1942-43; Cleveland Baptist Assoc, 1943-45; Univ of Louisville, Lectr Philosophy, 1946; Indiana Univ SE, Lectr English, 1946-52; Radio Stations, CHLO, WAKY, WC11, WUHE, Twenteith Century Questions, 1955-91. *Publications incl:* Basic Issues of the War and Peace; American Dialectics in Action; Personal Dialectical Idealism as a Philosophy of Educ; Intergration of the Historic Theories of the Atonement. *Memberships:* Academy of Politcal Sci; American Academy of Political & Soc Sci; Republican Nat Com; Republican Pres Task Force; Nat Republican Senatorial Inner Circle; Heritage Foundation. *Honours incl:* Pres Commission Republican Presidential Task Force; Presidential Order of Merit and Medal; Honorary Friend and Supporter of Afghan Mercy Fund. *Hobbies:* Flower Gardening; Walking; Historical Pres of Canadian Vacation Residence. *Address:* 1356 S. Brooke Street, Louisville, KY 40208, USA.

BRIGHTON Raymond Arthur, b. 6 Aug 1914, Boston, MA USA. Retired Researcher, Local History. m. (1)Mary J Pridham, 24 July 1942, (2)Betty J Nelson, 9 Dec 1989, 1 s, 1 d. *Education:* Antioch Coll, 1932-35; Ohio State Univ, 1935-38; BS in Ed, Army OCS, 1942. *Appointments:* Tchr, State Ind Sch, 1938-41; Army of US, 1941-46; Portsmouth Herald, 1946-79. *Publications:* They Came To Fish; Frank Jones, King of Alemakers; Clippers of Port of Portsmouth; The Checkered Career of Tobias Lear. *Memberships:* Portsmouth Athenaeum; Portsmouth Historical Soc; NE Assoc Press News Exec Assn; New England Soc of Newspaper Editors. *Honours:* Editorial Writing, Thomson Newspapers; Yankee Quill Award. *Hobbies:* Historical Research; Travel; Golf; Fishing. *Address:* 13 Hampshire Road, Portsmouth, NH 03801, USA. 6.

BRIMBLECOMBE Frederic Stanley William, b. 10 Sept 1919, Martock, Somerset. Physician. m. Esther Mary Stone, 25 Sept 1948, 1 s, 1 d. *Education:* Blundells Sch, 1933-37; St Marys Hospital Med Sch, 1938-43; London Univ; MD, FRCP, DCH, 1948, 1950, 1962. *Appointments:* Conslt Paediatrician, 1954-79, Royal Devon, Exeter Hospital, 1978-. *Publications:* Children in Health and Disease; Early Separation and Special Care Baby Units; The Story of Honeylands Papers, Handicapped Children and Young Adults. *Memberships:* Paediatric Sec RSM; British Paediatric Assoc; Visiting Prof Univ Southern Califonia; Chmn, Childrens Comm DHSS and DES; Pres, League of Friends, Royal Devon and Exeter Hospital. *Honours:* CBE; Hon Member Royal Soc for Mentally, Handicaped Children and Adults; External Examiner, many Univs. *Hobbies:* Classical Music; Medical History; Cricket; Golf; Countryside. *Address:* Coxes Farm, Clyst St Mary, Exeter, EX5 1DN, England.

BROADBENT Edward Granville, b. 27 June 1923, Huddersfield. Visiting Prof, Imperial Coll London, Maths. m. Elizabeth Barbara Puttick, 7 Sept 1949. *Education:* Huddersfield Coll, 1934-41; St Catharines Coll, Cambridge, 1941-43; BA, 1944; MA, 1947; ScD, 1975. *Appointments:* Govt Scientist, 1943-83. *Publications:* The Elementary Theory of Aeroelasticity, 1954; Burnhill Publications; Various Scientific Papers. *Memberships:* FRAeS; FIMA; FRS; FEng; FRSA. *Honours:* Simms Medal; Wakefield Gold Medal; Royal Aeronautical Society, Society Gold Medal. *Hobbies:* Garden; Walking; Music; Theatre; Chess; Bridge. *Address:* 11 Three Stiles Road, Farnham, Surrey, GU9 7DE, England. 1, 34.

BROADBENT Geoffrey Haigh, b. 11 June 1929, Huddersfield. Prof of Arch. m. Anne Barbara Sheard, 25 June 1955, dec 1985, 2 s. *Education:* Univ of Manchester, 1949-54. *Appointments:* Arch, Fairhursts, 1955-59; Lectr, Univ of Manchester, 1959-61; York, 1961-62; Sheffield, 1963- 67; Head of Sch of Arch, Portsmouth Poly, 1967-88; Prof of Arch, 1988-. *Publications:* Design in Arch; Emerging Concepts in Urban Space Design; Deconstruction. *Memberships:* RIBA; ARCUK; RSA; Intl Assoc of Semiotic Studies; British Sch of Rome Memb Appointing Board. *Honours:*

Prof Honorario Sto Dominqo; Dr Honoris Cause Tucuman Argentina; Prof Visitante, Univ Nacinal de Jnqenievia. *Hobbies:* Music; Fine Arts; Travel; Photgraphy. *Address:* 11 Hereford Road, Southsea, Hants PO5 2DH, England.

BROADHURST Alan Desmond, b. 24 Feb 1926, Birmingham. Med Practitioner, Univ Tchr. m. Lotte Zingrich, 11 Oct 1969, 2 s. *Education:* Univ London. Sheffield, Cambridge, MB ChB, 1955; MRCS, LRCP, 1955; DPM, 1963; MRC Psych, 1971; MIBiol, 1983; CBiol, 1986. *Appointments incl:* Clinical Pharmacol, Manchester and Basle, 1955-60; Reg in Pychol Med, Fulbourn Hosp, Cambridge, 1960-62; Med Reg, Papworth Hosp, 1964-66; Sen Reg in Psych and Sen Reg in Medicine, Addenbrookes Hosp, Cambridge, 1966-70; Sr Conslt Psych, West Suffolk Hosp, 1970-; Conslt Phys, Addenbrookes Hosp, Cambridge, 1970-89. *Publications:* Papers in Pharmacology, Psychopham, The Effects of Drugs on Human Performance and in Aviation Medicine. *Memberships:* Royal Coll of Psychiatrists; E. Anglian Thoracic Soc; BMA; Aero Med Intl; Oxford Postgraduate Inst of Psychiat; Britich Assoc for Psychopharacology. *Hobbies:* Motor Cruising; Sailing; Travelling. *Address:* Vicarage Grove, The Park, Great Barton, Suffolk IP31 2SU, England. 170.

BRODIE Don Edward, b. 8 Sept 1929, Bracebridge, Ontario. Prof of Physics. m. Naureen Elizabeth Petch, 27 Aug 1955, 1 s, 2 d. *Education:* BSc 1955; MSc, 1956; Type A High Sch Tchr Cert, 1957; PhD 1961. *Appointments:* Elemtary Sch Tchr, 1948-51; High Sch Tchr, 1957-58; Lectr, Waterloo Coll, 1958-59; Asst Prof, 1961-64; Assoc Prof 1964-68; Prof, 1968-. NCR, Grant Selection Com for Publications, 1973-76; Int Dir, Le Groupe de Recherches sur les Semiconducteur et less Dielectriques; Dean, Faculty of Sci, 1982-90; Board of Dir, Ontario Centre for materials Research, 1988-90. *Publications:* Sci and Prof Publications; Editor of Physics in Canada, 1969-73. *Memberships:* Canadian Assoc of Physicists; New York Academy of Sci; Solar Enery Soc of Canada; American Assoc for the Advancement of Science, ASM International. *Honours:* Deans Honour Role, 1955; Dupont of Canada Scholarship, 1956-57; Woodrow Wilson Memorial Fellowship, 1959; Nat Research Council of Canada Scholarship. *Hobbies:* Gardening; Woodworking; Cross Country Skiing. *Address:* Dept of Physics, Univ of Waterloo, Waterloo, Ontario, Canada, N2L 3G1. 142, 143.

BROEDNER-VON BEERFELDE Erika B, b. 19 Aug 1913, Muenster, West Falia. Archt Ret'd. m. Ernst Broedner, 26 Apr 1940, 1 s, 1 d. *Education:* Maturum (Abitur) Staatl Augustaschule (Greek, Latin, French, Engl), 1932; Study Archt, Archeology; Dipl Ing TU Berlin, Charlottenburg, 1937; Dr Ing, 1939. *Appointments:* Asst, Univ. Archt. Archtl researches in Turkey, Yugoslavia, Italy, Africa. *Publications:* Modernne Kuchen, 1950; Die Kuche als Arbeitsplatz, 1951; Modernes Wohnen, 1954; Co-author technik in der Wohnung, 1955; Immanuel Kroeker: Moderne Schulen, 1951; Immanuel Kroeker: Schulbauten, 1951; Die Frau und ihre Wohnung, 1956; Co-author Heimgestaltung-Form und Funktion der Wohnung; Stadtformung und Lebenswert, 1977; Untwersuchungen an den Caracallathermen; Die romischen Thermen und das antike Badewesen, eine kuilturhistorische Betrachtung, 1983; Wohnen in der Antike, 1989. *Memberships:* YDI; BDA; Koldewey Gesellschaft; Deutsche Orient Gesellschaft; Soroptimist Int. *Honour:* Stipendiat DAF 1940. *Hobbies:* Travelling around the World, Gardening, Art. *Address:* Am Muehlenberg 33, D-4800 Bielefeld 1, Germany.

BROMKE Adam, b.11 July 1928, Warsaw, Poland. Univ Prof. 2 s. m. (2) Ewa Boniecka, 2 s. *Education:* MA, St Andrews Univ 1950; PhD, Univ of Montreal, 1953; PhD, McGill Univ, 1964. *Appointments:* Lectr Univ of Montreal, 1952-54; Ed in Chief, Polish Overseas Project, Free Eur Cttee, NY; Lectr, McGill Univ, 1957-60; Rsch Fellow, Russian Rsch Centre, Harvard Univ,

1960-62; Asst Prof of Polit Sci, Carleton Univ, 1962; Chmn Soviet and East European Studies, 1963-66; Assoc Prof, 1964; Prof, 1967; Chmn of Dept, 1968-71; Prof of Pol Sci, McMaster Univ, 1973-89; Chmn of Dept, 1973-79; Prof Emeritus, 1989; Prof Hum, Polish Acad of Scis, 1990-. *Publications include:* The Communist States at the Crossroads, The Communist States and the West, Poland's Politics, Idealism vs Realism; Poland; The Protracted Crisis, Eastern Europe in the Aftermath of Solidarity, The Meaning and Uses of Polish History. *Honours include:* Lifetime Hon Mbr, Intl Cncl of Soviet and E Eur Studies; Canadian Assoc of Slavists; Polish Order of Merit Commander's rank. *Hobbies:* Reading; Music. *Address:* Bernardynska 22/26, 02-904 Warsaw, Poland.

BROOK Adrian Gibbs, b. 21 May 1924, Toronto, Canada. Univ Prof of Chemistry. m. Margaret Ellen Dunn, 18 Dec 1954, 2 s, 1 d. *Education:* Univ of Toronto, BA, 1947; Univ of Toronto, PhD, 1950. *Appointments:* Lectr, Dept of Chem, Univ of Saskatchewan, 1950-51; Univ of Toronto, 1953-; Lectr, 1953-56; Asst Prof, 1956-60; Assoc, 1960-62; Prof, 1962-89. *Publications:* Papers and Chapters, Organic Chemistry. *Memberships:* Chemical Inst of Canada; American Chem Soc. *Honours:* Gold Medal in Physics; Frederick Stanley Kipping Award (ACS); CIC medal; Fellow, Royal Soc of Canada. *Hobbies:* Computors; Windsurfing. *Address:* Dept of Chemistry, Univ of Toronto, Toronto, Canada M5S 1A1. 88.

BROOK David Conway Grant, b. 23 Dec 1935, Jerusalem. Civil Emergencies Adviser to Home Sec. m. Jessica, 14 Jan 1961, 1 s, 1 d. *Education:* Marlborough Coll, 1949-53; RAF Coll, Cranwell, 1954-56. *Appointments:* Fighter and Ground Attack Pilot RAF, 1956-89; Command of Harrier Squadron and Air Base, Joint and Airstaff Appointments, 1973-85; Retired, Air Officer Scotland, N Ireland, 1989. *Publications:* Construction to Bratseys Annual, 1973; Rolls Royce Magazine, 1979. *Membership:* NIL. *Honours:* CBE, 1983; CB, 1990. *Hobbies:* Music; Canals; Golf; Walking. *Address:* Cherry Orchard Cottage, Broad Campden, Glos, GL55 6UU, England. 1.

BROOK Greville Bertram, b. 30 July 1926, Nottingham. Conslt. m. Mary Rose Saunders, 12 Sept 1953, 2 s, 1 d. *Education:* B Met, Univ of Sheffield, 1947; FIM, Fellowship of Inst Metals, 1970; F Eng, 1987; FRSA, 1988; D.Met, Univ of Sheffield, 1992. *Appointments:* Investigator, 1949-56; Principle Metallurgist, 1956-75; Visiting Reader, Univ of Surrey, 19674-86; Dir, Fulmer Reasearch Labs, 1975-90; Conslt Metallurgy and Materials, 1990-. *Publications:* Diecasting Handbook; Conf in Physical Metallurgy in Engineering; Papers and Publications. *Memberships:* London Metallurgical Soc; Inst of Materials; ECRO. *Honours:* Sir Robert Hadfield Medal, Prize; TP Marsden Award; Master of Univ of Surrey. *Hobbies:* Music; Theatre; Wine; Gardening; Photography; Travel; Science and Technology; Hill Walking. *Address:* 9 Whitfield Road, Hughenden Valley, High Wycombe, Bucks HP14 4NL, England.

BROOKE Ralph Ian, b. 25 April 1934, Leeds. Vice Provost Health Sciences, Dean of Dentistry. m. Lorna Shields, 11 Mar 1963, 2 s. *Education:* Leeds Univ, Degree, Medicine and Dentistry; Fellowship, Oral Surgery, Pathology. *Memberships:* Pres, Canadian Acad of Oral Medicine; Chmn, Commision on Dental Accreditation of Canada. *Honours:* Intl Academy of Dentistry. *Address:* Vice Provost Health Sciences, Univ of Western Ontario, London, Ontario, Canada, N6A 5C1. 2, 88.

BROOKE-LITTLE John Philip, b. 6 Apr 1927. m. Mary Lee Pierce, 1960, 3 s, 1 d. *Education:* Clayesmore Scho; New Coll, Oxford, MA; Earl Marshal's Staff, 1952-53. *Appointments incl:* Bluemantle Pursuivant of Arms, 1956-67; Richmond Herald, 1967-80; Norroy and Ulster King of Arms, 1980-; Reg, Coll of Arms, 1974-82; Ass Dir, Heralds Museum, 1983-90; Director 1990-; Hon Editor The Coat of Arms, 1950-; Pres English Language

Literary Trust, 1985-. *Publications:* Royal London, 1953; Pictorial History of Oxford, 1954; Boutells Heraldry; Knights of the Middle Ages; Prince of Wales; Fox Davies Complete Guide to Heraldry;Kings and Queens of Great Briton; The British Monarchy in Colour; Royal Arms, Beats and Badges; Royal Ceremonies of State. *Hobbies:* Cooking; Painting. *Address:* Heyford House, Lower Heyford, Bicester, Oxon OX6 3NZ, England.

BROPHEY Peter M, b. 5 Oct 1928, Montreal, Canada. Public Affaris Conslt. m. Helena D Burrows, 22 Sept 1951, 3 d. *Education:* McGill Univ, 1949. *Appointments:* Deloitte Haskins and Sells, 1949-54; Johnson and Johnson, 1954-70; Xerox Canada, 197088; Vice Prs Coporate Affairs; Public Affairs Conslt, 1989-. *Memberships:* Inst of Chartered Acc; Ontario Chamber of Commerce. *Address:* PO Box 45, Bond Head, Ontario, Canada LO6 1BO.

BROUGHTON John Renata, b. 19 Mar 1947, Hastings, NZ. Univ Lectr. *Education:* BSc Massey Univ, 1971; BDS Otago Univ, 1977. *Appointments:* Dental House Surgeon, 1978; General Dental Practice, 1979-89; Clinical Tuote, 1979-90; Lectr maori Health, 1989-. *Publications:* The Return Home; The Sin; The Hills; Michael James Mania; A Time Journal for Halleys Comet. *Memberships:* New Zealand Dental Assoc; New Zealand Territorial Force. *Honours:* Dominion Sunday Times Bruce Mason Playwrighters Award; Efficiency Decoration, 1992. *Hobbies:* Contemporary New Zealand Art; Tikanga Maori; Life and Works of Captain Bruce Bairnsfather. *Address:* Te Maraenui, 176 Queen Street, Dunedin, Otago, New Zealand.

BROWICZ Kazimierz, b. 17 Dec 1925, Czestochowa, Poland. Retired 1991. m. 1948, dec 1986, 1 s. *Education:* MSc, Faculty of Agri and Forestry, 1949; PhD, Forest Botany, 1959; Degree, Field of Systematics and Geography, 1963; Assoc Prof, Polish Academy of Sci, 1970; Prof, Polish Academy of Sci, 1978; Corresponding member, Polish Academy Sci, 1983. *Appointments:* Inst of Tree and Forest Research, 1947-49; Poznan Univ, Agri Univ, Dept of Forest Botany, 1949-56; Inst of Dendrology, Polish Acad Sci, 1956-1991; Asst Dir of Sci Affairs, 1965-73, 1982-91; Chairman, Botanical Com, Polish Academy of Sci, 1981-86. *Publications incl:* The Genus Colutea, 1963; The Genus Periploca, 1966; Participation In: Flora Iranica, 1969-90 and Flora of Turkey, 1972-82; Chorology of Trees ans Shrubs in South West Asia, 1982-92. *Memberships:* Polish Botanical Soc; Intl Dendrology Soc; OPTIMA; Czechoslovakian Botanical Soc. *Honours:* Intl Honour Award for Outstanding Contributions to the worlds knowledge of woody plants. *Hobbies:* Philately; Bibliophile; Travelling. *Address:* Przybyszewskiego 66/6, 60-357 Poznan, Poland.

BROWN Allan Gordon, b. 8 Aug 1934, Victoria BC. Poet, Editor, Tchr. m. Patricia Elizabeth, 15 May 1965. *Education:* BA, MA, Univ of British Columbia. *Appointments:* Literary Editor, Quarry Mag 1982-84; In house Editor, Quarry Press, 1983-85; Tchr Master, Prof, Saint Lawrence Coll. *Publications:* Figures of Earth; Locatives; This Stranger Wood; Winter journey; The Almond Tree; The Burden of jonah ben Amittai; Forgetting. *Memberships:* Freelance Editors Assn of Canada. *Hobbies:* Classical Music; Theology. *Address:* 85 Baiden Street, Kingston, Ontario, Canada K7M 2K2. 142.

BROWN Blanche Rachel, b. 12 Apr 1915, Boston, USA. Prof of Art History. m. Milton w Brown, 15 July 1938. *Education:* BA, New York Univ, 1936; MA NYU Inst of Fine Art, 1938; Paris Inst d'Art et d'Archeologie, 1937; PhD NYU Inst of Fine Arts, 1967. *Appointments:* Metropolitan Museum of Art, Staff Lectr, 1942-66; New York Univ, Assoc Prof, 1967-73; Prof, 1973-85; Prof Emeritus, 1985-. *Publications:* Ptolemaic Paintings and Mosaics; Five Cities, An Art Guide to Athens, Rome, Florence, Paris, London; Anticlassicism in Greek Sculpture of the Fourth Century BC. *Memberships incl:*

Archacological Inst of America, New York Soc; American Numismatic Soc; New York City Audubon Soc. *Honours:* Fellowships: American Council of Learned Soc; American Council of Univ Women; National Endowment for the Humanities; JS Guggenheim Memorial Foundation. *Hobbies:* Sailing; Seashoring. *Address:* 15 West 70 Street, New York, NY 10023, USA.

BROWN Delores Elaine Robinson, b. 10 Dec 1945, Wildwood, Florida, USA. Minister, Humanitarian. m. Marshall L Brown, 21 December 1966, 1 d. *Education:* Fla, A&M Univ, Pre Engrg, 1962-64; Tuskegee Univ, BSEE, 1965-67. *Appointments:* General Electric, Engrg, 1967-68; Fla Power Corp, Engrg, 1968-70; Honeywell Aerospace, Engr, 1971-75; Sperry Univac, 1975; E-Systems, ECI Division, 1976-78. *Memberships:* Lakeview Presbyterian Church; The Replican National Committee, 1991-92; The Republican Presidential Advisory Board, 1991-92. *Honours:* Help Hospitalized Veterans Certificate of Apprec; Woman of the Year, 1991; The Republican Presidential Legion of Merit, The Republican Presidential Trust, 1992. *Hobbies:* Studying the Bible; Coin Collecting; Collecting Miniature Antiques; Writing Poetry and Short Stories of Inspiration. *Address:* 2630 Queen Street, South St Petersburg, FL 33712, USA. 138, 155.

BROWN George Gordon, b. 17 Feb 1925, Leatherhead. Barrister. m. Wendy Margaret Clark, 16 Aug 1968, 1 s, 1 d. *Education:* Eastbourne Coll, 1938-43; Queens Coll, Oxford, 1943; Sch of Tank Tech, 1952; Staff Coll, Camberley, 1958; Called to Bar, 1966. *Appointments:* ADC Gen McCeery, 1946-48; 12th Royal Lancers, 1948-60; 9/12 Royal Lancers, 1960-65; Barrister, 1966; Barrister, London and Western Circuit, 1966-. *Publications:* The New Divorce Laws; Getting A Divorce; Brown on Divorce; Brown on Seperation; Brown on Divorce, 2 ed; Finding Fault in Divorce. *Memberships:* Tylers and Bricklayers Livery; Inner Temple; Conserv Lawyers; Nat Campaign for Family; Nat Family Trust. *Hobbies:* Golf; Gardening; Reading; Cavalry and Guards Club; Hampshire Club. *Address:* 2 Kings Bench Walk, The Temple, London, EL4Y 7DE, England.

BROWN Howard Bernard, b. 2 Jan 1924, Chicago. Management Exec, Pres. m. Barbara Ann Lowe, 27 Dec 1952, 3 s, 2 d. *Education:* Armstrong Coll, Savannah, GA, BA 1946; BS Engr, GA Tech, 1948; Engr, 1949; LLB and Doc of Law, Emory Univ, 1953. *Appointments incl:* RAMM Ind, RAMM Foods; RAMM Electronics; RAMM Vending promotions; Pres, Chm of Board, 1976-; South Money Pub, 1976-; Computerized Marketing and Research. *Memberships:* Federal Bar Assoc; Cape Kennedy GA Tech Club; Nat Contract Manag Assoc; March of Dimes; Nat Manag Club; Prof Engr; Georgia Bar Assoc. *Honours:* Engr of Year; Chamber of Commerce Man of The Year; Fund Raiser of the Year. *Hobbies:* Military Pilot; Boat Racing; Prof Salvage Diver; Swimming; Running. *Address:* 420 South Orlando Ave, Winter Park, FL 32789, USA. 7.

BROWN James Anthony, b. 10 May 1932, Cleveland. Teacher; Author, Conslt. *Education:* BA Latin, 1955; Phl. Philosophy, 1957; MA English, 1959; Loyola Univ, Chicago; PhD Commun, Univ Southern Calif, 1970. *Appointments incl:* Asst Prof, Chm, Radio Television Dept, Univ Detroit, 1967-70; Conslt, Pres, CBS TV Network, 1971; CBS Inc, 1976; Asst Prof, Chm, Telecommunications Dept, Univ of Southern Calif, 1971-74; Exec Dir, Human Family Inst, 1974-76; Assoc Prof, Sch of Journalism, Univ Southern, Calif, 1978-82; General Manag, WVUA FM, 1982-88; Assoc Prof, Chm, Telecommunication & Film Dept, Univ Alabama, 1982-. *Publications:* Broadcast Management; Profits of Doom; Critical Viewing Skills Education; Encyclopedia Articles, New Catholic Encyl. *Memberships:* Broadcast Educ Assoc; Hollywood Radio and Telv Soc; Assoc for Educ in Journalism and Mass Communs; Pacific Pioneer Broadcasters; American Journ Historian Assoc; American Assoc of Univ Prof. *Honours:* KNXT CBS Graduate Scholar; Research Grant, Nat'l Assoc of

Broadcasters. *Address:* 4614 Overlake Circle, Northwood Lake, Northport, AL 35476, USA.

BROWN Judith Margaret, b. 9 July 1944, India. Prof of Commonwealth History, Oxford. m. 21 July 1984, 1 s. *Education:* Sherbon Sch for Girls, Dorset, 1957-61; Girton Coll, Cambridge, 1962-68; BA, 1965; PhD, 1968; MA, 1969. *Appointments:* Girton Coll, Cambridge, Fellow, 1968-71; Dept of History, Manchester, 1971-90; Lectr, 1971-82; Senior Lectr, 1982-90; Univ of Oxford, Prof of Commonwealth History, 1990-. *Publications:* Gandhi Rise to Power; Gandhi and Civil Diodedience; Men and Gods in a Changing World; Modern India; Gandhi Prisoner of Hope. *Memberships:* Royal Historical Soc; Balliol Coll, Oxford. *Hobbies:* Gardening; Reading; Classical Music; Craftwork. *Address:* Balliol College, Oxford, OX1 3BJ England.

BROWN Lillian, b. 8 Aug 1914, Ohio. Author, Lectr, Media Consult. 2 d. *Education:* Bowling Green State Univ, 1931-33; Ohio State Univ, 1933-36. *Appointments:* DTR Radio and TV, George Washington Univ, ,1956-66; DTR Radio and TV, American Univ, 1966-76; Lectr, George Town Univ, 1991. *Publications:* Your Public Best. *Memberships:* Nat Academy of TV, Arts and Sci. *Honours:* Intl Broadcasters Soc, Honours list, 1967; Nat Academy of TV Arts and Sci, Pres Enmy, 1966; Golden Mike Award, McCalls Mag. *Address:* 1003 Gelston Circle, McLean, VA 22102, USA.

BROWN Ollie Dawkins, b. 30 May 1941, Stanton, Texas, USA. Sci Researcher; Author; Psychotherapist; Educator. m. Robert Jerry Brown, 28 Sept 1958, div. 2 s. *Education:* BS Texas Tech Univ, 1965; MEd Univ of Noth Texas, 1973; MS East Texas State Univ, 1983. *Appointments:* School Tchr, 1965-73; Diagnostician, with Dr Lillian Solomon, 1973-82; Medical Researcher, Enviromental Health Centre, Psychotherapist, Inst, Univ of Texas, 1987-. *Contributions to:* Prof Journals and Medical Textbooks; Death and Dying; Relationship Between Length of Birth Labour and Learning Problems; Enviromental Aspects of Health and Disease; Food and Chemical Sensitivities with Emphasis on Cardiovascular Effects. *Memberships incl:* Current American and Texas Psychological Assoc; Texas Assoc of Marriage and Family Therapists; New York Academy of Sci; Dallas Museum of Art. *Hobbies:* Birding; Gardening; Family and Friends; Dance; Theatre; Art; Gourmet Food; Travel. *Address:* 634 Williams Way, Richardson, TX 75080, USA.

BROWN Stephen Ira, b. 14 July 1938, Brooklyn NY. Prof. m. Eileen Thaler, 12 June 1960, 1 s, 1 d. *Education:* Coumbia Coll, AB, 1960; Harvard Univ, MAT, 1961; Harvard Univ, EdD, 1967. *Appointments:* Simmons Coll, Boston MA, 1962-65; Harvard Univ, Cambridge MA, 1966-72; Syracuse Univ, 1972-73; Univ at Buffalo, 1973-. *Publications:* Some Prime Comparisons; Student Generations; Readings from Progestive Education; The Art of Problem Posing; Problem Posing: Elaborations and Applications. *Memberships:* John Dewey Soc; Philosophy of Educ Soc; Nat Council of Tchrs of Maths. *Honours:* Phi Beta Kappa; Phi Delta Kappa; John Dewey Senior Research Fellow. *Hobbies:* Tennis (Watching Wife play). *Address:* Graduate Sch of Education, 431 Baldy Hall, Univ of Buffalo, Amherst, NY 14260, USA. 2, 52.

BROWNING Frank Sacheverel Chips, b. 28 Oct 1941, Oxford. Pastic Surgeon. m. Carol Angela, 9 July 1966, 1 s, 2 d. *Education:* Dulwich Coll, 1952-60; Univ of St Andrews, 1960-66; MB ChB, FRCS, 1971. *Appointments:* Conslt Plastic Surgeon, St James's Univ Hospital and General Infirmary, 1980-; Microsurgical Research, St Vincents Hospital, Melbourne, 1975-76; Senior Reg, Plastic Surgeon, 1971-80. *Contributions to:* Rob and Smiths Operative Surgery; Surgical Review. *Memberships:* British Assn Plastic Surgeons; British Assn Aesthetic Plastic Surgeons; Medical Equestrian Assoc. *Honours:* Freeman City of London. *Hobbies:*

Rugby; Equestrian. *Address:* 4 Thornfield Road, Leeds, LS16 4AR, England.

BRUCE John Anthony, b. 8 Apr 1931, Los Angeles, California, USA, Artist. m. Barbara Jean Kennedy, 29 May 1967. div. June 1988, 3 s, 3 d. *Education:* BA Psychology Art, California State Univ, 1965. *Appointments:* US Army, 1949-52; Commercial Artist, Aerojet General Corporation, 1957-59; Advertising Manager, Flow Equip Co, 1959-63; Art Dir, Barnes Cahmp Advertising, 1963-66; Art Dir, Long Beech, 1970-73; Freelance Art Conslt, 1973-. *Creative Works:* Lithographs in permanent coll, Smithsonian Inst; Ghormley Gallery, 1966; Les Li Art Gallery, 1970; Upstairs Gallery, 1973; El Prado Gallery, 1987; Group Shows. *Memberships:* Knickerbocker Artists; American Indian and Cowboy Artists. *Honours:* John B Grayback Award; Philip Isinbwerg Award; Eagle Feather Award. *Address:* 5394 Tip Top Road, Mariposa, CA 95338, USA. 9, 52.

BRUCE RADCLIFFE Godfrey Martin, b. 19 June 1945, Rugby. Solicitor. m. Anita Claire miller, 5 Oct 1974, 1 s, 1 d. *Education:* Kings Coll, Tunton, 1958-64; Coll of Law Guildford, 1966, 69-70. *Appointments:* Articled with Trower Still and Keeling, Lincoln Inn; DJ Freeman & Co. of London, 1977; Partner, 1978-. *Memberships:* Law Soc. *Honours:* Freeman of the City of London. *Hobbies:* Sailing; Music; Investment. *Address:* Ellacombe, 21 Anstey Lane, Alton, Hampshire, GU34 2NR, England.

BRUEMMER Fred, b. 26 June 1929, Riga, Latvia. Writer; Photographer. m. Maud Van Den Berg, 31 Mar 1962, 2 s. *Education:* High Sch, Germany. *Appointments:* Journalist, Gazette, Montreal, 1964; Self Employed Writer, Photographer. *Publications incl:* The Long Hunt; The Arctic; Children of the North; The Arctic World; Seasons of the Seal; World of the Polar Bear. *Memberships:* Royal Canadian Academy of Art; Travel Journalists Guild; Arctic inst of North America. *Honours:* Silver Jubilee Medal; Order of Canada; Sandford Fleming medal, Royal Canadian Inst; Dr Lit h c Univ of New Brunswick. *Hobbies:* Photography; Travel. *Address:* 2 Strathearn South, Montreal West, Canada, H4X 1X4.

BRUMBY Donna Trotter, b. 26 July 1955. Athens, TN. Brach Libn, Andrews Public Lib. m. Edward Hunt, 16 Sept 1989, 2 stepson, 1 stepdaughter. *Education:* BA, Shorter Coll, Rome, 1977; M Ed, Brenau Coll, Gainsville, 1983; M Ln, Emory Univ, Atlanta, 1986. *Appointments:* Fannin County Board of Educ, 1979-85; Lake Lanier Reg Lib, 1985-86; Nantahala Reg Lib, 1986-. *Publications:* Co-author, The Glory That Was, Is and Shall be; A History of Blue Ridge First Baptish Church. *Memberships:* American Lib Assoc; Southeast Booksellers Assoc; Murphy First Baptist Church. *Honours:* Alpha Sigma Honour Soc. *Hobbies:* Reading; Collecting, David Winter Cottages, Bugs Bunny Memorabilia, Football Cards. *Address:* 112 Mauney Street, Murphy, NC 28906, USA. 7.

BRUNEAU Angus Andrew, b. 12 Dec 1935, Toronto, Canada. Chairman, Pres & CEO, Fortis Inc. m. Jean L McInnis, 16 May 1959, 3 s. *Education:* BA Sc Engr Physics, 1958; DIC, Physical Metallurgy, Imperial Coll, London, 1962; PhD, Physical Metallurgy, Univ of London, 1962. *Appointments:* Prof & Dean of Engr, Newfoundland, 1967-78; Pres & COE, Bruneau Resources Mgmt, 1978-86; Chmn, Pres & CEO, Fortis Inc, 1987-; Pres & CEO, Newfoundland power, 1986-90. *Publications:* Over 50 Reports. *Memberships:* Assoc Of Prof Engr of Nfld; Engr Inst of Canada; Conference Board of Canada; Canadian Academy of Engr; YM/YMCA Nat Advisory Council; Business Council on Nat Issues. *Honours:* Officer of the Order of Canada; Dr of Engr; Fellow of Engr Inst of Canada; Fellow of the Canadian Academy of Engr; Canadian Council of Prof Engr Gold Medal. *Hobbies:* Woodworking; Gardening;

Reading. *Address:* Fortis Inc, PO Box 8837, St Johns, Newfoundland, Canada. A1A 3T2. 88.

BRUNELLE Dorval, b. 8 Sept 1941, Montreal. Prof. m. 29 Oct 1970, 1 d. *Education:* Univ of Montreal, LLB, 1962; Univ of Madrid, 1963; Ecole Pratique des Hautes Etudes, Paris, Doctorate in Sociology, 1973. *Appointments:* Exec Sec, Municipal Affairs, 1964-66; Jour, CBC, 1967- 68; Prof Univ du Quebec a Montreal, 1970-. *Publications:* Le Code Civil et les Rapports de Classes; La Desillusion Tranquille; La Raison du Capital; Socialisme, etatisme et democratie; Les Trois Colombes; Le Libre Echange Par Defaut; Also, Articles, Interviews, Commontaries. *Honours:* Assoc de economie politique; Ligue des droits et libertes. *Hobbies:* Bibliophily; Skating; Jogging. *Address:* UQAM Dept of Sociology, PO Box 888, Montreal QC, Canada H3C 3P8. 142.

BRUTIAN Georg, b. 24 Mar 1926, Sev Kar, Armenia. Academician, Admr. m. 26 May 1955, 1 s, 2 d. *Education:* Diplomas, Yerevn Poly Inst, 1947; Yerevan Univ, 1950; Degree, Cand Phil Sci, 1951; Dr Phil Sci, 1962. *Appointments:* Assoc Prof Yerevan Univ, 1951-62; Prof Head of Chair, Yerevan Brusov Inst, 1962-70; Prof Head of Chair, Yerevan Univ, 1970- 86; Academician Sec of Div of Philosophy, Philology, 1977; Founder and Pres, Academy of Philosophy, Lake Sevan, 1987. *Publications:* 48 Books and Booklets; 200 Articles on Philosophy. *Memberships incl:* Academy of Sci of Armenian SSR; Academician; Academy if Sci; philosophical Soc of the USSR; European Centre for the Study of Argumentation; Intl Soc for Communications and Cognition; Advisory Board of the Intl Soc for the Study of Argumentation; Intl Biographical Assoc; American Biographical Inst Research Assoc; World Inst of Achievement; World Literary Academy; Intl parliament for Safety and Peace. *Honours:* Honorary Citizen, Masterton Borough Council, New Zealand; Lenins 100th Birthday Anniv medal; Komensky Medal; Sign of Honour 1st Class Medal; Veteran of Labour Medal; Vavilov Medal; Order of Friendship of peoples. *Address:* Pushkin Street 40, Apr 90, Yerevan 375010, Armenia, Russia. 52.

BRUVERIS Jonas Vytautas, b. 19 Mar 1939, Lithuania.Musicologist, Prof of the Lithuanian Couservatoize Vitnius. m. Rita Dauksaite, 30 Dec 1970, 1 s. *Education:* Lithuanian Conservatoize, 1960-65, 1966-69; Candidate of Art Criticisum. *Appointments:* Lectr of the Lithuanian Conservatoize, 1969-; Guest Lectr, Bzatislava Univ. *Publications:* Mikalojus Konstantines Ciuzlioms Kaunas;Ciuzloniui 100 Vilnius; Kiprui Petrauskui 100 v; Lietuvos Operos in Baloto Teatres. *Memberships:* Composers Union of Lithuania. *Hobby:* Reading. *Address:* Subaciaus 8-18, 232024 Vilnius, Lithuania.

BRUWER Anna Marie, b. 24 Sept 1949, South Africa. Nurse. *Education:* Dimploma, Gen nursing, Midwifery, 1970-72; B.Cur, 1975; M.Cur, 1982; D.Cur, 1986. *Appointments:* Ward Sister, Westcoppies Hos, 1972-75; Psychriatric Nursing, 1975-88; Deputy Dir, Tygenberg Hos. *Publications:* 15 Nat Prof Journals, 1975-88; 3 Int Prof Journals, 1984-89. *Memberships:* SA Nursing Assoc; SA Nursing Council; Int Soc for Quality Assurance; Exec Business Womens Club. *Honours:* Sttgn Bursary. *Hobbies:* Theatre; Music; Tennis. *Address:* 45 Woodbridge Drive, Woodbridge Island, Milnertan 7441, South Africa.

BRYAN Elizabeth Mary, b. 13 May 1942, Halifax. Conslt Paediatrician; Medical Dir, Multiple Births Foundation. m. Ronald Higgins, 16 Sept 1978. *Education:* St Thomas Hospital Med Scho, 1960-66; MBBS, 1966; MRCP, 1970; MD, London, 1976; FRCP, 1989. *Appointments:* Honorary Conslt Hammersmith Hosp; Queen Charlottes and Chelsea Hosp; Med Dir of the Multiple Births Found, 1988. *Publications:* Nature and Nurture of Twins; Twins in the Family; Twins, Triplets and More; Twins and Higher order Births, A Guide to their Nature and Nurture. *Memberships:* Royal

Soc of Medicine; British Paediatric Assoc; Vice-Pres, Intl Soc for Twin Studies; Trustee of the British Infertility Counselling Assoc. *Address:* Little Reeve, Vowchurch Common, Hereford, HR2 ORL, England.

BRYANT Alan W Jr, b. 17 Aug 1940, Glen Ridge, New Jersey, USA. Mgr Human Resources. m. Beverley Brown, 28 Dec 1963, 1 s, 1 d. *Education:* AB Dartmouth Coll, 1962; MBA Amos Tuck Sch, 1963; Law St Marys U/San, Antonio, 1964-65. *Appointments:* Specialist profl placement spacecraft dept Gen Electric Co. 1965-66; Foreman, methods analyst TV Dept, Gen Electric Co, Syracuse 1966-67; Spec Salaried empl armament Dept, Gen Electric Co, 1967-68; Spec profl and slaried compensation info systems equip div, Gen Electric Co, 1968-70; Mgr Personnel Relations, Nuclear Energy Dept, 1970-72; Mgr Relations Practices, TV Receiver Products Dept, 1972-76; Mgr Employee and Community Relations, Meter Bus Dept, 1976-85; Mgr Nuclear Energy, Gen Electric Co, San Jose, Calif, 1985-. *Publications:* Replacing ountive discipline with a positive approach, 1984; Speaker at meetings. *Memberships include:* Sr Staff Positive Mgmt Leadership Course; Adj Staff Exec Asses and Devel; Bay Area Human Resource Exec Council; Soc for Human Recource Mgmt. *Honours:* Govenors Award for Public Serv; Distinguished Serv Award, Rotary Intl. *Hobbies:* Sailing; Photography; Art; Civic Activities. *Address:* 17325 Parkside Court, Monte Sereno, CA 95030 USA. 9, 59.

BRYANT Allyn Gordon, b. 5 Jan 1913, Orange, NSW. Retired Anz Bank Mgr. m. Nellie Walter, 11 Apr 1960, 3 s. *Education:* Intermediate Cert, 1928, New South Wales, Import/Export Cert, Tech Coll, 1958. *Appointments:* The Union Bank, Australia Ltd, 1929-51; Jnr Clerk, Sydney, New South Wales, 1929-31; Clerk, Parramatta NSW Branch, 1931-36; Clerk, Casino NSW Branch, 1936-37; Ledgerkeeper, Cootamundra NSW, 1937-38; Staff Clerk, Insp Dept NSW, and Queensland, Sydney; Asst Bill Clerk, George St Sydney, 1946; Chief Clerk, Insp Dept, Perth, 1946-51; Australian Imperial Forces, 1942-46; Australia, New Zealand Bank, 1951-73; Insp Accountant, Perth, 1951-52; Audit Officer, Western Australia, 1952-55; Mgr, new branch, Mt Hawthorn, Western Australia, 1955-61; Mgr 223 William St Branch, 1961-69; Mgr Subiaco Western Australia Branch, 1969-73; Co Dir Pangbourne Nominees Pty Ltd, 1974-; Justice of the Peace. *Creative Works:* Watercolour Paintings, 1928-36. *Memberships include:* Austrian Inst of Bankers; Lions Clubs Intl; Lions Club of Wanneroo Inc; AAMR Inc; SLCG Inc; Vic Assoc on Intellectual Disability Inc; Australian Legion of Ex Servicemen and Women Inc; Royal Assoc of Justices of Western Australia Inc; Nulsen Haven Foundation; ANZ retired Officers Club. *Honour:* MBE. *Hobbies:* Philately; Gardening; Photography; Community Service; Numismatics; Fortified Wines:- Collectors Items. *Address:* 6B Stocker Court, Craigie, WA 6025, Australia. 139.

BRYANT James Montgomery, b. 27 July 1954, Dallas, TX. Dir, Museum of Nat History. m. Judith Ann Lawrence, 20 Nov 1988. *Education:* BA Biology, Austin Coll, Sherman, 1976; MAT in Sci, Univ Tex, 1979; Postgrad So Meth Univ, Dallas, 1989; Geo Wash Univ, DC, 1980. *Appointments:* Adj Instr, Brookhaven Comm Coll, 1988; Sci Ed Cons, Dallas Mus Nat Hist, 1988-89; Grad Fellow Geo Sci, So Meth Univ, 1989; Ed Dir, VA Mus Nat Hist, 1990; Dir, Pember Mus, At Hist, 1990-. *Publications:* Articles to profl journals. *Memberships include:* Am Assn Mus Dallas Paleontal Soc; Smithsonian Inst; Woodrow Wilson Ctr Assocs; Costeau Soc. *Honours:* English Award, Brown U Alumni Assn. *Hobbies:* Music; Illustration; Photography; Hiking. *Address:* PO Box 52, Granville, NY 12832, USA. 117.

BRYER Anthony Applemore Mornington. b. 31 Oct 1937, England. Prof of Byzantine Studies. m. 2 Aug 1961. *Education:* Canford Sch; Sorbonne Univ; Balliol Coll; Oxford BA, MA, DPhil. *Appointments include:* Nat Service, RAF; Univ of Birmingham, 1964-65; Lctr, 1965-

73; Sen Lctr, 1973-76; Reader in Byzantine Studies, 1976-79; Public Orator, 1991-; Dir of Byzantine Studies, 1969-76; Visiting Fellow, Dumbarton Oaks, Harvard, 1971-; Merton Coll, Oxford, 1985; Founder and Dir, annual British Byzantine Symposia, 1966-; Chm, British Nat Ctee, Internat Byzantine Assoc, 1989-. *Publications:* Byzantium and the Ancient East; Iconoclasm; The Empire of Trebizond and the Pontos; The Byzantine Monuments and Topograph of the Pontos, 2 vols; Continuity and Change in late Byzantine and Early Ottoman Soc; Peoples and Settlement in Antolia and the Causasus 800-1900. *Memberships:* Buckland; Lochaline Social; Black Sea. *Hobbies:* Travel; Gastronomic Adventure. *Address:* Centre for Byzantine, Ottoman and Modern Greek Studies, Univ of Birmingham, PO BOx 363, Birmingham B15 2TT, England.

BRYK William Michael, b. 12 Mar 1955, Troy, New York, USA. Lawyer. *Education:* BS Manhattan Coll, 1977; JD, Fordham Univ, 1989. *Appointments:* Staff Analyst and Special Projects Coordinator, New York City Controller's Office, 1977-82; Asst to the President of the Borough of Manhattan, 1982-85; Chief of Staff, New York City Council Member Walter L McCaffrey, 1986-87; Asst, Pres of the New York City Council, 1987-89; Attorney associated with, Law Firm, Bondy & Schloss, 1989-90; Court Attorney, New York City Civil Court, 1990-91; Asst Counsel to Pres, New York City Council, 1991-; Attorney in private practice, NY 1991-. *Contributions:* Articles to New York Newsday; The Wanderer; Reflections. *Memberships include:* Augustan Soc; Confederation of Chivalry; G K Chesterton Soc; Knightly Assoc of St George the Martyr. *Honours include:* Knight Grand Cross; Militia of the Holy Sepulchre; Knight Grand Officer, Sovereign Military Order of the Temple of Jerusalem; Knight Commander, Orthodox Order of the Knights Hospitaller of St John of Jerusalem. *Hobbies:* Writing; Reading; Politics; Literature; History; Military and Political Affairs; Music; Philately. *Address:* PO Box 6549, FDR Station, New York, NY 10150, USA. 139.

BRYLEVSKAYA Larisa Ivanovna, b. 27 Oct 1960, Leningrad. Univ Tchr. *Education:* Faculty Mathematics, 1977-82; Postgraduate, 1982-85. *Appointments:* Researcher, 1985-87; Lctr, 1987-. *Publications:* History and Mathematics; Functional Analysis, Theory of Integration, Mesure Theory, Set Theory. *Memberships:* Soviet Nat Committee for History and Philosophy of Sci. *Honours:* Doc of Mathematics, Moscow Acad Sci, USSR. *Hobbies:* Sewing; Traveling. *Address:* Proizerskoe Shosse, Osinovaya Roshcha G Fl 25, 194902, Leningrad, Russia.

BRYNJULFSDOTTIR Anna Kristin, b. 23 Dec 1938, Reykjavik. Tchr, Writer. m. Elias Sneland Jonnson, 24 June 1967, 3 s. *Education:* MR, 1958; Tchr Univ, 1960; BA latin, Greek, Univ of Iceland, 1987. *Appointments:* Journalist; Writer; Tchr of Latin, Mathematics, Flensborg, 1988-. *Publications:* Four Little Teddybears; Matti Patti; Glidingdown the Rainbow; Trille, Being from Outer Space; Julia and Snorri. *Memberships:* Assoc of Icelandic Writers; Icelandic Tchrs Assoc. *Hobbies:* Photgraphy; Painting; Drawing; Animals; Classics. *Address:* Box 24 Brekkutun 18, 200 Kopavogur, Iceland. 3, 138.

BRZOSKO Witold Jozef, b. 16 May 1929, Warsaw, Poland. Physn. m. Hanna Siedlanowska, 17 Apr 1952, 2 d. *Education:* MD, Med Acad, Warsaw, 1952; Dr's Thesis, 1959; Assoc Prof, 1966; Prof, 1975. *Appointments:* Dept of Pathology, Med Acad, Warsaw, 1952-65; Dept of Immunopathology, State Inst of Hygiene, Warsaw, 1965-74; Dept of Immunopathology, Inst of Infectious and Parasitic Diseases, Med Acad, Warsaw, 1974-82; Lab of Clin Immunology Communicable Hosp in Warsaw, 1982-90. *Publications:* First author and or co-worker of 430 papers and articles dealing with human pathology and/or immunopathology published in Polish, Russian, French,

German and Engl Jrnls. *Memberships:* Polish Natural Med Soc; Polish Immunological Soc; Polish Pathological Soc. *Honours:* State Prize 2nd Class; Award of Polish Ministry of Health and Welfare; Award of Polish Academy of Sciences. *Hobby:* Antiques Collection. *Address:* Willowa 8-10 Apt 18, 00-790 Warsaw, Poland.

BRZUSKIEWICZ Jerzy, b. 28 Mar 1946, Lingen, Germany. m. Barbara, 2 s, 1 d. *Education:* Matriculatin, Torun Municipal H. Sch 1964; Academy of Fine Arts, Gdansk, 1964. *Appointments:* Int Architecture; Painting, Running Art Galleries, Berlin, Torun; Pres, Polis Artists Assoc, Torun. *Creative Works:* Exhibitions. Cracow, 1978; Berlin. 1981; Leyden, 1990; Gdansk, 1991; Gottingen, 1992. *Address:* ZPAP ul Ducha Sw 8/12, PL 87-100 Torun, Poland.

BU Peter, b. 26 May 1940, Bratislava, Czechoslovakia. Theatre Histn and Critic; Theatre Festivals and Theatre Tours Organiser. m. Daniela Andrei, 8 Jan 1972, 1 s, 1 d. *Education:* Doct of Theatre, Bratislava, 1968; Study 3rd Cycle (Doct) Sorbonne, Paris, 1968-72. *Appointments:* Theatre Histn, Acad Slovak of Sciences, Bratislava, 1962-68; Researches into St Theatre, Ctr of Arts G Pompidou, Paris, 1980-81; Theatre Advsr, Culture House of Rennes, 1982-84; Freelance Cultural Cons, 1984-. *Publications:* Stanislavsky's System by the Communise Power, 1968; No Violence: Dream or Reality? (essay), 1971; Mime in Europe, 1983; Festival Mgr in the Field of Mine, Street Theatre, Drama in France and Europe, eg, Avignon's Festival Mimes and Clowns, 1977; Other Theatre in Paris, Barcelona, Modena, 1982; Mimos of Perigneux 1987-92. *Hobbies:* Chess, Go, Reading, Sport. *Address:* 14 Avenue Pascal, F-78600 Maisons Laffitte, France.

BUBNICKI Zdzislaw, b. 17 June 1938, Lwow, Poland. Prof, Dir of the Inst. *Education:* M Sc, 1960; PhD, 1964; Doc of Sci, 1967; Prof, 1972, Auto Control and Computer Sci. *Appointments:* Dir of the Inst of Control and Systems Sci, Tech Univ of Wroclaw, 1981; Pres of Automation Com, Polish Academy of Sci, 1989. *Publications:* Identification of Control Plants; Introduction to Expert Systems; Control Theory. *Memberships:* Polish Academy of Sci; Systems Sci; General Assembly and Artifical Intelligence Com, IFIP. *Hobbies:* Music; Films. *Address:* Tech Univ of Wroclaw, Inst of Control and Systems Engr, 50-370 Wroclaw, Poland.

BUCHAN James Alexander Bruce, b. 4 May 1947, Spenborough. Solicitor. *Education:* Birmingham Univ, 1965-68. *Appointments:* Partner Dibb Lupton Broomhead, 1975-92. *Memberships:* The Leeds Club; Leeds Law Soc; Headingley Golf Club; Govenor Fulneck Boys School; Church Warden, St Johns Baptist Adel. *Hobbies:* Walking; Fresh Air; Golf. *Address:* 8 St Helens Croft, Adel, Leeds LS16 8JY, England.

BUCHANAN Ronald Hull, b. 18 Dec 1931, Belfast, N. Ireland. Univ Tchr. m. Gwendelyn Moorhead, 19 Aug 1958, 1 s, 1 d. *Education:* Queens Univ, Belfast, BA, 1953; PhD, 1958. *Appointments:* Asst Lectr, Queen Univ, 1955-58; Asst Prof, State Univ, USA, 1958-59; Lectr, 1959-68; Sen Lectr, 1968-81; Reader, 1981-85; Prof, 1985-. *Publications:* Man and His Habitat; Fields, Falls and Settlement in Europe; Pravnice, City ans people; The World of man. *Memberships include:* Int of Powtish Geographers; Geographical Assoc; Agri History Soc; Folklife Soc. *Honours:* Fulbright Scholar; Research Fellow, American Council of Learned Sci; Nat Trust, N. Ireland Reg Com. *Hobbies:* Gardening; Reading; Sailing; Walking; Travel. *Address:* Inst of Irish Studies, Queens Univ, Belfast BT7 1NN, N. Ireland.

BUCKAWAY Catherine Margaret, b. 7 July 1919, N Battleford, Sask. Poet. m. 1 April 1941, 2 d. *Education:* Bronze medal and Bar; Silver Medal and Bar; First Class Inst Cert, RL55. *Appointments:* Lifeguard, 1940-41; Jaught Swimming, Watrous, 1941; Post Office; Local Government Offices. *Publications:* Books, plays and

3301 published poems. *Memberships:* League of Canadian poets; Sask Writers Guild; Canscalp. *Honours include:* Canada Council Grant; Saskatchewan Arts Board Grants; Don Mac Intosh Award. *Hobbies:* Judge Poetry Contests. *Address:* Porteous Lodge, 833 Avenue P North, Saskatoon, Saskatchewan, Canada S7L 2W5.

BUDAGOV Rowlen, b. 5 Apr 1910, Rostov Don. Philologist. m. Alla Bragina, 30 May 1950. *Education:* Diploma, Doc of Philology; Sci Academy USSR. *Appointments:* Keningrad Univ, 1933-52; Moscow Univ, 1952-. *Publications include:* Sravnitelno Semasiologisheskissledorania; Portrety, Lingvistov. *Hobbies:* Letters; Classical Music. *Address:* Alabyan Street 12 Ap 101, 125080 Moscow, Russia.

BUDRAITIS Juozas, b. 6 Oct 1940, Lithuania. Actor. m. Vita Paleckyte, 28 Feb 1968, 1 s, 1 d. *Education:* Diploma Vilnius Univ, Dept of Law, 1973; Cinema Dir, Moscow, 1977-79. *Appointments:* Films, 1965-91; Theatre Plays, 1979-90; Chairman, Lithuanian Theatre Union, 1990-91. *Creative Works:* Compositions. *Memberships:* Lithuanian Theatre Union; Cinema to Graphic Union of Lithuania; Unionof Photographic Art of Lithuania. *Honours:* Peoples Actor of the Republic; Best Theatre Actor; Best Film Actor. *Hobbies:* Painting; Photography; Reading. *Address:* Crirlionio 16-2, Vilnius, Lithuania.

BUDREVICS Alexander, b. 3 Jan 1925, Riga Latvia. Landscape Arch. m. Milija d Roberts Vite, 8 Apr 1948. *Education:* State Horticultural Sch, 1944; St Albans Sch of Art, 1949; London Coll of Art, 1951. *Appointments:* Pres, Alexander Budrevics and Assoc ltd, 1965-; Prc Landscape Arch, Latvia, Germany, Belgiu, England; Ptnr Golf Course Devel Assn, 1969. *Memberships include:* Fellow Canadian and Am Soc of Landscape Arch; Am Inst of Landscape Arch; Latvian Nat Found in Can; Edn and Cutural Found; Candn Latvian Bus and Profl Assn; Latvian Boy Scots Assn. *Hobbies:* Gardening; Travel; Golf; Clubs; Bd of Trade; The Empire of Club of Can. *Address:* Two Park Centre, 895 Don Mills Road, Suite 808, Don Mills, Ontario M3C 1W3, USA. 2, 142.

BUDZINSKA Alina Julia, b. 27 April 1927, Bielsko Biala. Journalist; Master of Ceremonies; Author of Biographies. m. 2 Sept 1948, 1 d. *Education:* Matriculation of Mathematics, Natural Lyceum, 1948; Humanistic Faculty, Jagiellonian Univ, 1952; Diploma of Art, Ministry of Culture and Art, 1976. *Appointments:* Governemental Radio and TV, 1960-63; Literary Chief of Silesian Operete, 1963-64; Weekly Magazines, 1968-. *Publications include:* Rodzynki Migdaly, Vol 1 & 2; The Facts, The Grossips, the Anecdotes; Bel canto not only; Susanne the Blond and Otpress. *Memberships:* Polish Journalist Assoc; Cracow Animal Care Assoc. *Honours:* Silver Cross of Merit; Gold Cross of Merit; Journalistic Prizes. *Hobbies:* Guitar Music; Domestic Animal Care. *Address:* Sw Jana Str 1/10 , Krakow, Poland.

BUDZINSKI Roman Marian, b. 8 Aug 1927, Limanowa. Doc of Medicine. m. 2 Oct 1948, 1 d. *Education:* Medicine Study, Jagiellonian Univ, Krakow, 1945-50; Doc of Medicine, 1951; Spec of Laryngology, 1954. *Appointments:* Otholaryngological Clinic Univ of Cracov, 1950-65; Head of Dept, Oto Laryngology PKP Hosp Cracov, 1965-. *Publications:* 19 Articles, Poland, England, Swedeen, Germany. *Memberships:* Germany Otorinolaryngological Soc; polish Otorinolaryngological Soc. *Hobbies:* Music; History. *Address:* ul Jana 1/10, 31 017 Cracov, Poland.

BUFORD Thomas Oliver, b. 17 Nov 1932, Overton, Texas. Prof of Philosophy. m. Delores Jean phife, 27 Dec 1954, 2 s, 1 d. *Education:* BA, Univ of North Texas, 1955; BD, Southwestern Baptist Theological Seminary, 1958; PhD, Boston Univ, 1963. *Appointments:* Assoc Prof, Kentucky Southern Coll, 1962-68; Assoc prof, U of N Texas, 1968-69; Prof, Furman Univ, 199-. *Publications:* Toward a phil of Education; Personal

philosophy; Ambushed on the Road to Glory; The Personalist Forum. *Memberships:* American Philosophical Assoc; South Atlantic Philosophy of Educ Soc; SC Soc for phil; Baptist Assoc for Phil Tchr. *Honours;* Summer Research Grant; Academy of Distinguished Alumni. *Hobbies:* Jogging; Playing Cello. *Address:* Philosophy Dept, Furman Univ, Greenville, SC 29613, USA.

BUI Khoi Tien, b. 23 Dec 1937, Binh dinh, Vietnam. Poet. m. Yen Kim Nguyen, 7 Dec 1962. *Education:* BS. MBA. PhD Univ of New York, Paris, London; Doc of Literature; Nat Panner Training, Taiwan, Phillippines, Japen, Thailand. *Appointments:* Ministry of Agri, Republic of Vietnam; Chief of Agri Econmics Office, 1960-65; Chief of Intl Relations Serv, 1966- 69; Chief of Cabinet, 1969-73; Dir of Training Centre, 1973-75; Prof, Business Mgmt Inst, 1970-75; Counselor, Houston Community Coll, 1976-; Indochinese Culture and Refugee Information Centre, Houston Com Coll, 1981-; Xulture Lectr at Univ of Texas, 1982-. *Publications:* America, My First Fellings; Novel, Text Books, History Books, Poetry Books. *Memberships include:* PEN Vietnamese Centre; Nat Devlop Council Vietnam; Vietnamese Ameerican Assoc; Vietnamese Australian Assoc; Vietnamese Japanses Assoc; PEN American Centre; Leadership Houston Assoc; American poetry Soc. *Honours include:* Medals and Decorations, Government of the Republic of Vietnam; Nat Literature Prize; Houston Poet Leaueate Award; Golden Poet Awars; Ambassador to Vietnamese and American Culture Award; Distinguished Leadership Award. *Hobbies:* Writing Poetry; Reading; Swimming. *Address:* PO Box 720236, Houston, TX 77272, USA. 2, 7, 139.

BUJA Giuseppe, b. 5 Mar 1946, Padova, Italy. Full Prof, Univ of Trieste. m. Baracco Naldina, 30 Jan 1972, 1 d. *Education:* Degree, Electronic Engr, Univ of Padova. *Appointments:* Resear Asst, 1971-74; Assoc Prof, 1975-86; Full Prof, Univ of Trieste, 1986-. *Publications:* 70 Papers on Industrial Electric Applications; Co Editor, Advanced Motian Control. *Memberships:* IEEE; IEEE-IES; Electrosoft; Italian Electrotech Com; Microprocessor Control of Electric Divices. *Hobbies:* Reading; Cycling; Ping-pong. *Address:* Univ of Trieste, Dept of Electrotechnics, Electronics, Informatics, Via Valerio 10, 34127 Trieste, Italy.

BULLMORE George Hilary Lanyon, b. 23 Mar 1912, Wisbech, Cambs. Medical Practitioner. m. Kitty Dedman, 25 May 1948, 2 s. *Education:* Oriel Coll, Oxford, 1930-34; BA, 1933; BM BCh, 1938; MA, 1984; UCH London, 1934-38; LMSSA, 1938; DPM, 1949. *Appointments:* Miller General Hosp, Greenwich, 1939-40; RAMC, 1940-45; Captain, 1941-45; India 1943-45; St Ebbas Hosp, Epsom, 1946-77; Deputy Physician Supt, 1957-77. *Publications:* Books and Articles, Medical Press on Schizophrenia, Endocrinology, Mental Handicap. *Memberships:* British Epilepsy Assoc; Employment Committe; Medical Advisory Committe; Sec, Psycho Endocrine Assoc; Pres, Kingston Numismatic Soc. *Honours:* Welsh Memorial Univ Prize. *Hobbies:* Genealogy; Numismatics. *Address:* 12 Portsmouth Road, Kingston, Surrey, KT1 2LU, England. 170.

BUNDU Abass Chernor, b. 3 June 1948, Sierra Leone. Lawyer, Intl Civil Servant. Khadija Allie, 11 Jan 1976, 2 s, 3 d. *Education:* LLB, 1969; Barrister at Law, 1970; LLM, 1971; PhD, 1974. *Appointments:* Legal Officer, Australia, 1969; Asst Dir, Commonwealth Secretariat, 1975-82; Cabinet minister sierra Ledne, 1982-85; Exec Sec, Ecowas, 1989-92. *Memberships:* Assoc of African Jurists. *Honours:* Yorke Award. *Hobbies:* Tennis; Jogging; Reading. *Address:* 40 United Nations Drive, PO Box 1107, Freetown, Sierra Leone. 34.

BUNN Joe Millard, b. 20 Jan 1932, Wayne Countu, North Carolina. Prof of Agricultural Engr. m. F Marie Baker, 26 June 1955, 2 s. *Education:* BS N. Carolina State Univ, 1955; MS N. Carolina State univ, 1957; PhD, Iowa State Univ, 1960; Agri Engr and mathematics;

Reg Prof Engr. *Appointments:* Univ of Kentucky, Assis prof of Agricultural Engr, 1960-66; Assoc Prof of Agricultural Engr, 1966-78, 1968-70; Kentucky Team, Khon Kean, Thailand; Prof of Agri Engr, 1978-. *Publications:* Tech Articles, Monographs; 6 Books inc. Digital Data Acquisition; American Soc of Agricultual Engr; Solar Drying of Specialty Crops; Solar Engery in Agriculture. *Memberships include:* American Soc of Agri Engr; ASAE Special Activities Comm; ASAE State Sec; ASAE Program Comm;Conference Steering Comm. *Honours:* Student Honor Award; Gamma Sigma Delta Agri Honor Soc; Sigma XI the Research Honor Soc. *Hobbies:* Gardening; Boating; Quail hunting; Computor utilization in Tchr working and playing. *Address:* Room 233, McAdams Hall, Agri Engr Dept, Clemson Univ, Clemson SC 29634 0357, USA. 7, 143, 125.

BUNZA Muhammad Mustapha, b. 3 Feb 1941, Bunza. Civil Servant. m. 5 Oct 1963, 6 s, 11 d. *Education:* Ahmadu Bello Univ, BA, 1971-74; M Ed, 1976; Univ of Wales, PhD, 1984. *Appointments:* Classroom Tchr, 1965-70; Sch Admin, Principal, 1970-84; Commuissioner of Educ, 1984-87; Registrar, 1987-89. *Memberships:* Inst of Admin Management of Nigeria; West African Examination Council. *Honours:* Committee of Prinicapls of Nigeria Secondary Sch. *Hobbies:* Sports; Squash; Reading. *Address:* Dir and Cheif Exec, National Tchrs Inst, PMB 2191, Kaduna, Nigeria.

BUONOMANO Vincent, b. 15 May 1941, USA. Prof. m. Judith louiss Williams, 7 Dec 1964, 1 s, 1 d. *Education:* PhD, Mathematics, McMaster Univ of Canada. *Appointments:* State Univ of Sao Paulo, Campinas, 1972-. *Publications:* Various Sci Articles. *Hobbies:* Foundations of Physics; Computor Sci. *Address:* Inst of Mathematics, Univ Estadual de Campinas 13081, Campinas, Sao Paulo, Brazil.

BURACK Sylvia E Kamerman, b. 16 Dec 1916, Hartford. Editor; Publisher. m. Abraham S Burack, 28 Nov 1940, 3 d. *Education:* BA Magna cum laude, Smith Coll,, 1938; Boston Univ, 1985. *Appointment:* Editor, Publisher, Plays; The Grama Mag for Young people; The Writer Mag. *Publications include:* Little Plays for Girls, 1955; Blue Ribbon Plays for Graducation, 1957; Dramatized Folk Tales of the World, 1971; On Stage for Christmas, 1978; Holiday Plays Round the Year, 1983; Plays of Black Americans, 1987; Plays from Favorite Folk Tales, 1987; The Big Book of Holiday plays, 1990. How To Write and Sell Mystery Friction, 1990. *Memberships include:* Brookline Sch Com; Mass Bd Higher Edn; Mass Hist Soc Library. *Honours:* Service Award Brookline Rotary Club; Freedoms Found Award. *Address:* 72 Penniman Rd, Brookline, MA 02146, USA. 2.

BURBIDGE John Leonard, b. 15 Jan 1915, Toronto, Canada. Visiting Prof. Mgnt Systems, Cranfield Inst of Tech. m. Elizabeth Newton Claret, 1947, 4 s. *Education:* Wellington Sch Som, 1926-30; Cambridge Univ, 1931-32; Dr HC, Novi Sad Univ, 1990; D Sc, Strathclyde Univ, 1991. *Appointments:* Apprentice Bristol Aero Co, 1934-37; RA Lister, 1937-39; Ministry of Supply, HMG, 1939-40; RAF, 1940-46; David Brown, 1952-57; Brit Ref Works Dir, 1957-59; Darlington Wire, MD, 1959- 61; ILO, 1962-76. *Publications:* Std Batch Control, 1960; The Principles of Production Control, 1962; Production Planning, 1971; The Introduction of Group Technology; Group Tech in Engr Ind; IFIP Glossary; Prod Flow Analysis. *Memberships:* Hon F I Prod E; Hon F. IEE; FBIM; M I Mech E. *Honours:* MID, 1945; Hon Fellow Inst of Prod Engr, 1989; Hon Fellow Inst of Elec Engr, 1991; OBE, 1991. *Hobbies:* Chess; Golf. *Address:* Wild Goose Leys, Abbotts Ripton, Huntingdon, Cambs. PE17 2LB, England.

BURCHARDT Clara Chavez, b. 20 Oct 1932, Colorado, USA. Prof of Spanish. m. William R, 29 Dec 1971. *Education:* BA Music, 1957; MA Spanish, 1966; PhD Spanish, 1972. *Appointments include:* Instr, Cedar Catholic High Sch, 1957-62; Instr, Dept Head, Mount

Marty Coll, 1966-68; Dir, Inter American Inst, Oklahoma, 1973-75; Dir, Prof of Spanish, Univ of Oklahoma, 1983-86; Prof of Spanish, Mount Marty Coll, 1988; Prof of Spanish, Southern Nazaiene Univ, Oklahoma, 1989-. *Publications:* Bi lingual materials, Economy Pub Co. *Memberships:* American Assoc of Tchr of Spanish, Portuguese; Oklahoma Foreign Language Tchr Assoc. *Honours:* Outstanding Young Woman of America, 1967; Nat Reg of Prominent Americans. *Hobbies:* Music; Sewing; Reading; Needle Work. *Address:* 127 East Shore Drive, Lake Hiwassee, Arcadia, OK 73007, USA. 7, 15.

BURCHETT Sandy Curtis, b. 6 Feb 1942, El Reno, Ok USA. Hairdresser. m. Ronald Burchett, 26 June 1960, 2 s. *Education:* Univ of Arkansas, 1959-1963; Paul Barnes Hair Styling, Ok; Paul Mitchell, Hono Lulu; Eclpse, London. *Appointments:* Vice Pres, General Manager, Barboras Hair and Dress Fashions, 1963-; Pres, Super Six Haircuts. *Publications:* Biography of Famous Father Eddie Curtis. *Memberships:* Okla Cosmetologist Assn; Jayceettes Phi Beta Kappa; Thunderbird Hair Fashions Comm. *Honours:* Hairsylist of the Year, Okla; Oklahoma State Womens Hairstyling Champion. *Hobbies:* Golf; Tennis; Snow Skiing; Travel; Pupeteer at Church Methodist. *Address:* Rt2 Ridge Road, The Coues Grand Lake, Afton, OK 74331, USA. 7, 76.

BURDEN Clive Albert, b. 1 June 1934, Ealing, London. Antiquarian Bookdealer. m. Pauline Elain Dean, 22 Mar 1958, 1 s, 1 d. *Education:* Univ Coll of SW, 1952-55; London Univ, B Sc, Physics, 1955; Flying Officer, RAF, 1955-58. *Appointments:* Research Sci, 1958; Mngr Automatic Welding Dept, 1959; Asst Mngr Welding Dept, 1962; Trainee Mngr Production, 1965; Equipment Sales Mngr, Eastern Region, 1968; Nat Sales Mngr Equip, 1971; Dir Irish Ind Gases, 1971; Gen Mgr, Automatic Welding Prod, 1971; Antiqarium Book and Print Business, 1973. *Memberships:* M Inst W, 1959; M Inst P, 1965; ABA, 1980. *Honours:* Harvey Shacklock Award, best Tech paper, 1964. *Hobbies:* Sports; English County Atlases and Maps. *Address:* 26 Sandy Lodge Road, Moor Park, Rickmansworth, Herts, WD3 1LJ, England.

BURDISON Evonne, b. 2 Oct 1947, Greenwood MS. Coll Prof. *Education:* BA Univ of Mississippi, 1969; MA Univ of Mississippi, 1971; PhD Univ of Mississippi, 1987. *Appointments:* Univ of Central Arkansas, 1978-80; Indiana State Univ, 1981-84; Univ of Mississippi, 1987-88; Limestone Coll, 1988-90; Wood Coll, 1991-92. *Memberships:* MLA; NCTE; AAUP; AAUW; ACLU. *Hobbies:* Reading; House Plants; Cats; Needlework. *Address:* PO Box 231, Mathiston, MS 39752, USA.

BURESOVA Dagmar, b. 19 Oct 1929, Prague. Pres of the Czech Nat Council. m. Radim Bures, 31 July 1950, 2 d. *Education:* Faculty of Law, Charles Univ, Prague, 1948-52. *Appointments:* Lawyer, Solicitor, 1956-; Minister of Justice, Czech Republic, 1989-90. *Publications:* Prof Essays, Bulletin of Czech Lawyers. *Memberships:* Mayor of Cesky Junak; Sokol, Masaryk Democratic Movement; Club of Rome. *Hobbies:* Books; Nature; Skiing; Sports; Scouting. *Address:* Na Orechovce 59, 160 00 Praha 6, Czechoslovakia. 1.

BURGESS John Herbert, b. 24 May 1933, Montreal. Physician. Prof of Medicine. m. Andrea Clouston Rutherford, 30 May 1958, 1 s, 3 d. *Education:* B Sc, McGill, 1954; MD, McGill, 1958; FRCPC Royal Coll, 1963; FACP, 1972; FACC, 1975. *Appointments:* Asst Prof, 1966-69; Assoc Prof, 1969-75; Prof, 1975-. *Publications:* 42 Original Publications, Medical Journals; Int Abstracts in Cardiology. *Memberships:* Royal Coll Of Physicians; Sugeons of Canada; American Coll of Physicians; American Coll of Cardiology; Hon Fellow, Royal Aust Coll of Phys; Hon Fellow, Coll of Med, South Africa; Pres, Royal Coll of Phys and Sur of Cda, 1990-92; Canadian Cardiovascular Soc. *Honours:* Wood Gold Medal; Nuffield Travelling Fellowship; Order of Canada; RS McLaughlin Travelling

Fellowship. *Hobbies:* Photography; Cross County Skiing. *Address:* The Montreal General Hosp, 1650 Cedar Avenue, Montreal, Quebec, Canada H3G 1A4. 2, 142.

BURGHARDT Gordon M, b. 11 Oct 1941, Milwaukee, Wisconsin. Distinguished Service, Prof of Psychology, Zoology. m. Sandra Twardosz, 6 July 1983, 1 s, 2 d. *Education:* SB Univ of Chicago, 1959-63; PhD Univ of Chicago, 1963-66. *Appointments:* Instr, Biology, Univ of Chicago, 1966-67; Asst Prof to Prof, Psychology, Univ of Tenessee, 1968-; Dir Grad, Program in Ethology, 1981-91. *Publications:* 90 Journal Articles; 37 Book Chapters; The Development of Behavior; Iguanas of the World; Foundations od Comparative Ethology. *Memberships:* Amer Psy Assoc; Amer Psy Soc; Animal Behav Soc; Inter Iguana Soc; Int Sox of Chemical Ecology; Amer Soc of Ichthyologists, Herpetologists. *Honours include:* NSF Research Grants; Sci Alliance, Univ of Tennessee, Knoxville Centre of Excellence. *Hobbies:* Hiking; Gardening; Reading; Poker. *Address:* Dept of Psychology, Univ of Tennessee, Knoxville, TN 37966, USA. 54.

BURGIN Richard Arlen, b. 12 Dec 1944, Manila, AR. Vice Pres; Compliance Conslt. m. Sharon K Avey, 8 Aug 1965, 2 d. *Education:* TCU, 1968; Academy of Life Underwriting, 1978; TCJC, 1980-88; International Claims Assoc, 1982; The American Coll, 1988. *Appointments include:* Southern Union Life Ins Co, Mngt Life Dept,1965-66; Goodwill Ind Inc, Truck Driver, 1966-68; Pioneer American Ins Co, Asst UP, 1968-79; Central Sec Life Ins, Vice Pres, 1980-; Champions Life Ins Co, Vice Pres, 1989-; Western Reinsurance Co, 1990-; Pres, Owner, Arlem Academy Inc, 1985-. *Publications:* Business related Manuals. *Memberships include:* Southwest Ins Assoc; Imperial Boys Club; Texas Home Office Life Inderwriters Assoc; Inst of Home Office Underwriters; North Texas FLMI Soc; Dallas Claims Assoc; CLU & ChFC Life and Health Compliance Assoc. *Honours:* Commissioned a Kentucky Colonel; Extroordinary Member Award, Southwest Ins Assoc; Phi Theta Kappa; Junior Achievement. *Hobbies:* Reading; Drawing; Hiking; Spanish. *Address:* 125 NE Timber Ridge Drive, Burlecon, TX 76028, USA. 7.

BURKE Ronald John, b. 22 Oct 1937, Winniped, Canada. Prof; Conslt; Lectr. Div, 1 s, 2 d. *Education:* BA, Univ of Manitaba, 1960; MA Univ of Michigon, 1962; PhD, 1966. *Appointments include:* Tchr Asst, Univ of Manitoba, 1959-60; Tchr Fellow, 1960-62; Research Asst, 1962- 66; Asst Prof, Univ of Minnesota, 1966-68; Asst Prof, York Univ, 1968-69; Assoc Prof, 1969-72; Prof, York Univ, 1972-. *Publications include:* Psychological Reports; Journal of Genetic Psychology; Journal Of Educational Research; Trainign and Developement Journal; The School Guidance Worker; Business Horizons; Journal of Health and Human Resources Admin; Problem Solving Articles. *Memberships include:* American psychological Assoc; Midwestern psychological Assoc; Western Psychological Assoc; Admin Sci Assoc of Canada; Canadian Psychological Assoc; Soc for Ind and Org Psychology; Intl Congree of Psychology. *Honours include:* Inst of Labour and Ind Relations Fellowship. *Hobbies:* Reading; Movies; Theatre; Travel. *Address:* Faculty of Administrative Studies, York Univ, 4700 Keele Street, North York, Ontario, M3J LP3, Canada. 14, 142.

BURKETT Marjorie Theresa, b. 21 Mar 1931, Jamaica, West Indies. Nurse Educator. m. Antoine Burkett, 4 April 1962, 1 d. *Education:* Cert Nursing, 1953; Cert Midwifery, 1954; Kingston Sch of Nursing, Jamaica, West Indies; Cert Nursing Studies, Univ of Edinburgh, 1963; BA Univ West Indies, Jamaica, 1975; MSN, 1977; PhD, 1990, Univ of Miami, Florida. *Appointments:* Staff Nurse, Ministry of Health, Jamaica, 1954-61; Sister Tutor, Kingston Sch of Nursing, 1963-75; Asst Prof, Indian River Comm Coll, Florida, 1977-86; Tchr Assoc, Univ of Miami, Florida, 1987; Asst Prof, Flordia Intl Unic, 1988; Adult Health Nurse Practioner, Florida International Univ, Florida, 1992. *Memberships:* Florida

Nurses Assoc; American Nurses Assoc; Nat Council on Aging; FNA District 24 President; Nat League of Nursing; Sigma Theta Tau Iner Honor Soc of Nursing; Phi Lambda Pi Scholastic Frat; New York Academy of Sci. *Honours:* Princess Alexandra Overseas Nursing Scholarship; PAHO/WHO Fellow; Pan American Health Org/WHO Fellow; Prof Nurse Traineeship Award; Phi Delta Kappa, Florida Chapter, 1992. *Hobbies:* Plays; Reading. *Address:* 4041 Greenwood Drive, Fort Pierce, FL 34948, USA.

BURNETT David Grant, b. 1 Oct 1940, Lincoln. Writer. m. Marilyn, 16 Dec 1983, 2 s, 1 d. *Education:* Birkbeck Coll and Courtauld Inst of Art, Univ of London; BA, 1965; MA, 1967; PhD, 1973. *Appointments:* Lectr, Univ of Bristol, 1967-70; Assoc Prof, Carleton Univ, Ottawa, 1970-80; Curator, Art Gallery, Ontario, 1980-84. *Publications:* Paul Klee, 1979; Contemporary Canadian Art, 1983; Harold Town, 1986; Anton Cetin, 1986; Jeremy Smith, 1989; Masterpieces from Nat Gallery of Canada, 1990. *Hobbies:* Reading; Flying. *Address:* Drabinsky Gallery, 86 Scollard Street, Toronto, Ontario, Canada M5R 1G2. 88.

BURNEY Ansar, b. 14 Aug 1956, Karachi. Advocate. m. 1981, 2 s, 1 d. *Education:* BA; LLb; Phd. *Appointments:* Lawyer, Advocate, Chairmen; Ansar Burney Welfare Trust; Prisoners Aid Soc, Pakistan; Bureau of Missing and Kidnapped Children. *Publications:* Articles, succeded in getting the release of more than 52000 illegally confirmed prisoners in 10 yrs. *Memberships:* Ansar Burney Welfare Trust; Prisoners Aid Soc; Bureau of Missing & Kidnaped Children; Prisons Reforms Comm, Government of Pakistan; Comm for Child Welfare; Ministry of Social Welfare. *Honours:* 124 Awards inc, Gold Medals; Silver Medals; Certificates; Shields and Degree in PhD, Philosophy, Sri Lanka. *Hobbies:* Human Rights; Social Work. *Address:* C 95 Block A, North Mazimabad, Karachi, Pakistan.

BURNS Maretta Jo. b. 7 Nov 1941, San Antonio, TX, USA. Retd Acc. *Education:* Bachelor Business Admin, Baylor Univ, Maretta, 1962. *Appointments include:* United States Federal Government, Dept of Defense, Pueblo Army Depot, Supervisory Acc Asst, 1962; Dept of Labor, Manpower Admin, Denver, Employment Sec Advisor, 1965; Budget Analyst, 1970; Budget and Accounting Officer, 1976; Senior Systems Acc, 1983. *Memberships:* Baylor Alumni Club; Intl Biographical Assoc; American Biographical Inst; Advisors of the American Biographical Inst. *Honours:* Number of awards and certificates of Recognition; Letters of commendation, 1978-80. *Hobbies:* Church Choir; Sundry Sch Class; Swimming; Crocheting; Knitting; Sewing. *Address:* 3784 South Quince Street, Denver, Co 80237, USA. 5, 8, 9, 138, 151, 152, 156.

BURR Brooks Milo, b. 15 Aug 1949, Toledo, Ohio, USA. Prof of Zoology. *Education:* BA Greenville Coll, 1971; MS Univ of Illinois, 1974; PhD Univ of Illinios, 1977. *Appointments:* Lab Inst, Dept of Biology, Greenville Coll, 1971-72; Research Asst, Illinois Natural History Survey, 1972-77; Asst Prof, 1977-81; Assoc Prof, 1987-; Prof of Zoology, Southern Illinois Univ, Carbondale. *Publications:* A Distributional Atlas of Kentucky Fishes; A Field Guide to Freshwater Fishes, North America North of Mexico; Sci articles. *Memberships include:* American Soc of Ichthyologists and Herpetologists. *Honours:* Paper of the Year Award from the Ohio Academy of Sci; Sigma XI Leo Kaplan Memorial Award for Outstanding Contibutions to the Biology of North American Freshwater Fishes. *Hobbies:* Scuba; Sci Writing; Travel; Photography; Pottery. *Address:* Dept of Zoology, Southern Illinios Univ, Carbondale, IL 62901, USA. 8, 14, 164, 176.

BURRIDGE Simon St Paul, b. 20 Mar 1956, London. Board Acc Dit, Advertising Agency. m. Camilla Rose Barkes, 13 Sept 1986, 1 d. *Education:* Sherborne Sch, 1969-73; Queens Coll, Oxford, 1974-77. *Appointments:*

Ayer Barker Megemann, 1979; Minden Luby & Assoc, 1979-81; Dewe Rogerson, 1981-87; J Walter Thompson, 1987. *Membership:* Turf Club. *Hobbies:* Horse Racing, Family Own Desrt Ochid, amongest others. *Address:* 52 Elbe Street, London SW6, England.

BURSTEIN Elias, b. 30 Sept 1917, New York City. Physicist; Prof of Physics Emeritus. m. Rena Ruth Benson, 19 Sept 1943, 3 d. *Education:* AB Brooklyn Coll, 1938; AM Univ of Kansas, 1941; Postgrad, MIT, 1941-43; Catholic Univ, 1946-48; D Tech, Chalmers Univ, Goteborg, 1982; D Sc, Brooklyn Coll, 1985. *Appointments:* Physicist Crystal br US Naval Res Lab, 1945- 58; Head Semiconductor br, 1958; Prof Physics, 1958-; Mary Amanda Wood Prof physics, 1982-88. *Memberships:* Solid State Scis; NRC Nat Acad Sc; Solid State Scis Com; Phys Soc; Nat Acad Scis; AAAS; Phi Beta Kappa; Sigma Xi; Comments on Condensed Matter Physics. *Honours:* Navy Civilian Meritorious Serv Award; John Price Wetherill medal Franklin Inst; Isakson Prize Am Phys Soc; Alexander Von Humboldt Sr U S Sci Award. *Hobbies:* Music; Hiking; Sailing. *Address:* Dept of Physics, Univ of PA, Philadephia, PA 19104, USA. 2.

BURTON Frances Rosemary, b. 19 June 1941, Bury St Edmunds, Suffolk. Barrister; Acadmic Lawyer. m. (1) Alexander of Weedon QC, 26 Oct 1963, Div. 2 s, 3 d. *Education:* Tortington Park, Arundel, 1953-8; Lady Margaret House, Cambridge, 1959-60; St Annes Coll, Oxford, 1960-61. *Appointments:* Called to the Bar, Middle Temple, 1970; Lincolns Inn Adeudem, 1972; Practised at the Chancery Bar, 1972-1975; Tutor, Bar & Law Soc Exam, 1975-86; Lectr Dept of Law, City of London Poly, 1998-; Course Director, BPP Final Course, CADMUS Legal Education, 1992-. *Publications:* Solicitors Finals Family Law Textbook; Bar Final General paper II; Documents, Forms & Precedents in Family Law. *Memberships:* Justice; British Section of the Intl Commission of Jurists; Soc of Conservative Lawyers; Anglo Spanish Soc. *Honours:* Harmsworth Major Entrance Exhibition. *Hobbies:* History; Archaeology; Opera. *Address:* Ground Floor, 10 Old Square, Lincolns Inn, London WC2A 3SU, England.

BURTON Margaret Ann Gideon, b. 23 Mar 1926, Washington, Pennsylvania, USA. Archivist, Exhibits Coordinator. m. Foster Moore Burton, 18 June 1949, 1 s, 2 d. *Education:* Arizona State Univ, BFA 1972; Arizona State Univ, MFA 1980; Post Grade Work, 1981-86. *Appointments:* Founding Dir, Temple Hist Museum, 1972-78; Ceramic Tchr, Special Educ Children; Dir, Stevens House, ASU Heritage Sq Proj, 1980-86; Asst to Exec Dir, public Events, 1986-89; Archivist, 1990-. *Creative Works:* Coordinator Documentary, KAET TV, An Arizona Album; Video Documentary Southwest Heritage; Weaving Exhibit Heritage Sq. *Memberships:* Adult Continuing Educ; ASU; Women Interest Now; Central Arizona Museum Assoc; Women in Higher Educ Admin Advisory Council. *Honours:* Merito Award; Citizen of the Year; Merit Award; Temple Year of the Women, Communication & Education. *Hobbies:* Politics; Cermacs; Spinning & Weaving; English Bulldogs. *Address:* Arizona State Univ, public Events, Gammage 105, Tempe, AZ 85287, USA. 9, 176.

BURTON Samuel Richard Manfred, b. 3 Jan 1960, Eschwege, Hessen, Germany. Chemist. m. Victoria Dawn Hassey, 15 Aug 1985, 1 d. *Education:* BS, Biochemistry, Univ of Arizona, 1983. *Appointments:* Plant Chemist, Exell Helium, 1983; Analytical Chemist, US Bureau of Mines, 1987-. *Publications:* Ripples, Poem, 1989; Report of Investigations, 1989. *Memberships:* Amarillo 99/4A Users Group; MS DOS Users Group; Nat Rifle Assoc; American Chemical Soc. *Honours:* Special Achievement Award; SVC Award; Suggestion Award. *Hobbies:* Computor Programming; Chess; Target Shooting; Hiking; Camping; Stamp & Coin Collecting; Sci Fiction. *Address:* 1323 Callahan, Amarillo, TX 79106, USA. 7.

BURTON-ROCHE Marlie, b. 15 Nov 1935, Rural Alberta, Canada. Visual Artist and Pol Activist. m. Leo Burton, 21 Mar 1957, div 1968, 1 s, 2 d. *Education:* Visual Arts Prog, Banff Schl of Fine Arts, 1950-53; BA (Hons), Art and Archaeology, Univ of Toronto, 1957; MA, Art, Univ of Calgary, 1973. *Appointments:* Visual Artist; Art Educator, Calgary, 1969-92; Pol Activist with El Salvador in opposition to US and Can Govt involvement in Ctrl America, since 1986 has worked in solidarity for-with ANDES 21 de junio, the nat tchrs Assn of El Salvador. *Creative works:* 1986-present a series of pol paintings and ceramic sculptures titled You Don't Want to be the Horses Hoofprints, You've Got to be the Hooves; Exhibs of Art Works: Banff Ctr, 1954; Hart House Gall, Toronto, 1956; Ctrl Gall, Toronto, 1959; Can Art Galls, Calgary, 1967; Mona Lisa Gall, Calgary, 1969; Adams Gall, Toronto, 1970; Toronto Outdoor Exhib, 1971; Nickle Art Gall, Calgary, 1975, 81, 83; Muttart Gall, Calgary, 1988; Alberta Coll of Art, 1990; Toronto Int Exhib, 1991; Montserrat Gall, Soho, NY, 1992; Chapelle de la Sorbonne, Paris, 1992; Commanderie Mus d'Unet, Bordeaux, France, 1992. *Memberships:* Alta Tchrs Assn, Pres and Fndr, Action Comm for Educ in El Salvador, 1987-92; Project Off, Change for Children, 1987-92. *Honours:* Art Scholarship, Int Order of Daughters of the Empire, 1951; Art Scholarship, Banff School of Fine Arts, 1952, 53; Travelling Art Scholarship to Europe, 1954; Art Research Award, Calgary, 1969-70. *Address:* 430 Capri Avenue, NW, Calgary, Alberta, Canada T2L OJ8.

BURWASH Paul Clifford, b. 16 Aug 1955, Gibson City, Illinois. Minister. m. Trina R Cruse, 17 May 1974, 2 d. *Education:* US Navel Reserve, 1973-76; Univ of New Mexico, 1977-83; Golden Gate Bapt Theological Seminary, 1983-85. *Appointments:* Paster of Latrinidad Spanish Mission, 1979-81; Assoc Paston, St Andrews Presbyterian Church, 1983-85; Assoc Paster, First Baptist Church, 1985-86; Paster, Grady Baptist Church, 1987-92. *Memberships:* New Mexico Emergency medical Serv. *Hobbies:* Golf; Hunting. *Address:* PO Box 64, Grady, NM 88120, USA.

BUSH George Herbert Walker, b. 12 June 1924, Milton, Massachusetts, USA. 41st Pres of USA. m. Barbara Pierce, 6 Jan 1945, 4 s 1 d. *Education:* Phillips Acad, Andover, MA; Graduated Yale Univ, 1948. *Appointments:* Navy Pilot, Lt, 1942-45; Oilfield Supply Salesman, Dresser Inds-IDECO, 1948-51; Co-Fndr, Bush Overbey Dev Corp, Midland, TX, 1951-53; Co-Fndr, Zapata Petroleum, Midland, TX, 1953-59; Co-Fndr, Zapata Offshore Co, Houston, TX, 1959-66; Exec Comm Chmn, First Int Bank of Houston, TX, 1977-78; Adjunct Prof of Bus, Rice Univ, 1977-78; US Rep, TX 7th Dist, 1967-71; US Amb to UN, 1971-73; Chief, US Liaison Off in People's Republic of China, 1974-75; Dir, Ctrl Intelligence Agcy, 1976-77; VP of US, 1981-89; Pres of US, 1989-92. *Publication:* Looking Forward w Victor Gold, 1987. *Memberships:* Delta Kappa Epsilon; Phi Beta Kappa; St Martin's Episc Ch, Houston; Bd Mbr, Episc Ch Fndn; Vestryman, St Ann's Episc Ch, Kennebunkport, ME. *Hobbies:* Fishing, Tennis, Golf, Jogging, Horseshoes, Boating.

BUSH Robin James Edwin, b. 12 Mar 1943, Hayes, Middlesex. Archivist; Historian; Lectr. m. Iris Maude Reed, 21 Sept 1968, div. 1 s, 1 d. *Education:* Exeter Coll, Oxford Univ, 1962-65; Hons BA Modern Hist, 1965; MA, 1984; Univ Coll, London Univ, 1965-66. *Appointments:* Asst Archivist, Surrey Record Office, 1965-67; Asst Archivist, Somerset Record Office, 1967-70; Asst Editor, Victoria Hist of Somerset, 1970-78; Deputy County Archivist, Somerset Record Office, 1978-. *Publications include:* Book on Taunton; Book for Exmouth; Jeboults Taunton; The Story of the County Hotel; A Portrait in Colour; Christianity in Somerset; Archaeology of Taunton. Film Scriptwriter & Narrator. The Land of Summer. *Memberships:* Oxford Union Soc; West Country Writers Assoc; Somerset Archaeological and Nat His Soc; Taunton Deane Archaeological and Research Com; Taunton Operatic Soc; Council member, Brewhouse Theatre and Arts Centre; Somerset Record

Soc; Devon and Cornwell Record Soc; Devonshire Assoc. *Honours:* Intl Pandit Nehru Prize for Poetry; Trevelyan Trust Scholarship; Stapledon Exhib; John Allen memorial Trophy. *Hobbies:* Performing Grand and Light Opera; Exploring the English Countryside; Interior Decorating. *Address:* Monksilver, 2 Kilkenny Villas, Kilkenny Avenue, Taunton, Somerset, TA2 7PJ, England. 3, 139, 156.

BUSSE Friedrich Hermann, b. 30 Sept 1936, Berlin. Prof. m. Cordula Dorothea Braun, 22 Dec 1976, 1 s, 2 d. *Education:* Diploma in Physics, 1961; Dr Rer Nat, Univ of Munich, 1962. *Appointments:* Sci Asst, Univ of Munich, 1961-65; Research Assoc, MIT, 1965-66; Ass Research Geophysicist, UCLA, 1966-67; Sci, Max Plank Inst Munich, 1967-70; Prof of Geophysics, UCLA, 1970-84; Prof of Physics, Univ of Bayreuth, 1984-. *Publications:* Nonlinear Evolution of Spatio-Temporal Structures in Dissipative Continuous Systems. *Memberships:* American Geophysical Union; American Physical Soc; Deutsche Geophysikalische Gesellschaft; American Academy of Arts and Sci. *Honours:* Guggenheim Fellowship; Richard Merton Visiting Professorship; Elected to Honorary Foreign Member American Academy of Arts and Sci. *Hobbies:* Bicycling; Hiking. *Address:* Inst of Physics, Univ of Bayreuth, Postfach, 8580 Bayreuth, Germany.

BUSZKO Jozef, b. 2 Sept 1925, Debica. Prof of Univ. m. Elzbieta Orcykowska, 1 s, 1 d. *Education:* Master of Arts, Jagellonien Univ; Docotr; Prof Asst; Assoc Prof; Pull Prof. *Appointments:* Chairman of the Chair, Contemporary History of Poland. *Publications include:* Sejmowz reforma uyboresa Yaligi; Warszava; Dzige rachu robotmiczegow Zachodmig Geligi, Krikou; Univ during world war II. *Memberships:* Assotiation d Historic Contemporaire, Geneve Strassbourg; Komitet Nauk History Oriych Polikig; Akademi Nauk, Warsava; Edit in Chief of Quaterly, Studia Historyorne; Polska Akademia Nauk; Intl Council of Museum Auschwitz Birkena. *Honours:* Krzyz Komandorski Ordera Odrodzenie; Medal Komisp Edukayi Nerodovey; Prize of the Ministry of Educ. *Hobbies:* Hiking, walking. *Address:* ul Kochanowskiego 11/11, 31-127 Krakow, Poland.

BUTLER Arthur William, b. 20 Jan 1929, London. Parliamentary Conslt. m. Evelyn Mary Luetchford, 3 May 1958, 1 d. *Education:* B Sc Econ, London Sch of Economics, 1952. *Appointments:* Graduate Trainee, Kemsley Newspapers, 1952-55; political Correspondent, News Chronicle, 1956- 60; Political Editor, Reynolds News, 1960-62; Political Corres, Daily Express, 1963-69; Political Editor, Dailey Sketch, 1969-71; Parliamentary Conslt, 1971-. *Publications:* No Feet to Drag; The First Forty Years, History of Parliamentary and Scientific Comm; Lobbying in the British Parliament; Articles in various Journals. *Memberships:* Royal Institution; Liveryman, Worshipful Company of Tobacco Pipe Makers; Nat Union of Journalists; Parliamentary and Sci Comm. *Honours:* Royal Asiatic Soc Univ Prize Essayist; Emergency Reserve Decoration; Freeman of City of London. *Hobbies:* Travel; Collecting Books; Military Prints and Militaria; Politics. *Address:* 30 Chester Way, Kennington, London, SE11 4UR, England. 1, 52.

BUTLER Rohan D'Olier, b. 21 Jan 1917, London. Historian. m. Lucy Rosemary nee Bynon. *Education:* Eton, 1930-35; Balliol Coll, Oxford, 1935-38; BA, 1938; MA, 1942. *Appointments:* Fellow of All Souls, Oxford, 1938-84; Editor of Documents on British Foreign Policy, 1945- 65; Historical Adviser to sec of state for Foreign Affairs, 1963-82. *Publications:* The Roots of National Socialism; Choiseal. *Memberships:* Fellow Emeritus of All Souls, Oxford; Royal Historical Soc. *Honours:* CMG; Laureate of Inst de France. *Address:* White Notley Hall, Nr Witham, Essex, England. 1.

BUTSON Arthur Richard Cecil, b. 24 Oct 1922, Hankow, China. Surgeon. m. Eileen De Witt, 30 June 1967, 1 s, 2 d. *Education:* Cambridge Univ, 1940-42;

BA, MA, MB, B Chir, 1945; MD, 1950; Univ Coll Hospital Medical Sch, 1942-45; FRCS, 1951; FRCSC, 1953. *Appointments:* House Surgeon, 1945-46; Med Officer Falkland Islands Dependenceies Survey, 1946-48; Lectr Univ Coll; Resident Queen Mary Vetereans Hosp, 1949-53; House Surgeon, Royal Cancer Hospital and Royal National Arthopedic Hospital, 1949-50; Surgical Registrar Univ Coll Hospital, 1950-52; Conslt General Surgeon, Hamilton, Ontario, 1953-92; Clinical Prof, 1983-91; Medical Officer, Canadian Militia, 1956-; Capt Major, Lt Col Presently Honorary Colonel, 1956-92. *Memberships:* Defence medical Assn; Asst Sec Gen Interallised Confederation Med Officers of Reserves; Ontario Med Assn. *Honours:* George Cross; Polar Medal; Officer of the Order of Military Merit Canada; Queens Honorary Surgeon; Canadian Forces Decoration and Bar. *Hobbies:* Skiing; Mountain Climbing; Raising Belted Galloway Beef Cattle. *Address:* 24 Auchmar Road, Hamilton, Ontario, Canada, L9C 1C5.

BUTT Margaret, b. 16 July 1921, Toronto, Canada. Horticultural Historian; Garden Restoration Conslt. m. Gene Willard Butt, 25 Nov 1950. *Education:* Artist, designer, Central Tech Scho, Toronto, 1937; Art, Humanities, Botany, York, 1974-76; Horticulture, 1970. *Appointments:* Reg Fashion Designer, 1941; Maggie Butt Interiors Ltd, 1958-77. *Creative Works:* Designed Gardens for macpherson House Museum; Victoria Hall, Cobourg; Doone House Herb Garden; Pioneer Cabin, Tor Historical Board; Montgomery Inn; Barnum House Museum; Blk Creek Pioneer Village; 17th Century Gardens. *Memberships:* Royal Ontario Museum; Colour Council of Canada; Arch Conservancy of Ont; Ward Two & Seven Business Assoc; Toronto Exec Assoc. Educ Comm, George Brown Coll; Southern Ontario Unit, Herb Soc of America; Toronto Heliconian Club; Royal Horticultural Soc; Brooklyn Botanical Soc; Soc for Psychical Research; American Soc for Psychical Research; Spiritual Frontiers Fellowship; Assoc for Research And Enlightenment. *Hobbies:* Old Roses; Collecting Old Varities of Plants; Gardening; Gourmet Cooking; Nature Conservation; Classical Music; Old Motion Pictures; Antique Books on Horticulture. *Address:* Lindisfarne, PO Box 70, La Have, Nova Scotia, Canada BOR 1CO.

BUTT Muhammad Zakria, b. 9 Apr 1949, Lahore. Tchr; Research. m. Rukhsana Butt, 26 Dec 1980, 2 s. *Education:* BSc, MSc, Government Coll, Lahore, 1964-70; PhD, Brunel Univ, London, 1975-78. *Appointments:* Punjab Educ Service, lectr, 1971-83; Asst Prof, 1983-84; Prof, Vice Principal, Principal, 1984-85; Prof & Dir, CASP, 1985-. *Publications:* over 60 original research papers; Text Book Physics for class IX & X; Assoc Editor, Phys, 1978-80; Editor Phys, 1980-84, 91-; Mngr Editor, 1986-; Journal of Nat Sci and Mathematics. *Memberships:* Pakistan Physical Soc; Ravian Physical Soc; Pakistan Inst of Physics; Intl Centre for Theoretical Physics. *Honours:* Academic Roll of Honour; Merit Certificate; Certificate of Honourable Mention. *Hobbies:* Gardening; Reading; Writing. *Address:* Centre for Advanced Studies in Physics, PO Box 1750, Government College, Lahore 54000, Pakistan. 50, 139.

BÜTTEMEYER Wilhelm, b. 21 May 1940, Brüsewitz, Germany. Philosophy Educator. *Education:* MA, Univ Münster, 1966; Diploma di Perfezionamento in Filosofia, 1968; PhD Univ Bochum, 1970; Habilitation, Univ Oldenburg, 1978. *Appointments:* Asst, Jnr Lectr, Univ Oldenburg, 1971- 82; Vis Prof, Univ Milan, 1982, 1986; Temp Prof, Univ Oldenburg, 1982-88; Apl Prof, Since 1988; Replacement of Full Prof, 1990-92. *Publication:* Roberto Ardigò e la psicologia moderna; Der erkenntnistheoretische Positivismus R Ardigòs; Wissenschaftstheorie für Informatiker. *Memberships:* Foreign Corresponding Member, Accademia Patavina di Scienze; Allgemeine Gesellschaft für Philosophie in Deutschland; Soc Filosofica Italiana; American Philosophical Assoc. *Address:* Staulinie 11, D 2900 Oldenburg i O, Germany. 52.

BUYUKLIISKI Dimiter Mitchy, b. 7 Sept 1943, Sofia, Bulgaria. Artist. m. Maia Bassileva, 4 Sept 1973, 1 s, 1 d. *Education:* HS for Arts, 1957-62; Art Acad, Sofia, 1964-69. *Creative Works:* One-man Exhibs: Bulgaria, Sofia, Rakovsky 125, 1978; Sewiskley, PA, USA, Int Images Ltd, 1987; Antwerp, Belgium, Vandergeeten Art Gall, 1991; Paintings: Interior, 1985 The Pushkin Mus of Fine Arts, Moscow, USSR; Theme 6, 1987, Pittsburgh, USA: Composition 1-26 Oct 1989, Sotheby's, London, Compositions 2-22 Feb 1990, Sotheby's, London. *Honours:* The Bulgarian Artists Union Award for Overall Participation, 1978; Meduza Aurea Second Prize at the Annual Competition in Rome, Awarded by the International Jury of the Academia Internacionale de l'Arte Moderna, Italy, 1980; Prize for Painting of the Municipality of Boecchout, Belgium, 1991. *Hobbies:* Reading, Hiking in Mtn, Fishing. *Address:* Bul. Vasil Levsky 87, Sofia 1000, Bulgaria.

BYRKIT Donald Raymond, b. 19 Mar 1933, Indianapolis IN. Prof of Mathematics and Statistics. m. (1) 16 Aug 1958, (2) Marnette Cook, 28 Nov 1975, 1 s, 1 d. *Education:* BS, Illinois Inst of Tech, 1955; MS, Illinois State Univ, 1958; PhD, Florida State Univ, 1968. *Appointments:* West Chicago Comm H S, 1958-63; Fort Myers, 1963-66; Univ of W Fl, Pansacola, 1967-. *Publications:* Elements of Number Theory; Elements of Statistics; Elemtary Business Statistics; Calculus for Business & Economics; Statistics Today. *Memberships:* Mathmatical Assn of America; Nat Council of Tchrs of Mathmatics; Florida Council of Tchrs of Mathmatics; Vp for College Math; Dir, Florida Assn of Mathmatics Educators; Pres, American Statistical Assn; Sch Sci and Mathmatics Assn. *Honours include:* Univ of West Florida, Distinguished Research/Creative Actvity award; Distinguished Tchg Award; Distinguished Service Award; Outstanding Inst Award, Excellence in Undergraduate Instruction. *Hobbies:* Travel; Classical Music; History; Wine. *Address:* 4995 Woodcliff Drive, Pensacola, FL 32504, USA. 7, 125, 143.

BYRNE John Edward Thomas, b. 16 Feb 1935, Kilkenny. Conslt Otolaryngologist. m. Margaret Elizabeth Ross Wilson, 23 Nov 1963, 2 d. *Education:* Kilkenny Coll; Mountjoy Scho, Dublin; Trinity Coll, Dublin; BA. MB. BCl. BAO, 1961; FRCSI, 1970; Fellow in Otology, Wayne State Univ, Detroit, 1972. *Appointments:* House Surgeon & Physician, Dr Steevens Hosp, 1961-62; House Surgeon, Nat Childrens Hosp, Dublin, 1963; House Surgeon, Royal Nat TNE Hosp, 1963; Cons in Otolaryngology, Belfast City Hosp, 1974-. *Publications:* Scott/Browns otolaryngolgy. *Memberships:* Otological Research Soc; Irish Otolaryngological Soc; Proceedings of Irish Otolaryngological Soc; Ulster Medical Soc; TCD Assoc. *Hobbies:* Maritime History; Sailing; Theatre; Gardening. *Address:* Mulroy Lodge, Ballymenoch Park, Hollywood, N Ireland. BT18 0LP.

BYROM Jack Edwards, b. 2 Mar 1929, San Antonio, TX. President, San Marcos Baptist Academy. m. Bobbie LaRue Massey, 30 Aug 1953, 1 s, 2 d. *Education:* BA, Baylor Univ, Waco, 1950; Master of Divinity, Southwestern Baptist Theology Seminary, Fort Worth, 1954; Doctorate of Divinity, Univ of Mary Hardin Baylor, Belton, 1972. *Appointments:* Pastor, First Baptist Church, Christine, 1947-50; Pastor, First Baptist Church, Maypearl, 1950-52; Pastor, Water St Baptist Church, Waxahachie, 1952- 55; Pastor, Grace Temple Baptist Church, Corpus Christi, 1955-57; Pastor, First Baptist Church, Carrizo Springs, 1957-61; First Baptist Church, San Marcos, 1961-65; Pres, San Marcos Baptist Academy, 1965-. *Publications:* Article, Educ Register, 1982; Student Handbook; Faculty Handbook. *Memberships:* Accrediting Commission/Texas Assoc of Baptist Sch; Christian Educ Coordinating Board; Baptist General Convention of Texas; San Marcos Chamber of Commerce; Texas Baptist Sch Admin Assoc; Lt Colonel, Texas State Guard; San Marcos Bicentennial Comm; Heritage Assoc, San Marcos; San Marcos United Fund. *Honours:* Outstanding Graduate Student; Beautify San Antonio Award; Outstanding Prof Man; outstanding Ex

Student. *Hobbies:* Golf; Hunting; Boating. *Address:* 2801 Ranch Road 12, San Marcos, TX 78666, USA. 7, 125.

C

CABARET Bernard, b. 7 June 1938, Montargis, Loiret. Vice Chairman and Chief Exec. m. Marie Madeleine Andre, 19 Dec 1964, 4 s. *Education:* Polytechnique Sch, 1958; Grad, Nat Univ of Petroleum, Motors, 1963; Engr , Mines Corps, 1964. *Appointments:* Engr, Ministry of Ind, Marseille, 1964-67; Delegate, Perrotorial planification, 1967-70; Tech Advisor, Cabinet of Andre Bettancourt, 1971-72; Tech Advisor, Cabinet of Robert Galley, 1972- 73; Tech Advisor, Defence Ministers Cabinet of Robert Galley, 1973-77; Dept of Military Products Equip, Renault Veh, 1977-79; Deputy Gen Mngr, Societe Lyonnaise des Eaux, 1980-82; Exec Vice Pres, Lyonnaise des Eaux, 1982-91; Chairman of Eau et Force, 1988-91; Admin of Degremont, 1984-; Vice Chairman, Chief Exec of Dumez, 1992-; Chairman, Mngr Dir of Dumez France, 1991-. *Honours:* Chevalia de l'orde National du Meute. *Hobbies:* Skiing; Sailing. *Address:* 55 Bd Glatigny, 78000, Versailles, France.

CACERES German Gustavo, b. 9 July 1954, San Salvador. Composer; Conductor; Prinicpal Conductor of El Salvador Symphony Orchestra. Div, 1 d. *Education:* Diploma, Juilliard Sch, New York, 1977; Post Grad Diploma, Juilliard Sch, 1978; Doc of Musical Arts, Univ of Cincinnati, ohio, 1989. *Appointments:* Principal Conductor, El Salvador Chamber Orch, 1979-82; Musical Adv, ministry of Culture, San Salvador, 1983-84; Principal Conductor, El Salvador Symphony Orch, 1985-. *Creative Works include:* Yulcuicat; STring Quartet no.1 & 2; Three Song for Soprano and String Quartet; Concerto for Viola and nine Instruments; Sonata for Viola and Piano; Symphony for large Orchestra;Sonata for Organ; Concerto for Violin and Orchestra; Trio for Violin, Cello and Piano; Partitas for Flute, Oboe, Clarinet, Cembalo, Violin and Cello. *Honours:* Guggenhiem Found Fellow; Fulbright Found Fellow; Meet the Composer inc Yrantee; Nat Prize of Culture; Intl Prize Gertued Ramdohr Found Hamburg; Rockfeller Found Fellow. *Hobbies:* Literature; Painting. *Address:* Apartado Postal 2979, Correo Central, San Salvador, El Salvador. 72.

CAI Hanwen, b. 19 Feb 1936, Hubei, China. Prof. m. Wu Laingging, 7 Aug 1965, 2 s, 1 d. *Education:* Beijing Inst of Tech, 1959. *Appointments:* Asst inst, Research Inst, Beijing Inst Tech, 1959-63; Inst, Mech & Engr Dept BIT, 1963-83; Assoc Prof, BIT, 1983-90; Prof, BIT, 1990-. *Publications:* Theory of Engr Design; Sci Papers, A Method for Calculating the Kill; Probability of Anti Aircraft Weapon with Touch Initiation; Design Method for Ballistic Match of Projectiles; Investigation on Fragments & Shock Wave Effect. *Membership:* China Ordnance Soc. *Honours:* Nat Significant Sci & Tech Achievement Award; Sci & Tech AA; Inventive patents, Patent Office of China. *Hobbies:* Chinese Chess; Music. *Address:* 7 Baishiqiao Road, Haidian District, Beijing 100081, China.

CAI Jingfeng, b. 22 Aug 1927, Fujian, China. Sci Researcher. m. Xie Haizhu, 1 Oct 1949, 3 s, 1 d. *Education:* Hsiang Yale Medical Coll, Changsha China, 1946-53; Research Class of Traditional Chinese Medicine, Peking China, 1956-58. *Appointments:* Res Physician, Central People's Hosp, Peking, 1954-55; Asst Researcher of Medical History, Academy of Trad Chinese Medicine, Beijing, 1958-80; Assoc Researcher, 1980-85; Research Fellow, 1985-; Prof Assoc, ICC, East West Centre, USA, 1985. *Publications:* World Records in Traditional Chinese Medicine; Tibetan Medical Thangka of the Four Medical Tantras; Chinese Medical Encyclopaedia, Fasciculus of Medical History; Dictionary of Chinese Medical Biography. *Memberships include:* Soc of History of Medicine, Chinese Medical Assoc; Medical History of Minority, Chinese Medical Assoc; Soc Sci & Med; Journal of Trad Chinese Medicine (English Edition); Medicine's Geographic Heritage. *Honours:* Best publication; Progress in Sci and Tech, Tibet, China; Best Sci Writer. *Hobbies:* Classical Music; Sci Writing.

Address: China Inst for the History of Medicine & Medical Literature, China Academy of Traditional Chinese Medicine, Beijing, 100700, China.

CAI Lianzhen, b. 1 Aug 1929, Wuxian, Jiangsu, China. Prof Research Lab for Archaeology. m. Qiu Shihua, 15 Feb 1956, 1 d. *Education:* Suzhou Middle Sch, 1945-48; Dept of Medicine, 1950-51; Physics, Zhejiang Univ, 1951-52; Dept of Physics, Fudan Univ, 1951-55. *Appointments:* Inst of Physics, CAS, 1955-59; Inst of Archaeology, 1959-; Radiocarbon Dating, 1959-. *Creative Works:* Setting up First Chinese C-14 Dating Lab; Chinese Prehistory Chronological Series, Applications of C-13 measurements in Chinese Archaeology; C-14 Dating in Chinese Archaeology. *Memberships:* C-14 Dating Soc, Chinese Quaternary Research Assoc; Chinese Soc of Archaeometry; Chinese Archaeology Soc. *Honours:* C-14 Dating Award, Chinese Academy of Soc Sci; Chinese Surcrose Charcoal Standard, GBS A650001 87. *Address:* Research Lab for Archaeology, The Institute of Archaeology, CASS, 27 Wangfujing Dajie, Beijing, 100710, China.

CAI Renkui, b. 29 Oct 1933, Zhejiang, China. Co Dir. m. Tao Shuri, 1 May 1959, 2 s. *Education:* Shanghai Fisheries Univ, 1953-57. *Appointments:* Dept Hd, Changjiang Fisheries Inst, 1957-78; Dept Hd, Dpty Hd, Dir of Freshwater Fisheries Rsch Ctr and Asian-Pacific Regl Rsch & Trng Ctr for Integrated Fish Farming. *Publications:* 13 books on Fisheries; Freshwater Fishculture Handbook; History of Chinese Freshwater Fishculture Technology; Rice Field Fishculture; Freshwater Fish Farming; Answers to Questions on Freshwater Fisheries Technology; Practical New Technology of Pond Fish Farming. *Memberships:* China Fisheries Soc; Rsch Assn for Chinese Fisheries Hist; Asian Fishery Soc; Chmn Bd of Trustees, China Freshwater Aquarium Dev Ltd; Ed-in-Chief, Scientific Fish Farming; VP Jiangsu Provincial Fisheries Soc; Ed, Freshwater Fisheries Studies. *Honours:* Second Prize for Lake Fisheries Resources Survey from Ministry of Agriculture, 1983; Second Prize for Fisheries Economics from Ministry of Agriculture, 1985; First Prize for Lake Fisheries Enhancement from Chinese Academy of Fisheries Sciences, 1987; Second Prize of Best Works for Answers to Questions on Freshwater Fisheries Technology; First Prize for Editing Journals Freshwater Fisheries Studies and Scientific Fish Farming, 1992. *Hobby:* Writing. *Address:* Freshwater Fisheries Research Center, Wuxi City, Jiangsu Province, China.

CAI Yun, b. 6 June 1942, Beijing. m. Sun YanFen, 4 Apr 1968, 2 d. *Education:* Beijing Sch of Handicrafts, Fine Arts, 1961. *Appointments:* Research Centre of the Decorative Designs, 1961; Beijing Serv Dept, Handicrafts, Fine arts, 1962; Beijing Enbroidery Factory, 1964; Beijing Jewelry Factory, 1983. *Publications:* Calender Pictorials, Chang e Fly to The Moon; The Dragon Girl Tending Sheep; Dream of the Red Chamber; Biblograhy of Modern Chinese Painters; Participated, Exhibition of Contemporary Chinese Painters. *Members:* Beijing Brach , China assoc of Artist; Inst of Chinese Paiting Research; Beijing Fine Brushwork, Deep Colour Painting Soc. *Honours:* Beijing Art Exhibition, Second Award, Third Award. *Hobbies:* Football; Classical Music; Folk Music. *Address:* 26 Shang San Tiao, ChunShu, XuanWu District, Beijing 100052, China.

CAI Zhen Xing, b. 7 Nov 1940, Gongxian County. General Mangr; Economist. m. Fan Sucai, 10 May 1961, 3 s, 1 d. *Education:* Gongxian Sec Sch, Jnr 1953-56; Snr 1956057. *Appointments:* Dir, Gongxian Comm Shop, 1957-60; Acct, Tech, Gongxian, 1961-69; Dir, Nanhedu Portray Commune of Gongxian, 1969-83; Gen Mangr, Gongxian Huaxian Information Serv Co, 1984-89. *Publications:* Huaxia Travels. *Memberships:* Equip Manage Soc of Zhengzhou City; Sci and Tech Information Inst of Zhengxhou City; Public Relationship Assoc. *Honours:* Excellent Enterpreneur of Zhengzhou City. *Hobbies:* Table Tennis; Fishing; Cooking; Touring;

Peking Opera; Chinese Classics. *Address:* 52 Jianshe St, Gongxian County, Heran 451200, China.

CAINE Francesca Mary, b. 12 Dec 1956, Luton. m. Philip Michael Caine, 11 June 1988, 1 d. *Education:* Churchill Coll, Cambridge, BA Engr, 1975-78; MA, 1982. *Appointments:* Rolls Royce Ltd, 1975-78; BBC, 1978-91; Toshiba Coroporation, 1991-. *Membership:* MBIM. *Hobbies:* Singing; Music; House Renovation. *Address:* Toshiba Europe Office, Audrey House, Ely Place, London EC1, England.

CAINE Michael, b. 14 Mar 1933, Actor. m. Shakira Khatoon Baksh, 8 Jan 1973, 2 d. *Education:* Army Serv, Berlin and Korea, 1951-53; Repertory Theatre, Horsham, Lowestoft, 1953-55; Theatre Workshop, London, 1955. *Appointments:* Over 100 TV plays, 1957-63; Films incl: A Hill in Korea, 1956; How To Murder a Rich Uncle, 1958; Alfie, 1966; Gambit, 1966; Funeral in Berlin, 1966; Billion Dollar Brain, 1967; Play Dirty, 1968; The Italian Job, 1969; Battle of Britain, 1969; Too Late the Hero, 1969; Get Carter, 1971; Kidnapped, 1971; Pulp, 1972; Sleuth, 1973; The Black Windmill, 1974; The Man Who Would Be King, 1975; The Eagle Has Landed, 1976; The Silver Bears, 1977; Ashanti, 1978; The Swarm, 1979; The Island, 1979; Dressed to Kill, 1980; Deathtrap, 1981; Educating Rita, 1982; The Jigsaw Man, 1982-83; Blame It On Rio, 1983; Water, 1984; Mona Lisa, 1985; The Fourth Protocol, 1986; Surrender, 1986; Sherlock and Me, 1987; Jack The Ripper (for Thames TV), 1988. *Publications:* Not Many People Know That, 1985; Not Many People Know This Either, 1986. *Honours:* Num honours and awards: Best Film Actor Award, BAFTA, 1983; Best Supporting Actor, Oscar, 1986. *Hobbies:* Reading, Tennis. *Address:* Dennis Selinger, 388-396 Oxford Street, London W 1, England.

CAIRNS Hugh Alan Craig, b. 2 Mar 1930, Galt, Ontario, Canada. Prof. m. Patricia Ruth Grady, 17 July 1958, 3 s. *Education:* Univ of Toronto, BA, 1953; MA, 1957; Oxford Univ, D Phil, 1963. *Appointments:* Instr to Prof, Dept of Political Sci, Univ of British Columbia, 1960-; Visiting Prof, Edinburgh, 1977-78; Harvard, 1982-83. *Publications:* Prelude to Imperialism; Constitution, Government and Soc in Canada; Disruptions, Constitutional Struggles from the Charter to Meech Lake. *Membership:* Canadian Political Sci Assoc. *Honours:* Queens Silver Jubilee Medal; Royal Soc of Canada; Canada Council 25th Aniv Molson Prize; Canada Council Killam Scholarship. *Hobbies:* Golf; Swimming; Theatre; Travel. *Address:* 4424 West 2nd Ave, Vancouver, BC, Canada V6R 1K5. 34, 142.

CALAM Derek Harold, b. 11 May 1936, London. Head, Chemistry Division. m. Claudia Summers, 15 Sept 1965, 2 s, 1 d. *Education:* Christs Hosp, 1946-54; Wadham Coll, Oxford Univ, BA, 1960; D Phil, 1962; MA, 1963. *Appointments:* Nat Inst for Medicine Research, 1962-66, 1969-72; Rothamsted Experimental Station, 1966-69; Nat Inst for Biological Standards and Control, 1972-. *Publications:* Numerous Sci Journals. *Memberships:* British Pharmacopoeia Comm; European Pharmacopoeia Comm; Expert Advisor World Health Organ. *Honours:* Chartered Chemist Fellow, Royal Soc of Chemistry; Hon Mbr, Roy Pharm Soc of GB. *Hobbies:* Walking; Travel. *Address:* Nat Inst for Biological Standards and Control, Blanche Lane, South Mimms, Potters Bar, Herts, EN6 3QG, England.

CALDER Andrew Alexander, b. 17 Jan 1945, Aberdeen. Prof and Head of Dept, Obstetrics and Gynaecology, Univ of Edinburgh. m. Valerie Anne Dugard, 1 s, 2 d. *Education:* Univ Glasgow, MBChB, 1968; MD 1978; Research Fellowship Univ Oxford, 1972-75. *Appointments:* Lectr, Snr Lectr, Obstetrics, Gynaecology, Univ of Glasgow, 1975-86; Prof, Head of Dept, Obs and Gynae, Univ of Edinburgh, 1986-. *Publications:* Research Publications in Medical and Sci Journals; Chapters in Postgraduate Textbooks. *Memberships:* Royal Coll of Obstetricians,

Gynaecologists; Royal Coll of Physicians; Royal Soc of Medicine; Munro Kerr Soc for the Study of Reproductive Biology. *Honours:* William Blair Bell Memorial Lectr for RCOG; Bernard Barron Travelling Fellow RCOG; World Health Organisation Travelling Fellow to South America; British Exchange Prof Univ of California in Los Angeles. *Hobbies:* Rugby Union Football; Golf; Curling; Piano and Organ Music. *Address:* Dept of Obstetrics and Gynaeocology, Univ of Edinburgh, Centre for Reproductive Biology, 37 Chalmers Street, Edinburgh, EH3 9EW, Scotland. 184.

CALDERINI Renata, b. 30 Nov 1955, Udine, Italy. Ballet Dancer. *Education:* Teatro Allo Scala Ballet Sch, 1966-71; Moscow Ballet Sch, 1971-73; Teatro Alla Scala Baller Sch, 1974. *Appointments:* Teatro Alla Scala, 197681; London Festical Ballet, 1981-86; Bayerische Staatsoper, Munich 1986-89; English National Ballet, 1990-. *Honours:* Premio Bordighera, Italy; Premio Positano, Italy; Premio Quadrivio, Italy. *Hobbies:* Pen Nibs Collecting; Hyacinths Vases. *Address:* c/o E N B. Marova House, 39 Jay Mews, London, SW7, England.

CALDERON Hernan, b. 20 Sept 1925, La Paz, Bolivia. Airline Exec. m. Aida Osorio, 27 Feb 1949, 1 s, 2 d. *Education:* Bach in Economics, San Andres Univ, 1947; Postgrad, Fin, Auditing, 1948-51. *Appointments:* Admin Asst, Pan Am, Grace Airways, La Paz, 1945-47; Acct Braniff Airways, La Paz, 1951-55; Sr Acct, 1956-60; Mgr Acctg, 1961-67; Fin Mgr, 1968-75; Controll, 1976-82; Country Contr, Eastern Air Lines, 1983-87; Board Dir, Lloyd Aereo Boliviano, 1988-; Area VP Aviation Svs & Mktg Systems Inc, Miami, 1987-; Bus Rep Fin Times, London, 1976-78; Coor Econ, Survey, 1977; Bus Rep In Herald Tribune, London 1979-81. *Membership:* Skal Club World Assn; Tennis Club L Paz. *Honours:* Civil Aviation Medal, Bolivian Ministry Aereonautics. *Hobbies:* Tennis; Swimming. *Address:* PO Box 7973, La Paz, Bolivia. 52.

CALDWELL Thomas Howell Jr, b. 5 Feb 1934, Wichita Falls, Tx, USA. Accountant. m. Bernell Irons, April 1968, Div. 1 s. Dec. *Education:* BA in Religion, Baylor Univ, 1956; Postgrad, Tex Christian Univ, 1958-63; North Tex State Univ, 1973-75. *Appointments:* Cert Internal Auditor, Tech Writer Gen Dynamics, Ft Worth, 1956-60; Asst Dir Pers, Harris Hosp, Ft Worth, 1960-62; Fiduciary Tax Sect, 1st Nat Bank, Ft Worth, 1962-64; Jnr Acctl Various CPA's, Dallas, 1964-65; Auditor Def Contract Audit Agy, Dallas, 1965-74; Tax Appraiser, Mcpl Acct, City of McKinney, 1974-75; Systems Acct, USDA, 1975-83; Auditor, US Army CE, Dallas, 1983-86; Acct Rep IRS, Dallas, 1986-87; Systems Acct, Defence Finance And, Acct Serv, Dallas, 1987-. *Memberships:* Bd Dir, Desc Vets, Mexican War; Baylor Univ, Ex Students Assn; Masons, Shriners Republican. *Hobbies:* Flying; Dogs; Watching Football; Church. *Address:* 10822 Pagewood, Dallas, TX 75230-4468, USA. 7, 132, 214.

CALHOUN Mary Diane Mason, b. 2 Sept 1954, Shreveport, LA. TV/Radio Prod, Writer, Talent. m. Richard, 25 Aug 1987, 4 d. *Education:* Graduate, Captain Shreve High, 1972; Louisiana State Univ, 1972-74; Ayers Business Sch, 1974. *Appointments:* Copywriter, KSLA TV, Shreveport, 1976-78; Disc Jockey, KROK FM, Shreveport, 1978-79; Secy, Aztec Pipe, Lafayette, 1979-80; ADM Asst to Snr VP, Vidal Sassoon, Los Angeles, 1980-81; Actres, Film & Stage, Los Angeles, 1981-84; Int Deisgn, Self Employed, 1984- 86; Producer, Writer, talent, TV & Radio, 1986-. *Publications:* Uston; Margo. *Memberships:* Nat Assoc for Female Exec; Intl platform Assoc; American Fed of TV & Radio Artists. *Honours:* 2 Bronze Awards for TV Commercials; Merit for Acting; Best Supportive Actress for Stage; Silver Award for TV Commericals. *Hobbies:* Golf; Writing; Song Writing; Piano; Decorating; Making Videos. *Address:* 1910 Hidden Creek Drive, Kingwood, TX 77339, USA. 5, 7.

CALLIGARIS Sergio, b. 22 Jan 1941, Rosario, Argentina. Prof of Piano, State Conservatory Alfredo

Casella, L'Aquita; Concert Pianist; Composer. *Education:* Prof Piano, Theory, Solfege Degree, 1955; Prof Harmony, Composition Degree, Amigos del Arte, 1957; Artists Diploma Piano, Cleveland Inst of Music, 1966. *Appointments:* Piano Faculty, Cleveland Inst of Music, 1966-67; Piano Faculty California State Univ, Los Angeles, 1968-69; Piano Faculty, San Peitro a Majella, Naples, 1974-77; Alfredo Casella, L'Aquita, 1977-79; Luisa D Annmunzio, Pescara, 1979-80; Alfredo Casella, L'Aquita, 1980-. *Creative Works include:* Concertizing South and North America; Europe; Africa; Recording Artist, Italian EMI; Composer, Concerto for strings; Concerto for piano and Orchestra Danze Sinfoniche (Symphonic Dances); Second Suite of Symphonic Dances; Concerto for twelve Violoncelli; Sonata for Cello, Piano; Organ Music; Vocal Settings; Choral Works; Editor: Carisoh SpA of Milan, a Warner Bros. Chappell Co. *Memberships:* The American Academy of the Arts in Europe; State Univ of Los Angeles; Piano Tchrs Assoc, Rome. *Honours:* Best Recordings of the Season. *Hobby:* Reading. *Address:* Viale Libia 76, 00199, Roma, Italy.

CALVIN Wyn, b. 28 Aug 1927, Narberth, Pembrokeshire. Theatre; Radio; TV. m. 13 Sept 1975. *Education:* Canton High Sch, Cardiff. *Appointments:* ENSA Revues, 1945; Weekly Repertory Seasons, 1945-52; Pantomine, Summer Shows, Revues and Variety Prod, 1955-; Radio & TV Series, BBC, 1974-. *Memberships:* Grand Order of Water Rats; MBE. *Honours:* Order of the British Empire; Honorary Freeman, City of Macon, Georgia; King, Grand Order of Water Rats, 1991; Freeman, City of London, 1992. *Hobbies:* Travel; Dinner Conversations. *Address:* 121 Cathedral Road, Cardiff, CF1 9PH, Wales.

CAMACHO Décio de Oliveira Lopes, b. 2 Oct 1916, Funchal. Univ Tchr. m. Olga Cerrilho Lopes Camacho, 21 June 1958, 3 s, 2 d. *Education:* Liberture, Soc Sci, by Technic Univ Lisbon, 1970; Master, Doc, Social and Cultural Anthropology in Third Age Univ of Lisbon, 1982. *Appointments:* Master & Dir, Research Training Unit, Social and Cultural Antropology. *Publications:* Pedagogie Works; Thesis, Academic Works; Collaboration upon Soc Sci in Papers and Mag. *Memberships include:* SNESUP; Soc of Portuguese Language; Assoc Luso-Spanish of Pedagogiy. *Honours:* Degree Doctor Honoris Causa in Anthropology; Internacia Ordeno de Minerva. *Hobbies:* Tec-Tac; Music and dance. *Address:* Rua Silvae Albuquerque, 9, 3 Dt, 1700 Lisboa, Portugal.

CAMBRIDGE Robert Adam, b. 26 Nov 1958, Minneapolis. Physician. *Education:* BA, Univ of Minnesota, 1983; MD, Univ of Minnesota, 1987; Graduate, Wright State Univ Sch of Business, Ohio, 1990. *Appointments:* Resident Pychiatry, Wright State Univ, 1987-91. *Memberships:* American Medical Assoc; American Psychiatric Assoc; Ohio Psychiatric Assoc; Plyton Psychiatric Soc; American Soc of Addiction Medicine; Golden Key Nat Honor Soc; Wests Whos Who. *Honours include:* Golden Key Nat Honor Soc; Wests Whos Who. *Hobbies:* Scuba Diving; Skiing; Squash; Portuguese Literature; Computors; Salt Water Fish; Ballroom Dancing; Biking; Travel. *Address:* 968A Great Vien Circle, Centerville, OH 45459, USA. 9.

CAMERON Donald James Gray, b. 4 July 1927, Melbourne. Artist; Art Tchr. m. Audrey Olga Smith, 10 Jan 1958, 2 s, 1 d. *Education:* Indust Design, Melbourne Tech, 1944-45; Slade Sch of Art, London, 1966; Diploma of Art, Caulfield Tech, 1969. *Appointments:* Artist/ Engraver, Commonwealth Bank Note, Stamp Printing, Melbourne, 1946-59; Art Tchr, Caulfield Tech Coll, Melbourne, 1960-69. *Publications:* Art is Adventure; Black White and Grey With Colour Added; Paints Portraits, Landscapes, Oil and Water Colour. *Memberships:* People Against Drink Driving; Victorian Artists' Soc; Old Water Colour Soc. *Honours:* French Government Tech Scholarship; Numeous Prizes, Water Colour & Oil Paintings. *Hobbies:* Music; Amatuer

Theatricals; Golf. *Address:* 15 Grandview TCE, N Kew 3101, Victoria, Australia. 139.

CAMERON Eric, b. 18 Apr 1935, Leicester, England. Prof/Head Dept of Art; Artist. m. Margaret Harrold, 23 June 1963, 2 s, 1 d. *Education:* Art, Kings Coll, Newcastle On Tyne, 1953-57; Art History, Courtauld Inst, London, 1957-59; Academic Diploma, History of Art, 1959. *Appointments:* Taught Art History, Leeds Univ, 1959-69; Univ of Guelph, Canada. 1969-76; Nova Scota Coll, 1976-87; Univ of Calgary, 1987-. *Creative Works:* Process Paitings; Videotapes; Thick Paintings; publications, Bent Axis Aproach; Divine Comedy. *Memberships:* Univ Art Assoc of Canada; Intl Assoc of Art Critics. *Honours:* Fellow of the Royal Soc of Arts. *Address:* 327 Hawkwood Blvd, N W Calgary, Alberta, Canada T3Q 3G7.

CAMERON Ian Robert, b. 26 July 1931, Ross Shire, Scotland. Prof of Physics. m. Heather Beatrice Colville, 21 Mar 1957, 1 d. *Education:* BSc, Edinburgh, 1953; PhD, Edinburgh, 1958. *Appointments:* Snr Sci, UK Atomic Energy Auth, 1958-63; Principal Sci, UK AEA, 1963-67; Assoc Prof, Univ of New Bruns, 1967-73; Prof, UNB, 1973-; Dean of Faculty, UNB, 1979-84. *Publications:* Nuclear Fission Reactors; From Quark to Quasar, An Exploration of the Physical Universe. *Memberships:* New York Academy of Sci. *Hobbies:* Music; Poetry; Climbing. *Address:* 128 Dunedin Road, Saint John, New Brunswick, Canada E2H 1P7. 142.

CAMP James John, b. 14 Dec 1943, Canada. Lawyer. m. B Anne Ross, 2 July 1966, 1 s, 1 d. *Education:* BA, Univ of Victoria, 1965; LLB, Univ Of BC, 1969. *Appointment:* Ladner Downs, Partner. *Memberships:* Cdn Bar Assn, Treas; Vice Pres; Pres. *Honours:* Sir Isaac Pitblado Law Lectr. *Hobbies:* Skiing; Golf; Gardening. *Address:* 2876 W King Edward Avenue, Vancouver, BC, Canada. 142.

CAMPBELL John Duncan, b. 4 July 1940, Melbourne. Chief Esec. m. Mary Veronica Comerford, Dec. 18 Jan 1964, 1 s, 2 d. *Education:* MB BS, Univ of Adelaide, 1965; DTM & H, Univ of Sydney, 1970; Master of Health Admin, Univ of NSW, 1975; Bach of Laws, Univ NSW, 1977; Master of Laws, Univ Sydney, 1985. *Appointments:* RMO Royal Adel Hosp, 1964; RMO IRAR Sol Vict, 1965; 7 Camp Hosp, Kapooka, 1966; SMO HQ PNG Cond, 1967-70; Ass Dir Gen Med Services AHQ, 1971-73; Com opp 2 Mil Hosp, 1975; Dir of Mcd Admin, Prince Henry, Prince of Wales, 1976,79; Dir Dofile Health, 1980; Dir of Medicine, 1981-82; Reg Dir of Health, Northern, 1983-84; Reg Dir, Southern, 1985-76; Admin St George Area Health, 1988-; Chief Esec, 1988-; Monograph, NSW, 1985. *Memberships:* Barister of Law, Supreme Court NSW; Roual Aushalia Coll of Med Admin; Admin Appeal Tribonal; Medical Swiss Comm of Enq; Vis Prof of Univ of Tech; Treas, Post Grad, Medical Council. *Honours:* Commonwealth Scholarship. *Hobbies:* Golf; Reading; Collecting; Sport. *Address:* 12 Morella Road, Clifton Gardens, NSW 2088, Australia. 23, 52.

CAMPBELL Lucy B, b. 26 Jan 1940, Philadelphia, PA. Art Dealer. 2 s, 2 d. *Education:* New York, Calidornia; Boston Mass Coll. *Appointments:* owner, Antique Print & Painting Gellery, 1984-. *Hobbies:* Collecting Art and Antiques; Reading; Travel. *Address:* 123 Kensington Church Street, London W8 7LP, England.

CAMPBELL Michael Jeffrey, b. 9 Jan 1948, Newark, NJ, USA. Music Prof. m. Mary Carol Hicks, 16 July 1988, 1 s. *Education:* Bach of Sci, Lebanon Valley Coll, 1969; Master of Arts, Trenton State Coll, 1973; Doc of Arts, Ball State Univ, 1984. *Appointments:* Prof Saxophonist; Band Dir, Hanover Park HS, Hanover, 1975-84; Music Prof, Armstrong State Coll, Savannah, 1984. *Memberships:* Clan Campbell Soc; Coll Band Dir Nat Assoc; Nat Band Assoc; Coll Music Soc; Ph Mu Alpha SinFonia. *Honours:* ASBDA, Stanbury Award for North

East; NBA Citation of Execellence; Phi Delta Kappa; Pi Kappa, Lambda; Doctoral Fellowship, Ball State Univ. *Hobbies:* Golf; Snow Skiing; Ice Hockey. *Address:* 124 E 46th Street, Savannah, GA 31405, USA. 7.

CAMPBELL Robin Bruce, b. 4 July 1944, Calgary, Alberta. Hospital Admin. m. Vicky, 14 June 1969, 2 d. *Education:* BPHE, Univ of Toronto, 1968; MS, Indiana Univ, 1972; HSM Diploma, Canadian Hosp Assoc, 1991. *Appointments:* Asst Prof, Sch of Physical & Health Educ, Univ of Toronto, 1976; Programme Coordinator, Cardiac Dept, Toronto Rehabilitation Centre, 1981-. *Memberships:* Marina Lodge; R Tait McKenzie soc; Canadian Assoc of Cardiac Rehabilitation; Canadian Coll of Health Serv Exec; Cheshire Homes Foundation. *Honours:* General Mangr Canadian Olympic Swimming Team; World Aquatic Games. *Hobbies:* Jogging; Skiing; Swimming. *Address:* 347 Rumsey Road, Toronto, Ontario, Canada, M4G 1R7. 142.

CAMPBELL Roger Keith, b. 1 Jan 1951, Johnson City, Tenn. Educator. m. Peggy Ann Holtsclaw, 18 April 1973, 2 s. *Education:* East Tennesse State Univ, BS Degree, 1975; Tennessee Military Academy, Commissioned Officer, 1983. *Education:* Carter County Sch Systems, 1975-; Captain TN Army Nat Guard, Maintenance Control Officer, 176 MT BN; Commander 776th Maintenance Co. *Publications:* Currently working on Campbell Family History. *Membership:* Hampton Lodge 750 F&AM. *Hobbies:* Genealogy; Photography; History Buff; Coach Youth League Basketball; Play Guitar; Being a Father. *Address:* RFD 7, Box 1690, Elizabethon, TN 37643, USA. 2.

CAMPBELL Ross, b. 4 Nov 1918, Toronto, Canada. Business Conslt. m. Penelope Grantham-Hill, 6 June 1945, 2 s. *Education:* BA, Law Faculty, Univ of Toronto Trinity Coll, 1940. *Appointments:* Served RCN, 1940-45; Dept of Ext Affairs, Canda, 1945; Third Sec. Oslo, 1946-47; Second Sec, Copenhagen, 1947-50; European Div, Ottawa, 1950-52; First Sec, Ankara, 1952-56; Head of Middle East Div, Ottawa, 1957-59; Special Asst to Sec of State, Ext Aff., 1959-62; Asst Under Sec of State, Ext Aff., 1962-64; Advisor Canadian Delegations to UN Gen Assemblies, 1958-63; North Atlantic Coun, 1959-64; Ambassador to Yugoslavia, 1964-67; Ambassador to Algeria, 1965-67; Ambassador and Perm Rep to NATO, 1967-73; Ambassador to Japan, 1973-75; Republic of Korea, 1973; Chm Atomic Energy of Canada Ltd, 1976-79; Pres Atomic Energy of Canada Intl, 1979-80; Canus Tech Serv Corp, Ottawa, 1981-83; Dir MBB Helicopter (now Eurocoptor) Canada Ltd 1984-; UXB Intl Inc. 1986-. *Memberships:* Prof Assoc of Foreign Service Officers; Naval Officers Assoc of Canada; Canadian Inst of Intl Affairs. *Honours:* Distinguished Serv Cross. *Hobby:* Gardening. *Address:* Partner, Intercon Consultants, Suite 1003, 275 Slater Street, Ottawa, Ontario, Canada K1P 5H9. 1, 2, 142.

CAMPION Edmund John, b. 28 Aug 1949, New York City. Prof of French. m. Mary Ellen Gallagher, 2 Sept 1978, 1 s, 1 d. *Education:* AB, Fordham Univ, 1971; MA, Yale Univ, 1973; PhD, Yale Univ, 1976. *Education:* Asst Prof of French, Univ of Tennessee, 1977-83; Assoc Prof of French, Univ of Tennessee, 1983-. *Publication:* Philippe Quinault's Tragedies Astrate; Bellerophon; Pierre Du Ryers Tragedy Esther. *Memberships:* Tennessee Chapter of the American Assoc of Tchr of French; American Assoc of Tchr of French. *Honours:* Lindsay Young Endowed Prof of the Humanities, Univ of Tennessee. *Hobbies:* Gardening; Swimming; Reading. *Address:* Dept of Romance Languages, Univ of Tennessee, Knoxville, TN 37996, USA.

CAMPO-TIMAL Francoise Tailhardat, b. 30 Sept 1938, Argentevil, France. Lit Transl, Playwright, Lit Dir. *Education:* Baccalaureat Classical and Lit Studies (Latin and Greek). *Appointments:* Tchr in Dakar, 1957-58; Tchr in Montevideo, 1960-63; Radio Prod at France Culture, 1967-72. *Memberships:* Membre du Comite de Parrainage de la Maison des Ecrivains a Paris; Membre

de l'association Atlas. *Honours:* Grand Prix National de la Traduction pour l'ensemble de l'oeuvre, 1991; Chevalier de l'Orche du Merite, 1992. *Hobbies:* Gardening, Travelling, Mtn Hiking. *Address:* Rue Mountplaisir, 31000 Toulouse, France.

CAMPOS Luis Manual Braga da Costa, b. 28 Mar 1950, Lisbon, Portugal. Prof of Mechanics & Mathematics. m. Maria Isabel Carreira de Vila- Santa Braga, 7 Aug 1978, 1 s. *Education:* Diploma Mech Engr, Inst Sup Tecn, 1972; PhD, Cambridge Univ, 1978; ScD, Inst Sup Tecn, 1982. *Appointments:* Asst, 1974; Auxilliary Prof, 1978; Assoc Prof, 1980; Full Prof, 1985, Inst Superior Tecnico. *Contributions to:* Professional Journals; Communications to Symposia Reports. *Memberships:* Cambridge Philosophical Soc; Soc of Ind and Applied Mathematics; American Mathematical Soc; London Mathematical Soc; American Soc of Mech Engr; Intl Astronomical Union; Advisory Group for Aerospace Research and Development; Space Sci Comm; Engr Sci Conn; Nat Inst of Sci Research; LEEC V Chmn, Royal Astro Soc, Aero Rsch & Tech Adv Cttee. *Honours:* Snr Rouse Ball Scholarship, Trinity Coll, Cambridge, 1977-79; Snr Visit, Cambridge Univ, 1982-83; Alexander von Humbold Schol, Max-Planck Inst fur Aeronomie, 1991-92. *Hobbies:* Classical Music; Plastic Arts; Photography; Swimming. *Address:* Inst Superior Tecnico, 1096 Lisboa Codex, Portugal.

CANGEMI Joseph Peter, b. 26 June 1936, Syracuse, New York, USA. Prof of Psychology. m. Amelia Elena Santalo, 2 d. *Education:* BSc, Engl, SUNY, 1959; MA, Educ, Syracuse Univ, 1964; Adv Graduate Study, Western KY Univ, 1969-71; EdD, IN Univ, 1974; Dipl, American Bd of Voc Experts, 1985. *Appointments:* Cons var Univs and Cos; Instr, Pub Schls; Chmn and Lectr, SUNY, 1962-66; Supvsr of Educ and Trng and Dev, US Steel Corp, Venezuela, 1965-68; Project Dir, Universidad de Los Andes, Venezuela, 1975-77; Assoc Prof, Asst Prof, Prof of Psychology, Western KY Univ, Bowling Green, 1968-. *Publications:* Author or Co-author 8 books; Num articles published in USA and abroad in periodicals and books; more than 300 papers. *Memberships:* Fellow, American Autogenic Soc; American Assn for Counselling and Dev, Life Mbr; AACD; APA; Nat Voc Guidance Assn; Phi Delta Kappa; Pi Kappa Delta; Psi Chi; Sigma Delta Psi; Sigma Tau Delta. *Honours:* Num awards and honours for teaching. *Address:* 1409 Mt Ayr Cirle, Bowling Green, KY 42101, USA. 2, 132.

CANNON Herbert Seth, b. 3 Dec 1931, NYC, NY, USA. Investment Banker. m. Edith Marilyn Marks, 20 June 1954, 2 s. *Education:* Cheshire Academy, 1949; Washington & Jefferson Coll, BA, 1953; Fordham Law Sch, LLB, JDS, 1960. *Appointments:* Stockbroker, Hirsch & Co, 1956-61; Stockbrokwer, Wineman, Weiss & Co, 1961-62; Pres, Weis, Voisin, Cannon Inc, 1963-70; Chm Brd, Elgin Nat Ind Inc, 1967-70; Pres, Cannon, Jerold & Co, 1970-73; Chm, Citowide Capital Corp, 1983-86; Pres, Cannon Enterprises Inc, 1976-. *Membership:* US Army. *Honours:* Trustee, Washington & Jefferson Coll; Young Presidents Organization, Member; Metropolitan Presidents Assoc, Member. *Hobbies:* Tennis; Golf. *Address:* 23402 Savona Court, Boca Raton, FL 33433, USA. 2.

CANNON Thomas, b. 20 Nov 1945, Liverpool, England. Univ Prof, Dir of Manchester Bus Schl. m. 7 Aug 1979, 1 s, 1 d. *Education:* BSc (Hons) London, 1968. *Appointments:* Rschr, ASKE Rsch; Rschr, Warwick Univ; Lectr, Middlesex Polytechnic, Grand Mgr, Imperial Grp; Lectr, Durham Univ; Prof, Stirling Univ; Dir, Manchester Bus Schl. *Publications:* Basic Marketing; Enterprise; The World of Business; Small Business Development; Small Firms Research; Advertising: The Economic Implications; Advertising Research; num learned papers. *Memberships:* Companion, Brit Inst of Mgmt; Fellow, Chartered Inst of Mktng; Fellow, Inst of Phys Distbn Mgmt; FRSA. *Hobbies:* Walking, Writing, Supporting Everton Football Club. *Address:* Manchester

Business School, Booth Street West, Manchester, England.

CAO Chusheng, b. 2 June 1926, Hankou, China. Chief Engr; Hydroelectric Engr. m. Zhao Xian Ping, 3 Nov 1957, 1 s, 2 d. *Education:* BE Structure Div, Dept of Civil Engr, Chiao Tung Univ, 1944-48, Asst Tchr, Chiao Tung Univ, 1948-51. *Appointments:* Chief Engr, Tianjin Prosp &Design Inst, Tech Commit Minitry of Water of China, Prof of Tianjin Univ, 1951-92; *Achievements:* Chief Design of many famous dams and power projects, Fuzilling, Yanguoxia, Bikon, Panjiakou. *Publications:* The Dam Engineering in China; The Hydraulic Structure Branch of Chinese Encyclopadia; Papers on the Aspects of Stress; Seismic Stress; Stability Analysis of the Dam and Roch Foundation; Dev of Water Resources; Pumped Storage plates. *Memberships include:* Int Water Res Assoc; Dir of Soc of Chinese Hydraulic/Hydroelectric Engr; Vice Pres, Tianjin Hydraulic/Hydroelectric Engr; China Intl Engr Conslt Corporation; Conslt Centre of the Hydraulic Engr in China; Bohai Engr Conslt Corp; Registered Conut of Asian Develope Bank. *Honours:* China Engr Design Master; Nat Advanced Worker/ Employee; Man of the 1st Class Merits in Harnessing the Huaihe River. *Hobbies:* Reading; Writting; Photographing. *Address:* Tianjin Design & Prosp Inst, 60 Dongting Road, Tianjin, China.

CAO Keqing, b. 19 June 1939, Qingdao, China. Palcontology; Museology. m. Zhaohui Lei, 1 Feb 1969, 2 s. *Education:* Palcontology Dept of Geology, Nanjing Univ, Graduated 1964. *Appointments:* Dept of Palcontology, Shanghai Museum of Nat Hist, 1964-913 Asst, 1964-79; Lectr, 1980-86; Research Assoc Prof, 1987-91. *Publications:* Book on the Mi- deer, Elaphurus davidianus; More than 150 Compositions. *Memberships include:* Academic Comm in Shanghai Museum of Nat Hist; Chinese Assoc of Nat Sci Museums in Beijing Museum of Nat Hist; Palcontological Soc of China; Educ and Pepularization Comm, Palcontological Soc of China; Editoral Board of Academic Periodical Shanghai Geology. *Honours:* Active Element of Palcontological Soc of China; Advanced Worker of Geological Popularization of Geological Soc Of China; Sci Technique Achievement of Shanghai Academy of Sci; STA of Shanghai City. *Hobbies:* Chinese Handwriting; Chinese Literature. *Address:* Dept of Palcontology, Shanghai Museum of Natural History, 260 East Yan an Road, Shanghai 200002, China. 139, 162.

CAO Pierre, b. France. Orchl Conductor. *Appointments:* Conductor of orchs w renowned int soloists; Permanent Conductor of the orch Les Musiciens, Grand Duchy of Luxembourg; Permanent Conductor of three choir groups: La Psallette de Lorraine, France; le Choeur de Chambre de Namur, Belgium and l'Ensemble Vocal du Conservatoire de Luxembourg, Grand Duchy of Luxembourg; Artistic Dir of Institut Europeen de Chant Choral, to which some 45,000 choristers belong, coming from Lorraine, Wallonie and the Grand Duchy of Luxembnourg, 1991-; as well as his symphonic repertoire he is concerned with works for choir and orch which explains his interest in lyrical works; although not a specialist in ancient music, he is especially interested in baroque music, interpreting such works with vocal ensembles and groups playing the instruments of the time. *Creative Works:* Recordings for radio, record cos and TV. *Address:* Institut Europeen de Chant Choral, 57 Rue Chambiere, 57000 Metz, France.

CAO Zi Fang, b. 25 Feb 1934, Jiangshu, China. Univ Prof. m. Zou Zurong, 11 Nov 1959, 3 s. *Education:* E China Normal Univ, 1952-53; Beijing Inst of Russian, 1953-54; H Tchrs Coll, Leningrad, USSR, 1954-56; B.Ed, Leningrad Univ, 1959. *Appointments:* Tchng Asst. Beijing Normal Univ, 1959-62; Prof, V-Chmn of Dept of Educ, N-E China Normal Univ, 1962-89; Prof, V-Dir of Ctr for Educ Science, Shanghai Normal Univ, 1989- . *Publications:* More than 30 works and articles: Child Development Psychology; An Investigation of the

Development of the Concept of Intersection Set among Children Aged 5-12 in China. *Memberships:* Int Soc for the Study of Behavioral Dev; Chinese Psychological Soc; Chinese Educl Soc. *Honours:* Honoured with Advanced Scientist by Jiling Province, 1984; Honored with Outstanding Article by Chinese Educational Society, 1986; Honored with Outstanding Works by Jiling Province, 1987. *Hobbies:* Travel, Music, Art. *Address:* Department of Educational Administration, Shanghai Normal University, Shanghai, China.

CAPDEVIELLE Jean Noel, b. 24 Dec 1944, Lhez, France. Dir de Recherche, NRS. m. Wisniewska Lidia, 22 Feb 1991, 1 s. *Education:* Licence es Scienes, 1967; DEA Physique Nucleaire, 1968; Doc es Physique, 1969; Doc es Sci, Paris, 1972. *Appointments:* Asst Physique, 1970-71; Toulouse Attache Recherche CNRS, 1971-74; Charge de Recherche CNRS, 1974-83; Dir de Recherche CNRS, 1983-91; Mayor of Lhez, 1971-91; Vice Deputy in French Parliament, 1973-78. *Creative Works:* Les Rayons Cosmiques, no 729 collection, Lene Saiz Je; Echos, 16mm movie SFRS. *Memberships:* IUPAP; Intl Comm on Emulsion Chamber and High Energy Inteructions. *Honours:* Fondition de la Vocution, for Sci Research; Diplmo of FAI; Merit Order. *Hobbies:* Economical Sci; Diplomacy; Litterature; Juda; Car Racing. *Address:* Laburtaire de Physique Theorique, 19 Rue de Solarium, 33175 Gradignan Cedex, France.

CAPLAN Verla Louise Van Voorhis, b. 1 Nov 1914, Oskaloosa, Iowa, USA. Educator; Resource; Volunteer Inst. m. Lewis H Caplan, 4 Mar 1939, 3 s, 3 d. *Education:* Training Cert, Lowa Normal, 1932; Cert Nursery-Primary, Ann Reno Tchrs Inst, 1938; BA History & Govt, KCMU, 1961; Master Ed, UMKC, 1969. *Appointments:* Rual Sch, Iowa, 1933, 1943, 1944-45; Kohut Boys Sch, NY, 1938; Organised Pre Sch, NYC, 1939-42; Sub Tchr, KCMO, 1959-60; Tchr, Independence Missouri, 24 yrs. *Publications:* Recipies-Indian- Pioneers-Mexican-Africa; Title 111 Curriculum Sci; History in Painting Bicentennial Foyer; Show Case to Malawi, Africa; Pysical Setting Curriculum Gifted Sci. *Memberships:* Indep MO State Tchrs Assoc; Historian Intl Reading Assoc; Sci Tchrs of MO; Nat Sci Tchrs; Math Tchr of MO; Early American Childhood Banquet Speaker. *Honours:* Community Award, Independance; Numerous Sci Fair Awards; Radio Program, People to People Program; Numerous Write Ups, Kansas City Star; Cert of Merit; NS Foundation Grant. *Hobbies:* Writing Books; Collecting Rocks; Fossils; Books; Objects for Teaching; Sharing Ideas. *Address:* 6017 Wornall Road, Kansas City, MO 64113, USA. 15, 138.

CAPLINGER Debra, b. 15 Nov 1954, Pell City, AL. Chm, Natural Sci, Mathematics, Computor Sci Dept; Mathematics Instr, Patrick Henry Coll. *Education:* Bach Sci, Mathematics, Livingston Univ, 1975; Master of Arts, Tchr, Mathematics, Livingston Univ, 1977; Mathematics, Auburn Univ, 1985. *Appointments:* Math, Chemistry, Physics Tchr, Marengo Co, HS, Thomaston AW, 1975-80; Mathematics Instr, Patrick Henry Coll, Monroeville, AL, 1980-; Chm, Nat Sci, Mathematics, Computor Sci Dept, Patrick Henry Coll, *Memberships:* Alabama Mathematical Assoc. *Honours:* Killebrew 1991-, Scholarship, Mathematics; Magna Cum Waud Graduate; Summa Cum Laude Graduate. *Hobbies:* Travelling; Walking; Swimming; Reading. *Address:* 1423 Clairmont Avenue, Monroeville, AL 36460, USA. 7.

CAPPE Melvin Samuel, b. 3 Dec 1948, Toronto. Public Servant; Economist. m. Marline Linda Pliskin, 14 Nov 1971, 1 s, 1 d. *Education:* BA, Univ of Toronto, 1971; MA, Univ of Western Ontario, 1972; PhD, Univ of Toronto, 1975. *Appointments:* Chief Tresury Bd, 1975; Sr Economist, Dept of Finance, 1978; Dep Dir of Investigation & Research, 1982; Asst Deputy min, Consumer & Corporate Affairs, 1985; Deputy Sec Tresury Bd, 1990. *Hobbies:* Travel; Sports; Reading; Computers. *Address:* 483 Highland Avenue, Ottawa, Ontario, Canada. K2A 2J5. 142.

CAPPELLETTI Vincenzo, b. 2 Aug 1930, Roma. m. Maurizia Alippi, 4 Oct 1956, 1 s, 1 d. *Education:* Degree Medicine, 1954; Philosophy, 1966. *Appointments:* Dit I1 Veltro, 1956; Dir Gen Enciclopedia Italiana, 1970; Pres Domus Galilaeana, 1970; Full Prof Hist of Sci Univ, Rome, 1980; Pres Societe Europeenne de Culture, 1988; Pres Academie Intl d'Historie des Sci, 1989-. *Publications:* Entelechia; Helmholtz; Freud; Scienze tra storia e societa; Alle origini della Philosophia Anthropologica. *Honours:* Honorary Degree Univ, Polytech El Salvador; Montaigne Prize, 1991. *Address:* Istituto della Enciclopedia Italiana-piazza Paganica 4 - I 00186 Roma, Italy.

CAPPON Daniel, b. 6 June 1921, England. Physician; Prof. m. Donna Coral Bolick, 1 Apr 1972, 5 s, 2 d. *Education:* LMSSA, London; LRCP MRCS, UK; MBBS, London; FRCP, Edinburgh & Canada; DPM, UK. *Appointments:* C/O Psychiatric & Medical Units, RAMC, India, 1945; Ass Prof Psychiatry, 1949; Prof Psychiatry, 1969; Prof Environmental Studies, 1970-. *Publications:* Understanding Homosexuality; Perception & Technology; Eating, Living & Dying; Coupling; Intuition. *Memberships:* BMA; CMA; APA; CPA; PWAC; ACTRA. *Hobbies:* Invention of Board Games; Hockey; Skiing; Tennis; Skin Diving; Horse Back Riding; Sailing; Astronomical Soc. *Address:* 32A York Valley CR, Willowsdale, Toronto, Canada.

CAPUTA Lewis Anthony, b. 20 May 1921, Hartford. Headmaster; Gulliver Preparation Sch. m. Jean Tierney, 16 Aug 1952, 2 s, 2 d. *Education:* AB, Univ of Miami, 1950; MA, Univ of Miami, 1955; Univ of Rhode Island Guidance Cert, 1962. *Appointments:* Foreign Lang, Instructor, Univ of Miami, 1951; Foreign Lang Tchr, Coral Gables High Sch, 1952; Asst Prin Killian High Sch, 1963; Dir of Student Serv, Dade County Sch, 1974; Headmaster, Gulliver Preparatory Sch, 1982. *Publications:* An Analysis of the Works of Rogelio Sinan. *Memberships:* Coral Gables Country Club; Univ of Miami Alumni Club; Sch Admin Assoc; Guidance Counselors Assoc; St Vincent de Paul Soc. *Honours:* Kappa Sigma Man of the Year; Club Scholarship, Univ Bd of Miami; Univ of Miami Graduate Asst. *Hobbies:* Numismatics; Gardening; Mountain Hiking; Traveling; Reading; Swimming. *Address:* 528 Alcazar Avenue, Coral Gables, FL 33134, USA. 7, 125.

CARAMAN Petru, b. 20 June 1930, Bucuresti.Snr Research Fellow, Mathematical Inst of the Academy. m. Fraga Colombina Ciocârdia, 29 June 1954, 2 d. *Education:* Faculty, Mathematics, 1949-53; Licentiate Degree, 1953. PhD, 1962; Scholarship, USA, 1971; Doc, a post doctoral Thesis, 1973. *Appointments:* Tchr Mathematics, 1953-55; Research Fellow, Inst of Mathematics of the Romanian Academy, 1955-92. *Publications:* Homeomorfisme cvasiconforme n dimensionale; n dimensional quasiconformal mappings. *Memberships:* American Math Soc; Univ Solidarity; League for Human Rights Defense; Civic Alliance Party. *Honours:* Simion Stoilow, Prize of the Romanian Academy. *Hobbies:* Tourism. Address: Str Palade, 12 Iasi, Romania.

CARAMASCHI Enzo, b. 11 May 1927, Mantova. Prof, French & Comparative Literature. m. Marie Carmen de Arbeloa. *Education:* Laurce in Kekou, Milan, 1950; French Literature, RDM, 1960; French Literature, Venise, 1966, 69. *Appointments:* Research, CNRS, Paris, 1955-58; Lectr, Univ Clermont, 1959-61; Prof, Univ Cagliaro, 1961-65; Venice, 1965-71; Florence, 1971-. *Publications include:* Techisma at Impressiommsme des loeuve des fuies Gonount; Arts visual at LiHeuture. *Memberships include:* ICLA Exec Comm. *Address:* Via Del Parione 7, 50123 Florence, Italy.

CARAPETYAN Armen, b. 11 Oct 1908. Musicologist. m. Hariette Esther Noris, 4 Nov 1937, 1 s, 1 d. *Education:* Music Studies, Paris, France, 1927-28; Studied Philosophy, Theology, Musicology, Andover Newton Theological Sch, 1932-43; MA PhD Harvard Univ. *Appointments:* Founder, Dir, American Inst of Musicology, 1945-; Dir of Series Corpus Mensurabilis Musicae; Corpus Scriptorum de Musica Renaissance Manuscripts Studies; Musicological Studies, Documents; Musica Disciplina Miscellanea. *Contributions to:* Corpus Mensurabilis Musicae; Corpus Sciptorum de Musica; Renaissance Manuscripts Studies; Musicological Studies & Documents; Musica Disciplina Miscellanea. *Memberships:* Intl Musicological Soc; American Musicological Soc. *Hobbies:* Romanesque Architecture; Reading; History. *Address:* Monte de los Almendros, 18680 Salobrena, Spain. 2, 52, 139.

CARDWELL Thomas A III, b. 25 July 1943, Oklahoma City. US Air Force Officer. m. to the former T J Hopkins of Alexandria, Virginia, 1 s, 1 d. *Education:* BBA Texas A&M Univ, 1965; MS Univ of Southern Calif, 1976; PhD, Pacific Western Univ, 1988; Tuck Exec Program Dartmouth Coll, 1989. *Appointments include:* 2nd Lieutenant, USAF, 1965; Advances thru to Col, 1982; F4 Fighter Pilot, Tactical Fighter Squadron USAF. 1967; F106 Pilot, Fighter Interceptor Squadron USAF, 1968-72; Dep Chief Staff for sys, logistics, 1973-74; Dep Comdr for Operations, 323d Flying Tng, 1982-84; Chief Strategy Div, 1984-85; Comdr 601st Tactical Control Wing, 1985-87; Dep Asst Chief Staff & Vice Comdr, Air Force Studies and Analysis Ctr, 1988-91, Comdr, Air Force Studies and Analyses Agency, 1992. *Publications:* Quest for Unity of Commond; Airland Combat; Global Reach, Global Power; Contributing, Pergamon Brasseys Intl Military Encyclopedia; Garlands Encyclopedia of WW11; Encyclopedia of the Korean War. *Memberships:* Texas State Soc of Washington; Texas Breakfast Club of Washington; Order of Daedalians; Army and Navy Club; Nat Aviation Club; The Military Order of the World Wars; Air Force Assoc; Military Operations Research Soc; Red River Valley Fighter Pilots Assoc; Assoc of Old Crows. *Honours:* 25 yrs operational flying & Staff Experience; Aircraft; Military Aircraft; Fighter, Trainer and Helicopter; Legion of Merit; Distinguished Flying Cross; Air Medal. *Hobbies:* Tennis; Jogging; Reading; Writing; Refurbishing Furniture. *Address:* 2385 N Danville St, Arlington, VA 22207, USA. 2.

CARDY Peter John Stubbings, b. 4 Apr 1947, Gosport, England, Dir, Motor Neurone Disease Assoc, UK. *Education:* Prices Sch, Fareham, 1958-1965; Univ Coll, Durham, BA, 1965-68; Cranfield Inst of Technology, MSc, 1981-83. *Appointments:* Adult Tutor, Cromwell Comm Coll. Cambs, 1968-71; Tutor Organ, WEA North of Scotland, 1971-73; Dis Sec, WEA North of Scotland, 1973- 77; Deputy Dir, Volunteer Centre, UK, 1977-87; Dir Motor Neurone Disease Assoc, 1987-; Sec Gen, Int Alliance, ALS/MND Assn, 1991-. *Memberships include:* Training for Comm Educ in Scotland; Reform Club; Broadcasting and Voluntary Action; Local Development Agencies Fund; Nat Assoc of Volunteer Bureaux; Charities Effectiveness Review Trust. *Hobbies:* Conversation; Travel; Sailing. *Address:* MNDA, David Niven House, PO Box 246, Northampton NN1 2PR, England.

CAREVIC Olga, b. 9 Apr 1925, Novisad. Prof, Univ of Zagreb, Crotia. m. Kolja, 28 Oct 1950, 1 s. *Education:* PhD Biochemistry, 1950; DSc Biochemistry, 1961; Habilitation, 1964; Prof, 1979. *Appointments:* Inst of Pharmacology, 1953-67; Univ of Birmingham, 1967-68; Inst of Rudjer Bošković. Retired, 1989. *Publications:* 89 pubs in foreign and in Croatian scientific journals and human and peace activities; Help Serbian People in Crotia; Letters in Crotian Journals. *Memberships:* Crotian Pugwash Group for Peace; Croatian League for Peace; Croatian Group for Help and Reconstruction of Croatia; European Group for Cell Biology; EG for Toxicology; EG for Lysosomology. *Honours:* Recognition Research Work from Croatian Assoc. *Hobbies:* Reading; Writing; Walking. *Address:* Palmoticeva 7/IV, U 1000, Zagreb, Croatia.

CAREY George Leonard, b. 13 Nov 1935, Bow, London, England. Anglican Bishop. m. Eileen Harmsworth Hood, 25 June 1960, 2 s, 2 d. *Education:* London Univ; London Coll of Divinity; BD Hons, MTh, PhD, ALCD, 1961-71. *Appointments:* Nat Serv, RAF, 1954-56; London Elec Bd, 1956-58; Univ, 1958-62; Curate, St Mary's Islington, London, 1962-66; Theology Tutor, Oakhill Theological Coll, 1966-70; Theology Lectr, St John's Coll, Nottingham, 1970-75; Vicar, St Nicholas Ch, Durham, 1975-82; Prin, Trinity Theological Coll, 1982-87; Bishop of Bath and Wells, 1987-. *Publications:* I Believe in Man, 1977; God Incarnate, 1980; Great Acquittal, 1981; Church in the Market Place, 1982; Meeting of the Waters, 1986; Gate of Glory, 1987; Great God Robbery, 1988; Cons Ed, Message of the Bible, 1987. *Contributions to:* num jrnls. *Memberships:* Soc of Theological Studies; Chmn, Faith and Order Advsry Grp, Ch of England. *Honours:* Univ prizes, Hebrew, Greek, Church History. *Hobbies:* Walking, Reading, Music, Assn Football. *Address:* The Palace, Wells, Somerset BA5 2PD, England. 1, 146.

CAREY Paul Richard, b. 17 June 1945, Dartford, England. Biophysicist. m. (1) Julia Smith, 4 Sept 1966, (div), 1 s, 2 d, (2) marianne Puszlai, 7 Mar 1991. *Education:* BSc, Univ Sussex, 1966; PhD, Univ Sussex, 1969. *Appointments:* Post Doctoral Fellowship, Nat Res Council, 1969-71; Head Protein Lab, Mngr Centre for Protein Structure and Design, 1987-; Adjunct Prof, Univ Ottawa, 1987-. *Publications:* Sci Publications; Reviews; Biochemical Applications of Raman and Resonance Raman Spectroscopies. *Memberships:* Intl Advis Comm for Intern Confs; Admin Body; Canadian Protein Engr Network; International Network of Protein Engr Centies; Chemical Inst of Canada. *Hobbies:* Literature; Music; Birding. *Address:* Inst for Biological Sciences, Nat Research Council, Ottawa, Canada K1A 0R6. 2, 143.

CARLIER Anthony Neil, b. 11 Jan 1937, Middlesex, England. Dir, Housing Assn. m. Daphne Kathleen Humphreys, 18 May 1954, 1 s, 1 d. *Education:* RMA Sandhurst, 1958; RMCS, Shrivenham, 1962; BSc; RCDS, 1986. *Appointments:* Cyprus, 1962-64; Borneo, 1965-66; Instr, Sandhurst, 1967-70; Staff Courses, Shrivenham, Greenwich, 1971-72; Sqn, Regt, RE GP Comdr, 1975-85; Comdr Br Forces, Falklands, 1987-88; Chief Joint Serv Liaison Offr, Bonn, 1989-90; Ministry of Defence, 1991. *Memberships:* Inst of Royal Engr; Royal Horticulural Soc; Int Assn of Cape Horners. *Honour:* CB; OBE. *Hobbies:* Offshore Sailing; Fly Fishing; Gardening; DIY. *Address:* Farnham, Surrey, England. 1.

CARLSON Wilda, b. 10 Dec 1920, Rome NY. Retired Prof Nurse. m. LeRoy E Carlson, 14 June 1947, 2 d. *Education:* Diploma, Buffalo Deasoness Nursing Sch, 1942; Buffalo Public Health Cert, 1961-62. *Appointments:* WCA Hosp, James Town, NY. 1942-46; James Town Visiting Nurse Assoc, 1960-63; Ind Nurse ProtoTool, 1942-46,1972-74; Marlin Rockwell, 1959-60; Retired, 1982. *Memberships:* Nursing Organization; IANA; PTA James Town Public Sch. *Hobbies:* Sewing; Fishing. *Address:* 512 Barr Street, Jamestown, NY 14701, USA. 52.

CARLSTROM Anders Johan Harald, b. 28 Apr 1933, Stockholm, Sweden. Medical Dir of the Armed Forces, Colonel. m. Birgitta Gustavsson, 24 June 1984. *Education:* Undergr ex Stockholm, 1952; MD Lund, 1962; MA Gothenburg, 1974; Specialist Psychiatry, 1975; SR Psychologist, 1981; MPH Gothenburg, 1985; USASAM, 1985. *Appointments:* MO Army part time, 1958- 83; Hosp Serv, 1962-73; PMOH Jonkoping, 1974-79; Research Psychologist FOA, 1976-83; FS 1986-89; CMO 1989-91; Chief Psychiatrist Armed Forces, 1992. *Publications:* Papers in Military Psychiatry and Military Psychology. *Membership:* Swedish Medical Assoc. *Honours:* SRK Silver Medal; AF1 Silver Medal; KNBLO Silver Medal; UNEFM; ONUCUM; UNIFICYPM; UNIFILM. *Hobbies:* Ethnology; Technical History. *Address:* 2 Baronvagen, S 574 00 Vetlanda, Sweden.

CARMICHAEL Robert Ralph, b. 20 Dec 1937, Sault Ste Marie, Ontario. Artist; Designer. m. Gwendolene Ann Keatley, 28 Aug 1964. *Education:* Ontario Coll of Art, 1959; Carleton Univ, 1964. *Appointments:* Coins Minted by Royal Canadian Mint: Loon, 1987; Black Smith, 1988; Bowhead Whale, 1988; Lancaster, 1990. *Creative Works:* Major Paintings; Moonchild; Resurrection; The Promise; The Ghost; The Woodsman; The History of Sault Ste Marie; Delta Warrior; Publications. The Seed Pod Book of Joy. *Hobbies:* Canoeing; Snow Shoeing. *Address:* RR1 Echo Bay, Ontario, Canada POS 1CO. 142.

CARNEGIE James Gordon, b. 22 Oct 1934, Toronto. Assoc Exec. m. Gail Elizabeth Jarvis, 25 June 1955, 1 s, 2 d. *Education:* Forest Hill Collegiate Upper Canada Coll. *Appointments:* Investment Dealer, 1955- 72; Exec Dir, Ontario Chamber of Comm, 1972-; Exec Dir, Ontario Bus Advis Council, 1979-; Pres Canada Opp Inv Network, 1986-. *Memberships include:* Toronto Bond Traders Assoc; Ontario Assoc of Chiefs of Police; International Assoc of Chiefs of Police; Inst of Corp Dir; St Johns Amb; Chamber of Comm Execs of Canada. *Honours:* Officer, Ven Order of St John; Gardiner Award; Ontario Auxilary Police Medal. *Hobbies:* Metropolitan Toronto Auxilary Police (Deputy Chief, Cmmdg); Police Badge Collecting; Model Soldier Painting; Gilbert & Sullivan. *Address:* Suite 1615, 45 Wynford Hts Cres, Toronto, Ontario, Canada M3C 1L3. 142.

CARNEGIE Margaret Frances, b. 14 Mar 1910, Melbourne, Australia. Author; Voluntary Worker. m. Douglas Howard Carnegie, 11 Mar 1931, 1 s, 3 d. *Education:* Secondary Scho, Australia & Switzerland. *Publications:* Friday Mount, 1973; Morgan the Bold Bushranger, 1979; In Search of Breaker Morant with Frank Shields, 1979; In Step with Sturt, with Keith Swan, 1979; Wildlife of the Australian Bush, 1985; Victorias Colonial Years, 1986. *Memberships:* Patron, State Library; Fellow, Royal Historical Soc of Victoria; Life Member, Nat Gallery of Victoria; Trustee, Telematics Course Dev Fund; Committee, Victoria Health Promotion Foundation. *Honours:* BA Degree; Queens Silver Jubilee Medal; Order of Austrlia Medal; Officer of the Order of Australia. *Hobbies:* Collecting Aboriginal Art; Writing; Historical Research. *Address:* 99 Spring Street, Melbourne, Victoria 3000, Australia. 138, 171.

CARNEY Thomas Francis, b. 7 Feb 1931, Brooklyn, NY. Univ Prof. m. Barbara P Parr, 17 Aug 1954, 1 s, 1 d. *Education:* BA, Univ of London, 1953; PhD, Univ of London, 1957; D Litt et Phil, Univ of S Africa, 1959. *Appointments:* Lectr, Classics, Victoria Univ, 1953-7; Snr Lectr, Prof, Classics, Univ Coll, Rhodesia & Nyasaland, 1957-62; Assoc Prof History, Univ of Sydney, 1962-66; Prof, History, Univ of Manitoba, 1966-77; Prof Communications, Univ of Windsor, 1977-. *Publications:* Biography of Caws Marius; Terence Hecyra; Bureaucracy in Traditional Soc; Content Analysis; Shape of the Past; Career Karate; Job Smarts. *Memberships:* Research Fellow, Ancient History, Univ of Pisa; Research Fellow, Brickbeck Coll, Univ of London; Visiting Fellow, Classics, Princeton Univ; Distinguished Visitor, Sch of Journalism, Univ of Western Ontario. *Honours:* Italian Govt Award; Snr Fulbright Scholarship; Killam Award; Canada Council Post Doctoral Fellowship; Zubeck Award; Rh Inst Award, Univ of Manitoba; Teaching Awards. *Hobbies:* Yoga; Meditation; Walking; Organic Gardening; New Paradigm Research Method; Creative Problem Solving Methodology; Pre-Press Microcomputerized Book Publishing: Layout; Typesetting; Graphics; Indexing. *Address:* Dept of Communication Studies, Univ of Windsor, Windsor, Ontario, Canada N9B 3P4. 3, 8, 133, 139, 154.

CARON H Marcel, b. 16 Sept 1919, Montreal, Quebec, Canada. Bus Exec. m. Madeleine Dussault, 26 Nov 1949, 3 s, 2 d. *Education:* Mount St Louis Coll; Ecole des Hautes Etudes Commerciales de Montreal; Univ of Montreal, L.s.Comm. *Appointments:* Jr Audit Clerk 1943, Mgr 1947, Ptnr 1949-84, Clarkson, Gordon, Montreal; Ptnr,

Woods Gordon, Montreal, 1957-84; Ret'd Exec Ptnr, Clarkson Gordon, Chartered Accts; Pres, Exec Comm, La Presse Ltee; TransCan Newspapers; Gesca Ltee; VP, Corp Financiere Canassurance; Dir: Can Deposit Ins Corp; Blue Cross; Canassurance-Vie Inc; Canassurance, Compagnie d'Assurance Generales Inc; Gentec Inc; Shearer Bock Rutherford; Chmn, Advsry Bd of Acctcy, Univ of Montreal; V-Chmn, Clin Rsch Inst of Montreal. *Memberships:* Past Pres, Can Tax Fndn; Order of Chartered Accts of Quebec; La Chambre de Commerce du dist de Montreal; Revue Commerce; Can Comm; Advsry Bd of Quebec Min of Revenue; Can Inst of Chartered Accts; Dir and Treas, La Salle Fndn; Jules and Paul Emile Leger Fndn; Past Pres, Hon Mbr and Advsr, La Corporation de l'Ecole des Hautes Etudes Commerciales; Past Pres, L'Opera du Quebec; Mbr Panel of Sr Advsrs of Auditor Gen of Can. *Honours:* Honorary Doctorate, University of Montreal; Officer of Order of Canada, 19890. *Hobbies:* Golf, Fishing, Sailing, Skiing. *Address:* 115 Chemin Cote Ste Catherine, Outremont, Quebec, Canada H2V 2A6.

CAROTHERS Robert Lee, b. 3 Sept 1942, Sewickley, Pennsylvania, USA. University President. m. Mary Patricia Ruane, 2 Nov 1974, 2 s, 1 d. *Education:* BS, Edinboro Univ, PA, 1965; MA 1966, PhD 1969, Kent State Univ; JD, Univ of Akron, 1980; Barrister, PA, 1981. *Appointments:* Prof of Engl, Dean, VP, Edinboro Univ, 1968-83; Pres, SW State Univ, Marshall, MN, 1983-86; Chancellor, MN State Univ System St Paul, 1986-91; Pres, Univ of Rhode Island, Kingston, 1991-; Cons, US Off Civ Rights, 1978-79. *Publications:* Freedom and Other Times, 1972; John Calvin's Favorn, 1980. *Hobby:* Fishing. *Address:* 56 Upper College Road, Kingston, RI 02881, USA.

CARPENTER Charles Elford Jr, b. 3 Nov 1944, Greenville, SC, USA. Attorney at Law. m. Nancy Townsend, 8 June 1968, 1 s, 1 d. *Education:* Furman Univ; BA Econ, Bus Admin, 1966; Univ of Virginia, J D, 1969; Univ of South Carolina, MPA, Public Admin, 1976. *Appointments:* Deputy General Counsel, US Army Procurement Agency, 1970-71; Attorney, Leatherwood, Walker, Todd & Mann, 1969; Attorney, Richardson, Plowden, Grier & Howser, 1974-. *Publications:* Products Liability - An Analysis of the Law Governing Design & Warning Defects in Workplace Products; Federal Appellate Practice; Article on New Appellate Court Rules for The Defense Line. *Memberships:* Board of Commissioners on Greivences & Discipline, SC Supreme Court; 4th Cir American Bar Assoc; Amicus Curiae Comm; Defense Trial Attys Assoc; American Judicature Soc. *Honours:* ABA ALI Appellate Process Program; ABA SC Bar Assn; mbr Richland County Fee Dispute Comm; Appellate Practice; proposed Rules of Appellate Practise for SC Bar Annual Meeting; Mbr Practice and Procedure Comm Health & Hospital Law Subcomm; *Hobbies:* Forest Lake Club; Palmetto Club; St Andrews Soc; Tarantella Club; The Columbia Ball; Torch Club; Fishing; Reading; Hunting; Tennis. *Address:* Richardson, Plowden, Grier & Howser, 1600 Marion Street, PO Drawer 7788, Columbia, SC 29202, USA. 7, 52, 162.

CARPENTER Donald Blodgett, b. 20 Aug 1916, New Haven, Ct, USA. Retired. m. (1) Barbara Marvin Adams, 28 Jun 1942 (dec 1978), (2) Lee Burker McGough, 28 Dec, 1980, Div. 5 s, 1 d. *Education:* PhB Univ of Vermont, 1938; Sonoma State Univ, 1968-69; Mendocine Comm Coll, 1977; Coll of the Redwoods, 1984-85. *Appointments:* Newspaper Reporter, 1938-39; NY Worlds Fair, 1939; Insurance Underwriter, 1939-40; Pencil Manufacturer, 1940-42, 1946-52; Insurance, 1952-61; Maintenance Conslt, 1961-68; Tchr Coach, 1968, 1985-87; Property Appraiser, 1968-88. *Creative Works:* Editor, Univ of Vermont Class of 1938 50th Year Renuion Souvenir Handbook; Rotary Blub of Mendocino Historian; Univ of Vermont Newspaper. *Memberships:* Legion Post Cmdr; Past Cmdr of California; Kappa Sigma Intl Fraternity; Mendocino Cardinal Booster Club; Rotary Intl. *Honours:* Kappa Sigma Intl Fraternity Scholarship Leadership Award; Boosters Comm Sportsman of the

Year; R I Paul Harris Fellow; Sec Navy Commendation; Com 12th Naval District Commendation; Rotarian of the Years; IBA, Life Fellow. *Hobbies:* Geneology; Historian; Philately; Football; Tennis; Writing; Youth. *Address:* 10801 Gurley Lane, Mendocino, CA 95460, USA. 9, 52, 59, 162, 179.

CARPENTER Miriam Charlotte, b. 30 Aug 1932, Milbrooke, Ala. Psychiatric Nurse; Asst Dir for Lamar County Mental Health Centre. m. Ovan Herald Caysenter, 23 Jan 1970, 1 s, 2 d. *Education:* AAS Galneston Coll, TX, 1974; AA Coll of Maniland, TX, 1977; BS East Salas State Univ, 1979; BSN, Univ of Texas, 1982; MS, East Texas State Univ, 1985; TWU, Denton TX, Student Doctoral Program. *Appointments include:* House Supervisor, Intl Medicine, 1974; Nurse Training Coordinator, 1977-79; House Supervisor, Nursing Quality Assurance Coordinator, 1984-85; Psychiatric Nurse, 1989-. *Publications include:* Class Book;Resigned and Implemented Employee Health Program; Resigned and Implemented Ward Clerk Mains Program. *Memberships:* Lions Club; AARP, Texas; LTSU; UTA; Kappi Delta Pi Honor Soc; Phi Keta Kappers Honor Soc; Soc of American Nurses; Hospital Auxillers Member; Intl Platfordm ASNN. *Honours:* Home Health Advisory Board; Member Advisory Comm; South Western Reporter Book; Phi Keta Kappa Honor Soc; Kappi Delta Pi Honors Soc. *Hobbies:* Choir Member; Sunday Sch Tchr; Fund Raising; Reading; Speaker to various organisations. *Address:* 200 Keywest Rd, Paris, TX 75460, USA. 5, 7.

CARR Leonard Barrett, b. 6 Oct 1930, Detroit, USA. HRSH The Prince of Lithuania; Medical Doctor. m. Ileana Garcia Ramirez de Arellano, 3 Mar 1961. *Education:* BSc, Birmingham, 1953; PhD, Ohio State Univ, 1958; MD Puerto Rico, 1980. *Appointments:* Puerto Rican Economy, Construction, Sugar, Planatation Operations, Coffee Growing, Finance, Banking, 1961-80; Medical Doc, Alt Medicine, 1983-; Apostolic Envoy, Ambassador, West Indies, Patriarchate of Antioch, 1987-; Ambassador for the Crown of Bohemia, 1988. *Memberships:* World Medical Assoc; World Mental Health assoc; Travel Century Club; Royal Overseas Club; Royal Commonwealth Soc. *Honours:* Austrian Albert Schweitzer Award in Medicine; Knight Grand Cross; Honorary Commodore; Honorary Vice Consul; Knight of the Royal Order; Lord of Livonia; Marquess of Kaunas. *Hobbies:* Opera; Travel; Cambodian Facial Medical Diagnostic Tech; Chinese Medicine; Iridology; Homeopathy; Korean hand acupuncture; Art; Ancient History; Tropical Argcult; Economics; Astronomy; Fishing. *Address:* PO Box 2045, Mayaguez, PR 00681, USA. 130, 155.

CARR Peter Derek, b. 12 July 1930, Mexborough, Yorkshire. Chmn, Northern Reg Health Auth; Chmn, County Durham Development Com. Chmn, Northern Screen Commission. m. Geraldine Pamela Ward, 12 Apr 1955, 1 s, 1 d. *Education:* Fircroft Coll, Birmingham, 1956-57; Ruskin Coll, Oxford, 1957-59; Garnett Coll, London, 1959-60. *Appointments:* Cabinet Maker, 1944-56; Lectr, Percival Whitley Coll, 1960-64; Snr Lect, Thurrock Coll, 1964-67; Indl Rels Advsr, Nat Bd for Prices and Incomes, 1967-69; Dir Commission on Ind Relations, 1969-74; Dir Advisory Conciltation Arbitrations Ser, 1974-78; Diplomatic Serv, 1978-83; Reg Dir, Dept of Employment, 1983-89; Chmn Northern Regional Health Auth; Chmn County Durham Development Co; Snr Partner Peter D Carr and Assoc; Visiting Fellow, Durham Univ. *Honours:* CBE; Honorary Fellowship; Northumberland Univ. *Hobbies:* Cabinet Making; Photography; Cycling; Cooking. *Address:* Corchester Towers, Corbridge, Northumberland. NE45 5NR. England. 1.

CARRASCO Maria Auxiliadora Luque, b. 8 Mar 1957, Jaen, Spain. P.Enterprise-Agric, Writer, Poet. *Education:* Dips in Admin, Hlth and Child Care. *Appointments:* P Enterprise Agric; Asst Admnstr, Asst Hlth Care; Writer; Poet. *Publications:* Poems in Anthology of Poetry, Nat and Int jrnls and sev other publs; Narrations, Stories. *Memberships:* Assn of World Writers; Assn of Spanish Writers. *Honours:* Honours and Awards from Univs in USA and Spain. *Hobby:* Oil Painting. *Address:* c/o Constitucion No 10-1 A, 11692 Setenil de ls Bodegas, Cadiz, Spain.

CARRASCO AGUILAR Isidoro Antonio, b. 14 May 1939, Huelva, Spain. Poet, Pres and Dir, Asociacion Jesus Abandonado y F Magnificat. m. 26 July 1984, 2 s, 1 d. *Education:* Dip in Catechism (Relig Doctrine), Salamanca, 1956; Lic in Theology, 1968; Doct in Theology, 1970, Salamanca; Scientific Mgmt, 1990; Hlth Techn, Seville, 1991. *Appointments:* Diocesan Delegate and Dir, Obviam Christo, 1971; Instr of Theologians and Tchr of Inst, 1972-; Deleg, Marginados Sociales and Fndr, Asociacion Jesus Abandonado. *Publications:* Renovacion de la D y M de Pastoral Vocacional, 1970; Sabes tu Camino?, 1972; Jesus Abandonado, 1981; Un Virrey y un Martir, 1984; Charles Espirituales, 1985; Ed, Hombre Nuevo periodical; Author: Sentimientos Rimados, 1986; Contemplando; Como de Parte del Senor and Marginacion, 1990; Dentro diti and Asi Sucedio, 1992; included in two Anthologies of Poets. *Hobbies:* Contact with Nature, Reading, Writing, Classical and Romantic Music. *Address:* C/S Pablo 1, 30B, 41001 Seville, Spain.

CARRIER W David III, b. 21 Dec 1943, Allentown, PA, USA. Geotechnical Engr. m. 9 July 1965, 2 d. *Education:* SB MIT, 1965; SM MIT, 1966; ScD MIT, 1969. *Appointments:* Johnson Space Centre, NASA, Houston, 1968-73; Specialist Lunar Soil Mechanics, Bechtel, San Francisco, 1973-77; Asst Chf Soils Engr, Woodward-Clyde Consultants, 1977-78; Mgr Solid Waste Systems, BCI, Lakeland, 1978-, Pres. *Publications:* Lunar Sourcebook; 50 Tech Papers. *Memberships:* Prof Engr in CA; CO; FL; GA; ND; TX; Geotech Engr; Chartered Engr; European Engr; American Soc of Civil Engr; Inst of Civil Engr. *Honours:* Norman Gold Medal ASCE; Cert of Commendation, Johnson Space Centre; Middlebrooks Award ASCE; Lunar Sample Principal Invest, NASA; Principal Investigaor Florida Inst of Phosphate Research. *Hobbies:* Stamp Collecting; Swimming; Flying. *Address:* BCI, PO Box 5467, Lakeland, FL, 33807, USA. 7, 14.

CARROLL Billy Roberta Price, b. 27 Nov 1920, Memphis, TN. Artist; Painting & Sculpture. m. David Donald Carroll, 25 Dec 1964, 1 d. *Education:* Diploma, Hutchison Sch, 1939; Art Course, Memphis Academy of Art, 1939-40; Farnsworth Sch of Painting, 1949,50,51; Academia Della Belle Arts, Florence, 1959. *Appointments:* Portaiture, Landscape, 1949-91; 36 One Man Exhibititions. *Creative Works:* Painting for Courtrooms; City Halls; Univ; Prof Buildings; Chinese Ink; Water Colour Sketches for Poetry Books. *Memberships:* Brooks Museum League; Nat League of American Pen Women; Nat Museum of Women in the Arts File, Slides, Data, NMWA Library. *Honours:* Brooks Art Gallery Bi Centennial; Fellowship Jay Hambidhe Art Found; Painting of the Year; Fellowship Huntingdon Hartford Found; TV Chan Interview. *Hobbies:* Flower Gardening; Travel; Adventure; Out Door Sports. *Address:* 1956 Central Avenue, Memphis, TN 48104, USA. 2, 52, 138.

CARROLL David Roger, b. 14 July 1932, Dewsbury. Prof of English. m. Dorothy Knox, 2 Apr 1956, 2 d. *Education:* Dewsbury, GS, 1943-50; Durham Univ, 1950-53; London Univ, 1955-57. *Appointments:* Lectr, English, Fourah Bay Coll, 1957-63; Asst, Assoc, Full Prof, Univ of Toronto, 1963-72; Reader, Prof, Univ of Lancaster, 1972-. *Publications:* Chinua Achebe; George Eliot: Critical Heritage; Richard Simpson As Critic; Middlemarch; Longman Literature in English. *Memberships:* Postgraduate Awards Comm. *Hobbies:* Travel; Walking; Sport. *Address:* Dept of English, Lancaster Univ, Lancaster, LA1 5ED, England.

CARROLL Janice Ann Hicks, b. 1 Sept 1957, Cameron, OK. Undergraduate Coordinator. m. Johnny Carroll, 27 May 1976, 1 s, 1 d. *Education:* Seosu, 1975-76, 1979-80; Osu, OK State Univ, 1076-78; UNM, 1979. *Appointments:* InformationSpec, Kerr Ind Applications Centre, 1981-81; CSCI Tchr, Sherman High Sch, 1982; Math Tchr, 1982-84; Tchr Fellow, UNT, 1985-86; Graduate Advisor, 1986-88; Undergraduate Coordinator, 1988-. *Publications:* ABC's, 123's. *Membership:* IEEE; ACM. *Honours:* UPE Honorary CSCT Fraternity; William R Pogue Math Exec Award; Full Scholarship. *Hobbies:* Crochet; Knitting; Reading; Computor Journals. *Address:* CSCI Dept, Univ of North TX, Denton, TX 76203, USA. 2, 7, 15.

CARROLL Kenneth Kitchener, b. 9 Mar 1923, Carrolls, NB Canada. Dir, Centre for Human Nutrition, Univ of Western Ontario. m. Margaret Aileen Ronson, 26 Aug 1950, 3 s. *Education:* Univ of New Brunswick, BSc, MSc, 1943,46; Univ of Toronto, MA, 1946; Univ of Western Ontario, PhD, 1949; Post Doctoral, 1949-52; Post Doctoral, Cambridge Univ, 1952-54. *Appointments:* Asst Prof, Prof and Acting Head, Dept of Medical Research Univ of Western Ontario, 1954-68; Prof Dept of Biochem, 1968-88; Emeritus, 1988; Dir, Centre for Human Nutrition, 1990-. *Publications:* Lipids & Tumors; Diet Nutriton and Health McGill; Numerous Report Papers. *Memberships include:* Royal Soc of Canada; Chem Inst of Canada; Nutr Soc of Canada. *Honours:* Canadian Life Insurance Officers Assoc Fellowship; Merck Fellowship; Earle Willard McHenry Award. *Hobbies:* Curling; Sailing. *Address:* Dir Centre for Human Nutrition, Dept of Biochemistry, Univ of Western Ontario, London, Ontario, Canada N6A 5C1. 2, 14, 34, 142.

CARROLL Raymond J, b. 21 Apr 1949, Tokohama, Japan, Prof of Statistics. m. Marcia Gail Ory, 13 Aug 1972. *Education:* PhD, Pudne Univ, 1974. *Appointments:* Univ of North Carolina, 1974-87; Texas A & M Univ, 1987-. *Creative Works:* Transformation & Weighting in Regression. *Honours:* Copss Pres Award; Wilcoxon Award; Fellow, American Statistics Assoc; Fellow, Inst of Math Statistics. *Hobbies:* Fishing; Golf. *Address:* Dept of Statistics, Texas A & M Univ, Coll Staton, TX 77843-3143, USA.

CARRUTHERS Leo Martin, b. 24 Nov 1949, Dublin, Ireland. Univ Prof. *Education:* Univ Coll Dublin, 1968-72, BA, MA; Univ de Paris: PhD, 1980, Docteur d'Etat, 1987. *Appointments:* Asst Lectr, English, Univ de Paris, 1978-83; Lectr, English, Univ d'Amiens, 1983-89; Prof of English Language, Literature, Univ d'Amiens, 1989-. *Publications:* La Somme Le Roi et Ses Traductions Anglaises; Etude Comparee, Paris; Articles in Learned Journals. *Memberships:* Pres, Intl Medieval Sermon Studies Soc. *Hobbies:* Reading; Music; Walking; History; Nature. *Address:* Faculte de Langues, Univ de Picardie, Campus Univ, 80025 Amiens Cedex, France.

CARSON Leta Nelle, b. 4 Apr 1937, Gorman, Texas, USA. m. John P Carson, 17 June 1967, 1 s. *Education:* Bach of Music, Tex Christ Univ, 1959; M Mus, TCU, 1960; PhD, Mich St Univ, 1965. *Appointments:* Intr Cottey Coll, 1963-64; Stt Prof, 1964-67; Farimont State Coll, Prof, Chairman, Div of Fine Arts, 1978-90; Prof of Music, 1990-; Assoc Prof, 1973- 78. *Memberships:* MTNA; MENC; WVMTA; AF. *Honours:* Both Baccalaureate Degrees Summa Cum Laude; Snr Achievement Award. *Hobbies:* Reading; Exercise; Walking; Sewing; Travel. *Address:* 111 Rosewood Avenue, Fairmont, WV 26554.

CARSON Maclem Kennedy, b. 24 July 1925, Canada. Retired Labour Relations Conslt, Mediator. m. Shirley Faith Adams, 28 Aug 1946, 2 d. *Education:* Sec Sch, 1939-43. *Appointments:* Clerk Canadian Nat Railway, 1943-56; Organizer, Negotiator, Dir, Organizing & Servicing, 1957-69; Nat Vice Pres, 1970-71, Canadian Brotherhood of Railway Trans and General Workers; Conciliation Officer, 1972-75; Ind Relations Conslt,

Mediator, 1975-89. *Memberships:* Prof Devel Comm; Assoc of Labour Relations Agencies; Prof in Dispute Resolution; Msonic Order Presbyterian Church. *Hobbies:* Golf; Fishing; Bridge. *Address:* PO Box 69 Tweed, Ontario, Canada, K0K 3J0.

CARTER Claire Phyllis Ducharme, b. 13 Feb 1933, Irvington, New Jersey, USA. Ret'd. m. Ralph E Carter, 19 Sept 1981. *Education:* MA, Smith Coll, 1958; BS, Univ of MA, 1954; MT, Newton-Wellesy Hosp Schl of Technology, 1955. *Appointments:* Microbiologist, NYS Dept Hlth, 1959- 81; Tchng Fellow, Smith, 1957-59; Mt Holyoke Soldiers' Home, 1956-57. *Memberships:* ZXi; ASMT (ASCP); ASM. *Hobbies:* Hiking, Canoeing, Skiing, Photography, Travel. *Address:* RR4 Box 43, 5555 Wormer Road, Voorheesville, NY 12186, USA. 6.

CARTER David, b. 6 Apr 1934, Moose Jaw, Saskatchewan. *Education:* Univ of Manitoba, Bach Arts, 1958; Licentiate Theology, St Johns Coll, Winnipeg, 1961; nglican Theological Coll, Univ of British Columbia, 1968; DOc in Divinity, St John Coll, 1968. *Appointments include:* Chaplin, Univ of Calgary, Southern Alberta Inst Tech, Mount Royal Coll, 1965-69; Rector, cathedral Church, Redeemer; Dean Anglican Diocese Calgary, 1969-79; Diocesean Archivist, 1966-88; Snator Univ of Calgary, 1971-77; Elected Rep, Calgary Millican, Legislative Assmby of Alberta, 1979, re-elected in 1982, 1986; Elected mbr, Calgary Egmont, 1989; Spkr, Leg Assmby, Alberta, 1986, 1989; Nova, Alberta Corporation, 1982-86. *Publications:* 7 Books, Western Canadian History; Poetry. *Memberships include:* Lupus Erythematosus Soc of Alberta; Calgary Chamber of Comm; Trinity Place Foundation of Alberta; Calgary Canucks Jnr Hockey Team. *Hobbies:* Dragooning Volunteers to Assist Restoring, Maintaining St Margarets Church. *Address:* 325 Legislature Building, Edmonton, Alberta, Canada T5K 2B6.

CARTER Peter Basil, b. 10 Apr 1921, England. University Teacher; Barrister. m. (1) Elizabeth Maxwell Ely, 1960 (dec.), (2) Lorna Jean Sinclair, 1982. *Education:* BA 1st Class Hons, MA, 1946, BCL 1st Class Hons, Vinerian Scholar, 1949, Oriel Coll, Oxford; Called to Bar, 1947, Hon Bencher, 1981, Middle Temple, London; QC, 1990. *Appointments:* Fellow, 1949-88, Sr Bursar, 1965-78, Emeritus Fellow, 1988-, Wadham Coll, Oxford; Delivered Gen Course, Pvte Int Law, Hague Acad Int Law, Netherlands, 1981; Vis Prof, var univs, Australia, Can, USA. *Publications:* Essays on Law of Evidence (w Sir Z Cowen); Cases and Statutes on Evidence; Articles, pvte int law, law of evidence, in var legal jrnls; Jt Ed, International and Comparative Law Quarterly. *Membership:* Fellow, Inst Dirs. *Honours:* Croix de Guerre, 1944. *Hobby:* Architecture. *Address:* Wadham College, Oxford OX1 3PN, England.

CARTER Robert Daniel, b. 1 Oct 1927, Vero Beach, FL. Research Chemist. m. Dorothy C Downey, 9 Sept 1972, 2 s, 1 d, 1 Stepson, 3 Stepdaughters. *Education:* BS Agricult Chemistry, Univ of FL, 1949. *Appointments:* Processed Prod Inspector USDA, Winter Haven, FL, 1949-54; Var FL processors, Dir, Rsch & Quality Cont, 1954-69; FL Dept of Citrus, Rsch Chem, 1969-; Univ of FL, Adj Fac Food Sci and Human Nutn Dept, 1969- . *Publications:* Over 70 including: Reconstituted Florida Orange Juice; Florida Orange Juice; The Structure of Citrus Fruits and Processing in Citrus Science & Technology, vol I AVI. *Memberships:* Bd of Dir, Lakeland, Presbyterian Apts; Presbyterian Housing Foundation, St Petersburg; Inst of Food Tech (IFT); FL State Horticultural Soc; American Chemical Soc. *Honours:* IFT Distingued Serv Award; Sigma XI, Honorary Sci Research Soc. *Hobbies:* Trailbuilding; Hiking; Swimming. *Address:* 2522 Helms Road, Winter Haven, FL 33884, USA.

CARTWRIGHT Ian David, b. 28 Mar 1952, Dukinfield, Cheshire, England. Photographer; Managing Dir. m. Christine May Lennie, 4 Sept 1976, 1 s. *Education:* Ashton-U-Lyne Coll, Art & Design, 1970-71; BA Graphic Design, Leeds Poly. *Appointments:* Asst Photographer,

Graham Powell Studios, 1975-78; Woburn Studios, Photographer, 1978-82; Photographer, Montage, 1982-87; Photographer, MD, Avalon, 1987-. *Memberships:* British Inst of Prof Photography; Assoc Photographers; Ski Club of Manchester; Ski Club of Great Britain. *Honours:* FBIPP; AFAEP; IPC Comm Photography Trophy, 90-91, 91-92. *Hobbies:* Skiing; Tai Chi; Painting; Drawing. *Address:* Cheadle Hulme, Cheshire, England.

CARUBELLI Raoul, b. 17 June 1929, Cordoba, Argentina. Research Biochemist. m. Barbara R Waken, 24 Jan 1959, 1 s, 1 d. *Education:* Pharmacist, 1953; Biochemist, 1955; Doc of Pharmacy & Biochemistry, 1960; Cordoba Univ, Agentina. *Appointments:* Lab Instr, Univ of Cordoba, 1953-6; Research Biochesmist, Oklahoma Medical Research Foundation, 1957-; Snr Scientist, DA McGee Eye Inst, 1986. *Creative Works:* Process for Lactulose, US Patent; Process for Lactulose, Canadian Patent. *Memberships:* American Soc for Biochemistry & Molecular Biology; Sigma Xi; American Chemical Soc; Assoc for Research in Vision and Ophthalmology; Academy of Medical Sci of Argentina. *Honours:* Graduate Sch of Pharmacy; Honor Graduate Sch of Biochemistry; University Prize, Univ of Cordoba; Research Career Dev Award. *Hobbies:* Swimming; Fishing; Hunting; Gardening. *Address:* 3626 NW 53rd Street, Oklahoma City, OK 73112, USA. 7, 143.

CASE Janet, b. 29 June 1943, Ashby de la Zorich. Barrister at Law. m. Jeremy David Michael, 1965, Div. 1 s, 1 d. *Education:* Durham Univ, LLB, Dunelm, 1965. *Appointments:* Called to Bar, 1975; Wales & Chelsea Circuit, 1975; Chmn Medical Appeals Tribunal. *Hobby:* Gardening. *Address:* Croeswylan, Oswestry, Shropshire, England.

CASSELLE Dawne Astride, b. 16 Apr 1943, Phila, PA, USA. Attorney at Law, Private Practice. m. (1) Frank Poindexter, 1968, div, (2) Raymond Spurlock, 1980, 1 s. *Education:* Assoc of Arts, Los Angeles Pierce Jr Coll, 1973; Bach of Arts, UCLA, 1975; Juris Doctr, Univ of California, 1980. *Appointments:* DA Casselle & Assoc, 1975-89; Attorney at Law, Private Practice, 1989-. *Creative Works:* Yarn Art; Wall Hangings & Tapestries. *Memberships:* The Bar Assoc; The PA Bar Assoc; PA Trial Lawyers Assoc; American Bar Assoc; Wilshire Chamber of Commerce; Nat Assoc of Female Exec. *Honours:* Newton Mfg Co, Nat Sales Topper Award; UCLA Law Moot Court Honors Program; Staff Writter, UCLA Black Law Journal; UCLA Letters & Sci Honors Program. *Hobbies:* Real Estate; Marketing; Public Speaking; Writing; Computors; Gardening; Horseback Riding; Swimming; Snow Skiing; Interior Decorating. *Address:* 1104 Walnut Street, Allentown, PA 18102, USA. 59, 138, 179.

CASTAING Raimond Bernard Rene, b. 28 Dec 1921, Manaco. Prof Emeritus, Univ of Paris-Sud, Orsay, France. m. Jeanne Gadrat, 7 July 1947, 2 s, 1 d. *Education:* Coll of Condom, 1940-46; Doc in Physics, Univ of Paris, 1951; Doc Honoris Causa, Univ of Tübingen, 1963. *Appointments:* Research Engr, ONERA, 1947-51; Lect, Univ of Toulouse, 1952-55; Univ of Paris, 1956-59; Prof, Univ of Paris-Sud, 1960-87; Dir Gen of ONERA, 1968-72. *Publications:* Initiation of new Methods of Microanalysis of Solids; Electron Probe Microananlysis; Secondary Ion Microscopy; Magnetic Energy Selecting Microscopy. *Memberships:* French Physical Soc; French Elec Micr Soc; French Metallurgical Soc; Royal Microscopical Soc; Franklin Inst. *Honours:* Albert Sauveur Achievement Award; Comm Leg d'Honneur; Gd off Ordre Nat Du Merite; Acad Sc Paris; Acad Leopoldina; Royal Swedish Acad of Sci; Acad of Astronautics; John Price Wetherill Medal; Holweck Prize; Gold Medal CNRS; Brinell Medal; Roebling Medal; Grand Medal Le Chatelier. *Hobbies:* Mountaineering; Family Tree. *Address:* Lab de Physique des Solides, Batiment 510, Univ de Paris-Sud, 91405 Orsay, France. 34, 52, 91.

CASTELEYN Mary Teresa, b. 28 Sept 1941, London. Genegalogist; Chartered Librarian. m. Ludwig Emil, 24 Feb 1965, 1 s. *Education:* Assoc of the Library Assoc, 1970; Fellow of the Library Assoc, 1984. *Appointments:* Westminster City Libraries, Staff & Training Officer, 1976-85; City of Westminster Leisure Dept, Personnel Officer, 1985-89; External Examiner Malawi Library Assoc, 1979-85. *Publications:* Planning Library Training Programes; Pre Licentiate Training Guidelines; Evaluation of Training in Library Training; Promoting Excellence: Personnel Management and Staff Developments in Libraries. *Memberships:* Council for the Library Assoc; Irish Genealogical Research Soc. *Honours:* Fellow of the Irish Genealogical Research Soc. *Hobbies:* Irish Genealogy; Book Collecting; Reading. *Address:* 253 Peach Road, Queens Park, London, W10 4DX, England.

CASTILLO Jaime Del, b. 14 Apr 1951, Santander, Spain. Gen Dir of Informacion y Desarrollo, S L. m Mercedes Ugedo, 12 Sept 1980, 1 s, 1 d. *Education:* Cert in Econs, Fac Econs, Bilbao, Spain, 1975; MA, IREP Grenoble, France, 1981; PhD, Econ Science, Bilbao, 1985. *Appointments:* Asst Prof, Bus Schl, Santander, Spain, 1974-75; Asst Prof, of Econ, Bilbao, 1975-80, 1980-85, Prof, 1985; Chief Operating Off, Informacion y Desarrollo, S L. *Publications:* Medidas ayudas a la Inversion, 1986; Ed, Regional Development Policy, 1989; Spatial Aspects of Technological Change, 1989; Econs Columnist, El Correo, 1986-. *Contributions to:* articles to profl jrnls. *Memberships:* European Assn Devel Insts, working grp, EADI, convenor 1988; Assn Reg Science Basque Country, Pres, 1988. *Hobbies:* Reading, Music, Travel, Gastronomy. *Address:* Informacion y Desarrollo S L, Diputacion 4-BIS 6o, 48009 Bilbao, Spain. 52.

CASTRO Brian Albert, b. 16 Jan 1950, Hong Kong. Author. m. Josephine Mary Gardiner, 10 Aug 1976. *Education:* St Josephs Coll, Hunters Hill, 1962-7; Univ of Sydney, BA Dip Ed, 1971; Univ of Sydney, MA, 1976. *Appointments:* Tchr, NSW State High Sch, 1972-76; Tchr, Lycee Technique, Aulnay, 1976-7; Tchr, ST Josephs Coll, 1978-9; Lectr, Univ of Western Sydney, 1988-89; Journalist, Asiaweek Mag, Hong Kong, 1980-87. *Publications:* Birds of Passage; Pomeroy; Double Wolf. *Membership:* Australian Soc of Authors. *Honours:* Australian Vogel Literary Award; The Age Fiction Award; Victorian Premier's Award. *Hobbies:* Golf, Skiing; Chess. *Address:* c/o Allen & Unwin Australia, 9 Atchison Street, St Leonards 2065, NSW, Australia. 52.

CATASUS Jose Magin Perez, b. 18 Jan 1942, Santiago de Cuba, Cuba. Sch Psychologist. m. Lina Teresa Jubran, 13 Nov 1982, 1 s, 1 d. *Education:* Inst Pre Univ de Santiago de Cuba, BS, 1960; Miami Dade Jnr Coll, 1971; Florida Intl Univ, BS, 1974; MS, 1976; Florida State Univ, PhD, 1989; Nat Cert Sch Psychology, 1989. *Appointments:* General Clinical Lab, Coral Gables Gen Hosp, 1961-65; Pediatric Clinical Lab, 1965-74; Psychometrist, 1974-77; Specialist Sch Psychology, Dade County Sch, 1974-76; Palm Beach County Sch, 1977-78; Doc Fellowship, Florida State Univ, 1978-80; Clinical Instr, Florida Intl Univ, 1980-82; Visiting Instr, Univ of Florida, 1982083; Lead Sch Psychologist, 1983-. *Memberships:* Psychoeducational Ser Graduate Students Assoc; Florida Intl Univ; Assoc of Sch Psychologists; Florida Assoc of Sch Psy; Hispanic Human Resources Council; Official Representative to State Legislature Latinos in Public Radio of Florida. *Honours:* US Dept of Educ Doc Fellowship to Florida State Univ; Dept of Educ Research, Development, Foundations. *Hobbies:* Field Reader, US Dept of Educ. *Address:* Alachua County Sch District Psychological Services, 620 East Univ Avenue, Gainesville, FL 32601, USA. 7, 176.

CATE Dietra Elaine, b. 19 Jan 1945, Hannibal, Missouri, USA. Receptionist, Model. 1 s 1 d. *Education:* Elem Educ, MO State Univ, 1963-65; Investments and Banking, Black Hawk Coll, 1980; Sales and Human Rels,

Dale Carnegie-Pub Speaking, 1976. *Appointments:* Stan Wynott Agcy, Ins Investing, 1974-; Fin Teller, Community Saving Bank, E Moline, IL, 1984-88; Hospitality Coord, McKenna & Cuneo, Attys, 1989-90; Model, Giorgio Corp, Washington Metro Area, 1990-; Off Admnstr, First Model Mgmt, Arlington, VA, 1991-; Receptionist, GPC Systems Inc, Vienna, V, 1992-. *Memberships:* Moline Task Force Against Drugs and Alcohol, 1980-87; Moline PTA Assn, 1970-80; Minitheater Chmn, 1978-80; PTA Legislation Chmn, 1975-80; First Christian Ch, var comms; Beta Sigma Phi, Tau Chi Chapt, Pres; Delta Sigma, Pres; Charter Mbr, Nat Mus of Women in the Arts, Wash D C. *Honours:* Beta Sigma Phi, Girl of the Year, 1987; Dale Carnegie Best Speaker, 1976. *Hobbies:* Reading, Skiing, The Arts, Music, Community Theatre, Travelling, Water Sports, Modelling and the Movie Industry. *Address:* 8760 Old Colony Way 2C, Alexandria, VA 22309, USA.

CATEDRAL Alfredo Perla, b. 9 Feb 1909, Philippines. Retired Dean, Graduates Sch, Western Inst of Technology. 3 s, 2 d. *Education:* MA, Math, Physics, Univ of Missouri, 1934; BD, Colgate Rochester Divinity Sch, 1947; Doc of Educ, Columbia Univ, 1949; EdD, Tchr Coll, Columbia Univ, 1949. *Appointments include:* Grade 2 Tchr, Bingawan Inst, 1924-25; Ordained Baptist Minister, Rochester, 1937; Pastor, Central Philippine Coll Baptist Church, 1940-41; Acting Dean, Coll of Educ, 1945-46; Exec Secr, Assoc of Christian Sch & Coll, 1960-67; Dean, Coll of Educ, West Negros Coll, 1967-68; Vice Pres Convention of Philippine Baptist Church. *Memberships include:* Philippine Theological Assoc; Phi Delta Kappa; Bacolod Ministerial Fellowship; CPBC Ministerial Fellowship. *Honours:* Asst in Physics; Graduate Scholarship in Guidance; Practical Theology Scholarship; Post Grad Scholarship, Student Personnel Admin. *Hobbies:* Gardening; Hiking; Reading; Tennis; Pingpong; Badminton. *Address:* 6672 130A Street, Surrey, British Columbia, Canada V3W 8PT.

CATLETT James C, b. 29 June 1957, Chattanooga, Tennessee, USA. Mental Hlth Admnstr, Cons, Lectr. m. Deborah Kaye Green, 13 Oct 1983, 1 d. *Education:* BA, Psychology (Hons), Lee Coll, 1978; MS. Clin Psychology, Univ TN, 1981. *Appointments:* Therapist 1981-82, Satellite Dir 1982-84, Assoc Dir 1984-90, Dir of Extended Care 1990-, Hiwassee Mental Hlth Ctr, Cleveland, TN; Cons, NWGA Mental Hlth Ctr, 1989-; Consultations, Trng, Lectures, var mental hlth ctrs, convens, colls in TN. *Creative Works:* Co-ed, Insane Jealousy by Vijai P Sharma, 1991; Profl Vocalist; Composer; Conceptual Artist. *Memberships:* Licensed Psychological Examiner, TN; Mbr Effective Advocacy for Citizens with Handicaps; TN Mental Hlth Consumers Assn; TN Conf on Social Welfare; TN Assn of Suicide Prevention; TN Assn of Psychological Examiners; TN Psychological Assn. *Hobbies:* Music, Racquetball, Reading, Photography, Computers, Writing, Theatre. *Address:* 3527 Brandon Lane NE, Cleveland, TN 37312, USA. 7.

CATON Shaun Vincent, b. 11 Jan 1965, Winchester. Performance Artist; Painter; Writer. *Education:* Peter Symonds College; Winchester School of Art; Goldsmiths' College, London. *Appointments include:* The Edinburgh Festival, 1985; Riverside Studios London, 1986; Nat Review Live Art Nottingham, Midland Group Gallery, 1986; Hyde Park, London, 1986; Galerie Paranorm, Berlin, 1987; Festival Plagiarism, London, 1988; The Diorama Gallery, London, 1989; Commerce Street Artists Warehouse, Houston, TX; Tokyo Art Fair, 1990; Braunschweig Filmfest, Galerie Fisch, 1991; Tour of Poland funded by British Council in Poland, 1991. *Creative Works:* Exhibition, DNA Galerie Rotterdam, Holland, 1990; Publications, ND Mag, Austin, Texas; Metro Riquet Mag, Paris; Weast Mag, Berlin; Sensoria, Toronto, Canada; Performance Mag; Braunschweig Filmfest Catalogue; Galerie Paranorm Cat; Films, DeadMan Decay Talk; Nocturnes; Human Soup, 1992. *Honours:* Greater London Arts Grant; The Scottish Arts Council; British Council; Jacob Mendelson Scholarship. *Hobbies:* Baroque Music; Zen Buddhism; Collecting

Primitive, Tribal Art; Travel, Orient. *Address:* 12 B Compton Terrace, Islington, London, N1 2UN, England.

CATTO Charles Robert, b. 7 June 1929, Torronto. Exec Dir, Frontiers Foundation. m. Barbara Jean Loveys, 25 Sept 1954, 2 s, 2 d. *Education:* BA, Univ of Toronto; M Dir, Univ of Toronto. *Appointments:* United Church, Canada, Home Mission Bd, 1954-57; Bd of World Mission, 1957-62; Postoral Charge, 1964-68; Frontiers Foundation, 1968-. *Honours:* Order of Canda; Commendation, Pickering; Guest of Honor, Native Council, Canda; Aboriginal Order of Canda; Diplomas Honor from Bulivia. *Hobbies:* Piano; Banjo Ukelele; Model Ships; Planes; Skating; Skiing. *Address:* 712 Kingfisher Drive, Pickering, Ontario, Canada. LIW IXS. 142.

CAULFIELD James B, b. 1 Jan 1927, Minneapolis, MN. Physician. m. Virginia Walsh, 11 Feb 1950, 1 s, 2 d. *Education:* Miami Univ, Oxford, 1947; Univ of Illinois, Coll of Medicine, BS, 1948; MD, 1950. *Appointments:* Prof, Chmn, Dept Pathol, Univ So Car Sch of Med, 1975- 85; Asst Dean, Univ So Carolina Sch Medicine, 1976-77; Prof, Dept Pathol, Univ Al at Birmingham, 1985-. *Publications:* Articles various Medical Journals; Calcium Antagonists. *Memberships:* ISHR; Am Soc of Cell Biologists; NY Acad Sci; Am Soc Nephrology; Am Assoc Pathology; Int Acad Pathology. *Honours:* Phi Eta Sigma; NIH Fellowship. *Hobbies:* Reading. *Address:* Univ of Alabama at Birmingham, UAB Station, Volker Hall G023, Birmingham, AL 35294, USA. 2.

CAVANAGH Charles Terrence Stephen, b. 29 July 1949, USA. Merchant Banker. *Education:* B Litt, Univ of Oklahoma, 1970; BA, Univ of Cambridge, 1974; MA, 1977; Cert Thel, Univ of Oxford, 1977. *Appointments:* Church of England, Curate, 1977-78; Heddenwisks, Stockbroker, 1978-81; SG Warburg & Co, Mercury Asst Mgmt, 1981-91; Hon Curate St Peters, 1980-84; Hon Curate, St Peters, 1985-; Kldinwolt Benson Gp Plc, 1991-. *Address:* Extemporary Dance Theatre; St Georges Crypt Gallery. *Hobbies:* Wine; Cooking; Modern Ballet; Contemporary Art. *Address:* 34 Tasman Road, London, WS9 9LU, England.

CAWLEY Charles Nash, b. 21 Aug 1937, Shreveport, LA. Enviromental Sci. *Education:* BA, Math Univ of Oklahoma, 1960; MA Economics, Univ of Oklahoma, 1970; MS, Env Sci, Univ of TX, 1976; PhD, Env Sci, Univ of TX, 1978. *Appointments:* Project Leader, TX Womans Univ Research Inst, 1964-73; Gen Partner, Southwest Textile Lab, 1973-76; Research Assoc, Univ of TX, 1977- 79; Asst Prof Cornell Univ, 1979-84; Principal Sci, Westinghouse Hanford Co, 1984-88; Licensing Supervisor, Bechtel Nat Inc, 1988-. *Publications:* Sci and Tech Papers, Environmental Transport; Consequences, Evaluation of Environmental Compliance; Performance of Waste Disposal Systems. *Memberships:* American Nuclear Soc; American Assoc for Advancement of Sci; American Statistical Assoc; Soc for Risk Analysis; Sigma Xi; NY Academy of Sci; Health Physics Soc. *Hobbies:* Reading; Gardening; Bridge; Travel; Swimming. *Address:* 130 Brandeis Lane, Oak Ridge, TN 37830, USA. 7, 9.

CAZEAUX Isabelle Anne Marie, b. 24 Feb 1926, NY. Prof Emeritus of Musicology. *Education:* BA, Hunter Coll, NY, 1945; Smith Coll, MA, 1946; Ecole Normale de Musique, Paris, 1950; Conservatore National de Musique, Paris, 1950; Columbia Univ, MS, 1959; Columbia Univ, PhD, 1961. *Appointments:* NY Public Library, Hd Music Cataloguer, 1957-63; Bryn Mawr Coll, Faculty of Music, 1963-92; Douglass Coll, Visiting Prof, 1978; Manhattan Sch of Music, 1969-82. *Publications:* The Chansons of Claudin de Sermisy; Translator, The Memoires of Philippe de Commynes; Author, French Music. *Memberships:* American Musicological Soc; Comm on the Status of Women; Intl Musicological Soc; Nat Opera Assoc; Soc Theophile Gautiers. *Honours:* Libby vab Arsdale Prize for Music; Fellowships;

Scholarships; Grants. *Hobbies:* Attending Concerts, Opera. *Address:* 415 East 72nd Street, New York, NY 10021-4412, USA.

CEBUC Alexandru, b. 5 Apr 1932, Pausesti. Art Historian. m. Turcu Florica, 5 Apr 1958, 1 d. *Education:* History, Bucharest Univ, 1957. *Appointments:* Research Wrker Bucharest, 1957-70; Vice Pres, Culture Comm, City of Bucharest, 1970-77; Dir Art Museum of Romania, 1977-91; Chmn Arch, 1991. *Publications include:* The Repertoire of Historical & Art; Dialogue of the Arts Flemish & Dutch Schools; Paintings & Graphics. *Honours:* Oder of Cultural Merit; Knight of Italian Republic. *Hobbies:* Art Collector. *Address:* 36 Spatarului Street, sector 2, Bucharest, Romania. 34.

CECIL Aurelia Margaret Amherst, b. 19 July 1966, London. Public Relations. m. Giles Crewdson, 20 Dec 1990. *Education:* Queensgate; Heathfield; Priorsfield. *Appointments:* MD of Aurelia Public Relations, 1990- . *Hobbies:* Reading; Walking. *Address:* Aurelia Public Relations Ltd, Victoria House, 1A Gertrude Street, London, SW10 OJN, England.

CELA TRULOCK Jose Luis, b. 7 Feb 1930, Madrid, Spain. Dr Engr. m. 7 Feb 1959, 1 s, 1 d. *Education:* Dr Engr, 1958; Diploma, Monograph Courses. *Appointments:* Chief Engr, Tool Room, Enasa, 1959-60; Dir Div Toll Room & Special Machinnery, 19660-63; Dir Quality, Reliability Chrsler Espana, 1963-66; Dir of Costs Anylisis of Chesa, 1966-71; Dir Chassis, Power Train Design Chesa, 1971-75; Dir Tech Advisor, Ind Operations, 1975; Dir Total Quality Programm, 1986. *Publications:* Numerous Papersin Seminars, Congessess. *Memberships:* Spanish Comm for Tooling Standardization; Spanish Assoc for Quality; Reliability Comm of the AECC; Camilo Jose Cela Foundation; Nat Counselor of the AECC; Honors & Awards Comm; AECC. *Hobbies:* Reading; Music; Fishing. *Address:* Avda Pio Xii 96, 28036 Madrid, Spain. 52.

CELANI Maria Antonieta Alba, b. 9 Dec 1923, Sao Paulo. Univ Lectr. *Education:* BA, Catholic Univ, Sao Paulo, 1946; TEFL, London, Univ, 1956; Doc of Letters, Catholic Univ, Sao Paulo, 1960. *Appointments:* Tch of English, Secondary Sch, 1947-58; Lect, Tchr Trainer, Catholic Univ, 1954. *Publications:* Get Ahead 1,2; The Brazilian Esp Project; Co Author, Take off 1,2,3; Particularly Verbs. *Memberships:* Assoc Intl Delinguistrue Apliruee; Intl Assoc of Tchr of English as a Foreign Language; Braz TESOL; Assoc de Linguistica Aplicada Dobrasil ALAB. *Honours:* Officer of the British Empire OBE. *Hobbies:* Reading; Cookery Books; Needle Work; Travel. *Address:* AV Higienopolis 318, Apt 42, 01258 Sao Paulo 3P, Brazil.

CELEM Huseyin E, b. 28 Sept 1937, Istanbul, Turkey. Ambassador of Turkey to Greece. m. 7 Mar 1962, 1 s, 1 d. *Education:* Faculty of Political Sci, Univ of Ankara, 1959. *Appointments:* Ministry of Foreign Affairs, 1959; Dept of Econmonic Affairs, 1960; Military Serv, 1960-61; Turkish Embassy, Washington DC, 1963-64; First Sec, Turkish Embassy, Buenos Aires, 1965-67; Dir of Sect, Dept of Bilateral Ecomomic Affairs, 1967-69; Cnslr, Turkish Embassy, Moscow, 1969-73; Acting Hd, Dept of European Security Affairs, 1973-75; Turkish Delegation CSCE, 1973-75; Deputy Hd, Turkish Parmanent Del OECD, 1975-78; Hd, Dept of Strategic Studies and Disarmement, 1978-79; Dir Gen Bilateral Political Affairs, 1979-81; Ambassador to Saudi Arabia, 1981-83; Ambassador to Kenya, 1983-86; Dir Foreign Serv Training Centre, 1987-89; Dep UnderSec for Bilateral Political Affairs, 1989-91. *Hobbies:* Music; Reading. *Address:* Turkish Embassy, 8 Vassileos Gheorchiou B Street, 106 74 Athens, Greece.

CELIC SVABEK Marija, b. 17 Feb 1927, Koprivnica. Ophthalmologist; Prof of Ophthalmology. m. 10 Apr 1952. *Education:* Medical Faculty, Univ of Zagreb, 1952; Spec of Ophthalmology, 1960; Doc of Sci, 1978;

Habilitation for Univ Lectr, 1981; Prof, Ophthalmology, 1983. *Appointments:* Physician, 1952-57; Specialisation in Ophthalmol, 1957-60; Univ Eye Clinic, Zagreb, 1960-77; Hd Strabological Centre, Univ Eye Clinic, 1977-. *Publications:* Diagnostics of Strabismus; Treatment of Amblyopia; Co-author, A Medicine of Sch & Prof Orientation; Co-author, Ophthalmology, A Textbook for Medical & Stomatol Students; Articles in Med Periodicals. *Memberships:* Croatian Medical Assn; Österreichische Ophthalmologische Gesellschaft; European Strabismological Assoc; Julius Hirschberg Gesellschaft; Croatian Medical Accademy. *Honours:* Clinical Medical Centre, Zagreb; Medical Faculty of Zagreb. *Hobbies:* General History; History of Ophthalmology; Travel. *Address:* Univ Eye Clinic, Kispaticeva 12, 41000 Zagreb, Croatia.

CELMI Carlos Emilo, b. 27 Feb 1935, Buenos Aires, Argentina. Tech Conslt. m. Mady Haimovict, 18 Sept 1976, 2 d. *Education:* PhD Chemistry, Univ of Cuenos Aires, 1957; Various Courses, Languages, Computing Systems foe Exec, Ind Organ, Business Admin, 1953-82. *Appointments:* Chemist, Textile Ind, 1953; Prod Mngr, Vegtable Oils Factory, 1953-56; R&D Mngr, Coca Cola Export Corp, 1957-67; Assoc Vice Pres, Asesoramientos Tecnios SA, 1967-82; Development Dir, South American Consol Enterproese, Panama, 1968- 76; Indept Tech Conslt, 1976-; Dir/Assoc Dir numerous other Business Concerns. *Creative Works:* Several Projects inc. Sodium Tetborate Plant, Brazil. *Memberships include:* Agentine Chemical Assoc; Intl Airlines Passanger Assoc; British, French, Swedish, Swiss Chamber of Comm. *Honours:* Otto Krause Silver Medal; Albert Einstein Intl Academy Foundation Bronze Medal; Life Fellow; Life Patron; Intl Biographical Assoc. *Hobbies:* Yachting; Cinematography; Music. *Address:* Rua Sao Vincente de Paulo, 638 Apt 84, CEP 01229, Sao Paulo, Brazil.

CEPIK Jerzy, b. 11 Dec 1929, Poznan, Poland. Writer, Histn. m. Wanda Krzyzaniak-Walinska, 16 Mar 1957, 1 s. *Education:* Tech Schl, Nat Inst of Progress, HS, Study of Med. *Appointments:* Soldier and Scout WWII; Imprisoned in Nazi concentration camp, arrested by NKWD; Instr of Polish Scouting until 1947; Histn and Writer, Mbr of the Mgmt ZLP in 1981 (Polish Writers Assn). *Publications:* Lit works (monographs, biogs and novels): Giordano Bruno, 1958; Cross and Crown, 1967; Vikings, 1969, 74, 85; Bison from Altamira, 1974, 87 (novel of prehistoric painters in France and Spain); Slaves, 1970 (historic novel from time of Roman Empire); Kopernik, 1977; History of Writing, 1979, 87; History of Religion, 1980, 85; Cristoforo Colombo, 1981; Leonardo da Vinci, 1983; The Prehistoric Civilisation and Culture, 1983; Rembrandt, 1985; Michelangelo, 1989, Rafael Santi, 1990; History of Art, 1991; Rubens, 1991; Hieronymus Bosch, 1992-93. *Memberships:* Polish Writers Assn; Epigraphic Soc; IBC; ABI; Int Hall of Leaders IBA. *Honours:* Polish Gold Order of Merit, 1977; Honorary Citizen of Poznan, 1980; Knight of the Order Polonia Restituta, 1986. *Hobbies:* Hist, Archaeology, Hist of Art, Relig and Arch, Biog Works, Drawing, Photography, Skiing, Swimming. *Address:* ul Sciegiennego 57 m 8, Poznan 60-136, Poland. 3, 57, 139, 152.

CERVENY Vlastislav, b. 26 Apr 1932, Drachov, Czechoslovakia, Prof of Geophysics. m. Eva Cervena, 1 Sept 1967, 2 d. *Education:* Graduated Charles Univ, Prague, 1956; PhD Geophysics 1961, RN Dr Physics 1966, DrSc Geophysics 1978, Charles Univ. *Appointments:* Inst of Geophysics, Charles Univ, Prague, 1955-; Long-term visits at world univs (USA, Can, Brasil, England, Germany, France, Netherlands). *Publications:* 2 books and about 200 scientific papers in field of seismology related to the propagation of seismic waves. *Memberships:* Seismological Soc of America; Soc of Exploration Geophysics; Academia Leopoldina, Germany. *Honours:* State Prize, Czechoslovakia, 1970; Honorary Member, Society of Exploration Geophysics, 1992. *Hobbies:* Reading; Travelling. *Address:* Institute

of Geophysics, Charles University, Ke Karlovu 3, 121 16 Praha 2, Czechoslovakia.

CETINBUDAKLAR Ahmet Gurer, b. 29 Sept 1944, Izmir, Turkey. General Mngr; Chmn Bd of Dir. m. Havva Hassan, 12 Feb 1971, 1 s. *Education:* Imperial Coll, London, Adv Chemical, Engr MSc, DIC, 1967- 68; Chemical Engr, BSc, ACGI, 1964-67. *Appointments:* Faculty of Sci, Univ of Ankara, Turkey, 1973; Chemical Engr Coll, 1971-73; Prime Ministry's State Planning Organ, Turkey, 1970-73; Tech Advisor, Dir, Haci Omer Sabanci Holdings AS, 1973-80; Coordinator, Dir, Yasar Holding AS, 1980-84; General Mmgr, Chmn, Bd of Dir, 1984-. *Publication:* Chemical Engr Science; Cocurrent Gas Liquid Flow. *Memberships:* Turkish American Businessman Assoc; Turkish Ind Mangerial Inst; Chamber of Comm; Turkish Foreign Trade Assoc; Agean Union of Olive and Olive Oil Exporters; Aegean Chamber of Ind; Basak Insurance Corp. *Honours:* Hinchley Medal. *Hobbies:* Reading; Football; Astrophysics; Mathematics. *Address:* 16 Sokak, 5 KAT 4 DA 8, Guzelyali Izmir, Turkey. 104.

CHAI Chung Chuan, b. 14 Sept 1931, Wuhu, Anhwei, China. Admin Vice Minister of Ministry of Justice. m. Tan Li-Yuan, 11 Nov 1962, 2 s, 1 d. *Education:* Bach of Law Sch, Nat Taiwan Univ, 1954. *Appointments:* Judge District Court, 1957-65; Judge High Court, 1965-67; Pres Kinmen District Court, 1967-69; Pres Hualian District Court, 1969-73; Attorney General Chang Hau District Court, 1973-78; Tainan District Court, 1978-83; Kaohsiung District Court, 1983-85; Taiwan High Court Tainin Branch, 1985-89; Admin Vice minister, 1989-; Part time Prof, 1974-. *Publications:* Prof Papers on Law. *Memberships include:* Taiwan ROC Chapter of Intl Assoc of Penal Law; Chinese Const Assoc; Drafting Comm for Law of Wire Tapping Control; Bd of Assoc of Ind Relations ROC; Legal Advisors of Private Int. *Honours:* Outstanding Youths Selected by ROC Jnr Chamber; Several Medals, Outstanding Achievement. *Hobbies:* Reading; Gardening; Discussion & Debate; Mountain Climbing; Golf; Stamp & Coil Collecting. *Address:* 130, Sec 1 Chungking S Road, Taipei, Taiwan, China.

CHAKRABORTY Pratima, b. 6 May 1940, Darjeeling. High Sch Tchr. m. 14 Dec 1966, 2 d. *Education:* Loreto Convent, Darjeeling, 1947-56; St Josephs Coll, Dartjeeling, 1956-60; BA, Calcutta Univ, 1960; Cert of Educ, Sheffield, 1976; BEd, Sheffield, 1977. *Appointments:* Tchr, St Helens Convent, Darjeeling, 1961-62; St Josephs Sch, 1962-66; Nuneaton Sch, Warwicks, 1968; Crofton High Sch, York, 1978-. *Publications:* The British Acquisition of Bengal. *Membership:* Nat Union of Tchrs. *Honours:* Inter Univ Elocution Contest in Shakespearean Drama. *Hobbies:* Stock Market Analysis; Painting. *Address:* Santi, West Edge Road, Kirk Smeaton, Pontefract, W. Yorkshire WF8 3JS, England.

CHAKRABORTY Sucharu Kumar, b. 1 June 1932, Culcutta. Doctor; Business Dir. m. Pratima Mookerjee, 14 Dec 1966, 2 d. *Education:* Jiaganj EC Inst, Calcuta Med Coll, MBBS, 1955; FFARCS, 1969; Royal Coll of Surgeons; Fellow Coll of Anaesthasia. *Appointments:* House Officer, 1955-67; Registrar, Snr Reg, 1967-71; Conslt, Pontefract Gen Infirmary, 1971-. *Publications:* Research Paper in British Journal of Anaesthesia. *Memberships:* BMA; Yorkshire Soc of Anasthetists; Intractable Pain Soc. *Honours:* 1st Place Order of Merit. *Hobbies:* Photography; Listening to Rabindra Sangeet. *Address:* Constl Anaesthetist, General Infirmary, Pontefract, W. Yorkshire, England.

CHALKER Robert P, b. 16 Mar 1914, Linden, Ala, USA. Exec Dir. m. (1)Edna V Wood, 1946, dec 1985, 1 s, 1 d, (2) Louise Studley, 23 Apr 1990. *Education:* Birmingham Ala Coll, 1929-31; Duke Univ, AB, 1933; MA, 1935; Post Grad, Columbia Univ, 1950-51; US Naval War Coll, Newport, Rhode Island, USA. *Appointments:* Tchr Sec Schs, 1934-38; US Diplomatic,

Consular Serv, 1939-69; Sec Embassy, Berlin, 1939-42; Interned Bad Nauheim, Germany, 1941-42; Vice Consul, Lisbon, 1942; Consul Birmingham, 1942-44; Sec Embassy, London, 1944-47; Consul Madras India, 1948-49; Bremen, 1949-50; Duesseldorf, Germany, 1951-54; Pers Operations, Dept of State Washington, 1954-56; Consul Gen Amsterdam, 1956-59; Kobe Osaka, 1959-63 Counsellor, Deputy Chief of Misson, Dublin Ireland Embassy, 1964-69. *Memberships:* Alpha tau Omega; Stephens Green Club; Milltown & Woodbrook Golf; Rotary Club; Paul Harris Fellow. *Hobbies:* Golf; Theatre; Limericks. *Address:* US Chamber of Commerce in Ireland, 20 Coll Green, Dublin 2, Ireland. 2, 52.

CHALLIS Chris, b. 11 Feb 1952, Essex, England. Writer, Lectr. *Education:* BA (Hons) 1973, MA (Distinction) 1974, PhD 1979, Leicester Univ. *Appointments:* Prior to Univ Copywriter, Docker, Tech Author, Hodcarrier etc; Full-time Writer, 1979-, Extensive Tchng. *Publications:* Quest for Keromac, 1984; 6 Slim Vols of Poetry; 12 Plays; 6 Anthologies Edited; Contbr to Anthologies in USA, Germany, Belgium, Holland. *Memberships:* Lit Panel, E Midlands Arts Assn, 1979-85; Drama Panel, 1982-83. *Honours:* NANDA Award Winner, 1979; EMA Writers Travel Bursary, 1979; EMB Writers Bursary, 1986; Short-listed for Heineman Fiction Award, 1990. *Hobbies:* Photography, Cats, Brit Mythology, English Civ War, Traditional Ale. *Address:* 65 High Street, Ingatestone, Essex IM4 OAT, England.

CHAMBERLIN Robert Joseph Tracy, b. 4 July 1929, Texas, USA. 2 s. *Education:* BA Mrktg, BS, Psych, Duke Univ, 1951. *Appointments include:* Salesman, Broker NASD, 1951-62; Dir of Sales, Haeai Clay Prod Inc, 1963-68; Auto Sales, Leasing Mngr, 1969-80; All American Fin Serv Ins, 1981-; Clasped Hands Inc, Golden Wilderness Nat Artesian Water, 1988-. *Memberships:* American Veterans Alliane; Am Vets; American Legion; Gene Autry Western Heritage Museum; Los Angeles World Affairs Council; The Passport Club; Intl Bottled Water Assoc; Smithsonian Inst; American Film Inst; Museum of Nat History; Citizen of Boys Town. *Address:* 27778 Avenue Hopkins, Valencia, CA 91355, USA. 125, 155.

CHAMBERS J K (Jack), b. 12 July 1938, Ontario. Prof of Linguistics; Jazz Critic; Biographer. m. Susan E L'Heureux, 9 Sept 1961, 1 s, 2 d. *Education:* BA, Univ of Windsor, 1961; MA, Queens Univ, 1963; PhD, Univ of Alberta, 1970. *Appointments:* Sec Sch Tchr, English, Dept Hd, 1963- 67; Prof of Linguistics, Univ of Toronto, 1970-; Departmental Chair, 1986-90. *Publications include:* Canadian English, Origins & Structures; Milestones I & II, The Music and Times of Miles Davis; Dialects of English, Studies in Grammatical Variation; Canadian Dictionary for Children; Articles on Jazz, Linguistics. *Memberships:* Canadian Linguistic Assoc; American Dialect Soc; Philological Soc; English World Wide; Intl Jl of American Linguistics. *Honours:* Visiting Prof, Linguistics; ASCAP; Deems Taylor Award; Fellowships for Research and Publication. *Hobbies:* Squash; Gothic Arch. *Address:* Dept of Linguistics, Univ of Toronto, Toronto, Canada M5S 1A1. 142.

CHAMBERS Richard Dickinson, b. 16 Mar 1935, W Stanley, Co. Durham, England. Prof of Chemistry, Univ of Durham. m. Anne Boyd, 17 Aug 1959, 1 s, 1 d. *Education:* Stanley GS, Univ of Durham, BSc, PhD, DSc, 1953-59. *Appointments:* Research Fellow, Univ of BC, Canada, 1959-60; Visiting Lectr, Fulbright Fellow, Case Western Reserve Univ, Cleveland, 1966-67; Reader, 1968; Prof, 1976; Hd of Dept, 1983-86; Univ of Durham, Foundation Fellow, 1988-89. *Publications:* Fluorine in Organic Chemistry. *Memberships:* Royal; Soc of Chemistry; American Chemical Soc. *Honours:* American Chemical Soc Award, Creative Work in Fluorine Chem. *Hobbies:* Opera; Soccer; Jogging. *Address:* 5 Aykley Green, Whitesmocks, Durham DH1 4LN, England.

CHAN Man-Wah Luke, b. 29 Nov 1948, Shanghai. Prof of Finance & Business Econ; Assoc Dean. m. Yuen Pui Raphael, 22 June 1974, 1 s, 1 d. *Education:* BSc, UPEI, 1973; MA, McMaster, 1974; PhD, McMaster, 1978. *Appointments:* Asst Prof, Univ of Toronto, 1977-81; Asst Prof, Assoc Prof, Prof, 1981-83, 1984-88, 88-. *Publications:* Sunzi on the Art of War and its General Application to Business. *Memberships:* Hamilton & District Chamber of Comm; The Hamilton Lung Assoc; Hamilton Wentworth United Way; Beijing Energy Soc. *Honours:* Advisory Prof, Fadan Univ, Shanghai; Naukai Univ, Tianjin. *Hobby:* Music. *Address:* Faculty of Business, McMaster Univ, Hamilton, Ontario, Canada L8S 4M4.

CHANA Balvinder Singh, b. 3 Apr 1958, Garh Padhana, India. Marketing manager Network South East, Thames & Chiltern Division, Reading. m. Jasvir Kaur, 30 Dec 1979, 1 s, 1 d. *Education:* BSc Physics, Chemistry & Mathematics, 1976-79. *Appointments:* British Rail, Passanger Serv, Mngr Slough, 1980-85; Travel Mngr Colchester, 1986-87; Travel Centre Mngr Leeds, 1988-89; Area Passanger Mngr, South East Wales, Cardiff, 1989-91; Station Manager, Intercity Swansea, 1991-92. *Memberships:* Chairman, Sikh Assoc South Wales; Gurdwara Cardiff; Chambers of Commerce Cardiff; British Jnr Chamber of Commerce. *Hobbies:* Hockey; Badminton; Squash; Swimming; Travel. *Address:* 55 Beale Close, Danes Court, Cardiff, CF5 2RU, Wales.

CHANDLER Danny Ricardo, b. 4 Apr 1962, Columbia, MS. Data Processing Tech, Specialist. m. Reta Cazette Boone, 6 Sept 1987. *Education:* BA Mathematics, 1984; AA Bus Admin, Accounting, 1989; Graduate Studies, Statistics, 1984-86. *Appointments:* Graduate Tchr Asst, Miss State Univ, 1984-86; Miss State Highway Dept, 1987-88; Miss State Dept of Health, 1988-. *Memberships:* Mississippi Academy of Sci; South Central Conference Exec Comm. *Honours:* CE Musely Pioneer Serv Award; Scholastic Achievement Award; Cum Lande Graduate; 3rd Place Oratorial Contest; Snr Most Likely to Succeed. *Hobbies:* Tennis; Soft Ball; Public Speaking; Community Serv; Writing Editorials. *Address:* PO Box 68052, Jackson, MS 39286, USA. 2, 7.

CHANEY Robert Eugene, b. 31 July 1957, Ada, Oklahoma, USA. Owner, The Ultimate Network; Telecommunication Exec. m. Connie Jean Clevenger, 14 July 1978. *Education:* Oklahoma Univ, 1957-77. *Appointments:* Paramedic City of Midland, TX, 1978-80; Nat Mngr, Long Distance Resale, 1982-84; Sales Mngr, American Telephone Sales, 1984-87; Reg Mngr, Telecom USA, 1987-89; Reg Mngr, Harmony Systems, 1989-91; Owner, The Ultimate Network, 1982-. *Memberships:* South OKC; Nat Assoc Jnr Coll; Metro Nat Networking; Nat Tae Kwon Do; South OKC Chamber of Comm; Metrocrest Chamber of Comm. *Hobbies:* Bicycle Racing; Golf; Training Dogs; Water Skiing; Private Pilot; Tae Kwan Do. *Address:* 1204 Lune Wolf Trail, Carrollton, TX 75007, USA. 7, 117, 132.

CHANG Allison, b. 29 Jan 1933, Tainan, Taiwan. Prod Mngr; Chemical Engr. m. Patricia A Holliday, 1 Dec 1990, 1 s, 1 d. *Education:* BS, 1957; MS, 1959; PhD, 1969. *Appointments:* Amer Cyanamid Wayne, NJ, 1970-75; Novamont Corp, Kenova, WV, 1975-77; Amer Cyanamid, WV, 1977-82; Alcon Lab, Sanford, NC, 1983-89; Microsi Inc, Phoenix, AZ, 1990-. *Creative Works:* Invented VISCOAT Viscoelastic Solution for use in Opthalmic Surgery. *Membership:* American Inst of Chem Engr; Soc of Biomaterial; Assoc of Research in Vision & Opthalmology; American Chem Soc. *Honours:* Phi Kappa Phi, Research Fellow. *Hobbies:* Sports; Flying. *Address:* 10028 South 51st Street, Phoenix, AZ 85044, USA.

CHANG Janice May, b. 24 May 1970, Loma Linda, CA. Pres, JMC Enterprises Inc. *Education:* Bach of Arts, California State Univ, 1990; Cert for Paralegal Studies, CSUSB, 1990; Cert in Creative Writing, CSUSB, 1991;

Student, Western State Univ of Coll of Law. *Appointments:* Pres JMC Enterprises Inc. *Publications:* Am Poetry Anthology; World Treasury of Golden Poems; Great Poems of the Western World; The Pacific Review; The piquant; The Best poems of the 90's; On The Threshold of A Dream; Quiet Moments; Love's Greatest Treasures; Am Anthology of Contemporary Poetry. *Memberships:* American Poetry Assoc; Nat Library of Poetry; World of Poetry; Alpha Gamma Sigma Mu; Nat Honor Soc, Loma Linda Chapter. *Honours:* Deans List Dept of Humanities; Golden Poet Award; Poet of Merit Award; Editors Choice Award; Publishers Choice Award. *Hobbies:* Writing Poetry; Works of Fiction; Literature; Drama; Music. *Address:* 11466 Richmont Road, Loma Linda, CA 92354, USA. 59.

CHANG Po-Ya, b. 5 Oct 1942, Chia-Yi City, Taiwan. Dir Gen, Dept of Health, Exec Yuan, ROC. m. Dr Tsan-Nan Chi, 1 s, 1 d. *Education:* MD Kaohsiung Medical Coll, 1968; MPH Inst of Public Health, Nat Taiwan Univ, 1970; MPH Sch of Hygiene & Public Health, The Johns Hopkins Univ, 1974. *Appointments:* Dir, Prof, Kaohsiung Medical Coll, 1974-83; Mayor, Chia-Yi City, Taiwan, 1983-89; Legislator, Legislative Yuan, ROC, 1990; Dir Gen, Dept of Health, The Exec Yuan, 1990-. *Publication:* Study of Occupational Lead Poisoning in Southern Taiwan. *Honours:* Outstanding Intl Alumni in Public Health Leadership, The Johns Hopkins Univ. *Hobbies:* Travel; Photography. *Address:* 4 Fu-Hsin Road, Ping-Tong, Taiwan, ROC.

CHANG Tien Chun, b. 22 Mar 1950, Taiwan, ROC. Doctor. m. Mei Chen Hong, 28 May 1977, 1 d. *Education:* MB, 1975; PhD, 1984; Medical Coll, Nat Taiwan Univ. *Appointments:* Asst Prof, 1983-85; Assoc Prof, 1985-90; Prof, 1990; Medical Coll Nat Taiwan Univ, Taipei. *Publication:* Hormones & Disease 1,11 & 111. *Memberships:* Endocrinology Soc of ROC; Intl Academy of Cytology. *Honours:* Taiwan Medical Promotion Foundation Award; Best Paper Award; Endocrinology Soc of ROC. *Hobby:* Painting. *Address:* 7 Chung Shan South Rd, Nat Taiwan Univ Hospital, Taipei, Taiwan 10016, China.

CHANNON Gordon Anthony, b. 2 July 1926, Exeter, England. Chartered Acct; Univ Lectr; Author. m. 3 Sept 1966, 1 s, 1 d. *Education:* John Stocker Sch, Exeter, Univ of Exeter, MA, 1959; Chartered Acct, 1957. *Appointments:* Articled Student, 1952-57; Partner, Yeo & Co, 1959-69; Tax Partner, Simpkins Edwards, 1969-; Lectr, Taxation Univ of Exeter, 1975-. *Publications:* Inheritance Tax; Economics of Taxation Work Book; Disincorporation; Articles in Taxation Journals. *Memberships:* Inst of Chartered Acct; SW Tax Comm; Exeter District Soc; SW Soc Chartered Acct; Inst of Taxation Fellowship by Thesis; Assoc of Certified Accts. *Hobbies:* Arts; Walking; Wine. *Address:* Dept of Economics, Univ of Exeter, Amory Building, Renness Drive, Exeter EX4 4RJ, England.

CHANO Fouad Georges, b. 8 June 1947, Cairo. Hd Personal Office, Services in Economical Conslt & Editing. *Education:* St Georges Coll, Cairo, 1954-56; Coll Sacre Coeur, 1956-59; Switzerland Inst, Blinds in Lauanne, 1959-63; Sch of Commerce, 1963-67. *Appointments:* Univ Asst, Lausanne, 1970-73; Co editor in Mktg Maz, 1973-78; Staff Econmonst Economical, Financial Studies, 1978-88. *Publication:* Better Understandin of Economy; Murger as Managment Tool. *Memberships:* Jr Chamber Internat; Senator, Chapter Lausanne, Switzerland; Intl Assn French Speaking Economists. *Honours:* Award in Econmoics Discipline; Award of Nat President Switzerland; Senat Membership; JCI Switzerland Award; Special Congratulations form the Jury. *Hobbies:* Walking; Tandem Biking; Music; Theatre; Gastronomy. *Address:* Redaction et Conseil Economiques, 2 Ch de Verdonnet, CH 1010 Lausanne, Switzerland. 52.

CHAO Yunyu, b. 1 Feb 1916, Langzhong, Sichuan, China. Vice Dir, Sichuan Research Inst, Painting &

Calligraphy. m. DiShu Yan, 8 June 1935, 4 s, 3 d. *Education:* Consistent Self Educ; Famous Artist Dagian Chang. *Appointments:* Tchr, Middle Sch for History, Chinese, Art, 1939-44; Prof Chinese Painting, Mingyun, 1945; Sichuan Museum, 1952-76. *Creative Works:* YY ZHao's Painting Selection; YY Zhao's One Hundred Fan Surface Paintings; YY Zhao's Collection Paintings of Cats. *Memberships:* Chinese Research Inst of Calligraphy & Painting; Chinese Artise Assoc; Chinese Calligraphy Assoc; Chinese Poen Inst. *Honours:* First Grad CertJiannan Calligraphy; Golden Dragon Award. *Hobbies:* Fonding of Poem; Chinese Traditional Music; Playing Trad Instruments; Sward Dancing; Peiking opea. *Address:* Sichuan Museum, Chengdu, China 610041.

CHAPKANOV Georgy, b. 23 Jan 1943, Vulchi, Dol. Prof Fine Arts, Academy of Fine arts; Sculptor. m. Chapkanova Snegana, 21 Nov 1977, 2 s. *Education:* Sch for Fine Arts, Sofia, 1956-61; Academy of Fine Arts, Sofia, 1964-69. *Appointments:* Chief Artist, Ministry of Sci, Sofia, 1969-74; Lectr Drawing, Academy of Fine Arts, 1974-88. *Memberships:* Intl Foundation Humor for Nations. *Honours:* Golden Aesop; Marke Martov; Grand Prix for Sculptor on Sports Thematic; 3d Roden Grand Prix. *Hobby:* Hunting. *Address:* bul Makedonia no.29, 1606 Sofia, Bulgaria.

CHAPMAN Colin, b. 3 Apr 1935, Kingston Upon Hull, England. Schoolmaster; Lilac Grower & Breeder. m. Shelagh Margaret McCann, 29 Sept 1962, 1 s. *Education:* Malet Lambert High Sch, Kingston upon Hull; Keele Univ, BA, 1957; Cam Inst of Educ, 1977; Univ of East Anglia, MA, 1983. *Appointments:* Prospecting Geologist NCB Opencast Exec, 1957-60; Schoolmaster, Mathematics, 1960-; Asst Chief Exam, 1967-70; Sci Advisor, Suffolk County Council, 1976-91. *Creative Works:* Trumpet Player Blackshaw's New Orleans Jazz Band; Quarterley Journal Intl Lilac Soc. *Memberships:* MCC; Intl Lilac Soc; Royal Horticultural Soc; Arboricultural Assoc. *Hobbies:* Cricket; Early 20th Century Popular Music; New York Humour; Oak Furniture; Trout Fishing; Real Educ; Growing Antique Fruit; Devel the Pan Meadow Hist & Intl Lilac Colection. *Address:* Norman's Farm, Mill Road, Wyverstone, Stowmarket, Suffolk IP14 4SF, England.

CHAPMAN John Newton, b. 21 Nov 1947, Sheffield, England. Prof Physics, Glasgow Univ. m. 23 Sept 1972, 1 s, 1 d. *Education:* King Edward VII Sch, Sheffield, 1959-65; St Johns Coll, Cambridge Univ, MA, 1966-69; Cambridge Univ, PhD, 1969-72. *Appointments:* Research Fellow, Fitzwilliam Coll, Cambridge Univ, 1971-74; Lectr, Reader, Sub Prof, Glasgow Univ, 1974-. *Publications:* Sci Papers; Quantitative Electron Microscopy. *Memberships:* Inst of Physics; Royal Microscopical Soc; Inst of Electl and Electncs Engrs. *Honours:* Fellow of Royal Soc of Edinburgh. *Hobbies:* Photography; Walking; Racquet Sports. *Address:* Dept of Physics and Astronomy, Univ of Glasgow, Glasgow, G12 8QQ, Scotland.

CHAPPELL Miles Linwood, b. 6 June 1939, Norfolk, Virginia, USA. Art Hist; Prof. 1 s, 2 d. *Education:* BS Chemistry, Coll of William & Mary, 1960; PhD Art & Hist, Univ of North Carolina, 1971. *Appointments:* US Navy, Lieutenant, 1960-65; Coll of William & Mary, 1971-. *Publications:* Co Author, Disegni dec Toscani a Roma, Florence, 1979; Form, Function & Finesse: Drawings from the Hermun Coll, 1983; Cristofano Allori Florence, 1984; Disegni di Lodovico Cigoli, Florence, 1992; Cigoli tra manierismo e barocco, Florence, 1992; Articles on Art. *Memberships include:* Kunsthistorisches Inst, Florence; Phi Beta Kappa Soc; South eastern Coll Art Assoc; Interlochen Centre for the Arts, Art Advisory Board. *Honours:* Phi Beta Kappa Soc Award; Numerous grants. *Hobbies:* Paintings; Drawing; Music. *Address:* Dept of Fine Arts, Coll of William & Mary, Williamsburg, VA 23185, USA. 2, 13, 139.

CHARLTON Clive Arthur Cyril, b. 30 Sept 1932, Surrey, England. Surgeon. m. Jennifer Sheelagh Price, 9 July 1960, 3 s, 1 d. *Education:* Kings Coll, Taunton, 1946-51; St Bartholomews Hosp Medical Coll, 1952-58; MB, BS, FRCS, MS. *Appointments:* Research Fellow, Univ of Kentucky, USA, 1965-66; Conslt Urological Surgeon, St Barholomews Hosp, London, 1968-72; Royal United Hosp, Bath, 1972-. *Publications:* Urological System; Chapters in Urological & Medical Hist Books. *Memberships:* Royal Soc of Medicine; Council of British Assoc of Urological Surgeons. *Honours:* Asst Editor, British Journal of Urology; Court of Examinations, Royal Coll of Surgeons of England. *Hobbies:* Golf; Theatre; Biographies; Medical Hist. *Address:* Radford Villa, Timsbury, Nr Bath, BA3 1QF, England.

CHARLTON Thomas Alfred Graham, b. 29 Aug 1913, Purley, Surrey, England. Retired Civil Servant. m. Margaret Ethel Furst, 22 June 1940, 3 d. *Education:* Rugby Sch, 1927-31; Corpus Christi Coll, Cambridge, 1932- 35; BA Modern Languages, 1935. *Appointments:* Asst Principal War Office, 1936; Asst Private Sec, Sec of State for War, 1937-39; Principal, 1939; Cabinet Office, 1947-49; Sec NATO Council, 1950-52; Command Sec BADR, 1952-55;Sec, Ministry of Defence, 1960-73; Sec Federation, 1973-84. *Honours:* CB. *Hobbies:* Golf; Gardening. *Address:* Victoria House, Elm Road, Penn, Bucks HP10 8LO, England. 1.

CHARTERS D'AZEVEDO Ricardo Manuel, b. 29 July 1942, Lisboa, Portugal. Hd of Div Educ & Training for Technological Change; Manag Bd of the European Centre for the Development of Vocational Training CEDEFOP, Berlin. m. Helena, 3 Oct 1970. *Education:* Univ Degree, Electronics & Telecommunications Engr, Tech Univ Lisbon, 1970; Masters Degree, 1970. *Appointments include:* Tchr Sec Tech Sch, Lisbon, 1969-71; Univ Researcher, Portuguese Nat Inst of Cientific Research, 1970-78; Deputy Dir Gen, Higher Educ Portuguese Ministry of Educ, 1978-83; Dir Gen Studies & Planning Office, Ministry of Educ Portugal, 1983-88; Portuguese Educ Reform Comm, 1986-88; Hd of Div, Educ & Training New Tech, CEC, 1988-. *Publications include:* Sistemas de Segunda Ordem, Resposta no Tempo e na Frequencia; Acesso ao Ensino Superior guia do Estudante; Guia do Ensino Superior; A Legistlacao do Ensino Superior Politecnico. *Memberships:* Statistical Adviser Body Portuguese Ministry of Educ; Portuguese Nat Body; Interministerial Employment Comm; Portuguesse Nat Comm for Planning; Schools Network Planning Body. *Honours:* Portuguesse Honors & Awards. *Address:* Commision of the European Communities, Task Force Human Resources Education, Training & Youth, Rue de la Loi 200, B 1049 Brussel, Belguim.

CHATTOPADHYAY Ashoke, b. 15 Sept 1943, Singur, Hooghly, WB. Service. m. Rina, 6 Dec 1977, 1 s, 1 d. *Education:* BA, CU, 1967. *Appointments:* Calcutta Docklabour Bd, 1971-. *Publications:* Elokacha Kachi; Uttartirisha Essay; Samudrik Nonagandha; Kabba Sankalan; Apar Opar Kichu kabita; Ed & Publisher, Godhulimome: A Bengali Literary Monthly, 1958-. *Memberships:* All India Small & Medium Newspaper Assoc; Press Council of India; Little maz Editors Assoc; Waist Pir Memorial Assoc; Press Club, Calcutta. *Honours:* Inst de Chandannagore; Bharat Chadra Library; Nikhil Banga Sahitya Sammelon; Young Writers at Togore Castle; Uttar Probashi Award. *Hobbies:* Gardening; Reading; Music. *Address:* 40 Banerjee Para, Barasat, PO Chandanmagore 712136, Dist Hooghly, W. Bengal, India.

CHATTOPADHYAY Gouranga P, b. 29 Apr 1931, Calcutta. Organization Conlt. m. Arati Roy, 14 Feb 1954, 3 s. *Education:* BSc, 1952; MSc, 1954; PhD, 1960. *Appointments:* Anthropological Survey of India, Snt Tech Asst, 1955; Research Assoc, 1956; Lectr Sociology, Delhi Sch of Econ, 1960-62; Urban Sociologist, Calcutta Metropolitan Planning Org, 1962-63; Leverhulme Fellow, Univ Coll of Swansea, 1963-

64; Prof Behavioural Sci, Indian Inst of Mngt, Calcutta, 1964-91; Visiting Snr Lectr, Manchester Business Sch, 1970-72; UNDP Advisor Modern Mgmt Techs, East Africa, 1976-78. *Honours:* Sir Asutosh Memorial Prize; Univ Prize, Univ Gold Medal; Sarat Mitra Gold Medal. *Hobbies:* Making Walking Sticks; Translating Bengali Literature into English; Writing Letters. *Address:* 2 Palm Place, Calcutta 700019, India. 93, 139, 156.

CHAU Raymond Ming-Wah, b. 28 Nov 1946, Hong Kong. Univ Prof. m. Rebecca Chan-Mui Ng, 27 Dec 1972, 1 d. *Education:* BSc, Microbiology and Chem, CA State Univ, Fresno, 1971; PhD, Cellular and Molecular Biology, Univ TX Hlth Science Ctr, Dallas (The Southwestern Med Schl), 1976. *Appointments:* Rsch Fellow, Pathology, Harvard Med Schl, 1977-78; Vis Assoc Scientist in Pathology, Nat Cancer Inst, NIH, Bethesda, MD, 1979; Lectr in Anatomy, Univ of Hong Kong, 1980-; Vis Prof in Histology and Embryology, Guangxi Med Univ, Nanning, People's Repub of China, 1985; Vis Scientist in Biochem, Biology, Cell Biology, Shanghai Inst of Cell Biology, Univ CA, San Diego Biology Dept. *Publications:* Over 60 publs on immunology and neuronotrophic factors. *Memberships:* Alumni Mbr, NIH, USA; Life Mbr, NY Acad of Sciences; Life Mbr, Soc of Chinese Bioscientists in America; Int Brain Rsch Org, France; American Soc for Cell Biology; Hong Kong Soc of Neurosciences; Soc for Neuroscience, USA; Trustee and Mbr, Asian-Pacific Org for Cell Biology, Japan. *Honour:* Honorary Lecturer, Fudan lectures in Neurobiology, Shanghai, 1990. *Hobbies:* Reading, Sports, Photography, Antiques Collections. *Address:* Department of Anatomy, University of Hong Kong, 5 Sassoon Road, Pokfulam, Hong Kong. 139, 152.

CHAUHAN Jagadish Narabheram, b. 8 Feb 1950, Belur Karnataka. Engr, RF Antenna Designer. m. Rekha, 20 Nov 1984, 1 d. *Education:* Bach of Engr, 1972; Diploma in Business Mgmt, 1984. *Appointments:* Engr, MS Kadevi Engg Co, Hyderabad, 1975-79; Tchnical Mgr, Electronics Cop, 1979-. *Membership:* Inst of Engr Hyderabad; The Planetary Society, USA. *Hobbies:* Reading Hindu Literature as Humanist; Watching Ameture TV. *Address:* 5 2 12 hyderbasti, GND Floor, Opp Jabbar Complex, Secunderabad 500 003, India.

CHAVARRIA Ernest M. *Education:* Grad, Univ of Texas, Austin, BBA; MBA. *Appointments:* Pres, Chief Exec Officer, ITBR, A World Trade & Business Conslt Co, Auston, Texas, 1976-; Over 19 yrs Hands on Ext as Conslt in, Business, Intl Trade, Finance, Mngt, Strategic Mktg, Investments, Business Devel. *Memberships include:* Small Business Admin Advisory Council; Texas Business Council; TEXAS; Austin Chamber of Commerce Sml Business Council; Austin Metropolitan YMCA; US SBA/San Antonio District Intl Trade Task Force. *Honours:* SBA Minority Advicate of the Year; SBA Exporter of the Year; Regional Public Speaking Award; American Award; Intl Award for Good Service and Quality; Forum of Distinguished Americans Award; Top 100 Most Influentials in USA, Hispanic Bus Mag. *Address:* 1250 Capital of Texas Highway South, Two Cielo Centre, Third Floor, Austin, TX 78746, USA. 7, 132, 139.

CHAWLA Shanti L, b. 26 Oct 1936, Lahore. Medicl Doc. m. 12 May 1967, 2 d. *Education:* BSc, 1957; LSMF, 1963; MBBS, 1966; DMRT, 1972. *Appointments:* Conslt, Clinical Dir, Radiothesapy Oncology, 1980-; Clinical Lectr, Radiotherapy, Newcastle Univ; Asst Surgeon, Delhi Central Govt; Reg in Radiotheraphy, Cookridge Hosp, Leeds; Snr Reg, Radiotheraphy, Clatterbridge Hosp, Bebington Wirral. *Publications:* Articles in Medical Journals. *Memberships:* BMA; BAO; RCR; MAC, Drug & Therapy; Indian Assoc; Hindu Cultural Soc; Middlesbrough & Cleveland County Panels. *Honours:* Fellowship, Radiotheraphy & Oncology; Gold Award, North Reg Health Auth, 1990; Bronze Medallion, Medical Community Award, ABI, Newcastle, 1991. *Hobbies:* Badminton; Dancing; Golf;

Music; Jogging. *Address:* South Cleveland Hospital, Marton Road, Middlesbrough, TS15 4BW, England. 1.

CHECKLAND Sarah Jane, b. 14 June 1954, Cambridge, England. Art Market Correspondent, The Times. *Education:* The Mount Sch, York, 1969- 72; Univ of East Anglia, 1973-76; BA in Fine art. *Appointments:* London Tour Guide, Nightclub Singer, 1976-78; Deputy Editor, Homes & Jobs Mag 1979; The Press Officer, Nat Gallery, 1979-83; Art Critic, Sunday Today, 1986; Times Galleries Correspondant, 1984-86; Art Critic, London Daily News, 1986-87; Art Market Correspondant, The Times, 1987-. *Hobbies:* Music; Art. *Address:* 12 Highbury Grange, London, N5 2PX, England.

CHELES Luciano, b. 7 Sept 1948, Cairo, Egypt. Univ Lectr. *Education:* BA, French and Italian, Reading Univ, 1973; PGCE, Cardiff Univ, 1974; MPhil, Hist of Art, Essex Univ, 1980; PhD, Lancaster Univ, 1992. *Appointments:* Lectr in Italian Studies, Lancaster Univ, 1978-. *Publications:* The Studiolo of Urbino: An Iconographic Investigation, 1986, Italian transl, 1991; Neo-Fascism in Europe, Co-Ed, 1991; sev articles on italaian Renaissance Art and Contemporary Propaganda. *Memberships:* Soc of Italian Studies; Istituto di studi Rinascimentali (Ferrara); Assn for the Study of Modern Italy; Soc for Renaissance Studies. *Hobbies:* Travel, Art and Design, Cinema, Classical Music. *Address:* Italian Studies, Department of Modern Languages, Lonsdale College, Lancaster University, Lancaster LA1 4YN, England. 3, 30, 139.

CHEN Bing Cong, b. 10 Oct 1921, Shandong, China. Prof. m. 20 July 1948, 1 s, 2 d. *Eduction:* BE, Northwestern Univ of Tech, Peiyang Univ, China, 1943; ME, AE, Mechanical Sch of China Airforce, 1945; MA, AE, Mechanical Sch of US Airforce, Snr Class, 1947. *Appointments:* Assoc Prof, Hd of Auto Vehicle Dept, Shandong Univ of Tech, 1949-55; Prof, Vice Pres of Jilin Univ of Tech, 1955-87. *Publications:* Therory of Tractor; Mechanics of Soil Vehicle System; Theory and Design of Walking Vehicle; Thesis about Tractor & Walking Mechanisum. *Memberships:* The Soc of Agriclt Engr of PRC; The Engr Group of the Comm of Academic Degree of PRC; Intl Soc for Terrain Vehicle System; Asian Assoc for Agricultureal Engr. *Honours:* Half Walking Wheel of the Paddy Field Award; Mechanical Walking Wheel of Paddy Field; Gold Price, Intl Inventive Exhibition, Montorea, Canada. *Hobbies:* Music, Classical, Symphony, Chinese Opera. *Address:* College Agricultural Machinery, Jilin Univ of Technology, Changchun, Jilin 130025, China.

CHEN Bing Fu, b. 10 Dec 1920, Anhui Province, China. Academic Chmn of Dept, Dir of Research Centre, Naukai Univ. m. Tsai, Mai Ru, 31 Dec 1948, 2 s. *Education:* Foreign Language Dept, Zhejiang Univ, 1940-41; Dept of Ecenomics, South West Assoc, 1941-45. *Appointments include:* Tchr, Research, Nankai Univ, 1940-50; Research, Economic Efficiency, How to Maximize useful output while minimizing labour & capital costs, 1950's; Research, Evolution & Development of the Philosophies & Thoughts of Chinese Mgmt, 1984. *Publications include:* Research on the Index Number Theory with Respect to the Relation, Complication & Establishing Methods & Demonstration of the Formula; Sino European Technological & Ind Policies; Papers on Science Technology & Ecnomic Development. Applied Economic Efficiency; Management of Tourism; Marketing Management. *Memberships:* Intl Journal of Research in Marketing; Nankai Canadian Studies Centre; China Nat Foundation of Natural Sci; EMAC. *Honours:* Distinguished Citizen of Tianjin City; Person of Achievement of Modern China; Distinguished Scholars of Auhui Province. *Hobbies:* Western Classical Music; Chinese Traditional Calligraphy; Chinese Traditional Poetry. *Address:* Dept of Management, Nankai Univ, Tianjin 300071, China. 139, 152.

CHEN Chang Shu, b. 8 July 1932, Shanghai, China. Tchr, Vice Dean of Grad of Northeast Univ of Tech. m. Luo Qian, 30 Sept 1956, 2 d. *Education:* Northeast Univ of Tech, 1950-54; Chinese People's Univ, 1954-56. *Appointments:* Northeast Univ of Tech, 1956-. *Publications:* Progress of Nature Sciences & Epistemology; History of Sci & Tech; On Technology; On Choice of Tech; A Course in Philosophy of Sci and Tech. *Memberships:* Inst of Tech and Phil; NEUT; China Soc of Philosophy of Nature, Sci & Tech; Liaoning Research Soc of Phil of Nature Sci & Tech. *Honours:* Academic Evaluation Group; Prof Chinese People's Univ; 1st Award of the Social Sci Research, Liaoning & Shenyang; Advanced Worker. *Hobbies:* Music; Stamp Collecting. *Address:* Inst of Tech & Sci, Northeast Univ of Tech, Liaoning, Shenyang 110006, China.

CHEN Chang, b. 26 Mar 1929, Shanghai. Surgeon. m. Wenwei Liu, 3 Aug 1962, 2 d. *Education:* Premedical Courses, St Johns Univ, Shanghai, BS Biology, 1945-49; St Johns Univ Medical Sch, 1950-54. *Appointments:* Surgeon, Tianjin Second Central Hosp, 1954-66; Surgeon in Charge, Tianjin North Suburban Hosp, 1966-79; Chief Surgeon, Tianjin Nankai Hosp, 1979-92. *Publications:* A Guide to Reading Medical Literature in English; Practice in Abdominal Surgery. *Memberships:* Tianjin Surgical Soc; All China Transfusion Assoc; Tianjin Medical Journal; Tianjin Journal of Traditional Chinese Medicine; China Acupunture Assoc. *Hobby:* Photography. *Address:* Tianjin Nankai Hospital, Intl of Acute Abdominal Diseases, 122 Sanwei Road, Nankai District, Tianjin 300100, China.

CHEN Chin, b. 15 Apr 1927, Foochow, China. Prof. m. Concordia Chad, 2 July 1960, 1 s, 2 d. *Education:* Nat Tai Won Univ, 1951; BS, Wayne State Univ, Michigan, 1956; MS, PhD, Boston Univ, Massachussetts. *Appointments:* Research Assoc, Lawont Doherty Geological Observatory, Columbia Univ, 1962-69; Western Connecticut State Univ, Prof, Coordinator of Grad Program of Earth Sci, 1969-. *Publications:* Stratigraphy, Paleogeography and Techonics; Geology of China Seas; Stratigraphy & Tectonics of China. *Memberships:* Geological Soc of America; Geological Soc of China; American Assoc for the Advancement of Sci. *Honour:* Solio Scholarship Award. *Hobby:* Travel. *Address:* Graduate Programe Of Oceanography & Limnology, Western Connecticut State Univ, Danbury, CT 06810, USA. 143.

CHEN Chun Jung, b. 28 Sept 1959, Chia Yah, Taiwan. Gen Editor, Rock Publishing Intl. *Education:* Dept of Political Sci, Nat Cheng Chi Univ, 1978-82; Grad Sch of Political Sci, MA, Nat Cheng Chi Univ, 1984-87. *Appointments:* Editor, China Times, 1987-89; Vice Gen Editor, Laureate Book Co, 1984-89; Chief Editor, China Times Publishing Co, 1989-92; Lectr, Coll of Medic ine, Fu Jen Univ, 1991-. *Publications:* Study of Justice Conference; Postmodern Syndrome; Image Society; Drinking a Cup of Soul Calling Wine; SL and Purple Notebook. *Membership:* Phi Tau Phi Scholastic Honor Soc. *Honours:* Outstanding Thesis for Masters Degree. *Hobbies:* Reading; Watching Video Tapes; Collecting Classical Films; Sing in the KTV; Travel. *Address:* 5F, 53, Min Lih Street, Chung-ho City, Taipei County, Taiwan, China.

CHEN Chung Yi, b. 11 Mar 1942, Taitung, Taiwan, China. Prof. m. Ying Ying Chen, 4 ch. *Education:* MBA, Waseda Univ, Tokyo, Japan, 1970; Doc, Bus Admin, John Dewey Univ Consort, 1992; Doc of Laws, The London Inst, Appl Rsch. *Appointments:* Certiified Securities Analyst; Prof, Grad Sch of Bus, Nat Chung-Shiun Univ; Chmn, Lai Lai Securities Investment Conslt Co Ltd; Chmn, Chung Lai Investment Mngt Conslt Co Ltd; Chmn, Chung Hui Securities Mag Co; Chmn, Chung Lu Investment Co Ltd. *Publication:* Securities Investment & Tech Analysis, 1979. *Memberships:* Dir, Securities Investment Trust & Advisory Assoc of Taipai, 1989; Baron, Royal Ord Boh Crown; Cmdr, Knight Lofsensic Ursinius Ord; Knight of the Templars; Hon Prof of Inst

De Doc Et D'EtuDes EuROPÉENNes; E Dir, Asian Am Rep Nat Fed (Taiwan Chap), 1992. *Honours:* Edison Award for Excellent Youth in Sci; Chia-Hsin Prize for Outstanding Pub, 1979; Attended Bush Breakfast Prayers, White House. *Hobbies:* Investment; Swimming; Writing. *Address:* Lai Lai Securities Investment Advisory Co, 4th Fl, no.111, Sec 2, Nan King E Road, Taipei 10409, Taiwan, China. 152.

CHEN Cimao, b. 8 Dec 1929, Shanghai. Pres, Snr Fellow, Shanghai Inst for Intl Studies. m. Shao Yuehua, 1 May 1958, 1 d. *Education:* Dept of Commerce & Ind, Gein Nan Univ, 1947-48; Grad, Dept of Chemistry, Shanghai Jiao Tong Univ, 1948-52. *Appointments:* Sec, Shanghai Municipal Comm of China Communist Youth League, 1962-66; Snr Fellow, Foreign Affairs Office, Shanghai Municipal Government, 1972-78; Sec, Shanghai Municipal Comm, China Communist Youth League, 1978-81; Pres, Snr Fellow, Shanghai Inst for Intl Studies, 1981-91. *Publications:* Survey of Intl Affairs; World Outlook; War and Peace, A New Reappraisal. *Memberships:* Shanghai Assoc of Intl Relations; Shanghai Centre of Intl Studies. *Hobbies:* Classical Music; Travel. *Address:* 1 Lane 845, Julu Road, Shanghai 200040, China. 139, 152.

CHEN Cong Yun, b. 18 Dec 1936, Sichuan Prov. Sedimeto Tectonics. m. 5 Feb 1962, 1 s, 1 d. *Education:* Grad, Chongquing Univ, 1956. *Appointments:* Sedim Deposits, CAGS, 1956-61; Sedimentology & Sedim Deposits, 1962-83; IGMR, Shenyang, Plate Tectonic & Sedimentation, Sedimento Tectonics, IGMR, 1983-. *Publications:* 28 Papers, Phospherite Desposits; Geolo of Cont Marg; The Discovery of Ophiolite and Fossil Zone; Sed and Maching Tectonic; The Cont Tec Geol in N. China. *Memberships:* Geological Soc of China; Shenyang Inst of Geology & Mineral Resources. *Hobbies:* Music; Reading. *Address:* Shenyang Inst of Geology & Mineral Resources, no.25 Beiling St, 11032 Shenyang, China.

CHEN Dai Sun, b. 20 Oct 1900, Foochow, China. Prof of Econs, Peking University, China. *Education:* BA Univ WI, USA, 1922; MA 1924, PhD 1926, Harvard Univ, USA. *Appointments:* Prof of Econs, Tsing-Hua Univ, 1929-52; Prof of Econs, SW Univ, 1937-45; Prof of Econs, Peking Univ, 1954-. *Publications:* From Classical School of Econ to Karl Marx, 1981; Selected Works, 1989. *Memberships:* Beijing Econs Assn; Western Econs Thought Assn. *Address:* School of Economics, Peking University, Beijing, China.

CHEN De Kun, b. 5 Dec 1933, China. Vice Pres of Shanhai Inst of Urban Const; Prof. *Education:* Undergrad, Tsinghua Univ, China, 1951-55; Postgrad, Tong Ji Univ, Shanghai, 1955-58. *Appointments:* Mathematical Tchr, Bei Jing Coll of Constr Ind, 1958-79; Mech Tchr, SIUC, 1979-; Snr Visiting Scholar, NJIT, USA, 1988-90. *Publications:* Study of the Crack Resistance of Waterproof Coating; Restrained & Non Restrained Deformation of Visco Elastic Bodies; Theoretical Model for Vacuum Absorption of Felt. *Memberships:* Royal Soc of Chemical Ind of UK; Shanghai Branch of Mathematical Soc of China; Shanghai Branch of Mech Soc of China. *Honours:* A Study of Crack Resistance etc, Reputed as one of two must execelent these among symposing. *Hobbies:* Literature; Poems; Table Tennis; Chinese Chess. *Address:* Shanghai Inst of Urban Construction, 71 Chi Feng Road, Shanghai 200092, China.

CHEN Guanlie, b. 22 Dec 1920, Chaoyang, Guangdong, China. Prof of Econs, Fudan Univ, Shanghai, China. m. Qin Yanan, 31 Aug 1947, 1 s, 1 d. *Education:* BA, Econs, Ctrl Univ, Chungking, 1942; MA, Econs, Harvard Univ, USA, 1947. *Appointments:* Fellow, Inst of Econ Rsch, Nat Resources Commn, Nanjing, 1947-48; Prof of Econs 1948-, Dean, Schl of Econs, 1985-87, Fudan Univ, Shanghai; Vis Prof of Econ, OH Univ, USA, 1989. *Publications:* Industrial Economics, 1965; Co-author, World Economics, 1983; Co-author, Contemporary

Western Econ Thoughts, 1986; Outlines of Western Monetary Theories and Financial Policies. *Memberships:* Bd of Execs, Soc of World Economy, China; Hon Mbr of Bd, Chinese Fin Assn; Advsr, Soc of Int Trade, China. *Honours:* Distinguished Teacher, Shanghai, 1985; Prize for Excellent Teaching Achievements, Shanghai, 1989. *Hobbies:* Swimming; Table Tennis; Travelling. *Address:*)School of Economics, Fudan University, 220 Handan Road, Shanghai 200433, China.

CHEN Guorui, b. 23 Aug 1936, Jiangsu. Prof Microwaves & Electromagnetics. m. Chunhui Li, 14 Feb 1961, 2 s, 1 d. *Education:* Eastern China Inst of Aeronautics, 1955-56; Northwestern Poly Univ, 1956-60; Diploma Electronic Eng, 1960; Advanced Study Univ of Sheffield, England, 1966-67. *Appointments:* Deputy Hd, Research & Teaching Sec, Microwaves, 1962-65, 1974-78; Deputy Dir, Univ Office, Intl Exchange Affairs, 1979-83; Vice Chmn, Dept Electronic Eng, 1983-87; Prof, 1988-. *Publications:* Ultrahigh Frequency Techniques; Solutions to Engineering Electromagnetic Fields & Waves; Papers on MM Wave Measurements, Microwave Control Devices, Antennas. *Memberships:* Chinese Soc of Electrostatics; Electromagnetic Metrology Group; Soc of Electronics Educ Shaanxi Prov; Reviewers, Nat Natural Sci Foundation of China; Aeronautic Sci Foundation of China. *Hobby:* Reading on History. *Address:* Dept of Electronic Eng, Northwestern Poly Univ, Xi'an 710072, Shaanxi Prov, China.

CHEN Hanping, b. 23 Nov 1937, Fujian Prov. Medicine; Acupuncture. m. Cao Cui-e, 1 Feb 1966, 2 s. *Education:* Shanghai Coll of Traditional Medicine, 1957-63; Diploma Paris Univ, Necker Hospital Nephrological Clinic, 1979-81. *Appointments:* Dr Shanghai Longhau Hosp, 1963-72; Dr Chinese Medical Team, Algeria, 1972-74; Dir, Shanghai Research Inst of Acupuncture & Medicine, 1981-91. *Publications:* Acupunture Therapeutics; Approach to the Method of Thinking Acupunture Immunological Research. *Memberships:* Chinese Acupuncture Assoc; Chinese Experimental Acupuncture Soc; Shanghai Acupuncture Soc; Who Collaborating Centre for Traditional Medicine. *Honours:* Clinical Effect and Immunological Mechanism of Moxibustion Treatment of Hashimotos Disease; British Acupuncture Soc; Argentine Acupuncture Assoc. *Hobbies:* Sports; Chinese Handwriting. *Address:* Shanghai Research Inst of Acupuncture & Meridian, 650 South Wanping Road, Shanghai 200030, China.

CHEN Hao Zhu, b. 6 Nov 1924, Guangdong, China. Prof of Medicine; Dir of Inst; Medical Doctor. m. Huei Hua Han, 5 Feb 1956, 1 s, 1 d. *Education:* Nat Chung Cheng Medical Coll, MD, 1949; Zhong Shan Hosp, Nat Shanghai Med Coll, 1948-49; Red Cross Soc First Hosp, 1949-53; Cardiology, Medical Sch of Chinese Academy of Medical Sci, 1957. *Appointments:* Chief, Dept of Cardiology, Zhong Shan Hosp, 1972-88; Assoc Prof of Med, Zhong Shan Hosp, Shanghai Med Univ, 1978-80; Deputy Dir, Shanghai Inst of Cardiovasc Diseases, 1978-84; Prof of Med, Shanghai Med Univ, 1980-; Dir Shanghai Inst of Cardiovasc Diseases, 1984-; Assoc Chief, Nat Med J Chin, 1981-; Chin J Card, 1988-; Chin J Int Med, 1990-. *Publications:* 248 Papers Chinese Med Journals, American & European Med Journals; 7 Books, Internal Medicine, Cardiology, Cardiac Catheterization, Electrocardiography. *Memberships:* Expert Advisory Panels of World Health Organ; The North American Soc of Pacing & Electrophysiology; The New York Academy of Sci; The Intl Soc of Cardiovascular Pharmacotherapy; Exec Comm of the Chinese Soc of Cardiovascular Diseases; Exec Comm of the Chinese Soc of Intl Medicine. *Honours:* Outstanding Research Work Award; Excellent Med Article Award; First Prize of Technical Advance, The Ministry of Health; Third Prize of Research Achievement; Distinguished Tchr Award; Third Prize of Sci and Technical Advance. *Hobbies:* Reading; Light Music; Travel. *Address:* Zhong Shan Hospital of Shanghai Medical Univ, 136 Yi Xie Yuan Road, Shanghai 200032, China. 139.

CHEN Heng Hong, b. 30 Oct 1937, Ganzhou, Jiangxi, China. Tchr; Prof. m. Xiao Hui Zhang, 1 Oct 1965, 3 d. *Education:* Zauho Elementary Sch, 1943-49; Ganzhou Middle Sch, 1949-55; Univ Tsinhau, Mech Engr, 1955-61; Univ Siegen, Visiting Scholar, 1981-83. *Appointments:* Inst of Aeronautical Matericals Beizing Tech, 1961-69; Compressor Plant Jiangxi Tech, 1969-73; Inst of Metallurgy, Jiangxi, Lectr, 1973-86; Inst of Metallurgy South, Prof, 1986-91. *Publications:* A Summary of Manufacturing Tech in Air Colled Gas Turhine Blade; A Comprehensive English-Chinese Dictionary of Metallurgical Industry; non Ferrous Metal Progress; A Study of Deformation in High Pressure Flange. *Memberships:* Chinese Assoc of Non Ferrous Metal; The Chinese Assoc of Mechanics. *Honours:* Second Prize Advance in Sci & Tech; Prize of Scientific Comm in Chinese Nat Defence. *Hobbies:* Football; Fishing; Tour; Classicl Music; Foreign Languages. *Address:* Dept of Electrical and Mechanical Engineering, Beijing Univ of Iron and Steel (Branch), Beijing, 10041, China. 139, 152.

CHEN Jian Hong, b. 13 Mar 1937, Hangzhou, Zheijiang, China. Engr; Educator. m. 1 May 1977, 1 d. *Education:* Grad 6 yr Course, 1961; 4 yr Course, 1967; Quing Hua Univ Beijing. *Appointments:* Asst Prof, Beijing Inst of Machinery, 1961-63; Instr, 1968; Assoc Prof, 1978; Prof, 1987-; Pres, 1986-; Gansu Univ of Technology. *Publications include:* 20 Tech Papaers, Micro Fracture Behaviour Induced by M A Constituent in Simulated Welding HAZ of HSLA Steel; Hygiene & Safety. *Memberships:* China Welding Inst. *Honours:* Named Nat Expert, State Comm of Sci & Tech. *Hobbies:* Reading; Singing; Table Tennis. *Address:* Gansu Univ of Tech, Lanzhou Gansu, China.

CHEN Jianhua, b. 16 July 1947, Shanghai, China. Poet, Scholar of Chinese Lit and Culture. m. Wei-Xing Wang, 26 Apr 1981, 1 s. *Education:* MA, Chinese Lit 1982, PhD, Chinese Lit, 1988, Fudan Univ, Shanghai, China. *Appointments:* Tchr, Coll of Liberal Arts, Shanghai Univ, 1982-85; Lectr, Chinese Classics Rsch Inst, Fudan Univ, Shanghai, 1988-90; Vis Scholar, Univ CA Berkeley, USA, 1988-91. *Publications:* On Ming Poet Li Meng-Yang, 1986; On Late Qing Poetry Revolution, 1987; Elegy for June 4th Massacre, 1990; Poetry and Death, 1991; The Literature of Jiangsu and Zhejiang in the Ming Dynasty, 1991. *Memberships:* Ctr for Mod China, NY, USA: American Assn of Chinese Comparative Lit; Classical Drama Assn of China; American Assn for Asian Studies; Classical Lit Assn of China, Shanghai Br; Int Ctr for Asian Studies, Hong Kong. *Honours:* Academic Award, Fudan University, Shanghai, China, 1987; Zhao Jingshen Chinese Classics Award, Shanghai, China, 1988; Liang Shuh--Ch'iu Literary Award, Taipei, Taiwan, 1990. *Hobbies:* Chinese Calligraphy, Collecting Stamps, Reading. *Address:* 220 Miller Court, Santa Cruz, CA 95065, USA. 11, 139, 152.

CHEN Jichang, b. 2 Apr 1935, Zhejiang, Jiaxing, China. Geologist. m. Sun Cruilan, 1 Oct 1967, 1 s, 1 d. *Education:* Beijing Inst of Geology, 1956-61. *Appointments:* Regional Geological Survey, Beijing, 1961-62; Diamond Exam 7th Geological Brigade, 1962-87; 7th Geological Brigade Found Kimberlites, 1965; Snr Geological, Ministry of Geology & Mineral Resources, 1988; Sapphire Identification 7th Brigade, 1987-91; 7th Brigade Found Sapphire Deposite, 1988. *Publications:* Papers Diamond; Reconnaissance and Exploration of Diamonds; Papers Diamond Structure; Appoaches to Genesises of Wide Crystal Edge Diamonds; Diamond Crystal Forms and Thier Orientations of Hardness. *Memberships:* Geological Soc of Shandong; China Assoc for Gem Stones and Jade. *Honours:* Best Scientist Award. *Hobby:* Painting. *Address:* 7th Geological Brigade of Shandong Prov Bureau of Geology & Mineral Resources, China.

CHEN Jin, b. 26 Mar 1967, Hal'an, Jiangsu, China. Sales Exec. m. Ding Ju Xiang, 1 Oct 1991, 2 ch. *Education:* Grad, Jiangsu Foreign Trade Sch, 1984-86.

Appointments: Documentation Mgr, Jiang Su Minmetals, Jiangsu, Nanjing, 1986-87; Transportation Mgr, 1987-88; Rep, Jiangsu Minmetal, Frankfurt, Germany, 1989; Sales Mngr, Jiangsu Minmetals Grp, Nanjing, 1988, 1989-92; Snr Sales Mgr, 1992-. *Hobbies:* Geography; History; Biography. *Address:* 10 Xia Cha Villiage, Ying Xi Town, Hai An County, Jiangsu Prov, China.

CHEN Jiujin, b. 12 Dec 1939, Jiangsu, China. Assoc Dir, Inst of History for Nat Sciences, Academica Sinica. m. 10 Oct 1969, 1 s, 1 d. *Educations:* Grad, Astronomy Dept, Nanjin Univ, 1964. *Appointments:* History of Astronomy, Inst of History for Nat Sci, Chinese Academia of Nat Sci, 1964-. *Publications:* These on ten month solar calender of Yi Nationality; History of Astronomy in Yi Nationality; Sources of Festival; Study on the Calendar of Tibetan. *Memberships:* Soc for History of Sci & Tech in China; Chinese Astronomy Soc; Soc for History of Sci and Tech in the Minoriy Nationalities of China. *Honours:* Nat Sci award. *Address:* Inst of History of Nat Sci, Chinese Academy of Nat Sci, 137 Chao Nei Main Street, Beijing 100010, China.

CHEN Junming, b. 15 Mar 1937, Jingyang County, Shaanxi. Geologist; Snr Engr. m. Shuxian Qu, 15 Feb 1962, 2 s, 2 d. *Education:* Xian Geological Sch, 1954-57. *Appointments:* No.214 Geological Party, Shanxi Bureau of Geology & Mineral Resources, 1957-65; No.211 Geological Party, BGMR, Shanxi, 1965-85; Shanxi Inst of Geological Sci, 1985-. *Publications include:* Basis of Petrochemical Method; Mineral Resources in the Coal Measure Strata, Shanxi; Study of Geology of Gold Deposits in Archean Greenstone Belt; Depositional Conditions and Geochemistry of the Greenstone Type Stratabound Gold Deposits in Beishan Mountain, Lingqiu County, Shanxi. *Honours:* 4th Prize Paper, Mineral Resources on the Coal Measure Strata; 3rd Prize Study of Geology of Gold Deposites in Archean Greenstone Belt. *Hobby:* Reading. Address: Shanxi Inst of Geological Science, China.

CHEN Lai, b. 20 Aug 1952, Beijing. Prof. m. Yang Ying, 30 Apr 1981, 1 s. *Education:* BA, Central South Univ of Ind, 1976; MA, Peking Univ, Dept of Philosophy, 1981; PhD, Peking Univ, Dept of Philosophy, 1985. *Appointments:* Asst Prof, Peking Univ, 1981-85; Assoc Prof, Peking Univ, 1986-89; Prof, Peking Univ, 1990-. *Publications:* Research on Chu Hsis Philosophy; Chronological Dating Chu Hsis Letters; The Spirit of Wang Yang Mings Philosophy; Song Ming Neo Confucianism. *Memberships:* China Confucius Soc; Research Assoc of History of Chinese Philosophy; The Int Soc for Chinese Philosophy. *Hobbies:* Reading; Walking; Swimming. *Address:* Bld 21, Wei Xiu Yuan, Hai Dian, Beijing 100871, China.

CHEN Lingzhi, b. 20 Jan 1933, China. Prof of Plant Ecology, Inst of Botany. m. Qian Ying Qian, 28 Dec 1959, 1 s, 1 d. *Education:* Grad, Dept of Biology, Fu Den Univ, 1954. *Appointments:* Inst of Botany, Chinese Academy of Sci, 1954-79; Inst of Terrestrial Ecology, Merlewood Research Station, UK, 1979-81; Inst of Botany, CAS, 1981-86, Asst Prof, Prof, 1986-. *Publications:* Enviromental Contamination and Plants; Study of Biological Ecology in Beijing, Tinjing Region. *Memberships:* Inst of Botany CAS; Beijing Forest Ecosystem Research Station; Committee on Plant Ecology & Geobotany, Chinese Soc of Botany; Acta Phytoecologica et Geobotanica Sinica. *Honours include:* SCi & Tech Achievement First Award; Sci & Tech Achievement Second Award. *Hobby:* Reading. *Address:* 100044 Xizhimenwai Road, Inst of Botany, Chinese Academy of Sciences, Beijing, China.

CHEN Meidong, b. 19 Feb 1942, Fujian, China. Dir of Inst for Hist of Natural Sciences; Prof of Hist of Science. m. Yu Lishang, 4 Feb 1970, 1 d. *Education:* MS, Inst for Hist of Natural Sciences, Academia Sinica, 1967; BS, Dept of Astro-Geodetic Survey, Wuhan Inst of Survey and Drawing, 1964. *Appointments:* Probation

Rschr, 1967-78; Assoc Prof 1978-86, Dpty Dir 1986-88, Dir, Prof, 1988-, Inst for Hist of Natural Sciences, Beijing. *Publications:* Scientific Achievements in Ancient China, 1978; History of Astronomy in China, 1981; Stories of History of Science in China, 1990; More than 50 papers on the history of astronomy, calendars and science in China. *Memberships:* China Astronomy Soc; Int Soc for the Hist of E Asian Science, Technology and Med; China Soc of Hist of Science and Technology, V-Chmn of Coun; China Assn for Science and Technology, Comm Mbr. *Honour:* Five Writings including A draft of the History of Science and Technology in China co-authored with others have been awarded the National Prize for Excellent Publications in China. *Hobbies:* Reading, Listening to Music. *Address:* 137 Chaonei Avenue, Beijing 100010, China.

CHEN Min-Chu, b. 30 June 1949, Hsiang Hsiang, Hu Nan, China. Exec Vice Pres; Engr. m. Yuh Mei Chung, 1 Aug 1975, 2 s. *Education:* BS, Nat ocean & Marine Univ, 1971; MS, Nat Taiwan Univ, 1975; PhD, Oregon State Univ, 1979. *Appointments:* Snr Engr, Brown & Root Inc, Houston, 1978-80; Snr Research Engr, Exxon Prod Research Co, 1980-81; Snr Engr, Sonat Offshore Drilling Inc, 1981-85; Vice Pres, C & C Intl Services Inc, 1985-. *Publications:* 25 Technical Papers in Journals, Symposium. *Memberships:* ASME; Sigma Xi. *Hobbies:* Bridge; Reading. *Address:* 11427 Wickershaw, Houston, TX 77077, USA. 7, 132.

CHEN Qiang, b. 3 May 1942, China. Coll Tchr; Prof. m. Zhong Ren Huang, 8 Dec 1969, 1 s, 1 d. *Education:* Changsha No.11 Middle Sch, 1953-59; Bach Hunan Univ, 1959-64. *Appointments:* Tchr, Hunan Univ, 1964-83; Prof, Inst of Military Engr, Changsha, 1983-. *Creative Works include:* Compositions. A Method of Comparative Decision of Stability of Functional Differential Equations; The Method of Two V Functionals for the Asymptotic Stability; The Criterions of Stability of Functional Differential Equations; Razumikhin Type Theorems of Total Asymptotic Stability of Functional Differential Equations. *Membership:* Hunan Maths Academy. *Hobbies:* Reading; Appreciating Music; Drama. *Address:* Inst of Military Engr, Changsha, Hunan, China. 152.

CHEN Shiwen, b. 1 Mar 1934, Yuyao, Zhejiang Province, The People's Republic of China. Prof of Electronics. *Education:* Dept of Physics, Peking Univ, 1952-56; BSc and Dip of Physics, 1956. *Appointments:* Asst, Physics Dept 1956, Lectr of Geophysics Dept 1958, Assoc Prof, Geophysics Dept 1985, Prof, Geophysics Dept 1991-, Peking Univ. *Publications:* The Transient, 1981; The Foundations of Electronic Circuits, 1991; The Electronic Circuits in the Communication Systems (in press); num papers in the field of maths, geophysics, electronics and pedagogics. *Honours:* A Prize for the Chinese Handwriting National Competition, 1986; An Honour of the Excellent Teacher of Beijing City, 1989. *Hobbies:* Lit, Reading, Writing, Chinese Handwriting, Music, Playing Chinese Musical Instruments, Erhu, Bamboo Flute. *Address:* Department of Geophysics, Peking University, Beijing 100871, China.

CHEN Shiyi, b. 6 Apr 1937, Guangdong, China. Prof. m. Zhou Fang, 20 Jan 1966, 1 s, 2 d. *Education:* BS, Geology, Central South Univ of Tech, 1962. *Appointments:* Elemtary Research Fellow, Central South Inst of Geotectonics, 1962-72; Geology Engr, Hunan Bureau of Geology, 1972-79; Lect, Assoc Prof, Prof, CSUI, 1980-. *Publications:* Discovered a Large Gibbsite-Type Bauxite in Guixian, Guangxi; Essays, Mesco Cenozoic Napples ix Southwestern Hunan and Their Signicicance; Discovery and Significance of Gibbsite. *Memberships:* Geology Soc of China; Tectonic Special Comm of Hunan; Metal Soc of China; Hunan Soc of Mineralogy Petrology & Geochemistry; Standing Council of Diva Theory Soc of China. *Honours:* Excellent Tchr of Central South Univ of Tech; 1st, 3rd Prize Chen Guoda Diwa Theory Fund. *Hobbies:* Travel; Watching TV; Family. *Address:* Geology Dept of Central South Univ of Tech, Changsha, Hunan, China. 139.

CHEN Shu Lan, b. 2 Dec 1931, Chang Chun, China. Chief Physician; Prof; Coll Pres. m. Shan Li Liu, 4 May 1953, 1 s, 1 d. *Education:* Grad, Zhongguo Medical Univ, 1952. *Appointments:* Resident, Attending Physician, Chief Dept of Medicine, Affiliated Hosp, Ningxia Medical Coll, 1953-70; Chief Dept of Internal Medicine, Yinchuan Municiple Hos, 1972- 79; Assoc Prof, Prof, Chief Physician, Pres, NMC, 1979-. *Publications:* Articles inc. Sinus Node Electrogram & Measurement of Sinoatrial Conduction Time; Sinus Node Electrogram Studies in Patents with Sick Sinus Syndrome; Epidemiological Survey of Hypertension in Wu Zhong; Doppler Echocardiography for Measuring Pulmonary Pressure; Echocardiography & Clincal Manifestation of Cardiac Tumors; Diagnosis of Aortic Sinus Aneurysos. *Memberships:* Chinese Medical Assoc; Assoc of Medical Educ; Chinese Cardivascular Assoc. *Hobbies:* Music; Literature. *Address:* Ningxia Medical Coll, Yinchuan, Ningxia, China.

CHEN Tian Sheng, b. 15 Mar 1953, Hubai, China. President; Assoc Prof. m. Jiang Zhong Lian, 4 May 1981, 1 d. *Education:* Economic Dept of Wuhan Univ, 1974-77. *Appointments:* Tchr, Wuhan Univ, 1977-79; Reporter, Guang Ming Daily, 1979-83; Chief Editor, Sci and Man, 1983-86; Pres, High SGI Tech Ind Park, Ding Lake, 1989-. *Publications:* Course on the Sci of Leadership. *Membership:* China Writers Assoc. *Honours:* Entitled As Pioneer of the Reform Time; Strong Man on Chinese Economy; Selected, One of the Ten Chinese Youth Talents. *Hobbies:* Reading Books. *Address:* 76 Tai Kang Road, Guang Zhou City, Guang Dong Pro, China.

CHEN Wan Chun, b. 11 Nov 1938, Jiang Su, China. Assoc Research Scientist; Prof. m. Mi Xin, 1 Feb 1970, 1 s, 1 d. *Education:* Grad, Physics Dept of Jiang Su Educ Coll, 1960; Grad, physics Dept of Nanking Univ, 1964; USA, 1983-85. *Appointments:* Intl Cooperation Bureau, Chinese Academy Sci. 1964-70; Inst of Physics, 1970-91; State Univ, NY, 1983-85. *Publications include:* The Crystal Growth of Lithium Iodate; New Process for Growing a Lilos Crystals; The Growth and Dissolution of Calcinm and Phosphates, Seventh Chinese Conference on Crystal Growth; The Kinetics of Dissolution of Tooth Enamel; The Habit of Likso Crystal Growth; A Advanced Subject of Matherials Sci in Space Crystal Growth under Microgravity Conditions; Gel Growth of KBs Crystal in Pure Diffusion Systems. *Memberships include:* Chinese Space Sci Soc; Chinese Optical Soc; Chinese Ceramic Soc. *Honours:* Nat Invention Prize; Gold Plated Medal Prize Award; Silver medal Prize Award. *Hobbies:* Reading; Tour; Cooking; Climbing. *Address:* Inst of Physics, Chinese Academy of Sci, PO Box 603, Beijing, 100080, China.

CHEN Xue Ya, b. 22 Mar 1943, Shaxian County, Fujian. Editor. m. Jiang Ming Dun, 1 July 1968, 1 d. *Education:* Grad, Composition Dept, Shanghai Conservatory of Music. *Appointments:* Music Editor, Shanghai Literature & Art Pub House, 1973-; Lectr, Shanghai Conservatory of Music, 1983-87; Vice Gen Editor, Shanghai Lit & Art Pub House, 1985-; Editor in Chief, Yinyue Aihaozhe & Do Re Mi, 1985-; Sec Gen, Shanghai Intl Music Cimp, 1987. *Publications:* Chinese Traditional Music; Guitarists Companion; Chinese Folk Songs; Paris Commune. *Memberships:* Chinese Musicians Assoc; Soc for Oriental Musicology; Soc for Music Educ in China; Shanghai Musicians Assoc; Shanghai Musicians Copyright Comm; The Guitarists Companion Club. *Honours:* East China Best Publications Award. *Hobbies:* Literature; Tourism. *Address:* 74 Shaoxing Lu, 200020 Shanghai, China.

CHEN Yadan, b. 13 Jan 1942, Xinchang, Zhejiang, China. Painter; Prof. m. 14 Feb 1967, 1 s. *Education:* Fine Art Sch, Annex of Central Academy of Fine Art, Beijing, 1958-60; Central Academy of Fine Art, 1960-65. *Appointments:* Beijing Diapositive Factory, creator, 1965; Central Academy of Art & Design, Prof, 1975. *Publications:* White-Black Art on the Plane; On

Charateristic in Illustration of Litterature; My Tour on Antactic. *Memberships:* Chinese Assoc of Fine Artists; Soc of Chinese Engravess. *Honours:* Prize of 9th Exhibition of China Engraving; Silver Medalist of the National Contest of Small Engraving and ExLibris Collections. *Address:* Dept of Book Decoration, Central Academy of Art & Design, No 34, Dongsan Huan Beilu, Beijing 100020, China.

CHEN Zhen Guang, b. 11 Aug 1925, Pingtan, Fujian, China. Prof; Tutor of Doctor Degree Postgraduate of the Horticultural Dept, Fujian Agri Coll. m. Xie Xi Yu, 21 Jan 1955, 1 s, 1 d. *Education:* Grad, Fujian Agri Coll, Bach of Agri, 1950. *Appointments:* Asst Lectr, Assoc Prof, 1950-92; Vice Chmn, Dept of Hort iculture, 1959-78; Vice Chief of Deans Office, 1977-78; Chmn Dept of Horticulture, 1978-84; Dir Inst of Subtropical Fruit Trees, 1982-92; Tutor of Doctor Degree, Postgrad, 1990-; Fujian Argi Coll, 1985-92. *Publications include:* Fruit Tree Breeding Science; Fruit Tissue Culture; A Study on Induction of Citrus Pollen Plants; A study on Consanguineous Relationship Between Nai & Other Species of Prunus; Recent Advances in Protoplast Culture in Fruit Trees; Birotechnology in Agri & Forestry. *Memberships:* Intl Soc of Citriculture; Fujian Horticultural Sci Soc; Fujian Genetics Soc; Flowers Assoc, Fujian, PRC. *Honours:* 1st Prize Sci and Tech Award; 2nd Prize of Sci & Tech Award; 3rd Prize of Sci & Tech Awd; Specialist of Outstanding Contribution. *Address:* Dept of Horticulture, Fujian Agri Coll, Fuzhou, China.

CHEN Zhi Ming, b.13 Mar 1934, Cizao, Jinjiang, Fujian. Research Fellow of geomarphology; Prof. m. Qi Ping Zhi, 15 July 1966, 1 s, 1 d. *Education:* Geomorphology, Dept of Geography, Nanjing Univ, 1954-58. *Appointments:* Nanjing Inst of Geography, CAS, 1958-; Physiographical maps of Jiangsu Atlas, 1959-75; Qinghai Xizang Comprehensive Expedition Sponsored CAS, 1976-80; Research Program of China Mega Geomorphology, Nat Geomorphic Map, 1987-92. *Publications:* 3 Theses & Translation Works; 50 Treatises; A Trial Discussion on Systematic Structure and Development Tendency in Geomorphology; Lake Retrogression and its Climatic Significance in the Tibetan Flateau; An Outline of China Landform. *Memberships:* Comm of Geomorphic Survey and Mapping, IGU; Study Group of Geomorphic Hazards, IGU; Enviroments of the Nat Comm of Sci; Nat Geomorphic Map. *Honours:* 1st Class Prize of the Nat Natural Sci; Special Prize of Natural Sci of Acadmia; 1st Class Prize of the Academy in the Cooperative Compilation of Chinas Gemorphic Map. *Hobbies:* Sport; Music; Landscape Sketch; Violin; Table Tennis. *Address:* Nanjing Inst of Geography & Limnology, Academia Sinica, 73 East Beijing Road, Nanjing 210008, China. 139, 152.

CHENG Andrew Francis, b. 15 Oct 1951, USA. Physicist. m. Linda Sun Hu, 29 Nov 1979, 1 s, 1 d. *Education:*AB, Princeton Univ, 1971; MA, 1974; PhD, Columbia Univ, 1977. *Appointments:* Post Doc Fellow, Bell Lab, 1976-78; Asst Prof, Physics, Rutgers Univ, 1978-83; Applied Physics Lab, Johns Hopkins Univ, 1983-. *Publications:* 90 Articles, Book Chapters; EoS Transactions of the American Geophysical Union. *Memberships:* American Geophysical Union; American Physical Soc; American Astronomical Soc; NASA; Nat Academy Advisory Comm. *Honours:* Outstanding Young Sci Award; NASA Group Achievement Award. *Hobby:* Piano. *Address:* Applied Physics Lab, Johns Hopkins Univ, Laurel, MD 20723, USA.

CHENG Chi ping, b. 17 June 1914, Hunan, PRC. Prof in Physiology, Medical Univ, PRC. m. 13 June 1944, 3 s, 1 d. *Education:* Hunan Yale Medical Coll, Bach of Medicine, 1940; Central Univ, 1944; Ms Continued Educ Univ, Utah, 1947-49. *Appointments:* Huan Yale Medical Coll, 1946-47; Hurbin Medical Univ, 1956-. *Publications:* Endorine Physiology; Experimental Design and Tech in Reaproductive Research; Contributor in Hsu

and Zhang Texbook of Physiology. *Memberships:* Chinese Physiological Soc; Chinese Reproductive Biology Soc; American Assoc for Advancement of Sci and Sigma Xi Soc. *Honours:* Harbin Model Worker; Provincial Model Worker; 1st Prize Award of Provincial Family Planning Research; Honor of Magnicient Work; Honor Award of Advanced Worker; Distinguished Returned Oversea Chinese. *Hobbies:* Classical Music. *Address:* Dept of Physiology, Harbin Medical Univ, Harbin, 150086, China.

CHENG Enhong, b. 26 Nov 1935, Taizhou, Jiangsu. Tchr English as a Foreign Language. m. Zhou Daokun, 1 Aug 1962, 1 d. *Education:* Grad, Shanghai Inst of Foreign Languages, 1956; English studies, Anhui Univ, 1959- 61; Beijing Inst of Foreign Languages, 1961-63. *Appointments:* Boston Univ, 1981-82; Huazhong Univ, Sci and Tech, 1956-. *Publications:* A Chinese Collegiate Dictionary of English Usage; The Schema Theory and Reading Instruction; A Chinese-English Dictionary of Usage for Scientists and Engineers. *Memberships:* Coll English Supervision, State Educ Commission. *Honours:* Awards for Improving the Tching of Reading in the Chinese Context. *Hobbies:* Cultures; Art. *Address:* Dept of Foreign Languages, Huazhong Univ of Sci & Tech, Wuhan, Hubei, China 430074.

CHENG Fu Zhen, b. 15 Mar 1942, Wuhan, Prof. m. 26 Jan 1971, 2 s. *Education:* BA, Dept of Physics, USTC, 1965; PhD, Dept of Astrophysics, ISAS, 1984. *Appointments:* Assoc Prof, USTC, 1986-90; Prof USTC, 1990-. *Publications:* 50 Papers, Nat & Intl Academic Physical, Astrophysical Journals; 3 Books. *Memberships:* IAU; Chinese Astronomical Soc. *Honours:* 2nd Class Prize for Nat Sciences. *Hobbies:* Sports; Literature. *Address:* Center for Astrophysics, Univ of Sci & Tech of China, Hefei, Anhui 230026, China. 139.

CHENG Guangzhi, b. 4 Jan 1934, Sicchuan Prov. Prof. m. Liu Suyun, 1 Aug 1957, 2 d. *Education:* BA, Chinas Southwest Normal Univ, 1957. *Appointments:* Asst Prof, Physics Dept, Guangxi Normal Univ, 1957; Lectr Physics Dept, GNU, 1960; Prof & Dean of Physics Dept, GNU, 1982; Vice Pres, GNU, 1984; Pres GNU, 1986; Pres GXU, 1991. *Publications:* State of Material; The Introduction of Theoretical Physics; Ehnilibrium & Nonequilibrium Stateistical Mechanics; Thermdyanmics & Statistical Physics; Papers & Thesis. *Memberships:* China Physics Soc; Guangxi Branch, CPS; Mngt Soc of Chinas Normal Univ; Guangxi Procincial Soc of Higher Educ; Guangxi Prov Soc of Sci. *Honours:* Advanced Worker of Sci & Tech in Minority Areas; Advanced Educ. *Hobbies:* Calligraphy; Swimming; Keeping Pigeons. *Address:* Guangxi Univ, Nanning, Guangxi, China.

CHENG Nansen, b. 23 Mar 1935, China. Marketing & Communications Exec. m. Agatha Menard, 3 Sept 1972, 2 d. *Education:* Shanghai Intl Studies Univ, 1957; Nat Taiwan Univ, LLB, 1961; Univ of Neuchatel, Switzerland, 1985; Inst des Hautes Etudes Intl, Nice, France, 1967; Diplomatic Academy, Post Doctorate, 1969. *Appointments:* Pres, Richelieu Asia Investment Inc, 1988-; Pres, Vice Chmn, Ossun Intl Trade & Investment Corp; Chmn & Chief Exec Officer, Paramex Corp; Pres Exec Ctte CIAC, North America Inc; Dir Gen Overseas Office China Chang Jiang Energy Corp; Special Adv to Comm Del Vienna, 1967-69; Prof of Chinese Studies, Diplomatic Acad of Vienne, 1967-69; Legis Adv to Govt of Can & Quebec, 1970-86; Pres & Gen Mgr, BCP China Mkgt Communications Inc, 1986-87. *Honours:* French Govt Fellowship; European Economic Community Fellowship; Wiener Diplomatische Akedemie Fellowship. *Hobbies:* Gardening; Reading; Photography. *Address:* 360 Rue Logan, St Lambert, Quebec, Canada J4P 1J2. 88.

CHENG Tsu Yu, b. 18 Mar 1916, Chin. Prof, Snr Research Fellow. m. Ting Kwee Choo, 1944, 1 s. *Education:* Diploma, Tchr Training Program, 1937; Diploma Rhetoric, Inst of Language Tchr, Wasada Univ,

Tokyo, 1964-65. *Appointments:* Visiting Prof, The Graduate Division of Literature, Wasada Univ, 1964-65; Full Prof, The Daito Bunka Univ, Tokyo, Japan, 1978-80; Visiting Prof, Amoy Univ, 1986-; Peking Univ, 1992-; Snr Research Fellow, Inst of Chinese Studies, Chinese Univ, Hong Kong, 1984-. *Publications:* Poetry and Poetics fo Lu Xun; Criticism of the Works of Huang Zunxian; Tokyo Lectures; Evolution of Chinese Rhetoric; Sindogical Research in Japan; The History of Chinese Rhetoric; Dr Sun Yat Sen at his Days as a student of Medicine. *Memberships:* Editor South Seas Soc; The Intl Order of Merit. *Honours:* Advisory Prof, Fudan Univ; Hon Advsr, China Rhetorical Soc; Hon Advisor of the American Biographical Inst USA; Hon Advisor IBS. *Hobbies:* Reading; Writing. *Address:* Inst of Chinese Studies, The Chinese Univ of Hong Kong, Shatin, NT Hong Kong. 3.

CHENG Zenghou, b. 28 Sept 1937, Wuxi, The People's Republic of China. Prof. m. Jiang Rong, 17 Aug 1968, 1 s. *Education:* Graduated Peking Univ, 1961; Completed 3 yr Postgrad Prog specializing in French Romanticism at Peking Univ, 1965. *Appointments:* Lectr, Nanjing Univ, 1965-68; Vis Scholar, Laval Univ, Can, 1978-80; Vis Scholar, Univ Paris VII 1989-; Full Prof. *Publications:* A Translation of Victor Hugo's Poems, 1986; Lexicometrics, 1987; Victor Hugo and Criticism, 1992. *Memberships:* Chinese Soc of French Lit, Cnslr; La Societe d'Histoire Litteraire de la France, Corres Mbr. *Honour:* China Distinguished Books in Foreign Literature Prize, 1991. *Hobbies:* Travelling, Photography. *Address:* 21-604 Suo Jin Er Cun, Nanjing 210042, China. 139, 151, 152.

CHERNIGOVSKAYA Tatiana V, b. 7 Feb 1947, St Petersburg. Neurolinguistics; Sensory Physiology. m. Nikolai Sulkhaniantz, 29 Nov 1974, 1 s. *Education:* Grad, St Petersburg Univ, Humanities, Physiology, 1970; PhD Human Physiology, 1977. *Appointments:* Lectr at St Petersburg Univ, 1970-72; I Sechenov Inst of Evol Physiol Russian Acad Sci, 1972-. *Publications:* 80 Pub on Sensory Perception, cerebal asymmetry. *Memberships:* Russian Assoc of Artifical Intelligence, Physiology, Psychology, Neuropsychology; Internat Soc of Language Origine, Phonetic Sci. *Hobbies:* Literature; History; Music; Art. *Address:* Torez Ave 44, I Sechenov Inst of Evol, Physiol & Biochemistry Russian Acad Sci, St Petersburg 194223, Russia.

CHERRY William Ashley, b. 25 Oct 1924, Halls, Tennessee, USA. Private Medical Practice. m. (1) 3 s 1 d, (2) Jacqueline Guidry, 2 June 1989. *Education:* Tulane Univ Coll of Arts & Sci, New Orleans, 1943-46; Tulane Univ Sch of Medicine, New Orleans, 1945-49; Philadelphia Gen Hosp, 1949-51; Gen Surgery Res, Loisianna State Univ, 1953-56; Thoracic Surgery Res, Louisiana State Univ, 1956-57. *Appointments include:* Asst Clinical Dir for Surgery, Charity Hosp, New Orleans, 1956-57; Clinical Prof of Surgery, Tulane Univ Sch of Medicine, 1970-80. *Publications include:* Beribert Heart Disease, Snr Medical Student Thesis; Management iof Chest Injuries; Legislative and Health Initiatives of Concern in DHEW Region Vi. *Memberships include:* Blockley Medical Soc; Orleans Parish Medical Soc; Iberia Parish Medical Soc; American Medical Assoc; Mouisiana State Medical Soc; American Lung Assoc of Louisiana; American Thoracic Soc of Louisiana; American Coll of Surgeons. *Hobbies:* Carpentry; Coin Collecting; Stamp Collecting; Photography. *Address:* 12674 South Highmeadow Court, Baton Rouge, LA 70816, USA.

CHEVRIER Jean-Marc, b. 2 Mar 1916, Cheneville. Pres, Gen Dir, Inst of Psychological Research. m. Madeleine Telesphore Bourassa, 4 Jan 1941, 2 s, 3 d. *Education:* Lic Sc Ped, 1942; Bacc en Psychologie, 1943; Licence en psychologie, 1945; PhD, 1949. *Appointments:* Exec Dir, JMC Press Ltd, 1968-; Founder & Chief Psychologist, Guidance Bureau Ministry of Youth Quebec Government, 1947-53; Conslt, Commission of Apprenticeship, Printing Trades, 1947-

73; Laval & Chambly Coll, 1949-58; Hopital Pasteur de Montreal, 1953-60; Prof, Inst de Psychologie, Univ of Montreal, 1951-57; Sch of Rehabilitation, Faculty of Medicine, 1953-57; Sch of Educ, 1959-61; Founder, Dir Psychology Dept, Rehabilition Inst of Montreal, 1953-62; Dir of Guidance, Montreal Catholic Sch, 1962-64; Prof Ecole Normale Secondaire, 1962-63; Admin, Pres, Edi Quebec, 1973-75; Dir, Treasurer, Vice Pres, Le Centre de Psychologie et de Pedagogie, 1945-57; Articles for the Educational Review; Numerous Textbooks; Psychological Tests. *Memberships:* APA; ABEPP; CPA; CPPO; CPCOQ; CGCA; OPA; NSTA. *Honours:* Silver Medal, Ecole Normale Jacques Cartier; Bronze Medal Graphic Arts Ind; Graphic Arts Ind Award; Stothers Exceptional Child Foundation Scholarship; Ministry of Health and Social Welfare Canadian Grant; CPCCOQ, Provinical Award, 1990; CGCA, Counselling Resources and Training Material Award, 1991; OSCA, Frank Clute Award for Professional Research, 1991; Distinction in psychometry from the psychology professors of the University of Montreal. *Hobbies:* Photography; Skiing; Golf. *Address:* 34 Flewry Street West, Montreal, Quebec, Canada H3L 1S9. 2, 6, 52, 88.

CHIANCONE Aldo, b. 30 Oct 1936, Bari, Italy. Univ Prof. *Education:* Liceo Parini, Milan; Univ Degli Studi Milano; MA, Univ of California, Berkeley. *Appointments:* Univ Padova, Lectr, 1967-75; Univ Padova, Chmn Publ Fin, 1976-77; Univ Venice, Chmn Publ Fin, 1978-84; Univ Brescia, Chmn Publ Fin and Law Fin, 1985-. *Publications:* Ammortament Anticipati Fiscali e Investmenti; L Efficacia Della Politicao Di Bilancio; La Programmazione di Bilancio; Changes in Revenue Structures. *Memberships:* Soc Ital Degli Economisti; Soc Ital Di Economia Pubblica; Intl Inst of Public Finance, Exec-Vice Pres. *Honours:* Fulbright Scholarship; Fubini Prize. *Hobbies:* Swimming; Tennis; Music; Art; Travel. *Address:* Via Mauro Macchi 33, I-20124 Milano, Italy. 52.

CHIANG Pin Kung, b. 16 Dec 1932, Nantou, Taiwan. Political Vice Minister, Ministry of Economic Affairs. m. Chen Mei Huey, 2 Feb 1960, 2 s, 1 d. *Education:* Doc Agri, Nat Tokyo Univ, Japan, 1962-69. *Appointments:* Economic Counsellor, Office Economic Counsellor, Embassy of the Republic China, 1979; Dir Gen, Bd of Foreign Trade, 1988; Admin Vice Minister, MOEA, 1989; Political Vice Minister, MOEA, 1990. *Hobbies:* Reading; Music; Sport. *Address:* Ministry of Economic Affairs, 15 Foochow St, Taipei, Taiwan, China.

CHIBA Mototsugu, b. 1 Feb 1935, Okayanna, Japan. Prof of Pharmacology, Tsurumio Univ. m. Sumie Kobayashi, 24 Apr 1959, 2 d. *Education:* Zoology Course, Tekyo Univ of Educ, BSc, 1954-58; Zoology Course, Tokyo Univ of Educ, MSc, 1958-60; D DSc Tokyo Mod & Deut Univ, 1967. *Appointments:* Asst, Tokyo Med & Demt Univ, 1964; Lectr, 1969; Asst prof, 1972; Prof, Tsurumi Univ, 1973. *Publications:* Numerous in the Field of Oral Biology. *Memberships:* Japanese Pharmacological Soc; Japanese Assoc for Oral Biology; Intl Assoc for Dental Research; American Assoc fo Advancement of Sci. *Honours:* British Council Scholarship. *Hobby:* Reading. *Address:* Dept of Pharmacology, Sch of Dental Medicine, Tsurumi Univ, 2 1 3 Tsurumi, Tsurumi Ku, Yokohama, Japan, 230.

CHIBUNDU Victor Nwazichi, b. 30 Dec 1930, Umojima Ukwu, Isialangwa. m. Catherine Ekpendu, 1 s, 4 d. *Education:* Federal Civil Srvice Entrance Exam, 1951; Fellow, Chartered Inst of Sec, 1964; Post Grad, Intl Relations, Cambridge Univ, 1965; PhD Political Sci, 1968; Nigerian Inst of Mngt, 1985. *Appointments include:* Private Sec, Ministry of Foreign Affairs, Commonwealth Relations, 1961-64; First Sec, Embassy of Nigeria, 1972; Charge D'Affairs, Ambassady of Nigeria Teheran, Iran, 1976-77; Ambassador, Embassy of Nigeria, Luanda, Angola, 1984-87; Dir, Arab Affairs Dept, Ministry of Ecternal Affairs, 1987-88; Contract Appointment, Nigerian FS, 1988-90. *Memberships:*

NGWA Soc Club; Owerrinta Development Assoc. *Honours:* Olu Oha 1 NKE MBTU Amairiniisii; Udo Ala Nke Mbutu Amairiniissii. *Hobbies:* playing Lawn Tennis; Reading; Academic Research. *Address:* PO Box 4346, No.11 Badaru Street, Surulere, Lagos, Nigeria.

CHICHESTER Dermot Michael Claud, b. 22 Nov 1953, London, England. Auctioneer. m. Shan McIndoe, 14 July 1982, 1 s, 2 d. *Education:* Harrow Sch, 1967-71. *Appointments:* Man Dir, Christies Scotland, 1983; Man Dir, Christies South Kensington, 1987; Man Dir, Christies Europe, 1990. *Memberships:* Royal Soc of Arts; Whites Club. *Hobbies:* Shooting; Golf; Skiing; Tennis; Cricket; Architecture; Furniture. *Address:* Lowick House, Lowick, Kettering, Northamptonshire, NN14 3BL, England.

CHIEN Frederick F, b. 17 Feb 1935, China. m. Julie Tien Chien, 22 Sept 1962, 1 s, 1 d. *Education:* BA, Nat Taiwan Univ, 1956; MA, Yale Univ, 1959; PhD, Yale Univ, 1962; Nat War Coll; LLD, Sung Kyun Kwan Univ. *Appointments include:* Sec to the Premier Exec Yuan, 1962-63; Deputy Dir, Dept of North American Affairs, Ministry of Foreign Affairs, 1967-69; Dir Gen, Government Information Office, 1972-75; Rep, CCNAA Office in USA, 1983-88; Minister of State, Chmn, Council for Economic Planning & Devel, 1988-90; Ministry of Foreign Affairs, 1990-. *Publications:* The Opening of Korea; A Study of Chinese Diplomacy; Speaking as a Friend; Faith and Resilience; The Republic of China Forges Ahead. *Honours include:* Order of Brilliant Star with Grand Cordon of the ROC; Order Nat Del Merito en el Grado Del Gran Druz de la Republica del Paraguay; L'Ordre Nat Honneur et Merite Grand Officier de la Republique D'Haiti; Orden Merito en el Grado de Gran Curz Extraordinarion de la Republica del Paraquay. *Hobbies:* Reading; Golf. *Address:* 2 Chieh Shou Road, Taipei, Taiwan, China.

CHILD John Frederick, b. 18 Apr 1942, Swindon, England. Barrister. m. Jean Alexander Cunningham, 2 Sept 1972, 2 s. *Education:* King Edward's Sch, Bath, 1950-61; Univ of Southampton, 1961-64; Sidney Sussex Coll, Cambridge, 1964-66; Univ of Columbia, 1964. *Appointments:* Supervisor in Law, Sidney Sussex Coll, Cambridge, 1966-78; Chancery Barrister, Lincoln's Inn, England, 1966-. *Publications:* Main Contributor Vol 19, Encyclopedia of Forms & Precedents; Forms of Accumulation and Maintenance Settlements, Encyclopaedia of Forms & Precedents. *Memberships:* Soc of Lincoln's Inn, London, England; Chancery Bar Assoc; Revenue Bar Assoc. *Honours:* BA Scholar; Tancred Common Law Student; Droop Scholar. *Hobbies:* Theatre; Lanugages; tennis; Badminton. *Address:* 17 Old Buildings, Lincoln's Inn, London WC2A 3UP, England.

CHIN James Kee-Hong, b. 2 Sept 1934, Burma. Physician; Surgeon. m. Julia Yu Siu Chin, 5 May 1964, 2 s, 1 d. *Education:* I SC, 1955; MB, BS, 1961; FCCP, 1965; CA CaS, 1965. *Appointments:* House Physician, Surgeon, 1961; Civil Asst Surgeon, 1962; Medical Officer, 1963-64; Research Fellow, 1965-66; Physician & Surgeon, 1966-. *Memberships:* Hong Kong Medical Assoc; Assoc of Fine Arts & Antiques. *Hobbies:* Medical Research; Sports; Swimming; Shooting; Fine Arts & Antiques. *Address:* Flat 3 Grand Court, 135 Kadoorie Avenue, Kowloon, Hong Kong.

CHIN Michael Kuo hsing, b. 19 Sept 1921, Singapore. Admin. m. Edith Tzu Lin Fang, 3 Feb 1951, 4 d. *Education:* BSc, Yencing Univ, Chengtu, China, 1945; Various Cources, New York, China, Taiwan, 1975. *Appointments:* Asst Proctors Office, Yenching Univ, 1945-46; Bureau of Relief, Chinese Nat Rural Rehabilitation Admin, 1946-48; Statistician in Charge, Chief Peronnel Officer, Nan King Physical Rehabilitation Centre, MOI, 1948-50; Tech, Soil Analysis, Public Health Research Inst, 1950-51; Snr Admon Asst, 1960-72; Joint Commission on Rural Reconstruction, Exec Officer, 1971- 83; Dir of Admin, 1983-91. *Publications:* Article, Admin of Research Centre Under Constraints;

Ways of Cutting Costs. *Memberships:* Recreation Comm; Transition Comm; AVRDC; Yenching Univ Alumni Club. *Honours:* 10 yrs outstanding Service, AVRDC. *Hobbies:* Music; Literature. *Address:* c/o TCM 6/F-3, 102 Chung Shan N. Road, sec 2, Taipei, Taiwan, China. 52, 132, 139, 156.

CHINEKE Sylvester Chukwunonyelu Roxy, b. 24 Nov 1948, AWHA. Resident Partner; Surveyor. m. 18 Aug 1979, 5 s. *Education:* BSc, Estate Mngt, 1975. *Appointments:* Nat Service, Knight Frank & Rutley, 1975-76; Pupil Survey KFR, 1976-78; Branch Mngr KFR, 1978-83; Resident Partner, 1984-. *Memberships:* Nigerian Inst of Estate Surveyors & Valuers; Nat Exec Council of the Inst; Intl Real Estate Federation. *Hobbies:* Travel; Music; Meeting People. *Address:* Knight Frank & Ruthley, NIDB House, 6th Floor, 18 Waff Road, PO Box 899, Kaduna, Nigeria.

CHINH Kiell Nguyen, b. 3 Sept 1939, Hanoi, Vietnam. Actress. m. Nguyen Nang Te, 1955, div. 1980, 2 s, 1 d. *Education:* Completed HS at French Cath Saint Paul Schl of Hanoi, 1955 and continued in Saigon, 1967. *Appointments:* 1st Movie 1957, The Bell of Thiem Mu Pagoda, filmed in Hue Ctr of Vietnam; After more than 20 films formed own movie co Giao Chi Film, 1970 and produced Warrior, Who Are You. *Memberships:* Screen Actors Guild; American Fedn of TV and Radio Artists; Assn of Asian Pacific American Artists. *Honours:* Best Actress Award Prize from President of South Vietnam, 1969; Most Popular Actress Award from Asian Film Festival, 1972; Best Leading Actress Award, Asian Film Festival, 1973; Woman Warrior Award by Asian-American Pacific Women Network of America, 1986; Certificate of Recognition Refugee of the Year by House of Congress, Washington DC, 1990. *Hobbies:* Cinema, Music, Reading, Gardening, Cooking. *Address:* 4233 Farmdale Avenue, Studio City, CA 91604, USA.

CHINWUBA Walter Nnaedozie, b. 13 Dec 1941, Enugu. Post Primary Sch Mngr. m. Lois Expe, 31 May 1975, 1 s, 3 d. *Education:* St Petus Sch, Ogbete, 1947-54; DMGS Onitsha, 1955-59; Fed Sci Sch Lagos, 1961-63; Univ of Ibadan, 1963-67; Univ of Lagos, BSc, 1976. *Appointments:* Bank Clerk, Union Bank, 1960; Bank Clerk, ACB Lagos, 1962; Graduate Tchr, 1967; Sch Mngr, 1978. *Publications:* WAEC Examiner in Biology. *Memberships:* Anambra State Conference of Principals; The Nigerian Assoc for Educ Admin & Planning. *Hobbies:* Table Tennis; Swimming; Taking A Walk. *Address:* Flat 4, 13 Igbariam Street, Achara Layout, Enugu, Nigeria.

CHITTARANJAN Mohapatra, b. 17 Aug 1937, Janardanpur,India. Conservator of Forests, Indian Forest Serv. m. Anjali Tripathy, 2 Feb 1964, 5 d. *Education:* Assoc of Indian Forest Coll (AIFC) Dehradun; Dr. Rer.Silv, Tech Univ, Dresden, Germany. *Appointments:* Asst Conservator of Forest, 1960; Dpty Conservator of Forest, 1966; Specialist, Forest Utilization and Ind, Asst Insp Gen of Forest, Govt of India, 1975-82; Conservator of Forest, 1984-. *Publications:* Melody of Cacesea (poetry), A Collection of English Poems; Gianga Siuli, A Collection of Oriya Poems; Num tech papers and lit compositions. *Memberships:* IUFRO; Indian Inst of Pub Admin, New Delhi; Alumni of Staff Coll of India, Hyderabad, HCM Inst of Pub Admin, Rajasthan; Rotary Int. *Hobbies:* Photography, Gardening, Tree Planting, Music, Collection of Coins of Different Countries, Writing Poems and Stories. *Address:* N-IV-19 Nayapalli, Bhubaneswar 12, Orissa, India 750012.

CHIU Ray Chu Jeng, b. 13 Mar 1934, Tokyo, Japan. Surgeaon. m. Jane Mong Hau Tan, 17 Apr 1962, 1 s, 1 d. *Education:* MD, Nat Taiwan Univ, 1959; Diploma American Bd of Surgery & Thoracic Surgery, 1968-69; PhD McGill Univ, 1970; FRCSC, 1969. *Appointments:* Chmn, Div of Cardiovascular and Thoracic Surgery, McGill Univ, 1992-; Prof Surgery, McGill Univ, 1981-; Snr Cardiovascular & Thoracic Surgeon, Montreal Gen Hosp, 1983-. *Publications:* 2 books on Myocardial

Protection; 2 books on Cardiomyoplasty & Biomechanical Cardiac Assist; 195 Scientific Papers, Chapters & Editorials. *Memberships:* Royal Coll of Surgeons of Canada; American Surgical Assoc; American Assoc for Thoracic Surgery; The Soc of Univ Surgeons; The Soc of Thoracic Surgeons. *Hobbies:* Reading; Classical Music. *Address:* The Montreal Gen Hosp, 1650 Cedar Avenue, Montreal, Quebec, Canada H3G 1A3. 17, 88.

CHLOPECKI Andrzej, b. 21 Jan 1950, Bydgoszoz, Poland. Musicologist; Music Critic; Music Publisher. m. Beata, 8 Aug 1978, 2 s, 1 d. *Education:* Grad, Music Lyceum, Bydgoszcz, 1969; MA, Warsaw Univ, Inst of Musicology, 1975; Scholarships, Intl Summer Courses of New Music, Darmstadt, Germany, 1980, 1982; Inst fur die Wissebschaften vom Merschen, Vienna, 1984; Alban Berg Stiftung, Vienna, Austria, 1986. *Appointments:* Hd of New Music Dept, Polish Radio & TV, Warsaw, 1985-81; Promotion Mngr, Polish Music Publishers, Warsaw, 1982-; Asst Prof, Academy of Music, Cracow, 1982-; Commentator, Polish Radio, Warsaw, 1991. *Memberships:* Bd Member, Intl Soc of Centemporary Music, Polish Section; Polish Composers Union; Lectrs in Poland, Soviet Union, Lithuania, Germany, Austria, Norway, Netherlands; Polish Composers Union; Intl Soc of Contemporary Music; Assoc of Polish Journalists. *Publications:* Essays; Articles; Reviews; Radio & TV Programmes; Contributions to Bi Weekly Muzyczny, Warsaw; Musik Texte, Zeitschrift fur Neue Musik. *Honours:* Artistic Prizes. *Hobbies:* Skiing; Chess; Astrology; Current Mngt; Polish Music Publishers. *Address:* Naleczwska 54 52, Warsaw, Poland.

CHLOSTA Jan, b. 27 Dec 1938, Olsxtyn. Journalist. m. Maria Idamska, 28 Oct 1968, 1 s, 1 d. *Education:* Trainign Sch Olontyn, 1963; Polish Faculty, Coll Educ Gdanisk, 1964-68; Doctors Degree of the Arts, Wrollaw Univ, 1975. *Appointments:* Inspector Financial Dept, Olzstyn, 1955-60; Mngr PAX Assoc Olzstyn, 1960-84; Editor in Chief, Inst of Publication, Warsaw, 1984-86; Tutor, Centre of Research Olzstyn, 1987-88; Mngr, PAX Assoc Clzstyn, 1989; Lectr, Coll of Educ, 1990. *Publications:* Gazeta Olsxtynska; Seweryn Pieujzing; Kasimierz Jaronyl; Around Waruias Matters About Staff Members of Gaxeta Olsxtynska. *Memberships:* Polish Authors Soc; Polish History Soc; Scientific Soc in Olsztyn. *Honours:* Knight of the Cross of Order of Penaissance of Poland. *Hobbies:* Reading; Films. *Address:* ul Pana Tadeusza 15 54, 10-460 Olsztyn, Poland.

CHMIELEWSKI Tadeusz Ludwik, b. 21 July 1922, Unin, Poland. Economist; Town and Country Planner. m. Izabella Warczewska, 26 Dec 1948, 1 s, 1 d. *Education:* Masters Deg, Lublin Catholic Univ, Fac Soc and Ec Scis, 1950; Postgrad Dipl, Planning Sch, Warsaw Tech Univ, 1966. *Appointments:* Designer, Hd of Planning Gp, Hd of Ofc, Lublin City Planning Ofc, 1956-74; Chief Designer, Hd Specialist in Spatial Planning, Voivodship Planning Ofc, Lublin, 1979-91. *Creative works:* Many works on town and regional planning, mostly as chief designer; Regional Plan of Lublin voivodship, 1977-89; Over 40 articles and treatises. *Memberships:* Ctl Comm on Town Planning and Arch, 1984-90; Polish Town Planners Soc, 1957-, VP Bd of Control, Pres Bd, Lublin Branch, Com for Experts Qualification; Polish Ec Soc, 1958-. *Honours:* Cross of Merit, Silver 1958, Gold 1968; Polonia Restituta Order Knight's Cross, 1983; Partisan Cross, 1984; First Class Awards from: Townplanning and Arch Min, 1959, City of Lublin, 1972, Union of Design Offices, 1988. *Hobbies:* Reading; Tourism; Philately. *Address:* 20-607 Wallenroda 2/107, Lublin, Poland.

CHODOROWSKI Zygmunt, b. 16 Feb 1938, Swieciany, Poland. Physn. *Education:* Univ Med Schl of Gdansk, 1955-62; MD, 1968; Assoc Prof, 1980; Prof, 1992. *Appointment:* Clin of Internal Diseases, 1962-. *Publications:* A Case of Nephropathy and Neurogenic Deafness with Thrombocytopenia, Aminoaciduria and Impairment of Urine Acidification, 1972; Serum Uric Acid Level and Urinary Uric Acid Excretion in Patients with Polycystic Kidney Disease, 1978; Alport's Syndrome with Mental Retardation and Disorders of Uric Acid Metabolism, 1979; Patient bed-rest supervision device approved in 1991 by Main Patent Office in Warsaw. *Honour:* Award of Polish Minister of Health, 1981. *Hobbies:* Gardening, Reading, Rsch. *Address:* ul Wilenska 24, 80-215 Gdansk, Poland.

CHODUBSKI Andrzej Jan, b. 1 Jan 1952, Grabienice Małe, Poland. Historian; Prof of Gdansk Univ. *Education:* MA, History, Univ of Gdansk, 1976; PhD, History, Univ of Baku, 1981; Asst Prof, Univ of Gdansk, 1986. *Appointments:* Sci, Univ of Gdansk, 1977-; Univ of Baku, 1979-80; Univ of Vien, 1987; Univ of Amsterdam, 1990. *Publications:* 150 Publications; Articles; Books. *Memberships:* Sci Soc of Plock; The Assoc of Interest in Armenian Culture; Polish Political Sci Assoc. *Honours:* Gdansk Honor Medal of Merit; Culture Worker of Merit; Bronze Cross of Merit. *Hobbies:* Collecting Caucasica; Armenica, Azerbaijanica, Georgica; Collecting Stamps; Intl Tourismus. *Address:* Bądkowskiego 15/5, 80-137 Gdansk, Poland.

CHOJNACKI Jakub, b. 22 Aug 1922, Sierpc, Poland. Ret'd. Pres of Scientific Soc of Plock. m. Anna Danielewska, 21 Oct 1946, 1 s, 1 d. *Education:* Lodz Univ, 1949; LLM; The Main Schl of Country Econ in Warsaw, 1953; Wood Technology Engr; Doctor of Pol Science, Warsaw Univ, 1975. *Appointments:* Worker in Plock Sawmill, 1939-61; VP of Plock, 1961-73; Mgr of Bldg Woodwork Instn in Plock, 1973-82. *Publications:* Bibliography of Science Works: Plock . . . in counts; Petrochemica and Development of Plock (2 Eds); The Romanesque Door of Plock. *Memberships:* Scientific Soc of Plock, Pres, 1968-; Comm of Explorations Industrialization Regions PAN, 1971-85; The Gazonian Ctr of Scientific Rschrs. *Honours:* Silver Order of Merit, 1954; Gold Order of Merit, 1969; 3 Orders Polonia Restituta; Knighthood, 1974; Commanders, 1980 and Commanders with Star, 1982; Prize of Science and Higher Education, Minister for Science Achievements, 1986. *Hobbies:* Hist, Pol, Travelling. *Address:* Zdunska 10-3, 09-400 Plock, Poland.

CHOLAJ Henryk, b. 1 Jan 1927, Osiny. Scientist. m. Krystyna Chokaj, 26 Nov 1960. *Education:* Master of Art, 1953; Doc, 1959; Habil Doc, 1961; Prof Extraoridnar, 1968; Prof Ordinar, 1972; Polish Academy of Sci, 1973. *Appointments:* Univ Lublin, Dir of Dept of Poutical Economy, 1963-67; Dir of Inst Cooperative, Warsaw, Vice Sec Polish Academy of Sci, 1966-86; Dir of Dept of Economy, High Sch & Planning & Statistics, 1973-89, 1977-79. *Publications:* 15 Books; 240 Scientipical Reasearches. *Memberships:* Polish Academy of Sci; Polish Soc of Economy. *Honours:* Scientific Award of Oscar Lange; Sci Award of the Sec of Polish Academy of Sci. *Hobbies:* Bridge; Poetry of Homer & Horatius. *Address:* Bruna 34-53, Warsaw, Poland.

CHOLAKOV Dimitar Nikolov, b. 25 July 1954, Popovo. Artist; Painter. m. Maria Vassileva Vulcheva, 15 Aug 1976, 1 s. *Education:* Art Sch, 1973; Grad, Painting , The Academy of Fine Arts, 1987. *Appointments:* Bulgarian Artist Assoc, 1982; Sec, Young Artists Assoc, 1985; Pres, Artists Assoc Targovishte, 1986; Pres, art Gallery Targow, 1989. *Creative Works:* Plovchv; Budapest; Sofia; Berlin; Warsaw; Collective Exhibitions, Cairo, Autumn Saloon, Paris; Tours, Amsterdam; Hague; Berlin; Moscow; Wien. *Memberships:* Admin Council of the Belief Hope And Love Intl Foundation. *Honours:* Prize for Painting, Miketi. *Hobby:* Travel. *Address:* 9 Episkop Sophromy street, 7700 Targovishte, Romania.

CHOME Maryse Ingrid, b. Bergerac, France. Prof; Performer of Violoncello. m. Frank Ernest Wilson, 1958, 2 s. *Education:* LRAM, ARCM, Royal Academy of Music, London, 1951; Paris Conservatoire, France, Private

Tuition, Paul Tortelier. *Appointments:* Sub Prof, Royal Academy of Music, London, 1951-52; Solo Tour South Africa, 1953; Principal Cellist, Walter Gore Ballet Orch, 1954; Principal Cellist, Soloist, Alexander Orch, Switzerland, 1955; Festival of Ballet, UK, 1955-57; Royal Ballet, 1957-58; BBC Concert Orch, 1958-59; Grissell Piani Quartet, 1963; Prof, Jnr Exhibitions, Royal Academy of Music, 1964; Prof Violoncello, Trinity Coll of Music, 1965. *Memberships:* London Violoncello Club; Ealing Music Tchrs Assoc; Royal Academy of Music Club; Trinity Coll of Music Tchring Staff Assoc. *Honours:* Recipient of numerous Awards, Scholarships. *Hobbies:* Gardening; Genealogy; Art. *Address:* 61 Twyford Avenue, Acton, London W3 9PZ, England.

CHOO Jimmy, b. 15 Nov 1952, Penang, Malaysia. Shoe Designer. *Education:* Cordwainers Coll, London Cert in Art & Design with Distinction. *Appointments:* Design Shoes for Coutowriers; Marc Bocan; Bruce Oldfield; Anouka Hemple; Tomasz Starlewski; Fashion Designers, Jasper Conran; Edina Ronay; Alister Blair. *Creative Works:* Consult & Feature on the Cloths Show. *Memberships:* Diploma Soc of Ind Artists & Ind Designers. *Honours:* The Bridal Award for Accessory. *Hobbies:* Sports; Travel; DIY. *Address:* Studio 50, The Metropolitan, Enfield Road, London N1 5AZ, England.

CHOUE Young Seek, b. 22 Nov 1921, Seoul, Korea. Chancellor, Kyung Hee Univ. m. Chung Myung Oh, 2 s, 2 d. *Education:* LLB, Seoul Nat Univ, 1950; LLD, Univ of Miami, USA, 1959; DHL, Univ of Manila, Philippines, 1971; LLD, Pusan Nat Univ, Korea, 1972; DHL, North Carolina Univ, USA, 1983; Honorary Causa Univ Autonoma De Guadalajara, Mexico, 1984; Dr of Commerce Nihon Univ, Tokyo, 1988, Dr of Peace Philosophy, Moscow St Univ, Russia, 1991. *Appointments include:* Pres, Kyung Hee Univ; Pres, Intl Assoc of Univ Presidents; Govenor, Korean District of the Civitan Intl; Founder & Chancellor, Kyung Hee Univ; Pres, Inst of Brighter Soc; Club Intl. *Publications include:* Democratic Freedom; Creation of the New Civilized World; World Peace through Educ; The Great Imperative; Peace in the Global Village; White Paper on World Peace. *Memberships include:* Assembly for Peaceful Reunification of Korea; 6th Triennial Confernce IAUP. *Honours include:* Highest Award of Humanities; UN Peace Medals; World Citzenship Award. *Address:* Office of the Chancellor, Kyung Hee Univ, 1 Hoiki Dong, Dongdaemoon Ku, Seoul 130-701, Republic of Korea. 129, 139, 151, 152, 154, 156, 162, 191.

CHOW Wen Tsao, b. 13 Oct 1929, Foochow, China. Master Mariner, US Marchant Ship. m. Ju Hsien Tang, 24 June 1950, 1 s, 2 d. *Education:* Foochow Mercant Marine Academy, 1947. *Appointments:* Merchant Marine Cadet & Officer, 1947-60; MM Master, 1961-72; Oprs Mgr Iran Destiny Carriers Inc, 1973-76; US MM Master, 1979-. *Creative Works:* The First Chinese MM Master has been Licensed by both British & US Authorities; The First US MM Master with all Civilian Crew Participated US Navel Exercise. *Memberships:* MEBA-AMO; AFL CIO; Fed Des Combattants Allies en Europe, UK; The Royal Life Saving Soc, Canada. *Honours:* Honorary Harbormaster of port of Galveston; Letters of Merit, US Navy; US Maritime Admin; Knight Grand Cross of the Order of the Star of Peace; The Allied Cross with MEF & FEF Bars; The Sphinx Cross; The Commomorative War Medal of Gen Dwight D Eisenhower; Silver Benefactor of the Royal Life Saving Soc, Canada. *Hobbies:* Photography; Chinese Opera. *Address:* 188 Ocean Dr E, Stamford CT 06902-8134, USA.

CHOYCE David Peter, b. 1 Mar 1919, London. Ophthalmic Surgeon. m. 3 Sept 1949, 3 s. *Education:* Stowe Sch, 1932-36; Univ Coll Hosp, 1937-42; Moorfields Eye Hosp, 1948-58; BSc, 1939; MB, 1963; MS, 1962; FRCS, 1947; FCOPHTH, 1988; Hunterian Prof, RC Surgeons, 1962. *Appointments:* Conslt Ophthalmologist Hosp Trop Dis London, 1953-88; Southend Group of Hosp, 1954-84; Henry Ford Hosp

Detroit, 1980-; Rec Tchr Univ of London, 1958-. *Publications:* Intraocular Lenses & Implants; 200 Papers. *Memberships:* Pst Pres, Internal Intraoc Implant Club; UN Kingdon Intraoc Imp Soc; Kerato Refractive Soc. *Honours:* Distinguished Achievement Award; ASCR 40th Anniversary pioneer Award; Intl Award for Excellence in Ohthalmology. *Hobby:* Golf. *Address:* 9 Drake Road, Westcliff On Sea, Essex SS0 8LR, England.

CHRISTEA Mihaela, b. 2 Oct 1946, Bucharest, Romania. Philologist; TV Journalist. m. Vladimir Ciobanu, 23 June 1984, 1 s. *Education:* Dipl Philology, Fac of French and Italian, Bucharest Univ. *Appointments:* Dir of TV studio, 1972-88; Collaborations with teh LUMEA magazine and literary magazines; TV literary editor, 1990-. *Creative works:* Critical anthologies on the writer Aurel Baraga and on art critic Petry Comarmercu; Monumental Sculpture in Romania; The Reality of Illusions. *Memberships:* Nichita Stanescu Foun; Romanian Jours Soc; Romanian Professional Journs Assn. *Honours:* Cultural Merits Medal, Czech and Slovak Fed Republic, 1989. *Hobbies:* Music; Cooking; Plastic art. *Address:* Str Urali No 2 et I Ap 2, 70186 Bucharest I, Romania.

CHRISTENSEN Doran Charles, b. 10 June 1937, Beaver City, Nebraska, USA. Minister of Christian Educ. m. Willa Sue Lacy, 13 June 1964. *Education:* Minnesote Bibles Coll; Cincinnati Christian Seminary Univ of Colorado, Indiana, Ohio State, Minnesota, 1955-78. *Appointments:* Minister of Educ, River Park Church of Christ, South Bend, 1960-64; Minister of Educ, Beechwold Church of Christ, Columbus, 1964-91. *Publications:* The Christian Standard; The Lookout Magazine; Key Magazine. *Memberships:* North American Christian Convention; Prof Assoc of Christian Educ; Nat Assoc of Evangelicals; Curriculum Evaluation Comm; Lifeline Christian Missions Intl; ISSA; Tree of Life Christian Sch. *Honours:* All Conference, Football; Estral Award; Outstanding Serv Awards. *Hobbies:* Music; Agriculture; Snr Adult Volunteers Serv. *Address:* 201 Piedmont Road, Columbus, OH 43214, USA.

CHRISTENSEN Lars, b. 19 Sept 1945, Horup. Mangaging Director. m. Karin Hoffmann, 2 Aug 1985. *Education:* M Sc Univ of Capenhagen, 1974. *Appointments:* Intl Sec, Danish Youth Council, 1970-72; Assoc Dir, Dis Congress Serv, 1974; Dir, Dis USA Inc, 1979-86; Founder, Mngr Dir, ICS Full Conference Serv Ltd, 1987-; Dir, INCON Ltd, London, 1990-. *Memberships:* Intl Assoc of Prof Congress Organisers; BOD Intl Congress Of Convention Assoc; Danish Convention Bureau. *Honours:* Meeting Planners Intl; Intl Relations Comm. *Hobbies:* Gardening; History; Reading. *Address:* 29 Hjortekaerbakken, DK 2800 Lyngby, Denmark. 1.

CHRISTIAN A John, b. 28 Apr 1938, Stourport, Worcs. Prof Endowed Chair Holder; Chartered, Prof Civil Engr. m. Veronica Cummins, 28 Aug 1965, 2 s. *Education:* B Eng, 1959; C Eng, 1964; PhD, 1974; P Eng, 1979. *Appointments:* London Transport, 1959-62; Ove Arup & Partners, 1962- 64; R Costain, 1964-67; Univ of Bradford, 1967-77; Memorial Univ, 1977-87; Univ of New Brunswick, 1987-. *Publictions:* Management Machines & Methods in Civil Engr; 50 Refereed Papers, Intl Nat Journals. *Memberships:* MICE; MCSCE; FICE; Constr Tech Advisory Bd. *Honours:* Listed in Dir of Experts in Constr CIB; First Constr Engr & Mngt Chair in Canada; Personally Endowed Chair in Engr in Canada. *Hobbies:* Jogging; Skiing; Hiking; Bridge; Camping. *Address:* M Patrick Gillin Chair in Const, Dept of Civil Engr, PO Box 4400, Univ of New Brunswick, Fredericton, New Brunswick, Canada E3B 5A3.

CHRISTIAN Edwin Ernest, b. 28 Dec 1953, Portsmouth, Virgina. English Prof. m. Margaret Foster, 19 Dec 1982, 2 s, 1 d. *Education:* BA, Union Coll, 1977; MA, Loma Linda Univ, 1979; PhD, Univ of Nebraska, 1983. *Appointments:* Exchange Prof, Beijing Languages Inst, Beijing, 1983-84; Instr, Loma Linda Univ, 1984-

85; Instr, Univ of Nebraska, 1985-86; Asst Prof, Kutztown of Pennsylvania, 1988-92. *Publications:* Joyce Carys Creative Imagination. *Memberships:* The Joyce Cary Soc; The Soc for Detective Fiction. *Honours:* Fulbright Sholarship, Oxford Univ. *Address:* Dept of English, Kutztown Univ of Pennsylvania, Kutztown PA 19530, USA. 6.

CHRISTIAN Gary Dale, b. 25 Nov 1937, Eugene, Oregon, USA. Prof. m Suanne Coulbourne, 16 June 1961, 1 s, 1 d. *Education:* BS, Univ OR, 1959; MS 1961, PhD 1964, Univ MD. *Appointments:* Rsch Aanalytical Chem, Walter Reed Army Inst of Rsch, 1961-67; Asst Prof 1967-70, Assoc Prof 1970-72, Univ of KY; Prof, Univ of WA, 1972-. *Publications:* Atomic Absorption Spectroscopy, 1970; Analytical Chemistry, 4th Ed, 1986; Instrumental Analysis, 2nd Ed, 1986; Trace Analysis: Spectroscopic Methods for Molecules, 1986; Problem Solving in Analytical Chemistry, 1988; 300 publs in chem jrnls and books. *Memberships:* American Chem Soc, Chmn, Puget Sound Sect, 1982- 83; ACS Div of Analytical Chem, Chmn, 1989-90; Soc for Applied Spectroscopy, Sec-Treas. 1977-78, Chmn, 1979-80, Pacific NW Sect; Spectroscopy Soc of Can; Soc for Electroanalytical Chem. *Honours:* Fulbright-Hays Scholar, 1978- 79; Medal of Honour, Universite Libre de Bruxelles, 1978; American Chemical Society Division of Analytical Chemistry Award for Excellence in Teaching, 1988; Editor-in-Chief, Talanta, 1989-. *Hobbies:* Reading, Fishing, Gardening. *Address:* Department of Chemistry, University of Washington, Seattle, WA 98195, USA. 2, 7, 9, 14, 30, 125, 129, 130, 139, 151, 155, 162.

CHRISTIAN William Edward, b. 24 Aug 1945, Canada. Univ of Toronto. m. Mary Barbara Lotton, 26 July 1969, 2 s. *Education:* BA, Univ of Toronto, 1966; MA, Univ of Toronto, 1967; PhD, London Sch of Economics, 1970. *Appointments:* Mount Allison Univ, 1970-78; Univ of Guelph, 1978; Visiting Prof, Univ of Toronto, 1987-88, 1988-89, 1990-91; McMaster Univ, 1990-91. *Publications:* Political Parties & Deologias in Canada; Idea File of Harold Adams. *Honours:* Academic Visitor, London Sch of Economics. *Hobbies:* Music; Wine; Computors; Reading; Watching Baseball. *Address:* Dept of Political Studoes, Univ of Guelph, Guelph, Ontatio, Canada N1G 2W1. 88.

CHRISTO Javacheff, b. 13 June 1935, Gabrovo, Bulgaria. Artist. m. Jeanne Claude de Guillebon, 1 s. *Education:* Academy of Fine Arts. Sofia, 195356; Academy of Fine Arts, Vienna, 1957. *Appointments:* Self Employed Artist, 1957-. *Creative Works:* 18 lgr scale temporary works of art; 25 Books title, Christo. *Address:* 48 Howard Street, New York, NY 10013, USA.

CHROSCIELEWSKI Tadeusz, b. 3 Mar 1920 Minsk Mazowiecki, Poland. Writer, Transl. m. Honorata, 1 s, 1 d. *Education:* Polish and Russian Philology at Univ of Warsaw; PhD 1945. *Appointments:* Asst Prof, Dept of Philology, Univ of Lodz, 1945-52; Sev Tchng Posts; Mbr of Transls Comm of the Writers Union, Ed in Lodz; Ed-in-Chief, Osnowa, Lit Quarterly. *Publications:* Over 20 vols of poetry: Feast of Aurelian; The Hidden Month; The Empty Chair; The Draft Card; Identity; The Concert in from Bork; Autumn and Autumn; Constelations in Four Colours; A Short Prayer in St Jacob's Church in Sandomierz; Fondest Places; Novels: Family Jedncrozec; The School of Two Girls; The Scarlet Hour; Matulem's Stick; The Jug of Life; My Marriage in the Land of Feakow and Others; sev short stories. *Memberships:* Polish Writers Union; ZAIKS; Scientific Soc of Lodz; Polish Transls Soc; Philologist Soc; Polish-Soviet Friendship Soc; Friends of Minsk Mazowiecki. *Honours:* Ministry of Culture and Art Officers Cross and Prize; City of Lodz Prize; Cavalier's Cross; Golden Cross of Merit; Warmia's Mazury's Prize; Lodz Province Prize. *Hobbies:* Tourism, Polish Hist. *Address:* al Kosciuszki 98 m. 5, 90-442 Lodz, Poland.

CHU Petra J A, b. 15 Oct 1942, Zeist, Netherlands. Art Historian. m. Fen Dow Chu, 10 Apr 1971, 1 s, 3 d. *Education:* Diploma, Municipal Gymnasium, Utrecht, 1960; Diplôme Supérieur, Cours de Civil Franç, Sorbonne, Paris, 1961; Doctoraal Degree, Art History, Univ of Utrecht, 1967; PhD Art History, Columbia Univ, NY, 1972. *Appointments:* Prof, Hd, Dept of Art & Music, Seton Hall Univ, So Orange, 1972-; Visiting Prof, Princetown Univ, 1990-91. *Publications:* French Realism and the Dutch Masters; Courbet in Perspective; Dominique Vivant Denon; Im Lichte Hollands; The Letters of Gustave Courbet; Unsuspected Pleasures in Artists' Letters. *Membership:* Inst for Advanced Study, Princetown. *Honours:* Guggenheim Fellowship; Nat Endowment for the Humanities Research Grant. *Hobbies:* Music; Travel. *Address:* 22 Park Place, So Orange, NJ 07079, USA.

CHU Sing Y, b. 5 Mar 1921, Tinghai, ROC. Fcaulty Member; Art Show Coordinator. m. Grace Chen, 9 Sept 1950, 2 s. *Education:* PAFA, 1984; BFA, Univ of Pennsylvania, USA, 1985; MA, Univ of the Arts, USA, 1988. *Appointments include:* Lectr, Intl Trade, Tunghai Univ, Taiwan, 1979- 80; Lectr, Chinese Arts & Culture, Public Sch, USA, 1984-88; Instr, Chinese Calligraphy, PAFA, 1985; Instr, Chinese Painting, PCOP, Philadelphia, 1987- 89; Faculty Member, Workshop Instr, Allens Lane Art Centre, Philadelphia Museum of Art, 1988-. *Creative Works:* Author Various Research Works; Various Oil Paintings; Non Traditional Sculptures & Brush Drawings. *Memberships:* USA East, Craft Assoc; Woodland Presbyterian Church; CIF Rotary Intl; Intl Trade Fairs; Inlt Marketing Conslt, Taiwan; Provincial Handicrafts Research Inst; Chinese Intl Marketing Assoc. *Honours:* Gold Medal; Oustanding Ward; 2nd Award, Art in Action. *Hobbies:* Painting; Sculpture; Handicrafts; Photography; Video; Travel. *Address:* 300 S, 41 st St, Philadelphia, PA 19104, USA. 15.

CHU Tin Chi Thomas, b. 3 Nov 1950, Hong Kong. Resident Financial Conslt, China Merchants Group, Hong Kong. m. Regina C W Leung, 2 Mar 1991. *Education:* Cat State Univ of Dominque, MBA, 1972. *Appointments:* AVP Citibank NA, 1973-81; Dir, Gen Mngr, Far East Bank, HK, 1982-86; Gen Mngr, Union Bank Ltd, 1986-88; Chmn of UB Gen Insurance Co Ltd, 1986-88. *Memberships:* Public Relations Assoc; Chitung Veteran Banker Assoc; HK Gov't Registered Securities Assoc; HK Gov't Registered Investment Adviser. *Honours:* Cash Award for Distinguished Performance by Citybank. *Hobbies:* Body Building; Tennis. *Address:* Unit B 11 Floor Tower 3, Robinson Heights, 8 Robinson Road, Hong Kong.

CHUDGAR Ashok, b. 18 June 1951, Cambay, India. Certified Public Accountant, Solo Practitioner. m. Mala, 3 Dec 1980, 1 s, 1 d. *Education:* B. Com Accounting, 1971; M Com, Accounting, 1973; Financial Planner, 1989; Public Accountant, 1991. *Appointments:* Bank of India,Cahsier, 1971-73; Avalon Ind, Brookeyn, NY, 1974-81; Almazon Tile, Charlotte, NC, 1981-86; Carpet Land, Charlotte, 1987-89; VP Pactising Accountant, Financial Planner, 1989-. *Memberships:* NC ACPA; AICPA; Charlotte Area CFP; Charlotte Area Indian Business Assoc. *Honours:* Nat Merit Scholarship; English Essay Competition Coll; Mutual Benetit Lite Squab Club. *Hobbies:* Sitar; Harmonium. *Address:* Ashok B Chudgar, 8246 Oakley Lane, Charlotte, NC 28270, USA.

CHUNDER Pratap Chandra, b. 1 Sept 1919, Calcutta. Supreme Court Advocate. m. Leena Roy Chowdhury, 3 Dec 1940, 4 s. *Education:* BA, History, 1940; MA, Ancient Indian History, 1942; LLB, 1943; Attorneyship, 1945; PhD, 1957. *Appointments:* Attorney, Cal High Court, 1945-77; Supreme Cour Advocate, 1953-; Law Lectr, Cal Univ, 1046-77; Minister, Finance & Judicial Dept, Govt of West Bengal, 1968; Union Minister of Educ,Soc Welfare & Culture, 1977-78. *Publications:* Kautilya on Love & Morals, Socialist Legality & Indian Law; The Sons of Mystery; Job Charnock & His Lady

Fair; Brother Vivekananda; Novels; Plays; Articles. *Memberships:* Incorporated Law Soc; Bar Assoc. Cal High Court; West Bengal Legislative Assem; Indian Parliament; Senate Cal Univ; Rabindra Bharati Univ; West Bengal Congress; Indo American Soc; Writers Guild of India; Indian Inst of Soc Welfare & Business Mngt. *Honours:* Fellow Artist Soc; Hon D S Sc, Special Medallist; Hon Citizen of New Orleans; Reg Grand Master of Eastern India. *Hobbies:* Reading; Writing; Painting; Social Work. *Address:* 23 Nirmal Chunder Street, Calcutta 700 012, India. 1.

CHUNG Cho Man, b. 3 Mar 1918, Hong Kong. Psychiatric Conslt in Private Practice. m. (1)18 Jan 1947, dec, (2) Lillian Auyang, 27 Sept 1968, 1 s, 2 d. *Education:* Lingnan Univ, MD, 1943; Inst of Psychiatry, London Univ, 1955-57; DPM Eng, 1956; LRCP, Edin, LRCS, Edin, LRFPS, Glasg, 1956; MCPS Manitoba, 1968; MRC Psych, Uk, 1972; MRANZCP, 1981. *Appointments:* Lt Col, Med Coprs, China, 1943-45; Tch Expert, Kwongtung Provincial Health Admin, China, 1945-49; Med Superintendent, Canton Municipal Hosp, China, 1948-49; Casulty Officer, Kowloon Hosp, Hong Kong, 1950-53; Psychiatric Resident, HK Mental Hosp, 1954-55; Psychiatric Conslt, 1957-58; Lectr Psychiatry, Hong Kong Univ, 1957-58; Psychiatric Conslt, Private Practice, 1961-; Dir, Bd, Hong Kong Central Hosp, 1961-. *Publications:* Independent Research in Field Psychiatric Problems of Entrepeneurs and Geriatrics in Hong Kong. *Memberships:* World Psychiatric Assoc; American Assoc for Soc Psychiatry; Hong Kong Psychiatric Assoc; Soc of Physicians; Hong Kong Coll of Psychiatrists; Royal Hong Kong Golf Club; World Trade Centre Club. *Honours:* Fellowship, World Health Organ; Fellow, Royal Coll of Psychiatrists; Honorary Member, World Psychiatric Assoc; Corresponding Fellow, American Psychiatric Assoc; Fellow, Royal Australian & New Zealand Coll of Psychiatrists. *Hobbies:* Golf; Carpentry; Classical Music. *Address:* 611 Melbourne Plaza, 33 Queens Road Central, Hong Kong. 52.

CHUNG Hyungkun, b. 26 July 1945, Masan, ROK. Snr Public Prosecutor. m. Myungjin Choi, 6 Sept 1972, 1 s, 2 d. *Education:* LLB, Seoul Nat Univ, 1964-68; LLM, The Univ of Michigan, USA, 1979-80; Nat Fire Academy, Virgina, USA, 1981; PhD, Seoul Nat Univ, 1991. *Appointments:* Snr Public Prosecutor, Seoul & Pusan District Presecutors Office, 1975-83; Chief of Bureau, Agency for Nat Security Planning, Seoul, 1983-. *Publications:* A Study on Legal Regulation of Intl Terrorism. *Memberships:* Intl Assoc of Arson. *Honours:* The Nat Award of the Order of Nat Security Merit. *Hobbies:* Tennis; Golf. *Address:* 1629 17 Secho Dong, Seocho Gu. Seoul 137 071, Republic of Korea. 52.

CHUNG Julie Jiyoon, b. 20 Feb 1972, Seoul, Korea. Student. *Education:* UCSD, Graduation, 1994. *Publications:* Poetry, Quiet moments; Awaken to a Dream; Best Poems of the 90's. *Memberships:* Jnr Classical League; World of Poetry; World Wildlife Fund; Student for Christ; Delta Delta Delta. *Honours:* Publishers Choice Award; World of poetry Golden Poet Award; Essay Contest, 1 st Prize; California Scholarship Federation Sealbearer; Nat Latin Exam, Magna Cum Laude Award. *Hobbies:* Writing poetry; Short Stories; Playing Piano; Swimming; Nature; History; Political Sci. *Address:* 6762 Vista Del Sol Drive, Huntingdon Beach, CA 92647, USA.

CHUNG Keng, b. 10 Oct 1928, Xingning, Guangdong, China. Snr Geologist. m. Jiang Lijuan, 2 Feb 1954, 2 s, 1 d. *Education:* SunYetson Univ, Canton, 1946-50. *Appointments:* Tch, Central South Geologic Survey, 1950-54; North Western Geologic Bureau, 1955-56; Vice Dir, Engr, Guangxi Geologic Bureau, 1957-62; Geologic Sci Inst of Centrol South China, 1963-66; GCB, 1967-80; Chief Engr, Snr Geologist, 1980-89; Tech Adviser, 1989-. *Creative Works include:* 50 papers inc. Regional Geology; Oil Geology; Mineral Deposits; Geologic Map of Guangxi; Studied the Reg Geology, Mineral Resources of Guangxi, Oil & Gas of Beibu Gilf.

Honours: Several Advanced Workers of the Geologic Soc of China & Guangxi; The Sci & Tech Assoc of Guangxi; Personal Super Honor of Marine & Bench Survey of Guangxi; Second Chmn of Meizhou Kakka Fellowship of Guangxi; Prof of Doctor - Student Conslt of Tongzi Univ. *Hobbies:* Reading; Gardening. *Address:* Guangxi Bureau of Geology & Mineral Resources, 1 Jianzheng Road, Nanning, Guangxi 530023, China.

CHURAEV Nikolai Vladimirovich, b. 1 Oct 1920, Moscow. Prof, Snr Scientist. m. Fedosejeva Marina, 14 Sept 1947, 1 d. *Education:* Moscow Univ, 1939-40; Army Serv, 1941-45; Moscow Peat Inst, 1946-51; Diploma Engr Mech; PhD, 1956; Dr Sci, 1962; Prof of Physics, 1964. *Appointments:* Moscow Peat Inst, Sci Docent, Prof, 1953-64; Moscow Inst Chem Engr, Prof, 1964-65; Inst Phys Chem Russian Acad Sci, Det Surf Phenomena Lab Thin Liquid Layers, Hd of Lab, Snr Sci, 1965-. *Publications:* 350 Papers in Sci Journals; Books. Wetting Films, Moscow; Surface Forces, Moscow, NY, London; Water in Disperse Systems; Phys Chem of Processes of Masstransfer in Porous Bodies; Masstransfer in Natural Disperse Systems. *Memberships:* Mbr, Russian Acad Natur Sci; Council Colliod Sci; Russian Acad Sci; Colloid Interface Sci; Council Intern Assc Colloid and Interface Sci. *Honours:* Medal for Batle Merits; Honoured Scientist of Russian Federation; Order of Patriotic War. *Hobbies:* Fishing; Reading; Art; Music. *Address:* Volgina St, 25 2 Apt 101, 117437 Moscow, Russia.

CHURCH Robert Bertram, b. 7 May 1937, Calgary, Alberta. Prof Emeritus, Dept of Medical Biochemistry. m. Joyce Maryanne, 2 May 1959, 1 s, 1 d. *Education:* Diploma, Olds Coll, 1956; Diploma, Univ of Upsalla, Sweden, 1961; BSc, Univ of Alberta, Edmonton, 1962; MSc, Univ of Alberta, Edmonton, 1963; PhD, Univ of Edinburgh, Scotland, 1965. *Appointments include:* Affilliate & Visting Prof, Animal Reproduction Lab, Colorado State Univ, 197278; Vis Prof, Sch of Vet Sci, Murdoch Univ, Australia, 1977; Hd, Dept of Med Biochemistry, Fac of Medicine, Univ of Calgary, 1969-83; Vis Prof, Soviet Academy of Sci, Moscow, 1972; Prof & Sci Assoc, Dept of Medicine, Foothills Hosp, 1971-90; Prof, Depts of Medicine Biochemistry, Biological Sci, Univ of Calgary; Assoc Dean, Faculty of Medicine, Univ of Calgary, 1981-88; Asst Dean, Faculty of Medicine, Univ of Calgary, 1990-92. *Publications include:* Transgenic Models. *Memberships:* The Biochemical Soc of Canada; The Canadian Genetics Soc; The Genetics Soc of America; The Soc for Developmental Biology; The Soc for the Study of Reproduction; The American Assoc for the Advancement of Sci; Calgary Council on Advanced Tech. *Honours include:* Gold Medal, Univ of Alberta; Recognition Award, Agri Inst of Canada; canadian Agri Hall of Fame; Medical Research Council of Canada, Member of Bd. *Hobbies:* Study of the Genetics of Domestic Animals. *Address:* The Univ of Calgary, Faculty of Medicine, Dept of Medical Biochemistry, 3330 Hospital Drive NW, Calgary, Alberta, Canada T2N 4N1. 9, 88, 158.

CHWIEDUK Edward Zbigniew, b. 18 Feb 1961, Goscino. Palaeontologist. m. Agnieszka Pawtowska, 25 Aug 1990, 1 d. *Education:* Dept of Biology, Adam Mickiewecz Univ, 1974; Dept of Geology, Warsaw Univ, 1989; MSc Palaeontology, 1990. *Appointments:* Tech Worker, Photographer, Dept of Geology, 1983-; Biologist, 1985; Palaeoutologist, 1989. *Publications:* Description of the Deutonymph & Protonymph, Prozenon Lutulentus in Badania Fizjopaf; Conodent & Stratiography of Frasmian in Wtetrznia. *Memberships:* The Archarology & Ethnography Soc of Asia & Pacific Ocean; Guard of Nat protection; Polish Soc of Geology. *Hobbies:* Photography; Collecting Stamps; Music; Travel. *Address:* ul Dworcowa 14, 73-115 Dolice, Poland. 139, 152, 162.

CH'EN Jerome, b. 2 Oct 1921, Chengdu, China. Distinguished Research Prof Emeritas. 1 d. *Education.* BA, 1943; MA, 1945; PhD, 1956. *Appointments:* Snr

Lectr, Leeds Univ, 1963-71; Prof, York Univ, 1971- 83; Distinguished Research Prof, 1983; Emeritus, 1987. *Publications:* Yuau Shih K'ai; Mao and the Chinese Revolution; China and the West; The Military Gentry Coalition; Highlanders and Central China. *Membership:* Royal Soc of Canada. *Honours:* Visiting Prof, Univ of Kansas, Australian Nat Univ; Univ of Adelaide; Keio Univ, Italy. *Hobbies:* Music; Theatre; Travel; Reading. *Address:* 208 MCaul Street, Toronto, Ontario, Canada, M5T 1W5. 142.

CIECHALSKI Arkadiusz Henryk, b. 1 Jan 1958, Chocen, Poland. Tchr. m. Agnieszka Barbara Osmalek, 12 May 1990. *Education:* MA, Polish Linguistics, Universitas Nicolai Copernici, Torun, 1978-83; Postgrad course of Polish Philology, Universitas Nicolai Copernici, Torun, 1984-85. *Appointments:* Tchr, Primary Schl iin Chodecz, 1983-88, Schl of Agric in Chodecz, Schl of Agric in Kowal, 1991-. *Creative Works:* Photographs and Paintings exhibited in Poland (Warsaw, Slupsk, Olsztyn, Starachowice, Chodecz) and in Germany (Griefswalder); Publs in 9 mags. *Memberships:* Tchrs Arts Club in Wloclawek; Chodecz Regl Assn. *Honours:* Prize Winner; Children's Painting, Warsaw, 1972; Youth Photography, Warsaw, 1978; Photographic Competitions: Child, Torun, 1978, Chocen, 1987, Warsaw, 1988, Goleniow, 1989, Slupsk, 1989; Regl Photographic Competitions: Wloclawek 1985, 89, Chodecz 1992. *Hobbies:* Lit, Films, Travelling. *Address:* Plac Kosciuszki 1, 87-860 Chodecz, Poland.

CIENSKI Andrzej, b. 27 Nov 1931, Lwow, Poland. Prof of Librarianship. m. Helena Leputa, 1959, 1 s. *Education: MA, 1955; PhD, 1968; Docent, 1981; Prof, 1989. Appointments:* Instytut Badan Literackich, 1953; Wydawnictwo Ossolineum, 1954-59; Instytut Badan ; Literachick, 1959-65; Univ of Wroclaw, 1965-. *Publications:* 5 books, 4 scientific, 1 prose fiction. *Membership:* Wroclawskie Towarzystwo Naukowe. *Hobbies:* Polish Songs, Walks. *Address:* Mikulskiego 10, 52-420 Wroclaw, Poland.

CINADER Bernard, b. 30 Mar 1919, Vienna. Univ Prof. div,1 d. *Education:* BSc, Univ of London, 1944; PhD, Univ of London, 1948; DSc, Univ of London, 1958. *Appointments include:* Research Asst, Lister Inst of Preventive Medicine, 1945-46; principal Sci Officer, Lectr, Inst of Aminal Physiology, Babraham Hall, Cambridge, 1959-58; Prof, Clinical Biochemistry, Univ of Toronto, 1970; Pres, Royal Canadian Inst, 1989-90; Member Academic Bd, Univ of Toronto, 1988-92. *Publications:* Over 300 original Sci Papers & Reviews; 6 Books inc. Progress in Immunology; series editor of Volumes on Receptors and Ligands in Intercellular Communication; Intercellular and Intracellular Communications. *Memberships include:* World Health Organization Task Force on Standardization of Immune Reagents; Nat Comm for Immunology; Health & Welfare Canada; Iroquoian Inst; WHO; Task Force for Birth Control Vaccines. *Honours include:* Old Student Prize; Jubilee Medal, Govenor Gen of Canada; Order of Canada; Hardi Prize for the Best Graduate Student in the Dept of Immunology; Bernard Cinader Annual Lectureship of the Canadian Society of Immunology; Jan E Purkine Medal, Czechoslovak Soc Of Immunology & Allergology. *Hobbies:* Art; Culture of Canadas First Nations. *Address:* Dept of Immunology, Medical Sci's Building, Univ of Toronto, Toronto, Ontario, Canada M5S 1A8.

CIRCEO Louis Joseph Jr, b. 31 Aug 1934, Everett, Mass, USA. Principal Research Scientist & Dir, Construction Research Centre, Georgia Inst of Tech. m. Brigitta H Rockstroh, 26 Jan 1961, Dec. 1 s, 1 d. *Education:* US Military Academy, West Point, BS Engr, 1957; Iowa State Univof Sci & Tech, MS Soils Engr, 1961; PhD Civil Engr, 1963. *Appointments:* US Army Corps of Engr, 1957-87; Dir, Constr Engr Research Lab, Champaign IL, 1979-83; Dir, Const Research Centre, Georgia Inst of Tech, 1987-. *Memberships:* American Soc of Civil Engrs; Soc of American Military Engrs; Soc

of Sigma XI; Assoc of the US Army. *Honours:* Engr of the Year. *Hobbies:* Reading; Travel. *Address:* Dir, Constr Research Centre, Georgia Inst of Tech, Atlanta, GA 30332, USA. 7, 143.

CIRENEI Anacleto, b. 19 July 1913, Loano. Surgeon. m. Cavallari Valeria, 10 Apr 1944, 1 d. *Education:* Med & Surgeon, Doc, 1935; Lib doc Surgery Univ, Rome, 1942; id Clinic, 1940; id, Semeiology, 1958. *Appointments:* Assist Univ, Rome, 1936-48; Chief Surgeon, 1949-75; Full Prof, Emergency Surgery, Rome, 1975-; Dir of Post Graduate Sch, 1980-. *Publications include:* Propedeutica e Metodologia Chir, 2 Vols; Surgery of the Liver, Biliary Tree and Pancreas. *Memberships include:* Lancisiana Academy of Rome; Med Academy of Rome. *Honours:* Order Merit Italian Republic; Honour Member, Hellenic Soc Surgery; Alger Soc Suregery; Cross First Class Order Meliteusis. *Hobbies:* Historical Studies; Classical Music. *Address:* Policlinico, Umberto 1, 00161, Roma, Italy. 43.

CISZEWSKI Bohdan, b. 23 Dec 1922, Grodno. Prof of Material Science. m. Zofie Klemczynske, 29 July 1950, 1 s, 1 d. *Education:* Tech Hight Sch, Lodz, 1947; Doc of Tech Sci, Tech Military Akademie, Warsaw, 1956; Prof Extrard, 1964; Prof Ord, 1970; Coresp Member of the polish Academy of Sci, 1973; Ord Member, Polish Academy of Sci, 1986. *Appointments:* Tech Hight Sch, Ledz, Asst, 1945; Tech Hight Sch, Warsaw, Asst, 1947; Prof, 1964; Tech Military Academy, Lectr, 1951; Prof Extrord, 1964; Prof Ordin, 1970; Dept Tech Sci, Chief Prof, 1981-86,89-. *Publications:* Powder Metalury; Technology of Metals; Metal Science; Heat Treatment; Defects of Cristal Structure; New Materials. *Memberhips:* Intl Inst Sintering Sci. *Honours:* Dr Hon Cause Tech Military Academy; Dr Hon Cause Hight Sch Tech. *Hobbies:* Gardening; Sport. *Address:* Swietojerska 2424, 00-202 Warsaw, Poland.

CIVASAQUI Jose, b. 2 Jan 1916, Satamaken, Japan. Author. m. Setsuko Hirose, 18 Sept 1940, 2 s, 1 d. *Education include:* Studied Poetry, Edmund Blunden, 1947-50. *Appointments:* Snr Examiner, Translator, Civilian Employee, US Army, 1946-48; Advisor, Laison Dept, Hakodate Dock Co Ltd, Tokyo, 1948-51; Mngr, Laison Sect, Watanabe Confectionary Co Ltd, Tokyo, 1951-54; Literary Staff, Toshiba EMI Ltd, 1955-76; Lectr, Japan Translation Academy, 1978-84; Sunshine Business Coll, 1985-. *Creative Works:* Numerous Translations from English to Japanese; Poems, In His Bosom; In Thy Grace; Beyond Seeing; Living Water; Doshin Shien, Translation of A Childs Garden of Verses; Invitation to the World of Haiku; Numerous Songs. *Memberships include:* Intl Shakespeare Assoc; Japan Song Translators Soc; United Poets Laureate Intl; Japan Guild of Authors & Composers; Japan League of Poets; Shakespeare Globe Centre of Japan. *Honours include:* World Poetry Award; Diploma of Merit; Fellow, Intl Academy of Poets. *Address:* Honcho 2 12 11, Ikebukuro, Toshima Ku, Tokyo 170, Japan. 52, 152, 156.

CLAGETT Arthur Frank Jr, b. 3 Dec 1916, Little Rock, Arkansas. USA. Qualitative Rsch Writer. m. Dorothy Ruth Pinckard, 23 Dec 1954. *Education:* BA, Chem, Baylor Univ, 1943; MA, Psychology, Univ AK, 1957; PhD, Sociology, LA State Univ. *Appointments:* Shift Chem, Celanese Corp, Cumberland, MD, 1942-44; Shift Supvsr, Commercial Solvents Corp, Terre Haute, IN, 1944-45; Rsch Supvsr, Schenley Labs, IN, 1945-48; Asst Mgr, Clagett's Feed and Seed Store, Donna, TX, 1948-40; Med Serv Rep, Blue Line Chem Co, MO, 1952-56; Prison Classification Off, 1956-59, Classification Supvsr of New Admissions Ctr, 1959-60, LA State Prison; Cons Psychologist, Baker, LA, 1960-64; Asst Prof, Sociology, Lamar State Coll of Technology, Beaumont, TX, 1964-66; Assoc Prof 1968-82, Full Prof, 1983-85, Prof Emeritus, 1986-, Stephen F Austin State Univ, TX; Consulting Sociologist, Social Psychologist, Criminologist, 1986-91. *Publications:* 24 rsch articles in profl jrnls. *Memberships:* sev univ and profl assns. *Honours:* Outstanding Educator of America, 1974-75;

Outstanding Sociology Graduate Professor by Alpha Kappa Delta, SFASU Chapter, 1977-78. *Hobbies:* Reading, Qualitative Rsch, Fishing, Classical Music. *Address:* Professor Emeritus, Sociology, Stephen F Austin State University, Nacogdoches, TX 75962, USA. 2, 7, 15, 52, 125, 139, 140, 143, 151, 152, 179.

CLAMPITT Amy Kathleen, b. 15 June 1920 New Providence, Lowa, USA. Writer. *Education:* BA, English, Grinnell Coll, 1941. *Appointments:* Editor, EP Dutton, 1977-82; Writer in Residence, Coll of William & MAry, 1984-85; Visiting Writer, Amherst Coll, 1986-87. *Publications:* The Kingfisher; What the Light Was Like; Archaic Figure; Westward; Predecessors, Et Cetera. *Memberships:* Nat Inst of Arts & Letters; Academy of American Poets; Poetry Soc of America. *Honours include:* Phi Beta Kappa; Guggenheim Fellowship; DHL Honoris Causa, Grinnell Coll; Award in Literature, The American Academy of Arts and Letters; Fellowship Award for Distinguished Poetic Achievement, The Academy of American Poets. *Address:* c/o Alfred A Knopf Inc, 201 East 50th Street, New York, NY 10022, USA. 2.

CLARFIELD Avram Mark, b. 21 Dec 1949, Toronto. Physician; Writer. m. Ora Paltiel, 25 Dec 1977, 1 s, 1 d. *Education:* MD, Univ of Toronto, 1975; CCFP, Canadian Coll of Family Practice; FRCPC, Royal Coll of Physicians of Canada, 1983. *Appointments:* Chief, div of Geriatrics, Jewish General Hosp, Montreal, 1984-92; Asst Dean, Faculty of Medicine, McGill Univ, 1989-92; Prof, Faculty of Medicine, McGill Univ, 1990. *Publications:* NY Times; In Grandfathers Room; 100 Articles. *Memberships:* Canadian Medical Assoc; Canadian Soc of Geriatric Medicine; American Geriatrics Soc. *Honours:* Upjohn Postgraduate Study Award; Osler Scholarship of the Canadian Medical Assoc; Zitter Comm Award; Munk Geriatric Award; Snr Medical Fellowship; Royal Canadian Legion Fellowship in Geriatrics. *Hobbies:* Reading; Hiking; Folk Music; Writing. *Address:* Division of Geriatrics, Sir Mortimer B Davies - Jewish Gen Hosp, 3755 Cote Ste Catherine, Montreal, PQ, Canada H3T 1E2. 1, 88.

CLARK Bonnie L, b. 2 Feb 1961, Washington DC. College Prof. *Education:* MA in Speech, Bowling Green State Univ, 1981; BS Communication Arts, Defiance Coll; PhD, Education, Univ of South Florida, in progress. *Appointments:* Radio Announcer, Disc Jockey, WBNO AM-FM, Bryan, 1977-84; Coll Prof, Dir of News, WRUF AM-FM, Univ of Florida, 1984-85; Dir of Communications, Defiance Coll, 1985-86; Coll Speech, Public Speaking prof, Dir of Forensics, St Petersburg Jnr Coll, Clearwater, Florida, 1987-. *Memberships:* Speech Communication Assn; Florida Comm Assn; Delta Kappa Gramma Tching Honorary; Alpha Xi Delta Nat Sorority. *Honours:* Nat Panel Presentations, Speech Comm Assn Convention; Named Master Tchr. *Hobbies:* Public Speaking; Music; Principal Tympanist, Clearwater Symphony Orchestra. *Address:* 2465 Drew Street, Clearwater, FL 34625, USA.

CLARK Eileen, b. 8 Jan 1924, Twechar, Scotland. Homemaker; Volunteer Guide, Mecord Museum of Canadian History. m. Edward Ritchie Clark, 11 Oct 1945, 1 s, 3 d. *Education:* BSc, St Andrews Univ, Scotland, 1945. *Appointments:* Redar Tech Officer, Womens Auciliary Air Force, 1943-45. *Publications:* Articles for Journal of Canadian Federation of Univ Women. *Memberships:* Canadian Federation of Univ Women; Intl Fed of Univ Women; Member of Senate, Presbyterian Coll; Virginia Gilderseeve Intl Fund for Univ Women; St Andrews Soc of Montreal. *Honours:* Honorary Citizen, City of Winnipeg. *Hobbies:* Reading; Downhill Skiing; English Smocking; Antique Porcelain; Swimming; Gardening. *Address:* 65 Franklin Avenue, Town of Mount Royal, Quebec, Canada H3P 1B8. 88, 138.

CLARK Judith Wells, b. 28 Dec 1943, Washington DC. Exec Dir of Southwest Virginia Opera. m. Richard Lee Clark, 1 July 1967. *Education:* Bach of Arts, Mary

Washington Coll, 1966; Master of Music, Northwestern Univ, 1967. *Appointments:* Public & Private Sch Music Tchr, 1967-74; Private Piano Tchr, 1974-78; Dir, Preparatory Div of Music, Olin Hall Coord, Arts Admin, 1979-88; Hollins Coll, Lectr in Music, 1988-89. *Creative Works:* Affiliate Artist Accompanist. *Memberships:* Mortar Bd; Thursday Morning Music Club. *Honours:* Alpha Phi Sigma Award; Soutstanding Snr Music Award; Woodrow Wilson Foundation Honorable Mention; Outstanding Yound Women of America. *Hobbies:* Gardening; Swimming; Piano; Biking. *Address:* 4510 Stonewall Road, Boanoke, VA 24017, USA. 7.

CLARK Robin Jon Hawes, b. 16 Feb 1935, Rangiora, New Zealand. Prof of Chemistry. m. Beatrice Rawdin Brown, 30 May 1964, 1 s, 1 d. *Education:* BSc, MSc, Canterbury Univ Coll, Univ of New Zealand, 1955, 57; PhD, DSc, Univ Coll, Univ of London, 1961, 69. *Appointments include:* Prof Chemistry, Univ Coll London, 1982-; Dean of Science, 1988; Sir William Ramsay Prof, Hd, Dept of Chemistry, Univ Coll London, 1989-. *Publications:* The Chemistry of Titanium &Vanadium; The Chemistry of Titanium, Zirconium & Hafnium; The Chemistry of Vanadium, Niobium & Tantalum; Advances in Spectroscopy; Raman Spectroscopy; over 300 Sci Research Papers. *Memberships:* Fellow, Royal Soc of Arts; Fellow, Royal Soc of Chemistry; Hon Fellow, Royal Soc of New Zealand. *Honours:* Tilden Lectr & Medalist; Nyholm Lectr & Medalist; Thomas Graham Lect; Harry Hallam Lect. *Hobbies:* Golf; Tennis; Swimming; Skiing; Bridge; Music; Theatre; Travel. *Address:* 3A Loom Lane, Radlett, Herts, WD7 8AA, England. 1.

CLARK Terrence Michael, b. 5 May 1946, Walton on Thames, Surrey. m. 29 May 1976, 2 s, 1 d. *Appointments include:* Editor, British Blacksmith Mag, British Artist Blacksmiths Assoc, 1980; Vice Chairman, British Artist Blacksmith Association, 1992; Victoria & Albert Museum, Towards a New Iron Age, 1982; Addy Cup, Worshipful Co of Blacksmiths, most Original & Well Made Piece of Work, 1983; Memphis & Wisconsin, USA, 1984; Guildford Cathederal, 1985. Artsmith, Royal Academy Comm under Sculpture, 1986; Forgemaster, First Intl Forge In, Ireland, 1991. *Creative Works include:* British Artist Blacksmiths Assoc Exhibition; New Ashgate Gallery; Heavy Metal Touring Exhibition. *Hobbies:* Skiing; Flying; Competition Shooting. *Address:* Wildfields Farm, Woodstreet Village, Nr Guildford, Surrey, GU3 3DT.

CLARK William Bedford, b. 23 Jan 1947, Oklahoma City, Okla, USA. Prof of English, Texas A&M Univ. m. Charlene Kerne, 22 Dec 1972, 2 d. *Education:* BA, Univ of Oklahoma, 1969; MA, Louisiana St Univ, 1971; PhD, Louisiana St Univ, 1973; Poctdoctoral Fellowship, Yale Univ, 1973-74. *Appointments:* Asst Prof, North Carolina A&T St Univ, 1974-77; Asst Prof, Prof, Texas A&M Univ, 1977-; Editor, South Central Review, 1984-87. *Publications:* Critical Essays on R P Warren; Critical Essays on Amer Humor; KA Porter and Texas; Amer Vision of R P Warren. *Memberships:* Conference on Christianity & Literature; American Literature Assoc; Nat Assoc of Scholars; South Central Mod Lang Assoc; Robert Penn Warren Circle; Phi Kappa Phi. *Honours:* Distinguished Achievement Award for Tching; Synod Delegate, Diocese of Austin. *Hobbies:* Classical Piano; Collecting Western Americana. *Address:* 2304 Burton Drive, Bryan, TX 77802, USA.

CLARKE Christopher David, b. 4 July 1971, Blackburn. Student. *Education:* Queen Elizabeth Grammer Sch, Blackburm 1979-80; Univ of Essex, 1989-. *Honours:* Presidents Cup; British Open Doubles Champion; App Bowl, Most Improved Player; Oregon Invitational, Full International Honors; Ranked 12th in the World, 1988. *Hobbies:* Ten Pin Bowling; Bridge; Chess; Golf. *Address:* 77 Mellor Lane, Mellor, Nr Blackburn, Lancs, BB2 7EW, England.

CLARKE Garry Kenneth Connal, b. 6 Oct 1941, Hamilton, Canada. Prof of Geophysics. m. Nora Kelly, 25 Aug 1973, Div. 1 s. *Education;* BSc, Univ of Alberta, 1963; MA, Univ of Toronto, 1964; PhD, Univ of Toronto, 1967. *Appointments:* Asst Prof, 1967-71; Assoc Prof, 1971-77; Prof, 1977; Univ of British Columbia. *Publications:* Numerous Research pub on Glaciology. *Memberships:* Arctic Inst of North America; Intl Glaciological Soc; Canadian Geophysical Union. *Honours:* Fellow, Arctic Inst of North America; Killam Snr Fellowship; Fellow, Royal Soc of Canada. *Hobbies:* Skiing; Hiking; Jazz Piano. *Address:* 1980 McNicoll Avenue, Vancouver, British Columbia, Canada V6J 1A6. 2, 88.

CLARKE Richard Gordon, b. 13 May 1949, Johnson City, TN, USA. Risk Mgmt; Financial Institution Insurance. m. (1) Jane Moore, 4 Oct 1975, div. (2) Sharon Winters, 29 Feb 1988, 1 s. *Education:* BS English, East Tenn State Univ, 1971; Prog Tech Mgrs, Univ of North Carolina, 1984. *Appointments:* Underwriter, Continental Ins Co, 1971-74; Underwriter, Royal Ins Co, 1974-75; Mgr, Wallace Ins Agency, 1975-76; American Ins Mgmt Corp, 1976-77;VP, McNeary Conslt Brooke & Co, 1977-89; VP, FINPRO Reg Cord, Marsh & McLennan Cos, 1989-. *Publications:* Articles; Maximizing Cov, Minimizing Costs. *Memberships:* Soc of Chartered Property Casualty Underwriters; Chmn, CPCU Risk Mgmt Section, 1989-92; East Tenn State Univ Nat Alumni Assoc, Pres 1989-90; Sigma Phi Epsilon Fraternity. *Hobbies:* Volunteer Work; Photography; Travel. *Address:* 3524 Billingsly Drive, Marietta, GA 30062, USA. 7.

CLARKE Stewart, b. 12 Mar 1936, Heanor, Derby. Conslt Physician. m. Gillian Mary Acres, 9 June 1962, 2 s. *Education:* univ of Birmingham, 1954-59; MB, CHB, 1969; MD, 1965; MRCP, FRCP, 1974. *Appointments:* Jnr Medical Posts, 1959-66; MRC Research Fellow, 1966- 69; Queen Elizabeth Hosp, Birmingham; Asst Prof CVRI, San francisco, 1970; The Royal Free Hospital, 1971-. *Publications:* Aerosols & The Lung; Fibreoptic Bronchoscopy; Book Chapters & Papers on Respiratory Medicine. *Memberships:* European Medicine Soc; The Thoracic Soc; Assoc of Physicians of Great Britian & Ireland; American Thoracic Soc. *Honours:* MD with Honors; Tudor Edwards Memorial Lectr. *Hobbies:* Rugby; Football; Saralens; Golf; Squash; Motor Cycling; Pointer Dogs. *Address:* Oak House, 13 Hadley Grove, Hadley Green, Barnet, Herts, EN5 4PH, England.

CLARKE Thomas Sydney, b. 29 Apr 1939, Sipson, Middlesex. Sports Editor, The Times. m. Margaret Jean Morgan, 12 Sept 1961, 1 s, 2 d. *Education:* Isleworth Grammar Sch, 1950-56. *Appointments:* Reporter, Hayes Chronicle, 1956-57; Sports Reporter, Herts Advertiser, 1957-59; Sports Reporter, Bulawago Chronicle, 1959-61; Sports Editor, Daily Nation and Sunday Nation, Nairobi, Kenya, 1961-63; Sports Sub Editor, Daily Express, London, 1963-67; Asst Editor, Queen Mag, 1967-69; Women's Features, Evening Standard, London, 1970-71; Sports Editor, Evening Standard, London, 1972-74; Sports Editor, Daily Mail, London, 1975-86; Sports Editor, The Times, 1986-. *Hobbies:* Travel; Watching Sport; Playing Golf. *Address:* 11 Thorndon Hall, Ingrave, Brentwood, Essex CM13 3RJ, England.

CLAS Andre, b. 1 June 1933, Laning. Prof. m. 19 July 1955, 1 s, 1 d. *Education:* MA, Linguistics, Montreal, 1960; PhD, Tubingen, 1967. *Appointments:* Prof of Linguistics, 1963-91; Editor of Meta, 1967-91. *Publications:* Phonetique Appliquee; Le Francais Laugue des Affaires; Dictiomaire Compact des Sciences et de la Technique. *Memberships:* Soc de Linguistique; Correspondant du TLF de I INALF. *Honours:* Honoary Member, Translation Soc of Quebec. *Hobbies:* Stamp Collecting Dictionaries. *Address:* 7405 Maynard, Montreal, Canada H3R 3B3.

CLAUDON Jean-Louis Rene, b. 28 Sept 1950, Nancy, France. Space Business Exec. m. Tadokoro Haru, 19 July 1977. *Education:* Engr, Ecole Nat Superieure d'Arts et Metiers, Paris, 1972; Master of Sci, Brown Univ, Providence RI USA, 1974; Doc of Engr, Tokyo Univ, 1981. *Appointments:* Structural Analyst, Peugeot, 1974-75; French Peace Corps Tech Adviser, Sousse, Tunisia, 1975-76; Commercial Attache Embassy of France, Japan, 1981-86; Rep for Japan, Arianespace, 1986; Rep for Asia Pacific, Arianespace, 1989. *Publications include:* Journal de Mecanique; Theorectical & Applied Mechanics; Computers & Structures; Optimization Methods in Structural Design. *Memberships:* European Business Comm in Japan; Aeronautics & Space Comm. *Hobbies:* Tennis; Swimming. *Address:* Yayoi 1-5-10-602, Bunkyo Ku, Tokyo 113, Japan. 52.

CLAUS Carl Christer Thure, b. 3 Feb 1955, Stockholm. Lincensed Psychologist; Psychotherapist. *Education:* Bach of Sci, 1980; Master of Sci, 1983; Licensed Psycghologist, 1985; Educ in Hypnotherapy, 1978-81. *Appointments:* Swedish Labour Market Inst, 1984; Karsudden Mental Hosp, 1985-87; Inst of Psychogenetics, 1987-90; Columbia Caerulea, 1990. *Publications:* Thesis, Dreamwork a Metamethodological Study. *Memberships:* The Intl Soc of Hypnosis; The Soc of Stockholm. *Honours:* Knight of the Order of the Temple. *Hobbies:* Yoga; Karate; Gnosticism; Globetrotting; History of Art & Sci. *Address:* Valhallavagen 124, S-114 41 Stockholm, Sweden.

CLAYTON David J, b. 22 Dec 1954, Paris, TN. Minister. m. Sharon Clayton, 28 Dec 1976, 2 s, 1 d. *Education:* David Lipscomb Univ, BA, 1975; Bethany Thedogical Seminary, MBs, 1991. *Appointments:* Burmette Chapel, Antiech, TN, 1979-83; Broadway Church of Christ, Paducah, 1983-87; Central Church of Christ, Spartanbury, SC, 1987-. *Publications:* Commentary ion Matthew; Mag Articles for Chritian Mag. *Hobbies:* Golf; Chicago Cubs. *Address:* 2052 N Church Street Place, Spartanbury, SC 29301, USA.

CLAYTON James Lee, b. 2 Mar 1934, Finger, Tennessee, USA. Chmn of the Bd, Chief Exec Officer & Pres, Clayton Homes Inc. 2 s, 2 d. *Education:* Electrical Engr Degree, UT, 1957; J D Degree, Univ of Tennessee, 1964; PhD in Business Admin, Cumberland Coll, 1990. *Appointments:* Obtained Volvo Franchise, Knoxville, TN, 1958; Television Show Host, Claytons Star Time, 1960; Opened Maunfactured Home Sales Centre, Knoxville, 1966; Opened Manufactuered Home plant, Hallis, TN, 1970; Clayton Homes Public as Pres, 1983. *Memberships include:* Dollar Gen Corp; First American Bank; Eat Tennessee Foundation; Knoxville Symphony Endowment Comm; Tennesse and American Bar Assoc. *Honours:* Sigma Phi Epsilons Career Distinction Award; Transcript Gold Award; Coopera & Lybrand Enterpreneur of the Year; TMHA Hall of Fame; Jnr Achiement Business Hall of Fame; Engr of Distinction; Horatio Alger Award. *Hobbies:* Pilot; Snow Skiing; Wine Connisseur; Health Enthusiast; Workaholic. *Address:* Clayton Homes Inc, PO Box 15169, Knoxville, TN 37901, USA.

CLEMENT Kathleen Ruth, b. 28 May 1928, Ord, Nebraska, USA. Artist (Painter). m. Richard Sibley, 28 Aug 1955, div 1972, 1 s, 2 d. *Education:* BA, Univ NB, 1960; Painting, Frank Gonzalez, 1967-69; Art Critic Seminars, Toby Joysmith, 1977-79; Mus Studies, Paris, France, 1980; Handmade Paper Course, 1984. *Appointment:* Self-employed Profl Painter. *Creative Works:* Individual Exhibs: Margolis Galls, 1985; Rossi Gall; Kin Gall; San Angel Gall; Stuhr Mus; Casa de la Culture, Puebla, Mexico, 1991; Toluca, 1992; Mus of Fine Arts, Mexico, 1992; Grp Exhibs: Centro Cultural Jose Marti, 1987; V Bienial Iberoamericana of Still Life, Domecq Cultural Inst; Siempre Ninos, Nat Mus of Hist, Chapultepec Castle, Mexico; Banamex, Mexico; Sheldon Mem Art Gall, Lincoln, NB, USA. *Memberships:* Delta Phi Delta; SOMART; Foro de Arte Contemporaneo; Pres

1985, Churubusco Book Club; Mexico City Chapt, Panhellenic. *Honours:* Prizes Graphic, 1949; Statue of Victory, World Culture Prize, Panma, Italy; Honorary Commercial Attache, State of Nebraska to Mexico. *Hobbies:* Reading, Swimming, Corale Singing. *Address:* Prolongacion Nayarit 120, Tizapan, Mexico 01080 DF, Mexico.

CLIFFORD ROSE Frank, b, 29 Aug 1926, London. Neurologist. m. Angela, 16 Sept 1963, 3 s. *Education:* Kings Coll, London, 1944-46; Westminster Medical Sch, 1946-49. *Appointments:* Conslt Neurologist, Charina Cross Hosp, London, 1965-91. *Publications:* 50 Books on Neurological Subjects. *Memberships:* Royal Soc of Medicine; Medical Soc of London. *Honours:* Harold Wolff Award; Dostinguished Clinical Award. *Hobbies:* Reading; Travel. *Address:* London Neurological Centre, 110 Harley Street, London W1N 1AF, England. 1.

CLIFTON John Ernest, b. 26 Aug 1932, East Lothain. Civil Servant. m. Margaret Govenlock Hepburn, 15 June 1957, 1 d. *Education:* Skerrys Coll, Edinburgh, Open Univ. *Appointments:* Telephone Mngr Office, 1950-55; Nat Service, 1950-52; HM Customs & Excise, 1955- . *Memberships:* Edinburgh Southern Harriers; Scottish Cross Country Union; UK Cross Country Commission; Scottish Amateur Athletic Assoc; Scottish Commonwealth Games Council; UK Civil Service Athletic Assoc; Scottish Civil Serv Athletic Assoc; Scottish Civil Serv Sports Council; Edinburgh Area Civil Serv Sports Assoc. *Honours:* Open Univ, Bach of Arts. *Hobbies:* Reading; Hill Walking; Athletics; Cross Country Running. *Address:* 8 Craigshannoch Road, Wormit, Fife, DD6 8ND, Scotland.

CLIFTON HADLEY Christopher Breen, b. 16 Dec 1948, Esher. Chiropractor. m. Virginia Fiona Clifton Duck, 1 Mar 1980, 2 s, 1 d. *Education:* Reeds Sch, Cobham Surrey, Guildford Tech Coll, 1965-68; Anglo Europea Coll of Chiropractic, 1968-72. *Appointments:* Self Amployed, 1971-; Hadley Chiropractic Clinic, Richmond, 1973-86; Centros Chiropracticos Hadley, Spain, 1981-. *Publications:* Procedure Manuals; Videotapes Instr. *Memberships:* Intl Chiropractic Assoc; American Chiropractic Assoc; British Chiropractic Assoc; Spanish Chiropractic Assoc; European Chiropractic Union; Parker Chiropractic Foundation; Acupunture Soc of America. *Honours:* Chiropractor of the Year; GTO Award; NACC Putstanding Contribution Award. *Hobbies:* Windsurfing; Carpentry; Clinic Systems; Collecting Limited Edition Porcelain Plates. *Address:* Centros Quiropracticos Hadley SA, Calle Asdrubal, Edificio Tharsis, Bajo 3, Cartagena, Murcia, Spain. 139, 152.

CLINTON Bill, b. 19 Aug 1946. President of USA. m. Hillary Rodham Clinton, 1 d. *Education:* BS, Georgetown Univ, Washington, 1964-68; Rhodes Scholar, Univ Coll, Oxford, 1968-70; JD, Yle Univ Law Sch, New Haven, CT, 1970-73. *Appointments:* Univ of Arkansas, Law Sch Prof, 1974-76; Attorney Gen, State of Arkansas, 1977-79; Governor, State of Arkansas, 1979-81; Wright, Lindsey & Jennings Law Firm, 1981-83; Governor, State of Arkansas, 1983-; Elected President, USA, November 1992. *Memberships:* Domocratic Leadership Council; Nat Governors Assoc, Task Force on Educ; Democratic Governors Assoc; Nat Governors Assoc; Southern Growth policies Bd. *Honours:* Nat Conference of Christians & Jews Humanitarian Award; Assoc award, Nat Council of State Human Service Admin; Nat Energy Efficiency Advocate Award; Recognition Award; US News and World Report, Selected one of Nations Best Governors; Newsweek, one of five Most Effective Governors in the Nation. *Address:* The White House, Washington DC, USA.

CLUTTER Gayle Ann, b. 14 Sept 1945, Homstead, Florida, USA. Radiological Technologist; Certified Tumor Registrar. *Education:* Reg'd Radio Technologist, Menorah Med Ctr, Kansas City, MO, 1967; Assn of Sci Advanced Radiological Tech, Hillsborough Com Col,

Tampa, FL, 1983. *Appointments:* Staff Radio Technologist, Baptist Hosp, Kansas City, 1967-71; Dir Radiation Oncol, 1971-90; Cancer Prog Dir, 1975-; S.E Mktg Dir, Elm Sers Inc, Rockville, MD, 1987-90. *Creative works:* Author; Editor, Professional Review for Tumor Registrars: A Study Guide, 1989. *Memberships:* Am Cancer Soc, 1980-; FL Tumor Registrars Assn, 1980- , Pres, 1977-79; Cancer Control and Res Adv Bd, 1981-90; West FL Soc for Radiation Therapy Technols, Pres, 1987-88; Nat Tumor Registrars Assn; Advanced Statistical Processes, audio-visual course, 1992; Cancer Epidemiology, audio-visual course, 1992; Principles of Biostatistics, audio-visual course, 1992. *Address:* 9764 Lake Sminole Dr E, Largo, FL 34643, USA.

COAKLEY Carolyn Jeanne Gwynn, b. 8 May 1943, Fairmount, West Virginia, USA. Consultant; Author. *Education:* BA Ed, Fairmont State Col, WV, 1965; MA Speech Communication, Univ Maryland, Col Pk, 1973. *Appointments:* Eng Tchr, Glen Burnie HS, 1965-67; Speech Tchr, Hg Point HS, 1981-90; Speech and Listening Instr, Univ of Maryland, 1981-84. *Creative works:* Listening Instruction, 1979; Experientia Listening, 1989; Listening, 4th ed, 1992; Perspectives in Listening, 1993; Teaching EEffective Listening, 1993. *Memberships:* Intl Listening Assn, Pres, 1987; Ed Testing Sers Adv Bd on Listening, 1986-; Maryland State Dept of Ed Lang Arts Curr Task Force, Listening Co-Chm, 1983-85. *Honours:* Speech Communication Assn Marcella K Oberle Awd for Outstanding Teaching, 1990; Intl Listening Assn's Listening Hall of Fame, 1988; US Dept of Ed Christa McAuliffe Fellow, 1987; Washington Post Agnes Meyer Outstanding Tchr Awd, 1987. *Hobbies:* Swimming; Biking; Writing. *Address:* 1110 Beasley Way, Sonoma, CA 95476, USA.

COATS Charles F, b. 31 Oct 1949, La Junta, Colorado, USA. Assistant Professor of Physics and Mathematics. *Education:* BS Phys & Math, 1970; MA Maths, 1977; MS Phys, 1979; PhD Phys, 1982. *Appointments:* US Army Lat Bech, 1971-73; McPherson Col Asst Prof of Math, 1979-80; Asst Prof Phys and Math Univ of Pittsburgh at Bradford, 1980-86; Coats Photographic Sers, 1986-; Asst Prof, Maths, S.E Oklahoma State Univ, 1987- 89; Asst Prof Phys and Math, Univ of Montevallo, 1989-. *Memberships:* AAPT; Sigma Xi; Pi Mu Epsilon; Kappa Mu Epsilon; ASSA; MAA. *Hobbies:* Art; Music; Reading; Photography; Computers; Chess; Ecology. *Address:* Mathematics and Physics Station 6490, University of Montevallo, Montevallo, AL 35115, USA.

COATS David Jervis, b. 25 Jan 1924, Edinburgh, Scotland. Civil Engineer. m. Hazel Bell Livingstone, 24 Mar 1955, 1 s, 2 d. *Education:* HS of Glasgow, 1938-40; BSc Hons Civil Engrg, Univ Glasgow, 1940-43. *Appointments:* Royal Elec & Mech Engrs, 1943-47; Babtie Shaw & MOrton, Consltg Engrs, Glasgow, 1947- , Partner, 1962-87, Sr Partner, 1979- 87, Sen Conslt, 1987-. *Memberships:* FICE, 1964, VP, 1987-89; Scottish Constrn Gp, 1980-88, Chm, 1986-92; Assn of Conslt g Engrs, Chm, 1979- 80; Glasgow Univ Trust, Chm, 1985-92; Intl Comm on large Dams, VP, 1983-86. *Honours:* CBE 1984; Telford Medal of ICE, 1983; Hon DSc, Glasgow Univ, 1984. *Hobbies:* Swimming; Hill walking. *Address:* 7 Kilmardinny Crescent, Bearsden, Glasgow G61 3NP, Scotland.

COBBOLD Anthony Alan Russell, b. 15 Mar 1935, Winchester, England. m. (1) Margaret Elizabeth Turner, 15 Aug 1959; (2) Jillianne Bridget Gibbs, 25 Apr 1974, 3 s. *Education:* Marlborough Col, 1948-53; Ba Gonville & Caius Col, Cambridge. *Appointments:* Duke of Edinburgh's Royal Regt, 1953-55; W & T Avery Ltd, 1958-66; W D & H O Wills, 1966-71; Evode Gp Plc, 1971-87; Cobbold Mgmt Conslts, 1987-89; Evode Gp Plc, 1989-. *Memberships:* FID; FBIM; Chartered Inst of Mktg; Inst of Roofing. *Hobbies:* Genealogy; Woodland Management. *Address:* The Vineyard, Weston under Redcastle, Shrewsbury SY4 5JY, England.

COBLE Daniel Bruce, b. 3 Nov 1949, Spangler, Pennsylvania, USA. Director Medical/Surgical Nursing. *Education:* BMus, Westminster Col, PA, 1971; AA Nsg, Indiana Univ S.E, 1974; BSc Nsg, Regents Col Prog, Albany, NY, 1982; MSc Nsg Admin, State Univ of NY, Buffalo, 1983. *Appointments:* Tampa Gen Hosp, 1985-; Bethesda Com Hosp, Nornell NY; United Com Hosp, Grove City, PA; Olean Gen Hosp, NY; VA Hosp, Bath, NY; Lock Haven Hosp, PA; Humanan Univ Hosp, Louisville, KY. *Creative works:* Articles on bedside computers. *Memberships:* ANA; FL Nures Assn; Sigma Theta Tau; FL Org of Nurse Execs; ANA Coun on Compter Applications; S.Nursing Res Soc; Phi Mu Alpha. *Honours:* Info Sers Awd, Signa Theta Tau, 1991. *Hobbies:* Baseball; Church Music; Organist. *Address:* Director, Medical/Surgical Nursing, The Tampa General Hospital, Box 1289, Tampa, FL 33601, USA.

COCKCROFT John Anthony Eric, b. 9 Aug 1934, Todmorden. m. Victoria Mary Hartley, 5 Sept 1965, 2 s, 1 d. *Education:* FTI, Burnley Col of Sci & Tech, 1951-54; BA, MA, Hist, Ec, St John's Col, Cambridge, 1956-59; MLitt, Polit, Strategic Studies, Aberdeen Univ; PhD Strategy, Sci & Tech Policy, Manchester Univ. *Appointments:* Army Comm, 1954, RAC & Air Desptach, Germany; OECD Paris, Athens, 1965; FCO Kabul, 1970; UN Amman, 1973, Dar es Salamm, 1980; Dalhousie Univ, Centre for Foreign Policy Studies, Canada, 1983; Prof Ec & Mgmt, Nigeria, 1982; Team Leader, Mgmt Conslt Team, Price Waterhouse, World Bank Proj BD-1205, 1985; MD, UK, 1986-90 (1974-78 Anglo-German manufacturing co); Currently, Stoddard Sekers Plc, Glasgow. *Creative works:* OECD Pilot Teams SCi & Devel, Greece, 1968; NATO Intra Alliance Ec co-op Military Asst SE Flank; Soviet Strategy, Directed Energy and Space (thesis). *Memberships:* C.Text Chartered Technologist; MCSD Chartered Designer, 1980' RIIA, London; IISS, London; RUSI, London; Textile Inst, Manchester; Calvary and Guards Club, London. *Honours:* Cambridge Univ Scholarship, 1956; Sword of Hon, Cadet Sch, 1955; Textile Inst and Bradford Textile Soc Design Prizes, 1953, 1954; NATO Fellow, 1979-80; Killam Fellow, Canada, 1983-84. *Hobbies:* Music; Prints; Painting; Leeds and Manchester Utds; Classic Cars and Motor Racing; Horse Racing; Walking; Travel; Mountains. *Address:* The Old Vicarage, Ledsham, South Milford, Leeds LS25 5LT, England.

CODY Sebastian, b. 6 Oct 1956, London, England. TV Producer; Writer. *Education:* King Alfred Sch, Hampstead, 1974; Univ of Vienna; BA Hons, Univ of York, 1978; Nat Film Sch. *Appointments:* BBC TV Reschr, 1979; Royal Opera Hse Staff Producer, 1985; TV Producer, including 4 years as the editor of After Dark for Channel 4, 1986-. *Creative works:* Producer and Director of Films: Why Do I Believe You?, 1983; Before His Very Eyes, 1984; Writer for numerous newspapers and magazines. *Honours:* Exec Producer of The Secret Cabaret, nominated Best Light Entertainment Prog, Royal TV Soc, 1991. *Address:* 9 Leamington Road Villas, London W11 1HS, England.

COE Anthony George (Tony), b. 29 Nov 1934, Canterbury, England. Musician (Clarinet, Saxophone), Composer, Writer. m. (1) 2 s, (2) Sue Stedman Jones, 7 Nov 1984. *Education:* Simon Langton, Canterbury; Army Serv in Africa and Germany; Composition w Donald Leggatt, Alfred Nieman, Richard Rodney Bennet, Glo Bokar. *Appointments:* Lyttelton, 1956-60; John Dankworth, 1963-67; Kenny Clarke, Francy Boland and Stan Tracey (at var times), 1967-69; Matrix w Alan Hacker, 1970-74; The Lonely Bears w Tony Hymas, 1991-. *Creative Works:* Compositions: Zeit Geist; The Buds of Time; The Jolly Corner and many shorter pieces; Var Films: Camomille, Mer de Chine; Writings: Essays on Hobsbawm in Culture Ideology, Politics; Articles in Die heimliche, Liebe des Jazz eur euro, Paischen Moderne and Jazz Ensemble. *Memberships:* Musicians Union; CASS; SACEM, Paris; PRS, London. *Honour:* Honorary Doctorate, University of Kent, 1989. *Hobbies:* Walking, Reading, Vintage Films, Chess, Alternative Therapy, Ecology, Anthroposophy. *Address:* 35 Mandeville Road, Canterbury, Kent CT2 7HD, England.

COFFENG John Adrianus, b. 22 Apr 1948, Amsterdam, Holland. Advertising Agency Managing Partner. m. Frances Ellen Keijer, 4 Dec 1978. 1s, 2d. *Education:* Grad Psycho, Univ Amsterdam, 1974; Emmanuel Col, Cambridge, England, 1975; Hamburgerology, McDonald's Univ, Oakbrook, Illinois, USA, 1984. *Appointments:* Asst Prof, Univ Amsterdam, 1974- 75; Mkt Reschr, InterViewer, 1975-79; Dir, Advrs Gp, 1980-83. *Creative works:* Dir, Go/Needham, 1983-85; Mng Ptnr, S6F, 1985-86; Mng Ptnr, GO/RSCS, 1986-1991; Grey Amsterdam, 1991-, Dir Client Services; Author: Buying Labour or Selling a Job? Grip on Direct Marketing. *Memberships:* The Marketing of Personality, 1984; Intl Adv Assn; Nederland Centrum von Dirs; Genootschap van Reklame. *Honours:* Art Dirs Club Nederland Awds, 1983-85; Effie Nederlandie Advisers Bureau, 1984- 89. *Hobbies:* Tennis; Skiing; Catamaran Sailing. *Address:* Witzand 19, N-Holland 1261BM, Blaricum, The Netherlands.

COGGESHALL Norman David, b. 15 May 1916, Ridgefarm, Illinois, USA. Research Director; Physicist; Private Investor. m. Margaret Danner, 22 Aug, 2 s, 2 d. *Education:* BA 1937, MS 1938, PhD 1942, Phys, Univ of Illinois. *Appointments:* Scist, 1943-55, Res Exec, 1955-70, VP, 1970- 81, Gulf Oil Co; Private Investor, 1981-. *Creative works:* Many research papers and patents in physics and chemistry; Contributing author to Colloid Chemistry; Physical Chemistry of Hydrocarbons; Organic Analyses; Advances in Mass Spectrometry. *Memberships:* FAPS; ACS; Mass Spectrometry Soc, Pres; Pres, Pittsburgh Spectroscopy and Physical Socs; Res Adv Coms. *Honours:* ACS Awd, 1970; Am Petroleum Inst Resolution of Appreciation, 1970; FAPS, 1951. *Hobbies:* Music composition; History; Science. *Address:* 701 Driftwood Drive, Lynn Haven, FL 32444, USA.

COHEN Janet, b. 4 July 1940, Oxford, England. Director, Charterhouse Bank. m. 18 Dec 1971, 2 s, 1 d. *Education:* South Hampstead HS, 1949-59; Hons Deg Law, Newnham Col, Cambridge, 1959-62; Qualified as a Solicitor, 1965. *Appointments:* Frere Cholmeley Nicholsons, 1963-65; Consultancy Work, 1965-69; Principal then Asst Sec, Dept of Trade & Industry, 1969-81, Charterhouse Bank, 1981-91. *Creative works:* Death's Bright Angel, 1988; Death on Site, 1989; Death of a Partner, 1991 (as Janet Neel); The Highest Bidder, 1992 (as Janet Cohen). *Memberships:* Fellow, RSA; Member, Schools Exam and Assessment Coun. *Honours:* Governor, National Institute for Economic and Social Research; John Creasey Prize for best first crime novel, Death's Bright Angel, 1988. *Hobbies:* Writing; Politics; Broadcasting. *Address:* 50 Blenheim Terrace, London NW8 OEG, England.

COHEN Philip, b. 3 July 1907, New York City, USA. Certified Public Accountant; Tax and Insurance Consultant. m. (1)Rhoda Gish, 6 June 1938; (2)Pauline Weber, 21 Dec 1984, 1 s, 1 d. *Education:* BBA, Col City of NY, 1929. *Appointments:* Self employed Acct, 1929-91; Gen Ins Broker Agent, 1927-78; The Cohen Brokerage, 1927-36; Public Affiliates Corp, 1936- 67; Levy Adler Cohen Ltd, NYC and Long Island, 1967-77; President & Owner, World Metal Spinning Corp, 1942-55; War Plant, 1942-45; Owner, Partner, Treas, Pres, World Hand Forged Products Mfg. *Creative works:* Lets Talk Taxes, monthly contribution to various condominiums and civic publications, 1984-91. *Memberships:* Pythian Order - Chancellor Commander (all lodges), Loyal Am Lodge, 1933-60, Life Mbr, Grt Am Lodge, 1960-72, Life Mbr, Onward Lodge, 1972-; NE Dade Coalition, Exec Comm, Treas, 1984-; Am Red Magen David of Israel Pres Admls Port Chap, 1989-; Admls Port Condo Assn, Exec Bd, Treas, 1983-; B'nai B'rith, Dir Col Marcus Lodge N.Miami Fl, 1985-; Admirals Port Social Club, Admirals Port Mens Club;

KP Onward Lodge. *Address:* 2801 NE 183 St 2116, North Miami Beach, FL 33160, USA.

COHEN Ruben David, b.4 Aug 1956, Bahrain. Associate Professor of Mechanical Engineering. *Education:* MBE, Concordia Univ, Montreal, 1978; MSME, Univ Massachusetts, 1979; PhD, Mass Inst of Tech, 1985. *Appointments:* Research Assoc, MIT, 1985; Mech Engrg, Rice Univ, 1985-. *Creative works:* Research publications in technical and scientific journals. *Memberships:* ASME; AIChE; Am Filtration Soc; Sigma Xi. *Address:* Dept of Mechanical Engrg & Mats Sci, Rice University, Houston, TX 77251, USA.

COKER Terry Andrew, b. 24 Oct 1959, Honolulu, Hawaii. Minister. m. 30 June 1984, 1 d. *Education:* BS Recreation and Leisure Studies, Midwestern State Univ, Wichita Falls, Texas, 1983; MDiv, S.W.Baptist Theol Sem, Ft Worth, Texas, 1987. *Appointments:* Youth Dir, 1980-82; Recreation Asst, 1982-83; Campus Minister, 1983; Youth Minister, 1984-87; Ed and Youth Minister, 1988-. *Creative works:* Satan in Scripture, 1990; Women in Ministry, 1983. *Memberships:* Missouri Baptists Youth Minister Assn; S.Baptist Religious Assn. *Honours:* Outstanding Student in Recreation and Leisure Studies, 1983; Student, Texas parks and Recreation Soc Chapter Pres, 1982. *Hobbies:* Golf; Gardening; Reading; Computer hacking; Collecting baseball cards. *Address:* First Baptist Church, 412 New Smizer, Mill Road, Fenton MO 63026, USA.

COLBORN Gene Louis, b. 23 Nov 1935, Springfield, Illinois, USA. Clinical Anatomist. m. Sarah Ellen Crockett, 14 Aug 1976, 4 s, 1 d. *Education:* BA Hons, Kentucky Christian Col, 1957; BS Hons, Milligan Col, 1962; MS 1964, PhD, 1967, Anatomy, Wake Forest Univ & Bowman Gray Sch of Med. *Appointments:* Post-Doctoral Fellow, Univ of New Mexico Sch of Med, 1967-68; Asst Prof, Univ of Texas Health Sci Centre, (UTHSC), San Antonio, 1968-72; Assoc Prof, 1972-75; Assoc Prof, Med Col of Georgia, 1975-87; prof, 1987-; Dir, Centre for Clin Anatomy, Med Col of Georgia, 1987-. *Creative works:* Books: Surgical Anatomy, 1989; Hernia, 1988; Practical Gross Anatomy, 1990; Surgical Anatomy of the Liver, 1988; Numerous publications in scientific and medical journals on clinical and surgical anatomy. *Memberships:* AAA; AACA, Nat Mem Chm, 1982-86. *Honours:* Outstanding Sci Student, Milligan Col, 1962; Golden Apple Awd in Tchg, UTHSC, 1975; Med Educator of the Year, Med Col of Georgia, 7 times, 1976-90; Dist'd Fac in Teaching, Med Col of Georgia Fac Senate, 1978. *Hobbies:* Agusta Opera Co; Church Soloist; Chorales; Gardening; Tennis; Camping; Chess. *Address:* Centre for Clinical Anatomy, Medical Col of Georgia, Augusta, GA 30912, USA.

COLDREN Dale Harold, b. 3 Sept 1953, Lancaster, Pennsylvania, USA. Pres, Computer Communication Solutions. 1 s, 1 d. *Education:* BS BA, The American Univ, 1971-75; MBA, Southeastern Univ, 1978-80; Additional Graduate work at George Washington Univ. *Appointments:* Burroughs Corp, 1980-81; Wong, 1981-84; Nat Sales Mgmt, Memorex-Telex, 1984-86; VP, Sales, Fed Computer Div, 1986-90; Pres, Computer Communication Solutions, 1990-. *Publication:* PC Magazine, Portable Computing. *Memberships:* Shriners; Scottish Rite; Masonic Lodge; Rotary Club; Chmbr of Comm. *Honour:* Outstanding Young American, 1979. *Hobbies:* Running, Weight Lifting, Tennis, Pol. *Address:* 1610 Dauphin Avenue, Wyomissing, PA 19610, USA.

COLE Anthony Paul, b. 23 Jan 1939, Plymouth, England. Consultant Paediatrician. m. Elizabeth Vaughan-Shaw, 24 July 1970, 2 s, 2 d. *Education:* MBChB, St Boniface's Col, Bristol Univ, 1963; RCP, Edinburgh, 1968; FRCP Edinburgh, 1983. *Appointments:* Registrar, Paed, Westminster Childrens Hosp, 1969-70; Sr Registrar, Paed, St Georges Hosp, 1970-74; Conslt Paed, Worcester Royal Infirmary, 1974. *Creative works:* 30 publications on paediatrics, law and ethics in Lancet, BMJ, Acat Paediatrica, Archives Ch

Health, CMQ, The Newman, Christian Law Jour. *Memberships:* Fdr, Pres, Worcestershire Medico Legal Assn; Brit Paed Assn; BMA; Coun, Catholic Union of GB. *Honours:* Knight Equestrian Order of the Holy Sepulchre of Jerusalem, 1991. *Hobbies:* Music; Golf; Sailing. *Address:* Downside, 106a Battenhall Road, Worcester WR5 2BT, England.

COLEMAN Alice Mary, b. 8 June 1923, London, England. University Professor. *Education:* Tchrs Cert, 1943; BA Hons, London Univ, 1947; MA Dist, London Univ, 1951. *Appointments:* Tchr, Geog, Northfleet Central Sch, 1943-48; Asst Lectr to Prof, King's Col London, 1948-; Sabbaticals in USA, Canada and Japan; Dir of DICE, Govt sponsored housing research proj, 1988-. *Creative works:* 245 scientific papers, reports and articles including: The Planning Challenge of the Ottawa Area, 1969; Utopia on Trial, 1985, 1990; Land Use Maps in eleven colours, 1961-67. *Memberships:* RGS, Coun; Geog Assn; Inst of Brit Geogs; Brit Urban Regeneration Assn, Coun; Brit Inst of Graphology. *Honours:* Gill Mem Awd, RGS, 1963; Woman in a Man's World Awd, 1974; First holder of visiting professorship for Distinguished Women Social Scientists, Univ of W.Ontario, 1976; Busk Gold Medal, RGS, 1987. *Hobbies:* Reading; Teaching of reading; Writing; Graphology; Genealogy. *Address:* Kings College, Strand, London WC2R 2LS, England.

COLEMAN Brenda Anne, b. 28 Sept 1959, Brazil. Solicitor. m; Tarquin Gorst, 7 Sept 1991. *Education:* Harrow Co Girls Sch, 1971-78; LLB Hons, AKC, Kings Col, London, 1978-81; Col of Law, 1981-82; Admitted as a Solicitor, 1984. *Appointments:* Slaughter and May, Solicitors, 1982-89; Herbert Smith, Solicitors, 1989, Partner, 1991, specialising in Corporate Tax. *Memberships:* Law Soc; City of London Solicitors Assn. *Hobbies:* Dance; Squash; Music; Reading. *Address:* 76 Holland Park, London W11 3SL, England.

COLEMAN Gordon Barton, b. 10 July 1924, Langdon Hills. Managing Director. m. Marie Jessie Terese Vogt, 2 d. *Education:* Brentwood Sch, 1935-39. *Appointments:* Army Capt, Royal Welch Fusiliers; Wounded in Normandy, 1944; Brazil, 1948-1961; Gen Mgr, Brazil FS Hampshire Co Ltd, 1959-61; Chm, Mng Dir, Intl Licensing Ltd (Tech Transfer, publication of monthly bulletin, Intl Licensing), 1964-90; Mng Dir, Projects for Industry Intl Ltd, 1990-, assisting developing countries in setting up new industries. *Hobbies:* Equestrian sports; Golf; Gardening; Antiques; Classic cars. *Address:* 17 Farm Avenue, Harrow, Middlesex HA2 7LP, England.

COLEMAN Richard Walter, b. 10 Sept 1922, San Francisco, California, USA. Professor Emeritus of Science. m. Mildred Coleman, 1949, dec, 1 d. *Education:* BA 1945; PhD 1951, Univ of California, Berkeley. *Appointments:* Asst, Res Div of Entomology and Parasitology, Univ of California at Berkeley, 1946-47; 1949-50; Prof, Chm, Dept of Biol, Curry Col, Milton, Mass, 1961-63; Prof of Sci, Dept of Biol, 1965-89; Prof Emeritus of Sci, 1989-, Upper Iowa Univ. *Contributions to:* various professional journals. *Memberships:* Life Mem, Am Malacological Union; Life Mem, Nat Assn Biol Tchrs; Life Fellow, Iowa Acad of Sci; Life Mem, Am Assn for the Advance of Sci; Am Inst of Biological Sci; Am Byrological and Lichenological Soc; Artic Inst of N.Am; Ecological Soc of Am; Nat Health Fed; Nat Sci Tchrs Assn; Sigmx Xi; Annual member of five other societies. *Honours:* Explorer for 1966 appointed by Commr of N.W.Territories, Canada. *Address:* US PO Box 156, Fayette, IA 52142, USA.

COLEMAN Sylvia May, b. 10 Dec 1957, Sao Paulo, Brazil. Director. *Education:* LLB Hons, Birmingham Univ, 1976-79; Solicitors Finals, Col of Law, Lancaster Gate, 1979-80. *Appointments:* Stephenson, Harwood, 1980-85; Co Lawyer, Gallaher Ltd, 1985-86; Sony Music Entertainment UK Ltd, Dir, Corp Bus Affairs and Co Sec, 1986-; Dir, Ceroc Enterprises Ltd, The Entertainment Zone Ltd. *Memberships:* The Law Soc; Action Aid; The

Kesington Close. *Hobbies:* Dance (Ceroc); Music; Entertainmeng. *Address:* Flat 1 20 Courtfield Gardens, London SW5 OPD, England.

COLES Bryan Randell, b. 9 June 1926, Cardiff, Wales. University Professor; Pro-Rector; Chairman, Taylor and Francis Ltd, (Scientific Publishers). m. 27 July 1955, 2 s. *Education:* BSc Wales, 1947; DPhil, Oxon, 1951. *Appointments:* Lectr, 1950-62, Reader in Phys, 1962-66, Prof of Solid State Physics, 1966-, Dean, Royal Col Sci, 1984-86, Pro-Rector, 1986-91, Imperial Col; Visiting Prof, Univ of California, 1969, Univ of Minnesota, 1983; Dean, Royal Col of Sci, 1984-86. *Creative works:* More than 100 scientific papers including co-author of: Electronic Structure of Solids; Atomic Theory for Students of Metallurgy. *Memberships:* Fellow and Former VP, Inst of Physics, UK; Mem, Coun of The European Physical Soc; Sci Bd of Sci and Engrg Res Coun, 1973-76, 1985-88. *Honours:* Fellow of the Royal Soc, 1991. *Hobbies:* Natural history; Mediaeval architecture; Opera. *Address:* Imperial College, London SW7 2AZ, England.

COLLAN Yrjo Urho Ilmari, b. 23 June 1941, Kauniainen, Finland. Professor, University of Turku. m. Era Lehto, 9 Oct 1971, 2 s, 1 d. *Education:* MD, 1968, Dr Med Sci, 1972, Univ of Helsinki; ECFMG Exam, 1974. *Appointments:* Instr, Univ Helsinki, 1968-74; Int Postdoc Res Fellow, Univ Maryland, 1974-75; Assoc Prof, Univ Helsinki, 1975-78; Lab Supvr, Inst of Occ Health, Helsinki, 1978-80; Prof of Path and Chm, Univ of Kuopio, 1980-88; Dic of Histopath, Univ Central Hosp, Turku, 1988-89; Acad of Finland and Nat Sci Foun, USA grantee, 1988-89; Prof, Univ of Turku, 1989-. *Creative works:* Editor and co-author: Medical English, 1975; Finnish Med Biographies, 1974; Morphometry in mophological diagnosis, 1982; Stereology and morphometry in pathology, 1984. *Memberships:* Soc for Stereology and Morphometry in Finland, Pres, 1982-87, 1990-; Intl Acad of Path, Councillor, 1982, 1986, Pres of Finnish Section, 1986-87; Int Soc Stereology, Reg Rep, Scandinavia, 1983-87; European Soc of Path, Com for Diagnostic Quantitative Path, Pres, 1988-. *Honours:* Golden Badge of Merit, Nature Youth Soc, 1963; First Class Badge of Merit, Order of the White Rose of Finland, 1982; Medal of City of Milan, 1986, City of Ancona, 1991. *Hobbies:* Ornithology; Languages; Decision making in life and research. *Address:* Department of Pathology, University of Turku 20520, Turku, Finland.

COLLIER Richard Hughesdon, b. 8 Mar 1924, London, England. Author. m. Patricia Eveline Russell, 24 July 1953. *Education:* Whitgift Sch, Croydon, Surrey, 1935-41. *Appointments:* Assoc Edit, Phoenix Magazine, South East Asia, 1945-46; Edit, Town and Country Magazine, London, 1946-48; Features Staff, Daily Mail, 1948-49. *Creative works include:* Ten Thousand Eyes, 1958, 1971; The City That Wouldn't Die, 1959, 1967; The Sands of Dunkirk, 1961, 1974; The General Next to God, 1965, 1976; Eagle Day, 1960, 1980; Duce!, 1971, 1983; 1940: The World in Flames, 1979; The Warcos, 1989. *Memberships:* Authors Guild and Author's League of America; Royal Horticultural Soc; Soc for Theatre Research. *Honours:* Newspaper World Journalist of the Year, 1948; Knight, Order of Mark Twain, 1972. *Hobbies:* Travel; Theatre-going; Cats; Gardening. *Address:* c/o Curtis Brown Ltd, 162-168 Regent Street, London W1, England.

COLLINGS Peter Glydon, b. 4 Nov 1942, West Midlands, England. m. Rosemary Anne Wesley-Harkcom, 1 Sept 1967, 2 d. *Education:* Worksop Col, 1956-60. *Appointments:* Asst Regional Mgr, Old Broad Street Securities Ltd, 1970-75; Regional Mgr, Grindlays Indust Fin Ltd, 1976-82; Int Chf Exec, West Midlands Enterprise Bd Ltd, 1982-; Directorships: Aston Manor Brewery Co Ltd, 1986-; Fairne Textile Holdings Ltd, 1986-; Tangya Ltd, 1986-87; Raydyot Ltd, 1987-; E R Hammersley & Co Ltd, 1989-91; Jeenay plc, 1990-; D H Haden Ltd, 1991-; Airfield Estates Ltd, 1992-; G R

Smithson & Co Ltd, 1992-; Somers Handling plc, 1992-. *Memberships:* Fellow, Inst of Chartered Accts in England and Wales. *Hobbies:* Rugby; Cricket; Theatre; Opera; Jazz. *Address:* Squirrels Leap, 15 Oaklands Road, Four Oaks, Sutton Coldfield, W. Midlands B74 2TB, England.

COLLINS Andrew Seymour, b. 2 Nov 1944, Northwich, Cheshire, England. Solicitor. m. (1) Susan Lucretia Chase, 17 July 1971 (2) Virginia Mary Crisp (neé Craik-White), 28 Nov 1986, 3 s, 1 d. *Education:* Radley Col, 1958-62; British Inst, Florence, 1963; Col of Law, 1964-68. *Appointments:* Solicitor: Partner, Cripps Harries, 1969-84; Partner, Walker Martineau, 1986-; Chmn, Multilaw Eastern & Central European Group, 1992-. *Creative works:* Lecturer and articles various commercio-legal subjects including Central Europe and Information Technology. *Memberships:* Territorial Army, Commissioned HAC, 1970; Inns of Ct and City Yomenry, 1971; Worshipful Co of Fanmakers; Holborn Law Soc; City of London Law Soc; Brit Czech and Slovak and British Hungarian Law Soc. *Honours:* Awarded Territorial Decoration, 1978. *Hobbies:* Country Sports; Sailing; Tennis. *Address:* The Old Rectory, Eydon, Daventry, Northants NN11 6QE, England.

COLLYMORE Peter Keith, b. 20 Apr 1929, London, England. Architect. *Education:* MA, Marlborough Col; AA Dipl, Cambridge Univ; RIBA, Arch Assn Sch. *Appointments:* Skidmore Owings & Merrill, NY, 1955-57; Robert Mathew Johnson-Marshall, 1957-59; Own Practice, 1959-. *Creative works:* House Conversion and Renewal, 1974; The Architecture of Ralph Erskine, 1982; Various articles for the Architectural Press. *Memberships:* RIBA; Architectural Assn; Profl Lit Com. *Hobbies:* Cricket; Painting and Sculpture. *Address:* Barrington Cottage, Byworth, Petworth, West Sussex GU28 0HJ, England.

COLMANO Germille, b. 22 Aug 1921. Professor Emeritus; Biophysics Researcher. m. Miranda Sobol, 12 Jan 1947, 2 s, 1 d. *Education:* BA Ed, 1942; DVM, 1949; PhD, Physiol-Biochem, 1950; MS, 1952. *Appointments include:* Instr Physiol, 1949-50, Asst Prof, Physiol-Biochem, 1950-51, Univ Bologna, Italy; Asst Vet, Phillips Vet Hosp, Denver, CO, 1951-52; Res Asst Physiol, Univ Wisconsin, 1952-53; Proj Asst, Inst Enzyme Res, Univ Wisconsin, 1954-56; Scist, Biophysicist, Res Inst Advanced Study, Baltimore, 1956-61; Visiting Fellow, Univ Pitts Sch of Med, 1961-62; Prof Physiol, Col Agric & Life Scis,1962-78, Prof Physiol-Biophysics, VA MD Reg Col Vet Med, 1978-86, VA Poly Inst & State Univ, Blacksburgh; Dept Vet Bioscis, 1986-89; Dept Biomed Sci, 1989-92; Prof Emeritus Biomed Sci, 1992-; Pres & CEO BioSpectro Co, 1992-. *Creative works include:* Inventor of patent on Isolation and purification of Chlorophyll, 1960; Over 370 Research Reports and 120 articles in professional journals. *Memberships:* Am Soc Vet Physiols and Pharmacols, 1968-; Bio Phys Soc, Charter and Emeritus Mem, 1957-; NYAS, 1962-; S.W.Virginia Vet Med Assn, 1975-; Vet Physiols Pharmacols, 1968; VA Acad of Sci, 1963, *Honours include:* Fellow, Royal Soc of Health, England, 1960; Nominated Mem, Pratt Animal Nutrition Fac, VA Poly Inst and State Univ, 1978; Horsley Res Awd in Med, VA Acad Sci, 1984; Phi Zeta Chi, 1984. *Hobbies:* Music; Intellectual pursuits; Dance. *Address:* Virginia/Maryland Regional College of Veterinary Medicine, Department of Biomedical Sciences, Southgate Drive, Blacksburgh, VA 24061-0442, USA.

COLUMBRO Madeline M, b. 16 Mar 1934, Aurora, Ohio, USA. University Professor. *Education:* BA Notre Dame Col, Cleveland, 1956; MA, Cath Univ of Am, 1966; Phd Case Western Reserve Univ, 1974; Cert in Lifelong Ed, Grad Sch of Ed, Harvard Univ. *Appointments:* Prof of Music, Notre Dame Col, 1963-; Adjunct Prof of Humanities, Lakeland Com Col, 1979-81; Adjunct Prof of Music, Borromeo Col, 1982-84; Music Dir, N.Am Col, Rome, 1990-91. *Creative works:* Articles incuded in: Studies in Med Culture; Music and Man; Music:

American Music Teacher; Pastoral Music. *Memberships:* Am Musicological Soc; Cleveland Mediaeval Soc; Am Assn of Higher Ed. *Honours:* Newberry Res Fellowship, 1973; Rainey Foun Awd, 1973-74; Nat Endowment for Humanities, 1977, 1978, 1980; Danforth Assoc, 1981; Kulas Foun Grants, 1970, 1976. *Hobbies:* Reading; Hiking; Mediaeval music manuscripts. *Address:* 4545 College Road, Cleveland, OH 44121, USA.

COMM Dorothy Minchin, b. 17 Oct 1929, Wichita, Kansas, USA. Professor of English. m. Walter O Comm, 22 July 1951, dec, 1 s, 1 d. *Education:* BA Eng, Atlantic Union Col, Mass, 1950; MA Eng Lit, Andrews Univ, MI, 1963; PhD Eng Lit, Univ of Alberta, Canada. *Appointments:* Secondary Eng Tchr, Canada and W.Indies, 1951-55; Chm, Dept of Eng, W.Indies Col, Jamaica, 1956-64; Chm, Dept of Eng, Philippine Union Col, 1970-77; Prof of Eng, La Sierra Univ, California, 1978-. *Creative works:* Books: Yesterday's Tears, 1968; T Persia with Love, 1980; His Compassions Fail Not, 1982; Modern Mosaic, 1981; Encore, 1989; Gates of Promise, 1989; The Paper House, 1990. *Memberships:* Modern Lang Assn; Inland Christian Writers Guild. *Honours:* MA magna cum laude, 1963; Canada Coun Fellowship (Doctoral) in Humanities. *Hobbies:* Travel; Writing; Reading; Music; Swimming; Family History. *Address:* 34395 Olive Grove Road, Lake Elsinore, CA 92330, USA.

CONDE Maria Victoria, b. 30 Mar 1949, Madrid, Spain. Physiology Educator. m. Julian Blazquez, 12 Oct 1974, 1 s, 1 d. *Education:* Lic Pharm, 1972, PhD Pharm, 1979, Complutense Univ, Madrid, Spain. *Appointments:* Prof, 1972-84, Assoc Prof, 1985- Physiol Autonoma, Univ Madrid. *Contributions to:* articles to journals and book chapters. *Memberships:* Sociedad Espanola de Ciencias Fisiologicas; Sociedad Espanola de Neurociencia; European Soc Microcirculation. *Hobbies:* Gardening; Music; Reading; Travelling. *Address:* Autonoma U. Faculty of Medicine, Physiology, 29029 Madrid, Spain.

CONDON James Michael, b. 9 June 1914, Portland, Oregon, USA. Owner of J M Condon & Co Commercial Real Estate. *Education:* BS Geol, Univ of Houston, TX, 1949; Real Est Brokers License, Midland, Texas, 1964. *Appointments:* Salesman, Zingary Map Co, Houston, 1937-40; Salesman in Commercial Real Est, Real Est Exchange, 1940-41; 41st Infantry Div, Washington State, Australia and New Guniea (Combat) G2 Intelligence HQ; Gulf Coast Explorer, Draftsman, Hd Draftsman, Standard Oil Co of Texas. *Memberships:* Am Assn of Pet Geols, 1945-65; Toasmasters Club, San Angelo, Pres, 1957; Houston Bd of Realtors, 1965-74; Am and Houston Assns of Pet Landmen, 1974-86. *Honours include:* Top Commercial Real Est Salesman: Gary Greene Realtors, 1970-74, Main Street Realty, Houston,1 1965-70. *Hobbies:* Golf; Swimming; Reading. *Address:* 5730 Creekband, Houston, TX 77096, USA.

CONESA Eduardo Raul, b. 27 June 1937, Buenos Aires, Argentina. University Dean, Economic and Legal Consultant. m. Ana Maria Pochat, 17 Sept 1965, 3 d. *Education:* LLB, Univ Buenos Aires, 1963; MA Ec, Williams Col, 1969; MA, 1971, PhD 1982, Ec, Univ of Pennsylvania; CPA, Univ of Buenos Aires, 1960. *Appointments:* Economist, World Bank, 1972-76; Exec Dir, World bank, 1976-78; Dir, Inst for Latin Am Integr, 1978-84; Fellow, Centre Int Affairs, Harvard Univ, 1984; Dean, Univ of Bellrono, Argentina, 1988-. *Creative works:* Books: Argentina: Policy Reform for Development, 1989; Terminos ie Intrerismbio, 1983; Capital Flight, 1986; External Debt, 1989. *Memberships:* Jockey and Rotary Clubs of Buenos Aires; Tennis Club of Argentino; Carilo Tennis Ranch. *Honours:* Fellowship, Fulbright Comm, 1968; Fellowship, Di Tella Inst, 1969. *Hobbies:* Tennis; Music; Theatre; Opera. *Address:* M T Alvear 636, 1058 Buenos Aires, Argentina.

CONHYEA Dyanane, b. 2 Feb 1926, Mauritius. Director, of the Sun and Sunday Newspapers and The

Sun Advertising and Marketing Agency. *Education:* Dipl, Ed Studies, Leeds, 1966; Maths Tchr Cert, Macquarie, 1972. *Appointments:* Principal Inspector of Schs, Ministry of Ed, Arts and Culture, 1981-86; Primary Inspectorate, 1969-81; Tchr, Dep Hd Tchr, Hd Tchr, 1947-69. *Creative works:* English Exercises for Junior Scholarship Pupils, 1969; Multiple Choice Maths for CPE, 1980; Maths for CPE (graded exercises), 1981; A Tale of Four Cities, 1989. *Memberships:* Gen Sec, Govt Tchrs Union, 1960-69; Fdr Mem, Pres,Port Louis Coop Hsg Soc, 1954; Editor n Chief, Fdr, The Amaranth, half-yearly magazine, 1953-58; Ct, Univ of Mauritius, 1990-92. *Honours:* MBE, 1986. *Hobbies:* Reading; Travel. *Address:* 12 Inkermann Street, Port Louis, Mauritius.

CONN Paul Harding Jr, b. 30 Oct 1955, Cairo, Illinois, USA. *Education:* BS 1977, MBA, 1979, Murray State Univ. *Appointments:* Gen Mgr, Controller, Smallgas, 1980-81; Dir of Admin, Miscofleet, 1982-84, Controller, GRMS, 1984-. *Memberships:* Nat Rifle Assn; Mo Sul Kwan; Sons of the Am Revolution; Am Police Hall of Fame and Museum. *Honours:* Ky Col, 1989; Ky Admiral, 1990; Ky Ambassador of Goodwill, 1990; Tenn Col, 1990; Georgia Lt Col, 1990; New Mexico Col, 1990; Top Ten High Sch Grad class, 1974. *Hobbies:* Martial Arts. *Address:* PO Box 6, 311 4th and 6um, Wyatt, MO 63882, USA.

CONNAUGHTON Richard Michael, b. 20 Jan 1942, Chelmsford, Essex, England. m. Annis Rosemary Georgina Best, 12 June 1971, 1 s, 1 d. *Education:* Duke of Yorks Royal Military Sch; Royal Military Acad, Sandhurst; MPhil, Defence Fellow, St John's Cambridge. *Appointments:* RASC, 1961; Brigade of Gurkhas, Far East, 7 years; Dir staff Brit and Australian Staff Cols; Currently, Hd of British Army's Defence Studies. *Creative works:* The War of the Rising Sun and Tumbling Bear, 1989; the Republic of the Ushakovka, 1991; Military Intervention and the Logic War, 1992. *Memberships:* Fellow, Chartered Inst of Transport; FBIM; Royal United Sers Inst; Intl Inst for Strategic Studies; Royal Inst for International Affairs. *Hobbies:* Family; Tennis; Writing. *Address:* Wallhayes, Nettlecombe, Bridport, Dorset, England.

CONRAD David Paul, b. 11 Jan 1946, Greensboro, North Carolina, USA. Vice-President; Director of Operations, Libby Hill Sea Food Restaurant Inc. *Education:* BSBA, E.Carolina Univ, 1970; N C Broker's Real Est License, Forsyth Tech Col, 1979. *Appointments:* Cashier, Cook, Ngt Mgr, Libby Hill Seafood, Summit Ave, 1962-64; Plant Mgr, Libby Hill Seafood Inc, 1970-76; Opened/Proprietor - Libby Hill Seafood, Silas Creek, Northpoint and Peter's Creek, 1976-85; VP, Dir of Ops, Bd of Dirs and Major Stock Holder, Libby Hill Seafood Restaurants Inc, Greensboro, 1985-. *Memberships:* Staff Sgt, NC Nat Guard, 1968-74; 32nd degree Scottish Rite Mason; A Methodist; Mbr, Greensboro Jaycees, 1973-81; St Jude's Children's Research Hospital. *Hobbies:* Family; Electronics; Computers; Golf; SNow Skiing; Astronomy. *Address:* PO Box 5091, Greensboro, NC 27435, USA.

CONROY Stephen Alexander, b. 2 Mar 1964, Helensburgh. Painter. *Education:* BA Hons, Glasgow Sch of Art, 1982-86; Postgrad, 1986-87. *Creative works:* Solo Exhibition, Marlborough Fine Art, London, 1989. *Address:* c/o Marlborough Fine Art, 6 Albemarle Street, London W1X 4BY, England.

CONYERS-SILVERTHORN Paul Rex, b. 6 Sept 1943 Hampshire, England. International PR Consultant. m Jacqueline Elizabeth Conyers, 1 s, 1 d. *Education:* Univ of Susex, 1961-63; London Poly, 1968. *Appointments* Mktg Mgr, Swans Tours, 1969-74; Man Dir, JFP Int 1974-79; Gen Mgr, Sally Line, 1987-91; Mng Dir Promotions Deux Mille. 1991-. *Creative works:* Author of articles on transfrontier trade, gastronomy, tourism as a service industry, radio TV and seminar speaker on international travel and tourism and business

Memberships: FRGS; MCIT; Dist Coun; Sch Govr; Dunkerque Tourist Office Col of Profls. *Hobbies:* Music; Crosswords; Gastronomy; Books. *Address:* Little Holland House, Kingsgate Bay, Broadstairs, Kent CT10 3QL, England.

COOK Desmond C, b. 19 Oct 1949, Geelong, Victoria, Australia. University Professor; Physicist. m. Patricia Sue Via, 16 May 1987. *Education:* BS Hons,1972, PhD Phys, 1978, Monash Univ, Melbourne, Australia. *Appointments:* Asst Prof, Phys, Old Dominion Univ, Norfolk, VA, 1981-87; Assoc Prof, 1987-; Conslt, Bethlehem Steel Corp, 1989- ; Conslt, Dreadnought Marino Inc, Norfolk, VA, 1988. *Memberships:* Life, AIP; Australian Inst of Phys; Virginia Acad of Sci; Sigma Xi; Commadore, Southern Chesapeake Bay NACRA Fleet, 1988. *Honours:* Ayrton Premium Awd, IEE, London, 1985. *Hobbies:* Sailing. *Address:* 4537 Lauderdale AVenue, Virginia Beach, VA 23455, USA.

COOK James Winfield Clinton, b. 23 Nov 1908, Camden, New Jersey, USA. Retired Sales Executive. m. Isabelle Killian, 28 Oct 1933, 2 s, 2 d. *Education:* AB Dickinson Col, 1932; Grad work at Univ Penn, 1942 and Univ Maryland, 1943; Dr HL, Combs Col, 1972. *Appointments:* Aluminum Co Am Supervisor, 1932-39; Pres, Vita Craft PA1939-59; Pres, Homec Inc, 1959-77. *Memberships:* Trustee: Dickingon Col, Suburban Gen Hosp, US Jaycee Foun, Pop Warner Little Scholars; Pres, Nat Assn of Direct Sales; Dir, Sales and Mktg Exec Intl; Dir, Chamber of Com. *Honours:* DR HL, Combs COl, 1972; Alumnus of the year, US Jaycee, 1985; Outstanding World Alumnus Jaycee 1990; Civic Leader, Chamber of Commerce, 1990. *Hobbies:* GOlf; Boating; Fishing. *Address:* 4235 Gulf of Mexico, Longboat Key, FL 34228, USA.

COOK James, b. 7 July 1948, Bonne Terre, Missouri, USA. Concert Pianist; Associate Professor of Music. *Education:* BA 1970, MA 1973, Univ of Missouri at Kansas City Conservatory of Music; DMA, Univ of Texas at Austin, 1979. *Appointments:* Columbia Col, South Carolina, 1983-85; Assoc Prof, Univ of Nebraska, Kearney, 1986-. *Honours:* Represented USA at Expo 92, Seville; Piano Recital Debut in Madrid, 1992, Warsaw, 1990, Minsk, Belarus, 1990, Vienna, 1989, Mexico City, 1984, Montreal, 1984. Piano Recitalist throughout USA. *Address:* Department of Music, University of Nebraska, Kearney, NE 68849, USA.

COOK Sue (Susan Lorraine), b. 30 Mar 1949, Ruislip, Middlesex, England. Broadcaster; Writer. m. John C Williams, 20 May 1981 dis 1987, 1 d. *Education:* BA Hons II, Psycho & Eng, Leicester Univ. *Appointments:* Radio Producer and Broadcaster, Capital Radio, 1974-76; Radio Presenter, Radio 4, BBC and World Service, 1976; BBC TV Presenter, 1979-. *Creative works:* Accident Action, 1978; Crimewatch UK, 1987; The Crimewatch Guide to Home Security and personal Safety, 1988. *Memberships:* Citizenship Foun, Coun; Patron, Zoo Check; Friend of Turning Point. *Hobbies:* Tennis; Badminton; Choral Singing; Listening to music, classical and rock; Spending time with the family. *Address:* c/o Sue Freathy, 162 Regent Street, London W1R 5TB, England.

COOKE John William, b. 14 Sept 1930, Barnstaple, Devon, England. Adviser, Church Music. m. (1) Mona Bennett, 1953, 2 sons, (2) Valerie Hollows, 1984. *Education:* Royal Col of Music, GRSM, 1952, ARCM, 1951, ARCO, 1953. *Appointments:* Music Tchr, Sandroyd Sch, 1952-54, Cottesmore Sch, 1954-63, Wood Green Sch, E.Barnet Grammar Sch, 1963-65, Cheshunt Grammar Sch, 1965-75; Church Posts: St Mary's Southgate, Crawley, 1958-63; St Paul, Winchmore Hill, 1964-66; Cheshunt Parish Ch, 1966-75; Conductor, various choirs; Currently Northern Commr, RSCM; Musical Dir, RSCM, Northern Cathderal Singers; Frequent RAdio and TV Broadcasts; Tours as Choral Conductor and Lectr on Ch Music, Canada, USA Australia, New Zealand, Belgium, Holland, Luxembourg;

Music Adjudicator, Brit Fed of Festivals. *Membership:* ISM. *Honours:* ARSCM, 1987; FGCM, 1990. *Address:* 3 Beckwith Road, Harrogate, North Yorkshire HG2 0BG, England.

COOKE Jonathan Gervaise Fitzpatrick, b. 26 Mar 1943, London, England. Captain, Royal Navy, Naval Attache, Paris. *Education:* Summerfields Sch, Oxford, 1951-56; Marlborough Col, 1956-61; Royal Naval Col, 1961-64; Qual Intalian Interpreter, 1966; French Interpreter, 1991; Joint Ser Defence Col, 1984. *Appointments:* Royal Navy, 1961, Far East, 1962-64, Submarine Serv, 1966, Qual Comdg Ofr, 1974, Capt of HMS Rorqual, Churchill & Warspite; Cmdr, Submarine Sea Training, 1984-86; Capt, SM, 3rd Submarine Squadron, 1986-89; Naval Attache, Paris, 1990-92; RCDS, 1993. *Membership:* Inst of Linguists. *Honours:* OBE, for Service in the Falklands, 1984. *Hobbies:* Skiing; Theatre; Family. *Address:* Downstend House, Morestead, Winchester, Hampshire SO21 1LF, England.

COOMBS Brian William James, b. 2 July 1932, Bristol, England. International Business Consultant. m. Joyce Margaret Higgs, 23 June 1956, 2 s, 1 d. *Education:* Lesisham Sch, 1940-48; Articles to Chartered Acct, 1948-53; RAF Statistics Branch, 1954-56. *Appointments:* Price Waterhouse & Co, 1957-58; Lauminium Bronze Co Ltd, 1958-60; Co Sec, Halladays Ltd, 1960-66; Mgmt Acct, Tubes Ltd, 1966-69; Sec and Fin Acct, Ti Steel Tube Div Ltd, 1970-73; Fin Dir, Tiaccles & Pollock Ltd, 1973-84; Fin Dir, Lewish Woolf Griptight Ltd, 1985-90; Chief Fin Ofr, LWG Holdings Ltd, 1985-90; Intl Bus Conslt, 1991-. *Memberships:* FCA; FCMA; London Bus Sch Alumni Assn; Walsall Family Health Sers Auth, 1990-. *Hobbies:* Sculpture; Classic Cars; Genealogy; Walking. *Address:* 12 Gorway Road, Walsall, W.Midlands WS1 3BB, England.

COOPER David John, b. 4 July 1951, London, England. Investment Banker; Entrepreneur. m. Jane Cnatrell, 20 Jan 1979, 1d. *Education:* Green Sch, 1967; BEd, pt 1, Univ of London, 1974. *Appointments:* Career Analyst, Unilever Plc, 1967-71; Chem Tchr, Barking Abbey, 1974-75; Bus Devpt and Mktg Exec, Baxter Inc, 1975-79; Mktg Exec, Smith and Nephew Ltd, 1979-82; Bus Devel and Mktg Exec, LIG Int Ltd, Dir Pfizer Inc, 1984-87; Corp Financier, Robert Flemings, 1987-88; Principle DCA, 1972-1988; MD, Protean Enterprises Intl Ltd. *Creative works:* Medical Device Design Work, 1975-. *Memberships:* Worshipful Co of marketors; FCIM; FBIM; FID; FRSA; Fellow, The Chem Soc; Chartered Inst of Bankers. *Honours:* Liveryman, Worshipful Co of Marketors. *Hobbies:* Opera; Theatre; Reading; Cooking. *Address:* The Savage Club, 1 Whitehall Place, London SW1 2HP, England.

COOPER Frederick Douglas, b. 22 June 1933, Victoria, BC, Canada. Principal, F D Cooper & Associates, Planning Consultants. *Education:* Sir George Williams U, Montreal, BA (Eng & Soc) Public Ser Comm Jr Mgmt, 1962, Middle Mgmt, 1968, Sr Mgmt (MA equiv), 1972. *Appointments:* RCAF Telecom, 1951-58; Admin Ofr, personnel Ofr, Canada Agric, 1962-66; Asst Chief Class'n & Pay CDA Agric, 1966-69; Chief Class'n & Comp Sol Gen CDA, 1969-72; Chief Admin Security Brss CDA, 1972-73, 1972-73; Chief Emergency Supply Planning, Supply and Sers CDA; Dir, Plans and Analysis, Emergency Preparedness CDA, 1979-; Regional Director BCI Yukon EP CDA, 1980-90; Principal, FD Cooper and Assocs, Emergency Planning Conslts, 1990-. *Creative works:* The Nevado del Ruiz Volcano, A Case Study, 1987; The Prediction no one wants to Hear: The Great Quake, 1988; Co-author, Wartime Public Protection in the 1980s, Final report of the Task Force on War Planning and Concept of Operations. *Creative works:* Co-author of report, Development of a Departmental Emergency Preparedness Strategy for Indian and Northern Affairs Canada, 1990. *Memberships include:* Conslt to Gvt of Colombia on Disaster Planning, 1986; Cdn Mem, Ed Adv Com Nat

Cen for EQ Engrg Res, State Univ of NY at Buffalo; Chm Fed Prov Task Force on War Planning; Royal Utd Sers Inst of Vancounver Island; Allied Armed Forces Communications and Elect Assn; Royal Victoria Yacht Club; Assoc Mem, Cdn Assn of Chiefs of Police; Fellow, UK Ist of Civil Defence, 1989-. *Honours:* Fellow, UK Inst of Civil Def, 1989. *Hobbies:* Sailing; Rockhounding; Reading; Travel. *Address:* 134 Linden Avenue, Victoria , BC, Canada V8V 4E1.

COOPER Joan Davies, b. 12 Aug 1914, Lancashire, England. Social Worker. *Education:* BA 1935, Tchg Dipl, 1937, Manchester Univ; Nat Inst for Social Work, London, 1976-77. *Appointments:* Tchg and social work, 1936-41; Asst Dir of Ed, Derbyshire, 1941-48; Children's Ofr, E. Sussex, 1948-65; Chief Insp, Children's Dept, Home Office, 1965-71; Dir, Social Work Serv, Dept of Health and Soc Security, 1971-76. *Creative works:* Patterns of Family Placement, 1978; Groupwork with Elderly People, 1980; Creation of the British Personal Social Services, 1983. *Memberships:* VP, Nat Children's Bureau, 1965-; Social Sers Res Coun, 1972-76; Ch, Central Coun for Ed and Training in Social Wk, 1984-86; Chair, NACRO, Com on Juvenile Crime, 1979-87; V-Chm, Lewes Tertiary Col, 1989; Chm, E.Sussex Care for the Carers, 1989. *Honours:* Companion, Order of the Bath (CB), 1972; Fellow, Royal Anthropol Inst, 1972; Awd, Social Sci Res Coun, 1980; Leverhulme Fellowship, 1984; Hon Visiting Res Fellow, Univ of Sussex, 1979. *Hobbies:* Walking; Reading. *Address:* 44 Greyfriars Court, Court Road, Lewes, Sussex BN7 2RF, England.

COOPER John Thomas, b. 31 Mar 1945, Georgia, USA. Licensed Psychologist. m. Sandra Jean page 2 June 1972, div, 1975. 1 d. *Education:* BA 1967, MS, 1973, Florida State Univ; PhD Atlanta Univ, 1989. *Appointments:* Psycho, VP of Prog Sers, 1989-91;Bayles and Assocs, Psycho Sers, 1987-; Psychi, The Psycho Centre, 1991-; Psychi, Cooper Psycho Sers, 1991-. *Memberships:* Am and Georgia Psycho Assns; Am Assn for Counselling & Devel; Georgia Mental Hlth Counsellors Assn; Soc for Personality Assessment; Intl Res Soc; Atlanta Metropolitan Mental Hlth Assn. *Honours:* The Nat Dean's List, 1987-88; Scholastic All-American, 1988; Friend of the Juvenile Ct Awd, Gwinnett Juvenile Ct, 1988. *Hobbies:* Movies; Television; Reading; Tennis; Basketball. *Address:* 145 Copeland Road Unit H1, Atlanta, GA 30342, USA.

COOPER Leon Earl Jr, b. 3 May 1944, Alabama, USA. Counsellor; Merchant Banker; Judge. m. Mary Patricia Ann Wood, 20 Aug 1977, 3 s, 1 d. *Education:* BS Phys & Math, 1965, LLB, 1967, JD, 1967, Univ of Alabama; MBA, Harvard Bus Sch Fin, 1973. *Appointments:* Patent Atty, NASA, 1967; Capt USAF Jag, 1968-71; VP, Sr VP, Blyth Eastman Paine Webber, 1975-80; Man Dir, Dean Witter, 1981; Man Dir, ECO, 1983; Man Dir, DLP Co, 1985-. *Memberships:* KA; ODK; Jasons; PAD; IFC; US Sup Ct Bar; US Ct of Appeals, 2nd Cir Bar; Counselor, Alabama Bar; MP PS; A&O. *Hobbies:* Energy, Weather, Platetectonics, Creation, End, Everlasting Cords. *Address:* Box 874, Southport, CT 06490, USA.

COOPER Paul Michael, b. 28 Sept 1958, Thirsk. Managing Director, Fonavieu Ltd. *Education:* Institut de Brittanique, Paris, France. *Appointments:* MD & Chm, Fonavieu Ltd and Paul Cooper Ltd and Tennen Fine Vines Ltd since inception on 25 May 1987, being the fourth to start up BT Premium Lines in U.K. *Memberships:* Racehorse Owners Assn. *Honours:* Won $250,000 for $16.50 on a multiple bet with Ladbrookes! - a record. *Hobbies:* Shooting; Tennis; Travel; Horseracing; Pon-Gou Poker. *Address:* Fonavien Ltd, St Nicholas House, The Mount, Guildford, Surrey GU2 5HN, England.

COOPER Rosemary Anne, b. 6 Apr 1925, Surrey, England. Physician. m. Walter van't Hoff, 14 Jan 1956, 3 s. *Education:* Girton Col, Cambridge, 1943; Kings Col Hosp Med Sch, 1950; MA MB BChir (Camb), 1951;

FRCP, 1977; MRCP, 1953. *Appointments:* House Phys, SHO: KCH, Royal Hammersmith, 1951-53, Nat Hosp For Neurol, 1953-54; Med Registrar, Westminister Hosp, 1955-56, London Hosp, 1959-62; Res Fellow, Paediatrics, Harvard Univ, 1956- 57; Conslt Clin Neurophysiol, N.Staffs Hosp Centre, 1968-89; Sr Res Fellow, Keele Univ (ret'd), 1980-89. *Creative works:* Papers in scientific journals on clin neurophsiology, neurology and sleep. *Memberships:* FRSM; Jt Comm on Higher Med TRG, 1976-84; Hon Adv Neurol Panel Dept of Transport, 1988-; Brit Soc Clin Neurophysiol, 1961-, Pres, 1982-84; Assn of Brit Clin Neurophysiols, 1972, Pres, 1984-87; Electrophysiol Tech Assn, 1972, Pres, 1986-91. *Honours:* Fulbright Scholar, 1956-57. *Hobbies:* Music; Painting; Travel; Sailing. *Address:* Granida, 9 East Street, Hambledon, Hants PO7 4RX, England.

CORBET Richard Hugh, b. 18 Nov 1936, Perth, Australia. Journalist and Writer. *Education:* BA, Polit & Ec, Univ Adelaide, Australia, 1957- 60. *Appointments:* Res ASst: Sprod & Co, Adelaida, 1961, Cazenove & Co, London, 1961-62, Conservatice Com on the European Community, Hse of Commons, London, 1962; Flnancial Corres, Thomson Newspapers, 1963-65; Specialist Writer, The Times, London, 1965-68; Dir, Trade Policy Res Centre, London, 1968-89; Mng Edit, The World Economy, Oxford, 1977-89. *Creative works:* Agriculture's Place in Commercial Diplomacy, 1974; Beyond the Rhetoric of Commodity Power, 1975; Co-author, Trade Strategy and the Asian-Pacific Region, 1971; On How to Cope with Britain's Trade Position, 1977; Co-Edit, Europe's Free Trade Area Experiment, 1970; Commonwealth Policy in a Global Context, 1971; In Search of a New World Economic Order, 1974; The European Community and the GATT Trading System, 1990. *Memberships:* Middlesex Co Cricket Club. *Hobbies:* Reading; Cinema; Theatre. *Address:* Flat E, 85 Warrington Crescent, Little Venice, London W9 1EH, England.

CORBETT Peter George, b. 13 Apr 1952, Rossett, North Wales. Artist. *Education:* Liverpool Col of Art & Design, 1970-71; BA Hons, Reg Col of Art & Design, Manchester, 1974. *Creative works include:* Paintings and drawings, oil on canvas, pencil, charcoal; Articles, New Humanity Journal, Artspool Magazine, 1987-; Lectures in creativity etc, Workers Ed Assn, 1986-; Exhibitions: Solo and group, various Liverpool galleries, 1979-, including 'Alternative 17' Merkmal Gallery, Liverpool (one man), 1991; Angelus Gallery, Winchester (mixed), 1992; Senate House Gallery, Liverpool University (one man), 1993; Sol, Ch Gallery, London W1, 1988; Two-man: Liverpool Univ, Sch of Arch, 1990; Unity Theatre, 1990. Work in various private collections in Liverpool, Manchester, and London. *Memberships:* Ch, 1988-89, Meryside Branch, Nat Artists Assn; Com, 1978-81, Creative Mind Arts Gp; Life Mem, Design and Artists Copyright Soc; Fdr mem, 1988, Mgmt Com, Merseyside Contemporary ARtists; Fdr mem, 1988, Order of St Francis; Ch, 1989-90, Fdr mem, 1990, Merseyside Visual Arts Festival. *Honours:* Awd, Liverpool Col, 1964-70; Intl Directory of Dist Leadership, 1989; Special Leadership Awd, ABC; Man of the Year, ABI, 1990. *Hobbies:* Playing the piano; Musical composition; Yoga; Meditation; Contemporary Dance. *Address:* Flat 4, 7 Gambier Terrace, Hope Street, Liverpool L1 7BG, England.

CORBIN John Albert Alleyne, b. 23 Sept 1931, Barbados, West Indies. Investment and Marketing, CEO Cariban Ltd. m. Dallison Melville, 30 June 1990, 1 d, from previous marriage. *Education:* Grad, Harrison Col, Barbados, 1950. *Appointments:* Fdr, 1952, Chm, Corbin Compton Caribbean Advg, ret'd 1986; CEO, Cariban Ltd, 1987, Investment and Mktg Conslt. *Membership:* IAA. *Honour:* First Advg Man of Caribbean Coun of Advg Agencies Assn, 1971. *Hobbies:* Reading; Music; Travel. *Address:* 8 St Andrews Terrace, Maraval, Trinidad, West Indies.

CORDRAY Sandra Elizabeth, b. 17 Sept 1956, Mississippi, USA. Public Affairs Specialist; Media and Consumer. *Education:* BA, Loyola Univ, New Orleans, 1978; Master of Jour, summa cum laude, Lousiana State Univ, 1989; MA, Univ of Wales, Cardiff, 1989. *Appointments:* Publicity Mgr, Public Info Ofc, Mississippi Gulf Coast Com Col, 1978-82; Mgr, Special Projs, Loyola Univ, 1982-89; Public Affairs Specialist; Media and Consumer Relations, Ochsner Med Insts, New Orleans, 1989-. *Memberships:* Bd, New Orleans Artists Against Hunger and Homelessness, 1990-; Intl Assn of Bus Communicators, (IABC); PR Soc of Am. *Honours:* Fellowship, The Rotary Foun of Rotary Intl, 1986-87; Awd of Merit, 1989, Achievement Awd, 1990, IABC; Awd of Excellence in Organizational writings, Press Club of New Orleans, 1978; Rev Louis J Twomey St Awd for Oustanding Social and Humanitarian Concern, Loyola Univ. *Hobbies:* Video Production; Tai Chi; Photography. *Address:* 3724 Napoleon Avenue, New Orleans, LA 70125, USA.

CORINTHIOS Michael Jean Georges, b. 19 Jan 1941, Cairo, Egypt. Professor. m. Maria Scigalski, 18 Nov 1967, 1 s, 2 d. *Education:* Art Dipl, Leonardo Da Vinci Sch, Cairo, Egypty, 1956; BSc Ain Shams Univ, Cairo, 1962; MScA, 1968, PhD Elec Engrg, 1971, Univ of Toronto, Canada. *Appointments:* Engr, Radio Transmission, Abu Zaabal, Cairo, 1962-65; Engr, Bell Telephone Co, Toronto, 1965-66; Res Engr, Litton Systems, Toronto, 1968-69; Asst Prof, 1971, Assoc Prof, 1974, Prof, 1977-, Elec Engrg, Ecole Polytech de Montreal, Univ of Montreal. *Creative works:* 40 scientific papers; chapters in books; Five patents of invention on high speed computer architecture; Investor of Ministers symmetric chess; Paintings and sculptures in art galleries and exhibitions. *Memberships:* IEEE. *Honours:* Mary H Beatty Fellow, Univ of Toronto, 1969; Invited Prof, Univ of Nice, France, 1979-80; Invited Acad Visitor, Imperial Col, London, 1991-92; First Prize Art Exhibition, IEEE Montreal, 1978. *Hobbies:* Painting; Sculpture; Chess; Tennis. *Address:* 5999 Monkland Ave No 1204, Montreal, Canada H4A 1H1.

CORMACK Ian Donald, b. 12 Nov 1947, Dundee, Scotland. Bank Executive. m. Susan Tallack, 14 Sept 1968, 1s, 1d. *Education:* BA Hons Oxford, 1969. *Appointments:* Citibank NA, 1969-1975; Dir, Scam, Paris, 1975-78; Dir, Training Europe, 1979-80; Personnel Dir, N. Europe, 1980-84; Div Exec, Financial Institutions Gp Europe, 1985-. *Memberships:* Coun of APACS, 1985-; Settlement Bd, Stock Exchange, 1989-; Bd of Cedel, Luxembourg, 1985-; Chm, Woolnoth Soc, 1989-. *Hobbies:* Sports; Theatre; Music; Travel; Books. *Address:* Holy Lodge, Lammas Lane, Esher, Surrey KT10 8PA, England.

CORNELIUS Deborah Alison, b. 25 July 1966, Epping, Essex, England. Trainee Accountant. *Education:* Mark Hall Comp Sch, Harlow, 1977-84. *Appointments:* Asst Acct, Wander Ltd, Kings Langley, Herts. *Memberships:* Student Mem, Inst of Mgmg Accts; Crocquet Assn, 1985-. *Honours:* Croquet: Brit Mixed Doubles Champion, 1987; Brit Women's Champion, 1988; New Zealand Women's Champion, 1990; US Nat Doubles Champion, 1990; 1990 World Ranking (Mixed), 33rd. *Hobbies:* Tennis; Bridge; Table Tennis. *Address:* Pear Tree Cottage, Hobbs Cross, Harlow, Essex CM17 ONN, England.

CORNILLE Patrick, b. 23 Nov 1942, Seclin, France. Research Scientist. *Education:* Bachelor, 1961 Master, 1965, PhD, 1968, Univ of Lille, France. *Appointments:* Post-PhD position at Berkeley Univ, 1969; Res Scist, French Energy Comm, CEA/DAM, 1970. *Memberships:* Soc of Exploration Geophysicists, USA; Intl Tesla Soc, USA. *Hobbies:* Reading; Swimming; Res in Physics. *Address:* Centre d'Etudes De Liemeil-Valenton 94195 Villeneuve St Georges, Cedex, France.

CORRIGAN Timothy Patrick Pennington Blake, b. 13 Mar 1957, Minnesota, USA. Advertising Executive.

Education: AB Deg, Eng Lit, Vassar Col, NY, USA. *Appointments:* Acct Exec, Leo Burnett Co, Chicago, 1979-81; Sr VP, Ted Bates Worldwide, NYC, 1982-87; Exec VP, European Bus Dir, BSB Worldwide, Paris, 1987-90; Multinat Mng Dir, BBS Intl, Paris, 1990-. *Memberships:* Eng Speaking Union; Am Club of Paris; Vassar Club of NY, Bd of Dirs, 1983-87. *Honours:* Visiting Prof, Univ Paris, Sorbonne, 1987-88; Guest Lectr, RSCG Campus, Paris, 1989; Pres, Young Reps, Chicago, 1982; Bd Dirs, Chicago Intl Film Festival, 1980-82; Chicago Mus Contemporary Art, 1981. *Address:* 3 Rue Bellini, 92806 Puteaux La Defense, France.

CORSI Patrick, b. 11 Aug 1951, Arzes, France. m. Chantal Chopin, 6 Dec 1986, 1 d. *Education:* Diatrise Maths, Mouseilles, 1974; Engr Ensirag, Grenoble, 1977; Phd Inst Nat Poly Grenoble, 1979. *Appointments:* Visiting Scst, San Jose Res Lab, IBM Copr, 1979-81; Prod Devel, IBM France, 1981-84; Dept Mgr, Adv to Pres, European Progs Coor, Cognitech, Paris, 1984-89; Dept Mgr, Syseca, Paris, 1989-90; Proj Ofr, CEG Brussels, 1990-. *Creative works:* Amateur Design of Logos. *Memberships:* IEE, New YOrk; AAAI, Palo Alto; Vendome Bus Club, France. *Honours:* Col Scientifique et Technique of Thomson Group, 1989-. *Hobby:* Golf. *Address:* 38 rue de Tourville, F-78100, St Gerdain en Laye, France.

COSH E E Mary. Architectural Historian. *Education:* Clifton Hg Sch for Girls, Bristol; BA, 1949, MA, 1955, St Anne's Col, Oxford. *Appointments:* Coun of Indust Design, 1950-52; Inst of Classical Studies, 1958-70; Library of the Order of St John, 1977-; Transcriber, Hansard Official Report, 1980-. *Creative works:* The Real World, 1961; Inveraray and the Dukes of Argyll, 1973; With Gurdjieff in St Petersburgh; Various Islington Walks Series, 1978-89; The Square of Islington, Part I, 1990, Part II, 1992. *Memberships:* Soc of Arch Historians of GB; Georgian Gp; Victorian Soc; V-Chm, Islington Soc, 1984-; Chm, Com Mem, Islington Arch and Hist Soc. *Honour:* FSA, 1988. *Hobbies:* Historical research; Architecture; Art history; Opera. *Address:* 10 Albion Mews, London N1 1JX, England.

COSOVEANU Dorana Maria, b. 9 June 1934, Bucharest, Romania. Dir of Mus, Art Histn. Widow. *Education:* Hist and Theory of Art, Fine Arts Acad in Bucharest; Graduation Dip: Dutch Engravings in the Prints and Drawings Department of the Nat Mus of Art. *Appointments:* Art Histn, The Nat Mus of Art in Bucharest, 1966-92; Guide and Lectr, Pub Rels Dept, Curator of Hiondt Arachion Collection, Ed in Charge all mus publs, Art Histn in Western Art Dept, Dpty Dir of Mus standing, 1990. *Publications:* Landscape in Dutch Engravings of the 17th Century, 1975; French Engraving in the 17th Century, 1983; Octav Grigoresca, Bucharest, Ed, 1985. *Membership:* Romanian Artists Union, Art Critics Sect. *Hobbies:* Music, Sports, Dogs. *Address:* The National Museum of Art, Calea Victoriei 49-53, Sect 1 70107 Bucharest, Romania.

COSSINS Edwin Albert, b. 28 Feb 1937, Havering, Essex, England. Professor or Botany. m. Lucille Jeanette Salt, 1 Sept 1962, 2 d. *Education:* BSc First class Hons, 1958, PhD, 1961, DSc, 1981, Univ of London. *Appointments:* Res Assoc, Purdue Univ, 1961-62; Asst Prof, 1962-65, Assoc Prof, 1965-69, Prof, 1969-, Assoc Dean of Sci, 1983-88, Univ Alberta. *Creative works:* Over 100 scientific publications in journals and textbooks regarding folate biochemistry in plants. *Memberships:* Fellow, Royal Soc of Canada; Canadian Soc of Plant Physiols, Pres, 1976-77; Am and Japanese Socs of Plant Physiols. *Honours:* Centennial Medal, Govt of Canada, 1967; Elected Fellow Royal Soc of Canada, 1972; McCalla Res Professorship, Univ of Alberta, 1982-83; Invited Prof, Univ of Geneva, 1972-73. *Hobbies:* Gardening; Golf; Cross country skiing. *Address:* 99 Fairway Drive, Edmonton, ALberta Canada T6J 2C2.

COSTEA Constanta, b. 2 July 1951, Butimanu, Romania. Researcher; Art Historian. *Education:*

Currently studying for PhD in Art Hist, Fine ARts Acad, Dept of Hist and Theory of Art, Bucharest. *Appointments:* Art Historian, Nat Cultural Patrimony, Bucharest, 1975-90; Reschr, Inst of Art History, Romanian Acad, Bucharest, 1990. *Creative works:* Papers on mediaeval art in Romania: Funeral Stone Marks in the Danube Valley, 1974; The Museum of Romanian Patriarchate at Bucharest, Catalogue of 16th-18th centuries Icons, 1978; The Imaginary in the Gorj County, Romania, 1980; Works of Mediaeval Art (17th century) from Moldavia in Private Collections at Bucharest, 1980; Post Byzantine Painting, Recent Discoveries, 1983; Catalogue of late 17th-early 18th century Icons in the Churches of Bucharest, 1983; A New Item for the Cataloge of Byzantine Painting in Romania, 1989; A Palaeologan Icon in Moldavia, 1989; The Narthex at Dobrovat: Addenda et Corrigenda, 1991; Catalogue of the Patrimony, Mediaeval Art, Bucharest, 1990; Bookish References in the late 15th century Moldavian Frescoes, 1991; A Late Aristocartic Psalter in Moldavia, 1992. *Memberships:* Romanian Cultural Anthropol Soc. *Hobbies:* Travelling; Reading. *Address:* Institute of Art History, 196 Calea Victoriei, Bucharest, Romania.

COTEA D Valeriu, b. 11 May 1926, Vidra-Vrancea. University Professor. m. Victoria Cotea, 8 Feb 1959, 1 s. *Education:* Fac of Agronomy, Iasi, 1951; Doctorate in Agronomy, 1965. *Appointments:* Prof's Asst, 1951-59; Chief Asst, 1959-63; Lectr, 1963-71; Prof, 1971-91. *Creative works:* 240 publications on Oenology: Treatise of Oenology, Vols I, 1985, II, 1988. *Memberships:* Mbr, Acad of Agriculture and Forest Sci of Romania; Corr mem, Acad of Romania, Int and Italian Acads of Vine and Wine, Swiss Acad of Wine; Mbr, Sci Soc of Oenology and Viticulture, USA; Soc of Viticulture and Wine Making, Yugoslavia. *Honours:* Prizes, Int Office of Vine and Wine, 1982, 1988; Cofradía del Vino de Rioja (Spain), diploma and medal, 1992. *Hobbies:* Reading historical books. *Address:* Laboratory of Oenology, Aleea M Sadoveanu nr 9, Iasi 6600, Romania.

COTRAN Eugene, b. 6 Aug 1938, Jerusalem. Circuit Judge. m. Christiane Avieriho, 6 Oct 1963, 3 s, 1 d. *Education:* Victoria Col, Alexandria, Egypt, 1948-54; LLB, LLM, Univ of Leeds, 1955-59; Dip in Intl Law, Trinity Hall, Cambridge, 1959-60. *Appointments:* Lectr, Sch ofOriental and African Studies, Univ of London, 1961-76; Hg Ctr Judge, Kenya, 1977-82; Visiting Prof of Law, SOAS, Univ of London; Chm, Centre of Islamic Middle East Law, 1988-; Circuit Judge, 1992-. *Creative works:* Several books and articles on laws of Africa, the Commonwealth, the Middle East and Immigration Law. *Memberships:* Lincoln's Inn Barister at Law; FCIArb; Bd mem, several African Commonwealth countries. *Honours:* LLD, Univ of London, 1972. *Hobbies:* Current affairs; Family; Horse racing. *Address:* 16 Hart Grove, Ealing, London W5 3NB, England.

COULTER Elizabeth Jackson, b. 2 Nov 1919, Baltimore, Maryland, USA. Economist; Biostatistician. m. Norman Arthur Coulter Jr, 23 June 1951, 1 s. *Education:* AB, Hons, Social Sci, Swarthmore Col, Pennsylvania, 1941; AM, 1946, PhD, 1948, Ec, Radcliffe Col, Cambridge, Massachusetts. *Appointments include:* Lectr, Ec, 1954-55, Clin Asst Prof, Prev Med, 1963-65, Ohio State Univ; Assoc Prof, 1965-72, Prof, 1972-90, Emeritus, 1990-, Biostatistics; Assoc Prof, Economics, 1965-78, Assoc Dean for Undergrad Public Hlth Studies, 1979-86, all at Univ of N.Carolina at Chapel Hill. *Contributions to:* articles in professional journals. *Memberships include:* Am Public Hlth Assn, Gov Coun, 1970-72; Am Ec Assn; Assn for Hlth Sers Res; Biometric Soc; Am Statistical Assn; Am Acad of Polit and Social Sci; Am Assn for the Advancement of Sci; Delta Omega; Sigma Xi. *Address:* 1825 North Lake Shore Drive, Chapel Hill, NC 27514, USA.

COULTER Myron L, b. 21 Mar 1929, Albany, Indiana, USA. Chancellor. m. Barbara Bolinger, 21 July 1951, 1 s, 1 d, (twins). *Education:* BS Indiana State Tchrs Col,

1951; MS, 1956, EdD, 1959, Indiana Univ. *Appointments:* Chancellor, W.Carolina Univ, 1984-; Pres, Idaho State Univ, 1976-74; Interim Pres, W.Michigan Univ, 1974; VP for Admin and Prof, W.Michigan Univ, 1974-76; Prof, 1958-74. *Creative works: Textbooks:* Sightings and Soundings; Young American Basic Reading Programme. *Memberships:* Am Assn of State Cols and Univs, Chm; N.Carolina Center for the Advancement of Tchg, Bd of Trustees; PVO/Univ Center for Collobaration in Devel, Bd of Dirs; N.Carolina Arboretum, Bd of Dirs; Phi Delta Kappa; Omicron Delta Kappa; Phi Kappa Phi; Beta Gamma Sigma; Intl Reading Assn; Nat Soc for Study of Ed. *Honours:* Hon Dr of Humane Letters, Col of Idaho, 1982; Master's Day Awd, 1969, Distinguished Alumnus Awd, 1975, Indiana State Univ; Resolution of Tribute, Michigan State Legislature, 1976. *Hobbies:* Reading; Horseback riding; Golfing; Woodworking; Fishing; Hunting. *Address:* 10 Chancellor's Drive, Cullowhee, NC 28723, USA.

COUNTRYMAN Charles Casper, b. 6 Oct 1913, New York City, USA. Analytical Research Chemist (retired). m. Veronica Mae Lenz, 3 Oct 1953. *Education:* BS Chem, 1934, MS Chem, 1935, Univ of Michigan. *Appointments:* Analytical Chem, West End Chem Co, California, 1935- 40; Res Chemist, Truesdail Lab, Los Angeles, 1940-45; Man Chem, Wm T Thompson Co, Los Angeles, 1945-50; Analytical Res Chem, Dart Industries Inc, Los Angeles, 1950-75. *Memberships:* Boy Scouts of Am; Pres, Chem-Phys Club; Searles Lake Gem and Mineral Soc; Soc of Cosmetic Chems; ACS, Pacific Railroad Soc, San Marino, California; Magic Castle, Hollywood. *Honours:* Nat Hon Soc, 1931. *Hobbies:* Photography; Model trains; Astronomy; Dancing; Travel. *Address:* 19404 Shelford Drive, Cerritos, CA 90701, USA. 59.

COUSSIOS Dimitrios, b. 30 June 1938, Bucharest Air Transport and Civil Engineer. *Education:* MSc Civ Engrg, Nat Tech Univ of Athens, 1962; MSc Airporting Eng, Univ of California at Berkeley, 1966; MSc Trans Engrg, Univ of Birmingham, UK, 1971; DSc, Technior Inst of Tech, 1978. *Appointments:* Dir, Greek Civil Aviation, 1962-63; Prof, Air Force Acad, 1968-83; Princ Admn in the Comm of European Communities (Transport), 1983-; Visiting Prof, Loughborough Univ UK, 1990-. *Creative works:* Books and articles in the field of transport including: A Methodology of Airport Location, 1975. *Memberships include:* Greek Tech Chamber, 1962- ; Fellow, Am Soc of Civil Engrg, 1966, ICE, UK, 1971; Fellow, Charter Inst of Transport, 1972, Athinai North Rotary Club, 1967. *Honours:* Doctor of Science in Technology, 1978. *Hobbies:* Painting; Tennis, Collecting coins and notes. *Address:* Avenue des Ombrages 8A, 1200 Brussels, Belgium.

COUTURE Pamela Del, b. 16 Nov 1951, Washington DC, USA. Assistant Professor of Pastoral Care. m. Car D Schneider, 3 July 1987, 1 s, 3 d. *Education:* BA Ashland Col, 1972; MDiv, Garett Evangelical Theo Seminary, 1982; PhD, Practical Theol, Univ of Chicago 1990. *Appointments:* Tchr, Ontario Hg Sch, 1971-73 Parish pastor, Utd Methodist Ch, 1978-84; Pastora Counsellor, Samaritan Centre on the Ridge, 1984-89 Candler Sch of Theol, 1989-. *Creative works:* Blessed are the Poor? Women's Poverty, Family Policy and Practical Theology, 1990. *Memberships:* Oxford Inst of Wesleyan Studies; Am Acad of Religion; Soc for Pastora Theol; N.Illinois Conf, Utd Methodist Ch. *Hobbies* Canoeing; Camping. *Address:* Candler School of Theology, Emory University, Atlanta GA 30322, USA.

COVINGTON Branice Ella, b. 19 July 1932. Compute Analyst. *Education:* Ms, Mass Inst of Tech, Cambridge MA, 1955. *Appointments:* Technical Staff, Bellcore; Div Mgr, Melpar; Fashion Conslt, B C Moore's *Memberships:* Math Assn of Am; Am Assn of Univ Women; IEEE Computer Soc; World Foun of Successful Women; Assn of MIT Alumanae; Sixma Xi; NAFE: Nat Org for Women; Nat Abortion Rights Action League

Planned Parenthood Fed of Am; Nat Museum of Women in Arts. *Honours:* Into Woman of the Year, 1991-92; Medal of Honour, 1990; Women's Profl Achievements Awd, 1991. *Address:* 16 Wedgewood Avenue, Colts Neck, NJ 07722, USA.

COX John B, b. 20 July 1932, Rochester, Texas, USA. Senior Pastor, Christian Counsellor. m. Karen D Scott, 12 Dec 1989. 3 s, 3 d. *Education:* Bachelor of Theol, 1965; BA, 1979; Doctor of Ministry, 1980; Candidate, Juris Doctor, 1992. *Appointments:* Pastor: Yankton Baptist Ch, 1965-68; Bethel B C, Linc, Nebraska, 1968-72; FBC Papillion, Nebraska, 1972-83; Missionary HMB, Omaha, 1983-87; Pastor UBC, Lubbock, TX, 1987-. *Creative works:* Prayer in the first Degree, book; Missions Study Guide for Adults. *Memberships:* Bd of Dirs, Home Mission BRD, 1979-85; VP Kan/Ben Baptist Foun, Topeka, Kansas, 1980-83; Bd of Dirs, Kan/Neb Convention S.Baptist, 1972-81; Com on Bds, S.Baptish Convention, 1982. *Honours:* Certified Tchr/Councillor, Inst of Adolescent Studies, 1981-. *Hobbies:* Golf; Reading. *Address:* 4905 11th Street, Lubbock, TX 79416, USA.

COX Robin Anthony Frederick, b. 29 Nov 1935, Leicester, England. Occupational Physician. m. Maureen Moore, 8 Sept 1962, 1 s, 1 d. *Education:* Gonville & Caius Col, Cambridge, 1954-57; Guy's Hosp, 1957-60, MA, MBBChir; FRCP; FFOM. *Appointments:* Gen Practice and Dir, North Sea Med Centre, 1964-76; Med Dir, Phillips Petroleum Co, Europe/Africa, 1976-86; Chief Med Ofr, CEGB, and Nat Power, 1986-. *Creative works:* Edit, Offshore Medicine, 1982. *Memberships:* FRSM, Pres, Occup Med Section; V-Dean, Fac of Occup Med; Pres, Intl Assn of Physicians for Overseas Sers; Soc of Occup Med. *Hobbies:* Ornithology; Fly fishing; Gardening; Photography. *Address:* Linden Housee, Long Lane, Fowlmere, Royston, Herts, SG8 7TG, England.

COX William Martin, b. 26 Dec 1922, Bernardsville, New Jersey, USA. Attorney at Law. m. Julia Sebastian, 1952, 1 s, 3 d. *Education:* BA Syracuse Univ, 1947; JD, Cornell Univ, 1950. *Appointments include:* Mem, Dolan and Dolan law firm, New Jersey; Tchr, Zoning Admin, Rutgers Univ, 1968-. *Creative works:* Author, New Jersey Zoning and Land Use Administration, 11th ed 1992; Contributor to various professional journals. *Memberships include:* Life, Past Pres, Sussex Co Hist Soc; The Monarchist League; Past Pres, Newton Bd of Ed, Sussex Co Vocational Tech Bd of Ed; Sussex Co Bar Assn; past Chm, Local Govt Law Section, NJ State Bar Assn; Dir, Gen Counsel, NJ FEd of planning Ofrs; Local Govt Section, ABA; Moderator, Panel on Zoning, NJ League of Municipalities; Land Use Com, ibit, 1969-; Past mem, Legislation Com, ibid; Past Dir, NJ Herald Newspaper; Newton Cemetery Assn; NJ Inst of Municipal Attorneys; Newton Rotary Club; Alpha Chi Rho. *Honours:* Man of the Yearl Alpha Chi Rho, 1976; Cert of Merit, NJ Red of Planning Ofrs, 1977; Chm, Dist Ethics Com, 1977-78; Dist Fee Arbitration Com, 1978-80; Presidents Dist Ser Awd, NJ League of Municipalities, 1980; Paul Harris Fellow, Rotary, 1988. *Address:* Newton, New Jersey, USA. 6, 52, 139, 163.

COXHILL Lowen, b. 19 Sept 1932. Musician (saxophones), Composer, Actor. *Education:* Bookbinding Apprentice, Hazell Watson & Viney, Aylesbury, 1946-53, 55; RAF, 1951-52; Music Educ: Pvte study w Aubrey Franks, 1959, 60; Derek Gilbey Rehearsal Orch, 1960, 61. *Appointments:* Solo Soprano Saxophone Perfs, 1956-92 throughout Europe, USA, Can and Japan; collaborations w. Chessmen, Rufus Thomas, Little Walter, Gass, 1962-67; Delivery, Alexis Korner, Otis Spann, Lowell Fulson, Champion Jack Dupree, 1968-70; MD Welfare State Theatre, 1972-73; Henry Cow, Caravan, Gong, G F Fitzgerald, 1972-74; Derek Bailey's Co, 1974; Dave Green's Fingers, 1979-85; Trevor Watts' Moire Music Orch, 1982-86; New Arts Consort, 1989-90; Music, Theatre Work: Matchbox Purveyors, IOU, Jeff Nuttall, Rose Maguire, Welfare State, People Show,

John Bull, Stephen Cochrane, Forkbeard Fantasy. *Creative Works:* Own recordings, 1971-92; Continuation CDs; Music for films; Music, Acting for TV; Music only for TV; Mag Articles. *Memberships:* London Musicians Collective; Clarinet and Saxophone Soc of GB; Sonic Arts Network; Assn of Brit Jazz Musicians; Brit Actors Equity Assn; Brit Film Inst; Ken Colyer Trust. *Hobbies:* Film, Theatre, Swimming, Art, Walking. *Address:* 17 Laney House, Portpool Lane, London EC1N 7UL, England.

CÔTÉ Richard Norman, b. 3 June 1945, Connecticut, USA. Author. *Education:* BA, Butler Univ, Indianapolis, 1965. *Appointments:* Writer and Photographer, Manitowoc, Wisconsin, 1971-78; Special Projs Dir, S.Carolina Hist Soc, 1979-80; Dir of Micrographics, County of Charleston, S.Carolina, 1982-85; Writer and Archivist, Charleston, 1979-82, Mt Pleasant, 1983-. *Creative works include:* The Genealogist's Guide to Charleston County, S.Carolina, 1980; Local and Family History in S.Carolina: A Bibliography, 1981; Renegade: The Biography of the Rev William Hammet, 1756-1803, 1982; The Dictionary of South Carolina Biography, 1983; Guide to the Alston-Pringle-Frost Manuscript Collection, 1990; Miles Brewton's Land: A History, 1694-1990, 1990; Guide to the Edward Middleton Manigault Collection, 1990; Guide to the John Julius Pringle Manuscript Collection, 1991; Spirit Tells me: Psychics and their Clients in New Age America, 1992; Love by Mail: The International Guide to Personal Advertising, 1992. *Memberships:* Nat Trust for Hist Preservation; S.Carolina Hist Soc; preservation Soc of Charleston; Soc of Am Archivists. *Honours:* Res Grants: S.Carolina Com for the Humanities, 1980, 1982, Post Courier Foun, 1989, 1990, 1991, Henry Yaschik Foun, 1990; Historical Writing Grant, Post Courier Foun, 1991. *Hobbies:* Ballroom Dancing; Art Collecting; Jogging. *Address:* PO Box 1898, Mt Pleasant, SC 29465, USA.

CRABBE Jean, b. 12 Aug 1927, Brussels, Belgium. Professor of Physiology. m. Marie de Guchteneere, 10 Aug 1954, 3 s, 2 d. *Education:* Aggregation de l'Enseignement Superieur, UCL, Belgium, 1962. *Appointments include:* Dept of Med, Univ Hosp of Louvain , 1954; Res Asst, Univ Hosp of Geneva, 1954; Asst in Med, Peter Bent Brigham Hosp, Mass, USA, 1955-58, Intern, 1958-59; Clin and Res Fellow, Mass Gen Hosp, Boston, 1959-60; Asst, Dept of Med, Univ Clinics St Raphael, Louvain, Belgium, 1961- 62; Conslt Physician, Endocrinol, Univ Clinics St Pierre, 1964; Dept of Phisiol, UCL, 1966; Assoc Prof, 1967, Prof of Physiol and Med, 1972; Visiting Prof, Dartmouth Med Sch, Hanover, USA, 1974; Bd or Dirs, Cercle des Alumni de la Foun Univ, Belgium, 1974-78; Guest Prof, Pahlavi Med Sch, Iran, 1978; Pyhsiol Inst der Univ Munchen, 1978-81, 1984-87, 1990-; Sabbatical, Nat Insts of Health, Bethesda, MD, USA, 1982-83. *Creative works:* Edit Bd, Jour of Steriod Biochemistry and Archives Intl de Physiologie et Biochimie. *Memberships include:* Am Soc for CLin Res; Endocrine Soc, US, 1958; Belgian Societies of Internal Med, Physiol, Gastroentrol (hon) and Endocrinology; European Soc for Clin Investigation; Assn des Physiols; NYAS (life); Am Assn for the Advancement of Sci (life); French Soc of Endocrinol. *Honours:* Rene Beckers Awd, Belgium, 1955; Prix des Alumni, Found Univ, Belgium, 1963; Chevalier 1969, Commandeur, 1990, de l'Ordre de Leopold, 1969; Spa Foun Awd, European Community, 1988.

CRADDOCK Malcolm Gordon, b. 2 Aug 1938, London, England. Film Producer and Director. m. Jenni Maclay, 29 May 1965, 2 s, 1 d. *Education:* St ALbans Sch, 1949-56; Queens Col, Cambridge, 1959-62; Open Exhibitioner in History; MA. *Appointments:* Asst Dir, Film Edit, 1962-66; Film Dir, 1966-86; Foun and Owner, Picture Palace Productions, 1970-. *Creative works:* Mr Lewis, 1965; The Beach, 1967; TV commercials and documentaries, 1968-88; Producer of TV Drama: Tandoori Nights, 1985; Ping Pong, 1986; 4 Minutes, 1987; Eurocops, 1988-90; When Love Dies, 1989; The Orchid House, 1991; Sharpe's Rifles, 1993; Sharpe's Eagle, 1993. *Honours:* 24 intl awds for TV commercials incuding: Cannes Advg Awds, Silver Lion, Sunday Times, 1978; Hollwood Advg Awds, Intl Broadcast, Sunday Times, 1979; CLIO Awds, Winner, Sunday Times Campaign, 1979; NY Gold Awd, Degrees of Excellence, 1984; Venice Film Festival, Ping Pong, 1986; Gold Awd Drama, NY, 4 Minutes, 1987. *Hobbies:* Gardening; Tennis; Watching Tottenham Hotspur FC. *Address:* 13 Randolph Road, Little Venice, London W9 1AN, England.

CRAIG Robert Michael, b. 29 May 1944, St Louis, Missouri, USA. m. 20 Dec 1975, 1 s. *Education:* BA, Principia Col, 1966; MA, Univ Illinois, 1967; PhD, Cornell Univ, 1973. *Appointments:* Instr Meremac Com Col, 1967-68; Asst Prof, 1973-78, Assoc Prof, 1978-, Georgia Inst of Tech. *Creative works include:* From Plantation to Peachtree: A Century and a Half of Classic Atlanta Homes, 1987; The American Dream: A Collection of Essays, 1983; Essays and chapters in: Victorian Britain: An Encyclopaedia, 1988; John Portman, 1989; Roadside America: The Automobile in Design and Culture, 1990. *Memberships include:* Soc of Arch Historians, Life; Soc of Arch Historians, S E Chapter, Pres, 1984-85; Treas, 1986-, Found Mem; S.E.Col Art Conf, Bd of Dirs; SE 19th Century Studies Assn, Bd of Dirs; SE American Society for 18th Century Studies, Bd of Dirs; Col Art Assn; Soc of Commercial Arch; Nat Trust for Hist Preservation; Atlanta Hist Soc; Atlanta Preservation Centre. *Honours:* Book, Plantation in Peachtree, on Atlanta's Best Seller List, 1987; Georgia Tech Foun Grant to China, 1985; Illinois and Cornell Univs Fellowships; Vietnam Sers Medal, US Navy, 1968; Cert of Appreciation, Mayor of Miami Beach, FL, 1990. *Hobbies:* Architectural Photography; Watercolour Painting; Piano. *Address:* College of Architecture, Georgia Institute of Technology, Atlanta, GA 30332, USA.

CRAIG-COOPER Frederick Howard Michael Sir, b. 28 Jan 1936, International Management Consultant. m. Elizabeth Snagge, 8 Mar 1968, 1 s. *Education:* Horris Hill; Stowe; Col of Law, London. *Appointments:* Nat Serv, 1954-56; Territorial Army, 1956-88; Jacques & Lewis, 1956-61; Allen & Overy, 1962-64; Craig Lloyd Ltd, 1968-; Intl Nickel Co of Canada, 1964-84; Carre Orban & Paul Ray Int, 1984-. *Memberships:* Law Soc; Solicitors Benev Assn; FCIArb; FRSA; Drapers Co, Ct of Assts; Coun, Order of St John, London, (Chm); Greater London TAVRA. *Honours:* Dep Lt, Greater London, 1986; Rep Lt, Royal Borough of Kensington and Chelsea, 1987-; Knight Bachelor, 1991; CBE, 1982; TD; Officer, 1978, Knight, 1990, Order of St John; Ofr Order of Merit with Swords, 1986; Sovereign Military Order of Malta. *Hobbies:* Walking; Reading; Travel in UK; Gardens. *Address:* Carre Orban and Paul Ray International, 44 St James's Place, London SW1A 1NS, England.

CRAIK Elizabeth Mary, b. 25 Jan 1939, Portmoak, Scotland. University Teaching. m. Alexander Craik, 25 July 1964, 1 s, 1 d. *Education:* MA Classics, Univ St Andrews, 1960; MLitt, Girton Col, Cambridge, 1963. *Appointments:* Res Fellow, Univ of Birmigham, 1963-64; Asst Lectr, Latin, 1964-65, Lectr, Sr Lectr, Greek, 1965, Univ of St Andrews. *Creative works:* The Dorian Aegean, 1980; Marriage and Property (ed), 1984; Euripides Phoenician Women, 1988; Owls to Athens, (ed), 1990; Articles in journals. *Memberships:* Classical Assn; Hellenic Soc; Cambridge Philological Soc. *Address:* Department of Greek, University of St Andrews, Fife, Scotland KY16 9AL.

CRAINZ Franco, b. 18 May 1913, Rome, Italy. Emeritus Professor of Obstetrics and Gynaecology. *Education:* MD, Roma, 1936. *Appointments:* Prof, Obs & Gynae, Novara, 1956-64; Cagliari, 1964-66; Messina, 1966-67; Bari, 1967-72; Roma, 1972-88; Emeritus since 1988. *Creative works:* Books: An Obstetric Tragedy, 1977; The Birth of an Heir to the 5th Duke of Devonshire, (1790), 1988; Over 100 papers. *Memberships:* Fellow ad Eundem, RCOG; Hon Mem, Past Pres, Italian Soc of Gynae & Obs; Hon Mem, Austrian, Portuguese,

Romanian, Spanish and Swiss Socs; Corr Mem, German Soc. *Honours:* Past VP, Italian Soc of the Hist or Med. *Hobbies:* History; Archaeology; Music. *Address:* Via P Mascagni 124, 00199 Rome, Italy.

CRAINZ Vittorio, b. 1 Dec 1918, Rome, Italy. Journalist; PR Consultant. m. (1)Laura Bachetoni Rossi Vaccari, 24 Jan 1945, div 1972; (2) Pauline Anne Douglass, 16 Nov 1972. 2 d. *Education:* Law Deg, Univ of Rome, 1940. *Appointments:* Edit Staff, Giornale d'Italia, 1942-43; Edit, Chief Edit, Domenica, 1944-46; Chief Edit, Jr, 1947-48, and Elefante, 1949-50; Jt Dir, SIPR, 1957-66; Man Dir, EPI, 1961-66; Man Dir, SEPA, 1951-, and SIPR, 1966-; VP, AISSCOM, 1984-. *Memberships:* Intl PR Assn; Federazione Relazioni Pubbliche Italiana; Federation Intl Presse Gastronomique et Vinicole; Centro Intl Stampa Turistica. *Honours:* Cross of War. *Hobbies:* Sailing; Climbing; Historical Studies. *Address:* SEPA/SIPR Via Tomassetti 5, 00161 Rome, Italy.

CRAMER Friedrich D, b. 20 Sept 1923, Institute Director. *Education:* Dr rer nat, Univ Heldeberg, 1949. *Appointments include:* Lectr, Heidelberg Univ, 1953; Res Fellow, Cambridge Univ, 1953- 54; Prof, Technische Hochschule, Darmstadt, 1959; Hd Dept, Max Planck Inst for Experimental Med, Gottingen, 1962; Dir, ibid. *Creative works include:* Author, Paperchromatography, 1952; Einschlussverbindugen, 1953; Fortschritt durch Verzicht, 1975; Chaos and Order, 1989; Erkennen, 1991; Amazonas, 1991; Natur der Schönheit, 1992; Zeitbaum, 1993; Over 400 papers on biochem. *Memberships:* Chm, Biol Med Section, max Planck Assn, 1976; German and Am Chemical Socs; Gottingen and Heidelberg Acads of Sci; Polish Acad of Scis; EMBO. *Honours:* Bavarian State Prize for Lit, 1990. *Address:* 400, Hermann Rein Str 3, 3400 Gottingen, Germany.

CRAMMER Bernard, b. 30 Apr 1939, Leicester, England. Head patent Examiner and Senior Project Leader, Organic Chemistry. *Education:* BSc Univ of London, 1963; MSc Org Chem, Hebrew Univ of Jerusalem, 1975; PhD, Org Chem, Univ of Bar Ilan, Israel, 1985. *Appointments:* Hd Patent Examiner, Israel Patent Office, 1968-; Supvsr in Chem for Summer Prog for Overseas Students, Hebrew Univ of Jerusalem, 1977-80, 1985, 1986; Sr Res Chemist, Teva Middle East Pharm & Chem works Ltd, Jerusalem, 1964-68. *Creative works:* 16 scientific publications; 2 book reviews; chapter in Encyclopaedia of Physical Sci and Tech, and, Developments in Sweeteners; 6 patents. *Memberships:* MRSC, 1976-; Israel Rep, 1989-; Israel chem soc, 1985-; Soc of Chem Engrs and chemists in Israel, 1968-; Asst Edit, Israel Jour of Chem and Chem Engrg. *Honours:* Res grant, RSC, London, 1980; Efficiency Prize from Dir Gen of The Israel Ministry of Justice; Res Grants, 1978-85. *Hobbies:* Photograpy, Bridge, Reading & Russian Classical Music. *Address:* 7 Rehov Yam Sof, Ramot Eshcol, Jerusalem 97701, Israel.

CRANCH Arthur Graeme, b. 10 Aug 1910, Ewell, Surrey, England. Retired Company Director. m. Molly Pernelle Pryce, 10 Aug 1940, 2 d. *Education:* King's Col Sch, 1924-29. *Appointments:* Mgmt Trainee, Mktg Exec, Rowntree, York, 1929; Res Exec, London Press Exchange, 1936; War Ser, 1939-45; Res Exec, Dir, 1954-67, Mather & Crowther, later Ogilvy & Mather, 1946-67; Conslt, UN/FAO, Rome. *Memberships:* Mkt Res Soc, UK, Past Pres; ESOMAR, Netherlands, Past Pres; ICC, Paris, Former Com Chm; Inst practitioners in Advtg, (London) Fellow. *Hobbies:* Antiquities; Gardening; Watching Cricket; Travel. *Address:* Summerlea, Beverley Lane, Coombe Hill, Kingston upon Thames, Surrey KT2 7EE, England.

CRANE Kathleen Renee, b. 5 Nov 1946, Erie, Pennsylvania, USA. RN Patient Care Produce Specialist. *Education:* Nsg Dipl, St Vincent Sch of Nsg, PA, 1967; BS, Villa Maria Col of Gannon Univ, PA, 1977; MSN, Edinboro Univ of Pennsylvania, 1989. *Appointments:* Staff Nurse, St Vincent Hosp, 1967-68; Staff Nurse,

Mill Creek Commun Hosp, 1968-70; Staff Nurse, Hoag Mem Hosp, 1970-72; Instr, St Vincent Sch of Nsg, 1972-75, 1977-82; System Anal, Training Coor, St Vincent Hlth Ctr, 1982-85; TDS Hlth Care Systems, Product Specialist, 1985-1987, 1988-1992; Nsg Conslt, TDS Ltd, UK, 1987-88; Sr Prod Specialist, Hlth Quest, 1991-92; Snr Applications Spec, CHC, Houston, TX, 1992-. *Memberships:* Sigma Theta Tau; Nat Neague for Nsg; Am Assn of Univ Women. *Honour:* Who's Who in American Nursing. *Hobbies:* Reading; Walking; Crochetting; Sewing; Travel; Aerobics. *Address:* 3310 Cherry Forest Drive, Houston, TX 77088-6951, USA.

CRANSTON Maurice (William), b. 8 May 1920, London, England. Professor of Political Science. m. Baroness Maximiliana von und zu Fraunberg, , Nov 1958. 2 s. *Education:* BA, 1948, MA, BLitt, 1951, St Catherines Oxford. *Appointments:* Lectr in Social Phil, Univ London, 1951-59; Lecter, Reader, Prof, Polit Scis, LSE, 1959-75; Prof Emeritus, 1985-. *Creative works:* Feeedom, 1953; John Locke, a biography, 1957; Sartre, 1962; What are Human Rights?, 1963; Political Dialogues, 1968; The Mask of Politics, 1972; Jean-Jacques, 1983; The Noble Savage, 1991. *Memberships:* Inst Intl de Philosophie Politique Paris, Pres, 1978- 81; Royal Lit Fund, Registrar, 1975-78. *Honours:* James T Black Meml Prize, 1957; Fellow, Royal Soc of Lit, 1959; Hon Foreign Mem, AAAS, 1966; Cmdr de l'Ordre de Palmes Academiques, Paris, 1988. *Hobby:* Walking. *Address:* 1a Kent Terrace, Regents Park, London NW1 4RP, England.

CRAWFORD Carl Benson, b. 2 Oct 1923, Canada. Adjunct Professor, Civil Engineering. m. Adah May Shanks, 6 Sept 1948, 2 s, 2 d. *Education:* BSc Queen's Kingston Canada, 1949, MSc N.W.Illinois, 1951, Civil Engrg; DIC, Imperial Col, London, 1957. *Appointments:* Res ofr, nat Res Coun, 1949-53; Hd, Soil Mechanics Section, 1953-69; Asst Dir, 1969-74; Dir, 1974-85. *Creative works:* More than 90 articles on civil engineering and building construction. *Memberships:* Can Geotech Soc; Engrg Inst of Canada; Assn of Profl Engrs of Ontario; Am Soc for Testing and Materials; ASCE; Intl Soc for Soil Mechs and Foun Engrg. *Honours:* Hogentogler Awd, ASTM, 1961; Special Serv Awd, ASTM, 1968; Robt F Legget Awd, Can, Geotech Soc, 1975; Hon Mem, ASTM, 1977; Fellow, Eng Inst of Canada, 1983; Julian C Smith Medal, EIC, 1989; Jean P Carriere Awd, Standards Coun of Can, 1990. *Hobbies:* Hiking; Skiing; Woodworking and Building Construction; Engrg Res. *Address:* 108-2556 Highbury Street, Vancouver, BC, Canada V6R 3T3.

CRAWFORD Iain Padruig, b. 21 Jan 1922, Inverness, Scotland. Author; Playwright. m. Kathy Hay, 23 Dec 1985, 3 s, 1 d. *Education:* Inverness Acad, Jordanhill; Col Sch, Glasgow. *Appointments:* Cadet, Merchant Navy, Ofr Royal Navy, 1939-46; Journalist, 1947-51; BBC, 1951-55; Freelance writer, 1955-59; Journalist and writer in Scotland and London, 1959-64; Film critic and travel Ed S Express, TV Plays and programmes for ATV and BBC, Publicity Dir, Edinburgh Festival, 1973-80; Scottish Opera, 1980-81. *Creative works include:* Plays, Broomstick and Badenoch, Under the Light, The Cruel Deadline; The Frewintosh Formula; Books: The Burning Sea; The Sinclair Exclusive; Scared of the Gentle Citizen; Cafe Royal; The Profumo Affair; London Man; The Havana Cigar; What About Wine; Gateway to Wine, Wine on a Budget; Make a Wine Connoisseur; Open Guide to Royal St George's and Sandwich; Open Guide to Royal Troon and Kyle; Open Guide to Old Course and St Andrew; Open Guide to Turnberry and Carrick; Open guide to Royal Lythan and St Annes; Held in Trust (book of TV series); The Sea Dominies; Gourmet Golf; TV Held in Trust. *Hobbies:* Music; Golf; Watching rugby; Archaeology; French; Italian. *Address:* 1 Church Road, North Berwick, EH39 4AD.

CRAWLEY Brenda, b. 30 July, Birmingham, Alabama, USA. Associate Professor. *Education:* BA Sociol, magna cum laude, California State Univ, 1971; MSW, 1973,

PhD, 1981, Univ of Illinois at Urbana. *Appointments:* Asst Prof, W.Michigan Univ, 1974-76; Prog Assoc, nat Coun on Aging Inc, 1981-84; Assoc Prof, Univ of Kansas, 1984-. *Creative works:* Articles: The Transformation of the American Labour Force: Elder African Americans; Impact of National Housing Policy on Adult Foster Care and Residential Care Facilities, 1990; Black Familes in a Neo Conservative Era, 1988. *Memberships:* Coun on Social Work Ed; Comm on Women; Nat Assn of Social Workers. *Honours:* Chancellors Teaching Awd Nominee, 1991; HOPE Tchg Awd Nominee, 1988, 1989; US Dept of HEW, Doctoral Dissertation Awd, 1979-80. *Hobbies:* Race walking; Travel; Writing poetry. *Address:* PO Box 1861, Lawrence, KS 66044, USA.

CRAWSHAY Martin Richard Charles, b. 16 Jan 1928, Norwich, England. Racing Liaison Executive, Horserace Betting Levy Board. m.Joanna Deborah Grania Bevan, 24 Oct 1967, 1 s. *Education:* Orwell Pk Prep Sch, 1937-41; Eton Col, 1941-46; RMA Sandhurst, 1948-49. *Appointments:* Comm, 16th/5th The Queens Royal Lancers, 1948; Adjutant, 1955-57; Ret'd, 1961; Raising Liaison Exec, Horserace Betting Levy Bd, 1963-91. *Memberships:* Hon Mem Brit Equine Vet Assn. *Hobbies:* Racing; Shooting; Croquet; Preservation of wildlife. *Address:* The Old Vicarage, Leavenheath, Colchester, Essex CO6 4PT, England.

CREESE Richard, b. 4 Dec 1919. Retired professor of Physiology, University of London. *Education:* Clifton Col, 1934-39; Kings Col London, 1939-41; MB, Westminster Hosp, 1941-44; PhD, Kings Col, London, 1948- 49. *Appointments:* Lectr 1950, Sr Lectr, 1957, London Hosp Med Col; Reader, 1961, prof, 1968-82, St Mary's Hosp Med Sch; Visiting Prof, Pharmacol, Univ California, LA, 1955-56, 1983-85. *Creative works:* Author, Recent advances in Physiology, 1963. *Memberships:* Physiol Soc; Brit Pharmacol Soc; Brit Biophys Soc; RSM, Pres, Hist of Med Section, 1992. *Honours:* TD, 1965; Mickle Fellow, Univ London, 1960. *Hobbies:* Travel; History; Drama; Running. *Address:* 93 Lonsdale Road, London SW13 9DA, England.

CREWE Candida Annabel, b. 6 June 1964, London, England. Novelist; Freelance Journalist. *Education:* St Mary's Sch, Calne, 1978-80. *Appointments:* Jr Edit, Quartet Books, 1983-86. *Creative works:* Focul, 1985; Romantic Hero, 1986; Accommodating Molly, 1989; Mad about Bees, 1991. *Memberships:* Pen Intl. *Honours:* Winner of Catherine Pakenham Awd for Journalism, 1990. *Hobby:* Photography. *Address:* c/o Imogen Praker, AP Watt Ltd, 20 John Street, WC1N 2DR, England.

CRICKMAY Anthony John Edward, b. 20 May 1937, Woking, Surrey, England. *Education:* Belmont Sch, Westcott, 1946-51. *Appointments:* Wallace Heaton, 1952-54; Lotte Meitner Graf, 1955-58; Freelance Photographer, 1961-. *Creative works:* Principles of Classical Dance, 1979; Lynn Seymour, 1980; Dancers, 1982; A Portrait of the Royal Ballet, 1988. *Honours:* Photography comm'd by HM Queen Elizabeth the Queen Mother Official 90th Birthday Pictures; HRH Princess Margaret; HRH Princess Alexandra and TRH, Prince & Princess Michael of Kent. *Hobbies:* Sports; Dinner with friends; Travel; Photography. *Address:* 74 Farm Lane, London SW6 1QA, England.

CRILLY Eugene Richard, b. 30 Oct 1923, Philadelphia, Pennsylvania, USA. Engineering Consultant, Nonmetallic materials and Processes. m. Alice Royal Roth, 16 Feb 1952. *Education:* BA Central Hg Sch, Philadelphia, 1941; Mech Eng, 1944, MSc, 1949, Stevens Inst of Tech; MSc, Univ of Pennsylvania, 1951; Courses, Univ of California, 1956-58. *Appointments:* Res Engr, Keasbey & Mattison, 1951-54; Sr Res Engr, N.American Aviation, 1954-57; Process Engr, Northrop Corp, 1957-59; Proj Engr, and Quality Control Mgr, HITCO, 1959-62; Sr Res Engr, Rocketdyne & Space Divisions, N.American Aircraft, 1962-66; Sr Res Specialist, Lockheed, 1966-74; Engrg Specialist, Rockwell Intl, NAA, 1974-89. *Creative works:* Various papers and reports, structural bonding and advanced composites. *Contributions to:* various handbooks, advanced composites. *Memberships:* Profl, military and civic organisations including numerous offices, Soc for Advancement of Material and Process Engrg, SAMPE. *Honours:* Awd of Merit, SAMPE, 1986; Sigma Xi, 1984; Citations, Military Order of World Wars, 1986-88; Cmdr, Ret'd, US Naval Reserve, 1975; Numerous appreciation certificates. *Hobbies:* History, USA, and World Warr II. *Address:* 276 J Avenue, Coronado, CA 92118, USA. 9, 26, 59.

CRIPPS Cyril Humphrey Sir, b. 2 Oct 1915, London, England. Chairman, Manufacturing Businesses; Foundation Chairman. m. Dorothea Casson Cook, 5 June 1942, 3 s, 1 dec, 1 d. *Education:* BA, MA, St John's Col, Cambridge. *Appointments include:* Dir, 1963-, Chm, 1973-, Velcro Industs NV; Fdr Mem, Chm, Cripps Foun; Chm, MD, Pianoforte Supplies Ltd, Roade, Northampton; Elected Mem, 1963-81, Leader of Independents, 1963-74, Former V-Chm, Ed and Plan Comms, Northamptonshire Co Coun; Bd, Northampton Devel Corp, 1968-85; Hg Sheriff of Northamptonshire, 1985-86; Dep Lt, 1986. *Memberships include:* Fellow, Chem Soc; RSC; Fellow, Chartered Chem, RIC; Life Mem of Ct, Univ of Nottingham; Former Gov, Northampton Grammar Sch, Chm, Old Grammar Sch Foun; Gov, Former Chm, Govs of Northampton Hg Sch for Girls; Former Foun Gov, Bilton Grange Prep Sch; Trustee, Pres, Postgrad Med Centre, Sports and Recreation Residence, Northampton Gen Hosp; Trustee: Trusts for Preservation of the fabric of Peterborough Cathedral; Trust for the Reconstruction of All Saints Ch, Northampton; Master Liveryman, Worshipful Co of Wheelwrights; Liveryman, Worshipful Co of Tallow Chandlers. *Honours:* Freeman, City of London, 1957; Hon Fellow, Cripps Hall, Univ of Nottingham, 1959-; St John's Col, 1966-; Magdalene and Selwyn Cols, 1971-; Queens Col, 1979-; Cambridge Univ, DSc (hon), Nottingham, 1975; LLD (hon) Cambridge, 1976; Knight Bachelor, 1989. *Hobbies:* Travel; Photography; Philately; Natural History. *Address:* Bull's Head Farm, Eakley Lanes, Stoke Goldington, Newport Pagnell, Bucks, England. 1.

CRISCOE Arthur H, b. 21 Feb 1939, Alabama, USA. Educator. m. Joy Orten, 4 Apr 1987. *Education:* BA Samford Univ, 1964; MDiv, 1968, MRE, 1969, EdD, 1975, Southwestern Baptist Theol Seminary; MAE, Cumberland Univ, 1993. *Appointments:* Prof, Acad Dean, Columbia Bible Col, 1971- 76; Dir, Mgmt Support, Sunday Sch Bd, 1976-; Adj Prof, Cumberland Univ, 1988-. *Creative works:* Author of 10 books and over 75 articles; Creator and writer of over 20 television programmes. *Memberships:* World Future Soc; Intl Brotherhood of Magicians; Am Soc of Magicians; Assn for the Supvn of Curriculum Devel. *Hobbies:* Magic; Reading; Walking. *Address:* Sunday School Bd, 127 9th Ave North, Nashville, TN 37234, USA.

CRISMOND Linda F, b. 1 Mar 1943, Burbank, California, USA. Exec Dir, American Lib Assn. 1 s. *Education:* BS, Univ of CA, Santa Barbara, 1964; MLS, Univ of CA, Berkeley, 1965; Cert Assn Exec, 1991. *Appointments:* Chief Dpty Co Libn, Los Angeles Co Pub Lib, 1980-81; Co Libn, Los Angeles Co Pub Lib, 1981-89; Exec Dir, American Lib Assn, 1989-. *Publications:* The Future of Public Library Services, Library Jrnl, 1986; Information Services in the Public Library, The Future of the Public Library, 1988; Library Readers, Public Libraries, 1988; Elbow Room for Editors, Association Management, 1992. *Memberships:* ALA; American Soc of Assn Execs; Chicago Soc of Assn Execs; IL Lib Assn. *Honours:* Outstanding Staff Member of the Year, San Francisco Public Library, 1968; Los Angeles County Department Head of the Year, 1986; Top Ten Public Librarians, Public Libraries, 1988; 100 Chicago Women Making a Difference, 1991. *Hobbies:* Sailing, Reading, Cooking. *Address:* 50 East Huron Street, Chicago, IL 60611, USA. 2, 9.

CRISWELL Susan J, b. 22 June 1952, Greensburgh, Pennsylvania USA. Assistant Professor of Education; m. John R Criswell, 15 June 1991, 2 step sons. *Education:* BS Ed, Slippery Rock Univ, 1973; MEd, Indiana Univ of PA, 1977; EdD W.Virginia Univ, 1989. *Appointments:* Tchr, 1974-84; Instr, Shepherd Col, 1986-89; Asst Prof, Edinboro Univ of PA, 1989-. *Memberships:* Phi Delta Kappa; Delta Kappa Gamma; Assn of Supervision and Curriculum Devel; Assn of Tchr Edrs; Am Assn of Univ Women; Eric Reading Coun; Keystone Reading Conf. *Hobbies:* Gardening; Reading. *Address:* 2085 Charleston Ave, Erie, PA 16509, USA.

CRNJAKOVIC Aleksa, b. 1 Apr 1949, Porec, Croatia. Jrnlst. m. Miroslav Crnjakovic, 2 Apr 1977, 1 s, 1 d. *Education:* Fac of Pol Science, 1973. *Appointments:* Jrnlst in Vjesnik, Zagreb; Reports from Parl, 1974-. *Creative Works:* Selected Interviews. *Membership:* Croatian Assn of Jrnlsts. *Honour:* State Award for Professional Achievements.. *Hobbies:* Fashion, Ceramics. *Address:* Hebrangova 28, Zagreb, Croatia.

CROCKER John, b. 18 June 1951, Luton, Beds, England. Histopathologist. m. Catherine Barbara Tombs, 1 s. *Education:* Sevenoaks Sch, Kent, 1961; MA (Cantab) Path, 1974; Kings Col Cambridge, MD (Cantab), 1983; MRCPath, 1981. *Appointments:* SHO Path, E.Birmingham Hosp, 1975-76; Lectr in Path, Univ Birmingham, 1976-83; Conslt Histopath, Hon Sr Lectr in Path, E.Birmingham Hosp, 1983-. *Creative works:* Papers, reviews and editorials on malignant lymphomas, Hodgkin's disease, immunohistochemistry, morphometry and neucleolar pathology. *Memberships:* RCPath; Assn Clin Paths; Intl Acad of Paths; Royal Microscopical Soc; Brit Lymphomas Path Gp; Hon Sec, W.Midlands Oncol Assn; Affil Mem, W.Midlands Otolaryngol Assn; Brit Interplanetary Soc. *Honours:* Barcroft Prize for Physiol, Univ Cambridge, 1969; King's Col, Cambridge, Travelling Prize, 1970; Graham McCollough Path Prize, Cambridge, 1971. *Hobbies:* English literature; Photography; German and English Opera and Classical music in general; Computing; Pre-Raphaelite painting. *Address:* Chiltern, 226 Blossomfield Road, Solihull, W.Midlands B91 1NT, England.

CROCKFORD Kenneth Harold, b. 16 July 1923. Retired Army Officer; Charity Worker. *Education:* Winslow C of E, Vauxhall Evening Inst. *Appointments:* Military Ser incl: Rgmt Platoon Cmdr, Co Cmdr, UK, France, Belgium, Holland, Germany, 1944-47; Aide de Camp to GOG, HQ 5 Div, Brunswick, Germany, 1947-48; Gen Staff Ofr, HQ Hamburg Sun Area, 1948-49; Instr, Army Mech Transp Sch, 1949-53; Ofr Cmdg Transp Co, 3rd Infantry Div, Egypt, 1953-54; Staff Ofr, Personnel, HQ Middle East Land Forces, 1954-56; Adjutant, 3rd Infantry Div, UK, 1956-58; Ofr, Cmdg Jr Leaders Unit, War Ofc Training Estab, 1959-60; Ofr Cmdg Transp Unit, HQ 24 Infantry Brig, Kenya 1960-62; Staff Ofr, Gp Maj, HQ Maritime Transp, Portsmouth, UK, 1963-66; Staff Ofr, Transp HQ 99 Gurka Infantry Brig, Borneo, 1966; Staff ofr, Plans Ops, HQ Far East Land Forces, Singapore, 1966-68; Ret'd, 1969; HQ Save the Children Fund, 1971-87; Overseas Supplies Ofr, 1971-78, UK Controller, 1978-82, Vehicle Insurance and Exec Mgr, 1982-87, Ret'd, Dec 1987. *Memberships:* Past Assoc Mem, BIM; Inst of Indust Transp; Inst of Adv Motorists; Order of the Road. *Honours:* Military Cross, 1946; Chevalier de l'Ordre de Leopold II avec Palme, 1946; Croix de Guerre 1940, avec Palme; Clayton Essay Prize Winner, 1959. *Hobbies:* Country walking; Photography; Philately; Gardening; Travel; Research on history of the 11th Armoured Div, Normandy to the Rhine, 1944-45; Classical music. *Address:* 21 Home Farm Road, Godalming, Surrey GU7 1TX, England.

CROCOMBE Graham Taturoanui, b. 7 Mar 1960, Apia, Western Samoa. Business Economist. *Education:* Dipl of Chinese Lang, Beijing Lang Inst, 1979; BA, Univ of South Pacific, 1982; MBA, Harvard Bus Sch, 1989. *Creative works:* Joint author with Michael J Enright and

Michael E Porter of Upgrading New Zealand's competitive Advantage, 1991. *Hobbies:* Outdoor pursuits; Philosophy; Teaching. *Address:* PO Box 6798, Wellesley Street, Auckland 1, New Zealand.

CROFT Ivor John, b. 6 Jan 1923, London, England. Painter. Retired Civil Servant. *Education:* MA Christ Church, Oxford, 1948; Tchr's Dipl, Inst of Ed, Univ of London, 1949; MA London Sch of Ec, ibid, 1953. *Appointments:* Home Office: Insp, Children's Dept, 1952-66; Sr Res Ofr, 1966-72; Hd, Res Unit, 1972-81; Hd, Res & Planning Unit, 1981-83. *Creative works:* Various studies of crime, criminological research and administraton of justice; Paintings in various group and one-man shows. *Memberships include:* Mem, 1978-83, Chm, 1981-83, Criminological Sci Coun, Coun of Europe. *Honour:* CBE, 1982. *Address:* 30 Stanley Road, Peel, Isle of Man, UK.

CROLL James George Arthur, b. 16 Oct 1943, New Zealand. Professor of Engineering. m. ELisabeth Joan Sprackett, 16 Dec 1966, 1 s, 1 d. *Education:* BEng, 1st class hons, 1964, PhD, 1967, Univ of Canterbury, New Zealand; Post Doctoral Scholar, Univ Col London, 1967-68. *Appointments:* NZ Ministry of Works: Engrg Asst, 1962-65; Asst Engr, 1965-67; Univ Col London: Res Fellow, 1968-70; Lectr, 1970-81; Reader, 1981- 85; Prof, 1985-; Head of Dept of Civil Engng, 1992-; Visiting Prof to Univs of: Rio de Janeiro, Cordoba Argentina, Hong Kong, Shanghai, Tohoko and Princeton. *Creative works:* Elements of structural stability, 1973; Force Systems and Equilibrium, 1975; 120 technical papers. *Memberships:* FISE; Fellow, Inst of Maths and Applic; Fellow, Royal Academy of Engrg. *Honours:* Telford Premium, ICE, 1982; Thomas B Hall Prize, IMechE, 1983; NZ Scholarships, 1961, 1964, 1967. *Hobbies:* Sailing; Music; Piano and choral singing; Painting and Drawing; Travel. *Address:* Dept of Civil Engng, Univ College of London, Gower St, London WC1 E 68T, England.

CROMER Charles Marion, b. 15 Sept 1943, Jefferson, Texas, USA. Poet. *Education:* Hon Grad, Hallsville Hg Sch, Texas, 1962; Le Tourneau Col, Longview, Texas, 1962, 1963. *Appointments:* Office worker at Cromer Steel, 1981-82. *Creative works:* Many books of verse and several books of prose. *Memberships:* The Poetry Soc of Texas, 1966-, Coun, 1966, 1967; Intl Platform Assn. *Honours:* Scholarship from Le Tourneau Col, 1962. *Hobbies:* Poetry; Music; Singing; Reading; Walking; Social Studies; Science; Art; Literature; Philosophy; Religion. *Address:* 3118 Robin Lane, Texarkana, TX 75503, USA.

CROMPTON Michael Robin, b. 19 Mar 1938, Manchester, England. Diplomat. div. *Education:* Hon Deg Modern Langs, 1959, MA, 1962, Jesus Col, Cambridge, 1956-59; Various Dipls, Trinity Col of Music, London, 1947-51. *Appointments:* Eng Lector, Heidelberg Univ, W.Germany, 1964-71; HM Diplomatic Serv, 1971-. *Creative works:* Translations: Britain's Relations with S.W Germany, 1965; The History of Heidelberg Univ, 1967; Goethe: Visits to Heidelberg, 1966; Fontane: Wanderings through Berlin, 1968. *Memberships:* Nat Coun of Civil Liberties; Anti-Apartheid Movement; Friends of the Earth; Charter 88; The European Movement; Commonwealth Trust; Fabian Soc. *Honours:* Scholarships: State 1955; Jesus Col, Cambridge 1956-59; Brit Coun 1959-60; State Studentship, 1960-63. *Hobbies:* Music; Reading; Walking; Writing; Motoring; Africa. *Address:* c/o Foreign and Commonwealth Office, King Charles St, London SW1, England.

CRONIN Robert Francis Patrick, b. 1 Sept 1926, London, England. Medical Consultant to the Secretariat, H H The Aga Khan. m. Shirley Gian Robertson, 19 June 1954. 1 s, 2 d. *Education:* Princeton Univ, 1943- 44, 1947-49; RCAF and Brit Army, 1944-47; MD, CM, 1953, MSc Exp Med, 1960, McGill Univ. *Appointments:* Fac of Med, McGill Univ, 1959-84, Prof, 1972, Dean, 1972-77, Conslt Cardiol, Montreal General Hosp, 1981-.

Creative works: Numerous contributions to professional journals in the field of cardiovascular physiology. *Memberships:* Royal Col of Phys and Surg, Canada; Fellow, 1959, Coun, 1979; Am Col of Phys, Fellow, 1962; Med Res Coun, VP, 1971; Gov, McGill Univ, 1982; Dir, Aga Khan Univ Hosp, 1985-. *Honours:* Fellowship, RCP, London, 1974. *Hobbies:* Skiing; Golf; Fishing. *Address:* En Champ Riond, 1815 Baugy sur Clarens, Switzerland.

CROOKALL John Roland, b. 5 May 1935, London, England. Consultant in Intellectual Property and Patents. m. Gretta Mary Inger, 19 June 1965, 2 s, 1 d. *Education:* Dipl,Imperial Col, 1963; PhD Univ of Nottingham, 1966. *Appointments:* Performance Engr, De Havilland Engine Co Ltd, 1958-61; Mgr, Prod Tech, MSc Course, Imperial Col, London, 1965-74; Prof of Mfg, 1965-74; Cranfield Inst of Tech, 1974-90; Conslt, J R Crookall & Assocs, 1990-. *Creative works:* Book: Numerically controlled machine tools, 1970; Over 100 publications on manufacturing systems, automation, integration and management. *Memberships:* Fellow, Royal Acad of Engrg; FIMechE; Brit Acad of Experts; Assoc Mem, IoD; Intl Inst for Prod Eng Res, Coun; Royal Col of Organists; Sr Mem, Soc of Mfg Engrs, USA. *Honours:* James Clayton Fellowship, 1962, Prize, 1965, IMechE; Industry Year Awd, 1986. *Hobbies:* Music - organist at St John's Bedford. *Address:* 12 Hall Close, Harrold, Bedford MK43 7DU, England.

CROSBY John Rutherford, b. 1 May 1933, Colchester, England. Personnel Director. m. Rosalind Elizabeth Williams, 10 Mar 1962, 2 s, 1 d. *Education:* BA Durham, 1954; Dipl in Personnel Mgmt, cardiff, 1958; MA London, 1968; CIPM, 1980; FInstD, 1984; CBIM, 1983. *Appointments:* Personnel Ofr, EMI, 1958-62; Personnel Mgr, Costain Gp, 1962-68; Sr Conslt, HAY/MSL, 1968-76; Personnel Dir, Bd Mem, Brit Am Tobacco Ltd, 1976-88; Dir of Gp Personnel, BAT Industries Plc, 1988-. *Creative works:* Various articles in professional magazines. *Contributions to:* The Handbook of Management Development, 1986, 1991. *Memberships include:* IPM, VP, 1979-81, Pres, 1985-87, Dir, IPM Sers Ltd, 1985-87, Chm, Adv Com on Nominations, 1987-89; Coun, Voluntary Ser Overseas, 1983-; CBI, Employment Policy Com, 1988-; Employment Appeal Tribunal, 1991-; Trustee, Overseas Students Trust, 1988-; V-Chm, Croydon Col, 1989-. *Hobbies:* Music; Opera; Theatre; Reading. *Address:* 70 Woodcote Valley Road, Purley, Croydon CR8 3DB, England.

CROSSLEY Paul Christopher Richard, b. 17 May 1944, Dewsbury, England. Concert Pianist. *Education:* Silcoates Sch, Wakefield, 1952- 63; MA Mansfield Col, Oxford, 1966. *Appointments:* Concert Pianist; Artistic Dir, London Sinfonietta, 1988-. *Creative works:* 15 films for television on prominent composers. *Honours:* Hon Fellow, Mansifield Col, Oxford, 1991. *Hobbies:* Reading; Mah-Jonng. *Address:* c/o Van Walsum Management, 26 Wadham Road, London SW15 2LR, England.

CROW Richard Thomas, b. 31 Aug 1939, Summit, Illinois, USa. Professor and Associate Dean. m. Carolyn Sue Carr, 11 Aug 1962, 2 d. *Education:* AB Wheaton Col, 1962; MA Indiana Univ, 1964; PhD, 1974, MPA, 1976, Univ of Denver. *Appointments:* Probation Ofr, 1962-66, Asst Supt, 1967, Marion County; Asst Dir, Youth Devel Inc 1967-70; Instr, Rockland Com Col, 1970-72. *Creative works:* Management for the Human Services, 1987; the PhD or the DSW, 1975; Is the Court Remaking the American Prison System, 1976; Management in the Human Service Organization, 1980; Planning and Management professions, 1987. *Memberships:* Nat Assn of Social Workers; Acad of Cert Social Workers; Am Public Welfare Assn; Alabama Conf of Social Work, Exec Com. *Honours:* Phi Alpha Alpha, 1979; Alabama Judicial Col Fac Assn, Hon Mem; Alabama Dept of Youth Sers Bd, 1982-91, Chm, 1988-91; Standing Com on Juvenile Procedures, Alabama Supreme Ct, 1985-. *Hobbies:* Skiing; Racquetball;

Reading; Movies. *Address:* 9138 Enterprise Avenue NE, Tuscaloosa, AL 35406, USA.

CROWE Brenda Stone, b. 24 May 1946, Anniston, Alabama, USA. English Professor. m. Robert Larry Crowe, 19 Dec 1964, 1 s. *Education:* BS 1968, MA 1970, PhD, 1992, English. *Appointments:* Litchfield Jr HS, 1968-73; Gadsden State Com Col, Alabama, 1973-. *Creative works:* Freelance magazine articles; Master's thesis and PhD Dissertation. *Memberships:* Nat Ed Assn; Alabama Ed Assn; Southern Assn of Modern Languages; Delta Kappa Gamma, Pres. *Honours:* Gadsden State Outstanding Tchr, 1990; Chancellor's Awd, State of Alabama, 1990; NISOD Intl Awd for Tchg Excellence, 1991. *Hobbies:* Reading; Oil Painting; Car Racing. *Address:* 111 Staci Lane, Gadsden, AL 35906, USA.

CROWSON Richard Borman, b. 23 July 1929, Gainsborough, England. Retired Diplomat. m. (1) Sylvia Cavalier, 29 Feb 1960; (2) Judith Elaine Turner, 21 May 1983, 1 s, 1 d. *Education:* MA, Downing Col, Cambridge, 1949-52. *Appointments:* HM Overseas Civil Serv, Uganda, 1955-62; Foreign Office, London, 1962-63; First Sec, Brit Embassy, Tokyo, 1963-68; Dep High Commr, Barbados, 1968-70; FCO, London, 1970-74; Counsellor Brit Embassies in Jakarta, 1975-77, Washington, 1977-82, Berne, 1982-85; Brit Hg Commr, Mauritius, HM Ambassador, Fed Islamic Republic of Comoros, 1985-89. *Memberships:* FCIS. *Honours:* CMG, 1986. *Hobbies:* Music; Writing. *Address:* 67 Crofton Road, Orpington, Kent BR6 8HU, England.

CROWTHER Leslie Douglas Sargent, b. 6 Feb 1933, Nottingham, England. Actor; Entertainer. m. 27 Mar 1954, 4 s, 1 d. *Education:* Thames Valley Grammar Sch, 1945-47; Ripman Sch, 1947-48; Royal Acad of Music, 1945-49. *Career includes:* Open Air Theatre, Regents Park, 1949-51; TV shows include: High Summer, 1960; The Black and White Minstrel Show; Crackerjack, 1960-68; Saturday Crowd; Crowther's in Town; The Leslie Crowther Show; The Golden Shot; Jocker's Wild; My Good Woman, 1970-73; Bud Flanagan & Chesney Allen Show; Hi Summer, 1977; Who's Baby?, 1983; The Price is Right, 1984; Deja Vu; Stars in Their Eyes, 1990; Birds of a Feather, 1990; Theatre includes: Let Sleeping Wives Lie, 1967-69; Aladdin, 1970; Royal Variety Show, 1970; Summer seasons and pantos, 1978-82; Bud 'n' Ches, 1982; Underneath the Arches, 1983; Robinson Crusoe, 1988-89, 1989-90. Radio includes: Are You Sitting Comfortably, 1991. *Memberships:* Pres, The Lords Taveners; V-Chm, Stars Org for Spastics; Grand Order of Water Rats; Variety Club of Great Brit. *Hobbies:* Antiques; Cricket; Wild life; Gardening; Philately. *Address:* Temple Court, Corston, Bath, Avon BA2 9EX, England.

CRYER William Jefferson, b. 19 Sept 1943, Meridian, Mississippi, USa. Hospital Administrator: Professor. m. (1)Delores Mclendon, 1964, 1 d; (2)Joyce Stovall, 1969, 1 s, 1 d. (3)Pamela Johnson, 25 Sept 1982, 1 s. *Education:* BA Sociol & Behavioural Sci, California State Univ, 1972; MA, 1974, PhD, 1976, Univ of Minnesota. *Appointments include:* Student Affairs Ofr, Asst Dean, Admissions and Records, California State Univ, 1977; Chancellor, Tech Health Careers Sch, Los Angeles, 1977-79; Dir, Res Planning and Evaluation, Central City Community Mental Health Ctr, 1979-83; Admr, Obs & Gynae, King/Drew Med Centre (KDMC), 1983-84; Hd, Mental Health Clin Prog, County of Los Angeles, 1984-85; Chief, Res Unit, UCLA/Drew Univ of Med and Sci, KDMC, 1985-; Dir, Reg Planning, Co of Los Angeles, 1985-; Asst Prof, 1985-90, UCLA/Drew Univ of Med and Sci. *Memberships include:* Nat Mgmt Assn, 1986-88; Alpha Kappa Delta, 1972-74; Black Psycho Assn, VP Los Angeles Chapter, 1977-82; Alumni Assn, Bd of Dirs, Pres for Fin, CSU, 1978-82. *Honours include:* Fellowship, Univ of Minnesota, 1972-74, 1974-76; Dean's Scholar, Univ Minnesota, 1972-74, 1974-76; Cert, Midwest Soc of Ed Admrs, 1975; Leadership Cert, Jack & Jill Inc of Am. *Hobbies:* Golf; Swimming; Reading;

Spectator sports. *Address:* 3754 West 58th Place, Los Angeles, CA 90043, USA.

CSENDES Ernest, b. 2 Mar 1926, Satu-Mare, Romania. Consultant Chemist; Businessman. m. Catharine Vera Tolnai, 11 Feb 1953, 1 s, 1 d. *Education:* BA, Prostestant Col, Hungary, 1944; BSC 1948; MSc Org Chem, 1951; PhD, 1951, Univ of Heidelberg; Res Assoc, Tulane Univ Med Sch and fellow, Chem, Harvard Univ, US, 1952-53. *Appointments:* Reschr, E I du Pont de Nemours Y Co, 1953-61; Dr, R&D, Agric Chems Armour & Co, 1961-63; Exec VP, Occidental Petroleum Corp, Exec VP and Chief Exex, Occidental Res & Engrg Co, 1963-68; Fdr, Pres, and Cheif Exec, TRI Gp, 1968-84; Mng Partner and Owner, Inter-Consult Ltd, 1984-. *Creative works include:* Books, reports, prospectuses, scientific journal and trade magazine articles numbering 250 in total; 29 patents. *Memberships include:* FRSC; AIC; AAAS. *Honours:* Gold Medal, Brazilian Acad of Humanities, 1974; Acclaimed for regional agricultural and industrial developments worldwide; Pioneered new types Eurodollar Investments. *Hobbies:* Decorative arts, 18th & 19th Century France; Chamber music; Hiking; Swimming. *Address:* 514 Marquette Street, Pacific Palisades, CA 90272, USA. 9, 52, 59, 132, 143.

CSERMELY Thomas John, b. 25 June 1931, Szombatheley, Hungary. Prof. m. 17 June 1961, 1 s. *Education:* Dip, Mech Engrng, Chem Indl Br, Polytechnic Univ of Budapest, Hungary, 1953; PhD, Syracuse Univ, NY, 1968. *Appointments:* Instr, Inst of Theoretical Phys, Polytechnical Univ of Budapest, Hungary, 1953-56; Rsch Engr, Rsch Div, Carrier Corp, Syracuse, 1957-67; Rsch Assoc, Phys Dept, Syracuse, 1957-67; Asst Prof, Physiology Dept, SUNY, Upstate Med Ctr, Syracuse, 1968-76; Asst Prof, Phys Dept, LeMoyne Coll, 1976-77; Assoc Prof, Bioengineering Dept, Syracuse Univ, 1977-88. *Contributions to:* Int Mtgs and Scientific Jrnls; Author or Co-author of about 35 reports and papers. *Memberships:* Sr Mbr, Biophysical Soc and IEEE; NY Acad of Sciences; American Phys Soc; American Assn of Phys Tchrs; AAAS. *Honours:* Wolverine; ASHRAE; Diamond Key Award for Outstanding Publication, American Society of Heating, Refrigeration and Air Conditionind Engineers, 1965. *Address:* Bioengineering Department, 417 Link Hall, Syracuse University, Syracuse, NY 13244, USA.

CU Huy Can, b. 31 May 1919, Vietnam. Poet; Pres of Nat Coun of Arts and Lit of Vietnam. m. (1) 14 July 1951, (2) 4 Oct 1964, 2 s, 2 d. *Education:* Agronomist, Agric Higher Schl, Hanoi, 1942. *Appointments:* Min of Agric, 1945-46; Vice-Min of the Interior, 1946 Gen Sec, Coun of Mins, 1949-55; Vice-Min of Culture, 1956-84; Min for Cultural Affairs, 1984-87; Pres, Nat Coun of Arts and Lit, 1984-. *Publications:* 18 Poetry Anthologies and many essays. *Memberships:* Assn of Writers, Vietnam; Pres, Nat Coun of Arts and Lit; Asian-African Writers Assn; Exec Bd, UNESCO, 1978-83; VP, ACCT, 1981-87; VP, Coun for Redaction of Vietnamese Ency. *Honours:* Ho-Chi-Minh Order; Twice Decorated Resistance Order, First Class. *Hobbies:* Reading, Movies, Theatre, Plastic Arts. *Address:* President of the National Council of Arts and Literature, 51 Tran Hung Dao Street, Hanoi, Socialist Republic of Vietnam. 52.

CUCUIANU Mircea Petru, b. 22 June 1928, Sibiu, Romania. Professor of Clinical Chemistry. m. Felicia, 28 June 1957, 1 s, 1 d. *Education:* Graduated 1953; Phd, 1966, Docent, 1971, Fac of Med, Cluj, Romania; WHO Trainee, McMaster Univ, Canada, 1968-69. *Appointments:* Lectr, Dept Pathophysiol, 1953-66, Lectr, 1966, Asst Prof, 1971-81, Prof, 1981-, Clin Chem, Univ of Cluj Med Sch. *Creative works:* Clinical Biochemistry II & II; Clinical Biochemistry of Haemostasis; 214 articles, 44 in English, in international journals in the area of fibrinolysis, platelets, hyperliproproteinemia, hepatic protein synthesis. *Memberships:* Romanian Union of Med Sci Socs; Pres, Romanian Biochem Soc. *Honours:* Prize, Romanian Acad for studies on Platelet function and pharmacology. *Hobbies:* Literature (fiction);

Swimming; Tourism. *Address:* Medical Clinic No 1, R-3400 Clum-Napoca, Romania.

CUDE Bobby Lee, b. 21 Apr 1925, Oklahoma, USA. Music Producer; Chief Executive Officer of Hard Hat Records. *Education:* Oklahoma Grad Col and State Univ. *Appointments:* Writer and composer of 800 songs partner in Cude and Pickens Music Publishing Co, BMI, Music Producer, Hard Hat Records; Writer and creator of the popular slogan, DJ's do it on request as well as the public service message, It's Twelve O'clock! Do you know where your children are?; Writer of the song/march, Los Angeles Town, and many more. *Memberships:* Fdr: Nat Hg Sch Band Dirs Hall of Fame, Nat Hg Sch Choral Dirs Hall of Fame, Nat Col Band and Choral Dirs Hall of Fame. *Address:* 519 Halifax Avenue, Daytona Beach, FL 32118, USA.

CUI Binhua, b. 30 Mar 1963, Hebei, China. Geochemical Engineer. m. Wang Aiping, 15 Nov 1988, 1 d. *Education:* BSc, Exploration Geochem, Wuhan Geol Col, 1979-83. *Appointments:* Geochem Engr, Shanxi Bureau of Geol and Mineral Resource,1983-88; Geochem Engr, Shanxi Inst of Geosci, 1988-. *Creative works:* Over 10 papers or technology reports in cluding: Regional Geochemistry of Zhongtiao Mountains, 1987; Regional Geochemistry of Northern Shanxi, 1988; Geochemistry of Tongkuangyu Copper Deposit, 1990. *Membership:* Geologic Assn of China. *Honours:* Geochem maps of Northeast Shanxi was given the third class technology prize by the Ministry of Geol and Mineral Resource of China, 1989. *Hobbies:* Reading; Touring. *Address:* Shanxi Institute of Geoscience, 4 Xuefu Street, Taiyuan, Shanxi 030006, China.

CULYER Richard C III, b. 12 Feb 1939, Baltimore, Maryland, USA. Professor; Writer; Consultant. m. Gail Blake, 9 Aug, 1969, 1 d. *Education:* BS, 1959, MA, 1964, Appalachian State Univ; PhD, 1973, Elem Ed, Florida State Univ. *Appointments:* Tchr, Kings Mountain, NC, 1959-66; Reading Coor, Kings Mountain, 1966; Fac Appalachian State Univ, Boone, NC, 1966-72; Fac Coker Col, SC, 1976-. *Creative works include:* Over 600 works including: Preventing Reading Failure: A Practical Approach; Teaching Reading to Adults; Materials on comprehension, higher order thinking skills, vocabulary and phonics. *Memberships include:* NC Council of the Intl Rgd Assn, Co-Fdr, Pres, Bd of Dirs; Intl Rgd Assn; Montgomery Co Council of the IRA, Pres; Applachian Rgd Coun, Pres; Col Rdg Assn, Life; Phi Delta Kappa, Life; Nat Coun of Tchrs of Eng, Life. *Honours:* Dist Ser Awd, Young Man of the year, Kings Mountain, NC, 1965; Ten Yr Awd for Dist Serv to Reading, NC Coun of Intl Reading Assn, 1979. *Hobbies:* Reading; Genealogy. *Address:* 401 Gandy Drive, Hartsville, SC 29550, USA.

CUMMINS Joseph Edwards, b. 5 Feb 1933, Montana, USA. Professor of Genetics. m. 23 Sept 1962, 1 s. *Education:* BS Washington State Univ, 1955; Phd Univ of Wisconsin, 1962; Postdoctoral Univ Edinburgh, 1964, McArthur Lab Cancer Res, 1966, Karolinska Inst Stockholm, 1969. *Appointments:* Asst Prof: Rutgers Univ, 1966-67, Univ of Washington, 1967-71, Western Ontario, 1972-. *Creative works:* Author of numerous scientific publications, environmental reports and legislative briefs. *Memberships:* Genetics Soc; Soc for Environmental Mutagenisis; Am Soc for Cell Biol; Dri, Greenpeace, Canada, 1985-88; Dir, Londoners to Eliminate PCBs, 1990-; Canada Genetics Soc. *Honours:* Dir, Dept of Planet Earth, Urban League green Umbrella Awd, 1985; Cert of Merit, Ministry of Environment, Ontario, 1988; Optimist Intl Community Ser Awd, 1990. *Hobbies:* Ju-Jitsu and other Martial Arts. *Address:* Dept of Plant Sciences, Univ of Western Ontario, London, Ontario, Canada N6A 5B7.

CUMMINS Walter (Merrill), b. 6 Feb 1936, USA. Professor; Editor in Chief, The Literary Review. *Education:* BA Rutgers Univ, 1957; MA, 1962, MFA, 1962, PhD, 1965, Univ Iowa. *Appointments:* Edit, Gen Electric, 1957-59; Edit, Renwar Inc, 1959-60; Instr of Eng, Univ of Iowa, 1962-65; Fairleigh Dickinson Univ, 1965-. *Creative works:* Story collections: Where We live, 1983; Witness, 1975; Novels: A Stranger to the Deed, 1968; Into Temptation, 1968; Short stories in more than 40 magazines. *Memberships:* Am Assn of Univ Profs, Chapter Pres; Col Eng Assn; Nat Coun of Tchrs of Eng. *Honours:* New Jersey State Coun on the Arts Fiction Fellowship, 1982-83. *Hobbies:* Travel; Reading; Computers; Music. *Address:* Fairleigh Dickinson University, 285 Madison Avenue, NJ 07940, USA.

CURE Susan Carol, b. 18 Aug 1940, Los Angeles, California, USa. Microbiologist; Lecturer; Scientific Collaborator. m. Michel Y M A Cure, 20 July, 1963. 1 s, 2 d. *Education:* BA Dist, 1962, PhD, 1966, Biol and Med Microbiol, Stanford Univ. *Appointments:* Postdoctoral Fellow, Calif Det of Health, Berkeley, 1965-68; Reschr, Centre des Etudes de la Biologie Prenatale, 1970-74; Lectr, Am Col Paris (now the Am Univ in Paris), 1970-74; Lectr, Hong Kong Univ, 1978-86; Sci Coor, Ass Franc contre les Myeopathies, 1989-. *Memberships:* AAAS; Am Soc ofr Microbiol; Sigma Xi; Bd of Dirs: Stanford Club of Paris and Stanford Sch Bd. *Hobbies:* Skiing; Horseback Riding. *Address:* 13 Chemin des Maigrets, 78160 Marly-le-Roi, France.

CURI Kriton, b. 19 Oct 1942, Istanbul, Turkey. Prof of Environmental Engrng. *Education:* BS, Civ Engrng, 1966, MS, Sanitary Engrng, 1967, Robert Coll, Istanbul; PhD, Environmental Engrng, Tech Univ of Istanbul, 1974; Dotzenship, Environmental Engrng, InterUniv Coun of Turkey, 1980; Dip, Acad of Turkish Naval Res Offs, Istanbul, 1974. *Appointments:* Cons, primarily on pollution control and wastewater treatment; Vis Prof, Inst of Marine Sciences, Univ of Istanbul, 1986-; Advsr to the Municipality of Izmir, 1987-; Prof of Environmental Engrng, Bogazici Univ, Istanbul, 1988-; Pres, Turkish Nat Comm on Solid Wastes, 1989-; Nat Coord for Earth Day Int, 1990, 91; Coord of the Volunteers for the Environment Movement, 1990; Short- term Advsr to WHO, presently preparing the Guidelines for Monitoring of Land Based Marine Pollution Sources. *Contributions to:* profl jrnls; proceedings, presentations. *Memberships:* Supreme Environmental Coun of Turkey; Soc of Civ Engrs, Turkey; Hon Mbr, Turkish Soc for the Protection of Nature; Environment and Woodlands Protection Soc of Turkey; Green Peace Int; Tech and Scientific Comm for Protection of Mediterranean Sea; Advsry Comm, Int Juridical Org for Environment and Dev; Rotary Int. *Honours:* Bogazici University Rector's Honor Award, 1981; Award of Research and Education Foundation, 1984. *Address:* Bogazici University, School of Engineering, Department of Civil Engineering, 80815 Bebek, Istanbul, Turkey.

CURRAN Charles E, b. 30 Mar 1934, Rochester, NY, USA. University Professor; Catholic Priest. *Education:* BA St Bernards Col, Rochester, NY, 1955; STL, Licentiate in Sacred Theol, 1959, STD Doctorate in Theol, 1961, Gregorian Univ, Rome; STD with spec in Moral Theol, Acad Alfonsiana, Rome, 1961. *Appointments include:* Prof, St Bernards Seminary, 1961- 65, Ast Prof, Assoc Prof and Prof, Moral Theol, Catholic Univ of Am, 1965-87; Visiting Prof: Cornell Univ, 1987-88, Univ of S.California Sch of Religion, 1988-90, Auburn Univ, 1990-91; Elizabeth Scurlock Univ Prof of Human Values, Southern Methodist Univ. *Creative works:* Books include: Christian Morality Today; A New Look at Christian Morality; Contemporary Problems in moral Tehology; Cahtolic Moral Theology in Dialogue; The Cirsis in Priestly Ministry, Politics, Medicine and Christian Ethics; A Dialogue with Paul Ramsey; Medical and Sexual Ethics; Faithfull Dissent. *Memberships:* Pres, Catholic Theol Soc of Am, 1969-70; Pres, Soc of Christian Ethics, 1971-72; Pres, Am Theol Soc, 1989-90; Mem, Cod Theol Soc. *Honours:* John Courtney Murray Awd for Dist Achievement in Theol, first recipient, from Catholic Theol Soc of Am, 1972; Hon Doctorate, Univ of Charleston, 1987; ABC-TV Person of the Week, Aug 1986. *Hobbies:* Golf; Swimming; Reading. *Address:* 317 Dallas Hall, Southern Methodist University, Dallas, TX 75275, USA.

CURRY Jilliain Mary, b. 29 Nov 1961, Cobham, Surrey, England. Freestyle Skier. m. Robin J Wallace, 1 Sept 1990. *Education:* Royal Naval Sch, Queen Anne's Sch, Caversham, Reading; Diplome Secretaire Bilingue, Inst Francais due Royaume Uni. *Appointments:* First elected to Brit Ski Team, 1984 and then every year subsequently. *Honours:* Evian Sports Jouranlist Awd for Winter Achievement, 1991; 4th Place, Aerials Skiing, Albertville, Winter Olympic Games, 1992; Winner of 3 Freestyle Skiing World Cups - La Clusaz, 1990, La Plagne, 1990 and Oberjoch, 1992; Ranked No 2 in 1990-91 World Cup Freestyle; Winner of 18 national titles in Freestyle Skiing to date. *Hobbies:* Tennis; Squash; Trampoline; Water-skiing; Foreign Languages; History of Revolutions. *Address:* Garden Flat, 61 Inverness Terrace, London W2 3JT, England.

CURTIS Deborah Sarah, b. 24 May 1965, London, England. Dental Technician. *Education:* BTec Dipl, 1986; HNC, 1988; Harley Street, 1989. *Honours:* Dental Technician of the Year, 1986. *Hobbies:* Competitive Horse Riding. *Address:* 118 Harley Street, W1N 1AG, England.

CURTIS James Robert, b. 4 Oct 1905, Fort Worth, Texas, USA. Lawyer; Radio Broadcaster; Entrepreneur. m. (1) Sarah DeRue Armstrong, 30 June 1935, dec 1977, 1 s 1 d, (2) Margaret H Gale, 1 Jan 1988. *Education:* BA 1927, Be 1928, Texas Christian Univ; MA. Southern Methodist Univ, 1929; JD Cumberland Univ, 1930; Banking Dipl, Rutgers Univ, 1945. *Appointments include:* Texas Bar, 1930, City Judge, Longview, Texas, 1933-35; Sec, Mgr, 1934, Dir, 1935, VP, 1955-78, First Fed Savings and Loan Assn; Pres, Voice of Lingview Radio Station KFRO, 1934-; Nat Security Ins Co, 1947-57; Courtesy Life Ins Co, 1955-57; Trans Security Investment Co, 1955- 60; Owner, Etex Sales Co, 1937-59; Dir, VP, Rogers Nat Bank, 1942-50. *Memberships include:* AIM; Texas Broadcast Assn; Nat Assn of Broadcasters; Texas Bar Assn; Fed Communications Bar; Oil belt Assn of Life Underwriters. *Address:* 2118 East Marshall Avenue, Longview, TX 75601, USA. 132.

CUSIC Donald F, b. 13 Nov 1948, Maryland, USA. m. Jacqueline Frantz, 25 June 1977, 3 s, 1 d. *Education:* St Marys Col, 1969-70; BS Jour, Univ of Maryland, 1972; MA Eng, 1982, Doctor of Arts, 1988, Middle Tennessee State Univ. *Appointments:* Assoc Prof, Middle Tennessee State Univ, 1982-. *Creative works:* The Sound of Light: A History of Gospel Music, 1990; Randy travis, 1990; Sandi Patti, 1988; Hear that Lonesome Whipperwill, 1991. *Memberships:* Nat Assn of Rec Arts & Scis; Popular Culture Assn; Gospel Music Assn; Tennessee Folklore Soc; Tennessee Philological Assn. *Hobbies:* Baseball; Reading; The Civil War. *Address:* Box 120751, Nashville, TN 37212, USA.

CZAJKA Anna, b. 7 Feb 1952, Ciechanow, Poland. Visiting Lecturer in Aesthetics and Theory of Literature. Gerardo Cunico, 4 June 1987, 1 d. *Education:* BA German, Univ of Warsaw, 1969-74; Acad of Scis, Berlin, 1975-76; Univ of Tuebingen, 1980-81; PhD, Polish Acad of Scis, PAS, Inst for Phil an Sociol, 1987. *Appointments:* Res Asst, Univ of Warsaw, 1974- 75; Res Ass, Inst of Phil and Sociol, PAS, 1975-84; Lecrt, Inst for Rhetoric, Univ of Tuebingen, 1991. *Creative works:* Book, Man Means Hope, WArsaw, 1991; Articles on contemporary philosophy, philosophical anthropology, theory of literature, politics; translations of German literature and Philosophy into Polish. *Memberships:* Ernst-Bloch Assn, Bd. *Honours:* Ernst-Bloch-Forderpreis of the City of Ludwigschfen, Rhine, 1988. *Hobbies:* Creating a home ambience for family and friends in which everyone can realize himself or herself; Taking reflective walks. *Address:* vico Barnabiti 27/11, I-16122 Genova, Italy.

CZAJKOWSKI Eva Anna, b. 4 Sept 1961, Connecticut, USA. Senior Aerospace Engineer. *Education:* BSc, 1983, MEng, 1983, Aero Engrg, Rensselaer Poly Inst (RPI), NY; MSc Mass Inst of Tech, Aeronautics and Astronautics, 1985; PhD, Aerospace Engrg, Virginia Poly Inst and State Univ, Virginia, 1988; Diploma, ICS Pennsylvania, Legal Assistant, 1992. *Appointments:* Part in sev US (tech) delegations to six European nations, 1991, 1992; Res Asst, 1985-88, Tchg Asst, 1985-88, VPI & State Univ; Res Asst, Mass Inst of Tech, 1984-85; Engrg Analyst, Pratt & Whitney Aircraft, 1984; Res Asst, US Army Res Ofc, RPI, 1982-83; Tchg Asst, RPI, 1983; NY State Assembly Intern, 1983. *Creative works:* Journal, Article, Spillover Stabilization of Large Space Structures, 1991; Conf papers include: Stabilizing the Neglected Dynamics in Active Control of Vibrarion, 1988; The Prediction of Force Coefficients for Labyrinth Seals, 1984; Encyclopaedia Entry, Space Station, 1992. *Memberships include:* IPA; IBA, Fellow; NYAS; Hon Advr, ABI Res Bd of Advrs; Am Helicopter Soc; Am Astronautical Soc; Hn Mem, IBC Adv Coun, 1989-; Sigma Gamma Tau; Phi Kappa Phi; Tau Beta Pi; Sigma Xi; Gamma Beta Phi; Nat Space Soc; Am Inst of Aeronautics and Astronautics; Assoc Mem, Nat Air and Space Museum; NAFE. *Honours include:* Woman of the Year, 1990; International Woman of the Year, 1991-92; Amelia Earhart Fellowship Awds, Zonta Intl, 1983-85; Rensselaer Medal for Excellence in Maths and Sci, 1978; Pratt Presidential Engrg Fellow, 1985-88; Sikorsky Scholarship, Am Helicopter Soc Vertical Flight Foun, 1983; Commemorative Medal of Honor, 1987. *Hobbies:* Skiing; Swimming; Tennis; Piano Music; Horseback Riding; Travel; Art. *Address:* 170 Carlton Street, New Britain, CT 06053, USA.

CZEKALSKI Marek, b. 6 June 1953, Lodz, Poland. Politician, Mktng Mgr. m. Liliana Pawlowicz, 19 Jan 1980, 1 d. *Education:* Graduated Tech Univ of Lodz, 1980. *Appointments:* Connected w circles of Polish Dem opposition, 1978-; Active part in creating Solidarity, 1980; Hd of All Polish Textile Workers Sect in Solidarity, 1980; Deleg for first Congress of Solidarity in Gdansk, 1981; Intered and freed after a year and started underground activity, 1981; Co-fndr of conspirational structures of trade union, 1982; Hd of Solidarity Comm for Interventions and Law-and Order, 1985; Fndr of Lodz Co of Social Initiatives, 1989; Elected Dpty to City Coun in Lodz and Cand for Pres of Lodz, 1990; Chief of Presidential campaign of Tadeusz Mazowiecki in region of Lodz, 1990; Co-fndr of Democratic Union, 1991; Elected Chmn of Democratic Union, 1991; Mktng Mgr in CIN-CIN, 1991-. *Membership:* Int Advt Assn. *Hobbies:* Pol, Jogging, Classical Music. *Address:* Unia Demokratyczna, ul Piotrkowska 157, 90-950 Lodz, Poland.

D

D'AMATO Jean Marie, b. 20 July 1945, Boston, Massachussets, USA. Associate Professor, Classics and Art History. m. Fleming Arden Thomas, 12 Mar 1989. *Education:* AB Tufts Univ, 1967; MA Middlebury Col, 1969; PhD Johns Hopkins Univ, 1975. *Appointments:* Asst Prof of Classics, Univ of S.California, 1976-81; Dir and Prof, Intercollegiate Ctr for Classical Studies in Rome, Administered by Stanford Univ, 1981-82; Adjunct Prof Prof of Classics, Brandeis Univ, 1983; Humanist Admr, Nat Endowment for the Humanities, 1984-87; Dir, Liberal Arts Progs for Adults, Tufts Univ, 1987-88; Assoc Prof, N.Western State Univ, 1988-; Director, Northwestrn Summer Session Abroad, 1992. *Creative works:* A new fragment of Eustatius of Matera's Planctus Italie and the Planctus Urbium in Classical and Mediaeval Literature, 1984. *Memberships:* Am Philological Assn; Louisiana Classical Assn, VP, 1990-91, Pres, 1991-92. *Honours: include:* Am Phil Soc, 1991; Res Nat Endowment for the Humanities, Travel to Collections, 1989; Northwestern State Univ, Res, 1989; Grants, Mass Foun for Humanities and Public Policy, 1987; Assocs Awd for Tchg Excellence, Univ of S.California, 1978; Am Coun for Learned Socs, Res, 1978; Am Assn of Univ Women, 1972; Mildred Hart Bailey, Res Awd, Northwestern State University, 1992. *Hobbies:* Biking; Photography; Squash. *Address:* 332 Henry Avenue, Natchiotches, LA 71457, USA.

D'AMICO Joseph Allen, b. 25 Mar 1962, Charlotte, NC, USA. Attorney, International Law and Trade. m. Mary Ellen Lawson, 29 Feb 1992. *Education:* BA Hons, Univ N.Carolina, 1984; JD, 1991, Harvard Law Sch; ALM, 1991, Harvard Univ. *Appointments:* Arnall Golden & Gregory, 1987- 89; Churchill and Ferguson, 1989-91; D'Amico Habib & Shapiro, PA, Atlanta, 1991-. *Creative works:* Institutional lending for Housing Development in Third World Nations, 1987; The Origins, Unintended Consequences and New Directions of the Intersteces of Law and Mental Health Policy, 1991. *Memberships include:* Belgian and French-Am Chambers of Commerce, Atlanta; Am and Atlanta Bar Assns; State Bar of Georgia; Young Lawyer's Intl Steering Com; World Trade Club Atlanta; Japan-Am Soc of Georgia; Democratic Party of Georgia: State Com, 1990-, Exec Com, 1990-91. *Hobbies:* Golf; Tennis; Photography; Languages; Bonsai; Civic Affairs and Politics; Rare political, legal and southern US Books. *Address:* Suite 304, 2480 Briarcliff Road NE, Atlanta, GA 30329, USA.

DABIC Milena, b. 11 June 1957, Warsaw, Poland. Artist; Abstract Painter. *Education:* Grad, Warsaw Art Col, 1977; MA Painting, Cracow and Warsaw Acad of Fine Arts, 1982. *Appointments:* Freelance Journalist, 1983-. One man shows include: Gallery Lot, Warsaw, 1987; Gallery brama, Warsaw, 1989; Gallery Dijkstra, Amsterdam, 1989; Gallery Test, Warsaw, 1990; One Man Shows Include: Daler Rowney Gallery, Warsaw, 1992; Group shows include: Arsenal 88, Warsaw, 1988; 100 Kleuren, Amsterdam, 1989; Red and White, Warsaw and Amsterdam, 1989; Schilders uit Oost Europa Utrecht, Holland, 1990; Kunsthuis 13 Velp Holland, 1990; XVI Akcja Swiat, Air Terminal Lot, WArsaw, 1990; Obraz i Ruch, Lodz, Poland, 1991; Gallery Sign, Gronigen, Holland, 1992. *Creative works:* Many articles on art, culture and antiques, paintings in private collections in Poland, Holland, France and Canada. *Membership:* Polish Artists Union, 1982-. *Hobbies:* Reading; Travelling; Antiques; Collecting Dutch tiles. *Address:* Berezynska 28m 7, 01-908 Warsaw, Poland.

DABIPI Ibibia Karisemie, b. 22 Apr 1955, Nigeria. Associate Professor. m. Jeneba, 9 Jan, 1981. *Education:* MSc 1981, PhD, 1987, Elec Engrg, Louisiana State Univ; BSc EE, BS Phys & Maths, Texas A & I Univ, 1979. *Appointments:* Assoc Prof, Elec Engrg, 1988-; Asst Prof 1981-87, Southern Univ & A & M Col; Tech Staff, Bell Communications Res, 1984, 1985 (summers); AT&T Bell Labs, Tech Staff, 1987 (summer). *Memberships:* Sigma Xi; IEEE; Assn of Computer Machinery; HKN, Elec Engrg Hon Soc. *Honours:* Fed Rep Germany Scholar, 1975-76; Rivers State of Nigeria Scholar, 1976-79; Grantee, Nat Sci Foun Awd for Digital Communications Lab, 1987, State of Louisiana, 1989. *Hobbies:* Tennis; Table Tennis; Music; Nature. *Address:* Electrical Engineering Department, Southern University, Baton Rouge, LA 70812, USA.

DABOV Borislav, b. 7 June 1954, Sofia, Bulgaria; Opthmalogist. m. Julietta Dabova, 2 May 1976, 2 s. *Education:* German Gymnasium Sofia, 1968-73; Med Acad Sofia, 1975-81; DAAD Fellowship, Munich, 1985-86; PhD Med, 1988. *Appointments:* Ophthalmol, Dist Hosp, Blagoewgrad, Bulgaria, 1981-82; Asst, Res Inst of Ophthalmol, Sofia, 1983-85; Urgent Eye Clinic, Sofia, 1987-88; Sr Asst, Res Inst of Ophthalmol, Sofia, 1988-92. *Creative works:* Thesis: Fundusperiphery of the Eye: Normal Variants, degenerative and proliferative processes. *Memberships:* Bulgarian Ophthalmol Soc; Union of Bulgarian Sci Socs. *Hobbies:* Reading; Skiing. *Address:* Bulgaria Str 55 Bl 51, 1000 Sofia, Bulgaria.

DABROWSKA Milena Izabela, b. 30 Sept 1959, Olecko, Poland. Haematologist. m. Andrej Dabrowski, 19 Sept 1981, 1 s. *Education:* Med Acad of Bialystok, Poland, Pharm Fac, 1978-83; MSc, 1983, PhD, 1986. *Appointments:* Asst, 1983-85; Sr Asst, 1985-90, Asst Prof, 1990-, Inst Lab Diagnostics, Univ Hosp; Specialist in Clin Diagnostics, Postgrad Med Ed Ctr, Warsaw, Poland, 1990-. *Creative works:* Five publications on Ethanol abuse and cell immunity; 10 publications on Granulocyte function inneoplastic disease. *Memberships:* Polish Soc of Lab Diagnostics; Polish Soc for Haematol and Transfusiol. *Honours:* Scientific Awds: Rector of Med Acas, 1984, 1986, 1987, 1991; Polish Ministry of health, 1985. *Hobby:* Touring. *Address:* Dept of Haematology Diagnostics, Institute of Laboratory Diagnostics Medica School, ul M Sklodowskiej-Curie 24a, 14-276 Bialystok, Poland.

DABROWSKI Andrzej Jan, b. 12 June 1939; Business Executive; Physicist. m. Irina Rymyantzeva, 7 Oct 1978, 1 d. *Education:* MS Solid State and Nuclear Phys, Univ of Warsaw, 1963; Fellow, Int Atomic Energy Agency, W.Germany, 1969-70; PhD Phys, Inst of Nuclear Res, Swierk, near Warsaw, 1973. *Appointments:* Physicist, Central Radiol Lab, 1963-69; Hd Comound Semiconductor Gp, Semiconductor Dector Lab, Inst of Nuclear Res, Warsaw, 1969-77; REs Assoc Prof, Univ of S.California, Los Angeles, 1977-89; Fdr, Chm and CEO, Xsirius Inc, 1985-91; Pres and CEO, 1988-89, Chm, 1989-91, Advanced Photonix Inc; V-Chm, Xsirius Inc, 1991-; Voluntary Fac Mem, Univ of S.California, 1989-. *Memberships:* IEEE; AAAS. *Hobbies:* Music; Playing the piano; Swimming; Family life. *Address:* 10869 Via Verona Bel Air, Los Angeles, CA 90077, USA.

DABROWSKI Andrzej, b. 15 Oct 1956, Bialystok, Poland. Gastroenterologist. m. Milena Izabela Syroka, 19 Sept 1981, 1 s. *Education:* MD 1981, Phd, 1984, Med Acad, Med Fac; Internal Med specialist, Postgrad Med Ed, Centre, Warsaw, Poland. *Appointments:* Sr Asst, Biochem, 1981-85, Gastroenterol Dept, 1985-, Asst Prof of Med, 1990-, Med Acad, Bialystok. *Creative works:* 4 publications on Biochemistry of connective tissue and 11 publications on Role of oxygen radicals in the pathogenisis of acute pancreatitis. *Memberships:* Polish Internist Soc, Warsaw; Polish Gastroenterol Assn, Wroclaw. *Honours:* Scientific Awards from Polish Ministry of Health, 1985, 1989, 1991. *Hobbies:* Sport; Judo; Cooking. *Address:* Gastroenterology Department Medical School, ul Sklodowskiej 24a, 15-276 Bialystok, Poland.

DAGDEVIREN Emre, b. 5 July 1946, Eskisehir, Turkey. Video Specialist; Director General, Ulusal Group. *Education:* BA Bus Admin, Univ of Anatolia, Eshisehir, 1974; PhD Communications, 1988, Elec Eng Deg, 1980,

Intl Corr Schls, London, 1980. *Appointments:* Mgr, Emre Elektrik, Eskisehir, 1968-74; Tech Mgr Ins of Ed TV, Eshisehir, 1976-80; Lectr, Univ Anatolia, Eskisehir, 1980-82; Tech Coor, Ulusal Video Film, Istanbul, 1982-90; Asst Gen Dir, Intl TV Co, INTV, 1990; Dir Gen, Ulusal Gp, 1991-. *Creative works:* Communications Over the Air, 1988; Columnist of major newspapers and weekly journals; Cable and Satellite yearbook, 1990-91, co-author. *Memberships:* European Satellite TV assn; European TV Sers Assn; Soc of Motian Picture and TV Engrs; Sec of Broadcast Engrs; Turkish-French Chambre of Commerce; Turkish-Canadian Assn for Bus Promotion; Istanbul Chamber of Indust; Rotary Club; Soc for Media Res; Royal TV Soc. *Honours:* Certs of Achievement: TV Tech, Studio Hamburg, 1979, Broadcast Mgmt, Japan Intl Coop Agy, 1980. *Hobbies:* Archaeology; Philosophy; Classical Music; Paintings; Cycling. *Address:* Ulusal Group, Kodaman Cad No 106 80220, Nisantasi, Istanbul, Turkey.

DAHLBACK Bjorn, b. 12 July 1949, Stockholm, Sweden. Professor of Blood Coagulation Research. m. Karin Dahlback, 24 Jan 1976, 1 s, 2 d. *Education:* MD, 1974, PhD, 1981. *Appointments:* Internship, 1974-76; Asst Phys, 1977-82; Fogarty Postdoctoral Fellow,1982-83; Asst Prof, 1983-85, Assoc Prof, 1986-89, Prof, 1989-. *Creative works:* Over 60 original works in basic biomedical research journals. *Memberships:* Swedish Soc of Med; Swedish med Assn; Intl Soc of Thrombosis and Haemostatis; NYAS. *Honours:* Astrup Legat 3rd prize, 1984, First Prize, 1988; Odd Fellow Awd for younger medical researchers, 1984; Erik K Fernstroms Awd for younger researchers, 1988. *Hobbies:* Music; Tennis. *Address:* Dept of Clinical Chemistry, University of Lund, Malmo General Hospital, S-21401 Malmo, Sweden.

DAHRENDORF Ralf, Sir, b. 1 May 1929, Hamburg, Germany. Warden, St Antony College, Oxford; Chmn, Newspapers Publishing Plc, The Independent. m. Ellen Joan Krug, 1980. *Education:* Several schools in Berlin and Hamburg; Studies in Phil and Classical Philology, Hamburg, 1947-52; DrPhil, 1952; PhD, 1956, Habilitation and Univ Lectr, Saarbrucken, 1957. *Appointments:* Fellow, Ctr for Advanced Study in Behavioural Scis, Palo Alto, USA, 1957-58; Prof of Sociol, Hamburg, 1958-60; Vis Prof Columbia Univ, 1960; Prof of Sociol, Tubingen, 1960-64; V-Chm, Foun Com of Univ of Konstanz, 1964-66; Prof of Sociol, Konstanz, 1966-69; Parly Sec of State F.O, W.Germany, 1969-70; Mem, EEC Brussels, 1970-74; Dir, 1974-78; Gov, 1986-, LSE; Prof of Social Sci, Konstanz Univ, 1984-87. *Creative works include:* Class and Class Conflict, 1958; Society and Democracy in Germany, 1965; The New Liberty, 1975; Life Chances, 1979; On Britain, 1982; Law and Order, 1985; The Modern Social Conflict, 1988; Reflections on the Revolution in Europe, 1990. *Memberships include:* Hansard Soc Comm on Electoral Reform, 1975-76; Royal Comm on Legal Sers, 1976-79; Com on Review Functioning of Fin Insts, 1977-80; Trustee, Ford Foun, 1976-88; Bd Chm, Friedrich naumann Stiftung, 1982-88; Non Exec Dir, Glaso Holdings Plc, 1984-92. *Honours:* Foreign Hon Mem, AAAS, 1975-; NAS, USA, 1977; Am Philosophical Soc, 1977; FRSA, 1977; Hon FRCS, 1982; 20 Hon-Degrees from Universities in England, Ireland, USA, Belgium, Canada, Malta; Grand Crois de l'Ordre du Merite du Senegal, 1971; Luxembourg, 1974; Grand Croix de l'order de Leopold II, Belgium, 1975. *Address:* St Anthony's College, Oxford OX2 6JF, England.

DAIBER Joachim Hans, b. 1 Apr 1942, Stuttgart, Germany. University Professor. m Helga Daiber-Brosamler, 17 July 1971 - 27 June 1991, 1 s, 1 d. *Education:* PhD, Saarbruecken Univ, 1968; Dr Habil, Univ Heidelberg, 1973. *Appointments:* German Oriental Inst, Beirut, 1973-75; Lectr, Univ Heidelberg, 1975-77; Prof of Arabic and Islam, Free Univ Amsterdam, 1977-. *Creative works:* Das theologisch-philosophische System des Mu'ammar Ibn 'Abbad as-Sulami, 1975; Ein Kompendium der aristotelischen Meteorologie, 1975; Aetius Arabus, 1980; Catalogue of the Arabic

Mss in the Daiber Collection, 1988. *Memberships:* Royal Netherlands Acad of Arts and Scis, 1981-; Am Oriental Soc; Middle East Studies Assn of N.Am; Societe Intl pour l'Etude de la Philosophie Medievale; Oosters Genootschap; Deutsche Morgenlaendische Gesellschaft; Union Europeene des Arabisants et Islamisants; Soc Intl d'Histoire des Scis et de la Philosophie Arabes et Islamiques. *Honours:* Best thesis of the Year, 1968. *Hobbies:* Collecting Arab manuscripts. *Address:* Am Huettenhof 10, 4000 Duesseldorf 31, Germany.

DAIGRE Denise Odell, b. 24 July 1952, Lafayette, Lousiana, USA. Geologist. m. David Dean Reimers, 16 Oct 1982, 1 d. *Education:* BSc Geol, Univ Southwestern Louisiana,, 1979-81; Postgrad studies at Oklahoma State, 1981 and Southwestern Louisiana, 1990 Univs. *Appointments:* Sr Geol, H J Gruy & Assoc, 1982-89; Geol, ERM Southwest, 1989-90; Envir Geol, Dominque SZabo & Assoc, 1990-91; Principal, Daigre-Neef & Assoc, 1991-. *Creative works:* Needlework displayed in private collections. *Memberships:* Nat Water Well Assn; Am Assn of Petroleum Geols; Lafayette Geol Soc; Houston Geol Soc; Sigma Gamma Epsilon; Jr League of Lafayette; Lafayette Chamber of Commerce. *Honours:* W A Tarr Awd, 1981. *Hobbies:* Reading; Jogging; Needlework. *Address:* Daigre- Neef and Assocs Inc, PO Box 51915, Lafayette, LA 70505, USA.

DALLMEYER Mary Dorinda Gilmore, b. 11 Sept 1952, Macon, Georgia, USA. International Law Specialist. m. Ray David Dallmeyer, 15 Mar 1975. *Education:* BS Geol, magna cum laude, 1973, MS Geol, 1977, JD cum laude, 1984, Univ Georgia. *Appointments:* Res Tech, Dept Zoology, Univ Georgia, 1978-81; Res Dir, Dean Rusk Centre for Intl and Comparative Law, Univ Georgia, 1984-. *Creative works:* Strategic Defense Initiative, 1986; Rights to Oceanic Resources, 1989; Conflict Resolution and the Futur of NATO, 1989; Chinese Economic Law, 1988; US-Japan Trade Relations, 1986. *Memberships:* Coun on Foreign Relations; ABA; Am Soc of Intl Law; State Bar of Georgia; Lawyers Alliance for World Security. *Honours:* Grants: Canadian Embassy, 1985, 1986, 1988, 1991; MacArthur Foun, 1989-90; Ford Foun, 1990-92; Hewlett Foun, 1988-92; Alton Jones Foun, 1985; Woman of the Year, UGA Law Sch, 1984. *Hobbies:* Gardening; Bird watching; Beekeeping. *Address:* Dean Rusk Centre for International & Comparative Law, Univ of Georgia, Athens, GA 30602, USA.

DALRYMPLE Brian, b. 23 Sept 1947, Toronto, Canada. Senior Forensic Analyst. m. Johnna Lee Thompson, 3 Nov 1973, 2 s. *Education:* AOCA, Ontario Col of Art, 1970; Grad, Biol Photography, Sheridan Col, Oakville, 1979. *Appointments:* Forensic Analyst, 1979, Sr Forensic Analyst and Assoc Section Hd, 1980, Ontario Provincial Police. *Creative works:* Inherent Luminescence of Fingerprints Detection By Laser, 1977; Narrow Band Pass Filters in Laser Photography, 1982; Document Photography By Laser, 1983. *Memberships:* Intl Assn for Identification; Canadian Identification Soc; Fellow, The Fingerprint Soc; Life, Michigan-Ontario Identification Assn. *Honours:* John Dondero Awd, IAI, 1980; Foster Awd, CIS, 1982; Awd of Merit, Inst of Applied Sci, NY, 1980; Lewis Minshall Awd, Fingerprint Soc, 1984. *Hobbies:* Hunting; Fishing; Canoeing. *Address:* c/o Ontario Provincial Police, 90 Harbour Street, Toronto, Ontario, Canada M7A 2S1.

DAMASKENIDES Anthony Nicholas, b. 17 Aug 1910, East Thrace, Turkey. Emeritus Professor. m. Argyro Tavouktsoglou, 16 July 1950, 1 d. *Education:* BComm, Inst Superieure de Commerce de l'Etat a Anvers, Belgium; BEcon, Univ Brussels; PhD, Aristotle Univ of Thessaloniki (AUT). *Appointments:* Sec, 1932-50, Lectr in Econ, 1948-54, Asst Prof, 1954- 60, Assoc Prof, 1960-65, Prof in Bus, 1965-78, Emeritus Prof, 1978-, Sch of Law & Ec, AUT. *Creative works:* The Problem of Industrial Credit, 1942; Aims and Limits of Monetary Policy, 1949; A Contribution to the Theory of Prices,

1953; Economics of Business Enterprise, 1956; An Introduction to Economic Science, two vols, 1985-88, all in Greek. *Memberships:* Royal Ec Soc; Am and Greek Ec Assns; Soc of Macedonian Studies in Thessaloniki. *Honours:* Two volumes of essays in honour of myself, edited by Prof Marmatakis, issued by the Fac of Law and Ec, AUT. *Hobbies:* Swimming; Gardening. *Address:* 3 Mitropolitou Josif St, Thessaloniki 546.22, Greece.

DAMBIS Pauls Miervaldis, b. 30 June 1936, Riga, Latvia. Composer; Organist; Choir Conductor. m. Zaiga Vinerte, 5 Oct 1975, 1 d. *Education:* Grad, Composition and Conducting, Music Sch of Jelgava, 1957; Grad, Composing and Orchestrating, Latvian Nat Conservatory, 1962. *Appointments:* Organist, 1951-55; Choirs Conductor 1954-75; Audio Producer, Latvian TV, 1954-75; Prof of Composition, 1972-; Chm, Latvian Composers Union, 1984-89; Chm, Latvian Musical Ed Assn, 1990. *Creative works:* Three operas: Wings, 1970; Letters on the future: King Lear, 1987- 88; Oratorios: Stanza di Michelangelo, Lamento Jesaie; Cantatas: Winter Games, 1981; Shepherds Voices, 1974; Conarto Fantasia on in nomine Albrecht Dureri, 1983. *Memberships:* Latvian Composers Union, 1965; Latvian Musical Edrs Assn, 1990; Latvian Nat Independence Movement, 1990. *Honours:* 1st Prize, USSR Young Composers Competition, 1971; 2nd Prize, Am Choral Competition, 1991; People's Artist of Latvian Republic, 1986. *Hobbies:* Philosophy; East Asia Folk Music. *Address:* Nesetas Str 8-5, Riga 226013, Latvian Republic.

DAMINATO Vanda Piera Marinelli, b. 24 May 1951, Mezzolombardo-Trento, Italy. Painter. *Education:* Dipl, Accademia Arti del'Incisione, Pisa, 1980; Dipl, Foerderung von Kunst und Kultur Ets, Vaduz, Liechtenstein, 1987; Independent Professional painter, 1970; Work includes oil paintings, acrylics, collages, fine prints, sculptures, art ceramics, advertising posters for industry, book covers, etc. Principal shows: Palazzo Grassi Venice, 1979; Galerie Internationale, NY, 1981; Museo de la Scienza e della Tecnica Leonardo da Vinci Milan, 1987; Villa Olmo, Como, 1987; Palazzo della Gran Guardia, Verona, 1987; Museo Internationale G. D'Annunzio Pescara, 1988; Museo d'Arte Moderna, Malta, 1988; Creator of the Image of The Groups: Maristel - Sirti - Pirelli, Telecom' 91, Geneve 1991; Ambroveneto - La Centrale Fondi S.P.A; Goglio Luigi - Milano S.P.A. *Memberships:* Galerie Koch, Bonn, Germany, 1978; Galerie Internationale NY, USA, 1980; MD Fine Prints, Milan, Italy, 1985; La Permanente, Milan, 1990. *Honours:* Gran Premio Città di Pompei; Premio Orginalità e Validità, Ferrara; Premio Filippo de Pisis, Ferrara; Premio Targa Oro, La Spezia, 1978; Int 1st Prize, original graphics, Düsseldorf; Oscar, 1979, Nice; Primo Gran Prix Intercontinentale, d'Arte Venice. *Hobbies:* Collecting modern art; Archaeology; Animals. *Address:* Corso XXII Marzo 28, 20135 Milano, Italy.

DAMM Guy France, b. 12 Feb 1945, Strasbourg. International Manager. m. Francoise Louis, 18 Dec 1975, 1 s, 1 d. *Education:* Eugr: Ecole Centrale Lyon, 1968; MBA, Insead Fontainebleau, 1972. *Appointments:* Country Mgr, Sandoz, Basle, Switzerland, 1972-74; Hd Planning, Sandoz, Sao Paulo, Brazil, 1974-76; Regional Mgr, Sandoz, Rio de janeiro, 1976-78; Intl Mgr, Laboratoires Biocodex, Paris, 1978- . *Memberships:* French Exporters Assn Pharm Indust, 1986. *Hobbies:* Antiques; Cooking. *Address:* 22 Place Saint-Georges, 75009, Paris, France.

DAMMANN Erik, b. 9 May 1931, Oslo, Norway. Author. m. Ragnhild Ostby, 8 Oct 1955, 4 s, 3 d. *Education:* Psychol, Univ of Oslo, 1950- 52; Advg, Nat Art Sch, 1952-55; MIFM, Norwegian Inst of Mktg IFM, 1958-61. *Appointments:* United Advg Agencies, 1955-56; Kittelsen & Kvaerk/Norman, Craig & Cummel Advg Agency, 1956-72; Fdr and Leader, Intl Movement, The Future in Our Hands, 1972-78; Freelance author, 1978. *Creative works:* 14 books published in 7 languages including: The Future in our Hands, 1972; The Day is

Yours, 1978; Revolution in the Affluent Society, 1979; Talofa Samoa, 1981; Beyond Time and Space, 1986; Your Money or your Life, 1989. *Memberships:* Norwegian Union of Non-Fiction Writers. *Honours:* The Right Livelihood Hon Awd, 1982; Permanent Govt Grant, 1987-. *Hobbies:* Rowing; Skiing; Carpentry and Wood carving; Inventions; Outdoor life. *Address:* Loftuveien 48, 1456 Nesoddhogda, Norway.

DAMMULLA Siripala, b. 29 May 1949, Galle. Secretary; Deputy Press Commissioner. m. 10 Jan 1979, 3 d. *Education:* BA Special West Hist, 1972; BPhil, 1st class hons, 1973; Grad Dip in Mass Media, 1984. *Appointments:* Bank Ofr, Peoples bank, 1970-73; Res Ofr, Srilanka Press Coun, 1973-85; Sec, Asst Press Commr, Sri Lanka Press Coun, 1986-. *Creative works:* Labour Movement of Sri Lanka; Analytical Study on Sri Lankan and Australian Press. *Memberships:* Com Mem, Sri Lanka Press Assns; Colombo Plan Assns. *Honours:* Best All-round Student; Elocution Contest Prizes. *Hobbies:* Reading books and newspapers; Politics. *Address:* Sri Lanka Press Council, 37 Keppetipola Road, Colombo 5, Sri Lanka.

DAMOUR Thibault Marie Alban Guillaume, b. 7 Feb 1951, Lyon, France. Physicist. *Education:* Ecole Normale Superieure, 1970-74; Agregation and Doctorat de Troisieme Cycle in Phys Sci, 1974; Doctorat d'Etat en Scis, 1979. *Appointments:* Jane Eliza Procter Fellow, 1974; European Space Agency, Intl Fellow, 1975; Attache, 1977; Charge, 1981 and Dir, 1985, De Recherche at Centre Nat de la Recherche Sci (CNRS); Prof, Inst des Hautes Etudes Sci, 1989-. *Creative works:* 100 scientific papers in the field of gravitational physics, black-hole physics, n-body problems in general relativity and gravitational waves. *Memberships:* Intl Soc of General Relativity and Gravitation, 1989-. *Honours:* Laureate of the Singer- Polignac Foun, 1978; Bronze Medal, CNRS, 1980; Paul Langevin Prize, French Phys Soc, 1984; Mergier-Bourdeix Prize, French Acad of Scis, 1990. *Hobby:* Piano. *Address:* Institut des Hautes Etudes Scientifiques, 91440 Bures sur Yvette, France.

DANDRIDGE Rita, b. 16 Sept 1940, Richmond, Virginia, USA. English Professor. *Education:* BA Virginia Union Univ, 1961; MA, 1963, PhD, 1970, Howard Univ. *Appointments:* Instr, Morgan State Col, 1964-71; Asst Prof, Univ of Toledo, 1971-74; Assoc Prof and Prof, Norfolk State Univ, 1974-. *Creative works:* Ann Allen Shockley: An Annotated Primary and Secondary Bibliography, 1987; Black Women's Blues: A Literary Anthology, 1935- 88, 1991. *Memberships:* Modern Lang Assn; Col Lang Assn; Soc for the Study of Multiethnichit; Am Studies Assn. *Honours:* Grant, Virginia Centre for the Humanities and Public Policy, 1987. *Hobbies:* Real estate management; Gardening; Quilting. *Address:* English Department, Norfolk State University, 2401 Corpren Avenue, Norfolk, VA 23504, USA.

DANE Christopher John, b. 30 Sept 1952, Pittsburgh, PA, USA. Mngng Dir, American Airlines. divorced, 1 s, 1 d. *Education:* BS Bus Admin, St Louis Univ, 1974. *Appointments:* Mgr, Passenger and Freight Sales, Albuquerque NM, 1979; Dist Sales Mgr, DFW, TK, 1980; Mgr, Travel Agency Sales, 1983; Div Mgr, Mktg Automation Sales & Serv, 1985; Managing Director Agency Sales Progs, 1987-. *Memberships:* Am Soc of Travel Agents; LAS Colinas Sports CLub. *Hobbies:* Golf; Travel; Reading; Cooking. *Address:* American Airlines Inc, P Box 619616, MD 5324, DFW Airport, TX 75261, USA.

DANEV Stoyan, b. 10 Jan 1932, Sofia, Bulgaria. Professor in Clinical Laboratory Medicine. m. 11 Aug 1963, 1 d. *Education:* Eng Philology, 1953; Bibliography, Sofia, 1954; Med, Med Fac, Sofia, 1964; Postgrad training: Clin Chem, Copenhaven, 1968; Clin Lab, Sofia, 1970. *Appointments:* Chm, Asst, 1965-72, Chm, Asst Prof, 1973-78, Assoc Prof, 1978-71, Prof, and Chm, 1991-, Clin Lab, Postgrad Med Inst Sofia; WHO Advr, Geneva, 1984; Lectr, Lisbon, 1985. *Creative works:* 120

works in clinical enzymology and clinical chemistry including several monographs, theses and 12 technical innovations. *Memberships:* Bulgarian Clin Lab Soc, Sec, 198-191, Pres, 1991-; Intl Soc of Clin Enzymol, Fdg Mem, 1975-; NYAS; IFCC, 1982-, Nat Rep, 1991-; Assn of Clin Biochems, England, 1991-; Culture Centre de Rougemont, Sofia, VP, 1991. *Honours:* Medals: 100 yrs of Bulgarian Health Care, 1979, Profl and Tchg Achievements, 1987. *Hobbies:* Music; Art; Pet animals (cocker spaniel, cats); Skiing; Swimming; Linguistics. *Address:* Chairman, Chair of Clinical Laboratory, Medical Academy, 1413 Sofia, Bulgaria.

DANIEL Andrey, b. 28 Mar 1952, Rousse. Associate Professor. m. Iliana Sotirova, 4 Mar 1977, 1 s, 1 d. *Education:* Nat Acad of Fine Arts, 1972-77. *Appointments:* One man exhibitions include: Sofia, 1979; Varna, Sofia, 1982; Delhi, India, Nicosia Cyprus, 1983; Plovdiv, 1987; Club of the Sofia Philaharmonic Orchestra, 1987; Dobrich, 1986; Apolonia Sozopol, 1987; Samokuv1988; Veliko Turnovo, 1989; Botevgrad, 1990; Hotel Sheraton, 1991. *Memberships:* Union of Bulgarian Painters, City Gp; Pres, Club Fourm Jewish Thought, Sofia. *Honours:* Intl Competition for Young Painters Prize, Sofia, 1985; First Place, Portrait prize, Bulgaria, 1988. *Address:* ul Luben Karavelov no 55, Sofia, Bulgaria.

DANIEL Joseph, b. 2 May 1966, Nigeria. Civil Servant; Engineer. *Education:* Govt Tech Col WAEC Tech Cert; Nat Dipl Elec Engrg; Higher Nat Dipl, Elec Engrg. *Appointments:* Elec Supvr, Water Co, 1989-90; Supvr, Nat Telecommunication, 1985; Lectr, Fed Poly, 1990-. *Creative works:* Investigation into electrical power distribution in the manufacturing industry. *Memberships:* NANISS Sec, 1989; KAPSSA Mem, 1990. *Honours:* Best Elect Engrg Student, 1987-88, 1988-89; Nigerian Breweries Awd for Best Student, 1988-89. *Hobbies:* Travelling; Reading; Games; Making friends. *Address:* PO Box 26, Kutigi, LLG Niger State, Nigeria.

DANIELS James Maurice, b. 26 Aug 1924, Leeds, England. Retired Professor of Physics. 3 s, 2 d. *Education:* BA 1945, MA 1969, DPhil, 1952, Oxon. *Appointments:* RRDE Malvern, 1944-46; Tech Ofr, ICI Explosives, 1946-47; Asst Prof, Prof, Univ of Brit Columbia, 1953-61; Prof of Phys, Univ of Toronto, 1961-87. *Creative works:* Oriented Nuclei Polarized Targets and Beams, 1964; 100 works in refereed journals. *Memberships:* Phys Soc of London; FIP, London; Chartered Physicist, UK; Am Phys Soc; Fellow, Royal Soc of Canada; FRSA London; NYAS; Canadian Assn Univ Tchrs, VP, 1979-80. *Honours:* Sloan Fellowship, 1962-64; Guggenheim Fellowship, 1978-79. *Hobbies:* Mountaineering; Skiing. *Address:* 40 Cranbury Road, Princeton Junction, NJ 08550, USA.

DANIELSON Anders Jerker, b. 28 Dec 1957, Karlskrona. Economics Educator. m. Annica Wallenhelm, 16 Aug 1988. *Education:* BA Ec, Univ Gothenburg, Sweden, 1981. *Appointments:* Res Asst: Univ Gothenburg, 1981-89, Univ Lund, 1984-. *Creative works:* Articles in professional journals. *Memberships:* Am Ec Assn; Assn for Res of Central Am and the Caribbean; Union of Radical Polit Ecs. *Hobbies:* Literature; Music. *Address:* Stora Sodergatan 63, S-22357 Lund, Sweden.

DANNEMARK Francis Henri, b. 13 Apr 1955, Macquenoise, Belgium. Writer. 1 s. *Education:* Licence en Philosophie & Lettres, Univ de Louvain, 1977. *Appointments:* Tchr, Col St Louis, Brussels, 1977-80; Attache culturel, Cabinet du Ministre de la Region de Bruxelles Capitale, 1990. *Creative works:* Novels: Le voyage a plus d'un titre, 1981; La nuit est la derniere image, 1982; Memoires d'un ange maladroit, 1984; L'hiver ailleurs, 1988; Choses qu'on dit la nuit..., 1991; Poems and short stories: Heures locales, 1977; Antarctique, 1978; Perimetres, 1981; Les Eaux territoriales, 1983; Sans nouvelles du paradis, 1988.

Hobbies: Music; Movies. *Address:* c/o Ed. Laffont, 6 place St-Sulpice, 75006 Paris, France.

DANUBRATA Mohammad Noor, b. 20 Sept 1932, Bogor. Chairman, Istiqamah Foundation. m. Miti Djoemiarti Djoemarma, 23 June 1962, 3 d. *Education:* Bus Mgmt; Fin Mgmt. *Appointments:* V-Dir, Sidik NV, 1953-55; Dir, Transito Co, 1954-58; Dir, Riloeny Co 1962-69; Dir, Rigas Co, 1970-76; Dir, H Penna Corp, 1983-90. *Memberships:* Exex, Indonesian Sugar Traders Assn; Exec, W.Java Chamber of Commerce; V-Chm, W.Java Entrepreneurs; V-Chm, W.Java Film Producers Distributors and Importers; Fdr, Advr, Indonesian Students Assn. *Hobbies:* Travelling; Reading. *Address:* Jalan Siliwangi No 6, Bandung 40135, West Java, Indonesia.

DARAKCHIEV Beila Stoyanov, b. 3 May 1957, Sofia, Bulgaria. Operator of Minilab. m. Maya Dimitrova Gaidarska Darakchieva, 3 Sept 1982, 1 d. *Education:* Tech Sch of Woodworking and Interior Decoration, 1975; Col Inst of Tchrs Lanbi Kandev, Intrerior Decoration, 1979-81. *Appointments:* Cabinet Maker, 1978-79; Tchr, Tech Sch of Interior Decoration,1981-86; Operator Minilab, Fotoservice Co Ltd, 1989. *Creative works include:* One man show, Sofia, 1984; Intl Saloon Act and Protrait, Poland, Venus, 1985; Festival of Amateur Art Activities, 1983, 1984; Republican Festival of the Amateur Art Activities, 1984. *Memberships:* Bulgarian Photographic Workers CLub. *Honours include:* : Dipls, 6th & 7th Saloons for Experimental Photography, Yambol, 1986-87; Dipl, 4th Saloon for Act Photography; Dipl and Plaquette, 10th Saloon for Experimental Photography. *Hobby:* Nude Photography. *Address:* 64 Luben Karavelov Str, 1000 Sofia, Bulgaria.

DARBY Michele Leonardi, b. 17 Aug 1949, New Kensington, PA, USA. College Professor. m. Dennis A Darby, 10 June 1972, 1 s, 1 d. *Education:* Cert in Dental Hygiene, Univ Pittsburgh, 1967-69; BS 1969-71, Ms 1971-72, COlumbia Univ, NY. *Appointments:* Prof, 1984-86, Chair, 1982-89, Eminent Scholar and Grad Prog Dir, 1989-, Sch of Dental Hygiene, Dominion Univ, Norfolk, VA. *Creative works:* Research methods for Oral Health Professionals, 1980; Comprehensive Review of Dental Hygiene, 1991. *Memberships:* Am Dental Hygienists Assn (ADHA); Am Assn of Dental Schs; Phi Kappa Phi. *Honours:* Phillip E Blackerby Awd, Columbia Univ, 1971; Alan Rufus Tonelson Dist Fac Awd, Alumni Assn, Old Dominion Univ, 1991; Warner Lambert and ADHA Awd for Excellence 1991. *Hobbies:* Reading; Cooking; Gardening; Travel. *Address:* School of Dental Hygiene, College of Health Sciences, Old Dominion University, Norfolk, VA 23529, USA.

DARLING John Rothburn Jr, b. 30 Mar 1937, Holton, Kansas, USA. Chancellor. m. Melva Jean Fears, 20 Aug 1958, 2 s, 1 d. *Education:* BA 1959, MS 1960, Com and Bus Admin, Univ Alabama; Phd Mktg, Univ of Illinois at Urbana-Champaign, 1967. *Appointments include:* Assoc Prof, Mktg, Univ Missouri, 1968-71; Prof of Admin, Wichita State Univ, Kansas, 1971-76; Dean and Prof of Mktg, S.Illinois Univ, Carbondale, 1976-81; VP, Acad Affairs and Res, Prof Intl Bus, Texas Tech Univ, 1981-86; Provost, VP for Acad Affair, Prof Mktg and Intl Bus, Mississipi State Univ, 1986-90; Chancellor and Prof of Mktg and Intl Bus, Louisiana State Univ, Shreveport, 1990-. *Creative works include:* Numerous publications including: Exporting to the US Market, 1983; International Management Excellence and Leadership Strategies, 1989; Deming: New Directions for Improving Quality, Public Acceptance and Competitive Positioning in Colleges and Universities, 1990. *Memberships include:* Am Assn for Higher Ed; Acad of Intl Bus; Intl Coun for Small Bus; Am Ec Assn; Am Mgmt Assn; Am Mktg Assn; Soc for the Advancement of Mgmt; Pi Sigma Epsilon; Alpha Phi Omega. *Honours:* Medal for Excellence in Admin Leadership and Direction of the Univ, Texas Tech Univ, 1984; Presidential Leadership Awd, Missippi State Univ,

1990. *Hobbies:* Tennis; Racquet ball; Golf. *Address:* 8925 Creswell Road, Shreveport, LA 71106, USA.

DARRAH Katherene Simpson, b. 7 Aug 1937, Los Angeles, California, USA. 1 s, 1 d. *Education:* Banking, Bus Col, 3 years. *Appointments:* City of Cheney, working in the Elec Dept, Office work and Bids in Court. *Memberships:* NAFE; Intl Platform Assn; US Senatorial Com; Presidential Task Force; Republican Nat Com; Order of Eastern Stars. *Honours:* Proclamation of Traffic Awareness; Medal of Merit; Presidential Order of Merit; Life Mem, Charter Fdr, Ronald Reagan Centre in Washington DC. *Hobbies:* Reading; Writing; Golf; Singing. *Address:* SO 1412 Warren Road, Veradale, WA 99037, USA.

DARSARTHY Belur Venkatchalan, b. 3 Apr 1944, Bangalore, India. Engineer. m. Harini Garudachar, 8 Feb 1973, 2 s. *Education:* BEng, Mysore Univ India, 1963; MEng, 1965, PhD, 1969, Indian Inst of Sci, Bangalore. *Appointments:* Sr Mem, Tech Staff, Comp Sci Corp, Huntsville, 1969- 71; Asst Prof, Indian Inst of Sci, 1971-74; Comp Scist, Comp Sci Corp, Huntsville, AL, 1974-76; Sr Tech Mgr, Intergraph Corp, 1976-89; Sr Principal Engr, Dynetics Inc, Huntsville, AL, 1989-. *Creative works:* Book: Nearest Neighbour (NN) Norms, NN Pattern Classification Techniques, 1991; Over 100 technical papers in various intl journals. *Memberships:* IEEE, Sr Mem, Chmn. Huntsville Section (IEEE); Am Soc of Engrs from India, Edit Huntsville Chapter Newsletter. *Honours:* Govt of India Scholarship; Comp Sci Corp awards. *Hobbies:* Writing; Stamp collecting; Tennis; Cricket. *Address:* Dynetics Inc, PO Drawer B, Huntsville, AL 35814, USA.

DAS Jagannath Prasad, b. 20 Jan 1931. University Professor. m. Gita d. R C Dasmohapatra Jamirapalgarh, 1 s, 1 d. *Education:* BA Hons, Utkal Univ, India; MA Patna Univ, India; PhD London Univ, UK. *Appointments:* Tchr, George Peabody Col, Univ of California; Prof, Ed Psychol and Dir Develop Disabilities Centre, Univ of Alberta, Canada. *Creative works include:* Simultaneous and Successive Cognitive processess, 1979; Intelligence and Learning, 1981; Theory and Research in Learning Disabilities, 1982; A Textbook of Psychology, 1985. *Memberships:* Assn of Cross-Cultural Psychol; FAPA; FCPA; Fellow, Intl Assn for Res in Learning Disabilities. *Honours:* Kennedy Foun Fellowship, 1963-64; Nuffield Fellowship, 1972; Harris Awds of Intl Reading Assn; Univ Res Prize, 1987. *Hobbies:* Translating poetry. *Address:* 11724-38A Avenue, Edmonton, Alberta, Canada T6J 0L9.

DASTYCH-SZWARC Elzbieta, b. 25 Mar 1939, Cieszyn. Musician; Flutist; Prof. m. Marek Szwarc, 1 July 1962, 1 d. *Education:* Cert with distn, State High Sch of Music, 1961; Santa Cecilia Conservat, Rome, 1962-63; King's Conservat, Brussels class of chamber music, 1967-68; Masters class, Siena, 1967-68. *Appointments:* 1 flutist, Orch of the Great Theatre and Nat Philharmony, Warsaw, 1962-84; Soloist in the chamber ensemble, Con moto ma cantabile, Radio, TV concerts, Perf, Componist's conc, Chamber music, home and abroad 1966-82; Prof, Acad of Music, Warsaw, 1972-; Prof, Acad of Music, Poznan, 1984-. *Publication:* Elaboration of flute compositions of Polih contemporary composers. *Membership:* Assn of Polish Musicians. *Honours:* Awds of the Rector, Acad of Music, Warsw, 1978, 1982, 1984, 1989; Certs of Merit, Great Theatre (Opera), Warsaw, 1981, 1983. *Hobbies:* Antiquities; Theatre; Literature. *Address:* ul Mickiewicza 70 m 21, 01-650 Warsaw, Poland.

DATE Toshihiro, b. 25 Apr 1931, Hiroshima, Japan. Professor of English. m. Gita 29 Apr 1960, 1 s, 1 d. *Education:* BA Horishima Univ, 1957; Postgrad, Edinburgh Univ, Scotland, 1981-82. *Appointments:* Elem Sch Tchr, 1951-53; Jr Sr Hg Sch Tchr, 1957-69; Asst Prof, Eng, Ohtani Women's Col, 1969-74; Asst Prof, 1975-78, prof, 1978-; Prof, Grad Sch, Eng, Ohtani Women's Univ, Osaka, Japan, 1985-. *Creative works:* Author: The Swan of Avon, 1985; Co-author: Works and Readers, 1977; Evil in Literature, 1981; Charles Dickens: Our Mutual Friend, 1983; Essays in Honour of Prof Kazuso Ogoshi, 1990. *Memberships:* Shakespeare Soc, Japan; Eng Lit Soc of Japan. *Hobbies:* Go-game; No, Bunraku (Japanese Traditional Theatre); Reading. *Address:* B404 2-5 Dairyo, Symiyoshi-Ku, Osaka 558, Japan.

DAUDEL Raymond, b. 2 Feb 1920, Paris, France. President of the European Academy. m. Salzedo Pascaline, 28 June 1944, 2 s. *Education:* Ingenieur, 1940; Docteur es Scis, 1944. *Appointments:* Asst, Pz Irene Joliot-Curie, 1943; Chef de Travaux of Pz Frederic Joliot, 1956; Maitre de Conferences of Pz de Broglie, 1957; Prof at the Sorbonne, 1962. *Creative works:* Author of 20 books including: Quantum Chemistry, 1959; Chemical Carcinoesgen is and Molecular Biology, 1966; L'Empire des Molecules, 1991. *Memberships:* Hon Pres, Intl Acad of Molecular Sci; Hon Pres, World Union of Theoretical Chemists. *Honours:* Ofr, Legion of Honour, Nat Order of Merit, Acad Palms; Dr Hon Causa, Univs of Uppsala, Leuven and Barcelona. *Address:* 60 Rue Monsieur Le Prince, 75006 Paris, France.

DAVENPORT Peter, b. 24 Mar 1961, Birkenhead, England. m. Lesley Jayne Reid, 5 Dec 1988, 1 s. Professional Footballer. *Education:* Corpus Christi Hg Sch. *Appointments:* Nottingham Forest, 1982-86; Man United, 1986-88; Middlesbrough, 1988-90; Sunderland, 1990-. *Honours:* England B Intl Cap v New Zealand; England Full Intl Cap v Eire; Zenith Data System Cup Runners Up, 1990; FA Cup Runner Up, 1992. *Hobbies:* Marine Art; Golf; Cricket; Tennis; Reading. *Address:* c/o Sunderland AFC, Roker Park, Sunderland, England.

DAVEY Christopher Julian Tudor, b. 9 Apr 1942, England. Commercial Balloonist. m. Deborah Ann, 6 Jan 1979, 1 s. *Education:* Beaudesert Park, 1951-55; Eton Col, 1955-60; MA, Jesus Col, Cambridge, 1961-64. *Appointments:* Comm'd: 2nd Royal Tank Rgt, Service in Baor and N. Ireland, 1964-; Ret'd as Major, 1983. *Creative works:* Zanussi: Transatlantic Balloon, 1982. *Memberships:* Inst of Advanced Motorists, HGV I, II, III; Royal Channel Island Yacht Club; Leander Club; Brit Balloon and Airship Club; Cambridge Univ Boat Club. *Honours:* Gen Ser Medal, 1972; Ladies plate: Henley Royal Regatta, 1960; Univ Boat Race, 1962, 1964; Channel, 1975; Royal Aero Club Gold Medal, 1978, for Atlantic Hot Air Rozier Balloon Flight; North Sea, 1980. *Hobbies:* Viticulture; Ballooning; House building; Sailing; Writing; Family. *Address:* The Wine House, Bathsprings Vineyard, Bailbrook Lane, Bath BA1 7AB, England.

DAVID Oladele Abiodyn, b. 28 Dec 1959, Kaduna, Nigeria. Electrical Engineer. m. Victoria Fummilayo, 22 Dec 1984, 1 s, 1 d. *Education:* Nat Dipl, 1980; HND, 1989, Kaduna Poly. *Appointments:* Utility Op, NNPC, Kaduna Refinery, 1979-82; Elec Supvr, Nigerian Paper Mills, Jebba, 1984-87. *Memberships:* Kaduna Poly Almuni; Otts Kano Old Boys Assn. *Honours:* Gold Medal, All Tech Games, 1979; Football medals: Gold 1983, Silver Nepa Games, 1986; Silver, Challenge Cup Nigera State, 1986. *Hobbies:* Sports; Reading; Travelling. *Address:* AY6 Calabar Street, Kaduna, Nigeria.

DAVID Sheila Jane Yorke, Lady, b. 29 Aug 1914, Witham, Essex, England. Trustee, Foundation of Chinese Art. *Education:* Challone Sch and Courtauld Inst, Univ of London; Dipl Chinese Art & Archaeol, 1936-40. *Appointments:* Curator, Librarian, Sir Percival David Collection of Chinese Art, 1931-40; Asst, Exhibition of Chinese Art, Burlington Hse, 1935- 36; Aircraft Production of de Haviland Mosquito. *Creative works:* Precisely Dated Chinese Antiques, 600-1644, 1970; Various papers contributed to oriental ceramic society; On retirement as Curator, established additional display area, Seminar Centre and Lecture Hall as well as donating own considerable library to the Percival David Foun of Chinese Art. *Memberships:* FRPSL; RIIA Oriental Ceramic Soc of London; Soc of Orientalists, Stockholm,

Sweden. *Honours:* Fellow School of Oriental and African Studies, Univ of London; Curator of Percival David Foun of Chinese Art, 1950-59. *Hobbies:* Ballet; Opera; Music; International Affairs.

DAVIDGE Christopher Guy Vere, b. 5 Nov 1929, Northampton, England. Company Director. *Education:* Maidwell Sch, 1938-43; Eton Col, 1943-48; MA, Trinity Col, Oxford, 1948-52. *Appointments:* Dir, Mixconcrete Holdings Plc, 1964-82; Coun of Lloyds, 1982-88; Dir, 1985, Chm, 1989, Lloyds of London Press Ltd. *Memberships:* Pres, Amateur Rowing Assn, 1977-85; VP, Brit Olympic Assn, 1976-; VP, Commonwealth Games Coun for England, 1974-; Cun of FISA (Intl Rowing Fed), 1976; Chm, Regattas Commn of FISA; Chm, Leander Club, 1968-78; Chm, Three Shires Hospital, Vice-Chmn St Andrews Hospital, Northampton; Pres, Northants Branch, British Red Cross. *Honours:* Desborough Medal, 1957; FISA Medal of Hon, 1973; OBE, 1982; High Sheriff of Northamptonshire, 1988-89; Freeman, City of London, 1982; Rowed for Eton, 1947-48, Oxford, 1949-52, GB, 1952-63 *Hobbies:* Chm, Northants Record Soc; Steward Henley Royal Regatta. *Address:* Little Houghton House, Northampton NN7 1AB, England.

DAVIDSON Greg Stuart, b. 6 Oct 1961, Philadelphia, PA, USA. m. Tamah Alyss Kushner, 9 Sept 1984, 1 s. *Education:* BA Hons, Swarthmore Col, 1983; Masters in Public Policy, Kennedy Sch of Govt, Harvard Univ, 1985. *Appointments:* NASA Office of Space Sci and Applications, 1985-. *Creative works:* Economics for a civilized Society, 1988. *Memberships:* Treas, Consumer Adv Bd of the Maternity Ctr. *Honours:* Kennedy Fellowship, Harvard, 1983, 1984; Presidential Mgmt Internship, 1985-86; NASA HQ Exceptional Performance Awd, 1990. *Hobbies:* Theatre; History; Operation research; Philosophy; Volleyball. *Address:* NASA HQ, Office of Space Science and Applications, 600 Independence Avenue SW, Washington, DC 20546, USA.

DAVIES Anthony John, b. 29 Oct 1936, Woodhall Spa, Lincs, England. Consultant in Management and Engineering. m. Mary Josephine Crook, 12 Sept 1959, 2 s. *Education:* RN Colls, Dartmouth 1953-54, Manadon 1956-59, Greenwich, 1962-69; Royal Col of Defence Studies, 1984. *Appointments:* Royal Navy, 1953; CDR, 1972; Capt, 1979; Fleet Weapon Engr Ofr, 1981-83; Dir, Ship Refitting, Policy MOD, 1985-87; Capt: HMS Collingwood, 1987-88; Man Dir, Davies Management Ltd, 1991-; Dir, ASC Ltd, 1989-92; Senior Consultant, Log Sec Ltd; Consultant, Int Quality Services, inc; Kanosha, Wisconsin, USA. *Creative works:* Systems Management Consultancy, 1990. *Memberships:* European Engr, FEANI; CEng; FIEE; FIMarE; FIMgt; IOD; RUSI: USNI; MENSA: Mem, Am Soc Quality Control; Batti-Wallahs Soc, Com, 1990-; Chichester Conservative Assn; Dist Coun for East Wittering & Chicester District Council, 1991; Vice-Chmn, Public Services Comittee; Ashridge Col Assn, Bd; Mem, Courts of Sussex Univ, Southport Univ. *Honours:* Prendergast Prize, HMS Excellent, RN Gunnery Sch, 1961. *Hobbies:* Climbing; Sailing; Golf; Working with Mentally Handicapped People. *Address:* North House, West Wittering, Chichester, West Sussex P020 8QG, England.

DAVIES David Ioan, b. 28 Aug 1936, Ibambi, Zaire. University Professor; Writer. m. Diane Gilda Bellan, 19 May 1975, 4 s, 1 d. *Education:* BSc Ec, London, 1961; PhD, Essex, 1972. *Appointments:* Cambridge Univ, 1962-65; Univ of Essex, 1965-70; Queens Univ, Canada, 1970-72; York Univ, Canada, 1972-. *Creative works:* Africa Trade Unions, 1966; Social Mobility and Political Change, 1970; Writers in Prison, 1990. *Memberships:* Intl PEN; Intl Sociol Assn; Canadian Sociol and Anthropol Assn; Writers Union of Canada; Canadian Communications Assn; Inst of Contemporary Arts. *Honours:* Various research awards from Canada Coun, Social Scis and Humanities Res Coun of Canada, Ontario Arts Coun and Social Sci Res Coun, (UK).

Hobbies: Gardening; Reading; Music; Travel. *Address:* 162 Roselawn Avenue, Toronto, Ontario, Canada M4R 1E6.

DAVIES Gerald Keith, b. 18 June 1944, Alberta, Canada. Vice President Marketing Services. m. Mary Lou Bethers, 22 Jan 1966, 1 s, 1 d. *Education:* BS Ec, Utah State Univ, 1968; PhD Ec, Washington State Univ, 1971. *Appointments:* Ec, Fed Railroad Admin, 1970-74; Asst to Pres, US Railway Assn, 1974-76; Asst VP Mktg, Burl Northern, 1976-78; Asst VP, Coal Mktg CSX Transp, 1984-85; VP Mktg Ser, CSX Transp, 1985-. *Memberships:* Elec Data Interchange Assn, Dir; The Dransportation Res Forum; The Western Ec Assn; The Nat Frt Transp Assn. *Address:* CSX Transportation Inc, 500 Water Street, Jacksonville, FL 32202, USA.

DAVIES Ivor John, b. 9 Nov 1935, Wales. Artist. *Education:* Intermediate Dipl, Cardiff Col of Art, 1952-56; Nat Dipl of Design, 1956, Art Tchr Dipl, 1957, Swansea Col of Art; Hist of Art, Aesthetics, Univ of Lausanne, 1959-61; PhD Univ Edinburgh, 1975. *Appointments:* Asst Tchr of Eng, Univ of Lausanne and Gymnases, 1959-61; Lectr, Dept of Fine Art, Univ of Edinburgh, 1963-78; Principal Lectr Hist of Art and Hd of Sch of Cultural Studies, Gwent Col of Higher Ed, 1978-88. *Creative works:* Articles include: Giorgio de Chirico: The Sources of Metaphysical Painting in Schopenhauer and Nietzsche, 1983; Chagall's Origins, 1985; Diego Rivera and Mexican Art, 1987; Only a Step Away - Museums of Nord-Pas de Calais, 1990; David Jones - Arlunydd a Bardd, 1989; Arlunio yn Saudi Arabia, 1990-91. *Memberships include:* Assn of Art Historians, 1975; Intl Assn of Art Critics, 1985-; GWELED, 1984-. *Honours:* Grant, Univ of Edinburgh, 1968; German Acad Scholarship, (DAAD), 1977; Numerous one-man and group exhibitions, and black and white and full colour illustrations;Work in several museum and public collections as well as private collections all over the world. *Hobbies:* Languages; Celtic Studies. *Address:* 99 Windsor Road, Penarth, South Glamorgan CF6 1JF, Wales.

DAVIES Robert John, b. 12 Oct 1948, Sheffield, England. Company Director. m. Eileen Susan Littlefield, 28 Aug 1971, 1 s. *Education:* LLB Law and Ec, Ediburgh Univ, 1970; Fellow, Chartered Inst of Mgmt Accts, 1976. *Appointments:* Ford Motor Co: UK and USA, 1970-83, Dir of Fin, Spain, 1983-85; Dir, Mgmt Conslt, Coopers and Lybrand Assocs, 1985- 87; Fin Dir, Wedgwood Ltd, 1987-88; Dir, Gp Chief Fin Ofr, Waterford Wedgwood Plc, 1989-1991; Group Finance Director, Ferranti International plc, 1991-. *Hobby:* Golf. *Address:* Netherwood, Shut Lane Head, Butterton, Newcastle, Staffordshire ST5 4DS, England.

DAVIES Susan Elizabeth, b. 14 Apr 1933, Abadan, Iran. Freelane Photography Consultant. m. 11 Sept 1954, 2 d. *Education:* Nightingale Bamford Sch, New York, 1944-46; Eothen Sch, Surrey, 1946-50. *Appointments:* Various, 195-68; Inst Contemporary Arts, 1968-70; Fdr, Dir, The Photographers Gallery, 1971-. *Membership:* Hon Fellow, Royal Photographic Soc. *Honour:* OBE, 1988. *Hobbies:* Gardening; Reading; Jazz. *Address:* 53 Britwell Road, Burnham, Bucks SL1 8DH, England.

DAVIN James M, b. 13 Sept 1958, New York, USA. Attorney. *Education:* BS Acct Mgmt, Syracuse Univ, 1976-80; JD, Loyalw Univ, 1980-83; Currently on MBA, Univ Houston, 1988-. *Appointment:* Julian & Seele, 1984-. *Creative works:* Bar Assn of the 5th Circuit; The maritime Law Assn. *Memberships:* Texas, Houston and NY Bar Assns; Syracuse Univ Mgmt Assn; Phi Alpha Delta; Houston Mariner Club; Ancient Order of Hibernians, State Sec. *Honours:* Regents Scholarship, 1976; Deans List, Syracuse Univ, 1976. *Hobbies:* Tennis; Biking; Cross Country Skiing; Swimming; Darts; Philately; Sailing; History. *Address:* 2322 Lexford, Houston, TX 77080, USA.

DAVIS Anthony Michael John, b. 5 Dec 1939, London, England. Professor of Mathematics. m. Roberta Susan Mallett, 11 Dec 1965, 1 s, 1 d. *Education:* BA 1960, PhD, 1964, Cambridge; DSc, London, 1977. *Appointments:* Nat Coal Bd, 1963-65; Univ Col London, 1965-84; Univ of Alabama, 1985-; Various visiting positions. *Creative works:* 80 journal articles on applied maths, principally water waves and slow viscous flows. *Memberships:* Amer Phys Soc; Soc for Indust and Applied Maths; Canadian Applied Maths Soc. *Hobbies:* Tennis; Golf; Rugby; Bridge. *Address:* Department of Mathematics, The University of Alabama, Tuscaloosa, AL 35487, USA.

DAVIS Billy Michael, b. 21 June 1955, Tennessee, USA. m. Leesa R Roberson, 2 Sept 1979, 2 s. *Education:* High Sch, 1973; BArch, Univ Tennessee, 1977. *Appointments:* Baddour Inc, 1978-83; Federal Express, 1983-. *Memberships:* IRDC; Intl Real Est Inst. *Hobbies:* Sport; Photography; Home construction and design. *Address:* 8294 Cedartrail Cv, Condova, TN 38018, USA.

DAVIS Bobbye Hudson, b. 17 Aug 1950. Professor of Psychology. div. 1 s. *Education:* BA Human Relations, BA Psycho, Kansas Univ, 1970; MEd, Counselling and Guidance, E.Central State Univ Ada, Oklahoma, 1973; PhD Counselling Psycho, Oklahoma Univ, 1976. *Appointments:* Grad Asst, Fin Aids, N.Eastern State Univ, 1971; Human Relations Counsellor, E.Oklahoma State Col, 1972-73; Grad Tchg Assoc, Oklahoma Univ Col of Ed, 1973-75; Prof of Psycho, S.Oklahoma City Jr Col, 1975-78; Asst Prof of Psycho, N.Eastern St Univ, Oklahoma, 1978-. *Creative works:* Books include: Predictive Strength of Academic Related Indicators of Potential Drop-Outs, 1977; Assessing Minority Children in a Public School Environment, 1982; Aspects of Cross-Cultural Communication, 1984; Testing Competency; Skill of the Future, 1986; Descriptive Study of the Effect Helper Response Style has on Cross-cultural Communication, 1990. *Memberships:* Am Bus Women's Assn; Phi Delta Kappa; Am Ed and Res Assn; Oklahoma Ed Assn; Alpha Kappa Alpha; Am Assn of Black Psychos; Nat Assn of Black Profl Women. *Honours:* Regent's Scholar, Doctoral, 1976; Non-traditional Career Women Awd, Muskogee Bus Assn, 1983; Exec Coun for Exceptional Children, 1985; Outstanding Educators Awd, Nat Educators Guild, 1989; NAACP Merit Scholar, 1990; Outstanding Educator, Race and Ethnic Relations Bd in Higher Ed, 1990. *Hobbies:* Computer Programme Design; Painting; Reading. *Address:* Northeastern State University, Education 1031, Tahlequah, OK 74464, USA.

DAVIS Christopher, b. 23 Oct 1928, Philadelphia, Pennsylvania, USA Writer; Teacher; Graphic Artist. m. Sonia Fogg, 6 June 1953, 4 d. *Education:* BA, Univ of Pennsylvania, 1951-55. *Appointments:* Univ of Pennsylvania, 1958-69; Bryn Mawr Col, 1977-continuing. *Creative works:* Novels: Lost Summer, 1958; First Family, 1989; A Kind of Darkness, 1962; Belmarch 1964; The Savour of Dachau, 1968; Ishmel, 1967; A Peep into the 20th Century, 1971; The Sun in Mid Career, 1975; Suicide Note, 1977; Dog Horse Rat, 1990; Non Fiction: The Producer, 1972; Waiting for it, 1980; Plays: Private Territory, 1984; A Peep into the 20th Century, 1988. *Memberships:* Authors Guild; Dramatists Guild; PEN. *Honours:* O'Henry Prize Story, 1966; Best Magazine articles, 1968; Nat Book Awd Nominee, 1971; Am Acad and Inst of Arts and Letters Career Awd, 1991; NEA Grants, 1967-74; Guggenheim Grant, 1972. *Hobbies:* Sculpture; Drawing (exhibited at Bryn Mawr Col). *Address:* c/o Curtis Brown Ltd, 10 Astor Place, New York City, NY 10003, USA.

DAVIS Coy A Jr, b. 6 June 1930, Arkansas, USA. Social Worker. m, 19 Nov 1960, 2s, 2 d. *Education:* BSc, Sociol, Texas Wesleyan Univ, 1959; MSc Social Work, Univ of Tennessee, 1963; PhD, Sociol of Deviance, study at Univ of New Mexico, 1987-91. *Appointments:* Univ Ark Med Sch, 1963-65; USPHS Indian Health, 1965-91; N.M Dept of Health, 1992- . *Creative works:*

Juvenile alcohol abuse in Native Americans, research paper; Child abuse in Native American Families; Theories of Sigmund Freud on Society and Culture; Life and Works of Erich Fromm; Social work with Indians: A history, 1965-81; Interviewing Skills, Techniques, and Pitfalls. *Memberships:* Nat Assn of Social Workers; Commd Ofrs Assn, USPHS; Nat Assn of Christians in Social Work. *Honours:* Honor Grad, Texas Wesleyan Univ; Commendation Medal, USPHS; Commendation Cert, Navajo Indian Tribe; Alpha Chi, Natl Scholarship Soc; Commendation Medals, US Air Force. *Hobbies:* Music; Writing; Bible Prophecy. *Address:* 4220 Penelope NE, Albuquerque, NM 87109, USA.

DAVIS Edward Mott, b. 24 Nov 1918, Massachusetts, USA. Archaeologist. m. Beth Ogden, 3 Feb 1943, 2 s. *Education:* BS 1940, MA 1942, PhD, 1954, Anthropol (Archaeol), Harvard Univ. *Appointments:* Dept of Anthropol and Museum, Univ ov Nebraska, 1948-56; Res Scist,, Univ of Texas at Austin, 1956-65; Assoc Prof, Prof Anthropol, 1965-89; Prof Emeritus, 1989-, Dir Radiocarbon Lab, 1966-89, in charge, Archaeal Studies, 1973-89. *Creative works:* Archaeology of the Lime Creek Site, 1963; Film, Early man on the Plains, 1954; Film series: Spadework for History, 1964. *Memberships:* Am Anthropol Assn; Am Assn Advancement of Sci, fellow; Soc for Am Archaeol, Sec, 2964-68; Soc of Profl Archaeols; Texas Archaeol Soc, Pres, 1961, 1972. *Honours:* Phi Beta Kappa, 1940; Texas Awd for Hist Preservation, 1988; Pres's Assocs Tchg Excellence Awd, Univ of Texas, 1987. *Address:* Dept of Anthropology, University of Texas at Austin, TX 78712, USA.

DAVIS Laura, b. 30 Dec 1959, Wilmington, USA. Marketing Manager. *Education:* MBA, Emory Univ, 1985; BA Sociol and Journalism, Univ Delaware, 1981; Univ Massachusetts, 1977-79. *Appointments:* Prod Mgr, 1986-87, Sr Res Analyst, 1988-89, Proj Dir, 1990-91, Dir, Indust Mktg, Equifax Inc, 1991-; Adjunct Bus Prof, Mercer Univ, 1988-. *Memberships:* Atlanta Chamber of Commerce, Toastmasters (Sgt at Arms); NAFE; AMA; World Future Soc; Amnesty Intl; Save the Children; Planning Forum; Sierra Club. *Honours:* High Hons Grad, Univ of Delaware; Kappa Delta 1981; Scholarship, Emory's MBA Prog, 1983-85. *Hobbies:* Reading; Writing; Drawing; Painting; Skiing; Church Activities; Foreign languages. *Address:* 1101 Collier Road NW Apt u-5, Atlanta, GA 30318, USA.

DAVIS Marian Lee, b. 10 Oct 1934, Ohio, USA. Professor. *Education:* BSc, Home Ec Ed, Ohio State Univ, 1956; MA, Intl Relations, NY Univ, 1960; PhD, Comparative and Intl Ed, UCLA, 1971. *Appointments:* Patternmaker, McCall's Patterns, NY, 1959-61; Home Ec Prog Spec, Girl Scout USA HQ, 1961-64; Lectr, Univ Nigeria, 1964-67; Home Ec Ed Spec, UNESCO, Philippines, 1969-70; Florida State Univ, Col of Human Scis, Tallahassee, 1971-; Conslt, Fujian Hwa Nan Women's Col, China, 1989-. *Creative works include:* Visual design in Dress, 1980; Home Economics Heritage and Promise in China: A College Reborn, 1991; Pina Fabric of the Philippines, 1991. *Memberships:* Intl Fed of Home Ec; Am Home Ec Assn; Fla Home Ec Assn; Comparative and Intl Ed Soc, Assn for Women in Devel; Intl Textile and Apparel Assn; Textile Musum; US Nat Comm for UNESCO, 1956-61. *Honours:* Ohio 4- H Alumni Recognition Awd, 1977; Diamond Anniversary Ohio State Univ Sch of Home Ec Outstanding Alumna Awd, 1971. *Hobbies:* Stained glass; Art; Nature; Swimming; Folk dancing; International food and textiles. *Address:* College of Human Sciences, Florida State University, Tallahassee, FL 32306, USA.

DAVIS Michael Todd, b. 3 Apr 1963, Charleston, South Carolina, USA. Process Improvement Specialist, Yarn Manufacturers. m. Cynthia Ann Baxley, 25 May 1985, 1 s, *Education:* BSBA, Citadel Military Col of S.Carolina, 1985; MS Ops Mgmt, Univ of Arkansas, 1987. *Appointments:* US Air Force, Ops Support Ofr, Fuels Mgmt Ofr, Material Mgmt Ofr, 1985- 89; Prod Mgr,

1989-91, Process Improvement Coor, 1991-, Cushman Plant, Milliken and Co, 1989-91; Process Improvement Coor. *Memberships:* Hammerton Masonic Lodge; Air Force Assn; March of Dimes; Pres, First Baptist Ch, Williamston SC; Co Grade Ofrs Coun; Williamston Republican Party. *Honours:* Commandants Dist Sers List, 1982; Deans List, 1984; Ofr of the Quarter, 1986-88 (3 times); Citadel Hon Com. *Hobbies:* Sunday School Teacher; Water Skiing; Golf. *Address:* 14 Dacus Drive, Williamston, SC 29697, USA.

DAVIS Muller, b. 23 Apr 1935, Chicago, Illinois, USA. Attorney. m. Jane Strauss, 28 Dec 1963, 2 s, 1 d. *Education:* Hons, Philips Exeter Acad, 1953; BA Magna cum laude, Yale Univ, 1957; JD Harvard Law Sch, 1960. *Appointments:* Assoc, Jenner and Block, 1960-67; Partner, Davis Friedman, Zavett, Kane & McRae, 1967-. *Creative works:* Law Review articles; Co-author, The Parental Couple in a Successful Divorce, 1983; Editorial Bd, Journal, Eqitable Distribution. *Memberships:* Tavern Club; The Chicago Club; Lake Shore Country Club; Fellow, Am Bar Foun; Am Acad of Matrimonial Lawyers; Am, Illinois, and Chicago Fed Bar Assns; Past Pres, Infant Welfare Soc; Law Club, City of Chicago. *Hobbies:* Reading; Writing; Tennis; Horseback riding. *Address:* 140 South Dearborn Street, Suite 1600, Chicago, IL 60603, USA.

DAVIS Reginald, b. 5 Mar 1925, London, England. Photographic Journalist. m. Audrey Fields, 20 June 1948, 1 d. *Appointments:* Photog, RN, FAA; Dist'd Photog of Royalty, accompanied the Brit Royal Family on over 50 State visits and Royal tours. *Publications:* Royalty of the World, 1969; Princess Anne, 1973; Elizabeth Our Queen, 1977; Monarchy in Power, 1977, 1978; Charles, Prince of Wales, 1978; Royal Families of the World, 1978; The Persian Prince, 1979; The Royal Family of Thailand, 1981; The Royal Family of Luxembourg, 1989; Photographed many intl dignitaries and film celebrities around the world. *Memberships:* FBIPP; FMPA; FRPS. *Honours:* Order of Taj (Iran), Personal Decoration by the Shah of Iran; won 1st & 2nd Ency Britannica awds for colour photography, 1962; 1st prize, Rothmans Awds, 1971. *Hobbies:* Gardening; Video-ing; Rotary; Soccer; Cricket. *Address:* 64 Totteridge Village, London N20 8PS, England.

DAVIS Ruth Carol, b. 27 Oct 1943, Wilkes-Barre, PA, USA. Reg Pharm; Conslt. *Education:* Pharm D, Ohio, 1970. *Appointments:* Mgr, Rea & Derrick Inc, 1961-75; Mgr, Peoples Drug, 1974-77; Mgr, Adams-Cumberland Med Ctr, 1978-80; Dir, Rombro Hlth Ser, 1981-84; Conslt, Fairview Prof Pharm, 1985-92. *Memberships:* Intl Platform Assn; APhA; NRHA; AQHA; YCPA. *Honours:* Pres, Ex Ofcr, PCP & S Dormitory Coun, 1964-67; Chairperson, Alumni Re-union Comm, 1967. *Hobbies:* Music; Riding and training quarter horses; Lecturing support groups for terminal ill patients; Teaching students of pharmacy. *Address:* 90 Lion Drive, Hanover, PA 17331, USA.

DAVIS Walter Stewart, b. 31 Mar 1924, Evanston, IL, USA. Chm of Bd. m. Betty M Grede, 19 Apr 1947, 3 s, 2 d. *Education:* BS 1941-42, 1945-47, JD 1947-50, Northwestern Univ. *Appointments:* Gen Atty, Butler Bros, 1950-51; USAF, Judge Advocate Gen Staff, Moody AFB, 1951-52; Davis & Kuelthau, 1952-; Chm of the Bd, Thomas Industries Inc, 1987-. *Memberships:* IBA; ABA; Wisconsin Bar Assn; Milwaukee Bar Assn. *Hobbies:* Golf; Reading. *Address:* 111 East Kilbourn Avenue, Milwaukee, WI 53202, USA.

DAVIS William Maxie, b. 7 June 1932, NC, USA. Trial Atty; Lawyer. m. Shirley Jane Smith, 24 Mar 1987. *Education:* Bachelor of Gen Ed, Univ of Nebraska at Omaha, Nebraska, 1965; MA, Univ of So California, Los Angeles, 1970; JD, N Carolina Ctl Univ, Durham, 1986. *Appointments:* Lt Col, USAF, 1950-75; Asst Co Mgr, Dir of Planning, Dir of Pers, Bladen Co, 1977-83; Trial Atty, 1986-. *Memberships:* Mem of Bar, Supr Ct of the USA; ABA; Nat Assn of Crim Def Lawyers; N Carolina

Bar; Intl Pltform Assn. *Honours:* Mil Decorations for Meritorious Ser and Outstg Perf, 1966, 1967, 1969, 1971, 1973, 1975; Nat Dean's List, USA, 1985-86. *Hobbies:* Chess; Working with the poor and underpriviledged; Pres, HELP. *Address:* 301 Queens Road, Charlotte, NC 28204, USA.

DAWE Donald Bruce, b. 15 Feb 1930, Geelong, Victoria, Australia. Assoc Prof. m. Gloria Desley Blain, 27 Feb 1930, 2 s, 2 d. *Education:* BA 1969, MA 1975, PhD 1980, Univ of Queensland; LittB, UNE, 1973. *Appointments:* Sec'dy Tchr, Downlands Coll, Towoomba, 1969-71; Lectr 1971-78, Sr Lectr 1978-90, DDIAE, Towoomba; Assoc Prof, UCSQ, Towoomba, 1990-. *Publications include:* No Fixed Address: Poems, 1962; Over Here, Harv! and Other Stories, 1983; Sometimes Gladness: Collected Poems 1954-78, 1978; Sometimes Gladness: Collected Poems 1954-82, 2nd rev edit 1983; Towards Sunrise, 1986; Speaking in Parables (ed), 1987; This Side of Silence, 1990; Bruce Dawe: Essays and Opinions, 1990. *Memberships:* Right to Life Assn, Queensland; AATE (Hon); VAATE (Hon); Assoc Mem, CSAL; Paul Harris Fellow, Rotary Intl; Patron, PEN, Melbourne. *Honours:* Myer Poetry Prize, 1966, 1969; Ampol Arts Awd for Creative Lit, 1967; Dame Mary Gilmore Gold Medal, Australian Lit Soc, 1973; Grace Leven Poetry Prize, 1978; Braille Book of the Year, 1979; Patrick White Lit Awd, 1980; Christopher Brennan Awd, Fellowship of Australian Writers, 1984; Order of Australia (AO), 1992. *Hobbies:* Reading; Gardening; Watching TV; Writing. *Address:* 30 Cumming Street, Towoomba 4350, Australia.

DAWSON Mary Martha, b. 30 Aug 1908, Anderson, IN, USA. Min; Tchr; Writer. m. John Franklin Dawson, 19 Apr 1950. *Education:* Colorado Univ, 1927-33; Denver Univ, 1933; DSB, Brooks Divinity Coll, 1947-51. *Appointments:* Freelance Writer, 1935-91; Owned & Operated 4 Sales Rms, 1959-68; Writer, Maginot Advtg Co, 1968-71; Tchr, Brooks Divine Sci Divinity Coll, 1971-91; Wrote Column ASPIRE, 1978-81; Ordained Min, Divine Sci, 1980. *Memberships:* Pres 1973-74, Denver Womans Press Club; Pres 1977-79, Colorado Poetry Soc; Secy 1978, Altrusa Club. *Honours:* Poetry, 1972, 1973, 1980; Short Story, Denver Post, 1973; Honorary Doctorate, Divine Sci, Brooks Divinity Sch, 1985. *Hobbies:* Reading; Music; Dancing. *Address:* 1255 19th Street 710, Denver, CO 80202, USA.

DAWSON Wiliam Johnson, b. 7 Oct 1925, Newark, OH, USA. Prof of Humanities and Social Sci. m. Evelyn Cardwell, 8 Sept 1948, 1 s, 3 d. *Education:* BS 1949, MS 1950, Virginia Tech; MA, Presb Sch of Ch Ed, 1962; MA, Appalachian State, 1966; EdD, NC State, 1972. *Appointments:* High Sch Tchr, Prince Edward Co, VA, 1950-52; Merchandising Mgr, Presb Book Store, Richmond, 1952-57; Asst Book Edit, John Knox Press, Richmond, 1957-62; Instr, Rel & Sociol, Lees McRae Coll, 1962-66; Instr, Soc & Rel, Rockingham Com Coll, 1966-72; Div Chair 1972-83, Prof 1983-1991, Humanities and Social Scis, New River Com Coll. *Memberships:* Pulaski Co Bd of Supvrs, 1983-87; Gov's Adv Bd on Aging; Chancellor's Fac Adv Com, 1988-90; Vice Chair, New River Com Action; Pres 1989-90, 1992-93, Pulaski Co Emer Needs Task Force; Fdg Vice Chair, Rural Virginia. *Honour:* State of NC doct internship, 1970-71. *Hobbies:* Political activities; Social service activities. *Address:* 46 Aldrin Street, Dublin, VA 24084, USA.

DAY Kenneth Arthur, b. 18 July 1935, London, England. Conslt Psychi; Sr Lectr; Mental Hlth Act Commr. m. Sheila Mary Torrance, 27 June 1959, 2 s, 1 d. *Education:* MB, ChB 1961, Bristol Univ & Med Sch; DPM 1964; MRCPsych 1972; FRCPsych 1978. *Appointments:* Psychiatric Tng, Bristol and Newcastle, 1962-69; Conslt Psychi, Northern RHA & Newcastle HA, 1969-92; Med Dir, Northgate NHS Trust, Northumberland, 1992-; Sr Lectr, Dept of Psychi, Univ of Newcastle, 1986-; Mental Hlth Act Commr, 1988-; Scientific Adv, Mem Standing Med Adv Com, DHSS.

Publications: The Special Child, 1977; The Special Child - The Teenage Years, 1979; Behaviour Problems in the Mentally Handicapped, 1988; Author of 40 chapts, papers & scientific articles on mental handicap; Writer, Conslt, Presenter of 9 television series and documentaries on mental handicap for BBC & ITV, 1977-82. *Memberships:* Mem of Coun, Exec & Fin Com & num other coms, RCPsych; Chm, Sect for the Psychi of Mental Handicap, 1983-87; Secy 1983-89, Vice Chm Mental Retardation Sect 1989-, World Psychiatric Assn; Vice-Pres, 1992, Intl Assn for the Scientific Study of Mental Deficiency; Secy, Coun Mem 1985-; Yeomam, Worshipful Soc of Apothecaries, 1988-. *Honours:* Winston Churchill Mem Fellowship, 1972; Burden Gold Medal & Res Prize, 1985-86; Blake Marsh Lectr, RCPsych, 1989; Winner, Animal Portraits Category, Wildlife Photog of the Year, 1989; Freeman, City of London, 1989; World Hlth Org Med Fellowship, 1990. *Hobbies:* Squash; Badminton; Tennis; Natural history; Painting; Carving; Photography. *Address:* Northgate Hospital, Morpeth, Northumberland NE61 3BP, England.

DAY Peter William, b. 22 Sept 1944, Oak Ridge, TN, USA. Assoc Dir for Res and Planning. m. 17 June 1967, 1 s. *Education:* MS, Emory Univ, Atlanta, 1966; PhD, California Inst of Tech, Pasadena, 1970. *Appointments:* Post Doct Fellow, Carnegie Mellon Univ, 1970-72; Mgr OSS 1972-74, Mgr User Sers 1974-75, Coor 1975-80, Asst Dir 1980-85, Assoc Dir 1985-, Emory Univ. *Publications:* Author and Prodr of 3 films 1964-89; Composer of 3 songs 1964-91; Author of: 4 math journ articles 1973-80; 10 computing articles 1975-81; Author of widely distributed computer prog, 1980. *Memberships:* Am Mathematical Soc; ACM; AAAS; Coor - Ed SIG 1980, Dir Ed SIG 1981, Am Univac Users Assn. *Honours:* Phi Beta Kappa, Alpha Epsilon Upsilon, Stipe Scholar, Career Scholar, Undergrad Math Awd, Hamilton Watch Awd in Sci, NSF Fellowship, Woodrow Wilson Fellowship, 1962-66; NSF Post Doct Fellowship, 1970-72; NSF Grant, 1988. *Hobbies:* Magic; Motion picture filming; Videos; Piano; Guitar; Recorder; Stamp collecting; Science; Mathematics; Computing. *Address:* 1183 Houston Mill Road, Atlanta, GA 30329, USA.

DAY Richard Bruce, b. 22 July 1942, Toronto, Canada. Edr. m. Judith D Day, 5 Aug 1969, 1 s, 2 d. *Education:* BA 1965, MA 1967, Dip REES 1967, Univ of Toronto; PhD, Univ of London, 1970. *Appointments:* Asst Prof 1970, Asst Chm of Pol Sci Erindale Campus 1973-76, 1981-84, 1991-, Assoc Prof 1974, Prof of Pol Sci 1979-, Univ of Toronto. *Publications:* Leon Trotsky and the Politics of Economic Isolation, 1973, Italian trans 1979; The Crisis and the Crash - Soviet Studies of the West 1917-1939, 1981; Selected Writings on the State and the Transitition to Socialism, by N I Bukharin (ed and transl), 1982; The Decline of Capitalism by EA Preobrazhensky, 1985; Democratic Theory and Technological Society (co-ed), 1988. *Memberships:* Canadian Assn of Slavists; Canadian Pol Sci Assn; Intl Soc for the Study of European Ideas; Assoc Ed, Canadian Slavonic Papers, 1982-88; Contbtg Ed, Intl Journ of Polit Economy, 1989-. *Honours:* Killam Sr Res Fellow, 1978, 1979; Mem, Appraisals Com, Ontario Coun Grad Studies, 1983-86; Mem, Res Grants Adjudication Com of Soc Sci and Humanities Res Coun of Canada, 1987-88; Democratic Theory and Technological Society, selected by Choice as an Outstg Acad Book of the Year, 1988-89. *Hobbies:* Skiing; Ratepayer activities; Municipal politics. *Address:* 2601 Truscott Drive, Mississauga, Ontario, Canada L5J 2B6.

DE BERNIERE-SMART Reginald Piers Alexander, b. 3 Mar 1924, Eltham, England. Ret'd Regular Army; Charity Dir. m. Jean Ashton Smithells, 7 June 1951, 1 s, 2 d. *Appointments:* Commissioned The Queen's Bays (2nd Dragoon Guards) 1943, Ret'd from 1st The Queen's Dragoon Guards (Major) 1959; Exec ecy, BR Diabetic Assn, 1960-65; Gen Secy 1971, Dir 1988, Shaftsbury Homes. *Memberships:* IAM, 1959-; NCVCCO, 1971-89; Mgmt Com, Bradfield Club, Peckham, 1989, Chm 1990-92; Council 1992-; SSAFA/FHS Case Wkr, 1990-; Life Gov, Imperial Cancer Res

Fund, 1990-; Intl Leag for Protection of Horses (Life); IFAW; P.C.C West Wittering, 1991-. *Honours:* Mentioned in Dispatches, Italian Campaign, 1944-45. *Hobbies:* Open air activities; Photography; Steam and model railways; Theatre; Poetry; Militaria. *Address:* 9 The Wad, West Wittering, West Sussex PO20 8AH, England.

DE CADAVAL Rudy, b. 1 Jan 1933. Pres; Mgr; Video Info Profl. m. Corsini Grazia, 31 Mar 1962, 1 s, 1 d. *Career:* Poet, Essayist, Writer; Dir, Grolier Intl Inc, 1972-82; VP, Kronos Europea, SPA, Rome, 1983- 85; Pres, Mgr, Video Informatics Profl. *Publications include:* Et apres .... 1980; Dove senza di loro, 1981; Poesie d'amore, 1983; Simboli e realta nella poesia di Salvatore Quasimodo, 1983; Colloquio con la pietra, 1985; L'albero del silenzio, 1988; Una vita recitata: Oscar Wilde, 1989. *Memberships include:* Bd of Dir, Intl Writers and Artists Assn of Moorhead State Univ; Ctr Study of Poetry and Poetics, Rome; Intl Burckhardt Acad, Basilea; Free World Acad, Deaborn; Intl Acad de Lutece, Paris; Acad de Perigold, Bordeaux; Acad di Filologia Classica, Milano. *Honours include:* Kt Cmdr, Sovereign Order of St John of Jerusalem; Kt of Malta; Kt Ordre Souverain Imperial Byzante de Costantin Le Grand; Prize Lago d'Iseo, Anni 80, 1980; Prize de la Critique, Paris, 1980; Prize Verona, 1981; Prize Montesacro, 1985; Poetry of '900 Prize, 1988; Gold Lion of Town Hall of Venice, 1989; Gold Plume, Acad des Poetes de France; Man of Year 1990, The Key of Success 1990, ABI, N Carolina. *Address:* via Mascagni 5, 37024 Loc Montericco Negrar, Verona, Italy.

DE CHASTELAIN Alfred John Gardyne Drummond, b. 30 July 1937, Bucharest, Romania. Chief of Def Staff, Nat Def. m. MaryAnn Laverty, 9 Sept 1961, 1 s, 1 d. *Education:* BA, Royal Mil Coll Can, Kingston, 1960; Grad, Brit Army Staff Coll, Camberley, 1966. *Appointments:* Commd 2nd Lt 2 Bn PPCLI, Edmonton, 1960; promoted Capt, named aide-de-camp to Chief of Gen Staff, Army HQ, Ottawa, 1962-64; Co Cmdr, 1 PPCLI Hemer, Germany, 1964- 65; promoted Maj, Co Cmdr, 1 PPCLI Edmonton, later served with 1 Bn UN Force Cyprus, 1967-68; Bgde Maj, 1 Combat Group Calgary, 1968-70; Cmdg Ofcr, 2 PPCLI Winnipeg 1970-72, promoted to Lt Col; Fed Bicultural Prog, Laval Univ, 1972-73; Sr Staff Ofcr, Quartier Gen Dist 3 Que (Milice), Quebec City, 1973; Col, Cmdr, Canadian Forces Base, Montreal, 1974; Dep Chief of Staff, HQ UN Forces Cyprus, Cmdr, Canadian Contingent, 1976; Brig Gen 1977, Commandent, Royal Mil Coll Can, Kingston; Command, 4 Candn Mechanized Bgde Group Lahr, Germany, 1980-82; Dir Gen, Land Doctrine & Operations 1982-83; Maj Gen 1983, Dep Cmdr, Mobile Command, St Hubert; Lt Gen 1986, Asst Dep Min (Pers), NDHQ, Ottawa; Vice Chief, Def Staff, 1988; Gen 1989, Chief of Def Staff, NDHQ, 1989-. *Memberships:* VP, Nat Coun, Boy Scouts of Canada; Pres, Dominion of Canada Rifle Assn; Royal Mil Coll of Canada Club; Royal Kingston Un Sers Inst; Royal Canadian Legion; St Andrews Soc of Montreal; Royal Scottish Country Dance Soc. *Honours:* Cmdr 1984, Prin Cmdr 1989, Order of Mil Merit; Ofcr 1987, Cmdr 1991, Order of St John. *Hobbies:* Fishing; Painting; Jogging. *Address:* National Defence Headquarters, Major-General George R Peakes Building, Ottawa, Ontario, Canada K1A 0K2.

DE CLOPPER Edmond, b. 29 Sept 1922, Antwerpen, Belgium. Rep Mgr. *Memberships:* Pres, Fdr, Movement of Flemish Folklore, 1948; Intl Com of the Europeade for European Folk-culture, 1964; VP, Coun of Flemish Cultural Fdn, 1990. *Honours:* Senator of Hon, Movement US of Europe, 1964; Mark of Honour of the City of: Madrid 1969, Paris 1975, Vienna 1978, Annecy 1972, Rennes 1984, Turin 1985, Autonomous Reg of Sardinia 1973; Mark of Hon: Coun Dutch Culture 1971, Min of Dutch Culture 1982; Intl Price Dag Hmmarskjold, 1988; Price Prudens van Duyse, 1991. *Address:* Merksemsebaan 264, B-2110 Wijnegem, Belgium.

DE FERRANTI Sebastian Basil Joseph Ziani, b. 5 Oct 1927, Alderley Edbe. Dir. m. (1)Mona Helen, 1953, (2)Naomi Angela Rae, 1983, 1 s, 2 d. *Education:* Ampleforth, 4th/7th Dragoon Guards, 1947-49; Brown Boveri, Switzerland and Alsthom, France, 1949-50. *Appointments:* Pres: Elec Rsch Assn 1968-69; BEAMA 1969-70; Ctr for Ed in Sci, Ed & Tech, Manchester and reg 1972-82; Chm, Int Elec Assn 1970-72; Dir: Brit Airways Helicopters 1982- 84, Nat Nuclear Corp 1984-88. *Creative works:* Lectures: Granada, Guildhall, 1966; Royal Instn, 1969; Louis Bleriot, Paris, 1970; Faraday, 1970-71. *Memberships:* Nat Def Industries Coun, 1969-77; Coun, IEE, 1970-73; Trustee, Tate Gall, 1971-78; Chm, Civic Trust for the NW, 1978-83; VP, RSA, 1980-84; Comr, Royal Commn for Exhib of 1851, 1984-; Chm, Halle Concerts Soc, 1988-. *Honours:* Hon DSc, Salford Univ, 1967; Cranfield Inst of Tech, 1973; High Sheriff of Cheshire, 1988-89; Hon Fellow, Univ of Manchester Inst of Sci & Tech. *Address:* Henbury Hall, Macclesfield, Cheshire SK11 9PJ, England.

DE HENSELER Maximilien Charles, b. 7 Nov 1933, Geneva, Switzerland. Dir-Curator Swiss Audiovisual Mus Audiorama, Montreux. m. Renate Urbich. 11 Mar 1975. *Education:* Bachelor-es-letters, Univ Fribourg, Switz; BSc, George Washington Univ, USA; Computer Mapping Cert, Harvard Univ, USA; DSc, Lorand Eotvos Univ, Hungary. *Appointments:* UN Serv, 1958, Sr Econ Affairs Off; Ret'd 1989 after 30 yrs as a surveying and mapping expert at UN HQ and at ECE and ECA as Chief of Cartography Sect, Dept of Tech Coop for Dev in NY; Exec Sec, sev UN Reg Cartographic Confs for Asia and the Pacific and the Americas as well as UN Confs on Standardization of Geographical Names; Sec, UN Grp of Experts on Geographical Names; Dir and Curator of Swiss Audiovisual Mus Audiorama in Montreux, Switz, 1989-. *Publications:* num articles in tech and histl radio jrnls; The Hallicrafters Story, 1991. *Memberships:* Fellow, Royal Geographical Soc; Fellow,. Radio Club of America. *Hobbies:* Amateur Radio, Preservation of Radio Hist. *Address:* Av de Florimont 9, 1820 Montreux, Switzerland.

DE KNYFF Henri Wynandus, b. 23 June 1931, Enschede, Holland. Tchr. m. Magdalena Dorothea De Jong, 16 Oct 1959, 3 s, 1 d. *Education:* Doct Ex Theol, Univ of Amsterdam; SW, Univ of Basel; Theol Dr, Univ of Leiden. *Appointments:* Min: Dutch Ref Ch, Hem-Venhuizen 1959-64; Prot Ev Ch of Belgium (Gent) 1964-69; Spykenisse 1969-74; Univ Tchr, Dep Theol, Utrecht, 1974-. *Publications:* ONoordmans' Bibl Interpr, 1970; History of Bibl Hermeneutics, 1980; Sexual Ethics and European Culture, 1988; Coll Essays, 1990. *Memberships:* Wiss Gesellsch fur Theol, Germany; European Soc of Sci & Theol; Theol Res Foun, Stegon, Holland. *Honour:* Mallinckrodt Prize, Univ of Groningen, 1975. *Hobbies:* History and philosophy of culture; Art history; Painting. *Address:* Theol Faculty, University of Utrecht, Heidelberglaan 2, 3584CS Utrecht, Holland.

DE LA LLAVE Rafael, b. 15 June 1957, Madrid, Spain. Mathematician. m. Ramona Gonzalez, 28 Apr 1989. *Education:* Licenciado, Univ Complutense, 1979; PhD, Princeton Univ, 1983. *Appointments:* Univ Minnesota, 1982-83; I H E S, 1983-84; Princeton Univ, 1984-89; Univ of Texas, 1989-. *Publications:* Over 20 Research Papers. *Memberships:* AMS; IAMP; APS. *Honour:* Fulbright Scholar. *Hobbies:* Reading; Theatre; Hiking. *Address:* Dept of Maths, Univ Texas, Austin, TX 78712, USA. 1.

DE LA MARE Albina Catherine, b. 2 June 1932, London, England. *Education:* BA, MA, Lady Margaret Hall, Oxford; PhD, London, 1966. *Appointments:* Temp Cataloguer 1962-64; Asst Libn 1964-88, Dept of Western MSS, Bodleian Llb, Oxford; Prof of Palaeography, King's Coll, London. *Publications:* Catalogue of the Italian Manuscripts of Major J R Abbey (with J J G Alexander), 1965; Catalogue of the Lyell Manuscripts, Bodleian Lib, 1971; Handwriting of Italian Humanists I, 1973; Articles in learned periodicals,

exhibitions and catalogues. *Memberships:* FRHistS; Comite Internationalde Paleographic Latine, 1986, Bur Mem 1990-; FBA, 1987; Fellow, Soc of Antiquaries, 1990; Assn of Univ Profs. *Honours:* Jr Res Fellow, Warburg Inst, 1957-59; Susette Tayor Res Fellow 1964, Hon Res Fellow 1979-88, Hon Fellow 1989-, Lady Margaret Hall; Guest Scholar, J P Getty Museum, Malibu, California, 1992. *Hobbies:* Cooking; Gardening; Listening to music; Travel. *Address:* Department of English Language and Lterature/Palaeography, King's College London, Strand WC2R 2LS, England.

DE LA TORRE Jack C, b. 2 Dec 1937, Paris, France. Phys; Neuroscist. *Education:* BS, Am Univ, 1961; PhD summa cum laude, Univ of Geneva, 1968; MD, Univ Cd Juarez, 1979. *Appointments:* Asst Prof in Neurosurg & Psychi 1969-75, Assoc Prof 1975-77, Univ of Chicago; Prof of Neurosurg & Pharm, Univ of Ottawa, 1983-. *Publications:* Dynamics of Brain Monoamines, 1972; Biological Actions and Medical Applications of DMSO; Translation The Neuron and the Glial Cell by Ramon y Cajal. *Memberships:* Soc for Neurosci; Cajal Club; IBRO; RSM; Am Heart Assn; Coll of Phys & Surgs, Ontario; Interam Coll of Phys & Surgs; Am Acad of Neurol. *Honours:* Fellow, Am Heart Assn, Stroke Coun; Conf Chm, Intl Conf on Med Uses of Dimethyl Sulfoxide, 1982. *Hobbies:* Chess; Tennis; Music. *Address:* University of Ottawa Faculty of Medicine, Division of Neurosurgery, 451 Smyth Road, Ottawa, Ontario, Canada K1H 8M5.

DE LA VEGA Aurelio, b. 28 Nov 1925, La Habana, Cuba. Composer; Writer (on music); Edr. m. Sara Lequerica, 26 Jan 1947. *Education:* BA, De La Salle Coll, Havana, 1944; MA, Univ of Havana, 1946; MA 1956, PhD 1958, A Iglesias Inst, Havana. *Appointments:* Music Critic, newspaper Alerta, Havana, 1952-57; Prof of Music, Chm, Music Dept, Univ of Oriente, Santiago de Cuba, 1953-59; Advr, Nat Inst of Culture, Havana, 1955-59; Guest Prof of Music, So California, Summer 1959; Dist'd Prof of Music, Dir, Elect Music Studio, California State Univ, 1959-1992. *Publications:* Legend of the Creole Ariel, cello, pno, 1953; Elegy, str orch, 1954; Interpolation, cl tape, 1965; Labdanum, fl vibr vla, 1970; Intrata, orch, 1972; Septicilum, cl, chamber orch, 1974; Adios, orch, 1977; Galandiacoa, cl, guitar, 1982; Tropimapal, chamber orch, 1983; Asonante, sopr, chamber orch, tape, 1985; Testimonial, mezzo sopr, chamber ensemble, 1990; Madrigales de Entones, S.A.T.B. chorus, 1991; Bifloreo, guitar, 1992. *Memberships include:* Past Pres, Cuban Coun of Music, UNESCO, 1952-55; Am Assn of Univ Profs, 1960-; NACUSA, 1962-; Soc of Composers Inc, USA, 1974-; Chilean Acad of Fine Arts, 1990. *Honours include:* Medal of the Order of Eloy Alfaro, Colombia, 1961; Outstg Prof Awd, The Californian State Univ & Colls, 1971; Dist'd Prof Awd 1974, Creativity Awd, Calif State Univ, Northridge, 1984, 1991, California State Univ, Northridge; Friedheim Awd, The Kennedy Ctr for Performing Arts, Washington, 1978, 1984; Nat Fdn of Music Clubs Awd of Merit, USA, 1985; Fulbright Res Awd, Washington-Rio de Janeiro, 1985. *Hobbies:* Painting; Reading; Comparative literature; Philosophy; History of World War II. *Address:* 18800 Stare Street, Northridge, CA 91324, USA.

DE LAETER John Robert, b. 3 May 1933, Western Australia, Australia. Dep Vice Chancellor (Res & Devel). nı. Robin, 28 Dec 1957, 2 s, 1 d. *Education:* BEd Hons; BSc Hons; PhD; DSc. *Appointments:* Hd, Dept of Physics 1968-74, Dean of Applied Sci 1974-80, Western Australia Inst of Tech; Dep Vice Chancellor (Engrg & Sci) 1980-90, Dep Vice Chancellor (Res & Devel) 1990-, Curtin Univ of Tech. *Memberships:* Chm, CSIRO Adv Com, WA, 1983-86; Sec 1983-87, Chm, Comm on Atomic Weights and Isotopic Abundances Intl Union of Pure and Applied Chemistry, 1987-91; Chm, Wesley Coll Coun, 1988-; Mem, Higher Ed Coun, 1990-; Mem, Bd of Mgmt, CSIRO, 1991-. *Honours:* Hon, Fellow, Australian Inst of Physics, 1970; Fellow, Brit Inst of Physics, 1970; Fellow, Australian Acad of Technological Scis & Engrg, 1984; Citizen of the Year for Western

Australia, 1986; Ofcr, Order of Australia, 1992. *Hobbies:* Hockey; Tennis. *Address:* 4 The Parapet, Willetton, WA 6155, Australia.

DE LAUNAY Leon David Ward, b. 30 Mar 1950, Ottawa, Ontario, Canada. Exec Asst. *Education:* Royal Conservatory of Music. *Appointments:* Res Assoc, 1986-90; Coor, Hlth & Safety Clin, 1990; EA Govt Hse Ldr, 1990-91; Exec Asst, Min of No Devel and Mines, 1990-. *Creative works:* Music and lyrics for album by Horn - On the Peoples Side, 1973; Soundtrack for chd's movie - In the Jungle, There's Lots to Do, 1975. *Memberships:* Soc of Composers, Authors and Music Pubrs of Canada, 1972-; United Steelwkrs of Am, 1982-85; Proj Ploughsharers, 1982-90; Ontario Public Ser Employees Union, 1986-90; Dir, Peace Mag, 1986-87. *Hobbies:* Music; Film; Reading. *Address:* 119 Gore Vale Avenue, Toronto, Ontario, Canada M6J 2R5.

DE MATRAN Hugo, b. 27 July 1941, Switzerland. Sculptor. *Education:* Lic.Phil; Lic.Theol; Lic.Pedagogic; Lic.Fine Arts. *Appointments:* Allemagne, Munich, Germany; Luxembourg, France; Lausanne, Switz; Rome, Italy; Matran-Fribourg, Switz. *Creative Works:* Large works, sculptures, drawings, throughout Europe and elsewhere; Portals, S Teresa, Lugano, Switz; Exhibs in Europe, Czechoslovakia, The Netherlands, Switz and Dayton, USA, 1992-93. *Membership:* l'Institut CSSR. *Hobbies:* Fine Art, Sculpture, Creative Work. *Address:* Atelier de la Fontaine aux Petits Cochons, CH-1753, Matran, Switzerland.

DE MEIRA PENNA Jose Osvaldo, b. 14 Mar 1917, Rio de Janeiro, Brazil. Diplomat. m Dorothy Ann Hessee. *Education:* Bach Juridical and Social Sciences, Univ of Brazil, 1939; Courses Dept of Anthropology, East Asian Inst and Latin American Seminars, Columbia Univ, USA, 1954-56; Analytical Psychology, C G Jung Inst, Zurich, 1961-63; Brazilian War Coll, Escola Superior de Guerra, 1965, refresher courses 1975, 80. *Appointments:* Entered For Serv, 1938; Vice Consul, Calcutta, 1940; Shanghai, 1941-42; Second Sec of Embassy in Ankara, Turkey, 1944-47; Charge d'Affaires in Nanking, China, 1947-49, San Jose, Costa Rica, 1951; First Sec of Embassy in Ottawa, Can, 1952; Asst to Brazilian Mission to UN, NY, 1953-56; Mbr of Delegations to Gen Assemblies, 1953-55, Security Coun and Econ and Social Coun; Represented Brazil in var comms; Consul Gen in Zurich, 1960-63; First Brazilian Amb to Nigeria, 1964-65; Amb to Israel and Cyprus, 1967-70; Amb to Norway and Iceland, 1974-77; Amb to Ecuador, 1978-79; Amb to Poland, 1980-81; Ret'd June 1981. *Publications:* Articles in jrnls and newspapers; sev books. *Memberships:* Mbr Tech Coun, Nat Confederation of Commerce, Rio de Janeiro, 1985; Co-fndr and Acting Pres, Tocqueville Soc; VP, Liberal Inst, Brazil. *Address:* SMPW Quadra 15-6-7, Brasilia 71700, Brazil.

DE MOOR Bart Lodewijk Rene, b. 12 July 1960, Halle, Belgium. Prof; Res Assoc. m. Hilde E Devoghel, 9 July 1988, 1 s. *Education:* Latin-Mathematical studies, Sint-Jan Bergmanscollege, Brussels; Electro- Mech Engrg specialisation control engrg 1983, PhD, Dept of Elect Engrg 1988, Katholieke Univ Leuven. *Appointments:* Visiting Res Assoc, Info Systems Lab and Numerical Anal Group, Stanford Univ, California, 1988-89; Res Assoc, Belgian Nat Foun for Scientific Res, 1989-; Assoc Prof, Dept of Elect Engrg, Katholieke Univ Leuven, 1990-; Chief Ministerial Ofcr, Belgian Nat Min of Budget & Sci, 1991-92; Scientific Adv of the Flemish Min of the Budget Wivina Demeester-De Meyer, 1992-. *Publications:* ssa 00Author of about 50 scientific papers in intl journs. *Memberships:* Assoc, ORSA; Am Mathematical Soc; Intl Linear Algebra Soc; SIAM; IEEE; KVIV, Koninklijke Vlaamse. *Honours:* The Leybold-Heraeus Prize, 1986; Leslie Fox Prize in Nummerical Anal, Cambridge Univ, England, 1989; Guillemin-Cauer Awd 1990 of IEEE Transactions on Circuits and Systems. *Hobbies:* Music; History of Science. *Address:* ESAT -

KULEUVEN, Kardinaal Mercierlaan 94, B-3001 Leuven, Belgium.

DE ROOSTER Lucien, b. 28 Jan 1943. Commercial Engineer; Managing Director, Du Pont de Nemours (Belgium); Comptroller, C & S Europe; Chairman, Board of Directors: Du Pont de Nemours (Belgium), Du Pont Coordination Center, Du Pont Engineered Parts, Du Pont de Nemours Investments (France); Board Member: Du Pont Conoco Technologies (France), Supply Chain Software. m. Danielle De Wachter, 1 d. *Education:* Commercial Engr, Univ Leuven. *Appointments:* Employee, Insp Serv, Banque de Paris et des Pays-Bas, 1965; Reserve Off, Mil Serv, 1966; Asst Auditor, Pub Acct, Arthur Andersen, 1967; Internal Auditor, 1969, Audit Mgr, BeNeLux, 1972, Comptroller, 1976, Du Pont de Nemours (Belgium); Asst Credit Mgr, Subsidiary Rels, 1977, Asst Mgr, Int Fin, 1978, E I du Pont de Nemours & Co, USA; European Credit Mgr, Du Pont de Nemours Int, Switzerland, 1979; Dir, Auditing N-Europe, 1981, Dir Fin, 1984, Du Pont de Nemours (Belgium); Dir Fin, Du Pont de Nemours (France), 1988. *Hobbies:* Tennis; Soccer; Reading. *Address:* Du Pont de Nemours (Belgium), A Spinoystr 6, B-2800 Mechelen, Belgium.

DEAKIN John, b. 4 Mar 1965, Bedford, England. Sales Rep. m. Mary Elizabeth Blacklidge, 7 Sept 1991. *Education:* HNC Bus & Fin, Bedford F E Coll, 1984; Open Univ Undergrad, Sharnbrook Sch, 1992-. *Appointments:* Commercial Trainee 1981-84, Asst Contracts Engr 1985-86, W H Allen Engrg, Bedford; Sales Rep, A R Wilson, Nottingham, 1989-. *Publication:* Simple Secrets of Successful Coxswain, 1991. *Membership:* Coxswain, Asst Coach, Nottinghamshire Co Rowing Assn. *Honours:* Represented Gt Britain in Rowing at Intl Level, 1987-; Bronze Medal, World Rowing Championships, Tasmania, 1990; Olympic Games Coxed Four, 1992. *Hobbies:* Sketching; Books; Wine; All Sports. *Address:* NCRA, National Watersports Centre, Holme Pierrepont, Nottingham, England.

DEAN Beale, b. 26 Feb 1922, Ft Worth, TX, USA. Atty at Law. m. Margaret Ann Webster, 3 Sept 1948, 1 s, 1 d. *Education:* BA 1944, LLB 1947, Univ of Texas. *Appointments:* Asst Dist Atty, Dallas Co, 1947- 48; Martin, Moore, Brewster & Dean, Ft Worth, 1948-51; Brewster, Parnell, Dean & Kerry, Ft Worth, 1951-61; Parnell, Dean, Parnell & Kerry, 1961-65; Brown, Herman, Scott, Young & Dean, 1965-71; Atty at Law, Brown, Herman, Scott, Dean & Miles, 1971-. *Memberships:* Am Coll of Trial Lawyers, 1964-; Pres 1971, Ft Worth Tarrant Co Bar Assn; Dir 1973-76, State Bar of Texas; Nat Coll for Dist Attys, Regent, 1985-; ABA; Texas Bar Foun; Am Bar Foun. *Honour:* Blackstone Awd, Tarrant Co Bar Assn, 1990. *Hobbies:* Reading; Racketball; Travel. *Address:* 203 Fort Worth Club Building, 306 West 7th Street, Fort Worth, TX 76102, USA.

DEAN James E, b. 14 Mar 1944, Atlanta, GA, USA. Govt Ofcl; Social Wkr; Edr. m. Vyvyan C Coleman, 6 Dec 1966, 2 d. *Education:* BA, Clark Coll, Atlanta, 1966; MSW, Atlanta Univ, 1968. *Appointments include:* Dir of Alumni Affairs, Clark Coll, Atlanta, 1971-78; MBO Contract Procument Spec 1978-80, Asst Dir, MBO Proj - So Reg Ofc 1980-82, Nat Urban Leag, Inc; Mgmt Rep, BMC Realty Co, Atlanta, 1982; Equal Employmt Opportunity Ofcr 1982-88, Equal Employmt Opportunity Review Ofcr 1988-, State of Georgia Dept of Trans. *Publication:* A Study of Community Organization Techniques Utilized by Three Self-Help Projects in Securing Low-Income Involvement. *Memberships include:* Intl Platform Assn; Nat Tech Assn; So Ctr for Study of Intl Issues; Ctr for Study of Presidency; Nt Assn of Social Wkrs; Acad of Certified Social Wkrs; Am Fdn of Police. *Honours include:* Admiral of the GA Navy, Lt Col, Aide de Camp, Gov's Staff; Presidential Cit, Clark Coll; One of Five Outstg Young Men of Atlanta by Atlanta Jaycees; NASW Awd for Social Action; Nat Urban Leag Fellowship. *Hobbies:* Reading; Listening to music;

Walking; Travelling; Sport activities. *Address:* 87 Burbank Drive NW, Atlanta, GA 30314, USA.

DEAN Sonya Velika, b. 21 Nov 1969, Atlanta, GA, USA. Tchr. Cashier; Asst Mgr. *Education:* BA, Spelman Coll, 1991. *Appointments:* Summer Intern, Georgia Dept of Agri, 1986-89; Tchr Asst, Spelman Coll Nursery, 1990; Cashier; Asst Mgr, Soul Source Bookstore, 1990- . *Memberships:* Friendship Bapt Ch; Nat Ed Assn; Friendship of Leag; Hunters Hill; Vols Against Crime; NAACP Urban Leag. *Honours:* David Watts Ednl Scholar, Nat Hons Soc, Dean's List, Spelman Coll. *Hobbies:* Reading; Walking; Travelling; Listening to music; Sewing. *Address:* 87 Burbank Drive NW, Atlanta, GA 30314, USA.

DEAN Vyvyan Coleman, b. 6 Nov 1945, Fort Benning, GA, USA. Edr. m. James E Dean, 6 Dec 1966, 2 d. *Education:* BA, Clark Coll, 1966; MA, Atlanta Univ, 1973. *Appointments:* Tchr, Atlanta Public Sch System, 1966- ; Dir of Summer Reading Prog, John F Kennedy Middle Sch Media Ctr, 1986; Tchr, Atlanta Metro Coll, 1988. *Memberships:* Christians in Action, Friendship Bapt Ch; Delta Sigma Theta Sorority; Gate City Day Nursery Aux; NAACP; GA Presch Assn; Dekalb Housing Res Com; GA Adult Lit Assn; Atlanta Fdn of Tchrs; The Inquirers Lit Club; Atlanta Circle Lets; The Decatur/Dekalb Drifters Interest Group; Vol, United Negro Coll Fund; Vol, Clark Coll Alumni Assn; Vol, NAACP Voter Registration. *Honours:* Spec Recog for Outstg Tchr of Chd in APS. *Hobbies:* Reading; Listening to music; Sports spectator. *Address:* 87 Burbank Drive NW, Atlanta, GA 30314, USA.

DEAN William George, b. 29 Nov 1921, Toronto, Canada. Prof of Geog. m. Elizabeth Elfveda Johnston, 18 Sept 1948, 1 s, 1 d. *Education:* BA Hons, Trinity Coll 1949, MA 1950, Univ of Toronto; PhD, McGill Univ, 1959. *Appointments:* Res Asst, Thelon R Keewatin, NWT, 1948; Res Geog, Intelligence, DND, 1949; Res Asst, Southampton, NWT, 1950; Asst Prof, United Coll, WPG, 1953-56; Asst, Full Prof, Univ of Toronto, 1956- 86. *Publications:* Economic Atlas of Ontario, 1969; Historical Atlas of Canada, 3 vols, 1979-93. *Memberships:* Am Assn of Geographers, 1951- 80; Rand Corp, Santa Monica, Res Conslt, 1954-1956; Canadian Assn of Geographers, 1955-57; Edit, The Canadian Geographer, 1960-67; Inst of Environmental Studies, Univ of Toronto, 1978-79. *Honours:* Trinity Coll Prize, 1949; Carnegie Arctic Res Fellow, 1950-52; US Nat Sci Fdn Fellow, 1963; Visiting Fellow, Univ Coll, Cambridge, 1969-70; Gold Medal, Leipzig, 1970, 1971; Pan Am Inst of Geographers & Hist, 1973; Sigma Xi, 1984; CAG Awd, 1985; Gold Medal, Royal Canadian Geog Soc, 1988; AAG Awd, 1990. *Hobbies:* Sailing; Curling; Music; Woodworking. *Address:* Department of Geography, University of Toronto, Toronto, Canada M5S 1A1.

DEAS Richard Ryder III, b. 19 Jan 1927, Birmingham, AL, USA. Prof of Music. *Education:* BFA in Mus, UNM, Albuqueque, 1949; BS 1949, MS 1951 in Piano, Julliard Sch of Music; EdD in Music & Music Ed, 1968. *Appointments:* Prof of Music, Bennett Coll, Millbrook, 1960-70; Prof of Music, UNC, Wilmington, 1970-. *Creative works:* Carnegie Recital Hall, 1964, 1968; The Unfinished Piano Sonatas of Pranz Shubert (Doct thesis); Presented recitals in Wilmington, performances with the Wilmington Symph Orch. *Memberships:* Pres Piano Sect 1977-79, Cape Fear Chapt, Pres, VP, Coor of Music Prog, N Carolina Music Tchrs Assn; AAUP. *Honour:* Albert Schueity Medal for Artistry, 1989. *Hobbies:* Travel; Languages. *Address:* 510 Upland Drive, Wilmington, NC 28405, USA.

DEBAKEY Lois, b. Lake Charles, LA, USA. Prof of Scientific Communication; Writer; Lectr; Edit; Scholar. *Education:* BA, MA, PhD, Tulane Univ. *Appointments:* Asst Prof, Eng, Tulane; Asst, Assoc, Prof, Scientific Communication, Tulane Med Sch, 1963-68; Lectr 1968- , Adj Prof 1981- , Prof Sci Comm, Baylor Coll of Med,

1968-. *Publications:* The Scientific Journal: Editorial Policies and Practices, 1976; Medicine: Preserving the Passion, 1987; Author of num articles in med and popular periodicals on scientific writing, publishing, editing, literacy, ethics. *Memberships incl:* Biomed Lib Reb Com 1973-77, Nat Lib of Med; Bd Regents 1982- 86, Conslt 1986-; Co-Chm, Permanent Paper Task Force, 1986-; Lit Selection Rev Com, 1992-93; Ed Bd, Jrnl AM Med Assn, Intl Angiology Excerpta Med Core Jrnls-Cardiology; Chm, Friends NLM Media Award; Usage Panel, Am Heritage Dict; Fellow, Am Coll of Med Informatics; Legal Writing Com, Conslt, ABA; Soc for Preservation of En Lang and Lit. *Honours:* Phi Beta Kappa; Dist'd Ser Awd, Am Med Writers Assn, 1970; Fellow, Roy Soc for Encouragement of Arts; Honorary Mem, Golden Key Nat Hon Soc, 1982; John P McGovern Awd, Med Lib Assn, 1983; Bausch and Lomb Sci Awd for outstg acad perf; Univ of Houston, Clear Lake Women's Assn Awd, Bay Area Med Wives, 1987. *Address:* Baylor College of Medicine, One Baylor Plaza, Houston, TX 77030, USA.

DEBAKEY Michael Ellis, b. 7 Sept 1908, Lakes Charles, LA, USA. Prof; Chm, Dept of Surg; Chancellor. m. Katrin Fehlhaber, 4 s, 1 d. *Education:* BS 1930, MD 1932, MS 1935, Tulane Univ. *Appointments:* Instr, Dept of Surg 1937-40, Asst Prof 1940-46, Assoc Prof 1940- 46, Tulane Univ; Prof, Chm, Dept of Surg, Baylor Coll of Med, 1948-; Pres 1969- 79; Chancellor, 1979-. *Publications include:* The Living Heart, 1977; The Living Heart Diet, 1984; Over 1200 articles in profl journs, textbooks, public press. *Memberships include:* RSM; Acad of Med Scis, USSR; Hon FRCS; Pres 1983, Assn of Intl Vascular Surgs; Pres 1990, So Surg Assn. *Honours incl:* USSR Acad of Sci 50th Anniv Jubilee Medal, 1973; Am Surg Assn Dist'd Ser Awd, 1981; Nat Medal of Sci, 1987; Acad of Surg Res Markowitz Awd, 1988; Am Soc of Mec Engrs Michael DeBakey Medal, first issue, 1989; Univ of Strasbourg Medal of Hon, 1990.

DEBAKEY Selma, b. Lake Charles, LA, USA. Prof of Scientific Communicaiton; Writer; Editor; Lecturer. *Education:* BA Languages, Newcomb Coll and Postgrad Studies, Tulane Univ, New Orleans. *Appointments:* Dir, Dept of Med Communication, Alton Oschner Med Foun, New Orleans, 1942-68; Prof of Scientific Communication, Baylor Coll of Med, Houston, Texas, 1968-. *Publications:* Current Concepts in Breast Cancer, Co-author, 1967; Numerous articles on scientific writing. *Memberships:* Bd of Dirs, numerous comms, American Med Writers Assoc; Assoc of Teachers of Tech Writing; Training in Sci Writing Comm, Council of Biology Editors; Soc of Tech Communication; Soc for Health and Human Values; Comm on Judges, Modern Med Monograph Awds; Judge, AORN DuPuy Writers Awd; American Assoc for the Advancement of Sci; Consultant Nat Assoc of Standard Medical Vocabulary; Former Editor: Cardiovascular Res Cancer Bulletin, Oschner Clinic Reports, and Selected Writings from the Oschner Clinic. *Address:* Baylor College of Medicine, One Baylor Plaza, Houston, TX 77030, USA. 5, 7, 15, 52, 125, 129, 130, 143, 155, 156.

DEBRECZENI Attila, b. 9 Nov 1959, Debrecen, Hungary. Sr Lectr. m. Andrea Kerekes, 7 May 1983, 2 s, 1 d. *Education:* BA 1984, PhD 1987, Klte Debrecen. *Appointments:* Asst Lectr 1984-90, Sr Lectr 1990-, Dept of Old Hungarian Lit, Univ of Arts and Scis, Debrecen. *Publications:* Mihaly Csokonai's Prose Fiction, 1990; Mihaly Csokonai Vitez, 1992. *Memberships:* Intl Soc for Eighteenth-Century Studies; Intl Assn of Hungarian Studies; Hungarian and European Age of Enlightenment and Romanticism. *Hobbies:* Theatre; Cinema; Excursion; Tennis. *Address:* Kossuth Lajos University, Institute of Literature, 4010 Debrecen, PO Box 52, Egyetem Square 1, Hungary.

DECHENNE James Allen, b. 7 Jan 1943, Centralia, IL, USA. Edr. m. Doris Jane Easley, 17 Apr 1964, 2 d. *Education:* AA, Kaskaskia Com Coll, 1968; BS 1970,

MS 1971, So Illinois Univ; EdD, Virginia Polytech Inst and State Univ, 1976. *Appointments:* Grad Tchg Asst, Instructional Mat(s) Dept, Coll of Ed, So Illinois Univ, 1970-71; Instructional Mat(s) Dir, Illini Jr High Sch, Jerseyville, 1971-72; Dist Media Dir, Carlyle (IL) Unit Sch Dist, 1972-74; Grad Tchg Asst, Virginia Polytech Inst and State Univ, 1975-76; Asst Prof, Coll of Ed, Kansas State Univ, 1976-78; Dir of Curr and Instructional Devel, Oklahoma City Com Coll, 1978-; Adj Prof of Ednl Tech (Grad Fac), Univ of Oklahoma, 1980-88. *Publications include:* Study Indicates Kansas Teachers Lack a Working Knowledge of the New Copyright Law, 1978; Let Microcomputers Cure Your Scheduling Headaches (with B Evans), 1982; Educating Incarcerated Students Through Technology, 1982-83; Reaching Out with Cable Television to New Student Populations (with B Gellman-Buzin), 1983; Computer Authoring Systems: Things to Consider, 1984-85. *Membership:* Assn for Ednl Communications and Tech. *Honour:* Federally Funded Doct Fellowship Grant, 1974. *Hobbies:* Reading; Jogging; Backpacking. *Address:* Oklahoma City Community College, 7777 South May Avenue, Oklahoma City, OK 73159, USA.

DECKER Dorothy Sexton, b. 29 Nov 1922, Albany, Shackleford Co, TX, USA. Libn; Public Sch. m. Clifton Henry Decker, 21 Feb 1942, 1 s, 2 d. *Education:* BA, Sul Ross Univ, 1957-60; Mast Lib Ser, North Texas State Univ, Denton. *Memberships:* Pres 4 yrs, Federated Womens Club; Pres 4 yrs, Texas Classroom Tchrs Assn; Pres 4 yrs, Texas State Tchrs Assn; Delta Kappa Gamma; Daughters of the Repub of Texas; Nat Assn for Picpetation and Preservation of Storytelling; Texas Libn Assn. *Honours:* Am Studies Scholarship, 1964; Delta Kappa Gamma Summer Scholarship, 1968; Bd of Dir, C of C, 1976-77; Outstg Citizen by Area C of C, 1980; State Com Person for Texas State Tchrs Assn 1984-85, Texas Lib Assn 1989-91; Appt Gov A Richard to Texas Schs Assembly, 1991. *Hobbies:* Travel; Reading; Gardening; Politics; Church work; Community service. *Address:* 506 SW 14th Street, Seminole, TX 79360, USA.

DEEIK Khalil George, b. 12 Nov 1937, Bethlehem, Jordan. Fac Mem; Prog Dir. m. Jalileh Mary Marzouka, 22 Aug 1965, 3 s. *Education:* BA, Sacramento State Univ, 1961; MA 1964, PhD 1972, Univ of So California. *Education:* Prin Admr, Manzanita Sch, California, 1964-65; Mgr, Gen Trading Co, Al-Khobar, Saudia Arabia, 1966-69; Prog Dir, Instr, Krebs Coll, N Hollywood, 1969-72; Mng Dir, VP, Sr Advr, Exec Asst to the Chm, The Olyan Group, 1973-; Fac Mem, Prog Dir, Century Univ, California, 1978-; Exec Com Mem, Saudi Arabian Constrn & Repair Sers Co, Jeddah, 1984-85; Bd of Dir, Saudi Polyester Prods, Jeddah, 1984-85. *Publications:* Author of several incentive plans, sales and marketing programs for different companies. *Membership:* VP 1970-73, Intl Edrs' Assn; Am Biographic Inst Res Assn's Bd of Govs, Adv Coun. *Address:* PO Box 8772, Riyadh 11492, Saudi Arabia.

DEGNER Robert Louis, b. 20 Jan 1942, Malone, TX, USA. Prof. m. Janet Louise Dunphy, 29 May 1976, 3 s, 1 d. *Education:* AA, Navarro Coll, 1961; BS 1963, MS 1970, PhD 1974, Texas A & M Univ. *Appointments:* Asst Cty Agri Agent, Texas Agri Ext Ser, 1963-67; Res Assoc 1971-74, Asst Prof 1974-76, Texas A & M Univ; Asst Prof 1976-81, Assoc Prof 1981-86, Prof 1986-, Univ of Florida; Dir, FL Ag Mkt, 1982-. *Publications:* Author of over 130 scientific reports and articles to profl journs. *Memberships:* Pres 1986-87, Food Distribution Res Soc; Am Ag Econ Assn; So Ag Econ Assn; Am Mktg Assn. *Honours:* Dist'd Student, Texas A & M Univ, 1962, 1963; Wall St Journ Student Achmt Awd, 1963; Nat Def Ed Act Fellowship 1967-70; Honorary Dir, Florida Dairy Prods Assn, 1985-; Past Pres's Awd, Food Distribution Res Soc, 1987. *Hobbies:* Antique cars; Woodworking. *Address:* 2842 NW 28th Place, Gainesville, FL 32605, USA.

DEGUILLAUME Jean-Charles, b. 23 July 1949, Paris, France. Biophysicist. m. Marie-Claude Lavedrine, 12 May 1979, 1 s, 1 d. *Education:* BS 1967; Superior Math degree, 1968; Spec Math degree, 1969; Res, various hosps, Paris, 1970-78; MD, PhD, Univ of Paris, 1977. *Appointments:* Phlebology and Biophysics. *Publication:* Fluid Mechanisms for Biologists. *Contributions to:* Articles to scientific journs. *Memberships:* French Soc for Biophysics; French Soc for Phlebology; French Soc for Angiology. *Honours:* Thesis Prize, 1977; Honorary Maj, French Hlth Forces, 1988. *Hobbies:* History of mathematics and medicine; Mathematical games; Piano. *Address:* 12 Avenue des Sapins, 95290 L'Isle-Adam, France.

DEL BUONO Vincent, b. 16 May 1949, Casacalenda, Italy. Law Reformer. m. Jennifer Pothier, 26 June 1976. *Education:* BA, Glendon Coll, 1972; MA 1974, LLB 1975, LLM 1976, Univ of Toronto; Alberta Bar, 1977. *Appointments:* Asst Prof, McGill Univ, Montreal, 1977-80; Conslt, Law Reform Comm of Canada, 1980-82; Sr Counsel, Dept of Justice, Canada, 1982-91; Adj Prof in Law, Sch of Grad Studies, Univ of Ottawa, 1982-; Pres, Intl Ctr for Crim Law Reform, Crim Justice Policy, Vancouver, 1991-. *Membership:* Fdr, Pres, Soc for Reform of Crim Law, 1987-. *Honours:* Duff- Rinfret Scholar in Law, 1975; Mem, Drafting Team, New Crim Code for Canada, Law Reform Comm of Canada, 1984-86. *Hobbies:* History; Music. *Address:* 19 Coupal Street, Ottawa, Ont, Canada K1L 6A2.

DEL MAR Michael. b. 6 June 1946, Chalfont St Giles, England. Stock Broker. m. Anthea Noel Van Der Gucht, 9 Jan 1971, 3 s. *Education:* 1st BSc Hons, Birmingham Univ, 1965-68. *Appointments:* Metallurgist, de Beer, 1968-71; L Messel & Co 1971 which became Shearson Lehman -1990; S G Warburg, 1990. *Membership:* City Club. *Hobbies:* Fishing; Shooting; Tennis; Reading; Gardening. *Address:* Avenue Farm, Herriard, Hampshire RG25 2PP, England.

DELANEY Cornelius Francis, b. 30 June 1938, Waterbury, CT, USA. Univ Prof. m. Helen Prescott, 17 Aug 1962, 1 s. *Education:* MA, Boston Coll, 1962; PhD, St Louis Univ, 1967. *Appointment:* Prof, Univ of Notre Dame, 1967-. *Publications:* Mind and Nature, 1969; The Synoptic Vision, 1977; Rationality and Religions Belief, 1979; Science and Reality, 1984; Science, Knowledge and Mind, 1992. *Memberships:* Exec Com, Am Philosophical Assn, 1983-85; Pres, Am Cath Philosophical Assn, 1985; Pres, C S Peirce Soc, 1986. *Honours:* Madden Awd for Tchg, 1974; Bicentennial Awd, 1976; Pres Awd, 1984; Sheedy Awd for Tchg, 1987. *Hobby:* Tennis. *Address:* Philosophy Department, University of Notre Dame, Notre Dame, IN 46556, USA.

DELANEY Robert Vincent, b. 1 Oct 1934, NYC, NY, USA. Conslt in Ofc Devel. m. Marie Josephine Monaco, 13 Oct 1956, 4 s, 1 d. *Education:* BS, Fordham Univ. *Appointments:* Various positions incl: VP 1980, Sr VP 1987, Group Sr VP, Chief Adm Ofcr 1989, Brooklyn Union Gas Co. *Publications:* Tech articles. *Memberships:* Bd of Dirs of: Queens Overall Ec Devel Conponation; Queens Symph Orch; New York Hall of Sci; Harvard Bus Sch Club of NY; NY State Bd of Profl Engrg; Chm, Greater Jamaica Devel Conponation Bd of Dir. *Honours:* Beta Gamma Sigma Hon Soc, Fordham Univ; Am Gas Assn Awd of Merit; Awd of NY State Soc of Profl Engrs; Am Red Cross; Queens Symph Orch; Queens Child Guidance Conp. *Hobbies:* Tennis; Opera; Fishing. *Address:* 133 Locust Road, Garden City, NY 11530, USA.

DELEKTA Eugeniusz, b. 8 Sept 1946, Maziarnia, Nisko, Poland. Pract in artistic graphic, easel painting. Edr. m. Olga Trzeciak, 4 Sept 1971, 2 s. *Education:* MA, Acad of Art, Katowice, 1972. *Career:* Asst, Graphic Arts Fac, Cracow Fine Arts Acad, Katowice Br, 1972-78; Dr, Lectr, Artistic Pedagogical Fac, Br in Cieszyn 1987-, Docent, Silesian Univ, Katowice. *Creative works include:* Individual exhibitions of graphic painting: 42 in Poland, 2 abroad; Participated in over 100 all-Polish exhibitions, over 40 exhibitions of Polish art aborad and intl exhibitions incl: Cracow, Katowice 1980, 1984; Ibiza, Baden-Baden 1981; London-Oxford 1983; Budapest 1985, 1989; Lublin-Majdanek 1988; Menton 1990. *Publications:* Monographic works and catalogues published together with individual exhibitions; 3 monographic films presented by Polish TV, 1978, 1989, 1990. *Honours include:* 3rd prize, 1st Nat Graphic Competition, 1975; 3rd prize, People's Poland 30th Anniv Exhibition, 1975; 2nd prize, 3rd Polish-Finnish Marine Art Competition, 1979; 2nd prize, VIII All-Polish Painting Exhibition, 1980; 1st prize, All-Polish Graphic Competition, Source, 1986. *Hobbies:* History of art; Historical literature. *Address:* ul Zywiecka 252, 43-310 Bielsko-Biala, Poland.

DELEU Jozef Hugo Maria, b. 20 Apr 1937, Roeselare. Author; Publisher. m. Annemarie Deblaere, 22 Oct 1960, 2 s, 1 d. *Appointments:* Fdr, Edit-in-Chief, Ons Erfdeel, 1957; Tchr, Moeskroen & Menen, 1960-70; Co-fdr, Dep Mgr, The Flemish-Netherlands Foun, Stichting Ons Erfdeel, 1970; Fdr, Edit-in-Chief, Septentrion, 1972; Fdr, Edit-in-Chief, De Franse Nederlanden/Les Pays-Bas Francais, 1976; Founder, Ed-in-Chief, series of brochures in 15 different languages about the language and culture of Flanders, Netherlands, 1981; Founder, Editor-in-chief, The Low Countries; Arts and Society in Flanders and the Netherlands, 1993. *Publications include:* De handen voor de bruid, 1979; Lees maar, 1980; Frans-Vlaanderen, 1982; Tekenen van tijd, 1984; De hazen aan de kim, 1985; Groot Gezinsverzenboek, 1985; Vlaams Leesboek, 1986; Nooit zag ik eerder, 1987; Citoyen de la Frontiere, 1988; Een beetje Columbus zijn, 1989; Voorbij de grens, Lyrisch proza, 1990. *Memberships:* Maatschappij van de Nederlandse Letteren; Zuidnederlandse Maatschappij voor taal, letterkunde en gechiedenis, Brussels; Pres, kommissie letteren van de provinciale kultuurraad van West-Vlaanderen. *Honours include:* Zilveren Medaille Robert Schuman, Metz, Frankrijk, 1973; G H's Gravesande-prijs van de Jan Campert Stichting, 1981; Lieven Gevaert-prijs, Antwerpen, 1989; Grote Cultuurprijs van Oost- Vlaanderen, 1989. *Address:* Stichting Ons Erfdeel VZW, Murissonstraat 260, 8931 Rekkem, Belgium.

DELIDES George, b. 14 Sept 1936, Athens, Greece. Prof of Path. m. Alice Eleftheriades, 2 s. *Education:* MB CHB, Univ of Athens Med Sch, 1961; MD, Univ of Athens, 1969. *Appointments:* Asst, Dept of Path 1963, Sr Lectr 1973, Asst Prof 1975, Univ of Athens; Registrar, 1965; Lectr, 1968; Lectr, Univ of Sheffield, 1970; Hd, Dept of Path, Metaxas Cancer Inst, 1975; Scientific Dir, Metaxas Cancer Inst of Pireus, 1982-85; Prof of Path, Univ of Crete Med Sch, 1990. *Publications:* Author of 2 monographs, 2 books, over 100 papers in scientific journs. *Memberships:* Br Soc of Path, 1971; ACP; European Soc of Path, 1980; Pres 1986-90, Hell Soc of Path; Gen Secy, Hell Cancer Soc, 1987; Scientific Coun, ESP, 1990; Coun, Intl Union Against Cancer, 1990. *Hobby:* Sailing. *Address:* University of Crete Medical School, Department of Pathology, Stavrakia, Heraclion, Crete, Greece.

DELLINGER Charles Wade, b. 25 Feb 1949, Lincolnton, NC, USA. Sr Min. m. Lynn Baxter, 20 July 1969, 1 s, 1 d. *Education:* AA 1969, BA 1971, Gardner-Webb Coll; Master of Divinity, Southeastern Bapt Theological Sem, 1975; Dr of Ministry, 1983. *Appointments:* Pastor, Roseland Bapt Ch, Lincolnton, 1968-71; Pastor, Temple Bapt, Gastonia, 1971-74; Pastor, Mulls Mem Bapt, Shelby, 1974-87; Sr Min, Old Town Bapt, Winston-Salem, 1987-. *Publications:* Personal Reflections; A Study in Theodicy: A Preventive Tool in Grief Ministry. *Memberships:* Am Assn of Pastoral Counsellors; Chm Eagle Bd of Review, Boy Scouts of Am; Moderator, Kings Mountain Bapt Assn, 1985-87; Chm of Cooperative Min Com, Bapt State Conv of NC; Bd of Assocs, Gardner-Webb Coll. *Honours:* Appointed to State Prison Comm, 1986; Dist'd Ser Awd, Boy Scouts of Am, 1990. *Hobbies:* Hunting; Fishing; Softball; Writing poetry; Gardening. *Address:* 1625 Turfwood Drive, Pfafftown, NC 27040, USA.

DEMARAY Leonard Allen, b. 23 Aug 1946, Chicago, IL, USA. Ret'd Mil; Conslt. m. Renee Hartley, 20 Aug 1990. *Education:* Assoc of Sci 1977, AA 1978, BSc 1980, Univ of the State of New York; Assoc of Applied Sci, Univ of Alaska, 1979; Assoc of Applied Sci, Pikes Peak Com Coll, 1981; Assoic of Sci 1981, BSc 1982, Regis Coll; BSc, So Illinois Univ, 1983; Assoc, Ctl Texas Coll, 1987; currently working on a dual Master degree prog, Webster Univ. *Appointments:* Entered US Army 1963, discharged 1970, re-entered active duty 1972, ret'd in 1991 as Logistics Sgt. *Memberships:* Life Mem of: Nat Geographic Soc; NRA; Veterans of Foreign Wars; Am Assn of Individual Investors; Nat Trappers Assn; Fur Harvesters of Tennessee; Alaska Trappers Assn. *Honours include:* Silver Star W/1 OLC; Dist'd Flying Cross w/3 OLC; Meritorious Ser Medal; Army Commendation Medal w/V w/7 OLC; Good Conduct Medal w/8th Awd; Armed Forces Expeditionary Medal; NCO Profl Devel Medal w/3; Republic of Vietnam Campaign Medal w/60 device; Parachute Badge. *Hobbies:* Flying and sport parachuting; Working with computers; Hunting and trapping. *Address:* PO Box 13170, El Paso, TX 79913, USA.

DENG Jingyang, b. 5 May 1916, Quangdong, China. Reschr. m. Yongyi Huang, 20 Oct 1948. *Education:* Dr of Natural Sci, Geneva Univ, Switzerland, 1959. *Appointments:* Sr Reschr, Chinese Acad of Agricultural Scis, 1960-; Hd of a res group of 120 members in China, 1981-. *Publications:* Taigu Genic Male-Sterile Wheat (Edit), 1987. *Memberships:* Genetics Assn, China; Cereal Assn, China. *Honours:* Foreign Mem, Acad of Agri of France, 1989; Hon Mention, Rolex Awds for Enterprise, 1990; Exec Com Mem, Sci & Tech Comm, CAAS; Local Com Mem, 8th Intl Wheat Genetics Symp, will be held in Beijing, 1993. *Hobbies:* Reading; Photography; Gardening; Tourism. *Address:* c/o Institute of Crop Breeding and Cultivation, Chinese Academy of Agricultural Sciences, 30 Bai Shi Qiao Lu, Beijing 100081, China.

DENG Weizhi, b. 10 Nov 1938, Anhui Province, P R China. Prof. m. Yaoxin Zhang, 26 Feb 1968, 1 d. *Education:* Economy and Trade Dept, Shanghai Fin and Economy Inst, Shanghai, 1956-60. *Appointments:* Res trainee, Shanghai Social Sci Inst, 1960-62; Reschr, Edit, East China Bur, 1962-78; Edit, China Ency Publishing Hse, 1978-88; Prof, Shanghai Social Sci Inst, 1988-; concurrent Prof in Pedagogical Univ of East China and 5 other Universities. *Publications include:* Various Aspects of Family Life, 1983; Awakening of Life, 1985; Tomorrow's Family, 1986; The Evolution of Chinese Families, 1987. *Memberships:* Standing Com, China Social Sci Assn; Vice Chm, Shanghai Social Sci Assn; Vice Chm, China Assn for Promoting Democracy; Hd, Shanghai Overseas Chinese Economy Study Inst. *Honours:* Chosen as one of the Ten Figures in Shanghai who made the headlines in Cultural World, 1986; Prize for excellent prog host for the broadcast, Deng Weizhi Post Box; Awded excellent reading prize 10 times. *Hobbies:* Calligraphy; Painting; Travel; Playing ping-pong. *Address:* Room 593, No 7, Lane 622, Huai-hai Zhong Road, Shanghai Social Science Institute, Shanghai 200020, China.

DENG Yu-Cheng, b. 4 May 1930, Jiangin City, Jiangsu Province, China. Prof. m. Ji-Fang Chui, 5 Aug 1962, 2 d. *Education:* Bachelor, Beijing Agricultural Univ, 1954. *Appointments:* Res Asst, Asst Prof, Assoc Prof 1954-89, Prof 1989-, Inst of Applied Ecol; Ldr of Phytochemistry Group and Res Projs for 33 years. *Creative works:* Introduced oil plant Chufa (Cyperus esculentus) into 14 Provinces, 1962-65; Studies on Evening Primrose (Oenothera biennis L) Oil as an Antihyperlipemia Med (Soft Capsules), 1980-86; Relationship Between the Fatty Acids and Plant Taxa, 1987. *Memberships:* Scientific Coun 1982-, Acad Degree Coun 1987-, Inst of Applied Ecol, Academia Sinica, 1982-; Phytochemistry Sci Coun, Chinese Botanical Soc, 1984-. *Honours:* The Oil Plants of Northeast China and Analytic Methods of Composition was awded the 3rd Class Prize of Natural Sci of

Academia Sinica, 1981; The Oil Plants in China was awded the 2nd Class Prize of Natural Sci of Academia Sinica, 1990 and the 3rd Class Prize of the Nat 5th Natural Sci, 1991; Studies on Evening Primrose (Oenothera biennis L). *Hobbies include:* Touring by bicycle; Sketching; Playing piano. *Address:* Department of Plant Resource ad Phytochemistry, Institute of Applied Ecology, Academia Sinica, 72 Wenhua Road, Shenyang 110015, China.

DENG Zaijun, b. 26 Jan 1937, Sichuan, China. Sr Scenarist; Dir. m. Erjun Zhou, 30 Jan 1958, 1 s, 3 d. *Education:* China Cinema Coll, Beijing, 1986. *Appointments:* Singer, Dancer, Leading Actress, Army Cultural Troupe, 1950-59; Dir, Dir in Chief, Sr Scenarist, Dir, CCTV, 1959-; Honorary Prof, Joint Arts Acad, Shanxi Univ of Sci & Tech, 1987. *Creative works:* The East is Red, 1964; Flowers and Songs, 1982; Wish You a Good Health, 1984; Performance on Spring's Festival Eve, 1987, 1988; Opening and Closing Ceremony of the 11th Asian Games, 1990. *Memberships:* China TV Art Comm; China Assn for Musicians; China Assn for Dancers; China Assn for TV Art; China Assn for Vocal Music of Minority Nationalities. *Honours:* Spec Awd, China State Univ, Affairs Comm, 1980; Commendation, Min of Radio and TV, China, 1984; Best Prog Awd, Scenario & Directing Awd, The First Star Light Awd for TV Art, 1987; Spec Awd, 2nd, 3rd, 4th Star Light Awd for TV Art, 1988, 1990, 1991. *Hobbies:* Cooking; Swimming; Painting. *Address:* Art Department, CCTV, 11 Fuxing Road, Beijing 100859, China.

DENHAM Bertram Stanley Mitford, Lord, b. 3 Oct 1927, Weston Underwood, England. Pear of the Realm. m. Jean McCorquodale, 14 Feb 1956, 3 s, 1 d. *Education:* BA, Kings Coll, Cambridge. *Appointments:* Lord in waiting to HM The Queen, 1961-64, 1970-72; Capt of the Yeoman of the Guard, 1972-74; Capt of the Gartar at Arms, 1979-91. *Publications:* The Man Who Lost His Shadow, 1979; Two Thy R Des, 1983; Fox Hunt, 1987. *Honours:* Priory Cmdr, 1981; KBE, 1991. *Hobbies:* Field sports. *Address:* The Laundry Cottage, Weston Underwood, Olney, Buckinghamshire, England.

DENIKER Pierre G, b. 16 Feb 1917, Paris, France. Prof of Psych. m Nadine Vincent, 6 Dec 1941, 2 d. *Education:* MD, 1945; Hd Physn, Psychiatric Hosps, 1949; Prof-agrege, Neuropsych, 1961; Chef de Service, St Anne Hosp, 1962. *Appointments:* Prof of Psych, 1971-85; Mbr, Acad of Med, 1982. *Publications:* Methodes chimitherapiques en psychiatrie, w Jean Delay, 1962; La Psychopharmacologies, 1966; Le Maniement des Medicaments Psychotropes, 1980; Precis de psychiatrie de l'adulte, w T Lemperiere and J Guyotat, 1990; La Depression. Fin du Tunnel, 1987; Les Drogues. Trafic et Contagion, 1988. *Memberships:* Royal Acad of Belgium; Acad of Catalonia; Soc of Therapeutics, Pres, 1971; Soc Psychological Med, Pres, 1985; Fndr Mbr and Past Pres, 1974-76, Int Coll of Psychopharmacology; Disting Fellow, American Psych Assn; Congres de Psychiatrie et Neurologies de Langue Francaise, Pres, 1984; Pres, Fondation de l'Association Francaise de Psychologie Biologique, 1974. *Honours:* Croix de Guerre, 1939-45; Prix Lasker, 1957; Legion d'Honneur, 1964; Ordre du Merite, 1968. *Hobby:* Yachting. *Address:* 17 rue de la Ville l'Eveque, F 75008 Paris, France. 91.

DENISOVA Raisa, b. 30 Aug 1930, Latvia. Scist; Phy Anthropology. m. Mirons Margulis, 28 Jan 1958. *Education:* Dr of Biol 1958; PhD 1973. *Appointments:* Scientific Wkr, Dept of Archaeology 1957-84, Chief of Lab of Phy Anthropology 1985-, Inst of Latvian Hist. *Publications:* Physical Anthropology of Ancient Balts, 1975; Ethnogenesis of Latvians, 1977; Bronze Age Cemetary of Kivutkalns (with J Graudonis, R Gravers), 1985; Physical Anthropology of Latvians and Lithuanians; Over 100 scientific articles. *Honours:* The Best Books, Latvian Acad of Scis, 1977, 1979. *Hobbies:* Gardening; Reading; Sports. *Address:* Latvian Academy of Sciences, 19 Turgenev Street, Riga 226524, Latvia.

DENKTAS Rauf Raif, b. 27 Jan 1924, Paphos, Cyprus. Pres, Turkish Republic of Northern Cyprusm. m. Aydin Munir, 17 July 1949, 2 s, 2 d. *Education:* Barrister-at-Law, Lincoln's Inn, London, England, 1947. *Appointments include:* Private law pract, 1947-49; Law Ofcr, Atty Gen's Ofc, Acting Solicitor Gen, 1949-57; Orgr, resistance to Cyprus unification with Greece, as Chm, Fdn of Turkish Assns, 1957; Est'd Turkish resistance movement, organised aid to refugees; Ldr, Turkish Cypriot delegation, various confs on future of Cyprus, UN; Represented Turkish Cypriots (& Greek Cypriots, on refusal of Greek Cypriot advocates to act), Supreme Constitutional Ct; Defender, communal rights; Pres, Turkish Communal Chamber, 1960-68, re-elected to 1973; Pres, Turkish Federated State of Cyprus, 1975-83, Turkish Republic of Northern Cyprus, 1983-; Cont'g assistance of all kinds to refugees, particularly in Northern Cyprus; Arranged agreement with Greek Cypriots, voluntary population exc (half Turkish Cypriot population), 1975; Rehabilitated nearly 65,000 Turkish Cypriots; Undertook welfare, 2,000 orphan chd. *Publications include:* Secrets of Happiness, 1941, 4th ed 1981; Hell Without Fire, 1943; Cyprus Problem, 1969; Talking with Youth, 1980; Cyprus Triangle, 1981. *Membership:* Turkish Cypriot Bar Assn. *Honours include:* Honorary PhD, Middle East Tech Univ, Ankara, Turkey, 1984. *Hobby:* Photography. *Address:* President's Office, Lefkosa, c/o Mersin 10, Turkey. 1, 12, 34, 52, 152.

DENNY Edward Joseph, b. 20 Nov 1962, Glasgow, Scotland. Chef; Co Dir. m. Alison Sheila Macintyre Denny, 1 s. *Education:* HCE, Macleod Tech Coll, Melbourne, Australia; City & Guilds, Newry Catering Coll, 1979-82; Dip Hlth & Hygiene, Leeds Polytech, 1989. *Appointments:* L'Auberge, Edinburgh, 1982-83; Chef; Dir, Box Tree Restaurant, Ikley, 1984-; Le Gouroche, London, Roux rests; Le Moulin de Mougins, 1991, Roger Verge. *Honours:* Recipient of: Egon Ronay Rosette; AA Rosette; Rosette Michelin; 4/5 for Cooking, Good Food Guide; Student of the Year, Newry Coll, 1980; Awd of Distn. *Hobbies:* Cooking; Reading; Eating out; Spending time with wife and son; Meeting people. *Address:* 20 Cambridge Drive, Otley, West Yorkshire LS21 1DD, England.

DENT Edward Eugene, b. 14 Oct 1948, Charleston, WV, UA. Mfg - Textile Fibres. m. Karen Sue Smith, 21 Nov 1968, 2 s. *Education:* BA cum laude (with hons), West Virginia Inst of Tech, 1973; MA, Virginia State Univ, 1988. *Appointments:* US Army: 1st Inf Div, Vietnam, V Corps, Germany, 1967-69; Union Carbide Corp, 1971-72; Bus Mgr, Broyhill Fond, Strosnider Chevrolet, 1973-78; Adm, Brown & Root, 1978-80; Mfg 1981-, Union Ofcl 1989-91, DuPont Co, Richmond. *Publication:* Race Relations in Hopewell Virginia: 1635-1932. *Memberships:* Treas 1972-73, Phi Alpha Theta, WV Tech; Alpha Chi - WVIT; WV Tech Alumni Assn; VA State Univ, Chesterfield Alumni, Public Relat Ofcr, Histn; So Historical Assn; Soc of the First Div; The Am Legion. *Honours:* Combat Infantry Badge; Vietnam Ser Medals and Ribbons; Army Commendation Medals with Clusters; Presidential Unit Cits; DuPont Corp Recog Awd for Envir Commitment. *Hobbies:* Reading; Writing; Relic hunting; Genealogical research; Travelling. *Address:* 1105 Walnut Drive, Chester, VA 23831, USA.

DESCAMPS Johan Jozef Arthur, b. 26 Apr 1951, Roeselare. Quality Control Virology. m. Cludts Maria, 1 s, 2 d. *Education:* Chem Engrg, Industrial Biol and Microbiol, Univ of Leuven, Belgium; Grad in Informatics, Leuven; Mgmt Devel Cert, Univ of Nebraska, Lincoln; Master in Management, Univ of Brussels, Belgium. *Appointments:* Asst Virology, Univ of Leuven, 1975-80; Res Asst, Yale Univ, 1980-81; RD Smith Kline, Rixensart, Belgium, 1981-85; Norden Labs, Lincoln, 1985-86; Smith Kline Beecham, 1986-. *Publications:* Author and Co-author of articles in Virology, Antivirals, Bacteriology. *Memberships:* Belgian Immunulogical Soc; Belgian Biochem Soc; Am Soc of Microbiol. *Hobbies:* Reading; Photography; Sports. *Address:* 89 Rue de l'Institut, B- 1330 Rixensart, Belgium.

DESOMOGYI Aileen Ada, b. 26 Nov 1911, London, England. Ret'd Libn. m. (1) Leslie Kuti, dec, (2) Joseph DeSomogyi, dec. *Education:* BA Hist 1936, MA 1939, Royal Holloway Coll, Univ of London; Assoc, Lib Assn, 1946; MALS, Univ of Western Ontario, Canada, 1971; Cert, Archival Principles & Adm, Carleton Univ, Ottawa, 1969; Dipl, Computer Programming, Career Learning Ctr, Toronto, 1980. *Appointments:* Libn, spec & public libs, England, 1943-66; Sr Instr, Eng, Nat Coal Bd, 1956-57; Staff, Lawson Mem Lib, Univ of Western Ontario, Canada, 1966-71; Cataloguer, Cooperative Book Ctr of Canada, 1971; Staff, East York Public Lib, Ontario, 1971-74; Mgr, Mgmt & Info Sers Lib, Ontario Min of Govt Sers, 1975-78; Libn, Sperry Univac Toronto Ctl Lib, 1980-81. *Contributions to:* Canadian Lib Journ; Sch ib Journ; Am Libs; Studies in Islam. *Memberships include:* Canadian Org for Devel through Ed, Canadian Wildlife Fdn; Consumers Assn; Eng Speaking Unino; Intl Platform Assn; Biographical Assns. *Honours:* Represented Univ of Western Ontario, World Conf on Records, Salt Lake City, UT, 1969; Nat Bd of Advrs, Am Biographical Assn; Dep Gov, ABI Res Assn; Medals, ABI, 1985, 1986, 1987; Dep Dir Gen, IBC; IBC World Decoration of Excellence, 1989; ABI 1990; Silver Medal of Cong, 1990. *Hobbies:* Reading; Travel; Work for animals; Collecting plates. *Address:* 9 Bonnie Brae Boulevard, Toronto, Ontario, Canada M4J 4N3.

DEUTSCH Antonia Sara, b. 24 June 1957, England. Photog. m. Colin David Guy Robinson, 31 May 1980, 1 s. *Membership:* AFAEP. *Honours:* Silver Awd 1989, Gold & Merit Awds 1991, AFAEP; Print of the Year, Ilford Ltd, 1989. *Hobbies:* Independent travel; Family; Photography; Contemporary British art. *Address:* 14A Hesper Mews, London SW5 0HH, England.

DEVANE John Anthony, b. 17 Aug 1954, Blackpool, England. Artist. m. Jane Anne Cross, 7 Oct 1988, 1 d. *Education:* BA Hons, Liverpool Polytech, 1972-75; MA, Royal Coll of Art, 1977-80. *Appointments:* Pt- time Lectr: Falmouth Sch of Art 1980-82, N Staffordshire Polytech 1981-84; Assoc Lectr, Newcastle-upon-Tyne Polytech, 1984-85; Assoc, Sr Lectr, Coventry Polytech, 1988-. *Creative works:* Mural Painter for Public Bldgs in Liverpool, 1976-77; Commissioned by the Imperial War Mus to make an Artistic Record of Mil Life in Cyprus, 1978; Drawing and Painting the Portrait, published by Phaidon, 1983. Solo Exhibitions: Riverside Studios Hammersmith, London, 1980; Paton Gallery, London, 1981, 1989, 1991. *Honours:* John Moores Scholarship, Liverpool, 1976; Artist in Residence, Brit Coun, Oviedo, Spain, 1990; Artist in Residence, Brit Coun, Las Palmas, Gran Canaria, 1991; Paintings in: Unilever Collection, London; Brunel Univ; Ocean Transport and Trade, London. *Hobbies:* Gardening; Reading. *Address:* 27 Riversley Road, Elmbridge, Gloucester GL2 0QU, England.

DEVARAJ Ramasamy, b. 4 Dec 1941, Sankaralingapuram, India. Tchr of Phys. m. Rukmani, 16 Sept 1973, 1 s, 2 d. *Education:* MSc, Phys, 1969, MPhil, Phys, 1977, BL, 1982, MEd, 1984, Madras Univ. *Appointments:* Prof of Phys, Madras Christian Coll, Tambaram, Madras; Subject Tchr in Phys, Govt Model Higher Second Schl, Madras. *Publications:* Poetry, published in Poet Int Monthly, Puthia Kavithai, Tamil Poetry Monthly. *Memberships:* Fndr, Pres, World Tamil Poetry Soc, Madras; Ed, Puthia Kavitai, New Poem, Tamil Poetry Monthly. *Honour:* Honorary Doctorate, D.Litt, World University, Tucson, Arizona, USA, 1984. *Hobby:* Writing Poetry. *Address:* 22 East Railway Gate Road, Avvai Nagar, Butt Medu, Madras 600 009, India.

DEVEREUX Richard, b. 3 Apr 1956, Lincolnshire, England. Artist (Sculptor). m. Christine Anne Holmes, 20 Aug 1977, 1 d. *Education:* Portsmouth Coll of Art, 1974-77. *Creative works:* Selected Group Exhibitions: Rufford Arts Ctr, Nottinghamshire, 1982; Ogle Gallery, Cheltenham, 1984; Sculpture to Touch: Usher Gallery, Lincoln, Ferens Gallery, Hull, Normanby Hall, Scunthorpe, 1986; Sacred Sites, Spotted Fawn Visual

Arts, California, 1987; 20th Century Brit Sculpture, Roche Ct, Wiltshire, 1988, 1989, 1990, 1991; Salisbury Fest, 1988; Dartington Hall Gallery, Devon, 1988; New Art Ctr, London, 1989, 1990; Sotherby's 20th Century Brit Sculpture, 1990; The Journey, Lincoln, 1990; Southampton City Art Gallery, 1990-91; Shared Earth Peterborough Art Gallery, 1991. One Person Exhibitions: Recent Works, Axis Gallery, Brighton, 1979; Recent Works, Hiscock Gallery, Portsmouth, 1980; Circles, Usher Art Gallery, Lincoln, 1984; Assembled Rites, Artsite, Bath, 1987; On Sacred Ground, Cairn Gallery, Gloucestershire, 1988; Beyond the Hall of Dreams, New Art Ctr, London, 1989. *Publications:* Quiet Flame, 1986; Assembled Rites, 1987; The Bowl of Grain, 1989-90; In Stillness and in Silence, 1991. *Honour:* Portsmouth Coll Scholarship, 1976. *Hobby:* Walking. *Address:* 21 North Parade, Lincoln, Lincolnshire LN1 1LB, England.

DEVINE Douglas, b. 23 Aug 1962, Louisville, KY, USA. Dir. m. 16 May 1986, 1 s. *Education:* BSBA 1986, MBA 1988, Univ of Louisville. *Appointments:* Area Mgr, Hycite Corp, 1982-84; Dir: Telecommunications Res Ctr, Bellsouth Telecommunications Inc, 1988-. *Publications:* Education Necessary to Compete in KY's Future; Published, Courier Journ & Times, 1988. *Memberships:* Bd, KY Assn for Older Persons, 1986-; Chm, Youth Involvement Comm, United Way, 1986-; Fdr, Pres 1986-88, Bd Mem 1988-90, Univ of Louisville Student Fed Credit Union, 1986-88 Pres, Univ of Lousville Student Body, 1987-88; Secy, Quality Care Trust, 1988; Citizens for Better Judges, 1988; Louisville Task Force on AIDS, 1988; Univ of Louisville Bd of Trustees, 1988; Univ of Louisville Bd of Dir, Athletic Assn, 1988. *Honours:* Excellence in Student Govt Awd, US Achmt Acad; KY Cite Corp Hall of Fame, 1984; Resolution in Apprec of Ser, KY State Senate, 1988; Finalist, Univ of Louisville Young Alumni of the Year, 1990; Allen Soc, Com Ser Awd from United Way, 1990. *Hobbies:* Reading; The Arts; Golf; Real Estate; Wildlife; Photography; Coin collecting. *Address:* 2712 Windsor Forest Drive, Louisville, KY, USA.

DEVLIN Brian, b. 30 June 1919, Liverpool, England. m. Dr Esther Margaret Carr, 1 Jan 1948, 3 s, 1 d. *Education:* MB ChB 1941, DPH 1951, Univ of Liverpol; DTM&H, Royal Army Med Coll, 1952. *Appointments:* Surg MN, 1942; Lt 1942, Capt 1943, Major 1946, Lt Col 1959, RAMC; 1 Airborne Div, served N Africa, Italy, Holland, Norway 1943-45; 60th Rifles, Tripoli, 1945-46; SMO, Brit Mil Mission to Saudi Arabia, 1946-49; DADAH, London, 1951-52; Singapore, 1952-55; War Office, 1955-58; PMO Min of Def, Malaya, 1958-62; RAMC)TA), 1966-72; MPNI, MSS, DHSS: MO 1963-71, SMO 1971-84, Adjudicating Med Practitioner 1984-89. *Memberships:* Somerset Co Coun (Conservative) 1985-89; NADFAS; Royal Brit Legion; Nat Trust. *Honours:* MBE 1959; OBE 1963. *Hobbies:* Golf; Bridge; Fishing. *Address:* Rectory Stables, Mells, Frome, Somerset BA11 3PT, England.

DEXTER Bunny Katherine Weston, b. USA. *Career:* Journalist, writer of num film scripts incl Flora, The New Taboo, 1992; European Games Agy, 1988; Invented bd game SHRINK; Mgr, polit campaign, New York State Election; SOS Charity. *Memberships:* BAFTA Chelsea Arts Acad. *Honour:* Best short subj film for Flora Chicago Film Fest. *Address:* 37 Lennox Gardens, Londor SW1, England.

DEYANOV Biser, b. 11 Mar 1949, Svoge. Premier Dancer. m. Katia Petrovska, 20 Sept 1989, 1 s. *Education:* Grad, Vaganova's Acad Ballet Sch, S Petersburg, 1968. *Career:* Premier Dancer, Nat Opera 1968-; Ballet Tchr, Bulgarian Nat Ballet Sch, 1978-87 *Creative works:* Prin Roles in the Ballets: Swan Lake Sleeping Beauty; Nutcracker; Gisselle; Don Quichot Romeo and Guliet; Spartacus; Carmen. *Honours:* 1s' Prize and Gold Medal: Jr Group 1968, Sr Group 1974 Intl Ballet Competition, Varna; Partnership, Dipl Moskow Intl Ballet Competition, 1973. *Hobbies:* Music

Books; Agriculture. *Address:* Lulin B2 541 vh A Ap 15, Sofia 1359, Bulgaria.

DEYO Steve, b. 26 July 1949, Columbus, OH, USA. Edit; Pubr; Speaker. m. Graciela Olivia Guerrero, 15 Feb 1975, 2 s, 1 d. *Education:* BA, Miami Univ, 1971. *Appointments:* Rocky Mountain Mktg, 1971; Nationwide Ins, 1975; Mkt Mgr, Azrock Industries, 1978; Account Mgr, Mercer Plastics, 1986; Fdr, La Vista de Mexico, 1988. *Publication:* La Vista de Mexico, Intl Newsletter. *Memberships:* VP, Beta Theta Pi; Toastmasters Intl; Intl Platform Assn. *Honours:* Outstg Speaker Awd, 1985, 1988; Nat Sales Ldr, 1985. *Hobbies:* Travel; Running; Backpacking; Reading; History. *Address:* 5289 Aurora Court, Lilbura, GA 30247, USA.

DHANJAL Surjeet Singh, b. 19 Mar 1923, Kisumu, Kenya. Conslt Paediatric Cardiologist. 2 s, 1 d. *Education:* MBBS, Univ of Madras, 1954; DCH, London, 1956; MRCP, Glasgow, 1962; MRCP, Edinburgh, 1963; FRCP, Glasgow, 1980. *Appointments:* Conslt Paediatrician, 1956-61; Asst Dir, Paediatric Cardiology Clins, 1963-76; Dir, Paediatric Residency Training, Dir, Paediatrics & Newborn Sers, 1966-76. *Publications:* Hamartonma of Liver in Infancy & Childhood; Ebstein's Anomaly in Trisomy 13, Sporotrichosis. *Memberships:* Kenya Br, BMA, 1957-61; AMA, 1972-79; Jeff Co Med Soc, 1972-; Kentucky Med Assn, 1972-; Louisville Ped Soc, 1975-85; Pres, Louisville Paediatric Soc, 1984. *Honours:* Gold Medal In Med, Gold Medal in Surg, Gold Medal in Ob & Gyn, Gold Medal, Best Outstg Grad, Univ of Madras, 1954. *Hobbies:* Wildlife Photography; Fretwork; Interior Decorating; Cooking. *Address:* Humana Heart Institute International, Humana Hospital Audubon, Louisville, KY 40217, USA.

DHEUR Patrick, b. 28 Mar 1960, Liege, Belgium. Concert Pianist. m. Nathalie Hosay, 9 Nov 1988. *Education:* Num hons 1976-, Dipls, Mozarteum, Salzburg, Austria, 1978, 1985; Diplome superior (Piano), Royal Conservatory of Music, Liege, 1982; Dipl, Univ Menandez Pelayo, Santander, Spain, 1983; Dipl, Geneva Conservatory, Switzerland, 1984. *Appointments:* Concert pianist, Europe, Japan, USA, Africa; Prof, Music Conservatory, Liege, 1978-. *Creative works incl:* Discography (LP & compact disc): 5 Aspects of Karol Szymanowski's Music, 1986; Brahms & Chopin, 1987; Post- Romantiques Liegeois (Franck, Lekeu, Jongen), 1988; Integral Schnittke Music for Violin & Piano, 1989. *Memberships:* Rotary Club; Artistic Dir & Admr, Fest de Wallonie; VP, Belgian Liszt Soc; Gen Secy, Cesar Franck Soc; Pres, Rendez-vous musicaux liegeois. *Honours:* 1st prizes, Solfege 1976, Piano 1977, Chamber Music 1979, Prize Marie 1982, Royal Conservatory of Music, Leige; 1st prize, Szymanowski Competition, Brussels, 1982; Scholarship, Rotary Intl (Capelle Foun), 1983; Cenacle Giacomo Fauser Awd, Italy, 1986; 1st prize, Musical Inst of Europe, Besancon, France, 1985; Crystal Record, 1987. *Hobbies:* Reading books on arts; Cinema; Exhibitions, painting & sculpture. *Address:* Rue Bassenge 27, 4000 Liege, Belgium.

DHIR Krishna Swaroop, b. 21 Mar 1944, Calcutta, India. Edr. m. Shailaja Nair, 3 July 1983, 2 d. *Education:* BTech, Indian Inst of Tech, Bombay, 1966; MS, Michigan State Univ, 1967; MBA, Univ of Hawaii, 1968; PhD, Univ of Colorado, 1975. *Appointments include:* Assoc Prof of Mgmt 1982-87, Adj Prof of Intl Studies 1985-86, Dir, MIM degree Prog 1986-87, Univ of Denver, Denver; Prodr & Host, KGNU, Boulder Pubic Radio, Boulder, 1984-86; VP for Strategic Planning, BioStar Med Prods, Inc, 1984-86; Visiting Prof of Mgmt & Statistics, Univ of Bombay, Bombay, 1985; Hd, Dept of Bus Adm 1987-89, Prof of Bus Adm 1987-91, The Citadel: The Mil Coll of S Carolina, Charleston; Prof of Hlth Sers Adm, The Med Univ of S Carolina, Charleston, 1987-; Prof of Mgmt 1991-, Dir, Sch of Bus Adm 1991-, Pennsylvania State Univ - Harrisburg, Middletown. *Publications:* Author of num profl papers in journs and forums, chapts in books. *Memberships include:* Acad of Mgmt, 1985-; MIIE, 1985-; Acad of Intl Bus, 1987-

; Adv Bd 1988-, Chm Adv Bd 1990-91, Info Resources Mgmt Assn; Track Chm, Southeastern Reg 1990-91, TIMS. *Honours include:* Sigma Iota Epsilon, Nat Honorary for Mgmt, 1973; Awded res grants by: CIBA-GEIGY AG 1979-82; Univ of Denver 1983, 1986; The Citadel Devel Foun, Inc 1987-91; The Notre Dame Ctr for Study of Religious and Ethical Values in Bus 1990; Med Univ of S Carolina 1991; AMP Inc, 1992-93; 1st Prize in Radio-Journalism (with J Holloway, Ali Ansari & Prodr, D Barsamian), Art of Peace Competition for the recording of GANDHI, broadcasted on KGNU, 1983; Lt Col, S Carolina Militia, 1987-91. *Hobbies:* Cricket; Photography; Philatelics; Travel; Camping. *Address:* School of Business Administration, Pennsylvania State University, Harrisburg, Middletown, PA 17057, USA.

DI LELLA Alexander A, b. 14 Aug 1929, Paterson, NJ, USA. Prof of Biblical Studies. *Education:* BA, St Bonaventure Univ, St Bonaventure, 1952; STL 1959, PhD 1962, Cath Univ of Am, Washington DC; SSL, Pontifical Biblical Inst, Rome, 1964. *Appointments:* Instr in Eng, St Bonaventure Univ, 1956-58; Lectr in Old Testament 1964-69, Lectr in New Testament Greek 1964-67, Holy Name Coll; Lectr in Syriac 1965, Asst Prof of Semitic Langs 1966-68, Assoc Prof of Semitic Langs 1968-76, Assoc Prof of Biblical Studies 1976-77, Prof of Biblical Studies 1977-, Cath Univ of Am; Adj Prof of Old Testament, Washington Theological Coalition, 1969-72. *Publications include:* The Book of Daniel (with Louis F Hartman), 1978; Proverbs in The Old Testament in Syriac according to the Peshitta Version, 1979; A Wise and Discerning Heart: Studies Presented to Joseph A Fitsmyer, SJ in celebration of His Sixty-Fifth Birthday (ed with R E Brown), 1986; The Wisdom of Ben Sira (with Patrick W Skehan), 1987; Edit, Assoc Edit and on the Editorial Bd of a number of Quarterlys. *Memberships:* Cath Biblical Assn; Soc of Biblical Lit; Corporate Rep for the Cath Univ of Am in the Am Schs of Oriental Res. *Honours:* Fellow, Am Sch of Oriental Res, Jerusalem, 1962-63; Guggenheim Fellow, 1972-73; Fellowship, Assn of Theological Schs in the US and Canada, 1979-80. *Hobbies:* Photography; Fishing; Computers. *Address:* 212 Curley Hall, Catholic University of America, Washington, DC 20064, USA.

DIAKONOFF Igor Mikhailovich, b. 12 Jan 1915, St Petersburg, Russia. Histn; Linguistics. m. Nina Diakonova, 22 June 1936, 2 s. *Education:* PhD 1946; Dr Hab of Historical Scis, 1960. *Appointments:* The Hermitage, 1936-41, 1946-59; Asst Prof, Leningrad Unv, 1937-41, 1946-49; Army Ser, Karelia & N Norway 1941-45; Hd Scist, Leningrad Br, Oriental Inst, Acad of Sci, 1952-. *Publications include:* Hurro-Urartian as an Eastern Caucasian Language (with S A Starostin), 1986; Afrasian Languages, 1988; Archaic Myths of the Orient and Occident, 1990; Men of Ur, 1990; Early Antiquity (ed), 1991; Proto-Afrasian and Old Akkadian, 1992; Author of over 200 journ articles. *Memberships:* Corpus Inscriptionum Iranicarune, 1954; Hon MRAS, 1962; Hon FBA; Hon, Am Acad of Art & Scis; Hon, Am Oriental Soc; Hon, Societe Asiatique. *Honours:* Dr Honoris Causa, Univ of Chicago; Order of the Red Star; Order of the Patriotic War, 2nd degree; Life Honorary Mem, Mun Coun of Kirkenes, Norway. *Hobbies:* Long range linguistic comparison; Lying on the sofa; Work. *Address:* Institut Vostokovedeniya, St Petersburg Branch, Dvortsovaya Naberezhnaya 18, 191065 St Petersburg, Russia.

DIAMOND Stephen Earle, b. 2 Dec 1944, San Fran, CA, USA. Investor Exec; Inventor Neuro Physicist. *Education:* Computer Progr, SCIE/BUS, 1969; Univ Supe, 1974-76; PhD 1976; Adva Univ Supe AUS, 1978; Adva PhD, 1980; Mind Advanced PhD, 1980; MA, Universal Suportorty, 1980. *Appointments:* Exec Chm, Gondia Corp, 1976-78; Chief Exec Ofcr 1978- 80, CAO 1980-85, Gondia Corp Inc Cos; CFO 1985-86, Owner 1986-, Exec Owner, Prin Dir, S'n E'e Diamond Assn. *Creative works:* Scientific Directive, Enviro-Quality Control, 1973-; Inventor, The Anatomic 48 Letter Alphabet & Font of Type 1975; Medical Treatise, 1976; Inventor, The Diamond Electric Engine, 1978; Economic

Product Tool, Real Authentic Gen Money, 1979; The Ballet of Life, performing arts, 1980; Residential Architecture Layouts and Legends, 4 vols; One Million Five Hundred Thousand Spoken and by Hand, Written Words Text. *Memberships:* Royal Soc of Lichtenstein; US Senate Club; Lawyers Book Club; Strategic Def Initiative, Con1 Disst Ldr; Chm, Ams for the High Frontier; Fdr Mem, Friends of the R'd R'n Lib; Sponser, Concerned Women for Am; Charter Fdr, Sponsor, The Ronald Reagan Repub Ctr; Charter Fdr, The Battle of Normandy Mus; Card Carrying Comm; Mem, The Grace Comm; Mem, The Edgewood Home for Chd; Card Carrying Mem the Committee to Save Social Security. *Honours:* Good Conduct Awd, USAF, 1964; National Defense Medal, 1964, United States Armed Forces, 1964; Achmt Awd, United Inventors and Scist(s), 1975; List of Friends, San Fran Symph Orch; Cert of Merit, Repub Nat Com, 1984; Cert of Polit Merit, Repub Party, 1985; Desk Plaque Paperweight, St Mary's Hosp Med Soc, 1988; Citizen of the Year Awd, Com for the Right to Bear Arms, 1988. *Hobbies:* Direct Ancestor: Picture, Painting, Portrait collecting, Coin Image Numsimatics; Economic data uses. *Address:* PO Box 4361, Zephyr Cove Stateline, NV 89449, USA.

DIANZINGA Scholastique, b. 7 Nov 1952, Brazzaville, Congo. Historian; Cultural Attache. *Education:* Lic, History, 1978; Maitrise, Hist, 1979; Dip, Adv Studies Hist of African Socs, 1980. *Appointments:* Asst, Hist, Marien N'Gouabi Univ, Brazzaville, 1981-; Cultural Attache to Presidency, Repub of Congo, 1985-90. *Publication:* Memorial illustre du Congo. *Memberships:* Assn Congolese Histns; Assn Women Researchers Congo; VP, Fedn Congo Women for Dev. *Honours:* Chevalier, Congolese Order of Merit, 1990. *Hobbies:* Reading; Music. *Address:* 73 rue Pere Drean, Bacongo, Brazzaville, Congo.

DIAS-AGUDO Fernando Roldao, b. 25 Nov 1925, Mouriscas, Abrantes. Prof of Maths. m. Elia Farinha Raposo, 2 Sept 1953, 2 d. *Education:* BA 1947, PhD 1955, Univ of Lisbon; MCE, Tech Univ of Lisbon, 1951. *Appointments:* Asst Tchr, Tech Univ of Lisbon, 1948-49; Asst Prof 1955-65, Assoc Prof 1965-68, Prof 1968-75, 1980-, Univ of Lisbon; New Univ of Lisbon, 1975-82. *Publications:* Author of 7 books and several papers on Linear Algebra, Analytical Geom, Advanced Calculus, Real Analysis, Differential Equations, Hilbert Spaces; Several articles on Science Policy. *Memberships:* Sigma Xi; Port Math Soc; Soc of Geog, Lisbon; Treas, Acad Scis of Lisbon; The New York Acad of Scis; AAAS. *Honours:* 2 Nat Prizes for the Best Classification on High Sch Exams, 1942-43; Nat Prize at the Univ for Best Paper in Maths, 1947. *Address:* AV 25 De Abril 35, P-2780 Oeiras, Portugal.

DICK Frank William, b. 1 May 1941, North Berwick. Dir of Coaching - Athletics. m. Linda Elizabeth Brady, 18 Feb 1980, 1 s, 2 d. *Education:* DLC Hons, Loughborough Coll, 1962-65; BSc, Univ of Oregon, 1967-68. *Appointments:* Asst Dir of Phy Ed, Worksop Coll, 1965, 1966, 1967, 1969; Scottish Nat Athletics Coach, 1970-79; UK Dir of Coaching - Athletics, 1979-. *Publications:* Winning Principles of Training; Training Theory; Strength Training; High Jump: Sprints and Hurdles; But First ---. *Memberships:* Pres, European Athletics Coaches' Assn, 1983-; Chm, Brit Assn of Nat Coaches, Pres, British Inst if SPorts Coaches, 1983-87; Chm, Brit Olympic Assn Coaches Adv Group, 1989-. *Honours:* OBE 1989; Fellow, Inst of Brit Sports Coaches, 1989. bb2Hobbies: Jogging; Coaching; Music; Public speaking. *Address:* Abingdon Sports Management, 22 Suffolk Street, London SW1Y 4HS, England.

DICK Paul W, b. 27 Oct 1940, Kapuskasing, Ontario, Canada. Min of Supply & Sers. *Education:* BA, Univ of Western Ontario; BL, Univ of New Brunswick. *Appointments:* Pres, PC Club, Univ of New Brunswick, 1965-66; Nat VP, PC Student Fdn of Canada, 1966-67; Mem of Nat Exec, PC Party of Canada; Asst Crown

Atty for the Co of Carleton, Ontario, 1969; Practiced Law, Ottawa Law Firm; Elected to the Hse of Commons, 1972; Chm, Fed Ontario PC Caucus; Fed PC Spokesperson on youth issues; Dep Opposition Ldr; Parliamentary Secy to: the Govt Hse Ldr and Pres of the Privy Coun, Pres of the Treas Bds; Served on the: Standing Com on Justice and Legal Affairs, Standing Com on Fin, Trade and Ec Affairs, Privileges and Elections, Reg Ec Expansion; Assoc Min of Nat Def, 1986; Min of Supply and Sers, 1989. *Address:* c/o Office of the Minister of Supply and Services, Ottawa, Canada K1A 0S5.

DICK Thomas Michael, b. 17 July 1955, Norfolk, VA, USA. Proj Control. m. Barbara Schuster, 28 May 1989. *Education:* AA, Hillsborough Com Coll, 1982; BA with hons 1984, MBA 1986, Univ of S Florida. *Appointments:* Dept Supvr, Truly Nolen Inc, 1980-82; Prog Controller, Harris Corp, 1986-88; Proj Control Team Ldr, Oglethorpe Power Corp, 1988-. *Memberships:* Assn of MBA Exec; Am Mgmt Assn; Audobon Soc; Georgia Nature Conservancy. *Honours:* Phi Kappa Phi, 1984; Grad Fellowship, 1985. *Hobbies:* Sports; Gardening; Reading; Investing. *Address:* 920 Scott Circle, Decatur, GA 30033, USA.

DICKE Klaus J, b. 1 Dec 1953, Koblenz, Germany. Sr Lectr. *Education:* Dr rer soc, Tuebingen, 1986. *Appointments:* Res Asst, Dept of Phil, Univ of Fubingen, 1979-83; Res Asst, Sr Lectr, Kiel Univ, Inst of Intl Law, 1983-91; Asst Prof, Kiel, 1991; Berlin, 1992; Mainz, 1992. *Publications:* Menschenrechte und europaeisohe Integration, 1986; About 30 articles on Intl Relat, the UN System, Polit Phil. *Memberships:* Res Unit 1987-, Governing Bd 1989-, German Assn for the UN; Deutsche Gesellschaft fur Politik-wissenschaft. *Hobbies:* Photography; History; Romanesque art. *Address:* Holtenauerstrasse 270 A, D-2300 Kiel, Germany.

DICKENS Barnaby John, b. 9 June 1954, London, England. Advtg. m. Lucy Anne Millar, 13 Oct 1983, 2 s, 1 d. *Education:* MA Cantab. *Appointments:* Account Exec, The Creative Bus, 1978-79; Account Mgr, WS Crawford, 1979-81; Account Dir, Marstfeller, 1981-85; Bd Account Dir, GGK, 1985-. *Hobbies:* Architecture; Badminton. *Address:* EGK London, 76 Dean Street, London W1V 5HA, England.

DICKERSON Graham David, b. 14 Dec 1951, March, Cambridgeshire, England. Registered Music Therapist; Accompanist; Piano Tchr. *Education:* Royal Northern/Manchester Coll of Music, 1970-74; Guildhall Sch of Music & Drama, 1975-76; Bretton Hall Coll, Univ of Leeds, 1976-77; GRNCM; ARMCM; ARNCM; LGSM(MT); PGCE; RMTh. *Appointments:* Music Therapist in Hlth and Ed Auth with learning difficulties, special needs (adult/child) and Mental Hlth (adult & child Psychi), 1977-93; Speciality-Group Psychodynamic Music Therapy Trainer, NZ, 1989, 1990. *Publications:* Articles in Brit Journ of Music Therapy; Therapy. *Memberships:* Assn of Profl Music Therapists; Brit Soc for Music Therapy; Assoc, West Midlands Inst of Psychotherapy; Nat Trust; Woodlands Trust; Former Chm, Vice Chair, Birmingham Music Fest Com; ISM. *Hobbies:* People; History; Eating out; Gardening. *Address:* 67 Mass house Lane, Kings Norton, Birmingham B38, England.

DICKEY John Sloan Jr, b. 24 Jan 1941, Washington DC, WA, USA. Edr. m. Lynn McMath, 7 June 1968, 1 s. *Education:* AB, Dartmouth Coll, 1963; MSc, Otago Univ, 1966; PhD, Princeton Univ, 1969. *Appointments:* Res Assoc, Carnegie Inst, 1970-72; Asst, Assoc Prof, MIT, 1972-79; Prog Dir, NSF, 1979-81; Prof, Syracuse Univ, 1981-88; Dean, Trinity Univ, 1988-. *Publications:* Lectures in Earth and Planetary Sciences; 40 Tech Papers. *Memberships:* AAAS; Am Geophys Union; FMSA; Treas, Geochem Soc; Geol Soc. *Honours:* Fulbright Scholar, 1964-65; Best Paper Awd, Geol Soc, Washington, 1972; Superior Achmt

Awd, NSF, 1980. *Hobby:* Earth and Planetary Science. *Address:* Trinity University Box 42, 715 Stadium Drive, San Antonio, TX 78212, USA.

DICKSON Katharine Hayland, b. 4 Dec 1904, E Hartford, CT, USA. Writer of Family Histories; Dance Tchr. m. (1) Harry Ashenden, 28 June 1928, dec 1967, (2) Theodore Brown, 26 Oct 1968, dec'd 1973, (3) Charles Alverson, 18 Feb 1978, dec'd 1985, 1 s. *Education:* Dipl, Boston Sch of Phy Ed, 1925; BEd, Boston Univ, 1948. *Appointments:* Tchr, Ballroom Dance, Model Sch Dance, Boston, 1923-26; Tchr, Ballroom, Ballet, Tap, Hazel Boone Sch of Dancing, Boston, 1926-28; Tchr, Mus Comedy and Tap, Knickerbocker Sch, Boston, 1928-31; Dir, Katharine Dickson Dance Studio, Cambridge, MA, 1934- 68; Headed Dance Depts, ballet, tap & chd's work at: Newton Com Ctr, Newton, Hayden Rec Ctr, Lexington & Ballroom at Boston Ctr for Adult Ed, 1943-74; Chd's work, Wellesley Rec Dept, 1967-74; Tchr, Ballroom Dance, Englewood & Venice, FL, 1974-. *Publications:* Stockman-Gallison Ancestral Lines, 1985; Downeast Dicksons, 1988; Burton-Tyler Ancestral Lines, 1990; The Stockman Story, 1992. *Contributions to:* Articles to profl journs. *Memberships:* Pres 1949-51, 1969-71, Dance Tchrs' Club of Boston; Chm, Convention Comm; Tng Sch; New York Soc of Tchrs' of Dancing; Dance Masters of Am. *Honours:* Awd of Merit, Boston Post Music Fest, 1959; Honorary Mem, Dance Tchrs' Club of Boston Inc with the Am Soc, 1974. *Hobbies:* Gardening; Swimming; Genealogical study of ancestors in old England. *Address:* RFD 1 Old Warner Road, Henniker, NH 03242, USA.

DIEBEL Donald R, b. 12 June 1947, Galveston, TX, USA. Pubr. m. Michele Rowland, 29 Sept 1990. *Appointments:* Owner, Germini Publishing Co, 1978- . *Publications:* How to Pick up Women in Discos; The Complete Guide to Meeting Women; Finding Mr Right; The Houston Entertainment and Dating Guide. *Memberships:* Key West Coll of Millionaires; Am Book Dealers Exc; Mail Order Assoc; Pubrs Mktg Assn. *Honours:* Doctorate of Publishing, The Publishing Workshop, 1988; Grad, Key West Coll of Millionaires, 1990. *Hobbies:* Astrology; Writing; All Sports; Inventing; Canoeing; Mountain climbing; Travel. *Address:* 11543 Gullwood Drive, Houston, TX 77089, USA.

DIETL Jerzy Jozef, b. 28 Apr 1927, Inowroclaw, Poland. Prof of Mktg; Hd of Dept; Pres. m. Janina Spychala, 30 May 1969, 1 s, 1 d. *Education:* MSc 1950, PhD 1958, Poznan Sch of Ec. *Appointments:* Asst Lectr, Asst Prof, Assoc Prof, Poznan Sch of Ec, 1950-68; Assoc Prof, Ctl Sch of Planing and Stats, 1961; Full Prof, Dir, Inst of Mktg, Lodz Univ, Fac of Ec and Sociol, 1969- ; Senator, Republic of Poland, Chm, Senate's Extraordinary Comm for Ec Legis, 1989-91. *Publications:* Marketing of Agricultural Products, 1959; Marketing, 1985; Industrial Product-Buyer Behaviour in a Centrally Planned Economy, 1986; Distribution in Central- Planned and Market Oriented Economy, 1988; Trade in Contemporary Economy, 1991. *Memberships:* Bd Mem, Com on Agricultural Ec, Polish Acad of Scis; Bd Mem, Polish Ec Soc; Bd Mem, Mgmt Soc; Trade Union Solidarity Advr; Editorial Bds of: Journ of Global Mktg, Intl Journ of Res in Mktg, Ofcl Journ of the European Mktg Acad, The Journ of European Res; European Soc for Opinion and Mktg Res; European Acad of Advanced Res in Mktg. *Honours:* Polonia Restituta: IV and V Class. *Hobbies:* Travelling; Reading; Mountains; Gardening. *Address:* 95-050 Konstantynow Lodzki, Klonowa 36, Poland.

DIETRICH Richard Farr, b. 16 Jan 1936, Sandusky, OH, USA. Prof of Eng; Edit. m. Lori Ruse, 2 s, 1 d. *Education:* AB, Miami Univ of Ohio, 1958; MA, Bowling Green State Univ, 1960; PhD, Florida State Univ, 1965. *Appointments:* Tchg Asst, Bowling Green State Univ, 1959-60; Tchg Asst, Florida State Univ, 1960-63; Asst Prof, Dir of Freshman Eng, Univ of Delaware, 1963- 68; Asst Prof 1968-70, Assoc Prof 1970-76, Prof 1976-

, Univ of S Florida. *Publications:* The Art of Fiction, 1967, 1974, 1978, 1983; The Art of Drama, 1969, 1976; Portrait of the Artist as a Young Superman: A Study of Shaw's Novels, 1970; The Realities of Literature, 1971; Annotated Bibliography of G B Shaw (Contbtg Edit), Vols II & III, 1986-87; British Drama 1890-1950, 1989; Author of many articles. *Memberships:* MLA; The Shaw Soc of England; The Shaw Soc of Am; The Shaw Fest Theatre Assoc; The Ibsen Soc of Am; The Stratford Theatre Fest Assoc; The Asolo Theatre Assn. *Honours:* Selected to teach at Florida State Univ - London Study Ctr, 1980; Coll of Arts and Lttrs Scholar of the Year, 1989-90; Editorial Bd, The Annual of Bernard Shaw Studies, 1990-; Edit, USF Press; 5 Univ Res Grants; 12 Departmental Res Awds. *Hobbies:* Tennis; Swimming; Racquet ball; Film; Travel; Gardening; Woodworking; Remodeling. *Address:* English Department, University of South Florida, Tampa, FL 33620, USA.

DIETZ Arno Kurt Wolfgang, b. 30 Aug 1921, Leipzig, Germany. Libn. m. Gisela Selige, 31 Oct 1963, 1 s, 2 d. *Education:* Univ of Leipzig, 1950-54; Deutsche Staatsbibliothek Berlin, 1954-56. *Appointments:* Libn, Univ Lib, Leipzig, 1956; Dir, Dept of Univ Pubs, Deutsche Bucherei Leipzig, 1957-58; Bibliothek des Deutschen Bundestages, Bonn 1958-86, Dir 1973-86; Consultee to Div Institutions, 1987-. *Publications include:* Bibliotheksarbeit fur Parlamente und Behorden (Edit), 1980; World Dictionary of Nat Parliamentary Libs, 1985, 1987, 1989; Verzeichnis der Parlaments und Behordernbibliotheken der Bundesrepublic Deutschland, 1985; Die Bibliothek des Deutschen Bundestages, 1989. *Memberships include:* Verein deutscher Bibliothekare, 1958-; Chm 1975-85, Assn of Parliamentary and Adm Libs of Germany; Chm 1979-83, Intl Fdn of Lib Assn and Institutions, Sect of Parl Libs; VP 1990-, Deutsch-Japanische Gesellschaft. *Honours:* Fed Cross of Merit, 1st Class, 1986; Silver Medal of the German Diet, 1986; Parlament und Bibliothek, Intl Festschrift für W. Dietz zum 65. Geburtstag, 1986. *Hobbies:* Classical music; International Politics; International Relations and Exchange Programmes; Travel. *Address:* Am Wolfsbach 50, 5300 Bonn 3, Germany.

DIETZE Peter, b. 10 Dec 1955, Castine, ME, USA. Ordained Min. m. Sharon Joy Hazzard, 9 Oct 1976, 2 s, 1 d. *Education:* Min's Course of Study, Wesleyan Ch of Am, 1976-82; Dipl, Emmanuel Bible Coll, 1988-89; ThB, Emmanuel Theological Sem, Nashville, 1988-89; STD, AMerican Bible Inst & Coll, 1991; Th.M., Amdersonville Baptist Coll & Sem, 1992. *Appointments:* Pastor, First Wesleyan Ch, Stony Creek, 1977-81; Pastor, Lynch Wesleyan Ch, Lywch, 1981-84; Pastor, Westwood Wesleyan Ch, Seattle, 1984-86; Pastor, First Free Meht Ch, Savannah, 1986-88; Supply Pastor, New Hope Free Meth Ch, Deville, 1988-89; Pastor, Erie Chapel & North East PA Free Meth Chs, 1989-. *Memberships:* Oil City Conf of the Free Meth Ch; North East PA Clergy Coun; Greater Erie PA Ministerial Fellowship; Pennsylvania Assn of Evang. *Honours:* Honoured for work in Christian ed 1987, Ordained to the Min 1987, by the Atlantic Southeast Conf of the Free Meth Ch; Outstg Young Am in the field of religion, 1988; D.Div London Inst for Applied Research, 1992; Baron, Royal Order of the Bohemian Crown, 1992; Knight Commander Iofsensic Ursinius Order, 1992. *Hobbies:* Reading; Coin collecting; Model train collecting. *Address:* 901 E 38th Street, Erie, PA 16504, USA.

DIGBY Dione Marian, b. 23 Feb 1934. m. Edward, 12th Baron Digby, 1952, 2 s, 1 d. *Appointments:* Fdr Chm, Hon Secy 1963-, Summer Music Soc of Dorset; Chm 1966-75, Dorset Assn of Youth Clubs; Mem 1971, Chm 1976- 81, Bath Fest Coun of Mgmt; Mem 1975-80, BBC/IBA Ctl Appeals Adv Com; West Dorset Dist Councilor representing the Cerne Valley, 1976-86; Chm 1977-79, Dorset Com Coun; Chm 1977-79, Standing Conf of Rural Com Couns and Couns of Voluntary Ser; Gov 1977-83, Dorset Coll of Agri; Mem 1980-86, South

West Arts Mgmt Com; Mem 1981-, Exeter Univ Coun; Mem 1982-86, Chm, Tng Com, Vice Chm, Dance Panel, Mem, Music Panel, Arts Coun of GB; Chm 1982-85, Dorset Small Industries Com of COSIRA; Mem, Wessex Water Auth, 1983-89; Chm, Avon and Dorset Customer Consultative Com; Trustee 1984-, Tallis Scholars Trust; Trustee 1985-, Royal Acad of Music Foun; Mem 1985-88, Gov 1988-90, South Bank Bd; Non Exec Dir, Western Adv Bd, Nat Westminster Bank, 1986-; Gov 1987-, Sherborne Sch; Chm, NRA Wessex Reg Adv Bd, Bd Mem 1989-, Nat Rivers Auth; Chm 1989-, South and West Concerts Bd; Bd of Mgmt, Mem 1990-, Dorset Respite and Hospice Trust; Pres of Coun 1991-, Mem Bd of Mgmt 1991-, Bournemouth Orchs. *Honours:* Pres: Dorset Opera, Dorset Craft Guild, Bournemouth Intl Fest; Patron, Friends of the Bath Fest; Dep Lt, Co of Dorset, 1983; DBE, 1991. *Hobbies:* Skiing; Sailing; Tennis; Music and the Arts; History; Politics. *Address:* Minterne, Dorchester, Dorset DT2 7AU, England.

DIKOV Anton, b. 29 Aug 1938, Sofia, Bulgaria. Performing Pianist; Piano Prof. m. Krassimira Dantcheva, 30 May 1964, dec 1989, 1 s, 1 d. *Education:* Musical Acad, Sofia, 1961; Specialising with Nadia Boulanger, Paris, 1964-65. *Career:* Pianist-Soloist, Sofia Philharm Orch, 1962-; Piano Prof, Musical Acad, Sofia, 1982-. *Creative works:* Recordings of piano music from Bach to contemporary composers incl: Integral recordings of Bartok's works for piano and orch, 1973; Beethoven's piano concerts, 1984, 1990. *Memberships:* Chopin Soc, Warsaw-Vienna- Sofia; Contemporary Music Soc, Sofia. *Honours:* VI prize, Liszt Competition, Budapest, 1956; Harriet Cohen Bach Medal, London, 1960; IV prize, III Intl Competition, Rio de Janeiro, 1962; III prize, M Long Competition, Paris, 1963; Bulgarian State Awds, 1971, 1974, 1981, 1983. *Hobbies:* Hiking; Gardening. *Address:* Ami Boue St 3, 1606 Sofia, Bulgaria.

DILL Harold Bernard, b. 6 March 1959, Rochester, NY, USA. Supvr, Horticultural Design & Maintenance. m. Sandra Marleen Ryman, 4 May 1985, 2 d. *Education:* AA in Liberal Arts, Monroe Com Coll, 1977-78; BA in Communication, Journalism, St John Fisher Coll, 1979-81. *Appointments:* Feature Writer, Webster Herald, 1979-80; Scriptwriter, Cameraman, Am Cablevision, 1982; Sales Conslt, Anderson-Little, 1983-90; Supvr, Ward West Planta, 1990-. *Publications:* Poems published in several anthologies and many in literary pubs and periodicals. *Memberships:* Lit Ed 1977- 78, Assoc Ed 1978-79, Cabbages and Kings; Fine Arts Reporter 1977-78, Fine Arts Edit 1978, MCCNews pub, Monroe Doctrine; Fdr, Pres, Webster Table Tennis Assn, 1977-81; Pres, Rochester Sports Collectors Assn, 1977-78; Assoc Edit 1979-80, Lit Edit 1980-81, Fisher Art pub, The Angle; Feature Reporter, Fisher news pub, The Pioneer, 1979-80; Broadcaster, Radio Sta WJFR, 1979-81; Rochester Poetry Soc 1982-, VP 1987-91; Pres, Rochester Poets, 1991-. *Honours:* Certs of Commendation for Editing and Writing, MCC, 1977-78; Deans List, Monroe Com Coll, 1978; Medalist, Cabbages and Kings, Lit Art Pub, 1978, 1979; Frank Rice Mem Awd for Writing Excellence, 1979; Dean's List, St John Fisher Coll, 1980. *Hobbies:* Music; Gardening; Reading; Nature; Photography. *Address:* 3209 Pine View Drive, Walworth, NY 14568, USA.

DILLINGHAM Marjorie Carter, b. 20 Aug 1915, Bicknell, IN, USA. m. William Pyrle Dillingham, dec, 2 s, 1 dec, 1 d. *Education:* PhD, Florida State Univ, 1970. *Appointments include:* Tchr, Duke Univ; Univ of Georgia; Florida State Univ; Panama Canal Zone Coll; St George's Sch, Havana, Cuba; Various sec'dy schs, Florida; Former Dir, travelling Spanish conversation classes, through-out Spanish-speaking world for many years, has lived, studied or travelled in every Spanish-speaking country except Dominican Republic. *Creative works:* Paper on original method of teaching Spanish, presented to Am Assn of Tchrs of Spanish & Portuguese, in New York; Res in Spain on Spanish Reference Grammar. *Memberships include:* Past Nat Pres, La Sociedad Honoraria Hispanica; Past Pres, Foreign Lang Div,

Florida Ed Asn; Pres, Florida chapt, Am Assn of Tchrs of Spanish & Portuguese; State Legis Chm, Delta Kappa Gamma. *Honours include:* Putnam Co Ednl Archives Hall of Fame, 1986. *Address:* 2109 Trescott Drive, Tallahassee, FL 32312, USA. 7, 52, 138, 152, 155, 156, 179.

DILOV Ljuben, b. 25 Dec 1927, Cerven brjag. Writer. m. Milka Vuchkova, 21 June 1953, 1 s, 1 d. *Education:* Slavic Philology, Univ of Sofia, 1953. *Appointments:* Writer's Union of Bulgaria, 1953-58; Lit Journ, Septemvri, 1962-74; Cartinna galeria, 1974-82. *Publications:* Author of 41 books; Edit of 14 short story-anthologies; Translator of several German books. *Memberships:* Writer's Union of Bulgaria; PEN - Ctr of Bulgaria; Assn of Bulgarian Journalists; WORLD-SF. *Honours:* Intl Awd for SF, Poland, 1973; Spec Awd for Sci-Fiction of the EUROCON III, 1976. *Hobby:* Fishing. *Address:* Major Tompson-str, block 13 w, 1407 Sofia, Bulgaria.

DIMITRAS Panayote Elias, b. 15 Dec 1953, Athens, Greece. Asst Prof of Polit Sci. m. Emily Sclivaniotis, 30 June 1980, 1 s, 1 d. *Education:* BA in Ec with highest hons, Athens Sch of Ec & Bus, 1975; MPA 1977, PhD in Polit Economy & Govt 1979, Harvard Univ. *Appointments:* Dir, Eurodim, 1979-89; Lectr, Univ of Laverne, Athens, 1980-89; Lectr, Univ of Maryland, Athens, 1984-89; Edit, Greek Opinion, 1984-90; Lectr, Southeaste RN Coll, Athens, 1987-89; Asst Prof of Polit Sci, Athens Univ of Ec & Bus, 1989-. *Publications:* Political Background, Parties and Elections in Greece, 1991. *Contributions to:* Many articles to profl journs and collective vols. *Memberships:* Intl Polit Sci Assn; Am Polit Sci Assn; Greek Polit Sci Assn; Nat Rep for Greece, World Assn for Public Opinion Res; Amnesty Intl; Greenpeace; Nat Secretariat & Rotating Presidium 1990, Ecologists-Alternatives; Minority Rights Group. *Honours:* US Ed Foun ITT Scholar, 1975-77; Krupp Foun Fellow, Harvard Univ, 1978- 79; Fulbright Fellow, 1984. *Address:* PO Box 31344, GR-10035 Athens, Greece.

DIMITROV Ivelin Ivanov, b. 18 Jan 1931, Silistra, Bulgaria. Composer; Conductor; Tchr. m. Mariana Stefanova Kudreva, 9 Dec 1970, 2 s, 1 d. *Education:* Nat Music Acad, Sofia, 1948-52. *Appointments:* Tchr, Nat Music Sch, 1952-56; Tchr, Bodra Smiana Chd Choir, 1956-; Conductor, P Penev (renamed Polyphonia Chamber a Cappella Choir), 1968. *Creative works:* Little Naive Symphony; Guasi Simph; Day of Sacrifice; Intimate Music; The Sunset; Improvised Suite; Frescos; Symphonies; Verses of Gratitude; Parting Melodies; Instrumental Chamber Music; Choir Music for ladies, mixed and chd choirs. *Memberships:* Union of Bulgarian Composers; Bulgarian Choir Union. *Honours:* Order Kiril i Methody, II degree, 1968; Anniv Medal, 25 years People Power, 1969; Kiril i Methody, I degree, 1972, 1974; Order of Labour, Golden, 1980; Mark Excellent Artist, 1981; Title, Honoured Artist, 1985. *Address:* Ap 29, Entr B, bl 31, Mihail Bubotinov str, 1408 Sofia, Bulgaria.

DIMITROVA Margarita Alexandrova, b. 20 Oct 1947, Sofia, Bulgaria. Ballet Dancer. div, 1 s. *Education:* Ed, Cert, Kirov Theatre, Leningrad, 1971. *Career:* Soloist Ballet Dancer, Nat Sofia Opera, 1966-; Athens Ballet, 1985; Ballet Tchr, Ballet Intl De Ochi, Japan, 1988. *Creative works:* Ballet Composition for Graduating Class, Nat Ballet Sch; Waltz - Straus. *Honours:* 4th prize, Bronze medal, 1968; 3rd prize, Bronze medal, Intl Ballet Competition, Varna, 1970; Medal, Awd of 2nd World Competition, Ballet, Japan, 1978. *Hobbies:* Music; Books; Theatre; Ballet. *Address:* Str Struga, bl 71, A Ap 1, Sofia 1233, Bulgaria.

DIMITROVA Roza, b. 4 Mar 1938, Sofia, Bulgaria. Res Engr. m. Zubomir Dimitrov, 29 Jan 1966, 1 d. *Education:* BSc 1956-58, MSc 1958- 61, PhD 1972-77, Acad of Mining and Geology, Sofia. *Appointments:* Asst, Mineral Engrg Fac, Acad of Mining & Geology, 1962-65; Hd of Mineral Dressing Dept, Sofia, 1966-90; Mineral Engrg Dept, IMI - Israel, Haifa, 1990-. *Creative works:* Res studies on the Benefication of Mineral Raw Mat(s); Author of 33 pubs, 1 book on Selection flocculation, 4 patents in Ore Dressing. *Memberships:* Assn of Mining Engrs, Bulgaria; Soc of Engrs & Archs, Israel; Nat Geographic Soc, USA. *Hobbies:* Archeology; History; Reading; Skiing. *Address:* IMI, POB 10140, 26 111 Haifa Bay, Israel.

DIMOV Michael, b. 8 May 1967, Varna, Bulgaria. Student. m. Donja Stefanova Dimov, 19 Oct 1989, 1 s. *Education:* Eng Lang Sec'dy Sch, 1981-86; Higher Ed in Logopaedics 1988-92, Psycho 1990. *Career:* Army Ser, 1986-88. *Publication:* Joint Solution of the Problems of Speech Therapy, 1991. *Memberships:* Assoc Mem, Brit Coll of Speech & Lang Therapists (A-74); Profl Union of Logopaedists in Bulgaria; Bulgarian Assn for Res in Fluency Disorders. *Honour:* Spec Scholarship for high acad results and merit, 1991. *Hobbies:* Football; Photography. *Address:* Macedonia 164 V, Varna 9004, Bulgaria.

DINERSTEIN Efim Abramovich, b. 17 May 1924, Moscow, Russia. Researcher in Book Sci. m. Kresina Larisa Markovna, 2 Nov 1958, 1 d. *Education:* Cand of Sci, 1969; DSc, 1990. *Appointments:* Moscow Lib for the Blind, 1950-53; State Lib Mus, V Mayakovsky, 1954-63; All-Union Book Chamber, 1964-92. *Publications:* Those who put the foundation stone: Gosizdat and its leaders 1972, I D Sytin, 1983; Factory for readers: A F Marx 1986, Mayakovsky and books 1987, A P Chehov and his pubrs 1990. *Honours:* Order of the Red Star, Order of the Patriotic War, 1945; Honorary Wkr of Culture, RSFSR, 1988. *Address:* ul Ostrovityanova 45/1/488, Moscow 117342, Russia.

DING Cong, b. 6 Dec 1916, Shanghai, China. Cartoonist. m. Jun Shen, 31 Dec 1956, 1 s. *Education:* Grad, Lowrie Inst, Shanghai, 1935. *Appointments include:* Dep Edit-in-Chief, People's Pictorial, 1949-59; No work, not allowed to paint, 1958-79; Cartoonist for the mag Book Reading, 1980-92. *Creative works include:* Selected Cartoons of Ding Cong, 1982; The Child Bride (Illustrators), 1982; Things That Happened Yesterday, 1984; Wit and Humor from Ancient China - 100 Cartoons, 1987; Children's Songs of Tao Xinzhi (Illustrations), 1987; Best Chinese Idioms II (Illustrations), 1988; 100 Glimpses into China (Illustrations), 1989. *Memberships:* Coun Mem, Chinese Artists' Assn; Dir, China Com of the Art of Caricature; Editorial Mem, Satire and Humor. *Honours:* Nat prize for excellent illustrations for illustrating Camel Xiangzi, 1979; Nat prize for the design and layout of Four Generations Under One Roof, 1980; Golden Monkey Prize for Outstg Contributions to the Art of Chinese Caricature, 1988. *Hobbies include:* Reading; Peking opera. *Address:* Xi San Huan Bei Lu, Chang Yun Gong 4th Building, Room 1105, Beijing, China.

DING Junde, b. 28 June 1932, Qingdao, China. Chief Geologist. m. Caiqin Zeng, 1 Apr 1956, 1 s, 2 d. *Appointments:* BSc, Dept of Mineral Geology, Changchun Coll of Geology, 1953. *Appointments:* Asst Engr 1953-59, Engr 1960-82, Sr Engr 1983-86, North China Exploration Co; Prof, North China Non Ferrous Metals Exploration Bur, 1987-. *Creative works:* Metallogenetic Regularity and Prediction of Skavn-Type Iron Ore in North Platform, 1986; On the Distribution Regularity of Largest Non Ferrous Metals Deposit at Home and Abroad and the Exploration Problem at Home, 1989. *Memberships:* VP, Geol Assn of Hebei Province; Dir, Chinese Soc of Non Ferrous Metals. *Honours:* Prize of Nat Scientific Conf, 1978; Advanced Scientific Wkr in Metallurgical Min and Hubei Province. *Hobbies:* Playing basketball; Dancing. *Address:* North China Non Ferrous Exploration Bureau, Guangning Road, Tianjin, China.

DING Tiping, b. 22 July 1941, Huan, China. Prof, Chief of Div. m. Xiaqui Zou, 28 Mar 1970, 2 s. *Education:* Bach, Central South Univ of Tech, China, 1964; Master, Chinese Academy of Geological Sci, 1967.

Appointments: Research Asst, Inst of Mineral Deposits, CAGS, 1979- 85; Assoc Prof, Inst of Mineral Deposists, CAGS, 1985-91; Prof Inst of Mineral Deposists, CAGS, 1991-. *Publications:* Oxygen and Hydrogen Isotope Geochemistry; Typical W Sn Pb Zn Ore Deposists in the South Range Area, China. *Memberships:* Comm of Isotape Geology; Geological Soc of China. *Hobbies:* Tour & Play Chinese Chess. *Address:* Inst of Mineral Deposists, Chinese Academy of Geological Sci, Baiwanzhuang Road, Beijing 100037, China.

DINGLI-ATTARD de BARONI INGUANEZ Marcel Vincent, b. 21 July 1951, Floriana, Malta. m. Mary Ann Bohnert, 1981, 2 d. *Education include:* B Phil, Degree in Philosophy, Vatican State, 1796; PhD Philosophy, US, 1979. *Appointments include:* Deputy Sec General, Assoc of Self Employed & Employers, Malta, 1978-80; Vice Pres, Academic Affairs Intl Univ, 1980-82; Hon Vice Chancellor, Intl Univ, USA, 1981-82; Hon Consul Republic of Malta, State Missouri; Gen Editor Univ Intelligence Data Bank of America; Special Envoy Intl Assoc of Educators for World peace, NGO. *Honours:* Commissioned Notary public within County of Jackson, State of Missouri; Diploma in Recognition Sci and Research Activity, Field of biocenotics; Appointed Research Prof Inst for Intl Relations & Intercultural Studies; Alabama Agricultural & Mechanical State University. 99.

DINKEL-KEET Emmy Gerarda Mary, b. 5 Sept 1908, The Hague, Netherland. Artist. m. Prof E Michael Dinkel, 25 Oct 1941, 2 s, 2 step-d. *Education:* Palmers Coll, Grays Essex, 1918-27; Southend On Sea Coll of Arts & Crafts, 1927-30; Bd of Educ, Diplomas in Drawing, 1928; Engraving, 1929; A.T.D, 1930; Royal Coll of Art, 1930-33. *Appointments:* LCC Evening Inst, 1932-34; Sherborne Sch for Girls, 1934-37; Freelance Illustrator & Designer, 1937-39; Snr Asst, Malvern Coll of Art, 1939-41; Supply Tchr of Art, Edinburgh Schs, 1957-61. *Creative Works:* Dream Children; Babe Eternal; Funeral of Mozart; Dream Cloud; Aconites in Duntisbourne; Into Spring; Hungarian Peasant Women; Jane Eyre, Flight to Freedom & Peace; Portraits. *Memberships:* Elected RWA. *Honours:* The Essex County Art Scholarship; RWA. *Hobbies:* Theatre; Ballet; Music; Travel; Languages; Exhibitions. *Address:* 1 The Mead, Cirencester, Gloucs, GL7 2BB, England. 19.

DITTMANN Lorenz, b. 27 Mar 1928, Munich. Univ Prof. m. Marlen Dittmann, 28 Aug 1965, 1 s, 1 d. *Education:* Univ of Munich, History of Art, Archeology, Philosophy. *Appointments:* Tech High Sch Aachen Asst, 1958-65; Dozent, 1965-70; Prof, 1970-77; Univ des Saarlandes, Full Prof, 1977-. *Publications:* Die Farbe bei Grünewald; Studien zu Kategorien der Kunstegschichte; Farbgestaltung and Farbtheorie in der abendländischen Malerei. *Memberships:* Verband deutscher Kunthistoriker. *Address:* Mecklenburgring 31, D-6600 Saarbrücken, Germany.

DITTMERS Manuel Ludwig, b. 15 Apr 1961. German Economist; Author; Founder of World Wide Peace. *Education:* LSH, Studio Sch Cambridge; Davies Tutorial Coll, London; Mander Portmann Woodward, London; Eurocentre, Paris; Univ of Nice; Univ of Lille; Univ of Buckingham; US Int Univ; BA, Med, London School of Economics (MSc). *Appointments include:* Dimen Corp, Conslt, 1985-; Mngmt Conslt, 1986-87; Sr Mgmnt Conslt, 1987-89; Sr Strategic Mgmnt Conslt, 1990; Hd of Strategy, 1991-; Fndr World Wide Peace; World Citizen Passport; Founder WWP Animal Rights, 1987. *Publications:* Charter of World Wide Peace; The Green Party in West Germany; World & Environment; Impressions of Fuerteventura; European Poems; Crisis Management; Sieseby & Schwansen. *Memberships:* Royal Ocean Racing; Silverstone Racing; LSH Bund; Norddeutscher Regatta Verein; British Institute of International and Comparative Law; Prof Socs and Assns: PEN 1987; British Inst of Management, 1990; Phi Delta Kappa, 1989; Convocation of Univ of London, 1990; Fellow Inst of Directors; Award: Fellow Royal

Society of Arts, 1990. *Hobbies:* Sailing; Golf; Motor Racing; Photography; Painting. *Address:* Buckingham MK18 1BS, England.

DITTON Robert Browning, b. 22 Jan 1943, New York, NY. Prof. m. Penelope Jane Wheeler, 28 Aug 1966, 2 d. *Education:* BS, Recreation Educ, State Univ of New York Cortland Coll, 1964; MS, Recreation & Park Admin, Univ of illinois, 1966; PhD, Recreation & Park Admin, Univ of Illinois, 1969. *Appointments:* Asst Assoc of Leisure Sci, Regional Analysis, Univ of Wisconsin Green Bay, 1969-74; Assoc Prof of Recreation & Parks, Texas A&M Univ, 1974-81; Prof of Recreation & Parks, Texas A&M Univ, 1982-; Prof of Wildlife & Fisheries Sci, Texas A&M Univ, 1988-. *Publications:* 125 Journal Articles, Tech Reports. *Memberships:* American Fisheries Soc; Nat Recreation & Park Assoc; Soc for Park & Recreation Educ; Academy of Leisure Sci; The Coastal Soc; Phi Kapp Phi; Sigma Xi. *Honours:* Charles K Brightbill Award; Allen V Sapora Research Award for Ecellence in Research; Theodore & Franklin Rossevelt Award for Excellence in Recreation & Park Research; Distinguished Alumnus. *Hobbies:* Travel; Photography; Stamps. *Address:* Dept of Wildlife & Fisheries Sci, Texas A&M Univ, Coll Station, TX 77843, USA. 139, 143.

DIXON Joe Boris, b. 15 Nov 1930, Clinton, KY. Prof of Soil Mineralogy. m. Martha Jane Duke, 27 Jan 1952, 2 s. *Education:* BS, Univ of KY, 1952; MS, Univ of KY, 1956; PhD, Univ of Wisconsin, 1958. *Appointments:* NSF Postdoctoral Fellow, Univ of WI, 1959; Asst Prof, Auburn Univ, 1959-63; Soil Scientist, Soil Conservation Serv, 1961; Assoc Prof, Auburn Univ, 1963-68; Prof, Texas A&M Univ, 1968-. *Publications:* J B Dixon & S B Weed; Minerals in Soil Environments; Sci Papers; Book Chapters. *Memberships:* Soil Sci Soc of America; Soil Mineralogy Div; Clay Minerals Soc; Intl Soc of Soil Sci; Soil Mineralogy Comm; Intl Assoc for the Study of Clays; Teaching Clay Min Comm; Soil Mineralogy Div Bd Represtative. *Honours:* American Assoc for Advancement of Sci; Fellow, ASA; Fellow, SSA; Faculty Distinguished Achievement Award in Research; SSSA Soil Sci Research Award; Distinguished Member Award, The Clay Mineral Soc. *Hobbies:* Photography; Gardening; Travel. *Address:* Soil & Crop Sci, Texas A&M Univ, Coll Station, TX 77843, USA. 143.

DJEROV Dimitar, b. 16 May 1934, Sofia, Bulgaria. Orthopaedic Surgeon. m. Maria Djerova, 11 Aug 1963, 2 s. *Education:* Med Faculty, MD, 1958; Conferrec Spec Degree Anatomy, 1971; Sugrery, 1966; Orthop & Traumatology, 1986. *Appointments:* Asst Prof of Anatomy, 1961; Asssoc Prof, Med Academy, 1981; Prof, Hd of Orthop, Dept in Inst Orthop & Trauma; dir, Inst of Orthop & Traumatology, Sofia. *Publications:* Methoden fur Osteosynthese; Orthopaedic Surgery; Special Surgery Textbook; Ultrastruktur Veranderungen in den Restlunge nach Pulmonektomie. *Memberships:* Bilgarian Assoc of Orthopaedics & Traumatology; Orthopedia i Travmatologia, Medical Journal. *Hobbies:* Music; Reading; Sports. *Address:* 6 Dante Street, Sofia 1000, Bulgaria.

DO Dinh Tron, b. 1 Apr 1960, Pleiku, Vietnam. Dir & Prod of Editor of Vietnamese Newspaper, Vietnamese TV Program & Films. *Education:* Vietnam Univ of Forrestry in Ban Me Thuot, Vietnam. *Appointments:* Editor, Yeu, Mag, 1984-; Pres, Vietnamese Dir, USA, 1984-; Dir, Editor, producer of Vien Thao Films & Vietnamese TV Progrm, 1988-. *Publications:* Noi Niem Mang Theo; Huong Dan Nguoi Moi toi; Mua Pho Nui; Hon Em Gia Biet. *Memberships:* Vietnamese Chamber of Commerce in Northern California; Vietnamese Youth Assoc; Promoter for Vietnamese Concerts & Opera. *Honours:* Writing; Promotions Works; Bright Ideas; Helping Vietnamese Refugees. *Hobbies:* Making Movies; Writing Books, Novels; Serving the Communities. *Address:* 874 E Santa Clara Street, San Jose, CA 95116, USA.

DOBBELAERE Karel M T C, b. 16 Sept 1933, Nieuwpoort. Univ Prof. m. 17 Dec 1959, 2 s. *Education:* Licentiate Political & Social Sci, 1956; Doc Political & Social Sci, 1966; Catholic Univ of Leuven. *Appointments:* Asst Prof, 1962-66; Assoc Prof, 1966-68; Prof, 1968-; Catholic Univ of Leuven; Assoc Prof, 1966-70; Prof, 1970-; Univ Antwerp; Dean, 1971-75, 1990-93. *Publications:* Sociologische Analyse van de Katholiciteit; Secularization; A Multi Dimentional Concept; Het Volk Gods de Mist in; Numerous Articles. *Memberships:* Intl Soc for Sociology of Religion; Belgian Sociologieal Assoc; Mem, Koninlijke Academie Voor Wetenschrappen, Letteren En Schone Kunsten Van België. *Honours:* Jan Marie Huyghe Prize; Ministry of Educ Belgium; Member Academia Europaea; Fellow, Soc for Sci Study of Religion. *Hobby:* Travel. *Address:* Dept of Sociology, Van Evenstraat 2c, B-3000 Leuven, Belgium. 43, 52.

DOBBIN David Michael, b. 23 Mar 1948, Calgary. Producing Dir, Alberta Theatre Projects. *Education:* B Ed, 1971. *Appointments:* Founding Artistic Dir, Palisade Arts, 1968; Theatre Mgr, Round House London, 1971; Man Dir, Vancouver Playhouse, 1972; Artistic Dir, Western Cdn Theatre Co, Kamloops, 1979; Prod Dir, Alberta Theatre Projects, 1983-. *Creative Works:* Co Founder Vancouver Playhouse Acting Sch; Playrites Festival of New Cdn Plays AIP. *Memberships:* Professional Assoc of Candian Theatres; BC Touring Council for Performing Arts; Candian Conference of the Arts; Nat Theatre Sch; Calgary Economic Devel Advisory Council; Advisory Comm to Theatre Dept, Mount Royal Coll and Banff Sch of Fine Arts. *Honours:* Alberta Achievement Award; Queens Jubilee Medal; Award of Merit from Federal Govt; Citation from House of Commons; Member, Governor Generals Canadian Study Conference, 1991. *Address:* Alberta Theatre Projects, 220 9 Avenue SE, Calgary, Alberta, Canada T2G 5C4.

DOBRE Ioan, b. 26 Aug 1930, Caracal, Romania. Orthopaedic; Traumatological Surgeon; Chief of Orthopaedic Dept, Colentina Hosp. m. Dobre Romanita Christina, 10 Aug 1967. *Education:* Cluj Medical Faculty, 1949-55; Spec in Orthopaeic & Traumatology, 1963; Doc of Medical Sci, 1975; Primarius in Orthop & Traumatology, 1980. *Appointments:* Conslt Physician, Constanta, Romania, 1955-59; Specialist Orthopaedic & Truamatology, Bucarest, Colehtina Hosp, 1980-89; Chief of Orthopaedic Dept, 1989-. *Publications:* Surgery & Prosthetic Appliance of Locomotor System; Post Traumatic Instabilities of the Knee; Numerous Other Publications. *Memberships:* The Romanian Orthepaedic Traumatological Soc; The Francophone Ortheopaedic Soc. *Honours:* Sanitar Merit. *Hobbies:* Travel; Photography; Automobiles. *Address:* 70 778 Str Transilvania No.39, Bucharest, Romania.

DOBROWOLSKI Jozef Andrzej, b. 22 Sept 1939, Lodz, Lodza. Research Worker, Docente. m. Jolanta, 22 Oct 1964, 2 s. *Education:* Philosophy, History of Art, Univ of Warsaw, 1964; Amdiploma Philosphy, 1985; Doc of Philosophy, M Sklodowska Curie. *Appointments:* Tchr Philosophy, Secondary Schs, Lodz, 1964-70;Research Worker, Medical Academy, Lodz, 1970; Research Work, polish Culture, Research of the Polish Culture philosophy Soc, 1974-84; Philosophy Dept, Univ of Lodz, 1983-87; Univ of Lublin, Sci Scholarship, Italy, 1985-86. *Creative Works include:* Giambattisha Della porta i Laicyzacja pojecia, Magil Naturalnej; Euhemer Przeglad Religioznawczy; Atheismus Triumphatus. *Memberships:* Polish Soc of Philosophy; Polish Soc for the Religions; Cooperation with the Polish Soc of Philosopy and History of Medicine. *Honour:* Rektors Award; Ministerial Awards for long Research Work; Othe Sci Awards. *Hobbies:* Mountain Tourism; Swimming; Gardening. *Address:* Ul Matejki 16 m 3, 91 402 Lodz, Poland.

DOBSON Harold, b. 25 Aug 1922, Manchester, England. Metrologist. m. Eliane Marthe Henriette Edmée

Decoeur, Oct 1949, 2 s, 2 d. *Education:* Tchr Diploma; Univ Gottingen, 1945; Ord Nat Cert, Coll Tch, Manchester, 1947; Higher Nat Cert, Univ Manchester, 1948. *Appointments:* Army Serv Europe, 1942-47; Sci Tchr, 1945-47; Statistician Manch Corp Tras Dept, 1947- 49; Electronic Engr, Comp Gen De Metrologie, France, 1949-64; Metrology Mgr Itte Inst Div, 1964-82; Metrology Advisor, 1982-; Advisor Singapore inst of Stds, 1975-. *)Contributions to:* Articles to prof Journals; Metrology in Industry; Industrial Measurement. *Memberships:* Annecy le Vieux Lake Zone Residents Assn; Precision Measurements Assoc; Metrology Section of French Assoc for Quality. *Hobbies:* Gardening; Electric Trains. *Address:* 17 Rue Des Muses, 74940 Annecy Le Vieux, France. 52.

DOBSON Wendy, b. 23 Nov 1941, Vernon, Canada. Economist. m. H Anthony Hampson, 13 Dec 1986. *Education:* B ScN, Univ British Columbia, 1963; MPA, Harvard Univ, 1971; SMHyg, Harvard Univ, 1972; PhD, Princeton Univ, 1979. *Appointments:* Sp Asst to Pres, Intl Devel Research Centre, Ottawa, 1973-75; Economist, C D Howe Inst, 1979-81; Pres & Exec Dir, CD Howe Inst, 1981-87; Assoc Dep Minister of Finance, Government of Canada, 1987-89; Professor, Fac of Management, Univ of Toronto, 1990-. *Publications:* Japanese Trade and Investment in East Asia; Intl Economic Policy Coordination Requiem or Overture; Canadian-Japanese Economic Relations in a Triangular Perspective; Shaping Comparative Advantage; Editor and Author of more than 50 Publications and articles on economic policy. *Memberships:* Directorships: Du pont Canada Inc, IBM Canada Ltd; Working Ventures Canadian Fund; Toronto-Dominion Bank and Trans Canada Pipelines Limited; Mem, Canadian Economics Assoc; American Economics Assoc. *Hobbies:* Tennis; Skiing; Gardening; Reading; Photography; Music. *Address:* Faculty of Management, Univ of Toronto, 246 Bloor St West, Toronto, Canada M5S 1V4. 88.

DOCKERY David Samuel, b. 28 Oct 1952, Tuscaloosa, AL. Theologian; Editor. m. Lanese Huckeba, 14 June 1975, 3 s. *Education:* BS, Univ of Alabana, 1975; M Div, Grace Seminary, 1979; M Div, Southwestern Seminary, 1981; MA, Texas Christian Univ, 1986; PhD, Univ of Texas, 1988. *Appointments:* Pastor, Metropolitan Bapt Church, Brooklyn, NY, 1981- 84; prof of Theology, Criswell Coll, Dallas, TX, 1984-88; Asst Prof of New Testament, Southern Baptist Seminary, Louisville, 1988-91; Editor, Broadman Press, Nashville, 1990-. *Publications:* Doctrine of the Bible; Baptist of God; People of God; Southern Baptist and American Evangelist; New Testament Criticism & Intepretation. *Memberships:* Inst of Biblical Research; Evangelical Theological Soc; Soc of Biblical Literature; American Academy of Religion; Southern Baptist Historical Soc; Nat Assoc of Baptist Prof of Religion. *Honours:* Greek & NT Award. *Hobbies:* Sports; Basket Ball; Jogging; Music; Table Games; Family. *Address:* 139 Woodvale Drive, Hendersonville, TN 37075, USA. 125.

DODSON Daryl Theodore, b. 9 Oct 1934, Warrensburg, MO, USA. Theatrical Manager. *Education:* Bach of Sci, 1956, Central Missouri State Univ. *Appointments include:* US Army, 1957-59; Asst Dir, The Nikado, NY City Opera, 1959; Prod Mngr, American Ballet Theatre, 1963; Mngr, Opera House Kennedy Centre Washington, DC, 1981; Mngr, New York Engagement The Golden Land, 1985; Mngr New York Engagement & United States Tour, Paris Opera Ballet, 1987; Mngr United States Tour, Les Miserables, 1988-92; Manager, US Tour of The Phantom of The Opera, 1992. *Memberships:* Theta Chi; Theta Alphi Phi. *Honours:* Member, Govenor of South Carolina Council on the Arts; Advisory Panel, Vermont Council of the Arts. *Hobbies:* Antique Collecting; Travel. *Address:* 328 West 86th Street, New York, NY 10024, USA. 2.

DOE Alice Delores, b. 25 Sept 1952, Danville, VA. Rockingham County Head Start, Tchr. *Education:* BA, Livingstone Coll, Salisbury, 1971-75; Tech Coll,

Alamance, Burlington, 1972-83; NC A&T State Univ, Greensboro, 1983-87. *Appointments:* Tchr, Danville VA, 1975-77; US Air Force, SA, 1978-81; Substitute Tchr, Caswell Co Sch, 1984-86. *Memberships:* Caswell County Rescue Squd, EMT; Gwynns Chapel Baptist Church; Choir Dir, Chaplin; Young Childrens Choir Leader. *Hobbies:* Singing; Drawing; Learning new things; Volunteer Work, Danville Memorial Hosp. *Address:* Route 2, Box 190, Pelham NC 27311. 76.

DOLCET BUXERES Luis, b. 2 Aug 1909, Spain. Prof of Ophthalmology. Retired. m. Maria de la Concepcion Cort Lozano, 1 s. *Education:* Grad, Barcelona Univ; Doctorate, Madrid Univ. *Appointments include:* Prof of Ophthalmology Universidd Authonoma, Barcelona; Hd Ophthalmology Serv, Hebron Valley Soc Security Dept. *Publications:* Over 100 Research Articles in Sci Journals & Reviews; Over 100 Sci Papers. *Memberships include:* Numerous Orders of Chivalry; Circulo de la Amistad. *Honours:* Numerous Honors from Various Orders of Chivalry incl, Supreme Council, Grand Collar, Grand Cross of Justics, Military & Hospitaller Order of St Lazarus of Jerusalem; Knight Grand Cross of Justice; Ambassador Extraordinary & Plenipotentiary, Aztec Crown to Celestial Empire of Great China. *Hobbies:* Painting; Sculpture; Collecting Stamps; Aviation; Yachting. *Address:* Muntaner 350 08021, Barcelona, Spain. 1, 15, 43, 139, 151, 152.

DOLIN Michele Irene, b. 5 May 1951, Perth, Australia. Bank Exec. m. Robert Maskell. 2 s. 2 d. *Education:* BA, Univ of Maryland, USA, 1972; MA, Michigan state Univ, USA, 1978; MBA, Univ of Melbourne, Australia, 1984. *Appointments:* Colonial Mutual Life Assur Soc, 1979-85; Price Waterhouse Urwick, 1985-87; Challenge Bank Ltd, 1988-. *Memberships:* Australian Inst of Company Directors; Australian Inst of Bankers; Australian Inst of Management; Bd Mem, King Edward Memorial Hosp for Women; Bd Mem, Meerilinga Young Children's Foundation; Council Mem, Australian Inst of Management. *Honours:* Australian Inst of Managements; Excellence in management Award for Women, 1991. *Hobbies:* Sailing; Canoeing; Tennis; Cycling; Hiking; Gardening; Reading. *Address:* 7 Richmond Avenue, Claremont, WA, Australia.

DOMBROVSKY Victor Joseph, b. 3 Aug 1946, Brest, USSR. Hd, Pathology Dept, Belarussien Maternity & Child Care Inst, Minsk. m. Ann Leonova, 1 July 1970, 1 d. *Education:* Physician, State Medical Inst, Minsk, 1970; Paediatrician, postgrad Staff Courses, Belarussien Maternity & Child Care Inst, Minsk, 1972; MD, Sci Council, State Medical Inst, Minsk, 1979. *Appointments:* Staff Physician, Belarussien Maternity & Child Care Research Inst, 1970-72; Staff Researcg Sci, 1972-77; Snr Staff research Sci, 1977-79; Hd of Pathology Dept,1979-. *Publications:* Children & Dietetic nutrition; Manual for Paediatricians; Your Child & Nutrition; Young Family Encyclopedia; Medicamentous Properties of Some Agricultural Plants; Paediatric Handbook; 100 Research papers in Sci Journals. *Memberships:* Belarussien Maternity & Child Care Fund; Belarussien Physicians Against Nuclear Disaster. *Honours:* Gold Medal, High Sch Academic Achievements; First Class Diploma; Graduate First Class Honors Degree Diploma; Decoration, For Excellent Results in Public Health Serv; Bronze Medal, USSR Exhibition of Nat Economic Achievements. *Hobbies:* Tourism; Reading; Computer Games. *Address:* 52 Prityski Str, Apt 104, Minsk 220121, Republic of Belarus.

DOMVILLE Eric William, b. 27 Apr 1929, Liverpool, England. Prof of English, Univ of Toronto. m. Jean Mac Phail, 13 July 1987, 1 d, 1 Stepson, 2 Stepdaughters. *Education:* BA, English, Univ of London, 1961; PhD, Univ of London, 1965. *Appointments:* Univ of Toronto, Dept of English, 1964-. *Publications:* The Collected Letters of W B Yeats; 5 Novels Awaiting Pub; Children's Books; Stories & Poems. *Hobbies:* Music; Badminton; Tennis;

Walking; Writing on Music. *Address:* 342 Brunswick Avenue, Toronto, Ontario, Canada M5R 2Y9. 88.

DONALD Craig Reid Cantlie, b. 8 Sept 1914, Lumphanan, Aberdeenshire. Retired Civil Servant. m. Mary Isabel Speid, 2 June 1945, (dec 1 Dec 1989) 1 d. *Education:* BA, MA, Fettes, Emmanuel Coll, Cambridge. *Appointments:* Admin Officer, Cyprus, 1937; Military Serv, Middle East & Central Mediterranean, 1940-46; Lieut Colonel, Commissioner, Famagusta, 1948; Registrar, Cooperative Soc, 1951; Deputy Financial Sec, 1951; Sec to the Treasury, 1956-63; Member Legislative Council, Busar, Malvern Coll, 1964- 79. *Memberships:* Economic Development Inst, World Bank. *Honours:* CMG; OBE. *Hobbies:* Country Pursuits. *Address:* 55 Geraldine Road, Malvern, Worcs WR14 3NU. 1.

DONATELLI Luciano, b. 24 Oct 1947, Biella. Managing Dir. m. Chiorino Franca, 20 June 1970, 2 d. *Education:* Diploma Perito Sch, Eugenio Bona, 1968; Master Gen Sch Istud, 1974. *Appointments:* Sls Mgr, Astrum France, 1968-69; Sls Mgr, E Zegna Taylor Div, 1969-71; Mkt Mgr, Emilio pucci, 1971-73; Project Mgr, Accessory Div, E Zegna, 1974-78; Mkt Mgr, Knitware Div, E Zegna, 1978-79; Mngr Dir, Accessory Div, E Zegna, 1979-88; Mngr Dir, Acc & Informal Div, E Zegna, 1989-. *Memberships:* Italian Ties & Scarves Mfg, Milan; Calzemaglie, Italian Knitware Assoc, Milan. *Hobbies:* Collector of Ancient Fabrics. *Address:* Via Novara 71, 28047 Oleggio, (Novara) Italy.

DONCHEV Anthony Kirilov, b. 5 Feb 1959, Bourgas, Bul. Composer; Pianist. m. Nadia Doncheva, 8 Oct 1983, 1 s. *Education:* Sofia Sch of Music, 1973-78; Academy of Music, 1980-84. *Appointments:* Academy of Music, 1990; Theatre of Sofia, 1992. *Creative Works:* Music for Plays & Feature Films. *Memberships:* Assoc of Bulgarian Jazz Musicians. *Honours:* First Prize, Best Soloist Prize, Intl Jazz Comp; Main Prize, Yound European Jazz Artist. *Hobbies:* Diving; Fishing. *Address:* 31 Emil Markov Blud, BL 76, Apt 99, 1612 Sofia, Bulgaria.

DONG Nai Qiang, b. 18 May 1941, City of Guilin. Librarianship. m. Du Shu Xian, 1 May 1970, 1 s, 1 d. *Education:* No.1 Middle Sch, Beijing Normal Univ, 1957; Beijing NOT Middle Sch, 1960; BA, Beijing Univ, Bei Da, 1968. *Appointments:* Sch Tchr; Editor; Writer; Farmer; Dir of the Dept of History, Beijing Normal Univ, 1986-; Dir of the Acquisition Department at the University Library. *Publications:* The Lates Bibliography of the Study of Red Chamber; The Concise Dictionary of Confucian Studies; Xiang Fai; Women & Football; The Males Changing Status in History; Confucian's viewpoint of women and its historival significance, delivered in the International Conference of the Confucian School and its Modern Perspective, China, 1992. *Memberships:* Assoc of China Confucius; China Library Assoc; China Index Assoc; Beijing Womens Theory Studies Soc. *Honours:* Chosen as an Outstanding Faculty of Beijing Normal Univ; Advanced Individual of Nat Unity of Beijing. *Hobbies:* Chess; Cycling; Reading. *Address:* Beijing Normal Univ Library, Beijing, China 100875.

DONLEAVY James Patrick, b. 23 Apr 1926, USA. Author. (1) m. Valerie Heron (div) 1 s, 1 d, (2) m. Mary Price, Div (div), 1 s, 1 d. *Education:* Prepatory Sch, New York; Trinity Coll, Dublin. *Publications include:* The Ginger Man, novel, 1955; Fairy Tales of New York, play, 1960; What They Did In Dublin With The Ginger Man, introd & play, 1961; A Singular Man, novel, 1963, play, 1964; Meet My Maker The Mad Molecule, short stories, 1964; The Saddest Summer of Samuel S, novel, 1966, play, 1967; The Beastly Beatitudes of Balthazar B, novel, 1968, play, 1981; The Onion Eaters, novel, 1971; The Plays of J P Donleavy, 1972; A Fairy Tale of New York, novel, 1973; The Unexpurgated Code: a complete manual of survival and manners, 1975; The Destinies of Darcy Dancer, Gentleman, novel, 1977; Schultz,

novel, 1980; Leila, novel, 1983; De Alfonce Tennis: the superlative game of eccentric champions, its history, accoutrements, rules, conduct and regimen, sports manual, 1984; Ireland, in all her Sins and in some of her Graces, 1986; Are you Listening Rabbi Low, novel, 1987; A Singular Country, 1989; That Darcy, That Dancer, That Gentleman, novel, 1990; contribs to num jrnls inclng, The Observer; The Times, London; NY Times; Washington Post; Esquire; Envoy; Punch; Guardian; Satuday Evening Post; Holiday; Atlantic Monthly; Satuday Review; The New Yorker; Queen; Vogue; Penthouse; Playboy; Architectual Digest; Vanity Fair; Rolling Stone. *Honours:* Brandies Univ, Creative Arts Award; Evening Std Drama Award; American Academy & Nat Inst of Arts & Letters Award. *Hobbies:* Tennis; Dry Stone Wall Building. *Address:* Levington Park, Mullingar, Co Westmeath, Eire. 1, 2, 3, 34, 43.

DONNET Jean Baptiste Alexio, b. 28 Sept 1923, Pontgibaud, France. Prof; Scientific Conslt. m. Suzanne Ritiman, 21 Dec 1968, 1 s, 2 d. *Education:* Sci Grad, Chemical Engr, 1946; PhD, 1953. *Appointments:* Asst, then in charge Research, Centre Nat de la Recherche Scientifique, 1946-53; Prof, Dir, Chemical Sch Mulhouse, ibid, 1953-; Faculty, 1975-, Pres, 1977-82, Univ of Haute Alsace; Dir, Research Centre Surface Physical Chemistry, 1967-86. *Publications:* Numerous Books inc Synthetic Rubber; Carbon Back; Translated Chinese, Russian, Japanese; Carbon Fibre; Sci Works; Various Journals. *Memberships include:* Rubber Div, American Chemical Soc; Intl Union of Pure & Applied Chemistry; Chemical Soc of France; Nat Com of Chemistry; French Polymers Group; European Fed of Polymers; French Chemical Soc. *Honours include:* Nat Order of Merit; Officer, French Legion of Honor; Commander, French Order of Academic Palms; Georges Skakel Memorical Award; Commemorative Medal, French Assoc Of Robber Engr; Na Academy of Sci Award; Harries Medal, Deutsche Kautshuk Gesellshaft; Georges Stafford Whitby, American Chemical Soc. *Hobbies:* Walking; Skiing. *Address:* 24 rue Zwiller, Didenheim, 69200 Mulhouse, France. 43, 52, 91, 139.

DONTCHEV George, b. 18 Aug 1967, Bourgas. Musician. *Education:* Bulgarian Academy of Music, 197-91. *Membership:* Bulgarian Jazz Soc. *Hobbies:* Theatre; Skiing; Reading. *Address:* 55 Hemus Str, 1111 Sofia, Bulgaria.

DORAIS Leo A, b. 21 Sept 1929, Montreal. Prof, Univ Ottawa. m. Suzanne Danserean, 3 Sept 1955, 2 s, 2 d. *Education:* BA, 1952; B PR, 1953; LB, 1955; MBA, 1962; PhD, 1964. *Appointments:* Prof, Univ of Montreal, 1956-67; Vic Pres, SHA Inc, 1967-69; Rector, Univ Quebec Montreal, 1969-74; Vice Pres, Cida, 1974-79; Asst Deputy Minister, Communications, 1979-83; Autogestion Universitaire, Montreal PUQ, 1974; Sec Gen, Nat Museum, 1983-87; prof Fac, Admin, 1987- . *Publications:* Chapters in Books; Articles. *Memberships:* Corporation Psychologues Quebec; Canadian Psychological Assoc; Admin Sci Canada; Can Assoc Art Admin Educators. *Hobbies:* Skiing; Photography. *Address:* 261 River Road, Vanier Ontario, Canada K1L 8B8. 88.

DORN Vjekoslav, b. 9 Sept 1939, Hrtkovci, Ruma. Ophthalmologist; Prof of Ophthalmology. m. Ljubica Sostarec, 9 June 1990. *Education:* Medical Faculty, Univ of Zagreb, 1963; Spec of Ophthalmology, 1970; Doc of Sci, 1979; Habilitation, Univ Lectr, 1988; Prof of Ophthalmology, 1988. *Appointments:* Physician, 1963-64; Asst in Inst for Medical Research & Occuptional Medicine, 1965-70; Univ Eye Clinic, 1970-76; Faculty of Medicine, Univ of Zagreb, 1976-. *Publications:* Co-author, Ophthalmology, A Textbook for Medical & Stomatol; Co-author, Diagnostic Ultrasound in Developing Countries; Articles in Med Periodicals. *Memberships:* SIDUO; Österreichische Ophthalmologische Gesellschaft; Julius Hirschberg Gesellschaft. *Hobbies:* History of Ophthalmology & Medicine; Christian Iconography; Hagiology; History of

Arts; Medical Herbs. *Address:* Univ Eye Clinic, KBC Rebro, Kispaticeva 12, 41000 Zagreb, Croatia.

DORNEMAN Eugene T, b. 26 July 1938, Hazleton, PA, USA. Snr Quality Engr. m. Sharon L Smith, 28 Dec 1968, 2 d. *Education:* Assoc of Engr, Penn State Univ, 1963; BS, Mech & Ind Engr, Letourneau Coll, 1969; MS, Ind Engr, Texas Tech Univ, 1971. *Appointments:* US Army, USA & Canada, 1957-61; Sandia Nat Laboratory, Snr Draftsman, 1963-67; Letourneau Corporation, Ind Engr, 1968-69; Atomic Energy Commission, Gen Engr, 1971-76; Energy Research & Devel Admin, Program Mgr, 1976-81; US Dept of Energy, Snr Quality Engr, 1981-. *Creative Works:* Tchr, Biblical Skills of Leadership & Scout Oath, Law, Motto & Slogan as Found in the Bible. *Memberships include:* Boy Scouts of America; Creation Research Soc; Reg Prof Engrs; Awana Intl Youth Assoc; Certified Snr Engr Tech. *Honours:* Eagle Scout; Explorer Silver Award; Door Olive Scholarship; Intl Wood Badge; Vigil Honor Award; State of Texas Research & Tching Assistantship; Silver Beaver Award; District Award of Merit; US Doe Recognition for Contribution to community Activities; God & Serv Award. *Hobbies:* Reading; Bible Study & Tching; Serv to Youth as an Adult. *Address:* 3517 Parsifal St, NE, Albuguergue, NM 87111, USA.

DOROFEEVA Alla, b. 14 Sept 1935, USSR. Mathematician. m. (1) 8 Feb 1954, (2) 26 Oct 1973, 2 d. *Education:* Moscow Univ, 1957; post Grad Courses, Moscow Univ, 1960; Candidat of Fisico Math Sci, 1963; Docent, 1968. *Appointments:* Asst of Chai, Members Theory in Moscow Univ, 1960; Docent, Moscow Univ, 1968. *Creative Works:* Creative Courses of Higher Mathematics. *Hobbies:* Reading; Skiing. *Address:* Paustowskogo Street 3, Flat 277, 117463 Moscow, Russia.

DORSETT Charles Irvin, b. 25 Sept 1945, Lufkin, Texas, USA. Univ Lectr. *Education:* BS, Austin State Univ, 1967; MS, Austin State Univ, Texas, 1968; PhD, North Texas State Univ, 1976. *Appointments include:* Tchr, State Univ, Nacogdoches, 1967-68; Lectr, North Texas State Univ, Denton, 1976-77; Lectr, Texas A&M Univ, Coll Station, Texas, 1979-82; Louisiana Tech Univ, 1982-. *Publications include:* Cyanide Analysis of Peaches, Economic Botany; Semi Compact, R & Product Spaces, Bulletin of the Malaysian Mathematical Soc; Semi Compactness, Questions & Answers in General Topology; Semi T, & Semi Ro Spaces, Ranchi Univ Mathematical Journal; Semi Normal Spaces, Kyungpook Mathematical Journal; Numerous other Mathematical Journals. *Memberships:* Americal Mathematical Soc; Bharata Ganita Parisad; Nat Academy of Sci, India; Sigma Xi; Intl Platform Assoc; American Biographical Inst Research Assoc; the Indian Academy of Mathematics. *Honours include:* Nat Honor Soc; Alpha Chi; Kappa Delta Pi. *Hobbies:* Mathematics Research; Farming. *Address:* Dept of Mathematics & Statistics, Louisiana Tech Univ, Ruston, LA 71272, USA. 2, 7, 52, 139, 152, 155, 156, 162.

DOSSETOR Roberts Simon, b. 20 Oct 1942, Wells, Somerset, England. Neuroradiologist. m. Helen Kalantidou, 19 Oct 1968, 1 s, 1 d. *Education:* BA, Oxon, 1964; BM BCh, 1968; DMRD, 1972; FRCR, 1974. *Appointments:* Registrar Radiology, 1971-74; Snr Reg Radiology, 1974- 75; Radcliffe Infirmary, Oxford; Conslt Rediologist, The Royal Sussex County Hosp, Hurstwood Park, Neurological Centre, Haywoods Heath, 1975-. *Publications:* A Simple New Formula for Relating Changes in Renal Lenght to Changes in Renal Volume; Computerised Tomography Lymphangiography an Ultra Sound in the Diagnosis of Lymph Node Enlargement; A Comparison in Total Body Computerised Tomography; Some Medical Aspects of Holography in Proceedings of XVth Intl Congress Radiology. *Memberships:* British Inst of Radiology; Royal Coll of Radiologists; British Soc of Neuroradiologists. *Hobbies:* Reading; Music; Painting; Sailing. *Address:* 8 Orpen Road, Hove, East Sussex BN3 6NJ, England. 158.

DOSTAL Elisabeth, b. 26 Apr 1948, Linz, Austria. Futurist; Conslt on Societaltrans Formation. m. Pauel Rafael Dostal, 25 Jan 1974. *Education:* Masters Degree, Social Sci, Kepler Univ, Linz; PhD, Univ of Cape Town. *Appointments:* Asst Economist, FVB, 1972-75; Researcher, CDC, 1975-77; Snr Researcher, Univ of Stellenbosch, 1977-91; Conslt, Vision Devel & Social Transformations, 1991-. *Publications:* Books; Articles; Speeches. *Memberships:* World Future Soc; Long Rauge Planning Soc; South Africa Assoc of Training & Devel; South Africa Market Research Assoc. *Hobbies:* Personal Transformation Activies; Painting; Sailing. *Address:* PO Box 5109, Helderberg, 7135, RSA.

DOUGLAS James, b. 4 July 1932, Dumbarton. Composer. m. Helen Torrance Fairweather, 16 Apr 1968, 2 s, 1 d. *Education:* Edinburgh Lram Arcne, London; Paris Conservatore; Hochschule, Munich; Mozarteum, Salzburg. *Appointments:* Accompnis, 1952-; Composer, 1952-; Dir, Eschenbach Editions, 1986-; Dir, Caritas Records, 1990-. *Creative Works:* Published Musical Compositions; Symphonies; 20 Orchestral Works; STring Quartets; Chamber Music; Piano Music; Organ Works. *Memberships:* Incorporated Soc of Musicians; Royal Coll of Organists. *Honours:* W B Ross Composition Prize; Arezzo Composition. *Hobbies:* Reading; Art; Theatre. *Address:* c/o Eschenbach Editions, 28 Dalrympie Crescent, Edinburgh, EH9 2NX, Scotland.

DOVE John, b. 24 July 1944, Hoylaux, Cheshire. Theatre Dir. *Education:* Ampleforth Coll; Durham Univ, BA, MA; Manchester Univ. *Appointments:* Freelance Dir, 1974-76; Assoc Dir, Old Vic, 1977-78; Assoc Dir, Hampstead Theatre, 1984-91. *Creative Works:* Over 80 Plays in London, Bristol, Manchester; New Plays for Hampstead, The Royal Court, The Bush; Revivals for the Old Vic, Manchester Royal Exchange. *Hobbies:* Music; Painting; Writing; Sport. *Address:* Simpson Fox Assoc, 52 Shaftesbury Avenue, London W1, England.

DOW Clista Mary Etta, b. 27 July 1931, Purcell, Oklahoma, USA. Tchr, Gifted & Talented program. *Education:* BA, Tufts Univ, 1953; MEd, Boston Univ, 1954; Tching the Talented Program, Univ of Connecticut, 1976-79. *Appointments:* Sharon Public Sch, 1954-; Adjunct Faculty, Lesley Coll, 1980-81; Fitchburg State, 1978-79; Bridgewater State, 1979, 1984; Anna Maria, 1977; Stonehill, 1966-67. *Publications:* Numerous Curriculum Projects; Once Upon a Building; Building A Differntiated Learning Environment for the Gifted & Talented; Triad Prototype Series; Power Over Words; An Inductive Approach to the Teaching of Spelling. *Memberships:* Nat Educ Assoc; Massachusetts Tchrs Assoc; Norfolk County Tchrs Assoc; Sharon Tchrs Assoc; Massachusetts Assoc for Advancement of Individual Potential; World Council for Gifted & Talented. *Honours:* Boston Edison Scholar; Horace Mann Award; Norfolk County Tchrs Assoc Award of Merit; Massachusetts Assoc for Advancement of Individual potential Public Service Award. *Hobbies:* Travel; Bridge; Reading; Theatre; Painting; Writing; Cirriculum Projects. *Address:* 18 Paul Revere Road, Sharon, MA 02067, USA. 15.

DOW Marilyn Schoeman, b. 28 June 1942, Cedar Falls, Iowa, USA. Business Owner; Prof Speaker; Author. m. Francis Shannon Dow, 6 June 1965. *Education:* BA, Univ of Northern Iowa, 1964; MA, Univ of Southern California, 1973; Post Grad, Kent State Univ; Ball State Univ. *Appointments include:* Tchr, Cedar Falls, Iowa, 1965-66; District Mgr, Field Enterprises, Cedar Falls, 1967-68; Tchr, Escola Americana, Belo Horizonte, brazil, 1974-75; Conslt, Gifted Educ Cooperative, 1982-84; Prof Speaker, Creative Thinking, 1984-; Adjunct Prof, Western Washington Univ, 1984-; pres, Schoeman Dow & Assoc, Seattle, 1984-. *Publications:* Teaching Techniques That Tantalize; Young Authors Conference: Kids Writing for Kids; Audio Tapes; Video Tapes. *Memberships:* Nat Assoc of Gifted Children; Nat Speakers Assoc; American Creativity Assoc; Washington Inventors Assoc; Minnesota Inventors

Assoc; Assoc for Quality & Participation. *Honours:* Scholarship Established in my name. *Address:* Schoeman Dow Assoc, 2515 39th Avenue SW, Seattle, WA 98116, USA.

DOW William Gould, b. 30 Sept 1895, Faribault, Minnesota, USA. Electrical Engr. Retired; Part Time Conslt. m. (1) Edna ois Sontag, 24 Oct 1924 dec 1963, 2 s, (2) Katherine Bird Keene, 2 Apr 1968, 1 Stepson, 2 Stepdaughters. *Education:* BS, EE, 1916; Electrical Engr, 1917; MSE, Univ of Michigan. *Appointments include:* Lieutenant US Army Engr, 1917-19; Westinghouse Electric Corporation, 1920-26; Faculty, 1926-64; Prof, 1945-64; Dept Chmn, 1958-64; Dept of Electric Engr, Univ of Michigan, Ann Arbor; Part Time Geophysicist, Ibid, 1966-71; Research Radar Countermeasurers, Harvard Univ, 1943-45; Members, US Panel, Rockets & Satelites for Outer Space Research, 1940-60. *Publications:* Fundamentals of Engeering Electronics; Very High Frequency Techniquesl Various Articles, physical Electronics; US Patents, Controlled Nuclear Fusion. *Memberships include:* Cosmos Club; Inst of Electrical & Electronics Engr; American Inst for Advancement of Sci; American Astronautical Soc; American Soc for Engring Educ; American Welding Soc. *Honours:* Recognition, US Nat Defence Research Comm for War Research; Distinguished Alumnus, Univ of Minnesota; Medal Award in Elet Eng Education, Inst of Electrical & Eletronics Engrs; Honorary ScD, Univ of Colorado. *Hobbies:* Intl Travel; Photography. *Address:* 915 Heatherway, Ann Arbor, MI 48104, USA. 2, 52.

DOWD Diane, b. 11 Mar 1953, San Francisco, California, USA. Communications/Finance Exec; Lawyer. m. Scott Allen Spiro, 8 Aug 1984, 1 s, 1 d. *Education:* BS, Arizona State Univ, 1976; JD, Pepperdine Univ Sch of Law, 1984. *Appointments:* WPVI TV producer, ABC Cap Cities Communications, Philadelphia, 1979; Producer, Cable New Netwrork, Los Angeles, 1980; Law Clerk, Times Mirror Corp, Los Angeles, 1983; Law Clerk, Federal Communications Commission, Washington DC, 1983; Sole Practice, 1986; Chief Exec, pharos Comm, Morgan Taylor. *Contributions to:* Editor, American Bar Assoc Securities Glossary. *Memberships:* American Bar Assoc; District of Columbia Bar Assoc; Nat Academy of Television Arts & Sci; Arizona Press Club. *Honours:* Arizona State Univ Deans List; Special Olympics Cert of Appreciation. *Hobbies:* Sailing; Tennis. *Address:* 9025 Wilshire Blvd, Suite 309, Beverly Hills, CA 90211, USA. 9, 59.

DOWGIALO Jan-Tadeusz, b. 7 Jan 1940, Lithuania. Tchr of Mathematics; Dir of Secondary Sch, no.19 in Vilnius. m. Maria Czesokajte, 20 Apr 1968, 2 s. *Education:* Tchr Inst, Vilnius, 1958-60; Pedagogical Inst, Grodno, 1970-75. *Appointments:* Eight Yr Sch, Korwie, Vilnius District, Tchr of Mathematics, 1960-70; Eight Yr Sch in Egliszki, Vilnius District, Dirs Asst, 1970-80; Secondary Sch, Lawaryszki, Vilnius Dis, Dir, 1980-82; Sec Sch no.19 Vilnius, Dir, 1982. *Memberships:* Counsil of ir Assoc, Vilnius. *Honours:* Ministry of Culture & Educ, Honourable Diploma. *Hobbies:* Reading; Gardening. *Address:* Architektu 200-39, 2049 Vilnius, Lithuania.

DOWNIE Mary Alice Dawe (Hunter), b. 12 Feb 1934, USA. Writer. m. John Downie, 27 June 1959, 3 d. *Education:* BA, English Language & Literature, Trinity Coll, Univ of Toronto. *Appointments:* Book Review Editor, Kingston Whig Standard, 1973-78. *Publications:* The Wind has Wings; Poems from Canada with Barbara Robertson; Seared Sarah; Dragon on Parade; The Last Ship; Jenny Greenteeth; A Proper Acadian with George Rawlyk; The Wicked Fairy Wife; Alisons Ghosts with John Downie; Stones & Cones with Julian Gillilan; Stories, Four Short Stories; La Belle et La Laide; Chapters from Honor Bound reprinted in inside & outside and Measure me Sky; Stories from the Witch of the North; Crossroads 1; Out and About; The Wellfilled Cupboard, with Barbara Robertson; How the Devil Got his Cat, 1988; The Buffalo Boy and the Weaver Girl, 1989; Doctor Dwarf and Other Poems for Children,

1990. *Memberships:* Writers Union of Canda; PEN. *Address:* 190 Union Street, Kingston, Ontario, Canda K7L 2P6.

DOWNIE Robert Silcock, b. 19 Apr 1933, Glasgow. Univ Prof. m. Eileen Dorother Flynn, 15 Sept 1958, 3 d. *Education:* Univ of Glasgow, MA, 1951-55; Queens Coll, Oxford, B Phil, 1957-59; Russian Linguist, Intelligence Corps, 1955-57. *Appointments:* Lectr in Philosophy, Glasgow Univ, 1959-69; Prof of Philosophy, Syracase HY, 1963-64; Prof of Moral Philosophy, Glasgow Univ, 1969-. *Publications:* Government Action and Morality; Respect for Persons; Roles And Values; Healthy Respect; Health Promotion; The Making of a Doctor. *Memberships:* Royal Soc of Edinburgh. *Hobbies:* Playing Piano; Hill Walking. *Address:* Dept of Philosophy, Glasgow Univ, Glasgow G12 8QQ, Scotland. 1, 34.

DOWNS Thomas, b. 27 June 1946, Huddersfield, Yorkshire. Univ prof; Engr. m. Tanya Nikitin, 18 June 1976, 1 s, 1 d. *Education:* BTech, 1968, PhD, 1972, Univ of bradford. *Appointments:* Research Engr, Theoretical Sci Lab, Marconi Co, Essex UK, 1968-73; Lectr, 1973-77; Snr Lectr, 1978-82; Reader, 1982-87; Prof, 1987-; Dept of Electrical Engr, Univ of Queensland, Australia. *Publications:* Textbook, Logic Design with Pascal, with M F Schulz; Over 100 Tech Papers. *Memberships:* Inst of Engr, Australia; Australian Computer Soc; Inst of Electrical & Electronics Engrs; Inst of Mathematics & its Applications, UK. *Honours:* Travelling Scholarship, Inst of Electrical Engrs. *Hobbies:* Opera; Ballet; Classical Music; Squash; Cricket; Running; Reading Novels. *Address:* Dept of Electrical Engr, Univ of Queensland, St Lucia, Queensland 4067, Australia.

DOWSON Jonathan Hudson, b. 19 Mar 1942, Leeds, England, Conslt Psychiatrist; Univ Lectr. m. Lynn Susan Dothie, 29 Dec 1965, 2 s, 1 d. *Education:* The Leys Sch Cambridge; Queens Coll, Cambridge, 1960-63; St Thomas Hospital, 1963-66; MA, MB, B Chir, MD, DPM, PhD, FRC Psych. *Appointments:* Lectr Anatomy, Univ of Edinburgh, 1969-72; Lectr Psychiatry, Univ of Edinburgh, 1973-75; Conslt Psychiatrist, Addenbrookes Hosp, Cambridge, Univ Lectr, Cambridge, 1977-. *Publications:* Treatment & Mgmt in Adult Psychiatry; Papers on Ageing; Brain Lipopigment; Drugs in Psychiatry; personality Disorder. *Memberships:* Royal Coll of Psychiatrists. *Honours:* Visiting Prof, Univ of Florida; Fellow Commoner, Queens Coll, Cambridge. *Hobbies:* Squash; Theatre. *Address:* c/o Univ Dept of Psychiatry, Level E4, Addenbrookes Hospital, Hills Road, Cambridge CB2 2QQ, England.

DRABBE Jheke, b. 13 July 1947. Rotterdam. Pianist. *Education:* Royal Conservatory of Music, The Hayges, Netherlands, 1963-68. *Appointments:* Prof, Conservatory, Rotterdam, 1980; Member of the Contemporain Chamber Music Ensemble. *Memberships:* Chamber Music Soc, Rotterdam. *Address:* Simon Vistdykleans, 2343 KW Oegstgeast, The Netherlands.

DRAGOSTINOV Stefan, b. 11 Apr 1948, Sofia. Composer; Gen Artistic Dir of the Philip Koutev Nat Folklore Company. m. Elene Konstantinova, 22 Aug 1978, 1 d. *Education:* State Sch of Music, Sofia, 1963-67; Bulgarian State Conservatory, 1967-70; Leningrad Conservatory, 1970-72; Army Service, 1972-74; DAAD Foundation, Cologne, 1982. *Appointments:* Conductor, Philip Koutev, Nat Folklore Co, 1974-86; Chief Conductor, 1986-88; General Artistic Dir, 1988-. *Creative Works include:* Six Symphonies; Two Vocal Cycles; Over 150 Songs, Nat Falklore Co; Film & Scenic Music; Books; Paintings. *Memberships:* Bulgarian Composers Union; Rotary Club, Sofia. *Honours:* First Prize, Karlheinz Stockhausen, Italy; Grand Prix, Arthur Honegger, Foundation de France; Second Prize, Simon Bolivar, Venezuela; Fernando Pessoa, Portugal. *Hobbies:* Fine Arts; Automobilism. *Address:* ul Persenk, Blok 24, Vhod B, 1126 Sofia, Bulgaria.

DRAPER Line Bloom, b. 10 Nov, Verviers, Belgium. Artist; Painter; Engrosser-Illuminator; Printmaker; Enamelist; Tchr; Jnr Lectr. m. Anthony Rubba. *Education:* Ecole des Arts Decoratifs, Verviers; Academie Royale de Tournai, US Bowling Green State Univ; Skowegan Sch of Art, Maine. *Appointments:* One Artist Shows inc: Cinema Gallery, Toledo, Ohio; Edison; Toledo; Ohio; Spectrum Friends of Fine Arts, Toledo, Ohio; Unitarian Church, Toledo, Ohio; Wauseon Historical Soc, Ohio; Toledo Museum of Art, Gallery 8. *Creative Works:* Touring Exhibitions. American Artist Assoc Traveling Exhibition; Casein Intl Touring Exhibition; Nat Painters in Casein Touring Exhib; Printmakers Nat Traveling Exhib; Spectrum Friends of Fine Art; 32nd Circuit Exhib of Ohio Water Colour Soc. *Memberships include:* Athena Art Soc; Prof Art Guild; Toledo Artists Club; Womens Republican Club of Boca Raton; Nat Museum of Women in the Arts; Inlt Soc of Artists; Soc of Scribes & Illuminators. *Honours include:* Broward Art Guild, Ft Lauderdale; Nat Casein Show, New York; Ohio Gold Medal Show, Toledo; Toledo Museum of Art, Ohio. *Address:* 401 East Linton Blvd 668, Delray Beach, FL 33483, USA. 2, 7, 8, 52.

DREES Gerd Udo, b. 29 Apr 1933, Breslau. Hd of Section, Commission of European Communities. m. Ingrid Schultz, 7 Apr 1959. *Education:* Economics & Business Admin, Betriebswirt, 1954-57. *Appointments:* Ind, 1957-58; High Authority of European Coal & Steel Community, Luxemburg, 1958-67; Sec of Interinst, Group Research, 1967-68; Civil Servant, Commission of European Communities, Brussels, Activities in Research and industrial pol, information netwrokls, steel, 1968-. *Publications:* Several Relating to Economics. *Hobbies:* Gardening; Sailing; Photo/Video. *Address:* Rue du Cortil Bailly 51, B-1380 Lasne, Belgium.

DREW Wallace Thomas, b. 16 Sept 1917, Wausau, Wisconsin, USA. Investment Banker. m. Katherine Connell House, 26 Jan 1942, 1 s, 2 d. *Education:* BA, Univ of Wisconsin, 1937. *Appointments:* Major, US Army, 1941-46; Asst Ad Mgr, Norwich Pharm Co, 1946-48; Advertising Mgr, Bristol Myers Co, New York, 1948-57; Vice Pres Cunningham & Walsh, New York, 1957-59; Vice Pres, Dir, Coty, 1959-64; Pres, Lander Co, 1964-68; Mngr Dir, Revlon Intl, London, 1968-71; Vice Pres, Smith Barney Harris Upham & Co, Santa Barbara, 1972-. *Memberships:* Drug Chemical & Allied Trades Assn; Nuclear Age Peace Foundation; St James The Less, Epis Church; All Saints By The Sea Epis Church. *Honours:* Outstanding Jnr Man; Phi Kappa Phi; Bronze Star, US Army; Distinguished Citizen Award; ADL, B'Nai B'Rith; Man of the Year Award; Lifetime Achievement Award. *Hobbies:* Sailing; Book Collecting; Intl Travel; Intl Relations. *Address:* 142 Northridge Road, Santa Barbara, CA 93105, USA. 59.

DREYER Inge, b. 12 June 1933, Berlin. Writer. *Education:* Univ, Coll of Educ, 1952-55; First State Exam passed with Distinction, 1955; Second State Exam, 1959; Degree Rektorin, 1968. *Appointments:* Tchr, 1956-68; Headmistress, 1968-78. *Publications:* Achtung Stolperstelle; Schule mit Dachschaden; Toenende Stille; Dic Streuner von Pangkor. *Memberships:* Writers Union; GEDOK; NGL; World Acad of Arts & Culture. *Honours:* World Poets Award Golden Crown; Doktor of Literature, confered by London Inst for Applied Res. *Hobbies:* Dance; Painting; Illustration; Dress Design; Skiing; Mountaineering; Sailing; Windsurfing. *Address:* Winkler Str 4A, Berlin 33, Germany. 30.

DRIVER David John, b. 4 Aug 1942, Cambridge. Hd of Design, The Times. m. Sara Penelope Rock, 27 Nov 1976, 1 s, 1 d. *Education:* Perse Sch, Cambridge, 1949-59; Cambridge Sch of Art, 1959-63. *Appointments:* Art Editor, Farm & Country, 1963-67; Asst Art Editor, Women Mirror, 1967-68; Art Dir, Cornmarket Press, 1968-69; Art Dir & Deputy Editor, Radio Times, 1969-81; Hd of Design & Asst Ed, The Times, 1981-. *Creative*

Works: Illustration. Town Queen, Vogue; Penguin Books; Observer; Sunday Times; Re Designed. Harpers Bazaar; The Listener; Art dir, Francis Kyle Gallery; Design work for Post Office inc Stamps for Christmas; Books. The Art of Radio Times; Graham Greene Country; The Windsor Style; The Mediterranean Shore. *Honours:* Design & Art Dir Gold & Silver Awards; Editorial Award of Excellance; Features Design Award; british Press Awards for the Times. *Hobbies:* Cricket; Collecting. *Address:* 56 Milton Park, London, N6 5QA, England.

DROBENA Thomas John, b. 23 Aug 1934, Chicago, Ill. Educator. m. Wilma S Kucharek, 27 Dec 1980, 1 s. *Education:* BA, Valparaiso Univ, 1964; ThB, Concordia Theological Seminary, 1961; M Div, 1974; MA, Herbrew Univ, Jerusalem, 1968; STM, Lutheran Theological Seminary, 1986; PhD, California Grad Sch, 1975. *Appointments:* Slavic Heritage Inst, Dir, 1965-; State Univ, Binghamton, Adj Prof, 1975-77; Holy Trinity Church, Torringdon,Co Pastor, 1986-. *Publications include:* Heritage of the Skus; Numerous Articles & Journals. *Memberships:* Inst Slovacco; Amer Assoc for the Advancement of Slavic Studies; Amer Tchrs of Slavic and East European Languages; Czechoslovak Soc of Arts & Sci; Slavic Heritage Inst. *Honours:* DSc London Univ; Russian & East European Centre, Univ of Illinois; US State Dept to Isreal. *Address:* c/o Slavic Heritage Inst, PO Box 1882, Torrington, CT 06790, USA.

DRUJININ Vladimir, b. 15 Aug 1908, Russia. Writer. m. Penko Tatiana, 1 Mar 1959, 1 d. *Education:* Univ of Leningrad, 1926-31. *Appointments:* Journalist, 1931-43; Radio News Asst, 1941043; Army Service. *Publications:* 35 Books; Novels; Detective Stories; Books of Travel. *Memberships:* Union of Writers; Various Commissions, Lectr, Editing. *Honours:* War Decorations. *Hobbies:* Travel; Languages; Educin early Infantcy. *Address:* Leningrad Post Off 197136, Lenin Street 34, Apt 70, Nehuhzpad Yu Nehuha 34 KB70, Russia.

DRUMMOND Carol Cramer, b. 5 Mar 1933, Indianapolic, Indiana, USA. Prof Singer; Voice Educ & Tchr; Artist; Writer. m. Roscoe Drummond, 1 June 1978. *Education:* Butler Univ, Indianapolis. *Appointments:* Singer, American Light Opera Co, Washington; Appreaded Numerous Opera Co inc. The Washington Opera; Lake George Opera Co, Glens Falls, NY; Arlington Opera Co, Arlington, Virginia; Charter Performer Concerts; Washington Performing Arts Soc, 1966-; Soloist, 5th Church of Christ Sci, Georgetown, Washington; May Ontario Co; Appearences with Symphony Orchestras in. Nat Symphony Orch; Fairfax Symphony & Buffalo Orch; Concerts in the Park; Private Voice Tchr, Mt Desert Island, Maine, USA; Painters, Artist, 1980; Voiccover Radio & TV Commercials, 1975-85; Host, The Sounding Bd, Stat WGTS FM Washington, 1972-78. *Publications:* Various Articles; Animal Crackers, A Newspaper Column; Lead Articles for Forecast Mag. *Memberships include:* Nat League of American Penwomen; Intl Reunion Registry; Intl Neighbours Club; Maine State Soc; Nat press Club; Kappa Kappa Gamma. *Honours:* Nat & Intl Awards for Writing; Scholarship to Coll. *Hobbies:* Cat; Gardening; Reading; Concerts; Painting; Travel. *Address:* Dream Come True, PO Box 791, Clerk Point Road, South West Harbour, ME 04679, USA.

DRUMMOND Rhona Jean, b. 25 Sept 1953, Aberdeen. Publisher, Observer Communications. *Education:* Regis Sch, Tettenhall; MA, Univ of Edinburgh; CAM Diploma, London, 1982. *Appointments:* St Marys Coll, St Lucia, WI, 1977-78; Express Newspaper, London, 1979-82; Observer Newspaper, London, 1982-91. *Publications:* Several Books for The Observer inc. The Observer, Observed; Small Business, Sucess, Succeed; Sayings of the 80's; Observer Book of Profiles; Great Green Limericks; Tearing Down The Curtain. *Membership:* IPI. *Honours:* Commended: Environment Exhibitons, McEwan Hall, Edinburgh, 1975. *Hobbies:* Sailing; Tennis; Painting.

Address: 231 Ladbroke Grove, London W10 6HG, England.

DRURY Ruth Elizabeth, b. 19 June 1927, Bridgend. Housewife. m. Denis Gordon de Courcy Drury, 11 Dec 1948, 2 s, 2 d. *Education:* Private. *Creative Works:* Fashion photography; Officer, The Military & Hospitaller, Order of St Lazarus of Jerusalem; Royal Henley Regatta; Lady Taveners. *Memberships:* Freeman City of London; Guild of Freemen City of London; Royal Soc of St George; United Wards Club; City of London Cripplegate Ward Club; White Lion Sec. *Hobby:* Genealogy. *Address:* 8 Evelyn Mansions, Carlisle Place, Westminser, London SW1 PINH, England.

DU Ding Zhu, b. 21 May 1948, Qigihar, China. Research prof. m. Shu Mei Li, 21 Jan 1977, 1 s. *Education:* MS, Inst of Applied Math, Chinese Acad of Sci, 1982; PhD, Univ of California, 1985. *Appointments:* Post Doc Fellow, MSRI, 1985-86; Asst Prof, MIT, 1986-87; Research Prof, Inst of Appl Math, Chinese Acad of Sci, 1987-. *Publications:* Convergence Theory of Feasible Direction Methods. *Memberships:* Soc of China; AMS. *Honours:* Wilder Fund Award; Third Class Prize, Nat Natural Sci of China; Prize of Young Sci in Acad Sithea. *Hobbies:* Swimming; Table Tennis. *Address:* Inst of Applied Mathematics, Chinese Acad of Sci, PO Box 2734, Beijing 100080, China. 2.

DU Xintian, b. 19 May 1925, Dengfeng, Henan, China. Prof. m. Mingjie Bai, 2 Jan 1977, 1 s, 1 d. *Education:* Henan Univ, 1945-49. *Appointments:* Asst, 1950-56; Lectr, 1956-78; Dir of Teaching & Research Sec, Crop Cultivation, Henan Agricl Coll; Vice Prof, prof, Vice dir, Agronomy Dept, Henan Agricl Univ. *Publications include:* Cultivation of Crops; Oil Crops; Cultivation of Sesame; Sesame; Farming System; Stero Agriculture; Numerous Articles. *Memberships:* China Cotton Soc; Henan Agric Soc; Henan Ecology Soc; Henan System Engr Soc. *Honours:* Elected Advanced Worker, Henan Agricl Soc; 2nd & 3rd Prizes, Nat Sci & Tech Improvement; 1st, 2nd & 3rd Prizes Henan Province Sci & Tech Improvement. *Hobbies:* Music; Beijing opera; Calligraphy; Basket Ball; Ping Pong. *Address:* Dept of Agronomy, Henan Agricl Univ, Zengzhou 450002, Henan, China. 139.

DU Yao Xi, b. Jan 1935, Xiping County, Henan Province, China. Prof. m. Ruizhen Lu, 2 d. *Education:* No.1 Snr Middle Sch, Xuchang; China Northwest Univ, Xian. *Appointments:* Nat Museum of Chinese History, Beijing; Sec, 1965; Vice Research Fellow, Chinese History of primitive Soc, 1983-; Hd of Dept Archacology; Vice Chmn, 1987-. *Publications:* History of Chinese primitive Soc; Take part in Editing (w 2 others), Seven Thousand Year Old China in Venice; Illustration of the 5000 yr Chinese History; Chinese Cuture and Art in A Thousand Yrs; More Than 20 Essays. *Honours:* Many Scholars from Difference Countries, Academic Exchanges. *Address:* History Museum of China, Tian en men, Beijing, China.

DUAN Guo Sheng, b. 4 Apri 1919, Liao ning. Doctor; Neurosurgery. m. Zan Feng chin, 20 Sept 1944, 3 s, 1 d. *Education:* Wen hui Higher Middle Sch, 1938; Liaoning Medical Coll, 1939-43. *Appointments:* Affiliated Hosp, Liaoning medical Coll, 1941-49; General Hosp of Chinese PLA, Sheng Yong Unit, 1949-69; Gen Hosp of Chinese PLA, Military Postgrad Medical Sch, Beijing, 1969-91. *Contributions:* War Surgery; Neurosurgery of Chinese Encyclopedia; Neurosurgery; Editor. Practical Neurosurgery; Operative Neurosurgery; 120 Papers. *Memberships:* Chinese Medical Assoc of Surgery; Chinese Assoc of Neurosurgery; Euro Asian Assoc of Neurosurgery; Military Ministry of Health; Sci Comm Chinese PLA Gen Hosp. *Honours:* Advanced Worker Awarded, State Sci Conference; 1 State 3rd Class Award on Advancement in Sci & Tech; 7 Army 2nd Class Awards; 15 Army 3rd Class Awards of Advancement in Sci & Tech. *Hobbies:* Basket Ball;

Reading; Gardening. *Address:* Dept of Neurosurgery, Gen Hosp of Chinese PLA, Beijing, China.

DUBAS Andrzej Filip, b. 29 Oct 1932, Wagrowiec, Poland. Accademic Prof of Plant Husbandry, Agricl Univ of Poznan, Poland. m. 26 Dec 1965, 3 d. *Education:* MS, Agronomy, 1955; Doc of Agricl Sci, 1963; Prof Agricl Sci, 1979; Full prof Agricl Sci, 1990. *Appointments:* Tech Asst Agricl Experimental Station, Swadzim, 1955-63; Adjunct, Agricl Univ, poznan, 1964-79; Prof, Agricl Univ Poznan, 1980-. *Publications:* 120 Research Publs; Maize; Maize in the Big Farms. *Memberships:* Polish Academy of Aci; Polish Union of Maize Producersu. *Honours:* Crosses of Polish Renaissance Order. *Hobbies:* Hunting; Touring; Tennis. Address: Grunwaldzka 33a m 13, 60 783 Poznan, Poland.

DUBERSTEIN Helen, b. 3 June 1926, NYC, USA. Writer. m. Victor Lipton, 10 Apr 1949, Dec, 2 d. *Appointments include:* The Circle Theatre Repertory Co; The Theatre for the New City; Many Off Broadway Houses; Produced Festivals of New Plays; Dir Own Work; Led Poetry & Playwriting Workshops, from Kindergarden,Coll, Snr Citizen Centes & Nursing Homes. *Publications include:* Essays; Reviews; Short Stories; Poetry; In Persuit of the Goddess; Hotel Europe & Other Tales; The Dream of Rewards. *Memberships:* PEN; American Centre; The Dramatists Guild; Poetry Soc of America; league of Prof Theate Women. *Honours include:* The Tenth Annual Editors Book Award; Theatreworks, Univ of Colorado, Special Praise; Interlochen Awards for Best Play; Iowa Sch of Short Fiction Award. *Address:* 463 West Street, New York City, NY 10019, USA.

DUBOIS Ivo, b. 26 May 1931, Eindhoven. Hd of Delegation of the Commission, European Communities, Stockholm. m. Hedvig Margareta Ingelson, 2 s, 2 d. *Educations:* Meester in de Rechten, 1955; Diplome d'etudes sup eur, 1957. *Appointments:* Admin, Euratom Commission, 1958-60; Principal Admin, 1960-68; Delegation, Commission of the EC, Washington, 1968-74; Secreteriat Gen, Commission of the EC, 1974-77; Dir personnel, Admin & Translation, Commission of the EC, Lux, 1977-85; Dir Translation, Commission of the EC, 1985-89. *Membership:* Christen Democratisch Appel. *Hobbies:* Riding; Swimming; Skiing; Violin. *Address:* Hamngatan 6, Box 7323, 103 90 Stockholm, Sweden. 1.

DUCA Sergiu, b. 3 Jan 1936, Dej, Romania. Prof of Surgery. m. Cornelia, 5 Aug 1959. *Education:* MD, 1959; PhD, 1975. *Appointments:* Lectr, Surgical Cl III, 1970-78; Snr Lectr, Surgical Cl III, 1978-89; Prof Surgery, Cluj. *Publications:* The Common Bile Duct; The Sphincter of Oddi, Pathology & Sergical Therapy. *Memberships:* Int Soc of Surgery; World Assoc of Hepate Pancreate Biliary Surgery. *Hobbies:* World Literature; Symphenic Music; Tourism. *Address:* Str Firiza nr 2 Ap 17, R-3400 Cluj Napoca 15, Romania. 139.

DUCAT-AMOS Barbara Mary, b. 9 Feb 1921, London, England. Retired Reg General Nurse. *Education:* Higher Sch Certificates; State Reg Nurse. *Appointments:* Sister, Gen Wards, Princess Marys Royal Air Force nursing Serv, UK, Aden, 1944-47; Midwifery Student, Nurse, St Thomas Hosp, 1947-48; Gen Nurse, South & South West Africa, 1948-52; Rejoined Princess Marys Royal Air Force Nursing Serv, 1952; Gen Ward Sister, Theatre Charge Sister, UK Federal Republic of Germany, Cyprus, Aden; Matron, RAF Hosp, Nocton Hall, 1967; Snr Matron, RAF Hosp, Changi, Singapore, 1968-70; Principal Matron, Ministry of Defence, London, 1970-72; Matron in Chief, Princess Marys Royal Air Force; Dir, RAF Nursing Serv, 1972-78; Nursing Sister, Cable & Wireless PLC, London, 1978-85; National Chmn, Girls Venture Corps Air Cadets, 1982-91; Vice-Pres, Girls Venture Corps, 1992. *Honours:* Royal Red Cross 1st Class; Queens Honorary Nursing Sister; Campanion of the Bath; Commander, Order of St John. *Hobbies:* The

Arts; Stage; Music; Painting; Cinema; Travel. *Address:* c/o Barclays Bank PLC, 75 High Street, London SW19 5EQ, England. 1.

DUCHESNE-GUILLEMIN Jacques Alfred Maurice Alphonse, b. 21 Apr 1910, Jupille, Liege. Univ Prof, Retired. m. Marcelle Guillemin, 5 Feb 1935, 2 s. *Education:* Doc Philosophy & Letters, 1931; Diploma Inst Linguisitique, Paris, 1937. *Appointments:* Charge de Cours, Univ of Liege, 1937; Prof, 1944; Distinguished Prof, Santa Barbara, 1987. *Publications:* Zoroaster; The Western Response to Zoroaster; La Religion de l' Iran Ancien; Engl Transl; Etudes pour un Paul Valery. *Memberships:* Soc Asiatique; Intl Assoc for the History of Religion; Cercle Belge de Linguistque. *Honours include:* Medaille Richeliea, Academie Francaise; Doc Honoris Cause, Tehran Univ; Correspondent of Royal Academy of Denmark and of the Inst de France. *Hobbies:* Flute; Astronomy. *Address:* 54 Avenue de l'Observatoire, Liege, Belgium.

DUCHESNE-GUILLEMIN Marcelle Marie Sophie, b. 5 July 1907, Liege. m. Jacques Duchesne, 5 Feb 1935, 2 s. *Education:* Doc Archeology & Art History, Liege, 1932. *Publications include:* Déchiffrement de la Musique Baby Ionienne; Music in Ancient Mesopotamia & Egypt, in World Archeology; Variations on the Scraper in Mankind Quarterly, 1982; Pukku and Mekku, Iraq, 1983; A Hurrian musical score, Ugarit: the Discovery of Mesopotamian Music, Undera Malibu, 1984. *Address:* 54 Avenue de l'Observatoire, Liege, Belgium.

DUCKWORTH Geoffrey Loraine Dyce, b. 24 May 1930, Valletta, Malta. Retired Army Officer; Now Hd of Admin, The Game Conservancy. m. Philippa Ann Rugg, 16 Dec 1961, 1 s, 1 d. *Education:* Stowe Sch; Staff Coll, Camberley. *Appointments:* Commissioned Royal Tank Regiment, 1950; Service in Germany, Korea, Libya, N Ireland, Cyprus, Australia, Canada, Gibraltar; Brigadier, 1980; Admin Mngr, Quilter Goodison Stockbroker, 1986; Hd of Admin, The Game Conservancy, 1987. *Memberships:* Armourers & Brasiers Co; Knight of the Round Table; Army Cadet League; PCC. *Honour:* CBE. *Hobbies:* Fly Fishing; Gardening; Making Music. *Address:* Weir Cottage, Bickton, Fordingbridge, Hants SP6 2HA, England.

DUCKWORTH Walter Eric, b. 2 Aug 1925, Blackburn. Retired Metallugist. m. Emma Evans, 16 Apr 1949, 1 s. *Education:* Cambridge Univ, MA, PhD, 1943-46. *Appointments:* Research Mngr, Glacier metal, 1949-60; Asst Dir, BISRA, 1960-68; Mngr Dir, Fulmer Ltd, 1968-91. *Publications:* Guide to Operational Research; Statistical Techniques in Technological Research; Electro slag Refining; Manganese in Ferrous Metallurgy. *Memberships:* Inst of Metallurgists; Assoc of indept Research & Tech Org. *Honours:* Honorary D Tech Brunel Univ; Honorary D Surrey Univ; OBE. *Hobbies:* Gardening; photography. *Address:* Orinda, Church Lane, Stoke Poges, Slough SL2 4PB, England. 2, 52.

DUDAS Lajos, b. 18 Feb 1941, Budapest. Clarinetist; Saxophonist; Composer; Music Thr. m. Reni Stojanowa, 15 Nov 1965, 1 d. *Education:* Bela Bartok Conservatory, Franz Liszt Academy of Music, 1958-63. *Appointments:* Freelanc Musician, 1963-73; Tchr, Sch of music, Neuss, Gemany, 1973-; Lectr Pedagogical Academy, Rheinland, 1975-85. *Creative Works:* Over 25 Singles; LPs; MCs; CDs; Numerous Radio, TV Productions. *Honours:* 1st Prize 11 Intl Comp for Jazz Themes in Monaco; Nominated for Top People Poll. *Address:* Am Sudpark 11 B, D 4040 Neuss 1, West Germany.

DUDEK DÜRER Andrzej, b. Nurnberg. Artist Graphic; Interior Decorator; Painter; Photographer; Drawer; Musician; Lectr; Sculptor; Performance Artist. *Education:* Sch of Music, Wroclaw, 1962-68; Sch of Art, Wroclaw, 1968-73. *Appointments:* Pop, Jazz Experimental Music Collaboration, 1966-; Active with Painting, Graphic, Drawing, Performance; Collaboration,

Polish Film, 1973-74; Wallpaper Activity, 1974-78; Books, Magazines, Graphic Posters Activity, 1978; Lectr Workshops, Intermediate Arts Activity, 1981-. *Creative Works include:* Art Shoes, Art Trousers, Art A Dudek-Dürer; Selfcrucifiction, Wroclaw; Intervention; Existence; Information-Disinformation; The Present The Past; All Is Only In Imagination. *Memberships:* All Plstic Music Hochart Ltd; One Person Assoc; Intl Metaphysical Telepathic Union; Union of Polish Artists & Designers; Intl Union of Traveling Artist; Other Media Artists Association; Hot Bip; Black Panel World Foundation; Inst of Fatuous Research. *Honours:* Arts Works, Nat Museum, Warszawa; Books & Arts Objects, Centro de Arte Actual, Barcelona; Tate Gallery London; Museum of Modern Art, NYC; The Sch of art, Inst of Chicargo; City Art inst library Sydney. *Hobbies:* Graphic; Drawing; Photography; Painting; Sculpture; Action; Music; Enviroment; metaphysical Telepathic Activity; Antypoetry. *Address:* ul Kolbuszewska 15/1, 53404, Wroclaw, Poland.

DUDKA Irina A, b. 4 Dec 1934, Ukraine, Kharkov. Mycologist; Chief of Mycological Dept of Inst of Botany, Ukrainian Academy of Sci. m. Kozuschko Voldemar K, 13 Oct 1960, 1 d. *Education:* Grad Biol, Dept of Jiev State Univ, 1957; Defended Thesis on Degree of Bach of Sci, 1965; Doctorate, 1978; Prof, 1986. *Appointments:* Inst of Botany, Ukr Academy of Sci; Reserch student, 1963; Snr Sci Worker, 1967; Chief Mycological Lab, 1975-. *Publications:* 271 Papers & Books inc. Aquatic Hyphomycetes of Ukraine; The Mushrooms of Genus Pleurotus. *Memberships:* Ukrainian Botanical Soc; Intl Mycological Assoc. *Honours:* Order of the Red Banner of Labour; State Prize of Ukraine, Fundamental Editor; State Prize of Ukraine, Cycle of Works in Submerged Cultivation of Edible. *Hobbies:* Tennis; Mountain Skiing; Gardening. *Address:* N G Kholodny Inst of Botany, Ukrainian Academy of Sci, Repin Street, 2, Kiev-GSP- 1, Ukaine 252601.

DUDKIEWICZ Zofia, b. 10 May 1942, Wrecza, Poland. Paediatric Surgeon. m. Ryszard Dudkiewicz, 30 July 1960, 1 d. *Education:* Medical Academy, Warsaw, 1960-65; Midal Faculty, 1966-69. *Appointments:* Asst, Snr Asst, Medical Academy, Warsaw, 1966071; Snr Asst, Dept of Paediatric Surgery, inst of Mother & Child, Warsaw, 1971-80; Asst Prof, 1980-. *Publications:* Osteogenesis of Rat Mandibule During Development; Choice of Time for Operation on Secondary Palate Cleft in Children; Congenital Diaphragmic Hernia; Bone Craft Value in the Treatment of Unilateral Cleft of Primary & Secondary Palet; Use of Skin Flap Craft for Reconstruction of Urethra in Boys with Hypospadiasis; One stage Treatment of Cleft Lip & Palate. *Memberships:* Polish Soc of Paediatric Surgeons; Polish Soc of Plastic & Reconstructive Surgery. *Honours:* Honorable Prize for Achievement in Sci Work. *Hobbies:* Theatre; Reading. *Address:* ul Kozia 9/16, 00-070 Warsaw, Poland.

DUDLEY Norman Alfred, b. 29 Feb 1916, Birmingham, England. Emeritus Prof of Engr Prod. m. Hilda Florence Miles, 1 s, 2 d. *Education:* BSc, London; PhD, Birmingham. *Appointments:* Ind Appts, 1932-46; Tech Coll Lectr, 1946-52; Univ of Birmingham Lectr, 1952-55, Reader, 1955-59, Lucas Prof, 1959-80; Hd of Dept of Engr Prod, 1955-80. *Publications:* Intl Journal of Prod Research, 1961-80; Work Measurement, 1968; Production & Ind Systems (co-Editor), 1978; Various papers on Eng Prod. *Memberships:* Cncl Inst of Prod Engrs; West Midlands Economic Planning Council, 1970-78; UK Delegation to UNCSAT, Geneva. *Honours:* CBE; Fellow, Royal Academy of Engrs; Hon DTech, Loughborough: Hon FIMfgE, Hon FIEE, Hon Mbr, Intl Foundation of Prod Rsch; Emeritus member, CIRP. *Hobbies:* Genealogy; Gardening. *Address:* 37 Abbots Close, Knowle, Solihull, West Midlands B93 9PP, England. 1.

DUFF Donald James, b. 18 Sept 1926, Calgary, Canda. Fund Raising; Communications Conslt. m. Beth Elinor Edwards, 19 Feb 1948, 2 s, 1 d. *Education:* BEd, Univ of Alberta; MS, Columbia Univ, NY; FRSA. *Appointments:* Chmn, The Duff Conslt Group. *Memberships:* Gallery Assoc; Kingston Symphony; St Andrews Soc of Kingston. *Hobbies:* Gardening; Golf; Photography. *Address:* Point of View, Bateau Channel Estates, Box 152 RR1, Kingston, Ontario, Canada K7L 4V1. 88.

DUFOUR Marie-Jeanne, b. 12 Mar 1955, Gumligen, Switzerland. Conductor. *Education:* 12 yrs Rudolf Steiner Sch, 1974-78; Flute Diploma, Berne Conservatory, 1978. *Appointments:* Asst, Conductor, Zurich Opera House, 1981-87; Asst Gen Conductor, Wiesbaden State opera, 1990-92; Guest Performances, Hamburg State opera, Mozart Festival Würzburg, Carinthische Sommer Ossiach; Concerts: Tonhalle Orchestra, Zurich, Netherlands Philharmonic Orchestra, Amsterdam, Orchestre de la Suisse Romande, Prague Chamber Orchestra; Orchestre de Chambre Lausanne; Radio TV Orchestra del la Suizzera Italian Medlen Burgische Staatsgappelu Schwerin; Guest Conductor: Hannover, Bienfeld, Aachen, Gelsenhirchen, Oldenburg. *Honours:* 1st Prize Hans Haring Competition for Conductors; Scholarship Schweizerischer Tonkunstlerverband. *Address:* Litschstrasse CH-8852 Altendorf/be Zürich, Schweiz.

DUGACKI Vladimir, b. 26 Feb 1939, Zagreb. Clinical Asst, Univ Dept of Ophthalmology, Zagreb. m. Dubravka Zidarevic, 22 Feb 1975, 1 s, 1 d. *Education:* Faculty of Medicine, Zagreb, 1957-64; Spec in Ophthalmology, Zagreb, 1972-75. *Appointments:* Asst of the Inst, History of Sci, Zagreb, 1966-69; Physician, Centre for Urgent Medicine, 1969-72; Clinical Asst, Zagreb, 1975-. *Publications:* Croatian Medical Bibliography; From the Medical History. *Memberships:* Croatian Medical Assoc; Intl Soc for History of Medicine; Assoc of the Julius Hirschberg Soc for History of Ophthalmology. *Honours:* Charter Croatian Medical Assoc. *Hobbies:* History of Medicine; Medical Bibliography; Medical Terminology. *Address:* Resetarova 30, 41090 Zagreb Susedgrad, Croatia.

DUGAW Dianne Mary, b. 24 Aug 1948, Seattle, Washington, USA. Literary Scholar; Tchr. *Education:* BA, Univ of Portland, 1972; M Mus, Univ of Colorado, 1974; PhD, Univ of California, Los Angeles, 1982. *Appointments:* Visiting Lectr in English, UCLA, 1982-85; Asst Prof, Univ of Colorado, 1985-89; Mellon Faculty Fellow, Harvard Univ, 1989-90; Assoc Prof, Univ of Oregon, 1991-. *Publications:* Warrior Women and Popular Balladry; Essays on Folklore, Music, Literture, Womens Studies. *Memberships:* Modern Language Assoc; American Folklore Soc; American Soc for 18th Century Scholars; Pi kappa Lambda Nat Honor Soc for Music Scholars; California Folklore Soc; Oregon Folklore Soc; Western Soc for 18th Century Studies. *Honours:* Eugene Kayden Book Manuscript Award; Clark Library Research Fellowship; Huntington Library Fellowship; NEH Summer St'pend; Newberry Library Fellowship; Danforth Foundation Fellowship. *Hobbies:* Folksinging; Guitar playing; Keyboard Music; Hiking. *Address:* Dept of English, Univ of Oregon, Eugene, OR 97403, USA.

DUGMORE Jean Montgomery, b. 7 Apr 1949, Walsall. Project Worker, Barnardos, Midlands Div; Advising, Informing, Counselling, Parents & Families with Life Limited, Sick Children. m. Roger Sidney Dugmore, 18 July 1970, 1 s, 1 d. *Education:* Sch of St Mary & St Anne, Abbots Bromley, 1960-67; St Marys Coll Cheltenham, 1967-70; Diploma of Community Work, Westhill Coll, Selly Oak, 1988-90. *Appointments:* Tchr, 1970-72; Walsall MBC, Tchr, Nursery Sch, 1975-78; Tchr Primary Sch, 1978-81; Intermediate Treatment Officer, 1983-86; YTS Tutor, YMCA, 1986-87; Jutice of the Peace, 1980-. *Memberships:* Magistrates Assoc, Vice-Chmn. West Midlands Branch, 1990; SOS; Action Group to Retain Open Space. *Hobbies:* Idsability Issues; Juvenile Justice; Walking; Inland Waterways. *Address:* Barnardos, Grosvenor Terrace, 90 Broad Street, Birmingham B15 1AU, England.

DUKA Dominik Jaroslav, b. 26 Apr 1943, Hradec Kralové. Provincial of the Dominican Order in CSFR; Asst Biblical Studies, Theol Fac, Univ Palacky, Olomouc. *Education:* Secondary Sch, 1965-70; Ordained, 1975. *Appointments:* Worked in Factory, Škoda Plzen, 1975-89; Simultaneously religious Dominican activity in illegality/exams for The Lic Mag of novices & Stud of Theole Vicar of Prov; Imprissoned for Rel Activity & Cooperation with Foreign Lands, 1981-82. *Publications:* Introduction to the Study of the Scriptures; School of Prayer; Fight for Man; Participation in the Czech edition of the Bible of Jerusalem. *Memberships:* Pres of Conference of the Superiors Majors CSFR; Vice-Pres of UCESM; Accredit Commission by the Government. *Hobbies:* History; Literature. *Address:* Konvent Radu dominikanu, Husova 8, 110 00 Praha 1, CSFR.

DUKHIN Stanislav, b. 6 Nov 1931, Kharkov, Ukraine. Inst of Colloid & Water Chemistry, Dept of Theoretical Electrochemistry of Colloid & Membranes, Hd of Physical Chemist. *Education:* Kharkov State Univ, 1948-53; PhD, Inst of Physical Chemistry, Moscow, 1956; Dr Sc, Inst of of Physical Chemistry, Moscow, 1965; Prof, 1971. *Appointments:* Jnr Research Assoc, Krivoj Rog, 1953-57; Snr Research Assoc, Krivoj Rog, 1957-58; Snr Research Assoc, Kharkov, 1958-59; Dept Hd, Ukrainian Academy of Sci, Kiev, 1959-68; Dept Hd, Inst of Colloid & Water Chemistry, Kiev, 1968-. *Creative Works include:* Dielectric Phenomena & Douvble Layer in Disperse Systems & Polyelectrolytes; Membrane Electrochemistry & Reverse Osmosis; Electrosurface phenomena & Electrofilration; 300 Publ. Colloid Chemistry, Membrane Sci, Aerosol Sci, Technologies of Water Purification & Flotation. *Memberships include:* Colloids & Surfaces, Advisory Bd; Colloid Chemical Foundations of Water Purification Technologies; Scientific Consil for Theoretical Biophysics; Membrane Sci & Tech. *Honours:* Discovery Diffusiophoresis Award; Founders Plaque in Recognition of Outstanding Contributions, advancement of Intl Cooperation in Sci Exchange. *Hobbies:* Classical Music; Tennis; Travel. *Address:* Inst of Colloid & Water Chemistry, Ukrainian Academy of Sci, Vernadsky Boulevard 42, Kiev 252680, Ukraine.

DUMBRILLE Sarah Jane, b. 13 Sept 1942, Chicago, Ill. Housewife. m. Richard M Dumbrille, 5 Apr 1969, 2 s, 1 d. *Education:* Queens Univ, BA, 1962-65; Katherine Gibbs Sch, NYC, 1966-67. *Appointments:* Exec Sec, 1967-69. *Publications:* Royal Visit to Prescott, Its Preparation & Staging. *Memberships:* May Court Club of Brockville; Queens Univ Council; Bd of Govenors, Brockville Gen Hosp; The Military & Hospitaller Order of Saint Lazarus. *Hobbies:* Collecting Royal Commencoiatives; Gardening; Travel; Swimming; Music. *Address:* Sprucelawn, PO Box 1, Maitland, Ontario, Canada K0E 1PO.

DUMITRESCU Anca, b. 14 Oct 1950, Bucharest. Main Scientifical Researcher, Educ Sci. m. Lorin, 6 July 1974, 2 s. *Education:* Germanic Languages, Univ of Bucharest, 1968-73; Doc Degree in Philology, 1989. *Appointments:* Tchr of English, High Sch, 1973-79; Adult Educ, 1979-86; Lectr of English, Univ of Bucharest, 1987-; Main Sci Researcher, Romanian Inst for Educ Sci, 1990-. *Publications:* The Noun Phrase in Contemporary Romanian & English; Over 30 Articles & Works; Over 25 Sci Papers & Reports. *Memberships:* Modern Languages in Sch; League for Sci, Culture and Art; Educ Pedagogical Sci; BAAL; Societas Linguistica Europaea, ENWS. *Honours:* PhD, Univ of Bucharest; Int Woman of the Year, 1991. *Hobbies:* Romanian Folklore & Historical Traditions; Scandinavian Languages & Culture; Man's Life in the Outer Space. *Address:* Inst for Educ Sci, 37 Stirbei Voda Street, 70732 Bucharest, Romania.

DUMITRESCU Monica, b. 27 Mar 1949, Blaj, Romania. Mathematician; Associated Prof. m. Horia Dumitrescu, 27 July 1981. *Education:* Faculty of Mathematics, Univ of Bucharest, 1966-71; Doc in

Mathematics, Univ of Bucharest, 1976. *Appointments:* Univ of Bucharest, Faculty of Mathematics, Asst, 1971-78; Asst Prof, 1978-90; Assoc Prof, 1990-. *Publications:* Sci work in Mathematicial Statistics, Publ 8 Courses; 25 Sci Papers. *Memberships:* Bernoulli Soc for Mathematical Statistics & Probability. *Hobbies:* Mountaineering; Music. *Address:* Univ of Bucharest, Faculty of Mathematics, Str Academiei no.14, RO 70 109 Bucharest, Romania.

DUMVILLE David Norman, b. 5 May 1949, Hillingdon, Middx. Historian & Palaeographer; Reader in the Early Mediaeval History & Culture of the British Isles, Univ of Cambridge. m. (1) Sally Lois Hannay, 23 Nov 1974, dec, 1 s, (2) Yoko Wada, 29 Dec 1990. *Education:* Emmanuel Coll, Cambridge, BA,1971; MA, 1974; Univ of Munich, Germany, 1971-72; Univ of Edinburgh, PhD, 1976. *Appointments:* Univ of Wales, Swansea, 1976-77; Asst prof, Univ of Pennsylvania, 1977-78; Lectr, Dept of Anglo-Saxon, Norse & Celtic, Univ of Cambridge, 1978-91; Reader, Early Mediaeval History & Culture British Isles, Cambridge, 1991-. *Publications:* Chronicles & Annals of Mediaeval Ireland & Wales; Annuals of St Neots; The Historia Brittonum; Histories & Pseudo-Histories of the Insular Middle Ages; Wessex & England from Alfred to Edgar; English Caroline Script and Monastic History. *Memberships:* Royal Historical Soc; Royal Soc of Antiquaries of Ireland; Centre Intl de Recherche et de Documentation sur le Monachisme Celtique; Sch of Celtic Studies, Dublin Inst for Advanced Studies. *Honours:* Hon MA, Univ of Pennsylvania; O'Donnell Lectr in Celtic Studies, Oxford, Edinburhg, Wales; Jeremiah Dalziel Prize for Best Thesis on British History (Edinburgh); British Academy Research Reader in History. *Hobbies:* Politics; Current Affairs; History of the French Fourth Republic. *Address:* Girton Coll, Cambridge, CB3 0JG, England.

DUNCAN Denis MacDonald, b. 10 Jan 1920, Bedlington. Minister; Author; Journalist; Company Dir. m. Henrietta Watson McKenzie, 1 s, 1 d. *Education:* George Watson Boys Coll, Edinburgh; Edinburgh Univ, MA; BD, Hons, PhD, Somerset Univ. *Appointments:* Minister St Margarets Parish, Juniper Green, Edinburgh, 1943-49; Minister, Trinity Duke St Parish, Glasgow, 1950-57; Mngr Dir, British Weekly, 1958-70; Assoc Dir, Westminster Pastoral Foundation, London, 1971- 79; Dir, The Churches Council for Health & Medicine, London, 1983-88. *Publications include:* Creative Silence; Love, The word that Heals; The Way of Love; The After Word to The Greatest Thing in The World. *Memberships:* Inst of Journalists; FICS; FIBA; IDEC; Forum Chmn, World Assoc for Care & Conselling. *Address:* One Cranbourne Road, London N10 2BT, England. 1, 139.

DUNCAN Kenneth Sandilands, b. 26 Apr 1912, Crawshawbooth, Lancs, England. Conslt; Librarian. m. (1) 4 June 1941, dec, (2) 20 August 1957, Div, 1 s. *Education:* Malvern Coll, Worcs; New Coll, Oxford. *Appointments:* Master, Bradfield Coll, 1936-48; Gen Sec, Univ Athletic Union, 1949-51; Hon Sec Achilles Club, 1948-81 and Commonwealth Games Federation, 1948-82; Gen Sec British Olympic Assoc, 1948-75 and Commonwealth Games England's Council, 1945-72. *Publications:* The Oxford Book of Athletic Training; Athletics, Do It This Way. *Honours:* OBE; Gold Medal, World Univ Games; Silver Medal, Common Wealth Games Sydney; Member Whits Rose & Lion, Finland; Olympic Order. *Hobbies:* Reading; Opera; Opera Singers; History of Sport; Memorabilia. *Address:* ssa 00Flat 1, 57 Gloucester Road, London SW7 4QN, England.

DUNDORE Dwight Arthur, b. 18 Jan 1922, Reading, PA, USA. Registered Prof Engr, Montgomery County Dir of Commerce & Economic Devel. m. Janet Styer Kitzmiller, 24 Dec 1943, 1 d. *Education:* BA, Albright Coll, Reading, 1943; US Navel Res, Midshipmens Sch, Annapolis, 1943; BS, Drexel Inst of Tech, Philadelphia, 1953; MBA, Drexel Inst of Tech, 1963. *Appointments:* Philadelphia Gas Works, Asst Supt, 1954-56; Proccess

& Maint Eng, 1956-64; Asst Mngr & Exec, 1964-70; Mngr Gas Supply, 1970-81; Vice Pres, Planning, 1981-84; Bd of Safety & Fire Prevention, 1976-81; Dir of Commerce & Ec Dev, 1984-. *Publications:* Numerous Papers for the american Gas Assc; Design & Constrn of a Carillon Practice Console; Safety Considerations for Liquefied Natural Gas. *Memberships include:* Soc of Gas Operators; Colonial Sch Auth; Mont Co Private Ind Foundation; Carillonneurs of North America. *Honours:* Operating Serv Award; Operating Serv Award of Merit; Nat Council Alumni Award; Drexel Alumni Assc, Honor Man of the Year; montgomery County Community Coll Founders Day Award; Nominee for Engr of the Year. *Hobbies:* Music; Playing Timpani, Local Symphony Orchestra; Woodworking; Skiing; World Travel. *Address:* 806 Penn Street, Flourtown PA 19031, USA. 7, 139, 176.

DUNN-MEYNELL Hugo Arthur, b. 4 Apr 1926, Streatham, England. Exec Dir, The Int Wine and Food Soc. m. Alice Wooledge Salmon, 20 Dec 1980. *Education:* John Fisher Schl, Purley. *Appointments:* Wine and Food Writer and Cons; Pres, Lonsdale Advt Int, 1978-89; Chmn, 1978-80, Exec Dir 1983-, The Int Wine and Food Soc. *Memberships:* Liveryman, Worshipful Co of Innholders; Grand Officier les Chevaliers du Tastevin; FRGS; Atheneum Club. *Honours:* Fellow of the Institute of Practitioners in Advertising, 1967; Gold Medal, International Wine and Food Society, 1972. *Hobbies:* Wine, Travelling. *Address:* 125 Mount Street, London W1YY 5HA, England.

DUNN-THOMAS Paula, b. 3 Dec 1964, Bradford, Yorkshire. Sports Development Officer. m. Peter Thomas, 26 May 1990. *Education:* Sociology; B/Tech Nat in Admin. *Appointments:* Clerical Officer, Housin Dept, Manchester City Council, 1985-89; Sports Devl officer, Recreational Serv Manchester City Council, 1989-91. *Memberships:* Intl Athletic Club; Sports Aid Foundation. *Honours include:* Young Mancunian of the Year; UK Champion & British Champian; UK Indoor Champion; Common Wealth Games, Silver Medalist; Medalist European Finals; Olympic Games Semi Finalist. *Hobbies:* Reading; Music. *Address:* 141 St Anns Road, Phestwich, Manchester M35 8QN, England.

DUPERROY Georges Camille Ambroise, b. 3 Oct 1923, Lodelinsart, Belgium. Gyneclogist. m. lise Schirmer, 16 Apr 1981. *Education:* MD, Louvain Univ, Belgium, 1947; M Sc D, Columbia Univ, NY, 1952; Agrége De Enseignement Superieur Louvain Univ, Belgium, 1954. *Appointments:* Res Dept Gynecology Obstetrics, Louvain Univ, Belgium, 1947-50; CRB Belgium American Educ Foundation, Sloane Hosp for Women, Columbia Presbyterian Med Centre, NY, 1950-52; Loans from Belgium Funds for Sci Research, 1953-55; Chief Dept Gynecology Obstetrics, Elisabeth Inst, Brussels, 1954-89. *Publications:* Numerous papers. *Memberships:* Pres, Prof Union of Belgium Gynecologists; Pres, Gynecological Sec European Union of Specialists; Intl Union of Gynecologists; Pres, Ministerial Admitting Comm of Belgium Gynecologists. *Honours:* Prize: Cambier, 1937; Belgian Government, 1940; Rufin Schockaert, 1950; Francois Empain, 1953. *Hobbies:* Reading; Gardening; Microscopical Research. *Address:* 75 Bosveldweg, 1180 Brussels, Belgium. 152, 162.

DURAKOVIC Zijad, b. 4 Mar 1943, Prijedor. Physician; Internist; Cardiologist; Nephrologist; Prof of Internal Medicine, Chief Dept of Cardiology. *Education:* Medical Faculty, Univ of Zagreb, 1968; Master of Sci Degree, 1971; Spec in Internal Medicine, 1976; Doc of Phylosophy, 1978; Cardiologist, 1985; Nephrologist, 1985. *Appointments:* Asst Prof of Internal Medicine, 1971; Assoc Prof of Intl Med, 1982; Prof of Intl Med, 1986; Chief, Intensive Care Unit, 1986; Chief, Dept of Cardiology, 1987. *Publications:* Many Books; 279 Papers in the Field of Medicine. *Memberhips:* New York Academy of Sci; The American Medical Assoc; The American Coll of Physicians; The Intl Soc of

Cardiovascular Pharmacotherapy; The Medica Conslt, The World Life Inst, USA; Fellow, American Coll of Physicians. *Honours:* Medal, Clinic Hosp Centre, Rebro, Zagreb; Medical Faculty Univ of Zagreb. *Hobbies:* Poetry; Phylosophy; Research in Medicine Cardiology & Neuphrology; Tchring. *Address:* Div of Cardiology, Dept of Intl Medicine, Rebro Univ Hospital, Zagreb, Croatia. 139, 152.

DURLACHER Gerhard Leopold, b. 10 July 1928, Baden Baden. Writer; Sociologist. m. J A P Durlacher Sasburg, 22 Dec 1959, 3 d. *Education:* HBS, B, 1947; Cand Ex Medical Sc, 1952; Cand Ex, Social Sci, 1959; Doc, Social Political Sci, 1964. *Appointments:* Research Fellow, Inst Preventive Medicine, 1960-61; Research, Dr Wiardi Beckman Stichting, 1961-64; Jnr Lectr to Prof, Univ of Amsterdam, 1964-84. *Publications:* Books on Poverty; Numerous Articles on Social problems, Income Policy, Sociology; Literary Books: Strepen aan de hemel, 1985; Drenkeling, 1987; German Transl: Streifen am Himmel, 1988; Engl Transl; Stripes in the Sky, 1991; De Zoektocht, 1991; Engl Transl: Drowning, awaiting publication. *Memberships:* Maatschappij Nederlandse Letterjunde, PEN Intl. *Hobbies:* Literature; Chamber Music; Visiting Museums; Politics; History. *Address:* Oosterduinweg 31, 2015 KH Haarlem, The Netherlands. 52.

DURMANOV Parel Victorovich, b. 29 Jan 1970, Berezniky City, Perm Region. *Eduction:* Faculty of Biology, Perm Univ, USSR. *Appointments:* Studing Taxonomy, Ecological & Zoogeography Problems of Staphylinid Beetles. *Hobbies:* Insect Collections for Sci Research; Sport; Body Building; Photography. *Address:* Dept of Biology, Perm Univ, Rubirev Str 15, 614000 Perm, Russia.

DURRETT Dewey Bert, b. 16 May 1929, Belington, West Virginia, USA. m. Pauline Ann Stefanik, 3 May 1958, 3 s. *West Virginia Univ, BS; Univ of Massachusetts, MS; Air Univ, Maxwell Air Force Base, Alabama; Cert of Nat Security Mgmt, Imesh Coll of Armed Forces.* Appointments: Lieutenant Colnel, USAFR, 1951-79; Captain, Delta Airlines, 1957-85; Owner, Chief Exec Officer, Durrett Enterprices, Salem, New Hampshire, 1967-; Rancher, West Virginia; Owner, Ind plant, Wood Products, West Virginia. *Publications:* Fruit & Vegetable Mkting. *Memberships include:* Credit Bureau of Greater Lawrence; Armed Forces Assoc; Reserve Officers Assoc; Aircraft Owners & pilots Assoc; Salem Contractors Assoc; Greater Lawrence Rental Assoc; Foundation for North American Wild Sheep; Safari Club Intl; Cub Club; Marmon Club; Intl 180-185 Club; Aulation Assoc of New Hampshire; Classic Car Club of America. *Honours:* American Farmer Degree Award, Future Farmers of America; Durrett Hall was named after him at Erickson Alumni Centre. *Hobbies:* Antique Automobiles; Skiing; Flying; Hiking; Boating; Driving. *Address:* 377 Main Street, Salett, NH 03079, USA. 6, 52, 132, 139, 152, 156.

DUVAL Dorothy Zinaida, b. 26 Sept 1917, Torquay, Devon. Artist; Painter. *Education:* Bedford Park Coll; Slade Sch of Fine art. *Appointments:* Artist Tchr, Public Schs; Kent Educ Adult Classes. *Creative Works:* Paintings; General Subjects, Portrait, Still Life, Sea & Lanscapes. *Memberships:* United Soc of Artists; Royal Marine Artists; FBA Mall Gallery Sco. *Honours:* Silver Medaille D'Argent, Paris Salon, Elysee Palace exhibition; Art Merit Diploma. *Hobbies:* Painting; Swimming. *Address:* 166 Percy Avenue, Kingsgate, Nr Broadstairs, Kent, CT10 3LF, England.

DUVIEUSART Pascaline Suzanne, b. 18 Mar 1940, Paris. m. Philippe 18 Dec 1963, 3 s, 1 d. *Education:* Law Sch, Paris; Political Sci. *Appointments:* French Cultural Centre, French Embassy, 1961-62; Press Serv, Mali Embassy, Washington, 1963-64. *Creative Works:* Water Colours; Paintings; Drawings. *Memberships:* Pres Tournant Europenne. *Honours:* Medal for Painting,

Assoc Royal Artists. *Hobbies:* Painting; Art; Travel. *Address:* Av du Maréchal 27, 1180 Brussels, Belgium.

DUZYK Jozef, b. 14 Mar 1928, Krakow. Historian; Historian of Polish Literature; Writer. m. Mieczystawa Rozycka, 5 Aug 1961, 1 s, 1 d. *Education:* Jagell Univ, 1948-52; Master Of Arts, 1978. *Appointments:* Asst, Jag Univ, 1951-52; Librarian Dipl, Bibl Polish Acad of Sci, Krakow, 1952-74; Libraian Dipl of Bible polish Acad of Sci, Rome, 1974-82; Bibl pol Acad Krakow, 1983. *Publications include:* Opowiesc o Lucjanie Rydlu; Stawa Panie Wfodzimierzu Opowiesco o Wtodzimierzu Tetmajerze. *Memberships:* Polish Authors Assoc. *Honours:* The Prize of City Krakow in Sci. *Hobbies:* Reading; Tourism. *Address:* ul Friedleina 28c m 37, 30-000 Krakow, Poland.

DVORETZKY Rachel Leah, b. 17 Apr 1960, Houston, Texas, USA. Curator; Musician. *Education:* HS Performing and Visual Arts, Houston, 1978; BA, Rice Univ, Houston, 1983. *Appointments:* Asst Slide Curator, 1983-88, 1988-, Dept Art and Art Hist, Rice Univ, Houston, TX; Musician, Blue Moon Quartet, Houston, 1987-. *Publications:* Songs: You're The One He Married; The Carrot and Stick of Love; Var cartoon illustrations. *Memberships:* Visual Resources Assn; Col Art Assn; Int Bluegrass Music Assn; Houston Profl Musicians Assn; Am Fedn Musicians. *Honours:* Nat Merit Scholar, 1978; Official Perf: Galveston (TX) Mardi Gras, 1989; Houston Int Fest, 1990, 1991; Kerrville (TX) Int Folk Fest, 1990. *Hobbies:* Blues and jazz music; Sacophone study; Political and satirical cartooning; International cuisine cookery; Organic gardening; Domestic and international travel. *Address:* 407 Cordell, Houston, TX 77009, USA. 76.

DWYER Timothy Edward, b. 29 Dec 1951, Albany, New York, USA. *Education:* AA, HUCE, 1976; BA, SUNY Stony Brook, 1978; MSW, Univ of Hawaii, 1983; ACSW, Nat Assn of Social Workers, 1987. *Memberships:* Nat Assn of Social Workers; Acad of Cert Social Workers, 1987. *Address:* Castle Medical Center, Human Services Unit, 640 Ulukahiki Street, Kailua, HI 96734, USA.

DYER Paul William, b. 11 Sept 1958, Australia. Professional Musician; Harpsichordist; Conductor; Lecturer; Artistic Director. *Education:* Studies, 1970-81, DipMus Ed, 1979, BMus, high distinction, 1982, Conservatorium Music, Univ Sydney; ATCL (London), Piano Perf, 1979; Studies, 1983-86, Dip, Harpsichord, Early Music Perf, Royal Conservatory, Hague, Netherlands, 1986; Harpsichord w Bob van Asperen, Ensemble Conducting w Sigiswald Kuijken, Orchestral studies w Frans Bruggen. *Career:* Tchng, pvte studio, 1975-80; Australian Piano Tchr Rep, Suzuki Talent Educ Conf, Munich, FRG, 1980; Rsch study-perf tour, Maligaya Music Co, Philippines, 1980; Perf num orchs, Europe, incl La Grande Ecurie et la Chambre du Roy, Nederlandse Bachvereniging, Groupa Bandistra, Imperial Consort, 1983-86; Recitals, Holland Fest, 1985; Appeared, Keline Zaal, Concertgebouw, Amsterdam, 1985; Tour, early opera perfs, Rome, Verona, Genoa, 1986; Resident Harpsichordist, Lectr, Newcastle Conservatorium Music and Conservatorium Music Sydney, Australia, 1986-; Appeared w Sydney and Queensland Symph Orchs, Australia Ensemble, Sydney String Quartet, Australian Opera, and Acad Ancient Music, London; Fndr-Dir, Sounds Baroque, Musica Viva Perf Schools Project, 1988-; Invited Dir, Australian Chamber Orch Mostly Mozart Concert, Sydney Opera House, Jan 1989; Fndr, Artistic Dir, Brandenburg Orch Of Australia 1990-; Student Rep, Bd Govs, NSW State Conservatorium Music, 1981; NSW School Friends Australian Opera; Early Music Assn NSW; Music Students Overseas Study Fndn, NSW, Sr VP 1972-92; Music Advancement Fndn, NSW, Sr VP 1982-92. *Honour:* Awarded: Netherlands Govt Scholarship, 1983. *Hobbies:* Music; Composing; Opera; Languages; Swimming; Sailing; Travel; Helping parents with charity work. *Address:* Villa Maria, 3 Inverallan Avenue, Pymble, NSW 2073, Australia.

DYRCZ Andrzej, b. 9 Jan 1933, Cieszyn, Poland. University Lecturer; Zoologist, Ornithologist. m. Alina Kowalska, 2 Feb 1959, 1 s. *Education:* MSc, 1955, PhD, Natural Hist, 1960, Full Prof, 1982, Univ Wroclaw. *Appointments:* Tchng Asst, Zool, 1955-60, Asst Prof, Zool, Ecol, 1960-71, Assoc Prof, Zool, Ecology, 1971-82, Curator, Dept Birds and Mammals, Mus Natural Hist, 1971-74, Hd, Dept Avian Ecol, 1975-, Full Prof, Zool, Ecol, 1982-, Univ Wroclaw. *Publications:* 108 sci papers in ornithology incl monographs of avifauna of Biebrza marshes and Karkonosze Mtns Nat Pk; Birds of Silesia - Faunistic Monograph (sr author); Series of more important papers on mating system in genus Acrocephalus; Ecol of birds of Peruvian Amazonia and Panama. *Memberships:* Corres Mem, Brit Ornithologists Union; Zool Com, Polish Acad Scis; Int Assn Ecol. *Honours:* Individual Awd, Rsch Accomplishment, Min Educ, 1971, 1974. *Hobbies:* Bird watching; Mounting hiking; Cycling. *Address:* Dept of Avian Ecology, Wroclaw University, ul Sienkiewicza 21, 50-35 Wroclaw, Poland.

DZIENIA Stanislaw, b. 1 Jan 1934, Boczkowice, Poland. Professor of Soil and Plant Cultivation. *Education:* MA, Agric, 1960, PhD, 1968, Dr hab, 1978, Prof, 1988, Univ Szczecin. *Appointments:* Asst Lectr, 1960-68, Lectr, 1969-78, Dept Hd, 1979, Sr Lectr, 1978-88, Fac Dean, 1981-90, Prof, Soil and Plant Cultivation, 1988-, Univ Szczecin. *Publications:* Some 60 papers concerning soil tillage and crop rotation. *Memberships:* ISTRO; ESA; PSAS; PSS. *Honours:* Min Educ Awds, 1972, 1977, 1989. *Hobby:* Ethnography. *Address:* ul Chopina 92 m 3, 71-450 Szczecin, Poland.

E

EASTERLING William Ewart III, b. 2 Oct 1953, Chapel Hill, North Carolina. University Professor. 2 d. *Education:* BA, Geog, Hist, 1976, MA, Geog, 1980, PhD, Geog, 1984, Univ NC. *Appointments:* Asst Prof, Agri Meteorology, Univ NE, Lincoln, 1981-; Profl Scientist, IL State Water Survey, 1984-87; Fellow, Resources for the Future, 1987-91. *Publications:* Planning for Drought; Greenhouse Warming: Abatement and Adaptation; Num scholarly articles on consequence of climate change for system of natural resources. *Memberships:* Am Meteorological Soc; Assn Am Geogs; AAAS; Bd Dirs, Renewable Natural Resources Fndn. *Honours:* Andrew Mellow Fndn Fellowship, Nat Acad Scis/Nat Rsch Coun; W R Boggers Award, Best Paper Published in Water Resources Bulletin in 1989, 1990. *Hobbies:* Cross country skiing; Tennis; Golf; Hunting; Fishing; Raquet ball; Basketball; Backpacking. *Address:* 237 L W Chase Hall, Department of Agricultural Meteorology, University of Nebraska-Lincoln, Lincoln, NE 68583, USA.

EASTON Earnest, b. 1 May 1943, South Bend, Indiana, USA. Adviser; Inventor; Composer; Consultant; Teacher; Manager; Writer; Researcher; Singer; Athlete; Scholar. *Education:* AA, Loop Coll, Chgo, 1968; BA, German, 1970, BA, Pol Sci, 1970, Univ IL, Chgo Circle; MPA, Pub Admin, Syracuse Univ, 1971; MA, Govt, 1975, PhD, Govt, 1978, Cornell Univ. *Publications:* Poems Representative of the Human Being from the Mind and Body, 1983; Wrapped Up in Nature, 1983; The Nightrider, 1983; The Knight Rider and the Helicopter Pirates, 1984. *Memberships:* Hollywood Chaparral Poetry Soc; CA State Poetry Soc; Naval Reserve Assn; Am Legion; Am Guild Authors and Composers; Concerts for Humanity. *Honours:* Winner, Best Singer of Yr, Koenigsbau Restaurant, Augsburg, FRG, 1964; Hon Student, Loop Coll, 1967; Scholarship, Univ Salzburg, Austria, 1969; Fellowship, Syracuse Univ, 1970; Pol Sci Hon Student, Univ IL, 1970. *Hobbies:* Walking; Writing; Theatre. *Address:* 605 South Normandie Street, Los Angeles, CA 90005, USA.

EATON Peter, b. 24 Jan 1916, London, England. Antiquarian Bookseller. m. (1) Ann Wilkinson, (2) Valerie Carruthers, 2 s, (3) Margaret Taylor, 2 d. *Education:* Municipal School (later Coll) Technology; Rochdale School Art; Manchester Univ. *Career includes:* War service, Rescue Squad, London; Started bookselling, London, 1945; Fndr, Dir, Peter Eaton Booksellers Ltd, Weedon, Aylesbury, Bucks; Painter; Exhibited, Rochdale School Art and Redfern Gall, London; Owner, historic house Lilies, 1969-. *Publications:* History of Lilies; Marie Stopes, A Preliminary Checklist of Her Writings. *Memberships:* Antiquarian Booksellers Assn; Historic House Assn; Pres, Pvte Lib Assn; FRGS; Reform Club. *Honours:* Univ Lib named after him, Japan. *Hobbies:* Reading; Listening to classical music; Theatre; Ballet; Foreign travel; Buying books; Painting; Cultural things in general; Watching other people. *Address:* Lilies, Weedon, nr Aylesbury, Buckinghamshire HP22 4NS, England. 1.

EBASHI Setsuro, b. 31 Aug 1922, Japan. President of Research Institute. m. Fumiko Takeda, 20 May 1956. *Education:* Fac Med, Univ Tokyo, 1940-44; MD, 1944; DMedSc, 1954. *Appointments:* Prof, Univ Tokyo, 1959-83; Vis Prof, Univ CA, San Fran, 1963, Harvard Univ, 1974; Prof, 1983-88, Dir-Gen, 1985-90, Nat Inst Physiological Sci; Currently Pres, Okazaki Nat Rsch Inst, Okazaki. *Creative works:* Establishment of the essential role of Ca ion in muascle contraction; Discovery of alpha-Actin, 1963; Discovery of Troponin. *Memberships:* Mitglieder, Deutsch Akad Leopoldina, 1971; Hon Mem, Am Soc Biological Chems, 1973; Hon For Mem, Am Acad Arts and Scis, 1975; For Mem, Royal Soc, London, 1977; Belgian Royal Acad Med, 1985; Accad Nazionale dei Lincei, Roma, 1985; Japan Acad, 1978. *Honours:* Prize, Yamaji Sci-promoting Fndn, 1965; Asahi Prize, Asahi Newspaper Publng Co, 1968; Imperial Prize, Japan Acad, 1972; Order Cultural Merit (Bunka-Kunsho), 1975; Peter Harris Award, 1986. *Address:* 17-503 Nagaizumi, Myodaiji, Okazaki 444, Japan. 50.

EBELING Werner, b. 15 Sept 1936, Bad Suderode, Germany. Professor of Theoretical Physics. m. Barbara Kuerschner, 14 Apr 1960, 1 s, 1 d. *Education:* Dip, Phys, Univ Rostock, 1959; Additional studies, Moscow Univ, 1960-61; Dr rer nat, 1963; Dr rer nat habil, 1968. *Appointments:* Prof, Theoretical Phys, Rostock Univ, 1970-79; Prof, Theoretical Phys, 1979-, Dean, Fac Maths and Natural Scis, 1985-90, Humboldt Univ, Berlin. *Publications:* Bound States, 1976; Self-organization and Evolution, 1982; Turbulence, 1984; Transport, 1984; Quantum Statistics, 1986; Complex Systems, 1989; Physics of Evolution, 1990. *Membership:* Acad Scis, Berlin. *Honours:* Humboldt Medal; Leibniz Medal; Haeckel Medal; Rostock Univ Prize; Nat Prize for Sci. *Hobbies:* Reading; Gardening. *Address:* Humboldt University, Institute for Theoretical Physics, Invalidenstr 42, 0-1040 Berlin, Germany.

EBERHARDT Cornelius, b. 3 Jan 1932, Oberaudorf, Germany. Conductor. m. Ursula Schade, 7 Aug 1957, 1 d. *Education:* Univs Munich and Hamburg, 1950-53; State Acad Music, Munich, 1953-56; Accad Chigiana, Siena, Italy, 1958. *Career:* Chorus Master, Municipal Opera, Ulm, FRG, 1956-60; Assoc Conductor, Munich State Theatre, 1960-69; Music Dir, Regensburg Symph and Opera, 1969-77; Fndr, Regensburg Music School; Co-Fndr, Bavarian Fest Mod Composers, 1973; Music Dir, Corpus Christi Symph, TX, USA, 1975-; Prof Opera, Conductor, 1977-, Pres, 1991-, State Acad Music, Munich, 1977-; Music Dir, Am Inst Musical Studies, Dallas, TX, 1978-; Vis Prof, 1979-80, Prof, Music Dir, 1984-87, Univ TX, Austin; Vis Prof, Corpus Christi State Univ, 1981-82; Music Dir, Mozart Fest Int, 1991-; Guest Conductor, Europe, N and S Am. *Publications:* Das Regensburger Orchester, 1972; Volksmusik und Kunstmusik in Sudosteuropa, 1988; Der Dirigent in Handbuch der Musikberufe, 1987. *Memberships:* Sci Cnslr, SE Europe Soc; Artistic Cnslr, Bavarian Assn Pub Educ. *Honours:* Bavarian State Award for Young Artists, 1969. *Hobbies:* Astronomy; History of art. *Address:* Darmstaedterstr 11/VII, D-8000 Munich 50, Germany. 4.

ECCLESTON Harry Norman, b. 21 Jan 1923, Coseley, Staffordshire, England. Artist. m. Betty Doreen Gripton, 5 Aug 1948, 2 s. *Education:* School of Art, Bilston/College of Art, Birmingham, 1937-42; ATD, Coll Art, Birmingham, 1946; Engraving School, Royal Coll Art, 1947-51; ARCA (1st class), 1950. *Career:* Served RN, 1942-46; Temporary Commn, RNVR, 1943; Lectr, Illustration, Printmaking, SE Essex Tech Coll, 1952-58; Freelance Graphic Design; Artist Designer, Bank England Printing Works, 1958-83; Full-time Painter, Printmaker, 1983-. *Creative works include:* Bank of England's Series D notes: 1 Newton, 5 Wellington, 10 Nightingale, 20 Shakespeare, 50 Wren; Prints and watercolours exhibited home and abroad, 1949-. *Memberships:* Royal Soc Painter-Etchers and Engravers, Assoc 1948, Fellow 1961, Hon Sec 1962-75, Pres 1975-89; Royal Watercolour Soc, Assoc 1964, Fellow 1975; Art Workers Guild, 1984; Hon Fellow, Royal Birmingham Soc Arts, 1989; Fellow, Royal West of England Acad, 1990; FRSA, 1972. *Honours:* OBE for work on Bank Notes, 1979. *Hobby:* Reading. *Address:* 110 Priory Road, Harold Hill, Romford RM3 9AL, England. 1, 19.

ECKENFELDER W Wesley Jr, b. 15 Nov 1926, New York City, New York, USA. Environmental Engineer; Consultant; Educator. m. Kathleen Hurley, 17 Nov 1974, 1 s, 1 d. *Education:* BCE, Manhattan Coll, NY, 1946; Postgrad, Chem Engrng, NC State Univ, 1947; MS, Sanitary Engrng, PA State Univ, 1948; MCE, Sanitary Engrng, NY Univ, 1954. *Appointments include:* Ptnr, Weston Eckenfelder & Assocs, 1952-56; Asst Rsch Prof, 1956-57, Assoc Prof, 1957-65, Manhattan Coll; Pres, Hydroscience Inc, 1962-65; Prof, Civil Engrng, Univ TX,

1965-69; Disting Prof, Environmental and Water Resources Engrng, 1970-89, Exec Dir, Ctr Environmental Quality Mgmt, 1974-89, Vanderbilt Univ, Nashville, TN; Pres, 1970-72, Chmn, Bd Dirs, 1972-89, AWARE Inc, Nashville; Cons, State of Israel, 1879-72; Chmn Emeritus, Sr Tech Dir, Eckenfelder Inc, Nashville, 1989-. *Publications:* 22 books incl: Industrial Water Pollution Control, 1989; Principles of Water Quality Management, 1990; 25 chapts; Over 200 sci and tech papers. *Memberships include:* Pres, Pan- Am Hlth Org; WHO, Copenhagen, 1965-75; Pres, Hon Mem, Int Assn Water Pollution Rsch Control; Fellow, Am Soc Civil Engrs; Fellow, Inst Water and Environmental Mgmt; Fellow, Am Inst Chems; Diplomate, Am Acad Environmental Engrs; Fellow, AAAS; NY Acad Scis; Water Pollution Control Fedn; Am Chem Soc. *Honours include:* Indl Wastes Medals, Water Pollution Control, Wash DC, 1957; Gold Medal, Environmental Chem, Wash DC, 1974; Thomas Camp Medal, Water Pollution Control, Wash DC, 1980; Thaddeus Kasciuszko Medal, Tech Univ Cracow, Poland, 1989; Karl Imhoff-Pierre Koch Medal, Int Assn Water Pollution Rsch Control, London, 1990; Hon DSc, Manhattan Coll, 1990; Hon Mem, Chi Epsilon; Mem, NYU Chapt, Sigma Xi. *Address:* Eckenfelder Ind, 227 French Landing Dr, Nashville, TN 37228, USA.

ECKERSLEY Michael Dean, b. 5 Mar 1954, Ogden, Utah, USA. Designer; Professor. m. Michelle Patterson. *Education:* BA, Hons, Fine Art, Weber State Coll, 1978; MFA, Painting, Washington Univ, St Louis, 1980; Doct Fellow, 1983-85, EdD, Art Educ, Cognitive Science, 1985, Ball State Univ. *Appointments:* Visual Merchandising Mgr, The Bon, Allied Stores Corp (Seattle), 1980-83; Dept Housing and Design, Univ MD, College Pk, 1985-91. *Publications:* The Form of Design Processes, 1988; Thoughts on a Computer-Based Design Apprentice, 1990; Rules, Randomness, and Compositional Structure in Design, 1990; On Heuristics and Design-Problem Solving Behaviour: Cracking the 'Black Box' 1990; Factors of Meaning, Chance, and Utility in Shape Production Systems, 1991. *Memberships:* American Center for Design; Design Methods Grp; Am Inst Graphic Arts; Coll Art Assn. *Address:* University of Minnesota, Design Communication, 240 McNeal Hall, 1985 Buford Av, St Paul, MN 55108, USA.

ECKMANN Augustyn, b. 25 May 1941, Ostrowite, Poland. Assistant Professor. *Education:* Philosl-Theological studies, Pelplin, 1959-65; Master's degree, Biblical Scis, 1974, Lic Theol, 1975, Master's degree, Classical Philology, 1976, DTheol, Biblical Scis, 1978, Asst Prof, Old Christian Lit Specialist, 1987, Cath Univ Lublin. *Appointments:* Parish Priest, Brodnica Gorna and Fordon, 1965-71; Trng, 1976-77; Jr Asst, Classical Philology, 1977-79; Asst Lectr, 1979-81, Lectr, 1981-88, Asst Prof, 1988-, Cath Univ, Lublin. *Hobbies:* Reading; Tourism. *Address:* ul Obroncow Pokoju 9/3A, PL 20-030 Lublin, Poland.

EDBERG Rolf F, b. 14 Mar 1912, Lysvik, Sweden. Author. m. Astrid Persson, 7 July 1937 (dec), 1 s, 2 d. *Education:* DrPhil. *Appointments:* Chief Ed: Oskarshamns Nyheter, Oskarshamn, 1934-37, Ostgoten, Linkoping, 1938-45, Ny Tid, Gothenburg, 1945-56; MP, 1941-44, 1948-56; Deleg: Coun Europe, 1949-52, UN, 1952-57, 1960-61, No Coun, 1953-56, Disarmament Conf, 1961-65; Ambassador to Norway, 1956-57; Gov, Varmland, 1967-77. *Publications:* Nansen - The European, 1961; On the Shred of a Cloud, 1966; At the Foot of the Tree, 1972; Letters to Columbus, 1973; On Earth's Terms, 1974; A House in the Cosmos, 1974; Dream of Kilimanjaro, 1976; Shadows across the Savanna, 1977; Land of Glistening Waters, 1980; Drops of Water Drops of Life, 1984; And They Sailed All The Time, 1986; Born with the Pleiades, 1987; Sunday is too Late (w Alexey Yablokov), 1988; The Eye of the Earth, 1989; To live with Words, 1990. *Memberships:* Pres, Swedish Press Club, 1951-53; Pres, Stockholm Int Peace Rsch Inst, 1973-78; Swedish Acad Scis, Chmn Environmental Comm 1974-81. *Honours:* Liberty Cross

of King Haakon, 1945; Grand Cross, Order of St Olav, 1962; Socrates Prize, 1972; Gold Medal, Pro Mundo Habitabile, Swedish Acad Scis, 1974; Dag Hammerskjold Medal, 1978; Kings Gold Medal, 1980; Govt's Gold Medal, Illis quorum meruere labores, 1984; Premio Mondiala della Cultura, 1985; Several other awards. *Hobbies:* Wildlife; Music. *Address:* Hybelejens gata 4, 653 40 Karlstad, Sweden. 3, 12, 30.

EDELMAN Colin Neil, b. 2 Mar 1954, London, England. Barrister. m. Jacqueline Claire Seidel, 26 Oct 1978, 1 s, 1 d. *Education:* Haberdashers Askes School, 1961-72; Clare Coll, Cambridge, 1973- 76; MA (Cantab); Called to Bar, 1977. *Appointments:* Mem, Devereux Chambers, London, 1979-. *Hobbies:* Badminton; Skiing; Walking. *Address:* Devereux Chambers, Devereux Court, London WC2R 3JJ, England.

EDELMAN David Laurence, b. 7 Apr 1948, London, England. m. Sandie Freeman, 4 July 1971, 1 s, 1 d. *Education:* Haberdashers Askes School, 1955-66; BCom (Hons), Leeds Univ, 1970; FCA, MCT. *Appointments:* Tax Ptnr, Gerald Edelman & Co, Chartered Accts, 1976-81; Dir, City Trust Ltd, Bankers, 1981-86; Dir, Moorfield Estates PLC, Bushey, Herts, 1983-. *Hobbies:* Skiing; Art; Classical music; Running; Theatre. *Address:* Moorfield Estates PLC, Shern House, 16 Melbourne Road, Bushey, Herts WD2 3LN, England.

EDMONDS Douglas Keith, 23 July 1949, London, England. Consultant Obstetrician and Gynaecologist. m. Gillian Linda Edmonds, 13 Oct 1990. *Education:* The Ecclesbourne School, Derbyshire, 1962-68; Univ Sheffield, 1968-73; MB ChB; FRCOG; FRACOG. *Appointments:* Jessop Hosp for Women, Sheffield, 1975-77; Southampton Gen Hosp, 1977-79, 1981-82; Queen Elizabeth Hosp, Adelaide, Australia, 1979-81; Queen Charlottes and Chelsea Hosp, Gt Ormond St Hosp for Sick Children, London, 1982-. *Publications:* Practical Paediatric and Adolescent Gynaecology; Spontaneous and Recurrent Abortion; Num chapts in other books; Extensive sci and med papers. *Memberships:* Gynaecological Club GB; Brit and Am Fertility Socs; Ovarian Club; Coun Mem, World and European Fedns Paediatric and Adolescent Gynaecology. *Hobbies:* Sport esp golf, Rugby Union, cricket, tennis; Wine. *Address:* 78 Harley Street, London W1N 1AE, England.

EDWARDS Clive Arthur, b. 16 June 1925, Worcester, England. Research Professor; Chairman, Department of Entomology. m. Elvira Tormen, 4 Apr 1964, 1 s, 1 d. *Education:* BSc, MSc, DSc, Univ Bristol, England; MS, PhD, Univ WI, USA. *Appointments:* Govt Entomologist, Min Agric, Fisheries and Food, 1951-60; Sr Prin Sci Off, Rothamsted Expmtl Station; Prof, OH State Univ, Columbus, USA, 1985-91; Tech Dir, Brit Earthworm Technology. *Publications:* Principles of Agricultural Entomology, 1964; Biology of Earthworms, 1972, 2nd Ed, 1977; Persistent Pesticides in the Environment, 1970, 2nd Ed, 1973; 220 sci papers; Ed, 8 books. *Memberships:* Fellow, Inst Biology; FRSA; Fellow, Royal Entomological Soc; Ecological Soc Am; Entomological Soc Am; Coun Mem, Assn Applied Biologists; Int Soc Soil Sci, Soil Biology Comm Mem; Int Assn Ecology; Soil and Water Conservation Assn; Sec, US Soil Ecology Soc; Co-Organiser, World Soc Sustainable Agric; Nat Rsch Coun Comm Sustainable Agric; Admin Coun, N Ctrl USDA Sustainable Agric Prog; Several ed bds. *Honours:* Fellowship, Kellogg Fndn, 1955-56; Fellowship, 1956-57, NSF, Sr For Scientist Fellowship, 1966-67, NSF; Medal, Int Soc Pesticide Chem, 1974; Pollution Abatement Award, RSA/Confedn Brit Industry, 1983; Medal, Univ Helsinki, Finland, 1985; Creative Programming Award, Nat Univ Continuing Educ Assn, 1989; Farming Systems Award, MI State Univ, 1990. *Hobbies:* Collecting old cameras and photographica; Old books; Sports. *Address:* Department of Entomology, The Ohio State University, 1735 Neil Avenue, Columbus, OH 43210, USA. 50.

EDWARDS John, b. 3 Mar 1938, London, England. Painter; Sculptor. *Education:* Hornsey Coll Art, London, 1953-56, 1958, 1960; Leeds Inst Educ, 1962-63; Ecole Superieure d'Arch et d'Art Visual, Brussels, 1963-64. *Career:* Hd, Painting, 1980-86, Hd, Painting, Sculpture, 1986-88, St Martins School Art, London; Participant, gp exhibs incl: Britische Kunst Heute, Hamburg, 1968; Sebastian de Ferranti Collection, Manchester, 1969; Contemporary British Art, Cleveland, 1976; British Painting 52-77, Royal Acad, London, 1977; The British Art Show, Arts Coun Exhib, 1979-80; British Art Now, Guggenheim Mus, NY, US tour, 1980; British Contemporary Art, Tokyo Metropolitan Mus, Japan tour, 1982; Aspects of British Art, Guggenheim Mus, 1983; Pintura Britanica Contemporanea, Madrid, 1983; New Works on Paper, Brit Coun Tour, 1984-86; Twenty-Five Years, Juda Rowan Gall, London, 1985; English Art, Bokhoven Wenneker, Doorn, Netherlands, 1988; Beelden, Galerie Bokhoven Wennekes, Amsterdam, 1989; International Architectureworkshop, Atelier W G, Amsterdam, 1989; From Prism to Paintobox, Oriel Gallery, Clwyd, Wales, touring, 1989; Four Abstract Painters, 1989, Homage to the Square, 1990, Flaxman Gall, London; Recent Directions, London, Amsterdam, 1990; Works in public collects incl: Arts Coun; Brit Coun; Contemporary Arts Soc; Gulbenkian Fndn; Power Inst Contemporary Art, Sydney; Solomon R Guggenheim Mus, NY. *Creative works include:* Painted steel wallworks, ceramic sculptures, larger constrns of laminated aluminium and wood, works using refractory cement w stove enamel.*Honours:* Brit Coun Scholarship to Brussels, 1963; Leverhulme Rsch Grant, 1988; Gtr London Arts Award, 1988; Winston Churchill Travelling Fellowship to Netherlands and Germany, 1989. *Address:* 52 Isledon Road, London N7 7LD, England.

EDWARDS Paul Geoffrey, b. 31 July 1926, Birmingham, England. Professor of English and African Literature. m. Maj Ingbritt Nilsson, 31 July 1952, 2 d. *Education:* 1st Class Hons, Engl Lang and Lit, Durham Univ, 1952; 1st Class, Archaeology, Anthropology (Celtic, Icelandic), Emmanuel Coll, Cambridge, 1954; MA, 1957. *Appointments:* St Augustine's Coll, Ghana, 1954-57; Univ Sierra Leone, 1957-63; Univ Edinburgh, Scotland, 1963-91, incl Prof, Engl and African Lit; Vis Prof: SUNY, Binghamton, 1970-71, univs, CA, Singapore, Bangkok, Benghazi, var times. *Publications:* Legendary Fiction in Medieval Iceland (w H Palsson), 1972; Black Personalities in the Era of the Slave Trade (w J Alvin), 1983; Black Writing in Britain 1760-1890 (w D Dabydeen), 1991; Eds: 18th Century black Brit authors Equiano, Cugoano, Sancho; Translations w H Palsson, 15 vols, Icelandic Sagas incl: Egilssaga, Orkneyinga, Eyrbyggja, 7 Viking Romances, Vikings in Russia; Articles mainly on black writing, 19th century lit.*Honours:* Olaudan Equiano Award, contbn to African Am Studies, Univ UT, 1989. *Hobbies:* Relaxing; Translating sagas; Reading dead poets.*Address:* 82 Kirk Brae Road, Edinburgh EH16 6JA, Scotland. 184.

EDWARDS Peter Stuart Allenby, b. 28 May 1948, Beckenham, Kent, England. Solicitor; Notary Public. m. Helene de Cabrol de Moute, 10 Oct 1981, dec. 16 Sept 1988. *Education:* Magdalen Coll, Oxford, 1966-69; BA, 1969; MA, 1972. *Appointments:* Asst Solicitor, Richards, Butler & Co, London, 1972-75; Asst Solicitor, 1975-79, Ptnr, 1979-, Johnson, Stokes & Master, Hong Kong. *Publications:* HK Profits Tax, and Anti-Avoidance Provisions in Hong Kong, in Strategy in International Taxation, 1987; Contbr to Cahiers de Droit Fiscal International, 1985, 1987, 1989, 1992. *Memberships:* Chmn, 1987- Int Fiscal Assn, Hong Kong Br, Dpty Chmn 1979-87; Royal Soc St George, Hong Kong Br, VP 1987-89, Pres, 1989-90; Hong Kong Jt Comm Taxation; Law Soc Revenue Law Comm; V-Chmn, Taxation Comm; Inter Pacific bar Assn; Argentier, Commanderie de Bordeaux, Hong Kong Br; Law Soc, England and Wales; Law Soc Hong Kong. *Address:* 34B Mount Kellett Road, The Peak, Hong Kong. 52.

EFIMIK Viktor Evgenjevich, b. 21 Dec 1963, Perm, USSR. Zoologist (Arachnologist). m. Alexandra Anatoljevna Starkova, 6 Sept 1991. *Education:* Grad, Fac Biology, Perm Univ. *Appointments:* Rsch, fauna, taxonomy, ecology and zoogeog of spiders of So Ural (Baschkiria), Zoology Lab, Univ Perm. *Publications:* About the fauna of spiders of Baschkirian National Park, 1988. *Hobbies:* Sport esp ideko; Photographing insects. *Address:* Mira st 66.5-24, 614066 Perm, Russia.

EFRAIMOGLOU Lazaros, b. 30 Jan 1932, Athens, Greece. Member of Parliament. m. Ourania Kli, 26 Aug 1964, 1 s. *Education:* Athens Coll; Grad, Hons Econs and Textiles, Univ Leeds, England, 1952. *Appointments:* Bus positions, textiles, constrn, portfolio mgmg; Fndr, Mamaging Dir, many firms; Fndr Mem, VP, Ergobank SA; Fndr, Pres, Ergo Investment SA; Fndr, Bd Mem, Ergodata SA; Ldr, num Greek Econ and Commercial Delegations, countries in Europe, N and S Am, Asia, Africa; Elected MP, Athens Central, 1989, re-elected 1990; Mem, Parly Comm Econs; Mem, Parly Comm Prod and Commerce; Hd, Greek-Brit Inter-Parly Grp; Mem, Coun Europe; Mem, Coun Europe Comm Econ Affairs and Dev; Coun Europe Com Environment, Reg Planning and Local Auths. *Creative works:* Fndng Mem, 2 orphanages; Financed preservation of Byzantine Monastery in Stemnitsa, Peloponnesus *Memberships:* Past Pres, Soc Textile Engrs; Bd Mem, Hon Pres, Athens Chmbr Comm, Gen Sec 1974, VP 1977, Pres 1978, 1983-88; Fndr, Hon Pres, Union Greek Chmbrs Comm, Pres 1981-88; VP, Assn European Chmbrs Comm, 1985-87; Assoc Mem, Textile Inst; Fndr Mem, Soc Ch Property Mgmt; Life Mem, Archaeological Soc Greece, Past Treas of Bd Dirs; Past Mem, Bd Dirs, St Paul Gen Hosp Accidents. *Honours:* Prizes: Hellenic Mgmt Soc, 1987; Athens Chmbr Comm and Industry, 1988; Union Greek Chmbrs Comm, 1988; Soc Descendents from Sparti, Asia Minor, 1989. *Hobbies:* Music; Reading; Swimming. *Address:* 44 Eleftheriou Venizelou str, 15237 Filothei, Athens, Greece.

EFRON Samuel, b. 6 May 1915, Lansford, Pennsylvania, USA. Attorney. m. Hope Bachrach Newman, 5 Apr 1941, 2 s. *Education:* BA, LeHigh Univ, 1935; LLB, Harvard Law School, 1938. *Appointments:* Atty, Forms and Regulations, Registration Div, SEC, 1939-40; Off Solicitor, Dept Labour, 1940-42; Asst Chief, Real and Personal Property, 1942-43, Chief, Debt Claims, Asst Chief, Claims Br, 1946-51, Off Alien Property Custodian, Dept Justice; Asst Gen Counsel, Int Affairs, Dept Def, 1951-53; Cons, Depts Int Affairs and Def, 1953-54; Ptnr, Surrey, Karasik, Gould & Efron, Wash, DC, 1954-61; Exec VP, Parsons & Whittemore, NYC, 1961-63; Ptnr, Arent, Fox, Kintner, Plotkin & Kahn, Wash, DC, 1968-. *Publications:* Creditors Claims Under the Trading With Enemy Act, 1948; Foreign Taxes on US Expenditures, 1954; Offshore Procurement and Industrial Mobilisation, 1955; Operation of Investment Incentive Laws with Emphasis on USA and Mexico, 1977. *Memberships:* Am, Fed, NYC, DC and InterAm Bar Assns; Am Soc Int Law; Phi Beta Kappa. *Honours:* Order of Lion of Finland, 1st Class, 1975. *Address:* Arent, Fox, Kintner, Plotkin & Kahn, Washington Square, 1050 Connecticut Avenue NW, Washington, DC 20036, USA.

EGBULEFU Christopher Akuwudike, b. Minna, Nigeria. Legal Practitioner. m. Regina Ibari Nkwocha, 15 Oct 1960, 2 s, 5 d. *Education:* Tchrs Higher Elem Cert, 1952; LLB (Hons), 1966; Dip, Nigerian Law School, 1971. *Appointments:* Primary School Tchr, Kano, 1953-54; Tutor, St Malachy's Trng Coll, 1955-56; School Hdmaster, St Theresa's, Zaria, 1957-63; Pvte Legal Practitioner, 1971-91. *Memberships:* Nigerian Bar Assn, Sec Owerri Br 1981-85; Mbaise Welfare Club, Port Harcourt; Legal Advsr, Ahiara Forum Owerri; Legal Advsr, Akabor Ahiara; Progressive Union Commandery 422, Treas; Knights St John. *Honours:* Best Boy Scout, 1st Minna Troop, 1943. *Hobbies:* Lawn tennis; Reading magazines esp Master Dictative; Cycling. *Address:* Akubudike Chambers, 46 Wetheral Road, PO Box 621, Owerri, Imo State, Nigeria.

EHARA Shozo, b. 5 May 1928, Otaru, Japan. Professor. m. Reiko Hirano, 10 June 1957, 1 s. *Education:* BSc, 1951, DSc, 1960, Hokkaido Univ, Sapporo. *Appointments:* Asst, Fac Sci, Hokkaido Univ, 1951-67; Assoc Prof, Fac Educ, 1967-71, Prof, Fac Educ, 1971- , Dir, Lib, 1984-86, Tottori Univ. *Publications:* An Introduction to Agricultural Acarology, 1975; Illustrations of the Mites and Ticks of Japan (editor), 1980. *Membership:* Ed Bd, International Journal of Acarology, W Bloomfield, MI, 1975-. *Honours:* Award, Japan Soc Applied Entomology and Zoology, 1969. *Hobby:* Gardening. *Address:* Biological Institute, Faculty of Education, Tottori University, 4-101 Koyama-cho Minami, Tottori 680, Japan. 52.

EICHLER Hans Joachim, b. 9 Nov 1940, Berlin, Germany. Professor. m. Renete Eichler, 26 Dec 1966, 2 d. *Education:* Abitur, 1959; DiplIng, 1965; Dr, 1967; Habilitation, Phys, 1970. *Appointments:* Asst to Prof Boersch, 1965-70; Full Prof, Technical Univ Berlin, 1972-; Mem, Tech Staff, Bell Labs, USA, 1981-83. *Publications:* Books: Laser-Induced Dynamic Gratings (w Guenter, Pohl); Laser-Grundlagen, Systeme, Anwendung (w J Eichler); Ed, special issue, IEEE Journal of Quantum Electronics. *Memberships:* Deutsche Physikalische Gesellschaft, Quantum Electronics Div Chmn; Deutsche Gesellschaft fuer Angewandt Optik; European Phys Soc; Hochschulverband: ASC, BSC. *Honours:* Dean, Phys Dept, Tech Univ Berlin, 1972-80; Invited talks, var confs; Hon Co-Ed, Journal of Nonlinear Optics and Journal on Optical Materials. *Hobbies:* Tennis; Skiing; Jogging. *Address:* Optisches Inatitut, Technische Universitaet Berlin, 1 Berlin 12, Germany. 43, 52.

EISENBACH Michael, b. 10 Apr 1945, Tel-Aviv, Israel. Scientist. m. Lea Eisenbach, 5 Sept 1967, div. 1985, 2 s. *Education:* BSc, Chem, 1969, MSc, Biochem, 1971, PhD, Biochem, 1975, Tel-Aviv Univ; Postdoct Rsch Fellow, Weizmann Inst, Rehovot, 1975-76. *Appointments:* Scientist, 1976-78, Sr Scientist, 1980-84, Assoc Prof, Membrane Rsch, 1984-, Chmn, Dept Membrane Rsch and Biophys, 1989-, Weizmann Inst Sci, Rehovot; Vis Scientist, Madison, USA, 1978-80. *Publications:* 47 papers in sci jrnls; Sensing and Response in Micro-organisms (editor). *Memberships:* Am Soc Microbiology; Am Biophys Soc; AAAS; Israel Biochem Soc; Israel Soc Microbiology; Am Soc Cell Biology. *Honours:* Shenkar Fndn Award, Disting Rsch, Tel-Aviv Univ, 1971, 1974; Prize, MSc w distinction, Tel-Aviv Univ, 1971; Rsch Grant, Bat-Sheva de Rothschild Fndn, 1976-77; H Dudley Wright Rsch Award, Outstanding Work in Membrane Studies, 1986. *Hobbies:* Photography; Tennis. *Address:* Dept of Membrane Research and Biophysics, The Weizmann Institute of Science, 76100 Rehovot, Israel. 52, 156.

EJIOFOR Michael Anthony Njide, b. 6 May 1949, Obeledu, Nigeria. Civil Servant; Research Officer. m. 8 Sept 1984, 1 s, 2 d. *Education:* BSc Hons, Botany, 1974; MSc, Microbiology, 1979; PhD, Microbiology, 1984; Postgrad Cert Educ, 1990. *Appointments:* Rsch Scientist: Pupil Rsch Off, 1975-77; Sr Rsch Off, 1981-87; Prin Rsch Off, 1987-88; Asst Chief Rsch Off, 1988-91. *Memberships:* Nigerian Inst Food Sci and Technology, Sect Chmn; Int Soc Tropical Root Crops, Africa Br. *Honours:* Cert of Hon, Univ Nigeria Football Team, 1973-74; Distinction, Overseas Tchr Trng Award, 1990. *Hobbies:* Sports (football, table tennis); Watching films. *Address:* Pre-National Diploma (Science and Technology) Programme, National Root Crops Research Institute, Umudike, Umuahia, Imo State, Nigeria.

EKBLAD Stig-Henrik Johan, b. 25 Oct 1952, Turku, Finland. Neonatologist. m. Satu Hakala, 21 Sept 1985, 1 s, 2 d. *Education:* MD, Univ Turku, 1977; Speciality, Paediatrics, 1985; PhD, 1987; Subspeciality, Neonatology, 1988; Snr Lectr in Paediatrics, 1992; Postgrad Fellow, Dept Paediatrics, St Goran's Children's Hosp, Karolinska Inst, Stockholm, Sweden, 1989-90. *Appointments:* Dept Paediatrics, Univ Turku, 1979-88;

Neonatologist, Dept Obstetrics, Turku City Hosp, 1989-. *Creative works:* Expmtl rsch in field of dev nephrology. *Honours:* Rsch Grants, Emil Aaltonen Fndn, Finland, 1988-91. *Hobbies:* Gardening; Travel. *Address:* Kaurakatu 17, SF-20740 Turku, Finland. 52.

EKE Kenoye Kelvin, b. 1 Sept 1956, Rivers State, Nigeria. Educator. m. Joy Grimes Eke, 24 June 1989, 2 s. *Education:* BA w highest hons, AL A&M Univ, USA, 1980; MA, Pol Sci, 1982, PhD, Pol Sci, 1985, Atlanta Univ; Postdoct study, Harvard Univ and Univ WI. *Appointments:* Asst Prof, Bethune-Cookman Coll, Daytona Beach, FL, USA, 1985-89; Assoc Prof, Pol Sci, Dir, Int Progs, Savannah State Coll, Savannah, GA, 1989-. *Publications:* Nigerian Foreign Policy under Two Military Governments, 1966-1979; Media Coverage of Terrorism: Methods of Diffusion (co-ed); Several jrnl articles. *Memberships:* Exec Bd, African Assn Pol Sci, N Am Chapt; Bd Dirs, Savannah Coun World Affairs; So Ctr Int Studies; Benefits Advsry Bd, Chatham Co Dept Family and Children's Servs; Several profl assns. *Honours:* Ja-Flo Davis Fac Mem of Yr Award, Fac Bethune-Cookman Coll, 1988-90; Summer Rsch Fellow, Ctr African Studies, Univ FL, 1991; Pew Fac Fellow Int Affairs, Harvard Univ, 1992-93. *Hobby:* Tennis. *Address:* Savannah State Coll, Savannah, GA 31404, USA. 152.

EKSTEDT John Wilford, b. 2 June 1938, Bremerton, Washington, USA. Professor of Criminology. m. Kay Louise Bryant, 28 Aug 1960, 2 s, 2 d. *Education:* BSc, Seattle Pacific Coll, 1962; BDiv, 1965, MDiv, 1973, Concordia Theological Sem; MA, Univ Chgo, 1971; PhD, Univ CA, 1977. *Appointments:* Exec Dir, Justice Dev Commn, BC, Canada, 1975; Dpty Min Corrections, Acting Dpty Atty-Gen, BC, 1975-78; Assoc Prof, Criminology, 1979, Dir, Inst Studies in Criminal Justice Policy, 1980-, Prof, Criminology, 1986-, Simon Fraser Univ, Burnaby. *Publications:* Corrections in Canada, textbook, 1984; Custody, Care and Control, hist book, 1990; Num articles, reports, reviews on justice related topics. *Memberships:* Fndg Dir, Int Ctr Criminal Law Reform and Criminal Justice Policy, Vancouver, 1990-. *Honours:* Martin Luther King Mem Award, USA, 1971; Gov-Gen's Award, Silver Jubilee Medal, Canada, 1977; Australian Bi-Centennial Cert Merit, 1988; Freedom Award, Am Soc Int Peace and Justice, USA, 1990. *Hobbies:* Basketball; Gardening; Running. *Address:* School of Criminology, Simon Fraser University, Burnaby, British Columbia, Canada V5A 1S6.

EKSTRAND Lars Henric, b. 30 July 1933, Gavle, Sweden. Educator. m. Gudrun Ylinentalo, 1 Jan 1959, 1 s, 1 d. *Education:* MA, Educ, 1958; PhD, Educ, 1964; PhD, Int Educ, 1978; PhD, 1992. *Appointments:* Min Educ, 1958; School Psychologist, Nat Bd Educ, 1958-66; Assoc Prof, Acting Prof, Malmo School Educ, 1966-; Currently on leave, Project Coord, Orissa Social Forestry Project, India, 1990-93. *Publications:* About 150 monographs and sci articles incl: Ethnic Minorities and Immigrants in a Cross-Cultural Perspective, 1985; Guest Ed, several jnls; Contbr to International Encyclopedia of Education. *Memberships:* Int Assn Cross-Cultural Psychology, 1980-88, Exec Comm 1984-87; Int Assn Applied Psychology, 1974-86; Int Assn Applied Linguistics, 1974-86; Am Psychological Assn, 1974-84. *Hobbies:* Downhill skiing; Tennis; Cooking. *Address:* Dept of Education, Malmo School of Education, University of Lund, S-20045 Malmo, Sweden.

EKSTROM Bjorn Fredrik, b. 22 Nov 1950, Uddevalla, Sweden. Medical Doctor. m. Helene Lundqvist, 26 Apr 1980, 1 d. *Education:* Grad, Med School, 1975; MD, 1977; Specialist, Urology, 1984; Specialist, Gen Surg, 1987. *Appointments:* Intern, 1975-77, Resident, 1978-82, Assisting Prof, 1983-85, Helsingborg Gen Hosp, Helsingborg; Rsch Fellow, Strong Mem Hosp, Rochester, NY, USA, 1982-83; Assisting Prof, Rschr, Dept Urology, Lund Univ Hospital, Lund, Sweden, 1985-. *Contributions to:* med jnls in surg and urology. *Memberships:* Swedish Med Assn; Swedish Soc Med; Swedish Surg Assn; Swedish Urology Assn; Scandinavian Urology Assn; Int

Continence Soc. *Honours:* Upjohn Achievement Award, 1983. *Address:* Toftagatan 6B, S-26035 Odakra, Sweden.

EL-AYASHY Mamdouh Mahmoud, b. 3 Mar 1954, Port Said, Egypt. Computer Senior System Analyst. m. Hala Mohamed Zanaty, 18 Aug 1984, 2 s. *Education:* BSc, Commerce, Cairo Univ, 1975. *Appointments:* Programmer, Egyptian Sugar and Refinery Co, Cairo, 1976-78; Project Ldr, CAP Saudi, Riyadh, Saudi Arabia, 1978-84; Cons, Saudi Ports Auth, Riyadh, 1981-84; Senior System Analyst, TAIC, Riyadh, 1984-. *Memberships:* Inst Bankers, London; The British Computer Soicety (BCS) London; Fellow, Riyadh Computer Grp; S/38-AS/400 User Grp, Riyadh. *Hobbies:* Travel; Visiting new countries; Swimming. *Address:* The Arab Investment Co (TAIC), PO Box 4009, Riyadh 11491, Saudi Arabia.

EL-BASSIOUNY Mahmoud Youssef, b. 13 Aug 1920, Damietta, Egypt. Professor Emeritus. m. 13 Aug 1952, 1 s, 1 d. *Education:* Dip, School Applied Arts, 1939; Dip, Inst Educ, 1942; MA, 1947, PhD, 1949, OH State Univ, USA. *Appointments:* Instr, Art Educ, Model Schools, Cairo, 1942-46; Mission to USA, 1946-49; Staff Mem, Dean Coll Art Educ, Hilwan Univ, Cairo, 1965- 75; Chmn, Dept Art Educ, K Abdulaziz Univ, Mecca, Saudi Arabia, 1975-80; Prof, Art Educ, Qatar Univ, 1980-86; Prof Emeritus, Hilwan Univ, 1986-. *Creative works:* Author or co-author, 43 books in Arabic, 1 in Engl; Articles in mags; 7 1-man shows, paintings, incl Cairo, 1992. *Memberships:* Pres, Egyptian Int Soc Educ through Art; Former World Councillor, Int Soc Educ through Art; Egyptian Artists Syndicate; Former Mem, 14 comms. *Honours:* Encouraging Prize, Egyptian State, 1971; Egyptian President's 1st Award, Sci and Art, 1973; Cert Appreciation, Cert Recognition, Mynia Univ, 1988; Cert Recognition, Hilwan Univ, 1989; Cert Merit, BIB, 1989. *Hobbies:* Writing; Painting; Teaching of art. *Address:* 8 Ahmad Mahmoud St, Heliopolis, Cairo 11351, Egypt. 139, 154, 191.

EL-NADI Fathi M A, b. 4 July 1940, Mansura, Egypt. Director of Human Resources. m. Amal A El-Tonnamly, 10 Dec 1964, 1 s, 1 d. *Education:* BSc, Commerce, Mansoura Commerce Inst, 1962; BA, Engl Lit, 1967, Ma, Mass Communication, 1973, Cairo Univ; PhD, Bus Admin, Pacific Wn Univ, Los Angeles, CA, 1988; Sr Execs Workshops, Univ MI, Univ WI, 1983-89. *Appointments:* Mgr, Union Carbide Corp, 1960-62; PR and Advt Mgr, NASCO, 1962-69; Bus Dir, Skidmore, Owings & Merill, 1975-82; Personnel and Admin Mgr, Johnson Wax, 1983-85; Dir, Personnel and Indl Rels, General Motors, 1985-89; Sr Mgmt Cons, MERIC Int, 1989-90; Dir, Human Resources, Bristol-Myers Squibb, 1990-. *Publications:* Writer, Short Stories Collection, 1959; Ed, Nasr Automotive Magazine, 1969. *Contributions to:* Theatre Magazine, 1963- 67; Contbr, articles to profl jnls. *Memberships:* Soc Human Resources Mgmt, USA; Chmn, Personnel Dirs Grp, Egypt; Maadi Sporting and Yacht Club, Egypt; Cons, Am Univ Cairo; Am Chmbr of Comm. *Honours:* Best Report-Writer Prize, Johnson Wax Corp, 1984; Rated Sr Profl in Human Resources, Am Soc Personnel Admin, 1985; Cert Instr, Crosby Quality Coll, 1986. *Hobbies:* Reading; Travel; Sports (tennis). *Address:* 5th floor, Apt 11, 103 Misr, Helwan Road, Maadi, Cairo, Egypt.

ELIAS-JONES Peter John, b. 29 May 1943, Wales. TV Programme Controller. m. Elinor Mair Owens, 10 Apr 1971, 2 d. *Education:* BA, Univ Leeds; Dip, Univ Manchester. *Appointments:* Sr Floor Mgr, TWW, 1966-68; Prod, Dir, News and Current Affairs, Sport, Light Entertainment, 1968-71, Hd, Children's Progs, Mem, ITV Network Com, 1971-81, Asst Prog Controller, Entertainment, 1982-88, Prog Controller, Entertainment, 1988-, HTV Ltd, Cardiff; Newspaper and Mag Columnist; Int Guest Speaker; Music and Drama Adjudicator. *Publications:* 4 books for young people; Num articles. *Address:* HTV, TV Centre, Culverhouse Cross, Cardiff, S Glam CF5 6XJ, Wales.

ELKAYAM Shelley Rachel, b. 18 Nov 1955, Haifa, Israel. Poetess; Literary Editor; Organisational Counsellor. *Education:* Qualified Tchr, Bet Berl, 1976; BA, Educ Counselling, Jewish Hist, 1980, MA studies, Educ Counselling, 1980-86, Hebrew Univ Jerusalem. *Appointments:* Army serv, Israeli Def Force; Nat Coord, Scouts Israel, 1980; Project Cnslr, Young Ldrship Prog, 1981; Spokesperson, E for Peace Movement, 1983; Organisational Cnslr, Israeli Def Force School Ldrship, 1986-91; Tchng Hebrew to gifted students, 1990; Chief Ed, Tarmil, Israeli Def Force and Min Def publ for Israeli soldiers, 1991. *Publications:* Poetry books: The Essence of Oneself, 1981; The Bud of the Lemon's Light, 1983; Song of the Architect, 1986; When the Mouse and the Snake First Met, 1987; Simple Days (in Engl), 1984; Selected Poems, 1984. *Memberships:* Exec Bd, Hebrew Writers Union; Co-Fndr, E for Peace Movement; Int Youth Coord, World Conf Relig and Peace; Pres, World Conf Relig and Peace, Israel; Ed Bd, Shdemot kibbutz movement publ; Advsry Bd, New Options, Wash, DC; Exec Bd, Youth Against Racism. *Honours:* 1st Prize, Young Poets Contest, Haifa Univ, 1980; Invited Israeli Rep and Deleg, Poetry Int, Rotterdam, 1984, 1985, 1987; Invited Speaker, opening assemblies and panels: Int Writers Conf, Belgrade, 1985; World Conf Relig and Peace, Nairobi, 1984, Korea, 1986, Beijing, 1986, Melbourne, 1989; Assembly World Religs, San Fran, USA, 1990. *Hobbies:* Hebrew Bible and teachings; Physical immortality; Reading and writing poetry; Radio programmes (literature and poetry), 1985-92. *Address:* 9 Kdoshei Struma Street, Malcha, Jerusalem 96910, Israel.

ELLERY Nina, b. 9 June 1913, Archangel, Russia. Writer; Broadcaster. m. (John) Edger (Eggi) Ellery, 31 July 1937, dec. 1970. *Career includes:* Broadcaster, BBC Overseas Radio; Writes as Nina Petrova. *Publications:* Books: Russian Cookery, 1968; Best of Russian Cookery, 1978. *Memberships:* Russian Refugee Relief Assn; Sec, Local Leasehold Assn, 1970-71; Soc Authors; USSR Assn, GB; Conservative Party. *Hobbies:* Making hats and clothes; Gardening. *Address:* 106 Edith Road, London W14 9AP, England.

ELLIOTT George Arthur, b. 30 Jan 1945, Montreal, Canada. Research Mathematician. m. Noriko Yui, 20 July 1974. *Education:* BSc (Hons), 1965, MSc, 1966, Queen's Univ, Kingston, Canada; PhD, Univ Toronto, 1969; Postdoct Fellow: Univ BC, 1969-70, Queen's Univ, Kingston, 1970-71. *Appointments:* Mem, Inst Adv Study, Princeton, USA, 1971-72; Lektor, Univ Copenhagen, Denmark, 1972-; Rsch Assoc, Ctr Nat Recherche Sci, Marseille, France, 1972-73, 1984-85; Guest Scholar, Rsch Inst Math Scis, Kyoto Univ, Japan, 1974, 1977; Assoc Prof, 1978-79, Adj Prof, 1979-81, 1982-85, Univ Ottawa, Canada; Vis Prof, Univ NSW, Australia, 1979; Vis Fellow, Univ Warwick, England, 1982; Adj Prof, 1984-, Vis Prof, 1986, 1988, 1990, 1991, Univ Toronto, Canada; Vis Fellow, Australian Nat Univ, 1984; Mem, Math Scis Rsch Inst, Berkeley, CA, USA, 1984-85; Vis Fellow, Univ Coll Swansea, Wales, 1988, 1989, 1990; Vis Prof, Univ Trondheim, Norway, 1990; Vis Rschr, Ctr Recherches Math, Univ Montreal, Canada, 1991. *Publications:* Abt 100 incl: On approximately finite-dimensional von Neumann algebras, 1976; Gaps in the spectrum of an almost periodic Schroedinger operator, 1982; The characterization of differential operators by locality: classical flows (w O Bratteli and D W Robinson), 1986; Dimension groups with torsion, 1990; Gauss polynomials and the rotation algebra (w M-D Choi and N Yui), 1990; The Atiyah- Singer index theorem as passage to the classical limit in quantum mechanics (w R Nest and T Natsume). *Memberships:* Am, Canadian, Danish, London and European Math Socs; Int Assn Math Phys. *Honours:* Elected Fellow, Royal Soc Canada, 1982. *Hobbies:* Reading; Listening to music. *Address:* Department of Mathematics, University of Toronto, Toronto, Canada M5S 1A1. 2, 52.

ELLIS Albert James, b. 27 Dec 1929, Dunedin, New Zealand. Retired Science Director. m. Dawn Evelyn

McMillan, 4 Apr 1954, 1 s, 3 d. *Education:* BSc, 1951, MSc, 1953, PhD, 1957, Otago Univ, Dunedin; Postgrad study, Southampton, England, 1964. *Appointments:* Geochemist, 1953-71, Director, Chem Div, 1971-79, Asst Dir-Gen, 1979-84, Dir-Gen, 1984-89, Dept Sci Indl Rsch, NZ; Chmn, NZ Polytechnics Prog Comm, 1991- ; Chmn, Energy Resources and Conservation Auth, 1992-. *Publications:* Over 100 papers, books, chapts, on geochem, phys chem, geothermal power, sci mgmt and hist. *Memberships:* NZ Inst Chem, Past Pres; NZ Geochem Grp, Past Pres; Geological Soc, NZ; Royal Soc NZ, Past Councillor. *Honours:* Fellow, NZ Inst Chem; ICI Medal, 1962; Nuffield Travelling Fellowship, 1963- 64; Fellow, 1969, Hector Medal, 1987, Royal Soc NZ; Chmn, C'wlth Sci Coun, London, 1984-86; NZ Jubilee Medal, 1977; OBE, 1989; NZ 1990 Medal. *Hobbies:* Travel; Old cars; Woodwork; Gardens; Science priorities management. *Address:* 775 High Street, Lower Hutt, New Zealand. 38, 52.

ELLIS Andrew Steven, b. 19 May 1952, Luton, England. Public Affairs and Political Consultant. m. Helen Prudence Drummond, 7 July 1990. *Education:* BA, Maths, Trinity Coll, Cambridge, 1972; MSc, Statistics, Univ Newcastle-upon-Tyne, 1973; BA, Law, Newcastle-upon-Tyne Polytechnic, 1983. *Appointments:* Proprietor, Andrew Ellis (Printing and Duplicating), Newcastle-upon-Tyne, 1973-81; Freelance Polit Organiser, 1981- 85; Sec-Gen, Liberal Party, 1985-88; Chief Exec, Social and Liberal Dems, 1988-89; Pub Affairs and Polit Cons, 1989-. *Publications:* Algebraic Structure (w Terence Treeby), 1971; Let Every Englishman's Home Be His Castle, 1978; General Election Agent's Handbook (ed, co-author), 1987. *Honours:* OBE, 1984. *Hobby:* Travel. *Address:* 19 Hayle Road, Maidstone, Kent ME15 6PD, England. 1.

ELLIS Jonathan Richard, b. 1 July 1946, Hampstead, London, England. Physicist. m. Maria Mercedes Martinez, 11 July 1985, 1 s, 1 d. *Education:* Kings Coll, Cambridge, 1964-67; BA (Cantab), 1967; Dept Applied Maths and Theoretical Phys, Cambridge Univ, 1967- 71; PhD, 1971. *Appointments:* Rsch Assoc, Stanford Linear Accelerator Ctr, Stanford, CA, USA, 1971-72; Richard Chase Tolman Fellow, Caltech, 1972-73; CERN, Geneva, Switzerland, 1973-. *Publications:* Over 380 sci publs. *Honours:* Maxwell Medal, Inst Phys, 1982; Elected FRS, 1984; Elected Fellow, Inst Phys, 1991. *Hobbies:* Hiking; Listening to music; Watching films; Amateur theatre. *Address:* 5 Chemin du Ruisseau, Tannay, 1295 Mies, Switzerland.

ELM Ludwig, b. 10 Aug 1934, Greussen, Germany. University Teacher (retired). m. Helga Elm, 22 Dec 1960, 3 d. *Education:* Studies, Hist, Philos; Dip Tchr, 1956; Asst, 1956; Dr Phil, 1964; Dozent, 1969; Prof, 1970. *Appointments:* Asst, 1956-69; Dozent, 1969-70; Prof, 1970-91. *Publications:* Zwischen Fortschritt und Reaktion. Geschichte der Parteien der liberalen Bourgeoisie in Deutschland 1893-1918, 1968; Hochschule und Neofaschismus, Zeitgeschichtliche Studien zur Hochschulpolitik in der BRD, 1972; Der neue Konservatismus, 1974, Polish Ed, 1979, Russian Ed, 1980; Aufbruch ins Vierte Reich, 1981; Konservatives Denken 1789-1848/49, 1989; Nach Hitler. Nach Honecker, 1991. *GDR Nat Prize, 3rd Class, Sci and Technology, 1987.* *Hobbies:* History; Music. *Address:* Schillbachstr 2, D-6900 Jena, Germany.

ELSTON John David, b. 2 Aug 1946, Darlington, England. m. Victoria Ann Harding, 27 Sept 1980, 2 s, 1 d. *Education:* BA, Econ, Univ Newcastle-upon-Tyne, 1968; ACA, Cooper Deloitte (formerly Deloitte, Plender and Griffiths), 1970-73. *Appointments:* Mgmt Trainee, Marks and Spencer, 1968-69; Mktng Planning Off, Skefko Ball Bearing Co, 1965-70; Sr Exec, James Capel and Co, 1973-. *Memberships:* FCA; Assoc, Soc Invemtment Analysts; Stock Exchange. *Hobbies:* Squash; Tennis; Bridge. *Address:* The Dene, 9 Kippington Road, Sevenoaks, Kent TN13 2LH, England.

ELWING Karl Ake Fredrik, b. 17 Oct 1954, Lund, Sweden. Corporation Vice-President. m. Jane Elizabeth Chorney, 29 Jan 1990, 1 d. *Education:* BA, Stockholm School Econs, 1979; MBA, INSEAD, Fontainebleau, France, 1984. *Appointments:* Army, serv, Sweden, 1975-76; Asst Dir, Benteler AG, FRG, 1980-83; Telesis SARL, Paris, France, 1985-86; VP Banking, First Boston Corp, London, England, 1987-. *Memberships:* Sallskapet, Stockholm; Royal Automobile Club, London; Annabel's, London; Wentworth, Virginia Water. *Honours:* Acad Prize, essay or paper on European Monetary System, O Sillen's Mem Fund, 1979; Scholarship, Int Studies Bus and Econs, Dr M Wallenberg's Mem Fund. *Hobbies:* Wine; Bridge; Dogs; Golf. *Address:* 12 St Johns Wood Road, London NW8 8RE, England.

ELYAN David Asher Gremson, b. 4 Oct 1940, Cork, Republic of Ireland. Company Director. *Education:* BA, BComm, 1962, MA, 1965, Trinity Coll, Dublin. *Appointments include:* Dir: Elyan Estates Ltd, 1983; Corp Lease Mgmt Ltd, 1984; Communication Investments Ltd, 1987; Langton Videotex Ltd, 1987; The Bankside Gallery Ltd, 1992. *Publications:* Occasional articles, poems and other publs; The Story of School Prints (ed), 1991. *Memberships:* FRSA; Treas, Friends Royal Watercolour Soc; Treas, TCD Dining Club; Comm, Friends of Royall Acad of Music; FCIS. *Honours:* Freeman, City of London, 1978; Liveryman, Worshipful Co Chartered Secs, 1978. *Hobbies:* Tennis; Squash; Music; Collecting first editions and original cartoons; Bridge. *Address:* 49 Chester Court, Regent's Park, London NW1 4BU, England. 32.

EMMONS Terence Leroy, b. 4 Feb 1937, Salem, Oregon, USA. Professor of History. m. Victoria Bellone, 10 Aug 1964, 2 s. *Education:* BA, Univ WA, 1959; MA, 1960, PhD, 1966, Univ CA, Berkeley. *Appointments:* Hist Dept, Stanford Univ, Stanford, CA, 1965-. *Publications:* Books: The Russian Landed Gentry and the Peasant Emancipation of 1961, 1968; The Formation of Political Parties and the First National Elections in Russia, 1983; Around California in 1891, 1991. *Membership:* Am Assn Advancement Slavic Studies. *Honours:* Fulbright Fellowship, 1969-70, 1973; ACLS, 1972-73; Geggenheim Fellowship, 1973-74; Ford Fndn Grant, 1976-78; Vucinich Annual Prize, Best Book in Slavic Studies, 1983-84. *Hobbies:* Carpentry; Book collecting. *Address:* Department of History, Stanford University, Stanford, CA 94305, USA.

EMREALP H Sadun, b. 4 Oct 1954, Istanbul, Turkey. Director, International Union of Local Authorities, Section for the Eastern Mediterranean and Middle East. m. Havva Gurlek, 22 Sept 1978, 2 d. *Education:* BS high hons, 1979, MS high hons, 1981, Mid E Tech Univ; MA, Ankara Univ, 1982; Rsch, Univ Kent, Canterbury, England, 1984. *Appointments:* Instr, Mid E Tech Univ, 1981-84; Cons, World Bank Izmir Project, 1985; Dpty Dir, Cukurova Reg Urban Dev Project, 1986-87; Cons, Metrop Municipality Istanbul, 1988; Dir, IULA-EMME, Istanbul, 1989-. *Publications:* Books incl: States in Transition (in Turkish), 1984; Metropolitan Management: A Global Perspective (co-ed), 1988; Local Government Institutions: A World-wide Directory, 1988, 1991; From Social Democracy to 'Social Democracy' (in Turkish), 1991. *Memberships:* Int Union Local Authorities; Int City Mgmg Assn, Acting Sec-Gen, Mid E Sect. *Honours:* Brit Coun Scholarship, 1983-84; Municipal Award, 2nd Summit Conf Maj Cities of the World, 1988. *Hobbies:* Fish-farming; Water sports; Basketball. *Address:* Gomec Sok s Sabanci Sitesi 2, A-3 Blok D-20, Kosuyolu, Kadikoy, Istanbul, Turkey. 52, 186.

ENACHESCU Dan, b. 19 Nov 1930, Braila, Rumania. Professor of Social Medicine; Institute Director. m. Liliana Clara Mirescu, 9 Jan 1955. *Education:* MD, 1954, PhD, 1972, Fac Med; Free Univ Brussels, 1968. *Appointments:* Paediatrician, village, 1954; Several positions, pub hlth, 1954-89: Dist Chief Phys, Dpty Dir, hosp, Dir, Town of Bucharest Hlth Directorate; Asst, Social Med Dept, 1959, to Prof, 1974-; Min Hlth, 1969-72, 1990; Dean, Gen Med Fac; Chief, Social Med Lab, Inst Hygiene and Pub Hlth, Bucharest; Rumanian Ambassador to Switzerland; WHO Expert; Hd, WHO Collaborating Ctr Primary Hlth Servs; Ed-in-Chief, Sante publique mag; Currently Gen Dir, Nat Inst Hlth Servs and Mgmt. *Memberships:* Rumanian Soc Hygiene and Public Hlth; Swiss Soc Social and Preventive Med; Assn French-Speaking Epidemiologists; Int Epidemiology Assn; European Assn Med Educ; ALASS; Rumanian Acad Med Scis. *Honours:* Several Rumanian and West German medals. *Hobbies:* Reading; Photography. *Address:* Str Dr Leonte 1-3, R-76256 Bucharest, Romania.

ENDLER Norman Solomon, b. 2 May 1931, Montreal, Quebec, Canada. Professor of Psychology. m. Beatrice Kerdman, 26 June 1955, 1 s, 1 d. *Education:* BSc, 1953, MSc, 1954, McGill Univ; PhD, Univ IL, USA, 1958; Registered Psychologist, Ontario. *Appointments:* Psychologist, PA State Univ, USA, 1958-60; Lectr, Psychology, 1960-62, Asst Prof, 1962-65, Assoc Prof, 1965-68, Prof, 1968-, York Univ, N York, Ontario, Canada; Cons, Clarke Inst, Toronto, 1972-81. *Publications:* Holiday of Darkness, 1982, Revised Ed, 1990; Personality and the Behavioral Disorders (w J McV Hunt), 2nd Ed, 1984; Electroconvulsive Therapy: The Myths and the Realities (w E Persad), 1988; Coping Inventory for Stressful Situations (w J D A Parker), 1990; Endler Multidimensional Anxiety Scales (w J Edwards and R Vitelli), 1991. *Memberships:* Fellow, Am Psychological Assn; Canadian Psychological Assn; Am Psych Assn, Fellow Divs 8, 9, 12; NY Acad Scies; Ontario Coun Acad Psychologists, Govng Bd Mem; Fellow, Soc Psychological Study of Social Issues. *Honours:* Sr Fellow, 1967-68, Killam Rsch Fellowship, 1987-89, Canada Coun; Canadian Silver Jubilee Medal (Queen Elizabeth II), 1978; Award of Merit, Ontario Psychological Assn, 1988; FRS (Canada). *Hobbies:* Tennis; Reading mysteries; Travel; Classical music. *Address:* 52 Sawley Drive, Willowdale, Ontario, Canada M2K 2J5. 2, 3, 139, 142, 143, 155, 164.

ENFLO Anita Margareta Henriksson, b. 2 Aug 1943, Helsingfors, Finland. Prin Scientist. m. Bengt Enflo, 29 July 1972, 1 s, 2 d. *Education:* Phil.Lic, Phys Chem, 1970; PhD, Theoretical Phys, 1986. *Appointments:* Rsch Assoc, Univ of Helsingfors, Finland, 1967-70; Univ of Stockholm, 1970-; Swedish Radiation Protection Inst, 1986-. *Publications:* Publs in Phys Chem, Quantum Chem and Radio Phys. *Memberships:* Finnish Chem Soc; Swedish Chem Soc; American Chem Soc; NY Acad of Sciences. *Honour:* Woman of the Year, American Biographical Institute, 1991. *Hobbies:* Family, Pol (Freedom and Democracy), Our Environment. *Address:* Institute of Theoretical Physics, University of Stockholm, Vanadisuageng, S-11346 Stockholm, Sweden.

ENGEL Juergen Kurt, b. 31 Aug 1945, Gerbitz, Saxony, Germany. Chemist; Researcher. m. Rita Busset, 7 Jan 1972, 1 s, 1 d. *Education:* Dip, Engrg, Naturwissenschaft-Technische Akad, Isny-Allgau, 1969; Dip, Chem, 1972, Dr rer nat, 1975, Tech Univ, Braunschweig; Habilitation, Pharm, 1985, Prof, School Pharm, 1990, Univ Regensburg. *Appointments:* Lab Ldr, Pharm Div, 1976080, Hd, Rsch Coordination, 1980-87, Hd, Medicinal Chem Synthesis, 1982-87, Hd, Chem Rsch, 1984-87, Degussa, Frankfurt; Hd, Chem and Pharm Rsch and Dev, 1987-, Div Dir, 1990, ASTA Medica AG subsidiaries, Degussa, Frankfurt; Prof, School Pharm, Univ Regensburg, 1990-. *Publications:* Pharmazeutische Wirkstoffe, 1982, 2nd Ed, 1987; Arzeinmittel (ed), 1987; Over 100 publs in profl jnls; Over 50 patents. *Memberships:* Bundesverband der Pharmazeutischen Industrie, Comm Drug Synthesis; BAH Drug Comm; Phylocher Comm, German Chem Soc; German Pharm Soc; Int Soc Heterocyclic Chem; NY Acad of Sci. *Honours:* Galileo Galilei Silver Medal, 5th Int Symp Platinum and Other Substances; Several others. *Hobbies:* Literature; History. *Address:* ASTA Pharma AG

Frankfurt, Weismullerstr 45, D-69 Frankfurt, Germany. 52, 92.

ENGEL Zbigniew Witold, b. 1 Apr 1933, Zawady, Poland. Professor of Applied Mechanics and Acoustics. m. 21 Apr 1957, 2 s. *Education:* MSc, Politek Cracow, 1954; PhD, 1962, DSc, 1966, Stanislaw Staszic Univ Mining and Metallurgy, Cracow. *Appointments:* Asst Lectr, 1952-57, Lectr, 1957-63, Assoc Prof, 1963-73, Prof, 1973-, Dir, Inst Mech and Vibroacoustics, 1974-, Stanislaw Staszic Univ Mining and Metallurgy, Cracow. *Publications:* Books: Mechanics, 1968, 2nd Ed, 1990; Vibration and Sound, 1973; Noise and Vibration Control, 1980; Noise Control, 1982, 85, 88, 92; Noise Control (ed), 1988; Over 270 other publs; Ed Bds: Archives of Acoustics, AVRA, Noise Control Engineering Journal; Ed-in-Chf, Mechanika. *Memberships:* Polish Theoretical and Applied Mech Soc, Cracow, Chmn 1969-70; Polish Acoustical Soc, Bd Mem 1979-81; Inst Noise Control Engrng, USA, 1984; Int Inst Noise Control Engrng, Bd Mem 1982-85; Coun Sci and Univs Poland, VP 1988-90; Deutsche Gesellschaft für Akustik; Gesellschaft für Angewnadte Mathematik und Mechanik. *Honours:* Hon Mem, Noise Abatement League, Poland, 1988. *Hobbies:* Gardening; Reading; Tourism. *Address:* ul Br A Kosiby 25, 32020 Wieliczka, Poland. 50.

ENGELBRECHT Richard Stevens, b. 11 Mar 1926, Ft Wayne, Indiana, USA. Environmental Engineering Educator. m. Mary Condrey, 21 Aug 1948, 2 s. *Education:* AB, IN Univ, 1948; MS, 1952, ScD, 1954, MIT. *Appointments:* Tchng Asst, IN Univ School Med, Indianapolis, 1949-50; Rsch Asst, 1950-52, Instr, 1952-54, MIT, Cambridge, MA; Asst Prof, 1954-57, Assoc Prof, 1957-59, Prof, Environmental Engrng, 1959-, Dir, Adv Environmental Control Technology Rsch Ctr, 1979-91, Ivan Racheff Prof, 1987, Univ IL, Urbana; Cons, US EPA, WHO, NSF. *Publications:* Author or co-author, over 120 contbrs to tech lit. *Membrships:* Nat Acad Engrng, 1976; Water Pollution Control Fedn, Pres 1978, Hon Mem 1986; Int Assn OH Water Quality, Pres 1980-86, Hon Mem 1990; OH River Valley Water Sanitation Comm, 1976-, Chmn 1980-82; Anwassertechnische Vereinigung, Hon Mem 1978; Life Mem, Am Water Works Assn, Chmn IL Sect 1970; Am Soc Microbiology; AAAS. *Honours:* Harrison Prescott Eddy Medal, Noteworthy Rsch, 1966, Arthur Sidney Bedell Award, 1972, Gordon Maskew Fair Medal, 1987, Water Pollution Control Fedn; George W Fuller Award, 1974, Publ Award, 1975, Am Water Works Assn; Named Ernest Victor Balsom Commemoration Lectr, 1978, Eric H Vick Award, 1979, Inst Pub Hlth Engrs, UK; Halliburton Award Excellence, Engrng Educ Ldrship, Univ IL, 1984; Benjamin Garver Lamme Award, Am Soc Engrng Educ, 1985; George J Schroepfer Award, Ctrl States Water Pollution Control Assn, 1985. *Address:* 2012 Silver Court West, Urbana, IL 61801, USA. 2, 26, 143.

ENGERRAND Doris D, b. 7 Aug 1925, Chicago, Illinois, USA. College Professor. m. Gabriel H Engerrand, 26 Oct 1946, dec. 1987, 2 s, 1 d. *Education:* BS, Bus Admin, 1958, BS, Elem Educ, 1959, N GA C oll; MBE, 1966, PhD, 1970, GA State Univ. *Appointments:* Tchr, Lumpkin Co HS, 1960-63, 1965-68; Asst Prof, Troy State Univ, 1969-71; Asst Prof, 1971-74, Assoc Prof, 1974-78, Prof, 1978-90, Chairperson, Dept Bus Info Systems and Communications, 1979-90, Prof Emerita, 1990, GA Coll, Milledgeville. *Contributions to:* ABC Bulletin. *Memberships include:* Am Bus Communication Assn, Bd Dirs 1978-80, 1982-85, 1989-92, VP SE 1978-80, 1983-85; Nat Bus Educ Assn; Delta Pi Epsilon; AAUW. *Honours:* Pilot of Yr, N GA Chapt, Ninety-Nines Int, 1973; Exec of Yr, Milledgeville Chapt, Profl Secs Int; Selected Fellow, Am Bus Communication Assn, 1983; Educator of Yr, Bus, GA Voc Assn, 1983-84; Post-Second Tchr of Yr, GA Bus Educ Assn, 1983-84. *Address:* 1674 Pine Valley Road, Milledgeville, GA 31061, USA. 5, 138.

ENGWALL Lars Otto Victor, b. 5 Apr 1942, Gävle, Sweden. Professor of Business Administration. m

Gunnel Jansson, 28 Jan 1968, 2 s. *Education:* Mas Polit Sci, 1966, PhD, 1970, Stockholm. *Appointments:* Assoc Prof, 1972-81, Prof, Bus Admin, 1981, Uppsala Univ, Uppsala. *Publications:* Models of Industrial Structure, 1973; Newspapers as Organizations, 1978; Från vag vision till komplex organisation, 1985; Mercury meets Minerva, 1992. *Memberships:* Royal Swedish Acad Scis, 1984-; Royal Swedish Soc Scis, 1985-; Royal Swedish Acad Engrng Scis, 1989-; Royal Swedish Acad Letters, Hist and Antiquities, 1991-. *Address:* Bergviksvägen 32, S-161 39 Bromma, Sweden. 154.

ENNES Adylson de Albuquerque Col, b. 18 Mar 1940, Rio de Janeiro, Brazil. Psychologist; Air Force Officer. m. Tania Marcia Pereira de Albuquerque Ennes, 5 July 1974, 1 s, 2 d. *Education:* Brazilian Air Force Acad, 1961; Bach, Psychology, 1969; Psychologist, Rio de Janeiro Univ, 1970; Specialisatiion, Psychoanalytic Therapy, Santa Ursula Univ, Rio de Janeiro, 1984; Specialisation courses, Brazilian Air Force; Pol, Strategy, Air Command and Staff Coll. *Appointments:* Brazilian Air Force, adv through grades to Col: Chief, Personnel Selection and Profl Guidance Div, 1972-73, Chief, Rsch Div, 1973-76, Vice-Dir, Dir, 1974-84, Air Force Inst Psychology, Chief, Admin Div, Air Force Acad, 1984-89, Admin Dir, Sao Paulo Depot, 1989- 91; Tech Advsr, Inst Personnel Selection, ITASE, Rio de Janeiro, 1974-81; Tchr, Social Psychology, Santa Edwiges Univ, Rio de Janeiro, 1985-80; Tech Dir, Trng and Managerial Advsrs Associated, EXTAE, Rio de Janeiro, 1976-82´ Tchr, Managerial Dev, Candido Mendes Univ, Rio de Janeiro, 1979-80; Pvte Prac, Rio de Janeiro and Sao Paulo, 1982-91; Tchr, Gen and Expmtl Psychology, Mackenzie Univ, Sao Paulo, 1990; Support, terminal AIDS patients and relatives, Rio de Janeiro, 1991. *Publications:* Articles in profl jnls. *Memberships include:* Air Force Club; Army Club; Civilian clubs; Masonry, Rep Rio de Janeiro Lodge 1983-91, Rosae Crucis. *Honours:* Decorated, Silver, Bronze and Gold Medals, 1973, 1979, 1988; Santos Dumont Merit Medal, 1979; Mem of Hon, Aeronautical Order, 1988. *Hobbies:* Music; Painting; Tennis; Aerobic gymnastics; Photography. *Address:* Rua Santa Clara no 212/304, Copacabana, Rio de Janeiro, Brazil ZIP 22041. 52.

ENNS James Theodore, b. 7 Jan 1957, Canada. Associate Professor of Psychology. m. Janet May Loewen, 15 July 1978. *Education:* BA Hons, Winnipeg, 1980; PhD, Princeton Univ, USA, 1984. *Appointments:* Asst Prof, Dalhousie Univ, 1984-87; Assoc Prof, Dept Psychology, Univ BC, Vancouver, 1987-. *Publications:* The Analysis of Variance (w C Collyer), 1986; The Development of Attention, 1990; Over 20 sci abstracts. *Memberships:* Sigma Xi; Psychonomic Soc; Am Psychological Soc; Canadian Psychological Soc. *Honours:* Gov-Gen's Gold Medal, Arts Hons, Winnipeg, 1980. *Hobbies:* Laser sailing; Tennis; Basketball. *Address:* Dept of Psychology, University of British Columbia, Vancouver, BC, Canada V6T 1Z4.

ERB Louise Josephine Bruning, b. 30 Sept 1918, Rawlins, Wyoming, USA. Bus Owner. m. Lester Dale Erb, 30 Aug 1940, 1 s, 1 d. *Education:* CO State Coll of Educ, Greeley, CO, 1936-37; RN, Children's Hosp, Denver, CO, 1937-40; Graduate Gemologist, Gemological Inst of America, 1981. *Appointments:* Children's Hosp, Denver, CO, 1948-55; Schl Nurse, 1970- 71; Gemologist, 1977-81; Self-employed and Author, 1981-92; ERBGEM Co. *Publication:* Western Americana Book, The Bridger Pass Overland Trail 1862-69. *Memberships:* Gemological Inst of America Alumnae; CO Gemological Assn; Nat League of American Pen Women. *Honour:* L C Bishiop Award from the Wyoming State Historical Society for the Promotion and Preservation of Western History, 1990. *Hobbies:* Reading, Travel, Writing. *Address:* 5727 South Hickory Way, Littleton, CO 80120, USA.

ERDELYI Csaba, b. 15 May 1946, Budapest, Hungary. Viola Player; Professor of Viola and Chamber Music. m. Ju-Ping Chi, 8 Oct 1989, 1 s. *Education:* Artist-Tchr Dip, Franz Liszt Acad, Budapest, 1970. *Career:* Mem, Franz Liszt Chamber Orch, 1968-72; Prin Violist, Philharmonic Orch, 1974-78; Violist, Chilingirian School of Music, 1981-87; Solo viola concerts, worldwide; Prof, Viola, Guildhall School Music, London, England, 1980-87; Prof, Viola, Chamber Music, IN Univ, Bloomington, USA, 1987- ; Master classes, worldwide. *Creative works:* Creator, Univ course: The History of the Viola and Viola Players; Rsch and publs of viola repertory. *Memberships:* Brit Musicians Union; Inst Dev Interculture Rels through the Arts; Am Viola Soc; Amnesty Int. *Honours:* Only viola player ever to win Carl Flesch Violin Competition w viola, 1972. *Hobbies:* Massage; Yoga; Acupuncture; Rebirthing; Body-mind control; Mountain walking; Bird-watching. *Address:* School of Music, Indiana University, Bloomington, IN 47405, USA. 4.

ERIJMAN Mauricio Oscar, b. 9 Sept 1944, Buenos Aires, Argentina. Medical Doctor. m. Nelida Dorotea Trakinski, 20 June 1972, 1 s, 1 d. *Education:* Grad, Fed Univ Med, 1970; Resident, Internal Med, Fimochietto Hosp, Buenos Aires, 1970-73; Fellow, Cardiology, Bellinson Med Ctr, Israel, 1974-80; Biophys, Auxiliary Prof, School Med, Univ Salvador, 1984. *Appointments:* Med Dir, Cardiovascular Lab, Buenos Aires, 1980-. *Publications:* Lymphocytopenia in Patients with Tricuspid Insufficiency; Haemodynamics and Echo Cardiographic Changes in Membraneous Type Subaortic Stonosis; Thermodynamic Interpretation of Stress. *Memberships:* Sociedad Argentina de Cardologia; Am Soc Echocardiography; NY Acad Scis; AAAS; Asociacion Medica Argentina. *Hobbies:* Gardening; Golf; Tennis. *Address:* Juncal 1062 6/K, Buenos Aires 1962, Argentina.

ERMA Reino Mauri, b. 8 Apr 1922, Tampere, Finland. Lawyer. m. Hilkka Marjatta Ahjo, 5 Jan 1946, 2 s, 2 d. *Education:* LLM, 1944, Lic Laws, 1948, LLD, 1955, Helsinki Univ. *Appointments:* Dir, Kansallis-Osake-Pankki Bank, Helsinki, 1947-70; Prof, 1960-70, Rector, 1970-84, Chancellor, 1984-90, Univ Tampere, Tampere. *Publications:* Books: Contract of Work, 1955; General Conditions for the Building Contracts, 1974, 1991; Legal Aspects of Subcontracting, 1975; General Conditions for the Delivery of Goods between Finland and CMEA countries, 1980; Arbitration practice relating to the construction industry according to awards of Finnish Arbitration Tribunals 1957-1980; Banking Laws, 1969, 1986; Legal Handbook of Foreign Trade, 1989. *Memberships:* Int Law Assn; Am Arbitration Assn; Finnish Arbitration Assn, Chmn; Gesellschaft fuer Rechtsvergleichung. *Honours:* Medal of Freedom, 1941; Cross of Freedom, 1942; Decorated Cmdr, 1st Class, Order of Finnish White Rose, 1990. *Address:* Mustanlahdenkatu 1 B 87, 33210 Tampere, Finland. 43, 52, 90.

ERSEVIM Ismail Hakki, b. 11 Oct 1929, Istanbul, Turkey. Adult and Child Psychiatrist. div., 1 s, 1 d. *Education:* MD, Istanbul Univ School Med, 1952; Bd Cert, Psych, Neurol, 1955; Grad, Istanbul Conservatory Music, 1955; Psych Intern, Ottawa, Canada, 1957; Resident: Buffalo Univ, USA, 1958, Medfield State Hosp, MA, 1959-63; Piano Cert, US School Music, NYC, 1961; Fellowship, Child Psych, Harvard Univ, 1963-65. *Appointments:* Staff Psych, Bradley Hosp, RI, USA, 1965; Dir, Newport Co Mental Hlth Ctr, RI, 1966; Chief, RI Mental Hygiene Servs, 1967-70; Adj Prof, Psychology, Salve Regina Coll and Univ RI, 1967-70; Staff Psych, Mystic Valley Mental Hlth Str, Lexington, MA, 1971; Dir, En Middlesex Guidance Ctr, Melrose, MA, 1971-73; Dir, Narcotics Programme, Harvard Univ, Cambridge, MA, 1976-77; Instr, Lynn Hops, Boston Univ School Med, MA, 1978; Sr Psych, NH Hosp, 1982-84; Pvte Prac, Manchester and Bedford, NH, 1984-90; Currently: Pvte Prac, Turkey; Staff, Amiral Bristol Hosp, Istanbul; Dramaturge, Analyst, under Beklan Algan, Istanbul Belediyesi Tiyatrolari Arastirma Laboratuari. *Publications:* Num translations from La Presse Medicale, 1952-55; No 8 writer, Short Stories in Turkey, 1955; Ed, poems, Suha Publ, Cambridge, USA, 1976; Prophet

Eshref, short stories, 1984; Several poems in US anthologies, 1983-90; I, Shaman: The Wheelwright. *Memberships:* Formerly: World Med Assn; AMA; Am Psych Assn; Am Orthopsych Assn; Royal Soc Hlth; New England Coun Child Psych; Dramatists Guild; Nat Writers Club; Fndn Shamanistic Studies; Turkish Neuro-Psych Soc. *Honours:* Poet of Merit, Am Poetry Assn, 1989. *Hobbies:* Turkish and classical music; Poetry; Theatre; Writing; Ballet; Opera; Reading; Travel; Languages. *Address:* PO Box 52, Tesvikiye, Istanbul, Turkey 80212. 6, 158.

ERSGAARD Hans V, b. 13 Jan 1946, Copenhagen, Denmark. Private Medical Practitioner (Anaesthesia and Pain Clinic). m. Kirsten Ellen Ersgaard, 20 Feb 1982, 1 s, 1 d. *Education:* Lab Tech, 1968; MD, Copenhagen Univ, 1982; Registrar: Surg, Med, 1982-83, Anaesthesia, 1984; Trainee, Sweden, Norway, USA, 1985-87; Specialist, Anaesthesis, Intensive Care, 1987. *Appointments:* Cons, Aalborg, Denmark, 1987-91; Pvte Prac, Anaesthesia, Pain Clinic, Esbjerg, 1991-. *Publications:* Several papers in med rsch. *Memberships:* Am Soc Anaesthesiology; Int Ass Study of Pain; Jr Chmbr Int. *Honours:* Rsch Scholarship, Microbiology, 1980. *Hobbies:* Veteran cars; Computers; Horses; Dogs; Foreign literature; Greek and Nordic mythology. *Address:* 9 Hybenvaenget, 7700 Thisted, Denmark.

ERSGAARD Ole Kristian, b. 9 Sept 1948, Copenhagen, Denmark. International Development Consultant; Management Consultant. *Education:* Dip, Pub Rels, NKI, Stockholm, 1971; Dip, Mktng, Danish Commercial Colls, Copenhagen, 1975; Postgrad: Danish Coll Commerce, London, 1979, London School For Trade, 1981, London Poly, 1982, DMC/INSEAD, France, 1988-89; DG, FABI, FIBA; Recipient, The International Cultural Dipl (Hon); Erhvervsoekonom MDM (Danish profl bus qualification), 1980. *Appointments:* Commercial Trainee, Advt and Mktng Trainee, var commercial enterprises and advt agcys, Denmark, 1966-76; Advt Mgr, worldwide, Ostermann Petersen Bros Ltd, Copenhagen, 1977-79; Group Advt Mgr, IN-WEAR A/S, Denmark, 1979-82; Group Mktg Dir, Carli Gry Int A/S, Denmark; Mgmt Cons, Denmark, 1984-; Dir/ CEO, Centergruppen, Viborg, 1991-. *Memberships:* Inst of Dirs; Int Advt Assn; Am Mgmt Assn; Int Mgmt Ctr Europe; Danish Mercantile Assn, Bd Chmn So Reg Br 1989-91; Bd Dirs, DBG INVEST A/S, 1990-92; Politcal Party Centrum Demokraternes, 1990-92; Life Mbr, WIA. *Address:* Pile Alle 2, Hjerting, DK 6710 Esbjerg V, Denmark. 52, 132.

ERSKINE George Saint Vincent, b. 24 Oct 1905, Springs, Transvaal, South Africa. Professional Electrical Engineer. m. Huê Thi Erskine, 16 Mar 1968. *Education:* Elec Engrng, Engrng Econs, Engrng Law, Int Correspondence Schools, Scranton, PA; Illumination: Holophane School Lighting; Pacific Coast Elec Assn; Maths: Balboa Coll, Canal Zone, Coll San Mateo, Foothill Coll; Univ CA Ext Div; USDA School Elec Engrng, Los Angeles; Registered Elec and Mech Engr. *Appointments:* Owner, Engr, Erskine Elec Works, Redwood City, CA, USA, 1926; George S Erskine Assocs, Redwood City, 1937-41; Currently Alfa Tech Engrs, San Jose, CA; Chief Elect Mech Engr: Frank E Lyon Assocs, Vietnam, Liberia, Africa; Daniel, Mann, Johnson, Mendenhall, Korea; Oscar Larsson & Assocs, Eureka, CA; Chief Elec Engr, Winzler & Kelly, Eureka; Cons: USAID, NRECA, Ecuador, Panama; Min Educ, Korea; Bur Reclamation, CA Water Plan; Elec Designer, pump storage generating facilities, San Luis Reservoir and O'Neill Forebay, pumping plant, Tracy-Mendota Canal; Project Elec Engr, Light Rail System, San Jose, CA, 1983-85; Cons Elec Engr, N Fork Stanislaus River hydroelec project, 1985-88. *Publications:* Gold in Our Lives. Tales of a Construction Stiff; A Future for Hydropower, 1978; Small Hydroelectric Power. Vol One, 1978; Electrical Generation and Hydrogen and Oxygen Production, 1979; Water to Hydrogen-A Self Replenishing Non Polluting Source of Energy, 1978; Small Hydroelectric Generation-A Dam Good Idea, 1982; Tidal Power, 1983; Earthquake Preparedness and Potable Water, 1986; Selecting, Specifying and Installing Cables, 1989; Our

Man in Vietnam, article series, 1967, 1968, 1969, 1970. *Memberships:* Indep Order Oddfellows, Past Dist Dpty Grand Master; CA Soc Profl Engrs, Past Pres; Life Mem, Nat Soc Profl Engrs; IEEE; Mbr, CA Link Number 130; Order of the Engineer, 1992. *Hobbies:* Philatelist, 70 yrs; OddFellow, 65 yrs; Author (published). *Address:* 961 Pershing Avenue, San Jose, CA 95126, USA. 59.

ESCHENBURG Emil Paul, b. 26 Dec 1915, Macomb County, Michigan, USA. Real Estate Broker. m. (1) Betty G Eschenberg, 5 June 1943, div. July 1975, 2 s, 2 d, (2) Dolly Woar, 27 Dec 1977. *Education:* BS w high hons, MI State Univ, 1939; Grad, Nat War Coll, Wash DC, 1957; MBA, Harvard Univ, 1960; MA, Int Rels, George Washington Univ, 1971; Cert, Real Estate Residential and Investment Specialist. *Appointments:* Served 2nd Lt to Brig Gen, US Army 1939-70, incl; Asst Cmdr, 101st Airborne Div, 1963-65; Chief Jt Mil Asst, US Mil Mission, Ethiopia, 1965-67; Acting and Asst Cmdng Gen, 1st Inf Div, US Army, Vietnam, 1967-70; Real Estate Salesman, Crows Nest Harbor, Wash, DC, 1971-72; Salesman, Sandy McPherson Realty, Helena, MT, 1973-80; Broker, Mgr, Century-21/ Heritage Realty, Helena, 1980-89; Pres, Century-21 Brokers Coun MT, 1988-89; Assoc Broker, Ahmann-Heller Realtors, Helena, 1990-. *Memberships:* Helena Bd Realtors, Pres 1976-77; YMCA, Pres 1988; Helena MLS, Pres 1986; Elder, Luth Ch 1981-83; Bd Dirs, MT State Bd Realtors, 1977- 80; Exec Comm, Support of Guard and Reserve, MT; Nat Assn Realtors; State of MT Investment Soc; Million Dollar Sales Club; Nat Mktng Assn; Helena Chmbr Comm; Disabled Am Veterans; Purple Heart; VFW; Helena Navy League, Pres 1985-86; Kiwanis, Disting Pres, Helena Chapt, Pres 1980-81, Bd Govs 1983-87, Dist Lt-Gov 1990); Bd Dirs, Model Cities Dev Corp, 1976-80; Chmn, Nat Fun Drive MT; Chmn, Vietnam Vets Mem, Wash DC, 1983-85; Crimestoppers, 1982-83. *Honours:* 117 mil decorations incl 77 valour awards; Top in commissions, all CO21 Real Estate Salespersons, State of MT, 1987; Realtor of Yr, 1987. *Hobbies:* Golf; Family history. *Address:* 2108 8th Ave, Helena, MT 59601, USA. 52.

ESCOBAR Roberto, b. 11 May 1926, Santiago, Chile. Composer; Humanist. m. Marta Cruchaga, 19 Mar 1950, 2 s. *Education:* Escuela Moderna de Musica, Chile; Manhattan School Music, USA; MA magna cum laude, Philos, Univ Catolica Valparaiso. *Appointments:* Rsch Fellow, Columbia Univ, USA, 1972; Chmn, Ext, 1974-75, Chmn, Sociology and Anthropology, 1981- 84, Sr Prof, 1985-, Univ de Chile; Vis Prof, Univ MO, USA, 1975; Chancellor, UTE, 1975-79. *Creative works:* 10 books on art and culture incl: Musicos sin Pasado, 1971; Filosofia en Chile, 1976; Teoria del Chileno, 1981; Estudios de Etica, 1986; Over 60 music compositions performed publicly; 3 LPs; 3 cassettes. *Memberships:* Asociacion Nacional de Compositores, Pres 1974-77, Treas 1972-73; Soc Chilena de Filosofia, Pres 1985-88, Dir 1980-84; Inst Geopol Chile; Soc Cientifica Chile; Int Soc Pol Sci; Int Soc Legasl and Social Philos. *Honours:* Fulbright Fellowship, Rsch, Columbia Univ, 1972, Lecturing, Univ MO, 1975; Prof Extraordinary, Univ Catolica Valparaiso, 1981; Goethe Prize, Music Composition, 1982; Hon Prof, Univ MO, 1989; Prize, Music Essay, 1992. *Hobbies:* Cooking; Mountaineering. *Address:* Casilla 16360, Santiago 9, Chile.

ESPINOLA Aida, b. 18 Apr 1920, Rio de Janeiro, Brazil. University Professor; Chemical Engineer. Indl Chem, 1941, Chem Engr, 1954, Univ Brazil; MSc course, Univ MN, USA, 1957-58; PhD, Chem, PA State Univ, USA, 1974. *Appointments:* Chem, Lab Mineral Prod, Min Mines and Energy, 1942-70; Assoc Prof, Chem, 1955-81, Full Prof, Grad Progs Engrng, 1975-, Full Prof, Chem, 1981-90, Fed Univ Rio de Janeiro; Sci Cons, Geochem Inst, Fed Univ Bahia, Bahia, 1960-62; Rshcr, Chem, Fuel Cells, Inst Space Activities, Aerospace Ctr, Brazilian Air Force, S Jose dos Campos, 1973-74; Vis Prof, School Chem, FL Atlantic Univ, USA, 1966, School Pharm, Fed Univ Pernambuco, 1973, Inst Chem, Fed Univ Bahia, 1973. *Publications:* Voltammetry of Dissolved Water in Fused Salts, 1978; Separacoes Analiticas e Preconcentracao, 1989; Brazil Fuel Cell Report, World Energy Coun, 1990; Articles; Papers. *Memberships:* Am Chem Soc; Brazilian Chem Soc, Rio de Janeiro Br, Treas 1955, VP 1956, Pres 1957; Iota Sigma Pi, 1969-70; Sigma Delta Epsilon, 1969-70. *Honours:* Best Grad Asst, Dept Chem, PA State Univ, 1969; Fellow, Dept Chem, PA State Univ, 1969; Gold Retort, Syndicate Chems, Rio de Janeiro, 1979; Hons, Inst Chem, Fed Univ Rio de Janeiro, 1984; Brazilian Rep, Fuel Cell Comm, World Energy Coun, London, 1988. *Hobbies:* Music; Swimming. *Address:* R Souza Lima 289, Ap 1002 Copacabana, 22081-010 Rio de Janeiro, Brazil.

ESPOSITO John Vincent, b. 25 Dec 1946, Logan, West Virginia, USA. Lawyer. *Education:* BA cum laude, WV Univ, 1968; Dr Jurisprudence, WV Univ Coll Law, 1971. *Appointments:* Legis Aide, Congressman Ken Hechler, US Congress, 1971; Sr Ptnr, Law Offs Esposito & Esposito, Logan, WV and Hilton Hd Island, SC, 1972-; Counsel to Senate Pres, WV Senate, 1972; Lectr, Speaker, Writer, Philos, 1985-. *Publications:* Laws for Young Mountaineers; Num articles and speeches regarding law, int law, int trade, trade regulations, space law; New World Order. *Memberships:* Am Bar Assn; Am Trial Lawyers Assn; Am Judicature Soc; World Peace Through Law; Int Platform Assn; WV State Bar Assn; SC Bar Assn. *Honours:* Special Judge, Circuit Ct Logan Co; Commissioner in Chancery, Circuit Ct Logan Co and Mingo Co, WV; Municipal Judge, Town of Chapmanville, WV; Citizen Ambassador to China and Soviet Union. *Hobbies:* Music; Art; Literature; Drama; Tennis; Sailing; Exercise; Writing; Meditation. *Address:* 409 Stratton Street, Logan, WV 25601, USA. 7, 52, 139, 152, 155.

EUTSLER Steve Dwight, b. 8 Jan 1958, Springfield, Missouri, USA. Pastor. m. 10 Jan 1977, 1 s, 1 d. *Education:* Dip, Galena HS, 1976; BA, Ctl Bible Coll, 1982; MA, Assemblies of God Theological Sem, 1987. *Appointments:* Asst Pastor, Galena Assembly of God, Galena, MO, 1979; Pastor, W Grand Assembly of God, Springfield, MO, 1982-87; Pastor, 1st Assembly of God, Sparta, MO, 1987-88; Pastor, 1st Assembly of God, Aurora, MO, 1988-. *Publications:* Book reviews; Sermon outlines; Commentary; Greek word studies; Theological jnl articles. *Memberships:* Former Pres, Springfield Area Ministerial Alliance; Former Bd Mem, Univ Christian Fellowship; Pres, Aurora Ministerial Alliance. *Honours include:* Commencement Speaker, graduating class, Bible coll, 1983; Nat Dean's List; Delta Epsilon Chi, Am Assn Bible Colls. *Hobbies:* Reading; Genealogy; Parenting; Hiking. *Address:* 215 E Walnut, Aurora, MO 65605, USA.

EVANS David Richard John, b. 5 June 1938, Tanzania. Bishop in the Church of England. m. Dorothy Evelyn Parsons, 25 July 1964, 1 s, 2 d. *Education:* Christ's Hosp, 1950-57; Gonville & Caius Coll, Cambridge, 1959-63; MA, Mod Langs, Theology. *Appointments:* 2nd Lt, Middlesex Regt, 1957-59; Ordained, St Paul's Cathedral, London, 1965; Curate, Christ Ch, Cockfosters, 1965-68; Mission Priest, Argentina, 1969-77; Bishop of Peru, 1978-88; Bishop of Bolivia, 1982-88; Asst Bishop of Bradford, England, 1988-. *Publication:* Encounter with God (Spanish book), 1976. *Membership:* Int Coord, Evangelical Fellowship Anglican Communion. *Hobbies:* Squash; Golf; Ornithological philately. *Address:* 30 Grosvenor Road, Shipley, W Yorks BD18 4RN, England. 1.

EVANS David Robert Howard, b. 27 Feb 1950, Bristol, England. Solicitor. m. Janet Lea Kanarek Kollek, 7 May 1989, 1 s, 1 d. *Education:* LLB, Univ Exeter, 1971; King's Coll and LSE, 1971-72; LLM, Univ London, 1972; Brasenose Coll, Oxford, 1973-74; Dip Law, Univ Oxford; Admitted as Solicitor, 1976. *Appointments:* Solicitor: Freshfields, 1975-77; Brit Railways Bd, 1977-79; Linklaters & Paines, 1980-82; Berwin Leighton, 1982-83; Ptnr, Berwin Leighton, 1984-87; Ptnr, D J Freeman & Co, 1987-91; Snr Partn, D Evans & Co, 1991-; P R & Mktng Trustee, Statute Law Trust, Balliol Coll,

Oxford Univ. *Publications:* Var articles in legal periodicals. *Memberships:* Law Soc, 1976; Liveryman, Worshipful Co of Solicitors of the City of London. *Honours:* Freeman, City of London, 1981. *Hobbies:* Playing clarinet; Tennis; Skiing; Riding; Keeping fit. *Address:* 51 Drayton Gardens, London SW10 9RX, England.

EVANS John Alfred Eaton, b. 30 July 1933, Bristol, England. Headmaster. m. Vyvyan Margaret Mainstone, 9 Aug 1958, 2 s, 1 d. *Education:* Bristol G.S, 1941-52; City Sr Scholar, Worcester Coll, Oxford, 1954-58; MA (Lit Hum). Appointments: Nat Serv, commissioned, 1952, served RAOC and AER, 1952- 54; Asst Master, Classics, House Tutor, Old House, Blundells School, Tiverton, 1958-63; Asst Master, Classics, House Tutor, School House, Rugby, 1963-68, 1969-73; Housemaster, Kilbracken, 1973-81; Asst Master, Housemaster, Phillips Acad, Andover, MASE, USA, 1968-69; Hdmaster, Brentwood School, Brentwood, England, 1981-. *Publications:* Var articles on community serv in educ. *Memberships:* FRSA, 1983-; JACT; CMC Selection Panel, 1982-88; Admiralty Interview Bd, 1985-; Army Scholarship Bd, 1990-; Bishops's Advisory Board of Ministry, 1992. *Hobbies:* Sport esp Rugby, cricket, Rugby Fives; Music esp piano, singing, composition; Theatre; Reading; Walking. *Address:* Brentwood School, Ingrave Road, Brentwood, Essex CM15 8AS, England. 1.

EVANS Martin Charles William, b. 31 Aug 1942, Southport, Lancashire, England. Schoolmaster. *Education:* Liverpool Coll, 1956-61; BA, Durham Univ, 1967; DipEd, Pembroke Coll, Oxford, 1968. *Appointments:* Schoolmaster, Marlborough Coll, Wiltshire, 1968-. *Memberships:* Marylebone Cricket Club; Royal Birkdale Golf Club; Marlborough Golf Club; Not Under Command Club (Naval). *Honours:* Kitchener Scholarship, 1963- 68; Pres, Union, Durham, 1966; CCF Medal, RNVR, 1982. *Hobbies:* Politics; Debating; Cricket; Golf. *Address:* Marlborough College, Wiltshire SN8 1PA, England.

EVANS Robert William, b. 18 Jan 1958, Oakland, California, USA. Clinical/Medical Psychologist and Neuropsychologist. m. Kamrin Judith Korsmeier, 3 Aug 1991. *Education:* BA, Psychology, UCLA, 1981; MA, Clin Psychology, Wn Sem, Portland, OR, 1983; Grad, Top Cadet, CA Police Acad, 1985; PhD, Clin Psychology, Profl School Psychology, San Fran, CA, 1988; Intern, Resident, Dept Psych and Dept Neurology, Kaiser Hosp and Med Ctr, Sacramento, CA, 1987-89. *Appointments:* Med Psychologist, Penrose Hosp, Colorado Springs, CO, 1989; Pvte Prac, Med Psychology, Med Neuropsychology, 1989-; Fndr, Pres, Rocky Mountain Clin Assocs PC, CO; Invited speaker. *Memberships:* Am Psychological Assn; CO Psychological Assn, Sunset Comm Mem, Legis Comm Mem; El Paso Co Psychological Assn; CO Neuropsychological Soc; Nat Acad Neuropsychology; Int Neuropsychological Soc; Am Bd Med Psychologists; Int Acad Behavioural Med; Am Coll Forensic Psychology; Chmn, Elder Bd, Austin Bluffs Evangelical Free Ch, Colorado Springs; Former Jr Asst Scoutmaster. *Honours include:* Eagle Scout, 1970; 1st Place, CA Judo Tournament; 1st Place, Nat Soloist Competition; 1 of Outstanding Young Men of Am, Jaycees Int, 1984; 1 of 20 doctors to represent USA, int exchange to Russia, 1993. *Address:* 455 East Pikes Peak Avenue, Suite 301, Colorado Springs, CO 80903, USA. 139, 152, 155.

EVANS Roger Kenneth, b. 18 Mar 1947, Cardiff, Wales. Barrister. m. June Rodgers, 6 Oct 1973, 2 s. *Education:* Trinity Hall, Cambridge, 1966-70; MA (Cantab). *Appointments:* Barrister, 1970-; Conservative Candidate, Gen Elections: Warley W, Oct 1974, 1979, Ynys, Môn, 1987, Monmouth By-Election, 1991; Elected MP for Monmouth, General Election, 1992. *Memberships:* Pres, Cambridge Union, 1970; Pres, Cambridge Georgian Grp, 1969; Chmn, Cambridge Univ Conservative Assn, 1969; Coningsby Club, Chmn 1977, Treas 1984-88; Carlton Club; Abergavenny

Constitutional; Chepstow, Monmouth and Usk Conservative Clubs. *Honours:* Schlar, Trinity Hall; Astbury Scholar, Middle Temple. *Hobbies:* Architectural history; Computers; Gardening. *Address:* 2 Harcourt Buildings, Temple, London EC47 9DB, England.

EVANS William Eugene, b. 11 Oct 1930, Elkhart, Indiana, USA. President of Texas Institute of Oceanography; College Dean. m. Phyllis J Roberts, 27 Dec 1952, 2 s. *Education:* BS, Sci Educ, Bowling Green State Univ, 1953; MA, Audiology, OH State Univ, 1954; PhD, Biology, Biophys, UCLA, 1975. *Appointments:* Lt, US Army, 1954-56; Lab Rsch Analyst, Bioacoustics, Thor and Mike Missile Systems MacDonald-Douglas, Santa Monica, CA, 1956-59; Sr Scientist, Bioacoustic Project Ldr, Lockheed Aircraft Corp, Burbank, CA, 1960-64; Rsch Scientist, UCLA, CA, 1964-66; Rsch Scientist, Sr Scientist, Assoc Hd, Marine Biomed Div, Naval Undersea Ctr, Point Mugu and San Diego, CA, 1966-72; Vis Scientist, Nat Marine Fisheries Serv, SW Fisheries Ctr and Scripps Instn Oceanography, La Jolla, CA, 1972-74; Hd, Bio-Analysis Gp, Biosystems Div, Naval Undersea Ctr, San Diego, 1974-76; Pres, Exec Dir, Sr Scientist, Hubbs-Sea World Rsch Inst, San Diego, 1977-86; Chmn, Marine Mammal Commn, 1983-86; Asst Adminstr, Fisheries, NOAA, 1986-88; Under-Sec Commerce, Oceans and Atmosphere, Adminstr, NOAA, 1988-89; Dean, TX Maritime Coll, 1989-, Pres, TX Inst Oceanography, 1991-, TX A&M Univ, Galveston; Var professorial positions. *Publications:* Over 100 scientific papers, chapts in several books; Co-author, 4 books; Patents: Underwater broadband acoustic source: a device for tagging and tracking marine animals, 1967; Oceanographic platform, NUC Catamaran (w L McKinley), 1972; Underwater protection habitat for divers (sea cage) (w L McKinley and C S Johnson). *Memberships include:* US Commnr, Int Whaling Commn, 1988-91; Fellow, Zoological Soc San Diego; Fndg Mem, Int Soc Marine Mammalogy; Fellow, Am Assn Zoological Pks and Aquariums, 1984-86; Am Soc Zoologists; Sigma Xi; Fndg Mem, San Diego Oceans Fndn. *Honours include:* Man of Yr, Portuguese Historical Soc San Diego, 1982; Co-recip, Silver Medal, contrbns to protection of Nature, All Union Sci Exposition, Moscow, 1982; Disting Alumnus, 1985, Hon Doct Pub Serv, 1989, Bowling Green St Univ, 1985; Revelle Award, Oceans Fndn, San Diego, 1988; NOAA Corps Commendation Medal, 1989. *Address:* Texas Inst of Oceanography, Texas A&M University at Galveston, P O Box 1675, Galveston, TX 77553, USA.

EVERITT William Norrie, b. 10 June 1924, Birmingham, England. Professor Emeritus of Mathematics. m. 25 July 1953, 2 s. *Education:* BSc, Univ Birmingham, 1945; BA, 1952, MA, 1955, DPhil, 1955, Balliol Coll, Univ Oxford. *Appointments:* Royal Mil Coll Sic, 1954-63; Baxter Prof, Maths, Univ St Andrews, Dundee, Scotland, 1963-82; Prof, Maths, 1982-89, Prof Emeritus, 1989-, Univ Birmingham, England. *Publications:* Num in math periodicals. *Memberships:* Royal Soc Edinburgh, Fellow 1965, Coun 1967- 79, VP 1970-73; London Math Soc, Mem 1957, Coun 1984-89; Edinburgh Math Soc, Mem 1963, Pres 1970-71; Inst Maths and Applications, Fellow 1964. *Honours:* For Mem, Royal Soc Scis, Sweden, 1971; For Mem, Soc Arts, Letters and Scis, Palermo, Sicily, Italy, 1972; Maths Medal, Czechoslovak Soc Maths and Phys, 1990. *Hobbies:* Music; Walking; Reading; Parson Woodforde Soc. *Address:* School of Mathematics and Statistics, University of Birmingham, Edgbaston, Birmingham B15 2TT, England.

EVROV Nikolay, b. 18 Nov 1936, Sliven, Bulgaria. Concert Pianist; Lecturer in Piano. m. Roumiana Valtcheva-Evrova, 20 June 1971, 1 d. *Education:* Full-time course, speciality Piano, 1955-60, Dip, 1960, Bulgarian State Conservatoire, Sofia; Piano Specialisation, Moscow State Conservatoire, USSR, 1963-64. *Appointments:* State Performing Artist, Sofia Philharmonia, 1962-76; Assoc Prof, Piano, 1976-85, Prof, Piano, 1985-86, Bulgarian State Conservatoire, Sofia; Artist-in-Residence, Piano Lectr, Sydney

Conservatorium Music, NSW, Australia, 1986-. *Creative works:* Var publs in Bulgarian Music and other periodicals; Nearly 20 records; CDs: Haydn-Concertos for Piano and Orch in G maj and D maj; Liszt-Concerto for Piano and Orch No 2 in A maj, 1989; Passionata, classical piano pieces, 1992. *Memberships:* Union Bulgarian Composers, 1948-; Union Musicians in Bulgaria, 1965-; Music Tchrs Assn NSW, 1990-. *Honours:* 2nd Prize, 1st Nat Competition, young pianists and violinists, Sofia, 1949; 1st Prize, Gold Medal, Int Piano Competition, World Youth Fest, Warsaw, 1955; 5th Prize, Marguerite Long Int Piano Competition, Paris, 1959; 4th prize, Liszt-Bartok Int Piano Competition, Budapest, 1961; Title of Honoured Artist, Presidium, Nat Assembly, Bulgaria, 1971; Title of Nat Artist, State Coun, Republic of Bulgaria, 1982; Cyril and Methodius Medal, 1st degree, gt achievements in dev of nat culture, Bulgaria; Republic of Bulgaria Medal, 3rd degree, gt achievements in dev of nat culture, 1986; Awarded Reader acad rank, 1976; Awarded Prof acad rank, 1985. *Hobbies:* Reading; Nature walks. *Address:* 143 Haydouchka Gora str, 1404 Sofia, Bulgaria.

EWERT Brita Louise, b. 31 May 1929, Stockholm, Sweden. Physician; Otolaryngologist. m. Gosta Ewert, 1 Feb 1954, 1 s. *Education:* MD, Karolinska Inst, Stockholm, 1960; Resident, Depts Otolaryngology, Surg, Plastic Surg, Karolinska and Sabbatsberg Hosps, Stockholm, 1960-72; Specialist Cert, Otolaryngology, 1972. *Appointments:* Maj, Armed Forces Med Staff, 1966-68; Phys, Radiology Depts, Sabbatsberg Hosp and Oncology Radiumhemmet, Karolinska Hosp, 1973-74; Asst Chief Surg, Otolaryngology Depts, Sabbatsberg and Danderyd Hosps, 1974-89. *Publications:* Sci papers in profl publs. *Memberships:* Swedish Med Assn; Swed Soc Oncology; Swed Soc Otolaryngology; Halmstad Golf Club. *Hobbies:* Cultural history; Gardening; golf. *Address:* Radjursvagen 31, S-302 73 Halmstad, Sweden.

EWERT Gosta, b. 6 June 1927, Gothenburg, Sweden. Associate Professor of Otolaryngology. m. Brita Ewert, 1 Feb 1954, 1 s. *Education:* MD, 1952, PhD, 1965, Karolinska Inst; Rsch Fellow, Memphis Fndn Otolaryngology, USA, 1959-60; Specialist, Otolaryngology, 1959. *Appointments:* Surg, ENT Clin, Karolinska Hosp, Stockholm, 1961-67; Assoc Prof, Otolaryngology, Karolinska Inst, Stockholm, 1966-; Surg Lt-Cmdr, Royal Swedish Navy, 1967-74; Asst Chief Surg, ENT Clin, Sabbatsberg Hosp, Stockholm, 1967-75; Chmn, Chief Surg, ENT Clins, Sabbatsberg and Danderyd Hosps, 1975-89; Asst Chief Med Off, W Dist, Stockholm, 1975-84. *Publications:* On the Mucus Flow Rate in the Human Nose, thesis, 1965; Sci articles in profl publs; History of the ENT-clinic Sabbatsberg Hospital, 1990. *Memberships:* Swedish Med Assn; Swedish Soc Med; Swedish Soc Otolaryngology, Sec 1971-75; Swedish Soc Oncology; Stockholm Cancer Assn. *Hobbies:* Cultural and modern history esp World War II; Natural science; Model ship building; Golf. *Address:* Radjursvagen 31, S-302 73 Halmstad, Sweden.

EWERT Janina, b. 19 Jan 1938, Lida, Poland. Professor of Mathematics; Dean of Science Department. m. Andrzej Ewert, 27 June 1961, 1 d. *Education:* MSc, Maths, 1961; DSc, Maths, 1975; Habilitation, 1986; Prof, Maths, 1990. *Appointments:* Tchg: Grammar School, Slupsk, 1961- 65; Tchrs Coll, Slupsk, 1965-69; Pedagogical Univ, Slupsk, 1969-, currently Prof, Math and Dean, Sci Dept. *Publications:* Homotopical properties and the topological degree for gamma-contraction vector fields, 1980; Fuzzy- valued maps, 1988; On measurability of quasi-continuous and some related maps, 1989. *Memberships:* Polski Towarzystwo Matematyczne (Polish Math Soc); Am Math Soc. *Hobbies:* Flowers; Knitting. *Address:* ul Garncarska 5/22, 76-200 Slupsk, Poland.

EWING Maria, b. Detroit, Michigan, USA. Opera and Concert Singer. *Education:* Cleveland; NYC. *Career:*

Debut as Cherubino, Marriage of Figaro, Metro Opera, NYC, 1976; Num debuts w maj US orchs incl NY Philharmonic and Chgo Symph; European debut as Melisande, Pelleas et Melisande, La Scala; Covent Garden debut as Salome, 1988; Australian debut, Carmen, 1990; Debut as Madame Butterfly, Los Angeles, 1991; Other operatic perfs incl: Composer in Ariadne auf Naxos, 1985; Title role, Carmen, 1986; Title role, Salome, Los Angeles Opera, 1986-87; Blanche in Poulenc's The Dialogues of the Carmelites, 1987; Dorabella in Cosi fan tutti, Susanna and Cherubino in Figaro, title roles, La Perichola and La Cenerentola; Concerts w Concertgebouw, London Philharmonic Orch, Cit of Birmingham Symp Orch, BBC Symphony Orch, NY Philharmonic, Chamber Orch of Europe, Royal Philharmonic Orch, Berlin Philharmonic Orch; Appeared, Glyndebourne, Brighton Fest, Salzburg Fest, BBC Proms, Luzern Fest; Recitals incl: European tour, 1985; Paris, Vienna, Florence, 1988; Paris, Vienna, 1991; Recordings; Prodn of Carmen, Royal Opera House, Covent Garden filmed for TV, 1991. *Address:* c/o Harold Holt Limited, 31 Sinclair Road, London W14 0NS, England.

F

FABBRINI Sergio, b. 21 Feb 1949, Pesaro, Italy. Pol Science Educator. m. Manuela Cescatti, 16 June 1985, 2 s. *Education:* Laura cum Lauden in Sociology, Trento Univ, Italy, 1973. *Appointments:* Asst in Pol Econ, Fac of Econ, 1974-76, Asst in Pol Econ and Pol Sociology, Fac of Sociology, 1977-81, Rsch Prof in Pol Studies, Fac of Sociology, 1982-, Trento Univ. *Publications:* Neoconservatism and American Politics; Politics and Social Changes; The Politics of Democratic Citizens; 50 articles in scientific jrnls. *Memberships:* American Pol Science Assn;; Italian Pol Science Assn; Int Pol Science Assn. *Honours:* Fellowship in Political Economy, Cambridge University, England, 1977-78; NATO Senior Fellowship in Political Studies, University of California, Berkeley, USA, 1981-82; Fulbright Fellowship in American Studies, Harvard University, 1987-88; CNR/IGS Fellowship in American Studies, University of California, Berkeley, 1991; Promoter of the ECPR Standing Group on American Politics, 1989-. *Hobbies:* Sport, Poetry, Nature. *Address:* via Milano, 13-38100 Trento, Italy. 52.

FABREGA Jorge, b. 19 Apr 1922, Panama, Republic of Panama. Atty at Law, Univ Prof of Law. m. Gloria Sanchez, 5 Jan 1960, 2 s, 2 d. *Education:* BA, 1945; MA (P S); Licenciado en Derecho, 1954. *Appointments:* Founding Mbr of Law Firm Moreno Y Fabrega; Alternate Justice (Supreme Ct of Justice). *Publications:* Unjustified Enrichment on Cassation; Estudios Procesales (3 vols); Attorneys and Judges: Labor Code. (All Books ibn Spanish). *Memberships:* Acad of Law; (Panama) Bar Assn; Iberoamericanm Inst of Labor; Procedural Law Interamerican; Inst of Procedural Law; Spanish Bar Assn, Hon Mbr; Inter-American Bar Assn. *Honours:* Spanish Jurista Order, San Rimundo de Penafort; Ordem do Merito Judiciario do Trabalho, Brasilia. *Hobbies:* Reading, Travelling. *Address:* Bancomer Building, Second Floor, 50th Street, Panama City, Republic of Panama.

FABRIKESI Eugenia Theodora, b. 2 Oct 1950, Athens, Greece. Hd of Phys Dept, Nat Def Rsch Ctr. m. Alex a Serafetinides, 27 Dec 1979, 2 s. *Education:* Dip Phys, Univ of Athens, 1973; MSc, Optoelectronics, 1974, PhD, High Power Lasers, 1981, Univ of Essex, England. *Appointments:* Rschr, Nat Def Rsch Ctr, 1978-84; Hd of Phys Dept, Nat Def Rsch Ctr, 1984- *Publications:* Var articles in profl jrnls; transl of book: Optics and Lasers, 1986. *Memberships:* Inst of Phys UK and Greece. *Honour:* Grantee for post studies by NATO, 1975-78. *Hobbies:* Stamp Collecting; Coin Collecting; Matches Collecting; Swimming. *Address:* Riga Fereou 11, Pefki, Athens 15121, Greece.

FABRY Laszlo Georg, b. 26 Apr 1947, Budapest, Hungary. Hd of Ctrl Analytical Labs, Silicon Chem. m. Judith Anna Englander, 3 Jan 1970, 3 s, 1 d. *Education:* Dip, Chem Technology, Eotvos Univ, Budapest, 1970; PhD, Silicon Chem, 1973; Dip, Plastics, Polytechnic Univ, Budapest, 1976. *Appointments:* Rsch Assoc, Chem Dept, Eotvos Univ, Budapest, 1970-76, 1978-83; Monbusho Fellow in Synthetic Chem, Univ of Kyotot, 1976-78; Rsch Assoc, Inorganic Chem, Techn Hochschule, Darmstadt; Vis Schlr, Max-Planck Inst in Mulheim-Ruhr, 1984-85; Univ of Utah, SLC, 1985-87; Corp Scientist, Wacker- Chemitronic, Burghausen. *Publications:* Reaction of H-atoms at Si, 1986; Patentee in field. *Memberships:* German Chem Soc; American Scientific Affiliation; Wacker Sailing Club; Int 420 Assn. *Honour:* Candidate of Chemical Society, Hungarian Academy of Science, 1981. *Hobbies:* Children, Bach and Mozart, Sailing. *Address:* Wacker- Chemitronic GmbH, PO Box 1140, D-8263 Burghausen, Germany. 52.

FACTOR Regis Anthony, b. 8 Sept 1937, Ellwood City, Pennsylvania, USA. Prof. m. Deborah Bliss, 25 Jan 1969, 2 s. *Education:* BA, Washington and Jefferson Coll, 1955-59; MA Schl of Adv Int Studies of The Johns

Hopkins Univ, 1964-66; PhD, Univ of Notre Dame, 1968-71. *Appointments:* Mil Serv, 1960-64; Off of Emergency Planning, US Govt, 1967-68; Univ of S FL, 1971-92. *Publications:* Max Weber and the Dispute Over Reason and Value; Guide to the Archiv fur Sozialwissenschaft und Sozialpolitik Group, 1904-33. *Memberships:* American Pol Science Assn; German Studies Assn; Fellowship of Cath Schlrs; Natural Law Soc; Pol Science Assn Study Grp in Greek Pol Thought; N American Soc of Social Philosophy. *Honours:* J Adolph Schmitz Award in Languages, 1958; Var schlrships and fellowships; National Endowment for the Humanities Fellowship for Teachers and Independent Scholars, 1989. *Hobbies:* Athletics, For Lang. *Address:* 167 Almedo Way NE, St Petersburg, FL 33704, USA.

FADEJEVA Tatiana Michajlovna, b. 14 Mar 1938, Moscow, USSR. Histn, Hist of Culture, Relig, Symbolism, European Civilisation. m. 10 Aug 1960, 1 s. *Education:* Moscow Inst of Pedagogy, 1960; Dip of histn- philologist, Inst of World Economy and Int Rels; Dr Hist of Sciences, 1971. *Appointments:* Inst of World Econ and Int Rels, Acad of Sciences of USSR, 1961-71; Inst of Info on Social Sciences, Acad of Sciences of USSR, Hist Dept, 1971-. *Publications:* Strategy of Reformism in Contemporary France, 1975; articles on liberal-conservative trends of social thought; Books: Mountain Crimea; Image and Symbols in History of Culture; art critic articles. *Membership:* Mbr of Dirs Coun of Louis Ortega Fndn, NY, Paris, Madrid, Moscow Sect. *Hobbies:* Travelling, Reading, Gardening. *Address:* Academ. Varga Street 24-54, Moscow, Russia.

FADYN Joseph Nicholas, b. 9 Sept 1947, Peckville, Pennsylvania, USA. Coll Prof, Author. m. Karen Ann Rashko, 24 Aug 1976. *Education:* BA Maths, 1971, MS Maths, 1974, PhD Maths, 1977, Lehigh Univ; MS Decision Sciences, GA State Univ, 1988. *Appointments:* Asst Prof of Maths, Oglethorpe Univ, Atlanta, GA, 1981-85; Asst Prof of Maths, Southern Coll of Technology, Atlanta, 1985-. *Publications:* Math Textbooks: Study Guide for College Algebra, 1989; Study Guide for College Algebra and Trignometry, 1989; A Brief Calculus for Business, Economics, Social and Life Sciences, 1991. *Memberships:* American Math Soc; Math Assn of America; Beta Gamma Sigma; Sigma Zeta. *Honour:* George Melanos Graduate Award for Academic Excellence from Georgia State University, 1989. *Hobbies:* Tennis, Chess, Billiards, Classical Music. *Address:* Southern College of Technology, 1100 South Marietta Parkway, Marietta, GA 30060, USA. 7.

FAINGUERSCH Julio, b. 26 Sept 1936, San Luis, Argentina. Choir Conductor. m. Alicia Aurora Carnaval, 5 Jan 1970, 3 s. *Education:* Dip Piano, Nat Conservatory, 1962; Dip Higher Studies in French, Alliance Francaise and Sorbonne, Paris, 1962; Dip Conducting, Inst of Higher Art Studies, Colon Thjeatre, 1964; Music study w: Luiggi Castelazzi, Erwin Leuchter, Hubert Brandenburg, Enrique Sivieri, Robert Kinsky, et al. *Appointments:* Dir, Colon Theatre Choir, 1974-87; Dir, Alliance Francaise Choir, 1966-; Dir, Nat Conservatory of Music, 1983-; Dir, Nat Poliphonic Choir, 1991-; Tchr Choir Conducting and French Phonetics. *Creative Works:* Music for the First Grade, 1962; Survey of Choral Activity in Argentina, 1977; Radio and TV Progs; Master Classes for Choir Conductors; First perf of works by ancient and mod French Composers; Conductor, Chmbr Music Grps. *Memberships:* ISME; Argentine Soc for Music Educ; Int Fedn for Choral Music; VP, Argentine Br, Internationale Heinrich Schutz Gesellschaft; Rep, Argentine Assn of Choir Conductors; Regular Jury for local and int music competitions. *Honours:* Academics Palms, French Government, 1978; Merit Award, Choir Conductor, Konex Foundation, 1989; num awards in local and international Choir Competitions. *Hobbies:* Reading, Gardening, Stamps. *Address:* J A Pacheco de Melo 1837, 6A, 1126 Buenos Aires, Argentina.

FAINLIGHT Ruth Esther, b. 2 May 1931, New York City, USA. Writer. m. Alan Sillitoe, 19 Nov 1959, 1 s,

1 d. *Education:* Elem and Second Educ in England and USA; Acad in GB. *Appointment:* Poet-in-Res, Vanderbilt Univ, Nashville, TN, USA, Spring Semester 1985-90. *Creative Works:* Poems: Cages, 1966; To See the Matter Clearly, 1968; The Region's Violence, 1973; Another Full Moon, 1976; Sibyls and Others, 1980; Fifteen to Infinity, 1983; Climates, 1983; Selected Poems, 1987; The Knot, 1990. Short Stories: Daylife and Nightlife, 1971. Transls: All Citizens Are Soldiers, 1969 (w Alan Sillitoe), play by Lope de Vega; Marine Rose, 1987, poems by S de Mello Breyner; Libretti: The Dancer Hotoke, 1991, chmbr opera, composer Erika Fox. *Membership:* PEN. *Hobbies:* Reading, Geography. *Address:* 14 Ladbroke Terrace, London W111 3PG, England. 3, 5, 11, 52, 138.

FAJUMI James Oladiran, b. 28 Oct 1943, Ilesha, Nigeria. Biomed Scientist, Univ Acad. m. Foluke Folashade, 26 Oct 1968, 1 s, 4 d. *Education:* Wesley Coll, Ibadan, 1962-64; UCH Ibadan, 1965-69; Napier Univ, Edinburgh, 1969-72; St Andrews Univ, 1972-74; Manchester Univ, 1976-78; MSc, PhD. *Appointments:* Rsch Fellow, Univ Ibadan, 1975-76; Demonstrator in Med Biochem, Manchester Univ, 1976-78; Lectr, Univ of Jos, 1978-80; Sr Lectr, Univ of Ilorin, 1984-86; Vis Fellow, Univ of Liverpool, 1986. *Creative Works:* Scientific Rsch Findings in field of Contraception expt. Cancer and Transplantation Rsch. *Memberships:* Brit Soc of Immunology of UK; Biochem Soc of UK, V-Chmn local branch Ilorin, Nigeria; Planned Parenthood Fedn, 1983-84. *Honours:* New York Population Council Award Recipient, 1975-76 via UNIBADAN; Federal Nigerian Government Scholarship recipient, 1976-78; British Council University Academic Staff Fellowship recipient 1986 tenable at the University of Liverpool. *Hobbies:* Football, Table Tennis, Squash, Rugby Football, Gardening, Christian Fellowship. *Address:* Cardiff Business School, University of Wales, College of Cardiff, P O Box 921, Cardiff CF1 3EU, Wales.

FALASE Ayodele Olajide, b. 4 Jan 1944, Nigeria. University Professor of Medicine and Cardiology. m. Adelola Omolara Omonijon 30 Dec 1967, 2 s, 2 d. *Education:* MBBS, Univ of Ibadan, Nigeria, 1968; MRCP, 1971, FRCP, 1982, RCP, London; MD, Univ of Ibadan, 1977. *Appointments:* Hs Ofr, Sr Hs Ofr, Univ Col Hosp, Ibadan, 1968-70; Hs Phys, Mt Vernon Hosp, 1970; Sr Hs Ofr, Dudley Rd Hosp, 1970-71; C'wlth Scholar, Kings Col Hosp, London, 1973; Registrar, Sr Registrar, Univ Col Hosp, Ibadan, 1974; Conslt, Univ Col Hosp, 1974-. *Publications:* An introduction to clinical diagnosis in the tropics; Clinical Medicine in the tropics series: Cardiovascular Disease; Over 100 scientific publications and five technical reports. *Memberships:* FRCP, London; WHO Adv Panel on Cardiovas Dis; Coun on Cardiomyopathies of the Intl Soc and Fed of Cardiol. *Honours:* Univ Dept Prizes in Biochem, 1965, Path, 1966; Sir Samuel Manuwa Gold Medal in Med, 1968; Sr Kofo Abayomi Prize in Med and Path, 1968. *Hobbies:* Table Tennis; Organ Music; Organist; All Saints Church, Jericho, Ibadan. *Address:* Department of Medicine, University College Hospital, Ibadan, Nigeria.

FALCON BLASCO Juan Antonio, b. 1 Mar 1959, Zaragoza, Spain. International Manager and Consultant. *Education:* Law, 1976-83; Sch Dipl, 1983; Master in Intl Mktg. *Appointments:* Prof of Intl Law, 1983- 85; Intl Mgr of Univ Indust Foun, 1985-89; Intl Mgr of Confed Reg de Empresarios de Aragon; Dir: Intl MBA OF/CREA, 1990; Dir, Inst de Relaciones, Geopolitca y Economic Intl, 1991; Pres, Ctr de Desarrollo Economico y Empresarial, 1990. *Publications:* Relaciones entre la comunidad europea y los paises ACP; LA CEE Co-Mo opportunidad commercial; Cooperation innovation between large and small firms; Articles about international economy and relations. *Memberships:* Ctr de De Desarrollo Economico y empresarial; Inst de Relaciones Geopolitica y Economic Int. *Hobbies:* Astronomy; International relations; Atheletics; Swimming; Aid and cooperation for the third world. *Address:* Alonso V 29-31, 50002 Zaragoza, Spain. 52.

FALK Haim, b. 20 Aug 1929, Berlin, Germany. Professor of Accounting. m. 24 Nov 1955, 1 s, 1 d. *Education:* BAcct, 1962, Dipl Bus Admin, 1967, PhD, 1971, Hebrew Univ; MBA Tel Aviv Univ, 1969; CPA, 63, CGA, 89. *Appointments include:* Instr; Lectr, Hebrew Univ, 1969-73; Vis Prof, Indiana Univ, 1972-75; Assoc Prof, McGill Univ, 1975-82; Prof, Univ of Calgary, 1982-86; Dist Prof Chair in Acctg, McMaster Univ, 1986-. *Publications:* 5 scholarly research books in business accounting; 80 articles in scholarly and professional journals. *Memberships include:* CGA, Ontario, Can; Dir, Can Cert Gen Accts Res Foun; Can Acad Acctg Assn; Fdg Ed, Jt Ed, Ed Bd, Contemporary Acctg Res; Am and European Acctg Assns; Am Econ Assn. *Honours:* Haim Falk Awd established by the Can Acad Acctg Assn for dist contrib to accounting, 1989. *Hobbies:* Swimming; Reading. *Address:* 10 Lennard Crescent, Dundas, Ontario, Canada L9H 6S5. 142, 154.

FALKNER Ann Coody, b. 2 Sept 1933, Shannon, Texas, USA. Educator; Consultant; Author; Researcher. m. Felix Lee Falkner, 31 July 1954, 2 d. *Education:* BA Maths, Texas Woman's Univ, 1954; MA Maths & Ed Psych, Univ Texas at Austin, 1957; Postgrad, Univ of Wisconsin, 1965-66; PhD work, Univ of Arizona, 1966-72, Adv Inst Princeton, 1985-86, 1988-89. *Appointments:* Prof of Maths, Univ of Arizona, 1966-72; Res Assoc, Arizona State Dept of Educ, 1971-72; Instr, Maths for Corpus Christi, TX Independent Sch Dist, 1974-. *Publications:* Arizona needs Assessment, 1973; Management by Objectives, 1968; Lyrics to Broadway Musical, I do, I do; Poems incollected works; Numerous articles to travel publications and professional journals. *Memberships:* MAA; AMA; IPA; NCTM; Texas Aerospace Tchrs Assn; Civil Air Patrol. *Honours include:* Fulbright Tchrs Exchange to Can, 1982-83, 1989-90; Coastal Bend Community Fund Fellowships, 1985-86, 1988-89; Nat Sci Foun Fellow, Univ of Wisconsin; VS Ofc of Educ Fellow, 1967-68; Special Asst to Commn of Educ, Wash DC. *Address:* 830 St Martin Street, Corpus Christi, TX 78418, USA. 2, 7.

FALKOWSKI Wojciech, b. 17 June 1930, Poland. Medical Practitioner. m. 8 Sept 1959, 2 s. *Education:* MBBCh, BAO (NUI), 57; LM, 1959; MRCGP, 1960; DPM, 1969; MPhil, 1970; MRCPsych, 1971; FRCPsych, 1983; Dipl Fine Art, Polish Univ, 1981. *Appointments:* Conslt in Psycho Med and Hon Sr Lectr, St George's Hosp and Med Sch, Univ of London. *Creative Works:* Held several solo exhibitions of oil paintings. *Memberships:* Prof and Pro-Rector, Polish Univ Abroad; Past VP, Ctr for Analytic Psychotherapy, Chm, Res Foun, Alcohol Community Ctr for Educ Prevention, Treatment and Res; Past Chm, Polish Med Assn; FRSM. *Honours:* Polonic Restituta. *Hobbies:* Painting; Music; Literature; Scouting. *Address:* 1 Earldley Road, London SW16 6DA, England.

FALLA David Frank, b. 1 June 1934, Guernsey, Channel Islands. University Lecturer. *Education:* Elizabeth Col, Guernsey, 1947-52; BSc Phys, 1955, PhD, 1960, Univ of Bristol. *Appointments:* Tchg Fellow and Res Asst, Univ of Manchester, 1958-61; Res Fellow, Queen Mary Col, London, 1961-65; Lectr in Phys, Univ Col of Wales, (UCQ), 1965-; Warden, Padarn Hall, UCW, 1969-84. *Publications:* About 25 papers in scientific journals on meson (elementary-particle) physics, astrophysics, quasars, synchrotron, radiation theory, supranuclear densities and black holes. *Memberships:* MInstP; Fellow, Royal Astro Soc; UCW Staff Hse, Acad Staff Club; Fdr, Astron Sect, Coun, 1972-85, La Soc Guernesiaise; Treas, Aberystwyth Biblio Gp; Royal Overseas League. *Hobbies:* Music; Travel; Wine and food; Gardening. *Address:* (1)1 Trefor Road, Aberystwyth, Dyfed, Wales. 161.

FALLACI Oriana, b. 29 June 1930, Florence, Italy. Author. *Education:* Grad, Liceo Classico Galileo, Italy; Univ of Florence, Fac of Med, 1946-48; Lit Doc, hon, Columbia Col, Chicago, 1977. *Appointments:* Ed and Special Corres, Europeo Mag, Milan, Italy, 1958-77;

Collaborator with major publications throughout world including: Look Mag, Life Mag, Wahington Post, NY Times, London Times, Corriere della Sera, Milan, Europeo. *Publications include:* The Egotists, 1965; Penelope at War, 1966; If the Sun Dies, 1967; Nothing and so be it, 1972; Interview with history, 1976; Letter to a child never born, 1977; A man, 1979, Insciallah, 1990. *Honours:* St Vincent Awd for Jour, 1971, 1973; Bancarella Awd, 1972; Two Viareggio Prize Awds, 1979; Hemingway prize for Literature and Super Bancarella Prize, 1991. *Address:* c/o Rizzoli, 31 West 57 Street, NY 10019, USA. 2, 3, 52, 138.

FALLIS Albert Murray, b. 2 Jan 1907, Ontario, Canada. Retired Professor Emeritus. m. Ada Ruth Bastock, 21 Sept 1938, 3 s. *Education:* Harriston Hg Sch, 1919-25; Toronto Normal Hg Sch, 1928-32; PA, 1932; PhD, 1937. *Appointments:* Tchr, 1926-28; Res Fellow, Ontario Res Foun, 1932- 47; Hd of Parasitol, 1947-66; Lectr, Parasitol, 1938-43, Assoc Prof, 1944-48, Prof, 1948-75, Emeritus, 1975-, Assoc Dean, Grad Studies, 1967-70, Govt Coun, 1972-73, Univ of Toronto; Erskine Fellow, Univ of Canterbury, 1975. *Publications:* Numerous papers, and chapters in books. *Memberships:* Am Soc of Parasitols, Emeritus VP, 1976, Pres, 1979; Can Soc Zoologists, Hon Wildlife Dis Assoc Emerit; Royal Can Inst Hon Ed, 1949-54, Pres, 1954-55; Am Soc of Trop Med and Hyg. *Honours:* FRSC, 1958; Pres, ICOPA V, 1982. *Hobbies:* Gardening; Furniture Refinishing; History of Medicine. *Address:* Caledon East, RRI Ontario, Canada LON 1EO.

FALLIS Alexander Graham, b. 20 Aug 1940, Toronto, Canada. Professor of Chemistry. m. Wanda Lee Wiley, 7 Oct 1967, 1 s, 1 d. *Education:* Hon BSc, Univ of Toronto, 1963; MA, 1964, PhD, 1967. *Appointments:* Asst Prof, 1969-74, Assoc Prof, 1974-78, Prof of Chem, 1978-88, Nfld Meml Univ; Prof of Chem, Univ of Ottawa, 1988- ; Dir, Ottata- Carleton Chem Inst, 1990-93. *Publications:* Numerous research articles. *Memberships:* RSC; ACS; CIC; CSC; Reg Coun, CIC, 1979-82, Dir Sci Affairs, 1983-84, Chm Bd of Dirs, 1984-86. *Honours:* Ontario Grad Res Fellowship, 1963-67; NRC Postdoc Fellowship, 1967-69; Fellow, CIC, 1980. *Hobbies:* Photography; Squash; Gardening. *Address:* Department of Chemistry, University of Ottawa, Ontario, Canada.

FALUYI Akinsola Olusegun, b. 13 Nov 1934, Ibadan, Nigeria. Human Resources Development Consultant. m. Teresa Ololade Ajai, 20 June 1965, 7 s, 1 d. *Education:* BEng, Loughborough Univ of Tech, 1953-58. *Appointments:* Hosp Engr, Univ Col Hosp, Ibadan, 1960-62; Asst to Chief Engr, Dunlop Nig Indust, 1962-64; Sers Engr, 1964-65; Chief Engr, Lagso Univ Tchg Hosp, 1965-75; Principal Ptnr, Edison Gp & Ptnrs, 1976-79; MD, Atess Ltd, 1980-; Dir of Studies, Atess Inst, 1984- ; Dir, Aries Nigeria Ltd, 1987-. *Publications:* The Nigerian Engineer and the challenges of a depressed economy, 1986; Lectures and papers on engineering management and hospital engineering. *Memberships:* Hon Sec, AAN, 1966-71; Pres, Nig Assn of Hlth Engrs, 1974-78; Sec Gen, 1978-81, 1st VP, 1984, Pres, 1985-86, Nig Soc of Engrs. *Honours:* Hon Fellow, NAHE; NSE Merit Awd, 1983. *Hobby:* Reading. *Address:* Atess institute, 16 Ogunlana Drive, Surulere, Nigeria. 52.

FAMADAS Jose, b. 10 Apr 1908, Rio de janeiro, Brazil. Linguist, Educator; Journalist. m. 1 s. *Education:* BSc, BLit, Col Pedro II & Col St Vincente; CPA, Dept of Bus Educ, Brazil; MA, Univ of Michigan, USA. *Appointments include:* Instr, Columbia Univ, 1943-47, City Col of NY, 1947-58; Radio commentator, actor, panel member, weekly progs, NBC, 1944-45; Ofc of War Info, 1944-45; Columbia Broadcasting Sys, 1944-47; Voice of Am, 1952-53; WRUL Radio, 1953-54; Ed in chief, Reader's Digest Brazil and Portugal Ed, 1947-50; Press Ofr, Brazilian Mission to UN, 1950-55; Film Translator and Narrator, 20th C Fox, 1950-56; US Dept of State, 1951-53; US Info Agy, 1953- 78; Universal Pictures, 1953-74; Utd Artists, 1956-83, Paramount Pictures, 1971-74; MGM, 1972, *Contributions to:* various book chapters

and journal articles. *Memberships include:* Past VP, NY Chap, Life mem, Am Assn of Tchrs of Spanish and Portuguese; Past Pres, Soc of Lang Specialists; Life, AAAS; Lang Soc of Am; Modern Lang Assn; Am Econ Assn; Soc of Am Magicians; Acad of Polit Sci, Columbia Univ. *Honours include:* Fellowships: Inst of Intl Educ, 1941, Rockefeller Foun, 1942; Order of Merlin Excalibur, Intl Brotherhood of Magicians, 1976. *Hobbies:* Travel; Stage magic. *Address:* PO Box 752, Flushing, NY 11352, USA.

FAN Zheng, b. 23 Feb 1929, Tianjin, China. Professor/Senior Research Librarian. m. Li Xueting, 1 Oct 1961, 2 s. *Education:* Dept of Mech Engrg, Hobei Inst of Tech (HIT), Tianjin, 1947-50. *Appointments:* Draftsman, HIT, 1950-52; Archivist, Personnel Div, TU, 1952-55; Lib, Hd of Catalogue Div, 1955-81; ASsoc Prof, 1981-87, Prof, Sr Res Lib, TUL, 1987-; Acting Dir, Tech Info Ctr, TU, 1990-. *Publications:* Science and Technical Information Sources, 1985; Practice Sci-Tech Literature Searching, 1988; The Searching and Use of Mechanical Engineering Literature, 1989; Selections from Fan Zheng, 1989. *Memberships:* Lit Searching & Res Com, China Soc of Lib Sci; Chm, Tianjin Assn of the Deaf; The China Soc of Sci and Tech Info, 1979-; Ed-in-Chief, Science Abstracts of Tianjin Univ Annual; Acad Com, TUL. *Honours:* Nat Deafness Model Worker, 1983; Nat Sci Info Adv Worker, 1986; Nat Exampliary Tchr, 1989. Adv Worker, 1986; National Exemplary Tchr, 1989. *Hobbies:* Chinese chess; Reading novels. *Address:* Tianjin University Library, Tianjin 300072, China. 152.

FANG Chaochen, b. 14 Feb 1934, Baoshan, Shanghai, China. Professor of Maths. m. Yuan Yuling, 25 Feb 1958, 2 s, 1 d. *Education:* Shanghai Tchrs Co, 1950-53; BA Maths, E.China Normal Univ, 1953-57; Vis Fellow, Inst of Math, Acad Sinica, 1958-61. *Appointments:* Tchg Asst, 1957-79, Lectr, 1979-87, Assoc Prof, 1987-91, Hd of Algebra Tchg and Res Ofc, 1961-88, Supervisor, Grad Students, 1985-, Qufu Normal Univ. *Publications include:* 14 papers in profession journals and magazines including: A proof of the fundamental property for a non-transitive groups, 1982; A class of algebras related to BCK algebras, 1984; Modules on BE algebras and semiprimitive be algebras, 1989. *Memberships:* Assn of China Math Soc; Assn of BCK BCI Algebra Soc of China; Ed, Chinese Jour of Communication in Algebra. *Honours:* Sci Res Awds, Qufu Normal Univ, 1985, 1986, 1990, Jinin City, 1980. *Hobbies:* Taijiquan; Bridge; Badminton; Music. *Address:* Dept of Maths, Qufu Normal University, Qufu, Shandong 273165, China.

FANG Cheng-Shen, b. 29 Mar 1936, Taipei, Taiwan. Professor. m. Fei-Ying Cheng, 2 Oct 1972. *Education:* BS 1958, MS 1965, PhD, 1968, Chem Engrg. *Appointments:* Shift-supervisor of Ammonia Plant Taiwan Fertilizer Co, 1960-62; Univ of S.Western Louisiana, Prof, 1969-. *Publications:* 2 books and 43 papers published or presented. *Memberships:* AICE: Sor of Petroleum Engrs; Phi Kappa Phi. *Honours:* Eloi Girard Professorship in Engrg, 1987-; Outstanding Achievement in Sci Res Awd, , 1989-90, Dist Prof, 1986, Univ of S.Western Louisiana; Sigma Xi, 1990. *Hobbies:* Water Colour painting. *Address:* 215 N Philo Dr, Lafayette, LA 70506, USA.

FANG Yuan, b. 6 Jan 1947, Shanghai, China. Musician. m. Zhang Zhen Shan, 6 Feb 1975. *Education:* Grad, Acad of Shanghai Conservatory of Mus, 1965. *Appointments:* Cultural Troupe of the Dong Hai Sea Fleet, 1965-69; Shanghai Phil Orch, 1973-84; Acad of Fine Arts, Nan Yang, 1991-. *Creative works:* A hundred birds singing to the Phoneix (Accordion solo piece); and other arrangments for the accordion. *Memberships:* China Musicians Assn; Standing Dir, China Accordion Assn; VP, Shanghai Accordion Assn. *Honours:* Outstanding Performance at Youth Competition, Shanghai, 1976; National Compostion Competition Prize, 1990. *Hobbies:* Travelling; Reading. *Address:* 10 Anson Road, International Plaza 42-14, Singapore 0207. 4, 152.

FANG Zheng, b. 18 Jan 1930, CHina. Professor of Medical Information. m. Chang Jin, 20 Aug 1955, 3 d. *Education:* Peking Inst of Foreign Lang, 1949-53; Chinese Inst of Chinese Med, 1972-73; Col of Trad Med, 1975-80. *Appointments:* Res Fellow, Prov Inst of Drug Control; Prof, Shanxi Inst of Trad Chinese Med. *Publications:* The method of research on info of Traditional Med, 1991; Prediction of Development of Chinese Med, 1988. *Memberships:* Chinese Soc for Info of Trad Med; COun, Prov Soc of Med Sci; Prov Com for Info. *Honours:* Nat Adv Res Fellow, Chinese Com of Sci and Tech. *Hobbies:* Listening to music; Watching football. *Address:* Shanxi Institute of Traditional Chinese Medicine, Bingzhou W. Street, Taiyuan, Shanxi 030012, China.

FARADAY Bruce John, b. 9 Dec 1919, NY, USA. Scientific Research Company Executive. m. Beverly Anne Hartzell, 4 Feb 1950, 3 s, 2 d. *Education:* AB Fordham Col, 1940; MS, Fordham Grad Sch, 1947; PhD, Catholic Univ, 1963; US Army Serv Pacific Theatre, 1943-46. *Appointments:* Res Phys, 1948-60; Supervisory Res Phys, 1960-80; Prog Mgr, Low Observable TEch, 1980-86; Naval Res Lab, Wash DC; Pres, Faraday Assocs, VA, 1986-; Lectr in Maths, Prince George's Com Coll, MD, 1960-79; Adj Prof, Maths, Virginia Com Col, 1980-87. *Publications:* Articles to professional journals; inventor of battery holder for satellites, solar cell mouting technology. *Memberships:* Fellow, APS; NYAS; Sigma Xi, Pres, 1974-76; Assoc of Old Crows; Am Legion. *Honours:* Navy Spec Achievement Awd, 1973, 1975, 1981; Superior Civ Ser Awd, 1981; Dir Awd for Improved Govt Ops, 1985. *Hobbies:* Reading; HIking. *Address:* 8670 Sinon Street, Annandale, VA 22003, USA. 7, 14, 28.

FARARA Katharine Georgia, b. 19 Nov 1962, Kingston-upon-Thames, England. Advertising Executive. m. Richard Michael Bruges, 7 Sept 1991. *Education:* Woking Co Grammar Sch for Girls, 1974-79; Woking 6th Form Col, 1979-81; Newnham Col, Cambs Univ, 1981-84. *Appointments:* Trainee Advtg Exec, J Walter Thompson, 1984, Bd of Dirs, 1989. *Memberships:* Gen Mgmt Com, Nat Ad Benevolent Soc. *Honours:* MA Cantab 2(i) History. *Hobbies:* Riding horses; Flute; Piano; St Kitts, West Indies. *Address:* c/o Mr C J Farara, 24 Guildown Road, Guildford, Surrey.

FARHA Bryan, b. 18 Nov 1957, Oklahoma City, USA. Assistant Professor of Counselling. *Education:* EdD, 1985, Med, 1981, Counselling Psychol; BS, Med, Univ of Ctl Oklahoma, 1980; EdD, Univ of Tulsa. *Appointments:* Lectr, Univ Ctl Oklahoma, 1985-86; Psychol Adj Prof, Oklahoma State Univ, 1987-88; Pvte Practice, 1985-90; Dir of Grad Study in Counselling, Asst Prof of Counselling, Oklahoma City Univ, 1988-. *Memberships:* Am and Oklahoma Assns for Coun and Devel; Oklahoma Mental Hlth Counsellors Assn; Oklahoma Assn for Counsellor Ed and Supervision; Assn for Multicultural Counselling and Devel; The Planetary Soc. *Honours:* Alpha Chi, 1980; Post Secondary Counsellor of the Year, Oklahoma, 1991. *Hobbies:* Space studies; The Physical Universe; Pocket billiards; Astronomy. *Address:* Oklahoma, USA. 7.

FARMER Norman Kittrell Jr, b. 24 Aug 1934, San Antonio, Texas, USA. University Professor. m. Cora Jane Barratt, 4 Jan 1959, 2 s, 1 d. *Education:* BA, Principia Col, 1955; MA, Trinity Univ, 1960; PhD, Univ of Pennsylvania, 1966. *Appointments:* US Air Force, 1956-59; Tchr, Texas Milit Inst, 1959-60; Univ of Texas at Austin, 1964-; Conslt, Ctr for Intl leadership, Wash DC, 1989-; Dir, The Humanities Prof, Univ of Texas, 1991-. *Publications:* Numerous articles on Renaissance Lit and culture, art and literature; Book, Poets and the Visual Arts in Renaissance England, 1984; Ed, The Worthy Tract a Paulus Iovius, 1976. *Memberships:* Renaissance Soc of Am. *Honours:* The Jean Holloway Awd for Excellence in Tchg, 1984; Grad Sch Awd for Tchg Excellence, 1988; Am Coun of Learned Soc Awd, 1989; Folger Shakespeare Lit Fellowship, 1966. *Hobbies:*

Tennis; Gardening; Cooking; Hunting. *Address:* 3220 Clearview Drive, Austin, TX 78703, USA. 7, 15.

FARNEL Frank Jacques, b. 12 Mar 1962, Boulogne, France. Director of Corporate Affairs. m. Laurence Gutenmacher, 24 Mar 1991. *Education:* Dipl of Law, Univ of Paris, 1983; Lic es Info et Communication, French Inst of Press, 1984; MS Foreign Ser, Georgetown Univ, Wash, 1988; Cert Exec Prog in Intl Bus Dipl, Georgetown Univ, 1991. *Appointments:* Asst Chef de Pub, Havas Deutsu Marsteller, Paris, 1985; Fin Analyst, Banque de l'Union Maritime et Financien, Paris, 1987; Res Dir, The Nat Ctr for Pub Policy Res, Wash DC, 1986; Charge de Mission, Def and Foreign Affairs Comm, Assemblee Nat, Paris, 1988; Corp Affairs Mgr, Switz, 1989, Mgr, Corp Affairs, Paris, 1991-, Philip Morris. *Publications:* Vers une nouvelle donne de Conduito de l'administration Reaga- Evenements et Perspectives, 1987; Chronology US/Nicaragua: 1977-87, 1992. *Memberships:* Sec Gen, Goun for Europe, 1985; Pres, Assn Jeunes Repubs, 1985; Pres, Assn Devel de la Communication, 1985; Pres, Inst Francais des Relations Intl Union des Sennes Responsables Econmiques, 1982-84; Georgetown ALumni, 1988; Foreign Affairs Coun, 1988. *Honours:* Hon Ambassador at Large, Repub of Poland in Exile, 1985. *Hobbies:* Sports; Reading. *Address:* 62 Rue du Rocher, 75008 Paris, France. 52.

FAROOQI Najeeb Mohammad, b. 22 June 1970, Rawalpindi. Student. *Education:* BA, 1989; BCom, 1990; Currently undertaking MBA in Mgmt Info Sys. *Creative works:* Composer of music as a hobby. *Memberships:* Bus Admin Students Coun; VP, Pioneers Youth Org; Gen Sec, Youth Power Youth Org. *Honours:* Capt Hockey Team, 1991; VP, Cricket Team, 1986-88, 1991; Gen Sec, Inventor's Club and Computer CLub, 1986-88; Runner up in Squash Torunament, 1986-88; Bowling Champion of Col, 1989. *Hobbies:* Cricket; Squash; Music; Snooker; Bowling; Hockey; Reading. *Address:* Bait-a;, Naeem, Hill ROad F-6/3, Islamabad, Pakistan.

FAROOQI Sakhi Qabool Muhammad IV, b. 19 July 1962, Daraza Sharif. Sufi Spiritual Master of the Holy Shrine of Saint Poet Hazrat Sachal Sarmast of Shah Daraza. m. Bibi Afshan Sultana, 20 Dec 1985, 1 s, 2 d. *Education:* BA Sociol & Eng Lit, 1987; MA Polit Sci, 1980; LLB 1990; Alim-Fazil 1990; Hon Deg of Shahadatal al Mia, equiv of MRelig, 1991. *Publications:* Eternal path of peace and love; Numerous essays and lectures on inward and outward human life and divine light. *Memberships:* Life Pres, Hazrat Sachal Sarmast Charity Trust London; Fdr and Chief Patron, Hazrat Sachal Sarmast Acad and Cultural Foun; Res Ctr of Shah Abdul Latif Univm KHP; Sindh Grad Assn. *Honours:* Meritorius Awe, 1983; Sporst Awd, 1987; Cultural Awd, 1989; Lit awd, 1989; Cert of Merit, 1990. *Hobbies:* Practice and research of religion and social service; Sport. *Address:* Sakhi Q M Sajjada-Nashin, Dargah Hazrat Sachal Sarmast, via Rani Pur PO Daraza Districe, KHP Mir'S, Sindh Pakistan.

FARR Richare Peter, b. 8 July 1954, Weston, England. Chartered Surveyor. m. 12 May 1979. *Education:* Bedford Sch, 1967-72; Ecole de Commerce Neuchatel, 1973; Univ of Bristol, 1973-74; BSc Est Mgmt, Univ of Reading, 1974-77. *Appointments:* Negotiator, Knight Frank & Rutley, 1977-80; Sr Surveyor, Richard Ellis, 1980-83; Assoc Dir, Greycoat Plc, 1983- 88; CEO, New Cavendish Est Plc, 1988-90; CEO, Park Square Devs, 1990-. *Memberships:* Assoc, RICS; Chm, UK Corp Team, The Hunger Proj. *Hobbies:* Snow skiing; Vintage Bentleys. *Address:* Park Square Developments Ltd, 41 Bedford Square, London, England.

FARRAR Austin Packard, b. 21 Feb 1913, Felixstowe, England. Consultant Naval Architect. *Education:* Imperial Ser Col, Windsor, 1925-30. *Appointments:* Maring Engrg Apprenticeship, Philip & Sons Ltd, Dartmoutj, 1930-36; Design Ofc, J S White Ltd, 1936; Yacht Des, Robert Clark, London, 1937-39; Tech Mgr, Sussex Yacht Works Ltd, Shorham, 1939-41; Dept of

Torpedos and Mining, Admiralty Tech Ofr, 1941-46; MD, Wolverstone Shipyard Ltd, 1946-54; Seahorse Sails, later Austin Farrar Sailmakers Ltd, 1954-82. *Memberships:* Fellow, RINA, Co-Chm, Small Craft Gp; Soc for Nautical Res, Hon VP, Res and Tech Com; Amateur Yacht Res Soc, VP; Royal Yachting Assn, Life Mem; Intl Yacht Raching Union, Tech Conslt. *Honours:* RINA Small Craft Gp Medal, 1988; IYRU Silver Medal,1990. *Hobbies:* Sailing; Developing rigs and sails for racing yachts; Designing and producing medals. *Address:* Orchard House, Stutton, Ipswich, Suffok IP9 2RY, England.

FARRER (John) Philip (William), b. 12 Mar 1958, Haslemere, England. Stockbroker. m. Maria Jane Margaret Bowlby, 19 July 1986, 3d. *Education:* Stone House, Broadstairs, 1966-69; Westbourne Hse, Chichester, 1969-71; Eton Co,, 1971-76; Sandhurst, 1978. *Appointments:* Lt, 2nd Battalion Coldstream Guards, 1978-82; Grievson Grant & Co, 1982- 84; UBS Phillips and Drew, 1985; SBC Stockbroking, 1986-89; Merrill Lynch Intl Ltd, 1989-. *Memberships:* Telford Pk Lawn Tennis CLub; Liphook Golf Club. *Hobbies:* Golf; Tennis; Skiing; Gardening. *Address:* 25 Killieser Avenue, London SW2 4NX, England.

FARTHING Stephen Frederick Godfrey, b. 16 Sept 1950, London, England. Artist. m. Joni Farthing nee Jackson, 5 July 1975, 1 d. *Education:* BA Hons, St Martins Sch of Art, 1969-73; MA RCA, RCA, 1973-75; Anney Scholar, Brit Sch at Rome, 1975-76. *Appointments:* Tutor, RCA, 1979-85; Hd of Painting, Col of Art, 1985-90; Ruski Master, Oxford Univ, 1990. *Creative works include:* Selected one-man exhibs: Edward Totah Gal, London, 1986, 1987, New Ashgate Gal, Farnham, 1987; Mus of Modern Art Oxford, 1988; Queen Elizabeth Hall, London, 1989; Paco Imperial Rio de Janeiro Nat Mus of Art, Museo de Monterray Mexico, 1990; Museo de Gil Mexico, 1990; Selected exhibs include: Advent Calendar Gal, N.Lancs, 1989-90; Haywood Gal, London, 1990; RA Sumemr Exhib, 1990; Heritage Exhib Cornerhouse, Manchester, 1990; Collections at Leics City Mus, Nat Mus of Wales, Bradford Art Gals and Mus, Govt Art Collection Fund, Granada; Edmund Hall, Oxford. *Memberships:* Fellow, St Edmund Hall, Oxford. *Hobbies:* Photography; Travel. *Address:* Ruskin School of Drawing, 74 High Street, Oxford OX1 4BG, England.

FARUQI Shamsur Rahman Faruqi, b. 15 Jan 1936, India. Chief Postmaster General, Lucknow, India. m. 26 Dec 1955, 2 s, 2 d. *Education:* MA Eng, Allahabad Univ, 1955. *Appointments:* Lectr, Eng Lit, 1955- 58; Managerial Positions in Indian Post Ofc, 1958-77; Dir, Postal Res and Planning, Posts and Telegraphs Bd (P&TB), New Delhi, 1977-80; Dir, Bureau for the Promotion of Urdu, Min of Educ, 1980-81; Dpty Dir Gen, Postal Materials Mgmt and Mechanization, P&TB, 1981-83; Jt Sec, Dept of Nonconventional Energy Sources, Govt of India, 1983-87; Postmaster Gen, Bihar, Patna, 1987-89; Dpty Dir Gen, Dept of Posts, 1989-90; Chief Postmaster Gen, UP, Lucknow, 1990-. *Publications:* Fdr and Ed of Shabkhoon (Allahabad), Urdu lit jour, 1966- ; Works in literary criticism, translations, edited volumes and poetry. *Honours:* Nat Coun of Letters Awd in Urdu, 1986; Delhi Urdu Acad Awd, 1985; 3 Uttar Pradesh Urdu Acad Awds; Hon Citizen of the City of Baltimore, MD, USA; Fakhruddin Ali Ahmad Ghalib Awd 1987. *Hobbies:* Reading thrillers; Reciting and listening to poetry; Indian Classical music; Observation and conservation of wild life; Raising and keeping pets. *Address:* Chief Postmaster General UP Circle, Lucknow 226001, India. 93, 52.

FATHAUER Theodore Frederick, b. 5 June 1946, Oak Park, Illinois, USA. Meteorologist in Charge. m. Mary Ann Neesan, 8 Aug 1981. *Education:* BA Geophys Sci, Univ of Chicago, 1968. *Appointments:* Res Aide, USDA N.Dev Labs, Peoria, 1966; Cloud Phys Lab, Univ of Chicago, 1967; Meteorol, Nat Meteorol Ctr, 1968-70; Nat Weather Ser (NWS)Alaska Reg, 1970-; Instr, Univ

of Alaska, 1975-76. *Publications:* Several presented papers and articles on arctic meteorology and oceanography, hydrology and oceanography in professional journals and magazines. *Memberships:* AMA, Sec/Treas, Fairbanks Chap, 1975-76; Chm, Anchorage Chap, 1977-78, Sec 1981-82, VP, 1984-86, Sec/Treas, 89-, Fairbanks Chap; AGU; AAAS; Royal Meteorol Soc; The Oceanography Soc; W.Snow Conference Bd of Dirs, Fairbanks Concert Assn. *Honours:* 6 Outstanding performance Awds, NWS; Fed Employee of the Yr, Anchorage, 1978; NWS EEO Awd, 1976-81; NOAA Unit Citations, 1972, 1988; Am Meteorol Soc TV Seal of Approval, 1978; Cert Conslt Meterol, 1979. *Hobbies:* American Literature; Classical music; Downhill skiing; Canoeing. *Address:* National Weather Service Forecast Office, 101 12th Avenue Box 21, Fairbanks, AK 99701, USA. 9, 52, 139.

FATTAH Ezzat A, b. 1 Jan 1929, Assiout, Egypt. University Professor. m. Jenny Sloveig Fattah, 31 Dec 1971, 1 s, 1 d. *Education:* LLL, Univ of Cairo, 1948; MA magna cum laude, 1965, PD, 1968, Univ of Montreal, Can. *Appointments:* Prof, Sch of Criminol, Simon Fraser Univ, Vancouver, 1974-; Fdr and Chm, Dept of Criminol, SFR, 1974-78; Asst and Assoc Prof, Sch of Criminol, Univ of Montreal, 1968-74; Prosecutor, several cities including Cairo, Egypt, 1949-61. *Publications:* co-author and Ed of 10 books including: Understanding Criminal Victimization, 1991; From Crime Policy to Victim Policy; 100 scholarly papers published in ten languages. *Memberships:* FRC, Can; Bd, Intl Soc of Criminol, Paris; Am Soc of Criminol; Can Assoc of Crim Justice. *Honours:* Beccaria Prize, Quebec Soc of Criminol, 1969; Presidential Citation, ASC, 1975; Alex Edmison Awd, Can Assn of Profl Criminols, 1977. *Hobbies:* Swimming; Fishing; Tennis; Classical music; Opera. *Address:* School of Criminology, Somon Fraser University, Vancouver, Canada V5A 1S6. 142.

FAULKNER Douglas, b. 29 Dec 1929, Gibraltar. University Professor. m. Isobal parker Campbell, 11 Aug 1987, 3 d. *Education:* Cert, Royal Corps of Naval Construction, (RCNC), 1954; BSc Hons, Glasgow, 1973; PhD, Shipstrength, MIT, 1976. *Appointments:* Asst Constr, Prod Engr, 1954-59; Constr, Asst Prof, RNC, Struc Advr, Constr Cmdr, BNS, Wash, Defence Fellow, MIT, 1959-71; Chief Constr, Submarines, 1971-73; John ELder Prof and Hd of Dept of Naval Arch and Ocean Engrg, Univ of Glasgow, 1973-; Dean of Engrg, 1978-81; Conoco Vis Res Fellow, 1981-82; Vis Prof, VPI Blacksburg, 1986. *Creative works:* Structural design HM Submarine Dreadnaught, 1960-63; Chm, Conoco-ABS Tension Leg Platform Design Code. *Memberships:* VP, FRNIA; FIStructE; MSNAME: MIESS: FRSA: CEng; FEng. *Honours:* Various medals and prizes from RINA and IESS for published papers; Elected FRSA, 1983; Elected FEng, 1981. *Hobbies:* Hillwalking; Swimming; Music; Chess. *Address:* 57 Bellshaugh Place, Kirklee, Glasgow G12 OPF, Scotland. 1, 184.

FAULKNER Thomas L, b. 20 Aug 1952, Rochester, New York, USA. Author; Computer Operator. m. Debra L Dugan, 21 June 1975, 1 d. *Education:* Dipl, Gates Chili HS, 1971; Monroe Com Col, 1971-74. *Appointments:* Eastman Kodal Co, 1973-. *Publications:* Basic Bible Truths for Young People, 1988; A learning Testamony, 1991; Poem, We do not say goodbye, 1990. *Hobbies:* Genealogy of my family; Reading and studying the bible; Writing books on religion and showing the truth of God's gospel. *Address:* Leroy, New York, USA.

FAYARD Cecil Aden Jr, b. 7 Aug 1951, Biloxi, Mississippi, USA. Pastor; Minister; Conference Speaker. m. Myrtl Denise Bowen, 15 Sept 1973, 2 s, 3 d. *Education:* Mid-Continent Bible Col, KY, 1977; BS Theol, Beth Haren Col, KY, 1979; MA Theol, Kentucky Bible COI, 1986; DMin, Patriot Univ, Colorado Springs, 1990. *Appointments:* US Air Force, Korea, Vietnam, 1971-75; Min of Youth and Music, 1st Bapt Ch, Fredonia, KY, 1975; Pastor: Repton Bapt Ch, Marson, KY, 1976-77; New Horizon Bapt Ch, Ward, Arkansas, 1980-87, Ctl

Bapt Ch, Marion, KY, 1987-. *Publications:* Preachers Guide to First Peter, 1990; Preachers guide to Titus, 1990; Palm Tree Christians, 1987, tape; Numerous tape series collections. *Memberships:* Disabled Am Veterans; Bd of Dirs,River City Mission, Paducal, KY; Chaplain Sons of Confed Veterans, Mayfield, KY. *Honours:* Arkansas Cert of Merit, 1983; Cert of Appreciation, Sons of Confed Veterans, 1990, 1991; Letter of Commendation, 49th Tactical Fighter Wing; Hollomom AFB New Mexico, 1973. *Hobbies:* Book collecting; Classical music; Progressive jass; Southern Gospel Music. *Address:* Rt 2 Box 178, Marion, KY 42064, USA.

FEATHERSTON Charles Ronald, b. 30 Dec 1938, Doniphan, Missouri, USA. Vice-President of Engineering, Petroleum Engineering Consultants. m. (1) Alana Rogers, 9 June 1961, 2 d, (2) Joann Garrison, 4 Sept 1985. *Education:* BS, MO School Mines, Rollo, MO, 1961. *Appointments:* Field Engr, Div Drilling Engr, Texaco Inc, S LA, 1961-76; Served to Capt, US Army Cors Engrs, Germany, 1961-64; Ops Mgr, En Div, Houston Oil and Minerals Corp, Houston, TX, 1976-80; VP Engrng, Eaton Industries of Houston Inc, 1980-. *Publications:* Casing Designs Analysis System (co-author), 1976; Some Unique Deep Sea Drilling Problems of the National Science Foundation's Ocean Margin Drilling Program, conf paper, 1982; How A Joint Effort Helped One Operator (Mesa) Drill A Well Faster, 1985; Restoration of an Obandoned Gas Well for Geopressured-Geothermal Energy Extraction, Part 1 co- author), 1990. *Memberships:* Am Petroleum Inst, Advsr 1979-81, 1981-82; Soc Petroleum Engrs; Sigma Gamma Epsilon; Registered Profl Engr, TX. *Honours:* Army Commendation Medal, 1964. *Hobbies:* Hunting; Fishing; Diving; Photography; Computers. *Address:* 6210 Rutley Circle, Spring, TX 77379, USA. 2, 7.

FECHO Cecelia Anne Hodges, b. 12 May 1960, Washington, NC, USA. Industrial Engineer. m. Jeffry Allen Fecho, 1 June 1985, 1 s. *Education:* BS Indust Tech, E.Carolina Univ, 1987. *Appointments:* Engrg Intern, Robert Bosch Power Tool Corp, 1985-86; Engrg Tech, Support Intern, Burroughs Wellcome, 1986-87; Mfg Engr, Robert Bosch Power Tool, 1987-88; IE Ametek Lamb Elect Div, 1988-89; IE, GKN Auto, 1989-. *Memberships:* Inst Indust Instrs; NAFA; Episolon Pi Tau. *Honours:* One of the first five recipients of ECU, Burroughs Wellcome Fellowship. *Hobbies:* Fitness training; Gardening; Travel; Water sport; Stained glass. *Address:* 2322 Lavista Drive No 23, Burlington, NC 27215, USA. 7.

FEI Qi, b. 20 Feb 1938, Jiangsu, China. Professor of Geology. m. (1) 1 s, 1 d, (2) Ruan Tianjin, 4 May 1990. *Education:* Beijing Coll Geology, 1955-60; Univ Chgo, USA, 1981-83. *Appointments:* Geological Survey, Hebei, 1960-73; Beijing Coll Geology, 1973-81; Wuhan Coll Geology, 1981-87; China Univ Geoscis, Wuhan, 1987-91. *Publications:* Growth Faults and Hydrocarbon Accumulation, 1985; Structural Analysis in Petroleum Exploration, 1988; Surface Geochemical Exploration, 1991. *Memberships:* Active Mem, Am Assn Petroleum Geologists; China Geological Soc; China Petroleum Soc. *Honours:* 1st Nat Sci and Technology Conf Awards, 1978; Best Paper, Am Assn Petroleum Geologists Annual Conven, USA, 1983; Sci and Technology Achievement Awards, Min Geol and Mineral Resources, 1985, 1989, 1990, 1991 (2). *Hobby:* Stamp collecting. *Address:* China University of Geosciences, Wuhan 430074, China.

FELDBRUGGE Ferdinand Joseph Maria, b. 10 May 1933, The Hague, Netherlands. Professor of Law. m. Mary B Lawlor, 12 Sept 1959, 3 d. *Education:* MLaw, 1955; Dr Law, 1959; Netherlands Army Russian Lang School, 1956. *Appointments:* Staff, Fac Law, 1959-67; Prof, Law, 1967- 73, 1989-; Prof, Soviet Law, 1973-87, Univ Leiden, Leiden; Sovietologist-in- Residence, NATO HQ, 1987-89. *Publications:* Soviet Criminal Law, 1964; Samizdat and Political Dissent in the SU, 1975; Encyclopedia of Soviet Law, 1973, 1985. *Memberships:*

Pres, Dutch Assn Slavists; Exec Comm, Int Coun Soviet and E European Studies; Dutch Govt For Policy Advsry Coun. *Hobby:* Forestry. *Address:* Mariahof, Frans Baantje 22, 4881 MG Zundert, Netherlands. 34, 100.

FELDMAN NEBENZAHL Bernardo, b. 28 Sept 1955, Mexico City, Mexico. Music Composer. m. Judy Goldwater, 22 May 1983, 2 d. *Education:* Adv Music Studies, Conservatorio Nacional de Musica, 1978; BFA, 1983, MFA, 1985, CA Inst of the Arts, USA. *Appointments:* Directing Mgr, Ex-Machina Publs, USA, 1985-; Fac Mem, School of Music, CA Inst of the Arts, 1988-89; Hd, Music Dept, Coll of the Canyons, Santa Clarita, CA, USA, 1989-. *Creative works:* Compositions: In Red And Black, 1984; Manel Xochitl, Manel Cuicatl, 1985; Disolvencias en Cristal, 1986; Still Life, 1987; Oh, Cetecho, 1987; Onirica, 1988; Koliding-Scopes, 1989; Portraits of Friends and Relatives, 1990; Caudal de Poesia, 1991-92. *Memberships:* Am Music Ctr; Pacific Contemporary Music Ctr; Soc Electro-Acoustic Music, Pres Los Angeles Chapt 1987-90; ASCAP. *Honours:* Meet the Composer Inc, 1980, 1986; DAFCA Grant, 1985; Ahamanson Fndn, 1985; ASCAP Standard Award, 1989, 1990, 1991. *Hobbies:* Art films; Outdoor activities; Food. *Address:* College of the Canyons, Music Department, 26455 North Rockwell Canyon Road, Santa Clarita, CA 91355, USA.

FELMAN Marc David, Lt-Col, b. 19 June 1954, Biloxi, Mississippi, USA. US Air Force Pilot. m. 6 Feb 1978, div. 14 Sept 1987, 1 s. *Education:* BS, USAF Acad, 1976; MS, Systems Mgmt, Univ So CA, 1982; Student, Air Command and Staff Coll, 1990; Grad, 1st Class, School for Adv Airpower Studies, 1992; (ABO) DPA, Univ AL, 1992. *Appointments:* USAF incl: KC-135 Instr-Pilot, Kadena Air Base, Okinawa, Japan, 1978-82; Seymour Johnson AFB, Goldsboro, NC, 1983-85; KC-10 Evaluator/Flight Examiner (also NC), 1985-89; Fac, Air Command and Staff Coll, 1991; KLYO Asst Operations Off (NC), 1992-. *Memberships:* Daedalians; Air Force Assn; Phi Sigma Alpha. *Honours:* Mackay Trophy, Most Meritorious Flight of Yr, Air Force and Nat Aeronautics Assn, 1986; Kalberer Trophy, Outstanding Airmanship, Strategic Air Command, 1987; DFC, 1987; Air Force Flying Safely 'Well Done' Award, 1987; Jabara Award, Greatest Contbn to Aviation, USAF Acad, 1988; Promoted to Lt-Col 2 yrs ahead of Peer Grp. *Hobbies:* Music; Reading; Soccer; Golf. *Address:* 102 Powers Court, Goldsboro, NL 27534, USA. 7.

FENDALL Neville Rex Edwards, b. 9 July 1917, New Zealand. Emeritus Professor; International Health Consultant. m. Margaret Doreen Beynon, 11 July 1942. *Education:* BSc (hons), 1939, MRCS, LRCP, 1942, MB, BS, 1943, MD, DPH, 1952, Univ London; FFCM (now FFPHM 1989), London, 1972. *Appointments:* House positions, UK, 1942-44; H M Overseas Med Serv, Nigeria, Malaya, Singapore and Dir, Med Serv, Kenya, 1944-64; Rockefeller Fndn, NYC, USA, 1964-67; Population Coun Inc, NYC, 1967-71; Prof, Hd, Dept Int Community Hlth, 1971-82; Vis Prof, Pub Hlth, Boston Univ, 1983-. *Publications:* Auxiliaries in Health Care, 1972; Co-author, 2 books. *Contributions to :* Several books; Num published papers. *Memberships:* Brit Med Assn; Faculty Pub Hlth Med; Soc Pub Hlth; Royal C'wlth Soc; C'wlth Human Ecology Coun. *Honours:* Mem, WHO Panel of Experts, 1957-82; Cons, var int and nat orgs; Corres Mem, Soc Natural, Phys and Med Scis, Guatemala; Gold Medal, Migrendra Trust, Nepal. *Hobbies:* Public health; Travel; Gardening; Reading; Ecology. *Address:* Berwyn, North Close, Bromborough, Wirral L62 2BU, England. 1, 43.

FENECH Joseph Michael, b. 2 Apr 1931, Malta. Minister of Justice. m. Marlene Ellul, 1 May 1957, 2 s, 1 d. *Education:* Dipl legal Procurator, 1951, BA Hons Eng, 1952; Dipl Fine Arts, Univ of Perugia, Italy, 54; LLD, 1955, Univ of Malta. *Appointments:* Practiced law doing litigation and later specialised in conveyances and company law before becoming Parliamentary Sec and recently Min of Justice; Assisted Baristers in the London

Hg Courts and Arbitration Tribunals, (Lloyds). *Memberships:* Com, B'Kara FC, 1953; VP, Malta Football Assn, 1954-62; VP, Pres, Duke of Connaught Own Bank Club, 1955-; Casino Maltese and Union Club of Malta; Intl Bar Assn. *Hobbies:* Reading; Swimming; Sport. *Address:* Villa San Anton, Birkirkara Road, Attard B2N 02, Malta.

FENECH Raymond Mario Paul, b. 6 Jan 1958, St Julian's, Malta. Managing Director. m. Angela Azzopardi, 1987. *Education:* Dipl Jour and Profl Writing, CACC, UK, 1979; London Educ Cert in Jour, LEA, UK, 1982. *Appointments:* Freelance Reporter, Independence Press Ltd, 1978-79; Jour, The Times of Malta, 1980-85; Sales Exec, TNT Skypak Ltd, 1986-88; PRO-CSB Ltd, 1988-90. *Publications:* various articles, short stories and poetry in Malta, UK, Italy and USA, in magazines, newspapers and anthologies. With the Edges of Immortality, a book of peotry, 1992. *Memberships:* Freelance Press Sers, UK; Nat Authors Registry, USA: Intl Soc of Poets, USA; Lions Club, Malta; The Red Cross Soc of Malta; PRO of Lions Club, Malta, 1992. *Honours:* Hon Mention for poem, The City of Darkness; Best Poem of the 90's for The Silent City; Poet of Merit Awd, Intl Soc of Poets, USA: Leo Awd of Hon, Lions Intl, USA. *Hobbies:* Reading; Fishing; Clay pigeon shooting; Gardening. *Address:* No 2, Carmen Flats, C. Von Brockdorff Street, Msida, MSDO2, Malta G.C. 152.

FENG Litian, b. 3 Dec 1928, Tianjin, China. Professor of Economics of Population; Institute Director. m. Lin Yi, 28 Mar 1953, div. 1 Feb 1991, 1 s, 1 d. *Education:* Grad, Shanghai Acctng Coll, 1950; Planned Econs, Grad School, People's Univ China, 1951; Cert, Mid Career Trng Prog, Coll Pub Admin, Ctr Policy and Admin Dev, Univ Philippines, Manila, 1987. *Appointments:* Instr, Dept Planned Econs, People's Univ China, Beijing, 1951-62; Dir, Commercial Econs Div, Beijing Ind Mgmt Coll, 1962-72; Instr, For Lang Div, Beijing Ind Univ, 1972-74; Rschr, Population Studies Div, 1974-78, Assoc Prof, Dept Indl Econs, 1978-84, Prof, Dir, Inst Population Econs, 1984-, Beijing Coll Econs. *Publications:* About 2 dozen incl: A Preliminary Discussion about the Object of Comprehensive Balance in the National Economy, 1963; The Principles of Population (co-author), 1977; The Relationship between Planned Economy and Market Economy, 1982; Situation of China's Working Population, 1986; Population Control-the Historical Inevitability, 1991; Working Population, 1991; Feasibility Studies on Current Policy of Family Planning in China, 1991; Theory of Population Control and Its Practice (ed-in-chief), 1991. *Memberships:* Standing Coun, China Population Assn; Int Union Sci Study of Population; Profl Cons, Beijing Municipal People's Govt; Population Advsry Comm, State Family Planning Commn; Vice-Chmn: Beijing Population and Family Planning Assns. *Honours:* Adv Rschr Grade B, 1985, Excellent Paper, 1991, Beijing Coll Econs; Excellent Work Grade B, Planned Econs, Beijing Sci Commn, 1986; Adv Individual for Population Studies, Beijing Municipal Govt, 1991. *Hobbies:* Listening to classical and popular music; Watching football and basketball; Swimming. *Address:* Room 802-2, Building 28, Jintaili, Chaoyang District, Beijing 100026, China. 139, 190.

FENG Shizuo, b. 8 Mar 1937, Tianjin, China. Professor and Director, Institute of Physical Oceanography, Ocean University of Qingdao. m. Dalan Wang, 17 Jan 1966, 1 d. *Education:* Majored in Fluid Mech, Dept Engrng Mech and Maths, Qinghua (Tsinghua) Univ, Beijing, 1956-62. *Appointments:* Asst, 1962-78, Lectr, 1978-80, Assoc Prof, 1980-85, Dept Phys Oceanography and Marine Meteorology, Ocean Univ Qingdao; Prof, Dir, Inst Phys Oceanography, Ocean Univ Qingdao, 1985-. *Publications include:* A 3-D Nonlinear Model (NM) of Tides, 1977; An Introduction to Storm Surges, 1982; On the f- and beta-coordinates, 1982; Tide-induced Lagrangian Residual Current (LRC) and Residual Transport (RT)m I and II, 1986; A 3-D Weakly Nonlinear Model of Lagrangian Residual Current and Residual Transport, 1987; On the Fundamental Dynamics of Barotropic Circulation in Shallow Seas, 1990;

Computational Physical Oceanography, 1992. *Memberships:* Sci and Technology Comm, State Educ Commn China; Sci and Technology Comm, SOA; China Nat Comm, IAPSO; China Nat Comm, SCOR; China Nat Comm, WOCE; Standing Comm, Chinese Soc Oceanology and Limnlogy; Vice-Chmn, China Union of Storm Surge and Tsunami; Chmn, China Soc Computational Marine Phys. *Honours:* China Nat Prize, 1st Class, Best Sci Monograph, 1983; China 2nd Nat Natural Sci Prize, 3rd Class, Shallow Water Storm Surge Dynamics and Prediction, 1982; China 4th Nat Natural Sci Prize, 3rd Class, On LRC and LT - A 3d Weakly Nonlinear Theory, 1989. *Hobbies:* Reading; Enjoying music; Walking and musing; Travel. *Address:* Institute of Physical Oceanography, Ocean University of Qingdao, 5 Yushan Rd, Qingdao 266003, Shandong Province, China. 139.

FENG Shunshan, b. 18 Aug 1952, Shanghai, China. Professor; Vice-Chairman of Mechanics and Engineering Department. m. Xu Yun July 1980, 1 s. *Education:* Grad, Beijing Inst Technology; BSc, 1976; MSc, 1982. *Appointments:* Asst Instr, 1976-80, Instr, Dir, Lab 811, 1982-87, Assoc Prof, 1987-89, Prof, Vice-Chmn, Mech and Engrng Dept, 1990, Beijing Inst Technology. *Publications:* 24 papers, int confs and int and domestic jnls incl: A Study of Interrelated Effect of Blast and Fragments on Aircraft, 1986; Optimum Design for Antiaircraft Missile Warhead, 1989. *Memberships:* China Ordnance Soc; China Calamity Prevention Soc. *Honours:* State Sci and Technological Progress Awards, 1 State level, 1985, 1 Min level and 3 Beijing Inst Technology level, 1987-90; Outstanding Sci and Technological Worker, Colls and Univs in China, China State Educ Commn and State Coun Degree Commn, 1990. *Hobbies:* Music appreciation; Travel; Furniture design. *Address:* Mechanics and Engineering Department, Beijing Institute of Technology, No 7 Baishiqiao Road, Beijing, China.

FENG Xin Wei, b. 9 Feb 1923, Shanghai, China Teacher; Researcher. m. Jian Qing Lin, 23 May 1954, 1 s. *Education:* Div Premed Scis, Soochow Univ, 1941-42; German Med Acad, Shanghai, 1942; Nat Jiang Su Med Coll, 1943-45; Grad, Dipl, MB, Med Coll, Nat Tongj Univ, 1949. *Appointments:* Physn, 1949-55; Tchr, Rschr, Tong Ji Med Univ, 1956-, currently Prof; Vis Scholar, Inst Immunology, Univ Heidelberg, FGR, 1981-82. *Publications:* Textbook of Pathophysiology (chief ed) 1st ed, 1979, 2nd ed, 1985, 3rd ed, 1991 Pathophysiology, vol of Chinese Med Encyclopedia (dpty chief ed), 1985. *Memberships:* Disciplinary Appraisa Grp, Acad Degree Comm, State Coun; Coun Mem Chinese Soc Pathophysiology; Former Coun Mem Chinese Soc Physiological Scis; Former Chmn, Hor Chmn, Soc Pathophysiology Wuhan City and Hube Province. *Honours:* 1st Class Prize, Achievements in Sc and Technology, Study on Hypokalemic Flabbiness Disease, Min Hlth and People's Govt Hubei Province 1984; 2nd Class State Prize, Improvement of Sci and Technology, Investigation of Raw Cotton Seed O Poisoning, 1985. *Hobbies:* Classical music of the Western world; Poetry, novels and literature of ancien and mediaeval China, and mediaeval Europe; Beijin Opera; Chinese calligraphy; Painting. *Address* Department of Pathophysiology, Tong Ji Medica University, 13 Hangkong Road, Wuhan 430030, Hube Province, China. 139, 152, 162, 190.

FENG Zhi-Jun, b. 22 Apr 1937, Beijing, China Specialist in Policy Studies, Planning of Strategy an Science of Sciences. m. Dong Li-hui, 23 Dec 1963, s. *Education:* Grad, Dept Archtl Engrng, Shanghai Ins Railway Technology, 1962. *Appointments:* Lectr, Asso Prof, 1962-84, Dir,1981-84, Rsch Unit Mgmt Sic Shanghai Inst Railway Technology; Dpty Dir, 1984-86 Dir, Prof, 1986-, Shanghai Inst Sci of Scis; VP, Ctl Comm China Democratic League, 1986-; Mem, Standin Comm, Nat People's Congress, 1988-. *Publications* Foundation of the Science of Sciences, 1983 Foundation of Leadership Science, 1983; Moder Thinking Tank, 1984; The Science of Sciences an

Modernization, 1985; Pillar of Modern Civilization Society, 1986; A New Outlook on Soft Science, 1987; Modern Leadership jnl (ed-in-chief), 1986-. *Memberships:* China Acad Mgmt Sci, VP 1987-; Chinese Assn Sci of Scis and Sci and Technology Policy, VP 1988-. *Honours:* 1st Class Prize, Shanghai Sci and Technology Progress, 1988; Hon Prize, for book Meeting the New Revolution of Science and Technology, 1988. *Hobbies:* Chinese and Western music; Peking Opera. *Address:* No 1, Dong Chang Bei Xian, Wang Fu Da Jie, Beijing 100006, China.

FENG Zhong Yan, b. 9 Sept 1930, Tianjin City, China. Professor of Geology. m. Zhang Mu Ju, 25 Mar 1954, 1 d. *Education:* BA, 1952, MA, 1961, Dept Geology, Peking Univ. *Appointments:* Geologist, Geological Min, 1953-56; Lectr, 1960-79, Assoc Prof, 1979-85, Full Prof, 1985-, Peking Univ. *Publications:* The principles of mineral deposits, 1984; The Genesis and Metallogeny of Skarn in Northern Taihang Mountains, China, 1987; The Genesis of iron skarn deposits in Southern Taihang Mountains, China, 1990. *Memberships:* Chinese Soc Mineralogy, Petrology and Geochem; Geological Soc China; Ed Comm, Acta Geologica Sinica; Ed Comm, Geological Review. *Hobbies:* Kino; Reading old Chinese novels; Travel. *Address:* Department of Geology, Peking University, Beijing 100871, China. 190.

FENLEY Joe B, b. 20 Oct 1948, Springfield, Missouri, USA. Educator; Associate Professor of Honours Interdisciplinary Studies. m. Pamela Sue Madole, 11 Sept 1971, 1 s. *Education:* BA, Philos, SW MO State Univ, 1973; MA, Lit, 1976, MA, Hist, 1979, Ctl MO State Univ; MDiv cum laude, Theology, Midwn Theological Sem, 1977; PhD, Philos, Lit, Emory Univ, 1990. *Appointments:* Tchg, Ctl MO State Univ, 1976-80; Pt-time tchg, Emory Univ, 1981-83; Assoc Prof, Hons Interdisciplinary Studies, St Petersburg Jr Coll, Clearwater, FL, 1983-; Speaker, community and profl orgs. *Publications:* Reflections - A History of St Petersburg Junior College; Acad articles. *Memberships:* Am Philosl Assn; So Humanities Coun, Vice-Chmn, Chmn, Immediate Past Chmn; FL Philosl Assn; Rep, FL Hons Coun; N Am Nietzche Soc; Int Platform Assn; Historian, OV-1 Mohawk Assoc, 1991-. *Honours:* Emory Univ Scholarships; Presby Educl Scholarship; Sigma Tau Delta; Phi Theta Kappa; Hon Col, ROTC Progs, 1979. *Hobbies:* Private pilot, airplane; Travel; Military history esp Vietnam War; Parachuting. *Address:* 3266 Centerwood Drive, Tarpon Springs, FL 34689, USA. 7, 15.

FENNER Gary Eugene, b. 30 Mar 1954, Wilmington, Ohio, USA. Minister of Religion. m. Deborah Lynn Bream, 13 May 1978, 2 s, 1 d. *Education:* HS Dip, Wilmington, OH, 1972; BA, Cinn Bible Coll, 1977; MA, Cinn Christian Sem, 1979. *Appointments:* Min, Bethany Christian Ch, Foster, KY, 1978-79; Assoc Min, 1979-80; Sr Min, 1980-86; Fairmount Christian Ch, Richmond, VA; Fndg Min, Calvary Christian Ch, Sellersburg, IN, 1986-. *Publications:* Articles in Restoration Herald, The Christian Standard, Leadership 100. *Memberships:* Nat Forensic League, 1971; Jr Rotarian, Rotary Inc, 1972; Tidewater Christian Serv Camp, Dir, Trustee, Chmn, Dean, 1979-86; Richmond Community Easter Sunrise Servs, Chmn 1984-86; Sellersburg Ministerial Assn, 1986-. *Hobbies:* Sports esp softball, basketball, fishing. *Address:* Calvary Christian Church, 605 Norman Drive, Sellersburg, IN 47172, USA. 46, 117, 145.

FERDOUS Murshida, b. 1 July 1970, Bagerhat, Bangladesh. Student. *Education:* HSC Humanities; SSC Humanities; Currently on BA Hons Psychol course at Rajshahi University. *Publications:* Articles in monthly magazines and journals at school, college and university. *Memberships:* Bangladesh youth Red Crescent Soc; Bangladesh Psycho Soc. *Honours:* Jr Scholarship; Educ Bd; Merit Scholarship, DPI Bangladesh; Best TV Debator, Taposhi Rabeya Hall 1990. *Hobbies:* Collecting rare stamps; Gardening;

Modern music. *Address:* Dept of Psychology, Rajshahi Univ, Rajshahi 6205, Bangladesh.

FERGUSON Constance Marie Dowling, b. 20 May 1954, Bamberg, SC, USA. Instr. m. Willie E Ferguson Sr, 8 Sept 1990, 2 stepsons, 3 stepdaughters. *Education:* BA magna cum laude, Benedict Coll, 1976; MA, Ohio State Univ, 1977. *Appointments:* Instr in Eng and Reading, Voorhees Coll, Denmark, 1977-85; Instr in Eng, Speech and Reading, Denmark Tech Coll, Denmark, 1985-. *Memberships:* Worthy Matron, Bethlehem Chapt No 50, Order of Eastern Star, Bamberg; Dist Dep, Williams Grand Chapt, State of SC Order of Eastern Star; Pres, AAUW; ecy, Williams Grand Lodge & Chapt Scholarship Fund; Treas, Bethlehem Bapt Assn Women's Aux; Asst Secy, Bethlehem Bapt Sunday Sch & BTU Conven; Fac Coun, Rep from the Div of Arts & Scis, Denmark Tech Coll, Denmark. *Honour:* Edr of Yr, Denmark Tech Coll, Denmark, 1986. *Hobbies:* Reading; Writing; Cooking. *Address:* Rt 2, Box 42, Bamberg, SC 29003, USA.

FERGUSON Edward Trevor, b. 23 May 1933, Utica, NY, USA. Dir of Pers; Univ Prof. m. Dorothy Croce, 13 May 1956, 1 s. *Education:* BS 1956, MS 1962, SUNY; PhD, Michigan State Univ, 1967. *Appointments:* Ohio State Univ, 1968-73; Univ of Maryland, 1975-86; Collier Co Sheriff's Ofc, 1989-. *Publications:* Problems & Projects in Retailing, 5th ed 1968, 6th ed 1974, 7th ed 1980. *Memberships:* Soc of Human Mgmt; Pers Testing Coun of S FL; Am Soc for Trng & Dev; Pers Assn of Collier Co. *Honours:* Rsch Fellow: Fulbright-Hays, Coun for Int Exc of Scholars, Germany, 1973. *Hobbies:* Fishing; Scuba diving;.Woodworking. *Address:* Collier County Sheriff's Office, 3301 Tamian's Trail E, Building J, Naples, FL 33962, USA.

FERGUSON Frederick Drummond, b. 28 July 1949, Ottawa, Canada. Chm, CEO Inventor-Designer. 1 d. *Education:* Applied Photo & Design, Sheridan Coll, Ontario, 1971. *Appointments:* VP, Interact Communications, 1971; Pres, APH Ltd, 1972-77; Pres, DJP Cartography, 1976-77; Pres, Moqnus Aerospace, 1978-88; Chmn, Nord-Am Corp, 1989-. *Creative works:* Invented and Patented: Magnus Rotating Sphere Airship; LEAP Airship; Van Dusen Solar Concentrator; HAPP, high altitude aircraft; Papers incl: The Mars air surveillance vehicle. *Memberships:* SD1 Sole Source Prime Contractor, USAF; Past Dir, Aerospace Industries Assn of Can, 1983-88; Past Chmn, Can Civil Airworthiness Coms, 1984-88. *Honours:* Can Awd of Excellence for Invention, 1984; Awd of Merit, Aerospace Industries Assn of Can, 1988; Cert of Hon, Am Inst of Aeronautics and Astronautics, 1990; Awd of Merit for Mars Outreach Proj - Mars vehicle. *Hobbies:* Photography; Video; Art collecting; Flying; Sports; Helicopter pilot. *Address:* PO Box 599, Stn B, Ottawa, Ontario, Canada K1P 5P7.

FERGUSON Helen Mott, b. 2 Mar 1941, Sparta, TN, USA. Admnstv Asst. m. John Bainbridge Ferguson Jr, 16 Apr 1966, 1 d. *Education:* Mississippi State Univ, 1960-62. *Appointments:* Engrng Aide, Tennessee Valley Auth, Chattanooga, 1962-66; Tax Examr, Internal Revenue Ser, Atlanta, 1967-69; Acct, Sandpiper Enterprises, Inc, Greenville, 1979-88; Admnstv Asst-Fin, Palmetto Int Exposition Ctr, Greenville, 1988-. *Memberships include:* Bd of Dir 1976-79, Secy 1977, Am Cancer Soc; Bd of Dir 1983-86, Carolina Ballet Theatre; Treas 1985, Beautification Com 1985- 87, Hospitality Com 1986, Bd of Dir 1989-90, Social Com 1990, Stratton Pl Club; Greenville Women's Club, 1990- . *Honours:* The Ballew Awd, Greenville Jr Women's Club, 1976; The Ann Borris Mem State Cancer Awd, SC Fdn of Women's Clubs, 1978. *Hobbies:* Tennis; Bridge; Hiking; Bicycling; Gardening. *Address:* 12 Coventry Road, Greenville, SC 29615, USA.

FERGUSON John Hilton, b. 16 July 1946, Bernice, LA, USA. Profl Cnslr. m. Magdalen Bezenbach Ferguson, 8 Mar 1969, 1 s, 1 d. *Education:* BS 1969; MA 1972;

MA 1974; EdD 1980. *Appointments:* Dir, Margaret Roane Ctr, 1974-78; Owner, Pvt Profl Counselling Sers, 1974-; Ed Spec, State of LA Dept of Ed, 1980-86; Grp Facilitator & Therapist, Woodland Hills Hosp, 1988. *Publications:* Letter of Acommendation Outstanding Work (Co- author), 1981. *Memberships:* Adv Coun, I Care Prevention Against Drug & Alcohol, 1986-88; N LA Prevention Coalition Against Drug Abuse, 1986-88; Lincoln C of C, 1988-89; Pres 1989-90, Ruston Rotary Club. *Honour:* Outstg Awd to SAC,S, USAF, Barksdale Air Force Base, 1973. *Hobbies:* Working with computers; Tennis; Coin collecting; Photography. *Address:* 206 Reynolds Drive, Suite 33, Ruston, LA 71270, USA.

FERGUSON Roger, b. 23 Aug 1946, Nottingham, England. Conslt Physn & Gastroenterologist. m. Ruth Elizabeth Spencer, 12 Jan 1974. *Education:* MBChB 1965-69, MD 1977, Univ of Birmingham; MRCP 1972; FRCP 1987. *Appointments:* Hse Physn 1969, Med Registrar 1970-73, Worcester RI; Hse Surg 1970, Rsch Registrar 1973-75, Gen Hosp, Birmingham; Sr Med Registrar, Nottingham Gen Hosp & Derom Royal Infirmary, 1975-79; Conslt Physn & Gastroenterologist, Arrowe Park Hosp, Wirral, 1979-. *Publications:* Author of papers and books on Gastroenterological Subjs. *Memberships:* BMA; Coun, Liverpool Med Inst; Univ of Liverpool Postgrad Adv Panel Med. *Honour:* Arthur Foxwell Prize in Clin Med, Univ of Birmingham, 1969. *Hobbies:* Golf; Reading; Music; Oenology; Gardening. *Address:* 89 Bidston Road, Oxton, Birkenhead, Wirral L43 6TS, England.

FERGUSSON David Alexander Syme, b. 3 Aug 1956, Glasgow, Scotland. Prof of Systematic Theol. m. Margot Evelyn McIndoe, 5 Sept 1985, 1 s. *Education:* MA, First Class Hons, Glasgow Univ, 1973-77; BD, First Class Hons, Edinburgh Univ, 1977-80; DPhil, Merton Coll, Oxford, 1980-84. *Appointments:* Asst Min, St Nicholas Ch, Lanark, 1983-84; Assoc Min, St Mungo's Ch, Cumbernauld, 1984-86; Lectr in Systematic Theol, Edinburgh Univ, 1986-90. *Honours:* Denyer and Johnston Studentship, Oxford Univ, 1983; Jr Chap to Moderator of the Gen Assembly of the Ch of Scotland, 1989- 90. *Hobbies:* Soccer; Golf; Jogging. *Address:* Department of Theology & Church History, King's College, Old Aberdeen AB9 2UB, Scotland.

FERNANDO Tilak, b. 2 Apr 1945, Colombo, Sri Lanka. Rsch Asst. m. Padmi Bambarande, 6 Dec 1971, 2 d. *Education:* Tourism Mktng, Min of Transp, Japan, 1976; Tourism Mgmt, 1979; Dipl in Mgmt, 1989-90. *Appointments:* Staff Asst, Ceylon Tourist Bd, 1971-75; Mgmt Asst Mktng, 1976-86; Rsch Asst, Ceylon Tourist Bd, 1986-. *Publication:* 50 Do's & Don'ts - Keep Sri Lanka Tidy, 1974. *Memberships:* Overseas Assc, Inst of Pub Rels (UK); Pres, Envir Protection Soc of Sri Lanka; Gen Coun Mem, Projs Com Mem, Girl Guide Assn of Sri Lanka. *Hobbies:* Photograhy; Travelling; Reading. *Address:* 103 Hampden Lane, Colombo-6, Sri Lanka.

FERRAIOLI Armando, b. 19 Mar 1949, Foggia, Italy. Biomed Engr. m. Maria Teresa Kindjarsky-D'Amato, 30 Aug 1976, 3 d. *Education:* Dipl of Elec Engr, 1967; Dr of Elec Engrng, 1973; MSc of Bioengrng, 1974; PhD in Med Engrng, Univ of Southampton, 1981. *Appointments:* Reg Mgr, Soxil SpA, Bari, Italy 1979-83, Naples 1983-84; Fdr, AGA Biomedica Srl, Cava dei Tirreni, 1985-; Pvt Conslt in Biomed Engrng, 1985-. *Publications:* Author of about 50 scientific papers in various journs. *Memberships:* IEEE; BMES; AAMI, USA; IEE; BES, GB; Associazione Elettronica de Elettrotecnica Italiana; Associazione Italiana di Ingegneria Medica e Biologica; Centro Nazionale Edilizia e Tecnica Ospedaliera. *Honour:* Brit Coun Higher Ed Scholarship. *Address:* Corso Italia 232, 84013 Cava Dei Tirreni, Italy.

FERRELL Marion William, b. 17 July 1960, Morristown, TN, USA. Evangelist. m. Belinda Gordon, 16 May 1986. *Education:* AS, Walters State Com Coll, 1981; BA, Freed-Hardeman Univ, 1985; Harding Grad Sch of Relig, 1990-. *Appointments:* Computer Programmer/Operator, Reliance Elec Co, 1981-82; Charleston Ch of Christ, 1986-. *Membership:* Chap, Civil Air Patrol, 1990-. *Honour:* Outstg Young Men of Am, 1986. *Hobbies:* Reading; Hiking; Camping; Bicycling; Volleyball; American football. *Address:* 904 Shelby, Charleston, MO 63834, USA.

FERRIER Robert Patton, b. 4 Jan 1934, Dundee, Scotland. Prof of Natural Phil. m. Valerie Jane Duncan, 2 Sept 1961, 2 s, 1 d. *Education:* BSc, First Class Hons, 1956; PhD, 1959; MA (Cantab), 1963. *Appointments:* Scientific Ofcr, Aere Harwell, 1959-61; Res Assoc, MIT, Cambridge, 1961-62; Sr Asst in Rsch 1962-64, Asst Dir of Rsch 1964-70, Lectr in Physics 1970-73, Univ of Cambridge; Guest Scist, IBM, USA, 1972-73; Chair of Natural Phil, Univ of Glasgow, 1973-. *Publications:* Author of over 100 articles in scientific lit. *Memberships:* Fellow, Inst of Physics, 1966; FRSE, 1977. *Hobbies:* Reading crime novels; Tennis; DIY. *Address:* Glencoe, 31 Thorn Road, Bearsden G61 4RS, Scotland.

FERRIS John Charles, b. 26 Apr 1933, Temora, NSW, Australia. Edn & Psycho Cons; Writer; Tutor. m. Beverley Jean Boyd, 22 Dec 1956, 1 s, 1 d. *Education:* Grad as Tchr, Wagga Wagga Tchr's Coll, 1952; NSW Conserv Music, 1956-66; Macquarie Univ, 1979-81. *Appointments:* Tchr, Bathurst HS, 1953-; Lectr, Broadcaster, Various Tchng, NSW Dept of Ed, -75; Profl Concert, Opera, Oratorio Singer, 1956-90; Nat and Commercial Broadcaster, TV and Radio; Tutor, Ednl and Ed Psycho, Music, Applied Sci, 1960-. *Publications:* Teachers - Experts or Fakers and Quacks, 1989; Teaching Singing - An Applied Scientific Approach, 1989; The Acoustics of the Singing Voice, 1990; Neurovox - The Singing Teacher's Handbook of The Physiology of Voice, 1991. *Memberships:* Aust & NSW Tchrs' Fdns; AAAS; The Voice Fndn; Sr Cons, The Aust Coll of Applied Psycho. *Hobbies:* Electronics; Computer Science; Computer Music; All performing arts; Sailing. *Address:* 2 Greystone Road, Killarney Heights, NSW 2087, Australia.

FERSEN Alessandro, b. 5 Dec 1911, Lodz, Poland. Dir. m. Iona Noemi, 5 Sept 1938, 1 d. *Education:* PhD, Univ of Genoa, 1933; Cert, Coll de France, Paris, 1935. *Appointments:* Gen Sec, Liberation Nat Comm, Genoa, 1944-45; Dir in Theatrical and Opera Theatres, Genoa, Rome, Florence, Naples, Bolzano 1946-82; Fests Maggio Musicale Fiorentino, Spoleto Fest, Siracusa Classical Fest; Actor in many Italian Movies; Dir, Fersen Studio of Performing Arts, 1957-. *Creative works include:* Lea Lebovitz, 1947; The Merry Wives of Windsor, 1949; L'Avare, 1954; Golem, 1969; Oedipus Rex, 1972; Leviathan, 1974; Fuenteovejuna, 1975; Leonce und Lena, 1979; Dibbuk, 1982. *Publications:* The Univers as a game, 1936; The theater, after, 1980. *Honours:* Campione Fest for the Best Play in 1969; Mayor of Genoa for Philosl and Theatrical Activity. *Hobby:* Classical Music. *Address:* Via Garibaldi 88, 00153 Roma, Italy.

FERWERDA Hedzer Adam, b. 9 Oct 1933, Leeuwarden, Holland. Prof of Physics. m. Riek Van Leeuwen, 20 June 1957, 2 d. *Education:* Master's degree 1957, PhD 1964, Univ of Groningen. *Appointments:* Scientific Off 1957-64, Rsch Assoc 1965-66, Assoc Prof 1966-80, Prof 1980-, Univ of Groningen; Vis Fellow, Cornell Univ, 1964-65. *Publications:* Author of publs on inverse problems in Optics, scattering and propagation throughout random media. *Memberships:* Dutch Phys Soc; Chmn, Optics Sect, European Optics Soc; VP, Optics Soc Am. *Honour:* Stipend Netherland Org for the Advancement of Pure Rsch, 1964. *Hobbies:* Piano playing; Travelling. *Address:* Boterdijk 5, 9765 EA Paterswolde, The Netherlands.

FFOULKES David, b. 8 Dec 1950, N.Wales. Agricultural Research and Development Adviser; Ruminant Nutritionist. m. Theresia Sulistiarty, 9 Jan 1988, 2 d. *Education:* BSc Zoology, Liverpool Univ, 1969-73; MAgSci, Tropical Agric Devel, Reding Univ, 1976-77;

PhD, Univ of New England, Aust, 1981-84. *Appointments:* Asst Horti Res Ofr, Univ of Botswana, 1979-75; Student, FAD Livestock Prod Div, Min of Agric, Swaziland, 1976-77; Experiments Ofr, Ctr for Livestock Res with Sugarcane, Dominican Repub, 1978; Tech Advr, Livestock Devel Proj, St Lucia, W.I, 1979; Tutor, Vet Sch, Univ oof Yucatan Mexico, 1980; Res Scist, Proj for Animal Res and Devel, Indonesia, 1985-86; Sr Res Ofr, Res Coor, Dept of Primary Indust and Fisheries, Darwin, Aust, 1987-. *Publications:* Practical feeding systems for ruminants based on sugarcane and its by-products, 1986; Res and Development of nutrition strategies for Indonesian ruminant livestock, 1986; Improving the nutrition level of draught animals using available feeds, 1988; Dynamics of protozoa in the rumen of cattle, 1988; High Quality meat production from swamp buffaloes, 1992; Work and Environmental effects on the nutrition of draught animals, 1991. *Hobbies:* Gardening; Woodwork; Guitar. *Address:* Dept of Primary Industry and Fisheries, PO Box 79, Berriman, NT 0828, Australia.

FIECHTER Georges Andre, b. 12 Sept 1930, Alexandria, Egypt. Co Dir; Cons; Asset Mgr. m. Francoise Forest, 1955. *Education:* Dr es sc pol, Geneva; Licencie es sc pol, etudes internationales, Geneva; Sem for Sr IMEDE Exec, Annual Middle Mgmt Prog, IMEDE; Swiss Fed Inst of Tech, Zurich. *Appointments include:* Intl VP, Swiss Nat Union of Students, Zurich; VP, Swiss C of C & Ind, Sao Paulo; Mem of Govng Bd and Pres, Alumni Assn of Intl Sch of Geneva; Mem of Ed Bd, Annales d'Etudes Internationales, Geneva; Exec Sec, Intl Assn for Mass Communication Rsch, Swiss Sect; Ex Sec, Swiss Pol Sci Assn; Owner, Integrated Fiduciary Trust-Mgmt Servs, Geneva; Chmn, Atlanticomnium SA, Geneva; MKS Fin SA, Geneva; Europ Dir, Simonsen Assoc, Sao Paulo. *Publications:* Le Regimemmodernisateur du Bresil, 1964-72; Etude sur les interactions politico-economiques dans un regime militaire contemporain; UK ed Brazil since 1964, UK 1972; Modernisation under a Military Regime, 1975; Criteres d'evaluation des effets des investissements prives suisse on le development, 1971; Castelo Branco in Les Hommes d'Etat Celebres, 1977; Le Bresil bientot Grande Puissance in Relations Internationales, 1979; Various specialised papers. *Memberships:* Fellow, Inst of Dirs, London; FCIM; Mktng Communication Exec Intl, Geneva; Fdn Suisse des Journalistes, Geneva; Jockey Club, Sao Paulo; Golf Club, Geneva. *Honour:* Cmdr, Brazilian Nat Order of Rio Branco; OSJ. *Hobbies:* Golf; Historical research. *Address:* 49 Terrassière, 1207 Geneva, Switzerland.

FIECHTNER Urs M, b. 2 Nov 1955, Bonn, Germany. Author. *Publications:* 24 books including: Mario Rosas, 1986; Erwachen in der Neuen Welt, 1988; Notizen vor Tagesanbruch, 1990; Geschichten aus dem Niemandsland, 1990; Gesang fur America II, 1991; Im Auge des jaguars, 1991. *Memberships:* Anns of German Authors; Writers Collective. *Honours:* Peace Prize, AGV 1977; Buxtehuder Bulle, 1985; Bookwork Prizes, 1986, 1989, 1990; Thaddaus Troll Prize, 1991. *Address:* Wacholderweg 6, D-7907 Langenau Ho, Germany.

FIELDING Leslie Sir, b. 29 July 1932, London, England. Hon Pres, Univ Assn for Contemporary University Studies; Mbr, Cncl of Royal Geog Soc; UK, Japan 2000 Comm and Japan ET Assn Steering Comm. m. 5 Aug 1978, 1 s, 1 d. *Education:* 1st in Hist MA 1953- 56, Hon Fellow 1989-, Emmanuel Coll, Cambridge Univ; Sch of Oriental & African Studies, London Univ, 1956-57; Vis Fellow, St Antony's Coll, Oxford Univ, 1977-78. *Appointments:* Foreign Serv 1956-73, inclng: Teheran, Iran, 1957-60; Phnom Penh, Cambodia, 1964-66; Paris, France, 1967-70; Commn of European Communities, 1973-87 inclng: Brussels, Belgium, 1973-77; Hd of Delegation, Tokyo, Japan, 1978-82; Dir Gen for External Rels, Brussels, 1982- 87; Vice Chancellor, Univ of Sussex, England, 1987-92 (Hon LLD); UK Mem, High Coun, European Univ Inst, Florence, Italy, 1988-92; Mem of the Hse of Laity, Gen Synod, Ch of England, 1990-92. *Honours:* Kt Cmdr, Order of

St Michael & St George, UK, 1988; White Rose of Finland; Silver OM, Austria; Order of St Agatha of San Marino; FRSA; FRGS. *Address:* Sutton Court, Stanton Lacy, Ludlow, Shropshire, SY8 2AJ, England.

FIELDS James Edward Jr, b. 22 Sept 1963, Oklahoma City, OK, USA. Cartoonist; Evangelist. *Education:* Northeastern State Univ, 1981-89. *Appointments:* Various Freelance Art Jobs, 1981-91; Coll Dir, First Bapt Ch, Muskogee, 1982-85; Nursing Home Evangelist, Grand View Bapt Ch, Muskogee, 1989-91. *Creative works:* Muskogee HS Staff Cartoonist; Northeastern Staff Cartoonist; Short story in a Muskogee High Anthology; 2 Art Shows, Northeaster, 1988, 1989. *Memberships:* OK Repub Party; Nat Repub Comm; Ed Dir, VPres of Oklahomans for Life; Ostiogenisis-Imperfecta Fndn; Intl Platform Assn; VP 1991, Teens for Christ. *Honours:* Outstg Youth of the Yr, Muskogee Optimist Club, 1980; OK Hon Soc, Muskogee HS, 1981; Outstg Christian Teens for Christ, 1981. *Hobbies:* Painting/Art Critism; Writing short stories and essays; Reading Southern American Literature; Travelling. *Address:* 804 Grandview Road, Muskogee, OK 74403, USA.

FIGEN I Sevki, b. 26 Nov 1924, Istanbul, Turkey. Busman; Pres; Owner. m. (1)Evin Keseroglu, 29 June 1962, dec 1980, (2) Leyla Oksar, 7 Sept 1983, 1 s. *Education:* BS, Indiana Tech Coll, Ft Wayne, 1953; MS, Univ of Texas, Austin, 1955. *Appointments include:* Aviation Mgr 1963-65, Area Sales Mgr 1965-67, Mobil Oil Turk Co, Istanbul; Mktng Mgr 1967-69, Gen Mgr 1969-73, Mobil Gas Co, Istanbul; Trustee, Robert Coll of Istanbul, 1980-; Hon Mem, Local Exec Coun Am Collegiate Inst, Izmir, 1984-; Vice Chmn, Advsr 1986-89, Turyag Co, Izmir; Chmn Bd 1985-87, Turset Co, Izmir; Partner, Chm Bd 1987-, ERITENEL, Chem Tradg Co, Izmir; Partner, Chmn Bd 1990-, FEKOMQ Computer Ctr Ltd; Mem Bd 1990-, EGEFREN SAN TIC Co. *Memberships include:* Bd of Govs, Turkish-Am Assn, Izmir; Mem Bd 1988-, Cimentas ed and hlth foun, Izmir; Fdr, Bd Mem 1989-, Consumer protection union foun, Izmir; Past Pres, Izmir Rotary Club. *Honours:* Hon Awds: Izmir Press Assn; Gov of Izmir; Columnist, Yeni Asir Newspaper, 1985; Gunaydin Izmir Newspaper, 1989-. *Hobbies:* Classical music, Jazz and Flamenco guitar; Reading; Writing to newspapers; Discussions with Friends; Social work. *Address:* Ataturk Cad, Yeni Kordon Apt 328-8, Izmir 35220, Turkey.

FIJALKOWSKI Stanislaw, b. 4 Nov 1922, Zdolbunow, Poland. Painter; Printmaker; Professor. m. Waleria Walicka, 19 July 1951. *Education:* Dipl Graphic Arts, Acad of Fine Arts, Lodz, 1951. *Appointments:* Pedagogue, Acad of Fine Arts, 1949, Prof, 1975; Vis Prof, Giessen and Marburg, 1989-90. *Creative works:* More than 250 exhibitions in Poland an abroad including one-man shows; Works in collections in Nat Mus of Poland, Tate Gal, London, Tretiakowska Gal, Moscow, Kunsthallen Hamburg and Hannover; St Annen Mus, Luebeck; Mus des Jahrhunderts in Vienna, Nat Mus Prague, Mus in Skopje,and Zagreb, Mus in Lugano and McGraw Hill Collection, NY. *Memberships:* VP, Xylon Intl Soc of Wood Engravers, Switz; European Acad of Scis and Fine Arts, Salzburg; Pres, Polish Nat Xylon Section. *Honours:* Graphic Biennial Krakow, 1968, 1970; Bianco e Nero a Lugano, 1972; Graphic Biennial Frechen, 1978; Graphic Biennial Heidelberg, 1979; Intl Art Festival in Cagnes sur Mer, 1986; CK Norwid Prize, Warsaw, 1971; Cybis Prize, Warsaw, 1990. *Hobbies:* Super 8 film; Music. *Address:* Laurowa 2, 91486 Lodz, Poland. 1.

FIK Miroslaw, b. 8 Aug 1937, Turyczany, Volhynia. Prof of Food Tech. m. Anna Barbara Leszczynska, 24 Dec 1964, 2 d. *Education:* MSc, Agricl Univ Olsztyn, 1959-64; PhD 1971, DSc 1980, Agricl Univ Szczecin. *Appointments:* Asst, Asst Prof, Assoc Prof, Agricl Univ Szcecin; Hd of Refrigeration & Food Ind Engrng Dept 1982-, Dean of Food Tech Fac 1987-90, Prof 1989, Agricl Univ Cracow. *Publications:* Author of about 70 papers in scientific journs, 1 text-book for students, 8 patents and patent claims, 10 technological works for food ind. *Memberships:* Polish Soc of Nutritional Scis; Mem of Bd, Polish Food Technologists' Soc. *Honours:* Prize, 1st degree, Min of Sci & Ed, 1977; Golden Cross of Merit, 1987; Prize, 2nd degree, Ed Min, 1988. *Hobbies:* Gardening; Reading. *Address:* Golaska 15/47, 30-619 Krakow, Poland.

FILIOS Vassilios, b. 30 Jan 1952, Heraklion, Crete. Sector Mgr. m. Athanassia, 8 Jan 1983, 1 s, 1 d. *Education:* BBA, Econ Univ of Athens, 1975; MSocSc, Univ of Southampton, 1977; PhD, Univ of Birmingham, 1980. *Appointments:* Lectr on Acctng and Fin Mgmt, Univ of Birmingham, England, 1978-80; Res Assoc, London Grad Bus Sch, 1979-80; Com Mem, Greek Min of Econ Coordination, 1980-87; Hd of Dept of Studies & Org, Hellenic Breweries, Athens, 1982; Dep Dir, Internal Auditing and Controls Dept, Group of Cos J S Latsis, Athens, 1982-84; Group Exec in Fin Mgmt, S Michailides SA, Athens, 1984-86; Coord of Grad/ Post-experience Courses in Acctng and Fin Mgmt, Greek Productivity Ctr, 1984-86; Ass Prof of Acctng and Mgmt, Dept of Econ(s), Univ of Patra, Greece, 1985-92; Dir of Econ Studies Div, Greek Econ(s) Reconstruction Org, Athens, 1986; Mgr, Grp's Activities Supervision Sector, Commerical Bank of Greece, Athens, 1986-; Instr of Bank Mgmt & Acctng, Inst of Banking Studies, 1986- ; Greek Min of Nat Economy, 1987-89. *Publications:* Socioeconomic Accounting, 1984; Public Sector Accounting, Financial Management and Auditing, 1985; Management and Productivity, 1st ed 1987, 2nd ed 1991; Bank Accounting, 1989; Valuation and Inflation Accounting, 1989; Strategic Management, 1991; Group of Companies and the Consolidation of their Financial Statements, 1991; The Economics of Banking Enterprises, 1991. *Hobby:* Stamp collecting. *Address:* 6 Neofronos Street, Ilissia 161 21, Athens, Greece.

FINKEL Henry, b. 7 Nov 1910, London, England. Indl Designer. m. Rose Goldblatt, 28 Aug 1937, 1 s, 1 d. *Education:* Arch, McGill Univ, 1934; Indl Design Sem, Mass Inst of Tech, 1963; Sem, Art Inst, Boston, 1969. *Appointments:* Archt, David R Brown, 1928-31; Archt, Harold Dooran, 1936-38; War Parts Mfr, Conlin Engrng, 1941-46; Designer, Die Plast --- Plastics Molder, 1945- 47; Estab Ind Design Consultancy, 1947. *Creative works:* Articles and lectures on Indl Design; Lectures on Indl Design at: McGill Univ; Univ de Montreal; Univ de Quebec a Montreal; Univ of Manitoba. *Memberships:* Pres, Assn of Can Indl Designers; Past Mem Coun, Soc of Plastics Engrs; Assoc Chmn, Design Spec Interest Grp, SPE Mem 1991 Conven Comm; RCA; FRSA; Emeritus Mem, Assn des Designers Indl de Quebec. *Honours:* Prize Awd for Bus Shelter Design, 1965; Cit Awd, Design Can for Excellence, 1983; Man of the yr, Quebec Sect of Soc of Plastics Engrs, 1990. *Hobbies:* Photography; Theatre; Music; Writing; Travel. *Address:* 342 Elm Avenue, Westmount, Quebec, Canada H3Z 1Z5.

FINKELSTEIN Ludwik, b. 6 Dec 1929, Lwow, Poland. Univ Prof. m. Mirjam Emma Wiener, 1957, 2 s, 1 d. *Education:* BSc (Spec) Physics 1950, BSc (Gen) Pure Maths, Applied Maths and Physics 1951, MSc 1959, Univ of London; DSc, City Univ, 1988. *Appointments:* Scist, Instrument Br, Nat Coal Bd Mining Rsch Estab, 1952-59; Prof of Instru & Control Eng, Dean of Sch of Elect E Eng & Applied Physics, Hd of Dept of Physics, Hd of Dept of Systems Sci, Northampton Coll Ldn, City Univ, 1959-. *Publications:* The Mathematical Modelling of Metabolic and Endocrine Systems (with E Carson, C Cobelli); Mathematical Modelling of Dynamic Biological Systems (with E Carson); Author of Co-author of over 150 papers. *Memberships:* FEng; FIEE; CPhys; FInstP; Hon FInstMC; Pres, Instn of Measurement and Control; Chmn, Mgmt and Design Div, IEE. *Honours:* Sir Harold Hartley Medal, 1980; OBE 1990. *Hobbies:* Books; Conversation; Jewish studies. *Address:* City University, School of Engineering, Northampton Square, London EC1V 0HB, England.

FINLAY Audrey Joy, b. 18 Sept 1932, Davidson, Sask. Naturalist and Educ Cons. m. James Campbell Finlay, 18 June 1955, 2 s, 1 d. *Education:* BA, Univ of Man, 1954; Prof Dipl in Educ First Class Standing 1974, Masters of Educ 1978, Univ of Alberta. *Appointments:* Social Wkr: Edmonton Alta, 1951-59; Brandon, 1954- 55; Regina, 1955-57; Classroom Tchr, Outdoor Educ Cons, Curric Cons & Dir of Tchrs' Ctr for Edmonton Pub Sch Bd, 1974-88. *Publications:* Winter Here and Now, 1975; Parks in Alberta, 1987; Nature Guide to BC, 1992; Num profl articles in variety of mags; weekly articles in Edonton Journ. *Memberships:* Hon Life Mem, First Pres, Envir & Outdoor Educ Coun of Alta, 1975- 80; Life Mem, Past Exec, Bd Mem, N Am Assn for Envir Educ, 1981-89; Bd of Dir, VP, Can Nature Fedn, 1984- 90; Sec, Pres, Am Nature Study Soc, 1986-. *Honours:* Woman of Yr, Chatelaine Mag for Can, 1975; Loran Goulden Awd, Fedn of Alta Naturalists, 1980; Order of Bighorn Awd, Gov of Alta, 1987; Ralph D Bird Awd, Manitoba Naturalists, 1987; Can Park Servs Heritage Awd, Envir Can, 1990; Order of Can, 1990; Reeve's Awd of Distinction, Co of Strathcona, 1991. *Hobbies:* Pottery; Nature; Photography. *Address:* 61 East Whitecroft, 52313 Range Rd 232, Sherwood Park, Alberta, Canada, T8B 1B7.

FINLAYSON Judith Ann, b. 26 May 1941, Burlington, IA, USA. Writer. m. Michael George Finlayson, 10 June 1975, 2 s, 2 d. *Education:* BA, Boston Univ, 1964; MAT, Harvard Univ, 1965; MA, Univ of Toronto, 1974. *Appointments:* Freelance Researcher, Sociology & Urban Studies, 1968- 73; Freelance Ed, 1973-78; Researcher, Reporter, Writer, Maclean's Mag, 1978-88; Freelance Writer, 1988-. *Publications:* Whose Money Is It Anyway: The Showdown on Pensions, 1988; Author of co-author of over 200 mag articles. *Membership:* Writers Union, Can. *Hobbies:* Gardening; Golf; Tennis. *Address:* 440 Markham Street, Toronto, Ontario, Canada M6G 2L2.

FINLEY George Edward, b. 11 Jan 1950, Clarendon, TX, USA. Univ Prof. m. Nancy Louise Bordelon, 14 July 1979, 1 s, 1 d. *Education:* BSc 1971, MSc 1975, TX Tech; Doct of Educ, Oklahoma State, 1981. *Appointments:* Rsch Asst 1979-81, Prof of Agricl Educ 1982-, OK State Univ; Hd, Agric Dept, Vernon Reg Jr Coll, 1981-82. *Publications:* International Agriculture, Foundations and Philosophy of Teaching Agriculture, Author of 45 rsch and journ articles. *Memberships:* Bd of Dir - Southern Reg, Am Assn of Agricl Educ; Am Voc Assn; Nat Voc Agric Tchrs Assn; Gamma Sigma Delta; Omicron Delta Kappa; Phi Delta Kappa; Am Assr of Intl Agricl Educ. *Honours:* Alpha Zeta Disting Tchng Awd, 1986; Hon Am Farmer Degree, Nat Assn of Future Farmers of Am, 1990; Nat Voc Agric Tchr Assn's Disting Serev Awd, 1990; Gamma Sigma Delta Disting Tchng Awd, 1991. *Hobbies:* Farming and ranching (particularly cattle & horses); All sports; Music; Fine arts; Assisting with all types of youth programmes. *Address:* 1709 Windmill Drive, Stillwater, OK 74075, USA.

FIRBAS Jan, b. 25 Mar 1921, Brno, Czechoslovakia. Prof Emeritus. m. Helen Kučerová, 26 July 1949, 2 s. *Education:* Tchr's Dip in Eng & German, Brno, 1942; PhD 1948, DSc 1991, Masaryk Univ; CSc, Charles Univ Prague, 1959. *Appointments:* Tchr, Basic Tech Sch, Brno, 1942-45; Asst 1947-50, Sr Asst 1950-66, Docent 1966-87, Prof 1990-91, Dept of Eng, Masaryk Univ; Visiting Prof: Erlangen 1969-70; Buffalo 1971; Sofia 1979, 1981; Hyderabad 1979. *Publications:* On the Function of Word Order in Old English amd Mod E 1957; Thematic Subjects in Contemporary E, 1962; Scene and Perspective, 1981; On the Dynamics of Written Communication, 1986; FSP in Written and Spoken Communication, 1992. *Memberships:* Academia Europea; Intl Assn of Univ Profs of Eng; Societas Linguistica Europea; NIAS Fellows Assn Wassenaar; Prague Linguistics Circle; Linguistic Assr Prague; Vice Chmn, Circle of Modern Philologists Prague; Co-Ed, Brno Studies in Eng. *Honours:* Jose Dobrovský Silver Medal, awded by the Czechoslova Acad of Scis, 1986; Dr hon causa, Univ of Leeds, 1986.

Dr hon causa, Univ of Leuven, 1986. *Hobbies:* Foreign languages; Shorthand; Reading. *Address:* Grohova 63, 602 00 Brno 2, Czechoslovakia.

FIRESTONE Bruce Murray, b. 4 Dec 1951, Ottawa, Ont, Canada. Civil Engr. m. Dawn Marie MacMillan Firestone, 2 s, 3 d. *Education:* BEng (Civil), McGill Univ, 1972; MEng, Univ of NSW, Australia, 1976; PhD, Australian Nat Univ, 1982. *Appointments:* Chmn, Gov, Ottawa Sen Hockey Club; Chmn, Dir, Presidential Exec, Travel Apts Ltd; Councillor, Fin Servs Ltd; Terrace Corporate Ctrs Ltd; Dir, Grocery Express Ltd; Former Publr, Ottawa Bus News; Former Cons Rentalex Ltd; Ops Rsch, Mgr, Metrop Waste Dispoal Auth, Sydney, Australia, 1973-76; Rsch Scholar, Australian Nat Univ, Canberra, 1976-79; Mgmt Cons, Bur of Mgmt Cons, Supply and Sers Can, Ottawa, 1980-82; Chmn, Dir, Terrace Investments Ltd, 1982. *Publications:* Author or co-author of various reports, articles, papers. *Memberships:* Capt, Australian Nat Univ Soccer Team, 1976-79; Coach Park Soccer League, Ottawa, 1980-83; BOMA; Chmn, Bring Back the Senators' Campaign. *Hobbies:* Long distance running; Volleyball; Soccer; Windsurfing; Skiing; Hockey. *Address:* 22 Zokol Crescent, Kanata, Ottawa, Ontario, Canada.

FIRTH Peter James, b. 12 July 1929, Stockport, Cheshire, England. Bishop. m. Felicity Mary Wilding, 27 Aug 1955, 2 s, 3 d. *Education:* BA 1952; Dip Educ 1953, MA 1962. *Appointments:* Asst Curate, Barbourne St Stephen, Worcester, 1955-58; Priest in Charge, Ascension Ch, Malvern Link, 1958-62; Rector, St George Abbey Hey, Manchester, 1962-66; Asst Prod, Relig Progs, BBC Manchester, 1966-67; Sr Prod, Organiser, Relig Progs, TV & Radio, BBC in Bristol, 1967-83; Bishop of Malmesbury, 1982-. *Publication:* Lord of the Seasons, 1978. *Honours:* Seville Int Radio Prize, 1975; Shell Nat Poetry Reading Prize, 1988. *Hobbies:* Poetry; Drama; Music; Photography; Philately; Foreign travel; Manchester United. *Address:* 7 Ivywell Road, Bristol BS9 1NX, England.

FISEISKY Alexander, b. 27 Feb 1950, Moscow, Russia. Organist. m. Nadezhda Kovalchuk, 24 June 1972, 2 d. *Education:* Masters Degree in Organ Performance and Piano Perfomance; Doctorate Deg, Organ Performance, Moscow Conservatory, 1970-75. *Appointments:* Soloist of Bedorussia State Phil Soc, 1975-83; Soloist of Moscow State Phil Soc, 1984-. *Creative works:* Performances: J S Bach complete Organ works, (15 progs); Anthology of Russian Organ Music, (2 progs); Organ Music Anthology: From Antiquity to the XX Century (18 progs). *Memberships:* Pres, Moscow Assn of Organists; VP, Organists Assn of the USSR, 1987-91. *Honours:* Hon Dipl of XII World Festival of 90th and Students, Moscow, 1985. *Hobbies:* Charity activities in Russian Orthodox Church. *Address:* 54 Frunzenskaya emb Apt 82, Moscow 119270, Russia.

FISHER Caroline Jane MacFadyen, b. 24 June 1947, Detroit, MI, USA. Assoc Prof of Mktng. m. Daryl John Fisher, 20 Dec 1969. *Education:* BA, Kalamazoo Coll, 1969; MSc, Eastern Michigan Univ, 1972; PhD, Bowling Green St Univ, 1975; MBA, Univ of New Orleans, 1982. *Appointments:* Dir, Int Mkt Inst 1981, Visiting Asst Prof 1981-82, Univ of New Orleans; Mkt Analyst, Gulf South Bev, 1982-84; Mktng Cons, 1984-; Asst Prof 1987-90, Assoc Prof 1990-, Dir of Grad Prog, 1992-, Loyola Univ. *Publications:* Business Fundamentals, 1987; Case Studies, 1991; Author of 3 articles. *Memberships:* Chm, Bd of Dir, Comm Residential Ctr, 1986-91; Bd Mem 1987-91, Sec, Bd of Dir 1991, Vol of Am of New Orleans, 1987-91; Am Mktng Assn; N Am Case Rsch Assn; Southern Mktng Assn; Southwestern Mktng Assn. *Honours:* Fellowship, Nat Sci Fndn, 1972-75; Louisiana Land and Exploration Awd, 1982; Fac Rsch Awd, 1988, 1990. *Hobbies:* Singing; Golf. *Address:* Department of Marketing, Loyola University, 6363 St Charles Avenue, New Orleans, LA 70118, USA.

FISHER Charles Harold, b. 20 Nov 1906, Hiawatha, WV, USA. Chem Educ & Rsch. m. (1) Elizabeth Dye, Nov 1933, dec 1967, (2) Lois Carlin, July 1968, dec 1990, (3) Elizabeth Snyder Kiser, 29 Nov 1991. *Education:* BS, Roanoke Coll, Salem, 1928; MS 1929, PhD 1932, Univ of Illinois, Urbana. *Appointments:* Instr, Chem, Harvard Univ, 1932-35; Rsch Grp Ldr, US Bur of Mines, Pittsburgh, 1935-40; Rsch Grp Ldr, USDA Eastern Reg Rsch Ctr, Philadelphia, 1940-50; Dir, USDA Southern Utilization Rsch Div, Southern Reg Rsch Ctr, New Orleans, 1950-72; Adj Rsch Prof, Roanoke Coll, Salem, 1972-. *Publications:* Author of co-author of over 200 pubs; inventor or co-inventor of 72 patents. *Memberships:* Pres 1962-63, Cmn of Bd 1963, 1973-75, Am Inst of Chems; Mbr of Bd 1969-71, ACS; Am Inst of Chem Engrs; The Chem Soc, London; AAAS; Cosmos Club, Washington DC; C of C, Int Hse, Round Table Club, New Orleans; Chems Club, NY; Pres 1978-79, Roanoke Coll Alumni Assn; Intl Torch Club, Roanoke. *Honours include:* Hon DSc, Tulane Univ, 1953; Hon DSc, Roanoke Coll, 1963; Presidential Cit of Merit, Am Inst of Chems, 1986; Roanoke Coll estab the annual Charles H Fisher Lectures in his hon, 1990; Bd of Dir, Salem Educl Fndn, Salem, 1991-; Estab the Lois Carlin Fisher Scholarship, Roanoke Coll, 1991. *Hobbies:* Music; Photography; Travel. *Address:* Chemistry Department, Roanoke College, Salem, VA 24153, USA.

FISHER George Harold, b. 19 July 1943, San Antonio, TX, USA. Assoc Prof of Chem. *Education:* BS, Rollins Coll, 1965; MS, Univ of Florida, 1968; PhD, Univ of Miami, 1973. *Appointments include:* Rsch Asst Prof of Med & Chem, Univ of Miami Sch of Med, Miami, 1977-83; Pt-time Instr of Chem, Miami-Dade Comm Coll, S Campus, 1983-89; Visiting Assoc Prof of Chem, Florida Int Univ, Miami, 1987-88; Rsch Assoc Prof of Chem & Med 1983-89, Adj Assoc Prof of Chem & Med 1989-, Univ of Miami, Coral Gables; Assoc Prof of Chem, Barry Univ, Miami Shores, 1988-. *Publications:* Author of 50 scientific articles. *Memberships include:* Am Chem Soc, Chmn, Florida Sect 1981, Nat Councillor 1983-; Sigma Xi; AAAS; Bd of Dir, Dade Co Chem Tchrs Alliance; Inst Food Technol. *Honours:* Thomas R Baker Mem Prize in Chem 1964, Sigmz Xi Sr Sci Awd 1965, Rollins Coll; NSF Grad Rsch Fellowship, Univ of Miami, 1970-72; Welch Scientific Postdoct Fellowship, Univ of Texas, Austin, 1973-75; Phi Kappa Phi; Phi Lambda Upsilon; Epsilon Tau Lambda; Zeta Alpha Epsilon; Gamma Sigma Epsilon. *Hobbies:* Classical music; Theatre. *Address:* Department of Chemistry, Barry University, 11300 N E 2nd Avenue, Miami Shores, FL 33161, USA.

FISHER Norma, b. 11 May 1940, London, England. Concert Pianist; Tchr. m. Barrington Saipe, 3 Sept 1967, 2 s. *Education:* Guildhall Sch of Music, London, 1952-57; Privately with Ilona Kabos, London, 1957-70. *Career:* Concerts, Recitals, Chamber-music, Internationally; Master Classes, Brit, US, Can, Ireland, Switz. *Honours:* 2nd prize, Busoni Int Piano Competition, 1961; Joint Piano Prize (with Vladimir Ashkenazy), Harriet Cohen Intl Music Awds, 1963. *Hobbies:* Opera; Tennis; Crosswords. *Address:* 5 Lyndhurst Gardens, Finchley, London N3 1TA, England.

FISHER Richard Welton, b. 18 Mar 1949, Los Angeles, USA. Investor; Merchant Banker. m. Nancy Miles Collins, 8 Sept 1973, 2 s, 2 d. *Education:* BA cum laude, Harvard, 1969-71; Post-Grad Studs, Oxford, 1972-73; MBA, Stanford, 1973-75. *Appointments:* Brown Bros Harriman & Co 1975-76, Sr Mgr 1980-87; Exec Asst to Sec of the Treasury, US Treasury, 1976-79; Managing Ptnr, Fisher Capital Mgmt, 1987-; Co-ord of Frgn Policy Iss, Perot Pres Camp, 1992. *Publications:* Author of num articles in major periodicals. *Memberships include:* Chmn 1983-, Dallas Comm on Foreign Relat; Chmn 1986-, Inst of the Ams; Exec Cttee, Inter-American Dialogue, 1991-; Visitors Cttee, John F Kennedy Sch of Govt, Harvard Univ, 1992-; Visitors Cttee, Centre for Intl Affairs, Harvard Univ, 1992-; Standing Acad Cttee, Southern Methodist Univ, 1990-; Coun on Foreign Relat; Chmn of Bus Adv Comm, Am Coun on Germany; Bd of Dir, Inst for Contemporary German Studies. *Honours:* Stanford Univ Outstg Achmt Awd, 1986; Commissioned as Admiral of Texas Navy, 1987; US - Japan Ldrship Fellow, 1989-90. *Hobbies:* Writing; Ranching. *Address:* 4600 Texas Commerce Tower West, 2200 Ross Avenue, Dallas, TX 75201, USA.

FISHWICK Avril, b. 30 Mar 1924, Hindley, England. Ptnr. m. Thomas William Fishwick, 4 Feb 1950, 2 d. *Education:* LLB 1946; LLM 1948. *Appointments:* Admitted Solicitor, 1949; Ptnr, Frank Platt & Fishwick, 1958-. *Memberships:* Northern Adv Bd, Dir, Nat Westminster Bank Plc; Chmn, Tidy Brit Enterprises Ltd; Dir, Grounwork Trust Trading Co Ltd; Pres: Wigan Civic Trust; Wigan RSPCA; Wigan Little Theatre; Mbr of Ct, Manchester Univ; Chmn, Wigan & Leigh CT Scanner Appeal; Trustee, Skelton Bounty; Trustee, GMP Comm Charity; The Law Soc. *Honours:* DL, 1982-; High Sheriff of Greater Manchester, 1983-84; Vice Lord Lt of Greater Manchester, 1988-. *Hobbies:* Natural history; Countryside. *Address:* Haighlands, Haigh Country Park, Haigh, Nr Wigan WN2 1PB, England.

FISIAK Jacek, b. 10 May 1936, Konstantynow, Lodzki. Univ Prof. m. Jadwiga Fisiak Nawrocka, 27 Jan 1966. *Education:* MA, Univ of Warsaw, 1959; UC, London, 1961; PhD, Univ of Lodz, 1962; Fulbright Fellow, UCLA, 1963-64; D Litt A Mickiewicz Univ, Poznan, 1965. *Appointments:* Lectr, Adjunct prof, ocent, 1959-67; Prof, Hd of Sch of English, Poznan, 1965-; Visiting Prof, Univ Kansas, 1970; Univ Florida, 1974; State Univ of NY, 1975; Univ Kiel, 1979; the American Univ, 1979-80, 1991-92; Univ of Vienna, 1983,1988,1990-91; Univ of Zurich, 1984; Univ Tromso, 1985; Univ Jyvaskla, 1987; Minister of Educ of Poland, 1988-89. *Publications include:* Over 100 Books & Papers. *Memberships:* Intl Assoc of Univ Prof of English; Intl Soc for Historical Linguistics; Societas Linguistica Europaea; modern Languages Assoc of Poland. *Honours:* Dr H C, Commander of the Lion of Finland; Knight of the Order, Polonia Restituta; Officer of the Order of the British Empire; Cammander of the Order, Polonia Restituta; Officer of the Order, Palmes Academiques. *Hobbies:* Modern History; Sports. *Address:* Sch of English, Adam Mickiewicz Univ, 61-712 Poznan, Poland. 52, 139, 156.

FITZGERALD John Thomas Jr, b. 2 Oct 1948, Birmingham, AL, USA. Relig Studies Prof. m. Karol Westover Bonneaux, 23 May 1970, 2 d. *Education:* BA 1970, MA 1972, Abilene Christian Univ; MDiv, Yale Divinity Sch, 1975; PhD, Yale Univ, 1984. *Appointments:* Instr, Yale Coll, 1979; Instr, Yale Divinity Sch, 1980-81; Instr 1981-84, Asst Prof 1984-88, Assoc Prof 1988-, Univ of Miami; Visiting Assoc Prof, Brown Univ, 1992. *Publications:* The Tabula of Cebes, 1983; Cracks in an Earthen Vessel, 1988. *Memberships:* Chapt Pres 1988-89, Phi Kappa Phi; Chmn, Hellenistic Moral Philos & Early Christianity Consultation 1989-, Soc of Biblical Lit; Chm, Scholarship Comm, 1990-, Golden Key Nat Hon Soc; Omicron Delta Kappa. *Honours:* Two Brothers Fellowship, Yale Divinity Sch, 1974-75; Rotary Int Fellowship, Tuebingen, Germany, 1975-76; Max Orovitz Summer Rsch Awd 1985, 1987, Freshman Tchng Awd 1991, Univ of Miami. *Address:* 15215 SW 78 Ct, Miami, FL 33157, USA.

FITZSBBOM William E III, b. 21 July 1945, Cambridge, MA, USA. Prof. div 1 s. *Education:* BA 1968, PhD 1972, Vanderbilt Univ. *Appointments:* Asst Prof 1972-75, Assoc Prof -1981, Prof 1982-; Univ of Houston; Visiting Scientist, Argonne Nat Lab, 1980; Vis Assoc Prof, Univ of California, San Diego, 1980-81. *Publications:* Author of 75 scientific pubs. *Memberships:* Am Math Soc; SIAM. *Hobbies:* Reading; Athletics. *Address:* Department of Mathematics, University of Houston, Houston, TX 77204, USA.

FLAX Barry Melvin, b. 15 July 1938, Boston, MA, USA. Cons. m. 23 Mar 1963, 1 s, 1 d. *Education:* BS, BA, Northeastern Univ, 1962. *Appointments:* RCA, 1964-71; Northern Telecom, 1972-88; Cons to AT & T, 1989-

92; Tech Dir, Intell Buildg Inst, 1992. *Publications:* Intelligent Building, 1991; Intelligent Buildings, 1991. *Memberships:* Intelligent Bldg Inst; Chmn, Tc/Info Intecmated Patamans Sub-comm. *Hobbies:* Sports; Gardening. *Address:* 104 Saratoga Waye NE, Vienna, VA 22180, USA.

FLAX Florence Roselin Polinsky, b. 23 June 1936, Brockton, MA, USA. Photographer. m. Barry Melvin Flax, 23 Mar 1963, 1 s, 1 d. *Apointments:* Sec, Bursar's Off, Northeastern Univ, 1956-63; Artist & Art Dealer, Self Employed Artist, Represented 6 other Artists and ran exhibits, 1974-80; Specialist in Macro Photography of Flowers, Produce Portraits, Landscapes, Still Lifes, Copy works and slides for Corporate Work & Model Portfolios, Florence P Flax - Photographics, 1980-. *Creative works:* Mainly using low speed films, produce close up photographs of flowers which, due to the film types & equipment make quite big enlargements; These photographs are on display in several places. *Memberships:* AFI; Smithsonian Inst; MI Hammel Club; N Virginia Photographic Soc; The Wilderness Soc; The Sierra Club; World Wildlife Fund; Nat Wildlife Fndn; Friends of the Nat Zoo; The Int Sinatra Soc; The Int Platform Assn. *Honours:* Appointed to a 2 yr term on The Women's Cabinet, Northeastern Univ, 1962; Cert of Merit, Temple Rodef Shalom, 1978; 3 Ribbons in a Nat Photo Contest, Northern Telecom, USA, 1984. *Hobbies:* Figure skating; Collectibles; Audiofile; Videofile; Movie buff; Reader; Conservationist. *Address:* 104 Saratoga Waye NE, Vienna, VA 22180, USA.

FLERKO Bela, b. 14 June 1924, Pecs, Hungary. University Professor. m. Vera Bardos, 23 July 1951. *Education:* Masters Deg, Univ Med Sch, Pecs, Hungary, 1948; DSc, Hungarian Acad of Scis, 1967. *Appointments:* Instr, 1948-51, Asst Prof, 1951-61, Assoc Prof, 1961-64, Prof, and Hd of Dept of Anatomy, 1964-, Univ Med Sch of Pecs; Rector, 1979-85. *Publications:* Hypothalmic Control of the Anterior Pituitary, 1962, 1968, 1972, in English and Russian. *Memberships:* Pres, Intl Soc of Neuendocrinol, 1988; Ctl Coun, Exec Com, Intl Brain Res Org, 1973-85; Pres, Hungarian Soc of Endocrinol and Metabolism, 1973-81; Pres, Hung Soc of Anatoms, Histols and Embryols, 1982-86; Ctl Coun of the Intl Soc of Endocrinol, 1973-85. *Honours:* Mem, Hungarian Acad of Scis, 1970; Hon Dr, Univ of Kuopio, Finland, 1982; Hon Mem, Czech Soc of Endocrinol, 1977, Soc for Endocrinol and Metabolism of Germany and Polish Soc of Endocrinol, 1985; Nat Prize for Sci Achievements, 1978. *Hobby:* Classical music. *Address:* Department of Anatomy, University Medical School of Pecs, Szigeti ut 12, Pecs H-7643, Hungary. 57, 154, 162.

FLETCHER Martin Anthony, b. 7 July 1956, Knighton, Radnorshire. Journalist. m. Catherine Jane Beney, 10 Oct 1981, 1 s, 2 d. *Education:* Edinburgh Univ, 1974-78; Univ of Pennsylvania, 1976-77. *Appointments:* Po Reporter 1986-89, Washington Corres 1989-, The Times. *Publication:* The Good Caff Guide, 1981. *Hobbies:* Sport; Travel. *Address:* 3252 Juniper Lane, Falls Church, VA 22044, USA.

FLETCHER Riley Eugene, b. 29 Nov 1912, Eddy, TX USA. Ret'd Atty. m. Hattie Inez Blackwell, 11 June 1954. *Education:* BA 1950, LLB 1950, Baylor Univ, Waco. *Appointments include:* Asst Atty Gen, Texas, 1956- 62 Asst Gen Counsell, 1962-63; Gen Counsell, 1963-78 Special Counsell, 1978-; Texas Municipal League 1978-. *Publications:* Mag articles on municipal law *Memberships include:* Am, Texas and Travis Co Ba Assns; Am Judicature Soc; Judge Advocates Assn Reserve Offs Assn of USA; Baylor Law Sch Counsellors Am Acad of Polit and Social Scis; Austin World Affairs Coun; Mil Order of the World Wars; Assn of the US Army. *Honours:* Disting Serv Awd, Texas Municipal Cts Assn, 1980; Appreciation Awd, Texas City Attys Assn 1982; Appreciation Awd, Assn of Mayors, Councilmer & Commnrs of Texas, 1984. *Address:* 7201 Creekside Drive, Austin, TX 78752, USA.

FLETCHER Robin Anthony, b. 30 May 1922, Godalming. Ret'd. m. Jinny May Cornish, 2 s. *Education:* MA; DPhil. *Appointments:* Univ Lectr, Oxford in Modern Greek Lang & Lit, 1949-79; Fellow, Trinity Coll, Oxford, 1950-89; Sr Proctor, 1966-67; Sec to Rhodes Trustees, Warden at Rhodes Hse, 1980-89. *Publication:* Kostes Palamas, 1984. *Memberships:* Pres, Hockey Assn; Chmn, Brit Hockey Bd; Trustee, Oxford Preservation Trust; Treas, Vincents Club, Oxford; Bd of Govs: Kelly Coll; Marlborough Coll; Radley Coll; Cheltenham Coll; Sherborne Sch. *Honours:* DSC 1944; OBE 1984. *Hobbies include:* Golf; Listening to music; Modern designed silver. *Address:* Binglea, Quoyloo, Stromness, Orkney KW16 3LU.

FLETCHER William Adrin, b. 22 Apr 1948, Graham, TX, USA. Preacher. m. Terri Lynn Hoch, 19 June 1970, 2 s. *Education:* BS, Abilene Christian Univ, 1970. *Appointments:* Eliasville Ch of Christ, Eliasville, 1967-70; Sighthill Ch of Christ, Edinburgh, Scotland, 1970-75; Brookhollow Ch of Christ, Houston, 1975-83; Murray St Ch of Christ, Rockdale, 1983-. *Memberships:* Trustee 1979-, Chmn Bd of Trustees 1987-, Ctrl Texas Area Mus; Bd of Dir 1988-90, Pres 1988, 1989, S Milam Co United Way; Am Assn of Christian Cnslrs, 1988-; Bd of Trustees 1989-, Richards Mem Hosp, Rockdale. *Honour:* Outstg Young Men of Am, 1978. *Hobbies:* Gardening; Swimming; Photography; Reading. *Address:* 1603 Sager Road, Rockdale, TX 76567, USA.

FLICK Willi Gerhard, b. 30 July 1939, Osnabrueck, Lower Saxony, Germany. Exec Mfg Ind. m. Traudel Karrenbrock, 6 July 1962, 2 d. *Appointments:* GM (Opel) Distbr, Osnabrueck, 1956-59; Daimler Benz, AG (Mercedes), Duisburg, 1960-62; Asst Sales Mgr, C Behrens, AG Alfeld, 1962-64; Dir Sales Div 1964-86, Dir, Mktng Div 1986-92, Comm Dir, 1992-, Hoedtke & Boës, Pinneberg & Kiel; Lectr, Workshops, Univ of Hanover, 1988-. *Contributions to:* Articles to profl journs. *Memberships:* Chmn, Dep Chmn, FDP (Liberals) Germany, Hildesheim 1971, Alfeld 1978-. *Hobbies:* Local and State Politics; UK-German Youth Exchange; Skiing; Sailing. *Address:* Pestalozzi str 4, D-3220 Alfeld, Leine, Germany.

FLINN Charles Gallagher, b. 22 Feb 1938, Ft Lauderdale, FL, USA. Lawyer. *Education:* AB, Princeton Univ, 1959; LLB, Univ of VA, 1962; BD, Univ of London, 1980. *Appointments:* Bar: FL 1962; VA 1962; US Supreme Ct 1966; DC 1970; Assoc, Charles B Fulton Esq, West Palm Beach, 1962- 63; Asst Counsel Off Gen Counsel US Dept, Navy, Washington, 1963-71; Asst C'wlth Atty, Co of Arlington, 1971-72; Asst Co Atty 1972-75, Dpty Co Atty 1975-81, Co Atty 1981-; Atty, Arlington Sch Bd, 1981-. *Memberships:* BAB; Bd of Dirs 1988-, VA Local Govt Attys Assn; Arlington Co Bar Assn; Dir-at-large 1988-, VA Co Sch Bd Attys; Am Schs Oriental Rsch. *Address:* 5812 1st Street S, Arlington, VA 22204, USA.

FLOOD John Edward, b. 2 June 1925, London, England. Chartered Engr. m. Phyllis Mary Groocock, 23 Apr 1949, 2 s. *Education:* DSc, PhD, Queen Mary Coll, Univ of London, 1942-44. *Appointments:* Expmtl Off, Admiralty Signals Estab, 1944-46; Dev Engr, Standard Telephones & Cables Ltd, 1946-47; Exec Engr, Post Off Rsch Stn, 1947-52; Sect Hd, Siemens Bros Ltd, 1952-57; Chief Engr, Advanced Dev Labs, Assoc Elec Inds Ltd, 1957-65; Prof of Elect Engrng 1965-90, Hd of Dept of Elect and Electronic Engrng 1967-81, 1983- 89, Dean, Fac of Engrng 1971-74, Sr Pro-Vice Chancellor 1981-83, Prof Emeritus 1990-, Aston Univ; Chmn, Univs Comm on Integrated Sandwich Courses, 1978-79; Chmn, Brit Standards Comm for Telecommunications, 1981-92; Mem, Monopolis and Mergers Commn, 1985-. *Publications:* Telecommunication Networks, 1975; Transmission Systems, 1991; Papers in scientific and tech journs. *Memberships:* F Inst P; FIEE; Chmn, IEE Profl Grp on Telecommunications, 1974-77; Chn, IEE S Midland Ctr, 1978-79. *Honours:* CGIA, 1962; OBE, 1986; FCGI, 1991. *Hobbies:* Swimming; Wine making.

Address: 60 Widney Manor Road, Solihull, West Midlands B91 3JQ, England.

FLORESCO Jean D, b. 7 Oct 1939, Romania. Physn. 1 d. *Education:* MD, Bucharest, 1962; PhD, 1978. *Appointments:* Asst Prof 1968, Assoc Prof 1975; Cons, Hosp Lariboisiere, Paris & Hosp Stell, Rueil-Malmaison, France; Pvt Prac, Paris. *Publications:* Psychotropic Therapy (co-author), 1968; Textbook of Psychiatry, 1976; Scientific papers in journs, Nature, Int Journ of Angiology, World Journ of Urology. *Memberships include:* Pres, Fdr, Fndn of European Help, Paris; Pres, GRAFT, European Med Assn; Gen Sec, Romanian Atheneum, France; Sec, French Sect, World Free Rumanians; Int Psychogeriatric Assn, USA; Am Electroencephalographic Assn. *Hobby:* Reading. *Address:* 95 rue de Courcelles, Paris 75017, France.

FLÖTTMANN Wilhelm, b. 26 Feb 1921, Gütersloh, Germany. Pharm Chem. m. Inge Tinzmann, 16 Dec 1943, 5 s, 2 d. *Education:* Chem Coll, Wiesbaden, 1937-39; State Exam, 1939; Extramural and Autodidactic Studies in Biochem, Biometry, Pharmacology, Oncology and related subjs; Several Lang Schs, Köln & Danzig. *Appointments:* Pharm Chem, Bayer Leverkusen, 1941-45; Into-Eng Specialist Transl and Writer to drug Mfrs, Rsch Ctrs and Scientific Publrs; Fr K Schattauer Verlag, Stuttgart, 1961; LEBENDE SPRACHEN, Berlin-Schoneberg, 1963; Wissenschaftliche Verlagsgesellschaft, 1982-. *Creative works:* Illuminating Love, 1943; Essays on Faith and Morals, 1948; Invitation to Pilgrimage, 1949; Recovery of Faith, 1950; Official Handbook of the German Health Resorts Association, 1953; Biochemica Boehringer, 1955; The Myocardium, 1955; Materia Medica, 1956; Chemotherapy of Malignant Tumours, 1961; Cyclophosphamide in Chemotherapy of Cancer, 15 vols 1958-79; Num Scientific Film Scripts. *Memberships:* Soc of German Scientists and Physns; Assn of German Transl; Inst of Linguistics, London; Società Dantesca Florence, Italy; WFSW, London. *Honours:* Silver Needle & Hon Certs of Merit, Assn of German Transl, 1973; Silver Key Awd, Profile Hons Record, 1976; Gold Medal of Hon, Am Rsch Assn; LHD; DSc, Hon's Causa; Albert Einstein Medal for Peace; IOM. *Hobbies:* Philosophy; Literature; Art; Gardening; Hiking. *Address:* Schlüterstrasse 11, 4830 Gütersloh 1, Germany.

FLOWER Antony John Frank, b. 2 Feb 1951. Dir. *Education:* BA Hons, MA, Univ of Exeter; PhD, Univ of Leicester. *Appointments:* Graphic Designer, 1973-76; Co-fdr (with Lord Young of Dartington), First Gen Sec, Tawney Soc, 1982-88; Coord, Argo Venture, 1984-; Dir, Argo Trust, 1986-; Dir, Hlthline Hlth Info Serv, 1986-88; Dir, Hlth Info Trust, 1987-88; Coord, Campaign for Educl Choice, 1988; Assoc, Open Coll of the Arts, 1988-; Assoc, Redesign Ltd, 1989-; Assoc, Nicholas Lacey, Jobst & Ptnrs (Arch), 1989- ; Assoc, Inst for Pub Policy Rsch, 1989-; Dir, Environmental Concern Ctr in Europe, 1990-; Dir of Dev, the Green Alliance, 1991-; Consultant, Construction Industry Research and Information Assn, 1992-. *Publications:* Starting to Write (with G Mort), 1990; Co-ed with A Wright, B Pimlott, The Alternative, 1990. *Memberships:* Fdr Mbr, SDP, 1981; Coun for Social Democracy, 1982-84; FRSA; Ed, Tawney Journ, 1982-88; Co-fdr, Mng Ed, Samizdat Mag, 1988-; Trustee, Hlth Info Trust, 1988-; Coun Mbr, Gaia, 1988-; Trustee, Mutual Aid Ctr, 1990-. *Hobbies:* Boats; Collecting, making and restoring musical instruments. *Address:* 18 Victoria Park Square, London E2 9PF, England.

FLOYD Richard Eaglesfield, b. 9 June 1938, Purley, England. Chartered Acct; Insolvency Practitioner. 1 d. *Education:* Assoc 1962, Fellow 1972, ICA. *Career:* Fitch & Valance & Co, London, 1955-61; Audit Sr, Peat Warwick Mitchell & Co, 1962-63; Insolvency Mgr, W H Cork Gully & Co, 1964-71; Formed Floyd Harris, 1971-. *Publications:* Voluntary Liquidation & Receivership, 1st ed 1984, 2nd ed 1987, 3rd ed 1991; Personal Insolvency (with I Grier), 1987; Company Administration Orders and Voluntary Arrangements, 1988. *Memberships:* Insolvency Practitioners Assn; Soc of Practitioners of Insolvency; Assn Europeenne des Praticiens des Procedures Collectives; Guilde of Freeman of the City of London. *Address:* c/o Floyd Harris, Mitre House, 44/46 Fleet Street, London EC4Y 1BN, England.

FOCK Cornelia Willemina, b. 25 June 1942, Surabaia, Indonesia. Prof. *Education:* MA 1968, Doct 1975, Univ of Leiden; Grant of Rotary Fndn, Univ of Florence, Italy, 1968-69. *Appointments:* Asst Prof, Art Histl Inst 1970-82, Prof of Hist of Decorative Arts 1982-, Univ of Leiden. *Publications include:* Willem van Mieris en zijn mecenas Pieter de la Court van der Voort, 1983; Master-pieces and marks of the Leiden furniture guilds in the eighteenth century, 1985; Pietre Dure work at the Court of Prague and Florence: Some Relations, 1988. *Memberships include:* Bd, Mus De Lakenhal Leiden, 1980-90; Ed, Oud Holland, 1981-; Bd, Vereniging Rembrandt, 1981-; Bd, Soc of Dutch Lit, 1981-89; Bd, Gemeente Mus, The Hague, 1981-89; Dutch Comm, Corpus Vitrearum, 1982-88; Chmn, Mr J W Frederites Awd, 1982-; Dutch Comm on Monuments, 1983-; Bd, Netherlands Off Fine Arts, 1985-. *Honours:* Mr J W Frederiks Awd, Pub Decorative Arts, 1968; Karel von Mander Awd, Hist of Art, 1975. *Address:* Institute of History of Art, Leiden University, Doclensteeg 16, 2311 VL Leiden, Holland.

FOGG Gordon Elliott, b. 26 Apr 1919, Langar, Notts, England. Ret'd. m. Elizabeth Beryl Llechid Jones, 7 July 1945, 1 s, 1 d. *Education:* BSc, Queen Mary Coll, Univ of London, 1939; PhD 1943, ScD 1966, St John's Coll, Cambridge. *Appointments:* Asst, Seaweed Survey of Brit Isles, Marine Biological Assn, 1942; Plant Physiologist, Pest Control Ltd, Cambridge, 1943-45; Asst Lectr, Univ Coll, London, 1945-47; Lectr 1947-53, Reader in Botany 1953-60, Prof of Botany 1960-71, Westfield Coll, London; Prof of Marine Biology 1971-85, Emeritus Prof, Univ Coll of N Wales. *Publications:* The Metabolism of Algae, 1953; The Growth of Plants, 1963; Algal Cultures and Phytoplankton Ecology (with B Thake), 1965, 1987; Photosynthesis, 1968; The Blue-Green Algae (with WPD Stewart, P Fay, AE Walsby), 1973; The Explorations of Antarctica (with D Smith), 1990; A History of Antarctic Science, 1992. *Memberships:* Hon Sec 1954-57, Pres 1976-77, Inst of Biology; Hon Sec 1957-60, Soc for Experimental Biology; Fellow, Royal Soc, 1965; Gen Sec 1967-72, Pres, Sect K 1973, Brit Assn; Chmn of Coun 1974-85, Freshwater Biological Assn. *Honours:* Hon LLD, Uiv of Dundee, 1974; Fellow, Queen Mary Coll, 1976; CBE, 1983; Emeritus Fellow, Leverhulme Trust, 1986-88. *Hobbies:* Antarctic Literature; Walking; Photography. *Address:* Bodolben, Llandegfan, Anglesey, Gwynedd LL59 5TA, Wales.

FOLEY John Miles, b. 22 Jan 1947, Northampton, MA, USA. Prof. m. Anne-Marie Conlisk Foley, 30 July 1983, 3 s, 1 d. *Education:* AB, Colgate Univ, 1969; MA 1971, PhD 1974, Univ of Massachusetts. *Appointments:* Asst Prof of Eng, Emory Univ, 1974-79; Visiting Fellow, Harvard Univ, 1976-77; Assoc Prof, Full Prof, Byler Humanities Chair, Univ of Missouri, 1979-; Prof of Classics, Univ of Missouri, 1992-. *Publications:* Oral-Formulaic Theory and Research, 1985; Oral Tradition (Ed), 1986-; The Theory of Oral Composition, 1988; Traditional Oral Epic, 1990; Immanent Art, 1991; Author of 70 articles. *Memberships:* Anthropological Approaches to Lit Div Exec Comm 1985-90, Folklore & Lit Exec Comm 1986-91, Old Eng Lang & Lit Exec Comm 1989-94, MLA. *Honours:* Grantee, Nat Endowment for the Humanities, 1974, 1983, 1987, 1989, 1991; Fellowship, Am Coun of Learned Societies, 1976-77; Fulbright and IREX Fellowship, 1979-80; Guggenheim Fellowship, 1980-81; Elected Fellow, Am Folklore Soc, 1989. *Hobbies:* Languages; Fieldwork (Yugoslavia); Travel. *Address:* Centre for Studies in Oral Tradition, 301 Read Hall, University of Missouri, Columbia, MO 65211, USA.

FOLSOM Burton Whitmore, b. 14 Nov 1947, Lincoln, NE, USA. Tchr. m. Anita Prince, 8 Apr 1979, 1 s. *Education:* BA, Indiana Univ, 1970; MA, Univ of Nebraska, 1973; PhD, Univ of Pittsburgh, 1976. *Appointment:* Tchr, Murray State Univ, 1976-. *Publications:* Urban Capitalists, 1981; Entrepreneurs Vs The State, 1987; Myth of the Robber Barons, 1991. *Honour:* Ed of Continuity: A Journ of Hist. *Address:* Department of History, Murray State University, Murray, KY 42071, USA.

FOMICHEVA Valentina M, b. 25 May 1946, Kiev, Ukraine. Biologist; Cytologist. m. Gezel Nicola, 8 Oct 1966, 1 s, 1 d. *Education:* PhD, Kiev State Univ, 1975. *Appointments:* Tchr, Kiev State Univ, 1969-71; Sci Rschs (cytology), Inst of Botany, Acad Sci of Ukraine, 1971-. *Publications:* Functional State of Chromatin and Proliferativ Activity of Meristematic Cells in Pea Seedlings Under Various Clinostatic Conditions, 1983; Plant Call Upon Change of Geophysical Factors, 1984; The preprint: Physico-Chemical and Biological Aspects of Weak Magnetic Field effects on Plants, 1987; The Influence of the Geomagnetic Field, 1991. *Memberships:* Sci Coun, Inst of Botany; Acad Sci of Ukraine, Kiev. *Hobbies:* Literature; Belles-Lettres; Travelling; Swimming. *Address:* Institute of Botany, Academy Science of Ukraine, Repin Street 2, Kiev GSP 1, Ukraine 252601.

FONTINOY Charles Jean Marie Eugene Corneille, b. 12 Mar 1920, Stavelot, Belgium. Retired Oriental Studies Professor. *Education:* Lic Phil et Lettres, 1941; Agrege Enseignement Morgen degree superior, 1941; Dr Oriental Langs, 1963, Univ Liege. *Appointments:* Tchr, Athenee Royal Aywaille, Belgium, 1945-66; Prof and Ch of Dept of Oriental Studies, State Univ of Leige, Belgium, 1966-85. *Publications:* Le Duel Dans les Langues Semitiques, 1969. *Contributions to:* articles to several journals on linguistics, and history of religion. *Memberships:* Soc of Biblical Lit, USA; Belgian Soc of Oriental Studies; Grop for Phonician and Punic Studies. *Honours:* Various grants for travel abroad, 1954, 1955, 1957, 1959, 1966; Various decorations including: Grand Ofr de l'Ordre de Leopold II, 1981. *Hobbies:* Literature; Psychology; Ornithology. *Address:* Univ De Liege section Orientale, Place Du XX Adut 32, 4000 Liege, Belgium.

FORBES Daniel Merrill, b. 20 June 1954, Clergy; Cnslr. m. Wanda Iris Rosa, 25 Sept 1977, 1 s, 1 d. *Education:* BA, Southern Coll of Seventh-day Adventists, 1974-77; MA 1985-88, Postgrad studies 1988-, Univ of S FL. *Appointments:* Min, FL Conf of Seventh-day Adventists, 1977-. *Memberships:* Am Assn for Counselling and Dev; Assn for Relig Values and Issues in Counselling. *Hobbies:* Walking; Nature; Reading; Music. *Address:* First Seventy-Day Adventist Church, 822 W Linebaugh Avenue, Tampa, FL 33612, USA.

FORBES James, b. 2 Jan 1923, Farnborough, Hampshire, England. Co Dir; Chartered Acct. m. Alison M F Moffat, 14 Aug 1948, 2 s. *Education:* Christ's Hosp, Horsham, Surrey, 1934-41; Off's Trng Sch, Bangalore, S India, 1942. *Appointments:* Commissioned 1942, released 1947, Indian Army, Hon Maj; Peat, Marwick Mitchell & Co, London, England, 1952-58; Chief Acct, L Rose Ltd after joining Schweppes Org 1958, later Operational Rsch Mgr, Grp Chief Acct, Dir of subsidiaries of Schweppes Ltd; Sec, Fin Advsr, Cadbury Schweppes (merger) 1969, Main Bd Appt as Fin Dir, 1971; Sr Exec Dir, Tate and Lyle plc, 1978; Vice Chmn 1980-84, Tate and Lyle Grp Pension Fund, Chmn 1978-85; Non Exec Dir: Brit Transp Hotels 1978-83; Brit Rail Investments 1980-84; Forestry Commnr 1982-88; Steetley plc 1984-89; Compass Hotels 1984-. *Memberships:* Coun Mem 1971-78, Treas 1984-86, ICA; Treas, Chmn, Coun of Almoners of Christ's Hosp, 1987-; Highland Soc of London; Royal C'Wlth Soc; Caledonian Club. *Hobbies:* Travelling; Golf; Music. *Address:* Caledonian Club, Halkin Street, London SW1X 7DR, England. 53, 32, 1.

FORBES Sebastian, b. 22 May 1941, Bucks, England. Prof of Music; Composer. m. (1)Hilary Taylor, 29 June 1968, (2)Tessa Brady, 24 Sept 1983, 1 s, 3 d. *Education:* RAM, 1958-60; King's Coll, Cambridge Univ, 1960-64; ARCO, LRAM, ARCM, 1960; Mus B (Cantab), 1964; MA 1967; MusD (Cantab), 1977. *Appointments:* BBC Prod, Music Div, Sound, 1964-67; Dir of Music, Trinity Coll, Cambridge, 1968; Univ Lectr in Music: Univ Coll of N Wales, Bangor 1968-72, Surrey Univ 1972-; Prof of Music, 1981-. *Creative works:* Compositions include: Symphony in Two Movements, 1972; Essay for Clarinet and Orchestra, 1970; Sinfonia 3, Guildford 91 Fest; Many other instrumental works incl: 3 String Quartets, several Chamber Ensemble Sonatas; Choral works incl: Voices of Autumn, BBC, 1976; Bristol Mass, Bristol Cathedral, 1990. *Memberships:* PRS; Composers Guild of GB; Assn of Profl Composers; Sec 1989-, Nat Assn of Univ Music Staff. *Honours:* McEwan Mem Prize, 1962; Clements Mem Prize, 1963; Radcliffe Awd, 1969; SPNM Prize, 1980; ARAM, elected 1990. *Hobby:* Playing with the children. *Address:* 32 Wykeham Road, Guildford, Surrey GU1 2SE, England.

FORD Benjamin Thomas, b. 1 Apr 1925, London, England. Ret'd. m. Vera Ada, 30 Dec 1952, 2 s, 1 d. *Appointments:* Fleet Air Arm, 1943-47; Convener of Shop Stewards, The Marconi Co, 1955-64; Clacton UDC, 1959-62; Alderman & JP, Essex, 1959-65; MP for Bradford North, 1964-83. *Publication:* Piecework, the time saved system. *Memberships:* Freeman, City of London; Gunmaker's Livery; Chmn, Eng Shooting Coun; VP, Nat Rifle Assn; FAIA (Hon); Idle Working Men's Club, Bradford; Royal Soc of St George. *Honours:* Dep Lt, Co of W Yorks; Grand Off, Order of the Southern Cross, Brazil. *Hobbies:* Family; Shooting; Politics; Music; Reading. *Address:* 9 Wynmore Crescent, Bramhope, Leeds LS16 9DH, England.

FORD Lee Ellen, b. 16 June 1917, Auburn, IN, USA. Scientist; Edr; Lawyer (ret 1992). *Education:* BA, Wittenberg Coll, 1947; MS, Univ of Minn, 1949; PhD, Iowa State Univ, 1952; JD, Univ of Notre Dame, 1972. *Appointments include:* Exec Dir, Legis Bur Univ, Notre Dame Law Sch, 1969-72; Ed, New Dimensions in Legis, 1969-72; Bd Dirs, Mbr Coun, St Marks Luth Ch, Butler, 1970-76; Ed, Butler Record Herald, 1972-76; Bd Dir, Ind Coun Chs; Ed, Ford Assocs pubs, 1972-86; Admitted to Ind Bar, 1972; Exec Asst to Gov Otis R Bowen Ind, 1973-75; Bd Dir, Ind Commn on Status Women, 1973-74; Bd Dir, Ind Interreligious Comm on Human Equality, 1976-80; Mbr, Pres's Adv Coun on Drug Abuse, 1976-77; Mbr, DeKalb Co (Ind) Sheriff's Merit Bd, 1983-87; Fdr, Dir, Pres, Ind Caucus for Animal Legis and Ldrship, 1984-87. *Contributions to:* Over 2000 sci and popular pubs on Cytogenetics, Dog Breeding and Legal Topics; Articles to Am Kennel Club Gazette, 1970-81. *Memberships include:* AAUW; AAAS; Am Genetics Assn; Am Soc Zoologists; Bot Soc Am; Bd Dir, ABA; Fdr, Bd Dir 1970-76, DeKalb Co Humane Soc; Bd Dir, Nat Assn Women Lawyers; Bd Dir, Women's Equity Action League; Assn So Biologists; Phi Kappa Phi. *Address:* 336 Hickory Street, Butler, IN 46721, USA.

FORD Peter Fletcher, b. 3 June 1936, Harpenden, Herts, England. Author; Ed; Ed Cons; Creative Writing Tutor. m. 28 Aug 1960, div, 2 s, 1 d. *Appointments:* Nat Serv, Royal Artillery, Malaya, 1955-56; Ed, Cassell, 1958-61; Sr Copy Ed, Penguin Books, 1961-64; Sr Ed, Thomas Nelson, 1964-70; Freelance & Ed Cons to Quartet Books, 1971-. *Publications include:* All about Drugs (with Prof F Bergel, DRA Davies), 1970; The Fool on the Hill (with Max Wall), 1975; Scientists and Inventors (with A Feldman), 1979; The True History of the Elephant Man (with the late Dr M Howell), 1980, fully revised ed, 1992; The Elephant Man (a retelling for children), 1983; The Picture Buyer's Handbook (with J Fisher), 1988; A Collector's Guide to Teddy Bears, 1990; Rings and Curtains: the Personal and Family Memoirs of Albert Whiteley, 1992. *Memberships:* Soc of Authors; Soc of Freelance Eds and Proofreaders; Folklore Soc; Hon Mbr, Lit Panel, Eastern Arts Assn, 1982- 87. *Hobbies:* Walking collie dog; Theatre and

concert going; Reading. *Address:* 42 Friars Street, Sudbury, Suffolk CO10 6AG, England.

FORD Robert Eustace Paul, b. 21 Feb 1916, Waldo, KS, USA. Ret'd. *Education:* BS, State Univ, Hays, 1937; MA, Univ of Missouri, 1971; Extensive graduate work in Universities in Latin America and Europe. *Appointments:* State Univ, Hays, 1941; Pan Am World Airways, 1941-50; Lockheed Aircraft, Europe, 1950-51; Trans World Airlines, 1951-72; Univ of Maryland, Spain and Germany, 1972-83; Aviation Advr to the Kingdom of Saudi Arabia; Engr, Kennedy Space Ctr; Instr, Trans World Airlines Flight Sch; Flight Supt, Trans World Airlines, New York; Mgr, Ground Ops, Pan Am World Airways; Lectr, Univ of Maryland. *Publications:* 35 tech books on aerospace subjs; Many tech bulletins and translations. *Memberships:* Former VP European Reg, Life Mbr, Navy League League of the US; Former Ed, Navy League Mag; Liga Naval Espanola; Former Exec Sec, Am Club of Madrid; Former Pres, Pan Am Airways Mgmt Club, MLA and NY; Lt Cmdr WMG, Imperial Constantinian Mil Order of St George; Commander American Knights in Spain; Orden Soberana y Militar del Temple de Jerusalem (Templars); Pres, Irans Wrld Airlines Club in Spain and Mbr, Int Bd of Dirs. *Hobbies:* Information sciences; Literature; Aviation. *Address:* Plaza del Biombo 6, 28013 Madrid, Spain.

FORD Robert Webster, b. 27 Mar 1923, Burton-on-Trent, England. Ret'd Dipl. m. Monica Florence Tebbett, 2 June 1957, 2 s. *Appointments:* RAF WWII, 1939-45; Indian Govt Serv, 1945-47; Tibet Govt Serv, 1947-50; Pol Prisoner, China, 1950-55; HM Dipl Serv, 1957-83. *Publications:* Captured in Tibet, 1957, reprinted 1990. *Memberships:* FRGS; FRCSoc; Coun, Tibet Soc. *Honour:* CBE 1982. *Hobbies:* Gardening; Walking; Skiing. *Address:* Cedar Garth, Latimer Road, Monken Hadley, Barnet, Herts EN5 5NU, England.

FORDHAM Michael Scott Montague, b. 4 Aug 1905, London, England. Analytical Psychologist. m. 1 Sept 1928, 1 s. *Education:* BA 1917; B Chia 1931; MB 1932; MBCP 1932; MD 1947. *Appointments:* Hse Physn, St Bartholomews; Child Psych, London Child Guidance Clin, 1930-39; Med Off, Long Grove Mental Hosp, 1932-33; Analyst, 1940-. *Creative works:* Life of Childhood, 1944 (revised as Children as Individuals, 1969); New Developments in AP, 1957; The Objective Psyche, 1958; The Self and Autism, 1976; Jungian Psychotherapy, 1978; Explorations into the Self, 1985; The Making of an Analyst, 1992; Author of over 200 contributions to scientific and other journs; Co-ed, Collected Works of C G Jung; Ed, The Journ of Analytical Psychology. *Memberships:* Chmn, Dir of Tng, Soc of Analytical Psychol; Chmn of Psychotherapy Sect, Fdr Fellow 1971, RCPsych; Chmn of Med Sect, Hon Fellow 1974, BPsS. *Honours:* Sr Exhibition of Trinity, 1925; Schuters Scholar at Barts, 1927. *Hobbies:* Gardening; Reading; Musical appreciation. *Address:* Wilton Lane, Jordans, nr Beaconsfield, Bucks HP9 2RE, England.

FORMWALT Lee William, b. 19 Dec 1949, Springfield, MA, USA. Prof of Hist. m. Dorothea M Mumm, 30 Dec 1972, 1 s, 2 d. *Education:* BA 1971, PhD 1977, Catholic Univ of Am; MA, Univ of MA, 1972. *Appointments:* Papers of Benjamin Henry Latrobe, Rsch Asst, Maryland Histl Soc, Baltimore, 1974-77; Asst Prof 1977-82, Assoc Prof 1982-88, Prof 1988-, Albany State Coll. *Publications:* Co-ed, The Journals of Benjamin Henry Latrobe 1796-1820, 3 vols, 1977, 1980; Co-ed, The Correspondence and Miscellaneous Papers of Benjamin Henry Latrobe, vol I 1984, vol II 1986; Over a dozen articles published in Ga Hist Quarterly, Plantation Society in the Americas. *Memberships:* Am Histl Assn; Org of Am Histns; Southern Histl Assn; Bd of Eds, GA Assn of Histns; Bd of Eds, GA Histl Soc; AAUP; Bd of Dir, Thronateeska Heritage Fndn. *Honours include:* Penrose Fund Grant, Am Philos Soc, 1981; Thronateeska Heritage Fndn Dir of the Yr, 1984, 1991; NEH Fellow for Coll Tchrs, 1985-86; Hist Tchr of the Yr 1985, 1990, 1991, Rschr of the Yr 1990-91, Albany

State Coll; Albert J Beveridge Grant for Rsch in Hist of Western Hemisphere, Am Hist Assn, 1986-87; Grant in Aid for Rsch in State and Local Hist, Am Assn for State and Local Hist, 1988-89; NEH Summer Sem Grant, 1991. *Hobbies:* Philately; Walking. *Address:* 939 Barbragale Avenue, Albany, GA 31705, USA.

FORRESTER Ian Stewart, b. 13 Jan 1945, Glasgow, Scotland. Queens Counsel, Scotland; Scottish Advocate; m. Sandra Ann Therese Keegan, 7 Mar 1981, 2 s. *Education:* MA 1965, LLB, 1967, Univ of Glasgow; MCL, Tulane Univ of Louisiana, USA, 1969. *Appointments:* Chm, Brit Conservative Assn in Belgium, 1982-86; Chm, European Trade Law Assn, 1989-. *Publications:* Numerous articles on EEC customs, dumping and trade law, competition law. *Memberships:* Athnaeum; Intl CLub Chateau Sainte Anne, Brussels; Royal Yacht Club of Belgium. *Honours:* Queens Counsel, Scotland, 1988. *Hobbies:* Politics; Wine; Cooking; Antiques; Restoring old houses; Sailing. *Address:* Forrester Norall and Sutton, 1 Place Madou, Box 34, 1030 Brussels, Belgium.

FORSYTH Elliott Christopher, b. 1 Feb 1924, Mt Gambier, S Aust. Emeritus Prof of French. m. Rona Lynette Williams, 29 May 1967, 2 d. *Education:* BA Hons, 1947; Dip Ed, 1950; Docteur de l'Universitéde Paris, 1954. *Appointments:* Tchr, The Friends' Sch, Hobart, 1947-49; Lectr, Sr Lectr, Univ of Adelaide, 1955-66; Vis Lectr, Univ of Wisconsin, 1963-65; Fndn Prof of French 1966-87, Emeritus Prof of French, LáTrobe Univ, Melbourne, 1988-; Vis Prof, Univ of Melbourne, 1992. *Publications:* La Tragédie Française de Jodelle à Corneille (1553-1640): le Thème de la Vengeance, 1962; Saül le Furieux (Crit Ed), 1968; Concordance des 'Tragiques' d'A d'Aubigné, 1984; Baudin in Australian Waters (Ed), 1988. *Memberships:* Hon Sec, Modern Lang Tchrs' Assn of S Australia, 1958, 1960-63; Pres, Alliance Française S Australia, 1960-63; VP 1975-77, Fellow, Australian Acad of the Humanities; Chmn, Ministerial Educ Commn, Uniting Ch in Australia, 1977-86; FACE. *Honours:* French Govt Scholarship, 1951-53; Off 1971, Cmdr 1983, dans l'Ordre des Palmes Académiques. *Hobbies:* Music; Photography; Church Activities; Bushwalking. *Address:* 25 Jacka Street, North Balwyn, Victoria, Australia 3104.

FORTE Ronald Neil, b. 24 Dec 1944, Southport, Qld, Aust. Mng Dir. m. Marilynn Alister Schurmann, 7 Feb 1970, 1 s, 1 d. *Appointments:* AGC Ltd, 1968-: Mgr, Credit Corp Malaysia 1979, Credit Mgr for S Aust 1983, Sr Mgr for S Aust 1984, Nat Mgr Dealer Lending 1989; Mng Dir, AGC Fin (UK) Ltd, 1990. *Memberships:* MIPMA; AAMI. *Hobbies:* Golf; Watching sports; Travel. *Address:* 6A Fortuna Court, 25 Repulse Bay Road, Hong Kong.

FORTIN J H E Carrier, b. 9 Sept 1915, Beauceville, Quebec, Can. Ret'd Judge; Lawyer. m. Solange Gobeil, 9 Sept 1943, 2 s, 1 d. *Education:* BA, Sem of Quebec, 1937; LLL, Laval Univ, 1940; LLD, Univ of Sherbrooke, 1965. *Appointments:* Lawyer, 1940-69; Alderman, Ldr, City Coun of Sherbrooke, 1953-62; Sec, Law Fac, Lectr, Univ of Sherbrooke, 1954-62; Min of Labour, Quebec, 1963-66; Justice, Superior Ct, 1969-90. *Creative works:* Fdr of Weekly Newspaper L'Asbestos, 1941; Fdr, La Cooperative d'Habitation d'Asbestos, 1941. *Memberships include:* Treas 1950, Batonnier 1959, St Francis Dist Bar; Sr C of C, Sherbrooke, 1954-69; Dir, Rural Bar Assn; Sherbrooke CoLiberal Assn, 1960-69; Dir 1969, Can Bar Assn; Pres, Assemblee Generale des Juges Cour Superieure du Que, 1973-75. *Honours:* Dr Honris Causa, Univ of Sherbrooke, 1965; Medal Pierre B Migh Ault, Bar St Francis, 1984; Medal, Albert Le Blanc, Fac of Law, Sherbrooke, 1989. *Hobbies:* Golf; History; Politics. *Address:* 2040 Vermont, Sherbrooke, Quebec, Canada J1J 1H1.

FORTUIN Harold Frederick, b. 20 Oct 1964, Mt Clemens, MI, USA. Lectr. *Education:* Assoc, Royal Conservatory of Music, Toronto, 1986; BMus, Wayne State Univ, 1987; MMus 1989, PhD cand 1990, MI State Univ; PhD cand, Univ of Glasgow, 1991. *Appointments:*

Adj Prof, Composition, Olivet Coll, 1988-89; Tchng Asst in Composition, Electronic and Computer Music, Music Theory 1988-91, Instr, Computer Music, Evening Coll 1990, MI State Univ; Lectr, Composition and Computer Music, Univ of Glasgow, 1991-92. *Creative works include:* There for solo flute, 1984; Antiphone-Polyphone: A Multichronal Emergence for 5 saxophones, electriv guitar, percussion, 1988; Undertow for soprano, violin, cello, piano, 1989; Extremities for large orch, 1989; ZEN wRAP for magnetic tape, 1990; Epitaph for alto sax and piano, 1991. *Memberships include:* Soc of Composers Inc; Soc for Electro-Acoustic Music in the US; BMI; Pi Kappa Lambda; Phi Kappa Phi; Golden Key Nat Hon Soc; Treas 1985-86, Pres 1986-87, Gamma Omicron Chapt, Phi Pu Alpha; Treas 1990-91, Gamma Epsilon Chapt, Phi Mu Alpha. *Honours include:* Untitled 3 played at the Nat Conf of the Soc for Electro- Acoustic Music, Olympia, Washington, 1988; Recorded works chosen for nationally syndicated broadcast on The Difficult Listening Hour, produced by the Independent Music Network, USA, 1990; Epitaph published by Dorn/Needham Pubs, Medfield, MA, 1991; Exdremities on Vienna Modern Masters 3003 CD. *Hobbies:* Current events; Reading; Chess; Vegetarianism; Ethnic food. *Address:* 11265 Grenada, Sterling Heights, MI 48312, USA.

FORTUIN Johannes Martinus Hendrikus, b. 30 Sept 1927, Rotterdam, Holland. Prof of Chem Engrng. m. Wilhemina Josephina Theresia van de Ven, 28 Sept 1961, 1 s, 3 d. *Education:* Degree in Chem Engrng cum laude 1953, PhD cum laude 1955, Tech Univ, Delft. *Appointments:* Sci Asst, Delft Univ, 1952-54; Rsch, Cen Lab N V Dsm, Geleen, 1954-61; Hd Tech Dept, C L DSM, Geleen, 1961-82; Prof, Chem Engrng, Univ of Amsterdam, 1977-; Coord Ext Rsch in Process Tech, DSM Rsch BV, Geleen, 1982-87. *Publications:* Ed: Physical and Chemical Aspects of Adsorbents and Catalysts, 1970; Chemical Reaction Engineering, 1972. *Contributions to:* Art to profl journs. *Memberships:* Royal Neth Chem Soc; Royal Inst Eng; Bd Mem, Neth Found Chem Rsch; Sec, Working Party on Chem Reaction Engrng of the European Fndn of Chem Engrng. *Honours:* Process Tech Awd, Hollandsche Maatshappij der Wetenschappen, Haarlem, 1978; Named Off, Order of Orange-Nassau, 1987. *Hobbies:* History of Europe. *Address:* University of Amsterdam, Department of Chemical Engineering, 166 Nieuwe Achtergracht, 1018 WV Amsterdam, Holland.

FOSKETT Daphne, b. 23 Dec 1911, Kimpton, Hants, England. Author. m. The Rt Rev Dr Reginald Foskett, 7 Apr 1937, dec, 2 d. *Appointment:* Matron, St Ives Sch, Bexhill, 1932-36. *Creative works:* British Portraits Miniature, 1963; John Smart, 1964; Arts Coun Exlub Cat, 1965; Dictionary of Brit Miniature Painters, 1972; Samuel Cooper, 1974; Jon Harden, 1974; Cat of S Cooper, Scottish Art Coun, 1974; Collecting Miniatures, 1979; Miniatures, Dictionary and Guide, 1987. *Memberships:* Co Sec, Girl Guide Assn; ARSA; Hon RMS; Theta Sigma Phi. *Honours:* Commendation for The Colvin Medal, Lib Assn, 1972. *Hobbies:* Antiques; History; Travel. *Address:* 55 Riverside Drive, Solihull, W Midlands B91 3HR, England.

FOSS Ralph Scot, b. 19 Aug 1945, Perth Amboy, NJ, USA. Cons. *Education:* BSME, PA State Univ, 1965; BS, Parsons Coll, 1966. *Appointments:* Plant Engrng, Volkswagon Gonloff, 1966-69; Prod Mgr 1971-73, Systems Engr Mgr 1981-87, Ingersoll Rand Co; Systems Engr Mgr, Minn Inst Tech, 1973-75; Sales & Mktng Mgr, Sullair Corp, 1975-81; Pres, Plant Air Tech, 1987-; Pres, Winborn Assoc, 1988-. *Publications:* Compressed Air Systems Workbook; 13 Nationally Pub Aritcles on Compressed Air Sci; 7 Patents in Energy Mgmt of Compressed Air. *Memberships:* Nat Pres, Corp Mbrs Coun, Am Inst of Plant Engrs; Instrument Soc of Am; Int Platform Assn; Bd of Dir, Nat Educ Com; Assn of Energy Engrs; Bd of Dir, Amethyst Fndn; Pres's Coun, FL Hosp; Repub Presidential Task Force. *Hobbies:* Golf;

Writing. *Address:* 5121 Hunt Stand Lane, Charlotte, NC 28226, USA.

FOSTER Charles Arthur, b. 25 June 1926, Wells, Somerset, England. Ret'd Cons Anaesthetist. m. Virginia Caroline Delap, 9 Mar 1963, 1 d. *Education:* MB BS, 1948; MRCS; LRCP London, 1948; DA, 1951; FFARCS, 1954. *Appointments:* Casualty Off 1948-49, Hse Physn 1949, Res Anaesthetist 1949-51, Registrar Anaesthetist 1953-58, Cons Anaesthetist 1958-86, St Thomas's Hosp; Nt Serv, RAMC, 1951-53; Cons Anaesthetist, Royal Masonic Hosp, 1970-86. *Publications:* An Introduction to Anaesthetics, 1966; Anaesthetics for Theatre Technicians, 1968. *Memberships:* Assn of Anaesthetists; FRSM; Freeman, City of London Liveryman; Worshipful Co of Barbers, 1980. *Honour:* ERD 1969. *Hobbies:* Bird watching; Archaeology. *Address:* Glebe Farm, Sternfield, Saxmundham, Suffolk IP17 1ND, England.

FOSTER Charles William, b. 1 Jan 1939, Chattanooga, TN, USA. Prof of Eng & Linguistics; Folklorist; Performer. m. Anne Carey Brandon, 24 Mar 1962, 1 s, 1 d. *Education:* BS, Univ of Chattanooga, 1961; MA, East TN State Univ, 1963; PhD, Univ of AL, 1968. *Appointments:* Tchr, Hixson HS, 1961-62; Rschr, East TN State Univ, 1962-63; Instr, Univ of AL, 1963-68; Asst Prof 1969, Assoc 1971, Full Prof 1973, Dept Hd 1973, Univ of N AL. *Publications:* Bluegrass Roots, 1975; A Sense of Place: Folklore of North Alabama, 1977. *Memberships:* Am Dialect Soc; Am Folklore Soc; MLA; TN Folklore Soc; AL Folklife Assn; AL Coun on the Humanities. *Honours:* TN Valley Old-Time Banjo Champion, 1969, 1970, 1971, 1972; Champion Folksinger, 1970-76; Champion Banjoist of the Upper Cumberland, 1975; Ldr, Old-time String Band of the Yr, 1986-90; Fac Mbr of the Yr, 1989. *Hobbies:* Appalachian folklore and folk music; 5-string banjo; Fiddle; Woodworking; Writing; Performing as part of of Foster Family Band. *Address:* 820 Olive Street, Florence, AL 35630, USA.

FOSTER Dale Warren, b. 7 Mar 1950, Bryan, TX, USA. Coll Prof; Real Estate Broker; Cons. *Education:* BBA 1972, MA 1979, TX A&M Univ; BS 1981, MEd 1983, Univ of Houston; AAS, Houston Comm Coll, 1982. *Appointments:* Internal Auditor, Hermann Hosp, 1980-82; Prof of Govt, Houston Comm Coll, 1980-; HS Tchr, Cy-Fair Sch Dist, 1983-84; Adj Instr, N Harris Coll, 1983-91; Second Tchr, Alief Pub Schs, 1984-88. *Publications:* Why the Homeless?, 1989; Departmental textbook supplement (Co-ed), 1990; Annotated curriculum and media guide (Co-author), 1990; A Politics Reader (Contributing Ed), 3rd ed 1991; Various journ articles. *Memberships:* Vice Chmn for Confs, Alumni Advsr, Sectional Rep, Chapt Pres, Alpha Phi Omega; Phi Theta Kappa initiate; Kappa Delta Pi initiate; Int Platform Assn; TX Coun on Social Studies; Inst of Certified Mgmt Accts; TX Jr Coll Tchrs Assn; Assn for Supervision and Curric Dev. *Honours include:* Disting Fellow, Am Bd of Master Educators, 1987; Adj Tchng and Comm Serv Awd, N Harris Coll, 1990; Gt Tchrs Seminarian, Houston Comm Coll, 1991; Medal of Tchng Excellence, Nat Inst for Staff and Organisational Dev, 1991; Outstg Instr Awd, HCCS Fac Assn, 1991. *Hobbies:* Reading; Bowling; Travel; Outdoor recreation; Public speaking. *Address:* 11936 Bellaire Boulevard, PO Box 249, Alief, TX 77411, USA.

FOSTER Edwin Powell, b. 7 May 1942, Louisville, KY, USA. Civil Engrng Prof; Dir. m. Joyce Ann Lane, 25 June 1966, 1 s, 2 d. *Education:* BE 1964, MS 1966, PhD 1974, Vanderbilt Univ. *Appointments:* Am Bridge - US Steel, 1964; Brown Engrng, 1966; AVCO Aerostructures, 1967; Univ of TN, 1968. *Publications:* 20 rsch papers on structural engrng. *Memberships:* Middle TN Pres of Am ASCE; Educ Chmn, Civil Engrng Sect for Southeast, Am Soc for Engrng; Sec, Chattanooga Chapt, Nat Soc of Profl Engrs. *Honours:* UT-Nashville Tchr Excellence Awd, 1973; UT Alumni Outstg Tchr, 1977; Outstg Tchr 1984, Prof of the Yr 1987, UTC Sch of Engrng; Norbert Koch Fac Serv Awd,

1988. *Hobbies:* Restoration of MGA sports cars; Tennis; Architecture. *Address:* University of Tennessee, School of Engineering, 615 McCallie Avenue, Chattanooga, TN 37403, USA.

FOSTER Grace Peterson, b. 11 Oct 1947, Lenoir County, Kinston, NC, USA. Maths Instr. m. Dwight B Foster, 19 May 1967, 1 s, 1 d. *Education:* BS 1970, MAE 1977, E Carolina Univ. *Appointments:* Pitt Co Schs, 1969-73; E Carolina Univ, 1977-81; Beaufort Co Comm Coll, 1981-. *Publications:* Hands on Mathematics, 1979; Experiencing Mathematics, 1982; Mathematics Via Manipulatives, 1988. *Memberships:* Contest Comm, NC Coun of Tchrs of Maths; Nat Coun of Tchrs of Maths; VP, Pres elect, Pres, NC Math Assn of 2 Yr Colls; Nat Math Assn of 2 Yr Colls. *Honours:* NCCTM Cert of Appreciation, 1986; Serv Awd, Gamma Beta Phi Hon Soc, 1990; Tchr of the Yr, Beaufort Co Comm Coll, 1991. *Hobbies:* Proceeds of Mathematics Via Manipulatives used to set up scholarship at ECU for Prospective Math Teacher; Reading; Gardening. *Address:* Route 2, Box 567A, Ayden, NC 28513, USA.

FOSTER Maxie Elliott, b. 1 May 1950, Athens, GA, USA. Univ Prof. *Education:* BSEd 1972, MEd 1974, Univ of GA. *Appointments:* Tchr, Coach, Clarke Ctrl HS, 1972-73; Instr, Macon Jr Coll, 1975-82; Asst Prof, LA State Univ, 1982-. *Creative works:* Inspirational Writings; Fdr, Organiser, Exec Dir, Henry A Morse Bible Conf, Athens, GA; State Dir 1987-90, Camp Anytown, USA; Pub TV Documentary: Integration in the South. *Memberships:* Black/White Task Force, Shreveport, 1985-90; Assoc Dir 1987-89, Hlth Fitness, LSU-S; Ldrship, Shreveport/Bossler, 1987; Coun on Black Am Affairs of the Am Assn of Comm/Jr Colls; LA Assn of Hlth, Phys Educ, Rec & Dance; Bd of Dir - Via C of C, Shreveport Juvenile Justice Prog, 1988. *Honours:* First Black Scholarship Athlete & Team Capt, Univ of GA, 1968, 1972; World's List, Track and Field News Mag, 1970; Nat Big Brother of the Yr Cand Awd, 1981; Int Rotary Fellow, India, 1984; Pres, Kappa Delta Pi, 1988; Omicron Delta Kappa. *Hobbies:* Inspirational writing; Biblical expositions; Working with people; Music; Reading; Sports; Travel; Church work: Presenting seminars, workshops & programme training. *Address:* Department of Health and Physical Education, Louisiana State University in Shreveport, One University Place, Shreveport, LA 71115, USA.

FOSTER Norman, b. 1935, Manchester, England. *Education:* Dip Arch Cert TP Manchester Univ; Masters degree, Yale Univ; Hon Doctorates from Universities of E Anglia, Bath, Valencia and Royal College of Art. *Appointments:* Consultancy work on urban renewal projs, USA; Estab pvt pract with R Rogers & W Cheesman, 1963; Estab Foster Assoc, 1967; Estab Sir Norman Foster & Partners, 1992; worked with Buckminster Fuller, 1968-83; Lectr, UK, USA, Europe, Far East; Past VP, Mbr Council, Archtl Assn; External Examiner, Mbr, RIBA; Coun Mbr, Royal Coll of Art. *Publications include:* Norman Foster: Team Four and Foster Associates Buildings and Projects, 1964-73, vol 1; Norman Foster: Foster Associates Buildings and Projects, 1971-1978, vol 2, and 1978-85, vol 3; Foster Associates Buildings and Projects, 1991; Norman Foster Sketches, 1992. *Creative works incl:* Exhibitions: In London, New York, Paris, Lyon, Nimes, Tokyo, Berlin, Madrid, Barcelona, Venice, Bordeaux, Florence, Milan. Major buildings: Willis Faber Dumas, Ipswich, 1975; Sainsbury Centre for Visual Arts and Crescent Wing Extension, Norwich, 1978-91; Renault Centre, Swindon, 1983; Hong Kong Bank HQ, Hong Kong, 1986; Sackler Galleries, Royal Academy of Arts, London, 1991; Stansted, London's Third Airport, 1991; Century Tower, Tokyo, 1991; ITN HQ, London, 1991; Telecom Tower, Barcelona, 1992; Carré d'Art, Nimes, 1992. Masterplans for King's Cross and Greenwich, London, Nimes and Cannes, France, Berlin, Duisburg and Lüdenscheid in Germany and Rotterdam in Holland. Projects: Street furniture for Decaux, Paris; Headquarters for Commerzbank, Frankfurt; Airport at Chek Lap Kok, Hong Kong; Technology Centre, Duisburg; Metro Railway

System, Bilbao; Furniture for Techno, Italy; Houses in Corsica, Japan, Germany; Law Fac, Cambridge Univ, Cambridge; Canary Wharf Stn for the Jubilee Line underground extension, 1991; Musée de la Préhistoire, Verdon, France. *Memberships include:* IBM Fellow; ARA; Hon FAIA; FCSD; Hon, Bund Deutscher Architeken Royal Designer for Ind; French Order of Architects, 1989; Assoc, Academie Royale de Belgique, 1990. *Honours:* Royal Gold Medal for Arch, 1983; Japan Design Foundation Award, 1987; Kunstpreis, berlin, 1989; Knighthood in the Queen's Birthday Hons, 1990; Mies van der Rohe Pavilion Awd for European Arch, Barcelona, 1991; Gold Medal, French Acad of Arch, Paris; Arnold W Brunner Memorial Prize, New York, 1992. *Hobbies:* Flying; Cycling; Running; Skiing. *Address:* c/o Sir Norman Foster & Partners, Riverside Three, 22 Hester Road, London SW11 4AN, England.

FOTEV Georgi, b. 24 Aug 1941, Dimitrovche, Bulgaria. Dir; Min. m. Violetta, 16 Oct 1966, 1 s, 1 d. *Education:* Cand of Philosl Scis Degree, 1975; PhD, 1987. *Appointments:* Lectr in Hist and Philos, Sofia Univ, 1977; Sr Rsch Assoc 1983, Hd of Hist of Sociology 1986, Prof, Dep Dir 1989, Inst of Sociology. *Publications:* The Sociological Theories of E Durkheim, 1979; The Principles of Positivist Sociology, 1982; Social Reality and Imagination, 1986. *Memberships:* Int Sociological Assn; Sec, Mbr of Exec Comm, Mbr of Coun, Bulgarian Sociological Assn; Ed Bd, Sociologicheski problemi journ. *Honour:* The Best Sociology Monograph Awd, Bulgarian Acad of Scis and KI Ohridski, Sofia Univ. *Hobby:* Painting. *Address:* Institute of Sociology, Bulgarian Academy of Sciences, 13-A Moskovska Str, 1000 Sofia, Bulgaria.

FOTIADE Bradu Constantin, b. 14 Apr 1928, Bucharest, Romania. Dr in Med; Chief of Dept. m. Grant Irene, 4 July 1957, 1 s. *Education:* Fac of Med, Bucharest, 1946-52. *Appointments:* Med Specialist, Cardiology, 1960; Med Specialist, Cardiovascular Invest, 1963; Dr in Med, 1983. *Creative works:* 11 Monographies; 190 Publs; 319 Scientific Communications; 4 Scientific Films. *Memberships:* Pres, Med Appar, 1962; Olympic Comm, 1966; Phisiopatology Staff, Romania, 1972; European Phisiopatology, Brussels, 1972; Comm on Sports Med, 1973; VP, Romanian Cardiology Soc, 1990. *Honours:* Med Work Awd, 1961, 1980; Work Order, Med, III Class, 1962; Special Work in Sport Med, 1973; Corres Mbr, Romanian Acad of Med, 1991. *Hobbies:* Electronics; Mechanics; Fishing; Diving. *Address:* Department of Invest Cardiovascular, Spitalul Clinic Fundeni, 505 Fundeni 258, Bucuresti, Romania.

FOTSIS Stavros, b. 6 Mar 1937, Greece. Author; Stock Market Speculator. m. Ermioni G Gogolos, 16 Sept 1973, 1 s, 1 d. *Education:* Piraeus Nautical Schs and Sems, 1955-69; London Pitman Sch of Eng, 1964- 65. *Appointments:* Deck Off, Merchant Navy, 1957-69; Futures and Options on Various Commodity Exchanges, 1967-; Master Mariner, VLCC Vessels, 1970-86. *Publications:* Num Lyric Poems for Various Mags; Novel and Biography Books. *Memberships:* Master Mariners' Union of Greece; Various Lit Unions; Paphos C of C and Ind. *Honours:* Dangerous Ops Awd, N Vietnamese Govt, 1967; Dangerous and Skilful Ops Awd, Nautical Auths of Bangladesh, 1971. *Hobbies:* Hunting; Swimming; Stock Market Speculating. *Address:* Polydrosson Souliou Thesprotias, 44017 Vrossinis Epirus, Greece.

FOUGERE Paule, b. 16 June 1916, Nantes, France. Doctor of Pharmacy; Scientific writer. m. Jean Fougere, 1 Sept 1938, 1 s, 2 d. *Education:* Inst Chavagnes a Nantes; Higher Studies, Nantes and Strasbourg; Pharmacist, 1938; Doctorate, 1949. *Appointments:* Hd, important Dispensary in Paris, 1941-91; Reporter on Medical Scis in Revue des Deux Mondes, 1968-88. *Publications:* La Mort Blanche Grands Pharmaciens, 1956; L'Homme La Femme et l'age critique, 1968; Les Mediaments du bien-entre, 1970; Le Livre des parfums,

1972; Patmos, 1974; Initiation a l'Immunologie, 1980; Radio play; Film Script; Numerous articles and conference papers. *Memberships:* Corres Mem, Nat Acad of Pharm; VP, French Soc of Doctors of Pharm; Soc des Gens de Lettres. *Honours:* Literary prizes: Bineg-Sangle, French Acad, 1968; Brit Acad Prize, 1972; Prix Nicolas Missarel, 1980; Ofr de la Legion d'Honneur et de l'Ordre Nat du Merite. *Hobbies:* Hunting; Swimming; Crossword Puzzles. *Address:* 22 Quai de Bethune, 75004 Paris, France. 91.

FOURNIER Albert Edouard André, b. 26 Nov 1938, Calais, France. Prof of Med. m. Jacqueline Kaponas, 13 Apr 1973, dec 1988, 2 s, 1 d. *Education:* Residency, Univ Hosp of Paris, 1964-68; MD, 1968; Rsch Fellow, Mayo Clin, US, 1968-69; Chef de Clinique Hopitaux, Paris, 1969-71; Prof of Med, 1974. *Appointments:* Chief of Internal Med and Neprology, Univ Hosp of Amiens, Univ of Picardie. *Publications include:* La Defletion Potassique; Rein et Hypertension; Rinon E Hypertension arterial; Vitamin D; Hypertension Arteriella; Articles in int journs. *Memberships:* French, European, Am and European Soc of Nephocology, Hypertension, Internal Med, Intensive Care. *Honour:* Chevalier des Palmes Academiques, 1989. *Hobbies:* Piano; Tennis; Swimming; Skiing. *Address:* 46 rue broix, St Firmin, 80090 Amiens, France.

FOX Alan Martin, b. 5 July 1938, London, England. Civil Servant. m. Sheila Naomi Pollard, 20 June 1965, 1 s, 2 d. *Education:* BSc Hons 1959; PhD 1963. *Appointments:* Min of Aviation, 1963-73; Foreign & C'wlth Off, 1973-75; MoD, 1975-. *Hobbies:* Bridge; Chess; Rugby; Cricket; Watching TV. *Address:* c/o Ministry of Defence, Horseguards Avenue, London SW1, England.

FOX James Harold, b. 30 Nov 1941, Washington DC, WA, USA. Supt of Schs; Educ. m. 21 Jan 1973, 2 s. *Education:* BS in Educ, 1963; MS in Educ, 1967; EdD in Gen Adm, 1971. *Appointments:* Tchr, Hist, Econ(s), 1963-66; Vice Prin, 1966-69; Assoc Prin, 1969-71; Prin, Middle, HS, 1971-73; Supt Schs, 1977-. *Publications:* Comprehensive Long Range Planning/District Reorganisation Middle School Reorganisation; Complex Role of the Teacher; Collision Course for the 80s; Thous Shalt Not Leave Board of Education in Dust, 1979. *Memberships:* Phi Delta Kappa; NMSA; NSBA; GA Sch Supts Assn; AASA; ASCD; Am Educ Fin Assn; Bd Chmn, Supts, Atlanta Metro Assn of Schs; Nat Assn Second Sch Prins. *Honours:* Outstg Young Men, Am Jaycees, 1972; Disting Servs Awd, Jaycees, 1985; Southeast Consortium for Minorities in Engrng, 1989; Cert of Merit, City of Atlanta, 1990. *Hobbies:* Boating; Snow skiing; Travelling; History. *Address:* 786 Cleveland Avenue SW, Atlanta, GA 30315, USA.

FOX Ronald David, b. 27 Sept 1946, London, England. Solicitor. m. Sonya Claudine Birshan, 11 Feb 1973, 1 s, 1 d. *Education:* MA Hons Jurisprudence, Lincoln Coll, Oxford Univ, 1965-68. *Appointments:* Herbert Oppenheimer, Nathan & Vandyk, 1969-88; Denton Hall Burgin & Warrens, 1988-89; Sr Ptnr, Fox Williams, 1989-. *Publications include:* Payments on Termination of Employment, 1st ed 1981, 2nd ed 1984, 3rd ed 1990; Commercial publs: Due Diligence, Disclosures and Warranties in Corporate Acquisition Practice - the United Kingdom, 1st ed, 1988, 2nd ed, 1992; Legal Aspects of Doing Business in England and Wales, 1990. Articles: Going into Business, 1989; Does your Secretary Have a Future?, 1990; Report on the 1990 Law Society National Conference, 1990; Doing it by the book, 1991; Dealing with redundancies, 1991. *Memberships:* RAC; Inst of Dirs; IBA; Law Soc of England and Wales; City of London Law Soc; Brit-Israel C of C; Brit-German Jurists' Assn. *Honour:* City of London Solicitors' Co Disting Serv Awd, 1989. *Hobbies:* Opera; Theatre; Cinema; Swimming; Skin diving; Scuba diving; Motoring & other forms of transport; Management studies. *Address:* c/o Fox Williams, City Gate House, 39-45 Finsbury Square, London EC2A 1UU, England.

FRAKES Ronald Alfred, b. 2 June 1928, London, England. Heraldic Artist. m. Joan Heather Chamberlain, 27 May 1950, 2 d. *Appointments:* Wireless Operator, RAF, 1946-48; Freelance Heraldic Artist, 1972-. *Creative works include:* Painting Royal Arms & Badges on a Royal Charter Bearing the Seal of HM The Queen, presented to the Worshipful Co of Painter-Stainers, 1981; Painting a matching pair of Coats of Arms for the Nat Heart Hosp, London; Designing the layout and drawing the badges of the RAMC, the Royal Dental Corps & Queen Alexandra's Royal Auxiliary Nursing Corps for a bronze plaque to commemorate the opening of a new Mil Hosp at Woolwich by HM Queen Elizabeth the Queen Mother; Painting the badge of 11 Group HQ, RAF, Bentley Priory on a commemorative plaque for the new Off's Mess opened by HM Queen Elizabeth the Queen Mother; Line drawing of the Arms of Swaziland on the flyleaf of a book presented to the King of Swaziland at his Coronation. *Memberships:* FRSA; Heraldry Soc; Richard III Soc; Freeman, Liveryman, Worshipful Co of Painter-Stainers'; Freeman, City of London. *Hobbies:* Study of Mediaeval History; Model making. *Address:* 77 Highfield Road, Woodford Green, Essex IG8 8JB, England.

FRANCESCHINA John Charles, b. 18 Oct 1947, Holyoke, MA, USA. Prof of Music & Theatre. *Education:* Mus Dipl Composition 1964, MM Theory & Composition 1971, Hartt Coll of Music; BA 1969, MFA Playwriting 1974, Cath Univ. *Appointments:* Composer in Residence, Nat Shakespeare Bd, 1970- 73; Composer in Residence, Asolo State Theatre, 1976-80; Composer, Players State Theatre, Coconut Grove, 1980-81; Musical Dir, Pittsburgh Pub Theatre, 1981-83; Musical Dir, Composer, Geva Theatre, 1983-85; Prof, FL State Univ, 1985-. *Creative works:* Letters to Tolstoy, 1984; Fanfare for the Fiftieth, 1985; Voyages, 1986; Concerto for Accordion & Orchestra, 1987; To the Ends of the Earth, 1988; Satiromastix, 1989. *Memberships:* Am Fndn of Musicians; Dramatists Guild. *Honours:* Composition Prize, Hartt Coll of Music, 1964; 1st Prize, Int Composition Competition, 1976; 1st Prize, Nat Composition Contest, 1984; 1st Prize, Southern Theatre Fest, 1988; Tchng Awd, FL State Univ, 1989-90. *Hobbies:* Collecting 18th Century Operas; English Women Playwrights; The Work of Charles Dibdin, The Elder; Opera Parodies in France. *Address:* 2133 Harriett Drive, Tallahassee, FL 32303, USA.

FRANCIS Hazel, b. 12 Apr 1929, Cannock, England, Prof of Educl Psychology. m. Dr Huw W S Francis, 23 May 1953, 2 s, 3 d. *Education:* BA Hons 1950, MA 1953, Girton Coll, Cambridge; MA 1967, PhD 1971, Univ of Leeds. *Appointments:* Second Sch Tchr, 1951-54, 1963-64; Pt-time Lectr 1969-73, Lectr, Sr Lectr 1973-78, Univ of Leeds; Prof 1978-, Pro-Dir, Inst of Educ 1985-90, Univ of London. *Publications:* Language in Childhood, 1975; Language in Teaching and Learning, 1978; Learning to Read, 1982; Toys and Games of Children of the World, 1984; Learning to Teach, 1985; British Journal of Educational Psychology (Ed), 1985-89; Num published papers. *Memberships:* Mbr of Coun 1979-85, BPsS; Brit Educl Rsch Assn; European Assn for Rsch on Learning and Instruction; Am Educl Rsch Assn; C Psychol. *Honour:* FBPsS, 1980. *Hobbies:* Mountain walking; Swimming; Tennis. *Address:* Institute of Education, University of London, 20 Bedford Way, London WC1H 0AA, England.

FRANCIS Robert Douglas, b. 2 Sept 1944, Ont, Can. m. Barbara Lynne Grant, 21 July 1973, 2 s, 1 d. *Education:* BA Hons 1963-67, PhD 1976, York Univ, Toronto; MA, Univ of Toronto, 1968. *Appointments:* Tchr, West Hill Collegiate, Toronto, 1968-69; Vis Lectr, Univ of BC, 1975-76; Asst Prof 1976-81, Assoc Prof 1981-88, Prof 1988-, Univ of Calgary; Vis Prof of Can Studies, Univ of Tsukuba, Japan, 1991-93. *Publications:* Frank H Underhill: Intellectual Provocateur, 1986; Origins: Canadian History Before Confederation (co-author), 1988; Destinies: Canadian History Since Confederation (co-author), 1988; Images of the West: Responses to the Canadian Prairies 1690-1960, 1989.

Memberships: Can Histl Assn; Alberta Histl Assn; Assn for Can Studies; Can Assn of Univ Tchrs. *Honours:* Master Tchr Awd, Univ of Calgary, 1982; J W Dafoe Book Prize, 1986; Awd of Merit, Assn for Can Studies, 1989. *Hobbies:* Skiing; Tennis; Squash; Hiking. *Address:* 1432 - 5th Street NW, Calgary, Alberta, Canada T2M 3B9.

FRANCIS Timothy Duane, b. 1 Mar 1956, Chicago, IL, USA. Chiropractic Kinesiology. *Education:* BSc 1982, Dr of Chiropractic magna cum laude 1984, Los Angeles Coll of Chiropractic; MSc cand, Univ of Bridgeport, 1984-; FIACA, 1989; DICAK, 1990. *Appointments:* Profl Fac, Dept of Recreation & Phys Educ, Univ of Nevada-Reno, 1976-80; Tchg Asst, Dept of Prins & Pract, Tchg Asst, Dept of Diagnosis, Full Time Fac, Dept of Prins & Pract, Los Angeles Coll of Chiropractic, 1983-85; Pvt Pract, Las Vegas, 1985-; Asst Instr, Int Coll of Applied Kinesiology, 1990; Nat Olympic Tng Ctr, Beijing, China, 1990. *Publication:* Structural Corrections For Eyes Into Distortion Patterns, 1990. *Memberships:* Am Chiropractic Assn; Nevada State Chiropractic Assn; Nat Strength & Conditioning Assn; Couns on Sports Injuries, Nutrition, Roentgenology, Technic ACA; Int Coll of Applied Kinesiology; Gonsted Clin Studies Soc; Fndn for Chiropractic Educ and Rsch. *Honours include:* Scholar of the Yr, Univ of Nevada-Reno, 1980; Nat Dean's List, 1984; Rsch Bd of Advsrs, Am Biog Inst, 1989; Am Biog Inst's Commemorative Medal of Hon, 1990; Golden State Awd, 1990; Key Awd for Exellence in the Field of Med, 1990; Man of the Yr, Am Bio Inst Bd of Int Rsch, 1990. *Hobbies:* Karate-Do; Weightlifting. *Address:* PO Box 81961, Las Vegas, NV 89180, USA.

FRANCO Antonio L P Sousa, b. 21 Sept 1942, Lisbon, Portugal. Prof; Pres; Court of Audit. m. Matilde Figueiredo Sousa Franco, 17 Sept 1984, 1 d. *Education:* LIB 1964, PhD 1972, Univ of Lisbon. *Appointments:* Prof of Law 1965-74, 1977-, Dean of the Law Sch 1979-86, Univ of Lisbon; Top Mgr of Enterprises, SACOR, 1968-72; CNP, 1972-74; Caixa Geral de Depositos, 1974-75; Mbr of Parliment, 1976-79, 1980-81; Sec of State, 1976; Prof of Law 1976-, Den of Law Sch 1989-, Cath Univ of Portugal; Min of Fin, 1979. *Publications include:* Politicas Financeiras e formacao do capital, 1972; A revisao da Constituicao Economica, 1982; Nocoes de Direito da Economia, I, 1983; Fiscalidade Europeia, 1987; Financas Publicas portuguesas - os subsectores institucionais, 1989-91; Financas Publicas e Direito Financeiro, 5th ed 1991. *Memberships include:* Pres 1974-78, Portuguese Inst of Admnstv Sci; Inst Int des Scis Admnstv; Assn Int Droit Economique. *Honours include:* 5 Acad Awd, Univ of Lisbon, 1962-65; Mbr of Bds of Scientific Journs - Common Market Law Review, Leyden; Estado e Direito, Lisboa e Madrid; Direito e Justica, Lisbon. *Hobbies:* Historic studies; Travelling; Reading; Tennis. *Address:* Edificio S Bernardo, Rua de S Bernardo No 50, r/c Dto, 1200 Lisboa, Portugal.

FRANCO Carole Ann, b. 21 Dec 1948, Hartford, CT, USA. Film Exec; Cons. *Education:* BA in Spanish, Duke Univ, 1970; Grad Cert in Educ, Trinity Coll, Hartford, 1971; Postgrad Studies in French, Sorbonne, Paris, 1980; M Int Rels, Cambridge Univ, 1981. *Appointments:* Tchr, West Hartford Pub Schs, CT, 1970-76; Rschr on Biog of Suner Welles Washington, Wa, 1976-77; Admnstr, Ctr for Strategic & Int Studies, Washington, 1978-79; Broker, Mgr, Parks Capital Mgmt, NYC, 1981-83; Assoc, Cons, Burgess Mgmt Assoc, 1984-88; Advsr, Sangre de Cristo Fund, Sussex, England, 1987-89; Pol Advsr, N Am Petroleum Corp, Curacao, Netherlands Antilles, 1987-; Pres, Kingdom Prods Inc, New Paltz, 1988-; Cons, Dorchester Capital Grp, London, 1988-. *Memberships:* Duke Univ Alumni Assn, NY; Fdr, Bd of Dir 1987-88, Cambridge Univ Alumni Assn, NY; United Oxford-Cambridge Univ Club, London. *Address:* PO Box 36, New Paltz, NY 12561, USA.

FRANCO Matilde Pessoa Figueiredo Sousa, b. 8 July 1943, Lisbon, Portugal. Museum Curator; University

Professor. m. Antonio Sousa Franco, 17 Sept 1983, 1 d. *Education:* Lic course of Hist, Fac of Letts, Univ of Lisbon, 1962-67; Postgrad course in Museology, Hist of Art. *Appointments:* Prof of Hist of Art and of Hist of Portugal, Univ of Lisbon and Intl Univ of Lisbon; Curator and Dir of Museums and Palaces, 1968-; Dir , Nat Mus Machado de Castro, Coimbra; Nat Palace of Sintra; St Roch Mus of Religious Art in Lisbon, 1991- . *Publications include:* Riscos das obras da universidade de coimbra; O Palacio Nacional de Sintra, Residencia que Rida de de Ioao I E D Ricipa de Lencastre; Museum de S Roque; O Colegio Des Pedro E S Paulo (Dos Inglesinhos); Em Lisboa. *Memberships:* Assn of Art Historians of GB; Postuduese Assn of Museology; Nat Soc for Fine Arts, Portugal; Portuguese Assn of Art Historians; Intl Coun of Museums. *Honours:* Elected to: Nat Acad of Fine ARts, 1992; Sci Soc of the Catholic Univ; Awds from GB, Spain, Austria, Belgium, France, Sweden, Brazil, and Venezuela. *Hobbies:* Gardening; Rooting; Reading; Travelling; History; Cultural heritate; History of art; Museology. *Address:* Rua de Sao Bernardo 50, RC D Edificio Sao Bernardo, 1200 Lisbon, Portugal.

FRANK Joseph Nathaniel, b. 6 Oct 1918, New York, USA. m. Maguerite J Straus, 11 May 1953, 2 d. *Education:* Univs: New York, 1937-38, Wiscons, 1941-42, Paris, 1950-51, Chicago, 1952-54; PhD, 1960. *Appointments include:* Lectr, Eng, Princeton Univ, 1955-56; Asst Prof, Univ of Minnesota, 1958-61; Assoc Prof, Prof, Comparative Lit, Rugers Univ, 1961-66; Prof and Dir of Christian Gauss Seminars in Criticism, 1966-68, Prof Emer, 1983-85, Princeton Univ; Vis Mem, Inst for Adv Study, 1985-88; Prof of Comp Lit and Slavic Langs and Lits, 1985-89, Prof Emer, 1989-, Stanford Univ. *Publications:* Numerous anthologies, book chapters, articles and papers including: Dostoevsky in the 1860s, 1988; Yves Bonnefoy, 1988; Erich Kahler and the Predicament of our Age, 1989; Through the Russian Prism, Essays on Literature and culture, 1990; The Idea of Spatial Form, 1991. *Honours include:* Res Grants, Am Coun of Learned Socs, Rockefeller Foun, Nat Endowment for Humanities. Fellow, AAAS, 1969; Nat Book Critics Circle Awd, 1984; James Russell Lowell Prize, MLA, 1986. *Address:* Department of Slavic Languages & Literatures, Stanford University, Stanford, CA 94305, USA.

FRANKE Hans, b. 27 Oct 1911, Konigshutte, Germany. Physn; Educator. m. Waldtraut Hermann, 23 Mar 1912, 1 s, 1 d. *Education:* MD, Univ of Freiburg, 1936. *Appointments:* Registrar, Inst of Pathology, Freiburg, 1936-37; Dept of Internal Med, Univ of Breslau, 1937-39; Sr Registrar, Dept of Internal Med, Univ of Innsbruck, 1940-47; Sr Registrar, Dept of Internal Med, Univ of Wurzburg, 1948-54; Prof of Med 1954-81, Prof Emeritus 1981-; Dir, Med Poliklinik, 1954-81. *Publications:* Carotid Sinus Syndrome, 1963; Centenaraians, 1971; Longevity, 1985; People of Very Old Age, 1987. *Memberships:* German Soc of Int Med; German Soc of Circulation Rsch; Argentinian Soc Progr Intern, Buenos Aires. *Honour:* Merit Cross 1st Degree, Germany, 1979. *Hobbies:* Mountaineering; Classical music. *Address:* Fruhlingstrasse 9, 8035 Gauting, Germany.

FRANKHOUSER Homer Sheldon, b. 6 Sept 1927, Reading, PA, USA. Corporate Exec. m. 2 Sept 1972, 3 s, 2 d. *Education:* BSc in Civil Engrng, Lehigh Univ, 1952. *Appointments:* Dravo Corp, 1954-72, final position VP, Area Mgr; Dep Chmn, Chief Op Off, Brown & Root Ltd, 1972; Brown & Root UK Ltd; Sr VP, Brown & Root Inc; Pres, Frankhouser & Assocs Inc. *Creative works:* Tech Papers for Various Journs; Oil Paintings. *Memberships:* MASCE; Inst of Dirs, London; The Houston Club; Masons; The Forum Club. *Honours:* Mbr, Tau Beta Pi, Eng Hon Soc, 1952; Mbr, Chi Epsilon, Civil Engrng Hon Soc, 1952. *Hobbies:* Oil Painting; Antique Furniture. *Address:* 9065 Briar Forest Drive, Houston, TX 77024, USA.

FRANKLAND (Anthony) Noble, b. 4 July 1922, Ravenstonedale, Eng. Histn; Biographer. m. (1) Diana Madeline Fovargue, 28 Feb 1944, dec 1981, (2) Sarah Katharine Davies, 7 May 1982, 1 s, 1 d. *Education:* Open Scholar, Trinity Coll, Oxon, 1941-42, 1945-47, 1950-51; MA 1948; DPhil 1951. RAF 1941-45: Bomber Command, 1943-45; Narrator, Air Histl Br, Air Min, 1948- 51; Official Mil Histn, Cabinet Off, 1951-60; Dep Dir of Studies, Royal Inst of Int Affairs, 1956-60; Dir, Imperial War Mus, 1960-82. *Publications:* Documents on International Affairs for 1956, 1957, 1958; Crown of Tragedy, Nicholas II, 1960; The Strategic Air Offensive Against Germany 1939-45 (with Sir Charles Webster), 4 vols, 1961; The Bombing Offensive Against Germany, Outines and Perspectives, 1965; Bomber Offensive, The Devastation of Europe, 1970; Prince Henry, Duke of Gloucester, 1980; Prince Arthur, Duke of Connaught, 1993; The Encyclopedia of 20th Century Warfare; Num articles, reviews. *Memberships:* Nat Arts Collection Fund; Nat Trust; CPRE; Friends of the Imperial War Mus. *Honours:* DFC 1944; CBE 1976; CB 1983. *Address:* Thames House, Eynsham, Witney, Oxon OX8 1DA, England.

FRANKLIN Margaret Lavona (Barnum), b. 19 June 1905, Caldwell, KS, USA. Ret'd Tchr. m. Benjamin Franklin, 20 Jan 1940, dec 1983, 1 s, 1 d. *Education:* Univ of Northern IA, 1923-25; Univ of IA, 1937-38; BA, Washburn Univ, 1952. *Appointments:* Tchr, pub schs, Union, 1925-27; Advance Rep, Jr Supvsr, Redpath-Vawter, summer 1926; Tchr, pub schs, Kearney 1927-28, Marshalltown 1928-40. Summer employment: Assoc Chautauguga - summer 1927, 1928, 1929, 1930, advance rep. *Memberships include:* VP 1952- 54, Women's Club; Minerva Club; Chapt Pres 1956-57, PEO Sisterhood; Bd 1961- 70, Chmn 1965-67, Topeka Pub Lib; Past Sec, Dir, Shawnee Co Histl Soc, 1963- 75; Pres 1964-65, Co-op Bd; Chmn 1968-71, Rep to Northeast Kansas Lib System; Friends of the Pub Lib, Western Sorosis, 1970-79; Past State Mus Chmn, Daughters of the Am Revolution; 50-yr's Mbr, Am Assn of Univ Women; Native Sons & Daughters of KS; Topeka Pub Lib Fndn Bd, 1984-. *Honours:* Serv Hon Cit, Topeka Civic Symph Soc, 1960; Waldo B Heywood Awd, Topeka Civic Theatre, 1967; Nonoso, Washburn Univ Hon Soc, 1970; Awds, Bd of Dir, Topeka Pub Lib, 1970, 1977; Outstg Mother of KS, Alpha Delta Pi, 1971. *Hobbies include:* Travel; Children's literature; Genealogy; History; Stevengraphs; Dolls. *Address:* 4808 West Hills Drive, Topeka, KS 66606, USA.

FRANKLIN Roosevelt, b. 30 Aug 1933, Chattanooga, USA. m. Darnell Pinkston, 30 Sept 1972, 1 s, 2 d. *Education:* BS, Northeastern Univ, 1958; MA Hons, Savannah State Coll, 1962. *Appointments:* Capt, US Army, Korea, 1951-54; Pastor, Free For All Bapt Ch, Greenwood, 1959-61; Radio Min, Spiritual Ch, Aiken, 1961-63; Nat Lectr, United Coun Spiritual Ch, Raleigh, 1963-66; Min, Holy Trinity Hse of God, Macon, 1966- ; Youth Dir 1966-72, Talent Coord 1966-73, Dir Spiritual Singers 1966-, Organiser Voters Registration 1977, Holy Trinity Ch, Macon; Bd of Dir, Ret'd Persons Assn, 1980-; Pub Relations Vol Nat Dem Party, Atlanta, 1984. *Memberships:* NAACP (Life); SCLC (Life); Inner Circle Congl Aides; C of C; VP 1986-, Min's Alliance; Dist Dep 1970-, Smooth Ashlar Grand Lodge; Direct Sellers League; Coord 1980-, GA Black Am Pageant; Rolls Royce Club; Woodsmen of Am Club; Pioneer Club; Nat Amb, Shriners; 33 Deg, Sovereign Grand Gen Insp, Masons; Optimist; Kiwanis; Civitan; Elks; Treas 1987-, Nat Grand Lodge. *Honours:* Named Extrovert Promoter Music Workshop, 1979; Citizen's Awd, Min's Alliance, 1979; Hunts Bond Troop Awd, Ft Valley State Alumni, 1980; Ldrship Awd, GA Black Am Pageant, 1982; Afro Am Heritage Awd, Afro Am Heritage Mus, 1987; Golden Eagle Awd, Macon Courier, 1988. *Hobbies:* Martial arts; Billiards. *Address:* 1830 Redwood Drive, Macon, GA 31204, USA.

FRANZEN Charles Rice, b. 24 June 1957, Terra Haute, IN, USA. Proj Coord. m. Sharon Ann Billings, 17 Oct 1987, 2 s. *Education:* AB, Coll of William & Mary, 1975-

79; MA, Univ of Mississippi, 1979-81; KS State Univ, 1981. *Appointments:* US Peace Corps, Tanzania, 1981-85; Luth World Relief, Tanzania, 1985; World Vision, Sudan, 1986-87; Luth World Fndn, Zambia, W Province, 1987-89; Luth World Fndn, E Province, 1989-. *Hobbies:* Sports; Literature; Writing. *Address:* LWF/ZCRS, Box 511234, Chipata, Zambia.

FRANZKE Hans Herman, b. 18 Mar 1927, Clansthal. Univ Prof. m. Leonoe Geb Schomer, 27 Sept 1952, 2 s, 1 d. *Education:* Abitur Latina, Gymnasium Francke'sche Stiffengen, 1946; Diploma Mining Engr, 1957; Doc Degree, Engr Sci, 1957. *Appointments:* Hd Section, AEG Berlin, 1957- 62; Hd Dept AEG Essen, 1962-67; Mgr Projekta Dusseldorf, 1968-75; Prof Tech Coll Cologne, 1975-77; Prof Tech Univ, Berlin, 1977-. *Publications:* Maschinen u An Lagen. *Membership:* Berliner issenschaffliche Gasellschaff. *Hobbies:* Collecting Old Books; Gardening. *Address:* Hochboum Str 36, D-1000 Berlin, Germany. 37, 52.

FRASE Anthony Richard Greenville, b. 8 July 1954, Newcastle On Tyne. Solicitor. m. Srah Louise, 23 May 1990. *Education:* Repton Sch, 1969-72; Trinity Coll, 1973; BA, 1976; MA, 1980. *Appointments:* Articles Allen & Overy, 1978-80; Solicitor Allen & Overy, 1981-83; Solicitor, Denton Hll Burgin & Warrens, 1983-87; Partner, 1988; Seconded Assoc of Futures, 1989-90; Securities & Futures Authority, 1991. *Publications:* Various Articles on Financial law; Euromoney Guide to World Equity Market. *Memberships:* Intl Bar Assoc; City of London Solicitors Co; Cavalry & Guards; United Oxford & Cambridge Univ; Wig & Pen. *Honours:* Entrance Exhibition, Cambridge. *Hobbies:* Travel; Art; Literature; Financial History. *Address:* London SW11, England.

FRASER Colin Gall, b. 18 Feb 1934, London. Solicitor. m. Gabrielle Genista Holt Wilson, 14 Dec 1963, 1 s, 1 d. *Education:* Cottesmore Sch, 1940-47; Aldenham Sch, 1947-52; Trinity Hall, Cambridge, 1954-57. *Appointments:* Admitted Solicitor, 1960; Partner, Joynson Hicks, 1964; Partner, Taylor Joynson Garrett, 1989. *Creative Works:* Speaker at Seminars; Contributor of Articles on Copyright. *Memberships:* British Literary & Artistic Copyright Assn; Assoc Queen Mary Coll, London; Drating Council of Churches. *Honours:* TD; Army Serv, Subaltern in 1 BN Queen's Own Royal West Kent Regt; 4th/5th BN TA; Retired as Major. *Hobbies:* Golf; Cricket; Hockey; Reading History. *Address:* High Trees, South Drive, Dorking, Surrey RH5 4AG, England.

FRASER Frederick Murray, b. 18 Apr 1937, Liverpool, England. Pres & Vice Chancellor, The Univ of Calgary. m. Anne Fraser, 20 Aug 1960, 3 s. *Education:* BA, Dalhousie, 1957; LLB, Dalhousie, 1960; LLM, London, 1962. *Appointments:* Asst Prof, Faculty of Law, Queens, 1963-64; Practised Law, Halifax, 1964-66; Assoc Prof, Prof, Assoc Dean, Dalhousie Law Sch, 1966-74; On Leave, 1973-74 Law Reform Commission of Canada; Founding Dean, Faculty of Law, Univ of Victoria, 1974-80; Prof of Law, 1974-88; Vice Pres, Academic, 1983-88; Pres, Vice Chancellor, Prof of Law, Univ of Calgary, 1988-. *Contributions to:* Texts on Faculty Law. *Honours:* Queens Counsel; The Weldon Award, Distinguished Alumns. *Hobbies:* Reading; Swimming; Skiing; Tennis. *Address:* Univ of Calgary, 2500 Univ Drive, Calgary NW, Canada T2N 1N4.

FRASER John Keith, b. 18 Feb 1922, Ottawa, Canda. Geography Conslt. m. Joyce Elleen Tate, 1 Oct 1949, 1 s, 1 d. *Education:* BA, 1949; MA, 1954, Univ of Toront; PhD, Clark Univ, 1964. *Appointments:* Research Sci, 1950-68; Research Admin, 1968-82; Sc Gen 22nd Internat Geog Congress, 1972; Exec Dir, Royal Canadian Geog Soc, Ottawa, 1982-90. *Memberships:* Canadian Assoc Geographers; Royal Canadian Geographers Soc; Arctic Instl North America. *Honours:* Award for Serv to the Prof Canadian Assoc Geag; Paul Harris Fellow, Rotary Intl. *Hobbies:* Sketching; Oils; Canoeing; Photography. *Address:* 571 Fraser Avenue, Ottawa, Canada K2A 2R3. 88.

FRASER Raymond Morris, b. 16 Feb 1947, Edinburgh, Scotland. Advocate. *Education:* LLB Hons, Edinburgh Univ, 1969. *Appointments:* John Menzies and Co Ltd, 1965; Housepainter in Chicago, Illinois, 1968; Advg Exec, Madison, WI, 1968. *Publications:* pending: Rough Injustice - The Trial of the Angolan Mercenaries; Women and Murder in Scotland. *Memberships:* Scottish Bench and Bar; Bruntsfield Links Golfing Soc; Scottish Arts Club; Caldeonian Club; Mercedes-Benz Club; Edinburgh Pistol Club; Waverley Pistol Shooting Soc; Pentland Conservative Assn; Colinton Amenity Assn; Drumsbeugh Baths Club; All Sphere Club. *Honours:* Parl Conserv Cand for Orkney and Shetland, 1974; Initiator of 4-man Mission to Defent Brit Mercenaries facing executive in Angola for war ceimes, 1976; Hon Pres, Auchinleck Boswell Soc, 1989-90. *Hobbies:* Publi and after-dinner speaking; Arts; Shooting, handgun and game; Castles and country houses; Reading; Writing; Flying Travel; Painting; Golf; Cinema; Collectors cars; Victoriana and Edwardiana; Eccentrics. *Address:* Bonaly Tower, Edinburgh, Scotland.

FRAZER Oliver Haldane, b. 13 July 1913, Dulwich, London, England. Retired Sch Tchr m Dorothy Adeline Stevenson, 18 Feb 1950. *Education:* Dulwich Coll, 1926-30; Coopers Hill Training Coll, 1947-48. *Appointments:* Farming, New Zealand, 1930-34; London Soc for Tching & Training the Blind, 1934-36; Self Employed, 1936-39; War serv, 1939- 46; RASC, sergeant, Staff Sergeant, Glider Pilot Regiment, D Day & Arnhem; Biology & Sci Tchr, 1946-75. *Publications:* Wants in a Habitat?; 12 Educ Broadcasts, slides & Information Pks for Sch; BBC Radio Solent; Contributor AA leisure Guide Isle of Wight, 1988; The Island from Within, 1990; Author. The Natural History of The Isle of Wight, 1990. *Memberships:* Isle of Wight Natural History & Archaeological Soc, Pres 1960-63; Editor of Proceedings, 1963-83, Vice-Pres, 1963-. *Honours:* MBE, 1991; Commem Medal of Hon, ABI, 1991. *Hobbies:* Nat History; photography. *Address:* Mottistone Mill, Brighstone, Newport, Isle of Wight PO30 4AW, England.

FREDERICK Richard Andrew, b. 26 June 1948, Dayton, Ohio, USA. Horticulturist; Business Owner. m. Pamela Rose Ammon, 28 Aug 1971, Div, 2 d. *Education:* Bach of Sci, Wright State Univ, 1970. *Appointments:* Addressograph, Bruning, Sales, 1970-71; Lunkenheimer Value Co, Sales, 1971-72; AMP Inc, Sales, 1972-77; Arrow Hart, Sales, 1977-78; Terminal Supply, Sales, 1978-79; Ammon Landscape Supply, Owner, 1979-. *Memberships:* American Assoc Nurserymen; Kentucky Nurseymens Assoc; Southeastern Ohio Horticulture Assoc; Southern nurseymens Assoc; Prof Grounds Maint Assoc; Cinto Golf Course Superintents Assoc. *Hobbies:* Travel; Sports Cars; Golf; Tennis; Soft Ball; Art; Music; Biking; Hiking. *Address:* 6418 Linkview Court, Florence, KY 41042, USA. 7.

FREEMAN Chas Wellman Jr, b. 2 Mar 1943, Washington, DC. US Ambassador, Kingdom of Saudi Arabia; Diplomat. m. Patricia Margaret Trenery, 31 May 1962, 2 s, 1 d. *Education:* Nat Autonomous Univ of Mexico, 1961; Yale Univ, AB, 1963; Harvard Univ, JD, 1975; Foreign Serv Inst, Taichung, Taiwan, 1971. *Appointments:* US Foreign Serv, 1965; Madras, India, 1966-68; Taichung & Taiwan, 1969-71; Washington, State Dept, & USIA, 1971-81; Deputy Chief of Mission, US Embassy Beijing, 1981-84; DCM Bangkok, 1984-86; Prical Deputy Asst Sec, State for Africa, 1986-89; US Ambassador, Kingdon of Saudia Arabia, 1989-. *Publications:* Article, Foreign Affairs; The Angola Namibia Accord. *Membership:* American Foreign Serv Assoc. *Honours:* Superior Honor Award; Presidential Meritorious Serv Award; Participant Group Distinguished Honor Award. *Hobbies:* Sailing; Reading; Computors. *Address:* American Embassy, PO Box 94309, Riyadh 11691, Saudi Arabia.

FRENETTE Thomas Roderick Orville, Hon, b. 2 May 1927, Fort Francis, Ontario, Canada. BA; BCL; DSL; LLD;

JSC; Superior Court Judge. m. Jeannine Murray, 31 Dec 1949, 4 s, 2 d. *Education:* Carleton Univ, BA, 1949; McGill Univ, BCL, 1953; Que Bar, 1945; Ottawa Univ, DSL, 1958; Ottawa Univ, lld, 1960. *Appointments:* Law Prac, 1954-65; Part Time Lectr, Univ of ottawa, 1960-68; Que Bar Admission Course, 1974-75; Asst, Crown Attorney, Hull, 1960-63; Chief Crown Attorney, 1963-65; Judge of Prov, Court, 1966-78. *Publications:* Quantum of Damages in Quebec *Memberhips:* Hull Bar; Que Judge's Assn of Prov Court Judges; Canadian Bar Assc; Canadian Conf of Fed Judges. *Address:* Court House, 17 Laurier St, Rm 1 374, Hull, Quebec, Canada J8X 4Cl.

FREUND Eckhard, b. 28 Feb 1940, Dusseldorf, Germany.Full Prof; Hd of the Inst of Robotics Research. m. Dr Brigitte Keudel, 2 s. *Education:* DipIIng, 1965; Dr Ing, 1968. *Appointments:* Sci ESA Darmstadt; Guest Prof USC Los Angeles; Sci Coordinator, Fraunhofer Inst Karlsruhe; Full Prof, Univ of Hagen Electrical Engring Dept; Sci Advisor Jet Propulsion Lab, NASA. *Publications:* Zeitvariable Mehrgroessensysteme, Regelungssysteme, 1981; Regelungssysteme im Zustandsraum 1/11; About 100 Papers in Intern Journals & Intern Conferences in the Fields on Control & Robotics. *Address:* Otto Hahn Strasse 8, D 4600 Dortmund 50, Germany. 43, 52, 92.

FREYTAG LOERINGHOFF Bettina von, b. 26 Sept 1943, Stuttgart, Germany. Archaeologist. *Education:* Dr Phil, 1971. *Appointments:* Asst Staatliche Kunstammlungen, Kassel, 1971; Asst German Archaeological Inst, Athens, 1972-74; Asst, German Archaeological Inst, Olympia, 1975; asst, Eberhard Karls Univ, D Tnebingen, 1976-77; Conservator, 1977-; Dr.phil.habil, 1991. *Publications:* Das Giebelrelief von Telamon und Seine Stellnng innerhalb der Ikonographie der Sieben gegen Theben; Corpus Speculorum Etruscorum, Bundes republik Deutschland. *Memberships:* Accademia dei Sepolti, Volterra; German Archaeological Inst, Berlin; Inst Nazionale di Studi Etruschi ed Italici. *Address:* Archaeologisches Inst, Wilhelm str 9, D 7400 Tuebingen, Germany. 52.

FRICKERS Gordon Stuart Allen, b. 25 May 1949, Beckenham, Kent, England. Artist; Painter. m. Patricia Eileen, 26 Nov 1983, 1 s, 1 d. *Education:* Broomham, South Bromley Coll, Maidstone Coll of Art, 1966- 68; Medway Coll of Art, 1968-71; Falmouth Tech Coll, 1974. *Appointments:* Photographer; Advertiser, 1971-74; MD & SE Boat Builders, 1975-79; Artist, Painter, Marine & Aviation. *Ceative Works include:* Painting. CS Sovereign, British Telecom New Cable Ship; Tracey Edwards Yacht; Virgin Atlanic Challenge 11; Blue Arrow America's Cup Challengor. *Memberships:* Soc of Nauticl Research; Nat Maritime Hisorical Soc; Steamship Historical Soc of America World Ship soc; Royal Plymouth Corinthain Yacht Club; Royal Soc Marine Artists; Friends of Nat Maritime Museum; Friends of Maria Asumpta; Friends of the Earth; World Wildlife Fund. *Hobbies:* Sailing; Travel; Aviation; Maritime Historical Reseach. *Address:* Lakeside Studio, 94 Radford Park Road, Plymouth, Devon, PL9 9DX, England.

FRIGGIERI Oliver, b. 27 Mar 1942, Malta. Univ Prof; Writer. *Education:* BA, 1968; MA, 1975; PhD, 1978. *Appointments:* Univ Lectr, 1972-88; Prof, 1988-. *Publications include:* Kittieba Ta'Zmienna; Saggi Kritici; Dun Karm II Bniedem-Fil-poeta; Fil-Parlament ma Jikbrux Fjuri; Stejjer ghal Oabel Jidlam; Gesabeela i Druge Pripovijesti; Ribelle gentile. *Memberships:* Assoc Intl des Critiques Litteraires; European Union of Sci & Authors. *Honours:* Premio Hediterraneo; Premio Silarus. *Address:* Faculty of Arts, Univ of Malta, Msida, Malta.

FRIIS Ib, b. 12 Jan 1945, Denmark. Assoc Prof. m. Victoria Gordon, 1977. *Education:* MSc Botany, Univ of Copenhagen, 1970; Fil Dr, Univ of Uppsala, 1985; Dr Scient, Univ of Copenhagen, 1992. *Appointments:* Asst Prof, Dept of Botany, Univ of Copenhagen, 1970-

74; Assoc Prof, 1974- 87; Assoc Prof, Botanical Museum, 1987-. *Publications:* 100 Sci Papers & Books. *Memberships:* Assoc Pour L'Etude Taxonomique de la Flore D'Afrique Tropicale; Intl Assoc of Plant Taxonomists. *Honours:* Elected Member, Royal Danish academy of Sci & Letters. *Hobbies:* History of Sci; Art & History of Art; Tropical Flora & Vegetation; History of Botanical Museums & Collections. *Address:* 19a Selsoevej, DK-2720 Vanloese, Denmark.

FRITZHAND Marek, b. 12 Oct 1973, Buczacz. Prof Ameritus. m. 12 Apr 1948, 1 d. *Education:* Lwow Univ, 1936; Doc, 1952; Assoc Prof, 1954-66; Pfor, 1966-69; Dean, Faculty of Philosophy, 1962-65;Hd Morel Sci Dept, 1966-84; Sch of Sci, 1973-83. *Appointments:* Polish Army, 1941- 48; St Uzba Polisce, 1948-49; Univ of Warsaw, 1950-84. *Publications:* Numerous. *Memberships:* Polish Philosophical Soc; Intern Soc for Univ. *Honours include:* Gold Cross of Merit; Cross of Valour. *Hobby:* Photography.*Address:* Murek Fritzhand, Al Wyzwolenia 2 m 3, 00-570 Warsaw, Poland.

FROEBE Hans Albrecht, b. 3 Oct 1931, Stuttgart, Germany. Prof. Div, 4 s. *Education:* Biology, Chemistry, Geography, 1951-61; Dr Degree, Botany, 1964; Habilitation, 1970; Prof of Botany Ache, 1971. *Appointments:* Asst Prof, Univ Mainz, 1961-65; Univ AAchen, up to 1970; Dozent fuer Bot, 1970; Prof, fuer Botanik, 1971. *Publications:* Die Bluetenstaende der Hydrocoty Loideen. *Memberships:* Deutsche Botan; Gesellsch; Regens burger Botan Ges; Biologenverband. *Hobby:* Philosophy. *Address:* Botanische Inst, der RWTH Aachen, D-5100 Aachen, Germany. 43.

FROLOV Ivan Timofeevich, b, 1 Sept 1929, Lipetsk, Dir of the Inst of Man of the Academy of Sci, Russia. m. Gelina L Belkina, 21 July 1951, 2 d. *Education:* Moscow State Univ, 1953; Prof of the Dept of Philosophy, of MSU, 1968-; Full Member Academy of Sci of Russia, 1968-77. *Appointments:* Editor in Chief, Voprosy Filosofii, Journal, 1968-77; Ed in Chief, The Communist Journal, 1985-87; Asst of the Gen Sec of the Cent Comm of CPSU, 1987-89; Ed in Chief, Pravda News, 1989-91. *Publications:* 20 Books; 18 Booklets; More than 300 Articles. *Memberships:* Philosophical Soc of Russia; DLMPS/IUHPS; FISP; Inter Acad of the Hist of Sci. *Honours:* Roll of Honor, The Global 500; Number of Awards from the USSR's Government. *Hobby:* Reading. *Address:* Volkhonka 14, 119842, Russia.

FROMM Henri (Karl-Heinrich), b. 18 Dec 1947, Hamberg, West Germany. Prof of Psychology. *Education:* Various professors; Colleges; Private Tuition. *Appointments include:* Dir, Henri Fromm music Co, 1971-80; Prod, Intl Records & Discs; Co Dir, Onas Gallery, Italy, 1976-80; Art Advisor, Babylon, Brussel Gallery; Lectr, Various Acedemies & Univ; Freelance Artist, Writer, Poet, 1976-. *Creative Works include:* Exhibitions, One Man Shows, Paris, Brussels, Vienna, Berlin, Antwerp, Lyon, Munich; Publs inc. Art Book, Henro Fromm DJ; Dir of European Artists, Italy; Le Arte Illustrate. *Memberships include:* Noble Academy de Caspis; Academia Citta di Boretto; Accademia Leonardo da Vinci; Accademia il Machiavello; Accademia Danzig. *Honours include:* Gold Medal, Leonardo de Vinci; Prize of Italy; Peter Paul Rubens Prize; Raffaelo Sanzio Prize; Gand Cross St Brigitta; Grand Cross Templier; numerous other Heraldic Honours. *Address:* Ottostrasse 7, 8600 Bamberg, Germany. 19, 43, 92.

FRUECKERT Rolf Herbert, b. 31 May 1945, Meerane. m. Ute Hehn, 8 May 1970. *Education:* Gymnasium, Boken Iwestf; Diploma Engr, Gauss Berlin. *Appointments:* Mfg Planner, AE6 Offenburg, 1968-70; Sales Mgr, Siemens AG, Munich, 1970-90; Mktg mgr, Eupec Gmbh & Co, Munich and Warstein-Belecke, 1990-. *Memberships:* Liberal Dem Party, Munich; Judge Labour Ct, Munich; Examiner Chamber Ind & Commerce, Munich; Assc Engrs & Sci. *Hobbies:* Sports; Music;

Stamps; Special Coins. *Address:* Klusenerweg 17, D 4770, Soest, Germany.

FRUTKIN Mark Jamie, b. 2 Jan 1948, Cleveland, Ohio, USA. Writer. m. Faith Seltzer, 14 Dec 1984, 1 s. *Education:* Bach of Arts, political Sci, Loyola Univ, Chicago, 1969; Writing Studies, Narapa Inst, Colorado, 1976. *Appointments:* Editor, Art Action Mag, 1985-90; Prof of Creative Writing, 1991. *Publications include:* Invading Tibet Random House of Canada; The Growing Dawn Quadrant & Bridges Books. *Memberships:* The Writers Union of Canada; PEN Intl; Ottawa Dharmadhatu. *Honours:* Finalist for Governor Gen Literary Award. *Hobbies:* Tibetan Buddhism; Books; Fine Wines. *Address:* 874 Wingate Drive, Ottawa, Ontario, Canada K1G 1S5. 88.

FRY Anthony Michael, b. 20 June 1955, Sussex, England. Dir, Merchant Bank. m. Anne Elizabeth Birrell, 27 July 1985, 1 d. *Education:* BA, Modern Hist, Magdalen Coll, Oxford, 1974-77. *Appointments:* N M Rothschild & Sons, 1977-80; Rothschild Australia, 1980-85; N M Rothschild & Sons, 1985-. *Memberships:* Bonnetmakers Glasgow; Australian Club, Melbourne; Carlton Club, London; Armadillos CC. *Honours:* Demyship; Atkinson Prize. *Hobbies:* V-Chmn, British Lung Foundation; Dpy Chmn, Westminster Conservative Assoc; Fellow, Royal Soc of Arts. *Address:* 27a Warrington Crescent, London W9 1ED, England.

FRY John, b. 16 June 1922. Medicine, General Practitioner. *Education:* Univ of London. *Appointments:* Gen Practitioner, 1947-; Conslt Editor. *Publications:* Common Diseases; Prmary Health Care; Medicine in 3 Societies; Disease Data Book; General Practice: The Facts. *Memberships:* Gen Medical Council; Nuffield Provincial Hosp Trust. *Honours:* Hunterian Soc Gold Medal; Sir Charles Hastings Prize BMA; James MacKenzie Medal; Queen Elizabeth the Queen Mother Fellowship; World Health Organisation Fellow; Regents Lectr, Univ of CA, San Francisco; CBE. *Hobby:* Caring for Patients. *Address:* 3 Kings Court, Kelsey Park Avenue, Berkenham, Kent BR3 2TT, England. 1.

FU Jick Chong John, b. 26 Oct 1932, Wen Cheong, Hainan, China. Mngr Dir. m. Ladda, 9 Dec 1968, 1 s, 3 d. *Education:* Chinese Language & Litterature Dept, Shanxi Univ, 1957. *Publications:* Knots, an anthology of Poetry. *Memberships:* Chinese Writers Club of Thailand; Chinese Writers Assc of Thailand; Chinese literary Assc of Thailand. *Honours:* 2nd Prize Essay Writing Comp. *Hobbies:* Writing; Reading; Music; Calligraphy. *Address:* 248/2 Silom Road, Bangkok 10500, Thailand. 139, 152.

FU Kun, b. 17 Mar 1925, China. Tchring & Sci Research; Professor. m. 1 Oct 1955, 1 s. *Education:* Nat 1st Middle Sch, 1938-44; Flight Training Coll, Chinese Air Force, 1945; Peking Univ, Bach Sci, 1946-50. *Appointments:* Peking Univ, 1950-52; Peking Coll of Geology, 1952-58; Guizhou Inst of Tech, 1950-58. *Publications:* Observations on the Structure of Pei Piao Type in Pei piao Liaoning; Stratigraphy of China no.5 The Ordovician System of China; Atlas of the palaeogeography of China. *Memberships:* Palaeontological Soc of China; Special Subcommission on Ordovician System of Commission on Stratigraphy of China; Chinese Comm on Hist of Geological Sci of the Geological Soc of China. *Honours:* Advanced Worker; Deputy to the 7th Nat Peoples Congress of PRC; Standing Member to the 5th Guizhou Prov Comm of CPPCC; 3rd Nat Natural Sci Prize. *Hobbies:* Tourism; Opera. *Address:* Dept of Geology, Guizhou Inst of Tech, Guiyang, Guizhou 550003, China.

FU Xi-Hou, b. 12 Oct 1932, Zhijang, PRC. Snr Engr Prof; Dir of Vehicle Engine Research Dept, Automobile Coll, Shanghai Univ. m. Ren sun Wang, 1 June 1953, 1 s, 1 d. *Education:* Shanghai Jiao Tong Univ, 1963. *Appointments:* Shanghai Diesel Engine Works, Designer Engr, 1954-87; Vice Dir, Engine Design Dept; Snr Engr;

Chief Designer; Shanghai Univ, Engring & Sci, 1987-. *Creative Works:* Development & Research of B135 Series Diesel Engine of Second Generation. *Memberships:* The Design & Strength Comm of Shanghai Soc Inner Combustion Engine; SAE Intl. *Address:* Vehicle Engine Research Dept of Automobile, Eng Coll of Shanghai Univ of Eng & Sci, 350 Xian-Xia Road, Shanghai, China 200335. 139.

FU Yun-Feng, b. 7 Aug 1934, Hebei of China. Research Work on Biochemistry; Prof. m. 3 Feb 1954, 2 d. *Education:* Lawting Middle Sch, 1949-52; Tangshan Medical Sch,1952-54; Hebei Medical Coll, 1954-59; Advanced Study, Holland, Dept of Biochemistry, Univ of Nijmegen, 1982-84. *Appointments:* Hebei Academy of Medical Sci, Dept of Biochemistry, Asst Prof, 1978; Dir of the Dept; Assoc Prof, 1982; Prof, 1987. *Publications:* 95 pcs of Original Articles; 16 pcs of Reviews; 5 copies of monographs. *Memberships:* Chinese Soc of Biochemistry; Hebei Soc of Biochemistry; Chinese Assc of Medicine; Hebei Assc of Biochemistry in Medicine. *Honours include:* Prize of Sci & Tech Progress; Prize of Medical Progress. *Hobbies:* Reading; Fishing; Basket ball; Watching Animal World on TV. *Address:* Dept of Biochemistry, Hebei Academy of Medical Sci, 62 Qingyuan Street, Shijiazhuang 050021, China.

FUCHS Klaus Rüediger, b. 18 Oct 1954, Neünkirchen. Editor of Inscriptions, Medieval. *Education:* Univ of Saarbrücken, 1985; Dr.phil, Univ des Saarlandes. *Appointments:* Asst, Univ of Saarbrücken, 1981-82; Editor of Inscriptions, Akademie Mainz, 1982-. *Publications:* Das Domesday Book und Sein Umfeld; Die Inschriffen der Stadt Worms. *Memberships:* Historisches Inst der Univ des Saarlandes; Kommission für Saarländische Laudesgeschnichte u Volkskunde. *Honours:* Dr Eduard Martin Prize. *Hobbies:* Mountain Hiking; Shooting. *Address:* Südstr 18, 6501 Budenhein, Germany.

FUDENBERG H Hugh, b. 24 Oct 1928, New York, USA. Scientist. *Education:* AB, UCLA, 1949; MD, Univ Chicago, 1953; MA, Boston, 1957. *Appointments:* Rockefeller Univ, 1957-60; Univ Cal S.F and Berkeley, 1960-75; Med Univ, S.Casr, 1975-91; VP, Res Neuroimmunotherapeutic Res, 1991-. *Memberships:* Fellow, AAAS; AMPhys; Intl Soc Immunopharmcol; AAI. *Honours:* Medal, Inst Pasteur, 1962; Annual medals, Am Acad Allergy; Danish and Russian Cancer Socs; Decennial Lectr, Brit Soc Immunol; Catello di Petrorossa Awd, Italy. *Address:* Neuroimmunotherapeutic Research Foundation, 145 N Chuerx St, Spasrtanburg, SC 29301, USA. 2, 57.

FUJIMOTO Ichiro, b. 1 Oct 1951, Japan. Visiting Asst Prof in Mathematics. m. Junko Fujimoto, 2 Jan 1990. *Education:* BS Physics, Univ Tokyo, 1975; Mathematics, Kyoto Univ, 1978-80; MS Mathematics, Hiroshima Univ, 1982; Postgrad, Univ Rochester NY, 1985-86; PhD, Mathematics, Univ Florida, 1990. *Appointments:* Visiting Asst Prof, Mathematics, Univ Florida, 1990-92. *Publications:* the General Stone Weirstrass problem in Convexity Theory; CP Convexity & its Applications; Equivalent conditions for the general Stone-Weierstrass problem. *Memberships:* Mathematical Soc of Japan; American Mathematical Soc; Phi Kappa Phi. *Address:* Dept of Mathematics, Univ of Florida, Gainesville, FL 32611, USA. 7.

FUKAI Yuh, b. 1 Nov 1934, Chiba, Japan. Prof of physics, Chuo Univ. m. Reiko Nakakimura, 9 Jan 1960, 1 s, 1 d. *Education:* Univ of Tokyo, BA, 1958; DSc, 1963. *Appointments:* Visit Prof, Univ Illinios, USA, 1967-69; Hiroshima Univ, 1978-79; Chuo Univ, Asst Prof, 1963-71; Prof, 1971-; Prof Associe, Univ Grenoble, France, 1980. *Publications:* Physics of Diffusion Phenomena; The Metal Hydrogen System. *Memberships:* Physical Soc of Japan; Jpan Inst of Metals; Japan soc of Applied Physics; Japan Soc of High Pressure Sci & Tech. *Hobbies:* Various Fields of Sci with a bit of Poems.

Address: Dept of Physics, Chuo Univ, 1-13-27 Kasuga, Bunkyo Ku, Tokyo 112, Japan. 52.

FUKUZUMI Naoyoshi, b. 7 Aug 1924, Taipei, Taiwan. Emerltus Prof of Pathology, Kyorin Univ Coll Medicine, Tokyo, Japan. m. Noriko Fukuzumi, 15 Nov, 1960, 2 d. *Education:* MD, Nat Taiwan Univ, 1947; PhD, Chiba Univ, 1955; Research Fellow, Inst for Reseach Med Sci, Toyko Univ, 1972-78. *Appointments:* Prof Pathology, Nat Taiwan Univ, 1964-72; Cons Pathology, USA, Navel Rser Univ, 1964-72; Prof Pathology, kyorin Univ, Toyko, 1979-91. *Publications:* Experimental Kernicterus; Human Cholera, Virch Arch B. *Memberships:* AAAS; Ny Academy Sci, USA; Japanese Cancer Assc; Japanese Soc for Cancer Therapy; Japanese Path Soc; Intl Coll Surgeons. *Honours:* Prize Advances in Culture; Prize from Taiwan Medical Assoc; Prize from Japanese Assc of Medicine; Prize from E B Virus Studing Group. *Hobbies:* Reading; Sports. *Address:* Dept of Pathology, Kyorin Univ Coll of Medicine, Shinkawa 6 20 2, Mitaka 181, Tokyo, Japan.

FULKERSON Richard Paul, b. 9 Feb 1942, Carterville, Illinios. Prof of English. m. Sharon Ann Loveless, 30 June 1963, 1 s, 1 d. *Education:* Bach of Sci, Southern Illinios Univ, 1963; PhD, English, Ohio State Univ, 1970. *Appointments:* Graduate Assis, Ohio State Univ, 1963-70; English Prof, East Texas State Univ, 1970-. *Memberships:* Rhetoric Soc of America; Conference on Coll Composition & Communication; American Civil Liberties Union; Nat Council of Tchrs of English; Assc of Tchrs of Advanced Composition. *Honours:* Distinguished Faculty Award; Distinguished Teaching Award; Prof of the Year. *Hobbies:* Tennis; Racquetball; Pen Collecting. *Address:* Dept of Literature & Languages, East Texas State Univ, Commerce, TX 75429, USA.

FULMER Irene Elizabeth, b. 24 Apr 1922, Elkhast. Nursing, Retired. *Education:* Univ of Washington, BSN, Psychiatric Nursing, 1949-52; Northern Illinios Univ, Community Health Nursing, 1969-71; Post Grad, Pinal Foundation; Practice Teaching, Univ of Washington; NIU, one to one Counceling & herapy; Roseland Community Hosp. *Appointments include:* Columbus Ohio State Univ Receiving Psychiatric Hosp, 1952-53; Bethany Brethren Hosp, Illinios, 1954-61; Evangelical Sch of Nursing, 1961-62; Elkhart Gen Hosp, Indiana, 1965-67; Christ Hosp, Illinios, 1969-79. *Membership:* American Nurse Assc. *Honours include:* Developed a Venoclysis Procedure Book, Chrsit Hosp; Advise the WTTW TV Station in the Panning of Psychiatric Video Programming, Viewing used Teaching Stuents; Univ of Washington, Second Scholarship for Masters Degree. *Hobbies:* Sewing; Travel; Photography; Reading. *Address:* 60358 County Road 11s, Elkhart, IN 46517, USA. 138.

FULTON Jay David, b. 4 Sept 1960, Norman, OK, USA. Farmer; Rancher. m. Nancy Diane Trusty, 27 May 1989, 1 d. *Education:* BS, Animal Sci, Oklahoma STate Univ, 1982. *Appointments:* Pen Checker, Okla Beef Inc, stillwater, 1978-82; Mgr, Happy Hill Angus, Enid Okla, 1979- 81; Owner, Mgr, Fulton Farms, Chickasha, Okla, 1982-. *Memberships:* Am Soc of Animal Sci, Okla; Cattlemans Assc; Beef Improvement Fed, Okla; Okla State Univ Alumni Assc; Grady County Cattlemans Assc; Nat Cattlemans Assc. *Honour:* County Breeder. *Address:* RT3 Box 141, Chickasha, OK 73018, USA. 7.

FUSE Toyomasa, b. 20 Jan 1931, Sapporo, Japan. Univ Prof. m. Lois E Prochaska, 23 Dec 1961, 1 s, 1 d. *Education:* BA, Missouri Valley Coll, 1954; MA, Univ of Calif, 1956; PhD, Univ of Calig, 1962. *Appointments:* Antioch Univ, 1961-64; Carleton Coll, 1964-66; Carnell Univ, 1966-68; Univ de Montreal, 1968-72; York Univ, 1972-. *Publications:* Personal Crisis and Ethnotherapy; Profiles of Death; Introduction to Suicidology in Cross-Cultural Perspective; Suicide & Culture; Modernization & Stress in Japan. *Memberships:* Canadian Assc of Suicide Prevention; Intl Assc of Suicide Prevention;

Japan Assc of Suicidology & Suicide Prevention. *Honours:* Hubert H Humphrey Fellow; Contribution to Knowledge Award in Suicidology, 1992; Research fellowship, Ministries of Health in Hungary, West Germany, Japan, France, Netherlands. *Hobbies:* Foreign Languages; Music; Film; Martial Arts. *Address:* 8 Nina Street, Toronto, Ontario Canada M5R 1Z3. 88.

FUXA James R, b. 26 Jan 1949, Lincoln, Nebr, USA. Prof of Entomology. m. Diann M Treptow, 20 May 1972, 2 s. *Education:* BS Zoology, Univ of Nebraska, 1971; US Army, 1971-73; MS Entomology, Oregon St Univ, 1975; PhD Entomology, North Carolina St Univ, 1978. *Appointments:* Dept of Entomology, Louisiana St Univ. Asst Prof, 1978-81; Assc Prof, 1981-86; Prof, 1986-; Dept Hd, 1990-91. *Publications:* Epizootiology of Insect Diseases; 50 Sci Journal Papers; Book Chapters. *Memberships:* Soc for Invertebrate Pathology; Entomological Soc of America; Intl Organization for Biological Control. *Honours:* Environmental Sci & Engr Fellow; Sigma Xi; Phi Sigma. *Hobbies:* Kids Activities; Tennis; Genealogy. *Address:* Dept of Entomology, Louisiana State Univ, Baton Rouge, LA 70803, USA. 143.

FUZEK John Frank, b. 21 Dec 1921, Knoxville, TN, USA. Conslt. m. Bettye Lynn Bean, 31 May 1943, 1 s, 2 d. *Education:* BS Chem Engr, Univ of Tenn, 1943; MS Phys Chem,1945; PhD Phys Chem, 1947; Post PhD Fellow Office of Naval Research, 1947-48. *Appointments:* Chemist, Hercules Powder Co, 1943-44; Res Chemist, North Am Rayon Corp, subsidiary at Beaunit Corp, 1948-55; Hd Res Physics, Beaunit Fibers Div, 1955-66; Snr Res Chemist, TN Eastman Co, 1966-70; Res Assc Eastman Kodak Co, Chem Div, 1970-86. *Publications:* Chapter in. Clothing Comfort; ACS Symposium Series Water in Polymers; Numerous Papers publ. *Memberships:* Am Assc for the Advancement of Sci; Am Inst Chemists; Am Chem Soc; ASTM; Am Cryst Assc; NY Academy of Sci; Fiber Soc; Am Assc Textile Chemists & Colorists; Sigma Xi. *Honours:* Oak Ridge Inst of Nuclear Studies Sci Research award; NE TN Sect of Am Chem Soc Speaker of the Year; Fiber Soc Lectr of the Year; ASTM D13 Cert of Appreciation; ASTM Award of Merit. *Hobbies:* Travel; Solar Eclipse Chasing; photography; Gardening; Ballroom Dancing. *Address:* 4603 Mitchell Road, Kingsport TN 37664, USA.

FYLE Hilton Ebenezer, b. 29 Sept 1946, Freetown. Broadcaster; Film Maker. m. Janet Matilda Faith, 11 Apr 1980, 1 s, 1 d. *Education:* Milton Margay Tchrs Coll, Freetown, 1966-69. *Appointments:* Radio, TV Presenter, Sierra Leone Broadcasting Serv, 1970-73; presenter, BBC World Serv Programme, Network Africa, 1976-; Presenter, Pick of the Week, BBC Radio 4, 1990-91. *Publications:* Coronation in Africa; A Country in the Life of Africa; The Liberia Tragedy; Salut Africa. *Memberships:* US State Dept Visitors Programme; The Wellington Club, London. *Honours:* Disc jockey of the Year; The Pater Award for Best Breakfast Radio; The Sony Award; Crowned Chief of the Assiga Clan, West Africa; The Rex Image Award for serv to Music. *Hobbies:* Travel; Gentle Music; Reading. *Address:* PO Box 1508, London N15 6EE, England.

G

GAASENBEEK Matthew, b. 27 Feb 1930, Bloemendaal, Holland. Corporate Finance Specialist. m. Mary Smella, 3 June 1955, 1 s, 2 d. *Education:* Univ of W Ont, BA, 1956. *Appointments include:* Pres, Dir, Camreco Inc, 1983-; Pres, Northern Crown Capital Corp; Dir, Ievinter Silversmiths Inc; Ont Share & Deposit Insur Corp; Woods Gordon & Co. *Memberships:* Naturalists; past Chmn, Save our Streams; Canadian Sportsmens Funds; Ont Council Univ Affairs; Quetico Park Found. *Hobbies:* Reading; Farming; Skiing; Boating; Clubs; Royal military Inst; Beaver Valley Ski. *Address:* suite 1502, 30 Wellington St, E Toronto, Ontario, Canada M5E 1S3.

GABALDONI Luis Emilio, b. 26 May, Lima, Peru. Economist; Author. m. Gertrude Vanderbilt Whitney Henry, 19 Jan 1946, 1 s, 1 d. *Education:* BS, 1938; MA, 1939; Columbia Univ, NYC, USA; Consejo Superioe de Investigaciones Cientificas, Inst Salazar Castro Genealogy, Madrid, 1970. *Appointments:* Vice Consul, NYC, 1943-48; Vice Pres, Gurtiss Gabaldoni Gabal Domini Co Inc, NYC, 1946. *Publications:* 15 Books. *Memberships:* Blub Nat, Lima; Lima Golf Club; Ateneo Madrid. *Honours:* OD Sospitalis J Sieroslymitani, Denmark; Knight Commander, Ordine de la Corona d italia; Academician, Accadimia Pontzen, Naples; Union Cultural Americana, Buenos Aires; Grand Prix Humanitaire de France; Academician Acccademia Archeologica, Italiana. *Address:* Calle Dr Fleming 44, Madrid, Spain.

GABARA Barbara, b. 30 May 1938, Pabianice, Poland. Univ of Lodz. *Education:* Masters Degree, 1961; ScD, 1965; Lectr, 1977; Snr Lectr, 1990; Prof, 1991. *Appointments:* Tech Asst, 1961; Asst, 1962-65; Asst Lectr, 1966-76; Lectr, 1977; Snr Lectr, 1990-91; Prof, 1991-. *Publications:* Meiosis, Cell Wall In, Podstawy Cytofiziologii. *Memberships:* Polish Soc Histochem Cytochem; Polish Soc of Botany. *Honours:* Ministers of High Educ. *Hobbies:* Classical Music; Skiing; Mountain Touring. *Address:* Dept of Plant Cytology & Cytochemistry, Univ of Lodz, Banacha 12/16, 90 227 Lodz, Poland.

GABEL Detlef, b. 18 Nov 1946. Prof. *Education:* PhD, 1973. *Appointments:* Asst prof, Univ Bremen, 1977-79; Prof, Univ of Bremen, 1979-. *Memberships:* German Chemical Soc; IUPAC; German Biophysical Soc; Intl Soc for Neutron Capture Therapy. *Honour:* Snr Fulbright Travel Award. *Address:* Dept of Chemistry, Univ of Bremen, PO Box 330440, D W 2800 Bremen 33, Germany.

GABRIEL Peter, b. 13 Feb 1950. British Rock Singer & Songwriter. *Education:* Charterhouse. *Career:* Co-Founder of Genesis Rock Band, 1966; Solosit, 1975; Solo Albums PG 1-1V, PG Plays Live, So, Shaking The Tree, US; Soundtrack Albums, Birdy, Passion (Last Temptation of Christ). *Creative Works:* Songs inc. Solsbury Hill; 1 Dont Remember; Sledgehammer; Blood of Eden; Family Snapshot; Digging In The Dirt; Mercy Street; Shaking The Tree; Dont Give Up; San Jacinto; Steam; Big Time; In Your Eyes. *Memberships:* 1982, Founded World of Music, Arts & Dance (WOMAD); 1985, Real World Group to Dev projects in Arts & Tech Focusing on Interactive Experinces; Set up Real World Studios, recording studio complex, 1986; Launched Real World Record Label, 1989. *Address:* Real World, Box Mill, Box, Wiltshire, England.

GAERTNER Henryk, b. 23 Mar 1922, Lublin. Physician; Prof of Medicine. m. Ludwika Kuros, 28 Apr 1962, 1 s. *Education:* N Copernicus Univ of Medicine, MD, 1951; Jagellonian Univ, Musicology, 1953; Sch of Music, Krakow. *Appointments include:* N Copernicus Univ Sch of Medicine, Krakow, Asst, 1950; Snr Asst, 1951; Adjunct, 1962; Assc Prof, 1968; Extrordinary Prof, 1975;

Ordinary Full Prof, 1985. Founder, Dir, Chair & Clinic for Intl & Rural Medicine, 1984-; Hd of Hosp Dept of Medicine, Krakow, 1971-. *Creative Works include:* About 300 publ; Numerous Books or Chapters. *Memberships include:* World Soc of Hematology; Intl Soc of Blood Transfusion; Intl European Soc of Hematology; Scientific Council & Representative of Poland. *Honours:* Honorary Cross of Commander, European Academy of Arts; Polonia Restituta Order; Gold Medal, Columbus Assc, Intl Inst of Culture & Asst; Diploma for Merits for Public Health Serv; Diploma of Brothers of Mercy. *Hobbies:* Literature; Music. *Address:* J Lea 19a/4, 30 048 Krakow, Poland.

GAGNE Mireille, b. 8 Aug 1949, Montreal, Canada. Director of Canadian Music Centre. m. 30 Dec 1985, 1 s, 1 d. *Education:* Lic in Law, 1972, MA Musicology, 1981, Univ Montreal; BACC Music, Univ of Sherlrooke. *Appointments:* Proj Mgr, Can Intl Devel Agy, 1972-74; Dir, Promotion and Lib Sers, Can Mus Ctr, 1981-. *Publications:* Sons d'Aujourh'Hui, book; Collection on Quebec Composers and Electoacoustic Music. *Memberships:* Assn for the Adv of Res in Mus, Quebec. *Hobbies:* Literature; Painting; History; Cinema; Sport. *Address:* 430 Saint- Pierre No 300, Montreal, Quebec, Canada H2Y 2M5.

GAGO FERNANDEZ Luis, b. 21 June 1932, Almanza, Spain. *Education:* Dr Philos and Letts; Translator, French courses in English and Italian; Lic Hispano-American Lit. *Appointments:* Hg Sch (Secondary) Tchr in Spain and Am. *Publications:* Poetry: Huellas di mi sombra; Sombras de mis suenos; Memoria del silencio; Salmodia dolorida; La paz no aliza su vuelo; El aire ensombrecido. *Contributions to:* newspapers and poetry journals. *Honours:* Premio do Poesia, Acentor, 1989; Premio de Poesia, Aga, 1990. *Hobbies:* Reading; Music. *Address:* c/o Marques de Asprillas, 77-6 o 1.Esc. S, 03201 Elche, Alicante, Spain.

GAIND Rachunandan, b. 1 Oct 1934, Jammu, India. Physician in Psychological Medicine. m. (1) 2 s, 4 d, (2) Susan Lesley Davenport, 7 July 1989. *Education:* DPM, 1965; FRCP, 1975; FRc Psych, 1977. *Appointments:* Lectr, Neurology, India Inst of Medical Sci, 1961-62; Physicians in Psychological Medicine, Guys Hosp, London, 1969-88; Sec Gen, World Assc for Social Psychiatry. *Memberships:* BMA; Royal Soc of Medicine; Chmn, Inst of Soc Psychiatry; Medical Legal Soc. *Honours:* State Scholarship, Kashmir; Gold Medal, Punjal Univ. *Hobbies:* Gardening; Sailing; Fishing; Travel. *Address:* Suite 206, Emblem House, 27 Tooley Street, London SE1 2PR, England.

GALADIMA Baba, b. 12 July 1962, Shango Minna. Lectr; Engr. m. 17 May 1991. *Education:* Govt Tech Coll, Minna, 1976-82; Kaduna polytechnic, 1983-89. *Appointments:* Biwater Nig Ltd, 1982-83; Bouygues Nig Ltd, 1986-87; Site Supvst, Niger State COE, 1990-. *Hobbies:* Travel; Reading; Music; Friends. *Address:* PO Box 493, No.1 Shango Vill Minna, Niger State, Nigeria.

GALBALLY Francis William, b. 22 July 1953, Melbourne. m. Carolyn Joy Trewin, 7 Feb 1976, 2 d. *Education:* Xavier Coll, Melbourne Univ. *Appointments:* Mellesons, 1975; Galbarry & O'Bryan, 1977; Partner, Galbally & O'Bryan, Solicitors, 1978. *Publications:* many Legal Publ. *Memberships:* Law Inst of Victoria; Law Council of Australia; victorian Regional Galleries & Public Museums; Conservation Centre; Small Business Develop Corp; Lectr Law & Mkt Univ pf Tech, New Sales Wales & Victoria. *Hobbies:* Tennis; Show Skiing; Scuba Diving; Reading; Music. *Address:* 259 William Street, Melbourne, Victoria 3000, Australia. 139, 152.

GALDOS-BETHENCOURT Ana Maria Carolina, b. Camaguey, Cuba. Writer. m. 27 Sept 1936, 1 s. *Education:* Art & Humanities, 1930-34; Diploma Delineante, Havana, Cuba, 1949; Exchange Nice, France Contemporay European Literature, 1958-59; Florida

State Univ, Tallahassee, Florida, 1960; Comm Art, Miami, Florida, 1962; Journalism, 1963. *Appointments:* Art Editor Sun Colony Mag, 1966; Prof Reader, Broward County Sch Papers, Copublisher Bilingual Tabloid, Suns/Soles; Commerical Artist, Advertising Advisors; Editor, Unidad Latina; Art & Prod Mgr, The Coulevard mag, 1974; Instr, Prospect Hall Coll, 1975; Founder, dir, Instr, Spanish Bilingual Studio 1, 1980; Bilingual Studio 2, 1986-90; Dir, Bistud Correspondence Advanced Spainish Prog, Iowa, 1992. *Creative Works include:* The Initiation of a Writer; El Abra del Yumuri; Spanish Today; Irregular Verbs using the Hispanoamerican Nomenclature; Spanish Phenetics Phonology & Morphosintax; Two Horse Heads, Medussa; Dream of Sao Joao Bosco; Published Poems: Time Speaks, 1991; White, Blue & Green, 1992. *Memberships:* ASW; BBB; NAFE. *Honours:* Second Prize, Equestrian Comp. *Hobbies:* Horseback Riding; Writing; Reading; Research; Yoga Excercises; Painting. *Address:* 205 W Hempstead Avenue, Fairfield, IA 52556, USA. 162.

GALE Steven Hershel, b. 18 Aug 1940, San Diego, California, USA. Endowed Prof of Humanities Educ; Dir. m. Kathy L L Johnson, 20 May 1973, 3 d. *Education:* BA, Duke Univ, 1963; MA, UCLA, 1965; PhD, Univ Co, California, 1970. *Appointments:* Reading Asst, English, LA Met Coll, 1965-66; Tchr Asst, Univ of Calif, 1966; Instr, 1967-68; Assc, UCLA, 1968-70; Asst Prof, UPR, Rio Piedras, 1970-73; Fulbright Prof, Univ Liberia, Monrovia, 1973-74; Assc Prof, Univ Fla, Gainsville, 1974-80. *Publications include:* Butters Going Up; S J Perelman, A Critical Study; Critical Essays on Harold Pinter. *Memberships:* Harold Pinter Soc; MLA; Am Theatre Assc, Africanists; Fulbright Alumni Assc; Con on Coll Compositions; Coll Eng assc; Nat Collegiate Honors Council; Am Soc Theatre Research; Am Lit Assc; Coll Eng Assc; NCTE; Backett Soc; African Studies Centre; Nat Ret Tchrs Assc; Chi Delta Pi. *Honours:* Grante NEH; Ky humanities COuncil; Mo So State Coll; Danforth Assc; Recipient Golden poet Award; Silver Poet Award. *Hobbies:* Reading; Gardening; Writing; Swimming; Sports; Films; Theatre. *Address:* KY State Univ, Frankfort, KY 40601, USA. 7, 52.

GALEANO Eduardo, b. 3 Sept 1940, Montevideo, Uruguay. Writer. m. Helena Villagra, 19 June 1976, 1 s, 2 d. *Publications:* Open Veins of Latin America; Days & Nights of Love & War; The Trilogy Memory of Fire: Genesis; Faces & Masks; Century of the Wind; The Book of Embraces. *Honours:* Jose Carrasco; Ruben Dario; Felix Varela; Casa de las Americas; American Book Award. *Hobbies:* Graphic Design; Mural Painting; Football. *Address:* Dalmiro Costa 4462, Montevidio, Uruguay.

GALECZKI George, b. 12 Dec 1945, Lugoj. Physicist. m. Gaby, 20 Sept 1969, 1 s, 1 d. *Education:* Licence in Physics, 1968; Master of Sci, 1975; Doc of Sci, 1979; Army Serv, Roumania, 1968; Israel, 1974. *Appointments:* Inst for Electronics Research, Bucharest, 1969-70; Technion, IIT, Haifa, 1972-80; Rafael, Haifa, 1981-88; Cologne Univ, 1988-. *Publications:* 41 Publ. *Memberships:* European Physical Soc; Germany Physical Soc; Israeli Physical Soc. *Honours:* Michael Landau Prize for Research. *Hobbies:* Philosophy; Foundation of Physics; History of Religion. *Address:* Fuldaer Str 90, 5000 Cologne 91, Germany.

GALKOWSKI Andrzej Edmund, b. 1 Oct 1926, Gniezno, Poland. University Professor. m. Maria Wallis, 18 Feb 1957, 1 s, 1 d. *Education:* ME Arch, 1951; Dr Tech, 1962; Asst Prof, 1973, Assoc Prof, 1983, Prof, 1991, Tech Univ of Gdansk. *Appointments:* Chief Proj Arch, Miastoprojekt, Poznan, 1951-64; Sr Asst, Asst Prof, Tech Univ of Poznan, 1963- 73; Vis Prof, Univ of Florida, 1974-75; Hd of Dept, 1976-, Dir, 1979-91, Pro Rector, 1991-, Tech Univ of Poznan. *Publications include:* Blood Donors Ctr, Poznan; Sanatorium in Ciechocinek; Health care and welfare facilities; Facilities for leisure activities for disabled people. *Memberships:*

Intl Union of Archts Pub Hlth Gp; Rehab Intl Comm on Tech Intl Union of Archts, Pub Hlth Gp; Intl Hlth Policy and Mgmt Inst, Adv Bd; Polish Acad of Scis; Intl Rehab Comm on Technol and Accessibility. *Hobbies:* Tourism; Music. *Address:* ul Chmielna 7, PL 61464 Poznan, Poland. 50, 57.

GALLAGHER Vicki Lea Smith, b. 6 Dec 1950, Norfolk, Va, USA. Real Est Sales. m. Steven Robert Gallagher, 19 Nov 1977. *Education:* Old Dominion Univ, BS, Music, 1973. *Appointments:* Goodman Segar Hogan Residential Sales, 1979-85; Realty Conslt, 1985-90; Leading Edge Realty, 1990-. *Memberships:* Ridewater Bd of Reltors; Tidewater Builders Assc Sales & Mktg; Virginia Assc of Realtors. *Honours include:* Tidewater Builders Assc Million Dolla Circle; Gold Award, Bronze Award, Silver Award, Nat Assoc of Homebuilders; Realty Conslt New Homes Agent of the Year. *Hobbies:* Raising & Showing Maine Coon Cats & Household Pets. *Address:* 2236 Cross Road Trail Va. Beach VA 23456, USA.

GALLEGHAN Persia Elspbeth, b. NSW, Australia. m. 8 Dec 1969. *Education include:* Diploma, Social Studies, Univ of Sydney. *Appointments:* Hd Social Workes, Repatmation General of Dept Hosp, Sydney, Australia, 1953-62. *Publications:* Care of the Aged; History of Red Cross V A D. *Memberships include:* Australian Red Cross Soc; Nat Council of Women; Friends of Sydney; Keep Australia Beautiful. *Honours:* Hon Life Member, Australia Red Cross; Pres, St John Ambulance; Order of the British Empire. *Hobbies:* Opera; Drama; Ballet; Orchestral Music; Reading. *Address:* 22 High Tor, 24 Rangers Road, Cremorne 2090, Sydney, NSW, Australia.

GALLENO Humberto, b. 31 Oct 1943, Lima Peru. Chmn of the Board. m. Cecilia Pinillos Ashton, 6 June 1968. 2 s, 1 d. *Education:* Agronomist Engr, Univ Agraria, Lima, 1965; MBA Escuela de Administracion para Graduados. Lima, 1967. *Appointments:* Dir, Profit Panning Marcona, minning Co. Lima, 1967-73; Mgr, CIA Constructora Utah, Lima, 1974- 76; Pres, Bd of Dirs, TTX, Lima, 1976-83; Comml Mgr, Dafico, Lima, 1984-86; Prin Prof, Univ Del Pacifico, Lima, 1971-. *Creative Works:* Prof Univ Catolica Lima; Bechtel Civil & Minerals; Refrigerados Inysa; Jumbo Andino Tours SA; Intl Traders SA; Inmolilaria El Cortijo SA. *Memberships:* Assc Cultureal Sol Y Armonia; Univ Peruana Cayetano Heredia; Club Nacional; Lima Golf Club; Los Inkas Golf Club; Country Club Los Condores; La Honda Club; Club De La Banca Y Seguros. *Hobbies:* Golf; Tennis; Boating; Reading. *Address:* Las Tres Marias, 175 Monterrico, Lima Peru. 52, 132.

GALLINER Peter, b. 19 Sept 1920, Berlin, Germany. British Publisher. (1) Edith Marguerite Gold-schmidt 1948, d, (2) Helga Stenschke, 1990. *Education:* Berlin & London. *Appointments:* Reuters London, 1944-47; Foreign Man Financial Times, 1947-60; Chmn of Bd, Mgr Dir, Ullstein Publ Group, Berlin, 1960-64; Vice Chair, Mgr Dir, British Printing Corp, Publ Group, Lodnon, 1965-70; Int Publ Conslt, 1965-67, 1970-75. *Honours include:* Fed Cross of Merit; Orden de Isabel la Católica, Spain; The Commanders Cross, Order of Merit. *Hobbies:* Reading; Music. *Address:* 27 Walsingham Street, Johns Wood Park, London NW8 6RH, England.

GALLUP Lee, b. St Louis, Missouri, USA. Educator; Drama Coach; Dir; Actress. m. Arthur Feldman, 1 d. *Education:* PhD, Univ of Denver; MA, BA, Univ of Illinois. *Appointments include:* Founder of Acting Classes, Third Eye Theatre, 1967-73; Founder of Theatre, Theatre Under Glass, 1974-77; Acting Instr, Colorado Womens Coll, 1977-80; Acting Instructor, Arvada Center, for Arts and Humanities, 1978-; Freelance Dialects Coach; Stage Actress, Bonfils Third Eye Theatre, Theatre Under Glass; Radio & TV. *Publications:* For Whom the Belle Told; Rumple Stiltzskin & The Green Witch. *Memberships:* Zeta Phi Eta; American Federation of TV & Radio Artists;

The Brecht Soc of America; Arts Advisory Bd, regis Univ. *Honours:* Best Actress Award; Outstanding Faculty Member Loretto Heights Coll; Outstanding Woman in the Performing Arts. *Hobbies:* English History; Archeology; Astronomy; Travel; Reading. *Address:* 2045 S Fillmore St, Denver, CO 80210, USA.

GALPERIN Boris, b. 25 Nov 1952, Kiev, USSR. Assoc Prof. m. Shlomit Galperin, 31 July 1980, 1 s, 1 d. *Education:* Latvian State Univ, Riga, 1970-75; Technion, Israel Inst of Tech, 1977-82. *Appointments:* Research Staff Member, Princeton Univ, 1983-89; Assoc Prof, Univ of South Florida, Dept of Mavine Sci, 1989-. *Publications:* Lrg Eddy Simulation of Complex Engineering & Geophysical Flows; 30 Prof Publ. *Memberships:* APS; IAA; AGU; TOS. *Hobbies:* Reading; Music; Travel. *Address:* Dept of Marine Sci, MSL138F, Univ of South Florida, 140 7th Avenue South, St Petersburg, FL 33701, USA. 7.

GALSTER Ulrike, b. 27 Feb 1942, Fuerstenzell. Sr Managing Dir. m. Karl Heinz Galster, 25 Aug 1962, 1 s. *Education:* Comml Training; Sining Studies; Beautician. *Appointments:* Mgr Dir, G&M Handelsgesellschaft. *Memberships:* Order of Knights of the Holy Grail, Munich. *Hobbies:* Music; Tennis; Skiing; Travel; Reading. *Address:* Arnstorfer Strasse 12, 8340 Pfarrkirchen, Germany. 92.

GALTON Herbert, b. 1 Oct 1917, Vienna, Austria. Retired Univ Prof. Div, 1 s, 1 d. *Education:* Philosophical Faculty, Univ of Vienna, 1935-38; PhD, The Univ of London, 1951. *Appointments:* Univ of. Kansas, Lawrence, KS. Asst Prof, 1962-64; Assoc Prof, 1964-69; Full Prof, 1969-88. *Publications:* Aorist und Aspekt im Slavischen; The Main Functions of the Slavic Verbal Aspect; Freedom, from Illusions; Reisetagebuch. *Memberships:* American Assn Advancement Slavic Studies Assn; Tchrs Slavic & East European Languages; Wiener Sprachgesellschaft, Schopenhauer, Gesellschaft. *Honours:* American Guest Prof in Bulgaria; Czechoslovakia; Yugoslavia; Macedonian Gold Medal for Merits on Behalf of the Maced Language. *Hobby:* Swimming. *Address:* c/o Inst fur Slawistik, Liebiggasse 5, A-1010 Vienna, Austria.

GAMAGE Venetia Ethel, b. 16 Oct 1935, Colombo. Member World Committee, World Assn Girl Guiders & Girl Scouts. m. Nihal Ranjith Gamage, 13 Oct 1967, 1 d. *Education:* Tchrs Cert, Sci, 1959; Girl Guide Trainers Diploma, 1974. *Appointments:* Tchr, Sci, 1960-82; Vice Pre, Sri Lanka, 1982; Project Dir, Migrant Women Training, Women Chamber & Ind & Commerce, 1990; Exec Dir, Water & Sanitation Decade Serv, 1991-. *Publications:* Shared Experiences, for World Assn & Girl Guides. *Memberships:* Sr Lanka Girl Guides; World Comm, World Assn of Girl Guides & Girl Scouts; Water & Sanitation Decade Serv; Sri Lanka Sch & Social Work. *Honours:* Women of the Year; Hihest Award for Outstanding Serv, Sri Lanka Girl Guides.*Hobbies:* Gardening; Counselling. *Address:* 30 Daya Road, Colombo 6, Sri Lanka.

GAMBURTSEV Azarij, b. 24 Apr 1935, Moscow, Geodynamic; Seismologic. m. 23 May 1958, 1 s, 1 d. *Education:* Moscow Univ, 1953- 58; Bach of Sci, 1968; Doc of Sci, 1991; Correspond Mbr of Acad of Nat Sci of Russia, 1991. *Appointments:* Seismic Investigation Structure of Geophysical Media, 1958-76; Seismic Monitoring of the Litosphere, Geodynamic, Ecology, 1976-; Hd of Grp, Geophysical Monitoring of Inst of the Physics of the Earth of Russian Acad of Sci; Dir of Inst, Geomonitoring and the Regime Observations of Russian Acad of Nat Sci, 1992. *Creative Works:* Seismic Invest on Littoral Part of East Antarctic, 1960; Seismic Wave Propagation in Real Media, 1969; Seismic Monitoring of the Earth Crust, 1984; Seismic Monitoring of the Litosphere, 1992. *Memberships:* Assoc Predictions & Circles; Sci Bds of Acad of Nat Sci of Russia. *Hobbies:* Photography; Theatre; Reading.

Address: Inst of Physics of the Earth 10, B Gruzinskaja 133810, Moscow, Russia.

GAMKRELIDZE Thomas Valerian, b. 23 Oct 1929, City of Kutais, Republic of Georgia. Prof of Linguistics & Culturual History. m. Djavakhishvili Nina, 25 May 1968, 1 s, 1 d. *Education:* Oriental Faculty, Univ of Tbilisi, Georgia; Doc of the Philological Sci. *Appointments:* Dir, The Oriental Inst, Georgia Academy of Sci; Prof, Univ of Tbilisi. *Publications:* Theoretical Linguistics & Semiotics; Typology of Writing & Cultural History; Indo European, Semitic, Caucasian Languages & Cultures. *Memberships:* Georgian Academy of Sci; Academy of Sci, Moscow; American Academy of Arts & Sci, Boston; British Academy, Lon; Russian Academy of Sci, Vienna; Sächsische Akademie der Wissenschaften, Leipzig; Hon Mem Linguistic Soc of America; Societas Linguistica Europaea; Mem of Parliament, Republic of Georgia, Head of the Foreign Relations Comm. *Honours:* Alexander Von Humboldt Stiftung Prize; Lenin Prize; Djavakhishvili prize. *Hobbies:* Music; Tennis. *Address:* The Oriental Inst, Georgia, Academy of Sci Acad Tseretel Street 3, Tbilisi 38062, Georgia. 52.

GAMMIE Robert Christie, b. 26 Oct 1932, Chelmsford, Essex, England. Chartered Arrchitect. m. Julia, 23 Aug 1962, 1 s, 1 d. *Education:* St Josephs Coll, Ipswich, 1942-49; Mid Essex Sch of Arch, 1950-54; Nat Serv Army Comm RPC, 1955-57; Thames poly, 1969-72. *Appointments:* Lewis Solomon, Kaye, 1957-62; R Seifert & Partners, 1962-91. *Memberships:* Royal Inst of British Arch; Magistrates Assoc; Catenian Assoc. *Hobbies:* Rugby; Cricket; Squash; Gardening. *Address:* Hookers, 25 Priory Farm Road, Nounsley, Essex CM3 2NJ, England.

GAN Zhigeng, b. 28 Feb 1933, Yuyao City Jiejiang Province. Nat Historian; Archaelogist. m. Leng Hong Ju, 30 Sept 1960, 3 s. *Education:* BA, History Dept, Northern Peoples Univ, 1953-57. *Appointments:* Research in History Heilongjiang Provincial Museum, 1957-80; Deputy Dir, Editorial Dept of Heilingjiang Publ; Deputy Dir in Chief, Heilongjiang Journal of Historical Relics, 1981-83; Deputy Dir, Heilongjiang Prov Cultural Dept, 1983-84; Deputy Dir, Heilongjiang Prov Relics Mngt Committee, 1984-. *Publications include:* Outline of Ancient Nat History of Heilongjiang Prov; Witness of the History; Symposium of the Yihe Boxers Against Russia; Numerous Articles & Lectures. *Memberships:* China nat History Assoc; Historical Assoc of the Chinese Liao Jin Qidan & Nuzhen; Heilongjiang Prov Assoc of Relic Museum; History Dept of Harbin Normal Univ; Jilin Prov Academy of Social Sci. *Honours include:* Excellent Reseacher; Award, for the Achievement in Social Sci; Award for Excellent Books in Social Sci. *Hobbies:* Collecting Old Paintings; China; Jadeware; Gem; Knives. *Address:* 1 Yiyuan Street, Harbin, China.

GANDOLFO Giancarlo, b. 17 Nov 1937, Turin, Italy. Univ Prof. m. D'Alessandro Luciana, 19 May 1962, 2 d. *Education:* Laurea, Univ of Rome, 1960; Libera Docenza, Univ of Rome, 1968. *Appointments:* Research Dept, Bank of Italy, Rome, 1961-65; Asst Prof, Econs, Univ of Rome, 1965-68; Assoc Prof of Maths, Econs, Univ of Siena, 1968-70; Full Prof, Univ of Siena, 1970-74; Full Prof, Intl Economics, Univ of Rome, 1974- *Publications:* Economic Dynamics, Methods & models; Econometric Estimation of Continous Time Models; Intl Economics. *Memberships:* Soc Italiana Economisti; Soc for Economic Dynamics Control; American Economic Assoc; European Economic Assoc. *Honours:* Premio Stefano Siglienti per l'economia; Premio St Vincent per I' Economia. *Hobbies:* Byciciling; Underwater Hunting; Wine & Watch Collecting; Reading. *Address:* Via Rodolfo Benini 7, I 00191 Roma, Italy. 43, 52.

GANEV Valentine, b. 7 Apr 1956, Rousse. Actor. *Education:* Army Serv, 1975-77; State Univ for Cinematography, Moscow, 1977-87. *Appointments:* Over 30 Pays in Prof Theatres. *Memberships:* Nat Academy for Theatre & Film Art; Teaching An Actors

Class. *Honours:* Best Theatre Actor Award. *Hobbies:* Playing the Violine; Skiing. *Address:* Buck Stone, b1 31a Apt 13, 1618 Sofia, Bulgaria.

GANG Bao Qi, b. 19 Apr 1927, China. Tchr; Prof. m. Hui Fang Gan, 3 Mar 1951, 1 s, 1 d. *Education:* China Medical Univ, Bach of Medical Sci, 1943-49. *Appointments:* Asst, Dept of Occupational Health, China Medical Univ, 1949-55; Lect, Dept of Occupational Health, Harbin Medical Univ, 1955-62; Assoc Prof, Prof, Dept of Ocupational Health, 1962-. *Publications:* Practical Handbook of Occupational Health; Systematic Diagram of Health Standards of China; Sci Papers. *Memberships include:* Chinese Assn of Preventive Medicine; Intl Commission on Occupational Health; Intl Soc of Complex Enviromental Studies. *Honours include:* Archieves of Complex Enviromental Studies. *Hobbies:* Reding; Tennis. *Address:* Dept of Occupational Health, Sch of Public Health, Harbin Medical Univ, 41 Dazhi Avenue, Harbin 150001, China.

GANO John, b. 26 Sept 1924, Dallas, Texas. Attorney at Law. m. Betty Jeanne McIver, 21 Dec 1949, 1 s. *Education:* Texas Christian Univ, 1942,1946; Univ of Texas, Bach of Laws Degree, 1947-50. *Appointments:* United States Army, 1943-46; Phillipines, Okinawa, Korea; United States Army, 1950-53; Germany; Asst City Attorney, Fort Worth, 1953-59; Snr Asst City Attorney, Houston, 1959-63; Jamail & Gano Law Firm, 1964-78; Gano & Donovan, Pc Law Firm, 1979-85; Gano, Donovan & Gano, Law Firm, 1985-. *Memberships:* Board Certified, Personal Injury Trial Law; State Bar of Texas; Supreme Court of United States. *Honour:* Military, World War 11, Korean War Decoration. *Hobbies:* Ranching; Raise Horses, Miniature Donkeys; Antique Maps and Guns. *Address:* 715 Cinnamon Oak Lane, Houston, TX 77079, USA. 2.

GAO Ertai, b. 15 Oct 1935, China. *Education:* Grad, Fine Arts Dept, Jiangsu Tchrs Col; Hist of Chinese Fine Arts, Dunhuang Res Inst of Cultural Relics; Aesthetics, Philos Res Inst, China Social Scis Acad, 1978. *Appointments:* Tchr, Philos Dept, Lanzhou Univ, 1978-84; Prof, Sichuan Tchrs Univ, Dept of Chinese Lit; P-time Prof, Nankai Univ; Prof, Chinese Dept, Nanjing Univ, Jiangsu, 1986. *Publications include:* The Awakening of Art; Historical Materialsim and Humanism; Yang Jiqiang; What is Philosophy; Essays: Impressions on a Greening Tree; Let Tears Shed for the Nation and Play the Fate of Beauties; An Apology for Sociological Criticism; Random Thoughts on literary criticism; The cultural consciousness in contemporary literature; Book: Beauty: The Symbol of Freedom, 1986. *Honours:* State Expert with Dist Contributions, 1983. *Address:* History Department, Sichuan Normal University, Chengdu, Sichuan 610066, China.

GAO Guangang, b. 4 Sept 1958, Shanghai, China. Freelance writer; Consultant. m. Weihua Lu, 7 Oct 1989. *Education:* BA, Journalism, 1982, MA 1985, PhD 1988, Fudan Univ. *Appointments:* Tchg Asst, Fudan Univ, 1985-87; Asst Prof, 1988-89; Freelance writer, conslt for intl communications and PR. *Publications:* Journalism Fundamentals, 1985; Concise Journalism History of China, 1986; Persuasion and Propaganda, 1989; Advertising in china, 1990; World Broadcasting, 1991; Journalism and Publication Volume, Chinese Encyclopaedia, 1991; Chinese Journalism History, 6 vols, 1992; Author and coauthor of numerous articles. *Hobbies:* Reading; Personal Computer; Table Tennis; Tennis. *Address:* 142 Lloyd Avenue, Fremont, CA 94536, USA.

GAO Hong Xun, b. Aug 1924, He Bei Province, China. Prof of Methematics. m. Lu Yunshu, 15 July 1950, 2 d. *Education:* BSc Dept of Math & Physics, China Univ, 1948. *Appointments:* Asst of Math, Beiyang Univ, Tainjin, 1948-52; Lectr, Assoc Prof, 1952-80; Prof of Math, Nankai Univ, 1981-. *Publications:* Numerous mathematical Papers. *Memberships:* Operations Research Soc, Tianjin, China; Council of Math Soc;

Combinatoral Math Council of China Math Soc; Information Security Soc of China Computer Federation. *Honours:* Cert & Plaque Award for Teaching more than 30 yrs; Citation for Excellent Member of Tianjin Sci & Tech Federation; Certificate and Golden Galloping Horse Award, for Teaching over forty years, State Commission of P R China, 1990. *Address:* Dept of Maths, Nankai Univ, Ba Li Tai, Tianjin, China.

GAO Jin Rong, b. 20 Apr 1935, Beijing, China. Prof of Dance; Principal at Gansu Arts Coll. m. Xiong Xiang Liu, 12 June 1963, 2 s, 1 d. *Education:* Advanced Dance Class, Central Drama Academy of PRC, 1952. *Appointments:* Actress, Song & Dance Ensemble, Gansu Province, 1952-58; Tchr, Lanzhou Arts Coll, 1959-62; Dir, Song Ensemble, Gansu Province, 1962-74; Principle, Gansu Arts Coll, 1974-. *Creative Works include:* Initiate & Establish Dunhuang Dance System; Compile the Basic Tching & Training Material for Dunhuang Dance; Compose & Choreography About 40 Dunhuang Dances. *Memberships:* Standing Council, Chinese Dancers Assn; Chmn, Gansu Dancers Assn; Vice-Chmn, Dancers Branch of the Dunhuang & Turfan Inst. *Honours:* Dunhuang Literature & Arts Genre Award; Gardener Award; Provincial 1st Prize, Scientific Research in Educ; Distinguished Service Award of Ministry of Culture of PRC; 3rd Prize, Gansu First Provincial Theatrical Festival. *Hobbies:* Peking Opea. *Address:* Gansu Arts Coll, 71 Duanjiatan, Lanzhou, Gansu 730020, China. 138.

GAO Zhi, b. 1 Nov 1937, Qixian, Shanxi Province, China. Sci Research; Prof. m. Qi Chunyan, 22 Apr 1967, 2 d. *Education:* Snr Middles Scho of Qixian, China, 1955; Dept of Mathematics & Mechanics, Beijing Univ, 1960. *Appointments:* Research Asst, Inst of Mechanics, Chinese Acad of Sci, 1979-81; Asst Prof, Ibid, 1982-85; Assoc Prof, Ibid, 1984-; Member of Academic Committee, Ibid, 1986-; Doctorant Advisor, Ibid. *Publications:* About Seventy publ. *Memberships:* Intl Soc of Optical Engrng; Chinese Soc of Theoretical & Applied Mechanics; Chinese Soc of optics; Chinese Soc of Aerodynamics. *Honours:* Honorary Prof; Award for outcome of Sci Researches. *Hobbies:* Classical Music; Symphonic Music; Reading Novels. *Address:* Inst of Mechanics, Chinese Academy of Sci, Beijing 100080, China. 152, 162.

GARDARSSON Thorsteinn, b. 8 July 1952, Iceland. Manager. m. Birna Gudjonsdottie, 28 Apr 1979, 1 s. *Education:* Cand Econs, Univ, Iceland, 1973-77. *Appointments:* Major, Comunity Olfushreppur, Thorlakshofn, 1977-81; Cons, Various Communities, 1981-85; Mgr, The State & Municipal Data Processing Centre, 1985-. *Hobbies:* Reading; Salmon Fishing; Swimming. *Address:* Ljosamri 5, 210 Gardabaer, Iceland. 52.

GARETSKY Radim, b. 7 Dec 1928, Minsk. Geologist. m. Morozova Galina, 1 Jan 1990, 1 d. *Education:* Moscow Oil Inst, 1946-52; Mining Engr Geologist, 1952; Doc of Geol & Mineral Sci, 1969; Prof, 1980; Corresponding Member, Byelorussian Academy of Sci, 1972, Academician, 1977. *Appointments:* Sci Worker, Geological Inst of USSR Academy of Sci, 1952-71; Hd Lab of General & Regional Tectonics, Inst of Geochemistry & Geophysics, 1972-91; Dir, Inst of Geochemistry & Geophysics, Byelourussian Academy of Sci since 1977-. *Creative Works:* Monographs. Tectonic Analysis of Rock Thickness; Inherited Dislocations of the Platform Cover, Mugodzhar Province; Tectonics of Young Platforms of Eurasia; Tectonics of Byelorussia; Potassium Bearing Basins of the World. *Memberships include:* Moscow Soc of Naturalists; Committee for the Intl Geological Correlation Programme; Russian Comm for the Intl Lithosphere Programme; Nat Comm of Geologists of Russia. *Honours:* USSR State Prize; Prize, USSR Academy of Sci, Honor of Academician N S Shatsky. *Hobbies:* Reading; Gardening. *Address:* Inst of Geochemistry &

Geophysics of the Belarus Academy of Sci, Zhodinskaya 7, Minsk 220600, Belarus.

GARG Devendra P, b. 22 Mar 1934. *Education:* BSc, Agra Univ, India, 1954; BE, Univ of Roorkee, India, 1957; MS, Univ of Wisconsin, Madison, 1960; PhD, New York Univ, 1969. *Appointments:* Univ of Roorkee, Visiting Prof, Reader, Lectr, 1957-65; New York Univ, Instructor, 1965-69; Massachusetts Inst of Technology, Visiting Prof, Lectr, Assoc Prof, Asst Prof, 1960-80; Georgian Tech Univ, Tbilsi, USSR, Fulbright Snr Scholar; Duke Univ, Prof, Dir, 1972-; Dir, Dynamic Systems, Control Prog, Nat Sci Found, Washington DC, 1992. *Publications include:* Supervisory Control for Coordination of Multiple Robots; Neural Network Control of Robotic Manipulators; Vision Guided Tracking in Manufacturing; Books; Chapters; Technical Reports. *Memberships include:* Nat Nominating Committee; USA Symposium on Manufacturing Automation; American Soc of Mech Engrs. *Honours include:* TCM Merit Scholar; Sigma Xi; Pi Tau Sigma; ASME Fellow. *Address:* Dept of Mechanical Engrng & Matericals Sci, Duke Univ, Durham NC 27706, USA.

GARNOR Darlene M, b. 27 Aug 1943, Iowa. Poet. m. Robert Garnor, 17 Jan 1965, 1 s, 1 d. *Education:* Cruston Iowa High Sch. *Publications include:* The Last Game; Xhristmas Is Past; Baby Dear Please Dont Cry; Children Making Snow Men; All About the Baby; Why Mothers Hair Turns Grey; Miachel Gets A Ride on Santas Sled; Bingo Thats The Name of the Game; Children Need A Lot of Love; Have We Forgotten The True Meaning of Christmas; Tender Care; Mikie Went to See Big Bird Goes to Holly Wood. *Honours:* Golden Poet Award; The United Amateur Press Award. *Hobbies:* Bowling; Collecting Stamps. *Address:* 108 Cedar, Atlantic, IA 50022, USA.

GARRETT Timothy Richard Trelogan, b. 5 Oct 1966, New Orleans, LA, USA. Mathematician. *Education:* BS, Maths & Sci, Univ of New Orleans 1989; MS, Physics, Computer Sci, 1991. *Appointments:* Computer Sci Tchr, Isidore Newman Sch, 1984-89; Photographer Instr, Newman Sch, 1983- 88; Visiting Math Prof, Saint Martins Sch, 1990-91. *Publications:* Black & White Photography; Over 300 Monochrome Prints on Display in North America. *Memberships:* MAA; AMS; NCTM; GNOMT; PPA; IFPo; IFMO; GNOCC; NOPS. *Honours:* William L Putman Comp Finalist; Merit Scholarship Foundation Finalist; Phi Kappa Phi; Phi Eta Sigma; Anvilla Prescott Shultz Citzenship; Nicholls Tae Kwon Do Karate Championship. *Hobbies:* Soccer; Tennis; Karate; Weightlifting; Bike Riding; Hiking; Photography; Computers; Keyboard Music; Flying Kites; Poetry; Reading; Writing. *Address:* 251 Bellaire Drive, New Orleans, LA 70124, USA. 7, 176.

GARSIDE Roger Ramsay, b. 29 Mar 1938, London, England. Chmn Garside, Miller Assoc advisers to emerging securities mkts. m. 11 Oct 1969, 3 s. *Education:* Eton Coll, 1951-56; Clare Coll, Cambridge, 1959-62; Sloan Sch of Management, MIT, 1971-72. *Appointments:* 2nd lieut, 1/6 QEC Gurkha Rifles, 1958-59; HM Foreign Serv, 1962-71; Served Rangoon, 1964-65; Mandarin Chinese Lang Student, Hong Kong, 1965-67; Second Sec, Peking, 1968-70; FCO, 1970-71; World Bank, 1972-74; FCO, 1975; First Sec, Peking, 1976-79; Prof of East Asian Studies, US Navel Postgrade Sch, Calif, 1979-80; Dep Hd Planning Staff, FCO, 1980-81; Seconded, HM Treasury, 1981-82; Financial & Commercial Counsellor, Paris, 1982-87; Dir, Public Affairs, London Stock Exchange, 1987-90. *Publications:* Coming Alive, China After Mao. *Membership:* Royal Inst of Intl Affairs. *Hobbies:* Family; Tennis; Windsurfing. *Address:* 36 Groveway, London SW9 0AR, England. 1.

GARTON George Alan, b. 4 June 1922, Scarborough, England. Biochemist. m. Gladys Frances Davison, 21 Aug 1951, 2 d. *Education:* Univ of Liverpool, BSc, 1944; BSc, 1946; PhD, 1949; DSc, 1959. *Appointments:* Experimental Asst, Min of Supply, 1942-45; Rowett Research Inst, Aberdeen, 1950-83; Hd of Dept, Lipid Biochem, 1963-83; Deputy Dir, 1968-83. *Publications:* Many Papers in Sci Journals; Chapters in Several Books. *Memberships:* Biochemical Soc; Nutrition Soc; Intl Conferences on the Biochemistry of Lipids; British Nutrition Foundation. *Honours:* Johnston Research & Teaching Fellow; Fellow, Royal Soc of Edinburgh; Snr Foreign Fellow, US Nat Sci Foundation; Fellow, Royal Soc; Hon Res Fellow, Univ Aberdeen; Serving Brother, Order of St John. *Hobbies:* Gardening; Golf; Foreign Travel. *Address:* Ellerburn, 1 St Devenick Crescent, Cults, Aberdeen, AB1 9LL, Scotland. 1, 34.

GARZA Roberto Jesus, b. 10 Apr 1934, Hargill, Texas, USA. Univ Prof. m. Idelina, 24 Aug 1957, 1 s, 1 d. *Education:* BA, A&I Univ, Texas, 1959; MA, 1964; EdD, Oklahoma State Univ, 1975. *Appointments:* High Sch Tchr, Counselor, 1959-64; Jnr Coll, Instr, Adm,1964-68; Univ Admin, Univ of Notre Dame, Texas, 1968-. *Creative Works:* SET, Spanish Experimental Theatre; Publ. Contemporary Chicano Theatre. *Memberships:* American Assn of Univ Prof; Texas Assn of Coll Tchrs; Phi Delta Kappan; Assn of Supervision & Curr Devel. *Honours include:* Nat Defence Educ Act Award; John Hay Whitney Foundation Award; Outstanding Educator, Citizen in Texas. *Hobbies:* Theatre; Travel; Writing; Sports; Reading; Gardening; Grandchildren. *Address:* Dept of Education, The Univ of Texas Brownsville, 1614 Ridgely Rd, Brownsville, TX 78520, USA. 2, 155.

GASPARSKI Wojciech Wladyslaw, b. 10 Oct 1936, Warsaw, Poland. Scientist; Prof of Humanities, Polish Acad of Sci. m. Renata Debrowska, 31 Dec 1962, 2 s. *Education:* MSc, Silesian Tech Univ, Gliwices, 1959; PhD, Polish Acad of Sci, 1969; Dr Habilitated in Design Theory, Warsaw Tech Univ, 1978. *Appointments include:* Mgr in Industry, 1959-61; Research Fellow, Inst of Industry Organ, 1961-65; Polish Academy of Sci, Warsaw, 1965- *Publications:* Logic, Practice, Ethics; Philosophy of Practicality; Praxiology and the Philosophy of Economics; Polish Contributions to Design Sci; Praxilological Studies; Understanding Design; The Elements of Scientific Knowledge and Design. *Memberships:* Learned Soc of Praxilogy; Design Research Soc; Polish Cybernetic Soc; Int Federation of Systems Research; Soc for Philosophy & Tech; Int System Sci Inst. *Honours:* Fulbright Fellowship USA; Hon Mbrship Austrian Soc of Cybern St; Hon Mbrship UK Systens Soc; Polonia Restituta Knight Cross in Hon of 25th Aniv of Polish Cybernetical Soc. *Hobbies:* Tourism; Hiking. *Address:* Tolwinskiego Str no.10-15, 01 711 Warsaw, Poland. 139, 156.

GASSOWSKI Szczepan, b. 25 Dec 1927, Rzadkowo, Poland. Editor. m. Teresa Krzysztofowicz, 1 Feb 1969. *Education:* Polish Philology, Univ Jagiellonski, Krakow, 1949-52. *Appointments:* Chief Lit, Theatre, 1953- 78; Theatrical Critic, 1958-68; Translator of plays; Ed, PWN Warsaw, 1971-91; Chief Ed, Polish Philol. *Publications:* Translations of plays; book of Polish contemporary drama, 1979; Ed of the writings of Stefan Srebrny, 1984. *Memberships:* Soc of Polish Artists in the Theatre, Drama Section; Soc of Authors. *Hobbies:* Collecting theatrical books, programmes, graphics, stamps, photos; Gardening. *Address:* Opinogorska 1m 35, 04-039 Warsaw, Poland.

GATHERCOLE Patricia May, b. 5 Oct 1920, Pennsylvania, USA. Prof of Foreign Languages. *Education:* BA, Univ of British Columbia; MA, 1942; PhD, Univ of California, 1950. *Appointments:* TA, Univ of California, 1945-50; Lectr, Instr, Univ of British Columbia, 1950-53; Instr, Univ of Oregon, 1953-56; Asst Prof, Assoc Prof, Prof, Roanoke Coll, 1956-; Prof Emeritus, 1992. *Publications:* Des Cas de Nobles; Selected Poems of U Liberatore; Tension in Boccaccio; Many Articles & Reviews. *Memberships:* Mid Atlantic Representative of AATF; Medieval Soc of SAMLA; FLAVA; Humanities Assn. *Honours:* E V Paget Scholar in French; Fulbright to Italy; 2 Southern Univ Fellowships; 3 Southern Inst Fellowships; 2 Andrew

Mellon Fellowships. *Hobbies:* Stamp Collecting; Showing Persian Cats; Gardening; Piano. *Address:* 423 Highfield Road, Salem, VA 24153, USA. 7, 125, 138.

GATOS Nicolaos, b. July 1921, Amfissa, Greece. Exporter; President of Panhellenic Exporters Assn. m. Mary Bitha, 27 Dec 1948. *Education:* High Economical Sch, Athens, 1940. *Appointments:* Mgr, Exporting Firm, 1946-; Pres, Panhellenic Exporters Assn, 1980-; Writer; Painter. *Creative Works:* Publ. Many Articlesin Mag & Newspapers; May Paintings; Drawings; Pastels; Aquarelles. *Memberships:* Panellenic Exporters Assn; Hellenic Shippers Council. *Honours:* Prize of Greek Army for Exquisist Acts; Prize of Intl Olive Oil Council. *Hobbies:* Painting; Drawing; Stamp Collecting; Historical Books; Artistic Books; Travel. *Address:* 12 Aghiou Constantinou Str, 104 31 Athens, Greece.

GAUDIN Nicolas Vincent, b. 19 Mar 1959, Saumur, France. Translator; Reviser. m. Anne Lucie Cousin, 25 June 1983, 1 s, 1 d. *Education:* Licence, Lyon, France, 1980; Master of Arts, Romance, Languages, Univ of Pennsylvania, 1983; PhD, Univ of Pennsylania, 1986. *Appointments:* Tchr of French, American Sch, Paris, 1986-89; Prof of Translation, Intl Univ Paris, 1986-89; Mgr, Managing Dir, Emera Press Agency for Health Ind, Paris, 1988-89; Translator, Revisor, World Health Organ, Manila, 1989-. *Publications:* L'Envers et L'Endroit Dans Voyage Au Bout De La Nuit; L'Incertitude Medicale; Histoire De La Litterature Japonaise; Various Articles in French Review, L'Esprit Createur, Tussot Ed'Teur. *Memberships:* Modern Language Assn of America; American Assn of Tchrs of French; Soc Des Etudes Celiniennes. *Hobbies:* Reading; Gardening; Hiking; Health Economics. *Address:* Chief Translation, World Health Organisation, PO Box 2932, 1099 Manila Philippines. 52.

GAULDING Melvin Walker Jr, b. 6 Dec 1959, Richmond, Virginia. Christian Minister. m. Mary Bob Snavely, 26 May 1984, 1 d. *Education:* Cincinnati Bible Coll & Seminary, BA, Christian Ministry, 1987. *Appointments:* Fairview Christian Church, Johnsville, KY, 1984-87; Rappahannock Church of Christ, Warsaw, 1987-. *Memberships:* Delta Aleph Tau Honor Soc of Cincinnati Bible Coll; Nat Rifle Assn; Virginia Arms Collectors; Rappahannock Church of Christ. *Honours:* Preaching Festival Winner; Special Award in Homoletics; Named, Delta Aleph Tau Honor Soc; Class Orated Cincinnati Bible Coll; Outstanding Young Minister. *Hobbies:* Hunting; Canoeing; Camping; Woodworking. *Address:* Rt 1 Box 446, Warsaw, VA 22572, USA. 176.

GAVRILESCU Serban, b. 14 Mar 1943, Bucharest. m. Dana Gavrilescu, 14 June 1975, 1 d. *Education:* Medical Studies, Univ of Medicine, Bucharest, 1968; Medicine Doctor, MD, 1984; Primary Surgeon, 1989. *Appointments:* UN Asst Dept of Anatomy, 1968-75; UN Ass & Lectr Dept of Surgery, Clinical Hosp, Univ of Medicine, 1975-91. *Publications:* Internal Medicine, Gastroenterology; Surgery; Surgery of Extrahepatc Biliary Ducts; Invention. Method of Treatment for Supurative Diabetic Foot. *Membership:* Rumanian Soc of Surgeons. *Hobbies:* Mountain Climbing; History of Art. *Address:* 49 Jean Monnet Street, 71291 Bucharest, Romania.

GAVRILOV Anatoly Nikolayevich, b. 21 Jan 1946, Donetskaya Oblast Region, Russia. Postman. m. Jatyana Vaninen, 23 Feb 1972, 1 s, 1 d. *Education:* Army Ser, 1965-68; BLit, A M Gorky Lit Inst, Moscow, 1973- 79. *Appointments:* Modeller, Zhdanov Metallurgical Plant, 1964-65; Life saver, 1976-79; Shdanov Municipal Gas service, metal worker, 1968-69, 1971-86; Zhdanov railway station Coupler, 1979-84; Vladimir Chem Plant Worker, 1985-87; Vladimir Communication Dept, Postman, 1987-. *Publications:* At the preface of the new life, 1990; The Old Woman and the Idiot, 1992; articles published in magazines at home and abroad. *Honours:* Laureat of Annual Prize of Volga Mag, 1989. *Hobbies:*

Gardening; Fotball. *Address:* Bobkova str 7 flat 22, Vladimir 600015, Russia.

GAWKRODGER David John, b. 14 Nov 1953, Bristol. Physician. *Education:* King Edwards Sch, Bath, 1964-71; MB, ChB, Univ of Birmingham, 1976; MRCP, 1979; Dermatology, 1985; MD, Univ of Birmingham, 1988. *Appointments:* House Physician, Surgeon, Queen Elizabeth Hosp, Birmingham, 1976-77; SHO, Registrar, North Staffs Hosp, Stoke On Trent, 1977- 81; Registrar, Snr Reg, Lectr, Royal Infirmary, Univ of Edinburgh, 1981-88; Conslt Dermatologist, Royal Hallamshire Hosp, Sheffield, 1988-. *Publications:* Scientific Papers, Chapters for Books on Dermatology & General Medicine. *Memberships:* British Assn of Dermatologists; Royal Colleges f Physicians; North American Contact Dermatitis Soc. *Honours:* Sampson Gamgee Prize in Surgery; Bristol Myers Award; Faculty MD Prize. *Hobbies:* Art; Travel. *Address:* Dept of Dermatoloy, Royal Hallamshire Hosp, Glossop Road, Sheffield S10 2JF, England.

GAZDOV Ivan Edward, b. 2 Nov 1945, Bulgaria. Artist; Painter; Assoc Prof; Chief of the Graphical Dept, Academy of Fine Arts, Sofia. m. Vesselina Grantcharova Gazdov, 23 Apr 1986. *Education:* Art Coll, Sofia, 1964; Academy of Fine Arts, Sofia, 1970; Attendance at Course of Prof Metz, Holland, 1978. *Appointments include:* Over 150 Exhibitions, Bulgaria & Abroad in the Field of Graphics, Posters, Caricatures, Illustrations of Books. *Creative Works include:* Series of Posters: Play of Silhouettes and Hand; Cycles of Graphics: Black Touches and Something is Superflous; Own Authors Style, Graphicature-Style, established 1991. *Memberships:* Union of Bulgarian Artists, ICOGRADA. *Honours include:* 25 Prizes from Nat & Intl Contests, Exhibitions & Biennals. *Hobbies:* Drums; Chess; Table Tennis. *Address:* PO Box 442, 1000 Sofia, Bulgaria.

GAZE Nigel Raymond, b. 11 Feb 1943, Leamington Spa. Conslt Plastic Surgeon; Composer. m. Heather Winifred Richardson, 6 Aug 1966, 3 s. *Education:* Prescot Grammer Sch, Lancs; MB, ChB, Liverpool Univ, 1966; B Mus, London Univ, 1986; FRCS, FRCS Ed, FRCO, FTCL, FVCM, LRAM. *Appointments:* Surgical Registrar, Chester Royal Infirmary, 1972-73; Registrar, West Midland Plastic Surgery Centre, 1973-75; Snr Registrar, Yorks Region Health Auth, 1975-79; Conslt Plastic Surgeon, Royal Preston Hosp, & Victoria Hosp, Blackpool, 1980-. *Publications:* Various Papers on Medical Subjects; Record. And My Heart Shall Be There; Several Publ Works for Organ and Choirs. *Memberships:* BMA, British Assn of Plastic Surgeons; British Assn of Aesthetic Plastic Surgeons; British Inst of Organ Studies; Victoria Soc; Nat Trust CPRE; Preston Select Vestry Club. *Honours:* William Eastwood Prize; Convocation Prize. *Hobbies:* Conductor; Elizabethan Singers; Organist; Collecting Books; Interesting Junk; Architecture; DIY. *Address:* Priory House, 35 Priory Lane, Penwortham, Preston, Lancs PR1 0AR, England. 52.

GBEWONYO Sylvestre Kwadzo, b. 16 Mar 1942, Sekondi, Ghana. Finance & Admin Dir. m. Gifty Esi Ribeiro, 28 June 1969, 4 s. *Education:* Univ of Ghana, 1963-67; MSc, Univ of Southampton, England, 1984-85. *Appointments:* Hosp Admin, 1967-75; Accountant, 1975-78; Chief Acct, Admin Mgr, 1979-81; Finance Mgr, 1981-87; Reg Finance Mgr, 1987-89. *Memberships:* Inst of Chartered Secs & Admin; British Inst of Management; Strategic Planning Soc; Intl Biographical Asson. *Honour:* Norman Griffiths Prize Award. *Hobbies:* Golf; Tennis; Swimming; Rotary Club; Royal Nairibi Golf Club; Parklands Sports Club. *Address:* World Vision Intl, P O Box 50816, Nairobi, Kenya. 52, 132, 139.

GE Changcai, b. 15 Dec 1933, Shangdong. Dir of Plant, Automobile & Tractor. m. 1 May 1959, 1 s, 3 d. *Education:* Autombile & Tractor Coll, Liaoning Province, 1949. *Appointments:* Shop Dir, Changchun Machine tool Repair Plant, 1950-69; Dir, Changchun Engine Manufacturing Plant, 1969-85; Dir Changchun Airlight Component Factory, 1986-. *Publications:* Quality Control of Enterprise; First Automobile Group. *Memberships:* Jeifang Automobile United Coop; China Inter Combustion Engine Learned Assn. *Honours:* Advanced Dir Changchun Automobile Ind Bureau; Advanced Dir, Jinlin Province. *Hobbies:* Football; Basket Ball; Table Tennis Ball. *Address:* CAACF, 67-19 Tiebei 4th Street, Changchun, Tilin, China 130052.

GE Ge, b. 22 Jan 1922, Hobei, China. Prof in History of Physics. m. Li Shu Ching, 14 May 1939, 1 s, 1 d. *Education:* Peking Univ, Physics Dept, 1949; Qinghua Univ, Chrystallography, 1949-52. *Appointments:* Asst Prof, Full Prof, Inst of Petroleum. *Publications:* Niels Bohr; Macro Electrodynamics; Many Papers on Niels Bohr. *Hobbies:* History & Philosophy; Quantum Physics; Study Chinese Literature & Art; Archaeology. *Address:* Petroleum Univ Beijing, PO Box 902, Beijing, China.

GE Xian Kang, b. 25 Nov 1932, Shanghai. Prof & Deputy Chmn Automotive Engring Dept, Shanghai Univ of Engring Sci. m. Cai Li Yie, 25 May 1953, 1 s, 1 d. *Education:* East China Jiao Tong Coll, Shanghai, 1952. *Appointments:* Nanking Mech Coll, Chmn of Automotive Tchring Group, 1952-65; Hunan Univ, Chmn of Internal Combustion Engine & Automotive Tchring Group, 1965-85; Shanghai Univ of Engring Sci, Deputy Chmn of Auto Engr Dept, 1985-. *Publications:* Numerical Simulation of Combustion Process in SI Engines; A Study on the Accurate Calculation Method of Heat Release Rate in Swirl Chamber Indirect Injection Diesel Engine. *Memberships:* Tchring Guiding Comm for Chinese Technical Univ I C Engine Speciality; Chinese Soc for I C Engine Member of Combustion Dept; Standing Dir, Shanghai Soc for I C Engines. *Honours:* Sci Award of Hunan Province; Model Tchr of Hunan Province; Sci Award of Ministry of Mechanical In; Model Worker of Hunan Province. *Hobbies:* Literature; Art; Music; Sports. *Address:* Automotive Engring Dept, Shanghai Univ of Engring Sci, 350 Xian Xia Road, Shanghai 200335, China. 139.

GEERTS Victor Marcel Maria, b. 25 Mar 1917, Edegem, Antwerp. Prof Ordinarius Emeritus. m. dec 1977, 1 s, 3 d. *Education:* Univ of Louvain. Bach of Philosophy, 1942; Licentiate Educ, 1943; Licentiate Criminology, 1945; Doc Pedagogical, 1949. *Appointments:* Prof, Psychology & Educ, Dutch Section Univ, Louvain, 1943-75; Univ for Women Antwerp, 1945-48; French Section Univ, Louvain, 1950-66; High Inst, Admin & Comml Section, Brussels, 1966-75. *Publications:* De Humanistische Pedagogiek in Italie; Katholieke Encyclopaedie Voor Opvoeding En Onderwys; Articles to Prof Journals. *Membership:* Vereniging Van Vlaamse Professoren Leuven. *Honours:* Officer of Order of Leopold Belgium; Civilian Medal First Class; Commander of Order of the Crown. *Hobbies:* Reading; Drawing; Painting; Photography. *Address:* Artanstraat 87, B-1030 Brussels, Belgium. 52.

GEHANI Loku Takhitram, b. 20 May 1936, Kandiaro, Sind. Mgr; Writer. m. Kavita, 24 May 1963, 2 s, 1 d. *Education:* Kovid, Hindi,1953; High Sch Sci, Second in the Bd, 1955; Inter Sci, Second In The State, Bach of Arts, 1957. *Appointments:* Branch Mgr, Sarabhais, 1961- 68; Div Sales mgr, DCM, 1968-70; Sales Mgr, Bhor, 1970-74; Mkting Mgr, Calico,1974-88; Mkting Mgr, JCT Fibres, 1988-90. *Publications:* Poems; Articles. *Memberships:* Authors Guild of India; Indian Soc of Authors; Indian Heritage Soc; Inst of Mkting & Mngmt; Textile Assn; Plastics Inst; World Wild Life Fund. *Honours:* Second Position, High Sch; Second Position, Inter Sci. *Hobbies:* Photography; Writing; Poems. *Address:* 203A Pocket C, Siddhartha Extension, New Delhi 110014, India.

GEIGER Georg, b. 29 Sept 1933. Baroque Recorder Maker. m. (1) 2 s, 1 d, (2) Arceli Macaraeg, 17 Feb 1990, 1 s. *Education:* Doc Juris, Univ California, 1958.

Creative Works: Numerous Baroque Recorder Designs; Publ. A Strategy for Swedish Military Survival in the 21st Century; The Trench; Sinai Diary; Numerous Articles. *Hobbies:* Music; Reading; Gardening. *Address:* 1 Sunrise Court, River Park, Bundaberg, Qld. 4670, Australia.

GELLMAN Gloria Gae Seeburger Schick, b. 5 Oct 1947, La Grange, Illinois, USA. Actress; Mkting Professional; Real Est Exec. m. Irwin Frederick Gellman, 9 Sept 1989, 2 Stepsons, 1 Stepdaughter. *Education:* BA, Magna Cum Laude, Purde Univ, 1969; UCLA, UCI, 1989; Acting Training, Lee Strasbergs Inst, 1972. *Appointments:* Radio & TV Talk Shoe, 1964-66; Radio & TV Commercials, 1976; Seemac Inc, Carmel Indiana, 1968-69; Vice Pres, VIP Properties Inc, 1989-. *Memberships include:* Mensa; Pi Beta Phi; Univ of California, Irvine; Humanities Assn; Chancellors Club; American Assn of Univ Women; Actors Equity; Screen Actors Guild; American Federation of TV & Radio Artists; Opera Pacific; Orange Country Philharmonic Soc; Orange Country Dance Alliance; Satelites of the Starlight Foundation. *Honours:* Awarded Key to the City of Indianapolis; Indianapolis Jnr Miss Contest; Indianapolis 500 Queens Court; Nominated to california Council for the Humanities. *Hobbies:* Oil Painting; Needlework; Opera; Creative Writing; Gardening. *Address:* PO Box 1993, Newport Beach, CA 92659, USA. 5, 9, 52, 76.

GENAIN Marc Pierre, Louis Marie, b. 28 Sept 1950, Paris. Engring Mgr. m. Chaignon Catherine, 22 Oct 1977, 2 s, 1 d. *Education:* Sup Acro, France, 1973; MIT, Master of Sci, USA, 1975; New Jersey, Professional Engr, 1989; CPA, Paris, 1989. *Appointments:* South American Projects, Sofretu, 1976-78;. 1978-81; Southeast Asian Projects, Sofretu, 1981-84; LSTS Start Up, North American Activities, 1984-88; European Activities, 1989-91. *Publications:* La Creation de LSTS. *Memberships:* Sigma Xi. *Hobbies:* Golf; Hunting; Jogging; Skiing; Tnnis; Music. *Address:* 35 Rue Du Marechal Joffre, 78100 Saint German En Laye, France. 1

GENETET Berdard, b. 17 Dec 1931, Chaumont. m. (1) Francoise Bellevile, 25 Apr 1957, (2) Noelle Pierron, 29 Apr 1972, 1 s, 2 d. *Education:* Baccalaureat Philosophy, 1955; doc in Medicine, 1964; Bichemical, 1967; Hematologia Superio, 1968; Doc es Sci, 1973; Hematology Immunology Bacteriology Aereronautical Medicine, 1970. *Appointments:* PIT, 1951-53; Tech Officer, 1961-64; Asst CRTS Nancy, 1964-68; Chef of Lab, CRIS Nancy, 1968-73; Ched of Lab, Faculty of Medicine Nancy, 197-73; dir of Regional Centre of Transfusion Rennes, 1973-. *Publications:* La Transfusion; Aide Memoire de la Transfusion; Glossaire de la Transfusion; Immunology; Hematology; Glossario Transfusion; Transfusion n Europe. *Memberships include:* French Soc of Transfusion; French Assoc of Transplantation of Bone Marrow; Assn for Intl Cooperation in Blood Transfusion; NYAS. Intl Soc of Transplantation. *Honours:* Legion d'Honner; Order Nat du Merite; Tunisian Medal of Health; Silver Medal of French Red Cross; Silver Medal of Medical Officer; Colonel of Army Medical Serv. *Hobbies:* Music; Libary. *Address:* 28 Rue Baudelaire, 35700 Rennes, France.

GENKOV Georgi, b. 3 Mar 1929, Sofia. Composer; Conductor. m. Bistaa Atanasova, 8 May 1991, 1 s. *Education:* Academi of Music, Sofia, 1946-51. *Appointments:* Theate of Youth, Sofia, 1951-61; Central Puppet Theatre, Composer, 1962-81; Theatre, Tear & Laughter, 1981-91; Freelance, 1991-. *Creative Works:* 1 Opera; 5 Musicals; Theatre Music; Plays; Film Music; Cartoon Films; Songs. *Memberships:* Bulgarian Composers Union; Bulgarian Film Union; Bulgarian Theatre Union; GEMA. *Honours:* Best Bulgarian Film Music; Best Cartoon Film Music; Best Puppet Play Music; Best Music for Children Musical. *Hobby:* Tennis. *Address:* Dobri Woinikov Str N15, 1164 Sofia, Bulgaria.

GENT John David Wright, b. 25 Apr 1935, Wellingborough, England. Dir Gen. m. Anne Elaine Hanson, 19 Aug 1970. *Education:* Lancing Coll, 1949-54; Solicitor, 1959. *Appointments:* Soc of Royal Manufacturers & Traders, 1961-80; Legal Adrian, 1961-63; Asst Sec, 1964; Sec, 1965-70; Dep Dueets, 1971-80; Lucas Serv, 1981-82; Lucas Ind, 1983; British Road Federation, 1983-85; motor Agents Assn, 1985-. Chmn, Mots Ind Pensions Ltd, EPA Holdings Ltd, 1985. *Memberships include:* Inst of Highways; Freeman, City of London. *Hobbies:* Farming; Gardening. *Address:* 44 Ursula St, London, SW11 3DW. England. 1.

GEORGE Robert Earl, Vice Admiral, b. 6 Oct 1940, Prince Albert, Sask, Canada. Naval Ofcr. m. Lois Elwood, 6 Feb 1965, 3 s. *Education:* BSc 1962, Univ BC. *Appointments:* Joined RCN 1961; Full time Naval Svc 1962-; Commanding Ofcr HMC Ships, Margaree 1974-75, Iroquois 1977-79; Defence Attache Tokyo 1980-82; Commander Maritime Forces Pacific, Victoria 1987-89; Commander Maritime Command Halifax 1989-91; Dep Chf of Defence Staff 1991-92; Canadian Military Representative to the Miltary Cttee in Permanent Session, Brussels, 1992-. *Memberships:* Former Hon mem, Boy Scouts of Canada; Rotary Intl. *Honours:* Decorations: Commander, Milit Merit, CMM; Candn Forces Decoration, CD; Awds: Chf of Defence Staff Commend; Queen's Jubilee Medal. *Hobbies:* Skiing; Golf; Fishing; Sailing; Squash. *Address:* NATO HQ, Boulevard Léopold III, 1110 Brussels, Belgium. 88.

GEORGE Roy Edwin, b. 17 Feb 1923, Liverpool, England. Professor Emeritus; Business Consultant. m. Lydia Jean Morgan, 10 Sept 1949, 2 d. *Education:* BSc Econ, 1949, PhD, 1967, Univ of London; MA, Univ of Bristol, 1957. *Appointments:* Asst Personnel Mgr, S W Gas Bd, 1949-56; Area Staff Mgr, Nat Coal Bd, 1956-60; Asst Prof, St Mary's Univ, Can, 1960-63; Prof, Dalhousie Univ, Can, 1963-. *Publications:* Technological Redundancy, 1969; A leader and a laggard, 1970; The life and times of industrial estates, 1974; Targetting high growth industries, 1983; Understanding the Canadian economy, 1988. *Memberships:* VP, BGI Mgmt Conslts, 1964-; Dir, Mar Prov Chamber of Commerce, 1973-74. *Address:* School of Business Administration, Dalhousie University, Halifax, Nova Scotia, Canada B3H 1Z5.

GEORGE Sue Ann, b. 17 Sept 1948, Altoona. Echocardiol. *Education:* AS BS Agronomy, Penn State Univ 1968-70; MEd Biol Sc, Agronomy & Ed, Penn State 1972; PhD Biol Sc 1980, Columbia Pacific Univ; DS Echocardiol 1981, Columbia Pacific; Postgrad, Nat Inst Sonophyl, Bowman Guy Med Sch; Num Perceptorships in Ultrasound. *Appointments:* Internship, Echocardiography, West Penn Hosp 1979-80; Echo Technologist, Bronson Methodist Hosp, Kalamazoo 1981-82; Echo Tech, 1983-85; Tech Dir, Cawlim Cardiol, Asheville 1985-86; Chf Echo Technologist, Conslt, Savennal 1986-88; Chf of Echo & Clin Specialist, Self Memorial Hosp, Greenwood, SC 1988-. *Publications:* 2-D Clinical Echo, 1991. *Contributions to:* Num & 24 arts; Research, Lectures, Problems of Echo, Speaker at confs. *Memberships:* Am Registry of Diagnostic Med Sonographs; RDMS; RDCS; Soc Diagnostic Med Sonographers; Am Inst Ultrasound Med; Am Soc of Tech Specilaists; Am Women in Sci; Penn State Alumni; Columbia Pacific Alumni; IPTAP; Am Soc Echo Cardiography; Lupus Fed of Am. *Honours:* Recip ACP Awd; Berkeley-Whittings Awd for Res & Acad Excellence; SDMS 10 year Awd; Phi Epsilon Phi for Botany; Grad Awds; Pentathlon & Track Awds, Lupus Foun of Am. *Hobbies:* Music-playing horn, organ & drums, performing, singing; Physical fitness & activities-walking, hiking, aerobics, biking weights; Choir & quartet; Percussionist. *Address:* Self Memorial Hospital, Echo Lab- Special Services, 1325 Spring Street, Greenwood, SC 29646, USA. 7.

GERGELY Agnes, b. 5 Oct 1933, Endrod, Hungary. Writer. div. *Education:* MA 1957, PhD 1979, Budapest Univ of Liberal Arts. *Appointments:* Tchr, 1957-63; Radio Producer, 1963-71; Writer for, Life and Letters, 1971-74; Ed in a publishing house, 1974-77; Hd of Column, Great World, 1977-88; Freelance writer, 1988-. *Publications:* 8 volumes of poems; 4 novels; 2 volumes of essays, one of them on W B Yeats, 1991; Several reports, articles and translations. *Memberships:* Hungarian Writers Union; Hungarian Creative Artists Fund; PEN Club. *Honours:* Atilla Joszef Prize for Poetry, 1977, 1987; Tibor Dery Awd, 1985; Hon Fellow, Intl Writing prog, Univ of Iowa, USA, 1973-74. *Hobbies:* Listening to classical music; Translating limericks; Walking. *Address:* Pannonia utca 64B, 1133 Budapest, Hungary.

GERGOVA Ani, b. 10 Sept 1937, Russe, Bulgaria. Professor. m. George Gergov, 8 July 1962, 2 d. *Education:* Dipl, Bulgarian Philol, 1962, Dipl Lib Sci, 1961, PhD Hist, 1972, DSc, Philol, 1989, Sofia State Univ. *Appointments:* Tchr, Russe, 1961-64; Lib, Sofia Chamber of Commerce, 1964-67; Res Scist, 1972-81; Sr Res Scist and Sci Sec, 1981-90; Sr REs Scist, Dpty Dir, 1990-91; Prof of Book Sci, Chief of Chair on Lib and Info Scis, 1991-. Inst of Culture, Sofia. *Publications include:* About 120 papers and research projects in bulgaria and abroad and contributions to books: L Litterature et les Bulgares, 1991; The reading and readers casebook, 1990; Book Science in Bulgaria, 1987; Bases of Book editing, 1987; Bibliophily of Bulgarian Renaissance Men, 1985; Bookish and the Bulgarians during the Renaissance, 1984. *Memberships:* Assn of Intl Bibliologists, Paris; Union of Bibliophiles, Russia; Union of Librarians of Bulgaria; Chm of Nat Coun on Libraries at the Min of Culture, Bulgaria. *Honours:* St Ciril and Metodji Medal, 1984. *Hobbies:* Gardening; Tourism. *Address:* Chechov Str 19-B, 1113 Sofia, Bulgaria.

GERLACH Sebastian A, b. 17 Jan 1929, Berlin. Rtd Prof Marine Biol. m. Christine Hempel, 29 Mar 1960, 1 s. 2 d. *Education:* Kiel Univ 1948-51. *Appointments:* Res Fellow in Pisa, Sao Paulo, Kiel 1952-55; Lectr, Kiel, Hamburg 1956-64; Dir, Marine Res Inst, Bremerhaven, 1964-81; Prof Marine Biol, Copenhgen 1975-76; Dir, Marine Botany Dept, Inst Marine Sci, Kiel 1981-91. *Publication:* Marine Pollution, 1981. *Address:* Stubenrauchstrasse 14, D 2312 Moenkeberg, Germany.

GERMAINE Max, b. 18 July 1914, Melbourne, Australia. Arts Writer & Dir. m. Noel Huenerbein, 15 June 1940, 1 s. 3 d. *Education:* Melbourne Tech Col; Destroyer Ofcr, Royal Navy 1940-44; Royal Australian Navy 1944-46; Licensed Valuer & Auctioneer. *Appointments:* Dir, Max Germaine Pty Ltd, Hobart 1947-64; F R Strange Group, Sydney 1964-77; Arts Writer & Dir, Sothebys Australia Pty Ltd 1982-91. *Publications:* Artists & Galleries of Australia & New Zealand, 1979; Artists & Galleries of Australia, 1984, 1990; A Dictionary of Australian Women Artists, Craftsman House, Sydney, 1991. *Memberships:* Fellow, Australian Inst of Mgmt; Australian Soc Authors; The Australian Club, Sydney, NSW. *Hobbies:* Public speaking; Lawn bowls; Tennis. *Address:* 16 The Grange, McAuley Place, Waitara, NSW 2077, Australia.

GERMAN Franciszek Karol, b. 10 Apr 1911, Zloczow. Scist; Univ Lectr. m. Teresa Iwanicka, 31 Oct 1943, 2 s. 3 d. *Education:* Master's in Humane Scis 1961, Doctor's degree 1963; Jan Kazimierz Univ in Lvov; Jagiellonian Univ, Cracow; Lodz Univ. *Appointments:* Lectr in: Theol the Resurrectionists Seminary in Cracow 1946-79; States Col of Mus in Katowice 1968-75, and Wroclaw 1980-. *Publications include:* Chopin & Warsaw's Men of Letters, 1960; Jan III Sobieski during his way to Wienna, 1983; About 100 biographies to Polish biographical dictionaries, about 400 sci arts. *Memberships:* Polish Acad Scis 1990-; Fr Chopin Soc, Vice-Chmn of Department in Katowice, 1953-91; Soc Friends of Books, Fdr Silesian Dept, 1968-; Zofia Kossak Soc, 1980-91, Cieszyn; Soc of Lovers of Wisla, 1984-. *Honours:* Knight's Cross of Order of Polish Regeneration, 1976; Meritorious Culture Worker, 1975;

Medal of Fr Chopin Soc in Warsaw, 1975; J Ligon Prize, 1983 in Katowice Silesia; Priest A Skowronski Prize, 1987 in Opole Silesia. *Hobbies:* Books; Bibliophiling; Exlibrises; Stamp collecting; Classical music. *Address:* ul Chorzowska 37 m 5, 44-100 Gliwice, Poland.

GERNAND Dorota Zofia, b. 11 Aug 1964, Brezeziny, Poland. Student. *Education:* MSc Biol, Genetics, Univ of Lodz, 1988. *Appointments:* Postgrad student, Dept of Plant and Cytol and Cytochem, Univ of Lodz, Poland, 1988-; Aerobic Tchr. *Publications:* Three scientific articles on cytogenetics. *Hobbies:* Swimming; Photography. *Address:* Bratyslawska 6 m 30, 94-035 Lodz, Poland.

GERSON Mark, b. 3 Oct 1921, London, England, Photographer. m. Renee Cohen, 18 Sept 1949, 2 d. *Education:* Regent Poly 1939-40; Commercial Photography, 1st class pass. *Appointments:* Proprietor, Photographic Studio 1947-87; Freelance Photographer 1987-. *Membership:* Fellow, Brit Inst Profl Photography. *Hobbies:* Theatre; Books. *Address:* 3 Regal Lane, Regent's Park Road, London NW1 7TH, England. 34.

GERST Steven Richard, b. 20 Oct 1958, NYC, USA. Phsician; Dir in Insurance Ind. m. Isabelle Sylvie Meier, 29 July 1987, 1 d. *Education:* Grad 1977, Phillips Acad, Andover, Mass; BA 1981, Columbia Col; MPH 1987, Columbia Univ Sch of Pub Health; MD 1986, Col Physicians & Surgs of Columbia Univ. *Appointments:* Med Affairs Coord, Sunlkath Inc 1987-90; Med Dir, Dir, Preferred Provider Arrangements, Crawford & Co 1990- . *Publications:* Edit, Columbia's Literary Mag 1977-80; Edit, Columbian 1977-81; Handbook, College of Physicians & Surgeons of Columbia University, Ed, 1982-83. *Memberships:* AMA; Am Col Med Dirs; Am Col Physician Execs; Am Col Healthcare Execs. *Honours:* Robert Stellow Gerdy Prize, Columbia Univ, 1981; Alumni Awd, Col Physicians & Surgs, 1983. *Hobbies:* Golf; Tennis; Bicycling; AIT. *Address:* 965 Peachtree Dunwoody Ct, Atlanta, GA 30328, USA. 7.

GETTER Marek Kazimierz, b. 10 Jan 1930, Warsaw, Poland. Historian; Bibliographer. m. Anna Czudowska, 9 May 1961, 1 s. *Education:* Dipl from gymnasium 1948; Dept Polish Philology, Univ Warsaw 1948-52. *Appointments:* Library, Warsaw Univ 1950-52; Nat Lib, Warsaw 1953-57; Inst History, Polish Acad Scis, Warsaw 1957-. *Publications:* Over 50 pubs; Co-Ed of books of sources; Civilian Defense of Warsaw in September 1939, 1964; Occupation & Resistance Reflected in Hans Frank Diary 1939-45, 1970, 2nd ed 1972; The Civilian Population in the Warsaw Uprising of 1944, 4 vols, 1974; Reports of Ludwig Fischer, the governor of the District of Warsaw 1939-44, 1987; Co-Author voluminous Bibliography of the 19th c Polish History; Contbr voluminous Polish Biographical Dictionary. *Memberships:* Polish Historical Soc; Main Comm for Investigation of Nazi Atrocities. *Honours:* 3 awds of Secy of the Polish Acad of Scis for 3 pubs; 2 awds of the weekly Polityka; Awd of Minister for Justice. *Hobbies:* Comparative history of churches; Military history; History of the railroad system. *Address:* ul Baleya 7/38, 02-132 Warsaw, Poland.

GEYKO Valentin S, b. 3 Mar 1939, Nikopol, Ukraine. Senior Researcher. m. 7 May 1971, 1 s. *Education:* PhD, Geol, Dsc, Phys and maths, Inst of Mining Engrg, Dnepropetrovsk. *Appointments:* Geophys exped, Sr Engr, 1962-66; Post-grad student, 1967-69, Sr Reschr, 1969-92, Inst of Geophys Acad of Sci of Ukraine, Kiev. *Publications:* Inversion of seismic travel-time curves, 1974; Inversion of travel-time curve of a reflected wave, 1981; 80 papers and articles published in professional magazines. *Memberships:* Sci Coun of Inst of Geoph Acad of Sci, Ukraine; Edit Coun, Geophys Jour. *Hobbies:* Reading; Gardening. *Address:* Institute of Geophysics, Ukranian Academy of Sciences, Pr Palladina 32 2526890, Kiev, 142 Ukraine.

GHALI Boutros Boutros, b. 14 Nov 1922, Cairo, Egypt. Dep Prime Min for Foreign Affairs of Arab Repub of Egypt. *Education:* LLB 1946, Cairo Univ; Dipl of Higher Studies in Pub Law 1947, Dipl Higher Studies in Ec 1948, Dipl Polit Sci Inst 1949, PhD in Intl Law 1949, Paris Univ. *Appointments include:* Prof Intl Law & Intl Relats, Hd Dept Polit Sci, Cairo Univ, 1949-77; VP, Egyptian Soc Intl Law 1965-; Minister of State for Foreign Affairs 1977-91; Pres, African Soc Polit Scis 1980-; MP 1987-; Pres, Egyptian-Soviet Friendship Assn 1989-; VP, Socialist Intl 1990-; Dep PM for For Affairs 1991-Participation in innumerable confs & academic symposia; Lectr on Intl Law & Intl Relats at var univs. *Publications:* 13 books in English & French incl: Foreign Policies in a World of Change, co-Author, 1983; Will We Survive?, co-Author, 1989; 18 books in Arabic; 66 arts & studies in Arabic; 48 in English & French. *Memberships:* Extensive membership incl: VP, Senghor Univ, Alexandria 1990-; Mem Curatorium of Inst of Pub Intl Law & Intl Relats of Thessaloniki, Greece 1976-; Com on Application of Conventions and Recommendations of the Intl Labour Org 1971-79; Assoc mem, Academie des Scis morales rt Politiques, Acad Francaise, Paris 1989-; Former mem Intl Legal Ctr, NY; Mem Comm of Intl Law of UN 1979-; Mem Inst of Intl Law 1975-, Pres of the Inst 1985-87; Fdr & Edit Al-Ahram Iktisadi 1960-75; Mem Edit Bd Egyptian Review of Intl Law and Yearbook of Assn of Attenders and Alumni of the Hague Acad of Intl Law & Chf Edit of Al-Siyassa Dawlya, intl affairs quarterly. *Honours:* 2 hon Doctorates; 26 Decorations incl: Order of the Republic, First Class, Egypt; Grand Croix de l'Ordre de la Couronne, Belgium; Gran Cruz de la Orden de: Boyaca, Columbia, Antonio Jose de Irisarri, Guatemala, Quetzal, Guatemala; Grand Cross of the Order of Merit of Germany; Commander Grand Cross of the Order of the Polar Star, Sweden. *Address:* 2 Nile Street, Cairo, Egypt.

GHODSE Abdul-Hamid, b. 30 Apr 1938, Iran. Prof. m. Barbara Bailin, 30 June 1973, 2 s. 1 d. *Education:* MD 1965, Iran; PhD 1976, Univ London; DPM 1975, Royal Col of Physicians and Royal Col Surgs. *Appointments:* Lt Iranian Health Corps 1965; Conslt, St George's and St Thomas Hosp 1978-87; Prof Psychi of Addictive Behaviour, St George's Hosp Med Sch 1987-. *Publications:* Over 100 pubs; Misuse of Drugs, co-Author, 1986, 2nd ed, 1991; Psychoactive Drugs: Improving Prescribing Practices, 1988; Drugs & Addictive Behaviour: A Guide to Treatment, 1989; Drug Misuse & Dependence, co-Author, 1990. *Memberships:* UN Intl Narcotics Control Bd, Expert Advisory Panel WHO; FRCP, 1992; (MRCP 1988); FRCPsych 1985 (MRCPsych 1980); Dir, SW Thames Regl Drug Problem Team; Hon Secy Soc for Study of Addiction; Pres, Assn for Prevention of Addiction; Pres Wandsworth Alcohol Gp; Chmn Substance Misuse Section and mem Coun of Royal Col Psychis; Hon Secy Assn of Profs of Psychi. *Hobbies:* Cycling; Reading. *Address:* Division of Addictive Behaviour, St George's Hospital Medical School, Cranmer Terrace, London SW17 0RE, England.

GHOSH Malay K, b. 31 Dec 1953, Calcutta, India. Sr Scist. m. Runa, 18 Jan 1990. *Education:* BSc Chem Hons 1973, Burdwan Univ; MSc 1975, North Bengal Univ; PhD 1983, Indian Inst Tech, Kharagpur, India. *Appointments:* Post Doc, Indian Inst Tech 1983-84; Res Assoc, Stevens Inst Tech, NJ, USA 1984-90; Sr Scist, Schering-Plough Res, Fl 1990-91; Sr Scist, Schering-Plough, NJ 1991-. *Publications:* Author 25 sci pubs in peer reviewed intl & nat Res jours; Author 4 Chapts of Books; Book Reviewer of J, Polymer News; Mem Bd of referee, Journal of Polymer Material. *Memberships:* Am Chem Soc; Sigma Xi; Indian Sci Cong. *Honours:* Nat Sci Scholarship, Govt India 1970-74; Outstg Student Fellowship, North Bengal Univ, 1975; Outstg Student Awd, North Bengal Univ, 1975; Recip Gold Medal, North Bengal Univ, 1975. *Hobbies:* Classical music; Photography. *Address:* Schering-Plough Corporation, 2000 Galloping Hill Road, Kenilworth, NJ 07033, USA.

GIACALONE Robert Augustine, b. 25 Aug 1957, NYC, USA. Assoc Prof of Mgmt. m. Karen Leslie Kraft, 3 Aug 1985, 1 s. 1 d. *Education:* BA 1979, Hofstra Univ; PhD 1984, State Univ NY at Albany. *Appointments:* Asst Prof Mgmt, Bryant Col 1983-85; Asst Prof Mgmt, Univ SW La 1985-88; Asst then Assoc Prof Mgmt, Univ Richmond 1988-. *Publications:* Impression Management in the Organisation; Applied Impression Management; Both co-Edited with P Rosenfeld, 1989 & 1991 resp. *Memberships:* Acad Mgmt; Decision Sci Inst. *Honour:* Outstg Young Men in Am, 1985. *Hobbies:* Reading; Creative writing; Music. *Address:* Robins School of Business, University of Richmond, Richmond, VA 23173, USA. 7.

GIANNITSIS Anastasios, b. 4 May 1944, Athens. Prof Ec. m. Anna- Irene Stefanopoulou, 19 July 1968, 2 s. *Education:* Dipl Law; Dipl Ec; PhD Ec. *Appointments:* Prof Ec, Univ Athens 1984-; VP, Bank of Investment; Pres, Greek Productivity Ctr 1987-89; Pres, Council of Economic Advisors, 1989/90. *Publications:* In Greek: Foreign Banks in Greece, 1982; Greek Industry, Development and Crisis, 1983; The effects of Greece's integration to the EEC on industry & trade, 1988; In English: Colobalisation and the small less advanced countries: The Case of Greece (EEC/FAST, 1991). *Memberships:* Royal Ec Soc; Am Ec Assn. *Hobbies:* Travelling; Music; Arts. *Address:* Koritsas 9, 14561 Kifissia, Greece. 52.

GIBBON Maggie, b. 6 July 1949, Epsom, England. Publisher. *Education:* BA Hons, Univ Essex. *Appointments:* BBC Publications 1974-76; BBDO & CDP Advtg 1976-80; The Observer 1980-82; Condenast Publications 1982-84; United Newspapers 1984-88; Murdoch Magazines 1988-. *Hobbies:* Swimming; Sailing; Cooking; Theatre. *Address:* Murdoch Magazines, Fanum House, 48 Leicester Square, London WC2H 7FB, England.

GIBBON William Arthur, b. 9 Apr 1921, Altrincham, Cheshire, England. Conslt Arch. m. Judith Eleanor Lough, 22 July 1944, 2 s. 1 d. *Education:* BA 1948, MA 1956, Univ Manchester Hons Sch of Arch. *Appointments:* Arch 1948-58, Ptnr 1958-68, Sr Ptnr 1968-86, Cruickshank & Seward; Conslt Arch 1986-. *Creative Works:* Ashby Building, Queen's Univ Belfast; Renold Building UMIST; Lib Extension, Emmanuel Col Cambridge; Manchester Bus Sch; Royal London Assurance Co, Head Office, Colchester; Power Stations in England, Mexico & Argentina. *Memberships:* Fellow, RIBA; Mem RIBA Coun 1964-68; Mem Arch's Registration Coun 1964-68; Pres, Manchester Soc of Archs 1965-67. *Honours:* Truscon Travelling Scholarship 1954; RIBA Medal 1955; RIBA Rose Shipman Student, 1956; Annual Medal of Reinforced Concrete Assn, 1958; Hon Fellow of UMIST, 1976. *Hobbies:* Reading; English art & architecture; Music; Family. *Address:* 132 The Close, Salisbury, Wiltshire SP1 2EY, England.

GIBBS Beresford Norman, b. 27 Feb 1925, London, England. Chartered Surveyor; Land Agent. m. Mary Jane Thatcher, 22 Aug 1956, 2 s. 2 d. *Education:* Dipl 1952, Royal Agric Col, Cirencester, Glos. *Appointments:* Asst Land Agent to G C Laws, FLAS, FRICS 1952-58; Land Agent & Chartered Surveyor 1958-. *Memberships:* Fellow, Chartered Land Agents Soc, Chmn 3 Counties Br; Chmn, Young Conservatives in Cirencester Constituency 1954-55; Fellow, Royal Institution of Chartered Surveyors; Marylebone Cricket Club 1961-91. *Honours:* High Sheriff of Wiltshire 1989-90; Dep Lt of Wiltshire 1990-92. *Hobbies:* Lawn tennis; Cricket; History; Geneology. *Address:* Flintham House, Oaksey, Malmesbury, Wiltshire SN16 9SA, England. 35.

GIBBS Leonard James, b. 5 May 1929, Cranbrook, Canada. Artist. m. 3 Oct 1953, 1 s. 1 d. *Education:* Brandon, Manitoba; Edmonton, Alberta. *Career:* VP, Creative Dir, James Lovick Advertising 1956-68; Full Time Fine Artist 1968-. *Creative Works:* Num exhibitions Canada, USA, England & Denmark prior to 1980; Represented in major corporate collections; Co-Author, The Art of Len Gibbs, 1981; Yacht Portraits, 1987; Images, 1988; Many arts var mag & art jours; Half hour TV film, Len Gibbs, the Artists, 1989; Exhibitions incl travelling exhibition to Peking, Shanghai, Szchewan, 1981; Prairie Art Gallery, Grande Prairie, 1981; West End Gallery, Edmonton, 1981, 1983, 1985, 1988, 1991, 1992; Hollander York Gallery, Toronto, 1984, 1986, 1987, 1989, 1993; Candn Soc Marine Artists, Victoria & Vancouver, BC, 1984, 1986, 1987; Royal InstPainters in Watercolour, London, Eng, 1984, 1985, 1986, 1987, 1988. *Membership:* Union Club of BC. *Honours:* Hon Alberta Artist, 1983; Hon Citizen, City of Victoria, 1985. *Hobbies:* Antique cars; Sailing; Miniatures. *Address:* 1-416 Dallas Road, Victoria, British Columbia, Canada V8U 1A9. 142.

GIBSON Curtis A, b. 5 Nov 1929, Springfield, Ohio. Rtd. *Education:* CHE 1952, Univ Cincinnati, Ohio. *Appointments:* Chem Engr 1952-54, Sylvania Electric Products Co, Emporium, Penn; Recognized authority in Design of Aircraft Oxygen Systems & Standardisationof Aircraft Oxygen Equipment 1960-69; Expanded expertise to Life Support Systems 1970, and Aircraft Systems Engrg 1979; Chem Egr 1956-59, Mech Engr 1959-70, Life Support Systems Engr 1970-79, Aircraft Systems Engr 1979-, USAF at Wright-Patterson AFB in Ohio; Rtd 1986. *Memberships:* Am Defense Preparedness Assn; Intl Acad Profl Bus Execs; Air Force Assn; Life mem 26 assns & socs incl: Acad Polit Sci; Nat Geographic Soc; Knights Templar Eye Foun; Palestine 33 Knights Templar; Univ Cin Alumni Assn. *Honours:* Hon PhD & DD degrees, Universal Life Ch, Modesto, Calif 1979; Silver Bear Awd, Boy Scouts of Am. *Address:* 2806 Oxford Drive, Springfield, OH 45506, USA. 8, 52, 152, 139, 155.

GIBSON Dirk Cameron, b. 13 Oct 1953, Evergreen Park, Illinois. Univ Prof. m. Angela Peterson, 5 Dec 1987. *Education:* BS 1977; MA 1979; PhD 1983. *Appointments:* Assoc Prof, Augusta Col 1989-90; Assoc Prof, Ga State Univ 1990-. *Publication:* The Role of Communication in the Practice of Law. *Memberships:* Alabama Speech & Theatre Assn, Treas; Ga Speech Communication Assn, Pres; Speech Communication Assn; Srn States Communication Assn; Intl Communications Assn. *Honours:* Creative Ballot Awd, Univ NM debate tourney; Top Paper Awd, Applied Communication Div, Srn States Communication Assn, 1989; Top Three in PR, Speech Communication Assn, 1990. *Hobbies:* Intercultural communication; Reggae music; Philosophy; Golf; Animal rights. *Address:* Department of Communication, Georgia State University, University Plaza, Atlanta, GA 30303, USA. 7, 15, 117.

GIBSON Elizabeth Margaret, b. 7 Oct 1951, Thundersley, Essex, England. Tchr; Businesswoman. m. Keith Lander Best, 28 July 1990, 1 d. *Education:* Cert of Ed 1973, Maria Assumpta Col. *Appointments:* Primary Sch Tchr, ILEA 1973-90, Dep Hd 1988-90; P-time Tchr 1990-; Runs own business 1990-. *Publication:* Co-Author, pamphlet, Education & Ethnic Minorities, 1988. *Memberships:* Prospective Parliamentary Candidate, Birmingham, Hodge Hill; Chmn, Parliamentary Candidates Assn 1990-; Dep Chmn, Chelsea Conservative Assn 1987-90. *Hobbies:* Bridge; Music; travelling; Making things grow. *Address:* 15 St Stephen's Terrace, London SW8 1DJ, England.

GIBSON Ian Bennett, b. 10 June 1936, Leeds, England. Mng Dir. m. Jane Macvean Graham-Pole, 3 June 1961, 2 s. *Education:* Leeds Modern Sch 1945-52. *Appointments:* Navigating Ofcr, Merchant Navy Worldwide 1952-65; Ships Master, United Baltic Corp 1965; Sales Dir, Carron Co Falkirk 1965-69; Gen Mgr Tractors, British Leyland (UK) 1969-74; Conslt 1974-78; Mng Dir, United Baltic Corp GmbH, Kiel-Canal, Germany 1978-. *Memberships:* Agric Engrs Assn,

London, mem Gen Coun 1971-74; Farmers Club, London, Life mem. *Honour:* Hon Brit Consul, Kiel, Germany 1988-. *Hobbies:* Golf; Bridge. *Address:* Knooper Landstrasse 6, 2300 Kiel 17, Germany.

GIBSON Maureen, b. 31 Oct 1955, England. Nurse. *Education:* Enrolled Nurse, NZ, 1975. *Appointments:* Reg Com Nurse, Midlemore Hosp, NZ, 1973-75; REN, Kingseat Hosp, 1978-81; SEN, Onslow Dist Hosp, WA, 1981-82; RNA, Wyndham Dist Hosp, WA, 1982-83; Enrolled Nurse, Alice Springs Hosp, 1983-84; SEN, Onslow Dist Hosp, WA, 1985-86; EN, Psychopaedic; Braemar Hosp, Nelson, NZ, 19867-88, Seaview Hosp, NZ, 1988; EN, Extended Care, Numbala Nuga Hosp, Derby, WA, 1989; SEN, Boddington Dist Hosp, WA, 1989-90; EN, Mt Henry Hosp, WA, 1990; EN, Onslow Dist Hosp, 1990; EN, Fitzroy Crossing, WA, 1990-91. *Publications:* 2 poems published in NZ, 1991. *Memberships:* Melbourne Poetry Soc; Poetry Aust. *Honours:* Melbourne Poetry Soc, Cert of Commendation, 1991-92. *Hobbies:* Poetry; Travel; Reading; Music theory and learning classical guitar; Camping; Walking. *Address:* c/o Flat 2, 67 Leichardt Street, Tennant Creek, NT 0861, Australia.

GIERZOD Kazimierz, b. 6 Aug 1936, Warsaw, Poland. Musician; Pianist. m. Jolanta Zegadlo, 14 July 1974. *Education:* MA under Prof M Trobini-Kazuro, State Higher Sch of Mus; Dipl di Merito under Prof Guido Agosti, Chigiana Accad in Siena. *Appointments:* Tutor 1969, Asst Prof 1973, Prof 1986-, Dean Piano Dept 1975-87, Rector 2 terms 1987, 1990-, F Chopin Acad of Mus, Warsaw. *Memberships:* Polish Musical Assns, Artistic's Contest Com, VP; F Chopin Intl Foun, mem Coun; Mem of Hon, Japan Piano Tchrs Assn, Assn Europenne des Conservatoires, Acad de Mus et Musikchohschulen, mem Bd Dirs. *Honours:* 1st Prize, Young Musicians Festival in Gdansk, Poland, 1964; Min of Culture Awds, 1968, 1975, 1979, 1983; Hon Prof of Mus at Soai univ in Osaka, Japan 1988-; Intl Piano Compts, Juror. *Hobbies:* Tourism; Photography; Gardening. *Address:* ul Sygietynskiego 36, 05-85 Otrebusy, Poland. 4.

GIFFORD Edwin Chester, b. 16 July 1901, Albert Park, Victoria, Australia. Rtd Banker. m. Dulcie Edna Conkey, 20 Feb 1934, 1 s. 4 d. *Education:* Prince Alfred Col 1915-16. *Appointments:* C'Wealth Bank Australia 1918-64, var Mgmt & Admin posts incl Chf Mgr Tasmania 1959-64. *Memberships:* Fellow, Australian Soc Accountants; Hon Life Fellow, Australian Inst Mgmt. *Honours:* Order of Australia, 1976; Knight of Grace, Venerable Order of St John of Jerusalem, 1971; Grand Master of Freemasons 1971-74. *Hobbies:* Royal Hobart Bowls Club; Gardening; Var Masonic Orders. *Address:* 194 Churchill Avenue, Sandy Bay, Tasmania 7005, Australia. 157, 23, 149.

GILBERT Patrick Nigel Geoffrey, b. 12 May 1934, London, England. Gen Sec, Retired. *Education:* Merton Col, Oxford. *Appointments:* Lectr in Further Ed, South Berks Col 1959-62; Personal Asst to Sir Edward Hulton 1962-64; Oxford Univ Press, 1964-69; Westinghouse (Linguaphone Gp), Mng Dir within Group 1970, 1969-71; Gen Sec, Soc for Promoting Christian Knowledge 1971-92; Dir, Surrey Building Soc 1988-92. *Publications:* Arts in var jours. *Memberships include:* Gov: Ellesmere Col, Shropshire 1977-87, Fin Com 1979-87; S Michael's Sch, Petworth 1978-88, Rep to Gov Bodies of Girls' Schs Assn, Exec 1981-84, 1988-89; Rep of Ellesmere Col to Independent Schools' Careers Org 1980-87, Exec 1983-85; Gov, St Martin-in-the-Fields Sch 1971-92, Vice Chmn 1978-, ILEA Tertiary Ed Coun 1983-89; Gov, Roehampton Inst of Higher Ed 1978-, var offices; Fellow, Corp of SS Mary & Nicholas (Woodard Schools) 1972-92, Corp Exec 1981-92; Chmn, Greater London Arts, 1980-84; Sev Church committees and assns, and arts appointments; Brit Nat Com for UNESCO World Book Cong, 1982; Nat Ec Res Coun, 1982; Freeman of the City of London, 1966; Master Worshipful Company of Woolmen, 1985-86; Parish

Clerk of All Hallows, Bread Street, 1981; Mem Worshipful Company Parish Clerks; Mem, Court Guild of Freemen of City of London, 1991-; Lord of Manor of Cantley Netherhall, Norfolk. *Honours:* FRSA 1978; FBIM 1982; F Inst D 1982; Hon DLitt, 1982; Order of St Vladimir, 1977. *Hobbies:* Reading; Walking; Enjoying the arts; Golf. *Address:* 3 The Mount Square, London NW3 6SU, England. 1, 52.

GILLARD Jean, b. 6 June 1926, Newport, Gwent. County Councillor; Magistrate. m. John Lessimore Gillard, 9 June 1951. 1 s. *Education:* Matric, Solent Hse, Cowes, 1941; Stl Sch of Speech and Drama, Dipl Dramatic Art, London Univ. *Appointments:* Tchr: Alice Ottley Sch, Worcs, 1946; Westonbirt Sch, 1947-49; Lectr: Glos Cp;, 1947-49, Redland Col, Bristol, 1949-52; Tchr & Lectr: Bristol Educ Auth, 1960-68; Conservative Party: Area V-Chm, 1972-75, Bristol NW Constituency Chm, 1969-72; Bristol City Coun, 1968-74, Avon CC, 1973; JP, 1976; Govr: Bristol Poly, 1976-88, Redmaids Sch, 1974, Queen Elizabeths Hosp, 1977, Brunel Col of Tech, 1988, Chm, Avon Educ Com, 1986-89; V-Chm, CC, 1989-90; Nat Adv Com, Conservative Party: Women, 1972-75, Educ, 1980; Chm, Area Educ COm, 1981-84; V-Chm, Southend Com Hlth Coun, 1976-78; Southend Dist HA, 1989. *Honours:* Lag Strong Essay Prize, 1944; Central School MBE 1981 for Poli and Public Ser. *Hobbies:* Reading; Theatre; Swimming; Gardening; Art needlework; Foreign travel. *Address:* 2 The Haven, 27 Downs Park West, Henleaze, Bristol BS6 7QH, England.

GILLESPIE Anne Jacqueline Fleming, b. 12 Nov 1945, Doune, Perthshire. Med Dir. m. Major James Wood, 8 July 1968, 2 s. *Education:* The Royal Sch, Bath 1962-68; MB ChB Glasgow Univ. *Appointments:* House Surg, Glasgow Royal Infirmary 1968-69; Principal Gen Practice 1969- 89; Med Dir, Lifewatch Ltd 1989-. *Memberships:* Chmn, Conservative Med Soc, Scotland; Exec mem, Conservative Med Soc; Vice Chmn, Health Reform Group; Chmn, Scottish Bus Gp. *Hobbies:* Fine art; Horse Racing-Owner & breeder; Politics. *Address:* The Spittal, by Balfron, Stirlingshire G63, Scotland.

GILLESPIE Patti Peete, b. 26 Jan 1938, Bowling Green, Kentucky. Univ Prof. m. William C Gillespie, 7 Dec 1958, div 1981. *Education:* Wellesley Col 1955-56; BS 1958, Univ Kentucky; MA 1962, Western Kentucky Univ; PhD 1970, Indiana Univ. *Appointments:* Prof & Hd, Dept of Theatre & Speech, Univ So Carolina 1979-82; Prof & Chair, Dept Communication Arts & Theatre 1982-89, Prof of Theatre 1989-, Univ Md; Goodmon Vstg Scholar, Peace Col 1990; Mitchell Dist'd Prof, Trinity Univ 1987. *Publications:* Co- Author: Western Theatre: Revolution & Revival; Enjoyment of Theatre; Speech: An Important Skill; Over 50 arts in var jours. *Memberships:* Assn Communication Admin, Pres 1979; Am Theatre Assn, VP for Progs 1984-87; Speech Communication Assn, Pres 1986, 1987; Univ & Col Theatre Assn, VP for Admin 1980-83. *Honours:* Omicron Delta Kappa, 1983; ACT-NUCEA Nat Awd, Project SAETT, 1981; Dissert Fellow & Indiana Univ Fellow 1967-70; Alpha Psi Omega, 1962; Phi Beta Kappa, 1958. *Hobbies:* Canoeing; Camping; Hiking; Riding. *Address:* Dept of Theatre, University of Maryland, College Park, MD 20742, USA. 15.

GILLON Arie, b. 31 July 1946, Litomerice, Czechoslovakia. Sci Instruments Co Exec; Chemist. m. Ilana Rozei, 24 Sept 1969, 1 s. 2 d. *Education:* BSc 1970, MSc 1975, PhD 1981, Technion, Israel Inst of Tech. *Appointments:* Div Mgr, Eldan Electronic Instrument, Jerusalem 1981-86; Commercial Devel Mgr, Biokoor, Jerusalem 1986-87; Mktg Mgr, Horizon Computer Systems, Tel Aviv 1987; Mng Dir, Bargal Analytical Instruments & Software, Tel Aviv, 1988-. *Publications:* Arts to profl pubs in Chemistry; Art in Humoristic Sci Jour; Author, Gillon's Law, one of the Murphy Laws. *Memberships:* Jr Acad Staff Org of Technion, Haifa, Vice Chmn 1978, Chmn 1979; Am Chem Soc; Israel Chem Soc; Israel Chamber of Engrs,

Chem Sect. *Hobbies:* Chess; Humour. *Address:* 1A Rachel Street, Givatain 53482, Israel.

GILLUM Ronald L, b. 7 Feb 1938, Decatur, Illinois. Prof Pathology. m. Elizabeth L Feigel, 27 Dec 1960, 2 s. 1 d. *Education:* BA with distinction 1960, DePauw Univ; MD 1964, Univ III Col of Med; Internship, III Central Hosp, Chicago 1964-65. *Appointments:* Residency, AP/CP, Univ III R&E Hosp, Chicago 1965-69; Major, USAR-MC, AFIP, Wash DC 1969-72, Duty, Addis Ababa, Ethiopia; Asst Prof, UTMB, Galveston, Tex 1972-75; Assoc Prof, UTMSH, Houston, Tex 1975-77; Assoc Prof & Prof, Univ Okla Col of Med 1977-; Chf, Clin Path, OKC-VA 1977-; Dir, Clin Labs, Okla Med Ctr 1977-. *Memberships:* Okla State Assn Pathologists, Pres 1980; Col Am Pathologists, var coms, Vice Chmn, Chmn; Am Soc Clin Pathologists; Am Assn for Clin Chemistry; AMA; OSMA; OCMS; ACLPS. *Hobbies:* Photography; Electronics; Religion. *Address:* Director Clinical Laboratories, Oklahoma Medical Centre, PO Box 26307, EB402, Oklahoma City, OK 73126, USA. 7.

GIMENO Juan-Bosco, b. 6 Mar 1956, Barcelona, Spain. Pres CMSF; Prof of Bus Sch; Ptnr ITM. m. Maria-Cinta Calvo, 11 Oct 1982, 4 s. *Education:* Lawyer 1978, Univ de Navarra, Spain; MBA 1982, Inst de Estudios Superiores de la Empresa, Barcelona; Assoc Prof 1983, Sch of Journalism, Univ de Navarra. *Appointments:* Asst Edit, Nuestro Tempo, Pamplona 1979-80; Asst Admin, Clin Univ de Navarra 1982-87; Gen Dir, Massachusetts Inst de Espana, & Community Care Systems SA, Madrid 1987-89; Dir, Tajamar Foun, Madrid 1989-90; Pres, Centro Medico Santa-Fe, Madrid 1990-; Prof of Centro de Estudios Comerciales (CECO) 1987-; Ptnr, Info to Mgmt (ITM) Bus Consltg Firm 1990-. *Contributions to:* arts & manuals on Health care & Human Organizations in Business; Dir Med Videotapes Programmes, some prized & honoured. *Honour:* Mem, Spanish Assn Hosp Administrators. *Address:* Abedul 17, 28036 Madrid, Spain. 52.

GINCHEV Ivan, b. 19 Feb 1950, Rousse, Bulgaria. Assoc Prof Maths. m. Mariana Nedelcheva, 13 Feb 1950, 2 d. *Education:* MS 1973, Univ Wroclaw, Math Inst, Poland; PhD 1980, Tech Univ at Warsaw, Math Inst, Poland. *Appointments:* Asst Prof 1973-80, Adjunct 1980-85, Tech Univ Rousse; Adjunct 1985-89, Assoc Prof 1989-, Tech Univ Varna. *Publications:* Reviewer: Zentralblatt fur Mathematik 1977-; Mathematical Reviews 1986-; 28 pubs incl: Local approximation of higher order for multifunctions of one variable, 1991; A method to obtain Berge equilibriums in bi-matrix games, in the collection Multi-Criterial Dynamic Problems under Uncertainty, 1991; Strong and weak minima of functionals in a real Hilbert space, in press. *Memberships:* Am Math Soc; Bulgarian Union of Mathematicians; Polskie Towarzystwo Matematyczne. *Address:* Technical University Varna, Department of Mathematics, Varna 9004, Studentska Str, Bulgaria.

GINSZTLER Janos, b. 23 May 1943, Budapest. Prof; Dept Hd. m. Elvira Lers, 31 Aug 1968, 1 s. 1 d. *Education:* Dipl Mech Eng 1966; Dipl Welding Eng 1970; PhD 1973; CSc 1980; Doctor of technical scis 1988. *Appointments:* Asst Lectr, Sr Lectr, Prof 1989-, Dept Hd, Tech Univ Budapest, Inst of Mech Tech & Materials Sci, Dept Electr Engrg Materials. *Publications:* Co-Author 10 books; 102 pubs connected with subjects of materials sci-damage analysis and reliability problems of materials-operating at high temps. *Memberships:* Edit mem: High Temperature Technology, The International Journal of Pressure Vessels and Piping, The European Journal of Mechanical Engineering; Gen Secy, Hungarian Acad of Engrg; Pres, Sci Soc Mech Engrs; Pres, Hungarian Nat Com for FEANI; VP, FEANI; VP, Fed of Tech-Sci Socs. *Honours:* Sci Soc of Mech Engrs Medal, 1982; Pattantius Prize, 1986. *Hobbies:* Tennis; Swimming; Football; Literature; Music; Psychology. *Address:* Technical University of Budapest, H-1521 Hungary.

GIORDANO Dennis Nicholas, b. 19 Apr 1945, Orange, New Jersey, USA. Exec Dir; Edr. m. Susan Catherine Barrett, 25 Aug 1968, 1 s. 1 d. *Education:* BA 1967, MEd 1981, William Paterson Col. *Appointments:* Tchr 1967-85; Union Pres, NJ Ed Assn 1985-89; Exec Dir, WV Ed Assn 1989-. *Publications:* Sunday Column, Newark Star Ledger 1985-89; The Urban Challenge NJEA/NEA, 1988; Asstd arts for profl jours. *Memberships:* WV Ed Assn, Staff; NJ Ed Assn, Treas, VP & Pres; Passaic County Ed Assn, Pres; Nat Ed Assn, Staff. *Honours:* Dist'd Alumni Awd, William Paterson Col, 1987; Dist'd Svc, NJ Citizen Action Gp, 1988; Bd Resolution, Wayne Bd Ed, 1989; NJ Senate, Senate Resolution, 1989; Hon mem, Kentucky Colonel, 1986. *Hobbies:* Video movies; Bowling. *Address:* 222 Woodbridge Drive, Charleston, WVA 25311, USA. 7, 15.

GIROD Erwin Ernest, b. 1 Oct 1944, Los Angeles, Calif, USA. Physician Int Med. m. Jill Louise Johnson, 16 Dec 1967, 1 s. 1 d. *Education:* BA Calif State Univ, Los Angeles 1962-66; DM, Univ Calif, Calif Col Med 1966-70; Straight Med Internship 1970-71, Residency in Int Med 1971-73, Los Angeles County, Univ Srn Calif Med Ctr. *Appointments:* Naval Regl Med Ctr, San Diego 1973-75; Co-Dir, Intensive Care Unit, Christian Med Col & Brown Memorial Hosp, Ludhiana, Punjab, India 1976-77; Asst Prof of Med, Punjab Univ 1976-77; Asst Prof Med, Loma Linda Univ Sch of Med 1978-80; Chf, Gen Med Section 1978-80, Asst Chf Med Svc 1979-80, Jerry L Pettis Memorial Vets Admin Hosp; Huntington Memorial Hosp, Pasadena, Calif 1981-; St Luke Med Ctr 1982-; Methodist Hosp, Srn Calif, Arcadia 1986-. *Publications:* Shock, 1977; Cardiopulmonary Resuscitation, 1977; Guidelines to the Administration of Emergency Medications, 1978; Behcet's Syndrome Following Dengue Fever: Case Report & Review of the Literature, 1979; Intoxication with Alcohol-Containing Mouthwash: Case Report & Discussion of the Problem, 1980. *Memberships include:* Am Col Physicians; Am Bd Int Med; Calif Med Assn. *Honours include:* Admiral Stitt Awd, Naval Regl Med Ctr, San Diego, 1973-74, 1974-75; Intl Cultural Dipl of Hon, 1989; Legion of Hon, Alpha Gamma Omega Frat 1989-. *Hobbies:* Swimming; Music; Roses. *Address:* 8332 Huntington Drive, San Gabriel, CA 91775, USA. 59, 130, 139, 151, 152.

GITTELSON Abraham Jacob, b. 22 Oct 1928, NYC, NY, USA. Jewish Ed Admin. m. Shirley J Bakst, 11 Oct 1953, 1 s. 2 d. *Education:* BSS 1949, City Col of NY; BRE 1950, Yeshiva Univ, NY; MA 1953, Hunter Col; EdD 1985, Univ Miami, Miami. *Appointments:* Tchr, NYC Pub Schs 1950-54; Tchr, Jewish Ctr Univ Height's 1952-54; Ed Dir, Temple Menorah, Miami B 1954-56; Ed Dir, North Dade Jew Ctr, Miami 1956-58; Ed Dir, Beth Torah Cong, Miami 1958- 71; Exec Dir, VP, Central Agency for Jewish Ed 1972-; Ed Dir, Camp Ramah Canada 1968-72, 1974-75. *Publications:* Co-Author: Ten Lesson Plans in Teaching Jerusalem, Heb & Eng, 1980; Subject Integration in the Jewish Day School, 1985; Arts in profl jours. *Memberships:* Coun for Jewish Ed, Bd mem; Assn for Curriculum Devel & Supv; Phi Delta Kappa, Ed Hon Soc; Assn for Jewish Studies, Assoc mem; Jewish Edrs Assembly, former Bd mem. *Honours:* Honoree, Combined Jewish Appeal Dinner, Miami, Fl 1972; Honoree, Central Agency for Jewish Ed Annual Dinner, Miami, Fl 1985; Jewish Edr Awd, Dept of Ed & Culture, World Zionist Org, Israel 1991. *Hobbies:* Reading; Travel; Exercising; Jewish history. *Address:* 970 NE 172 Street, North Miami Beach, FL 33162, USA. 7, 15.

GJURCINOV Milan, b. 28 July 1928, Belgrade. Univ Prof. m. Ann Cilimanova, 3 Oct 1954, 1 s. 1 d. *Education:* PhD 1960, Cyril & Methodius Univ, Skopje; Belgrade Univ, Fac Philosophy, Dept Slavic Studies, 1951. *Appointments:* Positions held at Cyril & Methodius Univ, Skopje, Fac Philosophy: Prof of Contemporary Russian Lit 1961-80; Chmn, Dept Slavic Studies 1965-71; Chmn Dept Gen & Comparative Lit 1980-85; Prof in Theory of Lit & in Modern Res Methods in Lit 1980-. *Publications:* 12 Books incl: B L Pasternak, 1988;

Modern Macedonian Literature, 1987; Osmosis, 1987; On the Threshold of the Future, 1991; Also Author 8 anthologies of Contemporary Macedonian Poetry & Prose in the original Macedonian & translated into other langs. *Memberships:* Intl Slavic Com for Poetics & Stylistics; Intl Soc of Dostoevsky Studies; Exec Bureau of Intl Comparative Lit Assn 1985-91; Pres of the Macedonian Assn of Comparative Lit 1987-; Macedonian Acad of Arts & Scis 1988-. *Honour:* Macedonian Nat Awd for Lit, "19th October" 1971. *Hobby:* Chess. *Address:* ul Karaormau No 22, 91000 Skopje, Yugoslavia.

GLADYSHEV Georgy Pavlovich, b. 19 Sept 1936, Alma-Ata, Kazachstan, Russia. 1 s, 1 d. *Education:* DChem, 1966, Prof of Phys Chem, 1968, Prof of Med Syst, 1978, State Univ, Kazachstan, 1954-59. *Appointments:* Scist, Vis Lectr, St Univ, 1963-66; Hd of Lab, Vis Prof, Ufa, 1968-70; Hd of Lab, Vis Prof, Moscow, 1970-; Hd of Inst of Biophys Chem, Moscow, 1990-. *Publications:* Over 400 cientific works ncluding 8 monograms in the fields of phys chem and polymer chem including: Polymerization at high conversion, 1978; Stabilization of thermo-resistant polymers, 1979; Thermodynamics and Macrokinetics of Hierarchical processes, 1968; Ecological biophysical chemistry, 1989. *Memberships:* Mendeleev Soc, 1959; Am Chem Soc, 1977-; Acad of Creative Endeavours (ACE), 1989. *Honours:* Pres, Fdr, ACE 1989; Academician, 1989; Gold Medal, W Glbbs, ACE, 1991. *Hobbies:* Mountaineering; Tourism; Science; Arts. *Address:* Acad of Creative Endeavours, 18 Sadovaya Kudrinskaya, 103001, Moscow K-1, Russia.

GLANVILLE John Foster, b. 1 Jan 1918, Portsmouth, England. Solicitor. m. Judith Anne Durey, 26 Apr 1952, 1 s. 2 d. *Education:* Bradfield College 1931-36; Col of Law, 1936-47. *Appointments:* RNVR, War Svc 1939-46; Admitted Solicitor of the Supreme Crt 1947. *Memberships:* Law Soc; Srn Growers Soc, Pres; Royal Ocean Racing Club; Royal Albert Yacht Club, past Cdre. *Honours:* DSC 1942; VRD 1951. *Hobbies:* Sailing; Music; Country walking. *Address:* Fowley Cottage, 46 Warblington Road, Emsworth, Hants PO10 7HH, England.

GLARE Sylvia Marina, b. New Zealand. Profl Specialised Kinesiogist; Qualified Naturopath. m. Euan, 24 Mar 1972, 2 d. *Education:* Dipl, Dietetics & Nutrition, 1986; Grad Facilitater in Specialised Kinesiology, 1987; Advanced Facilitator in Spec Kinesiol, 1988; Naturopathy degree, 1989. *Appointments:* Principal, New Image Health Clinic 1985- 91; Principal, New Image Health Sch 1986-91. *Memberships:* Aust Trad Med Soc 1986; Pres, NA Touch for Health Assn 1986-91; Charter mem, Intl Assn Specialised Kinesiol 1987; Awd'd Profl Membership to Intl Assn of Specialised Kinesiol 1988; Pres, WA Kinesiol Foun 1991-92. *Honours:* Most Productive Specialised Kinesiol Instr, 1989; Recog Awd to Growth of Touch for Health, 1990; Awd for Vol Work in the Im Special Ed Prog, 1990-91; Salespeople with a Purpose, Recog Awd, 1990-92. *Hobbies:* Family; Creative cooking; Music; Walking; Travel; Entertaining; Voluntary educational work with youth; Personal development; Public speaking. *Address:* 10 Kintail Road, Applecross 6153, WA, Australia.

GLASS Alexander, b. 1 June 1932, Dunbar, Scotland. Rector of Dingwall Acad. m. Edith Margaret Duncan Baxter, 1 Aug 1959, 3 d. *Education:* Univ Edinburgh; Univ Heidelberg, Germany; Univ Aix-en- Provence, France. Moray House Col of Ed, Scotland; MA Hons 1953, 1955; DipEd 1956. *Appointments:* Nat Svc, Royal Army Ed Corps, 1956-58; Tchr of Modern Langs, Montrose Acad 1958-60; Special Asst Tchr of Modern Langs, Oban HS 1960-62; Principal Tchr of Modern Langs, Nairn Acad 1962-65; Principal Tchr of French, Asst Rector, Perth Acad 1965-72; Rector, Milne's HS, Fochabers 1972-77; Rector, Dingwall Acad 1977-. *Memberships:* Chmn, Com for Special Ednl Needs; Chmn, Highland Region Children's Panel; Chmn,

Children's Panel Chmen's Gp; Chmn, Inverness District, Scottish Community Drama Assn; Reader in Ch of Scotland; Trustee, Chmn and Secy, Scottish Secondary Schools' Travel Trsut. *Hobbies:* Amateur drama; Foreign travel; Rotary; Music; Church work. *Address:* Craigton, Tulloch Avenue, Dingwall, Ross-Shire IV15 9LH, Scotland. 184.

GLASS Nancy C, b. 21 Sept 1959, Columbus, Georgia. Tchr. m. James B Glass, 12 Oct 1985, 1 s. *Education:* BS 1981, MAT 1982, Livingston Univ. *Appointments:* Math Tchr, Sweet Water HS 1981-. *Membership:* Delta Kappa Gamma. *Hobbies:* Cross stitching; Swimming; Playing cards; Gardening. *Address:* PO Box 200, Nanafalia, AL 36764, USA.

GLASSMAN Rosslyn Angela, b. 13 May 1947, Hove, Sussex, England. Antiquarian; Dealer with Specialist Knowledge of Performing Arts; Exhibition Org. *Education:* Wistons Sch, Brighton. *Appointments:* The Witch Ball, Brighton 1967-79; Witch Ball, London 1979-91. *Memberships:* Soc of Theatre Res; Soc of Dance Res; Soc Am Th Res; Int Fed Th Res; Soc London Th Res; Domizetti Soc; Theatres Trust. *Hobbies:* Theatre; Dance; Opera; Theatre Preservation. *Address:* The Witch Ball, 2 Cecil Court, London WC2, England.

GLATZER Wolfgang, b. 15 Sept 1944, Hohenborau. Univ Prof. m. Veronika Hess, 4 Aug 1969, 1 s. 1 d. *Education:* Dipl in Sociol 1972, J W Goethe-Univ, Frankfurt; PhD 1978, Univ Mannheim. *Appointments:* Res Asst, Social Polit Decision and Indicator System, Frankfurt 1972-78; Dir of Special Res Dept, Microanalytical Foundations of Soc, Mannheim 1979-84; Prof Sociol, J W Goethe-Univ, Frankfurt am Main 1984-. *Publications:* Sociological Almanac, Author & Ed, 1975; Housing in the Welfare State, 1980; Quality of Life, Co-Author, 1984; Household Production, Author & Ed, 1986; Modernization of Modern Society, Ed, 1990; Recent Social Trends in West Germany, Co-Author, 1992. *Memberships:* Intl Sociol Assn; German Sociol Assns; Speaker of the Social Indicators Sect. *Hobbies:* Family; Playing cards. *Address:* Im Rothkopf 8, 6370 Oberursel, Germany.

GLAZOUNOV Constantin, b. 1 Aug 1964, Riga. Painter; Tchr of Painting. *Education:* J Rozentals Sch of Arts, finished 1982; Grad 1988, Acad of Arts, Dipl work, Builders. *Career:* Painter; Tchr Painting, Ctr of Children & Teen-Agers. *Creative Works:* Paintings: Morning, 1988; Crossing, 1989; Forest, 1989; At Summer Cottage, 1990; Refraction, 1991. *Hobbies:* Studying of English & Latvian Language; Architecture; Modern (Contemporary) art. *Address:* Riga, Kalnciema 48/50 FL 18, 226046 Latvia, Russia.

GLEASON Edward Hinsdale Jr, b. 20 May 1927, N Adams, Massachusetts. Chemist. m. 15 July 1950, 1 s. 3 d. *Education:* BS 1953, Northeastern Univ; PhD 1959, SUNY, Col of Environ Sci & Forestry. *Appointments:* Am Cyanamid, Stamford, CT 1953-56; Koppers Co, Monroeville, PA 1959-74; Arco Polymers, Monaca, PA 1975-80; Polysar Latex, Chattanooga, TN 1980-87; BASF Dispersions, Chattanooga, TN 1988-. *Publications:* 6 arts in sci jours; 8 US Patents. *Memberships:* Am Chem Soc; Tech Assn of Pulp & Paper Ind. *Hobbies:* Gardening; Golf. *Address:* 5627 Barrington Country Circle, Ooltewah, TN 37363, USA. 7, 132.

GLEDHILL Ruth, b. 15 Dec 1959, Loughton, England. Religious Affairs Correspondent, The Times. m. John Stammers, 10 June 1989. *Education:* HND 1982, London Col of Printing. *Appointments:* Birmingham Post & Mail 1982-84; Daily Mail 1984-87; The Times 1987-91, Religious Affairs Correspondent 1990-91. *Memberships:* NUJ; Reform Club. *Hobbies:* Riding; Opera. *Address:* 1 Pennington Street, London E1 9XN, England.

GLEESON Noel Martin, b. 5 Jan 1934, Ireland. Registrar General; Solicitor. m. 28 Dec 1966, 2 s. 2 d. *Education:* Pvt, CBS Ennis; St Flannan's Col, Ennis, Co Clare; Incorporated Law Soc of Ireland & Univ Col Dublin. *Appointments:* Solicitor, Supreme Crt of Ireland, 1957; Solicitor, Michael Tynan & Co 1957-59; Orr, Dignam & Co, Chittagong & Dacca, East Pakistan, Bangladesh 1959-62; Registrar General's Dept, Hong Kong Govt 1963-; Registrar General, 1982. *Honours:* Justice of the Peace; OBE. *Hobbies:* Sailing; Chess. *Address:* Registrar General's Department, Queensway Government Offices, Queensway, Hong Kong.

GLICKMAN Barry W, b. 6 July 1946, Montreal, Canada. Prof & Dir, Ctr for Environ Health. div, 1 s. 2 d. *Education:* BSc 1968, MSc 1969, McGill; PhD 1972, Leiden. *Appointments:* Univ Leiden 1969-80; NIEHS, Res Triangle Pk, NC 1980-84; Prof, York Univ 1984-91; Prof, Univ Victoria 1991-. *Publications:* Num pubs on mutagenesis & DNA repair. *Memberships:* Assoc Edit, Mutation Res; EMS; Genetic Soc of Can; Am Genetic Soc; Soc of Toxicologists; Am Soc for Microbiol. *Honours:* Steacie Memorial Fellowship 1982-84; Japan Soc for the Promotion of Sci 1974-75. *Hobby:* Sailing. *Address:* Biology Department and Centre for Environmental Health, University of Victoria, Victoria, BC, Canada. V8W 2Y2. 142.

GLODARIU Ioan, b. 1 Feb 1940, Sibiu, Romania. Main Reschr. m. Eugenia, 27 June 1963, 1 s. *Education:* Lic Gh Lazar, Sibiu 1953-56; Babes-Bolyai Cluj Univ 1957-62; Licentiate in History & Arch 1962; Doctor's in History 1973. *Appointments:* Assistance of Instruction, Babes-Bolyai Univ 1962-66; Reschr at the History & Arch Inst, Cluj 1966-71; Main Reschr & Dir, Arch Inst Cluj 1990-91. *Publications:* 11 books incl: Dacian Fortresses and Settlements in South-Western Transylvania, 1989; The Dacian Fortress at Capilna, 1989; 79 studies & arts publ in Romania & abroad. *Memberships:* Classical Studies Soc; Intl Assn of Greek & Latin Epigraphy; Intl Assn of Pre and Proto Historical Scis. *Honour:* Vasile Parvan Prize of the Romanian Acad, 1974. *Hobbies:* Reading; Tourism in the mountains. *Address:* P-ta Mihai Viteazul nr 1/9, 3400 Cluj-Napoca, Romania.

GLOMBIK Czeslaw, b. 8 Dec 1935, Zabrze. Univ Prof. m. Urszula Smigielska, 26 Aug 1970, 1 d. *Education:* MA in Philos 1958, Warsaw Univ; Dr Philos 1970, Jagiellonian Univ; Dr Habil. Philos 1978, M Sktodowska - Curie, Univ Lublin; Prof Philos 1985. *Appointments:* Tchrs' Sch, Raciborz 1958-66; Acad Ec, Katowice 1966-75; Silesian Univ, Katowice 1975-. *Publications:* Czlowiek i Historia, 1973; Tradycja i Interpretacje, 1978; Oblicza Szczescia, 1982; Metafizyka Kultury, 1982; Martin Grabmann i Polska Filozofia Katolicka, 1983; Zapomniani Krytycy, Nieznani Filozofowie, 1988; Tradycja Narodowa A Perspektywy Kultury, 1989; Poczatki Neoscholastyki Polskiej, 1991. *Memberships:* Polish Philos Assn; Polish Assn for Study of Religion; Upper Silesian Assn of Friends of Sci, Chmn Gen Coun. *Honours:* Bachelor's Cross, Polonia Restituta, 1986; 2nd degree Individual Sci Awd of Min of Nat Ed, twice, 1983, 1989. *Hobby:* Opera music. *Address:* Silesian University, Institut of Philosophy, ul Bankowa 11, PL-40-007 Katowice, Poland.

GLOTZNER Frank Ludwig, b. 20 Oct 1938, Berlin. Hosp Exec; Prof Neurol. m. Dr Gisela Herms, 16 May 1969, 3 s, 4 d. *Education:* Abitur 1958; Med State Exam 1963; MD 1966; Privatdozent 1975; Prof Neurol 1982; Hd Neurol Svc 1982. *Appointments:* Internship, Gottingen/ Berlin 1964-66; Lt, German Navy 1967-68; Residency, Neurol/Psychi, Munich 1968-71; Asst Prof Neurological Surg, Seattle, USA 1971-73; Privatdozent, Wurzburg 1973-82. *Publication:* Arts & books: Posttraumatic Epilepsy, 1975, 1991; Brain Injuries, 1983; Autonomic Nervous System, 1990; Treatment of Epilepsy, 1990; Myoklonus, 1990. *Memberships:* AAAS; Intl Ligue of Epilepsy. *Hobbies:* Tennis; Hiking; Skiing; Education. *Address:* Chefarzt d Neurologischen Abteilung am Krankenhaus Rummelsberg, W 8501 Schwarzenbruck, Germany. 52.

GLOVER Robert Finlay, b. 28 June 1917, Cambridge, England. Rtd Edr. m. Jean Muir, 28 June 1941, 1 s. 2 d. *Education:* MA 1939, Corpus Christi Col, Oxford. *Appointments:* Major RA, Army 1939-46; Asst Master, Anmpleforth Col 1946-50; Hd of Classics, King's Cantarbury 1950-53; HM, Adams' GS, Newport, Salop 1953-59; HM, Monmouth Sch 1959-76. *Memberships:* Dep Secy, Headmasters' Conf 1976-82; Liveryman, Habardashers Company 1975; Fellow, Woodard Corp 1982-87; East India Club. *Honour:* TD, 1954. *Address:* Brockhill Lodge, West Malvern Road, The Wyche, Malvern, Worcs WR14 4EJ, England. 1.

GLYN John Howard, b. 18 Mar 1921, London, England. Physician. m. Daphne Barbara Bayley, 2 Apr 1947, 1 s. 1 d. *Education:* Harrow 1934- 38; Jesus Col, Cambridge 1938-42; Middlesex Hosp Med Sch 1942-45. *Appointments:* Conslt Physician 1957-86. *Publications:* 2 books on Cortisone Therapy and History, and History of Rheumatology. *Memberships:* Heberden Soc, Secy; Med Soc of London, Secy; Brit Soc Rheumatology; Royal Soc Med; Athenaeum, past mem, Coun; Royal Col Physicians, Fellow. *Hobbies:* Golf; Tennis; Skiing; Photography; Music; Discussions; People. *Address:* 35 Sunen Square, London W2 2PS, England.

GOALEN Gerard Thomas, b. 16 Dec 1918, Birkenhead, England. Rtd Arch. m. Maria Malheiro, 29 Apr 1943, 2 s. *Education:* BArch, Univ Liverpool Sch of Arch. *Appointments:* Royal Artillery 1940-42; RE 1942- 46; Planning Ofcr, LCC 1946-48; Arch, Harlow Devel Corp 1948-55; Ptnr, Frederick Gibberd 1955-65; Arch, Gerard Goalen 1965-75; Arch, Gerard Goalen & Ptnr 1975-81. *Creative Works:* Church: Our Lady of Fatima, Harlow 1960; Good Shepherd, Nottingham 1964; St Gregory, S Ruislip 1967; St Gabriel, Upper Holloway 1967; RC Chaplaincey, Cambridge (Fisher House) 1970. *Memberships:* FRIBA; MRTPI. *Honour:* RIBA Arch Awd, East Midlands Region, 1966, Good Shepherd Church, Nottingham. *Hobbies:* Gardening; Building crafts; Swimming. *Address:* 53 Lyndhurst Court, Sandringham Road, Hunstanton, Norfolk, PE36 5DN.

GOCZOL Jan, b. 13 May 1934, Rozmierz. Padagoge; Schriftsteller; Redakteur. m. Malgorzata Witon, 6 June 1960, 2 d. *Education:* Magister der Philologie 1965 Absolvierung der Padagogischen Hochschule in Opole *Appointments:* Redakteur in der kulturellen Zeitschrift Poglady, Katowice 1965-70; Redaktionsekretar der Monatschrift Opole 1970-74; Chefredakteur der Monatschrift Opole 1974-90. *Publications:* Poesien Topografia intymna, 1961; Malgorzata, 1961; Sprzec drzwi, 1969; Manuskrypt, 1974; Poezje, 1985 *Memberships:* Mitglied des Polnischer Schriftstellerverbandes 1963-91; Prases der Abteilung des Polnischen Schriftstellerverbandes in Opole 1971 91; Mitglied des Hauptvorstandes des Polr Schriftstellerverbandes 1971-91. *Honours:* Rote Rose Gdansk, 1963; Stanislaw Pietak Preis, Warszawa, 1974 *Hobbies:* Gartenpflege; Touristik; Klassische Musik *Address:* ul Partyzancka 20 a, PL 45-850 Opole, Poland

GODEAUX Jean Eugene Auguste, b. 6 Mar 1920 Liege, Belgium. Rtd Marine Biol Edr; Emeritus Prof. m Rita Marie Berland, 27 Oct 1945, 1 s. 1 d. *Education* MS 1941, PhD summa cum laude 1948, Dr in Biol 1958 Univ Liege, Belgium. *Appointments:* Scholar, Belg Na Res Foun 1942-48; Chf Practical Works, Supply Tch 1948-59; Assoc, Belg Nat Res Foun 1955-59; Hd Lal Zool, State Univ Belgian Congo (later Zaire) Elisabethville, Lubumbashi 1959- 68; Dean Fac Agro Elisabethville, Lubumbashi 1959- 68; Dean Fac Agror 1961-62; Ass Prof, Liege 1968-70; Hd Lab Marine Bic 1970- 85; Hd Lab Gen Biol 1975-85; Rtd 1985 *Publications:* Over 130 papers pub in 12 countries Contbr to sev treatises; Convenor, also Ed Colloquiun Oceanographic Res in Medit, Liege 1988; id Compa study Levantine Basin, Suez Canal, Red Sea, Athens

Greece, 1988; Ed Bulletin Roy Sciences, S of Liege 1983-. *Memberships:* Intl Comm Sci Explor Medit Sea (ICSEM) Monaco, Plankton Com, mem 1958, Pres 1989-; Nat Belg Com Oceanography (R Acad Sc), mem 1972, Secy 1982-1992; Royal Soc Sci Liege, mem 1955, Pres 1981-82, Hon Secy 1983-; Belg Roy Soc Zool, mem 1939, Pres 1985-89; Fifty One Club, mem 1975, Pres 1982-84. *Honours:* Off Leopold Order 1962; Command Crown Order 1972; Gr Off Leopold II Order 1982; 35 year Svc Medal; Recip Friends of Univ Liege 1954, Roy Acad Belgium Agathon de Potter Prize 1954; Royal Acad Belgium Edmond de Selys-Longchamps Prize 1971. *Hobbies:* Middle East ancient history; Impact of man on nature; Philately. *Address:* Laboratory of Marine Biology, Department of Oceanography, Zoological Institute, University of Liege, Quai Edouard Van Beneden 22, B 4020 Liege, Belgium.

GODEC Zdenko, b. 14 Sept 1939, Nis, Yugoslavia. Sci Conslt in Elect Engrg. m. Urch Mirjana, 24 July 1965, 2 s. *Education:* Dipl Ing 1962, MSc 1970, Dr 1975, Univ Zagreb. *Appointments:* Devel Engr in Lab 1962-72, in Transformer Dep R&D Engr 1972-81, Ldr of Thermal Gp 1981-90, Rade Koncar-Electrotechnical Inst, Zagreb; Sci Conslt, Koncar-Inst for Electr Engrg, Zagreb 1991-. *Publications:* 40 sci & profl papers; 19 tech innovations. *Memberships:* Croatian Engrs & Techs Assn, Zagreb, Berislaviceva 6; Conf Intl des Grands Reseaux Electriques-Comite Nat Croatia, Zagreb, Berislaviceva 6; Croatian Metrology Assn, Zagreb, Berislaviceva 6. *Hobbies:* Mountain climbing; Reading. *Address:* Krndeljeva 3A, 41000 Zagreb, Croatia.

GODFRAIND Theophile, b. 18 Feb 1931, Bande, Belgium. Univ Prof; Pres Royal Acad. m. Anne De Becker, 12 July 1957, 1 s. 1 d. *Education:* Bachelor Med Scis, ULB 1951; MD 1955, PhD 1958, Univ Cath de Louvain; Cert Inst Trop Med, Anvers 1958. *Appointments:* Prof, Univ Lovanium, Congo 1958-65; Prof, Univ Cath de Louvain 1965-; Fellow, 1974-88, VP 1987-91, Pres 1991-, Royal Acad Med; Secy Gen IUPHAR 1987-. *Publications:* 359 reports; 153 abstracts 1978-91; Edit 9 books. *Memberships:* Mem var socs in Belgium, France & W Germany; Biochem Soc, UK; Brit Pharmacol Soc; Physiol Soc, UK; NY Acad Scis; Am Soc for Pharm & Exptl Therapeutics; Intl Study Gp for Res in Cardiac Metabolism; Corr Mem: Acad Royal de Med de Belgique 1974, Acad Nat de Pharmacie de France 1980; Regular mem, Acad Royale de Med De Belgique 1984; For Corr Mem Acad Nat de Med de France 1988; VP Acad Royale de Med de Belgique 1988; Mem Acad Europaea 1990; Pres of Acad Royale de Med de Belgique 1991. *Honours:* Laureat du Concours des Bourses de Voyage, 1955; Laureat du Prix Specia, 1955; Laureat du Prix J F Heymans, 1967; Laureat du Prix Quinquennal des Scis Therapeutiques, 1973; Laureat du Prix Smith Kline, RIT, 1982; Docteur h.c. of Univ Louis Pasteur Strasbourg, 1984; Peter Debye Prize, Univ of Limburg, Maastricht, 1987; Laureat du Prix de la Foun de Physiopathologie Prof Lucien Dautrebande, 1988; 1991 ASPET Awd (Am Soc for Pharm & Exptl Therapeutics), USA. *Address:* Laboratoire de Pharmacologie-UCL 7350, Av E Mounier, 73, B-1200 Brussels, Belgium.

GODFREY Gerald, b. 22 Aug 1926, London, England. Physician. m. 9 Apr 1951, 1 d. *Education:* Glasgow Univ 1945-51. *Appointments:* Srn Gen Hosp 1951-52; Asst MOH, Wandsworth, Croydon, Lewisham 1963-67; Civilian Med Ofcr, RAF 1953-60; Police Med Ofcr 1953-62; EP Dagenham, Streatham 1953-66, Harley Street 1966-. *Memberships:* BMA; Royal Col Gen Practitioners. *Hobbies:* Sailing; Shooting; Tennis; Anthropology. *Address:* 86 Eaton Square, London SW1W 9AG, England.

GODFREY Walter P Jr, b. 18 Feb 1944, Venice, Florida, USA. Fire & Explosion Expert. m. Barbara J Floyd, 16 Feb 1980, 2 d. *Education:* Cert Fire Investigator; Cert Fire Investigation Instr. *Appointments:* Dep State Fire Marshall, Fla State Fire Marshals Office 1974-76; VP, William Alvine Assoc Inc 1977-81; Pres, Fire/

Reconstruction Conslts Inc 1981-. Pres, BJs Pal Inc 1989-; Pres, Rand Res & Recovery Inc 1991-. *Memberships:* Nat Assn of Fire Investigators; Nat Dir, Nat Certification, Bd mem; Intl Assn of Arson Investigators; Am Boat & Yacht Coun. *Hobbies:* Sailing; Reading; Scuba diving; Skiing; Deep sea fishing. *Address:* Fire/Reconstruction Consultants Inc, PO Drawer 307, Cape Canaveral, FL 32920, USA. 2, 7.

GODLEY Georgina, b. 11 Apr 1955, London, England. Fashion Designer. m. Sebastian Conran, 18 Apr 1988, 1 s. *Education:* Wimbledon Sch of Art Foun 1973-74; BFA 1st class hons 1977, Brighton Poly; MA with distinction 1978, Chelsea Art Sch. *Appointments:* Picture Restorer 1978-79; Designer, Browns 1979-80; Designer, Crolla 1981-85; Designer, Own label 1985-. *Honours:* Voted Designer of the Year 2000, Evening Standard 1988; One of 10 best dresses this century, Mail on Sunday, 1988. *Address:* 2, Mundon St, London W14 0RH, England. 34.

GOEVA Elisaveta Elsa Borisova, b. 27 July 1928, Boljarovo vil, Bourgas district. Artist; Painter. *Education:* Grad 1953, Acad Fine Arts in Sofia, Prof Panajotoff, speciality painting. *Career:* Free artist. *Creative Works:* Portrait, alndscape and compositions mainly, also still lifes; Many one-man shows in Sofia and in the country, latest in Sofia 1988; One-man shows in Budapest & Berlin; Participation in representative exhibitions of contemporary Bulgarian art in Germany, France, Spain, Austria & Italy and others, and almost all group exhibitions in Bulgaria; Work represented in Nat Gallery, the City Gallery, Sofia and many in the country, and in pvt collections. *Memberships:* Union of Bulgarian Artists; Soc 19.90. *Hobbies:* Learning languages; Fashion; Literature; Music; Cinema; Theatre; Medicine; Animals. *Address:* 16/B Vishneva str, Sofia 1126, Bulgaria.

GOINS Michael Edgar, b. 14 Oct 1954, Winston-Salem, North Carolina, USA. Dr of Optometry. m. 28 July 1980, 2 d. *Education:* AB 1976, Univ NC; OD 1981, Srn Col of Optometry; Optometric Fellowship, Bascom Palmer Eye Inst 1982. *Appointments:* Dr M Katzin 1982-83; Self employed 1983-. *Publications:* Dictionary of NC Biographies, 5 sketches; Synopsis of Ocular Anatomy, 1979; Carcinoma-du-Situ, Srn Journal of Optometry, 1982; Contbr arts to profl & ednl pubs. *Memberships:* Am Optometric Assn; Beta Sigma Kappa; Gold Key Intl; NC State Optometric Soc; Am Optometric Student Assn, Nat Pres 1980; Wilmington East Rotary 1983-, Pres 1986; St Andrews Covenant Presbyterian Ch, Deacon 1991. *Honours:* AOA Cert of Merit, 1979; ADSA Past Pres Awd, 1981; Outstg Young Men of Am, 1983, 1989; New Hanover County Bd of Health 1988-94, Vice Chmn 1991; Jaycees Dist'd Svc Awd, 1990; One of 5 Outstg N Carolinian's, 1991. *Hobbies:* Audubon Birds of America Prints; Classical music; Gardening. *Address:* 5030 Randall Parkway, Wilmington, NC 28403, USA.

GOLD Alan B, b. 21 July 1917, Montreal, Quebec. Chf Justice- Superior Crt Quebec. m. Lynn Lubin, 14 Aug 1949, 2 s. 1 d. *Education:* BA 1938, Queen's Univ, Kingston, Ontario; LL L cum laude 1941, Univ Montreal, Montreal, Quebec. *Appointments:* Read Law with Marcus Sperber QC; Ptnr, Sperber, Berger, Godine, Gold & Lapin, later Sperber, Gold & Lapin, finally Gold & Lapin 1946-61; District Judge & Vice-Chmn, Quebec Labour Relats Bd 1961-65; Assoc Chief Judge of Provincial Crt of Province of Quebec 1965-70; Chf Judge of Provincial Crt of Province of Quebec 1970-83; Chf Justice of Superior Crt of Province of Quebec 1983-; Pres of Judicial Coun of Province of Quebec 1970-83; Chmn of Conseil du Referendum, Quebec 1980. *Memberships:* Pres, Jr Bar Assn Montreal 1951-52; Mem Coun of Bar of Montreal 1952-53; Mem Bd Examiners of Bar of Province of Quebec 1952-61; Fdr Dir & Ofcr, Legal Aid Bureau of Montreal 1956-60; Candn Bar Assn 1946-; Charter mem, Soc of Profls in Dispute Resolution (USA) and Recip of its Special Awd of Excellence, 1981; Hon mem, Corp Profl des

Conseillers en Relats Ind de la Province de Quebec; Phi Delta Phi, Intl Legal Frat; Nat Acad Arbitrators, USA; Misc affiliations incl: Gov of McGill Univ 1974-83, Chmn Bd Govs 1978-82, Gov Emeritus 1984-; Chancellor Concordia Univ 1987-. *Honours:* LLD h.c. 4 univs; Dist'd Bora Laskin Awd, Yeshiva Univ, 1987; Human Relats Awd of Candn Coun of Christians & Jews, 1985; Ofcr of Ordre Nat du Quebec, 1985; Mem Conseil de l'Ordre 1985-; Pres, Conseil de l'Ordre 1985-87, 1989-91; Recip Medaille du Premier ministre du Quebec, 1987. *Address:* Chief Justice- Superior Court, Court House 16.62, 1 Notre-Dame Street East, Montreal, Quebec, Canada H2Y 1B6. 2, 12, 88, 142.

GOLD Lorne W, b. 7 June 1928, Saskatoon, Sask, Canada. Glaciology. m. Elizabeth Joan L'Ami, 8 Sept 1951, 1 s. 3 d. *Education:* BSc Engrg Physics 1950, Univ Sask; MSc Physics 1952, PhD 1970, McGill Univ. *Appointments:* Res Ofcr, Div Building Res 1950-52, Hd Snow & Ice Sect 1952-69, Hd Geotech Sect 1969-74, Asst Dir 1974-79, Assoc Dir 1979-86, Reschr Emeritus 1988-, Nat Res Coun. *Publications:* Author over 50 sci & tech papers. *Memberships:* Intl Glaciol Soc, Pres 1978-81; Assn Profl Engrs of Ontario; Engrg Inst Can; Candn Geotech Soc; Candn Soc Civil Engrs; Artic Inst N Am. *Honours:* Fellow: Royal Soc Can, 1979; Engrg Inst Can, 1985; Candn Soc Civil Engrs, 1989. *Hobbies:* Reading; Skiing; Curling. *Address:* 1903 Illinois Avenue, Ottawa, Ontario, Canada K1H 6W5. 142.

GOLDBERG Montague Joshua, b. 5 Nov 1924, Johannesburg, South Africa. Emeritus Conslt Cardiologist. m. Daphne Margaret Clark, 22 Apr 1960, 3 s. *Education:* Univ Witwatersrand; MB BCh 1948; Dipl Med (Wits) 1957; MRCP 1964; FRCP (London) 1973; DSc (Hon) Leicester Univ 1989. *Appointments:* HP & SHO J'Burg Gen Hosp 1949-50; Tutorial Med Registrar, Dept Med, J'Burg 1953-58; SHO, Hammersmith Hosp 1959; Sr Registrar, Middx Hosp 1959-65; Conslt Cardiol, Hosp, Leicester 1965-89, Emeritus 1989-. *Publications:* Num papers in med jours. *Memberships:* Fellow, Royal Col Physicians; Brit Cardiac Soc, Coun mem 1980-84; Royal Soc Med. *Honour:* Hon DSc 1989, Leicester Univ. *Hobbies:* Painting; Ornithology; Golf; Fell walking; Music. *Address:* 45 Spencefield Lane, Leicester LE5 6PT, England. 170.

GOLDBLATT Barry Lance, b. 29 July 1945, Palo Alto, Calif, USA. Mktg Exec. m. Andrea M McLaughlin, 19 Dec 1986. *Education:* BS 1967, MBA 1968, Univ S Calif. *Appointments:* Mkt Res Brand Supvr, Procter & Gamble 1968-71; Dir Mkt & Consumer Res, Johnson & Johnson 1971-. *Memberships:* Am Mktg Assn; Advtg Res Foun; USC Skull & Dagger; USC Assocs; USC MBAs; USC NJ Alumni Club, Pres. *Honours:* USC Outstg Sr 1967; USC Awd of Appreciation 1981. *Address:* 20 Andrews Lane, Princeton, NJ 08540, USA. 6, 52, 132.

GOLDBLATT Rose, b. 28 Aug 1913, Montreal, Canada. Prof Music & Piano, McGill Univ. m. Henry Finkel, 28 Aug 1937, 1 s. 1 d. *Education:* Strathcona Scholarship for 3 yrs study at Royal Col Music, London and postgrad extension for 2 yrs; Studied with Kendall Taylor, and later in NY with Egon Petri; ARCM degree; FRSA, London, Eng. *Appointments:* Prof Piano, McGill Univ, Montreal, Can 1955-; Chmn, Keyboard Dept 1958-78. *Memberships:* Fac Coun, McGill, Mus Pres, Provincial Cncl QMTA; Quebec Music Tchrs' Assn, Past Pres; Candn Fed Mus Tchrs Assns, Quebec VP; Royal Soc Arts, Fellow; Arts westmount, Mus Advr; Montreal Classical Mus Festival, Artistic Dir; European Piano Tchrs' Assn, Candn Correspindent. *Honours:* Cecille Leger Scholarship 1929, 1935; Strathcona Scholarship to RCM, London, Eng 1930; Dedications by many Candn Composers of their Music to Rose Goldblatt, 1946; Woman of the Year, Montreal Press Club, 1954; Rose Goldblatt Trophy for Student Compt at Quebec Mus Tchrs' Assn, 1990. *Hobbies:* Theatre; Travel; Literature; Science; Geology. *Address:* 342 Elm Avenue, Westmount, Quebec, Canada H3Z 1Z5. 4, 88.

GOLDMAN Renitta Lee, b. 15 Aug 1938, St Louis, Missouri. Assoc Prof of Special Ed. m. Jay Goldman, 20 Dec 1959. *Education:* BA 1960, Wash Univ, St Louis, Mo; MS 1967, NC State Univ, Raleigh, NC; PhD 1978, Univ Mo-Columbia, Columbia, Mo. *Appointments:* Counsellor, Columbia Pub Schs 1968-85; Adj Asst Prof, Univ Mo-Columbia 1978-85; Conslt 1985-; Assoc Prof, Univ Alabama at Birmingham 1985-. *Publications:* Silent Shame: The Sexual Abuse of Children & Youth, 1986; Children at Risk: an Interdisciplinary Approach to Child Abuse, co-ed, 1990; Sibling Relationships in Mildly Handicapped Children, co-Author, 1989-90. *Memberships:* Coun for Children with Behaviour Disorders, Ala State Pres; Coun for Exeptional Children; Intl Assn of Children with Mental Deficiency; Assn of Children with Learning Disabilities; UAB Fac Women, Pres 1989-90; Assoc Scist, Injury Prevention Res Ctr, UAB. *Honours:* Phi Beta Kappa, awd'd jr year; 1990 Nominee for Res Achmt Awd, Nat Mental Health Assn; 4 year full tuition hon scholarship, Wash Univ; Phi Delta Kappa; Phi Kappa Phi; Pres, Mo State Future Tchrs of Am; Pres Student Body, Univ City Sr High Sch. *Hobbies:* Reading; Tennis. *Address:* 4631 Pine Mountain Road, Birmingham, AL35213, USA. 7, 15, 130, 155.

GOLDS Anthony Arthur, b. 31 Oct 1919, Macclesfield, England. Rtd Brit Amb, HM Diplomatic Svc. m. Suzanne Macdonald Young, 9 Oct 1944, 1 s. 1 d. *Education:* MA, New Col Oxford Open Scholar, 1938-39, 1946-48. *Appointments:* War Svc, Royal Armoured Corps 1939-46; HM Diplomatic Svc, CRO, FO, FCO, 1948-77; Brit Dir, Intl C of C 1977-83. *Publications:* Many manuscripts destined for posthumous publication, but mainly poetic & non-Political. *Memberships:* Oxford Soc; Diplomatic Svc Assn; Dulwich Soc, Chmn of Planning; and others. *Honours:* LVO 1961; CMG 1971. *Hobbies:* Modernising medieval English poetry; Crosswords; Cricket; Rugby; Golf. *Address:* 4 Oakfield Gardens, London SE19 1HF, England. 1, 34.

GOLDSCHEIDER Gabriele Maria (Gaby), b. 7 Mar 1929, Vienna, Austria. Antiquarian Bookseller; Pubr; Author. *Education:* Ruskin Sch of Art, Oxford Univ 1949-53. *Appointments:* Edit of Art Books, Hamlyn Publishing Gp 1967-73; Antiquarian Bookseller 1973-; Independent Pubr 1975-. *Publications:* Medallion Collectors' Series (Constable) Dolls, 1977; Bibliography of Sir Arthur Conan Doyle, 1977; Arts in Antiquarian Book Monthly Review. *Memberships:* Antiquarian Booksellers' Assn 1978-; Com mem of the Windsor Lit Soc; Pvt Libraries Assn. *Honour:* Isle-of-Wight Soc Prize for Conservation of the Charles Dickens Bookshop in Cowes, I-O-W 1987. *Hobbies:* Reading; Book & toy collecting; Theatre. *Address:* Deep Dene, Baring Road, Cowes, Isle-of-Wight PO31 8DB, England.

GOLDSCHMIDT Hans Detrich Alfred, b. 4 Nov 1914, Freiburg, Berlin. Emeritus Prof of Sociology. m. 16 June 1955, 2 s, 3 d. *Education:* Dipl Ing Tech, Univ Berlin, 1939; Dr rer pol, Univ of Goettingen, 1953. *Appointments:* Engr, DEMAG Motors, berlin, 1939-44; Labour Camp, 1944- 45; Ed, Goett Univ Zeitung, Asst, Univ Goettingen, Fellow, Univ of Birmigham, 1945-56. *Publications:* Stahl und Staat, 1955; Die gesellschaftliche Herausforderung der Univ, 1991; Co-author and editor of numerous books and articles in teh field of higher education, politics and religion. *Memberships:* Numerous associations in the fields of sociol, polit sics, Higher educ and religion. *Address:* Max Planck Institute for Human Development and Education, Lentzeallee 94, D-1000 Berlin 33, Germany.

GOLDSMITH Ulrich K, b. 19 Jan 1910, Freiburg, Germany. Professor Emeritus of Comparative Literature. m. (1) 1 s; (2) Bobra Goldsmith Ballin, 19 Dec 1966. *Education:* BA Hons French and German, Toronto, 1942; MA German Lit, 1946; PhD, 1950, Univ of Calif at Berkeley. *Appointments:* Lang Tchr and Instr: Beltane Sch, London, 1934-40; Cantab Col, Toronto, 1942-44; Univ of Sask, 1944-46; Univ of Calif at Berkeley, 1946-47; Princeton Univ, 1947-50; Asst Prof, Univ Manitoba,

1950-51, Asst Prof, Mass, 1950-55; Instr, Yale Univ, 1955-57; Asst Prof, Univ Colorado, 1957-59; Assoc Prof, 1959-62; Prof of German and Comp Lit, 1962-65; Chm of German and Comp Lit, 1961-71; Vis Prof, Univ of Calif at Berkeley, 1970; Prof Emeritus of German and Comp Lit, 1979-. *Publications:* Stefan George: A Study of his early work, 1954; Stefan George Columbia Essays on Modern Writers, 1970. *Memberships:* MLA; ACLA; AATG; ACLU; Goethe Soc of N.Am. *Address:* 7202 N 45th Street, Longmont, CO 80503, USA.

GOLDSTEIN Irwin Stuart, b. 12 July 1947, Can. Prof. m. Alison Smith, 15 Aug 1978, 2 d. *Education:* BA 1970, Carleton Univ, Can; M Litt in Philos1974, Univ Bristol, UK; PhD 1979, Univ Edinburgh, UK. *Appointments:* Vstg position, Srn Methodist, Univ Tex/Dallas, Loyola, Univ Chgo 1980-83; Asst Prof, Davidson Col 1983-87; Assoc Prof, Davidson Col 1987-. *Publications:* Arts on Philos in profl pubs. *Memberships:* Am Philos Assn; Intl Soc for Value Inquiry; Srn Soc for Philos & Psycho; NC Philos Assn. *Honours:* Carleton Univ Grant 1969-70, Can; Vans Dunlop Scholarship 1977-79, Univ Edinburgh; Postdoctoral Fellow 1984, Univ Edinburgh. *Hobbies:* Reading; Travelling; Swimming; Music; Art; Theatre. *Address:* Dept of Philosophy, Davidson College, PO Box 1719, Davidson, NC 28036, USA. 7, 15.

GOLDSTEIN Julia Sonia, b. 20 Mar 1923, Baltimore, USA. Rtd. m. Harold Goldstein, 5 Nov 1943, 2 s. *Education:* BS 1963, MLS 1968, Univ Ill; Fla State Univ Summer Prog, Univ Oxford, England 1988, 1990. *Appointments:* Tchr, Thomas Paine Sch, Urbana. Ill 1963-65; Librarian, Flossie Wiley Sch, Urbana 1965-67, State Lib of Fla 1968-71; Children's Conslt 1971-72, Ill 1972-76; Librarian, Fla Dept Commerce, Tallahassee 1976-78; Fla Dept Labour, Tallahassee 1978-80; Employment & Trng Specialist, Fla Dept of Labour 1980-85. *Memberships:* Intl Torch Club, Pres Tallahassee Chapt 1988-89; Univ Club of Fla State Univ, Pres 1989-90; Toastmasters Intl, Pres Fla Dept Transp Chpt 1983; Tallahassee Opera Guild, Bd mem. *Hobbies:* Tai Chi; Dancing; Reading; Listening to music; Tennis; Edinburgh Festival; Travel; World peace; Friendships. *Address:* 1911 Angel's Hollow, Tallahassee, FL 32308, USA. 7.

GOLDSWORTHY Ashley William, b. 2 Nov 1935, Australia. Prof & Dean. m. Shirley Anne Wilkinson, 11 May 1957, 3 s. 1 d. *Education:* B Com 1960, AAUQ 1960, Dip Pub Ad 1962, Univ Qld; MSc 1980, Griffith Univ. *Appointments:* Mgr, Mgmt Svcs, SGIO, Qld 1970-79; CEO, Suncorp Bldg Soc 1979-87; MD & CEO, Jennings Gp Ltd 1987-90; Prof & Dean, Sch Bus, Bond Univ 1991-. *Memberships:* Chmn, Ctr for Intl Res in Communications Info Tech; Chmn, Info Inds Roundtable; Chmn, Nat Info Tech Coun; Dir, Aust Ballet; Dir, Qld Ballet; Exec Dir, Aust Computer Soc; Fellow: Aust Soc of Cert Practicing Accts; Aust Computer Soc; Inst of Dirs; Aust Inst of Mgmt; Inst Fin Svcs; Fed Pres, Liberal Party of Aust. *Honours:* OBE 1982; AO 1991. *Hobbies:* Tennis; Jogging; Reading; Work. *Address:* 386 Wishart Road, Wishart, Brisbane 4122, Australia. 23.

GOLEMBIEWSKI Robert Thomas, b. 2 July 1932, Lawrenceville, New Jersey, USA. Res Prof of Polit Sci & Mgmt; Conslt. m. Margaret Mary Hughes, 1 Sept 1956, 1 s. 2 d. *Education:* BA cum laude 1954, Princeton Univ, Woodrow Wilson Sch of Pub & Intl Affairs; MA Pol Sci 1956, PhD Pol Sci 1958, Yale Univ. *Appointments:* Instr Pol Sci, Princeton Univ 1958-60; Asst Prof Mgmt, Univ Ill, Champaign-Urbana 1960-63; Vstg Lectr, Ind Admin, Yale Univ 1963-64; Assoc Prof Pol Sci 1964-66, Prof Pol Sci 1966-67, Res Prof Pol Sci & Mgmt 1967-, Univ Ga; Dist'd Vstg Scholar, Fac Mgmt, Fall terms of 1980- 86 & 1989, Univ Calgary, Can; Vstg Prof, Vanderbilt, Oregon State and other univs. *Publications:* Over 50 books incl: The Small Group, 1962; Men, Management & Morality, 1965; Pub Adm, 1966; Sensitivity Training and the Laboratory Approach, 1970; Approaches to Planned Changes, vols 1 & 2, 1979; Humanizing Public Organisations, 1985; Stress

in Organisations, 1986; Phases of Burnout, 1988; High Performance & Human Costs, 1988; Organisation Development, 1989; Ironies in Organisational Development, 1990; Handbook of Organizational Consultation; Over 400 res arts in profl jours. *Memberships include:* Past Pres, So Pol Sci Assn; Charter mem, Cert Conslts Intl; Adv Bd, Organisation Devel Inst; Fellow, NTL Inst for Applied Behavioural Sci; Past Hd, Org Dev Div, Acad of Mgmt; Intl Assn of Applied Social Scists; Am Soc for Pub Admin; Am Soc for Trng & Devel; Am Poli Sci Assn. *Honours:* Hamilton Book of the Year Awd, 1967; Named Social Scist of the Year by Eastern Acad of Mgmt, 1972; Douglas McGregor Memorial Awd for Excellence in Application of Behavioural Sci, 1976, 1986; Chester I Barnard Mem Awd, 1980; Univ Ga Creative Res Awd, 1984; Fellow, Acad Mgmt, 1988; Wm A Owens Jr Awd for Creative Res, Univ Ga 1988; Outstg Organization Devel Conslt 1989; Outstg Fac Awd by Ga Students of Pub Adm, 1990; Res Grants from Lilly & Falk Founs, NIMH & UMTA & other Awds. *Hobbies:* Numismatics; Mountain climbing; Fly fishing; Jogging; Softball. *Address:* Department of Political Science, University of Georgia, Baldwin Hall, Athens, GA 30602, USA. 2, 3, 52, 139, 155.

GOLIK Marek, b. 26 Sept 1954, Cracow, Poland. Orthopaedic Surg. m. Danuta, 4 Aug 1979, 2 s. *Education:* MD 1980, Nicolaus Copernicus Acad of Med, Cracow; DSc 1990, Acad Med, Warsaw. *Appointments:* Regl Ctr of Sick Children & Adolescents, Zakopane, Poland 1980-89; Hd Dept Orthopaedic Surg, Orthopaedic Surg, Regl Ctr or Rehab, Swiebpdzin, Poland 1989-. *Publications:* 12 pubs in profl jours. *Memberships:* Polish Orthopaedic & Traumatology Soc, Chmn Regl Div; Polish Med Soc. *Honours:* Nicolaus Copernicus Gold Badge, 1979; Pres of Cracow City Awd, 1979; Bronze Svc Cross, 1986. *Hobbies:* Yachting; Tourism; Bioengineering; Neurophysiology. *Address:* os Luzyckie 44 A/5,66-200 Swiebodzin, Poland.

GOLOS Krzysztof Maria, b. 9 July 1954, Warsaw, Poland. Assoc Prof. m. Jane Klawifer, 21 Apr 1990. *Education:* MB 1978, PhD 1982, DSc 1990, Warsaw Tech Univ. *Appointments:* Asst Prof 1980-90, Assoc Prof 1990-, Warsaw Tech Univ, Inst of Machine Design Fundamentals. *Publications:* Over 50 res arts in profl jours in the field of Mechanical Engrg, Materials Sci, Fatigue & Fracture. *Memberships:* Polish Soc Applied Mechanics 1985; Com of Machine Building, Fatigue & Fracture Mech Sect 1990. *Honours:* Killam Fellowship from Univ of Alberta, Can 1986-88; Res Awd of Min of High Ed, 1989. *Hobbies:* History of art; Gardening; Tennis. *Address:* Warsaw Technical University, Institute of Machine Design Fundamentals, ul Narbutta 84, 02-524 Warsaw, Poland.

GOLOVKO Anatolij Alexandrovich, b. 12 Dec 1925, Alekseevka, Russia. Dr of Law; Univ Prof. m. Nina Victorovna Ozol, 5 Mar 1952, 1 s. *Education:* Army Svc 1941-46; Kharkov Inst of Law 1946-50; Postgrad studies at Byelorussian Acad Scis 1950-53. *Appointments:* Jr Res Ofcr 1953, Sr Res Ofcr 1954-59, Byelorussian Acad of Scis; Sr Reader 1959-65, Hd of Chr of Constitutional Law 1965-91, Byelorussian State Univ. *Publications:* 45 books incl: The Experience of Byelorussian Rural Soviets Activities, 1958; Permanent Commissions of Rural Soviet in Action, 1962; BSSR-Sovereign Socialist State, 1986. *Memberships:* Intl Assn of Constitutional Law; Mem Permanent Crt of Arbitration, Hague. *Honours:* Order of the Red Star, 1944, 1945; Dr of Law, 1973; Prof, 1974; Order of Patriotic War, 1985; Emeritus Lawyer of Byelorussian SSR, 1989. *Hobbies:* Business tourism; Reading books on history; Gardening. *Address:* 17 Zaslavskaja Street, Flat 19, Minsk 220004, The Republic of Byelaruss, Russia.

GOLOVKOV Boris Yurievich, b. 24 June 1941, USSR. m. 28 Apr 1978, 1 s. *Education:* Grad, 1966, Candidate, 1973, Dr Tech Scis, Leningrad Tech Inst, 1988. *Appointments:* Sci Asst, 1967, Postgrad student, 1969-

73, Chief of Lab, 1974-75, Dpty Dir, 1975-87, Dir, Leningrad Tech Inst, 1987-. *Publications:* 150 scientific works, 3 scientific books on automation, technological processes in mineral processing plants and mines, and solution mining. *Memberships:* Pres and Chm of the Bd, Potash Producers Union; Coun, Intl Potash Inst, Switz. *Honours:* Corres mem, Russian Acad for Natural Sics, 1992. *Hobbies:* Gardening; Automobile Driving; Travelling. *Address:* VNIIG (R&D Institute of Halwegy), Narodnogo Opolcheniya Av 2, St Petersburg 198216, Russia.

GOMIDE Fernando de Mello, b. 4 June 1927, Rio de Janeiro. Vstg Prof; Rtd Prof. m. Luiza Mitiko Yamashita, 13 July 1990. *Education:* BSc 1951, Univ Federal do Rio de Janeiro; Scholarship, Cent Brasi Pesq Fisicas 1951-53; Fellowship, Inst Fis Univ Bologna 1962-63. *Appointments:* Inst Nacional Technologia 1953-54; Prof Aux 1955-62, Asst Prof 1962-73, Assoc Prof 1973-89, Rtd as Prof, Depto Fisica, Inst Tecnol Aeronautica; Vstg Prof, Catholic Univ of Patropolis. *Publications:* Sci arts in intl sci jours, philosophical arts in profl jours; Books: Relatividade Geral e Cálculo Tensorial; Introducao Cosmologia Relativistica; Filosofia do Conhecimento Cientifico; Dialogo Filosofia e Ciencia. *Memberships:* Soc Brasileira Progresso du Ciencia; Am Assn Progress of Sci; Soc Brasiliera de Fisica; Soc Astronomica Brasileira; NY Acad of Scis; Intl Astronomical Union; Soc Brasiliera de Filosofos Catolicos; The Planetary Soc; Am Phys Soc. *Hobbies:* Listening to classical music & British military music; Theology & Biblical exogesis; Archaeology. *Address:* R Angelica Lopes de Castro 71, 25655 Petropolis, RJ, Brazil.

GONG Shu-duo, b. 21 Mar 1921, Quanzhou City. Historian; Prof of History. m. Mrs Zhang Ping-zi, 12 July 1961, 1 s. 1 d. *Education:* Taiwan Tchrs' Col 1947-49; Beijing Normal Univ 1950-52. *Appointments:* Fac mem of History Dept, Beijing Normal Univ 1952-, currently Chmn of the Dept. *Publications:* Over 40 works and arts incl: Author, On Guan Han- qing, 1979; Probe into Modern Culture, 1988; Chf edit & Co-Author, Outline of Modern History of China, 1986. *Memberships:* Pres, History Assn of Beijing; Dir, Inst of Historiography, BNU; Fellow, Modern Culture Soc of China; Dramatist Assn of China; Standing Dir, Social Scis Union of Beijing; Chinese Res Soc of War Against Japanese Invasion, China. *Honours:* Best Treatise Awd of Nat Theory Symposium, 1988; Winner of Nat Medal of May Day, 1990; Best Edr Awd of China, 1990. *Hobbies:* Reading; Listening to Peking Opera. *Address:* Number 2, Living Building 19 for Staff & Workers, Beijing Normal University, Beijing 100875, China.

GONGORA-TREJOS Enrique, b. 4 June 1931, San Jose, Costa Rica. Mathematician; Univ Prof; Advr. m. (2)11 Sept 1991, 1 s. 2 d. *Education:* Licentiate Chem 1961, Univ de Costa Rica; Dipl Mathematiker Georgia 1966, Augusta Univ, Gottingen. *Appointments:* Chair Math & Math Logic, Univ Costa Rica 1966-76; Dean Fac Sci 1973-76, Hd Math Dept 1976-77, Univ National; Consellor Energy, Oficina de Planificacion Nacional y Polit Ec 1975-81; Academic Vice-Rector 1977-80, Res Vice-Rector 1980-86; Lectr Philos & History of Music, Univ Costa Rica 1980-89; Alternate Amb, Intl Atomic Energy Agency 1986-. *Publications:* Books: Introduccion al Pensamiento Logico Matematico, 1979; Falso Verdadero, 1983; ?Que son los Reactores Nucleares?, 1989. *Memberships:* Secy, Com Interamericano de Ed Matematica, 1972-82; Mem Bd Fdrs, Univ Nacional, 1974; Mem Bd Fdrs, Univ Estatal a Distancia, 1977; Bd Dirs, Atomic Energy Comm of Costa Rica, 1984-. *Honour:* Book, Introduccion al Pensamiento Logico Matematico awd'd Premio Jorge Volio. *Hobbies:* Early music-founder of the Collegium Musicum; Fencing; Medieval German Literature. *Address:* Comision de Energia Atomica de Costa Rica, Ap 6681, 1000 San Jose, Costa Rica.

GONTIER Jean Roger, b. 8 Mar 1927, Lens, France. Internist; Edr. m. Sylviane Prevost, 8 Dec 1969, 3 s.

1 d. *Education:* AB 1945, Col d'Etampes, France; MS 1947, Col Scic, Paris; MD 1965, Sch Med, Paris. *Appointments:* Prof Physiol, UGSEL, Paris 1957-62. Instr in Med, SchMed, Paris 1960-65; Dir Physiol, SchMed, Reims 1966-68; Prof Physiol, Univ de Montreal 1970-78; Conslt Edit, var pubrs, NYC 1975-78; Conslt Int Med, Paris 1979-. *Publications:* Author 9 works incl Physiologie de la Respiration, 1976; Digestion, 1969, 2nd ed 1982; La Respiracion, Spanish translation, 1986. Translator of 9 works incl: Traite de Physiologie, A C Guyton, 1980; Physiologie Humaine, Vander, 1989. *Memberships:* Am Physiol Soc; Can Physiol Soc; NY Acad Scis; Am Assn Scis; Assn des Physiol; Cercle de l'Etrier, Paris; Country Club, La Baule. *Honours:* Laureat Sch of Med of Paris, 1965; 1st Prize of Thesis: Rene Leriche, 1965; Silver Medal of Sch of Med, 1965. *Hobby:* Sailing. *Address:* 133 rue Michel-Ange, F-75016 Paris France. 52.

GONZALES Frank, b. 1 Aug 1933, Phoenix, Arizona USA. Minister; Counsellor. m. Jeanne Carol Peterson 4 June 1969, 3 d. *Education:* UCLA 1952; ELAJC 1952-53; BA 1958, MA 1959, Bob Jones Univ; Dr of Ministries 1991, Bethany Theological Seminary. *Appointments:* Pres, Insto Evangelico 1963-69; Fdr-Pres, Frank Gonzales Evang Assn 1963-91; Fdr, Casa de Ninos Frank Gonzales, 1970, orphanage; Fdr-Dir, Intl Choir 1960-90; Fdr-Dir, Breakthrough Ministries, and radio & television Outreach. *Memberships:* Hon mem of Rotary Club; Dir, Drug Rehab Ctr, East Los Angeles Elkhart, Indiana; Pub Sch Speaker for Anti-drug abuse. *Honour:* Hon degree, Univ of Vera Cruz, Mexico. *Hobbies:* Political Science; Basketball; Trumpet music; Gardening. *Address:* 13 Chimney Ct, LaGrange, GA 30240, USA.

GONZALEZ Wenceslao J, b. 21 Sept 1957, Ferrol, La Coruna, Spain. Univ Prof. *Education:* BA Philos 1979 Univ Salamanca; DPhil 1983, Univ Murcia. *Appointments:* Lectr 1979-82, Sr Lectr 1983-87, Titular Prof 1987-, Univ of Murcia. *Publications:* Author: La Teoria de la Referencia Strawson y la Filosofia Analitica 1986; Edit, Aspectos metodologicos de la investigacion cientifica, 1988, 2nd ed 1990; Edit, Action Theory, 1991. Author 25 arts. *Memberships:* Sociedad Espanola de Historia de las Ciencias y las Tecnicas; Aristotelian Soc & Mind Assn, UK; Brit Soc for the Philos of Sci; Austriar Ludwig wittgenstein Soc. *Honour:* Extraordinary Awc Doctoral Thesis, Univ Murcia, 1986. *Hobbies:* Soccer Jogging. *Address:* Alfonso X el Sabio s/n, Edificic Captesa 10o C, 30008 Murcia, Spain. 52, 139, 156.

GONZALEZ RAYNAL Bertha Elena, b. 10 Sept 1950 Havana, Cuba. Reschr; Geophysist. 2 s. *Education:* Fac of Physics 1968-70; Univ Bucharest 1970-75; Germany trng course 1982; Inst Seismoresistant Structures anc Seismology, USSR 1983-84. *Appointments:* Na Geophysical Enterprise 1975-77; Inst Geophysics & Astronomy, Seismological Dept 1977-. *Publications:* Over 20 sci reports on Applied Seismology; 22 pubs in Nat & Intl Reviews on Seismic Hazard & Microzoning. *Memberships:* Sci Coun, Inst of Geophysics & Astronomy; Cuban Soc of Geol. *Honours:* Nat Prize Andre's Poey, for best res work in sect of Earth anc Space Sciences, Havana, 1985; Mention in the first con on Applied Investigations, Havana, 1986. *Hobbies:* Reading; Movie; Music. *Address:* Calle 54, No 4517 Apto 5 entre 45AY47, Playa, Habana, Cuba.

GONZALEZ-DUENAS Hernan, b. 24 Apr 1949, NY USA. Sr Ptnr; CPA/Lawyer; Publ Acctg. m. Joanne M Welch, 2 June 1984, 2 s. 2 d. *Education:* BS Acctg & Ec 1971, Fordham Univ; MBA Fin & Acctg 1972 NYU; JD Tax Law 1980, George Wash Univ. *Appointments:* Special Agent, US Treasury Dept 1972-76; Sr Acct, Arthur Anderson & Co 1976-78; Asst Tax Mgr, Fla Power & Light Co 1978-79; Tax Dir & Ass Controller, Gulf States Utilities 1979-81; Ptnr, Deloitte Haskins & Sells 1981-89; Sr Ptnr, KPMG Peat Marwic 1989-. *Publications:* Author Chapt 17, Taxes o Accounting for Public Utilities; Over 20 arts on corporat taxation for jours; Expert Witness on utility taxation

Book, Taxation of Public Utilities, 1992; Edit, Utility newsletter for KPMG Peat Marwick; Over 300 speeches; Sev tax & acctg position & planning papers & arts. *Memberships:* Am Inst CPAs; NatAssn Accts; Fla/Oh/ NJ/NY/DC/Tex and La Inst of CPAs; Edison Electr Inst Taxation Com; Am Gas Assn; Fin Assoc & Tech Advr, Am Gas Assn; Tax Sect, George Wash Univ Law Sch Alumni Assn. *Honours:* Beta Alpha Psi 1967-71; Beta Gamma Sigma 1970-71; NYU Fellowship Awd 1971-72; Pres Task Force 1988-; Cont Mem Republican Party Inner Circle 1991; Grad cum laude, Fordham Univ, 1971; Full Scholarship to George Wash Univ Law Sch, 1976. *Hobbies:* Tower Club of Dallas; Lakewood Club of Dallas; Reading; Golf; Swimming; Suloflex exercise; Coin collecting-Roman Empire. *Address:* KPMG Peat Marwick, 1601 Elm Street, Thanksgiving Tower, Dallas, TX 75201, USA. 7, 163.

GONZI Lawrence (The Hon), b. 1 July 1953, Valleta, Malta. Speaker of the House of Reps, Malta. m. Catherine Callus, 18 Sept 1978, 2 s. 1 d. *Education:* Dipl as Notary Public 1974, Doctorate of Law, Lawyer 1975, Univ Malta. *Appointments:* Grad as Lawyer & established own firm 1976- 88; Chmn Bd Dirs of a Ldg Gp of Companies, 1987; Chmn Pharmacy Bd, 1987; Mem Prisons Bd 1987-88; Chmn, Nat Comm for the Handicapped 1987-; Speaker, House of Reps 1988-; C'Wealth Parliamentary Assn, Speakers' and Presiding Ofcrs, mem pn Exec Com 1992. *Publication:* Thesis: Unlawful Assembly, 1975, for Doctorate in Law. *Memberships:* Chmn, Nat Comm for the Handicapped; Chmn of Dar Il-Wens, a residential Home for the Handicapped; Mem Inter Parliamentary Union; C'Wealth Parliamentary Assn, Exec mem 1992-; On Presiding Ofcrs & Speakers' Com. *Honour:* Scholarship Fund, Simonds Farsons Cisk Scholarship for Univ Students, 1971. *Hobbies:* Sports-mainly football; Reading; Computer technology & applications to working environment; Main interest is matters relating to the rights of the disabled. *Address:* Settembrina, Zaffran Street, Marsascala, Malta.

GOOD Sherrie, b. 4 Nov 1952, Brooklyn, NY, USA. Journalist. *Education:* AA 1972, Miami-Dade Community Col; BA 1974, Colorado State Univ; MA 1976, Ball State Univ; PhD 1981, Srn Ill Univ. *Appointments:* Lectr, Communications Dept, Fla Intl Univ 1980-81; Asst Prof of Communication & Pub Affairs Reporting, Sangamon State Univ 1981-83; Copy Edit, Washington Post 1984-85; Assoc Mng Edit, Legal Times 1985; Asst City Edit, Copy Edit, Baltimore, News Am, 1985-86; Copy Edit, Detroit Free Press 1986-88; Lectr, Dept Communication, Univ Mich, Fall 1987; Asst Community News Edit, The Orange County Register 1988-1992; Exec Ed, South Orange County News, 1992-; Sr Lectr, Sch Journalism, Univ Sr Calif, spring 1992. *Publication:* Dissert: Newsworthiness as a Privacy Defense Against the Media, 1981. *Memberships:* Edit Bd, Newspaper Res Journal 1991-; Profl Dir, Orange Co Press Club 1991-92; Chmn, Ill First Amendment Cong 1983. *Hobbies:* Bicycling; Travelling; Writing. *Address:* South (Orange) County News, 23811 via Fabricante, Mission Viejo, Calif 92690, USA.

GOODDEN Robert Crane, b. 2 Apr 1940, Birmingham, England. Entomologist; Writer; Co Dir. m. Rosemary Bagwell Purefoy, 1 June 1968, 2 s. 1 d. *Education:* Salisbury Cathedral Choir Sch; Dauntsey's Sch. *Appointments:* Trainee L Hugh Newman, The Butterfly Farm Ltd, Bexley, Kent 1957; Harrods, Knightsbridge 1959; Fdr & Mng Dir, Worldwide Butterflies Ltd 1960; Co-Fdr, Trustee & Vice Chmn, Brit Butterfly Conservation Soc, 1968; Owner, Lullingstone Silk Farm. *Publications:* 10 books on lepidoptera and entomology incl Field Guide to Butterflies of Britain, 1978; Beningfield's Butterflies, 1978; Butterflies, 1971; Field Guide to Butterflies of Europe, 1991. *Memberships:* Mgmt Com, St John's Almshouse, Sherborne; Sherborne Chamber Choir; Amateur Entomologists Soc; Brit Ent Soc; FRHS; VP, Brit Butterfly Conservation Soc; Church Warden, St Michael's Church, Over Compton. *Hobbies:* Music; Gardening; Arts & crafts; Photography;

Audio & video; Walking; Botany; Entomology; Natural history; Travel; Computer programming. *Address:* Compton House, Nr Sherborne, Dorset DT9 4QN, England.

GOODE Anthony William, b. 3 Aug 1944, Newcastle Upon Tyne. Conslt Surg; Reader in Surg. m. Patricia Josephine Flynn, 26 Sept 1987. *Education:* Univ Newcastle Upon Tyne: MB BS 1968; MD 1978; FRCS England 1973. *Appointments:* Clin Surg posts in Newcastle Univ Hosp Gp 1968-70; Univ of London Tchg Hosps 1976-. *Publications:* Num sci pubs relating to surg nutrition & metabolism, endocrine disease & microgravity experimentation; Mem Edit Bd, Medicine Science and the Law. *Memberships:* Asst Secy Gen, Brit Acad Forensic Scis 1982-87; Hon Secy, Brit Assn Endocrine Surgs 1983-; Intl Soc Surg 1984-; Int Soc Endocrine Surgs 1984-; NY Acad Scis 1981-; Royal Soc Med 1972-. *Hobbies:* Music esp opera; Cricket; Literature. *Address:* The Surgical Unit, The Royal London Hospital, Whitechapel, London E1 1BB, England. 34.

GOODFELLOW Byron Beaton (Ike), b. 5 Mar 1931, Toronto, Canada. Asst VP Bus Devel. 1 s. 3 d. *Education:* BASc Engrg 1953, MASc Engrg 1954, Toronto. *Appointments:* IBM Can Ltd 1957-84; Ryerson Univ 1985- 87; Northern Telecom Can Ltd 1987-. *Memberships:* Assn Profl Engrs of Ontario; Exec Com, Ottawa Carleton Ec Devel Corp 1982-85; Le Cercle Univ d'Ottawa; Rideau Club of Ottawa; Engrs Club of Toronto; Can Info Processing Soc; Can Club of Ottawa. *Hobbies:* Fishing; Model railroads; Painting. *Address:* 451 Balliol Street, Toronto, Ontario, Canada M4S 1E1.

GOODFELLOW Mark Aubrey, b. 7 Apr 1931, London, England. Rtd UK Amb. m. 10 Oct 1964, 1 s. 1 d. *Education:* Higher Sch Cert 1949. *Appointments:* Foreign Office 1949; Milit Svc 1949-51; Foreign Office 1951-54; Brit Milit Govt, Berlin 1954-56; 2nd Secy, Khartoum, Sudan 1956-59; FCO 1959-63; 2nd Secy, Yaounde, Cameroon 1963-66; Brit Trade Commr, Hong Kong 1966-71; FCO 1971-74; 1st Secy, Ankara 1974-78; Consul, Atlanta 1978-82; Counsellor for Hong Kong at Wash DC, USA 1982-84; Counsellor (Commercial), Lagos 1984-86; Amb at Libreville, Repub of Gabon 1986-90. *Honour:* Commander Equatorial Star (Gabon), 1990. *Hobbies:* Travelling; Gardening; Visiting historic sites and places. *Address:* c/o Royal Over-Seas League, Park Place, St James's Street, London SW1A 1LR, England. 1.

GOODNER Homer Wade, b. 28 May 1929, USA. Reliability Engrg. m. Kathleen Annette Holland, 20 Oct 1950, 1 s. 3 d. *Education:* BS Mech Engrg 1959, Univ Al; Postgrad Matriculant (non-degree course) at Princeton 1961, Steven Inst 1969, Univ Tenn 1981-85. *Appointments:* Monsanto 1959-67; Dow-Badische 1967-73; Phillips Petroleum 1973-. *Creative Works:* Holder of Am & Foreign Patents; Devel Hara Methodology for Risk Analysis. *Contributions to:* Encyclopaedia & Tech Profl Jours. *Memberships:* Inst Elect & Elect Engrs Risk Soc; Instrument Soc of Am; Soc for Risk Analysis; Regd Profl Engr. *Honour:* Pi Tau Sigman 1958. *Hobbies:* Non-fiction reading; Study of history; Philosophy Science; Woodworking; Peregrinating. *Address:* 106 Brittany Park, Anderson, SC 29621, USA. 7, 132.

GOODWIN Richard Murphey, b. 24 Feb 1913, Newcastle, Indiana, USA. Rtd Prof. m. Jacqueline Wynmalen, 24 June 1937. *Education:* AB 1934, PhD 1941, Harvard; BA 1936, BLitt 1937, Oxford. *Appointments:* Lectr in Ec, Harvard 1938-50; Lectr in Ec, Cambridge 1965-80; Prof of Ec, Univ Sienna, Italy 1980-88; Fellow, Peterhouse, Cambridge 1958-. *Publications:* Elementary Economics from the Higher Standpoint, 1970; Essays in Dynamic Economics, 1983; Essays in Linear Economics, 1984; Dynamics of a Capitalist Economy, co-Author, 1989; Essays in Nonlinear Dynamics, 1989; Chaotic Economic Dynamics, 1990. *Membership:* Econometric Soc.

Hobbies: Painting; Music; Walking. *Address:* Dorvis's, Ashdon, Essex CB10 2HP, England.

GOODYEAR Nelson, b. 12 Jan 1912, NYC, NY, USA. Designer; Prof Ind Mgmt; Inventor; Investor. m. (2)Virginia B Goodyear, 2 s. 2 d. *Education:* BA 1933, MA Ed Admin 1939, Columbia Univ; PhD 197 , Cal Chris Univ, La, Ca. *Appointments:* Prof Ind Mgmt, Syracuse Univ, NY 1947-50; Prof Ind Mgmt, USC, La, Ca 1950-52; Tech Writer, Milit etc 1952-72; Dean, VP & PR, CalChris Univ 1972-80; Asst Dean, Woodbury Col 1964; Asst Dir, Frohme Sch, Pasadena, Calif 1969; Dean then Asst to Pres, Calif Christian Univ, La, Calif 1972-80; Apptd to Presidency at death of Dr Rummerfield; Rtd but ednl res continues. *Creative Works:* Inventions incl Office Organizer; Writer- Reschr: Life & Accomplishments of Charles Goodyear and 7 other Inventors of the Goodyear Family. *Memberships:* SIE Honorary; AAUP; Soc Applied Ind Engrg, VP; Sgt at Arms, Lambda Chapt of Psi Upsilon Frat 1930-. *Honours:* 87 Suggestion Awds from Pratt & Whitney & Brewster Aeronautical Corp pre 1943; US Patent, Office Org, 1987; Man of the Year, 1991. *Hobbies:* Chess; Profl fencing Instructor; Tennis. *Address:* 23/15111 Bushard, Westminster, CA 92683, USA. 59.

GOPAL R, b. 6 Aug 1952, Bombay, Indian. Businessman. m. Vijaya Lakshmi, 10 Sept 1979. *Education:* Engrg Deg in Elec; Postgrad Dipl in Computer Engrg. *Appointments:* Owner of marketing company since 1983 trading in RF & Microwave products. *Memberships:* IEEE (USA). *Hobbies:* Reading; Travel. *Address:* 1010/C 2nd Stage, Indira Nagar, Bangalore 560038, India.

GORAS Liviu, b. 20 Oct 1948, Jasi, Romania. Assoc Prof; Electr Engr. m. Alexandrescu Tecla Castelia, 21 Nov 1981, 1 s. *Education:* Tchg Asst 1971-78, Lectr 1978-90, Fac Elect Engrg, Assoc Prof, Fac Electr & Telecommunications 1990-, Poly Inst Jasi. *Publications:* About 50 papers in var tech res jours; Tchr, 2 semester course on Signals, Circuits & Systems. *Membership:* IEEE. *Hobbies:* Aphorisms; Music. *Address:* Polytechnic Institute Jasi, Faculty of Electronics & Telecommunications, Bd Copou 11, Jasi 6600, Romania.

GORDIENKO Vadim V, b. 20 Jan 1939, Kazan, USSR. Geophysicist. m. Lyudmila Gordienko, 29 June 1961, 2 s. *Education:* Dr of Geol and Minerol, 1978, Kiev State Univ. *Appointments:* Geophysicist, Geol Ser, 1961-63, Res Worker, Inst of Geophys, Ukrainian Acad of Scis, 1963-87, Head, 1987-. *Publications:* Keat anomalies of the geosynclines, 1975; Geophysical model of the Europe tectonosphere, 1987. *Memberships:* Tectonosphere Com of the Ukraine; Geodynamics and Earthquake Prognosis Com, Ukraine. *Honours:* State Prize of the Ukraine, 1984. *Hobbies:* Jogging; Slalom. *Address:* Institute of Geophysics, Ukranian Academy of Sciences, pr Palladina 32, 252680 Kiev 142, Ukraine.

GORDON Anthony George, b. 21 Apr 1925, London, England. Chmn Trade Assns. m. Sylvia Levers, 22 Apr 1966, 2 s. *Education:* Corpus Christi Col, Cambridge 1943-44, 1946-47; RAF Col, Cranwell 1945. *Appointments:* Pilot, RAF 1945-46; River Plate Freight Com & Intl Meat Trade Assn 1950-. *Memberships:* Assn Brit Meat Processors, Chmn 1986-1992; European Abattoir Union, Pres 1990-; Nat Assn of Catering Butchers, Exec Dir 1983-; London Meat Trades & Drovers Benevolent Assn, Pres 1979. *Honour:* MBE 1979. *Hobbies:* Tennis; Photography; Shooting. *Address:* 55 Fentiman Road, London SW8 1LH, England.

GORDON Eric Arthur, b. 3 Jan 1945, New Haven, Connecticut. Writer. *Education:* BA 1966, Yale Univ; MA 1969, PhD 1978, Tulane Univ. *Appointments:* Manchester Community Col 1972-75; Sephardic Home for the Aged 1982-84; G Schirmer 1984-86; Social and Public Art Resource Ctr 1990-. *Publications:* Mark the

Music: The Life and Work of Marc Blitzstein, 1989; Ballad of an American, co-Author with Earl Robinson-his autobiography. *Memberships:* Secy, Friends of Earl Robinson; Bd mem, Srn Calif Lib for Social Science & Res; Adv Bd, Jewish Currents magazine. *Hobbies:* Philately; Body culture; Music. *Address:* c/o Frances Goldin, Literary Agent, 305 E 11th Street 3F, New York, NY 10003, USA.

GORDON John Keith, b. 6 July 1940, Fleet, Hants, England. Environmentalist. m. Elizabeth Shanks, 14 Aug 1965, 2 s. *Education:* 1st class Hons in History 1961, Trinity Col, Cambridge; Yale Univ; London Sch Ec. *Appointments:* Entered FCO 1966; Budapest 1968-70; Seconded to Civil Svc Col 1970-72; FCO 1972-73; UK Mission, Geneva 1973-74; Hd of Chancery & Consul, Yaounde 1975-77, concurrently Charge d'Affaires, Gabon & Central African Repub; FCO 1977-80; Cutlural Attache, Moscow 1980-81; Office of UK Rep to European Community, Brussels 1982-83; UK Permanent Del to UNESCO, Paris 1983-85; Hd of Nuclear Energy Dept, FCO 1986-88; Acad Vstr, Ctr for Environ Tech, Imperial Col, London 1988-90; Deputy & Policy Dir, Global Environ Res Ctr, Imperial Col of Sci, Tech & Med, London 1990-. *Publication:* Co-Author, Institutions and Sustainable Development: Bridging the Gap. *Memberships:* Fellow, Royal Soc Arts. *Hobbies:* Walking; Jogging; Sailing. *Address:* Global Environment Research Centre, 56 Queen's Gate, London SW7 5JR, England. 1.

GORDON Michael, b. 7 May 1941, New York, USA. Physician. m. Gilda C Berger, 2 s. 2 d. *Education:* BA Chem 1962, Brooklyn Col; MB Ch B with commendation 1966, Univ St Andrews, Dundee, Scotland; MD; FRCPC. *Appointments:* Trng: Aberdeen City Hosp, Boston Univ Hosp, Royal Victoria Hosp (Montreal), Hadassah & Shaare Zedek Hosps (Jerusalem), Toronto Gen & Mt Sinai Hosps (Toronto) 1966-75; Asst Prof 1977-85, Assoc Prof Med, Univ Toronto 1985-; Geriatrician 1976-78, Hd Div Geriatrics 1984-, Mt Sinai Hosp; Sr Conslt 1976-89, Med Dir 1989-, Baycrest Ctr for Geriatric Care. *Publications:* Old Enough to Feel Better-A Medical Guide for Seniors, 1981, 1988, 1990; An Ounce of Prevention-A Canadian Guide to a Healthy & Successful Retirement. *Memberships:* Am Col Physicians; Royal Col Physicians & Surgs of Can; Am Geriatrics Soc; Gerpntological Soc of Am; Can Soc for Geriatric Med. *Honours:* Smoking and Health Action Foun & the Non-Smoker's Rights, 1985; Awd of Merit, Can Mental Health Assn, 1986. *Hobbies:* Music; Writing. *Address:* Baycrest Centre for Geriatric Care, 3560 Bathurst Street, Toronto, Canada M6A 2E1. 142.

GORDON LENNOX Ellinor Caroline Lila, b. 28 July 1952, London, England. Yoga Tchr; Dance therapist. *Education:* Elementary & Intermediate RAD, Elmhurst Ballet Sch, 1968; Pursuing Yoga Dipl Course. *Career:* Danced in Chichester Cathedral; Danced with John Curry in Coventry Cathedral, 1976; Taught ballet which developped into Dance Therapy for Children 1986. *Publications:* Written poetry; Painted nature in watercolour; Illustrated publication of Pat Chittananda's Meditation Book. *Memberships:* Patron of Meditational Arts of Sound & Light under Dennis Stoll; Royal Acad Dancing; Brit Wheel of Yoga. *Honour:* Won Mary Hayley Bell Cup for Writing. *Hobbies:* Singing; Reflexology; Any form of dance; T'ai Chi Chuan; The Alexander Technique; Painting; Drawing. *Address:* Goodwood House, Chichester, Sussex, England.

GORECKA Bozena, b. 11 Feb 1958, Sierpc, Poland. Graphic Artist; Art Painter. m. 13 June 1981, 1 s. *Education:* Studied painting at Acad Fine Arts in Lodz, Poland pvtly at the studio of Mr Wlodzistaw Sier, Lodz 1975-78; Studied painting under direction of Prof W Sliwinski in Warsaw 1988- 90; Studied the History of Art, Philosophy & Morphology at Acad of Scis, San Marino, Italy 1980-. Received the right to teach the Esperanto langs at lectorates 1984. *Career:* Managed own Advertising Studio and Photography in Ciechanow

1980-; Organised many exhibitions of her drawings & paintings; Participated in exhibitions of paintings at Barbakan Gallery in Warsaw. *Creative Works:* Miniatures of her paintings are in Museum of Kleinkunstin Holstebro, Denmark; Arts have been pub regarding Esperanto lang; 30 drawings & 2 paintings 1975-78; 7 paintings, 50 graphic art, 50 miniature of paintings, 10 drawings 1979-91. *Memberships:* Polish Artist Union, Warsaw 1979-91; Int Acad of Lutece, Beauty Art Sect, Paris 1989-91; Barbakan Gp, Warsaw 1989-91; World Esperanto Union, Rotterdam, Del 1989-91; Acad Sci, Art Sect, San Marino, Itlay 1990-91. *Honours:* Hon Dipl, Museum of Kleinkunst, Holstebro, Denmark, 1988; Hon fem mem, Centro Cultural, Literario e Artistico, Felqueiros, Portugal, 1989; Livre d'Or of Intl Acad de Lutece, Paris, 1990. *Hobbies:* Tourism; Gymnastics; Dance; Gardening. *Address:* Wyzwolenia 22, 06.400 Ciechanow, Poland. 152.

GORMAN William Moore, b. 17 June 1923, Kesh, N Ireland. Academic. m. Dorinda Maud Scott, 29 Dec 1950. *Education:* Mount Temple Sch, Dublin; Foyle Col, Derry; Naval Svc; BA 1948, Trinity Col, Dublin. *Appointments:* Asst, L, & Sr L, Univ Birmingham 1949-63; Prof Ec, Univ Oxford 1962-67; Prof Ec, LSE 1967-79; Fellow, Nuffield Col, Oxford 1962-67, 1979-90. *Publications:* Arts in var ec jours. *Memberships:* Econometric Soc, European Chmn, 1971-73, Pres 1972; Ec Study Soc, Chmn 1963-65. *Honours:* Fellows: Econometric Soc 1962, Brit Acad 1976; Hon f mem: Am Ec Assn 1987, Am Acad Arts & Scis 1986; Mem Academiae Europaea 1990; Hon Fellow, Trinity Col, Dublin 1990; Hon Doctorates: Birmingham 1973, S'Hampton 1974, Nat Univ of Ireland 1986. *Hobbies:* Talking; Reading. *Address:* 32 Victoria Road, Oxford OX2 7QD, England. 1, 2, 34, 43, 52.

GOROVEI Stefan-Sorin, b. 28 July 1948, Falticeni. Reschr; Historian. *Education:* Student, Fac of History 1966-71; MSc 1971. *Appointments:* Sub-Edit, Magazin Istoric, Bucharest 1971-77; Reschr, History Inst A D Xenopol 1977-. *Publications:* Books: Dragos Si Bogdan, 1973; Musatinii, 1976, 1991; Dragomirna, 1978; Petru Rares, 1982. *Memberships:* Comm of Genealogy, Heraldry & Sigillography, Bucharest, 1971; Assn of the European Historians, Rome 1985; Majestas Soc, Toronto 1985. *Honour:* N Balcescu Prize of Romanian Academy 1978. *Hobbies:* Music; Poetry. *Address:* History Institute A D Xenopol, Bd Lascar Catargi 15, RO-6600 Iasi 1, Romania.

GORSKI Andrzej, b. 11 Aug 1946, Wroclaw, Poland. Prof Med & Immunol. m. 16 Oct 1988, 2 d. *Education:* MD 1970, PhD 1973, Warsaw Med Sch; Fulbright Scholar, Sloan-Kettering Inst for Cancer Res, NY, USA 1974-76; Prof Med & Immunol 1988. *Appointments:* Warsaw Med Sch 1970-; Hd Dept Immunol, Transplantation Inst, Warsaw Med Sch 1984-. *Memberships:* Am Assn Immunologists; Transplantation Soc; Intl Soc Exptl Haematol; and others; Pres, Immunol Com, Polish Acad Scis; Hd, Senate Comm for Sci, Warsaw Med Sch; Hd, Nat Com for Coop with Intl Union Immun Soc. *Honours:* Meller Awd for excellence in cancer res, Sloan-Kettering Inst for Cancer Res, NY 1976; J Sniadecki Memorial Awd-highest awd in med scis in Poland, 1988. *Hobbies:* Languages; Ethymology; History; Bridge. *Address:* Dept of Immunology, Transplantation Institute, Warsaw Medical School, 02006 Warsaw 22, Poland.

GORSTKO Alexander Borisovich, b. 4 Feb 1934, Kharkov, USSR. Mathematician. m. Olga Mordvinkina, 18 Dec 1979, 2 d. *Education:* Dipl 1956, Kharkov Univ; Degree Candidate of Maths Scis 1967; Title Docent 1969; Degree Dr of Math Scis 1979; Title Prof 1980. *Appointments:* Asst Prof Eng Sch Kharkov 1956-62; Reschr, Inst Math, Siberian Div of Acad of Scis, USSR 1962-72; Chmn of Applied Math & Programming, Rostov Univ 1973-. *Publications:* Over 150 sci works incl 6 Books among them: Optimal Solutions in the Economy, Co-Author, 1972; Meet the Mathematical

Modeling, 1991. *Memberships:* Sci Coun, System Analysis of Water Problems, USSR Acad of Scis; Rostov Math Soc; Sci City Coun of Rostov for Environ Problems; Sci Coun of Rostov Univ. *Honours:* USSR State Prize, 1983; Fulbright Scholarship, USA 1990; Adj Prof of Maths, Univ of Wisconsin-Superior, USA 1990. *Hobbies:* Skiing; Jogging; Swimming; Yoga. *Address:* Zorge str 5, Rostov University, Math Faculty, Rostov-on-Don, Russia.

GORZELSKI Roman, b. 12 Apr 1934, Luck, Poland. Writer; Journalist. *Education:* Col, Lodz 1954; Univ Warsaw 1962. *Appointments:* Tchr of Secondary Sch 1962-70; Journalist & Writer 1960- 91. *Publications:* 4 plays; 5 books translated into Polish; 9 books poetry; 2 books of aphorism; Short story collections incl: Three Blueses, 1969; Western, 1970; H and G, 1973; The Town and the Poem, 1975; Pronunciation of Words, 1977; Policeman Brandy, 1982; The Pichna River, 1986; Affair in One Sentence, 1989; Tales Not Far From the Truth, 1991; Funny Tales, 1991. *Memberships:* Union of Polish Writers; Polish Soc of Authors; Assn of Authors and Composers. *Honours:* Nike Warszawska Awd, 1969; Merit of Polish Culture Awd, 1977; Merit of Lodz Town Awd, 1986. *Hobbies:* Serious music; Animals-cats & dogs; Cycling; Fencing; Swimming; Travelling. *Address:* ul Chodkiewicza 6, 94-028 Lodz, Poland. 3, 152.

GOSHEN-GOTTSTEIN Moshe Henry, b. 6 Sept 1925, Berlin. Philologist; Edr. m. Esther R Hepner, 27 July 1953, 2 s. *Education:* MA 1947, PhD 1951, Hebrew Univ, Jerusalem. *Appointments:* Prof Bibl & Semitic Philology, Hebrew Univ, Jerusalem 1950-91; Dir Bible Project 1955-91; Dir, Inst for Lexicography & Jewish Bible Resch, Bar Ilan Univ, Ramatgan, Israel 1970-91; Past VP World Union Bible Studies. *Memberships:* World Union for Jewish Studies; Soc for Bibl Lit. *Publications:* Author & Edit, 20 books & over 400 arts. *Honour:* Recip Israel Prize for Jewish Studies, Ministry Ed & Culture, 1988. *Address:* 17 Jabotinsky Str, Jerusalem, Israel.

GOTO Ken, b. 13 Dec 1952, Yokosuka, Japan. Assoc Prof. m. 18 Nov 1975, 1 s. 1 d. *Education:* BSc 1975, Kyoto Univ; MSc 1977, DSc 1980, Nagoya Univ. *Appointments:* Postdoc Res Assoc, SUNY 1982-83; Postdoc Res Assoc, Inst Applied Biochem, Mitake, Gifu 1984-86; Assoc Prof, Obihiro Univ 1986-. *Contributions to:* Models in Plant Physiol & Biochem, 1987; Contbr, Handbooks of Chronobiology, 1991. *Memberships:* Botanical Soc Japan; Jap Soc Plant Physiol; Am Soc Plant Physiol; Jap Soc Biochem; Intl Soc Chronobiol; Soc for Res on Biol Rhythms. *Honours:* Jap Soc for the Promotion of Sci Fellow, 1980-82; NSF Fellow 1982-83; Inst Applied Biochem Fellow 1984-86; Ministry of Ed, Sci & Culture Res Grantee 1987-88, 1990-91. *Address:* Biology Laboratory, Obihiro University of Agricultural & Vet Medicine, Obihiro, Japan 080. 52.

GOTO Kimio, b. 30 Mar 1926, Japan. Univ Prof Computer Sci. m. Yahoko Goto, 18 Dec 1958, 1 s. 1 d. *Education:* BEng 1951, PhD Elect Engr 1981, Tokyo Univ. *Appointments:* Reschr, Central Res Lab of Hitachi Ltd 1951-60; Chf of Design Sect, Totsuka Factory, Hitachi Ltd 1971; Tchr, Hitachi Keihin Tech Col 1971-84; Prof, Dept Compt Sci, Kanagawa Inst of Tech 1984-. *Publications:* Book, Pulse Circuit, in Japanese, 1978; 25 Japanese Patents; 1 US Patent. *Memberships:* Inst Electr Engrs of Japan; Inst Electronics, Info & Communication Engrs of Japan; Info Processing Soc of Japan; IEEE. *Hobby:* Reading. *Address:* 2-11-6 Honfujisawa, Fujisawa City, Kanagawa Prefecture, Japan 251. 52, 132.

GOTO Kunio, b. 3 Oct 1930, Japan. Univ Prof. m. Motoko Kuwaharda, 29 Mar 1958, 1 s. 1 d. *Education:* Dept Physics, Nagoya Univ 1950-55; MS in Physics 1957, Grad Sch of Physics, Nagoya Univ. *Appointments:* Res Asst of Physics Inst, Nagoya Univ 1960-61; Lectr 1961-, Prof 1968-, St Andrew's Univ, Osaka. *Publications:* Introduction to the History of Science Study, 1969; Civilsation, Technology & Human Beings,

1971. *Memberships:* Physical Soc of Japan; Fellow, History of Sci Soc of Japan; Fellow, Japan Soc of History of Indl Tech; Fellow, Liberal & Gen Ed Soc of Japan. *Hobby:* Go playing. *Address:* 5-1-47 Satsukigaoka, Ikeda, Osaka 563, Japan. 52.

GOTOH Hiroki, b. 21 Feb 1937, Osaka, Japan. Univ Prof. m. 1 Apr 1973. *Education:* BA 1961, Kyoto Univ of Foreign Studies; MA 1967, Univ Mich, Ann Arbor, Mich, USA. *Appointments:* Die, Eng Lang Inst, Osaka 1961-63; Assoc Dir, Tokyo YMCA English Lang Sch, Tokyo 1968-69; Lectr, Intl Col of Commerce & Ec, Kawagoe, Saitama 1969-71; Lectr 1971-73, Asst Prof 1973-79, Full Prof 1979-, Chuo Univ, Tokyo; Vstg Scholar, Univ Mich 1981-83; Pres of the Soc of Eng Lang & Lit, Chuo Univ 1986-87; Dir of Crescent Acad at Chuo Univ 1989-. *Publications:* Idiomatic English, 1968; Edit, American English, 1973; Co-Author, English-Japanese Dictionary, 1976; Senior English-Japanese Dictionary, 1970; A Historical Study of the Southwestern Dialect Used in Mark Twain's Works, 1976. *Memberships:* Soc English Lang & Lit; English Linguistic Soc of Japan. *Honour:* Rough Sea, a Japanese painting, was awd'd in 1975 under the auspices of the Bd of Ed at Matsudo City, Chiba, Japan. *Hobbies:* Travel; Painting; Photography; Tennis. *Address:* Chuo University, Room number 2919, 2nd Building, 741-1 Higashinakano, Hachioji City, Tokyo 192-03, Japan. 52.

GOTSEV Kiril, b. 10 Dec 1957, Sofia, Bulgaria. Video Engr. m. Krasimira, 17 Oct 1981, 1 s. *Education:* Dipl Engr of Electronics & Automation 1989, Tech Univ Sofia. *Appointments:* Bulgarian Television 1985-. *Creative Works:* Participation over 30 photo exhibitions, nat & intl. *Membership:* Bulgarian Photographic Assn 1986-. *Honours:* from nat compts of Bulgaria 1980-; FIAP 15th Intl Salon of Photographic Art; FIAP 18th Monochrome Biennial, San Marino, 1985. *Hobbies:* Applied electronics; Home movies. *Address:* 85 Tolbouchin Bld, Sofia 1000, Bulgaria.

GOTTLIEB A Arthur, b. 14 Dec 1937, USA. m. Marise S 1958, 2 d. *Education:* AB Chem, Columbia Col, 1957; MD, NY Univ Sch of Med, 1961. *Appointments:* ASst Prof of Med, Harvard Med Sch, 1969; Assoc Prof, 1969-72, Prof, 1972-75, Microbiol, Rutgers Univ, NJ; Prof and Chm, Dept of Mircobiol and Immunol, Tulane Univ SCh of Med, New Orleans, presently. *Publications:* Numerous patents, papers and articles including: Concepts in question regarding HIV infection, 1990; Development of Immunomodulators for treatment of HIV infection, 1990; Clinic and immunologic observations in patients with Aids related complex treated with IMREG-1, 1991. *Memberships include:* AAAS; AACR; AAI; ACS; ASBC; ASCB; ASCI; ASM. *Honours include:* Phi Beta Kappa; Alpha Omega Alpha; Frances Stone Burns Awd, Am Cancer Soc; Travelling Fellow, RSM; FACPhys; FAAMicro; Various visiting professorships; Mayor's Cert of Merit, City of New Orleans, 1985.

GOTTLIEB Paul, b. 29 June 1936, Budapest. Prof; Writer. m. Dr Erika Gottlieb, 19 Mar 1961, 1 s. 1 d. *Education:* BA 1964, MA 1970, Sir George Williams Univ, Montreal. *Appointments:* Creative Dir of major Toronto Advtg agencies 1977-86; Columnist, Mktg Mag 1986-. *Publications:* The Agent of Aquarius, thesis, 1970; Agency, novel, 1974; Screenwriter in Praise of Older Women, RSL Prod 1976. *Memberships:* Acad Can Cinema & Television; Writers Guild of Can; Writers Union of Can; Writers Guild of Am (East). *Honours:* Num adtg awds incl CLIOs, BESSIEs, NY Film & Television Festival, Hollywood Radio TV Festival. *Hobbies:* Film; Reading; Chess. *Address:* Toronto, Canada.

GOUGH Orlando Matthew Leslie, b. 24 Aug 1953, Brighton, Sussex, England. Composer. m. Joanna Osborne, 2 Dec 1989, 2 s. *Education:* Oxford, 1st in Maths, 1971-74. *Appointments:* Composer 1974-; Tchr, Lansdowne Tutors, London 1977-86. *Creative Works:* The Complete A Level Maths, 1987; Fdr Mem Bands The Lost Jockey & Man Jumping; Main Compositions:

Hoovering the Beach, 1979; Buzz Buzz Buzz Went the Honeybee, 1981; New Tactics, 1982; Further & Further into Night, 1984; Mozart at Palm Springs, 1984; Bogendorfer Waltzes, 1985; Weighing the Heart, 1987; Goes Without Saying, 1989; Currulao, 1990; Slow Walk Fast Talk, 1990; The Mathematics of a Kiss, 1990; Lives of the Great Poisoners, 1991; The Air Shouts, 1991; Touch Your Coolness To My Fevered Brow, 1992; The Empress of Newfoundland, 1992. *Hobbies:* Cooking; Juggling; Cricket; Squash. *Address:* 12 Spencer Rise, London NW5 1AP, England.

GOULD Cecil Hilton Monk, b. 24 May 1918, London, England. Keeper & Dep Dir of the Nat Gallery, London. *Education:* Pvtly in Germany 1936-37. *Appointments:* RAF Ofcr 1940-46; Nat Gallery, London 1946-78, Dep Keeper 1962, Keeper & Dep Dir 1973-; Vstg Lectr, Melbourne Univ 1978. *Publications:* Books: An Introduction to Italian Renaissance Painting, 1957; Trophy of Conquest, 1965; Leonardo da Vinci, 1975; The Paintings of Correggio, 1976; Bernini in France, 1982; Var pubs for the Nat Gallery incl 16th century Italian Schs catalogue; Arts in Encyclopaedia Britannica, Chambers's Encyclopaedia, Dizionario Biografico degli Italiani, and specialist art jours of Europe & USA. *Membership:* FRSA, 1968. *Hobbies:* Music; Travel. *Address:* Jubilee House, Thorncombe, Chard, Somerset TA20 4PP, England. 1.

GRABOIS Aryeh, b. 9 July 1930, Odessa. Prof Mediaeval History. m. Carmela Langleben, 20 Apr 1966, 1 d. *Education:* BA 1958, MA 1961, Hebrew Univ of Jerusalem; PhD 1963, Univ Dijon, France. *Appointments:* Lectr, Hebrew Univ of Jerusalem 1963-65; Prof, Univ Haifa, Israel 1963-, Dean Grad Sch; Vstg Prof, Univ Calif at Berkeley 1979-80. *Publications:* 7 books incl: Illustrated Encyclopaedia of the Middle Ages, 1980; Civilisation et Societe dans l'Occident Medieval, 1983; Les Sources Hebraiques du Moyen Age, 1988; 100 scholarly papers in English, French & Hebrew. *Memberships:* Israeli Historical Soc, VP 1983-86; Soc d'Etudes Medievales; Soc des Antiquaires de France; Soc for Study of the Crusades and Latin East Haskins' Soc, USA; Ben-Zwi Inst for Palestinography, mem Coun. *Honours:* Ordre Nat du Progres (France), Medaille Vermeil, 1976; Ordre des Palmes Academiques (France): Chevalier, 1980, Officier, 1990. *Hobbies:* Theatre; Politics & Economics. *Address:* University of Haifa, The Dean of Graduate School, Mt Carmel, Haifa 31999, Israel.

GRABOWSKA Dorota, b. 19 Jan 1968, Bielsk Podlaski, Poland. m. Piotr Grabowski, 2 Sept 1990, 1 d. *Education:* Masters Deg, Warsaw Univ, 1986-91. *Appointments:* Librarian in Primary Sch, Warsaw, 1990- 91; Asst Warsaw Univ Inst of Lib and Info Sci, 1992-. *Publications:* three papers in, Library and Guide Library, both Polish periodicals. *Hobbies:* Reading; Films; Embroidery. *Address:* Suwalska 40m 28, 03-252 Warsaw, Poland.

GRABOWSKA-HAWRYLAK Jadwiga, b. 29 Oct 1920, Tarnawce, Poland. Henryk Hawrylak, 16 Dec 1948, 2 s, 1 d. *Education:* MArch, Tech Univ of Wroclaw, 1950. *Appointments:* Dept of Freehand Drawing, Tech Univ of Wroclaw, 1948-49; Design Ofc, Arkady, 1948-51; Res Design Ofc, Miastoprojekt, Wroclaw, 1951-81; SARP Studio of Architectonic Sers, 1988-; Own studio, 1981-. *Creative works:* Solo and group exhibitions of drwings; Articles published in professional journals. *Memberships:* Wroclaw TP and Arch Comm, 1975-80; Min of Culture and Arts Comm on Arch Creativity, 1979-83; TP and Arch Comm of Polish Acad of Scis; Assoc of Archs SARP, 1951-; SARB Bd, 1978081, 1987-91. *Honours include:* Outstanding Architectonic Creation Awd, SARP, 1984; Golden Cross of merit, 1972; Knight's Cross of Merit, 1986. *Hobbies:* Travelling; Skiing. *Address:* 84a/1 Kochanowskiego Street, 51-601 Wroclaw, Poland.

GRAC Jan, b. 5 Apr 1930, Kovarce, Topolcany, Slovakia, CSFR. Psychologist. m. Zuzana Durisova, 15 Aug 1959, 1 s. 1 d. *Education:* Grad Psychol 1956; Grad Philos & History 1959; PhDr 1968; CSc 1966; DrSc 1991; Assoc Prof 1974; Prof 1992. *Appointments:* Employee in Bratislava: Regl Ednl Inst 1956- 61; Secondary Sch Tchr 1961-64; Ednl Res Inst 1964-66; Comenius Univ 1966-. *Publications:* 323 titles pub incl: 14 independent book monographs, 14 univ textbooks, 74 sci studies, 150 profl works; Most important book monographs: How to learn successfully, 1964; Youth in Society, 1966; Social Contacts and Psychology of Youth Education, 1968; School and Psychology of Satisfaction of the Youth, 1973; Psychology of Self-Learning, 1978; Insights into the Psychology of Value Orientation of Youth, 1979; Psychology of the University Student, 1981; Persuasion-Influencing of Man by Man, 1985; Exemplification-Examples and Models in Life of Man, 1990. *Memberships:* Mem in sev expert coms for ed and trng of central and governmental institutions and organs in CSFR incl: mem, Comenius Univ Sci Bd. *Honours:* Honours degrees in 1956 & 1959; Medal of the Czecho-Slovak Red Cross, 1981; Medal of Comenius Univ, 1990; Literary Prizes in the category of the lit of fact, 1973, and in the cat of sci lit, 1986; Prize for original work, 1988. *Hobbies:* Active stay in nature; Cottage works & gardening. *Address:* Katedra psychologickych vied, Filozoficka fakulta University Komenskeho, 811 02 Bratislava, Gondova 2, CSFR.

GRACE Sherrill Elizabeth, b. 18 Aug 1944, Ormstown, Quebec. Canada. Prof Eng; Assoc Dean Arts. *Education:* BA Eng 1965, Univ Western Ontario; MA Eng 1970, PhD 1974, McGill Univ. *Appointments:* Lectr in English 1974-75, Asst Prof Eng 1975-77, McGill; Asst Prof Eng 1977-81, Assoc Prof Eng 1981-87, Full Prof Eng 1987-, Assoc Dean Arts 1991-, UBC. *Publications:* Regression & Apocalypse: Studies in North American Literary Expressionism, 1989; The Voyage That Never Ends: Malcolm Lowry's Fiction, 1982; Violent Duality: An Introduction to Margaret Atwood, 1980; 2 edited books; 90 arts, review arts, chapts in books; Currently editing Collected Letters of Malcolm Lowry, 2 vols. *Memberships:* Can Assn Am Studies, Pres 1989-91; Assn Can Univ Tchrs of Eng; Can Comparative Lit Assn; Modern Lang Assn; Assn for Theatre History in Can; Assn for Can Studies. *Honours:* Elected Fellow of the Royal Soc of Can, 1991; Killam Res Prize 1990; Killam Res Fellow, 1990-91; Social Scis & Humanities Res Coun of Can Res Leave Stipend, 1989-90; DAAD Fellowship 1985; Can Coun Doctoral Fellow 1971-74. *Hobbies:* Art collecting; Music; Gardening; Wilderness activities. *Address:* Dept of English, 397-1873 East Mall, The University of British Columbia, Vancouver, BC, Canada V6T 1W5. 138.

GRACEY Peter Bosworth Kirkwood, b. 12 Dec 1921, Bannu, Pakistan. Dir; Mus Pubr. m. (1) 1 s, 2 d, (2) Jane Owen, dec May 1987, (3)Andra Julia Mary Duckworth, 4 Feb 1989. *Education:* BA Maths 1941, BA Ec with Stats 1948 (now MA), Brasenose Col, Oxford. *Appointments:* World War II, Commissioned RE 1941, 2nd Lt 280 Parachute Sqn, 81st Inf Div HQ, West African Engrs RWAFF; Capt RE OC Gold Coast FD Co 1946; Tate & Lyle Ltd 1948-62; London Mgr, TPT 1955; Gen Mgr & Dir Sturgeons TPT 1963; Gen Mgr, Marley Tile TPT 1968; Distn Dir, Lyons Bakery 1973; Dir, Bosworth & Co (Mus Pubrs) 1973; Hill Samuel Fin Svcs 1978-91; Harsard Financial, 1992-. *Memberships:* Com Nat Freight Transport Assn 1976; Pres Oxford & Cambridge Golfing Soc 1987-91; Hon Secy 1959-66; Capt 1970-71; Freeman City of London 1970; Worshipful Co of Wax Chandlers 1970; Capt Old Wellingtonian Golfing Soc 1970; Capt County Cricketers Golfing Soc 1960. *Honours:* German Recitation Prize, Wellington Col 1940; Gold Medal, Wellington Col, 1940; Hons degree (Oxon), 1941, 1948.Scholarships to Wellington Col & Oxford Univ. *Hobbies:* Sport; Music; Literature. *Address:* The Oast House, Houghton Green Lane, Playden, Rye, East Sussex TN31 7PJ, England.

GRACNER Miro, b. 16 Dec 1936. Electronic Engineering Research Management. m. Vesna, 26 Apr 1975. *Education:* BSE, Univ of Sagreb, 1961. *Appointments:* Tchr, Fac of Elec Engrg, Univ of Zagreb, 1969; TV Set Specialist, RIZ TV Prod, 1962-64; Div Mgr, RIZ Maintenance and Repair, 1965-68; Devel Specialist, 1969-7 Gp Leader, Reschr, 1972-75, Div Mgr, 1976-85, Sys Engr, 1986-90, RIZ Inst: Colour TV set and Profl Video Equipment Devel; Tech Conslt, Sistemprojekt Zagreb, 1991-. *Publications:* Co- author, TV Set Handbook for you, 1967, Family of professional video and data graphic monitors development: research project; TV-set course organizer, 1965- 68; Network planning applied on colour TV set pilot production, 1976-78; *Memberships:* Croatian Nat Sci Coun.1982-86; Chamber of Economy in Zagreb. *Honours:* Special Citation of Sci Proj Com for Dist Contrib in Devel of First Monochrome Monitor in Ex-Yugoslavia, 1982; Best Pruj Awd for Profl Colour Graphic Monitor. *Hobbies:* Table Tennis; Winter Skiing; Ecology; Hatha Yoga; Holistic recuperation methods. *Address:* Sistemprojekt, Rakusina 4, 4100 Zagreb, Croatia.

GRAHAM Alexander Michael, b. 27 Sept 1938, London, England. Lloyd's Insurance Broker. m. Carolyn Stansfeld, 6 June 1964, 3 d. *Education:* St Paul's Sch, London; FCII; FCIS. *Appointments:* Broker 1957-65, Gen Mgr 1965-67, Dir 1967-, Norman Frizzell Ptnrs Ltd; Mng Dir, The Frizzell Gp Ltd 1973-90, Dep Chmn 1990-. *Memberships:* FCII, VP 11 of London; FCIS; FBIIBA; FRSA; CBIM. *Honours:* JP 1978; DCL 1990; GBE 1990. *Hobbies:* Wine Genealogy; Music; Reading; Silver; Bridge; Golf; Tennis; Swimming; Shooting; Education; Lord Mayor of London 1990-91; Sheriff City of London 1986-87; Master Mercers Co 1983-84. *Address:* Walden Abbotts, Whitwell, Hitchin, Herts SG4 8AJ, England. 1.

GRAHAM Donald Ralph, b. 3 Aug 1947, Regina, Sask. Lighthouse Keeper. m. Elaine Mary Cawker, 4 Jan 1969, 2 s. *Education:* BA 1968, MA 1971, Univ Sask, 1973. *Appointments:* Economist, Exec Coun, Govt Sask 1968-69; Tchg Asst 1972; Cultural Conservation Coord, Province of Sask 1972-76; Lighthouse Keeper, Can Coastguard 1979-91. *Publications:* Keepers of the Light: A History of British Columbia's Lighthouses and Their Keepers, 1985; Lights of the Inside Passage: A History of British Columbia's Lighthouses and Their Keepers, 1986. *Memberships:* Chmn, French of Cypress; Dir, Heritage Forest Soc; Co-Fdr, Gulf Environmental Emergency Response Team; Dir, Regina Community Health Clinic. *Honour:* BC Book Prizes: Roderick Haig-Brown Regl Prize for best BC non fiction work. *Hobbies:* Deep Ecology; Peace. *Address:* Point Atkinson Lightstation, PO Box 91338, West Vancouver, BC, Canada V7V 3N9. 142.

GRAHAM Francis Walter, b. 28 Apr 1914, Ocean Island, Kiribati, Central Pacific. Physician; Psychi; Psychoanalyst. *Education:* MB, BS 1940, Sydney Univ, Aust; DPM 1944, Melbourne Univ; NYU, USA 1958-59.*Appointments include:* Work & study, Aust, England, India, USA; Hon Asst Psychi, 2nd in charge, Royal Melbourne (teaching) Hosp, 20 years; Currently: Hon Conslt Med Psychoanalyst, Prince Henry's Hosp, Melbourne (univ tchg); Assoc, Dept of Psychol Med, Monash Univ; Pvt Practice, p-time hosp work. *Publications:* Num profl papers, var jours & confs; Title include: Some Impressions of Group Psychotherapy; Psychotherapy with Psychotics; Psychiatry in General Practice; Yoga & Western Methods of Psychotherapy; On Repression. *Memberships include:* Past Pres, Aust Psychoanalytical Soc; Brit & Aust Med Assns; Aust & NZ Assn of Gp Psychotherapy; Aust Assn of Physical Med & Rehab; Soc for Res in Rehab, UK; Fellow, Royal Soc Med. *Honours:* Jessie Howard Gregg Fellow, NYU 1958- 59; FRC Psych (Foun); FRANZCP (Foun); FBPsS; FAPsS; FACRM; FAGPA; Mem Brit Psycho-analytical Soc; Mem of the Order of Australia (AM), 1991. *Hobbies:* Chess; Philosophy; Music. *Address:* 28 Pasley Street, South Yarra, Victoria 3141, Australia. 23.

GRAHAM Howard Lee Sr, b. 26 May 1942, Monroe, Michigan, USA. Company Pres. m. Bobbie Jo Hamilton, 2 Aug 1986, 2 s. 2 d. *Education:* Grad 1962, Dake Bibl Sch, Atlanta, Ga; Central Bibl Col, Springfield, Mo 1964-67; Lee Cpl, Cleveland, Tenn 1985; Life Underwriter Trng Course, 1964. *Appointments:* Debit Agt, Metro Life Ins Co 1963-68; Agency Mgr, Preferred Risk Ins Co 1968-72; Agency Owner, Howard Graham Ins Agency 1972-85; Spec Agt/Rep, Prudential Ins Co 1985-; Pres, Graham Enterprises 1985-; Pres, Graham & Graham Canvas Shoppe Inc 1976-. *Publications:* Author arts for periodicals on ins & investments. *Memberships:* Full Gospel Businessmen's Fellowship Intl 1963-; Pres & VP, Detroit, Mich Chapt 1972-80; Gideons Intl 1963-; Nat Assn Life Underwriters 1963-; Am Col 1985-; Indl Fabrics Assn Intl 1988-; Intl Platorm Assn 1989-; Am Entrepreneurs Assn 1989-. *Honours:* PR Dir & Fund Raiser for Real Life Childrens Ranch, a Protestant Home Mission) 1967-68; Nat & Regl Sales Ldr, Preferred Risk Ins Co 1969, 1970-72, resp; Prudential Ins Co hons: Central Regn Agent of the Year 1985; Million Dollar Round Table 1985; Hall of Hon 1986; Trustee, Repub Presidential Task Force 1984-. *Hobbies:* Avid reader; Pursuing a Business & a Bible degree; Presently researching & writing a book on end-time happenings/apocalyptic themes; Lectr on The Biblical Plan for Personal Finances, and God's Plan for the Family, and The Last Days. *Address:* 2853 Jonesboro Road, Abingdon, VA 24210, USA. 7, 52, 125, 132, 152.

GRAHAM Ian David, b. 9 May 1955, Alnwick, England. Barrister. *Education:* Christ Church, Oxford 1974-77, Open Exhibitioner, BA Hons Jurisprudence 1977, MA 1981. *Appointments:* Called to Bar, Middle Temple, 1978; Barrister, North Eastern Circuit 1979-. *Publications:* Arts in Catholic Periodicals 1988-. *Honours:* Harmsworth Exhibitioner, Middle Temple, 1977; Astbury Scholar, Middle Temple, 1978. *Hobbies:* Opera; Traditional Catholic music & liturgy. *Address:* 36 Burdon Terrace, Jesmond, Newcastle Upon Tyne NE2 3AE, England.

GRAHAM Neil Bonnette, b. 23 May 1933, Liverpool, England. Prof Chem. m. Marjorie Royden, 16 July 1955, 1 s. 3 d. *Education:* ALCM 1950; BSc 1953; PhD 1956; CChem; FRSC; FPRI; FRSE. *Appointments:* Can Inds Ltd, Can 1956-67; Imperial Chem Inds Ltd, UK 1967-73; Young Prof Chem Tech, Univ Strathclyde, Glasgow, Scotland 1973-84; Res Prof, Univ Strathclyde 1984-; Fdr & Dir of Polysystems Ltd 1980-90. *Publications:* Many sci papers & patents in fields of polymers & controlled drug delivery. *Memberships:* Fellow: Royal Soc Chem, Plastics & Rubber Inst, Royal Soc Edinburgh. *Hobbies:* Walking; Music; Sailing. *Address:* 6 Kilmardinny Grove, Bearsden, Glasgow G61 3NY, Scotland. 184.

GRAHAM Peter (pen name of Jaroslav Pokorny-Stastny), b. 1 July 1952, Brno. Composer. m. Julie Stastna, 6 Aug 1988, 2 d. *Education:* Conservatory, Brno, Organ 1975; Janacek Acad of Mus, Brno, Composition 1980. *Appointments:* Conservatory, Brno 1981; Theatre Divadlo na Provazku 1984; Radio Brno 1986; Czech Mus Fund, Prague 1989; Cernovice Mus Sch, Brno 1991. *Creative Works:* Compositions incl: 3 Orchestral with Soloists; 4 Chamber Music; 3 Instrumental; 4 for Percussion Instruments; 2 for Organ; 8 Solo Piano; 5 Vocal & Choral, most recently: Stabat Mater for mixed chorus, 1990; Ave Verum Corpus for soprano, clarinet & piano, 1990; Regen for soprano, flute & harp, 1991. *Membership:* Assn for New Music, 1990. *Hobbies:* Jazz; Oriental art; Gardening; Cooking. *Address:* Novodvorska 406/121, 142 00 Praha 4-Lhotka, Czechoslovakia.

GRAHAM Peter Walter, b. 14 Mar 1937, London, England. Lt Gen GOC Scotland; Gov Edinburgh Castle. m. Alison Mary Morren, 23 Mar 1963, 3 s. *Education:* RMA Sandhurst 1955-56; psc, Staff Col, Aust 1968; ndc, Nat Def Col, Can 1984-85. *Appointments:* Commd into Gordon Highlanders 1956; Regtl Appts, UK, BAOR,

Kenya 1957-63; Staff Capt, HQ Highland Bde, Perth 1962- 63; Adj, 1 Gordons, Kenya, Scotland, Borneo 1963-66; Staff Capt, HQ 1 (BR) Corps, BAOR 1966-67; Coy Comd, 1 Gordons 1969-70; BM, 39 Bde 1970-72; 2 ic, 1 Gordons, NI, Scotland, Singapore 1972-74; MA to the Adj Gen 1974-75; CO, 1 Gordons 1976-78; COS, HQ 3 Armd Div, BAOR 1978-82; Comd, UDR 1982-84; DMS 'B' MOD 1985-87; GOC Eastern District 1987-89; Comdt RMA Sandhurst 1989-91. *Creative Works:* Gordon Highlanders Pipe Music Collection vols I & II, with PM B Macrae; Art in RUSI jour. *Memberships:* Col The Gordon Highlanders 1986-; Col Commandant The Scottish Div 1991-; Royal Company of Archers, the Queen's Body Guard for Scotland 1985-. *Honours:* Mentioned in Despatches, 1966, 1984; MBE 1972; OBE 1978; CBE 1987; KCB 1991. *Hobbies:* Shooting; Fishing; Stalking; Hill walking; Reading; Bagpipe music; Gardening under wife's supervision. *Address:* c/o HQ Scotland Army, Craigie Hall, Edinburgh, Scotland. 1.

GRAHAM Peter William, b. 11 Feb 1951, Manchester, Connecticut, USA. Prof Eng. m. Kathryn Louise Videon, 28 Dec 1973, 2 s. *Education:* AB cum laude 1973, Davidson Col; MA 1974, PhD 1977, Duke Univ. *Appointments:* Asst Prof 1978-84, Assoc Prof 1984-90, Prof 1990-, Va Poly Inst & State Univ. *Publications:* Byron's Bulldog, 1984; Don Juan & Regency England, 1990; Articulating the Elephant Man, co-Author, 1992; Ed, Psychiatry & Literature, 1985; Fictive Ills, with Elizabeth Sewell, 1990. *Memberships:* Modern Lang Assn; Bd Edits, Literature & Medicine; Phi Beta Kappa; Intl Byron Soc. *Honours:* James B Duke Fellowship 1973-76; Lilly Postdoctoral Fellowship 1977-78; Mellon Postdoctoral Fellowship 1980- 81. *Hobbies:* Tennis; Walking; Gardening; Reading. *Address:* 208 Sunset Boulevard, Blacksburg, VA 24060, USA. 7.

GRANDE Zbigniew, b. 22 Nov 1946, Lutry, Poland. Mathematician. m. Eulalia, 24 Dec 1969, 1 s. *Education:* Master Maths 1968; Dr of Maths 1974; Habilitation 1978; Prof Math 1986. *Appointments:* Gdansk Univ 1964-75; Gdansk Tech Univ 1975-78; Bydgoszcz Pedagogical Univ 1978-89; Copernicus Univ in Torun 1989-91; Stupsk Pedagogical Univ 1991-. *Publication:* Dissert: La mesurabilité des fonctions de deux variables et de la superposition F(X,Ll(x)), 1979. *Membership:* Polish Math Soc. *Address:* ul Sandomierska 37/39, 85-830 Bydgoszcz, Poland.

GRANEAU Peter, b. 13 Mar 1921, Lissa, Poland. Physicist. m. Brigitte Weil, 24 Oct 1955, 1 s. *Education:* BSc with 1st class hons 1955, PhD 1962, Univ Nottingham, UK. *Appointments:* Dept Hd & Asst Mgr, BICC Res Lab, London 1955-67; Simplex Wire & Cable Co, MIT, Cambridge, MA, USA; Northeastern Univ, Boston. *Publications:* Books: Underground Power Transmission, 1979; Ampere-Neumann Electrodynamics, 1985; 80 pub papers. *Memberships:* Fellow, Brit Inst Physics; Sr mem, IEEE. *Hobbies:* Sailing; Tennis; Chess. *Address:* 205 Holden Wood Road, Concord, MA 01742, USA. 143.

GRANGER Derek Harold, b. 23 Apr 1921, Bramhall, Cheshire, England. Film, Television & Theatre Producer. *Education:* Eastbourne Col 1935-39. *Appointments includes:* Theatre & Film Critic, Financial Times 1952-68; Writer & Producer, Granada Television 1958-67; Producer, London Weekend Television 1967-69; Lit Conslt, Nat Theatre 1969-71; Producer, Granada Television 1971-81; Exec Producer, Goldcrest Films & Television 1982-84; Fdr Dir of Stagescreen Productions Ltd, 1984. *Creative Works:* Produced & script-edited 2 series of Country Matters 1972-73; Co-Produced a series of plays The Best Play of the Year 1976; Produced & Co-Scripted Brideshead Revisited 1981; Produced & Co-Scripted the feature films: A Handful of Dust 1989, Where Angels Fear to Tread 1991; Co-Produced in the West End The Normal Heart 1986, Drood 1987 & The Vortex 1988. *Memberships:* Drama Panel of Arts Coun of GB 1956-62; Coun of Eng Stage Company 1979-90; Co-Chmn, West End Cares; Chmn, Fund Raising

Com of Crusaid. *Honours include:* Brit Soc of Film & TV Arts, Best Drama Series, Country Matters, 1972; Critics Circle, Best Drama Adaptation, Country Matters, 1972, 1973; Intl Emmy, The Collection, 1977; Brit Acad of Film & TV Arts, Brideshead Revisited, 1982; Golden Globe Awd, Best TV mini-series, Brideshead Revisited, 1983. *Hobbies:* Reading; Swimming; Painting; Architecture; Cooking; Cats. *Address:* c/o Peters, Fraser & Dunlop, The Chambers, Chelsea Harbour, London SW10 0XF, England.

GRANT Delma P, b. 10 Sept 1939, Rugby, Warwicks. Artist; Writer; Business Woman. *Education:* City of Bath Trng Col; Dipl 1959, Principles & Practice of Ed. *Appointments:* Career Tchr 1959-74; Fdr Delma Design Collections Company 1974-. *Creative Works:* Annual Delma Design Collections, Exhibition Ctr, London 1974-88; Design & Ind Bd of Trade, Exhib London & touring 1984; Writer Children's books: Goodnight, New Nonsense, Good Morning, 1986; 9 Teddybear books, 1988. *Honour:* Selected by Brit Des Coun for touring exhibition. *Hobbies:* Restoration; Photography; Museum collation; Snouting in junk shops, interiors, museums; Mountains; Entertaining nieces; Art galleries; Moley Jingo Cairn; Horse and cart driving; Viewing beautiful and historic houses; Old churches; Nattering; Thinking; Good food; Pekin bantams; Fine architecture; Woodlands; Defying migraine; Reading autograph letters. *Address:* PO Box 99, 17 West Street, Alresford, Hants, England.

GRANT Franklin Dean, b. 20 Jan 1941, Athens, Tennessee, USA. Asst Supt Schs; Edr. m. Geraldine Marlowe, 14 June 1986, 2 s. 1 d. *Education:* BS 1962, Tenn Wesleyan Col; MEd 1970, EdS 1975, Univ Ga; Postgrad studies: Emory Univ, Ga State Univ & E Tenn State Univ. *Appointments:* DeKalb County Sch System 1962-92; Tchr 1962-68; Supv of Employment 1968-71; Asst Dir Personnel 1971-83; Dir Personnel 1983-89; Asst Supt for Staff Svcs 1989-92. *Publications:* Arts pub in profl jours; Num books pub by DeKalb Schs' Press. *Memberships:* Kappa Delta Pi; Phi Kappa Phi; Pi Kappa Delta; DeKalb Admnstrs Assn, Treas; Ga Assn of Sch Personnel Admnstrs, Pres; Nat Ed Assn; White House Conf for a drug-free Am. *Honours:* Nat Sci Foun Grant Recip, Emory Univ 1965; Barkley Forum Debate Coach Awd, Emory Univ 1966; Awd for most outstg personnel policies manual in the US 1978; Resolution of Commend by the Ga House of Reps 1986. *Hobbies:* Amateur radio; Photography; Tennis; Travel. *Address:* DeKalb County School System, 3770 North Decatur Road, Decatur, GA 30032, USA. 7, 15.

GRANT James Shaw, b. 22 May 1910, Stornoway. Author. m. Catherine Mary Stewart, 25 July 1951. *Education:* MA 1931, Glasgow Univ. *Appointments:* Edit, Stornoway Gazette 1932-63; Chmn Crofters Comm 1963-78. *Creative Works:* Plays: Tarravore, 1944; Magic Rowan, 1947; Legend is Born, 1948; Comrade The King, 1951; Books: Highland Villages, 1977; Their Children Will See, 1979; The Hub of My Universe, 1982; Surprise Island, 1983; The Gaelic Vikings, 1984; Stornoway and the Lews, 1985; Discovering Lewis & Harris, 1987; Enchanted Island, 1989. *Memberships:* Gov Pitlochry Festival Theatre 1954-84, Chmn 1971-83; Vice Chmn Eden Court Theatre 1987-. *Honours:* OBE 1956; CBE 1968; FRAgS 1973; LLD (Aberdeen) 1979; FRSE 1982. *Hobbies:* Walking; Photography. *Address:* Ardgrianach, Inshes, Inverness 1V1 2BQ, Scotland. 1, 43, 184.

GRANT Janet E, *Address:* International Young Author's Camps, Suite 2004, 99 Harbour Square, Toronto, Ontario, Canada, M5J 2H2.

GRANT William Frederick, b. 20 Oct 1924, Hamilton, Ontario, Can. Geneticist; Edr; Emeritus Prof Plant Sci. m. Phyllis Kemp Harshaw, 23 July 1949, 1 s. *Education:* BA 1947, McMaster Univ, Hamilton; MA 1949, PhD 1953, Univ Va, Charlottesville. *Appointments:* Botanist, Geneticist under Colombo Plan to Dept Agr, Malaysia 1953-55; Asst Prof, McGill Univ, Montreal, Quebec

1955-61; Assoc Prof 1961-66, Prof Depts Plant Sci & Biol 1967-90, Emeritus Prof 1990; In charge Genetics Lab, McGill Univ. *Publications:* Edit, Lotus newsletter 1970-85, Can Jour Genetics & Cytology 1974-82; Mem Edit Bd, Mutation Research 1978-85, Plant Species Biology 1985-. *Memberships include:* Mem joint WHO & Intl Prog on Chem Safety Collaborative Study on Short Term Tests for Genotoxicity and Carcinogenicity 1984-; Environ Contaminants Adv Com, Ministers of Environ & Nat Health & Welfare, Ottawa, Ontario 1978-86; Fellow AAAS; Linnean Soc, London; Royal Soc Can; Int Organization Plant Biosystematists, Pres 1981-86; Genetics Soc Can, Life Mem, Pres 1975, Presidential Citation 1991, Archivist 1984-; Environ Mutagen Soc; Can Bot Assn (George Lawson Medal 1989); Am Soc Plant Taxonomists; Soc for Study Evolution, VP 1972. *Honours:* Andrew Fleming Awd, 1953; Gov Gen Silver Medal Commemorating 25th Ann of Accession of HM Queen Elizabeth to Throne, 1977; Blandy Res Fellow 1950-53. *Address:* 43 St Andrews Road, Baie d'Urfe, PQ Canada H9X 2T9. 2.

GRASBECK Ralph Gustaf Armas, b. 6 July 1930, Helsinki, Finland. Prof; Chf Res Inst. m. Christina Stromberg, 11 Sept 1954, 2 s. *Education:* MD 1953, Dr med (PhD Biochem) 1956, Helsinki Univ. *Appointments:* Res Fellow, Dept Biochem, Sch Hygiene & Pub Health, Johns Hopkins Univ, Baltimore, Md, USA 1954-55; Res Fellow, Dept Biochem, Karolinska Inst, Stockholm 1957; Asst Instr, Dept Med Biochem 1958-59, Res, 4th Dept Int Med 1959, Docent Clin Chem 1959-, Univ Helsinki; Secy Gen 1959-, Chf 1971-, The Minerva Foun for Med Res, Helsinki; Chf Physician, Lab Dept Maria Hosp, City Helsinki 1960-90 (rtd); Edit, Scandinavian J of Clin & Lab Investigation 1965- 75; Exchange Vstg Prof, Univ Madison, Wis 1969; Chmn Bd, Oy Medix Ab (Clin Lab) Espoo 1969-, Chf Res Dept, Helsinki 1990-, Chmn Bd, Oy Medix Biochemica Ab (Mftr of monoclonals) 1985-; Edit, European J of Haematology 1975-. *Publications:* Approx 275 pubs in fields of clin chem, biochem, physiol, haematology & parasitology, esp metabolism of Vit B12, transport of haem, ref values, lymphocyte mitogens, intestinal receptors. *Memberships include:* European Soc Clin Investigation; Finnish Soc for Scis & Letters (Acad of Sci), Pres 1987-89; Am Chem Soc; Finnish Soc of Chem Pathologists, Pres 1962-63, 1965-66; Finnish Med Soc, Chmn 1977, Pres Grant Bd 1979-85; Secy, Clin Chem Div IUPAC 1975-77, Pres Elect 1977-79, Pres 1979-81; Scandinavian Soc Clin Chem & Clin Physiol, Pres 1967-69, VP 1969-73. *Honours include:* Jahre Price for young scists, Oslo Univ 1966; Invited Lectr to num congs, socs & acad insts; Medal of City of Nancy, 1986; Commander, Order of the Finnish Lion, 1988; Silver Medal, Finnish Soc of Scis & Letters, 1988. *Address:* Minerva Institute, Stockholm St 2, SF-00250 Helsinki, Finland.

GRATWICK John, b. 2 Mar 1923, England, Writer; Conslt. m. 23 Mar 1957, 1 s. *Education:* King's Col London 1941-42, 1946-48, BSc 1948; Royal Stat Soc Cert 1952. *Appointments includes:* Var positions 1942-69 incl RAF Radar Br 1942-46; Co-Chmn, Dept Task Force on objectives & structure for federal transportation 1969, Chmn Transportation Devel Agency 1970-72, Transport Canada; Com National Rlys; VP 1972-82, R&D 1972-78, Corp Affairs 1978-80, Exec 1981-82, Pres 1979-81, CN Marine; Exec Dir, Intl Inst for Transportation and Ocean Policy Studies 1987-88, Can Marine Transportation Ctr, Dalhousie Univ 1983-87; Ptnr, Hickling Corp Ltd 1983-; Assoc, Oceans Inst of Can, Dalhousie Univ 1988-; Chmn, Halifax-Dartmouth Port Development Commission, 1991-; Commissioner, Natl Transptn Act, Review Commission, 1992-93. *Publications:* 15 pubs incl: A Lady with a Past, 1985; Transportation: Theme Lecture, Can Engrg Cong Centennial, 1987; Canadian Transportation-Origins, Perspectives & Prospects, 1989, 1990. *Memberships:* Can Operational Res Soc, Pres 1969; Can Transportation Res Forum, Pres 1970; Ops Res Soc of Am; Royal Stats Soc, Fellow; Chartered Inst of Transport, Fellow. *Honours:* Can Op Res Soc Awd of Merit, 1986; Nat Transportation Week Awd of Achmt, 1990; Can Op Res

Soc Svc Awd, 1991. *Hobbies:* Food and wine; Flying; Theatre; Computers; Puppetry. *Address:* 984 Bellevue Avenue, Halifax, Nova Scotia, Canada B3H 3L7. 142.

GRATZ Norman Gerald, b. 16 May 1925, Minneapolis, USA. Conslt WHO. m. Catherine Thoeni, 15 Apr 1987. *Education:* BSc 1948, MSc 1950, Univ Calif; DSc 1965, Univ Geneva. *Appointments:* Chf, Vector Control Dept, Min of Health, Jerusalem, Israel 1953-58; WHO, Vector Control, Africa, Switzerland 1958-80; Dir, Vector Biol & Control Div, WHO, Geneva 1981-86. *Publications:* 88 sci pubs. *Memberships:* Am Mosquito Control Assn; Soc for Vector Ecol. *Honours:* Medal of Hon, Am Mosquito Control Assn, 1985; Nat Recog Awd, Pi Chi Omega Frat, 1986. *Hobby:* Collecting old travel books. *Address:* 4 ch du Ruisseau, 1291 Commvgny, Switzerland. 14, 54.

GRAUER Eva Marie Lyons, b. 13 Jan 1925, Memphis, Tennessee, USA. Sculptor. m. John J Grauer, 19 Sept 1945, 1 s. 2 d. *Education:* Southwestern Col; Memphis Col of Arts. *Career:* Artist & Sculptor, self employed; Art Instr; Arch Artifacts Restorer. *Creative Works:* 7ft statue, St Dominic Overbrook, Nashville; Childrens Garden, St Judes Hosp, Memphis; Monumental statues, St Mary's Cathedral; Lg Pr Eagles, Anheuser- Busch; Regan Memorial, St Judes Children Hosp, Memphis; Num pvt collections; Contbr arts to num publs. *Membership:* Brooks Art League. *Honour:* WWKNO Art Awd, Brooks (Museum) Art League. *Hobbies:* Reading; Gardening; Art related. *Address:* 1261 West Perkins Road, Memphis, TN 38117, USA.

GRAY Dulcie Winifred Catherine, b. 20 Nov 1920, Kuala Lumpur. Actress; Writer. m. Michael Denison, 29 Apr 1939. *Education:* England & Malaya. *Career:* Actress & Writer; Recent acting 1984-90 incl Kate in Howard's Way, TV series; Nat tours of Best of Friends, & The Importance of Being Earnest, 1991; Tartuffe, Playhouse, London, 1991-92; Nat Tour, An Ideal Husband, Globe Theatre, London, 1992. *Publications:* Latest book, Looking Forward, Looking Back, autobiography, 1991. *Memberships:* Fellow, Linnean Soc; Fellow, Royal Soc Arts; Mem Brit Equity; VP, Butterfly Conservation Soc. *Honours:* CBE 1983; The Queen's Silver Jubilee Medal 1977; The Times Ednl Supplement Sr Info Book Awd 1978. *Hobbies:* Swimming; Butterflies. *Address:* c/o Ronnie Waters, International Creative Management, Oxford House, 76 Oxford Street, London W1N 9HE, England. 1, 3, 43, 138.

GRAY Eileen, b. 25 Apr 1920, London, England. m. 24 Aug 1946, 1 s. *Education:* Matric 1937. *Appointments:* Amateur Administrator. *Publications:* Arts in sports mags. *Memberships:* Past Pres, Brit Cycling Fed; Women's Intl Comm for Cycling; Vice Pres, Brit Olympic Assn; Dep Grand Master, Hon Frat Women Freemasons; Mayor Royal Boro Kingston 1990-91; Vice Chmn Regl Sports Coun. *Honours:* OBE 1977; Sportswriters Assn Awd for Svcs to Sport, 1982; Freeman City of London 1987; Awd from Dept Ed, Taiwan; Gold Badge Hon for Svcs to Cycling; Int Olympic Assn Womens Year Awd, 1990. *Hobbies:* All sport especially women participation; Freemasonry; Local Govt; Gardening; Cooking; Sewing. *Address:* 129 Grand Avenue, Surbiton, Surrey KT5 9HY, England.

GRAY James Allan, b. 24 Mar 1935, Bristol, England. Conslt in Communicable Diseases. m. Jennifer Margaret Newton Hunter, 17 Sept 1960, 1 s. 2 d. *Education includes:* Flt Lt, SS Comm RAF Med Br 1960-63; Fac Med, Univ Edinburgh 1953-59; MB Ch B (Edinburgh) 1959; MRCP (Edinburgh) 1965; FRCPEd 1974. *Appointments:* NHS & Res Med Posts, Edinburgh, Bristol, London as SHO, Reg, Sr Reg 1964-69; Conslt in Communicable Diseases 1969-, Hon Sr Lectr, Dept Med 1969-, Univ Edinburgh. *Publications:* Antibacterial Drugs Today, Co-Author, 1983; Colour Guides: Infectious Diseases, Co-Author, 1984 & 1992; Fdr Edit, Res Medica 1957-58; Asst Edit, Journal of Infection

1979-86. *Memberships:* Fellow 1957, Sr Pres, Roy Med Soc 1958-59; VP 1987-89, Pres 1989-91, Brit Soc for the Study of Infection; Asst Principal MO 1979-90, Principal MO 1990-, Scottish Widows' Fund & Life Assurance Soc. *Hobbies:* Hill walking; Pottery collecting. *Address:* St Andrews Cottage, 15 Lauder Road, Edinburgh EH9 2EN, Scotland. 184.

GRAY Sidney John, b. 3 Oct 1942, Woodford, England. Prof Int Bus. m. Hilary Fenella Jones, 23 July 1977, 1 s. 1 d. *Education:* BEc 1971, Univ Sydney; PhD 1976, Univ Lancaster. *Appointments:* Peirce Leslie Co Ltd, London & India 1961-67; Burns Philp & Co Ltd, Australia 1967-68; Univ Sydney, Australia 1972; Univ Lancaster 1974-78; Univ Glasgow 1978-92; Univ Warwick, 1993- . *Publications:* Author or Co-Author 14 books incl: Information Disclosure and the Multinational Corporation, 1984; Mega-Merger Mayhem, 1989. *Memberships:* Chartered Assn Cert Accts, Fellow 1980; European Acctg Assn, Secy Gen 1982-83; Brit Acctg Assn, Chmn 1987; Intl Assn Acctg Ed & Res, Pres 1992- . *Hobbies:* Tennis; Golf. *Address:* Warwick Business School, University of Warwick, Coventry CV4 7AL, England. 184.

GREEN Bernard, b. 11 Nov 1925, Walgrave. Baptist Minister. m. Joan Viccars, 19 July 1952, 2 s. 1 d. *Education:* BA in Theol, Bristol Univ & Bristol Baptist Col 1947-50; MA, Oxford Univ, St Catherines & Regents Park Col; BD, London Univ External. *Appointments:* Ordained 1952; Minister, Yardley Baptist Ch, Birmingham 1952-61; Minister, Mansfield Road Baptist Ch, Nottingham 1961-76; Min, Horfield Baptist Ch, Bristol 1976-82; Gen Secy, Baptist Union of GB 1982-91; Rtd 1991. *Publications:* Co-Author, Patterns & Prayers for Christian Worship, 1991; Edit Com for Hymn Book, Baptist Praise & Worship, 1991. *Memberships:* Moderator of Free Church Fed Coun 1988-89; Frequent Broadcaster on BBC Radio Nottingham, VP, 1970-1976, BBC Radio Bristol 1976-82, BBC Radio Oxford 1989-1991; VP, Churches Council for Health & Healing, 1988- . *Hobbies:* Gardening; Walking; Swimming; Spectator sport; Reading; Listening to music. *Address:* 6 Alexander Close, Abingdon, Oxon OX14 1XA, England. 1.

GREEN Geoffrey Edward, b. 27 Mar 1929, Beaconsfield, England. Solicitor; Notary Public; Underwriter. m. Joy Anne Willcocks, 2 Jan 1954, 1 d. *Education:* Law Soc Col of Law; LLB Hons, London Univ. *Appointments:* Asst to Sir Cullum Welch Bart 1951-52; PA to Sir Frank Medlicott MP 1952-54; Sole Practice & Ptnr Central London 1954-61; Practice in Beaconsfield 1962-. *Memberships:* Fdr, Mem, Central & S Mddx Law Soc, former Coun Mem; Freeman City of London; Soc Conservative Lawyers, former Exec Coun mem; Liveryman, City of London Solicitors Co; Notaries Soc; Law Soc; Berks, Bucks & Oxon Law Soc; Arts Club; Wig & Pen. *Hobbies:* Reading; Travel; Theatre; Gardening; Politics-Parliamentary Candidate 1974. *Address:* Tumblers Chase, 8 Stratton Road, Beaconsfield, Bucks HP9 1HS, England.

GREEN Gordon Ralph, b. 10 Nov 1924, Englewood, NJ, USA. Conslt; Artist; Pubs Exec. m. Flora Schuler, 5 June 1948, 2 s. *Education:* Art Major, Acad Art, Newark, NJ 1946-48; Cert, Montclair Sch of Fine Arts, NJ 1948-50; Postgrad ITT & LTV Mgmt Courses 1968-75; Univ Ala Mgmt & Creative Writing & Speaking Courses 1981-85. *Appointments:* Art Dir, Renwar Inc, NYC 1952-57; Sr Tech Illustr, Proposal Prod Coord, Admin Art & DFTG, ITT Federal Electr Corp, Pakamus, NJ 1957-65; Data Production Mgr, ITT Fed Electr Corp, Houston, Tex 1965-71; Mgr Pubs, LTV/Kentron Intl, Houston 1971-79; Prog Mgr, Kentron Intl, Huntsville, Ala 1980-84; Dir Bus Devel, Mgmt Svcs Inc, Huntsville, Ala 1985-88; Conslt Pubs, Proposal Writer, Artist, Illustr 1989-. *Creative Works:* Speaker in Field; Artist/Illustr; Fine Art Painter-Juanita Green Parks Awd 1991, Cent & S Tenn for Oil Painting; Exhibitor, Mayor's Gallery; Huntsville Times Gallery; Exhibited Lake Worth, FLA; Tenn Valley Art Ctr, Tuscumbia, ALA; Presented papers on graphics mgmt, pubs at STC Seminars at Rice Univ, Univ Houston, Univ Tenn & 34th ITCC, St Louis. *Memberships:* Intl Soc for Tech Communications, Huntsville & Houston Chapt, Past Chapt Secy, Lectr; Bd mem, Huntsville Art League; Tenn Art League; Montgomery Art Guild; Past mem, Classification Mgmt Assn. *Honour:* Juanita Green Parks Memorial Awd for oil painting at Central & S Tenn Art Exhibition, Nashville, Tenn 1991. *Hobbies:* Photography; Music appreciation; Reading; Antique glass collection; Gardening. *Address:* 2519 Excalibur Drive SE, Huntsville, AL 35803, USA.

GREEN Helen J, b. 24 Feb 1942, Kent, England. Arch. *Education:* Arch Assn; Univ London; Dipl Arch & Distinction in Design; Dipl Restoration of Historic Buildings; Chartered Arch. *Appointments:* Historic Bldgs Divn, GLC 1968-70; Project Arch, Kent C C 1970-73; Arch Company of Designers 1973-76; Project Mgr, DOE Property Svcs Agency 1976-. *Creative Works:* Head Offices; Labs; Specialist Bldgs for HM Svcs; Restoration of Listed Bldgs. *Memberships:* Archl Assn 1960-; Royal Inst Brit Archs 1968; ARCUK Reg'd Arch 1968-; Soc for Protection of Ancient Bldgs 1969-; Assn for Studies in Historic Bldgs 1970-; Archs & Surveyor's Inst, Fellow 1979-. *Honours:* RIBA SE Regl Rep Woman of Kent, 1980, 1986. *Hobbies:* Country pursuits; Reading; Gardening; Historic Buildings. *Address:* Spinnakers, Nettlestead Green, Nr Wateringbury, Kent, England.

GREEN John Dennis Fowler, b. 9 May 1909, Stroud, Kent, England. m. Diana Judith Elwes, 2 May 1946. *Education:* Cheltenham Col; Peterhouse, Cambridge; Historical 1928, Law Tripos 1931; Entrance Scholar, Inner Temple. *Appointments:* Barrister at Law 1931; BBC 1934, established Agricultural Broadcasting; Agricultural Liaison Ofcr with MAFF 1940-45; Rep MAFF, Australia, NZ 1945-47; BBC, Chf Asst Current Affairs 1950; Controller, Talks Div 1956-61; Chmn, Agriculture's Ministers Adv Coun, MAFF 1963-69. *Publications:* Mr Baldwin: A Study in Post War Conservatism; Arts on historical & agricultural subjects. *Memberships:* Nat Pig Breeders Assn, Pres 1956; Royal Agric Soc Eng, Dep Pres 1984; Trustee, RASE 1985. *Honours:* Hon Fellow RASE, 1990; Hon Fellow RAS C'Wealth, 1991. *Hobbies:* Livestock breeding; Forestry. *Address:* The Manor, Chedworth, Cheltenham, Gloucestershire GL54 4AA, England.

GREEN Rachael Paulette, b. 28 Nov 1953, Shreveport, Louisiana, USA. Librarian. *Education:* BA Eng 1975, La Tech Univ; MLIS 1986, La State Univ. *Appointments:* Librarian, Shreve Memorial Lib, Shreveport 1976-78, 1979-89; Dep Clerk of Crt, Fed Crt House, Shreveport 1978-79; Librarian, La State Univ, Shreveport 1989-. *Memberships:* Am Lib Assn; IPA; La Lib Assn; Nat Assn Female Execs; N La Film Gp, Historian; Democratic Nat Com. *Hobbies:* Gardening; Bicycling; Reading; Film research. *Address:* 1005 Willow Drive, Shreveport, LA 71118, USA. 7, 15.

GREENE Charles Ian George, b. 28 Jan 1948, Alberta, Canada. Associate Professor. m. Eilonwy Anne Morgan, 30 July 1982, 1 d. *Education:* ARCT, Royal Conserv of Mus, Toronto, 1967; BA Hons, Univ Alberta, 1970; MA, 1972, PhD, 1983, Univ of Toronto. *Appointments:* Asst to Min of Consumer Affairs, Alberta, 1972-73; Lectr in Polit Sci and Soc Welfare, Univ of Lethbridge, Alberta, 1981-85; Asst to Reg Dir of Soc Sers, Lethbridge, 1982-85; Assoc Prof, 1985-90, Coor, Pub Policy and Admin Prog, 1998-91. *Publications:* The Charter of Rights, 1989; Judges and Judging, 1990; 11 articles in scholarly journals; 6 book chapters. *Memberships:* Can Law and Soc Assn, Sec/Treas, 1990-92; Can Polit Sci Assn; Can Eval Soc. *Honours:* Vis Phys Fellow, Cambs, 1992; Dean's Tchg Awd, 1987, 1989; IODE War Meml Scholarship, 1977-79; Univ of Toronto Open Fellowship, 1971. *Hobbies:* Mountain climbing; Skiing; Tennis; Classical Music. *Address:* Department of Political Science, York University, North York, Ontario, Canada M3J 1P3. 142.

GREENE Jaime S, b. 27 Aug 1958, Syracuse, NY, USA. Emergency Med Svcs Trng Ofcr. *Education:* Associates in Applied Sci 1978, Onondaga Community Col; BA 1983, Asbury Col. *Appointments:* Staff Office of Student Devel, Asbury Col 1981-86; Capt Jessamine County EMS 1987-90; Trng Ofcr, Woodford Co EMS 1990-. *Publication:* Transition and Guidance: Assimilation of the New Student into the College Campus, 1983. *Memberships:* Central Ky Firefighters Assn, EMS Com Chairperson; Ky EMT Instructors Assn. Bd Dirs; Ky Firefighters Assn; Ky Search Dog Assn. *Hobbies:* Hiking; Camping; Reading. *Address:* 117 Bell Ct, Versailles, KY 40383, USA. 117.

GREENHALGH Peter Andrew Livsey, b. 18 Oct 1945, Littleborough, Lancs, England. Merchant Banker; Author. m. Anna Mary Beatrice Dixon, 24 Aug 1968, 1 d. *Education:* King's Col, Cambridge; BA 1st class hons, Classical Tripos 1967; MA 1970; PhD 1971. *Appointments:* Res Student & Col Supvr in Classics & Ancient History, King's Col, Cambridge 1967-70; Mgmt trainee, Reckitt & Colman, Hull & London 1970-71; Articled Clerk, Thomas McLintock & Co, Chartered Accts, London 1971-72; Asst Mgr, Corporate Finance, Hill Samuel & Co Ltd, London 1972-76; Sr Lectr, subsequently Assoc Prof, of Classics (tenured), Univ Cape Town 1977-82; Conslt in Corp Fin Systems, QB On- Line Systems, Camberley, England 1979-; Asst Gen Mgr, Corporate Finance, Hill Samuel Merchant Bank (SA) Ltd, J'Burg 1982-84; Dir, Hill Samuel Securities Ltd, London 1985; Dir & Hd of Corp Fin & Mem Exec Com, Arbuthnot Latham Bank Ltd, London 1985-88; Chf Exec, AAF Investment Corp PLC, London 1989-90; Mng Dir, AAF Conslts Ltd, London 1989-90; Mng Dir, Corp Fin, Chartered WestLB Ltd, Merchant Bankers, London 1990-91; Chmn, Lister BestCare Ltd, 1991-; Many non-exec Directorships. *Publications:* 5 books in the field of Classics incl: Deep into Mani: a journey to the Southern tip of Greece, 1985, reprinted 1987, German transl 1987; 4 plays; 6 academic arts; Also many arts for the press on ednl, academic & fin matters & several radio talks. *Honours:* 4 scholarly prizes & 3 awds incl: Carrington-Koe Res Studentship1967-68; Acad Awd for Radio Drama, The Wrath of Achilles, 1985. *Hobbies:* Reading; Writing; Theatre; Travel; Dining with friends. *Address:* 138 Humber Road, Blackheath, London SE3 7LY, England.

GREENHALGH Robert, b. 15 Mar 1942, Lancaster, England. Specialist in Visual Disability. m. Elizabeth Higdon, 17 July 1965. *Education:* Home Tchg Cert, Col of Tchrs of the Blind 1965; Cert in Social Work 1970; BA (Open) 1978. *Appointments:* Social Worker, Manchester, Sr Social Worker, Wolverhampton 1965-74; Principal, Royal Nat Inst for the Blind's Nat Rehab Ctr 1975-83; Principal of Trng, S Regl Assn for the Blind 1983-1992; Snr Ptnr, Iridian, pecalists in Visual Disabilty, 1992-. *Publications:* Edit & Contbr Author, Light for Low Vision Handbook, 1979, 1991; Contbr Author, Nursing Elderly People. *Memberships:* Brit Assn of SW; Assn for the Ed & Welfare of the Visually Handicapped; Nat Light for Low Vision Com, Vice Chmn; Partially Sighted Soc, mem Bd Dirs. *Honour:* Freeman of the City of Lancaster, 1961; Mem, Royal Nat Inst, Blind Exec Cncl. *Hobbies:* Music; Good food & wine; Writing; All aspects of the rehab of people with poor sight. *Address:* 15 Belsize Park Mews, London NW3 5BL, England.

GREENOUGH Alan Edward, b. 14 July 1949, St Helens, England. Chmn & Chf Exec of Prime People plc. m. Sheila Mary Collins, 16 Aug 1975, 2 d. *Education:* Bristol Univ 1967-70; LLB Upper 2nd class; Qualified as Solicitor 1973. *Appointments:* Solicitor, Alsop Wilkinson 1974-90; Ptnr 1980-90; Sr Corp Ptnr 1989-90; Exec Dir, Doctus PLC 1990; Commercial Dir, Microvitec PLC 1990; Chmn and Chf Exec, Prime People Plc, 1991. *Memberships:* Law Soc; Inst Dirs. *Hobbies:* Rugby League; Tennis; Golf; Cinema; Travel. *Address:* Southcroft, 30 Hough Lane, Wilmslow, Cheshire SK9 2LH, England.

GREENWOOD (Arthur) Alexander, b. 8 Mar 1920, Corby Glen, Lincolnshire, England. Genealogist. m. (1)Betty Doreen Westrop, 20 July 1946, 1 s. 1 d. (2)Shirley Knowles-Fitton, 16 Sept 1976. *Education:* Oakham Sch & Sidney Sussex Col, Cambridge (incomplete due to war); Milit Intelligence Sch 1954-55; Fellow, Chartered Inst Secys 1970; Soc Co Accts 1970; Public Admin, Can 1981; PhD, USA 1987. *Appointments include:* Army: Commissioned, Royal Lincolnshire Regmt 1939, Major 1952, Rtd 1959; ADC to Field Marshal Sir Claude Auchinleck 1943-44; Served Norway, Iceland, India, Burma, Middle East; Civilian: Mem London Stock Exchange 1962-75; Fdr Chmn, Lincolnshire Chickens Ltd 1963-87; Fdr Dir, Allied City Share Trust plc 1964; Chmn, Alderney Offshore Svcs Ltd 1976-80; Emigrated to Can 1980; Dir, Reform Party of Canada, 1992-. *Publications:* Brief History of the 4th Battalion, Royal Lincolnshire Regiment (TA), 1948; Greenwood Tree in Three Continents, 1988; Field Marshal Auchinleck, 1990. *Memberships:* Life Fellow, RSA, Royal Ec Soc; Fellow, Royal Geographical Soc, Inst Dirs; Soc Genealogists; Assn Profl Genealogists, USA; Guild of One-Name Studies; Soc Authors; Carlton Club; MCC; The Pilgrims. *Honours:* Mentioned in despatches, 1944; Freeman, City of London, 1960; Pres, Old Oakhamian Club 1960-61; Liveryman, Pattenmakers Co, 1965; Chartered Secys Co, 1978; Mem Hon Company of Freeman of City of London (N Am), 1983. *Hobbies:* Cricket; Shooting; Genealogy (lectr Malaspina Col, BC, 1984-). *Address:* RR1 Box 40, Madrona Drive, Nanoose Bay, BC, Canada VOR 2RO. 1, 20, 32, 35, 41, 88, 123, 139, 146.

GREENWOOD Frank, b. 6 Mar 1924, Rio de Janeiro, Brazil. Prof. m. 24 Oct 1972, 2 s. 1 d. *Education:* BA 1950, Bucknell Univ, USA; MBA 1959, Univ Srn Calif; PhD 1963, Univ Calif at Los Angeles. *Appointments:* Var positions, The Texas Co, West Africa, Can & USA 1950-60; Prof & Computer Ctr Dir, several US univs 1961-89; Prof Mgmt Info Systems, Central Mich Univ, Mt Pleasant, Mich 1989-. *Publications:* Author or Co-Author 8 books & chapts in 4 others; 15 publ monographs & papers; 32 arts in profl jours; 43 misc pub pieces; Columnist for Computer World and other pubs. *Memberships:* Data Processing Mgmt Assn; Principal, Ctrs for Productivity. *Honours:* UCLA Alumni Scholar 1961; Ford Foun Fellow 1962-63. *Address:* School of Business Administration, Central Michigan University, Mt Pleasant, MI 48859, USA. 6, 8, 15, 52, 132, 139.

GREENWOOD Gordon Edward, b. 21 Aug 1935, Jasonville, Ind. Col Prof. m. 1 May 1982, 3 s. *Education:* BS Social Sci & Language Arts in Ed, MA in Secondary Admin, EdD in Ednl Psychology, Indiana State Univ. *Appointments:* Eng Tchr, Central HS, Dowagiac, Mich 1958-60; Social Studies Tchr, Wiley HS, Terre Haute, Ind 1960-65; Prof Ed, Foundations Dept, Col of Ed, Univ Fla 1967-. *Publications:* Books: Problem Situations in Teaching, 1971; Case Studies for Teacher Decision Making, 1989; Over 30 pubs in profl jours; Dir, 8 Res Grants. *Memberships:* Am Ednl Res Assn; Fla Ednl Res Assn; Am Soc Clin Hypnosis. *Honours:* Sch Bd Merit Awd, Alachua County, Fla 1979; Outstg Achmt & Performance Awd, Fla State Univ System, 1990; Dist'd Alumnus Awd, Jasonville, Ind HS 1990. *Hobbies:* Running; Volleyball; Racquetball. *Address:* College of Education, University of Florida, Gainesville, FL 32611, USA. 7, 15, 125, 129, 130, 139, 141, 158.

GREENWOOD Robert Walter, b. 1 Mar 1941, Hanover, NH. Actor; Dir. *Education:* BA cum laude 1963, Dartmouth Col, Hanover, New Hampshire; MFA Hons 1967, Yale Univ, Sch Drama, New Haven, Conn; Postgrad Work, Dartmouth Col, 1969; Repertory Acting, Directing, Tchg 1969-70; Laban Analysis, Labanotation, Laban Ctr for Human Movement Studies, Goldsmith's Col, London, England 1979; Festival Mgmt, Fund Raising & Bd Mgmt, The Banff Ctr, Sch of Mgmt, Banff, Alberta 1975, 1982. *Career:* Var tchng positions from tchg acting at Dartmouth Repertory Theatre Co 1969, to tchg emotional techniques to United World Col of S E Asia

in 1988, 1989; Adjuducator at Festivals; Participant at Workshops & Master Classes; Actor in modern & classical roles incl: Edmund in A Long Day's Journey Into Night, Hamlet, Mr Golightly in The Happy Haven; Theatre Director; Radio; Modelling; Community Theatre; Musicals & Childrens Theatre; Over 150 original roles 1977-; Poetry Readings; Television Roles; Opera; Plays; Choreography; Cabaret; Design Work; Art work (painting & sculpture) in one-man & group exhibitions, works represented in 20 pvt collections and also corporate collections; Tours to Czecho-Slovakia, 1991, 1992; 40 minute special for Slovakian Television, 1993; Int Theatre Festival, Nita, Slovakia, 1992; Two Tours to Croatia, to perform for Refugees, 1992; Tours to British Columbia, 1992/1993; Tours to Israel, 1989; Indonesia, 1988; Hong Kong, 1990. *Publications:* Currently writing book on acting and a book of poems; 9 original produced theatre pieces and adaptations of folk tales for Twinings and translations & adaptations for Fables; Art reviewer; Drama Reviewer & Critic; Editor, Advtg, Art-Layout, Centre Stage 1962-63. *Memberships include:* Fdr & Pres of Bd, Sun Ergos, a Company of Theatre & Dance 1977-; Fdr, Calgary Coun for All Arts Assn 1987-, Chmn Bd 1987-88; ACTRA; Can Actors' Equity Assn 1968-; Am Theatre Assn; Okla Community Theatre Assn; IPA; Humanities Assn of Can. *Honours:* The First Ina A Bolser Scholarship to attend Dartmouth Col, 1959; Rufus Choate Scholar, 1961, 1962, 1963; Marcus Heiman Awd for Theatre Arts, 1962; Adelbert Ames Awd for Art History, 1963; Actor of the Year Awd (The Albertan), 1976, 1979; Leonardo Da Vinci Awd Dipl of Recog, 1989; Dipl of Distinction: For 1 man show of Shakespeare, Pila, Poland, 1991; For duo show of Legends, Pila, Poland, 1991. *Address:* 2205 700-9th Street SW, Calgary, Alberta, Canada T2P 2B5.

GREER Gayle, b. 20 Mar 1956, Ft Worth, Tex. Musician. *Education:* Rice Univ, BMus 1981, MMus 1981. *Appointments:* Houston Ballet Orchestra 1978-82; Boston Pro Arte Chamber Orch 1983-85; Austrian Radio Orch 1985-86; Regensburg Philharmonic 1986-. *Publications:* Nightmare on L Street, 1990; Window Shopping, 1991. *Memberships:* Deutsche Orchester-Vereinigung; Fdr mem, Wulferode Liturature Discussion Group. *Hobbies:* Bridge; European History; Cooking. *Address:* Stadische Buhnen Regensburg, Bismarkplatz 7, D-8400 Regensburg, Germany. 52.

GREER Germaine, b. 29 Jan 1939, Melbourne, Australia. Broadcaster; Journalist; Columnist; Prof. *Education:* Melbourne Univ 1956-59; Sydney Univ 1960-62; Cambridge Univ 1964-67; BA Hons Eng & French Lang & Lit 1959; MA 1st class Hons 1962; PhD 1967, thesis on Shakespeare's Early Comedies. *Appointments:* Sr Tutor in Eng, Sydney Univ 1963-64; Asst Lectr then Lectr in Eng, Univ Warwick 1967-72; Vstg Prof, Grad Fac Modern Letters 1979, Prof Modern Letters 1980-83, Univ Tulsa; Fdr Dir, Tulda Ctr for Study of Women's Lit; Fdr Editr, Tulsa Studies in Women's Lit 1981; Dir, Stump Cross Books 1988-; Special Lectr & Unofficial Fellow, Newnham Col, Cambridge 1989-; Lectr throughout N Am with Am Prog Bureau 1973-78 and to raise funds for Tulsa Bursary & Fellowship Scheme 1980-83. *Publications:* Broadcaster, Journalist, Columnist, Reviewer 1972-79; Selected journalism pub as The Madwoman's Underclothes, 1986; The Female Eunuch, 1969; The Obstacle Race: The Fortunes of Women Painters and Their Work, 1979; Sex and Destiny: The Politics of Human Fertility, 1984; Shakespeare, OUP Past Masters series, 1986; Co-Ed, Kissing the Rod: An Anthology of 17th Century Women's Verse, 1989; Daddy, We Hardly Knew You, 1989; Ed, The Uncollected Verse of Aphra Behn, 1989; The Change: Women, Ageing & the Menopause, 1991. *Honours:* Jr Govt Scholarship 1952; Diocesan Scholarship 1956; Sr Govt Scholarship 1956; Tchr's Col Studentship 1956; C'Wealth Scholarship 1964; J R Ackerly Prize & Premio Intl Mondello for Daddy, We Hardly Knew You. *Address:* c/o Aitken & Stone, 29 Fernshaw Road, London SW10 OTG, England.

GREGO Mario Domenico, b. 20 June 1927, Bologna, Italy. Univ Prof. *Education:* Degree in Ec & Commerce; Qualified Tchr Eng Lang & Lit. *Appointments:* Prof Eng, Fac Ec & Commerce, Univ Venice; Journalist; Consul of Repub San Marino; Prof Tourist Sci, Intl Acad Scis San Marino; Prof Intl Relats; Formerly: Pres, Padua Province Tourist Bd; Municipal Councillor, Padua. *Memberships:* Pres, Intl Acad Tourism; Amb for Italy, mem World Grand Coun and Grand Master, Commandery of Tre Venezie, Intl Order of Anysetiers; FRSA; Soc Européenne de Culture; Ateneo Veneto; Accad dei Concordi; European Press Assn, mem Polit Com; and other acads & cultural insts in sev countries. *Honours include:* Grand Ofcr, Order of Merit of Italian Repub; Grand Ofcr, Knightly Order of St Agatha, Repub San Marino; Chevalier, Ordre des Palmes Académiques (French Repub); Dipl Hon as Italy's Freedom Fighter; Hon Crossbowman os San Marino; Knight with plaque, Sacred Milit Order of Constantine St George; Knight, Mil & Hosp Order of St Lazarus of Jerusalem; KSJ; Gold Medal, Arts-Scis-Lettres & Etoile Civique. *Hobby:* Fine arts. *Address:* Casella Postale 116, 30100 Venice, Italy.

GREGORY Calvin Luther, b. 11 Jan 1942, Bronx, NY, USA. Insurance & Real Estate Agent; Edr. m. (1) Rachel Anne Carver, 14 Feb 1970 div, (2) Carla Deaver, 30 June 1979, 2 d. *Education:* AA 1962, Los Angeles City Col; BA 1964, Calif State Univ; MDiv 1968, Fuller Theol Seminary, Pasadena; Master Religious Ed 1969, Southwestern Seminary, Fort Worth, Tex; PhD 1982, Universal Life Ch Inc, Modesto, Calif; DD 1982, Otay Mesa Col, San Diego. *Appointments:* Auxiliary Chaplain, Edwards AFB, Calif 1970; Pastor, 1st Baptist Ch, Boron 1971; Insurance Agent, Prudential Insurance Company, Ventura 1972; Insurance Mgr, Prudential 1973; Casualty Insurance Agent, Allstate Insurance Co 1974; Hd Youth Minister, Emanuel Presbyterian Ch 1974; Pres, Insurance Agency Placement Svc, Thousand Oaks 1975-; Owner, Mgr, over 50 apts, Calif 1971-; Developer, Owner, 700 acres, USA, Wales, Can, Australia. *Memberships include:* Calif Apt Assn. *Honours:* Top 20 Salesmen Southeastern Company, Nashville, Tenn 1967; President's Citation, Whole Life Round Table; Millionaire Awd, Prudential Insurance Company, Ventura 1972; Hon Cultural Doctorate, Sacred Philos, World Univ, Ariz, 1986. *Hobbies:* Travel; Video tapes; Jogging. *Address:* PO Box 4407, Thousand Oaks, CA 91359, USA.

GREGORY Michael Anthony, b. 8 June 1925, London, England. Journalist; Rtd Barrister. m. Patricia Ann Hodges, 11 Aug 1951, 3 s. 5 d. *Education:* LLB 1951, Univ Col London. *Appointments:* Navigator, RAF 1943-47; Called to Bar 1952; Practised 1952-60; Legal Dept Country Landowners' Assn 1960-90; Chf Legal Advr 1977-90. *Publications:* Angling and the Law, 1967, 2nd ed 1974, supplement 1976; Organisational Possibilities in Farming, 1968; Joint Enterprises in Farming, Co-Author, 1968, 2nd ed 1973; All for Fishing, Co-Author, 1970; Farm Partnerships, Co-Author, 1979; Essential Law for Landowners & Farmers, Co-Author, 1980, 2nd ed 1987, 3rd ed 1990; Num booklets, arts, short stories, contbr to compendiums. *Memberships include:* Middle Temple 1952-; Mgmt Com of Catholic Social Svc for Prisoners 1952-90 (Bourne Trust, 1990-), Hon Secy 1953-60, Chmn 1960-71, 1974-85; Hon Secy of Soc of Our Lady of Good Counsel 1953-58; BSI Com on Installation of Pipelines in Land 1965-83; Chmn, Intl Help for Children, Fleet & District Br 1967-77; Hon Legal Advr, Nat Anglers Coun 1968-91; Cove Angling Soc 1969-; Thames Water Authority Regl Fisheries Adv Com 1974-90; Agric Law Assn 1975-; Coun of Anglers' Coop Assn 1980-; Coun of Salmon & Trout Assn 1980-90; Trustee CLA Charitable Trust 1980-; Coun of John Eastwood Water Protection Trust 1982- ; Nat Rivers Authority Regl Fisheries Adv Com 1990-; Inland Waterways Amenity Council. *Honours:* Papal Medal Pro Ecclesia et Pontifice, 1988; Ofcr of the Order of the Brit Empire (OBE) 1990. *Hobbies:* Playing bowls, tennis & other ball games; Angling; Playing saxophones; Music of all ages; Wildlife watching; The family. *Address:* 63 Gally Hill Road, Church Crookham, Fleet, Hampshire GU13 0RU, England. 1.

GREGORY Robert George, b. 25 Sept 1939, Melbourne, Australia. Economist. m. Annette, 3 s. 1 d. *Education:* BComm 1st class Hons 1961, Univ Melbourne; PhD 1967, LSE & Polit Sci, Univ London. *Appointments:* Tutor,Asst Lectr, LSE1964-67; Vstg Asst, Asst Prof, Northwestern Univ 1967-69; First Asst Commr, Inds Assistance Comm 1973-75; Vstg Scholar, Bd Govs of Fedl Reserve System 1977; Sr Res Fellow, Sr Fellow, Professorial Fellow 1969-, Prof Ec 1987-, Australian Nat Univ; Dir, Ctr for Ec Policy Res 1987; Hd Div of Ec & Politics 1990. *Publications:* Author over 50 papers in profljours & chapts in books. *Memberships:* Mem Bd, Reserve Bank of Aust; Aust Sci & Tech Coun, 1986-92. *Honours:* Fellow, Aust Acad Social Scis 1983-84; Chair Aust Studies, Harvard Univ. *Hobby:* Gardening. *Address:* Economics Program, Research School of Social Sciences, Australian National University, GPO Box 4, Canberra, ACT 2601, Australia.

GREINER Walter Albin Erhard, b. 29 Oct 1935, Neuenbau, Germany. Physicist. m. Barbara Chun, 2 s. *Education:* MS 1959, Univ Darmstadt, Germany; PhD 1961, Univ Freiburg, Germany. *Appointments:* Res Asst, Univ Freiburg 1961-62; Asst Prof, Univ Md, Prof of Phys Univ of Frankfurt, Germany 1965-; Dir, Inst Theoretical Physics 1965-; Guest Prof at num univs; Adj Prof, Vanderbilt Univ, Oak Ridge Nat Lab 1975-; Perm Sci Conslt, Gesellschaft fur Schwerionenforschung, Darmstadt. *Publications:* Co-Author, Nuclear Theory, Nuclear Models, vol 1, 1970; Excitation Mechanism of Nuclei, vol 2, 1970; Theory of the Nucleus, vol 3, 1972, 3rd ed 1987-89; Theoretische Physik 12 Vols 1974-89; Edit, J of Physics 1975-89. *Memberships:* Fellow, Royal Soc Arts & Scis; mem European Physics Soc; Am Physics Soc; Sci Soc Johann Wolfgang Goethe Univ; Eotvos Lorand Soc, Hungary, hon mem; Acad of Sci, Romania, Hon Mem. *Honours:* Max Born Prize, Inst Physics, 1974; Otto Hahn Prize, 1982; Hon DSc 1982, Univ Witwatersrand, South Africa; Hon DSc 1990-91, Univ Tel Aviv, Israel; Dr hon Causa, Univ Lois Pasteur Strasbourg, 1991; Dr Hon Causa Univ of Bucharest, 1992; Hon Prof, Univ of Bejing, China, 1990; Mng Edit for Europe of Int Journal of on Nuclear Physics E, Singapore 1991-. *Address:* 44 Gundelhardtstrasse, Taunus, D-6233 Kelkheim, Germany.

GRESHOFF Peter Michael, b. 26 Nov 1948, Berlin, Germany. Univ Prof. m. Rosalyn Marie Williams, 24 Nov 1973, 2 s. *Education:* BSc 1970, Alta; PhD 1973, DSc 1979, ANU. *Appointments:* Res Fellow 1975-79, Sr Lectr 1979-87, ANU, Canberra; Prof, Racheff Chair of Plant Molecular Genetics, UT Knoxville 1988-. *Publications:* Edit, Molecular Biology of Symbiotic Nitrogen Fixation, 1990; Co-Edit, Nitrogen Fixation: Achievements and Objectives, 1990. *Memberships:* Am Soc Plant Physiol; Int Soc Plant Mol Biol; Sigma Xi; Phi Kappa Phi; Phi Beta Kappa. *Honours:* Queen Elisabeth Scholarship 1966-67; Alexander v Humboldt Fellowship 1973-75, 1985- 86; Doctorate of Sci, ANU, Canberra 1989. *Hobbies:* Chess; Tennis; Snooker; Fishing; Wind surfing; Classical music; Game design. *Address:* 801 Kempton Road, Knoxville, TN 37909, USA.

GRESSNER Axel M, b. 9 July 1943, Apolda. Dir; Prof Clin Chem. m. Dr Gabriele Gressner, 9 June 1972, 1 s. 1 d. *Education:* Dipl Human Med 1969; MD 1969; Res Asst Biochem, Univ Heidelberg, Germany; Chicago, USA; RWTH, Aachen, Germany. *Appointments:* Univ Heidelburg; Univ Chcgo, USA; Univ Aachen, Germany; Univ Marburg, Germany; Full Prof & Dir Clin Chem. *Publications:* Textbook of Clinical Chemistry and Pathobiochemistry, edit, 1989, 2nd ed; Over 200 pubs. *Memberships:* Germ Soc Clin Chem, VP; Germ Assn Study of Liver, Pres; Am Assn Study of Liver; Int Assn Study of Liver. *Hobbies:* History of science; Music; Anthropology. *Address:* Dept of Clinical Chemistry and Central Lab, Philipps University, Baldingerstr, 355 Marburg, Germany.

GREY Robin Douglas, b. 23 May 1931, London, England. Barrister. m. Berenice Anna Wheatley, 8 Aug 1972, 1 s. 1 d. *Education:* Eastbourne Col 1945-49; LLB Hons 1954, London Univ, King's Col; Barrister-at-Law, Grays Inn 1957. *Appointments:* Crown Counsel, Colonial Legal Svc, Aden 1959-63; Registrar General, Actg General for periods, Actg Atty; UK Practising Barrister 1963-; Dep Circuit Judge 1977; QC & Recorder of Crown Court 1979-. *Publications:* Joint pubs as mem of Conservative Study Gp on Crime, viz: Crime Revisited, Police, Criminal Policy, Criminal Waste. *Memberships:* Brit Acad of Forensic Med; Crime & Juvenile Delinquency Gp of Ctr for Policy Studies. *Honours:* QC 1979; Recorder of Crown Crt 1979. *Hobbies:* Tennis; Golf; Reading; People. *Address:* Dun Cottage, The Marsh, Hungerford, Berks RG17 0SN, England. 1.

GRIESSER Gerhard (Gerd), b. 31 July 1918, Stuttgart, Germany. Prof Emeritus, Med Informatics & Stats. m. Gisela Breuer, 7 Nov 1942. *Education:* Med studies, Friedrich Wilhelm Univ, Berlin, & Eberhard Karl Univ, Tuebingen; Distinction, Med State Bd Exam, Berlin, 1942; Dr med, Univ Tuebingen, 1942; Addtl study, ec & math stats, Tuebingen 1960-63. *Appointments include:* Med Ofcr, Russia 1943-45; Hosps in Bavaria, Switzerland, Tuebingen, Stockholm, Duesseldorf 1945-59; Lectr (Gen Surg), Sr Lectr (Surg & Med Stats), Univ Tuebingen 1959-63; Full Prof, Med Informatics & Stats 1964-79, 1985-86, Dept Hd 1976-, Lectr (Info Sci) Fac Sci 1976-, Univ Pres 1979-85, Full Prof Emeritus 1986-, Christian Albrecht Univ, Kiel; Co-Fdr, Ptnr 1985-, Mng Dir 1986-1991, ITK Info Tech Kiel Ltd. *Creative Works include:* Devel of heart-lung machine 1952-57; 5 books; Num papers, book chapts, surg topics/med informatics; Mem var Editl Bds. *Memberships include:* Offices past/present: German Socs for Medical & Biol Electronics, Med Stats, Informatics & Documentation, & Assn of Computer Users; Var local med assns; Intl Med Informatics Assn (IMIA); Wkg Gp on privacy & confidentiality. *Honours include:* Awd IMIA, 1980; Hon Senator, Med Univ Luebeck, 1980; Silver Core Awd, Int Fed for Info Processing, 1980; Cross of Merit, 1981, Knight of Merit, 1985, Fed Repub Germany; Hon memberships. *Hobbies:* Classical music; Reading history & English literature; Sailing. *Address:* Barstenkamp 51-Rammsee, D-2300 Molfsee, Germany. 92.

GRIFFIN Cassandra Jeanette, b. 27 June 1974, San Augustine, Texas, USA. Student. *Education:* Bancroft Elem, 1979; Lorena Oates Elem, 1980-82; George D Jones Elem, 1983-84; M B North Intermed Sch, 1985; W.Orange Middle Sch, 1986-86; W Orange Stark Hg Sch, 1988-92. *Honours:* Houston Cronicle Spelling Bee Champ, 1985; Best Actress Awd, 1987; Scholastic Bowl Team, 1987; Pres Acad Fitness Awd, 1987; Nat Hon Roll, 1992; Zeta Phi Beta; Outstanding Scholastic Achievement Awd, 1992. *Hobbies:* Reading; Dancing; Listening to music; Shopping. *Address:* 109 W Schley Avenue, Orange, TX 77630, USA.

GRIFFIN Henry Wesley, b. 14 Oct 1949, Paris, Tex, USA. Dentist. m. Stephanie Ruth Griffin, 4 Aug 1982, 1 d. *Education:* BS 1970, Tex A&M; DDS 1975, UT Health Sci Ctr, Houston. *Appointments:* Dentist in pvt practice. *Memberships:* ADA; TDA. *Honour:* Delta Delta Delta Frat, 1971. *Hobbies:* Reading; Travelling. *Address:* 1349 Lamar Avenue, Paris, TX 75460, USA.

GRIFFIN Keith Alastair, b. 11 Mar 1927, Manchester, England. Freelance Marine Artist. m. Barbara Elizabeth Sutton, 16 July 1955, 2 d. *Education:* Laird Col Art, Birkenhead 1942-45; Grenadier Guards, Germany 1945-48l Scenic Designer, Winsen & Hamburg 1946-48 (on detachment) to CSEU. *Career:* 2 Commercial Art Studios, Liverpool 1948-54; Display Designer, Birkenhead 1954-56; Still-Life, Fashion & Illustrator, Liverpool Studio 1956-67; Freelance Marine Artist. *Creative Works:* Works in pvt collections; Works in Shipping Co Collections: Westminster Dredging Co, Land & Marine Contractors Ltd, Blue Funnen, Elder

Dempster, New Zealand Shipping Co, Sealand Container Svcs, USA, and others; Williamson Art Gallery, Birkenhead; Over 300 works in oils & watercolour; 12 subjects in Fine Art Print; Exhibited, RSMA, GB, Can, Vancouver & USA. *Honours:* 3rd Prize Poster Exhibition, Wings for Victory Week, 1943, 1st Prize Poster Exhibition, Salute the Soldier Week, 1944, Laird Sch of Art, Birkenhead. *Hobbies:* Swimming; Model making; Stamp collecting; History of deep sea sail. *Address:* 2 Penrhyn Avenue, Thingwall, Wirral, Cheshire L61 7UP, England.

GRIFFIN Stephanie Ruth, b. 27 Apr 1955, Nevada, Missouri, USA. Marriage & Family Counsellor. m. Dr Henry W Griffin, 4 Aug 1982, 1 d. *Education:* Baylor Univ 1973; Richland Col 1975-76; AS 1983, PJC; BS 1983, MS 1984, ETSU. *Appointments:* US Women's Army Corps, Honourable Discharge 1974; Pvt Practice Marriage & Family Counsellor, Psychotherapist 1985-. *Memberships:* AACD; TACD; ACA; TCA; ABMP; IABMCP; AABT; AAMHC; TAMHC; NCFR; AAPH. *Honours:* Hon Discharged, US Army, 1974; Sci Scholarship, PUC, 1980; Psi Chi Nat Hon Soc of Psychol, 1983; Cert of Volunteer Work, Family Haven Women's Crisis Ctr, 1984. *Hobbies:* Gardening; Research; Reading; Playing flute. *Address:* 1349 Lamar Avenue, Paris, TX 75460, USA. 5, 138, 152.

GRIFFITH Edward Michael Wynne, b. 29 Aug 1933. m. Jill Grange Moseley, 30 Oct 1959, 2 s. *Education:* Eton Col; Royal Agric Col. *Appointments:* Agric Res Coun 1972-81; Reg Dir, Nat West Bank 1974-; Chmn, Clwyd Health Authority 1980-90; UFC Wales Com, Nat Trust, Chmn Wales 1984-91; Chmn, Countryside Coun Wales 1991-. *Honours:* CBE 1986; DL, Vice Lt Clwyd 1988. *Hobbies:* Countryside; Farming; Horses; Hunting. *Address:* Greenfield, Trefnant, Clwyd, Wales. 1.

GRIFFITH Emlyn I, b. 13 May 1923, Utica, NY, USA. Lawyer. m. Mary L Kilpatrick, 13 Aug 1946, 2 s. *Education:* AB 1942, Colgate Univ; JD 1950, Cornell Law Sch. *Appointments include:* US Army Air Corps 1942-46, Pvt to Major; General law practice, Lockport, NY 1950-52, Rome, NY 1952-; Atty, var towns & sch districts 1953-73; Pres, Oneida County Bar Assn 1974-75; House of Delegates, NY State Bar Assn 1974-76; Co-Chmn, Com on Lawyer Professionalism 1989-; Chmn, NY Conf of County Bar Ofcrs 1974-77; Dir, NY Bar Foun 1989-; Bd Editors, NY State Bar Journal 1986-; Pub Ed Com, Am Bar Assn 1974-; Var coms; Phi Alpha Delta Law Frat 1980-86. *Memberships include:* Osgoode Soc, Can; Selden Soc, UK; VP, Hon Soc of Cymmrodorian, UK; Past Pres, Nat Assn State Bds of Ed; Bd Trustees, Phi Gamma Delta Intl; Phi Gamma Delta Edn 2, Foun; Nat Welsh- Am Foun; Presbyterian Home for Central NY; Rome Area C of C, Community Concerts Assn, Past Chmn, Joint Com for Griffiss AFB; Past Dir, Colgate Univ Alumni Corp; Chmn, var coms, NY State Bd Regents 1973-; Treas, NY State Photonics Dev Corp, 1989-; Trustee, Aerospace Ed Foun; United Presbyterian Ch Bd of Pensions. *Honours:* Fellow, Am & NY Bar Founs; Alumni Awd, dist'd svc, Colgate Univ, 1975; Citation, Air Force Assn, 1980; Root-Stimson Awd, pub svc, NY State Bar Assn, 1986; Hon doctorates & citations, var ednl & profl insts, state & nat. *Address:* 225 North Washington Street, Rome, NY 13440, USA. 2, 6, 52, 129, 130, 132, 139, 163.

GRIFFITHS Gareth Lloyd, b. 28 Mar 1954, Rhondda, Glamorgan. Communications Conslt; Barrister. *Education:* MA Oxon 1975, Jesus Col, Oxford; Dipl in Law 1985, City Univ; Coun of Legal Ed 1985-86; Barrister at Law. *Appointments:* Grad Editl Trainee, Thomas Regl Newspapers 1975-78; Liverpool Daily Post 1978-79; Correspondent, Financial Times 1979-84; Dir, Shardwick Conslts 1985-90; Chmn & CEO, GCS 1991-. *Publications:* Opticians & Competition Policy, 1987; Brunei in Profile, 9 editions 1988-. *Memberships:* Royal Inst of Pub Admin; Royal Inst Intl Affairs; Reform Club; Hon Soc Cymrodorrion; Inst PRs. *Honours:* Donald Miller Awd for Public Speaking, 1972; Sword of Excellence for Outstg Contbr to PR, Inst of PRs, 1989. *Hobbies:* Fund raising for Bodleian library, Oxford Univ; Chmn, St Augustine's Appeal, Penarth; 19th century church & political history. *Address:* 2 St Donats House, Seaview Court, Kymin Road, Penarth, South Glamorgan CF6 1AS, Wales. 24, 52.

GRIMMEISS Hermann Georg, b. 19 Aug 1930, Hamburg, Germany. Prof in Solid State Physics. m. Hildegard Weizmann, 17 Nov 1956, 1 s. 1 d. *Education:* Arbitur 1950, Oberschule Nordlingen; Univ Munich 1950-57; Diplomphysiker 1957; Dr rer nat 1957. *Appointments:* Reschr, Philips Res Lab, Aachen, Germany 1951-65; Prof in Physics, Frankfurt Univ 1971-72; VP, RIFA, Stockholm, Sweden 1982-84; Prof in Solid State Physics, Hd of Dept, Univ Lund, Sweden 1965-71, 1973-81, 1984-; Director of Semiconductor Physics, Frankfurt (Oder), 1991-1992. *Publications:* Over 160 sci pubs in intl jours; 4 book chapts. *Memberships:* Royal Physiographic Soc, Lund, Sweden; The Swedish Nat Com for Physics; Royal Swedish Acad of Engrg Scis; Royal Swedish Acad Scis; Finnish Soc of Sci & Letters; NY Acad Scis. *Honours:* Order of North Star, 1969; Fellow Am Phys Soc, 1989. *Hobbies:* Tennis; Classical music. *Address:* Dept of Solid State Physics, University of Lund, Box 118, S-221 00 Lund, Sweden. 34.

GRIMSHAW James Albert Jr, b. 10 Dec 1940, Kingsville, Tex, USA. Tchr. m. Glenda Darlene Hargett, 10 June 1961, 1 s. 1 d. *Education:* BA 1962, MA 1968, Tex Tech Univ; PhD 1972, La State Univ. *Appointments:* USAF with duty in TX, Vietnam, CA, AL, and CO, rtd in rank of Lt Col 1963- 83; Prof & Hd, Dept Lit & Langs, East Tex State Univ 1983-90; Full-time Tchr, ETSU 1990-. *Publications:* The Flannery O'Connor Companion, 1981; Robert Penn Warren: A Descriptive Bibliography, 1982; RPW's Brother to Dragons, 1983; Time's Glory: Original Essays on RPW, 1986; Paul Wells Barrus Lectures, 1990. *Memberships:* Robert Penn Warren Circle, Pres 1991-93; Am Lit Assn; Bibliographical Soc of the Univ of Va; Tex Assn of Depts of Eng, Pres 1988-89; S Atlantic MLA; S Central MLA. *Honours:* Flannery O'Connor Vstg Prof, Ga Col, 1977; Vstg Fellow in Bibliography, Yale Univ 1979- 80; ETSU Fac Senate Dist'd Fac Awd, 1988; Ctr for RPW Studies Adv Bd 1989-. *Hobbies:* Swimming; Chess; Gardening; Five-string banjo. *Address:* Rt 2, Box 40T, Greenville, TX 75402, USA. 3, 7, 15, 30, 152.

GRIMSHAW John Stuart, b. 22 Sept 1934, Sheffield, England. Med Practitioner; Conslt Psychi. m. Anne Vince, 12 July 1958, 1 s. 1 d. *Education:* Jesus Col Cambridge 1952-55; UCH Med Sch 1955-58; MA, MB, BChir 1958; FRCP (Ed) 1977; FRCPysch 1977; MRCS (Eng) 1958; DPM 1962. *Appointments:* House Physician, House Surg, UCH 1959; House Physician, Whittington Hosp 1960; RAMC 1960-65 Major; Sr Registrar, Dept Psychological Med St Thomas' Hosp & Knowle Hosp 1965-67; Conslt Psychi, Southampton Univ Hosps 1967-90; Dep Med Dir, Marchwood Priory Hosp 1986-. *Memberships:* Royal Col Psychis Approval Exercise Convenor 1973-77; Examiner for MRCPsych 1977-81, 1983-87; Observer for MRCPsych 1987-; MH Act Comm 1983-89, Central Policy Com 1988-89; Fellow Royal Soc Med 1967-; MH Review Tribunal (Wessex) 1990-. *Honours:* Suckling Essay Prize for Obst, UCH Med Sch 1957; Sir William Gower's & Fellowes Gold Medal for clin med, UCH Med Sch, 1957; Conslt Emeritus, Southampton & South West Hants Health Authority, 1991; Mem, Worshipful Soc of Apothecaries, 1991; Freeman of the City of London, 1991. *Hobbies:* Long distance walking; History; Gardening; Numismatics. *Address:* The Orchard, Curdridge, Southampton SO3 2BH, England.

GRINBERG Daniel, b. 18 Mar 1950, Lodz, Poland. Historian. *Education:* MA History 1973, Dr Hum 1977, Doc dr hab 1987, Warsaw Univ. *Appointments:* Adj 1978-82, Docent 1988-90, Prof 1991-, Inst History, Warsaw Univ, Bialystok Br; Jewish Historical Institute 1988-, Dir 1990-. *Publications:* Book, Geneza

Apartheidv, 1980; Ruch Anarchistyczny i Europie Zachodniej 1870-1914, book; Translation into Polish of Russell B, Berlin I, Arendl H, Sartori 6. *Memberships:* Assn degli Storici Europei; Polskie Towarzystwo Historyczne; Assn Track & Field Statisticians; Chmn Stats Comm in Polish Assn of T&F Athletics 1983-89. *Hobbies:* History of film; Track & field athletics. *Address:* Putawska 176/178a m 71, 02 670 Warsaw, Poland.

GRIST Norman Roy, b. 9 Mar 1918, Doncaster, England. Emeritus Prof. m. Mary Stewart McAlister, 27 Feb 1943. *Education:* BSc 1939, MB ChB 1942, Univ Glasgow; M(1950)F(1958)RCPEdinb; M (1 9 5 9) F (1 9 6 7) R C P a t h o l ; M(1980)F(1983)RCPSGlasgow. *Appointments:* Armed Svcs: RAMC 1943-46; Res Asst, Lectr Virus Dis, Univ Glw 1948-62; Reader Viral Epidemiol, UG 1962-65; Prof Infectious Diseases, UG 1965-83, Emeritus 1983-. *Publications:* Diagnostic Methods in Clinical Virology, 1966, 1974, 1979; Infections in current medical practice, joint author, 1986; Diseases of Infection, 1987, 1993; Num pubs in med & sci lit. *Memberships:* Brit Soc for Study of Infectn, Pres 1982-83; Path Soc GB & Ireland; Soc Gen Microbiol; Assn Clin Path, Hon mem 1990-; Brit Med Assn; Scot Ornithol Club; Glasgow Nat Hist Soc, Gen Secy 1989-91; Arran Nat Hist Soc; Scott Diagnostic Virol Gp, Fdr mem. *Honours:* Bronze Medal Univ of Helsinki, 1972; Orden de Sanidad, cat Encomienda, Spain, 1974. *Hobbies:* Natural history; Bird watching; Music; Ecology- epidemiology; History of civilisations. *Address:* 5A Hyndland Court, 6A Sydenham Road, Glasgow G12 9NR, Scotland. 1, 43, 52.

GRISWOLD Wilburn Carnell, b. 16 July 1943, Camden, Texas, USA. Pastor. m. Patricia Aileen Tovey, 24 Jan 1964, 3 d. *Education:* BS 1966, Sam Houston State Univ; MS 1975, Fla Inst Tech; MDiv 1990, MidWestern Baptist Theol Seminary. *Appointments:* Ofcr, US Army 1966-87; Co- Pastor, Siloam Spring Baptist Chapel, Excelsior Springs, Md 1988-90; Pastor, Ogden Baptist Mission, Ogden, Kansas, USA 1990-. *Memberships:* Alphi Phi Omega, Nat Svc Frat; Nat Defense Transportation Assn; Assn US Army; Nat Milit Hon Soc of Scabbard & Blade. *Honours:* Bronze Star Medal, 1967, 1972; Army Meritorious Svc Medal, 4 awds, 1970, 1974, 1984, 1987; Defense Meritorious Svc Medal, 1981; Pres, Graduating Class of 1990, Midwestern Baptist Theol Seminary. *Hobbies:* Reading; Golf; Fishing; Hunting; Woodworking. *Address:* 3202 Chestershire Drive, Pasadena, TX 77503, USA. 176.

GROCHOWSKI Jan Antoni, b. 4 June 1930, Lvov, Poland. Paedoatric Surg. m. Elzbieta Rog, 18 Oct 1969, 1 s. 1 d. *Education:* Dipl of Physician, Fac Med 1955; MD 1962; Assoc Prof 1966; Prof 1973; Specialist in Gen Surg 1958; Io Specialist in Paediatric Surg 1962, Ilo 1965. *Appointments:* Asst Prof, Chair & Dept of Paed Surg, Acad Krakow, Poland 1955-65; Hd Dept Paed Surg, Inst Paediatrics, Med Acad, Krakow 1965-, Dir Inst Paed 1976-. *Publications:* 3 Chapts on paed surg in textbooks on gen surg, gynae & intensive care; 112 papers on gen surg, paed surg, surg trauma, epidemiol of congenit defects. *Memberships:* Polish Surg Assn; Edit of Paed Surg, Polish Surg Review; Vice Chmn, Polish Assn Paed Surg; German Assn Paed Surg. *Honours:* Silver Cross of Merit 1954; Golden Cross of Merit 1964; Medal Polonia Restituta 1969. *Hobbies:* Ornithology; Bird watching; Collecting figurines of owls-over 3000 items in collection; Ethnography of the Spisz Region, Poland. *Address:* Polish-American Children's Hospital, Medical Academy, 265 Wielicka Street, 30-663 Krakow, Poland.

GRODZINSKA Krystyna Aleksandra, b. 27 May 1934, Lwow, Poland. Prof Ecol. m. Wladyslaw Grodzinski, 3 Mar 1957, 1 s. 1 d. *Education:* MSc Biol 1956, PhD 1962, Prof Ecol 1975, Jagiellonian Univ, Krakow. *Appointments:* Asst 1956-62, Prof's Asst 1963-75, Assoc Prof 1975-85, Full Prof 1985-, Vice Dir Inst Bot 1984-91, Hd, Environmental Ecol Lab, Inst Botany 1991-

, Polish Acad Scis; Scholarships: Univ Wyoming 1973, 1982, Univ Lund, Sweden 1976, Phillips Univ, Marburg, Germany 1986, Spitsbergen Expedition (Polar Star Station) 1985. *Publications:* Author 75 papers and arts publ in Polish & foreign (European, Am) jours & books, main topics ecol-environmental pollution, acidification, monitoring, plant sociol, geography. *Memberships:* Mem Exec Bd European Ecol Fed 1989-; Intl Assn for Ecol, INTECOL, 1983; Mem sev nat socs & coms. *Honours:* Polish Acad Scis prizes: 1978, 1979, State Prize Poland 1988. *Hobbies:* Reading; Music. *Address:* Institute of Botany, Polish Academy of Sciences, Lubicz 46, 31 512 Krakow, Poland.

GROESSCHEN Heribert Johannes, b. 18 July 1943, Hennef, Germany. Mftg Co Exec. m. Heidemarie Spies, 30 June 1966, div 1979, 2 s. *Appointments:* Engr, Mech & Textiles, Col Wuppertal 1968; Mech Engr, Opti-Ion, London, Essen 1964-69; Secy, Gen Mgr Osto Prov, SJ, Frankfurt, Darmstadt 1969-70; EDP Project Mgr, Fuhr/Philips, Cologne 1970-72; Mgmt Cons Innovative Recycling Technologies, var locations 1973-; Cons in field. *Membership:* Mgr Mag Club. *Hobby:* Writing. *Address:* Ploesslgasse 11, A-1040 Vienna, Austria.

GRONOW Michael, b. 26 July 1937, Cardiff, S Wales. Company Director. m. Janet Ruth Tompkins, 21 Dec 1968, div, 1 s. 1 d. *Education:* BSc Hons, Univ Wales; PhD Cantab, Trinity Col, Univ Cambridge. *Appointments:* MRC Res Asst, Dept Radiotherapeutics 1963-65, Demonstrator Dept Chem 1962-65, Univ Cambridge; Res Assoc, Dept Pharmacol, Baylor Univ, Houston, Tex, USA 1965-66; Res Assoc & Demonstrator, Dept of Biochem, Univ Oxford 1966-69; Lectr Dept Experimental Pathol & Cancer Res, Univ Leeds 1969-75; Perm Sr Res Fellow, Cancer Res Unit, Univ York 1975-79; Conslt PA Tech Ctr Int 1979-80; Hd Bioscis PA Ctr for Advanced Studies 1980-81; Jt MD & Fdr, Cambridge Life Sci plc 1981-88; MD CRL Ltd 1989; Dir Aquamarine Scis & Kognos Ltd, 1992. *Publications:* Author 50 pubns; Edit, The Genetic Engr & Biotechnologist. *Memberships:* Biochem Soc 1967; Br Assn Cancer Res 1969. *Hobbies:* Music; Photography; Hockey; Chess; Wine. *Address:* Thornton House, 131 Waterbeach Road, Landbeach, Cambridge CB4 4EA, England.

GRÖNROOS Christian, b. 16 Jan 1947, Helsinki, Finland. Prof Mktg. m. (1) 1 s, 1 d, (2) Suvi Kilpelainen, 16 Mar 1981. *Education:* BBA 1969, MBA 1972, Lic BA 1974, Dr Econ (in business) 1979, Swedish Sch of Ec & Bus Admin, Helsinki, Finland. *Appointments:* Assoc Prof & Actg Prof Mktg 1974-84, Prof Mktg 1984-, Swedish Sch Ec & Bus Admin; Vstg Prof Mktg, Ariz State Univ, USA 1988, 1992. *Publications:* Strategic Management and Marketing in the Service Sector, 1983; Service Management and Marketing, 1990; 5 books in Finnish & 3 Scandinavian Langs. *Memberships:* Dist'd Mem of the Finnish Soc of Sci & Letters 1985-; Res Fellow of First Interstate Ctr for Services Mktg at Ariz State Univ 1989-. *Honours:* The Ahlsell Awd for Res into Mktg & Distribution in Scandinavia, 1985; The Erik Kempe Awd for Pubs in the Field of Mktg & Bus in Scandinavia. *Hobbies:* Travelling; Literature. *Address:* Swedish School of Economics & Business Administration, Arkadiagatan 22, SF-00100 Helsinki, Finland. 90.

GROOM Raymond John, b. 3 Sept 1944, Victoria, Australia. Political Premier of Tasmania. m. Gillian M Crisp, 21 Jan 1967, 4 s, 2 d. *Education:* LLB, Univ Melbourne, 1967. *Appointments include:* Elected, Hse of Reps, 1975; Environ Hsg Com Devel, 1977-78, Fed Min for Hsg and Constr, 1978-80; Chm, S.Pacific C'wlth and State Hsg Mins, NZ, 1980; Min for Forests, Sea Fisheries and Mines, Min Assting the Premier, 1986-89; Dpty Premier, 1988; Dpty Ldr of Lib Party, 1986-91; Ldr of Opposition, Shadow Treas, Shadow Min for C/wlth/State Relations, 1991-92; Premier, Treas, and in for Econ Devel, 1992. *Hobbies:* Family; Painting; Golf; Football. *Address:* 21 Cromwell Street, Battery Point Tasmania 7004. 1, 23, 152.

GROS-ESPIELL Hector, b. 17 Sept 1926, Montevideo. Minister For Relats. m. Mercedes Cibils-Puig, 5 Sept 1955, 1 s. 1 d. *Education:* Dr Law, Universidad de la Republica, Montevideo; Prof Constitutional Law, Univ de la Republica, Montevideo. *Appointments:* Vice Secy For Relats 1963-64; Amb Uruguay 1964-73; Dir Uruguayan Diplomatic Sch, Inst Artigas del Servicio Exterior 1989-90; Rep of Uruguay in: General Assembly of the UN 1965-67, General Assembly of OAS 1966-67, UNESCO Conf 1950, 1954, 1958, Conf of ILO 1967-72; Judge of Admin Tribunal of: UN 1961-70; ILO 1981-84; Judge of Interam Crt Human Rights, Costa Rica; Former Asst to Secy Gen of UN at the Western Saharas Affaires 1989; Secy Gen OPANAL. *Publications:* Dir Newspaper, La Tribuna, of Montevideo 1959-63; Course delivered at the Intl Law Acad of the Hague 1975; Chapt on Am System in the UNESCO Manual, Study on the Judge Elections at the Interam Crt Human Rights; Diplomacy & history; Democracy & human rights; Procedure at the Interam Crt of human rights; Books & arts publ in Uruguay, Argentina, Brasil, Chile, and many other countries. *Memberships include:* Inst Hispano-Luso-Am de Derecho Intl, Madrid; Mem of former Inst de Estudios Politicos, Madrid; Assn Uruguaya de Derecho Intl. *Honours include:* Great Cross, Order of: Libertador, Argentina; Condor de los Andes, Bolivia; Cruzeiro do Sul, Brazil; Merito, Colombia; Libertador d'Higgins, Chile; MatiasDelgado, Ecuador; the Republic, Egypt; FRG; Quetzal, Guatemala; Aguila Azteca, Mexico; Mariscal Francisco Solano Lopez, Paraguay; Merito, Paraguay; Merito, Peru; of the Sol, Peru; of Duarte, Suarez y Mella, RCA Dominicana; Isabel la Catolica, Spain; Alfonso X El Sabio, Spain; Merito Civil, Spain; Andres Bello, Venezuela; Encomienda, Order of Cedro del Lidano, Lidannon; Chevalier, Order of Republica, Italy; Mem of Hon, Inst de Cultura Hispanica, Spain. *Address:* Ministerio de Relaciones Exteriores, Colonia 1206, Montevideo, Uruguay.

GROSS Manfred Ferry, b. 22 Dec 1907, Berlin, Germany. Conslt Physician; Res Wkr. m. Sylvia Edna Webb, 17 Aug 1963. *Education:* Univs: Berlin, Heidelberg, Wurzburg, Edinburgh; MD, LRCP, LRCS, LRFP&S (Ed). *Appointments:* Brit Expat in Germany, Hufeland Hosp 1933-34; Virchow Hosp 1934-35; Hosp Persische Strasse 1935-36; Kerckoff Res Inst, Bad Nauheim 1936-38; New End Hosp, London 1942; War Svc RAMC 1943-46, 112 Br Gen Hosp, India, 23 ICCS Burma, M i Desp Burma; Com Ofcr, Milit Hosp, Kodaicanal, Mysore, S India; Hon Conslt Cardiol, New End Hosp 1948-51; Res Wk into xenogenic cell impl (cell therapy) 1952; Res Work, intl therapeut applic of ozone i cardio-vascular & other diseases 1965. *Memberships:* BMA 1942; FRSM 1952; Med Assn f Organo-Biotherapy, Germany 1964; Med Assn f Ozone Therapy, Germany, 1970. *Hobbies:* Music; Drawing cartoons. *Address:* 3 Loom Place, Radlett, Herts WD7 8AF, England. 170.

GROSS Michael Lester Phillip, b. 31 Mar 1952, Hertfordshire, England. Conslt Neurologist. m. Jennifer Ruth Hoffman, 30 July 1974, 2 d. *Education:* Sidney Sussex Col, Cambridge 1970-73, MA, MB, BChir, MD 1987; London Hosp 1973-76, MRCP 1978. *Appointments:* Sr Registrar, Nat Hosp, Queen Sq; Conslt Neurologist, Chmn, Div of Neurological Sci, Regl Neurol Ctr, Royal Surrey County Hosp & East Surrey Hosps 1990-. *Publications:* The Therapeutic Modification of Inflammatory Polyneuropathy, 1987; Sci papers & intl presentations; Treatment of Guillain Barre Syndrome, Inflammatory Polyneuropathy, EAN, Rejection Encephalopathy & General Neuro Topics. *Memberships:* Royal Col Physicians; BMA; Southwest Thames Regl Neuroscis, Adv Com; Assn Brit Neurologists; South of England Neurol Assn. *Honour:* Action Res Tng Fellowship, 1980. *Hobbies:* Tennis; Weightlifting; Theatre; Food. *Address:* Green Waters, Green Lane, Stanmore, Middlesex HA7 3AF, England.

GROSSETETE Bernard Louis Claude, b. 25 July 1938, France. Professor, University of Paris; Director, LPNHE Paris 6 & 7. 1 s, 1 d. *Education:* Alumnus Student,

1957-61; DSc, 1964. *Appointments:* Attache, 1962, Maitre, 1968, de Recherche au CNRS, 1968; Maitre de Conf a la Fac des Scis de Paris, 1968; Prof a l'Univ Paris 7, 1973. *Publications:* La representation des phenomenes physiques, 1981. *Memberships:* French Soc of Phys. *Honours:* Bronze Medal, Ctr Nat de la Recherche Sci. *Address:* Laboratoire de Physique Nucleaire et de Hautes Energies, Universite Paris 6, Tour 33 RdC, 4 Place Jussieu, 75252 Paris Cedex 05, France. 91.

GROTH Klaus, b. 8 Dec 1923, Dömitz, Germany. Univ Prof. m. Ruth Groth, 16 Sept 1950, 2 s. *Education:* Eng Ofcr, Naval Acad, Murwik & Kiel 1041-45; Dipl Mech Engrg 1950, Dr ing 1953, Lectr, Dr habil, 1958, Univ Hannover. *Appointments:* Chf Engr of a submarine, Navy 1943-45; Sci Asst 1950-53, Sr Engr, Lectr 1953-62, Univ Han; Chf Design & Devel Engr, MAN Corp, Augsburg 1960-67; Prof, Dir of Inst, 1967-, Guest Prof, China 1991, Japan 1992, Univ Han. *Publications:* 2 Books; Over 60 sci pubs in sci jours. *Memberships:* VDJ; Braunschweigische Wiss Gesellschaft, elected mem, engrs class; Navy Ofcrs Assn; GERM Lloyd Hamburg; Wiss Beirat (Sci Conslts Bd); Sci Bd AJF. *Honours:* Medal for Submarine Hunters & Minesweepers, 1942; Silver Hon Medal VDJ, 1978; Hon Medal, 1979; Stipendiat Studienstiftung des Deutschen Volkes, 1949; Prof. H.C., China Acad of Railway Sci, 1991. *Hobbies:* History; Sailing; Skiing; Do-It-Yourself work; Gardening. *Address:* Schaftrift 18, 3003 Ronnenberg, OT Benthe, Germany. 26, 43, 92.

GROVE William Dennis, b. 23 July 1927, Swansea, Wales. Company Chmn. m. Audrey Saxel, 10 Jan 1953, 1 s. 1 d. *Education:* BSc 1951, King's Col, London; Comm, S Wales Borderers, 1946. *Appointments:* Overseas Gen Mgr, Dunlop Gp 1953-70; Chmn, TPT & Sonoco Gp 1970-85; Chmn, North West Water 1985-. *Hobbies:* Travel; Golf; Spectator sports. *Address:* Wilmslow, Cheshire, England.

GROVES Sharon Darlene Maffett Pittman, b. 4 May 1951, Cleveland, Ohio. Conslt; Trainer; Writer. m. Robert Groves, 22 June 1974, div, 1 s. *Education:* BA Social Work 1973, Ohio Univ; MSc in Social Admin 1980; CWRU. *Appointments:* Social Svcs Dir, Emmanual Care Ctr 1974-76; Community Guidance & Human Svcs 1976-80; Trng Coord, Provider Liaison, Ga Dept Human Resources 1980-89; Pres, SDG Assocs, Mgmt Conslts 1986-. *Memberships:* Atlanta C of C; Atlanta Bus League; Am Soc for Trng & Devel, Chmn Multicultural Network 1988-89, Chmn Awds 1990; Delta Sigma Theta; Career Devel Support Gp, Fdr & Facilitator. *Honours:* Am Soc for Trng & Devel, Cert of Appreciation, 1988; Outstg Svc Awd, Southwest Middle Sch, 1988; Spelman Col, Cert Appreciation, 1991; Women in Community Svc, Cert of Appreciation, 1991. *Hobbies:* Reading; Painting; Cultural events; Walking. *Address:* SDG Associates, 2221 Peachtree Road, Suite 242, Atlanta, GA 30309, USA. 7, 76.

GRUNBAUM Adolf, b. 15 May 1923, Cologne, Germany. Edr. m. Thelma Braverman, 26 June 1949, 1 d. *Education:* BA 1943, Wesleyan Univ; MS 1948, PhD 1951, Yale Univ. *Appointments:* Andrew Mellon Prof Philos, Res Prof Psychi, Chmn Ctr for Philos of Sci, Univ Pittsburgh. *Publications:* Philosophical Problems of Space & Time, 1963, Russian translation 1969, 2nd enlarged ed, 1973; Modern Science and Zeno's Paradoxes, 1967, Brit Ed 1968; Geometry & Chonometry in Philosophical Perspective, 1968; The Foundations of Psychoanalysis: A Philosophical Critique, 1984; Validation in the Clinical theory of Psychoanalysis, 1993. *Contributions to:* over 250 arts to sci jours. *Memberships:* Fellow, Am Assn for Advancement of Sci; Am Acad Arts & Scis; Laureate Acad of Humanism. *Honours:* Pres, Am Philos Assn, Eastern Div 1982-83; Gifford Lectures, Univ St Andrews, Scotland, 1985; Werner Heisenberg Lecture, Bavarian Acad Sci, Munich, Germany, 1985; Sr US Scist Awd, Alexander von Humboldt Foun, Germany, 1985; Fregene Prize in

Scienc, Italian Parliament, 1989; Wilbur Lucius Cross Medal, Yale Univ, 1990. *Address:* 2510 Cathedral of Learning, University of Pittsburgh, Pittsburgh, PA 15260, USA. 3, 152.

GRÜNEWALD Björn Mikael, b. 2 Mar 1940, Stockholm. ILO Senior Adviser (Dir European Affairs). m. Ann Britt Jonsson, 2 June 1962, 4 s. *Education:* Ofcrs Dipl, R Sw Naval Acad 1960; Dipl in Bus Adm, Stockholm Sch of Ec 1968; Grad studies 1967-69; Dipls in Personnel Adm 1976, & from Swedish Armed Forces Staff & War Col 1987. *Appointments:* Secy, Stockholm Univ Stud Union 1967-68; Secy, Sw Nat Union of Studs 1968-70; Secy, Sw Fed of Industries 1970- 71; Sw Employers' Confederation 1971-93; Dir Ed & Trng 1978-88; Dir European Affairs 1988-93; Snr Advr, Intl Labour Org, 1993-. *Publications:* Num arts in newspapers & profl jours, mostly on ed, trng, human resource devel; Books & materials for the Confederation. *Memberships:* Chmn, Ed Com of BIAC; Advr to OECD, Paris, France; Chmn, Sw Naval Reserve Ofcrs Assn; Past, Chmn Coun of Sw ORT, affiliated to World ORT Union of London; Rotary Club of Osteraker, past pres. *Hobby:* The sea. *Address:* International Labour Office, Central and East European Team, Mozsár Utca 14, H-1066 Budapest, Hungary. 52.

GRUSAS Bronius, b. 20 Aug 1932, Gailiskiu Village, Skuodo Region, Lithuania. Artist; Painter. m. Tamara Baskakova, 24 Nov 1956, 2 s. *Education:* Dipl Artist & Painter 1963, Art Acad Lithuania. *Appointments:* Artist, Dept Culture of Lithuania 1963-70; Tchr Arts, Art Acad Lithuania 1970-73; Curator of Arts & Art Assns, Coun of Ministers of Lithuania 1973-91; Profl Artist 1991-. *Creative Works:* Works in stained glass; Oil paintings; Paintings in glass plastic technique. *Membership:* Assn Lithuanian Artists. *Honours:* Hon Artist of Lithuania 1982; 2 Jubilee Medals, 1970, 1984; Dipls of Lithuanian Supreme Soviet, 1975, 1982. *Hobbies:* Philosophy; Portraits of beautiful women. *Address:* 6-3 Stikliu Street, Vilnius 2001, Lithuania.

GRYKO Czeslaw, b. 16 Dec 1951, Lewsze. Philosopher. m. Danuta Skrzypczak-Gryko, 10 Jan 1976, 1 s. *Education:* Bachelor of Admin 1972, Warsaw Univ Fac Law & Adm; Master Admin 1974, Univ Wroclaw, Fac Law & Admin, & Fac Philos; MPhil 1978, Dr Humanistic Sci 1983, State Univ in Lublin. *Appointments:* Lectr in Philos of Culture Dept, State Univ Lublin 1975- . *Publications:* Time in Natural Science & Cultural Science, 1983; Axiological Differentiation of Social Space, 1984; Law & Culture: The Conception of Legal Culture, 1985; Jozef Chalasinski Sociological Theory of Culture, 1989. *Memberships:* Polish Philo Soc; Polish Soc of Sci of Religions; Lublin Sci Assn Nationwide Team for Res in Philos of Culture and Polish 20th Century Philos and Polish Sociological Assoc. *Honour:* Prize awd'd by Ministry Higher Ed, 1990. *Hobbies:* Studying maps; Collecting books. *Address:* ul Wierzbowa 11 m 23, 20-353 Lublin, Poland.

GU Fangchou, b. June 1926, Ninbo City, Zhejiang, China. Professor of Virology. m, 1951, 2 s, 1 d. *Education:* PhD, Inst of Virol, Acad of Med Scis, Moscow, 1950. *Appointments:* VP, 1976-84, Pres, 1985, Chinese Acad of Med Scis and Peking Union Med Col. *Publications:* Ed: Chinese Med Scis Jour; Acata Academiae Medicinae Sinicae; Chief Ed, Nat Med Jour of China; Assoc Ed, Chinese Jour of Immunol; Sci Com, European Jour of Epidemiol. *Memberships:* China Assn of Sci and Tech; Nat Natural Sci Foun of China; FRCP, London; Hon Col Fellow, Coun of Cumberland Col of Hlth Scis in Austr; Acad Europeenne, Paris; Chinese Med Assn; V-Chm, Beijing Assn of Sci and Tech; Pres, Chinese Soc of Biomed Engrg. *Honours:* Fdr of China Polio Vaccine. *Hobbies:* Classical music; Literature. *Address:* Chinese Academy of Medical Sciences, 9 Dong Dan San Tian, Beijing 100730, China.

GU Huanzhang, b. 11 Nov 1934, Jiangsu, China. Professor of Agricultural Economics. m. Neng, 6 Jan

1964, 2 s. *Education:* Grad, Agric Econ Dept, Nanjing Agric Col, 1956-60. *Appointments:* Ofr of Animal Husbandry Bureau of Nanhui County, Shanghai, 1951-56; Tchr of Agric Econ, Nanjing Agric Col, 1960-68; Dean of Agric Econ Dept, 1979-89; Prof and Dean of Agric Econ Inst, 1989-. *Publications:* Agricultural Technical Economics, 1990; On Stock Economics, 1990; 80 papers. *Memberships:* Agric Tech Econ Assn, Dpty Dir; Agric Econ Assn of Jingsu, Dir; Sci and Tech Com of Agric Min; Chief Ed, Rural Econ in Jiangsu; V-Chief Ed, Agric Tech Econs. *Honours:* Exempliary Tchr, 1985; Specialist with Outstanding Contribution, 1988; Second prize, social sci achievement, 1985; Third prize, Sci and Tech Progress, all Min of Agric. *Hobbies:* Reading; Writing. *Address:* College of Agricultural Economics and Trade, Nanjing Agric University, Nanjing 210014, China.

GU Ting-long, b. 10 Nov 1904, Suzhou. Res Librarian; Bibliographer; Lib Scist. m. Pan Cheng-gui, 8 Aug 1922, 2 s. *Education:* BA 1931, Shanghai Chizhi Univ; MA 1932, Beiping Yencheng Univ. *Appointments:* Hd Acquisitions Dept of the Library of Harvard Yenching Univ of Beiping 1933-39; Dir, Hezhong Lib 1939-53; Dir, Shanghai Municipal Lib of Historical Lit 1953-62; Dir, Shanghai Lib 1962-85; Hon Dir, Shanghai Lib 1985-. *Publications:* Chf Edit: Universal Bibliography of Chinese Rare Book Serials, 1962; Bibliography of Chinese Rare Books, 1992; A Chronological Sketch of the Life of Wu Ta-ch'eng, Author, 1935; Collection of Ancient Chinese Pottery Writings, 1939; Zhang's Si Dang Zhai Bibliography, 1938; Co- Edit: Collection of Illustrative Plates of Ming Edition Rare Books, 1941; Selection from Hanshu, 1956; Reading Guide to Erya, 1990. *Memberships:* VP, China Soc of Lib Sci; State Appraisal Com of Cultural Relic of the Cultural Ministry; Conslt of the Planning Gp of Rare Book Rectification & Publication of the State Coun; Municipal Com of Preservation of Cultural Relics of Shanghai; P-Time Prof of Fudan Univ & East China Normal Univ; Hon mem Council of China Assn of Calligraphers. *Honour:* 1991 Municipal Awd for Dist'd Svc in the Field of Incunabulogy & Lib Sci. *Hobby:* Chinese Calligraphy. *Address:* 325 Nanjing Road West, Shanghai 200003, China.

GU Tong Zeng, b. 6 Dec 1933, Jiangsu, China. Senior Architect, Professor. m. Qin Baozhen, 2 Feb 1962, 1 d. *Education:* Grad, Archt Dept, Tongji Univ, Shanghai, 1956. *Appointments:* Arch Design Work, Civil Arch Design Inst, Min of Constrn, China, 1956-57; Res Dept, Beijing Arch Design and Res Inst, 1957. *Publications:* Aerated Concrete application in building compositions, 1975-91; Cutting machine design with aerated concrete application, 1983; Impression on Buildings in USA, 1991; Glimpse of housing in South Korea. *Memberships:* Beijing Inst of Arch Design; Coun, Dpty Sec Gen, Beijing Arch and Engrs Assn; Coun and Sec Gen, Beijing Archt Assn. *Honours:* Outstanding Sci and Tech Prize, 1985; Beijing: Tech Progress Prize, 1986-87; Sci and Tech Assn prize, 1987-88; Outstanding Sci and Tech Person Prize, 1991; China Archts Soc Prize, 1991. *Hobbies:* Painting; Photography. *Address:* Beijing Institute of Architectural Design and Research, 62 Sough Lishi Road, Beijing, China.

GU Zhiyan, b. 17 Feb 1932, Beijing, China. Sr Edit; Prof. m. 10 Oct 1960, 1 s. 1 d. *Education:* Beijing Med Col 1950-55. *Appointments:* Tien-jin Med Col Hosp 1955-58; Xinjiang Med Col Hosp 1958-84; Chinese Med Assn 1984-. *Publications include:* Pollinosis in Xinjiang Area, 1980; Clinical Allergy, 1988; Clinical Allergic Diseases, 1991. *Memberships:* Soc Otolaryngol; Chinese Med Assn. *Honour:* Investigations into Pollinosis in Xinjiang Area, won Sci & Tech Awd of Xinjiang Province, China 1978. *Hobbies:* Reading; Travelling. *Address:* Chinese Medical Association, Dongsi Xidajie, Beijing 100710, China.

GUDE Gilbert, b. 9 Mar 1923, Wash DC. Writer; Lectr; Conslt. m. 19 June 1948, 3 s. 2 d. *Education:* BS 1948, Cornell Univ; MA 1958, George Wash Univ. *Appointments:* MD, House of Delegates 1953-58; MD,

State Senate 1962-66; Mem US House of Representatives, 8th Dist MD 1967-76; Dir, Congressional Res Svc, Lib of Cong 1977-86. *Publications include:* Where the Potomac Begins: A History of the North Branch Valley, 1984; Congressional Research Service: The Research & Information Arm of Congress, 1985; Small Town Destiny: The Story of Five Small Towns Along the Potomac Valley, 1989. *Memberships include:* Sr Fellow, Nat Acad of Pub Admin; Bd Trustees & Pres's Coun, St Mary's Col, St Mary's City, Maryland; Chmn, Anglo-American Conference on Africa, 1976; Parliamentary Libs Sect of Intl Fed of Lib Assns, 1977-85, Chmn 1983-85. *Honours:* Georgetown Univ, DSc h.c. 1977; George Wash Univ, Dist'd Alumni Awd; Mem Hon, Bd Trustees, US Capital Historical Soc; Lib of Cong Dist'd Svc Awd, 1985. *Address:* 5411 Duvall Drive, Bethesda, MD 20816, USA.

GUDEA Nicolae, b. 17 Oct 1941, Deva, Romania. Reschr; Arch. m. Emilia Kovacs, 3 Sept 1967, 2 s. *Education:* Univ Cluj, Fac History & Philos 1963-68; Doctorship 1978. *Appointments:* Arch 1968-72; Reschr 1972-. *Publications:* Der Romerlager von Rosenau, 1970; Der Romerlager von Bucium, 1972; Drei Munzhorte von Banat 4th, 1974; Asezări din epoca romanăa si Romană tîrzie la Gornea, 1976; Porolissum, 1989. *Memberships:* Soc de Studii Closice din Romania; Rei Cretariae Romanae Fautor 1978; Institutum Arch Germanicum. *Honour:* Nat Prize for Arch 1989. *Hobbies:* Reading; Sports. *Address:* Institutul de Arheologie si Istoria Artei, 3400 Cluj-Napoca, Str E Ilac 2, Romania.

GUDJONSSON Hermann, b. 17 Oct 1952, Iceland. Gen Dir. m. Bertha Sigurdardottir, 26 May 1976, 2 d. *Education:* BSc in Civil Engrg 1976, Univ Iceland; MSc Engrg 1979, Tech Univ Denmark. *Appointments:* Engr, Fjarhitun, Consltg Firm, 1979-83; Chf Engr 1983-86, Gen Dir 1986-, Icel Lighthouse & Harbour Authority. *Membership:* State Town Planning Coun 1986-. *Address:* Nokkvavogur K, 104 Reykjavik, Iceland.

GUDKA Naresh, b. 13 Jan 1942, Kisumu, Kenya. Stock Broker. m. Catherine Elizabeth, 1 Apr 1967, 2 d. *Education:* Balham & Tooting Col of Commerce 1960-61; Articled Clerk 1961-66, qualified as Chartered Acct 1966. *Appointments:* Articled Clerk, Lesley Furneaux & Co 1961-66; Peat Marwick McLintock 1967-68; J & A Scrimgeour & Co 1968-74; Paribas Capital Markets, 1974-82; Citicorp Scrimgeour Vickers & Co 1982-89; Paribas Capital Markets, 1989-. *Publications:* Var arts on property incl: Institutional & Foreign Investors' Attitude Towards Property Investments in the UK in Conjunction with Crooch & Wagstaff. *Memberships:* FCA 1967; AIIMR 1975; MSI 1975. *Honours:* Rated as No 2 Property Team by Extel Survey 1979-88; Rated as No 1 Property Analyser by Institutional Investor 1986-87, 1989; Asian City Club Achm't Awd 1989. *Hobbies:* Cricket; Gardening. *Address:* 2 Aston Avenue, Kenton, Middlesex HA3 0DB, England. 53.

GUDMUNDSSON Thorir, b. 18 Oct 1960, Reykjavik. TV Journalist. m. Steinunn Arnthrudur Bjornsdottir, 27 Aug 1988. *Education:* BS Journalism, Univ Kansas. *Appointments:* DV newspaper, foreign affairs 1984-85; State radio, foreign affairs 1985-86; Iceland TV Corp, foreign news dir 1986-. *Membership:* Assn Icelandic Journalists. *Hobbies:* Photography; Travel. *Address:* Thjorsargatal, 101 Reykjavik, Iceland.

GUERRA Maximiliano, b. Argentina. Ballet Dancer. *Education:* Superior Inst Arts, Buenos Aires. *Career:* Joined La Plata Argentine Theatre Ballet Co as Principal Dancer & performed var roles inclDon Jose in Alberto Alondo's Carmen; Later invited to dance for Teresa Carreno Foun in Venezuela; Joined Ballet of Teatro Colon, Buenos Aires 1985, performed complete version of Pierre Lacotte's La Sylphide in RJ's Third Festival, Brazil; John Clifford invited him to take part in SAm premiere of Dvorak Serenade, assigned principal role in The Four Temperaments of Balanchine, danced with

Eva Evdokimova part of Bournonville's La Sylphide; Invited in 1987 on a 30 city Am tour with Los Angeles Ballet; Principal Dancer, Eng Nat Ballet 1988; Toured with ENB in 1989; Role was created for him in Bruce's Symphony in Three Movements; Toured Russia 1989 dancing Giselle, Swan Lake & Don Quixote, 2nd visit performed Romeo & Juliet; Toured Siberia & Spain & danced full version of Grigorovich's Spartacus, the first non-Soviet dancer to perform in this; Invited twice to dance with the Kirov Ballet; Toured USA & Can with the Ballet of the Americas; Currently Principal Dancer with Deutsche Oper Berlin and Guest Artist with London City Ballet & other companies. *Honours:* Grand Prix Ciudad de Trujillo & Silver Medal at Trujillo Intl Festival in Peru, 1985; Silver Medal at NY Intl Ballet Compt, USA, 1987; Gold Medal at XIII Varna Intl Ballet Compt, Bulgaria, 1988. *Address:* 17B Edith Road, London W14 8NA, England.

GUEST George Howell, b. 9 Feb 1924, Bangor, Wales. Dir Mus; Univ Organist. m. Nancy Mary Talbot, 31 Oct 1959, 1 s. 1 d. *Education:* St John's Col, Cambridge 1947-51; Served in RAF 1942-46. *Appointments:* Asst Org, Chester Cathedral 1945-47; Org, St John's Col, Cambridge 1951- 91; Asst Lectr in Mus, Camb Univ 1953-56; Univ Lectr in Mus 1956-82, Univ Org 1974-91. *Contributions to:* learned jours. *Memberships:* Royal Col Organists, Pres 1978-80; Cath Orgs Assn, Pres 1980-82; Incorp Assn Orgs, Pres 1987-89. *Honours:* John Stewart Rannoch Scholar in Sacred Music 1948; Fellow, Royal Sch Church Music 1973; Aelod er Anrhydedd, Gorsedd y Beirdd, Eisteddfod Genedlaethol Cymru 1977; DMus Cantuar 1977; Hon mem Royal Acad Mus 1984; Hon Fellow, Univ Col of N Wales; CBE 1987; Hon DMus Univ Wales 1989; Fellow Royal Can Col of Orgs 1991; Fellow, Welsh Coll, Music & Drama, 1992. *Hobbies:* The Welsh Language; Professional football. *Address:* St John's College, Cambridge CB2 1TP, England. 1, 4, 21.

GUEST Gowan Thomas, b. 8 Feb 1929, Toronto, Canada. Businessman. m. (1) Patricia Ann Connell, 16 June 1961, (2) Michele Ida-Jane Shaw 6 May 1978, 3 s. 2 d. *Education:* BA 1950, Univ Toronto; LLB 1954, Univ BC. *Appointments:* Barrister & Solicitor 1955-58; Principal Secy to PM of Can 1958-60; Ptnr Law Firm 1961-86; Corp Exec 1986-91. *Publications:* Occasional arts & reviews. *Memberships:* Pres, Can MH Assn 1966-68; Chmn, York House Sch 1973-75; Pres, World Fed MH 1979-81; Chmn, Investment Funds Inst Can 1987-88; Regent, Can Inst Fin Planning 1989-91; Law Soc BC 1955-86; Law Soc Upper Can 1982-86; Bar Yukon Territory 1957-62. *Honours:* Centennial Medal, Can, 1967; Queen's Counsel, BC, 1985. *Hobby:* Family. *Address:* 1390 West King Edward Avenue, Vancouver, BC, Canada V6H 1Z9. 88, 142.

GUEST Michele Ida-Jane, b. 18 Jan 1944. Design Conslt. m. Gowan T Guest, 6 May 1978, 2 s. 1 d. *Education:* BID 1965, Fac Arch, Univ Manitoba; Nat Coun Interior Design Qualification (NY) Cert 1980. *Appointments:* SPACE Ltd 1972-85; Coord Interior Design, Kwantlen Col, BC 1979-85; Design Conslt, Guest Holdings Ltd 1986-91. *Creative Works:* Occassional profl art; Shown amateur paintings. *Memberships:* Interior Designers Inst of BC, Past Pres; Interior Designers Can, Past Pres; Nat Coun Interior Design Qualification, Past Pres; Design Vancouver, Chmn 1990-. *Honours:* Academician, Royal Can Soc Arts, 1975; Fellow, Interior Designers Inst of BC, 1980; Fellow, Interior Designers of Can, 1985. *Hobbies:* Gardening; Family; Professional activities. *Address:* 1390 King Edward Avenue, Vancouver, BC V6H 1Z9, Canada. 142.

GUILLIOUMA Larry Jay Jr, b. 23 Apr 1950, Massillon, Ohio. Mus Edr. *Education:* BS, MA Univ N Ala, Florence, Al; Postgrad, Univ Miss. *Appointments:* Phil Campbell, Al 1972-76; Univ Miss 1976-78; Victoria (Tex) Schs 1978-81; Harlingen (Tex) Schs 1981-87; McAllen (Tex) Schs 1991-. *Memberships:* Tex Mus Edrs Assn, Bd Dirs,

Region Vice Chmn, Region Band Chmn; Huntsville, Al Symphony; Victoria, Tex Symphony; Nat Band Assn; Phi Beta Mu Tex Band Masters' Intl Frat. *Honours:* Outstg Band Dir, Alamo Tournament of Bands, 1985; Harlingen Band Marched in Pasadena Tournament of Roses Parade, 1987; NatBand Dirs Hall of Fame, 1987; Harlingen Band invited to perform in Carnegie Hall, 1987. *Hobby:* Travel. *Address:* 1600 Tamarack 19, McAllen, TX 78501, USA. 7.

GUIMARAES Eduardo Lopes Pereira, b. 25 Oct 1941, Rio-Brazil. Arch; Bus Admin. m. Maria Consuelo M P Guimaraes, 28 July 1968, 3 d. *Education:* Col, Santo Inacio; Arch in FNA, Univ Brazil (Fundao), Grad 1966; Admin in Catholic Univ of Parana, Grad 1976. *Appointments:* Fdr, Klotz & Guimaraes Construction 1966-71; Hermes Macedo Gp 1971-. *Creative Works:* Created, Devel, Planned the Magazin Garcez in Curimba (Dept Store Bldg); Restoring a 1929 Art Deco Bldg. *Memberships:* Inst of Store Planners, NY Chapt; Inst Archs of Brazil; Inst Engrg of Parana, Pres; Assn Paranaense Reabilitacao, then VP. *Honours:* Trophy Awd on Worldstore 89, Atlanta, USA, Best Visual Presentation (1989) for Magazine Garcez, Curitiba, PR, Brazil. *Hobbies:* Dairy farm; Scuba diving (3 stars); Rehabilitation; Assn of Parana, VP. *Address:* Joao Negrao 595 Curitiba, 80010 PR-Brazil. 52.

GUINNESS ASCHAN Marit Victoria, b. 28 Jan 1919, London, England. Enamelist; Painter. m. Carl William Aschan, 21 July 1937, diss 1963, 1 s. 1 d. *Education:* PNEU Arts Schs in Munich, Florence & Paris. *Appointments:* Nat Svc, MOI 1939-45; Enamelist & Painter. *Creative Arts:* Ind exhibitions incl: Beaux Arts Gallery, London 1948, Van Diemen Lilienfield Galleries, NY 1949, 1955, 1957, 1959, 1962, 1966, 1968, Inter Art Gallery, Caracus 1973, Roy Miles Gallery, London 1979, Saga Gallery, London 1990, Gallery Galtung, Oslo 1974, 1981, 1984, 1990, 1991; Commns & collections in Eng incl: Victoria & Albert Museum, Worshipful Co of Goldsmiths, London; Focal Point on the Cross for the High Altar, Exeter Cathedral; Hugo & Reine Pitman Collection, Paul Oppe Collection, Royal Norwegian Embassy Collection, The Lord & Lady Iliffe Collection, John Studzinski Collection; in Norway: HM The King Olav V of Norway and the Queen of Norway; in USA: Brooklyn Museum, NY, Yale Univ Art Gallery, Nelson Gallery and Atkins Museum Kansas, New Orleans Museum of Art, NC Museum of Art Raleigh, Ian Woodner Family Collection, NY; Work in num other pvt collections worldwide. *Publications include:* Modern Jewellers, The Art of Jewellery, 1968; Enamels, ed 1983. *Memberships:* Chelsea Arts Club; Pres, Artist Enamellers 1969-. *Hobby:* Travelling. *Address:* 25 Chelsea Park Gardens, London SW3 6AF, England. 19.

GUL Mohammad, b. 6 Apr 1939, Lakkimarwat. Surgeon and Associate Professor of Surgery. m. 10 Nov 1971. *Education:* MBBS King Edward Med Col, Lahere, 1963; FRCS, Glasgow, 1970, Edinburgh, 1975. *Appointments:* MBBS King Edward Med & Hs Ofr, Mayo Hsp, 1963-65; Surg posts in UK, 1966- 72; Armed forces Surg, Pakistan, 1972, 1975; Dpty Surg, Middle East, 1976-82; Ayuh Med Col, Abbotab, 1983-. *Memberships:* Fellow, Intl Col of Surgs, Chicago; Fellow, Intl Col and of Angiol, Switz; Life, Am Soc of Vienna Univ; Asian Surg Assn, Hong Kong. *Honours:* Sec, Clin Confs, Ayah Med Col; Man Ed, Jour of Ayah med Col. *Hobbies:* Teaching; Gardening; Reading. *Address:* Lakki Marwat Dist Bannu, NWFP, Pakistan.

GULBENKIAN Boghos Parsegh (Paul), b. 23 Mar 1940, London, England. Solicitor; P-time Immigration Adjudicator; Asst Recorder. m. Jacqueline Seferian, 15 Dec 1990, 2 d. *Education:* LLB 1961, LSE. *Appointments:* Asst Solicitor 1966-70, Ptnr 1970-89, Sr Ptnr 1989-, Isadore Goldman; Sr Ptnr, Gulbenkian Harris Andonian 1989-. *Publications:* Arts in the Law Soc's Gazette on: US Immigration, Conciliation in Divorce, Specialised Referral Lists. *Memberships include:* Law Soc 1984-; Chmn, Camden CAB Svc, Mgmt

Com 1978-83; Pres, Holborn Law Soc 1984-85; Chmn, Monitoring of Arts Panel of the Law Soc 1986-89; Hon Auditor of Law Soc 1986-89; Apptd by Lord Chancellor as P-Time Immigration Adjudicator 1989-; Apptd by Lord Chancellor as Asst Recorder, 1992-; Fdr mem, Solicitors Family Law Assn, Immigration Law Practitioners Assn & European Immigration Lawyers Gp; Served on Com of the Principal Registry of the Family Div of the High Crt that set up the Conciliation Svc there. *Honours:* Three Encyclicals from His Holiness Vasken I, Supreme Catholicos of All Armenians, for svcs to the Armenian Community; St Mesrob Medal presented by His Holiness in 1978. *Hobbies:* Music-one of the organisers of Music Armenia 1978; Tennis; Squash; Walking. *Address:* 181 Kensington High Street, London W8 6SH, England.

GULBICKI William T, b. 17 July 1937, Pittsburg, PA. Communications Exec. m. Nora Lee Haller, 20 Jan 1968, 2 s. 1 d. *Education:* AB 1961, MA 1972, Seton Hall Univ, South Orange, NJ; Turkish, Defense Lang Inst, Monterey, CA 1968-69. *Appointments:* HS Tchr/Coach, Latin, Maths, Baseball, Basketball, NJ 1961-65; Special Agent, FBI, criminal assignments, Milwaukee, WI, Richmond, Alexandria, VA-Organised Crime Chf, NY-Inspection Div Chf, Terrorist Res Bomb Data Ctr, Dir, FBI Nat Acad 1965-89; Communications Exec 1989, Satellite Broadcasting & Communications Assn Anti-Piracy Task Force; Pres, Madison Intl, Consltg & Investigative Firm, 1989. *Memberships:* Intl Assn of Chfs of Police (IACP); Nat Sheriff's Assn; FBI Nat Acad Assocs; Seton Hall Univ Pirate Blue. *Honours:* Honor Grad, Seton Hall Univ Grad Sch; Pres's Awd, FBI Nat Acad Assocs for Establishment of. Intl Chapts. *Hobbies:* Jogging; Reading; Swimming; Travel. *Address:* 6707 Grey Fox Drive, Springfield, VA 22152, USA.

GUMMARAJU Srinivas Chakravarthy, b. 2 July 1967, Hyderabad. MD. *Education:* MB, BS 1989, Osmania Univ. *Creative Works:* Poems & arts on sev subjects incl The Japanese Theatre, Drugs for the Layman; Profuced, Directed & Acted in plays for Dramatic Circle of Hyderabad & Osmania Med Col, & Indian TV; Produced prize winning painting & Illustrates children's books; Held performances on the violin. *Memberships:* Life mem, Indian Med Assn; Joint Secy, The Children's Universe; Pres, Hi-Y Club of Hyderabad; Life mem, YMCA; Y's Men's Club of Hyderabad; Youth Hostel's Assn of India; Panel of Aksharajyoti Adult Literary Drive. *Honours:* Prizes in sev painting compts and awds in dramatics incl: The Andhra Pradesh State Children's Acad Awd 1979;Special Awd for Exemplary Svcs rendered during Violent Social Disturbances in 1990, by Osmania Gen Hosp; Commended for svc during cyclonic devastation of the Indian East Coast, by Govt of Andhra Pradesh; Del to represent Y's Men's Club of Hyderabad at Y's Men's Intl Convention in Kyoto, Japan 1988; Invited to address the Rotary Club of Hyderabad and the People-Police Friendship Soc, as a Young Person of Outstg Merit. *Hobbies:* Reading; Writing; Painting; Theatre; Music-studied violin; Travelling; Social work. *Address:* 3-4-491/1 Barkatpura, Hyderabad 500 027, Andhra Pradesh, India.

GUNN Alexander Ewen (Ben), b. 24 June 1923, Glasgow, Scotland. m. Geraldine Phillips, 23 Dec 1946, 1 s. *Education:* Whitehill, Glasgow; RAF Col, Cranwell. *Appointments:* RAF 1941-49, 501 Sqdn 11 Gp Fighter Command, 274 Sqdn 2nd TAF 1943-45; Test Pilot, A & A. EE, Empire Test Pilots Sch 1948; Chf Test Pilot, Bouaton Paul Ltd 1949-66; CTP Rover Gas Turbines 1966- 67; Mktg Regl Dir, Beagle Aircraft 1967-71; Airport Dir, Shoreham Airport 1970-90. *Publication:* Delta Dilemma (Vapour Trails). *Memberships:* Upper Freeman Guild of Air Pilots & Navigators; Royal Aeronautical Soc. *Honours:* MBE; 1939-45 Campaign Medals; Master Air Pilot (GAPAN); Silver Medal, Airport Operators Assn, and Hon mem; AOPA Sword. *Hobby:* Fishing. *Address:* Four Winds, 69 Offington Lane, Worthing, West Sussex BN14 9RJ, England.

GUNN John Charles, b. 6 June 1937, England. Prof of Forensic Psychi. m. (1) Celia Willis, 9 Sept 1959, (2) Pamela Taylor, 6 Nov 1989. *Education:* MB, ChB (Birm) 1961; MD (Birm) 1969; MRCPsychi 1971, F 1980. *Appointments:* House Ofcr, QEH, Birm 1961-63; Registrar, Maudsley Hosp 1963-66; Lectr, Inst Psychi 1969-78; Dir, Special Hospitals Res Unit 1975-78, Prof Forensic Psychi 1978-. *Publications:* Books: Violence in Human Society, 1973; Epileptics in Prison, 1977; Psychiatric Aspects of Imprisonment, 1978; The Mentally Disordered Offender, 1991. *Memberships:* Royal Col of Psychis; Royal Soc Med, Sect of Psychi, Royal Commission on Criminal Justice, 1991-93, VP. *Honour:* RMPA Bronze Medal, 1970; Pinel Prize, 1992. *Hobbies:* Opera; Theatre; Cinema; Walking; Photography. *Address:* Institute of Psychiatry, De Crespigny Park, Camberwell, London SE5 8AF, England. 1, 30, 34, 139.

GUNN Kenneth David, b. 28 May 1940, Tyler, Tex, USA. Explosives- Space Operations. m. (1) Roswitha Klein, 22 Sept 1964, div 1985, 2 s. 1 d. (2) Jutta Maria Hauser, 6 Jan 1986, div 1991. *Education:* AA in Bus & Mgmt 1978, Univ Md; BS in Bus & Mgmt 1982. *Appointments:* Enlisted USAF, advanced through grades to Sr Master Sgt, 1958, rtd 1986; Explosive Ordnance Disposal Specialist USAF, Vietnam 1971-72, Volk Field, Wis 1972-74, Spangdahlem AB, Germany 1974-77; Chf Explosive Ordnance Disposal USAF, Aviano AB, Italy 1977-80, Barksdale AFB, La 1980-81; Chf 7007th Explosive Ordnance Disposal Flight USAF, Spangdahlem AB 1981-85; Chg Explosive Ordnance Disposal Div, USAF, Patrick AFB, Fla 1985-86; Safety Supvr, Pan Am World Svcs Inc, Cape Canaveral, Fla 1986-89; Safety Specialist, NASA Safety, John F Kennedy Space Ctr, Fla 1989-90; Ordnance Foreman, Johnson Controls World Svcs, Cape Canaveral AFS, Fla 1990-. *Memberships:* Key mem, Search, Recovery & Reconstrn Team, Space Shuttle, Challenger, 1986; Narrator Nuclear Safety Films, 1969; Life mem, VFW; Air Force Assn; Soc Explosive Engrs. *Honours:* Meritorious Svc Medal; Joint-Svc Commend Medal; Air Force Commend Medal; Air Force Achmt Medal. *Hobbies:* Beekeeping; Photography. *Address:* 304 Arthur Avenue, Cocoa Beach, FL 32931, USA.

GUNNOE Nancy Lavenia Thompson, b. 7 Jan 1921, Southside, Tenn, USA. Secy-Treas R G Gunnoe Farms Inc. m. Raymond Glen Gunnoe, 6 Dec 1941, 1 s. 2 d. *Education:* Austin Peay Col 1939; Univ Charleston, 1973, 1987, p-time. *Appointments:* Cashier, Kroger Co, Charleston 1939-40; Superior Laundry Cleaning, Charleston 1940-41; File Clerk, Hancock Oil Co, Oakland, Calif 1942; Clerk Office, Price Adm Stockton, Calif 1943; Secy-Treas, R G Gunnoe Farms Inc 1947-. *Creative Works:* One man Art Show, WV Cultural Ctr 1979; One man Art Show, Univ Charleston 1980; One man Art Show, Chequers 1986; Miniature Show at: Sunrise 1974-80, Jackson, Tenn Pen Women. *Memberships:* Charleston Historical & Preservation Soc; Woman Bldrs of Univ of Charleston; Charleston Womans Club; Sunrise Museum; Presidential Task Force, Republican; Allied Artists of WV; Nat League of Am Pen Women Hospice. *Honours:* Rhodendron Festival Best of Show, 1977, Hon Mention 1990, First Place 1984, Second Place, 1981 & 1982; Parkersburg Art Ctr, Intl Show, Hon Mention Oils & Watercolour. *Hobbies:* Sculpture; Water aerobics; Porcelain; Painting; Personal shopper; Oil & watercolour painting; Fabric painting. *Address:* 2040 Oakridge Drive, Charleston, WV 25311, USA.

GUNTER John Forsyth, b. 31 Oct 1938, Billericay, Essex, England. Theatre & Opera Design. m. Micheline McKnight, 19 Dec 1969, 2 d. *Education:* Central Sch of Art & Design, London, Grad with Dipl with distinction 1961. *Career:* Worked for sev repertory cos; Became Resident Designer, Royal Crt Theatre, designed many productions incl: Peter Gill's production of D H Lawrence Trilogy, and Osborne's West of Suez; Designed many plays for the RSC incl: Trevor Nunn's productions of Juno and the Paycock, and All's Well That Ends Well;

For Broadway he designed David Hare's Plenty among others; He designed 8 plays for the National Theatre incl The Beggar's Opera, and Guys & Dolls; West End credits incl Trevor Griffith's Comedians, Alan Bennett's The Old Country, and the musical High Society; Also designed num operas incl The Greek Passion, Faust & The Meistersinger; His Am opera debut was Fidelio in San Francisco & Wash DC; Designed the Flying Dutchman at La Scala, Milan 1988 and Meistersinger for Australian Opera; Designed the sets for Tosca and Madame Butterfly for Los Angeles Opera; At Glyndebourne he designed for Peter Hall's productions of Simon Boccanegra, Albert Herring, La Traviata, Marriage of Figaro, and Falstaff; Hd of Design, Nat Theatre 1988-90. where he designed Mrs Klein, The Secret Rapture, and Hamlet; and Peter Wood's School for Scandal; Also been a Tchr; Recent Productions Incl: The Flying Dutchman and Porgy & Bess, Royal Opera House, Covent Garden; Peter Grimes at Glyndebourne directed by Trevor Nunn; RSC, All's Well That Ends Well & Gift of the Gorgon, both directed by Peter Hall. *Membership:* RSA 1982-. *Honours:* Best Designer Awd for Guys & Dolls, Royal Nat Theatre, Olivier Awd, 1982; Best Designer Awd for Wild Honey, Royal Nat Theatre, Olivier Awd, 1984. *Address:* c/o Peter Murphy (Agent), Curtis Brown & John Farquharson, 162-168 Regent Street, London W1R 5TB, England.

GUNTER Michael Martin, b. 22 Feb 1943, USA. Univ Prof. m. Lorene Judith Keeley, 22 Oct 1960, 1 s. 1 d. *Education:* BA 1964, MIA 1966, Columbia Univ; PhD 1972, Kent State Univ. *Appointments:* Asst Prof Polit Sci 1972-76, Assoc Prof 1976-81, Prof Polit Sci 1981-, Tenn Tech Univ. *Publications:* Books: A Study of Contemporary Armenian Terrorism, 1986; Transnational Armenian Activism, 1990; The Kurds in Turkey, 1990; The Kurds in Iraq, 1993. *Memberships:* Am Polit Sci Assn; Middle East Studies Assn; Intl Studies Assn; Nat Assn for Armenian Studies & Res; Turkish Studies Assn. *Honours:* Invited Guest Lectr, US State Dept, Can Govt, Turkish Govt, Univ Paris; Sr Fulbright Lectr in Intl Relats, Turkey 1978-79. *Hobbies:* Tennis; Travel; Swimming; Coin collecting. *Address:* Department of Political Science, Tennessee Technical University, Cookeville, TN 38505, USA.

GUNZEL-KOLBE Sigrid, b. 24 Oct 1931, Olbersdorf, Germania. Psychotherapist. m. Reinhard Kolbe, 24 Sept 1957, div 1975, 1 s. 1 d. *Education:* Univ Greifswald 1950-53, and Jena 1953-56, MD; Psychoanalytic Trng, Sigm Freud Inst, Frankfurt am Main 1971-79, Psychotherapist for Psychoanalyt Psychotherapy. *Appointments:* Med Asst, Univ Rostock, E Germany 1956-58; Med Asst different clinics Frankfurt am Main 1962-66; GP 1967-69; Psychotherapist, Psychosomatic Clinic, Hofheim 1971-79. *Publications:* Thesis: Pregnant-Anamnesis of mothers from newborn babies with Pylorospasmus, 1956; Ava & Edam, on partnership between man and woman, 1989; Participated in intl confs in Napoli, Munich & Assisi 1990, regarding self-development in man and women and the difference between the 2 sexes; Translations and reviewing German Authors. *Hobbies:* Taking care of plants and animals which epitomises her love for all creatures and all life in this world; Travelling to enlarge knowledge of people, their customs, emotions, feelings, thoughts. *Address:* Villa del Parco, Poggi d'Imperia, 18100 Italy.

GUO Daren, b. 1935, Harbin, China. *Education:* MD equiv, Beijing MEd Univ, 1959; State Univ of NY at Buffalo Sch of Med and Johns Hopkins Univ Sch of Med, 1980-83, post doc fellowship cert. *Appointments:* Resident, Tiajin Children's Hosp, 1959-69; Attending Paed, Tiajin E.Suburban Hosp, 1969-79; Attending Paed and Reschr, Paediatric Res Inst, Tianjin Children's Hosp, 1979-80, 1984-87; Dir, Parental Nutrit, 1988-. *Publications include:* Fat agglutination and acute-phase proteins in paediatric burn patients: Clinical significance, 1992; Fat agglutination and acute-phase proteins in paediatric burn patients, 1992. *Memberships:* Corres Mem, Am Acad Paed; Intl Mem, Soc of Critical Care Med, USA: Soc of Paeds; Chinese Med Assn; Conslt,

Chinese Assn of Nutrit and Hlth. *Honours:* The book, Paediatric Intensive Care Unit - its organization, equipment and techniques won 2nd prize fron Nat Sci and Tech Books of Excellence, 1988. *Hobbies:* Reading and studying English; Classical music and nature. *Address:* Tianjin Children's Hospital, Tianjin 300074, China.

GUO Fuxiang, b. 6 Aug 1935, Liaoning, China. Prof Geol. m. 1 Sept 1965, 1 s. *Education:* Grad from Palaeontologic-Stratigraphic Speciality of 6 study-year system, Geologic-Geographic Dept of Beijing Univ, 1964. *Appointments:* Engr, Geol Bureau of Yunnan Prov 1964-74; Sr Engr, Yunnan Inst of Geol Scis 1974-87; Prof, Guilin Col of Geol 1987-. *Publications:* Books: Fossil Bivalves of Yunnan; On Trigonioidaceans (non-marine Cretaceous Bivalves) and Asian Non-marine Cretaceous System; Over 30 papers. *Memberships:* Dir Bivalves Gp of Palaeontol Soc of China; Jurassic Gp of Stratigraphic Com of China; Geol Soc of China. *Honours:* Sci Res prizes of Yunnan Prov, a 3rd class 1979,, 2 2nd class prizes 1981, 1984; Model Worker of Yunnan Prov, 1983; Model Worker of Min of Geol & Min Resources of China, 1985; 3rd class prize of Progressive Sci & Tech of Guangxi Ed Com, 1989; 2nd class prize of Progressive Sci & Tech of Ed Com of China, 1990. *Hobbies:* Bivalves; Tectonics. *Address:* Guilin College of Geology, Guilin 541004, China.

GUO Yuxin, b. 25 Dec 1939. Sci Reschr. m. Jinqi Huang, 18 Jan 1968, 1 s. 1 d. *Education:* BSc 1963, Shandong Univ. *Appointments:* Energy Engr, Power Plant of Nanding 1963-72; Engr, Laiwu Iron & Steel Works 1972-83; Assoc Res Prof, Shandong Energy Res Inst 1983-. *Publications include:* Papers: Heat Pump Analysis, 1988; The Design Standard of Transmission of Marsh Gas, 1989; Heat Transfer Enhancement, 1991. *Memberships:* Tech Com of Energy Standardisation of Shandong; Shandong Energy Res Com; Applied Tech Assn of Jinan. *Honours:* Outstg Prize of Shandong, 1988; Outstg Prize 1989, First Prize of Shandong, 1991; Gold Prize of Spark Plan, 1989. *Hobby:* Music. *Address:* Shandong Energy Research Institute, Keyuan Road, Jinan 250014, China.

GUO Zonghai, b. 21 Dec 1932, Jiangsu, China. Professor. m. Wong Jiazhen, 1 Jan 1954, 3 s. *Education:* MAgric, Nanjing Agric Univ, (NAU) 1947. *Appointments:* Tchr, Dept of Agric Econ, NAU, 1954-83; Tchg Sec, 1957-83, Assoc Prof, 1983-88, Postgrad Tutor, 1984-, Prof, Doctor's Tutor, 1988-, Dir of Tchg and Res Section of Mgmt, 1983-. *Publications include:* Agricultural Economic Management, 1981; New technological revolution and strategy of rural economic development in Jiangsu Province, 1985; Management Science in Rural Enterprises, 1987; A study of Development of strategy of coastal rural enterprises organization and industrial structure, 1990. *Memberships:* Res Fellow, Res Ctr of Agric Devel Strategy, Min of Agric; Expert, Assesment Com, Jiangsu Province, Assessment of applicants for higher quals in Agric Economics. *Honours:* Exempliary Tchr: Nanjing Agric Univ, 1985, Inst of Ctl Agric Mgmt for Cadres, 1969, 1995; Second Prize, Tchr of Quality, Tiangsu Province, 1989. *Hobbies:* Music; Chinese classical literature; Philately. *Address:* College of Agricultural Economics and Trade, Nanjing Agric University, Nanjing, Jiangsu, China.

GUPTA Parmeshwari Lal, b. 24 Dec 1914, Azamgarh UP, India. Chmn, Governing Body, Indian Inst Res in Numismatic Studies. m. 6 Dec 1931, 2 s. 3 d. *Education:* MA 1950; PhD 1959. *Appointments:* Edit, weekly Hindi Sandesh, Azamgarh UP 1935-43; Asst Edit, Hindi daily AJ, Varanasi 1943- 50; Special Correspondent, English daily Amrit Bazar Batrika 1945; Asst Curator, Bharat Kala Bhavan (Museum of Art & Arch), Banaras Hindu Univ, Baranasi 1951-53; Numismatist, Asst Curator, Curator, Arch Sect, Prince of Wales Museum Bombay 1953-60, 1962-63; Asst Keeper, Dept Coins & Medals, Brit Museum, London 1951; Curator, Patna Museum, Patna 1963-73; Dir 1983-90, Chmn Governing Body

1990-, Indian Inst of Res in Numismatic Studies, Nasik. *Publication:* 47 Books incl: A survey of Indian Numismatography, 1964; Coin Hoards from Maharashtra, 1970; Numismatic History of Himachal Pradesh, 1989; Sodha aur Samiksha, 1990. *Memberships:* Life mem: Nagari Pracharni Sabha, Varanasi, Arch Soc of India, New Delhi; Hon Fellow: Numismatic Soc India, Varanasi, Royal Numismatic Soc, London, Indian Coin Soc, Nagpur; Contbr mem, Am Numismatic Soc, NY; Hon mem, Intl Numismatic Comm; Royal Asiatic Soc, London. *Honours include:* Hiralal Gold Medal, Kasi Nagari Pracharni Sabha, Varanas, 1951; Chakravikrama Medal, Numismatic Soc of India, Varanasi, 1952; Lhotka Memorial Prize, Royal Numismatic Soc, London 1971; Sir Jadunath Sarker Gold Medal, Asiatic Soc, Calcutta, 1977; Royal Numismatic Soc Medal, London 1977; Huntington Medal, Am Numismatic Soc, NY 1987. *Hobbies:* Reading; Writing; Travel. *Address:* Indian Institute of Research in Numismatic Studies, Anjaneri, Nasik 422 213, India.

GUPTA Raj Kumar, b. 17 Aug 1936, Kanpur, India. Prof English. m. Dr Priya Lakshmi Gupta, 4 Dec 1973, 1 s. *Education:* BA 1955, MA 1957, Agra Univ; MA 1962, Univ RI, USA; PhD 1964, Univ Pittsburgh, USA. *Appointments:* Robertson Col, Jabalpur 1957-61; Asst Prof, Memphis State Univ, 1969-70; Vstg Prof, Univ Ibadan, Nigeria 1983-84; Asst Prof 1965-73, Assoc Prof 1973-76, Prof 1976-, Indian Inst Tech, Kanpur. *Publications:* The Great Encounter: A Study of Indo-American Literary & Cultural Relations; Interpretations: Essays on American Literature; American Literature: Fundamentals of Research. *Memberships:* Intl Assn of Univ Profs of Eng; Modern Language Assn; Am Studies Assn; Indian Assn for Am Studies; Indian Assn Eng Studies; Am Studies Res Ctr. *Honours:* Fulbright Study Grant, Univ RI 1961; Andrew Mellon Fellowship, Univ Pitts 1962-64; Sr Fulbright-Hays Fellowship, Univ Penn 1977-78; Sr Fulbright Grant, Yale 1989. *Hobbies:* Travelling; Photography; Gardening; Chess; Music. *Address:* House No 611, Indian Institute of Technology, Kanpur 208016, India.

GUPTA Shakunchand Anya, b. 2 May 1935, India. m. 3 Mar 1953, 1 s, 2 d. *Education:* Vishand Exam, equal to BA, 1950. *Publications:* Adhunil Bhaiat Ki Mahan Bibhutiya; Stories, poems and letters published in newspapers. *Memberships:* Pres, Arysanaj. *Honours:* Lekhan Kala Visharad; Sahityashm Award; Sanskrit Sahitya Pamshad Mathuravid, 1979. *Hobbies:* Reading and writing books and short stories; Social work. *Address:* c/o Visharad Medical Stores, Towns PO, Lalganj Dist, Reubouli VP, India.

GUSEV Alexander, b. 5 Feb 1945, Moscow. Geophysicist; Seismologist. m. Eugenia Gusev, 25 Apr 1975, 1 d. *Education:* Candidate of Sci in Physics & Maths (MS & BS equiv) 1967, Moscow Univ, Phys Dept; Degree awd'd in 1977, Schmidt Inst of Physics of the Earth, Moscow; Sr Res Fellow degree 1984, Ac Sci USSR. *Appointments:* Jr Reschr, Scmidt Inst Phys of the Earth, Kamchatka Gp, Petropavlovsk-Kamchatsky, USSR 1967-72; Jr Reschr 1973-78; Hd Res Gp 1978-91, Inst of Volcanology, Petropavlosk-K; Learned (Sci) Secy, Inst Volcanic Geol & Geochem, Petropavlovsk-K 1991-. *Creative Works:* Distant aftershock. precursory seismicity pattern discovered in 1974; Coda envelope steepness anomaly, first actual successful prediction in 1983; Statistical model of earthquake source radiation, proposed 1981; Multiasperity fault model, proposed 1988; Preliminary design seismic loads for Kamchatka, published 1990. *Hobby:* Reading. *Address:* Institute of Volcanic Geology & Geochemistry, 9 Piip Blvd, Petropavlovsk-Kamchatsky 683006, Russia.

GUTH Deborah, b. 14 Feb 1950, Cardiff, S Wales. Lectr Eng & Am Lit. m. Michael B Cohen, 20 Oct 1982, 1 d. *Education:* BA Hons Eng Lit 1972, MA Comp Lit 1973, Sussex Univ; Doctorat de 3eme cycle Comp Lit 1980, Univ Paris IV-Sorbonne. *Appointments:* Lectr 1980-, BA

Advr 1985-, Dept Eng Lit, Tel Aviv Univ. *Publications:* Scholarly arts in profl jours. *Memberships:* MLA; Virginia Woolf Soc. *Honours:* French Govt Scholarship 1974-75; Cohen Foun Res Grant, Tel Aviv Univ 1988. *Hobbies:* Classical music; Handwork. *Address:* Department of English, Tel Aviv University, Ramat Aviv, Tel Aviv 69978, Israel.

GUTIERREZ Hipolito Felipe, b. 4 Feb 1931, Buenos Aires. Musician; Pvt Prof. m. Wimpy Ponce de Leon, 20 Oct 1960, 1 s. *Education:* Nat Arts Bachelor 1949; Graduated at Municipal Music Conservatory of the City of Buenos Aires 1953; Master of Composition with Jacobo Ficher 1966. *Appointments:* Pvt Prof, Jury at Nat Tribune of Composers 1982-; Mem Jury at Nat Fund of Arts of Argentina. *Creative Works:* Unamuniana Obertura, 1966; Music for Bows, 1975; Three Eternities, for mezzo sopr & orch, 1977; Nocturno y Scherzoso, 1991; ODA II, 1982; ODA, 1989, chosen by BBC for recording in London; 22 chamber works. *Memberships:* Past Pres, Young Composers Assn of Arg 1969; Dir, Argentina United Composers 1979-91; VP, Argentina Music Coun, UNESCO, Paris 1989-93. *Honours:* 1975 Awd of Municipality of the City of Bs Aires for Allusions; Awd'd 1st class Prize for Three Eternities by First Nat Tribunal of Composers, 1979; Jury of Nat Fund of Arts of Argentina requested a piece for Bows Orch, which was Chique, 1989. *Hobbies:* Painting; Poetry; Politics; Rugby; Ornithology. *Address:* COD 1419 San Nicolas 4248 3o Pisa, Dpt No 12, Buenos Aires, Argentina.

GUTTER Robert Harold, b. 16 June 1938, NYC, USA. Orch Conductor; Mus Edr. 3 d. *Education:* BMus 1959, MMus 1960, Yale Univ. *Appointments:* Asst Prof, Univ Wis at Madison 1964-67; Assoc Prof, Drake Univ 1988, Univ NC, Greensboro 1988-; Also Lectr, Wittenberg Univ 1969- 70; Condr, Des Moines Symph 1967-69, Springfield (Ohio) Symph 1969-71, Springfield (Mass) Symph 1970-86, Condr Emeritus 1986-; Condr, Mus Dir, Philharm of Greensboro, 1988; Guest Condr, Albuquerque Symphony, 1970, Colorado Springs, Colo, 1970, New Orleans Opera, 1969, Siena, Italy, 1970, Palazzo Pitti, 1970, Austrian Tonkunstler Orch, 1978, Leonard Bernstein Festival of Am Mus, 1978, Vienna Volksopera Orch, 1981, Sarajevo (Yugoslavia) Philharm, 1981, Orquesta Sinfonica de Xalapa, Mex, 1979, 1981, Seville Philharm, 1983, Bucharest Philharm, 1983, Ploesti Symph, 1983, Irish Nat Radio Orch, 1983, Stuttgart Philharm, 1984, Victoria Symphony, 1984, Santa Cruz County Symph, 1985, Hartford Symph, 1985, Istanbul State Orch, 1986, Cairo Philharm, 1986, R I Philharm, 1987, Slovenian Radio-TV Orch, Ljublana, 1987, CJRT Chamber Orch, Toronto, 1987, Tianjin Symph, China, 1989. *Memberships:* Am Fed of Musicians; Conductors Guild; Am Symph Orch League; AAUP; NC Music Edrs. *Honours:* Alice M Ditsou Awd, 1960; Semi-finalist Dimitri Mituopoulis Conducting Compt, 1969; Conductor Emeritus, Springfield, Mass, Symphony Orch, 1986. *Hobbies:* Gardening; Hiking; Sailing. *Address:* School of Music, 206 Brown Hall, University of North Carolina at Greensboro, Greensboro, NC 27412, USA. 2, 6, 7.

GUTZKE Karl N, b. 27 June 1933, Parma, Ohio, USA. Chemist. m. Mary Nella Hardy, 10 Aug 1963, 3 s. *Education:* BS Indl Chem 1956, Case Inst of Tech; Grad courses in Chem Engrg, Lamar State Univ. *Appointments:* Koppers 1956-63; Texaco 1963-72; Woodville, Tex ISD 1972-74; Livingston Tex ISD 1974-75; NCH 1975-. *Creative Works:* Devel turbine oils, gear oil additives, diesel fuel additives. *Memberships:* Region II, Tex, Okla, Rep & Mem Exec Comm of Div of Petrol Chem of Am Chem Soc 1991-92; Am Inst Chem Engrg; N Tex Sect Chmn of Soc of Tribologists and Lubrication Engrs 1987. *Honour:* Van Horn Scholarship 1951. *Hobbies:* Golf; Bridge; Chess. *Address:* PO Box 165118, Irving, TX 75016, USA. 7.

GUYON John Carl, b. 16 Oct 1931, Washington, PA, USA. Administration; President; SIUC; m. Elizabeth Joyce, 1 s, 1 d. *Education:* Ba Chem, Wash and

Jefferson, 1953; MS Phys Chem, Toledo Univ, 1957; PhD Analyt Chem, Purdue Univ, IN, 1961. *Appointments:* Asst Prof, 1961-64, Assoc Prof, 1965-69, Chm, Chem Dept, 1069-71, Univ of Missouri; Prof and Chm, Memphis State Univ, 1971-74; Dean, Col of Sci, S.Illinois Univ, Carbondale, (SIUC), 1974-76; Assoc VP, Res and Dean of Grad Sch, 1976-82, Act VP for Acad Affairs and Res, 1980-81, VP for Acad Affairs and Res, 1981-87, Act Pres, 1987, Pres, 1987-, SIUC. *Memberships:* Chm, Pres Coun, Missouri Valley Conf, 1990; Chm, Illinois Sci Lit Adv Com; S.Illinois collegiate Common Mkt. *Hobbies:* Golf; Racquetball. *Address:* President, Southern Illinois University, Carbondale, IL 62901, USA.

GUZEK Jan Wojciech, b. 28 Mar 1924, Lublin, Poland. Physiol; Univ Prof. m. Barbara Moskalewska, dec, 24 Oct 1952, 1 s. 2 d. *Education:* Fac Med, Jagellonian Univ, Cracow, grad in Med 1951; Doctoral thesis, Lodz, 1962; Habilitation, Lodz, 1968; Professorship 1979. *Appointments:* Asst, Lectr, Dept Gen Pathol, Fac of Med, Cracow, 1949-60; Sr Lectr, Reader, Asst Prof, Dept Physiol, Sch Med, Lodz 1960-74; Ord Prof & Hd 1974-, Dept Pathophysiol, Sch Med Lodz; Vice Dean, Fac of Med, Lodz 1972. *Publications:* Author & Co-Author 240 pubs; Expert Res Wk & Reviews, mainly on Neuroendocrinol; Edit & Co-Author 4 textbooks on pathophysiol; Author sev arts on history of physiol in Poland. *Memberships:* Polish Physiol Soc, Pres 1984-90; Int Soc Neuroendocrinol; Int Brain Res Org; Europ Neuroendocrine Soc; Europ Pineal Soc; Int Soc Pathophysiol, Coun mem & Chmn of ednl comm; Polish Endocr Soc; Mem sev coms of Polish Acad Scis. *Honours:* Hon title Tchr of Merit, 1975; Chevalier of Polonia Restituta, 1980; Sci Awd, Min of Health, Warsaw, 1987; Corr mem, Soc Pathol & Clin Physiol, GDR, 1987; Perpetual mem, Gen Sikorski's Inst Polish History, London, 1988; Mem Intl Parliament for Safety & Peace, Palermo, 1991; Knight, Sovereign Milit Templar Order, Jerusalem, 1991. *Hobbies:* Science in history; Classical painting; Old Polish maps; Long forest walking. *Address:* Dept of Pathophysiology, School of Medicine, ul Narutowicza 60, 90-136 Lodz, Poland. 139, 151, 162.

GWANDU Abubakar Aliyu, b. 20 Jan 1941, Gwandu, Nigeria. University Educator and Administrator. m. Aishah A Bande, 20 Feb 1966. 2 s,7 d. *Education:* BA Arabic and Islamic Studies, Ahmedu Bello Univ, 1966; MA Islamic Studies, Am Univ in Cairo, 1971; PhD, Univ of Durham, England, 1977. *Appointments:* Tutor, Asst Lectr, Sr Lectr, 1966-86, Ahmadu Bello Univ; Tutor, Univ of Sokoto, 1977-86; Dir of Higher Educ, Fed Min of Educ, Lagos, 1986-89; V-Chancellor, Usmann Danfofiyo Univ, Sokoto., 1989-. *Memberships:* Nigerian Assn of Tchr of Arabic and Islamic Studies. *Honours:* Prizes in Secondary, Middle and Elementary Schs for being best overall student. *Hobbies:* Farming. *Address:* Usmanu Danfodiyo University, PMB 2346, Sokoto, Nigeria.

GWIN James Ellsworth, b. 1 Mar 1947, Chattanooga, Tenn, USA. Col Librarian. m. Sheena Mckenzie, 5 Oct 1985, 1 d. *Education:* AB History 1969, Univ Tenn, Chatt; MLN Librarianship 1970, Emory Univ; MPA Public Admin 1984, Va C'Wealth Univ. *Appointments:* Librarian, US Army Logistics Lib, US Army Quartermaster Sch & Fort Lee 1970-72; Asst Dir of Cataloging Dept, Univ Tenn at Chatt 1972-75; Dir Cataloging Svcs, Univ Richmond 1975-85; Actg Univ Librarian, Univ Richmond 1985-86; Dir Learning Resources Ctr, Univ Richmond 1986-; Dir Tech Svcs 1987-90, Actg Univ Lib 1990-91, Univ Richmond. *Memberships:* Am Lib Assn; Potomac Tech Processing Librarians Assn; Assn Col & Res Libs; Am Soc Pub Admin; Va Lib Assn; Pres 1986-, Va Chapt, Assn Col & Res Libraries. *Honours:* Tommy Dora Barker Scholarship, Emory Univ 1969-70; Phi Kappa Phi 1984. *Hobbies:* Music-playsthe bass viole; Reading; Films; Gardening. *Address:* 1232 Windsor Avenue, Richmond, VA 23227, USA. 7.

GYEMANT Ladislau, b. 12 Sept 1947, Oradea, Romania. Prof History. m. Amalia Gyemant, 27 July 1981, 1 s. 2 d. *Education:* Univ Cluj, Fac History 1965-70; PhD History 1982. *Appointments:* Inst History of Romanian Acad Searcher, mem Sci Bd 1970-91. *Publication:* Repertory of the Romanian Printed Official Acts in Transylvania, Bucharest, 1981; The Romanian National Movement in Transylvania 1790-1848, 1986; I Bodai-Deleano, De Originibus Populorum Transylvaniae, Critical Ed I-II, 1991. *Memberships:* Dr Moshe Carmilly Inst for Jewish & Hebrew History, Cluj-Napoca, Sci Councellor; Inst History Cluj-Napoca, mem Sci Bd. *Honours:* N Balcescu Prize of Romanian Acad, 1981; Prize for Rigour & Erudition, of the Romanian Nat Book Exhibition, 1991. *Hobbies:* Literature; Music; Politics. *Address:* Str Tarnita No 1, Bl B5, Sc III, Ap 28, 3400 Cluj-Napoca, Romania.

H

HAAS Andreas Martin, b. 14 June 1963, Zofingen, AG. Theologian; Journalist. *Education:* BD 1987, Univ Berne, Switzerland; Scholarship, Univ Oxford; lic theol 1991, VDM 1992, Univ Berne. *Appointments:* Dir, Svc d'Information et de Presse, Kolliken 1983-; Gp Advr, Red Cross 1988-89. *Publication:* What Shall We Do with the Bible in Pastoral Care?, 1990. *Memberships:* Syndicat des Journalistes et Ecrivains, Paris. *Hobbies:* Politics; Reading; Music. *Address:* Kunzhubel 10, 5742 Kolliken, Switzerland.

HAASE Elisabeth, b. 13 Nov 1946, Copenhagen. Exec Dir. m. Svend Erik, 29 Mar 1969, 2 d. *Education:* Physiotherapist, Teilmanns Inst, Col of Physiotherapy 1969. LLD 1986, Univ Copenhagen. *Appointments:* Empl, Orthopaedic Hosp, Copenhagen 1969-73; Empl, Danish Assn Physiotherapists as Ed Conslt 1973-84, Exec Dir 1984-. *Memberships:* Danish Assn Physiotherapists; Danish Lawyers & Economists. *Honours:* Gen Secy 1979-89, 1st VP 1989-91, Pres 1991-, Standing Liaison Com of Physiotherapists within the EEC; Hon mem, Dutch Assn of Physiotherapists; Hon mem, Spanish Assn Physiotherapists. *Hobbies:* Badminton; Jogging; Gardening; Reading. *Address:* Danske Fysloterapeuter, Norre Voldgade 90, DK 1358 Kobenharn K, Denmark.

HAASE Otto Wolfgang, b. 25 Oct 1936, Reinholdshain. Prof Physical Chem. m. Dr Ingeburg Karer, 7 Sept 1963, 1 s. 1 d. *Education:* Ingenieur 1957, Magdeburg; Dipl Chemist 1960, Dr rer nat 1964, Jena; Habilitation 1970, Marburg. *Appointments:* Asst, Univ Jena 1961-68; Postdoc, Univ Stockholm 1966; 68; Asst, Univ Marburg 1969-70; Prof, T H Darmstadt 1971-. *Publications:* 10 book contrbs & 230 original sci contrbs. *Memberships:* Gesellschaft Deutscher Chemikar; Deutsche Bunsengesellschaft; Deutsche Physikalische Gesellschaft; Europäische Kolloidchemische Gesellschaft; Am Chem Soc. *Address:* Im Trappengrund 72, D 6107 Reinheim 1, Germany. 52.

HAAVELSRUD Magnus, b. 24 Apr 1940, Nord-Aurdal. Assoc Prof. m. 2 Dec 1967, div 1987, 1 s. *Education:* Cand Polit 1968, Univ Oslo; PhD 1970, Univ Wash, Seattle, USA. *Appointments:* Assoc Prof, Univ Tromsoe, Norway 1974-; Guest Prof, German Coun for Peace & Conflict Res 1978- 79. *Publications:* Edit: Education for Peace, 1975, Approaching Disarmament Education, 1981; Author, Fredslaering (Peace Learning), 1991. *Memberships:* Int Peace Res Assn; Int Sociol Assn. *Address:* Malselvgt 19A, 9007 Tromso, Norway. 52.

HABERMAS Jurgen, b. 18 June 1929, Dusseldorg, Germany. Prof Philos. m. Ute Wesselhoeft, 2 Aug 1955, 1 s. 2 d. *Education:* PhD 1954, Univ Bonn; Habilitation 1961, Univ Marburg. *Appointments:* Prof Philos: Univ Heidelberg 1961-64, Univ Frankfurt 1964-71; Dir, Max-Planck-Inst, Starnberg-Munich 1971-83; Prof Philos, Univ Frankfurt 1983-. *Publications:* 20 books incl: Knowledge & Human Interests, 1971; Theory of Communicative Action, 2 vols, 1983, 1985; Discourse of Modernity, 1989; Postmetaphysical Thought, 1991. *Memberships:* Acad Arts & Scis, Cambridge, Mass; Academia Europaea, London; Akademie Fur Sprache und Dichtung, Darmstadt; External Mbr, Max-Planck-Inst F Psycholojie, Munchen. *Honours:* 4 Academic Prizes; Hon degrees of New Sch F Soc Res, NY; Hebrew Univ of Jerusalem; Univ Utrecht; Univ Hamburg; Univ Buenos Aires; North-Western Univ, Evanston, Ill. *Address:* Department of Philosophy, University of Frankfurt am Main, Dantestrasse 4-6, D 6000 Frankfurt am Main, Germany.

HABIBUR RAHMAN Shah Muhammad, b. 25 Sept 1945, Khulna, Bangladesh. Edn. m. Sayyeda Quamarun Nessa Begum, 7 July 1968, 2 s. 2 d. *Education:* BA Hons in Ec 1966, MA 1967, Rajshahi Univ, Bangladesh; Residential Trng on Islamic Banking in Sonali Bank Staff Col, Dhaka, Bangladesh. *Appointments:* Lectr, P C Col, Bagerhat 1968; Lectr Dept Ec 1970, Asst Prof Dept Ec 1974, Assoc Prof Dept Ec 1985, Rajshahi Univ. *Publications:* Books: (in Belgali) Islamic Economics for the Children, 1980; Economic Revolution of Islam, 1980; Why & What Is Islamic Banking?, 2nd ed, 1984; Clarification of Some Misgivings About Islamic Banking, 1986. *Memberships:* VP, Bangladesh Ec Assn 1985-91; Fellow, Islamic Ec Res Bureau; Bangla Acad; Asiatic Soc Bangladesh; Bangladesh Nat Geographical Assn; Bangladesh Itihash Parishad; Bangladesh Soc for Intl Studies; Bangladesh Nat Assn Social Sci; Bangladesh Assn for Advancement of Sci. *Honours:* Edit, Thoughts on Ecoomics, quarterly journal; Champion, All Pakistan Inter-Univ Debate Compt, Lahore, 1966. *Hobbies:* Stamp collecting; Collecting old & rare books & journals; Travelling. *Address:* Department of Economics, Rajshahi University, Rajshahi 6205, Bangladesh.

HABY Vincent Andrew, b. 6 Dec 1940, Castroville, Texas, USA. Res Scist. m. Kathleen Adell Hagan, 28 Aug 1965, 2 s. 1 d. *Education:* BS Agronomy 1963, MS Soil Chem 1969, Tex A&M Univ; PhD Crop & Soil Sci 1975, Montana State Univ. *Appointments:* Tex Agric Extension Svc 1963-69; Montana Agric Expt Station 1969-82; Prof in Soil Chem, Res Scist in Soil Fertility, Chem & Plant Nutrition, Tex Agric Expt Station 1982-. *Publications:* Testing soils for potassium, calcium & magnesium, co- Author, in Soil Testing & Plant Analysis, 1990. *Memberships:* Am Soc Agronomy, Membership Com; Soil Sci Soc Am; Coun for Agric Sci & Tech; Srn Assn of Agric Scists; Texas A&M Former Students Assn; Reg'd as a Cert Profl Soil Scist with Am Registry Cert Profls in Agronomy, Crops & Soils. Tex A&M Univ System Awd for Excellence in Team Res for 1989; Tex-La Aglime & Fertilizer Assn 1990 Meritorious Svc Awd; Superior Achievement Awd for Research, TX A&M Univ Soil and Crop Scis Dept. *Hobbies:* Gardening; Boating; Fishing; Back packing; Environmental reclamation of soils. *Address:* Texas A&M University Agricultural Research & Extension Centre, PO Box E, Overton, TX 75684, USA. 7.

HACKETT David Kramer, b. 11 Nov 1948, Frankfort, Indiana, USA. Forensic & Failure Engr; Writer; Sci Advocate. m. 6 Jan 1972. *Education:* BSc Materials Sci & Metallurgical Engrg 1975, with addtl studies in Geol & Computer Sci, Univ Tenn. *Appointments:* Tech Advr to Dir, Univ Tenn 1973-75; Chf Engr, Aztech Res Svcs 1975-77; Welding Engr, Union Carbide Nuclear 1977-81; Forensic & Failure Engr, Aztech Res Svcs 1981-; Exec Dir, Pellissipi Sci Engrg Prog 1989-. *Publications:* Edit 4 books; Num awds photography; Author num jour arts. *Memberships:* Am Soc Metals, 25 year mem; Am Indian Sci & Engrg Soc; Orion Res Forum & Network, Bd Dirs; Foothills Craft Guild, Bd Dirs 1979-80; Pellissippi Sci Enrichment Prog, Bd Dirs. *Honour:* Licensed Profl Engr, 1982. *Hobbies:* Stone carving; traditional native American smoking pipes; Palaeontology-5 new species established; Photography-numerous awards; Genealogy; Hiking. *Address:* Aztech Research Services, 6500 Trousdale Road, Knoxville, TN 37921, USA. 7.

HACKETT John Charles Thomas, b. 4 Feb 1939, Epsom, Surrey. Dir Gen Trade Assn. m. Patricia Margaret Tubb, 27 Dec 1958. *Education:* London Univ, LLB Hons (External) 1969. *Appointments:* Production Planning Mgr, Rowntree Gp 1960-64; Production Controller, Johnsons' Wax 1964; Commercial Secy, Heating & Ventilating Contractors Assn 1964-70; Secy, Com of Assns of Specialist Engrg Contractors 1968-79; Dep Dir 1970-79, Dir 1980-84, Brit Construcional Steelwork Assn; Dir Gen, Brit Insurance & Investment Brokers' Assn 1985-. *Publication:* BCSA Members' Contractual Handbook, 1972, 1979. *Memberships:* Fellow, Brit Inst Mgmt (FBIM); Inst Dirs. *Hobbies:* Music; Reading; Motoring; Walking. *Address:* BIIBA House, 14 Bevis Marks, London EC3A 7NT, England. 1.

HAENDEL Ida, b. 15 Dec 1928, Chelm, Poland. Violinist. *Education:* Warsaw Conservatoire, gained gold medal aged 7; Studied in Paris under Carl Flesch & George Enescu. *Career:* Debut as child prodigy at Queen's Hall, London under baton of Sir Henry Wood, playing Brahms's Violin Concerto; Gave concerts for the troops during war; Since the war she has played internationally, appearing throughout Europe, Scandinavia, Turkey, Israel, US, Can, Central & S Am, the Far East & Russia; Regular visitor to all major orchs of GB, accompanying them on foreign tours; Also plays with major orchs worldwide; In UK makes regular appearances at major festivals incl Edinburgh & BBC Proms; On Jury of major compts incl the Carl Flesch in London, the Sibelius Compt in Helsinki, the Intl Violin Compt in Cologne and the 1991 Mozart Compt in Newfoundland, Can. *Publications:* 1st part of autobiography , Woman With Violin, pub; 2nd part in progress; 2-part TV documentary about her life. *Honours:* Sibelius Medal, 1982; CBE 1991. *Address:* c/o Harold Holt Ltd, 31 Sinclair Road, London W14 0NS, England.

HAERLE Wilfried, b. 6 Sept 1941, Heilbronn. Univ Prof. m. Elisabeth Pillmeier, 28 Oct 1964, 2 s. 1 d. *Education:* Heidelberg & Erlaugen Univs 1961-66; Dr theol 1969, Univ Bochum; Habil syst Theol 1973, Univ Kiel. *Appointments:* Wiss Asst 1966-73; Priv Dozent 1973-77; Dozent 1977-78, Groningen, Netherlands; Univ Prof, Marburg 1978-. *Publications:* Sein und Guade, 1975; Die Frage nach Gott, 1978; Rechtfertigung, 1980; Syst Philosophie, 1987; Lehrfreiheit und Lehrbeanstanding, 1985; Theologenlexikon, 1987; Kirche und Gesellschaft, 1989; Zum Beispiel Golfkrieg, 1992. *Memberships:* Wiss Ges fuer Theol; Martin-Luther Ges; Soc Ethica; Evang Bund; Landessynode der Ev Kirche; Von Kurhessen-Waldeck; Gen Synode der VELKD. *Honour:* Universitaetspreis Bochum, 1969. *Hobbies:* Music; Chess; Horse riding. *Address:* Lahntor 3, D 3550 Marburg, Germany. 43, 52, 92.

HAFEZ Salah Eldin, b. 8 Dec 1938, Egypt. Edit; Lectr of Journalism. m. Prof Nabila Khalifa, 6 Oct 1963, 1 s. 1 d. *Education:* BA Journalism 1960, Cairo Univ. *Appointments:* Al-Akhbar Daily Newspaper 1957-58; Al-Shaab daily newspaper 1958-60; Al- Taawon, weekly magazine, 1960-66; ALAHRum Daily Newspaper, 1968- ; Chf Edit, Information Studies Mag, 1984-; ALAHRam Deputy Chief Editor and supervisor of ALAHRAM Internation Edition; Lectr of Journalism, Cairo Univ, Mass Media Fac. *Publications:* Books: Horn of Africa, struggle of super powers; Bolizario Conflict on Western Desert; Afghanistan, Islam & Revolution; Democracy & Revolution; Democracy Shochk; Freedom of the Press, under print. *Memberships:* Egyptian Press Syndicate, Secy- Gen 1967-71, 1973-77; Fed of Pan Arab Journalists, Secy Gen 1976-77; African Union of Journalists; Intl Press Inst; fdr mem, Arab Org of Human Rights. *Honour:* Hon Medallion from Intl Org of Journalists, 1971. *Hobbies:* Reading in political science, journalism, world political development; Writing short stories; Researching on futute of the press. *Address:* 28-El Hussein Street, Mohandesseen, Cairo, Egypt.

HAFNER Klaus, b. 10 Dec 1927, Potsdam, Germany. Prof Org Chem. m. Dr Gisela Schneider. *Education:* Dr phil 1951, Univ Marburg; Res Asst with Prof Dr Karl Ziegler 1951-55; Habilitation 1956, Univ Marburg, Privat Dozent. *Appointments:* Assoc Prof, Univ Munich 1962; Full Prof, Technische Hochschule Darmstadt 1965. *Publications:* Over 160 papers in profl jours on preparative org chem. *Memberships:* Bd Trustees, Beilstein Inst; Com mem, German Inst Macromolecular Chem; Deutsche Akademie der Naturforscher Leopoldina; German Chem Soc; Am Chem Soc; Chem Soc of Brit; Assn Austrian Chemists. *Honours:* Adolf von Baeyer Memorial Coin, German Chem Soc, 1980; Carus Medal, Acad Sci Leopoldina, 1980; Carus Prize of the City of Schweinfurt, 1980. *Address:* Institut fur Organische Chemie, Technische Hochshule Darmstadt, Petersenstrasse 22, D-6100 Darmstadt, Germany. 34, 52, 92, 154, 162.

HAGBERG Arne, b. 5 May 1919, Partille, Sweden. Prof Emeritus Genetics & Crop Breeding. m. Gunborg Jonsson, 23 Mar 1946, 3 s. *Education:* Fil kand Chem & Biol 1942; Fil mag Chem & Biol 1944; Fil lic Genetics 1948; Fil dr Genetics 1953. *Appointments:* Asst Breeder, Hillerhog 1942-44; Asst Breeder 1945-51, Hd Cytogenetics 1951-60, Hd Barley Breeding 1960-71, Dir 1972-79, Svalov Inst; Asst Tchr Genetics 1949-52; Assoc Prof Genetics 1953-64; Prof Genetics 1965-79; Prof Genetics & Breeding Crops 1979-85. *Publications:* Books: Studies on Heterosis, 1953; Mutations and Polypoidy in Plant Breeding, 1961; Plant Breeding-Green Evolution, in Swedish, 1977; Edit, Journal of Swedish Seed Assn 1972-91. *Memberships include:* Royal Acad Sci, Sweden; Royal Acad Forestry & Agric; Royal Physiografic Soc, Lund; Mendelian Soc, Lund; Swedish Seed Assn; Hon mem Indian Soc Genetics. *Honours include:* Tammisto Medal, Finland, 1982; Engestrom Medal, Lund, Swden, 1990; Nilsson-Ehle Medal, Stockholm, Sweden, 1991. *Hobbies:* Sailing; Nature; Gardening. *Address:* S-26042 Molle, Sweden.

HAGENBUCHLE Roland, b. 13 Oct 1932, Homburg, Switzerland. Prof Am Lit. m. Dr Helen Imfeld, 30 Mar 1964. *Education:* Doctorate 1967, Habilitation 1975, Univ Zurich. *Appointments:* Guest Prof, Univ Gottingen, Germany 1974-75; John F Kennedy Inst, Berlin 1975-76; Univ Bern, Switzerland 1976-77; Prof Am Lit, Wuppertal 1977-80, Cath U Eichstatt 1981-. *Publications:* Choice and the Fall of Man in Milton's Paradise Lost; Self Encounter in the Poetry of Emily Dickinson; American Poetry Between Tradition & Modernism, ed; Poetic Knowledge: Circumference and Centre, ed; Poetry & Epistemology, ed; Poetry & the Fine Arts, ed; Das Paradox. Eine Herausforderung des abendländischen Denkens, ed. *Memberships:* Am Coun Learned Soc Fellow, Yale 1971-72; European Assn Am Studies; Modern Lang Assn; Milton Soc of Am; Soc for the Study of Midwestern Lit. *Hobbies:* Music; Mountain climbing. *Address:* Im Schilf 3, 8044 Zurich, Switzerland. 52, 92.

HAGENFELDT Jan Artur, b. 1 Oct 1931, Orebro, Sweden. Retail Exec. 2 s. 1 d. *Appointments:* CEO, Hagenfeld-affArerna AB, Orebro, Sweden 1966-; Bd Dirs, Nordbanken, Orebro, Sweden. *Memberships:* Swedish Commerce Employers' Orgn, Bd Dirs; Swedish Merchants' Assn Credit Ops, Chmn; Round Table, Nat Pres 1967- 68; World Coun of Young Mens Svc Clubs, Hon Secy 1965-66. *Address:* Hagenfeld-affArerna AB, Box 947, 701 31 Orebro, Sweden.

HAGER Nina, b. 1 Dec 1950, Berlin, Germany. Scist; Prof. 1 s. *Education:* Dipl Physics 1973; Dr phil 1976; Dr sc phil, habilitation 1987; Prof of Acad of Sci of GDR 1989. *Appointments:* Sci Asst, Zentralinst fur Philos, Acad of Sci of GDR 1973-90; Sci Asst, Zentralinst fur Philos, Berlin, FRG 1990-. *Publications:* Modelle in der Physik, 1982; Materialistische Dialektik in der Physikalischen und Biologischen Erkennteris, 1982, Co-Author; Philosophie-Wissenschaff-Politik, 1982, Co-Author; Experiment-Modell-Theorie, 1982, in Russian, 1982, Co-Author; Philosophie und Naturwissenschaften, 1978, 1983, 1991, Co-Author; Faszination Weltraumflug, 1985, Co-Author; Philosophie und Naturwissenschaften, 1986, Co-Author; Der Traum vorn Kosmos, 1988; Dialektika-Poznanie-Nauka, 1988, in Russian, Co-Author; Verantwortung aus Wissen, 1989, Co-Edit; Over 60 arts, annotations, translation of arts, from Russian to German, in sev sci jours in the GDR, FRG, Poland & Austria. *Membership:* Gesellschaft fur Weltraumforschung und Raumfahrd. *Hobbies:* Pieskower weg 52, D (0)-1055 Berlin, Germany.

HAGLUND Ann-Cathrine, b. 24 Aug 1937, Orebro, Sweden. MP. m. Finn Haglund, 18 Apr 1957, 1 s. 2 d. *Education:* MA. *Appointments:* Lang Tchr; MP 1979- . *Memberships:* Mem Moderate Party; Red Cross; Amnesty; Pres, Sweden-Israel Assn 1990-; Pres

Moderate Women's Assn 1981-90. *Address:* Riksdagen, 10012 Stockholm, Sweden.

HAGOEL David, b. 30 Jan 1929, Tripoli, Libya. Hd Youth Aliyah Dept, Jewish Agency. m. Hana, 1 s. 1 d. *Education:* LLM 1970; Undergrad & Grad Studies at Fac Law, Hebrew Univ in Jerusalem. *Appointments include:* Lawyer 1970-; Soldier at Independence War 1948 and holds rank of Brig Gen (Res); Served in var command, staff and trng positions; Commander, Jerusalem Brigade (District) 1969-73, Commander of the Independence Day events for the 25th Anniversary of the State of Israel; Chf of Planning and Organisation in the Ops Div of the General Staff of Israel Defence Forces 1973-76; Commander, Judea and Samaria Area and bore overall responsibility for the civil & military admin of this area 1976-78; Dir Gen, Min of Energy & Infrastructure 1979-82; Chmn Bd Dirs, Israel Electric Corp 1982-84; Chmn Bd Dirs 1984-88, Paz Oil Co Ltd; Chmn, Israel's Nature Reserve Authority 1988-; Hd Dept, Youth Aliya, mem Exec of Jewish Agency & the World Zionist Org; Head of Information Dept of the World Zionist Organisation; Current, Head of the Information Dept of the World Zionist Organization. *Memberships:* Chmn & Dir Gen, Nat Energy Authority; Chmn, Israel Nat Oil Co Ltd; Mem Bd Dirs, Oil Refineries Ltd; Mem Bd Dirs, Mediterranean Sea-Dead Sea Co; Chmn Bd Dirs, Company for Desalination of Sea Water; Mem US-Israel Steering Com for Desalination Project; Mem Supreme Emergency Authority for Economy, and Supreme Authorities for Energy & Fuel; Chmn Bd Dirs, Israel Electric Corp; Mem Atomic Energy Com. *Hobbies:* Gardening; Hiking. *Address:* Ben Maimon Street No 6, Jerusalem, Israel.

HAGRUP Knut, b. 13 Nov 1913, Bergen, Norway. Professor; Consultant. m. Ester Skaugen, 1944 (dec 1976), 2 d. *Education:* Coll Maths degree, 1933; Coll Econs, Oslo, 1934-35; Mil Coll, Royal Norwegian Air Force, 1935-36; Dip, Engrng Univ Darmstadt, Germany, 1940; DEcon, Univ Dresden, DRG, 1979; DTech, Univ Stockholm, Sweden, 1981. *Appointments include:* Pres, CEO, Scandinavian Airlines, Stockholm, , 1969-79; Chmn, Int Air Transport Assn, Geneva, Switzerland, 1976; Chmn, Assn European Air Transport, Brussels, Belgium, 1977; Chmn, Air Transport Commn, Int Chmbr of Comm, Paris, France, 1979-83; Bd Chmn, Saab-Fairchild Civil Aeroplane Enterprise, NYC, USA, 1980-84; Prof, Northrop Univ, CA, USA, 1981-91; Mem, var industry bds; Cons. *Publications include:* Flyet i Fare, 1976; Flyg utan Aatervando, 1976; Luftfarten, 1976; La Bataille du Transport Aerien, 1978; Die Heutige Luftfart, 1979; How the Aerospace Industry in Europe Will Survive, 1981. *Memberships:* Fellow, Royal Aeronautical Soc, England; RAF Club, England; Bd Mbr, Guggenheim Medal Bd, USA; Conquistadores, USA. *Honours:* Cmdr, St Olav's Order, Norway, 1975; Cmdr, No Star Order, Sweden, 1975; Cmdr, Legion d'Honneur, France, 1977; Cmdr, Oranje-Nassau Order, Netherlands, 1979; Cmdr, White Elephant Order, Thailand, 1982; Norwegian War Medal, 1946; Brit Def Medal, 1977; Hon DSc, Northrup Univ, USA, 1978; Hon LLD, Pacific L Univ, USA, 1978. *Hobbies:* Golf; Skiing; Hunting. *Address:* 14 rue St Jean, 1260 Nyon, Switzerland.

HAHN Werner, b. 7 Mar 1912, Trier, Germany. Professor; Consultant. Doctor of Medicine; Doctor of Dental Medicine; Head, Heinrich Hammer Institut (for Postgraduate Education). m. 24 Oct 1942, 1 s, 2 d. *Education:* Univ Bonn; Dr med dent, Univ Dusseldorf, 1936; Asst to Prof Axhausen, Dept Facial Oral and Maxillo-Facial Surg, Univ Berlin; Specialisation, Oral Surg, 1944; Dr med, Univ Munster, 1957; Specialisation, Oral Maxillo-Facial Surg, 1961. *Appointments:* O a, Dept Oral Maxillo-Facial Surg, Munster, 1951; Hd, Dept Oralmaxillofacial Surg, 1961, Hd, Dept Postgrad Educ, 1982, Kiel. *Publications:* Papers in all sci jnls of dentistry, topics incl oral med, cytology, prae canc cond diseases of the oral cavity, implantology, med law. *Memberships:* German Soc Dentistry, 1936; WG Maxillo Facial Surgery, 1938; FDI, 1976; Int Acad

Oral Surg, 1969; Fellow, Int Acad Dentistry, 1988. *Honours:* Gold Medal, Soc Italiana di od stom, 1960; Gold Medal, German Bd Dentistry; Gold Medal, Soc S Dentistry Germany; Hon Mbr, Acad Praxis und Wissenschaft. FDI, Mer Award. *Hobbies:* Sport; Sailing. *Address:* Westring 498, 2300 Kiel, Germany.

HAIN Violet Edna Hobbs, b. 23 Mar 1914, Washington, District of Columbia, USA. Artist; Painter; Teacher. m. John Adams Hain, 23 Dec 1939, 4 s. *Education:* BS, Wilson Tchrs Coll, 1935; Grad work, Art, MD Univ, Am Univ; Tchr of Art Cert, Bd Examiners, NJ; Studied watercolour w Eliot O'Hara. *Career:* Appts incl: Tchr, Oil Painting, Cape May Co Art League, NJ; Pvte tchng, Avalon, 1967-79; 1-artist shows: Cape May Co Art League, NJ, 1967; Avalon City Hall, 1970; Arts Club Wash DC, 1971; Galerie Int, NYC, 1973, 1979; 77 pictures, Chautauquam NY, 1975; Work as child exhibited Columbia Univ; As HS student participated in 4 travelling exhbns. *Contributions to:* World Biographical Hall of Fame, Historic Preservation of America Inc. *Memberships:* Wash DC Chapt, Artists Equity Assn; Corcoran Gall Art; Women's Civic Club, Stone Harbor; Cape May Co Art League; Centro studi e scambi, Leonardo da Vinci Int Acad, Italy; Life Fellow, ABI. *Honours:* Best in Show, Profl MD Fedn Women's Clubs, 1968, 1969; HQ Army Art Show, Pentagon, Wash DC, 1971; Dip di Benemerenza, Leonardo da Vinci Int Acad, 1980; Dip d'Onore La Gloire, 1982; Dip d'Onore Palme d'Oro, 1984; Num other art show awards; Commemorative Silver Medal, IBC, Hall of Fame, Personalities of Am, 1985; Commemorative Medal Hon, ABI, 1986. *Hobbies:* Music; Gardening. *Address:* 3530 Raymoor Road, Kensington, MD 20895, USA. 138, 151, 155, 178.

HAINES Andrew Paul, b. 26 Feb 1947, London, England. Professor of Primary Health Care. m. June Power, 12 Feb 1982, div. 12 Feb 1990. *Education:* MB BS, King's Coll, London, 1969; MRCP (UK), 1971; MRCGP, 1976; MD, Univ London, 1985; MFPHM, 1986. *Appointments:* Mbr, Sci Staff, Epidemiology and Med Care Unit, Med Rsch Coun, 1976-87; Prof, Primary Hlth Care, Univ Coll and Middlesex School Med, London, 1987-. *Publications:* Over 90 published papers on range of topics incl prevention, cardiovascular disease, alcohol, care of the elderly, hlth effects of global warming. *Memberships:* Coun Mbr, Int Physns for Prevention of Nuclear War, 1981-85; Coun, Pugwash Org Sci and World Affairs, 1987-91; Med Rsch Coun Hlth Sers Rsch Comm, 1989-. *Honours:* Hons, Pathology, Surg, Pharmacology, Therapeutics, MBBS Final Exams, Univ London, 1969; As Coun Mbr, Int Physns for Prevention of Nuclear War shared in Nobel Peace Prize, 1985; Vis Prof, Universiti Kebangsaan, Malaysia, 1991. *Hobbies:* Travel; International relations; Theatre. *Address:* Dept of Primary Health Care, University College and Middlesex School of Medicine, Whittington Hospital, London N19 5NF, England.

HAINES Arthur Barry, b. 13 Dec 1921, Middlesbrough, England. Consultant Aerodynamicist. m. Lilian May Brown, 15 Aug 1951, dec. 1989. *Education:* BSc Hons, Maths, Birmingham, 1941; CEng. *Appointments:* Aerodynamics Dept, Royal Aircraft Estab, 1941-55; Chief Aerodynamicist, 1955-78, Asst Chief Exec, 1978-80, Chief Exec, 1980-88, Aircraft Rsch Assn Ltd. *Publications:* Many papers and lectures on aerodynamics incl: Subsonic Aircraft Drag - An Appreciation of Modern Standards, 1968; European Pioneers Day Lecture, 1977; 27th Lanchester Lecture, Royal Aeronautical Soc, 1987. *Membership:* Fellow, Royal Aeronautical Soc, currently Chmn, Aerodynamics Grp Comm. *Honours:* Busk Prize, 1968, 1977, 1988, Soc Gold Medal, 1987, Royal Aeronautical Soc. *Hobbies:* Music; Walking; Reading. *Address:* 3 Bromham Road, Biddenham, Bedford MK40 4AF, England.

HAINING Thomas Nivison, b. 15 Mar 1927, Scotland. Retired Ambassador; Writer; Lecturer. m. Dorothy Patricia Robson, 26 Apr 1955. *Education:* Edinburgh

Univ; Univ Goettingen, Germany. *Appointments:* HM Diplomatic Serv, 1952-87: Served, Germany, Austria, USSR, Italy, and UK Mission to UN, NYC; HM Ambassador and Consul Gen, Ulan Bator, 1979-82. *Publications:* Between the Kremlin and the Forbidden City, 1989; Genghis Khan: His Life and Legacy (translator, ed), 1991; Problems of Mongolian Historiography, 1991; The Mongols: A European View, 1991; 'The Great Buddha of the Khalkha River', Jrnl of the Royal Asiatic Soc, vol 2, 1992. *Memberships:* Pres, Chinese Studies Grp, Univ Aberdeen; FRGS; Royal Soc Asian Affairs; Anglo-Mongolian Soc. *Honours:* CMG, Companion, Order of St Michael and St George, 1983; Hon Freeman, City of Rochester, NY, 1971; Hon Rsch, Hist, Univ Aberdeen, 1988-90; Hon Rsch Fellow, 1990-. *Hobbies:* Travel; Languages; Mongolia; Writing; Music; Golf; Reading. *Address:* Carseview, 7 The Banks, Brechin, Angus DD9 6JD, Scotland. 1.

HAIRSTON William Michael, b. 12 Oct 1947, Roswell, New Mexico, USA. Manufacturing Engineer. m. Margaret Cliff, 21 Aug 1970, 2 s. *Education:* BS, Engrng Sci, 1970, MS, Engrng Sci, 1973, TN Technological Univ, Cookeville. *Appointments:* Mech Engr, Naval Surface Weapons Ctr, Dahlgren, VA, 1972-77; Asst Plant Engr, Colonial Rubber Works, Kingstree, SC, 1977-79; Tyre Designer, Michelin Ams Rsch Corp, Greenville, SC, 1979-81; Staff/Indl Engr, Michelin Tire Corp, Greenville, 1981-84; Sr Engr, Raychem Corp, Fuquay-Varina, NC, 1984-. *Membership:* Rotary Int, Fuquay-Varina NC Chapt. *Hobbies:* Church activities; Classical music; Automotive and construction projects. *Addess:* 107 Nathaniel Court, Cary, NC 27511, USA. 7.

HAJIFANIS George, b. 25 Feb 1937, Larnaca, Cyprus. Architect; Town Planning Consultant. m. 11 Apr 1976, 2 d. *Education:* Dip Arch, Univ London, 1961; Dip Town Planning, Polytechnic Ctl London; MA, Hist and Theory Arch, Univ Essex, 1974. *Career includes:* Tchg, lecturing on arch. *Creative works:* Designed prototype Charlie Ratchford Ctr for physically handicapped in London, 1973; The Cypriot Communbity in the UK: Issues of Identity (co-ed w John Charalambous and Litsa Kilonis), 1988; Contbr to Parikaiki newspaper. *Memberships:* ARIBA; FRSA; Bd of Dirs' Govs, Univ N London; Chmn, Bd Dirs, Theatro Technis; Hon Sec, Nat Fedn, Cypriots UK. *Address:* 43 Hornsey Lane Gardens, London N6 5NY, England.

HAJNY Josef, b. 4 July 1941, Litovel, Czechoslovakia. Cultural Television Editor. m. 5 Sept 1969, 1 s. *Education:* Grad, Fac Philos, Charles Univ, Prague, 1963; Doct. *Appointments:* Odeon publng house, 1963-68; Ed, PH Melantrich, 1969; Translator, Roman Lit, 1970-89; Chief, Cultural Editing, Czech TV, 1990-. *Publications:* Translations, over 60 authors; Book about Italy; Num articles. *Memberships:* Assn Jours, Czechoslovakia; Ctr Europeen de la culture, Switzerland. *Honours:* Premio Europeo di Letteratura Giovanile, Univ Padova, Italy, 1978. *Hobby:* Tennis. *Address:* Puchovska 4, 141 00 Prague 4, Czechoslovakia.

HAKIM Seymour, b. 23 Jan 1933, New York City, New York, USA. Educator; Writer; Artist. m. Odetta Roverso, 18 Aug 1970. *Education:* AB, En NM Univ, 1957; MA, NY Univ, 1960; Postgrad studies, var univs incl Univ CA, Brigham Young Univ, Univ PA. *Career:* Served, AUS, 1942-54; Tchr, Art, Engl, NYC School System, 1957-60; Tchr, Art, Engl, 1960-70, Engl, Photography, 1972-, Chmn, Engl Dept, 1973-, Dept Def System, Vicenza, Italy; Tchr, London Ctl HS, 1971; Profl Artist and Writer; 1-man art exhbns, 1970, 1973, 1982-83, 1986, forthcoming May 1993; Grp showings, 1971, 1976, 1978, 1984, 1985, 1987, 1988, 1989. *Creative works include:* The Sacred Family, play, 1970; Poems: Manhattan Goodbye, 1970; Under moon, 1970; The Museum of the Mind, 1971; Wine Theorem, 1972; Substituting Memories, 1976; Iris Elegy, 1979; Balancing Act, a Congruence of Symbols, 1981; The Birth of a Poet, 1985; Eleanor Goodbye, 1988; Art works in pub and pvte collections, China, Rumania, Japan,

England, Korea, Germany, Italy, USA. *Honours:* Outstanding Superior Tchng Awards, Dept Def, DODDS-MED, 1976-79, 1981-86, 1988, 1989, 1990, 1991, 1992. *Hobbies:* Reading; Travel; Photography (semi-professional). *Address:* Via Chiesa Nuova No 1, Longare (VIC) 36023, Italy. 3, 52, 151.

HAKOLA Hannu Panu Aukusti, b. 22 Feb 1932, Lapua, Finland. Professor of Forensic Psychiatry. m. Maija-Leena Salo, 19 Apr 1954, 3 s, 1 d. *Education:* MD, Univ Turku, 1956; MA, 1960; MD, acad dissertation, 1972; Dip, Hlth Admin, Nat Bd Hlth, Finland, 1979. *Appointments:* Asst Physn, Neuropsych Clin, Turku, 1956-60; Chief Psych, Harjamaki Hosp, Siilinjarvi, 1960-69; Chief Psych, Niuvanniemi Hosp, Kuopio, 1969-83; Prof, Forensic Psych, Kuopio, 1983-. *Publications:* Books: On Environmental Conditions of Criminal Psychopaths, 1959; Clinical aspects of a New Hereditary Disease, 1972; PLO-SL. A Neuropsychiatric Follow-up Study, 1990. *Memberships:* Ed Bd, Med Jrnl Duodecim, 1975-81; Bd Mbr, Kuopio Univ Ctl Hosp, 1985-89. *Honours:* Grantee, Paulo Fndn, Helsinki, 1971; Grantee, Aaltonen Fndn, Tampere, 1973; Prize, Acta Psychiat Scandinaviae. *Hobbies:* Music; Elk hunting; Joutenlahti farm; Rotary. *Address:* Satamakatu 3 D 49, SF-70100 Kuopio, Finland. 52.

HAKSAR Aditya Narayan Dhairyasheel, b. 3 Dec 1933, Gwalior, India. Diplomat. m. Priti Raina, 19 Nov 1961, 1 s, 1 d. *Education:* MA, Allahabad Univ, 1954; BA, Brasenose Coll, Oxford, England, 1956; MA, Oxford. *Appointments:* Joined Indian For Serv, 1956; Served Jakarta, New Delhi, Brussels, Addis Ababa, Cairo, UN (NYC), 1957-73; Official Spokesman, External Affairs Min, New Delhi, 1974-77; High Commnr to Kenya and Seychelles, 1977-80; Min, Wash DC, USA, 1980-83; Amb to Portugal, 1984-87; Dean, For Serv Trng Inst, New Delhi, 1987-. *Publication:* Panchatantra translations from Sanskrit, 1988. *Memberships include:* Delhi Gymkhana Club. *Honours:* Elected Pres, UN Environment Prog (UNEP) Govng Coun, 1980-81. *Hobbies:* Reading; Writing; Travel. *Address:* c/o Ministry of External Affairs, New Delhi 110011, India.

HALADYNA Jeremy John, b. 4 Aug 1955, Louisville, Kentucky, USA. Composer. *Education:* BS, Radio, TV, Film, 1977, BMus, 1978, MA, Radio, TV, Film, 1980, Univ TX; Dip, Musical Composition, Schola Cantorum, Paris, 1979; MMus w distinction, Univ Surrey, England, 1988. *Appointments:* Radio Arts Prod, Univ TX, 1981-82; Radio Prog Dir, OK State Univ, 1982-87; Fac Assoc, Tchng Composition and Theory, Dept Music, Univ CA, Santa Barbara, 1989-. *Creative works:* Alibi for a Diamond Necklace, piano solo, 1986; A Colloquy of Fireflies, flute, piano, 1986; Just Plain Bob, small orch, 1988; Penguin Island, chamber quintet, 1989; Romanesca, o Il Trionfo del Solfeggio, voices, 9 instruments, 1990; El llanto de Izamal, viola, piano, 1991; Hearts of Yucatan, electronics, narrator, 1991. *Memberships:* Coll Music Soc; Am Guild Organists; Am Music Ctr; ASCAP. *Honours:* Rotary Int Fellowship, 1978; Lili Boulanger Prize, France, 1979; Joyce Dixey Prize, MCPS Ltd, England, 1988; Premieres, St John's, Smith Sq, Feb 1989, S Bank Ctr, June 1990; Prizes, Composition, Univ CA, 1990, 1991. *Hobbies:* Reading; Languages; Shortwave radio; Cycling. *Address:* PO Box 13823, Santa Barbara, CA 93107, USA.

HALAS Stanislaw, b. 9 July 1945, Stryjow, Poland. University Professor of Physics. m. Barbara Strakowska, 2 Sept 1973, 4 s, 2 d. *Education:* Master's degree, 1968, PhD, Expmtl Phys, 1973, Marie Curie-Sklodowska Univ, Lublin. *Appointments:* Asst Prof, 1968, Tutor, 1973, Assoc Prof, 1984, Univ Prof, 1991-, Marie Curie-Sklodowska Univ, Lublin. *Publications:* Over 130 sci publs in var jnls and maj contbns in 2 monographs on mass spectrometry and stable isotope effects in nature, 1968-. *Memberships:* Polish Phys Soc, Warsaw; Polish Chem Soc, Warsaw; Sci Soc Lublin; Isotope Sect, Polish Mineralogical Soc, Cracow; Polish Soc Amateur Astron, Cracow. *Honours:* Copernicus Medal, 1973; Golden

Cross, 1989; Medal State Geological Inst; Warsaw, 1990. *Hobbies:* Swimming; Driving. *Address:* ul Zelazowej Woli 17/20, 20-854 Lublin, Poland.

HALASZ Bela, b. 4 July 1927, Kalazno, Hungary. Professor of Anatomy; Physician. m. Etelka Karacsonyi, 17 Apr 1954, 2 d. *Education:* MD, Univ Med School, Pecs, 1954; Cand Sc, 1966; DSc, 1972. *Appointments:* Asst Prof, Adj, Assoc Prof, Dept Anatomy, Univ Med School, Pecs, 1954-71; Prof, Chmn, 2nd Dept Anatomy, Semmelweis Univ, Budapest, 1971-. *Publications:* 130 sci publs. *Memberships:* Hungarian Acad Scis, VO, Pres Med Sect; Exec Coun, European Sci Fndn; European Fedn Endocrine Socs, VP; Int Soc Endocrinology, Exec Comm; Acad Europaea; Int Soc Neuroendocrinology, VP. *Honours:* Ulf von Euler Award, Int Soc Endocrinology, 1976; Semmelweis Medal, 1986; Szechenyi State Award, 1990; Hon Mbr: Czechoslovakian Endocrine Soc, 1973; Polish Endocrine Soc, 1978; Am Physiological Soc, 1987; Am Acad Arts and Scis, 1989. *Address:* 2nd Department of Anatomy, Semmelweis Medical University, Tuzolto u 58, H-1094 Budapest, Hungary.

HALE Julian Anthony Stuart, b. 27 Nov 1940, Llandrindod Wells, Wales. Writer; Radio Producer. m. Helen Elizabeth Grace Likierman, 18 Apr 1987, 1 s, 2 d. *Education:* Winchester Coll, 1954-59; Christ Church, Oxford, 1959-63; Int Univ des Hautes Etudes Ints, 1965-57. *Appointments:* Text Ed, G G Harrap, 1963-65; FAO/ECE, Geneva, Switzerland, 1965-67; BBC World Serv, 1968-73; Ed, European Gazette, 1973; BBC Radio 3 and 4, 1979-. *Publications:* Non-fiction: Ceausecsu's Romania, 1971; Radio Power, 1975; Fiction: Snap Judgement, 1977; Vicious Circles, 1978; Midwinter Madness, 1979; Force Play, 1979; The London Affair, 1981; Russian Leave, 1981; Black Summer, 1982. *Hobbies:* European languages; Real tennis. *Address:* 11 Alexander Street, London W2 5NT, England.

HALIN Rudolf, b. 3 Feb 1934. Professor of Mathematics. *Education:* Phd, 1962, Habilitation, 1966, Cologne. *Appointments:* Asst, Univ Cologne, 1962-70; Prof, Maths, Hamburg, 1970. *Publications:* 60 Math jnls; Graphentheorie, book, 2nd Ed, 1989. *Address:* Kaiser-Friedrich-Str 4, 2410 Moelln/Lbg, Germany.

HALL Dinny, b. 28 Apr 1959, Hertfordshire, England. Jewellery Designer. *Education:* BA Hons, Jewellery Design, Ctl School Art, Holborn, London, 1982. *Career:* Started own Bus, London, 1984; Opened 1st shop, London, 1992. *Publication:* Creative Jewellery, book, 1986. *Membership:* Groucho Club, Soho. *Honours:* Brit Fashion Award, 1989; Brit Accessory Designer of Yr. *Hobbies:* Travel; Architecture; Walking; Ancient and tribal art. *Address:* 58 Brondesbury Villas, London NW6, England.

HALL Douglas Lee, b. 5 Feb 1947, San Antonio, Texas, USA. Chairman, Computer Science Department. *Education:* AA, San Antonio Coll, 1967; BA, Univ TX, 1969; MEd, Pan Am Univ, 1977; PhD, N TX State Univ, 1987. *Appointments:* Brownsville Indep School Dist, 1976-78; A B Dick Inc, 1978-79; Dallas Indep School Dist, 1979-82; N TX State Univ, 1983-86; Chmn, Computer Sci Dept, St Mary's Univ, 1986-. *Publications:* Introduction to Computer Languages, 1984; Introduction to IBM-PC COBOL, 1985; Learning Modalities and Programming, 1986; Intelligent Tutoring Systems Using CERA, 1987. *Memberships:* ACM; IEEE; Am Assn Artificial Intelligence; Alamo Area Assn Artificial Intelligence; Japan-Am Soc (Parl); German-Am Soc; Life Mbr, TSTA. *Honours:* Nat Merit Finalist, 1965; Dean's List, 1965-69, 1970-72, 1983-87; Top Ten, 1967; Tchr of Yr, 1971, 1974, 1975, 1977; Outstanding Computer Sci Grad, 1986. *Hobbies:* Folk dance; Languages; Genealogy. *Address:* 515 Marquis, San Antonio, TX 78216, USA. 15.

HALL Jane Anna, b. 4 Apr 1959, New London, Connecticut, USA. Poet; Writer. *Education:* Profl Mod, Barbizon School, 1976; Dip, Westbrook HS, 1977. *Career:* Model, Barbizon Agy, 1977; Sunday School Tchr, 1977-90, Asst Superintendent, 1979-84, 1st Congregational Church; Employed by Dir, Career Planning, Wesleyan Univ, 1985-86; Self-employed Poet, Writer, 1986-; Poetry reading, Congregational Ch, Broad Brook, CT, 1988; Fndr, Ed, Poetry in Your Mailbox Newsletter, 1989-; Participant, grp poetry reading and display, 1989, Reader, Night of A Thousand Stars Readathon, 1990, 1-woman show, 1989, 1990, Westbrook Pub Lib, Westbrook; Grp poetry display, Acton Pub Lib, Old Saybrook, CT, 1990. *Publications:* Chapbooks: Cedar and Lace, 1986; Satin and Pinstripe, 1987; Fireworks and Diamonds, 1988; Stars and Daffodils, 1989; Sunrises and Stonewalls, 1990; Mountains and Meadows, 1991; Moonlight and Waterlillies, 1992. *Memberships:* Bd Christian Educ, 1st Congregational Ch, Westbrook, 1979-84; CT Poetry Soc, World Poetry Chmn, Old Saybrook Chapt, 1989; Int Platform Assn; Romance Writers Am; Romance Writer of Am, CT Chapt. *Honours:* 2nd Prize, Post Dawn Enchantment poem, 1983, 2nd Prize, Polar Bear Frolic poem, 1986, CT Poetry Soc Contest, 1983; Hon Mention for In Your Arms, World of Poetry Contest, 1988; Poetry Contest Judge, Acton Plc Library Old Say Brook, Ct 25th Anniversary Celebration, 1992. *Hobbies:* Interior decoration and design; Fashion design; Tennis. *Address:* PO Box 629, Westbrook, CT 06498, USA. 3, 5, 6, 52, 138, 152, 155, 156, 162, 178, 191.

HALL Jonathan Michael Francis Cooper (Brigadier), b. 10 Aug 1944, Wilmslow, Cheshire, England. Army Officer. m. Sarah Linda Hudson, 5 Oct 1968, 2 d. *Education:* Royal Mil Acad, Sandhurst, 1964-65; Army Staff Col, 1976-77; Higher Command and Staff Course, 1988; Royal Col Def Studies, 1990. *Appointments:* Served regimental duty, Royal Scots Dragoon Guards, FRG, Singapore, Libya, Cyprus, No Ireland, 1966-76; Army Staff Coll, 1976-77; Instr, JDSC, 1978-80; BAOR, 1980-82; MOD, 1982-84; CO, Scots Dragoon Guards, 1984-86; Col MS2, 1986-88; Brig Cmdng, 12 Armoured Pode, 1989-90. *Membership:* Cavalry and Guards Club. *Honours:* OBE, 1987. *Hobbies:* Country pursuits; Travel; Skiing; Tennis; Walking; Gardening; Military history. *Address:* Home Headquarters, Royal Scots Dragoon Guards, The Castle, Edinburgh, Scotland.

HALL Laurance David, b. 18 Mar 1938, London, England. Professor of Medicinal Chemistry. m. Winifred Margaret Golding, 1 Aug 1962, 2 s, 2 d. *Education:* BSc 1st Class Hons, Chem, 1959, PhD, Chem, 1962, Bristol Univ; MA, Cambridge, 1990. *Appointments:* Fac positions, Chem Dept, Univ BC, Can, 1963-84; Herchel Smith Prof, Medicinal Biochem, Cambridge Univ, England, 1984-. *Memberships:* Fellow, Chem Inst Can; FRS Can; Fellow, Royal Soc Chem. *Honours:* C'wlth Bursar, Univ NSW, Australia, Royal Soc and Nuffield Fndn, 1967; Jacob Bielly Fac Rsch Prize, Univ BC, 1974; Tate and Lyle Award, Carbohydrate Chem, Chem Soc, 1974; Merck, Sharpe and Dohme Lecture Award, Chem Inst Can, 1975; Corday Morgan Medal and Prize, Chem Soc, 1976; I W Killam Sr Rsch Fellow, Univ BC, 1979-80; Barringer Award, Spectroscopy Soc Can, 1981; Can Coun Killam Rsch Fellow, 1982-84; 1987 Interdisciplinary Award, Royal Soc Chem, 1988; 1990 Royal Soc Chem Award, Chem Analysis and Instrumentation, 1990. *Hobbies:* Scientific research; Travel; Wine making from grapes. *Address:* Herchel Smith Laboratory for Medicinal Chemistry, Cambridge University Forvie Site, Robinson Way, Cambridge CB2 2PZ, England.

HALL Ralph Frederick, b. 19 Sept 1940, Sydney, New South Wales, Australia. University Professor. m. (1) Diane Everett, 15 Jan 1965, div. 1976, 1 s, 2 d; (2) Susan Moxham, Jan 1976, 1 d. *Education:* Acctcy Cert, St George Tech Coll, 1956; BA, 1966, MA, 1968, PhD, 1971, Univ Sydney. *Appointments:* Clerk, Sydney Co Coun, 1956-60; Asst Acct, Dairy Farmers Coop, 1960-64; Lectr, Psychology, Univ Sydney, 1969-72; Sr Lectr,

1972-74, Prof, 1975-, Univ NSW; Sr Lectr, Macquarie Univ, 1974-75. *Publications:* Global Issues, 1987; Impacts, 1991. *Memberships:* Australian Psychological Soc, Gen Sec 1967-68; Federated Australian Univ Staff Assn, VP 1987-88, Pres 1988-. *Honours:* Univ Medal, Psychology, 1968, H Tasman Lovell Mem Medallion, 1971, Univ Sydney. *Hobbies:* Swimming; Running; Chess; Wine. *Address:* School of Social Science and Policy, University of New South Wales, PO Box 1, Kensington, NSW 2033, Australia. 23.

HALL Rodney Thomas William, b. 15 Nov 1919, Weymouth, England. Retired; Formerly in Petroleum Research and Refining. m. Jean Hazel Burgoyne, 2 Apr 1945, 2 s. *Education:* BSc Hons (Spl Chem), King's Coll, London, 1940; PhD, Chem Engrng, Birmingham Univ, 1951. *Appointments:* Royal Ordnance Factories, 1940-45; Dev Lab, Courtaulds, 1945-47; Lectr, Chem Engrng, Birmingham Univ, 1947-52; Tech Mgr, Refining, Chief Chem, Univ Liaison, Esso, 1951-82. *Publications:* Review paper on explosives, 1947; Rsch papers, Vapour-Liquid Equilibria, 1955; About 10 patents (w Esso), bitumen, explosives, wax, jet fuel, caustic reg, 1956-65; Survey - Supply/Demand for Chemical Engineers (Instn Chem Engrs), 1980. *Memberships:* CChem; CEng; Fellow, Royal Soc Chem, Qualifications Comm 1978-82, Ind Higher Educ Comm 1975-82; Fellow, Instn Chem Engrs, Examiners Comm 1957-58; Fellow, Inst Petroleum, Standardisation, Ed Comm 1965-; Industry Acad Comms: Inst Energy, TEC, CIA; Chmn, S Bank Poly Comm; SRC (Chem) CASE Comm; Var other comms. *Hobbies:* Golf; Alternative medicine; Theatre, local and national; Dancing; Music, piano, organ, orchestral, big band, composing, orchestration, music criticism. *Address:* Sheaves, 6 Milldown Avenue, Goring-on-Thames, Reading RG8 0AG, England.

HALL Zaida Mary, b. 11 July 1925, London, England. Consultant Psychiatrist and Psychotherapist. m. (1) Ruthven O Hall, 13 May 1950, dec. 1983, 4 s, (2) Sir Peter Ramsbotham, 6 July 1985. *Education:* Somerville Coll, Oxford; St George's Hosp; BM, BCh, 1948; DM, 1955; FRCPsych, 1983; FRCP, 1984. *Appointments:* Gen and Chest Med, 1948-65; Trained as Psych, 1965-71; Cons Psych, Southampton Univ, 1971; Cons Psychotherapist, 1977, Hon Rsch Fellow, Univ Dept Psych, 1990, Royal S Hants Hosp, Southampton. *Publication:* Understanding Women in Distress (w Pamela Ashurst), 1989. *Memberships:* Ctee Grp Analytic Soc, London; Wessex Psychotherapy Soc. *Hobbies:* Choral singing; Opera; Theatre; Gardening. *Address:* East Lane, Ovington, Alresford, Hants SO24 0RA, England.

HALLAWELL Philip Charles, b. 31 July 1951, Sao Paulo, Brazil. Art Educator; Artist. m. Sonia Oz, 6 July 1974. *Education:* Rugby School, England, 1965-68; Haverford Coll, USA, 1968-70. *Career:* Exclusive Artist Contract, Galeria de Arte Andre, San Paulo, 1976-79; Organiser, Contemporary Collection Exhbn, SESC, Bertioga, 1980; Art Educator, 1983-89, Mem, Restructuring Comm, 1985, Liceu de Artes e Oficios, Sao Paulo; Art Educator, Revistinha prog, presenting, creating Drawing Workshop, Cultura TV, Sao Paulo, 1989-91; Dir, Hallawell School Art and Lang, Sao Paulo, 1989-; Art Educator, Guignard Art Workshop, Alphaville, Sao Paulo, 1991-. *Creative works:* Over 300 art works; 31 exhbns incl: Andre Galeria de Arte, 1976, 1977; Panorama Brazilian Art, 1976, 1977; Nat Salon, 1978, 1979; Iliad Series: Cafe Arte & Cia, Jau, Sao Paulo, 1990, Espaco Cultural Almeida Jr, Itu, Sao Paulo, 1991. *Honours:* Prix de Dibuix Joan Miro, Barcelona, Spain, 1980. *Hobbies:* Literature; Cinema; Music; Tennis; Swimming. *Address:* Rua Humaita 149, apt 61, 01321 Sao Paulo, Brazil. 34.

HALLEN Lars Gunnar, b. 11 Sept 1946, Uppsala, Sweden. Associate Professor. m. Elsy K Hoglund, 15 June 1985, 1 s, 1 d. *Education:* BA, 1968, MSc, Bus Admin, 1970, PhD, 1982, Docent, Bus Admin, 1989, Uppsala Univ. *Appointments:* Asst Prof, 1970-86, Assoc

Prof, 1986-, Dir, Int Bus Prog, 1987-, Uppsala Univ; Vis Lectr, Aarhus Univ, Denmark, 1984-85. *Publications:* Sverige pa Europamarknaden, 1980; International Industrial Purchasing, 1982; Networks of Relationships in International Industrial Marketing (ed w Jan Johanson), 1989; Several articles in profl jnls. *Memberships:* Int Mktng and Purchasing Rsch Grp; Advances in Int Mktng, Ed Bd Mbr; Acad Adv Grp of ERASMUS Bureau (EC Commn); Econs and Bus Stds Secn Bd of Euro Assn for Int Educ. *Hobby:* Violin playing. *Address:* Uppsala University, Department of Business Studies, Box 513, S-75120 Uppsala, Sweden. 52.

HALLIDAY William R, b. 9 May 1926, Emory Univ, GA, USA. Retired Physician; Author; Speleologist. m. (1) 1 s, 2 d, (2) Louise Baird Kinnaird, 7 May 1988. *Education:* BA, Swarthmore Coll; MD, George Washington Univ. *Appointments:* Pvte prac, Thoracic Surg, 1957-65; Med Cons, then Med Dir, WA State Dept L&I, 1965-76; Med Dir, WA State Div Voc Rehab, 1976- 82; Pvte prac, Voc Med, Seattle, Wa, 1983-84; Med Dir, Comprehensive Med Rehab Ctr, Brentwood, TN, 1984-87. *Publications:* Adventure is Underground, 1959; Depths of the Earth, 1966, 2nd Ed, 1976; American Caves and Caving, 1975, 2nd Ed, 1981. *Memberships:* Fellow, Am Coll Chest Physns; Fellow, Am Acad Compensation Med; Fellow, Explorers Club; Diplomate, Am Bd Voc Experts; Past Pres, Am Spelean Hist Assn; Dir Rsch, Past Dir, Wn Speleological Survey; Current Dir, Nat Speleological Soc; Num other orgs. *Honours:* Hon Mbr, Nat Speleological Soc; Gov's Award, Lit, WA State; Essay prize, Am Coll Chest Physns. *Hobbies:* Outdoor activities. *Address:* 308 Aaron Court, Sterling, VA 22064, USA. 2, 3, 9, 30, 165.

HALPER Edward Charles, b. 28 Sept 1951, Barberton, Ohio, USA. Professor of Philosophy. m. Jaroslava Tausinger Halper, 19 Aug 1979, 3 s. *Education:* BA, Ideas and Methods, Univ Chgo, 1973; MA, Philos, Columbia Univ, 1975; PhD, Philos, Univ Toronto, 1980. *Appointments:* Asst Prof, Gustavus Adolphus Coll, 1980-84; Asst Prof, 1984-87, Assoc Prof, 1987-92, Prof, 1992-, Univ GA, Athens. *Publications:* Books: One and Many in Aristotle's Metaphysics: The Central Books, 1989; Form and Reason: Essays in Metaphysics, 1993Num articles in philos jnls. *Memberships:* Am Philosl Assn; Soc Ancient Greek Philos; Metaphys Soc Am; Hegel Soc Am. *Hobbies:* Metaphysics; Ancient philosophy; 19th century philosophy. *Address:* Department of Philosophy, Peabody Hall, University of Georgia, Athens, GA 30602, USA. 117.

HALPER Jaroslava, b. 1 Aug 1953, Czechoslovakia. Physician; Scientist. m. Edward Charles Halper, 19 Aug 1979, 3 s. *Education:* MD, Univ Toronto, Can, 1980; PhD, Expmtl Pathology, Univ MN, USA, 1986. *Appointments:* Pathology Fellow, Mayo Clin, USA, 1982-86; Rsch Assoc, Dept Cell Biology, Vanderbilt Univ, Nashville, TN, 1985-86; Asst Prof, 1986- 91, Assoc Prof, 1991-, Dept Pathology, Coll Vet Med, Univ GA, Athens. *Publications:* Published rsch papers in cell biology esp in area of growth factors and cell proliferation. *Memberships:* AAAS; Am Soc Cell Biology; Am Assn Pathology; Int Acad Pathology. *Honours:* Diplomate, Am Bd Pathology, 1984; NIH Rsch Grantee, 1987. *Hobbies:* Music; Literature; Art. *Address:* Department of Pathology, College of Veterinary Medicine, University of Georgia, Athens, GA 30602, USA. 5, 7.

HAMADAH Kamel, b. 20 Apr 1929, Egypt. Consultant in Psychological Medicine. m. Brenda Olive Mullinger, 27 Mar 1969. *Education:* MB BCh, Cairo Univ; DPM and Neurology, Ain Shams Univ, 1959; MRCPsych, 1972, FRCPsych, 1977, Royal Coll Psychiatrists, England. *Appointments:* Cons, Psychological Med, St Thomas' Hosp, London, 1975- ; Recognised Tchr, United Med and Dental Schoolm Guy's and St Thomas' Hosps, 1982-. *Publications:* Jt author, several articles on biochem of depression and schizophrenia in Lancet, Brit Med Jnl, Brit Jnl Psych and other jnls. *Memberships:* Commnr, Mental Hlth Act Commn, 1986-; Sr Orgniser,

Mbrship Exam, Royal Coll Psychs, 1978-; Med Assessor, Hlth Comm, Ged Med Coun, 1980-, Examiner 1980-; Nat Advsr, Nat Counselling and Welfare Serv for Sick Drs, 1985-; Sn Div, Royal Coll Psychs, Chmn 1980-84, Sec 1977- 80; Dpty Reg Advsr, Psych, SE Thames Reg Hlth Auth, 1984-90; Wise Men Comm, St Thomas' Hosp, 1988-; Chmn, Psychs Comm, St Thomas' Hlth Dist, 1979-82; Med Adm, Tooting Bec Hops, 1973-75; Brit Assn Psychopharmacology; World Fedn Mental Hlth. *Honours:* WHO Fellowship, Psych, 1962-63. *Hobbies:* Walking; Music; Shooting. *Address:* Dept of Psychological Medicine, St Thomas' Hospital, London SE1 7EH, England.

HAMAL Prem Bikram, b. 22 Feb 1935, Kathmandu, Nepal. Pathologist. m. Shante Hamal, 10 May 1961; 2 s, 1 d. *Education:* MBBS, 1959; DPath, 1968; ECFMG, 1970; MRCPath, 1970; LRCP MRCS, 1975. *Appointments:* Med Off, Nepal, 1961-65; Registrar, Pathology, Portsmouth, England, 1965-66; Registrar, Pathology, Rochdale, 1966-69; Registrar, Pathology, 1969-71, Sr Registrar, Pathology, 1971-75, Birmingham; Cons, Wakefield, 1976-. *Publications:* Tuberculin Reaction in Kathmandu, 1964; Primary Pulmonary Nocardiosis, 1974; Leiomysarcoma of Penis, 1975; Granular Cell Myoblastoma, 1979. *Memberships:* Chmn, Nepalese Drs Assn, 1985-87; Chmn, Overseas Drs Assn, Wakefield, 1986-; Brit Med Assn; Fellow, Royal Coll Pathologists; Yeti Nepalese Assn, UK. *Honours:* Nepal Govt Scholarship, 1954-59; Colombo Plan Scholarship, 1965-66. *Hobbies:* Gardening; Travel; Badminton; Reading. *Address:* 9 Attlee Crescent, Sandal, Wakefield, West Yorkshire WF2 6RF, England.

HAMANN Ole Jorgen, b. 4 Feb 1944, Frederiksberg, Denmark. Professor of Botany; Botanic Garden Director. m. Michelle Marie Louise Worning, 1 Oct 1966, 1 d. *Education:* MSc, Bot, 1970, DSc, 1981, Univ Copenhagen. *Appointments:* Asst Prof, 1970-74, Assoc Prof, 1974-89, Prof, Dir Botanic Garden, 1989-, Univ Copenhagen; UNESCO Expert, Wildlife Ecology, Charles Darwin Rsch Station, Galapagos Islands, Ecuador, 1971-72; Plants Prog Off, IUCN, Switzerland, 1984-87. *Publications:* Over 90 sci and popular papers, contbns to books and others, on flora and vegetation of the Galapagos Isles, conservation and botanic gardens; Main works: Plant Communities of the Galapagos Islands, 1981; Botanic Gardens and the World Conservation Strategy (co-ed, co-author), 1987; Botanical Research and Management in the Galapagos Islands (co-ed, co-author), 1990. *Memberships:* VP, Europe, Charles Darwin Fndn for the Galapagos Isles; Bd Mbr: World Wildlife Fund, Denmark; Botanic Gardens Conservation Secretariat; Galapagos Darwin Trust, Luxembourg. *Honours:* Rasch's Legat, Danish Botanical Soc Award, best publ of yr, 1981; Topdanmark Prisen, initiative to create new genebank at Botanic Garden, Univ Copenhagen, 1989. *Hobbies:* Gardening; Mountainwalking; Skiing; Basketball; Reading. *Address:* Botanic Garden, University of Copenhagen, Oster Farimagsgade 2B, DK-1353 Copenhagen K, Denmark.

HAMAOKA Takashi, b. 6 Nov 1924, Hiroshima Prefecture, Japan. Professor of Electrical Engineering. m. 20 Mar 1954, 2 s, 1 d. *Education:* Grad, Fac Elec Engrng, Nagoya Univ, 1949; DEng, 1984. *Appointments:* Rsch Assoc, Nagoya Univ, 1949-53; Asst Prof, 1953-59, Assoc Prof, 1959- 61, Akita Univ; System Engrng Div, Hitachi Ltd, 1961-82; Prof, Hiroshima Denki Inst Technology, 1982-. *Publications:* Operations Research, 1962; System Engineering, 1987; An Outline of Contemporary System Engineering, 1991. *Memberships:* Inst Elec Engrs Japan; Soc Instrument and Control Engrs; Op Rsch Soc Japan; Japanese Agricl Systems Soc; Japan Soc Fuzzy Theory and Systems. *Honours:* Promotion of Sci Author Award for An Outline of Contemporary System Engineering, 1991. *Hobbies:* I-Go; Golf; Bowling; Classical music concerts. *Address:* Hiroshima Denki Institute of Technology, Electronic Dept, 26-20-1 Nakano Akiku, Hiroshima City, Japan 739-03.

HAMBLEN David Lawrence, b. 31 Aug 1934, London, England. Professor of Orthopaedic Surgery; Consultant in Orthopaedic Surgery. m. Gillian Frances Bradley, 16 Nov 1968, 1 s, 2 d. *Education:* MB BS, Univ London Med School, 1957; FRCS Edinburgh, 1962; FRCS England, 1963; PhD, Edinburgh, 1975; FRCS Glasgow, 1976. *Appointments:* Tchng/Rsch Fellow, Harvard Univ, USA, 1966-67; Lectr, Orthopaedics, Univ Oxford, England, 1967- 68; Sr Lectr, Orthopaedics, Univ Edinburgh, Scotland, 1968-72; Currently Prof, Orthopaedic Surg, Univ Glasgow and Hon Cons, Orthopaedic Surg, Gtr Glasgow Hlth Bd. *Publications:* Outline of Orthopaedics (w J C Adams), 11th Edition, 1990; Outline of Fractures (with J C Adams), 10th Edition, 1992. *Memberships:* Hon Cons Orthopaedic Surg to Army, Scotland; Brit Orthopaedic Assn, Pres 1990-91; Fellow, Royal Soc Med. *Honours:* Maj Co Scholarship, London Co Coun, 1952; Sr Fulbright Exchange Scholarship, 1966; Travelling Fellowship, Brit Orthopaedic Assn, 1970; Vis Prof'ships overseas: S Africa, 1982, Kuala Lumpur, 1987; Wn States AM, 1989; Melbourne, Australia, 1991; Montreal, Canada, 1992. *Hobbies:* Golf; Survival. *Address:* University Department of Orthopaedic Surgery, Western Infirmary, Glasgow G11 6NT, Scotland. 170, 184.

HAMBSCH Philip Parkinson, b. 28 Oct 1919, Philadelphia, Pennsylvania, USA. Naval Electronics Engineer; Statistician. m. (1) Norma Florence Laffin, 1 Jan 1950, dec, 2 s, 2 d; (2) Gladys Smead Magin, 3 May 1986, dec 1990. *Education:* BSc Naval Sci, US Naval Acad, 1942; MBA Mgmt Sci, San Diego State Univ, 1976. *Appointments:* Carrier Pilot, ret'd Cmdr, US Navy, 1962; Ops Res'Logistics, 1942-86, Repub Fairchild Aviation, Farmingdale, NY; Rockwell Aviation, Anaheim, Calif; Lockheed Missiles and Space Co, Calif; Teledyne Ryan Aeronaut, San Diego; Naval Aviation Logistics Ctr, MMD; Res Analyst, Co of San Diego; Logistics Support Analyst, Kaiser Elec, San Jose; Elec Engr, Nnaval Air Sys Command, Wash; Elect Engr, Naval Surface Weapons Ctr, MD; Ret'd from Fed Civil Ser, 1986. *Memberships:* Ops Res Soc of Am; Soc of Logistics Engrs; Nat Contract Mgmt Assn; Soc of Automative Engrs. *Honours:* Unit Commendation, S.Pacific Campaign, USS Taylor, 1942-43. *Hobbies:* Cross- country and acrobatic flying; Home workshop; gardening; Amateur auth machanics; Dancing; Music; Theatre. *Address:* 4990-A2 Dorsey Hall Drive, Ellicott City, MD 21042, USA.

HAMID Muhammad Abdul, b. 27 Dec 1939, Serajganj, Bangladesh. University Vice-Chancellor. m. Ayesha Hamid, 4 Dec 1962, 3 s. *Education:* BA Hons, 1961, MA (Econ), 1963, Rajshahi Univ; MA (Econ), 1969, PhD, 1972, Manchester Univ, England. *Appointments:* Lectr to Prof, Econs, Rajshahi Univ, 1963-91; Vice-Chancellor, Islamic Univ, Kushtia, 1991-. *Publications:* Rural Development in Bangladesh (in Bengali), 1988; 77 rsch-based articles and books. *Memberships include:* Rajshahi Univ Tchrs Assn, Pres; Bangladesh Econ Assn, EC Mbr, Treas; Common Property Network. *Honours:* Yasin Dr Scholarship, 1959; Scholarships, 1961-63, Prizes, 1963, Rajshahi Univ; C'wlth Scholarship, 1967-72; C'wlth Acad Staff Fellowships, 1978-79. *Hobby:* Reading creative works related to rural development. *Address:* Islamic University, Kushtia, Bangladesh.

HAMILTON (Charles) Nigel, b. 16 Feb 1944, Alnmouth, Northumberland, England. Author. m. Outi Helena Palovesi, 12 July 1976. *Education:* Westminster School; Trinity Coll, Cambridge, 1962-65; BA, Hons; MA. *Career:* Trainee, Andre Deutsch Ltd, 1965; Founded The Greenwich Bookshop, 1966; Indep Author, 1971-; Currently John F Kennedy Scholar and Assoc Prof, Univ MA, Boston, USA. *Creative works:* Books: Royal Greenwich (w Olive Hamilton), 1969; The Brothers Mann, 1978; Monty, The Making of a General, 1981; Monty, Master of the Battlefield, 1983; Monty, The Field-Marshal, 1986; Monty The Man Behind the Legend, 1987; JFK Reckless Youth, 1992; Writer, Presenter, BBC TV documentaries: Monty, In Love and War, 1987, Frontiers, Finland and the USSR: The Price of

Independence, 1990. *Honours:* Whitbread Lit Award, Best Biography, 1981; Templer Medal, Best Contbn to Mil Hist, 1987. *Hobby:* Lake sailing. *Address:* David Higham Associates, 5-8 Lower John St, Golden Square, London W1 4HA, England.

HAMILTON Alexander Gordon Kelso, b. 27 Aug 1945, Cardiff, Wales. Chartered Accountant. m. France Elisabeth Mary Colette Millet, 12 July 1980, 1 s, 1 d. *Education:* Charterhouse, 1959-63; Pembroke Coll, Cambridge; MA, Cambridge Univ. *Appointments:* Ptnr, Mann Judd & Co, 1973-79, merged into: Ptnr, Touche Ross & Co, 1979-. *Memberships:* FCA, Inst Chartered Accts in England and Wales; Royal Nat Inst for the Deaf, Coun Mgmt, Fin Comm. *Honours:* Fndn Scholar, Charterhouse, 1959-63. *Hobbies:* Golf; Gardening. *Address:* 19 Elm Park Road, London SW3 6BP, England.

HAMILTON Peter Brian, b. 7 Feb 1941, Chipping Norton, England. Public Relations Executive; Managing Director, Public Relations Consultancy. m. Rosalind Hamilton, 1 June 1979, 2 s, 1 stepson, 1 stepdaughter. *Education:* Beaumont Col, Windsor; Dip, Plymouth Coll Navigation. *Appointments:* Navigating Cadet, Shell Tankers Ltd, 1957-60; Reporter, Feature Writer, FinancialTimes, 1960-63; Mng Dir, Planned Pub Rels Int (Young & Rubicam), 1963-75; Dir, Pub Affairs, Gulf Oil Corp, Europe, Africa, Middle East, 1975-80; Dir, Good Rels PLC, 1980-84; Mng Dir, Hill and Knowlton Ltd, London, 1984-85; Mng Dir, The Communication Grp PLC, 1985-. *Publications:* Author, var articles and essays on pub rels. *Memberships:* Inst Pub Rels, 1967; Int Pub Rels Assn, 1971; Salcombe Yacht Club. *Honours:* Winner, var awards for UK community affairs; Prog for Gulf Oil. *Hobbies:* Sailing; Gardening; Music; French railways. *Address:* 5 Priory Close, Castle Cary, Somerset BA7 7DH, England.

HAMILTON Peter Williamson, b. 15 July 1941, Toronto, Canada. Architect. m. Linda D Kasen, 8 Jan 1967, 2 d. *Education:* BArch, Univ Toronto, 1963; MArch, Harvard Univ, USA, 1969. *Appointments:* Bengt Lundsten Architect, Helsinki, Finland, 1963-64; Andre Gomis Architect, Paris, France, 1964-66; John Andrews Architect, Toronto, Can, 1967-68; Pvte Prac: Hamilton Ridgely Architects, 1969-73; Hamilton Ridgely Bennett, 1973-78; Hamilton Kemp, 1978-83; Peter Hamilton Architects, Toronto, 1983-. *Creative works include:* Low cost stressed skin plywood housing system; Light chandelier, School Arch, Univ Toronto; Child's high chair; House, 2 Hedgewood Rd; Millcroft Inn (w Ridgelyte Bennett); Minaki Lodge (jt venture w Kemp and R V B Burgoyne; 136 Cumberland; Kramer Design Studio; Malvern Coll lib and cafeteria; House, 2 Cedarwood Ave; Muscatel Flats Condominium, Telluride, CO, USA; Design for Sheikh A Alissa Palace, Riyadh, Saudi Arabia. *Memberships:* Ontario Assn Archts; Royal Archtl Can; Councillor, Royal Can Acad Arts; Toronto Soc Archts. *Honours:* Toronto Historic Bd, 1970, 1985; Canadian Housing Design Coun, 1974; Awad Excellence, Ontario Assn Archts, 1978, 1990; Heritage Can Nat Award, 1978; Ontario Clay Brick Assn, 1987; Arbor Award, Univ Toronto, 1990. *Hobbies:* Skiing; Squash; Sailing (windsurfing, yacht racing); Children; Garden; Dogs; Sketching architecture; Painting; Sculpture; Music. *Address:* Peter Hamilton Architects, 21 Price Street, Toronto, Canada M4W 1Z1. 142.

HAMMARBERG Thomas Viktor Asmund, b. 2 Jan 1942, Ornskoldsvik, Sweden. Secretary-General, Charitable Organisation. m. Tia Itkonen, 30 June 1978, div., 1 s. *Education:* Civilekonom, Stockholm School Econs, 1969. *Appointments:* For Ed, Expressen daily, 1973-86; For Corres, Swedish Broadcasting, 1976-80; Sec Gen, Amnesty Int, 1980-86; Sec-Gen, Save The Children, 1986-. *Publications:* Book: Massmedia, 1980; Several other publs on human rights. *Memberships:* Govtl Advsry Bd Humanitarian Aid, 1986-; Govtl Coun Humanitarian Law, 1988-; UNICEF Bd, 1991; US Comm Rights of the Child, 1991-. *Honours:* Nobel Peace Prize on behalf of Amnesty Int, 1977; Hon Medal, Portuguese

Parl, 1980. *Hobbies:* Sports esp running. *Address:* Surbrunnsgatan 40, 11348 Stockholm, Sweden. 52.

HAMMOND-STROUD Derek, b. 10 Jan 1926, London, England. Concert and Operatic Baritone; Professor of Singing. *Education:* Studies w Elena Gerhardt and Gerhard Hüsch, Trinity Coll Music, London. *Career:* Debut, Haydn's Orfeo ed Euridice, London, 1955; Guest Artist w num opera cos; Prin Baritone, Engl Nat Opera, 1961-71, as Rossini's Bartolo, Verdi's Melitone, Wagner's Alberich and Beckmesser, Glyndebourne, 1973-; Royal Opera, Covent Garden, 1971-; Broadcasts, BBC and European radio; Opera and recital appearances, Netherlands, Denmark, Iceland, FRG, Austria, Spain, USA; Opera appearances: Metrop Opera, NYC, 1977-89; Teatro Colon, Buenos Aires, 1981; Nat Theatre, Munich, 1983; Recordings, HMV, RCA, Célèbre, Symposium. *Memberships:* Inc Soc Musicians; Pres, Univ London Opera Grp, 1971. *Honours:* Freeman, City of London, 1952; Hon RAM, 1976; HON FTCL, 1982; OBE, 1987; Sir Charles Santley Mem Gift, Worshipful Co Musicians, 1988. *Hobbies:* Chess; Philosophy. *Address:* 18 Sutton Road, Muswell Hill, London N10 1HE, England. 1, 4, 21, 52, 139.

HAMMONS Thomas James, b. Northampton, England. Chartered Engineer; Power Engineering Consultant; University Teacher. *Education:* BSc (Eng) 1st Class Hons, 1957, PhD, 1961, Imperial Coll, London Univ; ACGI, 1957; DIG, 1961. *Appointments:* Engr, Systems Engrng Dept, AEI, Trafford Pk, Manchester, 1961-62; Fac Engrng, Glasgow Univ, Scotland, 1962-; Prof, Elec and Computer Engrng, McMaster Univ, Can, 1978-79; Vis Prof, Silesian Polytechnic Univ, summer, 1978; Vis Scientist, Univ Saskatchewan, Can, summer 1979; Vis Acad, Czechoslovak Acad Scis, Prague, 1982, 1985, 1988; Vis Prof, Polytechnical Univ Grenoble, France, spring 1984; Cons: Mawdsleys, Dursley, Glos, 1965-78, NSHEB, 1965-70, GEC, 1975-84. *Publications:* Over 180 sci papers and articles in profl jnls. *Memberships:* Fndr Mbr, Univs Power Engrng, Conf Convenor 1967-68; Sr Mbr, IEEE; CEng; Inst Mech Engrng; CIGRE; IEEE Energy Dev and Power Generation Comm, Chmn Int Pracs, Synchronous Machinery Subcomm, Chmn, Station Control Subcomm; Var working grps; IEEE PES Standards Voting Comm; IEEE PES Power Generation Awards Comm; Registered European Engr, Fedn Nat Engrng Assns Europe. *Honours:* Dpty Dir Gen, Life Patron, IBA; State Scholar, 1954-57; DSc (Hon), London Univ; Cultural Doct, World Univ. *Hobbies:* Hillwalking; Travel; Music. *Address:* Clairmont, 11c Winton Drive, Kelvinside, Glasgow G12 0PZ, Scotland. 52, 139, 149, 152, 153, 154.

HAMNER Sharon Boone, b. 31 July 1939, Sandersville, Georgia, USA. Mental Health Counsellor. m. Charles Edward Hamner Jr, 17 June 1961, 1 s, 1 d. *Education:* BSHE cum laude, 1961, MEd, 1963, Univ GA, Athens; MEd, Counselling, Univ VA, 1988. *Appointments:* Pres, Hamner Rsch Serv, 1975-91; Creator, Owner, Forebears, 1979-91; Pvte prac, Mental Hlth Counselling, 1989-. *Memberships:* Am Assn Counseling and Dev; NC Assn Counseling and Dev; NC Career Dev Assn; Albemarle Co Histl Soc, VP. *Honours:* Phi Kappa Phi; Phi Upsilon Omicron. *Hobbies:* Reading; Travel. *Address:* 1304 Salem Lane, Chapel Hill, NC 27516, USA. 155.

HAMRICK Joseph Thomas, b. 20 Mar 1921, Carrollton, Georgia, USA. Engineer. m. Dorothy Jones, 19 June 1948, 1 s, 2 d. *Education:* BME, 1946, MSME, 1948, GA Inst Technology, Atlanta. *Appointments:* 1st Lt, USAF Tech Air Intelligence, Far East, World War II; Aeronautical Rsch Scientist, NACA, 1948-55; Chief Rsch Engr, TRW, Euclid, OH, 1955-61; Pres, Aerospace Rsch Corp, 1961-. *Creative works:* 40 published sci reports and papers; 23 patents; Designed and supervised constrn of only known direct fired wood burning gas turbine (3000 kw) power generating system, Red Boiling Springs, TN. *Memberships:* Am Soc Mech Engrs, Info Ctr Comm Mbr; Pres, N Franklin Co Pub Pk. *Honours:*

Pi Tau Sigma, 1946; Grantee: Dept Energy, 1978-89, NSF, 1980; Tech Achievement Award, US Dept Energy, 1984; Area Combat Ribbons, SW Pacific and Philippines, World War II. *Hobby:* Collectiong contemporary Impressionist paintings. *Address:* 4353 Windy Gap Drive, Roanoke, VA 24014, USA. 7, 52, 139, 164.

HAN Nairen, b. 24 Jan 1935, Beijing, China. Geologist. m. Zhou Youmin, 1 Aug 1962, 1 s, 4 d. *Education:* Beijian Coll Geology, 1954-59; Nanjing Univ, 1960-61. *Appointments:* E China Coll Geology, 1960-82; Guilin Coll Geology, Pingfengshan Guilin, 1982-. *Publications:* 42 palaeontological papers; 1 of Nat Natural Sci Fndn of China for Panderian Organ and Enrollment of Ordovician Trilobites. *Memberships:* Palaeontological Soc China; Geological Soc China. *Honours:* Cert Merit, Sci Conf China, 1978. *Hobbies:* Photography; Football matches; Swimmming. *Address:* Department of Geology, Guilin College of Geology, Pingfengshan Guilin, Guangxi 541004, China.

HAN Shangyi, b. 4 Nov 1917, Shangyu, Zhejiang, China. General art Director. m. Ji Bijun, Jan 1940, 3 d. *Education:* Shanghai Art Trng, 1933-37. *Appointments:* Art Dir, China Film Studio, Chongqing, 1940-45; Art Dir, Shanghai Kunlun Co, 1946-49; Art Designer, Shanghai Film Studio, 1949-53; Dir, Art Off, Shanghai Haiyan Film Studio, 1953-66; Chinese Govt Observer, Film Art, USSR, 1954; Chinese Govt Film Expert, Viet Nam, 1959; Dpty Dir, Gen Art Dir, 1978-88. *Creative works:* Art Dir, 40-odd films incl: Tears of Yangtze, 1940; The Spring River Flows East, 1946; The Concentration Camp in Shanrao, 1949; Conquer South, Conquer North, 1952; Mei Lanfang's Stage Art, 1955; The Opium War, 1957; Wangjiang Pavilion, 1958; Song Shijie, 1958; Nie Er, 1958; A Withered Tree Revives, 1961; Dr Bethune, 1965; From Slave to General, 1977; Nanchang Uprising, 1980; Midnight, 1982; Books: On Art Design in Films and Plays, 1960; Literary Notes on Art Design, 1978; Informal Essays on Art Design, 1983; Random Talks on the Beauty of Film Art, 1988; Essays, criticisms, in newspapers and mags incl: On Film Designing; On the Film 'Hibiscus Town'; Paintings: Ploughing, woodcut, 1981; Egret, watercolour, 1983; Album of Han Shangyi's Paintings, 1992. *Memberships:* Shanghai Fedn Lit and Art Circles; Assn China's Artists; Hon Dir, Assn China Film Artists; Hon Pres, Shanghai Rsch Soc Watercolour Paintings. *Honours:* 2nd Best Film, The Concentration Camp in Shangrao, 1955, Best Film, Nanchang Uprising, 1981, China's Min Culture; Biog Film Award, Nie Er, Karlovy Vary Fest, Czechoslovakia, 1950; Dr Bethune appraised, Mexico Film Fest, Italy, 1978; Golden Rooster Award, Best Art Design, Midnight, 1982; 1st Art Prize, From Slave to General, People's Liberation Army, 1983. *Address:* Rm 602, 1000 Cao Xi Bei Road, Shanghai 200030, China.

HAN Yujing, b. 23 Sept 1936, Shanghai, China. Associate Professor of Geology. m. Yang Weiran, 11 Feb 1964, 1 s. *Education:* Dip, Beijing Coll Geology, 1957. *Appointments:* Tchr, Zhengzhou School Geology, 1957-65; Tchr, Xian School Geology, 1965-70; Lectr, Wuhan Coll Geology, 1970-83; Vis Prof, Univ Liverpool, England, 1984-85; Assoc Prof, China Univ Geoscis, Wuhan, 1986-. *Publications:* Metamorphic Processes and Structural Analyses of Continental Orogenic Belts (w You Zhendong and others), 1991; P-I-t Path of Metamorphism, textbook, 1991. *Memberships:* Petrological Comm, Geological Soc China; Specialised Comm Metamorphic Rocks, Mineralogical, Petrological and Geochem Soc China; Fellow, Geological Soc London. *Honours:* Excellent Tchr Award, Hubei Province, 1979; 3rd Award, Achievements in Sci and Tech, Min Geology and Mineral Resources, 1985; 1st Award, Excellent Paper, Mineralogical, Petrological and Geochem Soc Hubei Province, 1990; 2nd Award, Natural Sci Thesis of Excellence, Hubei Province, 1990. *Hobbies:* Climbing; Reading; Classical music. *Address:* Dept of Geology, China University of Geosciences, Wuhan 430074, China.

HANAS Sven Ragnar, b. 3 July 1951, Vasteras, Sweden. Paediatrician. m. 1987, div 1990, 1 s, 2 d. *Education:* MD, Uppsala Univ, 1977; Internship, 1977-79; Residency, Paediatrics, 1979-83, Uddevalla Hosp; Paediatric Specialist, 1983. *Appointments:* Clin Fellow, Dept Paediatrics, Sect Endocrinology, Gothenburg Univ, 1984; Sr Registrar, Dept Paediatrics, Uddevalla Hosp, Uddevalla, 1985-. *Creative works:* Med articles in profl jnls; Inventor, indwelling catheter for insulin injections in diabetes treatment. *Memberships:* Study Grp Adolescent Med; Int Study Grp Diabetes in Children and Adolescents; European Assn Study of Diabetes; Swedish Study Grp Childhood Diabetes; Swedish Med Assn; Swedish Paediatric Assn. *Hobbies:* Canoeing; Hiking; Sailing; Diabetes camps. *Address:* Dept of Paediatrics, Uddevalla Hospital, S-45180 Uddevalla, Sweden.

HANCOX Tony, b. 1927. Chairman, Hancox Management Services. m. Doreen Hancox, 1949, 1 s, 1 d. *Education:* MA Hons (Oxon). *Appointments:* Retail Mgr, 1952-87, latterly in personnel mgmt and trng; Mbr, Employers Sides, Retail Wages Couns, 1965-80; Dpty Chmn, City of Westminster Employment Comm, 1969-72; Univ London Careers Advsry Bd, 1970-80; Assoc, Templeton Coll, Oxford, 1983-85; Mbr, City Univ Mgmt MBA Degree, 1986-87; Mgmt Bd, Univ Stirling Distance Learning MBA Degree, 1986-; Gov, London Inst, 1986-89; Dev Grp, Nat Coun Voc Qualifications, 1987-89; Fac, European School Mgmt, Oxford, 1987-; Nat Coord, Nat Retail Trng Coun, 1987-; Currently National Verifier, Pitman Exams Inst, 1991-; Chmn, Enterprise Steering Grp, Oxford Brookes Univ, 1991-. *Publication:* Selection Methods, 1972. *Memberships:* Fellow, Inst Personnel Mgmt, 1975; Fellow, Inst Trng and Dev, 1987; Coun Mbr, Assn Retail Distributors, 1970-72. *Honours:* Rowed for England, Bronze Medallist, Eights, VIth C'wlth Games. *Hobbies:* Music; Reading; Writing; Rowing. *Address:* Athenaeum Club, Pall Mall, London, England. 139, 162.

HANDA Urmil, b. 24 May 1940, India. Doctor (General Practitioner). m. Hawahar Handa, 13 Sept 1967, 2 s. *Education:* MBBS, 1964; Postgrad study, Chandigarh, 1967-69; MD, 1969; DRCOG, 1974. *Appointments:* Sr House Off, var places, 1970-76; Gen Practitioner, 1976-. *Memberships:* Brit Med Assn; Asian Art Soc, Glasgow; ODA. *Hobbies:* Reading; Cooking; Hill walking. *Address:* 26 Locksley Crescent, Greenfaulds, Cumbernauld G67 4EL, Scotland.

HANDS Hargrave Patrick, b. 2 Feb 1921, London, England. Artist; Illustrator. m. Daphne Mary Hands, 19 Aug 1949, 1 s, 1 d. *Education:* Art School; MSIA. *Career:* Considerable work, all fields of publng and advt, worldwide; Regular contbns to newspapers and mags, 1970-; Pioneer, realistic but decorative approach; Specialist, anatomical, entomological, ornithological and horticultural illustration. *Membership:* Soc Illustrators and Artists. *Honours:* Num incl Grenfell Medal, Royal Horticultural Soc. *Hobbies:* Music; Golf *Address:* Thatch End, Flempton, Suffolk IP28 6EG, England.

HANKINSON David Kyrle, b. 30 May 1928, London, England. Portrait Painter and Muralist. m. (1) 2 s, (2) Lavinia Joan Lascelles, 3 Sept 1969. *Education:* St Peter's Ct, 1935-41; Royal Naval Coll, Dartmouth, 1942-45; Naval Staff Coll, 1962; Studied picture framing craft under Robert Sielle, 1966-69. *Career:* Served RN, 1945-66, mostly destroyers; Specialised Gunnery, 1955; Promoted Cmdr, 1962; Commanded HMS Cambrian Near and Far East, 1962-64; Retired, RN, 1966; Prof Artist, 1969-; 1-man exhibs, London, Vienna and provinces; Occasional Exhib w Royal Soc Portrait Painters. *Creative works include:* Over 1000 portraits UK, USA and Europe including HRH The Princess of Wales; Murals, London, Vienna and provinces. *Hobbies* Listening to music; Landscape painting; Building things *Address:* 12A Barkston Gardens, London SW5 0ER England.

HANN Judith, b. 8 Sept 1942, Derby, England. Broadcaster; Writer. m. John Exelby, 17 Oct 1964, 2 s. *Education:* BSc Hons, Zoology, Durham Univ. *Appointments:* Westminster Press newspapers, 1965-70; Freelance Writer, 1970-; TV Presenter, BBC Serv, Tomorrows World, 1975-. *Publications:* But What About the Children, 1976; Family Scientist; Perfect Baby; Total Health Plan; The Food of Love; How Science Works. *Honours:* Glaxo Sci Writer Award, 1975, 1981. *Hobbies:* Walking; Cooking; Reading. *Address:* Tomorrows World, Kensington House, Richmond Way, London W14 0AX, England.

HANNA Judith, b. 10 Mar 1954, Nowra, New South Wales, Australia. Environmental Lobbyist; Transport Analyst. m. Joseph Nicholas, 1983. *Education:* BA, Univ WA; MA (Prelim), Univ Sydney. *Appointments:* Asst to Arthur Murch, artist and sculptor, 1978-82; Rsch/Admin Asst, Equal Opportunities, NSW Corrective Servs Dept, 1982; Co-Ed, Paperback Inferno mag, Brit Sci Fiction Assn, 1983-85; Personal Asst to Chmn and Gen Sec, Elections Worker, Campaign Nuclear Disarmament, 1984-87; Assoc Ed, Interzone Mag, 1984-86; Asst Dir, Transport 2000, 1987-92; Editor, Local Transport Today, 1992-. *Publications:* Travel Sickness: the Need for a Sustainable Transport Policy for Britain (co-ed), 1992; Num articles, reviews, short stories, poems. *Memberships:* Brit Sci Fiction Assn, 1982-; Coun Mbr, Sci Fiction Fndn, 1987-; Bd Dirs, Environmental Transport Assn, 1990-; VP, European Transport and Environment Fedn, 1992; Sec, Transport and Hlth Study Grp, 1990-92; Exec Comm, Pedestrians Assn, 1987-92. *Honours:* NOVA Award, 1990. *Hobbies:* Backyard ecology; Painting; Textile Arts; Walking; Reading; Writing. *Address:* Local Transport Today, Quadrent House, 250 Kennington Lane, SE11 5RD, England.

HANRAHAN John Patrick, b. 28 May 1939, Ballarat, Victoria, Australia. Freelance Writer. m. Helen Capel Roddis, 15 May 1971, 1 s, 2 d. *Education:* BTheol, 1965; BA, Australian Nat·Univ, 1968; MA, Melbourne, 1972. *Appointments:* Cath Priest, 1965-70; Lectr, Lit, Royal Melbourne Inst Technology, 1972-83; Freelance Writer, 1983-. *Publications:* News Items from Tiger Country, poems, 1972; Gerald Murnane (ed), 1988; O Excellent Virgin, 1990. *Membership:* Assn Study of Australian Lit. *Hobbies:* Family life; Theology; Genre novels and films (Westerns, thrillers). *Address:* 34 Monash Ave, Balwyn, Victoria 3103, Australia.

HANRATTY James Francis, b. 27 July 1919, Huddersfield, England. Retired Hospice Doctor. m. Irene Belton, 26 May 1945, 4 s, 1 d. *Education:* Stonyhurst; MB, ChB, Leeds, 1943; MRCGP, 1969. *Appointments:* Surg-Lt, RNVR, 1943-46; Gen Practitioner, 1946-78; Med Dir, St Joseph's Hospice, Hackney, London, 1978-89. *Publications:* Palliative Care in Terminal Illness, 1989; Monographs on terminal care. *Memberships:* Gov, Stonyhurst Coll, 1975-81; Pres, Stonyhurst Assn, 1989; Jt Chmn, Help the Hospices; Fellow, Royal Soc Med; Past Chmn, Chesterfield, Brit Med Assn; Past Master, Guild Cath Drs, Nottingham; Athenaeum; Naval Club; Hurlingham. *Honours:* Mentioned in despatches, 1944; Kt, Order St Gregory the Gt, 1988; OBE, 1989. *Hobbies:* Classical music; Watching cricket. *Address:* 44 Westminster Gardens, Marsham Street, London SW1P 4JG, England.

HANREZ Marc, b. 15 Aug 1934, Brussels, Belgium. University Professor. div., 1 s, 2 d. *Education:* Lic Philos, Lettres, Agrégé, Enseignement second supérieur, Univ Brussels, 1958; Dr, 3e cycle, Lettres modernes, Univ Paris-VII, 1973. *Appointments:* Asst Prof, Romance Langs, Univ MA, Amherst, USA, 1967-70; Vis Asst Prof, French, IN Univ, summer 1968; Assoc Prof, French, 1970-76; Prof, French, 1976-, Univ WI, Madison. *Publications:* Céline, 1961, 1969; Les écrivains et la guerre d' Espagne (ed), 1975; Sous les signes d'Abellio, 1976; Pierre Drieu la Rochelle (ed), 1982; La Grande Chose Américaine, 1992. *Memberships:* Enseigne de Vaisseau de 1ère classe des Services de Réserve (retired), Belgian Naval Force. *Honours:* Rsch Grant, Am Philosl Soc, 1971; Guggenheim Fellow, 1972- 73. *Hobbies:* Travel; Arts; Politics. *Address:* c/o Department of French and Italian, University of Wisconsin, Madison, WI 53706, USA. 13.

HANSEN Dennis M, b. 13 Dec 1952, Atchison, Kansas, USA. Minister; Pastor. m. Marcia L Allen, 27 Dec 1974, 1 s, 2 d. *Education:* BS, Communications, NW MO State Univ, Maryville, 1974; MDiv, Midwn Bapt Theological Sem, Kansas City, MO, 1977. *Appointments:* Pastor, Smithton Bapt Ch, Smithton, MO, 1978-81; Pastor, Immanuel Bapt Ch, Gt Bend, KS, 1981-86; Pastor, 10th St Bapt Ch, Trenton, MO, 1986-89; Dir, Evangelism-Stewardship-Communications, IA So Bapt Fellowship, Des Moines, 1989-. *Creative works:* Small Church Treasurers Workbook, 1987; 7 Basic Building Blocks for an Evangelistic Church, 1990; Developed Bivocation Pastor's Program Became National Prototype, 1991; Developed IA's 1st Annual Youth Evangelism Rally, 1991. *Memberships:* Midwn Sem State Alumni Off, 1983-85, 1989-; Bd Trustees, SW Bapt Univ, Bolivar, MO, 1988-; Rotary Club, Seg of Arms, Hway Test, 1986-89; Sem Extension Tchr, 1986-89; Bapt Student Union Dir, ·1981-82; Associational Camp Dir, 1982-89. *Honours:* Featured Speaker, Nat Alumni Banquet, Midwn Sem, 1986; Crusade Preacher, Chochi Wna, Korea, 1987; Speaker, Jericho Nat Missions Camp, 1991; Featured Speaker, many functions, IA and MO; Entertained through characterisations and impersonations, 6 US states, 1 for country; Produced radio commercials and half-hour Christian progs for radio and TV, 1982-. *Hobbies:* Weight- lifting; Fishing; Hunting; Gardening. *Address:* 3829 Hillcrest Dr, Des Moines, IA 50310, USA.

HANSEN Flemming, b. 16 July 1938, Copenhagen, Denmark. Professor of Economics. m., 3 children. *Education:* MBA, 1962, PhD, 1967, Copenhagen School Bus Admin and Econs; Columbia Univ, USA, 1962-63; Ekon dr, Lunds Univ, Sweden, 1972. *Appointments:* WA-Reklame/Mktng I'S advt agcy, 1960-64; Asst Prof, 1964-67, Prof, 1977-, Copenhagen School Bus Admin and Econs; Assoc Prof, Whitemore School Bus Admin and Econs, Univ NH, USA, 1967-70; AIM A/S Copenhagen, Denmark, 1940-74, also Pt-Owner, Bd Chmn, 1973-; Prof, Aalborg Univ Ctr, Aalborg, 1974-77; Vis Prof, Univ Los Angeles, USA, 1986; Chmn, Mktng Dept, Copenhagen Bus School, 1987-; Mbr, Bd Dirs, BRFkredit, 1987-; Difko Holdning, 1989-. *Publications:* Consumer Choice Behavior-A Cognitive Theory, 1972; Maleproblemer i samfundsvidenskaberne, 1979; Borns mediavaner, 1979; Forbrugeradfaerd og - beslutning, 1987; Reklame i Radio og TV, 1087; Over 80 articles in Journal of Consumer Research, Journal of Marketing Research, Journal of Economic Psychology, International Journal of Marketing, Scandinavian mktng jnls, Am Mktng Assns proceedings, European Soc Opinion and Mktng Rsch proceedings, others. *Memberships:* European Acad Adv Studies Mktng; European Soc Opinion and Mktng Rsch, Coun Mbr 1981-88, VP; World Assn Pub and Opinion Rsch; Assn Consumer Rsch, Advsry Bd Mbr 1982-; European Econ Psychologists; Assn Media Researchers Denmark; Danish Mktng Assn, Bd Dirs 1978-; Bd, Danish Bus Economists Publng Co Ltd, 1986-. *Honours:* Scholarship, A C Nielsen Fndn, 1962-63; Award, Rsch in Mktng, Danish Bus Soc, 1972; European Soc Opinion and Mktg Rsch Award, Best Corp and Strategic Planning Paper, Annual Conf, Stockholm, 1989. *Address:* Ordrupgardvej 12, DK-2920 Charlottenlund, Denmark.

HANSEN Will, b. 16 Jan 1953, Tonder, Denmark. University Professor. m. Ruth D Shaffer, 20 Aug 1983. *Education:* MS, Civil Engrg, Tech Univ of Denmark, 1977; PhD Civil Engrg, Univ of Illinois, Urbana, USA, 1983. *Appointments:* Adj Prof, Civil Engrg, Univ Michigan, 1982-83; Asst Prof, 1983-89, Assoc Prof, 1989-; Prof, Dept of Bldg Tech and Struc Engrg, Aalberg Univ, Denmark, 1990-. *Publications:* Articles in refereed journals and proceedings on time dependent deformation of concrete and fiber reinforced concrete.

Memberships: ACI, various posts; ASCE; ACS; Nordic Concrete Res Com; Danish Concrete Soc. *Honours:* Masuda Foun Fellowship, Vis Prof to Kobe Univ, Japan, 1989. *Hobbies:* Jogging; Photography. *Address:* 11279 Cloverlawn Drive, Brighton, MI 48116, USA.

HANSOTIA Anita, b. 21 May 1944. Communications Adviser. m. Minoo Hansoita, 21 Dec 1967. *Education:* BA, 1967; MA, 1968. *Appointments:* Kyoritsu Women's Univ, Tokyo, Japan, 1972; Ojo Paper Co, Tokyo, 1972; Kioritz Corp, Tokyo, 1984; Bunkyo Women's Univ, Tokyo, 1988; Seito-ku Jr Coll, 1990. *Publication:* English Through Letters, A Guided Study in English Language. *Memberships:* Coll Women's Assn; For Correspondents Club Japan. *Hobbies:* Watching Sumo wrestling; Reading; Travel; Collecting blue and white Imari pottery. *Address:* Towa Hakusan Co-op 703, 4-34-10-703 Hakusan, Bunkyo-ku, Tokyo 112, Japan.

HANSRAJ Prakash Hassanand, b. 26 Nov 1945, Karachi, Pakistan. Advertising Practitioner. m. Asha Prakash Hansraj, 27 May 1973, 1 s, 1 d. *Education:* Secondary School Cert, St Sebastain Goas HS, Bombay, 1965; Govt Cert, Applied Arts, Sir J J Inst Applied Arts, Bombay, 1970. *Appointments:* Trainee, M/S Dattram Advt Pvte Ltd, Bombay, India, 1970-71; Visualiser, 1971-73, Ptnr, 1971-86, Account Exec, 1973-86, Chief Exec, Creative Dir, Proprietor, 1986-92, M/S PH Advt, Bombay. *Memberships:* Int Advt Assn, India Chapt, Hon Sec 1989-90, 1990-92, 1992-93; Advt Agcys Assn India, Bombay, Exec Comm 1982-83, 1989-90, 1992-93, Hon Sec 1983-84, Chmn, Constitution and Legal Comm, 1990-91; Co-Chmn, Exhibitions Committee, 13th Asian Advt Congress, New Delhi, 1982; The ADvt Club, Bombay, Jt Sec 1977-78, 1978-79; United Servs Club; Otters Club; Pub Rels Soc India; BCA Garware Club; Bombay Presidency Golf Club Ltd, Rotary Club of Bombay Central. *Hobbies:* Golf; Cars. *Address:* M/S PH Advertising, 307 Ram Nimi, 3rd Floor, 8 Mandlik Road, Colaba, Bombay 400 039, India. 52, 93.

HANSZ Janusz, b. 22 Nov 1931, Poznan, Poland. Physician; Teacher; Researcher. m. Krystyna Madry, 21 Sept 1963, 1 d. *Education:* Acad Med, Poznan, 1951-57; MD, 1965; Hahnemann Med School, Philadelphia, USA, 1968-69; Habilitation, Med (PhD), 1973; MI State Univ, Lansing, USA, 1985. *Appointments:* Dept Anatomy, 1957-60, Dept Internal Med, 1962-68, Dept Haematology, 1968-, currently Hd, Dept Haematology, Acad Med, Poznan. *Publications:* Over 150 articles. *Contributions to:* med jnls and chapts in books on immunohaematology, pathophysiology, clin bichem, diagnosis and therapy of haematological disorders. *Memberships include:* Polish Soc Haematology and Blood Transfusion, 1970-, Chmn Poznan Div 1975-, Pres 1987-; Int Soc Haematology, 1982-, Nat Councillor 1987-; Sci Bd, Inst Haematology, Warsaw, 1984-, Pres 1984-91. *Honours:* Award, Sci Coun, Min Hlth and Social Welfare, 1970; Award, Nat Bd, Polish Soc Haematology, 1972; Awards, Min Hlth and Social Welfare, 1973, 1982; Gold Cross of Merit, 1978; Kt's Cross, Order of Polonia Restituta, 1983. *Hobbies:* Reading; Music; Skiing; Sailing. *Address:* 21A Miodowa Str, 60591 Poznan, Poland.

HAO Ke Ming, b. 12 July 1933, Xian, Shanxi Province, China. Director-General, National Centre for Education Development Research; State Education Commissioner. m. Hu Chi Li, 1 May 1955, 1 s, 1 d. *Education:* Grad, Chinese Lit Dept, Beijing Univ, 1951-55. *Appointments:* Ed-in-Chief, newspaper, 1956-65, Dpty Dir, Higher Educ Rsch Off, 1977-81, Beijing Univ; Dir, Dpty Sec-Gen, Educ Policy Rsch Dept, SEDC, 1982-85; Dir,Gen, Nat Ctr Educ Dev Rsch, 1986-; Currently Commnr, State Educ Commn and Vis Prof, Beijing Univ. *Publications:* Books: Study on the Structure of Chinese Higher Education, 1987; Current Situation and Prospects of Educational Development in China in the Context of Economic and Social Development, 1990; Study of Diversification of Training Approaches of High-level Specialised Personnel in Applied Disciplines, 1991;

Chinese Education facing 21st Century, 1991. *Memberships:* Standing Dir, Chinese Higher Educ Assn; Dir, Higher Educ Dev Strategy Study Assn. *Honours:* 1st Award, Humanitarian Social Sci, Beijing Univ, 1988; 1st Award, Educ Sci, Chinese Higher Educ Assn, 1989; 1st Award, Nat Educ Rsch Achievements, 1990. *Hobbies:* Reading literary works; Listening to music. *Address:* 37 Damucang Hutong, Beijing, China.

HAQ Kaiser Mohamed Hamidul, b. 7 Dec 1950, Dhaka, Bangladesh. University Teacher. m. Rowshan Haq, 21 Nov 1976. *Education:* BA Hons, Engl, 1972, MA, Engl, 1973, Dhaka Univ; PhD, Engl Lit, Warwick Univ, England, 1982. *Appointments:* Lectr, Engl, 1975-82, Asst Prof, 1982- 85, Assoc Prof, 1985-91, Prof, 1991-, Dhaka Univ. *Publications:* Starting Lnes, poems, 1978; A Little Ado, poems, 1978; Selected Poems of Shamsur Rahnan, translations, 1985; Contemporary Indian Poetry (ed), 1990. *Memberships:* Asiatic Soc Bangladesh. *Honours:* Pope Mem Gold Medal, 1972, Abu Hena Gold Medal, 1973, Dhaka Univ; C'wlth Scholar, 1978-81; Sr Fulbright Scholar and Vilas Fellow, 1986-87. *Hobbies:* Physical fitness; Yoga; Writing. *Address:* English Department, Dhaka University, Dhaka 1000, Bangladesh. 52.

HARA Minoru, b. 9 Sept 1930, Tokyo. Emeritus Professor of Sanskrit. m. Kineko Ueda, 30 May 1963, 2 s, 1 d. *Education:* BA, Univ Tokyo, 1953; PhD, Harvard Univ, USA, 1967; MA, Univ Cambridge, England, 1978. *Appointments:* Lectr, 1960, Assoc Prof, 1964, Prof, 1975, Univ of Tokyo; Guest Prof: Univ Vienna, Austria, 1987-88; Univ Hamburg, Germany, 1989-90. *Publications:* 'Tapas' in the Mahabharata, 1979; History of Indian Philosophy (co-author); About 45 articles in Engl, about 30 in Japanese. *Memberships:* For Mbr, Royal Swedish Acad (Letters, Hist, Antiquity); Int Assn Sanskrit Studies, VP. *Hobbies:* Classical Western music; Western paintings esp Impressionists; Japanese painting; Gardening. *Address:* 1-19-1-201 Ishikawa-cho, Ota-ku, Tokyo, Japan. 52.

HARAKAL Betty Maybee, b. 1 Jan 1939, USA. Convalescent Centre Supervisor; Consultant. 3 s, 2 d. *Education:* AASm 1976, BS, 1978, Youngstown State Univ; Grad School. *Appointments:* Cons, Coord, Hlth Care Mgmt, 1990-; Charge Nurse, 1984-85, Supvsr, 1990-, Hillhaven Convalescent Ctr, Delray Beach, FL; Staff Nurse, Charge Nurse, Youngstown Hosp Assn, 1985-86; Dir, Nursing Servs, Convalescent Ctr Palm Beaches, FL, 1987-90; Adj Prof, Palm Beach Community Coll, Larnworth, FL, 1991. *Publications:* Articles on prof jnls. *Memberships:* Am Nurses Assn; Am Nurses Fndn Century Club; OH Nurses Assn, Peer Assistance Prog for Nurses (for nurses w work perf impaired due to alcoholism, drugs or phys or mental dysfunction); Nat Nurses Soc on Addiction, Impaired Nurses Comm, Reg Liaison SE USA; Charter Mbr, Nursing Chapt, Youngstown State Univ Alumni Assn; Nat Coun on Alcoholism. *Address:* 2715 SE 1st Ct, Pompano Beach, FL 33062, USA. 151.

HARALDSSON Ingthor G(udmundur), b. 17 Nov 1932, Reykjavik, Iceland. Managing Director and Majority Owner of Import Firm. m. Thorbjorg Danielsdottir, 17 Nov 1957, 2 s, 2 d. *Education:* HS Flensborg, 1946-49; German, Berlitz School, 1950. *Appointments:* Automobile Agcy Salesman, 1949-53 Profl Harmonica Artist, stage, radio, 1950-55; Off Mgr USAF Warehouse Off, Keflavik NATO Base, 1953-55 Real Estate Mgr, 1956-60; Import Mgr, Vesam Impor Union, 1960-66; Owner, Mgr, Ingthor Haraldsson Ltd 1966-. *Contributions to:* num articles to Icelandic ane for Lions mags on youth exchange and travel *Memberships:* Auditor, local forestry assn, 1982-; Lions MD 109 Iceland, Youth Exchange Multiple Dist Chmr 1980-90. *Honours:* Lions Awards: DSA, 1982; In President's Award, 1986, 1991; Multiple (MD) Award 1987; MD Award, 1988, 1990; Melvin Jones Fellowship, 1990; Num local Lions Dists Awards *Hobbies:* Photography; Travel; Fishing; Forestry

Address: Vigholastigur 21, IS-200 Kopavogur, Iceland. 52.

HARALDSTED Hans H, b. 14 Apr 1942, Copenhagen, Denmark. Consulting Engineer. m. Karen E Haraldsted, 1969, 1 s, 1 d. *Education:* Engr (MSc), Machine, 1969; Cand Merc (MSc), Mktng, 1979; Cand Merc (MSc), Export, 1982; Master Bus, MDM/MBA, Mgmt, 1983. *Appointments:* Currently Dir, Owner, Hans H Haraldsted, Engrng and Trdng Co. *Publications:* Articles in newspapers; Ed, book; Inventor, patent application. *Memberships:* Soc Engrs; Danish Mercantile Assn; Danish Soc Engineers, VP. *Honours:* Gold Medal, Silver Medal, Eureka, Brussels, 1979. *Hobbies:* Inventions; Painting. *Address:* Ellegaardspark 19, Postbox 107, DK-3520 Farum, Denmark. 52.

HARASYM Zenon, b. 12 May 1941, Boryslaw, Poland. Art Photographer. m. Urszula Mielczarek, 18 Mar 1965, 2 d. *Education:* Studies, 1959-64, Doct, 1976, Wroclaw Inst Technology; Self-taught, Art Photography. *Career:* Inst Technology, 1964-66; Inst Computer Systems, Automatic and Measurements, 1966-78; Freelance Photographer, 1978-; 25 1-man exhibs incl: Gall Photo, Medium, Art, Wroclaw, 1978; Cultural Ctr, Tbilisi, Georgia, 1979; Liptov Mus, Ruzomberok, Czechoslovakia, 1980; Fotohuset, Gothenburg, Sweden, 1981; Galerie Slon, Ljubljana, Yugoslavia, 1983; Gall FCCB. Sao Paulo, Brazil, 1983; Gall Fritza Bokkafe, Kristiansand, Norway, 1984; Gall 1st Bank, Vienna, Austria, 1987; Gall KZT, Opole, Poland, 1988; Gall Kiek in de Kok, Tallinn, Estonia, 1990; Participant, over 300 grp exhibs incl: Interpressfoto 75, Berlin, 1975; Polish Landscape in Photography, Kielce, Poland, 1984; Polish Contemporary Art Photography, Warsaw, 1985; Faces of Earth, Tokyo, 1986; Polish Landscape and Its Photographers, Berlin, 1986; Photography, 40 Yrs of Union of Polish Art Photographers, Warsaw, 1987. *Creative works include:* Works in collections: National Museum, Wroclaw; Art Exhib Bur, Kielce; Liptov Mus, Ruzumberok; Mus Sport, Warsaw. *Membership:* Union Polish Art Photographers, 1978. *Honours:* Artist, 1976, Excellence, 1985, FIAP; Hon Mbr, Photographic Society Wroclaw, 1980; Meritorious Cultural Worker, Min Culture and Art, 1980; Hon Medal, Union Polish Art Photographers, 1987; Hon Medal, 15th Anniversary of Photography, Poland, 1989. *Hobbies:* Collecting old and ancient cameras and old photographs; Member of Club Daguerre, international collectings club, Germany. *Address:* Bulwar Ikara 31/24, PL 54-130 Wroclaw, Poland.

HARDER Kelsie Brown, b. 23 Aug 1922, Pope, Tennessee, USA. Distinguished Teaching Professor. m. Louise Marcia Maron, 9 Oct 1960, 5 s, 2 d. *Education:* BA magna cum laude, 1950, MA, 1951, Vanderbilt Univ; PhD, FL, 1954. *Appointments:* Youngstown Univ, 1954-64; SUNY Coll, Potsdam, 1964-. *Publications:* Names and Their Varieties (ed); Dictionary of Place Names: United States and Canada (ed), 1976; A Dictionary of American Proverbs (co-ed), 1991. *Memberships:* Am Name Soc; Mod Lang Soc; Nat Coun Tchrs of Engl; NY Folklore Soc; TN Folklore Soc; Am Soc Geolinguistics. *Honours:* Phi Beta Kappa; Phi Kappa Phi; Eta Sigma Phi; Sigma Delta Pi; Fulbright Professorship to India, 1962-63, to Poland, 1971; Disting Tchng Prof, SUNY, Best Fac, SUNY. *Hobbies:* Reading; Baseball; Football; Basketball. *Address:* 5 Lawrence Avenue, Potsdam, NY 13676, USA. 2, 52.

HARDER Rolf P, b. 10 July 1929, Hamburg, Germany. Graphic Designer; Painter. m. Maria-Inger Rumberg, 3 May 1958. 1 s, 1 d. *Education:* Hamburg Acad of Fine Arts, 1948-52. *Appointments:* Designer, Rolf Huhle Werbung, Hamburg, 1952-55; Art Dir, George Ferguson Assn, Montreal, 1956-57; Visualizer, Lintas GMBH, Hamburg, 1957-58; Designer, Prin, Rolf Harder Design, Montreal, 1959-65; Designer, Co-Fdr, Design Collaborative, Montreal, 1965-77; Designer, Pres, Rolf Harder & Assn Inc, Montreal, 1977-. *Creative works:* Author: Intro, Who's Who in Graphic Art, 1983; Intro,

World History of the Poster, 1988; Co-publisher: Pitseolak, Pictures out of my life, 1972; Arts of the Eskimo: Prints, 1974. *Memberships:* ssa OORoyal Canadian Acad of Arts; Alliance Graphique Intl; Am Inst of Graphic Arts; Fellow, Soc of Graphic Designers of Canada. *Honours:* Over 100 national and international design awards. *Hobbies:* Music; Tennis. *Address:* Rolf Harder & Assc Inc, 273-A Bord Du Lac, Pointe-Claire, Que, Canada H95 4L1. 88, 37, 2, 52.

HARDIE Miles Clayton, b. 27 Feb 1924, New York City, New York, USA. Health Care Management (retired). m. (1) Pauline Le Gros Clark, 22 July 1949, diss, 1974, 2 s, (2) Katherine Melissa Woelfel, 21 Nov 1974, diss. 1985, (3) Madeleine Elizabeth Spencer-Smith, 20 Apr 1985. *Education:* Charterhouse, 1937-42; Oriel Coll, Oxford, 1946-49; MA (Oxon). *Appointments:* Pilot, RAF, 1943-46; Sec, Victoria Hosp for Children, 1952-56; Sec, Bahrain Govt Med Dept, 1956-58; Joined King Edward Hosp Fund, 1958; Dir, King's Fund Ctr, 1966-75; Dir-Gen, Inr Hosp Fedn, 1975-87; Served, var couns and comms, 1970-87; Mind; Mental Hlth Fndn; Ctr Policy on Ageing; Spinal Injuries Assn; Vol Ctr. *Creative works:* Helped establish Brit Hosps Export Coun, 1964, Hon Sec, Counc Mbr. *Memberships:* Fellow, Inst Hlth Servs Mgmt; Liveryman, Worshipful Co of Salters, 1954-; Advsr to WHO, 1978-. *Honours:* WHO Hlth for All Medal, 1987; OBE, 1988. *Hobbies:* Gardening; Walking. *Address:* Tallow Cottage, Fishers Lane, Charlbury, Oxford OX7 3RX, England. 1.

HARDING Christopher Philip, b. 4 Aug 1944. *Education:* SFPE, 1977; DPhE, 1978; FIBA, 1985; AAABI, 1986; MCC, 1988; PhD, 1988, World Univ Rountable; KtMSS, 1989; SRFTp, 1990; MP, 1991; Dipl, Intl Fine Arts Counc, 1991. *Appointments:* CIAW, 1969-83; Good News, 1983-86; Eltran, 1985-87; Computer Conslts, 1987-88; Point One Adv Gp Inc, 1988-90. *Publications include:* Jt auth of computer progs, Londgold and HiQ- Solver; Poetry published as well as over 400 original ideas. *Memberships include:* MENSA, Intl and Aust; Intl Legion of Intelligence; Intl Soc for Philos Enquiry, various posts; Mega Soc; Intl Test Comm; Mega Soc; Omega Soc; Aust Mensa Inc. *Honours include:* Cert for Poetic Achievement, Am Poetry Assn, 1989, 1990; Life membership, INTERTEL, 1974; Biography of the Yr Awd, Hist Preservations of Am, 1987; Hon Life Mem, London Inst of Applied Res; Intl Fine Arts Coun. 3, 156, 191, 151, 152, 162, 139, 178, 190.

HARDING Geoffrey Wright, Solicitor in Private Practice. m. Margaret June Danger, 7 Oct 1972, 1 s, 1 d. *Education:* LLB, AKC, King's Coll, London, 1956; LLM, NWn Univ Sch Law, Chgo, 1965; Called to the Bar, Gray's Inn, London, 1957; PhD, Queen Mary Coll, London, 1982. *Appointments:* Served RAF, 1951-53; Asst Sec, Fedn Civil Engrng Contractors, 1958-60; Legal Advsr, Brit Ins (Atomic Energy) Comm, 1960-63; Ptnr, Wilde Sapte Solicitors, London, 1967-. *Publications:* Banking Act 1987 - Current Law Annotated, 1987; Encyclopaedia of Competition Law (European). *Memberships:* Law Soc; Bus Advsr, The Prince's Youth Bus Trust; Mbr, Exec Cttee of Nat Autistic Soc; Guild of Freemen of City of London. *Honours:* Exchange Lawyer with Isham, Lincoln & Beale, Chgo law firm, Harvard Law School Prog, 1963-64; Gen Elec Fndn Fellowship, NWn Univ School Law, 1964- 65; Freeman, City of London, 1986. *Hobbies:* Learning the piano; Scuba-diving; Mountain-biking; Understanding Autism; His family. *Address:* Wilde Sapte, Queensbridge House, 60 Upper Thames Street, London EC4V 3BD, England. 53.

HARDING Wilfrid Gerald, b. 17 Mar 1915, Berlin, Germany. Retired Community Physician. m. Hilary Harding. *Education:* Woodbrooke Coll, Selly Oak, England, 1933-34; Univ Coll and Hosp, London, 1934-41; MRCS, LRCP, 1941; House Surg and Physn, Univ Coll Hosp, 1941-42; Lond School Hygiene and Tropical Med, 1948-49; MRCP, 1968; FRCP, 1972; FFCM, 1972.

Appointments: Asst Med Off Hlth, City of Oxford, 1943-45; Served to Lt-Col, Royal Army Med Corps, 1943-46; Career posts, pub hlth, 1949-73; Med Off Hlth, Camden, London, 1965-73; Area Med Off, Camden/Islington, London, 1974-79. *Creative works:* Num papers and broadcasts; Parkes Centenary Mem Lecture, 1976. *Memberships:* Brit Med Assn, Past Chmn Pub Hlth Comm; Soc Med Offs Hlth, Past Coun Chmn, Past Pres; Co-Fndr, Past Pres, Fac Community Med; Dist Councillor, Sevenoaks, 1979-; Athenaeum, 1968-. *Honours:* CBE, 1978; Hon Fellow, Fac Community Med, 1986. *Hobbies:* Listening to classical music; Walking; Watching river birds; Drinking and talking wine. *Address:* Bridge Cottage, High Street, Farningham, Dartford DA4 0DW, England. 1.

HARDSTAFF Joseph, b. 28 Feb 1935, Kirkby-in-Ashfield, Nottinghamshire, England. County Cricket Club Secretary; Former Royal Air Force Officer. m. Olive Mary Nancekievill, 21 Dec 1963, 1 s, 1 d. *Education:* RAF Staff Coll, 1970; Royal Coll Def Studies, 1983. *Appointments:* General Duties, Pilot, RAF, 1953-88 incl: Off Cmdng, 47 Squadron, 1974-76; Off Cmdng, RAF Lyneham, 1979-81; Dpty Cmdt, RAF Staff Coll, 1983-85; Dir, PA, RAF, 1985-87; Currently Secretary, Middlesex Co Cricket Club. *Membership:* Fellow, Brit Inst Mgmt. *Honours:* MBE, 1967. *Hobbies:* Cricket; Golf; Most other sports; Reading; Walking. *Address:* 5 Dial Clos, Seend, Melksham, Wiltshire SN12 6NP, England.

HARDY Lance Walter, b. 20 June 1964, Longmont, Colorado, USA. Youth Minister. m. Elizabeth Ann Lendrum, 12 Aug 1989. *Education:* BSc, Christian Educ minor, NE Christian Coll, 1986. *Appointments:* Summer Youth Intern, 1st Christian Ch, Longmont, CO, 1985; Youth Min, Greeley Christian Ch, Greeley, CO, 1986-. *Publications:* 3 articles in Faith Perspectives, Greeley Tribune. *Hobbies:* Collecting baseball cards; A little computer work; Spending time with his wife. *Address:* 3451 23rd Avenue, Greeley, CO 80634, USA. 117.

HARE Frederick Kenneth, b. 5 Feb 1919, Wylye, England. University Chancellor. m. 26 Dec 1953, 1 s, 1 d. *Education:* King's Coll, London, 1939; PhD, Montreal, Can, 1950. *Appointments:* Asst Lectr, Univ Manchester, 1940-41; Meteorologist, UK Air Min, 1941-45; Asst Prof, 1945-49, Assoc Prof, 1950-52, Chmn, Geog Dept, 1950-62, Prof, Geog, Meteorology, 1952-62, Dean, Arts, Sci, 1962-64, McGill Univ, Can; Prof, Geog, King's Coll, 1964-66, Master, Birkbeck Coll, 1966-68, Univ London, England; Pres, Univ BC, Can, 1968-69; Prof, Geog, Phys, 1969-84, Dir, Inst Environmental Studies, 1974-79, Univ Prof, 1976-84, Univ Prof Emeritus, Geog, 1984-, Chmn, Advsry Bd, Inst Int Prog, 1990-, Univ Toronto; Provost, Trinity Coll, Toronto, 1979-86; Chmn, Climate Prog Planning Bd, Can, 1979-89; Commnr, Ont Nuclear Safety Review, 1986-88; Chancellor, Trent Univ, Peterborough, Ont, 1988-; Chmn, Can Global Change Prog, Royal Soc Can, 1989-90. *Publications:* About 40 books and chapts on geog, climatology esp environmental effects; About 100 in refereed jnls and conf proceedings. *Memberships include:* Arctic Inst N Am, Bd Chmn 1963, Gov 1971-76; Can Assn Geogs, Pres 1963-64, Past Councillor; Royal Meteorological Soc, Pres 1967-68, VP 1968-70; Sigma Xi, Pres 1986-87, Univ Toronto Chapt Treas 1983-84; AAAS, Sect W Chmn 1985-86; Past Councillor: Am Meteorological Soc; Assn Am Geogs; Glaciological Soc; Royal Geogl Soc; Soc geog Montreal; Am Geogl Soc; Num couns, bds, comms. *Honours:* Num incl: FRS Can, 1968; Companion, Order of Can, 1987; Dawson Medal, Royal Soc Can, 1988; Int Meteorological Assn Prize, 1988; Hon LLD: Queen's Univ, Can, 1964; Univ Wn Ont, 1958; Trent Univ, 1979; Univ Toronto, 1987; Hon DSc: McGill Univ, 1969; York Univ, 1978; Univ Windsor, 1988; DSc ad eund grad, Adelaide, 1974; DSLitt, iure dig, Thorneloe Coll, Laurentian Univ, 1984; DLitt hc, Mem Univ Nfld, 1985. *Hobbies:* Music; Gardening; Research. *Address:* 301 Lakeshore Road West, Oakville, Ontario, Canada L6K 1G2. 1, 142.

HARGIS Michele, b. 13 Jan 1947, Kansas City, Missouri, USA. Editor; Photojournalist. *Education:* Memphis Acad Art, 1965; Univ MS, 1965-67; Maj, Jrnlsm, Art, Memphis State Univ, 1968. *Appointments:* Freelance Jrnlst, Entertainment and Nightlife, Montreal, Can, 1984-85; Ed, Germantown News, Germantown, TN, 1985-92; Writer, Nine-O-One Music Mag, Memphis, 1988-90. *Publications:* Book of poetry, 1993; Rock'n'roll novel, 1993. *Memberships:* Nat League Am Pen Women, Chickasaw Br. Memphis, Newsletter Ed 1991-92; Int Soc Poets, 1992-93. *Honours:* Media Award, Shelby Co Govt, Memphis, 1988; Ed of Yr Germantown News, 1989, 1990; Published in On A Threshold Of A Dream anthology of poetry and songwriting, Nat Lib Poetry, 1992; Semi-finalist, poem No-One Really Knows What Gravity Is, N Am Oper Poetry Contest, 1992. *Hobbies:* Photography; Art; Music; Gardening. *Address:* 6043 Summer Ridge Drive, Suite 1, Memphis, TN 38115, USA.

HARGREAVES George Kenneth, b. 24 Oct 1928, Rossendale, Lancashire, England. Consultant Dermatologist. m. Hazel Nutter, 24 Mar 1956, 2 s, 2 d. *Education:* MB ChB, Edinburgh Univ, 1951; FRCP (Edinburgh), 1971. *Appointments:* Cons Dermatologist 1962-; Manchester and Salford Skin Hosp, Stockport, Macclesfield and Buxton Hosps. *Contributions to:* dermatological jnls. *Memberships:* Brit Assn Dermatologists; Royal Soc Med; N of England Dermatological Soc, Sec 1963-78, Pres 1981. *Hobbies:* Gardening; Walking; Music. *Address:* 23 St John St, Manchester M3 4DT, England. 170.

HARINGTON Charles Richard, b. 22 May 1933, Calgary, Canada. Vertebrate Palaeontologist. *Education:* BA, 1954, BSc, 1957, PhD, 1977, Univ Alta, Edmonton; MSc, McGill, Montreal, 1961. *Appointments:* Wildlife Biologist, Can Wildlife Serv, 1960-65; Curator Quaternary Zoology, 1965-, Chief, Palaeobiology Div 1982-91, Can Mus Nature, Ottawa. *Publications:* 180 sci and popular publs, 1959-, incl: Quaternary Vertebrate Faunas of Canada and Alaska and Their Suggested Geochronological Sequence, 1978; Editor 6 vols on Can and global change, 1 vol on Arctic sc and hist, 1977-. *Memberships:* FRGS; Fellow, Royal Can Geogl Soc; Fellow, Arctic Inst N Am, Chmn Devon Island Rsch Comm 1973-80. *Honours:* Can Assn Geogs Prize 1957; Massey Medal, Royal Can Geogl Soc, 1987. *Hobbies:* Travel; Camping; Reading; Canoeing; Cycling. *Address:* Canadian Museum of Nature (Paleobiology) Ottawa, Ontario K1P 6P4, Canada. 2, 142.

HARKER FARRAND Margaret Florence, b. 17 Jan 1920, Southport, Lancashire, England. Photographic Historian; Lecturer; Author. m. Richard Farrand, 20 Dec 1972. *Education:* Qualified in Photography, Polytechnic Ctrl London (now the Univ of Westminster), London 1940-43; Prof, Photography, 1972. *Career:* Self-employed Archtl Photographer, 1945- 58; Lectr Photography, 1945-59, Hd, School Photography, 1959-74, Dean, School Communication, 1974-75, Pro-Rector 1975-80, Polytechnic Ctrl London; Exhibitor, own photographs, 1945-75, incl: Photokina, Cologne, FRG 1958. *Publications:* Books: Photographing Architecture 1951; Victorian and Edwardian Photographs, 1975; The Linked Ring, 1892-1910, 1979; Henry Peach Robinson 1988. *Memberships:* Hon Fellow, Royal Photographic Soc, Pres 1958-60; Hon Fellow, Brit Inst Prof Photography, Pres 1964-65; European Soc for Hist of Photography, Pres 1985-. *Honours:* Hood Medal, 1945, 1948, Fenton Medal, 1990, Royal Photographic Soc; Pro Emeritus, 1987, Hon Fellow, 1988, Univ of Westminster; Hon Dr Art, Coun Nat Acad Awards, 1987. *Hobbies:* Swimming; Gardening; Collecting old photographs. *Address:* Egdean House, Egdean, near Pulborough, West Sussex RH20 1JU, England.

HARNEY Desmond Edward St Aubyn, b. 14 Feb 1929, London, England. Consultant; Banker; Borough Councillor. m. Judith Geraldine Downing, 10 July 1954, 1 s, 2 d. *Education:* BSc, King's Coll, Univ Durham, 1953

Postgrad, Univ Cambridge, 1953-54; Persian Studies, School Oriental and African Studies, Univ London, 1957-58. *Appointments:* Imperial Chem Inds, 1954-56; H M Diplomatic Serv, 1956-74; Morgan Grenfell & Co Ltd, 1974-88; Councillor, Royal Borough Kensington and Chelsea Dpty Mayor, 1991-. *Creative works:* Misc pol and travel articles; Freelance photographer. *Memberships:* Royal Soc Asian Affairs, VP; Brit Inst Persian Studies, Govng Coun; former Irano-Brit Chmbr of Comm, Chmn; Chelsea Conservative Assn, Chmn. *Honours:* OBE, 1968. *Hobbies:* Local Government; The Middle East; Photography; Astronomy; Skiing; Fishing. *Address:* 16 Stafford Terrace, London W8 7BH, England.

HARPER Anthony John, b. 26 May 1938, Bristol, England. University Lecturer. m. Sandra Harper, 4 Apr 1964, 1 s, 2 d. *Education:* 1sr Class Hons German, 1959, MA by dissertation, 1963, Univ Bristol; Cert Ed, Univ Exeter, 1961; PhD, Univ Edinburgh, 1975. *Appointments:* Lectr, Univ Edinburgh, Scotland, 1962-79; Prof, Univ Strathclyde, 1979-. *Publications:* David Schirmer - A Poet of the Baroque, 1977; Essays on German and European Literature, 1981; Schriften zur Lyrik Leipzigs 1620- 1670, 1985; The Song-Books of Gottfried Finckelthaus, 1988. *Memberships:* Soc Renaissance Studies; Soc Emblem Studies, European Treas. *Hobbies:* Tennis; Travel. *Address:* 101 Stirling Drive, Bishopbriggs, Glasgow G64 3PG, Scotland. 184.

HARPER Robert James, b. 7 Sept 1940, Belfast, Northern Ireland. Company Director. m. Sophie Heijndijk, 25 July 1969, 1 s, 1 d. *Education:* BSc 1st class Hons, 1962, PhD, 1965, Queen's Univ, Belfast; Tech Univ, Delft, Netherlands, 1965-67; McMaster Univ, Hamilton, Can, 1967-69. *Appointments:* Mng Dir, Lorimont Enterprises BW, Breda, Netherlands, 1969-; Geschaeftsfuehrer, Lorimont Enterprises GmbH, Koblenz, Germany, 1971-; Dir, Lorimont Enterprises (Pty) Ltd, Johannesburg, S Africa, 1972-; Gen Mgr, Europe, Homcare Int, Zug, Switzerland, 1975-81; Dir, Lorimont Cosmetics Belgium NV, Antwerp, Belgium, 1975-; Petrolon (Pty) Ltd, Johannesburg, 1979-; Oil Slick (Pty) Ltd, 1990-. *Contributions to:* articles to profl jnls. *Membership:* No Ireland Ptnrship. *Honours:* Kilwaughter Medal, 1961, Richardson Medal, 1962, Queen's Univ, Belfast. *Hobbies:* Automobiles; Antiques; Persian rugs; Tennis; Golf. *Address:* Hertog Hendriklaan 2, 4817 JV Breda, Netherlands. 52, 132.

HARPER William Thomas III, b. 10 Sept 1956, Newport News, Virginia, USA. Psychologist; Professor; Counsellor. *Education:* BS, VA State Coll, Petersburg, 1978; MEd, Counselling Psychology, VA State Univ, 1981; W&M, Adv Study, Hampton Univ; PhD, Old Dominion Univ. *Appointments:* Prof Asst: Norfolk State Univ, Old Dominion Univ, Hampton Univ; VP, Amcrest Diversified Inc; Educ Specialist, US Army Educ Ctrs; Dir, Student Support Serv, Hampton Univ; Counsellor, Man Power Trng Servs. *Creative works:* 15 proposals: Adult Educ Progs; Student at Risk Progs; Career Exploration Booklet; Student Dev Progs. *Memberships:* Assn Black Psychologists; VA and Mid-En Assns Educ Opportunity Personnel; Peninsula Lit Coun; So Coll Personnel Assn; Kappa Alpha Psi; Am Assn Counseling Dev. *Honours include:* Cert, Acad Achievement, 1975, Psychology Dept Award, Minority Student Biomed Rsch Scholarship, VA State Coll, 1978; VA Coll Personnel Assn Award, 1981, 1985; 2nd Place, Solo Ensemble, VA Band and Orch Dr Assn, 1977; Letters of Commendation from VP Acad Affairs, 1983, 1985, 1986, Mobil Oil Scholarship, 1985, Hampton Univ; Grad Scholarship, Old Dominion Univ, 1983, 1985; Outstanding Dir's Award, Student Special Servs Prog, Howard Univ, 1986; Opportunity Prog Personnel Planning Comm Award, VA Assn Educ, 1984, 1985, 1986; US Army Serv Award, 1985; VA State Univ Alumni Award, 1985; Black Coll Prog Counsellor Achievement Award, 1985; Brother of Yr, Kappa Alpha Psi 1986; Community Serv Award, Vets Admin Med Ctr, 1987, 1988, 1990; Hampton Roads Boys Club Serv Award, 1989, 1990; Num other achievement awards. *Hobbies:* Research; Reading; Basketball; Football;

Baseball; Writing; Skating; Boating; Cultural enrichment activities; Educational proposal writing; Travel; Community service work. *Address:* 1042 44th Street, Newport News, VA 23607, USA.

HARR Lorraine Ellis, b. 31 Oct 1912, Sullivan, Illinois, USA. Housewife; Writer; Poet; Haikuist. m. 18 Aug 1958, 2 s, 1 s dec. *Education:* HS Grad; Self-taught; Coll classes incl Lit, Engl, Writing; Tchr's Degree, Ikebana (Ryusei-Ha) freestyle flower arrangements. *Career includes:* Ed, Dragonfly, haiku quarterly, 1972-84; Fndr, Wn Wrld Haiku Soc, 1972; Ed, Wn World Haiku Soc Annual Award Winners, 1974-75, 1976-77, 1978, 1979, 1980, 1981; Judge, num State Poetry Contests; Talks on haiku. *Publications include:* Haiku: Cats, Crows, Frogs and Scarecrows; Tombo, about dragonflies; Snowflakes in the Wind; The Red Barn, Midwn haiku; A Flight of Herons, haiku seasons and seascapes; Sundowners, 1-line haiku; Pathways of a Dragonfly, haiku in sequence; Selected Senryu of Leh, senryu; Haibun: China Sojourn; Modern Narrows Roads to Matsushima; Children's poems: Poems for Peter K; Poems for Sarah J; Contbr: The Instructor; Writers Digest, East- West Journal, The Oregonian, The Journal, Beloit Journal, Modern Haiku, American Haiku, The Red Pagoda, Wind Chimes, Brussel Sprout, Janus/Scth, The Human Voice Quarterly, Hai, Cicada, Outch, many others; Writes under pen-name Tombo. *Memberships:* Oregon State Poetry Assn; Intl Ikebana Soc. *Honours:* Nat Finalist, Japan Air Lines Contest, 1964; Award, Black Ship Fest, Japan, 1967; 2nd Place, haiku article, Deep S Artists and Writers, 1969; Modern Haiku: Special Mention, Vol II, No 2, Hon Mention, Vol II, No 3, Vol III, No 1, Outstanding Achievement, Vol IV, No 1; 1st Place, haiku article, Ascent, MHCC; 3rd Place, New Year's Contest, Haiku Mag, Vol III, No V, 1969; Award, Mainichi daily newspaper Haiku Contest, 1982, 1983, 1984, 1985; Other awards incl short story, poetry, children's stories and poems, articles. *Hobbies include:* Writing; Painting; Reading; Cooking; Grandchildren; Tavel; Other cultures; World happenings. *Address:* 4102 NE 130th Place, Portland, OR 97230, USA. 34.

HARRE Alan Frederick, b. 12 June 1940, Nashville, Illinois, USA. Administrator; University President. m. 9 Aug 1964, 1 s, 2 d. *Education:* BA, Concordia Sr Coll, Ft Wayne, IN, 1962; MDiv, Concordia Sem, St Louis, MO, 1966; MA, Presby School Christian Educ, Richmond, VA, 1967; PHD, Wayne State Univ, Detroit, MI, 1976. *Appointments:* Asst Pastor, St James Luth Ch Grosse Pointe, Grosse Pointe Farms, MI, 1967-73; Asst Prof, Theology, 1973-78, Asst to Pres, 1981, Assoc Prof, Theology, 1982-84, Dean, Student Affairs, 1982-84, Acting Pres, 1984, Concordia Tchrs Coll, Seward, NE; Pres, Concordia Coll, St Paul, MN, 1984-88; Pres, Valparaiso Univ, Valparaiso, IN, 1988-. *Publication:* Close the Back Door, book. *Memberships:* Dir, MN Pvte Coll Coun, St Paul, 1984-88; Dir, NW IN Forum, Merrillville, 1989-; Dir, Independent Colls IN, Indianapolis, 1988-; Midway Civic and Commerce Assn, St Paul, 1984-88; Rotary Club, Valparaiso, 1988-; Chmbr of Comm, Valparaiso, 1988-. *Hobby:* Golf. *Address:* Valparaiso University, Valparaiso, IN 46383, USA.

HARRELL William Edward Jr, b. 18 Dec 1948, Columbus, Georgia, USA. Orthodontist. m. Joyce Tatum Jackson, 21 Dec 1974, 1 s, 1 d. *Education:* BS, Univ AL, Tuscaloosa, 1971; DMD, Univ AL School Dentistry, Birmingham, 1975; Orthodontic Postgrad Residency, Univ PA, Phila, 1975-77. *Appointments:* Pvte Orthodontic Prac, orthodontics for youth and adults, Temporomandibular jt disorders, surg orthodontics, facial orthopaedics, 1977-; Lectr, temporomandibular jt disorders. *Publication:* A Fixed Functional and TMJ Treatment Appliance, 1988. *Memberships:* Am Bd Orthodontics; Coll Diplomates, Am Bd Orthodontists; Am Assn Orthodontists; So Assn Orthodontists, Chmn New Mbr Comm 1988-90; AL Assn Orthodontics, Sec-Treas 1988-89, VP 1989-90, Pres, 1990-91; 9th Dist Dental Assn, State of AL, Pres 1987-88; Royal Soc Med, UK; Fndn Orthodontic Resh; Am Equilibration Soc;

Dental Hlth Coun, State of AL Comm Pub Hlth, 1991- ; AL Dental Assn, Bd Trustees 1988, House Delegs 1987-88, Special Comm on Temporomandibular Jt Disorders; Chmn, NASA Project Lazer, State of AL, 1991- ; Farrar-Norgaard Radiological Soc; Orthodontic/ Temporomandibular Jt Disorders Instr, Normandie Study Grp Temporomandibular Jt Dysfunction, Montgomery, AL, 1981-86; Am Dental Assn; Orthodontic Educ and Rsch Fndn. *Hobbies:* Golf; Swimming; Boating; Cub Scoutmaster; Involved with innovative research in regard to 3-D imaging with NIH. *Address:* Suite 1-A, Medical Arts Building, 1110 Alison Drive, Alexander City, AL 35010, USA. 7.

HARRIS Allen, b. 3 Feb 1929, Brooklyn, New York, USA. Lawyer; Educator. m. Susanne T Berger, 1 Sept 1957. *Education:* BA, NY Univ, 1949; JD, Columbia Univ, 1954. *Appointments:* Var positions, US Army, 1951-53; Newman & Newman, NYC, 1954-55; Carey & Carey, 1955-56; Dist Atty's Off, NY Co, 1956-59; Coord Comm on Discipline, 1st Judicial Dept, 1959-62, Supreme Judge's Off, 1962-63; NY State Supreme Ct; United Bd & Carton Corp, NYC, 1963; NY State Comm Investigations, 1963-65; Inst Judicial Admin, NY Univ, 1965-67; Prof, Law: Univ MO, 1967-69, Brooklyn Law School, 1969-72; Counsel, NY State Study Comm for NYC, 1972; Special Ast, NY State Atty Gen, 1972-76; Sole prac, NYC, 1976-79; Sr Law Asst, Appellate Div, 1st Judicial Dept, NY State Supreme Ct, 1979-. *Publications:* Num articles in encyclopaedias and law jnls. *Memberships include:* Cons, NY State Select Comm on Correctional Instns, 1971-72; Cons, KS City Police, 1968-69; Special Projects Dir, NYC Patrolmen's Benevolent Assn, 1978; Fac, Appellate Judges Sems, NY Univ, 1965-67; Num commitments, NY State proceedings; Num offc, Am, NY State, NYC Bar Assns; Int Assn Police Chiefs; Col, Judge ADvocate Gen Corps, US Army. *Honours:* Combat Infantrymans Badge; Serv Cross, NY State Companions. *Hobbies:* Reading; Sport. *Address:* 700 Victory Boulevard, Staten Island, NY 10301, USA. 6, 52, 146, 163.

HARRIS Grace P, b. 24 Oct 1928, Boston, Massachusetts, USA. Teacher. m. Melvin O Harris, 12 Oct 1952, 2 d. *Education:* AA 1975, BA 1980, MS Educ, 1985; Para Profl, 1967-81. *Appointments:* Spec Educ Reading Tchr, 1981; Reading Specialist, 1981-. *Memberships:* Protestant Tchr Assn; Delegate Nat Coun Negro Women; Ch person, Good and Welfare Com Educ Com; Tau Gamma Delta, VP; Unt Fed of Tchrs; Sch based Middle Sch Task. *Honours:* Dean's List, 1973,Manhattan Com Col. *Hobbies:* reading; Travelling; Community Service. *Address:* 235-17 148 Ave, Rosedale, NY 11422, USA.

HARRIS Herbert Irwin, b. 18 Dec 1926, USA. Natural Resources Consultant. m. Hava Novick, 28 Mar 1954, 2 d. *Education:* BA magna cum laude, Geology, Univ MN, 1948; MA, Geol, UCLA, 1950. *Appointments:* Texaco Inc, 1951-53; Pan Israel Oil Co, 1953-59; Magellan Petrol Corp, 1959-62; Ford, Bacon & Davis Inc, 1962-68; Nicolet Inc, 1968-77; Cons, 1977-. *Memberships:* Am Assn Petroleum Geologists; Am Inst Profl Geologists. *Hobbies:* Foreign affairs; Stock and metals markets. *Address:* 18/1 Davidson St, 93706 Jerusalem, Israel.

HARRIS Iain Grant Nicolson, b. 17 Mar 1946, Edinburgh, Scotland. Company Director. m. Jane Petrie Robertson, 8 Aug 1969, 1 s, 1 d. *Education:* MA Hons, Econs, Univ Aberdeen, 1968. *Appointments:* Grp Sales Promotion Mgr, RMC Grp, 1968-74; Dir, Parker PR Assocs, 1974- 80; Mayor, Royal Borough Windsor and Maidenhead, 1976-78; Dir, Shandwick Cons, 1980-82; Dir, Good Rels City, 1982-85; Chmn, Chief Exec, Lombard Grp plc, Chmn, Lombard Communications Ltd, Chmn Lombard PR Ltd, Chmn, Lombard Cons Ltd, Chmn, Wolfe Lombard Ltd, 1985-90; Pres, Lombard Communications Inc, USA, 1987-91-; Chmn, First Pacific Ltd, 1990-; Dpty Chmn, Grandfieldrork Collins Fin Ltd, 1991-. *Memberships:* Pres, Windsor Soc

Mentally Handicapped Children and Adults; Pres, Windsor Talking Newspaper for the Blind; Trustee, New Windsor Community Assn; VP, Royal Windsor Rose and Horticultural Soc; VP, Windsor and Maidenhead Sports Assn for the Disabled. *Honour:* Queen's Jubilee Medal, 1977. *Hobbies:* Gardening supervision; Rugby. *Address:* Chanonry, St Leonard's Hill, Windsor, Berkshire SL4 4AT, England. 53.

HARRIS Nigel Henry, b. 11 July 1924, Grimsby, England. Consultant Orthopaedic Surgeon. m. Dr Elizabeth Harris, 2 Aug 1951, 2 s. *Education:* Trinity Coll, Cambridge, 1943-45; Middlesex Hosp, 1945- 48; MA; MB BChir; Dipl, FRCS, 1958. *Appointments:* House Surg, Middlesex Hosp, London, 1948; Med Off, Sq Ldr, RAF, 1949-52; House Surg, N Middlesex Hosp, 1952-53; Orthopaedic Registrar, King Edwards Hosp, Ealing, 1953-55; Surg Registrar, Mile End Hosp, 1955-56; Surg Registrar, Fulham Hosp, London, 1958-59; Orthopaedic Registrar and Sr Registrar, Royal Nat Orthopaedic Hosp, London, 1960-63; Cons Orthopaedic Surg, St Mary's Hosp and London Foot Hosp, 1964-90; Currently Hon Cons Orthopaedic Surg, St Mary's Hosp, London, Pvte Cons, Orthopaedic and Medico-Legal Prac, Orthopaedic Surg to Arsenal Football Club, Med Examiner, Football League Underwriters. *Publications include:* Postgraduate Textbook of Clinical Orthopaedics (ed), 1983; Medical Negligence (ed w Michal Powers), 1990. *Memberships:* Fellow, Brit Orthopaedic Assn; Fellow, Royal Soc Med; Brit Orthopaedic Rsch Soc; Medico-Legal Soc; Brit Acad Experts; Hosp Consultants and Specialist Assn. *Honours:* European Travelling Fellow, Brit Orthopaedic Assn, 1962; Geigy Scholar, 1967. *Hobbies:* Flat and National Hunt racehorse owner; Cricket (Mbr, Marylebone Cricket Club); Gardening. *Address:* 72 Harley Street, London W1, England.

HARRISON Brian David Walter, b. 24 Apr 1943, Blackpool, England. Consultant Physician (Doctor). m. Jennifer Anne Stokes, 13 July 1968, 1 s, 1 d. *Education:* Shrewsbury School, 1956-61; St John's Coll, Cambridge, 1961-64; Guys Hosp, London, 1964-67; MA, MB, BChir, 1967; MRCP, 1970; FRCP, 1987; FCCP, 1990. *Appointments:* House Physn, 1967- 68, Jr Registrar, 1969-70, Guys Hosp; House Physn, Brompton Hosp, London, 1970-71; Registrar, Westminster Hosp, London, 1971-72; Sr Registrar, Abu Hosp, Nigeria, 1973-74; Lectr, Sr Registrar, Middlesex Hosp, London, 1974- 77; Cons Physn, Norfolk and Norwich/W Norwich Hosps, 1978-. *Creative works:* Publications in med jnls and lectures, UK and overseas, on pneumonia, smoking, asthma, pulmonary function, respiration failure, secondary polycythaemia, chronic airflow obstruction, lung biopsy, sarcoidosis. *Memberships include:* Fellow, Am Coll Chest Physicians; Brit Thoracic Soc, Rsh Comm Mbr 1980-86, Educ Comm 1986-89, Chmn Pneumonia Standing Subcomm 1987-89, Chmn Standards of Care Comm 1989-, Coun and Exec 1989-. *Honours:* Humphrey Davy Rolleston Exhibitioner, St John's Coll, 1961-64. *Hobbies:* Gardening; Sailing; Theatre; Skiing; Travel. *Address:* The White House, Church Avenue East, Norwich NR2 2AF, England.

HARRISON Frank Russell III, b. 11 Mar 1935, Jacksonville, Florida, USA. Professor of Philosophy. m. Dorothy G Harrison, Sept 1967. *Education:* BA w hons, Philos, Univ of the South, Sewanee, 1957; MA, Philos, 1959, PhD, Philos, 1961, Univ VA. *Appointments:* Instr, Philos, Roanoke Coll, Salem, VA, 1961-62; Asst Prof, Philos, 1962-66, Assoc Prof, Philos, 1966-72, Prof, Philos, 1972-, Univ GA, Athens; Vis Prof, Univ NC, Chapel Hill, 1963; Emory Univ, Atlanta, GA, 1965; GA Inst Technology, School Info and Computer Sci, Atlanta, 1965-66; Keele Univ, Keele, England, 1984. *Creative works:* About 50 contbns to jnls, proceedings and books incl: Wittgenstein and the Doctrine of Identical Minimal Meaning, 1962; What Kind of Beings Can Have Rights, 1972; Epistemological Dogma: A Need for Examination, 1980; On Hearing God, 1985; Language, Knowledge and God, 1987; Moore, Wittgenstein y los escepticos; About 100 papers. *Memberships include:* Am Philosl Assn, En Div; Soc Philos Relig, Sec- Treas 1965-, Pres

1984-85; So Soc Philos and Psychology, Chmn Prog Comm 1973, Chmn Epistemology Sect 1975, Coun Mbr 1973-75; GA Philosl Assn; Metaphys Soc Am; Am Guild Scholars, Pres 1968-69; Soc Christian Philosophers, En Div, Chmn Steering Comm 1986-, Sec-Treas 1986-, Sem and Workshop Comm 1988-; Assocs for Philos of Relig, Pres 1985-; Am Soc Value Inquiry; Am Soc Advancement Humanities; S Atlantic Philos Educ Soc; Soc Christian Philosophers, Chmn En Div Planning Comm 1985-88, En Div Sec-Treas 1985-88. *Honours:* Phi Kappa Phi; Phi Beta Delta; Phi Sigma Tau; Outstanding Educator; Gridiron Secret Soc; Outstanding Tchng, Univ GAS Hons Prog, twice; Honored Prof, Franklin Coll Arts and Scis; Sandy Beaver Prof, 1985-88; Mentor, Tchng Improvement Prog, 1988-90. *Address:* Department of Philosophy, University of Georgia, Athens, GA 30602, USA. 2, 7, 13, 15, 30, 52, 125, 129, 139, 154, 155, 156, 162, 179.

HARRISON Kenneth Cecil, b. 29 Apr 1915, Hyde, Cheshire, England. Writer; Editor; Lecturer; Former Librarian. m. Doris Taylor, 26 Aug 1941, 2 s. *Education:* Coll Technology, Manchester; Fellow, Lib Assn, 1938; Royal Mil Acad, Sandhurst, 1942. *Appointments:* Borough Libn, Hyde and Glossop, 1939-47; Borough Libn, Curator, Hove, 1947-50; Borough Libn, Eastbourne, 1950-58; Borough Libn, Hendon, 1958-61; City Libn, Westminster, London, 1961-80. *Creative works:* Author, ed, 22 books incl: First Steps in Librarianship, 5th Ed, 1980; Libraries in Scandanavia, 2nd Ed, 1969; The Library and the Community, 3rd Ed, 1977; Public Relations for Librarians, 2nd Ed, 1982; International Librarianship, 1989; Contbr to encyclopaedias and festschriften; Over 370 published articles; Over 1000 lectures, addresses, presentations. *Memberships:* Lib Assn, 1932-, Pres 1973; C'wlth Lib Assn, Pres 1972-75, Chief Exec 1980-83; Marylebone Cricket Club, 1962, Art and Lib Comm 1973-89. *Honours:* MBE (Mil), 1946; Kt 1st Class, Order of the Lion of Finland, 1976; OBE, 1980; Hon Mbr, Malta Lib Assn, 1986. *Hobbies:* Reading; Writing; Watching cricket; Travel; Oenophily; Crosswords. *Address:* 5 Tavistock, Devonshire Place, Eastbourne, East Sussex BN21 4AG, England. 1, 3.

HARRISON Philip Lewis, b. 30 Nov 1945, Lynn, Massachusetts, USA. Writer. m. Margaret Anne Taylor, 19 Aug 1977, 1 s, 1 d. *Education:* BS, Brooklyn Coll, 1969. *Appointments:* Assoc Ed, Ashrae, NYC, 1967-69; Assc Ed, Railway Age, NYC, 1969-71; Assoc Ed, Reader's Digest, NYC, 1971-72; Asst Dir, Alden Omnisphere, MA, 1972-74; Assoc Engr, Goodyear Aerospace, AZ, 1974-76; Freelance Writer, 1976-; VP, H W & E Creative Servs, 1991-. *Publications:* Hundreds of articles for local, reg, nat, int jnls; Ghost-writer, books; Speciality, sci and technology, bus, econs; Author, Official Evan Mecham Jokebook, 1987. *Memberships:* Make-a-Wish Fndn, Ctrl and So AZ, Comm Chmn 1985-90, Make-A-Wish Fndn of Am, Pub Rels Comm Mbr, 1991-. *Honours:* Copper Quill Award, Int Assn Bus Communicators, 1986, 1988, 1989, 1990, 1991; Gold Pen, Phoenix Gazette, 1986. *Hobbies:* Astronomy; Geology; Woodworking; Baseball cards. *Address:* 3370 W Grandview Rad, Phoenix, AZ 85023, USA. 3, 9, 139, 155.

HARRISON Reziya, b. Essex, England. Barrister. m. 11 June 1965, 1 s, 1 d. *Education:* Somerville Coll, Oxford; BA (Lit Hum), Oxford; MA, 1990; Called to Bar, Lincoln's Inn, 1975. *Appointments:* Prac as Barrister, Lincoln's Inn, 1975-. *Hobbies:* Reading; Listening to music; Domestic pursuits. *Address:* 11 Old Square, Lincoln's Inn, London WC2A 3TS, England.

HART Anelay Colton Wright, b. 6 Mar 1934, Leconfield, England. Solicitor. m. Margaret Gardner Dewing, 22 Mar 1979. *Education:* Stamford Sch, 1944-53; LLB, King's Col London, 1955-58; Solicitor, 1961. *Appointments:* Ptnr, Appleby Hope & Matthews, 1963-. *Memberships:* RSPCA: Chm of Coun, 1981-83, 1985-86, 1988-90; Mbr Coun, 1969-; Treas, 1974- 81; V-

Chm of Coun, 1983-84; Advr Dir World Soc for the Protection of Animals, 1982-. *Honour:* Queen Victoria Silver Medal, RSPCA, 1984. *Hobbies:* Hill walking. *Address:* Village Farm, Moulton, Richmond, N Yorks, DL10 6QQ, England. 1.

HART Edwin Robert Jr., b. 26 Mar 1953, Ft Benning, Georgia, USA. City Manager. m. Lois Anne White, 16 Aug 1980, 1 s, 4 d. *Education:* BS, Baylor Univ, 1975; MPA, Univ of N.Texas, 1978. *Appointments:* City of Grapevine, TX: Recreation Supt, 1975-76; Dir of Parks & Rec, 1976-78; Admin Asst, 1978-79; City of Claremont, CA: Admin Analyst, 1979-80; City of Sundown, TX, City Admr, 1980-82; City Mgr, TX Cities of: Sweetwater, 1982-85; Pampa, 1985-89; Georgetown, 1989-. *Creative works:* Author: Building Bridges for Emergency Management, 1992; Emergency Preparedness, 1989; Emergency Response, 1988; When Bids are too High, 1989; Privitization, 1987. *Memberships:* TX, Panhandle and Intl City Mgmt Assns; Texas Municipal eague Bd; Teaxas Mgt Assoc, Bd; Texas Public Assoc, Bd; Texas Found for the Improvement to Local Government, Sec-Treas; ASPA; Bd, Foreign Trade Zone of Central TX Inc; Rotary Intl. *Honours:* ssa 000Owen W Sherrill Award for Economic Development, 1992; ICMA Int Management, Exchange Program to Beechworth, Victoria, Australia; Paul Harris Fellow, 1990; Adj Fac Mem 1989-93, Be-a-Pro Appl Awd, 1988, EMI. *Hobbies:* Genealogy; History; Reading; Sunday School Teaching. *Address:* 607 Meadowbrook, Georgetown, TX 78628, USA.

HART Kevin John, b. 5 July 1954, London, England. Writer and Academic. *Education:* BA Hons ANU, 1976; PhD, Univ of Melbourne, 1986. *Appointments:* Assoc Prof, Dept Eng, Monash Univ, 1991; Lectr 1987, Sr Lectr 1990, Dept Lit Studies, Deakin Univ. *Creative works:* Poetry: The Departure, 1978; The Lines of the Head, 1981; Your Shadow, 1984; Peniel, 1991; The Buried Harbour, 1990; The Trespass of the Sign, 1989; A D Hope, 1992. *Honours:* Poetry Awds: Grace Leven, 1991; NSW Premier, 1985; Victorian Premier, 1985; Wesley Michel Wright, 1984; Harri Jones, 1983; John Shaw Neilson, 1977. *Hobbies:* Cooking; Reading; Walking. *Address:* Golvan Arts Management, 21a Mary Street, Hawthorn, Victoria 3122, Australia.

HART Michael D, b. 21 Dec 1959, Toronto, Canada. Economist; Trader; Arbitrater; Professor. *Education:* NHSS Hons, 1979; Combines Hons, Econ and Applied Sociol, York Univ, 1985; Certs: Canadian Securities Inst, 1985; Canadian Futures, 1987 and US Futures, 1987; RR Exam Qual, 1991. *Appointments:* Canadian Nat Railway, 1982-84; Friedberg Mercantile Gp, 1986-; Ryerson Univ, 1989-. *Creative works:* Friedberg Currency and commodity Comments, co-author; Various other economic and business articles. *Memberships:* Bd, Jewish Community Ctr of Toronto, 1990-; Canadian Nuclear Assn Imperial Club, Pres, 1989-; The Inst for Econ Equality, Treas, 1991. *Honours:* Sir Isaac Newton Phys Awd, 1979; Jerusalem Fellowship, 1985; Caesar Awd Nomination Ryerson Univ, 1989. *Hobbies:* Squash; Amateur Film Making; Woodworking; Videophile. *Address:* Friedberg Mercantial Gp, 347 Bay St Suite 207, Toronto, Ontario, Canada M5H 2R7. 88.

HARTLEY Frank, b. 5 Jan 1911, Lancashire, England. Consultant Scientist. m. Lydia May England, 22 Dec 1937, 2 s. *Education:* London Univ: PHC, Sch of Pharm, 1932, BSc Chem, 1936, PhD, 1941, FRPharmS, FRSC 1941, CChem, 1941. *Appointments:* Lectr, Sch of Pharm, London, 1932-40; Chief Chem, Organon Labs, 1940-43; Sec, Therapeutic Res Corpn, 1943-46; Dir or Res and Sci Sers, Brit Drug Houses Ltd, 1946-62; Dean, Sch of Pharm, London, 1962- 76; V-Chancellor, Univ of London, 1976-78; Chm, British Pharmacopoeias Comm, 1980. *Memberships:* Chm, Brit Pharm Conf, 1957; VP, 1963-65, 1967-69, Pres, 1965-67, Royal Inst of Chem; FRPS, 1932-; FRSC, 1970; SCI, 1941-. *Honours include:* Hon FRCP, 1979; Hon FRCS, 1980; Hon DSc, Warwick, 1978; CBE, 1970; Knight Bachelor,

1977. *Hobbies:* Spectator sports; Reading. *Address:* Flat 16 Town Thorns, Easenhall, Rugby CV23 0JE, England. 1.

HARTLEY Godfrey, b. 26 Aug 1937, Ulverston, Lancs, England. Chaplain. *Education:* Univs of Manchester and Nottingham; Cuddesdon Col, Oxford. *Appointments:* RAF, 1956-58; Deacon, 1964; Priest, 1965; Asst Curate, St Giles Balderton, Southwell, 1964-67; Missions to Seamen Chaplain and Rector, St George, Mozambique, 1968-73; Sr Chaplain and Sec for Scotland, Parish Priest, St Gabriels, Glasgow, 1973-89; Chaplain RNR 1973-; Chaplain the Missions to Seamen in Cornwall, 1989-. *Memberships:* Inc of Coopers of Glasgow, 1978; Soc of the Holy Cross; Skal Club of Scotland; Intl Christian Maritime Assn; Ski Club of GB; Hon Chaplain RNR Ofrs London CLub; Army and Navy Club. *Honours:* Freeman City of Glasgow, 1939; Hon Roughneck, City of Beaumont, TX, 1978. *Hobbies:* Painting; Photography; Travel; Skiing; Theatre; Gardening; Country life; Reading. *Address:* Sandoes Gate, Feock, Truro, Cornwall TR3 6QN, England.

HARTMANN Reinhard Rudolf Karl, b. 8 Apr 1938, Vienna, Austria. University Reader. *Education:* Translator's Dipl, Univ Vienna, 1960; BSc, Vienna Sch of Econ, 1960; MA S.Illinois Univ, 1962; Doctorate, Vienna Sch of Econ, 1965. *Appointments:* Lectr in Modern Langs, Univ Manchester Inst of Sci & Tech, 1964-68; Lectr, Applied Linguistics, Univ of Nottingham, 1968-74; Dir, Lang Ctr, Univ of Exeter, 1974-92; Hd, Dept of Applied Lings, 1992-. *Creative works:* Dictionary of Language and Linguistics, 1972; Contrastive Textology, 1980; Ed: Lexicography, Principles and Practice, 1983; LEXeter '83 Proceedings, 1984. *Memberships:* Brit Assn for Applied Linguistics; Linguistics Assn of GB; Societas Linguistica Europaea; Assn for Lit and Linguistic Computing; European Assn for Lexicography. *Honours:* Fellowships: Humanities Res Centre, Australian Nat Univ, 1977; Centre for the New OED, Univ of Waterloo, Canada, 1985; Erasmus Grant, 1990. *Hobbies:* Linguistics; Translation; Lexicography; Music; Travelling; Yoga; Table Tennis; Collecting Stamps and Dictionaries. *Address:* 40 Velwell Road, Exeter, Devon EX4 4LD, England.

HARTY Dwayne John, b. 23 May 1957, Saskatchewan, Canada. Artist; Painter; Sculptor; Dioramist. *Education:* Art Students League, NY, 1977-78, with Robert Loughheed, Santa Fe, NM, 1977-81, with Clarence Tiuenius, Winnipeg, Canada, 1975-88; Bob Khun Workshop, Jackson Hole, Wyoming, 1984. *Appointments:* Hardwood Forest Diorama, Royal Ontario Museum, 1985-86; Chief Dioramist, Sask Mus of Natural Hist, 1987-90; Long Point Diorama, Royal Ontario Mus, 1990; Five natural history Dioramas and one decorative mural for New Algonquin Pk Mus, 1991. *Creative works:* Art and The Animal Exhibition, Jameston, NY, 1992; WWF Stamps, NY, 1988-91; The Squirrels of Canada, Nat Mus of Canada, 1980; An Atlas of Endangered Species of Canada, 1989; Mammals in North America, 1986; One man Private Exhibition Sale, Toronto, 1991. *Memberships:* Salmagundi Club, NY, 1992; Soc of Animal Artists, 1980; Instructor Life Drawing and Anatomy, Royal Ontario Mus, 1985-86; Oil Painter and Animal Drawing Instructor, Univ of Regina, Canada, 1987-89; Judge and Lecturer on Wildlife Art; Instr Fine Arts, Wolfe Inst, Toronto. *Honours include:* Sasketchewan Arts Bd Scholarship, 1981; Canada Coun Grant, 1978; Canadian Nature Fed Scholarship, 1977; Paintings in many private and corporate collections. *Hobbies:* Bird watching; hunting; Basketball. *Address:* 8 Hemlock Crescent, Whitney, Ontario, Canada, KOJ 2MO. 88.

HARUTUNIAN John Martin, b. 29 Aug 1948, Watertown, MA, USA. College Teacher. *Education:* BM Composition, Wheaton Col, IL, 1969; Grad Study, Harvard Univ, 1969-90; MA Musicol, Univ of PA, 1975; PhD Musicol, UCLA, 1981. *Appointments:* Tchg Asst, 1977-78, Tchg Assoc, 1978-79, UCLA; Pvt Piano Tchr,

1983-88; Lectr in Music, Gordon Col, 1988-; Gordon-Conwell Theological Seminary, 1992-. *Creative works:* Fantasy-Gavotte for piano and orchestra, 1965; Nocturne, piano, 1974; Haydn and Mozart; A Study of their Mature Sonata-Style Procedures, 1981. *Memberships:* AMS; NGPT; New Englang Piano Tchrs Assn. *Honours:* Piano soloist with Boston Pops Orchestra, 1965, and Boston SO, 1966; Paderewski Medal, NGPT Auditions, 1966; Adjucator, NGPT Auditions, 1986; Semi-finalist, Competition of Young Keyboard Artists, Michigan, 1988. *Hobbies:* Reading Christian literature. *Address:* 355 Newtonville Avenue, Newtonville, MA 02160, USA. 4, 179.

HARVEY Andrew Sydney, b. 21 Sept 1939, St Stephen, NB, Canada. Professor of Economics. m. F Dawn Daly, 17 June 1961, 2 d. *Education:* Ricker Col, 1957-58; ba Univ of Maine, 1958-63; Clark Univ, 1963-65; MA, 1967; PhD, 1971. *Appointments:* Dalhousie Univ, 1966-79; Univ of Ottawa, 1978-81; Dalhousie Univ, 1981-83; St Mary's Univ, 1983-. *Creative works:* Time Budget Research, 1983; Where Does the Day Go, 1991; Blueprint for Social Indicators Research; Numerous articles and nonographs. *Memberships:* Canadian Reg Sci Assn; Charter Pres; Intl Assn for Time Use Res, Sec, Treas; Intl Sociol Assn; Atlantic Canada Econ Assn; Cdn Population Soc; Caribbean Studies Assn. *Hobbies:* Theatre; Jazz & Travel. *Address:* 19 Balcome Drive, Halifax, NS, Canada B3N 1H9. 6, 88.

HARVEY Michael Anthony, b. 22 Aug 1921, Kew, Surrey, England. m. A J Pike 30 Oct 1965, div. 1 s. *Education:* Intermediate Exam in Art and Craft, Nat Dipl in Design, Wimbledon Sch of Art. *Appointments:* Merchant Navy, 1943-55; QM Art Tchr in various schools and adult education, 1957-77; ARt Critic, Surrey Mirror, 1974-80; Art Corres, Croydon Advertiser, 1976-79. *Creative works:* Limehouse Reach, oil, 1968; Piercefield St, St Pancreas, pastel, 1968; St Aubyns Square, oil, 1978; Cabin Boy, short story, BBC Radio Brighton, 1985. *Memberships:* Chichester Art Soc; Soc of Graphic Fine Art; Intl Assn of Arts; FRSA. *Honours:* Linton Prize for Painting, 1972. *Hobbies:* Walking; Yachting. *Address:* 15 Waterloo Square, Bognor Regis, W.Sussex PO21 1TE, England. 19.

HARVEY Peter, b. 23 Apr 1922, Huddersfield, England. Asst Counsel to the Speaker of the House of Commons. m. Mary Vivienne Goss, 29 Mar 1950, 1 s, 1 d. *Education:* MA, BCL, St John's Col, Oxford; Called to the Bar, Lincolns Inn, 1948. *Appointments:* Legal Advr Branch, Home Ofc, 1948-77; Legal Advr, Dept of Educ and Sci, 1977-83; Conslt, Legal Advr Br, Home Ofc, 1983-86; Asst Counsel to the Speaker of the House of Commons, 1986-. *Contributions to:* 3rd and 4th edits of Halsbury's Laws of England. *Honours:* CB, 1980. *Hobbies:* Walking; History; Genealogy. *Address:* Old Avenue, Weybridge, Surrey KT13 OPS, England.

HARWOOD Giles Francis, b. 31 Jan 1934, Chairman Registered Homes Tribunal. *Education:* MA Christ Church, Oxford,; Called to the Bar, Inner Temple, 1956. *Appointments:* Barrister: London & Western Circuit, 1959-70; First Parly Counsel, Kenya, 1970-75; Legal Advr, St Vincent, 1976-78; Chief Parly Draftsman, Malawi, 1978-83; Chief Justice, Tonga, 1983-85; Law Revision Comm for Grenada, 1988-. *Creative works:* Odgers Principles of Pleading and Practice, 17-20 edns, 1960-71. *Membership:* ACIArb, 1985. *Honour:* JP, North Avon. *Hobbies:* Music; Travel. *Address:* Fernhill Hse, Almondsbury, Bristol BS12 4LX, England.

HARWOOD-NASH Derek Clive, b. 11 Feb 1936, Rhodesia, South Africa. Professor of Radiology; Paediatric Neuroradiologist. m. Barbara Jordan, 9 Mar 1963, 3 d. *Education:* MBChB, Capetown, 1960; FRCPC, 1967, DMR, 1965, Toronto; FCM(SA), 1991, Cape Town; FACR, USA, 1991. *Appointments:* Phys & Radiologist, 1968-, Radiologist in Chief, 1978-88, Hosp for Sick Children, Toronto. *Creative works:* Neuroradiology in infants and Children, 1976; Mylegraphy and CT in children, 1980; 200 scientific articles. *Memberships include:* Pres, ASNR, 1987; Soc of Paediatric Radiol, 1986; Prog Chm, Radiol Soc of N.Am, 1988-91. *Honours include:* BEIT Fellow, 1962-64; Presidential Medal, Brazil, 1978; Medal, Swedish Soc of Med Radiol; Hon Fellow, S.Africa Col of Med, 1991. *Hobbies:* Cross country skiing; Classical music; Opera; Pastel painting; Travelling. *Address:* Hospital for Sick Children, 555 University Ave, Toronto, Ontario, Canada M5G 1X8. 88.

HASEGAWA Yosinobu, b. 26 Sept 1930, Japan. Consultant. m. 1 May 1959, 1 s, 1 d. *Education:* BEng, Osaka Univ, 1956. *Appointments:* Dir, Hokushin Elec Co Ltd, 1977; Pres, Cosmo Keiso Co Ltd, 1981, Chm, Cosmo Eeiso Co Ltd, 1989. *Memberships:* Jour of Japanese Soc for Quality Control; Soc of Instrument and Control Engrg. *Hobbies:* Golf; Classical Music. *Address:* 233 6-36-3 Sasage Komamku, Yokohama, Japan.

HASHMI (Aurangzeb) Alamgir, b. 15 Nov 1951, Lahore. Professor; Editor; Broadcaster. *Education:* MA 1972; MA 1977; DLitt, 1984. *Appointments:* Lectureships and Professorships in Asian, American and European Univs, 1971-; Editor of several scholarly, literary and research journals and English Broadcaster with Radio Pakistan. *Creative works include:* Books: The Oath and Amen, 1976; America is a Punjabi Word, 1979; An Old Chair, 1979; My Second in Kentucky, 1981; Pakistani Literature, 1978; This Time in Lahore, 1983; Commonwealth Literature, 1983; Neither This Time-Nor That Place, 1984; The Worlds of Muslim Imagination, 1986; Ezra Pound in Melbourne, 1983; Inland and Other Poems, 1988; The Commonwealth, Comparative Literature and the World, 1988; The Poems of Alamgir Hashmi, 1992; Sun and Moon and Other Poems, 1992. *Honours include:* Cert of Acad Merit, Univ of Punjab, 1973; Academic Roll of Hon, Govt Col, Lahore, 1972; Nat Lit Prize, Pakistan Acad of Letters, 1985. *Hobbies:* Walking; Music; Films. *Address:* c/o Indus Books, PO Box 2905, Islamabad, GPO 44000, Pakistan. 52, 3, 11.

HASSANALI Noor Mohamed, b. 13 Aug 1918, San Fernando. President of the Republic of Trinidad and Tobago. m. Zalayhar Mohammed, 17 May 1992, 1 s, 1 d. *Education:* BA Hons Law, Univ of Toronto, 1947; Called to the English Bar, Grays's Inn, England, 1948. *Appointments:* Pvte Practice, Law, 1948-53; Magistrate, 1953-59; Sr Magistrate, 1960; Sr Crown Counsel, Ofc of Attorney Gen, 1961-64; Solicitor Gen, Min of Legal Affairs, 1965; Judge of the Hg Ct, Supreme Ct of Judicature, T&T, 1966-67; Judge, Ct of Appeal, T&T, 1978-84; Master of Moots, Hugh Wooding Law Sch, 1987-. *Memberships:* Bd of Control, Naparima Col, San Fernando, 1948-60; Judicial and Legal Ser Comm, 1985-87; Trinidad and Tobago Def Fore Comm Bd, 1985-87; Exec Mem, Scout Assn of Trinidad and Tobago, 1965-87. *Honours:* Cert of hons for contribution to football at Skinner Pk, San Fernando Borough Coun, 1984; Hon Doctorate, Univ of the W.Indies, 1989; Hon Doctorate of Laws, Univ of Toronto,Can, 1990. *Hobbies:* Walking; Football; Cricket; Soccer; Theatre. *Address:* The President's House, St Ann's, Port of Spain, Trinidad and Tobago, West Indies. 12, 52.

HASSE Rolf H, b. 18 Dec 1940, Berlin, Germany. University Professor. m. Christa, 3 Jan 1967, 1 s. *Education:* Dipl Volkswist, 1967; Dr rer pol, 1973; Habilitation, 1981. *Appointments:* Sci Asst, 1969-81; Prof in Econ, 1981. *Creative works:* Theory and Politics of Embargos, 1973; Multiple Reseerves, 1984; Econometrics in the Service of Economic Interests, 1986; European Central Bank, 1990. *Memberships:* Verein fur Socialpolitik; Western Econ Assn; Assn for Canada Studies; Studienkreis Intl Bezichungen. *Hobbies:* Collecting old engravings of towns and famous economists. *Address:* Dankwartstrasse 11, D 5030 Huerth, Germany. 52.

HASSID S b.19 June 1950, Athens, Greece. Professor of Environmental Engineering. Ernestine Nahmias, 25 Feb 1983, 1 s, 1 d. *Education:* BSc, MSc, Nuclear Engrg, Univ of London; DSc, Israel Inst of Tech. *Appointments:* Consltg Scist, Nat Energy Coun, Athens, Greece, 1978-79; Techn, Environmental & Water Resources, Engrg Dept, Haifa, Israel. *Creative works:* Co-author, Energy Saving Buildings, 1989. *Memberships:* Intl Solar Energy Soc; Euro Assn for the Sci of Air Pollution. *Honours:* DRORI Prize for best engineering textbook, Haifa Municipality, 1990. *Address:* Dept of Env & Water Resources Eng, Technion Israel Institute of Technology, Haifa 32000, Israel.

HATADA Kazuyuki, b. 23 Dec 1951, Maebashi City, Gunma, Japan. Mathematician; Educator. m. Kumiko (Yoshikawa) Hatada, 15 Dec 1985. 1 s. *Education:* BSc 1974, MSc 1976, Dr of Sci, 1979, Dept of Maths, The Univ of Tokyo. *Appointments:* Res Fellow, The Univ of Tokyo, Fac of Sci, 1979-80; Assoc Prof in Maths, Gifu Univ, 1981-. *Creative works:* Author of numerous mathematical papers including: Correspondences for Hecke rings and co-homology groups on smooth compactifications of Siegel modular varieties, 1990; On the action of Hecke rings on homology groups of smooth compactifications of Siegel modular varieties and Siegel cusp forms, 1990; On the Local Zeta functions of the Hilbert Modular Schemes, 1990. *Memberships:* Dep Dir Gen, 1989-, Life Fellow, 1987-, Hon Mem Adv Coun, 1991-, IBC; Dep Gov, 1989-, Res Bd of Advrs, 1988-, Grand Ambassador of Achievement Intl, 1990-, ABI; Reviewer of Math Reviews, 1989-; Life Mem, World Inst of Achievement, 1988-; Math Soc of Japan, 1976; Am Math Soc, 1979-; Astronomical Soc of Japan. *Honours:* Intl Cultural Dipl of Hon, 1988; Commemorative Gold Medal of Hon, 1988; Man of the Yr, 1990; Res Advr of the Yr, 1990; Personality of the Yr, 1991, ABI; World Decoration of Excellence, Raleigh, 1989; Dipl of Authority, 1989; Silver Medal, 1989; Insignia of Dedication, 1988; Gold Mdl for 1st 500, 1990; Intl Order of Merit, 1990; Intl Man of the Yr, 1991-92, IBC; The Bio Roll of Honor, 1989, HPA. *Hobby:* Music. *Address:* Dept of Maths, Faculty of Education, Gifu Univ, 1-1, Yanagido, Gifu City, GIFU Prefecture 501-11, Japan. 52, 139, 151, 152, 156, 178, 191, 192, 190.

HATCH David John, b. 11 Apr 1937, Hutton, Essex, England. Professor of Paediatric Anaesthesia. m. Rita Goulter, 4 June 1960, 2 s, 2 d. *Education:* MBBS London, 1961; MRCS LRCP, 1965; FFARCS, 1965; FCAnaes, 1988. *Appointments:* Fellow in Anesthesiol, Mayo Clinic, USA, 1968-69; Conslt, Anaes and Respiratory Measurement, Gt Ormond St Hosp for Sick Children, 1969-91. *Creative works:* Author: Neonatal Anaesthesia and Perioperative Care, 1986; Textbook of Paediatric Anaesthetic Practice, 1989; Over 60 scientific papers on paediatric anaesthesia, intensive care and respiratory measurement. *Memberships:* VP, Col of Anaes; Chm, Exam Com, 1988-90; Coun Mem, Assn of Anaes of GB and I, 1983-86; Hon Sec, Assn of Paed Anaes GB and I, 1979-84; Sub Dean, Inst of Child Health, 1974-83. *Hobbies:* Encouraging unity within the Christian Church; Sailing; Squash. *Address:* Institute of Child Health, 30 Guilford Street, London WC2N 1EH, England.

HATLEY Von Devin, b. 9 Jan 1959, Lake Charles, LA, USA. Operations Manager; Safety Engineer. 1 d. *Education:* BSBA, Univ of S.W LA, Lafayette, 1981; MBA, Loyola Univ of the South, LA, 1988. *Appointments:* Assembly Ops Mgr, Safety Dir, Intralox Inc, New Orleans, LA, 1984-; Safety Engr, STOP Inc, Bqaiq, Saudi Arabia, 1982-84; Prod Coor, Al George Inc, 1979-82. *Publications:* Ed, Newsletter, Crescent City Connection, 1989. *Memberships:* Am Safety Soc of Eng, 1987; APICS, 1984-; APICS Vp, Bd of Dirs, 1988-89. *Honours:* Dean's Hon Awd, Loyola Univ, New Orleans, 1988. *Hobbies:* Guitar; Piano; Hunting; Fishing; Basketball. *Address:* 927 Marengo, New Orleans, LA 70115, USA. 7.

HATZENBUEHLER Tony Ray, b. 24 Jan 1959, California, USA. Clinical Assistant; Pastor. m. Edwina Faith Taylor, 9 Aug 1978, 3 s. *Education:* BA Religion, CA Baptist Col, 1989. *Appointments:* Served in MSMC, 1977-85; Pastoral Intern, Grace Bap Ch, Riverside, CA, 1986-89; Youth Psychi Intensive Care Unit, Yellowstone Treatment Centre Billings, MT, 1990-. *Honours include:* Navy Achievement Medal and Marine Corps Expeditionary Ribbon. *Hobbies:* Back packing; Camping; Reading; Meeting the needs of youth and young adults. *Address:* 4121 Jansma Avenue, Billings, MT 59101, USA.

HAUGEN Paal-Helge, b. 26 Apr 1945, Valle, Setesdal, Norway. Author. m. Yngvil Molaúg, 28 Dec 1965, 1 d. *Education:* Med, Univ of Oslo, 1964-70; Film/Theatre studies, USA, 1970-72. *Appointments:* Dramaturg, Norway Broadcasting Corp/TV, Drama Dept, 1972-73; Prof, Col, Film/Lit, 1973-78; Freelance writer, 1978- . *Creative works:* 12 volumes of poetry; 1 novel, 3 children's books; collaborations with visual artists, opera libretti and oratorios, plays for the stage and TV; Translated into 20 languages. *Memberships:* Norwegian Authors Assn, Bd of Lit Advrs, Chm, 1982-85; Norway State Bd of Film Prod, Chm, 1980-85; Special Conslt to the Norwegian Cultural Coun (NCC), and the Norwegian Ministry of Culture. *Honours:* Dobloúg Lit Prize, 1968; Dobloúg Lit Prize, Swedish Acad, 1986; Richard Wilbur Prize for Poetry, USA, 1987; Norwegian Lit Critics Awd, 1990; The Norwegian Lit Awd (The BRAGE Awd), 1992. *Address:* J W Cappelen & Co Publishers, PO Box 350 Sentrum, N-0101, Oslo, Norway.

HAUPT Heinz Gerhard, b. 21 Mar 1943, Gottingen, Germany. Professor of Compemporary History. m. Heide Schimke, 28 May 1982, 1 s, 3 d. *Education:* Univs of Gottingen, Berlin and Inst d'Etudes Politiques, Paris; PhD, Berlin, 1971. *Appointments:* Asst, Berlin, 1972-74, Prof for W.Euro Soc Hist, Bremen; Visiting Prof, Univs of Paris, Lyon, Hautes Etudes en Sciences Sociales Paris; Prof, Euro Univ Inst, 1989-. *Creative works:* Nationalismus und Demokratie in Frankkreich der Restaurationszeit, 1974; Wirtschaft undd Gesellschaft in Frankreich seit, 1989, 1975; Die Pariser Kommune, 1978; Shopkeepers and Master Artisans in 19th Century Europe, 1984; Die Radikale Mitte (with G Crossick). Lebensweise und Politik von Handwerkern und Kleinhandlern in Deutschland, 1985; Sozialgeschichte Frankreichs seit, 1789, 1989. *Honours:* Prit de recherche Franco-allemand. *Address:* Via di Terzano 34, 50 012 Bagno a Ripoli, Italy.

HAUSMANN Albert Charles, b. 26 Jan 1932, Lakewood, Ohio, USA. Artist; Professor. m. Barbara Anne Bunge, 10 July 1955, 1 s, 2 d. *Education:* Kent State Univ, 1952; BA Capital Univ, 1955; MFA Bowling Green State Univ, 1967; Cmdr, US Navy, 1955-77. *Appointments:* Mgmt Trainee, Gen Fin Corp, 1958; Owner, Advert Conslt, Pensacola, 1958-60; Owner, Milo Bowling Lanes, Ohio, 1960-67; Art Prof, Univ Mississippi, 1967-69; Art Prof, Artist Univ N.Alabama, Florence, 1969-92; Prof Emeritus, 1992. *Creative works:* Advertising publications, TV production, radio commercial art, lifesize bronze sculptures, steel, stone, wood stained glass, painting, etching, engraving, relief, silk screen calligraphy, posters, set designer II plays at the Zodiac Theatre, Florence. *Memberships:* United Way, Pensacola, TV Chm, Florence Recreation Dept Coach, 1972-88; Alabama Reuinion - Mem Florence Beautification Bd, Chm, 1991; Friends of Florence Library - Publicity Chm, Shoals are Military Advy Coun, Sculptors Intl; Naval Res Assn; Ret Ofrs Assn; Rennaisance Faire; Phi Kappa Phi; Natchez Trace Genealogical Assn. *Honours include:* Artist for Alabama Music Hall of Fame, 1985-90; Artist for WC Handy Music Festival, 1982, 1983; Outstanding Achivievement Awd, Shoals Advt Fedn, 1986; Art Tchg Grant, at the Muscle Shoals Crippled children Centre, 1979; National Recognition for We are the Shoals, 1986. *Hobbies:* Sailboating; Tennis; Gardening; US Military affairs; Genealogy. *Address:* 126 Fairground Road, Florence, AL 35630, USA. 7.

HAVENGA COETZER Anna Aletta, b. Orange Free State, S Africa. Public Relations Executive. m. William Bedford Coetzee, 4 Sept 1979, dec 26 Sept 1989. *Education:* BA Hons, MA, DPhil, Univ of Pretoria; Dipl in Logotherapy, Vienna. *Creative works:* Various articles on logotherapy; Dissertations: Proofs for the Existence of God; The Anthrolopological concept in Logotherapy. *Memberships:* Hon Mem, Allgemeine Artzliches Gesellschaft fur Psychotherapie; Nat Bd of Adv, Am Bio Inst; Adv Coun, IBA; Viktor Frankl Foun of SA; Life, Am Med Soc of Vienna; Austrian Soc of Existentral Analysis of Logothreapy. *Hobbies include:* Philosophy; Logotherapy; Spy novels; Sculpture; Painting; Wildlife. *Address:* PO Box 65577, Benmore 2010, S. Africa.

HAW David William Martin, b. 17 Mar 1926, Batticoloa, Ceylon. Orthopaedic Surgeon (Retired). m. Marorie Elise Hetherington, 27 Mar 1948. 2 s, 3 d. *Education:* BSc Anat, 1948, MBChB 1951, FRCS, 1960, Leeds Univ Med Sch. *Appointments:* Hse Phys, 1951-52; RAF 1952-55; Demonstrator in Anat, Leeds Univ, 1955-56; Hse Surgeon, Leeds Gen Infirmary, 1956-57; SHO, Manchester Royal Infirmary, 1957-58; Registrar Surgeon, Ashton Under Lyne, 1958-59; SHO, Royal Nat Orthopaedic Hosp, 1959-60; Registrar, Lord Mayor Treloar Orthopaedic Hosp, 1960-61; Registrar, Guys Hosp, 1961-63; Sr Registrar, Leeds Regional Hosp Bd, 1963-65; Conslt Orthopaedic Surgeon, York Dist, 1965-91. *Memberships:* FRCS England; FBOA; Pres, Holdsworth Orthopaedic Travelling Club, 1989-91; Pres, Northern Veterans Athletic Club, 1975-77. *Honours include:* Represented England in 3 miles, 1947; Northern Counties 3 mile Champion, 1947; Suffolk Cross country Champion, 1954- 55. *Hobbies:* Athletics; Painting; Botany; Gardening; Hill Walking; Carving. *Address:* East Court, Shipton by Beningbrough, York YO6 1AR, England.

HAWK Robert Wayne, b. 13 Jan 1954, Collingswood, New Jersey, USA. Pastor. m. Debra Ann Toth, 21 Aug 1976, 3 d. *Education:* MDiv, Denver Seminary; BABL, N.Eastern Bible Col, NJ. *Appointments:* Pastor, Lynnfield St Bapt Ch, MA, 1985-; Youth Pastor, Bethel Bapt Ch, Denver, CO, 1981-85; Asst Pastor, Bapt Temple Ch, 1976-80, MA. *Memberships:* Evangelical Assn of Greater Lynn; Conservative Bapt Assns of Am, MA and Rhode Island. *Hobbies:* Vocal Music; Volleyball; Reading. *Address:* 1 Den Quarry Rd, Lynn, MA 01904, USA.

HAWKE Gary Richard, b. 1 Aug 1942, Napier, New Zealand. University Professor. m. Helena Joyce Pourie, 21 Aug 1965, 2 s. *Education:* BA Hons, BCom, Victoria Univ of Wellington, 1961-64; DPhil, Oxford Univ, 1965-68. *Appointments:* Lectr 1968-70, Reader, 1971-73, Prof, 1974-, Econ Hist, Dir, Inst of Policy Studies, 1987- , Victoria Univ of Wellington. *Creative works:* Railways and Economic Growth in England and Wales, 1970; Between Governments and Banks, 1973; Economics for Historians, 1980; The making of New Zealand, 1985. *Memberships:* NZ Planning Coun, 1985-91, Chm, 1986-91. *Honours:* Visiting Fellow: Stanford Univ, All Souls Col, Oxford, Australian Nat Univ; Lavney Lectr, UK Econ Hist Soc, 1978. *Hobbies:* Music; Reading; Armchair criticism. *Address:* Institute of Policy Studies, Victoria University of Wellington, PO Box 600, Wellington, New Zealand.

HAWKESWORTH John Stanley, b. 7 Dec 1920, London, England. Film and TV Writer and Producer; Painter. m. Hyacinthe Nairne M Gregson-Ellis, 10 Apr 1943, 1 s. *Education:* Rugby Sch; BA, Oxford Univ. *Appointments:* Grenadier Guards Ofr, 1941-46; Film industry, Art Dept and Designer, 1946-54; Film and TV Producer and Writer, 1955-; Painter. *Creative works:* Films: TV series: Producer writer: Tiger Bay; Upstairs Downstairs; Duchess of Duke Street; Danger UXB; The Flame Trees of Thika; The Tales of Beatrix Potter; Mrs 'Arris Goes To Paris, 1992; Painting exhibitions in 1989, 1991; Author of two novels. *Memberships:* BAFTA Writers Guild of GB. *Honours:* 3 BAFTA Awds, 1971, 1973; 2 Emmy Awds, USA, 1974, 1975; Peabody Awd,

Univ of Georgia, 1977; 2 Writers Guild of GB Awds, 1967-74; Critics Circle, USA, 1976, 1977. *Hobbies:* Painting; Gardening; Hunting; Tennis. *Address:* Fishponds House, Knossington, Oakham, Leics LE15 8LX, England.

HAWKSEY Brian, b. 22 Aug 1932, Manchester, England. Management Consultant. m. Patricia Anne Maginnis, 19 June 1965. *Education:* Douai Sch, Woolhampton, 1945-51. *Appointments:* Materials Mgr, Smiths Indust Ltd, 1973-77; Dep Dir of Training, Purchasing Economics Ltd, 1977-79; Partner, Brian Hawksey & Assocs, 1979-80; Mgr, Corp Ed and Training, Thorn EMI Plc, 1981-86; Purchasing & Materials Mgmt Sers, Dir, 1986-. *Memberships:* Fellow, Charter Inst of Purchasing and Supply, Nat Coun, 1975-87, 1988-91; MIMgt; Assoc Fellow, Singapore Inst of Purchasing and Materials Mgt. *Honours:* Meritorious Ser Awd, Inst of Purchasing and Supply. *Hobbies:* Music; Photography. *Address:* Tall Trees, Egypt Lane, Farnham Common, Bucks SL2 3LD, England.

HAWORTH Lionel, b. 4 Aug 1912, Edenburg, S Africa. Retired Formery Director of Design, Rolls Royce. m. Joan Irene Bradbury, 1 Dec 1956, 1 s, 1 d. *Education:* BSc Eng, Dist, Univ of Cape Town, 1933. *Appointments:* Apprentice, Assoc Equipment Co 1934; Rolls Royce Ltd: Designer, 1936, Asst Chief Designer, 1945, Dept Chief Designer, 1951, Chief Designer, civil engines, 1954, Chief Engr, turboprops, 1958; Bristol Siddeley Engines Ltd: Chief Design Conslt, 1963, Chief Designer, 1964, Dir of Design Aero Div Rolls Royce Ltd, 1966-77; Fdr and Sr partner, Lionel Haworth and Assocs, 1977. *Memberships:* FRS, 1971; Fdr Fellow, Fellowship of Engrg, FEng, 1976; GIMechE, 1936; FIMechE, 1954; FRAeS, 1959. *Honours:* OBE 1958; Bronze medal of RAeS, 1962; Brit Gold Medal for Aeronautics, 1971; Mem of the Royal Inst, 1972. *Hobbies:* Sailing; Walking; Gardening; Travel. *Address:* 10 Hazelwood Road, Sneyd Park, Bristol BS9 1PX, England. 1, 34.

HAY Andrew M, b. Apr 1928, London England. *Education:* MEcon, St John's Col, Cambs, 1950. *Appointments include:* VP Mktg, 54, VP & Treas, 1960, Pres and CEO, 1962, Calvert Vavasseur & Co Inc (CVC), NY; Merged CVC with Guiness Peat Gp, 1978-81; Non Exec Chm, Barretto Peat Inc, 1974-88; Consultancies in Intl trade, 1981-; Exec Sec, Portland Chapter, Am Assn of Exporters and Importers, 1982-; Exec Dir, Pacific Northwest Intl Trade Assn, 1986-91; HM Honorary Consul, Portland, Oregon, 1987-; Dean, Oregon Consular Corps, 1991. *Creative works:* Author of A Century of Coconuts; Appeared on over 125 radio and TV programmes in the USA, and has produced an educational film. *Memberships:* Pres, BACC, 1966-68; Pres, Philippine Am Chamber of Commerce, 1977-79, presently, Hon Dir; Pres, Am Assn of Exporters and Importers, 1977-79; NAS Com, 1979-81; Dir, Episcopal Bishop of Oregon Foun, 1985; Police Internal Investigations Auditing Com, Chm Appeals Sub-Com, 1984-86; Treas and Trustee, World Affairs Coun of Oregon, 1985-87. *Honours:* Trustee, Winston Churchill Foun of US; Dir, St Georges and St Andrews Socs of NYC; CBE, 1968. *Address:* 3515 S W Council Crest Drive, Portland, OR 97201, USA. 132.

HAY David William, b. 18 Aug 1905, Capetown, South Africa. Presbyterian Minister; Prof of Theology. m. Christina Crawford Reid, 26 July 1936, 1 s, 1 d. *Education:* MA hons Phil, 1929, Edin Univ; Dipl, New Col, Edin, 1929-32; Predigerseminar, Wupperthal, Germany, 1932-33. *Appointments:* Minister of St Margarets Ch of Scotland, 1933-39; Royal Army Chaplains Dept, UK and Italy; Prof of Syst Theol, Knox Col, Toronto, 1944-76; Server two parishes, 1976-83. *Creative works:* Articles in theological journals; Chm, Editorial Com, Canadian Jour of Theol, 1950-62; Lectr and Preacher widely. *Memberships:* Faith and Order Comm of WCC; Sec, N.Am Comm on Tradition; Pres, Can Coun of Chs; Moderator, Pres, Ch in Canada, 1976. *Honours:* Ferguson Scholar in Phil of the fours Scottish

Univs, 1929; Hon DD by 5 Canadian Univs and Cols viz: Queens Kingston; Trinity Toronto; Kings Halifax; St Michaels, Toronto; Knox, Toronto. *Hobbies:* Country cottage; Fishing; Golf. *Address:* Knox College, 59 St George Street, Toronto, Ontario, Canada M5S 2E6. 88.

HAY George Austin, b. 25 Dec 1915, Johnstown, Pennsylvania, USA. Film Actor; Director; Producer; Musician; Artist. *Education:* BS 1938, MLitt, 1948, Univ of Pitts; Postgrad, Univ of Rochester, 1939; MA, Columbia Univ, 1948. *Appointments include:* Producer, Dir, Off-Broadway Productions, 1946-50; PR Promotion Coor, Metropolitan Gp Advg, 1950-53; Motion picture casting Dir, US Govt Dept of Defence, 1955-70; Motion picture Producer and Dir, US Dept of Transportation, 1973-. *Creative works include:* Musical compositions, solo Pianist, concerts and recitals; Author and illustrator; Film appearances include: Pretty Boy Floyd; The Landlord; Chekov's The Bet; Being There; Child's Play; No Way out; Her Alibi; Network TV appearances include: Westinghouse Presents; As the World Turns; Another World; Adam's Chronicle; Edge of Night. Stage Appearances: Inherit The Wind, Broadway 2 yrs; What Every Woman Knows (J M Barrie); Originator, World Painting film, Museum of Modern Art; Dir, Documentary, Highways of Hstory; Painting and sculpture exhibitions in various galleries and permanent collections. *Memberships include:* NATAS; Arts Dir, English Speaking Union; Music Library Assn; Intl Bach Soc; Beethoven Soc; Am Arch Foun; Columbia Univ Club; Nat Press Club; The Players, Nat Naval Med Command; Bd of Govs and Trustee, Arts Club of Washington; Bd of Dirs, Victorian Soc; Bd, Washington Film Coun; NSAL. *Honours include:* Gold medal, Accademia Italia, 1980; Pictorial Awd, Smithsonian Inst, 1982; Fed Govt Hon Awd, 1990; Pres's Coun, Col of William and Mary; Book of Memorabilia, Austin Hay: Careers of a Christmas Child, catalogued NY Public Library. *Address:* 2022 Columbia Rd NW, Washington DC 20009, USA. 2, 6, 37, 52.

HAY Hamish Grenfell Sir, b. 8 Dec 1927, Christchurch, New Zealand. Former May or of Christchurch; Company Director. m. Judith Leicester Gill, 14 May 1955, 1 s, 4 d. *Education:* St Andrew Col, 1940-44; BCom, FCA, Univ of Canterbury, 1944-49. *Appointments:* Hays Ltd, later Haywrights Ltd, 1947-54, Sec, 1954-62; Dep MD, 1962-74; Mayor of Christchurch, 1974-89, longest serving Mayor; Chmn, Museum of New Zealand, 1992-. *Creative works:* Hay Days, 1989. *Memberships:* NZ Soc of Accts, Chm of Canterbury Branch, 1959; Christchurch City Coun, 1959-74; Lyttleton Harbour BD, 1983-89; Canterbury Univ Council, 1974-89; Queen Elizabeth II Arts Coun, 1975-78; Canterbury Museum Trust Bd, Chm, 1983-86; Christchurch Town Hall Bd, Chm, 1968-92. *Honours:* Knight Bachelor, 1982; Order of the Rising Sun, 1990; Queens Jubilee Medal, 1977; NZ 1990 Medal. *Hobbies:* Attending concerts; Gardening. *Address:* 70 Heaton Street, Merivale, Christchurch, New Zealand. 1, 38, 157, 69.

HAY Jocelyn, b. 30 July 1927, Neath, Wales. m. 26 Aug 1950, 2 d. *Education:* BA, Open Univ, 1982. *Appointments:* Writer and Broadcaster, 1953-; Hd of Press and PR, Girl Guides Assn, London, 1973-78; Principal, London Media Workshops, 1978-. *Memberships:* FIRP and former Cttee Mbr Soc of Authors; FRSA; Soc of Women Writers and Journalists; Chm, Voice of the Listener and Viewer. *Address:* Voice of the Listener and Viewer, 101 Kings Drive, Gravesend, Kent DA12 5BQ, England.

HAYAISHI Osamu, b. 8 Jan 1920, Stockton, California, USA. Director, Osaka Bioscience Institute. m. Takiko, 1 d. *Education:* MS 1942, PhD, 1949, Osaka Univ. *Appointments:* Asst Prof, Washington Univ Sch of Med, 1952-54; Chief, Toxicol, NIH, 1954-58; Prof, Dept of Med Chem, 1958-83, Prof Emeritus, 1983-, Kyoto Univ; Pres, 1983-89, Prof Emeritus, 1989- , Osaka Med Col; Dir, Osaka Bioscience Inst, 1987. *Creative works:* Edit, Oxygenase, 1962; Edit, Meolcular Mechanism of

Oxygen Activatioj, 1974; Co-edit, ADP ribosylation Reactions, 1981. *Memberships:* NAS, USA; Am Soc of Biol Chems; The Japan Acad; Deutsche Acad der Naturforscher Leopoldina; Hon MD, Karolinska Institutet, Sweden. *Honours include: ssa* 00Awd, Japan Acad, 1967; The Order of Culture, 1972; Ciba Foun Gold Medal, 1976; Jimenez Diaz Mem Awd, Spain, 1979; Wolf Foun Prize in Med, Israel, 1986; Gold Medal, Chez Acad of Scis, 1988; Laurea Hon Causa, Univ de Padova, Italy, 1988; Special Achievement Awd, Miami Bio/Tech Winter Symp, 1989; Intl Hon Citizen of New Orleans, 1990; Disting visitor Awds, Univ of New Orleans, USA; Kotake Memorial Award in Tryptophan Research. *Hobbies:* Golf; Music. *Address:* Osaka Bioscience Institute, 6-2-4 Furuedai Suita, Osaka 565, Japan. 34.

HAYAMI Yujiro, b. 26 Nov 1932, Tokyo, Japan. m. 11 May 1962, 1 s, 2 d. *Education:* BA Univ of Tokyo, 1956; PhD, Iowa State Univ, 1960. *Appointments:* Res Assoc, Nat Res Inst of Agric Econs, 1956-66; Prof: Tokyo Metropolitan Univ, 1966-67, Aoyama-Gakuin Univ, 1976-. *Creative works:* Agricultural Development: An International Perspective, 1971, 1985; Japanese Agriculture under Siege, 1988. *Memberships:* Agric Econs Soc of Japan; Am Agric Econs Assn, AAEA; Intl Assn of Agric Econs. *Honours:* Disting Res Awd, AES of Japan, 1969; Outstanding published research worker, AAEA, 1971; Best Journal article Awd, AAEA, 1976, 1978; Fellow, AAEA, 1987. *Hobby:* Tennis. *Address:* 6-8-14 Okusawa, Setagaya, Tokyo 158, Japan.

HAYASHI Mitsuhiko, b. 3 Sept 1930, Okazaki, Japan. m. Etsuko Ito, 18 Oct 1964, 2 d. *Education:* BS 1958, MS 1960, Nagoya Univ; PhD, Tokyo Inst Tech, 1971. *Appointments:* Res Assoc, 1960-70, Asst Prof, 1970-75, Assoc Prof, 1975-76, Nagoya Univ; Prof, Toyama Med & Pharm Univ, 1976-. *Creative works:* Author: Introductory Physics, 1966; Ultrafine particles, 1984; Invited and contributed articles to professional journals, 1960-. *Memberships:* Phys Soc of Japan; Crystallographic Soc of Japan; Biophys Soc of Japan; Surface Sci Soc of Japan. *Hobbies:* Concerts; Art museums. *Address:* 3-103, 2556-4, Gofuku Suehirocho, Toyama 930, Japan. 52.

HAYCRAFT John, b. 11 Dec 1926, Consultant, International House; Writer. m. Brita Langenfelt, 17 Oct 1953, 2 s, 1 d. *Education:* Wellington Col; Jesus Col, Oxford (Open Exhib); MA, ESU Fellowship Yale Univ. *Appointments:* Fdr: Academia Britanica Cordoba, Spain, 1953-58; Intl Hse, London, 1959-90, Paris, 1971-72, Rome, 1967; Affiliation of 92 schools world-wide to International House, 1963-90; Dir, Soros Eng Lang Prog, 1991-. *Creative works:* Babel in Spain, 1958; Getting on in English, 1964; Babel in London, 1965; Choosing your English 1972; Introduction to English Language Teaching, 1978; Italian Labyrinth, 1985; Search for the French Revolution, 1989. *Memberships:* Brit Coun, ETAC, 1974-80; Arels Coun, 1975-82. *Honours:* CBE, 1982. *Hobbies:* Films; History; Tennis; Travel; Swimming; Chess. *Address:* 79 Lee Road, London SE3 9EN, England. 1.

HAYES K William, b. 11 Mar 1943, Holyoko, Massachusetts, USA. Educator; Historian. m. Phyllis Marie Bichard, 1 Aug 1964, div Sept 1989. 1 s. 1 d. *Education:* US Military Acad, 1962-63; BA 1964, MA 1971, St Mary's Univ, San Antonio, TX. *Appointments:* Commd 2nd Lt US Army, 1964, advanced through grades to Lt Col, 1980; Ofr HQ 2nd Armoured Div, Ft Hood, TX, 1964-66; HQ 4th Army, Ft Sam, Houston, 1966; Prin Antonian Hg Sch, San Antonio, 1966-69; Prof Tex Mil Inst, San Antonio, 1969-76; Instr, San Antonio Col, 1971-78; with ops/investigations US Army, Ft Sam, Houston, 1976-79; Sales Franklin Watts Pub Co NYC, 1979-80; Educator, Leesburgh HS, FL, 1980-; Cons, Social Stuies, The Col Bd, TX, 1973-76; Advr, Lake Co Sheriff's Dept, FL, 1980-. *Contribution to: ssa* 00articles to professional journals; research on capital punishment. *Memberships:* Orgn Am Hists; FL Hist Soc; Reserve Ofr Assn; Optimist Club, Bd of Dirs,

1976-79; Lions. *Honours:* Teacher of the Yr, Valley Forge Freedoms Foun, 1970; Ednl Res Awd, Nat Endowment for the Humanities, 1976. *Hobbies:* Stamps; Guns; Historical research. *Address:* PO Box 492257, Leesburg, FL 34749, USA. 7.

HAYLEY Thomas Theodore Steiger, b. 4 Oct 1913, Colombo, Sri Lanka. Psychoanalyst. m. Audrey Cantlie, 7 Sept 1946, 3 s, 2 d. *Education:* MA Peterhouse Col, Cambs, 1933-36; 1st class Hon Deg, Soc Anthropol, 1936; Peterhouse Scholar and Prize, 1936; MA Hons Exeter Col, Oxford, 1937-38; PhD London Sch of Econ, London Univ. *Appointments:* Indian Civil Serv, 1938-50; Sec to Govt of Assam in Depts: under the Prime Minister, 1947-50; Brit Branch Inter Chamber of Commerce, Asst Dir, 1951; Physhoanalyst, 1955-. *Creative works:* Anatomy of Lango Religions and Groups, 1947; Ritual Pollution and Social Structure in Hindu Assam, 1963. *Memberships:* Brit Psycho-Analytical Soc, VP, Chm of Coun; Inst of Psycho-Analysis, Chm, Bd of Dirs; Edit, Intl Jour of Psycho-Analysis, 1978; Edit, Intl Review of Psycho-Analysis, 1978-. *Hobbies:* Farming; Gardening; DIY; Photography. *Address:* Old East Haxted, Edenbridge, Kent TN8 6PT, England.

HAYNES Edith M., b. 23 Jan 1934, Marshfield, Missouri, USA. Colleg Administrator. div. 1 s, 3 d. *Education:* Dr of Chiropractic, Cleveland Chiropractic Col (CCC) of Missouri. *Appointments:* Purchasing Agent, Missouri; Receptionist/Sec, CCC, Missouri, during education: Transferred to CCC, Los Angeles, 1977, working as Receptionist, Gen Ofc, Dir of Admissions, Dir of Postgrad Ed, Dir of Devel/Alumni Affairs, and Admin Asst to the Pres. *Memberships:* Intl, Am, and California Chiropractors Assns; Nat Assn of Fund Raising Execs; Nat Notary Assn; Sigma Chi Psi; Delta Tau Alpha; APHA. *Hobbies:* Reading; Meeting people. *Address:* Cleveland Chiropractic College, Los Angeles, CA 90004, USA.

HAYNES John Lenneis, b. 25 Mar 1934, Washington DC, USA. m. Technology Consultant. m. Alice Marie Sandi, 11 Sept 1955, 1 s, 2 d. *Education:* BEEng, Cornell, 1956; MEEng, Stanford, 1953. *Appointments:* Stanford Res Inst, 1956-61; Data Tech Corp, 1962; Pacific Commun & Elec, 1962-64; Becton Dickinson & Co, 1965-1992; The O'Donnell Group, 1993-. *Creative works:* Worlds first whole blood platelet Analyzer; 12 articles; 15 US patents, 40 worldwide. *Memberships:* Sr mem: IEE, Am Assn Med Instrumentation, Instrument Soc of Am; Pres, Focus Photographic Soc; Pres, Oaks Assn. *Honours:* Grant Awd in Circuit Design, EEE, 1960; 1st Prize, Fueltes Mem Stage, 1956; John R McMullen Scholar, 1955. *Hobbies:* Photography; Woodworking; Computers. *Address:* 20 Kendall Drive, CHapel Hill, NC 27514, USA.

HAYNES Teresa Wathenia, b. 2 Nov 1953, Kentucky, USA. Assistant Professor of Computer Science. m. Ben Buckner, 16 Apr 1990. *Education:* BS 1975, MA 1978, MS 1984, Maths, E.Kentucky Univ; PhD Comp Sci, Univ of Ctrl Florida. *Appointments:* Engr, Mgr, S.Central Bell, 1978-81; Instr of Comp Sci, Pikeville Col, KY, 1981-83; Asst Prof, PCC, KY, 1983-85; Asst Prof of Comp Sci, E.Tennessee State Univ, 1988-. *Creative works:* Extremal 2-2-insensitive Graphs, 1989; Same Remarks on k-insensitive graphs in Network design, 1990; The g-network and its inherent fault tolerant properties, 1990. *Memberships:* IEEE; ACM; Tennessee Acad of Sci; Kappa Mu Episilon. *Honours:* KY Tomorrow Com, 1980; Phia Kappa Phi. *Hobbies:* Running; Body building; Reading. *Address:* Dept of Computer Science, E. Tennessee State University, Johnson City, TN 37614, USA. 152.

HAYWOOD Richard Mowbray, b. 28 Apr 1933, Baltimore, Maryland, USA. Associate Professor of History. m. Piroska Molnar, 6 Sept 1965, 2 s. *Education:* BA, NY Univ, 1954; MA New Col, Oxford, 1956; PhD, Columbia Univ, 1966. *Appointments:* Asst, Assoc Prof,

E.Michigan Univ, 1965-69; Assoc Prof of Hist, Purdue Univ, 1969-. *Creative works:* The Beginnings of Railway Development in Russia in the Reign of Nicholas I, 1835-1842, 1969; The Development of Steamboats on the Volga River and its tributaries 1817-1856, 1981. *Membership:* Am Assn of Advancement of Slavic Studies. *Honours:* Nat Endowment for the Humanities Fellowship, 1969; Fulbright-Hays Fac Res Abroad Prog Grant, 1983; IREX Sr Scholar Fellowship, 1983; IREX Short-term Res Fellowship, 1990. *Hobbies:* Railways and train spotting; Baseball; Soccer. *Address:* Dept of History, Purdue University, W.Lafayette, IN 47907, USA. 3, 30.

HAZEWINKEL Michiel, b. 22 June 1943, Amsterdam. Professor of Mathematics. *Education:* PhD, Maths, Univ of Amsterdam, 1969. *Appointments:* Scist, Univ of Amsterdam, 1965-70; Lectr, 1970-72, Prof, 1972-82, Erasmus Univ, Rotterdam; Prof, & Hd of Dept, CWI Amsterdam, 1982-. *Creative works:* Over 100 published scientific articles; Books include Enclopaedia of Mathematics, Vols 2-7, 1988-91. *Memberships include:* Wiskundig Genootschap, Coun, 1974-78; London, France, Japan and Am Maths Socs; Unione Mat Italiana; SIAM; MAA; Deutsche Math Ver; NYAS; IEEE; Nederlandse Vereniging voor Natuurkunde; APS; EPS; IAMP; Inst of Maths Stats; Chm, Dept of Maths, Econometric Inst, Earsmus Univ, Rotterdam, 1972-84; Chm, Dept of Pure Maths, CWI, 1982-; Holland mem, European Math Soc Database Com, 1985-88. *Hobbies:* Tennis; Squash; Hockey; Golf; Literature; Travel; Hiking. *Address:* CWI, PO Box 4079, 1009 AB Amsterdam, The Netherlands. 52.

HE Daren, b. 20 Oct 1932, Xaimen, China. b. 20 Oct 1932. Professor. m. Sufei Jian, 1 Jan 1955, 1 s, 1 d. *Education:* BSc, Oceanography, Xiamen Univ, 1952; Advanced Studies, Dept of Biol, Leningrad Univ. *Appointments:* Trainee, Fishery Bureau of Fijian Province, 1947- 53; Asst Lectr, Dept of Biol, 1953-69, Lectr, Assoc Prof, Prof, Dept of Oceanography, 1970-, Xiamen Univ. *Creative works include:* Translation: Fish Physiology, 1959; Fish Behaviour 1984; Selected works on the phototactic physiology of fish and marine animals; Published more than 50 papers including: The Feeding intensity and its dynamics of juvenile mullet under different illumination; A study of the optomotor reaction of some young fish; Histological study of the retina of grey Mullet; Chief Edit, Basic Philatelics Textbook. *Memberships:* Chinese Icthyological Soc; Chinese Physiol Soc; Chinese Oceanographycal and Limnological Soc; Chinese Fishery Soc and Chinese Philatelic Soc; Pres, Philatelic Soc of Xiamen Univ. *Honours:* Nat Sci Conf of China prize, 1978. *Hobbies:* Philately, collecting for over 40 years, Chinese, Russian, Singaporean and fish stamps of the world. *Address:* Department of Oceanography, Xiamen University, Xiamen 361005, China.

HE Qingzhong, b. 1 Oct 1938, China. Director of Pulmonary & Critical Care Medicine. *Education:* Med Coll, Tong Ji, 1956-1961. *Appointments:* Pediatrician, 1961-1978; Pediatric attending physician, Lectr, 1978-1985; Assoc Prof, 1985-1992; Guilin Med Coll, Affiliated Hosp; Vstng Prof, Case Western Reserve Univ, Cleveland, Ohio, USA, 1986-1987. *Creative Works:* 15 Acad Theses on Critical Care Med & Pediatrics in various domestic Med Publs; Set up first ICU in Guangxi Province, being first man tointroduce Critical Care Med to the Province.

HE Wenchen, b. 1 July 1940, Hunan Province, China. Professor of Physical Chemistry. m. Li Xianlian, 7 Feb 1969, 1 d. *Education:* BSc Phys Dept, Shandong Univ, 1961. *Appointments:* Asst Prof, Beijing Poly Univ, 1961-73; Lectr 1977, Prof, 1986-, Hebei Chem Engrg Inst, Shikiathuang, China, 1973-. *Creative works:* Advances in the theory of Benzenoid Hydrocarbons, 1990; 40 papers published in professional journals and magazines. *Memberships:* Intl Soc for Math Chem; Coun of Hebei branch of Chinese Phys Soc. *Honours:*

Outstanding Scientific Achievement awd, Chinese Sci and Tech Comm, 1986. *Hobbies:* Swimming; Playing chess. *Address:* Hebei Chemical Engineering Instute, Shijiazhuang, China. 139, 152.

HE Wenjie, b. 22 Jan 1942, Fuzhou, China. Professor, Hebei Academy of Sciences. m. Liu Xiren, 25 July 1942, 2 d. *Education:* Grad, Math Dept, Qufu Normal Univ, China, 1960-64. *Appointments:* Tchr, Middle Sch, 1964-74; Tchr, Shijiazhuang Fin and Commerce Col, 1974-78; Prof, Hebei Acad of Sci, 1978-91. *Creative works:* Published over 30 papers on mathematical chemistry; Co-author of book: Advances in the theory of Benzenoid Hydrocarbons, 1990. *Memberships:* Intl Soc fo Maths Chem; Pres, Op Res, Hebei Province; Guest Prof, Hebei Tchr's Col. *Honours:* First Prize, Sci and Tech Achievement, Hebei Province, 1986; Outstanding Scist, Hebei Province, 1987. *Hobbies:* Smoking; Playing chess. *Address:* The Applied Mathematics Institute, Hebei Academy of Sciences, Shijiazhuang City, China. 152.

HE Wenwan, b. 26 Jan 1943, Hangzhou, China. Engineer. m. 1 Feb 1976, 1 d. *Education:* Grad, Shinghai Postal Telecom Col, 1963. *Appointments:* Asst Engr, 1963-78; Engr, 1978-82; Dir, Engr, 1982-83; Vice-Chief engineer 1983-; Sr Engr, 1987. *Creative works:* Design and research and made ST-1 model 1024 line telex exchange system, 1979-82. ST-2 model 16000 line low speed data and telex exchange 1983-88. *Memberships:* Dir of Communication's, Inst of China. *Honours:* Model Worker, Shanghai Muncipal Govt, 1983; First Class Prize, Sci and Tech Progress, Shanghai Municipal Govt, 1990; Second and Third Class Prizes, Sci and Tech Progress, Chinese Govt, 1985, 1990. *Hobbies:* Drawing pictures; Playing the Claranet. *Address:* Shanghai Long-Dis Telecomm Office, 333 Wusheng Road, Shanghai, China.

HE Xilin, b. 20 Aug 1924, Jiangxi Province, China. m. 10 Sept 1957, 1 s, 1 d. *Education:* Dipl, Geol Dept, Beijing Univ, 1948-52; PhD, 1986. *Appointments:* Tchr, Geol Dept, China Univ of Mining and Tech, 1952-79; Assoc Prof 1979, Prof, 1983, Stratigraphy & Paleontol. *Creative works:* Published more than 45 papers internationally; Books: A Textbook of general Paleontology; Research on the Late Paleonzoic Coal-bearing Stratigraphy and Biota in Jungar, Nei Mengol. *Memberships:* Geol Soc of China; Paleontol Soc of China; Prof Common Stratigraphy and Paleontol. *Honours:* Sci and Tech Progress Prizes, 1983, 1985, 1988. *Hobbies:* Swimming; Hunting. *Address:* Geologic Department, China University of Mining and Technology, Xuzhou City 221008, China.

HE Xiyuan, b. 27 Nov 1937, Beijing, China. Editor. m. Wu Vanzhen, 29 Sept 1962, 2 d. *Education:* Plant Protection Dept, Hebei Agric Univ, Boading, 1961-65. *Appointments:* Ed, Tchr, Hebei Agric Univ, 1961; Lectr, 1983; Assoc Prof, Chief Ed, 1987, Prof, Ed, 1990, Boading, Hebei. *Creative works:* Books include: The Pest of the Chinese Chestnut, 1985; Courtyard Strawberry, 1990; Practical Chinese English Dictionary of Economy, 1990; An outline of Journal of Editing, 1991; Agricultural Science Writing, 1991; Economy co-operation of Enterprises, 1990. *Memberships include:* Dir, Standing Jour Res Com of Natural Sci Cols and Univs of China; Chief Dir, Jour Res Com of Nat Agric Univs; Pres, Press Assn of Sci and Tech, Hebei Province; Chief Dir, Jour Res Com of Cols and Univs. *Honours:* Sci and Tech Progress Prizes, 1985, 1986; First Class prizes for Excellence in Journal Editing, 1989, 1990, 1991; Prize of Excellence as Editor of Natural Sci Jour of Nat Univs, 1989. *Hobbies:* Literature; Opera; Music; Photography. *Address:* Journal of Hebei Agricultural University, Baoding 071001, China.

HEALE Michael John, b. 29 Jan 1941, Paignton, Devon, England. University Teacher. m. Lesley Cooper, 4 July 1981. *Education:* BA, Univ of Manchester, 1962; DPhil, Oxford Univ, 1962-65. *Appointments:* Lectr, 1965-78, Sr Lectr, 1978-86, Rdr, 1986-92, Prof, 1992-, Lancaster

Univ. *Creative works:* The Making of American Politics, 1977; The Presidential Quest, 1982; The American Revolution, 1986; American Anticommunism, 1992. *Memberships:* Brit Assn for Am Studies, Exec Com, 1980-; Ed, Jour of Am Studies, 1992-. *Honours:* Rockefeller Fellowship, Colombia Univ, 1963-64; Am Coun of Learned Socs Fellowships: Rutgers Univ, 1972-73, Univ of Maryland, 1982-83; Visiting Scholar, Warren Centre, Harvard Univ, 1978-79. *Hobbies:* Eating; Drinking; Reading; Watching. *Address:* 41 Meadowside, Lancaster LA1 3AQ, England.

HEALEY Norman John b. 2 Sept 1940, England. Osteopathic Physician. m. Maureen Anne Brock, 24 June 1978, 3 d. *Education:* Epsom Col, 1953-58; Guy's Hosp, 1959-65; Univ of London, MRCS, LRCP, DA DRCOG, FLCOM, MRO. *Appointments:* Surgeon Lt, Royal Navy, 1966-71; HMS Albion service in the Far East, 1968-69; Full-time Private practice as Osteopathic Phys and specialist in musculo-skeletal medicine, 1975-. *Memberships:* Fellow, London Col of Osteopathic Med; FRSM; Brit Osteopathic Assn, ex Hon Sec; Brit soc Rheumatology; Brit Assn Manipulative Med; Hon Conslt, St Luke's Hosp, London. *Honour:* Kitchener Scholarship, 1959. *Hobbies:* Gardening; Country Walks and Swimming; Cricket and Rugby Football. *Address:* 37 Devonshire Place, London W1N 1PE, England.

HEAP Desmond, b. 17 Sept 1907, Burnley, Lancs, England. Solicitor; Consultant. m. Adelene Mai Lacey, 27 Oct 1945, 1 s, 2 d. *Education:* LLB, 1929, LLM, 1937, Hon LLD, 1973, Univ of Manchester. *Appointments:* Dep Town Clerk, Leeds, 1940-47 Comptroller and City Solicitor, Corp of London, 1947-73. *Creative works:* An Outline of Planning Law, (10th ed), 1991; Encyclopaedia of Planning Law and Practice, 1948-91. *Memberships:* Pres, The Law Soc; Pres, Royal Town Planning Inst; Assoc Royal Inst of Chartered Surveyors; Hon Mem, Inc Soc of Auctioneers and Valuers; Hon Assoc, City of London Solicitors Co. *Honours:* Gold Medal, RTPI, 1983; Gold Medal and Awd, Lincoln Inst of Land Policy, 1983; Hon Mem, Am Bar Foun; Hon Life Mem, Intl Bar Assn; Hon Life Pres, Section in Gen Practice, Intl Bar Assn. *Hobbies:* Opera; Ballet; Theatre; Writing; Reading; Swimming; Tennis; Pedal biking; Walking. *Address:* c/o Sweet & Maxwell Ltd, South Quay Plaza, 183 Marsh Wall, London E14 9FT, England. 1.

HEAPS Porter Warrington, b. 27 May 1906, Chicago, USA. Musician. m. Dorothy Hill, 22 July 1930, 2 d. *Education:* BM, 1927, BA, 1928, MA, 1931, Northwestern Univ, Evanston, IL. *Appointments:* Organist, and Univ of Chicago, and Sholem Temple, 1928-32; Organist and Choir Dir: First Methodist, Evanston, 1928-32, New England Congregational, Chgo, 1932-38, N.Shore baptist, Chgo, 1939-42, St Matthew's Episcopal, Evanston, 1943-70, Palo Alto Community Ch, CA, 1970-90; Douglas Aircraft and Precise Development Co, 1945; Organist, Chicago Radio and TV; Hammond Organ Co, 1936-70; Participant in concerts and workshops the world over. *Creative works:* Porter Heaps Music. *Memberships:* Am Guild of Organists, Dean, St Jose Chapter. *Honours:* Nat Assn of Women's Clubs Awd, 1926; Best Anthem Prize, 1935; Awd of Merit, Northwestern Univ; Hammond Excellence Awd, 1972; 70 year service award, AGO, 1991. *Hobbies:* Photography. *Address:* 4218 Pomona Avenue, Palo Alto, CA 94306, USA.

HEARNE Stephen Zachary, b. 18 Jan 1952, Burlington, North Carolina, USA. Assistant Professor of Religion. m. Mary Jaundrill, 31 Dec 1974, 2 s. *Education:* BE Religion, Elon Col, 1976; MDiv, 1979, ThM, 1981, Southeastern Bapt Theol Seminary. *Appointments:* Min of Ed, Hocutt Mem Bapt Ch, 1977-81; Instr, Col of Alamane, 1978-81; Instr, 1981-84, Asst Prof, 1984-, N.Greenville Col. *Creative works:* Articles in Mercer Dict of the Bible and the Bibilical Illustrator; Four papers on the controversy in the S.Baptist Convention. *Memberships:* Nat Assn of Bapt Prof of Religion; S.Carolina Acad of Religion, vp, 1991-92; S.Carolina

Baptist Hist Soc; S.Carolina Com on Humanities. *Honours:* S.Boston Ministerium Awd, 1976; Dean's List, Eton Col; N.Greenville Col Fac Minigrants, 1983, 1985; Fac Marshall, NGC, 1989-90; Fac Chiar, 1991. *Hobbies:* Family outings; Softball; Golf; Hunting; Fishing; Reading. *Address:* Department of Religion, PO Box 1892, North Greenville College, Tigerville, SC 29688, USA. 145, 7.

HEATH Dennis Ivan Ewart, b. 20 Nov 1915, Colchester, Essex, England. Retired. m. Vera Irene Wakeling, 16 Oct 1939. *Education:* Sir George Manoux Grammar Sch, 1926-30; Chelsea Col Tech Sci, 1930-33. *Appointments:* MD, Perivan Press ltd, 1937-64; MD and Dep MD, Williams Lea Gp, 1964-78. *Memberships:* Liveryman, Worship Co of Stationers and Newspaper Makers; Lloyd's of London; Hon Treas, Printers Charitable Corp. *Honours:* MID, 1943 (S/Ldr RAF). *Hobbies:* Golf; Finance; Charity work. *Address:* Acres Gate, 18 Woodside, Leigh-on-Sea, Essex SS9 4QU, England.

HEATH Michele Christine, b. 22 Sept 1945, Bournemouth, England. University Professor. m. Ian Brenth Heath, 23 Sept 1967, 1 d. *Education:* BSc 1966, PhD, 1969, Univ of London; DIC, Dipl, Imperial Col, 1969. *Appointments:* Post-Doc Res Fellow, Univ of Georgia, USA, 1969-71; Res Fellow, 1971-72, Lectr, 1972-73, Asst Prof, 1973-76, Assoc Prof, 1976-81, Prof, 1981-, Univ of Toronto. *Creative works:* Book: Ultrastructure of Rust Fungi, 1979; Over 70 scientific papers and publications. *Memberships:* Assoc Ed, Phytopathology, 1991-93; Sr Ed, APS Press, 1988-91; Ch, Prog Com, 6th Intl Congress of Plant Path, 1993; Sr Ed, Physiol and Molec Plant Path, 1982-89. *Honours:* Huxley Mem Awd, 1979; FAPS, 1982; Steacie Mem Fellowship, NSERCC, 1982; Gordon Green Awd, CPS, 1986. *Hobbies:* Lapidary; Painting; Horseriding. *Address:* Botany Department, University of Toronto, Ontario, Canada M5S 3B2.

HEBBLETHWAITE Margaret Isabella Mary, b. 16 June 1951, London, England. Writer. m. Peter Hebblethwaite, 21 July 1974, 2s, 1d. *Education:* St Paul's Girls Sch, 1968-70; BA, MA, Lady Margaret Hall, Oxford, 1970-75. *Appointments:* Assistant Editor, The Tablet. *Creative works:* The Theology of Penance, 1979; Motherhood and God, 1984; Through Lent with Luke, 1986; Finding God in All Things, 1987; My Secret Life, 1991; Our Two Gardens, 1991. *Hobby:* Riding. *Address:* 45 Marston Street, Oxford OX4 1JU, England.

HEBBLETHWAITE Peter, b. 30 Sept 1930, Ashton under Lyne, England. Writer. m. Mary Isabella Mary Speaight, 21 July 1974. 2 s, 1 d. *Education:* Xaverian Col, Manchester, 1942-48; Philos, Les Fontaines, Chantilly, France; Cert Ed, Manresa Col, Roehampton; MA 1st class, Modern Langs, Oxford, 1958; Licentiate in Theol, Heythrop Col, 1965. *Appointments:* Ed, The Month, 1965-73; Lectr in French Lang and Lit, Wadhum Col, Oxford, 1976-79; Vatican Affairs Writer, Nat Catholic Reporter, 1979-. *Creative works:* Articles in newspapers and 14 books including: The year of Three Popes, 1978; The New Inquisition, 1980; The Papal Year, 1981; Introducing John Paul II, the Populist Pope, 1982; John XIII Pope of the Council, 1984; Synod Extraordinary, 1986; In the Vatican, 1986; Paul VI, the First Modern Pope. *Honours:* Awd for US edition of John XXIII Shepherd of the Modern World, 1984. *Hobbies:* Piano playing; Singing; Gardening. *Address:* 45 Marston Street, Oxford OX4 1JU, England. 1.

HECTOR Peter John, b. 5 Sept 1934, Brigstock, England. Engineering Consultant. m. Ann Helen Elizabeth Hetterley, 24 Mar 1956, 1 s, 2 d. *Education:* HNC, Rugby Col of Tech and Arts, 1951-56; Chartered Engr, RAF Tech Col, 1959. *Appointments:* RAF Ofr, 1956-88, Ret'd Grp Capt; Engrg Conslt, 1988-; Asst Sec, Brit Nat Com for Intl Engrg Affairs, 1988-. *Creative works:* Magazine articles on military engineering training and engineering education. *Memberships:* Fellow, Royal Aeronautical Soc, Profl Standards Policy

Com; FIMgt. *Hobbies:* Painting; Reading; Eating; Wines. *Address:* 21 Cotterstock Road, Oundle, Peterborough PE8 5HA, England.

HEDDEN Robert, b. 22 Feb 1948, Okehampton, Devon, England. Solicitor. m. 10 Sept 1977, 1 s, 1 d. *Education:* LLB, AKC, 1969; Law Soc Profl Exams, Cliffords Inn Prizeman, 1970. *Appointments:* Ptnr, 1980-, Herbert Smith, Solicitors, 1970-. *Creative works:* Occasional Professional papers on commercial conveyancing and Town Planning Law. *Memberships:* Law Soc, IBA and UKELA; Liveryman, City of London Solicitors' Co Com Mbr Planning and Environmental Coun Sub Cttee, City of London Law Soc, and Brit Polish Legal Assn; Ass Mbr, Dir's Guild of GB; Athenaeum. *Hobbies:* Theatre and Music, (making and watching); Tennis; Skiing; Swimming; Travel. *Address:* Exchange House, Primrose Street, London EC2A 2HS, England.

HEDEGAARD Connie, b. 15 Sept 1960, Copenhagen, Denmark. Journalist. *Education:* Deg in Lit, Univ of Copenhagen, 1982. *Appointments:* Mbr Danish Parliament, 1984-90, the Conservative Party; Party Spokesperson in General Politics, 1989-90. *Memberships:* The Democracy Fund of the Danish Foreign Ministry. *Address:* Berlingskt Tidende, Pilestrade 34, DK-1147 Copenhagen K, Denmark.

HEGARTY George John, b. 20 July 1948, Cape May, New Jersey, USA. University Administrator; Professor. m. Joy Schiller, 9 June 1979. *Education:* Univ of Fribourg, Switzerland, 1968-69; BA Eng, La Salle Univ, 1966-70; Cert, Laval Univ, Canada, 1970; MA and Dr of Arts, Eng, Drake Univ, 1971-; Cert, UCLA, 1979; Cert, Univ of Pennsylvania, 1981. *Appointments:* Eng Tchr: Peace Corps Volunteer, Col de Sedhiou, Senegal, 1970-71; Belmore Boys' and Westfields HS, Sydney, Australia, 1972-73; Tchg Fellow, Drake Univ, Des Moines, USA, 1974-76; Mbr of Fac, Des Moines Community Col, 1976-80; Maitre de Confs, Fulbright prof, Univ of Yaounde, Cameroon, 1980-83; Fulbright Prof, Nat Univ of Cote d'Ivorie, 1986-88; Dir, Centre for Intl Progs and Sers, Drake Univ, USA, 1983-. *Creative works:* 25 articles, reviews, book chapters, mongraphs, fiction and peotry. *Memberships:* Inst Intl Educ; Coun for Intl Educ Exchange; NAFSA Assn of Intl Educators and Region IV, ADSEC Ch, 1986; Tchrs of Eng to Speakers of Other Langs and MidTESOL. *Honours include:* Academic Specialist, US Info Agency in 7 countries; Fulbright Sr Lectureships. *Hobbies:* Collecting non-Western Art; Travel; Lap swimming; Creative writing. *Address:* Director, Centre for International Programmes & Services, Drake University, Des Moines, IA 50311, USA. 8, 139, 154, 176.

HEIN Cheryl, b. 1 Aug 1945, Arkansas, USA. Professor of Accounting and Crea Co-ord for Acctg and Bus Law. *Education:* BS, 1967, MBA, 1977, PhD, 1983, Acctg. *Appointments:* KGPM Accts, 1971-72; Algoma Univ Col, 1970-80; Univ of Arkansas, 1979-82; Univ of Tulsa, 1982-83; Corpus Christi State Univ, 1983-. *Creative works:* Author of many accounting papers both at home and abroad. *Memberships:* AAA, 1980-; Inst of Mgmt Accts, VP Membership, 1990-; Beta Alpha Psi, 1980-. *Honours:* Awd for outstanding manuscript in Accounting, S.West Bus Symp, 1988. *Hobbies:* Travelling; Genealogy; Reading; Cooking. *Address:* College of Business Administration, Corpus Christi State University, 6300 Ocean Drive, Corpus Christi, TX 78412, USA. 7.

HEINE Willi Otto Paul, b. 6 Mar 1930. Director. m. Ursula Anita Margarete Borges, 13 Feb 1959, 1 s, 2 d. *Education:* Vet Col, Hannover, 1951-58; DVM, 1959; Specialist in Lab Animal Sci, Chamber of Vets, 1970; Privatdozent, 1970, Prof, 1976, Lab Animal Sci, Vet Col, Hannover. *Appointments:* Animal Caretaker, Zoological Garden, Hannover, 1951; Vet, small animal practice, Hannover, Frankfurt, Bochum, 1958; Jr Scst, 1959, Sr Scist, 1965, Dept Dir, 1967, Dir, 1971-, Central Inst for Lab Animal Breeding; Dir, WHO Calloborating Centre

for Defined Lab Animals, 1984. *Creative works:* Author: Gnotobiotechnik, 1968; Scientific articles and co author of several books and scientific publications. *Memberships:* SOLAS, Bd, 1973-76; German Res, Com for Lab Animal Sci, Sec, 1968-70, Chm of Advy Gp, 1970-82; AALAS; Gnotobiotic Assn; Intl Coun for Lab Animal Sci; Chinese Assn for Lab Animal Sci; Corres Mbr, Colegio Brasileiro de Experimentacao Animal. *Honours:* Dr Wilma von During Res Awd, 1980. *Hobbies:* Travelling; Motorcycling; Film and Photography; Geography; Ethnology. *Address:* Werlohweg 9, D-3004 Isernhagen F B, Germany. 50, 52.

HEINE-BAUX Manfred Michael, b. 24 Dec 1940, Munich, Germany. Artist. m. Marie France Gillet. *Education:* MFA, PhD, SCA; Grad, Acad of Fine Arts, Munich, 1964, MFA, PhD in Art Hist. *Appointments:* Assoc Prof, Acad of Fine Arts Munich, 1964-66; Self employed painter, 1966-. Exhibitions at: Goethe Inst, Tehran, Iran, 1975; Le Grant Palais, Paris, 1977; Ruf Gallery, Munich, 1983; The Ottawa Art Gallery, 1989, BMW Gall, Toronto, 1989, Circle Arts Gall, Ontario, 1990, Art Guild of Canada, 1990, The Hahn Gall, Philadelphia, 1991. *Creative works:* Paintings and aquatint etchings on international market scenes, landscapes and portraits; Portrait commissioned by King Faisal, 1974. *Memberships:* Soc of Canadian Artists, Toronto; Friend of the Royal Canadian Acad. *Honours:* First Prizes: Still life, Mus of Fine Arts, Munich, 1964-66; Paintings of exotic themes, Munich, 1973; Painting and etchings at Living Arts Biennale Johannesburg, S.Africa, 1976. *Hobbies:* Travelling; Studying native cultures. *Address:* 641 Queenston Road, Cambridge, Ontario, Canada N3H 3K2, Canada.

HEINRICHS Wolfhart Peter, b. 3 Oct 1941, Cologne, Germany. Professor of Arabic. *Education:* Habilitation, 1979, PhD, 1967, Univ of Giessen, Germany. *Appointments:* Asst, Islamic Studies and Semitic Langs, 1967-72, Dozent, 1972-78, Giessen Univ; Prof of Arabic, Harvard Univ, 1978-. *Creative works:* Arabische Dichtung und griechische Poetik, 1969; The Hand of the Northwind, 1977; Studies in Neo-Aramaic, 1990. *Memberships:* Am Oriental Soc; Middle East Studies Assn; Am Assn of Tchrs of Arabic; Deutsche Morgenländische Gesellschaft; Ed Bds of Encyclopaedia of Islam, Jour of Middle Eastern Studies and Al Arabiyya. *Hobbies:* Nature; Early music; Languages in general. *Address:* Department of Near Eastern Languages and Civilisations, Harvard University, 6 Divinity Avenue, Cambridge MA 02138, USA.

HEISS Wolf-Dieter, b. 31 Dec 1939, Zell a See, Austria. Physician. m. Brigitte Kroiss, 8 Aug 1965, 1 s, 1 d. *Education:* Realgymnasium Salzburg, 1950-58; MD, Med Sch, Univ of Vienna, 1965. *Appointments:* Resident Psych Neurol, Univ Klin, Vienna, 1966-68; Asst Prof, Dept of Physiol, State of NY, Buffalo, USa, 1968-69; Asst Prof, Hd of Hirnkrieslauflabor, Klin, Vienna, 1968-71; Neurol, Univ Klin, Vienna, 1971-74; Res Assoc, Univ of Minn, USA, Assoc Prof, Univ Klin, Vienna, 1974-78; Dir Max Planck Inst for Neurol Res and Neurol Clinic Koln Merheim, 1978-; Dir Neurol Univ Clinic Kolm Lindenthal and Dir MPI for Neurol Res, 1985-. *Memberships:* ANA; AAAS; Am Heart Assn; Soc Nucl MEd; NYAC; German Neurol Soc Assn; Austrial Soc Neurol and Psychis; Austrian Nucl Med Soc; Austrian Acad of Scis. *Honours:* Eiselberg Prize, 1969. *Hobbies:* Skiing; Class; Music; Archaeology. *Address:* MPI f Neurol Forschung, Gleueler Str 50, 5000 Koln 41, Germany. 52, 92, 43, 50, 139.

HELBERG Gunnar Ivar, b. 24 May 1922, Milwaukee, Wisconsin, USA. Chemical Engineer. m. 5 June 1954, 1 d. *Education:* BS Chem Engrg, Univ Wisconsin, 1949; Grad Work, Chem engrg, TX A & M Univ, 1956-58. *Appointments:* Chief Chem, Cities Serv Oil Co, 1949; Analytical Chem, Ladish Drop Forge, 1950-54; Prod Dev Engr, Dow Chem, 1955-58; Process and Oper Res Supv, Petro-Tex, 1958-64; Prod Supt Dow Chem Freeport, 1964-71; Tech Mgr, 1971-78, Proj Mgr, 1978-80, Dow

Chem Reg PE St of TX and WI. *Creative works:* 3 US patents; Composed and arranged music for small wind chamber groups; Army of US Pacific Theater of OP, 1943-45. *Memberships:* AIChE Fellow; Historian of Local Section, past Chm, By-Laws and Constitution Com; Chm, Inc of ALChE; Fellow, AIC; Alpha Chi Sigma; St Vincent de Paul Soc; Bd of Equalization, Beautification Comm, City of Lake Jackson; Brazosport Symphony Bd of Dirs, 1990-. *Honours:* Fellow, AIChE, 1988; Dep Gov, ABI Res Assn, 1989; Outstanding Ser Awd, Local Section, AIChE, 1986; Dow Engrg Excellence Awd, 1986; Energy Conservation TX Ops Awd, Dow Chemical, 1976. *Hobbies:* Music; Hiking; Fishing. *Address:* 310 Pine Street, Lake Jackson, TX 77566, USA.

HELGASON Haukur, b. 1 Dec 1936, Akureyri, Iceland. Editor. m. Nanci Arnold Helgason, 5 Jan 1968. *Education:* BBA, Univ of Iceland, 1960; MA Econ, Univ of Chicago, 1967. *Appointments:* Journalist, Editor, Dagbladid-Visir, 1968-. *Honour:* Fulbright Scholar, Chicago, 1963-64. *Hobbies:* Politics; Travel; Reading. *Address:* Lundarbrekka 6, Kopavogur, Iceland. 52.

HELMICK Charles G III b. 14 Oct 1950, Ann Arbor, Michigan, USA. Medical Epidemiologist. m. April Kristy Harrison, 19 June 1982, 1 s, 2 d. *Education:* BS Univ of Michigan, 1972; MD Johns Hopkins Univ, 1976. *Appointments:* Med Residency, Baltimore City Hosps, 1976-79; Nat Centres for Disease Control, 1979-. *Creative works:* Published Epidemiologic research on rabies, Rocky Mountain Spotted Fever, Lassa Fever, Q Fever, Cryptosporidiosis, Alzheimers Disease, multiple sclerosis, peptic ulcer disease, inflammatory bowel disease and other topics. *Memberships:* Soc for Epidemiol Res; APHA; Gerontol Soc of Am; Phys for Social Responsibility; Sig Xi Sci Res Soc; Intl Phys for the Prevention of Nuclear War. *Honours:* Bd Certified, Intl Med, 1979; Preventive Med, 1991. *Hobbies:* Soccer; Reading; Camping; Hiking; Astronmy; History. *Address:* c/o National Centres for Disease Control, 1600 Clifton Rd MS-K51, Atlanta GA 30333, USA.

HELMORE Roy Lionel, b. 8 June 1926, Perth, Australia. Retired. m. Margaret Lilian Martin, 5 Apr 1969. *Education:* Montrose Acad, 1938-44; BSc Eng, Edinburgh Univ, 1947; MA Cambridge Univ, 1986. *Appointments:* Crompton Parkinson Ltd, 1947-49; Asst Lectr, Peterborough Tech Col, 1949-53; Sr Lectr, Shrewsbury Tech Col, 1953-57; Hd of Dept, Exeter Tech Col, 1957-61; Principal: St Albans Col, 1961-67, Cambs Col of Arts and Tech, 1977-86; Fellow, Hughes Hall, Cambridge, 1982-. *Publications:* Book: CCAT - A Brief History, 1989. *Memberships:* Manpower Servs Comm, 1974-82; Assn of Principals of Cols, Pres, 1972-73, Hon Sec, 1968-71, Hon Treas, 1983-86; Tech Ed Coun, V-Chm, 1973-79; Assn of Cols of Further and Higher Educ, Chm of Coun, 1987-88; FIEE. *Honours:* CBE, 1980; JP, St Albans, 1964-83; Hon mem, City and Guilds of London Inst, 1987. *Hobbies:* Opera; Gardening; Watercolours. *Address:* 5 Beck Road, Saffron Walden, Essex CB11 4EH, England. 1.

HELZER Dorothy Beatrice, b. 3 June 1943, Santa Fe, Ohio, USA. Homemaker. m. Dan Lee Williams, 7 Aug 1959, 2 s, 1 d. *Education:* Mature Grad, 1989. *Appointments:* Marie's Candies, W.Liberty, OH, 1979; Sec, Kiser Lake Kennels, St Paris, 1989; Logan Co Classifieds, 1990; Bookkeeper and Sales person. *Memberships:* Hospitality Com, Grace Chapel Ch, W.Liberty, OH. *Hobbies:* Going to church; Fishing; Gardening; Grandchildren; Spending time with friends; Making the world a better place by serving God. *Address:* 2848 Rd 32 South, Bellefontaine, OH 43311, USA.

HENDERSON Edward Hugh, b. 21 Apr 1939, Atlanta, Georgia, USA. University Professor of Philosophy. m. Patricia Weems, 25 Aug 1973, 2 s, 2 d. *Education:* BA Rhodes Col, 1961; MA Philos, 1964, PhD Phil, 1967, Tulane Univ. *Appointments:* Asst Prof of Philos: Westminster Col, Fulton, MO, 1964-66, Louisiana State Univ, 1966-71, Assoc Prof, 1971-; Prof, 1992-.

Publications: Faith and Inquiry; Knowing Persons and Knowing God; Co- ed, Divine Action: Studies inspired by the Philosophical Theology of Austin Farrer. *Memberships:* Am Philos Assn; Am Acad of Religion; Scholarly Engagement with Anglican Doctrine; Soc of Christian Philos; Soc for Philos of Religion. *Honours:* Phi Beta Kappa, 1960; Dist Fac Awd, Louisiana State Univ, 1981; Omicron Delta Kappa, 1959; Grants for Humanities and Bus, 1978-91; LA Endowment for the Humanities Grant, 1986. *Hobbies:* Fishing; Home carpentry; Lawn Care. *Address:* Dept of Philosophy, Louisiana State University, Boston Rouge, LA 70803, USA. 7, 145.

HENDERSON Richard Wayne, b. 6 July 1953, Maybuery, West Virginia, USA. Baptist Minister. m. Billie Gail Kelley, 10 June 1972. 2 s, 1 d. *Education:* Elec Sch, US Navy, 1972; BTh, 1990. *Appointments:* US Navy, 1971-73; Meat cutter, Foodland, Hinton, WV, 1973-75; US Postal Ser, 1975-89; Ministry, 1973-. *Memberships:* Future Farmers of Am (FFA), Pres; Sch Advy Coun; Local Fire Dept, Sec; Kiwanis, Local VP; Bapt Ordination Coun, Moderator. *Honours:* Star Chapter Farmer, FFA, 1969; DAR Awd, 1971; Am Defence Medal, USN, 1971. *Hobbies:* Gardening; Reading Christian literature; Basketball; Football. *Address:* Rt.1 Box 129, Patrick, SC 29584, USA.

HENDRICKSON Benjamin S, Sir, b. 23 Jan 1931, Springlake, NJ, USA. Retired Lt Col, USAF/CAP. m. Princess Mary Rachel, 26 Mar 1989, 1 s, 2 d. *Education:* AA Antelope Valley Col, Lancaster, CA, 1961-63; ThB, STD, LIFE Bible Col, Los Angeles, 1968-70; MA, BA, Anzusa Pacific Col, 1970-71; ThD, FL State Theol Seminary, 1971-72; PhD, Am Intl Univ, Pasadena, CA, 1978- 79. *Appointments include:* Dir, Family Counselling Ctr of AV, 1973-75; Exex Dir, Valencia Counselling Ser, 1976-78, Lancaster Counselling Ser, 1975- 78; Prof, Univ of La Verne, 1978-79; Marriage, Family and Child Therapist, 1978-82; Conslt, Author, Tchr, 1983-91. *Memberships:* Am Psycho Assn; Am Bd of Examiners in Pastoral Counselling; Am Col of Clinic Orders of Chivalry, World Parliament Confederation of Chivalry Admrs; Nat Psycho Assn; Nat Allance for Family Life; Am Guild of Hypnotherapist; CA Assn of Marriage and Family Therapists. *Honours:* Medal of Hon; Presidential Medal of Merit; Biographical Medal of Hon; Knighted, House of Assington, 1991. *Address:* 5970 Gaskell Rd HCR-3, Rosamond, CA 93560, USA. 59, 152,

HENDRY Arnold William, b. 10 Sept 1921, Buckie, Scotland. Civil Engineer. m. (1) Sheila Mary Cameron Roberts, 27 June 1946, dec 1966; (2) Elizabeth Lois Alice Inglis, 28 Dec 1968, 2 s, 1 d. *Education:* BSc Eng, 1941, PhD 1946, DSc 1954, Univ of Aberdeen, Scotland. *Appointments:* Asst and Lectr, Univ of Aberdeen, 1943-49; Reader in Civil Eng, Univ of London, 1949-51; Prof of Civil Eng, Univ of Khartoum, 1951-57; Prof of Bldg Sci, Univ of Liverpool, 1957-63; Prof of Civil Eng, Univ of Edinburgh, 1964-88. *Publications:* Over 100 papers in technical journals; Several books on structural engineering including: Structural Masonry, 1990; Load Bearing Brickwork, 1989; Ed, Reinforced and Prestressed Masonry, 1991. *Memberships:* FICE; FISE; FRSA; FRS Edin; Pres, Scottish Assn for Public Transp. *Honours:* Bronze Medal, Inst Structural Engrs, 1948 and 1972; Jubilee Medal, Univ of Khartoum, 1981; Hon membership, Brit Masonry Soc, 1989; Distinguished Service Certificate, British Standards Inst, 1992. *Hobbies:* Conservation of buildings and the environment; Walking; Bird watching; DIY; Reading. *Address:* 146/6 Whitehouse Loan, Edinburgh EH9 2AN, Scotland. 1, 184.

HENKEL Kathy, b. 20 Nov 1942, Los Angeles, California, USA. Composer; Writer; Lecturer. *Education:* BA Hist, UCLA, 1965; BM Composition, CSUN, 1976; MA Music Composition, CSUN, 1982. *Appointments:* Music Reviewer, Los Angeles Times, 1979; Music Res & Clearance, Paramount Pictures Corp, 1977-81; Producer, Scripwriter, KUSC FM, 1984-89; Prog

Annotator, Educ Coor, Chamber Music/LA Festival, 1987-; Prog Annotator, Los Angeles Chamber Orch, 1988-. *Publications:* Compositions: Book of Hours, 1990, Solo Harp; River Sky 1988, Solo Guitar; Bass Clarinet Sonata, 1987; Piano Sonata, 1986; Moorland Sketches, 1985; Lost Calendar Pages, 1984, Flute & Harp; Pioneer Song Cycle, 1968; Trumpet Concerto, 1979. *Memberships:* Phi Beta Kappa; Phi Beta Womens Profl Fraternity; Chamber Music Am. *Hobbies:* Coastal path walking in Cornwall; Travelling; Cooking. *Address:* 2367 Creston Drive, Los Angeles, CA 90068, USA.

HENKEN Bernard S(amuel), b. 30 May 1919, Everett, Massachusetts, USA. Psychologist and Clinical Counsellor. m. Charlotte Popvsky, 20 Dec 1953, 2d. *Education:* Prelegal, Boston Col, 1938-41; BSc, 1947, Doctorate studies, 1953, Harvard Univ; MSc, Purdue Univ, 1950; DSc, Portia Grad Sch, 1955. *Appointments:* Psychologist, Carney Hosp, 1950-52; Psychologist, Medford Pediatric Assn, 1974-. *Memberships:* Am Psycho Assn. *Hobbies:* Sport; Swimming; Music; Playing the Bass. *Address:* 118 Wavery Avenue, Melrose, MA 02176, USA. 55,

HENNESSY Helen Adele, b. 5 June 1905, Duluth, USA. Homemaker; Writer; Genealogist. m. Harold Richard Hennessey, 24 July 1930, 1 s, 3 d. *Education:* Ba Carleton Col, 1927. *Publications include:* Co-author; Weinke, Krueger, Lounsberry Relationhips, 1975; The Hennessey Sketch, 1979; Helen Lounsberry Hennessy's Lineage Data, 1980; Ousman, Hennessy and Allied Families, 1980; Col Clement A Lounsberry, 1982; Ebenezer Hoskins, 1982; Lineage Laroy N Castor, PhD, 1983; The Hennessy Immigrants 1850, 1984; Our Grandchildren's Great Grand Parents, 1985. *Memberships include:* DAR; Nat Soc Daughter of Fdrs and Patriots of Am; Gen Soc, Mayflower Descendants; Nat Soc Magna Carta Dames; Colonial Order of the Crown, 1987; Plantagenet Soc, 1988; Flagon and Grencher Soc, 1990. *Honours:* Dakota Territory Pioneer Cert; Michigan Hist Comm Hon; Clan Stewart Awd, Duluth, 1922. *Hobbies:* Writing; Needlework; Travel. *Address:* 29549 N Waukegan Rd Apt 104, Lake Bluf, IL 60044, USA.

HENNINGSMOEN Gunnar, b. 17 Sept 1919, Oslo, Norway. Retired Professor Emeritus. m. Kari Egede Henningsmoen, 28 July 1962. *Education:* Phd, 1957, Oslo Univ. *Appointments:* Curator, Palaeont Mus, Univ of Oslo, 1948-67; Prof, 1957-85, Emeritus Prof, 1985-; Visiting Prof, Univ of Kansas, USA, 1966-67. *Publications:* Numerous scientific papers in journals in Norway and eleswhere on fossil ostracodes, trilobites, and other fossils and on stratigraphy. *Memberships:* Norwegian Acad of Sci; Geol Soc of Norway; Intl Comm on Stratigraphy, Gen Sec, 1960-65. *Honour:* Reusch Medal, 1955. *Hobby:* Gardening, especially growing vegetables. *Address:* Ingar Nilsens vei 3A, N-0568 Oslo, Norway.

HENRIKSEN Bent, b. 20 Mar 1938, Denmark. Chairman. m. Hanne Frederiksen, 12 Oct 1963, 2 s, 1 d. *Education:* Handelsskole, Horsens, Denmark, 1953-33; Forsvarets Gymnasium, Denmark, 1963-64; Copenhaven Bus Sch, 1967-68; Manchester Bus Sch, 1977; Imede Lausanne, Switzerland, 1980. *Appointments:* VP, Elmwood Sensors Inc, USA, 1971-83; MD, Elmwood Sensors Ltd, 1974-83; Chief Exec, TSL Gp PLC, 1983-87; Currently: Dir, Canford Audio plc; Chm, Pharma Nord (UK) Ltd. *Memberships:* IOD Com Mbr, 1975; RSA FRSA, 1982; Univ of Northumbria Governor; Chm, Export Com, Tyne & Wear Chamber of Commerce. *Honours:* OBE (Hon) for contribution to Brit Indust and Export, 1983; N.East Bus Man of the year, 1985. *Hobbies:* Gardening; Nutrition; Badmington. *Address:* Spital Hall, Mitford, Morpeth, Northumberland NE61 3PN, England.

HENRY Desmond Paul, b. 5 July 1921, Almondbury. Retired Reader in Philosophy. m. Louise Henriette Jeannette Bayen, 19 May 1945, 3 d. *Education:*

Huddersfield Col, 1931-37; Leeds Univ, 1946-49; BA Hons Philos, 1949; PhD, Philos, Univ of Manchester, 1960. *Appointments:* Lectr, Sr Lectr, Reader, Dept of Philos, Univ of Manchester, 1949-62; Visiting Prof, Brown and Penn Univs, USA. *Publications:* Numerous articles and reviews; 7 books on history of logic (mediaeval), including: That Most Subtle Question, 1984; Mediaeval Merelogy, 1991. *Memberships:* Past Pres, Manchester Mediaeval Soc; Soc Intl pour l'étude de la Philosophie Médiévale. *Honours:* Sr Emsley Scholar, Univ of Leeds, 1962; London Opportunity Art Prize Winner, 1962. *Hobbies:* Art (exhibitions and one- man shows since 1962; pioneer in computer art). *Address:* Dept of Philosophy, The University of Manchester, Manchester M13 9PL, England.

HENRY Martha, b. 17 Feb 1938, Detroit, Michigan, USA. Actress; Director; Artistic Director. m. Rod Beattie, 28 Dec 1989, 1 d. *Education:* Grad, Nat Theatre Sch, Montreal. *Career includes:* Murray Davis Repertory Season, Crest Theatre, Toronto, 1959-60; Manitoba Theatre Ctr, 1961; The Canadian Players, 1965-66 and Shaw Festival; Arena State Co, Wash DC, 1966-67; English TV, and London's West End, 1969, 1970; NY Lincoln Ctr, 1971; Manitoba Theatre Ctr, 1973; Montreal's Centaur Theatre, 1976; London, 1979-80; Radio appearances and CBC television; The Stratford Festival, 1962-80, productions include: Richard III, All's Well that Ends Well, Much Ado about Nothing, A Midsummer Night's Dream; The Winter's Tale, The Devils, Uncle Vany, The Second Part of Henry VI, Love's Labour's Lost, The Woman and King Lear. On leaving Stratford in 1980, has pursued a career in TV and film as well as directing for the theatre, and returned for the 1991 season to direct Ibsen's, An Enemy of the People at the Avon Theatre, The Odd Couple for the opening of The Grands 1991-92 season and A Walk in the Woods. A Tutor at the Nat Theatre Sch, Univ of Windsor, Tarragons Maggie Bassett Studio and Winipeg's Prairie Theatre Exchange, she also has a string of musical credits to her name. *Honours include:* 5 Hon university doctorates; Ofr of the Order of Can, 1982; Companion of the Order of Fan, 1991; Genie Awd, Best Actress, 1984, 1986; Gemini Awd for Best Guest Performance in a Series, 1989 *Address:* Artistic Director, The Grand Theatre, London, Ontario, Canada.

HENSHAW John Trueman, b. 26 Nov 1913, Salford, Lancs. Retired. m. Elsie Goddard, 14 May 1941, 1 s, 1 d. *Education:* HNC, Royal Tech Col, Salford, 1929-36; MSc 1970, PhD, 1975, Univ of Salford. *Appointments:* Structure Designer, Aircraft, 1935-50; Asst Ch, Stressman, 1950-54; Hd of Air Frame Design, Weapons Div, 1954-55; Sr Lectr, Univ of Salford, Aero Eng, 1955-79. *Publications:* Airframe Construction and Repair, 1943; Aircraft Mechanics Pocket Bk, 1944; Supersonic Engineering, Ed, 1962; Numerous papers in bio-engineering structures. *Memberships:* Fellow, RAes, 1965; Tech Dir, N.W. Orbbotic Inst, 1970-79; Fdr, Chm Whaley Br Amenity Soc (Civic Trust); Fdr, Chm, WB Branch of Action Res for the Crippled Child. *Honours:* OBE, 1976. *Hobbies:* Walking; Thinking. *Address:* Texal View, Fernilee, Whaley Br SK12 7HD, England.

HENTSCHEL Uwe, b. 23 Jan 1940, Greifsuald, Germany. Professor of Clinical Personality Psychology. m. (1) 1s, 1d, (2) Marleen van der Voort, 16 Sept 1987, 2 d. *Education:* Dipl in Psycho, Univ of Giessen, 1964; PhD, Univ of Freiburg, 1969; Habil Univ of Mainz, 1977. *Appointments:* Reschr, Marplan Frankfurt, 1965-67; Masius, Hamburg, 1970; Res Dir, McCann Hamburg, 1971; Asst Prof, Prof, 1975-87, Univ of Mainz; Chair of Personality Psycho, Univ of Leiden, The Netherlands, 1987-. *Publications:* Ed, Experimentelle Persönlichkeitspsychologie, 1980; Persönlichkeitsmerkmale and Familiensrtruktur, 1984; The Roots of Perception, 1986; Ausländerstudium in internationalem Kontext, 1991; Co-ed, Processes in Cognition and Personality, 1984. *Memberships:* Deutsch Gesellschaft für Psychologie; SOc for Psychotherapy Res; European Assn of Personality

Psychology; Intl Col of Psychosomatic Med; Gesellschaft zur Förderung persönlichkeits und sozialpsychologischer Forschung, Chm, 1984-. *Hobbies:* Skiing; Sailing; Modern art. *Address:* Leiden University, Dept of Psychology, Wassenaarseweg 52, 2333 AK Leiden, The Netherlands. 52.

HEPLER Lowell Eugene, b. 23 Dec 1950, Sligo, Pennsylvania, USA. Professor of Music. m. Juanita K Hubler, 31 Aug 1974, 1 s, 1 d. *Education:* BS Music Ed, Clarion univ of Penn, 1972; MFA Music, Carnegie Mellon Univ, 1974; PhD Case Western Reserve Univ, 1986. *Appointments:* Prof of Music, Allegheny Col, 1974-; Principal Tuba: Erie Phil Orchestra, 1982-, Erie Chamber Orchestra, 1983-; Erie Concert Bank, 1983-; Lake Erie Ballet Co, 1989-. *Publications:* Tuba Soloist: Erie Phil Orchestra and Erie Chamber Orchestra; Piano Soloist: Alleghney Summer Music Fest Orchestra and Clarion Univ Orchestra and Band; Concert Band of N.W Pennsylvania; Numerous solo and chamber performances. *Memberships:* College Band Dirs Nat Assn; PA Music Educators Assn; Music Educators Nat Conf; Meadville Rotary Club; Phi Beta Mu; Phi Mu Alpha Sinfonia; Kappa Delta Pi; Kappa Kappa Psi; Advy Bd, Meadville YWCA. *Honours:* Partners in Educ Awd, Crawford Ctl Sch Dist, 1989; Arion Awd, 1968; Nat Hon Sco, 1968. *Hobbies:* Reading; Walking; Bicycling; Travelling. *Address:* 944 Limber Road, Meadville, PA 16335, USA.

HEPPLE Keith Michael, b. 31 July 1965, York, England. Fashion Editor. *Education:* York Col of Arts and Tech, Fasion; BA Hons, Trent Poly. *Appointments:* Deputy Fashion Ed of Fashion Weekly, 1987; Style Ed, Dr, 1988-90; Fashion Ed, Dr, 1991-. Lectr, Nottingham Col. *Publications:* Written various freelance fashion articles for the Sunday Times paper, Esquire Mag, Image, London Illustrated News and the Independent Newspaper. *Honours:* BA Hons Deg in Fashion, 1986; RCA commendation in illustration, 1986. *Hobbies:* Browsing in bookstores. *Address:* 19 Bishops Road, Highgate, London N6, England.

HERBERT Arthur James, b. 24 Oct 1918, Melbourne, Australia. Company Chairman. m. 20 Nov 1948, 1 s, 3 d. *Education:* Knox Col, NSW, Australia, 1926-29; Sydney Ch of England Sch, NSW, 1929-31; Merchant Taylors Sch, 1932-37; Pembroke Cambridge, 1937-39. *Appointments:* Comm'd 1940; Royal Engrs, 1940-46; Major, 1945, Gibraltar, N.Africa, Italy, Austria; Joined Family Bus, Herbert & Sonc Ltd, 1946. *Memberships:* Pres, Nat Fed Scale and Weighing M/C Mfrs, 1966, 1982; Pres, E.Anglia Engrg Employers Assn, 1982, 1986; Chm and Pres, Bury St Edmunds Conservative Assn, 1972-86; Chm and Pres, Suffolk and S.E.Cambs Euro Con Assn, 1980-92; Pres, S Suffolk Con Assn, 1987-91. *Honours:* Mentioned in Dispatches, 1946; CBE, 1982; BA, 1940, MA 1942, Cambridge; Freeman, City of London, 1964. *Hobby:* Gardening. *Address:* 18 Rookwood Way, Haverhill, Suffolk, England.

HERBERT John Anthony, b. 10 Sept 1939, Coventry, England. Documentary Film Director and Scriptwiter. m. Michelle Forbes Dennis, 3 Aug 1963, 2 d. *Education:* Dean Close Sch, Cheltenham; Exeter Univ. *Appointments:* Rediffusion TV, 1962-65; Random Films, 1965-72; Self- employed freelance since, 1973 as documentary film maker and script writer. *Publications:* Number of documentaries in many subjects including conservation of buildings, archaeology in Arab world, military subjects, currently the II World War in Poland; Books on archaeological excavations and contributor to illustrated London News on Arabian Archaeology; Photo exhibs in London and Paris, 1986. *Memberships:* FRGS; The Georgian Gp; The Hist Hses Assn; The Anglo Arab Soc; English Vineyards Assn. *Honours:* Gold Awd for Excellence, Int Video and Cinema Awds Festival, London, for film, Fighting the Good Fight, 1991. *Hobbies:* Historical research and reading architectural and Arab world subjects; Travelling in France; Growing vines for

English wine-making. *Address:* Much Hadham Hall, Much Hadham, Herts SG10 6BZ, England.

HERBERTSON Robert Ian, b. 30 Dec 1953, Croydon, Surrey, England. Bank of England. m. Joanna North, 22 Mar 1985, 2 d. *Education:* BA Hons Philos, Birbeck Col, Univ of London, 1984. *Appointments:* Crown Agents, 1979-85; Bank of England, 1985-. *Memberships:* FIAP, 1986; Cert Dipl in Acctg and Fin, 1985; Aristotelian Soc, 1982-; Challoner Club, London; Conservative Club, Huntingdon. *Hobbies:* Philosophy; Literature; National Hunt Racing. *Address:* 21 Euston St, Huntingdon, Cambs PE18 6QS, England.

HERBUT Jozef Kazmierz, b. 1 Nov 1933, Barysz, Poland. Lecturer in Philosophy. *Education:* Philos and Theol, Catholic Univ of Lublin; Masters Deg, 1960; PhD, 1962; Ast Prof, 1976. *Appointments:* Lectr in Philos, Theol Seminary of Opole, 1961-76; Lectr in Philos of Religion and Methodology of Philos, Univ of Lublin, 1976-. *Publications:* Hypotheses in the Philosophy of Being, 1978; The Transscendental Method in metaphysics, 1987; More than 30 articles. *Memberships:* Polish Catholic Philos Assn, Sec; Sc Soc, Catholic Univ, Lublin; Societas Ethica. *Hobbies:* Sailing; Climbing; Skiing; Classic Poetry. *Address:* Wydzial Filozofii, Katolicki Uniwersytet, Lubelski, Al Raclawickie 14, P 20-950, Poland.

HERMANN Tadeusz Wladyslaw, b. 13 June 1937, Gniezno, Poland. Professor of Pharmaceutical Sciences. m. Irene Janowski, 28 Aug 1961, 1 s. *Education:* MS 1960, PhD, 1969, Col of Pharm, Poznan, Poland. *Appointments:* Asst, 1960, Asst Prof, 1969, Assoc Prof, 1979, Prof, 1989, Dean, 1987-93, Col of Pharm, Poznan; Post Doc, Univ of Florida, 1971-72; Hd, Dept of Phys Chem, Univ of Kentucky, 1980-81. *Creative works:* Bases of Drug Stability, 1982. *Memberships:* Polish Pharm Soc; Polish Acad of Sci; Chm, Comm of Drug Analysis. *Honours:* MSc Pharm, with distinction, 1960; Jan Wolfgang Awd for Best Paper in the field of drug analysis, Polish Pharm Soc, 1974. *Hobbies:* Gardening; Tennis; Poetry. *Address:* Department of Physical Chemistry, University School of Medical Sciences, 6 Swizcicki Street, 60-781 Poznan, Poland.

HERMET Guy, b. 14 June 1934, Paris, France. Political Scientist. m. Brigitte Devriendt, 3 July 1963. 2 s. *Education:* DLit, 1977; Dr Sociol, 1966; Grad, Paris Inst of Polit Sci, 1957. *Appointments:* Res Scholar, Nat Foun for Polit Sci, 1963-75; Dir, Ceri, Paris, 1976-85; Res Dir, 1985-. *Publications:* 10 books and 100 articles on the history of democracy and political culture. *Memberships:* Bd of Doctors without Borders; France; Ed Bd, Revue Francaise de Science Politique. *Honours:* Prize in History of the French Acad, 1974. *Hobby:* Travelling. *Address:* 139 Rue Pelleport, 75020 Paris, France.

HERNANDEZ Elise Ann, b. 31 Dec 1945, Hackensack, New Jersey, USA. Nurse. m. George Hernandez, 9 June 1979, 2 s. *Education:* Dipl Nurse, Scranton State Gen Hosp Sch of Nsg, 1966; BS Nsg, McKendree Col, Lebanon, IL, 1981; Nat Cert Trauma Nurse, 1989; Military courses including Flight Nurse Course, 1973; Advanced Staff Devel Ofr Course, 1989. *Appointments include:* USAF Serv with 11 years active duty, 1968- Charge Nurse, 1977-80, Ofr in Charge, Pediatric Unit, 1980-83, Nrsg Staff Devel Ofr, 1986-, Scott AF Base, IL, 1973-75; Flight Nurse, Flight Nurse Examiner and Instr, Pope AF Base, NC, 1975-77; Asst Chief Nurse, Battle Creek, MI, 1983-84; Grissom AF Base, IN, 1984086; Current, rank Lt Col; Civilian posts include Staff Nurse, Anderson Hosp, IL, 1980-83, 1986-90; Clin Nsg Instr, Indiana Univ, 1983-84; Staff Nurse, Dukes Hosp, Peru, IN, 1984-86; Ofc Nurse, Dr Dwyer-Hymowitz, Mt Laurel, NJ. *Memberships:* Assn of Trauma Nurses; Emergency Nurses Assn; Assn of Military Surgeons of the US. *Honours include:* USAF FLight Nurse Wings, 1973; Commendation Medal, 1980;

Humanitarian Serv Medal, 1983; Achievement Medal, 1984; Chief Nurse Badge, 1985. *Hobbies:* Bible study; Sewing; Crochet; Helping with school projects and elementary clss trips; Moulaging disaster victims for simulation exercises. *Address:* 2406 Craig Drive, Mt Holly, NJ 08060, USA. 8.

HERNAUT Kruno A, b. 8 Apr 1941, Zagreb. Doctor of Engineering Sciences; Deputy Director. m. Rosemarie Hernaut, 30 Apr 1970, 2 s. *Education:* Eng Dipl, Univ of Zagrey Fac of Elec Engrg, 1964; DEng, Univ of Dortmund, 1978. *Appointments:* Design Engr, Dept for Signalling Systems, 1966-68, Proj Leader, 1968-72, Reschr, 1972-79, Siemens AG, Munich, Germany; Lectr, 1968-85, Dep Dir, Dept of Ed Policy, 1979- .Siemens Ed Ctr, Munich. *Publications:* Numerous scientific publications in the fields of microelectronics, general questions of education policy with national and European aspects and recommendations fore engineering curricula. *Memberships include:* European Fed of Nat Engrg Assns; Intl Soc for Engrg Pedagogy; European Soc for Engrg Ed; European Round Table for Industs; European Community. *Honours:* FEANI Europa Ingenieur, 1988. *Hobbies:* Music; Literature; Theatre; Opera; Skiing; Hiking; Assembling, programming and playing electric organs. *Address:* Munchener Str 21, D-800 Munchen 70, Germany.

HEROUX Paul, b. 9 Jan 1951, Trois-Rivieres, PQ, Canada. University Professor and Medical Scientist. *Education:* BSc Laval Univ, 1972; MSc, 1975, PhD 1981, Phys, Inst Nat de la Recherche Scientifique, Univ du Quebec. *Appointments:* Res Scist, Inst Recherche d'Hydro, Quebec, 1976-87; Ass Prof,Sch of Occup Hlth, McGill Univ, 1987-; Med Scist, Dept of Surgery, Royal Victoria Hosp; Principal Investigatory Pathophysiol of ELec Burns, 1987-1991. *Publications:* Chapters in: Electromagnetics in Medicine and Biology, 1991; Electrical Shock Safety Criteria, 1985; Electrical Trauma, 1992. *Memberships:* Bioelectromagnetics Soc; Bioelectrical Repair and Growth Soc; Intl Comm on Occup Hlth; Am Aging Assn. *Honours:* MICA Prize, Conseil de l'Industrie Electronique du Quebec, 1988; First Awd, Plastic Surgery Educ Foun, 1986. *Hobbies:* Badminton; Riding; Fencing; Sailing. *Address:* 921 J P Vincent No 6, Longueuil, PQ Canada J4G 1V1. 142.

HERRINGTON Mark Bruce, b. 22 Dec 1959, San Antonio, Texas, USA. Architect. m. Amy Kathryn Hamm, 17 Nov 1990. *Education:* BArch, Mississippi State Univ, 1982. *Appointments:* Draftsman, Ronald L Lane Inc, 1981; Assoc Archt, Giattina, Risher & Co Architects Inc, 1982-. *Memberships:* AIA, 1985-. *Honours:* AIA Honour Awds: Birmingham Chapter,1989, Alabama Coun, 1989. *Hobbies:* Home renovation; Camping; Hiking; Backpacking. *Address:* c/o Giattina, Fisher & Co Architects Inc, 2031 11th Avenue South, Birmingham, AL 35205, USA. 132, 7.

HERRMANN Joachim, b. 19 Dec 1932, Lubnitz, Germany. Historian; Archaeologist. m. Ursula Becher, 3 July 1954, 2 s, 1 d. *Education:* Studies in Hist, Archaeol and Anthropol, Humboldt Univ, Berlin, 1951-55; Dipl, 1955; Doctorate, 1958, Habil, 1965, Prof, 1969. *Appointments:* Asst Lectr, Archaeol, 1956; Res Asst, 1958, German Acad of Scis; Hd Dept of Protohistory, Inst of Vor-rund Fruhgeschichte, Berlin, 1966; Dir, Zentralinstitut fur Alte Geschichte und Archaologie, Berlin, 1969-90. *Creative works:* 30 books on ancient history, archaeology, early mankind, slavic and germanic tribes in central and eastern Europe; About 100 scientific papers. *Memberships:* Deutsche Akademie der Wisenschaften, 1972; Deutsches Archaologisches Inst, 1984; Bulgarian and Polish Acads of Scis. *Honours:* Dr Honoris Causa, Univ of Athens, 1990; Prizes and medals of honour from German, Czech and Bulgarian Acads of Scis, and Univ of Bruxelles. *Hobbies:* Gardening; Reading. *Address:* Harnackstr 20, 0-1130 Berlin, Germany. 52.

HERRMANN John, b. 17 May 1931, Berkeley, California, USA. Writer; Editor. m. Andrea Watson, 25 May 1968, 3 d. *Education:* BA 1960; MA 1961; MFA 1964. *Appointments:* Eng Prof, Univ Montana, 1961-66; Univ of Iowa, 1962-63, State Univ of NY, 1966-69, Univ of Shiraz, Iran, 1969-70; Univ of Maryland, Europe, 1970-71; Cedar Crest Col, 1971-78; Lock Haven Univ, 1980- 81; Jrnst, 1979-, Ed, Health Systems Review. *Creative works:* **Publications include:** Summer will Rise, 1975; Office Automation, 1984; 25 stories in leading journals and 300 articles in magazines and journals. *Memberships:* Western Lit Assn; Bd of Dir, Modern Lang Assn; Assoc Writing Progs. *Hobbies:* Music; Travel; Photography. *Address:* ssa 0012 Echo Point, Little Rock, AR 72210, USA. 7.

HERSKOVITS Jean Frances, b. 20 May 1935, Evanston, Illinois, USA. Professor of African History. m. Robert Childres 22 Dec 1974, dec. *Education:* BA Swarthmore Col, 1956; DPhil, Oxon, 1960. *Appointments:* Lectr, Brown Univ, 1961-62; Instr, Asst Prof, Swarthmore Col, 1962-67; Asst Prof, City Col, City Univ of NY, 1967-71; Assoc Prof, Prof of Hist, State Univ of NY at Purchase, 1977-; Adjunct Prof, Columbia Univ, 1986; Dir, Nigeria Reinvestment Proj Citizens Energy Corp, 1984-91. *Creative works:* A Preface to Modern Nigeria, 1965; Nigeria: Power and Democracy in Africa, 1982; Articles in professional magazines and journals. *Memberships:* Coun on Foreign Relations; Near East Foun, Bd, 1980-; African Studies Assn, Bd, 1973-76; Am Hist Assn; Hist Soc of Nigeria. *Honours:* BA High Hons; Phi Beta Kappa, 1956; 6 Res Grants, 1958-80. *Hobbies:* Travel; Lecturing; Reading; Computer Science. *Address:* Dept of History, Humanities Division, State University of New York, Purchase, NY 10577, USA.

HERTZOG Christopher Barry, b. 21 Aug 1939, Cambridge, England. International Health Consultant. m. Jeanne Lovell Brough, 21 Aug 1963, 3 d. *Education:* MA Cantab, 1964; FBIM 1987; PhD 1988. *Appointments:* Sr Lectr in Law, Surrey CC, 1974-89; Vale Royal Stately Home Restoration Proj, 1982-89; Intl Healthcare Trident, UK Ltd, 1990-. *Creative works:* Various travel articles for newspapers, magazines and professional journals. *Memberships:* IOD; FBIM; Inst of Mktg; Aircraft Owners and Pilots Assn. *Honours:* Duke of Edinburgh Awd in Law, 1962. *Hobbies:* Flying; Skiing; Tennis; Photography; Travel; Archaeology. *Address:* 21 Grove Road, Havant, Hants PO9 1AR, England.

HESLIN Cathleen Jane, b. 24 Feb 1929, Brooklyn, NY, USA. Artist; Designer; Entrepreneur. m. John Thomas Heslin, 24 June 1950. *Education:* AA Packer Collegiate Inst Bklyn, 1950; Postgrad, Duke Univ, Pratt Inst. *Appointments:* Sr Artist, Designer, Klopman Mills, NJ, 1966-72; Freelance Designer, 1972-90; Propr, Quilters Corner, NY, 1978-90; Delegate, 114th Episc Convention, 1988; Borough of Rockleigh, NJ, Councilwoman, 1973-85, 1990-92; Chm, Environmental Com, 1974; Chm, Bicentennial Com, 1974-76; Chm, Shade Tree Comm, 1975; Chm, Fin Comm, 1977-78; Chm, Bldg Com, 1983-85; Chm, Hist Advy Com, 1977-86; Chm, Hist Preservation Comm, 1987-90; Planning Bd, 1973, 1987-89; Pres of Coun, 1983-85; Republican Mayoral Nominee, Borough of Rockleigh, 1990; Borough Historian, 1973-90; Trustee, Abram Demaree Homstead, 1982-84. *Creative works:* History of Rockleigh, NJ, 648-1973, 1973; Old Order Amish-The People and their Quilts, 1988; Inventor: Quilters Quarter measuring device. *Memberships:* Tappantown Hist Soc; Am Archtl Historians; Am Soc Planning Ofcls; BErgen Co Hist Soc, trustee, 1984-; Historic Homes Assn. *Honours:* Nat Historic Dist status, Borough of Rockleigh, 1976; Fdr, Cathleen Heslin Fdn, 1990. *Address:* Piermont Road, Rockleigh, NJ 07647, USA.

HESS Walter Otto, b. 16 July 1918, Zurich, Switzerland. Professor of Surgery. m. Charlotte Schmidlin, 25 May 1947, 1 s, 1 d. *Education:* Swiss Med Dipl, 1945; Swiss Res Inst Davos, 1945-46; Resident, 1946-49, First Resident, 1950-57, Surgical

Clinic Univ Basle; Resident, Univ Hedelberg, 1949-50. *Appointments:* Prof of Surgery, Univ of Alexandria, Egypt, 1957; Prof of Surgery, Univ of Basle, 1964-85. *Creative works include:* Chirurgie des pankreas, 1050; Operative Cholangiographie, 1954; Erkrankungen der Gallenwege, 1961, 1986; English, Italian, Spanish French, 1987-91; Over 200 papers on abdominal surgery. *Memberships:* Cantonal Parlament, Zurich, 1968-81; Delegate, Intl Red Cross, 1971; Capt Swiss Army, 1951-54; Swiss Socs of Surgery and Gastroenterology. *Honours:* Purkynje Medal, Prague, 1968; Hon Memberships include, Socs of Surgery in Italy, Sudan, and Cuba; Hon Prof, Univ of Ica, Peru. *Hobbies:* Politics; History. *Address:* Chalberweidstrasse 47, CH-8127 Forch, Switzerland. 52.

HESSABY Mahmoud, b. 25 Feb 1903, Tehran, Iran. Professor of Tehran University. m. Seddigheh Haeri, 1948, 1 s, 1 d. *Education:* BA, BSc, Am Univ of Beirut, 1920; Civil Eng Deg, French Engrg Sch of Beirut, 1922; Dr Deg in Phys, Sorbonne Univ, Paris, 1927. *Appointments:* Engr, Ministry of Public Works, Iran, 1927; Fdr, Tchr, Sch of Highway Engrg, 1928; Fdr, and Tchr, Tchr's Col, 1928; Fdr, Tehran Univ, 1934; Frd, Engrg Sch, 1934, Dean, 1936; Fdr, Fac of Sci, Dean, 1942-48, 1951-57, Tchr, 1957-; Prof of Phys, Tehran Univ, 1934-. *Creative works:* Books include:High School Physics, 1939; Physical Optics, 1961; Electromagnetic Theory, 1966; SOlid State Physics, 1969; Quantum Optics, 1979; Electrodynamics, in press. *Memberships:* European, Am and French Phys Socs; Life, Iranian Acad; NYAS; Univ Coun, 1924-; Educ Coun, 1953-; Soc for Sci Vocabulary; Intl Atomic Conf; Intl Space Conf; Fdg Chm: Space Res Org and Geophys Org. *Honours:* Legion d'Honneur Medal; Dr Hessaby Prize awarded by the Acad of Phys of Iran. *Address:* 8 Hessaby Avenue, Hessaby Sq, Tajrish, Tehran, Iran. 139, 50, 162, 139.

HESSE Helmut, b. 28 June 1934, Gadderbaum. Bank President. m. Hiltrud Hesse, 13 Apr 1962, 2 s. *Education:* Dipl Ec, 1958; Doctorate Ec, 1959; Habilitation, 1965. *Appointments:* Prof, Univ Gottingen, 1966-68; Prof, Georgetown Univ, 1983-84; Coun of Ec Advis, 1958-88; Pres, Land Central Bank, 1988-. *Creative works:* Books and articles on econonic affairs. *Memberships:* Club of Rome. *Honours:* 1989 Hon Senator, Univ of Gottingen. *Address:* Land Central Bank in Lower Saxony, Georgs Platz 5, D-3000 Hannover 1, Germany. 52.

HESTER Ronald Ernest, b. 8 Mar 1936, Slough, Bucks. Professor of Chemistry. m. Bridget Ann Maddin, 30 Aug 1958, 2 s, 2 d. *Education:* BSc 1959, DSc, 1979, London Univ; PhD, Cornell Univ, USA, 1962. *Appointments:* Res Fellow, Cambs Univ, 1962-63; Asst Prof, Cornell Univ, 1965-71; Sr Lectr, 1971-76, Reader, 1976-83, Prof, 1983-. *Creative works:* Books: Physical Inorganic Chemistry, 1965; Advances in Infrared and Raman Spectroscopy, 1975-85; Advances in Spectroscopy, 1986-93; 200 Research papers. *Memberships:* RSC, Chm, Environmental Gp, 1982-85; Ind Div Coun; Sci and Engrg Res Coun, Chm, Chem Com, 1988-90, Coun Mem, 1990-. *Honours:* FRSC, 1971; CChem, 1975. *Hobbies:* Tennis; Squash; Golf; Skiing; Travel; Reading. *Address:* Dept of Chemistry, University of York, York YO1 5DD, England. 1.

HEUER Helmut, b. 31 July 1932, Cuxhaven. University Professor. m. 22 Mar 1962, 1 s, 1 d. *Education:* State Exam and PhD, Munich Univ, 1958-59. *Appointments:* Lectr 1965, Prof of Eng Didactics, 1961, Col of Ed, Dortmund Univ; Ed, English, 1987-. *Creative works:* Die Englischstunde, 1968; Grundwissen der Englischen Fachdidaktik, 1977; Englischmethodik, 1987. *Membership:* Anglistentag. *Honours:* Univ Prize, Marburg, 1956. *Hobby:* Tennis. *Address:* University, Institute for English and American Studies, 4600 Dortmund 50, Germany.

HEVENER Fillmer Jr, b. 14 May 1933, Churchville, Virginia, USA. Portrait Artist; English Professor. m. 27 Aug 1954, 1 d. *Education:* BA Columbia Union Col, 1954;

MA James Madison univ, 1957; EdD Univ of Virginia, 1973. *Appointments:* Longwood Col, 1966-. *Creative works:* Books: Technical Writing: A Theoretical Basis; Successful Student Teaching; Hot Tips for Student Teachers; 19 published articles in professional journals. Graphite Paintings: Eve's Daughere, 2000 Ad; General George Weshington; Queen Esther; Prince of Life; General Robert E Lee; Graphite and Pastel portraits: American Cowpuncher. *Memberships:* Virginia Conf of Eng Educrs, Chm, 1989-90; IPA; Nat Coun for Tchrs of Eng; Univ Pros for Acad Order. *Hobbies:* Playing bluegrass fiddle and mandolin; Travel; Writing; Walking. *Address:* Route 2, Box 1425, Farmville, VA 23901, USA.

HEWITT Michael Earling, b. 28 Mar 1936, Southsea, Hants. Director of Central Banking Studies, Bank of England. m. Elizabeth Mary Hughes Batchelor 10 Aug 1961, 1 s, 1 d. *Education:* MA Modern Hist, Merton Col, Oxford, 1957-61; BSc Econ, London Univ, 1969. *Appointments:* Bank of England, 1961-70, Seconded, Econ Advr, Govt of Bermuda, 1971-74; Bank of England: Financial Forecaster, 1976-78, ADvr, Fin Insts, 1978-83, Hd of Fin Supervision, Gen Div, 1984-87, Hd of Fin and Indust Area, 1987-88, Sr Advrs Fin and Indust, 1988-90, Dir of Central Banking Studies, 1990-. *Creative works:* Chm of OECD Gp report, Systemic Risks in Securities Markets, 1991. *Memberships:* Assoc, Soc of Investment Analysts. *Honours:* Chancellor's Prize for Latin Prose, Oxford, 1958. *Hobbies:* Chess; Wine; Travel; Reading. *Address:* Bank of England, New Change, London, England. 1, 34.

HEWITT Thomas, b. 10 June 1950, Jarrow, England. Engineer; Civil Servant. *Education:* S.Shields Marine and Tech Col; City and Guilds, Gateshead Tech Col, 1969; Tec Further Ed, 1975-85; Computer Studies. *Appointments:* Engr, Energy Conservation, Civil Servant, Dept of Environment Property Sevrs Agy, 1992; Owner, Sherburn Electrics. *Memberships:* Trustee, St Pauls Jarrow Devel Trust; Treas, Friends of Jarrow Hall, 1986-92; Tyneside Energy Mgr Gp; Mbr, Tyne & Wear Small Bus Club. *Hobbies:* Gardening; Crosswords; Genealogy; DIY; Reading; Working for Charitable Trusts. *Address:* 65 Underwood Grove, Northburn Grange, Cramlington, Northumberland NE23 9UT, England.

HICKS David Gregory, b. 8 Sep 1958, Georgia, USA. Executive Pastor. m. Melanie Jon Ronas Hicks, 6 Sept 1986, 1 s, 1 d. *Education:* BS Ed, Auburn Univ, 1982; MDiv, S.Western Baptist Theol Sem, TX, 1986; Currently working towards DMin, Fuller Theol Sem, Pasadena, CA. *Appointments:* Students Ch Plnter, SBC Home Mission Bd, SWBTS Columbus, OH, 1985; Instr, Sheridan Hills Christian Sch, Hollywood, FL, 1986-87; Exec Pastor, Ch Growth, Orange Hill Bapt Ch, Austell, GA, 1988-91. *Memberships:* South Cobb Leadership Inst (Grad), 1991. *Honours:* Kappa Delta Pi, 1982; Nat Deans List, 1986. *Hobbies:* Photography; Gardening; Hiking; Camping; Travel; Reading; Walking; Water Skiing; Snow Skiing. *Address:* 1492 Ashlyn Court, Austell, GA 30001, USA.

HIGGINS John Dalby, b. 7 Jan 1934, Hong Kong. Journalist. m. Linda Christmas, 3 Sept 1977. *Education:* KCS, Wimbledon; MA Mod Lang, Worcester Col, Oxford. *Appointments:* Features Ed, 1962-64, Arts Ed, 1963-69, Financial Times: Arts Ed, 1970-88, Opera Critic, Obituaries Ed, 1988, The Times. *Creative works:* Publications include Travels in the Balkans, 1970; The Making of an Opera, 1977; Glyndebourne: A Celebration, Ed, 1984. *Memberships:* Com Royal Literary Fund, 1969-. *Honours:* Chevalier, 1973, Officier, 1990, De L'Ordre des Arts et Des Lettres; Ehrenkreuz fur Kunst und Wissenschaft, 1977; Goldenese Verdienstzeichen des Landes Salzburg, 1985; BP Special Award for Distinguished Services to Arts Journalism, 1992. *Hobbies:* Claret; Football; France. *Address:* The Times, Virginia St, London E1 9XY, England.

HIGGINS Ronald Trevor, b. 10 July 1929, London, England. Author. m. 15 Sept 1978. *Education:* BSc Sociol Hons, London, 1953. *Appointments:* Nat Serv, 1948-49; HM Diplomatic Serv, 1954-68; The Observer, 1968-76; Richmond Fellowship, 1978-79; Dir, Dunamis, St James Ch, Piccadilly, 1980-91. *Creative works:* The Seventh Enemy: The Human Factor in the Global Crisis, 1978; Plotting Peace: The Own's Reply to Hawks and Doves, 1990. *Memberships:* Ch, Champerowne Trust for Psychotherapy and the Arts; Bd, Guternational Sec Info Serv; Pupwash; Intl Inst for Strategic Studies; V-Chmn, Hereford Comm Hlth NHS Trust, 1992. *Honours:* Hon Fellow, Schumcher Soc, 1985; Hon Res Fellow, Richardson Inst, Lancs Univ. *Hobbies:* Music; Gardening; Travel; Tennis; Argument. *Address:* Little Reeve, Vowchurch Common, Hereford HR2 ORL, England.

HILDEN Patricia Jane Penn, b. 31 May 1944, Los Angeles, California, USA. Professor. m. Timothy J Reiss, 1 stepson, 1 stepdaughter. *Education:* BA Eng, 1965, MA Hist, 1977, Univ of Calif; Ma 1981, PhD Hist, 1981, Univ of Cambs. *Appointments include:* Caseworker, Yolo Co, CA, 1974; Tutor, Univ of Calif, 1974-75; Tchg Asst, Dept of Hist, Univ of Calif, 1976-77; Res Fellow, Trinity Hall, Cambs, 1980-81; Asst and Assoc Prof, Grad Inst of Liberal Arts, Emory Univ, Atlanta, GA, 1982-. *Creative works:* Working Women and Socialist Politics in France, 1986; Women, Work and Politics in Belgium, 1830-1914, in press. *Memberships:* Am Hist Assn; Indigenous Women's Network; Amnesty Insl; Am Friends Serv Com; Campaign for Peace and Democracy East and West. *Honours:* Fellowships: Am Assn of Univ Women, 1979-80, Am Coun of Learned Socs Humanities, 1983-84; Res grants: Brit Acad, 1980, Soc Sci Res Council, 1981, Nat Endowment for the Humanities, 1984-85; Fulbright Res Awd, 1985-86. *Hobbies:* Native American Politics and History; Poetry; Running; Feminist politics. *Address:* Graduate Institute of the Liberal Arts, Emory University, Atlanta, GA 30322, USA.

HILFER Anthony Channell, b. 19 Oct 1936, Los Angeles, California, USA. Professor of English. div. 1 s. *Education:* ba Middlebury Col, 1958; MA Columbia, 1960; PhD, Univ of N.Carolina, 1963. *Appointments:* Asst Prof, 1963-69, Assoc Prof, 1969-81, Prof, 1982-, Univ of Texas; Lectr, Keele Univ, UK, 1970-71; Assoc Prof, Univ Paul Valery, France, 1979; Lectr, Lancaster Univ, UK, 1982-83. *Creative works:* The Revolt from the Village, 1915-1930, 1969; The Ethics of Intensity in American fiction, 1981; The Crime Novel: A Deviant Genre, 1990. *Membership:* Modern Lang Assn. *Hobbies:* Film, especially film noir; History. *Address:* English Department, University of Texas, Austin, TX 78712, USA.

HILL (Michael) Hedley, b. 3 Feb 1945, Huddersfield, England. Solicitor; Public Notary. *Education:* Rydal Sch; St Johns Col, Cambs. *Appointments:* Solicitor, Admitted, 1964; Ptnr in Firm of Weightman Rutherfords in Liverpool, 1971-. *Memberships:* Past Pres, Old Rydalian Club; Pres, Liverpool Law Soc; Past Chm, 1992-93, Liverpool Young Sols; Law Soc; Liverpool Law Soc; Liverpool Racquet Club; Union Soc. *Hobbies:* Canal narrow boating; Oenology. *Address:* Fulwood Park Lodge, Liverpool L17 5AA, England.

HILL Archibald Govan IV, b. 5 Jan 1950, Louisville, Kentucky, USA. Associate Professor. m. Katherine C Powell, 21 Nov 1987, 1 s, 1 d. *Education:* MEng, Univ of Louisville, 1973; PhD, Lousiana Tech Univ, 1980. *Appointments:* Res Assoc, Louisiana Tech Univ, 1977-80; Asst Prof, Oklahoma State Univ, 1980-86; Assoc Prof, Uni of S.Western Louisiana, 1986-. *Creative works:* Artificial Intelligence in Control Valve Selection, 1988; Process and Disturbance Identification by Curve Fitting the Closed loop response, 1989; Using a spreadsheet for frequency response analysis, 1990. *Memberships:* AIChE; Am Soc for Engrg Educ; Instrument Soc of Am; Soc for Ind and Applied Math; Intl Ozone Assn; Am Soc of Sugarcane Technologists. *Honours:* Texaco Fellowship, 1974. *Hobbies:* Swimming; Golf; Hiking. *Address:* 1120 Marilyn Drive, Lafayette, LA 70503, USA. 143, 7.

HILL Christopher Richard, b. London, England. Sr Lecturer in Politics. *Education:* Radley Col; Trinity Col, Cambs, BA 1956, MA 1960. *Appointments:* Guthrie & Co, 1957-58; HM Foreign Serv, 1958-62; Inst of Race Relations, 1962-65; Univ Col of Rhodesia, 1965-66; Univ of York, 1966-; Sr Conslt, Jockey Club Ed Trust, 1991-. *Creative works:* Bantustans: The Fragmentation of S.Africa, 1965; Rights and Wrongs: Some Essays on Human rights, 1969; Change in S.Africa, 1983; Horse Power: The Politics of the Turf, 1988; Olympic Politics, 1991. *Memberships:* S.African Studies Trust, Trustee; Worshipful Co of Leathersellers, past third Warden; Royal Inst of Intl Affairs; Royal African Soc. *Hobbies:* Travel; Racing; Gardening; Writing. *Address:* Dept of Politics, Univ of York, Heslington, York YO1 5DD, England.

HILL James L, b. 12 Oct 1941, Meigs, Georgia, USA. Educator; Administrator. m. Flo J Hill, 16 Aug 1964, 2 s, 2 d. *Education:* BS Eng, Fort Valley State Col, 1963; MA Eng, Atlanta Univ, 1968; PhD Am Civilization, Univ of Iowa, 1976. *Appointments:* Tchr, Winder City Schs, 1964-65; Chm, Eng Dept, Hancock Central Hg, 1965-68; Ch of Eng Dept, Benedict Col, 1974-77; Ch, Eng Dept, 1977, Pres, Dean Arts and Scis, Pres, 1981, Albany State Col. *Creative works:* Ed, Studies in African and African American Culture; Ed, A Sourcebook for Teachers of Georgia HIstory; A Bibliography of Works of Himes, Petry and Yerby. *Memberships:* Nat Coun of Tchrs of Eng, Exec Com, 1981-82, Chair, CCC, 1981-82; Pres, SHADE, 1986-87; Nat Fed of State Humanities Coun, 1983-86. *Honours:* Gov Awd in the Humanities, 1987; Govs Appointee, Georgia; Desoto Comm; Govs Appointee, Christopher Columbus Comm. *Hobbies:* Reading; Travelling. *Address:* 2408 Greenmount Drive, Albany, GA 31705, USA. 7, 2.

HILL Jeri Linda, b. 6 Sept 1949, Texas, USA. Biomedical Research Scientist; Language Consultant. *Education:* BA Our Lady of the Lake Univ, 1971; MS, PhD, Univ of Calif at Berkeley, 1983. *Appointments:* Instr, Biomed Sci, 1979-80; Tchg Asst, Immunol, 1979-82; Instr, Microbiol, 1983-; Rheumatol Fellow, 1983-87; Res Assoc, 1987-. *Contributions to:* articles and reviews on professional journals. *Memberships:* Metro Harbour Fair Hsg Coun, Exec Com; Turku Microbiol Soc; Am Soc for Microbiol; NYAS; Am Col of Rheumatol; AAAS. *Honours:* Our Lady of the Lake Univ Scholar, 1967-71; Univ of Calif Fellow, 1973, Presidential Fellow, 1986; Ford Fellow, Nat Res Coun, 1985; Human Serv Awd of Los Angeles, 1986-; Image Builders Awd, 1980. *Hobbies:* Reading; Travelling; Music; Poetry; Cross-Cultural Interests. *Address:* 384 Lynbrook Drive, Pacifica, CA 94044, USA. 52.

HILL John Edward Christopher, b. 6 Feb 1912, York, England. Retired. m. Bridget Irene Sutton, 1 s, 1 d. *Education:* BA 1934, MA 1938, D Litt, 1965, Balliol Col, Oxford. *Appointments:* Fellow, All Souls Col, Oxford, 1934-38; Asst Lectr Hist, Univ Col Cardiff, 1936-38; Fellow and Tutor, Hist, 1938-65, Master, 1965-78, Balliol Col. *Creative works:* Economic problems of the church; Intellectual origins of the English Revolution; The World turned upside down; Milton and the English Rev; A Thinker and A Poor Man: John Bunyan. *Memberships:* FRHS; FBA. *Honours:* Milton Soc of Am Awds for Milton and the ENglish Rev, 1979; W H Smith Lit Awd for A Tinker and a Poor Man, 1989. *Hobbies:* 17th century theology. *Address:* Woodway House, Sibford Ferris, Banbury, OX15 5RA, England.

HILL Julian, b. 9 Aug 1932, India. Company Director. m. Ruth Monica Toll, 20 Mar 1956, 2 s, 1 d. *Education:* Rottingdean Sch; Eastbourne Col. *Appointments:* 2nd Lt, 22nd Cheshire Regt, 1952-54; Unilever Ltd, Overseas Allied Suppliers, Lipton Overseas Ltd, 1954-63; Unilever Ltd, Lipton Overseas Ltd, 1972-77; Dir of various

Unilever Cos since 1967; MD, Julian Hill Ltd, 1977-; Commercial Advr to UN, Geneva, 1977-; Commercial Advr to European Comm, Brussels, 1984-. *Memberships:* Fellow, BIM; Fellow, IOD CIM. *Honours:* Freedom, City of London, 1981; Liveryman, Marketors Co, 1984-. *Hobbies:* European Affairs; Opera; Cricket; Sailing; Skiing. *Address:* Huntsland Cottage, Huntsland Lane, Crawley Down, Sussex RH10 4HB, England.

HILL Ronald Charles, b. 4 Sept 1948, Parkersburg, West Virginia, USA. Associate Professor of Surgery. m. Lenora Jane Rexrode, 12 June 1971, 1 s, 1 d. *Education:* BA Liberal Arts,1970, MD Med 1974, WVU; Surg Residency, Duke Univ, 1974-85. *Appointments:* Instr, Surg, Duke, 1984-85; Asst Prof of Surg, 1985-90, Assoc Prof of Surg, 1990-, WVU. *Publications:* 85. *Memberships:* Southern Thoracic Assn; Assn for Acad Surg; Soc Univ Surgeons; Southeastern Surg Congress; Soc of Thoracic Surgs; Am Col of: Surgs, Cardiol, Chest Phys, Angiology. *Honours:* Alpha Epsilon Delta; Phi Beta Kappa; Alpha Omega ALpha; Lang Med Bk Awd, 1971, 1973, 1974; Roche Med Awd, 1972; Merck Manual Awd, 1974. *Hobbies:* Fishing; Photography; Collecting. *Address:* Dept of Surgery, 4060 Health Sciences Centre North, West Virginia Unversity, Morgantown, WV 26506, USA. 46, 7, 15.

HILL Shaun Donovan, b. 11 Apr 1947, London, England. Chef. m. Anja, 11 June 1966, 1 s, 2 d. *Education:* The London Oratory, 1957-61; St Marylebone Grammar Sch, 1962-65. *Appointments:* Carriers, Islington, 1967-71; Gay Hussar, Soho, 1972-74; Intercontinental Hotel, London, 1975-76; Capital Hotel, Knightsbridge, 1976-77; Gidleigh Park, Chagford, Devon, 1985-. *Creative works:* Shaun Hill's Gidleigh Park Cookery Book. *Memberships:* Acad Culinaire de France; Master Chefs Inst. *Hobbies:* Drinking; Trying to reconcile income with expenditure. *Address:* 14 Oaktree Park, Sticklepath, Sampford Courtnay, Devon EX20 2NB, England.

HILL Thomas Allen, b. 29 Mar 1958, Salem, Ohio, USA. Attorney at Law. *Education:* BA Hist and Polit Sci, Magna cum laude, Hiram Col, OH, 1980; JD, Nat Law Ctr, George Washington Univ, 1984. *Appointments:* Legislative Intern, Off of Hon John Conyers Jr, Washington, 1979; Asst to Dean, Campus Life for Hsg, Conf Dir, Hiram Col, 1980-81; Corp Counsel, Capital Oil & Gas Inc, Austintown, OH, 1984-; Sec and Gen Counsel, N.Coast Energy Inc, 1987-. *Creative works:* Co-author: The Politics of Principle and the Third Party System: Garfield, A Case Study, 1980. *Memberships:* ABA; Christian Legal Soc; Eastern Mineral Law Foun; Fed Energy Bar Assn; OH Land Title Assn; OH Oil and Gas Assn; Mahoning Co and Trumbull Co Bar Assns; SAR; Gen Soc of War of 1812; OH Genealogical Soc; Mahoning Valley Hist Soc. *Honours:* Admitted to the Bars of: OH, 1984, PA 1987, DC, 1988, US Supreme Ct, 1989, TX, 1990, OK, 1991; Appt to NOV Task Force by Chief, Div of Oil and Gas, OH Dept of Natural Resources, 1988-90; Kappa Delta Pi; Pi Gamma Mu; Eagle Scout, BSA 1973, Brotherhood, Order of the Arrow. *Hobbies:* Local history and genealogy; Local church affairs; Study of Amaranth. *Address:* 4841 Westchester Drive, Apt 102, Austintown, OH 44515, USA. 139, 163, 52, 8.

HILL SMITH Marilyn, b. 9 Feb 1947, Carshalton, Surrey, England. Soprano Singer. *Education:* AGSM Dist, Guildhall Sch of Mus, London. *Appointments include:* Cabaret, pantomime, concerts, 1971-74; Extensive concert touring, Gilbert & Sullivan for All, NZ and Aust, 1974, USA & Can 1976; Principal Soprano, Eng Nat Opera, 1978-84; Covent Gdn debut, Peter Grimes, 1981; Wels, Nat Opera debut, 1987; Also appeared with: Eng Bach Festival, Aldeburgh Festival, New Sadlers Wells, Can Opera, Scottish Opera, and festival seasons, Grenada, Athens, Belfast. Commercial recordings including rare operatta, works by Rameau to Ivor Novello, Meyerbeer. *Honours:* Young Mus of the Yr, 1975; Susan Longfield Prize, 1974; Young Mus of

the Yr, 1975; Susan Longfield Prize, 1974; Various student awards. *Hobbies:* Cooking; Gardening; Sleeping. *Address:* c/o Music International, 13 Ardilaun Road, Highbury, London N5 2QR, England. 34.

HILLENGASS Eugen Georges Walther, b. 14 Aug 1930, Frankfurt, Germany. General Treasurer; Priest. *Education:* Licenciates: Phil, 1953-56, Theol, 1959-63; Dipl, Bus Admin, 1963-68. *Appointments:* Socius to the Provincial in Munich, Germany, 1968-73; Gen Treas, Soc of Jesus in Rome, 1972-. *Membership:* Bd of Dirs, Ecumenical Devel Coop Soc, 1979-84. *Honour:* First class German Merit Cross, 1985. *Hobby:* Catholic theology. *Address:* Generals Curia of the Society of Jesus, Casella Postale 6139, I-00195 Roma, Italy. 2.

HILLERY Mary Jane Larato, b. 15 Sept 1931, Boston, USA. Television Hosp; Editor; Columnist; Reserve army Officer. m. Thomas H Hillery, 25 Feb 1961, 1 s. *Education:* BS, Univ Mass, 1962; Grad, Command and Gen Staff Col, 1982. *Appointments include:* Interpreter, Intl Conf Fire Chiefs, Boston, 1966; Tchr, Spanish, YWCA, Mass, 1966-67; Community Rels Cons Adv Bd Dirs Lectr for Migrant Educ Proj Div Mass Dept Community Affairs, 1967-69; Ed in Chief, Sudbury Citizen, 1967-76; Assoc Ed, The Beacons, 1976079; Contbtg Ed, 1979-83; Area Ed Advr, Becon Pub Co, Mass, 1970-80, Ed, 1976-80; Columnist Town Crier, 1987-; Contbtg Ed, Town Talk, 1975-79, Citizens Forum, 1975-81; Dir, Pub Affairs Mass Dept Eviron Qual Engrg, 1981-83; Producer, host TV interview show, For the Record. *Memberships include:* Nat Press Club; Nat Edit Assn; Nat Newspaper Assn; New Eng Press Assn; Various posts: Bus and Profl Womens Club, League Am Pen Women, Res Ofrs Assn; Omega Sigma. *Honours:* Meritorius Ser Medal; Jt Ser Achievement Medal, 1991; Ed of the Yr, Becon Pub Co, 1970; Medal of Appreciation, Intl Order DeMolay, 1969; Cert of Appreciation, US Def Civil Preparadness Agy, 1975; Appreciation Awd, US Milit Acd, 1976-86; Newswriting Awd, Media Contest, Air Force Sys Command, 1984. *Address:* 65 Willow Road, Sudbury, MA 01776, USA.

HILLIER Jack Ronald, b. 29 Aug 1912, London, England. Writer; Japanese Art Expert. m. Mary Louise Palmer, 28 May 1938, 1 s, 1 d. *Education:* Fulham Secondary Sch; Central Sch, Holborn. *Appointments:* Conslt, Sothebys for Japanese Art, 1953-77; Freelance Writer, 1977-. *Creative works include:* The Art of Hokusai in book illustration, 1980; Japanese Prints: 300 years of albums and books, 1980; The Art of the Japanese Book, 1987; Japanese and Chinese Prints in the Amstutz Collection, 1991; The Japanese Picture Book, 1991; Wood-engravings from 1933- 87, 1991. *Memberships:* Japan UKIYO-E Soc, Intl Ed Advy Bd. *Honours:* Uchiyama Prize, Japan, 1982, 1988; Ord of Rising Sun Awd, 1992. *Hobbies:* Wood engraving; Watercolour; Classical Music; Countryside. *Address:* 30 Clarence Road, Meadvale, Redhill, Surrey RH1 6NG, England.

HILSKY Martin, b. 8 Apr 1943, Prague, Czechoslovakia. Professor. Translator; Essayist. m. 4 July 1970, 2 s, 1 d. *Education:* Grad, Charles Univ, Prague, 1965. *Appointments:* Asst and Grad Student of Eng Lit, Charles Univ, 1965-71; Asst Prof, 1971-83; Assoc Prof, 1982-92; Prof, 1992-. *Creative works:* Angloamerican New Criticism, 1976; Contemporary British Novel, 1991; 100 essays, and translations. *Memberships:* The Circle of Modern Philologists; The Assn of Czech Translators; The Assn of Czech Americanists; The European Soc for the Study of Eng. *Honours:* Publishing House Odeon Awd for translation of D H Lawrence and J G Farrell, 1989; Czech Assn of Translators Awd for translations of Shakespeare and T S Eliot, 1991. *Hobbies:* Literature; Theatre; Drama; Music; Fine Arts; Skiing; Good company and conversation. *Address:* Charles University, Dept of English and American Studies, Nam Palacha 2, Prague 1, Czechoslovakia.

HINCHCLIFFE Ronald, b. 20 Feb 1926, Bolton, Lancs, England. Emeritus Professor of Audiological Medicine, University of London. *Education:* Manchester University MB ChB MD; Research Fellow Psycho-Acoustic Lab, Harvard University; London University PhD. *Appointments:* RAF MEd Branch Sqdn Ldr; RAF Acoustics Lab, 1951-55; Sci Staff, MRC, 1956-60; Assoc Prof, Univ of Iowa, USA, 1960-63. *Creative works:* Scientific foundations of Otolaryngol, 1976; Hearing and Balance in the Elderly, 1983. *Memberships:* First VP, Intl Soc of Audiol; Past Pres, Intl Assn of Phys in Audiol; FRCP, Edinburgh and London. *Honours:* Ciba Foun Awd for Res, 1959. *Hobbies:* Skiing; Sailing; Travelling. *Address:* Athenaeum, Pall Mall, London SW1Y 5ER, England.

HINDE Robert Aubrey, b. 26 Oct 1923, Norwich, Norfolk, England. Master, St John's College, Cambridge. m. (1) Hester Cecily Coutts, 1948, 2 s, 2 d; (2) Joan Gladys Stevenson, 1971, 2 d. *Education:* St John's Col, Cambs, 1946-48; Balliol Col, Oxford, 1948-50. *Appointments:* Res Asst, Edward Grey Inst, Dept of Zoology, Oxford Univ, 1948-50; Curator, Ornithol Field Station, Dept of Zoology, Cambs Univ, 1950-63; Royal Soc Res Prof, 1963- 89; Master, St John's Col, Cambs, 1989-. *Creative works:* Over 300 journal articles and chapters in books including: Essays on Violence, 1987; Relationships within Families: Mutual Influences, 1988; Education for Peace, 1989; Agression and War, 1989; Cooperation and Prosocial Behaviour, 1991; The Institution of War, 1991. *Memberships include:* FRS; Foreign Hon Mem, AAAS; Hon Fellow, Am Ornithologists Union; Hon Foreign Assoc of NAS; Hon Mem, Assn of the Study of Animal Behaviour; Hon Fellow, RCPsych. *Honours:* Huxley Medal, Royal Anthropol Inst; Mem, Academia Europaea; Hon Fellow, Trinity Col Dublin, 1990; Dist Sci Contribution Awd, Soc for Res in Child Devel; Dist Career Awd, Int Soc Study Res Relationships, 1992; Hon Doctorates: Univs of Brussels, Paris, Sterling, Goteborg and Edinburgh, 1991. *Hobbies:* Walking; Swimming. *Address:* St Johns College, Cambridge CB2 1TP, England. 1, 43, 2, 34.

HINGHOFER-SZALKAY Helmut G, b. 22 Jan 1948, Graz, Austria. University Professor. m. Irma Leber, 6 Apr 1979, 1 s, 1 d. *Education:* MD, 1974, Universitatsdozent, 1981. *Appointments:* Physiologisches Inst, Univ Graz, 1970-. *Creative works:* Book on applied physiology; 150 Scientific publications; reviews on space medicine. *Memberships:* Int Acad of Astronautics; Am and German Physiol Socs; Aerospace Med Assn. *Honours:* Hoechst Awd Graz, 1978, 1980, 1986; NASA Tech Brief Awd, 1986; Tit AO Univ Prof, 1987; VP, Austrain Soc for Aerospace Med, 1991-. *Hobbies:* Sports; Music; Talking about ideas. *Address:* Goethestra 47, A-8010 Graz, Austria.

HIRANSOMBOON Vajira James, b. 7 July 1945, Bangkok, Thailand. Managing Director. m. Sansanee Sandy Hiransomboon, 20 Apr 1979, 2 d. *Education:* Dipl, Assumption Col, Sriraja, 1962; Degree, Assumption Commercial Col, 1966. *Appointments:* Asst Mgr, S.East Ins Co Ltd, 1966- 69; Sr Exec, Heath Hudig Langevelot, 1975-78; Gen Mgr, Minet Janes Thailand Ltd, 1978-85; Wilson Ins Co Ltd, 1985-. *Memberships:* Gen Ins Assn of Thailand, Res and Tech Chm; Dir, Bd of Trade of Thailand; Sub-Com on Thai Dictionary of Insurance, Royal Inst. *Honours:* E.Asian Insurane Congress, Session Commentator, 1990. *Hobbies:* Swimming; Scuba Diving; Golf. *Address:* Wilson Insurance Co Ltd, 245-249 Rajawong Road, Bangkok, Thailand.

HIRVONEN Leo Leopold, b. 15 Nov 1924, Savonlinna, Finland. Professor of Physiology. m. Hellin Sucksdorff, 6 Aug 1950, 2 s, 1 d. *Education:* Matriculation, 1942; MD, Turku Univ, 1950; DMS, Helsinki Univ, 1955. *Appointments:* Asst, Univ of Helsinki, 1952-55, Univ of Turku, 1955-57; Assoc Prof, Univ of Turku, 1957-70; Prof Univ of Oulu, 1970- 91. *Creative works:* Publication on cardiovascular, neonatal and clinical physiology, smoking questions and temperance.

Memberships: Societas Physiologica Finlandiae, Chm, 1976-82; Hon Mem, 1991; Nordsisk Forenif for Fysiologi, Chm, 1976-79; Finnish Christian Med Assn, Chm, 1969-82. *Honours:* Cmdr: Order of the Holy Lamb, 1978, Order of the Finnish Lion, 1989. *Hobbies:* Photography; Carpentry. *Address:* Department of Physiology, University of Oulu, Kajaanintie 51A, SF-90220 Oulu, Finland. 90, 52, 43, 50, 139.

HISASHIGE Tadao, b. 6 Apr 1936, Tokyo, Japan. University Professor. m. 7 Dec 1976. *Education:* BA 1959, MLitt, 1961, Tokyo Univ; DLitts, Univ Paris, 1982. *Appointments:* Lectr, 1964-71, Asst Prof, 1971-77, Prof, 1977-, Fac of Letters, Senshu Univ. *Creative works:* Phenemenologie de la conscience de culpabilite, 1983, 1988, French and Japanese editions. *Memberships:* Philos Assn of Japan; The Japanese Soc for Ethica; Soc de Philos Franco-Japanese. *Honours:* Watsuji Prize, Soc for Japanese Ethics, 1967. *Hobbies:* Classical music; Reading. *Address:* Kokubunji-dai 5-8-19, Ebina, Japan. 52.

HLAWITSCHKA Eduard, b. 8 Nov 1928, Dubkowitz, Bohemia. University Professor. m. Eva Marie Schmidt, 29 May 1958, 1 s, 1 d. *Education:* PhD, Freiburg Univ, 1956; Habil. Saarbrucken Univ, 1966. *Appointments:* Univ Docent, Mediaeval Hist, Saarbrucken, 1966; Univ Prof, Dusseldorf, 1969, Munchen, 1975-. *Publications:* 10 scholarly books and voer 70 scholarly articles on mediaeval hitory. *Memberships:* Sudentendentschu Akademie der Wissenschafsen und Kunste, Pres, 1991-. *Honours:* Cultural Prize for Scholarly Learning, 1987. *Address:* Panoramastr 25, D-8036 Herrsching, Germany.

HNIK Pavel, b. 30 Nov 1927, Nachod, Bohemia. Scientist. m. Olga Hnikova, 30 June 1951, 1 s, 1 d. *Education:* MD Med Fac, Charles Univ, Prague, 1951; PhD , DSc, 1966, Inst of Physiol, CAS, Prague. *Appointments:* Rehabilitation Phys in Poliomyelitis, 1951-52; Inst of Physiol, Czechs Acad Sci, 1952-; Wellcome Foun Fellow, Aberdeen Univ, 1964-65; Visiting Prof, Salt Lake City, 1969-70. *Creative works:* Author of more than 200 scientific papers and monographs including: Muscle Atrophies, 1966; Electromyography in Chronic Animal Experiments, 1988. *Memberships:* Brit Physiol soc, 1965; NYAS, 1987; Ed-in-chief, Physiological Research and Ceskoslovenska fyziologie, 1991; V-Chm, Czech Physiol Soc, 1990. *Honours:* Purkinje Meml Medal, 1990; Laufberger Meml Medal, 1991. *Hobbies:* Chamber music playing (violin); Sport; Grandchildren; Teaching English to PhD students. *Address:* Institute of Physiology, Czechoslovak Academy of Sciences, Videnska 1083, 142 20 Prague 4, Czechoslovakia.

HO Chin Ko (He Jin Ke), b. 22 Aug 1919, Henan Province, China. Research Professor. m. Liu Tsai Pae (Liu Zai Pei), 17 May 1946, 2 s, 1 d. *Education:* BS Nat Central Univ, 1940-45; Res Student of Wood Chemistry, Div of Forest Products, CSIRO, Australia, 1948-50. *Appointments:* Engr, 1952, Assoc Prof, 1956, Res Prof, 1982, Section Hd, 1953-66, Dir, 1978-84, Res Inst of Chem Processing and Utilization of Forest Products (RICPUFP), Chinese Acad of Forestry. *Creative works:* Chief author and Ed, Black Wattle (Acacia Mearnsii) and Its utilization, 1991; Chief Ed, Chemistry and Industry of Forest Products, 1981, Communications of Science and Technology of Forest Chemical Products, 1981-87; Author of Many scientific papers; Chief Ed, Comprehensive Treatise on Forest Chemical Industries, 1990-. *Memberships:* IUFRO, 1981, Intl Coun, 1986-90; Chm, Chinese Soc of Chem and Chem Engrg of Forest Products, 1984-; Exec Bd, Chinese Soc of Forestry. *Honours:* Fellow, Intl Acad of Wood Sci, 1984-; Chief Sponsor, of Proposal concerning pulp production which was awarded first class national prize, 1991. *Hobbies:* Reading; Bejing Opera. *Address:* Research Institute of Chemical Processing and Utilization of Forest Products, Chinese Academy of Forestry, Long Pan Road, Nanjing 210037. China.

HO Eliot Ear-Shun, b. 10 Dec 1947, China. Gen Manager, Commercial Department. m. 13 Jan 1974, 2 s, 1 d. *Education:* BSc, Major in Marine Engrg, 1967-71. *Appointments:* Asst Section Chief of Iron Making Engrg Div, CSC, 1982-89; Gen Mgr, Admin, CSCC, 1989-91; Gen Mgr, Commercial in CSCC, 1991-92. *Creative works:* Paper presented at 1st Intl Coke Making Congress, Germany, 1987. *Memberships:* Soc of Naval Archs and Marine Engrs; Chinese Soc of Mech Engrs. *Honours:* Outstanding employee from govt enterprise, Ministry of Econ Affairs, ROC. *Hobbies:* Swimming; Table Tennis; Basketball; Reading; Enthusiasm for the unification of China. *Address:* 23 Tung-Ya South Road, Hsiao Kang District, Kaohsiung, Taiwan, China.

HO Shung Pun, b. 5 Dec 1938, Guangzhou, China. Principal Lecturer. *Education:* BSc Applied Maths, 1st class hons, 1963; BSc Phys, 2nd class hons, 1964, PhD, 1968, Univ Col of Wales, UCW; MSc Courant Inst, NY Univ, USA, 1966. *Appointments:* Dept Tutor, Dept of Applied Maths, Univ Col of Wales, 1966-68; Asst Lectr, Dept of math, 1968-69, Lectr, 1969-70, Univ of Leices; Asst prof, Dept Math, Laurentian Univ, Ontario, Canada, 1970-81; Principal Lectr, Hong Kong Poly, 1981-. *Memberships:* Candian Applied Maths Soc; NYAS. *Honours:* Col REs Fellow, UCW, 1976-77; Visiting Asst Prof, 1978-79, Visiting Assoc Prof, 1986, Div of Applied Math, Brown Univ, Providence RI, USA; Visiting Scholar, Dept of Math, MIT Cambs, Mass, 1979-80, *Hobbies:* Reading; Travelling; Jogging; Swimming; Classical music; Table Tennis; Badmington; Chinese Chess. *Address:* Department of Maths, Hong Kong Polytechnic, Kowloon, Hong Kong. 152.

HO YEN Darrel Orlando, b. 1 May 1948, Guyana. Conslt Microbiologist. m. Jennifer Nichols, 18 July 1975, 2 s. *Education:* BMsc, 1971; MB ChB, 1974; MD, 1983; MRC Path, 1986. *Appointments:* Conslt Microbiologist, Raigmore Hosp, Inverness, 1987-. Dir, Scottish Txoplasma Ref Lab; Dir, Scottish Hydatid Ref Lab; Hon Clinical Snr Lect, Aberdeen Univ. *Publications:* Better Recovery from Viral Innmesses; Diseases of Infection. *Memberships:* British Soc for Study of Infection; Assn of Clinical Pathologists; Pathological Soc of Great Britain & Ireland; Soc of Authors. *Address:* Microbiology Dept, Raigmore Hosp, Inverness IV2 3UJ, Scotland.

HOARE SaraJane b. 27 June 1955, London, England. Fashion Director. *Education:* BA Eng Lit, Warwick Univ. *Appointments:* Fashion Jrnist, Observer Newspaper, 1986-88; Fashion dir, Vogue Magazine, 1988-. *Honours:* Graduated with BA Hons. *Hobbies:* Playing the paino; Ballet; Opera; Scuba Diving; Tennis. *Address:* Vogue House, 1 Hanover Square, London W1, England.

HOBART Caroline, Lady, b. 17 May 1931, Jersey, Channel Islands. Artist working under the name of Caroline Leeds. m. (1) 11th Duke of Leeds, dec; (2) Peter Hoos, div 1975; (3) Lt Cdr Sir Robert Hampden Hobart, dec. *Education:* St Mary's Sch, Wantage; Croft Hse Shillingstone, Dorset; The Chelsea Sch of Commercial Art. *Appointments:* Profl Artist, painting in oils, watercolours, pastels, conte and silver point; Numerous exhibitions in England, France and USA. *Creative works:* Portraits and landscapes; Portraits include: HRH The Prince Andrew, The Duke and Duchess of Bedford; Landscape commission includes: Set of Watercolours for Moet et Chandon, France. *Memberships:* Assoc Lady Mbr, Royal Yacht Squadron; Arts Club, Dover St, London. *Hobbies:* Travelling and visiting old towns in Europe; Looking at Greek and Roman Remains. *Address:* 42 Egertons, London SW32 2BZ, England.

HOBBS Kenneth Edward Frederick, b. 28 Dec 1936, London, England. Professor of Surgery; Consultant Surgeon. *Education:* Guy's Hosp Med Sch, Univ of London, MBBS, 1960, FRCS, 1964, CHM, Bristol, 1970. *Appointments:* Lectr in Surg, Univ of Bristol, 1966-70; Surg Res Fellow, Harvard Univ, 1968-69; Sr Lectr in Surg, Univ Bristol, 1970-73; Prof of Surg, Royal Free

Hosp Sch of Med, Univ of London, 1973-. *Creative works:* Chapters on aspects of liver surgery in textbooks and multiple publications on surgical aspects of liver disease and transplantation. *Memberships:* Med Comm of Univs Funding Coun; Exec Com, World Assn of HPB Surg; Trustee and Bd, Stanley Thomas Johnson Foun, Berne; Sci Advr, Mason Med Res Foun, London. *Hobbies:* Gormet dining; The Countryside. *Address:* The Rookery, New Buckenham, Norfolk NR16 2AE, England. 1.

HOBSBAUM Philip Dennis, b. 29 June 1932, London, England. Writer; Professor of English Literature. m. Rosemary Philips, 20 July 1976. *Education:* BA 1955, MA 1961, Downing Col, Camb; RAM, Royal Acad of Music, 1956; PhD, Univ of SHeffield, 1968. *Appointments:* Tchr, Tulse Hill Sch, London, 1956-58; Lectr, Queen's Univ Belfast, 1962-66; Lectr, Sr Lectr, Reader, Prof of Eng, Univ of Glasgow, 1966-. *Creative works:* A Theory of Communication, 1970; A Readers Guide to Charles Dickens, 1973; Tradition and Experiment in English Poetry, 1979; A Readers Guide to Robert Lowell, 1988. *Memberships:* BBC Club, Glasgow; Assn of Univ Tchrs; Assn for Scottish Literary Studies. *Hobbies:* Playing the piano; Walking the dog; Cooking. *Address:* c/o Dept of English Literature, Univ of Glasgow, Glasgow G12 8QQ, Scotland. 184. 3.

HODAPP Volker Artur, b. 12 July 1944, Freiburg, Germany. Professor of Psychology. m. Christa Maria Luhr, 24 Apr 1970, 1 s. *Education:* Dipl Univ Freiburg, Germany, 1970; Dr rer nat, 1973, Habilitation, 1981, Univ of Mainz. *Appointments:* Res Asst, Univ of Mainz, 1970-81; Heisenberg Scholar Deutsche Forschungsgemeinschaft, 1982-83; Prof of Psychol, Univ of Düsseldorf, 1983-. *Creative works:* Author: Analyse linearer Kausalmodelle, 1984; Book chapters and articles to professional journals on stress, emotion, psychosomatics, and statistics. *Memberships:* Soc for Test Anxiety Res; Intl Soc for Res on Emotions; Deutsche Geselleschaft fur Psychologie; Deutsche Gesellschaft fur Psychophysiologie und ihre Anwendungen. *Hobbies:* Music; Chess. *Address:* Institut für Physiologische Psychologie, Heinrich Heine Universität, Universitätsstr 1, D-4000 Düsseldorf 1, Germany. 52.

HODGE Bobby Lynn, b. 14 Oct 1956, North Carolina, USA. Mechanical Engineer. m. Robin Mayhue Renegar, 8 June 1979, 1 s. *Education:* AAS, Mech Engrg Forsyth Tech Inst, NC, 1974-76; Bachelor of Engrg Tech, (Mechanical), Univ of NC at Charlotte, 1976-78. *Appointments:* Design Engr, 1978-79, Proj Engr, 1979-80, Gravely Corp, NC; Design Engr, Ingersol- Rand, Davidson, NC, 1980-83; Devel Engr, Ingersoll-Rand, 1983-85; Application Engr, 1985-87, Mgr Driveline Applications Gp, 1987-88, Mgr, 1988-90, Dir, 1990-, Automotive Application Eng, INA Bearing Co. *Creative works:* Six US patents; Papers include: INA Precision Design Double Coolant Pumps Efficiency, 1991; Anti-Friction System Design... The INA Approach to Automotive Engineering, 1991, INA Bearing Co Inc; Saturn in Orbit - The Rolling Element, 1991. *Memberships:* ASMechE, 1976; Soc of Automotive Engrs, 1985; Soc of Tribologists and Lubrication Engrs, 1989; Univ of North Carolina at Charlotte Engineering Advisory Council, 1992; Soc of Automotive Engrs, Manual Transmission, Automatic Transmission, and Clutch Standards Committees, 1990; Raintree Country Club, 1986. *Honours:* Hon Grad, 1976; Res Awds in Engrg, Ingersoll Rand, 1982, 1983. *Hobbies:* Hunting; Woodworking; Golf. *Address:* 10032 Whitethorn Drive, Charolotte, NC 28277, USA. 7, 26.

HODOUŠEK Eduard, b. 18 Sept 1921, Volyně, Czechoslovakia. Historian; Translator; Editor. m. Jaroslava Čabounová, 6 Feb 1949, 1 d. *Education:* Dr Dipl, Fac of Philos, Charles Univ, Praha, 1945-50. *Appointments:* Municipal Office at Volyně, 1940-42; Dist Hosp at Strakonice, 1942-45; Publishing Hse Melantrich in Praha, 1950-52; State Publishing Hse Odeon, Praha, 1953-62, 1971-82; Inst of Foreign Lits of Czech Acad in Praha, 1963-70; External Lectr, Fac of Philos of Charles Univ, Praha, 1982-90. *Creative works:* Various reviews and essays about Hispanic literatures, studies accompanying the published Czech translations; Czech version of many Spanish and Latin-American and French authors. *Memberships:* Assn of Czech Translators; Czech-Spanish Soc. *Honours:* Annual prize, Dictionary of Writers of Spain and Portugal, Publishing House Odeon, 1968; Annual Prize, Czech Literary Fund, 1977. *Hobbies:* Travelling; Touring. *Address:* Mánesova 20, Praha 1, Czechoslovakia.

HODSON Philip, b. 2 Oct 1944, Peterborough, England. Solicitor. m. Diane Elizabeth Stansfield, 3 Aug 1968. *Education:* BA (Juris Prudence) MA, St Edmund Hall, Oxford, 1963-66. *Appointments:* Articled Clerk, 1966-69, Asst Solicitor, 1969-73, Manchester Corp; Asst Solicitor, 1973-74, Partner, 1974-87, Leak, Almond and Parkinson; Partner, Cobbett, Leak & Almond, 1987-. *Memberships:* Manchester Young Solicitors Assn, Com Mem, Chm, 1980-81; Manchester Law Soc, Coun, Pres, 1988-89; Solicitors Disciplinary Tribunal, 1989-; Former Treas and Chm, S.Manchester Law Centre. *Hobbies:* Squash; Golf; Theatre; Collecting Art Deco Ceramics. *Address:* 12 Stafford Road, Eccles, Manchester M30 9HW, England.

HOEFER Milan Peter, b. 15 Feb 1936, Landskron, Czechoslovakia. Professor of Microbiology. m. Eva Kvasnickova, 1 s, 1 d. *Education:* Dipl Chem, 1959, RNDr, 1966, Charles Univ, Prague; CSC Biol, Acad of Scis, Prague, 1963; Venia Legendi in Microbiol, Univ of Bonn, 1971. *Appointments:* Inst of Microbiol, Acad of Scis, Prague, 1963-68; Res Assoc, Univ Pennsylvania, 1965-66; Scist, Gesellschaft fur Molekularbiol. Forschung, Stockheim/Braunschweig, Germany, 1968-70; Univ of Bonn, 1970; Privat-Dozent, 1971, Apl Prof, 1973, Prof, 1980; Visiting Profs: Univ of Alexandria, Egypt, 1979-80, Univ of MO, Columbia, 1985, Univ of CA at Berkeley, 1990. *Creative works:* Transport across Biological Membranes, 1981; 80 articles in professional journals. *Memberships:* Gesellschaft fur Biol Chem, Vereinigung fur Allgemeine und Angewandte Microbiol; AAAS; NYAS; Life Fellow, ABI. *Hobbies:* Tennis; Skiing; Handicrafts; Theatre. *Address:* Mirabellestrasse 2, 5309 Meckenheim, Germany. 43, 52.

HOEVE Anthon Roelof, b. 16 June 1953, Numansdorp, Holland. Retired Business Economist. *Education:* Bus Sch, 1970-73; Tchrs Sch, 1973-78; Fiscal Econ, Erasmus Univ, 1978-80. *Appointments:* Fiscal Advr and Tchr, 1980-82; Acct, Tchr, 1982-83; Course Leader, 1983-85; Bus Ptnr, Course Writer; Fdr of EKON, 1985-91. *Creative works:* Books: Basic Economics for textile shops, 1986; Basic Economics for Fashion Shops, 1991. *Hobbies:* Travelling; Cooking and eating; Music; Discussing. *Address:* De Breistroeken 5-7, 7938 PV Nieuw- Balinge, Holland. 52.

HOFFMAN Roy A, b. 31 Jan 1940, Natchez, Mississippi, USA. Professor. m. Jeanne M SNover, 18 Nov 1972, 1 s, 1 d. *Education:* AB Mississippi State Univ, 1962; PhD Univ of Alabama, 1968; Post grad work: Univs of Colorado and Ohio; SSPS Corp. *Appointments:* Doctoral Fellow, 1966- 68; Asst Prof of Psychol, N.West Missouri State Univ, 1968-69; Assoc Prof, Prof, 1969-; Assoc Dean of Educ, 1984-90, Florida Atlantic Univ. *Creative works:* More than two dozen research articles in measurement and teacher education published in research journals; numerous reports for federal and state agencies evaluating programmes. *Memberships:* Florida Educ Res Assn; Assn for Supvn and Curriculum Devel; Am Philatelic Soc. *Hobbies:* Philately; Reading. *Address:* 1760 SW 9th Street, Boca Raton, FL 33486, USA.

HOFFMAN Sharon Lynn Seaman, b. 24 May 1939, Chicago, Illinois, USA. Research Editor in Publishing. *Education:* BA Educ, (Lang Arts) Indiana Univ, 1961; Master of Adult Ed, National-Louis Univ, 1992; Publishing Prog, Univ of Chicago, 1988, 1989.

Appointments: Lang Arts Tchr, 1961-86; Co-Ed, Surgeon Generals Wives Club Newsletter, 1975-76; House Newsletter, Macmillan Info Sers, 1986-90; Res Ed; Special Projs Ed, Marquis Who's Who, Reed Reference Pub, 1986-1992; Currently, Adult Educator, Consultant, Bennett & Assocs, 1992-. *Memberships:* Am Assn of Univ Women; League of Women Voters. *Address:* 2270 Highmoor Road, Highland Pk, IL 60035, USA.

HOFFMEISTER Gerhart, b. 17 Dec 1936, Giessen, Germany. Professor of German and Comparative Literature. div. 1 s. *Education:* PhD, Univ of Maryland, USA, 1970. *Appointments:* Instr, Univ of Maryland, 1966- 70; Asst Prof, Univ of Wisconsin, 1970-74; Assoc Prof, Wayne State Univ, Detroit, 1974-75; Assoc Prof, Prof, Univ of California, 1975-. *Creative works:* The Renaissance and Reformation in GErmany, 1977; From the Nazi Era to the present, 1986; Goethe in Italy, 1988; European Romanticism, 1989. *Memberships:* MAL; Am Assn of Tchrs of German; Am Comparative Lit Assn; Goethe Soc of N.Am. Soc for the Study of Baroque Lit. *Honours:* Honnefer Model stipend, Germany, 1958- 62; Am Philos Soc grant 1974; German Acad Exchange Serv Stipend, Univ Col London, 1962-63. *Hobbies:* Gardening; Tennis; Swimming. *Address:* 117 Calle Alamo, Santa Barbara, CA 93105, USA.

HOGARTH Cyril Alfred, b. 22 Jan 1924, London, England. Emeritus Professor of Physics. m. Audrey Jones, 4 Sept 1951, 1 s, 2 d. *Education:* Queen Mary Col Univ of London, 1941-43, 1946-68; BSc Hons, 1944; PhD 1948; DSc, 1973, all in Phys. *Appointments:* Experimental Ofc, Lt (SP)RNYR 1943-46; Lectr, Chelsea Col, 1948-49; Res Physicist, Univ of Reading, 1949-51; Sr Sci Ofr, Roy Rad Est, 1951-58; Hd of Phys, Brunel Col, 1958-64; Prof of Phys, Brunel Univ, 1964-89. *Creative works:* Materials used in semiconductor devices, 1965; Techniques of non-destructive testing, 1960; Over 300 original scientific papers. *Memberships:* FIP, Coun, 1967-73, VP, 1969-73; FIEE; Life, FRSA; Chartered Engr and Physicist; Gerrards Cross Parish Coun; S.Bucks Dist Coun. *Hobbies:* Travel; Gardening; Music; Bridge. *Address:* Shepherds Hey, Orchehill Ave, Gerrards Cross, Bucks SL9 8QG, England.

HOGBEN Neil, b. 23 Mar 1923, Barnard Castle, Durham, England. Retired Marine Consultant. m. Edith Cornelia Leister, 10 Mar 1958, 1 s, 2 d. *Education:* BSc 1st class hons, 1951, PhD 1956, Naval Arch, Univ of Durham. *Appointments:* Mgmt Trainee, J L Thompson Shipbuilders, 1947- 51; Tech Asst, Rotol Propeller Co, 1951-52; Nat Phys Lab, Prin Sci Ofr, 1956, Sr PSO, 1967, Dep Chief Sci Ofr, 1979; NPL/NMI, 1956-85. *Creative works:* Co-author: Ocean Wave Statistics, 1967; Global Wave Statistics, 1986. *Contributions to:* Advances in Hydroscience Vol 4, 1967; The Sea, Vol 9, 1990; Encyclopaedia of Fluid Mechanics Vol 10, 1990. *Memberships:* Fellow, Royal Inst of Naval Archts; Assoc, NE Coast Inst of Engrs and Shipbuilders; Fellow, Royal Acad of Engrg. *Honours:* Medals for published papers from RINA and ICE; RINA Silver Medal, 1974; Bronze Medal, 1984; ICE George Stephenson Medal, 1977; Min of Defence/SUT Awd for Oceanography, 1989. *Hobbies:* Music and playing the piano. *Address:* 60 Foley Road, Claygate, Surrey KT10 0ND, England.

HOGGARD William Zack Jr, b. 2 Dec 1951, Albuquerque, New Mexico, USA. Amusement Caterer. m. Sandra K Walker, 22 Nov 1990, 1 s, 1 d. *Appointments include:* Asst Mgr, Lone Star Amusements, TX, 1969; Gen Mgr, Golden Spread Amusements, Hedley, Amarillo, TX, 1969-72; Bkg Agt, Monte Young Shows, Utah, 1972; Independent Concessionaire Gene Ledel Shows, Ft Worth, TX; Concession Mgr, Schaffer Shows Unit 2, Dallas, 1974; Person Enterprises, Ft Worth, 1975-76; Gen Agt Concession Mgr, Aero Space Shows, Dallas, 1977-80; W.Sales Mgr, Op Engr, Pretzel Ride Inc, NJ, 1981; Broker, Distributor of amusement rides, carnival operator, Joshua, TX, 1982-; Los Control Conslt, Allied Speciality Ins Co, FL, 1985-; State Bd of Ins, TX, 1985-; Cnslt Engr, Eli Bridge Co Inc, IL, 1985-89; Pretzel Ride Inc, NJ, 1981- ; Conslt Amusement Ride Safety Act, 1983, State of Oklahoma Carnival Org and fund raiser, 1969-89; Owner of Phoenix Amusements & Operator of Presidents Pk Amusement Pk, NM, 1991-. *Memberships:* Texas Assn Fairs and Expositions; Oklahoma Assn Fairs and Festivals; Outdoor Amusement Bus Assn; Nat Assn Amusement Ride Safety officials; Lone Star Showmen's Club. *Hobbies:* Refurbishing used and antique amusement rides. *Address:* 711 Muscatel Avenue, Carisgad, NM 88220, USA. 7, 132.

HOGWOOD Christopher Jarvis Haley, b. 10 Sept 1941, Nottingham, England. Conductor; Writer. *Education:* Cambs Univ; Charles Univ, Prague, MA; FRSA. *Career:* Fdr Mem, Early Music Consort of London, 1967-76; Fdr, Dir, Acad of Ancient Music, 1973-; Fac, Cambs Univ, 1975-; Dir, Handel and Haydn Soc, Boston, US, 1986-; Hon Prof of Music, Keele Univ, 1986- 89; Dir Music, St Paul Chamber Orch, Minnesota, 1987-92; Prin Guest Conductor, St Paul Chamber Orch, Minn, 1992-. *Recordings:* Many recordings of baroque and classical music including: CDs of Bach Double Concertos, Cantatas 211 and 212; Handel Messiah; Handel Italian Cantatas; Athalia; Pergolesi Stabat Mater; Stravinsky Dumbarton Orks and Pulcinella; Telemann Orchestral Works; Vivaldi L'estro Armonico and 12 violin concertos op 4 La Stravaganza; Mozart Symphonies; Beethoven Symphonies, Beethoven Piano Concertos, Haydn symphonies. *Creative works:* Author: Music at Court, 1978; The Trio Sonata, 1979; Haydn's London Visits, 1980; Co-author, Music in Eighteenth Century England, 1983; Handel, 1984; Ed, The Life of Mozart by Edward Holmes, 1991; Many editions of musical scores. *Contributions to:* New Grove Dictionary of Music and Musicians. *Honours:* Walter Wilson Cobbett Medal, 1986, CBE, 1989; Hon Fellow, Jesus Col, Cambs, 1989; Freeman, Worshipful Co of Musicians, 1989; Hon Doc of Mus, Univ of Keele, 1991; Hon Fel, Pembroke Col, Camb, 1992. *Address:* 10 Brookside, Cambridge CB2 1JE, England. 4.

HOLL-ALLEN Robert Thomas James, b. 3 Dec 1934, Leamington Spa, England. Consultant Surgeon. m. (1) Barbara Mary Holl, 1962, diss 1972; (2) Diana Elisabeth Toothill, 2 Mar 1974, diss 1990, 2 s, 1 d. *Education:* London Univ Col, 1953-56, Univ Col Hosp Med Sch, 1956-59; Harvard Med Sch, 1968-69: BSc HoOns, 1956; MRCS, LRCP, 1959; MBBS Hons, 1959; FRCS Eng, 1963; DLO (RCS & RCP), 1963; MS Lond 1971, MD Lond, 1972; FACS, 1974; FICS, 1974. *Appointments:* Conslt Surgeon, E.Birmingham Hosp, Solihull Hosp and Marston Green Maternity Hosp. *Creative works:* Numerous articles in scientific and medical journals. *Memberships:* Fellow, Assn of Surgs of Gt Brit and Ireland; Fellow, RSM; Intl Soc of Endocrine Surgs; Brit Assn of Endocrine Surgs; Surg Res Soc; Fellow, Am Col of Surgs. *Honours:* Suckling Prize, Univ COl, 1956; Geoffrey Duuben Prize, 1958; Tuke Medal, 1959; Atchinsion Prize, UCH, 1959; Wessex RHA, Res Prize, 1966; Peel Trust Travelling Fellow, 1968; Wellcome Travelling Scholarship, 1968. *Hobbies:* Collecting china; Reading; Golf; Travel; Good food. *Address:* Dept of Surgery, East Birmingham Hospital, Bordesley Green East, Birmingham B9 5ST, England.

HOLLINSHEAD Ariel C, b. 24 Aug 1929, USA. Professor Emeritus; Pres of HT Virus and Cancer Research. m. Hon Montgomery Hyon, 27 Sept 1958, 2 s. *Education:* AB Ohio Univ, 1951; MS 1955, PhD, 1957, George Washington Univ. *Appointments:* George Washington Univ Med Ctr: Asst Prof Pharmacol, 1959-61, Asst Prof Med, 1961-64, Assoc Prof Med, 1964-73, Prof Med, 1974-90. *Creative works:* 400 articles including professional paers, book chapters on scientific medical research in virology and oncology. *Memberships:* Am Acad Microbiol. NYAS; AAAS; Grad Women in Sci; Bd Dir, Nat Womens Econ Alliance; ISPO; SEBM; ASM; AACR: ASO; CIS; ISAR: IASLC: IUAC:

AMWA. *Honours:* PAI Beta Kappa; Med Woman of the Year, 1976; Star of Europe Medal, 1987; Outstanding Women of America; Cert of Merit, Med Col, PA; Hn DSc and Outstanding Alumni, Ohio Univ. *Hobbies:* Oil painting; Golf; Swimming; Hiking; Piano Playing. *Address:* 3637 Van Ness St NW, Washington DC 20008, USA.

HOLLOWAY Julia Bolton, b. 14 Apr 1937, London, England. Professor Emerita. m. Halbert H Holloway, 10 Aug 1957, separated 1967, 3 s. *Education:* BA San Jose State Univ, 1957; MA 1967, PhD, 1974, Univ of California at Berkeley. *Appointments:* Quincy Col, 1971-74; Princeton Univ, 1974-81; Prof, Dir Mediaeval Studies, Univ of Colorado, Boulder, 1981- 92. *Creative works include:* Il Tesoretto, 1981; Equally in God's Image: Women in the Middle Ages, 1990; The Life of St Birgitta of Sweden, 1991; Lichens for Vegetable Dyeing, 1991; Tales within Tales: Apuleius through Time, 1992. *Memberships:* Community of the Holy Family; Mediaeval Acad of Am; Dante Soc of Am; Bronte Soc; Formerly, Bd of Dirs, Colorado Endowment for the Humanities; Rocky Mountain Peace Ctr; V-Chm, Colorado Women's Agenda. *Honours:* NEH Seminar, 1973; NEH Stipend, 1983; Govr's Awd, Outstanding Contribution to Humanities Educ, 1987; AAUW; Fdrs Fellowship, 1987-88. *Hobbies:* Carpentry; Watercolour. *Address:* Holmhurst St Mary, 731 The Ridge, St Leonards on Sea, E. Sussex TN37 7PT, England. 5.

HOLM Jessica Lynn, b. 29 Mar 1960, Stratford upon Avon, England. Zoologist; Broadcaster. m. Gavin Bernard Chappell, 27 Feb 1988. *Education:* BSc Hons Zoology, 1981; PhD 1990, Royal Holloway and Bedford Univ London. *Appointments:* Inst Terrestrial Ecol, Biotrack, 1982; Freelance Zoologist and Broadcaster, 1987; BBC Natural Hist Unit and others; Presenter, Radio 4 natural history programme, 1987-1993; Currently: Professional Painter; TV progs include: The Case of the Vanishing Squirrel, 1987; Daylight Robbery 1988; Wild about the West, TSW, 1988; Badger Watch, 1991; Up Country, Tyne Tees TV, 1990, 1991 & 1992; Daylight Robbery II, 1991. *Creative works:* Books: Squirrels, 1987; The Red Squirrel, 1989. *Memberships:* Coun of Mammal Soc, 1989-92. *Hobbies:* Natural history; Dogs; Riding. *Address:* c/o Rachel Daniels, London Management, 2-4 Noel Street, London W1V 3Rb, England.

HOLMES-WALKER William Anthony, b. 26 Jan 1926, Horwich, Lancs, England. Director, Intl Tech & Innovation. m. Maire Anne Russ, 26 July 1952, 2 d. *Education:* BSc, PhD, Queens Univ, Belfast, 1947-53; DIC, Imp Col, 1953-54. *Appointments:* Visiting Prof, City Univ, 1981- 83; Sec Gen, European Brewers Assn, 1984-88; Reading Univ, Dir Ind Liaison, 1988-90; Assoc Dir, Inventions to Indust, 1990-91. *Creative works:* Book: Polymer Conversion, 1975; Numerous scientific papers in journals and lectures worldwide. *Memberships:* FRCS, 1966; FPRI, Chm Educ Com, 1969; FIM, 1972; Master Skinners Co, 1980-81. *Honours:* Emergency Reserve Decoration, 1974; TD, 1991. *Hobbies:* Music; Genealogy; Walking. *Address:* Blue Cedars, Sheethanger Lane, Felden, Boxmoor, Herts HP3 OBG, England.

HOLMSTROEM Gustat Werner Alexander, b. 13 July 1923, Pastor; Clergy for Social Help. m. Sonja Viola, 21 June 1947, 3 s, 2 d. *Education:* Bible School. *Appointments:* Work in Business, 1941; Bible work in Mission, 1941-43; Military Chaplain, 1945; Pastoral Work, 1945- 52; Free Ind Catholic Worker, 1952-88. *Creative works:* Poetry by ABI; Articles in magazines and the conservative press. *Address:* Syrengatn 1o Ltr, S 15146 Sodertalje, Sweden.

HOLOWIECKI Jerzy, b. 8 May 1937, Warsaw, Poland. Professor; Haematologist. m. Beata M Stella, 11 June 1975, 1 s, 1 d. *Education:* Univ Dipl, Silesian Med Acad, Katowice, 1955-62; MD, 1967 Habilitation, 1977, Assoc Pro, 1979, Prof of Med, 1988. *Appointments:* Dept of

Physiol, Silesian Med Acad, 1962-63, 1962-72, 1974-80; Dept of Internal Med, SMA, 1972-73; Univ Clin Zurich, 1974; Inst of Haematol, Vienna, 1980-; Hd of Dept of Haematol, SMA, Katowice. *Creative works:* 200 scientific publications and book chapters. *Memberships:* Polish Soc of Haematol, Sec Gen, 1975-88; Intl Soc of Haematol, Coun, 1980-84; Intl Soc of Haemoimmunotherapy, Study Chm, 1982-89. *Honours:* Scientific and educational prizes from the Polish Ministry of Health, 1981-90; Scientific Prize, Polish Acad of Sci, 1989; Order of Polonia Restituta. *Hobbies:* Tennis; Motoring; Joinery. *Address:* 10c Malachowskiego Str, Katowice 40-689, Poland.

HOLT Joan Patricia, b. 15 Jan 1920, London, England. Solicitor. m. Brian Alfred Whittell Holt, 12 June 1945, 1 s, 1 d. *Education:* Oakdene Sch, Beaconsfield. *Appointments:* Admitted Solicitor, 1943; Acct, Womens Auxiliary Air Force, 1942-45; Ofr, Ronaldsway Aircraft Co Ltd; Ronaldsway Aircraft Co Ltd, Isle of Man, 1959, Dir and Chm, 1984-. *Membership:* Fellow, BIM. *Honours:* Serving Sister of St John, 1989; JP, 1975. *Hobbies:* Reading; Needlework. *Address:* Balladoole House, Castletown, Isle of Man, England.

HOLZ Hans Heinz, b. 26 Feb 1927, Frankfurt, Main. University Professor. m. Silvia Elisabeth Markun, 20 Apr 1979. *Education:* Gymnasium Frankfurt, Main, 1937-45; Univs of Frankfurt and Mainz, 1945-52; Phd, Univ of Leipzig, 1969. *Appointments:* Freelance Journalist, 1952- 70; Chief Dept, Abendstiudio Hessischer Rundfunk Frankfurt, Main, 1962-64; Prof of Philos, Univ of Marburg, FRG, 1971-79. *Publications include:* Jean Paul Sartre,1951; Leibniz 1958, 1983; Lagos Spermatikos, 1975; Die abenteuerliche Rebellion, 1976; Dialektik und Widerspiegelung 1983. *Memberships:* Intl Assn for Legal and Soc Phil, Sec 1951-54; Intl Assn for Dialectical Phil, Societas Hegeliana, Pres, 1981-88, Hon Pres, 1992. *Honours:* Medal of Hon, Verein Deutscher Ingenieure, 1986. *Hobbies:* Literature; Theatre; Fine Arts. *Address:* Strada Cantonale, CH-6577 S Abbondio, Switzerland. 52.

HOMMEL Nicholas, b. 8 Oct 1915, Wolwelange, Grand Duchy of Luxembourg. Retired Diplomat. m. Denise Ruffie, 21 Sept 1959. *Education:* Univ Studies, Luxembourg, 1934-35; Law studies, Louvain, Paris, France, 1935-38; LLD, 1939. *Appointments include:* Called to the Bar, 1939; Polit Exile, 1941-44; Attorney at law, 1944-46; Foreign Serv, 1946-, including: Mbr, Luxembourg Military Mission, Berlin, 1946-48; Delegate, IARA, Brussels, 1946-49; Permanent Rep, OEEC, 1949-58; NATO, 1953-58; Hd, Luxembourg delegation, EDC negotiation, Paris, 1952-54; Ambassador, Belgium, 1959-62, France, 1963-67; Sec Gen, Min of Foreign Affairs, 1967-68; Ambassador, FDR, 1968-73, Denmark, 1973; Sec Gen, Coun of Ministers, EEC, 1973-80. *Memberships:* Luxemborg Soc of Foreign Affairs; Chm, Luxembourg Atlantic Com. *Honours:* Ofr, Order of Merit, Grand Duchy of Luxembourg. *Hobbies:* Painting; Reading politics and economics; Golf. *Address:* 100B Route d'Arlon, 1150 Luxembourg. 12, 34.

HONCIUC Maria, b. 30 June 1939, Balaci Teleorman, Romania. Physicist; Professor. m. Gheorghe Honciuc, 10 Dec 1966, 1 d. *Education:* Dipl, Physics Dept, 1964, Dr Dipl in Phys, Bucharest Univ, 1977. *Appointments:* Asst Lectr, Phys, 1964-77, Workings Leader, 1977-89, Prof, 1989-, Poly Inst of Bucharest. *Creative works:* 60 works published 1976-86, including: Investigations on the solid state of semiconductors, 1969-77. *Memberships:* Phys Assn of Romania and Ro-AMSE Assn. *Honours:* Hon Dipl for the industrial and biological iquid crystals research, 1984; Innovator Certs, 1987, 1988; Prizes from the Romanian Acad Constantiu Niculescu. *Hobbies:* Feminine Fashion; Classical music; Trips. *Address:* Polytechnical Inst of Bucharest, Splaiul Independentei 313, Bucharest 7000, Romania.

HONDA Yuzo, b. 13 Aug 1947, Tokyo, Japan. University Professor. m. Kazuko Honda, 14 Jan 1973, 1 s, 1 d. *Education:* BA Waseda Univ, Tokyo 1971; MA 1977, PhD 1980, Econ, Princeton Univ, USA. *Appointments:* Loan Ofr, Japan Devel Bk, 1971-75; Grad Student at Princeton, 1975-80; Asst Prof, Assoc Prof, Kobe Univ of Commerce, 1980-87; Assoc Prof, Prof, Kobe Univ, 1987-. *Creative works:* Large sample tests in econometrics, 1990; Testing the error components model with non-normal disturbances, 1985; Many articles in professional journals. *Membership:* Assoc Ed of the Econ Studies Quarterly. *Honours:* Nikkei Economic Books Awd, for Large Sample Tests in Econometrics, 1990. *Hobby:* Tennis. *Address:* Sch of Business Admin, Kobe University, Nada-ku Kobe 657, Japan. 52.

HONG Huang, b. 26 June 1923, Zhejiang, China. m. Su Hui-Zhen, 1 Jan 1956, 2 s, 1 d. *Education:* Grad of Fine Arts, Guangdong Provincial Art Col, 1944. *Appointments:* Sec in charge of Fine Arts Activities: Chongqing Soc Serv Ofc, 1944-46, Shanghai Youth Centre, 1947; Tchr of Fine Arts, Shanghai Bile Middle Sch, 1948-49; Chief of Fine Arts and Photography, Sr Ed, Wen Hui Bao Daily, 1950-89. *Creative works include:* Even Death would be too good for Mark Twain, 1956; Hello, we meet again, 1983; Stamp Design, 1985; Modern Weapons, 1988. *Memberships:* Shanghai Artists Assn, Bd of Dirs, 1950-; All China Artists Assn, 1959-; Shanghai People's Polit Conslt Coun, 1963-65, 1979-81; Standing Com, All China News Cartoon Res Soc; Pres, Shanghai News Cartoon Res Soc. *Honours:* Awd of Excellence, Shanghai Area, Nat Art Exhibition, 1985; Second Prize, Grand Competition of Cartoons on Shanghai Daily Life, 1988; Work included in collection of world cartoons published in Japan, and reprints made in Soviet magazine. *Hobbies:* Calligraphy; Drawing; Music appreciation; Touring. *Address:* 50 Hu Qiu Road, Shanghai 200002, China.

HONG Wenxue b. 27 May 1953, Yian County, China. Associate Professor. m. 20 Jan 1979, 1 s, 1 d. *Education:* Masters Deg, 1983. *Appointments:* Tchr, 1977-80; Asst Prof, 1980-86, Assoc Prof, 1987-. *Creative works:* Research: Set up and presented generalized transducer Construction and mathematical model: Author: Electrical Measurement Techniques. *Memberships:* Harbin Youth Assn; IM Soc; IEEE. *Honours:* Sci and Tech Progress Awds, for crystal transducer and calorimeter, 1985. *Hobbies:* Reading; Basketball. *Address:* 40 4th Fuhua Street, Nangan District, Harbin, China.

HONGO Kohei, b. 2 June 1939, Sendai, Japan. Consultant. m. 15 Oct 1968, 3 s. *Education:* BIEE, 1962, MEE 1964, DEE, 1967, Tohoku Univ. *Appointments:* Assr Reschr, Tohoku Univ, 1967; Lectr, Shizuoka Univ, 1968; Asst Prof, 1969; Prof, 1972. *Creative works:* Introduction to AC Circuit; Introduction to Radio Engineering; Introduction to Electromagnetic Field. *Memberships:* Sr Mem, IEEE, USA; Inst of Electronics, Info and Communication Engrs, Japan. *Hobbies:* Reading books on Buddhism. *Address:* 919-295 Tomitsukacho, Hamamatsu 432, Japan. 52.

HOOK Andrew Dunnet, b. 21 Dec 1932, Wick, Caithness, Scotland. Professor of English Literature. m. Judith Ann Hibberd, 18 July 1966, dec 1984, 2 s, 1 d. *Education:* MA Univ of Edinburgh, 1954; PHD, Princeton Univ, USA, 1960. *Appointments:* Lectr in Eng, Univ of Edinburgh, 1963-70; Sr Lectr in Eng, Univ of Aberdeen, 1970-79; Bradley Prof of Eng Lit, Univ of Glasgow, 1979-. *Creative works:* Scotland and America, 1750- 1835, 1975; American Literature in Context, 1865-1900, 1983; History of Scottish Literature, 660-1800, ed, 1987; Scott Fitzgerald, 1992. *Memberships:* Brit Assn for Am Studies; Assn for Scottish Lit Studies. 18th Century Scottish Studies Soc, Pres, 1990-92; CNAA, Chm, Comm for Humanities; Scottish Exam Bd Mem. *Honours:* ssa 00Vans Dunlop Scholar, Univ of Edinburgh, 1954; Jane Eliza Procter Fellow, Princeton Univ, 1957-58. *Hobbies:* Theatre; Opera; Reading.

Address: 5 Rosslyn Terrace, Glasgow G12 9NB, Scotland. 184.

HOOPER William Douglas, b. 26 Apr 1949, Huntington, NY, USA. Finance Company Executive. m. Cathleen Doreen Collins, 3 Oct, 1982. 1 s. *Education:* BA Engrg, 1971, MS Engrg, 1973, MBA, 1974, Columbia Univ. *Appointments:* Res Asst, Dr Seymour Melman's The Permanent War Economy, 1971-73; Sr Conslt, Arthur Andersen & Co, 1975-78; Sr Profitability Analyst, Am Airlines, 1978; VP, Devel, Citicorp, 1979-; Instr, New Sch'Parson Sch of Design, NY; Instr, Digital Imaging for Photography and Computers in Photography. *Memberships:* VP, ALumni Coun, St Paul's Sch, Garden City, NY; IPA; Assoc Mem, Profl Photographers of Am. *Honours:* Hons List, St Pauls Sch, 1966-67; Dean's List 1970, Res Asst Grant, 1971, Columbia Univ. *Hobbies:* Photography; Digital imaging; Sailing; Cycling. *Address:* 7 Kanes Lane, Huntington Bay, NY 11743, USA. 6.

HOORDE Ernest Eugene Van, b. 12 Oct 1922, Gent, Belgium. Professor. m. Renee Eugenie Decuyper, 23 Aug 1947, 1 s. *Education:* Drawing, 1945, Painting, 1952, Royal Acad, Antwerp; Laureat of the Nat Hoger Inst voor Schone Kunsten, Antwerp, 1958. *Appointments:* Prof, Royal Athenee, Renaix, 1958; Prof, Royal Athenee, Gent, 1981; Prof, Royal Acad of Fine Arts, Gent, to 1981. *Creative works:* Paintings; Drawings; Engravings. *Honours:* Min Camille Huysmans Prize, 1958; Prix Rotary de ATH 1959; Prix Anto-cartell 1965; Prix Aug Oleffe 1976; Prix Van Sevenbergen, 1990, all for painting. *Hobbies:* Visiting Museums; Architecture. *Address:* 13 Laurent Delvauxstraat, 9000 Gent, Belgium. 2.

HOPKINS Anthony Philip, b. 15 Oct 1937, Poole, Dorset, England. Consultant Neurologist; Researcher. m. Elizabeth Ann Wood, 10 Aug 1965, 3 s. *Education:* Guys Med Sch, 1954-60; BSc 1957; MBBS 1961; MD London, 1968; FRCP, 1976; FACP, 1991. *Appointments:* Med Registrar, Guys Hosp, 1962-3; Asst Etranger, Salpetriere Hosp, Paris, 1963-64; Resident Med Ofr, Nat Hosps for Nervous Diseases, 1967-68; Res Assoc, Mayo Clinic, 1969-70; Conslt Neurol, St Bart's Hosp, 1972-; Phys in Charge, Dept of Neurol Scis, 1976-88; Dir, Res Unit, Royal Col of Physns. *Creative works:* Epilepsy, 1987; Headache: Problems in diagnosis and managment, 1988; Measuring the quality of medical care, 1990; Clinical Neurology: a modern approach, 1993. *Hobbies:* Walking; Reading; Dining; Theatre. *Address:* 149 Harley Street, London W1N 2DE, England. 1.

HOPKINS Antony, b. 21 Mar 1921, Enfield, Middlesex, England. Musician; Author. m. Alison Purves, 12 Feb 1947 (dec 1991). *Education:* ARCM, LRAM, FRCM, Hon RAM, Royal Col of Music, 1939-42. *Appointments:* Freelance Composer and author; Regular Broadcaster, Talking about Music, since 1955. *Creative works:* Numerous scores for radio drama and features; also Theatre (especially Stratford upon Avon) and films; Seventeen books mostly on music including: The Nine Symphonies of Beethoven; Beating Time; Sounds of Music; Pathway to Music; The Concergoer's Companion. *Honours:* Tokyo City Medal for service to music; Hon Doctorate, Stirling Univ; Fellowship, Robinson Col, Cambs; Hon RAM; Fellowship, RCM, CBE, 1976. *Hobbies:* Golf; Sports cars. *Address:* Woodyard, Ashridge, Berkhamsted, Herts HP4 1PS, England. 4, 1.

HOPKINS Theodore Mark, b. 2 Jan 1926, Vermontville, Michigan, USA. Ordained Minister. m. Ruth Ann Allspaw, 10 Oct 1954, 4 d. *Education:* BA, Taylor Univ, IN, 1954; MRE, N.Bapt Theol Sem, 1957; BD, 1958 exchanged for MDiv, 1972. *Appointments include:* Pastorates: First Bapt Chs, Darlington, WI, 1958-60; Lexington, IL, 1960-61; Killdeer, ND, 1961-65; Hardin, MT, 1965-66, Centerville Walkenda Bapt Parish, Centerville, IL, 1966- 68; Interim Pastorate, Meml Bapt Ch, Chambers, NB, 1969-70; Bi Vocational Pastorates: 1st Bapt Ch, Mercer, MI 1976-78, Blytherdale, MO,

1979-90; Guidance Counsellor, Chambers HS, NB, 1968-71; Rosholt HS, 1971-73; Coon Rapids Com Sch, IA, 1973-75; Lineville Clio Community Sch, IA, 1976-90. *Memberships include:* N Dakota, Chm of State Convention Christian Ed Com, Chm of Leader Educ; Pastor, Counsellor, Am Bapt Men of Montana; S.Dakota, Sec, Centerville Ambulance Serv; N.Dakota Rep, Bapt Convention, First Open Theol Conf, 1968; Pres, Lineville Educ Assn, 1978-79, 1981-82; Dir, Music for N.Grant River Bapt Assn, 1986-. *Honours:* Hon Dr Sacred Theol, STD, 1991. *Hobbies:* Music; Walking; Photography; Reading. *Address:* 303 Brown Street, Lineville, IA 50147, USA. 145.

HOPPER David L, b. 28 Aug 1953, Memphis, Tennessee, USA. Clinical Director. *Education:* BS Lousiana State Univ, 1980; PhD, Columbia Pacific Univ, 1987. *Appointments include:* Private Practice, Centre for Interpersonal Studies, Las Vegas, 1989-90; MEd Psychol, Dept of Physical Med, Univ Med Centre of S. Nevada, 1989-91; Consltg Somnologist, W. Region Sleep Disorders Centre, Las Vegas, 1991-; Private Practice, Behavioural Med and Somnology Conslt, 1991-; Adjunct Fac, Dept of Sci and Health, Community Col of S. Nevada, 1990-. *Creative works:* Books include: Family Guide to Brain injury Rehabilitation; Psychobiology of Sleep Disorders; Alternative approaches to Treatment; Somnopathology; Children's Self Health & Stress Management Series; Tape: Self-helf through Hypnosis Series, 1984-85. *Memberships include:* Am Acad of Pain Mgmt; Am Pain Soc; NYAS; Assn of Applied Psychophysiol and Biofeedback; Nevada Assn of Alcohol and Drug Abuse Counsellors; Intl Acad of Behavioural Med, Counselling and Phycho; Am Acad of Somnology. *Honours:* Fellow, Am Bd of Med Psychos; Fellow, Intl Acad of Behavioural Med, Counselling and Psycho; Fellow, Am Acad of Somnology; Fellow, AM ASsn of Profl Hypnotherapists; Fellow, Am Acad of Behavioural MEd. *Hobbies:* Reading; Writing; Music; Hiking; Racquetball. *Address:* PO Box 29124, Las Vegas, NV 89126, USA. 7.

HOPPER Michael St John, b. 1 Apr 1927, Hoddesdon, Herts, England. Chartered Surveyor. m. Aline Mary Kingsford 2 June 1951, 1 s, 1 d. *Education:* Col of Est Mgmt, 1948-51. *Appointments:* Asst Surveyor, 1950-56, Ptnr, 1957-82; Jt Sr Ptnr, 1982-88, Conslt, 1988-92, Gerald Eve & Co; Mem, Lands Tribunal, 1994-. *Memberships:* Fellow, RICS; Past Pres, Rating Surveyors Assn; Anglo Am Real Property Inst. *Hobbies:* History; Travel. *Address:* Bamville Copse, Cross Lane, Harpenden, Herts AL5 1BU, England.

HORDER John Plaistone, b. 9 Dec 1919, Ealing, London, England. Visiting Professor. m. Elizabeth June Wilson, 20 June 1940, 2 s, 2 d. *Education:* Open Classical Scholar, Lancing Col, 1932 and Univ Col Oxford, MA, 1938; BMBCh, London Hosp Med ch, 1945. *Appointments:* Hse Ofr, Registrar, London Hosp, 1948-57; Various offices, 1954-82; Pres, RCGP, UK, 1979-82. *Creative works:* The Future General Practitioner Learning and Teaching, 1972; 14 Princes Gate; Papers on General Practice, education and psychiatry. *Memberships:* Conslt, WHO, 1960; Fellow, RCGP, 1970; FRCPhys, London, 1972, Edinburgh, 1981; FRCPsych, 1980; VP, RSM, 1988-90. *Honours:* OBE, 1971; Hon Mem, Canadian Col of Family Practice, 1980-; CBE, 1981; Life Hon Fellow, RSM, 1982; Hon MD, Free Univ of Amsterdam, 1985; Hon Fellow, Green Col, Oxford, 1988; Visiting Professorships, 1976-92; Pres, Med Art Soc, 1989-. *Hobbies:* Playing the piano and organ; Painting water colours. *Address:* 98 Regents Park Road, London NW1 8UG, England. 1.

HORI Toshikazu, b. 3 June 1924, Shizuoka, Japan. University Professor. m. Yoko Hagiwana, 8 Nov 1955, 2 d. *Education:* BA, Tokyo Univ, 1943-48. *Appointments:* Asst, Tokyo Univ, 1949-58; es Worker, Toyo Bunko, 1958-60; Prof, Meiji Univ, 1960-. *Creative works:* The Study of the Land Allotment System in Ancient China, 1975; The History of the World, Vol 4, Ancient China,

1977; The Status System of Ancient China, 1987. *Memberships:* Hist Sci Soc of Japan, Com, 1950-51, 1953-54, 1961-63; Hist Soc of Japan; Sundai Hist Assn, Chief Ed, 1966-79; Japanese Hist Coun, Com, 1964-66, 1980-84. *Hobbies:* Reading; History of Art; Photography. *Address:* 5-9-14 Minamizawa, Higshikurume-shi, Tokyo 203, Japan. 2.

HORIE Akio, b. 19 Dec 1931, Iki-gun, Nagasaki, Japan. University Professor. m. Masako Ishizuka, 3 Mar 1961, 2 s. *Education:* Med Sch, Kyushu Univ, 1953-57; MD, 1958; DMSci, 1962; ECFMG Cert, 1967. *Appointments:* Asst Prof Path, Kyushu Univ, Japan, 1964-65, Assoc Prof, 1965-72; Chier FEs Lab, Nat Kyushu Cancer Ctr, 1972-78; Prof, Path & Oncol, UOEH, 1978-91. *Creative works:* Co-author: Pancreatic Tumours in Childen, 1982; Progress in Nickel Toxiocology, 1985. *Memberships:* Japanese Path and Lung Cancer Socs; Japanese Cancer Assn; Clin Elec Mic Soc of Japan; Intl Assn for Study of Lung Cancer. *Honours:* Prize for Clinical Electron Microscopy Soc of Japan, 1988. *Hobbies:* Tennis; Photography. *Address:* 3-22-8 Mitsusadadai, Yahata-Nishiku, Kitakyushu, Fukuoka 807, Japan. 52, 1.

HORIOKA Charles Yuji, b. 7 Sept 1956, Boston, Massachusetts, USA. University Professor. *Education:* BA Ec, Harvard Col, 1977; PhD Bus Econ, Harvard Univ, 1985. *Appointments:* Lectr, 1983-85, Assoc Prof, 1985-87, Fac of Econ, Kyoto Univ Japan; Assoc Prof, Inst of Social and Econ Res, Osaka Univ, 1987-; Visiting Asst Prof, Econ, Stanford Univ, 1988; Visitg Assoc Prof, Econ, Columbia Univ, 1993. *Creative works:* Numerous articles in professional journals and books. *Memberships:* Am Econ Assn; Japan Assn of Econs and Econometrics; Assoc Ed, Economic Studies Quarterly. *Honours:* Fulbright Hays Fellowship, US Dept of Educ, 1982-83. *Address:* Institute of Social and Economic Research, Osaka University, 6-1 Mihogaoka, Ibaraki, Osaka 567, Japan. 52.

HORLOCK Henry Wimburn Sudell, b. 19 July 1915, Bath, England. Retired. m. Jeannetta Robin Tanner, 21 July 1960. *Education:* MA, Pembroke Col, Oxford, 1937-39. *Appointments:* WW II, Army, 1939-42; Civil Serv, 1942-60; Fdr, Dir, Steppingstone Sch, 1962-87. *Memberships:* Clubs: Athenaeum; Guildhall; City Livery. *Honours:* CDR Order of Merit, Germany, 1972; Cdr, Nat Order of Aztec Eagle of Mexico, 1973; Cdr Du Wissam Aloulite of Morocco, 1987. *Hobbies:* Travel; Country pursuits. *Address:* Copse Hill House, Lower Slaughter, Glos GL54 2HZ, England. 1.

HORN David Bowes, b. 18 Aug 1928, Edinburgh, Scotland. Clinical Chemist. m. Shirley Kay Riddell, 5 Oct 1963, 2 d. *Education:* Associateship in Applied Chem, Heriot Watt Col, Edinburgh (AHWC), dist, 1954, BSc 1967; PhD, Edinburgh Univ, 1956. *Appointments:* Sr Biochem, W.Infirmary, Glasgow; Hd of Clin Chem, Vale of Leven Hosp, Alexandria, 1956- 59, Queen Eliz Hosp, Birmingham, 1959; Principal Biochem, 1959-64, Dep Hd, Clin Hosp Serv, 1959-66, Top Biochem, 1964-66, Royal Victoria Infirmary, Newcastle upon Tyne; Hon Lectr, Univ of Newcastle upon Tyne, 1963-66; Biochem, Hd of Clin Chem, Edinburgh N.Hosps Gp W Gen Hosp, 1966-87; Hon Sr Lectr, Univ of Edin, 1966-67. *Creative works:* 64 publications covering a range of subjects in clinical chemistry and medicine of benefit to patient care and also involving laboratory information computer systems, education on both a Scottish and British basis. *Memberships:* FRSC; CChem; FRCPath; FRSE; FIBiol; CBiol; Assn of Clin Biochems; Past Ch, Coun of Sci and Tech Insts Registration Com of Scists in Health Care; Coun of Sci and Tech Insts Health Care Adv Com. *Honours:* Heriot Watt Col Medals: Chem, 1946, 1949, 1950, Applied Chem, 1954. *Hobbies:* Computing; Walking; Gardening. *Address:* 2 Barnton Park, Edinburgh EH4 6JF, Scotland. 184.

HORNE-ROBERTS Jennifer, b. 15 Feb 1949, Harrow on the Hill, England. m. Keith Michael Peter Roberts, 29 Apr 1987, 1 s, 1 d. *Education:* BA Hons, London;

Dipl in Italian, Perugia Univ. *Appointments:* Barrister; Called to the Bar Middle Temple, 1976; ad Eundem Mem, Inner Temple. *Creative works:* Trade unionists and the law, 1984; Justice for Children, 1992; Writer on political issues, family law, employment law, human rights; literature. *Memberships:* Chm, Assn of Women Barristers, UK; Ch, Holborn and St Pancras Liberal Democrata; Former mem, Young Bar Com; Justice, Amnesty lawyers; Exec Mem, Liberal Democrat Lawyers: Parl candidate: 1974, Fareham, Labour, 1987, Medway, Alliance, 1992, Holborn & St Pancras, Lib Democrats. *Hobbies:* Writing; Visual and literary arts; Politics; Travel. *Address:* 3 Paper Buildings, Temple, London EC4Y 6EU, England.

HORNER Sally McKay Melvin, b. 17 Nov 1935, Bladen County, North Carolina, USA. Academic Administration; Chemist. m. William Horner, 9 June 1953, 1 s, 1 d. *Education:* BS Chem, 1957, PhD Inorganic Chem, 1961, Univ N.Carolina. *Appointments:* Res Assoc, Instr, Univ of N.Carolina, 1961-67; Prof, Ch Chem Dept, Dir of Inst Res, Meredith Col, 1967-68; Dena, Provost, VP Admin & Fin, Acting Pres, Univ of Charleston, WV, 1968-84; V- Chancellor Planning and Fiscal Affairs, USC Coastal Carolina Col, SC, 1984-. *Creative works:* Author of 20 articles, 1962074; Presenter, 10 invited/submitted papers, 1962-74. *Memberships:* ACS, 1975-78; Sec, Chair Elect, NC Section; Sigma Xi, 1961-67; Bd of Dirs, NC Acad of Sci, 1976-79. *Honours:* Phi Beta Kappa, 1957; Order of the Valkyries, Univ of NC, 1957; NSF Predoctoral Fellow, Nat Sci Foun, Chapel Hill, 1957-60; Nat Forum, Am Coun on Educ Women Admnrs, Phoenix, AZ, 1980. *Hobbies:* Gardening; Jewellry making. *Address:* 608D 35th Avenue North, Myrtle Beach, SC 29578, USA. 7, 5.

HORNSBY Beve, b.13 Sept 1915. m. (1)Capt Jack Myddleton Hornsby, 14 July 1939, dec 1975, 3 s, 1 d; (2) John Hillyard Tennyson Barley, 21 Dec 1976, dis 1986. *Education:* MSc, PhD, Univ ofLondon; MEd, Univ Col N.Wales. *Appointments:* Ambulance Driver, FANY and Mech Transp Corp, 1939-42; Pilot, Civil Air Gd, 1938-39; Hd of Speech Therapy Clin, Kingston, 1969-71; Hd, Femedial Tchg, St Thomas's Hosp, 1970-71; Tchr, World Blind Clinic, Barts, 1969-71; Hd, Dyslexia Dept Bart's 1971-80; Dir, Hornsby Ctr for Learning Difficulties, 1980-; Prin, Hornsby Hse Sch 1987-. *Publications:* ALpha to Omega - The A to Z of Teaching Reading, Writing and Spelling, 1974; Alpha to Omega Flash Cards, 1975; Overcoming Dyslexia, 1984; Before Alpha - A pre-reading programme for the Under Fives, 1989; Alpha to Omega Activity Packs, 1990, 1992. *Memberships:* Gov All Farthing Primary Sch Wandsworth, mem, Wandsworth Common Mgmt Com. *Honours:* Hon Fel, Col of Speech Therapists, 1988,; Brit Dyslexia Assn, 1987; AFBPsS, 1983; Chartered Psychol, FRSA. *Hobbies:* Riding; Sailing; Golf; Reading; Walking; Theatre; Music. *Address:* The Hornsby Centre, Glenshee Lodge, 261 Trinity Road, Wandsworth, London SW18 3SN, England.

HOROSZEWICZ Michal, b. 3 July 1922, Warsaw, Poland. Journalist. m. Lidia Kocol, 27 Apr 1958. *Education:* Chem, Polytech HS, 1946-52; Dipl, Food Tech Engr, 1957. *Appointments:* Asst, HS Agric, Warsaw, 1949-; Staff Writer of periodicals: Voice of the Free Poeple, 1948-51; Arguments, 1957-81; Man and Philosophy of Life, 1976-89. *Creative works:* Author: Church in Contemporary Africa, 1962; Papacy and Church, 1980-83; Through Two Millennia Towards Roman Synagogue. *Memberships:* Free Thought Assn, 1948-51; Assoc of Atheists and Freethinkers, 1957-69, VP, 1962- 69; Soc of Dissemination of Lay Culture, 1969-83; Polish Soc of Sci of Religions, 1963-. *Honours:* Publicistic Awds, 1962, 1976. *Hobbies:* ssa 00British cartoons and humour up to 1950; Genesis of World War I; Hiking. *Address:* ul Raszynska 3-A m.3, 02-026 Warsaw, Poland.

HORSFALL Ernest John, b. 21 Apr 1918, Bradford, Leeds, England. Retired. m. Nora Teresa Gallagher,

1951, 1 s. *Education:* Secondary, Forster, Bradford Yorks. *Appointments:* Apprentice Trained Engr, Fitter, Machinist, Textiles, Motorist Industry; Experimental 8; Jowett Cars, Vauxhall Motors; Serv Mgr, Sales Mgr, Mktg Mgr, GM Ltd. *Memberships:* Popular Flying Assn, Executive Mgmt, 20 years; TEng (CEI); MIMI. *Hobbies:* Specialist amateur builder, reparer and servicing of aircraft; Pilot; Test Pilot, light aircrat; Specialist in Jodel Aircraft. *Address:* Sandel, 43 St Vincents Road, Preston, Lancs, England.

HORSFIELD Dorothy, b. 24 Nov 1932, Halifax, England. Consultant Chemical Pathologist. *Education:* Royal Free Hosp Sch of Med, 1951-57; MBBS London, 1957; MRCS LRCP London, 1957; MRCPath, London, 1970, FRCPath, 1984. *Appointments:* Hse Surg, Royal Free Hosp, Hse Phys, Royal Northern Infirmary Iverness, 1958; SHO, Chests and Geriatrics, St Luke's Hosp, Bradford, 1959; HSO Path, Royal Free Hosp, 1960; Registrar, Clin Path: Wittington Hosp, 1961, Guy's Hosp, 1963; Lectr, Chem Path, Inst of Neurol, 1966; Sr Registrar, Chem Path: Central Middlesex Hosp, 1973, Hammersmith Hosp, 1975; Conslt Chem Path, Barnsley Hosp Dist Gen Hosp, 1977. *Memberships:* RSM; RCPath; BMA; Assn of CLin Paths; County Landowners Assn. *Honours:* Yorkshire County Minor Scholarship, 1942; Halifax Major Borough Scholarship, 1950. *Hobbies:* Oraganic Gardening; Compassionate Farming; Wildlife Consevation. *Address:* Holly Farm, New Brighton, Birdsedge, Huddersfield HD8 8XP, England.

HORSFORD Cyril Edward Sheehan, b. 13 Mar 1929, London, England. Retired Barrister. m. Susan Frances Bolton, 31 Aug 1957, 1 s. *Education:* Marlborough Col 1943-47; Clare Col, Camb, 1949-52; MA Barrister Inner Temple, 1953. *Appointments:* Clerk of Arraigns, Central Crim Ct, 1954- 56; Sr Asst, Inner London Sessions, 1956-68; Dept Asst Registrar, Ct of Appeal, 1968-74; Dep Clerk, Privy Cncl, 1974-89. *Creative works:* The Assize and Quarter Sessions Handbook, 1958. *Contributions include:* Halsbury's Laws of England; Solicitors Jour. *Memberships:* VP, Medico Legal Soc of London; Fellow, Brit Interplanetary Soc; Mbr, Royal Soc of St George; Freeman, City of London; Dir, Intl Inst of Space Law, 1967-74. *Honours:* ssa 00CVO, 1984; Andrew G Haley Space Law Awd, 1964. *Hobbies:* Amateur theatre; Fly-fishing. *Address:* 32 Prairie Street, London SW8 3PP, England.

HORST Antoni, b. 4 June 1915, Zakrwewo, Poland. Scientist. 3 d. *Education:* Dip., 1945, MD, 1945; PhD 1947, Med Fac, Poznan Univ. *Appointments:* Sr Asst, Internal Med, Warsaw Univ, 1945-46; Assoc Prof, Poznan Univ, 1946-50; Dir, Gen Path Dept, Poznan Univ, 1950-74; Dir, Inst of Human Genetics, Polish Acad of Scis (PAS), 1974-86; Prof, Inst of Human Genetics, 1986-. *Creative works:* Molecular Pathology, 1991; Physiological Pathology - Handbook for students. *Memberships:* PAS: Pres, Sci Coun, Inst of Biogenic Amines; Sci Couns, Inst of Human Genetics and Inst of Immunol; Pres, Com of Cell Pathophysiol. *Honours:* Hon Mem, PASC, 1969-, Poznan Soc of Friends of Scis, Polish Socs of Genetics, Immunol and Histo and Cytochemists. *Hobbies:* Hunting. *Address:* ul Podhalanska 14, 60-615 Poznan, Poland.

HORTON Joseph Julian Jr, b. 7 Nov 1936, Memphis, Tennessee, USA. Professor and Dean. m. Linda Anne Langley, 30 May 1964, 2 s, 1 d. *Education:* BA New Mexico State Univ, 1958; MA 1965, PhD, 1968, Southern Methodist Univ. *Appointments:* Asst Prof, George Washington Univ, 1968-69; Univ of Maryland, 1969-70; Fin Econ, Fed Deposit Ins Corp, 1967-71; Prof and Chm, Dept of Econ and Bus, Slippery Rock State COl, 1971-81; Chm, Commerce Div, 1981-82, Dean W Fielding Rubel Sch of Bus, 1982-86; Bellarmine Col; Dean, Sch of Mgmt, Univ of Scranton. *Creative works:* Author of more than 80 publications including: The Political Econ of Henry Geroge, 1991; Labor Law: A Mandate for change, 1990; Ed, Jour of Economic Democracy, 1990; N.Am Review of Economics and Finance, 1988. *Memberships:* Pres, N.Am Econ and Fin Assn; Pres, Congress of Polit Econs; VP, Eastern Econ Assn; Pres, Pennsylvania Econ Assn; Prog Com, Fin Mgmt Assn. *Honours:* Clarence Lichefeldt Fellow, Bank Admin Inst, 1981; Outstanding Centennial Alumnus, New Mexico State Univ, 1988. *Hobbies:* Chess; Science fiction; History. *Address:* School of Management, University of Scranton, Scranton, PA 18510, USA. 8, 140, 143.

HOSCHL Cyril, b. 12 Nov 1949, Prague, Czechoslovakia. Director of Psychiatric Centre. m. Jitka Stenclova, 17 Sept 1976, 2 s, 2 d. *Education:* MD, 1974; CSc, 1982, DSC, 1990, Prof, 1991, Charles Univ Med Fac. *Appointments:* Psych Res Inst Res Fellow, 1974-81; Psych, 3rd Med Fac, 1977-; Dir, Prague Psych Centre, 1990-, Dean, 3rd Sch of Med, Charles Univ. *Creative works:* More than 100 publications including: book, Neuroendocrinology in Psychiatry, 1989. *Memberships:* World Fed of Socs of Biol Psych; Mbr, European Col of Neupsychopharmacol; Collegium Internationale Neuro-Psychopharmacologiam (CINP); NY Acad Sci; Czech Med and Psychi Socs; Czech Soc of Biol Psyc; Soc of Neurosci. *Honours:* Dipl of Hon, Czech Psychi Soc, 1985; Presidential Prize, Czech Med Soc, 1990. *Hobby:* Chamber music. *Address:* Rakovskeho 3143, 14300 Praha 4, Czechoslovakia. 139, 152, 162.

HOSELITZ Stephen, b. 12 Mar 1947, Sheffield, England. Editor. *Career:* Ed Asst on ILIFFE trade magazine 1965, Asst Ed of Utd Trade Press publication and subsequently for Central Press Features until 1968; Freelance journalist: UK, 1968-69, India, 1969-70; Ed Indian and Eastern Engineering, 1969-70; Chief Sub-Ed, W.Lancs evening Gazette until 1977, Sub-Ed 1970; Ed, S.Wales Argus, 1987-, Dpty Ed, 1977-87. *Address:* South Wales Argus, Cardiff Road, Newport, Gwent NP9 12W, Wales.

HOSIASSON Jose, b. 12 July 1931, Warsaw, Poland. Businessman; Jazz Writer. m. Gabriela Saavedra, 21 Dec 1957, 3 s, 1 d. *Education:* Arch, Univ of Chile, 1951-52, non grad. *Appointments:* Scandinavian Airlines, 1953-56; Alitalia, 1956-58; Koralek & Hosiassou Ltda, 1959-. *Creative works:* Articles in international arts and jazz publications; Radio Jazz programmes, 1948-80. *Memberships:* Fdr, Club de Jazz de Valparaiso; Club de Jazz de Santiago, Fdr and HOn Pres. *Hobbies:* Music; Reading; Gastronomy. *Address:* PO Box 2726, Santiago, Chile, S.America.

HOSKINS Cedric Howard, b. 25 May 1929, Cheviot, new Zealand. Anaesthetist. m. Doreen, 29 Oct 1955, 4 d. *Education:* MBCHB, Univ of NewZealand, 1954; FFA RCS, England, 1964; FFA, RACS, 1970; FANZCA, 1992. *Appointments:* Specialist Anaes, Auckland Area Health Bd, 1965-; Private Specialist, Anaes Practice, Auckland, 1969-; Dir, Auckland Surg Ctr Ltd, 1986-89. *Creative works:* History of Asian and Australasian Regional Section of the World Federation of Socs of Anaesthesiologists, 1962-90; Requirements for a Freestanding Day Stay Centre, 1990. *Memberships:* Exec Com, 1984-92, VP, 1992-, World Fed of Socs of Anaesthesiols; Chm and Sec, Bd of Asian and Australasian Regional Section of the WFSA, 1978-86; Mem, 1980-92, Chmn, 1990-92, NZ Regional Com, Fac of Anaes, RACS; Chm, NZ Regional Com, Fac of Anaes, RACS, 1980-; Sec, 1968-69, Pres, 1977-79, NZ Soc of Anaes. *Hobbies:* Racing and Trotting; Yachting. *Address:* 6 Appleyard Crescent, Meadowbank, Auckland 1005, New Zealand. 139.

HOSPITAL Janette Turner, b. 12 Nov 1942, Melbourne, Australia. Author. m. Clifford G Hospital, 5 Feb 1965, 1 s, 1 d. *Education:* BA Univ Queensland, Australia, 1965; MA Queen's Univ, Canada, 1973. *Appointments include:* Full Time Writer, 1982-; Writer in Residence: MIT Camb, MASS, 1985-86, Univ of Ottawa, 1987, Univ of Sydney, 1989, La Trobe Univ, Melbourne, 1990, 1991, Boston Univ, 1991; Currently, Adjunct Prof of Eng, La

Trobe Univ, Melbourne, Adjunct Prof, Eng, Univ of Ottawa. *Creative works include:* Novels: The Ivory Swing, 1982; The Tiger in the Tiger Pit, 1983; Borderline, 1985; Charades 1988; The Last Magician, 1992; A Very Proper Death, 1990. *Memberships:* PEN Intl; Writers Union of Canada; Am Authors Guild; Amnesty Intl. *Honours include:* Listed, Canada's 10 Best Young Fiction Writers, 1986; Seal First Novel Awd, Canada, 1982; Fiction Awd for Dislocations, Fellowship of Australian Authors, 1988; Charades: shortlisted for the Miles Franklin Awd, Nat Book Council Banjo Awd, NY Times List of Most Notable Books, 1989. *Address:* c/o MIC Cheetham, Sheil Land Association, 43 Doughty Street, London WC1N 2LF, England. 5, 2.

HOSSAIN Golam, b. 13 June 1954, Dhaka, Bangladesh. University Teacher. m. Samina Hossain, 29 Nov 1981, 2 d. *Education:* BA Hons, 1975, MA 1976, Dhaka Univ; PhD, Univ of Rajasthan, India, 1984. *Appointments:* Res Ofr, 1984-85, Asst Prof, Dept of Govt & Polit, 1985- 88, Assoc Prof, 1989-, Chm, 1990-, Bangladesh Inst of Intl and Strategic Studies. *Publications:* General Ziaur Rahman and the BNP - Political Transformation of a military regime, 1988; Civil Military Rleation in Bangladesh - a comparative study; Bangladesh - Govt and Politics. *Memberships:* Life, Assn of Brit Coun Scholars; VP, Bangladesh Polit Sci Assn; Former Treas, Bangladesh Polit Sci Assn; Inst of C'wlth Studies, London. *Honours:* Lions Club Intl Awd, India, 1983. *Hobbies:* Reading; Travelling; Gardening; Fishing. *Address:* Department of Government and Politics, Jahangirnagen University, Savar, Dhaka, Bangladesh. 52.

HOU Depeng, b. 25 July 1932, Taizhou City, Jiangsu, China. Chairman of Guangxi Education Commission. m. Xiaoling Huang, 20 Sept 1962, 2 s. *Education:* BSc, Phys Dept, Beijing Univ, 1956. *Appointments:* Lectr Phys, Guangxi Univ, 1958-79; Assoc Prof, 1979-85, Prof, 1985-, Dep Pres, 1980-91, Pres, 1981-86, Guangxi. *Creative works:* Many books and papers on nuclear physics and theoretical physics published in China and abroad and also some translations on philosophy including: The Resonance Theory, 1980; The Coupling Chnnel Equatrons and the Optical Theorem, 1983; Quantum Theory, 1982. *Memberships:* Pres, Coun of Guangxi Phys Soc, 1982-; Coun, Chinese Phys Soc, 1982-. *Honours:* Silver Prize for Scientific Progress of Guangxi, 1978. *Address:* Guangxi Education Commission, 3 Education Road, Nanning Guangxi 530022, China.

HOU Jingru, b. 29 Aug 1934, Shaanxi Province. Prof of Geostatistics & Mathemtical Geology; Vice Chmn of Dept of Geology. m. 6 June 1963, 1 d. *Education:* Dept of Geochemistry, Chinese Univ of Sci & Tech, 1960-64; Research Worker, Geomathematics, Beijing Geologicl Inst of the MMI, 1965-77; Engr, Capital Iron & Steel Co, 1978-86; Prof, Beijing Univ of Sci & Tech, 1987-. *Publications:* Geostatistics and Its Application in Ore Reserves Calculation; Introduction of Mathematical Geology; Quantitative Evaluation of Mineral Resources; Mining Geostatistics of A G Journal; Sci Articles. *Memberships:* Inst of Geology, The Chinese Soc of Metals; Inst of Geomathematics, Remote Sensing Geology & Computer Application of IGCSM; 1st of Mathematical Geology of the Chinese Soc of Geology; Inter Geostatistcs Assn. *Honours:* Prize of Sci & Tech of MMI; Advanced Worker of Sci Research in Beijing; Excellent Tchr Material Prizes. *Hobbies:* Music; Scenery; Tape Exercise. *Address:* Dept of Geology, Beijing Univ of Sci & Tech, 30 Xueyuan Road, Beijing 100083, China.

HOUSE H Wayne, b. 31 Aug 1948, Borger, Texas. Vice Pres, Academic Affairs; Prof of Theology. m. Leta Frnces, 22 July 1967, 1 s, 1 d. *Education:* Hardin Simmons Univ, 1970; Western Baptist Seminary, ThM, 1974, M div, 1973, Abilene Christian Univ, MA, 1983; Concordia Seminary, ThD, 1986; OW Coburn Sch of Law, JD, 1986.

Appointments: Highland Park Baptist Church, Asst Pastor, 1974-75; Le Tourneau Coll, Asst Prof, 1976-83; Dallas Theological Seminary Assn, Prof, 1986-90; Simon Greenleaf Sch of Law, Visiting Prof, 1989-; Western baptist Coll for Academic Affairs, Prof, 1990-. *Publications:* Death Penalty Debate; Divorce & Remarriage, Four Christian Views; Roleof Women in the Ministry Today; Civilization in Crisis; Theology, Blessing or Curse; Schooling Choices; Restoring the Constitution. *Memberships:* Evangelical Theological Soc; Biblical Manhood & Womenhood; Soc Of Biblical Literature; American Bar Assn; American Trial Lwyers Assn; Christian Legal Soc. *Honours:* Alpha Mu Gamme; Outstanding Young Men of America; Corpus Juris Secundum; American Jurisprudence Award for Corporation Law. *Hobbies:* Travel; Computer Games; Target Shooting. *Address:* Western Baptist Coll, 5000 Deer Park Drive SE, Salen, OR 97301, USA.163.

HOUSE Sherwood Nevin, b. 16 June 1959, Hartford, CT. Computer Conslt. *Education:* Bach of Arts, Williams Coll, MA, 1981; Master of Arts, George Washington Univ, 1987. *Appointments:* PIC, Fundraiser; PRC, Computer Conslt, 1989-. *Creative Works:* OI Sports TV Show, Producer; Koreen Development Paths. *Memberships:* Colonial Vill Commens Housing Cooperative; HUD Tanstmasters; Arlington Cable Advisory Comm; Arlington Recycling Coalition; Committee of 100. *Honours:* Intl Directory of Distinguished Leadership; Letter of Commendation, PRC; Outstanding Young Man of America; Nat Auduban Soc, Earth Defenders Award. *Hobbies:* Amatuer Athletics; Community; Recycling; Golf; Skiing; Raquet Sports. *Address:* 2018 N Key Blud 634, Arlington, VA 22201, USA. 117.

HOUSEGO-WOOLGAR William Michael, b. 3 July 1944, England. Snr Adviser ODA, London. m. Diana Lilian Woolgar, 13 July 1968, 1 s, 1 d. *Education:* Brighton Sch of Architecture; Leeds Sch of Town Planning; Brighton Sch of Mngt. *Appointments:* Warr & King Arch & Surveyors, 1966-67; Leeds City, Arch & Town Planner, 1969-72; Brighton Council, 1972-76; Sultanate of Brunel, 1976-79; Ministry of Foreign Affairs, 1980-83. *Publications:* Master Plans Brunei & Bandasen Bulgarian, Urban Decay. *Memberships:* ARIBA; FRTPI; FRSA; MBIM; MRIPA; Intl Development Forum. *Honour:* South Easter Soc of Arch joint Student Award. *Hobbies:* Tennis; Squash; Scuba; Bridge; ESP Panning. *Address:* Tobora, London Road, Brighton, BN1 8QA, England.

HOWARD Frances Marianne, b. 21 Aug 1946, England. Doc; Conslt Paediatrician. m. David Ivan Pearce, 5 June 1982, 1 d. *Education:* MB, BS, MRCS, LRCP, 1970; D Obst RCOS, 1972; DCh, 1973; MRCP, Paed UK, 1974. *Appointments:* RMO Middlesex Hosp, 1973-74; Scientific Officer, Hon Sen Reg, Gt Ormond St Hosp, 1978-80; Conslt Paediatrician, frimley Park Hosp, 1981-. *Publications:* 20 Papers on Genetic & Gen Paediatic Topics. *Memberships:* Academic Bd, British Paediatric Assn; Royal Coll of Physicians Committee on Glinical Genetics. *Honour:* British Council Tour of Russia. *Hobbies:* Reading; Gardening; Lapidory; Doctor, Dreamfight. *Address:* Orchard House, Glazier Lane, Normandy, Guildford, Surrey GU3 2DE, England.

HOWARD John Michael Henry, b. 23 May 1942, Harpenden, England. Clinical Biochemist. 1s, 1 d. *Education:* Manland Sch, Harpenden, 1953-58; Luton Coll of Advanced Tech, 1958-63; Various Post Graduate studies, London, 1963-67; State Univ, Florida, 1975-79; Fellow, American Coll of nutrition, 1989. *Appointments:* Research Asst, Laporte Chemicals, 1958-62; Sci Officer, Welwyn Hall Research Assn, 1962-65; Clinical Biochemist, London Clinic, 1965-84; Principal Clinical Biochemist, Research & Tech Dir, Biolab Medical Univ, London, 1984-. *Publications include:* Numerous Papers in Medical & Sci Journals. *Memberships:* Inorganic Biochemistry Discussion Group; American Coll of Nutrition; British Soc for

Nutritional Medicine; Luton Industrial Coll. *Honours:* Analyrical Lab Award; Carlton Coll award for Outstanding Sci Contribution to Nutritional Medicine. *Hobbies:* Church Organs; Buildings & Repairing; Healing & Personal Devel; Methodist Preacher; Radio & TV Broadcaster. *Address:* Biolab Medical Unit, 9 Weymouth Street, London W1N 3FF, England.

HOWELL John Newton, b. 20 Jan 1940, Franklin, NH. Assoc Prof of Zoological Biomedical Sci. m. Suzanne Hoviszny, 28 Jan 1961, 2 s. *Education:* Kalama Coll, BA, 1961; UCLA, PhD, 1968. *Appointments:* Asst Prof, Calif State Poly Univ; UCLA Physiology; Instr, Post Doc; Univ of Pittsburgh, PA, Asst Prof; Ohio Univ, Athens, Assoc Prof. *Memberships:* American Physiological Soc; Biophysical Soc; Soc of General Physiologists; American Coll of Sports Medicine. *Honour:* Danforth Foundation Fellowship. *Hobbies:* Playing French Horn. *Address:* Ohio Univ, Dept of Zoological & Biomed Sci, Athens, OH 45701, England. 1.

HOWELL Mary Elizabeth, b. 19 Feb 1942, Galesburg, Illinois, USA. Business Conslt. m. Murrell D Howell, 22 Dec 1969, 3 s, 1 d. *Education:* Degree, Alamo Beauty Sch, 1961; Janes Gates Sch of Dress Design, 1973; BS, Business Admin, 1985. *Appointments:* Accounting Serv, Howells Accounting, 1973-78; Gen Mgr, Gravel Products, 1978-80; Comptroller Bluebird Intl, 1981-83; Owner, Pres, Magnetic power Systems, Huntingdon Beach, 1984-. *Creative Works:* Developer of Honey Does it cosmetic cream; Prize Wining Designer Needlework; Thin Graille of Insanity, Etching; Research on Biomass Energy System with Pollution Controls. *Memberships include:* Nat Assn of Accountants; Orange Coast; Intl Committee Community Serv; Toastmasters Intl; Nat Assn of Exec Women. *Honours:* Letter of Commendation, Veterans Admin; 1st Prize for Needlework; Various Civic Awards. *Hobbies:* Sewing; Craft Design; Gold Minning; Hiking; Splunking; Skiing. *Address:* Magnetic Power Systems, PO Box 1115, Huntingdon Beach CA 92647, USA.

HOWORTH Michael John, b. 21 Oct 1949, Liverpool, England. Mkting dir, Copy king Group. m. Frances Rumney Samson, 16 July 1977, 1 s, 1 d. *Education:* HMS, Conway Merchant Navy Training Sch, 1964-67; Univ of Southampton Nautical Studies, 1972. *Appointments:* P&O Shipping Group, 1967-76; Michael Howroth Assoc, 1976; Merged, Copy King Group, 1981. *Publications:* Numerous Articles on Print Mkting. Quick Printers Guide. *Memberships:* RNR; Conway Cruising Assoc; Hurlingham Club; British Assn of Printers & Copy Shops; M Inst m; M Inst PR. *Honour:* Quick Printer of the Year. *Hobbies:* Sailing; Cruising; Gastronomy; Writing; Video; Editing. *Address:* 47 Napier Avenue, Hurlingham, London SW6 3PS, England.

HOYES Thomas, b. 19 Nov 1935, Horncastle, Lincs. Member Lands Tribunal; Chartered Surveyor. m. Amy Joan Wood, 27 Aug 1960, 2 d. *Education:* Queen Elizabeths G S Alford, Lincs; Ddowning Coll Cambridge. *Appointments:* Partner, Hallam Brackett Ch Surveyors, 1962-83; Prof, Land Mngt, Univ of Reading, 1983-88; Lands TV, 1989. *Creative Works:* The Practie of Valuation. *Memberships:* Royal Inst of Ch Surveyors; Planning Devel Div, RICS; Rating Surveyors Assn; Land Inst. *Honours:* Harold Samuel Studentship. *Hobbies:* Gardening; DIY; Education for Surveying . *Address:* 2 Braybrooke Gardens, Wargrave, Berks RG10 8DW, England. 1.

HOYLE Trevor, b. 25 Feb 1940, Rochdale, England. Author. m. Dorothy Lumb, 15 Sept 1962, 1 s, 1 d. *Education:* Rochdale Grammar Sch, 1951-57. *Appointments:* Actor, Repertory & TV, 1958-63; Advertising Cpoywright, 1963-70; TV Writer, Presenter, 1972-75; Author, 1970-. *Publications:* The Relatively Constant Copywriter; Rule of Night; The Man Who Travelled on Motorways; The Last Gasp; Vail. Radio Plays. Conflagration; Randles Scandals. *Memberships:* Soc of Authors; Amnesty Intl. *Honours:* Winning British

Entry in Transatlantic Review Short Story Comp; Judging Panel of Constable novel Prize; 1990 Radio Times Drama Award. *Hobbies:* Crown Green Bowls; Cycling; Cinema; Human Rights; Cosmology & Quantum Physics. *Address:* Sheilland Assoc Ltd, 43 Doughty Street, London WC1N 2LF, England.

HOYOS Arturo, b. 9 Dec 1948, Panama. Justice of the Supreme Court; Univ Lectr. m. Jinny Boyd, 28 Dec 1985, 2 s, 1 d. *Education:* Doctoris Scientiae Juridicae, Univ Javeriana, Columbia, 1972; MA, Univ of Sussex, 1974. *Appointments:* Supreme Court of Justice, 1990-. *Publications:* Dercho Del Trabajo; Numerous Articles. *Memberships inc:* Panamierican Bar Asson; Panamerican Academy of Law. *Honours:* Scholarships; Visiting Prof, Univ of Mexico; Participant, 1990 Intl Visitors Programe, United States State Dept. *Hobbies:* Reading; Writing Legal Essays; Literature; History. *Address:* PO Box 657, Zone 9A, Panama, Republic of Panama. 52.

HROUDA Frantisek, b. 28 Aug 1944, Praha. Geophysicist. *Education:* Physics, Geology, Univ of Brno, 1966; Mineralogy & Petrology Univ Brno, 1969; Mathematics & Physics, CSAV Praha, 1979. *Appointments:* Geofyzika State Co, Brno, 1966-. *Publications:* More Than 80 Original Papers in Intl & Nat Sci Journals. *Membership:* Czecholovak Soc for Mineralogy & Petrology. *Hobbies:* Gardening; Reading; Music. *Address:* Uranovska 29, CS 61400 Brno, CSFR.

HSIAO Roger C, b. 23 Aug 1955, Taichung, Taiwan. Asst Prof, Higher Educ. m. Hanling Hwang, 3 Jan 1981, 1 s. *Education:* BS, Taipei Inst of Tech, 1976; ME, Renselaer Poly Inst, 1981; MS, Rensselaer Poly Inst, 1985; PhD, 1985. *Appointments:* Engrng Officer, Chinese Army, Taiwan, 1976-78; Design Engr, China Engrng Conslt, 1978-79; Research Asst, Renesselaer Poly Inst, 1981-85; Asst Prof, Univ of South Carolina, Columbia, 1986-. *Publications:* Intl conference Proceedings, Robotics & Automation; Tech Reports; Journals; Confernce Proceedings, Artificial Intelligence in Manufacturing. *Memberships:* American Soc of Mech Engrng; Inst of Electrical & Electronics Engr; Soc of Manufacturing Engr; Nat Serv Robot Assn; American Assn for Artificial Intelligence. *Honours:* South Carolina Research & Productive Scholarship; Rensselaer Fellowship; Distinguished Graduate Award; Scholastic Merit Scholarship. *Hobbies:* Stamp Collection; Remote Controlled Aircraft Modeling. *Address:* Dept of Mech Engrng, Univ of South Carolina, Columbia, SC 29208, USA. 7, 132.

HSU Chao Fan, b. 7 Sept 1927, Shanghai, China. Insurance. m. Hsuch Hsuan Ku Hsu, 9 May 1952, 3 s, 1 d. *Education:* St Johns Univ, Shanghai, 1949; Clark Univ, Worcester, Massachusehs, 1957. *Appointments include:* Special Officer, Central Trust of China, 1959-65; Committee Member, Supervisory Committee on Reserve Against New Taiwan Currency Issue, 1972-73; Sr Vice Pres, Central Reinsurance Corp, 1978-83; Dir, Insurance Inst of the Republic of China, 1985-89; Pres, Chung Kuo Insurance Co, 1989-. *Publications:* A Study of Foriegn Trade of Teh Republic of China; A Study of Reinsurance System in the Republic of China; Improvement of Managment of Life Insurance in a Liberalized Insurance Market; Several Articles; Various Survey Reports. *Memberships include:* Nuclear Engery Insurance Pool of the Republic of China; Intl Insurance Soc. *Honour:* Civil Serv Award. *Hobbies:* Literature; Music; Drama; Photography. *Address:* No. 6-2 Nung An Street, 2nd Floor, Taipei, Taiwan, China.

HSU Ming-Yu, b. 4 Dec 1925, Kweiyang, Kweichow, China. Registered Prof Civil, Structure Engr; Prof. m. Chih Ju Yao, 1 Jan 1952, 2 s, 3 d. *Education:* Delft Tech Univ, The Netherlands, 1959; Nat Kweichow Univ, China. *Appointments include:* Prof, Cheng Kuan Univ, 1958-64; Dir of Structural Engrng, Hussey, Gay Bell & Deyoung, 1982-; Prof, Savannah Coll of Art & Design, 1985-. *Creative Works:* Hundreds of Buildings from

Single to 40 Stories; From Steel to Reinforced Concrete; Hundreds of Marine Structures & Bulk Materials Transportation Conveyor Systems Structures; Developed Thousands Hectargs Tidal Land. *Memberships:* Nat Soc of Prof Engrs; American Soc of Civil Engrs; Ref Prof Engrng in Illinois. *Address:* 1115 Wilmington Island Road, Savannah, Ga 31410, USA. 7.

HSU Yih Yun, b. 10 July 1930, China, Amoy. Chmn, Atomic Energy Council, ROC. m. Shiao Ying Chiang, 2 s, 1 d. *Education:* BSc, Nat Taiwan Univ, 1952; MSc, Univ of Illinois, 1957; PhD, Univ of Illinois, 1958; Northwestern Univ, 1958-59. *Appointments:* Snr Research Engr, NASA Lewis Research Centre, 1959-74; Snr Reactor Engr, AEC/NRS, USA, 1974-81; Prof Nuc Engr, Univ of Maryland, 1980-90; Chmn Atomic Energy Council, ROC, 1990-. *Publications:* Transport Processes of Bioling and Two Phase Flow System; Over 100 Articles. *Memberships:* Thermal Hydraulic Div; American Nucleat Soc; Heat Transfer & Energy Conversion Div; American Inst of Chem Eng. *Honours:* ASME Heat Transfer Memorial Award; LSNRC High Quality Award; Fellow, AICHE; Fellow, ANS; Tchrng Excellence Award. *Hobbies:* Swimming; Reading. *Address:* 67 Lane 144, Keelung Road, Section 4, Taipei, Taiwan 16, China.

HSU Zuey Shin, b. 13 Dec 1930, Shining, Taiwan, ROC. Prof of Physiology. m. Pan Tsu Wu, 1 Feb 1964, 1 d. *Education:* MD, Nat Taiwan Univ, 1949-56; Internal Medicine, NTU Hosp, 1956-57. *Appointments:* Asst, KMC, ROC, 1957-59; Instr, KMS, ROC, 1959-62; Ap of Legal Medicine, KMS, 1962-68; Ap of Physiology, KMS, 1968-72; Prof, KMS, 1972-; Dir, Dept of pharmacology, KMS, 1973-74; Dir, Dept of Physiology, KMS, 1972-85. *Creative Works include:* Invension of the Vaccine Prepared by Treating Homologous Tumor Cells with HCHO HAOH Mixture and CONA for Treatment of S 180 Ascites Tumor. *Memberships include:* Forosan Medical Assn; The Am Biographical Inst; IBC; ABI. *Honours:* Nat Sci Council Grant; World Decoration of Excellence Medallion; Gold Medal to Commemorate Biographical Induction in the First Five Hundred. *Hobbies:* Philosophy; Painting; Music; Travel. *Address:* Dept of Physiology, Kaohsiung Medical Coll, No.100 Shih Chuan 1st Road, Kaoshiung, Taiwan, China. 52, 139, 152, 156, 175.

HU Chun Sheng, b. 3 Jan 1938, Liuzhou. Chief Engr. m. Zhou Xunlian, 6 Jan1963, 3 s, 1 d. *Education:* Dept of Geology, Ind Univ of Changnan, 1962. *Appointments:* Geological Techm 1962-65; Geological Engr, 1966-83; Vice Chief Engr, no.7 Geological Team, Guangxi, 1984-85; Chief Engr, Petroleum Geological Team, Guangxi, 1986-. *Creative Works include:* First Discussion on the Geological Features and Genesis of Lead, Zinc and Pyrite in Beishan. *Memberships:* Geological Soc of Guangxi; China Sci & Tech Assn. *Honours include:* Advanced Member, Dept of the Minority Areas Sci; High Engr. *Hobbies:* Football; Photography. *Address:* Petroleum Geological Team, Liushi Road 470, Liuzhou, Guangxi Prov, China.

HU Jason Chih-Chiang, b. 15 May 1948, Kirin, China. *Education:* LLB, Nat Chengchi Univ, 1970; Master Soc Sci, Univ of Southampton, 1978; PhD, Oxford Univ,1984; Res Fellow, St Anthony's Col, Oxford Univ, 1985. *Appointments:* Dpty Sec Gen, Asian Pacific League for Freedom and Democracy, 1986-89; Dpty Sec Gen, Soc for Strategic Studies, China, 1989; Assoc Prof, Sun Yat-Sen Inst for Interdis Studies, Nat Sun Yat-Sen Univ, 1986-90; Sec Gen, China Chap, World League for Freedom Democracy, 1989-91; Dpty Dir, First Bureau Ofc of the Pres, China, 1991; Chief Conf Dept, Nat Unification Coun Ofc of the Pres, China, 1990-91; Dir Gen and Govt Spokesman, Govt Info Ofc, China. *Address:* Director General, Government Information Office, 2 Tien Tsin Street, Taipei, China.

HU Zhuanglin, b. 30 Mar 1933, Shanghai. Prof of English; Chmn of the English Dept. m. Wenqi Chen, 18 Feb 1960, 2 s. *Education:* St Francis Xaviers Coll, 1944-50; Tsinhua Univ, 1952-54; Western Language, Peking Univ, 1952-54; Sydney Univ, 1979-81. *Appointments:* Translator, Gen Staff PLA, 1954-58; 858 State Farm, Hulin; Translator, Chinese Academy of Agricl Sci, 1959-72; Tchr, Lectr, Assoc Prof, Prof, English Dept, 1973-. *Creative Works include:* A Companion to English Studies; Linguistics, A Course Book. *Memberships:* Intl System Congress Committee; China English Educ Assn; Beijing Linguistics Soc; English Group, Commission for the Compliation and Supervision of Foreign Language. *Honours:* Peking Univ Distinguished Social Sci Prize. *Hobbies:* Soccer; Table Tennis; Jogging; Swimming; Bridge. *Address:* English Dept, Peking Univ, Beijing 100871, China.

HUA Ding-Ke, b. 12 May 1931, Wu Xi City, Jiang Su Prov, China. Fish Patholoy Research. m. Cai Miao Lan, 7 Feb 1957, 1 s, 1 d. *Education:* Freshwater Agricl Major, Shanghai Fisheries Coll, 1950-53. *Appointments:* Tchr, jimei Fisheries Coll, 1953-73; Tchr, Zhanjiang Fisheries Coll, 1974-87; Research, Zhuhai Maricultural Research Centre, 1988- 91. *Publications include:* Studies on the Life History iof a Fish Louse; Diseases of Pond Fishes and Its Control; The Diagnosis and control of Diseases of Fish & Shrimps. *Memberships:* Asian Fisheries Soc; China Fisheries Soc; Guangdong Parasitology Soc. *Honours:* Honor Cert for Tchrng for over 30 yrs; Advanced Worker in Fisheries Sci & Tech; Reg Cert for Zhuhai & Guangdong Great Sci & Tech Research. *Hobbies:* Running; Swimming; Climbing; Table Tennis; Bridge; Travel. *Address:* 112 1 304 Xingfu Street, Xiangzhou Zhuhai, Guangdong, China. 139.

HUA Yong-feng, b. 20 Jan 1939, Yun Nan, China. Senior Geologist. m. 10 May 1944, 1 d. *Appointments:* Senior Geologist. *Publications:* Origin and prospecting prediction of Mercury in china, 1982; National Symp on Geology and Geochemistry or ore deposit, 1990. *Memberships:* Chinese Soc of Minerol, Petrol and Geochem; Chinese Guizhou Soc of Geol. *Hobbies:* Golf; Basketball; Reading. *Address:* Non-Ferrous Geological Exploration Company of Quizhou, Quizhou Quiyang, China.

HUANG Bao-Kui, b. 9 Oct 1926, Putain. Prof of Economics. m. Chen Xue Yin, 28 Sept 1949, 2 s, 2 d. *Education:* Putian Liqing Middle Sch, 1939-42; Putian High Sch, 1942-45. *Appointments:* Tchr, Hangjiang Middle Sch, 1949; Clerk, Putian Peoples Bank, 1950-76; Tchr, Putian 6th middle Sch, 1977-79; prof, Xianmen Univ, 1980-. *Publications:* Comparative Financial Systems; Financial System of Selected Countries; Comparative Banking Acts; Intl Finance & Investment. *Memberships:* Taiwan Affairs Researcher; Nat Financial soc. *Honours:* Excellent Creative Work. *Hobbies:* Poet; Handwriting; Painting. *Address:* Finance & Banking Dept, Xiamen Univ, Xiamen 361005, China.

HUANG Changqing, b. 26 Mar 1942, Nanping City, Fujian. Vice Pres of Yongan TV Univ; Assoc Prof. m. Wang Shuming, 24 Apr 1967, 1 s, 1 d. *Education:* Fujian normal Univ, BA. *Appointments:* Secondary Sch Tchr, Dean, 1966-85; Coll Tchr, Dean of Shanming Prof Univ, 1985-90; Vice Pres, Yongan TV Univ, Fujian, 1990-92. *Publications:* The Use of English Adverbs with Two Forms in Pairs; English Writing Skills for Snr; English Cloze Test for Snr; A Guide to Trainging for MET Test; Composition. English Tutorial ion TVU in China. *Memberships include:* Fujian Foreign Languages & Literature Soc; China Translation Assn; Intl Assn of Tchrs of English as a Foreign Language. *Hobbies:* Reading; Swimming; Qigong. *Address:* Yongan TV Univ, Fujian, China.

HUANG Chunyao, b. 9 Jan 1925, Sichuan, China. PRof. m. 18 Dec 1948, 2 s, 2 d. *Education:* BA, Art Dept Nat Central Univ, 1947. *Appointments include:* Dir of Tchrng Affair, no.8 middle Sch, Nanjing, 1949-51; Section

Member, Municipal Educ Admin, Nanjing, 1951-52; Dean of Studies, Nanjing Tchrs Training Coll, 192-55; Assoc Prof, Art Dept, nanjing Normal Univ, 1979-85; Prof , Sichuan Coll of Educ, 1987-. *Creative Works:* Selected Paintings by Huang Chunyao. *Membership:* China Artists Assn. *Honours:* Participated China Nat Arts Exhibition. *Hobbies:* Music; Drama; Calligraphy; Poetry. *Address:* Pox 3 of Sichuan Coll of Educ, 24 of Section 3, South Peoples Road, Chengdu, Sichuan, China.

HUANG Francis Fu-Tse, b. 27 Aug 1922, Hong Kong. Coll Prof. m. Fung Yuen Fung, 10 Apr 1954, 2 s. *Education:* BS, San Jose State Coll, 1951; MS, Stanford Univ, 1952; Columbia Univ, 1964. *Appointments:* Design Engr, M W Kellogg Co, NY, USA, 1952-58; Asst Prof, 1958-62; Assoc Prof, 1962-67; Prof, 1967-; Chmn, Dept of Mech Engrng, 1973-81. *Publications:* Engrng Thermodynamics; Fundamentals & Applications. *Memberships include:* American Soc for Engrng; Assn for Advancement of Sci; Intl Assn of Sci & Tech Development; Tau Sigma; Phi Kappa Phi. *Honours include:* Sci Faculty Fellow; Distinguished Tchrng Award; Honorary Prof; Cultural Docorate in Energy Sci. *Hobbies:* Travel; Sports; Reading. *Address:* 1259 Sierra Mar Drive, San Jose, CA 95118, USA. 2, 9, 52, 143.

HUANG Huo-Quan, b. 12 July 1933, Fujian, China. Tchr. m. (1) 18 Feb 1960, (2) 1 Mar 1984, 1 s. *Education:* Middle Sch, 1946-52; Xiamen Univ, 1952-56. *Appointments:* Tchr, Xiamen Univ, 1956-85; Lect, Prof, Xiamen Univ, 1986-91. *Publications:* A Theorem on a Stability Criterion in the Critical Case; The Sumary by Maths. *Memberships:* Standing Committee of Xiamen; System Research Assn. *Address:* Dept of Maths, Xiamen Univ, Fujian, China.

HUANG Ruihau, b. 13 Feb 1940, Hengyang. Research fellow. m. 1 Feb 1971, 2 d. *Education:* Geological Dept, Central Southern Inst, Mining, Metallurgy, 1956-61. *Appointments:* Geological Team, 1961-64; Geological Exploration & Mineral Prospecting. *Publications:* Tin Tectonogeochemistry in South East Part of China; Tin Tectonic Gathering Dispersing & Tectonic Ore Forming. *Memberships:* Soc of Enviromental Sci of Hunan; Soc of Mineralogy, Petrography & Geochemistry of hunan Prov; Council of Element Geochemistry & Regional Geochemistry. *Honours:* Model Tutor of graduate Students; Merit Award; 3rd Class Prize of Achievement in Sci Research. *Hobbies:* Reading; Taijiguan. *Address:* Changsha Inst of Geotectonics, Academia Sinica 410013, Changsha, Hunan, China.

HUANG Shun-Ji, b. 29 Jan 1932, Jinghua City, PRC. Prof of Electronic Engrng. m. 13 Feb 1961, 1 s, 1 d. *Appointments:* Asst, South China Univ of Tech, 1955-56; Assoc Prof, Prof, Lectr, Chengdu Inst of Radio Engrng, 1956-87; Prof, Univ of Electronic Sci & Tech, 1987-. *Publications:* Digital Signal Processing and its Applications; Digital Signal Processing. *Memberships:* Chinese Electronics inst; Signal Processing Soc of China; Radar Soc of China; Radar Soc of Province Sichuan, China. *Honours:* Outstanding Prof Award; Prize for Sci & Tech Achievement. *Hobbies:* Painting; Swimming. *Address:* Dept of Electronic Engrng, Univ of Electronic Sci & Tech of China, Chengdu, Sichuan 610054, China.

HUANG Yongren, b. 24 Feb 1936, Canton, China. Physics Prof. m. Xiuying Sheng, 18 Jan 1963, 1 s. *Education:* South China Normal Univ, 1952-56; East Chin Normal Univ, 1956-58. *Applications:* East China Normal Univ, 1958-. *Creative Works includde:* A Study of polypropylene Synthetic Fiber by Means of NMR; The Density Operator Theory of NMR; Improving the Resolution with Multiple Quantum Filter; Optimization of Pulse Technique for Solvent Suppression; The Foundation of NMR Theory. *Memberships:* Chinese Physics Soc; Chinese Physical Biology Soc. *Honours:* Two Medals of the Chinese 2nd Rank of Sport. *Hobbies:* Chinese Classical Literature. *Address:* 3663 Northern Zhong Shan Road, 200062 Shanghai China.

HUBEL Vello, b. 6 July 1927, Tallinn, Estonia. Chair, Ind Design & Ind Design Conslt. m. 10 Apr 1965, 2 d. *Education:* Ontario Coll of Art, 1955; Mit Summersessions, 1962,71,73. *Appointments:* Various Canadian Manuf, 1955-58; Design Conslt, 1958-; Tchr, Ontario Coll of Art, 1965-; Chair, Ind Design, 1991-. *Publications:* Focus on Designing; 300 Coloured Drawings of Toronto; Many Product & Exhibition Designs. *Memberships:* ACIDO; ACID; Royal Canadian Academy of Arts; Estonian Federation n Canada. *Honours:* Medal of Service; Community Citation; A J Casson Tchrng Award; Various Design awards. *Hobbies:* Landscape Sketching; Travel; Walking. *Address:* 531 Soudan Avenue, Toronto, Ontario, Canada M45 1X1. 88.

HUBL Lothar, b. 1941, Barn. Prof oe Economics. m. Ulla Hohls Hubl, 31 Dec 1987, 3 s. *Education:* Abitur Oberrealschule Weien, 1960; Tech Univ Berlin, 1966; Tech Univ Hannover, 1968; Tech Univ Hannover, 1972. *Appointments:* Rector, Univ Hannover, 1973-74; Dir, Inst for Systems Analysis, 1974-87; Dir, Inst for Economic Research, 1981-; Prof for Econmoncs, Univ of Hannover, 1972-. *Publications:* Kapitalmarktzins; Zinsentwicklung; Volkswirtschaftslehre; Mikrookonomie. *Memberships:* Verein fur Socialpolitik; Verband der Wirtschaftsingenieure Rotary Hannover. *Honours:* Stresemann Scholarship. *Hobbies:* Modern Art; Tennis; Skiing. *Address:* Univ Hannover, Inst fur Volkswirtschaftslehre, Konjunktur und Strukturpolitik, Wunstorfer Str 14, 3000 Hannover 91, Germany. 52.

HUBSCHMID Johannes, b. 14 Aug 1916, Kusnacht. Prof Univ Heidelberg & Barn. m. Erika Schori, 19 Jan 1946, 3 s. *Education:* Univ of Zurich, 1935-42; Ecole Practique des Hautes Etudes, 1937-38; Univ of Florence, 1943. *Appointments:* Linguist, Federal Toqogr Ser, Switzerland, 1944-52; Private Docent, Prof Hon, Univ of Barn, 1949-; Prof, Univ of Heidelberg, 1960-; Visiting Prof, Ecole Practique des Hautes Etudes, Paris, 1968-71. *Publications:* Praeromanica; Sard Studier; Schlauche und Fasser; Thesaurus Praeromanieus. *Memberships:* Collegium Romanicum Schweiz; Inst di Studi Etruschi. *Hobbies:* Oriental Carpets. *Address:* Romanisches Seminar, Univ of Heidelberg, Germany.

HUDD Nicholas Payne, b. 11 Oct 1945, Romford, essex. Physician. m. Gwendeleen Mary Johnstone, 11 Oct 1969, 2 s, 1 d. *Education:* Palmers Sch, Grays, 1957-64; Sidney Sussex Coll, Cambridge, BA,1967; MA, 1971; MB, 1971; Westminster Hosp, MRCP, 1976. *Appointments:* House physician, Harlow, 1971; Medical Reg, Basildon Hosp, 1972-74; Snr Medical Reg, Manchester, 1976-78; Conslt Physician, Benenden Hosp. *Publications:* Sundry Poems; Small Choral Compositions. *Memberships:* Ronney Marsh Historic Churches Trust; St Mildreds Church; Conductor, Benenden Hosp Choir; Royal Soc of Medicine; Royal Coll of Physicians; British Diabetic Assn. *Hobbies:* Golf; Cricket; Gardening; Music; History; Talking; Scotophile. *Address:* 54 Wimpole Street, London W1M 7DF, England.

HUDIK Martin Francis Joseph, b. 27 Mar 1949, Chicago, Illinois. Hosp Admin; Police Admin. 1 d. *Education:* Morton Coll, 1969; III Inst of Tech, BSMAE, 1971; Jackson State Univ, BPA, 1974; Loyola Univ of Chicagi, MBA, 1975; Univ of Sarasota, 1975-6. *Appointments:* Asst Admin, 1969-; Snr Aux, Cicero III Polick Dept, 1971-; Instr, Nat Safety Council, 1977-85. *Publications:* Various Short Stories; Oil Paintings; Video Training Programs. *Memberships:* Emergency Serv & Disaster Agency; Intl Assn for Hosp Security; CACI. *Honours:* Meritorious Ser Medal; Mensa; Alpha Sigma Nu; Council Mambers; Lieutenant. *Hobbies:* Photography; Videography; Watching My Daughter Grow Up. *Address:* 836 W Wellington Avenue, Chicage, IL 60657, USA. 2, 8, 52, 132, 139.

HUDSON Miles Matthew Lee, b. 17 Aug 1925, Belfast. Farmer. m. 19 May 1956, 3 s, 1 d. *Education:* Sherborne

Sch, 1939-43; Trinity Coll, Oxford. *Appointments:* Army, 1943-62; Conservative Research Dept, 1963-71; Political, Foreign Office, 1971-74. *Publications:* Triumph or Tradegy. *Honour:* OBE. *Hobbies:* Tennis; Golf; Shooting; Fishing; Politics; Reading; Writing; Local Government; Travel. *Address:* The Priors Farm, Mattinglby, Bassingstoke, Hants, England.

HUEBNER Peter, b. 12 Nov 1944, Apolda. Historian, Dr Sc Phil. m. Christe Degen, 7 Aug 1971, 1 d. *Education:* Univ Leipzig, 1965-72; Dr Phil, 1972; Acad Sci, German Dem Republic, Berlin, 1972-90; Inst German History, Berlin, 1990-. *Appointments:* Sci Cooperator, 1972-90; Mgr, Dept Contemporary History & Vice Dir, Inst of German History, Berlin, 1990-. *Publications:* Studies & Articles on Soc History of eastern Germany; Schwarze Pumpe. *Memberships:* Geselischaft fur Deutschland forschung; German Studies Assn. *Hobbies:* Geology; Mineralogy; Tramp the Mountains & Woods. *Address:* Heinrich Rau Str 360, 0 1143 Berlin, Germany. 52.

HUGHES George, b. 4 May 1937, England. m. Janet, 29 June 1963, 2 s. *Education:* Liverpoll Collegiate; Gonville & Cains Coll, Cambridge Univ. *Appointments include:* Ski Instr, Switzerland, 1959; Ld in Film, Holiday, 1959-60; Banking, Paris, 1960; IBA london, 1960-69; UK Strategy Unit Mgr, 1968-69; Merchant Banking, 1969-70; Willowbrook World Wide, 1971-83; Hampton Court Frms, 1975-87; Hughes Tech, 1984-. *Publications include:* The Effective Use of Computers; Military & Business strategy; Interigated Cattle Developement; Road to Recovery;Speed Thinking Kaleidoscpw. *Memberships:* Mensa; Derbys CCC; TCCB. *Honours include:* Liverpool City Snr City Scholar; British Open State Scholar; MA, Honours; MBA. *Hobbies:* Soccer; Cricket; Tennis; Renoir; Perception of Visual Patterns in Thinking & Creativity. *Address:* Xanadu, Matthews Green, Wokingham, England RG11 1JU. 1, 52.

HUGHES Gillian Mary, b. 12 Sept 1959, Reading, Berks. Accountant. *Education:* Haywards Heath Coll, 1970-77; Bedford Coll, univ of London, 1977-80. *Appointments:* Spicer & Pegler, Chartered Acct, 1980-81; Anzecs Exec Ltd, 1981-85; Fisons Instruments, 1985-86; Continental Reinsurance Corporation, 1986-89; CCL Financial Grou Plc, 1989- 91. *Memberships:* Chartered Assn of Ceritified Accountants. *Honours:* Honorary Life Govenor of the South of England. *Hobbies include:* Reading; Writing; Gardening; Spectating Agricult & Horse Shows; Horse Racing. *Address:* Penryn, Off High Street, Flihwell, East Sussex TN5 7PB, England.

HUGHES James Madison, b. 20 July 1897, Claysville, TN. Retired. m. Ella Turner, 4 s. *Education:* Bryan Coll, Dayton, TN; Baxter Inst, Baxter TN; Liscenced to Preach, 1920; Ordained to Ministry, 1932. *Appointments:* Pastorate. Maynardsville TN, 1923-24; Graysville TN, 1925-26; Peakland TN, 1927-28; Morgantown TN, 1929-31; Doyle TN, 1932-37; Spencer TN, 1938-40; Clay St Baptist, Drayton Oh, 1941; Christianburg Oh, 1944-45. *Address:* Crossville, TN, USA.

HUI Jacques Albert Pierre, b. 18 May 1933, Paris, France. Asst Gen Mgr, phone Poulene, Organic & Inorg Intermediates Sector. m. Francoise L Champille, 16 Apr 1959, 1 s, 4 d. *Education:* Ingenieur Ec Nat Sup Mines d Paris, 1955; Doct es Sci Univ De Paris, 1962. *Appointments:* Research Engr, 1961-65; Mfr Mgr, 1965-70; Research Mgr, 1070-75; Dept Asst mgr, 1975-78; Dept Mgr Org Chem, 1978-79; Snr Vice Pres, Div Gen Mgr, Phone Poulene Inc, USA, 1979-82; R & D Planning & Strategy Mgr, 1982-86; Dir, Valorisation CNRS, 1986-87; Dir, Strategy & Develop, 1987-90. *Publications:* Report for X Plan Commission for Education on Diversification and Personalization of Tchrng & Educ. *Contributions to:* Various News Paper & Magazines. *Memberships:* Parents D'Eleves Enseignement Public; Nat X Plan Commission for Educ. *Honours:* Croix de la Valeur Miuitaire; Order/Nat du Merite. *Hobbies:* Music; Hiking. Address: 25 Rue Stephane Proust, 95600 Eaubonne, France. 52, 91.

HUISGEN Rolf K J, b. 13 June 1920, Gerolstein, Eifel. Prof Emeritus, Univ of Munich. m. Trudi Schneiderhan, July 1945, 2 d. *Education:* Univ of Bonn & Munich, 1939-40. *Appointments:* Assoc Prof, Univ of Tubingen, 1949-52; Full Prof, Organic Chemistry, Univ of Munich, 1952-88; Prof, Emeritus, 1988-. *Publications:* More than 520 Research Papers; Handbook Articles. *Memberships:* Bavarian Acad of Sci; American Acad of Arts and Sci; German Acad of Naturforscher Leopoldina; Real Acad de Ciencias Exactas, Madrid; Heidelberg Acad of Sci; Nat Acad of Sci, Washington; Acad Nazinale deo Lincei, Roma. *Honours include:* Liebig Medal of German Chem Soc; Honorary Memberships. Real Soc Espanola de Frisica y Quimica; Royal Soc Chem London. *Hobbies:* Art of XX Century; Archeology. *Address:* Inst fur Organische Chemie der Univ Munchen, Karlstr 23, D-8000 Muncehn 2, Germany. 1, 52.

HUIZER Gerrit Jan, b. 6 Apr 1929, Arnhem. Prof. *Education:* Prop Civil Engrng, 1948; Cand Soc SC, 1952; Loet Soc SC, 1959; PhD, 1980. *Appointments:* Community Develop Worker, 1955-61; UN Asst Expert, 1962-65; Un Expert, Advisor, 1965-73; UN FAO Conslt, 1973-; Thirld World Centre, Catholic Univ, Netherlands, 1973-. *Publications:* Peasant Rebellion in Latin America; Peasant Movement and Thier Counter Forces in S E Asia; Politics of Anthropolgy; Popular Power in Latin American Relegions. *Memberships:* Intl Foundation SE Asian Mountain Peoples; Intl Foundation Comporative Ethics. *Hobby:* Walking. *Address:* Thirld World Centre, Catholic Univ, PO Box 9108, 6500 HK Nymegen, Netherlands. 52.

HULA Pavel, b. 23 Jan 1952, Praha. Musician. m. Helena Hilova, 29 June 1976, 1 d. *Education:* Acad of Music Arts, Prague, 1970-74; Acad of Chamber Music, 1980-82. *Appointments:* 1st Violin, Kocian Quartet, 1975-. *Creative Works:* CD Records, Supraphen Panton. *Honours:* Kocian Ciolin Compt, 1st Prize; Concertino Proza, 2nd Prize; Prize of Czech philharmonic. *Hobbies:* Photography; Sport. *Address:* Vyzlovska 2251, 100 10 Praha, Czechoslovakia. 1.

HULL Howard Antony, b. 26 Nov 1953, Trowbridge, England. Dir of Develop; Acad of St martin in the Fields. m. Janet Elizabeth Lacy, 2 Aug 1977. *Education:* Christs Hosp, Horsham, 1965-71; St Peters Coll, Oxford, 1972-75; BA, 1975; MA, 1978. *Appointments:* Schoolmaster, Gordonstoun Sch, 1976-79; Charity Fund, Raising & Develop Conslt, 1980-87; Dir of China Challenge Ltd, 1987; Dir of Develop, Acad of St Martin in the Fields, 1988-90; Dir, the Liverpool Poly Trust, 1990-. *Publications:* An Essay on John White, Elizabethan Water Colourist; An Unnamed Tree; Poems; The Shin King; Plays. Snowfall, Dava moor; A Brush with Infinity, Oxford. *Memberships:* Inst of Charity Fundraising Mgrs; The Royal Geographical Soc; portland Sculpture Trust; Thornham Field Centre; Advisory Council, The Butler Trust. *Hobbies:* West African Music; Painting; Sculpture; drama; The Nat World. *Address:* 6 Sandlea House, Sandlea Park, West Kirby, Wirral L48 0QF, England.

HULLEN Werner, b. 17 Oct 1927, Cologne. Prof for English Philology, Linguistics & Theory of Modern Language Tchrng. *Education:* Colgne Univ, 1946-52; Lektor, German Dept of Birmingham Univ, 1952-53; Tchr, German & English Grammar Sch, 1953-63. *Appointments:* Prof, Tchr Training Coll, Neuss, 1963-73; Full Prof, Trier Univ, 1973-77; Pull Prof, Essen Univ, 1977-. *Creative Works include:* Linguistik & Englischunterricht; Zeitschrift fur Fremdesprachforschung. *Memberships:* Deutsche Gesellschaft fur Fremdsprachenforschung; IAUPE; ISAPL; Linguistica Europea; EURALEX; EUROSLA; ESSE; GAL. *Address:* Fachbereich 3, Univ of Essen, Universitatsstrabe 12, 4300 Essen, Germany. 52, 92.

HUMPHREY Sandra Faye, b. 27 Jan 1945, Australia. Chief Exec Officer. m. Graham Humphrey, 7 June 1969. *Education:* BA, 1966; PhD, 1972; MEd, 1983. *Appointments:* Dept of Trade & Ind, 1963-65; Reserve

Bank of Australia, 1965-67; Univ of Syney, 1967-70; Head of Dept, Sch of Business & Admin Studies, New South Wales, 197078; Principal Petersham Coll, Tafe, 1978-79; Principal East Sydney Tech Coll, 1980-82; Dir of Panning Coll Research & Information, New South Wales, 1982-85; Principal Sydney Tech Coll, 1986-89; Chief Exec Officer, New South Wales Educ & Training Foundation, 1989-. *Memberships:* Univ of New South Wales Council; Commonwealth Committee for the Accreditation of Teritiary awards; Tech & Adult Tchrs Educ; New South Wales Bd of Architects; NSW Ind & Commercial Traning Council. *Hobbies:* Travel; Reading; Swimming. *Address:* NSW Educ & Training Foundation, GPO Box 170, Sydney, New South Wales 2001, Australia. 23, 138.

HUNKLER Dennis Francis, b. 3 Mar 1943, Oakland, California, USA. Artist; Painter; Sculptor. m. Dorothy Gillmeister, 19 Aug 1989, 1 s. *Education:* New Sch of Art, Toronto, 1965-70; BFA San Francisco Art Inst, 1972. *Appointments:* Asst Dir, Artists Resource Centre, California, 1973; Member, Advisory Committee, Jane Brown Foundation for Dance & Related Studies, 1979-. *Exhibitions:* Printmakers Council of Great Briton; 2nd Intl Text Sound Image Festival. *Honours:* Various Commissions; Works represented in Permanent Collections in US & Brazil. *Hobbies:* Experimenting with Transformations of Language; Reading; Conversation. *Address:* Art Dialogue Gallery, 80 Spadina Ave, ste 201, Toronto Ontario, Canada M5V 2J4. 37.

HUNT John Frederick, b. 2 Oct 1925, Scunthorpe. Chartered Accountant, Retired. m. Maria, 17 Feb 1947. *Education:* Scunthorpe C S; Queens Univ, Belfast; FCA, 1950; ATII, 1960; ACIARB, 1989. *Appointments:* Partner, Stephenson Smart & Co, 1949-90; Snr Partner, 1965-89. *Memberships:* Inst of Chartered Accountants; Inst of Taxation; Inst of Arbitrators. *Hobbies:* Travel; opera; Bowls; Reading. *Address:* 29 Audley Gate, Peterborough PE3 6PG, Cambs, England.

HUNT John Leslie, b. 24 Jan 1924, New Plymouth, New Zealand. Medical Editor. *Education:* Christs Coll, Christchurch, 1937-43; Canterbury Univ Coll, 1943; OTago Univ Medical Sch, 1944-50; MBChB, 1950; MRCP, 1972; FFCM, 1979; FFPHM, 1989. *Appointments:* Registrar, Guys Hosp, London, 1955-56; Medical Advisor, mgr, Medical Dept British Drng Houses Ltd, 1957-60; Principal, Medical Officer, Dept of Health, 1961-89. *Creative Works:* Editor in Chief, Medical Publ at Dept of Health; Foundation Editor, Presctribers Journal & Health Trends; Editor of Annual Report on the State of the Public Health. *Memberships:* Royal Coll of Physicians of London; Faculty of Public Health Medicine; Faculty of Community Medicine; Australia & NZ medical & Dental Assn. *Honour:* OBE. *Hobbies:* Philology; Language; Reading; Travel. *Address;* 109 Northcote Road, Battersea, London SW11 6PN, England. 3, 139.

HUNTER Charles Christopher, b. 2 Feb 1950, Nottingham, England. Conslt, Forensic Psychiatrist; Coordinator of the all Wales PForensic Psychiatry Serv; Advisor in Forensic Psychiatry, Welsh Office. *Education:* MB, BS, 1973; LRCP, 1973; MRCS, 1973; DPM, 1979; MRCPsych, 1980. *Appointments:* Surgeon Lieutenant Royal Navy, 1974- 79; Snr Reg Forensic psychiatry, 1979-82; Conslt Forensic psychiatrist & Deputy Medical Dir, park Lane Hosp, 1982-89. *Memberships:* Royal Coll of Psychiatrists; British Medical Assn; Clinical Tchr in Forensic Psychiatry; Univ of Wales Coll of Medicine; Exec Committee Forensic Section of Royal Coll of Psychiatrists. *Hobbies:* Reading; Travel; Theatre. *Address:* Dept of Forensic Psychiatric Serv, Whitchurch Hosp, Cardiff CF4 7XB, Wales.

HUNTER Jane Proud, b. 12 Jan 1939, Sarnia, Ontario, Canada. Artist. m. John Donald Hunter, 5 Aug 1961, 2 s, 1 d. *Education:* Doan Sch of Fine Arts, 1956; Ontario Coll of Art, 1959; Toronto Tchrs Coll, 1960; Schneider Sch of Fine Arts, 1974. *Appointments:* Elementary Sch Tchr, Sarnia, 1960-61, 1962-63; Elementary Sch Tchr, Wayne, ohio, 1961-62. *Creative Works:* Painter in Water Colour; Solo Exhibitions in Sarnia & London; Group Exhibitions. *Memberships:* Canadian Soc of Painters in Water Colour; Gallery in the Groue, Brights Grove, Ontario. *Honours include:* Painting Selected for Intl Waters; Several Juried Awards; Grants for Creative Artists in Schs. *Hobbies:* Walking; Swimming; Cross Country; Skiing; Bird Watching. *Address:* 440 Charlesworth Lane, Sarnia, Ontario, Canada N7V 2R2. 88.

HUNTER Judith Marylyn, b. 26 Jan 1938, Norwich. m. Roy Leslie, 1 Apr 1961, 2 d. *Education:* Blyth Sch, Norwisch, 1949-56; Univ of London, BSc, 1956-59; Univ of Reading, 1990-. *Appointments:* Adult Educ Tutor, OUESD and other 1969 Awards; Honorary Curator of Roya Borough Collection, Windsor, 1977. *Publications include:* The Changing Face of Windsor; From Tudor Inn to Trusthouse Hotel; The Streets of Windsor & Eton; Slough, a Practorial History. *Memberships:* Berkshire Local History Assn; Berkshire Archaeological Trust; Berkshire Archae Soc; Conslt Committee for Museums in Berkshire. *Hobbies:* Gardening; Walking. *Address:* 26 Wood Lane, Cippenham, Slough SL1 9EA, Berkshire, England.

HUNTER Rodney John, b. 8 Oct 1940, Detroit. Seminary Prof. m. Ann Covington, 17 May 1970, 1 s. *Education:* Yale Univ, BA, 1962; Princeton Theological Seminary, BD, 1965; PhD, 1974. *Appointments:* Candler Sch of Theology, Emory univ. Asst Prof, 1972-78; Assoc Prof, 1978-89; Prof, 1989-. *Publications:* Dictionary of Pastoral Care & Counseling. *Memberships:* American Acad of Religion Soc for Pastoral Theology; Assn for Clinical Pastoral Theology; Soc for the Sci Study of Religion; Cherokee Presbytery, Presbyterian Church. *Honours:* Book of the Year Award; Assoc of Theological Sch Research Grants; Presbyterian Graduate Fellow. *Hobbies:* Classical Piano; Carpentry. *Address:* Candler Sch of Theology, Emory Univ, Atlanta, GA 30322, USA.

HUNTER Tim Bradshaw, b. 15 Aug 1943, Baltimore, MD USA. Prof of Radiology, Coll of Medicine, Univ of Arizona. m. Carol K Ing, 29 Feb 1992, 1 s, 1 d. *Education:* DePauw Univ, BA, 1966; Northwestern Univ, MD, 1968; Univ of Arizonia, BS, 1980. *Appointments:* Asst Prod of Radiology, 1975-81; Prof of Radiology, 1987; Assoc Prof of Radiology, 1981- 87; Chief of Diagnostic Radiology, 1992-. *Publications:* The Computer in Radiology; Radiologic Atlas of Medical Devices. *Memberships:* American Coll of Radiology; Radiological Soc of north America; Arizona Radiological Soc; Assn of Univ Radiologists. *Honours:* Phi Beta Kappa; Alpha Omega Alpha; Fellow American Coll of Radiology. *Hobbies:* Astronomy; Flying; photography. *Address:* Dept of Radiology, AHSC, Tucson, AZ 85724, USA.

HUNTER William John, b. 5 Apr 1937, England. 2 s, 1 d. *Education:* Westminster Hosp Medicine Sch, London, MB, BS, LRCP, MRCS, 1961. *Appointments:* General Midical Pathology & Occupational Medicine, 1961-74; Commission of the European Communties, Principal Admin, 1974-83; Head of Div, Ind Med & Hygiene, 1983-88; Dir, Health & Safety Direct, 1988-. *Creative Works:* Editor of Several Books & Author of Numerous Articles. *Honour:* FFOm. *Hobby:* Swimming. *Address:* Commission of the European Communities, Health & Safety Directorate, Jean Monnet Building, Rue Alcide de Gasperi, L2920 Luxembourg.

HUSAIN Imtizaj, b. 21 June 1932, Meerut, India. Agricl Devel Commissioner/Additional Sec, Ministry of Food & Agricl. m. Shamima Husain 27 Dec 1957, 1 s, 3 d. *Education:* BSc Agronomy, Plant Breeding & Genetics, Argicl Ecomomics, 1950; MSC, 1953; PhD, 1964-67. *Appointments include:* Asst Dir, Ministry of Industiries, 1954-57; Deputy Dir of Research, Agricl Research Council, 1967-72; Dir General, Federal Seed Cerf Dept, 1980-85; Agriclt Devel, 1985-. *Memberships include:* Nat Seed Council; Pakistan Tobacco Board; Agricl

Business Inter Ministerial Wing Representing Agricl, Finance, Commerce, Ind. Islamabad Horticlt Soc. *Hobby:* Gardening. *Address:* House 41, Street no.13, F-7/2, Islamabad, Pakistan.

HUSAIN Sabir, b. 20 Sept 1935, Dabai. University Professor and Chairman. m. Zahida Khatoon, 16 Dec 1961, 1 s. *Education:* MLib Sci, Delhi; MA Sociol, BLibSci, Alig; BCom; Cert AVEduc, New Delhi. *Appointments:* Asst Libn, Gen Educ Ctr, Aligarh Muslim Univ (AMU), 1959-71; Lectr, Dept of Lib and Info Sci, (DLIS), AMU, 1971-75; Sr Lectr, EASL, Mak Univ, Kampala, Uganda, 1975-78; Rdr, 1978-86, Prof, DLIS, AMU, Alig, 1986. *Memberships:* Life, Indian Lib Assn; Soc for Info Sci; IASLIC and IATLIS: UCG Curric Dev Com Lib and Info Sci; UGC JRF Syllabi Com, 1990; Raja Rammohun Roy Lib Foun. *Hobbies:* Photography; Gardening. *Address:* Chairman, Department of Library & Information Science, Aligarh Muslim University, Aligarh 202 002, India.

HUSSAIN Mushtaq, b. 29 Oct 1954, Khulna. Researcg Officer; Statistician; Economist. m. Helena Wisiewska Hussain, 30 Mar 1978, 1 s, 1 d. *Education:* MA, Acad of Economics, Poland, 1979; PhD, Acad of Economics, Poland, 1982. *Appointments:* Research Officer, Study Group, Intl Analysis, Luxenburg, Uastria, 1982-89; Research Officer, Inst for Applied Statistics, 1990-. *Publications:* Structural Changes in Austrian Foreign Trade; Number of Articles to Prof Journals. *Memberships:* Intl Biometric Soc; Soc for Classification; Austrian Statistical Soc. *Hobbies:* Reading; Travel; Philosophy. *Address:* Instl for Applied Statistics, Joanneum Research, Steyregasse 25A, A8010 Graz, Austria. 1.

HUSSAIN Shamshad, b. 1 Jan 1940, Buxar. Prof of Psychology; Dir of Inst of Correspondance Courses. m. Nishat Abdin, 20 Sept 1961, 1 s, 1 d. *Education:* Matriculation, 1954; JA, 1956; BA, 1958; MA, 1960; PhD, 1970. *Appointments:* Lectr Psychology, Patna Univ, 1962; Reader Psychology, 1980; Prof Psychology, 1985; Dir of JCC, Patna Univ, 1987. *Publications:* Adjustment and Its Measurement; Creativity, Concepts & Bindings; Mohsin Shanshad Adaptationa of Bell Adjustment Inventory; Elementary Statistics in Psychology. *Memberships:* Indian Sci congress Assn; Convenour of India Acad of Applied Psychology; Central Advisory Bd on Handicapped. *Honours:* Sci & Tech Section, Member; Central Advisory Bd on Handicapped, Member; Produced 10 PhD Candidates. *Hobbies:* Music; Sports; Reading. *Address:* Univ Prof of Psychology, Dir of Inst of Correspondance Courses, Patna Univ, Patna 800005, Bihar, India.

HUTCHCROFT Paul Theodore, b. 18 Jan 1931, Burlington, Iowa, USA. Program Officer, Communication, Winrock Intl Inst for Agriclt Devel. m. Beverly Jane Walk, 14 June 1953, 3 d. *Education:* BS, 1953; MA, 1959; PhD, 1978. *Appointments:* Iowa Farm Bureau Federation, 1955-56; US Dept of Agricl, 1956-59; Nat 4H Foundation, 1959-75; Council for Agricl Sci & Tech, 1975-83; Winrock Intl, 1983-. *Publications:* World Atlas; Agricltural Research in Bangladesh; Ten Years of Agricl Research in Bangladesh; Evaluating Agricl Research Programs; Mngt of Human Resources in Agricl Research. *Memberships include:* Public Relations soc of America; Farm House Fraternity; Phi Kappa Phi; Gamma Sigma Delta. *Honours:* Agricl Communicators in Educ; Award of Excel in Intl Affiars. *Hobbies:* Reading; Potography; Agricl History. *Address:* Winrock Intl, Route 3, Morrilton, AK 72110, USA.

HUTCHESON Robert Bennett, b. 23 July 1933, Montreal, CDA. Conslt Obstetrician; Gynaecologist. m. Nicola Caroline Pumphrey, 30 Sept 1972, 4 d. *Education:* Lower Canada Coll, McGill Univ, 1956; London Univ, MB, BS, 1963; Royal Coll of Obstetricals & Gynaecologist, 1970. *Appointments:* Snr Reg, O&G Hammersmith Hosp, 1974-75; Conslt Obstetrician, Gynaecologist, Gloucester Royal Hosp, 1975-.

Memberships: Royal coll of Obstetrician & Gynaecologists; British Medical Assn; British Menopausal Soc; Gloucester Clinic. *Honours:* Elected Fellow of Royal coll of Obstetricians & Gynaecologists. *Hobbies:* Flying; Distinguished Peaope of Today. *Address:* 1 Burnet Close, Robinswood, Glouester, Glos GL4 9YS, England.

HUTCHINSON (John) Maxwell, b. 3 Dec 1948. PRIBA; Chmn, Hutchinson & Partners Arch Ltd; Pres, Royal Inst of British Arch. *Education:* Wellingborough Prep Sch; Oundle; Scott Sutherland Sch of Arch, Aberdeen; Archtl Assoc Sch of Arch. *Appointments:* Hutchinson & Partners, Chartered Arch, 1972; Chmn, Permarock Prod Ltd, Loughborough, 1985; Royal Inst of British Arch. *Publications include:* The Prince of Wales; Right or Wrong? *Memberships include:* Energy Policy Cttee; Industrial Bldg Bureau; Freeman, City of London. *Hobbies:* Composing; Recording; Playing the Guitar; Opera; Ballet; Theatre; Riding; Running. *Address:* 401 St Johns Street, London EC1V 4QE, England. 1.

HUTCHINSON Stephanie Belle, b. 27 June 1957, Los Angeles, CA. Pianist; Hymnwriter. *Education:* BM, Magne Cum Laude, 1978; MM, 1980; DMA, 1985; Univ of Southern California, 1990-91. *Appointments:* private Tchrng, Piano & Voice, 1975-; Faculty, Univ of Southern Calif, 1979-81; Accompanist, Los Angeles Childrens Chorus, 1988-; numerous Piano Solo Recitals. *Creative Works include:* 20 Original Psalmr; Hymns; Spiritual Songs. *Memberships:* The Hymn Soc in the United Studies and Canada; Pi Kappa Lambde; Mu Phi Epsilon; Phi Delta Gamma; Intl Congress of Women in Music; Christians in the Arts Networking. *Honours:* 1st Prize Mozart Festival Nat Young Artist. *Hobbies:* Opera; Museums; Theatre; Reading. *Address:* Shepherd Song Music, PO Box 27718, Los Angeles, CA 90027, USA. 138.

HUTT Michael Stewart Rees, b. 1 Oct 1922, Shresbury. Emeritus Prof of Geographical Pathology. m. 4 May 1946, 1 s, 3 d. *Education:* Eastbourne Coll, 1936-40; St Thomasa Hosp Medical Sch, 1941-45; MB BS, 1945; MRCP, 1946; MD, 1949; MRC Path, 1963; FRCP, 1967; FRC Path, 1967. *Appointments:* Lectr, Snr Lectr in Pathology, St Thomas Hosp Medical Sch, 1951-62; Prof of Pathology, Makerere Univ Coll, 1962-70; Prof og Geographical Pathology, 1970-83. *Publications:* Medicine in a Tropical Environment; Cardiovascular Disease in the Tropis; The Geography of Non Infectious Disease. *Memberships:* Tropical Medicine Research Bd; Council of Royal Soc of Tropical Medicine; Bd of Tropical Doctor; Action in Intl Medicine. *Honours:* Mavdg Abbott Lectr. *Hobbies:* Reading; African Affairs. *Address:* Gwernvale Cottage, Brecon Road, Crickhowell, Powys NP8 1SE. Wales. 139.

HUTTON James Thomas, b. 12 May 1923, Glasgow. sch Tchr; Visiting Specialist in Music. Retired. m. Anne Bowes, 15 Aug 1946, 1 s. *Education:* Glasgow Univ, Music Faculty, 1955-58; Scottish Acad of Music, 1958-59; Joroanhill Coll of Educ, 1959-60. *Appointments:* Renfrewhire Educ Auth, 1960-64; Lanarkshire Educ Auth, 1964-88. *Creative Works include:* Composer of Orchestral Music; 2 Symphonies; 2 Concert Overtures; Jazz Orchestral Compositions. *Memberships:* General Techng Scouncil; Educ Inst of Scotland; Soc of Composers. *Hobbies:* Reading; Improvising at th Piano. *Address:* 88 Warwick, East Kilbride, Scotland G74 3PY.

HVISC Jozef, b. 24 Apr 1935, Kurima. Assoc Prof. m. Edita Jaskova, 12 May 1962, 2 s. *Education:* Faculty of Arts, Univ Komensky, Bratislava, 1957-62; Master of Arts, 1968; Philosophy Doc, 1969; Assoc Prof, 1991. *Appointments:* Research Worker, Slovak Acad of Sci, Bratislava, 1968-90; Univ Tchr, Univ of Komensky, 1990-. *Publications:* Epic Literary Genres in The Slovak & Polish Romanticism; The Literary Evolution of Jan Cajak jr Slov Spisovatel; Problems of the Literary Genologie; Poetics of Literary Genres; The Slovak Historic Prose; Slovak Polish Literary Relations.

Memberships: Slovak Committee of Slavists; Union of Slovak Writers. *Hobbies:* Painting; Drawing. *Address:* Katedra Slavistiky FFUK, Gondova 2, 818 01 Bratislava, Czechoslovakia.

HVIZDALA Karel, b. 16 Aug 1941, Prague. Journalist; Writer. m. Allena Born Sebestova, 19 May 1970, 1 s. *Education:* Faculty of Engrng, CVUt Diploma, 1963; Politology Moscow, 1967-68; Gothe Inst German Lang, 1978-79. *Appointments:* Reporter, Chief of Columns, Mlady Suet, 1966-70; Editor, Objektiv, Editing House Albatros, 1970-77; Free Lance journalist, Writer, Editor in Chief, Daily Mlada Fronta, 1977-90; Pres, SA H & F, 1990; Pres, MA FRA, 1992. *Address:* MaFra A S Presidium, NA Porici 30, 112 86 Prague 1, Czechoslovakia. 1.

HWALETZ Otto Josef, b. 26 Oct 1951, Villach. Historian; Researcher. m. Christa Anna Trostheide, 3 May 1988. *Education:* Mag Philos,1978; PhD, 1981. *Appointments:* Instr, 1978-79; Staff, Inst for Hist, Univ of Graz, 1980-81; Lectr, 1983-. *Publications:* Johnsdorf, 1982; Bogmann oder Werkssoldat, 1984; Uber den Prozcys von Akkumulation und Kapitalverwertung in Osterreigh, 1990; Industriesysten Region und Arbeiterbewftsein, 1991. *Hobbies:* Reading; Football; Computing; Wandering. *Address:* Mariengasse 36, A-8020, Graz, Austria. 52.

HYLLEBERG Svend Anton Foged, b. 1 Sept 1944, Horup. m. Elly Norcard, 1 Mar 1969, 1 s, 2 d. *Education:* Univ of Darhus, 1964-71; Masters, 971; Doctorate, 1984. *Appointments:* Adjunt, Aarh Univ, 1972- 75; Visiting Sholar, MIT, USA, 1973-74; Lectr, Aarh Univ, 1975-86; Visiting Prof, UCSO, 1980; Prof, AArhus, 1986; Visiting Prof, VCSO, 1986-87. *Publications:* Seasonality in Regression; New Approaches to Empirical Macro Economics; Modelling Seasonaily; Articles in Leading Journals. *Memberhips:* Econometric Soc; American Statstical Assn; Danish Soc Sci Research Council. *Hobbies:* Badminton; Tennis; Soccer; Cooking; Nature; Opera. *Address:* Fasannej 4, DK 8450 Hammel, Denmark.

HYTNER Benet Alan, b. 29 Dec 1927, Prestwich, Lancs. Barrister. m. Joyce Hyers, 9 Dec 1954, 3 s, 1 d. *Education:* Manchester Grammar Sch, 1939-46; Trinity Hall, Cambridge, 1946-49. *Appointments:* Called to Bar, middle Temple, 1952; Bencher, 1977; QC, 1970; Recorder, 1972; Judge of Appeal, Isle of Man, 1980. *Memberships:* Gen Council of Bar; Senate of Inns of Court & Br; Leader, Northern Circuit. *Address:* 5 Essex Court, Temple, London EC47 9AH, England.

I

IACOB Crucita Glafira, b. 18 Feb 1928, Bucharest. Btructural Building Engr; Ind Engr. m. Grigore Mircea, 29 Oct 1953, 1 s. *Education:* Central Grils Coll, Bucharest; Civil Engrng Building Inst; United Nations Fellowship, Ind Building; Doctorate Stage; Doctors Degree. *Appointments:* Ind Building Structure Design Engr, 1950-56; Chieg Designer, Hd of Structural Design, 1957-74; Hd of Structural design, 1975-83. *Publications include:* Building Reviews; Various Papers. *Memberships:* Engr Building Assn; CAER; Structural Buildings in the Archt Faculty & Building Faculty. *Honours include:* Different Prizes at Several Design Competitions; Order of Destinction in Labour. *Hobbies:* Historical Literatue; Philosophy; Esthetics Reading; Computer Programs; Classical Music. *Address:* Boulevard Dinicu Golescu nr 15, on the 5th Floor, 24th Flat, sector 1, 77112 Bucharest, Romania.

IANNUCCI Flavio, b. 28 Dec 1955, Naples, Italy. Medicine Doctor. m. Maria Cesarone, 15 Mar 1981, 2 s. *Education:* Classic Maturity Diploma, 1973; Medicine Doctor Diploma, 1981; Nuclear Medicine Diploma, 1984; Radio Protectionist Diploma, 1986; Qualified Expert Phisical Radioprotection, 1986. *Appointments:* Dir, Radiomund Assay Unit medical Centre; Clinical Pathology, Asst Ascalesi Hosp. *Publications:* Agglornaments in Tisiologia; 45 Scientific Publ; Many Intl Reviews. *Memberships:* Italian Nuclear Medicine Soc. *Hobbies:* Musician For Keyboards & Guitar; Computers. *Address:* Via to Gliatti 50, 80046 S Glorgio A Cremano, Naples Italy.52.

IBRAHIM Michika Abdurrahman, b. 16 Apr 1964, Lokoja, Nigeria. Civil Engineer. m. Maryam Ibrahim, 10 Oct 1986, 1 d. *Education:* Nat Dipl, 1986; Hlgher Nat Dipl, 1989. *Appointments:* Min of Works & Transp, Yola, 1986-87; Gerid Nigeria Ltd, Yola, 1990-91; Jomm Engrg Sers Nig Ltd, 1991-. *Creative works:* Part structural design and detailing of a proposed multistorey library complex for Kaduna Poly. *Memberships:* Treas, Kaduna Poly Students Union; Pres, Gongola State Students Union Kad Poly Branch; Mem, Sec and Budget Com, Hse of Reps, KPTSU. *Honours:* Cert of Hon, Kaduna Poly Students Union; Mem, Rita Rochella Farl Club. *Hobbies:* Making friends; Reading; Badmington; Travelling. *Address:* 18 Jalingo Street, Old GRA, Jimeta-Yola, Gongola State, Nigeria.

IBRAHIMOVA Yildiz, b. 8 Apr 1952, Silistra, Bulgaria. Singer. *Education:* Secondary Sch of Music, Sofia, 1967-71; Conservatoiare, Bulgarian State Music Acad, 1971-75. *Appointments include:* Jazz Festivals; Concerts; Consert Tours; Discography; Radio & TV. *Creative Works:* Compositions.Ex ile; Improvization on Peasant Dance; On The Road to the Sunrise. *Honours:* Union of Musician of Bulgaria Award. *Hobbies:* Painting; Race. *Address:* Rakovski 145 G, Sofia 1000, Bulgaria.

ICONOMOV Stefan, b. 8 May 1937, Sliven, Bulgaria. Docent; Composer. m. Rumyana Tabacova, 10 Aug 1975, 1 d. *Education:* Dip, State Acad Music, Moscow, 1960. *Appointments:* Currently Docent, state Academy Music, Sofia. *Creative works:* Orchestral, chamber, ballet and choral music incl: Sonata, Ballad for Piano, 1966; Pastoral and Dance for Harp and Chamber Orchestra, 1969; Music for two Pianos and Percussions, 1971; Concerto for Piano and Orchestra, 1977; Sonata for 1 Pianos, 8 Hands, 1979; Dedication and Joke, for Piano Trio, 1981; Symphony for String Orchestra, 1982; Meditations, for Trio (clarinet, piano and percussion), 1985; Prelude, Choral and Fugue for Organ, 1988; Piano Cycle Images, 1988; Musica-concertante for two Pianos, String Orchestra and two Bongos, 1990; Wind Quintet, 1991. *Memberships:* Assn Composers, Bulgaria; Int Piano Duo Assn, Tokyo, Japan. *Honours:* Prize, 1st Int Competition for 2 Pianos Composition, Tokyo, 1990; 4 Prizes for Compositions, Assn Composers, Bulgaria.

Hobbies: Photography; Mountain walks. *Address:* Blrd Vitosha 42, 1000 Sofia, Bulgaria.

IENAGA Yasumitsu, b. 6 Mar 1925, Japan. Prof. m. Teruko, 21 Oct 1952, 1 s, 1 d. *Education:* Kyushu Univ, 1948; PhD, Univ of Tokyo, 1962. *Appointments include:* Asst Prof, Farm Elons, Kyushu Univ, 1948- 50; Tech Officer, Dept Farm Mgnt, Toyko, 1953-64; Visiting Scientist, Dept Agricl Ecoms, Intl Rice Research Inst, 1972-84. *Publications:* Intl Development of Food Resources; Intl Development of Agriculture; Plough & Farming Culture; Origin of Grain Culture; Numerous Other Books. *Memberships:* Agriclt Econ Soc Japan; Fram Mgnt Soc Japan; Intl Assn Agriclt Economists; Tropical Agriclt Research Assn; Agriclt Econs Soc, Southeast Asia. *Hobbies:* Oil Painting; Travel; Reading. *Address:* Nishikasai 4 Chone, 2-5-1220 Edogawd-Ku, Toyko, Japan.1.52.

IGI Keiji, b. 24 Sept 1933, Okayama Ken, Japan. Prof of Physics. m. Mariko Uyama, 30 May 1965, 2 s, 1 d. *Education:* Bach of Sci, Univ of Toyko, 1956; Master of Sci, 1958; Doc of Sci, 1961. *Appointments:* Research Assoc, Toyko Univ of Edn, 1961-66; Lectr, Univ of Toyko, 1966- 68; Assoc Prof, 1968-81; Prof, 1981-. *Publication:* Phenomenological Duality. *Memberships:* Japanesse Physical Soc; American Physical Soc. *Hobbies:* Tennis; Swimming; Skiing; Listening to Classical Music. *Address:* 4-42-7 Yoyogi, Shibuya Ku, Toyko 151, Japan.52.

IGLAUER Edith, b. Cleveland, Ohio. Writer. m. (1) Philip Hamburher, 24 Dec 1942, div 1966. (2) John Heywood Daly, 1 Mar 1976, Dec, 2 s. *Education:* Hathaway Brown Cleveland, 1934; Zimmern Sch, Geneva, 1937; Wellesley Coll, 1938; Sch of Journalism, Columbia Univ, 1939. *Appointments:* Grad Sch, Public & Intl Affairs, Princeton Univ, 1940; McCalls Mag, 1941; US Office of War Information, Radionewsroom, OWI Repres, 1941-44; War Correspondent, Mediterranean Theatre, Cleveland News, 1945; UN Correspondent, Harpers Mag, 1947-54; New Yorker Mag, 1961-. *Publications:* The New People; The Eskimos Journey inton Our Time; Denisons Ice Road; Inuit Journey; Seven Stones, A Portrait of Arthur Erickson, Architect; Fishing with John. *Memberships:* Authurs Guild Inc; Writers Union of Canada; Cosmopolitan Club; Federation of BC Writers; PEN; American, Canadian, BC Civil Liberties Union. *Honours include:* Woodrow Wilson Prize in Modern Politics; Cleveland Arts Prize. *Hobbies:* Travel; Art; Music. *Address:* RR1 5192 Claydon Road, Garden Bay, BC Canada VON 1S0.2.3.5.88.

IHONDE Ayodele, b. 1952, Afuze, Nigeria. Civil Servant. *Education:* Primary Sch Cert and Govt Trade Test, Gr II, Carpentry. *Appointments:* Crafstman Carpenter, 1977; Sr Craftsman Carpenter, 1979; ATO (Bridge), 1983. *Hobbies:* Watching football and athletics. *Address:* Bridge Engineering Department, Nigerian Railway Corporation, Kaduna Junction, PMB 2089, Kaduna State, Nigeria.

IHOR Toshihto, b. 25 Feb 1952, Kurashiki, Japan. Prof. m. Nami Ihori, 30 Mar 1981, 1 d. *Education:* BA, Univ of Toyko, 1974; MA, 1976; MA, Johns Hopkins Univ, 1979; PhD, 1981. *Appointments:* Assoc Prof, Toyko Metropolitan Univ, 1981-85; Assoc Prof, Osaka Univ, 1985-. *Publications:* Modern Public Economics; Government Deficits in Japan; Fiscal Policy in the World Economy. *Memberships:* American Economic Assn; Royal Economic Assn; Intl Int of Public Finance; Japanesse Economic Assn. *Honour:* Nikkes Prize. *Address:* Dept of Economics, Osaka Univ, Toyonaka, Osaka 560, Japan.1.

IIVANAINEN Matti Vilho, b. 25 July 1935, Leppavirta, Finland. Professor of Child Neurology. m. Mirja Pohto-Iivanainen, 25 Mar 1988, 4 s. 1 d. *Education:* MD, 1962; Neurol Spec, 1972; DMSci, 1974; Spec Phys for Mentally Retarded, 1989; Spec, Child Neurol, 1991.

Appointments: Hd, Vaajasalo Hosp for Epileptics, 1973-75; Assoc Hd, Neurol, Univ Hosp, Helsinki, 1975-77, 1980-83; Vis Scist, Nat Inst of Hlth, Bethesda, MD, USA, 1977-80; Assoc Prof, Neurol, 1983-91, Prof and Chief, Child Neurol, 1991-, Univ of Helsinki. *Publications include:* A study on the origins of mental retardation, 1974; Brain developmental disorders leading to metal retardation, 1985; 180 articles and chapters in the fields of developmental neurology, neuroimmunology and epilepsy. *Memberships:* Neurol Assn, Pres, 1986-88; Neuropaed Soc; Phys for Mentally Retarded; Med Assn; Intl Soc for Neuroimmunol; NYAS: Brain Res Soc of Finland. *Honours:* Ambassador, Epilepsy Intl, Wash DC, 1983. *Hobbies:* Fishing; Cross country skiing. *Address:* Mustankorventie 6, SF-01900 Nurmijarvi, Finland.

IKEDA Kazuyosi, b. 15 July 1928, Fukuoka, Japan. Prof of Theoretical Physics; Poet. m. Mieko Akiyama, 20 Nov 1956, 1 s, 1 d. *Education:* Postgrad Study, 1951-56; Dept of Physics, Kyushu Univ, 1957. *Appointments:* Asst, 1956-60; Assoc Prof, 1960-65; Dept of Physics, Faculty of Sci, Kyushu Univ; Assoc Prof, 1965-68; Prof, 1968-; Faculty of Engrng, Osaka Univ, Dept of Applied Physics, 1965-89; Dept of Mathematical Sci, 1989-. *Publications include:* Mechanics without Use of Mathematical Fornulae, From a Moving Stone to Halleys Comet; Basic Thermodynamics, From Entropy to Osmotic Pressure; Numerous Papers on Theoretical Physics; Serialised Peoms of Fixed Form; Essays on Poetry. *Memberships include:* Physical Soc of Japan Committee; Prof World Peace Acad; Nat Coalition for the Unification of North East West South; IBA; IBC; WIA. *Honours include:* Yukawa Scholarship Fund award; World Decoration of Excellence Medallion; Hall of Fame, American Biographical Inst; Intl Cultural Diploma of Honor; Grand Ambassador of Achievement; Intl Order of Merit; Man of the Year; One in a Million Award. *Hobbies:* Watching Kabuki & Noh Plays; Watching & Performing noh Farces; Chanting Noh Songs; Reading Japanesse Classical Literature. *Address:* Nisi 7-7-11 Aomadani, Minoo si, Osaka 562, Japan.11.139.151.152.156.162.178.191.

ILIC Ogor, b. 29 June 1961, Bjelovar. General Mgr; Economist. m. Gordana Kuzman, 1 June 1985, 1 s. *Education:* BSc, Univ of Economics, Zagreb, 1985. *Appointments:* Sales Dept Exec, 1986-89; Sales Dept Mgr, 1989-90; General Mgr, 1990-. *Creative Works:* Software for Clearing House; Software for Compensation Bourse. *Membership:* Business Club, Zagreb. *Honours:* Deans Award for the Best Student in the Generation. *Hobbies:* Fly Fishing; Philately; Financial Conslt. *Address:* Majevicka 12, 41000 Zagreb, Yugoslavia.

ILIZAROV Gavriill Abramovich, b. 12 June 1921, Belovezh, Belorussian SSR. General Dir of All Union, Kurgan Scientific Centre for Restorative Traummatology & Orthopaedics. m. Valentina Alekseevna Glotukhina, June 1984, 1 s, 2 d. *Appointments include:* Rural Doctor, Kurgan Region, 1944-50; Orthopaedic & Trauma Surgeon, Kurgan Regional Hosp, 1950-55; Hd of Orthopaedic & Trauma Research Inst, 1969-71. *Creative Works include:* 213 Inventions covered with Authors Certificate of the USSR. *Memberships include:* USSR Acad of Sci; Academician of Cuban Acad of Sci; Macedonian Acad of Arts; Bd of Children Lenin Fund; Charity Fund Bd. *Honours include:* Lenin Proze Winner; Honoured Inventor of the USSR; Medal for the Valient Labour; Golden Medals of the EEA; Order of Honor of Palestine; Medal of Mexican Inst for Soc Security. *Hobbies:* Work; Collecting Souvenirs, Corals, Shells; Gathering Mushrooms in the Forest. *Address:* VKNZ VTO, M Ulianova Str 6, Kurgan 640005, Russia.

ILLIS Leon Sebastian, b. 4 Mar 1930, London. Conslt Neurologist. m. Oonagh Mary, 14 Oct 1967, 3 s. *Education:* BSc, 1954; MD, 1964; MRCP, 1963; FRCP, 1975. Army Service, RAC & RA Germany, 1948-50. *Appointments:* Conslt Neurologist, Wessex Neurological Centre, Southampton, Clinical Snr Lectr in Neurology,

Univ of Southampton, 1967-. *Publications:* Herpes Simplex Encephalitis; Viral Diseases of the Central Nervous System; Rehabilition of the Neurological Patient; Spinal Cord Dysfunction; Numerous Papers in Sci Journals. *Memberships:* Sci Committee; Intl Spinal Research Trust; Intl Neuromoduction Soc. *Honours:* Gold Medal, Ceylon Coll of Physicians; Visiting Prof of Neurology. *Hobbies:* Skiing; Sailing; Walking; Reading. *Address:* Pond House, Sowley, Lymington, Hampshire, England.

ILMONEN Eino Ossian, b. 31 Mar 1908, Helsinki. Engrng Exec. m. Anna Railo, 30 Dec 1933, 1 s, 3 d. *Education:* MS, Mech Engrng, Helsinki Univ, 1931; D Tech, 1947; Chartered Engr; Major Engr, 1968. *Appointments:* Workshop Engr, Pietarsaaren, 1933-36; Hd Gun Dept, Oy Tampella, 1937-45; General Mgr, Lokomo Oy, 1947-61; Tech dir, Oy Soffco Ab, 1962-65; Hd Mech & El Div Metro Off, Helsinki, 1973-87. *Publications:* Fixing of Piece Work Rates in Engrng Ind. *Memberships:* Fellow Inst Mech Engrs; Finnish Acad Tech; Engrng Soc Tampere; Royal Over Seas League. *Honours include:* Cross of Liberty. *Hobbies:* Ind Economy; Firearms. *Address:* 3 Ehrensvardintie SF 00150, Helsinki, Finland.52.

ILMONIEMI Risto Juhani, b. 1 Aug 1954, Jyvasklan Mlk, Finland. Research Scientist. *Education:* Master of Sci, Dept of Tech Physics, Helsink Univ of Tech, 1981; PhD, Dept of Tech Physics, Helsonk, 1985. *Appointments:* Low Temperature Lab, Helsink Univ of Tech, 1978-85, 1987-; New York Univ, Dept of Physics, 1985-87. *Publications include:* Constr & Performance of a Large Volume Magnetic Shield; Magnetometer for Brain Research; Cerebral Magnetic Fields; Neuropsychobiology; Magnetometers for Lw Frequency Applications; Neuromagnetic Responses to Faces from Human Temporoparietal Cortex. *Memberships:* Finnish Brain Research Soc; AAAS; NY Acad Sci; Finnish Physical Soc; Neural Network Soc; Soc for Neuroscience. *Hobbies:* Philosophy; Skiing; Languages. *Address:* Otakuja 4 A 11, 02 150 Espoo, Finland.1

ILONZEH Ogechukwu Linda, b. 21 Feb 1968, Ogidi, Nigeria. Dental Surgeon. *Education:* Univ of Negeria, Bach of Dental Surgery, 1990. *Appointments:* Baptist Dental Centre, 1990-91; Univ of Nigeria Tchrng Hosp, 1991-. *Creative Works:* Over 35 Drama Shows; TV Plays. Immortal Wedlock; Bandit in Paradise; The Crucial Test. *Memberships:* Nigeria Dental Assn; Acts Theatre Enugu; Full Gospel Business Men Fellowships of Nigeria. *Honour:* Children Evangilism Ministry Distinction Award. *Hobbies:* Music; Reading; Gisting; Swimming. *Address:* 41 Edozie Street, Uwandi, Enugu, Nigeria.

ILUYOMADE Oyinlade Raphael Franklin, b. 4 Jan 1937, Ondo Nigeria. Business. m. Solayide Sabinah Olagundoye, 5 s, 2 d. *Education:* West Africa Sch, 1961; Military Training, Indian Acad, 1963-64. *Appointments:* Army Officer, 1964; Capt, 1967; Major, 1969; Lt Gen, 1972; Retired, 1977. *Memberships:* Philosophical Soc; Athletic Club of Ibadan; Retired Army Officers Club; 3 Church Soc; 3 Social Clubs. *Honour:* 1st Prize Officers Shooting Comp. *Hobbies:* Reading; Discussion on World Affiars; Fishing & Hunting; Music, Church & Classical. *Address:* 11 Ekiti Street, Old Bodija, Ibadan, Nigeria.

IMBODEN Roberta Ann, b. 11 July 1934, Buffalo, NY, USA. Prof of Literature. m. David Grimshaw, 4 June 1977. *Education:* Bach of Arts, 1956; Master of Arts, 1961; Master of arts, 1977. *Appointments:* Ryerson Poly Inst, English Dept, Toronto, 1965-. *Publications:* From the Cross to the Kingdom; Sartrean Dialectics & Liberation Theology. *Memberships:* Sartbean Soc; American Acad of Religion. *Honours include:* Delta Epsilon Sigma. *Hobbies:* Cinema; Classical Music; Travel. *Address:* Ryerson Polytechnical Inst, English Dept, 350 Victoria Street, Toronto, Ontario, Canada M5B 2K3.88.

IMRE Laszlo, b. 17 Nov 1944, Csorna, Hungary. Professor. m. Mezey Theodora, 8 Aug 1968. *Education:* Univ Deg, Hungarian, Kossuth L Univ, Debrecen, 1968; Doctorate, 1970, Candidates Deg, 1989. *Appointments:* Asst, 19th C Hungarian Lit, Kossuth L Univ, 1969-77; Lectr, 1977-87, Sr Lectr, 1987-, Chm, 1989, Dean of Fac of Arts, 1989-92. *Publications:* Monographs: Rakos Sandor, 1973; Brsuszov es as orosl slimbolista regeny, 1973; Arany janos ballada, 1988; A masyar verses resenty, 1990. *Memberships:* Assn of Hungarian Writers. *Address:* Kossuth L University, H-4010 Debrecen, Hungary.

INAN Ergin, b. 14 Nov 1943, Malatya, Turkey. Painter. m. Giler Inan, 13 Mar 1971, 1 d. *Education:* Painting, Coll of Applie Fine Arts, 1964-68; Salburg Intl Summer Acad, 1969; Munich Acad of Fine Arts, 1971-73. *Appointments:* Prof, Marmara Univ Faculty of Fine Arts; Berlin Artists Scholarship, 1983-84; Guest Prof, Berlin Coll of Fine Arts, 1985-86; Invited Leverkusen City Artist, 1988-89. *Creative Works:* Dahau, Concentration Camp; Cross Letter; Berlin; Righthand; Long Letter. *Membership:* Assn of Plastic Arts, Turkey. *Honours include:* Intl Graphic Biennial Medal; Sedat Simaui Trust, Pastic Art Award. *Hobby:* Reading. *Address:* Sadika Sabanci Sites 11, Gomec Sok, A4 Daire 5, Kosuyolu, Istanbul, Turkey.

INDECKI Krzysztof Leonard, b. 14 May 1952, Lodz, Poland. Senior Lecturer in Law. m. 30 Oct 1980. *Education:* LLM, Fac of Law and Admin, 1977, MSociol, Fac of Econ and Sociol, 1979; LLD, 1986, Univ of Lodz, Poland. *Appointments:* Univ of Law and Admin, Chm of Penal Law, 1978-80; Asst, 1980-86, Sr Asst, 1986-; Sr Lectr on Hist of Penal Law. *Publications include:* Numerous articles including: Humanitary and individual treatment of juveniles by courts, 1990; Torture and other cruel inhuman or degrading treatment in Polish Penal Law, 1991; The Nature of Terrorism, 1991; International law and the protection of human rights, 1992; Juvenile offenders, 1992; Receiving stolen property: A dogmatic analysis, 1990. *Memberships:* Penal Law Assn. *Honours:* 7 Awds, Rector of Lodz Univ, 1980-91. *Hobbies:* Bicycling; Sightseeing; Reading SF literature. *Address:* ul Jesionowa 12 m 15, 91-363 Lodz, Poland. 152.

ING Nancy Chang, b. 12 Sept 1920, Peiping, China. Writer; Translator & Editor, Chinese PEN. m. Glyn T H Ing, 1943, 1 s, 2 d. *Education:* BA, English Literature, West China Union Univ, 1943. *Creative Works:* Translations of Chinese Short Stories; New Voices; Greean Seaweed & Salted Eggs; Ivory Ball & Other Stores; The Execution of Mayor Yin; Collection of Own Poetry. *Memberships:* Intl PEN. *Hobbies:* Swimming; Reading. *Address:* 12th Floor no.28, Yi Shien Road, Taipei, Taiwan.

INGE Peter (Anthony), b. 5 Aug 1935. British Army Officer. m. Letita Marion Beryl Thornton Berry, 2 d. *Education:* Summer Fields; Wrekin Coll; RMA Sandhurst. *Appointments include:* Commissioned Green Howards, 1956; Served Hong Kong, Germany, Malaya, Libya, UK; Instr Staff Coll, 1973-74; CO 1 Green Howards, 1974-76; Chief of Staff, HQ 1 Corps, 1982-83; MOD, 1986-87; Commander Northern Army Group, Commander in Chief, British Army of the Rhine, 1989-. *Memberships:* Army & Navy Club; MCC. *Honours:* KCB; Aide De Camp General to the Sovereign. *Hobbies:* Cricket; Walking; Music; Reading; Military History. *Address:* c/o Barclays Bank, Leyburn, North Yorkshire, England.1.

INGRAM David Eric, b. 9 Jan 1939, Qld, Australia. Prof for Applied Linguistics. m. Nelly Nohokau Airi, 1 Aug 1981, 2 s, 1 d. *Education:* Queensland Tchrs Coll, Australia, 1957; Univ of Queensland, Brisbane, 1958-62; Bach of Educ, 1958-65; MA, Univ of Essex, 1970-71; PhD, Univ of Essex, 1975-78. *Appointments include:* Primary Sch Tchr, Queensland, 1958-60; Subject Master, Bremer state High Sch, Ipswich, 1967; Principal Lectr, Dir, Inst of Applied Linguistics, 1987-90; Prof of Applied Linguistics, 1990-. *Publications include:* The Australian Second Language Proficiency Ratings; Language in Education Planning. *Memberships include:* World Federation of Modern Language Assn; Applied Linguistics Assn of Australia; Queensland Assn for the Tchrng of English as a Second Language. *Honour:* Fellow of the Australian Coll of Educ. *Hobbies:* Family; Classical Music; Photography; Lawn Bowls; Travel. *Address:* Centre for Applied Linguistics & Languages, Griffith Univ, Nathan, Queensland 4111, Australia.52.

INGRAM James Charles, b. 27 Feb 1928, Australia. Exec Dir of the World Food Programme, United Nations. m. Odette MA Koven, 16 Oct 1950, 1 s, 2 d. *Education:* Univ of Melbourne, BA, 1954. *Appointments:* Australian High Commissioner, Canada Jamaica, Barbados, Guyana & Trinidad Tobago, 1973-74; 1st Asst Sec, Australian Dev Ass Bur, 1974-76; Dir, Australian Dev Ass Bureau, 1977-82; Exec Dir, United Nations World Foor Programme, 1982-. *Memberships:* Soc for Intl Development; Food Policy Research Inst; Intl Commission on Peace & Food; Tidewater Group; North South Roundtable; Commonwealth Club. *Honour:* AO, Officer in the Genral Div of the Order of Australia. *Hobbies:* Sailing; Music. *Address:* World Food Programme, Via Cristoforo Colombo 426, 00145 Rome, Italy.52.156.

INGRAM Jeffrey Eugene, b. 16 July 1966, Montgomery, AL. Youth Minister, Graymere Church of Christ. m. Dawn Davenport, 28 July 1990. *Education:* Westumpka High Sch, 1984; BA, Freed Hardeman Univ, 1988; David Lipscomb Univ, 1988-. *Appointments:* East Ridge Church of Christ, 1988-90; Graymere Church of Christ, 1990-. *Honours:* Outstanding Yound Men of America; Outstanding Coll Student of America. *Hobbies:* Golf; Tennis; Softball. *Address:* 228 Valley Dr, Columbia, TN 38401, USA.145.

INGRAO Charles William, b. 15 Mar 1948, New York, USA. Professor of History. m. Kathleeen Beloin, 28 Aug 1971, 1 s, 1 d. *Education:* BA Wesleya Univ, 1969; MA Hist, 1971, PhD, 1974, Brown Univ. *Appointments:* Instr, Brown Univ, 1974-76; Asst Prof, 1976-82, Assoc Prof, 1982-987, Prof, 1987-, Purdue Univ. *Publications:* The Hessian Mercernary State, 1987; In Quest of Crisis: Emperor Joseph I and the Habsburg Monarchy, 1979. *Memberships:* Am Hist Assn; Soc for Austrian and Habsburg Hist, Exec Sec, 1991; Conf Gp for Ctl European Hist; German Studies Assn. *Honours:* Phi Beta Kappa; Fulbright fellow, 1972-73; Bye Fellow, Robinson Col, Cambs, 1989; Humboldt Fellow, 1980. *Hobbies:* Tennis; Baseball; Classical Music. *Address:* Department of History, Purdue University, W. Lafayette, IN 47907, USA. 154, 8, 30.

INMAN James Charlton, b. 10 Nov 1945, Shreveport, LA, USA. Licensed Prof Counselor, Pain Mngt Conslt. m. Linda L Dugas, 20 Jan 1968, 1 s, 1 d. *Education:* McNeese State Coll, BS, 1969; McNeese State Univ, BA, 1981; MA, 981. *Appointments:* Master Counselor, Louisiana Office of Emp, 1976-87; Vocational Conslt, Crawford Health Serv, 1987-89; Profl Conselor, Self Employed, 1989-. *Publications:* Regular Contributor, Poetry; Telicon Journal of Intl Soc for Philosophical Enquiry. *Memberships:* American Acad of Pain Mngt; ISPE; Royal Anthropological inst of Great Britain, Ireland; Soc. of Antiquaries of Scotland. *Honours include:* Certified Rehabilitation Counselor; Medical Rehabilitation Therapist. *Hobbies:* Reading; Collecting Movies. *Address:* 1813 Rose Street, Lake Charles, LA 70601, USA.7.

INNS Harry Douglas Ellis, b. 4 June 1922, Ontario, Canada. Doctor of Optometry. m. Helen Mitchell, 3 Sept 1985. *Education: OD; FAAO; FACLP; FRSH.* *Appointments:* Private Optometric Practice, brantford, 1963-; Ind Conslt, Firms inc. Scotcon American Optical Soft Lens Div; Lomb Soflens Div, Cooper Vision Inc. *Creative Works:* Inventor. Inns Extension Disc, to Extend range of Keratometer; Author. Papers in Various journals; Lectrs, Various Profl Conferences. *Memberships include:* Canadian Assn of Optometrists; Canadian Soc of Saftely Engrng; Heraldry Soc of Canada; Royal Canadian Military Inst; Intl Platford Assn. *Honours include* 5 Awards, Ontario Assn of optometrists; Fellow, American Acad of Optometry. *Hobby:* Heraldry. *Address:* 36 King George Road, Brantford, Ontario, Canada N3R 5K1.6.52.129.130.139.156.158.

INOSE Hiroshi, b. 5 Jan 1927, Toyko, Japan. Dir General, Nat Centre for Sci Information Systems. m. Mariko Tsuchiya, 30 Sept 1960. *Education:* Bach of Engrng, Univ of Toyko, 1948; Doc of Engrng, Univ of Toyko, 1955. *Appointments:* Prof, Univ of Toyko, 1961; Dean of Engrng, Univ of Toyko, 1986; Dir General, Nacsis, 198. *Publications:* An Introduction to Digital Intergrated Communications System; Information Technology and Civilization. *Honours include:* Marconi Intl Fellowship; Foreign Member, Royal Swedish Acad of Engrng Sci. *Hobbies:* Fine Arts; Japanese Classics. *Address:* 39-9 Jingumae 5 Chome, Shibuya Ku, Tokyo 150, Japan.

INOUYE Arlene Ruth, b. 2 Jan 1954, Oakland, USA. Editor & Church Conslt. *Education:* BA, Sociology, Univ of California, 1976; MA, Univ of California, 1978; Master of Divinity, Fuller Theological Seminary, 1992. *Appointments:* California State Dept of Educ, Research Analyst & Conslt, Special Educ, 1977; Educational Testing Serv, Berkeley, 1978; McGraw Hill Book Co, Assoc Editor, 1978-81; Evergreen Baptist Church, Conslt, 1987-; Freelance Editor & Writer, 1981-. *Creative Works:* Technological Trends & National Policy; Level 1, & Level 11, Abilities in Asian, White & Black Children, Intelligence; Cultural Barriers to Church Renewal; The Ministry of Incorporation. *Memberships:* Phi Beta Kappa; Evergreen Baptist Church, Rosemead. *Honours include:* Appointed a Regents Fellow in Educ; China Cup Series, Offshore 5K Race, 2nd Prize; Award of Excellence in Christian Formation and Discipleship. *Hobbies:* Fishing; Camping; Bicycling; Walking; Reading; Time With Friends & Family. *Address:* Evergreen Baptist Church, 1255 San Gabriel Blvd, Rosemead, CA 91770, USA.76.

IOANNOU Susan, b. 4 Oct 1944, Toronto, Canada. Writer; Editor. m. Lazaros Ioannou, 28 Aug 1967, 1 s, 1 d. *Education:* BA, Univ of Toronto, 1966; MA, Univ of Toronot, 1967. *Appointments include:* Mgrng Editor, Coiffure du Canada, 1979-80; Assoc Editor, Cross Canada Writers Mag, 1980-89; Poetry Instr, Toronto Bd of Educ, 1982-; Poetry Instr, Sch of Continuing Studies, Univ of Toronto, 1989-. *Publications:* Spare Words; Motherpoems; The Crafted Poem; Familiar Faces; Clarity Between Clouds. *Memberships include:* The Arts & Letters Club of Toronto; Canadaian Council of Tchrs of English; Media Club of Canada. *Honours:* Norma Epstein Foundation Award for Poetry; The Book Cellar Mothers Day Poem Award; Arts Scarborough City Poetry Contest Winner. *Hobbies:* Reading; Watercolour Painting. *Address:* PO Box 456, Station O, Toronto, Ontario, Canada M4A 2PL.3

IONESCU Radu, b. 1 Feb 1930, Bucarest, Romania. Historian of Art; Critic. Div. *Education:* Faculty of History, Theory of Arts, 1948-52. *Appointments:* Research Worker, 1953-59; Keeper, Museum of the Cad, 1960-77; Keeper, Paint Room Library of the Acad, 1977-90; Vice Pres, Council of Museums & Collections, 1990-. *Creative Works include:* Art Monographs; Studies. Dissertations for Meetings & Congresses; articles & Chronicles. *Memberships include:* ICOM; Comission of Historical Monuments; Comission of the Old Town. *Hobbies:* Collect Works of Art & Old Books; Travel. *Address:* Str Brezoianu No.10, Sc C Et VI Ap 62, 70 627 Bucuresti, Romania.

IORDACHE Dan-Alexandru, b. 2 Sept 1939, Constantze. Univ Prof of General Physics. m. Viorica Ionescu, 27 July 1967, 1 s, 1 d. *Education:* Physics

Faculty, Bucharest Univ, 1960; Physics Doctorat in Optics, Spectroscopy, Bucharest Univ, 1971. *Appointments:* Physicist, Factory Electronics, Bucharest, 1960-65; Physics Dept, Poly Inst Bucharest, Asst Lectr, 1963-67; Univ Lectr, 1967-76; Univ Conf, 1976-82; Univ Prof, 1982-; Sci Leader, Romanian Team, Int Phys Olymp, 1988-90. *Publications:* Over 40 Publ, Sci Works; Over 20 Didact Books. *Memberships include:* Romanian Physics Soc; Romanian Soc of Magnetic Materials; Assn of Romanian Scientists. *Honours include:* Nat Prize Creativeness & Efficiency in Educ. *Hobbies:* Universal History; Classical Music; Tourism. *Address:* Physics Dept, Plytechnic Inst of Bucharest, Splaiul Independentzei, 313 Bucharest, Romania.

IORDANOVA Kostadina, b. 1 May 1960, Sofia, Bulgaria. Researcher in Humanities. m. Stanislav Kolev, 16 Oct 1985, div, 1992. *Education:* MA, 1983, PhD, 1985, Philos, Sofia Univ. *Appointments:* Vis Scholar, Univ of Ottawa, 1992; Res Fellow, Meml Univ of Nfld, 1991; Inst for Cultural Studies, Sofia, 1985-90. *Publications:* Over 100 papers and book reviews in Bulgarian and Canadian magazines and newspapers inthe fild of humanities; Also translator of 4 books. *Memberships:* Intl Assn for Women Philos; World Fed of Bus and Profl Women. *Honours:* Can Coun Translators Grant, 1992. *Hobbies:* Reading; Films; Knitting. *Address:* ul Zagore 5, 1124 Sofia, Bulgaria.

IOSIPESCU Sergiu, b. 17 Dec 1948, Bucharest, Rumania. Historian; Archaeologist. *Education:* Fac Hist, Univ Bucharest, 1966-71; BA, 1971; Dip, Universal Hist, 1971; Specialisation, Mediaeval Archaeology, Latin Palaeography, Slavonic; Cand for Doct. *Appointments:* Archivist, 1971- 74; Sci Rschr, 1974-89; Prof, Hist: Mil Acad Rumania, 1979-85, Polytechnic Inst, Bucharest, 1987-89; Dpty Dir (Sci Dir), Direction, Histl Monuments, Ensembles and Sites of Rumania, 1990-. *Publications:* Over 50 studies in sci reviews; Books in Rumanian: Formation of the Romanian Feudal States (co-author), 1980; The Military History of the Romanian People, vols I-IV (co-author), 1984-87; Balica, Dobrotita, Ioancu (A History of Romanian Sea Shore in 14th century), 1985; The Great Mircea (co-author), 1987; Romanian and European Cultural Confluence (90 years from the birth of the Romanian historian Gheorghe Bratianu) (co-author), 1998. *Memberships:* Rumanian Soc Classical Studies, 1978-; Pres, Rumanian Commn Archtl and Archaeological Photogrammetry, 1990-; Ed Staff, Review of Historical Monuments, 1990-; Ed Staff, Bulletin of the Commission of Historical Monuments, 1990-; Nat Commn Archaeology, Rumanian Acad, 1991-. *Honours:* Prize, Citation, Order Rumanin Army, for archaeological discovery of late mediaevel fortress and gt gold and silver hoard at Vadu, Rumanian Black Sea shore, 1987. *Hobbies:* Linguistics; Travel. *Address:* Str General Ipatescu, No 14, Apart 2, 70317 Bucharest 11, Romania.

IREDALE John Martin, b. 10 June 1939, England. Chartered Accountant; Insolvency Practitioner. m. Anne Jewell, 14 Sept 1963, 3 s, 1 d. *Education:* FCA. *Appointments:* Chartered Acct, 1962-; Insolvency Practitioner, 1965-; Ptnr, Cork Gully, 1971-; Coopers & Lybrand, 1980-. *Publication:* Receivership Manual, 1987. *Memberships:* Insolvency Practitioners Assn; Soc Practitioners of Insolvency; Gov, Royal Shakespeare Theatre. *Hobbies:* Family; Royal Shakespeare Theatre; Cricket. *Address:* Holybrook Farm House, Burghfield Bridge, Reading RG3 3RA, England.

IRIUCHIJIMA Juro, b. 28 June 1931, Tokyo, Japan. Professor of Physiology. m. Michiko Kumami, 8 Sept 1960, 1 s. *Education:* MD, 1955, PhD, 1962, Univ Tokyo. *Appointments:* Instr, 1962-64, Assoc Prof, 1964-79, Univ Tokyo, Prof, 1979-, Univ Hiroshima. *Publications:* Cardiovascular Physiology, 1972. *Membership:* Physiological Soc Japan. *Hobby:* Backpacking. *Address:* 4-14-704 Nakamachi, Naka-ku, Hiroshima, Japan.

IRMAGEAN, b. 9 Apr 1947, Detroit, Michigan, USA. Artist (Fine Art). div., 1 s. *Education:* AA, Grove St Coll; BFA, CA Coll Arts and Crafts, 1976. *Career:* Exhib Coord, Expo 1989-90, Ebony Mus Project; Artist Mentor, CA Coll Arts and Crafts; City Sites Prog, 1989; Instructor: Workshop, Koncepts Cultural Gall, 1989; Juror, Oakland Fest at the Lake, 1989. *Creative works include:* Exhibs: San Fran Mus Mod Art, 1981; Galerie Franz Mehring, Exchange Show, Berlin, Germany, 1981; The Aurora Fall, 1987; Hatley Martin Gall, 1990; Contbn to Daniel Mendelowitz' A Guide to Drawing, 1982, 2nd Ed 1988. *Memberships:* Hon Mbr, Sigma Gamma Rho. *Honours:* Drawing Award, CA Coll Arts and Crafts, 1976, 1982; Best of Show, 1st Place Purchase Award, Expo 89-90, Ebony Mus Project, CA, 1990; Sigma's Outstanding Woman of 20th Century, Sigma Gamma Rho; Assisted US Coord, II Bienal del Grabado de Am, Maracaibo, Venezuela. *Hobbies:* Writing; Acting. *Address:* PO Box 5602, Berkeley, CA 94705, USA. 138.

IRVINE Demar B, b. 25 May 1908, California, USA. Professor Emeritus of Music. m. Greta Eickenscheidt, 12 June 1934. *Education:* BA, 1929, MA, 1931, Univ CA; PhD. Harvard Univ, 1937. *Appointments:* Fac, School Music, Univ WA, Seattle, 1937-78. *Creative works:* Var compositions incl 2 symphonies; Writing About Music, 2nd Ed, 1968. *Publications:* Anton von Webern: Perspective, 1966; Massenet: A Chronicle of His Life and Times, 1974, New Ed, 1993. *Membership:* Am Musicological Soc. *Honours:* Prix de Paris, study in Europe, Univ CA, 1931-33. *Hobby:* Correspondenc with former students scattered far and wide, with successful careers. *Address:* 4904 NE 60th Street, Seattle, WA 98115, USA. 2, 4, 13, 156.

IRWIN Frederick George Ernest, b. 19 Nov 1933, Donegal, Republic of Ireland. Consulting Engineer. m. Juliet Faith Tatlow, 11 Sept 1964, 1 s, 2 d. *Education:* Trinity Coll, Dublin, 1951-55; BA, BAI 1st Class Hons; MSc, IA State Univ, USA, 1956. *Appointments:* Seelye Stevenson, Cons Engrs, NYC, USA, 1958; DuPont (UK) Ltd, England, 1958-61; Ove Arup & Ptnrs, 1961-64; Ove Arup & Ptnrs (Ghana), 1964-67; Ove Arup Ptnrship, 1968-. *Publication:* Chmn Comm, Instn Civil Engrs Report: Construction Research and Development, 1987. *Memberships:* Fellow, Instn Civil Engrs; Fellow, Instn Structural Engrs. *Honours:* MBE, 1989. *Hobbies:* b3Drawing; History; Golf; Walking. *Address:* 46 Selly Wick Road, Selly Park, Birmingham B29 7JA, England.

ISAACS Keith, b. 30 May 1921, Drummoyne, New South Wales, Australia. Aviation Historian; Retired Air Force Officer (Pilot). m. (1) Kathleen McQuillan, 23 June 1951, (2) Elizabeth O'Brien, 1 Sept 1974, 1 s, 1 d. *Education:* St Mark's, Drummoyne; St Joseph's, Rozelle. *Appointments:* Clerk, Dunlop Perdriau Rubber Co; Citizen Mil Forces, 1940-41; Australian Imperial Force, 1942; Served to Grp Capt, Royal Australian Air Force, 1942-71. *Publications:* Military Aircraft of Australia, 1971; The Golden Years - RAAF (pt author), 1971; 1000 Famous Australians (pt author), 1978; Contbr to: Australian Encyclopaedia; Australian Dictionary of Biography; Macquarie Book of Events, 1983. *Memberships:* Assoc, Royal Aeronautical Soc; United Serv Instn, NSW; Aviation Histl Soc Australia. *Honours:* Air Force Cross, 1961. *Hobbies:* Tennis; Cricket; Music; Australian aviation history. *Address:* 23 Garling Street, Lyneham, ACT 2602, Australia.

ISAACS Madelyn Lisa, b. 29 June 1953, Brooklyn, New York, USA. University Administrator. m. Christopher B Smith, 29 May 1978, 2 s. *Education:* BA, Hist, Social Studies, Univ Albany, 1974; MA, Counselling, Univ CT, 1977; PhD, Educl Rsch, Counselling Psychology, Hofstra Univ, 1985. *Appointments:* Var admin fac appts, New Coll, Hofstra Univ, 1977-86; Dir, Student Affairs, Univ S FL, Ft Myers, 1987-. *Memberships:* AACD; AMEG; NACD; AERA; ACPA; NASPA; Zonta, Sec, VP, Pres-Elect; SW FL Drowning Prevention Comm, Chair. *Hobbies:* Reading; Movies. 15, 76.

ISAEV Dmitry, b. 25 Oct 1929, St Petersburg, USSR. Professor of Child Psychiatry; Department Chairman. m. Galina Isaeva, 7 Jan 1956, 2 s. *Education:* Grad, Leningrad Paediatric Med Inst, 1953; Cand Med Sci, 1958; Dr Med Sci, 1971. *Appointments:* Med Dir, Psych Hosp, 1956-60; Asst of Prof, Assoc Prof, Prof, 1960-69, Chm, Dept Child Psych, 1970-, Paediatric Med Inst, St Petersburg. *Publications:* Bases Teoricas de los Problemas Centrales de la Psiciatria Infantile, 1966; Neuroses of Children and their Treatment, 1977; Sex Education, 1979, 1980, 1988; Mental Retardation, 1982; Prevention of Psychiatric Illness, 1984. *Membership:* Pres, Psych Soc St Petersburg. *Hobby:* Coin collector. *Address:* Department of Child Psychiatry, Paediatric Medical Institute, Litovskaja street 2, 194100 St Petersburg, Russia.

ISHIDA Yoichi, b. 2 June 1935, Osaka, Japan. University Professor. m. 12 Mar 1965, 2 s, 1 d. *Education:* BEng, 1959, DrEng, 1978, Univ Tokyo; MS, 1961, ScD, 1963, MIT, USA; Post-doct Fellow, Univ CA, 1963. *Appointments:* Rsch Assoc, MIT, USA, 1963; Sr Sci Off, Nat Phys Lab, England, 1965; Assoc Prof, 1966, Prof, 1980-, Univ Tokyo, Japan. *Publications:* Grain Boundary Structure and Related Phenonena, 1986; Fundamentals of Diffusion Bonding, 1987. *Memberships:* Bd Dirs, Japan Inst Metals; Bd Dirs, Electron Microscope Soc Japan; Bd Dirs, Japan Inst Materials Sci. *Honours:* Best Papers of Yr, Am Inst Mech Engrs, 1966; Setoh Award, Electron Microscope Soc Japan, 1971; Jefferys Award, 1976, Achievement Award, 1977, Inst Metals Japan. *Hobby:* Cross-country skiing. *Address:* Department of Materials Science, University of Tokyo, 7-3-1 Hongo, Bunkyo-ku, Tokyo 113, Japan.

ISHII Takashi, b. 17 Feb 1935, Nakaizu, Japan. University Professor. m. 22 Mar 1965, 3 d. *Education:* BS, Zoology, 1957, MS, Zoology, 1959, DS, Zoology, 1967, Tohoku Univ; MS, Entomology, Univ HI, USA, 1964. *Appointments:* Asst Prof, 1968, currently Prof, Univ Tokushima; Rsch Sect Mgr, Kyoto Prefecture Inst Pub Hlth, 1975. *Publications:* Co-author, 4 books on entomology. *Memberships:* Am Mosquito Control Assn; Entomological Soc Am; Soc Vector Ecology; Culex pipiens Soc; Japan Soc Sanitary Zoology. *Honours:* Soc Award, Japan Soc Sanitary Zoology, 1989. *Hobbies:* Philately; Photography; Travel; Gardening. *Address:* College of General Education, University of Tokushima, 1-1 Minamijosanjima, Tokushima, 770 Japan. 52.

ISKANDER Felib Y, b. 19 Sept 1949, Egypt. Radio Chemist; Manager of Nuclear Analytical Services. m. Soheir A Maximoss, 11 May 1972, 2 d. *Education:* BS, Pharm Sci, Cairo Univ, 1971; MSc, Chem, 1982, PhD, Chem, 1983; WA State Univ, USA. *Appointments:* Instr, Cairo Univ, 1977-78; Radiochemist, 1983-85, Rsch Assoc, 1985-90, Mgr, Nuclear Analytical Servs, 1990-, Univ TX, Austin, USA. *Publications:* Over 35 in profl jrnls incl: Specification of titanium in solvent refined coal using SESC-INAA (w R H Filby), 1984; Use of NAA to determining nutritive elements in immature and mature soybeans, 1986; Neutron activation analysis for assessing the concentration of trace elements in laboratory detergents, 1986; Neutron activation analysis for measuring the unsaturation in edible oils, 1987; Geochemistry of upper cretaceous classic sediments of Ifon area, S W Nigeria (w T R Ajayi, O I Asubiojo, D E Klein), 1989; Aluminium contest of Egyptian breads (w K R Davis, H Asheur, H F Hassan), 1990; Zinalco and Zircaloy-4 Nuclear Characterization (w H R Carrillom C R Martinez, L Q Torres, N E Hortel), 1991. *Memberships:* NY Acad Scis; Am Chem Soc; Am Nuclear Soc; TX Jr Coll Tchrs Assn; Egyptian Pharm Soc; TX Assn Radiation Rsch. *Honours:* Fellowships awards, acad excellence, WA Mining and Min Rsch Inst, Univ WA; Scholarship award, acad excellence, WA State Univ. *Hobbies:* Tennis; Biking; Camping; Fishing. *Address:* Nuclear Engineering Teaching Laboratory, Balcones Research Center Bld No 159, The University of Texas at Austin, Austin, TX 78712, USA. 7, 143.

ISLAM A K M Azharul, b. 2 Nov 1946, Bogra. Professor of Physics. m. Shamsunnahar Islam, 15 May 1968, 2 d. *Education:* BSc Hons, 1966, MSc, 1967, Rajshahi Univ; DIC, Imperial Col, 1970; PhD, London Univ, 1972. *Appointments:* Lectr, 1968, Asst, 1968, Assoc Prof, 1975, Prof, 1984, Rajshahi Univ; Dean of Sci, 1986; Chm of Phys Dept, 1988-91. *Publications:* Electricity, magnetism and modern physics, 1982; On Solid State matters, 1984; Introduction to Nuclear Physics, 1989; Electrodynamics, 1991. *Memberships:* Inst of Phys, UK; VP, The Phys Soc of Bangladesh, 1986- 88; NYAS; Asian Phys Soc. *Honours:* Habib Bank Gold Medal and Book Prizes, 1966, 6967; Gold Medal and Prizes, Pres of Pakistan, 1968. *Hobbies:* Reading; Gardening. *Address:* Department of Physics, Rajshahi University, Rajshahi 6250, Bangladesh.

ISLAM Muhammad Nazrul, b. 2 May 1945, Jehnidah. Professor of Physics. m. Tahera Begum, 8 Jan 1973, 1 s, 2 d. *Education:* BSc Hons, 1966, MSc 1967, Rajshahi Univ, Bangladesh; PhD, Southampton Univ, UK, 1972. *Appointments:* Lectr and Asst prof, 1968-75, Assoc Prof, 1975-79, 1982- 86, Prof of Physics, 1986-, Rajshahi Univ; Assoc Prof, Tripoli Univ, 1979-82. *Publications:* Electricity, Magnetism and Modern Physics, 1982, 2nd ed, 1992. *Memberships include:* Inst of Bio Sci; VPRU Tchrs Assn; Tras, Phys Assn, 1982-92; Bangladesh Phys Soc; Elec Soc; Bangladesh Assn for the Adv of Sci; Univ Grants Comm; Bangladesh Med Assn; Bangladesh Inst of Tech. *Honours:* Merit scholarship, Ctl Govt of Pakistan, 1969-71; Fellowship, Comm of European Communities, 1992-93. *Hobby:* Reading. *Address:* Department of Physics, Rajshahi University, Rajshahi 6250, Bangladesh.

ISONO Kunio, b, 18 Nov 1946, Japan. Neurobiologist; Researcher. m. 28 Oct 1973. *Education:* BS, 1969, MS, 1971, PhD, 1974, Tohoku Univ. *Appointments:* Lectr, Miyagi Women's Univ, Sendai, 1978-81; Rsch Assoc, Tohoku Univ, Sendai, 1978-; Rsch Fellow, Purdue Univ, USA, 1981-83. *Creative works:* Biological rsch on genetics and physiology of sensory system. *Memberships:* Biophys Soc Japan, Jnl Ed; Physiological Soc Japan; AAAS, USA. *Hobby:* Music. *Address:* 2-1-30 Mukaiyama, Taihaku-ku, Sendai 982, Japan. 52.

ITO Kentaro, b. 13 Nov 1939, Nagoya, Japan. Electrical Engineering Educator. m. Nobuko Nakashima, 21 Mar 1969, 1 s, 1 d. *Education:* BEE w hons, Nagoya Inst Technology, 1962; MEE, 1964, DEng, 1967, Tokyo Inst Technology. *Appointments:* Lectr, Engrng, 1967-68, Assoc Prof, 1968-80, **Prof,** 1980-, Chmn, Dept Elec and Electronic Engrng, 1983-84, 1988-89, Chmn, Grad Studies on Microdevices, 1991-92, Shinshu Univ, Nagano; Vis Fellow, So Meth Univ, Dallas, TX, USA, 1971-72. *Publications:* Handbook of Electrical and Electronic Engineering Materials (co-ed), 1987; Principles of Sensors (w K Takahashi), 1990; Contbr, articles to profl jrnls. *Memberships:* Japan Soc Applied Phys; Inst Electronics, Info and Communication Engrs; Inst Elec Engrs Japan. *Honours:* Shimizu Prize, 1962; Grantee: Iwatani Fndn, Tokyo, Misuzu Matsukoh Fndn, Matsumoto, 1981; Broadcasting Culture Fndn, Tokyo, 1984; Min Educ, Sci and Culture, Tokyo, 1984-92. *Hobby:* Go (Japanese national board game). *Address:* Department of Electrical and Electronic Engineering, Faculty of Engineering, Shinshu University, 500 Wakasato, Nagano 380, Japan. 52.

ITOKAWA Yoshinori, b. 27 Oct 1933, Tokyo, Japan, Professor of Medicine. m. 7 Dec 1965, 2 s. *Education:* Fac Med Kyoto Univ, 1955-59; MD, 1960; PhD, 1965. *Appointments:* Instr, 1969-74, Assoc Prof, 1974- 79, Prof, 1979-, Fac Med, Kyoto Univ, Kyoto; Rsch Assoc, Yale Univ, USA, 1967-70. *Publications:* Books: Fundamentals of clinical nutrition (in Japanese), 1986; Magnesium in health and disease, 1989. *Memberships:* Pres, Jap Soc Hygiene; VP, Int Comm Magnesium Rsch; Sec-Gen, Fedn Asian Nutrition Soc. *Honours:* Young Rschr Achievement Award, Vitamin Soc Japan, 1975; Journal of Applied Nutrition Award, USA, 1977; Bronze

Medal, Acad Nat de Medicine, France, 1985; Achievement Award, Japanese Soc Nutrition and Food Sci, 1987. *Hobbies:* Reading; Movies. *Address:* 33 Koyama-Itakuracho, Kitaku, Kyoto 603, Japan. 52.

IVANOV Sergey (Di-Xiong Yao), b. 3 May 1949, China, Artist. *Education:* High School. *Appointments:* Self employed professional artist. *Creative works:* Paintings include: Hundred Horses (4 metres long); Hundred Camels, (14 metres long); 200 kangaroos (63 metres long). *Memberships:* Victoria Art Soc; Aust-Chinese Art Assn; Chm, Aust, Chinese and Aboriginal Art Res Com. *Honours:* Wood Board Prints Awd, 1978; Guiness Book of records for the longest Chinese painting, 1988; The Marquis Who's Who Publications Board, 1989; All Chinese Calligraphy and painting competion Hon Awd, 1991. *Hobbies:* Singing; Swimming; Basketball; Table-tennis. *Address:* 3/252 Holden St N Fitzroy, Victoria 3068, Australia.

IVANOV Tomislav, b. 29 Oct 1929, Prilep, Yugoslavia. Retired University Professor of Geology. m. Vera Babic, 3 July 1960, 3 d. *Education:* PhD, Fac of Geol, Belgrade Univ, 1965; Specialiszation on Geochem in Franch, 1960-61. *Appointments:* Mgr, Geol Inst, Skopje, 1954-68; Docent and Prof, Fac of Tech and Metallurgy, 1968-79; UN Expert in Egupt, 1969-73; Prof, Fac of Mining and Geol, Stip, 1979-88. *Publications include:* The Metallogeny of the PB, ZN, BA Vein-type deposits in macedonia, 1982; Metallogeny of Serbian-Macedonian Massif and Pelagonian Massif, 1983; Mineral Resource basis of the metallic and non-metallic raw materials, 1986. *Memberships:* Union of Engrs and Techs, of Macedonia; Intl Org for Geol Res of SEV: Macedonian Geol Soc, Pres; Union of Geol Socs of Yugoslavia. *Honours:* Medal for trade of Third Order, 1960; Hon Mem, Soc of Mineral and Fossil Friends Trzii Slovenia, 1987. *Hobbies:* Mineral research and collection; Reading and translating poetry; Photography. *Address:* AW Karamanov 13, 91000 Skopje, Macedonia, Yugoslavia.

IVERSON Laurie Jean Wylie, b. 13 Mar 1951, Seattle, Washington, USA. Nurse Practitioner; Consultant; Executive. m. John William Iverson, 21 Sept 1974, 1 s, 1 d. *Education:* BSN, 1975, Adv Prog School Nurses, 1976-77, Univ WA, Seattle; MA, Nurse Execs, Columbia Univ, NYC, 1990. *Appointments:* School Nurse, Snohomish School Dist, 1976-80; Interim Shcool Nurse, Lake Stevens School Dist, 1980-81; Family Prac RN, Emergency Dept RN, Charge Nurse, Cons Nurses, Cons Nurs, Emergency Dept, Grp Hlth Coop Puget Sound, 1980-; Maternal Infant Nurs Cons, Prog Coord, Vis Nurse Assn, Snohomish Co, 1986-88; Nursing Prac and Govt Rels Coord, King Co Nurses Assn, 1987-90; Exec Dir, Wn WA Area Hlth Educ Ctr, 1990-. *Publications:* Articles: Pediatric Rashes; Home Phototherapy for Treatment for Neonatal Hyperbilirubinemia (w Elizabeth Reece), 1989; The Nursing Shortage, interview, 1988; Development and Implementation of a Home Phototherapy prog (w Elizabeth Reece), abstract, tapes, 1988. *Memberships:* Pres, 2nd VP, Shohomish Co Nurses Assn; Chair, Dist Presidents Coun, WA State Nurses Assn; Chaim, Comm Examiners for School Nurse Practitioners; Am Nurses Assn; Sigma Theta Tau. *Honours:* Tchrs Coll Scholarship, Columbia Univ, 1989, 1990; USPHS Nurse Traineeship, Columbia Univ Tchrs Coll, 1989. *Hobbies:* Music; Art; Ballet; Reading. *Address:* 12120 7th Place SE, Lake Stevens, WA 98258, USA.

IVORY Hugh Gordon, b. 13 Aug 1929, Wellington, New Zealand. Food Technology Consultant. m. Joyce Alfreda Willis, 29 Sept 1956, 2 s, 2 d. *Education:* MSc (Hons), Chem, Canterbury Univ Coll, Univ NZ, 1952; Dip Mgmt, N.Z, Inst Mgmt, 1975. *Appointments:* Chem, Dept Sci and Indl Rsch, 1950-56; Dev Chem, Soaps, Toiletries, Unilever NZ Ltd, 1957-63; Quality Control Mgr, Project Dev Mgr, Frozen Foods, Unilever NZ Ltd Foods, 1963-71; Rsch and Dev Mgr, 1971-89, Tech Mgr, Int Mktng, 1989-92, Tip Top Ice Cream Co Ltd, Retired.

Memberships: NZ Inst Food Sci and Technology, Br Pres (2 brs), Nat Pres 1977-79; Fellow, Profl Mbr, Inst Food Technology, USA. *Honours:* J C Andrews Award, Eminence in Food Technology, 1991. *Hobbies:* Sailing; Lawn Bowls; Carpentry; Boat-building; AFS intercultural programmes (student exchange); Home building and decorating; Hobby business printing business cards. *Address:* 97 Wirihana Raod, Titirangi, Auckland, New Zealand. 52.

IWAKI Hidehiro, b. 4 July 1956, Asahikawa, Japan. Senior Economist. m. Naomi Nagasawa, 3 May 1984, 3 s. *Education:* BA, Econs, Univ Tokyo, 1981; MBA, Fin, Univ Chgo, 1986. *Appointments:* Econ Forecasting, Nomura Rsch Inst Ltd, 1981-; Guest Scholar, Brookings Instn, USA, 1990-91. *Membership:* Assn Investment Mgmt and Rsch. *Honours:* Chartered Fin Analyst, 1990. *Hobbies:* Mountaineering; Skiing. *Address:* 1-8-2 Kamishakujii, Apt 602, Nerima-ku, Tokyo 177, Japan. 52.

IWASHIMIZU Yukio, b. 20 Aug 1943, Inazawa, Aichi, Japan. Professor of Mechanical Engineering. m. 8 Apr 1972, 1 d. *Education:* BEng, 1966, MEng, 1968, DEng, 1974, Kyoto Univ. *Appointments:* Rsch Assoc, Dept Aeronautical Engrng, Kyoto Unv, 1968-74; Assoc Prof, 1975-79, Prof, 1980-, Dept Mech Engrng, Ritsumeikan Univ, Kyoto. *Publications:* Rsch papers on applied mechs esp acoustoelasticity incl: Int J Solids Structures, 1968, 1971, 1973; J Acoust Soc Am, 1978, 1982; J Sound and Vib, 1972, 1975; ASME J Appl Mech, 1990. *Memberships:* Japan Soc Mech Engrs; Soc Materials Sci, Japan; Japanese Soc Non- destructive Inspection; Kyoto Sci Club. *Address:* Department of Mechanical Engineering, Faculty of Science and Engineering, Ritsumeikan University, Tojiinkita-machi, Kita-ku, Kyoto 603, Japan. 52.

IWASZKIEWICZ Joanna, b. 4 June 1928, Bydgoszcz, Poland. Journalist; Critic; Writer; Reporter; Poet. div. 1 s. *Education:* MA, Polish Philology, Jagiellonian Univ, Cracow, 1957; MEcon, Warsaw, 1968. *Appointments:* Radio reportages, Lit, Theatre, Critic, coop w cultural periodicals, poems, feuilletons, 1966-. *Creative works include:* Reportages: The daddy, report about an alcoholic, 1980; Then were blossoming the forsythias; Novels include: The nude mice, 1981; For so many beautiful days, 1984; Corkscrew, 1987; Near the dream; Poetry as Joanna Kybernet incl: Before the Entrance, selection of poems, 1990; Self- extermination, about ecological scandals in Poland, 1983. *Membership:* Polish Club Ecology. *Honours:* 1st Prize for Radio Reportage, I'm 21 years old, 1971; Gold Medal of Hon, Polish Assn Tourism and Country Vis, 1971; Gold Medal of Hon, Polish Ecology Club, 1990. *Hobbies:* Tourism incl kayak, skiing; mountain wandering, country visiting; Ecology; Protection of nature and culture; Judaica esp the holocaust; World War II; Tragic fate of Poland and all people of the present day; Medicine esp the tragedy of serious contemporary illnesses. *Address:* ul Nowolipki 22 m 125, 01- 019 Warsaw, Poland.

IWATA Yasuo, b. 25 Apr 1932, Tokyo, Japan. Professor of Philosophy. m. Makoto Ishii, 16 Oct 1960, 2 s, 6 d. *Education:* BA, Fac Letters, Tokyo Univ, 1956; MA, 1958, PhD, 1987, Fac Letters, Tokyo Univ Grad School. *Appointments:* Asst, Tokyo Univ, 1961-64; Lectr, Seijo Univ, 1964-67; Assoc Prof, Hokkaido Univ, 1967-73; Assoc Prof, 1973-76, Prof, 1976-, Fac Letters, Tohuku Univ, Sendai. *Publications:* Currents of Western Thoughts, 1964; The Ethics of Aristotle, 1985; The Vestige of God, 1989. *Memberships:* Philosl Assn Japan, Comm Mbr 1984-; Classical Soc Japan, Comm Mbr 1985-; Japanese Soc Medieval Philos, Comm Mbr 1982- ; Japanese Soc Ethics; Philosl Soc Tohoku, (Comm Mbr 1973-. *Honours:* Japan Fndn Sci Rsch Award, 1 yr rsch at Louvain Univ, Belgium, 1979-80; Fulbright Fndn Award, 7 months rsch at Harvard Univ, USA, 1986- 87. *Hobbies:* Go; Gardening; Walking; Classical music. *Address:* Kamisugi 4-4-16, Aoba- ku, Sendai, Japan. 52.

IYODA Mitsuhiko, b. 1 Oct 1943, Aichi Prefecture, Japan. Professor of Economics. m. Masako Chojahara, 7 Jan 1975, 1 s. *Education:* BA, Econ, Wakayama Nat Univ, 1965; MA, Econ, Osaka City Univ, 1968. *Appointments:* Assoc, 1972-82, Prof, 1982-, Dir, Rsch Inst, 1985-89, Dean, Fac Econs, 1990-92, Momoyama Gakuin Univ, Osaka; Vis Fellow, Lancaster Univ, England, 1982-83. *Publications:* Introduction to Economics (co- author), 1989. *Memberships:* Japan Assn Econs and Econometrics; Int Assn Rsch in Income and Wealth; Japan Soc Econ Policy. *Hobbies:* Tennis; Music. *Address:* 3-6-14 Momoyama-dai, Sakai-shi, Osaka 590-01, Japan. 52.

IZEZE Eluemuno Chukwuemeka, b. 11 Sept 1957, Ibusa, Nigeria. Journalist. m. 4 Oct 1986. *Education:* W African School Cert/Gen Cert Educ, Inst Continuing Educ, Benin City, 1980; Dip, Mass Communications, Univ Lagos, 1982. *Appointments:* News Ed, Sunday Graphic, Benin City, 1982; Correspondent, 1984, Mng Dir, 1986, The Guardian, 1984; News Ed, 1985, Dpty Ed, 1987, Ed, 1988-, The Guardian on Sunday, 1985. *Publications:* Chapter in book on death penalty. *Memberships:* Nigerian Guild Eds, Sec Gen 1990-92; Nigerian Union Jrnlsts. *Hobbies:* Reading; Horticulture; Sports. *Address:* PO Box 5525, Surulere, Lagos, Nigeria.

IZZIDIEN Yousif, b. 1922, B'aquba, Iraq. Professor of Arabic Literature; Academic Administrator. *Education:* BA (Hons), 1950, MA (Hons), 1953, Alexandria Univ, Egypt; PhD, London Univ, England, 1957. *Appointments:* Tchr, Second Schools; Lectr, 1956, Asst Dean, 1958, Fac Arts, Baghdad Univ, 1956; Sec Gen, Iraqi Acad, Baghdad, 1966?-; Dir Gen, Press and Guidance, Min Culture and Guidance, 1966; Prof, Arabic Lit, Univ Baghdad. *Publications include:* In the Conscience of Time (Poems), 1950; Ballads, 1953; Arabic Poetry in Iraq, in the Nineteenth Century, its Aims and Trends, 1958, 1965; Modern Iraqi Poetry, the Influence of the Political and Social Trends, 1960, 2nd Ed, 1965; Sighs of Life, poem, 1960; Literary Trends in Iraq and Al-Zahawi the Restless poet, 1962; Studies in the Manuscript of Al-Akhras's Poetry, 1963; Poetry and Iraqi Society 1900-1945 (in English), 1963; Khairi Al-Mindawi (An Iraqi poet), His Life and Poetry, 1965; Modern Arabic Literature, Essays and Studies, 1967; Dawud Pasha and the Decline of the Mamluk Dynasty in Iraq, 1967; Arabic Manuscripts in the Sofia National Library, 1968; Nationalism and Socialism, their Influence on Modern Poetry, 1968; Iraq Poets in the 20th Century, 1969. *Memberships:* Fndr Mbr, Iraqi Writers and Authors Assn, Sec, Chief Ed Al-Kitab Review; Admin Coun, Iraqi Red Crescent Assn; Royal Soc Lit, London; Bd, Al-Jamhuria House for Printing and Publng; Bd, Iraqi Acad Review; Sometime Mbr: Ed Comm, Al- Mu'allem Al-Jadid Review, Min Educ; Publng Comm, Al-Aqlam Review, Min Culture and Guidance. *Address:* Department of Arabic Literature, University of Baghdad, Baghdad, Iraq.

J

JABES Jak, b. 8 Oct 1945, Istanbul, Turkey. University Professor. m. Vicky Akohen, 28 Dec 1974, 2 s. *Education:* BA, Econ, Robert Coll, 1968; MA, Psychology, 1971, PhD, Social Psychology, 1973, KS Univ, USA. *Appointments:* Fac Admin, Univ Ottawa, Canada, 1973- . *Publications:* Individual Processes in Organizational Behavior, 1978; Traite des organisations (w J P Gruere), 1981; Gestion strategique internationale, 1988; The Vertical Solitude (w D Zussman), 1989; Management: Aspects Humains et Organisationnels, 1991; Over 50 articles and conf presentations. *Honours:* Special Mention, Best Books in Management, Harvard Extension, 1982. *Hobbies:* Gardening; Reading; Wines; Tourism. *Address:* Faculty of Administration, University of Ottawa, 136 Jean Jacques Lussier, Ottawa, Ontario, Canada K1N 6N5. 88.

JACKLIN Bill, b. 1 Jan 1943, Hampstead, London, England. Artist. m. Lesley Sarina Berman, 21 June 1979, div 1993. *Education:* NDD, Walthamstow School Art, 1964; MArt, Painting, Royal Coll Art, 1967. *Career:* Tchng, var art colls, 1967-75; 1-man exhibs: Nigel Greenwood Inc, London, 1970, 1971, 1975; Hester van Royen Gall, London, 1973; Marlborough Fine Art, London, 1980, 1983, 1988; Marlborough Gall, NYC, 1985, 1987, 1990; Num int grp exhibs internationally. *Creative works include:* Works in collections incl: Art Gall NSW, Sydney, Australia; Arts Coun GB; Brit Coun, London; Brit Mus, London; Irish Arts Coun, Dublin; Metrop Mus, NYC; Mus Mod Art, NYC; Mus Boymans van Beuningen, Rotterdam, Netherlands; Tate Gall, London; Victoria and Albert Mus, London; Yale Ctr Brit Art, New Haven, CT, USA. *Membership:* Royal Academician, Royal Acad London. *Honours:* Arts Coun Bursary, 1975. *Hobby:* Running. *Address:* c/o Marlborough Fine Art London, 6 Albemarle Street, London W1X, England. 1.

JACKSON Charles Wayne, b. 3 June 1930, Louisville, Kentucky, USA. Management Consultant. m. Elizabeth J Soptic, 1 June 1980, 1 s, 1 d. *Education:* BEE, GA Inst Technology, 1952. *Appointments:* 1st Lt, US Army, 1952-54; Student Engr, AT&T, Cinn, OH, 1954-55; Dist Plant Engr, AT&T, Jacksonville, FL, 1955-56; Commercial Rep to Acctng Asst, AT&T, Atlanta, GA, 1956-59; Transmission Systems Engr to Plant Design Engr, AT&T, Kansas City, 1963-66; Project Mgr to Dir, maj project, Wn Elec Co, NYC, 1966- 69; Engr, Dir, TWX Coord to Bus Rels Dir, AT&T, NYC, 1969-75; Dir, Pvte Lines Rates, Long Lines Co, Somerset, NJ, 1975; Dir, Pvte Lines Rates to Dir, Planning, Long Lines Co, Bedminster, NJ, 1975-81; Dir, Data Prog Serv Dev Mktng Dept, AT&T, Bedminster, NJ, 1981-87; Cons, Pvte Prac, Brandenburg, KY, 1987-. *Address:* 604 Strawberry Point, Brandenburg, KY 40108, USA. 32.

JACKSON David Edward Pritchett, b. Calcutta, India. Senior Lecturer in Arabic Studies. m. Margaret Letitia Brown, 9 July 1982. *Education:* Maj Scholar, Rossall School; For Off Scholar, Mecas, Shemlan, Lebanon; Fndn Scholar, Pembroke Coll, Cambridge; MA; PhD. *Appointments:* Rsch Fellow, Pembroke Coll, Cambridge, 1967-70; Asst Lectr, Arabic Lang and Lt, 1967-69, Lectr, Arabic Studies, 1969-84, Dir, School Abbasid Studies, 1979-, Ed, occasional papers, School Abbasid Studies, 1983-, Sr Lectr, Arabic Studies, 1984-, Univ St Andrews, Scotland; Served to Lt-Cdr, RNR, 1972-82. *Publications:* Saladin (w M C Lyons), 1982; Contbr, profl jrnls. *Memberships:* Brit Soc Mid Eastern Studies; Mid Eastern Studies Assn; Brit Soc Hist of Maths; Mid Eastern Mediaevalists; Royal Naval Assn, Comm Mbr 1984-86. *Hobbies:* The river; Music; Food; Golf. *Address:* c/o Department of Arabic Studies, The University, St Andrews, Fife KY16 9AL, Scotland. 52, 184.

JACKSON Douglas, b. 1 Sept 1916, Dublin, Republic of Ireland. Dental Surgeon (retired). m. Annie Bennett, 22 Sept 1961, 1 stepdaughter. *Appointments:* Very large dental prac, City of London. *Creative works:* Many musical compositions. *Memberships:* Brit Acad Songwriters, Composers and Authors; Brit Dental Assn; Elected, Guild of Freemen, London, 1978; Barber-Surgs Livery, 1967; Freeman, City of London. *Hobbies:* Composer; Music; Travel; Photography; Inventor; Bridge. *Address:* 1 Broad Walk, Winchmore Hill, London N21 3DA, England.

JACKSON G(eorge) Mark, b. 27 Aug 1952, Atlanta, Georgia, USA. Writer; Photographer. *Education:* Spring Hill Coll, 1971-75; BA, Univ AL, Birmingham, 1976; MA, Univ Ctl FL, 1988. *Appointments:* Writer: Jefferson Advertiser, Birmingham, AL, 1978-79; Southside News, Orlando, FL, 1979-80; Sentinel Star (now Orlando Sentinel), 1980-81. *Creative works:* Ninja - Men of Iga (as Kano Shinichi), novel, 1989; Articles; Photographs; Stories in mags; Martial arts movies; Action films; Black Belt, Fighting Stars Ninja; FL Automotive; Am karate. *Memberships:* FL Freelance Writers Assn. *Honours:* Jesse Hill Ford's Creative Writing Workshop, Univ AL, Birmingham, 1978; Robert M Young's Film Directing Workshop, sponsored by School of Visual Arts, 1981. *Hobbies:* Criticism; Historical research; Reading. *Address:* 2043 Southeast Isabell Road, Port St Lucie, FL 34952, USA. 30.

JACKSON Harper Scales Jr, b. 23 Feb 1951, Fort Smith, Arkansas, USA. Health Care Executive. m. Virginia Stack, 4 June 1976, 3 d. *Education:* BS cum laude, Bus Admin, Univ AR, Fayetteville, 1973; Master, Hlth Admin, Washington Univ School Med, St Louis, 1979. *Appointments:* Admin Resident, 1979-80, Asst VP, 1981-83, VP, 1983-85, Sr VP, 1985-, The Meth Hosp, Houston, TX; Admin Asst to Dr Michael E DeBakey, Houston, 1979-81. *Memberships:* Am Coll Hlthcare Execs; Hlthcare Forum; Am Hosp Assn; TX Hosp Assn; Gtr Houston Hosp Coun; Bd Dirs, Washington Univ Hlth Admin Prog Alumni Assn; Bd Dirs, Am Heart Assn, E Ft Bend Div; Beta Gamma Sigma; Omicron Delta Kappa; Sigma Iota Epsilon. *Honours:* Foster G McGaw Scholarship, Am Coll Hlthcare Execs, 1979; Nominated Emerging Leader in Hlthcare, Hlthcare Forum, 1989; Eagle Scout, Boy Scouts Am. *Hobbies:* Swimming; Weightlifting; Music; Travel. *Address:* 3007 West Steepbank Circle, Sugar Land, TX 77479, USA. 7, 132.

JACKSON Richard Anthony, b. 31 Mar 1932, Harrogate, Yorkshire, England. Theatrical Agent and Producer. *Education:* Cheltenham Coll, 1945-48. *Appointments:* Army Serv, Benghazi, 1950-52; Henry A Lane & Co Ltd, 1953-56; Walt Disney Prods, 1956-59; Richard Jackson Personal Mgmt Ltd, London, 1959- . *Creative works:* Stage prods: Jock on the Go, A Remnant, 1967; Chox, 1974; The Peter Pan Man, The Polynesian Prime Minister, Diaries, Madame De Sade, Jade, The Sound of Mime, Charles Trenet, 1975; Carol's Christmas, Quentin Crisp, Norm And Ahmed, Better Days, Better Knights, The Bitter Tears of Petra, 1976; Blind Date, Our Kid, Oedipus At The Crossroads, John Barrymore, Like Dolls Or Angels, 1977; An Evening With Quentin Crisp, The Singular Life Of Albert Nobbs, Alterations, Tribute To Lili Lamont, DHL-A Portrait Of D H Lawrence, 1978; Flashpoint, A Day In Hollywood, A Night In The Ukraine, The Square, La Musica, Portrait Of Dora, Tomorrow I'll Be Fifty, 1979; Night Duty, Appearances, A Galway Girl, 1980; An Evening With Quentin Crisp, Bar and Gee, 1981; Charity Show for mentally handicapped, 1982; Latin, 1983; The Human Voice, 1984-90; Swimming Pools at War, 1985; Matthew Mark Luke and Charlie, I Ought To Be In Pictures, 1986; Sally-Jape Heit Starts In The Middle, 1987; Creditors and Latin, 1989; Beached, 1990; Eden Cinema, 1991; Noonbreak, 1991; Beardsley, Don't Play With Love, 1992. *Memberships:* Brit Acad Film and TV Arts; Green Room Club. *Hobbies:* Theatre; Opera; Ballet; Cinema; Table tennis; Crosswords. *Address:* Richard Jackson Personal Management Ltd, 59 Knightsbridge, London SW1X 7RA, England.

JACOBS James Paul, b. 14 May 1930, Augusta, Arkansas, USA. Insurance Executive. m. Joan Gillum, 18 Aug 1956, 2 d. *Education:* Ins Trng School, Ins Co N Am, Phila, 1949; Chartered Property Casualty Underwriter, 1964. *Appointments:* Underwriter, 1955-58, Supervising Underwriter, 1958-64, Mgr, Underwriting, 1964-68, Ins Co N Am, Richmond, VA; Tchr, Univ Richmond Evening School, 1965-78; Mgr, Underwriting, Ins Co N Am, Detroit, MI, 1968-71; Casualty Mgr, Montgomery and Collins (Surplus Lines Broker), Los Angeles, CA, 1971-73; Ptnr, Tabb Brockenbrough and Ragland, Richmond, 1973-; Chmn, All Ind Day, Richmond, 1978; Bd Dirs, I Day Corp, Richmond, 1978-. *Publications:* Var articles in trade jrnls. *Memberships:* Soc Chartered Property Casualty Underwriters, Bd Dirs 1979-82, Reg VP 1981-82; Smithsonian Instn; Bd Dirs, Daily Planet non-profi org for homeless, 1990-91; Agents Advsry Couns, Ins Cos: Ins Co N Am, Phila, 1975-78; Firemens's Fund Ins Co, San Fran, 1981; Commercial Union Ins Co, Boston, 1984-89; Gt Am Ins Co, Cinn, 1989; PA Manufacturers Assn Ins Co, Phila, 1990-93; ITT Hartford, 1991-92; MD Casualty Co, Baltimore, 1991-92. *Hobbies:* Golf; Baseball; Football; Basketball; Colonial Williamsburg; Kennedy Center for Performing Arts. *Address:* 1510 Westshire Lane, Richmond, VA 23233, USA. 7, 132.

JACOBS Michael Edward Hyman, b. 21 May 1948, London, England. Solicitor. m. Ruth Simpson, 5 Mar 1973, 2 s. *Education:* Scholar, St Paul's School, London, 1961-66; LLB (Hons), Birmingham Univ, 1969. *Appointments:* Solicitor, 1972-, Ptnr, 1976-, Hd, Tax Dept, 1981-, Ptnrship Bd, 1988-, Nicholson Graham & Jones, London. *Publications:* Tolley's Tax on Takeover, 1990; Contbr to Tolley's Tax Planning, 1989, 1990, 1991, 1992, 1993-; Editor, Trust Law International, 1989-; Many articles on tax, trusts and share schemes. *Memberships:* Vice-Chmn, Co-Fndr, Share Scheme Lawyers Grp; Fellow, Brit Inst Mgmt, 1983; Int Bar Assn; Int Fiscal Assn; Int Tax Planning Assn; Law Soc. *Hobbies:* Reading; Writing; Photography; Sailing; Anything else which saves him from doing the gardening. *Address:* Nicholson Graham & Jones, 25-31 Moorgate, London EC2R 6AR, England.

JACOBSON Ronald Alan, b. 7 Nov 1935, Calgary, Alberta, Canada. Provincial Court Judge. m. (1) Sonja Currie, 19 Sept 1958, dec. 1981, 2 s, 1 dec, 1 d dec, (2) Mariette Celine Dufresne, 14 Dec 1985, 1 stepdaughter. *Education:* BA, 1958, LLB, 1959, Univ Alta, Edmonton; Admitted, Bar of Alta, 1960. *Appointments:* Assoc, Ptnr, Sole Practitioner, gen prac, Lethbridge and Ft Macleod, 1960-79; Sometime Agent: Atty Gen, Alta, 1963-69, Atty Gen, Can, 1967-69, 1971-79; Lethbridge Agent and Solicitor for Admnstr, Motor Vehicle Accident Claims Act, 1965-79; Judge, Provincial Ct, Alta, 1979-; Organiser, Chmn, lectr, judicial and legal sems, Can, 1979-; Dpty Territorial Judge, NW Territories, 1981-83; Served to Col, Can Militia; Colonel Commandant The Royal Regiment of Canadian Artillery, 1991-. *Memberships include:* Alta Provincial Judges Assn, Mbt Educ Comm 1979-90, Chmn Educ Comm 1980-82, Pres 1983-84; Can Assn Provincial Ct Judges, Educ Comm Mbr 1979, 3rd VP 1986-87, 2nd VP 1987-88, 1st VP 1988-89, Pres 1989-90; Canadian Bar Assn, Chmn Lethbridge Sect Commercial Law 1977; Life Mbr, Can Inst Admin Justice; Bd Dirs, Mgmt Comm, Chmn Servs and Ceremonies, 1975 Can Winter Games Soc, 1973-76; Presidents Advsry Bd, Lethbridge Community Coll; Life Mbr, Royal Can Artillery Assn, Exec Comm 1959-70, 1971-76, 1982-86, VP 1979-80, Pres 1980-81; Interallied Confedn Reserve Offs, (CIOR), 1984-90, Exec Comm, VP Can, 1988-89, 1989-90; Lethbridge United Servs Inst; Can Inst Strategic Studies. *Honours:* Queen's Jubilee Medal, 1978; Can Forces Medal, 1978; Co-Communicator of Yr, Toastmasters, 1986. *Hobbies:* Golf; Skiing; Hunting (upland and migratory birds); Fishing; Dog field and obedience training; Oldtimers hockey; Boating; Water-skiing. *Address:* Lethbridge, Alberta, Canada.

JACOBSON Werner Ulrich, b. 4 Jan 1906, Berlin, Germany, Sir Halley Stewart Professor of Medical Research. m. Gertrude Elena Ebler, 14 Feb 1934, dec. 1969. *Education:* MD, Univ Heidelberg, 1930; PhD, Univ Cambridge, England, 1940, ScD, 1960; FRCP, 1986; FRCPath, 1986. *Appointments:* Acad Assts Coun Grantee, 1933-35, Rockefeller Grantee, 1934-35, Strangeways Rsch Lab, Cambridge, England; Sir Halley Stewart Rsch Fellow, 1935-78, Sir Halley Stewart Prof, Med Rsch, 1978-, Univ Cambridge; Vis Sr Rsch Assoc: Univ TX Med Br, Galveston, USA, 1948-49, Harvard Med School, 1949-51; Vis Prof, Harvard Med School, 1969-70, 1972. *Contributions to:* var med publs and books. *Memberships:* Physiological Soc; Int Soc Haematology; Fellow, Cambridge Philosl Soc; Fellow, Royal Soc Med; Fellow, Royal Soc Tropical Med. *Honours:* Gedge Prize, Cambridge Univ. *Hobbies:* Classical music; Gardening; Limoges enamel. *Address:* Dept of Paediatrics, University of Cambridge, Level 8, Addenbrooke's Hospital, Cambridge CB2 2QQ, England.

JACQUES Peter Roy Albert, b. 12 Aug 1939, London, England. Trade Union Official. m. Jacqueline Anne Sears, 20 Aug 1965, 1 s, 1 d. *Education:* BSc, Newcastle-upon-Tyne Polytechnic; Univ Leciester. *Appointments:* Bldg Labourer, 1955-58; Market Porter, 1958-62; Asst, 1968-71, Sec, 1971-, TUC Special Adv, 1992-, Social Ins and Indl Welfare Dept, Trades Union Congress. *Publications:* Responsible for Trades Union Congress publs on hlth and safety, pensions, people w disabilities. *Memberships:* Hlth and Safety Commn; Royal Commn on Environmental Pollution; Indl Injuries Advsry Coun. *Honours:* CBE. *Hobbies:* Reading; Yoga; Walking; Camping; Vegetable growing. *Address:* Trades Union Congress, Congress House, Great Russell Street, London WC1B 3LS, England. 1.

JAENICKE Lothar, b. 14 Sept 1923, Berlin, Germany. Professor of Biochemistry. m. Doris Heinzel, 12 Dec 1949, 2 s, 2 d. *Education:* Dipl Chem Dr phil, 1948, Privatdozent, 1954, Univ Marburg; Rsch Fellow, Wn Reserve Univ, Cleveland, USA, 1954-56; Dozent, Univ Munich, 1957; a o Prof, 1962, o Prof, 1963, Univ Cologne. *Appointments:* Prof, Dir, Inst Biochem, Univ Cologne, 1963-88. *Memberships:* Hon Mbr, GBCh; Biochem Soc; RW Acad Scis; Bavarian Acad Scis; Dt Akademie d Naturforscher (Leopoldina). *Honours:* Paul Ehrlich-Ludwig Darmstaedter Prize; Otto Warburg Medal, GBCh; Richard Kuhn Medal, GDCh. *Address:* Kaesenstrasse 13, D-5000 Cologne 1, Germany.

JAFFE Irma B, b. New Orleans, Louisiana, USA. Emeritus Professor of Art History. m. (1) Donald Korshak, 16 July 1936, 1 d, (2) Samuel B Jaffe, 12 June 1941. *Education:* MA, 1960, PhD, 1966, Columbia Univ. *Appointments:* Rsch Curator, Whitney Mus Am Art, 1963-66; Prof, Art Hist, 1966-87, Emeritus Prof, 1987-, Fordham Univ, NYC. *Publications include:* Joseph Stella; John Trumbull; Patriot-Artist of the American Revolution; The Sculpture of Leonard Baskin, 1980; Ethics in Eighteenth Century American Art, 1986; Italian Presence in American Art, 1760-1860, 1989; Many articles in scholarly jrnls. *Memberships:* Coll Art Assn; Am Studies Assn. *Honours:* Phi Beta Kappa, 1958; Outstanding Achievement Award (OWL), Columbia Univ, 1965; Virgiliana Medal, Istituto della Enciclopedia Italiana. *Hobby:* Tennis. *Address:* 880 5th Avenue, New York, NY 10021, USA. 37, 138.

JAGADISH Shobhna, b. 20 Oct 1954, New Delhi, India. Television Newsreader. m. Shri G K Jagadish, 13 Feb 1977. *Education:* BA, Gen Engl, Hindi, Sanskrit, Pol Sic, Lucknow Univ, 1973; Visharad, Vocal Classical Music, Bhatkande Univ Hindustani Music, Lucknow, 1973; Theatre Trng, Acting, Uttar Pradesh Natak Acad, 1975; Postgrad Dip, Jrnlsm, Bhartiya Vidya Bhawan's R P Inst Communication and Mgmt, Bombay, 1981. *Career:* Radio Artist, music, 1965-; Appeared in 15 theatre plays in pivotal roles, TV plays and films, over 75 radio plays; Announcer, Lucknow TV Ctr, 1975-; Newsreader, Nat Prog, Indian TV System Doordarshan, 1989-; System

Consultancy, media planning for mass communications. *Publications:* Articles in Education monthly mag. *Membership:* Press Club India. *Honours:* Prizes, Vocal Competitions, 1965-; Best Actress Award, Theatre, U P Sangeet Natak Acad, Lucknow, 1973; Best Radio Play, Cactus Main Phool, Akashyani Govt India, 1985; Best Newsreader Award, 1989. *Hobbies:* Acting; Music; Kathak dance; Gardening. *Address:* 32 Sarojini Debi Lane, Maqboolganj, Lucknow 226018, India.

JAGAN Janet, b. 20 Oct 1920, Chicago, Illinois, USA. Journalist. m. Cheddi Jagan, 5 Aug 1943, 1 s, 1 d. *Education:* Univ Detroit; Wayne Univ, Detroit; MI State Coll, Lansing; Cook Co School Nursing, Chgo. *Appointments:* Gen Sec, 1950-70, Int Sec, 1970-85, Exec Sec, 1985-91, People's Progressive Party, Guyana; Ed, Thunder, 1950-57; Elected Mbr (1st woman), Georgetown City Coun, 1950-52; Dpty Speaker, House of Assembly, 1953; Min Labour, Hlth and Housing, 1957-61; Min Home Affairs, 1963-64; Mbr, Elections Commn, 1967-69; Mbr, Nat Assembly, 1976-92; Elected MP, 1992 Elections; First Lady-Wife og Pres, 1992 Elections; Ed, Mirror, 1973-. *Memberships:* Pres, Women's Progressive Org; Pres, Union Guyanese Jrnlsts. *Honours:* Univ Guyana Award for Disting Guyanese Women. *Hobby:* Writing children's stories. *Address:* State House, Georgetown, Guyana. 2, 52, 138, 189.

JAGANNATH Kannivelu, b. 19 May 1945, Madras, India. Doctor. m. Vasatha Kumari, 25 Jan 1974, 1 d. *Education:* MBBS, 1967; Dipl in Chest Diseases, 1971; MD, Gen Med, 1975. *Appointments:* Govt of Tamil Nadu, Asst Phys, 1969-81, Asst Supt, 1981-83, Supt TB Sanatorium Tambaram, 1983-86; Dir of Inst of Thoracic Med and Prof, Madras Med Col, 1986-. *Contributions to:* articles published in, Lung India, and Indian Jour of Tuberculosis; papers presented at international conferences in Madras, 1978, Nepal, 1985, USA, 1991. *Memberships:* TB Assn of India, Mem of Ctl and Tech Coms; Ed Bd, Lung India; Sci Adv Com, TB Res Ctr, Madras. *Honours:* Pres, Nat Conf in TB and Lung Dis; Participant in National Confs in Madras, 1988, 1989, and Madurai, 1988. *Hobbies:* Cricket; Gardening. *Address:* 53 Sterling Road, Madras, India 600034.

JAGUARIBE Emerson Freitas, b. 27 Oct 1947, Paraiba, Brazil, Teaching and Research Professor. m. Celia Lacerda Jaguaribe, 20 Jan 1984, 1 d. *Education:* Mech Engr, Fed Univ Paraiba, 1970; MSc, Cath Univ, Rio de Janeiro, 1972; Dr d'Etat, Aix-Marseille III, France, 1978; Postdoct Rsch, Univ MI, USA, 1982. *Appointments:* Lectr, Cath Univ, Rio de Janeiro (PUC/RJ), 1971-72; Lectr, Brazilian Navy School, Rio de Janeiro, 1972; Prof, Fed Univ Paraiba, Joao Pessoa, 1973-. *Publications:* Papers on solar energy and heat and mass transfer. *Memberships:* Int Solar Energy Soc, Vic, Australia; Coop Mediterraneenne pour l'Energie Solaire, Plagne, Switzerland. *Hobbies:* Chess, Travel. *Address:* Department of Mechanical Engineering, Centro de Tecnologia, Campus Universitario da UFPB, 58 059 Joao Pessoa, PB, Brazil.

JAHAN Anowara, b. 15 Dec 1937, Bangladesh. Director of Women's Training Project. m. Mohammed Shah Jahan, 8 Apr 1957, 2 s, 1 d. *Education:* BA, 1956, MA (Econ), 1958, MA (Sociology), 1966, Dhaka Univ; Postgrad Cert Educ, London Univ, 1975. *Appointments:* Tchng incl Dpty Hdship, Bangladesh, 1959-61; Lectr, 1961-62; Asst Dir, E Pakistan, Small Inds Corp, 1963-67; Community Rels Off, Islington, London, England, 1975-80; Pt-time Commnr, Commn Racial Equality, 1977-80; Tchr, Sr Tchr, Inner London Educ Auth, 1980-90; JP, 1980-; Deputy Head, South Camden Community School, 1992. *Publications:* A children's book of poetry; Textbook in Bengali (jt author). *Memberships:* Fndr Mbr, Bangladesh Women's Assn GB, 1971, Gen Sec and Chair, to 1990; Fndr Mbr, Bangla Educ and Cultural Ctr, 1974; Chair, Fedn Bangladesh Assns in UK and Europe; UK Rep, Migrants Forum of European Communities. *Hobbies:* Writing; Travel; Community

work. *Address:* 52 Ashmead Road, London SE8 4DX, England.

JAJA Nana Angelina, b. 8 Feb 1943, Madakiya, Zonkwa Local Government Area, Nigeria. Principal School Inspector; Demonstration School Principal. m. 2 children. *Education:* Nigerian Cert Educ, Adv Tchrs Coll, Kano, 1970; BA, Engl Lang and Lit, 1974, MEd, Educ Planning and Admin, 1987, Ahmadu Bello Univ, Zaria; Registered, PhD Prog, 1989. *Appointments:* Classroom Tchr, St Joseph's Cath Primary School, Kagoro, 1962; Tchr, Hist, Our Lady of Apostles Tchrs Trng Coll, Akwanga, 1965; Classroom Tchr, Ikeja and Kaduna Army schools, 1966-67; Taught, Women Tchrs Coll, Maiduguri, 1970-71; Prin, Govt Girls Second School: Yola, 1974-76, Bauchi, 1976-78, Gombe, 1978-79, Soba, Zaria, 1979-80; Special Advsr to Gov, Kaduna State, 1981; Permanent Sec, Min Social Dev, Youth and Sports, then Min Establishment, Kaduna State Govt, 1981-83; Prin Insp Schools, Kaduna Zone, Kaduna State Min Educ, 1983-; Prin, Demonstration Second School, Ahmadu Bello Univ, Zaria, 1985-. *Creative works:* Papers: Education in the Eighties in Kaduna State, 1981; The Dilemma of the Working Mothers: White Collar Jobs versus Child Rearing, 1982; A Juvenile Delinquency, A Major Social Problem, 1982; Home Economics and the Rural Woman, 1982; Women's Participation in Nation Building through Self Help, 1982; What Should Be the Role of Women, the Armed Forces and Labour Unions in Future Nigerian Politics, 1986; Child Abuse and Neglect: Its Effect on the School Child, 1988. *Memberships:* Coun, Univ Benin, 1976-80; Chmn, Kaduna State Sickle Cell Club; Nat Chmn, Sickle Cell Club; Treas, Kabyyeyan Club Nigeria; Nigerian Assn Univ Women; Interim Pres, Nat Exec Mbr, African Network Child Abuse and Neglect, 1987; Nat Coun Women's Socs; Kaduna State Scholarship Bd, 1987. *Hobbies:* Reading; Swimming; Music; Gardening. *Address:* Demonstrationm Secondary School, Ahmadu Bello University, Zaria, Nigeria.

JAKANDE Lateef Kayode, b. 23 Jul 1929, Lagos State, Nigeria. Company Chairman and Managing Director; Journalist. m. (3) Alhaja Sikirat Abimbola Jakande, 23 Mar 1968, 4 s, 4 d. *Appointments include:* Chmn, Ed-in-Chief, African News Serv, News and Feature Agcy, 1973-; Corres, Interco Press NY, 1975-; Chmn, Mngng Dir, John West Publications Ltd, John West Trading Ltd, John West Newspapers Ltd, John West Farms Ltd, John West Properties Ltd; Mngng Dir, John West Packaging Ltd, 1964; Chmn, Int Merchant Bank Ltd, 1978-1979; . *Publications:* Books: The Trial of Obafemi Awolowo; The Case for a Lagos State; West Africa Annual; Nigerian Oil Directory; Nigerian Educaion Directory; Nigerian Economic Review; The Sole of the mass media in a developing country; The Problems and Prospects of Free Education at all Levels; Action Years Books, I, II, III, IV; Numerous Papers. *Memberships include:* Chmn, Bd Govs, Nigerian Inst Jrnlsm, 1974-79; Chmn, World Press Freedom Comm, 1974; Co-Fndr, 1st Treas, Patron, Nigerian Union Jrnlsts; Fndr, 1st Pres, Nigerian Guild Eds, 1961-72; Co-Fndr, 1st Pres, 3rd Pres, Newspaper Proprietors Assn Nigeria, 1961-79; Fndr, Nat Sec, Nat Press Club Nigeria, 1960-78; C'wlth Press Union; Int Assn Mass Communication Rsch; Int Inst Communications; Int Press Inst, VP 1968-72, 1st African Pres, 1972-74; Int Fedn Jrnlsts; Int Fedn Publrs; In-Ca-Fiej Rsch Assn; Unity Party Nigeria, Co-Fndr 1978, Lagos State Chmn 1979-83; Num others. *Honours:* Nigerian Union Jrnlsts Award; Chieftaincies: Gbonyi of Ibeshe, Ikorodu Div Lagos State; Baba Adinni, Epe and Badagry Divs, Lagos State. *Hobbies:* Advocate, rapid mass transit public transportation; miniwater works, greatest good of greatest number, full employment, agrarian revolution, free education and health services for all, low cost housing for low income people, medium cost housing for others; Draughts; Reading; Walking; Travelling. *Address:* 2 Bishop Street, Ilupeju, Lagos State, Nigeria. 149, 152.

JAKOB Michel Alexandre, b. 28 Oct 1962, Creil (Oise), France. Theatre Consultant; Secretary-General

Auditing. *Education:* Bach, Furuch School System, 1981; Degree, German, Univ Strasbourg, 1985; Lic Theatre and Press, Univ Vienna, 1987. *Appointments:* Exec Bd Cons, 1986-88, Tchr, 1987-, Furuch School, Vienna, Austria; Asst Mgr, Div Theatres, 1988-91; Theatre Cons, Sec-Gen Auditing, 1991-. *Publications:* Vienna Coffeehouse, 1985; 200 Years French Revolution and Austria, 1989. *Memberships:* Surg Vol Hosp Vienna, 1985-88; Maltese Cross Union, France, 1982-87; Austrian Reserve Mil Offs, 1981-82; AAECFU, Pres 1982-89; Forum France-Austria; Maltese Lodge, TC Lobby; Rotary Int Youth Serv Vienna. *Honours:* Austrian Mil Cross, 1981; Maltese Hon Cross Brevet, France, 1982; Hon Citizenship, St Oswald, Austria, 1984; Med Hon Distinction, 1985; French Min Award, 1986. *Hobbies:* Skiing; Culture; Arts; Sports; Music; History. *Address:* Scheibenbergstr 49, A-1180 Vienna, Austria. 52.

JALALI Bushan L, b. 14 June 1943, Srinagar, Kashmir. Research and Teaching Professor; Head of Plant Pathology. m. Indu Jalali, 26 Nov 1970, 1 d. *Education:* BSc, Agric, 1963, MSc, Plant Pathology, 1965, Banaras Hindu Univ; PhD, Plant Pathology, Punjab Agricl Univ, 1968; Grundstufe, German Lang, Goethe Inst, FRG, 1973. *Appointments:* Asst Prof, 1968-71, Assoc Prof, 1971-82, Prof, 1983-, Chmn, Dept Plant Pathology, 1987-, Haryana Agricl Univ, Hisar. *Publications:* 2 books on: Current trends in mycorrhizal research; Plant pathology through the decades; 85 rsch publs on var aspects of phytopathology in int jrnls. *Memberships:* VP, Indian Soc Plant Pathologists; Pres, Assn Microbiologists India, Hisar; Fellow, Indian Phytopathological Soc; Advsr, Tech Advsry Comm on Mycorrhiza- Asia; Ed Bd: International Legume Research, Journal of Microbial Ecology; Several profl socs. *Honours:* Postdoct Rsch Fellowship, Fed Rsch CTr Agric, Braunschweig, FRG, 1973-74; Nat Narasimhan Acad Award, best original rsch in field of Plant Pathology, 1978; Vis Scientist, USA and FRG, 1978; Vis Prof, Hanover, FRG, 1987. *Hobbies:* Light classical music; Poetry; Photography. *Address:* Department of Plant Pathology, Haryana Agricultural University, Hisar 125 004, Haryana, India. 139, 149, 156, 181.

JAMES Arthur Montague, b. 27 Feb 1923, Parkstone, England. Retired; Professor Emeritus. m. 3 Apr 1954, 2 s. *Education:* Balliol Coll, Oxford Univ, 1941-47; MA, DPhil, 1947; DSc, 1965. *Appointments:* Snr Lectr, Reader, Phys Chem, Chelsea Coll Sci and Technology, 1949-64, Reader, Phys Chem, Queen Elizabeth Coll, 1964-70, Prof, Phys Chem, Bedford Coll, 1970-85, pt-time tchng, Royal Holloway Coll, 1985-91, Univ London. *Publications:* Practical Physical Chemistry (w F E Prichard), 1974; Dictionary of Thermodynamics, 1976; Dictionary of Electrochemistry (w D B Hibbert), 1984; Dictionary of Chemistry (w D B Hibbert), 1987; Macmillian's Chemical & Physical Data, W.M.P. Lord, 1992; Over 100 sci papers. *Membership:* Fellow, Royal Soc Chem, 1954-. *Hobbies:* Do-It-Yourself. *Address:* 50 Brodrick Road, Tooting, London SW 17 7DY, England.

JAMES Cynthia Delores Rembert, b. 13 Aug 1949, Birmingham, Alabama, USA. Minister; Psychologist. m. Alvin D James, 16 Aug 1969, 2 s. *Education:* Carneigie Mellon Univ; BA Psychol, Wesleyan Univ, CT, 1971; MA 1973, PhD, 1980, Rutgers Univ, MA; MDiv, Pacific Sch of Religion; J F Kennedy Law Sch, 1991. *Appointments:* Educ Testing Ser, Princeton, NJ, 1972-73; Staff Psychol, Pressley Ridge Sch, 1974; Asst Prof, Univ of Pittsburgh, 1974-77; Asst Dir of Planning and Ops, Alam Co Employment Bd, 1978-81; Principal: Dir of Educ, Fellowship Acad, 1980-82; Legislative Analyst, Alameda Co Equal Opportunity, 1984-. *Publications:* Paper, JACI scale - James Analysis for Classroom Interaction, 1985; Parent as child's first teacher; Numerous newspaper articles. *Memberships:* Fdr, Pastor, Landmark Mins, 1982-; VP, Col and Univ Div, YWCA: Nat Bd, Family Res Coun; Calif State Assembley Task Force on Family; Am Black Psychols; N.Calif Ch of God Ministers. *Honours include:* Pres Volunteer Awd, 1991; Women of the Year, 1977; Letters of Commendation; Ernestine Cleveland Reems Awds and Trophy, 1989; Nat Screnee Fellow, 1973; Ordained Min, Intl Ch of God, Anderson, Indiana, 1988. *Hobbies:* Writing; Playing the piano; Law Studies. *Address:* 4222 Roderick Road, Oakland, CA 94605, USA.

JAMES Eddie William, b. 2 Jan 1939, Kansas City, Missouri, USA. Pastor; Evangelist. m. Betty Broadrick, 29 May 1959, 3 s, 1 d. *Education:* Kansas City Bible Coll, 1957-58; Tulsa Univ, 1958; OK Bapt Univ, 1958-61. *Appointments:* Pastor: Immanuel Bapt Ch, Maysville, AK, 1962-66; Liberty Bapt Ch, Dutch Mills, AR, 1966-69; Calvary Bapt Ch, Hughes Springs, TX, 1969-71; Falfa Bapt Ch, Talihina, OK, 1971-72; Union Hill Bapt Ch, Purcell, OK, 1972-75; Meadowview Bapt Ch, Owassa, OK, 1975-86; Hillcrest Bapt Ch, Tulsa, OK, 1986-88; Immanuel So Bapt Ch, Wagoner, OK, 1988-. *Publications:* 50 printed messages through Immanuel Bapt Ch, Wagoner. *Memberships:* Eddie James Mins, Evangelism; Evangelical Comm, Muskogee Bapt Assn; Bapt Student Union; Tulsa Bapt Assn; Bapt Fndn; Rogers Bapt Assn; Child Care Rep, Union Bapt Assn. *Honours:* Pace Setter Award, led Rogers Bapt Assn in percentages of baptisms, Bapt Convention, 1976. *Hobbies:* Study of American history; Writing messages and tracts. *Address:* 611 N Gertrude, Wagoner, OK 74467, USA. 2, 145.

JAMES Maryam Sandy Jacobs, b. 30 Nov 1941, Bronx, New York, USA. Vocational Specialist; Director of Vocational Training Programmes. div., 1 s, 1 d. *Education:* Pratt Inst Art, NYC, 1961; Bus and Personnel Mgmt, NY Univ, 1961-63; Nursing degree, Phoenix Coll, 1977; Bus Mgmt, Bus Law, Nursing Law, AZ State Univ; Computers, Programming, Yavapai Coll, 1989. *Appointments:* Commercial Artist, 1961-64; Employment Specialist, Coleman Assocs, Phoenix, AZ, 1961-69; Div Mgr, Employment Specialist, Wn Personnel, Phoenix, 1969-72; Owner, Operator, Regency Personnel, Phoenix, 1972-74; Registered Nurse, St Joseph's Hosp, Phoenix, 1977-79; Intensive Care Nurse, Alternate Hd Nurse, 1979-81, Clin Coord, Med Ward, 1981-82, Hd, Voc Rehab Dept, Veterans Hosp, 1982-89, Dir, Trng Progs, Supvsr, Voc Rehab Serv, 1989-, Veterans Admin Med Ctr, Prescott, AZ. *Creative works include:* A Counselor's Guide, 1971; 9 trng manuals for apprenticeship trng; Prog on developing rural rehab programming, 1984; Var voc progs; Voc counselling coll progr, 1986; Developed Veterans Educ Trng and Support Serv, 1989. *Honours:* Outstanding Leadership in Prog Dev Networking, Gov's Off, State of AZ, 1990; Plaque, Outstanding Hospital Award for Prog Innovation, 1990; Num spec contbn awards, Veterans Admin. *Hobbies:* Enjoying outdoors; Painting; Woodwork; Horses; Passion for animals. *Address:* 2753 Kings Hwy E, Prescott, AZ 86314, USA.

JAMES Peter John, b. 22 Aug 1948, Hove, England. Author. m. Georgina Wilkin, 21 Apr 1979. *Education:* Charterhouse School, 1962-67; Ravensbourne Coll Arts and Design, 1967-69. *Appointments:* Dir, Cornelia James Ltd family bus, 1977-; Full-time self-employed author. *Creative works:* Films: Dead of Night (producer), 1973; Spanish Fly (writer, producer), 1976; Biggles (assoc producer), 1985; Novels: Possession, 1988; Dreamer, 1989; Sunset Heart, 1990; Twilight, 1991. *Memberships:* Royal Warrant Holders Assn; Soc Authors; Soc Psychical Rsch; Jaguar Drivers Club; Tramp; Crime Writers Assn. *Hobbies:* Golf; Skiing; Tennis; Food; Wine; Classic cars; Motor sport. *Address:* c/o Cornelia James Ltd, 123 Havelock Road, Brighton BN1 6GS, England.

JAMES Peter Maunde Coram, b. 2 Apr 1922, London, England. Emeritus Professor. m. Denise Mary Bond, 27 Nov 1945, 4 s. *Education:* Westminster School, 1936-40; LDSRCS (Eng), 1945, MDS, 1961, Royal Dental Hosp, Univ London; DPD, Univ St Andrews, 1949. *Appointments:* House Surg, Sr House Surg, 1945, Sr Lectr, 1955-64; Surg Lt (D), RNVR, 1945-48; Registrar, Hon Lectr, Inst Dental Surg, 1949-55; Reader,

Preventive Dentistry, Univ London, 1965; John Humphreys Prof, Dental Hlth, 1966-87, Emeritus Prof, 1987-, Univ Birmingham. *Contributions to:* Num dental lit; Community Dental Health (editor), 1984-. *Memberships:* Life Mbr, Brit Dental Assn, Pres Cen Counties Branch 1981-82; Hon Life Mbr, Brit Paedodontic Soc, Pres 1962; Fndng Pres, 1st Pres, Hon Life Mbr, Brit Assn Study Community Dentistry. *Honours:* Gibbs Travelling Scholarship, 1952; VRD, Royal Naval Vol Reserve Offs Decoration, 1964. *Hobbies:* Music; Photography. *Address:* The Pump House, Bishopton Spa, Stratford-upon-Avon CV37 9QY, England. 1.

JAMES Russell, b. 5 Oct 1942, England. Thriller Novelist. m. Gillian Redfern, 7 Oct 1978, 2 d. *Education:* Mil, 1953-60; 3 A Levels. *Appointments:* Broadcasting and Theatrical, 1960-67; IBM, 1967-70; Managerial, 1970-79; Bus Cons, 1979-. *Publications:* Num articles, theatre sketches, others; Underground, 1989; Daylight, 1990; Payback, 1991. *Memberships:* Crime Writers Assn; Fresh Blood. *Hobbies:* Travel to unlikely places; Drinking with friends. *Address:* c/o Victor Gollancz, Villiers House, 41-47 Strand, London WC2, England.

JAMES Simon Robert, b. 1 Apr 1952, Barry, South Wales. Economist. *Education:* BSc (Econ), 1973, MSc, 1974, London School Econs, Univ London; Assoc, Coll Preceptors, 1990; CDipAf, 1991. *Appointments:* Rsch Asst, London School Econs, 1974-76; Lectr, Econs, 1976-88, Sr Lectr, Econs, 1988-, Univ Exeter. *Publications:* Books incl: Self-Assessment for Income Tax (co-author), 1977; The Economics of Taxation (co-author), 1978, 4th Ed, 1992; A Dictionary of Economic Quotations, 1981, 2nd Ed, 1984; Pears Guide to Money and Investment, 1982; A Dictionary of Sexist Quotations, 1984; A Dictionary of Legal Quotations, 1987; The Comprehensibility of Taxation (co-author), 1987; A Dictionary of Business Quotations (co-author), 1990; Chambers Sporting Quotations, 1990. *Memberships:* FRSA; Trapped in Poverty? (co-author), 1992; FTII; Fellow, Coll Preceptors. *Hobbies:* Cookery, awarded City and Guilds Cook's Professional Certificate 1989; Rambling; Quotations. *Address:* Department of Economics, University of Exeter, Amory Building, Rennes Drive, Exeter EX4 4RJ, England.

JAMES Veronica Clare, b. 14 Sept 1950, London, England. Translator; English language consultant. div., 1 s. *Education:* St Hugh's Coll, Oxford, 1969; BSc (Econ), London Univ, 1976; Dip Tchng Engl as For Lang, RSA, 1979; Authorised Pub Translator, Sweden, 1987. *Appointments:* Tchr, Engl as For Lang: London, 1977-80, Stockholm, Sweden, 1980-85; Freelance Translator, Engl Lang Cons, Sprakverkstan AB/The Word Shop (own co), Stockholm, 1985-. *Creative works include:* Num translations incl plays for Swedish TV, tourist brochures, books, govt reports, The Body Victorious, and A Child is Born (w photographic illustrations, Lennart Nilsson). *Memberships:* Assn Authorised Translators, Sweden. *Hobbies:* Reading; Travel; Music. *Address:* Fräkenvägen 6, S-191 48 Sollentuna, Sweden.

JAMES William Stirling, b. 20 Nov 1941, Oxford, England. Merchant Banker. *Education:* Stonyhurst Coll, 1954-60; Magdalene Coll, Cambridge, 1961-64; MA (Cantab). *Appointments:* Morgan Grenfell & Co Ltd, 1964-65; Touche Ross & Co, 1965-69; Hill Samuel Bank Ltd, 1969-. *Membership:* FCA. *Hobbies:* Shooting; Bridge; Farming. *Address:* 12 Godfrey Street, London SW3, England. 32, 52, 53.

JAMIL Ahmad Khan, b. 12 May 1939, Takht Bhai, Pakistan. Physician. m. Taslim Sattar, 28 Mar 1968, 1 s, 1 d. *Education:* MB, BS, Univ Peshawar, 1965. *Appointments:* Capt, Pakistan Army Med Corps, 1965-67; Med Off, Lady Reading Hosp, Peshawar, 1967-68; Med Off, 1968-72, Anaesthetist, 1972-75, Nat Hlth Serv, England; Med Off, Anaesthetist, Nat Iranian Oil Co, Iran, 1976-80; Gen Prac, Pakistan, 1980-. *Creative works:* Articles in med jrnls; Speculations about Cancer,

1964; Magnetic Vacuum and Magnetic High Pressure, Laryngotracheal Toilet before Extubation, Easy Cooking, TST-Technique of Anaesthetic Induction and Intubation, 1974; My Father's Biography (active leader in freedom movements) 1925-47, 1985; Identification of National Interests and Creating Social Awareness about them, Experience and Views, 1988; My Autobiography With Reference to My Inventive and Creative Works, 1989; Attitude Towards Inventive and Creative Work in the Developing Countries, Appropriate Education for the Uneducated Skilled Workers in the Developing Countries, 1990; Author, designer: Possible Mechanism of Acupuncture, How Things are Invented, Simple Approach for Drawing Bridge Rectifier Circuit, Simpler Time-tables (Sheffield Departures, British Railway), 1973; Some Basic Requirements for Anaesthesia and Instructions for Recovering Unconscious Patients, A Simple Analogy of Dreams, 1974; A Simple Layout of Central and Autonomic Pharmacology, A Simple and Safer System of Case Notes for Hospital Patients, Information on Patients Due for Anaesthesia, 1975; North South Alignment of Magnet, 1987; Simple Approach Substituting Fleming's Rules and Lenz's Law, 1988; Invented med devices. *Membership:* Pakistan Med Assn. *Honours:* Tamgha-i-Jang, Pakistan Army, 1965. *Hobbies:* Research and development; Inventing; Designing; Writing; Medical engineering; Topology; Physics esp magnetism, electricity, electronics; Analogies; Links between phenomena; Methods and approaches leading to discovery. *Address:* Hakim Fazal Ahad Rd, Takht Bhai, District Mardan, Pakistan. 52, 139, 162, 190, 191.

JAMSHEER Hassan Ali, b. 21 July 1941. University Lecturer. m. 3 Mar 1973, 1 s, 1 d. *Education:* Gen Cert Educ, England, 1961-63; Master's degree, Hist, 1969, Doct degree, Hist, 1973, Poland. *Appointments:* Lectr, Baghdad Univ, Baghdad, Iraq, 1974-80; Lectr, Lodz Univ, Lodz, Poland, 1981-. *Publications:* National Insurrection of 1920 in Iraq, 1979; Suez conflict in international affairs, 1987; The League of Arab States, 1988; The Arab World - The World of Islam, 1990; The Arab Political Thinker Al-Kawakibi, 1990; Arab-Islamic Political Thought, 1991. *Memberships:* Iraqi Histns Assn; Polish Histl Soc; Polish Soc Pol Scis. *Honours:* Rector's Prize, Univ Lodz, 1987, 1988. *Hobbies:* Chess; Classical music and opera; Tourism. *Address:* Narutowicza St 75E/18, 90-132 Lodz, Poland.

JANES Violeta, Artist. *Education:* Chile; Art, Regent St Polytechnic, London, England; Watford School Art; London City and Guilds School Art. *Career:* Freelance, showcards, children's illustrations, textile designs; Position in advt studio; Dir, Art Studies, Alma Coll, Ontario, Can; Pvte art-classes; Commns, portraits in pastels and oils, flower paintings, landscapes; Exhibs: Soc Botanical Artists, Mall Galls, London; 2- man exhib, Mayfair Art Gall, Mayfair, London, 1954; 1-man exhib, Broomfield Mus, Broomfield Pk, London, 1975; Grp exhibs: Royal Acad Arts, London; Royal Soc Portrait Painters; Paris Salon, Paris, 1978-90, incl Bilan de l'Art Contemporain; Quebec Municipal Congress Ctr, Can; Num others, London, Paris, provinces. *Creative works include:* The Fiddler; Red River, New Mexico; The Cockney Character; Rosemary Cottage; The Old Shepherd; Pink Flowers; The Red Necklace; The Music Teacher; The Lady in Green; Distant Snow. *Memberships:* United Soc Artists, London; Milldon Art Soc; Inst Linguists; Anglo-Chilean Soc. *Honours:* Var prizes and medals as art student; Hon Mention, Paris Salon Exhib, 1990. *Hobbies:* Travel to distant lands; Antiquarian books; Languages; Reading. *Address:* 2 Salisbury Avenue, Harpenden, Hertfordshire AL5 2QQ, England. 19, 43, 52, 87, 138, 156.

JANG Shen Yang, b. 21 Dec 1927, Du Yung County, Guizhou Province, China. Educator; Researcher. m. Wang Jun Yuan, 29 Jan 1957, 4 d. *Education:* Guizhou Univ, 1951-52; Dip Metallurgy, Kun Ming Inst Technology, Yin Nan Province, 1955. *Appointments:* Tchng, Sci Rsch, Mining and Metallurgical Inst Ctrl China, 1955-58; Tchng, Sci Rsch, 1959-, formerly Hd

Tchng and Rsch Off, Dpty Hd of Dept, currently Assoc Prof, Dir of Master's degree students, Guizhou Inst Technology, Guiyang. *Publications:* Increasing Direct Extraction Rate of Electrolic Zinc through Membranes of Ion Exchange, 1979; Direct Leaching of Fine Zinc Ore under Normal Atmosphere, 1984; New Process for Extraction of Zing and Manganese Dioxide, 1988; Complete Wet Treatment of Fine Zinc Ore of High Ferrous Content, 1990. *Memberships:* Non-Ferrous Grp, Guizhou Sci and Technology Commn; Standing Mbr, Guizhou Assn Non-Ferroud Metals, Dpty Hd of Heavy Metal Acad Comm; Degree Comm, Guizhou Inst Technology. *Honours:* Nat Sci Conf Award, 1978; Adv Worker in Educl System, Guizhou Province, 1980; Copper Prize, Int Exhib of Invention, Beijing, 1988; Model Worker, Guizhou Province, 1989. *Hobbies:* Literature; Art; Calligraphy. *Address:* Metallurgical Department, Guizhou Institute of Technology, Guiyang, Guizhou Province 550003, China.

JANKOVIC Nikola, b. 12 May 1953, Zagreb, Croatia. Specialist in Internal Medicine (Nephrologist). m. Vera Katalinic, 27 May 1978, 1 s, 1 d. *Education:* Med Fac, Univ Zagreb, 1972-78; Postgrad study, Clin Pharmacology, Med Fac, Zagreb, 1978-80; Magister, Med Sci, 1990. *Appointments:* Emergency Med Dept, City of Zagreb, 1979-80; Internal Clin, Dept Nephrology and Haemodialysis, Sveti Duh Hosp, Zagreb, 1980-. *Publications:* Over 40 sci papers, 1 book, book chapts, mainly about haemodialysis. *Memberships:* Croatian Med Drs Assn, Nephrology Sect, Dialysis and Transplantation Sect; Int Soc Peritoneal Dialysis. *Hobbies:* Tennis; Skiing. *Address:* Jarnoviceva 40, 41000 Zagreb, Croatia.

JANOUŠEK Jaromír, b. 19 Mar 1931, Police nad Metuji, Czechoslovakia. Professor of Psychology. m. Marie Karlik, 15 July 1955, 1 s, 1 d. *Education:* PhDr, 1954, Habilitation as Docent, 1969, Habilitation as Prof, 1983, DSc, 1986, Charles Univ, Prague; Cand Sci, Lomonosov Univ, Moscow, 1957; Elected Corres Mbr, Czechoslovak Acad Scis, 1988. *Appointments:* Fac Philos, Charles Univ, Prague, 1958-59, 1980-; Czechoslovak Acad Scis, 1959-80; Fellow, Ctr Adv Study in Behavioral Scis, Stanford, CA, USA, 1990-91. *Publications:* Practice and knowledge, 1963; Social Communication, 1968. *Contributions to:* The context of social psychology (Ed J Israel and H Tajfel), 1972; Joint activity and communication, 1984; Methods of social psychology (ed), 1986; Communication and optimization of joint activity (ed w G M Andreyeva), 1987; Social Psychology (ed), 1988. *Memberships:* European Assn Expmtl Social Psychology, Exec Comm 1969-75; Comm Transnat Social Psychology, Social Sci Rsch Coun, 1968-74. *Honours:* Prize for Joint activity and communication, 1985, for Methods of social psychology, 1987, Comm Sci Lit, Czech Lit Fndn. *Hobbies:* History; Hiking. *Address:* Belohorska Street 139, Prague 6, 169 00 Czechoslovakia.

JANOWSKA Anita Halina, b. 2 Feb 1933, Lodz, Poland. Musician; Sociologist; Freelance Writer. widowed, 1 d. *Education:* HS Music, 1953; Warsaw Conservatoire, 1960; MD, 1965, PhD, 1974, Warsaw Univ. *Appointments:* Accompanist, Tchr, School Music, Warsaw, 1951-65; Asst, Dept Criminology, Polish Acad Scis, 1965-72; Adj and Dir, Dept Educ, Inst Youth Rsch, Warsaw, 1973-91. *Publications:* 7 books incl 3 brochures: Zabojstwa i ich sprawcy, 1974; Funkcjonowanie szkolne mlodziezy i jego uwarunkowania, 1982; Moj diabel stroz, 1988; 15 articles. *Contributions to:* various mags. *Memberships:* Polish Sociological Soc; Polish Authors Soc. *Honours:* Silver Crss, 1979; Polonia Restituta Cross, 1984; Lit awards, competitions organised by mags: Swiat, Kulisy. *Hobbies:* Sport (ping- pong); Jazz; Psychotherapy. *Address:* ul Grzybowska 16/22 m 1327, 00- 132 Warsaw, Poland.

JANSEN Gregory Johannes, b. 5 Dec 1946, Kew, Victoria, Australia. Secondary School Teacher. m.

Catharina Anna Maria Scholtes, 14 Dec 1968, 2 s, 3 d. *Education:* PSTC, Melbourne, 1967; BSc, Monash Univ, 1974. *Appointments:* Tchng positions, Victorian Min Educ, 1968-. *Publication:* A Modified Approach to Teaching Secondary School Mathematics, 1990. *Memberships:* Assoc, Inst Maths Educ, LaTrobe Univ; Victorian Affiliated Tchrs Fedn; School Mbr, Math Assn Vic. *Hobbies:* Reading; Gardening; Fishing; Walking. *Address:* 28 Oliver Street, Yea, Victoria, Australia.

JAQUES John Michael, b. 29 Sept 1930, London, England. Architect. m. Caroline Knapman, 27 Jan 1962, 2 s. *Education:* Dip Architecture, thesis distinction, Regent St Polytechnic, London, 1954. *Appointments:* Ptnr, Jaques, Muir and Ptnrs, Chartered Archts. *Creative works:* Housing schemes; Sports bldgs; Museums; Archt for major restoration work to Ch Holy Sepulchre, Jerusalem. *Memberships:* Royal Inst Brit Archts; FRSA; Coun Mbr, Anglo Jordanian Soc, 1980-87, 1991-; Comm Mbr, Friends of St John Ophthalmic Hosp, Jerusalem, 1982-86; Mbr, Appeal Comm, Royal Soc British Sculptors; Arts Club. *Honours:* Order of El Istiqlal, Jordan, 1977; Off, Order St John, 1985; MBE, 1988. *Hobbies:* Reading; Travel; The arts. *Address:* 8 Vine Yard, Sanctuary Street, London SE1 1QL, England.

JARDINE Betty June, b. 17 May 1930, Ballarat, Victoria, Australia. Clinical Consultant. m. John Jardine, 15 Jan 1955, 1 s. *Education:* BA, Sociology, Psychology, Vic, 1980; Cert Sterilisation and Infection Control, 1985; BEd (Second), Psychology, Bus, 1986. *Appointments:* Registered Psychologist; Registered Nurse; Registered Second Tchr; Accredited Counsellor, Pre and Pst HIV Antibody Testing; Lectr, community grps, HIV prevention; Currently: Clin Cons, Infection Control, Latrobe Reg Hosp, Moe Campus; Crisis Vol, Kalparrin Ctr Against Sexual Assault. *Publication:* Preoperative Nursing Interventions for Surgical Patients: Effects on Anxiety and Postoperative Recovery (w C O Fraser), 1989. *Memberships:* Fellow, Am Psychological Soc; Fellow, Royal Coll Nursing Australia; Affiliate, Australian Psychological Soc; Monash Univ Alumni; Australian Infection Control Assn; Victorian Infection Control Nurses Assn, Past Comm Mbr; Nat AIDS Counselling Assn; Operating Room Nurses Grp; Sterilization and Disinfection Soc; Reg 5, Gippsland AIDS Support and Update Grp; Reg 5, Country Infection Control Grp; Australian AIDS Nurse Resource Grp. *Honours:* Life Mb, GIAE Student Union, 1980; Life and Fndn Mbr: Past Grads Assn, Latrobe Valley Hosp; Yallourn Old Girls Assn; Life Gov, Latrobe Valley Hosp, 1991. *Hobbies:* Music; Computing; Research. *Address:* PO Box 29, Newborough, Victoria 3825, Australia. 138, 152.

JAROSZ Maria, b. 30 May 1931, Lodz, Poland. Professor of Sociology. m. (2) Boleslaw Korczak, 13 Mar 1982, 1 s. *Education:* MPh, Dept Philos, Warsaw Univ, 1955; Dr Humanities, 1965, Assoc Prof, 1986, Ordinary Prof, 1989, Inst Sociology, Polish Acad Scis. *Appointments:* Asst, Dept Sociology, Warsaw Univ, 1955-57; Adj, Inst Sociology, Polish Acad Scis, 1958-69; Lectr, Higher Engrng School, 1970-72; Chief Rsch Expert, Ctrl Statistical Off, 1973-78; Hd, Rsch Dept, Inst Criminal Problems, 1978-83; Docent, Assoc Prof, currently Ordinary prof, Inst Econs, Polish Acad Scis, Warsaw, 1983-; Vis Prof, var occasions, Univs Bologna, Italy, Budapest, Hungary, CNRS, Paris, France, Belgrade and Zagreb, Yugoslavia. *Publications:* 14 books in Polish incl: Workers Self-Management, 1967; Self-Destruction, 1980; Social Inequalities, 1984; Barriers in Life of Young People, 1986; Disorganisation of Family and Society, 1987; Workers Self- Government: Aspirations and Reality, 1988; Over 200 sci papers and articles, worldwide. *Memberships:* Sci Bd, Inst Econs, Polish Acad Scis; Comm Experts on Alcoholism, Coun Mins; Polish Sociological Soc; Polish Soc Authors; Int Rural Sociology Assn. *Honours:* For books: Stanislaw Ossowski Prize, 1980; 2 prizes, Sci Sec, Polish Acad Scis, 1981, 1989; State Prize, 1987; Youth Press Prize, 1987; Min Nat Educ Prize, 1988. *Hobbies:* Visiting exotic countries; Ethnography. *Address:* c/o Polish Academy of Sciences, Institute of Economic Science, Nowy Swiat 72, 00-330 Warsaw, Poland. 138, 152.

JÄSCHKE Kurt-Ulrich, b. 6 Mar 1938, Danzig. University Professor. m. Renate J Jaschke, 2 Jan 1964, 1 s, 1 d. *Education:* Greek, Hebrew, Univ Munster, 1957-58; Staatsexamen, 1963, Dr phil, 1964, Univ Bonn; Habilitation, Univ Marburg, 1969. *Appointments:* Prof, Univ Marburg, 1971; Prof, Mediaeval Hist, Auxiliary Scis, Univ Saarbrücken, 1975-. *Publications:* Die aelteste Halberstaedter Bischofschronik, 1970; Burgenbau und Landesverteidigung um 900, 1975; Wilhelm der Eroberer, 1977; Die Anglonormannen, 1981; Imperator Heinricus (VII), 1988; Nichtkoenigliche Residenzen, 1990; Notwendige Gefaehrtinnen, 1991; Zu Koeniginnen und Kaiserinnen der Salierzeit, 1992. *Memberships:* Deutsche Kommission fuer die Bearbeitung der Regesta Imperii, Akademie der Wissenschaften und der Literatur, Mainz; Kommission fuer saarlaendische Landesgeschichte und Volksforschung; Verein für Rheinische Kirchengeschichte. *Honours:* Dissertation Prize, Bonn Univ, 1964. *Hobbies:* Playing the violin and making chamber music, esp string quartet. *Address:* Historisches Institut, D-6600 Saarbrucken 11, Germany. 43.

JASINSKI Janusz, b. 4 Sept 1928, Wolomin, Poland. Historian specialising in 19th Century Warmia and Mazuria. m. Wieslawa Rajkowska, 7 Nov 1953, 1 s, 1 d. *Education:* MA, Cath Univ Lublin, 1954; Dr Humanities, Univ Warsaw, 1964; Asst Professorship, Univ Torun, 1982. *Appointments:* Rsch Station, Polish Histl Assn Olsztyn, 1954-62; Ketrzynski Inst Sci Rsch, Olsztyn, 1962-74; Inst Hist, Polish Acad Scis, Warsaw, 1974-. *Publications:* Reformy agrarne na Warmii na poczatku XIX w, 1967; Andrzej Samulowski 1840-1928. O narodowe oblicze Warmii, 1976; Swiadomosc narodowa na Warmii w XIX wieku, 1983; Franciszek Lieder: Warmia moich mlodych lat (ed), 1988; Ferdinand Gregorovius: Idea Polskosci (ed), 1991. *Memberships:* Vice-Chmn, Polish Histl Soc, Olsztyn Br; Vice-Chmn, Sci Coun, Ketrzynski Inst; Sci Soc, Cath Univ Lublin; Sci Soc Torun; Inst Wn Affairs Poznan. *Honours:* Hon Mbr, Ketrzynski Sci Soc, 1971; Award, Sci Sec, Polish Acad Scis, 1984; Jubilee Dip, Polish Histl Soc Centennial, 1986; Special issue of Komunikaty Mazursko-Warminskie quarterly dedicated to him on his 60th birthday. *Address:* Osrodek Badan Naukowych im W Ketrzynskiego, ul Partyzantow 87, 10-402 Olsztyn, Poland.

JASKEL Martin Stephen, b. 3 June 1946, London, England. Director of Global Marketing. m. Antone Sheila Jaskel, 15 May 1976, 1 d. *Education:* BA Hons, Econ, Univ Manchester, 1967. *Appointments:* Phillips and Drew, 1967-72; Capel Cure Carden, 1972-74; Capel Cure Myers, 1974-75; W Greenwell & Co, 1976-86; Greenwell Montagu Gilt Edged, 1986-88; Midland Montagu Treasury Sales, 1988-90; Currently Dir of Global Marketing, NatWest Gp Treasury, Natwest Mkts. *Hobbies:* Cricket (Member, Marylebone Cricket Club); Opera; Theatre. *Address:* 135 Bishopsgate, London EC2M 3UR, England.

JASON Julie, b. 14 May 1949, Kentucky, USA. Lawyer; Managing Director. m. Marius Mason, 19 Dec 1970, 2 d. *Education:* BA, Baldwin- Wallace Coll, 1971; JD, Cleveland State Univ, 1974; LLM, Columbia Univ, 1975. *Appointments:* Practised Law, NYC firms, 1974-78; Atty, then Asst Gen Counsel, Pres, Trust Co and Futures Mgmt Subsidiary, Paine Webber, 1978-88; Sr Fin Servs Atty, Donovan Leisure law firm, NYC, 1988-89; Co-Fndr, Mngng Dir, Jackson, Grant and Co stock brokerage firm serving long-term investors, Stamford, CT, 1989-. *Memberships:* Dir, Greenwich League Women Voters; Greenwich Jr League; AAUW; Am Pen Women; Corp Counsels Assn; Legal Div, Securities Ind Assn; Am Bar Assn Investment Co Comm. *Honours:* Var school acad hons; Award for plan to eliminate her function and dept by integrating systems, Pres of Paine Webber, 1985.

Hobbies: Writing monthly column on investing for Woman's Journal; Teaching community level courses on investing; Writing for journals on investment topics; Riding; Active in voluteer efforts in community and study of government. *Address:* Jackson, Grant and Company, 1177 High Ridge Rd, Stamford, CT 06905, USA. 163.

JAVERI Ratnakar Madhusudan, b. 5 Sept 1932, Bombay, India. Architect. m. Vimal Pandurang Vaidya, 20 Feb 1960, 1 s, 1 d. *Education:* Full-time Dip Course, Arch, 1950-55; Govt Dip, Arch, 1956. *Appointments:* Lectr, Archtl Hist, Bombay, 1956-69; Archt, pvte archtl firms, Bombay, 1956-59; Paper Setter, Examiner, Indian univs; Organiser, study tours; Pvte coaching classes, Arch, 1964-69; Asst Archt, Newmarket Urban Dist Coun, England, 1970-72; Asst Archt: Sir William Halcrow and Ptnrs, London, 1972-73; Coop Retail Servs Ltd, 1975-81; Pvte archtl prac, Ilford, 1982-. *Memberships:* Royal Inst Brit Archts, Corp Mbr 1960, Co-Deleg and Rep to Liverpool 1978, to Netherlands 1987; Fellow, Indian Inst Archts, 1985; Fellow, Fac Bldg, 1986; FRSA, 1987; Registered Archt, Archts Registration Coun, UK, 1970-. *Hobbies:* Travel; Reading; Photography; Music. *Address:* 32 Dike Road, Barkingside, Ilford, Essex, England.

JAVITCH Daniel G, b. 13 June 1941, France. Professor of Comparatve Literature. m. Leila Laughlin, Aug 1968, 2 d. *Education:* AB, Princeton Univ, USA, 1963; BA (Hons), Cambridge Univ, England, 1965; PhD, Harvard Univ, USA, 1971. *Appointments:* Asst Prof, Columbia Univ, NYC, NY, USA, 1970-78; Assoc Prof, Prof, NY Univ, 1978-; Dir, New Directions Publng Corp. *Publications:* Poetry and Courtliness in Renaissance England, 1978; Proclaiming a Classic. The Canonization of Orlando Furioso, 1991. *Memberships:* ICLA; ACLA; Mod Lang Assn; Exec Bd, Renaissance Soc of Am. *Honours:* Villa I Tatti Fellowship, Harvard, 1976-77; ACLS Fellowship, 1977, 1990; Rome Prize Fellowship, Am Acad Rome, 1989-90. *Address:* Dept of Comparative Literature, New York University, 19 University Place, New York, NY 10003, USA. 13.

JAVOR Istvan, b. 28 Feb 1954, Szeged, Hungary. Associate Professor of Sociology. m. Violetta Suveges, 1 Mar 1984, 1 s, 1 d. *Education:* Univ Dip, Budapest Univ Econs, 1977; Univ Doct, 1982; PhD, Sociology, 1989. *Appointments:* Lectr, int bus school, 1980-85; Univ lectr, Sociology, 1986-90, Assoc Prof, Sociology, 1991-, Lorand Eotvos Univ Sci, Budapest. *Publication:* Book in Hungarian: Intraorganisational Power Structure, 1988. *Membership:* Bd, Int Sociotech Assn. *Address:* ELTE Szociologiai Intezet, Pollack M ter 10, H-1081 Budapest, Hungary.

JA'VOR Tibor, b. 10 Apr 1926, Debrecen, Hungary. Professor of Medicine. m. Kornelia Terner, 18 Jan 1949, 1 s. *Education:* MD, 1951; Acad Dr Med Scis, 1968. *Appointments:* Asst Prof, 1951-58, Assoc Prof, 1958-68, Prof, Hd of Dept, 1968-, 1st Dept Med, Univ Med School, Pecs. *Publications:* Books: Hungarian Textbook of Medicine; Textbook of Diagnostics; Methoden der Klinischen Pharmakologie. *Membership:* Pres, Hungarian Soc Gastroenterology. *Hobby:* Music. *Address:* 1st Department of Medicine, University Medical School, Pecs, Hungary.

JAY Peter Aldred, b. 30 June 1930, London, England. Consulting Engineer. m. Jane Ohna Campbell Miller, 18 Oct 1986. *Education:* Cheltenham Coll; Oriel Coll, Oxford; BA, 1952; MA, 1955. *Appointments:* Fndr, Peter Jay and Ptnrs, Elec Consultants, later Cons Engrs Bldg Servs. *Publications:* Electrical Installations (w J Hemsley), 1962; Var articles and papers on lighting incl: Visual Perception and Apparent Brightness, 1971. *Memberships:* Sometime VP, former Illuminating Engrng Soc, 1974-77, M InstP, 1972; FIOA, 1976; FCIBSE, 1978; FRSA, 1989; MConsE, 1979; Advsr on Lighting and Elec, Ctrl Coun Care of Chs; Chmn, Paddington Waterways and Maida Vale Soc, 1974-88.

Hobbies: Music; Reading. *Address:* 1 Penfold Place, London NW1 6RJ, England.

JAYACHANDRA Chickaballapur Reddiyappa, b. 21 Nov 1928, India. Consultant Paediatrician. m. Sujaya Jayachandra, 6 Sept 1961. *Education:* MB BS, Mysore, India, 1954; DCH, London, 1958; MRCPE, 1968. *Appointments:* Var trainee appts, UK, 1955-68; Cons Paediatrician, 1968-. *Publications:* Child Management: Five Universal Basic Principles; Several articles on cure for persistent crying of infants. *Memberships:* Brit Paediatric Assn; Brit Med Assn. *Honours:* Fellow, Royal Coll Physicians, Edinburgh; Life Mbr, World Inst Achievement, USA. *Hobbies:* Gardening; Sports; Current affairs. *Address:* The Royal Oldham Hospital, Rochdale Road, Oldham, Gr Manchester, England. 191.

JAYANTHAN T K, b. 20 Apr 1933, Trichur, India. Bank Officer. m. M Arya, 7 Feb 1956, 1 s, 2 d. *Education:* BA (Stat); Cert AIIB. *Appointments:* Var positions, Indian Overseas Bank, incl Br Mgr, 1958-. *Publications:* 1st collection of poems forthcoming. *Memberships:* Kalari, Edappal, Kerala, India; Int Poets Acad, Madras; Writers Forum, Ranchi, India. *Hobbies:* Writing poetry; Farming; Reading. *Address:* Kadalayil, Kadalasseri, Vallachira, Trichur, Kerala, India.

JAYAWARDENE Kirikankanange Albert Thistlethwayte Wilhelm Perera, b. 9 Nov 1928, Sri Lanka. Consultant Anaesthetist. m. 28 Nov 1957, 1 s, 2 d. *Education:* MB BS (Ceylon), 1956; House Off, 1956-61; Postgrad, England, 1961-63; DA, London, 1962; FFARCS, England, 1963. *Appointments:* Cons Anaesthetist, Gen Hosp, Badulla, 1964-65; Cons Anaesthetist, Gen Hosp, Kurunegala, 1965; Cons Paedatric Anaesthetist, Children's Hosp, Colombo,1965-90; Cons Anaesthetist, Cardiothoracic Unit, 1965-, Anaesthetist in Charge, Surg Intensive Care Unit, 1968-, Gen Hosp, Colombo. *Memberships:* Sri Lanka Med Assn, Pres 1990-91, VP 1988-89; Coll Anaesthesiologists Sri Lanka, Pres 1984, 1985, 1986; Bd Mgmt, Postgrad Inst Med, 1979-; Chmn, Bd Study in Anaesthesiology, 1983-86, 1986-89; Standing Comm, Ch Ceylon, 1980-86; Bd Trustees, Deaf and Blind School Ceylon, 1983-; Bd Govs, St Thomas Coll, Mt Lavinia and brs. *Honours:* Fellow, Am Coll Cardiology, 1985. *Hobbies:* Photography; Orchid grower; Coconut planter. *Address:* 14 Albert Place, Dehiwela, Sri Lanka.

JAYSON Malcolm I V, b. 9 Dec 1937, London, England. Professor of Rheumatology. m. 1 July 1962, 2 s. *Education:* MB BS, Middlesex Hosp, Univ London, 1961; MRCP London, 1964; MD, Bristol, 1967; FRCP London, 1974. *Appointments:* Sr Lectr, Rheumatology, Univ Bristol, 1969; Hon Cons, Royal Nat Hosp Rheumatic Diseases, Bath, 1969; Prof, Rheumatology, Univ Manchester, 1977-. *Publications:* Author, Ed: Back Pain: The Facts; Rheumatism and Arthritis (w A St J Dixon); Lumbar Spine and Back Pain; Collagen in Health and Disease (w J Weiss); Systemic Sclerosis: Scleroderma (w C Black). *Memberships:* Int Back Pain Soc, Sec-Gen; Soc Chiropodists, Pres; Arachnoiditis Self-Help Grp, Pres; Assn Physicians; Brit Soc Rheumatology Int Soc Study of Lumbar Spine. *Honours:* Volvo Prize, Int Soc Study of Lumbar Spine; Vis Prof, Univs IA and Queensland. *Hobbies:* Antiques, esp sundials and clocks; Trout fishing. *Address:* The Gate House, 8 Lancaster Rd, Didsbury, Manchester M20 8TY, England.

JAZIC Zivojin, b. 14 Nov 1927, Osijek, Yugoslavia. Diplomat. m. Nevenka Susnjar, 5 May 1963. *Education:* BA Law, Univ Zagreb, 1950; Dipl, Inst of Soc Scis, Belgrade, 1952; Dipl Inst of Europen Studies, Univ of Saarbrucken, 1954; Doctorate, Intl Law, Univ of Zagreb, 1981. *Appointments:* Inst for Intl Polit and Econs, 1954-57; Fed Sec for Foreign Affairs, DPR, Yugoslav Mission to UN, 1967-71; Ambass to Cuba, 1978- 82; Foreign Pol Advr to Pres of Yugoslavia, 1983-84; V-Min, Foreign Ser, Ambass to India, 1986; Currently, Ambass, Fed Sec for Foreign Affairs, SFR of Yugoslavia. *Publications:* European Community Aspects of International Law,

doctoral thesis, 1981; Numerous essays, articles in Yugoslav professional journals and magazines. *Memberships:* Yugoslav Assn for Intl Law. *Honours:* Awd, Intl Affairs, Belgrade, 1988. *Hobbies:* Travel; Chess; History; Theatre; Films; Music. *Address:* Narodnih Heroja 41a, Apt 41/XX, Novi Beograd, 110076 Beograd, Yugoslavia.

JEFFCOCK David Philip, b. 8 July 1933, Little Bealings, Suffolk, England. Stockbroker. m. Josephine Anne Warde-Norbury, 14 Dec 1963, 2 s, 2 d. *Education:* Ampleforth, 1945-51; Scholar, Trinity Coll, Cambridge, 1951-54; BA (Cantab), 1954. *Appointments:* Conservative Rsch Dept, 1964; The Stock Exchange (Grieveson Grant, McAnally Montgomery, Laing and Cruickshank, Greig Middleton, Raphael Zorn Hemsley,), 1966-. *Publications:* Co-author, var publs on tax and law reform for Sir Alec Douglas-Home. *Memberships:* The Stock Exchange, 1971-92; MSI 1992-; Patron, Ct Jeffcock A O F. *Hobbies:* Books; History; Music. *Address:* Wellington House, Captains Row, Lymington, Hampshire SO41 9RR, England. 35.

JELENC Zoran, b. 2 Apr 1935, Ljubljana, Slovenia. Researcher in Adult Education; Department Head. m. Dorotea Jelenc, 26 Oct 1963, 2 d. *Education:* Dip, Violin, Music HS, Ljubljana, 1958; Dip, Psychology, Educ, Univ Ljubljana, 1960. *Appointments:* Child Psychologist, Dir, Child Guidance Ctr, Ljubljana, 1961-74; Viator Ljubljana, 1974-76; Counsellor, Instg Social Planning Slovenia, 1976-81; Rschr, Dept Hd, Inst Rsch in Educ, Ljubljana, 1981-. *Publications:* Var publs in child psychology and adult education incl 4 publs of rsch project on the conception of adult educ in Slovenia. *Memberships:* Assn Adult Educ Orgs Yugoslavia, Sec-Gen 1980-82; Assn Adult Educ Slovenia, Pres 1982-88; Slovene Psychology Assn, VP 1964-66; Slovene Sociology Assn. *Honours:* Preseren's Prize for Students, Ljubljana, 19761; Gold Medal, Friends of Children and Youth Assn Slovenia, 1969; Silver Medal, Trade Unions Assn Slovenia, 1980; Djuro Salaj Award, outstanding achievements in educ of workers, Trade Unions Assn Yugoslavia, 1988; Award, outstanding achievements in dev of theory and prac of adult educ, Assn Adult Educ Orgs Yugoslavia, 1990. *Hobbies:* Music; Mountain climbing; Mushroom picking and identifying. *Address:* Miklosiceva 34, 61000 Ljubljana, Slovenia. 152, 162.

JELÍNEK Milan, b. 1923, Brno, Czechoslovakia. University Professor. m. Jana Poláková, 1966, 5 s. *Education:* Fac Arts, Masaryk Univ, Brno, 1945-48; PhDr, 1950; Sr Lectr, 1960; Prof, 1964. *Appointments:* Ed, Publng House, 1949-53; Rsch Worker, Inst Czech Lang, 1953-58, 1970-83; Sr Lectr, 1958-64, Dean, 1962-65, Prof, 1964-70, 1989-, Fac Arts, Brno; Vice-Rector, 1966-69, Rector, 1989-92, Masaryk Univ; Lectures, Univ Greifswald, 1967-62; Sorbonne, Paris, 1965- 66. *Publications:* In Czech: On Newspapers Language and Style, 1957; Action Nouns, 1967; Sophist Aspects of a Grammatical System, 1974; On the Normative, Semantic and Stylistic Adequateness of Translation, 1980; On Everyday Czech (co-author), 1984; 160 articles; 600 essays. *Memberships:* Rsch Workers Union Czechoslovakia, Vice-Chmn 1968-71; Fndr Mbr, Masaryk Community, 1988-. *Honours:* Medal for Loyalty 1939-1945, 1951; Silver Medal, Masaryk Univ, 1966; Meda; 50th Anniversary CSR, 1968. *Hobbies:* Stylistics; Language culture of Slavic languages; History of Czech language, 19th and 20th centuries; Syntax; Swimming; Skiing. *Address:* Zborovska 39, 61600 Brno, Czechoslovakia.

JENKINS Aubrey Dennis, b. 6 Sept 1927, London, England. Professor of Polymer Science. m. Jitka Horska, 29 Dec 1987. *Education:* Sir John Cass Tech Inst, 1943-45; King's Coll, Univ London, 1945-50; BSc, 1948; PhD, 1951; DSc, 1961. *Appointments:* Rsch Chem, Courtaulds, 1950-60; Hd, Chem Rsch, Gillette, 1960-64; Prof, Polymer Sci, School Molecular Scis, Univ Sussex, Brighton, 1964-. *Publications:* Kinetics of Vinyl Polymerisation, 1958; Polymer Science, 1972;

Reactivity, Mechanism and Structure in Polymer Chemistry, 1974. *Membership:* Fellow, Royal Soc Chem. *Honour:* Heyrovsky Gold Medal for Chem, Czechoslovak Acad Scis, 1990. *Hobbies:* Music; Travel; Photography. *Address:* Shoe Box Cottage, 115 Keymer Road, Hassocks, West Sussex BN6 8QL, England. 1, 52.

JENKINS Bernard Stephen, b. 21 Dec 1939, Croydon, Surrey, England. Consultant Cardiologist. *Education:* MB BChir (Cantab), 1964; MA (Cantab), 1965; FRCP (London), 1974. *Appointments include:* Dist Gen Mgr, W Lambeth Hlth Auth, London, 1985-91; Chief Exec, St Thomas' Hosp, London, 1989-91. *Memberships:* Brit Cardiac Soc; FRSA. *Hobbies:* Music; Cooking. *Address:* Cardiac Department, St Thomas' Hospital, Lambeth Palace Road, London SE1 7EM, England.

JENKINS Dennis Robert, b. 19 June 1957, Williams Air Force Base, Arizona, USA. *Education:* BS, Computer Sci, 1979, MS, Rsch and Dev Systems Mgmt, 1982, Pacific Wn Univ. *Appointments:* Data Systems Specialist, Fed Aviation Admin, 1977-79; Software Engr, Martin- Marietta, 1980-83; Data Systems Mgr, OSHCO-PAE-SOMC, 1983; Sr Systems Engr, Lockheed Space Ops, 1984-86; Sr Systems Engr, Sand Hill Engrng Inc, 1986-89; Project Engr, Harris Space Systems Corp, 1989-. *Publications:* Author: Space Shuttle; EA-6A/EA-6B Prowler; F-15 Eagle/Strike Eagle; The History of Developing The National Space Transportation System; Co-author: F-14 Tomcat; Su-27; B-52G/H Stratofortress. *Memberships:* Am Inst Aeronautics and Astronautics; Flight Test Histl Soc; Air Force Mus Fndn. *Hobbies:* Photography; Driving; Writing; Reading. *Address:* 580 S Brevard Ave No 844, Cocoa Beach, FL 32931, USA.

JENKINS H Ann, b. 11 June 1945, Richmond, Virginia, USA. Licensed Professional Counsellor. *Education:* BS, Social Wellfare, 1970, MEd, Counsellor Educ, 1977, Adv Cert, Profl Counselling, 1988, VA C'wlth Univ, Richmond. *Appointments:* Social Worker-B, Dept Social Servs, Culpeper Co, then Caroline Co, VA, 1969-71; Tchr, Educably Mentally Retarded, Culpeper Co Pub Schools, Culpeper, VA, 1971-75; Document Analyst, Aspen Systems Corp, Germantown, MD, 1976-77; Rehab Servs Supvsr, Richmond, VA, 1977-81; Counsellor, 1981-82, Coord, 1982-86, Community Re-Entry Prog, United Meth Family Servs, Richmond; Dir, Counselling, Metrop Community Ch, Richmond, 1986-87; Exec Dir, pt-time Substance Abuse Therapist, Another Chance Counselling Serv Inc, Richmond, 1988-; Student Assistance Therapist, Burkeville, VA, 1989-90. *Memberships:* Nat Acad Cert Clin Mental Hlth Counsellors; Nat Child Care Workers Assn; VA Child Care Workers Assn, Sec 1983, Pres 1985-89; Nat Org Women; Am Assn Counseling and Dev; Am Mental Hlth Counselors Assn; Assn Specialists in Grp Work. *Honours:* Dean's List, 1987, 1988; Award, Outstanding Serv to Youth as Child Care Worker, VA Assn Youth and Child Care Educ. *Hobbies:* Travel; Golf; Music and listening to music; Spending time with friends. *Address:* 3117 Forest Hill Ave, Richmond, VA 23225, USA. 7, 132.

JENKINS James Sherwood Jr, b. 25 July 1941, Franklin, Tennessee, USA. Clinical Pharmacologist. *Education:* BS, David Lipscomb Univ, 1962; BSPh, 1964, PD, 1982, Univ TN. *Appointments:* Jim Jenkins Pharmacy, 1969-91-; Clin Pharmacology Consultants, 1980-91-. *Creative works:* 25 publs on hypertension and cardiovascular diseases; Rsch abstracts. *Contributions to:* profl jrnls on topical rsch; US FDA Licence, Ibuprofen Cream. *Memberships:* Nat Aeronautic Assn; Fellow, Am Coll Apothecaries; Diplomate, Am Acad Pain Mgmt. *Honours:* 45 world and USA aviation speed records, Nat Aeronatic Assn/Federation Aeronautique Internationale, 1978-88; Mbr, Ed Bd, Am Acad Pain Mgmt Jrnl, 1991-94. *Hobbies:* Aviation: USA/FAA licence commercial/instrument/multi and single engine land rating; Archaeology; Photography; Art; Theatre; Music; Antique furniture;

Gardening. *Address:* PO Box 772, 107 New Brick Church Pike, Goodlettsville, TN 37070, USA. 7.

JENNINGS Barry Randall, b. 3 Mar 1939, Purley, Surrey, England. Research and Development Director. m. Margaret Penelope Wall, 1 Sept 1964, 2 d. *Education:* BSc, 1964, PhD, 1964, ICI Fellow, 1965, DSc, 1976, Univ Southampton; Rsch Fellow, Strasbourg Univ, 1964. *Appointments:* Lectr, Phys, Queen Elizabeth Coll, London, 1966-71; Prof, Hd, Expmtl Phys, Brunel Univ, 1971-84; Prof, Phys/Optics, Reading Univ, 1985-90; Dir, Rsch and Dev, ECC Int Ltd, St Austell, 1990-. *Publications:* Electro-Optics of Macromolecules, 1969; Atoms in Contact, 1974; Colloid & molecular Electro-Optics, 1991; 200 papers in sci lit on colloid and molecular optics. *Memberships:* Fellow, Inst Phys; Fellow, Chem Soc; Past Chmn, Brit Biophys Soc; Past Chmn, Polymer Phys Grp, UK; VP, Minerals Ind Rsch Org; Hon Ed, Journal of Physics D; Pres, Cornish Fedn Male Voice Choirs. *Honours:* Cowan-Keedy Prize, Southampton Univ, 1961; Polymer Prize, Soc Chem Ind, 1969; Vis Prof, Univ Reading; Vis Prof Bristol Univ. *Hobbies:* Long-cased clocks; Church activities; Antiquarian books. *Address:* Luney Barton House, Lower Sticker, St Austell PL26 7JH, Cornwall, England. 32, 47.

JENRETTE Thomas Shepard Jr, b. 1 Feb 1946, Roanoke, VA, USA. Choral Conductor; Professor of Music. *Education:* BA, Music, 1968, MMus, Conducting, 1970, Univ NC, Chapel Hill; DMA, Voice Perf, Univ MI, 1976. *Appointments:* Choral Dir, Cummings HS, Burlington, NC, 1969-72; Dir, Cultural Arts, Burlington City Schools, 1972-73; Dir, Choral Activities, SW State Univ, Marshall, MN, 1976-79; Prof, Music, E TN State Univ, Johnson City, TN, 1979-; Special appearances as Choral Conductor: Am Choral Dirs Assn So Div Conven, 1986, 1988; Am Choral Dirs Assn Nat Conven, 1989; TN Educators Assn Conven, 1990, 1991; The White House, Wash DC, Christmas 1989. *Memberships:* Am Choral Dirs Assn; Int Fedn Choral Music; Nat Assn Tchrs Singing; Music Educators Nat Conf; Coll Music Soc. *Honours:* Omicron Delta Kappa; Hon Mbr, Phi Mu Alpha Sinfonia. *Address:* 2734 E Oakland Avenue, C-25, Johnson City, TN 37601, USA. 7.

JENSEN Elsabeth, b. 26 Apr 1950, Denmark. Registered Nurse. m. Leonard Douglas Kushnier, 27 Sept 1980, 1 s, 1 d. *Education:* Dip, Hamilton Civic Hosps School Nursng, Can, 1972; BA, 1981, BScN, 1989, Univ Wn Ont. *Appointments:* Staff Nurse, London Psych Hosp, London, Ont, Can, 1972-81; Staff Nurse, Univ Hosp, London, Ont, 1982-90; Nurse Mgr, Victoria Hosp Corp, London, Ont, 1990-. *Memberships:* Can Nurses Assn, Dir 1989- 90; Registered Nurses Assn Ont, Dir 1982-87, Pres-Elect 1987-89, Pres 1989-9-; Project Turnabout, Dir 1990-91; Sigma Theta Tau; Fndng Mbr, Soc Rogerian Scholars. *Honours:* M Josephine Flaherty Award, 1989; Dean's Hon List, Fac Nursing, Univ Wn Ont, London, 1989. *Hobbies:* Gardening; Reading; Travel; Camping; Hiking; Environmental issues. *Address:* 80 Archer Crescent, London, Ontario, Canada N6E 2A5. 142.

JENSEN Walter Godfried, b. 4 Mar 1932, Antwerp, Belgium. Executive Secretary and Director. *Education:* Schooling in Belgium; BA Hons, Univ of London, 1954; PhD, 1957. *Appointments:* Nat Coal Bd, 1956-67; Brit Petroleum, 1968-73; Brit Coal Corp, 1974-. *Publications:* Energy in Europe, 1967; The Common Market, 1967; Nuclear Energy, 1969; Energy and the Economy of Nations, 1971. *Memberships:* Inst of Energy; ESCS Consul Com. *Hobbies:* Chess; Reading. *Address:* Patrijzenlaan 7, 1950 Kraainem, Belgium.

JEPPESEN Knud Olav, b. 26 Sept 1938, Vodskov, Denmark. Lecturer/Associate Professor. m. Ida Marie Bang, 15 July 1961, 2 s, 1 d. *Education:* Gen Cert, Maths, Phys, Aalborg, 1957; Cand theol, 1965, Dr theol, 1987, Univ Aarhus. *Appointments:* Scholarships and tchng, 1965- 74, Lectr, Assoc Prof, Old Testament, 1974-88,

1991-, Univ Aarhus; Bible Translator, 1989-90; Guest Prof, Kiel Univ, Germany, 1992. *Publications:* Profeti og protest, 1971; Graeder ikke saa saare, I-II, 1987; Jesajas bog fortolket, 1988; Co-ed: Scandinavian Journal of the Old Testament, 1986-; Several essay collections. *Memberships:* Collegium Biblicum, 1972- , Comm Mbr 1988-; Soc Old Testament Study, 1988- ; Soc Biblical Lit, 1989-. *Honours:* Golden Medal, Univ Aarhus, 1967. *Hobby:* Literature. *Address:* Department of Old Testament Studies, Hovedbygningen, Universitetet, DK Aarhus C, Denamrk.

JEPPESEN Palle, b. 6 Aug 1941, Vordingborg, Denmark. University Professor. m. Trine Kirsten Just Jeppesen, 10 Apr 1974, 1 s, 2 d. *Education:* MSc, Elec Engrng, 1967, PhD, Microwave Electronics, 1970, DSc, Microwave Electronics, 1978, Tech Univ Denmark; PhD student, Tech Univ Denmark and Cornell Univ, USA, 1967-70. *Appointments:* Assoc Prof, Rsch Prof, Prof, Tech Univ Denmark, Lyngby, 1970-; Dir, Ctr Broadband Telecommunications, 1989-. *Publications:* Gallium Arsenide Transferred Electron Devices, doct thesis, 1978; Papers, int jrnls and confs on microwave electronics and optical communications. *Memberships:* IEEE, 1967-; Danish Acad Tech Scis, 1978-; Sci Coun, Great Danish Encyclopedia, 1991-; Bd Mbr: Terma Electronik AS, 1985-; ElektronikCentralen, 1989-; Telecom A/S, 1991-. *Honours:* Peter Gorm Petersens Mem Stipend, 1974; Esso Prize, 1978; Villum Kann Rasmussens Rsch Prize, 1988. *Hobby:* Tennis. *Address:* Elmevej 10, DK-2840 Holte, Denmark.

JERABEK Karel, b. 9 Sept, Prague, Czechoslovakia. Chemist; Researcher. m. Marta Cernohorska, 4 June 1969, 1 s, 1 d. *Education:* Engr, Technological Inst, Prague, 1966; PhD, Czechoslovak Acad Scis, Prague, 1972. *Appointments:* Mbr, Tech Staff, 1972-79, Sr Scientist, 1979-, Inst Chem Process Fundamentals, Prague. *Publications:* 30 sci papers; 17 patents. *Membership:* Ed Bd, Reactive Polymers sci jrnl, 1991- . *Honours:* Nat Prize, Czech Republic, 1989. *Hobbies:* Reading; Computers. *Address:* Kankovskeno 1241, 182 00 Prague 8, Czechoslovakia. 52.

JERMAKS Romuald S, b. 10 June 1931, Latvia. Assistant Professor. m. Ilma Grauzdina, 10 Nov 1973, 1 s, 5 d. *Education:* F Medins Music School, Riga, 1954-57; Hons Grad, specialising as Composer and Lectr Music Theory, F Vitols Latvia State Conservatoire, Riga, 1962. *Appointments:* Army serv, Moscow, Leningrad, 1951-53; Tchr, Rezekne Music Second School, 1962-64; Sound Prod, Latvian TV, 1964-71; Asst Prof, Latvia Music Acad, 1971-. *Creative works:* 5 cantatas, 1962, 1979, 1983, 1987, 1990; 3 symphonies, 1963, 1964, 1977; 3 oratorios, 1972, 1989, 1990; 4 concertos for organ and chamber orchestra; 3 solo concertos for organ, 1984, 1988, 1992; Latvian Music, 1985; 4 masses, 1989, 1991, 1992 (2). *Memberships:* Latvian Composers Union, Chmn Inspection Comm; Latvian Music Acad, Coun Chmn; Latvian Popular Front, Latvia Music Acad Grp Ldr. *Honours:* Dip, Praesidium, Supreme Coun Latvia, 1973; Dip, Pedagogic Achievements, 1981, Dip, Creative Success, 1985, Min Cultural Affairs, Latvia; F Ivanovs Prize, 1988; Hon Artist, Latvia, 1989. *Hobbies:* Organ building; Folklore; Astronomy; Fishing; Sports (jogging, skiing). *Address:* Kr Barona Str 12, 226011 Riga, Latvia.

JERMYN Helen Williams, Capt, b. 11 Nov 1957, Hong Kong. United States Air Force Officer; Environmental Research Officer. m. Richard Anthony Jermyn Jr, 26 Mar 1990. *Education:* BSc, Chem Engrng, Syracuse, NY, 1979; MSc, Chem Engrng, 1983, MBA, 1987, Univ Rochester. *Appointments:* Test and Dev Engr, Chrysler Corp, Highland Pk, MI, 1979-80; Sr Dev Engr, Mobil Chem Co, Macedon, NY, 1980-85; USAF, 1987-. *Publications:* 15 papers in area of hazardous waste minimisation published in var tech jrnls; 1 US patent application filed. *Memberships:* Am Chem Soc; Am Inst Chem Engrs; Air Force Assn; Soc Am Mil Engrs; Offs Club. *Honours:* Off of Quarter, July-Sept 1990, Off of

Yr, 1990, HQ AF Engrng and Servs Ctr, Tyndall AFB, FL; Off of Quarter, USAF Air Def Weapons Ctr, Tyndall AFB, July Sept 1990; 12 robbons for Bay Co Fair, Bay Co, FL. *Hobbies:* Reading; Swimming; Cross country skiing. *Address:* HQ Air Force Engineering and Services Center, Tyndall Air Force Base, FL 32403, USA. 7.

JERNDAL Jens, Sir, b. 5 Jan 1934, Gothenburg, Sweden. Doctor of Holistic Medicine. m. Ulla B Haggstrom, 16 Oct 1964, div 1974, 3 s. *Education:* MSc, Stockholm, 1958; BA, Uppsala, 1959; Univ courses, Int Law; DIC, Acupuncture, 1982, MD, Med Alternativa, 1987, Colombo, Sri Lanka. *Appointments:* Attache, 1960, 1st Sec, 1965, Royal Swedish Min For Affairs, 1960; Sec, Embassy, Copenhagen, Denmark, 1962; 1st Sec, Embassy, Karachi, Pakistan, 1964; Investment Broker, Pres, Investconsult SL, Real Lanzarote SA, Las Palmas, Spain, 1968-80; Pres, Cosmosophical Fndn, Stockholm, 1977-88; Fndr Pres, Dragon's Hd Ctr Holistic Med, Lanzarote, Canary Islands, Spain, 1983-; Vis Prof, 1987, Prof, Holistic Med, Sr Fac Mbr, 1991, Open Int Univ Complementary Meds. *Publications:* Booklet on Indonesia, 1958; Articles, var mags and newspapers; Lectures, int confs. *Memberships:* Canary Islands Deleg, Assn Swedish Citizens Residing Abroad; Int Coll Acupuncture, Sri Lanka; Medicina Alternativa; Astrological Assn, UK; Am Fedn Astrologers; Fndr Mbr, C'wlth Inst Acupuncture and Natural Meds. *Honours:* KT, Royal Order of Dannebrog, Denmark, 1963; DSc hc, 1988; Knight Commander of Justice, Sovereign Order of St John of Jerusalem, 1989; Kt Grand Cross, Ordre Souverain et Militaire de la Milice du Saint Sepulchre, 1990; Kt of Humanity, K C, Sovereign World Order of the White Cross, 1991. *Hobbies:* Music; History; Philosophy; Psychology; Heraldry. *Address:* Apartado 248, Arrecife de Lanzarote, Canary Islands, E-35500 Spain. 52.

JERNIGAN Michael, b. 22 Aug 1953, Honolulu, HI, USA. Instructional Dev Specialist. m. Peggy A Russell, 16 Apr 1988. *Education:* BS, Ctrl MO State Univ, 1978; MRE, Midwestern Bapt Theo Sem, 1986; Postgrad, Memphis State Univ, 1990-. *Appointments:* Cryptographic Communications Equipment Maintenance, USAF, Offutt AFB, NB, 1972-75; Programmer, Analyst, Electronics Realtors Assn, Shawnee Mission, KS, 1979-81; Electronic Computer Programming Inst, KS City, MO, 1980-82; Proj Mgr, Edutronics, McGraw-Hill, Overland Parks, KS, 1981-83; Instructironal Developer, Shelby State Comm Coll, Memphis, 1987-89; Instructional Dev Specialist, Univ of AR for Med Sci, Lt Rock, 1989-; Cons, AR Mus of Sci & Ind, Lt Rock, 1989-90. *Creative works:* Author, Designer: (video disk prog) Case Study for PTA and Prosthetics Students, 1988-89. *Memberships include:* ACM, 1990-; Int Interactive Communications Soc; AR State Computer Info Interchange; AR Soc for Computer & Info Tech; Soc for Applied Learning Tech; Soc for Computer Applications in Med Care. *Honours:* Kappa Delta Pi, 1990; Psi Chi. *Hobbies:* Reading; Fishing; Camping; Computer Games. *Address:* c/o UAMS/OED, 4301 W Markham, MS 595, Little Rock, AR 72205, USA. 7, 15.

JEROY Frederick Daly, b. 22 June 1937, USA. Int Cons. m. Joan Elizabeth Wickham, 6 Dec 1962. *Education:* BCS; AGSIM (Thunderbird); BFT; Grad Studies: Univ of NSW; Santo Tomas, Hong Kong. *Appointments:* Pacific Multiserves, 1972-79; Waste Mgmt, 1979-81; Corrintec, 1981-84; Venture Capital Fund, 1984-87; US Govt (AID), 1987-90; Pakistan Venture Capital Ltd, 1990-. *Publications:* Various Bus Articles; US and Foreign Publs. *Memberships:* World- wide Am C of C; Hong Kong Club; Army Navy Club; Am Clubs, Hong Kong, Sydney, Buenos Aires, Tokyo, Rio de Janeiro, Taipei, Bogota. *Hobbies:* Collector - Chinese Art; Modern Paintings. *Address:* 4944 Woodway Drive, Suite 5, Houston, TX 77056, USA.

JESSUP Richard Edward, b. 4 Nov 1932, San Fran, CA, USA. Ordained Min; Sch Admnstr; Tchr. m. Shirley

M Book, 18 June 1954, 2 s, 1 d. *Education:* BA, Southern CA Coll, 1955; BA, La Verne Univ, 1960; MA, CA State Polytech Univ, 1974. *Appointment:* Prin, Neighbourhood Christian Sch, Bellevue, 1989-. *Publications:* Poetry, The Pentecostal Evangel, 1981-90. *Memberships:* Chmn 1990-91, Prins Assn of Christian Schs; Northwest Assn of Christian Sch Admnstrs; Int Fellowship of Christian Sch Admnstrs. *Honour:* Tchr of the Yr, Atascadero Unified Sch Dist, Atascadero. *Hobbies:* Hiking; Running; Books; Christian art. *Address:* c/o Neighbourhood Church, 625 - 140th Avenue NE, Bellevue, WA 98005, USA. 15.

JEYE Peter Austin, b. 5 Sept 1959, Ridgewood, NJ, USA. Software Exec; Sr VP. m. Emy, 27 Oct 1990. *Education:* BA 1980, MA 1982, Univ of Ctrl FL. *Appointments:* WKIS Radio, Orlando, 1978-81; Acacia Grp of FL, Orlando, 1981-82; Kiachman Corp, Orlando, 1982-85; Newtrend, Orlando, 1985-. *Publications:* Inducing Resistance to Persuasion, 1981; How to Shop for Effective User Documentation, 1988; 10 Steps to Better Relations With Your Software Vendor, 1988. *Honours:* Miser Users Grp Outstg Achmt Awd, 1987; Newtrend Extraordinary Client Satisfaction Awd, 1988. *Hobbies:* Collectibles; Jazz music; Golf; Baseball; Writing. *Address:* 2600 Technology Drive, Orlando, FL 32804, USA. 7, 132.

JI Shanyu, b. 27 Apr 1955, Shanghai, China. Asst Prof; Maths Edr. m. Zhou Qien, 24 Sept 1983, 1 d. *Education:* BS, East China Normal Univ, 1982; MA 1986, PhD 1989, Johns Hopkins Univ. *Appointments:* Fac, East China Normal Univ, 1982-85; Vis Asst Prof, Johns Hopkins Univ; 1988-89; Asst Prof, Univ of Houston, 1989-. *Contributions to:* Articles to Profl Journs. *Membership:* Am Math Soc. *Hobbies:* Music; Reading. *Address:* 2811 Blue Mist Drive, Sugarland, TX 77478, USA. 7.

JI Xun-Jie, b. 12 Oct 1918, Huzhou, Zhejiang, China. Ret'd. m. Xue Zi Lu, 23 Apr 1950, 1 s, 1 d. *Education:* Dip, Soochow Univ Middle Sch, 1936-38; WuXi Inst of Chinese Classics, 1939-40. *Appointments:* San-Yu Commercial Sch, Huzhou, 1943-51; Shanghai No 64 Middle Sch, 1951- 56; Dept of Hist, Shanghai Educl Coll, 1956-70, 1978-84; Dept of Hist, Shanghai Normal Univ, HudDong Normal Univ, 1970-78. *Publications:* Some Corners of the Economic Situation in Liao Dynasty, 1980; The General Situation of Criminal Law in Liao Dynasty, 1982; Supplementary Explanation on the Tomb- Inscription of Liao Ja Liye, 1985; Some Problems Concerning the Nomenclature, Tribe Organisation and Origination of Qidan, 1985; Textual Criticism about the Emperor's Biography in Liao Dynasty, 1986; Study of Liao Ye-Li-Yuan-Nin's Tomb Inscription, 1987; On the Study of the Tribe of Liao Empress Xiao-Ruiti, 1987; Textual Criticism of Geographical Notes in Liao Dynasty History. *Membership:* Shanghai Hist Soc. *Honours:* Philos & Social Sci Rsch Thesis Prize, Shanghai Univs, 1984; Hon Cert for 40 yrs Tchng, 1985; Shanghai Philos & Social Sci Study Prize, 1986; Social Sci Acad Thesis Prize, 1988. *Hobbies:* Music; Sports News in TV; Literature. *Address:* 19/1295 Fu Xing Zhong Road, Shanghai 200031, China.

JIA Ping Wa, b. 21 Feb 1952, Danfeng, Shaanxi, China. Writer. m. 1 Jan 1979, 1 d. *Education:* Grad, Chinese Lit Dept, Northwestern Univ, 1975. *Appointments:* Ed, Shaanxi People's Pubing Hse, 1975-80; Fndn of Lit and Art Circles, Xi'an, 1980-91. *Creative works:* Shangzhou; Disturbance; Breed; First Mouth of the Year; Dog of Heaven; Taibai; Selected Proses of Ping Wa Jia; Author of over 40 books. *Memberships:* Dir, China Writers' Union; Vice Chmn, Shaanxi Writers' Union; Chmn, Fndn of Lit and Art Circles of Xi'an; Pres, Prose Writer Rsch, Shaanxi. *Honours:* Ful Moon, Prize for the First Excellent Short Novel, 1978; First Mouth of the Year, Prize for China's 3rd Excellent Novel, 1984; Brake, Prize for the First Comic Dialogues, 1987; Disturbance, Mobil Pegasus Prize for Literatuze Winning Novel, 1988; Prose Love's Course, Prize for the 1st Excellent Prose, 1989;

Over 30 prizes for Newspapers and Lit. *Hobbies:* Reading; Writing; Drawing; Playing all kinds of chess. *Address:* No 2 Lianhu Lane, Da Lianhua Chi Street, Xian Writers Union, China.

JIA Ping-Xi, b. 21 Dec 1937, Shandong Province, P R China. Profl Painter. m. (1) 2 d, (2)Ying-Chun Zeng, 25 May 1989. *Education:* BA, LuXun Acad of Fine Arts, 1959-64. *Appointments:* Profl Painter, 1979-; Official Full-time Artist, Heilongjiang Province, 1979-; Assoc Prof of Art, Heilongjiang Province, 1987-. *Creative works include:* Mountain Pearl, 1981; The Image of This World, 1990; Boundless and Indistinct, 1990; Day by Day, 1991. *Memberships:* Chinese Nat Artistss Assn, 1985-; Contemporary Chinese Fine Brushwork Painting Inst of P R China, 1987-; Chmn, Flower-and-Bird Painting Rsch Inst of Heilongjiang Province, 1987-; Sec Gen, Heilongjiang Provincial Traditional Chinese Painting Rsch Inst, 1989-; Dir, Chinese Nat Artists Assn, Heilongjiang Br, 1989-. *Honours include:* Nat Fine Arts Prize for Autumn Meditation, Chinese Art Gall, 1984; 2nd Prize for Endless Nights, Heilongjiang Provincial Painting Exhib, 1988; 1st Prize, Painting Exhib of Northeast China for Transcience, 1989; Excellent Art Prize for Water Mirror, Japan Int Arts Exchange Exhib, 1989. *Hobbies:* Running; Watching TV; Seeing films. *Address:* Chinese National Artists Association, Heilongjiang Branch, Harbin 150006, China.

JIANG Hesen, b. 18 July 1928, Haian, Jiangsu Province, China. Lit Histn; Novelist; Critic. m. Xiaocui Zhang, 8 Mar 1955, 2 s. *Education:* Grad, Dept of Journalism, Fudan Univ, 1952. *Appointments:* Reporter, Xinhua News Agcy, Beijing Br, 1952-53; Ed, Wenyibao (The Lit and Art Gazette), Beijing, 1953-56; Sr Rsch Fellow, Inst of Lit 1956-; Prof (Doct Tutor), Grad Sch, Chinese Acad of Social Scis, 1956-; Concurrent, Prof, Nanjing Normal Univ; Invited to do Lectures in Japan, 1982. *Publications:* Books: The History of Chinese Literature (co-author), 1965; A Treatise on A Dream of Red Mansions, 1959, revised ed 1981, 3rd ed 1990; Annotations on Selected Poems of Tang Dynasty, 1978; A Survey of A Dream of Red Mansions, 1979; The Howling Wind, 1981; An Introduction to A Dream of Red Mansions (translated into Japanese), 1985; The Intermittent Drizzles, 1985. Articles incl: Life and Work of Du Fu, A Great Singer of His Time, 1962; Tugging the Whale in the Blue Sea - the Boldness of Du Fu's Poetry, 1962. *Memberships:* Vice Chmn, China Soc of a Dream of Red Mansions; Chinese Writer's Assn; Comm Mbr, Chinese People's Pol Consultative Conf. *Hobbies:* Painting; Calligraphy; Music; Photography. *Address:* Institute for Literature, Chinese Academy of Social Sciences, Beijing 100732, China.

JIANG Jaryuan, b. 13 Aug 1932, Wuhu, China. Prof of Anatomy; Pres. m. Shunhua Cui, 7 Feb 1957, 1 s, 2 d. *Education:* Bach, Suzhou Med Coll, 1955; PhD, Anhui Med Coll, 1958. *Appointments:* Lectr, Anhui Med Coll, 1958-70; Prof, Bangbu Med Coll, 1970-80; Prof, Dean of Studies, Pres, Wannan Med Coll, 1980-. *Publications:* Author of 40 articles, 1958-91; Surgical Anatomy of Lungs, 1961; Minute Anatomy of Respiratory System, 1983; Clinical Anatomy of Lungs, 1989; Anatomy, 1991. *Memberships:* Standing Coun, Sec-Gen, Soc of Anatomy, Anhui Br; Hon Chmn, Coun of Forensic Med Soc, Anhui Province. *Honour:* Nat Model Wkr of Educl System. *Hobbies:* Basketball; Calligraphy. *Address:* 406 The 8th Building, Wannan Medical College, Wuhu, Anhui 241001, China.

JIANG Shaoyu, b. 25 Jan 1940, Shanghai, China. Prof. m. Xu Fulian, 1 Aug 1972, 1 s. *Education:* Grad, Dept of Chinese Lang and Lit, Peking Univ, 1962. *Appointments:* Tchr, Rschr 1962-82, Assoc Prof 1983, Vice Chmn 1987-89, Full Prof 1989, Chinese Dept, Peking Univ; Rsch Assoc, Sinological Inst, Leiden Univ, Holland, 1981-82; Vis Prof, Dept of Asian Langs, Stanford Univ, 1989-90; Rsch, OH State Univ, 1991. *Publications:* Dictionary of Frequently Used Words in Classical Chinese (co-author), 1979; An Outline of

Classical Chinese Vocabulary, 1989; A Study of the Language of Tang Poetry, 1990; Comprehensive Source Materials for the Study of Ancient Mandarin (co-author), 1990. *Membership:* Vice Sec Gen, All China Soc of Linguistics. *Honours:* Young Linguistics Prize, China Social Acad, 1984; Scientific Rsch Achmt Prize, Peking Univ, 1986, 1991. *Hobbies:* Reading Chinese Classical Poems. *Address:* No 110, Building 56, Changchun-yuan, Peking University, Beijing 100871, China.

JIANG Sheng, b. Taizhou, China. Maths Edr. m. Ruichen Chen, 2 d. *Education:* Dept of Maths, Yanzhou Tchrs' Coll, 1958-60; Inst of Maths, Fudan Univ, 1978-79. *Appointments:* Asst 1961-77, Assoc Prof 1978-85, Prof 1986-, Yangzhou Tchrs' Coll; Reviewer of Math Rev, 1981-. *Publications:* 25 articles on differential geometry; 5 articles on combinatorics; 10 books & about 40 articles on math educ. *Memberships:* Dir, Jiangsu Provincial Math Soc; Chinese Math Soc; Chinese Phys Soc. *Honours:* Scientific Awds, Jiangsu Province, 1978, 1979, 1985. *Hobbies:* Reading; Music; Drawing. *Address:* Department of Mathematics, Yangzhou Teachers' College, Yangzhou, Jiangsu 225002, China.

JIANG Shengyang, *Address:* Metallurgical Dept, Guizhou Institute of Tech, Guiyang, Guizhou, China.

JIANG Shi Wei, b. 16 Nov 1950, Shenyang, China. Poet. m. Huizhu Wu, 24 Apr 1991, 1 s. *Appointments:* Musticated Youth, 1969-76; Wkr, 1976-78. *Creative works:* Mang Ke Shiji; Mei you shijian de shijian; Ye shi. *Honour:* Translation of Mei you shijian de shijian was awded a prize in Japan for best transl. *Address:* 414 Lou 1 Mem 95 Mang Ke, Jingsong Sigu, Beijing, China.

JIANG Yi-Qing, b. 5 June 1929, Jiang-Shu, P R China. Med Dr; Prof of Cardiology; Dir of Cardiology. *Education:* Grad, Nanking Medical Univ, 1952; Postgrad study, PUMC. *Appointments:* Postgrad Dr, Dept of Med, 1952-54; Dr of Med, 1954-60; Chief Dr of Cardiology, 1960-80; Dr, Prof of Cardiology, 1980-91. *Publications include:* Experimental coronary spasm induced thrombosis & AMI prevented by intravenous nifecipine, 1988; Animal model of coronary spasm-thrombosis-AMI, 1990; A Clinco-Pathological Res of Sudden Death due to Coronary Heart Disease, 1991, Chinese Medical Sciences Journal, 1991; Nitroglycerin and heparin iv infusion in treating instable angina pectoris for prevention of acute myocardial infarction. *Memberships:* Chinese Assn of Cardiology, 1991; Int Soc of Cardiovascular Pharmacotherapy. *Honours include:* Outstg Prize of Chinese Women, 1980, 1988; won Scientific and Tech Awds of the Armed Forces, 1987-90; Outstg Invention Prize of Beijing, 1988; Outstg Tchr of Air Force, 1989. *Hobby:* Literature. *Address:* Department of Cardiology, General Hospital of Air Force, West Diao Yu Tai No 30, Beijing 100036, China.

JICHA Josef Ladislav, b. 7 Nov 1934, Plzen, Czechoslovakia. Painter; Graphic Artist. m. Marie Anna Kulasova, 13 Mar 1961, 2 d. *Appointments:* Libn, Municipal Lending Lib, Plzen, 1956-59; Graphic Artist, Park of Culture and Rest, Plzen, 1960-68; Freelance Artist, 1969-. *Creative works:* Traditional blue-white wall calendars have been made on linen with fairy-tale, architectural elements or folklore motifs for the Czechoslovak TV, Skoda Concern, Prague Investor of Transport Constructions, Czech State Insurance Co, Ale-Agency, Prague, 1960-; Ways to Princesses, 1961; Picture postcards, various illustrations, plenty of ex-libris, free and applied graphics, free drawings, architectural painting. *Memberships:* Chmn of the Artistic Bd for Painting, Sculpture and Graphic Arts, Assn on Czech Artists, 1962-; Hon Mbr, Czech Union of Fruit Growers and Garden Owners, 1980; Nat Geographic Soc, 1989; Union of Czech Creative Artists, 1990-. *Honours:* Reg Prize, West Bohemian Nat Com for exceptional results in applied and propaganda graphic arts, 1984; Hon Awd, Com of the Czech Fund of Fine Arts, Prague, 1984. *Hobbies:* Reading; Publicity;

Talks especially club house talks with the youth. *Address:* Sokolovska 133, 323 19 Plzen, Czechoslovakia.

JIMOH-ATOYEBI Nusirat Bolatito, b. 26 Dec 1966, Minna, Nigeria. Technologist. *Education:* Dip in Elec Engrng, 1984-87; Higher Nat Dip in Electronics & Communication Engr, 1990-92. *Appointments:* Tech Off, Nigerian TV Auth, Minna; Basic TV Engr Course at TV Coll, Jos, Nigeria, 1989. *Memberships:* Nigerian Red Cross Soc; Quater Mistress; Nigerian Assn of Media Women, Niger State Chapt. *Hobby:* Collection of International Stamps. *Address:* S W 326 Kwangila Road, Minna, Niger State, Nigeria.

JIN Guang Xi, b. 15 Feb 1936, Soochow, Jiangsu, China. Prof. m. 3 July 1966, 2 d. *Education:* BSc 1957, MBA 1959, Northeast Univ of Tech. *Appointments:* Asst 1959-63, Instr 1963-83, Assoc Prof 1982-87, Prof 1987, Northeast Univ of Tech. *Publication:* Econometrics, Productivity Improvements in Chinese Iron and Steel Industry. *Memberships:* Am Inst of Indl Engrs (Sr); Pres, Liaoning Mgmt Modernization Inst; VP, Liaoning System Simulation Inst. *Hobby:* Reading. *Address:* Department of Management Engineering, Northeast University of Technology, Cultural Road, Shenyang, Liaoning 110006, China. 156.

JIN Ling, b. 12 Nov 1959, Harbin, China. Chinese Painting Artist & Calligraphist; Art Ed. m. Wei-Jun Li, 14 Oct 1990, 1 d. *Education:* Bach's degree, Art Dept, Harbin Tchrs Univ, 1979-83. *Appointment:* Art Ed, Calligraphy Appreciation, Heilongjiang Calligraphist Assn, 1983-. *Creative works include:* Life, 1987; Black Peony, 1989; Long, Long Years, 1989; Blue Dream, 1991; The Attraction in Woods, 1991. *Memberships:* Chinese Artists Assn; Chinese Calligraphist Assn; Heilongjiang Chinese Painting Acad; Heilongjiang Art of Designing and Binding Book Assn; Coun, Heilongjiang Youth Artists and Calligraphist Assn; VP, Yia Xin Art Sch. *Honours:* Excellent Awd, The First and Second Youth Art and Calligraphy Exhib, 1985, 1986; 2nd Awd, The First Heilongjian Calligraphy and Seal-carving Match, 1987; Excellent Awd, Seal-carving Match of Chengfeng Cup, 1988; Two 2nd Awds, The Seventh Heilongjiang Art Exhib, 1989; 2nd Awd, Chinese Flower-bird Paintings Exhib; Excellent Awd, Guangdong Painting Exhib, 1991. *Hobbies:* Photography; Travelling; Singing. *Address:* Heilongjiang Calligraphist Association, No 16 Yue Jing Street, Nanggang District, Harbin, China.

JIRAL Jeannine Carol, b. 29 Apr 1955, Shiner, TX, USA. Acctng Mgr. div. *Education:* BBA, Univ of Houston, 1990. *Appointments:* Acctng Clerk 1979, Scctng Supvsr 1982, Acctng Mge 1985, ITT Snyder. *Honour:* Gen Mgr's Awd, ITT Snyder's Recognition for Outstg Effort and Achmt, 1991. *Hobbies:* Art; Music; Dance; Scuba. *Address:* 9807 Sage Aspen, Houston, TX 77089, USA. 7.

JIRANEK Jaroslav, b. 21 Aug 1922, Praha, Czech. Musicologist; Aestheticean. m. (1) Jarmila Konigova, 31 Mar 1950, (2) Milada Ladmanova, 8 Feb 1963, 1 s, 2 d. *Education:* PhD 1948, Doc habil 1961, Charles Univ, Prague; DrSc, Acad of Scis, 1966. *Appointments:* Dir of Artistic Prog, Radio Prague, 1950-52; Redactor en chief of mus journ Hudebni rozhledy, 1953-60; Dir, Musicological Inst, Acad of Scis, 1962-71; Prof, Acad of Music, Prague, 1990-91. *Publications include:* Assafiew's Intonation Theory, its Genesis and Import, 1967; Musicological Studies, 1981; Smetana's Operas, I 1984, II 1989; Zu Grundfragen der musikalischen Semiotik, 1985; Essays on Romanticism, 1989. *Memberships:* Czechoslovak Soc of Composers, Musicians, Musicologists, 1953-89; Deutsche Gesellschaft fur Musikforschung, 1965-; Aesthetic Soc, Acad of Scis, 1975-; Czech Musical Soc, 1980-; Czech Musicological Soc, 1990-. *Honours:* Czechoslovak State Prize, 1960; Prize of Czechoslovak Acad of Scis, 1967; Nat Prize of Czech Repub, 1987. *Hobbies:* Arts and

Sciences; Gardening. *Address:* U vinne revy 6, 106 00 Praha 10, Czechoslovakia. 21.

JIWA Asmina, b. 31 Mar 1952, Mombasa, Kenya. Applications Scientist. *Education:* BSc Hons 1973, MSc 1974, Univ of Karachi, Karachi, Pakistan; MS, Univ of MA, USA, 1986. *Appointments:* Clin Labs, Karachi, 1975-76; ILRAD, Nairobi, Kenya, 1978-82; Univ of MI, Ann Arbor, 1987-88; Meridian Instruments Inc, 1988-91. *Memberships:* FRSTM&H; Am Soc of Cell Biology; Am Assn of Women in Sci; Assoc, Inst of Med Lab; Pres, F-Tech, 1992. *Honour:* Outstg Young Women of Am, 1987. *Hobbies:* Travel; Cross cultural activities; Photography; Global village; Beyond War; Dancing; Classical music; Reading; Cooking. *Address:* 2124 Blue Lac Drive, Haslett, MI 48840, USA.

JODLOWSKI Marek, b. 5 May 1941, Kielce, Poland. Author; Journalist. m. Teresa Slowikowska, 13 Feb 1961, 1 d. *Education:* Grad, Wroclaw Univ, 1964. *Appointments:* Vice Chief, Opole, monthly mag, 1975-81, 1985-91; Vice Chief, Trybuna Opolska, daily, 1990-. *Publications:* Osad, 1973; Dowod osobisty, 1978; Psia fuga, 1990. *Membership:* Polish Writers Union, 1975-82. *Honours:* Polish Poetry Fest, Lodz, 1974; Voivode of Opole Province Awd. *Hobby:* Strolling. *Address:* ul Stefana Grota-Roweckiego, 45-256 Opole, Poland. 3, 11.

JOENSEN John Paul, b. 8 Oct 1952, NY, USA. Admnstv Dir of Geriatrics. m. Kim Langenbacher, 27 Sept 1982, 2 s, 1 d. *Education:* Bach's of Social Work, Stockton State Coll, 1982; Master of Social Work, Rutgers Univ, 1983. *Appointments:* Psychotherapist 1983-, Asst Dir of Geriatrics 1985-88, Dir of Geriatrics 1988-, Monmouth Med Ctr. *Publications:* Author of over 50 published articles. *Memberships:* Nat Assn of Social Wkrs; Fellow and Dipl, Bd of Med Psychotherapists. *Honour:* Nat Winner, Discharge Planning Prog, 1989. *Hobbies:* Tennis; Reading. *Address:* Monmouth Medical Centre, Department of Geriatrics, 300 Second Avenue, Long Branch, NJ 07740, USA. 176.

JOHANSEN Ulla Christine, b. 17 June 1927, Tallinn, Estonia. Ret'd Prof. 1 s. *Education:* PhD 1953. *Appointments:* Hd, Dept of Anthropological Mus, Hamburg, 1961-65; Asst, Assoc Prof, Univ of Heidelberg, 1965-73; Full Prof, Hd of Dept of Anthropology, Cologne Univ, 1973-90. *Publications:* Die Ornamentik der Jakuten, 1954; Gastarbeiterfamilien (with Barbara Wolbert), 1981; Ed of 2 Anthropological Series and Zeitschrift fur Ethnologie; 49 articles in scientific journs. *Memberships:* 6 Assns for Anthropology and Orientalistics; Pres, German Anthropological Assn, 1985- 89. *Address:* Institut fur Volkerkunde der Universitat, Albertus Magnus-Platz, D 5000 Koln 41, Germany. 43.

JOHANSEN-BERG John, b. 4 Nov 1935, Middlesborough, Eng. Min of Relig; Ldr: Comm for Reconciliation. m. Joan Scott Parnham, 17 July 1971, 2 s, 1 d. *Education:* BA, BD, Leeds Univ, 1954-58; MA, Cambridge Univ, 1958- 61. *Appointments:* Tutor, Westminster Coll, Cambridge, 1961-62; Min, St Ninian's, Luton, 1962-70; Fdr Min, St Katharine's, Dunstable; Rock Ch Ctr, Liverpool, 1970-77; St Andrew's, Ealing, 1977-86; Ldr, Comm for Reconciliation, 1986-; Minister-Beacon Church Centre, 1992. *Publications:* Prayers of the Way, 1987; Prayers of Pilgrimage, 1988; Prayers of Prophecy, 1990; Prayers on The Way, revised and enlarged, 1992. *Memberships:* Sponsor, Former Vice Chmn, Christian Concern for Southern Africa; Sponsor, Former Chmn, Clergy against Nuclear Arms; Mbr of Forum, Churches Together in England; Former Chmn, Christian Fellowship Trust; Trustee, Brit Irish Exchange. *Honours:* Moderator of Gen Assembly, United Reformed Ch, 1980-81; Fdr, Comm for Reconciliation, 1985; Moderator, Free Ch Fed Coun, 1987, 1988; Fdr, Romanian Concern, 1990; Fdr, Ecumenical Order of Min, 1990. *Hobbies:* Hill and mountain walking; Golf; Creative writing. *Address:*

Barnes Close, Chadwich Manor, off Money Lane, Nr Bromsgrive, Worcs B61 0RA, England.

JOHN Joshy, b. 9 Oct 1940, India. Cons Physn. m. Tersa, 25 Jan 1970, 2 s, 1 d. *Education:* BSc 1959, MBBS 1964, Kerala Univ; MD, Univ of Sheffield, 1984. *Appointments:* Cons Physn, Venereology, Trent reg Hlth Auth, 1976-81; Hon Lectr, Div Med Univ of Sheffield, 1976-81; Cons Physn, GU Med, North West Thames Reg Hlth Auth, 1981-; Hon Cons, Westminster Hosp, London, 1990-. *Publication:* Non-Gonococcal Urethritis Therapy, Asymptomatic Gonorrhoea in Men and Abnormal Forms of Trichomonas Vaginalis. *Memberships:* Examr PhD, Univ of Madras, India; Int Union Against Venereal Diseases & Treponematoses; Med Soc Study VD; Am VD Assn; Indian Assn Study Sexually Transmitted Diseases; FRSM; BMA. *Honour:* Gold Medal, BSc, Kerala Univ. *Hobbies:* Swimming; Reading; Travelling; Learning about foods, wines and spirits. *Address:* Jostre, 30 Magnaville Road, Bushey Heath, Watford, Herts WD2 1PP, England.

JOHNS Alan Wesley, b. 27 Mar 1931, Farnborough, Hants, Eng. Exec Dir; Pres of Sight Savers. m. Joan Margaret Wheeler, 17 Apr 1954, 1 s, 1 d. *Education:* Cert Ed, Univ of Southampton; BSc Econ, Univ of London. *Appointments:* Tchr, Second Schs, Wilts Lea, 1953-61; Ed Off, Govt St Helena, 1961-68; Dir of Ed, Govt Seychelles, 1968-74; Dir of Ed, Govt Gibralter, 1974-78; Dep Dir, Royal C'wlth Soc for the Blind, 1978-83. *Memberships:* Chmn, Partnership Comm of Int Non Govt Orgs in Blindness Prevention, 1983-91; Chmn, Consultative Grp of Int NGOs to WHO prog, 1986-90; VP 1986-90, Pres 1990-, Int Agcy for Prevention of Blindness; Fellow Royal Society of Arts; Pres, Sight Savers, 1984-. *Honours:* OBE 1973; CMG 1990. *Hobbies:* Travel; Sailing; Home maintenance; Rotary Club of Haywards. *Address:* Sitwell; Courtmead Road, Cuckfield, W Sussex RH17 5LR, England.

JOHNS Allan Thomas, b. 14 Apr 1942, Exeter, Eng. Prof of Elec Engrng. m. Marion Franklin, 23 Sept 1972, 2 d. *Education:* BSc first class hons 1966, PhD 1971, DSc 1982, Univ of Bath. *Appointments:* Ast Dist Engr, SWEB, 1963-68; Prof of Elec & Electronic Engrng, City Univ, London, 1984-91; Hd of Dept 1989-91, Prof of Elec Engrng 1991-, Univ of Bath. *Publications:* Author of over 130 Learned Soc Paper in major int journs on Elec & Electronic Engrng. *Memberships:* FIEE; C Eng; FRSA; Ed, IEE Power Engrng Books 1984-, Power Engrng Journ 1989-; IEE Power Divisional Bd, 1986-; Chair, SERC Elect, Rsch Comm 1989-; SERC Elect Power Ints Comm, 1989-; Pres, Swindon NE Bowling Club, 1990. *Honours:* 3 Learned Soc Premiums, IEE G&S Premium 1967, The Crompton Premium 1982, Power Divisional Bd Premium 1988. *Hobbies:* Ice dancing; Bowling; Walking; Singing; Piano. *Address:* School of Electronics & Electrical Engineering, University of Bath, Claverton Down, Bath BA2 7AY, England.

JOHNS Michael Stephen Mackelcan, b. 18 Oct 1943, Radlett, Herts, Eng. Solicitor; Mng Ptnr. m. (1) 2 s, (2) 10 Mar 1979, 1 d. *Education:* Marlborough Coll, 1957-62. *Appointments:* Theodore Goddard & Co, 1963-69; Allen & Overy, 1969-72; Nicholson Graham & Jones, 1972-. *Memberships:* Law Soc; Inst of Dirs. *Hobbies:* Cricket; Golf; Gardening; Theatre. *Address:* 22 Bowerdean Street, London SW6 3TW, England. 32.

JOHNSON Frederick Dean, b. 27 Feb 1911, Shreve, OH, USA. Ret'd Cons. m. Haulwen Elizabeth Richey, 19 June 1937, 1 s, 2 d. *Education:* Artium Baccalaureum, The Coll of Wooster, OH, 1935; Post Grad, Univ of Akron, OH, 1940-41. *Appointments:* Dir of Rsch, Dev, Quality Control, J M Smucker Co, Orrville, 1936-61; Ruling Elder, Presby Ch, USA, 1947-; Dir of Rsch & Quality Control, Bama Co, Birmingham, Alabama, Houston, Texas 1961-64; Bama Food Prods Div, Borden Foods Div, Borden Inc, Birmingham & Houston, 1964- 78; Cons, 1978-; Repub Precinct Chmn 1981-. *Publication:* Fruit Utilization, 1964.

Memberships: Mbr 50 yrs, Past Sec, Past Chmn, Wooster Ohio Sect, Southeastern TX Sect, ACS; Charter Mbr, Inst of Food Technologists, 1939; AAAS, 1968- . *Honours:* Dir, Afton Oaks Civic Club, 1967-70, 1982- ; US Delegate to WHO/WFO Codex Alimentarius Commn Comm on Processed Fruits (for the estab of world food standards), Dept of State, Washington DC, 1973, 1974, 1975; Cit and Plaque 1974, Hon Mbr 1978- , Int Jelly & Preserve Assn. *Address:* 4546 Shetland Lane, Houston, TX 77027, USA.

JOHNSON Fridthjofur O, b. 27 Feb 1956, Reykjavik, Iceland. Mng Dir. m. Kristin Amundadottir. *Education:* Hons, Commercial Sch of Iceland, 1976; Cand Oecon, Hons, Univ of Iceland, 1980; MBA, Hons, Babson Coll, MA, 1983. *Appointments:* Mktng Trainee, The Pilsbury Co, MPLS, 1981; Sales Mgr, HP Denmark, 1983; Mktng Mgr, Hewlett Packard, Iceland, 1984- 87; Mng Dir, Blikksmidjan, Ventilations, 1987-91; Mng Dir, O Johnson & Kaaber, 1991. *Creative works:* Thesis on Competing Airports on N- Atlantic, 1980; Office Automation, 1985; Lectures on Marketing, 1989;Co-author of programme for the school of marketing and sales under Management Assn of Iceland. *Memberships:* Beta Gamma Sigma; Pres, The Mktng Assn of Iceland, 1987-90; Ed Comm, Icelandic Assn of Economists and Bus People; PR Comm for Bd of Commerce, Iceland; Bd of Dir, Mgmt Assn of Iceland. *Hobbies:* Marketing & Management: Theories, Practice, Literature; Fly fishing; Soccer; Skiing; Travel. *Address:* Hoergshlid 2, 105 Reykjavik, Iceland. 52.

JOHNSON Michael David Clarke, b. 24 May 1938, East Bergholt. Asst Sec, Dept of Trade and Ind. m. Sarah Janet Francis, 5 Sept 1964, 2 d. *Education:* BA, Jesus Coll, Cambridge, 1957-60. *Appointments:* Bd of Trade, 1960-67; Min of Tech, 1967-70; Hon Treas, Handel Opera Soc, London, 1967-85; Prin, HM Treasury, 1970-73; Asst Sec, Dept of Trade and Ind, 1975-; Asst Sec to Dirs, Royal Opera Hse, Covent Gdn, 1985-. *Hobbies:* Travel; Walking; Books; Theatre; Gardening; Music. *Address:* 10 Avenue Road, London N6 5DW, England.

JOHNSON Winston Conrad, b. 27 Apr 1943, Wellborn, FL, USA. Maths Edr. *Education:* BA 1971, MEd 1977, EdS 1979, Univ of FL. *Appointments:* Math Tchr, Columbia HS, Lake City, 1971-76; Math Tchr, Jr HS, Lake City, 1979-80; Math Prof, Ctrl FL Comm Coll, Ocala, 1981-91. *Memberships:* FL Developmental Educl Assn; Treas 1990-92, Nat Assn for Developmental Educ; Nat Coun of Tchrs of Maths; Math Assn of Am; Am Math Assn of Two-Yr Colls. *Hobbies:* Music; Sports; Reading history. *Address:* Beach Street, PO Box 37, Wellborn, FL 32094, USA. 7, 15.

JOHNSON d'Elaine A Herard, b. 19 Mar 1932, Puyallup, WA, USA. Artist; Coutic; Writer; Edr; Lectr. m. John L Johnson, 22 Dec 1926. *Education:* BA, Ctrl WA State Univ, Ellensburg, 1954; MA, Univ of WA, Seattle, 1958. *Appointments incl:* Art Instrn, TV-9, Univ of WA, Seattle, 1968; Art Critic, Capuchin Fathers, Rome, Italy, 1976; Supvsr- Hostess for Japanese Artist-Instr, Seattle Pub Schs, Seattle, 1977; Art Cons, WA State Area, 1978-. Lectr: The Artist in Six Chapters, Kitsap Co Art League, Port Orchard, 1987; Evolution of d'Elain, the Artist, Nat League of Am Pen Women, Seattle Chapt, 1989; Featured Artist, 37 major paintings, Rosicrucian Egyptian Mus, Rosicrucian Park, San Jose. Art Juror: Poulsbo Art Fest, Poulsbo, 1978; Juror, Rite of Autumn Art Show, Prim Gall, Edmonds Comm Coll Campus, Lynnwood, 1988. *Creative works include:* Invitational Exhibit, Art Quest, San Fran, 1987; Thirtieth Annual Puget Sound Area Exhibit, Frye Art Mus, Seattle, 1988; Featured Artist, The Prince George Art Gall, BC, Canada, 1989; Juried Exhib, Episc Ch of St David, Seattle, 1989; Featured Artist, Nordic Heritage Mus, Seattle, 1990; Featured Artist, Peace Exhib in Japan, 1991. *Memberships include:* IBC Int Cong on Arts and Communication, New Orleans 1986, Madrid, Spain 1987; World Inst of Achmt, Raleigh, 1988-; Hon Appt, Rsch Bd of Advsr, Am Biog Inssst, Inc, Raleigh, 1988-

. *Honours include:* Hon Mention, Thirtieth Annual Puget Sound Area Exhibit 1988, Hon Mention, Nat League of Am Pen Women 1989, Frye Art Mus, Seattle; First Recipient, Nat League of Am Pen Women Art Scholarship, 1990. *Hobbies include:* Scuba-diving; Collecting sea shells and sea artifacts; Studying violin. *Address:* 16122 72nd Avenue W, Edmonds, WA 98026, USA. 5, 9, 15, 37, 52, 138, 152, 155, 156.

JOHNSON-LAIRD Philip Nicholas, b. 12 Oct 1936, Rothwell, Nr Leeds, Eng. Prof. m. Maureen Mary Sullivan, 1 Aug 1959, 1 s, 1 d. *Education:* BA Hon 1964, PhD 1967, Univ Coll, London. *Appointments:* Quantity Surveyor & Misc Jobs, 1952-64; Lectr, Dept of Psychology, Univ Coll London, 1967-73; Rdr, Prof, Lab of Expmtl Psychology, Sussex Univ, 1973- 82; Asst Dir, MRC Applied Psychology Unit, Cambridge, 1982-89; Prof of Psychology, Princeton Univ, 1989-. *Publications include:* The Psychology of Deduction (with P C Wason), 1972; Language and Perception (with G A Miller), 1976; Mental Models, 1983; The Computer & the Mind, 1988; Deduction (with Ruth Bryne), 1991. *Memberships:* FRS; FBA; BPsS; Expmtl Psychology Soc; Linguistics Assn, GB; Soc of Expmtl Psychologists; Govng Bd, Cognitive Sci Soc; Int Soc for Rsch on Emotion; Psychonomics Soc; Eastern Psychological Assn; Int Pragmatics Assn. *Honours:* Rosa Morison Medal, Univ Coll, London, 1964; James Sully Scholar, 1964-68; Spearman Medal 1974, Pres's Awd 1985, BPsS; Hon Doct, Univ of Gothenburg, 1983; Medaglia D'Onore, Univ of Florence, 1989. *Hobbies:* Conversation; Arguement; The Arts; Playing modern jazz piano. *Address:* Department of Psychology, Princeton University, Green Hall, Princeton, NJ 08544, USA.

JOHNSTON Thomas, b. 27 June 1927, Kintyre, Scotland. Dir; Chartered Engr. m. Gwendoline Jean Bird, 24 Dec 1949, 1 s, 3 d. *Education:* BSc, Univ of Glasgow. *Appointments:* Mng Dir 1979-89, Chmn 1989-90, BARR & STROUD Ltd; Dir, Scottish Amicable Life Assurance Soc; Dir, Glasgow Dev Agcy; West Bd, Bank of Scotland; Chmn, Sci Projs (Scotland) Ltd. *Memberships:* FIEE; Past Pres, Scottish Engrng Employees; FRSA. *Honours:* OBE 1982; Fellowship, Paisley Coll, 1990; D.Univ (Strathclyde) 1992. *Hobbies:* Cottage Gardens; Low Hills; Grand Opera. *Address:* 43 Strathblane Road, Milngavie, Glasgow G62 8HA, Scotland. 53.

JOLOWICZ John Anthony, b. 11 Apr 1926, London, Eng. Prof of Comparative Law. m. Poppy Stanley, 8 Aug 1957, 1 s, 2 d. *Education:* Law Tripos, Class I, BA, MA, Trinity Coll, Cambridge, 1948-51. *Appointments:* Barrister, 1952-; Fellow, Trinity Coll, Cambridge, 1952- ; Law Tchr, Cambridge, 1955-. *Publications:* Books and articles on legal subjs. *Memberships include:* Academia Europaea; Pres of the Common Law Grp, Int Acad of Comparative Law; Pres 1986-87, SPTL; Coun Mbr, Int Assn of Procedural Law. *Honours:* Yorke Prize, Cambridge, 1952; Prize Fellow, Trinity Coll, Cambridge, 1952; D (HC) Universidad Nacional Autonoma De Mexico, 1985; QC 1990. *Hobbies:* Music; Travel; Wine. *Address:* Trinity College, Cambridge CB2 1TQ, England.

JONES (Calvin) David, b. 16 Nov 1931, Erie, PA, USA. Edr; Clergyman. m. (2) Barbara Ann Hillman, 16 July 1971, 2 s, 1 d. *Education:* BA 1958, MA 1960, Northwest Coll; BTh, Am Divinity Sch, 1959; BEd, Seattle Univ, 1965; DMin, Drew Univ, 1976; Postdoct studies, Mansfield Coll, Oxford Univ, Eng, 1980. *Appointments include:* Ordained, 1955. Pastor: Various parishes, Washington 1955-71; Canton Ecumenical Parish 1971-74; Three Mile Island Meth Chapel, PA 1975-77; White Marsh, MD, 1977-78; St Andrew's, Annapolis, 1977-88; Sr Pastor, Charlestown Ecumenical Parish, Baltimore, 1988-. Also: Tchr, schs in Washington 1966-69, Pennsylvania 1972-73; Assoc Prof, Essex Comm Coll, Baltimore, 1977, 1979; Adj Prof, Drew Univ, NJ, 1980- 83; Fdr, Headmaster, St Andrew's Elem Sch, Annapolis, 1984-86; Charlestown Ecumenical Parish, Baltimore, 1988-91; St Luke's United Meth of Woodlawn, Baltimore, 1991-. *Publication:* The Pastoral

Mentor, 1980. *Memberships:* Past Pres: I B Inc, Seattle; Eta Alpha chapt, Kappa Delta Pi, Seattle Univ; Fine Arts Assn, Middletown; Dean of Advanced Pastoral Studies, Acad of Parish Clergy; Former Rotarian. *Honours include:* Fellow, Acad of Parish Clergy, 1979-. *Hobbies:* Golf; Yachting; Horses; Hunting; Fishing; Music. *Address:* 1085 Carriage Hills Court, Annapolis, MD 21401, USA.

JONES (Cyril) Gareth, b. 28 May 1933, Blaina, Gwent, Wales. Indep Cons; Co Dir. m. (1) Anne Pickard, 9 Aug 1958, 1 s, 2 d, (2) Helen Rahming, 7 Apr 1989. *Education:* MA, Christ's Coll, Cambridge, 1954; PhD, Birkbeck Coll, London, 1969. *Appointments:* Asst Master, Stationer's Sch, 1957-59; Asst Master, Dulwich Coll, 1959-63; Esso Petroleum Co, 1963-69; Booz Allen & Hamilton, 1969-85; Ernst & Whinney, 1985-89; Non Exec Dir, Gwent Hlth Auth, 1990-92; Dir, Welsh Nat Opera, 1990-, Gov, Univ of Glamorgan, 1991-, Chmn, Wales 2010, Inst of Welsh Affairs. *Publications:* Strategy for Schools (co-author), 1964; Perspectives in Manpower Planning (co-author), 1967. *Memberships:* Arthritis & Rheumatism Coun, 1973-86; Welsh Water Auth, 1981-85. *Honour:* Fellow, Int Acad of Mgmt, 1987-. *Hobbies:* Opera; Travel; Welsh language and culture. *Address:* Tre Graig House, Bwlch, Powys LD3 7SJ, Wales.

JONES Anne, b. 8 Apr 1935, Coventry, Eng. Cons Prof. 1 s, 2 d. *Education:* BA Hons 1956, Post Grad Cert 1957, Dip Sociology, 1967, Univ of London. *Appointments:* Asst Mistress: Malvern Girls' Coll 1957-58, Godolphin & Latymer Sch 1958-62, Dulwich Coll 1964; Sch Cnslr, (PT) Mayfield Sch, 1965-71; Dep Headmistress, Thomas Calton Sch, London, 1971-74; Headmistress, Vauxhall Manor Sch, London, 1974-81; Hd, Cranford Comm Sch, Hounslow, 1981-87; Dir of Educ Progs, Dept of Employment, 1987-; Vis Prof, Univ of Sheffield, 1990-; Prof, Head of Continuing Educ, Brunel Univ, 1991-; Freelance Cons, 1991-. *Publications include:* Counselling Adolescents in School, 1977; Time to Spare (co-author), 1980; Counselling Adolescents in School and Beyond, 1986; Leadership for Tomorrow's Schools, 1986, reprinted 1987; Author of chapts in edited books, book reviews, articles. *Memberships include:* Coun Mbr, RSA; Coun Mbr, Careers Rsch & Advsry Ctr; Cncl Mem, Queen Mary Westfield College, London Univ, 1991; Cncl, West London Inst of Higher Educ, 1991. *Honours include:* FRSA, 1984; Hon Mbr, City & Guilds Inst, 1985; Hon Mbr, Standing Conf on Schs Sci & Tech; Hon, Fellow of College of Preceptors, 1990; Fellow, Queen Mary & Westfield Coll, London Univ, 1992. *Hobbies:* Walking; Boating; Theatre; Gardening. *Address:* 23 Southerton Road, London W6 0PJ, England. 52.

JONES Barry Edward, b. 11 Mar 1940, Bristol, Eng. Prof of Mfg Metrology; Dir. m. Julie Pritchard, 7 Dec 1963, 2 d. *Education:* BSc (First Class Hons) 1963, MSc 1965, PhD 1969, DSc 1985, Univ of Manchester. *Appointments:* Govt Communications HQ, 1956-60; Univ of Mancheser, 1964-81; The Open Univ, Pt-time 1972-84; Inst of Sci & Tech, Univ of Manchester, 1981-86; Brunel Univ, 1986-. *Creative works:* Tchr, Practitioner, Rschr in the fields of measurement, instrumentation, metrology and allied aspects of control; Author & ed of 5 books and over 150 papers. *Memberships:* Chartered Engr, 1970; Fellow, Inst of Measurement and Control, 1979; Chn, IEE Profl Grp, 1980-81; Fellow, Inst of Physics, 1982; Hon Ed, J Physics E: Scientific Instruments, 1983-87; CNAA, 1983-85; FIEE, 1984; Chartered Physicist, 1986. *Honour:* Publs Awd, IEEIE, 1984. *Hobbies:* Music; Gardening; Meth Local Preacher. *Address:* The Brunel Centre for Manufacturing Metrology, Brunel University, Uxbridge, Middlesex UB8 3PH, England.

JONES Clem, b. 16 Jan 1918, Ipswich, Qld, Aust. Surveying, Town Planning and Property Cons; Former Lord Mayor. m. Sylvia Ada Jones, 25 Aug 1951. *Education:* BSc, Univ of Qld, 1940; Authorised Surveyor,

1940; FRGS, 1947; Postgrad studies, UCLA, 1955. *Appointments:* Surveyor, Town Planner, Qld, 1940-55; Local Govt cons, 1956-61; Lord Mayor of Brisbane, 1961- 74; Chmn, Darwin Reconstruction Commn, rebuilding Darwin after Cyclone Tracy, 1975-78; Surveying, Town Planning and Property Consultancy Bus, Brisbane, 1985-; Chmn, Western Qld Flood Rehabilitation Ctr, 1990-91. *Memberships include:* Life, Camp Hill Carina Welfare Assn; Qld Inst of Surveyors; Vice Patron, Endeavour Fndn; Hon Mbr, Rotary Club, Stones Corner; Chmn, Aged and Disabled Persons Hostel and Welfare Assn; Patron, Qld Model Railways; Bd, 4RPH Radio Stn for Blind. *Honours:* AO 1976; Advance Aust Awd for contribution to sport and community, 1983; Life Mbr, Aust Labour Party, 1984; Qldr of the Yr, 1990. *Hobbies:* Sport; Tennis; Cricket; Billiards; Snooker; Football. *Address:* 758 Old Cleveland Road, Camp Hill, Brisbane, Queensland 4152, Australia.

JONES David Ian Stewart, b. 3 Apr 1934, Blackburn, Eng. Dir. m. 19 Aug 1967, 1 s, 1 d. *Education:* BA 1957; MA 1960. *Appointments:* Commissioned, Royal Signals, 1952-54; Curate, Oldham Parish Ch, 1959-62; Vicar of All Saints, Elton, Bury, 1962-66; Sr Chap & Conduct, Eton Coll, 1966- 74; Headmaster, Bryanston Sch, 1974-82; Rector, Designate of Bristol City, 1982-85; Dir, Lambeth Endowed Charities, 1985-. *Memberships:* Hon Priest Vicar, Southwark Cathedral, 1985-; Gov, Forest Sch, 1987-; Chmn, Inner Cities Young People's Proj, 1988-; Spiritual Advsr, Nat Assn of Boys Clubs, 1990-. *Hobbies:* Reading; Theology; General interest in sport. *Address:* 127 Kennington Road, London SE11 6SF, England.

JONES Edward Scott, b. 6 June 1922, Liverpool, Eng. Artist. m. Althea Mary, 4 Jan 1947, 1 d. *Education:* Liverpool Art Coll. *Appointments:* Advt Agcy, 1938-41, 1946-65; RAF Serv, 1941-46; Full time Freelance Painter, Illustrator, 1965-. *Creative works:* Exhibited, RSMA, RI; Works in private and pub collections; Various one man exhibs throughout country. *Membership:* RCA. *Hobbies:* Photography; Bowls; Swimming teaching; Wine making. *Address:* 18 The Fairway, Knotty Ash, Liverpool LI2 3HS, England.

JONES Emlyn Bartley, b. 9 Dec 1920, Buckley, Clwyd, N Wales. Sport/Leisure Cons. m. Constance Inez Jones, 27 Mar 1944, 1 d. *Education:* Tchrs Cert, Bangor Coll, N Wales, 1941; Dip of Phys Educ Loughborough, 1947. *Appointments:* Hist/PE Master, Flint Modern Second Sch, 1945-46; Tech Rep 1947-51, Tech Advsr 1951-62, Ctrl Coun of Phys Recreation; TV Commentator (Sports), 1956-85; Dir, Crystal Palace Sports Ctr, 1962-78; Dir, Gen, The Sports Coun, 1978-83. *Publications:* Learning Lawn Tennis, 1960; Sport in Space, 1985. *Membership:* FBIM, 1984. *Honour:* MBE 1975. *Hobbies:* Reading; Newspapers; Conversation; Writing; Golf; Skiing. *Address:* Chwarae Teg, 1B Allison Grove, Dulwich, London SE21 7ER, England.

JONES Emrys, b. 17 Aug 1920, Aberdare, Wales. Prof Emeritus. m. 7 Aug 1948, 2 d (1 dec). *Education:* BSc 1941, MSc 1945, Fellow 1946- 47, PhD 1947, Univ of Wales; Fellow, Rockefeller Fndn, 1948-49. *Appointments:* Asst Lectr, Univ Coll London, 1947-50; Lectr, Sr Lectr, Queens Univ, Belfast, 1950-58; Rdr 1958-60, Prof 1961-85, Univ of London, The London Sch of Econ(s). *Publications:* Social Geog of Belfast, 1960; Intro to Human Geog, 1964; Towns & Cities, 1965; Atlas of London, 1970; Metropolis, 1990. *Memberships include:* Chmn 1968-70, Reg Studies Assn; VP 1978-83, RGS. *Honours:* Victoria Medal, RGS, 1977; Hon DSc, Queen's Univ, Belfast, 1978; Hon D Univ, Open Univ, 1990; Hon Fellow, Univ Coll of Wales, 1991. *Hobbies:* Books; Music. *Address:* 2 Pine Close, North Road, Berkhamstead, Herts HP4 3BZ, England. 139.

JONES Ethelene Dyer, b. 13 May 1930, Union Co, GA, USA. Libn; Media Specialist; Freelance Writer. m. Grover D Jones, 23 Dec 1949, 1 s, 1 d. *Education:* AA,

Truett McConnell Coll, Cleveland, 1949; BA, Mercer Univ, Macon, 1953; MA, Western Carolina Univ, Cullowhee, 1968; SEd, Univ of GA, 1971. *Appointments:* Classroom Tchr: Choestoe Union Co, GA 1949-50; Bibb Co, GA 1953; Hart Co, GA 1955-56; Fannin Co 1961-68; Libn, Media Specialist in HS, Fannin Co, 1968-90. *Publications:* Faith through Flood and Fire, 1983; The Singing in the Wood, 1984; Facets of Fannin: A History of Fannin County, 1989. Ed of: The GA Lib Media Dept Newsletter, 1983- 86; The GA Poetry Soc Newsletter, 1986-92. *Memberships:* Pres, GA Lib Media Dept, GA Lib Assn; Am Lib Assn; VP, Newsletter Ed, Pres, GA State Poetry Soc; Fannin Co Ret'd Tchrs' Assn; Histn, Reporter, Beta Upsilon Chapt of Alpha Delta Kappa Hon Soc for Women Edrs; Phi Beta Kappa. *Honours:* William Patterson Awd for profl serv to libs, 1986; GA Lib, Media Specialist of the Yr Awd, 1986; Publr's Awd of Exellence for Hist Book, 1989. *Hobbies:* Writing; Photography; Travel; Music. *Address:* PO Box 120, Epworth, GA 30541, USA.

JONES Geraint Martyn, b. 15 July 1948, Luton, Eng. Barrister. m. Caroline Mary Eyres, 29 July 1978, 1 s, 1 d. *Education:* MA, LIM, Christ's Coll, Cambridge, 1966-70; Inns of Ct Sch of Law, 1970-71; Admitted Barrister, 1972. *Appointments:* Practised London, 1972-74; South- Eastern Circuit, based Fenners Chambers, Cambridge, 1974-; Chn, Rent Assessment Comms, 1985-; Asst Commissioner, Parliamentary Boundary Commission, 1992-. *Memberships:* Gray's Inn; South-Eastern Circuit; Cambridge Bar Mess, Sr Circuit Rep; RNLI; RYA; OGA; Cruising Assn; Royal Norfolk & Suffolk YC; Little Ship Club; Bourn GC. *Hobbies:* Liveryman Worshipful Co of Glaziers, 1992; Sailing; Golf; Jazz; Carpentry; Reading. *Address:* Fenners Chambers, 3 Madingley Road, Cambridge CB3 0EE, England.

JONES Hazel Emma, Main, b. 6 Apr 1919, Footscray, Vic, Aust. Ret'd Libn; Vol Wkr. m. Clifford Henry Jones, 11 June 1945, dec, 2 s, 3 d. *Education:* BA, Melbourne Univ, 1943; Assoc, Lib Assn of Aust, 1974; Various certs, dress design, arts. *Appointments:* Cataloguer, Serials Libn, Med Libn, ref work, Univ of Melbourne, 1935-45; Cataloguing, Ch of Eng Roberts Ctr, 1969; C'wlth Dept of Works, 1970-71; Repatriation Hosp Greenslopes, 1971-72; Dep Libn, Acting Libn, State Dept of Hlth, 1973-84. *Creative work:* Painting. *Memberships:* Publicity Off, Chd's Book Coun; Sec, Aust Med Libns Grp, Sec, Treas, Comm Mbr, Cataloguer's Sect, Pres, Special Libs Sect, Auditor, Sch Libs Assn of Qld, Br Coun, ALIA; Comm, ARLISAM; Comm, Theological Libs; Sec, Visual Arts Comm, St John's Cathedral; Vol, Qld AG Soc; Com, Friends of Conservatorium. *Honours:* Sch leaving hons; 1st & 2nd class hons; Plaque, Int Biographical Ctr, 1984. *Hobbies:* Arts & crafts; Gardening; Singing, various choirs. *Address:* 35 Greer Street, Bardon, Queensland 4065, Australia. 149, 156.

JONES Herman Otto, Jr, b. 1 Dec 1933 Jacksonville, FL, USA. Pres. m. Marjorie Seaver Jones, 4 June 1955, 2 d dec. *Education:* BSA, Univ of FL, 1956. *Appointments:* VP 1962-71, Oak Crest Hatcheries; VP 1962- 68, Exec 1968-71, Oak Crest Enterprises, Inc; Pres: HermanO Enterprises, J&B Hatcheries 1971-73; Diversified Imports, 1973-75; Dir of Sales, BEC of Eng, 1975-78; Dir of Sales, Paul Revere Ins Co, 1978-80; Nat Sales Mgr 1980-85, VP 1982-85, Sales, Antiox Corp; Pres, Gateway Suppliers, Inc, 1986-. *Publications:* Articles for nat and int trade mags. *Memberships include:* Pres 1961, FL Poultry Prods Assn; State VP 1962-66, Southeastern Poultry and Egg Assn; Pres 1963-65, FL Poultry Fndn; Worthy Patron 1969, Order of Eastern Star; Bd of Dir 1971-81, Cystic Fibrosis Fndn; Deacon 1987- 90, Riverside Bapt Ch; Sunday Sch Dir 1989-91; Bd of Dir 1989-91, Rotary Club of S Jacksonville; Chmn of Sponsorship Comm 1989-91, Greater Jacksonville Agricl Fair; Sunday Sch Tchr, 1991-; Mason, Shriner, Royal Order of Jesters; Phi Gamma Delta. *Honours:* 4-H Alumni Awd, Co 1961, State 1962; Man of Yr, FL Poultry Ind, 1965; Outstg Young Farmer 1966-68, Disting Serv Awd 1970,

Jacksonville Jaycees; Outstg Young Farmer in State of FL, FL Jaycees, 1968- 69; Workhorse of Yr, Southeastern Poultry & Egg Assn, 1969. *Hobbies:* Golf; Travel; Staying at beach. *Address:* 2596 Edison Avenue, Jacksonville, FL 32204, USA. 7, 16, 81, 117.

JONES Hywel Francis, b. 28 Dec 1928, Morriston, Swansea, Wales. Former Commnr for Local Admin in Wales. m. Marian Rosser Craven, 10 Mar 1959, 1 d. *Education:* BA 1949; MA 1953. *Appointments:* Dep Co Treas, Breconshire CC, 1956-59; Asst Co Treas, Carmarthenshire CC, 1959-66; Borough Treas, Port Talbot CC, 1966-75; Sec - Commn 1975-85, Commnr 1985-1991, for Local Admin in Wales. *Memberships:* CIPFA, 1953-; Gorsedd of Bards; Chancellor's Advisory Cttee for West Glamorgan, 1990-. *Honour:* Hon Treas, Royal Nat Eisteddfod of Wales, 1975-; Hon Treas, Gorsedd of Bards, 1992-. *Hobbies:* Music; Reading; Gardening. *Address:* Godre'r Rhiw, 1 Lon Heulog, Baglan, Port Talbot, West Glamorgan SA 12 8SY, Wales. 1.

JONES Hywel Glyn, b. 1 July 1948, Merthyr, Wales. Econ & Mktg Advsr. m. Julia Claire Davies, 1 Aug 1970. *Education:* BA (Cantab); MA (Cantab); MA (Oxon). *Appointments:* Univ Lectr in Econ(s), Univ of Warwick, 1971-73; The Univ Lectr in the Econ(s) of the Firm, Oxford Univ, 1973-77; Dir, Henley Ctr for Forecasting, 1977-85; Chmn, Fixpoint Ltd, 1986-. *Publications:* Second Abstract of British Historical Statistics, 1970; An Introduction to Modern Theories of Economic Growth, 1974 (Translated into Japanese and Portuguese); Full Circle into the Future: Britain into the 21st Century, 1984. *Hobbies:* Conversation; Military History; Rock and Roll. *Address:* 59 Yarnells Hill, North Hinksey, Oxford OX2 9BE, England. 1.

JONES Idwal, b. 19 July 1913, Deiniolen, Caernarvon, Wales. Min of Relig. m. 14 June 1945, 2 s. *Education:* BA Hons, Univ of Wales; St Michael's Coll, Llandaff, Cardiff. *Appointments:* Hon Chap to the Forces, Normandy Campaign, 1943-50; Vicar of Cuddington, Diocese of Guildford, 1950-63; Vicar of Royal Leamington Spa All Saints, 1963-79. *Creative works:* Village Histories, Birdingburm & Grandborough. *Memberships:* Vice Chmn, Leamington & Warwick; UN Assn. *Honours:* Asst Chap, Order of St John of Jerusalem; Former Nat Vice Chmn, C of E Mens Soc; Former Pres, Leamington & Warwick Arthritic & Rheumatic Coun; Hon Canon, Coventry Cathedral. *Hobbies:* Local history; Nature studies; Reading; Country walking. *Address:* Leam Cottage, Birdingburm, Nr Rugby, Warwickshire CV23 8EL, England.

JONES Jimmie Clyde, b. 10 June 1900. Ret'd. m. (1) 1 s, (2) Sandra Jea Dudley, 11 Jan 1986, 3 d. *Appointments:* Farmer, 1908- 18; Mech, 1944-85. *Honour:* Blue Ribbon Cert in Mech. *Hobby:* Farming. *Address:* HC 77 Box 120, Licking, MO 65542, USA.

JONES John E, b. 28 Oct 1941, Odum, GA, USA. Real Estate Broker. m. Nellie Ann Dougherty, 21 June 1963, 1 s, 1 d. *Education:* Dip Valedictorian, Odum HS, Odum, 1959; BSBA, Univ of FL, Gainesville, 1967. *Appointments:* FBI: Washington DC 1959-61, Jacksonville 1961-64; Mgr, Fed Reserve Bank of Atlanta, Jacksonville, 1967-69; Asst Mgr, Blue Cross-Blue Shield of FL, Jacksonville, 1969-72; Mgr, Heavener Realty Co, Jacksonville, 1972-75; Pres, Owner, John Jones Realty, Jacksonville, 1975-77; Pres, Owner, ERA of Middle GA, Jacksonville, 1977-79; Pres, Owner, Jones Realty Co, Macon, 1979-81; Instr (Real Estate), Macon Coll, Macon, 1980-; Assoc Broker, McNair Realty Co, Macon, 1981-89; Assoc Broker, Sheridan, Solomon, Kernaghan Realtors, Macon, 1989-. *Creative work:* Video Sales Training Tape. *Memberships:* FL Bd of Realtors; FL Assn of Realtors; GA Bd of Realtors; GA Assn of Realtors; Nat Assn of Realtors; Dir, Macon Multiple Listing Serv; River N Country Club, Macon; Gideons Int, Macon; Vineville Bapt Ch, Macon. *Honours:* Top Prod Agent, Macon Multiple Listing Serv, 1983;

Hon Life Mbr, Macon C of C, 1989; State Treas, GA Assn Real Estate Edrs; Certified Real Estate Specialist; Grad, Realtors Inst; Life Mbr, Million Dollar Club, Macon Bd of Realtors. *Hobbies:* Bible study; Sel development reading and study; Travelling. *Address:* SSK Realtors, 2449 Vineville Avenue, Macon, GA 31204, USA, 7.

JONES John Elfed, b. 19 Mar 1933, Maentwrog, Wales. Chmn. m. Mary Sheila Rosser, 31 July 1957, 2 d. *Education:* Denbighshire Tech Coll, Wrexham, 1949-53; HND, Elec Engrng, Heriot Watts Coll, Edinburgh, 1953-55. *Appointments:* Commissioned Flying Off, RAF, 1955-57; Bldg & Running Power Plants, CEGB, 1957-69; Dep Mng Dir, RTZ, Kaiser Aluminium, Anglesey Aluminium, 1969-79; Under-Sec, Welsh Off, 1979-82; Chmn, Welsh Water, 1982-. *Publications:* Various articles in tech journs. *Memberships:* FIEE; C Eng; FRSA; Comp BIM; FIWO; Hon FIWEM; Fellow, Univ of Wales, Aberystwyth; Pres, Univ of Wales, Lampeter, 1992. *Honours:* CBE 1987; Dep Lt, Co of Mid Glamorgan DL, 1988. *Hobbies:* Fishing for Salmon and Trout; Attending Eisteddfodau; Music. *Address:* Ty Mawr, Coety, Penybontarogwr, Mid Glamorgan CF35 6BN, Wales. 1.

JONES Philip (Mark), b. 12 Mar 1928, Bath, Eng. Musician. m. Ursula Strebi, 1 Aug 1956. *Education:* ARCM, 1947. *Career:* Prin Trumpet with all major orchs in London, 1949-72; Fdr, Dir, Philip Jones Brass Ensemble, 1951-86; Hd of Dept of Wind and Percussion, RNCM, Manchester, 1975- 77; Hd of Wind and Percussion Dept, Guildhall Sch of Music, London, 1983-88; Principal, Trinity Coll of Music, London, 1988-. *Creative works:* Over 50 Gramophone Records; Just Brass Music Series. *Memberships:* Arts Coun of GB, 1984-88; Royal Soc of Musicians; Worshipful Com of Musicians; Musicians Benevolent Trust; Park Lane Group, Artists Committee; FRSA. *Honours:* OBE 1977; FRNCM 1977; Composers Guild Awd, 1979; FRCM 1983; FGSM 1984; CBE 1986; Cobbett Medal of the Worshipful Co of Musicians, 1986; Hon FTCL 1988; Freedom of the City of London, 1988; FRAM 1991. *Hobbies:* History; Skiing; Mountain walking. *Address:* 14 Hamilton Terrace, London NW8 9UG, England. 34.

JONES Prudence Heather, b. 19 Aug 1952, Bolton, Lancs, Eng. Writer; Cnslr. *Education:* BA, Girton Coll, Cambridge, 1970-73; MA (Cambridge), 1975. *Appointments:* Grad Tng Asst, Univ of Alberta (Anglophone) and College Universitaire Saint-Jean, Edmonton (Francophone), Alberta, Canada, 1973-74; Philos Supvsr, New Hall, Clare, Kings and Girton Colls, 1975-79; Wkr, Mbr, Arjuna Wholefoods Coop, Cambridge, 1978-81; Cnslr, Therapist (Freelance), Adult Educ Tutor, Cambs Village Colls, Writer, Lectr, 1980-. *Publications include:* The Shoemaker as Angel, 1983; Symbols, Signs and Superstition, 1983; Northern Mythology of the Constellations, 1987; Voices From the Circle; the Heritage of Western Paganism (ed), 1990; Creative Astrology: Experiential Understanding of the Birth Chart (ed), 1991; A History of Pagan Europe (with Nigel Pennick), 1993. *Memberships:* FRSA; AIL; Inst for Biosynthesis; Assn of Profl Astrologers; Hon Life Mbr, Pagan Fndn. *Hobbies:* Hillwalking; Amateur singing; Opera; Oriental martial arts. *Address:* 21 Shelly Garden, Cambridge CB3 0BT, England. 138.

JONES Richard Norman, b. 20 Mar 1913, Manchester, Eng. Analytical Rsch Spectroscopist. m. Magda Kemeny, 11 July 1939, 2 s. *Education:* BSc 1933, MSc 1934, PhD 1936, DSc 1954, Manchester; DSc (Hon), Univ of Poznan, 1972; DSc (Hon), Tokyo Inst of Tech, 1982. *Appointments:* Post Doct Fellow, Harvard Univ, 1937-42; Lectr, Asst Prof 1942-46, Adj Prof 1984, Queen's Univ, Kingston, Ont, Can; Assoc Rsch Off, Hd of Organic Spectro-chem Sect 1946-77, Guest Wkr 1978-92, Nat Rsch Coun of Can, Ottawa; Guest Prof 1979-82, Vist Rschr 1985-86, Tokyo Inst of Tech, Tokyo; Disting Vis, Univ of Alberta, Edmonton, 1982-83; Guest Scientist, Univ of Alberta, Edmonton, 1992. *Publications:* Author of 3 monographs and over 250 tech papers in chem

and spectroscopyic journs. *Memberships:* Hon Fellow, FCIC; MACS; FRS (Can); MRSC; Pres of Phys Chem Div, IUPAC; VP of Com on Data for Sci & Tech, ICSU; Pres, The Coblentz Soc; Can Sci & Tech Histl Assn; Am Soc for Testing and Mat(s). *Honours:* Fisher Scientific Lecture Awd, Chem Inst of Can, 1971; Gerhard Herzberg Awd, Spectroscopy Soc of Can, 1979. *Hobbies:* Travel; Photography; History of Science; Preservation of Spectroscopic Archival Material. *Address:* Claridge House, Suite 1003, 11027-87 Avenue, Edmonton, Alberta, Canada, T6G 2P9. 2, 142, 143.

JONES Stephen Richard, b. 24 Sept 1954, Chislehurst, Kent, Eng. Art Histn. *Education:* St Dunstan's Coll, London, 1963-73; Magdalene Coll, Cambridge, 1974-78. *Appointments:* Asst Curator, Victoria & Albert Mus, 1978-79; Curator, Gainsborough's Hse, 1979-81; Curator, Leighton Hse Mus, 1981-89; Ed of Publs NACF, 1989-91; Dir, Spencer Hse, 1991-. *Publications:* The Eighteenth Century, 1985; Ackermann's Repository of Art, 1985; Traditional Style, 1990; Power and Glory, 1991. *Memberships:* FRSA; Ed Advsry Bd, Hist Today Mag; Com, Byron Soc. *Honour:* Selwyn Brinton Lectr in Italian Renaissance Art, RSA, 1989. *Hobbies:* American Literature; Ecclesiastical History; Baroque Opera; Good Food. *Address:* Spencer House, 27 St James's Place, London SW1A 1NR, England.

JONES Timothy Arthur, b. 20 Apr 1951, London, Eng. Barrister. 1 d. *Education:* Christ's Hosp, Horsham; Jesus Coll, Cambridge; LSE; Coll of Law, Chancery Lane. *Appointments:* Called to the Bar, Inner Temple, 1975; Barrister, St Ives Chambers, Birmingham, 1975-; Dep Hd of Chambers, 1990-; Called to the Irish Bar, King's Inns, 1990. *Creative works include:* Counsel in Wyre Forest DC v Secretary of State; Rv Housing Benefit Review Board ex pL Smith; Rv S Herefordshire DC ex p Miles; Rv Secretary of State ex p T Smith; S Norhtants DC v Power. *Memberships:* Local Govt, Planning and Environmental Bar Assn; Admnstv Law Bar Assn; Midland and Oxford Circuit. *Honour:* Almoners' Nominee Scholarship to Christs Hosp, Horsham, 1962-69; Politics: Parliamentary Candidate, Liberal then Liberal Democrat, Warwick and Leamington 1974, Mid Staffordshire 1983, 1987, 1990 By Election; Pres, Cambridge University Liberal Club, 1970; Mbr Standing Comm, Cambridge Union, 1971; Mbr, Liberal Democrat Federal Policy Comm, 1990-. *Address:* St Ive's Chambers, 9 Fountain Court, Steelhouse Lane, Birmingham B4 6DR, England.

JONES Timothy Duncan, b. 16 Jan 1967, Birmingham, Eng. Swimmer; Sports Dev Off. *Appointments:* Sports Dev Off, Birmingham City Coun, 1991-. *Membership:* Birmingham Area Sports Internationalists Club. *Honours:* Brit & Eng Short Course 200 metres Butterfly Record Holder; Mbr of Eng C'wlth Games Team, 1986, 1990; Mbr of 1988 GB Olympic Team; Sandwell Sports Personality of the Yr, 1991. *Hobbies:* Playing golf; Eating out; Computers; Travelling; Electronic music. *Address:* 2 George Road, Great Barr, Birmingham B43 6LG, England.

JONES-TODD Pamela Louise, b. 9 Oct 1942, Spokane, WA, USA. Registered Nurse, Am Nurses' Assn Certification as Clin Specialist/Med - Surg Nursing. *Education:* BA, Duke Univ, Durham, 1964; BSN, Case-Western Reserve Univ, Cleveland, 1969; MSN, The Cath Univ of Am, Washington DC, 1974; DNSc, DSc, Widener Univ, Chester, 1991-. *Appointments:* Charge Nurse, Univ Hosps, Cleveland, OH, 1969-70; Charge Nurse, VA Hosp, Washington DC, 1970-73; Lectr, The Cath Univ of Am, Washington DC, 1974; Clin Nurse Specialist, VA Med Ctrs, Washington DC & Philadelphia, 1974-86; Neurology Nurse, VA Med Ctr, Philadelphia, 1987-; Instr, Dept of Nursing, Thomas Jefferson Univ, 1991-. *Publications:* Clinical Simulations in Patient Management in Extended Care Facility, 1987; Dysphagia Teams, 1987; Pressures Sores - Length of Stay, 1988; Dysphagia-Team Approach, 1989; Wound Healing and the Aged, 1990. *Memberships:* Am Nurses'

Assn; Nat League for Nursing; Washington DC Thoracic Soc; Chairperson, Nat ByLaws Comm, Am Assn of Critical Care Nurses, 1980-81. *Honours:* Sigma Theta Tau Int Nursing Hon Soc, 1969-; NCA/Am Heart Assn Awds for Comm Serv, 1977, 1980, 1981; VA Recognitions for Nursing Performances & Achmts, 1978, 1981, 1983, 1988, 1990; GWAC/Am Asn Critical Care Nurses Awds for Serv & Scholarship, 1980, 1981; VA Nursing Serv Commendation Plaque, 1984. *Hobbies:* Music, classical and jazz; Books; Computers; Original art works. *Address:* 408 Pine Vista, 4800 Pine Street, Philadelphia, PA 19143, USA.

JONKER Pieter, b. 12 May 1950, Amsterdam, Holland. Dep Mayor. m. 27 Aug 1975, 2 d. *Education:* Doct Exam in Econ(s), Free Univ, Amsterdam, 1967-73. *Appointments:* Asst Prof, Free Univ, Amsterdam, 1974-82; Dep Mayor, City of Amsterdam, 1982-. *Membership:* Koninklyke Vereniging voor de Staaathuishoudund, Amsterdam. *Address:* Nieuwe Purmerweg 8, 1025 VS Amsterdam, The Netherlands. 52.

JORDAN Barbara Leslie, b. 30 Sept 1915, New York, NY, USA. Writer; Vol in Civic & Cultural Projs. m. Dr John I Yellot, 2 June 1951 dec, 2 s 1 dec, 1 stepson, 1 stepdaughter. *Appointments:* Freelance Poet, Writer, 1934-; Sec, Treas 1958-86, Pres 1987-90, John Yellot Engrng Assn. *Publications:* Web of Days, 1949; Comfort The Dreamer, 1955; Silver Song, 1980; Collected Poems; Rsch Ed, Am Bio Soc, 1990-. *Memberships:* Pres, Eng Speaking Union, Phoenix Br, 1989-; Nat Soc of Arts and Letters, Phoenix Chapt; Charter 100; Chair, Progs, Womens Bd, All Saints Episc Ch; Life, San Pablo Inst. *Honours:* Bronze Medal, Nat Soc of Arts and Letters, 1987; Commemorative Medal, Am Bio Inst, 1989; Presidential Medal of Merit, 1989; Silver Shield of Valor, 1992-; English Speaking Univ of the US Bd of Dirs Awd furthering the goals of the ESu and helping the unique relationships between our two great Nations; Honoured with Dr John I Yellot, for distinguished service to Phoenix County Day School and this Community. *Hobbies:* Swimming; Travel; Cats. *Address:* 901 West El Caminito Drive, Phoenix, AZ 85021, USA. 5.

JORDAN F Gene, b. 3 Dec 1932, Carlton, TX, USA. Oil Field Mktg; Pres. m. Frances Irene Briggs, 1 Sept 1956, 2 s. *Education:* BBA, Howard Payne Univ, 1956; Student Modern Mgmt, Alexander Hamilton Inst, NYC, 1966-68. *Appointments:* US Army, 1953-55; Trainee, Continental Supply Co, Abilene, 1956-57; Bookkeeper, Continental Supply Co, Synder, 1957-58; Oilfield Salesman, Continental Supply Co, McCamey, 1958-60; Specialist Salesman, Continental Emsco Co, Kermit, 1960-63; Store Mgr, Continental Emsco Co, Monahans 1963-68, Pampa 1968-69; Mgr, Ea Venezuela Continental Emsco Co, 1969-76; Pres, Escuela Anaco, 1975-76; Sec, Bd of Dir, Escuela Belle Vista, Maracaibo, 1976-80; Sales Mgr, Venezuela Continental Emsco Co, Maracibo, 1976-80; Area Mgr, Latin Am LTV Energy Products Co, Houston, 1980-86; Pres, Chief Exec Off, Latin Am Int Sales Inc, Houston, 1986-91; Agt, Red Adair Co, Standco Industries, Lebus Int, Mexico City, 1987-. *Memberships:* Masons; Alpha Beta Sigma. *Honour:* Silver Plaque, Escuela Belle Vista, 1980. *Hobbies:* Football; Rodeos; Livestock. *Address:* 8215 Forest Ridge Road, Spring, TX 77379, USA. 7, 132.

JORDANOVA Daniela Liubomirova, b. 1 Mar 1961, Sofia, Bulgaria. Artist. m. Bisser Kostadinov, 28 Sept 1985, 1 d. *Education:* Special Artistic Sch of Fine Arts, Sofia, 1980. *Appointments:* Sphere of Stage and Costume Designing, Graphic, Drawing & Illustration; Costume Designer, Bulgarian TV, Sofia, 1987-90; Painting. *Creative works:* Produced over 50 TV plays, prods for Children & Rubrics, 1987-90. Opera: The Zograff Zahari, 1985-87; Marriage Misunderstanding, 1987; Don Carlo, 1988. Operette incl: Contess Mariza; Earl Fon Luksemburg; Princess of the Circus; Island Tuilipatan. Drama incl: Accident, 1983; Out, in Front the Door, 1985; Opera for Three Penny, 1986; Show in Planetarium Smolian, 1987; Electra My Love, 1988.

Gen Art Exhibs in Bulgaria for Graphic and Stage Design, Int Print Biennalles and Exhibs Abroad; Works are seen in the Nat Art Gall, the Nat Mus of Decorative Applied Arts and a number of pvt collections in Bulgaria and Abroad. *Membership:* Soc of Bulgarian Graphic Artists, 1989-. *Honours:* Grad with Gold Medal and Hon for Excellent Average Mark, Higher Inst of Fine Arts, Sofia, 1986; 1st Prize for Drama-play, Electra My Love from Hungarian Embassy, Sofia, 1989; Won a competition for course- specialisation in Lithography Workshop, Tamarind Inst for Colour Lithography, Albuque, NM, USA, 1990. *Hobbies:* Learning Foreign Languages: English, French, Germanic, Italian; Skiing; Windsurfing; Mountain climbing; Travelling. *Address:* Han Krum Str No 7A, Sofia 1000, Bulgaria.

JORGENSEN Bent Lauring Schiodte, b. 20 May 1936, Randers, Denmark. Mgmt Cons. m. Lene von Barner, 15 Oct 1981, 2 d. *Education:* Dipl in: Mktg 1974, Acctng 1980, Data Processing 1987, Personal Admin 1989; Cert as ERHVERVSOEKONOM, MDM, 1989. *Appointments:* Sgt, Danish Air Force, 1957-59; Off Mgr, Nestle & Broedrene GRAM, 1962-76; Admin & Personnel Mgr, State Lib Insp & Danish Chartered Acct Union, 1976-80; Sec, Funktionary Union, 1980-90; Mgmt Cons, JS Mgmt, Denmark, 1987-. *Publication:* Job-searching Tecnic, 1991. *Memberships:* Pres, Danish Mercantile Assn; Danish Assn for Commercial and Industrial Educ; Panel, Danish ERFA-prize. *Hobbies:* Hunting; Yachting; Travelling. *Address:* Lodsvej 51, 2650 Hvidovre, Denmark.

JORIS Jean-Louis, b. 3 Aug 1948, Wilrijk, Belgium. Lawyer. m. Annic Dopchie, 16 Sept 1977, 1 s, 2 d. *Education:* LIC JUR, magna cum laude, 1972; Master, Econ Law, magna cum laude, 1974. *Appointments:* Assoc, Janson, Baugniet, 1972-76; Assoc, Cleary Gottlieb, Steen & Hamilton, USA, 1975-76; Assoc, Cleary, Gottlieb, Steen & Hamilton, Brussels, 1976-83; Ptnr, European Counsel, 1986-. *Memberships:* NY Bar; Brussels Bar; ABA. *Address:* Avenue des Cattle Yas, 23, B-1150 Brussels, Belgium.

JORRE DE ST JORRE Danielle Marie-Madeleine, b. 30 Sept 1941, Seychelles. Min of Planning and External Rels. 2 s, 1 d. *Education:* MA Hons, Univ of Edinburgh, 1965; PGCE, Inst of Educ, Univ of London, 1966; B Phil, Univ of York, 1972. *Appointments include:* Prin, Tchr Tng Coll, Seychelles, 1974-76; Prin Educ Off, Min of Educ, Seychelles, 1976- 77; Prin Sec, Min of Foreign Affairs, Tourism & Aviation, 1977-79; Prin Sec, Min of Educ & Info, 1980-82; Prin Sec, External Rels, Min of Planning and External Rels, 1982-83; Accredited Ambassador for Seychelles to France, UK, Can, Cuba, Germany, Greece, USSR, 1983, 1984, 1985; Prin Sec, Planning & External Rels, 1983-86; Gov for Seychelles on the Bd of Govs, World Bank & African Dev Bank, 1984-; VP, Comite Int Des Etudes Creoles, 1984-; Sec of State for Planning External Rels, Dept of Planning and External Rels, 1986; Pres, Bannzil Creole, 1986- ; Dir, Bd of Dir, Int Ctr for Ocean Dev, 1987-; Min for Planning & External Rels, 1989-; Minister, Environment, Economic Planning & External Relations, 1992. *Publications:* Apprenons la Nouvelle Orthographie, 1978; Dictionnaire Creole Seychelles, 1982; Lexique des Specificites de la Langue Francaise aux Seychelles, 1989. *Hobbies:* Reading; Lexicography; Folklore; Arts & Crafts. *Address:* Ministry of Environment, Economic Planning and External Relations, PO Box 656, Victoria, Mahe, Seychelles. 1, 138, 152.

JOSCELYNE Richard Patrick, b. 19 June 1934, Bristol, Eng. m. (1) 1 s, 1 d, (2) Irangani Dias, 15 June 1988. *Education:* MA, Queen's Coll, Cambridge. *Appointments:* Brit Council since 1962: Montevideo 1962, Moscow 1967, Madrid 1969, London 1972, Colombo 1977; Controller Fin 1982; Rep (later called Dir), Spain 1987; Dir, Japan 1991-. *Hobby:* Painting. *Address:* c/o British Council, 10 Spring Gardens, London SW1, England.

JOSEPH Michael Anthony, b. 4 Nov 1944, Darlington, Vice President. m. Johanna Cornelia Niesje de Wijs, 15 Mar 1969, 2 d. *Education:* Lic es Sciences Economiques, 1963-67. *Appointments:* IBM UK Ltd, Croydon, 1968-70; Standard Chartered Leasing, Paris, 1974-77; Sr VP, Comdisco Inc & Europe, Paris & Switzerland, 1977-90; Meridian Computers Ltd, Paris, 1990-1991; AT & T Capital Ltd, London, 1992- . *Membership:* Pres, European Computer Trading and Leasing Assn, 1984. *Hobbies:* English Silver (18th Century); Gold & Porcelain Snuff Boxes (Continental - 18th Century); Golf; Skiing; Classic, Oldtimer Sports Cars. *Address:* Route de Mex, 1036 Sullens, Switzerland. 132.

JOSEPH Paul Philip, b. 3 Mar 1947, Niagara Falls, NY, USA. Min. m. Patricia Hoke, 4 May 1967, 2 d. *Education:* Assoc of Sc, Broward Co Jr Coll, Davie, 1967; BSc 1969, MEd 1973, 1974, 1977, FL Atlantic Univ, Boca Raton; Master of Divinity, Southeastern Bapt Theological Sem, Wake Forrest, 1980. *Appointments:* Deacon, First Bapt Ch, Brooksville, 1974-76; Cons for Tchr Tng and Special Fed Projs, Dept of Educ, FL, 1976-78; Dir of Ch Tng, Assoc Pastor for Visitation, Educ and Music, sponsored Bradfordville Bapt Ch, Thomasville Rd Bapt Ch, Tallahassee, 1977-78; Assoc Pastr of Educ, Youth & Music, Hester Bapt Ch, Oxford, 1979-80; Pastor, Northcliffe Bapt Ch, Spring Hill, 1980-89; Min of Educ & Admin, Seminole Heights Bapt Ch, Tampa, 1989-. *Creative works:* Composed several songs and performed them professionally incl: Here not there; Disappointed; There is a Reason; Lord. *Memberships:* Pres, FL Adult Educ Assn, 1976-78; Bd of Dir, FL Vocational Assn, 1977-78; Bd of Dir, FL Assn of Supvsr & Admnstr, 1978. *Hobbies:* Softball; Running; Tennis; Guitar. *Address:* 802 Settlers Road, Tampa, FL 33613, USA.

JOWITT Paul William, b. 3 Aug 1950, Doncaster, Eng. Prof. m. Jane Catriona Urquhart, 11 Aug 1973, 1 s, 1 d. *Education:* BSc (Eng) 1st Class Hons 1972; ACGI 1972; PhD 1978; DIC 1978. *Appointments:* Lectr in Civil Engrng 1974-86, Warden, Falmouth Hall 1980-86, Imperial Coll; Prof of Civil Engrng, Heriot-Watt Univ, Edinburgh, 1987-. *Publications:* Author of num acad papers. *Memberships:* MICE; Brit Hydrological Soc; Nat Conf of Univ Profs. *Honour:* Trevithick Premium, Instn of Civil Engrs, 1987. *Hobbies:* Restoring Morgan 3 wheelers; Renovating old houses; Water colours; Claret. *Address:* 22 Fountainhall Road, The Grange, Edinburgh EH9 2LW, Scotland. 184.

JU Qihong, b. 3 Sept 1941, Shanghai, P R China. Sr Archt. m. Shaoqiang Liang, 12 Feb 1969, 1s, 2 d. *Education:* Archt Bachalor, Tongji Univ, Shanghai, 1958-64. *Appointments:* Asst Archt 1964-65, Archt 1965-88, Sr Archt 1988-, Shanghai Municipal Inst of Civil Archtl Design. *Creative works include:* The Art Library of Fudan Univ, 1985; The Teaching and Researching Building of Arts Lib of Fudan University, 1988; Kun Shan Business Centre Planning, 1990; Library of Shanghai Communication University Minghang Branch, 1991. *Membership:* Vice Gen Sec, Archtl Soc of Shanghai. *Honours:* Design of Shanghai Municipal Lib Proj (Co-design with Yuen Tang), 1984; Selected winning projs of Ctrl Audio-Visual Educ Centre (Co-design with J Z Zhang), 1985; Fudan Lib awded 3rd prize of Fine Archtl Creative Design Projs of MOC, 1986; 2nd prize of Fine Archtl Creature Design Projs of MOC, 3rd prize of Sci Tech Projs, Tchng and Rsching Bldg of Arts Lib, Fudan Univ. *Hobbies:* Feeding cats; Touring. *Address:* 17 Guangdong Road, Shanghai 200002, China.

JUDD Judith Margaret, b. 18 Apr 1949, Walkden, Manchester, Eng. Journalist. m. 14 July 1973, 1 s, 1 d. *Education:* Degree in Modern Hist, St Anne's Coll, Oxford, 1968-71. *Appointments:* Birmingham Post, 1972-75; Times Higher Educ Supplement, 1975-79; The Observer, 1979-89; Education Correspondent, 1984-89; Educ Corres, Independent on Sunday, 1989-91; Educ

Corres, Independent, 1991-92. *Hobbies:* Walking; Music; Gardening; Reading. *Address:* The Independent, 40 City Road, London EC1Y 2DB, England.

JUNCO Mariha del Carmen, Countess del Vendrell, b. 21 Aug 1956, Spain. Writer; Transl, Supreme Ct of SC. div, 1 s, 1 d. *Education:* HS, Notre Dame de Sion; BA, Univ of Costa Rica; CR, Finishing Sch, San Jose; Communications, Clemson Univ. *Appointments:* Newscaster, SBTV, Schofield; Transl, Pub Defender's Off; Writer of Children's Books; Spanish Transl, US Supreme Ct of SC. *Publications:* Poem published in anthology, 1991; The Other Side of the Mirror; The Little Princess; Hen Adventures. *Memberships:* Vol, Red Cross; Active Sister Care; Org for the abused children; Vol, Spokeperson; Vol, Repub Party; Vol, Disabled Am Veterans. *Honours:* 2 Medals won in rifle competion, Am Rifle Assn; Best ArtWork Awd, East Coast Spartanburg Tech Coll; Mayor Area 4, Schofield, 1987-88. *Hobbies:* Historic Preservation Society; Shrewsbury Abbey Restoration Project, England; Portraiture; Gardening; Cooking; Riding. *Address:* PO Box 21441, Columbia, SC 29221, USA.

JUNDZILL Juliusz, b. 30 Sept 1952, Elk, Poland. Tchr. m. 5 July 1975, 1 s. *Appointments:* Asst 1976-80, Dr 1980-87, Dr Hab 1987-90, Prof 1990-, Acad of Pedagogy, Bydgoszcz. *Publications:* Monery in Latin Christian Literature of Later Roman Empire, 1984; St Ambrose Selections of Hist Prints, 1986; Theoretics Problems of Education in the Roman Family III Century BC - III Century AD, 1987; Romans and the Sea, 1991; Author of about 30 articles. *Memberships:* Polish Learned Soc of Hist; Learned Soc of Philology; Polish Learned Soc of Vautological; Numismatical Comm, Polish Acad of Sci; Comm of Pedagogy and Psychology of Learned Soc. *Honours:* Rector's prize, 1980, 1984, 1987; Min of Educ prize, 1988. *Hobbies:* Roman family in ancient Rome; the management of the sea environment under the ancient Romans. *Address:* Skarzynskiego 6e/13, 80463 Gdansk, Poland.

JUNG Samson P, b. 28 Sept 1963, Hong Kong. VP of Investment Firm. *Education:* AA, City Coll of SF, 1983; BA, SF State Univ, 1990. *Appointments:* Computer Cons, Brasswork, SF, 1980; Dir, Inst of Self Improvement, 1981-83; VP, Eagle Investment Co, 1983-; Computer Analyst, D W Smith & Assoc, 1988-; Owner, Agatha's Bloomers, 1989-. *Publications:* Holistic Enlightenment Learning Process; Inventor of Acupuncture Probe. *Memberships:* Life, Golden Key Soc; Computer Learning Ctr. *Hobbies:* Reading; Health Research; Fishing. *Address:* 1887 South Norfolk Street, San Mateo, CA 94403, USA. 9.

JUNG Timothy Tae Kun, b. 1 Dec 1943, Seoul, Korea. Prof; Physn; Rschr. m. Lucy Moon-Young Jang, 10 Sept 1972, 2 s, 1 d. *Education:* BS, Seoul Nat Univ, 1962-66; MD, Loma Linda Univ, 1969-74; PhD, Univ of MN, 1975-80. *Appointments:* Asst Prof, Dept of Otolaryngology, Univ of MN, 1980-85; Assoc Prof 1985-90, Prof 1990-1992, Clin Prof, 1992-, Div of Otolaryngology, Loma Linda Univ. *Publications:* Author of 32 book chapts, 40 scientific articles, 65 abstracts. *Memberships:* AMA; Am Acad of Otolaryngology; Soc of Univ Otolaryngologists; Assn for Rsch in Otolaryngology; Am Coll of Surgs; Am Laryngological Rhinological Otological Soc (Triological Soc); Am Otological Soc; Am Neurotology Soc. *Honours:* Awd for Basic Rsch in Otolaryngology 1979, Hon Awd 1990, Am Acad of Otolaryngology; Edmund Price Fowler Awd, The Triological Soc, 1988; Mbr of Deafness and Communications Disorder Review Comm, NIDCD, Nat Inst of Hlth, 1989-92; Mbr of Collegian ORLAS, 1992. *Hobbies:* Gardening; Photography; Reading. *Address:* 11790 Pecan Way, Loma Linda University Medical Centre, Loma Linda, CA 92354, USA. 9, 52, 59.

JUNIUS Frans, Marcel, b. 14 July 1930, Mollem, Belgium. Director, National Bank of Belgium. m. Paula Van Haute, 25 July 1958, 2 s, 3 d. *Education:* Lic Econ

Scis, Univ of Leuven, 1959. *Appointments:* Advr, Study Dept, Nat Bank of Belgium, 1965-77, Sec, 1978-80, Dir, 1980-. *Memberships:* Com du Fonds des Rentes; Com de Directin do l'Inst de Reescompte ed de Tarantie; Conseil d'Admin de la Caisse Nat de Credit Profl. *Honours:* Chevalier de l'Ordre de Leopola, 1972; Com de l'Ordre de la Couronne, 1982. *Address:* National Bank of Belgium, Boulevard de Berlaimont 5, B-1000 Brussels, Belgium. 52, 12.

JUNKER Hans Dieter, b. 6 Aug 1936, Hanau, Germany. Univ Prof; Artist. m. Traudel Newiger, 1964, 1 s, 1 d. *Education:* PhD, Univ of Bremen, Germany. *Appointments:* Prof for Art Pedagogy and Art Hist, Erziehungswissenschaftl Hochschule Rheinland-Pfalz, Worms and Koblenz, Germany, 1967-90; Prof for Art Educ and Art Hist, Univ of Koblenz-Landau, Germany, 1990-. *Publications:* Author of num articles and cartoons to mags and books. *Membership:* Co-ed, Zeitschrift fur Kunstpadagogik, 1973-75. *Address:* Riedstr 8, D 6458 Rodenbach, Germany. 43, 52.

JURECKI Krzysztof, b. 24 July 1960, Lubartow, Poland. Histn of Art; Art Critic. m. Mariola Grodzinska, 24 Sept 1983, 1 d. *Education:* Master's degree, Jagiellonian Univ, Cracow, 1979-85; Cand for Dr degree, Inst of Art, Polish Acad of Scis, 1990-. *Appointments:* Mus of Art, Lodz, 1985-89. *Creative works:* Organiser of the exhibs: Nie wider, Stadtmuseum, Dusseldorf, 1989; Changing of the Guards, Galleria FF, Lodz, 1991. *Publications:* Polish Photography of the 80, 1989; Photography the Past Tense and the Present (ed with Dariusz Berdys), 1991; Author of over 80 articles. *Membership:* Assn of Art Histns in Poland, 1987-. *Honour:* Prize-winner, Artistic Olympiad, Warsaw, 1977. *Hobbies:* Reading; Philosophy. *Address:* ul Krolewska 16, 99-300 Kutno, Poland.

JURTH Levente Attila, b. 20 Apr 1980, Vienna, Austria. *Education:* Cello, Piano, Percussion, Composition, Music Theory and Chamber Music studies, 1983-; Assoc Dip in Music, 1991. *Appointments:* Speaker, Cellist, LKGT Quartet, 1987-; Actor, Royal Qld Theatre Co, 1990; Pvt Cello Tchr, 1991-. *Creative works:* Compositions: Melody No 18 for strings, 1985; Melody No 29B for flute and cello, 1985; pieces for piano. *Memberships:* Australian Violoncello Soc, 1984-; Cub Scout, Second, Sixer, Scout, Scout Assn of Australia, 1988-; Convenor, Fans and Friends of Family Chamber Music, 1989-. *Honours:* Full Scholarship, Stoliarsky Sch of Music, Australia, 1985, 1986, 1987; Cert of Distinction in Cello, Australian Music Exam Bd, 1989. *Hobbies:* Electronics; Swimming; Scouting; Irish dance; Languages. *Address:* 17 Shannon Street, Redbank Plains, Brisbane, Queensland, Australia 4301.

JUVARA Ruxandra Polixenia Elena, b. 28 Nov 1942, Bucharest, Romania. Chief Rschr; Lectr. m. Minea Grigorie, 24 Feb 1964. *Education:* Art Hist and Theory, Acad of Arts, Bucharest, 1961-66; Postgrad, intensive eng course, Bucharest, 1975; Tng Course, Ctrl Inst of Informatics, Bucharest, 1977-78; Dr degree, 1990. *Appointments:* Asst Lectr, Acad of Arts, Bucharest, 1966-75; Art Histn, Ctr of Nat Cultural Patrimony, 1975-77; Analyst, Ctr of Informatics, Nat Cultural Patrimony, Bucharest, 1978-85; Rschr 1985-90, Chief Rschr 1990-, Inst of Art Hist, Romanian Acad, Bucharest; Lectr of Costume Hist, Acad of Arts, Bucharest, 1987-. *Publications:* Studii si cercetari de istoria artei; Revue Roumaine d'Histoire de l'Art; Arta; Studies about the presence of Romanian art in various exhibs abroad in the XIXth and XXth centuries; Pub Lectures on Modern Romanian Mag Graphic and Book Illustrations. *Hobbies:* Study of film and stage management; Stage design and costume design; Classical music; Modern literature. *Address:* 68 Jean Louis Calderon, II Section, Bucharest 70 203, Romania.

K

KAARSTED Tage, b. 27 May 1928, Silkeborg, Denmark. Prof. m. Soes Roenlev, 1955, 2 s, 1 d. *Education:* Cand mag 1955, Dr Phil 1968, Aarhus Univ. *Appointments:* Grammar Sch Master, 1955-68; Lectr, Aarhus Univ, 1961-68; Prof, Contemporary Hist, Odense Univ, 1968; Historiographer to HM Queen Margrethe II, 1976. *Publications:* Author of num books about Danish domestic and foreign politics, biographies, diaries. *Memberships:* Royal Danish Acad for Scis Humanities; Royal Danish Soc for Hist. *Honours include:* Radio Denmark Prize, 1968; Gyldendal Prize, 1970; Queen's Danish Prize, 1992; Cmdr of the Royal Order of the Dannebrog, Legion d'honneur. *Address:* Odense University, 5230 Odense, Denmark.

KABANOV Modest M, b. 19 Mar 1926, Leningrad. Psych; Dir. m. Lidiya V Kabanova, 23 July 1955. *Education:* Cand of Med Sci, 1962; Dr of Med Sci, 1972. *Appointments:* Hd of Psych Wardm 1948-1960; Psych-in- Chief of Leningrad, 1960-64; Dir, V M Bekhterev Psychoneurological Rsch Inst, 1964-. *Publications:* Rehabilitation of the Mentally Ill, 1978, 2nd ed 1985; Klinische und soziale Aspekte der Rehabilitation psychischen Kranker, 1981. *Memberships:* VP, World Assn for Dynamic Psych; Hon Chmn, Psych Soc of St Petersburg; Russia Psych Soc, the Mbr of Board; Hungarian & Bulgarian Psych Societies. *Honours:* V M Bekhterev Prize, Acad of Med Scis, 1984; Hon Scientist of RF. *Hobbies:* Reading; Music; Art; Tourism; Old architecture. *Address:* Reshetnikov St 13, Apt 115, St Petersburg 196105, Russia.

KABAT Elvin Abraham, b. 1 Sept 1914, NYC, NY, USA. Immunochem; Biochem; Edr. m. Sally Lennick, 28 Nov 1942, 3 s. *Education:* BS, CCNY, 1932; MA 1934, PhD 1937, DSc Honoris causa 1987, Columbia Univ; LLD (Hon), Univ of Glasgow, 1976; Doct degree (hon), Univ of Orleans, France; PhD (Hon), Weizmann Inst of Sci, Rehovot, Israel. *Appointments include:* Mbr Fac 1941-, Asst Prof Bacteriology 1946-48, Assoc Prof 1948-52, Prof Microbiology 1952-85, Prof Human Genetics & Dev 1969-85, Higgins Prof Microbiology 1984-85, Higgins Prof Emeritus Microbiology 1985-, Lectr, 25th Michael Heidelberger Lecture, Coll Physns & Surgs, 1986, Columbia Univ; Mbr Advsry Panel on Immunology WHO, 1965-; Off of Dir, NIH, 1989-. *Publications include:* Author, Experimental Immunochemisry, 2nd Ed, 1961; Blood Group Substances, Their Chemistry and Immunochemistry, 1956; Structural Concepts in Immunology and Immunochemistry, 1968, 2nd Ed, 1976; Variable Regions of Immunoglobulin Chains (with T T Wu, H Bilofsky), 1976; Sequences of Immunoglobulin Chains (with others); Sequences of Proteins of Immunological Interest, 1983, 5th ed (with T T Wu, H M Perry, K S Gottesman, C Foeller) 1991. *Memberships include:* FAAAS; NAS; Am Acad of Arts & Scis; ACS; Assn for Rsch in Nervous and Mental Diseases; Hon, Japanese Electrophoresis Soc; Phi Beta Kappa; Sigma Xi. *Honours include:* Ann Rsch Awd, City of Hope, 1974; Awd, Ctr for Immunology, SUNY, 1976; R E Dyer Lectr Awd, NIH, 1979; Philip Levine Awd, Am Soc Clin Pathology, 1982; Dickson Prize for Med, Univ of Pitts, 1986; Disting Serv Awd, Columbia Univ Coll of Physns and Surgs, 1988; Acad Medal, NY Acad of Med, 1989; Nat Medal of Sci, 1991. *Address:* 70 Haven Avenue, New York, NY 10032, USA.

KABIRO Zenon, b. 21 May 1956, Mwisale. Plant Breeder. m. Marcelline Kavungerwa, 2 July 1983, 2 s, 1 d. *Education:* BSc, Purdue Univ, USA, 1989. *Appointments:* ISABU, 1977-87, 1990-. *Creative work:* Synthese des travaux de recherche en riziculture dans le perimetre irrigue de l'IMBO-Centre (with P Nkikabajizi, J De Brabandere), 1978-85. *Membership:* Eastern Africa Rsch on Sorghum and Millet. *Honours:* The Keim Family Scholarship in Genetics, Purdue Univ Agronomy Dept, 1989; Sweat and Blister Awd, Heifer Proj Int, Lt Rock, 1989. *Hobbies:* Reading books; Jogging.

KACZMAREK Urszula Zofia, b. 31 Mar 1950, Mirkow, Poland. Dentist; MD; Asst Prof; Subdean. *Education:* Med Acad, Wroclaw, 1967- 72; MD 1978. *Appointments:* Asst 1972-75, Asst Lectr 1975-78, Lectr 1978-86, Asst Prof 1987-, Subdean of Stomatology 1990-, Katedra Stomatologii Zachowawczej. *Publications:* Author of 128 papers in biochemical researches of human saliva, epidemiology of dental caries, periodontal diseases and developmental enamel defects, diagnosis, therapy and prophylaxis of oral diseases. *Membership:* Polish Stomatological Assn, Lodz. *Honours:* Prize, Rector of Med Acad, Wroclaw 1976, 1979, 1980, 1982- 90; Wroclawska Stomatologia, 1983; Hons, Czasopismo Stomatologiczne, 1983, 1984; I prize, Czasopismo Stomatologiczne, 1986. *Hobbies:* Reading; Gardening; Tourism. *Address:* Katedra i Zaklad Stomatologii Zachowawczej, ul Kuznicza 43/45, 50/138 Wroclaw, Poland.

KADIISKI Kiril Krumov, b. 16 June 1947, Kjustendil. Publr. m. 18 Apr 1971, 2 d. *Education:* St Kliment Ohridski, Sofia Univ, 1965-70. *Appointments:* Radio Journalist, 1972-76; Freelance Journalist, Writer, 1977-79; Ed, Narodna kultura Pubing Hse; Estab own pubing hse Nov Zlatorog, 1991-. *Publications:* Concerts in heaven, 1979; Rider on marble horses, 1983; Sand time, 1987; In double abyss, 1990; Selected poems, 1991; Plume of phoenix, 1991; Transls of: Baudelaire, Verlaine, Mallarme, Apollinaire, Blok, Pasternak, Akhmatova, Voloshin. *Memberships:* Union of Transl in Bulgaria, 1975; Union of Bulgarian Writers, 1991. *Honour:* Annual Awd, Transls' Union for best transl, 1980-89. *Hobbies:* Painting; Artistic design and binding of books. *Address:* 24 Chervena iskra str, Sofia 1619, Bulgaria.

KADIJEVIC Djordje, b. 6 Jan 1933, Sibenik. Film & TV Dir; Histn of Art; Art Critic. m. Danica Kolasinac, 12 Aug 1962, 1 s, 1 d. *Education:* Fac of Philos, Dept of Hist of Art, Univ of Belgrade, 1959. *Appointments:* Indep Artist, 1980-. *Creative works:* Author of the films: Holiday, 1967; Visit, 1968; Torrid, 1971; Colonel's Wife, 1973; Holly place, 1990. TV films: Maria's Gifts, 1970; Miracle, 1971; The Oath, 1972; Protege, 1973; Butterfly, 1973; The man who ate a wolf, 1981; The Deat of Karadjordje, 1983. TV serials: Belgrade stories, 1980; Vuk Karadzic, 1987. Author of over 1000 articles in the fields of art criticisms, num art exhibs. *Membership:* Film Artists Assn of Serbia. *Honours:* Golden Wreath, Film Fest of Pula, 1967; David Brith Fndn Prize from film in Venice, 1969; Grand Prize of Rome TV Fest, Chianciano Terme for TV serials, Vuk Karadzic, 1987. *Hobbies:* Sports recreation; Bicycling; Table tennis; Playing classical music on guitar. *Address:* Praska str 35, 11000 Belgrade, Yugoslavia.

KADRI Kartono, b. 9 Dec 1928, Magelang, Indonesia. Ret'd Govt Official; Secretariate. m. R Sri Satiti Prasmini, 20 Jan 1957, 5 s. *Education:* LLM, Gajah Mada State Univ, Yogyakarta, 1958. *Appointments include:* Sr Official to the PM, 1958-65; Sec, Indonesian Rep at Hollandia, West New Guinea, 1962-63; Ret'd from the Cabinet Secretariate of The Republic of Indonesia, 1979; Nat Def & Security Coun, Repub of Indonesia, Non-residential staff, Mbr, Accumulating & Evaluating Comm for the state doctrine on The Nat Tenacity, Mbr, Accumulating and Evaluating Comm for the state doctrine on The Archipelegic State Concept, Mbr, Accumulating and Evaluating Comm on The State Guidance 1988-93, 1993-98. *Publications:* Paper works for assembling Govt Policy on Nation Bldg and Character Bldg. *Membership:* Indonesian Sawmillers and Wood Prod Mfrs' Assn. *Honours:* from The Nat Def and Security Coun, Repub of Indonesia. *Hobbies:* Sports; Out-door life. *Address:* Jl Kramat Batu I No 11, Cilandak, Jakarta 12420, Indonesia.

KAERJAE Juhani A, b. 25 Dec 1934, Kalajoki, Finland. Med Dir; Prof. m. Leena Niemi, 31 July 1960, 1 s, 1 d. *Education:* MD, Univ of Turku, 1960; Specialist in

Otolaryngol, 1966; Dr Med Sc, Univ of Oulu, 1968; Specialist in Audiology, 1979. *Appointments:* Asst Demonstrator in ORL, Univ of Oulu, 1965-72; Prof in ORL 1975-90, Hd Dept of ORL 1975-90, Pres 1984-90, Univ of Kuopio; Med Dir, Pohjois-Savo Hospitar Direct, 1990-. *Publications:* Audiology and Audiological Rehabilitation (co-author), 1978, 1984; Ear Nose and Throat Diseases (joint ed), 1980, 1984, 1990; University Research in Finland (ed), 1989. *Memberships:* Pres, Finnish Coun of Univ Rectors; Chmn, Finnish Coun of Higher Educ; Sci & Tech Policy Coun of Finland; Collegium Oto-Rhino-Laryngo - logicum amicitiae sacrum. *Honour:* Best Paper of the Yr, Ultrastructural Pathology, Hemisphere Pubing Corp, 1984. *Hobbies:* Old doctoral theses; Skiing. *Address:* Pohjois-Savo Hospital District, SF-70210 Kuopio, Finland. 52, 90.

KAFAROVA Elmira Mikail, b. 1 Mar 1934, Azerbaijan, Baku. Chmn. m. Salamov Fuad Mamedali, 10 Oct 1963, 1 s, 1 d. *Education:* Cand of Sci, Baku State Univ, 1958. *Appointments:* Instr, Baku State Univ, 1958-60; Sec 1961-66, 1st Sec 1966-70, Young Communist League; Sec, Baku City Party Comm, 1970-80; Min of Pub Educ, 1980-83; Min for Foreign Affairs, 1983-87; Vice Chmn, Coun of Mins, 1987-89; Chmn, Presidium of the Supreme Soviet of Azerbaijan SSR, 1989-90; Chmn, Supreme Soviet of the Azerbaijan Repub, 1990-. *Honours:* 3 orders of the USSR, the pupil dep of the Supreme Soviet of the USSR, Azerbaijan Repub. *Hobby:* Classical music. *Address:* Rashid Beibutov str 8-140, Azerbaijan Republic, Baku, Russia.

KAFETZ Kalman Meir, b. 3 Dec 1947, London, Eng. Cons Physn. m. Marion Linda Singer, 11 Oct 1972, 2 s, 1 d. *Education:* BSc 1970; MBBS 1973. *Appointments:* Cons Physn, Dept of Med for Elderly People, Whipps Cross & Chingford Hosps, 1982-; Recognised Tchr, London Univ, 1982-; Hon Lectr, Med Coll of St Bartholomews Hosp, 1986-. *Publication:* Clinical Tests - Geriatric Medicine, 1986. *Memberships:* Coun 1985-86, Brit Geriatric Soc; BMA. *Honours:* Wainwright & 1st Chair of S Box Prize, Med, 1972; Lord Riddle Surg Scholarship, 1973; Seymour Graves Coller Prize, Med, 1973. *Hobbies:* Gardening; Cornish history. *Address:* 22 Offham Slope, London N12 7BZ, England.

KAGAWA Yukio, b. 8 May 1935, Yamagata, Japan. Engrng Prof. *Education:* B Eng 1958, M Eng 1960, Dr Eng 1963, Tohoku Univ. *Appointments:* Instr, Tohoku Univ, 1963-66; Rsch Fellow, Tech Univ, Norway, 1966-68; Rsch Fellow, Southampton Univ, 1968-70; Elec Engrng Prof 1970-90, Prof Emeritus 1990-, Toyama Univ; Elec & Electronic Engrng Prof, Okayama Univ, 1990-. *Publication:* Introduction to Finite Element Method for Electrical Engineers, 1977. *Memberships:* Fellow, Inst of Acoustics, UK, 1975; Fellow, Inst of Elec Comm Eng, India, 1984; FIEEE, USA, 1986. *Honour:* Ishikawa Prize, Union of Japanese Scientists and Engrs, 1989. *Hobby:* Travelling. *Address:* Department of Electrical and Electronic Engineering, School of Engineering, Okayama University, Tsushima, Okayama 700, Japan. 52.

KAGEYAMA Kiichi, b. 8 Aug 1936, Kawasaki City, Japan. Prof. m. 4 May 1961, 2 s, 1 d. *Education:* BEc, Dept of Econ(s) 1959, Master, Post Grad Sch 1961, Cand, Post Grad Sch of Econ(s) 1976, Keio Univ, Tokyo. *Appointments:* Lectr 1975, Prof 1980, Prof, Grad Sch 1981, Chief, Fac of Econ(s) 1990-, Chiba Univ of Commerce, Ichikawa; Vis Scholar, Fac of Econ(s), Univ of Cambridge, Eng, 1988. *Publications:* Contemporary Theory on Automobile Industry, 1980; Theory on Economic Development, 1987; Contributor (Treaty), Corporate Groups in Japanese Automobile Industry (English), 1989. *Memberships:* Fuji Royal Country Club, 1978; Dir, Japanese Acad on Foreign Trade, 1981-84; MIT Rsch Proj of The Future of Automobile, 1981-85; Dir, Japanese Acad on Econ Policy, 1983. *Honour:* Medal with Dark, Prime Minister of Japan, 1981. *Hobbies include:* Golf; Tennis; Classical music. *Address:* 12 - 2, 6 Chome Takamatsu, Nerimaku, Tokyo, Japan.

KAIDA Ikuo, b. 27 Sept 1931, Ehime, Japan. Prof. m. 7 May 1960, 3 s. *Education:* BA 1955, MA 1957, PhD 1989, Kansai Univ. *Appointments:* Lectr 1960-63, Asst Prof 1963-73, Prof 1972-, Dean Fac of Econ(s) 1983-84, Kansai Univ. *Publications:* Western Public Finances and Meigi Japan, 1988; System of National Debt and Thought of Public Debt in Meiji Japan, 1989. *Memberships:* Japanese Assn of Pub Fin; Japanese Assn of Home Econ(s). *Honours:* Matsunaga Sci Fndn Grantee, Tokyo, 1965; Pub Mbr of Local Labour Rels Comm in Osaka Prefecture, 1989-. *Hobbies:* Touring; Cinema; Theatre; Museum. *Address:* 2-5-7-304 Hata, Ikeda 563, Japan. 52.

KAISER Gunther Willy Heinz, b. 27 Dec 1928, Walkentied. Prof; Dir. m. Charlotte knoblich, 1955, 1 s, 1 d. *Education:* Doct Law, 1962; Post grad dip of higher educ in Criminology & Penal Law, Tubingen, 1969. *Appointments:* Scientific Asst, Acad Adv Fac of Law, Tubingen, 1963-69; Scientific Mbr, Hd Criminology Rsch Grp 1970, Dir 1973-, MPI; Prof of Criminology and Penal Law, Univ of Freiburg, 1971-; Prof of Criminology and Penal Law, Univ of Zurich, Switzerland, 1982-; Doctoral hon degs: Univ of Miskole, Hungary and Univ of Wroclaw, Poland, 1991; Basque Univ of San Sebastian, Spain, 1992. *Publications:* Randalierende Jugend, 1959; Verkehrsdelingue und Generalprvention, 1970; Jugendkriminalität, 1982; Kriminologie Ein Lehrbuch, 1988. *Memberships:* Int Assn of Penal Law; Int Soc of Criminology; Neue Kriminological Gesellschaft; Rotary Club. *Hobby:* Gardening; Special Interests: Comparative Criminology; Criminal Justice; Juvenile Court Law; Corrections. *Address:* Burgstrasse 10, D-W7830 Emmendingen, Germany.

KAISER Wolfgang Albert, b. 22 Feb 1923, Schoental, Germany. Univ Prof. m. Klara Thoma, 15 Sept 1951, 2 d. *Education:* Dip Ing 1951, Dr Ing 1955, Univ of Stuttgart. *Appointments:* Rsch Engr 1954, R & D Dir 1963-67, Mbr Superisory Bd, Sel-Co, Stuttgart; Prof for Telecommunications, 1967-. *Publications:* Author of 12 books and 100 papers on Telecommunications. *Memberships:* Info Tech, Gesellschaft; Chmn Rsch Coun, Mnendiner Kreis; Chmn of Scientific Bd, Heinrich-Herlz Inst, Berlin. *Honours:* FIEEE, 1979; Mbr of Acad of Scis, Heidelberg, 1982; Serv Medal, State of Baden-Wuerffemberg, 1982; Dr Ing Eh, Univ of Munich, 1985; Serv Medal, Germany, 1987. *Address:* Florathweg 17, D 7000 Stuttgart - 80, Germany.

KAKKAD Sunil Shantilal, b. 19 May 1959, Kampala, Uganda. Solicitor. m. Darshna Hindocha, 23 Aug 1984, 1 s. *Education:* Alder Sch & Barnet Coll, 1972-78; Univ of Hull, 1978-81; The Coll of Law, Guildford, 1981-82. *Appointments:* Brecher & Co, Articled Clerk, 1982- 84; Hill Dickinson & Co, Solicitor, 1984-89; Hill Taylor Dickinson, Partner, 1989-. *Membership:* The Law Soc. *Hobbies:* Reading; Music. *Address:* Irongate House, Dukes Place, London EC3A 7LP. England. 1.

KALETA Jozef, b. 28 Feb 1925, Kasina, Weilka, Poland. Prof of Economics. m. Danuta Stankiewicz Keleta, 30 July 1955, 1 s, 1 d. *Education:* Univ of Wroclaw; Masters Degree in Law, 1954; PhD, 1960; Habilitatus Degree, 1967; Assoc Prof of Economics, 1971; Prof of Economics, 1976. *Appointments:* Mroclaw Regional Council, 1947-50, 1953-57; Oscar Lange Acad of Economics, Wroclaw, 1957-60; Snr Inst, 1960-67; Lectr, 1967-71; Asst Prof, 1971-76; Assoc Prof, 1976-. *Publications include:* Over 400 Publi; Regional Budget Planning; Budget Economic Organizations; Prospects for Overcoming the Crisis; The road to Market. *Memberships:* Economic Sci Committee of the Polish Acad of Sci; Forecasting Committee, PAN; Deputy of Parliament; Economic Section of the Central Committee on Acad Titles & Degrees; Main Bd of the Polish Economic Soc. *Honours:* Sveral State Decorations inc: Knoghts Cross of the Order of Polonia Pestituta; The First Degree Award of the Epoka Publi. *Hobbies:* Sports;

Travel; Grandchildren. *Address:* Kutnowska 26a, 53-135 Wroclaw, Poland. 152.

KALIAGUINE Serge Claude Francois, b. 4 July 1940, Sigoules, France. Prof. m. Kim In Young, 31 Oct 1980, 1 s, 2 d. *Education:* Ing IGG Toulouse, 1964; Doct Ing Univ de Toulouse, 1967. *Appointments:* Prof Adjoint, Univ Laval, 1967; Prof Agrere, Univ Laval, 1972; Prof, Titulaire, Univ Laval, 1977. *Publications:* Over 100 Publi in Sci Journals. *Memberships:* Chemical Inst of Canada; Canadian Soc of Chemical Engrng. *Honour:* Best Paper Award in Canada J Chem Engr. *Hobbies:* Travel; Cinema; Reading. *Address:* Dept de Genie Chimique, Pavillon Adrien Pouliot, Univ Laval, Ste Foy QC, Canada G1K 7P4.

KALIMI Isaac, b. 15 Dec 1952, Mieyandab, North Iran. Prof of Biblical Studies. m. Esther, 17 Mar 1982, 2 s, 1 d. *Education:* BA, Hebrew Univ, 1976; MA, Hebrew Univ, 1978; Post Grad, Biblical Historiography, Hebrew Univ, 1982-84; Post Doctorate, Ruprecht Karls Univ, Heidelburg, 1989- 90; PhD, Hebrew Univ of Jerusalem, 1989. *Appointments include:* Lectr, Biblical Studies, 1977-80; Researched, Wrote & Broadcast, series of Lectures on the Bible, 1980-83; Lectrs in Biblical Studies, 1991; Lectr, 1991. *Publications include:* Die Geschichtsschreibung des Chronisten; The Books of Chronicles. *Memberships:* Soc of Biblical Literature; Assn for Jewish Studies; Intl Organ for the Study of the Old Testament. *Honours include:* ssa 00Songs Prize for Biblical Researcher; World Sepharadhi Federation, Research Prize. *Hobbies:* Reading; Classical Music; Travel; Movies; Theatre; Swimming. *Address:* 7 38 Diskin Street, Jerusalem 91072, Israel.

KALIMO Esko Antero, b. 9 July 1937, Helsinki. Research Dir; Prof. m. Raija Moilanen, 20 Dec 1964, 1 s, 1 d. *Education:* Legitimate Psychologist, 1967; Doctor of Soc Sci, 1969. *Appointments:* Johns Hopkins Univ, Baltimore, 1969-70; Social Insurance Inst, Helsinki, Finland, 1964-; World Health Organ, Geneva, 1974-75, 1981-83; Mordic Sch of Public Health, 1989- . *Publications:* 250 Scientific Publi; Books; Sci Articles in Journals. *Memberships:* world Health Organ; Advisory Committee on Soc Security Research of Intl Soc Security Assn. *Honours:* Decoration Order of the Lion of Finland; Decoration, Order of the White Rose on Finland. *Hobbies:* Reading; Travel; Tennis. *Address:* Kilonkallionkuja 6, SF 02610 Espoo, Finland. 52.

KALITA Zdzislaw Jan, b. 6 Aug 1936, Lubnice. Philosophy Prof. m. (1) dec, 2 d, (2) Alicja Ordczynska, 24 Aug 1991. *Education:* BA, Philosophy, 1964; MA, 1977. *Appointments:* High Sch Tchr, 1964-90; Univ Prod, Wroclaw Univ, 1970-. *Publications:* In the Renaissance Regnum Hominis G Manetti and His Philosphy of Man; The Ethics of Renaissance, Humanity. *Memberships:* Polish Assn of Philosophy; Soc of History of Religion; Inst of Philosophy. *Honours include:* The Minister of Educ Award; Golden cross of Merit. *Hobbies:* Reading; Photography; Bridge. *Address:* ul Rogowska 34/24, 54 440 Wroclaw, Poland.

KALLAY Nikola I, b. 5 Sept 1942, Zagreb. Prof of Chemistry. m. Visnja, 12 Jan 1972, 1 s. *Education:* Faculty of Tech, Univ of Zagreb, BSc, 1967; Faculty of Sci, Univ of Zagreb, Master of Sci, 1972; Dr Sci, 1973. *Appointments:* Chemistry Dept, Faculty of Sci, Univ of Zagreb, Research Asst, 1969; Research Assoc, 1977; Asst Prof, 1978; Asso Prof, 1982; Full Prof, 1988; Asst Dean, 1982-83. *Publications:* Articles inc: Physical Chemistry of Colloids & Interfaces; The Extent of Reaction Concept; Extent of Reaction, Its Significance in Thermodynamics & Kinetics; Books inc. Novi pristup racunanju u kemiji; Quantities, Units & Symbols in Physical Chemistry. *Memberships:* Croatian Chemical Soc; American Chemical Soc; Intl Assn of Colloid & Interface Scientists; Commission on Quantities & Units, Intl Union of Pure & Applied Chemistry. *Honours:* Rudjer Boskovic Award Intl Advisory Committe, Intl Symposium on Surfactants. *Hobbies:* Hunting; Fishing; Painting.

Address: Laboratory of Physical Chemistry, Faculty of Sci, Univ of Zagreb, PO Box 163, 41001 Zagreb, Croatia.

KALLENDORF Craig William, b. 23 June 1954, Cincinnati, Ohio. Assoc Prof of English & Classics. *Education:* BA, Valparaiso Univ, 1975; MA, Univ of North Carolina, 1977; PhD, Univ of North Carolina, 1982. *Appointments:* Asst Prof of English & Classics, 1982-88; Assoc Prof, 1988-. *Publications:* Latin Influences on English Literature; Selected Letters; In Praise of Aeneas; Epistle of St Paul to the Romans. *Memberships:* Renaissance Soc of America; Intl Soc for Neo Latin Studies; American Philological Assn; Intl Soc for the History of Rhetoric; Modern Language Assn; American Dante Soc. *Honours include:* Nat Endowment for the Humanities; Delmas Foundation Grant for Study in Venice. *Hobby:* Music. *Address:* 1209 Haines Drive, College station, TX 77840, USA. 7.

KALLUM Bengt O, b. 21 Feb 1938, Malmoe. Asst Prof. m. Christina Eklund, 15 Dec 1989, 1 s, 2 d. *Education:* MD, Univ of Lund, 1966; Specialist in Gen Surgery, 1970; PhD, Univ of Lund, 1974; Specialist in Radiation Oncology, 1980. *Appointments:* Asst, General Surgery, Univ Hosp, Lund, 1970-74; Special Fellow General Surgery, memorial Sloan Kettering Cancer Centre, New York, 1974-75; Asst Prof, Radiation Oncology, 1980- . *Contributions to:* Articles to Profl Journals. *Hobbies:* Tennis; Wood Turning. *Address:* Dept of Oncology, Univ Hospital, 221 85 Lund, Sweden. 52

KALOWSKI Miron Serafin, b. 20 Dec 1929, Poznan. Prof of Medical Sci. m. Sabina Pawlowska, 16 Jan 1954, 1 s, 1 d. *Education:* Karol Marclinkoski Coll, Poznań, 1950; Sch of Medicine, Gdańsk, Dental Surgeon with Distinction, 1954; Doctor of Dental Medicine, 1960; Habilitate Doctor, 1971; Assoc Prof, 1972; Prof, 1980. *Appointments:* Sch of Medicine, Gdańsk, Dept of Conservative Dentistry and Med Microbiology, 1955-70; Bd of Medical Faculty, since 1971-; Head Dept Experimental Dentistry, 1971-82; Hd Dental Subfaculty, 1971-78; Hd Dept Oral Microbiology, 1982-92. *Publications:* Co-author of Four Editions of Pharmacology for Dental Students, Sections in Books; Author or Co Author of Numerous Papers; Published Sev 100 Abstracts in Oral Res Abstr, Amer; Dental Assn, Chicago. *Memberships:* Polish Dental Assn; Mem, Headquarters Plenum Board, 1981-89; Council on AIDS prophylaxis; Cieszunski Prizes Commision, VP, 1978-81 and Pres, 1981-89, Gdansk Branch of Polish Dental Assn; Polish Soc for Microbiology & Others Scientifici Soc. *Honours include:* Prize for Habilitate Doctor Dissertation; Special Awards, Dental Assn & Sch Scientific Bd. *Hobbies:* Fishing; Gardening; Dog. *Address:* ul Migowska 22, 80 287 Gdansk, Poland.

KALOYANIDES Michael George, b. 17 July 1950, Arlington, Massachusetts, USA. Prof of Humanities; Musician. m. Sheila Wade, 2 June 1979, 1 s, 2 d. *Education:* BA, Wesleyon Univ, 1972; PhD, Wesleyan Univ, 1975. *Appointments:* Prof of Humanities, Univ of New Haven, 1976-; Chmn, Dept of Visual & Performing Arts & Philosophy, Univ of New Haven, 1983-. *Publications:* Greek Music from the Isle of Crete; Turkish Folk Music; The Royal Archives of EBLA. *Memberships:* Audio Engrng Soc; Soc for Ethnomusicology; Modern Greek Studies Assn; Astronomica Soc of New Haven. *Honour:* Mellon Fellow, Yale Univ. *Hobbies:* Astronomy; Music. *Address:* Dept of Visual & Performing Arts & Philosophy, Univ of New Haven, West Havem, CT 06516, USA. 117.

KALTENIS Petras, b. 12 Nov 1937, Berzyte, Kedainiai District. Hd, Centre of Pediatrics, Univ of Vilnius; Prof of Pediatrics; Physician. m. Liudmila Steponaityte, 26 June 1965, 1 s, 2 d. *Education:* Medical Acad of Kaunas, Physician, 1961; Medical Sciences, 1970; Assoc Prof, 1972; Doc of Medical Sci, 1987; Prof, 1990. *Appointments include:* Editor, Lithuanian Encyclopaedia, 1961-63; Asst Prof, Dept of Pediatrics, Univ of Vilnius, 1963-72; Hd, Dept of Medical

Information, Res Inst Exptl Clin Med, Vilnius, 1972-74; Assoc Prof, Univ Vilnius, 1974-90; Hd, Centre of Pediatrics, 1991-. *Publications:* Functional Heart Murmurs in Children; Childrens Diseases; Renal Diseases in Childhood; Guide Book for Pediatricians; 150 Papers. *Memberships:* Intl Pediatric Nephrology Assn; Intl Soc Human Rights; Lithuanian Med Assn; Lithuanian Pediatrics Soc. *Hobbies:* Gardening; Reading. *Address:* Antakalnio Street 95-3, 2040 Vilnius, Lithuania.

KALTSOS Angelo John, b. 19 Aug 1930, Boston, Massachusetts, USA. Photographer; Educator; Mgr, Pampas Inc. m. Verna Kay Wilson, 1 s, 6 d. *Education:* Mass Radio & TV, 1955-57; Harvard Extension Coll, 1964; Boston State Coll, 1965-67; Univ of New Mexico, 1976; Fitchburg State Coll, 1977. *Appointments:* US Army, 1948-52; US Postal Clerk, Boston, 1954- 57; Eletronic Research Tech, Crosley Div of Avco Cincinnati, Ohio, 1957; Enviromental, research & Production Electronic Tech, Supervisor, Raytheon Mfg Co, Massachusetts, 1957-63; Educator, Cambridge Sch Dept, Cambridge, 1961-81; Mgr, Pampas Inc, Boston; Bd of Dir, Expansion Dancers, 1980-. *Creative Works:* Intl Brotherhood of Electrical Works; photo Exhibits. One Man Shows. *Memberships:* Appalachian mtn Club; No Thank Q Hydro Quebec. *Honours:* 5 Pueblo Indian Educ. *Hobbies:* Ethnology; Entomology; Cooking; Gardening; Hiking; Travel; Writing Prose & Poetry; Naturalist; Enviromentalist. *Address:* 10 Lesley Avenue, Somerville, MA 02144, USA. 6.

KAMENOV Zahary Petrov, b. 30 July 1949, Vidin, Bulgaria. Artist. m. 7 July 1972, 1 d. *Education:* Acad of Fine Arts, Sofia, 1974. *Appointments:* Free Artist, Take Part in Almost all Nat Exhibitions, Some Representative Contemorary Bulgarian Graphic Art. *Creative Works:* One Man Shows, Sofia, Vidin, Gabrovo, Varna, Bratislava, Mexico City; Autumn Exhibition in Plov Div; Group Exhib. *Membership:* Union of the Bulgarian Artists; Soc 33. *Honours include:* Award for Graphic Art. *Hobbies:* Archaelogy; Collecting Old Keys; Old Photos. *Address:* 1172, Compl Isgrev, Bl 11/D, Sofia 1172, Bulgaria.

KANAZAWA Takafumi, b. 5 Dec 1926, Toyko. Chemistry Educator. m. Taiko Suzuki, 8 May 1955, 1 s. *Education:* Bach, Univ Toyko, 1948; PhD, Univ Toyko, 1961. *Appointments:* Research Assoc, 1952-57; Lect, 1957-62; Assoc Prof, 1962-66; Prof, 1966-90; Prof Emeritus, 1990-; Toyko Metropolitan Univ; Prof, 1992- ; Chiba Inst of Tech. *Publications:* Industrial Mineral Chemistry; Tnorganic Phosphorus Chemistry; Inorganic Phosphate Materials. *Memberships:* Chemical Soc of Japan; Ceyamic Soc of Japan; Surface Sci Soc of Japan; Japanese Assn of Inorganic Phosphorus Chemistry; American Ceramic Soc. *Honours:* Scientific Award Ceram Soc Japan; Treatise Award Soc Gypsum and Lime; Jyotaki Award Soc Powder Technol Japan. *Hobbies:* Essay Writing; Modern Japanese Literature. *Address:* Sakura 1 62 12, Setagaya Ku, Tokyo 156, Japan. 1.

KANAZAWA Yoshiki, b. 25 Aug 1929, Toyko. Prof of Joetsu Univ of Educ. m. Kazue Saitoh, 28 Sept 1963, 2 d. *Education:* Toyko Univ of Educ, 1953; Univ of Toyko, MA, 1956. *Appointments:* Kotchi Nat Tech Coll, Kisarazu Nat Tech Coll, Univ of Tsukuba, Lectr, 1981-86; Joetsu Univ of Educ, Prof, 1984-. *Publications include:* The Outline of Histories; Questions on Alexander the Great; Egitto e Storia Antica Dallellenismo All'eta Araba. *Memberships:* The Classical Soc if Japan; The Historical Soc of Japan; The Soc for Near Eastern Studies in Japan; The Paleological Assn of Japan; Japan Greece Soc; Assn Intl de Papyrologues. *Hobbies:* Gardening; Interested in Men Of War, Both World Wars. *Address: ssa 00*Motoshiro 5 5 103 Joetsu Takada, J 943 Japan. 52.

KANIAVA Eduardas, b. 1 July 1937, Klaipeda, Lithuania. Singer. m. Barbora Abramaviciute, 8 Jan 1969, 2 s. *Education:* Student of Lithuanian Conservatoire, 1955-60; Probationes of Sofia Opera, 1966-67. *Appointments:* Solist, Lithuanian Opera, 1958; Prof, Lithuanian Conservatoire, 1979; Hd Dept, Lithuanian Conservatoire, 1989. *Creative Works:* Germont, Figaro Di Posa Rigoletto; Jago Onegin Porgy Alekko. *Memberships:* Intl Theatre Assn; Lithuanian Theatre Assn. *Honours:* Merrited Artist of the Republikin; Name of the Peoples Artist; Name of the Peoples Artist in the USSR. *Hobbies:* Driving; Hunting. *Address:* Blindziu 19-1, 23004 Vilnius, Lithuania.

KANNAPPAN P L, b. 28 June 1934, Nattorason Kottai, India. Prof of Mathematics. m. Renganayaki, 1952, 3 s, 2 d. *Education:* BSc, Annamalai Univ, 1955; MS, PhD, Univ of Washington, USA, 1964. *Appointments:* Lectr, 1955-61; Reader, 1964-66; At Annamalai; Research Asst, Univ of Washington, 1961-44; Assoc Prof, 1967-76; Prof, Univ of Waterloo, 1977-. *Publications:* Over 100 Papers in Profl Journals. *Memberships:* American Mathematics Soc; Ind Mathematical Soc; Indian Acad Sci; Ramanujan Maths Soc. *Honours:* Frist Rank Littlelail Maths Prize; Fulbright Scholarship. *Hobbies:* Stamps; Coins; Literature. *Address:* Dept of Pure Mathematics, Univ of Waterloo, Waterloo, Ontario, Canada N2L 3G1.

KANTOR Jeffrey Clair, b. 10 July 1954, Intl Falls, Minnesota, USA. Assoc Prof. m. Diane Bradley, 25 June 1977, 2 s. *Education:* BS ChE, Univ of Minnesota, 1972-76; Princeton Univ, PhD, 1976-81. *Appointments:* Univ of Tel Aviv, 1980-81; Univ of Notre Dame, 1981-91. *Publications:* More than 30 Papers. *Memberships:* American Inst of Chemical Engrs; Inst of Electrical & Electronic Engrs. *Honours:* Presidentual Young Investigator Award; Henry & Camille Dreyfus Tchr Scholar Award. *Address:* 1712 East Wayne, South Bend, IN 46615, USA.

KANWAL Harbans Singh, b. 5 Apr 1932, Indai. Hotelier; Company Chmn. m. Sheila Dharam Chand, 31 July 1971. *Education:* BA, Bach of Arts; BT, Bach of Tchrng; Panjab Univ. *Appointments:* Self Employed 1983-; Shop Owner; Hotelier. *Memberships:* TGWU; Indian Worlers Assn; Indian Social & Welfare Assn, Hounslow; Immigran Welfare Soc, Cranfor. *Honours:* Labour Councilor; Deputy Mayor; Vice Chmn, Transport & Cleaning Committee; Chmn, Enviromental Health & Renact Sub Committee. *Hobbies:* Classical Music; Gardening; Organize Social Events for Charity. *Address:* 43 Woodfield Road, Cranford, Middx TW4 6LL, England.

KAPERA Jan Kazimierz, b. 3 Mar 1968, Przenosza. 5th Yr Student, Jagiellonian Univ. *Education:* Theory of Film, 1989-91; Librarianship & Information Sci Dept, Jagiellonian Univ, 1987-92. *Creative Works:* Bibliography of Zygmunt Katuzynslu; Show Games by Jerry Andzejewski; In the World of Painting and Music of M K Curliomis; A Schzoid Man in the Garden of Love. *Hobbies:* Books; Literature. *Address:* 34 620 Jodlownik 22, Poland.

KAPKO Justyna Mapjozota, b. 20 Feb 1970, Kratoo, Poland. Student of Medicine. *Education:* Medical Acad in Kraboo. *Hobbies:* Sci Fiction; Reading; History; Biology; Medicine. *Address:* ul Opolske 53 142, Kratoo, Poland.

KAPTEYN Paul Joan George, b. 31 Jan 1928, Laren, Netherlands. Judge European Communities, Court of Justice. m. Ieteke Streef, 20 Mar 1956, 1 s, 1 d. *Education:* LLM Leiden Univ, 1945-50; Doctor of Law, Leiden Univ, 1960. *Appointments:* Official Min of Foreign Affairs, 1960-63; Prof on the Law of Intl Organization, Utrecht and Leiden Univ, 1963-76; Member, Council of State, 1976-90; Judge Court of Justice, 1990-. *Creative Works:* Introduction to the Law of the European Communities. *Memberships:* Royal Dutch Acad of Sci; Dutch Soc inf Intl Law. *Honour:* Commander of the Order of Ornjje Nassua. *Address:* c/o Court of Justice of the European Communities, Palais de Justice L 2925, Luxembourg. 43, 52, 139.

KAPUR Harish, b. 21 Feb 1928, Jhelum. Prof, Graduate Inst of Intl Studies, Geneva. div, 1 d. *Education:* BA, 1951; LLB, 1953; MA, 1955; PhD, 1964. *Appointments:* Asst Legal Adviser, UN High Commissioner, Refugees, 1957-62; Prof, Graduate Inst, 1962-. *Publications include:* Soviet Union & Asia; The Awakening Giant; The End of An Isolation; Distant Neighbours. *Hobbies:* Walking; Cooking. *Address:* 132 Rue de Lausanne, 1211 Geneva 21, Switzerland.

KAPUSCINSKI Ryszard, b. 4 Mar 1932, Pinsk. Writer; Journalist. m. Alicja Mielczarek, 6 Oct 1952, 1 d. *Education:* Ma, Faculty of History, Warsaw Univ. *Appointments:* Sztandar Mtodych, 1951; Polityka, 1957-61; Corr Polish Press Agency, 1962-72. *Publications:* Bush Polish Style; The Emperor; The Soccer War; The Shah of Shahs; Another Day of Life. *Memberships:* PEN Club Polish Centre; Polish Assn of Artistic Photographers; Mem, Nat Coun of Culture; Mem, Bd of Advs, New Perspective Quarterly. *Honours:* Gold Cross of Merit; Knights Cross; Order Polonia Restituta; Prize of Intl Journalists. *Hobby:* Photography. *Address:* ul Prokuratorska 11/2, 02-074 Warsaw, Poland.

KARACSONYI Sandor, b. 19 Apr 1932, Budapest. Surgeon. m. Adrienne Ferencz, 11 Aug 1957, 1 s. *Education:* Semmelweis Medical Univ, Budapest, 1956. *Appointments:* Semmelweis Medical Univ, 1st Dept of Surgery, 1957-81; Szent Gyorgyi Albert Medical Univ, Dept of Surgery, 1982-. *Publications include:* Lber Abdominalchir f die Praxis, Leipzig. *Memberships:* Intl Soc of Surgery; World Assn of HPB Surgery; German Surgical Assn; Gastro Surgical Club; Hungarian Surgical Soc. *Honours:* Honorary Member, Chechoslovakain Purkyne Surgical Soc; Surgical Soc of Poland. *Hobbies:* Tourism; Classical Music; Opera. *Address:* Albert Szent Gyorgyi Medical Univ, Dept of Surgery, PO Box 464, Szeged, 6701 Hungary.

KARATSU Osamu, b. 25 Apr 1947, Tokyo, Japan. Large Scale Integration Researcher. *Education:* BS, Tokyo Univ, 1970; MS, Tokyo Univ, 1972; PhD, 1975. *Appointments:* Reseacher, Musashino Labs, Tokyo, 1975-79; Staff Researcher, 1979-83; Snr Staff Researcher, NTT LSI Labs, Japan, 1983-86; Research Group Leader, 1987; Snr Mgr NTT Headquarters, Tokyo, 1988-89; Snr Research Mgr, NTT LSI Labs, 1989-90; Exec Mgr, 1991-. *Creative Works:* Introduction to Vary Learge Scale Integrations Design; Microelectronics Series; Encyclopedia of Information Science. *Memberships include:* American Physical Soc; IEEE: Japan Soc Applied Physics. *Honours:* Best Paper Award. *Hobbies:* Playing & Listening to Classical Music. *Address:* 5 19 2 Hiroo 501, Shibuya ku, Tokyo 150 Japan. 52, 132.

KARDJILOV Christo Rashov, b. 10 Sept 1952, Sofia. Artist. m. Gergana Dimitrova Kardjilova, 26 July 1981, 1 d. *Education:* High Art Sch, 1967-71; Army service, 1971-73; Art Acad, Sofia, 1978. *Appointments:* Art Editor, Advertisement Agency, 1983-90; Liberal Artist, 1990-. *Creative Works:* Is There Life in Island; Megalithes; Monument: A Great number of Illustrations of books for Children. *Memberships:* Uion of the Bulgarian Artist. *Honours include:* Prizes of Graphic; for Illustration; Book design. *Hobbies:* Music; French Language & Culture. *Address:* ul Rakovski 157A, Sofia 1000, Bulgaria.

KAREKLAS Petros M, b. 19 Apr 1949, Kythrea, Cyprus. Hd Dept of Industry & Econ Research. m. Ursula Vallo, 29 Oct 1979, 2 d. *Education:* Gynasium, 1967; Diplom Volkswirt, Univ of Freiburg, Germany, 1977; MA, Univ of S Carolina, 1983; PhD, Univ of S Carolina, 1986. *Appointments:* Cyprus Government Officer, 1969-86; Research & Teaching Asst, USC; Co Researcher, Project for the Bank of Jamaica; Hd, Dept of Ind & Econ Research. *Publications:* Studies in Econ Analysis; Many articles on Ecom; Book Reviews; Magazines. *Memberships:* Former Pres of Greek student Assn, Freiburg; Pres Cypriof-German Assoc; Movement for

Europe; Cyprus Soc for Sci; American Econ Assoc. *Honours include:* Scholarship from DAAD, CASP; Intl Honor Soc in Econ; Officer's Cross of Merit from F.R Germany. *Hobbies:* Reading; Classical Music; Football; Swimming. *Address:* 46 Arch Makarios Avenue, Aglandjia, Nicosia 123, Cyprus. 52.

KARKLINS Ludvigs, b. 19 Aug 1928, Latvia. Musicologist. m. Karklina Austra, 28 Nov 1964, 2 s, 2 d. *Education:* Leningrad, Art Sci, 1969; Moscow, Dr Art Sci, 1982; Dr. hab. art, 1992. *Appointments:* Asst Prof, Hd of the Chair of Music Theory, Latvian Acad of Music, 1963-80; Vice Chancellor, Research Work, 1980; Prof, 1983. *Creative Works:* Mjaskovskys Harmony; Symphonic Works in Latvian Music; Symphonism of Janis Ivanovs; Latvian Symphonic Music; Symphonic Music in Latvia. *Memberships:* Latvian Composers Union. *Honours include:* Laureate of the Janis Ivanovs Prize. *Hobbies:* Theatre; Flowers. *Address:* 1 Kr Barona St, Riga 226050, Latvia. 1.

KARKLISIISKI Tommy, b. 8 June 1955, Varna, Bulgaria. Musicologist; Asst in Music Analysis, State Acad of Music. *Education:* State Music High Sch, Varna, 1969-74; State Acad of Music, Sofia, 1976- 81; Faculty of Theory, PhD, 1988. *Appointments:* Asst in Music Analysis, State Acad of Music, 1982-. *Memberships:* Union of the Bulgarian Composers. *Honours:* 1st Prize for Piano Duet Players; awards from the Union of the Bulgarian Composers. *Hobby:* Technics. *Address:* State Acad of Music, 11 Klement Gotvald Boulevard, 1505 Sofia, Bulgaria.

KARL Robert H, b. 4 Sept 1947, Milwaukee, Wisc, USA. Physician. m. Nilza Karl, 14 Jan 1979, 2 s, 1 d. *Education:* BA, Northwestern Univ, 1965-69; MD, Washington Univ, 1969-73; Univ Miami, 1973-76. *Appointments:* Private Practice, Cardiology, 1978-; Chief Cardiology, Baptist Hosp, 1987-89; Assistant chief dept of Medicine Baptist Hospital, 1991-; Clinical Asst, Univ of Miami, 1978-. *Memberships include:* Dale County Medical Assn; American Coll of Cardiology; American Heart Assoc; Child Abuse Prevention Project. *Honours:* Intl Medicine; Cardiovascular Diseases, (board certified). *Hobbies:* Reading; Skiing; Piano; Horseback Riding; Karate; Tennis; Raquet ball. *Address:* 8950 N Kendall Drive, 302, Miami, FL 33176, USA. 1.

KARLINSKY Simon, b. 22 Sept 1924, Harbin, China. Prof of Slavic Languages & Literatures. *Education:* Belmont High Sch, 1941; Music Studies with Honegger, Paris, 1950-51; Blachen, Berlin, 1952-58; BA, UC Berkeley, 1960; MA, Harvard Univ, 1961; PhD, UC Berkeley, 1964. *Appointments:* US Army service, 1944-46; Conference Interpreter & Liaison Officer, 1946-58; Asst Prof, UC Berkeley, 1964; Assoc Prof, Harvard, 1966; Prof, Berkeley, 1967-91; Emeritus, 1991-. *Publications include:* Marina Tsvetaeva, Her Life & Art; Anton Chekhov's Life & Thought; Marina Tsvetaeva, The Woman, Her World & Her Poetry. *Memberships:* AAASS; AATSEEL. *Honours:* Woodrow Wilson Fellowship; Guggenheim Fellowship (twice); Humanities Research Fellowship. *Research Interests:* Russian Literature, Culture & Music; French & English Literature; Chekhov, Nabokov, Tsvetaeva; Theophile Gautier; Tchaikovsky, Stravinsky, Ravel, Gay Studies. *Hobbies:* Sailing; Opera. *Address:* Dept of Slavic Languages & Literatures, Univ of California, Berkeley, CA 94720. USA. 2.

KARPATI George, b. 17 May 1934, Hungary. Prof of Neurology. 2 s. *Education:* MD, Dalhousie Univ, Halifax, Nova Scotia, Canada, 1960. *Appointments:* Montreal Neurological Inst of McGill Univ & Royal Victoria Hosp. *Publications:* 200 Sci Articles; 1 Book, co author; 2 Books authored. *Honour:* Isaac Walton Killam Chair of Neurology. *Address:* 3801 Univ Street, Montreal, Quebec, Canada H3A 2B4.

KARPENKO Yuriy Alexandrovich, b. 29 Sept 1929, Malin, Ukraine. Philology; Linguistics; Onomastics. m. Musa, 1 Sept 1950, 1 s, 1 d. *Education:* Lvov Univ, 1953; Philologocial Sci, 1956; Snr Lectr, 1957; Doc of Philological Sci, 1967; Prof, 1968. *Appointments:* post Grad Chernovtsy Univ, 1953; Ukzainian Language Lectr, Chezn Univ, 1956; Hd of General Linguistics, 1958; Odessa Univ, 1968; Hd of Gen Ping, Hd of Russian Language Dept, 1979. *Publications include:* 273 Sci Works. *Memberships:* Intl Committee of Onomastic Sci; Ukzainian Slavistic Committee; Ozthographical Commission of Ukzainaian Acad of Sci; Onomastic Subcommission of Intl Slavistic Committee. *Hobbies:* Cats; Post Cards. *Address:* 24/26, Univ Philological Faculty, Russian Language Dept, Frantsuzskiy Blvd, 270056 Odessa, Ukraine.

KARPOWICZ Andrzej Mikolaj, b. 6 Dec 1948, Warsaw. Lawyer. m. 25 Oct 1991, 1 s. *Education:* Warsaw Univ, MA, 1966-70. *Appointments:* Arkady Publising House, Deputy of Dir, 1973-84; Polish Soc of Authors, Zaiks, Legal Adviser, 1984-89; Under Sec of State ministry of Culture & Arts, 1990-91; Juris Co, Ltd, Conslts, Barristers, Solicitors, 1991-. *Publication:* A Handbook of Copyright Law. *Memberships:* Polish Soc of Editors; Council of Polish Chamber of Book. *Hobby:* Reading. *Address:* ul Nowomiejska 21 m.30, 00-260 Warsaw, Poland.

KARSCH Christian, b. 25 Aug 1940, Warnsdorf. Economist. m. Gertraud Schneemayer, 9 Dec 1964, 1 d. *Education:* Dr Rer Pol, Univ of Vienna. *Appointments:* Univ Asst, Dept of Economics, Univ of Vienna, 1964-83; Chief Economist, Austrian Insurance Offices Assn, 1984-; Sec of Personal Ins, Mgr of Gesellschaft für Versicherrungsfachwissen, Austrian Ins Offices Assn, 1992-. *Contributions to:* More than 30. *Memberships:* Austrian Econ Assn; American Econ Assn; Regional Sci Assn; Carl Menger Inst; European Assn for Evol Pol Econ; Assn for Ins Math. *Hobbies:* Sailing; Contemp Fine Art. *Address:* Gruenentorgasse 12/15, A-1090 Vienna, Austria. 52.

KARUNATILAKE Halwalage Neville Sepala, b. 1 Mar 1930, Colombo. Governor, Central Bank of Sri Lanka. m. Malini Regina Bastian, 1966, 1 s, 1 d. *Education:* BA, 1952; MSc, London, 1957; MPA Harvard, 1964; MA, Harvard, 1965; PhD, London, 1972. *Appointments:* Snr Deputy Governor, 1979-85; Mgrng Dir, Sri Lanka Inst of Social & Economic Studies, 1985-87; Governor, Central Bank, 1988-. *Publications include:* English Publ in Ceylon in the nineteenth Century; The Banking & Financial System of Sri Lanka. *Memberships:* Society for Intl Development, Sri Lanka; Sri Lanka Economic Assn; Sri Lanka Assn for the Advancement of Sci. *Honours:* Univ Entrance Scholarship; Fulbright Scholarship; Research Fellow in Economics. *Hobbies:* Collecting Old Books, Coins & Currency Notes, Sri Lanka; Astrology; Carpentry; Metal Work; Growing Exotic Plants. *Address:* Governor, Central Bank of Sri Lanka, PO Box 590, Colombo, Sri Lanka. 1, 52.

KASTORY Andrzej, b. 14 Apr 1939, Poland. Historian; Asst Prof, Pedagogical Univ, Cracow. m. Stanislawa Kutiewicz, 30 Dec 1961, 3 d. *Education:* Jagiellonain Univ, Cracov, 1962; Pedagogical Univ, Cracov, 1971; Univ de Stesbourg, Inst des Hautes Etudes Europennes, 1974; Jagiellonian Univ, Cracov, 1982. *Appointments:* Archives, Wroclaw, 1962-64; High Sch, ystrzyca, 1964-66; Acad of Mining, 1966-80; Pedagogical Univ, Rzeszow, 1980-86; Pedagogoical Univ, Cracov, 1986-. *Publications include:* Romania, Bulgaria & Hungary in Policy of the Great powers. *Memberships:* Acad of Sci, central Europe Commission. *Honours:* The award of the Minister of Educ. *Hobbies:* Bicycle; Gardening; Reading. *Address:* ul SW Leonarda 22/38, 32-700 Bochnia, Poland.

KATO Hoichi, b. 18 Jan 1944, Imabari, Japan. Surgeon. m. 14 Feb 1971, 1 s, 1 d. *Education:* Univ of Tokyo, Sch of Medicine, 1964-71. *Appointments:* Fellow in Surgery, Univ of Toyko, 1971-77; Staff Surgeon, Nat Cancer Centre Hosp, Toyko, 1978; Lectr, Toyko Univ, 1987; Hd Surgeon, NCCH. *Publications include:* Papers; Superficial Esophageal Carcinoma. *Membership:* Intl Soc for Diseases of the Esophagus. *Hobbies:* Swimming; Spead Skating; Baroque Music. *Address:* Nat Cancer Centre Hosp, 1-1 Tsukiji 5 Chome, Chuo Ku, Toyko 104, Japan.

KATO Masanobu, b. 9 Sept 1946, Nagasaki. Prof of Law. m. Machiko Kawashima, 30 Sept 1973, 2 s. *Education:* Sch of Law, Univ of Toyko, 1969; Doc of Juridical Sci, 1986. *Appointments:* Research Fellow, Univ of Toyko, 1969-73; Assoc Prof, Univ of Nagoya, 1973-82; Visiting Fellow, Harvard Univ, 1980-81; Prof of Law, Univ of Nagoya, 1982-; Visiting Prof, Hawai Univ, 1985; Columbia Univ, 1986-87; Beijin Univ, 1991; Alternate Representative, The Delegate From Japan, Diplomatic Conference for Adoption of UNIDROIT Conventions on International Factoring and International Financial Leasing; Dept of Foreign Affairs, 1988. *Publications include:* The Civil Law System and Law of Unjust Enrichment; Japan Business Law Guide. *Memberships:* Private Law Soc of Japan; Comparative Law Soc of Japan; Japan Soc for Socio Legal Studies. *Hobbies:* Essay Writing. *Address:* Sch of Law, Nagoya Univ, Fiurecho, Chikusc Ku, Nagoya 464, Japan. 163.

KATO Shunsaku, b. 27 Feb 1923, Toyko. College Pres; Dean; Retired Educator. m. Chizuko Uozumi, 16 Oct 1958, 3 d. *Education:* BA, Keio Gijuku Univ, Tokyo, 1946; With Liason Sect, Cen Labor Coll, 1946-48. *Appointments:* Asst Prof, 1948-51; Prof, 1951-66; Research Fellow, Keio Gijuku Univ, 1961-62; Visiting Fellow, Australian Nat Univ, Canberra, 1965-66; Dean, Coll Econs, Kanto Gakuin Univ, 1967-68; Dean, Coll Humanitites, 1972-76; Dir, Intl Ctr, 1976-86; Prof Intl Rels, Prof Emeritus, Dean, Acting Pres, Kyoai Gaken Womens Jnr Coll, Japan, 1987-. *Memberships:* Japanese Assn, Intl Rels; Peace Study Assn, Japan; Keio Assn Lae, Politics & Sociology; Intl Peace Assn; World Assn for World Fedn; United Federalists Japan. *Hobby:* Pottery. *Address:* 4 2 15 Jomyoji, Kamakura 248, Japan. 1.

KATSABOURIS Alexander, b. 10 Oct 1959, Piraeus, Greece. Educator. m. Erika Gisele, 2 July 1988. *Education:* MA, 1986; B Ed, ontarion Techrng Cert, 1986; BSc, Univ of Toronto, 1983; MEd, Ontarion Inst for Studies in Educ, 1991. *Appointments:* Research Asst, 1981-85; Tchrng Asst, Univ of Toronto, 1982-83, 1985, 1987-; Research Coordinator, Ontario Advisory Council, Government of Ontario, 1987; Tchr, Scarborough Bd of Educ, 1987-. *Memberships include:* Assoc of Ed Res Offcr; Ontario Ed Res Coun; Phi Delta Kappa, UofT Chapter; World Conference on Religion for Peace, United Nations; The Empire Club of Canada. *Publications:* Reflections on Canadian Citizenship; Speech: Canada As World Leader. *Honours include:* ssa 00Serving Brother, and Service Medal, Most Venerable Order of the Hosp of St John of Jerusalem; Knight, Military and Hosp Order of St Lazarus; Gold Duke of Edinburgh Award; EdD (Honoris Causa), Australia; LLD (Honris Causa), England. *Hobbies:* Nature Walks; Music; Community Work. *Address:* Univ of Toronto, Dept of Anthropology, Toronto, Ontario, Canada M5S 1A1. 156.

KATSAMOUNSKI Jordan Parashkevoff, b. 30 May 1943, Pleven. Fine Artist. m. Wrasimira Naidenova Katsamounska, 25 Aug 1976. *Education:* Fine Art Acad, Belgrade, Yougaslavia, 1967-71. *Appointments:* Fine Art and Only Fine Art. *Creative Works:* Painting Exhib, Boucharest, Moskow, Bratislava, Cannessur Mec, US, Mexico, London, Roma, Basle, Belgium, Munich, Japan. *Membership:* Bulgarian Artists Union. *Honours:* Committee for Culture Award; The Vladimir Maistoca Award for Painting; The Valimir Maistora Award. *Hobby:* Art. *Address:* Levski Avenue 31, Sofia 1000, Bulgaria.

KATSURA Fumiko, b. 21 Feb 1944, Kyoto, Japan. Prof of English. *Education:* BA, Kyoto Univ, 1966; MA, 1968;

Visiting Scholar, UCLA, 1977-78; Visiting Scholar, St Edmunds Coll, Cambridge, 1989-90. *Appointments:* Asst, Kyoto Univ, 1970-72; Instr, Ryukoku Univ, 1972-76; Assoc Prof, Ryukoku Univ, 1976-91; Full Prof, 1991- . *Publications:* Euro; A History of English Poetry. *Memberships:* The English Literary Soc of Japan; The Japan Assn of Coll English Tchrs; The Browning Inst; Modern Language Assn of America. *Hobbies:* Mountaineering; Listening to Classical Music. *Address:* 51 Hatago Cho, Kameoka, Kyoto 621, Japan. 52.

KATTAN Naim, b. 26 Aug 1928, Baghdad. Writer; Assoc Dir, Canada Council. 1 s. *Education:* Law Coll, Baghdad. *Appointments:* Cauadian, Jewish Congress, 1954-66; Nouveau Journal, 1960-61; Royal Commission, 1966-67; Canada Council, 1967-1991; Univertié du Québec à Montreal, 1991. *Publications include:* Reality & Theatre; La Memoire et La Promess; Le Sable de l'ile; Le Perè, Fasida. *Membership:* Ryal Soc of Canada. *Honours:* Order of Canada; Order of Arts & Letters of France; Nat Order of Quebec. *Address:* 3463 rue ste Famille, No 2114, Montreal, PQ, Canada, H2X 2K7.

KATTEF Dora Baron, b. 15 May 1903, Slutzk, White Russia. Mosaic Artist. m. Sol Kattef, 20 May 1950, dec. *Creative Works include:* Mosaic Collages inc. My Bronx; Emmet Kelly; Joan of Arc; Flying Saucer; Ball Game; Fairy Tale; Still Life; The Challenge Tragedy, including, Self Portrait with President Ronald Reagan & Nancy; The Assassination of President J F Kennedy, including The Portrait of the President and the Artist; Exhibited in over 100 Solo Group Exhib. *Memberships include:* Composers, Authors & Artists of America; NYC Chapter, Foundationfor the Community of Artists; Long Beach Art Assn; Museum of Nat History. *Honours include:* Cert of Excellence for Mosaic Art; 33rd Anniversary Biennial Exhib of the Composers; Authors & Artists of America; Artist of the Year; Second Prize for the Big Apple Greeting The Hostages, 1992. *Address:* 2188 Creston Avenue, Bronx, NY 10453, USA. 37, 138, 155.

KATZAROV Tihomir, b. 8 Oct 1931, Samokov. Doctor of Medicine, Docent, Chief of Dept of Nucleat Medicine, Nat Oncology Centre. m. Milka Petrova Nikolova, 7 Nov 1970, 1 s. *Education:* 2nd Male Cymnasium, Sofia, 1945-49; Higher Medical Sch, Sofia, 1949-55; Medical Doc, 1956; Doc of Philosophy, 1977; Docent of Oncology, Nuclear Medicine, 1986. *Appointments:* General Practician, 1956-60; Chemotherapy of Cancer, 1960-68; Radiotherapeutist, Nuclear Medical Specialist, 1968-77; Cancer of the Thyroid Gland, 1977-86. Nat Oncology Centre,1968-. *Publications include:* Publi more that 60 Sci Papers; Co Authored in 4 Sci Monographs. *Memberships:* Bulgarian Soc of Radiology; Scientific Council of Oncology. *Hobbies:* Tourism; Mountain Climbing; Carpentry. *Address:* Chief of Dept of Nuclear Medicine, Nat Oncology Centre, Medical Acad, Sofia, Bulgaria.

KAUFMAN Asher Selig, b. 7 July 1925, Edinburgh, Scotland. m. Josephine Hilda Corman, 28 Aug 1950, 1 s, 1 d dec. *Education:* George Heriots Sch, 1937-42; Univ of Edinburgh, BSc, 1942-45; BSc Hons physics, 1947-48; PhD, 1951-54. *Appointments:* Nat Service, 1945-47; Sec of Bnei Akiva Youth Organ, 1948-49; Research, Ferranti Ltd, 1949-50; Research on Nuclear Fusion, Lab of Assoc Electrical Ind, 1954-59; Research & Tchr in Physics, The Hebrew Univ of Jerusalem, 1959-87, Retired. *Publications:* Physics Research, Especially on Plasma & Spectroscopy; Architecture & Precise Location of the Ancient Temples of Jerusalem; Ancient Metrology; Location of Mt Sinai & Tabernacle at Shiloh; The Temple of Jerusalem. *Memberships:* Inst of Physics; European Physical Soc; Soc for Archaeological Exploration & Judaic Studies. *Honours:* Newton Scholarship in Physics; Selection Committee for Jerusalem Prize on Archaeology of Jerusalem. *Hobbies:* Walking; Weather of the Holy Land; Development of Jewish Religious Law & Custom. *Address:* 54 Hehaluz Street, Jerusalem 96269, Israel.

KAUFMAN Martin, b. 6 Dec 1940, Boston, MA, USA. Prof of History. m. Henrietta Flax, 22 Dec 1968, 1 s, 1 d. *Education:* BA, Boston Univ, 1962; MA, Univ of Pittsburgh, 1963; PhD, Tulane Univ, 1969. *Appointments:* Instr, Worcester State Coll, 1968-69; Asst Prof, Westfield State Coll, 1969-73; Assoc Prof, 1974-76; Prof of History, 1977-. *Publications include:* Homeopathy in America; American Medical Education; Dictionary of American Medical Biography. *Memberships:* Amer Assn for History of Med; Organ of American Historians; Inst for Massachusetts Studies; Nat Educ Assn; History of Soi Soc. *Honours:* Westfield State Coll Distinguished Service Award; 3 Times, Commonwealth Citation for Distinguished Serv. *Hobbies:* Sports; Baseball; Tennis; Summers on Cape Cod. *Address:* 666 Western Avenue, Westfield, MA 01085, USA. 6.

KAUFMANN Jacobo, b. 20 Apr 1939, Buenos Aires, Argentina. Opera & Theatre dir; Playwright; Lectr; Translator. m. Luisa S Drimer, 1964, 2 s, 1 d. *Education:* Maestro in Theatre Direction, Stage Design & Theatre Admin, 1967; Graduated, Hons, Instituto Superior De Arte Del Teatre Colon, Argentina, 1967. *Appointments:* IPAL, Buenos Aires, 1970-71; Jerusalem Rubin Acad of Music, 1972-; Teatro Colon, Buenos Aires, Opera Houses, USA, Spain, Canada, Australia, Japan, New Zealand, Chile, and others. *Creative Works:* 20 Plays inc. Ferocious Banquet; Luciphers Journey; Fable of One Man and Other People; Fowl Play, The Testament of Joseph Lumbroso. *Memberships:* Argentores, Authors Assn of Argentina; Intl Theatre Inst; American Guild of Musical Artists; Nat Union of Actors & Dir, Israel; Canadian Actors Equity Assn. *Honours:* ITI, Best Dir of the Year, 1973. *Hobbies:* History; Archaeology; Photography; Design. *Address:* PO Box 1269, Jerusalem 91012, Israel. 94.

KAUL Avtar Krishna, b. 15 June 1940, Syinagar. Agricultural Scientist; Program Officer. m. Uma, 10 Oct 1959, 1 s, 2 d. *Education:* BSc, 1958; MSc, 1960; PhD, 1964. *Appointments:* Geneticist, 1966-71; Hd Nutrition Res Lab, Germany, 1971-75; Co Dir, IAEA UN, 1975-79; Coordinator, W Bank, Bangladish, 1979-81; Research Specialist, 1981-87; Program Officer, Winrock, 1987-. *Publications:* 7 Books; 112 Tech Publ; Paintings in Oil. *Memberships:* Rotary Club; Several Profl Soc. *Honours:* Merit Awards for Research. *Hobbies:* Oil Painting; Photography. *Address:* Winrock Intl, R3 Morrilton, AR 72110, USA.

KAUL Hari Krishen, b. 21 Dec 1941, Srinagar, Kashmir, India. Librarian; Poet. m. Kamal, 26 Feb 1964, 1 d. *Education:* BSc, 1962; B Lib Sc, 1967; M Lib Sc, 1992. *Appointments:* Yoga Research Asst, Gwalior, 1965-66; Tech Asst, India Intl Centre, 1967-70; Reference Asst, IIC, 1970-73; Librarian, IIC, 1973-; Project Dir, Course Dir of Literary & Bibliographical Projects, 1973-89; Sec Gen, The Poetry Soc, 1986-; Convener, Delnet, 1989-92; Dir, DELNET, 1992-. *Creative Works include:* Sri Aurobindo: A Descriptive Bibliography; Traveller's India; Historic Delhi; The Deep Seas; Poetry India: New Voices; Library Netwroks and others. *Memberships:* Indian Library Assn; Authors Guild of India; Indian Assn of Special Libraries & Information Centres; The Poetry Soc. *Honour:* Prof D N Marshall Felicitation Prize, 1992. *Hobby:* Yoga. *Address:* Librarian, India Intl Centre, 40 Lodi Estate, New Delhi-110003, USA. 52, 93.

KAWADE Yoshimi, b. 9 May 1924, Qingdao, China. m. Tamie Naito, 25 May 1951, 1 d. *Education:* Univ of Tokyo, Faculty of Sci, Dept of Chemistry, 1944-47; Doc of Sci, Univ of Tokyo, 1957. *Appointments:* Assoc Prof, Kyoto Univ, 1956-74; Prof, 1974-88; Dir of Inst Virus Res, 1985-87. *Publications include:* Co Editor, The Biology of the Interferon System. *Memberships:* Intl Soc for Interferon Research; The Soc of Japanese Virologists. *Honours:* Intl Soc for Interferon Research, Life Member; Ibero Latin American Soc for Interferon Research. *Hobbies:* Reading; Table Tennis. *Address:* 43-

6 Okazaki Minamigosho Cho, Sakyo Ku, Kyoto 606, Japan. 50, 52

KAWAMURA Sin'itiro, b. 6 June 1912, Nohezi, Aomori, Japan. Conslt Res Committee, Soy Protein in Nutrition, Osaka. m. Hideko Kasiwamura, dec, 15 Aug 1936, 2 s, 1 d. *Education:* Univ of Toyko, BS, 1933-36; PhD, 1961. *Appointments:* Nihan Yushi Co Ltd, 1936-45; Nihou Univ, Dept Agricl Chem, Asst Prof, 1945-52; Kagawa Univ, Prof, 1952-76; Meizen Jnr Coll, Prof, 1976-90. *Publications include:* Biochemistry of Foods; Chemical Research & Literature; About 300 Paper in Academic Journals. *Memberships:* Japanese Soc of Nutrition & Food Sci; Japanese Soc of Starch Sci; Agricl Chemical Sci of Japan; American Chemical Soc. *Honours include:* Award from Japanese Soc of Nutrition & Food Sci; Third Order of Merit in Research & Educ. *Hobbies:* Esperanto, Internacia Sci Assn. *Address:* Sakuragaoka Nakamati 5 5 12, Nisi Ku, Kobe Si, Japan 651 22.

KAYE William, b. 26 Feb 1914, Wakefield. Retired Civil servant; Land Owner; Lord of the Manor of Hulland, Derbyshire. m. Elizabeth Barnwen Elwy Williams, dec, 21 June 1949. *Education:* Thornes House Sch, 1931. *Appointments:* Civil serice, 1934-1970; RAF, 1942-44. *Memberships:* Governing Council Federation of Environment Soc; Nat Domesday Celebrations; Manorial Soc of GB. *Hobbies:* Music; Gardening; Golf; Travel. *Address:* Minffordd, Capel Garmon, Llanrwst, Gwynedd, Wales.

KAZMIERCZAK Wladyslaw, b. 27 June 1951, Psary. Painter; Art Performer. m. Joanna Pawlak, 14 June 1975, 1 d. *Education:* Coll for Tchrs, 1971; Acad of Fine Art, Cracow, 1971-76. *Appointments:* Free Artist, 1976-91; Dir of Bureau of Artistic Exhibitions, Slupsk. *Creative Works:* Numerous Pictures; New Action Painting; Installations Views; Performance Art. *Memberships:* Assn of Polish Artists & Designers; Artistic Assn of Alternative Art. *Honours include:* The Critics Award; Award of Honor; Medal of Honor. *Hobby:* Reading. *Address:* ul Teligi 30-/48, 30 835 Krakow, Poland.

KAZUBSKI Stanislaw Leszek, b. 2 Mar 1933, Mieporet, Nr Warsaw. Scientist; Editor. m. Bozena Grabda, 11 Oct 1960, 1 s, 1 d. *Education:* Univ of Nizhny Novogorod, Univ of Sanct Petersburg, MSc, 1956; Univ of Warsaw, DSc, 1963; Habilitate Doc of Biological Sci, 1984. *Appointments:* Inst of Parasitology Polish Acad of Sci, Warsaw, Asst, 1956; Snr Asst, 1958; Adiunkt, 1963; Docent, 1970; Prof, 1987; Vice Dir, Inst from 1984 to 1991; Medical Acad of Warsaw, Docent, 1975-79; Dir of Museum and Inst of Zoology Polish Acad Sci, 1992; Sec Gen of VI Intl Congress Protozoology, Warsaw, 1981; Editor Intl Journal, ACTA Protozoologica, 1966-. *Publications include:* More than 140 Sci Papers. *Memberhips:* Cytological, Parasitological, Zoological Committee of Polish Acad of Sci; Soc of Protozoologists; Polish Zoological Soc; Polish Parasitological Soc. *Honours:* Prizes of Polish Acad of Sci. *Hobbies:* Photography; Stamps. *Address:* Museum and Institute of Zoology, of the Polish Acad of Sci, Wilcza str 64, PO Box 2007, 00-950 Warsaw, Poland.

KAZUNO Mitsuko, b. 22 July 1928, Japan. Prof of Physics, Toho Univ. *Education:* BSc, Toho Univ, 1948; PhD, Trinity Coll, Univ of Dublin, 1967. *Appointments:* Asst Prof of Dublin inst for Advanced Studies, Ireland, 1967-72; Research Assoc, State Univ of New York, 1972-74; Research Assoc, Maryland Univ, 1974-76; Prof of Physics, Toho Univ, Faculty of Sci, 1982-. *Memberships:* Councillor of Toho Univ; Physical Society of Japan; Dir of Soc of Japanese Women Scientists; Pres of Trinity Coll, Dublin Assn; Chairperson of Japenese Women Engineers Forum; Assn Women in Science, USA. *Hobbies:* Oil Painting; Travel; Reading; Intl Exchange of Scientific Work. *Address:* 5-9-7 Shibayama, Funabashi, 274 Chiba, Japan.

KEARNEY J Stephen, b. 17 May 1945, Danville, Inninois, USA. Prof of Theology & Bible; Library Dir. m. Ann Mary Stonebanks, 26 July 1969, 1 s, 2 d. *Education:* Bach of Arts, 1973; Bach of Religious Educ, 1977; Master of Divinty, 1977. *Appointments:* Blue Cross & Blue Shield of Tennessee, 1973-78; Supervisor of Data Processing, 1981-82; Evangelical Baptist Mission, 1978-81; Faith Baptist Church, Florida, 1982-84; Riverdale Baptist Church, michigan, 1984-87; Spurgeon Baptist Bible Coll, Florida, 1987-. *Memberships:* Evangelical Tchr Training Assoc; Polk County Library Assn. *Honours:* Alfred E Cierpke Award; Aplha Episton Theta Honor Soc. *Hobbies:* Intl Motor Sports Assn; Moto Sports Club; Personal Computing; Genealogy. *Address:* 4360 Spurgeon Drive, Mulberry, FL 33860, USA. 7.

KEAY Ronald William John, b. 20 May 1920, Richmond, Surrey. Biologist Retired. m. Joan Mary Walden, 18 Aug 1944, 1 s, 2 d. *Education:* Kings Coll Sch, Wimbledon; St Johns Coll, Oxford; BA, 1942; MA, BSc, D Phil, 1963. *Appointments:* Colonial Forest Serv, Nigeria, 1942-62; Dir of Forest Research, 1960-62; Royal Soc of London, Deputy Exec Sec, 1962-77; Exec Sec, 1977-85. *Publications:* Flora of West Tropical Africa; Trees of Nigeria; Papers on Tropical African Ecology & Taxonomy. *Memberships:* Past Pres Sci Assn of Nigeria; African Studies Assn of UK; Inst of Biology. *Honours include:* OBE; CBE. *Hobbies:* Gardening. *Address:* 38 Birch Grove, Cobham, Surrey KT11 2HR, England. 1.

KEEFE Terence, b. 1 Feb 1940, Birmingham, England. Prof of French Studies. m. Sheila Parkin, 30 June 1962, 1 s 1 d. *Education:* King Edward Grammar Sch, 1951-58; Univ of Leicester, BA, 1962; MA, 1968; Univ of London, BA, Philosophy, 1966. *Appointments:* Lectr, Snr Lect in French, Univ of Leicester, 1967-88; Prof of French Studies, Univ of Lancaster, 1988-. *Publications:* Simone De Beauvoir; French Existentialist Fiction; Zola and the Craft of Fiction; Simone de Beauvior, Les Belles Images and La Femme Rompue. *Membership:* Assn of Univ Prof of French. *Hobby:* Golf. *Address:* 103 High Road, Halton, Lancaster LA2 6PS, England. 1, 52.

KEEGAN William James, b. 3 July 1938, London, UK. Journalist. m. (1) Tessa Ashton, 7 Feb 1967, div, 2 s, 2 d, (2) Hilary Stonefrost, 1992. *Education:* Wimbledon Coll; Trinity Coll, Cambridge, MA. *Appointments:* Financial Times, 1963-64; Daily Mail, 1964-67; Financial Times, 1967-76; Bank of England, 1976-77; The Observer, 1977-. *Publications include:* A Real Killing; Who Runs the Economy?; Mrs Thatchers Economic Experiment; Britain without Oil; The Spectre of Capitalism. *Membership:* Garrich Club, London. *Honours:* Visiting Prof of Journalism. *Address:* The Observer, Queenstown Road, London SW8 4NN, England. 1.

KEEL William Clifford, b. 22 Sept 1957, Jackson, Miss. Astronomer. m. Terri Gregory, 13 July 1985, 1 s. *Education:* BA, Vanderbilt Univ, 1978; PhD, univ of Calif, Santa Cruz, 1982. *Appointments:* Research Assoc, Kitt Peak Nat Observatory, 1982-85; Snr Research Astronomer, Leiden Univ, 1985-87; Asst Prof, Univ of Alabama, 1987- 91; Assoc Prof, Univ of Ala, 1991-. *Publications:* Translator, Binary Galaxies; 60 Research Papers; Co Editor, Paired and Interacting Galaxies. *Memberships:* American Astron Soc; Intl Astron Union; Astron Soc of the Pacific. *Honours:* Nal Sci Foundation Fellowship; Visitin Scientist, USSR Acad of Sci. *Hobbies:* Classical Music; Photography; Stamp Collecting. *Address:* Dept of Physics & Astronomy, Box 870324, Univ of Alabama, Tuscaloosa, AL 35487, USA. 7, 164.

KEELER Melvina Florence, b. 6 Nov 1902, Mitchell, South Dakota, USA. Partly Retired Tchr. m. Clyde Keeler, 8 July 1931, 1 d. *Education:* BA, Denison Univ, Ohio, 1924; Graduate Studies, Eastman Sch of Music, 1925; Harvard Univ, 1933; Cleveland State Univ, 1954; Ashland Coll, 1951, 1953; Hyannis State Tchrs Coll,

1941; Ohio Univ, 1961, 1962. *Appointments include:* Theory & Piano Tchr, Denison Univ, 1924-25, 1927-28; Tchr of Latin, Harding High, Marion, Ohio, 1927-38; Tchr & Principal of Orleans Elemtary Sch, 1940-47; Tchr of Music, Wellington, Ohio, 1951-59; Substitute Tchr in Many Areas, 1969-; Teacher of Latin, Oberlin High School, 1972-1974. *Creative Works:* Carols & Hymns, WPA Chorus, Boston. *Memberships include:* Boston Musical Guild; Denison Univ AAUW; Boston AAUW; Delta Omicron Alumni Music Fraternity; Fava Art Soc, Oberlin; Mem, AAUW Bd, Oberlin, Ohio, 1955-91. *Honours include:* Salutatorian Harding High; Honary Athletic Soc; Phi Beta Kappa; Delta Omicron Music Intl Fraternity. *Hobbies:* Music; Christian Sci Church; Gardening. *Address:* 172 North Prospect Street, Oberlin, OH 44074, USA.

KEET Marina Ingrid. b. 2 Sept 1934, Calvinia, South Africa. Prof Lectr, Dance & Ballet. m. Mikael Grut, 12 Mar 1959, 2 s, 1 d. *Education:* Univ of Cape Town Ballet Sch, 1951-55; Maestra de Baile, Spanish Dance Soc, 1975; Private Study, England & Spain. *Appointments include:* Own Studio, Cape Town & Stellenbosch South Africa, 1951-58; Univ of Cape Town, 1956-58; Stockholm, Sweden, 1959-60; George Washington Univ, USA, 1981-. *Publications:* Spanish Dance; History of Ballet in South Africa; Syllabi & Theory for Spanish Dance Soc; Various Articles. *Memberships:* Dance History Scholars; Spanish dance Soc; Hon Pres in Italy, Founded the Soc in 1977-1981. *Honours:* Dame of the Order of Isabel; Award, Hispanic Inst for Performing Arts; Honorary Life Vice Pres South Africa. *Hobbies:* Reading; Music. *Address:* 4201 Cathedral Avenue NW, Apt 814E, Washington, DC 20016 USA.

KEITH-LUCAS David, b. 25 Mar 1911, Cambridge. Retired Prof Emeritus. m. (1) Dorothy D Robertson 25 Apr 1942 dec, (2) Phyllis Marion Everard, 11 July 1981, 2 s, 1 d. *Education:* Gresham Sch, Holt, 1922- 29; Gonville & Cauis Coll, Cambridge, 1929-33; BA, 1933; MA, 1956. *Appointments include:* CA Parsons & Co Ltd, 1933-39; Short Brs Ltd, Chief Designer, 1949-64; Cranfield Inst of Tech, Prof of Aeronautics, 1965-73; Pro Vice Chancellor, 1970-73; Dir, John Brown & Co. 1970-77; Civil Aviation Authority, Chmn, Airworthiness Requirements Bd, 1972-81. *Publications:* Design of Britains First Jet Lift Vtol Aircraft. *Memberships:* Hon Fellow, Royal Aeronautical Soc; Fellow Inst of Mech Engrs; Fellow Royal Acad of Engineering. *Honours include:* Gold Medal; Royal Aeronautical Soc; Hon DSc Cranfield Inst of Tech; Hon DSc, Queens Univ Belfast; Hon Fellow, American Inst of Aeronautics & Astronautics. *Hobbies:* Vintage Cars; Vintage Motor Boats; Mending The Unmendable. *Address:* Manor Close, Emberton, Olney, Bucks MK46 5BX, England. 1.

KEKEDY Laszlo, b. 28 Nov 1920, Sighet. Univ Prof, Retired; Conslt Prof. m. Kiss Erfsebet, 16 Nov 1946, 1 s, 1 d. *Education:* Univ, Faculty of Chemistry, 1938-42; PhD, 1944. *Appointments:* Bolyai Univ, Cluj, Asst, 1944; Lectr, 1945; Snr Lectr, 1951; Hd of the Chair of Inorganic & Analytical Chemistry, 1954-59; Dean of Faculty of Chemistry, 1956-59; Babes Bolyai Univ, 1961-66; Prof, 1970; Retired, 1986. *Publications include:* Approx 100 Sci Papers; Texbooks; Selected Chapters from Modern Analytical Chemistry; Volumetric Analysis. *Memberships:* Transsylvanian Museum Soc; Dept of Natural Sci & Mathematics. *Honours:* Distinguished Univ Prof. *Address:* Str Memorandumului nr.8, RO 3400 Cluj Napoca Romania. 152.

KELEMEN Tomislav, b. 17 Feb 1932, Banja Luka. Deputy Dir; DSC Univ Prof. m. Dubravka Hropic, 23 Nov 1960, 2 s, 1 d. *Education:* Gymnasium, Banja luka, 1951; Faculty of Electrical Engrng, Zagreb univ, BSc, 1957; DSc, 1974. *Appointments:* Tranfs Fact, Rade Koncar, Zagreb, Designer, 1958-62; Koncar Inst, Zagreb, R&D Engr & Mgr, 1961-91. *Creative Works:* Patent, Improvement of Current Transformers; 25 Papers. *Memberships:* IEC; CIGRE. *Honours:* Silver & Golden Medals; Nikola Tesla Award. *Hobbies:* Tchrng Theory of Electricity & Trnsformers. *Address:* Koncar, Inst za Elektrotehniku d.o.o., Bastijanova bb, HR 41001 Zagreb.

KELL Richard Alexander, b. 1 Nov 1927, Youghal, Co Cork. Authorship & Musical Composition; Retired Polytechnic Snr Lectr. m. Muriel Adelaide Nairn, 31 Dec 1953, 2 s, 2 d. *Education:* Methodist Coll, Belfast, 1937-44; Wesley Coll, Dublin, 1944-46; Univ of Dublin, 1946-53; BA, 1952; Higher Dip in Educ, 1953. *Appointments:* Luton Public Libraries, 1954-56; Asst Librarian, Acton Tech Coll, 1956-59; Lectr, Isleworth Poly, 1960-65; Snr Lectr, Newcastle Upon Tyne Poly, 1970-83. *Publications:* Poems, Control Tower; Differences; The Broken Circle; In Praise of Warmth; Various Musical Compositions. *Membership:* Composers Guild of Great Britain. *Hobbies:* Country Walking; Pubs. *Address:* 18 Rectory Grove, Gosforth, Newcastle Upon Tyne, NE3 1AL, England. 11, 52, 139.

KELLEHER Bryan John, b. 17 Jan 1924, Caulfield, Victoria, Australia. Business Exec. m. Mary Teresa Clare, 18 May 1946, 1 s, 1 d. *Education:* Christian Brothers Coll, East St Kilda, 1936-40; B Comm, 1950; BA, 1952; Univ of Melbourne. *Appointments include:* Officer, Dept of Navy, 1941-59; Snr Research Officer, Federal Dept of Labour, 1960-64; Snr Inspector Public Serv Bd & Ind Advocate, 1964-70; mgr, Ind Relations Dept of Australia Post, 1975-82; Dir on Bd Australian Natives Assn, 1972-; Dir, Southern Community Broadcasters, 1984-87. *Publications include:* Federation and Constitutional Reform--The ANA's Interest; Australian Poetry and the ANA. *Memberships:* Old Colonists Assn of Victoria; Royal Historical Soc of Victoria. *Honours:* Queen Elizabeth 11 Silver Jubilee Medal; Award for 40 yrs Serv to the Community of Australia; Adam Lindsay Gordon 150th Anniv Oration at Memorial Cottage, Ballarat. *Hobbies:* Gardening; Carpentry; Travel; Philately; Australian History. *Address:* 47 Bowen Street, Chadstone, Victoria 3148, Australia. 52, 139, 152, 156.

KELLEHER Graeme George, b. 2 May 1933, Sydney, Australia. Commonwealth Public Servant. m. Fleur, 21 Nov 1959, 1 s, 2 d. *Education:* Bach of Engrng in Civil Engrng, Univ of Sydney, NSW. *Appointments include:* Project Mgr, Googong Project, Australian Government, 1955-72; Asst Sec, Dept Environment & Conservation, Australian Government, 1974-75; Examiner, OECD, 1980; Chmn Great Barrier Reef Marine Park Auth, 1979-; Prof of Systems Engineering, James Cook University, 1992-. *Publications:* Co Author, Guidelines for Establishing Marine Protected Areas; Ranger Uranium Environmental Inquiry. *Memberships include:* Acad of Tech Sci & Engrng (Fellow); World Wide Fund for Nature, Australia (Trustee); Environment Inst of Australia; Inst of Engineers Aust (Fellow); Queensland Marine Parks Consultative Committee. *Honours:* Churchill Fellow; Member of the Order of Australia; Monash Medal. *Hobbies:* Tennis; Squash; Badminton; Bush Walking; Scuba Diving; Swimming; Skiing; Windsurfing. *Address:* 12 Marulda Street, Aranda, ACT 2614, Australia.

KELLENS Jean Armand Christian Marie, b. 26 Jan 1944, Seraing. Prof, Liege Univ. 1 d. *Education:* Licence en Philologie Romane, 1966; Licence, 1967; Doctorat, 1974; Doctorat Special, 1980. *Appointments:* Prof, Comparative Indo European Linguistics, indo Iranian Philology, Liege Univ, 1986-. *Publications include:* Les Noms Racines de L'Avesta; Le Verbe Avestique; Zoroavtre. *Memberships include:* Soc de Linguistique de Paris; Indo Ger Manis Che Gesellschaft; Soc Iranologica Europaea. *Address:* Avenue des Jones 60, 4100 Seraing, Belgium.

KELLER C Graden, b. 10 Nov 1949, Poplar Bluff, Mo, USA. Mgnt Conslt. m. Humaira Kerai, 17 Dec 1977, 1 s. *Education:* Univ of St Thomas, 1988; The Union Inst, Cincinatti, 1977. *Appointments:* Mgr, Fins Admin, HCYFS Inc, Houston, 1973-77; Exec VP Mktng

Kinderfilm, 1977-80; Pres Co Owner, The Ben Shaw Agency, 1980-84; Mgr Dir, Gen Patnr, Kelcon Enterprices; Lectr, Mgnt, Econs Univ of Houston, 1988-; Univ of St Thomas, 1988-. *Publications include:* The Executives Series; Managing For Performance in Profits. *Memberships:* American Mngt Assn; American Soc for Training & Dev; American Assn of Univ Prof; North American Case Research Assn; MSO Foundation. *Honours include:* Jesse H Jones Scholar; Kenneth Know Scholarship. *Address:* PO Box 440562, Houston, TN 77244, USA. 2, 7, 132.

KELLETT Caroline Anne, b. England. Writer; TV Reporter. *Education:* Wycombe Abbey Sch; Wayham Coll. *Appointments:* Fashion Features Editor, Vogue, 1981-86; Contributing Editor, 1987-88; Fashion Editor, Evening Standard, 1988-89; Fashion Editor, Tatler, 1989-90; TV Reporter, Presenter, BSB, 1990-. *Membership:* History BA Hons, Olon. *Hobbies:* English Heritage, architecture; Art; Bonani; Travel. *Address:* 31, Eaton Mews North, London SW1, England.

KELLEY Patricia Marie, b. 8 Dec 1953, Cleveland, Ohio. Geology Educator; Program Dir, Nat Sci Foundation. m. Jonathan Robert Kelley, 18 June 1977, 1 s, 1 d. *Education:* BA, Coll of Wooster, 1975; AM, Harvard Univ, 1977; PhD, Harvard Univ, 1979. *Appointments:* New England Coll, Henniker NH, Instr, 1979; Univ Misiissippi, Asst Prof, 1979-85; Assoc Prof, 1985-89; Acting Assoc, Vice Chancellor, 1988; Prof, 1989-; Assoc Dean, 1989-; Nat Sci Foundation Program Dir, 1990-92. *Publications:* Articles in Profl Journals; Encyclopedias. *Memberships:* Paleontological Soc; Geol Soc Am; AAAS; Miss Acad; Sci Paleontol Research Inst; Sigma Xi; Phi Beta Kappa. *Honours include:* NSF Predoctoral Fellow; Outstanding Faculty Member. *Hobbies:* Family; Church Work; Writing; Music; Travel. *Address:* Program Dir, Geology & Paleontology, Nat Sci Foundation, Room 602, Washington DC 20550, USA. 7, 125, 138, 143, 164.

KELLIHER Henry Joseph, b. 2 Mar 1896, Clyde, New Zealand. Company Dir. m. Evelyn J Sproule, 1917, 1 s, 4 d. *Education:* Clyde Sch, 1903-14. *Appointments:* Founder & Mgrng Dir, Dominion Breweries, 1929-82; Ngrng Dir, mirror Publi Co, 1922-63; Dir, Bank of New Zealand, 1936- 42; Mgrng Dir, Kelliher & Co Ltd, 1922-82. *Publications:* New Zealand at the Cross Roads. *Memberships:* Inst of Directors; 1st NZ Expeditionary Force. *Honours:* Knight Bach; Knight of St John. *Hobbies:* Established. Puketutu Ayrshire Stud; Aberdeen ngus Stud; Suffolk stud; Puketutu Island Thoroughbred Stud; Fallow Deer Stud. *Address:* Puketutu Island, Manukau Harbour, Auckland, New Zealand.

KELLY Christopher William, b. 18 Aug 1946, London. Civil Servant. m. Alison Mary Collens Durant, 11 July 1970, 2 s, 1 d. *Education:* BA, Cambridge, 1968; MA, Manchester, 1970. *Appointments:* HM Treasury, 1971; Private Sec, Financial Sec, 1971-73; Sec, Wilson Committee, 1978-79; Asst Sec, 1980; Under Sec, 1987. *Hobbies:* Narrow Boating. *Address:* HM Treasury, Parliament Street, London SW1, England. 1.

KELLY Jane Maureen, b. 20 Sept 1948, England. Independant Management Conslt. *Education:* Notre Dame High Sch, Sheffield, 1958- 65; Univ of Birmingham, LLB, 1965-68; Admitted Solicitor, 1971. *Appointments:* Solicitor, Private Practice, England & Far east, 1971- 79; AMI Healthcare Group Plc, 1979-90; Legal Adviser, 1979; Company Sec, 1983; Dir of Corporate Health Serv, 1988; Dir AMI Healthcare Group Plc, 1987- 90. *Memberships:* Women in Management; General Council & Register of Osteopaths; Intl Womens Forum; Repem Club. *Address:* 26 Ramillies Road, London, W4 1JN, England.

KELLY Matthias John, b. 21 Apr 1954, Dungannon. Barrister. m. Helen Holmes, 5 May 1979, 1 s, 1 d. *Education:* Saint Patrick's Acad, Dungannon, Co Tyrone,

1969-73; Trinity Coll, Dublin, 1973-77; Council of legal Educ, london, 1977-78. *Appointments:* Private Practise, London, Barrister, 1979-. *Membership:* CAHAG; EVA Campaign; British Soc of Crimmology; Alcohol Recovery Project; Family Law BAC Assn; Criminal Bar Assn; Soc of Labour Lawyers; US Federal Bar, NY; Assn Personal Injury Lawyers; Grays Inn. *Honours:* Honorary Life Member British Soc of Criminology. *Hobbies:* Walking; Reading; Squash. *Address:* 15 Old Square, Lincoln's Inn, London WC2A 3UH, England.

KELLY Michael Howard, b. 19 Nov 1946, Hull. Prof of French. m. Josphine Ann Doyle, 3 Jan 1975, 2 s. *Education:* Grammar Sch, Hull, 1958-65; Univ of Warwick, BA, PhD, 1965-72. *Appointments:* Lectr, Univ Coll, Dublin, 1972-86; Prof Univ of Southampton, 1986-. *Publications:* Pioneer of the Catholic Revival; Modern French Marxism; Formes et Enjeu du Roman; Hegel in France. *Membership:* Assn of Univ Prof of French. *Honours:* Leverhulme Research Fellowship; Fellow, Royal Soc of Arts. *Hobbies:* Politics; Football; Sci Fiction. *Address:* Dept of French, Univ of Southampton, Southampton SO9 5NH, England.

KELSO Ann Breeding, b. 21 Sept 1945, Hollywood, FL. USA. Curator of Educ. m. John Russell Kelso, 22 July 1972, 1 d. *Education:* Foreign Language, BA, 1963; Art History, MA, 1971. *Appointments:* Curator of Ed: School, Teacher & Family Programs High Museum of Art, Atlanta; Lectr, Fine arts Conslt, Adjunct Faculty, Art History, 1972-; Curator of Educ, Centre for the Fine Arts, 1987-; Adjunct Faculty, Miami Community Coll, 1989-. *Publications:* Breaking Down Traditions; Jaspen Johns, Printed Symbols; Winslow Homen, Civil War Engravings; Three Centuries of French Paitings; Adventures in Art . *Memberships:* American Assn of Museums; Florida Art Educ Assn; Museum Division Dir; American Pen Women; Nat Art Education Assn; Very Special Arts; Visual & Performing Art; Children Cultural Coalihum. *Honours include:* Recoginition for Contributions in Field of Museum Educ; Award of Excellence. *Hobbies:* Music; Tennis; Swimming; Needlework; Collect Antuque Trains. *Address:* High Museum of Art, 1280 Peachtree St, NE, Atlanta, GA 30328, USA. 7.

KEMPER Hans Georg, b. 18 May 1941, Konigsberg. Prof of German literature. m. Liane Gentner, 31 May 1968. *Education:* Univ Tublingen & Conn, 1960-66; PhD, Tubingen, Habil, 1969; Tubingen, 1977. *Appointments:* Lectr, Univ Tubingen, 1969-77; Prof, Univ Bochum, 1978- 91; Prof, Univ Gieben, 1991-. *Publications:* Georg Traskl; Dadaism; Experssionism; Poetry of Baroque; Poetry of the Early Modern Age. *Address:* Fachbereich Germanistik, Univ Gieben, Otto Behaghel Str 10, D-6300 Gieben, Germany.

KENDALL Viona Ann Risheson, b. 28 Aug 1925, Berkeley, Calif USA. Artist. m. Giles A Kendall, 27 Oct 1943, div, 2 s. *Education:* Occidental Coll; Lukits Acad of Fine art; Sergel Bongart; Joe Mugnaini; Ernest Freed. *Creative Works include:* Exhibited. Los Angeles County Museum, California; Deauville, France; Grace Art, Toyko, Japan; One Man Shows. Honfleur, France; Salon D'Automne, paris, France; City of Argoura Hills, California; TV, Articles, Reproductions. One of a Kind; City of night. *Memberships:* Intl Inst of Arts & Letters; Nat Soc of Arts & Letters; Laguna Art Assn. *Honours include:* Fry Museum, Seattle Washington; All California Exhib, California; Las Vagas Art Festival, Neveda. *Hobbies:* Gardening; Reading; Collecting Antiques. *Address:* PO Box 8493, Universal City, CA 91608, USA. 9, 59.

KENDELL Robert Evan, b. 28 Mar 1935, Rotherham, England. Chief Medical Officer, The Scottish Office. m. Ann Whitfield, 2 Dec 1961, 2 s, 2 d. *Education:* Mill Hill Sch, 1948-53; Camb Univ, BA, 1956, MA, 1959, MB, B Chir, 1959, MD, 1967; Kings Coll Hosp Medical Sch, 1956-59. *Appointments:* Visiting Prof, Univ of Vermont, Coll of Medicine, USA, 1969-70; Reader in

Psychiatry, Inst of Psychiatry, London, 1970-74; Prof of Psychiatry, Univ of Edinburgh, 1974-91; Dean of the Faculty of Medicine, 1986-90. *Publications:* The Classification of Depressive Illness; Psychiatric Diagnosis in New York & London; The Role of Diagnosis in Psychiatry; Companion to Psychiatric Studies. *Memberships:* Medical Research Council; World Health Organisation Expert Advisory Committee on Mental Health; WHO Expert Committee on Problems Related to Alcohol Consumption. *Honours:* Gaskell Gold Medal of the Royal Coll of Psychiatrists; Paul Hoch Medal of the American Psychopathological Assn; CBE, 1992. *Hobbies:* Overeating; Hill Walking. *Address:* St Andrews House, Edinburgh, EH1 3DE, Scotland. 1.

KENNEDY Barry Lynn, b. 7 July 1946, Nebraska, USA. Assoc Exec. m. Diane Kay, 7 June 1969, 1 s, 1 d. *Education:* Univ of Nebraska; United State Army, 1967-68; Numerous Continuing Ed Programs. *Appointments:* Self Employed Political Conslt, 1984-87; Nebraska Chamber of Commerce & Ind, 1987-. *Publications:* Numerous Articles on Leaderhip Training & Devel. *Memberships:* United States Jnr Chamber of Commerce; Jnr Chamber Intl; VFW Post 52 89; Nat, Intl Jnr Chamber Offices. *Honours include:* M Keith Upson Memorial Award; US Jaycee Ambassadore Award. *Hobbies:* Politics; Golf; Tennis; Hunting; Reading. *Address:* PO Box 95128, Lincoln, NE 68509, USA.

KENNEDY Richard Paul, b. 17 Feb 1949, Brighton, England. Head Master, Highgate Sch, London. m. Joanna Alica Gore Kennedy, 21 July 1979, 2 s. *Education:* New Coll Sch, Oxford, 1957-62; Charterhouse, 1962-67; New Coll, Oxford, 1967-71; BA, Mathematics & Philosophy, 1970, MA, 1977. *Appointments:* Shrewsbury Sch, 1971-77; Westminster Sch, 1977-84; Deputy Hd, Bishops Stortford Coll, 1984-89; Hd Master, Highgate Sch, 1989-. *Memberships:* Governor, The Hall Sch, Hampstead; Wycombe Abbey School; Acad of St Martin in the Fields Chorus; Great Britain Intl Athlete. *Hobbies:* Choral Music; Reading Biographies. *Address:* Highgate Sch, North Road, London N6 4AY. England. 1.

KENNEDY Robert Emmet Jr, b. 19 Dec 1941, New York City. Prof of European History. m. 23 June 1968, 2 s, 2 d. *Education:* BA, Johns Hopkins, 1963; MA, Boston Coll, 1965; PhD, Brandies Univ, 1973. *Appointments:* Merrimack Coll, Instr, 1964-66; Kent State Univ, Instr, 1968- 69; Univ de Toulouse, Asst Assoc 1969-73; George Washington Univ, Prof, 1973- *Publications include:* A Cultural History of The French Revolution. *Memberships:* Soc for French Historical Studies. *Hobbies:* Walking. *Address:* Dept of History, The George Washington Univ, Washington, DC 20052, USA. 6.

KENNEDY Terence Leslie, b. 12 Dec 1919, Plymouth. Surgeaon. m. Bridget Frances Walker, 21 June 1949, 1 s, 2 d. *Education:* St Edwards Sch, Oxford, London Hospital Medical Coll, 1937-42; MS, London, 1949; FRCSI, 1976. *Appointments:* Horse Surgeon London Hosp, 1942; Surg Lieut RNVR, 1942-46; Registras & Snr Reg, 1946-50; Cors Surgeon Royal Victoria Hosp, Belfast. *Publications include:* Over 80 Papers on Gastric & Endocrime Surgery; Chapters in 8 Text Books. *Memberships include:* Assn of Surgeons of GB & Ireland; Royal Coll of Surgeons; Intl Assn of Endocrine. *Honours include:* James IV Traveling Fellow; K H Koster Prize. *Hobbies:* Sailing; Gardening; Cabinet Making. *Address:* 47 Saintfield Road, Killinchy, Newtownards, Co Down, BT23 6RL, N Ireland.

KENNEDY Tessa Georgina, b. England. Interior designer. m. (1) Dominick Elwes, 27 Jan 1958, (2) Elliott Kastner, 26 Jun 1971, 4 s, 1 d. *Education:* Oak Hall, Haslemere; Ecole de Beaux Arts, Paris. *Appointments:* Clients inc. Sam Spiegel; Ricahrd Burton; Michael Winner; HM King of Jordan; Candice Bergen; Rudolf Nureyev; Claridges & George Harrison. *Membership:* President, UK Chapter, IS ID. *Hobbies:* Tennis; Movies;

Watching American Football. *Address:* 1 East 62nd St, New York, NY 10021, USA.

KENNEDY Thomas Eugene, b. 9 Mar 1944, New York, USA. Author; Editor; Translator; Tchr; Administrator. m. Monique M Brun, 28 Dec 1974, 1 s, 1 d. *Education:* BA, Summa cum Laude, Fordha, Univ, New York; MFA, Vremont Coll of Norwich Univ, 1985; PhD, Copenhagen Univ, 1988. *Appointments:* Guest Editor, Frank, Intl Journal, 1987; European Editor, Cimarron Review, 1989; Contributing Editor, Pushcart Prize; Advisory Editor, Short Story Mag; Creative Writing Faculty, Vermont Coll, Norwich Univ, 1987-89; Fiction Faculty Emerson Coll Int Semminar, 1990, 92; Writer-in-Residence, W.I.C.E., Paris. *Publications include:* Crossing Borders; Andre Dubus: A Study; Robert Coover: A Study; New Danish Fiction; Index to American Short Story Awards; The American Short Story Today; 50 stories; 30 essays; 50 Poems and Translations. *Memberships include:* P.E.N. (Denmark); Danish Writers Union; Danish Assn for American Studies; Nordic Assn for American Studies; This World Poetry Foundation; American Soc of Composers, Authors & Publishers; Danish Writers Union; Modern Language Assn of America. *Honours include:* TB Goodman Fund Grant; Charles Angoff Award; Emerging Writer Award; Pushcart Prize; Cited in Best American Short Stories. *Address:* Fragariavej 12, DK 2900 Hellerup, Denmark.

KENNY Douglas Timothy, b. 20 Oct 1923, Victoria BC. Psycholoy Educ. m. Margaret Lindsay Little, 5 June 1976, 1 s, 1 d. *Education:* Victoria Coll, 1941-43; BA, Univ of BC, MA, 1947; PhD, Univ Washington, 1950; LLD, UBC, 1983. *Appointments:* Lectr, UBC, Vancouver, 1950-54; Asst Prof, Psychology, 1954-57; Assoc Prof, 1957-64; Prof, 1965-89; Hd of Dept Psychology, 1965-69; Acting Dean Faculty of Arts, 1969-70; Dean of Arts, 1970-75; Pres, Vice Chancellor, 1975-83; Pres Emeritus, 1989-. *Publications:* Numerous Articles on Profl Journals. *Memberships include:* Vancouver Gen Hosp; Arts, Sics & Tech Ctr, Vancouver; Intl Foundation of Learning. *Honours include:* Queens Silver Jubilee Medal; Park O Davidson Meml Award. *Address:* 4180 Crown Crescent, Vancouver, BC Canada V6R 2A9.

KENT Frederick James, b. 21 May 1928, Miami, FL, USA. Music Librarian. *Education:* BM, DePauw Univ, Indiana, 1950; MM, Univ of Illinois, Urbana, 1951; MLS, 1961; US Army, 1952-54. *Appointments:* Librarian I, Music Dept, Free Library of Philadelphia, 1961-63; Librarian III, Asst Hd, Music Dept, 1963-74; Hd Music Dept, 1974-89; Music Curator, Fleisher Collection of Orchestral Music, 1989-1992. *Publications:* Anthem. Come; My Way; My Truth; My Life; Editor, Crescendo, Philadelphia Chapter, A60. *Memberships include:* Music Library Assn; Organ Music Roundtable; Musical Fund Soc of Philadelphia. *Honours:* DePauw Univ, Rector Scholar; Phi Mu Alpha; Commission by Delaware Valley Composers. *Hobbies:* Cooking; Ballroom Dancing; Travel. *Address:* 229 Ridgewood Road, Coral Gables, FL 33133, USA. 4.

KEOHANE Desmond John, b. 5 July 1928, Sheerness, Kent. Educator; Training Conslt. m. Mary Kelliher, 13 Aug 1960, 2 s, 2 d. *Education:* Borden Grammer Sch; Univ of Birmingham BA, 1949; Univ of London, PGCE, 1955. *Appointments:* Research in History, Univ of Birmingham, 1949-50; RAF Educ officer, 1950-53; Tchr & Lectr, 1953-64; Hd of Dept of Social & Academic Studies, 1964-69; Vice Principal Havering Tech Coll, 1969-71; Prinipal Northampton Coll, of FE, 1971-76; Principal Oxford Coll of FE, 1976- 90; Part Time Lectr, Univ of Leicester, 1990-. *Membership:* British Inst of Mngt. *Honours:* Baxter Prize in History, Univ of Birmingham; Visiting Fellow in Educ; OBE. *Hobbies:* Cricket; Reading; Walking. *Address:* 14 Abington Park Crescent, Northampton, NN3 3AD, England. 1.

KERESZTESI Koloman, b. 7 Oct 1916, Gr Mutschen. Dentist. m. Maria, 5 Apr 1947, 2 s. *Education:* Obitur,

1935; Medical Studies, 1935-40. *Appointments include:* War Service, 1939-45; Clinic Doctor, 1945-46; Dental Clinic, 1976-. *Publications:* About 75 Sci Papers. *Honours include:* Prof Extandimary; Full Prof. *Address:* Gonzagagasse 13, A-1010 Vienna, Austria.

KERKER Milton, b. 25 Sept 1920, Utica, NY, USA. Prof of Chemistry. m. Reva Stemerman, 16 June 1946, 2 s, 2 d. *Education:* AB, Columbia Univ, 1941; MA, 1947; PhD, 1949. *Appointments:* Clarson Univ, Potsdam, NY; Instr-Prof, 1949-91; Dean of Arts & Sci, 1964-74; Dean of Sci, 1981-85; Prof Emeritus, 1991. *Publications:* The Scattering of Light & Other Electromagnetic Radiation. *Memberships include:* American Chemical Soc; Intl Union of Pure and Applied Chemistry; Sigma Xi. *Honours include:* American Chemical Soc Award in Culloid Chem. *Address:* Clarkson Univ, Potsdam, NY 13676, USA. 2.

KERR Alex Arthur Jr, b. 16 June 1952, Bethesda, Meryland, USA. Oriental Art Dealer; Real est Finance. *Education:* BA, Japanese Studies, Yal Univ, 1974; Keio Univ, Toyko, 1973; MA, Chinese Studies, Oxford Univ, 1977. *Appointments:* Intl Staff, Oomto Foundation, Kyoto, 1977-; Art Conslt, 1984-; Pres, Chiorl Ltd, 1984-; Japan Representavie, Trammell Crow Ventures, 1989-. *Publications:* Kyoto Rediscovered; Immortal Images; In Search of Lost Beauty. *Honours:* Rhodes Scholarship; Chancellors English Essay Prize. *Hobbies:* Japanese & Chinese Calligraphy; Kabuki Theatre; Travel. *Address:* Mubanchi, Higashi Kakiuchi, Kamiyada Cho, Kameoka Shi, Kyoto Fu, Japan 621. 52.

KERSHAW John Stephen, b. 21 Dec 1931, London. *Education:* Cheltenham Coll; New Coll, Oxford. *Appointments:* Investment Mngt; Former Dir, Bandanga Tea Plantations; Henckell Du Buisson & Co Ltd; Plantation Trust Co Plc. *Publication:* Referendum. *Memberships:* Stock Exchange Sailing Assn; Oriental Club. *Hobbies:* Reading; Travel; Old Cars. *Address:* 9 Heath Mansions, Hampstead Grove, London NW3 6SN, England.

KERSHAW Walter, b. 7 Dec 1940, Rochdale. Artist; Mural Painter. *Education:* Durham Univ, 1958-62; BA Fine Art. *Appointments;* Self Employed since 1962; Exhibitions of Paintings & Drawings, Oxford, 1962; Satford, 1969-90; Berlin, 1983; Sao Paulo, 1985; Brazilian Embassy, London, 1987; Nat Portrait Gallery, Tate, Whitechapel, Serpentine. *Creative Works:* External Murals for the British Council in Brazil; Manchester United FC; Science museum in Manchester; British Aerospace; Wensum Lodge Norwich; Italiam Consulate Manchester. *Honours:* Gulbenkian Foundation Award for Mural Painting. *Hobbies:* Travel; Cricket. *Address:* Studio, Todmorden Road, Littleborough, Lancashire OL15 9EG, England.

KERTESZ Imre, b. 9 Nov 1929, Budapest. Writer. m. Albina Vas, 12 June 1962. *Appointment:* Journalist, Vilagossag, 1948-50. *Publications include:* Sorstalansag; A Nyomkeveso; A Kudarc; Kaddis a Meguem Szuletett Gyeruekert. *Honour:* First Milan Dij Award. *Address:* Pasavet ut 45, H-1026 Budapest.

KESSLER Avraham A, b. 11 Sept 1924, USA. Consulting Economist. m. 3 June 1954, 2 d. *Education:* BS, City Coll, NY, 1946; MA, PhD, Univ of Wisconsin, 1947-49. *Appointments:* Conslt, Prime Ministers Office & Min of Finance, 1950-53; External Lectr, Hebrew Univ, Jerusalem, 1951-54; Economist, Economic Advisory Staff, 1953-55; Research Economist, Faolk Project for Economic Research, 1956-58; Indepent Conslt, 1958-62; External Lectr, Bar Ilam Univ, 1960-63; Exec Dir, Assn for Housing of the Aged, 1977- 83; Chmn, Exec Dir, Economic Research Corporation, 1962-. *Publications:* Books; Numerous Articles. *Memberships:* Assn of Americans & Canadians in Israel; American Economic Assn; Israel Economic Assn; Soc for Jewish Demography & Statistics; Israel Gerontological Assn;

Israel Mngt Assn; World Union of Jewish Studies. *Honours include:* Phi Beta Kappa. *Hobbies:* Bible & Talmudal study. *Address:* PO Box 981, 91009 Jerusalem, Israel. 52, 94.

KESSLER Minuetta, b. 15 Sept 1914, Gomel, Russia. Composer; Pianist; Teacher. m. Myer M Kessler, 14 Sept 1952, 1 s, 1 d. *Education:* Lic, Assoc Bd, UK, Scholarship to Ernest Hutcheson, age 15; Grad Dip, Piano, 1934, Postgrad Dip w dist, Artist, Tchr, 1936, Juilliard School Music, USA; Additional study: Piano w Ania Dorfman, Composition w Ivan Langstroch. *Career:* Tchr, Piano, Juilliard School Music, 1937-39; Concerts as Solo Pianist and Composer throughout Can and USA, incl: Boston Pops w Arthur Fiedler; Montreal CBC Orch; Radio and TV perfs incl CBC (incl CBC), Can, WNYC, NYC; Performed own compositions w Montreal and Toronto CBC Orch, Quebec, Calgary, Regina Symphonies, Boston Civic Symphony Orch; Appeared Boston: Jordan Hall, Boston Lyric Opera, Morning Pro Musica on WGBH Radio; 2 Town Hall concerts, NYC; Pvte tchng studio, 1952-; Creator, Minuetta Kessler Music Kindergarten Method, w annual courses for tchrs, 1965-; Dir, Fndr, Concerts in the Home, 1965-79; Fndr, Owner, Pres, Musical Resources Publs, Belmont, MA, 1977-. *Creative works include:* Alberta Concerto; Commns: Nocture in Purple, 1989; In Hours of Love, Yiddish song cycle, 1991. *Memberships:* New England Pianoforte Tchrs Assn, Pres 1965-67; Fndr, New England Jewish Music Forum, Bd Dirs, VP; Fndr, Friends of Young Musicians; MA Music Tchrs Assn, Pres 1982-83; Music Tchrs Nat Assn, Boston Chapt Pres 1984-86; Am Women Composers, Co-Pres MA Chapt 1987; Boston Juilliard Alumni Assn, Organiser, Fndr, Pres; Hon Mbr: NEPTA; Hon Mbr, Nat League Am Pen Women, Music Ed 1982- 86. *Honours include:* Key, City of Calgary, Can, 1951; 1st Master Tchr Cert, Piano, Composition, Music Tchrs Natl Assn, 1984; Cert Distinction, Boston Woman Mag, 1988; 1st Prize, Left Hand Piano Composition, Nat League Am Pen Women; Num other composition awards. *Hobby:* Hiking mountain trails in Canadian Rockies. *Address:* 30 Hurley Street, Belmont, MA 02178, USA. 4, 15, 129, 138, 155, 162, 179, 191.

KHABAROVA Natalia Arkadievna, b. 11 Aug 1951, City of Tutaev, USSR. Doctor. m. Vitaliy Stepanovich Khabarov, 19 Aug 1972, 2 s. *Education:* Econs, Moscow Inst Fin, 1970-75; Propagandist, Moscow Univ Marxism, 1975-77; MD, 3rd Moscow Inst Med, 1974-80; Specialist, Non-Contact Massage, Yuna Davitahvili's course, 1989-90. *Appointments:* Dir, Ctr Alternative Med, w SOKK and Cl, Russia. *Memberships:* Bd Assn Extra- Sensory Perception, USSR; Sci Consultative Comm Info Exchange on Bio-Energy Info, USSR Acad Scis. *Hobbies:* Chess; Reading; Swimming. *Adess:* Horoshevskoe Shosse, house 64, korpus 2, flat 343, Moscow 123007, Russia.

KHAITOV Rakhim Musaevich, b. 6 Jan 1944, Samarkand, USSR. Immunologist; Director of Institute of Immunology. m. Karima N Khigmatullaeva, 1 June 1965, 1 s, 2 d. *Education:* Dip, Physn, 1967, Cand Med Scis, 1968, Dr Med Scis, 1972, Samarkand State Med Inst. *Appointments:* Sci Researcher, Lab Hd, Samarkand State Med Inst, 1967-73; Sci Researcher, Lab Hd, Inst Biophys, USSR Min Hlth, 1973-83; Lab Hd, Dpty Dir, Dir, Inst Immunology, USSR Min Hlth, Moscow. 1983-. *Publications:* About 300 publns on immunology incl 9 monographs; Main books: Cell Interactions and Vaccines of Tomorrow, 1984; Artificial Antigens and Vaccines, 1988; Synthetic Antigens in Immunodiagnostics and Immunoprophylaxis, 1988. *Memberships:* Corres Mbr, USSR Acad Med Scis; Russia Acad Natural Scis; Active Mem, New York Academy of Sciences; VP, Soviet Union Immunological Soc; Int Gastro-Surg Club; Expert on Immunology, WHO. *Honours:* Lenin Komsomol Prize, 1973; USSR State Prize, 1983; Labour Red Banner Order, 1985. *Hobbies:* Reading; Hunting. *Address:* Institute of Immunology, Ministry of Health, 24-2 Kashirskoye Shosse, Moscow 115478, Russia. 34, 52.

KHAN M Shamsul Islam, b. 1 Dec 1949, Tangail, Bangladesh. Librarian; Information Specialist. m. Nilufar Akhter, 30 May 1976, 3 d. *Education:* BA, 1970, Dip, Lib Sci, 1972, MA, Lib Sci, 1974, Dhaka Univ; Cert, Lib Sci, Lbr Trng Inst, Lib Assn Bangladesh, 1970; Dip, Personnel Mgmt, Bangladesh Mgmt Dev Ctr, 1979. *Appointments:* Lib Asst, Sr Read Hall Asst, Sr Ref Asst, Bangladesh Ctrl Pub Lib, 1968-72; Asst Libn, 1972-75, Documentation Off, 1975- 76, Bangladesh Inst Dev Studies; Asst Libr, 1976-77, Acting Hd Libn, 1977-79, Cholera Rsch Lab; Hd Libn, 1979-84, Mgr, Int Diarrhoeal Disease Info and Documentation Ctr Project, 1982-89, Hd, Lib and Publ Br, 1984-89, Hd, Diarrhoeal Diseases Info Servs Ctr, 1989-, Int Ctr Diarrhoeal Disease Rsch, Bangladesh. *Publications:* Papers in area of info servs, esp for diarrhoeal diseases in Nat and Int Jls; Bibliog and indexes; Directory of Asian diarrhoeal disease scientists and practitioners (compiler w M A Matin, I Islam, M M Ali, H S Ahmed, M A Chowdbury), 1985. *Memberships include:* Life Mbr, Lib Assn Bangladesh (LAB), Asst Sec 1976-78, Gen Sec 1989-94, Sec Comm Standardisation of Libnship in Bangladesh 1989-91; Sec, Bangladesh Med Lib Assn; Life Mbr, Exec Coun Mbr, Editing and Publng Assn Bangladesh, Sec Nat Sem and Conf Organising Com 1992; Exec Coun Mbr Int Congress Muslim Libns and Info Scientists; Gen Mbr, Inst Lib Rsch and Dev, Dhaka; Life Mbr: Nepal Lib Assn; Population Assn Bangladesh; Bangladesh Assn Libns, Info Scientists and Documentalists; Bangladesh Soc Microbiologists; Bangladesh Assn Advancement Sci. *Honours:* Govt Jr Scholarship, 1963-65; Scholarship, Lib Assn Bangladesh, 1970; Project grants: Int Dev Rsch Ctr, Can, 1982-91; Swiss Dev Coop, 1988-91. *Hobbies:* Reading; Outdoor games. *Address:* Diarrhoeal Diseases Information Services Centre, International Centre for Diarrhoeal Disease Research, Bangladesh, GPO Box 128, Dhaka 1000, Bangladesh.

KHAN Majid Ali, b. 18 Nov 1942, Rampur, U P, India. University Teacher; Researcher. m. (1) 1 s, 3 d, (2) Shahnaz Begum, 8 Aug 1986, 1 s. *Education:* BSc, 1959, MSc, 1962, BTh, 1962, BEd, 1965, MTh, 1968, PhD, 1971, DTh, 1980, Aligarh Muslim Univ, Aligarh. *Appointments:* Lectr, I I Coll, Etawah, 1962-63; Lectr, Govt Coll, Agra, 1965-66; Lectr, Faize Am Coll, Meerut, 1966-70; Hd, Dept Islamic Studies, Asja Coll, Trinidad, W Indies, 1970-74; Lectr, Dept Sunni Theology, Aligarh Muslim Univ, Aligarh, India, 1975-76; Lectr, then Reader, Prof Dept Islamic Studies, Jamia Millia Islamia, New Delhi (Ctrl Univ), 1976-; Prof, Dean, F/o Islamic Studies and Humanities, Hamdard Univ, New Delhi, Apr-Aug 1990. *Publications:* 28 books; Over 100 rsch articles. *Memberships include:* Fellow, Nadwatul Musannifin, Delhi; Grand Coun, World Parl, Sydney, Australia; Life Mbr: Confedn Chilvalry, Sydney, Australia; Inst Hist, Brazil; Saulat Pub Lib, Rampur, UP; UWAI, Madras; Aligarh Muslim Univ Old Boys Assn, Delhi. *Honours include:* Merit Cert, Faize Am Coll, Meerut, 1967-68; Certs of Hon, TTMYO, Trinidad, 1971-72, 1972-73; Monetary Award for book Muhammad, The Final Messenger, Rabetat Al-Alam Al-Islami, Mecca, Saudi Arabia, 1979; D.Litt (hc), Univ Aeterna Lucina, Sydney; Gold Medal of Hon, ABI, USA, 1987. *Hobbies:* Writing books and research articles; Translating Arabic works into English. *Address:* 273 Zakir Nagar (Main Rd), Jamia Nagar, New Delhi 110025, India. 139, 151, 152, 191.

KHAN Muhammad Ali Asgar, b. 30 June 1938, Warshi, Tangail, Bangladesh. University Teacher and Researcher. m Dilara Khanam, 16 July 1961, 3 s, 1 d. *Education:* BA (Hons), 1960, MA, 1961, Dept Islamic Hist and Culture, Dhaka Univ; PhD, Univ Ankara, Turkey, 1971; Postdoct Rsch, C'wlth Acad Staff-Fellow, London Univ, England, 1975-76; Dipl, Turkish. *Appointments:* Lectr, Islamic Hist and Culture, P C Coll, Bagerhat, Khulna, 1962-64; Pt-time Tchr, Islamic Hist, Bagerhat Mahila Coll, 1963-64; Asst Prof, 1964-65, Assoc Prof, 1975-76, 1976-84, Prof, 1984-, Dept Islamic Hist and Culture, Rajshahi Univ; Pt-time Tchr, Dept Mil Sci, Rajshahi Univ, 1966-67. *Publications:* 24 Published Articles; Text-book on Middle East hist (1958-1914) (w

S M Lutfar Rahman), 4th Ed, 1975; Textbook on hist of Mod Europe, 1984; Textbook on hist of Mod Turkey, 1984; 1 parts (w M Rahman) of Muslim Shashan Babasthar Kramabikash; Var papers incl: Balkan War: Its repercussions in India, 1974; The Services of Amir Ali in Turkey, 1977; The First Palestinian Muslim Mission to India, 1980; The Lausanne Treaty, 1923: its socio-political impact in India, 1985; Gadar Movement in Burma and the role of Jahan-i-Islam Newspaper of Istambul, 1986. *Memberships:* Bangladesh Asiatic Soc, Dhaka; Bangladesh Itihash Samiltee, Dhaka; Itihash Paishad, Dhaka. *Hobbies:* Reading; Gardening; Visits to historical places. *Address:* Department of Islamic History and Culture, Rajshahi University, Bangladesh.

KHAN Munir Ahmad, b. 20 May 1926, Kasur, India. Nuclear Engineer; Retired Chairman, Pakistan Atomic Energy Commission. m. *Education:* BS, Phys, Pubjab Univ, 1946; BSc, Elec Engrng, Lahore Univ, 1946; MS, Elec Engrng, NC State Univ, USA, 1951; Postgrad, IL Inst Technology, 1953; Grand Dip, Nuc Engrng, 1957. *Appointments:* C'wlth Edison, Chgo, IL, USA. 1953-56; Argonne Nat Lab, 1956-57; AMF Atomic, 1957-58; Int Atomic Energy Agcy, Vienna, Austria, 1958-72; Chmn, Pakistan Atomic Energy Commn, 1972-91. *Memberships:* Am Nuclear Soc; Int Advsr, Comm Nuclear Energy; Int Coun, USCEA; Nat Coun Sci and Technology, Pakistan; Univ Grants Commn, Pakistan. *Honours:* Acad Roll of Hon, 1946; Rotary Int Fellowship, 1951; Fulbright Grant, 1951; Sigma Xi, 1952; Hilal Imtiaz Pakistan, 1990. *Interests:* Development of science and technology in the Third World; International cooperation programme in atomic energy. *Address:* c/o Pakistan Atomic Energy Commission, PO Box 1114, Islamabad, Pakistan.

KHAN Muzaffar Ali, b. 1937, Umraoti, India. Business Executive; Comptroller. *Education:* BCom, 1959; Assoc, 1965, Fellow, 1971, Inst Cost and Mgmt Accts Pakistan; ACIS, 1975; FCIS, 1976. *Appointments:* Acctng and Audit Clerk, Burmah Oil Co (PT) Ltd, Karachi, 1955- 62; Asst Cost Acct, Colony Textile Mills Ltd, Multan, 1963-64; Chief Acct, Mitchell's Fruit Farms Ltd, Renala Khurd, Sahiwal, 1965-68; Mgr, Shish Mahal Hosiery Ltd, Lahore, 1969; Chief Commercial Off, Lahore Improvement Trust, 1970; Chief Acct, 1971-73, Fin Mgr, 1974-77, Comptroller, 1978-, Petromin Lubricating Oil Co, Jeddah, Saudi Arabia; Currently Pres, Bloomington Trading Co, Flushing, NY, USA. *Publications:* Articles in var profl jrnls on cost and mgmt. *Memberships:* Brit Inst Mgmt; Am Int Mgmt (Int); Assoc: Assn Ins and Risk Mgrs in Ind and Commerce, UK; Inst Petroleum, UK; European Econ Assn, Belgium; Nat Geographic Soc, USA; Am Entrepreneur Assn. *Hobbies:* Reading about business, economics and related issues; sport. *Address:* 1633 157th St, Flushing, NY 11357, USA.

KHAN Sarbuland Bill, b. 11 Apr 1951, Zanzibar. Inventor; Entrepreneur. m. Stella Conner, 12 May 1979, div. 1989, 1 d. *Education:* Queensbridge School, Birmingham, England, 1964-67; Gen Cert Educ O Levels; GPO Birmingham, 1968-71; Telecommunications Dips; Phys A Level. *Appointments:* GPO, Brit Telecommunications, England, 1968-71; Owner, Aston School Martial Arts, Birmingham, 1972-75; Exec Dir, Birmingham Dianetics and Scientology Ctr, 1976-82; Rsch and Dev, 1982-84; Exec Dir, Am Sunsolar, Redondo Beach, CA, USA, 1984-86; Bus Cons, WISE Corp, Los Angeles, CA, 1986- 87; Rsch and Dev, 1987-89; Research, biodegradable diapers, 1989-. *Publication:* How to Invent & Get Rich. *Creative works:* 7 patents, new diaper technologies, 1989-. *Memberships:* Wilderness Soc, Washington; Father Flanagan's Boys Home, NA; Int Platform Assn, OH; Challenger Ctr, Washington; Planetary Soc; Children Int; Millionaires Club Hollywood. *Hobbies:* Karate; Ballroom and Latin American dancing; Reading; Writing. *Address:* 1539 N Alexandria Ave, Los Angeles, CA 90027, USA. 9, 59.

KHAVROSHKIN Oleg Borisovich, b. 13 May 1938, Voronezh, USSR. Geophysicist (Seismology). div., 1 d. *Education:* Dip Mech Engr, Moscow Higher Tech Coll, 1962; Postgrad courses, Impulse Moscow Rsch Inst, 1964-67; Cand Scis, Dip, Acoustics, 1976. *Appointments:* Test Engr, Design Ctr Aerospace Technology, 1962-64; Sr Researcher, Inst Phys Measurements, Gosstandart, 1970-78; Sr Researcher, USSR (currently Russian), Inst Phys of the Earth, Moscow, 1978-. *Creative works:* Monographs: Regional High- Frequency Seismic Noise Modulation, 1985; Temporal Structures of Seismic Emission, 1987; Nearly 80 scientific publs and papers incl: Modulation of high-frequency microseisms (co-author), 1978; Properties and Special Features of Powerful Acoustic Fields in Active Media; Problems of Search and Recording Gravitational Waves in the Framework of the Einstein Theory; Nature of Properties of Seismic Noise, Non-Linear Seismic Waves and the Chaos Problem of Geophysical Processess; Cycle of works: Seismic Noises Modulation and seismic emission, 1980-90; Research of Non-Linear Seismic Waves and Processes, 1980- 90; 70 inventions; Sci discovery of effect of modulation of high-frequency noises of the Earth. *Memberships:* Corres Mbr, Russian Acad Natural Scis; European Sub-Commn Seismic Noise; USSR Nuclear Soc; USSR Union Scientists. *Honours:* Dip for series of works on study of planets, Inst Phys of the Earth, USSR Acad Scis, 1979; USSR Dip for Sci Discovery, State Comm Discoveries and Inventions, 1983. *Hobbies:* Irrational inventing; Listening to classical music; Russian nature; Enjoying pure-bred dog society. *Address:* Institute of Physics of the Earth, Academy of Sciences, 10 B Gruzinskaya, 123810 Moscow, Russia.

KHAWAJA Liaquat Ali, b. 8 June 1953, Talagang, Pakistan. Service and Marketing Executive. m. Nigar Nazneen, 29 May 1984, 1 s, 2 d. *Education:* Grad, Punjab Univ, 1975. *Appointments:* NFC (USAID) Mkt Rsch Project, Lahore, 1975-76; Sales Mgr, ASIF Traders mktng co, 1977-78; NFML, Faisalabad, 1978-. *Creative works:* Souvenir of Gymkhana Club Nawabshah. *Memberships:* Dir Int Serv, Rotary Club, Nawabshah; Sec, Nawabshah Gymkhana Club. *Honours:* Winner: Gymkhana Badminton Championship; Billiards; Snooker. *Hobbies:* Indoor sports; Foreign educated penfriends; Tourists. *Address:* 13/2 Khawaja House, Imran Road, Khayaban No 2 (213 RB), Faisalabad, Pakistan.

KHAYATA Abdul Wahab, b. 24 Feb 1924, Aleppo, Syria. m. 2 s, 2 d. *Education:* French Law School, Beirut, Lebanon, 1946-49; London School Econs, 1949-51; Univ Louvain, Belgium, 1949-53; Doct, Fin, 1953. *Appointments:* Dpty Gov, other positions, Ctrl Bank Syria, Damascus, 1953-63; Prof, Lectr, Econs Fin Analysis, Univ Damascus, 1956-68; Undersec, Min Planning, Syria, 1963-68; Min Planning, Syria, 1965; Advsr, Planning, UN, Beirut, Lebanon, 1969-71, 1973-74; Dpty Dir, Europe and Mid East, UNDP, NYC, USA, 1971-73; Gen Mgr, Frab Bank Int, Paris, France, 1974-78; Pres, 1978-91, Dpty Chmn, 1978-90, Advsr to Dpty Chmn, 1991-1992, Ctrl Bank Oman, Ruwi. *Publications:* Principles of Economics, 1968; Balance Sheet Analysis, 3rd Ed, 1967; Planning Technology, lecture notes, 1966-68; Financial Planning, lecture notes, 1970, 1971. *Memberships:* Arab Econ Assn, Syria; Auditors Soc, Syria; Arab Bankers Assn, Amman; Arab Thought Forum, Amman; Union Arab Banks, Beirut. *Honours:* Order of Oman 3rd Class, H M Sultan Qaboos Bin Said, 14th Nat Day Oman, 1984. *Hobbies:* Playing chess; Tennis; Swimming. *Address:* PO Box 8424, Aleppo, Syria. 52.

KHE Tran Van, b. 24 July 1921, Mytho, Vietnam. Musicologist; University Professor. 2 s, 2 d. *Education:* Cert of Med, Univ of Hanoi, 1941-44; Dipl Int Relations, Inst of Polit Studies, Paris, 1951; PhD, Mus, Univ de Paris, Sorbonne, 1958. *Appointments:* Jour, Vietnam Newspaper, 1946-54; Musician; Radio Prod, 1954-58; French Nat Ctr for Sci Res, 1960-87; Attache de Res, 1960-64; Maitre de Res, 1968-71; Dir De Res, 1971-87; Prof, Univ de Paris, Sorbonne, 1966-87.

Publications: 3 books and more than 180 articles on Music in Asia, Vietnamese Music, and ethnomusicology. *Memberships include:* Life, Hon Mem, Intl Mus Coun; Intl Inst for Comp Mus Studies and Documentation; French Socs of Muscol and Ethnomusicol; Soc des Jens de Lettres; Soc for Ethnomusicol; Intl Soc for Mus Educ. *Honours:* Medals for Arts and Lettres, 1974, Culture, 174; DMus, Hon Causa, Univ of Ottawa, 1975; UNESCO Mus Awd, 1981. *Hobbies:* Collecting travel documentation; Music. *Address:* 44 Rue Clement Perrot, 9440 Vitry sur Seine, France. 4.

KHOL Andreas, b. 14 July 1941, Bergen, Germany. Politician. m. Heidi Nau, 3 s, 3 d. *Education:* Law, Univs Innsbruck and Paris, 1963; LLD, Innsbruck Univ; Habilitation, Vienna Univ; Prof, Vienna Univ, 1969. *Appointments:* Sec, Austrian Constitutional Ct, Sec-Gen, Austrian Soc For Policy and Int Rels, 1966-69; Int Civil Servant, Secretariat, Coun Europe, served European Commn Human Rights and Sec, Expert Comm Human Rights, 1969-74; 1st Pres, Staff Comm, Coun Europe, 1972-74; Dir, Pol Acad, Austrian People's Party ctrl instn rsch and studies, 1974-; Exec Sec, European Dem Union, 1978-; Prof, Vienna Fac Law, 1979-; MP for Tyrol, 1983-; Parly Spokesman, foreign affairs, Austrian People's Party, Dpty Chmn, For Rels Comm, Austrian Nat Coun, Dpty Chmn, Constitutional Comm, Austrian Nat Coun, 1990-. *Publications:* Books: Zwischen Staat und Weltstaat - die Internationalen Sicherungsverfahren zum Schutz der Menschenrechte, 1969; Die Gewerkschaften in Oesterreich, 1982; Oesterreichisches Jahrbuch fuer Politik (ed); Num books on human rights; Articles in int pol, European integration, Austrian constitutional law. *Memberships:* Bd Dirs, Austrian Soc For Policy and Int Rels; Bd Dirs, Austrian League for UN. *Hobbies:* Family; Gardening; Tennis. *Address:* Tivoligasse 73, 1120 Vienna, Austria.

KHOL Oldrich Vaclav, b. 17 Feb 1941, Prague, Czechoslovakia. Information Systems Consultant. m. Lenka Hejzlarova, 23 Nov 1967, 1 s, 1 d. *Education:* Fac Maths and Phys, Charles Univ, Prague, 1958-60; Dipl Ing, Coll Technology and Org, Inst Mech Engrng, Liberec, 1970. *Appointments:* Served Czechoslovakian Army, 1961-63; Home Servs Insp, 1967, For Servs Rep, 1971, After Mkt Systems Dev, 1972, Skoda Car Factory HQ, Mlada Boleslav; Commercial Systems Dev, Ford Motor Co HQ, Cologne, FRG, 1973; Commercial Systems Project Ldr, 1975; Chief Cons, Commercial Systems, 1977, Jagenberg Werke AG HQ, Dusseldorf; Project Ldr, Int Operative Systems, 1979, Responsible Cons, Constrn and Dev Integral Info and Operative Systems, 1987, Uni-Cardan Trust AG HQ, Siegburg; Chief Exec, CESORG Systems Cons, Hradec Kralovve, Czechoslovakia, 1990-. *Publications:* Num articles, Auto-Moto, 1969; World History of Motor Cars Producers, 1975. *Memberships:* Sci- Tech Soc, Prague; Mktng Soc, Prague. *Hobbies:* Mountain hiking; Paragliding; Special interest in theory of complex information systems management. *Address:* Sepp-Herberger Str 31, D-4018 Langenfeld, Germany.

KHOSHNOODI Mohammad, b. 20 Oct 1948, Bandar Abbas, Iran. Professor of Chemical Engineering. m. Faridah Badri, 7 Nov 1979, 2 d. *Education:* BSc, Petroleum, Gas Engrng, Abadan Inst Technology, Abadan, 1971; MSc, Chem Engrng, DIC, 1974, PhD, Chem Engrng, 1978, Imperial Coll Sci and Technology, London. *Appointments:* Plant Engr, Bid Boland Gas Refinery, Nat Iranian Gas Co, Agha Jari, 1971-73; Sr Lectr, Chem Engrng, 1978- 85, Hd, Dept Chem Engrng, 1979-80, Assoc Prof, Chem Engrng, 1985-, Dena, 1987-, School Engrng, Univ Sistan and Baluchestan, Zahedan; Tech Mgr, Bank Sistan and Baluchestan Province, Zahedan, 1980-82; Acad Vice-Chancellor, Univ Sistan and Baluchestan, 1987-; Sabbatical Rsch prog, School Engrng, Inst Interdisciplinary Rsch, Univ Tokyo, Japan, 1986; Postgrad Rsch Examiner, Dept Mech Engrng, Univ Ferdowsi, Mashdad, Iran, 1989; Guest Prof, Dept Chem Engrng, Sharif Univ Technology, Tehran, 1990. *Publications:* Solved Problems in Physics, 1979; Heat Transfer, Vol 1, Conduction, Vol 2, Convection and Radiation, 1980; Engineering Thermodynamics with solved Porblems, 1987; Engineering Thermodynamics; 3 books in press; 3 books translated into Farsi incl: Flame and Combustion (J A Barnard and J N Bradley), 1990; About 18 papers. *Memberships:* Ed Bd, Journal of Engineering, Iran; Chem Engrng Comm, Bd Postgrad Educ Exam to Iranian Engrng Univs; Fellow, Matsumae Int Fndn, Tokyo; Combustion Inst, Pittsburgh, USA; Am Inst Chem Engrs. *Honours:* Bursaries: Esso Petroleum Co, England, 1974, Ctlr Elec Generating Bd, England, 1977; Rsch Fellowship, Matsumae Int Fndn, Tokyo, 1986; Book of Yr Prize, Iran, 1991. *Hobby:* Volleyball. *Address:* University of Sistan and Baluchestan, PO Box 98135-161, Zahedan, Iran. 190.

KIELAN-JAWOROWSKA Zofia, b. 25 Apr 1925, Sokolow, Poland. Palaeontologist. m. 8 May 1958, 1 s. *Education:* Master of Zoological Scis, 1949, PhD Palaeontol, 1953; Prof, Inst of Palaeobiol, Polish Acad of Scis (PAS), 1961. *Appointments:* Asst, Univ of Warsaw, 1948-52; Sr Scist, 1952-60, Prof and Dir, 1961-82, Hd, Vetebrate Paleontol Lab, 1984-87, Inst of Paleobiol, PAS; Vis Prof, Nat Natural Hist Mus, Paris, 1982-84; Prof of Paleontol, Univ of Oslo, 1987-. *Publications:* 130 scientific papers and monographs on Mesozoic mammals, trilobites and fossil polychaete jaw apparatuses; Books include: Hunting for Dinosaurs, 1969; Mesozoic Mammals: The first two-third of mammalian history, 1979. *Memberships:* Polish Geol Soc; Palaeontol Assn of the UK; Paleontol Soc, USA; VP, Intl Union of Geol Scis, 1980-89; VP, Intl Paleontol Assn. *Honours:* Hon Doc, Univ of Camerino, Italy, 1989; Polish State Prize for work on early mammals, 1974; *Hobby:* Downhill skiing. *Address:* Paleontologisk Museum, Universitetet 1, Oslo, Sars Gate 1, 0562 Oslo, 5 Norway. 138, 162.

KIGOSHI Kunihiko, b. 7 July 1919, Tokyo, Japan. Professor Emeritus. m. Noriko Hayashi, 14 Oct 1944, 2 d. *Education:* MSc, 1942, PhD, 1954, Univ Tokyo. *Appointments:* Rsch Asst, Phys and Chem Rsch Inst, Tokyo, 1942-46; Rsch Asst, Meteorological Rsch Inst, Tokyo, 1946-50; Asst Prof, Geochem, 1950-54, Prof, 1954-90, Dir Radiocarbob Lab, 1959-, Dean, Fac Sci, 1969-71, 1982-84, Prof Emeritus, 1990-, Gakushuin Univ, Tokyo. *Publications:* Radiochemistry, 1956; Age Determination, 1965. *Memberships:* Chem Soc Japan; Geochem Soc Japan; Japanese Assn Quaternary Rsch, Tokyo; Am Geophys Union, Wash DC. *Honours:* Award, Nishima Mem Fndn, 1970. *Hobbies:* Music; Handcraft work. *Address:* Shibuyaku Higashi 3-8-4, Tokyo 150, Japan. 50, 52.

KIJIMA Kiyohiko, b. 19 Feb 1917, Tokyo, Japan. Music Composer. m. 5 July 1949, 2 s. *Education:* Grad, Coll Arts, Nihon Univ, 1939; Studied w Prof T Ikenouchi. *Appointments:* Chief Prof, Music Course, Coll Arts, 1973-75, Dean, Coll Arts, 1974-79, Dir, 1974-79, Nihon Univ. *Creative works include:* Satsukino for Soprano, Flute and Piano, 1940; Symphonic Overture in A, 1942; Prelude and Fugue for Orch, 1948; Sonata for Violin and Piano, 1951; 5 Meditations for Orch, 1956; Divertimento on Sairei- bayashi for Orch, 1963; Piano Quintet, 1965; Trio on Saibara for Flute, Violin and Piano, 1970; Anthology of 15 songs, 1980; Yoriai I, II, III for 2 instruments, 1980-82; Sonata for Cello and Piano, 1981; 2 Movements for Koto, 1983; Unintentional Emotion in Autumn for Voice, Flute, Cello and Piano, 1983; 2 Poems for Piano, 1984; Paraphrase on Japanese Antique Ode for Cello Solo, 1985; String Quartet No 2, 1986; Trio At the Vale of Times for Clarinet, Cello and Piano, 1987; Trio for Violin, Cello and Piano, 1990. *Memberships:* Japan Fedn Composers; Japan Inst Musicology; Chmn, Seijusha (Coterie of Music Composers). *Honours:* 1st Class Hons, Composition, Japan Music Competition, 1948; Hon Mbr, Japan Assn Contemporary Music. *Hobbies:* Field work of folk music, esp in respect of Okinawa Islands; Enjoyment of the arts. *Address:* 6-13-6 Oizumigakuen-cho, Nerima-ku, Tokyo 178, Japan.

KIKKAWA Jiro, b. 15 Dec 1929, Yokohama, Japan. Ecologist. m. Naoko Yamaya, 25 Oct 1957, 1 s, 1 d. *Education:* BSc, Tokyo Univ Fisheries, 1950; Postgrad Matriculation, Jesus Coll, Oxford, 1955; DSc, Kyoto Univ, 1961. *Appointments:* Tchng Fellow, Zoology, Otago Univ, NZ, 1958- 61; Demonstrator, Temporary Lectr, Univ New England, Australia, 1961-64; Sr Lectr, Reader, Zoology, 1965-79, Prof Zoology, 1980-, Univ Qld, Brisbane. *Publications:* Editor, books: Comparative Ecology, 1980; Community Ecology, 1986; Australian Tropical Rainforests, 1990. *Memberships:* Fellow, Inst Biology; Brit Ecological Soc; Ecological Soc Am; Past Pres, Ecological Soc Australia; Brit Ornithologists Union; Corres Fellow, Am Ornithologists Union; Royal Australasian Ornithologists Union; Int Ornithologists Comm; Past Pres, Qld Ornithological Soc. *Honours:* Gold Medal, Ecological Soc Australia, 1986. *Hobbies:* Bird watching; Music; Language study; Writing. *Address:* Department of Zoology, The University of Queensland, St Lucia, Brisbane, Queensland 4072, Australia.

KIKUCHI Hiroshi, b. 6 May 1926, Sendai, Japan. University Professor. m. Kazuko Kikuchi, 29 June 1958, 1 s. *Education:* BS, Engrng Sci, 1949, PhD, Engrng Sci, 1959, Univ Tkyo. *Appointments:* Chief, Microwave Lab, Electrotech Lab, MITI, Tokyo, 1956; Sr Rsch Fellow: Univ Oxford, England, 1961; Univ Toronto, Can, 1965; Max-Planck Inst Aeronomy, Lindau/Harz, FRG, 1967; NASA/ Goddard Space Flight Ctr, USA, 1969; Prof, Fac Sci and Technology, Nihon Univ, Tokyo, Japan, 1973-; Guest Prof: Inst Plasma Phys, Nagoya Univ, 1974-80; Max-Planck Inst Aeronomy, 1975. *Publications:* Ed: Relation between Laboratory and Space Plasma, Astrophysics and Space Science Library, Vol 84, 1981; Power Line Radiation and Its Coupling to the Ionosphere and Magnetosphere, 1983; Nonlinear and Environmental Electromagnetics, 1985; Laboratory and Space Plasmas, 1989. *Memberships:* Chmn, Int Union Radio Sci Commn E, 1987-90; Mbr, Electromagnetics Acad, 1990; Int Coun Sci Unions; NY Acad Scis; Ch-Chmn, Tokyo Chapt, IEEE, Nat Phys Soc; Instn Elec Engrs; Am Phys Soc; AGU; Inst Elec Engrs Japan; IECI Japan; Japan Phys Soc. *Honours:* Prize for Promotion Sci, Award for Paper, Inst Elec Engrs, Japan, 1956; Inada Mem Prize, Inst Elec Communications Engrs, Japan, 1959; Ford Fndn Fellow, 1965; Dept Sci Indl Rsch Fellow, UK, 1961; Fellow, IEEE, 1984; Golden Hon Award of Distinction, Polish Assn Elec Engrs, 1988. *Hobbies:* Reading; Travel; Appreciation of fine arts; Baseball. *Address:* Nihon University, College of Science and Technology, 8-14 Kanda Surugadai, 1-chome, Chiyoda-ku, Tokyo 101, Japan. 139, 152.

KIKUCHI Masahiro, b. 21 Mar 1934, Fukuoka, Japan. Medical Doctor; Haematopathologist. m. Makiko Nakagawa, 16 May 1963, 1 s, 1 d. *Education:* MB, 1968, Postgrad Student, 1959-63, DrMedSc, 1963, Kyushu Univ School Med. *Appointments:* Asst, 1963-64, Lectr, 1964-71, Assoc Prof, 1971-73, Kyushu Univ; Prof, 1973-, Dean, School Med, 1983-87, Fukuoka Univ; Dir, Fukuoka Univ Hosp, 1989-. *Publications:* Histiocytic Necrotizing Lymphadenitis, 1977; Ed: Pathology Research and Practice, 1988-; Virchows Archiv B, 1990- . *Memberships:* Fellow, Japanese Soc Pathology; Fellow, Japan Haematological Soc; Fellow, Japanese Soc Reticuloendothelial System. *Honours:* 1st Prize, Fukuoka Cancer Soc, 1978. *Hobby:* Trekking. *Address:* First Department of Pathology, School of Medicine, Fukuoka University, Jyonanku, Nanakuma 7-45-1, Fukuoka 814-01, Japan. 52.

KILIANSKA Zofia Maria, b. 14 Sept 1945, Sandomierz, Poland. Biochemist. m. Edward Kilianski, 19 Aug 1971, 1 s, 1 d. *Education:* MSc, Biology, 1968, PhD, 1975, Habilitation, 1987, Univ Lodz. *Appointments:* Rsch Assoc, 1968-75, Adj, 1977-87, Assoc Prof, 1988-, Univ Lodz, 1968-75; Rsch Assoc, Vanderbilt Univ, Nashville, TN, USA, 1976-77; Asst Prof, Univ VT, Burlington, 1988. *Publications:* Author or co- author, over 80 rsch articles and communications (incl 10 reviews) concerning nuclear proteins structure and function, and molecular biology of HIV. *Memberships:* European Assn Cancer

Rsch; Polish Biochem Soc; Polish Soc Oncology. *Honours:* Sec's Award, Polish Acad Sci, 1984; Golden Badge, Univ Ldz, 1987; Golden Cross, Polish People's Republic, 1989. *Hobbies:* Literature; Films; Gardening. *Address:* Department of Cytobiochemistry, University of Lodz, ul Banocha 12/16. 90-237 Lodz, Poland.

KILLALA Neal John Patrick, b. 20 Jan 1945, Balham, London, England. Consultant Psychiatrist. m. Jennifer Ann Lee, 3 Feb 1973, 2 s, 5 d. *Education:* Dulwich Coll; St John's Coll, Cambridge; MA, 1970; BChir, 1971; MB, 1972; St Mary's Hosp Med School, London; MRCS England, LRCP London, 1971; DCH England, 1973; DObsRCOG, 1974; DPM England, 1976; MRCPsych, 1978. *Appointments:* Sr House Off, Queen Mary's Hosp for Children, 1972-73; Sr House Off, Kingston Hosp, 1974; Registrar, Belmont Hosp, 1974-76; Registrar, Maudsley Hosp, 1976-80; Sr Registrar, N Middlesex Hosp, London, 1980; Cons, Runwell and Southend Grp Hosps, 1981-. *Publications:* Papers in Lancet and other jrnls on hazards of exposure to lead in paediatrics. *Memberships:* Brit Med Assn; Soc Study Addiction; New Directions in Study of Alcohol Grp; NE Thames Reg Hlth Auth, Reg Consultants and Hosp Specialists Comm, Reg Drug Advsry Comm, Reg Drug Team, Reg Alcohol Advsry Comm; Coopted, Essex Probation Comm. *Hobbies:* Reading; Swimming; Music; Member, Acorn Apostulate (Church's Ministry of Healing); Committee Member, The Other Ministry of Health; Honorary Consultant, St Luke's Hospital to the Clergy; Lecturer for Crowhurst Home of Healing. *Address:* 16 Drake Road, Westcliff-on-Sea, Essex SS0 8LP, England. 170.

KIM Soo Ryun, b. 25 July 1934, Kwang Ju, Korea. Professor of Medicine; Medical Doctor (Acupuncture). m. 2 Jan 1959, 3 s, 2 d. *Education:* BA, Law, 1958; MA, Admin Instrn, Jun Nam Nat Univ, 1969; PhD (MD), 1982; Dip, MD TM, Med Alternativa; Dip, Dr Acupuncture, Int Acupuncture Coll. *Appointments:* Served to Col, Korean Army, 1958-81; Tchng: World Tae Kwon Do Fedn, Black Belt 8th degree; Viet-nam Mil Acad; Viet- Nam Nat Police Coll; USA Special Forces; Iranian Ground Forces; Prof, Korea Traditional Med Acad, 1982-91; Vis Prof: India Acupuncture Coll and Int Univ Complementary Meds; Co Dir, 1989-91. *Publications:* The Guide of Taekwondo and Acupuncture; The Human Weapon; Persian Language; The Method of Acupuncture and Moxibustion Treatment. *Memberships:* Int Acupuncture Assn; Sri Lankan Acupuncture Assn; Australian Acupuncture Soc; NCCA; USA; C'wlth Inst Acupuncture, UK; Paxmundi Diplomatic Corres Master, World Tae Kwondo Fedn; Prof, Int Univ. *Honours:* Mil Merit In-Hun, Viet Nam War, 1969; Iranian Medal, Educl Merits; Viet Nam Medal, Educl Merits; Letter Commendation, Educl Merits, USA; Nobel Award, Natural Med (Alternativa), 1984; Dag Hammerskjold Award, Human Merit, 1986; Albert Schweizer Award, Med, 1989. *Hobbies:* Sports (Tae Kwon Do art); Medical research. *Address:* 331-11 Sang Chon Dong, Kwang Ju City, Korea.

KIMMENADE Thijs Van, b. 3 Jan 1946, Geldrop, Netherlands. Sculptor. m. Marianne Clerk, 8 Apr 1982, 1 s, 1 d. *Education:* Acad of Sculpture, Breda, Holland. Kunste Kassel, Germany. *Appointments:* Tchr, Acad of Art, Univ Tilburg, 1976-; Dir Musee D'Air Moderne, 1981-. *Creative works:* Sculptures in a conceptual way of art. *Memberships:* BBK Amsterdam; Buldsrecht Amsterdam NBKS. *Hobbies:* Classical Music, (Bach, Handel, Purcell). *Address:* Schutsroomsestraat 16, 5763 BR Milheeze, The Netherlands.

KIMOTO Yasuo, b. 28 Mar 1929, Nara Prefecture, Japan. Professor of Manufacturing System. m. Kazuyo Ikeda, 25 Jan 1958, 1 s. *Education:* Grad, Elec Engrng, Fac Engrng, 1952, Dr Eng, 1962, Osaka Univ. *Appointments:* Rsch Engr, Chief Researcher, Tech Rsch Inst, Hitachi Shipbldg and Engrng Co Ltd, 1952-81; Prof, Dept Indl Mgmt, Osaka Inst Technology, Osaka, 1981-. *Creative works:* Rsch projects: Measuring apparatus for weak terrestial magnetic field around a ship and

its Degaussing, 1953-56; Elec discharge machining phenomena, 1952-65; Dev of electro-hydraulic servo-system E D Machine and Optimal System (HYDREX-R), 1965-75; Electrolytic- abrasive combined mirror finish grinding, 1975-81; Ultra-precision electrolytic analysis, 1981-; Next generation manufacturing (necessary conditions, system analysis and developing technologies intelligent factory automation), 1990-; Books: Precision Machining by Electro-Physico-Chemical and Combined Method, 1982; Micro Application Machining, 1984. *Memberships:* Sr Mbr, Soc Manufacturing Engrs; Dir, Japan Soc Elec Machinging Engrs; Japan Soc Precision Engrng, Instrument/Control Engrng and Indl Mgmt. *Honours:* Kurafuji Award, Japan Soc Elec Machining Engrs, 1974. *Hobby:* Golf. *Address:* 1-2-8 Gakuenmae, Habikino City, Osaka 583, Japan.

KIMURA Yoshimasa Frank, b. 1 Mar 1936, Tokyo, Japan. Chief Executive Officer. m. Kazuko Horioka, 22 Apr 1967, 2 s. *Education:* Sophia Univ, Tokyo, 1954-56; BBA, Gonzaga Univ, USA, 1958; MBA, Marquette Univ, USA, 1960. *Appointments:* Stewart Warner Corporation, USA, 1960; S Kimura & Co Ltd international trade co, Tokyo, Japan, 1961-. *Memberships:* Am Japan Soc; Am Chmbr of Comm Japan; Tokyo Chmbr of Comm; Japan External Trade Org; Japan Productivity Ctr. *Honours:* Scholarship, Sophia Univ, 1954-56; Scholarship, Gonzaga Univ, 1956-58; Scholarship, Marquette Univ, 1958-60. *Hobbies:* Music; Travel; Camera. *Address:* S Kimura and Company Ltd, CPO Box 461, Tokyo, Japan.

KINDERMANN Udo, b. 19 July 1941, Breslau, Germany. Educator. m. Elisabeth Falkner, 6 Aug 1965, 1 s, 1 d. *Education:* Dr phil, 1969; Dr phil habil, 1974. *Appointments:* Asst Prof, 1968-74, Akad Rat, 1974-75, Akad Oberrat, 1975-82, Akad Dir, 1982-1991, ap Prof, 1982-1991, Univ Erlangen, Full Prof, 1991-, Univ Cologne. *Publications:* Books: Laurentius von Durham, 1969; Satyra, 1978; Zwischen Epos und Drama, 1987; Der Dichter vom heiligen Berge, 1989; Editor of Mittellateinisches Jahrbuch (Int Journal of Medieval Studies). *Membership:* German Mediaevelists Assn, Cons Latinist. *Hobby:* History of geology. *Address:* Hutweide 9, 8520 Buckenhof, Germany. 52, 92.

KING Allan Winton, b. 6 Feb 1930, Vancouver, British Columbia, Canada. Film Maker. m. (1) Phyllis April Leiterman, 10 May 1952, 1 d, (2) Patricia Watson, 30 June 1970, 1 s, 1 d, (3) Colleen Murphy, 15 Apr 1987, 1 s. *Education:* BA, Philos, Univ BC. *Appointments:* CBC, 1954-58; Indep Film Prod and Dir, 1958-; Fndr, Allan King Assocs Ltd, 1961, then Allan King Assocs England Ltd. *Creative works:* Films incl: Skidrow, 1956; Rickshaw, 1960; Warrendale, 1967; A Married Couple, 1970; Who Has Seen the Wind, 1976; One Night Stand, 1977; Silence of the North, 1981; Who's In Charge, 1983; Termini Station, 1989. *Memberships:* Dirs Guild Can, Past Pres; Assn Cinematograph and TV Techs, UK; ACFTP; Can Coun Film Makers. *Honours:* Skidrow, 3 awards, Can and USA; Rickshaw, Leipzig and Vancouver Fests awards, 1961; Warrendale, Cannes Critics Prize, 1967, Top Can Film, 1967, shared Best For Film Award, Brit Critics, 1967, 2 prizes, Australia, Best Documentary, US Film Critics, 1968; A Married couple, Dirs, Fortnight, Cannes; One Night Stand, 4 Can Film Awards; Who Has Seen the Wind, Grand Prix, Paris Fest; A Bird in the House, 4 Can Film Awards; Var others. *Hobbies:* Music; Reading. *Address:* 965 Bay Street No 2209, Toronto, Ontario, Canada M5S 2A3. 142.

KING Carl Darlington, b. 26 Jan 1939, Washington, Kansas, USA. Associate Professor of Vocal Music Education. m. Helen Johnson, 14 Aug 1965. *Education:* BA, Ministerial, 1960; Bach Sacred Music, 1961; BA, Music Educ, 1962; MS, Music Educ, 1965; PhD, Music Educ, 1972; Summer Cert, Kodaly Music, 1979; Level III Orff-Schulwerk Cert, 1986. *Appointments:* Choral Dir, Farragut HS, Knoxville, TN, 1963-65; Vocal-

Instrumental Dir, Newport, TN, 1965-69; Tchng Assoc, OH State Univ, 1969-72; Vocal-Music Educ Prof, Univ S FL, 1972-74; Chair, Cinn Bible Sem, Cinn, OH, 1974-77; Vocal Music Specialist, Cinn Pub Schools, 1977-85; Assoc Prof, Vocal Music Educ, E TN State Univ, Johnson City, 1985-. *Creative works:* Publications: The Conservation of Melodic Pitch Patterns by Elementary School Children as Determined by Ancient Chinese Music; Discipline and the Elementary Music Class; Charles Faulkner Bryan: America's Reality; Review of the 1986 Dalcroze Society of America National Conference, Cullowhee, North Carolina - An Educator's Viewpoint; Resources for Classroom Teachers - a conceptual approach, book, 1985; Choral arrangements: Charlie, American folksong, SSA, 1979; I Wonder As I Wander, Appalachian carol for SSA, 1983; Christmas Trilogy, 1988; Banjo Sam, American folksong, SSA, 1989; We Hear, from Judas Maccabeus, 1989; Solo song: With This Ring, 1965. *Memberships:* Nat Assn Tchrs Singing; Music Educators Nat Conf; Coll Music Soc; Org Am Kodaly Educators; Dalcroze Soc Am; Int Soc Music Educ; Life Mbr: Am Choral Dirs Assn; Phi Delta Kappa. *Honours:* HS Valedictorian; 3 Presidential Grants-in-Aid for Rsch, E TN State Univ; Collaborative Educ Grant, TN Dept Educ. *Hobbies:* Woodworking; Dulcimer making; Folk music of the Appalachian Mountains. *Address:* 15 Foxxborough Lane N, Johnson City, TN 37604, USA.

KING Julian Rex, b. 31 Mar 1944, Shrewsbury, Shropshire, England. Book Publisher. m. Gillian Mary Hemmett, 1 Mar 1969, 2 s, 1 d. *Education:* Kingston Polytech, Surrey,1 1962-64. *Appointments:* Mgr, Regency Bookshops, Surbiton and Kingston, 1964-69; Co-Proprietor, Ctr Bookshop, Croydon, 1969-73; Mng Dir, Co-Proprietor, Prism Press Book Publrs, 1973-91. *Hobbies:* Reading; Music; Cinema. *Address:* 2 South Street, Bridport, Dorset DT6 3NQ, England. 52.

KINGSTON Beryl Alma, b. 28 Jan 1931, Tooting, London, England. Writer. m. Roy Kingston, 29 July 1950, 1 s, 2 d. *Education:* BA, 1952, AKC, 1952, King's Coll, London. *Appointments:* Tchng: Var Inner London Educ Auth Schools, 1952-54, 1964-75; Hd, Engl, Felpham Comprehensive School, Felpham, West Sussex, 1975-85. *Publications:* Hearts and Farthings, 1985; Kisses and Ha'pennies, 1986; A Time to Love, 1987; Tuppenny Times, 1988; Fourpenny Flyer, 1989; Sixpenny Stalls, 1990; London Pride, 1990; War Baby, 1991. *Memberships:* Soc Authors; Nat Childbirth Trust. *Address:* c/o Darley Anderson, 11 Eustace Rd, Fulham, London SW6 1JB, England.

KINGSTON Frederick Temple, b. 30 Dec 1925, Toronto, Canada. Priest; Professor of Philosophy. m. Pauline Boyd Smith, 15 June 1951, 2 s, 2 d. *Education:* BA, Philos, Engl, 1947, MA, Philos, 1950, Toronto Univ; LTh, 1950, BD, 1952, Trinity Coll, Toronto; DPhil, Oxford Univ, England, 1954. *Appointments:* Professor, Theology, Anglican Coll, Univ BC, 1953-59; Prof, Philos, 1959-91, Prin, Canterbury Coll, 1965-91, Univ Windsor. *Publications include:* French Existentialism, a Christian Critique, 1961; The Metophyics of George Berkley, 1685-1953, Irish Philosopher, 1992; Anglicism and Principles of Christian Unity (ed), 1972; The Church and Ethics in Public Life, 1975; The Reality of God in the Contemporary World, 1982; Friendship and Dialogue Between Ontario and Quebec, 1985. *Memberships:* Humanities Assn Can, Nat Pres 1985-87; Can Philosl Assn; Aristotelian Soc; Royal Inst Philos. *Honours:* Co-recipient, John H Moss Mem Scholarship, Univ Toronto, 1947; Can Coun Leave Fellowship, 1968-69; Cultural Exchange to France, 1974; Can Coun Rsch Grant to France, 1975; Hon Fellow, Huron Coll, Univ W Ontario, Van Mildevt Coll, Durbam; Recipient, Ontario-Quebec Exchange, 1980-91; Vis Prof, Laval Univ, 1983. *Hobbies:* President, Llewellyn Beach Association, 1983-88; Tennis. *Address:* 833 Kildare Road, Windsor, Ontario, Canada N8Y 3H3. 2, 142.

KINLOCH Henry Stewart, b. 28 Mar 1916, Rosewell, Midlothian, Scotland. Retired Master Baker. m. Florrie Louise Allen, 6 Feb 1945, 3 s, 2 d. *Education:* Rosewell Purlie School, Midlothian; Evening classes, Bakery Coll, Edinburgh. *Appointments:* Played football, Vogrie Dundas, Scottish 1st Class Juvenile Team, 1937; Profl, Thorntree United (Scottish Jr Football Club), 1938-41; Served RN, 1941-46: Joined HMS King George V battleship; Convoys to Russia, then Mediterranean; Covered Sicily landing, 1943; Joined HMS Aire frigate, Bay of Biscay; Far East ops, Pacific and South China Sea, 1944; Foreman, Gen Foreman, var firms, England; Bakery Mgr, Kunzle, Birmingham, 1954-69; Owner, Master Baker, Croyland Bakery, Kettering, 1969-87; Past Chief Examiner, City and Guilds Examining Brds. *Memberships:* Brit Chapt, Am Soc Bakery Engrs; Fellow, Inst Brit Bakers; Nat Assn Master Bakers. *Honours:* Winner, 300 prizes incl: Cardiff Cup; John Macadam Shield; Swansea Cup; Confectioners Trophy; Played for HMS King George V Football Team, 4 times, for RN Football Team, 2 times; Winner, bowling: Mijas Singles and 2- wood Pairs, 1989-90; Santa Maria Singles and Triples, Hambros Open Triples, 1990-91. *Hobbies:* Bowling: Member, Mijas Bowling Club, Santa Marie Golf and Country Club Bowling Section, Wellingborough Town Bowling Club; Formerly football. *Address:* 4 Northampton Road, Orlingbury Road, Kettering, Northants NN14 1JF, England.

KINNEY Abbott Ford, b. 11 Nov 1909, Radio Executive; Writer; Historian. *Appointments:* Ed, Publr, Dermott News; Ptnr, Delta Drug Co; Broadcasting Inc, USA, 1951. *Memberships include:* Nat Broadcasters Assn; AR Broadcasters Assn; Ed, Advsry Bd Mbr, Int Broadcasters Soc; AR Econ Assn; MS River Pkway Commn, 1961-72; AR State Planning Commn, 1963-; Dermott City Planning Commn, 1961-; Ruth Vassey Educ Fndn, 1962-; Var offs, Boy Scouts Am. *Honours include:* Silver Beaver Award, Boy Scouts Am, 1951; Abbott Kinney Day named, SE AR, 1955; AR Man of Yr, 1969; Dermott Man of Yr, 1977. *Address:* 202 South Trottet Street, PO Box 111, Dermott, AR 71638, USA. 7, 12, 16, 52, 128, 130.

KINSMAN Robert Preston, b. 25 July 1949, Cambridge, Massachusetts, USA. Biomedical Plastics Engineer. *Education:* BS, Plastics Engrng, Univ Lowell, 1971; MBA, Pepperdine Univ, 1982; Cert, Biomed Engrng, Univ CA, Irvine, 1984. *Appointments:* Served to Capt, USAF, 1971-75; Product Dev Engr, Plastics Div, Gen Tire Corp, Lawrence, MA, 1976-77; Manufacturing Engr, 1978-80, Sr Engr, 1981-82, AM Edwards Labs, Div Am Hosp Supply Corp, Irvine, CA; Manufacturing Engrng Mgr, Edwards Labs Inc, Anasco, PR, 1983; Project Mgr, 1984-87, Engr, Prod Mgr, 1987-, Baxter Edwards Div, Baxter Hlthcare Corp, Irvine. *Memberships:* Sr Mbr, Soc Plastics Engrs; Am Mgmt Assn; Plastics Acad; VFW; Am Legion; Elks; Pres, Bd Dirs, Lakes Homeowners Assn, Irvine; Bd Dirs, Paradise Pk Owners Assn, Las Vegas; Mgmt Advosry Panel, Modern Plastics Mag, NYC; 1st Aid Instr, Am Red Cross; Vol Worker, VA; Am Heart Assn; Chmn, Heart and Sole Classic Fundraiser. *Honours:* Elected Nat Hon Soc, 1967; VA Cert Appreciation, AM Heart Assn, Cert of Appreciation 1991, 1971; Cert Merit, Contbn and Serv to Mission, USAF, 4 times, 1971-75; Admitted Am MENSA Ltd, 1986; Mbr of Month, So CA, Soc Plastics Engrs, 1989. *Hobbies:* Skiing; Scuba diving; Marathon running; Golfing; Music; Reading; Philately; Numismatics; Automobile restoration. *Address:* 124 Lakepines Drive, Irvine, CA 92720, USA. 9, 52.

KINYOMI Babatunde Olayide, b. 3 May 1927, Lagos, Nigeria. Agriculture and Management Consultant; Certified Internal Auditor. m. 4 Nov 1954, 2 s, 4 d. *Education:* Bus Studies, Yaba Coll Technology; Profl Educ, Acctcy, AR State Univ, USA, 1975-76. *Appointments:* Indent and Stores Controller, CFAO, Lagos, 1944-55; Accounts Controller, G Gottschalk (WA) Ltd, 1956-59; Acct, Sepulchre Bros Nig Ltd, 1960-63; Internal Auditor, Nigerian External Telecom Ltd, 1964-76; Currently Pres, B O Kinyomi Assocs, Agric Servs and Mgmt Consultants. *Creative works:* Art works of enamel and earthenware designs; Papers on: Accountancy and Internal Auditing in Particular; The Accountancy Profession and Practice in Nigeria, 1982; Internal Auditing in Nigeria Compared to Other Countries. *Memberships:* Inst Internal Auditors Inc, USA, Int Rels Comm; Assn Govt Accts, USA, Int Consortium on Govt Profl Mgmt; Nat Assn Accts, USA; Am Acctng Assn, USA; YMCA, Lagos; Sec, Eko Lions Club; Fellowship Prayer Grp; Govng Coun, Fed Poly, Sokoto; Sec, Soc Welfare Multiple Birth; Ctr Audit Rsch, J M Tull School, Univ GA, Athens, USA. *Honours:* Prize, 1st position, 100m race, Primary School. *Hobbies:* Swimming; Football (soccer); Acknowledgement for paper presented to Beta Alpha Psi WY CHAP, Univ WY Coll Commerce and Ind, 1982. *Address:* Asesewon House, 11 Gbeto Street, off Iwaya Road, Onike, Yaba, Lagos State, Nigeria. 52.

KIRBY Ian John, b. 15 Feb 1934, Ilford, Essex, England. Professor of English. m. Pamela Jean Wren, 22 July 1961, 1 s, 1 d. *Education:* BA, 1955, PGCE, 1956, King's Coll, London; PhD, London, 1973. *Appointments:* Engl Master, Fletton HS, 1956-57; Engl Master, Barking Abbey School, 1957-61; Lectr, Uppsala Univ, Sweden, 1961-67; Prof, Engl, Univ Iceland, 1967-71; Prof, Engl, Univ Lausanne, Switzerland, 1971-. *Publications:* Biblical Quotation in Old Icelandic-Norwegian Religious Literature, 2 vols, 1976, 1980; Bible Translation in Old Norse, 1986; Var articles, reviews, others. *Memberships:* Int Assn Univ Profs Engl, Bulletin Ed 1978-89, Exec Comm 1983-, Pres 1986-89; Engl Assn; Mod Humanities Rsch Assn; Viking Soc No Rsch; Swiss Assn Univ Tchrs Engl. *Hobbies:* Mountain walking; Drama; Tennis; Bridge. *Address:* University of Lausanne, BFSH 2, 1015 Lausanne, Switzerland. 52.

KIRCHHOF Paul, b. 21 Feb 1943, Osnabruck, Germany. Professor in Consultutional Lae. m. Jutta Kirchof geb Hellbrugge, 1 Aug 1968, 2 s, 2 d. *Education:* Humanistiches Gym Karlsruhe, 1953-62; Stadium der Rechtswissenschaften an den Univ Freiburg und Munchen: Promotion, 1968; Habil, 1974. *Appointments include:* Sci Asst, Inst for German and Intl Fiscal Law, 1970-75; Univ Prof, Public Law, especially financial and fiscal law; Dir, Inst of Fiscal Law, Munster Univ, 1975-81; Prorector, Rector's Depty, 1979-81; Jt Dir, Inst for Coop Concepts, 1979-81, Corresp Mem, 1981-; Judge, Magistrate, Sub Ofc, Higher Reg Ct, 1980-81; Prof Pub Law, Dir Inst of Fin and Fiscal Law, 1981, Dean, Fac of Law, 1984-85, Univ Heidelberg; Ct, Judge, Fed Constit Ct, Mem 2nd Univ Senate. *Publications include:* Die Steuerwerte des Grundbesitzes, 1985; Wissenschaft in verfasster Freiheit, 1986; Die Bestimmtheit und offenheit der rechtssprache, 1987. *Memberships:* VP, German Sect, Intl Juristenkommission; Deutsche Staatsrechslehrervereinigung; Acad Adv Bd, Deutsche Stueuerjuristische Gesellschaft. *Hobbies:* Music; Theatre. *Address:* Inst fur Finanz und Steurrecht, Friedrich-Ebert- Anlane 6-10, 6900 Hidelberg 1, Germany. 52.

KIRCHHOFF Helga, b. 10 Nov 1930, Eidlitz, Czechoslovakia. Scientist; Professor. m. Klaus Kirchhoff, 5 May 1955, 2 s, 1 d. *Education:* Dip, Biology, 1955; PhD, 1957; Dr Habil, 1974. *Appointments:* Scientist, Inst Hygiene, 1958-63; Scientist, Prof, Inst Microbiology, Vet School, Hanover, 1963-. *Publications:* Arthritis, Models and Mechanisms, 1981; Infections Caused by Mycoplasmatales, 1985; Veterinary Microbiology (co-author), 1986; Pathomechanisms of Inflammatory Rheumatoid Disease, 1989; Mycoplasmas: Molecular Biology and Pathogenesis, 1992. *Membership:* Int Org Mycoplasmalogy, Sec Gen 1986-88. *Address:* Institute fuer Mikrobiologie, Tieraerztliche Hochschule, Bischofsholer Damm 15, D 3000 Hannover, Germany. 52.

KIRILOV Georgi, b. 12 Feb 1951, Sofia, Bulgaria. Medical Doctor. m. Nadija Javorska, 19 Dec 1987, 1 d. *Education:* Med Acad, 1974; MSc, 1980; DAAD

Scholar (Asst Prof), Heidelberg Univ, 1982; Docent, 1992. *Appointments:* Med Dr, Gen Prac, 1975; Specialist, Internal Med, 1981; Specialist, Nuclear Med, 1989. *Publications:* Radioimmunology and Immuno Assay, 1980; Handbook of Endocrinology, 1981, 1992; Sci papers in field of neuroendocrinology esp vasopressia and oxytocin. *Memberships:* Bulgarian Endocrine Soc; German League High Blood Pressure. *Honours:* Sec, Bulgarian Endocrine Soc, 1982-89. *Hobbies:* Mountaineering; Reading; Boating on wild rivers. *Address:* Stefan Milenkov Str 30, 1619 Sofia, Bulgaria.

KIRJUCHIN Leonid Grigorjevich, b. 25 Feb 1936, Klinci, Bryansk Region, USSR. Oil Resources Geologist. m. Irina S Emelyanova, 30 Oct 1958, 1 s, 1 d. *Education:* Grad, Moscow Geology Prospecting Inst, 1958; PhD, 1967; Dr Geology, Mining Sci, 1974; Prof, 1984. *Appointments:* Chief, geological party, Airgeology, 1958-67; VNIGNI, Moscow, 1967-91; Lectures, Univs Berlin, Leipzig, Gracefald, DDR; Chief, contract, DRR. *Creative works:* 220 articles; 15 monographs; 3 inventions. *Memberships:* Sci-Tech Oil and Gas Soc; Sci Coun, VNIGNI. *Honours:* Order of Soviet Govt; Gold Medal, 3 Silver Medals, Bronze Medal, USSR Exhib; 2 Prizes for 2 oil and gas fields discoveries: Karachaganac, USSR, Pekenzen-Zalcvedal, DDR. *Hobbies:* Reading; Music; Garden. *Address:* Tverskaya-Yamskaya d 2/11 kv 75, 125047 Moscow 4, Russia.

KIRK Jerry Alvin, b. 22 May 1939, Martins Ferry, Ohio, USA. Pastor-Teacher; Consultant. m. Geraldine Ann Stottlemire, 13 Aug 1983, 2 s, 4 d. *Education:* MI State Univ, 1957-59; Dr Biblical Philos, 1985, PhD magna cum laude, Relig Educ, 1991, Int Sem; BTh summa cum laude, currently Doct degree prog, Sacred Theology, Bethany Bible Coll and Theological Sem, Dothan, AL. *Appointments:* Served US Army Security Agcy, 1961-64; Cert Techn, Parts Mgr, automotive ind incl Gen Motors and Am Motors, 1972; Specialist Cons, Scott Fluid Power Products Inc, Wheeling, WV, 1976-; Co-Pastor, 3 chs, United Meth Ch; Pastor, Nazarene Chu; Pastor-Tchr, Elm Grove Christian Ch, Wheeling, 1991-. *Publications:* Var tech articles in automotive trade mags. *Memberships:* Int Sem Alumni Assn; Int Ministerial Assn; Indep Christian Chs Int, Bd Bishops 1986-89; St Clairsville Christian Ch, Elder, Trustee, Supt 1989-91. *Honours:* Letter of Commendation, Ldrship, US Army; Good Conduct Medal, US Army; S-K Hands Hall of Fame Award, 1972; Mech of Yr Award, Motor Age, 1972; Hon degrees: DDiv; DLitt. *Hobbies:* Roller skating; Wood working; Biblical studies. *Address:* 43358 National Road, Belmont, OH 43718, USA.

KIRK Raymond Maurice, b. 31 Oct 1923, Beeston, England. Consulting Surgeon; Director of Training Scheme. m. Margaret Schafran, 2 Dec 1952, 1 s, 2 d. *Education:* King's Coll, London, 1946-47; Charing Cross Hosp, 1947-52. *Appointments:* RN Exec Br, 1942-46; Anatomy Lectr, King's Coll, London, 1953-54; Surg Registrar, Charing Cross Hosp, Royal Postgrad Hosp, Royal Free Hosp, London, 1955-61; Cons Surg, Willesden Gen Hosp, Hampstead Gen Hosp, Royal Free Hosp, 1962-90; Currently Dir, Overseas Drs Trng Scheme, Royal Coll Surgs England. *Publications:* A Manual of Abdominal Operations, 1967; Basic Surgical Techniques, 1973, 1978, 1989; General Surgical Operations, 1978, 1987; Complications of Upper Gastrointestinal Surgery, 1986; Sci papers on peptic ulceration, gastric and oesophageal surg. *Memberships:* FRCS England, Coun Mbr, Ed Annal RCS; Med Soc London, Past Pres; Royal Soc Med, Past Pres Surg Sect; Surg Rsch Soc; Brit Soc Gastroenterology. *Hobbies:* Squash; Cycling; Opera; Travel. *Address:* 10 Southwood Lane, Highgate Village, London N6 5EE, England. 1, 52.

KIRKOV Ivan Nikolov, b. 18 Jan 1932, Asenovgrad, Bulgaria. Professor of Painting. *Education:* Grad Painting, Acad of Fine Arts, Sofia, 1949-54. *Appointments:* Lectr, Acad of Fine Arts, 1966-69; Assoc Prof, 1979-85, Prof, 1985-; Works cover all aspects of imitative, fine, plastic and figurative arts; Illustration, mosaic, mural printing and theatrical decoration. *Publications:* A biographical sketch with reproductions. *Memberships:* Alliance of Bulgarian Printers. *Honours:* Andersen Prize for illustration, Rio de janeiro; Series of Bulgarian prizes. *Hobbies:* Jazz, classic and modern music. *Address:* Cul Gililev 44, Bl 35, Sofia 1111, Bulgaria.

KIRKWOOD Antoinette, b. 26 Feb 1930, London, England. Composer; Publisher. m. Richard Phibbs, 14 July 1961, dec. 1987, 1 s, 2 d. *Creative works:* Orchl works incl 1 symphony: 2 ballet scores: Suite for Strings; 3 Fantasies on Irish themes; Chamber music; Songs. *Memberships:* Composers Guild GB, Exec Comm 1969-73; Performing Right Soc; Inc Soc Musicians. *Address:* 56 Sutherland Street, London SW1V 4JZ, England. 1, 4.

KIROV Dimitar Nikolov, b. 20 May 1935, Istanbul. Artist. m. Rozalia Spassova Kirova, 15 Jan 1965. *Education:* Grad, Decorative- Monumental Art of Painting Studio, N. Pavlovitch Acad Fine Arts, Sofia, Bulgaria, 1959. *Appointments:* Creative Sec, Dist Grp Plovdiv Artists, Bulgaria, 1970-76, 1987-89; Chmn, Plovdiv City Coun Art and Culture, 1980-86; Chmn, State Commn Fine Arts, Min Culture, 1986-90. *Creative works:* Cycles of paintings: Burned Icons; Alafrangi; Music; Ballet; Plovdiv; Japan; Greece; Portraitsd of Contemporaries; Monumental works: Mosaics, frescoes, graphites; Works in Nat Art Gall, Pushkin Mus, Moscow, Hermitage, St Petersburg, Erevan Nat Mus, Tbilisi Nat Mus, Dresden Nat Mus, Prague Nat Gall, Munich Mus Mod Art, Wiesbaden Rathaus, Ludwig Mus, Cologne, Okayama Town Hall. *Memberships:* Soc Bulgarian Artists; Hon Mbr, Japanese Grp Artists Higashi. *Honours:* Honoured Artist, 1974-; Nat Artist, 1985-; Zl Boyadzhiev Grand Prize, 1986. *Hobby:* Interested in ballet. *Address:* 3 Khan Omurtag St, 4025 Plovdiv, Bulgaria.

KISIEL Andrzej, b. 11 Dec 1930, Zdolbonow, Poland. Physicist; Professor in Physics. m. Zofia Kossakowska, 2 Sept 1957, 1 s, 2 d. *Education:* Master's degree, Phys, 1952, Dr's degree, 1960, Specialised Dr's degree, 1972, Extraordinary Prof, 1982, Jagellonian Univ, Cracow. *Appointments:* Asst Prof, 1952-60, Adj, 1960-74, Docent, 1974-82, Hd, Gen Phys Div, 1974-, Dpty Dean, Maths, Phys and Chem Fac, 1976-79, Extraordinary Prof, 1982-, Jagellonian Univ, Cracow; Contract Prof, Trento Univ, Italy, 1985-86. *Publications:* Over 120 sci articles in int circulated jrnls, on atomic spectroscopy, optical spectroscopy of semiconductors using XANES and crystalline local structure by EXAFS. *Memberships:* Polish Phys Soc, Chmn Cracow Div 1991-; European Phys Soc; European Synchroton Radiation Soc, Exec Comm Mbr 1991-; Ed Bds: Acta Phisica Polonica and Postepy Fizyki, 1960-65, Dpty Ed 1965-72, Ed 1972-74; Ed Bd, Optica Applicata. *Honours:* Gold Cross of Merit, 1973; Medal, Nat Educ Commn, 1979; Kt Cross, Polonia Restituta, 1983; 3rd Class Prize, 1979, 2nd Class Prize, 1986, Nat Educ Min; Prize, Sec of Polish Acad Scis. *Hobbies:* History; Sociology; Camping; Canoe touring. *Address:* K Nitscha 4a, 30 225 Cracow, Poland.

KISLING Norbert Erwin, b. 20 Jan 1959, Vienna, Austria. Marketing Manager. *Education:* Fed Tech Coll, 1973-78; Univ Economy and Trade, Vienna, 1978-82; MA, Econs, 1982. *Appointments:* Army Serv, 1983; Product Mgmt, Henkel Austria, 1984-86; Mktng, Savings Bank Grp, 1986-89; Mktng Mgr, Neusielder AG, 1989-90; Mktng Mgr, Bank Austria AG, Vienna, 1990-. *Address:* Thurnbergstrasse 47, A-2344 Ma Enzersdorf, Austria.

KISYNSKI Jan Maria, b. 24 June 1933, Warsaw, Poland. Mathematician; Mathematics Educator. m. (1) Krystyna Pawlak, 14 Jan 1967, dec. 1979, 2 s, (2) Maria Nowacka, 3 Jan 1991. *Education:* MS, Maths, 1955, PhD, 1960, Univ M Curie-Sklodowska, Lublin;

Habilitation, Inst Maths, Polish Acad Scis, 1964; Polish State Council nominations: Extraordinary Prof Maths, 1973, Ordinary Prof Maths 1983. *Appointments:* Asst, Univ M Curie- Sklodowska, Lublin, Univ Warsaw and Inst Maths, Polish Acad Scis, Warsaw, 1955-61; Adj, Inst Maths, Polish Acad Scis, 1962-65; Docent, 1965-73, Extraordinary Prof, Maths, 1973-83, Inst Maths, Polish Acad Scis and Univ Warsaw; Ordinary Prof, Maths, Univ Warsaw, 1983-85; Ordinary Prof, Maths, Tech Univ Lublin, 1985-; Cons, Inst Nuclear Rsch, 1972-76. *Publications:* 44 papers in profl math jrnls, on hyperbolic PDE in 2 indep variables, semigrp theory of linear operators, measure theory, Markov processes; Lecture notes: Semigrps of operators and some of their applications, 1976. *Memberships:* Corres Mbr, Polish Acad Scis; Fellow, Sci Soc Warsaw; Polish Math Soc; Ed Comms: Studia Mathematica; Commentationes Mathematicae. *Honours:* Awards, Polish Math Soc, 1958, 1969; Awards, Polish Acad Scis, 1971, 1979, 1987; Awards, 1st degree, Min Nat Educ, 1973, 1978; Golden Cross of Merit, 1975, Cavalier Cross, Polonia Restituta, 1980, Polish State Coun. *Hobbies:* Physical exercise esp jogging, swimming, downhill and cross country skiing; Formerly canoe excursions; Music; Nature; Interested in physics, natural sciences, philosophy and religion; Antihobbies - longing for power, political parties of communistic type and present Polish type. *Address:* ul Tymiankowa 56 m 4, 20-542 Lublin, Poland. 52.

KITAJIMA Heiichiro, b. 18 May 1925, Kyoto, Japan. Professor of Law. m. Takae Kitajima, 30 Oct 1959, 1 s, 1 d. *Education:* LLB. Univ Kyushu, 1948; Postgrad, Univ Kyoto, 1948-54; Univ IL, USA, 1961; MA, Univ PA, USA, 1962. *Appointments:* Assoc Prof, Kansai Univ, 1957-67; Prof, Fac Law, 1971-80, 1989-, Pres, 1980-89, Osaka Univ Econs and Law. *Publications:* Modern Diplomatic History (in Japanese), 1975; Contemporary Diplomatic History (in Japanese), 1979; Japan Diplomacy (in English); Contbr, articles to profl publs. *Memberships:* Japan Assn Int Law; Japan Assn Int Pol. *Hobby:* Listening to classical and popular music. *Address:* Uehommachi 1-chome 2-11, 4th Fl Kitajima Bldg, Tennoji-Ku, 543 Osaka, Japan. 52.

KITAMURA Takashi, b. 19 Aug 1925, Amagasaki City, Japan. Professor of Physics. m. 5 May 1948, 1 d. *Education:* Dept Phys, Osaka (Imperial) Univ, 1944-47; Grad course, 1947-50; Dr Nat Sci, Osaka Univ, 1963. *Appointments:* Asst, Phys, 1950, Lectr, Phys, 1956, Assoc Prof, Phys, 1960, Osaka City Univ; Prof, Inst Nuclear Study, 1972-73; Prof, Inst Cosmic Ray Rsch, 1973-86, Univ Tokyo; Prof, Rsch Inst Sci and Technology, Kinki Univ, 1986-. *Publications:* Over 100 papers in English on nuclear interaction of cosmic ray muons, measurements of cosmic ray muon energy spectrum by var devices, astrophys phenomena, rapporteur's papers in int cosmic ray confs, DUMAND works, bioluminescence in oceanology. *Honours:* Emeritus Prof, Univ Tokyo, 1987. *Hobbies:* Reading; Overseas travel. *Address:* Habikigaoka 5-4-9, Habikino City, Osaka Prefecture 583, Japan.

KITANI Osamu, b. 1 Apr 1935, Tokyo, Japan. Professor of Agriculture. m. Shigeko Tanaka, 12 July 1964, 2 d. *Education:* BAgri, 1959, MAgri, 1961, DAgri, 1964, Univ Tokyo; PhD, MI State Univ, USA, 1966. *Appointments:* Rsch Asst, MI State Univ, USA, 1964-66; Assoc Prof, Mie Univ, Japan, 1966-78; Guest Prof, Tech Univ Munich, FRG, 1972-73; Prof, Fac Agric, 1978-, Chmn, Dept Agricl Engrng, 1980, 1980, 1988, Univ tokyo, Japan. *Publications:* Books: Biomass, 1981; Energy in Agriculture, 1983; Introduction to Agricultural Machinery, 1984; Biomass Handbook, 1989; Agricultural Machinery, 1991. *Memberships:* Pres, Japan Agricl Systems Soc; Dir, Japanese Soc Agricl Machinery; VP, Japan Int Assn Agric Engrng; Am Soc Agric; Am-Japan Assn; Mbr, Mgmt Mbr, Club of Bologna. *Honours:* Gov's Award, Gov, Kagawa Prefecture, 1950; Fulbright Grant, Fulbright Commn, 1964; Fellowship, Alexander von Humboldt Fndn, 1972; Acad Award, Japanese Soc Agricl Machinery, 1976.

Hobbies: Appreciation of art; Appreciation of classical music; Swimming. *Address:* Agricultural Engineering Department, Faculty of Agriculture, University of Tokyo, Yayoi 1- 1-1, Bunkyo-ku, Tokyo 113, Japan. 52.

KITANO Hirohisa, b. 28 Jan 1931, Toyama, Japan. Professor of Tax Law. m. Hachie Aoyama, 28 Jan 1962, 3 s. *Education:* LLB, 1055, LLD, 1974, Ritsumeikan Univ, Kyoto; LLM, Waseda Univ, Tokyo, 1962; Vis Scholar, Univ CA, Berkeley, USA, 1975-76. *Appointments:* Mbr, Bur Tax, Min Fin, Tokyo, 1055-60; Lectr, Univ Tokyo, 1963-64, 1977-79; Lectr, 1964-66, Asst Prof, 1966-71, Prof, 1971-, Fac Law, Nihon Univ, Tokyo. *Publications include:* Books: Structure of Modern Tax Law, 1972; Rights of Taxpayers, 1981; Japanese Constitution and Public Finance Law, 1983; General Consumption Tax, 1987-89; Direct Tax and Indirect Tax, 1987. *Memberships include:* Dir, Japan Civil Liberties Union, Tokyo; Pres, Taxpayers Union, Tokyo; Pres, Tac Legis Com for People, Tokyo, 1977-79; Int Fiscal Assn; Tokyo Bar Assn; Japan Tax Jurisprudence Assn, Exec Dir 1969-75; Dir, Japanese Soc Tax Law; Chief Dir, Japan Assn Pub Fin Law; Exec Dir, Japan Assn Land Law; Exec Dir, Japan Assn Sociology of Law; Chief Dir, Japan Assn Sci Taxation. *Honours:* Onoazusa Prize, Waseda Univ, Tokyo, 1962; Prize, Japan Assn Tax Cons, 1973, 1977, 1983; Award, Nihon Univ, 1977. *Hobbies include:* Literature; Baseball. *Address:* 5-9-25 Kitamachi, Kokukubunji, Tokyo 185, Japan. 52.

KITANO Masanori, b. 24 Oct 1935, Kagawa, Japan. Professor of Mechanical Engineering. m. Mineko Nasuno, 17 Mar 1964, 1 s, 2 d. *Education:* BS, Nat Def Acad, 1958; MS, 1964, DEng, 1967, Osaka Univ. *Appointments:* Chief Researcher, Tech Rsch and Dev Inst, Def Agcy, 1967; Assoc Prof, 1972-77, Prof, Mech Engrng, 1977-, Dean, Grad Sci and Engrng, 1984-85, currently Chmn, Dept Mech Engrng, Nat Def Acad, Yokosuka; Vis Prof: Mil Univ, Hamburg, FRG, 1982; Mie Univ, Japan, 1988. *Publications:* Books: Metal Cutting Theory; Traction Mechanics; Handbook of Agricultural Engineering. *Memberships:* Int Soc Terrain-Vehicle Systems, Dir and Dpty Gen Sec Asia Pacific Area, Assoc Ed Journal of Terramechanics; Soc Automotive Engrs; Japan Soc Mech Engrs; Japan Soc Precision Engrng; Japan Soc Agricl Engrng. *Honours:* VP, Int Soc Terrain-Vehicle Systems; Fellow, Japan Soc Terramech. *Hobbies:* Golfing; Swimming; Gardening; Painting. *Address:* 4-43-8 Hairando, Yokosuka 239, Japan. 52.

KITAYAMA Katsuhiko, b. 13 Dec 1937, Osaka, Japan. Professor of English. *Education:* BA, Tokyo Univc For Studies, 1960; MA, Tokyo Metrop Univ, 1964. *Appointments:* Asst to Asst Prof, Engl, Tokyo Univ Mercantile Marine, 1965-71; Asst Prof, Engl, 1971-77, Prof, Engl, 1977-, Rikkyo Univ. *Publications:* Co-author/ contbr, in Japanese: An Introduction to Modern English Literature, 1975; 30 Readings of American Literature, 1981; Translations to Japanese: Hurry On Down (John Wain), 1971; Dandelion Wine (Ray Bradbury), 1971; Making It (Norman Podhoretz), 1973; Bright Book of Life (Alfred Kazin), jt translation, 1974; In Hazard, Richard Hughes, 1975; Beggarman, Thief (Irwin Shaw), 1980; The Ebony Tower (John Fowles), 1986; The Fall of Public Man (Richard Sennett), jt translation, 1991. *Memberships:* Engl Lit Soc Japan; Am Lit Soc Japan; Int Assn Study of Anglo-Irish Lit; Dir, Japan-Ireland Soc. *Hobby:* Swimming. *Address:* 6-24-5-502 Maeno-cho, Itabashi-ku, Tokyo 174, Japan. 52.

KITO Shozo, b. 29 Jan 1927, Nagoya, Japan. Educator; Pharmacologist; Neuroscientist. m. Sachiko Wada, 16 May 1955, 1 s. *Education:* MD, 1951, PhD, 1959, Tokyo Univ School Med. *Appointments:* Instr, Tokyo Univ School Med, 1968; Asst Prof, Tokyo Women's Coll, 1971; Prof, 3rd Dept Internal Med, Hiroshima Univ School Med, 1973; Prof, Univ of the Air Japan, Chiba, 1990-. *Publications:* Ed: SYNAPSE; Acta Histochemica et Cytochemica; Ed; author: Neurotransmitter Receptors, 1984; Neuroreceptors and Signal Transduction, 1988; Neuroreceptor Mechanisms in

Brain, 1991. *Memberships:* Emeritus Mbr, Am Soc Neurosci; NY Acad Scis; Int Brain Rsch Org; Int Basal Ganglia Soc; Int Soc Developmental Neurosci; Councillor: Japanese Soc Pharmacology; Jap Soc Geriatric Med; Japanese Soc Internal Med; Others. *Honours:* Japanese Med Assn award, 1976; Mitsukoshi Med Award, Mitsukoshi Co Ltd, 1977. *Hobby:* Reading. *Address:* The University of the Air Japan, 2-11 Wakaba, Chiba 260, Japan. 34.

KITTEL (Ernst) Wolfram, b. 12 June 1940, Jaegerdorf, Czechoslovakia. Professor of Physics. m. 24 Apr 1965, 1 s, 1 d. *Education:* PhD, Univ Vienna, 1967. *Appointments:* Inst fuer Hochenergie phys der OEAW, Vienna, 1966; Joined, 1968, Staff, 1969, CERN; Phys Dept, Univ Nijmegen, Netherlands, 1974-. *Publications:* Co-author, about 200 reviews and publs; Ed, var conf proceedings. *Hobbies:* Skiing; Mountaineering. *Address:* Physics Dept, Toernooiveld 1, NL-6525 ED Nijmegen, Netherlands. 52.

KJELDSEN-KRAGH Soren, b. 7 Mar 1938, Copenhagen, Denmark. Professor of Economics. m. Elisabeth Kjeldsen-Kragh, 8 Aug 1964. 1 s, 1 d. *Education:* PhD, Univ Copenhagen, 1964. *Appointments:* Assoc Prof, Copenhagen School Econs and Bus Admin, 1964-73; Prof, Royal Agricl Univ, 1973-; Econ Advsr: African Dev Bank, European Community, UNDP, FAO, Danish Min Agric, Danish Min Environment. *Publications:* Specialization and Competitiveness, 1973; International Trade and Investments, 1977; Economics, 1987; What is the Optimal Size in Danish Agriculture, 1988; Denmark in the Union, 1992. *Memberships:* The Board of Dirs at The Competition Coun, 1990. *Honours:* Knight of the Order of Dannebrog, Queen of Denmark. *Hobbies:* History; Music; Travel. *Address:* Ingersvej 31, DK-2920 Charlottenlund, Denmark. 52, 156.

KLAAR Richard, b. 6 Oct 1941, Novi Vrbas, Yugoslavia. Manufacturing Engineering Specialist. m. Kay Murray, 26 Apr 1964, 2 s. *Education:* Dip, Metals Engrng Inst, 1986, USA. *Appointments:* Welding Techn, Seatrain Shipbldg, NYC, USA, 1973-75; Foreman, Welding, 1975-76, Gen Foreman, Welding, 1976-77, Welding Engr, 1977-82, Sr Welding Engr, 1982-87, Nat Steel and Shipbldg Co, San Diego, CA; Sr Manufacturing Tech Engr, 1987-88, Manufacturing Engrng Specialist, 1988-, Gen Dynamics Space Systems Div, San Diego. *Memberships:* Welding Advsry Bd, San Diego Community Coll, 1980-90; Am Welding Soc, Chmn San Diego 1979; Am Soc Non- Destructive Testing; Am Soc Metals; Nat Mgmt Assn. *Hobbies:* Soccer; Camping; Shooting; Hunting; Chess; Exploring; History (American West); Science fiction. *Address:* Route 1, Box 100K, Loranger, LA 70446, USA. 9.

KLAHR M Carol DeClue, b. 10 June 1937, Crystal City, Missouri, USA. Business Owner. m. Saulo Klahr, 29 Dec 1969, 2 s. *Education:* Dip, Nursing, Maryville Coll, 1958; BS, St Louis Univ, 1960; MS, Washington Univ, St Louis, 1965; Cert, Woman Entrepreneur, St Louis Community Coll, 1990. *Appointments:* Hd Nurse, Washington Univ Clin Rsch Facility, St Louis, MO, 1960-65; Dir, Nursing, CRC, Univ Miami School of Med, 1975; Coord, Med Oncology, Washington Univ School Med, St Louis, 1974-80; Fac, St Louis Community Coll, 1981-85; Currently Owner, Send A Hug. *Publications:* Amphotericin B Induction of Sensitivity to Adriamycin, (BCNU-NSC 409462) Plus Cyclophosphamide in Human Neoplasia, 1977. *Memberships:* Nat Assn Women Bus Owners; Amnesty Int; Better World Soc; Chmbr of Comm; St Louis Symph Soc; Friends St Louis Art Mus; Pub Interest Rsch Grp. *Honours:* USPHS Trainee, Washington Univ, St Louis, 1963-65; Rsch Assoc, Washington Univ School of Med, 1975-80. *Hobbies:* Reading; Gardening; Walking; Photography. *Address:* 11544 Ladue Road, St Louis, MO 63141, USA.

KLAUI Wolfgang, b. 28 Apr 1945, Zurich, Switzerland. Professor of Inorganic Chemistry. m. Johanna

Schuettloeffel, 4 Mar 1971, 1 s, 1 d. *Education:* Diplomkemiker, 1971, DrPhil, 1973, Univ Zurich; Postdoct rsch w Sir Jack Lewis, Univ Cambridge, England, 1973-74; Dr rer habil, Univ Wuerzburg, FRG, 1979. *Appointments:* Oberasst, Univ Zurich, 1974-78; Privatdozent, 1980-81, Prof, Inorganic Chem, 1981-82, Univ Wuerzburg, FRG; Prof, Inorganic Chem, Technische HS Aachen, 1982-91; Prof, Inorganic Chem, Univ Dusseldorf, 1991-. *Address:* Institut fuer Anorganische Chemie und Strukturchemie, Lehrstuhl I, Universitaet Duesseldorf, Universitaetsstr 1, D- 4000 Duesseldorf, Germany.

KLAUSSNER Burghart, b. 13 Sept 1949, Berlin, Germany. Actor. m. Jenny Naarding, 18 Dec 1988, 2 s. *Education:* Max Reinhard Actors School, Berlin, 1972. *Career:* Schiller Theatre, Berlin, 1972; Theatre Cologne, 1974; Theatre Stuttgart, 1976; Theatre Frankfurt, 1978; Schauspielhaus, Hamburg; Worked w dirs: Palitzsch, Lietzau, Wendt, Rudolph, Nel, Minks, Bogdanov, Mouchtar-Samorai; Films: Das Beil von Wandsbek, 1981; Das Raetsel der Sandbank (The Riddle of the Sands), 1985; Die Staatskanslei, 1989; Kinderspiele, 1992; French Film: Un tank dans Les lilas. *Hobbies:* Sailing; Reading. *Address:* 14 Lenbachstr, D-2000 Hamburg 52, Germany.

KLEIN George, b. 28 July 1925, Budapest, Hungary. Professor of Tumour Biology. *Education includes:* Rsch Fellow, 1947-49, MD, 1951, Karolinska Inst, Stockholm, 1951. *Appointments:* Instr, Histology, 1945, Instr, Pathology, 1946, Budapest Univ, 1945; Guest Investigator, Inst Cancer Rsch, Phila, PA, USA, 1950; Asst Prof, Cell Rsch, 1951-57, Prof, Tumour Biology, Hd, Dept Tumour Biology, 1957-, Karolinska Inst Med School, Stockholm, Sweden; Vis Prof, Stanford Univ, CA, USA, 1961; Fogarty Scholar, NIH, 1972; Vis Prof, Hebrew Univ, Hadassah Med School, Israel, 1973-88. *Publications:* Books: Installet for Hemland, 1984; Ateisten och den Heliga Staden, 1987; Pieta, 1989; The Atheist and the Holy City, 1990; Over 1000 papers in fields of expmtl cell rsch and cancer rsch. *Memberships:* Royal Swedish Acad Scis; For Assoc, Nat Acad Scis, USA; Hon Mbr: Hungarian Acad Scis; Am Assn Immunologists; French Soc Immunology; Am Assn Cancer Rsch; For Mbr, Am Philosl Soc; Sci Advsry Coun, Swedish Med Bd; Hon For Mbr, Am Acad Arts and Scis; Ed, Advances in Cancer Research; Sci Comm, Ludwig Inst Cancer Rsch, NYC, 1990; 1st Hon Mbr, Israel Immunological Soc, 1991. *Honours:* Mbr, Nobel Assembly, Karolinska Inst, 1960-; Hon DSc: Univ Chgo, 1966; Univ NE, 1991; Hon MD, Univ Debrecen, Hungary, 1988; PhD hc, Hebrew Univ, Jerusalem, 1989; Dunham Lectr, Harvard Univ, 1966; Clowes Mem Lectr, Am Assn Cancer Rsch, 1967; Lennander Lectr, Swedish Med Assn, 1967; Harvey Lectr, 1973; Num prizes and awards incl: Rabbi Shai Shacknai Prize, Tumour Immunology, 1972; Sloan Prize, Gen Motors Cancer Rsch Fdnd, 1979; Letterstedt Prize, Royal Swedish Acad Scis, 1989; Dobloug Prize, Swedish ACad Lit, 1990; Lisl and Leo Eitinger's Prize, Oslo Univ, 1990. *Address:* Institution for Tumorbiologi, Karolinska Inst, Box 60400, 104 01 Stockholm, Sweden.

KLEKOWSKI Romuald, b. 1 Jan 1924, Pinsk, Poland. Professor of Ecology; Division Secretary, Academy of Sciences. m. Krystyna Ramlau, 1961, 1 s, 1 d. *Education:* MSc, Univ Lodz, 1950; Dr Natural Sci, 1960, Asst Prof, 1966, Extraordinary Prof, 1970, Inst Expmtl Biology, Polish Acad Scis; Ordinary Prof, Inst Ecology, Polish Acad Scis, 1978; Corres Mbr, Polish Acad Scis, 1979. *Appointments:* Asst to Adj position, Univ Lodz, 1945-52; Rsch, 1952-75, Hd Dept Expmtl Hydrobiology (renamed Dept Ecological Bioenergetics, Dpty Dir, 1970-73, Inst Expmtl Biology, Polish Acad Scis; Co- Organiser, Polish Polar Studies, esp Antarctic, 1969-, Project Coord, Polar Rsch Prog, 1970-80, Project Coord, Ecological Basis Environment Mgmt, 1973-85, Dir, 1973-82, Nat Projects Hd, Dept Ecological Bioenergetics, 1975-90, Inst Ecology, Polish Acad Scis; Hd, Polish grps, 5 oceanological cruises; Dpty Sec, 1970-73, 1984-86, Sec, 1987-, Biological Div, Polish Acad Scis.

Publications: About 135 contbns in Polish, Engl or German to jrnls, proceedings and books, esp in field of ecology, hydrobiology, oceanology, bioenergetics and ecological physiology of pojkilotherms. *Honours include:* Medal of Victory and Freedom, 1947; Companion, 1971, Commander, 1977, Commander w Star, 1986, Polonia Restituta. *Hobbies:* Polar expeditions; Loony oceanological cruises. *Address:* ul Jaktorowska 2 m 50, 01-202 Warsaw, Poland.

KLIKA Jiri, b. 18 Sept 1947, Liberec. Musician. m. Bela Boserova, 20 Jan 1979, 2 s. *Education:* Grad, Conserv of Mus, Prague; Grad, Acad of Mus & Arts, Prague; Postgrad study at Chamber of Mus, Acad of Mus & Arts. *Career:* Violinist in trio originating in Prague Acad of Arts under the guidance of Prof Antonin Kohout, a member of the Smetana String Quartet. Intl Concert Tours, 1970-; Has performanced in most European countries, India, Mexico, Egypt, Cuba, The Far East, Japan, USA, and has made recordings in Czechoslovakia. *Honours:* Special Prizes, Intl Competition of Piano Trios, Fed Intl des Jeunesses Musicales, Belgrade. *Address:* Branicka 1569/122, 147 00 Praha 4, Czechoslovakia.

KLINKOVA Galina Furievna, b. 25 Mar 1960, Hsino. Botanist. *Education:* Grad, Volograd Pedagogic Inst, 1983; PhD, Moscow Main Botanial Gardens, 1992. *Appointments:* Secondary Sch Tchr, 1983-85; Botany Dept Asst, 1985-88; Postgrad Student, 1988-81; Volgograd Pedagogic Inst Botanic Dept, 1992-. *Publications:* A number of scientific papers in Bulletin of Mian Botan Garden and Bulletin of Moscow Soc of Naturalists. *Memberships:* Russian Botanical Soc; Moscow Soc of Naturalists. *Hobbies:* Gardening; Music; Reading. *Address:* Botanical Department, Volgograd Pedagogical Institute, Lenin Prosp 27, 40013 Volgograd, Russia.

KLIPPSTATTER Kurt L, b. 17 Dec 1934, Graz, Austria. Music Director; Director of Opera. m. Mignon Dunn, 22 July 1972. *Education:* Graz Conservatory; Mozarteum, Salzburg; Private study w von Matacic, von Zallinger, von Karajan. *Career:* Opera Graz, 1954-58; Raimundtheater, Vienna, 1958-60; Opera Dortmund, Germany, 1960-62; Opera Pforzheim, 1962-64; Opera Saarbrucken, 1964-66; Deutsche Oper am Rhein, Dusseldorf, 1967; Music Dir, Raimundtheater, Vienna, 1968-70; Opera Krefeld, FRG, 1970-72; Memphis Opera Theatre, TN, USA, 1972-76; Music Dir, AR Orch, 1973-80; Fac, Memphis State Univ, 1973-76; Fac, Hartt School Music, 1977-90; Music Dir, Gtr Trenton Symph Orch, 1984-90; Dir, Opera Univ IL, 1990-; Guest appearances, Germany, Poland, Austria, France, Italy, USA, Mexico; Vis Fac: AIMS, Graz, 1983-87, MCI, 1985-89, Grad Vocal Arts Inst, Tel Aviv, Israel, 1989-, IVAI, 1990-. *Memberships:* Conductors Guild; ASOL; Opera America. *Honours:* Musician of Yr, Nat Fedn Music Clubs, 1976; AR Musician of Yr, AR Fedn Music Clubs, 1977; Hon Citizen, Tupelo, MS; Hon Citation, ASCAP, 1977. *Address:* 1002 Ross Drive, Champaign, IL 61821, USA.

KLOOSTER Willem Gerrit, b. 10 Aug 1935, Medan, Sumatra. Full Professor of Dutch Language. m. Julia Louisa Maria de Vreese, 10 Aug 1973, 2 d. *Education:* Grad, Dutch Lang and Lit, Univ Amsterdam, 1962; Doct, Linguistics, Univ Utrecht, 1971. *Appointments:* Second School Tchr, Netherlands, 1959-65, Univ Tchr, 1965-72, Full Prof, 1972, Univ Amsterdam; Dir, Inst voor Neerlandistiek, Amsterdam, 1972-89. *Publications:* Vuurwerk en wiskunde, poems, 1955; Zonder het genadige einde, twin novelettes, 1956; The Structure Underlying Measure Phrase Sentences, dissertation, 1972; Num articles on linguistics; 3 books on Dutch grammar. *Memberships:* Fndr, Pres, Landelijke Vereniging van Neerlandici; Rotary Club, Amsterdam-Sloterdijk, Pres 1987-88. *Honours:* Reina Prinsen Geerligs Award for Young Lit Authors, 1955. *Hobbies:* Piano playing; Reading; Writing. *Address:* Van

Eeghenstraat 169, 1071 GC Amsterdam, Netherlands, 52.

KLUGE Jürgen, b. 2 Sept 1953, Hagen, Germany. Management Consultant. m. Gabriele Holz, 28 July 1987. *Education:* Dip, Phys, Univ Cologne, 1979; PhD, Phys, Univ Essen, 1984. *Appointments:* Sci Asst, Univ Cologne, 1975-79; Asst, Univ Essen, 1980-84; Mgmt Cons, McKinsey and Comp, Düsseldorf, 1984-. *Hobbies:* Reading; Tennis; Motorracing (cars). *Address:* McKinsey and Comp, Koenigsallee 60c, D-4000 Düsseldorf, Germany. 34, 52.

KLUSSMANN Rudolf, b. 19 June 1937, Osnabruck, Germany. University Professor. m. Barbara Thiele, 1975, 1 s, 2 d. *Education:* State Exam in Med, Univ Munich; Specialist, Psychosomatic Med, Univ Munich; Psychoanalyst; Habilitation, 1980. *Appointments:* Hd, Psychosomatic Hlth Ctr, Med Outpatients, Univ Munich, 1976; Prof, Univ Munich, 1983. *Publications:* Monographs: Psychosomatische Aspekte der Gicht, 1983; Psychosomatische Medizin - eine Uebersicht, 2nd ed 1992; Psychoanalytische Entwicklungspsychologie, Neurosen lehre, Psychotherapie - eine Uebersicht, 1988, 1989; Ed or co-ed: Psychosomatische Medizin im interdisziplinaeren Gespraeche, 5 vols, 1987, 1987, 1988, 1989, 1990; Aktuelle Themen der Psychoanalyse, 1988; Over 80 articles, papers, abstracts, book chapts. *Memberships:* DGPT; DPG; DAGG; DKPM. *Hobbies:* Music; Painting; Literature. *Address:* Medizinische Poliklinik der Universitaet, Pettenkoferstr 8 a, 8000 Munich 2, Germany.

KNAUF Ernst Axel, b. 6 Aug 1953, Dusseldorf, Federal Republic of Germany. Research Scholar. 2 d. *Education:* Dr Theol, Kiel, 1982; Dr Theol Habil, Heidelberg, 1985. *Appointments:* Instr, Old Testament Studies, Univ Tubingen, 1977-80; Instr, Old Testament Studies, Univ Kiel, 1980-82; Asst Dir, German Prot Archaeological Inst, Amman, 1982-85; Asst Prof, Yarmouk, 1985-87; Heisenberg Rsch Scholar, Univ Heidelberg, Germany, 1987-. *Publications:* Books: Midian, 1988; Ismael, 2nd Ed, 1989. *Memberships:* Deutsche Verein zur Erforschung Palaestinas; Deutsche Morgenlaendische Gesellschaft; Am Schools Oriental Rsch. *Honours:* Fac Award, Fac Theology, Kiel, 1982; Heisenberg Rsch Scholarship, 1987. *Hobbies:* Mountain biking; Travel; Toy soldiers. *Address:* Wissenschaftlich-Theologisches Seminar, Kisselgasse 1, D-6900 Heidelberg, Germany.

KNETIG Jerzy Jan, b. 18 Nov 1950, Warsaw, Poland. Singer (Tenor). m. Anna Maria Zlotkowska, 24 Sept 1977. *Education:* Master, Sanitary Engr, Warsaw Polytech School, 1973; Hochschule fuer Musik, Vienna, 1984; Solo Singer, class of Prof Kurt Equiluz, High Acad Music, Cracow, 1987. *Career:* Tech Dir, Warsaw Ctrl Hosp, 1979-82; Solo Singer, oratorio concerts and opera perfs, throughout Europe and Japan, 1980-; Warsaw Chamber Opera, 1986-; High Acad Music, Warsaw, 1991-; Records, compact discs w classical music; Records for Polish Radio and TV film music; Repertory, 86 oratorio, 25 operas, esp Bach, Haydn, Mozart. *Membership:* Assn Polish Artists Music. *Honours:* 1st Prize, Singing Competition, Jelenia Gora, 1971; 3rd Prize, Singing Competition, Lodz, 1973; Medal, Didura Singing Competition, Bytom, 1973; Artistic Medal Szymanowski Music Yr, 1982; Artistic Medal, Fest Classical Music, Torun and Loretto (Italy), 1983; Medals, Vramslavia Cantans Fest, 1984-87, 1989-91. *Hobbies:* History; Painting. *Address:* Jagiellonska Street 2.21, 03-721 Warsaw, Poland.

KNIE-ANDERSEN Bent, b. 14 Nov 1942, Horsens, Denmark. Chief General Manager. m. Lisbeth Knie-Andersen, 28 Jan 1967, 1 s. *Education:* Cand oecon, Aarhus Univ, 1968. *Appointments:* Mgr, Jyllands Kreditforening, 1971-77; Gen Mgr, 1977-80, Chief Gen Mgr, 1980-, Alm Brand af 1792, Lyngby. *Publications:* Insurance Accounting, 1983; Var books and articles of social and econ nature. *Memberships:* Comm Mbr, AISAM; Comm Mbr, Danish Ins Soc; Bd, Danish Assn

Gen Ins; Chmn, Danish Assn Mutual Ins Cos. *Address:* Alm Brand af 1792, Lyngby Hovedgade 4, DK-2800 Lyngby, Denmark. 52.

KNIGHT Jeffrey Russell, b. 1 Oct 1936, Bristol, England. Consultant. m. Judith Marion Delver Podger, 12 Dec 1959, 4 d. *Education:* St Peter's Coll, Oxford, 1957-60; MA (Oxon). *Appointments:* The De La Rue Co Ltd, 1960-62; Fuller Wise Fisher and Co, Chartered Accts, 1962-67; Stock Exchange, London, 1967-90. *Membership:* FCA. *Hobbies:* Music; Cricket. *Address:* Robin Haye, The Drive, Godalming, Surrey GU7 1PH, England. 1.

KNIGHT Teman Willis III, b. 27 Mar 1964, Bogalusa, Louisiana, USA. Baptist Minister. m. Darlana Bobbette Adams, 11 Aug 1984, 1 s. *Education:* Bach, SEn LA Univ, Hammond, 1985; Master's degree, 1988, PhD, 1992, New Orleans Bapt Theological Sem. *Appointments:* Pastor, Sunnyhill Bapt Ch, 1985-87; Pastor, Bethel Bapt Ch, Kentwood, LA, 1987-89; Pastor, Hillsdale Bapt Ch, Amite, LA, 1989-; Fellow, Dept Old Testament and Hebrew, New Orleans Bapt Theological Sem; Prof, Sem Extension Prog, So Bapt Conven. *Honours:* Ordained So Bapt Min, 1985. *Hobbies:* Basketball; Sports; Reading. *Address:* Rt 1, Box 94, Amite, LA 70422, USA. 1, 117.

KNILL John Lawrence, b. 22 Nov 1934, Wolverhampton, England. Chairman, Natural Environment Research Council. m. Diane Constance Judge, 16 July 1957, 1 s, 1 d. *Education:* Imperial Coll, Univ London, 1952-57; BSc; PhD; DSc, 1981. *Appointments:* Geologist, Sir Alexander Gibb & Ptnrs, Tehran, Iran, 1957; Lectr, Reader, Prof, 1957-88, Imperial Coll, Univ London; Chmn, Natural Environment Rsch Coun, 1988-. *Publication:* Industrial Geology, 1978. *Memberships:* Fellow, Royal Academy Engrng; Fellow, Inst Civil Engrs; Fellow, Hong Kong Inst Engrs; Chartered Engr; Chartered Geologist. *Honours:* Murchison Medal, 1954, Watts Medal, 1955, Imperial Coll; Whitaker Medal, Instn Water and Environmental Mgmt, 1969; Hon Fellow, City and Guilds, London Inst, 1988; Aberconway Medal, Instn Geologists, 1989; Hon Mbr, Geologists Assn, 1990; Hon DSc, Kingston Univ, 1992. *Hobby:* Viticulture. *Address:* Highwood Farm, Shaw-cum-Donnington, Newbury, Berks RG16 9LB, England. 1.

KNOBEL Dale Thomas, b. 14 Sept 1949, East Cleveland, Ohio, USA. University Administrator; Associate Professor of History. m. Tina Hess Jamieson, 19 June 1971, 1 s, 1 d. *Education:* BA, Yale Univ, 1971; PhD, NWn Univ, 1976. *Appointments:* Asst Prof, Hist, NWn Univ, 1976-77; Asst Prof, Hist, 1977-84, Assoc Prof, Hist, 1984-, Dir, Univ Hons Prog, 1987-91, Exec Dir, Hons Progs and Acad Scholarships, 1991-, TX A&M Univ, Coll Station. *Publications:* Prejudice (co-author), 1982; Paddy and the Republic: Ethnicity and Nationality in Antebellum America, 1985. *Memberships:* Nat Coll Hon Coun; Org Am Histns; Immigration Hist Soc; Soc Histns of Early Am Republic; Gt Plains Hons Coun. *Address:* The University Honors Program, Texas A&M University, College Station, TX 77843, USA. 7, 13, 15.

KNOBLOCH Johann Josef Pius, b. 5 Jan 1919, Vienna, Austria. Professor Emeritus. m. Gertrud Edelmann, 28 Apr 1947. *Education:* PhD, Univ Vienna, 1944. *Appointments:* Privatdozent (Univ Lectr), 1951-55, Prof, 1957-63, Univ Innsbruck; Full Prof'ship, Univ Greifswald, DRG, 1955-57; Prof, Univ Bonn, FRG (now Germany), 1963-. *Publications:* Sprache und Religion, 1, 1979, 2, 1983, 3, 1986; Kulturhistorische Wortforschung 1, 1991. *Memberships:* For Mbr, Instituto Lombardo, Milan; Hon Mbr, Gesellschaft fuer deutsche Sprache, Wiesbaden. *Address:* Venusbergweg 34, D-5300 Bonn 1, Germany.

KNODT Gerrit Janus, b. 5 Mar 1938, Germany. Registered Organizational Development Professional

(RDDP). div., 2 s, 1 d. *Education:* BA, Hist, King's Coll; MA, Psychology, Villanova Univ; PhD, Human Resources Dev, Columbia Pacific Univ. *Appointments:* Lehigh Portland Cement, 1963-65; Omnicrete Constructors Corp, 1965-68; Temple Univ, 1979-80; Univ Tampa, FL, 1980-83; Citicorp/Citibank, 1983-91; Dir, Organisational Dev, Right Assocs, Tampa, FL, 1991-. *Publications:* The Effect of Coaching and Feedback on the Transfer of People Skills from the Cognitive to the Behavioral State, book. *Memberships:* Am Soc Trng and Dev; Organizational Dev Inst. *Honours:* Walter Clausen Award, State of FL, 1989; HRD Profl of Yr, Am Soc Trng and Dev, 1990. *Hobbies:* Tennis; Soccer; Photography; Chess; Fishing; International travel. *Address:* DHL Worldwide Express, 124 Rue Colonel Bourg, 1140 Brussels, Belgium. 7.

KNOPS Robin John, b. 30 Dec 1932, London, England. Professor of Mathematics; University Vice-Principal. m. Margaret Mary MacDonald, 2 Sept 1965, 4 s, 2 d. *Education:* BSc, 1955, PhD, 1958, Univ Nottingham. *Appointments:* Asst Lectr, Maths, Nottingham Univ, 1956-59; Lectr, Maths, 1959-62, Lectr, Applied Maths, 1962-68, Reader, Continuum Mech, 1968- 71, Univ Newcastle-upon-Tyne; Prof, Maths, 1971-, currently VP, Heriot-Watt Univ, Edinburgh. *Publications:* Uniqueness Theorems in Elasticity (co- author), 1971; Theory of Elastic Stability (co-author), 1973. *Memberships:* Curator, Royal Soc Edinburgh; Int Soc Interaction of Maths and Mech, Pres 1991-94; RSA; Edinburgh Maths Soc, Pres 1974-75. *Hobbies:* Walking; Reading. *Address:* Heriot-Watt University, Edinburgh EH14 4AS, Scotland. 184.

KNOTT Herbert Espenett (Herbie), b. 11 Mar 1949, Manchester, England. Photojournalist. *Education:* Rugby School, 1962-67; BA, MA, Univ Coll, Oxford. *Appointments:* Mgmt Trainee, Atlas Express Co Ltd, 1972-73; Photojrnlst (as Herbie Knott): The London Standard, 1977-80; Now Mag, 1980-81; The Sunday Times, 1981-86; The Independent, 1986-. *Publications:* Illustrator: Diary of an Election (Carol Thatcher), 1983; How They Made Piece of Cake (w Robert Eagle), 1988; Black and White, 1990; Glasmoth (w Jonathan elwees), 1990. *Membership:* Brit Press Photographers Assn. *Honours:* Contbr to: Telegraph Mag 25th Anniversary Exhib, Brit Press Photographers Exhibs, 1986-89, World Press Photo Exhibs, 1987, 1989, Witness Exhib, NT, 1990; Nikon Photographer of Month, June 1983, Dec 1990; Nikon Photographer of the Election, 1987. *Hobbies:* Skiing; Tennis; Supporting Winmbledon Football Club; Veteran shooting at Bisley for Old Rugbeians. *Address:* c/o The Independent, 40 City Road, London EC1, England.

KNOX-JOHNSTON William Robert Patrick (Robin), b. 17 Mar 1939, London, England. Master Mariner; Author. m. Suzanne Singer, 6 Jan 1962, 1 d. *Education:* Berkhamsted School; Masters Cert, 1965. *Career:* Merchant Navy, 1957-69; 1st person to sail single-handed non-stop round world, 14 June 1968-21 Apr 1969; Author, 1969-. *Publications:* A World of my Own, 1969, in 9 other langs, republd, UK, 1988, USA, 1990; Robin Round the World, 1969; Sailing, 1974; Twilight of Sail, 1978; Last but not least, 1978; Bunkside Companion, 1982; Seamanship, 1986; The BOC Challenge, 1988; Yachtsmans Guide to the English Channel (ed), 1988; The Cape of Good Hope, 1989; The History of Yachting, 1990; The Columbus Venture, 1991; Cape Horn, 1992; Contbr to: The Times, Guardian, Field, Yachting World, Yachting Monthly, High Life, Telegraph Colour Supplement, Cruising World (USA), Classic Boats, France, Financial Times, others. *Memberships:* Younger Brother, Trinity House; Hon Co Master Mariners; FRGS; Royal Inst Navigation. *Honours:* CBE, 1969; Yachtsman of Yr, 1969; Seamanship Award, Royal Yacht Assn, 1991; Hon DSc, ME Maritime Acad, USA. *Hobbies:* Sailing; Navigation; Outdoor pursuits. *Address:* c/o Curtis Brown, 157-162 Regent Street, London, England. 1, 52.

KNUDSEN Morten, b. 21 Jan 1926, Silkeborg, Denmark. Professor of Forestry; Executive Advisor. m. Julie Tauson, 17 Dec 1949, 1 s, 1 d. *Education:* Master of Forestry, 1951. *Appointments:* Prof, Dept Forestry, Copenhagen Univ, 1952-58; Hd, Wood Dept, 1959, Dir Gen, 1970- 89, Exec Advsr, 1990-, Technological Inst, Copenhagen; Prof, Roskilde Univ, 1990-. *Publications:* Rsch reports and articles on wood technology, rsch and educl policy. *Memberships:* Danish Acad Tech Scis; Danish Design Coun; Chmn, Advsry Bd for Continuing Educ; Chmn, Advsry Bd for Danish Tech Dev Assistance; Chmn, Advsry Bd, Fedn European Industrial Coop Rsch Orgs; Sec Gen World Assoc of Jud and Tech Rsch Org, 1991. *Honours:* Otto Bruun Prize. *Interests:* Development assistance; Industrial design; Research and education policy; Environment. *Address:* Danish Technological Institute, PO Box 141, DK 2630 Taastrup, Denmark.

KOŚCIELAK Jerzy, b. 6 Sept 1930, Lodz, Poland. Biochem; Scientist. 1 d. *Education:* MD 1960, DSc 1969, Med Acad, Warsaw. *Appointments:* Asst, Dept of Biochem 1953, Hd of Dept 1969, Inst of Hematology, Warsaw; MA Gen Hosp, Boston, 1964-65; Assoc Prof 1973, Full Prof 1982, Med Acad, Warsaw. *Publications:* Author of over 150 scientific articles in Polish and int scientific journs, mostly on the subj of chem and biol of glycoconjugates. *Memberships include:* Polish Acad of Scis, 1982; Polish Rep, Int Glycoconjugate Org; NY Acad of Sciences, 1992. *Honours:* Parnas Scientific Awd, Polish Biochem Soc, 1977; Sniadecki Awd, Polish Acad of Sci, 1977; State Scientific Awd, 1980. *Hobby:* History. *Address:* Institute of Hematology, 00957 Warsaw, Poland.

KOBAYASHI Isao, b. 14 Oct 1945, Yokohama, Japan. Professor of Law. *Education:* Univ Tokyo, 1964-68; LLD. *Appointments:* Asst, Univ Tokyo, 1968-71; Assoc Prof, 1971-78, Prof, 1978-, Fac Law, Rikkyo Univ. *Publications:* Rational Choice and Contract, book, 1990; Many articles on legal philos and mediaeval pol thought in Europe. *Memberships:* Bd Dirs, Japanese Assn Legal Philos; Int Assn Social and Legal Philos. *Hobbies:* Opera; Islamic arts. *Address:* 3-4 Shimo-cho, Isogo- ku, Yokohama-shi, Japan.

KOBAYASHI Manji, b. 29 Mar 1931, Tokyo, Japan. Professor of English Literature. m. Fumiko Uchiyama, 11 Mar 1967, 1 s, 1 d. *Education:* BA, 1954, MA, 1957, Doshisha Univ, Kyoto; MA, Columbia Univ, NYC, 1966. *Appointments:* Lectr, Engl, 1961-64, Assoc Prof, Engl Lit, 1964-68, Doshisha Univ, Kyoto; Assoc Prof, Fac Letters, 1968-79, Prof, 1979-, Kobe Univ. *Publications:* The Climate of Modern Poetry, collection of essays on Brit and Am poetry; Num articles in profl jrnls. *Memberships:* Engl Lit Soc Japan, Ed 1970-76, Dir 1989-91; Yeats Soc Japan, Comm Mem 1979-. *Honours:* Fulbright Scholarship, 1963-65. *Hobbies:* Gardening; Detective fiction. *Address:* 1-6-9 Kofudai, Toyono-cho, Toyono-gun, Osaka-fu, Japan 563-01. 52.

KOBAYASHI Tsunehiro, b. 4 Mar 1932, Tokyo, Japan. English Language Educator. m. Fusako Santo, 15 Nov 1961, 2 d. *Education:* BA, 1954, MA, Keio Univ, Tokyo. *Appointments:* Sub-Asst, 1957, Asst, 1958, Instr, 1962, Assoc Prof, 1966, Prof, Present-day Engl, 1973-, Dpty Dir, Inst Audio-Visual Lang Educ, 1989-1991, Keio Univ, Tokyo; Pt-time Instr, Tokyo Univ of Foreign Studies, 1979-. *Creative works:* Translator, screenplays incl: The Third Man, 1963; A Rage to Live, 1965; North by Northwest, 1966; Picnic, 1966; The Red Pony, 1973; Paris, Texas, 1990. *Memberships:* Engl Lit Soc Japan; Japan Soc Mediaeval Engl Studies; Lang Lab Assn Japan. *Honours:* Audiovisual Instruction Grantee, The Asia Fndn, San FRan, 1962. *Hobby:* Canoeing. *Address:* Keio University, 2-15-45 Mita, Minato-ku, Tokyo, Japan 108. 52.

KOCH Friedrich, b. 19 Feb 1936, Goettingen, Germany. University Professor. m. 14 Aug 1970, 1 d. *Education:* HS Music and Theatre, Hamburg, 1954-57;

Paedagogical HS, Oldenburg, 1963-65; Univ Hamburg; Dr phil, 1970. *Appointments:* Tchr, Niedersachsen, 1965-, 1968; Asst, Paedagogical HS, Luneberg, 1970; Prof, Univ Hamburg, 1970-. *Publications:* Negative und positive Sexualerziehung, 1971; Sexualpaedagogihk und politische Erziehung, 1975; Gegenaufklaerung, 1979; Sexuelle Denunziation, 1986; Schule im Kino, 1987; Christian Fürchtegott Gleert, 1992.. *Memberships:* Deutsche Gesellschaft fuer Erzeihungswissenschaft, Goettingen; Deutsche Gesellschaft fuer Sexualforschung, Hamburg. *Hobbies:* Walking; Cinema. *Address:* Vom-Melle-Park 8, 2000 Hamburg 13, Germany. 43, 52, 92.

KOCH Jan Maciej, b. 25 Feb 1931, Kobylnica, Poland. University Professor. m. Anna Teresa Hladowska, 12 July 1952, 2 s. *Education:* Grad, 1956, PhD, 1964, D habil, 1972, Tech Univ, Wroclaw. *Appointments:* Univ Asst, 1953-64, Lectr, 1964-69, Asst Prof, 1969-76, Vice-Dir, Institute, 1971-80, Assoc Prof, 1976-, Pro-Rector, 1984-87, Dir, Inst Mech Engrng and Automatization, 1987-, Full Prof, 1990-, Tech Univ Wroclaw. *Publications:* Books: Machine Tools-Spindles, 1982; Calculation of Machine Tool Structure, 1984; Over 100 sci works in Polish and German sci papers about constrn and investigation of machine tools. *Memberships:* Ed Bds: Tech Mag and Sci Jrnl, Polish Acad Scis. *Honours:* Medal of Sci Educ; Prize, Min Educ; Kt Cross, Polonia Restituta. *Hobbies:* Gardening; Reading. *Address:* Technical University of Wroclaw, Institute of Mechanical Engineering and Automatization, ul Lukasiewicza 3/5, 50-371 Wroclaw, Poland.

KOCH Joanne Barbara, b. Chicago, USA. Author; Playwright. m. Lewis Z Koch, 1 s, 2 d. *Education:* BA Cornell Univ, 1961; MA Columbia Univ, 1962. *Appointments:* Dir of Publications, Roosevelt Univ, IL, 1964-66; Dir of Advg, Educ Methods Inc, 1969; Ptnr, Parents in Touch Proj, 1989-. *Publications:* Good parents for hard times, 1992; The Familes In Touch Series, 1990; Children: Development through adolescence, 1983; The Marriage Savers, 1976; Marriage and the Family, 1983; Plays: Haymarket, 1986; Teeth, 1988; Nesting Dolls, 1989; Hearts inthe Wood, 1991; Sophie Toitie and Belle, 1992. *Memberships:* Pres, Soc of Midland Authors, 1978080; Pres, Chicago Alliance for Playwrights, 1990-. *Honours:* Illinois Art Coun Playwrighting Fellowship, 1992; 1st Prize, 8th Intl Playwriting Contest; Women in the Theatre Awd, 1981; Harris Media Awe, 1978; Family Ser Assn Awd, 1975. *Address:* 343 Dodge Avenue, Evanston, IL 60202, USA. 5.

KOCKBERG Mats Borje, b. 25 Oct 1950, Helsinki, Finland. Managing Director; Management Consultant. m. Jannica Fagerholm, 8 Nov 1986, 3 s, 1 d. *Education:* BA, Univ Helsinki, 1975. *Appointments:* Dist Dir, 1975-78, Int Sec, 198-83, Nat Coalition Party; Ed-in-Chief, Forum for ekonomi och teknik, 1978-80; Dir, The Uusi Suomi Grp, 1983-85; Mng Dir, Scandinavian Serv School, 1985-88; Mng Dir, Oy Interpersona Ab, Helsinki, 1988-. *Publication:* Det andra Finland, book, 1984; Dey nya Europa, Book, 1992. *Memberships:* Borsklubben; Handelsgillet. *Hobby:* Yachting. *Address:* Oy Interpersona Ab, Lonnrotsgatan 19 A, SF-00120 Helsinki, Finland. 52.

KODAMA Junzo, b. 10 Aug 1927, Mikage, Kobe, Japan. Medical Director. m. Akiko Takagi, 15 Oct 1956, 2 s, 1 d. *Education:* Grad, Dept Sci, Himeji Higher School, 1948; Grad, School Med, 1953, completed med trng course, University Hosp, 1954, Osaka Univ, 1953; Nat Dip, med prac, 1954; DMed, 1959. *Appointments:* Asst, School Med, Osaka Univ, 1959; Asst, School Med, Julius-Maximilians Univ, Wuerzburg, FRG, 1963; Hd Physn, 4th Div (Cancer) Internal Med, Nat Osaka Hosp, 1967; Dir, Clin Lab Div, 1979, Dir, Comprehensive Outpatients Div, 1981, Nat Cardiovascular Ctr; Med Dir, Inst Med Care and Hlth Maintenance, SANYO Elec Grp, Hlth Ins Assn, 1986-. *Creative works:* Clin med rsch on metabolism of haematopoeitic vitamins,

erythrokinetics assessed by metabolism of bile pigment, side effects of anticancerous drugs esp those of 1-asparaginase, biochem abnormality in hereditary angioneurotic edema patients esp in vivo functions of Cl-esterase inhibitor, early recognition of preparedness for onset of cardiovascular diseases and prevention of them; Pubns incl: Intracellular distribution of vitamin B12, folic and folinic acid in the bone marrow tissue of rabbit, 1959. *Memberships:* Japanese Soc Haematology; Japanese Soc Internal Med; Int Soc Haematology; Japan Soc Clin Haematology; Japanese Circulation Soc; Japan Med Assn. *Honours:* Award, Studies of untowards reactions of 1-asparaginase, Rsch Fndn Cancer and cardiovascular Diseases, Osaka, 1972. *Hobbies:* Cameras; 8mm video; Japanese swords; Hobby carpenter; Gardening; Classical music; Reading articles in field of medical science and clinical practice to prevent adult disease. *Address:* Institute for Medical Care and Health Maintenance, SANYO Electric Group, Health Insurance Association, 2-16 Kaneshita-cho, 570 Moriguchi-shi, Osaka, Japan.

KODZUHAROVA Ruth Borisova, b. 18 Jan 1958, Bansko, Bulgaria. Paediatrician. m. Atanas Paunov Paunov, 10 Sept 1985, 1 d. *Education:* MD, Med Acad, 1983; Trng, Hosp, Razlog, 1983-85. *Appointments:* Paediatrician, Haskovo, 1985-. *Membership:* Med Drs Union Bulgaria. *Hobbies:* Reading; Collection of antique books, newspapers and magazines; Publications of bibliographical value. *Address:* c/o fam Tanakiev, Vasil Zevski Blvd No 1-A-1, Hasko, Bulgaria.

KOFIE Nicholas, b. 17 May 1946, Tamale, Ghana. Senior Lecturer. m. Susanna Hagan, 14 May 1988, 1 d. *Education:* Gen Dipl in Mus, Univ of Ghana, 1971; PhD, Univ of Hamburg, 1978. *Appointments:* Tchr, Navrongo, 1966-67; Asst Mus Tutor, WA Tchr Trng Col, 1971-72; Mus Tutor, Wiawso Trng Col, 1972-73; Mus Master, Aggrey Meml Secondary Sch, Cape Coast, 1978-80; Piano Tchr, Musikschule Lubbecker Land, Germany, 1980-91; Lectr, Sr Lectr, Univ of Cape Coast, 1987; Vis Sr Lectr, Kenyatta Univ, Nairobi, 1991-. *Creative works:* Three piono compositions; Book: Contemporary African music in world perspectives: some thought on systematic musicology and acculturation. *Memberships include:* Ghana Mus Tchrs Assn; St Frangs Cathedral Choir; External Exmr, Nat Acad of Music. *Honours:* Organ scholarship, Univ of Ghana, 1969-71; Res Scholarship, Staatliches Inst fur Musikforschung, Berlin, 1975-76. *Address:* Department of Music, University of Cape Coast, Cape Coast, Ghana. 52.

KOH Siak Khee Kenneth, b. 6 June 1963, Singapore. Corporate Lawyer. m. Kumi Arakawa, 16 June 1990. *Education:* LLB, Nat Univ of Singapore, 1988; LLM, Cambs Univ, England, 1989; Singapore Intl Monetary Exchange, 1990. *Appointments:* Asst Mgr, Nitto Funka Pte Ltd and KK Tan Enterprise Pte Ltd; Proprietor, Standard Producs, 1985-91; Proprietor, Emergent Bus Ventures, 1990; Allen & Gledhill, 1988-. *Memberships:* Singapore Law Acad; Law Soc of Singapore; Inner Temple, London, Hon Mem; Cambs Soc, Fellow; Anglo-Chinese School Old Boys Assn; Nat Univ of Singapore Grads Soc; Singapore Armed Forces Reservist Assn. *Honours:* Cambs Overseas Devel Asst Scholarship, 1988; Young Scist of the Yr, Nat Sci Fair, 1980; Pegasus Scholarship of the Inner Temple and Clifford Chance, 1984, 87. *Hobbies:* Reading; Mathematics; Swimming; Travel. *Address:* Chay Yan Street, 04-12 Blk 80, Singapore 03160.

KOHEN Sami, b. 14 July 1928, Istanbul, Turkey. Journalist; Foreign Affairs Columnist. m. Mirka Barzilay, 29 May 1960, 1 s, 1 d. *Education:* Sch of Jour, Istanbul Univ, 1951. *Appointments:* Asst Night Ed, Yeni Instanbul, 1951-52; Foreign Ed, Istanbul Ekspress, 1952-54; Foreign Ed, 1954-81, Foreign Affairs Columnist, Sr Ed, 1981-, Milliyet. Corres in Turkey for: Newskweek mag, Christian Sci Monitor, Daily Mail, Maariv, ABC Radi, Radio Suisse Romande. *Publications:*

Articles to variety of foreign publications; Books: Today's Japan, 1980; Changing China, 1982; Frequent lecturer and speaker at home and abroad, at academic and professional organizations. *Memberships:* Exec Bd, Intl Press Inst, 1980-84; Turkish Press Assn and Foreign Press Assn. *Honours:* Holder of serveral awards given by the Turkish Press Assn for best reporting, best series of articles and best columns, 1960-. *Hobbies:* Music; Fishing. *Address:* Maya Sitesi 2/2, Camlik, Etiler, Istanbul. 104.

KOHL Ernst, b. 20 Nov 1935, Elbing, Germany. Librarian. m Ingeburg Wendhausen, 8 Oct 1973, 1s. *Education:* Univ of Goettingen, 1955-57; Univ of Kiel, 1958-64; PhD, 1964. *Appointments:* Reschr, German Africa Soc, 1965-66; Staff, Bavarian State Lib, 1967-78; Lectr, Bavarian Civil Servants Col, 1979-80; Proj Mgr, Lib Network of Supreme Fed Auth, 1981-85; Lib, German Bundestag Admin, 1986-. *Publications:* Zeichensatz und Zeichenverschulesselung fuer die elektr, 1977; Bibliog of Bibliog Sers of European Parliamentary Libs, 1990; Ed, World Dir of Nat Parliamentary Libs, 1991. *Memberships:* Intl Fed of Lib Assoc, Profl Bd, Chm, Parl Libs and Div of Gen Res Libs. *Hobbies:* Environmental issues. *Address:* Deutscher Bundestag, Verwaltung, Bundeshaus, D-5300 Bonn 1, Germany. 52.

KOHL Helmut, b. 3 Apr 1930, Ludwigshafen, Germany. German Politician (CDU). m. Hannelore Renner, 1960, 2 s. *Education:* Frankfurt Univ; PhD, Heidelber Univ, 1958. *Appointments include:* Mem, Parl of Rhineland Palatinate, 1959-76; Ldr, Christian Democratic Union (CDU) Parl Party in Rhineland Palatinate Parl, 1963-69; Chm, CDU Rhineland Palatinate, 1966-74; Min, Pres, Rhineland Palatinate, 1969-76; Mem, Fed Exec Com, CDU, 1964-; Chm, CDU, Germany, 1973-; Mem, Bundestag, 1976-; Ldr of Opp, Bundestag, 1976-82; Chancellor, FRG, 1982-, re-elected, 1991. *Honours:* Grosskreuz Verdienstorden, Germany; Numerous foreign decorations. *Address:* Marbacher Strasse 11, D-W 6700 Ludwigshafen, Germany. 1.

KOHNER Eva Maria, b. 23 Feb 1929, Budapest, Hungary. Professor of Medicine. m. Steven J Warman, 2 Nov 1962, div. *Education:* Matriculation, 1947; SRN, 1952; BSc, 1956; MBBS, 1959; MRCP, 1964; MD, London, 1969. *Appointments:* Jr Hosp Post, 1959-69; Alexander Wernhes Piggott Fellowship, 1969-70; Conslt Phys, hammersmith and Moofields, 1977; Prof, 1989. *Publications:* Over 300 articles and book chapters, mainly on diabetic eye disease. *Memberships:* BMA; Brit and Am Diabetes Assns; FRCM; FCOpthal; Assn for Res in vision and Opthalmol; European Assn for the study of Diabetes. *Honours:* Vis Prof, Univ of Wisconsin, 1972; Parker Hlth Lectr, Am Acad of Ophthalmol, 1983; Kellion Lectr, Aust Diabetes Assn, 1987; Madras Gold Medal for Diabetes res, 1985. *Hobbies:* Art; Archaeology. *Address:* 32 Monckton Ct, Strangways Terrace, London W14 8NF, England.

KOHOUT Ladislav, b. 22 Apr 1941, Prague, Czechoslovakia. Scientist. m. Eva Titerova, 23 Jan 1988, 1 s, 2 d. *Education:* Fac Natural Scis, Charles Univ, 1958-63; PhD, Czech Acad of Scis, 1963-67. *Appointments:* Czech Acad Scis, 1967-73; Prof, Univ Central de Venezuela, 1973-74; Sr Leading Scist, Czech Acad Sci, 1974-. *Publications:* Scientific articles inprofessional journals; Patents. *Memberships:* Czech Trade Unions; Czech Union of Philatelists; Sci Tech Soc. *Hobbies:* Gardening; Philately. *Address:* Inst of Organic Chemistry and Biochemistry, Czechoslovak Academy of Sciences, Fleminogovo nam 2, 166 10 Prague 6, Czechoslovakia. 52.

KOKT Gerard Johannes, b. 31 Dec 1953, Carnarvon. Managing Director; Interior Designer. *Education:* BA Rand Afrikaans Univ, Johannesburg. *Appointments:* David Hicks S.Africa, 1973; Buyer, Levinsons Gp, Jhb, 1973-75; Div Merchandise Mgr, Edgars Gp, 1976-83; Liaison Dir for Clavin Klein SA.A, 1983-85; MD Design,

Gerard Koks. *Publications:* Numerous magazine articles on design projects; Local and Overseas TV programmes on inerior design of homes and hotels. *Memberships:* Overseas Mem, Brit Interior Decorators and Designers Assn. *Hobbies:* Collecting contemporary American and European Art Antiques; Gardening; Extensive world travel; Reading. *Address:* 54 Greenway, Greenside, Johannesburg 2193, S. Africa. 52.

KOLCZAK Tadeusz, b. 20 June 1938, Wielopole, Poland. University Professor. m. Irena Juszczynko 6 Mar 1973, 1 d. *Education:* MSc, 1961, DSc, 1968, Agric Univ, Krakow. *Appointments:* Sci Ofr, Dept of Animal Physiol, Inst of Zootechnics, 1961; Asst Prof, Dept of Animal Sci, Agric Univ Krakow, 1978; Hd, Dept of Animal Prod Tech, 1984, Prof, 1991. *Publications:* Biologiczne Podstawy Technol Migsa, 1983; 71 papers published in professional magazines and journals. *Memberships:* Animal Sci Com, Polish Acad of Sci (PAS); Protein Section, Food Tech Com, PAS: Fellow, Polish Soc of Animal Breeding; Fellow, Polish Soc of Food Tech. *Honours:* Two prizes for the Min of Educ. *Hobbies:* Philately; Gardening. *Address:* Nad Sudolem 12/36, 31-228 Krakow, Poland.

KOLDAMOVA Krasimira, b. 8 Dec 1938, St Sagora, Bulgaria. Ballerina Pedagogue. m. Stojan Ljubomirov Nanchev, 11 Nov 1973, 1 s. *Education:* Nat Choreographic Sch, Sofia, 1954; Moscow Choreographic Sch of Bolshoi Theatre, 1958. *Appointments:* Nat Ballet, 1954-91; Ballet Contemporain, 1968-69; Grand ballet Classic de France, 1972-73; Choreodran Elinic, Greece, 1973. *Creative works:* Lead role: Gizel, Romeo and Juliet, Swan Lake, Odet-Odil, Sleeping Beauty, and Karmen. *Memberships:* Chm, Ballet Actors League, Assn of Mus and Dancers in Bulgaria. *Honours:* 2nd prize, Intl Youth Festival, Moscow, 1957; 1st prize, Intl Youth Festival, Vienna,, 1959; 2nd Prize, Best Actor, First Ballet Festival, Varna, 1964; Prima Ballerina Abssoluta of the Nat Ballet. *Hobbies:* Music; Nature; Architecture; Padagogue activities. *Address;* Vela Blagoeva Str 18, Sofia 1463, Bulgaria.

KOLESSOV Vladimir, b. 10 Apr 1934, Ussurijsk. Linguist. m. Olga Sergejevna Rosa, 19 Dec 1956, 2 d. *Education:* Unvi of Leningrad, 1957; Cand of Arts, 1962; Dr of Arts, 1969; Prof of Russian, 1973; Prof Tutilaire de la Chaire de Langue Russe, 1978. *Publications:* The History of Russian Accent, 1972; An Introduction to the Historical Phonology, 1974, 1982; The History of Russian Language in stories, 1976;, 1982; Russian Historical Phonetics, 1980; The man's World in the World of Old Rus' 1986; The Old Russian Literary Language, 1988; The Culture of Speech - The Culture of Behaviour, 1988; The Language of the City, 1991; Domostroy, 1990, 1991, 1992; Lev V Shcherba, 1987. *Membership:* Independent Acad of Humanities, St Petersburg, 1989. *Honour:* Best Book of the Yr, Univ of Sanct, Petersburg, 1974, 1988. *Hobbies:* Gardening; Reading; Walking. *Address:* Torzhkovskaya Street, 6 Apt 22, St Petersburg 197342, Russia.

KOLLAR Istvan, b. 2 June 1954, Budapest, Hungary. Associate Professor. m Agnes Michelberger, 18 June 1982, 1 s, 2 d. *Education:* Enec Engrg, Tech Univ of Budapest (TUB), 1977; Candidate, Hungarian Acad of Scis, 1985; DTech, TUB, 1985. *Appointments:* Meas and Instrument Engrg, TUB, 1977-; Vis Prof, Vrije Univ, Brussels, 1989-90. *Publications:* 40 scientific papers published as well as thesis, Inviestigation of Fourier Analyzers. *Memberships:* IEEE, 1987-; Intl Measurement Confed; Ed, Periodica Polytechnica, 1988-91; Chief Ed, 1991-. *Honours:* Intl Olympiad in Maths, 2nd Prize, 1972; 1st prize, Intl Math competition for Students of Tech Univs, Bulgaria, 1977. *Hobby:* Reading. *Address:* Department of Measurement and Instrument Engineering, Technical University of Budapest, H-1521 Budapest, Hungary.

KOLLONTAY (YERMOLAYEV) Mikhail Georgiyevitch, b. 21 Aug 1952, Moscow, USSR. Composer; Pianist. m. Irina Yevgenyevna Lozovaya, 18 Nov 1973. *Education:* Studied Piano, 1971-77, Composition, 1971-78, Moscow Conservatoire. *Appointments:* Dept Folk Music, 1972-73, Prof, 1977-85, Moscow Conservatoire; Soloist, Mosconcert, 1982-85; Prof, Moscow State Musical and Pedagogical Gnesins Inst, 1989-91; Concerts, USSR, 1982-85, 1991-; Repertory incl Bach, Beethoven, Liszt, Purcell, Tchaikovsky, Mousorgsky, Glinka. *Creative works:* Orchestral works incl: Concerto for viola, 1980; Concerto for piano, 1985; Catechisis, 1990; Chamber works incl: Praise to the Virgin, 2nd string quartet, 1988; Trio-Symphony for organ, 1986; Vocal and choral works incl: Village Choruses for mixed chorus and 6 soloists to traditional Russian words, 1973; Plantain for bass and piano to poems of N Roubtsov, 1981; Under the Canopy of the Bird Cherry Trees and Acacias, little cantata for children's chorus, string orchestra and flute to poem of K Batyushkov, 1985; Action on Ten Leprous Men for mixed and children's choruses, 10 soloists and oboe to texts of the Bible, 1991; Author, articles for periodicals and radio progs on Russian composers and gen problems of contemporary music. *Memberships:* Union Soviet Composers; Chmn, Soc Musical Heritage; Fndr, Biennale Heritage, 1990, 1992. *Honours:* USSR Pianist Competitions, 1st degree, 1981; Prize, Composers Union Russia, 1981; Dip, Special Prize, VII Int Tchaikovsky Competitions, 1982. *Hobby:* Participation in church services. *Address:* 9/11, 14 Zoologitchesky pereulok, Moscow 123242, Russia.

KOLUDROVIC Ciril, b. 27 Oct 1931, Stomorska, Yugoslavia. Prof. m. Virginia Radosinic, 4 Aug 1956, 1 s, 1 d. *Education:* BSc, Coll of Indl Pedagogy, 1966. *Appointments:* Second Sch, Rijeka, 1955-62; Prof, Coll of Indl Pedagogy, 1962-. *Creative works include:* Technical Drawing in Pictures with Basic Exercises, Beograd, 1985; Group Exhibition of Professors of the Art Department, Rijeka, 1987; Insulation Jackets with Computer Applications (with Rudolf Koludrovic), 1988; Basic Exercises in Technical Drawing with Computer Applications (with Irena and Rudolf Koludrovic), Rijeka, 1990; Technical Drawing in Pictures with Computer Applications - Map of Graphofoils (with Irena and Rudolf Koludrovic), Rijeka, 1991. *Memberships:* Yugoslav Team for Robotics and Flexible Automatics; Yugoslav Assn for Descriptive Geometry and Engrng Graphics. *Honours:* 2nd prize of the Belgrade Book Fair for the 4th ed of Technical Drawing in Pictures, 1985; City of Rijeka Prize, 1989. *Hobbies:* Member of the Old Timer Club of the Croatian Wood Shipbuilding; Sailing; Computer Graphics. *Address:* Olge Ban 40, 51000 Rijeka, Yugoslavia. 139, 152.

KOM Ambroise, b. 15 Dec 1946, Cameroun. Prof of Lit. m. Dorothee Njuidje, 30 Aug 1969, 1 s, 2 d. *Education:* Lic es lettres, Univ of Yaounde, 1970; DES, Univ Federale du Cameroun, 1971; Doct 3e cycle, Univ of Pau, France, 1975; Doct es lettres, Sorbonne, Nouvelle, Paris III, 1981. *Appointments:* Taught in various Universities in USA, Canada, Africa, 1972-: Brown Univ, USA 1972-75, Dalhousie Univ, Univ of Ottawa, Univ of Montreal, Univ of Quebec in Montreal, Univ of Laval, Univ of Sherbrooke, Univ of Rabat, Morroco. *Publications include:* Le Harlem de Chester Himes, 1978; Dictionnaires des oeuvres litteraires negro-africaines, 1983; George Lamming et le destin des Cara ibes, 1986; Litteratures africaines, 1987; Le cas Chester Himes, 1991. *Address:* PO Box 7915, Yaounde, Cameroun.

KOMAI Dale S, b. 19 Aug 1952, Santa Monica, CA, USA. Computer Consultant. *Education:* BSc, Univ of SC, 1974. *Appointments:* Bank Examiner, Fed Home Loan Bank Bd, 1974-80, 1984-85; Photographer, 1980-84; Cons, 1983-84; Field Mgr 1985-88, Sr Prog Dev Analyst 1988-89, Computer Programmer, Analyst, Off of Thrift Supervision 1989- 91,Computer Cons 1991-, Fed Home Loan Bank of San Fran. *Creative works:* Photographs published in Jugglers World, Daily Trojan, San Diego Union, Access to Learning newspaper; Contributing writer: American Dance Friendship Tour newsletter. *Memberships:* Int Platform Assn; Bay Area Country Dance Soc; Ctr for Citizen Initiatives; Int Interactive Communications Soc. *Honours:* Bowling trophies, 1968, 1969, 1971; Cert Awd, Entrepreneur Club of San Diego, 1983, 1984; Dance Participant, San Fran Ethnic Dance Fest Audition, 1988; Dep Gov, Am Biographical Inst Rsch Assn, 1989. *Hobbies:* Photography; Fine art; Music; Dancing; Theatre; Russian culture; Hiking; Travel. *Address:* 4090 Twin Peaks Terrace, Fremont, CA 94538, USA. 59, 139, 165.

KOMAKI Hisatoki, b. 29 Aug 1926, Kyoto, Japan. Fdr-Pres; Pres. m. Yoriko, 24 Jan 1954. *Education:* PhD, Kyoto Univ, 1959. *Appointments:* Prof, Mukogawa Univ; Prof, L'Universite Transnational; Pres, Japanese Campus of World Univ of Am; Fdr, Pres, Komaki Peace Fndn. *Publications:* Selected Works of Prof Dr Hisatoki Komaki, vol 1-8; Four Steps to Absolute Peace. *Memberships:* Japan Soc for Biosci; Japanese Soc of Nutrition; Paul Harris Fellow, Rotary Int, Evanston, USA; Japanese Acad of Sci. *Honours:* Nobel Prize Nominee, 1975-; Acad Grand Prize, Univ Alum Assn, Japan; Highest Gold Medal, Red Cross of Japan; Medal of Hon with Dark Blue Ribbon, Japanese Govt. *Hobbies:* Camera; Poems; Painting; Gardening. *Address:* 12 Donokamicho, Matsugasaki, Sakyo, Kyoto, Japan. 166.

KOMATSU Noboru, b. 26 Sept 1919, Taiwan. Advsr. m. 1 May 1955, 1 d. *Education:* BSc 1941, Dr of Engrng 1960, Kyushu Univ. *Appointments:* Prof, Tohoku Univ, 1969; Dir 1969, Exec VP 1971, Dir, Pres 1975, Pres, COO 1977, Dir, Hon Pres 1989, Advsr 1991, Toyota Ctrl R&D Labs Inc. *Publications:* Author and co-author of num tech articles; Has been awded 241 domestic and foreign patents. *Memberships include:* Pres 1988, 1989, Hon Mbr 1990-, Japan Inst of Metals; Sr Advsr, Japan Manesium Assn, 1991-; Cons, Japan Info Ctr of Sci & Tech, 1991-93; Dir, Multidisciplinary Rsch Coun of Chubu, 1991-. *Honours:* Persons of Scientific and Technological Merits, Sci & Tech Agcy of Japanese Govt, 1975; Fellow of ASM Int'l, 1989-; The Okochi Mem Prize, Tech Prize, Nat Medals of Hon with Purple Ribbon, 1981; 3rd Class of the Order of the Sacred Treasure, 1990. *Hobbies:* Playing various sports. *Address:* 41-1, Aza-Yokomichi, Oaza-Nagakuate, Nagakute-cho, Aichi-gun, Aichi 458, Japan.

KOMATSU Yoshitaka, b. 1 Apr 1906, Tokyo, Japan. Prof Emeritus. m. Yoshiko Fujino, 26 May 1947, 3 s. *Education:* Grad, Waseda Univ, Tokyo, 1928; D Econ(s), 1960. *Appointments:* Prof of Econ Hist, Waseda Univ, 1942-76; Vis Prof, Univ of Melbourne, 1964. *Publications:* The Image of an Entrepreneur in the Age of the Industrial Revolution, 1979; The Birth of the Railway and Its Influence on the Growth of the British Economy, 1984. *Memberships:* Chmn of Coun 1960-70, Socio-Econ Hist Soc, Japan; Exec Comm 1974-78, Int Econ Hist Assn; Japan Acad, 1983-. *Honour:* The Nikkei Prize for Cultural Books on Econ(s), 1980. *Address:* 6-15-14-306 Shirokane, Minato-ku, Tokyo 108, Japan.

KOME Penney, b. 2 Nov 1948, Chicago, USA. Writer. m. Robert S Pond, 25 July 1987, 2 s. *Education:* Rsch Assoc, Can Rsch Inst for the Advancement of Women. *Appointments:* Self-employed work has appeared in major publs: Maclean's, Saturday Night, Columnist 1976-88, Homemaker's Mag, currently Columnist for Calgary Herald. *Publications:* Somebody Has to Do It, 1982; The Taking of Twenty-Eight, 1983; Women of Influence, 1985; Every Voice Counts, 1989; Peace: A Dream Unfolding (co-ed). *Memberships:* The Writers' Union of Can; Can Assn of Journalists; PEN Int; Writers Guild of Alta. *Honours:* Robertine Barry Prize, 1984; Toronto YWCA Women of Distinction, 1987. *Hobbies:* Gardening; Cycling. *Address:* 2319 Uxbridge Dr NW, Calgary, Alberta, Canada T2N 327. 142.

KOMIYA Ryutaro, b. 30 Nov 1928, Kyoto, Japan. Prof; Dir-Gen. m. Midori Taniawa, 30 May 1954, 3 d. *Education:* BA, Sch of Econ(s), Univ of Tokyo, 1949-52. *Appointments:* Assoc Prof of Econ(s) 1955-69, Prof of Econ(s) 1969-89, Dean of the Fac of Econ(s) 1978-80, Dep Pres 1981-83, Univ of Tokyo; Rsch Assoc, Harvard Econ Rsch Proj, Harvard Univ, 1957-59; Vis Prof of Econ(s), Stanford Univ, 1964-65; Dir Gen, Rsch Inst of Int Trade and Ind, Min of Int Trade and Ind, 1988-; Prof of Econ(s), Aoyama-Gakuin Univ, 1989-. *Publications:* Postwar Economic Growth in Japan, 1966; Industrial Policy of Japan, 1987; The Japanese Economy: Trade, Industry and Government, 1990; Japan's Foreign Exchange Policy: 1971-1982 (with M Suda), 1991. *Memberships:* Am Econ Assn 1965-, Foreign Hon Mbr 1988-; Pres 1983-84, Japan Assn of Econ(s) and Econometrics; Royal Econ Soc, UK; Econometric Soc; The Acad of Japan, 1990-. *Hobby:* Tennis. *Address:* 8-35-16 Shakujii-machi, Nerima-ku, Tokyo 1977, Japan.

KOMORI Hiroo, b. 3 June 1925, Nagoya, Japan. Sci Edr. m. Noriko Matsushita, 16 Mar 1958, 1 d. *Education:* Sci Course, Grad Sch 1951-58, DSc 1962, Nagoya Univ. *Appointments:* Rsch Asst, Dept of Aeronautics, 1958-59; Assoc Prof, Dept of Phys, Yamanashi Univ, 1959-68; Prof, Phys Lab 1968-89, Prof Emeritus 1989-, Tokyo Univ of Fisheries; Prof, Dept of Scis, Yamanashi Gakuin Univ, 1990-. *Publications include:* Anomalous Magnetic Moment of Muons, 1956; Effect of Prompt Muons in High-Energy Cosmic Rays, 1982; Energy Spectrum of Cosmic-Ray Neutrinos in the Atmosphere, 1986; monte Carlo simulation for multiple-muom distributions of cosmetic rays, 1991. *Memberships:* Phys Soc of Japan. *Honours:* Yukawa Fellowship grantee, 1952, 1956; Yukawa-Yomiuri Fellowship grantee, 1952. *Hobbies:* Classical music; Reading; Walking; Art. *Address:* Department of management Information, Yamanashi Gakuin University, 2-4-5 Sakaori, Kofu, Yamanashi Prefecture 400, Japan. 52.

KONAN Uladzimir Mikhajlovich, b. 23 Apr 1934, Vereskovo, Grodn Obl, Belarus. Writer; DP; Chief of Dept. m. Zvonorjova Lola Utkirovna, 27 Oct 1981. *Education:* Byelorussian Univ, 1954-59; Postgrad, 1962-64; DP, Prof Philos, 1980. *Appointments:* Tchr, 1959-61; Scientist, Nat Acad of Scis, 1965-91. *Publications:* Author of 8 books and 400 articles incl: From Rennaissance to Classicism, 1978; At the Springs of Self-Consciousness, 1989; The Light of Poetry: Lirics by Bagdanovich, 1991. *Memberships:* The Union of Byelorussian Writers; Pres, Byelorussian Assn of Byelorussists. *Honour:* Byelorussian State Prem, 1981. *Hobbies:* Reading; Picking mushrooms; Folklore. *Address:* vul Malinina 14, kv 110, Minsk, Belarus 220085.

KONDIC-BELOS Ksenija, b. 13 July 1934, Brcko, Yugoslavia. Professor of Psychopathology of Childhood and Adolescence. m. (1) 31 Dec 1955, (2) Mirko Belos, 2 Jan 1987, 1 s. *Education:* Clin Psycol, 1958; MA, Clin Psychol, 1971; Doctorate, 1981; Psychoanalyst, 1970. *Appointments:* Ctr for Cerebral Palsy, 1959-62; Sch Guidance Clin, 1962-70; Fac of Phil, Dept of Psychol, 1970-. *Publications:* Connectedness between childhood neuroses and their parents pathology, 1983; DST Interview, 1985; ECO Psychlology, 1987; Over 50 artivles and monographs on child and adolescent psychopathology and psychotherapy. *Memberships:* Psychol Circles Pvte Guidance Clinic; Inst for Mental Hlth. *Honours:* Ziza Visic Awd for popularisation of contemporary psychology, 1975. *Hobby:* Literature. *Address:* Department for Psychology, Faculty of Phylosophy, Cika-Ljubina 16-18/II, 11000 Beograd, Yugoslavia.

KONIECZNY Zygmunt, b. 3 Jan 1937, Cracow, Poland. Music Composer. m. Elzbieta Baranska, 17 June 1982. *Education:* Grad: Musical Coll, Cracow 1958; Acad of Music, Cracow 1963. *Appointments:* Coop with the Cracow Cabaret, Cellar at the sign of Rams, 1959-; Lectr in Theatre Music, State Coll of Theatrical Arts, Cracow, 1986-; Freelance Composer; Polish Lit Songs; Music for theatre and films. *Creative works include:* Music to: The Devils by F Dostoevski; Dybuk by Anski; All Souls' Day by A Mickiewicz; The Master and Margaret by M Bulhakov; Affabulazione by P Passolini; Snow-storm by S Przybyszewski & A Osiecka; Cracow Crib for the Pompidou Ctr in Paris. Music to Films: Valley of Issa; Free riders; The Steward; Joanna; The Taboo; Funeral of a Potatoe; The Fly-Paper, ballet. *Membership:* Polish Assn of Authors and Composers. *Honours include:* Gold Cross of Merit, 1979; 1st Prize for Music to the film Bruno Schultz, 1985; Awd for Contribution to the Jewish Culture, Int Fest of Jewish Culture, Cracow, 1990; The Golden Lions' Awd, 1st Prize for Music, Polish Feature Film Fest, Gdansk, 1990; Awd, Min of Culture and Arts, 28th Opole Song Fest, 1991. *Hobby:* Sport. *Address:* ul Nowowiejska 37 m 21, 30-052 Cracow, Poland. 1, 139.

KONIGOVA Radana, b. 31 July 1930, Praha, Czechoslovakia. m. Dr Jan Placht, 21 Dec 1959, 2 s. *Education:* Grad, Med Fac, Charles Univ, Prague, 1955. *Appointments:* Gen Hosp, Karlsbad, 1955-61; Univ Dept of Plastic Surg, Prague, 1961-66; Univ of Uppsala, 1966; Edinburgh, 1966-67; Karolinska, Stockholm, 1969; ICU 1969, Hd 1978-, Prague Burn Ctr. *Publications:* Extensive Burn Trauma, 1978; Reconstruction and Rehabilitation in Burn Trauma, 1983, updated 1990; European Text Book on Burn Care (co-wkr). *Memberships:* Int Soc for Burn Injuries, 1965; Int Confed Plastic and Reconstruction Surg, 1966; Tord Skoog Soc, 1967; Inst for Postgrad Educ of Physns and Pharmac, Prague, 1979; Exec Comm, European Burn Assn, 1981; World Fndn of Soc of Intens & Crit Care Med, 1984. *Honours:* Hon Mbr, Soc Chir et Traumat, Hungarica, 1983; Martin Ramelot Prize for Psycho-social rsch on burns, Lobbes, Belgium, 1985; James Laing Mem Essay on Facial Disfigurement following Burns, 1987; Hon Mbr, Sociedad Cubana de Cir Plastica yCaumatologia, 1989; Sci & Rsch Bd, Med Fac, Charles Univ Prague, 1991. *Hobbies:* Music; Walking in forests; Travelling. *Address:* 3 rd Medical Faculty, Charles University, Srobarova 48, CS-10000 Praha 10, Czechoslovakia.

KONKEL Kazimierz Gerard Edward, b. 27 Aug 1950, Rotterdam, Holland. Police Official; Novelist. m. Robin Devine, 17 Feb 1979, 1 d. *Education:* BA Hons 1972; MA 1973. *Appointments:* Insp of Police, Royal Hong Kong Police, 1974-76; Staff Sgt, Metropolitan Toronto Police Off of the Chief of Police, 1976-. *Publications:* The Glorious East Wind; Author of num profl papers which have become the basis for policing stand in N Am. *Memberships:* Fellow, Royal Soc of Arts and Letters; Imperial Offs Assn; Can Comprehensive Auditors Fndn; Int Police Assn; Empire Club of Can; Hon Life Mbr, The Hamilton Club, 1989. *Honours:* Recipient of several police awds for bravery. *Hobbies:* Internationally acknowledged expert in Chinese Criminal Triad Societies; Regular book reviewer for two national newspaper chains; Lectr, Canadian Police College; Lectr, Ontario Police College; Regular Panelist, Life Time, National TV Talk Show. *Address:* 15 Douglas Crescent, Toronto, Ontario, Canada M4W 2E6. 142.

KONONENKO Tatyana, b. 24 Dec 1945, Minsk, USSR. Prof. 1 s. *Education:* Grad, Minsk State Pedagogical Inst of Foreign Langs, 1967; PhD, 1988. *Appointments:* Lectr 1967-89, Sr Lectr 1989-90, Asst Prof 1991-, Minsk State Pedagogical Inst of Foreign Langs. *Publications:* Author of 18 publs incl univ textbooks and articles on methods of tchng foreign langs. *Hobbies:* Reading; Travelling; Caring for pets; Knitting. *Address:* 20 K Marx Str, Apt 10, Minsk, 220050 Belarus, Russia.

KONONOWICZ Andrzej Kiejstut, b. 28 July 1950, Wroclaw, Poland. Scientist; Prof. m. Halina Michniewicz, 20 Mar 1976, 1 s. *Education:* MSc 1973, PhD 1978, Habilitation in Cell Biology 1989, Univ of Lodz. *Appointments:* Rsch Asst 1973-78, Sr Rsch Fellow 1978-81, 1983-89, Dept of Plant Cytology and

Cytochem, Univ of Lodz; Postdoct Fellow 1981-83, Vis Prof 1990-, Dept of Horticulture, Purdue Univ, West Lafayette. *Publications include:* Factors affecting in vitro fatty acid content and composition in a sexual embryos of Theobroma cacao (with D C Wright, J Janick), 1984; Cytochemical analysis of changes in nuclear DNA content in leaves from young and flowering plants of Vicia faba L (with M J Olszewska, B Damsz), 1986; Localization of 5S DNA by situ hybridization in metaphase chromosomes of Vicia faba L (with M J Olszewska, C J Madrzak, A B Legocki), 1990; Cell cycle duration in tobacco cell adapted to NaCl (with P M Hasefawa, R A Bressan), 1992; Gene expression in genetically engineered tobacco plants (with D E Nelson, NK Singh, PM Hasegawa, R A Bressan), 1992. *Memberships:* Comm for Cytobiology, Polish Acad of Scis; Am Soc of Plant Physiol; Intern Soc of Plant Mol Biol; Polish Genetical Soc; Polish Soc for Histochem and Cytochem. *Honours include:* Min of Scis, Higher Educ and Technics (for PhD Dissertation), 1979; Grant, Bd of the Fndn of European Societies for Histochem and Cytochem (participation in the VIth Intl Cong of Histochem and Cytochem, Brighton, Eng, 1980; Awd, Polish Genetical Soc (for monography, Methods in Chromosome Research), 1983. *Hobbies:* History; Politics; Reading. *Address:* Department of Horticulture, Purdue University, West Lafayette, IN 47907, USA.

KONONOWICZ Halina, b. 7 July 1947, Lublin, Poland. Prof of Cell Biol. m. Andrzej Kononowicz, 20 Mar 1976, 1 s. *Education:* MS 1971, PhD 1977, Habilitation in Cell Biol 1987, Univ of Lodz. *Appointments:* Rsch Assoc, Univ of Torun, Poland, 1971-76; Rsch Assoc 1976-77, Sr Rsch Assoc 1977- 81, 1983-87, Asst Prof of Cell Biol 1987-, Univ of Lodz; Rsch Assoc, Purdue Univ, USA, 1981-83. *Publications:* Author of num original papers and reviews dealing with plant cell biol. *Memberships:* Polish Soc of Histochems & Cytochems; Polish Boton Soc. *Hobbies:* Art collection; Travelling; Hiking. *Address:* Lermontov st 18/33, Lodz, Poland.

KONOPKA Lech Jerzy, b. 3 Feb 1938, Wilno, Poland. Prof of Haematology and Internal Diseases MD. m. 21 July 1960. *Education:* Med Acad, Warsaw, 1955-60. *Appointments:* Internship of Med, 1961-62; MD 1968, Assoc Prof 1975, Prof of Med 1987, Dept of Haematology, Inst of Haematology, Warsaw; Dept of Haematology, Royal Postgrad Med Sch, Hammersmith Hosp, London, 1973-74. *Publications:* Author of co-author of 220 papers and 6 books on haematology incl: Isotopical Diagnostic of Haematology, 1972; Laboratory Diagnostic in Haematology, 1983, 2nd ed 1990; Diagnostic and Therapy in Haematology, 1985; Surgery of the Spleen, 1987; Internal Diseases, 1991. *Memberships:* Int Soc of Haematology and Blood Transfusion; Int Gesellschaft fur Chemo- und Immunotherapie, Vienna; Gen Sec, Polish Soc of Haematology. *Hobby:* Social work. *Address:* Bonifacego 79/42, Warsaw 02-945, Poland.

KONSTANTINOV Gennady N, b. 18 Jan 1952, Irkutsk, USSR. Educl Specialist; Scientist. 1 d. *Education:* Cand of Scis, Uralskiy Univ, 1979; DSc, Acad of Sci, Moscow, 1989. *Appointments:* Lectr 1967-89, Hd, Dept of Theory of Systems 1989-91, Irkutsk Univ; Prof, Societ-Am Jt Fac of Mgmt, Maryland-Irkutsk, 1991. *Publications:* Models of control of natural resources (co-author), 1981; Normalizing signals to a dynamic systems, 1983; Ecology-economic strategy of development of a region (co-author), 1990; Methods of decision of problems of control theory based on the principle of enlargement (co-author), 1990; Author of a number of articles. *Membership:* Math Soc of Siberian Dept, Acad of Sci, USSR. *Hobbies:* Painting; Skiing; Philosophy. *Address:* Irkutsk State University, 1 K Marx Street, Irkustsk 66403, Russia.

KOOISTRA VAN CAMPENHOUT W John, b. 26 Apr 1951, Utrecht, Holland. Dir. m. Anne Marg Potter, 30 Dec 1987, 2 s, 2 d. *Education:* BA, York Univ, Toronto, 1979; Dip Herbalism, Dominion Herbal Coll, Burnaby,

1982. *Appointments:* Mbrship Sec, Pollution Probe Fndn, Toronto, 1979-80; Student Advsr, Site Coord, Dept of Computing Servs, Queens Univ, Kingston, 1982-83; Rschr, Freelance Writer, Kingston, 1983-; Dir, Fdr, Inst for Johannine Christianity, Toronto, 1985-; Private Scholar, 1984-. *Publications:* Essays and lectures on Christian Mysticism, Gnostic Christianity, Catharism, Rosicrucianism and Christian Communal Societies. *Membership:* Chartered Herbalist, BC Herbalist Assn, 1982. *Honours:* Int Man of the Yr, 1991-92; Licientiate in Sacred Theology (S.T.L.), Honorary, Sophia Divinity School, Georgia, 1992; Ordained, Atlanta, 1992. *Hobbies:* Classical music; Travel; Sailing. *Address:* c/o Institute for Johannine Christianity, 295 Shuter Street, Suite 1611, Toronto, Ontario, Canada M5A 1W6.

KOONS Robert Charles, b. 22 Feb 1957, St Paul, MN, USA. Univ Prof. m. Deborah Leslie Good, 29 Dec 1979, 2 d. *Education:* BA, MI State Univ, 1979; BA, Oxford, 1981; PhD, UCLA, 1987. *Appointments:* Asst Prof of Philos, Univ of TX at Austin, 1987-. *Publication:* Paradoxes of Belief and Strategic Rationality, 1991. *Memberships:* Assn for Symbolic Logic; Am Philosl Assn; Soc of Christian Philos. *Honours:* Disting Alumni Scholar, MI State Univ, 1979; Marshall Scholar, 1981; Danforth Fellow, 1981; Gustave O Arlt Prize, 1992. *Hobbies:* Running; Gardening. *Address:* Department of Philosophy, University of Texas, Austin, TX 78712, USA.

KOOY Gerrit Andries, b. 9 Mar 1926, Kedichem, Holland. Prof Emeritus. m. Onni Hondius, 4 Nov 1981, 2 s, 1 d. *Education:* MA, Utrecht Univ, 1949-53; PhD, Leiden Univ, 1957. *Appointments:* Scient Collab 1953-59, Sr Lectr 1959-64, Full Prof 1985, Prof Emeritus, Agricl Univ, Wageningen. *Publications incl:* Het echec van een volkse beweging, 1964; Het modern-Westers gezin, 1967; Seksualiteit, huwelijk en gezin in Nederland, 1978; Author of num articles. *Memberships:* Pres 1970-74, Comm on Family Rsch, Int Sociological Assn; Chmn 1972-80, Hon Mbr, Netherlands Assn for Demography; Chmn of Bd 1981-88, Netherlands Inst for Interdisciplinary Demographic Rsch; Social-scientific Coun, Royal Acad of Scis, 1982-90. *Honour:* Kt of the Dutch Lion. *Hobbies:* Chicken breeding; Gardening. *Address:* Knoppersweg 22, 6668 AV Randwijk, Holland. 52.

KOPIEC Jan, b. 18 Dec 1947, Zabrze, Poland. Cath Priest. *Education:* Ordination, Theological Sem, Nysa, 1972; DTheol, Cath Univ, Lublin, 1982; Dip, Scuola Vaticana di Paleografia, 1985. *Appointments:* Vicar, Zabrze, 1972-78; Lectr of the Hist of Ch at: Theol Sem, Nysa 1982-, Theol Sem in the Cong of the Divine Word (SVD), Nysa 1985-; Br of the Cath Univ of Lublin, Opole 1985-; Dir, Diocesan Archives, Opole, 1986-. *Publications:* Historiograpahy of the Diocese of Wroclaw until 1821, 1983; Acta Nutiatura Polonae: Julius Piazza 1706-1708, vol I, 1991; The History of the Cath Church in the Opolian Silesia, 1991. *Memberships:* The Learned Soc of the Cath Univ of Lublin, 1983-; Gorres - Gesellschaft zur Pflege der Wissenschaft, 1989-. *Hobbies:* History of ancient Rome; Visiting Italian monuments of the past. *Address:* ul Kard Kominka la, PL-45032, Opole, Poland.

KOPP Maria S, b. 14 Jan 1942, Budapest, Hungary. Rsch Psych; Psychophysiologist. m. Arpad Skrabski, 15 Aug 1965, 2 d. *Education:* MD, Semmelweis Med Sch, 1968; Clin Psychologist, Eotvos Lorand Univ, 1977; Cand Med Sci, Hungarian Acad of ci, 1982; Postgrad, Med Univ, Budapest, 1984. *Appointments:* Ldr of Clni Epidemiological Rch Grp, Nat Inst of Occupational Hlth, 1968-73; Ldr of Clin Epidemiological Grp 1973-82, Ldr of Lab Psychophysiology, Dept of Psych, 1982-, Semmelweis Med Sch. *Publications:* Author of 29 publs. *Memberships:* Ed, Digest Journ of Hungarian Psych Assn; Vegeken, Journ of Mental Hlth; Pres, Hungarian Hlth Psychology & Psychophysiology Assn, 1989-; Presential Bd, Hungarian Psych Assn. *Hobbies:* Writing; Reading; Theatre. *Address:* Bela kiraly u 19, H-1125 Budapest, Hungary. 52.

KOPPEL Lone, b. 20 May 1938, Copenhagen, Denmark. Opera Singer. m. Bjorn Asker, 23 July 1983, 2 s, 1 d. *Education:* Royal Acad of Music, Copenhagen, debut 1961. *Career:* Royal Theatre, Copenhagen, 1962-; Sydney, Australia, 1973-78; Guest appearances in Scandinavia, GB, Germany, Iceland, New Zealand. *Creative works:* Performed almost 40 lead roles, incl: Tosca, Salome, Elektra, Jenufa, Masked Ball, Macbeth, Ariadne, Manon Lescaut, Parsifal, Lohengrin, Katarina, Ismailowa. *Honour:* Knighted of the Danish Queen Margrethe the 2 to: R1. *Address:* Aboulevard 50, 2200 Copenhagen N, Denmark.

KOPYLENKO Moisey, b. 25 Nov 1920, Odessa, USSR. Linguist; Rsching Slavonic Langs & Gen Linguistics. m. Poline Kopylenko, 22 June 1941, 2 d. *Education:* Odessa State Univ, 1938-41; Middle Asia State Univ, Tashkent, 1944-45; Cand of Philol Scis, Kuybyshev, 1954; Dr of Philol Scis, Leningrad, 1967. *Appointments:* Tchr, Asst Prof, Odessa Univ, 1945-57; Asst Prof, Dep Dir, Hd of Dept, Alma-Ata Inst of Foreign Langs, 1957-78; Hd of Dept, Leading Rschr, Inst of Linguistics, Acad of Scis, 1978-. *Publications:* Issledovaniye v oblastistavyanskoy phrazeologiyi drevneyshey pory, 1967; Ocherki po obshchey phrazeologiyi, 1972, 1978, 1989; Sochetayemost lexem v rysskom yazyke, 1973; Russko-kazakhskiy phrazeologich slovar, 1989; Kazakhskoye slovo v russkom khudozhestvennom texte, 1990. *Honours:* Order of the Patriotic War 1st degree; Medals. *Hobbies:* Esperanto; Reading; Tourism. *Address:* 29 A Baytursynov Institute of Linguistics, Academy of Sciences of Kazakhstan, Alma Ata 480021, Kazakhstan.

KORDYUM Elizabeth L, b. 3 Nov 1932, Kiev, USSR. Cell Biol; Space Bot. m. Vitaly A Kordyum, 6 Nov 1954, 1 s, 1 d. *Education:* PhD, Kiev Univ, 1960; ScD, Bot Inst of USSR Acad of Sci, Leningrad, 1968. *Appointments:* Jr Scientist of Bot Gdn 1955-59; Jr Scientist 1959-64, Sr Scientist 1964-76, Chmn of Dept for Cell Biol 1976-, Prof for Cell Biol 1986-, Inst of Bot, Ukraine Acad of Sci, Kiev. *Publications:* Cytoembryological Aspects of Sex Problem of Angiosperms, 1976; Cytoembryology of Umbelliferae Family, 1967; Evolutionary Cytoembryology of Angiosperms, 1978; Plant Cell in Processes of Differentiation and Dedifferentiation, 1980; Plant Cell under Changes of Geophysical Factors, 1984; Microorganisms in Space Flight, 1986; Fungi and Algae - Objects for Space Biology, 1991. *Memberships include:* Sci Coun, Inst of Bot, Ukraine Acad of Sci; Comm for Grav Physiol of Intern Union of Physiol Sci; Cospar ISC F, Comm for Space Res, Acad of Sci of Ukraine; Sci Coun, Plant World; Corrsponding Mem, int Acad of Astronutics, IAA, 1991. *Honours:* Gold, 2 Silver, 4 Bronze Medals, Exhib Achiev Nat Economy, Moscow, 1978-89; State Prize for Sci and Tech, Ukraine, 1979; N G Kholodny Prize, Ukrainian Acad of Sci 1979; Hon Scientist of Ukraine, 1984. *Hobbies include:* Reading; Travelling; Listening to music; Mechanisms of cell adaptation to microgravity. *Address:* N G Kholodny Institute of Botany, Ukrainain Academy of Sciences, Repin str 2, 252601 Kiev 4, Russia. 162.

KORHERR Edgar Josef, b. 12 June 1928, Wien, Austria. Univ Prof. m. Eleonor Korherr, 28 June 1955, 4 s. *Education:* Univ of Vienna, Austria, 1955-63. *Appointments:* Prof, Paedagogische Akademie, Wien, 1966-76; Prof, Univ of Graz, 1976-. *Publications:* Praktisches Worterbuch der Katechetik und Religious Padagogik, 1974, 1977; Methodik des Religiousunterrichts, 1977; Paedagogische Psychologie fur Theologen, 1990; Belen Lehren (Gebetspaedagogik), 1991. *Memberships:* Wiener Katholische Akademie, 1972; Aktion Gegen Den Antisemitismus in Oesterreich, 1972; Int Catechetical Coun, Rome, 1977. *Honours:* Commendatore des Silvester Ordens, 1985; Grosses Ehrenzeichen fur Verdienste Um No. *Hobby:* Literature. *Address:* Universitaetsplatz 3, A-8010 Graz, Austria.

KORNEGAY Roy Aubry, b. 15 Aug 1937, Shreveport, LA, USA. Dir of Missions. m. Janette Sewell, 27 Dec 1958, 3 d. *Education:* BA, Howard Payne Univ, Brownwood, 1959; MRE 1961, MA 1983, Southwestern Bapt Theological Sem, Ft Worth. *Appointments:* First Bapt Ch, Dumas, 1961-64; First Bapt Ch, TX City, 1964-67; First Bapt Ch, Pampa, 1967-70; Bapt Ch Phoenix, N Phoenix, 1970-71; First Bapt Ch, Amarillo, 1971-86; Amarillo Bapt Assn, 1987-. *Publications:* Articles and units of study for Southern Bapt SS Bd for Bible Searcher, Chd's Ldrship Mag, Adventure, VBS Curr 1975, WMU Acteens Mag, Ch Tng Mag, SS Ldrship Mag. *Memberships:* Southwestern Bapt Rel Ed Assn 1961-, Pres 1993; Metro Rel Ed Assn 1973-, Chmn 1984; Exec Bd 1973-78, Bapt Gen Conv of TX; Trustee, Howard Payne Univ, 1977-86, 1988-91. *Honour:* World Champion Pony League Baseball, 1951. *Hobbies:* Stamp collecting; Fishing; Softball; Racquetball; Music; Travel; Biblical archaeology and geography. *Address:* 1800 S Western, Amarillo, TX 79106, USA. 7, 145.

KOROL Abraham, b. 18 Oct 1946, Moldavia, Bendery, USSR. Prof. m. Bella Fishman, 12 Aug 1967. *Education:* MS, Leningrad Polytech Inst, 1971; PhD, USSR Acad of Sci, Moscow, 1976; Dr of Biol Sci, Leningrad State Univ, 1988. *Appointments:* Sr Engr-Programmer 1971-74, Sr Res Assoc 1974-77, Moldavian Inst of Vegetable Growing, Tiraspol; Sr Res Assoc 1977-83, Hd of Lab of Induced Recombinogenesis 1983-85, Dept of Plant Genetics, Hd of Lab of Genetic Control of Recombination 1985-87, Leading Res Assoc, Dept of Recombinogenesis 1987-89, Ecological Genetics Inst, SSRM Acad of Sci, Kishinev; Assoc Prof, Dept of Genetics, Moldavian State Univ, Kishinev, 1981- 90; Sr Rsch Fellow, Med Ctr of Child and Mother Hlth, Kishinev, 1989-91; Hd of Population Genetics Lab, Ecological Genetics Inst, Mold Acad of Sci, Kishinev, 1989-91; Prof, Inst of Evolution, Haifa Univ, 1991-. *Publications:* Author of about 150 publs incl: Marker analysis of quantitative characters (with I A Preigel), 1989; Sex difference in recombination frequency in Arabidopsis (with I Yu Vizir), 1990; The effect of hybrid dysgensis factors of the T-007 chromosome on the recombination system of Drosophila melanogaster (with N M Vereschchagina), 1991; The effect of genotype x cytoplasm interacton on meiotic behaviour of maize chromosomes (with M M Kruleva, T G Dankov, V G Scorpan, I A Preigel), 1992. *Membership:* Presidium of Moldavian Genetic Soc, 1982-86. *Honour:* Moldavian Repub State Prize in Sci & Tech, 1985. *Hobbies:* Reading; Classic music. *Address:* Institute of Evolution, Haifa University, Mount Carmel 31905, Israel.

KORSHAK Yvonne, b. 30 May 1936, Chicago, IL, USA. Prof of Art Hist. m. 18 Aug 1977, 1 d. *Education:* BA cum laude, Radcliffe Coll, Cambridge, MA, 1958; MA 1966, PhD 1973, Univ of CA, Berkeley. *Appointments:* Asst Prof 1975-79, Dir Hons Prog 1977-79, Chairperson of Dept 1978-81, Dir Mus Studies Prog 1979-89, Assoc Prof 1979-85, Prof 1985-, Dept of Art & Art Hist, Adelephi Univ, Gdn City. *Publications include:* Selections from the Permanent Collection of the Arkansas Arts Centre (co- ed), 1983; Frontal Faces in Attic Vase Pointing of the Archaic Period, 1987; Paris and Helen by Jacques Louis David, 1987. *Memberships:* Coll Art Assn of Am; Sec, San Fran Soc 1969-70, Archaeological Inst of Am; Chair, Clifford Prize Comm 1989; Am Soc for Eighteenth-Century Studies; Am Classical League; Am Philological Assn; Assn of Ancient Histns. *Honours:* Bella K Zellerbach Fndn Grad Fellowship, 1968-69; Samvaltt Kress Fndn Rsch Grant, 1970-71; Am Assn of Mus Awd of Merit; Runner Up Clifford Prize, Am Soc for Eighteenth-Century Studies, 1986-87; Pres's Aed for Disting Grad & Undergrad Tchng, Adelphi Univ; Proj Dir, Nat Endowment for the Humanities Summer Sem on the Modern Condition, 1990. *Address:* Department of Art and Art History, Adelphi University, Garden City, NY 11530, USA. 5, 6, 15.

KORZENIOWSKI Andrzej, b. 18 Sept 1939, Kolo, Poland. Scientist. m. Grazyna Jaworska, 25 Dec 1967, 1 d. *Education:* MA, Acad of Economy, Poznan, 1962; PhD, Adam Mickiewicz Univ, 1966. *Appointments:* Acad of Economy, Poznan, 1962-67; Inst of Stock Mgmt, 1968-90; Asst Prof 1979, Full Prof 1984, Acad of Economy, Cracow; Chair of Indl Commodity Sci, Acad of Poznan, 1991-. *Publications:* 149 bibliographic items on indl comm sci, packaging and storage incl 4 books on storage mgmt. *Memberships:* IGWI, Vienna; Polish Soc of Commodity Sci Comm of Chem; Polish Acad of Sci. *Honours:* of the Min of Commodity Mgmt, 1976, 1990; Individual Awd, Poznan Dist for Outstng Achmt in Sci, 1981. *Hobbies:* Hunting; Skiing; Horse riding. *Address:* Sloneczoa 11, 60-286 Poznan, Poland.

KOSARY Domokos, b. 31 July 1913, Selmecbanya, Hungary. Pres. *Education:* Pázmany Péter Univ, Budapest; PhD, 1936, Sorbonne, Paris, 1937; Inst of Historical Rsch, London, 1938-39. *Appointments:* Prof, Eotvos Coll, 1937-50; Fdr, Ed-in-Chief, Revue d'Histoire Comparee, published in French in Budapest, 1943-48; Dir, Inst of Hist, Teleki Inst, 1945-49; Prof of Modern Hist, Univ of Budapest, 1946-49; Pres, Revolutionary Coun of Histns, 1956; sentenced to 4 yrs prison, 1957, released 1960; Archivist; Scientific Rschr, Scientific Cnslr, Inst of Hist, Elected Corresponding Mbr 1982, Ordinary Mbr 1985, Pres, 1990, Hungarian Acad of Scis; Pres of Nat Comm, Hungarian Histns, 1985-90. *Publications include:* Author of a number of essays; Introduction to the Sources and Literature of Hungarian History, 3 vols, 1951-58; Napoleon and Hungary, 1979; History of the City of Budapest, vols II-III, History of the Hungarian Press, vols I-II, 1979-85; Author of num papers on different problems of the 18th century. *Memberships:* Acad Europaea, London, 1990; Acad Europeenne, Paris, 1990; Brit Acad, London, 1991. *Honours:* Laureate of the Hungarian State Prize, 1988; Off of the Ordre des Palmes Academiques de a Republique Francaise, 1988. *Hobby:* Gardening. *Address:* Hungarian Academy of Sciences, Roosevelt ter 9, 1051 Budapest, Hungary. 34.

KOSCIELNIAK Cyprian Milosz, b. 27 Sept 1948, Kalisz, Poland. Tchr; Illustrator; Designer. m. Joanna Wnuk, 23 Sept 1984, 1 s, 1 d. *Education:* Graphic Art Dept, Copernicus Univ, 1967-70; State Coll of Arts, Gdansk, 1970-71; Acad of Fine Arts, Warsaw, 1971-74. *Appointments:* Graphic Designer, Acad of Fine Arts, Warsaw, 1980-84; Graphic Designer, State Coll of Arts, Gdansk, 1983-87; Acad Minerva, Groningen, Holland, 1988-; Rhode Isl Sch of Design, Providence, USA, 1990. *Creative works:* Grahic designs for Polish film and TV, foremost for Andrzej Wajda's films, 1973-81; All Poland rsch over vernacular design and naive signing, around 1500 dias - shows and lectures, 1978-86; Free arts period, painting pastels, making sculptures, 1985-87; Subs two exhibs, Warsaw, 1986, 1987; Illustrations for mags incl: Avenue, Quote, Elle, Inter, 1987-. *Honour:* Cultural poster of the yr, Warsaw, 1981. *Hobbies:* Profession; Ethnography. *Address:* Keizersgracht 66, The Rep's, 1015 CS Amsterdam, Holland.

KOSHI Masaki, b. 16 Nov 1934, Tokyo, Japan. Prof. m. Yoko Sato, 10 Oct 1959. *Education:* BS 1953-57, MS 1957-59, Dr Eng 1969, Univ of Tokyo. *Appointments:* Rschr, Min of Constrn, Tokyo, 1959-64; Lectr 1964-66, Assoc Prof 1966-78, Prof 1978-90, Inst of Indl Scis, Prof, Fac of Engrng 1990-, Univ of Tokyo. *Publications:* Road Safety - Success and Failures in Japan, 1987; Tokyo's Traffic Congestion Can be Unraveled, 1989; Cycle Time Optimazation in Traffic Signal Coordination, 1989; Explanation of and Countermeasures against Traffic Congestion, 1989. *Memberships:* Japan Soc of Civil Engrs; VP, Japan Soc of Traffic Engrs; VP, Int Assn of Traffic and Safety Scis. *Honours:* Article Awd, Int Assn of Traffic & Safety Scis, 1984, 1991. *Hobbies:* Skiing; Sailing. *Address:* 4- 40-1-601 Yoyogi, Shibuya-ku, Tokyo 151, Japan. 1, 52.

KOSIDEO Krzysztof, b. 28 July 1959, Krasnik. Tchr. m. 19 Nov 1983, 1 s. *Education:* MSc, Fac of Pedagogics & Psychology, 1983. *Appointments:* Tech Asst, Fac of Pedagogics & Psychology, Lublin Univ, 1982-86; Tchr, Primevy Sch No 1 Konskie, 1986-. *Membership:* Polish

Sci Film Assn, 1985-. *Hobbies:* Photography; Reading. *Address:* 3 Maja 7/16, 26-200 Konskie, Poland.

KOSKINA Katerina, b. 30 July 1959, Corfu, Greece. Art Historian. *Education:* Dip, Athens Univ; DEA in Hist of Art, DEA in Modern Greek Lit, Sorbonne. *Career includes:* P Picassos's Mus, Paris, 2 mths; Participated in the org of the Hommage a Teriade; TV Mag CHROMATA; Special Cons ECCD; Curator, I Kostopoulos Fndn. *Creative works:* Collaboration with the French Art Mag, KANAL and the Eng Art Int; Articles in cataloguescerues and newspapers; Articles in the book Tsarouchis APANTA and TETRADIA TEHNIS; Mbr of Ed Comm, European Art Review KANAL EUROPE. *Memberships:* AICA; ICOM (CIMAM); KOSMOPOLIS; The Piereus Cultural Soc. *Hobbies:* Music; Travelling; Good food. *Address:* 25 Neofronos St, 161 21 Athens, Greece.

KOSLOWSKI Peter Franziskus Theodor, b. 2 Oct 1952, Gottingen. Director. *Education:* MA 1977, PhD, Philosophy, 1979, MEcon 1980, Univ of Munich. *Appointments:* Asst Prof of Philos, Univ of Munich, 1977-85; Dir, Inst of Philos 1985-87, Prof of Philos and Polit Economy 1985-, Univ of Witten/Herdecke; Dir, Forschungsinstitut fur Philosophie Hannover, 1987-. *Creative works include:* Die Kulturen der Welt als Experimente richtigen Lebens, Entwurf fur eine Weltausstellung, 1990; Nachruf auf den Marxismus-Leninismus, 1991; Der Mythos der Moderne, Die dichterische Philosophie Ernst Juengers, 1991. *Memberships:* Am Econ Assn; Verein fur Socialpolitik; Allgemeine Gesellschaft fur Philosophie in Deutschland; Leibniz-Gesellschaft; Gorres-Gesellschaft; Dep Chmn 1979-82, Chmn 1982-, Civitas Soc for Advancement of Sci & Art; Rheno-Bavaria. *Hobbies:* Playing piano; Skiing. *Address:* Forschungsinstitut fuer Philosophie Hannover, Lange Laube 14, 3000 Hanover 1, Germany. 52.

KOSOWSKI Stanislaw Wincenty, b. 27 July 1940, Zarki, Near Cracow, Poland. Unemployed; Indep Rschr; Physicist. 1 s, 2 d. *Education:* Master of Physics, Jagiellonian Univ, Cracow, 1958-63; Dr of Tech Scis 1963-68, Habilitated Dr of Tech Scis 1974, Inst of Fundamental Technological Rsch, Polish Acad of Scis (PAS). *Appointments:* Adj 1968-74, Docent 1974-75, Inst of Fundamental Technological Rsch; Postdoct Fellowship 1975-76, Assisting Prof 1976-77, Mem Univ of Newfoundland, St John's, Canada; Docent 1977-85, IFTR of PAS. *Publications include:* Interaction of two spheres in a free-molecular medium, 1973; A new theory of distant variable stars brightness, 1991; Balceroyvicz plan and a free market in Poland, 1991; Poetry and fiction. *Hobbies:* All domains of human creativity; physics - nature of light, electricity and magnetism; variable starts; fundamental forces; economics; philosophy; Writing poetry and fiction; Sport; Swimming in the sea; Long distance running; Physical exercises. *Address:* ul Pereca 2 m 1214, 00-849 Warsaw, Poland.

KOST Arnulf, b. 16 Mar 1941, Berlin, Germany. Prof. m. 3 Aug 1966, 1 s, 3 d. *Education:* Dipl Ing 1967, Dr Ing 1973, Techn Univ of Berlin. *Appointments:* Rsch Asst 1967-73, Prof of Elec Engrng 1979-, Mng Dir, Inst of Elec Machines 1984-86, 1990-, Techn Univ of Berlin; Acad Coun, Univ of Dortmund, 1973-79. *Publications:* Author of articles on Electromagnetic Field Calculation, 1967-. *Hobby:* Photography. *Address:* Am Sandwerder 44, D-W1000 Berlin 39, Germany. 52.

KOST Glen Edmond, b. 29 May 1936, Gt Falls, MT, USA. Exec Dir; Dir. m. Elva Valverde, 7 June 1969, 2 s. *Education:* BA, McNeese State Univ, 1962; MPH, Tulane Univ, 1969; PhD, Walden Univ, 1978. *Appointments:* Pastor, Chaffee Comm Bapt La, Denver, 1957-58; Asst Supt, Muller Co, Lake Charles, 1958-61; Tchr, Calcasieu Parish Sch, Lake Charles, 1961-63; Traffic, Pgm News Dir, KRMD, Shreveport, 1963-; Med Sci Ed, Marshall News Messenger, 1963-66;

Admnstr II, TX State Dept of Hlth, 1966-70; Coord, Proj MEDHIC, UT Sch of PH-Tex, 1970-71; Dir, Comprehensive Hlth Plng, Coastal Bend Coun of Govts, 1971-73; Dean for Hlth Scis, Del Mar Coll, 1973-85; Exec Dir, DMC Fndn, Dir of Devel, DMC, 1985-. *Publications include:* Author of 263 articles, 67 columns, 1964-66; Immunization Reports in Texas Medicine, 1968- 69; Student Evaluattion of a Public Health Curriculum, 1971; Dental Manpower i Texas, 1972; Early Childhood Development - Pilot Programme, 1973; Relationship of Selected Personality & Value Indices to the Retention of Freshman Spanish- Surnamed and Anglo Health Science Students at Del Mar College (Doctoral Dissertation), 1978. *Memberships include:* Affairs Comm, Trustees Comm, AOHA; Pres, Treas, DMEA; Bd of Dir, Gov's Urban Dev Commn, Tulane Univ Med Alumni Assn. *Honours include:* Presidential Awd of Hon, 1962; Jaycee of the Month, Key Man Awd, 1962; Nat Classroom Tchr of Yr, Valley Forge Freedoms Fndn, 1962; Co-fdr, Pres, Treas, Coastal Bend Chp, Phi Delta Kappa, 1973; Paul Harris Fellow, Rotary Int, 1986. *Hobbies:* Reading; Sailing; Sea shell collecting; Travel. *Address:* 9726 Wilkins Drive, Corpus Christi, TX 78410, USA. 7.

KOSTELANETZ Richard, b. 14 May 1940, New York, NY, USA. *Education:* AB with hons, Brown Univ, 1962; Fulbright Scholar, King's Coll, Univ of London, 1964-65; MA, Columbia Univ, 1966. *Appointments:* Co-fdr, Pres, Assembling Press, 1970-82; Assoc, Thematic Studies Prog, John Jay Coll, CUNY, 1972-73; Sr Staff, IN Univ Writers Conf, 1976; Lit Dir, The Future Press of the Cultural Coun Fndn, 1976-; Vis Prof of Am Studies and Eng, Univ of Texas at Austin, 1977; Co-ed, Publr, Precisely: A Critical Mag, 1977-; Sole Proprietor, RK Eds, 1978-; Coord, Interviewer, Am Writing Today, Voice of Am Forum Series, 1979-81. *Publications include:* On Innovative Music(ian)s, 1989 Unfinished Business: An Intellectual Nonhistory, 1990; Politics in the African-American Novel, 1991; The New Poetries and Some Old, 1991; On Innovative Artists, 1992; Solos, Duets, Trios & Choruses, 1992; Wordworks: Poems New and Selected, 1993; A Dictionary of the Avant-Gardes, 1993; On Innovative Performances, 1994; New books edited include, Mercie Cunningham, 1992; Writings About John Cage, 1993; John Cage, Writer, 1993; New Discs: Americas' Game, 1993. Author of num booklets, anthologies, collections edited & co-authored, booklets edited, essays, reviews. *Creative works:* Group Exhibs: An Exhib of Artists' Books and Portfolios from the USA, Book Fair, Leipzig, Germany, 1983; Ams in Print, Guttenberg Mus, Germany, 1989; Inst of Contemporary Art, Boston, 1990. *Memberships include:* Am PEN; Int Asn of Art Critics; Audio Indeps; Fndn for Indep Video & Film; Nat Artworkers; ASCAP; Nat Writers Union; Soc for Origination of Horspiel in Am. *Honours include:* Numbers: Poems & Stories, selected as one of the Best Books of 1976, Am Inst of Graphic Arts, also included in its 1977 exhib. *Hobbies:* Swimming; Reading. *Address:* PO Box 444, Prince Street, New York, NY 10012, USA. 2, 6, 13, 37, 52.

KOSTOV Dimiter Iliev, b. 11 July 1958, Plovdiv, Bulgaria. Archt; Specialist. m. Anelia Nikolchina, 15 Aug 1987, 1 s. *Education:* Higher Inst of Arch & Constrn, Archt, Theory & Hist of Arch, Sofia, 1979-86. *Appointments:* Dist Bldg-Design Agcy, 1986-87; Nat Inst for the Monuments of Culture: Conservation of historic urban areas, designer, Plovdiv, 1987-90; Mayor of the Old City, Plovdiv, 1990-91; Expert, Sofia, 1991. *Creative works include:* Special focus on the development and implementation of a modern methodology of Urban Development for the Conservation and Rehabilitation of Cultural Heritage; Pioneering development of Conservation Programme under Master Plan for Plovdiv. *Contributions to:* International fora organized by ICOMOS, ICCROM, UN HABITAT, the Int Acad of Arch, the Working Group on the Restoration of Monuments and Museum Pieces. *Memberships:* Working Grp on the Restoration of Monuments & Mus Pieces, Prague; Planning Hist Grp; Mng Bd, Philippopol Fndn, Plovdiv. *Honour:* Plovdiv Ctrl Area Dev Proj, World Biennale of

Arch, Sofia, 1989. *Hobbies:* Oil painting; Music; Reading; Applied sociology; philosophy. *Address:* 54 Ivan Vazov Street, 4000 Plovdiv, Bulgaria.

KOSTUCH Ryszard Walerian, b. 25 Mar 1929, Krakow, Poland. Prof. 4 s, 1 d. *Education:* PhD, Wroclaw, 1963; Prof of Agric awded by State Coun, 1976. *Appointments:* Lectr, Univ of Wroclaw, 1953-58; Hd of Grassland Dept, Wroclaw, Inst for Reclamation and Grassland Farming, Krakow, Head of Mountain Grassland Dept, 1959-88; Vis Prof, Mexico, 1985-87; Prof of Agric Univ, Krakow, 1988-. *Publications:* Author of 2 sci books on mountain grassland & 500 sci publs on popular sci. *Memberships:* Mexican Pasture Assn; Brit Grassland Soc; European Grassland Fedn; Polish Agric Assn; Polish Engrs and Technics of Agric Assn. *Honours:* Cross of Merit, State Coun, 1978; Bach Cross of Polonia Restituta, 1984; Decoration, Min of Environment Protection, 1986; Decoration, Merit of Agric, Agric Univ, 1987. *Hobbies:* Theatre; Classical music; Ancient Indian history; Poetry; Sport; Mountain hiking. *Address:* ul Naczelna 19, 31-421 Krakow, Poland.

KOSZTOLNYIK Zoltan J, b. 15 Dec 1930, Heves, Hungary. Prof. m. Penelope Louise South, 15 June 1966, 2 d. *Education:* BA cum laude, St Bonaventure Univ; MA, Fordham Univ; PhD with hons, NY Univ. *Appointments:* Instr in Hist, 1967-68; Asst Prof of Hist, 1968-72; Assoc Prof of Hist, 1972-81; Prof of Medieval Hist, 1981-. *Publications:* Five Eleventh Century Hungarian Kings, 1981; From Coloman the Learned to Bela III (1095- 1196): Hungarian Domestic Policy and its Impact upon Foreign Affairs, 1987. *Memberships:* Am Histl Assn; Am Cath Histl Assn. *Honours:* Fulbright Scholar, Univ of Vienna, 1963-65; NY Univ Founders Day Awd, 1969; Phi Kappa Phi Hon Soc, 1979-. *Hobbies:* Music (harpsichord); Walking. *Address:* Department of History, Texas A&M University, College Station, TX 77843, USA. 7, 13.

KOTARBINSKI Adam, b. 3 Dec 1914, Warsaw, Poland. Town Planning. m. Jadwiga Piotrkowska-Kotarbinska, 21 Oct 1945, 1 s. *Education:* Master's degree in Arch 1948, Dr's habil in theory of urban planning 1969, Fac of Arch, Tech Univ, Warsaw. *Appointments:* Dir, Inst of Town Planning and Arch, Warsaw, 1958-62; Scientific Sec, Comm of Arch and Town Planning, Polish Acad of Scis, 1978-80. *Publications:* Development of Polish town planning and architecture 1944-1964, 1967; Typology of towns for the long-range physical planning of the settlement network, 1967; Appreciation of the condition of architecture and town planning in Poland, 1980; Introduction to the researches on architecture as the domain of activity, 1987. *Memberships:* Fellow, Polish Town Planners Soc, 1949-; Soc of Polish Archts, 1949-; Fellow, The Learned Soc of Praxiology, Warsaw, 1990-. *Honours:* Prize, Dept of Tech Scis, Polish Acad of Scis, 1968; The Off's Cross of Polonia Restituta, 1973; The Standard of Labour I Class, 1985. *Hobby:* Painting. *Address:* Al Wyzwolenia 10 m 127, 00-570 Warszawa, Poland. 139.

KOTILAINEN Markku Kustaa, b. 23 Sept 1953, Raakkyha, Finland. Rsch Fellow. m. Eija-Maija Kotilainen, 1 Sept 1985, 1 s. *Education:* MSc, Univ of Helsinki, 1983; Lic. Sc, Univ of Helsinki, 1992. *Appointments:* Pellervo Econ Rsch Inst, PTT, 1983-85; Econ Dept, Min of Fin, 1985-86; Rsch Fellow, Rsch Inst of the Finnish Economy, 1986-. *Publications:* Author of books and articles in the fields of int macroecon(s) and foreign trade. *Membership:* Finnish Econ Assn. *Hobbies:* Gardening; Reading; Jogging. *Address:* Arentitie 14 as 7, 00410 Helsinki, Finland. 1.

KOTULSKI Piotr Jan, b. 26 July 1923, Wojkowice, Poland. Engr. 1 s,1 d. *Appointments:* Asst, Poznan Univ, 1948-50; Las Olsztyn, 1950-52; Gen Dir, Las Koszalin, 1952-56; Gen Dir, Las Opole, 1956-67; Gen Dir, Las Katowice Co Ltd, 1967-91. *Memberships:* Chmn of Students Org Forestwkr, Poznan Univ; Chmn of Hunters Coun, Polish Hunters Assn; Chmn, Nat Coun of Las

Org, 1980-88. *Honours:* Silver Cross of Merit, 1964; Gold Cross of Merit, 1972; Polonia Restituta Cross, 1979; 2nd Awds for Serv, Local Communities, 1988. *Hobby:* Bee-keeping. *Address:* 19 Nowa Street, 42-580 Wojkowice, Poland.

KOTYK Arnost, b. 11 July 1930, Melnik, Czech. Sr Rsch Scist; Univ Tchr of Biochem. m. Helena Kotorova, 10 June 1965, 1 s, 2 d. *Education:* MSc, Charles Univ, Prague, 1950-54; PhD 1958, DSc 1978, Czech Acad of Scis, Prague. *Appointments:* Inst of Microbiol 1958-84, Inst of Physiology 1985-, Czech Acad of Scis. *Publications:* Cell Membrane Transport, 1970, 2nd ed 1975; Membrane Transport, 1977; Enzymova kinetika, 1977; Biophysical Chemistry of Membrane Functions, 1988. *Memberships:* Czech Biochem Soc; Czech Biophysical Soc; Czech Microbiol Soc; Exec Comm, Int Union of Biochem and Molec Biol; Gen Comm, Int Coun of Sci Unions; UNESCO Comm for Molec and Cell Biol; Brit Biochem Soc; Deutsche Botanische Gesellschaft. *Honours:* Czech State Prize in Biochem, 1978; J G Mendel Medal, 1980; J E Purkyne Medal, 1988; Mbr, Czech Acad of Scis, 1989. *Hobbies:* Choir singing and conducting; Comparative etymology. *Address:* Institute of Physiology, Czechoslovak Academy of Sciences, Videnska 1083, 142 20 Prague 4, Czechoslovakia. 1.

KOTZAMANIS Triantafyllos, b. 29 Mar 1959, Athens, Greece. Archbishop; Writer. *Education:* Fac of Law, Univ of Athens. *Appointments:* Entered the Ch, 1980; Priest, 1987; Bishop, 1987; Archbishop, 1988; Archbishop Primate, 1990. *Publications:* The Bridge of Search, 1983; Esoteric Testimony, 1987; Dictionary of Esotecism, 1988; Confession of Faith, 1990; An Introduction to Gnosticism, 1991. *Memberships:* Charter Pres, Lions Club; Order of Serv. *Honours:* Grand Cross of the Order of St Dennis; Grand Cmdr of the Order of St Constantine the Gt; Hon Ambassador, Govt of Poland in Exile; Grand Cross Stom of Europe. *Hobbies:* Reading; Gardening; Travelling. *Address:* 27A Voulgaroktonov Str, GR 114 72 Athens, Greece.

KOUNEVA Penka Dinkova, b. 25 Feb 1967, Sofia, Bulgaria. Composer. *Education:* BA, Sofia Conservatory, 1990; BA, Sofia Univ, 1990; Ph.D Duke Univ, 1992. *Career:* Pianist, Sofia Ballet Sch; Singer-soprano, Pipkov Sofia Chamber Choir, 1987-90; Composer, Music Dir, Pianist, Tchr, Alba Pantomime Theatre, Sofia, 1988-90; Composer, ATF Experimental Theatre, Sofia, 1990. *Creative works:* Music Compositions: Rhapsody, for piano, 1987; Raga, for harpsichord, 1989; Wild and Humble, for flute and strings, 1989; Windscape, piano trio, 1990; Voices and Spells, for organ, 1990; Beyond Words, for flute, viola and harpsichord, 1992; Simulacrum, for strings, 1991; Music for synthesizers for theatrical shows and performances. *Membership:* Int League of Women Composers. *Honours:* Union of Bulgarian Composers Awd for chd's work, 1979; Grand Prix of Second World Chd's Music Competition, Tokyo, 1984; Ellen Zwilich Special Awd of Int League of Women Composers, Search for New Music Competition, 1989; Mary Duke Biddle Fellowship for studying composition at Duke Univ, 1990; William Klenz Award for Composition, 1992. *Hobbies:* Films; Theatre; Fine art; History; Jogging; Babysitting. *Address:* 814 Berkeley Street, Durham, NC 27705, USA. 138.

KOURI Donald Jack, b. 25 July 1938, Hobart, OK, USA. Disting Univ Prof. m. Shirley A Kouri, 9 Apr 1965, 1 s, 1 d. *Education:* BA, magna cum laude, OK Bapt Univ, 1960; MS 1962, PhD 1965, Univ of WI; Fellow, Jt Inst for Lab Astrophysics, Univ of CO, 1965-66. *Appointments:* Asst Prof of Chem and Phys, Midwestern Univ, 1966-67; Asst Prof of Chem 1967-71, Assoc Prof 1971-73, Prof of Chem and Phys 1973-88, Disting Univ Prof of Chem and Phys 1988-, Univ of Houston. *Publications:* Author of lyrics to choral music for chd's choirs and adult ch choirs. *Memberships:* Steering Comm, Few Body Tropical Group, Fellow, Am Phys Soc; ACS; ASCAP; Am Assn of Phys Tchrs. *Honours include:* ACS Southeastern TX Sect Awd, 1981; Esther Farfel

Awd, Univ of Houston, 1982; US Sr Scientist Summer Fellowship, Humboldt Fndn, Germany, 1985; Special Creativity Awd, US Nat Sci Fndn, 1991-93. *Hobbies:* Hebrew; Collecting ancient coins; Piano; Writing poetry and music lyrics; Collecting US coins; Reading; Singing choral music; Teaching Sunday School; Archaeology (Middle East). *Address:* Department of Chemistry, University of Houston, Houston, TX 77204, USA. 2, 7, 117, 143.

KOUSAKOV Sergei, b. 12 Aug 1950, Irkutsk, Russia. Dr Prof of Phys. m. Larissa Kozlova, 5 Dec 1975, 1 d. *Education:* MSc, PhD, Univ of Irkutsk; DSc, Inst of Phys, Latvian Acad of Sci, Riga, 1988. *Appointments:* Rsch Fellow 1972-78, Asst Prof 1978-80, Assoc Prof 1980-88, Full Prof 1988-90, Univ of Irkutsk; Vis Scientist 1984-85, Vis Prof 1990- 91, Univ of Amsterdam. *Publications:* Electron Excitation and Radiation Defects in the Lanthanum Halides Crystals, 1987; Point Defects of the Crystals Studied by Laser and Optical-Microwave Double Resonance Spectroscopy, 1991. Author of over 70 papers incl: Optical-Microwave Double Resonance on the Excited States of the Point Defects in Crystals, 1988; Picosecond Spectroscopy of the Defects in Ionic Crystals, 1991; Energy Transfer between F-tyrpe Defects in CaO, studies by Optical-Microwave Double-Resonance Spectroscopy, 1992. *Membership:* Phys Soc of the USSR. *Hobbies:* Reading; Travelling; Alpine skiing. *Address:* Dzerjinsky str 35-7, 664026 Irkutsk, Russia.

KOVACHEVA Nina, b. 19 Dec 1960, Sofia, Bulgaria. Artist. m. Stefanov Valentin, 14 Apr 1985, 1 d. *Education:* BA, Acad of Fine Arts, Sofia, 1985. *Career:* Freelance Artist. *Creative works:* Solo Exhibs: Prints in Rakovski 108 Gall, Sofia, 1988; Prints in Hemvs Gall, Sofia, 1989; Prints in NDA Gall, Sapporo and Tokyo, Japan, 1990; Watercolours in NDA Gall, Sapporo, Japan, 1991. Int Exhibs and Biennals incl: IIIth, IVth, VIth, Int Print Bienale, Varna, 1985, 1987, 1989, 1991; Vth, VIth, Int Print Bienale, Digne-les-Bains, France, 1986, 1988; Intl Drawing Exhib, Ferrol, Spain, 1989; Art of Today - III, Budapest, Hungary, 1990; 1st Annual Int Miniprint Exhib, Napa Art Ctr, Napa, USA, 1991; Int Memori Collection, Brussels, Belgium, 1991. Rep Exhibs of Bulgarian Art: Modena, 1988; Moscow and Leningrad, 1988; Paris, 1990; Brussels, 1990. *Membership:* Union of Bulgarian Artists Assn 33. *Honours:* Prize from the Vth Int Print Bienale Digne-les-Bains, France, 1986; From 1st Annual Int Miniprint Exhib, Napa, USA, 1991. *Hobbies:* Gardening; Travelling. *Address:* str Dimitar Stoianov BL 65 A, Sofia 1407, Bulgaria.

KOVALSKI Maryann, b. 4 June 1951, NYC, NY, USA. Chd's Book Author; Illustrator. m. Gregory Sheppard, 31 Aug 1975, 2 d. *Education:* Sch of Visual Arts, NYC. *Creative works:* Wrote and Illustrated: Brenda & Edward; Wheels on the Bus; Jingle Bells; Frank & Zelda. Illustrated: Mother Goose; Alice & The Birthday Giant; Junkpile Jennifer (Author John Greene); Grandma's Secret (Paulette Bourgeois); The Cake That Mack Ate (Rose Robart). *Memberships:* Can Soc of Chd's Authors, Illustrators & Performers; Art Dirs Club of NY; The Writers Union, Canada. *Hobbies:* Swimming; History; Gardening; Screen writing. *Address:* c/o Steven Jack, 14 Monteith Street, Toronto, Ontario, Canada M4V 1J4.

KOWAL David Martin, b. 17 Jan 1950, NYC, NY, USA. Prof; Curator; Scholar. *Education:* BA, Brandeis Univ, 1972; MA 1974, PhD 1981, Univ of MI, Ann Arbor. *Appointments:* Lectr, Dept of Art, Emmanuel Coll, 1977-78; Lectr, Dept of Hist of Art, Univ of MI, 1978-79; Asst Prof 1979, Assoc Prof 1985, Coord of Art Hist 1985, 1988-91, Dir of the Halsey Gall of Art 1988-91, Coll of Charleston. *Publications:* Ribalta y los Ribaltescos, 1985; Francisco Ribalta and His Followers, 1985; Author of num scholarly articles for art hist journs on Spanish 17th c painting and sculpture and Portuguese colonial arch in India. *Contributions to:* Int Dictionary of Arts and Artists, 1990. *Memberships:* Coll Art Assn; Am Soc or Hispanic Art Histl Studies; Southeastern Coll Art Conf;

Carolina Art Assn; Dir, Halsey Gall of Art. *Honours:* Fulbright Fellow, Spain, 1976- 77; Fellow, Am Coun of Learned Societies, 1983-84; Indo-Am Rsch Fellow, Smithsonian Inst, 1986-87; Rsch Fellow, Fundacao Oriente, Lisbon, Portugal, 1991-92; Fellow, Netherlands-Am Commn for Educl Exchange, 1991. *Hobbies:* Travel; Sailing. *Adress:* Department of Art History, School of the Arts, College of Charleston, Charleston, SC 29424, USA.

KOWALSKA Alina, b. 19 Aug 1932, Czeladz, Poland. Linguist. *Education:* MA 1955, PhD 1964, Jagiellonian Univ. *Appointments:* Lectr, HS of Pedagogics, Katowice, 1955-68; Assoc Prof 1968-88, Prof, Dir, Pol Lang Inst 1988-, Silesian Univ, Katowice. *Publications:* Author of 50 publs incl: The Polish language in XVI century civic records of Tarnowskie Gory, 1970; Evolution of analytical verbal forms with participle in -1 in the Polish language, 1976. *Memberships:* Polish Linguistics Assn; Linguistics Comm, Polish Acad of Scis. *Honours:* Gold Cross of Merit, 1976; Medal of the Commn of Nat Educ, 1984; Kt's Cross of the Order of Polish Renascence, 1986. *Hobbies:* Linguistics; History; Literature; Moutain tourism. *Address:* Uniwersytet Slaski Instytut Jezyka Polskiego, Plac Sejmu Slaskiego 1, Katowice, Poland.

KOWALSKI Stefan, b. 30 Mar 1940, Osieczna, Poland. Forest Pathologist. m. 19 Sept 1964, 2 s, 1 d. *Education:* MSc, 1964; DSc, 1972; Dr habilit, 1979. *Appointments:* Asst, Agric Univ, Poznan, 1964- 73; Adj 1973-80, Asst Prof 1980-, Hd of Forest Pathol Dept 1986-, Agric Univ, Krakow. *Publications:* Author of over 60 scientific publs concerning soil fungi, mycorrhiza of forest trees and pathogenic root fungi. *Memberships:* Comm of Forest Sci, Polish Acad of Scis; Polish Forestry Soc; Vice Chm, Krakow's Br 1975-84, Chmn 1984-90, Polish Phytopathological Soc. *Honours:* Of the Min of Sci & Educ for the dr's degree dissertation, 1973; of the Min of Sci & Educ for the habilit dr's degree dissertation, 1981. *Hobbies:* Gardening; Christian philosophy. *Address:* Agricultural University, Department of Forest Pathology, 29 Listopada 46, 31-426 Krakow, Poland.

KOZAK Stefan, b. 11 Aug 1937, Wierzbica, Poland. Prof. m. Irena Drotiak, 17 Feb 1967, 1 d. *Education:* PhD, Kiev and Warsaw Univ, 1967; Habilitacja, Wroclaw Univ, 1977. *Appointments:* Journalist, Nasze Slowo, Warsaw, 1962-63; Polish Acad of Scis, Warsaw, 1968-81; Prof, Univ of Warsaw, 1981-. *Publications:* Typology of Polish-Ukrainian Lit Rels, 1967; Sources of Romanticism in Ukraine, 1978; Ukrainian Conspirators & Messianists, 1990; Author of 160 articles, essays and reviews. *Memberships:* Mbr of Bd, Int Ukrainian Assn; Pres, Polish Ukrainian Assn; Slavic Comm, Polish Acad of Scis. *Honours:* Rector's Awd, 1989, 1991. *Hobbies:* History; Politics; Sightseeing; Walking fast. *Address:* University of Warsaw, Ukrainian Department, ul Szturmowa 4, 02-678 Warsaw, Poland.

KOZHEVNIKOV Dmitry A, b. 21 Mar 1935, Moscow, Russia. Mining Engr; Geophysicist. 2 d. *Education:* PhD, Inst of Nuclear Rsch, Moscow State Univ, 1964; State Dr Sc, All-Union Rsch Inst of Nuclear Geophys, 1983. *Appointments:* Assoc Prof, Full Prof of Well Logging Dept, Complete prog lectures in the theory and applications of elec, electromagnetic, nuclear, acoustic and thermal logging, Gubkin State Acad of Oil and Gas. *Publications:* Author of over scientific publs incl 5 monographs, 5 inventions. *Membership:* Mineral and Geotech Logging Soc, USA; Chmn of Nuclear Geophys Sect, USSR Acad of Scis; VP, Nuclear Geophys Assn. *Hobbies:* Swimming; Skiing; IBM-PC; Classic art. *Address:* Russia State Academy of Oil & Gas Mocow, 65 Lenin Avenue, 117917 Moscow, Russia.

KOZLOV Jurij, b. 15 May 1935, Kiev. Scientist. m. Dmitrieva Tamara, 6 Oct 1957, 2 d. *Education:* Postgrad Student, Moscow State Univ, 1958-61; DPh, 1962; DSc, 1969. *Appointments:* Sr Scientific Specialist 1961-71, Hd of Lab 1971-77, Moscow State Univ; Rector 1977-89, Hd of Physico-Chem Biol Chair 1977-89, Irkutsk

State Univ; Prof of the Environmental Protection Chair 1990-92, Hd of the System Ecology Chair 1992, Hd of the Ecological Dept 1992, Russian People's Friendship Univ. *Publications:* Free Radical Oxidation of Lipids in Biological Membranes, 1972; Free Radicals in Biological Systems, 1973; Phospholipids in Biological Membranes, 1982. *Memberships:* Int Union of Pure and Applied Biophys; Scientific Coun on Biophys, Scientific Coun on Biochem, Scientific Coun on Biomembranes, Russian Acad of Sci. *Honours:* State Awd Laureate, Russia, 1983; Sci Honouresman, Russia, 1985. *Hobbies:* Fishing; Hunting; Gardening; Autoamateur; Theatre; Music. *Address:* Russian People's Friendship University, System Ecology Chair, 6 Miclucho- Maclaya Street, 117198 Moscow, Russia.

KOZLOWSKI Jerzy, b. 25 Jan 1931, Krakow, Poland. Prof. m. Zofia Kubala, 1 Apr 1956, 1 s. *Education:* BArch 1953, MArch 1955, Fac of Arch, Dr Hab 1981, Tech Univ, Krakow; Dip Urb, Ministere de la Constrn, Paris, 1963; PhD, Univ of Edinburgh, 1971. *Appointments:* Planner, Vonodship Town Planning Off, Krakow, 1955-65; Rsch Fellow, Planning Rsch Unit, Univ of Edinburgh, 1965-71; Dir, Rsch Inst of Environment, Krakow, 1971-81; Prof, Hd of Dept, Univ of Qld, St Lucia, 1982-. *Creative works:* Freelance Archt, Ch and several Hses; 12 Town Plans; 1 Plan for Nat Park; 10 books; Over 60 articles; Several rsch projs; Over 60 papers at Nat and Int Confs. *Memberships:* Assn of Polish Archts; Soc of Polish Town Planners; Royal Aust Planning Inst; C'wlth Human Ecology Coun; Comm on Environmental Strategy and Planning, IUCN (Int Union for Conservation of Nature). *Honours:* Nat Awds for Achmt in Planning, 1959, 1961, 1973; Silver Hon Badge, Polish Soc of Town Planners, 1975; Nat Awd, Polish Acad of Sci for Achmts in Rsch, 1979; Gold Cross of Merits, 1981. *Hobbies:* Tennis; Pastel painting; Photography. *Address:* 118 Mildura Drive, Helensvale, Queensland, Australia. 52.

KOZLOWSKI Ryszard, b. 28 July 1938, Uniejow, Poland. Dir. m. Jadwiga Grygorowicz, 13 June 1964, 2 d. *Education:* MSc, 1961; Dr of Chem Scis, 1970. *Appointments:* Hd of the Particle Bd Dept 1961-76, Dep Dir for Scientific Affairs 1976-87, Gen Dir 1987-, Inst of Natural Fibres; Hd of the Wood Protection Dept, Inst of Wood Tech, 1976. *Publications:* Method of Flax Straw Retting with Addition of Urea (Co-author), 1967; The Efects of Nuclear Radiation on Polymers, Especially Fibre-creating ones as Well as Application of Radioactive Isotopes for Fibre Modification (Co- author), 1967; Methods of Flax Straw Retting Process Degree Estimation, 1969; Retting of Flax With Addition of Ures Apaint, A Background of Classical Method, Taking Into Special Consideration the Liberation of Fatty Acids from Retting Liquid and in Sheaves, As Well as Liberated Gases, and Nitrate Compounds, 1970; Tables of Calculating Coefficients of Some SI System Units for Linen Industry (Co-author), 1970; Author of about 100 scientific publs. *Memberships:* Coord, FAO Flax Grp in Europe, Rome Italy; Comm, The Textile Inst, Manchester, Eng; Int Juste Org, Dekka, India; Exec Bd, Gdyniz Wool Fndn; Vice Chmn of Chem Sci Comm, Polish Acad of Scis, Poznan; Wood Protection Comm, Min of Agric. *Honours include:* Chem and Textile Ind Min Prize for Autiflame Protection of Finishing Materials for Aviation, 1981; Min of Sci, Higher Educ and Technics Special Awd for Tech of Indation Bd Protection on the basis of Stramit Method from Wood and Plant Refuse, 1984. *Hobbies:* Gardening; Fruit farming; History of chemistry. *Address:* Institute of Natural Fibres, ul Wojska Polskiego 71 B, 60-630 Poznan, Poland.

KOŽMÍN Zdeněk, b. 28 Feb 1925, Hnevice, Czech. Prof. m. Drahomira Šimkova, 6 Aug 1952. *Education:* PhD, 1949; CSc, 1962. *Appointments:* Second Sch Tchr, Stary Jicin, Breclav, 1949-56; Pedag Fac Lectr, As Prof, Brno, 1956-70; Tchr, Zastáva, 1970-85; As Prof, Ped Fac 1990-91, Prof, Phil Fac 1991-, Masaryk Univ, Brno. *Publications:* Author of over 450 lit articles and studies, 1955-70, incl: 2 Czech Lit Reading Books, 1961, 1970; Umenl stylu, 1967; Styl Vancurovy prozy, 1968; Interpretace-basni, 1986; Zvetseniny ze-stylu bratri

Capku, 1989; Vmeni basne, 1990. *Memberships:* Svaz c spisovatelu, 1967-69; Obec spisovatelu, 1990-; Assn Int des Critiques Littéraires, Paris, 1991-. *Honour:* Medal of the Min of Culture on the occasion of 100 yr anniv of Karel Capek's birth, 1990. *Hobbies:* Philosophy; Art; Hiking. *Address:* Kounicova 11, 60200 Brno, The Czech Republic.

KOZMINYKH Vladislav Olegovitsch, b. 3 Jan 1957, Perm, USSR. Pharmaceutist; Chem. m. Manelova Elena Nikolajevna, 26 July 1984, 1 s, 1 d. *Education:* Cand of Chem Sci Degree, 1985; currently working on Doctorship studies. *Appointments:* Aspirant Special Course, Organic Chem, 1979-80, 1981-84; Army Serv, 1980-81; Chair of Drug Tech and Analytical Chem, Perm Pharm Inst, 1984-. *Contributions to:* Papers, Communications, Reviews in journs incl: Zhurn Obstsch Khim, 1985; Zhurn Org Khim, 1985; Khim Geterotsikl Soedin, 1989, 1990. *Memberships:* All- Union Chem Soc; Ural Dept, All-Union Entomological Soc. *Hobbies include:* Entomology; Taxonomy; Faunistics; Bicycle sports. *Address:* PO Box 52, Perm 51, 614051, Russia.

KRAEV Zdravko Emilov, b. 1 Oct 1947, Sofia, Bulgaria. Surg. m. Mariana Kraeva, 8 Aug 1971, 1 s, 1 d. *Education:* PhD, 1986. *Appointments:* Dept of Gen Surg, Mihailovgrad, 1971; Asst Clin of Gen Surg, Med Acad, 1973; Ctr of Hemodialysis Vascular Surg, 1981. *Publications:* Author of over 50 publs about Gen Surg and Vascular access for patients on hemodialysis. *Membership:* European Assn for hemodialysis, nephrology and kidney transplantation. *Hobbies:* Skiing; Swimming; Stamp collecting. *Address:* Nadejda 636 B, Ap 82, 1231 Sofia, Bulgaria.

KRAINTZ Leon, b. 3 Oct 1924, Johnstown, PA, USA. Lectr; Physiologit; Prof Emeritus. m. Frances Draper Whitcomb, 26 Aug 1949, 1 s, 2 d. *Education:* AB, Harvard, 1950; MA 1952, PhD 1954, Rice Inst. *Appointments:* Rsch Assoc, Dept of Psych, Harvard, 1946-47; Rsch Assoc, Sloan Kettering Inst, NYC, 1948-50; Rsch Scientist, M D Anderson Hosp, Houston, 1950-52; Assoc Prof, Univ of TX, Houston, 1954-62; Prof of Biol 1962- 64, Hon Prof 1964, Rice Univ, Houston; Prof, Hd of Oral Biol 1964-81, Prof Emeritus 1987, Lectr in Nutrition 1991, Univ of BC. *Publications:* Author, Co-author of 80 scientific papers, book chapts incl: The Parathyroids, 1961; Salivary Glands and Their Secretions, 1967; Biological Mineralization, 1973. *Memberships:* Scientific Rsch Soc; Pres, UBC Chapt, Sigma Xi; Endocrine Soc; Am Physiol Soc; Can Physiol Soc; Soc for Exp Biol and Med; Univ Speakers Bur; Sci World, Vancouver; Scientists in the Sch Prog of BC. *Honours:* Bausch & Lomb Hon Sci Awd, 1942; Nat Sci Fndn Fellow, 1952-54; FAAAS, 1958; Sr Fellowship, USPHS, 1969-70. *Hobbies:* Native American Arts & Crafts; Wood carving; Gardening; Public understanding of science; History of science. *Address:* 6478 Dunbar Street, Vancouver, BC, Canada V6N 1X6. 2, 50, 52, 142, 143, 154.

KRAJDEN Sigmund, b. 9 Apr 1946, Germany. Physn; Univ Prof. m. Jeanie Cohen, 31 Mar 1974, 3 s, 1 d. *Education:* BSc, 1967; MDCM, 1971; FRCP(C), Internal Med, 1976; FRCP(C), Microbiol, 1980. *Appointments:* Cons: St Michael's Hosp, Branson Hosp (Toronto), Govt of Canada (Hlth and Welfare), Life Ins Ind; Univ Prof, Univ of Toronto; Chief Microbiol, Infection Diseases, Infection Control, St Joseph's Hlth Ctr, Toronto, 1980-. *Publications:* Author of over 60 scientific articles and chapts in books. *Honour:* Fungus named in his hon, recognizing contributions in mycology/medical TRICHOPHYTON KRAJDENII. *Hobbies:* Tennis; Swimming; Jogging. *Address:* Department of Microbiology, St Joseph's Health Centre, 30 The Queensway, Toronto, Ontario, Canada M6R 1B5. 142.

KRAMER Lorenz, b. 24 Nov 1941, Naples, Italy. Prof. m. Wilma Kramer, 20 Sept 1970, 1 s, 2 d. *Education:* Vordiplom, Univ of Heidelberg, 1962-64; Dip, Univ of Hamburg, 1964-67; PhD, Stanford Univ, USA, 1967-

69; Habilitation, Cologne Univ, 1973. *Appointments:* Postdoct Rsch Assn, Rutgers Univ, USA, 1969-71; Wiss Mitarbeiter an IFF d KFA Julich, 1971- 74; Prof (C3), Tech Univ, Munich, 1974-78; Prof (C4), Universitat Bayreuth, 1978-. *Publications:* Author of 80 articles in journs, 1967-91. *Memberships:* Deutsche Physikalische Gesellschaft; Deutsche Gesellschaft fur Biophysik; Ed Bd, Phys Review A, 1991-93. *Honours:* Fellowship from Studiemsbiffung des Deutschen Volkes, 1962-68; Offer of Chair, Tech Univ of Munich, 1981 (declined); Recipient of many travel awds and guest positions in foreign countries. *Hobbies:* Mountaineering; Cayaking; Music. *Address:* Physikalisches Institut, Universitat Bayreuth, D-8580 Bayreuth, Germany.

KRAMER Paul R, b. 6 June 1936, Baltimore, MD, USA. Atty. m. Janet Amitin, 1 Sept 1957, 3 d. *Education:* AB, Am Univ, Washington DC, 1959; JD, Am Univ, Washington Coll of Law, 1961. *Appointments:* Staff Atty, Dep Dir, Legal Aid Agcy, DC Fed Pub Defender's Off, Washington, 1962-63; Asst US Atty 1963-69, Dep US Atty 1967-83, Off; Exec Bd, Baltimore Area Coun Boy Scouts Am, 1970-83; Instr, Univ of Md, Sch of Law, 1975-80; Assoc Prof of Law, Villa Julie Coll, 1976-80; Assoc Professorial Lectr, George Washington Univ, 1979; Instr, Nat Coll of Dist Attys, 1979; Adv Counsel to Exec Bd, Boy Scouts, 1983-; Permanent Mbr, 4th Cir fed Jud Conf. *Memberships:* ABA; Pres Baltimore Chapt 1973-74, Nat Cir VP 1973-81, 1985-86, 1992-1993, Mbr Nat Coun 1973-, Chmn Nat Cir VP 1978-80, Nat Dep Sec 1981-82, Fac Fed Practice Inst 1981-, Nat Sec 1982-83, Fed Bar Assn; Md Bar Assn; Baltimore Bar Assn; Nat Assn Criminal Trial Attys; Md Trial Lawyers Assn; Md Criminal Def Atty's Assn; US Atty Alumni Assn; Past Master, Masons. *Hobby:* Aerial Boy Scouts of Am. *Address:* 231 St Paul Place, Baltimore, MD 21202, USA. 6, 52, 163.

KRAMER Walter, b. 21 Nov 1948, Ormont. Univ Prof. m. Doris Caspari, 17 Mar 1977, 1 s, 1 d. *Education:* Univ of Mainz, 1969-76. *Appointments:* Lectr, Univ of Mannh; Asst Prof, Vienna; Assoc Prof, Hannover; Full Prof, Dortmund. *Address:* Fuhrenweg 42, D-3050 Steinhude, Germany.

KRAUS Andreas, b. 5 Mar 1922, Erding. Prof Emeritus. m. Maria, 27 Dec 1947, 1 d. *Education:* Dr phil, 1952; Dr phil habil, 1960. *Appointments:* Gymnasium, St Ottilien, 1948-52; Weilheim, 1952-53; Pasing, 1953-60; Phil Theol Hochschule Regensburg, 1967; Univ Regensburg, 1967-77; Prof, Univ of Munich, 1977, Emerit, 1989. *Publications:* Author of a number of publs. *Memberships:* Kommission f bayer Landesgeschichte; Marstallplatz 8, Munchen 22; Bayerische Akademie der Wissenschaften. *Honours:* Bayerischer Verdienstorden, 1983; Bayerische Verfassungsmedaille, 1984. *Address:* Nederlingerstrafse 30a, D 8000 Munchen 19, Germany. 34, 52.

KRAUS Heinrich, b. 21 Aug 1923. *Education:* Univ of Lektor am Theatrewiss; Inst d Univ Wein. *Appointments:* Mitarb d Dion d Burgtheatersm 1945-48; Stellv Ltr u Lehrer am Max Reinhardt-Sem, 1949-51; Cultural Activities, Dir, US-Info Serv, Austria, 1951-56; Dir d ungar Fluchtlingsorchesters Philharmonica Hungarica, 1957-59; Chefdisponent d Dt Oper am Rhein, 1959-61; Wr Burgtheater: Verw Dir anschl viele J VDir, 1961-77; Gschf Dir am Theater in d Josefstadt, 1977-84; Gschf Alleindir d Theaters in d Josefstadt, 1984-. *Memberships:* Osterr Ehrenkreuz f Wiss u Kunst I Kl; Gr Silb Ehrenz f Verd um d Rep Osterr; Gold Ehrenz f Verd um d Bundesland Wien; Offz Kreuz Kl d Kgl Schwed Wasa Ordens; Kommandeur d Kgl Schwed Nordsternordens. *Honours:* Paul Harris Fellow Rotary Intern; VP, d Intern Nestroyges; Vorst Mtgl d Osterr-Amerikan Ges; Mtgl d Ver ehemaliger Theresianisten. *Hobby:* Theatre.

KRAWCZYK Waclaw Waldemar, b. 18 June 1926, Sosnowiec, Poland. Dr of Humanistic Scis. m. Izabella Strzalkowska, 16 May 1949, 1 s, 1 d. *Education:*

Jagiellonian Univ, Cracow, 1953; Main Coll of Social Scis, Warsaw, 1963; Studies, 1965-72, Inst of Philosophy and Socjology of the Polish Academy of Science. *Appointments:* Journalist, Nat Def Publs, 1950-67; Journalist 1967-72, Mgr of Publs, Ed-in-Chief 1973-84, Nat Def League. *Publications:* Masters thesis, Positivists towards workers questions and socialism; Dr's dissertation, Philosophical views of Kazimierz Czapinski, 1971; Struggle Against Clericalism in the Columns of Robotnik in 1918-1928; The Anticlerical Journalism of Kazimierz Czapinski 1882-1941; Philosophy ob Culture by Kazimierz Czapinski; Totalitarianism the main enemy of Democracy, 1991. *Honours:* Medal of Nat Educ, Order Polonia Restituta; Medal named after Dr Henryk Jordan of Chd's Friends Soc; Num dips and decorations. *Hobbies:* Activity in the sphere of development of secular culture and Aspiration of working people to political and social emencipation and realization of their humanistic ideals. *Address:* Nowolipie 2B, Ap 18, 00-146 Warsaw, Poland.

KREGLEWSKI Marek, b. 28 Nov 1949, Poznan, Poland. Prof. m. Maria Szydlowska, 5 Jan 1982, 1 d. *Education:* MSc, 1972; PhD, 1978. *Appointments:* Adam Mickiewicz Univ, Poznan, 1972-, Solidarity Pres of the Revisory Bd 1980-81, Dozent 1989-91, Prof 1991-; Alexander von Humboldt Fellow, Univ of Kiel, Germany, 1988-89. *Publications:* Problems in Quantum Chemistry; Author of 30 papers on Quantum Chem and Molecular Spectroscopy. *Membership:* Pres, Poznan Br, Polish Chem Soc, 1991. *Hobbies:* Skiing; Reading. *Address:* Os Boleslawa Chrobrego 9/31, PL 60 683 Poznan, Poland.

KRETZSCHMAR Jan G V, b. 24 June 1942, Oostende, Belgium. Div Hd. m. Trees Segier, 4 Sept 1965, 1 s, 1 d. *Education:* Elec Engr, Nuclear Engr, K U Leuven; Dr in Applied Sci. *Appointments:* Asst, Cath Univ, Leuven, 1965-71; Rschr, Sect Hd, Div Hd of Energy and Environment, Nuclear Energy Rsch Ctr, Mol, 1972-91. *Publications:* Author of 150 papers in nat and int journs and books. *Memberships:* Royal Flemmish Inst of Engrs; Int Microwave Power Inst; European Assn for the Sci of Air Pollution; Orde van de Prince; Verbond der Vlaamse Academici. *Honours:* Hon Rsch Assoc, Univ of London, 1969; Postdoct Fellowship, Univ of CA, Berkeley, 1970-71; Rsch Prize, Royal Soc of Flemmish Engrs, 1989. *Address:* Vareselaan 13, B-2400 Mol, Belgium. 43.

KREUTER Jorg Wilheim Rudolf, b. 4 Jan 1948, Gelnhausen. Prof. m. Susan Szabo, Dec 1971, 1 s, 1 d. *Education:* PhD 1974, Habilitation 1982, ETH, Zurich. *Appointments:* Univ Asst 1975, Chief Asst 1976-84, ETH, Zurich; Assoc Prof 1984-90, Full Prof 1990-, Univ of Frankfurt. *Publications:* Author of over 100 scientific publs. *Memberships:* Arbeitsgemeinschaft fur Pharm Verfahrenstechnik; Reticuloendothelial Soc; Gov 1987-90, Controlled Release Soc; Deutsche Pharmazeutische Gesellschaft; Deutsche Gesellschaft fur Nuklearmedizin. *Honours:* ETH Silver Medal; APV Prize. *Hobbies:* Skiing; Mountain climbing. *Address:* Institut fur Pharmazeutische Technologie, Georg-Voigt-Str 16, D-6000 Frankfurt/Main, Germany. 52.

KRIDALAKSANA Harimurti, b. 23 Dec 1939, Ungaran. Prof. m. Kusmarlinah, 27 Jan 1968, 2 s, 1 d. *Education:* MA 1963, DLitt 1987, Univ of Indonesia; Dip, Univ of Pittsburg, 1970; Dip, Nat Def Coll, 1975. *Appointments:* Transl of lit and scientific works, 1961; Tchr of HS, 1961; Tutor 1961, Lectr, Prof 1963, Univ of Indonesia. *Publications:* Author of 25 books on linguistics and over 90 tech papers. *Memberships:* Linguistic Soc of Am; Societas Linguistica Europeae; Pres 1974-78, Soc for the Promotion of Indonesian; Pres 1988-91, Linguistic Soc of Indonesia. *Honour:* Satyalencana Dwijasistha for tchng at Indonesian Navy Command Sch, 1975. *Hobbies:* Active in social works helping underprivileged people with their education; International affairs. *Address:* Perumahan UI No 45, Ciputat, Jakarta Selatan 15419, Indonesia.

KRIDEL Craig, b. 31 July 1951, USA. Curator. *Education:* PhD, OH State Univ, 1980. *Appointments:* Prof, OH State Univ, 1980- 84; Prof, Univ of SC, 1984- . *Publications:* Ed, Tchng Educ; Ed, Curr Hist. *Memberships:* Pres, Soc for the Study of Curr Hist; Dir, Inst for the Adv of the Arts in Educ, OH State Univ; Pres, United Serpents; Dir, The First Int Serpent Fest. *Address:* Museum of Education, McKissick Museum, University of South Carolina, Columbia, SC 29208, USA.

KRILIC Zlatko, b. 19 Aug 1955, Osijek. Writer. m. Tatjana Spincic, 5 Sept 1987, 1 s. *Career:* Writer. *Publications:* Prvi Sudar, 1979; Cudnovata Istina, 1980; Pocetak Plovidbe, 1982; Veliki Zavodnik, 1984; Zabranjena Vrata, 1985; Zivi Pijesak, 1987; Zagonetno Pismo, 1987; Kazaliste Lutaka I Drugi Igrouazi, 1989. *Memberships:* Assn of Croatian Writers, 1980-; Croatian Pen Ctr, 1990-. *Honours:* Ivana Brlic Mazuranic Awd, 1980; Grigor Vitez Awd, 1982; 7 Sekretara Skoja Awd, 1984. *Hobbies:* Photography; Collecting Antiquities. *Address:* Put Vladimira Nazora 107, Kastav/Kolarova 16, Zagreb.

KRING Jonathan Edward, b. 27 May 1956, Lansing, MI, USA. Automotive Body Designer. m. Elizabeth Anne Prince, 14 June 1980, 2 d. *Education:* BA, Olivet Nazarene Univ, 1979. *Appointments:* Mental Hlth Techn, Chicago Hgts Terrace, 1979-80; Res Dir, Olivet Zazarene Univ, 1980-83; Automotive Draftsman, Carron & Co, 1983-87; Automotive Designer, Modern Eng, 1987-88; Automotive Designer, Gen Motors Design Staff, 1988-. *Memberships:* Chmn of the Bd of Christian Life 1985-88, Plymouth Ch of the Nazarene; Chd's Ministeries Dir, Ch Bd Mbr 1990-, Warren Woods Ch of the Nazarene. *Honours:* HS Nt Hon Soc; Res Asst, ONU; Capt of Coll Soccer Team; Top Salesman Awd, Southwestern Co, Nashville, 1976. *Hobbies:* Golf; Tennis; Reading. *Address:* 29244 Nottingham Circle, Warren, MI 48092, USA.

KRIPPENDORFF Ekkehart, b. 22 Mar 1934, Eisenach, Germany. Prof. m. Eve Slatner, 9 Sept 1962, 2 s. *Education:* PhD, 1959; Dr phil habil, 1972. *Appointments:* Fulbright Fellow, Harvard Univ, 1960-61; Tchng Asst, Yale Univ, 1961-62; Rockefeller Fndn Fellowship, Columbia Univ, NY, 1962-63; Asst Prof, CUNY, Queens Coll & Columbia Univ, 1968-69; Prof of Int Rels, Johns Hopkins Univ, Bologna Ctr, Italy, 1969-78; Prof of Polit Sci, Free Univ Berlin, John F Kennedy Inst for N Am Studies, 1978-. *Publications:* Reisebuch Italien I-II (with P Kammerer), 1981; Staat und Krieg, 1985; Internationale Politik, 1986; Wie die GroBen mit den Menschen spielen, 1988; Politische Interpretationen, 1990; Politik in Shakespeares Dramen, 1991. *Hobby:* Viola playing.

KRISTO NAGY Istvan, b. 16 June 1921, Sandorfalva. Essayist; Ed. m. Marta Koncz, 7 Jan 1959, 1 s. *Education:* Univ of Szeged, 1944. *Appointments:* Official in charge, Min of Info, Budapest, -1944; Ed, several periodicals, -1991; Ed 1959-69, Ed in Chief 1970-73, 1982-90, Magveto Pub, Budapest. *Publications:* Author, ed, transl of several works of art and lit criticism. *Memberships:* Active in youth orgs, Hungary; Budapest Bd of Patriotic People's Front, 1973-; Nat Coun of Patriotic People's Front, Hazafias, 1980-90; Supr Hungarian Chapt 1989, PEN Club. *Honours:* Order of Work by Hungarian Govt (twice). *Hobby:* Art collecting. *Address:* Terez korut 18, H 1066 Budapest, Hungary. 52.

KRIVOSHIEV Stephan, b. 24 June 1949, Pleven. Nephrologist; Assoc Prof. m. Anna-Maria Borissova, 30 Sept 1973, 1 s. *Education:* PhD, 1987. *Appointments:* Gen Practitioner, 1974-81; Asst 1981-, Hd Asst 1986, Assoc Prof of Nephrology 1991- Med Fac, Haemodialysis Ctr, Sofia. *Publications:* Author of over 50 publs in the field of nephrology. *Memberships:* Full Mbr, European Dialysis and Transplant Assn; European Renal Assn, 1983-. *Hobbies:* Numismatics; Reading. *Address:* University Hospital, Queen Giovanna, Hemodialysis Centre, Sofia 1527, Bulgaria.

KRIZEK Raymond John, b. 5 June 1932, Baltimore, MD, USA. Prof. m. Claudia Stricker, 8 Aug 1964, 2 s. *Education:* BE, Johns Hopkins Univ, 1954; MS, Univ of MD, 1961; PhD, Northwestern Univ, 1963. *Appointments:* Lt Corps of Engrs, US Army, 1955-57; Instr, Univ of MD, 1957-61; Rsch Asst 1961-63, Asst Prof 1963-66, Assoc Prof 1966-70, Prof 1970-, Chmn 1980-92, Northwestern Univ. *Publications:* Author of over 300 tech papers, about 50 tech reports; Ed. *Contributions to:* about 10 books. *Memberships:* Chmn, Awds Comm, Geotech Engrng Div, ASCE; Int Soc of Soil Mechanics & Fndn Engrng. *Honours:* Hogentogler Awd, ASTM, 1970; Huber Rsch Prize, ASCE, 1971; Stanley F Pepper Endowed Chair, Northwestern Univ, 1987. *Address:* 1366 Sanford Lane, Gleview, IL 60025, USA. 2, 8, 26, 143.

KROCHMAL Arnold, b. 30 Jan 1919, NYC, NY, USA. Assoc Ed; Adj Prof. m. Connie Brite, 27 Nov 1970, 3 . *Education:* BSc, NC State Coll; MSc, PhD. *Appointments:* Dir, Expt State, Univ of Wyoming, Afghan, 1957-59; Chair, Hort Escue Agr Panam, Honduras, 1960-61; Prin, Econ Bot, US Forest Svce, 1966-83; Asst Off, US Dept of Ag, Virgin Isl, 1961-66. *Publications include:* Let There be Forest; A Field Guide to Medicinal Plants; Uncultivated Nuts of the US; A Guide to Appalachian Medicinal Plants; Gardening in the Carolinas; Complete Book of Dye from Natural Sources; Alternate Energy; Acid Rain; World Hunger; Aging. *Memberships:* Soc of Sigma Xi; Disabled Am Veterans. *Honours:* 2 silver, campaign· stars; Amphibious arrows, 1943-46; Combat Infantry Badge, 1944; Grants, 1987-92, Alfred Burnham Fund; Bronze Star, 1989; Fulbright Awd, Greece; Nat Acad of Scis, Romania (2); Hon Rsch Assoc, Inst of Econ Bot, NY Bot Gdn; Adj Prof of Forestry, NCSU; Tropical Forestry Foundation, Holland, 1982. *Hobbies:* Travel abroad; Corresponding; Writing. *Address:* 119 Bell Road, Asheville, NC 28805, USA. 7, 30.

KROGER Dawn Virginia Dodd, b. 19 Oct 1941, St Louis, MO, USA. Reading Specialist. m. Allen B Kroger, 26 July 1968, 1 s. *Education:* BA, Southern Meth Univ, 1963; MEd, East TX State Univ, 1978. *Appointments:* Dallas Ind Sch Dist, 1963-72; Highlander, Carden Sch, 1972-75; Mesquite Ind Sch Dist, 1975-91. *Memberships:* Alpha Delta Pi; Pres 1975-76, 1990-92, Dist Chap, Alpha Delta Kappa; Int Reading Assn; TX Assn for Improvement of Reading; Assn TX Prof Edrs; Sec, VP, Social Comm, PTA. *Honours:* Petroleum Inst, Univ of Houston, 1967; Magic Circle, 1970; Learning Disabilities Symposium, Dallas ISD, 1971; Alpha Delta Kappa Scholarship, 1978. *Hobbies:* Flower arranging; Needle point; Sewing; Reading. *Address:* 6516 Brook Meadow Drive, Mesquite, TX 75150, USA. 7.

KROHN Edward John, b. 14 Dec 1942, Detroit, MI, USA. Prof; Chmn. m. Johanna Akins, 23 Dec 1989. *Education:* BS, FL State Univ, 1964; AAB, Univ of FL, 1965; MEd, FL Atlantic Univ, 1967. *Appointments:* Peat Marwick Mitchell & Co, 1969-72; Miami Dade Comm Coll, 1972-. *Publications:* Noble's Catalog of Cachected Presidential Inaugural Covers; Eisenhower Philatelic Catalog; Basic Finance. *Membership:* Inst of Certified Financial Planners. *Honours:* Outstg Prof, 1967; Fac Senate Pres, 1982, 1983, 1985; Consortium Pres, 1984; Awdrd Southeast Banking Endowed teaching Chair, 1992; Vice-Chmn, Dade County School Employees Federal Credit Union Bd of Dirs. *Hobbies:* Philately; Nusmismatics. *Address:* Box 570699, Miami, FL 33257, USA.

KROHN Leena Elisabeth, b. 28 Feb 1947, Helsinki, Finland. Writer. 1 s. *Education:* Helsinki Univ. *Publications:* Vihrez vallankumous, 1970; Viimeinen kesavieras, 1974; Ihmiawn vaatteissa, 1976; Metsanpeitto, 1980; Donna Quijote, 1983; Tainaron, 1985; Oofirin kultaa, 1988; Rapina, 1989; Umbra, 1990. *Address:* Timonkuja 2, 00730 Helsinki, Finland.

KROHNE Heinz Walter, b. 5 Feb 1939, Herford. Prof. m. Sigrid Munster, 27 Apr 1973. *Education:* Dip in Pychology, Berlin, 1966; Dr rer nat, Marburg, 1971. *Appointments:* Asst 1970, Asst Prof 1972, Univ of Marburg; Prof of Psychology, Univ of Osnabruck, 1973; Prof of Psychology, Univ of Mainz, 1982. *Publications:* Angst und Angstverarbeitung, 1975; Theorien zur Angst, 2nd ed 1981; Achievement, Stress and Anxiety, 1982; Angstbewaltigung in Leistungssituationen, 1985; Attention and Avoidance, 1993. *Memberships:* Deutsche Gesellschaft fur Psychology; Am Psychological Assn; Int Soc for Rsch on Emotions; Stress and Anxiety Rsch Soc. *Address:* Johannes Gutenberg - Universitat, Psychologisches Institut, PO Box 3980, D-6500 Mainz 1, Germany.

KROL Joseph, b. 14 Jan 1911, Warsaw, Poland. Chartered Engr; Emeritus Edr; Lloyd's Underwriter. m. Evelyn Swingland, 15 Apr 1952. *Education:* MME, Tech Univ of Warsaw, 1937; PhD(ME), Univ of London, 1947. *Appointments:* Assoc Prof of Mech Engrng, Univ of Man, Can, 1951- 56; Prof of Indl and Systems Engrng, GA Inst of Tech, Atlanta, 1956-79; Prof Emeritus, GA Tech, 1980-. *Contributions to:* Articles on engrng and mgmt to profl journs. *Memberships:* FIMechE (UK); ASME, USA; Order of Engrs, Quebec; AAAS; AAUP; USS Naval Inst; Sigma Xi; Underwriting Mbr, Lloyd's of London, 1985-; Royal Overseas League, London. *Honours:* George Stephenson Prize, Instn of Mech Engrs, 1951; Centennial Medallion, GA Inst of Tech, 1987. *Hobbies:* Reading; Cruising. *Address:* 311 Tenth Street NW, Atlanta, GA 30318, USA. 7, 52, 132, 139.

KROLL Robert Melvyn, b. 15 June 1947, Montreal, Can. Speech Pathologist; Edr. 2 s. *Education:* BSc, Sir George Wiliams Univ, Montreal, 1969; MSc, McGill Univ, Montreal, 1971; PhD, Bowling Green Univ, OH, 1974. *Appointments:* Royal Victoria & Jewish Gen Hosp, Montreal, 1971; Proj Evaluator, Toledo, OH, 1972; Hd, Dept of Speech Pathology, Clarke Inst, 1974-; Univ of Toronto, 1975-; Hadassah Univ Hosp, Israel, 1984-85. *Publication:* Manual of Fluency Maintenance: A Guide for Ongoing Practice, 1986. *Memberships:* Can Assn of Speech-Lang Pathologists; Exec Coun 1975-77, Ont Assn of Speech-Lang Pathologists; Advsry Bd 1982-84, She'arim Hebrew Day Sch; Advsry Bd 1988-, Georgian Coll; Advsry Bd, Inst for Stuttering Treatment & Rsch; Int Fluency Assn. *Honours:* of the Ont Speech and Hearing Assn, 1982. *Hobbies:* Squash; Travel; Hiking; Camping; Nature; Photography. *Address:* Speech Pathology Department, Clarke Institute of Psychiatry, 250 College Street, Toronto, Ontario, Canada M5T 1R8. 142.

KROLOPP Wlodzimierz Jan, b. 24 June 1928, Zdunska, Wola, Poland. Prof; Rector. m. (1) Anna Barbara Max, 16 July 1957, (2) Teresa Barbara Blachnio, 31 Aug 1985, 2 s, 1 d. *Education:* ME, 1956; DE, 1972; DSc, 1980. *Appointments:* Jr Scholars 1954-60, Asst Prof 1967-74, Lodz Tech Univ; Advsr, Textile Inst, Lodz, 1956-60; Cons, Design Off of Synthetic Fibres, Lodz, 1956-62; Hd of Automatics Dept, Ctrl Tech Off of Paper Ind, Lodz, 1960-67; Assoc Prof, Hd of Elec Metrology Dept, Swietokrzyska Tech Univ, Radom, 1974-83; Prof, Hd of Chair of Elec Metrology 1983-, Rector 1989-, Lublin Tech Univ, Lublin. *Publications:* Author of 60 papers, articles and patents dealing with rsch of properties of paper, 1962-91; Measuring Methods and Instruments in Paper Industry, 1968; Research of Optical Properties of Paper, 1980; Foundation of Electrtechnics, 1982; Electrical Measuring Methods, 1985. *Memberships:* Maria Sklodowska-Curie Polish Soc for Radiation Rsch; Pres of Swietokrzyska Br 1976-81, Polish Cybernetics Soc; Lublin Scientific Soc; Solidarity 1980-; Pres 1989-90, Solidarity of Lublin Tech Univ. *Honours:* Gold Awd of Meritorious Railwayman, Min of Transp, 1976; Medal of Nat Educ, Min of Educ, 1979; Gold Cross of Merit, Pres of The Repub of Poland, 1990. *Hobbies:* Classical music; Sports; Tourism; Painting. *Address:* M Brzeskiej 11/15, 20-640 Lublin, Poland.

KRONEN Peter Heinrich, b. 17 Oct 1921, Rheydt, Germany. Prof. m. Elisabeth Ruland, 29 Apr 1950, 2 s, 1 d. *Education:* Dr phil, Cologne Univ. *Appointments:* Schtchr, 1947-64; Asst at Univ Level 1964-68; Lectr 1968-70; Professorships (Education), Freiburg, 1970-73, Bonn, 1973-75; Cologne, 1975-. *Publications:* Author of: 10 books, ed of K W E Mager; Collected Works, 10 vols, 1984-91; Co-author of 8 books; Articles in 2 Encyclopedias; about 60 articles in profl journs. *Contributor to:* Many newspapers, 1948-56. *Membership:* Rotary. *Interests:* Cultural sciencies especially Modern Media; History, especially 19th Century. *Address:* Adolf-Kolping Str 11, D 5020 Frechen, Germany. 52.

KROSS Jaan, b. 19 Feb 1920, Tallinn, Estonia. Writer. m. Ellen Hiob Niit, 13 Sept 1960, 2 s, 2 d. *Education:* Fac of Law, Univ of Tartu, 1944. *Career:* Estonian writer of prose and poetry; Transl; Critic. *Publications:* Between Three Plagues, I-IV, 1970-80; Celestial Stone, 1975; The Third Range of Mountains, 1975; The Tzar's Madman, 1978; The Novel of Rakvere, 1982; Professor Marten's Departure, 1984; Sailor Against the Wind, 1987; The Wikman Boys, 1988; Under Cleo's Eye. *Memberships:* Kalevala Soc, Finland; Hon Mbr, Finnish Writers' Union; Acad Soc of Native Lang, Estonia; Estonian PEN Club; Vice Chmn, Estonian Writers' Union; Acad Soc of Jurisprudence, Estonia. *Honours:* Eeva Joenpelto Prize, Finland, 1988; Best Translated Book of the Yr, France, 1988 for the French Transl of The Tzar's Madman; Hon Dr, Univ of Tartu, Estonia, 1988; Lit Prize, Amnesty Int, 1990; Univ of Helsinki, Finland, 1990. *Address:* Harju 1- 6, Tallinn, 200001 Estonia. 3, 139.

KRUEGER Robert Kenneth, b. 22 Nov 1941, Watertown, WI, USA. Dir. m. Margie E Leonard, 31 Aug 1963, 1 s, 3 d. *Education:* BS, IN Inst of Tech, Ft Wayne, 1963. *Appointments:* Sect Hd, Organic Chem, Jos Schlitz Brewing Co, Milwaukee, 1964-72; Rsch Grp Ldr, Krause Milling Co, Milwaukee, 1972-79; Quality Control Mgr, Armira Co, Sheboygan, WI & Bolivar, TN, 1979-85; Dir of Quality Assurance, Martha White Foods, Jackson, 1985-. *Memberships:* ACS; Am Assn of Cereal Chems; Am Corn Millers Fedn; MI Bean Shippers Assn. *Hobby:* Bass fishing. *Address:* 100 O'Hara Lane, Jackson, TN 38305, USA. 1, 7.

KRUESSELBERG Hans-Guenter, b. 31 May 1929, Wuppertal. Prof of Econ(s). m. Gisela geb Zeppenfeld, 10 June 1958, 1 s, 1 d. *Education:* Dipl, Volkswirt 1957, Dr rer pol 1962, Habilitation 1968, Univ Cologne. *Appointments:* Rsch: Investment Behaviour 1957-60, Asst 1960-68, Univ of Cologne; Guest Prof, 1968-69, Univ of Bochum; Guest Prof 1968-69, Full Prof 1969-, Dean 1971-72, 1989-90, Dep Mng Dir, Forschungsstelle fuer Systemvergleich 1973-, Dir, Inst fuer Sozial und Familienpolitik 1979-, Univ of Marburg. *Publications:* Marktwirtschaft und okonomische Theorie, 1969; Vermogen im Systemvergleich (ed), 1984; Markt, Staat und Solidaritat bei Adam Smith (co-ed), 1984; Verhaltenshypothesen - Familienzeitbudgets, 1986; Zur Transformation von Wirtschaftssystemen: Von der Sozialistischen Planwirtschaft zur Sozialen Marktwirtschaft (co-ed), ed 1991. *Memberships:* Chmn 1978-84, Coun for Advsrs for Family Policy, 1978-; Advsry Bd, Gesellschaft fur Sozialen Fortschritt, 1981-; Synod of the Protestant Ch of Kurhessen-Waldeck, 1986-; 5th Family Report Commn, 1991-; Am Econ Assn; Int Joseph A Schumpeter Soc; List Gesellschaft; Verein fur Socialpolitik. *Hobbies:* Literature; Tennis; Hiking. *Address:* Philipps- Universitat Marburg, Fachbereich Wirtschaftswissenschaften, Wirtschaftspolitik II, Am Plan 1, 3550 Marburg/Lahn, Germany. 43, 52, 92.

KRUGER Hans Peter Walter, b. 18 Mar 1954, Potsdam. Philos. *Education:* Dip Phil 1976, PhD 1980, Humboldt Univ; Phil Habilitation, Acad of Scis, East Berlin, 1987. *Appointments:* Asst Lectr, Humboldt Univ, Berlin, 1976; by polit order out of tchng and publishing in East Germany, 1976-79; Lectr, Colls of Econ(s) and Theatre Prod, Berlin, 1979-82; Rschr, Acad of Scis, East Berlin, 1981-91; Acad Prof for Philos of Humanities, 1989; Dir, Acad Inst for Philos & Hist of Sci, Berlin, 1990. *Publications:* Wissenschaft Das Problem ihrer Entwicklung (Ed), vol I 1987; Kritik der kommunikativen Vernunft, 1990; Objekt und Selbst Erkenntnis (Ed), 1991; Demission der Helden, 1992; Perspektivenwechsel, 1992. *Membership:* Fellow, Wissenschaftskolleg, Inst for Advanced Study, 1990-91; Fellow, Univ of Pittsburgh, PA, 1992-93. *Hobbies:* Modern or post-modern literature and movies; Classical and modern music; Multi-median performances. *Address:* Banschstr 72, 01035 Berlin, Germany.

KRUSE Lise Fiaux, b. 23 May 1947, Copenhagen, Denmark. Banker. m. Michel Fiaux, 22 Aug 1981, 1 s. *Education:* MA, Univ of Copenhagen, 1974; MBA, INSEAD, Fontainebleau, France, 1976. *Appointments:* EC Commn, Bruxelles, 1975; Chase Manhattan Bank, London, 1977-78; Hd of Fin Instns, Citibank, Copenhagen, 1978-81; Mktng Mgr, Credit Suisse, Zurich, 1981- 87; VP, Mitsubishi Bank, Zurich, 1987-. *Memberships:* Co Pres, INSEAD Alumni Assn; Past Pres, ZONTA; Bd Mbr, CH 700 Years. *Hobbies:* Sailing; Skiing; Opera. *Address:* Langackerstrasse 127, CH-8704 Herrliberg, Switzerland. 52, 132.

KRYCZYNSKI Selim Piotr, b. 15 Feb 1941, Wilno, Poland. Plant Pathologist; Acad Staff. m. Anna, 20 Jan 1976, 3 d. *Education:* MSc 1963, PhD 1969, Habilitation 1980, Warsaw Agricl Univ. *Appointments:* Rsch Asst, Rsch Inst of Pomology, Skierniewice, 1963-64; Dept of Plant Pathology, Warsaw Agricl Univ 1964-. *Publications:* Author of 2 handbooks; Co-author of 3 handbooks in plant pathology; Author of 35 rsch papers. *Memberships:* Leading Comm, Polish Phytopathological Soc; Leading Com, Int Plant Viroid Working Grp. *Honours:* of the Polish Acad of Sci, 1981; of the Min of Educ and Sci, 1983. *Hobbies:* Swimming; Music. *Address:* Madalinskiego St 39/43, Apt 1, 02-544 Warsaw, Poland.

KRZYMUSKI Jerzy, b. 26 May 1927, Warsaw, Poland. Scientific Worker of Agric. m. Izabela, 6 Aug 1950, 1 d. *Education:* Agricl Fac, Univ Wroclaw, Agricl Engr, 1950; Agricl Acad, Olsztyn, Dr Agricl Science, 1962; Prof 1979. *Appointments:* Profs Asst, Agricl Acad, Olsztyn, 1955- 69; Mgr of Dept, Cons, Rsch Ctr of Cultivars Test, Slupia Wielka, 1969-77. *Publications:* 227 works inclng 89 original creative works, 52 science and popular science articles, 17 chapts in handbooks, 28 train instrn, recommendations. *Memberships:* Scientific Coun: Inst of Soil Science and Plant Cultivation; Pulawy Rsch Ctr of Cultivars Testing, Slupia Wielka; Plant Breeding and Acclimatization Inst, Radzikow; Inst of Agricl Economy and Food Economy, Warsaw. *Honours:* Medal of Victory and Freedom, 1946; Medal of Grunwald, 1946; Honorary Medal of Agricultural Academy in Olsztyn, 1965; Golden Cross of Merit, 1973; Medal for Meritorious Worker of Agriculture, 1975. *Hobbies:* Bridge, Tennis, Heraldry, Skiing. *Address:* Mickiewicza St 20-18 a, Warsaw, Poland.

KŠICOVÁ Danuše, b. 26 Apr 1932, Brno, Czechoslovakia. Prof of Slavic Langs and Lit. m. Dr Petrov Evzen, 29 Apr 1977, 1 d. *Education:* Brno Univ, Fac of Arts, 1951-56; PhD 1969; CSc 1970 DrSc 1991. *Appointments:* Masaryk Univ in Brno, Czechoslovakia, Fac of Arts, Dept Slavic Lits: Lectr 1956, Sr Rsch Asst 1961, Asst Prof 1990. *Publications:* Books in Czech: Russian Poetry in F Tabortsky's Interpretation, 1979; The Romantic and Neoromantic Long Poems, 1983; Russian Literature of 19th and Early 20th Century, 1988; In Russian: Russian Poetry at the Turn of the Twentieth Century, 1990. *Memberships:* Lit Assn; Assn of Russian Studies; Assn of Slavonic Studies; Czech Comm of Slavists; Participated in int symposia, congresses, lecturing in Soviet Union, GB, USA, Germany, Austria, Poland, Hungary, Yugoslavia. *Honours:* Silver Plaque of

Brno Univ, 1982; Memorial Plaque of Brno Skauting, 1990. *Hobbies:* Lit, Art, Music, Theatre, Swimming, Skiing. *Address:* E Machove 37, Brno 16, 616 00, Czechoslovakia.

KUBRYK David, b. 5 Apr 1912, Cluj, Romania. Can Pub Servant. m. Marion Willey, 1 s, 2 d. *Education:* Liceul Mihaiu Viteazul, Bucharest, BA 1929; Ecole des Sciences, Rouen, France, BSc 1931; Ecole de Medecine, Rouen; Faculte de Medecine, Paris; Univ de Bologna, Italy, MD 1936; Univ of Montreal, DPH 1956. *Appointments:* Med Off (Pt-time), London Heathrow Airport, 1977-; Med Off, Can Embassy, Paris, France; Gen prac UK; var positions with Dept Nat Hlth and Welfare; Med Off i/c Med Servs, Hlth and Welfare, Can, Can High Commn, New Delhi, India; Lt Col RCAMC (ret'd); served in WWII with French Army, For Legion and Brit Army. *Memberships:* Brit Med Assn; Royal Soc of Hlth; Can Pub Hlth Assn; Assn Mil Surgs of US; Def Med Assn Can; Assn des med de langue francaise. *Address:* 15 Colonel Butler Court, RR3, Grp 14, NOTL, Ontario, Canada LOS 1JO.

KUC Joseph A, b. 24 Nov 1929, New York City, USA. Prof, Dept of Plant Pathology, Univ of Kentucky. m. Karola Maywald, 17 July 1991, 1 s, 2 d. *Education:* Purdue Univ, BS, Biochem 1951, MS Biochem 1953, PhD Biochem 1955. *Appointments:* Purdue Univ, Asst Prof 1955, Assoc Prof 1959, Prof 1963; Univ of Kentucky, Prof 1974-. *Publications:* 24 book chapts; 215 publs; 40 PhD Students; 11 MS Students. *Memberships:* American Chem Soc; American Soc Plant Physiologists; American Phytopathological Soc, Fellow; American Soc for Biochem and Molecular Biol; Phytochem Soc; Sigma Xi; American Inst Chems, Fellow; Kentucky Acad of Science; NY Acad of Science. *Honours:* Medal for Outstanding Achievement in International Plant Protection; Fulbright Fellow; Alexander von Humboldt Senior Scientist; Awards: Distinguished Alumni Professor, University of Kentucky; Sturgill Award; Campbell Award; Thomas Poe Cooper Award. *Hobbies:* Gardening; Hiking; Conversation. *Address:* Department of Plant Pathology, University of Kentucky, Lexington, KY 40546, USA. 28, 50.

KUCZYNSKI Maciej Czeslaw, b. 15 Apr 1929, Warsaw, Poland. Freelance Writer. m. Barbara Schiller, 4 Oct 1976, 1 s. *Education:* Arch Dept, Cracow Inst of Technology, Engr Arch. 1953. *Appointments:* Arch Design Studios, Cracow, 1952-56; Mgr Scientific Expeds, Polish Acad of Sciences, 1956-57. 1963-75. *Publications:* Fiction novels: Alarm at the Foot of Andes, 1961; Goodbye Sun, 1962; White Palms, 1962; Stars of the Dry Steppe, 1965; Atlantis, Island of Fire, 1967; Catastrophe, 1968; Cold Coast, 1969; Kayum, 1970; The Robbery, 1972; The Winner, 1976; The Globetrotter, 1976; The Invention, 1978; The Crash Helmet, 1978; The Year of the Ram, 1989; Non-fiction: The Abyss, 1972; Tropic of Dinosaur, 1977; The Mysterious Plateau, 1979; Where Children Come From, 1986; Worshippers of the Serpent, 1990. *Memberships:* Polish Alpinists Assn, Hon Mbr; The Explorers Club, NY; Union of Polish Authors. *Honours:* Polish Scout Literary Award, 1976; UNESCO's International Board on Books for Young Men List of Honour, 1978; Polish Prime Minister's Literary Award, 1980. *Hobbies:* Mountaineering, ancient petroglyphs. *Address:* Woronicza 14 m.17, 02-625 Warsaw, Poland.

KUEHR Gerd, b. 28 Dec 1952, Luggau, Austria. Composer, Conductor. *Education:* Music Acad Mozarteum, Salzburg, Austria: Dips: Music Educ 1976, Conducting 1978, Composition 1979; Univ of Salzburg, Mag.Phil 1978; Music Acad, Cologne, Germany, Diploma Composition 1983; Var courses in conducting with H Swarowsky and S Celibidache, composition and piano. *Appointments:* Coach, Opera House, Cologne 1981-84; Graz 1984-86; Tchr, Music Acad, Graz, Austria, 1985; Artistic Dir, Youth Music Festival, Deutschlandsberg, Styrian Autumn, 1987-89; Tchr, Univ of Graz, 1988-90; Composer and Conductor in var

countries. *Creative Works:* For String Quartet, 1980-81; Lamento E Conforto for Orch, 1983; Walt Whitman for President, 1984; Stallerhof, Opera on play by F X Kroetz, 1986-87; ESO ES for orch, 1989; Palimpsest, 1989-90; Concertare for solo clarinet and orch, 1990-91. *Honours:* Foerderungspreis fuer Musik des Landes Kaernten, 1979; Oesterreichisches Staatsstipendium fuer Komponisten, 1984, 88; Foerderungspreis fuer Musik des Bundesministeriums fuer Unterricht und Kunst, 1990. *Address:* Dietersdorf 1, A-8142 Wundschuh, Austria.

KUHN Douglas Scott, b. 29 May 1956, Decatur, Indiana, United States of America. Psych Techn m. Susan Elaine Bradbury, 26 Sept 1981, 2 s, 1 d. *Education:* Assoc of Science, Vincennes Univ, IN, 1976; Faith Bapt Bible College, IA, BS; Fed Law Enforcement Trng Ctr, GA; US Army, 1977-80. *Appointments:* Fed Protective Serv, 1980-84; Prin, Fin Grp, 1984-85; IA Luth Hosp, 1986-. *Creative Works:* Formation and beginning of Four K Concepts Inc. Company developing equipment to be used in Mental Hlth Units. Pres, Four K Concepts. *Memberships:* IA Police Offs Assn; Evangelical Tchr Trng Assn; Former Mbr of Ctrl TX Peace Offs Assn. *Honours:* Letters of Commendation, US Army and Fed Protective Serv. *Hobbies:* Golf, Gardening. *Address:* 1606 N W Fourth Street, Ankeny, IA 50021, USA.

KUJUMDZIEVA Svetlana Emilova, b. 1 Aug 1949, Sofia, Bulgaria. Musicologist, History of Music. m. Alexander Angelov Kujumdziev, 22 May 1972, 1 d. *Education:* State School of Music, Sofia; Fac of Music Theory, Bulgarian State Conservatoire, 1968-72. *Appointments:* Since 1972 working on problems of Medieval Bulgarian and Balkan music at Inst of Music by Bulgarian Acad of Sciences; 1988 Inst of Art. *Publications:* Over 30 publs in Bulgarian and For Eds, Poland, Germany, Greece, Hungary; Books: The Rila Monastery School of Singing in the First Half of the 19th Century; Vocative verses in Balkan Singing Prac from 14th to Early 19th Century; Music of Bulgarian National Revival. *Memberships:* Union of Bulgarian Composers; Union of Bulgarian Scientists. *Honours:* Youth Award for Scientific Projects, 1974; Defended PhD Thesis and became Dr, 1980, Reader, 1991; Award for Second Competition of Young Researchers, 1980; Award of Bulgarian Jubilee Comm 13 Centuries of Bulgaria, 1981; Award of Bulgarian Radio, 1983; Award of Bulgarian Acad of Sciences, 1983. *Hobbies:* Music, Res Work, Travelling. *Address:* Dunay 35, Sofia 1000, Bulgaria.

KUKHAR Valery Pavlovich, b. 26 Jan 1942, Kiev, Ukraine. Scientist; Dir and Hd of Lab of Fine Organic Synthesis, Kiev. m. Miryan Nataly, 1 Oct 1964, 1 s, 1 d. *Education:* Chem Technol Inst, Dipl Ing, 1963; Inst of Organic Chem, 1963-66. Cand of Chem Science 1967, Dr of Chem Science, 1973. *Appointments:* Inst of Organic Chem, Ukrainian Acad of Science, Scientist 1966-68, Sr Scientist 1968-74, Head of Lab, 1974-84; Acad of Science, Ukrainian SSR, Kiev 1978-88; Academician-Sec, Hd of Chem Div, VP 1988-; Bioorganic Chem Dept, Inst of Organic Chem, UKR Acad Science, Head 1984-87; Inst of Bioorganic Chem and Petrochem, Dir and Hd of Lab of Fine Organic Synthesis, Kiev, 1987-. *Publications:* 450 publs in phosphorous and fluorine-organic chem and organic synthesis; 50 USSR patents and 2 monographs. *Memberships:* Corres Mbr, UKR Acad Science, 1978-85; Pro of Chem, 1979-; Academician of Ukrainian Acad of Science, 1985-. *Honour:* A Kiprianov Prize in Organic Chemistry of UKR Academy of Science, 1989. *Hobbies:* Gardening, Reading. *Address:* Stretinskaya Str 17 F 34, Kiev 25, Ukraine.

KUKKONEN Pertti Tapani, b. 26 Dec 1931, Hiitola, Finland. Prof, Mng Dir, Pellervo Econ Rsch Inst, Espoo, Finland m. Taina Tellervo Tapanila, 1 Nov 1958, 2 s. *Education:* Univ of Helsinki, MA 1959, PhD (Econ) 1968. *Appointments:* Mathn, Post and Telegraph Admin,

1959-60; Rsch Fellow, Bank of Finland Inst of Econ Rsch 1960, Hd of Dept 1969, Dir of Inst 1970, Dir of Planning 1973-82; Mng Dir, Pellervo Econ Rsch Inst, 1982-; Docent (Lect), Helsinki Univ, 1971-, Turku Schl of Econs, 1972-83. *Memberships:* The Econometric Soc; European Econ Assn; Finnish Econ Assn, Chmn 1981; Rsch Coun for Social Sciences of Acad of Finland, 1986-91. *Honour:* Knight First Class of the Order of the White Rose of Finland 1977. *Hobby:* Jogging. *Address:* Pellervo Economic Research Institute, Revontulentie 8A, 02100 Espoo, Finland. 52.

KULA (Jan) Marcin, b. 24 Mar 1943, Warsaw, Poland. Histn and Sociologist m. Malgorzata Ciszecka, 2 Dec 1972, 1 s, 1 d. *Education:* Univ of Warsaw, MA Hist 1965, MA Sociology 1967; Inst of Hist, Polish Acad of Sciences, Warsaw, PhD 1968, Habil 1976. *Appointments:* Inst of Hist, Polish Acad of Sciences, Warsaw, 1968-90; Prof, Warsaw Univ, 1990-. *Publications:* Beginnings of the Black Slavery in Brazil, 1970; The 1933 Revolution at Cuba, 1978; The Brazilians of Polish Descent, 1981; The History of Brazil, 1987; The National and the Revolutionary, 1991 (all in Polish). *Memberships:* Polish Histl Assn; Polish Sociological Assn. *Honours:* Polityka Award, 1974; Znaniecki Awards, 1980, 84; Halecki Award, 1988; Swastek Award, 1990. *Address:* University of Warsaw, Institute of History, Krakowskie Przedmiescie 26-28, 00-325 Warsaw, Poland.

KULAKOWSKI Andrzej, b. 10 Aug 1929, Warsaw, Poland. Prof of Oncological Surg m. Barbara Bolinska-Kulakowska, 1 s. *Education:* Stefan Batory, Warsaw, Baccalaurate Degree 1948; Med Acad, Warsaw, MD 1953; Dr Sci Med, 1964, Dozent 1969, Prof Oncological Surg 1978. *Employment:* Inst of Oncology, Dept of Surg, Warsaw, 1953; Municipal Hosp, Gen Surg, Warsaw, 1955-56; Churchill Hosp, Dept Plastic Surg, Oxford, England, 1960-61; Roswell Pk Mem Inst, USA, 1965-66. *Publications:* 136 publs in field of oncological surg; co-author 6 books. *Memberships:* Polish Surgs Assn; Surg Oncology Sect of PSA; Polish Oncological Soc; Brit Assn Plastic Surgs; Pan-Am Med Assn; Bulgarian Oncological Assn; European Assn for Cancer Rsch; European Soc of Surg Oncology Exec Comm Mbr, Hon Sec; European Schl of Oncology; Polish Fndn of ESO; WHO Melanoma Project. *Hobbies:* Tourism, Sailing, Skiing. *Address:* Cancer Center of the Maria Sklodowska-Curie Institute, 15 Wawelska Street, 00-973 Warsaw, Poland.

KULCSAR-SZABO Erno, b. 27 Mar 1950, Debrecen, Hungary. Prof and Hd of Dept (Theory of Lit) m. Eniko Varnay, 22 Feb 1973, 1 s, 1 d. *Education:* Kossuth Lajos Univ, Debrecen, BA 1973, MA 1978; Hungarian Acad of Sciences, PhD 1987. *Appointments:* Inst of Lit Studies of the Hungarian Acad of Sciences, 1978-84; Univ of Bayreuth, 1984-88; Hungarian Acad of Sciences, 1988-90; Janus Pannonius Univ, Pecs, 1990-. *Publications:* A zavarbaejto elbeszeles, 1984 (The Surprising Narration), Mualkotas szoveg hatas, 1986 (Work Text Effect). *Memberships:* Assn Hungarian Authors; Int Hungarian Philological Assn; Ed Bd, Literatura, Mng Ed. *Hobbies:* Driving, Travelling. *Address:* MTA Irodalomtudomanyi Intezet, Menesi ut 11-13, H-1118 Budapest, Hungary.

KULDANOVA Pavlina, b. 16 Mar 1967, Frydek-Mistek. Student of English. m. Radek Kuldan, 9 Sept 1989. *Education:* Philos Rac, Univ of Masaryk, Brno, Chzch, 1985-90; Grad in Czech and Russian Lang and Lit, 1990. *Appointments:* Tchr, Czech and Hist, Hg Sch in Ostrava, 1991; Mgr and Eng Lang Tchr, Lang Agy, 1991-92, presently, Student of Eng in London, 1992. *Publication:* Roman Jakobson and his relationship with Czechoslovakia. *Honours:* Univ Masaryk Prize for Res, 1989; Czech-Russian Assn in Prague for Res, 1989. *Hobbies:* Foreign languages; History; Music; Sport; Reading. *Address:* Oracova 11, 70500 Ostrava 3, Czechoslovakia.

KULINKOVICH Arnold Yevgenyevich, b. 8 May 1932, Moscow, USSR. Geophysicist m. Logvinova Tamara Ivanovna, 20 Oct 1956, 3 d. *Education:* Graduate Moscow Geological Survey Inst, Geophysical Fac, 1955; Dip Mining Engr-Geophysicist; Dr Tech Sciences, 1970; Prof 1982. *Appointments:* Scientific Worker, All-Union Geophysical Inst, Moscow, 1955-63; Ukrainian Geological Inst, Geophysical Br, Kiev, 1963-73; Chief of Dept, Inst of Cybernetics, Kiev, 1974-78; Chief of Dept, Ukrainian Geological Inst, 1979-. *Publications:* Over 200 scientific publs in geophysics, geology, cybernetics, maths, phys, logic, heuristic pedagogy. *Membership:* Co- chmn, Ukrainian Br Assn Prognosis and Cycles. *Honours:* Anniversary Medals for Distinguished Labour, centenary of Lenin's birthday, 1970; City of Kiev's 1500 years, 1982; Medal Veteran of Labour, 1985. *Hobbies:* Gardening, Reading, Collaboration of Science and Relig. *Address:* Str Revutsky 29 B Ap 44, 253068 Kiev, Ukraine.

KULKARNI Arun Digambar, b. 14 Dec 1947, Poona, India. Assoc Prof. m. Vasanti, 15 Oct 1978, 1 s, 2 d. *Education:* BE Electronics and Comm, 1969; MTech, Elec Engrng, 1971; PhD, Elec Engrng, 1978. *Appointments:* Design Engr, SERC, 1971-73; Sr Scientist, NRSA, India, 1977-84; Res Assoc, VPI, Blackburg, 1984-85; Vis Fac, Univ of South, MS, 1985-86; Asst Prof, Univ of Texas, Tyler, 1986-91, Assoc Prof, 1991-. *Publications:* Two chapts in books; 30 papers in jrnls and/or proceedings. *Memberships:* Inst of Elec Engrng; Assn Computing Machinery; Int Soc of Neural Networks. *Honour:* Fulbright Fellowship Award for post doctoral studies, 1984. *Hobbies:* Reading, Chess, Swimming. *Address:* 5105 Old Bullard Road E-6, Tyler, TX 75703, USA. 7, 15.

KULL Bryan Paul, b. 23 Jan 1960, Newark, New Jersey, USA. Sales Exec. m. Lindsay P, 26 Nov 1983, 1 s. *Education:* BS Univ of NH, 1982; MBA Southern IL Univ, 1986. *Appointments:* Territory Mgr, Warner- Lambert Co, 1982-83; Key Account Mgr, Clorox Co, 1984-85; Dist Mgr, Alberto Culver Co, 1986-89; Area Mgr, Schering-Plough Corp, 1989-90, Nat Sales Mgr, 1991-. *Memberships:* Assn MBA Execs; Soc for Advancement of Mgmt. *Honour:* Pres's Club, Schering-Plough Corp, 1991. *Hobbies:* Golf, Tennis, Skiing, Wines. *Address:* 16 Ranney Road, Long Valley, NJ 07853, USA.

KULL Ulrich Otto, b. 26 July 1938, Stuttgart Bad Cannstatt, Germany. Prof of Biology. m.Marga Buehler, 16 Jan 1981. *Education:* Scientific Exam for tchr 1962; Dr.rer.nat 1964; Habil 1969. *Appointments:* Asst, 1964-69; Univ of Stuttgart, Lectr, 1969-77, Prof 1977-78; Prof and Ldr of Dept of Plant Physiology, 1978-. *Publications:* Books on evolution, 1977, evolution of man, 1979, genetics, co-author, 1980, biology, co-author, 1989, general botany, 1993. *Memberships:* Gesellschaft fur Naturkunde in Wuettemberg, Chmn 1983-89, & since 1992; sev profl orgs. *Hobbies:* Geology, Archeology, Hist. *Address:* Biologisches Institut, University of Stuttgart, Pfaffenwaldring 57, D-7000 Stuttgart 80. Germany.

KUMAMARU Takahiro, b. 28 Mar 1936, Japan. Prof. Dept of Chem, Faculty of Science, Hiroshima Univ, Japan. m. Taeko Shinagawa, 15 May 1966, 2 d. *Education:* Kyoto Univ, Japan, BSc 1959; Hiroshima Univ, Japan, DSc 1969. *Appointments:* Chief Rsch Team, Rsch Inst, Mitsui Chem Ind Co Ltd, 1960-65; Hiroshima Univ: Asst Prof, Dept Chem, Fac of Science, 1965-68, Instr, 1968-69, Assoc Prof, 1969-76, Assoc Prof, Dept Environmental Science, Fac Integrated Arts & Sciences, 1980-86, Prof 1976-80, Prof, Dept Chem, Fac of Science, 1986-; Rsch Assoc, Biophysics Rsch Lab, Harvard Med Schl, USA, 1978-79. *Publications:* Co-author, Environmental Science, 1983; Ed. Co-author, Current Atomic Absorption Spectrometry, 1989. *Contributions:* Analytical Chem Articles to profl jrnls (130 papers); Assoc Ed, Bull of Chem Soc of Jpn, Tokyo, 1983-85; Analytical Science, Tokyo, 1989-91. *Memberships:* American Chem, Soc, USA; Japan Soc for Analytical Chem; Chem Soc of Japan; Spectroscopical Soc Japan. *Address:* Department of Chemistry, Faculty of Science, Hiroshima University, 1-3-1 Kagamiyama, Higashi-Hiroshima 724, Japan. 52.

KUMAR Devendra, b. 14 Sept 1944, Delhi, India. Associate Professor, Rsch. m. Usha Srivastava, 20 Nov 1969, 1 s. *Education:* Delhi Univ: BSc (Hons) 1963, MSc (Physics) 1965, PhD (Physics) 1976. *Appointments:* Asst Lectr, Physics, K M Coll, Delhi, 1965-68; Lectr 1968-78; Post-Doct Rsch Assoc, LA State Univ, 1978-85, Asst Prof 1986-91, Assoc Prof 1991-. *Publications:* About 30 rsch papers in scientific jrnls; 1 patent. *Memberships:* IEEE, Sr Mbr; Optical Soc of America; American Chem Soc. *Hobbies:* Electronics, Chess, Cricket. *Address:* Dept of Chemistry, Louisiana State University, Baton Rouge, LA 70803, USA. 7, 54.

KUMOR Boleslaw S, b. 1 Dec 1925, Szymanowice, Poland. Professor of Catholic Univ of Lublin, Poland; Catholic Priest. *Education:* ThM 1951; ThD 1954; MSH 1957; Docent 1959; Extraordinary Prof 1969; Ordinary Prof 1978. *Appointments:* Prof, Church Hist, Theol Inst Tarnow, 1957-60; Prof, Cath Mod Hist, Cath Univ of Lublin, 1960-91; Prof, Church Hist, Pont Acad Theol, Krakow, 1967-91. *Publications:* Historia Kosciota, vols 1-4 1974-79, vols 1-7 1972-91. *Memberships:* sev profl orgs; European Science Fndn. *Honour:* Pratat Papieshi Monsignior. *Hobby:* Reading -- histl books. *Address:* Katolichi Uniwevstytet Lubelshi, Al Ractawichie 14, Lublin, Poland.

KUNAEV Dzhavdat. b. 7 Mar 1927, Bashkir Autonomous, Soviet Socialist Republic. Mining Engr; Geologist. m. Raisa Iskhakovna, 2 Oct 1955, 1 s, 1 d. *Education:* Kazakh Mining and Metall Inst, Alma-Ata, 1945-50; Kazakh SSR Acad of Sciences, Cand of Science, Geology, 1953, DSc 1974. *Appointments:* Kazakh Mining and Metall Inst, 1945-50, Jr Rsch Worker, 1951-56, Sr Rsch Worker, 1957-64; Chief, Sect Mine and Quarry Geology, Kazakh Rsch Inst of Mineral Raw Materials, 1964-69; Assoc Prof Kazakh Polytechnic Inst, 1970-74; Acad Sec, Inst of Geological Sciences, Kazakh Acad of Sciences, 1974-76; Chief, Sect Sedimentary Ore-info, 1976-79; Hd of Chair of Hist and Reg Geology, Kazakh Polytechnic Inst, 1979-. *Publications:* Minerals of Kazakhstan, 1956; Geology and Minerals of Cuba, 1991. *Memberships:* All-Union Sect Metallogeny of Pre-Cambrian, Acad of Sciences USSR; Nat Comm of Geologists, USSR, Moscow; Scientific Coun in ore-formation, Inst of Geological Sciences, Acad of Sciences of Kazakh SSR. *Honours:* USSR Govt Award Labour Veteran, Moscow, 1987; Honoured Scientist Medal, Alma-Ata, 1984. *Hobbies:* Sociology, Culture and Pol. *Address:* F 35 109b Lenin Avenue, Alma-Ata, Russia.

KUNNAPU Vilen, b. 30 June 1948, Tallinn, Estonia. Archt, Installation Artist, Philosopher, Essayist, Poet. *Education:* Archtl Dept, Estonian State Univ, Dipl 1971. *Appointments:* Archt, EKE Project Planning Inst, 1971-90; Estab w Archt Ain Padrik pvte off Kunnapu & Padrik Ltd; Freelance Artist, Writer and Essayist; Vis Prof, Estonian State Univ of Art, Univ of Oulu, Finland, 1991; Vis Lectr, Tech High Schl, Zurich, 1989; Chief Architect of City of Tallin, 1992. *Contributions to:* mags and books; Exhibs in Tallinn, Moscow, USA, Paris, Stockholm, Helsinki, Zurich, Kiel and Leeuwarden, Holland. Main Bldgs: Sanatorium, Parnu, Estonia; Estonian Embassy, Moscow; Rural clubs w offs, Polva, Peetri, Valgu, Kehra and Laekveere; Mercedes-Benz Ctr, Tallinn; Estonian Pavillion in Exhib of 11 cities, 11 nations, Leeuwarden, Holland. *Honours:* First Prize, Sanatorium in Parnu, Estonia, 1975 (built 1986); Honorable Mention, Int Comp for Arctic Ctr, Rovaniemi, Finland, 1984; State Award of Arch, Estonia; Second Prize, Int Comp for W Coast Gateway, Los Angeles, USA, 1988; Shared First Prize in Nordic International Competition for New Town for 30,000 people near Helsinki, 1992. *Hobbies:* Poetry, Music, Films, Walking, Sleeping. *Address:* Raua 8-3, Tallinn EE0010, Estonia.

KUNZ Michelle B (Riemann), b. 9 June 1955, Hoisington, Kansas, USA. Asst Prof, Clothing and Textiles, Fashion Merchandising. m. dale L Kunz, 22 Nov 1974. *Education:* KS Wesleyan Univ, BA 1977; KS State Univ, MS 1987; Univ of TN, PhD Cand. *Appointments:* Design Cons, Interiors Unlimioted, 1980-83; Dept Chair, Fashion Merchandising, The Brown Mackie Coll, 1983-87; Asst Prof, Morehead State Univ, 1988-. *Creative Works:* Owner, Operator, The Image Manager. *Memberships:* American Collegiate Retailing Assn; Americanm Home Econs Assn; American Assn of Textile Chenms & Colorists; Int Textile and Apparel Assn; KY Home Econs ASssn; Nat Assn of Female Execs. *Hobbies:* Music, Piano and Organ, Computers. *Address:* 69 Cardinal Way, Mount Sterling, KY 40353, USA. 2, 15, 138.

KURCYUSZ Helena Maria, b. 10 May 1914, Sandomierz, Poland. Town Planner, Archt. div. *Education:* Polytechnic, Warsaw; M.Engr Archt Dip, 1939. *Appointments:* Prison in Warsaw and Nazi Concentration Camps, 1942-45; 1945 settled in Szczecin as Town Planner Archt rebldg 74 towns ruined in war in Province of Szczecin. *Memberships:* SARP (Polish Archts Assn) of UTA (Int Union of Archts of TUP (Polish Town Planners Soc). The Club 13 Muses and Tourists Soc. *Honours:* Two Grand Prizes in contests of projects of living districts of Szczecin, 1972, 74; Polonia Restituta Order for professional and social life and activity in Szczecin, 1975; First Prize, writing memory on profl and social work in Szczecin. *Hobbies:* Water- colour painting (portraits, landscapes, arch, flowers), on invitation of Mrs Sue Ryder in England painting English and Scottish landscapes, Mountain touring, Yachting, Travelling, Short gun shooting (championship), two displays of paintings in Szczecin, 1970, 80. *Address:* ul Wyspianskiego 7, 70- 497 Szczecin, Poland.

KURIATA Czeslaw, b. 29 Apr 1939, Marcelowka, Poland. Author. m. Ludmila Janusewicz, 24 Apr 1974, 1 s, 1 d. *Education:* MA Polish Lit and Lang, A Mickiewicz Univ, Poznan. *Appointments:* Mgr, Lit Unit, local broadcasting stn, Koszalin, 1965-83; Staff Mbr, monthly Pobrzeze, 1969- 75; Jrnlst wkly Morze i Ziemia, 1985-87. *Publications:* Six books of poetry: The Sky Levelled with the Earth; Five books stories and selected short stories, 2 long poems, novel Gallop to the Big Forest, 1965; 2 children's books. *Memberships:* Assn of Polish Writers, Chmn Koszalin Dept; Mbr main staff Warsaw Assn of Authors ZAIKS. *Honours:* Many awards; Poznan Poetry November for best poetry book of 1961; Two prizes from National Radio Committee for radio dramas, 1966, 82; Two prizes for Red Rose for poetry, 1960, 63; Prize of Lodz Spring for poetry, 1960, 62; Prize of a monthly Pobrzeze and others. *Hobbies:* Lonely pondering over the sense of human existence, Scientific lit concerning life beyond the earth. *Address:* ul Emilii Plater 2c-33, PO Box 79, 75-348 Koszalin 9, Poland.

KURITA Chushiro, b. 16 Apr 1910, Shitaya-ku, Tokyo, Japan. Pres, Gakujutsu Bunken Shuppankai. m. 8 Dec 1947, 1 s. *Education:* Elec Engrng Dept, Schl of Science and Engrng, Waseda Univ, Tokyo, B.Engrng, 1935. *Appointments:* Elec Dept, Special Engrng Schl, Waseda Univ, 1945, Lectr, Elec Dept of Second Schl of Sci and Engrng (Asst Prof), 1959, Elec Dept of First Schl of Science and Engrng, 1968, Retd 1981; Lectr, Elec Dept of Schl of Engrng, Kokushikan Univ, 1977-89. *Publications:* Thermo- Electrical Refrigerator (Patent), 1960; Thermo-Electrical Engineering (in Japanese), 1963; Principle of Contact relating to Solids (in Japanese), 1977; Kanze School Suutai Programs, A Combinative Table (Japanese Table), 1978; Principle of Contact relating to Solids (in English), 1979; Electronic Contact Properties relating to Solid States (in Japanese), 1979; Essay Then and Then (in Japanese), 1981; The Principles of Electron Theory (The True Values of e, IC and 1A and The Others) (in Japanese), 1987. *Memberships:* Inst of Elec Engrng of Japan, Life Mbr; The Electro-Chem Soc of Japan. *Hobbies:* Kanze Schl

No Song, Camera. *Address:* 6-19 Kohinata 2-Chome Bunkyo ku, Tokyo, Japan 112. 52.

KURNIK Wlodzimierz, b. 20 Nov 1950, Poland. Scientist, Univ Tchr, Prof of Mech. m. Ewa Kosiarek, 13 July 1974, 2 s. *Education:* Warsaw Univ of Technology, MSc 1974, PhD 1978, DSc 1988. *Appointment:* Inst of Machine Design Fundamentals, Warsaw Univ of Technology, 1977-. *Publications:* Over 40 papers on stability and vibration problems in mech systems w applications in machine bldg, 1980-91. *Memberships:* Gesellschaft fur Angewandte Mathematik und Mechanik, Germany; Polish Soc of Theoretical and Applied Mech. *Honours:* Polish Min of Educ Award for Habil, 1989; Polish Min of Educ Award for the book Tasks on Theory of Vibrations (in Polish), 1990. *Hobbies:* Tourism, Hiking, Cycling. *Address:* Institute of Machine Design Fundamentals. Warsaw University of Technology, Narbutta 84, 02-524 Warsaw, Poland.

KURODA Tatsuaki, b. 11 Mar 1955, Shirakawa, Japan. Assoc Prof of Econs, Nagoya Univ, Japan. m. Junko Otani, 18 Oct 1980, 2 d. *Education:* Kyoto Univ, BS 1978, MS 1980; Univ of PA, USA, PhD 1989. *Appointments:* City Planner, Japan Reg Dev Corp, 1980-85; Asst Prof, Nagaoka Univ of Technology, 1984-86. Kyoto Univ, 1985-89, Toyohashi Univ of Technology, 1989- 91. *Publications:* Book: City Planning with Amenity, 1982; Articles: Location of Public Facilities, Jrnl of Reg Science, 1989; Provision of Residential Infrastructure, Studies in Reg Science, 1989. *Memberships:* American Econ Soc; Reg Science Assn Int. *Honours:* Graduate Prize, Regional Science Department of University of Pennsylvania, 1987; Grants for Scientific Research, Ministry of Education, Japan, 1989, 91. *Hobbies:* Swimming, Applications of microeconomics. *Address:* Takamoridai 4- 4-18, Kasugai 487, Japan. 52.

KUROSAWA Kazukiyo, b. 26 July 1926, Chingtao, China. Prof. m. 24 Jan 1956, 1 d. *Education:* B.Econ 1953; M.Econ 1955; DSc 1971. *Appointments:* Rsch Fellow, Fisheries Inst, Japan, 1955-56; Prof of Productivity Science, Tokyo Inst of Technology, 1956-85, Prof Emeritus, 1985; Prof, The Univ of the Air, Japan, 1988-. *Publications:* Measuring Producivity, 1984; Productivity Measurement and Management, 1991. *Memberships:* Prof Emeritus, Beijin Metall Mgmt Inst, Beijin; Prof, Northeast Univ of Technology. *Honours:* Prize of Japan Brewery Inst, 1969; Acad Prize, Japan Industrial Mgmt Assn, 1976; Science Prize, Tezima Fndn, 1977. *Address:* 4 cho-me, 18-6, Jyo-Myo-Ji, Kamakura City 248, Japan.

KUSCHINSKY Klaus b. 9 Oct 1939, Berlin, Germany. Prof of Pharmacology and Toxicology. *Education:* Med and Biochem; Graduated in Med, Univ of Freiburg, Germany, 1963; MD, Free Univ of Berlin, 1965. *Appointments:* Rsch Asst in Pharmacology: Univ of Kiel 1966-68, Max Planck Inst for Expmtl Med, Gottingen 1969-83; Prof of Pharmacology and Toxicology, Univ of Marburg, 1983-. *Memberships:* Soc of Neuroscience, For Mbr; European Behavioural Soc, Comm Mbr 1986-88; Coll Int Neuro-- Psychopharmacology. *Hobbies:* Lit, Hist. *Address:* Institute for Pharmacology and Toxicology, Faculty of Pharmacy, University of Marburg, Ketzerbach 63, D-W 3550 Marburg, Germany. 1.

KUSENBERGER Sherry Lynne, b. 1 Nov 1967, San Antonio, TX, USA. Student. *Education:* BS Speech (Hons), Univ of TX, Austin, 1991; presently working on BS Educ. *Appointments:* Internship in PR, Southwest Meth Hosp, 1991; Internship in Dev, Univ of TX Austin, 1991. *Publication:* Learning Disabled Children Can Become Our Future Resources, Texas PTA Communicator, 1991-92. *Membership:* Women in Communications Inc; Gamma Beta Phi; Phi Beta Kinsolving. *Honours:* Univ hons. *Hobbies:* Int Travel, Acting; Dancing; Singing, Sailing, Rowing, Needlework,

Histl Preservation, Brit Hist. *Address:* 2719 Northland, San Antonio, TX 78217, USA.

KUSHNER David Zakeri, b. 22 Dec 1935, Ellenville, New York, United States of America. Musicologist; Lectr; Educator. 4 s, 1 dec. *Education:* BM, Boston Univ, 1957; MM, Univ of Cinn, 1958; PhD, Univ of MI, 1966. *Appointments:* Asst Prof of Music, MS Univ for Women, 1964- 66; Assoc to Full Prof, Radford Univ, 1966-69; Prof, Doct Rsch Fac, Coord Graduate Studies in Music, Coord of Musicological Studies, Univ of FL. *Publications:* Ernest Bloch and His Symphonic Works, 1966; Ernest Bloch and His Music, 1973; Ernest Bloch: A Guide to Research, 1988; articles and reviews. *Memberships:* American Liszt Soc (co-fndr, charter life mbr, pres, Southern Div, Bd Dirs); American Musicological Soc (1st VP Southern Chapt); College Music Soc; Music Tchrs Nat Assn, Life Mbr; Sonneck Soc for American Music; Ernest Bloch Soc; Pi Kappa Lambda; Phi Mu Alpha Sinfonia; Phi Beta Delta; Phi Kappa Phi; FL State Music Tchrs Assn; Fndn for Promotion of Music. *Honours:* Pro Mundi Beneficio Medal, Brazilian Academy of Humanities, 1975; Master Teacher Certs, Music Teachers Nat Assoc, 1984; Nat Arts Associate, Sigma Alpha Iota; Musician of tthe Year, Foundation for the Promotion of Music, 1992; Teacher of the Year, University of Florida College of Fine Arts, 1988; Most Noted Speaker Award American Biographical Institute, 1990, Man of the Year,American Biographical Institute, 1990. *Address:* Dept of Music, University of Florida, Gainesville, FL 32611, USA. 2, 4, 52, 130.

KUSUI Toshiroh, b. 1 Feb 1932, Nagasaki, Japan. Prof of Econ Hist, Yokohama Nat Univ, Japan. m. 6 Apr 1965, 1 d. *Education:* Bach. Wakayama Univ, 1961; Tokyo Univ: MA 1963, Dr Econ, 1970. *Appointments:* Asst Prof, Tokyo Univ, 1965-68; Yokohama Nat Univ: Assoc Prof, 1968-79, Prof, 1979-. *Publications:* A Study of English Agricultural Revolution, 1969; A Study of American Industrial Revolution, 1970; American Economic History I, 1971, II, 1988; American Capitalism and Democracy, 1986. *Memberships:* Socio-Econ Hist Soc, Japan; Tochi Seido-shi-Gakkai (The Agrarian Hist Soc, Japan). *Hobbies:* Listening to classical music, Writing essays. *Address:* 1495-3 Shinohara-Cho, Kohoku-ku, Yokohama 722, Japan.

KUSY Robert Peter, b. 19 Oct 1947, Worcester, Massachusetts, USA. Prof, Univ of N C, USA. m. Gisela Bauer, 27 June 1969, 1 s, 1 d. *Education:* BS Mech Engrng, Worcester Polytechnic Inst, 1969; Drexel Univ: MS Metall 1971, PhD Materials Science and Engrng, 1973. *Appointments:* Prin Investigator, Dental Rsch Ctr, Univ NC, 1972-; Asst Prof, Orthodontics, 1974-79; Assoc Prof, Orthodontics, 1979-89; Prof, Biomed, Engrng and Orthodontics, 1989-. *Publications:* Over 120 articles in profl dental, med and basic science jrnls; Textbook chapters. *Memberships:* American Soc for Metals; American Chem Soc; Int Assn for Dental Rsch; Int Metallographic Soc; Soc for Biomaterials; Soc of Plastic Engrs; N American Thermal Analysis Soc. *Hobbies:* Autos. Brewing, Chess, Basketball, Fishing, Boating, Carpentry, Pool (billiards). *Address:* University of North Carolina, Building 210-H, Room 313 DRC, Chapel Hill, NC 27599, USA. 7, 152, 164.

KUTEK Jan, b. 5 Jan 1935, Rakszawa, Poland. Prof of Geology. m. Barbara Wroczynska, 2 Feb 1974, 1 s. *Education:* Univ of Wroclaw, 1952- 53; Univ of Warsaw, MSc 1957, DSc 1962. *Appointments:* Univ of Warsaw, 1955-, Prof 1976-, Dir, Inst of Geology 1973-78, Dean of Fac of Geology 1980-- 84. *Publications:* Papers on Mesozoic stratigraphy and geology of Poland. *Memberships:* Polish Acad of Sciences, Comm of Geological Sciences, mbr 1978-, VP 1984-90; Acta Geologica Polonica, Pres Ed Bd 1979-; IUGS, Int Subcommn on Jurassic Stratigraphy, corres mbr 1979-. *Honours:* Polish Academy of Sciences, Scientific Secretary's Awards, 1986, 89. *Hobbies:* Reading, Philos. *Address:* ul. Swietojerska 4/10 m.33, PL-00-236 Warsaw, Poland.

KUZICHEVA Zinaida Andreevna, b. 3 June 1933, Vill Kochelevo, Altai District, USSR. Mathn, Sr Scientific Assoc. m. Alexandr Sergeevich Kuzichev, 7 Apr 1933, 1 s. *Education:* Degree Grad mech-math, Moscow State Univ, 1979; Cand degree phys-math sciences. *Appointments:* Moscow State Univ: Jr Scientific Assoc 1972-86, Scientific Assoc 1987-91, Sr Scientific Assoc 1991-. *Publications:* The Mathematic Logic in Mathematics in 19th Century, 1978; Algebra of Logic in A De Morgan's Formal Logic; Symbolic Logic of I Lambert, 1980; N I Styazhkin: The Sketch of the Life and Activity, 1992. *Membership:* Div of Hist of Science and Technol Soviet Nat Comm on Hist and Philos of Science and Technol of Acad Science of USSR. *Hobbies:* Walking, Nature, Classical Music, Art, Market gardening. *Address:* Leninskie Gory, Moscow State University, Dept of Mathematics, 119899 Moscow, Russia. 138, 151.

KUZUYA Fumio, b. 23 July 1928, Japan. Prof, Dept of Geriatrics, Nagoya Univ Schl of Med. m. Misako, 25 Nov 1954, 2 s. *Education:* Graduated Nat Matsumoto Med Coll, 1954; Postgrad Dr Course, Nagoya Univ Schl of Med, 1959. *Appointments:* Nagoya Univ Hosp: Asst Prof 1960-, Assoc Prof 1970-; Prof, Dept of Geriatrics, Nagoya Univ Schl of Med, 1980-. *Publications:* Ed, Japanese Journal Geriatrics, 1980-; Ed, Drugs and Aging, 1990-. *Memberships:* Dir, Japan Geriatrics Soc, 1980-; Dir, Japan Gerontological Soc, 1983-; Dir, Japan Atherosclerosis Soc, 1980-; Dir, Japan Clin Nutrition Soc, 1985-; Nagoya E Rotary Club. *Honour:* Merit Award (Pt B-2) in Hanamoon Campaign Photography Competition by Government of Ontario, Canada 1990. *Hobbies:* Photography, Golf. *Address:* 38, 5-chome Motomiya-cho, Showa-ku, Nagoya 466, Japan.

KVAM Oddvar S(chirmer), b. 26 Sept 1927, Oslo, Norway. Composer; Supreme Court Attorney-at-law. m. May 1964, 1 s. *Education:* LLB, Oslo, 1949; MCJ, NY Univ, 1958; Music Conservatory, 1944-48. *Appointments:* Dpty Judge, 1950-51; Min of Justice, 1951-59; Solicitor Gen's Off, 1959-61; Pvte prac, 1961-; Pres, Norway's Council of Cultural Affairs, 1985-92. *Creative Works:* 1 Opera; 2 Symphs; Chmbr and Choral Music; Piano works. *Memberships:* Norwegian Bar Assn; Norwegian Composers Assn, V-chmn 1978-85. *Honours:* 1st Prize Competition Contest Male Chorus and Orchestra, 1967; Two Prizes: Competition for Orchestra in connection with inauguration of Oslo Concert Hall, 1977; several prizes in choral competition contests. *Hobbies:* (European) Handball, Bridge. *Address:* Breidabliknv 12 E, N 1169, Oslo, Norway. 52.

KWAMENA-POH Michael Albert, b. 14 Oct 1932, Mamfe-Akuapem, Ghana, W Africa. Univ Prof. 3 s, 1 d. *Education:* BA (Hons) London, 1962; MA London, 1968. *Appointments:* Univ of Science and Technology, Kumasi: Lectr 1964-72, Sr Lectr 1972-76, Assoc Prof, 1976-84, Hd Dept of Gen and African Studies 1979-84, Dean of Fac of Social Sciences, 1982-84; Hd, Dept of Hist, Ogun State Univ, Ago-Iwoye, Nigeria, 1984-91; Vis Fellow, Univ of Birmingham, England, 1972-73; Fulbright Vis Prof of Hist, Talladega Coll, AL, USA, 1980-81. *Publications:* Government and Politics in the Akuapem State, 1973; Co-author, The Development of Education in Ghana, 1975; Co- author, African History in Maps, 1982; Monographs and Articles. *Memberships:* Fellow, Histl Soc of Ghana; Histl Soc of Nigeria, Fellow. *Honours:* British Council Award for Research, Public Records Office, U K, 1966; Danish Government Award for archival study, Copenhagen, 1968; British Council Award, 1970; Commonwealth Fellowship, University of Birmingham, England, 1972-73; Ghana Book Development Council Award for Published Works, 1979; Visiting Fulbright Professorship, 1980-81. *Hobbies:* Gardening, Farming. *Address:* Department of History, University of Ghana, Legon. 30.

KWO Charles Chin, b. 28 Oct 1926, Loyang, Henan, China. Physn, Surg, Acupuncturist. m. Toa-Tzu Dorothy Chen, 8 July 1961, 1 s, 2 d. *Education:* MB, MD, Nat Def Med Coll, Taipei, Taiwan, 1952; MSc, McGill Univ, Montreal, Can, 1969. *Appointments:* NDMC Hosp, Taiwan, Chief Res, 1963-58; Acting Chief in Surg and Specialist in Surg, Taiwan, 1958-61; Med, Surg, Orthopaedic Surg, Expmtl Surg and Acupuncture, Quebec, Can, 1962-91; Dir, Can Inst of Chinese Med and Acupuncture, a pioneer Can in use of acupuncture, analgesia for Surg and Dental Surg, 1973-91. *Memberships:* Pres, Inst of Chinese Lang and Culture, Quebec, 1988-91; Med Coun of China, Taipei, 1952; Gen Med Coun of London, England; VT Med Bd, USA; Can Med Coun; Corp Prof des Med du Quebec. *Honours:* National Republic of China, Taipei, Taiwan Government Award Surgical Achievement, 1958; Best Dissertation Award and Paper Prize, Chinese Language Education, People's Republic of China, 1990. *Hobbies:* Photography, Chinese Painting, Oil Painting; Chinese Calligraphy. *Address:* 1414 Drummond Street, Suite 517, Montreal, Quebec, Canada H3G 1W1. 6, 88, 151.

KWOK Pui Lan, b. 16 Apr 1952, Hong Kong. Lectr, Dept Relig, Chinese Univ of Hong Kong. m. Wai Pang Lau, 1 d. *Education:* BA, Chinese Univ of Hong Kong, 1976; BD 1978, MTh, SE Asia Graduate Schl of Theology; ThD Harvard Univ, USA, 1989. *Appointments:* Asst Lectr, Chinese Univ of Hong Kong, 1980-84; Fac, Women's Theological Ctr, Boston, USA, 1985-87; Lectr, Chinese Univ of Hong Kong, 1988-; Lectr, Union Theological Sem, New York, 1991-92. *Publications:* Ed, 1997 and Hong Kong Theology, 1983; Co-ed, The Fullness of the Gospel, 1984; Co-ed, Inheriting Our Mothers' Gardens, 1988; Chinese Women and Christianity 1860-1927, 1992. *Memberships:* Exec Comm, Assn of Theological Educ in SE Asia; Cons, Int Review of Mission; Commn Mbr on Theological Concerns, Christian Conf of Asia; Ecumenical Assn of Third World Theologians. *Hobbies:* Cooking, Reading, Writing. *Address:* 99 Brattle Street, Cambridge, MA 02138, USA.

KWOK Sun, b. 15 Sept 1949, Hong Kong. Prof Univ of Calgary, Canada. m. Shiu-tseng Emily Yu, 16 June 1973, 2 d. *Education:* BSc, McMaster Univ, 1970; MS 1972, PhD 1974, Univ of MN, USA. *Appointments:* Postdoct Fellow, Univ BC, 1974-76; Rsch Assoc, York Univ, 1977-78; Rsch Assoc, Nat Rsch Coun, 1978-83; Univ of Calgary: Asst Prof 1983-85, Assoc Prof 1985-88, Prof, 1988-. *Publications:* over 100 articles in scientific jrnls; Book: Co-author, Late Stages of Stellar Evolution. *Memberships:* Int Astronomical Union; Can Astronomical Soc; American Astronomical Soc. *Honour:* JILA Vis Fellowship, Nat Inst of Standards and Technol. *Hobbies:* Piano, Simulation Games, Model Railroad. *Address:* Department of Physics and Astronomy, University of Calgary, Calgary, Alberta, Canada T2N IN4. 142, 143, 164.

KYLE Donald Gordon, b. 26 June 1950, Westmount, Quebec, Canada. Assoc Prof of Hist. m. Adeline Marie Schiller, 22 Aug 1980, 2 s. *Education:* BA, York Univ, 1973; MA, McMaster Univ, 1974; BEd, Univ of Toronto, 1977; PhD, McMaster Univ, 1981. *Appointments:* Lectr, Classics, Univ of Winnipeg, 1980-81; Asst Prof, Hist & Classics, Univ Sask, 1981-84; Asst Prof. Hist, 1984-89, Asst Chair, Hist, 1987-, Assoc Prof, Hist, 1989-, Univ of TX, Arlington. *Publications:* Athletics in Ancient Athens, 1987; Co-Ed, Essays on Sport History and Sport Mythology,. 1990; articles in profl jrnls. *Memberships:* Ed Bd, Jrnl of Sport Hist Stadion; Classical Studies Ed, Int Jrnl of the Hist of Sport; Exec Bd Mbr, N American Soc for Sport Hist, 1989-91; Book Award Selection Comm, 1988-90; N American Soc for Sport Hist; Publs Bd Mbr, 1984-87, N American Soc for Sport Hist. *Honours:* Dalley Fellowship,McMaster Univ, 1974-78; Canadian Council Fellowship and Queen Elizabeth II Ontario Scholarship, 1978-79; Social Science and Humanities Research Council of Canada Fellowship, 1979-80; Chancellor's Council Award for Excellence in Teaching, UTA, 1990; UTA Faculty Development Leave, 1991. *Hobbies:* Sports, Antiques, Gardening. *Address:* 917 Bert Drive, Arlington, TX 76019, USA. 7, 15.

KYLIN Anders Olof, b. 25 July 1925, Lund, Sweden. Prof of Plant Physiology. m. Elsa B Bengtsson, 1 June 1957, 1 s, 2 d. *Education:* Fil.mag 1947, Fil.lic 1954, Fil.dr 1960, Univ of Lund. *Appointments:* Teaching and Rsch Asst, Dept Plant Physiology, Univ Lund, Sweden, 1949-60; Lectr, Biol, HAL, Umea, Sweden, 1960-61; Docent and Rsch Docent, Botan Inst, Univ Stockholm, 1961-73; Prof, Plant Physiology, Copenhagen, Denmark, 1973-76; Prof, Plant Physiology, Univ of Lund, 1976-91; Prof Emeritus 1992-. *Publications:* Ed-in-Chief, Physiologia Plantarum, 1971-91; approximately 90 publs in physiology anmd biochem of plants and 15 publs on theory and prac of scientific publ. *Membership:* Hon Mbr, Scandinavian Soc for Plant Physiology, 1991. *Honour:* Dip of Fedn of European Socs of Plant Physiology, 1986. *Address:* Dept of Plant Physiology, Univ of Lund, Box 7007, S-220 07 Lund, Sweden. 52, 139.

L

LAAJOKI Kauko Veikko Olavi, b. 3 Apr 1940, Helsinki, Finland. Prof of Geology and Mineralogy. m. Aila-Maija, 4 Sept 1963, 1 s. *Education:* BA 1963; MSc 1966; Lic.Ph 1971; PhD 1973. *Appointments:* Geologist, Geological Survey, Finland, 1966-72; Rschr, Geological Survey, Finland, 1972-78; Prof of Geology and Mineralogy, Univ of Oulu, Finland, 1978-. *Publications:* Num articles on Precambrian Geology and Mineralogy in var scientific jrnls and books; 3 monographs and num edited works on geology of Finland. *Memberships:* Geological Soc of Finland, Sec; Geological Soc, London; Geological Socs of Sweden, Norway and India; Mineralogical Soc of Finland; Vuorimiesyhdistys; Geol Soc of America, Euopean Union of Geol Sci. *Honours:* Numerous scholarships from the Academy of Finland and the Ministry of Education of Finland; Adjunct Prof of Geol Sci, Unvi of Tennessee, Knoxville, TN, 1992-1993. *Hobby:* Living Christian faith. *Address:* Department of Geology, University of Oulu, Linnanmaa, 90570 Oulu, Finland. 52.

LAASONEN Pentti, b. 24 Dec 1928, Kitee, Finland. Prof of Ch Hist. m. Aino Larikka, 25 May 1953, 4 d. *Education:* ThD, Univ Helsinki, 1967. *Appointments:* Sr Tchr, Gymnasium of the State, Savonlinna, 1957- 74; Asst Prof of Ch Hist, 1974-81, Prof, 1981-,Dean Fac of Theology, 1987-90, Univ of Helsinki. *Publications:* Two books of folk cultural life in the E of Finland, 1967, 71; Johannes Gezelius Jr and the Orthodoxy of Finland, 1977; Die Rezeption des deutschen Pietismus in Finnnland, 1988. *Memberships:* Fellow, Finnish Acad Science; Finnish Histl Soc; Finnish Ch Hist Soc; Finnish Soc for Hist of Science and Learning; Finnish Lit Soc. *Hobbies:* Lit, Bibliophily, Fishing. *Address:* Runoilijanpolku 2 A, SF 00650 Helsinki, Finland. 52.

LABELLE Huguette, b. Rockland, Ontario, Canada. Dpty Min, Transp, Can. *Education:* B.Ed, 1967; BSc, Nursing Educ, 1968; M.Ed, 1968; PhD, Educl Admin, 1980. *Appointments:* Asst Dpty Min, Indian and Inuit Affairs, 1978-80; Under Sec of State, 1980-84; Assoc Sec to Cabinet and Dpty Clerk of Privy Coun Off, 1985; Chmn, Pub Serv Commn of Can, 1985-90; Dpty Min of Transp, Can, 1990-, Govt of Can. *Memberships:* Past Pres, Can Red Cross Soc; Chmn of Bd, Algonquin Coll; Chmn of Bd, Ottawa-Carleton United Way; Chmn of Bd, Ottawa Hlth Sciences Ctr Inc; Pres, Mgmt Consulting Inst; Pres, Can Nurses Assn; VP, Can Safety Coun; Mbr Bd of Govs, Carleton Univ and Can Comprehensive Audit Fndn; Mbr Coun of Govs, Can Ctr for Occupational Hlth and Safety; Bd Dirs, Collaboration Sante Internationale; Exec Comm, Inst of Pub Admin of Can; Master of Pub Mgmt Advsry Coun; Fac of Bus, Univ Alta; Advsry Bd, Schl of Pub Admin, Dalhousie Univ; Currently Past Chmn, Bd Trustees, Ottawa Gen Hosp; Pres, Transportation Assoc of Canada; Mbr, Bd Govs, McGill Univ; Bd Dirs, Pub Policy Forum; Fac Admin Advsry Bd, Univ Ottawa. *Honours:* LL.D, Honoris Causa: Brock Univ 1982, Univ Sask 1984, Carleton Univ 1986, York Univ 1990, Univ Windsor 1990; Univ Manitoba, 1992; Off of Order of Can, 1990. *Address:* 330 Sparks Street, Ottawa, Ontario, Canada K1A ON5. 138, 177.

LABELLE Jean-Paul, b. 21 June 1920, Montreal, Canada. Prof; Priest; Mbr Soc of St Sulpice (Can Prov). *Education:* BA Montreal Univ, 1943; LCL, Canon Law, St Thomas Pontifical Univ, Rome, Italy, 1950; Dip, Japanese Lang, Franciscan Inst of Japanese Studies, Tokyo, Japan, 1955. *Appointments:* Stagiaire Ecclesiastical Provincial Tribunal, Montreal, 1950-51; Prof, Canon Law and Moral Theology, St Sulpice Reg Sem, Fukuoka, Japan, 1951-; Defender of the Bond, Diocesan Tribunal, Fukuoka, 1957; Sec, Episcopal Commn on Ch Admin and Legis, Japan, 1978-87; Mbr, Episcopal Commn for transl of Code of Canon Law into Japanese, 1983-92; Promoter of the Faith in the cause of Saints, Tokyo, 1985-. *Publications:* Marriage Registration and Naien in Japan, 1958; Commentary of the Apostolic Faculties, 1964; Guide for Education of the Faith, 1978; Christian Family, 1984; The Faith and the Life of the Christian, 2 vols, 1990; 250 articles, USA and Japanese encys, reviews, France, Japan, Philippines, Italy. *Memberships:* Can Canon Law Soc; Societe Internationale de Droit Canonique et de Legislation Religieuse Comparees, France; Cath Theological Soc of America. *Hobby:* Stamp Collecting. *Address:* St Sulpice Seminary, Matsuyama 1-1-1, Jonnan-ku, Fukuoka 814-01, Japan.

LACEY Peter William, b. 13 Nov 1945, Westminster, England. Dir Community Coun for Somerset; Regl Bd Mbr (Wessex) Nat Rivers Auth. m. Pamela Muriel Nicholl, 22 Nov 1969, 3 s. *Education:* The Old Hall, Wellington, Salop; Solihull, Warwicks. *Appointments:* Chas Richards Co, 1964-68; Pepper Rutland Cotterill Co, 1968-69; Goodland Bull Co, 1970-83; Robson Rhodes, 1983-88; Apsleys, 1988-90; Community Coun for Somerset, 1990-. *Memberships:* Fellow, Inst Chartered Accts in England and Wales (FCA); Chmn, Court Fields Schl Governors -1990; Chmn, Regl Rivers Advsry Comm; Chmn, Wessex Water Auth Customer Consultative Comm - 1989. *Hobbies:* Gardening; Co Sec (formerly Chmn) Somerset Assn of Local Couns. *Address:* The Old Forge, West Buckland, Wellington, Somerset TA21 9JS, England.

LACKO Andras Gyorgy, b. 10 Nov 1936, Budapest, Hungary. Prof of Biochem. m. (1) 2s, 2 d, (2) Terri Mann, 27 May 1984. *Education:* BSA 1961, MSc 1963, Univ BC; PhD, Univ Wash, Seattle, 1968. *Appointments:* Temple Univ Med Schl, Phila, PA, 1971-75; Assoc Prof, TX Coll, 1975-83; Prof, Biochem, Univ N TX, 1983-. *Publications:* over 50 publs in refereed scientific jrnls. *Memberships:* American Soc Biochem-Molecular Biology; American Heart Assn. *Hobbies:* Tennis, Piano, Bridge, Stamp collection. *Address:* Department of Biochemistry and Molecular Biology, 3500 Camp Bowie Blvd, Fort Worth, TX 76107, USA. 2, 7.

LACOSTE Paul, b. 24 Apr 1923, Montreal, Canada. Univ Admnstr. m. Louise Marcil, 31 Aug 1973, 1 s, 2 d. *Education:* BA 1943, MA 1944, L.Ph 1946, LL.L 1960, Universite de Montreal; Fellowship, Univ Chgo, 1946-47; Doct, Unmiversite de Paris, 1948. *Appointments:* Vis Prof, Fac Law, 1960-70; Practicing Lawyer, 1964-66; Full Prof, 1958; Prof, Fac of Philos, 1948; Vice-Rector, 1968-75; Rector (Pres), 1975-85, Univ Montreal. *Publications:* Num articles on educl problems and collaborator on sev publs. *Memberships:* Bd Mbr: I musici Orch, Can Schlrship Trust Fndn; Quebec Bar Fndn; Mbr: Can Human Rights Fndn; Commn de Toponymie du Quebec; Hon Pres: Assn des Universites partiellement ou entierement de langue francaise (AUPELF). *Honours:* Honorary Doctorate: McGill Univ, 1975, University of Toronto, 1978, Universite Laval, 1986; Officer, Order of Canada, 1977; Human Relations Award of the Canadian Council of Christians and Jews, 1981; Chevalier de la Legion d'honneur, 1984. *Hobbies:* Travel, Music. *Address:* 356 Woodlea, Mont-Royal, Quebec, Canada H3P 3J7. 2, 6, 13, 15, 52, 139, 142.

LADELL John Lindsay, b. 30 Sept 1924, Bangkok, Thailand. Writer; Environmental and Histl Cons. m. Monica Southey, 8 Oct 1955, 1 s, 1 d. *Education:* Munro Coll, Jamaica, W Indies; BSc, Forestry, Univ Toronto, 1951; D.Phil (Oxon), 1961. *Appointments:* RN, Lt RNVR, 1942-46; Forest Products Lab, Ottawa, 1952-57; Ont Rsch Fndn, 1962-72; Self employed, 1972-. *Publications:* num tech articles in forest products field and variety of subjects; Books: Inheritance: Ontario's Century Farms Past and Present, 1979, 86; A farm in the family, 1985. Both books co-authored with Monica Ladell; They Left Their Mark: Surveyors and Their Role in the Settlement of Ontario, 1993. *Memberships:* Writers Union of Can; Periodical Writers Assn of Can; Ont Profl Foresters Assn; Can Inst of Forestry; Oxford Soc. *Honour:* Ontario Bicentennial Award of Merit, 1984. *Hobbies:* Gardening, Acting. *Address:* 247

Warden Avenue, Scarborough, Ontario, Canada M1N 2Z9.

LADIZESKY Kathleen Ann, b. 14 Oct 1941, Wem, Shropshire, England. Libn. m. 28 Mar 1978, 2 d. *Education:* BA, Libnship, Russian, 1980. *Appointments:* BLDSC, Boston Spa, 1980-85; S Island Schl, Hong Kong, 1986-. *Contributions to:* profl jrnls. *Memberships:* Assoc, Lib Assn, GB; ALA; Hon Sec, Hong Kong Lib Assn, 1990-91. *Hobby:* Travel. *Address:* Library, South Island School, 50 Nam Fung Road, Hong Kong. 52.

LAFORTUNE Louise, b. 24 May 1951, Montreal, Canada. Prof of Maths. *Education:* BSc, Maths, MEd, 1988, Univ Montreal; PhD, Educ, Univ Quebec, 1992. *Appointments:* Coll Manitou, 1975-76; CEGEP du Vieux, Montreal, 1973-74, 1976; Prof of Maths, CEGEP Andre Laurendeau, LaSalle, Quebec, 1977-. *Publications:* Ed, Femmes et Mathematique, 1986; L'enseignement des Mathematiques d'appoint aux Adultes, 1988; Ed, Quelles differences? Les Femmes et L'enseignement des Mathematiques, 1989; La Demythification de la Mathematique, Materiel Didactique, 1990; Adultes, Attitudes et Apprentissage des Mathematiques, 1990; Dimension Affectiv en Mathematiques, Recherche-Action et Matieral Didactique, Modulo, 1992; Les Fennes Font des Maths, Remue-Menage, 1992 . *Memberships:* HOIFEM Movement Int pour les femmes et l'enseignement de la Mathematique; Assn Mathematique du Quebec. *Honours:* Award Bourse de Doctorat (1988- 89) en education from University of Quebec in Montreal for the Quality of Record; Prix Marie Therese (1990) for work of a woman in teaching and promoting Mathematics; Priz de la Ministre for Res on Affective Domain in Mathmatics, 1992. *Hobbies:* Skiing, Canoeing, Bridge, Reading, Writing. *Address:* CEGEP Andre Laurendeau, 1111 Lapierre, LaSalle, Quebec, Canada H8N 2J4.

LAFRENIERE Rene, b. 13 July 1953, Shawinigan, Quebec, Canada. Surg Oncologist. m. Zam Zam Saad, 8 Oct 1981, 2 s, 1 d. *Education:* DEC, St Jean Coll, 1970-72; MD,CM, McGill Univ, 1972-77; Residency Gen Surg, Jackson Mem Hosp, 1977-82; FRCSC; FACS; Fellowship, Surg Oncology, 1982-84; Fellowship in Tumor Immunology, NIH, 1984-86. *Appointments:* Instr of Surg, Univ Miami, 1982-86; Asst Prof, Surg, Univ Calgary, 1986-88; Assoc Prof, Surg, Univ Calgary, 1988-1992; Prof, Surg, Univ Calgary, 1992-. *Publications:* Author and Co-author of over 70 med publs. *Memberships:* Southern Surg Congress; Can Oncology Soc, Educ Comm; American Radium Soc; American Assn for Cancer Rsch; American Soc Clin Oncology; Soc Surg Oncology. *Honours:* American Cancer Society Fellowship Award, 1982-84; Alberta Heritage Foundation for Medical Research Scholarship, 1986-93. *Hobbies:* Flying, Antiques, Woodworking. *Address:* Univ of Calgary, Health Science Center, 3330 Hospital Drive N W, Calgary, Alberta, Canada T2N 4N1. 142.

LAI In-Jaw, b. 24 Aug 1946, Taiwan, Republic of China. Vice-Min, Min of Fin, Rep of China. m. Lai Chang, Huey-Jiuan, 30 June 1987, 1 s. *Education:* LL.B, Nat Chung-Hsing Univ, 1973; LL.M, Nat Taiwan Univ, 1976; LL.M, 1977, SJD, 1981, Harvard Univ, USA. *Appointments:* Prof of Law, Nat Chung-Hsing Univ, 1981-; Chmn, Graduate Schl of Law, Nat Chung-Hsing Univ, 1982-84; Dir Gen, Customs Dept, Min of Fin, Rep of China, 1984-89. *Publications:* Legal Problems of Parent-subsidiary Corporations in Taiwan, 1981; Essays on Corporate Law, 1986; Annotations of the ROC Securities Exchange Act, 4 vols, 1984, 85, 86, 91. *Memberships:* Chmn, Accounting Rsch anmd Dev Fndn of ROC; Dir, Tax Rsch Assn of ROC; Dir, Alumni Assn of Nat Taiwan Univ; Supvsr, Alumni Assn, Nat Chung-Hsing Univ. *Honours:* Outstanding Alumnus, National Chung-Hsing University, 1982; Awarded Great Merit in 1988 by Ministry of Finance for the accomplishment of ROC tariff reforms; Awarded one of the Best Government Officials in 1988, by the Premier of the Executive Yuan; Awarded Great Merit in 1989 by the Ministry of Finance for the establishment of ROC Harmonized Commodity Description and Coding System. *Address:* Ministry of Finance, No. 2, Ai-kuo West Road, Taipei 10729, Taiwan, China.

LAI Tsung Hui, b, 26 June 1953, Tainan, Taiwan, Republic of China. Assoc Prof, Econs. m. Shu-Chin W, 26 June 1982, 1 s. *Education:* BA, Pub Fin, Nat Chengchi Univ, Taiwan, 1976; PhD, Econs, OH State Univ, Columbus, OH, USA, 1984. *Appointments:* Rsch Asst, Taiwan Econ Rsch Inst, 1978-79; Lectr, Econs, OH State Univ, 1984-85; Asst Prof, Liberty Univ, Lynchburg, VA, USA, 1985-88, Assoc Prof, 1988-. *Publications:* Profl Publs and Papers. *Membershsips:* American Econ Assn; Southern Econ Assn, USA; VA Assn of Econs, USA; Int Assn of Bus Forecasting, USA. *Hobbies:* Fishing, Walking, Reading. *Address:* 208 Cheyenne Drive, Lynchburg, VA 24502, USA. 7, 15.

LAI Xinghua, b. 2 July 1942, Jakarta, Indonesia. Assoc Prof, Dpty Dir of Guangxi Plant Protection Inst of Guangxi Acad of Agricl Sciences. m. 21 Mar 1967, 1 d. *Education:* Guangxi Agricl Coll, 1960-64. *Appointments:* Guangxi Acad of Agricl Sciences, 1964-. As Sr Scientist sent by Chinese Govt to USA, 1984-85 and Aust, 1990. *Publications:* 22 articles in Chinese or English in Chinese and American mags or books; 4 articles translated from English to Chinese. *Memberships:* Standing Comm Mbr, Guangxi Comm of Chinese People's Consultative Conf; Exec of Standing Comm, Mbr of Guangxi oversea exchange comm; Exec of Standing Comm of Guangxi Plant Protection; Chinese Agricl Soc; Chinese Plant Protection Soc. *Honours:* 14 research items of scientific results awarded special awards from Chinese or Guangxi Provincial Scientific and Technology Conference or Bur, 1980-91; Title An exemplary intellectual of returned oversea Chinese conferred by Chinese Government, 1989; Title having outstanding contribution of returned Scientist going abroad, conferred by Chinese Government, 1991. *Hobbies:* Music, Reading Novels, Gardening (flower). *Address:* Guangxi Academy of Agricultural Sciences, Nanning, Guangxi 530007, China.

LAI Yim Shik Daniel, b. 4 Nov 1955, Hong Kong. Lawyer. m. Anne L L Peng, 31 July 1982, 2 s. *Education:* LL.B (Hons) 1978, PC.LL 1979, Schl of Law, Univ of Hong Kong; Cert of Qualification in Laws, Osgoode Hall Law Schl, York Univ, Can, 1990. *Appointments:* Pvte Prac, Hong Kong, 1981-; Pvte Prac, Ont, Can, 1988-90; Solicitor, Supreme Ct of Hong Kong, 1981; Solicitor, Supreme Ct of England and Wales, 1984; Barrister and Solicitor, Supreme Ct of Vic, Vic, Melbourne, 1985; Barrister and Solicitor, Supreme Ct of Ont, Can, 1990; Notary Pub, Ont, Can, 1990; Law lectures for Practitioners, Hong Kong, 1984; Int Bar Assn Conf Speaker, 1991; Chalice Bearer, St John's Cathedral, Hong Kong; Server, St John's Cathedral, Hong Kong. *Memberships:* Law Soc of Hong Kong; Law Soc of England and Wales; Law Soc of Upper Can, Ont, Can; Soc for the Rehab of Offenders, Hong Kong, Exec Comm and China Comm; Hong Kong Sea Schl, Bd of Mgmt, 1986-87; Chief Justice's Working Party on use of Chinese Lang in Cts of Hong Kong, 1987; Hon Law Lectr, Schl of Law, Univ of Hong Kong, 1983-87. *Hobbies:* Singing; Automobiles appreciation; Boating. *Address:* D2, 8 Cornwall Street, Kowloon, Hong Kong.

LAI Yonghai, b. 26 July 1949, Pinghei, Fujian, People's Republic of China. Prof of Philos. m. Wu Yuan, 20 July 1977, 1 s. *Education:* MA. Chinese Acad of Social Science, Beijing, 1981; PhD, Nanjing Univ, 1985. *Appointments:* Ed. Jrnl of Zhongshan Univ, 1976-78; Ed, Jrnl of Chinese Social Science, 1981-82; Assoc Prof, Dept Philos, Nanjing Univ, 1986-. *Publications:* On the Nature and Character of Buddha in China; An Introduction to Religiology; Chan Poetry in Buddhism; Zhang Ren: The Collection of Books of World Philosophers; Research on Chinese Buddhism Thoughts. *Memberships:* Council, Nat Acad Soc of Religiology; Chairperson, Jiang Nan Chan Acad Soc;

Chief Ed, Chan Science Collect; Dpty Ed, Classical Works on Buddhism. *Honours:* Award by the Wang An Sinology Foundation of the American Computer Company, 1988; Award by National Scientific Foundation of America, 1988; A New Star Scientific Award from Nanjing University, 1988; Awarded First Prize for Good Teaching, 1988; Chinese Doctor of Excellent Achievement Award, 1991. *Hobbies:* Buddhism, Religiology, Music, Sport. *Address:* Department of Philosophy, Nanjing University, China 210008. 139, 152.

LAIRD Margaret Heather, b. 29 Jan 1933. Third Ch Estates Commnr. m. The Rev Canon John Charles Laird, 14 Jan 1961, 2 s. *Education:* Westfield Coll, Univ of London, 1951-54; BA (Hons) Mediaeval Hist, Kings Coll, London, 1954-55. *Appointments:* Tchr: The Grey Coat Hosp 1955-59, Newquay Grammar 1959-61; Hd of Relig Studies, The Dame Alice Harpur Schl, 1969-88. *Memberships:* Mbr Gen Synod of The Ch of England; Oxford and Cambridge Club. *Hobbies:* Mediaeval Art, Cornish and Celtic Studies. *Address:* 1 Millbank, London SW1 3J2, England. 1, 146.

LAIRD Paul Robert, b. 26 Oct 1958, Louisville, Kentucky, USA. Musicologist. m. Joy Ellen Thomas, 10 July 1982. *Education:* B.Mus.Ed, 1980, MA, Music Hist, 1982, OH State Univ; PhD, Music, Univ NC, Chapel Hill, 1986. *Appointments:* Vis Asst Prof of Music Hist, PA State Univ, 1987- 88; Asst Prof, Music Hist, SUNY-Binghamton, 1988-91; Asst Prof, Music Hist, Lamont Schl of Music, Univ of Denver, 1991-. *Creative Works:* Dissertation: The Villancico Repertory at San Lorenzo El Real del Escorial 1630-1715, 1986; Scholarly articles on aspects of the Spanish villancicos; Articles on jazz festivals in The New Grove Dictionary of Jazz, 1988; Column on early string instruments(1989-present), That Gut Feeling: The World of Early Strings, Continuo Mag; Reviewer of Early Music Recordings for American Record Guide; Dir, computer database: International Inventory of Villancico Texts; Scholarly papers given to American Musicological Society and International Musicological Society. *Memberships:* American Musicological Soc; Coll Music Soc; Early Music America; Sociedad Espanola de Musicología; Viola da Gamba Soc of America. *Honour:* National Endowment for the Humanities Travel to Collections Grant, 1989. *Hobbies:* Early Music Perf (baroque cello, viola da gamba), Sports fan, Hist buff. *Address:* Lamont School of Music, University of Denver, 7111 Montview Boulevard, Denver, CO 80220, USA.

LAJOS Tamas, b. 31 Jan 1944, Eger, Hungary. Univ Prof. m. 16 Aug 1969. 2 d. *Education:* MSc, Mech Engrng, 1968, PhD, Fluid Machinery, 1972, Tech Univ of Budapest; Candidate of Tech Sciences, 1977; Dr Tech Sciences, Hungarian Acad of Sciences. *Appointments:* Asst 1968-72, Asst Prof 1972-78, Assoc Prof 1978-89, Prof, Fluid Mechanics 1989-, Tech Univ of Budapest; V-Rector, 1987-91. *Publications:* More than 90 publs in Fluid Mechanics, Aerodynamics, Fluid Machinery, Engrng Educ, Internationalization of Higher Educ. *Memberships:* European Soc of Engrng Educ, Admnstv Coun Mbr; European Distance Educ Network, VP; Hungarian Fulbright Commn; Hungarian Comm of European Cultural Fndn; Dir, Hungarian TEMPUS Supervisory Bd; Pres, FEANI Hungarian Qualification Bd; Hungarian Acad of Engrng; Hungarian Nat Comm of Distance Educ VP. *Hobbies:* Skiing, Hist, Lit. *Address:* Mandula u.35, H-1025 Budapest, Hungary.

LAJOUS Roberta, b. 6 Feb 1954, Mexico DF, Mexico. Ed, Diplomat, Writer. *Education:* BA, El Colegio de Mexico, 1975; MA, Stanford Univ, CA, 1976. *Appointments:* Dir Gen America del Norte, Secretaria de Relaciones Exteriores, 1979-89; European Ed, monthly Examen, Mexico City., 1989-. *Publications:* La politica exterior de porficio stey, 1990; articles in profl jrnls. *Memberships:* Mexican For Serv Assn; Int Inst for Strategic Studies; Pantido Revolucionanis Institucional (PR) Nat Exec Comm. *Honour:* Minister, Mexican Career Foreign Service. *Hobbies:* Hiking,

Tennis, Reading. *Address:* Nieve 171, Jardines del Pedregal, Mexico SF 01900, Mexico. 34.

LAL Deepak Kumar, b. 3 Jan 1940, Lahore. Prof of Econs. m. Barbara Ballis, 11 Dec 1971, 1 s, 1 d. *Education:* St Stephen's Coll,. Delhi, 1957-60; Jesus Coll, Oxford, 1960-63, 1964-65; BA (Hons) Delhi, 1959; MA, B.Phil, Oxford, 1962, 65. *Appointments:* Indian For Serv, 1951-57; Lectr, Christchurch, Oxford, 1966-68; Rsch Fellow, Nuffield Coll, Oxford, 1968-70; Lectr, 1970-79, Rdr 1979-84, Prof, Pol Economy 1984-, Univ Coll, London; James Coleman Prof of Dev Studies, Univ CA, Los Angeles, 1991-; Rsch Admnstr, World Bank, 1981-87; Cons 1970- ILO, UNCTAD, OECD, World Bank, Min of Planning, S Korea and Sri Lanka; Cons, Indian Planning Commn, 1971-74. *Publications:* Wells and Welfare, 1972; Methods of Project Analysis, 1974; Appraising Foreign Investment in Developing Countries, 1977; Men or Machines, 1978; Prices for Planning, 1980; The Poverty of Development Economics, 1983, 85; Co-author Labour and Poverty in Kenya, 1986; Co-editor, Stagflation, Savings and the State, 1986; The Hindu Equilibrium, 2 vols, 1988, 89; Co-editor, Public Policy and Economic Development, 1990; Ed, Development Economics,4 vols, 1991. *Hobbies:* Opera, Theatre, Tennis. *Address:* Department of Economics, University College London, Gower Street, London WC1E 6BT, England. 52.

LALWANI Narendra D, b. 25 Sept 1952, Kandla, India. Rsch Scientist. m. Leena Kishinchand Hingorani, 26 Apr 1985, 1 s. *Education:* BSc, Gujarat Univ, Ahmedabad, India, 1973; PhD, Bombay Univ, India, 1979; Postdoct trng, Northwestern Univ, Chgo, USA, 1979-83. *Appointments:* Rsch Fellow, Cancer Rsch Inst, Bombay, India, 1973-79; Postdoct Assoc, 1979-83, Asst Prof, Rsch Science, Northwestern Univ, Chgo, 1984-87; Asst Prof, Med Coll VA, Richmond, 1987-90; Sr Scientist, Parke-Davis, Ann Arbor, MI, 1990-. *Publications:* Rsch papers, book chapts, review papers in peer reviewed scientific jrnls. *Memberships:* AAAS; American Assn of Cell Biology; American Assn for Cancer Rsch; Soc of Toxicology; American Soc for Microbiology. *Honour:* Young Investigators Research Award, National Cancer Institute, NIH, 1984-87. *Hobbies:* Painting, Music. *Address:* Parke-Davis Pharmaceutical Research Division, Warner-Lambert Company, 2800 Plymouth Road, Ann Arbor, MI 48106, USA.

LAMB Hubert Horace, b. 22 Sept 1913, Bedford, England. Meteorologist, Climatologist. m. 7 Feb 1948, 1 s, 2 d. *Education:* Trinity Coll, Cambridge Univ, 1932-35; BA (Hons) 1935; MA 1947; ScD 1983. *Appointments:* Meteorological Off, 1936-40, 1945-71; Irish Meteorological Serv, 1940-44; Dir and Fndr, Climatic Rsch Unit, Univ of E Anglia, 1972-78. *Publications:* Climate: Present, Past and Future, 1972, Vol 2 1977; Climate, History and the Modern World, 1982; Weather, Climate and Human Affairs, 1988; Historic Storms of the North Sea, British Isles and Northwest Europe, 1991. *Memberships:* Hon Life Fellow, Royal Meteorological Soc; Fellow., Royal Geogl Soc; Corres Mbr, Danish Natural Hist Soc; Corres Mbr, Royal Acad of Arts and Sciences, Barcelona. *Honours:* L G Groves Memorial Prize, Meteorological Office, UK, 1960, 71; Murchison Award, Royal Geographical Society, 1974; Professor Emeritus, University of East Anglia since Retirement 1978; Hon.D.Sc, University of East Anglia, 1981; Hon. LL.D, University of Dundee, 1981; Vega Medal, Royal Swedish Geographical Society, 1984; Symons Memorial Medal, Royal Meteorological Society, 1987. *Hobbies:* Travel, Hill Walking, Skating, Cross-country skiing, Social history, Scandinavia and Northern Lands, Seafaring, Central Europe and the Alps, Antarctic, Social Democracy and Liberal Democratic Politics. *Address:* Climate Research Unit, University of East Anglia, Norwich NR4 7TJ, England. 30, 43, 47, 52, 139, 161.

LAMBERMONT Jeannette Monique, b. 31 Dec 1956, The Netherlands. Theatre Dir. m. Jeffrey Charles Boyce,

13 Sept 1986. *Education:* BFA, Theatre, York Univ, 1978. *Appointments:* Co-Artistic Dir, Next Stage Inc, 1984-87; Dir: Easter, Equity Showcase, 1987; The Great Lover, Stratford Fest, 1988; Titus and Andronicus, Stratford Fest, 1989; The Miracle Worker, Citadel Theatre, 1989; Doctor Faustus, Ryerson Theatre Schl, 1990; Grand Inquisitor and Swan Song, Stratford Fest, 1990; Bon Ton and Lying Valet, Geo Brown Coll, 1990; Winters Tale, Univ Alta, 1991; The Tempest, Dartmouth Coll, NH, 1991. *Memberships:* Can Actors Equity Assn; American Actors Equity Assn; Anthroposophical Soc of Can. *Honours:* Jean Chalmers Award, 1988; Tyrone Guthrie Award, 1988. *Hobbies:* Reading, Hiking, Film-making. *Address:* c/o Christopher Banks and Associates, 219 Dufferin Street, Suite 305, Toronto, Ontario, Canada M6K 1Y9. 88.

LAMBERT Andrew David, b. 31 Dec 1956, Norfolk, England. Lectr in War Studies, Kings Coll, London, England. m. Zohra Bouznat, 27 Nov 1987, 1 d. *Education:* BA (Hons) Law, 1978; MA, War Studies, 1979; PhD, Hist, 1982. *Appointments:* Lectr in Hist, 1983-87; Lectr, Royal Naval Coll, Grenwich, 1987-89; Sr Lectr, RMA, Sandhurst, 1989-91; Lectr in War Studies, Kings Coll, London, 1991-. *Publications:* Battleships in Transition, 1984; HMS Warrior, 1987; The Crimean War, 1990; Maintaining Naval Mastery, 1991. *Memberships:* Fellow, Royal Histl Soc; Cnslr, Navy Records Soc; Cnslr, Int Commn for Maritime Hist. *Hobbies:* Vintage Motorcycles; Travel. *Address:* Department of War Studies, Kings College, Strand, London WC1R 2LS, England.

LAMBERT Denis Clair, b. 26 Apr 1932, Lyon, France. Prof of Econs, Univ Lyon, France. m. Yvonne Lambert-Faivre, 10 July 1956, 2 s, 1 d. *Education:* Law degree, 1954; Econs Doct, 1960; Agregation, 1962. *Appointments:* Rsch Fellow, ISEA Paris, 1957-61; Univ Prof, Morocco, Rabat, 1962-66, Lyon, 1962-; Vis Prof, Univs of Rabat, Algiers, Benghazi, Tunis, Dakar, Yaounde, Abidjan, Tamatave, Saint-Denis in Africa, Warsaw, Lwowch, Poland, Buenos Aires, Santiago del Chile, Montevideo, Rio de Janeiro, Sao Paulo, Lima, Quito, Bogota, Medellin, Caracas, San Jose de Costa Rica, Pointe a Pitre, Mexico, Guadalajara, in Latin America and Stanford, Minneapolis, 1985 and Athens, GA, 1991 in USA. *Publications:* (mostly in French): 100 papers relating to econ dev, demography, econ hist, money, ins, hlth and social security; Books: South American Inflations, 1960; Algeria's Traditional Sectors, 1962; French-English Monetary Dictionary, 1970; Latin America, 1971; The Economics of Third World, 1974; Technological Mimetism among Developing Countries, 1979; 19 Latin Americas, 1984; Dictionary of Health Economics, 1985; Welfare State Questioned, 1990; The World AIDS economic impact 1980-2000, CNRS, 1992. *Hobby:* Painting. *Address:* 23 Rue Sala, 69002 Lyon, France.

LAMBERTSON Wingate Augustus Jr, b. 29 June 1920, Rich Square. North Carolina, United States of America. Inventor; Cons, Zero-point Energy Conversion. m. Helen Eileen Hall, 27 Apr 1946, 2 s, 1 d. *Education:* BS, Ceramic Engrng, NC State Univ, 1941; MS, Ceramics, 1948, PhD, Ceramics, 1949, Rutgers Univ. *Appointments:* Rsch Assoc, Argonne Nat Lab, Chgo, 1949-52; Prof, Univ Toledo, Ohio, 1952-55; Mgr, Applied Rsch, Carborundum Co, Niagara Falls, NY, 1955-63; Mgr, Phys Science Rsch, Spindletop Rsch, Lexington, KY, 1963-66; Exec Dir, KY Science and Tech Commn, Lexington, 1966-69; Pres, Solvex Corp, Louisville, KY, 1969-74; Watersol Yarns, Winchester, KY, 1974-76; Quality Control Mgr, Confederate Plastics Inc, Lexington, 1977-80; Pres, Inventive Ideas Inc, Holmes Beach, FL, 1980-. *Creative Works:* Inventions in specialty thermoplastic threads, ambient temp superconductivity and zero-point energy conversion. *Hobbies:* Energy Conversion Research, Swimming, Reading, Island Players Theatre. *Address:* 216 83rd Street, Holmes Beach, FL 34217, USA.

LAMM Zvi, b, 15 Jan 1921, Jaroslaw, Poland. Prof. m. Daphna Sirota, 9 Nov 1969, 2 s. *Education:* BA, Sociol and Educ, 1960, MA, Educ, 1962, PhD, 1967, Hebrew Univ, Jerusalem. *Appointments:* Prin, D Yelin Coll of Educ, Jerusalem, 1957-64; Lectr, 1964, Sr Lectr, 1971, Assoc Prof, 1974, Prof, 1981, Hebrew Univ, Jerusalem; Vis Prof to Columbia Univ, NY, Boston Univ and Harvard Univ, Cambridge, MA, USA. *Publications:* Conflicting Theories of Instruction, 1976; War and Education, 1976; articles in profl jrnls. *Address:* Hebrew Univ, School of Education, Mount Scopus, Jerusalem 91-905, Israel. 52.

LAMOUREUX Lucien, b. 3 Aug 1920, Ottawa, Canada. Barrister, Solicitor. m. 13 July 1980, 1 d. *Education:* Univ of Ottawa, BA 1940, L.Ph 1941, MA 1942, Osgoode Hall Law Schl, Toronto, 1946. *Appointments:* Speaker, House of Commons, Can, 1965-74; Amb, Belgium, Luxemburg, 1974-80, Portugal, 1980-85; Res, Counsel in Brussels, Fasken Martineau, 1989. *Contributions to:* legal publs in Can. *Memberships:* Can Bar Assn; Law Soc of Upper Can; Assn European Lawyers. *Honours:* QC, 1965; PC, 1974; Hon. LLD, Ottawa Univ, 1970, Windsor Univ, 1971, Western Univ, 1972, Dalhousie Univ, Halifax, 1974. *Hobbies:* Golf, Skiing, Reading. *Address:* 96A Franklin Roosevelt Avenue, 1050 Brussels, Belgium.

LAMPITT Dinah, b. 6 Mar 1937, Essex, England. Author. m. L F Lampitt, 28 Nov 1959, dec, 1 s, 1 d. *Education:* Putney HS; Regent St Polytechic, 1945-55. *Appointments:* Asst, Woman Magazine, The Times, The Evening News, late 50's. *Publications:* Sutton Place, 1983; The Silver Swan, 1984; Fortune's Soldier, 1985; To Sleep No More, 1987; Pour the Dark Wine, 1989; The King's Women, 1992. *Membership:* Soc of Authors. *Hobbies:* Drama; Swimming. *Address:* Rupert Crew Ltd, Kings Mews, London WC1N 2JA, England. 30.

LAMPLUGH Diana Elizabeth, b. 30 July 1936, Cheltenham, England. Tchr; Author; Dir-Trustee, the Suzy Lamplugh Trust. m. Paul Crosby Lamplugh, 18 Oct 1958, 1 s, 3 d, one presumed murdered. *Education:* W London Inst of Higher Educ, City and Guilds 730, Double Distinction in Tchng; Adult Educ, 1980; Dip.Ed. ASE/FEE 1982-84; Swimming Tchrs Dip, ASA. *Appointments:* Tchr Swimming, children and adults, 1968-; Fndr Dir, British Slimnastics Assn, 1973-89; Tchr, Slimnastics and Relaxation, Richmond Adult and Community Coll, 1974-88; Tutor and Assessor, Slimnastics Tchrs, 1973-89; Fndr-Dir, The Suzy Lamplugh Trust, 1986-. *Publications:* Slimnastics, 1970; Slimnastics, 1972; Stress & Overstress, 1974; The New Penguin Slimnastics, 1980; The Whole Person Approach to Fitness, 1984; Body & Soul, 1986; Beating Aggression, 1988; Survive the 9-5, 1989; Physical Activities for Visually Handicapped People, 1989; Without Fear, 1991. *Memberships:* Fndr Mbr, Exec Comm, ISTCS, UK; Hlth and Safety Execs Comm on Violence; Inst of Dirs; Soroptimists Int. *Honour:* OBE for her work with The Suzy Lampugh Trust, 1992. *Hobbies:* Opera, Boats, Riding, Swimming, Teaching, Speaking, Enjoying her children, Being alone with husband. *Address:* 14 Sheen Avenue, London SW14 8AS, England.

LAN Xi-chun, b. 21 Feb 1907, China. Prof of Surg. m. Min-zhen Zhuang, 11 Feb 1940, 1 s, 4 d. *Education:* Dip, Schl of Med, Qi Lu Univ, China, 1933; MD, 1933; Toronto Univ, Can; Schl of Med, Liverpool Univ, England, 1938-39. *Appointments:* Surg, Ren Ji Hosp, 1933-38; Dir, Surg Dept, St Johns Univ, 1939-52; Prof of Surg, Shanghai Second Med Univ, 1952-; Pres, SSMU, 1978-84; Dir, Shanghai Inst, BME, 1985-88. *Publications:* Cardiac Surgery, 1959, 64; Vascular Surgery, 1963; Surgery, 1973, 76; Cardiovascular Surgery, 1985. *Memberships:* Hon Dir, Chinese Inst, BME; Hon Dir, Chinese Med Assn; Hon Dir, Artificial Organs, Chinese Inst of Biomedical Engrng. *Honours:* Hon Prof: Osaka Dental University, Japan, University of Missouri, Kansas City, USA; Prize for Mitral Commissurotomy, 1954; First

Award for Artificial Heart-Lung Machine, 1966; Prize for Treating Schistosomiasis, 1985. *Hobbies:* Sports (tennis, basketball, motor- cycle driving), Classical Music, Chinese Opera. *Address:* Shanghai Second Medical University, 280 Chong Wing Nan Road, Shanghai, 200025, China. 139, 151, 152.

LANCASHIRE Ian, b. 27 Nov 1942, Winnipeg, Manitoba, Canada. Prof of Engl. m. Anne Charlotte Begor, 25 May 1968, 1 s, 2 d. *Education:* BA (Hons) Univ Man, 1964; MA 1965, PhD 1969, Univ Toronto. *Appointments:* Instr, Dept Engl, Univ Man, Summers 1965, 67; Univ Toronto: Asst Prof, Dept Engl, 1968-74, Assoc Prof, 1974-81, Prof, 1981-. *Publications:* Two Tudor Interludes, 1980; Computer Applications in Literary Studies, 1983; Dramatic Texts and Records of Britain, 1984; Microcomputer Text-Analysis System, co-author, Ms-Dos Software, 1985; Humanities Computing Yearbook, co-author, 1988; Humanities Computing Yearbook, 1989-90; A Comprehensive Guide to Software and Other Resources, 1991. *Memberships:* Ed Bd, Records of Early English Drama, 1976-; Fndg Dir, Centre for Computing in the Humanities; Pres, Toronto Semiotic Circle, 1987; Exec Bd, Assn for Lit and Linguistic Computing, 1987-; Exec Bd, Centre for Machine Readable Texts in Humanities, 1991-; Emerging Technologies Comm, MLA, 1990-. *Honour:* Queen Elizabeth II Scholar, Woodrow Wilson Fellow. *Hobbies:* Rsch in Computational Stylistics, Chaucer, Early Brit Drama, Lit and Dictionaries, Bibliography, Travel, Golf, Film, Reading. *Address:* Department of English, Weymore Hall, New College, University of Toronto, Toronto, Ontario Canada M5S 1A5. 88.

LANCASTER SMITH Michael John Laurence, b. 4 Sept 1941, Hastings, Sussex, England. Cons Physn. m. 11 Apr 1964, 1 s, 2 d. *Education:* London Hosp Med Coll, 1960-66; MBBS 1966, MD 1980, Univ London; MRCP 1969; FRCP 1982. *Appointments:* House Physn, House Surg, 1966-67; Sr House Physn, 1967-68, London Hosp; Med Registrar, Southend Hosp and London Hosp, 1969-71; Sr Registrar, London Hosp, 1971-73; Sr Lectr, St Bartholomews Hosp, 1973-74; Cons Physn, Queen Mary's Hosp, Sidcup, Kent, 1974-91. *Publications:* Problems in Practice -- Gastroenterology, 1987; Problems in Management, Gastroenterology, 1989; num med and scientific papers. *Memberships:* BMA; Brit Soc of Gastroenterology. *Honour:* State Scholar, 1960. *Hobbies:* Playing Cricket, Skiing, Listening to Music, Theatre. *Address:* Stableside House, 36 Southborough Road, Bickley, Bromley, Kent BR1 2EB, England.

LAND Betty Lou Jackson, b. 22 Mar 1947, North Carolina, USA Prof of Reading Educ. m. James Philip Land, 25 June 1970, 1 s, 1 d. *Education:* BA, Samford Univ, 1969; MA, Univ AL, 1979; EdS, Winthrop, 1979; PhD, Univ SC, 1983. *Appointments:* Tchr, Birmingham Bd of Educ, 1970-72; Prof, Winthrop Coll, 1975-; Writer, Bapt Sunday Schl Bd, 1984-. *Contributions to:* profl jrnls; Parent-Child Educational Interaction: A Longitudinal Study of the Effects of a Kindergarten Parent Involvement Program, 1983. *Memberships:* Cnslr; Kappa Delta Pi; Phi Kappa Phi; Omicron Delta Kappa; IRA; Phi Delta Kappa. *Honours:* Excellence in Teaching Award, 1978, 85, 87, 91; Outstanding Young Woman of the Year 1981; Winthrop College's Nominee South Carolina Professor of the Year 1991. *Hobbies:* Reading, Baking Bread, Walking, Role of Parents, Spiritual Developmenmt of Children. *Address:* 304B Withers, School of Education, Winthrop College, Rock Hill, SC 29732, USA.

LAND Ming Huey, b. 10 July 1940, Hsinchu, Taiwan, Republic of China. Dean and Prof, Coll of Fine and Applied Arts, Appalachian State Univ, NC, USA. m. Whei-ing Yang, 30 July 1970, 1 s, 1 d. *Education:* BS, Taiwan Normal Univ, 1963; MS, Northern IL Univ, USA, 1968; EdD, UT State Univ, 1970. *Appointments:* Asst Prof, Eastern IL Univ, 1970-71; Prof, Miami Univ, 1971-83; Chair, Technol Dept, 1983-89, Dean, 1989-,

Appalachian State Univ. *Publications:* Bk Chapt Author, Industrial Arts Education: Retrospect, Prospect, 28th Yearbook of ACIATE, 1979; More than 50 published articles in profl jrnls. *Memberships:* Int Coun for Fine Arts Deans; American Soc for Engrng Educ; American Voc Assn; Int Technol Educ Assn; Nat Assn of Indl Technol; Phi Kappa Phi; Epsilon Pi Tau. *Honours:* Fulbright Lectureship, Chungnam National University of Korea, 1981; Honorary Professor, Northeast University of Technology, China, 1986; Laureate Citation, Epsilon Pi Tau, 1987; Special Recognition Award, International Technology Education Association, 1990. *Hobbies:* Classical Music, Travel, Tennis. *Address:* 115 University Circle, Boone, NC 28607, USA. 7, 15, 139, 141, 143.

LAND Rebekah Ruth, b. 5 Feb 1946, Columbus, Georgia, USA. Univ Prof. m. Richard Dale Land Sr, 29 May 1971, 1 s, 2 d. *Education:* AB, Samford Univ, 2967; M.Relig Educ, New Orleans Bapt Sem, 1970; MSW, Tulane Univ, 1971; PhD, TX Woman's Univ, 1988. *Appointments:* Adj Fac, Criswell Coll, 1976-90; Asst Dir, Counseling, Dallas Theol Sem, Therapist, Minirth-Meier Psych Clin, 1988-90; Pvte Prac, Coord of Trilogy Prog, Parthenan Pavilion Psych Hosp, 1990-. *Publications:* Num articles in profl publs. *Memberships:* American Assn of Marital and Family Therapy, Clin Mbr; American Assn of Sex Educators, Counselors anmd Therapists; Dipl, Am Bd of Sexology; American Assn for Counseling and Devel; Learning Disability Assn; American Mental Hlth Assn. *Honour:* National Institute of Mental Health Scholarship, 1971. *Hobbies:* Arts and crafts, Sewing. *Address:* Parkview Towers, Suite 1010, 210 25th Avenue North, Nashville, TN 37203, USA. 7, 46.

LANDERS Vernette Trosper, b. 3 May 1912, Lawton, Oklahoma, USA. Ret'd Tchr. m. Newlin Landers, 2 May 1959, 2 s. *Education:* BA (Hons) 1933, MA 1935, EdD, Univ CA, LA; 4 Tchng Credentials State of CA. *Appointments:* Tchr Pub Second Schls, Montebello, 22 yrs; Sponsor, Assemblies, parades, sing clubs and other student activities; Prof, Long Beach City Coll, 1 yr; Asst Prof, LA State Coll; Dean of Girls, Twentynine Palms HS; Dist Cnslr; Dir, Guidance Project; Coord, Adult Educ, Morongo Unified Schl Dist; Clerk i/c, Landers Post Off, 1962-84. *Publications:* Articles in newspapers and mags; poems in jrnls and anthols; Books of verse: Impy's Children, 1975; Slo-Go, 1977; Sandy the Copydog, 1979; The Kit Fox and the Walking Stick, 1980. *Memberships:* Life Fellow, IBA, ABIRA; Int Acad of Poetry; mbr and off holder var local and nat civic orgs; Alpha Xi Delta. *Honours:* num awards for poetry; Cert of Apprec, Morongo Unified Schl Dist for Outstanding Serv to Students, 1984; Landers area Chmbr of Comm, Presidential Trophy for Outstanding Serv, 1986. *Hobby:* Raising Bobcats and crossbreeds. *Address:* P O Box 3839, Landers, CA 92285, USA

LANDRUM Diedra Gansloser, b. 29 Mar 1952, San Francisco, CA, USA. Cnslr. m. Gene Landrum, 6 June 1987. *Education:* BA, Psychology, 1973, Educ Credential, 1973-74, San Jose State Univ; MA Counseling, Rider Coll, 1988. *Appointments:* Tchr, 1974-85, Cnslr, 1985-87, San Jose, CA; Tchr, 1989-91, Cnslr, 1990, Naples, FL. *Memberships:* American Assn for Counseling and Dev; Collier Co Assn for Counseling and Dev. *Address:* 7065 Villa Lantana, Naples, FL 33963, USA. 7, 15, 138.

LANDRY Edmond E, b. 12 July 1931, Caraquet, Canada. First Magistrate of Grande-Anse. *Education:* Universite du Sacre-Coeur, Bathurst; Ottawa Univ. *Appointments:* Former owner of Edmond E Landry Assurances Ltee; Grand-Anse Beverages Ltd; Gallian Night Club; Bonbons de l'Acadie Ltee; Propane Baie des Chaleure Enrg; Irving Serv Stn; Owner, Grande- Anse Servs Ltee and Salon des Pecheurs Ltee. *Memberships:* First Municipal Coun, Caraquet; Provincial Municipal Coun; Acad Gentium Pro-Poche, Rome; Can Heraldric Soc; Chmn, Econ Expansion Commn, Peninsula Inc, 2 yrs; Provincial Chmn, St Johns Ambulance; Bd Dirs, Can Automobile Assn; Bd Dirs, St Joseph Nursing Schl,

Bathurst; Prin Org of Youth Club, Ste Anne du Bocage; Chmn and Prin Org of corp, Initiative and Dev Grand-Anse Inc. *Honours:* Hon Citizen, Madawaksa, NB; Municipality of Paspebiac. Quebec; Village of Bas Caraquet; Kt of Columbus, 4th degree; Commandeur of Ordre Equestre du Saint-Sepulcre of Jerusalem; Order of Can; Knight & Commandeur of Most Venerable Order of St John of Jerusalem; Dr Honoris Causa, Humanitarian Science, St Thomas Univ; Decorated, France-Can Assn; Medaille de l'Etoile Civique of France. *Address:* CP 14, Site 6, 613, boul St-Pierre O, Caraquet, New Brunswick, Canada EOB 1KO.

LANDSBERGIS Vytautas, b. 18 Oct 1932, Kaunas, Lithuania. Musician; Musicologist. m. Grazinas Rucyte, 28 May 1960, 1 s, 2 d. *Education:* Grad Pianist, Conserv of Lithuanian SSR, Vilnius, 1955; Cand Scis, Musicol, 1969. *Appointments:* Piano Tchr, Teenage Mus Sch, Vilnius, 1952-57; Piano Tchr, Vilnius Conserv, 1957-63; Piano Tchr, Pedagog Inst, 1957-74; Fac, Vilnius Conser, Klapeda, 1974-78; Mus Hist, Conser of Lithuanian SSR, 1978-. *Publications:* Sonata of the Spring, 1965; Ciurlionis work, 1971, 1975; The Art of Ciurlionis, 1976; The Life and wor of Ceslovas Sasnauskas, 1980; The Music of Ciurlionis, 1986. *Memberships:* Union of Soviet Composers; Union of Composers of Lithuanisn SSR, Bd, 1967-, Chm, Musicol Branch, 1979-85; MK Ciurlionis Soc, Chm, 1987. *Honours:* State Prize, 1975, Hon Art Worker, 1982, Lithuanian, SSR 1975; Prize for Critics, Union of Soviet Composers, 1981. *Hobbies:* History of Arts; Aesthetics; Poetry; Films. *Address:* Eidukevicius Street 15-129, Vilnius, 232051 Lithuania.

LANE David John, b. 12 June 1935, Huddersfield, Yorkshire, England. Prin, Coll of the Resurrection, Mirfield, England. *Education:* Hurstpierpoint Coll, Sussex, 1948-53; Magdalen Coll, Oxford, 1955-60; Coll of the Resurrection, 1960-61; Codrington Coll, Barbados, 1961-62; BA 1958; MA 1962; BD 1988 (Oxon). *Appointments:* Royal Signals, 1953-55; Codrington Coll, Barbados, 1961-65; Pembroke Coll, Oxford, 1966-71; Univ of Toronto, 1971-83; Coll of Resurrection, 1983-. *Publications:* Articles in learned jrnls; Ed, Leiden Peshitta. *Membership:* Soc for Old Testament Study. *Honours:* Hall Houghton Syriac Prize, Oxford, 1961; Kennicott Hebrew Fellowship, 1966. *Hobbies:* Gardening, Reading. *Address:* College of the Resurrection, Mirfield, West Yorkshire WF14 OBW, England.

LANE William Arthur, b. 16 Sept 1958, Nashville, Tennessee, USA. Atty. m. Brenda Diane Kinamon, 5 Dec 1981, 2 s. *Education:* BS, Middle TN State Univ, 1980; JD, Nashville Schl of Law, 1984. *Appointments:* Pvte Prac of Law, Smyrna, TN, 1987-; Atty, Travelers Ins Co, Nashville, 1990-91; Atty, U S F & G Ins Co, Nashville, 1991-92; Atty, Willis-Corroon Admnstv Servs Corp, 1992-. *Memberships:* TN Bar Assn; US Dist Ct, TN, 1986; US Ct of Appeals (6th circuit), 1986; US Supreme Ct, 1990; Nashville Bar Assn; Assn of Trial Lawyers of America; Masons; Shrine; Sigma Delta Kappa; NRA. *Honours:* TN Squires Association, 1979; Tennessee Colonel, Governor's Staff, 1979; Honorable Order of Kentucky Colonels, 1983; George Dickel Tennessee Whiskey Water Conservation Society, 1986. *Hobbies:* Golf, Swimming, Hunting, Shooting. *Address:* PO Box 291587, Nashville, TN 37229, USA. 7, 52.

LANG Bernhard, b. 12 July 1946, Stuttgart, Germany. Prof of Relig. *Education:* Dip Theology, Tubingen, 1970; Elève titulaire de l'Ecole biblique, Jerusalem, 1971; ThD, Tubingen, 1975; ThD, habil, Freiburg, 1977. *Appointments:* Prof, Ancient Judaism, Tubingen, 1977-82; Prof, Old Testament, Mainz, 1982-85; Prof Relig, Paderborn, 1985-; Guest Prof: Berlin Univ, 11980, Temple Univ, Phila, 1982, Ecole des Hautes Etudes en Sciences Sociales, Paris, 1991, Sorbonne, Paris, 1992/1993. *Publications:* Kein Aufstand in Jerusalem, 1978; Monotheism and the Prophetic Minority, 1983; Wisdom and the Book of Proverbs, 1986; co-author, Heaven: A

History, 1988 (sev transls). *Membership:* Soc of Biblical Lit. *Hobbies:* Anthropology, Social Sciences. *Address:* Universitat. Fb 1, Warburger Str 100, D-W4790 Paderborn, Germany. 30, 52, 145.

LANG Shao-jun, b. 24 Dec 1939, Heibei, China. Art Critic. m. Xu Gai, 14 Feb 1969, 2 s. *Education:* Graduate, Art Coll of Tianjin, 1961; Graduate, Graduate Schl in Acad of Arts of China with MA, 1981. *Appointments:* Lectr, Art Hist and Theory, Art Coll of Tianjin, 1961-78; Assoc Rsch Fellow, Fine Arts Rsch Inst, Acad of Arts of China, 1982-91. *Publications:* Early Murals at Dunhuang, 1985; SuShi and the Aesthetics of Chinese Painting, 1985; On Modern Chinese Art, 1988; Study in Qi Bai-shi, 1991. *Memberships:* Dir, Mod Art Rsch Sect, Fine Arts Rsch Inst in Acad of Arts, China; Chinese Artists Assn; Outer Fellow, Acad of Dun Huang. *Honour:* The First Award of Research Achievement of the Academy of Arts of China, 1989. *Hobbies:* Traditional Chinese Painting, Classical Western Music, Poetry. *Address:* Fine Arts Research Institute, Academy of Arts of China, No.17 Qianhai Xijie, Beijing 100009, China.

LANGE Robert Dale, b. 24 Jan 1920, Redwood Falls, Minnesota, United States of America. Med Rschr. m. Mary Jane Adams, 16 Sept 1944. *Education:* BA, Macalester Coll, St Paul, MN, 1941; MD, Washington Univ, St Louis, MO, 1944. *Appointments:* Maj, MD, Walter Reed Army Inst Rsch, 1954-56; Asst Prof of Med, Washington Univ, St Louis, MO, 1956-61; Assoc Prof of Med, Med Coll of GA, 1962-64; Prof, Dept Med Biology, 1964-85, Dir and Chmn, 1975-81, Prof Emeritus, 1985-, Univ of TN Med Ctr. *Publications:* Author or co-author of 180 publs and book chapts related to hematology. *Memberships:* Alpha Omega Alpha; Southern Soc of Clin Investigation; American Fedn of Clin Rsch; American Soc of Hematology; Int Soc of Expmtl Hematology; Phi Pi Epsilon; Sigma Xi. *Hobbies:* Photography, Golf. *Address:* 8116 Bennington Drive, Knoxville, TN 37909, USA. 2, 17.

LANGER Ralph Ernest, b. 30 July 1937, Benton Harbor, Michigan, United States of America. Newspaper Ed. m. Katherine B McGuire, 25 June 1960, 2 d. *Education:* BA, Jrnlsm, Univ MI. *Appointments:* Grand Haven Daily Tribune, 1959-60; US Army, 1960-62; Managing Ed, Port Angeles Daily News, 1962-66; Copy Ed, Detroit Free Press, 1966-67; Managing Ed, Dayton (Ohio) Jrnl Herald, 1968-75; Ed, Everett (Washington) Herald, 1975-81; Sr VP and Exec Ed, Dallas Morning News, to present. *Memberships:* Assoc Pres Managing Eds Assn, Pres, 1990-91; Pres, Freedom of Info Fndn of TX, 1987-89; Pres, Coun of Pres's, 1991-92; Pres, Press Club of Dallas, 1984-85; Pres, Nat Freedom of info Coalition, 1992-93. *Hobbies:* Photography, Writing, Fishing. *Address:* c/o Dallas Morning News, Communications Center, Dallas, TX 75265, USA. 2, 7.

LANGER Salomon Z, b. 14 Oct 1936, Argentina. Med Dr. m. Martha Faigelbaum, 4 Aug 1960, 3 d. *Education:* MD. summa cum laude, Buenos Aires Med Schl, 1960; MD, Buenos Aires Med Schl, 1962; Rockefeller Fndn Fellow, 1962-64; Instr in Pharmacology, Harvard Med Schl, 1965-66; Sr Rsch Fellow, Wellcome Trust Fndn, Cambridge, England. 1967-68. *Appointments:* Dir, Instituto de Investigaciones Farmacologicas, Buenos Aires, Argentina, 1969-76; Hd, Dept Pharmacology, Wellcome Rsch Labs, England, 1976-77; Dir of Biology, Synthelabo Recherche Labs, Paris, France, 1977-. *Publications:* Rsch publs in area of neurotransmission and receptor pharmacology. *Memberships:* Pres, Latin American Soc of Pharmacology, 1974-76; Pres, Argentine Soc of Pharmacology, 1975-77; Pres, European Coll of Neuropsychpharmacology, 1989-92; Chmn, Fellowship Comm, Collegium Internationale Neuropsychopharmacology, 1987-. *Honours:* John Simon Guggenheim Foundation Fellowship, 1976; Fellow, High Blood Pressure Research Council, American Heart Association, USA, 1977; Sixth Gaddurn Memorial Lecture, London of George Brown Memorial Lecture, 1977; American Heart Association, 1980; First

Prize Anna Monika Foundation, Germany, for Research in Endogenous Depression, 1981. *Hobbies:* Bicycling, Tennis. *Address:* Synthelabo Recherche, 58 rue de la Glaciere, 75013 Paris, France. 152.

LANGFELDT Bent, b. 23 Nov 1923, Aarhus, Denmark. Chief of Radiology. m. Lea Esteri Rantanen. 22 Oct 1953, 2 s, 1 d. *Education:* MD, Univ Copenhagen, 1953; Residency: State Hosp, Aarhus, 1953, Co Hosp, Holstebro, 1953-54, Randers, 1954-56; Sr Resident, Municipal Hosp, Aarhus, 1956-65; Specialist, Diagnostic Radiology, 1965. *Appointments:* Chief, Radiology, Co Hosp, Aarhus, 1965-; Asst Prof, Univ Aarhus, 1969-; Cons, Royal Dental Coll, Aarhus, 1974-; Sr Cons, Gizan, Saudi Arabia, 1985-86. *Publications:* Ed Books Breast Cancer, 1984, 86, 89. *Contributions to:* textbooks and jrnls on med hist. *Memberships:* Danish Radiology Soc; Scandinavian Radiology Soc; European Assn Radiology; Int Soc Radiology; Swedish, Norwegian and Finnish Radiology Socs; Swedish Drs Soc; The Danisk Baker St Irregulars,The Sherlock Holmes Club in Denmark. *Honours:* Schlrship, Danish State, 1959-61; Legacy, Danish Kodak, 1973, 79; Legacy, Prof Krebs, 1977; Legacy, Polack, 1975; Legacy, Ellen Nielsen, 1976; Fndn for Advancement of Radiology, 1973. *Hobbies:* Hist of Med; Sherlock Holmes invest. *Address:* Tretommervej 20 A, DK-8240 Risskov, Denmark. 52.

LANIER Anita Suzanne, b. 21 May 1946, Talladega, Alabama, United States of America. Organist, Piano anmd Organ Tchr. *Education:* BS, Music Educ, Jacksonville State Univ, 1969. *Appoinmtments:* Elem Music Tchr, Talldega City Schls, 1969-81; Libn, Elem Music Tchr, Talladega Acad, 1981-84; Tchr, Piano and Organ, Talladega, 1981-; Organist, Trinity United Meth Ch, 1981-. *Memberships:* Talladega Commun Chorus Pilot Club, Sec, 1977-78; Delta Omicron; Music Tchrs Nat Assn; Nat Assn for Female Execs; World Inst of Achievement; ABI Rsch Bd of Advsrs; Women's Inner Circle of Achievement, FIBA; World Fndn of Successful Women; Nat Guild Piano Teacher's; Int Platform Assoc; Am Pianists Assoc. *Honours:* World Decoration of Excellence Medallion, American Biographical Institute, 1990; Commemorative Medal of Honor, American Biographical Institute, 1990. *Hobbies:* Collecting Dolls, Walking. *Address:* 601 North Street, Talladega, AL 35160, USA. 5, 7, 130, 138, 156, 162.

LANTOS Peter Laszlo, b. 22 Oct 1939, Hungary. Prof of Neuropathology. *Education:* Med Univ of Szeged, Hungary, 1958-64; PhD 1973; MRCPath 1975; FRCPath 1987; DSc, 1992. *Appointments:* Prof of Neuropathology, 1980-; Hon Cons of Neuropathology. *Memberships:* Brain Rsch Assn; The Pathological Soc of GB and Ireland; The Pontish Neuropathological Soc; Royal Soc of Med, Coun Mbr, Sect Neurology; Cncl Mbr, Int Soc of Neuropathology; Assn Clin Pathologists; Royal Coll of Pathologists; Brit Assn for Cancer Rsch. *Hobbies:* Fine Arts, Travel, Music. *Address:* Institute of Psychiatry, Department of Neuropathology, De Crespigny Park, Denmark Hill, London SE5 8AF, England.

LANZANO Ralph E, b. 26 Dec 1926, New York City, United States of America. Profl Engr. *Education:* BCE, NY Univ, 1959; Profl Engr, NY State Educ Dept, 1966. *Appointments:* Engrng Aide, Seelye Stevenson Value and Knecht, 1957-58; Jr Civ Engr, 1960-1963, Asst Civ Engr, 1963-66, NYC Dept Pub Works; Civ Engr, NYC Dept Water Resources, 1967-71; Sr Sanitary Engr, Parsons Brinkerhoff Quade and Douglas, 1971-72; Civ Engr, NY Dept of Water Resources, 1972-80; Civ Engr, NY Dept of Environmental Protection, 1981-; Retired, 1990. *Creative Works:* Paintings; Plays. *Memberships:* American Soc Civ Engrs; American Water Works Assn; Water Environment Fedn; American Pub Hlth Assn; US Inst for Theatre Technology; American Soc for Testing and Materials; Nat Soc Profl Engrs; American Fedn of Arts; Int Wildlife Assn; Life Mbr, Nat Rifle Assn; AAA; American Nat Theatre and Acad; Bklyn Botanic Garden; Film Soc-Lincoln Center; Life Mbr, US Tennis Assn; Nat

Parks Assn; Chi Epsilon. *Hobbies:* Painting, Writing, Walking, Swimming, Record and Book Collecting, Reading, Films, Theatre, Sports. *Address:* 17 Cottage Court, Huntington Station, NY 11746, USA. 2, 6, 26, 52, 132, 139, 153.

LAPOINTE-CRUMP Janice Deane, b. 27 Mar 1942, Chicago, Illinois, United States of America. Assoc Prof of Dance. *Education:* BS, 1964, MA, 1968, Northwestern Univ, Evanston, IL; PhD, TX Woman's Univ, 1980. *Appointments:* Instr, Univ IL, Chgo, 1968-71; Instr, Univ of N TX, 1973-76; Faculty, Arts Magnet HS, Dallas, 1979-80; Fac, TX Woman's Univ, 1980-. *Creative Works:* Var periodical writings; Choreography and staging of dances by August Bournonville, 1971-; In Balance: Fundamentals of Ballet, 1985; Encore II, A Spectrum of Dance Writings, 1978-87, 1990; Jazz II: Introduction to an American Art Form, 1992. *Memberships:* Congress for Rsch in Dance, Ed Review Bd; Nat Dance Assn, Chair, Rsch Comm, 1981-86; Jrnl for Hlth, Physical Educ, Recreation and Dance, Chair, Educ Comm; Task Force on Dance Educ; Soc for Dance Hist Schlrs. *Honours:* Fulbright Hays Fellowship, 1977; TX Doct Schlrship, 1979; George Marshall Award, American Scandinavian Fndn, 1978; Mary Mason Lyons Award for Excellence in Tchg from TWU. 1985; TAHPERD Schlr, 1991. *Hobbies:* Gardening, Reading, Children and Husband. *Address:* Texas Woman's University, Department of Performing Arts: Dance, P O Box 23747, Denton, TX 76204, USA. 15, 18, 46.

LAPPERT Michael Franz, b. 31 Dec 1928, Brno, Czechoslovakia. Prof of Chem. m. 14 Feb 1980. *Education:* Northern Polytechnic London, BSc, PhD, DSc; FRIC (now FRSC). *Appointments:* Asst Lectr, Lectr, Northern Polytechnic, 1953-55; Lectr 1959-61, Sr Lectr 1961-64, Univ Manchester Inst Science and Technology; Rdr 1964-69, Prof 1969-, Univ Sussex. *Publications:* Metal and Metalloid Amides, 1980; Chemistry of Organo-Zirconium and Hafnium Compounds, 1986; more than 50o rsch papers. *Memberships:* Royal Soc of Chem, Pres, Dalton Div, 1989-91; American Chem Soc; FRS,1979. *Honours:* First Award of Royal Society of Chemistry in Main Group Element Chemistry, 1970; Tilden Lecturer, Royal Society of Chemistry, 1972; Kipping Award, American Chemical Society, 1976; Organmetallic Chemistry Medal, Royal Society Chemistry, 1979; Dr Rer Nat (Hon Causa) University of Munchen, Federal Republic of Germany, 1989; Nyholm Lecturer, Royal Society of Chemistry, 1993. *Hobbies:* Theatre, Opera, Art, Tennis, Walking. *Address:* 4 Varndean Gardens, Brighton BN1 6WL, England. 1, 52.

LAPTEV Rumen, b. 20 May 1957, Sofia, Bulgaria. Artist, Painter. *Education:* Arts Coll, Sofia, 1972-76; Dip, Artist Painter, Acad of Fine Arts, 1982-88. *Appointments:* Selecting and Performing all Exhibs (from Bulgaria and abroad) in Nat Fine Arts Gall, 1978-82. *Creative Works:* Participated in all exhibs of Union of Bulgarian Artists, 1988-; One-man show in Plovdiv, Bulgaria, 1991; Participated in Autumn Saloon in Paris and symposia abroad, 1991-. *Membership:* Union of Bulgarian Artists. *Honour:* Diploma from International Youth's Exhibition in Painting, Sofia, 1989. *Hobbies:* Music, Photography, Bicycling. *Address:* 15 Pavel Lilov Str, 1111 Sofia, Bulgaria.

LAQUEUR Walter, b. 26 May 1921, Breslau, Germany (now Wroclaw, Poland). Histn and Pol Commentator. m. Barbara Koch, 1941, 2 d. *Appointments:* Ed Survey, 1955-65; Dir, Inst Contemporary Hist and Wiener Lib, London, 1964-91; Ed, Jrnl of Contemporary Hist, 1965; Prof of Hist, Brandeis Univ, 1967-72; Prof of Hist, Tel Aviv Univ, 1970-87; Prof of Govt, Georgetown Univ, 1979-1992; Chair, Int Rsch Coun, Ctr for Strategic and Int Studies, Wash DC, 1973-; Ed, Washington papers, 1973-; Washington Quarterly. 1978-; Vis Prof of Hist, Harvard, 1977; Rockefeller, Guggenheim Fellow. *Publications:* Young Germany, 1962; The Road to War, 1967, 68; Europe since Hitler, 1970; A History of

Zionism, 1972; Confrontation, 1974; Weimar, 1974; Guerilla, 1976; Terrorism, 1977; A Continent Astray: Europe 1970-78, 1979; The Missing Years (novel), 1980; The Terrible Secret, 1981; Farewell to Europe (novel), 1981; Germany Today, 1985; A World of Secrets, 1985; Breaking the Silence, 1986; The Age of Terrorism, 1987; The Long Road to Freedom, 1989; Stalin, 1990. *Hobby:* Swimming. *Address:* Center for Strategic and International Studies, 1800 K Street, N W, Washington, DC 20006, USA.

LAREDO Jaime, b. 7 June 1941, Cochabamba, Bolivia. Violinist. m. Sharon Robinson. *Education:* Studied w Antonio de Grassi and Frank Houser, San Fran, 1948; w Josef Gingold, Cleveland, 1953; Ivan Galamian at Curtis Inst. *Appointments:* Recital at age 8 in Sacramento; Appearances with maj orchs in USA, Can, Europe and Ctrl and S America; Summer festivals at Spoleto, Tanglewood, Hollywood Bowl. Dir of Chamber Music at 92nd St Y Series, NYC. Dir Solist w int chmbr orchs inclng St Paul and Scottish Chmbr. Distguished Artist, St Paul Chamber Orchestra. Took St Luke's Chamber Orchestra on their debut tour of Japan a director/soloist, 1992. Mbr of Kalichstein-Laredo-Robinson trio and tours widely in USA and Australia giving recitals in maj music ctrs of Europe. *Creative Works:* recordings w Brahms String Sextets, Isaac Stern, Co-Liang Lin, Michael Tree, Yo-Yo Ma and Sharon Robinson. *Honours:* Stadium in La Paz named after him and commemorative set of postage stamps issued in his name; Awarded Handel Medallion, USA. *Address:* c/o Harold Holt Ltd, 31 Sinclair Road, London W14 ONS, England.

LARGE John Barry, b. 10 Oct 1930, Droitwich, England. Professor; Director. m. 18 Oct 1958, 2 s. *Education:* BSc Hons, Queen Mary Col, 1953; MSc Purdue Univ, 1954; Cornell Univ, 1956-58; Harvard Univ Bus Sch, 1963. *Appointments:* Aerodynamicist, Cissna Aviation, 1956-58; Chief Acoustics Engr, The Boeing Co, 1958-70; Univ of Southampton: Prof and Dir, Inst of Sound and Vibration Res, 1970-80, Dean of Engrg, 1980-84, Dir of Indust Affairs, 1984-92, CEO, Univ of Southampton Holdings Ltd, 1988-. *Memberships:* Pres, Assn of Noise Conslts; FRAS; FID; Fellow, Inst of Acoustics; Acoustical Soc of Am; FRSA; Soc of Automotive Engrs, USA; Corr Mem, Inst of Noise Control Engrs, USA. *Honours:* Pres, Southampton Chamber of Commerce; Hon Chief Sci Ofr, Defense Research Agency. *Hobbies:* Horticulture; Viticulture. *Address:* Chinook, Southdown Road, Shawford, Hampshire SO21 2BY, England. 1, 50.

LARKINS Ernest Radford, b. 13 Oct 1955, Nashville, Tennessee, USA. Accounting Professor. m. Nancy Kaye DeBusk, 22 Aug 1981, 1 s, 2 d. *Education:* BS Acct, Bob Jones Univ, 1977; MAcct, Virginia Tech, 1978; PhD Bus, Virginia Tech, 1982. *Appointments:* Tutor and Part-time Instr, Virginia Poly Inst State Univ, 1980-81, Fac Intern, Coopers & Lybrand, 1983; Faculty, Sch of Acct, Georgia State Univ, 1982-, currently Accounting Professor. *Creative works:* Numerous articles to professional journals including: The Effect of the Tax Reform Act of 1986 on Economic Efficiency; Social Security arrangements of US employees who work outside the US; Tax Havens: Their Selection and Use by US Multinationals in the 1990s; Taxation and the Future of Offshore insurance Companies. *Memberships:* AAA; ATA; Beta Alpha Psi; Tau Alpha Chi. *Honours:* Financial Writers Awd, Inst of Cert Fin Planners, 1984; Res grants from Col of Bus Admin, Georgia State Univ, 1983-, 1985-. *Hobbies:* Church activities; Home schooling; Reading fiction; Landscaping; Photography. *Address:* 1840 Galilee Court, Tucker, GA 30084, USA. 7, 52, 43.

LARSEN Kai, b. 15 Nov 1926, Hillerod, Denmark. University Professor of Botany. m. Supee Saksuwan, 24 June 1971. *Education:* MSc, Copenhagen Univ, 1952. *Appointments:* Sci Asst, Bot Lab, Copenhagen Univ, 55-62, Asst Prof, Pharm HS, Copenhagen, 1962-

63; Assoc Prof, 1963-; Prof of Bot, Fdr and Dir, Bot Inst, Aurhus Univ. *Creative works:* Over 200 books and articles on botany, particulary plant geography and biodiversity of tropical Asia. *Memberships:* Royal Danish Acad of Sci and Letts; Royal Norwegian Acad; Fellow Linn Soc, London; Dan Sci Assn; Collegium Polynologicum; Ed-in-Chf, Nord Journ Botany and Opera Botanica; Ed, Fl Thailand and Fl Nordica; Ex-bd, Flora Mulesiand Fndn (Leiden); Ed bd, Flora of China. *Honours:* Knight of Dannebrog; Knight of Crown of Thailand. *Hobbies:* Classical music, especially playing the piano; Far East art and culture. *Address:* GraastenveJ 6, Soften, DK 8382 Hinnerup, Denmark.

LARSKI Zdzislaw Bogumil, b. 5 Jan 1919, Rzeszow, Poland. Prof of Microbiology. m. Janina Berger, 29 Dec 1945, 1 s, 1 d. *Education:* Grad, 1947, Doctorate, 1958, Asst Prof, 1962, Assoc Prof, 1969, Prof, 1979, Fac of Vet Med, Univ of Wroclaw *Appointments:* Jr Asst, Physiol Dept, Fac of Med, Univ Wroclaw, 1946-47; Practising Vet, 1947-49; Sci Worker, 1949-67, Hd of Lab of Gen Virol, 1959-67, Vet Res Inst, Pulawy; Hd, Dept of Vet Microbiol, Acad of Agric and Tech, Olsztyn, 1967-89; Ret'd, 1989. *Creative works:* 150 publications including books: Veterinary Viral Diagnostics, 1971, 1977, in Hungarian and Russian; Veterinary Virology, 1968, 1980, 1989, in Bulgarian, English and Spanish. *Memberships:* Polish Soc of Vet Scis; Polish Microbiol Assn; Virol Com, Polish Acad of Scis, (PSA), Chm, 1976-81; Microbiol Com, PAS; Edit Bd, Archivum Veterinarium Polonicum. *Honours:* Prizes from the Polish Ministers of Agric and Ed; Cert of Appreciation, US Dept of Agric, 1967; Medal Pro Scientia Veterinaria Polona, 1983. *Hobbies:* Tourism; Skiing; XX Century Polish History. *Address:* ul A Puszkina 8 m 10, 10-294 Olsztyn, Poland.

LARSSON Lars-Inge, b. 11 Dec 1950, Helsingborg, Sweden. Professor. m. Benedikte Traasdahl, 11 July 1987. *Education:* Med Deg, 1971; DSc, 1975; Docent, 1976. *Appointments:* Jr Lectr, Histol, Univ of Lund, Sweden, 1970-75; Sr Lectr, Biochem, Univ of Aarhus, 1976-82; Res Prof, Copenhagen DK, 1982-88; Dept Hd, State Serum Inst, Copenhagen, 1988-. *Creative works:* 230 scientific works including: Histochemistry of the Gastrin Cells, 1974; Peptide Immunocytochemistry, 1981; Immunocytochemistry: Theory and Practice, 1988; Regulatory Peptides and Amines during development and cancer over the years; Edit, Histochemistry. *Memberships:* NYAS; Histochem Soc; Edit Bd, Histochemical Jour. *Honours:* Boehringer Ingelheim Awd, 1983; Mack Forster Awd, Euro Soc Clin Invest, 1986; Anders Jahre Awd, 1987; Lundbeck Awd, 1987; Robert Fuelgen Lecrt, 1988; PV Petersen Awd, 1991. *Hobbies:* Photography; Art; Poetry. *Address:* Grundtvigsvej 34 4th, 1867 Frederiksberg C, Denmark.

LASBURY Leah Bartlett, b. 4 Nov 1915, Boca Grande, Florida, USA. Retired Business Woman and Community Worker. m. CLyde P Lasbury, 16 Sept 1939, dec 1989, 3 d. *Education:* BS, Simmons Col, Boston, MA, 1937. *Appointments include:* Organizing Chm, Englewood Bus and Profl Women, 1961; Charter Dir, Asolo Theatre Festival Assn, 1963-72; Pres, Florida's Artists Gp, 1972-74, 1978-80; Mission Chm, Englewood Utd Methodist Ch, 1982- 84; Dir, Historical Comm of Sarasota Co, 1985-87; Sarasota Co Library Adv Bd, 1990-; Public Relations Com Englewood Chapter, 1991. *Memberships:* Nat Soc Magna Carta Dames; Phi Mu; IPA; Englewood Utd Methodist Ch, 1954-. *Honours:* Patriot's Awds, Sarasota Co, 1976, Englewood, 1976; Hon Life, Englewood Bd of Realtors, 1985, Florida Artist Gp, 1981. 7, 132, 129,

LASDUN Denys (Louis) Sir, b. 8 Sept 1914. Architect. m. Susan Bendit, 1954, 2 s, 1 d. *Education:* Rugby Sch; Arch Assn, London, RIBA. *Appointments:* Royal Engrs, 1939-45; Practised with Wells Coates Tecton & Drake, 1935-48. Prof of Arch, Univ of Leeds, 1962-63; Private Practice, Peter Softley & Assocs, London; Assessor, Belgrade Opera Hse, 1971, New Parliamentary Bldg, London, 1971-72. *Creative works include:* Housing and

Schools for Bethnal Green & Paddington; London HQ, NSW Govt; Flats at 26 St James's Place; Royal College of Physicians; Fitzwilliam College, Christ's College extension, Cambridge; New Univ of East Anglia, works for Univs of London (SAS, Inst of Ed, Law Inst), Leicester, Liverpool; Nat Theatre and IBM, South Bank; EEC HQ for European Investment Bank, Luxembourg; Design for new Hurva Synagogue, Jerusalem; Cannock Comm Hosp; Genoa Opera HGouse Comp; Offices, Fenchurch St, EC4 and Milton Gate, EC2. *Publications:* An Architects approach to Architecture, 1965; A Language and a Theme, 1976; Architecture in an Age of Scepticism, 1984. *Contributions to:* architectural and other papers; Lectures worldwide. *Memberships:* Trustee, Brit Mus, 1975-85; CIAM and MARS Gp, 1935-59; Jerusalem Town Planning Committee, 1970; Victoria and Albert Adv Coun, 1973-83; Slade Com, 1976-92; Arts Panel, ACGB, 1980-84; Academie d'Architecture, Paris, 1984; Accademia Nationale di San Luce, Rome, 1984; Academician, Intl Acad of Arch, Bulgaria, 1986. *Honours:* MBE; CBE, 1965, KT, 1976; Hon Fellow, AIA, 1966; Hon DA, Manchester, 1966; Hon DLitt, E.Anglia, 1974, Sheffield, 1978; Hon FRCP, 1975; London Arc Bronz Medallist, 1960, 1964, Royal Gold Medal for Arch, 1977, Arch Awd for London Region, 1978, RIBA; Civic Trust Awds: Class 1, 1967; Gp A, 1969; Special Awd, Sao Paulo Biennale, Brazil, 1969; Concrete Soc Awd, 1976; RA, 1991; Wolf Foundation Prize in Arts (Architcture), 1992; RIBA Trustees' Medal, 1992. *Address:* 146 Grosvenor Rd, London SW1V 3JY, England. 1, 43, 52, 139.

LASOK Karol Paul Edward, b. 16 July 1953, London, England. Barrister. m. Karen Bridget Morgan Griffith, 23 Feb 1991. *Education:* MA Jusus Col, Cambs, 1972-75; LLM, PhD, Exeter Univ, 1975076; Inns of Ct, Sch of Law, 1976-77. *Appointments:* Called to the Bar, England and Wales, 1977; Legal Sec, Ct of Justice of The European Communities, 1980-84, 1985; Private Practice, Brussels, 1985-87, London, 1987-. *Creative works:* Publications include The European Court of Justice: Practice and Procedure, 1984. *Contributions to:* Halsburys Laws of England; The Law of the European Communities; Stair Memorial Encyclopaedia of the Laws of England; Weinberg and Blank on Takeovers and Mergers; Numerous articles on European Community Law. *Memberships:* Middle Temple; Newman Assn; Bar European Gp; UK Assn for European Law. *Hobbies:* Music; Military History; Travel. *Address:* 4 Raymond Buildings, Grays Inn, London WC1R 5BP, England.

LAST Frederick Thomas, b. 5 Feb 1928, Wembley, England. Applied Biologist. m. 12 Sept 1952, 2 s. *Education:* Imperial Col of Sci and Tech, London, 1945-51; BSc, ARCS, 1948; PhD, DIC, 1951, DSc, London Univ, 1965. *Appointments:* Rothamsted Experimental Station, Herts, 1951-61; Chief Plant Pathologist, Sudan Govt, 1956-58; Hd, Mycology and Bacteriol, Glasshouse Crops Res Inst, 1961-69; Vis Prof, Pennsylvania State Univ, 1969- 70; Directorate, inst of Terrestrial Ecol, 1970-86. *Creative works:* Jt Ed, Tree physiology and yield improvement, 1976; Land and its uses, actual and potential, 1986; Acidic deposition: Its nature and impacts, 1991. *Memberships:* Assn of Applied Biols, Gen Sec 1961-67, Hon Tres 1967-72, Pres 1977-78, Hon Mem 1982-; Brit Mycol Soc; Inst of Biol; Inst of Chartered Foresters. *Honours:* Fellow, Royal Soc of Edinburgh, 1975. *Hobbies:* Gardening; Philately; Travel. *Address:* Furuly,Seton Mains, Longniddry, East Lothian EH32 OPG, Scotland.

LATHAM Edward Michael Locks, b. 7 Jan 1930, Hadley Wood, England. Timber Merchant. m. Joan Doris Coubrough, 15 Oct 1955, 1 s, 2 d. *Education:* Modern Langs Scholarship, BA Ec, 1952, MA 1956, Clare Col, Cambs. *Appointments:* James Latham plc, 1952-91, (Chm 1973-87); Chm, Trebartha Estates Ltd, Dir Bloomsbury Properties Ltd. *Memberships:* Pres, Sandringham Assn 1982-83, and Council 1987-91, Royal Warrant Holders; Pres, The Timber Trade Fed, 1984-85; Pres, The Intl Tech Assn for Tropical Timber, 1987-91; Exec Com, Nat Coun of Bldg Material

Producers, 1985-91; Chm, The Lanlivery Trust, 1989-; Gov, St Dunstans Abbey Sch, 1988-; Pres, Royal Cornwall Agric Assn, 1992-93; Non-Ex Dir Royal Cornwall Hospitals Trust, 1991-; High Sheriff of Cornwall, 1992-93. *Hobbies:* The countryside; Tennis; Classic cars; History; Books. *Address:* Trebartha Lodge, Launceston, Cornwall PL15 7PD, England. 1

LATHAN Samuel Robert, b. 28 Apr 1938, Charlotte, N.Carolina, USA. Physician. m. Mary Amelia Hudson, 19 Mar 1966, 1 s, 2 d. *Education:* BS Davidson Col, 1959; MD Johns Hopkins Univ Sch of Med, 1963; Internship Med, Duke Hosp, 1963-64; Fellowship, 1964-65, Residency, 1965-67, Grady Mem Hosp. *Appointments:* Lowance Clinic, 1969-73, Colony Med Gp, 1973-80, Solo Practice, 1980-, Atlanta, Georgia. *Creative works:* 10 scientific papers published in medical journals. *Memberships:* Med Assn of Atlanta Bd of Trustees; Ed, Atlanta Medicine; Atlanta Clin Soc; Gen Heart Assn; Am Soc Int Med; Med Assn GA; AMA; GA Thoracic Soc; Am Col of Sports Med; Am Med Joggers Assn. *Honours:* Diplomate, Am Bd of Intl Med, 1969, REcertified, 1977-; FACP, 1974, ACCP, 1976; AMA Phys Recognition Awds, 1969-; WS Beaver Awd, 1977. *Hobbies:* Long distance and Marathon running; Reading; Travel; Golf. *Address:* 1938 Peachtree Road, Atlanta, GA 30309, USA. 7, 17,

LATORRE Robert George, b. 9 Jan 1949, Toledo, Ohio, USA. Professor of Naval Architecture and Marine Engineering. m. Erika Y Yoshino, 5 Sept 1980. *Education:* BSe, 1971, MS, 1972, Univ of Michigan; MSE 1975, DrEng, 1978, Univ of Tokyo. *Appointments:* ASst Prof, Navel Arc and Marine Eng Univ of Michigan, 1979-84; Reschr, French Navy, Paris, 1984; Prof Naval Arch, Univ of New Orleans, 1984-, Chm of Naval Arch, 1989. *Creative works:* Naval Architecture, Encyclopaedia of Science and Technology, 1987, 1991; Design of Univ of New Orleans Towing Tank Laboratory. *Memberships:* RINA; Soc of Naval Arch and Marine Engrs; ASME; ISNA, Ocean and Marine Engr Div Chm; Am Soc of Engrg Ed. *Honours:* Tau Beta Pi, 1970; Grad Scholarship, SNAME, 1973-78; Japanese Govt Ministry of Ed Scholarship, 1985; Halburton Tchg Awd. *Hobbies:* Travel; Writing. *Address:* 300 Lake Marina Dr No 7BE, New Orleans, LA 70124, USA. 50, 26.

LATTEA Kathleen M, b. 30 Jan 1954, Washington DC, USA. Psychotherapist. m. 4 June 1977, 1 s, 1 d. *Education:* BA Psycho, Am Univ; MA Counselling Psycho, Wheaton Col. *Appointments:* Private Practice, Psycho, 1983-; Prof, Washington Bible Col, 1983-84; Grad Asst Wheaton Col, 1982-83; Res Assoc, Conslt firm, 1977-81. *Creative works:* Co-author, Christian Faith and Community Psychology, 1983. *Memberships:* Am and Maryland Psycho Assns; Frederick Co Mental Health Assn; Christian Assn of Psycho Studies. *Honours:* Nat Dean's List; Magna cum laude grad; Rech Awd for outstanding Grad Psycho Student; Outstanding Young Woman of Am. *Hobbies:* Workshop presentations on the prevention of personal, marital and family problems; Studying and teaching the Bible. *Address:* 5300 Westview Dr, Suite 108, Frederick, MD 21701, USA.

LATZ Dorothy Lenore, b. 9 Dec 1930, New York, USA. Professor and writer. *Education:* BA Eng, Col of New Rochelle, NY, 1953; MA Eng, Fordham Univ, NY, 1962; French Lic, Univ Grenoble, 1971; Doctorates: Comparative Lit, Univ de Paris, 1969, Catholic Theol, Univ Strasbourg, France, 1986. *Appointments include:* Instr, Eng, Seton Hall Univ, NJ, 1964-66; Asst Prof, Eng and French, Marywood Col, PA, 1969-70; Assoc Prof, Humanities, St Thomas Aquinas Col, NY, 1975-78; Adj Assoc Prof, Humanities, Poly Univ, NY, 1987, 1988; Prof Theol, St Joseph;s Sem Grad Div, Yonkers, NY, 1990-. *Creative works:* Books include: Glow Worm Light: Writings of 17th C English Recusant Women, 1989; The Building of Divine Lone as Translated by Dame Grace Agnes More, 1991; The World of St Angela Merici, translated nto English, 1991; Articles include: Angeli Merici; Marie of the Incarnation, 1991; Le

Theatre du Moyen Age, 1980; Poetry. *Memberships:* Dir, Intl Recusant Manscript Soc, Co Dir, Intl Conf, 1991-93; other literary, theological and historical associations. *Honours:* Elected Assoc of Renaissance Sems, Columbia Univ, NY, 1980-; Various other scholarships for undergrad and grad work. *Hobbies:* Creative writing, especially poetry. *Address:* PO Box 265, New Rochelle, NY 10802, USA. 11, 3.

LAUFS Kurt Wilhelm, b. 29 Nov 1948, Krefeld, Rhine, Germany. Psychologist; Artist. *Education:* Psycho Dipls, 1974, 1977; Clinical Psycho, 1981; Clini Psycho and Psychotherapist, 1990; PhD, 1990; DPsych, 1991. *Creative works:* Parapleis, 1989; Short stories, poetry, science, paintings and ink drawings which have been exhibited. *Memberships:* Berufsverband Deatscher Psychologen; Intl Parliament for Safety and peace; Alliance Univ pour la Pai par la connaissance; Madras Cultural Corres Club. *Honours:* Res Scholarship, 1975-76; Coptic Cross, Ethiopia; Dr in Comp Religion; Prof in Paris and Brussels; Grandmaster, Lofsensic Ursinius Order; Knight of the Templars. *Hobbies:* Reading; Writing; Painting; Structuralism; Swimming; Alpine Skiing; Canoeing; Gardening; Meditating; Freudian psychoanalysis. *Address:* Atelier fur Kuust und Wissenschaft, Sittard Str 41, D-4050 Mouchengladbach 1, Germany. 152.

LAUREL Salvador, b. 18 Nov 1928, Manila, Philippines. Vice President, Republic of the Philippines. m. Celia Franco Diaz, 2 Sept 1950, 4 s, 4 d. *Education:* AA, pre law, 1946, LLB, 1952, Univ of the Philippines; LLM, 1953, JSD, 1960, Yale Univ. *Appointments:* Sanator, Repub of the Philippines, 1967-73; Assemblyman, Batasang Pambansa, 1978-83; Sec, Dept of Foreign Affairs, 1986-87; Prime Minister, Feb - March 1986, V- Pres, 1986-, Repub of the Philippines. *Creative works include:* Socio- Legal Determinants of the Philippines Labour Policy, 1961; Laurel Reports: Central Luzon, 1971, Mission to China, 1972, Penal Reforms, 1969, Military Unrest, 1987, Towards the Centre - Or the Best of Two Worlds, 1988; Resilience and Realism, 1989; Proceedings of the Philippine Constitutional Convention, 1934-35, Ed in 7 vols, 1970. *Memberships:* Pres, Nacionalista party, Utd Nat Democratic Org; Partner, Laural Law Offices; Chm, Fdr, Citizens Legal Aid Soc of the Philippines; Integrated Bar of the Philippines; Yale Club of the Philippines; Upsilon Sigma Phi. *Honours:* Outstanding Legal Aid lawyer of th Wordl Intl Bar Assn, 1976; Dangal ng Batangan Awd, 1976; Outstanding Senator, 1968-71; Lawyer of the year, Justice and Ct Reporters Assn of the Philippines, 1967. *Address:* 515 Shaw Blvd, Mandulyuong, Metro Manila, Philippines.

LAURITZEN Christian, b. 6 Dec 1923, Rendsburg, Germany. Professor of Gynaecology and Obstetrics. m. Brigitte Schoreit, 18 Mar 1954, 2 d. *Education:* MD, 1949; Prof, 1961; Chm, 1968, Univ Ulm. *Appointments:* Gynae Dept, Univ of Kiel, Germany, 1950-68, Univ Stockholm, 1958-61, Univ Ulm, Germany, 1968. *Creative works:* Oestrogee Blimenschen Springer, 1961; Lehrbuch Geburtshilff Gynakologie Springer; Gynakol Endokrinologie Urban Schuarzenberg, 1988. *Memberships:* Dean Med Fac; VP Univ Ulm; Pres Fed Intl Children Adolescent Gynaec; Pres, Menopause Soc German Speaking Countries. *Honours:* Bundesverdienstureuz I Class, 1988; Ernst von Bergmann Medal, 1988; Ernst Laqueur Medal, 1990. *Hobbies:* Poetry; Collecting autographs. *Address:* Alpenstrasse 49, D-7900 Ulm, Germany.

LAURSEN Axel Norskov, b. 23 Mar 1951, Denmark. m. Winnie Laursen. 2 d. *Education:* BEcon & Bus Admin, 1975; BSc, 1978; BCommerce, 1981. *Appointments:* Sales Mgr, 1979-82, Product Mgr, 1982, General Mgr, 1983-84, Sabroe Refrigeration; VP, Atlas Danmark AS, 1985-86; Pres, Atlas Industries AS, 1987-. *Memberships:* Danish Employers Confed Gen Assembly. *Address:* Egestien 6, 2950 Vedbaek, Denmark.

LAURSEN Finn, b. 17 June 1944, Romlund Sogn, Denmark. Professor of International Politics. m. Maria Berenice Lara, 20 Aug 1983, 1 s. *Education:* PhD Polit Sci, Univ of Pennsylvania, 1980; Cand Scient Pol, Aarhus Univ, 1974; Dipl, Inst Européen des Hautes Etudes Intl, Nice, 1967. *Appointments:* Assoc Prof, Odense Univ, 1982-85; Lectr, London Sch of Ec, 1985-88; Prof of Intl Polit, European Inst of Public Admin, 1990-. *Creative works:* Books: Superpower at Sea, 1983; L'Europe Bleue, 1986; Danmark og Havretten, 1988. *Memberships:* Dir of Inst of Global Policy Studies, Amsterdam; Bd of Centre Intl De Formation Europeenne, Paris. *Honours:* Fulbright Grant, 1985-76; Penfield Scholarship, Univ PA, 1977; John Parker Compton Fellowship, Princeton Univ, 1980-81; Res Fellowship, Comm of EC, 1983-84. *Hobbies:* Travelling; Gardening. *Address:* Camerig 14, NL 6294 NB Vijlen, The Netherlands. 52.

LAWLEY Kenneth Larry, b. 13 Dec 1932, Harrisburg, Pennsylvania, USA. Vice President, Texas Medical Instruments. m. Arlene Evans Lawley, 30 Dec 1976, 2 s, 3 d. *Education:* BS Metallurgy,Pennsylvania State Univ, PhD, Ohio State Univ. *Appointments:* Bell Telephone Labs, 1962-68; Tech Dir, Monsante, 1968-72; Gp Leader, Texas Instruments, 1972-82; Chief Engr, Honeywell Corp, 1980-86; VP, Texas Med Instruments, 1986-. *Memberships:* IEEE: Electrochem Soc. *Hobbies:* Choral Music: San Antonio Symp Mastersingers, Boston Symp Tanglewood Chorus, Dallas Symp Chorus, Masterworks Chorus. *Address:* 16 Cheshire Court, San Antonio, TX 78218, USA. 7, 14.

LAWNICZAK-JABLOVISKA Krystyna Maria, b. 24 Mar 1950, Warsaw, Poland. Solid State Physicist. m. Alexander Jabtonski, 7 June 1979. 2 d. *Education:* Grad, Dept of Solid State Phys, Warsaw Univ, 1973; PhD, Inst of Pys, Polish Acad of Scis (PAS). *Appointments:* Asst, 1973, Adjunct, 1981, Reschr, 1992, Inst of Phys, PAS. *Publications:* 40 in international scientific journals and proceedings of conferences in the field of x-ray and lectron spectroscopy. *Memberships:* European and Polish Synchrontron Rediation Socs. *Honours:* Awds from: Sec of PAS, 1980, 1983, and the Dir of Inst of Phys, PAS, 1988. *Hobbies:* Growing exotic flowers indoor and out; Swimming; Bicycling; Cross country skiing. *Address:* Institute of Physics, Polish Academy of Sciences, Al Lotnikow 32/46, 02668 Warsaw, Poland. 138.

LAWRENCE John Wilfred, b. 15 Sept 1933, Hastings. Book Illustrator and Wood Engraver. m. Myra Gillian Bell, 14 Dec 1957, 2 d. *Education:* Salesian Col, Cowley, Oxford; Hastings and Central Schls of Art. *Appointments:* Vis Lectr, Illustration, Brighton Poly, 1960-68; Camberwell Sch of Art, 1960-, External Assessor in Illustration, Edinburgh Col of Art and Kingston Poly. *Creative works:* Illustrated more than 100 books. *Memberships:* Art Workers Guild, Master, 1990; Soc of Wood Engravers; Double Crown CLub. *Hounours:* Francis Williams Book Illustration Awd, 1971, 1977. *Address:* 22a Castlewood Road, London N16 6DW, England. 1.

LAWRENCE Roderick John, b. 30 Aug 1949, Adelaide, Australia. Architect; Consultant to ECE; Master of Teaching and Research. m. Clarisse Christine Gonet, 30 Sept 1977, 3 s. *Education:* BArch, 1st class hons, Univ of Adelaide, 1972; ARAIA, 1973; ARIBA, 1975; Postgrad Res Fellow, St John's Col, Cambs, 1975-77; MLitt, Cantab, 1977; DArch, Ecole Poly Fed de Lausanne, (EPFL),1983. *Appointments include:* Tutor, Arch, EPFL 1978-84; Conslt, Com on Hsg Bldg and Planning, Ec Comm for Europe, Geneva, 1984-85; Guest Lectr, Reschr, Sch of Arch, Univ of Geneva, 1984- 85; Vis Lectr, Univ of Adelaide, 1985; Vis Res Fellow, Sch of Soc Scis, Flinders Univ of S.Australia, 1985; Master of Tchg and Res, Centre for Human Ecol and Environ Scis, Univ of Geneva, 1986-; Expert to Soc and Human Scis Div of Swiss Natl Sci Fndn, 1992-. *Creative works:* Books: Le Seuil franchi: Logement populaire et vie quotidienne en Suisse romande, 1860-1960, 1986; Housing Dwellings and Homes: Design Theory, Research and Practice, 1987; Numerous chapters, articles and reviews. *Memberships:* Environ Design Res Assn, Washington DC; People and Phys Environ Res Assn, Sydney; Bd, Intl Assn for the Study of People and their Phys Surroundings; Ed Bd, Open Hse Intl Assn; Reg Ed, Intl Sociological Assn Newsletter; Ed Bd, Jour Arch and Behaviour. *Honours:* Recipient of several prizes, fellowships and travelling scholarships. *Hobbies:* Skiing; Photography; Bushwalking. *Address:* Centre for Human Ecology and Environmental Sciences, University of Geneva, 102 Boulevard Carl-Vogt, 1211 Geneva 4, Switzerland. 52, 139, 151, 191.

LAWSON Donald S, b. 18 Jan 1935, Liverpool, England. President, Atomic Energy of Canada Ltd. m. Rosanne, 10 Aug 1957, 3 c. *Education:* Grad, Aeronaut Engrg, Univ of Bristol, 1956. *Appointments:* Design, Testing and Engineering Mgmt of nuclear equipment, English Elec Co, 1958-76; VP Power and Desalination projts, Saudi Arabia, Sanderson & Porter Inc, NY, 1977-78; AECL CANDU, 1978, Pres, 1984; Pres, AECL Technologies, Rockville, Maryland. *Memberships:* Assn of Profl Engrs of Ontario; Canadian Nuclear Soc; Dir, Nuclear Proj Mgrs Inc; Past Bd, Brit Nuclear Energy Soc. *Honours:* Recipient of the James Clayton Fund Prize, 1969; Assn of Profl Engrs of Ontario Engineering Medal, Management Category, 1992. *Address:* AECL CANDU, 2251 Speakman Drive, Mississauga, Ontrario, Canada L5K 1B2. 88.

LAY David John, b. 15 Aug 1948, Oxford, England. Journalist. m. Tamara Said Mufti, 1 Sept 1973, 1 s, 3 d. *Education:* Magdalen Col Sch, 1959-67; MA Modern Hist, Corpus Christi Col, 1967-70, Oxford. *Appointments:* BBC: News Trainee, 1970-72, News Sub Editor, 1982-74, News Reporter, 1974-79; Presenter, 24 hrs BBC World Service, 1979-91; Mng Ed, Oxford Analytica, 1988-. *Hobbies:* Tennis; Foreign Travel; Middle East Politics. *Address:* 215 Ashburnham Rd, Ham, Richmond, Surrey TW10 7SE, England.

LAY K Edward, b. 2 Dec 1932, Carlisle, Cumberland Co, Pennsylvania, USA. m. Margaret Jane Fleming, 28 Dec 1955. 1 s, 1 d. *Education:* MArch, Kansas State Univ, 1965; BArch, Penn State Univ, 1955; NCARB, 1965-. *Appointments include:* Fac, Univ of Virginia, 1967-, Prof of Arch, Assoc Dean, 1981-82, Asst Dean, 1974-81, Acting Dean, 1976, Dir of Undergraduate Architecture, 1992-, Univ Senator, 1973-81, Historic Preservation Conslt, 1990; Supervisory Archt for HABS/HAER of NPS, Am Indust Heritage Proj, 1988-89; Vis Prof, Edinburgh Col of Art, 1977. *Creative works include:* A Virginia Family and its Plantation Houses, 1987; Jeffersons Master Builders, 1991; Dinsmore and Neilson, 1991. *Memberships include:* Local Branch, APVA, Bd of Dirs, 1986-90; Victorian Soc of Virginia, VP, 1982-86; Pioneer Am Soc, Bd, 1975-81; Charlottesville Historic Landmarks Comm, Chm, 1975-87, and Bd of Arch Review, Chm, 1972-78. *Honours include:* Omicron Delta Kappa; Tau Sigma Dalta; Hon Awds: Nat Trust for Hist Preservation, 1982; Am Soc of Landscape Archts, 1983; Mayoral Awd for Historic Preservation Efforts, 1984; APVA Award for Outstanding Achievement in Hist Preservation, 1991; Grants: Am Philos Soc, 1978, 1990, German Acad Exchange 1978. *Hobbies:* Lecturing; Conducting Historic Tours; Hiking; Racquetball; Badminton; Genealogy; Photography. *Address:* Campbell Hall School of Architecture, University of Virginia, Charlottesville, VA 22903, USA. 7, 131.

LAYSON Ruby Lee, b. 1 Oct 1927, Henderson, Kentucky, USA. Writer and Editor. m. Mason Sexton, 22 Nov 1952, div 1985, 1 s, 1 d. *Education:* AB Wesleyan Col, GA, 1949; AM Indiana Univ, 1952; Grad Study, Ed and Eng, California State and UC Extension, Los Angeles. *Appointments:* Writer and Ed, Ky Dept of Ed, 1984-; Copy Ed, Lexington Ky Gerald Leader, 1981-84; Writer and Comms Supervisory, Ky Dept of Public Info,

1978-81; Reporter and Consumer Affairs Writer, San Diego Union, 1974-78; Los Angeles Bureau Chief, Copley News Ser, 1971-74; Reporter, City Ed, Alhambra Post Advocate, 1968-71. *Creative works:* Co-ed, From the Fort to the Future: Educating the Children of Kentucky; articles in professional and travel publications. *Memberships:* Ky and National Community Ed Assns; Proj 21 Com of Ky Chamber of Commerce; Appalachia Ed Lab; Ky Assn of Govt Communicators; Soc of Profl Jours. *Honours:* Copley newspapers Ring of Truth Awd, 1970; Pres's Awd, Ky Community Ed Assn, 1990; Harlan Alumni Hall of Fame, 1991. *Hobbies:* Archaeology; Playing and Teaching Appalachian Dulcimer. *Address:* 616 Polsgrove St, Frankfort, KY 40601, USA. 5, 7,

LAZENBY David William, b. 13 Oct 1937, Frimley, England. Consulting Engineer. m. Valerie Ann Kent, 2 Sept 1961, 1 s. 1 d. *Education:* Battersea Col of Tech, 1955-59; DIC, Imperial Col, London, 1960-61; DipCU, City Univ, London, 1975-78. *Appointments:* Andrews, Kent & Stone, 1962-, Assoc 1968, Partner, 1972, Chm 1983. *Creative works:* Structural Steelwork, 1975; Structural Mechanics, 1974; Cutting for Construction, 1978. *Memberships:* FICE; FIStructE, Pres, 1990-91; Assn of Consltg Engrs. *Honours:* European Engineer, Euro Ing; Pres, IStructE. *Hobbies:* Travel; Tennis; Opera; Good food and wine. *Address:* Paddock House, 11 Bennett Way, W.Clandon, Guildford GU4 7TN, Surrey, England. 26.

LE Masaji, b. 5 Oct 1937, Ishikawa. Prof Intl Law. m. Takeko Inoue, 12 Feb 1972, 2 d. *Education:* Rakuho Ku High Sch, 1956; Doshisha Univ, 1962; Kyoto Univ, 1964. *Appointments:* Asst, Kobe City Univ of Foreign Studies, 1966; Instr, 1967; Assoc Prof, 1969; Prof, 1979; Dean of Students, 1990-. *Publications:* Evolution of the Systems of Non Self Governing Territories; The Unit of Nations and the Application of the Right to Self Determination; The Namibian Problem and the United Nations. *Memberships include:* Japanese Assn of Intl Law; Intl Law Assn; American Soc of Intl Law; Intl Assn for the Future of Humanity. *Honours:* Letter of Appreciation by Democratic Proples Republic of Korea. *Hobbies:* Reading; Swimming; Appreciation of Movie. *Address:* 1-2-17 Suzurandai Kitamachi, Kita Ku, Kobe, Japan.1.52

LE DAIN Gerald Eric, Hon, b. 27 Nov 1924, Montreal, Canada. Retired Judge, Supreme Ct of Canada. m. Cynthia Roy 13 Sept 1947, 1 s, 5 d. *Education:* BCL, McGill Univ, 1949; D de l'Univ, Univ de Lyon, 1950. *Appointments:* Walker Martineau & Co, 1950-53; Fac of Law, McGill Univ, 1953-59; Legal Dept, Canadian Intl Paper Co, 1959-61; Riel, Le Dain & Co, 1961-66; Fac of Law, McGill Univ, 1966-67; Dean, Osgoode Hall Law Sch, York Univ, 1967-72, Prof of Law, 1967-75; Chm, Comm of Inquiry into the non-Med use of Drugs, 1969-73; Justice Fed Ct of Appeal, 1975-84; Justice, Supreme Ct of Canada, 1984-88. *Honours:* Elizabeth Torrance Gold Medal and Macdonald Travelling Scholarship, McGill Univ, 1949; QC, 1961; Hon LLD's, York Univ, 1976; Concordia Univ, 1976; McGill Univ, 1985; Hon DCL Acadia Univ 1978; Companion of the Order of Canada, 1989; The Justice Gerald Le Dain Award for Achievement in the Field of Law, Drug Policy Foun, 1990. *Address:* 263 Island Park Drive, Ottawa, Ontario, Canada K1Y OA5. 88, 2.

LE ROUX Jean-Louis, b. 15 Apr 1927, France. Orchestra Conductor. m. Marta Bracchi, 13 Dec 1957, 2 s, 1 d. *Education:* Ecole Superieure Commerce Paris, 1946; Dipl, Conservatoire Nat de Musique Paris, 1949. *Appointments:* Principal Oboe: Belo Horizonte, Brazil, 1950-54; Montevideo, Uruguay, 1954-59; San Francisco Symph, 1960-80; Music Dir, San Francisto Contemporary Music Players, 1975-87; Conductor, SF Ballet, Music Dir, SF Chamber Symph, 1980-. *Creative works:* Various recordings of contemporary work on CRT lebel; Recording of music for The Tempest by Paul Chillara. *Honours:* Chevalier de l'ordre des Arts et des

Lettres, 1981; Emmy, 1984. *Address:* 2874 Washington Street, San Francisco, CA 94115, USA. 2.

LEACH Catherine Frances, b. 26 July 1956, Sringfield, Vermont, USA. Trumpet Professor. *Education:* BM Music Educ, Univ of Michigan, 1978; MM Applied Trumpet, Univ of New Mexico, 1981. *Appointments:* Prof of Trumpet, Univ of Tennessee, 1981-; Principal Trumpet, Knoxville Symphony Orch, 1981-. *Memberships:* Intl Trumpet Guild, Bd, 1991-; Pi Kappa Lambda; Clinician for Bach Selmer Corp. *Honours:* Stanley Medal, (Outstanding Sr), Univ of Michigan, 1978. *Hobbies:* Tennis; Swimming; Jogging; Reading; Languages; Dogs; Birds; Computer. *Address:* 3421 Luwana Ln, Knoxville, TN 37917, USA.

LEADBETTER Martin John, b. 6 Apr 1945, London, England. Fingerprint Expert and Adviser. m. Ivy Georgina, 7 June 1969. 2 s. *Education:* Assoc and Licentiate, Trinity Col of Music, London. *Appointments:* Fingerprint Expert: New Scotland yard 1966; herts Police, 1974-91; Morpo Systemes Fountainebleau, France. *Creative works:* 150 compositions including: An English Requiem, 1982; Symphony No 1, 1982; 3 String Quarters; Southampton: Portrait of a City, 1991. *Memberships:* The Fingerprint Soc, Hon Life; Intl Assn for Identification, Bd of Dirs and Dist Mem; The Performing Right Soc; The Composer's Guild of GB; Chorale Laudate Dominum de Fontainebleau; The Forensic Science Soc; Canadian Indentification Soc; British Acad of Forensic Sciences; The Police History Soc. *Honours:* Lewis Minshall Awd, 1978. *Hobbies:* Classical music; Natural Sciences; Travel; Cooking; Arts. *Address:* c/o Morphd Systèmes, 33 Route de la Bonne Dame, France.

LEAKE Larry Bruce, b. 19 May 1950, Asheville, N.Carolina, USA. Attorney. *Education:* BA 1972; JD, 1974. *Appointments:* Assoc Attorney, 74-77, Partner, 1977-80, Uzell & Dumont; Partner, Attorney, Harrell & Leake, 1980-. *Memberships:* Buncombe Co Bar Sec, 1975-76; Am and N.Carolina Bar ASsns. *Honours:* Phi Beta Kappa, Univ N.Carolina, Chapel Hill, 1971; Order of the Long Leaf Pine, 1980; Outstanding Young Democrat, Young Democrat of Am, 1981. *Hobbies:* Spectator sports and bowling. *Address:* Harrell & Leake, 701 BB&T Bank Building, Asheville NC 28801, USA.

LEAPER David John, b. 23 July 1947, York, England. Consultant Sr Lecturer in Surgery. *Education:* Leeds Univ, 1965-60; MBChB Hons, 1970; FRCS Edin, 1974; FRCS England, 1975; MD, 1979; ChM, 1982. *Appointments:* Registrar, Leeds and Scarborough Hosps, 1972-75; Res Fellow, Kings Col Hosp, 1975-76; Sr Surg Registrar, Westminster Hosp, 1977-81; Prof of Surg, Univ of Hing Kong, 1988-90. *Creative works:* Original articles on wound infection, wound healing and breast cancer; Books and chapters in surgical texts; Chief Ed, Surgical Research Communications. *Memberships:* Surg Res Soc; RSM, Surg Section, VP; Assn of Surgs; Surg Infection So of Europe, Coun. *Honours:* Surg Res Soc European Fellowship; Past MRC and CRC Fellow, Leeds and London; Hunterian Prof, RCS, 1981. *Address:* University Department of Surgery, Medical School Unit, Southmead Hospital, Bristol BS10 5NB, England.

LEARY Nancy, b. 25 Mar 1952, Massachusetts, USA. Marketing Consultant. *Education:* AA Mass Bay Community Col, 1979; BS Org Behaviour, Lesley Col, Cambs, MA, 1988; MA Ed, Univ of S.Florida, 1992. *Appointments:* Admin Mgr, Cullinet Software, 1985-86; Mktg Specialist, 1986-89; Supervisor, Tech Support, Arthur Andersen, Fla, 1989-90; Mktg Consultant, 1990-. *Memberships:* NAFE; Florida Community Assn Mgrs. *Honours:* Phi Kappa Phi, 1991. *Hobbies:* Reading; Travel; Community Volunteer work. *Address:* PO Box 181, Bradenton, FL 34206, USA. 132, 5.

LEBLANC Roger M, b. 5 Jan 1942, Quebec, Canada. Professor in Physical chemistry. m. Micheline Veillette, 26 June 1965, 2 s, 2 d. *Education:* BSc Chem, 1964, PhD Phys Chem, 1968, Univ Laval, Quebec, Canada; Posdoc Fellow, Royal Inst of GB, 1968-70. *Appointments:* Prof, Chem Biol Dept, Univ of Quebec Trois Rivieres (UQTR), 1970-; Dir, Photobiophys Res Ctr, UQTR, 1981-91; Chm, Chem Biol Dept, UQTR, 1971-75; Analytial, Phys Chem, Grant Selection Com, NSERC, 1990-91. *Creative works:* Co-author of more than 200 scientific papers and 230 scientific communications. *Memberships:* ACS; Am Soc for Photobiol; Assn Canadienne-Francaise pour l'Advancement des Scis; Biophys Soc; Brit Photobiol Soc; European Photochem Assn; Protein Soc; Spectroscopy Soc of Canada. *Honours include:* John Labatt Ltd Awd, Canadian Soc for Chem, 1992; Medale of Merit, UQTR, 1987; Barringer Awd, Spectroscopy Soc of Canada, 1983; Noranda Awd, Chem Inst of Canada, 1982; Fellow, Chem Inst of Canada, 1980. *Hobbies:* Hockey; Reading; Music. *Address:* 5539 rue Marseille, Trois Rivieres Quest, Quebec G8T 3Z6, Canada. 2, 164, 6.

LECONTE Frederick James, b. 27 Nov 1941, Castle Donnington, England. Artist; Painter. m. 22 Sept 1962, 2 s. *Education:* Islington Green School, Islington, London, England. *Appointments:* Scenic Artist, Royal Opera House, Covent Gdn, 1963-77; Scenic Artist, English Natl Opera, 1977-85, Scenic Artist Hd of Dept, Royal Opera House, 1985-. *Creative works:* One man painting shows at Gallery Cathedral Place, 1968; Alpine Gallery, 1977; Black Heath Gallery, 1988; Ansdell Gallery, 1975. *Hobbies:* Music; Sport; Snooker; Country walks. *Address:* 60 Warland Road, Plumstead, London SE18 2EU, England.

LECROY Hoyt Franklin, b. 8 Oct 1941, Cherokee County, Alabama, USA. Music Administrator. m. Karen Allene Adams LeCroy, 6 June 1964, 2 s, 1 d. *Education:* BA, Jacasonville State Univ, AL, 1963; MM E.Carolina Univ, 1966; PhD Univ of S.Miss, 1978. *Appointments:* Coordinator of Instrumental Music Education; DeKalb County Sch System, ATlanta, 1988-; Asst Prof of Music Ed, Kennesaw State Col, GA and Mercer Univ, Macon, GA; Supervisor of Music, Coweta Sch Dist, GA; Assoc Dir of Bands, Tennessee Tech Univ; Dir of Instrumental Music GA Public Schools; Performer with regional and community orchestras and bands. *Creative works:* Publications in major professional journals relate to aspects of pedagogy, graduate study, history and literature of the concert band; History of Music Education; also music published for percussion instruments; Presenter of educational research at state, regional, and national conferences. *Memberships:* Georgia Music Educators Assn; Music Educators Nat Conf; Soc for Res in Music Ed; Nat Band Assn; Phi Beta Mus; United Methodist Ch. *Hobbies:* Reading; Gardening. *Address:* 1185 Meadow Oaks Drive, Acworth, GA 30101, USA. USA. 7.

LEDERIS Karolis (Karl) Paul, b. 1 Aug 1920, Lithuania. Professor Emeritus. m. Hildegard Gallistl, 28 Feb 1952, 1 s, 1 d. *Education:* Teachers Col, Lithuania, 1939; BSc, 1958, PhD 1961, DSc, 1968, Bristo, Univ, UK. *Appointments:* Lectr, Reader, Bristol, UK, 1961-69; Prof, 1969, Emeritus Prof, 1989, Univ of Calgary, Canada. *Creative works:* Ed 5 books; 400 scientific papers, reviews and book chapters; Ed in chief, Pharmacology, 1977-89. *Memberships:* Socs of Pharmcol, Physiol, Biochem, Endocrinol in UK, Canada and USA; Pres, W.Pharmacol Soc, 1985-86; Med Res Coun, Canada, 1983-90; Med MRC Exec, 1984-90; Chm, various MRC Coms, 1977-. *Honours:* Visiting Prof, Vilnius Univ, 1976, Univ Kyoto, japan, 1979-80, Univ Bristol, UK, 1979; CAreer Investigtor, MRC, Canada, 1970-89; Fellow, Royal Soc, Canada, 1987; Upjohn Achievement Awd in Pharmacol, 1990. *Hobbies:* Choral Music; Violin; Brass Instruments; Cabinet Making; Sailing; Fishing; Hunging; Skiing. *Address:* Department of Pharmacology and Therapeutics, Faculty of Medicine, health Sciences Centre, University of Calgary, Alberta, Canada T2N 4N1. 161, 149, 88.

LEDWARD Rodney Spencer, b. 30 June 1938, Liverpool, England. Consultant Gynaecologist. m. Lady Jane Annabella Seth-Smith, 26 Aug 1983, 1 s, 1 stepdaugher. *Education:* DM, 1975; FRCOG, 1983; FRCS, 1974. *Appointments:* Conslt, Obs & Gynae: Riyadh Military Hosp, 1979-80; S.E.Kent Health Dist, 1980-. *Creative works:* Drug Treatment in Obstetrics, 1991; Drug Treatment in Gynaecology, 1984; Handbook of Obstetrics and Gynaecology, 1985. *Memberships:* Royal Soc Med; Royal Commonwealth Soc; Mosimans, London. *Hobbies:* Riding; Old Cars; Swimming. *Address:* Beaulieu, Riviera, Sandgate, Kent CT20 3AB, England.

LEE B Kyun, b. 20 Sept 1952, Taegu, Korea. Assistant Professor. m. Mi Sook Lee (Park), 3 Oct 1980, 1 s, 1 d. *Education:* BS Yeung Nam Univ, Korea, 1980; MS Oregon Stae Univ, USA, 1985; MS Northwest Christian Col, USA, 1988; PhD Oregon State Univ, 1988. *Appointments:* Engr, Hyun-Dai Motor Co, Korea, 1980-82; Tchg Fellow, Oregon State Univ, 1983-88; Engrg Prof, LeTourneau Univ, USA, 1988; Reg Professional Engr, Texas, USA; Active in Res and Consulting in Engng. *Creative works:* Engineering Research on Adaptive control of robotics and in the area of system dynamics and controls; Author of several technical papers. *Memberships:* Am Soc of Mech Engrg; Am Soc for Engrg Ed; Soc of Mfg Engrs, Regional V-Chm, and Dir of Continuing Ed. *Hobbies:* Soccer; Golf; Travel; Camping. *Address:* 1805 Rodden, Longview, TX 75604, USA. 7.

LEE Burtrand Insung, b. 20 Jan 1952, Korea. Professor. m. Connie W Min, 6 Dec 1979, 1 s. *Education:* BS Chem, Southern Col, 1976; MS Chem, Westerm Michigan Univ, 1979; PhD Materials Engrg, Univ of Florida, 1986. *Appointments:* Analytical Chemist, Biosphetics Inc, 1976-77; Assoc Prof, Clemson Univ, 1986-. *Creative works:* Chemical Processing of Ceramics, Ed. *Memberships:* Am Chem So; Am Ceramic Soc; Materials Res Soc; Florida Acad of Sci. *Honours:* Fulbright Scholar Awd, 1989; Norwegian Marshall Fund Awd, 1990; Material Res Soc Grad Student Awd, 1986; Dist Vis Prof, Pusan Nat Univ, Korea, 1991. *Hobbies:* Gardening; Boating. *Address:* 179 Falling Spring Road, Central , SC 29630, USA. 176, 7.

LEE David Michael, b. 22 Apr 1955, Ft Wayne, Indiand, USA. Director, Alloys Blends and Compounds. m. Debra Ann Shappell, 11 Aug 1973. *Education:* BSChE, Indiana Inst of Tech, 1977; MS Macromolec Sci, 1980, PhD 1981, CAse Western Reserve Univ. *Appointments:* Owens Corning Fiberglass, 1982-87; Supervisor, 1988-89; Dir of Alloy Blends, Phillips Petroleum Co, 1988-91. *Creative works:* 6 US Patents; 14 Technical publications. *Memberships:* Soc of Plastics Engrs; Sr mem, Pres, VP, Bd, local branch; Pres, Sr Class, 1977. *Honours:* Pullam and Goodyear Scholarships, 1975, 1980. *Hobbies:* Golf; Camping; Reading.

LEE David Wayne, b. 13 Aug 1948, Crockett, Texas, USA. Pastor. m. Carolyn Sue Landers, 11 Nov 1989, 2 s, 1 d. *Education:* BCA, Dallas Bapt Univ, (DBU), 1977; MDiv, 1981, D.Min, 1986, Southwestern Bapt Theol Sem. *Appointments:* Assoc Pastor, Lancaster Pk Bapt, TX, 1977-79; Pastor, First Bapt, Red Springs of Texarkana, TX, 1981. *Creative works:* Doctoral project: Preparation for Evangelism through establishing theological foundations. *Memberships:* VP, Ministerial Alliance of DBU, 1976-77. *Honours:* Alpha Chi, 1976-77; Awds for Academic Excellence, DBU, 1976, 1977; Grad magna cum laude, DBU, 1911. *Hobbies:* Study of Theology; Golf; Snow Skiing; Weight lifting. *Address:* 1202 FM 991, Texarkana, TX 75501, USA. 46.

LEE Jordan, b. 20 July 1956, Taiwan. Group Executive and Director. m. Feei-Tsuey Chang, 1 s, 1 d. *Education:* Michigan State Univ. *Appointments:* Group Executive Dir. *Memberships:* Am Acad of Advt; Am Mktg Assn. *Honours:* Outport Ad of the Year, 1985; Clio 1987; China Times Ad Awds, 1982-84. *Hobbies:* Karate; Shooting.

Address: 3F 8 LN 252, Sung-Chiang Road, Taipei, Taiwan, China. 52.

LEE Joseph, b. 23 June 1980, Taiwan. Senior Investment Management Analyst. m. Pauline Lee, 24 Dec 1988, 3 d. *Education:* BSc Maths, 1972; MBA, 1977; PhD Econ, 1975. *Appointments:* Bishoptrust W Ltd, 1975; Conahan & Conahon, Law firm, 1977; Peat Marwick Mitchell, CPA, 1979; Pension Consultants Co, 1981; Kemper Consulting Gp, 1989. *Creative work:* Composer and producer of several music records. *Memberships:* Assn of Investment Mgmt and Res; Investment Mgmt Conslts Assn; Inst of Cert Fund Specialists; Hawaii Assn of Public Accts; Intl Assn for Registered Fin Planners. *Honours:* Swasseful Buglene Hon, State of California, 1991. *Hobbies:* Music; Tennis; Golf. *Address:* 945 Makaiwa Street, Honolulu, HI 96816, USA.

LEE Kenneth Stuart, b. 23 July 1955, Raleigh, N.Carolina, USA. Neurosurgeon; Clinical Assistant Professor of Neurosurgery. *Education:* BA, Wake Forest Univ, 1973-77; MD, E.Carolina Univ, 1977-81. *Appointments:* Resident in Neurol, Bowman Gray Sch of Med, 1981-82; Resident in Neurosurg, Bowman Gray, 1982-88; Neurovascular Fellow, Barrow Neurological Inst, 1988-89; Practising Neurosurgeon, 1989-; Clin Asst Prof of Neurosurg, Sch of MEd, 1989-. *Creative works:* Author and co-author of over 30 articles and 5 book chapters in the neurosurgical literature; Ed Bd, Jour of Current Surgery. *Memberships:* NC Med Soc; AMA; NYAS: Congress of Neurol Surgs; Am Assn of Neurol Surgs; Fellow, Stroke Coun, Am Heart Assn; NC Neurosurg Soc. *Honours:* Athletic Coast Athletic Conf Acad Hon Roll, 1977; Path Awd E.Carolina Univ Sch of Med, 1981; Bucy Fellowship in Neurosurg, Gray Sch of Med, 1988. *Hobbies:* Reading; Jogging; Golf; Medical History. *Address:* 3600 Baywood Lane, Greenville, NC 27834, USA. 7.

LEE Kim Shin, b. 28 Feb 1950, Sarawak, Malaysia. Senior Administrative Officer. *Education:* BSocSc Hons, Polit Sci. *Appointments:* Tchr, 1968; ASst Sch Affairs Ofr, 1969-74; Asst Sec, 1983-84; Pvt Sec to Minister in Sarawak Govt, 1984-. *Creative works:* Politics in Sarawak, Malaysia. *Memberships:* Malaysian Social Sci Assn; Malaysian Red Crescent Soc, Sarawak Branch, Dist Sec, Branch Quartermaster; Hoppoh Assn Miri; Farmers Assn, Miri, Advr. *Honours:* Sarawak Govt Hons Awd, 1985; Outstanding Young Malaysian Awd, 1986; Meritorious Ser Medal, Red Crescent Soc, 1979; Sarawak Govt HOns Awd, 1991; Meritorious Ser to Vietnamese Boat People, MRCS, 1980. *Hobbies:* Reading; Swimming; Photography; Exercise. *Address:* 39 Lai Pau Garden, Miri, Sarawak, Malaysia. 98.

LEE Sung Man, b. 8 Dec 1947, Suwon, S. Korea. Director; Designer. Journalist. *Education:* Grad Sch of Admin, Sung Kyun Kwan Univ, 1985- 87. *Appointments:* Pres, Art Centre Inc 1984-; Design Jour, 1988-; Pres, Lee Man Motion Picture Prod Co, 1989-. *Creative works:* Movie, Chaos, 1991. *Memberships:* Am Soc of Interior Designers; Intl Inst for Info Design, 1989; Am Inst of Graphic Arts; Art Dirs Club, 1989-. *Honours:* Meritorious Ser Awd, Commr of Seoul, 1986; Special Prize, 28th Annual Baek Sang Awds,1992; Best New Dir Awd, 30th Grand Bell Awds Film Festival, 1992; Invited Intl Jury at 6th Intl Competition of the Art Dirs Club of NY, 1992. *Hobbies:* Movies. *Address:* 70-9 Art Center Bldg, Kalwol-Dong, Yongsan-Ku, Seoul, S.Korea. 140 150.

LEE Wen-Jong Philo, b. 14 Jan 1954, Kaohsiung, Taiwan. Marketing manager. m. Mei-Mei Chen, 29 Nov 1987, 1 s. *Education:* Cheng Shiu Inst of Tech, 1974. *Appointments:* Imperial Chemical Industries PLC, UK: ICI Taiwan Ltd, Dulux paints Div; Colour Matcher, 1977; Mfg Plant Supervisor, 1978-82; TND Techno-Commercial Rep, 1983-85; Mkt Mgr Motor Paints, 1986-87; Market Mgr, Refinish Paints, 1988-90; ICI Swire Paints Hong Kong: Mktg Mgr, Industrial Paints, 1991-. *Memberships:* Chinese Inst of Engrs. *Hobbies:*

Swimming; Reading. *Address:* 12 Lane 73, Te Yu Road, Ping Chen City, Taoyuan County, Taiwan, China.

LEE-POTTER Jeremy Patrick, b. 30 Aug 1934, Great Missenden, Bucks, England. Consultant Haematologist. m. Lynda Higginson, 26 Oct 1957, 1 s, 2 d. *Education:* Epsom Col; Guys Hosp Med Sch; MMBS, London, 1958; MRCS LRCP, Eng, 1958; DTM & H, Eng, 1964; DCP, London, 1965; FRCPath, 1978; M, 1967. *Appointments:* Pre-Reg Hse posts, 1958-59; RAF Med BR, 1960, Sr Specialist in Path, RAF Inst of Path and Tropical Med, 1966-68; Lectr, Haematol, St George's Hosp Med Sch, Univ of London, 1968-69. *Memberships:* BMA, Chm, Coun, 1990; Past D-Chm, Central Conslts & Specialists Com; Assn ofClin paths; Brit Soc of Haematol. *Hobbies:* Printing; Printmaking; Visual Arts. *Address:* British Medical Association, Tavistock Square, London WC1H 9JP, England. 1.

LEE-STEERE Ernest Henry, Sir, b. 22 Dec 1912, Perth, Australia. m. Jessica Margaret Venn, 1942, 2 s, 3 d. *Education:* Hale Sch, Perth; St Peter's Col, Adelaide. *Appointments:* Capt, Army/Air Liaison Gp, AIF, SW Pacific Area, 1944-45; Pres for WA, Pastoralist and Graziers Assn, 1959-72; Boy Scout Assn, 1957-64; Nat Trust, 1969-72; VP, Coun of Royal Flying Doctor Ser ov WA, 1954-59, 1962-74; Chm, State Adv Com, CSIRO, 1962-71, Coun, Fed Adv Coun, 1960-71; WA Soil Conservation Adv Com, 1955-72; Aust Capital Cities Secretariat, 1975-76; WA Turf CLub, 1963-84, V-Chm, 1959-63. *Memberships:* Nat Coun for Aust Boy Scouts Assn, 1959-64; Exec Com of WA State Com, Freedom from Hunger Campaign; WA State Adv Com, Aust Broadcasting Comm, 1961-64; Aust Jubilee Com for the Queen's Silver Jubilee Appeal for Young Australians, 1977; Aust Wool Indust Conf, 1971-74; Coun, Aust Wool Growers and Graziers Coun, Pres, 1972-73; St George's Col, Univ of WA, 1945-81; Leader, Trade Mission to India, 1962; JP, Perth, 1965. *Hobbies:* Polo, Competed for the Australisian Gold Cup. *Address:* 26 Odern Crescent, Swanbourne, WA 6010, Australia.

LEECH John Cooper, Major, b. 25 Feb 1928, Loughton, Essex. State Invitations Assistant, Lord Chamberlains Office, Buckingham Palace, 1979-91. m. Pauline Mary Forth, 25 Apr 1964. *Education:* Northgate Grammar Sch, Ipswich, Suffolk, 1939-46; Inst of Ed, Univ of London, 1951-53. *Appointments:* Army Ser 1946-49, 1951-78; Australia, Malaya, Borneo, Malta, N.Africa and Cermany; Chamberlain Lincoln Cathedral, 1978-79. *Honours:* Chevalier du Wissam Alouite, Morroco, 1970; Ordine al Merito Della Republica Italiana, 1991. MVO, Birthday Hons List. *Hobbies:* Video; Photography; Restoration of old furnigure; History; Swimming; Travel. *Address:* 1 Hartley Russel Close, Church Way, Iffley, Oxford OX4 4EA, England.

LEGON Anthony Charles, b. Sudbury, Suffolk, England. Professor of Physical Chemistry. m. Deirdre Anne Rivers, 20 July 1963, 2s, 1d. *Education:* BSc 1963, PhD 1967, Univ Col London. *Appointments:* Fellow, Univ of London, 1968-70; Lectr, 1970-83, Reader, 1983-84, Chem, UCL; Prof of Phys Chem, Exeter, 1984-89; Prof of Chem, UCL, 1989-90. *Publications:* More than 190 refereed papers in scientific journals of international repute. *Membership:* FRSC. *Honours:* Tilden Medal and Lectureship, RSC, 1990; Doctor of Sci, London Univ, 1981. *Hobbies:* Reading; Cricket. *Address:* Dept of Chemistry, University of Exeter, Stocker Rd, Exeter EX4 4QD, England.

LEHMANN L Olga M, b. 10 Feb 1912, Chile. Designer; Artist- Portrait Painter. m. 13 Oct 1939, 1 s. *Education:* Santiago Col; Portraiture; Theatrical Design, Slade Sch of Fine Art; Slade Dipl. *Career:* Scenic Artist, Gainsborough Studios, Islington, 1941; Film credits include: Kidnapped: The man in the Iron Mask; Les Miserables; Little Lord Fauntleroy; Portraits include: H E Bates: Prince Harry Faucigny-Lucinge; James Mason; Dirk Bogarde; Marlene Dietrich; Michael York; Jane Seymour; Charlton Heston; Stephanie Beecham;

Exhibitions with the Suffolk Art Soc; Contemporary Portrait Soc; Wright Hepburn Webster Gallery, New York; Graphic Fine Art Soc, London; Solo exhibitions include: The AIA Gallery; The John Whibley Gallery; Gainsborough's House, Suffolk; The Rushmore Rooms, St Catherine's Col, Cambs; The Guildhall, Thaxted; War sketches at the Imperial War Mus, the RAF Mus and in private collections. *Memberships:* Soc of Graphic Fine Art; Nat Soc; FRSA. *Hobbies:* Picture Galleries; Films; Theatres; Painting. *Address:* 1 Artisans Dwellings, Saffron Walden, Essex CB10 1LW, England.

LEHNER Paul Michael,b. 5 Dec 1941, Mishawaka, Indiana, USA. International Business Executive and Consultant. *Education:* BBA summa cum laude, Univ Notre Dame, 1963; MBA dist, Harvard Univ, 1969. *Appointments include:* VP, Irwin Mgmnt Co, Columbus, Ind, 1968-1984; Pres, Dir, Nashville Intl Trading Co Ind, 1977-80; Exec VP Tipton lakes Co, Columbus, 1981-84; Pres, 1985-86, VP, Southmark Corp, Dallas, 1986-88; N.Am Mortgage Investors, 1986-88; Nat Partner, Trammell Crow Residential Co, Dallas, 1988-90; Ptnr, Trammell Crow Realty Advrs, 1990-1992; Pres, Contron Lehner Barrett Inc, 1992-; EVP Consultors Intercionales CLB, SA de CV Cuernavaca, Morelos Mexico, 1992-; Dir, Cen Ind Homeowner Warranty Corp Pres Tlpton Lakes Community Asssn, Columbus, 1981-86, Lookout Condominium Owners Assn, Columbus, 1984-86; Brown Co Bd Zoning Appeals; Bd Dirs, Steeplechase Corp, Ctr Owner Assn Sterling VA, 1987-88; V-Chm, Brown Co Planning Comm; Bd, Columbus Econ Devel Bd, 1983-86; Governing Com, All Saints Sch, 1984-86. *Memberships:* C of C Intl Coun Shopping Ctrs; Nat Assn Homebuilders; Ind Homebuilders Assn, Dir; Bartholomew Co Homebuilders Assn, Dir, Pres, 1984-86; Bd Realtors, Urban Land Inst; Nat Assn Indsl and Office Parks, Dallas Coun; Beta Gamma Sigma; Beta Alpha Psi. *Address:* 10701 Inwood Road, Dallas, TX 75229, USA. 132, 8.

LEHTINEN Seppo Ilmari, b. 10 July 1937, Helsinki, Finland. Management Consultant; Educator. m. Kaija Annikki Karki 3 Nov 1962, 1 s, 1 d. *Education:* Grad Engr, Eekninen Opisto, Helsinki, 1967. *Appointments:* Military Ser, Lt, 1957-58; Aynokia AB, 1965-87: Chief Engr, 1965-67, Proj Chief, 1967-68, Prod Mgr, 1968-70, Mgr Prod Res, 1970-77, Prod Devel Mgr, 1973-77, Mgr Educ, 1978-79; Principal of Norsk Acad, 1979-87; Col Leadership Regional Executing, 1977; Univ of Tampere, 1974-, Tchr in Org Psychology; Man Dir, PVKS palvelut Ky, 19787-. *Publications:* Co- author, Managment and Leadership, 1972; Articles to professional journals. *Memberships include:* Tech Com IEC Europe, 1974-86; Finnish Red Cross, 1980-; Finnish Scout Union, 1944; Chamber of Commerce, 1988-; Finnish Chief Educator, 1970; Pres, finnish Reserve Officer Union, 1956-; Member of Hon, Leadership CLub, 1975-. *Honours:* Knight Order of the White Rose, 1988; Blue Cross, 1991; Silver Badge of C of C Gen Helsinki, 1987; Defence of the Country Bronze Medal, 1970. *Hobbies:* Reading; Social work; Politics; Scouting. *Address:* Pahkinamaenkatu 5C 16, SF 33840 Tampere, Suomi, Finland. 52, 132.

LEHTO Sakari Tapani, b. 26 Dec 1923, Turku, Finland. Writer; Chm, Bd of Directors. m. Karin Hilden 29 Apr 1950, 3 d. *Education:* BSc Econ, Helsinki, 1945; LL.B, univ of Helsinki , 1948; Tech Dr h.c., 1981; MIT/Sloan Sch, Sr Execs, 1971; Econ Dr h.c. Hels Sch of Econ, 1991. *Appointments:* Chief Legal Advr, Utd Paper Mills, Finland, 1952-63; Man Dir, Fed of Finn Industries, 1963-71; Pres and CEO, Partek Corp, 1972-87; Minister for Foreign Trade, 1975, 1976. *Creative works:* Book, Managing Change, 1990; Art in the fields of law, national economy, industrial policy in Finland and elsewhere. *Memberships:* Finn Assn; Club of Rome Chm, 1981-86; Supervisory Bd, Foun of Club of Rome, Switzerland; Finn Assn for Futures Studies, Hon mem, 1987; Finn Law Assn; Finn Nat Econ Assn. *Honours:* 1st cl. with star, Order of Liberty of Finland; Commander 1st cl., The White Rose of Finland; Commander 1st cl., The Polar Star of Sweden; Commander, The Lion of

Finland; Title of Minister, from Pres of the Rep of Finland, 1977. *Hobbies:* Water sport; Skiing; Golf; Languages; Literature. *Address:* Puistokatu 9 A, 00140 Helsinki, Finland.

LEI Maofa, b. 17 May 1951, Harbin, China. Worker, Harbin Institute of Technology. m. 28 Jan 1978, 1 d. *Education:* Long-Boxing, 1956-75, Harbin; baguazhang, 1966-; Gao Style Baguazhang in Qin Dao City, 1975-80; Wu Dang Kong Fu, 1980-. *Appointments:* Countryside worker, 1961-71; Harbin Inst of Tech, 1971-. *Publications:* The characteristics of Banguazhang, 1988; Eliminating ills and strengthening health by practising Baguazhang, 1988. *Memberships:* Harbin Martial Arts Assn; Dir, Govt Com for Harbin Martial Art Schs; Pres, Baguazhang Res Soc of Chinese Gong Fu Assn in Harbin; Nat II Coacher for Martial Arts. *Honours:* Distinguished Coach of Excellence in Martial Arts, Harbin Phys Educ Assn, 1988; High Hon in Nat Farm Games for Martial Arts, 1988; Championship of Baguazhang in Heilongjiang. *Hobbies:* Fishing; Handwriting; Bird and Fish Breeding; Gardening. *Address:* 34 Hexing 3rd Street, Nangang District, Harbin City 150080, China.

LEIGHTER Murel Jean Mowder, b. 9 Dec 1945, Bartlesville, Oklahoma, USA. Quality Assurance Manager. m. Gordon R Leighter Jr, 25 Jan 1975, 1 d. *Education:* BSN, Graceland Col, Iowa, 1975; MSN, Univ of Missouri, Kansas City, 1978. *Appointments:* Staff Nurse, Med, Medical Ctr of Independence, Missouri, 1975-77; Clinical Nurse Specialist, Truman Med Ctr, Kansas City, 1978-79; Clin Nurse Specialist, 1979-81, Quality Assurance Coor of Nursing, 1981-88, St Mary's Hosp, Kansas City; Quality Assurance Mgr, Independence Reg Health Ctr, 1988-. *Publications:* Evaluating your indicator: Criteria Mix, 1989. *Memberships:* Nat Assn of Quality Assurance Profls, Region IV Nominating Com; Missouri Assn of Quality Assurance Profls, Pres Elect, Pres, past Pres; Kansas City Area Quality Assurance Profls, Jr Ser League. *Honours:* CPQA, Nat Assn of Quality Assurance Profls, 1986-. *Hobbies:* Genealogy; Gardening; Volunteerism; Boy Scouts Counsellor; Roller Skating; Gymnastics. *Address:* 9755 Winner Road, Independence, MO 69052, USA.

LEINER Wolfgang, b. 21 Oct 1925, Saerbrucken, Germany. University Professor. m. Jacqueline Lecocq, 13 Apr 1953, 1 s. *Education:* PhD, 1955; Habilitation, 1963. *Appointments:* Priv Docent, 1963; Saarbrucken Vis Prof, Univ of Washington, Seattle, 1963-64; Asst Prof, 1965; Prof,1966; Prof, Univ Tubingen, 1975-. *Publications:* Numerous books and articles on French literary criticism; Ed of two professional journals. *Memberships:* Modern lang Assn; Assn Intl des Eludes France, VP; Hon Mem, Univ Italiana di lingua e letter francese; Centre Intl des Rencontres sur le 17e Siecle, Pres. *Honours:* Officier de Plumes Academiques. *Address:* Wilhelmstrasse 50, 7400 Tubingen, Germany. 1.

LEITE Silvio Carlos, b. 20 Sept 1952, Rio de Janeiro, Brazil. Airline Information Technology Consultant. m. Monika Schwager, 27 May 1976, div 1983. 2 d. *Education:* Grad in Commercial and Bus Admin, Zurich, Switzerland, 1972. *Appointments:* Stock Broker, Various banks in Zurich, 1972-73; Swissair, 1973-. *Publications:* Some novels. *Hobbies:* Reading; Writing. *Address:* Hardackerstr 29, 8302-Kloten, Switzerland. 1.

LEITZMANN Claus, b. 6 Feb 1933, Dahlenburg, Germany. Professor of Nutrition. m. Ilse Wachenhusen, 30 Apr 1957, 2 s, 2 d. *Education:* BSc Chem, Capital Univ, Columbus, OH, 1962; MSc Microbiol, 1964, PhD Biochem, 1967, Univ of Minnesota. *Appointments:* Res Asst, Univ California, 1967-69; Lectr, Biochem, Mahidol Univ, Bangkok, Thailand, 1969-71; Chief of Labs, Malnutrition and Anaemia Res Ctr, Univ of Chiang Mai, Thailand, 1971-74; Prof of Nutrition, Univ of Giessen, Germany, 1974-. *Publications:* Wholesome Nutrition,

1981; Dictionary of Nutrition, 1988; Human Nutrition, 1988; Nutrition Ecology, 1992; Vegetarainism, 1993. *Memberships:* German and Am Socs of Nutrition; Eden Foun, Bd; Soc of Profl Nutritionists; Vegetarian Soc. *Honours:* Zabel Prize, 1986. *Hobbies:* Gardening; Travel; Jogging. *Address:* Inst of Nutrition, Univ of Giessen, Wilhelmstrasse 20, 6300 Giessen, Germany. 1.

LEKKAS Stefanos, b. 27 May 1947, Athens, Greece. Music Teacher; Chairman. *Education:* Dipl, 1970, Tchr, 1971, Byzantine Music; Dipl, Classic Song of Nat Conservatory, 1975. *Appointments:* Tchr of Music, Nat Conservatory, 1975; Hg Sch Music Tchr, 1979-. *Publications:* Author: Theory of Byzantine Music, 1975; Compositions of Classic Music. *Memberships:* Fdr and Chm, CHON; Fdr, Culture Ctr of Pol Faliro, Athens, Greece; UNISEF; Fed of Tchrs and Union of Presenters. *Honours:* First Awd in Byzantine Music, Nat Conservatory, 1975; Dipl of Hellenic Union of Writers, 1988; Cert, Univ Show Prods Inc, 1988; Hon of Culture Ctr, City of Athens. *Hobbies:* Reading; Singing; Gardening; Swimming. *Address:* Delphon 6, Poleo Faliro, PO Box 17562, Athens, Greece.

LEKTOZSKY Vladislav, b. 23 Aug 1932, Moscow, Russia. m. Ludmila Saveljera, 31 Dec 1988. 1s. 1d. *Education:* Philosophical Fac, Moscow State Univ, 1950-55; Post Grad Student, Inst of Philos, USSR Acad ofScis, 1957-59; Philos Scis Candidate, 1964; Dr of Philosophical Scis, 1978. *Appointments:* Res Fellow, Inst of Philos, USSR Acad of Sci, 1959-67; Hd of Epistomology Dept, Inst of Philos, 1968-; Ed-in-chief, Problems of Philosophy Jur, 1987-. *Publications:* Problem of Subject and object in contemporary philosophy, 1965; Subject, Object, Cognition, 1982; Introduction to Philosophy, 1989. *Memberships:* Steering Com, Intl Fed of Philos Socs; VP, Intl Soc of Universalism; Presidium of Intl Soc of Activity Theory. *Honours:* Order of the Sign of Hon, 1986. *Hobbies:* Gardening; Skiing. *Address:* Str 19 fl 123, Moscow 121002, Russia.

LELENTAL Stefan, b. 2 Nov 1935, Lodz, Poland. m. 25 Dec 1965, 1 s. *Education:* LLM, 1958; LLD, 1964; Asst Prof, 1973, Prof, 1984. *Appointments:* Univ of Lodz: 1959-62, Asst, Criminal Law Dept, 1963-64; Sr Asst, 1965-73, Sr Lectr, 1984-; Prof, 1984-, Hd of Criminal Law Dept, 1989-. *Publications:* Individualization of carrying out the penalty of imprisonment,1970; Carrying out the penality of imprisonment in European Socialist Countries, 1975; Executive penal law, 1990. *Memberships:* Assn of Intl Criminal Law; Sci Assn of Lodz; Sci Assn of Criminal Law. *Honours:* Hons and Awds, Minister of Ed, 1974-86; Awds, Rector, Univ of Lodz, 1977-91. *Hobbies:* Pet dog; Philately; Collecting postcards. *Address:* ul Zachodnia 101/7, 90-723 Lodz, Poland.

LELIE Martinus Christoffel (Christo), b. 28 Dec 1956, Dordrecht, Netherlands. Musician; Author. *Education:* Rotterdam Conservatory, Teachers Deg; Piano, 1982, Organ, 1984. *Career:* Organist, Musical Dir, Reformed Chs, The Hague, Delft; Critic, Trouw Newspaper 1981; Pianist, Rotterdam Dansacademy, 1983; Ed, EPTA Piano Bulletin, 1984; Ed, F. Liszt, Kring; Freelance Writer on Music; Numerous organ recitals; Played Liszt organ works in Liszt Cycles, Rotterdam, 1990; Accompanist, (piano, organ, harpsichord) in vocal and instrumental concerts and dance performances, Netherlands, Germany; Staff Mem, Liszt Festivals: Utrecht, 1988, Amsterdam, 1990; Staff Mem, Gina Bachauer Audition, Amsterdam, 1991; Lectures on Liszt, Scarlatti, Italian Organs; BRT Radio Commentary on Harpsichord and Fortepiano 1986, Bruges, Belgium; Pres, Hist Dance Ensemble Volta. Compositions: Roman Variations, Study of (piano); Fantasie ine, Passacaglia, 3 Renaissance Dances transcribed for organ, Choral Preludes (organ); Several Religious works for Choir. *Publications:* Numerous articles on piano and organ music in several music journals and newspaper Trouw; Co-author, Book, Scarlatti, 1985; Book, Van Piano tot forte, 1993.

Contributions to: Numerous reviews, interviews, articles in Trouw; Articles on Liszt, Alkan, Scarlatti, Boëly, history of the piano, the pedalier, piano pedagogy, music and the brain in: Mens en Melodie; Muziek en Dans; Piano Bulletin; Piano Wereld; Franz Liszt Kring; Disk; Glenn Gould Soc. *Memberships:* EPTA Netherland, Coun; Franz Liszt Krig Nederland, VP; Nederl Toonkunstenaarsraad; Kon Nederlandse Organisten Vereniging; Liszt Soc; Am Liszt Soc. *Hobbies:* Antiquarian books; Bird watching. *Address:* Havenstraat 12, 2613 VK Delft, Netherlands.

LELYVELD Gail Annick, b. 22 May 1948, Boston, Massachusetts, USA. Performing Artist; Stage Manager. *Education:* BA Polit Sci, Boston Univ, 1970; MA Goddard Cambridge, 1974; Am Conservatory Theatre, summer, 1978; London Acad M & Drm Art, summer, 1983. *Career:* Films include: The Gentle Creature, 1991, Mr Clown Says, 1990, White Noise, 1991; Theatre includes: Toby Tyler, Littletop Theatre Co, 1990; Alice in Wonderland, Not so Grimm Fairytale Players, 1989; Spanish Scenes, Bohemian Nights Prostitute, USA Productions, 1986; Singing (choruses) include: PALA Opera Assn, 1991; St Patricks Cathedral Choir, 1990; Musicum Collegium Hofstra Univ, 1988- ; Stage Mgr, Light and Sound Operator, USA Productions at Hofstra, 1986. *Memberships:* Am Fed of Radio and TV Artists. *Honours:* Grey Wig Achievement Awd, 1987; Inner Circle Awd, 1990; Review, Newsday for lighting, Breaker Morant, 1991. *Hobbies:* Reading; Walking; Knitting. *Address:* c/o USA Productions, 464 Macatee Place, Mineola, NY 11501, USA. 5, 52.

LEMANN Jean (Juan), b. 7 Aug 1928, Vendome, France. Composer and Professor of Composition. m. Maria Luisa Herreros, 28 Sept 1957, 2 d. *Education:* BA Maths, 1948; Piano Studies, Univ of Chile, Nat Conservatory of Music, 1942-54, 1955-59; Composition, Univ of Chile, Catholic Univ of Chile, Visiting Fulbright Scholar, Juilliard Sch of Music, NY, 1970- 71; Arch, Catholic Univ of Chile, 1948-50. *Appointments:* Prof of Piano, Music Theory, Choral Conductor, Experimental Sch of Arts, 1957-61; Prof of Piano, Harmony, Counter Point Composition (Hd Prof), V-Dean, 1981-82, Univ of Chile Fac of Arts; Pianist, Lectr and Adjudicator. *Compositions include:* Orchestral, Chamber and Choral Music, including works for mimes, theatre, ballet and movies: Leyendd del Mar; Obertura de Concierto; 3 Variables para piano; Recordings Include: Variaciones para piano; Puentes, Maestranza de niche (wds P Neruda); Leyendd del Mar. *Contributions to:* several professional journals. *Memberships:* Academic Chilena de Bellas Artes; Nat Assn of Composers of Chile, past Pres; Foun mem, Contemporary Music Assn; AMCA; Fulbright Almni Assn. *Honours include:* Orrego Carvallo prize, 1950; Rosita Renard Prize, 1951; Festivals of Chilean Music Prizes, 1962, 1969, 1979; Adriazola Award, 1992. *Hobby:* Photography. *Address:* Laura de Noves 460, Santiago, Chile.

LEMCHE Niels Peter, b. 6 Sept 1945, Copenhagen, Denmark. Professor of Theology. m. Elsebeth Skovby, 12 June 1966, 4 s. *Education:* MA Copenhagen, 1971; DTheol, Copenhagen, 1985. *Appointments:* Res ASst, Univ Copenhaven, 1972-78, Sr Lectr, Univ of Aarhus, 1978-87; Prof of Theol, Copenhagen, 1987-. *Publications:* Israel I Dommertiden, 1972; Det Gamel Israel, 1984; Early Israel, 1985; Ancient Israel, 1988; The Canaanites, 1991. *Memberships:* Collegium Biblicum, Tres; Nathansoderblom Selskabet; Wissenschaftliche Gesellschaft fur Theol; Soc of Biblical Lit. *Honours:* Silver medal, Univ of Copenhagen, 1969. *Hobbies:* Captain, Danish Home Guard, and Nat Guard; Gardening; Reading. *Address:* Smedebakken Gurre, Smedebakken 12, DK-3490 Kvistgaard, Denmark.

LEMER Andrew Charles, b. 25 Dec 1944, Alabama, USA. Engineer Economist; Consultant. *Education:* SB, 1967, SM, 1968, PhD, 1971, Massachussets Inst of Tech (MIT). *Appointments:* Sr Assoc, Principal, mgr, Alan

M Voorhees Assos, 1971-77; Chief Planner, PRC Nigeria Ltd, 1977-81; Div VP, PRC Engrg, 1981-85; Pres, Matrix Gp Inc, 1985-; Dir, Bldg Res Bd, Nat Acad of Sci, 1988- . *Publications:* Numerous articles and professional publications including: Macro-Project in West Africa; Planning Nigeri's Federal Capital; Macro Engineering Revisited, Co-ed, 1980; Batam Centre: Spearhead for Economic Development, 1984. *Memberships:* ASCE; AICP; Com on Transportation and Land Devel; Transportation Res Bd; Educ Coun, MIT. *Address:* c/o Building Research Board, National Academy of Sciences, 2101 Constitution Avenue, Washington, DC 20418, USA.

LEMP Liselotte (Annemarie), b. 4 Apr 1916, Oppein, Germany. Writer. div. *Education:* Private and public schools, 1922-34; Private training with Frank Thiess, 1934-36. *Appointments:* Posts in publishing and banking, 1971-75. *Publications:* Plays: Die Augen 1946; Performed, 50; Das Dunkle Jahr, 1947; Die Lilith 1981; Zwei Maenner, 1982; Poems: Magischer Raum, 1988; Poems in 25 anthologies; author of radio plays, 1944-47. *Memberships:* Freier Deutscher Autorenverband; Life Fellow, IBA. *Honours:* Travel Grant, Vereinigung Deutscher Schriftstellerverbaende and Foreign Office, Bonn, 1958. *Hobbies:* Reading; Hydroculture. *Address:* Alexander-Zinn Str 6, DW 2000 Hamburg 52, Germany. 138, 3, 52.

LENGYEL Peter, b. 4 Sept 1939, Budapest, Hungary. Novelist. *Education:* Univ of Arts and Scis of Budapest, 1957-62; Dipl Spanish and Italian Lit and Langs. *Appointments:* Dramaturgist in drama theatre in Budapest, 1959-60; Ed staff of literary magazines, 1965-75; Redactor of an electric bill board, Gr Blvd of Budapest, 1975-88; Freelance writer and teacher, creative writing at the Univ of Budapest of Arts and Scis, 1988-. *Publications:* Books: Two Twilights, 1967; The Second Planet of Ogg, 1969; Secondary Characters, 1972; Back to Base, 1978; Rondo, 1982; Cobblestone, 1988; The Day before Tomorrow, 1992. *Memberships:* Intl Pen CLub; Assn of Hungarian Writers; Magistrate, City of Budapest, 1990-. *Honours:* Short Story Competition Prize, Intl PEN and Intl Writers Foun, 1965; Literary Achievement prize, Attila Jozef, 1983; Golden Meteor Prize, 1985; Novel of the year, Cobblestone, 1989; Pro Urbe Budapest Prize, 1990. *Hobbies:* Writing novels; Cosmology; Anthoropology; Theory of evolution; Travelling; Teaching. 3.

LENNARD-JONES John Edward, b. 29 Jan 1927, Bristol, England. Consultant Physician. m. Verna Margaret Down, 19 Feb 1955, 4 s. *Education:* Corpus Christi Col, Cambs, 1944-46, 1948-50; Univ Col Hosp; BA 1947; MA 1951; MBBchir, 1953; MD 1965; FRCP Lond, 1968; FRCS Engl, 1992. *Appointments:* Conslt PHys, UCH, 1965-74; Prof of Gastroenterol, London Hosp, 1974-87; Conslt Gastroenterol, St Mark's Hosp, London, 1965-92. *Publications:* Papers on medicine, gastroenterology and clinical nutrition. *Memberships:* Brit Soc of Gastroenterol; RCPhys; Nat Assn for Colitis and Chron's Disease; Nutrition Soc, Brit Assoc for Parental and Enteral Nutrition. *Honours:* Aitchinson Scholarship, 1953, Fellowes Gold Medal, 1953, UCH; Cunning Prize in Med, Corpus Christi Col, 1953; Res Prize, Central Middlesex Hosp, 1964; Bryan Brooke Awd, Ileostomy Assn, 1991. *Hobbies:* Ornithology and Natural History; Gardening; Golf; Pres, Brit Digestive Foundation. *Address:* 55 The Pryors, East Heath Road, London NW3 1BP, England. 170.

LENNOX Edward N, b. 27 July 1925, New Orleans, Louisiana, USA. m. Joan Marie Laundry of Houma, 4 d. *Education:* Grad, Georgia Military; Acad Col Pk, AG, 1943; Col of Com and Bus Admin; Tulane Univ of Louisiana, 1949. *Appointments include:* Military Ser, 1943-46; VP, Public Affairs, S.Industries Corp, 1971-88; Pres, Tideland Indust Inc, 1982-85; VP, Public Affairs, Dravo Natural Resources Co, 1982-; VP, Dravo Corp, Public Affairs, 1989-. *Memberships include:* Construction Industry Legislative Coun, Bd, 1968-85;

Gov's Adv Coun on Econ State of AL, 1971-72; Public Affairs Res Coun of LA, Area VP, 1972-73; Bd of Trustees, 1970-79; LA Good Roads Assns Inc, Exec Com, 1972-74; LA Civil Ser League, Bd of Govs, 1974-, Pres, 1977-78, Hon Life Chm, 1980. *Honours include:* Times Picayune Loving Cup Selection Com, 1972; ConstructionIndustry Assn of New Orleans Inc, Cert of Appreciation, 1972; Hon Mem, Bd, Metropolitan New Orleans Safety Coun, 1985-87. *Address:* 862 Topaz Street, New Orleans, LA 70124, USA. 7, 132, 2, 125, 132.

LENOIR Gloria Irma Cisneros, b. 18 Aug 1951, Monterrey, Nuevo Leon, Mexico. Business woman. m 6 June 1975, 2 d. *Education:* French and Art Studies, Inst of Am Univ, Aix-en-Provence, France, 1971-72; BA, MA, French & Art, Austin Col, TX, 1969-74; MBA Fin, Univ of Texas at Austin, 1977- 79. *Appointments:* HS Tchr, Austin, TX, 1974-77; Legislative Aide, TX State Capitol, 1977-81; Stock Broker. Merrill Lynch, Pierce, Fenner & Smith, 1981-83; Scheider Barnets & Hickman, 1983-84; Mgr, Owner, Holleman Photographic Labs, 1984-; Stockbroker. Eppler Guerin & Turner Inc, 1987-88; Independent Distributor, 1990-; Prof, St Edwards Univ, 1991-. *Publications:* Photographs in: Women in Space, 1977, REview, 1988; Exhibitions throughout Texas; One woman shows, Imperfect Images, Austin, TX, 1989. *Memberships:* Austin Col Volunteer Liason Leads Prog; Central Presbyterian Ch; Bryker Woods Elementary Sch PTA; Austin City Coun PTA Bd. *Honours:* Scholarship, Inst for Am Univs, 1971-72; Brinegar Fellowship, Austin Col, 1973-74; D L Mosle Scholarship, Univ of Texas, 1979; Volunteer Awd, Hispanic Chamber of Commerce, Austin, 1986. *Hobbies:* Walking; Reading; Embroidery. *Address:* 1202 W 29th , Austin, TX 78703, USA. 3, 132, 5, 52, 138.

LENZ Hanfried Wilhelm, b. 22 Apr 1916, Munich, Germany. Retired University Professor. m. 24 July 1943, 2 s, 2 d. *Education:* Grad, Maths & Phys, Univ of Leipzig, 1941; Dr rer nat 1951, Habilitation, 1953, Maths, Munich. *Appointments:* Military Ser, 1935-37, 1939-43; Res Asst, German RADAR Prog, 1943-45; Hg Sch Tchr, 1947-48; Asst, 1949, Lectr, 1953, Assoc Prof, 1958, Technische Hochschule Munich; Vis Prof, Ohio State Univ, 1967-68; Prof, Free Univ, Berlin, 1969; Dr h.c. Munich, 1991. *Creative works:* 4 books and 80 research papers in mathematics. *Memberships:* Deutsche mathematiker-Vereinigung. *Hobbies:* Politics; Go - Japanese Board Game. *Address:* Oldenbourgstr 17, D 8000, Munchen 60, Germany.

LEON Bruce Frederick, b. 6 Nov 1952, Los Angeles, California, USA. Manager, Environmental Studies. m. Linda Gail Gloss, 7 Jan 1990. *Education:* BS Univ Michigan, 1974; MA Ecology, 1976, PhD, 1979, Princeton Univ. *Appointments:* Ecol Sci Inc, Milwaukee, WI, 1978-80; Asst Prof, Landscape Arch & Urban Planning, Univ Illinois, 1981-85; Quadrant Conslt Inc, Houston, TX, 1985-90; Mgr, Environmental Studies, Brown Root Inc, Houston, 1990-. *Creative works:* Creative works in professional journals include essays, research reports and environmental impact assessments. *Memberships:* Ecological Soc of Am. *Honours:* Fellowship, Nat Sci Foun, 1975-77; Res Grant, Univ Illinois, 1983. *Hobbies:* Music performance; Photography; Cycling. *Address:* Brown Root Inc, PO Box 3, Houston, TX 77001, USA. 7.

LEONHARD Lapin, b. 29 Dec 1947, Rapina, Estonia. Artist; Architect. *Education:* Arch, Tallinn Art Univ, 1966-71. *Appointments:* Estonian Artists Union, 1977; Estonian Archt Union, 1982; Printmaking and Painting Tchr, Tallin ARt Univ; Prof, Hasilki Art School, MAA Editor-in-Chief, Estonian Architecture Magasin, EHITUSJUNST. *Creative works:* Graphic scenes: Machines 1973-79; Processes, 1980-92; Signs, 1979-82; Conversation of Signs, 1989-91; Rhythm and Melody, 1991. *Honours:* Lublana 1973, Japan, 1974, Print Biennial Prizes; Estonian Artist of the year, 1987; Soviet Arch Competition Prize, 1987; Tallinn City Prize,

1989; Estonian Arch Prize, 1991; Estonian Book Graphic Prize, 1992. *Hobbies:* Zen Buddism. *Address:* Liivalaia 7-41, Tallinn EE 0106, Estonia.

LEONOY Alexander, b. 16 Sept 1943, Moscow, USSR. Oceanologist; Hydrochemist. m. Evgenia Leonova Dmitrieva, 1 Apr 1972, 1 s. *Education:* Geog Fac, Oceanol Dept, Moscow Univ, 1961-66; Post Grad, State Oceanographic Inst, Moscow, 1971-74; Deg, 1975; DChemSci, 1991, Hydrochem Isnt, Rostov on Don, USSR. *Appointments:* Jr Res Sci, Atlantic Res Inst for Fisheries & Oceanography, Kaliningrad, 1966-71; Jr then Sr Res Scist, State Oceanographic Inst, Moscow, 1974-77; Res Scholar, Intl Inst for Applied Sys Analysis, Laxenburg, 1981; Sr then Chief Res Scist, Water Problems Inst of USSR Acad of Sci, 1982-. *Creative works:* A Review of mathematical models of phosphorus release from sediments, 1985; Modelling and explaining the phosphorus dynamcs of lake Balaton, 1976-79; Mathematical modelling the phophorus transformation i freshwater ecosystems, 1986. *Hobbies:* Travelling; Photography; Reading; Classical Music. *Address:* The Water Problems Inst of USSR Academy of Sciences, Sdovaya Tchernogriazskaya 13/3, Moscow 103064, Russia.

LEOTARD Francois Gerard Marie, b. 26 Mar 1942, Cannes, France. m. France Reynier, 22 Dec 1976. *Education:* Fac of law, Inst of Polit Studies, Pari; Lic Laws, Nat Sch of Admin, 1971-73. *Appointments:* Nat Ser, 1964-65; Sec, Chancellors Ofc, Min of Foreign Affairs, 1968-71; Civil Admnr, Urbanism and Environ, Prefect of Paris, 1973-75; Dpty Prefect: Dordogne, Perigueux, 1975-76, Ofc of Min of State, Min of Interior, 1976-77; Mayor of Frejus; Var, 1977, 1983; Polit Bureau Repub Party Mem, 1977; Pres, Dept Fed, Repub Party, 1977-78; Dpty, 1978, 1981, Var Reg Coun, Provence Alpes Cote d'Azur; Coun Gen Cauton of Frejus, 1979, 1984; VP, 1979, Pres, 1985, Assn Mayors of France; Dpty Sec Gen, 1981, Deleg Gen, 1982, Sec Gen, 1982, 1984, Pres, 1988, Hon Pres, 1990, Repub Party; Min of Culture and Communication, 1986. *Publications:* A Mots Decouverts, 1987; Les Chetins de Printemps, 1988; M Ville Aimee, 1989; Adresse au President des Republiques Francaises, 1991. *Honours:* Chevalier Nat Order of Merit, 1977. *Address:* 5 Fbg St Honore, 75008 Paris, France. 91.

LEROY Claude, b. 30 Sept 1947, Charleroi, Belgium. University Professor. *Education:* Math Speciale, St Louis Fac Brussels, 1967; Univ of Louvain: Licence en Sci 1971, PhD Phys, 1976. *Appointments:* Res, IISN, Univ Louvain, 1971-77; Res Assoc Phys: McGill, 1977-80, NW Univ, 1980- 81; Louvain 1981-83; Res Sci Inst of Particle Phys, McGill, 1983-90; Assoc Prof, McGill, 1983-90; Prof; Dir of Nucl Phys Lab, Univ Montreal, 1990-. *Creative works:* Author and coauthor of more than 200 scientific papers published in international scientific reviews. *Memberships:* Sci Assoc Euro Ctr for Nucl Res, Geneva, 1980-; Fellow, Inst of Particle Phys of Canada, 1983-; Fellow, Royal Soc of Canada, (RSC), 1989-. *Honours:* Rutherford Prize for Phys, RSC, 1988. *Hobbies:* Egyptian Hieroglyph; History; Fishing. *Address:* 5155 Boulevard Lasalle, Verdun, Quebec H4G 2C1, Canada. 142.

LERSNER Heinrich Ludwig von, b. 14 July 1930, Stuttgart, Germany. President of Umweltbundesamty. m. Uta von Weyhe, 19 Apr 1968, 1 s, 3 d. *Education:* LLD, Univ of Tubingen, 1959. *Appointments:* Public Admin, State Baden Wurttemberg, 1959-61; Fed Ministry of Interior, 1961-73; Pres of the Fed Environ Agy, 1973-. *Creative works:* Law of Waste Management, 1972; Handbook of German Water Law; The Ecological Turn, 1991. *Memberships:* Synode of the Protestant Ch, Berlin Brandenburg. *Honours:* Order of St John Fed Merit Cross. *Hobbies:* Genealogy; Walking. *Address:* Murtener Str 1, D 1000 Berlin 45, Germany.

LESKA Oldrich, b. 16 June 1927, Jablonec nad Nisou, Czechoslovakia. Senior Research Worker. m. Zlata

Hacklova, 5 Jan 1964. *Education:* PhD, Russian Philology, Charles Univ, Prague, 1951; CSc, Moscow State Univ, 1956. *Appointments:* Reschr, Slavic Philology and General Lings, Czech Acad of Scis, 1956- ; Lectr, Extern, Charles Univ, 1956- 68; Vis Prof, Univs of Colorado and Chicago, 1968-70. *Creative works include:* Contrastive studies in Ukrainian, Czech and Russian, 1987; Dynamics in the structural make up of Russian morphology, 1989; Topical problems of Russian Morphology, 1988; The Structure of language: Jan Baudouin de Courteney and present-day linguistics, 1989; The Ressurection of the Prague Linguistic Circle, 1990. *Memberships:* Soc Intl de Ling Fonctionnelle, Paris; Cercle Ling de Prague, Chm; Ling Soc of the Czech Acad of Scis. *Hobbies:* Painting; Birdwatching. *Address:* Haskova 14,m 170 00 Praha 7, Czechoslovakia.

LESNIAK Janusz Marian, b. 12 June 1947, Krakow, Poland. Photographer. m. Anne Witowska, 13 Sept 1969, 1 s. *Education:* Dipl, Union of Polish Art Photographers, Warsaw, 1977. *Appointments:* Film recorder, TV, 1967-69; Studio Dir, St Staszic Univ, Krakow, 1970-85; Freelance Photographer, 1985-. *Creative works:* Numerous publications, one-man and group exhibitions at Foto-Video Gallery, Krakow 1988; Gallery BWA, Szczecin, 1988, Bolzano/Ortisei, italy, 1990, Gniezno, 1990; CSCE Symp on Cultural Herigate, Cracow, 1991; Work in private and public collections internationally. *Memberships:* Union of Polish Art Photographers. *Honours:* Prizes for: Wenus, 1974; Polish Sunlight, 1975, 1976; Preservation of Human Habitat, 1975, 1976; Apollo 75, 1975. *Hobbies:* Photography. *Address:* Czarnowiejska 893, 30-049 Krakow, Poland.

LESTCHENKO-SOUKHOMLINA Tatiana Ivanovna, b. 19 Oct 1903, Tchernigov, USSR. Singer; Writer; Translator. m. (1) 1923, (2) 1931, (3) Vassili Soukhonlin, 1957, 1 s, 1 d. *Education:* Inst St Catherine, 1912-17; Moscow Soviet Sch, Piatigorsk, Caucasus, 1917-21; Sch of Journalism, Comumbia Univ, NY, 1925-27. *Appointments:* Actress, Newplaywrites Theatre, NY, 1926-27; Actress, Goulag Theatre, Vorkouta, 1947-54; Translator and Singer (with guitar), all life long. *Creative works:* A long future, 1991; Two concerts a month in Moscow and Petersborg since 1987; two autobiographical films, 1989, 1992; Two records, 1989, 1991. *Memberships:* LITFOND (Lit Foun of Russia); Admitted to Actor's Union, NYC, 1929. *Hobbies:* Playing the guitar; Singing. *Address:* Novopeschana ul 8j apt 52 , 125057 Moscow, Russia.

LESTER Andrew D, b. 8 Aug 1939, Coral Gables, FLorida, USA. University Professor. m. Judith A Laesser, 8 Sept 1960. 1 s, 1 d. *Education:* BA Mississippi Col, Clinton, MS, 1961; BD 1964, PhD 1968, S.Bapt Theol Sem, Louisville, KY. *Appointments include:* Asst 1964-66, Grad Tchg Fellow, 1966-67, Special Instr, 1967-69, Psycho of Religion Dept, S.Bapt Theol Sem; Vis Lectr Religion, Wake Forest Univ, NC, 1972-77; Vis Prof of Pastoral Care and Counselling, S.E.Bapt Theol Sem, Wake Forest, NC, 1972- 77; Prof, Psycho of Religion, S.Bapt Theol Sem, 1977-91. *Creative works:* Articles and books including: It Hurt so Bad Lord? The Christian Encounters Crisis, 1976; Understanding Aging Parents, 1980; Coping with Your Anger: A Christian Guide, 1983; Pastoral Care with Children in Crisis, 1985; Spiritual Dimensions of Pastoral Care: Witness to the Ministry of Wayne E Oates, 1985; When Children Suffer; A Sourcebook for Ministry with Children in Crisis, 1987. *Membership:* Soc for Pastoral Theol. *Address:* Pastoral Care & Psychology, Texas Christian University, Brite Divinity School, Ft Worth TX 76129, USA.

LESTER W Bernard, b. 9 Jan 1939, Havana, Florida, USA. Executive VP, Alico Inc. m. Elaine Purnell, 30 Mar 1961, 1 s. *Education:* BS Agric, Univ of Fla, 1961; MS Agric Econ, 1962; PhD Agric Econ, Texas A & M Univ, 1965. *Appointments:* Res Asst, 1962-65, Agric Econ, 1965-67, Texas A & M Univ; Res Econ 1967-68, Econ Res Dir, 1969-76, Dep Exec Dir, 1976- 78, Exec Dir,

1979-86, Fla Dept of Citrus, Univ of Fla; Dep Exec VP and Chief Op Ofr, 1986-87, Exec VP, 1988-, Alico Inc, La Belle, Fla. *Creative works:* Author of numerous research reports and articles related primarily to the Florida citrus industry, but also including reports and articles related to other food commodity groups. *Memberships:* Overall Extension Adv Com, hendry Co; S.Fla Agric Coun, 1991; Corkscrew Reg Ecosystem Watershed, Alternate Trustee; Gulf Citrus Growers Assn: Bd, Sec, Exec Com, Long Range Policy and Planning Com, Processed Mktg Com. *Honours:* Boss of the Year, Profl Secs Intl, Winter Haven Chap, 1982; Bus Assoc of the Year, 1989, Am Bus Women's Assn, Caloosahatchee Charter Chap. *Hobbies:* Hunting; Reading; Sport. *Address:* B-201 Villas River Run, LA Belle, FL 33935, USA. 7, 132, 155, 125, 152.

LESZCZYNSKI Waclaw Kazimierz, b. 11 Apr 1936, Warsaw, Poland. Scientist; Food Technologist. m. Danuta Grys, 26 June 1961, 1 s, 2 d. *Education:* BSc Agronomy, 1957, MSc Food Tech, 1959, PhD, 1969, DSc, 1977, Prof, 1987, Agric Univ of Wroclaw. *Appointments:* Asst, 1959, Sr Lectr, 1969, Asst Prof, 1978, Prof, 1987, Dean Fac Food Tech, 1980-87, V-Rector, 1990, Agric Univ of Wroclaw; Exec Supervisor, Bakery of Wroclaw, 1989. *Creative works:* Textbooks for students, book: Potato Science a Technology; 56 Research papers and 51 research communiques; 2 patents. *Memberships:* Com of Food Tech and Chem, Polish Acad of Sci. *Honours:* Knight Cross Order Polonia Restituta, 1988; Golden 1983 and Silver 1975 Crosses of Merit; Nat Educ Bd Medal, 1991; Minister of Nat Educ Prizes, 1986, 1987, 1990. *Hobbies:* Reading; History; Polish scouting. *Address:* Agricultural University of Wroclaw, ul Norwida 25, 50-375 Wroclaw, Poland.

LETT James William, b. 29 Sept 1955, Augsburg, Germany. Anthropologist. *Education:* BA Col of William and Mary, 1977; MA 1980, PhD, 1983, Univ of Fla. *Appointments include:* Instr, Univ of Fla, 1977-81; Adj Prof, Philos, Barry Univ, Fla, 1984; Adj Instr, Social Scis, 1985-86, Asst Prof, 1986-89, Assoc Prof, 1989-, Indian River Community Col, Fla, 1985-86; Adj Prof, Humanities, Fla Inst of Tech, 1986; Guest Lectr, Anthropol, Univ Utah, 1989; Adjunct Assoc Prof, Anthropol, Fla Atlantic univ, 1990. *Creative works:* Numerous articles in professional publications including: Practicing Anthropology, Communicator, Anthropology Newsletter, Annals of Tourism Research, Journal of Anthropological Res, Skeptical Inquirer, Current Anthropology, Human Organization and Anthropology and Humanism Quarterly; Book, The human Enterprise; Chapters in books, Emics and Etics, The Hundredth Monkey, World Class Service. *Memberships:* Fellow, Am Anthropol Assn; Fellow, Soc for Applied Anthropol; Exec Coun, Tampa Bay Skeptics. *Honours:* Outstanding Acad Bd of the Yr, Choice Magazine, 1987-88; Awd of Excellence, Fla Tchg Profession and Nat Educ Assn Newsmaker, 1986; Fellowship, Inter-Am Foun, 1979. *Hobbies:* Boating; Golf; Tennis; Racquetball; Travel. *Address:* Department of Social Sciences, Indian River Community College, 3209 Virginia Avenue, Ft Pierce, FL 34981, USA. 15, 7.

LETTS Quentin Richard Stephen, b. 6 Feb 1963, Cirencester, England. Journalist. *Education:* Haileybury; Bellarmine Col, Kentucky; BA Trinity Col, Dublin; Dipl Class Arch, Jesus Col, Cambs. *Appointments:* Published and edited various independent magazines in Dublin, 1982-86; Specialist Publications, Cardiff, 1987; Diarist, Sketch writer, Foreign Correspondent, The Daily Telegraph, 1988-; Cuurrently, Ed, Peterborough Column. *Memberships:* Frogs Cricket Club; Savile Club. *Hobbies:* Restaurants; Watching Cricket. *Address:* 16 Chilworth Street, London W2 6LL, England.

LEUNG Raymond Chung-Chun, b. 2 June 1952, Guangzhou, China. Computer Professional. m. Amy Li-Tian Zhao, 29 Feb 1984, 1 s. *Education:* BS Geol, Hebei

Inst of Geol, China, 1977; MS Maths & Comp Sci, Emory Univ, USA, 1989. *Appointments include:* Res Trainee, Nanjing Res Inst of Geol and Paleontol, China, 1977-80; Sales and Mktg Posts, Hong Kong, 1981-85; System Op, Acad Comp Ctr, Atlanta Univ, 1986; Computing Lab Rep, Math Dept, 1986-88, Computing Lab Conslt, 1988-89, Emory Univ, Atlanta; Programmer Analyst, Industrial Comp Corp, Atlanta, 1989-91; Systems Adminr, Quaker Oaks Co, Jackson, TN, USA. *Memberships:* Am Math Soc; Atlanta Unix Users Gp. *Honours:* Grad Fellow, Emory Univ, 1986-89. *Hobbies:* Jogging; Swimming; Table Tennis; Tennis; Weight Lifting; Martial Arts; Reading; Philately; Painting; Playing the Piano. *Address:* 842 North Parkway Apt C5, Jackson, TN 38305, USA. 7.

LEVENE Victor, b. 20 Feb 1939, London, England. Barrister. m. Jacqueline Anne Perry, 17 Feb 1980. 3 s, 1 d. *Education:* Latymer Upper Sch, Hammersmith, 1950-57; LLB Hons, Univ Col London, 1961. *Appointments:* Called to the Bar, Middle Temple, 1961; Inner Temple, 1978; Practising, *Membership:* Brit Film Inst. *Hobbies:* Numismatics; Philately; Films; Crusing. *Address:* Lamb Building, Temble, London EC4Y 7AS, England.

LEVER Eric Gilbert, b. 5 Apr 1947, Hampton Court, England. Consultant Physician. m. Nicola Langdon, 26 Aug 1985, 2 s. *Education:* BSocSc, Univ Birmingham, 1968; BA 1972, MB BChir, 1975, Trinity Col, Cambs; MRCP, UK, 1978. *Appointments:* Univ Col Hosp, 1975; Nottingham Gen Hosp, 1976-77; Royal Marsden Hosp, 1977; Hammersmith Hosp, 1978; Kings Col Hosp, 1979-80; Univ of Chicago Res Rellowship, 1981-83; Conslt Endocrinologist, 1984-. *Creative works:* Many papers on endocrinology and diabetes. *Memberships:* RCPhys; RSM. *Hobbies:* Painting; Music; Mountain climbing. *Address:* 136 Harley Street, London W1, England.

LEVESON Richard Cecil, b. 25 Feb 1941, England. Entrepreneur. m. Mei Lam, 1967, 2 s. *Education:* BSc Hons Phys, 1963; DIC Imperial Col, 1973; PhD Materials Sci, 1973. *Appointments:* Pres and Foun, Photovac Inc, 1975-; VP, Intraspace Intl, 1974-75; Conslt, Apollo Prog, 1974. *Creative works:* Paper, Sputtered thin film solid lubricants, Journal of Applied Physics, 1974. *Membership:* Ontario Assn of Profl Engrs. *Honour:* Instrument Soc of Am Gilmer Thomason Fowler Awd, 1981. *Hobbies:* Playing classical guitar; Reading; Swimming; Travel. *Address:* c/o Photovac Inc, 330 Cochrane Dr, Markham, Ontario, Canada L3R 8E5. 88. 142.

LEVETO-JABR Paula Denise, b. 13 Mar 1950, Canonsburgh, Pennsylvania, USA. Associate Professor. 1 s, 1 d. *Education:* BA Georgia State Univ, 1971; MA 1978, PhD 1985, Indiana Univ. *Appointments:* Assof Prof, Georgia State Univ, 1986-; Asst Prof, Univ of Georgia Studies Abroad, summer, 1990. *Creative works:* Articles in Art Bulletin, 1990; Intl Dictionary of Architects and Architecture, 1991; The Dictionary of Art, 1994; Gesta, 1987; Indiana Univ Art Mus Bulletin, 1979. *Memberships:* Col Art Assn; S.E.Col Art Conf; Intl Ctr of Mediaeval Art; Am Acad of Religion; Am Assn of Univ Women. *Honours:* Andrew W Mellon Fellow, Metropolitan Mus of Art, 1981-82; Kress Fellow, Dept of Fine Arts, Indiana Univ, 1980-82. *Hobbies:* Gardening; Movies. *Address:* School of Art and Design, Georgia State University, University Plaza, Atlanta, GA 30303, USA.

LEVINE Benjamin, b. 22 May 1931, New Haven, Connecticut, USA. Trial Attorney. m. Arleen E Rosenblatt, 14 Jan 1962, 1 s, 1 d. *Education:* BA, 1953, Univ of Connecticut, 1953; JD, Rutgers Univ, 1963. *Appointments:* Clk, Supreme Ct, State of New Mexico, 1964; Special Asst, NJ Commr of Econ Devel, 1965-67; Dep Attorney Gen, NJ, 1967-70; Private Practice, 1970-. *Creative works:* Co-author: Medical Malpractice, Zoning and Land Use Guide for Public Officials; Other articles in professional journals on medical malpractice.

Memberships: Trial Attys NJ; Assn Trial Lawyers am: NJ Bar Assn; Summit Bar Assn; NY State Trial Lawyers Assn; NY County Lawyers Assn; Am Arbitration Assn. *Hobbies:* Photography; Hiking; Geography. *Address:* 1 Riverfront Plaza 5th Fl, Newark, NJ 07102, USA. 52, 163, 132.

LEVINSON Charles, b. 19 Oct 1920, Canada. Economist; Professor; Author. m. Marie Rose de Gunzburg, 3 d. *Education:* BBA St Johns Univ, Myc, USa; MA Univ Toronto; PhD Univ of Paris; DBA Univ Bus Sch, Lusanne. *Appointments:* Asst Dir, CIO Euro Ofc, Paris, 1953; Dep Gen Sec Intl Metal Workers Fed, 1955; Dir Tech Ast, World Ort Union, 1961-79; Sec Gen, Intl Fed of Chem Workers, 1964; Asst Dean Bus Sch, Lausanne. *Creative works:* Capital inflation and multinations, 1964; International trade unionism, 1966; Industrys democratic revolution, 1960; Multinational pharmaceutical industyr, 1969; Global Health hazards, 1970; Vodka Cola, 1972. *Memberships:* Dir, Dupont de Nemours-Germany, 1975-1980; Dir, Western Airlines, USA, 1984-87; Assoc Dir, Global Conslts; Ass Intl Labour Inst, NYC, 1990; Conslt, Brotherhood of Termsters: Assoc Che Workers Fed; UN Com on Sustainable Devel, 1988. *Honours:* Sec Gen Emeritus, Intl Chem Workers Fed, 1985; Hon pres, Turkish metal Workers Fed, 1964; Tchg Awd, Bus Sch, Lusanne, 1990; RCAF decorations, 1945; Hon Pres, Greek metalworkers Fed, 1962. *Hobbies:* Sport; Golf; Skiing; Music; Theatre. *Address:* 27 Ave de Bude , PO Box 345, 1202 Geneva 19, Switzerland. 88, 94,

LEVITZKY Michael Gordon, b. 3 Jan 1947, Elizabeth, New Jersey, USA. Professor of Physiology. m. Elizabeth Gouaux, 13 Mar 1985, 1 s. *Education:* BA Univ Pennsylvania, 1969; PhD Albany Med Col Union Univ, 1975. *Appointments:* Instr, Physiol, Albany Med Col, 1974-75; Asst Prof 1975-80, Assoc Prof, 1980-85, Prof, 1985-, Physiol, LSUMC. *Creative works:* Pulmonary Physiology, 1991; Introduction to Respiratory Care, 1990. *Memberships:* Am Physiol Soc, Ed Com, 1988-91; Am Thoracic Soc; Assn of Am Med Col Gp on Educ Affairs; Am Heart Assn, Basic Sci and Cardiopulmonary Couns. *Honour:* Sigma Xi. *Address:* Department of Physiology, Louisiana State University Medical Centre, 1901 Perdido St, New Orleans, LA 70112, USA. 7, 15,

LEVSHOUNOVA Svetlana Pavlovna, b. 29 Mar 1938, Kujbishev District. Geochemist. m. V Zavragnov, 7 Mar 1964, 1 s, 1 d. *Education:* Dipl, Univ, 1960; Dr of Geol and Minerol Scis, 1968. *Appointments:* Geol Expedition at Choukotka, N.E, 1960-64; Aspirant, VNIGNI, 1964-68; Scientist, VNIGNI, 1968-. *Creative works:* More than 80 articles, 2 monografs and two inventions. *Memberships:* Sci Tech Soc in oil an dGas. *Honours:* Gold 1955, Silver 1980, 1990, medals, All Union Exhibition; Third Deg Dipl, 1978; Second Deg Dipl, 1987; Silver Dipl, Intl Exhibition, 1984; Medal for labour, 1988. *Hobbies:* Ballet; Tourism; Travelling. *Address:* Shosse Enthousiastos, 36 Vnigni, Moscow 105819, Russia. 138.

LEVY Alan Joseph, b. 10 Feb 1932, New York City, USA. Editor in Chief, The Prague Post. *Appointments:* Reporter, Cour-Jour, Louisville, KY, 1953-60; Investigator, Carnegie Comm on Educ TV, 1966-67; Foreign Corr, 1967-, Life and Good Housekeeping Mags in Prague, 1967-71; NY Times and International Herald Tribune in Vienna, 1971-. *Creative works:* Draftee Confidential Guide, 1957, Revised, 1966; Operation Elvis, 1960; The Elizabeth Taylor Story, 1961; Wanted Nazi Criminals at Large, 1962; Interpret Your Dreams, 1962, 1975; Kind Hearted Tiger, 1964; The Culture Vultures, 1968; God Bless You Real Good: My Crusade with Billy Graham, 1969; Rowboat to Prague, 1972; Revised as So Many Heroes, 1980; Good Men Still Live, 1974; The Bluebird of Happiness, 1976; Forever Sophia, 1979; 1986; The World of Ruth Draper, play, 1982; Ezra Pound: The voice of Silence, 1983; W H Auden: In the Authm of the Age of Anxiety, 1983; Treasures of the Vatican Collections, 1983; Just an Accident? Libretao for Symphonic Requiem by Composer René Staar, Chamber Version, 1983, Orchestral Version; Vladimir Nabokov: The Velvet Butterfly, 1984; Erza Pound: A Jewish View, 1987. *Contributions to:* International Herald, Tribune, Paris; Art News, NY City; NY Sunday Times; Readers Digest; Travel and Leisure. *Address:* c/o Serafina Clarke Literary Agent, 98 Tunis Road, London W12 7EY, England.

LEVY Michael H, b. 2 Oct 1947, Newburgh, NY, USA. Environmental Consultant. m. Judith Linenbroker 28 Aug 1971, 2 s. *Education:* BS Civil Engrg, 1969, ME Civil and Environmental Engrg, 1972, Rensselaer Poly Inst; MBA Prog, Personnel Admin, Fairleigh Dickinson Univ, 1977-78. *Appointments include:* Asst Sanitary Engr, NY State Dept, 1972-73; Sr Air Pollution Engr, 1973-76; Environ Engr allied Chem Co Div Semet Solvay, Morristown, NJ, 1976-78; Supt Environ and Quality Control Div, Allied Chem Co, Detroit, 1979; Mobile Chem Co, 1979-83; Mgr, Environ Affairs Mobil Chem, NY and NJ, 1984-87; Mgr, Legis and Regulatory affairs, Mobil Chem Co, Fairfax, VA, 1987-89; VP Franklin Assocs Ltd, McLean, VA, 1990-. *Memberships:* Chem Mfrs Assn; Coun on Plastics and Packaging in the Enviroment; Coun for Solid Waste Solutions; Flexible Packaging Assn; Foodservice and Packaging Inst; Polystyrene Packaging Coun; Soc of Plastics Indust, Inc; Styrene Info and Res Ctr. *Honours:* Chi Epsilon; Registered Profl Engr, 1975; Certified Environmental Auditor, 1991. *Hobbies:* Sport; Travel; Volunteer organizations. *Address:* 744 Ridge Drive, McLean, VA 22101, USA. 132, 7.

LEVY Philip Marcus, b. 4 Feb 1934, Redcar, Yorks, England. Professor of Psychology. m. 8 Mar 1958, 2 d. *Education:* BA Univ Leeds, 1952-55; PhD Univ Birmingham, 1960. *Appointments:* Psychol, Royal Air Force, 1959-63; Sr Res Fellow, Lectr, Sr Lectr, Univ Birmingham, 1962-72; Prof of Psychol, Univ Lancaster, 1972-. *Creative works:* Ed, Brit Jour of Math and Stats Psychol, 1975-80; Tests in Education: A book of Critical Reviews, 1984; Cognition in Action, 1986. *Memberships:* Pres, Brit Psychol Soc, 1978-79; Econ and Socil Res Coun, various posts, 1979-89, Coun, 1983-89. *Honours:* Fellow, Brit Psychol Soc, 1970. *Hobby:* Bridge. *Address:* Department of Psychology, Lancaster University, Lancs LA1 4YF, England. 1, 154,

LEW Sip Hon (Dato), b. 27 June 1925 Malaysia. Company Director. m. Molly Goh, 25 Sept 1945, 1 s, 4 d. *Education:* BA Hons, Econ, Univ of Malaya, 1952. *Appointments:* Malaysian Civil Ser, 1952-66; Dpty Controller of Rubber Res, 1967-72; Chm, Malaysian Rubber Exchange and Lic Bd, 1972-74; Dpty Min of Primary Industs, 1975-77; Dpty Minister of Trade and Indust, 1978-83; Malaysian Ambassador to USA, 1983-86; Exec Chm, Universal Cable Holdings Bhd, 1986-92; Exec Chm, Tomen Intl Malaysia Sdn Bhd, 1986-92; Chm, Long Huat Timber Industs Bhd, 1989-92; Chm, Kuala Lumpur Fin Berhad, 1988- 90. *Membership:* Fellow, Royal Econ Soc, London. *Honours* Titles conferred by the King of Malaysia: Kesatria Mangku Negara, 1962; Johan Mangku Neagra, 1976; Datoship, Sultan of Selangor, 1977; Hon LLD, Golden Gate Univ, CA, 1986. *Hobbies:* Photography; Golf; Tennis. *Address:* 25 Jalan 14/3, Taman Tun Abdul Razak, 68000 Ampang Jaya, Salangor, Malaysia.

LEWIN Christopher George, b. 15 Dec 1940, Poole, Dorset, England. Pensions Mgr. m. Robin Lynn Stringham, 1 Nov 1985, 2 s. *Education:* Coopers Company's Sch, Bow, London, 1951-55; Actuarial Exams, Inst of Actuaries, 1956-62. *Appointments:* Actuarial Asst: Equity and Law Life Assurance Soc Ltd, 1956-63, London Transport, 1963-67, British Rail, 1967-88, Controller Corp Pensions, 1970-80, Coor Private Capital, 1980-88; Pensions Dir, Associated Newspapers Holdings Ltd, 1989-92; Hd of Grp Pensions, Guiness plc, 1992-. *Creative works:* Articles in professional journals on the history of actuarial science, investment, and manpower planning. *Memberships:*

Fellow, Inst of Actuaries, 1963; Fellow, Pensions Mgmt Inst; Fellow, Royal Stats Soc; Coun, Occ Pensions Adv Ser; Chm, nat Fed of Consumer Gps, 1984-86. *Honours:* Joseph Burn Prize, 1962, Messenger and Brown Prize, 1968, Inst of Actuaries. *Hobbies:* English social history pre 1700; Old books and manuscripts; Old table games; Family life. *Address:* Guiness plc, 33 Pinkhill, Edinburgh EH12 7BA, Scotland. 52.

LEWIS Arthur Roland, b. 9 May 1920, Kingsley, Cheshire, England. Retired Anglican Priest. m. Gladys Rhodes 26 Apr 1958, 1 s. *Education:* MA St Edmund Hall, Oxford, 1941; Dipl of Theol, St Stephens Hse, Oxford, 1942. *Appointments:* English curacies, 1943-47; Univs Mission to Central Africa, Tanganyika/Zanzibar, 1947-58; Priest i/c Rhodesian missions, 1958-69; Rector of Rusape, Rhod, 1958-60; Priest i/c Plalaborwa, SA, 1984-87. *Creative works:* Christian Terror in Southern Africa, 1978; Too Bright The Vision, forthcoming. *Memberships:* Archdeacon of Inyanga, Rhodesia, 1966-69; Rhodesian Senator, 1976-78. *Honours:* Hon Pres: Rhodesia Christian Gp, 1984; Good Hope Chirstian Gp, 1988-. *Hobbies:* Writing; Poetry; Music. *Address:* PO Box 430, Chingford, London E4 9SQ, England. 39.

LEWIS Brent Renault, b. 23 May 1958, Mineapolis, Minnesota, USA. President of Integration Plus. *Education:* Cert, Computer Prog, Brown Inst, 1978. *Appointments:* DP Coor, Dakotu County, 1979-82; Analyst Programmer, Compucare, 1981-84; DP Mgr, Golden Valley Health Ctr, 1985-86; Computer Consultation, 1986-87; Pres, Integratin Plus, 1987-90. *Memberships:* Corp Adv Bd and Bd of Dirs, Epilepsy Soc of Arizona; Bd of Dirs of Integration Plys; Data Processing Management Assn. *Hobbies:* Racquetball; Caribbean travel; Public speaking. *Address:* Integration Plus, PO Box 3289, Scottsdale, AZ 85271, USA.

LEWIS Clifford Thomas, b. 29 Aug 1923, Newport, Gwent, Wales. Emeritus Professor. m. Joan Lewis Willey, 19 July 1949, 1 s, 1 d. *Education:* BA 1948, Ma 1952, Queens Col, Cambs; PhD, Imperial Col, London, 1954. *Appointments:* Lectr in Insect Physiol, Imperial Col, London, 1955-65; Sr Lectr, 1965-74, reader, 1974-78, Royal Holloway Col, London; Prof of Zool, 1978-88, V-Principal, 1981-85, Emeritus Prof, 1988-, Royal Holloway and Bedford New Col; Vis Prof: UCLA California, 1975; Ghana, 1976; Latrobe, Australia, 1986. *Memberships:* Royal Entomological Soc; Soc of Experimental Biol; The Athenaeum Club. *Hobbies:* Painting; Sculpture; Fell Walking. *Address:* 9 Silwood Close, Ascot, Berkshire SL5 7DX, England.

LEWIS Geoffrey David, b. 13 Apr 1933, Brighton, Sussex, England. m. Frances May Wilderspin, 7 July 1956, 3 d. *Education:* MA Univ of Liverpool. *Appointments:* Asst Curator, Worthing Mus and Art Gall, 1950-60; Dpty Dir, 1960-65, Dir, 1966-72, Sheffield City Mus; Dir: Liverpool City Mus, 1972-74; Merseyside County Mus, 1974-77, Mus of Studies, Univ of Leicester, 1977-89; Assoc Tchr, Univ of Leicester, 1989-92. *Memberships:* Intl Coun of Mus, Pres, 1983-89; Mus Assn, Hon Fellow, pres, 1980-81; Soc of Antiquaries of London, Fellow; Trustee, Royal Armouries. *Honours:* Hon FMA, Hon Fellow of the Mus Assn. *Hobbies:* Walking; Computing. *Address:* 4 Orchard Close, Wolvey, Hinckley LE10 3LR, England. 43.

LEWIS Jason A Jr, b. 17 Aug 1941, Clarksville, Texas, USA. System Technician. *Education:* Stockton Col, 1959-60; San Jose Jr Col, 1962- 63. *Appointments:* Telephone Installer, 1966-83, Field Engr, 1983-84, Pacific Bell; System Technician, AT&T, 1984-. *Creative works:* Invention of an audio visual signal to work with an ACD Commnication System. *Memberships:* IPA: The Cousteau Soc; Astronomical Soc of the Pacific; San Francisco Zoological Soc. *Honours:* Man of the Year, ABI, 1990; Dpty Governor, The American. *Hobbies:* Photography; Astronomy; Study of Quasars and their cosmological redshift. *Address:* 139 Pecks Lane, South San Francisco, CA 94080, USA. 9

LEWIS John Arthur, b. 4 Oct 1934, Tanganyika. Archdeacon of Cheltenham. m. Hazel Helen Jane Morris, 6 June 1959, 1 s, 1 d. *Education:* MA, Jesus Col, Oxford, 1953-56; Cuddesdon Col, Oxford, 1958-1960. *Appointments:* Nat Ser, 1956-58; Asst Curate: Prestbury Glos, 1960-63; Wimborne Minister, 1963-66; Rector, Eastington w. Frocester, 1966-70; Vicar of Nailsworth, 1970-78; Vicar of Cirencester, 1978-88; Rural Dean of Cirencester, 1984-88; Hon Canon Glos Cathedral, 1985; Archdeacon of Cheltenham and Canon of Glos Cathedral, 1988. *Memberships:* Chmn, Gluster Diocesan Bd of Education, 1988; Chmn, Glouster Diocesan Stewardship Committee, 1988; Chmn, Gloucester Diocesan Redundant Church Uses Committee, 1988; Mem, Council, Cheltenham Ladies' College. *Hobbies:* Travel; Music; Gardening; Walking. *Address:* Westbourne, 283 Gloucester Road, Cheltenham, Glos GL51 7AD, England. 1.

LEWIS Kenneth Paul Jr, b. 9 July 1947, Quayaquil, Ecuador. Social Work Administrator. m. Sue Lewis, 29 Aug, 1970, 1 s, 1 d. *Education:* BSW, 1973, MSW, 1975; LSW, 1989; Dipl in Clin Social Wk and ABECSW. *Appointments:* Dir, Social Ser and Activity Depts, Lakeside Place Nsg Home, Kentucky, 1975-76; Assoc Dir, Human Sers Dept, Philadelphia Geriatric Ctr, 1977-86; Dir, Dept of Social Ser and Pastoral Care, Inglis Hse, Philadelphia, 1987-. *Creative works:* 36 articles in leading journals and magazines regarding institutionalised aged, the physically disabled and the theory and practice of social work. *Memberships:* Acad of Cert Social Workers; Nat Rehab Assn; Register of Clin Social Workers; Social Ser Workers Assn for Nsg Homes, Pres, 1988, 1989; Nat Assn of Social Workers. *Honours:* Outstanding Ser Awd, Philadelphia Geriatric Ctr, 1984; Ed Bd, A Positive Aproach Magazine; Lectr and facilitator, workshop and seminars on varied topics realted to long-term care. *Hobbies:* Reading; Sport; Philately; Classical music. *Address:* 2809 Lillian Avenue, Willow Grove, PA 19090, USA.

LEWIS Mary Etta McMakin, b. 23 Oct 1928, Ontario, California, USA. Special Education Teacher. m. Charles Jesse Lewis, 15 Dec 1946, 1 s, 1 d. *Education:* AA Chaffey Col, Alta Loma, CA, 1963; BA, Laverne Col, 1965; MA, Calif State Univ, 1979; Cert, Elem Tchr, Learning handicapped Specialist. *Appointments:* Tchr, Chino Unified Sch Dist, CA, 1965-67; Tchr, Ontario-Montclair Sch Dist, 1967-79; Spl Edn Tchr, 1979-80; Resource Specialist, 1980-88; Resource Specialist, Math Cadre Morongo Unified Sch Dist, Yucca Valley, CA, 1988-; Tchr Presby Ch Upland CA, 1956-78. *Memberships:* Delta Kappa Gamma Awd Tchg Colleagues, 1982-88; AAUW, Sec, 1967-69; NEA Pilot's Intl Assn; Calif Tchrs Assn Coun for Exceptional Children; ZONTA, Calif Assn Resource Specialists, Co-Chm, Hi Desert Chpt; 99ers Club; Assistance League Club. *Address:* PO Box 2349, Yucca Valley, CA 92286, USA. 15, 52.

LEWIS Mervyn K, b. 20 June 1941, Adelaide, Australia. Midland Bank Professor of Money and Banking. m. Kay Judith Lewis née Wiesner, 24 Nov 1962, 4 d. *Education:* BEc 1st class Hons, 1960-64, PhD 1978, Univ of Adelaide. *Appointments include:* Tutor in Econ, 1965-66, Lectr, 1967, Sr Lectr, 1973, Reader, 1980-84, Assoc Dean, Fac of Econ, University of Adelaide; Vis Scholar, Econ Div, Bank of England, London, 1979-80; Univ of Nottingham, 1984; Vis Prof, Flinders Univ of S.Australia. *Creative works:* Books include: Australia's Financial Institutions and Markets, 1985; Personal Financial Markets, 1986; Domestic and International Banking, 1987; Money in Britain, 1991; Current Issues in Financial and Monetary Eonomics, 1991; Co-Ed, The Australian Financial System, 1993. *Memberships include:* Royal Econ Soc; Am Econ Assn; E.India Club, London; Research Assoc, Center for Pacific Basin Studies, Fed Res Bank of San Francisco. *Honours:*

Fellow, Acad of Social Sers in Australia, 1986; Winner of Essay Competition, Inst of Bankers, 1963. *Hobbies:* Rambling; Gardening; Tennis; Music; Hi Fi. *Address:* Sarum Chase, 13 Rostrevor Road, Stirling 5152, SA, Australia. 30.

LEYDEN Donald Elliott, b. 26 June 1938, Alabama, USA. Scientist. m. Alice J Trowbridge, 10 June 1961, 1 s, 1 d. *Education:* BS Kent State Univ, 1960; MS 1961, PhD 1964, Emory Univ. *Appointments:* Asst Prof, Univ of Georgia, 1965-76; Prof, Univ of Denver, 1976-82; Prof, Colorado State Univ, 1982-88; Philip Morris, USA, 1988-. *Creative works:* Co- author of 175 Scientific papers. Served on many editorial boards. *Memberships:* Am Chem Soc; Soc for Applied Spectroscopy. *Hobbies:* Sailing; Skiing. *Address:* Philip Morris USA, PO Box 26583, Richmond, VA 23261, USA. 2, 7.

LHOTKA John Francis, b. 13 May 1921, Butte, Montana, USA. Professor Emeritus of Anatomical Sciences. m. Lois Katherine Clysdale, 22 Sept 1951. *Education:* BA Univ of Montana, 1942; MS Anatomy, N.Western Univ, MS, 1947; MB 1949; MD 1951; PhD 1953; Internship, Minneapolis Gen Hosp, 1950- 51. *Appointments:* US Army, 1942-46; Asst Prof, 1951-55, Assoc Prof, 1955-69, Prof, 1969-86, Emeritus Prof, 1986-, Anatomy, Oklahoma Med Sch. *Creative works:* Over 60 papers in histochemistry research, articles and book chapters, 5 texts on medieval coinage of the Byzantine Empire, Feudal France, Bracteates, Iberian States and Bohemia. *Memberships:* AAA; Histochem Soc; Intl Acad of Path; ACS; Am Numis Assn; Hon Fellow, Royal Numis Soc; Fellow, Am Numis Soc; Fellow, Royal Soc of Hlth. *Honours:* Military Awds, WW II, and Yugoslav War Cross; Media Productions Awd, Univ Oklahoma, for series of tapes in microanatomy. *Hobbies:* Classical and Medieval numismatics; Military Firearms, 1871-1918; Military history and insignia (medical). *Address:* University of Oklahoma Health Sciences Centre, PO Box 26901, BMSB Anat Sci, OK 73190, USA. 7, 52,

LI Bao Zhen, b. 15 Oct 1916, Tianjin. Professor. m. Shi Zhu Zhen, 11 Feb 1938, 4 d. *Education:* Ba Commerce, Hautes Etudes Indust et Commercialles, 1932-36; MA Econ, nankai Univ, 1936-37. *Appointments:* Lectr, Acctg, Hautes Etudes, 1937-42; Prof, Hd of Acctg Dept, Adam Smith Inst, 1942-52; Prof in Nankai Univ, 1948-58; Prof and Dean of Acctg Fac in Tianjin Col, 1958-91. *Creative works:* 140 books and theses on Accounting and auditing; Author of: Income Tax in China, 1937; Auditing, 1942; Commercial Accounting in Soviet Enterprises, 1953; Encyclopaedia of B.Adm 1984; Contemporary Accounting in China, 1990. *Memberships:* Exec Dir, Acctg Soc of China, 1980-91; Chm of Res Com of Hist of Acctg,; Dir of Auditing Soc of China, 1984-91; Canadian Comprehensive Auditing Foun; Inst of Internal Auditors; Pres of Acctg Soc of Tiajin. *Honours:* Model Laborer of Tianjin, 1984-88; Dist Tchr of China, 1988; Advanced Hg Sch Prof of China, 1989. *Hobbies:* Drama; Reading; Table Tennis. *Address:* Tiangin College of Finance and Economics, 25 Zhujiang Road, Hexi District, Tianjin 300222, China.

LI Baolin, b. 20 Aug 1936, China. Artist; Division of Creation and Res, Chairman, Academy of Chinese Paintings. m. Chen Yadan, Feb 1967, 1 s. *Education:* BA, Fine Arts, China Nat Inst of Fine Arts, 1958-63. *Appointments:* Profl Painter, Chinese Navy, 1963-90; Painter, Acad of Chinese paintings, Dept of Culture of China, 1990-. *Creative works:* Chief Ed, Li Keran on Arts; Essays in various art magazines, and international museums and private collections; Exhibited in 8 countries. *Memberships:* Chinese Artists Assn; VP, China Soc of Langscape paintings; Dpty Pres, China Soc of Oriental Arts Exchanges; Mem, Evalative Cttee of Fine Art, Senior Academic Ranks, Culture Dept, Chinese State Cncl *Honours:* Recipient of seven national awards for achievement. *Hobbies:* Gardening; Travelling;

Drama. *Address:* Academy of Chinese Paintings, 54 Xisanhuan Beilu, Beijing 100044, China.

LI Chujie, b. 30 Dec 1926, Guangdong, China. Professor. m. Cai Dao Hui 20 June 1927, 1 s, 1 d. *Education:* MD Med Sch, Zhongshan Univ, China, 1951. *Appointments:* Asst Prof, Asst Chm, 1955-68; Assoc Prof, 1969-78, Prof of Pathophysiol, 1979-, Dean of Med Col, 1984-89, Jinan Univ. *Creative works:* Book: Methodology of Medical Research, 1980; Cold Injury, 1987; Edema, 1990; Clinical Pathophysiology, Ed-in-chief; Over 70 research papers in the fields of cold injury and fever. *Memberships:* Chief Ed, Chinese Jour of Pathophysiol; VP, Chinese Soc of Pathophysiol; Pres, Soc of Inflammation, Fever and Infection; Chm, Acad Com of Med Col, Jinan Univ. *Honours:* Chinese Outstanding achievement for reseach in Frostbite, 1978, Cold Injury, 1986; Sci Contribution Awd for Fever Res, 1986; Hon Awd, Nat Educ Com of China, 1990. *Hobbies:* Gardening; Reading. *Address:* Department of Pathophysiology, Medical College, Jinan University, Guangzhou, China.

LI Ji-ren, b. 6 Nov 1931, Anhui, China. Physician of Traditional Chinese Medicine. m. 6 Feb 1957, 4 s, 1 d. *Education:* Grad, Anhui Acad of Trad Chinese Med, 1956. *Appointments:* Tchr, Doctor and Reschr, Annui Col of TCM and Anuhi Med Univ, 1958-72; Yi Ji Mountain Hosp, 1972-. *Creative works:* Publications: The General Theory of Rheumatoid Arthritis; On Empirical Cases of Tumours; Time Medical Science of TCM; Published One Hundred Papers in his field. *Memberships:* Profl Com of Rheumatism of the China Soc of TCM: Experts Com, Nat Admin Bureau of TCM: VP, Annui Provincial Com of Tech Identification of Med Accidents; Academic Board of South Anhui Medical College; One of 1st group of professors, authorized to give Master's Degree in China. *Honours:* Outstanding Educator, Anhui Province; Outstanding Physn of TCM, Health Ministry of China, 1990; Special Allowance, awarded by China Government, 1991; Praised by Sevrl Newspapers, Guangming Daily, Health Daily, China Daily TCM, Anhui Daily. *Hobbies:* Collecting antiques; Painting; Calligraphy. *Address:* Yi Ji Mountain Hospital, S.Anhui Medical College, Wuhu, Anhui Province, China.

LI Jiaxi, b. 26 Aug 1924, Wuhan, Hubei, China. Professor of English. m. Peilin Wen, 2 Feb 1954, 1 s. *Education:* Yale in China, Hunan, 1944; BA Dept of Jour, Yenching Univ, Beijing, 1949. *Appointments:* Interpreter, Liaison Ofr, US Army, CBI Theatre, Kunming, 1945; Liaoning Ribao, Shenyang, Reporter, 1949-54; Instr, Lu Xun Col of Fine ARts, 1955-59; Sr Staff, Liaoning Library, 1959-66; Sch Tchr, 1966-78; Chem Engrg Inst, Shijiazhuang, 1978-82; Prof, Xiangtang Univ, 1982-91. *Creative works:* Art translator of: Jour of Delacrois; Biography of Cellini; Diary of an Art Dealer; Folk art of Yugoslavia. *Memberships:* The Translators Assn of Hunan; Chm , Fed of Translators, Xiangtang City; Nat Geographic Soc, USA. *Honours:* Hon Tchr, Xiangtan Univ, 1990. *Hobbies:* Swimming; Calligraphy; Reading. *Address:* 6-301 Beidou Bldgs, Xiangtan University, Hunan 411105, China.

LI Jinlin, b. 15 Aug 1932, Guangzhou, China. Chief Engineer. m. Zheng Meihua, 16 Feb 1968, 2 s. *Education:* Bachelor of Elec Engrg, S.China Univ of Tech, 1956. *Appointments:* Acad Sinia: Reschr, Inst of Applied Phys, 1958; Asst Reschr, Inst of Phys, 1958; Dpty Res Prof, Res Prof, Inst of Semiconductors, 1960; Chief Engr, China Xiao Feng Tec Equipment Corp, 1985. *Publications:* Electronic measurement instruments sampling theory; A number of technical books and papers. *Memberships:* Commr: Chinese Socs of CAS and of MI; Sr Mem, IEEE. *Honours:* Sci and Tech Achieve Awds, 1964, 1978, 1991; Paper of Excellence, Chinese Transaction on Meas & Instrument, 1991. *Hobbies:* Reading; CLassical music; Chinese Calligraphy. *Address:* 92 Dongzhimennei St, Beijing 100007, China.

LI Juan, b. 15 June 1943, Tianjien, China. Professor, Chief Station Announcer of CCTV. m. Zhou Guoxing, 2 May 1968, 1 s. *Education:* Grad, Beijing Broadcast Col, 1961. *Appointments:* Radio Announcer, Central People's Broadcast Station, 1961-73; Chief Station Announcer, Chinese Central TV Station, 1973-; Hd of Dept, Station Announcers of CCTV, 1985-87. *Creative works:* Books; On the image and language-feature of TV broadcasters, 1983; On developing direction of TV broadcasters, 1986. *Memberships:* Assn of Chinese Reciting Artists; Soc of Chinese Broadcast and TV, Bd of Dirs. *Hobbies:* Reading; Reciting. *Address:* Chinese Central Television Station, 11 Fuxing Road, Fuxingmenwai, Beijing 100859, China.

LI Jun, b. 15 Feb 1928, Xian, China. Editor in Chief, The Family Periodical. m. Cheng Xiu-feng, 15 Mar 1953, 1 s, 2 d. *Education:* BAgric Chem, Northwest Agric Col, 1950. *Appointments:* Ed: Guangdong Zhujian Peoples News, 1949-52, Yuezhong Peasants News, 1952-53, Guangzhou Daily, 1956-61, Yangchen Evening News, 1961-68, Nanfang Daily, 1978- 84. *Creative works:* Chief Ed, The Family; Main compiller of Enduring Love, A Collection of Essays of Love, Romantic Women, Arts and Love, Love of Sports Stars. *Memberships:* Pres, Guangdong Periodical Publicaton Assn; VP, Family Sociol Res Com of China Sociol Inst; China Writers Assn, Guangdong Branch. *Hobbies:* Editing and compiling; News-writing. *Address:* The Family Periodical, 14 Siheng Road, Sinhepu, Guangzhou 510080, China.

LI Kui Wai, b. 25 July 1952, Hong Kong. Senior Lecturer; Economist. m. Cecilia Kau Wah Fong, 21 Nov 1984, 1 s, 1 d. *Education:* BSc 1976, MSc 1980, Univ of London. MDevel Studies, Holland, 1982; PhD, City Univ London, 1993. *Appointments:* Lectr, Univ of Maiduguri, Nigeria, 1977-79; Lectr, Lingnan Col, HK, 1982-84; External Reschr, ILO, Geneva, 1982; Conslt, ESCAP, Thailand, 1984; Sr Lect, City Poly, HK, 1984-; Conslt, ESCAP, Thailane, 1990-91. *Creative works:* Fdr and Exec Ed, Jour of Economics and Inter Relation, HK, 1987-89; Author: Advanced Microeconomics, 1987; HK Econ System, 1988; Ed Bd, Methodus, 1990-; Ed, Intellectus, 1990-. *Memberships:* Am Econ Assn; Royal Econ Soc; Hon Sec, 1989-90, HK Econ Assn; BIM; Exec Mem, HK Inst of Econ Sci; Atlantic Econ Assn. *Honours:* Full scholarship, Camb Educ Authority, 1973-76. *Hobbies:* Driving; Photography; Reading; Squash. *Address:* Department of Economics and Finance, City Polytechnic of Hong Kong, 83 Tat Chee Avenue, Kowloon, Hong Kong. 52

LI Li, b. 11 Feb 1925, Xiangtan, Hunan, China. Professor, Hunan Training School of Light Industry. m. Xie Xiaoyin, 6 Feb 1951. 1 s, 3 d. *Education:* Sch of Fine Arts, Hunan Huazhong, 1938-40; Nat Training Sch of Fine Arts, Hangzhou, 1948-49. *Appointments:* Tchr, Wenyi Middle Sch, Hunan Jinye Hg Sch of Commerce, 1950-53; Pt-time Prof, Changsha Railway Inst, 1984-87; Prof, Hunan Training Sch of Light Industry, 1988-. *Creative works:* A Collection of Impressions of Seals based on poems and Ci poetry by Chairman Mao, 1979; Chinese Calligraphy Painting and Seal Carving, 1985; A Collection of Impressions of Seals based on Eulogy of the Sense of Right by Wen Tianxiang, 1990; Seal Cutting of Modern China. *Memberships:* Dir, Chinas Calligraphers Assn; V-Chm, Hunan Branch; Dir, Chinas Artists Assn, Hunan Branch; Chm, Hunan Assn of Arts and Craft, Calligraphy and painting; Xiling Seal Cutting Soc; Hon Chm, Nanchu Seal Cutting Assn. *Honours:* Exhibitions in Japan and Taiwan; Silver Plate Awds; Mayor of Hsintian City, Legislative Assembly of Taipei County, and Pres of Chungching Magazine. *Hobbies:* Collecting calligraphy, paintings and lithographic stones; Music; Dancing; Travelling; Motor-cycles. *Address:* 50 Xi Yuan Bei Li, Xiangchun Road, Changsha, Hunan 410005, China.

LI Mingqi, b. 20 Apr 1920, Canada. Professor. m. Xu Pengru, 25 Oct 1952, 1 s, 1 d. *Education:* BS Lignan Univ, 1946-49. *Appointments:* Horticultural Asst,

Lingnan Univ, 1951-52; Asst, Plant Physiol, 1953-56, Instr, 1957-77, Prof 1978-, S.China Agric Col. *Creative works:* Author: Fruit Physiology; Assoc Ed, Basic Biochemistry; Articles in professional journals. *Memberships:* Ed Bd, Acta Phytophysiologica Sinica; Acad Com of S.China Botanical Inst; Chinese Socs of Plant Physiol, Botany and Biochem. *Honours:* Best Tchr Awds: Guangdong Province, 1982, Dept of Agric, 1983-84, Nat Educ Com, 1989. *Hobbies:* Reading; Gardening; Music appreciation. *Address:* Department of Agriculture Biology, South China Agricultural University, Guangzhou 510642, China.

LI Musun, b. 16 July 1930, Shanghai, China. Professor of Electronics. m. Chuanxiang Zhang, 1 May 1965, 1 s, 2 d. *Education:* Grad, Elec Engrg, Jiaotung Univ, Shanghai, China, 1952. *Appointments:* Asst, Dalien Navigation Inst, 1952-54; Changchun Col of Geol, 1954-78, Assoc Prf, 1978-83, Prof, 1983-92; Changchun Col of Geol, Chairperson, Dept of Instrumentation, 1978-91; CCG, Guest Prof, Col of St Rose, USA. *Creative works:* Design of integrators in track type instrumention, 1979; Analysis and design of optical pumping magnetometer, 1980; Geological instrumentation terminology, National Standard, 1989; ISR and Window Techniques, 1990; Geological Instrumentation, 1991. *Memberships:* D-Chm, China Electronics Assn; Jilin Div, 1985-90, Standing Mem of Bd, 1991; Bd, Nat office Automation Assn, 1984; IEEE, 1987. *Honours:* Outstanding worker in Sci and Tech, 1983, Outstanding Tchr, 1984, Outstanding Awd for Achievements, 1980, Jilin Province. *Hobbies:* Music; Violin. *Address:* Room 502, 14-3 Wan Bao Lane, Changchun, Jilin 130026, China.

LI Qiao, b. 10 Aug 1909, Shipin, Yunnan, China. Writer. m. Li Fengzhen, 5 Oct 1932, 4 d. *Education:* Middle Sch Grad; A year's study at prep class in Univ. *Appointments:* Tchr, 1931-49; Section Chief, Yunnan Nat Inst, V-Chm, Writers Com of Yunnan Lit and Art Fed, 1952-55; Prof Writer, 1956-; V-Chm, All China Minority Soc, 1978-88; Hon Chm, Yunnan Weiters Assn, 1989-. *Creative works:* Over 100 short stories, poems, folk tales, collected works; Novel, The Merry Jinsha River, published in Chinese, English Russian and Japanese; Novels include: The Unfinished Dreams; The Legend of Zhang Chong, a Yi Hero. *Memberships:* Dir, All China Writer's Assn; Intl Pen; All China Minority Nat Weiters Assn; Yunnan Contemporary Lit Inst; Yunnan Yi Studies. *Honours:* Deputy to 4 sessions of the Yunnan Peoples Congress; Deputy, Nat People's Congress; Yunnan People's Political Consultative Conf. *Hobbies:* Reading; Writing; Gardening; Rearing Birds; Walking. *Address:* Yunnan Writers Association, 3 East Cuihu Lake Road, Kunming 650031, China.

LI Quingzhen, b. 13 June 1936, Ping Yi, China. President and Professor. m. 18 Jan 1961, 1 s, 2 d. *Education:* Grad, Peking Univ, 1960. *Appointments:* Dir of Pres's Ofc, 1978; V-Dir of Res Inst of Culture and Hist, 1982; Chief Ed, Publishing Assn, 1984, Shandong Univ. *Creative works:* Science Theory of Knowledge: Leading Remarks; Great Balance Beam-New Earth-Shaking technical Revolution; Large motive four-on Science of Technical Motion. *Memberships:* Chinese Res Assn of the Dialectics of Nature; Res Inst of Mgmt Sci of China; V-P, Publishing Assn in Shandong Province. *Honours:* The Pick of the Talents of Shandong Province, 1987; Chinese Young and Middle-aged Experts of Outstanding Achievement, 1988. *Hobbies:* Photography; Listening to drama on the radio; Writing prose; Reading. *Address:* Yantai University, Yantai City, Shangdong 264005, China.

LI Renke, b. 19 June 1934, Shangdong, China. Senior Engineer and Vice President. m. Zhang Jun, 1 Jan 1957, 2 s, 1 d. *Education:* Grad, Changcun Geol Sch, 1954. *Appointments:* Chief, Petrologic and Mineralogic Section, Changsa Geol and Exploring Co, 1956-57; Capt, Guangxi 215 Geol Prospecting party, 1960-65; Chief Engr, Guangxi 271 Geol Prospecting party, 1966-85;

Chief of Section, VP, Guangxi Geol Inst for Nonferrous metals, CNNC, 1986-. *Creative works:* A Study on the constituent of Denfuxian Tungsten Deposits, Hunan Province; A Study on the constituent and genesis of X mechanical accumulation maganese deposit, 1968; A study on the geological characteristics and mineralization regularity of X granite-type tantalum and niobium deposits, 1972; Tin bearing granite and vertical zonation of Limu tin deposits. *Memberships:* Geol Soc of China; Nonferrous metal Soc of China; Mineralol, Petrological and Geochem Soc of China. *Honours:* Two Ministry of Metallurgical Indust awds, and one CNNC awd for research studies. *Hobbies:* Sport; Reading. *Address:* Guangxi Geological Institute for Nonferrous Metal, 9 Dancun Road, Nanning 530031, P.R. China.

LI Renzhi, b. 5 June 1956, Baishui, Shaanxi, China. Professor of Linguistics and Computer Science. m. Li Lian, 14 Jan 1984, 1 s. *Education:* BA Eng Lang, Xi'an Jiaotong Univ (XJTU), China, 1979-83; MA Ling and Applied Ling, Essex Univ, England, 1985-86. *Appointments:* Asst Lectr, 1983-87, Lectr, 1987-88, Assoc Prof, 1988-92, XJTU; Vis Prof, Shantou Univ, 1990. *Creative works:* Microcomputer translation of library catalogues; Development and Problems of machine Translation; A Computer-based approach to the translation of foreign Biographical names; The wonderful world of Maths, translation; A selected vocabulary of the latest TOEFL. *Memberships:* Sec Gen: Acad Com of Xian Translators Assn; Xian Intl Conf on Texts and Lang Res, 1989. *Honours:* Dist Young Tchr, Fok Ying Tung Ed Foun, 1990; First Prize for Progress in Sci and Tech, XJTU; Univ Tchr of Excellence. *Hobbies:* Table Tennis. *Address:* Dept of Foreign Languages, Xian Jiatong University, Xian 710049, China.

LI Rong, b. 25 Aug 1941. Professor. m. Sa Ren Qi Qi Ge, 3 Sept 1968, 2 d. *Education:* Inner Mongolia Univ, 1960-65. *Appointments:* Assoc prof, Dir of Natural Sci, 1983-; Prof, 1991, Inner Mongolia Mus, 1965-. *Creative works include:* Author: Ancient History of Erdos, 1981; Study of Paleogeography of Erdos Plateau, 1982; The Biggest Mammoth in China discovered at Zalanor, Inner Mongolia, 1988; Fossils of Equidae in the Gobi Desert in Inner Mongolia, 1990; Mammoth's Ecological Environment of Zhalanor, 1990; Book, The Dinosaur Fossils of Inner Mongolia, 1991. *Memberships:* Soc of Vertebrate Paleontol, N.Am, 1980; Chinese Paleontol Soc; Coun Mem of Chinese Assn of Natural Sci Mus; Chinese Mus Soc; Coun, Chinese Vertebrate Paleontol Soc; Dir of Inner Mongolia Stratigraphic Paleontol Soc; The China Canada Dinosaur Proj, 1986-90. *Honours:* Six Model Worker Awds, 1979-89; Middle Aged Expert Awd for Outstanding Contributions, 1991. *Hobbies:* Literature; History; Fine Arts. *Address:* Inner Mongolia Museum, Huhhot, Inner Mongolia, China. 152.

LI Shi-Lian, b. 5 Jan 1934, China. Professor; Technical Director. m. Zhang Shu-Ying, 30 Nov 1961, 1 s. *Education:* MS Mech Engrg, Dresden Tech Univ, Germany, 1953-60; DEng, Prod Info Sys, Aachen Tech Univ, Germany, 1979-82. *Appointments:* Res Engr, Hd of Dept of Inst of Machine Tools, 1979-82; Vis Scholar in FRG, 1982-; Prof, Tech Dir of Res Inst of Automation; Proj Dir, State High Tech, CIM. *Creative works:* Books: CIM technology for Chinese Enterprises, 1991; CAD/CAM Technology and its application in the machinery industry, 1989; Enterprise management Information System, 1988; Planning of Production Information System, 1982; German Chinese Dictionary, 1978. *Memberships:* German Assn of Engrs, VDI; Bd of Dirs, Assn of Mgmt of Chinese Mech Engrg Soc; Standing Com, Assn of Machine Design and CAD. *Honours:* Prize, Nat Congress of Sci, 1978; Sci Key Achievements Prize, 1986; Outstanding Software, Beijing Region, 1986; Nat Sci & Tech Progress Awd, 1989. *Hobbies:* Reading; Jogging; Volleyball; Bicycling. *Address:* Beijing Research Institute for Automation for Machine Building Industry, Ministry of Machinery and Electronics, 1 Jiao Chang Kou, De Sheng Men Wai, Beijing, 100011, China.

LI Sifa, b. 4 Apr 1938, China. Professor in aquaculture and fish ecology. m. Cai Wanqi, 4 Feb 1967, 1 s. *Education:* BS, Dept of Aquaculture, Shanghai Fisheries Col, 1960; Vis Scist, Freshwater Inst, Dept of Fisheries and Oceans, Canada, 1979-81. *Appointments:* Asst Tchr, 1960- 67, lectr, 1976-86, Prof, 1986-. *Creative works:* Books: Fish Culture and Capture in Reservoirs, 1988; Population Ecology of Freshwater Fishes, 1990; Comprehensive Genetic Study on Chinese Carps, 1990. *Memberships:* Am Fisheries Soc; China and Asian Fisheries Socs; China Soc of Ecol; Ed Mem, Aquaculture, Asian Fisheries Sci, Jour of Fisheries of China; Jour of Aguaculture in the Tropics. *Honours:* Naga Awd, Intl Ctr for Living Aquatic Resources Mgmt, 1988; Sci and Tech Awd, City of Shanghai, 1987; Sci and Tech Progress Awd, Ministry of Agric of China, 1989. *Hobby:* Reading. *Address:* Dept of Aguaculture, Shanghai Fisheries University, 334 Jun Gong Road, Shanghai 200090, China. 152.

LI Sijing, b. 8 Feb 1933, Ninghe County, Tiangin, China. Deputy Editor in Chief, Commercial Press. m. 6 Feb 1971, 1 s. *Education:* Grad, Chinese Lang and Lit, Peking Univ, 1955; Hist of Chinese Lang, Grad Sch of Peking Univ, 1955-59. *Appointments:* Ed Staff: Zhong Hua Book Store, Beijing, 1963, Commercial Press, Beijing, 1974; Dpty Ed in Chief, Commercial Press, 1989-; Prof of Nankai Univ, Tianjin, 1991-. *Publications include:* Phonology of the Chinese Language; Co-ed, A New Chinese-Japanese Dictionary, A Pocket Japanese-Chinese Dictionary; Dpty Ed in Chief of A Chinese Encyclopaedic Dictionary, A Study of Traditional Chinese Speech Sounds, A Scheme of Phonetic Combinations; Translations: Crab Catcher's Boad, Walnut Wood, The Other Shore, The Clan. *Memberships:* Chinese Lang Inst, Coun Mem, Chinese Phonol Inst. *Honours:* Wang Li Philology Awd, 1989. *Hobbies:* Peking opera; Writing poems; Calligraphy. *Address:* The Commercial Press, 36 Wangfujing Street, Beijing, China 100710, China.

LI Suping, b. 2 Mar 1937, Shanxi, China. Senior Engineer. m. He Ruzhen, 1 Feb 1962, 4 s, 1 d. *Education:* Majored in Mineral Geol, Taiyuan Minig Sch, 1955-58. *Appointments:* Geol Engr, Shanzi Bureau of Geol and Min Resource, 1958-76; Geol Sr Engr in Shanxi Inst of Geosci, 1977-. *Publications:* 10 papers including: Structural interpretation on Shanxi satellite photography, 1979; Analysis of nappe and overthrust, 1986; Application of remote sensing to evaluation of engineering geology, 1987; Perspectives of Zhongtiaoshan copper deposits, 1989. *Memberships:* Geol Assn of China; Seismic Assn of Shanxi Prov. *Honours:* 2nd Tech Prize, and 4th Class prizes for outstanding works, Min of Geol and Min Reosurces of China. *Hobby:* Touring. *Address:* Shanxi Institute of Geoscience, 4 Xuefu Street, Taiyuan, Shanxi 030006, China.

LI Ta-Tsien, b. 20 Nov 1937, Jiangsu, China. Professor. m. Xu Yu-ling, 1 Oct 1962, 1 s. *Education:* Student, Maths Dept, 1953, Grad Student, 1962-66, Fudan Univ; Vis Scholar, College of France, Paris, 1979-81. *Appointments:* Prof, Fudan Univ, 1980-; Dean, Grad Sch of Fudan Univ, 1991-. *Creative works:* Boundary value problems for quasilinear hyperbolic systems, 1985; Global Classical Solutions for nonlinear evolution equations, 1992. *Memberships:* VP, Chinese SIAM; Standing Com, Shanghai Assn for Sci and Tech; Pres, Shanghai SIAM; VP, Shanghai Math Soc. *Honours:* National Natural Sci Prize, 1982; Sci and Tech Progress Prizes: Beijing, 1985, 1986, 1992, Shanghai, 1987. *Hobby:* Reading. *Address:* Department of Maths, Fudan University, Shanghai 200433, China.

LI Tong, b. 3 Oct 1923, Guangdong Province, China. Professor of economic geology and geochemistry. m. Van Yixin 1 July 1952, 1 s, 2 d. *Education:* SB National Peking univ, 1949; DSc, Inst og Geol, Academic Sinica, 1960. *Appointments:* Geologist, Exploration Units, 1949-57; Prof, Univ of Sci and Tech, China, 1960-84;

Prof Iron and Steel Tech, Beijing Univ, 1984-87; Prof, Univ of Sci and Tech, Beijing, 1987-. *Memberships:* Com of Mineral Deposit, Geol Soc of China. *Honours:* First Prize Winner, Nat Com of Educ, 1989. *Hobbies:* Reading, Gardening. *Address:* Department of Geology, USTB, Beijing 100083, China.

LI Xincan b. 12 Jan 1934, Sichuan, China. Professor of Mathamatics. m. Zhengjin Zhou, 2 Nov 1963, 1 s, 1 d. *Education:* Grad Dipl, Sichuan Univ, 1956. *Appointments:* Asst, 1956-62, Lectr, 1962-80, Assoc Prof, 1980-86, Chm, Dept of Maths and Phys, 1983-89, Prof, 1986, Beijing Univ of Aero and Astronautics. *Creative works:* Books: Curves surfaces fairing; Encounter with Higher mathematics; Systems of Ordinary Differential Equations and Stability of Motion; Computer Aides Geometric Design; Translations: Mathematics and Plausible Reasoning; Mathematics for the Million; Computational Geometry for Design and Manfacture. *Memberships:* Chinese Socs of: Maths, Computational Maths, Aero and Astronautics; IBA; Hon Mem, IBC Adv Coun; Res Bd of Advrs, ABI. *Honours:* Nationwide Worker of Excellence, China; Special Grade Model Worker, Teacher of Excellence, Sci and Tech Specialist of Outstanding Contribution, Ministry of Aeronautics Indust of China. *Hobbies:* Music; Travelling. Swimming. *Address:* Maths and Physics Dept, Beijing University of Aeronautics and Astronautics, Beijing, China. 162, 156.

LI Ya, b. 7 Feb 1926, Yan Cheng, Jiangsu, China. Professional Painter. m. He Wei, 20 July 1950, 1 s, 1 d. *Education:* Painting Faculty, Jiang Ning Normal Sch, Nanjing, 1946-49. *Appointments:* The Painting Unit, Inst of Art & Lit, Nanjing, 1950; The Workers Palace, Fu Shun City, 1951; North Mus, Shenyang, 1952; Artists and Writers Assn, Wuxi, 1959; Jiangsu Acad of Chinese Trad Painting, Nanjing, 1960-. *Creative works:* Master pieces: Rape Flower, 1964; Spring 1985; Birds among the willows, 1985; A Group of Happy Golden Fish, 1986; Autumn Mood, 1986; Meditation, 1991; Kidnap, 1991; International exhibitions of paintings. *Memberships:* Assn of Cinese Artists; Painter of Jiangsu, Acad of Chinese Trad Painting; Dir of Assn of Jiangsu Artists; VP, Jiangsu Flowers and Birds Painting Soc; Hon Chm, Yan Zemqing Painting and Calligraphy Gallery. *Honours include:* Chinese Trad Painting Prize, The Culture Ministry, 1979; Hon Prize, Jiangsu Printing and Calligraphy Exhibition, 1986. *Hobbies:* Pot-flower Cultivation Art; Kun Opera. *Address:* 202 Apt 3E Mu Xu Yuan, Nanjing 210014, China.

LI Yan, b. Nov 1943, Beijing, China. Artist; Professor. m. Sun Yan hua, 1970, 1 d. *Education:* The Central Acad of Fine Arts, 1958-66. *Appointments:* Prof, Qi Bai Shi Corres Col of Arts; VP, Central Inst of Arts and Crafts; Appraizing Specialist, entitled by Bejing Auction, 1992, of the Appraizing Committee of the Chinese Arts of Calligraphy and Painting. *Creative works:* Selection of Li Yan's Sketches; Chinese Emperor; Zhou Wen Emperor; Lai Zi: Confucian Worry About Taois; Lao Zi and Einstein; Five-Colour Earth; Start Sailing; Tiger Cub. *Memberships:* VP, Flowers and Birds Painting Assn, Beijing; VP, Li Ku Chan Mus; Chinese Artists Assn; Yi Jing Assn. *Hobbies:* Writing poetry; Qigong; The Book of Changes (Iching the Oracle). *Address:* 2-1 Bldg 15, Nan Sha Go, San Li He, Xi Cheng District, Beijing, China.

LI Zehou, b. June 1930, Changsha, Hunan, China. m. 1963, 1 s. *Education:* Grad, Phil Dept, Peking Univ, 1954. *Appointments:* Res Fellow, Inst of Philos, Chinese Acad of Scis, 1955; Sr Res Fellow, Prof, Chinese Acad of Social Scis, 1978-. *Creative works:* Books include: A Path of BEauty; Chinese Aesthetics; Four Lectures on Aesthetics; Ancient Chinese Intellectual History; Modern Chinese Intellectual History; Contemporary Chinese Intellectury History; Critique of Critical Philosophy: A Study of Kant; Outline of my Philosophy. *Memberships:* VP, Chinese Assn of Aesthetics, 1980; Bd of Dirs, Writers Assn of China, 1984; Bd of Dirs, Confucius Foun of China, 1985; Inst Intl de Philosophie,

Paris, 1988. *Honours:* Vis Prof, Invited Lecturer at international conferences in Japan, Singapore, Europe and USA. *Address:* c/o AI Li Wb 1228, Worner Centre, 902 N Cascade, Colorado Springs, CO 80946, USA.

LI Zhi-yu, b. 4 Dec 1936. Acting Associate Professor. m. Ma Zho- zhi, 2 d. *Education:* BA 1958, MA 1962, Shanghai Theatre Acad. *Appointments:* Asst Prof, Lectr, Assoc Prof, Shanghai Theatre Acad, 1958-; Participated in many films and TV as an actor. *Creative works:* Book: On film acting, 1991; Films: Fu Bing in the Smile of a Vexed Man, 1979; Qi-shi in Night Rain in Ba Mountains, 1980; Zhou-Hong in Forget-me-not, 1982; Zhu Shi-Yi in Well, 1987. *Memberships:* Film Assn of China; Film Performing Art Assn of China; Theatre Assn of China. *Honours:* Best Actor nomination, Golden Cock Prize of China, 1981; Best Actor, Golden Eagle Prize, China, 1985. *Address:* 630 Huashan Road, Shanghai 200040, China.

LI Zuo Zhi, b. 31 Jan 1933, Nanjing, China. Professor of Archaeology. m. Zhuang Shun Fang, 22 Feb 1972, 1 s, 1 d. *Education:* Dipl, Dept of Hist and Archaeol, Peking Univ, 1959. *Appointments:* Lectr, Univ of Inner Mongolia, Dept of Hist, 1962-78; Archaeol team,inner Mongolia, 1978-; Res Fellow, Hist Mus of China, Peking. *Creative works:* Author: The Discovery of Yulin Town of Sui Tang Period, 1976; Construction of Shang-Jing City of Liao period, essay, 1985; The Problem of Liatiuhe River, 1985; Prehistoric Man and Culture in China. *Memberships:* Chinese Assn of Archaeol. *Hobbies:* Chinese Calligraphy; Painting and Carving. *Address:* Historical Museum of China, Peking, China.

LIANG Chia-pin, b. 29 May 1910, Peking, China. Retired Professor. *Education:* BA Nat Tsing-Hua Univ, 1932; Grad Sch, Oriental Hist, Tokyo Empire Univ, 1937; DLitt, Tokyo Univ, Japan, 1971. *Appointments:* Compiler, Lectr, Pt-time Prof, to 1955; Prof, Tung Hai Univ, 1955-62; Vis Prof, Sr Scholar, Univ Hawaii and East West Ctr, Honolulu, USA, 1962-63; Prof, Grad Sch of Diplomacy, Nat Chengchi Univ, Taipei, 1965-75; Res Prof, Chengchi Univ, 1970-71; Prof, Grad Sch of Chinese Culture Univ, Tapei, 1975-87, R'td. *Creative works include:* Intl Relations of the Ming Dynasty 1968; Hong Merchants of Canton Prior to the Opium War, 1937; An Investigation into the Origin of Modern Sin-Japanese Relations, 1968; Sino-Japanese Conflict and Negotiations during the Downfall of the Ryakyu Kingdom, 1974; Li Hang-chang and the Sino-Japanese War, 1894-95, 1975; The Chi-txu's Korea, 1980. *Honours:* Taiwan Provincial Govt, 1953; Ministry of Ed, 1975, 1976; Nat Sci Comm, China, 1970; Fellowships, Japanese Nat Comm for UNECO, 1969; Hon PhD, 1987, Hon DH, 1990. *Hobbies:* Reading; Research; Writing. *Address:* 4 Lane 82 Ching Jen Street, Ching-mei District, Taipei 11702, China.

LIANG Jigang, b. 24 July 1933, Sichuan, China. m. Zhang Peihua, 1 Oct 1961, 2 d. *Education:* Grad, Changchun Col of Geol, Mineral Geol Exploration Fac. *Appointments:* Dep Dir, Chief Engr, China Coal Geol Bureau. *Creative works:* Directions of Coalfield expectations of Shandong Province; Atlas of Shandong Coal Resources; Detailed exploration geological report of Jining Coal Filed, Shandong Province; The Reformation of Permo-Carboniferrous coal measures after deposition, and coal expectation. *Memberships:* Geol Soc of China, Dep Dir of Coun; China Coal Soc, Coun; Li Siguang Geoscis Awd Com. *Honours:* Sci Progress Awd, Shandond Province, 1978; Geol Report of Excellence Awd, All China Coal Geol Exploration, 1983; Paper of Excellence Cert, China Coal Soc, 1990. *Hobby:* Light Music. *Address:* 9 Bldg 11 S.Residential Area, China Coal Geol Bureau, Fanyan Rd, Zhuozhou, Hebei, China.

LIANG Jihua, b. 14 Oct 1953, Sichuan, China. University Professor. m. 20 Aug 1979, 1 d. *Education:* BA, Basic Math, 1977; MA, Topology, 1982. *Appointments:* Lectr, 1977-78; Prof, 1988-, Math Dept,

Sichuan Univ. *Creative works:* Works on metrization in Fuzzy topological spaces. *Memberships:* Math Assn of China; Sysmetical Engrg Assn of China. *Honours:* Prize of Excellence for Sci Res, Sci Assn of Sichuan, 1988; Devel of Sci and Tech Prize, Govt of Sichuan Province, 1989. *Hobby:* Music. *Address:* Math Dept, Sichuan University, Chengdu, Sichuan 610064, China.

LIANG Xiangji, b. 5 Dec 1937, Zhejiang, China. Research Professor. m. 1 May 1968, 1 s. *Education:* Dipl, Beijing Col of Geol, 1964. *Appointments:* Reschr, Rocks and Deposits, 1963-72; Ed, The Monograph oflron and Copper mineral deposits, 1972-76; Built a high temperature and high pressure Laboratory, 1976-91; Res, Experimental Petrol, Minerol and Geochem; Lecturer in FRG, 1988; Vstng Acad of Sci, USSR, Attending Int Symposium of Granites and Geodymanics in ISSR and Investigating the South Tienshan in USSR by Helipcopter, 1991; Attending Secnd Int Symposium of Thermodynamics of Natural Processes, Russia, 1992. *Creative works:* 25 papers about experimental petrology, minerology and geochemistry in professional magazines; A book on physico- chemical conditions for gold deposit of Honglazi type in China. *Memberships:* Intl Assn of Geochem and Cosmochem; Geological Soc of China; Chinese Soc of Experimental Petrol, Minerol and Geochem. *Honours:* Sci and Tech Awd, Sichuan Province, 1976; Awds for Achievements in Sci Res, Ministry of Geol and Mineral Reserves, 1982, 1986, 1988, 1991, 1992. *Hobbies:* Literature; Poems; Calligraphy. *Address:* Institute of Geology, Chinese Academy of Geological Sciences, Baiwanzhuang Rd 26, Beijing 100037, China. 152.

LIANG Yongming, b. 9 July 1942, Shanghai, China. Research Engineer. m. Qihui yang, 1989. *Education:* Shanghai Metallurgical Vocational Sch, 1958-62; Higher Acupuncture Training Course, Assn of Trad Chinese Med, 1985-86. *Appointments:* Steel Rolling Technician, Taiyuan Steel and Iron Co, 1962-79; Steel Rolling Engr, Shanghai Baosan Steel and Iron Factory, 1979-85; Rehab Expert Dr, Ghanghai Res Centre of Qigong, 1985-92. *Creative works:* Successes in curing infantile Cerebral Paralysis; Cerebella Ataxia; Parkinson's Disease; Sequelae of encephalitis and other various chronic diseases. *Memberships:* Local branch, World Acad Soc of Med; Dir, Gigong Doctors Assn in Shanghai; First Rank Gigong Doctor of Shanghai Res Centre; Qugong Phys Therapy Res Inst; Gigong Massage Doctor of Shanghai Yangzijiang. *Hobbies:* Breathing exercises; Reading; Taijiquan. *Address:* 24 Lane 322, Zizhong Road, Shanghai, China.

LIANG Yuerong, b. 5 Sept 1957, Guangxi, China. Food Scientist. m. Ma Weiyang, 1 May 1986, 1 d. *Education:* BSc 1981, MSc 1985, Zhejiang Agric Univ. *Appointments:* Tchg Asst, Zheijiang Agric Univ, 1985- 87; Lectr, 1987-90; Food Scist, Unilever Plc UK, 1990- 91. *Creative works:* Tea Genetics and Breeding, 1989; A Study on Chemical Composition of two special green teas, 1990. *Memberships:* Chinese Assn of Agronomists; Chinese Tea Assn. *Honours:* First Prize of Excellence, Zhejiang Tea Assn, 1987, 1989; Third Prize, Outstanding Scientific Thesis, Zhejiang Assn of Sci and Tech, 1987. *Hobbies:* Bridge; Photography. *Address:* Dept of Tea Scienc, Zhejiang Agricultural University, Hangzhou 310029, China

LIAO Ying-Ming, b. 22 Dec 1912, Kwangtung, China. Chairman of the Board of Trustees, Feng Chia University. m. Meng-Yen Chen, 3 Dec 1939. 6 s, 1 d. *Education:* BA Nat Sun Yat Sen Univ, 1937. *Appointments:* Prof, Central Military Acad, 1955-62; Dean of Studies, Feng Chia Col of Eng & Bus, 1962-73; Pres, Feng Chia Univ, 1973-88; Chm, Bd of Trustees, Feng Chia Univ, 1988- . *Creative works:* The Way to a Harmonious Family; My Trip Around the World; Words from Shanhsing Garden; A Detailed Report of Political Consultation; The Strategical Position of Taiwan. *Memberships:* Phi Tau Phi; Central Evaluation and Discipline Comms, Juomingtang; VP, Chinese Strategical Assn; Private

Colls and Univs Assn, Taiwan Branch. *Honours:* John Dewey Medal of Hon for Dist Sers in Intl Educ and Devel, USA, 1979; Hon PhD: Univ ov Mindanao, Philippines, 1979, Ming Ji Univ, Korea, 1981. *Hobbies:* Reading; Hiking; Taichui Chuan (Chinese shadow boxing). *Address:* 100 Wenhwa Road, Seatwen, Taichung, Taiwan 40724, China. 50, 162.

LIBIGER Jan, b. 16 June 1948, Usti n Labem, Czechoslovakia. Psychiatrist and Associate Professor of Psychiatry. m. Eva Zikmundova, 7 June 1975, 1 s, 1 d. *Education:* MD, 1972, Csc, 1985 Charles Univ, Prague; WHO Fellow in Psychi, Vanderbult Univ, Nashville, 1978-79. *Appointments:* Psychi Hosp Horni Berkovice, 1972-75; Dept of Psychi and Psych Clinic, Med Sch, Charles Univ, 1975-99; Nath Kline Inst ofr Psych Res Orangeburgh, NY, Vis Scholar, 1990-92. *Creative works:* Over 50 articles in professional journals and monography on Schizophrenia, 1991. *Memberships:* Czech Psychi Soc, Exec Bd; European Col of Neuropshcyopharmacol. *Honours:* Prize, Czech Psychi Soc for Publ on Schizophrenia, 1991. *Hobbies:* Hiking; Outdoor activities; Reading. *Address:* Dr E Benese 1525, Hradec, 500 12, Czechoslovakia.

LIBRACH Israel Mayer, b. 23 Nov 1914, Belfast, N.Ireland. Retired Hospital Physician. m. 11 Apr 1945. *Education:* Royal Belfast Acad Inst, 1926-32; MB, BCh, BAO, 1938; DPH, 1942; DCH 1947; MRCGP 1986; MFCH, 1988. *Appointments:* RMO, City Hosp Nottingham, 1942-45; Med Supt, City Isolation Hosp, Nottingham, 1945-47; Phys, Chadwell Heath Hosp, Essex, 1947-77. *Creative works:* Numerous papers in medical journals, Asst Ed, Brit Jour of Clin Practices. *Memberships include:* BMA; RSM. *Honours:* Freeman City of London, 1966; MRCGP, 1986. *Hobbies:* Antiques; Reading; Gardening; Motoring; Book collecting. *Address:* 2 Fauna Close, Chadwell Heath, Romford Essex RM6 6AS, England.

LIBROWSKI Stanislaw, b. 26 Apr 1914, Krzemieniewice, Poland. Professor; Editor. *Education:* MHist, Univ of Varsovian, 1948; Dr of Hist, 1951; Asst Prof, 1965. *Appointments:* Assoc Prof, Catholica Univ Lubliniensi, 1970; Prof, 1975-. *Creative works:* 12 works, 10 editions of sources historics, 200 dissertations and articles, 60 volumes magazines Archiva, Bibliothecae et Musea Ecclesiastica. *Memberships:* Societatis Sci Catholicae Univ Lubliniensis, 1969; Sci Soc of Lublinensis. *Honours:* Combatant, 1939-45; Consecration into Priesthood, Paris, 1945, Prelate papal, 1963, Order of the Cross Polonia Restituta, 1974; Sci Awd, Wlodzimierza Pietrzaka, 1976. *Hobbies:* Collecting; Keeping memoirs. *Address:* ul Faraona 6 m 15, 20-635 Lublin, Poland.

LICHKO Andrei E, b. 8 Nov 1926, Luga, Russia. Psychiatrist. *Education:* Physician, 1st Leningrad Med Inst, 1951; DMS, 1963; Prof of Psychi, 1969; RSFSR Hon Scist, 1977, Bekhterev Leningrad Psychoneurol Inst. *Appointments:* Pavlov Inst of Physiol, Leningrad, 1951-54; Inst Exper Med, 1954-56; Sechenov Inst Evolut Physiol and Biochem, 1956-66; Bekhterev Psychonevrol Inst, Dpty Dir, Chief Dpt Adolescent Psychia, 1967-. *Creative works:* Psychopathies and character accentuation in Adolescents, 1977, 1983; Adolescent Psychiatry, 1979, 1985; Schizophrenia in Adolescents, 1989; Adolescent Narcology, 1991. *Memberships:* Hon Mem, Leningrad Psychia Soc. *Honours:* Bekhterev Prize, USSR Acad of Med Scis, 1978. *Hobbies:* Pathobiographical studies of eminent personalities; History of St Peterbourg, Russia. *Address:* Bekhterev Institute, ul Bekhtereva 3, 193019 Leningrad, Russia.

LICHT Victor, b. 12 Aug 1944, Moscow. Musicologist; Critic; Violinist. m. Nina Blecher Licht, 30 Dec 1978, 2 d. *Education:* Grad Violinist, 1969, Musicologist, 1975, Sazatov Conservatory; Postgrad, Moscow Conservatory, 1976-79. *Appointments:* Saratov Symph Orch, 1962-71; Tchr, Musical Schools, Colleges, Conservatory,

1971-86; Ed, Chief of Dept, Sovetskaya Muzika magazine, 1986-91; Ed, Russia Music Newspaper, 1991-. *Creative works:* Many articles in professional journals and magazines including: The Confirmation of the Good, 1983; There are no Draws, 1983; The Successful Beginning, 1989; Mozart for the Poor People, 1991; The December Nights on Volkhonka Street, 1992; Revaz Gabitchvadze, 1988, book. *Memberships:* Union of Composers of Russia. *Hobbies:* Conductor of children's String Orchestra; Poetry. *Address:* Licht Victor, Pobeda Str 6 flat 9, 143900 Balashicha, Moscow, Russia.

LICHTENHELD Frank Robert Heinz, b. 11 Apr 1923, Weimar, Germany. Retired Chief, Clinic for Plastic Surgery. div. 1 s, 1 d, 4 adopted. *Education:* DM, 1951 Johann Wolfgang Goethe Univ, Frankfurt. *Appointments:* German Navy, 1941-45; Internship and Surg Residency, 1951-52, Presbyterian Hosp, Newark, NJ, USA; Fellow, Surg Mayo Clinic, Rochester, Minn, USa, 1953-56; Asst Chief of Urol, USAF Hosp, Wiesbaden, 1956- 64; Med Dir, Winthrop Pharm GmbH, Frandfurt, 1964-65; Ausland 1965-66, Chief of Clinic for Plastic and REconstructive Surg, 1966-88. *Creative works:* Author of over 45 publications in the field of plastic and reconstructive surgery including new methods in face lifting and surgery by transsexual patients. *Memberships:* ssa OOCertified Surg, Plastic Surg and Urologist; Ventnor Alumni Foun, USA: Alumni Assn of Mayo Foun, Military Surg, USA: Deutsche Gesellschaft fur Asthetisch-Plastische Chirurgie, Germany, Pres, 1976, 1980; Deutsche Gesellschaft fur Plastische-und Wiederherstellungschirurgie. *Hobbies:* World politics and economics. *Address:* Panoramaweg 11, 6200 Wiesbaden, Germany. 143, 52.

LICHTENTHALER Frieder W, b. 19 Jan 1932, Heidelberg, Germany. Professor of Organic Chemistry. m. Evemaria von Ihfeld, 15 Apr 1966, 2 s, 1 d. *Education:* Diplomchemiker-Hauptexamen, 1956; Dr rer Nat Chem, 1959, Univ of Heidelberg; habilitation in Org Chem, 1963. *Appointments:* Docent, Org Chem, Tech Univ of Darmstadt, 1963, Prof, Org Chem, 1972-. *Memberships:* Royal Chem Soc; Chem Socs of Japan, Germany and Am. *Hobby:* Classical music. *Address:* Inst fur Organische Chemie, Technische Hochschule Darmstadt, Petersenstr 22, D-6100 Darmstadt, Germany.

LICHTENTHALER Hartmut Karl, b. 20 June 1934, Weinheim, Germany. Professor of Biology. m. Regine Schneider, 1966, 3 s. *Education:* MPharm, Univ of Karlsruhe, 1958, PhD Botany, Univ of Heidelberg, 1961; Res Fellow: Grenoble, France, 1961, Univ CAlifornia, Berkeley, 1962-64. *Appointments:* Sci Asst, Docent, Assoc Prof, Univ Munster, Germany, 1964-70; Prof, Dir, Botany Dept, Univ of Kharlsruhe, Germany, 1970-. *Creative works:* Ed, Co-Ed: Lipids and Lipid Polymers in Higher Plants, 1977; Praktikum der Photosynthese, 1978; Das Waldsterben aus botanischer Sicht, 1984; Applications of Chlorophyll Flourescence, 1988. *Memberships:* European Soc of Plant Physiols, FESPP Pres, 1984-86; Chm, Sektion Pflanzenphysiologie, 1978-86. *Hobbies:* European history and art; Classical Music; Tennis. *Address:* Botanisches Institut, University of Kharlsruhe, Kaiserstr 12, D-7500 Karlsruhe, Germany. 52.

LICHTIGER Monte, b. 12 July 1939, New York, USA. Anesthesiologist. m. Barbara Zuker, 25 Aug 1962, 1 s, 2 d. *Education:* AB, Columbia Col, 1961; MD Albert Einstein Col of Med, 1965; NIH Fellow, Anaesth, Univ of Miami Sch of Med, 1966-69; Intern, Mt Sinai of Miami, 1965- 66. *Appointments:* Asst Prof, 1971-76, Assoc Prof, 1976-82, Clin Prof, 1982-, Univ of Miami; USAF, Wilford Hall USAF Hosp, 1969-71. *Creative works:* Intro to practice of Anaesth, 1975; 1978; Multiple contributions to journals and textbooks in anaesthesiology. *Memberships:* Am and Florida Socs of Anaesth. *Honours:* Phi Beta Kappa; Academic Scholarships to Columbia and to Med Sch; Ed, Current

Reviews in Clin Anesth and Curren Reviews for Nurse Anesthetists. *Hobbies:* Boating; Scuba Diving; Fishing; Flying; Marine Biology; Giariatric and Ambulatory Anaesthesia. *Address:* Dept of Anaesthesiology, Mt Sinai Medical Centre, Miami Beach, FL 33140, USA. 17.

LICHTIGFELD Don David, b. 25 May 1941, Johannesburg, S.Africa. General Manager. m. Corinae Gilda Averbuch, 2 July 1967, 1 s, 3 d. *Education:* BSc 1964, BSc HOns, 1965, Univ of Pretoria; HED, JHB Col of Educ, 1967. *Appointments:* Tchr, Lectr, 1979-81; Mgr, Ge Kendall Pty Ltd, 1981-84; Mgr, AGS/MS, 1984-90; Self employed Conslt, 1990-. *Creative works:* Articles on biology in the Star and Sowetan, S.Africa. *Memberships:* Hon Mem, NJ PMI. *Honours:* First student to receive BSc Hons in Genetics at Univ of Pretoria, 1965. *Hobbies:* Numismatics; Chess; Sports. *Address:* 5 Tiburon Lane, Malvern, PA 19355, USA. 55

LICKORISH Adrian Derick, b. 29 Oct 1948, London, England. Solicitor. m. Vivien Mary Gould, 16 May 1987. *Education:* Highgate Sch; London Univ, LLB, 1970, LLM, 1971. *Appointments:* Freshfields, 1972-80; Durrant Pierse, 1980-88; Lovell White Durrant, 1988-91. *Hobbies:* Fishing; Shooting; Farming; Military history. *Address:* Woodhouse Farm, Avening, Tetbury, Glos, England.

LIEB Hans-Heinrich, b. 13 Nov 1936, Hannover, Germany. Linguist. *Education:* PhD, Univ of Cologne, 1963; Habilitation, 1969. *Appointments:* Lectr, Prof of Gen Lings, Univ of Cologne, 1969-71; Vis Assoc Prov, UBC Vancouver, 1970-71; Prof of Lings, Fachbereich Germanistik, Freie Univ Berlin, since 1971. *Creative works:* Books: Communication complexes and their stages, 1968; Sprachstadium und Sprachsystem, 1970; Integrational Linguistics; 1983, ed Oberflachensyntax und Semantik, 1980; Bevaton, Berliner Verfahren zur aauditiven Tonhöhenanalyse, 1988; Prospects for a New Structuralism, 1992. *Memberships:* Fdg Mem, Intl Assn of Semostics; German Soc of Lings. *Honours:* Prize, Univ of Cologne; Res Grant, Deutsche Forch, 1967-69, 1970, 1980-81, 1984. *Address:* Free University of Berlin, Fachbereich Germanistik, Habelschwerdter Alle 45, D-1000 Berlin 33, Germany. 52.

LIEBER Ian Steven, b. 14 July 1941, Hertfordshire, England. Interior Designer. *Education:* Waverly Prep, Nottingham, 1947-52; Cottesmore Gram, 1952-56. *Appointments:* Time and Motion and Mgmt Prods, Jersy Fabrics, Nottingham, 1957-59; Display and Sales, Jessops Nottingham, 1959-62; Own Antique shop, 1962-63; Antique Training Trevor Antiques, Brighton, 1963-69; Rings of Hove Fabrics and Interior Design, 1964-66; Ken Moore Designs, 1966-69; Own practice, 1969; Lectr for ICI, The Inchbald Sch of Design, The Design Acad. *Memberships:* Chm of Interior Designers an dFurnishing Suppliers Assn, Prince of Wales Jubilee Appeal, 1977. *Hobbies:* Travel; Chinese Porcelain. *Address:* The Shop, 29 Craven Terrace, Lancaster Gate, London W2 3EL, England.

LIEBERMAN Stuart, b. 4 Oct 1942, USA. Consultant Psychotherapist and Honorary Senior Lecturer. m. Sybil Margarte Battersby, 30 Oct 1986, 3 s, 3 d. *Education:* MD Univ of Miami, 1966; MRCPsych, 1974, FRCPsych, 1983, London. *Appointments:* Internship, David Grant USAF Hosp, CA, 1966-67; Gen Med Ofr, Capt USAF, RAF Bentwater nr Woodbridge, Suffolk, England, 19767- 70; Resident in Psychi: Boston City Hosp, 1970-72, Medfield State Hosp, 1972- 73; Postgrad Student, Inst of Psychia, 1973; Sr Registrar, Westminster Tchg Hosp and Netherne Hosp, 1973-75. *Creative works:* Book, Transgenerational Family Therapy, 1979; Articles include: A Family with four bulimic Children, 1989; A Survey of Psychosocial problems of parents of children with cancer, 1990; The Birth Pains of Establishing a family therapy clinic in the NHS, 1989; Family Features associated with normal weight Bulimia, 1990. *Memberships include:* Hd of Psychotherapy, Acad Dept

of Mental Health Scis, St George's Hosp Med Sch; VP, Ctr for Analytical Psychotherapy; BMA; Fdg Mem: Assn of Family Therapy and Inst of Family Therapy. *Hobbies:* Golf; Swimming. *Address:* St Georges Hospital Medical School, Dept of Mental Health Sciences, Cranmer Terrace, Tooting, London SW17 0RE, England.

LIEBOWITZ Shelly, b. 2 Feb 1946, Brooklyn, New York, USA. Advertising and Entertainment Executive. *Education:* Francis Lewis Hg Sch, NYC. *Appointments:* Mgr, Robert Hall, 1965-67; Promotion of Capitol Prod, Roulette Records, 1967-70; Pres, Belvedere Records, 1975-80; Pres, AAT, 1982-87; Pres, Creative Media, 1988-; VP, Fresh Squeezed Records, 1990; Pres, Saturn Records, 1991. *Creative works:* Author: Anything goes; Just for Laughs; Commercial Madness. *Memberships:* Hollywood and North Dade Chambers of Commerce; Downtown Redevelopment Coun; Armada, Assoc Dir; BeachSprots Com; Artists Against Drugs, Chm. *Honours:* Best Promotion of New Group, Reording Coun, 1979; Man of the Year, Entertainment Assocs, 1981. *Hobbies:* Music; Writing; Old Movies; Baseball. *Address:* 120 Golden Siles Drive, Hallandale, FL 33009, USA. 7, 132.

LIENARDY Pierre Marie Constant Delphin, b. 6 Nov 1952. Inspector General of Finances. m. Anne Chantal Ghils, 11 Apr 1987, 3 s. *Education:* CEP, St Joseph Sch, 1964; MAT, St Julien Sch, 1970; CAnd, St Louis Univ, 1972; Lic Droit, 1975, Postgrad, 1876, Univ of Louvain. *Appointments:* Auditor: VAT Admin, 1976; VAT Direction-Mons, 1977; Revisor, Credit Public Diror, Brussels, 1978; InspectionDes Finances, 1979-; Lecturer at the FUCAM (Mons), 1992-. *Creative works:* Various articles in Public Law and Budgeting. *Memberships:* Belgian Inst of Public Fin; CIFE, Brussels, Bd of Dirs; CIFE, Nice, France, Bd. *Honours:* Medaille de la Ville d'Ath (Musique), 19677; Medaille du Gouvernement (Declamation), 1972. *Hobbies:* Gardening; Reading. *Address:* Avenue Astronomie 14 BTE 23, B1030 Brussels, Belgium. 1.

LIESENFELD Vincent Joseph, b. 16 Feb 1947, St Paul, Minnesota, USA. Cultural Studies Educator. 1 s, 1 d. *Education:* BA summa cum laude, Univ Minnesota, 1970; PhD Univ Wisconsin, Madison, 1978. *Appointments:* Writer: Minnesota State Employment Ser, 1970, Univ Wisconsin News and Pubs, 1972; Asst Prof, 1977-83, Assoc Prof, 1983-, English Univ Oklahoma; Res Conslt, Civil Rights Law, 1982-. *Creative works:* Author: The Licensing Act of 1737, 1984; Ed, The Stage and the Licensing Act, 1981; Author of articles and reviews in professional journals. *Memberships:* S.Central Soc for 18th Century Studies, Exec Bd, 1979-80; Greenpeace; Phi Kappa Phi; Amnesty Intl; Am Radio Relay League; Inst of Hist Res, Univ of London. *Honours:* Fulbright Scholar, UK, 1973-74; Woodrow WilsonFellow,1969; W A Clark Library Fellow, 1980; Nat Endowment for the Humanities Res Fellow, 1980-81; Phi Beta Kappa, 1968. *Hobbies:* Running; Amateur radio; Computer programming. *Address:* Dept of English, University of Oklahoma, 760 Van Vleet Oval Room 113, Norman OK 73019, USA. 7, 13.

LIEVENS Stefan Rene Jozef, b. 15 Feb 1940, Nazareth. Professor of Psychology. m. Rita Niemegeers, 9 Sept 1968, 1 s, 1 d. *Education:* Dr in Applied Psychol, Univ of Ghent, 1969. *Appointments:* Asst, 1963, Chief Asst, 1969, Assoc Prof, 1980, ; Dept of Med Psychol, State Univ of Ghent. *Creative works:* Is testen pesten, 1980; Psychology and Dentistry, 1986; Graffiti, 1987; Graphology, 1990; Psychology and Sport, 1987. *Memberships:* Belgische Vereniging Psychologen, Intl Union of Psychol Sci. *Honours:* Selected by Minister of Employment to prepare legislation on selection, head hunting and outplacement services. *Hobbies:* Lecturing; Travelling. *Address:* Service of Medical Psychology and Neuropsychology, University of Ghent, De Pintelaan 185, 9000 Gent, Belgium.

LILLIE Thomas H, b. 2 Apr 1954, Lafayette, LA, USA. Lieutenant Colonel, USAF. m. Michelle J Hamblet, 29 May 1976, 2 d. *Education:* Bs Wildlife Mgmt, 1976; MS, 1978, PhD, 1985, Med Entomol. *Appointments:* Entomol Conslt, USAF, Occup and Environm Health Lab, 1978-82; Grad Student, Univ of Florida, 1982-85; Med Entomol, USAF, Sch of Aerospace Med, 1985-87; Chief Ecol Function, USAF, 1987-88; Dpty CHief Environ Planning, Space Sys Div, 1988-91; Prog Mngr Natural and Cultural Resources, Headquarters USAF, 1991-. *Creative works:* Over 30 scientific and technical reports. *Memberships:* Entomol Socs of Am, Florida and CAnada; Air Force Assn; Am and Louisiana Mosquito Control Assns; Sigma Xi; Phi Kappa Phi; Alpha Zeta; Phi Eta Sigma. *Honours:* Meritorious Serivce Medal, 3 Commendation Medals, Air Force; Company Grade Ofr of the Quarter, 1986, and of the Year, 1979; First, Florida Entomol Soc Student Paper Contest, 1984; Leadership Awd, Col of AGric, 1985. *Hobbies:* Jogging; Cabinet-making; Photography; Bowling; Reading Biographies; Computers. *Address:* Headquarters United States Air Force, Environmental Planning Division, Pentagon 5D-381, Washington, DC 20330-5140, USA. 176.

LILLYWHITE Harvey B, b. 1 Dec 1943, Arizona, USA. Professor of Zoology. m. Jamie L Johnson, 31 Aug 1967, 1 s, 1 d. *Education:* BA, 1966; MA 1967, PhD, 1970, Univ of California. *Appointments include:* Asst Prof, 1971-76; Assoc Prof, 1976-82, Prof, 1982-84, Physiol and Cell Biol, Univ of Kansas,; Prof, Dept of Zool, Univ of Florida, Gainesville, 1985-. *Creative works:* Articles to professional journals, books and magazines including: Arboreal specializations of snakes, 1993; Cadiovascular Adaptations of Pitvipers, 1992; Reptilian models for the study of cardiovascular homeostasis, 1987; Physiological constraints of vertical posture in viperid snakes, 1990; Pulmonary blood flow regulation in snakes, 1989. *Memberships include:* Am Soc of Zoologists; Am Physiol Soc; Am Soc of Ichthyologists and Herpetologists; Soc for the Study of Amphibians and Reptiles; AAAS; Ecol Soc of Am. *Honours:* Recipient of 5 undergraduate scholarships; Phi Alpha Mu; Phi Beta Kappa; NIH Predoctoral Fellow, UCLA: NSF Postdoctoral Fellow, UC Berkeley; Vis Lectr, Monash Univ, Australia, 1975-76. *Hobbies:* Photography; Scuba Diving; Camping; Exploring. *Address:* Department of Zoology, University of Florida, Gainesville, FL 32611, USA.

LIM David Chee Seng, b. 1 Jan 1963, Hong Kong. *Education:* Bsc Arch Studies, Univ of Wales Inst of Sci and Tech, England, 1985; Dipl of Arch, City or Birmingham Poly. *Appointments:* Computer Drafting, Hodson Assocs in Cardiff Wales, 1984-1990; Designing and Erecting Architectural Monumental work, Architects Firm in London, 1985-86; Apostle of Christ, 1983; Commg Photographer; Currently Self-Styled Preacher, author of Biblical Message Tracts; Canadian Artist with 8 exhibitions in 1992, exhibited, London, 1990-1991. *Memberships:* RIBA; Token Society of Gt Britain, FCCP Canada, Visual Arts Ontario; ARCUK. *Honours:* Paintings exhibited in Hong Kong and Somerset, England. *Hobbies:* Research Theology; Martial Art Systems; Survivalism; System Planning; Chinese Medicine; Graphology; Travelling. *Address:* 57 Northolt Crescent, Markham, Ontario, Canada L3R 6P2.

LIM Hong Sup, b. 15 Jan 1941, Korea. Scientist. m. Kwang Ja Kim, 5 Oct 1969, 1 s, 1 d. *Education:* BS Chem, 1965, MS Chem, 1967, Seoul Nat Univ, Korea; PhD Chem, California Inst of Tech, 1971. *Appointments:* Hughes REs Lab, Malibu, CA, 1972-87; Sr Scist, Energy Storage Product Line, Electron Dynamics, Div Hughes Aircraft Co, Torrance, CA, 1988-. *Creative works:* Developed superior nickel-cadmium battery cell for satellite application; Developed a superiof nikel-hydrogen batter cell for staellite application. *Memberships:* Electrochem Soc; Korean Scist and Engrs Assn. *Honours:* Lawrence A Hyland Patent Awd, 1986; Principal Investigator for Project Awded to Hughes Aircraft Co by R & D Magazine, 1988, 1990. *Hobbies:* Mountain hiking; Fishing; Golf; Woodwork; Gardening.

Address: 30446 West Rainbow Cres Dr, Agoura Hills, CA 91301, USA.

LIN Baorong, b. 20 July 1952, Fujian, China. manager and Senior Engineer. m. 1 Oct 1980, 1 d. *Education:* Grad, Indust Elec Automation, Fujian Mech & Elec Sch, 1979. *Appointments:* Seed Multiplication Farm, 1969-75; Tchr, Middle Sch, 1975-76; Mgr and Sr Engr, Power Co of Zhenghe Co, Fujian, 1980-82. *Creative works:* 37 compositions including: Incresing economic benefit of the county's electric network, 1987; The operation and adjustments of hydropower station during the dry season, 1986; Troubleshooting water turbogenerator's circular scarping, 1988; Low voltage wattless power compensation for China's countryside electric network, 1991; Registered patents. *Memberships:* Chinese Peoples Polit Consultative Conf, Com of All China Staff and Workers Tech Assn, V-Chm, Polit Consultative Conf Mgr, Power Co of Zhenghe, all of Fujian Province. *Honours:* Model Worker of Fujian Province, 1988; Advanced Acad Activities prize, National Countryside Electrification, 1989; Bronze Medal for invention of electric meters non- loading dissipation Eliminator, 1992. *Hobbies:* Painting; Calligraphy; Mechanisms. *Address:* Power Company of Zhenghe County, Fujian, China.

LIN Feng Qing, b. Oct 1939. Painter; Teacher. m. 18 Feb 1969, 2 s. *Education:* Dept of Trad Chinese Painting, Guangzhou Acad of Fine Arts, 1956-60. *Appointments:* Dept of Indust Art, 1960-86, Dept of Fine Arts, 1986-, Guangzhou Acad of Fine Arts. *Creative works:* Chief ed of the book, Tree Peony; Paintings include: Quiet night in star crags; A banyan at dawn; A Long roll of Poeny; Beautiful Five Mountains. *Honours:* Works or art in collections helf by Guangdong Peoples Political Consult Conf, Beijing Peoples Great Hall, State Sec of California. *Hobbies:* Qi-Gong; Football; Music; Travelling. *Address:* Department of Fine Arts, Guangzhou Academy of Fine Arts, Guazghou 510261, China.

LIN Guangheng, b. 6 Sept 1938, Fuzhou, China. Professor of Genotoxicology. m. Yuwen Li, 15 Jan 1969, 1 s, 1 d. *Education:* Fudan Univ China, 1957-62; Vis Scholar, W.Illinois Univ, USA, 1981-83. *Appointments:* Inst of Oceanol, Academic Sinica, 1962-; Etats Lies Moleculaires n CNRS, France, 1987; DTI Cantanduanes, Philippines, 1990; Inst of Oceanol, AS, 1991-. *Creative works:* A Trad MCN Image Computer Analysis System, 1990; The Mutagenesis of Benzocaspyrene in 1990; Cadmium FLux and its Genotoxicity, 1991. *Memberships:* Standing Mem: CEMS, Shanghai, CMBS, Qingdao; Dir, Biotech Div of QHNTCC, Qingdao; AM Genetics Soc; AEMS, USA. *Honours:* Sci and TEch Achievement Awd, 1987; Res Paper of Excellence Awd, 1983. *Hobbies:* Reading; Travelling; Photography. *Address:* Institite of Oceanology, Academic Sinica, Qingdao, Shangong, China.

LIN Jun, b. 3 Aug 1954, China. Associate Professor and Deputy Head of Department. m. Jiang Min 30 Sept 1982, 1 d. *Education:* BSc, 1982, MSc, 1985, Changchun Univ of Earth Sci. *Appointments:* School Tchr, Jilin and Liaoning, China, 1970-78; Lectr, Changchun Univ of Earch Sci, 1982-89; Vis Scholar, Univ of Leiscester, England, 1989-90; Guest Res Prof, Groby Rd Hosp of Leicester, 1991; Assoc Prof, Dpty Hd of Dept, Changchun univ of Earth Sci, 1991-. *Creative works:* More than 60 papers, two books and 15 novel microcomputer based measurement and control systems, 1986-. *Memberships:* China Portable Computer Soc; China Geol Instrument Soc; China Inst of Electronics; China Signal Processing Soc; China Geophys Soc. *Honours:* China Excellent Teacher, China Education Committee, 1989, Young Geologist, Univ of Earth Sci, 1988; Sci and Tech Awds, Jilin Province, 1985, Shanghai, 1987, 1988, Ministry of Geol and Minerals of China, 1988, 1989; Best Design Ideas, Electronic Design, USA, 1990, EDN, USA, 1991. *Hobbies include:* Reading; Writing; Travelling; Chess;

Bridge; Computer based instrumentation, digital signal processing, graphic image processing; Geophysics. *Address:* Dept of Instrumentation, Changchun University of Earth Science, Jilin 130026, China. 1.

LIN Kung-hsun, b. 21 Apr 1922, Fuzhou, China. Professor of plant pathology. m. Shun-yeh Liu, 15 Oct 1951, 1 d. *Education:* BS Agric, 1947; Dipl in Agronomy, Lingnan Univ, 1947; Grad Student, Agric Col, Zhong Shan Univ, 1950-51. *Appointments:* Asst of Plant Path, 1947-51, Lignan Univ; Lectr, Prof of Plant Path, Dept of Plant Protection, S.China Agric Col (now Agric Univ). *Creative works:* Co-author of Chemical Control of Plant Pests; Chinese Tranlations of Principles of Fungicidal Action of G J Horsfall and Systemic Fungicides; 50 papers on agricultura fungicides, plant disease, epidemiology and physiological plant pathology, on peanut diseases. *Memberships:* Bd of Dirs, Plant Path Soc of China, Guangdong Branch; Epidemiol Com, Plant Path Soc of China. *Honours:* Elected, Dist Prof, 1985. *Hobbies:* Music; Tennis; Badminton; Playing Bridge; Social Dance. *Address:* Dept of Plant Protection, S.China Agricultural University, Guangzhou, China. 152.

LIN Sui, b. 14 Jan 1929, Zhejiang, China. Professor of Engineering. 2 d. *Education:* BS, Ordinance Eng Col, Taiwan, China, 1948-53; Dipl Ing, 1958-62, DrIng, 1962-64, Univ of Karlsruhe, W.Germany. *Appointments:* Res Assoc: Inst for Refrigeration, 1963-65, Inst for Fluid Mechs and Machinery, 1965-69, Univ Karlsruhe; Postdoc Fellow, Inst for Aerospace Studies, Univ Toronto, 1969-70; Vis Asst Prof, Mech Eng, Sir George Williams Univ, 1970-72; Asst Prof, 1972-75, Assoc Prof, 1975-81, prof, 1981-, Mech Engrg, Concordia Univ. *Creative works:* Over 140 scientific and technical papers published in the fields of heat and mass transfer and fluid mechanics. *Memberships:* Engrg Inst of Canada; Canadian Soc of Mech Engrg; Am Soc of Heating, Refrigeration and Air Conditioning Engrs; Deutsche Gesellschaft fur luft und Raumfahrt eV. *Hobbies:* Qi-gong exercises. *Address:* Department of Mechanical Engineering, Concordia University, 1455 de Maisonneuve Blvd West, Montreal, Quebec, Canada H3G 1M8. 154.

LIN Weicheng, b. 31 Aug 1942, Guangzhou, China. Polyglot Translator. m. Zhi Linlin, 22 Jan 1970, 1 d. *Education:* Dipl, Shanxi Periodicals Instr Univ, 1985; Dipl, Chinese Lang and Lit, Fujian Tchrs Univ, 1989; Dipl, Eng and Am Lang and Lit, 1991. *Appointments:* Tchr, Fujian Labour Bureau, Skilled Wkrs Sch, 1960; Tracer and Latheman, Fujian Tractor Plant, 1960- 70; Latheman and Cheker, Jianou Gear Plant, Fujian, 1970-84; Polyglot Translator, Des and Res Inst, Minjiang Construction Bureau, Ministry of Energy, 1984-91. *Creative works:* Translations from or into English, Japanese, French, Russian, German, Spanish, Esperanto and from Portuguese and Italian; work published in newspapers and magazines. *Memberships:* Translators Assn of China; Ed Bd, Fujian Translators Post; Contributing Ed, Intl Financiers, Hong Kong; Contributing Translator, World Science. *Honours:* Theses Awds, 1985; Self-taught Talent Awd, Fujian Trade Union Coun, 1986; Translation Prize, Fujian Translators Post, 1990. *Hobbies:* Music; Philately. *Address:* Design & Research Institute, Minjiang Construction Bureau, Huangdun, Nanping, Fujian 353000, China. 152.

LIN Yi-Pu, b. 7 July 1927, Quang-xi, China. Researcher in Palaeoanthropology. m. 15 Aug 1962, 2 s, 1 d. *Education:* BA, Inst Paleontol Vertebrate and Paleoanthropol (IPVP), Academia Sinica, 1962; MA, Quang-xi Med Col, 1952. *Appointments:* Tchr, Kun-min Nsg Sch, 1952-57; Asst Reschr, IPVP, Academic Sinica, 1962-87. *Creative works:* Book, Anatomy of the Gibbon, 1978; Homo Orientalis, 1987; Over 40 compositions including: The Study of Djlai-nor man, 1962; The Study of Yuanmao Fauna, 1976; First Discovery of Dryophithecus in E.China, 1984. *Address:* PO Box 643, Beijing 100044, China.

LIN Yifan, b. 28 Jan 1939, Shanghai, China. m. Shao Haoming, 17 Dec 1967, 1 s, 1 d. *Education:* Grad, Dept of Textile Chem Engrg, E.China Textile Inst, (now China Textile Univ), 1960. *Appointments:* Ministry of Textile Indust, Beijing, 1960, Res of Finishing Fabrics and Trial of new products, 1964-80; Dir, Inst of Applied Chem; Prof, Inst of Textiles, Shanghai Univ of Engrg Sci, 1980- . *Memberships:* All Chinese Coun of the China Assn of Inventors. *Honours:* Completed independently, new kinds of Conductive Fabric, numerous awards by the Ministry of Central Government; Prize of City of Geneva, Cold Prize, 15th Int Exhib of Inventions, New Techniques of Geneva, 1987; Nat Invention 2nd prize, 1987; Advanced Technico-scientific Worker of Chinese Higher Ed Awd, Sci and Tech Comm and Ed Comm, 1990. *Hobbies:* Sport; Literature. *Address:* Inst of Textiles, Shanghai University of Engineering Science, 435 Xin Cun Road, Shanghai 200061, China.

LIN Yuanzhang, b. 30 May 1935, Fujian province, China. Astrophysicist. m. 9 Sept 1959, 2 d. *Education:* BS, Astronomy Dept, Nanjing Univ, 1956. *Appointments:* Res Asst, Purple Mountain Observ, Nanjing, 1956-57; Res Assoc, Assoc Prof, Beijing Astro Observ, Beijing, 1957- 85; Vis Prof, Herzberg Inst of Astrophys, Ottawa, Canada, 1985-86; Prof, Beijing Astro Observ, 1986-. *Creative works:* More than 60 research papers on solar physics published in professional journals, nationally and internationally; Co-author, Solar Flares, 1983. *Memberships:* Coun, Chinese Astronomical Soc; Intl Astronomical Union; Chinese Space Sci Soc. *Honours:* Principal Prize for Res, Chinese Nat Congress of Sci and Tech, 1978; First class prize, Chinese Acad of Sci, 1988. *Hobbies:* Philately. *Address:* Beijing Astronomical Observatory, Chinese Academy of Sciences, Beijing 100080, China.

LINCOLN Clifford, b. 1 Sept 1928, Mauritius. m. Lise Margeot, 15 July 1953, dec, 5 s, 2 d. *Education:* Fellow, Chartered Ins Inst, FCII, London; Fellow, Chartered ARbitrators Inst, FCIArb, London; Fellow, Ins Inst of Canada, FIIC. *Appointments:* Pres, Lincoln Manson Ltd and Lincoln Manson Inc, USA, 1964-80; Mem, Nat Assembly of Quebec for Nelligan, 1981-88; Minister of the Environment of Quebec, 1985; Pres, Canadian Coun of Environment Ministers, 1986. *Memberships:* Pres, LARC, Intellectually Handicapped, 1970-75; Pres, Cild Care and Child Devel Sers, 1979-85; Dir Emeritus, Canadian Arbitrators Inst; Dir, Ctr for the Great Lakes. *Honours:* Citation by AMA, NY for contribution to educational management, 1977; Nomination, Paul Harris Fellow, Rotary Intl, 1989; Nomination, Dir Emeritus, Canadian Arbitrators Inst, 1978. *Hobbies:* Reading; Tennis; Cycling; Hiking; Travel. *Address:* 186 Westcroft, Beaconsfield, Quebec, Canada H9W 2M3. 142.

LINCOLN John Francis, b. 30 July 1916, Australia. Retired Judge. m. Joan Alison Scott, 24 Jan 1952, 1 s, 1 d. *Education:* Newington Col, NSW, Australia; Balliol Col, Oxford, 1939-40; Admitted Barrister at Law, Hon Soc of Lincoln's Inn; LLD, Hon Causea, Macquarie Univ, Australia. *Appointments:* Dpty Asst Judge Advocate Gen, 1945-46, India and Singapore; ASsoc to Chief Justice of NSW, 1949; Practising Mem, NSW Bar, 1949-68; Acting Judge Supreme Ct of NSW, 1967; Judge Dist Ct NSW, 1968-86; Chm, Parole Bd, NSW, 1984-85; Chm, Elec Dists Commrs, 1990-91. *Memberships:* Dpty Chancellor, Macquarie Univ, 1976-, Univ Coun, 1963-; Chancellor Diocese of Newcastle, 1978-; Mayor of N.Sydney, 1956-58; Dpty, Chm Municipal Conf, 1957; NSW State Treas, Liberal Party of Australia, 1966-68; Hon Sec, Order of Australia Assn, NSQ, 1987-88; VP, 1988-92. *Honours:* Order of Australia, 1985; Hon Rotarian, 1986; Fellow, Australian Inst of Welfare and Community Worker, 1984-. *Address:* Stone Lodge, 30 Stanley Street, St Ives, NSW 2075, Australia. 23, 157, 128, 162, 149, 52, 186, 156.

LIND Niels Christian, b. 10 Mar 1930, Denmark. Professor of Engineering. m. Virginia Cano Reynoso,

26 Jan 1985, 3 s. 1 d. *Education:* MSc, Tech Univ of Denmark, 1953; PhD, Univ of Illinois, 1959. *Appointments:* Engr, Dominia Ltd, 1953-54; Bell Telephone Co of Canada, 1954-55; Univ of Illinois, Res Asst, Res Prof, 1956-60; Assoc Prof, Prof, Univ of Waterloo, 1960-91. *Creative works:* Co-author of 3 books: Methods of structural safety; Managing risks in the public intersts; Energy for 300 years; 200 scientific papers. *Memberships:* FRSC; Canadian Acad of Engrg; Am Acad of Mech, Pres 71-82; Int Assn cor Civil Engrg, Reliability and Risk Analysis, Pres, 1987-91. *Honours:* Ostenfeld Gold Medal, 1979. *Address:* Institute for Risk Research, University of Waterloo, Ontario, Canada N2L 3G1. 2, 43, 142, 6.

LIND Sven-Gunnar, b. 9 Oct 1954, Dorotea, Sweden. Dentist. m. Marilou Lind Jabellana, 10 July 1981. *Education:* DDS, Dept of Dentistry, Univ of Umea, 1979; Courses in English, Univ of Eskilstauna, Vasteras, A, B & C level exams, 1981-86. *Appointments:* Dist Dentist, Klostergatan and Rappe Vaxjo, 1979-80; Dist Dentist, Vardcentralen City, Eskilstuna, 1980-86; Gen Dentist, Dental Clinic, ARmed Forces Hosp, Tabuk, Saudi Arabia, 1986-88; Gen Dentist, Airbase Dental Clinic, Tabuk, Saudi Arabia, 1988-90; Gen Dentist, Sodermanlands Co Coun, Eskilstuna, Sweden, 1990-. *Memberships:* Swedish Dental Assn. *Hobbies:* Literature; Table Tennis; Badminton. *Address:* Forsbomsgaten 14, 632 27 Eskilstuna, Sweden. 55.

LINDBERGH Diana St Leger, b. 7 Feb 1957, Johannesburg, S.Africa. Marketing Director. *Education:* Student, various language schools, colleges and universities, 1974-84; Dipl di Conoscenza della Lingua Italiana, Centro Linguistico Italiano, FLorence, 1977; BA Intl Rels and Hebrew Studies, U Witwatersrand, Johannesburg, 1984; BA Hons, Hebrew Studies, 1985; Postgrad, Hebrew Univ Jersslalem, 1986-87. *Appointments:* Translator and News Reader, Italian TV Station, Florence, 1978; General Ofc Wk,Gibb Hawkins and Partners, Consltg Engrs, Johannesburg, 1978-79; Lecturer and Lang Lab Monitor, Univ of Witwatersrand, Hebrew Studies Dept, 1984-85, Lang Lab Monitor, 1986; Mktg Dir, Lindbergh Lodge, Wolmaransstad, S.Africa, 1988-. *Creative works:* Brochures and advertising copy for Lindbergh Lodge. *Memberships:* S.Africa Foun; S.Africa Inst for Intl Affairs; S.African Inst of Race Relations; Inst for Multiparty Democracy; Life, Women for Peace; Deomcratic Party; Inst for Am Studies. *Honours:* Cert of Merit in Hebrew Studies, 1983, 1984, 1985; Scholarships: Haymann-Gordon 1984, Nat Postgrad Scholarship, 1985; Ben Tsion, 1986; Travel Mix Laurel for Ser, Lindbergh Safaris, July 1991. *Hobbies:* Riding; Tennis; Piano; Guitar; Skiing; Foreign Languages; Swimming; Wildlife; Golf; Flying; Bridge Building; Politics. *Address:* Vaalboschfontein Estates, Private Bag X1010, Wolmaransstad 2630, W Transvaal, S.Africa. 52.

LINDE Robert Hermann, b. 22 July 1944, Schlewecke, Germany. Professor of Economics. m. Ingrid Windus, 30 June 1987, 1 s, 1 d. *Education:* Dipl, Econ, 1969, Dr Rer Pol, 1977, Dr Habil, 1981, Univ Gottingen. *Appointments:* Asst, 1976-81, Univ Gottingen; Lectr, Univs Gottingen and Mannheim, 1981-86; Prof of Econs, Univ Gottingen, 1986; Prof, Univ Luneburg, 1987-. *Creative works:* Theory of Product Quality, 1977; Pay and Performance, 1984; Introduction to Microeconomics, 1988, 1992; Co-author: Theory of Production, 1976. *Memberships:* Am Econ Assn; Verein for Socialpolitik. *Address:* Luneburg University, Postfach 2440, 2120 Luneburg, Germany. 52.

LINDEGAARD Hans, b. 29 June 1934, Copenhagen. Financial Executive. m. Kirsten Wegener-Thomsen, 1 s, 2 d. *Education:* Law Deg, Univ of Copenhaven. *Appointments:* Ministry of Foreign Affairs, 1959; Pvte Law Practice; Appointed to the Superme Ct, 1960; Exec VP, Den Danske Bank, 1970; Co Kreditforeiningen Denmark, 1991. *Creative works:* Co- author: Branches

and Subsidiaries in the EEC. *Address:* Gralen 2, 4780 Stege, Denmark. 52.

LINDENBERGER Herbert Samuel, b. 4 Apr 1929, Los Angeles, California, USA. Writer; University Professor. m. Claire Elizabeth Flaherty, 14 June 1961, 1 s, 1 d. *Education:* BA, Antioch Col, 1952; PhD, Univ of Washington, Seattle, 1955. *Appointments:* Instr to Prof, Univ of California, Riverside, 1954-66; Prof, Washington Univ, 1966-69; Avalon Prof of Humanities, Stanford Univ, 1969. *Creative works:* On Wordsworth's Prelude, 1963; Georg Buechner, 1964; Georg Trakl, 1971; Historical Drama, 1975; Saul's Fall: A Critical Fiction, 1979; Opera: The Extravagant Art, 1984; The History in Literature, 1990. *Memberships:* Modern Lang Assn. *Honours:* Fellowships: Fulbright, 1952-53; Guggenheim, 1968-69; Nat Endowment for the Humanities, 1975-76, 1982-83, Stanford Humanities Ctr, 1982- 83. *Address:* Dept of English, Stanford University, CA 94305, USA. 9, 2.

LINDGREN C E, b. 20 Nov 1949, Coeburn, Virginia, USA. Educational Consultant; Photographer; Writer. m. Penni Bolton, 18 Nov 1990. *Education:* AEduc, Hons, N.West Community Col, 1970; BA Educ, 1972, MEduc, 1977, Postgrad work, 1990, Univ Mississippi; FCP (TBA); Col of Preceptors, Essex. *Appointments:* Coor, Handicap/Educ Sers, Delta Hills Educ Assn, 1976- 79; Lectr, Photography, Univ of Mississippi, 1980-81; Lectr, Health Educ, Batesville Job Corps, 1980; Pres, Educ Conslts of Oxford, 1981-. *Creative works:* Photography for the Educator, 1991; Publications in professional journals and magazines; Numerous photographic exhibits including the Ctr for the Study of Southern Culture; Various saloon showings in Washington, NY, TX and CA. *Memberships:* Fellow Royal Soc of Arts; Fellow Royal Soc of Health; Col of Preceptors; Fellow, Royal Asiatic Soc; Phi Delta Kappa; Phi Alpha Theta; Kappa Delta Phi; Phi Theta Kappa; Photographic Soc of Am. *Honours:* Acad Achievement Scholarship, 1970; Educ Devel Proj Fellowship, 1973; Robert A Taft Fellow, 1977; Associateship, India Intl Photographic Coun, 1991. *Hobbies:* Writing; Computers; Reading; Archaeology. *Address:* PO Box 8161, The University of Mississippi, MS 38677, USA. 7, 15.

LINDHARDT Margarita Agcaoili, b. 25 Feb 1947, Philippines. Legal Sec, Sales. m. Wilbur J Linhardt, 21 Nov 1979, 1 d. *Education:* BSc Med Tech, Univ of Santo Tomas, Manila, 1967; Postgrad, Divine Word Col, 1967; Speedwriting Shorthand, Sch of Speedwriting, NY, USA, 1973; Legal Res, The Paralegal Inst, Phoenix, AZ, 1982; Fin Counsellor, Jerical Col of Fin Profls, Anaheim, CA, 1982. *Appointments:* Legal Sec, Wellington-Hall, LA, 1975-1976; Wyman Bautzer Rothman Kuchel & Silbert, LA, 1979-80; Kindel & Anderson, LA, 1981-82; Hufstedler, Miller Carlson and Beardsley, LA, 1985-86; McKenna Conner and Cuneo, LA, 1987; Pryor and Benson Inc, Torrance, CA, 1988-89; Outside Public Contract (Promotion) Royal Reservations, Las vegas, NV, 1983; First American Travel, Las Vegas, 1983-; Financial Counselor, Jerical Financial, 1982-83; Mgmt Trainee, Sales, Encyclopaedia Britannica, PI Branch, 1969-70; Sales, UBI/Southwest Bus Sales, Long Beach, CA. *Memberships:* The Smithsonian Assoc; Nat Trust for Hist Preservation; Am Mus of Natural His; The Cousteau Soc; NAFE; National Parks; Conservation Assn; World Wildlife Fund; LA County Museum of Natural History; the Colonial Williamsburg Foundation. *Honours:* First Hons Grades, 1-4; Valedictorian Elementary, 1959; Salutatorian HS, 1963. *Hobbies:* Museums; Galleries; Opera; History; Films. *Address:* 1648 W 218th Street 9, Torrance, CA 90501, USA.

LINDQUIST Robert John, b. 10 July 1948, Pennsylvania. m. Ann S Kennedy, 23 Aug 1990. *Education:* BS, Civil Engrg, PA State Univ, 1971; MBA Hons, Roy E Crummen Grad Sch of Bus, Rolling Col, 1990; Registered Profl Engr; Cert Contractor. *Appointments:* Field Engr, Cebor Constrn Corp, Pitts, 1972-73; Proj Engr, Chicago, 1973-75; VP Engrg,

Estimating, Peabody Midwest Inc, Chgo, 1975-81; Pres, Peabody Southwest Inc, Houston, 1981-84; VP, The Argee Corp, Denver, 1984-87; VP; Div Mgr, Hubbard Constrn Co, Orlando, FL, 1987-. *Creative works:* Author: Municipal and Industrial Heavy Construction-Market Survey and 5 Year Plan, 1984; Privitization-Introduction and Concept Outline, 1984. *Memberships:* Chm, Constrn Devel Div, Heart of Fla Utd Way, Orlando, 1990; Corp Coun Exec Bd, Crummer Grad Sch of Bus, 1991; Fla Engrd Soc; Profl Engrs in Constrn; Nat Soc Profl Engrs; ASCE; Calif, and Colo Contractors Assns; Fla Transp Builder's Assn; Alpha Gamma Rho, Social Chm, 1969-71; Beta Gamma Sigma. *Hobbies:* Golf; Running; Weight Training. *Address:* 537 Birdsong Court, Longwood, FL 32779, USA. 7.

LINDSEY William Byron, b. 3 Sept 1947, New Orleans, Louisiana, USA. Professor. 2 s, 1 d. *Education:* BA Hons, Univ Girginia, 1969; MBA, Boston Col, 1979; PhD, Mass Inst of Tech, 1987. *Appointments:* Pillsbury Corp, 1975-77; Boston Col, Prof, 1982-86; Prof, Vanderbilt Univ, 1986-. *Memberships:* Acad of Mgmt; Straregic Mgmt Soc; Planning Forum, Pres, nashville Chapt; Phi Beta Kappa. *Honours:* Outstanding Prof, Exec MBA, Vanderbilt, 1986; Webb Tchg Awd, MBA, Vanderbilt, 1987. *Hobbies:* Tennis; Drawing; Outdoors. *Address:* 1905 Harpeth River Drive, Parentwood, TN 37027, USA.

LINDSTROM Jan-Ingvar, b. 3 Feb 1936, Malmde, Sweden. Area Manager, Telematics and Disability. m. Karin Margareta, 29 June 1962, 2 s. *Education:* Higher Cert, 156; MEE, 1964; DTech, 1967. *Appointments:* Res ASst, Microwaves, 1962-66; Res Engr, Med Electr, 1967-69; Res Engr, Handicap Techn, 1970-77; Hd, R & D Dept, Handicap Techn, 1978-90; Hd, R & D Conslt, Visual Imp, 1987-86; Area Mgr, Telematics and Disability, 1987-. *Creative works:* Lectr at various conferences in the field of technology and disability; Issues in Telecommunication and Disability, 1991. *Memberships:* Rehabil Intl, Intl Com on Tech and Accessibility; World Blind Union, Res Com; World Fed of the Deaf, Comm on Technical Aids; Coor on Scientific and Tech Res. *Hobbies:* Technology and environment; Art; Classical Music; Sailing. *Address:* Trakvista Bygata 40, S-17837 Ekero, Sweden.

LINEBARGER James Morris, b. 6 July 1934, Abilene, Texas, USA. Professor of English; Poet in Residence. m. 1958, div 1979, 2 s. *Education:* AB, 1956; MA Hons, 1957, Columbia; PhD Emory Univ 1963. *Appointments:* Georgia Tech, 1957-62; Univ of N.Texas, 1963-. *Creative works:* Books: Five Faces, poems, 1976; John Berryman, criticism, 1974; Texas Blues, poems, 1989; Arthur Sampley, criticism, 1978; The Worcester Poems, 1991. *Memberships:* Poetry Soc of Am; S-Central Modern Lang Assn; Conf of Col Tchrs of Eng; The Yeats Soc. *Hobbies:* Cycling in Ireland; Writing poems. *Address:* English Department, University of North Texas, Denton, TX 76203, USA. 7, 11, 30, 13, 3.

LINKE Hansjürgen, b. 23 Nov 1928, Görlitz, Lower Silesia. Professor of German. m. Tamako Yamada, 1978, 2 d. *Education:* PhD, Cologne Univ, 1955; Univ of Göttingen, 1955-56; Univ of Hamburg, 1956-58, Eng and French; State Exam, 1958. *Appointments:* Master of Grammar Sch, Hamburg, 1959-60; Asst, Univ Giessen, 1960-66; Habilitation Giessen, 1966; Prof, Chm, German Dept, Univ Cologne, 1969-. *Creative works include:* Das Kultische in der Dichtung Stefan Georges, 1960; Epische Strukturen in der Dichtung Hartmanns von Aue, 1968; Die österlichen Spiele aus der Ratsschulbibliothek Zwickau, 1990; Contributor to professional journals and magazines. *Memberships:* Intl Assn of Germanic Studies; Mediävistenverband; Intl Soc for the Study of Mediaeval Theatre. *Address:* Institut für Deutsche Sprache und Literatur, Universitat Köln, Albertus-Magnus-Plaz, D-5000 Köln 41 (Lindenthan), Germany. 52, 92.

LINSTEAD Stephen Guy, b. 23 June 1941, Chesterfield, England. Director, Department of Trade

and Industry. m. (1) 1971, diss, (2) Rachel Marian Feldman, 3 Apr 1982, 2 s, 2 d. *Education:* King Edward VII Sch, Sheffield; Corpus Christi Col, Oxon, 1959-63: MA, Modern Hist; Dipl Public and Social Admin, Carleton Univ, Ottawa: MA, Polit Sci, 1963-64. *Appointments:* Asst Principal, Bd of Trade, 1964-69; Pvt Sec to Minister of State, 1967-69; Principal 1969; Asst Sec, 1976; Under Sec DTI, 1990. *Creative works:* The Law of Crown Privilege in Canada and Elsewhere, 1968. *Memberships:* Assn of First Div Civil Servants, Nat V-Chm, 1982-84. *Hobbies:* Biblical Criticism; Swimming; Travel; Entertainment. *Address:* DTI-WM, 6th Floor, 77 Paradise Circus, Birmingham B1 2DT, England.

LIPIEN Jozef, b. 6 Feb 1949. Trainer. m. 30 June 1973, 2 d. *Education:* Trainer. *Appointments:* Unemployed Businessman. *Creative works:* Automobile Assn Motor Sports. *Honours:* The Silver Cross of Merit, 1978; Great Cross Order Renaissance of Poland, 1983; Sports master, 1972; Distinguished Sports Achievement Medal, 1973. *Hobby:* Sport. *Address:* 103 Sportowa Street, 39-200 Debica, Poland.

LIPKA Judy Ann, b. 28 Dec 1960, Detroit, Michigan, USA. Chiropractor. *Education:* Dr of Chiropractic Degree, Magna cum laude, 1982; Assoc Deg in Arts, hons, 1979. *Appointments:* Owner West Bay Chiropractic Ctr, 1983-; Owner Quality Imaging, 1987-. *Memberships:* Baldwin Chiropractic Soc,Sec and Treas; Alabama State Chiropractic Assn, C-Pac Sec, Treas; Int Chiropractic Pediatric Assn; Am Chiropractic Assn. *Honours:* Cert in computed tomography, 1990; Fellowship in Magenetic Resonance Imaging, 1991; Baldwin Chiropractic Soc Chiropractor of the Yr, 1990. *Hobbies:* Travel; Sports; Interior Decorating; Music. *Address:* 2501-C Dauphin Island Pky, Mobile, AL 36605, USA. 138, 7, 76.

LIPOU-MASSALA Albertine Anne Honorine, b. 16 May 1953, Brazzaville, Congo. Judge. m. A Lipou, 22 Oct 1975, 3 d. *Education:* BA, Law, Univ of brazzaville, 1976; Dipl, Magistrature, Nat Sch of Magistrature, Paris, 1979; Postgrad Deg, Criminol, Univ of Paris X, France, 1981. *Appointments:* Juvinile Ct Judge, 1981; Pres, Judge of the Juvenile Ct, 1981-83; General Substitute for Attorney Gen, 1982-90; Attorney Gen Ct of Appeals, 1990-91. *Memberships:* Congolese Jurist Women Assn; Congolese Women Fed for Devel. *Honours:* Crossroads Africa's Visitor, 1986. *Address:* PO Box 2883, Brazzaville, Congo.

LIPSCOMB John Bailey, b. 25 July 1950, Virginia, USA. Priest. Rector. m. Marcia Hinton Mason, 28 Dec 1968, 1 s, 1 d. *Education:* BA Univ of N.Carolina, 1973; MDlv, Univ of the South, 1974; DMIN GTF, Notre Dame, 1986. *Appointments:* Vicar, St Paul's, St Thomas, 1974-76; Asst to the Rector, St James, 1976-78; Rector, Ch of the Good Shepherd, 1978-81; Rector, Christ Ch, 1986-89; Rector, Good Shepherd Parish, 1989-. *Memberships:* Fellow of the Grad Theol Foun, 1986-. *Honours:* Am Bible Soc Awd for Public Interpretation of the Scriptures; Army Commendation Awd; Army Achievement Medal; Nat Defense Ser Ribbon, (Dessert Shield). *Hobbies:* Golf; Computers; Reading; Weaving; Fishing. *Address:* Episcopal Church of the Good Shepherd, 715 Kirkman Street, Lake Charles, LA 70601, USA.

LIPSON Andrew, b. 3 Dec 1956, Voronezh, Russia. Physicist. m. Dorofeeva Natalia, 20 Dec 1985, 1 d. *Education:* Voronezh State Univ, 1973-79; USSR Acad of Sci, Moscow, 1982-86; PhD, 1987. *Appointments:* Jnr Scientist, Lab of Mechanochemistry of Solids, USSR Acad of Sci, 1986- 90; Snr Sci, 1990-. *Publications:* Titanium Fracture... Nature; Excitation of Nuclear Reaction; Electrical & Magnetic Properties. *Memberships:* Mechanochemical Assn of the USSR; Adhesion Assn of the USSR. *Hobbies:* Books; Swimming; Football. *Address:* Inst of Physical Chemistry USSR Acad of Sci, Leninsky Prs 31, Moscow 117915, Russia.

LISCHKE Gottfried, b. 18 Aug 1938. Prof. m. Gabriele Lischke Naumann, 13 Mar 1974, 1 s, 1 d. *Education:* Univ of Mannheim, 1968; Faculty of Sci, Univ of Freiburg, 1969. *Appointments:* Sci Asst, with Prof Bender, 1968; Scientific Asst, with Prof Heiss, 1969-70; Prof, Pedagogical Acad of Berlin, 1970-71; Univ Prof, Free Univ of Berlin, Psychological Inst, 1971-. *Publications:* Aggression and the Overcoming of Aggression; Several Articles in Books & Journals. *Memberships:* German Soc for Psychology; Soc for the Renewal of Psychology. *Hobbies:* Reading; Writing; Photography. *Address:* Quastenhornweg 28, 1000 Berlin 22, Germany.52.

LISIEWICZ George Richard, b. 5 Apr 1935, Lvov. Clinician; Hematologist. m. 6 Feb 1982, 1 s. *Education:* Univ Sch of Medicine, Cracow, BSc, 1960; MD, 1967; Assoc Prof, 1976. *Appointments:* Asst of Dept of Internal Medicine, 1960-69; Jnr Prof, Dept of Hematology, 1970-76; Assoc Prof, 1976-90. *Publications include:* Lymphocytes; Industiral Hematology. *Memberships:* Polish Hematological Soc. *Honour:* Gold Cross of Merit. *Hobbies:* History of Art; History of Philosophy. *Address:* Str 55, Apt 34, 30 081 Krolewska, Poland.

LISIEWSKA Maria, b. 2 Jan 1934, Poland. Mycology, The Specialist in Mycocoenology, Ecology, Phenology of Macrofungi. *Education:* Studies of Biology, Poznan Univ, 1952-57; Master of Sci, 1957; Doc of Sci, 1964; Asst Prof, 1974; Prof, 1985. *Appointments:* Asst, 1957-60; Asst Lectr, 1960-64; Lectr, 1964-74; Asst Prof, 1974-85; Assoc Prof, A. Mickiewicz Univ, Poland, 1985-. *Publications include:* Over 70 Publi. *Memberships:* Polish Botanical Soc; Polish Hygienic Soc; Alliance of Nature Protection; Pozan Scientific Soc. *Honours:* Golden Cross of Merit; Prizes of the Minister of Nat Educ. *Hobbies:* Radiestesia; Psychotherapy; Applied Mycology. *Address:* Os Kosmonautow 7 m 63, 61 624 Poznan, Poland.

LISINSKA Grazyna, b. 8 Jan 1941, Poland. Scientist; Food Tech. m. 25 Dec 1961, 1 s, 1 d. *Education:* Univ of Wroclaw, MD, 1963; PhD, 1972; DSc, 1982; Prof, 1992. *Appointments:* Univ of Wroclaw, Asst, 1963-72; Lectr, 1972-81; Reader, 1981-92; Prof, 1992-. *Publication:* Potato Sci & Tech. *Hobbies:* Gardening; Reading; Skiing. *Address:* Glogowczyka Street, 51 604 Wroclaw, Poland.

LISOVIK Leonid, b. 6 Oct 1948, Turiysk, Ukraine. Mathematician. m. Artemenko, 2 Aug 1974, 2 s. *Education:* Lutsk, Ukraine, 1966-67; Kiev Univ, 1967-72; Post Grad Course, 1972-74; Candidate of Sci, 1975. *Appointments:* Asst Prof, 1975-79; Assoc Prof, 1979-91; Doc of Sci, 1990; Full Prof, Kiev Univ, 1992-. *Creative Works:* Regular Events in Semigroups; Algorithms and Formal Systems; Logical Properties of Partial Continous Functions. *Membership:* AMS. *Hobbies:* Poetry; Philosophy; Basket Ball. *Address:* Dept of Cybernetics, Kiev State Univ, Vladimirskya Street 64, 252017 Kiev, Ukraine.

LIST Anneliese, b. 6 Jan 1922, Heroldsberg, Soubrette. m. Huldreich List, 28 Feb 1945, dec. *Education:* State Exam, Dancer, Munich, 1939. *Appointments:* Dancer, Municipal Theatre, Guben, 1939- 41; Soubrette, Municipal Theatre of Landsberg Warthe, 1941-42; Municipal Theatre, Thorn, 1943, 1944; Municipal Theatre, Elbing, 1944, 1945; Clerk, US European Exchange System, 1954; Sec, Refugee & Migration Section, Field Office Nuremberg, American Conslt General, US Embassys Escape Program, 1955- 60; Clerk in Charge, Foreigners Office of the City of Nuremberg, 1960-82. *Publications include:* The Tree; Stories & Poems in Various Publi; Zenit. *Memberships:* World Literary Acad. *Honours:* 2nd Prize, Contest for Best Story in True Stories Mag; Intl Cultural Diploma of Honor; Cultural Doctorate of Literature; Intl Order of Merit. *Hobbies:* Reading; Theatre; Cinema; TV; Travel. *Address:* Ritter Von Schuh Plaz 15, 8500 Nuernberg 40, Germany.

LISTER David, b. 18 Apr 1930, Grimsby, England. Solicitor, Retired. m. Margaret Crampin, 6 Sept 1956, 2 s 1 d. *Education:* Downing Coll, Cambridge, 1950-53; BA, 1953; MA, 1957; Law Soc, 1956. *Appointments:* Nat Service RAF, 1948-50; Solicitor, Articled Clerk, 1953-56; Asst Solicitor, 1956-62; Partner, Wilkin & Chapman Solicitor, Grimsby, 1962-90. *Publications:* Various Articles in Specialized Journals. *Memberships:* Law Soc; Grimsby & Cleethordes Law Soc; British Origami Soc; Flag Inst. *Hobbies:* Heraldry & Flags; Origami; Arthurian Origins & Literature; Folklore; Study of Playing Cards; History of Roses; Swimming. *Address:* 21 Vaughan Avenue, Grimsby, South Humberside, DN32 8QB, England.

LISTER Herbert Keith Norton, b. 5 Dec 1922, Croydon, England. Medical Practitioner, Retired. m. (1) Esther Wigram Arkwright, 6 May 1950, 2 s, 2 d. (2) Caroline Lawrence, 25 June 1980, 1 s, 1 d. *Education:* Eastbourne, 1936-41; Queens Cabridge, 1944-46; St Thomas Hsp, 1946-49; BA, 1946; MA, 1950; MRCP LRCP, 1949. *Appointments:* General Practioner, Harlow, 1951-60; General Practioner, Porlock, 1960-83; Divisional Med Officer, Essex Red Cross, 1951-55; MOTA, 1952; Founder Member, Committee Riding For Disabled, 1959; TV Document MOI Community Care, 1983; TV Document Gardem, 1990. *Membership:* Intl Dendrological Soc; Internat Camellia Soc; Royal Hortic Soc. *Honours:* Holder Several. *Hobbies:* Gardening; Horticulture; Tennis; Art. *Address:* Chapel Knap, Porlock Weir, Somerset, England.

LITTLE Douglas Irvine, b. 3 Apr 1948, Saint John, NB, Canada. Marketing Exec. m. Robata Major, 15 Mar 1969, 1 d. *Education:* Univ of New Brunswick; Perdue Univ; Georgian Coll. *Appointments:* Journalist & Editor, 1968-77; Founder & Owner, Little services PR, 1977-82; Mgr Huronia Tourist Assn, 1983-86; Mgr, Downtown Orillia Bus Improvement Area, 1989-; Founder & Owner, Little & Assoc Mktng, 1986-. *Publications:* Limerick Awards Collection. *Memberships include:* Festials Ontario; Leocock Heritage Festival; Leocock Memorial Home. *Honours:* Canadian Assn of Festivals; Mktng Awards. *Hobbies:* Writing; Reading; Event Production. *Address:* 12 Lankin Blvd, Unit 30, Orillia, Ontario, Canada L3V 6T2.88.

LITTLECHILD Stephen Charles, b. 27 Aug 1943, m. Kate Crombie, 1974, Dec. 2 s, 1 d. Dir General of Electricity Supply; Prof of Commerce; Hd of Dept of Industrial Economics & Business Studies. *Education:* Univ of Birmingham, BCom; Univ of Texas, PhD. *Appointments include:* Asst Lectr in Ind Econs, Univ of Birmingham 1964-65; Harkness Fellow, Stanford Univ, 1965-66; ATT Post Doctoral Fellow, UCLA & North Western Univ, 1969; Prof of Apploed Econs, Hd of Econs, Econometrics, Statistics & Mktng Subject Gp, Aston Mngt Centre, 1972-75; Sec of State for Energys Adv Council on R&D, 1987-89. *Publications:* Operational Research for Managers; The Fallacy of the Mixed Economy; Elements of Telecommunications Economics; Energy Stratagies for the UK; Regulation of British Telecommunications' Profitability; Economic Regulation of Privatised Water Authorities; Over 50 Articles. *Hobbies:* Football; Genealogy. *Address:* Office of Electricity Regulation, Hagley House, Hagley Road, Birmingham B16 8QG, England.

LITTMAN Anthony Frank, b. 23 Aug 1933, London, England. Chartered Accountant. m. (1) Valerie A Singer, 1 s, 2 d, (2) Pamela Leila Lewis, 24 Oct 1986. *Education:* Dagenham CHS, 1944-47; Latymers Edmonton, 1947-49. *Appointments:* Tubbs, Clarke & Co, Whetstone, 1949-54; Deloitte, Piender Griffiths, London, 1955-58; Chalmers, Impey, London, 1958-64; Self Employed, Prof Practice, 1965-. *Memberships:* Intl Mensa Committee; British Mensa Committee; Local Committies of Inst of Taxation. *Hobbies:* Theatre; Music; Literature; Travel; Skiing; Numismatics. *Address:* 16 Stanhope Gardens, Mill Hill, London NW7 2JD, England.

LIU Bai Bi, b. 1 May 1925, Sichuan, China. Prof of Law. m. Shu Qing Liu, 30 Jan 1956, 4 d. *Education:* Law Dept of Chaoyang Univ, 1946; Hua Bei Univ, 1948. *Appointments:* Chief Editor; Chief Edito, Technical Post; Public Procurator, Supreme Procuratorate PRC; Research Fellow, Narv Kai Univ; Prof of Law, Mngng Cadre Inst of Chinese Acad of Sci. *Publications include:* Economical Criminal Law; Dissertation on Crime Committed by Legal Person; Chinese Procuratorial System. *Memberships:* Chinese Inst of Law; Inst of Civil & Economic Law of the CIL; Chinese Poem Inst; Beijing Inst of Chinese poem; Chinese Painting for Snr Public Procurator of Supreme procuratoration. *Hobbies:* Chinese Painting; Chinese Writing; Chinese Poems; Swimming. *Address:* 5 East Unit 13 Building, 13 Block, He Ping Street, Beijing 100013, China.

LIU Chuan Zhi, b. 29 Apr 1944, Jangsu, China. Pres, Beijing Legand Computer Group Co; Exec Dir, Hong Kong Legand Computer Group Co. m. Gong Guoxing, 1 Aug 1969, 1 s, 1 d. *Education:* Xian Military Electronic & Communications Coll, 1961-66. *Appointments:* Technician, Chengdu Communication Inst, 1967-70; Researcher of Inst of Computing Tech, Chinese Acad of Sci, 1970-83, 1984-. *Honours:* Silver Medal; Gold Medal, Nat Best Industrialist. *Hobby:* Chinese Chess. *Address:* PO Box 2704, Beijing Legand Computer Group Co, Beijing, China.

LIU Ciquan, b. 30 Oct 1937, Yibin, Sichuan. Theoretical Biology & Biochemistry. m. Chen Lili, 16 Apr 1966, 2 d. *Education:* Univ, 1955- 59, Diploma; Graduate Study, 1959-61, Diploma. *Appointments:* Yunnan Aquatic Sch, 1961-71; Kunming Inst of Zoology, Academia Sinica, 1972-. *Publications:* Introduction to Quantum Biology; Quantum Biology & Its Application; Study on the Carcinogenic Polycyclic Aromatic Hydrocarbons. *Membership:* Chinese Biochemical Soc. *Honours:* Four Research Achievement Prizes. *Hobby:* Painting. *Address:* Kunming Inst of Zoology, Academia Sinica, Kunming 650223, Yunnan, China.

LIU Dun-yi, b. 13 Mar 1937, China. Professor of Geochronology. m. Wu Yu-Yhang, 20 Aug 1965, 2 d. *Education:* Bachelor of Phys, Yunan Univ, Kunming. *Appointments:* Reschr, Isotope Geothromology, Chinese Acad of Geol Scis, 1962-. *Publications:* Precambrian Geochromology of China; Geochromological technique development in China; Discovery of the oldest crust in China (pre 3.8 Ga). *Honours:* Geoscience prizes, Min of Geol and Mineral Resources of China, 1984, 1986, 1988. *Hobbies:* Baseball; Swimming; Photography. *Address:* Institute of Geology, Chinese Academy of Geological Sciences, Baiwanyhuang Road, Beijing 100037, China.

LIU Ji Ren, b. 22 Aug 1955, China. Prof. m. 10 Aug 1981, 1 s. *Education:* Northeast Univ of Tech, 1976-80; Graduate Sch of NEUT, 1980-82; PhD, 1984-87. *Appointments:* Asst of NEUT, 1982-84; Visiting Scholar, Nat Bureau of Standard USA, 1986-87; Lectr, Prof, 1988-. *Publication:* First Local Area Computer Network Product of China. *Memberships:* China Soc of Automation; Young Scientific Worker Soc of Liaoning Province, China. *Honours:* Sci Advanced Awards; Honors of Outstanding Achievement PhD of China. *Address:* Dept of Computer Sci & Engrng, Northeast Univ of Tech, Liaoning, Shenyoung, China.

LIU Jianjun, b. 6 Aug 1935, Xian. m. (1) Mao Licun, 27 July 1962, (2) Zhou Merying, Feb 1988, 2 s, 2 d. *Education:* Northwestern Univ, 1953-57; Chinese People Univ, 1959-63. *Appointments:* Chinese Dept, Northwestern Univ, Asst, 1957-59; Lectr, 1963; Assoc Prof, 1981; Prof, 1986. *Publications:* On Liu Qings Artistic Outlook; Another Outlook On Life; Essays on Researching Chinese Contemporary Literature. *Memberships:* Chinese Writers Union; Chinese Novel Soc; Northwestern Univ Academic Committee. *Honours include:* First Honor Prize of Chinese Contemporary Literature Research. *Hobbies:* Reading; Nature; Chinese

Chess. *Address:* c/o Dept of Chinese Language & Literature, Northwestern Univ, Xian, Shaanxi, China.139.

LIU Jin Wu, b. 29 Aug 1935. Vice Chmn Standing Committee Yunnan Natl Culture. m. Jiang Fang, 20 Aug 1955, 1 s, 1 d. *Education:* Yunnan Song & Dance Ensemble, 1950. *Appointments:* Dancer & Editor, Song & Dance Ensemble of Yunnan Prov, 1949-60; Dean of the Dance Dept, Yunnan Arts Sch, 1961-76; Dir of Yunnan Minority Natl Dance, 1979; Stresemt Vice Chmn, Standard Committee of Yunnan Natl Culture, 1980-. *Publications include:* Coming From Kingdom of Dance; Dance of Han Nationality; 100 Essays in Newspapers. *Memberships include:* The Intl Organ of Folk Art; Standing Committee of Yunnan Natl Culture. *Honours include:* Natl First Class Play Wright Award; Natl Excellent Works Award. *Hobbies:* China Minority Nationality Dance & Music; European Ancient Ballet & Opera; Travel; Fames Scenic Spots & Historical Cultural Sites. *Address:* 3 Greenlake West Road, Kunming 650031, Yunnan Province Dances Assn, China.

LIU Junjun, b. 15 Jan 1933, Tianjin, China. Prof of Sociology & History of Sci; Chair of Dept of Sociology, Nankai Univ. m. Jiang Zhe Shi, 9 Sept 1962, 2 s. *Education:* Dept of Western & Russian Language, Beijing Univ, 1950-54; Dept of Philosophy, Chinese Peoples Univ, 1955-57; Indiana Univ, USA, 1987-88. *Appointments:* Nankai Univ, Lectr Philosophy and Nat Dialectics, 1960-80; Assoc Prof, History & philosophy of Sci, 1981-87; Prof, Sociology & History of Sci, 1988-; Chair Dept of Sociology, Nankai Univ, 1990-. *Publications include:* Questions & Answers in Natural Dialectics; Sociology & Science; Numerous articles. *Memberships:* Chinese Assn of the History of Sci & Tech; Chinese Research Soc of Nat Dialectics. *Honours:* Outstanding Articles of Social Sci Award; Outstanding Translations Award. *Hobbies:* Swimming; Dancing. *Address:* Dept of Sociology, Nankai Univ, Tianjin 300071, China.

LIU Lang, b. 26 Feb 1933, Xiushan, Sichun Chn. Cinematographer; Editor. m. Sun Wei, 26 Mar 1968, 1 s, 1 d. *Education:* Southwest Art Inst, 1951-52; Beijing Film Inst, 1954-56. *Appointments:* Cinematographer, Editor, Central Newsreal & Documenting Film Studio, Beijing, 1956-. *Creative Works include:* Many Films, Newsrels & Documenting; The Works Exhibition of Documenting Film for Liu Lang. *Memberships:* Council of Chinese Film Artist Assn; Council of Chinese Cinematographer Assn; Mem of Chinese Cinematograph Artist Assn; Mem of Painting & Calligraphy Research Committee, Beijing; Painter of Kunming Inst of Trad Chinese Paints. *Honours include:* The Research for Earth Forest; Jiuzhaigou Fantasia, Travel in Southwest Chn. *Hobbies:* Music; Physical Trainning; Travel. *Address:* The Central Newsreel & Documenting Film, Studio of Beijing, No 15 West Road of Beihua, Beijing, China.

LIU Ray Ho, b. 3 Apr 1942, Taiwan. Prof. m. Hsiu Lan Lin, 4 Dec 1965, 2 s, 1 d. *Education:* Central Police Coll, 1965; Southern Illinois Univ, 1976. *Appointments include:* Univ of Illinois, Chicago, Asst Prof, 1977-80; US Dept of Agric, Eastern Regional Research Centre, 1982- 83; Univ of Alabama at Birmingham, Assoc Prof, 1984-89; Prof, 1989-; Graduate Program of Forensic Science, Dir, 1991-; Environmental Health Research & Testing, Technical Director, 1987-91; Environmental Chemical Corporation, Technical Director, 1992-; Forensic Science, Review, Editor-in-Chief, 1989-. *Publications include:* Approches to Drug Sample Differentation; Book Chapters. *Memberships:* American Acad of Forensic Sci; American Chemical Soc; American Assn of Clinical Chemistry; American Soc for Mass Spectrometry; Sigma Xi. *Address:* Dept of Crimincal Justice, Univ of Alabama at Birmingham, Birmingham, AL 35294, USA. 7.15.143.

LIU Shi-Yue, b. 2 Aug 1935, Tientsin, PRC. Music Archaelogist; Musicologist; Pianist; Violinist; Poet; Translator. *Education:* Univ of Logic & Language Peking, 1982-83; Self Taught Piano, Violin, 1956-66; V Ashkenzy, 1965; J Squier, Tientsin, 1982; Self Culture in Music Archaeology, 1983-86. *Appointments include:* Translato, Editor, Tchr, Typist, Tianjin Museum of Nat History, 1983-87; Tianjin Activities Centre for Disabled , 1988-. *Creative Works include:* on Music of P Tchaikovsky; Bone Flutes of Hemudu in Chekiang China; Praise You; my Dreams. *Memberships include:* ICTM; UNESCO; ABIRA; Ancient Philharmonic Soc. *Honours include:* Diploma for English Competition; Excellent Green Star for Music; Lu Hsun Literature and Art Prize, 1988. *Hobbies:* Classical Music; Fine arts; Art Appreciation; Stamp Collecting; Playing Piano & Violin. *Address:* 87 Changsha Road, Tientsin 300050, China.4.139.152

LIU Shu Chang, b. 8 June 1938, Gu Ye, Tang, Shan City, Hebei, China. Vice Dir, Dept of Animal Husbandry & Aquatic Products of Hebei Prov. *Education:* Hebei Agricl Univ, 1958-62. *Appointments:* Animal Husbandry, Vet Medicine Station in Ji County, 1962-72; Profl Sch in Ji County, 1973; Chief of Animal Husbandry, Vet Medicine Station in Ji County, 1974-78; Dir & Engr, 1979-83; Deputy Gen, Dept of Livestock & Aquatic Products of Hebei Prov, 1983-85; Vice Dir, 1985-. *Publications include:* Chinese Veterinary Acupuncture & Moxibustion; Numerous Papers Publ by Natl Grade Mag. *Memberships include:* Council of Chinese Veterinary Medicine Research Assn of China; Council of Chinese-Veterinary Medicine Res Assn of Hebei Prov; Animal Husbandry and Vetinary Medcine Assn of Hebei Prov; Poultry Ind Assn of Hebei Prov. *Honours include:* Prize for Excellent Paper Given by Hebei Sci & Tech Assn; New Star of Sci & Tech given by Hebei Government; Second Prize for Science and Technology Advance given by Agriculture Ministry of China. *Hobbies:* Classical Music; Chinese Ancient Poems. *Address:* No.13, Yuhua Mid Road, Shijiazhuang City, 050011 Hebei, China.139.152.

LIU Shukai, b. 24 Aug 1921, Yanshi County, China. Prof & Tchr of Doctoral Students in Agricl Resource Economics & Land Economics of Agricl Economics & Trade Coll. m. 20 May 1943, 2 s, 2 d. *Education:* Nat Northwest Agricl Coll, 1940-43; Nat Central Univ, 1944-49; Chinese Peoples Univ, 1960-62. *Appointments:* Asst, Agricl Economics & Land Economics, Nat Northwest Agricl Coll, 1943-46; Nat Central Agricl Coll, 1955-80; Assoc Prof, Agricl Regionalization & Resource Economics, 1980-85; Prof, Tchr of Doctoral Students, 1986-. *Publications include:* Agricltural Regionalization, National Textbook of Agricl Coll & Univ; An Approach to Some Problems of Agricl Resource Economics. *Memberships include:* Soc of Chinese Agricl Resource & Regionalization; Soc of Chinese Ecological Economics. *Honours include:* Certificate of Government Allowence from the State Council of the P R China, Outstanding Attributes to the Higher Educ of China. *Hobbies:* Studing; Writing; Travel. *Address:* Agricl Economics & Trade Coll, Nanjing Agricl Univ, Nanjing, China.

LIU Shuoren, b. 6 Dec 1930, Beijing, China. Stamp Designer; Snr Ind Artist. m. Lu Tianjiao, 6 Feb 1960, 1 s. *Education:* Jinghua Acad of Fine arts, 1949-50; Central Acad of Fine Arts, 1950-53. *Appointments:* Stamp Designer, Snr Ind Artist, China Nat Stamp Corportion, 1953-; Dir of Editorial Dept, 1986-89. *Creative Works:* Stamp Deisgns of Lu Xun, V I Lenin; Mao Zedong; Stamps Featuring Animal & Plant, Historical Relics, Importants Events; Thesis on Stamp desinging. *Memberships:* Chinese Artists Assn; Beijing Watercolour Painting Soc; Soc of Chinese Bookplates; China Council for Promotion of Old People; Culture Exchange & Orient Collectors assn. *Honours include:* Best Stamp Contect Awards; First Day Cover Awards; Gold Medal and a Certification in 24th Olympic Art festival. *Hobbies:* Collect Bookplates, Post Stamps; Music; Poems; Dancing; Swimming; Skating. *Address:*

China Nat Stamp Corporation, Hepingmen, Beijing 100051, China.

LIU Wen Wei, b. 27 July 1936, Shanghai, China. Assoc Prof in Otorhinolaryngology. m. Chen Chang, 3 Aug 1962, 2 d. *Education:* Beijing Medical Coll, 1955-60. *Appointments:* Instr, Dept of Anatomy & Histology, Tianjin Medical Coll, 1960-62; Dept of ENT, Tianjin 1st Central Hosp, 1962-69; Dept of ENT, Tianjin Medical Coll Hosp, 1970-74; Lectr, Surgeon in Charge, 2nd Affiliated Hosp of Tianjin Medical Coll, 1975- 85; Assoc Prof, 2nd Affiliated Hosp of Tianjin Medical Coll, 1986-92. *Memberships:* Tainjin Soc of Otorhinolryngology; Chinese Medical Assn; Hexi Chapter of Tianjin Soc of Otorhinolarynology, CMA. *Address:* Dept of Otorhinolaryngology, The 2nd Affliated Hosp of Tianjin Medical Coll, Weidong Road, Hexi District, 300211 Tianjin, China.

LIU Xiao-Cheng, b. 26 July 1949, Jiamusi, China. Dir of Mudanjiang Cardiovascular Hospital; Prof of Cardiac Surgery. m. Hong Yi Shu, 13 Feb 1977, 1 s. *Education:* Harbin Medical Univ, China, 1972-77; Cardiovascular Inst, Chinese Acad of Medical Sci, Beijing, 1979-82; The Prince Charles Hosp, Brisbane, Australia, 1984-85. *Appointments:* General Surgeon, Thoracic Surgeon, Jiamusi Medical Coll, 1977-79; Cardiac Surgeon, Fu Wai Hosp & Cardiovascular Inst CAMS, Beijing, 1979-87; dir of Mudanjiang Cardiovascular Hosp, Prof of Cardiac Surgery, 1987-91. *Publications:* Eleven Articles Publ Chinese Nat Medical Journals. *Memberships:* Chinese Medical Assn; Heilongjiang Medical Assn; Mudanjiang Medical Assn. *Honours include:* Chinese National Scientist with Outstanding Contribution; Chinese National Outstanding Worker. *Hobbies:* Swimming; Playing Piano Accordion. *Address:* Dir of Mudanjiang Cardiovascular Hosp, Mudanjiang 157011, Heilongjiang Province, China.

LIU Xiao Chun, b. 5 Mar 1941, Luo Yang, China. Art Critic. m. Li Shao Hua, 5 Jan 1947, 1 s. *Education:* Acad of Central Fine Arts, Beijing, 1961-66; Graduate Sch, Acad of Arte of China, 1979-82; Litt D, 1982- 85. *Appointments:* Tchr, Acad of Central Fine Arts, 1966-73; Editor, Fine Arts, 1976-77; Chief Editor, Fine Arts in China, 1985-89; Research Fellow, Fine arts Research Inst, 1985-. *Publications include:* From Animal Pleasant Sensation to Human Sense of Beauty; Over 100 articles. *Memberships:* Learning Committee of the Fine Arts Research Inst in the Acad of Arts of China; Chinese Artists Assn; Oriental Art Exchange Soc. *Honours:* Award of Research Achievement. *Hobbies:* Music; Photo. *Address:* Fine Arts Research Inst in the Acad of Arts of China, No.17 Qianhai Xijie, Beijing, China.

LIU Xiaoliang, b. 5 Mar 1923, Hebei Province, China. Research Fellow; Prof, Shenyang Inst of Geology & Mineral Resources, Stratigraphy & Palaeontology. m. 20 Jan 1955, 1 s, 2 d. *Education:* Dept of Geology, Coll of Sci, Beijing Tchrs Univ, 1941-45. *Appointments:* Tchr, Middle Sch Beijing, 1945-49; Ministry of Fuel Ind, 1949-53; Changchun Geological Sch of Ministry of Geology, 1953-62; Shenyang Inst of Geology & Mineral Resources of Chinese Acad of Geological Sci, 1962-. *Publications include:* Medusoid Fossils of Jinxian Fauna. *Memberships:* Profl Group of Late Precambrian pf Stratigraphical Commission of the Whole Nation of China; Acta Palaeontologica Sinica. *Honours:* Prizes in Scientific Researches of Bryozoa; Stratigraphical Record of Liaoning Province Award. *Hobbies:* Gardening; Sport; Travel; Beijing Opera. *Address:* Geological Publishing House, Xisi, Beijing, China.

LIU Xijun, b. 7 Mar 1923, Lian Jian, Fujian, PRC. Prof of Economics. m. Zhuang Luzhu, 17 Oct 1956, 2 s. *Education:* Xiamen Univ, 1946. *Appointments:* Lectr, Dept of Economics, Xiamen Univ, 1952; Assoc Prof, Economics Dept, Xiamen Univ, 1963; Prof, Economics Dept, Xiamen Univ, 1985. *Creative Works include:* A New Explanation on the Interrelation of the Scope of Accumulation and the Speed of Growing Between the

Two Great Categories. *Membership:* Fujian Inst of Agricl Economy. *Honour:* Advanced Educationlist, Fujian Province. *Hobbies:* Literary works; Chinese Chess. *Address:* Campus Box 807, Xiamen Univ, Xiamen, Fujian 361005, China.

LIU Yi-Lun, b. 11 May 1913, Fukien, China. Educator. m. Xiao Qian Wang, 10 Oct 1942, 2 d. *Education:* BSEE w distinction, 1936, MSE, Grad School Engrng, 1937, Purdue Univ, USA; MS, Communications Engrng, Grad School Engrng, Harvard Univ, 1938; Mil: Lt Chinese Navy, 1932-38, Tech Staff W Rank Corres to Col, 1942-44. *Appointments:* Prof, Hd, Elec Engrng Dept, Chongqing Univ, 1941-55; Prof, Rsch Inst Telecommunications, Chongqing Jiaotong Univ, 1945; Vice-Dir, Chief Engr, 4th Dist (Sichuan, Xikang, Tibet), Telecommunications Admin, Min Communications, 1946-50; Dpty Dir, Chongqing Telecommunications Bur, Min Posts and Telecommunications, 1953; Prof, Asst Pres, Beijing Univ Posts and Telecommunications, 1955-63; Prof, VP, Pres, Advsr, Chongqing Inst Posts and Telecommunications, 1963-; Dpty Dir, Chief Engr, 9th Rsch Inst, Min Posts and Telecommunications, 1973-79. *Publications:* Radio for Navigation, 1945; Theory of Network Synthesis, 1962; Over 30 papers concerning electronic engrng, network theory, digital transmission and telecommunications policies, mostly in var Chinese and Am periodicals, 1938-. *Memberships:* Exec Mbr, China Nat Popular Sci Assn; Exec Mbr, China Nat Instn Posts and Telecommunications; Vice-Chmn, Hon Exec Mbr, Chongqing Sci and Technology Assn; Hon Dir, Chongqing Inst Posts and Telecommunications; Advsr, Sichuan Inst Posts and Telecommunications; Standing Mbr, Beijing Instn Electronic Engrs; Standing Mbr, Sichuan Instn Electronic Engrs; Eta Kapp Nu; Tau Beta Pi; Sigma Xi; Dpty, 3rd Chinese Nat People's Congress; 5th, 6th, 7th Chinese People's Pol Consultative Conf. *Honours:* Scholarship, Harvard Univ; Prize, PCM transmission system rsch project, China Nat and Sichuan Provincial Sci Conf; Medal, Disting Work in Sci and Technology, Sichuan Provincial Govt and Chongqing City Govt; Prize 10 Yrs Excellent Work as Hon Dir, Chongqing Instn of Poets & Telecoms, 1992; Award for a paper, the 3rd Chongqing Social Sci Excellent Res Result Comm, 1992. *Hobbies:* Football; Bridge. *Address:* Chongqing Institute of Posts and Telecommunications, Chongqing, Sichuan, China. 139.

LIU Yick Wah Edmund, b. 28 Sept 1953, Hong Kong. Hotelier. m. Chan Lai Ting, 4 Dec 1983, 1 s. *Education:* Queens Coll, 1969-73; Hong Kong Poly, 1977-79; Haking Wong Tech Inst, 1980; Hong Kong Tech Tchrs Coll, 1980. *Appointments:* Holiday Inn Golden Mile Hotel, Snr Asst Mgr, 1979-81; East Lake Hotel, Gen Mgr, 1981-83; Right Ease Ltd, Mng Dir, 1983-. *Publications:* Supervisory Developemnt. *Memberships:* Inst of Personnel Mngt; Inst of Training & Devel; Inst of Purchasing Mngt; Inst of Supervisory Mngt; Royal Soc of Health; Hotel Catering & Institutional Management Assoc Cookery & Food Assoc; American Hotel & Motel Assn; Hong Kong Computer Soc. *Honours:* Certified Hotel Admin; Pei Hua Educ Foundation; Hong Kong Caritas Adult Educ Centre. *Hobbies:* Gardening; Fishing; Reading; Housekeeping; Travel. *Address:* PO Box 8, Tai Po Market. N T Hong Kong.52.

LIU Yilun, b. 20 Oct 1926, Shexian, Hebei Province, China. Tchr. m. Pan Zhengqi, 27 Aug 1952, 2 s, 2 d. *Education:* Dept of Chemistry, Northwest Univ, 1952. *Appointments:* Asst, 1952; Lectr, 1956; Asst Prof, 1979; Prof, 1985. *Publications include:* 8 Books; 73 Papers. *Memberships:* Chinese Chemical Soc; Xian Human Body Function Research Division; Southwest Normal Univ. *Honours include:* Commemorative Cert, Educ Commission; Citation of Merits, Shaanxi Province Higher Educ Bureau. *Hobbies:* Playing Chess; Reading; Tourism; Chemical Educ Research; Human Body Antiaging Research. *Address:* New Village 4304, Northwest Univ, Xian, Shaanxi, China.

LIU Yingxin, b. 26 Apr 1919, Muping County, Shandong Province. Scientific Research; Prof Researcher in Botany. m. 1 Jan 1944, 1 s, 2 d. *Education:* Beiman Girls Middle Sch, 1931-34; Middle Sch, 1934-37; Peking Tchrs Univ, Beijing, 1940-44; NW Agricl Coll, 1944. *Appointments:* Tchr, Several Middle Schs, 1944-47; Asst Researcher, Inst of Forestry & Pedology, 1950-61; Prof, Inst of Desert Research, 1961-. *Publications include:* About 20 Papers, Sand Fixation & Characteristics of Sand Fixators. *Memberships:* Botanical Assn of Gansu Province; Council of the Desert Assn. *Honours include:* Nat Top Grade Prize, Advancement of Sci. *Hobbies:* Traditional Peking Opera. *Address:* Inst of Desert Research, Acad Sinica, West 174 Donggang Road, Lanzhou, Gansu 730000, China.

LIU Yuan, b. 16 Dec 1954, Shanxi, P R China. Vice Principal, Peoples Acad of Fine Arts. m. Zhang Yubo, 1979, 1 s. *Education:* Shanxi Peoples Acad of Fine Arts, 1971-86; Drama Specialist, Peking Central Acad, 1986-88. *Appointments:* Vice Principal, Peoples Acad of Fine Arts. *Creative Works include:* The Lead in. Life of a Women; Avant garde technique. *Memberships:* All China Profl Drama Assn; Shanxi Drama Assn. *Honours include:* China's Most Prestigious plum Blossom Award; Shanxi Drama Competition. *Hobbies:* Reading, European Classical Literature; Russian Literature. *Address:* 11 Jianxi Road, Shanxi Peoples acad of Fine Arts, Shanxi Province, China 710054.

LIU Yuzhu, b. 2 July 1937, Rongcheng, Shandong. Pres, Shandong Poly Univ. m. Chen Jihuan, 19 Oct 1968, 1 s, 1 d. *Education:* Shandong Univ, 4 yrs. *Appointments:* Shandong Polytechnic Univ, 1991. *Publications include:* Analysis of Using Computers in Students Marks; Rustic Opinion to Principal of Tchrng Students by Aptitude. *Memberships:* Higher Educ Mgnt Assn in Eastern China; Higher Educ Mngt Assn in china; Higher Educ Mngt Assn in Shandong. *Honours:* Excellent Educator of China. *Hobbies:* Chinese Classic Poetry. *Address:* Shandong Poly Univ, Jinan, Shandong 250014, China.

LIU Zhan Qiu, b. 20 Nov 1935, Auhui Province, China. m. 1963, 1 d. *Education:* BA, Inst of Foreign Languages, 1955. *Appointments:* Snr Editor, 1984; Editor in Chief, Chinas Largest Poetry Journal, 1986- 89. *Publications include:* On the Early Spring Writting Paper; The Secret of Poetry. *Memberships:* China Assn of Prose Poetry; World Acad of Arts & Culture; World Congree of Poets; Federation Intl Poetry Assn. *Honours:* China New Poetry Award. *Hobbies:* Playing Guitar; Piano; Swimming. *Address:* No.10 Longzhanguan Lanli, Beijing, China.11.139.

LIU Zhongde, b. 11 May 1914, Hunan, PRC. Prof of English; Tutor to Post Graduates; Adviser to the Translatology Studies Group. m. shufeng Chen, 1942, 3 s, 1 d. *Education:* Provincial Joint Graduation Exam, 1934; BA, Natl Peking Univ, 1938. *Appointments:* Tchr of English, Snr Middle Sch, 1938-41; Officer, Bureau of the Yunnan Burma Highway, 1941-42; Offical, Central Organ Ministry, 1942-44; Lectr, Assoc Prof, Full Prof, 1944-. *Publications include:* A Study of The Various Uses of the English Word As; Ten Lectures on Literary Translation. *Memberships:* Translators Assn of China; Assn of Hunan; Provincial Foreign Literature Soc; Hunan Linguists Assn; Linguists Assn of China; Provincial Research Inst of Culture & History. *Honours include:* Merit Cert given by Provincial Foreign Literatture Soc; Univ Merit Cert for the Achievements Scored in old age. *Hobbies:* Tennis; Ping Pong; Morning Exercise; Gardening; Reading; Writing. *Address:* Foreign Languages Dept, Hunan Tchrs Univ, Changsha 410006, Hunan, China.

LIU Zunquan, b. 4 Apr 1940, Harbin, China. Prof. m. 13 Feb 1967, 2 s. *Education:* BS, Ind Univ of Northwest, Xian, 1957-62. *Appointments:* Visiting Research Scientist, INRIA, Paris, 1982-83; Adjunct Prof, Queensland Univ of Tech, 1992; Full Prof, Computer Centre, Chinese Acad of Sci, Beijing, 1986-92.

Publications: Sixty Articles; Intl Conference Papers; Ten Books. *Memberships:* Beijing Computerland Inst. *Honours include:* Gold Medal Award; Expertise Cert for Important Results of Sci & Tech. *Hobbies:* Music; Sport; Computer Security; Computer Aided Design; Scientific Calculation & Computer Simulation. *Address:* Computer Center, Chinese Acad of Sci, PO Box 2719, Beijing 100080, China.

LIU-LENGYEL Hongying, b. 5 Aug 1950, Beijing, PRC. Librarian; Book Review Editor. m. Alfonz Lengyel, 21 July 1984. *Education:* Anhui, China, 1981; MSLS, Villanova Univ, USA, 1986; PhD, USA, 1991. *Appointments:* Tchr, The Third Highschool, Huaibei, Anhui, 1982-84; Librarian, Gwynedd Mercy Coll, USA, 1987-91; Librarian, Fudan Museum Foundation, USA, 1991-. *Publications include:* Articles & Book Reviews; The Development & Use of the Chinese Classification Systems. *Memberships:* American Library Assn; Assn of College & Research Libraries; Michigan Acad of Sci, Art & Letters; Assn for Asian Studies Nat Assn of Scholars. *Honours include:* Merit for Distinguished Service; Award for Outstanding Serv. *Hobbies:* Pocelain Painting; Water Colour; Playing Chinese Musical Instrument; Photograph Making; Travel. *Address:* 1522 Schoolhouse Road, Ambler, PA 19902, USA.

LIVINGSTON Dorothy Kirby, b. 6 Jan 1948, Gosforth, Northhumberland, England. Solicitor. m. Julian Millar, 11 Sept 1971, 2 d. *Education:* Central Newcastle High Sch, 1953-66; St Hughs Coll, 1966- 69; Univ of Oxford, 1970. *Appointments:* Articled Clerk, 1970-72; Asst Solicitor, 1972-80; Partner, Herbert Smith, 1980-. *Publications:* Competition Law Matgrails Longmans. *Memberships:* Law Soc; City of London Solicitors Co; City of London Law Soc Banking Law Sub Committee; Friends of the Girls Public Day Sch Trust. *Hobbies:* Gardening; Reading; Theatre; Family Life. *Address:* Exchange House, Primrose Street, London EC2A 2HS, England.

LIXL-PURCELL Andreas, b. 9 Sept 1951, Austria. German Prof. m. Amy Purcell, 21 June 1986, 1 s. *Education:* PhD, Univ of Wisconsin; MA, Univ of Wisconsin; BS, Univ of Wisconsin. *Appointments:* Wabash Coll, 1984-87; Univ of North Carolina at Greensboro, 1987-. *Publications:* Erinnerungen deutsch jüdischer Frauen; Stimmen eines Jahrhunderts, Autobiog‑aphien, 1888-1990; Women of Exile; Ernst Toller. *Memberships:* Leo Baeck Inst; Modern Language Assn; American Assn of Tchrs of German; Amnesty Intl. *Honours:* Robert Bosch Foundation Award; DAAD Award; Byron Trippet Research Award. *Hobbies:* Photography; Skiing; Travel; Reading. *Address:* Dept of German & Russian, Univ of North Carolina, Greensboro, NC 27412, USA.7.

LLANES BURON Carlos, b. 24 Aug 1953, Havana. Univ Prof. m. 25 July 1977, 2 s, 1 d. *Education:* Civil Engr, 1972-78; Sport Reporter, 1979; Doc in Tech Sci, 1985. *Appointments:* Prof of the Fac of Civil Engrng, 1978-; Hd of Analysis of Sructures Dept, 1985-87; Hd of Structural Lab of Cecat, 1987-89; Hd of Structural Div of Cecat. *Publications include:* Over 60 Tech Papers in Natl & Intl Journals; 2 Video Films; Sport Papers in the Newspapers, Tribune of Havana & Workers. *Memberships:* Normalization of Structural Analysis Committee; Nat Union of Construction Engrs & Arch of Cubs. *Honours include:* Gold Medal in Fencing; Best Graduate of Civil Engrng Faculty. *Hobbies:* Baseball; Softball; Tennis; Fencing; Karate; Reading. *Address:* Centro de Estudios De Construction Y Arquitectura Tropical, Cecat, Ispjae, Calle 127 S/N Marianao CP 19390, Cuidad De La Habana, Cuba.

LLEWELLYN Sam, b. 2 Aug 1948, Isles of Scilly. Author. m. Karen Wallace, 15 Feb 1975, 2 s. *Education:* Eton Coll, St Catherines Coll, Oxford, BA Modern Languages, 1968-71. *Appointments:* Editor, Pan Books, 1973-76; Snr Editor, McClelland & Stewart, Toronto, 1976-79. *Publications include:* Novels. Hell Bay; Death Roll; Blood Knot; Rip Tide; Clawhammer; Pegleg; Pig in the Middle; Non Fiction. The Worst Journey in the Midlands. *Hobbies:* Sailing; Gardening; Accompanying Mrs Llewellyn on the Guitar. *Address:* 45-47 Clerkenwell Green, London EC1R 0HT, England.

LLOMPART Jose, b. 3 Mar 1930, Plma de Mallorca. Cath Priest, Jesuit. *Education:* Licentiate in Phil, Barcelona, 1954; Licentiate in Theol, Frankfurt, 1962; Doctorate in Law, Bonn, 1967. *Appointments:* Lectr, Fac of Law, Sophia Univ, Toyko, 1968; Asst Prof, 1970; Prof of Law, 1975. *Publications include:* Die Geschichtlichkeit in der Begruendung des Rechts im Deutschland der Gegenwart; Philosophy of Law; The seven Wonders of Penal Law; The Vignity of Mon & the Power of the State. *Memberships:* Japan Assn of Legal Philosophy; Japan Assn of Penal Law; Intl Assn for Phil of Law & Social Phil. *Honours:* Das grosse Silberne Ehrenzeichen fuer Verdienste um dir Republik Oesterreich. *Hobby:* Hiking. *Address:* S J House, 7-1 Kioiche, Chiyoda Ku, Toyko 102, Japan.2.

LLOYD Denys David Richard, b. 28 June 1939, Brighton, England. *Education:* Brighton Coll, 1953-57; Trinity Hall, Cambridge, 1958-61; BA, 1961; MA, 1965; MA, Leeds, 1969. *Appointments:* Asst Curate, St Martins Rough Hills, Wolverhampton, 1963-67; Tutor, Coll of The Resurrection, Mirfield, 1970-75; Vice Principal, 1975-84; Principal, 1984-90. *Membership:* Community of the Resurrection, 1969-90. *Address:* 7 Whitfield Hill, Kearsney, Dover, Kent CT16 3BQ, England.1.

LLOYD Geoffrey Ernest Richard, b. 25 Jan 1933. Prof. m. Janet Elizabeth Lloyd, 1956, 3 s. *Education:* Chaterhouse, 1946-51; Kings Coll, cambridge, 1951-54; BA,1954; MA, 1958; PhD, 1958. *Appointments include:* Fellow, kings Coll, Cambridge, 1957; Asst Lectr, Cambridge Univ, 1965-67; Lectr in Classics, 1967-74; Snr Tutor, Kings Coll Cambridge, 1969-73; Fellow, Japan Soc for the Promotion of Sci, 1981; Fellow, The British Acad, 1983-; Visiting Prof, Peking Univ Acad of Sci, Beijing, 1987-; Master, Darwin Coll, Cambridge, 1989-. *Publications include:* Books. Translations. Spanish; French; Italian; Greek Sci After Aristotle; The Revolutions of Wisdom, 1987; Demystifying Mentalities, 1990; Methods and Problems in Greek Science, 1991; Numerous Articles. *Contributions to:* Books. *Honour:* Sarton Medal. *Address:* 2 Prospect Row, Cambridge, CB1 1DU, England.

LLOYD Geoffrey Gower, b. 7 June 1942, Carmarthen. Conslt Psychiatrist. m. Margaret Hazel Rose, 19 Dec 1970, 1 s, 2 d. *Education:* Queen Elizabeth GS Carmarthen Emmanuel Coll, Cambridge, 1963; MB, B Chir, 1966; MD, 1983; Westminster Medical Sch, 1963-66; Inst of Psychiatry, 1970-1973. *Appointments:* Snr Registrar, Maudsley Hosp, london, 1974-76; Lectr, Inst of Psychiatry, 1977-79; Conslt Psychiatrist, Royal Infirmary, Edinburgh, 1979-85; Conslt Psychiatrist Royal Free Hosp, 1985-. *Publications include:* Textbook of General Hosp Psychiatry; Papers & Chapters on Various Pychiatric Topics. *Memberships:* Royal Coll of Physicians of London; Royal Coll of Physicians of Edinburgh; Royal Coll of Psychiatrists. *Hobbies:* Golf; Piano; Watching Rugby Football. *Address:* 148 Harley Street, London W1N 1AH, England.52

LLOYD Richard Hey, b. 25 June 1933, Cheshire, England. Musician. m. Morwenna Willmott, 29 Dec 1962, 4 d. *Education:* Lichfield Cathedral Sch, 1942-47; Rugby Sch, 1947-51; Cambridge Univ, 1951-55; Natl Service, 1955-57. *Appointments:* Asst Organist, Salisbury Cathedral, 1957-66; Organist, Hereford Cathedral, 1966-74; Organist, Durham Cathedral, 1974-85. *Creative Works:* Church Music. Anthems; services; Responses. *Hobbies:* Reading; Walking; Cricket; Theatre. *Address:* Refail Newydd, Pentraeth, Anglesey, Gwynedd IL75 8YF, Wales.1.

LLOYD JONES Joseph, b. 23 Sept 1944, Karachi. Prof; Univ Admin. m. Joanne Lloyd Jones, 27 Oct 1973, 2 s. *Education:* BA, Dalhousie Univ, 1971; Carleton Univ, MA, 1974; Univ of Iowa, MBA, 1976; PhD, 1978. *Appointments:* Asst Vice Rector, Univ of Ottawa, 1987- ; Adjunct Prof of Hosp Admin, 1988-; Dir, Inst Research & Acad Planning, Univ of Ottawa, 1978-87; Adjunct Prof, Strategic Mgmt, 1982-88; Chmn, Primary Card Bd, Ottawa Carleton Dist Health Council, 1978-81; Ottawa Carleton Bd of Trade; Dir, Treas, Shastri Indo Candn Inst, 1988-90. *Publications:* Strategic Mngt in the Health Care Sector; Mktng Strategies for the Health Admin; Co Author. *Memberships:* Canadian Evaluation Soc; Evaluation Soc. *Address:* 6078 Meadowglen Dr, Gloucester, Ontario, Canada.88.

LOBKOWICZ Nicholas, b. 9 July 1931, Prague, Czechoslov. Pres of the Ctholic Univ of Eichstatt. m. Josephine Waldburg Zeil, 23 Aug 1953. *Education:* Univ of Fribourg, Switzerland, 1958. *Appointments:* Assoc Prof, Philos, Univ Notre Dame, 1960-67; Ch for Political Philos, Univ of Munich, 1967-91; Pres, Univ Munich, 1971-92; Pres of Catholic Univ, Eichstatt, 1982-96. *Publications include:* Marxismus Leninismus in der CSR; Am Ende aller Religion; Jan Zahradnicek Der Haftling Gottes, Gedichte; Was Ware eine geistige Wende. *Memberships:* German Writers Assn; Pontifical Council for Culture. *Honours include:* Bavarian Order of Merit; L Thoma Medal of Twon of Munich; Order of Merit of Rep of Senegal. *Address:* Kue, D 8078 Eichstatt, Germany.

LOCK Robert (Robin) Christopher, b. 14 Aug 1925, London, England. Visiting Research Prof in Aerodynamics. m. Ruth Margaret Pembrooke, 14 Aug 1965, 2 s, 2 d. *Education:* Goncille & Caius Coll, Cambridge, 1943-45. *Appointments:* Research Fellow, Gonville & Cauis Coll, 1951- 54; Aerodynamics div, NPL, 1954-70; Aerodynamics Dept, RAE, 1970-85; Snr Principal, Scientific Officer, Visiting Research Fellow, City Univ, London, 1985-; Conslt Engrng Sci Data Unit, 1985-. *Creative Works include:* Design of Aircraft Wings for Transonic Speeds. *Memberships:* Royal Aeronautical Soc; Inst of Mathematics and its Applications; American Inst of Aeronautics & Astronautics. *Honour:* Silver Medal. *Hobbies:* Music; Gardening. *Address:* 74 Ormond Avenue, Hampton, Middlesex TW12 2RX, England.

LOCKE Stephen Charles, b. 30 May 1953, London, England. Mathematics Prof. m. 25 Aug 1974, 2 s. *Education:* B. Math, 1975; M. Math, 1976; PhD, 1982; Univ of Waterloo, Ontario, Canada. *Appointments:* Asst Prof, 1981-86; Assoc Prof, 1986-; Florida Atlantic Univ. *Publications include:* 22 Articles in Refereed Journals. *Memberships:* MAA; USJA. *Honours:* Honorable Mention, 10th Place Overall, William Lowell Putnam Mathematical Comp. *Hobby:* Judo. *Address:* Dept of Mathematics, Florida Atlantic Univ, Boca Raton, FL 33431, USA.7.

LOCKE Thomas Bernard, b. 3 Nov 1948, Bridgeport, Connecticut, USA. Law Enforcement. m. Gina Rae Robinson, 21 May 1983, 2 s, 1 d. *Education:* Bach of Arts, Catholic Univ of America, 1970. *Appointments:* Special Agent, Federal Bureau of Investigation, 1971-77; Field Supervisor, 1977-80; Headquarters Supervisor, 1980-85; Supervisor, Exchange Program, Drug Enforcement Admin, Washington, 1985-87; Asst Special Agent in Charge, 1987-. *Publications:* Black Tar Heroin in the United States. *Memberships:* American Soc for Industrial Security; Honor Legion Police Dept of New York; Intl Platform Assn; FBI Agents Assn; Eastern District Narcotics Unit, Tennessee. *Honours:* Achievement Award, NY City Police Dept; United States Secret Service Plaque; Honor Legion, Valor Award. *Address:* 1532 Pine Springs Road, Knoxville, TN 37922, USA.7.139.

LOCKLAIR Dan Steven, b. 7 Aug 1949, Chalotte, NC.Composer; Prof of Music; Organist. m. 23 July 1983, Paula Welshimer Locklair. *Education:* BM, Mars Hill Coll,

1971; SMM, Sch of Sacred Music, 1973; DMA Eastman Sch of Music, 1981. *Appointments:* Lectr in Music, Hartwick Coll, 1974, 1977-82; Church Musician, First Presbytarian Church, Binghamton, NY, 1973-82; Composer-in-Residence, and Assoc Prof of Music, Wake Forest Univ, 1982-. *Creative Works include:* Numerous Publ Works for Orchestra; Selo; Chamber Ensembles; Chorus; Ballet; Opera; Represented on a number of compact disc recordings. *Memberships:* ASCAP; American Music Center; American Guild of Organists; Coll Music Soc. *Honours include:* Top Barlow Intl Comp Award; An Alienor Award; A Kennedy Center Friedheim Award. *Hobbies:* Collecting Smoking Pipes; Swimming. *Address:* c/o Dept of Music, Wake Forest Univ, PO Box 7345, Winston Salem, NC 27109, USA.

LODGE Brian Robert William, b. 15 May 1925, Golders Green, London, England. Conslt Psycho Geriatrician Medicine. m. Lynn Mary Brown, 16 Feb 1991, 1 d. *Education:* Univ Coll Sch, London Hosp Medical Sch, MRCS, LRCP, 1949. *Appointments:* Temp Conslt Physician, Geriatric Medicine, 1965-71; Conslt Physician, Geriatric & Psycho Geriatric Medicine, Leicestershire District Health Auth, 1971-. *Publications:* Coping with Caring; Handbook of Mental Disorders in Old Age. *Memberships include:* BASE; Age Corcern; British Medical Assn. *Honours:* Health & Social Services Journal Joint Care Award. *Hobbies:* Walking; Theatre; Concerts; Books; Genealogy. *Address:* 25 St Georges Avenue, Hinckley, Leicestershire, LE10 0TE, England.

LOEFFLER William Robert, b. 31 Aug 1949, Cleveland, Ohio, USA. Quality & Productivity Specialst. m. Beth Ann Manderfield, 1 s, 2 d. *Education:* BA, Wittenberg Univ, 1971; MA, SUNY at Stony Brook, 1972; Post Grad Research Fellow, Clare Coll, Cambridge Univ, 1975-76; Ed Spec, Univ of Toledo, 1979; PhD, Univ of Michigan, 1984. *Appointments:* Dir, Chemical & Metallurgical Serv, Toledo Testing Lab, 1979-82; Vice Pres, Benchmark Technologies, 1983-85; Ford Motor Co, Endowed Chair for Statistics, Eastern Michigan Univ, 1985-86; Pres & CEO, The Loeffler Group Inc, 1986- . *Publications include:* Over 200 Publ on Quality Control, Robotics, Group Process. *Memberships include:* Tech Soc of Toledo; American Chemical Soc Chapter. *Honours:* Harvard Prize Book Award; Fellowship to Cambridge; Appointed Examiner & Trainer for the Malcolm Baldridge Natl Quality Award. *Hobbies:* Photography; Squash. *Address:* The Loeffler Group Inc, 3018 S Republic Blvd, Toledo, OH 43615, USA.52.132.

LOEPPERT Richard Henry Jr, b. 26 Sept 1944, Raleigh, NC. m. Sara Vela, 11 Mar 1989, 1 s. *Education:* BS, North Carolina State Univ, 1966; MS, Univ of Florida, 1973; PhD, 1976. *Appointments:* Asst County Agent, Florida Agricl Ext Serv, 1966-69; Post Doctoral Fellow, Michigan State Univ, 1978-79; Asst, Assoc, Full prof, Texas A & M Univ, 1979-. *Publications:* Refered Journal Articles; Book Chapters; Numerous Invited Lectures. *Memberships include:* Soil Sci Soc of America; American Soc of Agonomy; American Assn for the Advancement of Sci. *Hobbies:* Reading; Bicyling; Tennis; Photography. *Address:* Soil & Crop Dept, Texas A&M Univ, Coll Station, TX 77843, USA.

LOEV Bernard, b. 26 Feb 1928, Phila PA, USA. Conslt; Chemistry, Pharmaceuticals & Patents. m. Pearl Winter, 28 Feb 1954, 3 s. *Education:* BSc, Univ Penna, 1949; MSC, Columbia Univ, 1950; PhD, Columbia Univ, 1952. *Appointments:* Pennwalt, Snr Chemist, 1952-58; Smith Kline Fronch, Dir of Medicinal Chemistry, 1958-75; VP Chemical, Revlon Health Care, 1975-82; VP Scientific Affairs, 1982-86; Pres, Sci Conslts ves, 1986-. *Publications:* 200 US Patents; 100 Journal Articles. *Honours:* American Chemical Soc Award. *Hobbies:* Travel; Fishing. *Address:* 42 Penny Lane, Scarsdale, NY 10583, USA.2.6.14.

LOGAN James, B. 28 Oct 1927, Haddington, Scotland. Theatre Dir. m. Anne Brand, 27 Dec 1958, 1 s, 1 d. *Education:* Robert Gordans Inst, Aberdeen, 1948-52; C

Chem, MRIC. *Appointments:* Macanlay Inst, Aberdeen, 1948-81; Dir, Scotland The What, 1979-. *Creative Works:* Many Products of Scotland the What? *Memberships:* Friends of Aberdeen Art Gallery & Museums; Scotland Arts Council; Art Council of Great Britain; Voluntary Serv Aberdeen. *Honour:* OBE. *Hobby:* Theatre. *Address:* 53 Fountainhall Road, Aberdeen AB2 4EU, Scotland.1.

LÖKÖS István, b. 10 Nov 1933, Eger. Assoc Prof; Hd of Dept of World & Comparative Literature, Univ at Debrecen. m. Éva Jakab, 28 Mar 1959, 1 s. *Education:* Lajos Kossuth Univ, 1953-57; Univ of Zagreb, 1966-67; 1971-73. *Appointments:* Asst Prof, Tchrs Training Coll, Eger, 1959-65; Snr Lectr, 1965-75; Assoc Prof, 1975-85; Assoc Prof, Hd of the Dept of World & Comparative Literature, 1985-. *Publications include:* Hidak jegyében; Magyar és délszlávirodalmi tanulmányok; Over 100 Compositions. *Memberships include:* Intl Soc of Eighteenth Century Studies. *Hobby:* Hunting. *Address:* Vizimolnár u 12 11 6, H-3300 Eger, Hungary.

LOMAN M LaVerne, b. 10 June 1928. Prof of Mathematics. m. Coy E Loman, 23 Dec 1944, 1 d. *Education:* The Univ of Oklahoma. BS, 1956; MA, 1957; PhD, 1961. *Appointments:* Grad Asst, Maths Dept, Univ of Oklahoma, 1956-57; Instr, 1957-61; Asst Prof, Central State Univ, 1961-62; Assoc Prof, 1962-66; Prof, 1966-91; Prof, Univ of Central Oklahoma, 1991-. *Memberships:* Mathematics Assn of America; Natl Council of Tchrs of Mathematics; Oklahoma Council of Tchrs of Mathematics; Delta Kappa Gamma; Higher Educ Alumni Council of Oklahoma. *Honours include:* Fellow, Natl Sci Foundation; Tchr of the Year, Central State Univ. *Address:* 2201 Tall Oak Trail, Edmond, OK 73034, USA.5.7.15.125.143.

LOMAS Jonathan, b. 30 Apr 1944, Farnham, Surrey, England. Architect. *Education:* Belmont Coll, Bickington; North Devon Coll; Barnstaple Poly South West. *Appointments:* Partner, Dyer Feesey Wickham, 1976; Diocesan Archt & Ecclesiatical Archt, 1988; Commissioned Archt to English Heritage, 1988; archt to Ruman Catholic Diocese of Plymouth; Natl Trust Constl Archt. *Creative Works include:* Devons Traditional Buildings; Transactions of the Devonshire Assn; Archts Journal; Building Design. *Memberships:* Exeter Diocesan Advisory Committee; Assn for the Conservation of Historic Buildings; Inst of Archaelogy; Devonshire Assn; Soc for the Protection of Ancient Buildings; RIBA; FRSA; Devon County Council Historic Buildings Trust; North Devon Athenaeum Trustee. *Honours:* Arnold Sayers, RIBA Commendation for House Design; Devon & Cornwall Soc of Archt Travel Scholarship. *Hobbies:* Archaeology; Local History; History of Architecture; Photography; Travel; Garden design; Japanese Gardens; Steam Railways; Antiques; Swimming; Walking. *Address:* Sheraton Cottage, Old Sticklepath Hill, Barnstaple, North Devon, EX31 2BG, England.

LONEY Hazel Monica, b. 30 Nov 1927, Colon, Republic of Ranama. Cytotechnologist. *Education:* Licenciate & High Sch Tch, Mathematics & Physics, Univ of Panama, 1955; Post Grad Studies, London Univ Inst of Educ, 1961; Cytotechnologist, Memorial Hosp, NY, 1974. *Appointemnts:* Tchr, Mathematics & Physics, Schs in Panama, 1956-73; Cytotechnologist, Memorial Hosp, 1974-76; Montefiore Hosp, 1976-86. *Creative Works include:* Organist 1st Cytology Lab; Cytology Workshop, Peoples Republic of China. *Memberships:* Assn of Asst Masters & Mistresses in Secondary Schs; Intl Acad of Cytology; Assoc American Soc of Clinical Pathologists; Greater N Y Assn of Cytotechnologists. *Honours:* Recognition, Services in Foreign Country; Distinguished Women of the Year. *Hobbies:* Volunteer Cytotechnologist; Church & Community Work; Singing; Piano; Sewing; Baking. *Address:* 218 Midwood Street, Brooklyn, NY 11225, USA.152.

LONG Dale Hawkins, b. 31 July 1952, Alabama, USA. Project Engr; Constl. m. Ellen Scott, 2 d. *Education:* Bach of Sci, Texas Southern Univ, 1974. *Appointments include:* Assoc Engr, McDonnel Douglas Tech Serv, 1974-79; Supervisor, Texas Instruments Inc, 1979-86; Design Review & Interface Specialist, Parsons Brinckerhoff Centec, 1987-88; Health & Housing Serv Liason, City of Garland, 1989-90; Project Engr, O'Brian Krietzberg & Assoc, 1990-. *Memberships include:* Big Brothers & Sisters of Metropolitan Dallas; United Way Speakers Bureau; Alpha Phi Alpha. *Honours include:* Outstanding Serv to Youth and the Dallas Community; Reflected Glory Award; Distinguished Serv Award. *Address:* 1614 Darado Street, Garland, TX 75040, USA.7.

LONG Derek Albert, b. 11 Aug 1925, Gloucester, England. Emeritus Prof of Structural Chemistry. m. Moira Hastings Gilmore, 8 Aug 1951, 3 s. *Education:* Jesus Coll, Oxford, MA, D.Phil, 1943-49. *Appointments:* Research Fellow, Univ of Minnesota, 1949-50; Univ of Oxford, 1950-55; Lectr, Snr Lectr, Reader, Univ Coll Swansea, 1956-66; Prof of Structural Chemistry, Univ of Bradford, 1966-92; Dir Molecular Spectroscopy Unit, Univ of Bradford, 1982-88; Visiting Prof, Univ of Paris VI, Reims, Lille, Bordeaus, Bologna, Florence. *Publications include:* Raman Spectroscopy; Co Editor of 9 Other Books; Papers in around 200 Sci Journals; Co-Editor, Journal of Raman Spectroscopy. *Memberships:* FRCS; European Lab for Non Linear Spectroscopy, Florence, Italy. *Honours:* Docteur es Sci; Foreign Member Lincei Acad Rome, Italy. *Hobbies:* Intl Sci; Collecting Antique Woodworking Tools; History of Sci; Pembrokeshire. *Address:* 19 Hollingwood Rise, Ilkley, W Yorks, LS29 9PW, England.1.

LONG Madalyn Shannon, b. 5 Mar 1938, El Dorado, KS, USA. Dir of Elem Educ; Principal. m. James E Long, 9 June 1960, 1 s. *Education:* BS, 1960; MT, 1967; EdD, 1982. *Appointments:* Tchr, 1960-70; Univ of Dkla Grad Asst, 1975-77; Counselor, 1977-81; Asst Prof, 1981-83; Counselor, Bithany Univ, 1983-86; Middle Sch Principal, 1986-90; Dir of Elem Educ, 1990-. *Memberships include:* CCOSA; Phi Delta Kappa; NASSP. *Honours:* Tchr of the Year; First Lady Member in Kiwanis; Staff Person of the Month. *Hobbies:* Reading; Family; Friends; Latch Hook; Needlepoint. *Address:* 7208 Crown Point Road, OKC, OK 73132, USA.7.15.

LONG Martyn Howard, b. 1 May 1933, Teddington, England. Chmn of Mid Downs Health Auth; West Sussex County Council; Vice Chmn Natl Assn of Health Auth & Trusts. m. Veronica Mary Gascoigne, 4 Oct 1958, 4 d. *Education:* Univ Coll Sch; Surrey Agricl Coll. *Memberships:* Inner Magic Circle; Intl Brotherhood of Magicians; Sussex Club; Inst of Hlth Servs Mgt. *Honours:* Deputy Lieutenant, West Sussex; Commander of the Order of the British Empire. *Hobbies:* Art of Magic. *Address:* Lunces Cottage, Church Lane, Wivelsfield, West Sussex, RH17 7RD, England.

LONGLEY James Timothy Chapman, b. 21 May 1959, Leeds, England. Chartered Accountant; Corporate Finance. m. 2 Sept 1989. *Education:* Workshop Coll, Notts, 1972-77; Leeds Poly, 1977-81. *Appointments:* Finnies, 1980-82; Freedman Ross & Co, 1983; Arthur Anderson & Co, 1984- 85; Creditanstalt, Bankuerein, 1986-88; Touche Ross & Co, 1989-90; The Wilcox Group Co, 1990; Partner, Longleys, Chartered Accountants, 1991-. *Memberships:* Inst of Chartered Accountants in England & Wales. *Hobbies:* skiing; Horse racing; Tennis; Gardening. *Address:* 24/25 Cromwell Place, South Kensington, London, SW7 2LD, England.

LOPATKA Adam, b. 10 Nov 1928, Szlachcin. Prof of Consitutional Law. m. Helena Kania, 2 July 1952, 2 s. *Education:* Adam Mickiewicz Univ, 1951; Doctor of Law, 1958; Doc of Habilitatus of Law, 1962; Prof of Law, 1968; Full Prof, 1973. *Appointments include:* Adam Mickiewicz Univ, Faculty of Law, 1950-73; Asst Prof, Assoc Prof, Full Prof; Polish acad of Sci, 1969;

Full Prof, Dir, 1969-87; Member of Parliament, 1976-1985, Minister for Religious Affairs, 1982-1987; First Pres, Supreme Court of Poland, 1987-90. *Publications:* The state and the Communist Party; The State and the Trade Unions; Introduction to Jurisprudence; Human Rights in Poland; The Political System of Poland. *Memberships include:* Intl Acad of Comparative Law; Inst Assn for Philosophy of Law & Soc Philosophy. *Honours:* Honorary Doctor of Law, Florida Univ; United Nations Award for Outstanding Achievements in the Field of Human Rights; Many Natl Distinctions. *Hobbies:* Political History; Walking. *Address:* Oleandrów 4 m 2, 00-629 Warsaw, Poland.

LOPEZ PINA Antonio, b. 4 June 1937, Murcia, Spain. Prof for Constitutional Law & Politics. m. Annegret Pietsch, 28 July 1964, 2 d. *Education:* PhD, Univ Munich, 1960-61; Free Univ of Berlin, 1961-63; Univ de Paris, 1963-64; Univ of Michigan, 1964-66; Harvard Univ, 1966. *Appointments:* Senator Constituent Assembly, 1977-79; Prof Political Law, 1977-79; Univ Valladolid, 1979-82; Univ Complutense Madrid, 1982-; Counselor of State, 1983-91. *Publications include:* Escritos Politics. *Memberships:* Assn Espanola de Ciencia Politicay Derecho Constitucional; Assn Espanola de Dercho Humanos. *Honours include:* American Council of Learned Societies Award; Alexander Von Humboldt Award. *Address:* Catedra de Derecho Constitucional, Faculted de Ciencias Economicas, Univ Complutense, Ciudad Univ de Somosaguas, 28023 Pozuelo, Madrid, Spain.52.

LOPEZ-CARMONA Antonio, b. 28 Nov 1954, Granada, Spain. m. Marisa Garcia Valverde, 3 Sept 1988, 1 s. *Education:* Lectr, Mathematics, Univ of Granada, 1877; PhD, Univ of Granada, 1982. *Appointments:* Tchr, Univ of Granada, 1977-82; Full Prof, 1987-. *Publications include:* Numerical Methods to Optimisation Theary. *Memberships:* Real Sociedad Matematica Espanola; American Mathematical Soc; Soc for Ind & Applied Mathematics; Consultor de Caicyt. *Honours:* Mathematical Reviews; Zentralblock fur Mathematik. *Hobbies:* Reading; Tennis; Trains. *Address:* El Sos del Rey, Catolico N 14 6 D, 18006 Granada, Spain.1.52.

LOPPINET Alain Louis Georges Marie, b. 30 June 1940, Cognac, France. Technical Coordinator/Director. m. Jacqueline Tomas, 19 Nov 1971, 4 d. *Education:* Baccalaureat Mathematics, 1958; Civil Engrs, Ecole Natl Des Donts Et Chaussees, 1964; Ecole Natl Des Mines De Paris, 1965. *Appointments:* Soletanche, Site Engr, 1967; CFP Equipment Engr, 1967071; CFP Drilling Engr, 1971-75; CFP Operation Mngr, 1975-85; Total CFP Hd of Procusement, 1986-89; Hd of Logistics Procurement & Drilling, 1989-1992; Total Exploration Production, Russie/CEJ; Technical Coordinator, Tatol Petro Director. *Memberships include:* IFI; SPE; AFTP-CEDAF. *Honours:* Communication 2nd Proze. *Hobbies:* Mountain Trekking; Downhill Skiing; Committee for Culture. *Address:* 3 Rue De La Fontaine, 78870 Bailly, France.1.

LORD Mia W, b. Dec 1920, New York City, New York, USA. World Peace Activist for Abolition of War & Armaments. m. Robert P Lord, 2 d. *Education:* BA cum Laude, Liberal Arts, Brooklyn Coll; Currently Grad Student, Second Baccalaureate in Fine Arts, San Francisco State Univ. *Appointments:* Honorary Sec, Commonwealth of World Citizens, London; Secretariat of World Citizens, USA; Sec, British Assn for World Government. London; Sec, Group 68, Americans in Britain for US Withdrawal from SE Asia; Organiser, Vietnam Vigil to End the War, London; Honorary Sec, Natl Exec Committee Member, Assn of World Federalists, UK; Founder & Dir, Crusade to Abolish War & Armaments by World Law; Founder & Pres, Lets Abolish War. *Publications include:* The Practical Way to End War and Other World Crises; War, The Biggest Con Game. *Memberships:* Assn of World Federalists; World Government Organ; World Federal Auth Committee; Campaign for UN Reform; Citizens Global

Action; World Constitution & Parliament Assn; World Public Forum; Intl Registry of World Citizens. *Honours:* Nominated for Nobel Peace Prize, 1975, 1992; Officially invited to Vietnam; Four Merit Awards: Nominated for Nobel Peace Prize, 1992. *Address:* 174 Majestic Avenue, San Francisco, CA 94122, USA.9.138.152.155.156.162.

LOTT Bernard Maurice, b. 13 Aug 1922, Woodford, Essex, England. Research Fellow. m. Helena Winkup, 17 Sept 1949, 2 s, 1 dec, 1 d. *Education:* Bancrofts Sch, 1932-40; MA, Keble Coll, Oxford, 1946-48; BA, MA, PhD, Univ of London, 1950-60; Dip Ling, Univ of Edinburgh,1957-58. *Appointments:* Lectr, Univ of Ankara, 1949-55; Asst Rep, British Council, Finland, 1955-57; Dir of Studies, Indian Central Inst of English, 1961-66; Controller English Studies, British Council, 1966-75; British Council Rep, Poland, 1975-77. *Creative Works:* Gen editor, New Swan Shakespeare; Editor of Macbeth; Twefth Night; Merchant of Venice; Much Ado; Hamlet; King Lear. *Memberships:* Research Fellow, Univ Coll, London; British Assn for Applied Linguistics; Assn of Tchrs of English as a Foreign Language. *Honour:* OBE. *Hobbies:* Music; Local Studies. *Address:* 8 Meadway, London, NW11 7JT, England.1.

LOUGHBOROUGH Derek Ralph, b. 5 Mar 1927, Thornton Heath, England. Dir (Retired 1991), Lautro Ltd; Councilor London Borough of Croydon. Retired. m. Hazel Hilda Benn, 1 Sept 1951, 2 s. *Appointments:* Mngr, Sun Life Assurance Soc, 1943-77; Royal Navy, 1945-47; Councillor LB of Croydon, 1974-; Sec, Chief Exec, Post Office Insurance Soc, 1977-88; Dir, Lautro Ltd, 1985-91; Assoc Member, Croydon DHA, 1989-. *Memberships:* ACII; APMI; MBIM; Natl Conference of Friendly Soc; NCFS; Mayor of Croydon. *Hobbies:* Walking; Reading; Music; Essential DIY. *Address:* 45 Cheston Avenue, Croydon CR0 8DE, England.1.

LOUSTAU LALANNE Bernard Michel, b. 20 June 1938, Mahe, Seychelles. Sec Gen; Barrister. m. Debbie Elizabeth Temple Brown, 15 Mar 1974, diss, 1 d. *Education:* Seychelles Coll, 1955; St Marys Coll, Southampton, 1955-57; Imperial Coll, London, 1957-59; Middle Temple, London, 1965-69; Called to Bar, London, 1969. *Appointments:* Asst Inspector, Northern Phodesia Police, 1962-65; Asst Attoney Gen, Seychelles, 1970-76; Attoney Gen, Seychelles, 1976-78; Seychelles High Commissioner to UK, 1978-80; Intl Rep PRS, 1980-90; Sec Gen, FEACO, 1990-. *Memberships:* Honorable Soc of the Middle Temple; Bar Assn for Commerse Finance & Ind; British Actors Equity. *Hobbies:* Intl Affiars; Theatre; FRench/English Literature; Tennis; Skiing. *Address:* European Federation of Mngt Consultancy Assn, 79 Avenue De Cortenbergh, 1040 Brussels, Belgium.1

LOUX Joseph Anthony Jr, b. 2 Oct 1945, Albany, NY, USA. Cleryman; Reformed Church in America. m. Marjorie Anne Bronk, 5 May 1973, 1 s. *Education:* AA cum laude, Jnr Coll of Albany, 1965; BA, Suny Albany, 1967; M Div cum laude, New Brunswick Theol sem, 1970; Doctorandus in de Godgeleerdheid in Church History, Univ of Leyden, Netherlands, 1972; PhD, Philosophy, Roosevelt Univ, Leyden Univ, 1985. *Appointments:* Ordained, 1970; Pastor, Tchr, Pilgrim Fellowship, Hervormed Kerk, Dordrecht, Netherlands, 1971-73; Helderberg Ref Ch, Guilderland Ctr, NY, 1973-86; 2nd Ref Ch, Coxackie, NY, 1986-; Pres, Loux Music Publ Co, Hannacroix, 1984-; Pres, Dovehouse Music Editions, Ottawa, 1988-. *Publications include:* Boels of Hilversum; Boels Complaint Against Frelinghuysen; Numerous Articles in Profl Journals. *Memberships include:* Capital District Council of Churches; Classis of Schenectady; Catskill Mt Housing Devel. *Hobbies:* Antiques; Painting; Music; Gardening. *Address:* Fairview, 2 Hawley Lane, Hannacroix, NY 12087, USA.6.

LOVAS Istvan, b. 1 Oct 1931, Gyonyoshalasz. Physicist; For Gen of the Central Research Inst for Physics. m.

Erika Muller, 6 Sept 1958, 1 s. *Education:* Master of Physics, 1955; PhD, 1963; Docent of Physics, 1969; Doc of Sci, 1971; Prof of Physics, 1974. *Appointments:* Inst for Nuclear Physics, 1954-56; Central Research Inst for Physics, Budapest, 1956-; Niels Bohr Inst, Copenhagen, 1964-65; Joint Inst for Nuclear Res, Dubna, 1966-68; Kernforschungsanlage, Julich, 1974-75; Gesellschaft fir Schwerionenforschung, 1980; Lajos Kossuth Univ, Debrecen, 1986. *Publications include:* Scientific Papers in Journals; Physical Review; Physics Letters. *Memberships:* Hungarian Acad of Sci; European Acad of Arts, Sci & Humanities; European Physical Soc; Roland Eotvos Physical Soc. *Honours:* Gold Medal of Labour; Rezso Schmid Prize of the Physical Soc; Acad Prize; Eotvos Medal. *Hobby:* Gardening. *Address:* Central Research Inst of Physics, H 1525 Budapest, PO Box 49, Hungary.1.

LOVE Malcolm Barr, b. 1 Nov 1929, Paisley, Scotland. General Medical Practitioner. m. 31 Oct 1961, 1 s, 2 d. *Education:* Worcester Royal Crammer Sch; Birmingham Univ Medical Sch. *Appointments:* RMO Childrens Hosp, Birmingham, 1956-57; Trainee General Practitioner, Edinburgh, 1957-59; Registrar, General Hosp, 1960-61; Reg, Brook Hosp, 1961-64; General Prochice, 1964-. *Memberships include:* Royal Soc of Medicine; Flyfishing Club; Reform Club; Caledonian Club. *Hobbies:* Fishing; Music. *Address:* The Old Manor House, Milston, Salisbury, Wilts SP4 8HT.

LOVE Philip Noel, b. 25 Dec 1939, Aberdeen, Scotland. University Administrator. m. Isabel Leah Mearns, 1963, 3 s. *Education:* Aberdeen Univ, MA, 1961, LLB, 1963. *Appointments include:* Bar, Scotland, 1963; Partner, Campbell Connon, Aberdeen, 1963-74; Conslt, 1974-; Dean Faculty of Law Univ of Aberdeen, 1979-82, 1991-1992, Vice-Prin, 1986-90; Vice-Chancellor, Univ of Liverpool, 1992-; Chmn, Scottish Conveyancing and Executry Svcs, Bd, 1991-; Commr, Scottish Law Commn, 1986-; Local Chmn, Rent Assessment Panel for Scotland, 1972-1992; Chmn, Sec of State for Scotland's expert com, house purchase, 1982-84; Chmn, Standing Com on Legal Edn in Scotland, 1976-80; Mem, rules coun, Court of Session, 1968-92; Chmn, Customer Adv Group, Registers of Scotland, 1990-; Aberdeen Home for Widowers' Children, 1971-92; Pres, Aberdeen Grammar Sch, Former Pupils Club, 1987-88; Hon Sheriff of Grampian, Highland and Islands, 1978-; Trustee, Grampian and Islands Family Trust, 1988-92; Gov, Inst, Occupational Medicine Ltd, 1990-. *Memberships:* Mem, Law Soc, Scotland, pres, 1981-82; Scottish Law Agts Soc, vice-pres, 1970; Internat Bar Assn, coun, 1983-87; New Club, Edinburgh; Royal Aberdeen Golf Club. *Hobbies:* Rugby; Physical Fitness.

LOVE Robert Malcolm, b. 9 Jan 1937, Paisley, Scotland. Controller of Drama, Scottish TV Plc. *Education:* MA, Glasgow Univ, 1957; Dip American Studies, Washington Univ, St Louis, 1959. *Appointments:* Royal Air Force, Flt Lt, 1959-61; Actor, Dir, Nottingham Playhouse, 1962-65; Producer Drama, Thames TV, 1966-76; Freelance Producer, 1976-79; Controller of Drama, Scottish TV, 1979-. *Memberships:* Royal TV Soc; Directors Gents: Cath Priest, Tchr, St Gregorys Coll, 1959-69; Banker, First Natl Bank of Chicago, 1970-80; Banker, Lasalle Natl Bank, 1980-83; Bank Consl, 1984-88; Novelist, 1988-. *Publications:* The Chartreue Clue; The Fundamentals of Murder; Bloddy Ten. *Memberships include:* Mystery Writers Of Americal Intl Assn of Crime Writers; Private Eye Writers of

America; Soc of Midland Authors. *Honous:* Agatha Award; MaCavity Award. *Hobbies:* Acting; Tennis; Skiing; Reading; Singing. *Address:* 940 Cleveland, Hinsdale, IL 60521, USA.

LOVELL Mary Sybilla, b. 23 Oct 1941, N Wales. Writer. m. 22 Oct 1960, diss, 1 s. *Education:* Notre Dame Coll, Liverpool. *Appointments:* Baron Intruments Ltd, 1970-77; Yachting Provance Ltd, 1977-79; Yachting Provence Sarl, 1977-; Baron Computers Ltd, 1979-82; Tabs Ltd, 1982-86. *Publications:* A Hunting Pageant; Cats As Pets; Boys Book of Boats; Straight on Till Morning; The Splendid Outcast; The Sound of Wings; Cast on Shadow. *Memberships:* New Forest Hunt Club; MFHA; Royal Overseas League; RS Surels Soc; Bournemouth Flying; Rhinefield Polo Club. *Hobbies:* Yacht Racing; Flying; Fox Hunting; Travel; Polo; Reading. *Address:* Laura Cottage, Romsey Road, Lyndhurst, Hampshire, SO4 7AR, England.

LOVELL Walter Carl, b. 7 May 1934, Springfield VT, USA. Design Engr; Inventor. m. Patricia Lawrence, 6 May 1951, 5 d. *Education:* BS, Mech Engrng, Hillyer Coll, Hartford; Prof Design, Electrical Electronic Engrng, Mass, USA. *Appointments:* Design Engr, 196-62; Pres, Lovell Eng Co, 1963-64; Conslt Engr, 1965-66; Treasurer, Egg Stlr Corp, 1970-72; Pres, Crestwood Intl, 1973-; Pres, Chmn, Kady Kaks Corp, 1976-78; Conslt, Intl Corp, 1979-. *Publications:* Over 85 Copyrights inc. Country Songs-Show Tunes. *Membership:* BMA Composers & Writers. *Honours include:* Over 50 World Patients. *Hobbies:* Music; Guitar; Piano; Singing; Bicycling; Target Shooting; Artist Drawings; Oil Painting. *Address:* MA, USA.6.52.132.139.

LOVELOCK Lynn Carole, b. 4 Sept 1956, London, England. Parliamentary Officer. *Education:* BA (Hons), Univ of Sydney, 1978; Dip Ed, Univ of Sydney, 1979. *Appointments:* Research Officer, Dept of Defence, Canberra, 1980; English/History Tchr, 1981-86; Parliamentry Admin Officer, 1987-88; Usher of the Block Rod, 1988-89; Clerk Asst, 1989-90; Deputy Clerk NSW Legislative Council, 1990-. *Memberships:* Soc of Clerks at the Table; Austrlian Study of Parliment Group. *Hobbies:* Bridge; Swimming; Travel; Classical Guitar; Snow Skiing. *Address:* Legislative Council, Macquarie Street, Sydney, NSW 2000, Australia.138.

LOVING Jerome MacNeill, b. 25 Dec 1941, Philadelphia, PA, USA. Prof of American Literature. m. Cathleen C Loving, 3 July 1965, 1 s, 1 d. *Education:* BA, English Penn State Univ, 1964; MA, English Duquesne Univ, 1970; PhD, Duke Univ, 1973. *Appointments:* Leningrad State Univ, 1978; Univ of Paris, 1984, 1989; Univ of Texas, 1986; Texas A&M Univ, 1973-; Cal State Univ, Fresno, 1990-92. *Publications include:* Leaves of Grass; Walt Whitmans Champion; Civil War Ltrs of G W Whitman. *Memberships:* American Literature Assn; Intl Assn of Univ Profs of English. *Hobbies:* Gardening; Reading; Walking. *Address:* Dept of English, Texas A&M Univ, Coll Station, TX 77843, USA.7.13.

LOW Donald Anthony, b. 22 June 1927, Naini Tal, India. Pres, Clare Hall & Smuts Prof of the History of the British Commonwealth, Univ of Cambridge. m. Isobel Smails, 1952, 1 s, 2 d. *Education:* Open Scholarship, Oxford, 1944; BA, Exeter Coll, Oxford, 1948; MA, Oxon, 1952; D Phil, Oxon, 1957; Fellow, Australian Acad of the Humanities, 1974; Fellow, Acad of the Soc Sci in Aus, 1975; FRHistS; PhD, Cantab, 1983. *Appointments include:* Makerere Coll, Africa, 1951-58; The Australian Natl Univ, 1959-64; Univ of Sussex, 1964-72; The Australian Natl Univ, 1973-82; Univ of Cambridge, 1983-. *Publications include:* Buganda & British Overrule; Soundings in Modern South Asian History; Buganda in Modern History; Lion Rampant; Congress and the Raj; The Mind of Buganda; Sovereigns & Surrogates; The Political Inheritence of Pakistan; Eclipse of Empire. *Address:* Clare Hall, Cambridge, England.

LOW City, OK, USA. Novelist. m. Joyce M Athman, 30 May 1970, 2 d. *Education:* St Johns Univ, 1955; Univ of Chicago, 1970-72; M Business Admin, 1972. *Appointments:* Cath Priest, Tchr, St Gregorys Coll, 1959-69; Banker, First Natl Bank of Chicago, 1970-80; Banker, Lasalle Natl Bank, 1980-83; Bank Consl, 1984-88; Novelist, 1988-. *Publications:* The Chartreue Clue; The Fundamentals of Murder; Bloddy Ten. *Memberships include:* Mystery Writers Of Americal Intl Assn of Crime Writers; Private Eye Writers of

LOW Philip Funk, b. 15 Oct 1921, Carmangay, Alberta, Canada. Prof of Soil Chemistry, Purdue Univ. m. Mayda Stewart, 11 June 1942, 2 s, 4 d. *Education:* BS, Brigham Young Univ, 1943; MS, Califonia Inst of Tech, 1944; PhD, Iowa State univ, 1949. *Appointments:* US Dept of Agricl, 1949; Purdue Univ, Asst Prof, Assoc Prof, Prof, 1949-. *Publications:* 125 Scientific Articles. *Memberships include:* Clay Minerals Soc of America; Soil Sci Soc of America; Intl Soc of Soil Sci; Sigma Xi; Gamma Sigma Delta; Blue Key. *Honours include:* Annual Research Award, Purdue Chapter Sigma Xi; Herbert McCoy Award of Purdue Univ; Soil Science Achievement Award, Soil Science Soc of America; Pres, Soil Science Soc A, 1973; Fellow, Soil Science Soc America; Fellow, American Soc Agronomy; Bouyoucou Distinguished Career Award, Soil Science Soc of America; Distinguished Visitor Award to Australia; Distinguished Service Award of Brigha, Young Univ; Thurburn Visiting Fellow and Guest Professor, Univ of Sydney; Honorary Prof, Zhejiang Agricultural Univ, China; Distinguished Mem, Clay Minerals Soc; Mem, Nat Acad of Sciences of USA. *Hobbies:* Collecting Oil Paintings; Oriental Rugs; Crystal & Jade; Hiking; Cicycling; Camping; Listening to Opera; Classical Music; Reading. *Address:* 340 Hollowood Drive, West Lafayette, IN 47906, USA. 2.

LOWE Gordon, b. 31 May 1933. Prof of Biological Chemistry, Univ of Oxford. m. Gwynneth Hunter, 1 Sept 1956, 2 s. *Education:* Royal Coll of Sci, Imperial Coll, Univ of London, 1951-54; ARCS, BSc,1954-57; PhD, DIC, Oxford Univ, 1957-59; MA, 1960; DSc, 1985. *Appointments:* Univ Demonstator, Oxford Univ, 1959-65; Weir Jnr Research Fellow, Univ Coll, 1959-61; Official Fellow, Tutor, Lincoln Coll, 1962-; Univ Lectr, Oxford Univ, 1965-88; Sub Rector, Lincoln Coll, Oxford, 1986-89; Aldrichian Praelector in Chemistry, 1988-89; Prof of Bilogical Chemistry, Oxford Univ. 1989-. *Publications:* Over 180 Articles & Reports. *Memberships:* FRS; FRSC; FRSA; Oxford Enzyme Group; Oxford Centre for Molecular Sci. *Honours:* Governors Prize; Edmund White Prize; Charmian Medal. *Address:* Lincoln Coll, Oxford OX1 3DR, England.1.52.

LOWE Richard Grady, b. 5 July 1942, Eunice, Loisiana, USA. Prof of History. Widower, 3 s, remarried, 1992. *Education:* BA, Univ of Southwestern Louisiana, 1964; AM, Harvard Univ, 1965; PhD, Univ of Virginia, 1968. *Appointments:* History Faculty, Univ of North Texas, 1968-; Visiting Asst Prof, Univ of Virginia, 1970. *Publications include:* Wealth & Power in Antebellum Texas; Republicans & Reconstruction in Virginia. *Memberships:* Southern Historical Assn; Soc of Civil War Historians; Texas State Historical Assn. *Honour:* Phi Beta Kappa. *Address:* Dept of History, Univ of North Texas, Denton, TX 76203, USA.7.

LOWEN Allen Wayne, b. 8 Nov 1946, Covington, VA. Pres, Florida Christian Coll. m. Sharon Kay Tyler, 23 Aug 1969, 3 d. *Education:* BS, Cincinnati Bible Ceoll, 1969; MA, Christiran Seiminary, 1971; M Div, 1972; PhD, Univ of Missouri, 1985. *Appointments:* Minister, Delhi Church of Christ, 1969-73; Prof, Central Christian Coll, 1973-76; Acad Dean, Central Christian Coll, 1976-87; Pres, Florida Christian Coll, 1987-. *Publications:* 22 Articles; New Bible Dictionary Booklet; A Bright Light on Moonism; Adam Newsletter; Numerous Jounral Articles. *Memberships:* Adv Cttee, FL State Bd of Indep Colls and Univs; Regal Shores Homeowners; Commission on Computers of the American Assn of Bible Colleges; American Assn of Higher Educ; Phi Delta Kappa. *Honours include:* Eagle Scout; Kappa Delta P. *Hobbies:* Coin Collecting; Karate; Balkpacking; Shooting. *Address:* 1011 Osceola Blvd, Kissimmee, FL 34744, USA.7.15.139.145.

LOWENTHAL Armand, b. 7 Sept 1919, The Hague, Netherlands. Prof of Neurology & Neurochemistry. Widower, 1 s, 1 d. *Education include:* ULB, Fleurice Mercier Award, 1941; Univ of Geneva, faculty of Medicine, 1944; Univ of Geneva, Doctorate Thesis,

1945; Aggregation faculty of Medicine, 1959. *Appointments include:* Asst Internal Medicine, Geneva, 1944-45; Conslt Neurologist, Medico Surgical Inst, Charleroi, 1948-62; Conslt Hd of Dept of Neurology, Acad Hosp, Univ of Antwerp, 1984-85; Sec Treasurer Gen, World Federation of Neurology, 1985-. *Memberships include:* Belgian Soc of Neurology; Founding Mem European Soc for Neurochemistry; Honorary Mem Acad Brasillera de Neurologia; Hon Mem Gesellschaft Österreichischer Nervenärzte u Psychiater; American Soc of Neuroimaging. *Honours:* Chevalier, Order of Leopold II; Order of the Crown; Commander, Order of the Crown; Great Officer, Order of Leopold 11. *Address:* AZM, Lindendreef 1 2020 Antwerpen, Belgium.

LOWMAN John, b. 14 July 1950, Dorking, England. Prof. *Education:* BA, Sheffield, 1971; MA, York, 1976; PhD, Univ of British Columbia, 1983. *Appointments:* Simon fraser Univ, Asst Prof, 1983-87; Assoc Prof, 1987-91; Prof, 1991-. *Publications include:* Regulating Sex; Realism in Criminology; Crime Control and Policing in the 1990's. *Memberships:* Canadian Law & Soc Assn. *Honours:* Canada Council Doctoral Scholarship; Soc Sciences & Human Research Council Doctoral Scholarship; Killam Doctoral Scholarship. *Hobbies:* Tennis; Fishing; Birding. *Address:* Sch of Criminology, Simon Fraser Univ, Burnaby, BC, Canada, V5A 156.88.

LOWNIE Andrew James Hamilton, b. 11 Nov 1961, Kenya. Literary Agent. *Education:* Fettes; Westminster; Magdalene Coll, Cambridge, MA; Edinburgh Univ, MSc. *Appointments:* Dir, John Farqharson Literary Agents, 1986-88; Andrew Lownie Literary Agents, 1998-; Denniston & Lownie, 1991-. *Publications:* The Edinburgh Literary Companion; Essays in American Espionage. *Memberships:* Trustee; Iain Macleod Memorial Award; Frm Pres, Cambridge Union Soc; Parl Cand, Marklands West, 1992; VChmn, Conserv Grp for Eur; FRSA; FRGS. *Hobbies:* Music; Hill Walking. *Address:* 122 Beford Court Mansions, Bedford Square, London WL1B 3AH, England.

LOWRANCE Robert Stuart, b. 12 Feb 1906, Sansaba, Texas. Tchr. m. Willa Beckham, 29 Nov 1934, 1 d. *Education:* BS, Davidson Coll; MS, Emory Univ; PhD, World Univ. *Appointments:* Gaston IA, NC, High Sch, 1928-29; Troy, NC, High Sch, 1930-31; North Fulton High, 1931-71. *Publications:* Three Books of Poetry; Vesper Song. *Memberships:* Kiwanis; Presbyterian Church. *Honours:* Track Letter; Boxing Championship; Camp McClellan Wrestling Championship. *Hobbies:* Stamp Collecting. *Address:* 3747 Peachtree 1503, Atlanta, GA, 30319, USA.

LOWREY Robert Edward, b. 30 Aug 1940, Jacksonville, Texas. Prof of American Literature; Univ Press Dir. m. Pamela, 28 Apr 1983, 2 s, 1 d. *Education:* Texas A&M Univ, BA, 1958-62; MA, 1962-64; PhD, Louisiana State Univ, 1966-74; John Hopkins univ, 1976. *Appointments:* Instr, Louisiana State Univ, 1972-74; Asst Prof, Assoc Prof, Full Prof, Univ of Central Arkansas, 1976-; Dir, UCA Press, 1985-. *Publications include:* Thors Hammer; Hier & Prototype; Essays on the Poetry of Anne Sexton. *Memberships include:* Modern Language Assn; Natl Desktop Publ Assn; Ducks Unlimited. *Hobbies:* Painting; Hunting; Fishing; Reading. *Address:* UCA Press, 312 Augusta Street, Conway, AR 72032, USA.7.15.139

LOWRY John Patrick, b. 31 Mar 1920, Sydenham, Kent, England. Conslt. m. Sheilagh Mary Davies, 5 Apr 1952, 1 s, 1 d. *Education:* Wyggeston Grammer Sch; London Sch of Economics, 1949-52; Bach of Commerce. *Appointments:* Engrng Employers Federation, 1938-39, 1946-70; Various Posts British Leyland, 1970-81; Dir, Industrial Relations, Dir Personnel, advisory Conciliation & Arbitration, 1981-87. *Publications:* Employment Disputes & the Third Party. *Memberships:* Inst of Peronnel Mngt; British Inst of Mngt. *Honours:* CBE; Knight Bach. *Hobbies:* Theatre; Travel. *Address:* 31

Seaton Close, Lynden Gate, London SW15 3TJ, England.1.

LOYNMOON Yusef Noman, b. 6 Mar 1929, Bombay, India. Partner Founder, Intl Electronics Dir; Signet Electronics PVT Ltd; Mgr, Sound Tech Services. m. 26 Feb 1952, 1 s, 1 d. *Education:* Di Stxaviers Coll, 1952. *Appointments:* Mgrng Family Business; Founder Intl Electronics; Manufacture Elect Instr; Soundtechnical Serv PVt Ltd; Signet Electronics PIT Ltd. *Memberships:* Local Trade Assn; IERE. *Honours:* Instruments Mfr By Intel, Wisitex Award. *Hobbies:* Reading; Music. *Address:* Intl Electronics, 202 Champak Indl Estate 105, Sion East, Bombay 400 022, India.1.

LOZOVAYA Galina, b. 20 Nov 1935, Kiev, Ukraine. Biochemist. m. Alexander I Sidenko, 24 Apr 1970, 1 d. *Education:* Dip, Plant Physiologist, 1958, Postgrad studies, 1960-63, Cand biol sci, 1964, Dip, Sr Sci Worker, 1969, Kiev Univ. *Appointments:* Sr Lab Asst, 1958-60, Jr Rsch Student, 1963-68, Sr Sci Worker, 1968-, Inst Bot, Kiev. *Publications:* Over 120 incl: The principles of the evolutionary biochemistry of plants, 1982; Early evolution of photobiological systems, 1990. *Memberships:* All-Union Biochem Soc; Ukrainian Biochem Soc; Ukrainian Boton Soc. *Hobbies:* Music; Reading. *Address:* Institute of Botany, Academy of Sciences of Ukraine, Repin street 2, 252601 Kiev-GSP-1, Ukraine. 138, 152.

LU Chengxin, b. 12 Aug 1938, Wenzhou, China. Senior Engineer. m. 9 Apr 1967, 2 s, 1 d. *Education:* Grad, Engrng, Zhejiang Univ, Hangzhou, 1961. *Appointments:* Techn, Wenzhou Elec Machinery Factory, 1961-78; Asst Engr, 1978-79, Engr, 1980-84, Chief Engr, 1985-, Sr Engr, 1988-, Wenzhou Submersible Motor Pump Factory; Cons Engr, Wenzhou Mech Seals Factory. *Contributions to:* articles to profl jrnls. *Memberships:* Fellow, Chinese Sci Assn; Zhejiang Soc Elec Machinery and Power; Zhejiang Soc Agricl Machinery; Wenzhou Computer Soc; Wenzhou Power Soc; Wenzhou Chief Engrng Rsch Inst; Wenzhou Rsch Assn Mgmt and Sales; Chinese Jiu San Soc. *Hobby:* Table tennis. *Address:* 2-406, 17 Hetongqiao Rd, Wenzhou 325005, China. 52.

LU Chong Liang, b. 26 Dec 1938, Vietnam. Hospital Vice-Director. m. 23 Aug 1963, 2 s. *Education:* Med Coll, Tong Ji, 1957-63. *Appointments:* Surgeon, Tchr, 1963-78, Physn-in-charge, Lectr, Surgery, 1978-85, Assoc Prof, 1985-89, Guilin Med Coll and attached Hosp; Vice-Dir, Guilin Med Coll Hosp, 1989-. *Creative works:* 49 acad theses on gen surg in var domestic med publs; Has successfully improved operation method for thyroidectomy. *Memberships:* Dpty, Nat People's Congress; Coun, Guangxi Surg Soc; Vice-Chmn, Standing Comm, Xiu Feng Dist, Guilin People's Congress. *Honours:* Adv Element, Guiling Med Coll, 1978-90; Exemplary Tchr, Guilin City, 1984; Excellent Thesis Award, 1990. *Hobbies:* Gardening; Cooking. *Address:* Guiling Medical College Hospital, Guilin City, Guangxi Province, China.

LU Frank K, b. 17 Oct 1954, Taipei, Taiwan. University Educator and Consultant. m. Jean C Yang, 29 Oct 1983, 1 s. *Education:* Cambridge Univ, 1973-76; BA (Cantab); MA (Cantab); MSE, Princeton Univ, 1982; PhD, PA State Univ, 1987. *Appointments:* Served Singapore Armed Forces, 1976- 79: Army Off and Admin Asst, Min Def; Project Engr, ICOS Corp Am, NYC, USA, 1982-83; Asst Prof, Univ TX, Arlington, 1987-. *Publications:* Author or co-author, num jrnl articles and conf papers. *Memberships:* Sr Mbr, Am Inst Aeronautics and Astronautics; Am Phys Soc; Am Soc Engrng Educ; IEEE; Sigma Xi; Sigma Gamma Tau. *Honours:* UK and Singapore Govt Scholar, 1973-76; Guggenheim Fellow, Aeronautical Engrng Dept, 1979; John de Young Outstanding Tchng Award, 1991. *Hobbies:* Gardening; Travel; Reading. *Address:* Mechanical and Aerospace Engineering Department, University of Texas at Arlington, PO Box 19018, Arlington, TX 76019, USA. 7, 15, 143.

LU Guoyao, b. 14 Nov 1937, Taixian County, Jiangsu Province, China. Full Professor. m. Lian Dihua, 16 Jan 1963, 1 s, 1 d. *Education:* BA, 1960, MA, Grad School, 1964, Beijing Univ. *Appointments:* Dept Chinese Lang and Lit, Nanjing Univ, Nanjing, 1965-: Currently Full Prof and PhD Advsr for Hist of Chinese Lang. *Publications include:* The Cihai Dictionary (principal co-ed), 1979, 1989; On the Origin of the Standard Speech of the Ming Dynasty, 1985; A study on the history of the Taizhou and Nantong Dialect, 1988; Nancun Chuogeng Lu and the Wu Dialect of the Yuan Dynasty, 1989; The Rhyming of the Ci-poems of the Song Dunasty and its Comparison with the Rhyming of the Ci-poems of the Jin and Yuan Dynasties, 1991. *Memberships:* Trustee, Linguistic Soc China; Trustee, Phonology Assn China. *Honours:* Wang Li Mem Award, Disting Linguistic Contbn, 1986, 1989. *Hobby:* Reading, esp history. *Address:* Dept of Chinese Language and Literature, Nanjing University, Nanjing 210008, China.

LU Huan-zhang, b. 23 Feb 1934, Hebei, China. Surgeon. m. Xu Dong- qing, 1 July 1960, 2 s. *Education:* MD, Hebei Med Coll, 1959. *Appointments:* Surg Residency, 1959-64, Chief Resident, 1964-65, Tianjin Nankai Hosp; Jing Co Med Team, Hebei Province, 1965-66; Vis Surg, Dpty Chief Surg, Chief Surg, Prof, Tianjin Nankai Hosp, 1966-. *Publications:* Practice of Abdominal Surgery (co-author), 1990; A Manual of Laser Therapy (ed-in-chief), 1990; Clinical Duodenoscopy (ed-in-chief), 1991. *Memberships:* Tianjin Surg Soc; Standing Comm, Chinese Med Assn; Integration Traditional Chinese and Wn Med Soc; Standing Comm, Digestive Endoscopy Soc. *Honours:* City Adv Sci Tech Worker, 1984; 2nd Class Award, Sci and Technology, Herbal Medicine and Endoscopic Sphincterotomy in Choledocholithiasis, 1986; 3nd Class Award, Acute Severe Cholangitis Treated by Integrated Medicine, 1989; Nat Middle-Aged Expert, 1990; 2nd Class Award, National Admin Bur, Traditional Chinese Med, 1990; Moral Award, Municipal Pub Hlth Bur, 1990. *Hobby:* Tourism. *Address:* Tianjian Nankai Hospital, 122 Sanwei Road, Nankai District, Tianjin 300100, China.

LU Huiqiong, b. 14 July 1937, Fuzhou, Fujian, China. Professor in Computer Science. m. Chongguang Yang, 11 Mar 1967, 1 s. *Education:* Grad, Dept Maths, Beijing Univ, 1958. *Appointments:* Rsch, Computer Sci, 1958-85; Prof, Dept Dir, Inst Software Rsch, Chinese Acad Scis, Beijing, 1985-. *Creative works:* Designed and implemented list of software tools; Set up computer aided software environment; Many papers and collections of papers. *Memberships:* Comm Soft Engrng Technology, Nat Comm Standards on Computer and Info Processing Technology; Comm, Chinese Soc Off Automation; Hd, Working Grp Microcomputer Software, Chinese Assn Microcomputers. *Honours:* Adv Rschr, Inst Software Rsch, 1977, 1978; 2nd Prize, Acad Achievement, Chinese Acad Scis, 1980; 3rd Prize, Inst Software Chinese Acad Scis Software Tools Project, Nat Electronic Promoting Leading Grp, 1986. *Hobbies:* Classical music; Sightseeing. *Address:* No 1201, Bldg 901, Zhong Guan Cun, Beijing 100080, China. 152.

LU Qi-Hui, b. Mar 1936, Shanghai, China. Professor of Sculpture and Painting. m. Fang Zen-Xian, Jan 1960, 1 s. *Education:* Grad, Ctrl Art Acad, E China Br, 1955. *Career:* Sculptress, China Sculpture Factory, E China Br, 1955-61; Tchr, Shanghai Art School, 1961-65; Profl Sculptress, Shanghai Oil Painting and Sculpture Inst; Prof, 1988-; Exhibited: Nat Art Show, 20th Anniversary Chmn Mao's Speech, Yunnan, 1962; Large Show, Centenary of Lu Xun's birth, 1980; Contemporary Oil Painting of People's Republic of China, NYC; Chinese Art Fest Art Show, 1986; 7th Nat Art Show, 1989. *Creative works include:* Transplanting Rice Seedlings; Statue of Children Labourers, 1974; Statue of Lu Xun, Lu Xun Mus Shanghai, 1979; Angrily Seeking Verses against the Reign of Terror, 1980; Bada - an ancient Chinese Artist, bronze; Plateau in the Morning Sun, 1986, stone, 1986; Emotion at Plateau, 1989; A portrait statue of Zhang Zhong-Jing, bronze, 1990; A Portrait statue of Tibit Youth Sangji - Cairang, stone, 1990;

Assisted in design of man and woman workers sculpture, Nat Industry Exhib, 1960; Participant, creation sculpture for Chmn Mao Mem Hall, 1977; Statue of Wang Ge-Yi, Chinese Artist, Wang Ge-Yi Mus Nan-Tong, 1992, Bronze. *Membership:* Chinese Artists Assn. *Honours:* Merit Prize, Transplanting Rice Seedlings, Shanghai Youth Art Show, 1957; Prize, Bada - An Ancient Artist, Shanghai; Plateau in the Morning collected by Chinese Art Mus, 1988. *Hobby:* Chinese painting. *Address:* 100 Nong-Gong Alley, Hong Qao Road, Shanghai, China. 34, 190.

LU Tan, b. 23 Feb 1932, Changshu County, Jiangsu Province, China. Professor of Astrophysics; Director of Astrophysics Institute. m. Jingyu Zhou, 20 Jan 1966, 2 s, 1 d. *Education:* Grad, Dept Phys, Beijing Univ. *Appointments:* Rsch Asst, Nuclear Phys Inst, Beijing, 1957-58; lectr, Engrng Inst, 1958-69; Telecommunications Instruments Factory, Nanjing, 1969- 78; Assoc Prof, 1978-81, Full Prof, 1981-, Dept Astron, Nanjing Univ; Dir, Astrophys Inst, Nanjing Univ, 1979-; Vis Prof, Dept Applied Sci, City Polytechnic Hong Kong, Kowloon, 1991. *Publications:* Over 100 papers on particle phys and astrophys, mainly on hadron structure, weak processes, neutron star phys and cosmology, 1962-; 2 books: Particle Physics; From Electron To Quark. *Memberships:* Int Astronomical Union; Chinese Astronomical Soc, Pres High Energy Commn 1982-85, Mbr 5th and 6th Coun 1985-. *Honours:* Prize, Nat Sci Meeting China, 1978; 1st Prize, Sci Rsch Neimenggu, 1980; 3rd Nat Prize, Natural Sci China, 1987; Silver Medal Hon, 1990, Gold Medal Hon, 1991, Outstanding Lifelong Achievements, ABI. *Hobby:* Listening to music esp classical music. *Address:* Department of Astronomy, Nanjing University, Nanjing 210008, China. 139, 151, 152.

LU Tianjiao, b. 10 Dec 1934, Shanghai, China. Stamp Designer; Senior Industrial Artist. m. Liu Shuoren, 6 Feb 1960, 1 s. *Education:* Hangzhou Nat Art School, 1950-53; Ctrl Acad Fine Arts, 1953-54. *Appointments:* Stamp Designer (1st woman in China), Min Post and Telecommunications, 1954-. *Creative works:* Stamp designs of Dr Sun Yat-sen, Mme Song Qingling, Zhou Enlai, Dr Norman Bethune; Stamps featuring women and children, sports, historical relics, important events; Thesis on stamp designing. *Memberships:* Chinese Artists Assn. *Honours:* Best Stamps Prize for Anniversary of Zhou Enlai's Death, Tri-coloured Pottery of Tang Dynasty, 30th Anniversary of the Founding of the PRC, and Peony, 1980; National Annual Prize for Ancient Coins of China, Am Philatelist and Numismatic Assn, 1982; Prize for Selected Paintings of Wu Changshuo, and Song Qingling, 1982. *Hobbies:* Loves collecting folk toys; Toy making; Music lover; Watching sports and dance performances. *Address:* China Stamp Corporation, Hepingmen, Beijing 100051, China.

LU Wan-zhen, b. 29 Sept 1924, Tienjin, China. Chemist. m. Min Enze, 14 June 1950, 1 d. *Education:* BS, Nat Ctrl Univ, 1946; MS, Univ IL, USA, 1948; PhD, OH State Univ, 1951; Postdoct, Chem Dept, NWn Univ, 1951-53. *Appointments:* Analytical Chem, Corn Products Refining Co, 1953-55; Dept Dir, Petroleum Rsch Inst, 1955-83; Chief Engr, Rsch Inst Petroleum Processing, 1983-. *Publications:* Evaluation of Chinese Crudes; Petroleum Analysis. *Memberships:* Chinese Petroleum Soc; Int Union Pure and Applied Chem; Vice-Chmn, Chinese Assn Chromatography; Standing Comm, Chinese Women's Assn. *Honours:* Disting Alumnus, OH State Univ, 1983. *Hobbies:* Reading; Music. *Address:* 18 Xue Yuan Road, Beijing 100083, China.

LU Yaochen, b. 6 Feb 1940, Yixing, Jiangsu, China. Pottery Artist. m. Li Hefeng, 1 Oct 1963, 2 s. *Education:* Gaocheng Primary School, 1948-53, Gaocheng Middle School, 1954-56, Yixing. *Appointments:* Violet Sand Arts and Crafts Factory, Yixing, 1958-71; Violet Sand Pottery Art Rsch Inst, 1972-88; Hd, Lu Yaochen Studio, Ceramic Mus, Yixing, 1988-. *Creative works:* Over 1000 pottery art works incl some collected by China Palace

Mus, Ziguangge of State Coun, Tianjin Mus, Yixing Mus; Created technique of Violet Sand Twisted Roughcast; A Collection of Lu Yaochen's Pottery Art, publication; Theses: On the characteristics of the formation of Violet Sand Pottery Art; On the Inheritance and Originality of the Violet Sand Pottery Art; The Body Change of the Violet Sand Pot. *Memberships:* China Ancient Ceramic Rsch Soc; China Artists Assn Arts and Crafts; China Soc Ind Design. *Honours:* 2nd Award, Combined Bamboo Teapot with Cups, Comparison and Appraisal of Chinese Ceramics, 1980; Fine Award, Bamboo Circle Wien Pot with Cups, Chinese Tourism Products, 1982; 1st Prize, Chinese Ceramic Art Design, 1985; Named: Master of Fertile Prod; Magician of Pot Technique. *Hobbies:* Billiards; Wushu; Acting in plays. *Address:* Lu Yaochen Studio, The Ceramic Museum, Yixing, Jiangsu Province, China.

LU Yaoru, b. 27 May 1931, Fuzhou City, Fujian Province, China. Professor of Geology. m. 11 Jan 1963, 2 d. *Education:* Dept Geology, Tsinghua Univ, Peking, 1950-52; Dept Hydrogeology and Engrng Geology, Beijing Geological Coll, 1952-53; Learning from for and Chinese experts, 1953-55. *Appointments:* Ldr, Hui River, Guangting, 3 Yangtze River Gorges, SW China, other Engrng Geology or Karst Rsch teams, 1955-62; Dir, Karst Rsch Sect, 1963-82, Dir, Engrng Geology Rsch Sect, 1975-82, Prof, 1984-, Inst Hydrogeology and Engrng Geology, Min Geology and Mineral Resources, Zhengding; Sr Expert, Albania, 1973; Prof: Chinese Acad Geological Scis, 1984-; Rsch Ctr, State Nationalities Affairs Comm, 1988-. *Publications:* The Development of Karst in China and some of its Hydrogeological and Engineering Geological Conditions, 1973; Karst in China, 1976; Karst in China - Landscapes, Types, Rules, 1986; Over 50 papers, 1958-91; 5 volumes, 1959-91. *Memberships:* Geological Soc China, Karst Geological Comm 1978-, Engrng Comm 1988; Sec, Speleological Soc, Geological Soc China; Chinese Working Grp, 299 Project, Int Geological Comparison Prog. *Honours:* Cert Merit, Nat Sci and Tech Conf, 1978; Medal, Cert Merit, Geological Scis, Min Geology and Mineral Resources, 1987; Cert Merit, Nat Splendid Sci and Tech Publs, State News and Press Admin, 1988. *Hobbies:* Reading; Field investigation; Travel; Photography; Symphony music; Swimming; Ballroom dancing. *Address:* Institute of Hydrogeology and Engineering Geology, Ministry of Geology and Mineral Resources, Zhengding, Hebei 050803, China.

LUBUSKA Adam Zbigniew, b. 14 Dec 1925, Lwow, Poland. Chairman of Metal Science and Heat Treatment Chair. m. (1) 1 d, (2) Elzbieta Wieczorek, 9 June, 1984, 1 d. *Education:* BSc, Mech, 1952, MSc, Mech, Silesian Polytechnic; DSc, 1962; Prof, State nomination, 1976. *Appointments:* Served Polish Army, Mid East, 1942-43; Pilot, Polish Air Force, UK, 1943- 47; Asst, Silesian Polytechnic, 1951-52; Hd, Metal Sci Dept, Inst Ferrous Metall, Gliwice, 1952-77; Hd, Steel Application Dept, Inst Materials Economy, Dabrowa Gornicza, 1977-80; Hd, Metal Sci and Heat Treatment Chair, Saint-Cross Polytechnic, Kielce, 1980-92. *Publications:* Books in Polish on phys of metals and on high strength low-alloy steels; About 70 others incl results of work on dev of microalloyed steels in Poland and dev of controlled rolling in Poland. *Memberships:* VP, Org Solidarity of Polish Combattants; Formerly: Polish Metal Sci Assn, Polish Register of Shipping; Some consultative grps. *Honours:* Polish Air Force Medal, 1946; Brit War Medal, 1946; Medal of Victory and Freedom, 1974; 2 Golden Crosses of Merit, 1975; Cross, Polonia Restituta, 1989; 8 State Prizes for tech achievements, 1970-77. *Hobbies:* Literature concerning history, archaeology, religions of the people of various countries in the world; Painting incl cultivation of painting. *Address:* Politechnika Swietokrzyska, Al Tysiaclecia 7, 25-314 Kielce, Poland.

LUCIUK Lubomyr Yaroslav, b. 9 July 1953, Kingston, Ontario, Canada. Assistant Professor of Geography. m. Alexandra Chyczij, 13 May 1990, 1 d. *Education:* BSc Hons, Geog, 1976, MA, Geog, 1979, Queen's Univ; PhD, Geog, Univ Alta, 1984; Postdoct Fellow, Dept Geog, Univ

Toronto, 1984-88. *Appointments:* Rsch Fellow, 1988-90, Adj Asst Prof, 1990-, Dept Geog, Queen's Univ, Kingston; Asst Prof, Dept Pol and Econs, Royal Mil Coll Can, Kingston, 1990-. *Publications:* 13 books incl: Ukrainians in the Making: Their Kingston Story, 1980; Anglo-American Perspectives on the Ukrainian Question 1938-1951: A Documentary Collection, 1987; A Time for Atonement: Canada's First National Internment Operations and the Ukrainian Canadians 1914-1920, 1988; Creating A Landscape: A Geography of Ukrainians in Canada (w B Kordan), 1989; Searching For Place: Canada's Ukrainians and their Encounter with the Displaced Persons of Europe, 1992; 3 book chapts; 2 booklets; 5 articles in refereed jrnls; 10 popular articles; 14 book reviews. *Memberships:* Can Assn Goegs; Can Ethnic Studies Assn; Can Inst Int Affairs; Can Slavists Assn; Can Comm Study of 2nd World War; Assn Am Geogs; Chmn, Ukrainian Can Centennial Comm Inc, 1988-91. *Honours:* Grad Scholarship: Queen's Univ, 1976-77, Ont, 1977-78; Doct Fellowship: 1979-82, Postdoct Fellowship, 1985-87, Can Rsch Fellowship, 1988-90, Social Scis and Humanities Rsch Coun Can; Doct Thesis Fellowship, 1982-84, Neporany Postdoct Fellowship, 1984-85, Can Inst Ukrainian Studies, Univ Alta; Edward Scheyer Fellowship, Ukrainian Studies, 1984-85; Postdoct Fellowship, Sec State Multiculturalism, 1986-87; John Sopinka Award, Excellence in Ukrainian Studies, Ukrainian Studies Fndn Chair, 1989. *Hobbies:* Writing; Jogging; Herpetology; Travel; Reading. *Address:* Department of Politics and Economics, Royal Military College of Canada, Kingston, Ontario, Canada K7K 5LO. 142.

LUDWINIAK Zdzislawa, b. 2 Aug 1958, Wolomin, Poland. Painter. *Education:* Grad, Fac Graphic Art, Acad Fine Arts, Warsaw, 1987. *Appointments:* Drawing Studio, Acad Fine Arts, Warsaw, 1987-. *Creative works:* Paintings; Drawings; Graphic Art. *Address:* ul Matejki 2, 05-200 Wolomin, Poland.

LUE Fu-hua, b. 31 July 1907, Shandong Province, China. Professor of Pharmacology. m. Gu Yi-qi, 6 June 1955, 3 s, 1 d. *Education:* Grad, Med Fac, Tung-chi Univ, 1932; Dr med, Univ Freiburg, Germany, 1934. *Appointments:* Prof, Pharmacology, Dir, Pharmacological Dept, Tong-ji Med Univ, Wuhan, 1936-86. *Creative works include:* 1st proved experimentally carcinogenity of tobacco, 1934 (results confirmed by Schuerch and Winterstein, 1935); Experimental production of Carcinoma by Tobacco on Rabbit, article, 1934; Developed Divasid, cardiotonic derived from Chinese Strophanthus (divaricatus), accepted by Chinese Pharmacopoeia, 1963. *Memberships:* Mbr, then Hon Mbr, Chinese Pharmacopoeia Comm, Hlth Min; Dpty, 3rd Nat People's Cong; Rep to 2nd to 7th Municipal People's Congress, Wuhan; Chinese Pharmacological Soc, VP 1979-84, Chmn 1st Advsry Comm 1984-90; Hon Chmn, Cardiovascular Pharmacological Comm, Chinese Pharmacological Soc, Chmn 1980-86. *Honours:* Awards, dev of Divasid, Nat Sci Meeting, 1978. *Hobbies:* Phonology; Poetry; Flowers. *Address:* Dept of Pharmacology, Tong-ji Medical University, Wuhan 430030, China. 139.

LUECKEN Peter Grant, b. 18 Jan 1950, Brooklyn, New York, USA. Doctor of Chiropractic. m. Roxanne Sammis, 20 Sept 1975. *Education:* BA, Hofstra Univ, 1972; DC, NY Chiropractic Coll, 1975; Dipl, Nat Bd Chiropractic Examiners; Fellow, Am Chiropractic Coll. *Appointments:* Dir, Prog Dev and Alumni Affairs, NY Chiropractic Coll, 1975-78; Assoc, Rockaway Chiropractic Clin, 1976-78; Practising Chiropractic Phys, Dir, Fairfield Chiropractic Off, Fairfield, CT, 1978-; Pres, Roxy Realty; Pres, Luecken Arabians. *Publications:* Chiropractic and Sports Medicine, article; Attitudes of Health and Success, lecture tapes. *Memberships:* Advsry Bd, Kentuckiana Children's Ctr; NY Chiropractic Coll Alumni Assn, Past Dir; Fairfield Chmbr of Comm, Past VP Profl Div, Past Dir; Parker Chiropractic Rsch Fndn; Am Chiropractic Assn; Ct Chiropractic Assn; Int Chiropractic Assn; Fndn Chiropractic Educ and Rsch; Am Hlth Assn; Int Assn Chiropractic Industrial Injury Consultants; Am Assn

Chiropractic Ins Consultants; Fairfield Rotary Club, Past VP Int Affairs; Int Arabian Horse Assn; CT Arabian Horse Assn; Pyramid Soc. *Honours:* KY Col, C'wlth KY, 1976; Disting Serv Citation, NY Chiropractic Coll, 1977; Outstanding Serv Award, Fairfield Chmbr of Comm, 1981; Disting Ldrship, Nat Fndn-March of Dimes; Kt, Sovereign Mil Order Temple of Jerusalem. *Hobbies:* Breeding Egyptian Arabian horses; Opera. *Address:* 527 Tunxis Hill Road, Fairfield, CT 06430, USA. 117.

LUGON Jerome, b. 10 Oct 1937, Martigny, Switzerland. International Civil Servant. m. Therese Frizon, 16 May 1964, 1 s, 1 d. *Education:* Law degree,, Univ Geneva, 1961; Coll Europe, Bruges, Belgium, 1962; High Studies Dip, European Studies, Univ Saarbrucken, FRG, 1963. *Appointments:* Fed Off for Econ Rels in Bern, Integration Serv, 1964-70; Swiss Permanent Mission to UN, Geneva, 1970-74; Dept Dir, Secretariat, European Free Trade Assn, Geneva, 1980-. *Address:* EFTA Secretariat, CH-1211 Geneva 20, Switzerland.

LUH Jiang, b. 24 June 1932, Chejiang, China. Professor of Mathematics. m. Tsu-yunn Ma, 25 July 1956, 2 s, 1 d. *Education:* BS, Nat Taiwan Normal Univ, 1955; MS, Univ NE, USA, 1959; PhD, Univ MI, 1963. *Appointments:* Assoc Prof, IN State Univ, USA, 1963-66; Assoc Prof, Wright State Univ, 1966-68; Assoc Prof, 1968-71, Prof, Maths, 1971-, NC State Univ, Raleigh. *Publications:* Over 50 articles in math jrnls. *Memberships:* Am Math Soc; Math Assn Am. *Hobby:* Collecting stamps. *Address:* Department of Mathematics, North Carolina State University, Box 8205, Raleigh, NC 27695, USA.

LUI Ming Wah, b. 4 Apr 1938, China. Industrialist. m. Adeline, 1970, 1 s, 1 d. *Education:* Univ of NSW, Australia, 1968; Univ of Saskatchewan, Canada, 1973. *Appointments:* Chief Mgtallurgist, Chiap Hua Ind, 1963-65; Research Fellow, Univ of Sask, 1973-76; Deputy Gen Mgr, Meyer Aluminium Ltd, 1976-81; Mgrng Dir, Keystone Electronics, 1981-. *Memberships include:* Inst of Metallurgists; Chinese Mfrs Assn of Hong Kong; Royal Golf Club; Pacific Club. *Hobbies:* Reading; Chinese Poetry; Music. *Address:* A2, 12F 67 Beacon Hill Road, Kowloon Tong, Hong Kong.52.132.

LUKASIK Seweryn Jan, b. 27 Mar 1919, Chwalibogowicz, Poland. Physician. m. Walentyna Kasperek, 25 Dec 1948, 3 d. *Education:* Dipl Physn, 1948; Dr Med Sci, 1951; Asst Prof, 1963; Prof, 1970; Full Prof, 1980. *Appointments:* Asst, Dept Internal Diseases, 1948-51, Lectr, Dept Internal Diseases, 1951-63, Asst Prof, 1963-70, Hd, Clin, Dept Cardiology, 1970-90, Med Acad Wroclaw. *Publications:* About 150 comprising 20 monographs or handbooks, 130 articles in nat and int med jrnls in field of internal and cardiological diseases. *Memberships:* Nat Supvsr, Internal Diseases Poland, 1971-91; Presiding Off, Drug Comm, Hlth Min, 1974-92; Polish Soc Internal Diseases, Pres 1976-82; Bd, Polish Cardiological Soc, 1980-90; Ed Bd, 3 med jrnls, 1970-92. *Honours:* Decorated w several orders and medals of merit; Hon Mbr: Polish Soc Sports Med, 1984; DRG Soc Internal Diseases, 1985; Polish Cardiological Soc, 1990; Polish Soc Internal Diseases, 1991. *Hobbies:* Tourism; Tennis. *Address:* ul Szymanowskiego 10, 51-609 Wroclaw, Poland.

LUMPE Adolf Ingo, b. 20 October 1927, Falkenau, Bohemia, Czechoslovakia. Academic Director. m. Johanna Reingruber, 18 July 1967, 1 d. *Education:* 1st Pub Exam, Munich, 1951; Dr phil, Univ Munich, 1952. *Appointments:* Fellow, Thesaurus linguae Latinae, Munich, 1954-71; Acad Instr, Acad Dir, Univ Augsburg, 1971-. *Publications:* Several articles in Reallexikon fur Antike und Christentum, 1959-; Die Elementenlehre in der Naturphilosophie des Joachim Jungius, 1984. *Membership:* Verein fur Lubeckische Geschichte und Altertumskunde. *Hobbies:* Philology; History of sciences, philosophy and religion. *Address:* Auenweg 20 a, D-8900 Augsburg 22, Germany.

LUMSDEN OF CUSHNIE David Gordon Allen d'Aldecamb, b. 25 May 1933, Quetta, Baluchistan. Herald; Garioch Pursuivant of Arms. *Education:* Bedford School; Jesus Coll, Cambridge, 1955-58; MA (Cantab). *Appointments:* Exec, BAT, serving Africa, India, En Europe, Far East, 1959-82; Dir, Heritage Porcelain Ltd; Dir, Heritage Recordings Ltd. *Contributions to:* The Muster Roll of Prince Charles Edward's Army 1745-46, 1984. *Memberships:* Co-Fndr, Castles of Scotland Preservation Trust, 1985; Co-Fndr, Scottish Historic Organs Trust, 1991; 1745 Assn and Scottish Mil Hist Soc, Pres 1991; Coun Mbr, Royal Stuart Soc; Lloyds, 1985; Clubs: Brooks's; Pitt (Cambridge); Leander, Puffins (Edinburgh); Hidalgos (Madrid). *Honours:* Kt of Justice, Sacred Mil Constantinian Order of St George, 1978; Kt of Malta, Hons Devotion, 1980; FSA (Scot), 1984. *Hobbies:* Music; Architecture; Heraldry; Scottish History; Rowing. *Address:* Leithen Lodge, Innerleithen, Peeblesshire EH44 6NW, Scotland.

LUNSFORD Julius R Jr, b. 22 Jan 1915, Weston, Georgia, USA. Attorney. m. Mary Vann, 24 Aug 1941, 3 s. *Education:* Mercer Univ, Macon, GA, 1931-34; JD, Univ GA Law School, 1936; Admitted: GA State Bar, 1936; US Ct Custom and Patent Appeals, 1953; US Ct Mil Appeals, 1955; US Supreme Ct, 1955; DC State Bar, 1975; US Ct Appeals for Fed Circuit, 1982. *Appointments:* Asst VP, Mgr, Trademarks and Unfair Competition Dept, Coco-Cola Co, 1936-75; Capt. US Navy, 1942-45; Adj Prof, Emory Univ Law School, Atlanta, GA, 1960-63; Ptnr, Beveridge, DeGrandi, Kline & Lunsford, Atlanta, 1975-79; Sr Ptnr, Hurt, Richardson, Garner, Todd & Cadenhead, Atlanta, 1980-87; Ptnr, Jones, Askew & Lunsford, Atlanta, 1987-; Adj Prof, Mercer Univ School Law, Macon, 1990, 1991; Lectr in field. *Publications:* Over 60 articles in var trademark publs and Law Reviews. *Memberships:* US Trademark Assn, Pres 1971-72, Exec VP 1970-71, VP 1964-65, 1967-69, Chmn Exec Comm 1971-72, Bd Dirs 1959-66, 1967-72,1974-77, Hon Chmn, Bd Dirs, 1972-73; Atlanta Bar Assn; Am Bar Assn, Chmn, Trademark Div, 1962-63, Chmn, Unfair Competition Comm, 1957-58, 1959-61, Chmn, State Trademark Rights and Statutes Comm, 1968-69; Lawyers Club Atlanta; GA Bar Assn; Kiwanis Club Atlanta; Kappa Alpha Order; Bd Trustees, Mercer Univ; Phi Delta Phi. *Hobbies:* Reading; Sports fan and spectator. *Address:* Jones, Askew & Lunsford, 37th Floor, 191 Peachtree Street, Atlanta, GA 30303, USA. 7, 16, 163.

LUO Chenglie, b. 9 May 1935, Jining City, China. Professor of History; Research Institute Administrator. m. Liu Guilin, 1 Oct 1970, 2 s, 1 d. *Education:* Grad, Dept Hist, Shandong Normal Univ, Jinan, 1956. *Appointments:* Asst, Lectr, Assoc Prof, Dept Hist, 1956-83, Assoc Prof, Prof, Dpty Dir, Rsch Inst Confucius, 1983-, Qufu Normal Univ, Qufu. *Publications:* Jinan Massacre, 1956; From Juye Religious Case to Shandong Yihotuan, 1959; Stories About Festivals and Folk Customs, 1959; A Collection of Archives in Confucius Mansion, 23 vols (dpty ed-in-chief), 1980- 83; Confucius, 1985; Qufu, 1986; The Annals of Jining, 1990; 200 essays on hist, archaeology, other fields. *Memberships include:* Coun, China Confucius Funds; Deputy Dir, Histl Relics Assn; Dpty Hd, Yanzi Study Assn; Deputy Hd, China Sunzi and Qi Culture Study Assn. *Honours:* Title of Adv Worker, Shandong Province, 1958. *Hobbies:* Beijing opera; Classical Chinese poetry. *Address:* Research Institute of Confucius, Qufu Normal University, Qufu, Shandong 273165, China.

LUO Fu Wu, b. 30 Oct 1930, Suzhou, China. Professor of Civil Engineering. m. Wang Cun Yan, 10 July 1953, 1 s, 1 d. *Education:* BEng, Tsinghua Univ, 1952. *Appointments:* Hd, Constrn Site, 1952, Sect Chief, Bldg Design, 1954, Asst, Lectr, Assoc Prof, Prof, Civil Engrng Dept, 1953, 1957, 1979, 1989-, Dpty Dir, Educ Inst, 1982, Tsinghua Univ, Beijing. *Creative works:* Author: Case Study of Quality in Building Design and Construction, 1976; Elementary Members of Reinforced Concrete Structure, 1978, 1985, 1987; Design of Masonry Building Structure, 1979, 1990; Design of Single-Storey Factory Structure, 1986, 1989; Theory of Teaching/Learning in Higher Engineering Education, 1988; Concepts, Systems and Estimate of Building Structure for Architects and Engineers, 1990; Accreditation and Evaluation of Colleges and Universities, 1990; Chief Designer: Students Hostel, Classroom Hall, Hydraulic Dept Hall, Tsinghua Univ Main Hall, 1954, 1955, 1957; Factory bldgs, Beijing Heavy Machinery Factory, 1958; Structure design of State Theatre, 1959; Hostels and meeting halls for mil use, 1972-73. *Memberships:* Beijing Su-Ping Scholarship Assn, Pres 1984; Educ Soc, Tsinghua Univ, Sec Gen 1986; Dpty Sec Gen, Int Symposium Higher Engrng Educ, 1989. *Honours:* Special Hon Award, Capital Constrn, Tsinghua Univ, 1954; Model Worker, Beijing, 1959; Adv Worker, Civil Engrng Dept, 1980, Adv Worker, 1982, 2nd Class Award, Tchng Reformation, 1988, 1st Class Award, Textbook Evaluation, 1989, Tsinghua Univ; Hon Award, Imparting Knowledge and Educating Students, 1984; 2nd Class Award, Excellent Theses, Higher Engrng Educ Soc, 1987; 1st Class Award, Outstanding Achievement, Educ Sci, China, 1990. *Hobbies:* Table tennis; Calligraphy; Literature. *Address:* Civil Engineering Department, Tsinghua University, Beijing 100084, China.

LUO Rong-qu, b. 29 Aug 1927, Chengdu, Sichuan, China. Professor of History; Educator. m. Zhou Yin-ru, 3 Feb 1950, 2 d. *Education:* SW Associated Univ, 1945-46; BA, Peking Univ, 1949. *Appointments:* Rsch Fellow, Ed, Nat Assn Sino-Soviet Friendship, Beijing, 1949-56; Lectr, Assoc Prof, Prof, Dept Hist, Peking Univ, 1956-. *Publications:* The Great Anti-fascist War, 1980; The Mystery of Discovery of America by the Chinese, 1988; From Westernization to Modernization, 1990. *Memberships:* VP, Beijing Histl Assn; Chmn, Assn Study of Latin-American Hist China; Coun, Chinese Soc Pacific Reg Hist; Comm Mbr, China Assn Oriental Culture Studies; Assoc Mbr, Inst Hist of European Expansion, Leiden Univ. *Honours:* Special Stipend, State Coun, 1991. *Hobbies:* Chinese calligraphy and painting. *Address:* 46-407 Zhong Guan Yuan, Beijing 100080, China.

LUO Yu-ming b. 8 July 1951. m. Ruan Shu-qing, 1978 *Education:* Grad, Classic Chinese Lit, Dept of Chinese Lang and Lit, Fudan Univ, 1977. *Appointments:* Tchr, Lectr, Dept of Chinese Lang and Lit, Fudan Univ, 1977-. *Publications:* A commentary on Xu Wen-chang, 1987; Outrageous Schemes and Plots in Chinese History, 1989; The Wailing of the Pathtic Songs - Talented Poets in Southern China during the Middle of the Ming Dynasty, 1990; Literature during the Southern and Northern Dynasties, 1991; Co-ed, Ci Hai, an all inclusive Chinese Dictionary, 1989; 30 essays on classic Chinese literature and philosophy published in various professional periodicals. *Memberships:* Shanghai Assn of Classic Chinese Lit. *Hobbies:* Playing Weiqi; Reading; Travelling. *Address:* Department of Chinese Language and Literature, Fudan University, Shanghai 200433, China.

LUSH Denzil Anton, b. 18 July 1951, Southsea, England. Solicitor. *Education:* BA, 1973, MA, 1974, Univ Coll, London; Coll Law, Guildford, 1978; Admitted as Solicitor, 1978; Corpus Christi Coll, Cambridge, 1982-83; LLM, 1983. *Appointments:* Ptnr, Anstey Sargent & Probert, Solicitors, Exeter, 1985-. *Publications:* The Encyclopaedia of Forms and Precedents, 5th Ed: Vol 26, Minors; 2nd Vol 31, Powers of Attorney. *Memberships:* Law Soc; Medico-Legal Soc. *Hobbies:* Admitted as Reader (Church of England), Wells Cathedral, 2 Oct 1982; Watching football and cricket. *Address:* 5 Barnfield Crescent, Exeter EX1 1RF, England.

LUSIS-GRINBERGA Elina, b. 1 Dec 1966, Riga, Latvia. Textile Artist. m. Gints Lusis-Grinbergs, 15 Mar 1992. *Education:* Latvian Acad Arts, 1984-89. *Appointments:* Chief, Mus Fund, Latvian Acad Arts, 1990-. *Creative works include:* Tapestries: Dark Night, Green Grass; Fashion Theatre; The Flight; The Sisters; Composition

I, II. *Memberships:* Young Artists Union Latvia. *Hobbies:* Knitting; Working in the garden. *Address:* A Pumpura Street 5-7B, 226010 Riga-10, Latvia.

LUSSKY Warren A, b. 16 Apr 1919, Chicago, Illinois, USA. Professor Emeritus. m. Mildred Joann Island, 12 June 1948. *Education:* BA, Univ CO, 1946; MA, Dip Lib Sci, Univ Denver, 1948. *Appointments:* Asst Libn, Pacifie Luth Coll, 1948-49; Libn, Hopkins Tn Lib, Stanford Univ, CA, 1950; Libn, Rocky Mt Coll, 1950-55; Lib Dir, NE Wesleyan Univ, 1955- 56; Lib Dir, 1956-85, Prof Emeritus, 1985-, TX Luth Coll, San Antonio. *Creative works:* Rsch and publs on design and functions of coll lib bldgs; Prin contbr to design of TX Luth Coll Lib Bldg. *Membership:* Am Lib Assn. *Honours:* Mbr, accrediting teams for coll libs, TX Educ Agcy, several times; Lib Cons on coll libs; Chmn, Vice-Chmn, TX Lib Assn Dist, 1965-66; Dir, 1968-85, Pres, 1976-78, Coun Rsch and Acad Libs. *Address:* 359 Irvington Dr, San Antonio, TX 78209, USA. 7.

LUSTIG Ernst, b. 12 Sept, 1921, Gleiwitz, Germany. Chemist. m. 9 Feb 1951, 1 s, 2 d. *Education:* Dr Chem, Univ Buenos Aires, 1948; PhD, MIT, 1957. *Appointments:* Tchng Asst, Phys Chem, Univ Buenos Aires, Argentina, 1948-49; Chief, Rsch and Dev Lab, Sylvania Lix-Klett, Buenos Aires, 1949-53; Tchng Asst, 1953-54, Rsch Asst, 1954-57, MIT, USA; Rsch Chem, DuPont Co, Wilmington, DE, 1957-58; Hd, Div Phys Chem, Off Saline Water, WAsh DC, 1958-59; Sci Researcher, 1959-62, Hd, Sect Instrumental Analysis, 1962-69, Rsch Div, Dept Rsch, Food and Drug Admin; Pt-time Lectr, Georgetown Univ, Wash DC and Grad School, Nat Insts Hlth, Bethesda, MD; Hd, Div Molecular Structure, Temporary Vice-Dir and Pres, Coun Scientists, 1970-86, Emeritus, 1986-, Gesellschaft fur Molekularbiologische Forschung (later Gesellschaft fur Biotechnologische Forschung), Braunschweig-Stockheim, Germany; Pub Translator, English, Spanish, German. *Publications:* Book: Computer Assistance in the Analysis of High-Resolution NMR Spectra (co-author); About 35 publs in int jrnls. *Memberships:* Am Chem Soc; Gesellschaft Deutscher Chemiker; Fellow, Sigma Xi; Fellow, Wash (DC) Acad Scis, Fndr, Div Magnetic Resonance; Fndr, Former Bd Mbr, Assn Old-Town Wolfenbuttel. *Honours:* Award of Merit, Food and Drug Admin, 1965. *Hobbies:* Piano; Mushrooms; Application of EDP in the humanities; History of Jews of Upper Silesia esp of Gleiwitz. *Address:* Rossittenweg 10, D;3340 Wolfenbuttel, Germany. 43, 92.

LUX Jonathan Sidney, b. 30 Oct 1951, London, England. Solicitor. m. Simone Ittah, 3 Sept 1979, 1 s, 2 d. *Education:* LLB, Univ Nottingham, 1973; Postgrad, Law, Univ Aix-Marseille, France, 1973-74; Law Soc Profl Exams, Pt II, 1974-75; Admitted as Solicitor, 1977; Admitted as Solicitor, Hong Kong, 1986. *Appointments:* Articled Clerk, 1975-77, Asst Solicitor, 1977-83, Ptnr, 1983-, Maritime Solicitors, Ince & Co, City of London. *Publications:* The Law of Tug, Tow and Pilotage, 1982, The Law and Practice of Marine Insurance and Average, co-author, 1987; Var articles. *Memberships:* Law Soc; Supporting Mbr, London Maritime Arbitrators Assn; Freedom, City of London; Liveryman, Worshipful Co Solicitors; Int Bar Assn, Vice-Chmn Maritime and Transport Law Comm; Assoc, Chartered Inst Arbitrators. *Honours:* Nottingham Univ Law Dept Exhib, 1972; French Govt Scholarship, 1973-74. *Hobbies:* Single-seater motor racing; Golf; Gardening; Opera; Reading. *Address:* 7 Holt Close, London N10 3HW, England.

LUXMOORE Christopher Charles, The Rgt Revd, b. 9 Apr 1926, Boroghbridge, Yorkshire, England. Assistant Bishop; Provost. m. Judith Johnstone, 12 Apr 1955, 4 s, 1 d. *Education:* Sedbergh School, 1940-44; Trinity Coll, Cambridge, 1947-50; BA, 1950, MA, 1953, Cambridge; Chichester Theological Coll, 1950-52. *Appointments:* Army, 1944-47; Asst Curate, S John the Bapt, Newcastle-upon-Tyne, 1952-55; Priest-in-charge, S Bede's Ecclesiastical Dist, 1955-57, Vicar, 1957-58,

Newsham; Rector, Sangre Grande, Trinidad, 1958- 66; Vicar, Headingley, Leeds, 1967-81; Proctor in Convocation, Mbr, Gen Synod, 1975-81; Hon Canon, Ripon Cathedral, 1980-81; Precentor, Canon Residentiary, Chichester Cathedral, 1981-84; Bishop, Bermuda, Dean, Bermuda Cathedral, 1984-89; Archdeacon, Lewes and Hastings, 1989-91; Currently Asst Bishop, Diocese of Chichester, and Provost, So Div, The Woodard Schools. *Hobbies:* Opera; Church history; Winemaking. *Address:* 42 Willowbed Drive, Chichester, West Sussex PO19 2JB, England. 1.

LYALL Fiona Jane, b. 13 Apr 1931, Inverness, Scotland. Medical Practitioner (retired). m. Alan Richards Lyall, 20 July 1957, 1 s, 1 d. *Education:* MB ChB, 1954, DPH, 1958, DL, 1982, Aberdeen Univ. *Appointments:* Fam Med Practitioner; Retired, 1990; Dir, Grampian TV PLC. *Memberships:* Princes Trust, Grampian Comm; Coun, Templehill Community, Dir. *Hobbies:* Provincial silver; Victorian glass; Skiing. *Address:* Melrosebank, Laurence Kirk, Kincardineshire AB30 1AL, Scotland. 184.

LYNCH Thomas Dexter, b. 19 June 1942, San Angelo, Texas, USA. Professor of Public Administration. m. Sherry Ann Lynch, 30 Dec 1965, 1 s, 1 d. *Education:* BA, 1964, Grad Study, Pol Sci, 1965, Univ ID; MPA, 1966, PhD, Pol Sci, Rockefeller Coll, SUNY, Albany. *Appointments:* Prog Analyst: Urban Mass Transp Admin, US Dept Transp, 1969-72; Maritime Admin, US Dept Commerce, 1972-74; Adj Prof, George Washington Univ, 1972-73; Asst Prof, Pub Admin Dept, Maxwell School Citizenship and Pub Affairs, Syracuse Univ, NY, 1974-77; Assoc Prof, Pol Sci Dept, MS State Univ, 1977-81; Adj Prof: Fed Exec Inst, Charlottesville, VA, and Naval Postgrad School, Monterey, CA, 1980, Univ OK, Norman and overseas exts; Prof, Pub Admin, Dept Pub Admin, School Pub Affairs and Servs, FL Int Univ, 1981-84; Prof, Pub Admin, School Pub Admin, Coll Urban and Pub Affairs, FL Atlantic Univ, Ft Lauderdale, 1984-; Cons, Palm Beach Co, FL, 1985. *Publications:* Policy Analysis in Public Policymaking, 1975; Organization Theory and Management, 1984; Public Budgeting in America, 1979, 3rd Ed, 1990; Contemporary Public Budgeting, 1991; Exercises in Public Budgeting, 1983; Public Budgeting and Financial Management, 1993; Budgeting amd Financial Management, 1991; Var articles, book chapts, papers; Ed, several books. *Memberships:* Am Soc Pub Adm, Nat Pres 1992-93, num other positions, chapt and nat; Nat Assn Schools of Pub Admin and Affairs, Rsch Sect Chmn 1985-86; Govt Fin Offs Assn; Int Inst Admin Scis; Fndr, Pres, The Bureaucrat Inc, 1972-82; several ed bds. *Honours:* Phi Gamma Mu, 1961; Pi Sigma, 1964; ID Bar Assn Law Award, 1964; Pi Sigma Alpha, 1967; Nat Capital Area Chapt Award, Am Soc Pub Admin, 1970, 1971, 1972; Outstanding Perf Award, Urban Mass Transp Admin, US Dept Transp, 1972; Pi Alpha Alpha, 1981; The Bureaucrat Inc Award, 1982. *Hobby:* Travel. *Address:* School of Public Administration, Florida Atlantic University, 220 SE 2nd Avenue, Ft Lauderdale, FL 33301, USA.

LYNFORD Jeffrey Hayden, b. 7 Oct 1947, New York City, New York, USA. Investment Banker. 1 s, 1 d. *Education:* BA w hons, Hist, SUNY, Buffalo, 1969; MPA, Woodrow Wilson School, Princeton Univ, 1971; JD, Taxation, Real Estate, Fordham Univ School Law, 1975; Admitted to practice, NY State Bar. *Appointments:* VP, Real Estate, Int Paper Co sub, 1974-77; Assoc, White Weld & Co Inc, 1977-78; Mng Dir, A G Becker Paribas Inc, 1978-84; Ltd Ptnr, Assoc Dir, Bear Stearns & Co Inc, 1984-86; Chmn, CEO, Wellsford Grp Inc, Merchant Bankers, NYC, 1986-. *Publications:* Project Financing 1985: Power Generation, Waste Recovery and Other Facilities; Real Estate Syndications 1986: Current Techniques and Investment Vehicles; Contbns to Real Estate Finance and other jrnls. *Memberships:* Am Bar Assn; NY State Bar Assn; Assn Princeton Grad Alumni, Bd Mbr; Ed Bd, Real Estate Finance jrnl; Trustee: Lynford Family Charitable Trust, NYC; Nat Trust Historic Preservation; Bd Chmn, Quality Hill Redev Corp; Bd: Alan Guttmacher Inst; Cohen & Steers Realty Shares

Inc, NYC; Keaau Macadamia Corp, Hilo, HI; Real Estate Securities Income Fund Inc, NYC; Chmn, Wellsford Residential Property Trust, NYSE Listed Real Estate Investment Trust, 1992-. *Honours:* NY State Regents Scholarship; Woodrow Wilson School Fellowship, Princeton. *Address:* Wellsford Group Inc, 375 Park Avenue, New York, NY 10152, USA. 132.

LYONS Jonathon Edward, b. 1 May 1951, London, Leeds, Yorkshire, England. Company Director. m. 30 Dec 1975, 2 s, 1 d. *Education:* Carmell Coll. *Appointments:* Sales Exec, Alexandra Ltd, Leeds, 1968-71; Chief Exec, John David Mansworld Ltd, London, 1971-89; Dir, Ptnr, Int Investments Ltd, 1978-; Chief Exec, H Alan Smith Ltd, London, 1983-85; Dir, JLC Ltd, London, 1986; Jt Chief Exec, J E London Properties Ltd, 1988-; Pvte Investment Cons, Jonathon E Lyons & Co, 1988-; Dir: Britimpex Ltd, Can, Art Leasing Inc, Can. *Memberships:* Conservative Industrial Fund; Fedn Jewish Relief Orgs; Jt Chmn, Hyde Pk Comm, Ctrl Brit Fund, London, 1975-80; Comm Mbr, Royal Coll Music, London; Fellow, Inst Dirs; HMBRA; Bentley Owners Club; Hon Mbr, Insignia Club; Trustee, Sir Jack Lyons Charitable Trust, 1989-. *Hobbies:* Art; Music; Sports Writer; Classic postwar cars. *Address:* 35 Loudoun Rd, St John's Wood, London NW8 0NE, England. 52.

M

MA Bo-Huang, b. 20 Dec 1913, Hai-Cheng County, Liao-Ning Province, China. Professor of Economics and History. m. 27 Apr 1947, 1 d. *Education:* BA, Nat Univ Peking, 1938; MA, School Higher Studies, Fac Philos, Johns Hopkins Univ, USA, 1946. *Appointments:* Prof, Chmn, Dept Pol Sci, NEn Univ, Liao-Ning Province, 1946-48; Prof, Law School, Univ Soochow, Shanghai, 1950-52; Prof, Shanghai Fin and Econ Coll, 1952-58; Prof, Inst Econ Rsch, Shanghai Acad Social Scis, 1958-. *Publications:* Chief Ed: Documentary History of Dr Ong-Seng Liu's Enterprises, 3 vols, 1981; History of Economic Thoughts in Modern China, 3 vols, 1988; Author, theses: The Exploration, Sorting Out and Application of Ancient Chinese Ideas on Management, 1986; National Character of the Open Type and the Closed-Door Policy in Chinese History, 1988; Traditional Culture and Feudalism in Chinese History, 1989; A Brief Discussion of the History of Confucianism, 1991; The Unbalanced Development of the Geographical Economy History in China, 1992. *Memberships:* Hon Coun Mbr, Econ Thoughts Hist Soc China; Histl Sci Soc Shanghai; Advsr to: Rsch Soc Chinese Ancient Mgmt Thoughts; Soc Econ Sci Hist Shanghai. *Honours:* Authorship Prize, Shanghai Municipality, 1986; 2 Authorship Prizes and Sci Work Prize, Shanghai Acad Social Scis, 1991. *Hobbies:* Writing Chinese characters with Chinese writing brush; Chinese operas esp Peking and Hobei Operas; Western classical music. *Address:* Institute of Economic Research, Shanghai Academy of Social Sciences, 622/7 Huai-Hai Rd, Shanghai 200020, China.

MA Feicheng, b. 30 Oct 1947, Guiyang, China. University Faculty Member. m. Shaoying Shi, 1 Oct 1975, 1 s. *Education:* Trainee, Guiyang Gear Factory, Guiyang, 1965-68; MS, Wuhan Univ, 1982. *Appointments:* Worker, Guiyang Gear Factory, 1968-75; Translator, Japanese and Engl, Techn, Guizhou Inst Info, 1975-79; Fac Mbr, School Lib and Info Sci, Wuhan Univ, 1982-; Vis Prof, GMD-Informationszentrum fur Informationswissenschaft und Praxis FI-Schulung, Darmstadt, Germany, 1991. *Publications:* 5 books incl: Introduction to Information Science; Economics of Information; Strategies of Development and Utilization of Information in Modern Enterprises; 35 papers. *Memberships:* Standing Dir, China Soc Econs of Info; China Soc Sci and Technological Info. *Honours:* 5 prizes incl: Excellent Paper Prize, J Info China, 1982; 1st Prize, Excellent Paper, Hubei Province, 1982; 1st Prize, Excellent Tchng Achievement, 1982. *Hobbies:* Reading; Classical music; Jogging; Walking; Weiqi. *Address:* School of Library and Information Science, Wuhan University, Wuhan 430072, China.

MA Feng-shi, b. 13 Nov 1939, Beijing, China. Professor of Statistics. m. Fu Jing-zhen, 12 Sept 1967, 1 s, 1 d. *Education:* BA, Dept Maths, Peking Univ, 1963. *Appointments:* Tchng Asst, 1963-79, Lectr, 1979-83, Assoc Prof, 1983-87, Prof, 1987-, Tianjin Univ. *Publications:* Applied Probability and Statistics, book, 1989; Over 20 rsch papers in jrnls. *Membership:* Int Statistical Inst. *Honours:* Best Textbook Prize, China, 1991. *Hobbies:* Classical music; Swimming. *Address:* 18-3-101 N 5 Village, Tianjin University, Tianjin 300073, China.

MA Tongchang, b. 1954, m. 4 Feb 1975, 1 s, 1 d. *Education:* Anyong Med Sch, 1976-79. *Appointments:* Doctor: Neihuang Liquor Factory, 1973-75, Anyong Med Sch, 1979-74, Anyong Angitis Hosp, Hd of Hosp, 1984-. *Publications:* Vasculitis; New Theory on Vasculitis; New Theory on Heart Disease; New Theory on Treating Apoplexy. *Memberships:* Henam Youth Union, China. *Honours:* Sci Tech Prize for Youth, Henan Prov, 1991. *Address:* Anyang City Angitis Hospital, Anyang City, Henan Province, China.

MA Xiwen, b. 23 May 1939, Hebei, China. Mathematician; Computer Scientist. m. 4 May 1968, 1 s, 1 d. *Education:* Grad Dip, Dept Maths, Peking Univ, 1959. *Appointments:* Tchng, Rsch, 1959-80, Dir, Computer Ctr, 1981-83, Vice-Dir, Inst Computer Sci, 1984-, Peking Univ; Vis Scientist, Aptronix Inc, Santa Clara, CA, USA, 1991. *Publications:* Mathematical Theory of Orthogonal Design, 1981; In the Garden of Mathematics, 1981; Introduction to Theoretical Computer Science, 1990; Over 10 pieces of ballet music for orch, 1971-78. *Membership:* Vice-Chmn, China Assn Artificial Intelligence. *Honours:* Award, Best Book for Jr Readers, 1983. *Hobbies:* Reading; Music; Biking; Martial arts. *Address:* Institute of Computer Science, Peking University, Beijing 100871, China.

MA Yuanliang, b. 15 July 1938, Sichuan, China. Professor of Acoustic Engineering. m. Zheng Xingyuan, 20 July 1962, 1 s. *Education:* NWn Polytechnical Univ, 1956-61, transferred, Harbin Inst Technology, 1958-60. *Appointments:* Tchng, Rsch, 1961-, Assoc Prof, 1980, State Approved Doct Supvsr, Full Prof, 1986-, Dean, Coll Marine Engrng, 1991-, NWn Polytechnical Univ; Vis Scholar, Loughborough Univ Technology, England, 1981-83. *Publications:* Beampattern Optimization for Arbitrary Array of Sensors, 1984; Array Design and Processing Methods for Underwater Sound Measurement, 1990; Advances in Acoustic Signal Processing, 1991. *Memberships:* Councillor, Acoustical Soc China; VP, Xi'an Acoustical Soc; VP, Xi'an Marine Engrng Soc. *Honours:* Nat Sci Congress Award, 1978; Pioneering Educators Award, Shaanxi Province, 1985; Excellent Tchrs Award, 1989; Disting Contbn Award for Scholars Who Studied Abroad, 1991, Min Aero-Space Inds; Keynote Speakers Prize, W Pacific Reg Acoustics Conf IV, 1991. *Hobbies:* Reading; Taking photos. *Address:* Institute of Acoustic Engineering, Northwestern Polytechnical University, Xi'an, China.

MA Zhen Shen, b. 25 Oct 1939, Beijing, China. Painter. m. 19 Sept 1968, 1 s, 1 d. *Education:* Grad Dip, Ctrl Inst Fine Arts, 1966. *Appointments:* Ctrl Inst Fine Arts, 1966-73; Profl Painter, Artists Assn, Sichuan Br, 1973-91. *Creative works include:* Paintings: Salute Mother, 1959; State Affairs, 1964; Welcome to Liang Sha, 1976; Singing and Drinking, 1979; Journey, 1981; Lu You of Patriotic Poet, 1984; Racing Yak, 1985; Market Day, 1989; Loath to Part from Each Other, 1990. *Membership:* Artists Assn China. *Honours:* 3 Prizes, Min Culture China and Arts Assn China, 1979; Silver Medal, Min of Culture China and Artists Assn China, 1984. *Hobby:* Tai-jiquan. *Address:* ssa 00Artists Association of Sichuan Branch, No 116 Lan Jie Dong Cheng, Chengdu, Sichuan, China.

MAAS Robert William, b. 13 Feb 1943, London, England. Chartered Accountant. *Education:* FCA, 1965; Assoc, Inst Taxation, 1965. *Appointments:* Tax Ptnr, Stoy Hayward, 1970-77; Ptnr, Robert Maas & Co, 1977-83; Tax Ptnr, Casson Beckman, 1983-87; Tax Ptnr, Blackstone Franks & Co, London, 1987-. *Publications include:* Tax Planning for Entertainers, 1987; Tax Planning for the Smaller Business, 1990; Tolley's Anti-Avoidance Provisions, 2nd Ed, 1991; Tolley's Schedule E, 2nd Ed, 1991; Tolley's Property taxes, 5th Ed, 1992. *Memberships:* Tech Comm, Inst Chartered Accts in England and Wales Tax Fac; Tax Comm, London Soc Chartered Accts; Former Chmn, Ctrl London Small Practitioners. *Hobbies:* Reading; Walking; Listening to jazz; Drinking; Watching West Ham United Football Club. *Address:* Blackstone Franks & Co, Barbican House, 26-34 Old Street, London EC1V 9HL, England.

MAASILTA Timo Tuomas Mikael, b. 21 Dec 1954, Finland. Company President. m. Tiina Suhonen, 15 Apr 1985, 2 d. *Education:* MSc, Civil Engrng, 1979. *Appointments:* Off Engr, Helsingin Vesipiiri, Helsinki, 1978-80; Project Mgr, Vesi-Pekka Oy, Es Sider, Libya, 1980-82, Helsinki, 1982- 84; Pres, Tukinvest Oy, Helsinki, 1984-. *Memberships:* Bd Dirs: Amer Grp Ltd; Maa- ja vesitekniikan tuku ry; Tuen Kiinteistot Oy; Amerin Kulttuurisaatio; Teknillis-Yhteiskunnallinen Tutkimussaatio; Supervisory Board: orion Corporation.

Address: Tukinvest Oy, Annankatu 29 A 5, 00100 Helsinki, Finland. 52.

MABEE Sandra Ivonne Noriega, b. 13 Jan 1955, Hato Rey, Puerto Rico. Music Professor. m. Carl David Mabee, 2 Aug 1980, 1 d. *Education:* BA summa cum laude, Biblical Studies, Patten Coll, USA, 1977; BM magna cum laude, Percussion Perf, San Fran Conservatory Music, 1983; MA cum laude, Music, CA State Univ, 1985. *Career:* Debut, Hellman Hall, San Fran Conservatory; Percussionist, Timpanist, Prin Timpanist, Bay Area Women's Philharmonic, San Fran, 1983-; Prof, Music, 1983-88, Chairperson, Profl Studies Div, 1986-88, Patten Coll; Timpanist, Redwood Symph, 1985-88; Concerto Soloist, 1988; Percussionist, var orchs; Min Music, El Cerrito Christian Ctr, 1988-91; Hd, Music Dept, Hayward Christian School, 1988-91; Clergy, Avangelical Church Alliance, 1991; Trinity Church, Intern Pastor, 1991-92; Unvieled Chirst Ministries, Assoc Pastor, 1992-; Prof, Landmark School of Ministries; Recorded World Premiere, The Great Instruments of the Geggerotts, 1989, and var other world premieres. *Publication:* Rsch article on Bowed Percussion. *Memberships:* Treas, Patten Coll Student Body, 1977; Percussive Arts Soc; Hymn Soc Am; Cert, Evangelical Tchr Trng Assn; Follow-up Mins. *Honours:* Valedictorian, Patten Coll, 1977; Scholarships, San Fran Conservatory, 1980-83; Winner, Redwood Symp Concerto Competition, 1988. *Hobbies:* Music, various choirs; Volunteer, Prison Ministry; Teaching seminars; Counselling. *Address:* 2153 Santa Clara No C, Alameda, CA 94501, USA. 4, 9, 76.

MACCALLUM Norman Ronald Low, b. 18 Feb 1931, Walston, Lanarkshire, Scotland. Titular Prof in Mech Engrng. m. Mary Bentley Alexander, 23 June 1964, 1 s, 2 d. *Education:* BSc 1st Class Hons 1948-52, PhD 1956, Glasgow Univ. *Appointments:* Asst Lectr 1952-55, Lectr 1957-61, Lectr, Sr Lectr, Acting Hd of Dept, Reader, Titular Prof, 1962-, Glasgow Univ; Nat Serv RNVR, Final Rank Sub Lt, 1955-57; Performance Engr, Rolls Royce, 1961-62. *Publication:* The Transient Behaviour of Aircraft Gas Turbines, 1989. *Memberships:* FIMechE; Pres 1964-66, Hon VP 1991-, Orpheus Club; Pres 1991-93, Glasgow Univ Engrs Soc. *Honour:* Winner of Glasgow Univ Engrng Soc Prize for Best Grad in Engrng, Glasgow Univ, 1952. *Hobby:* Singing. *Address:* Department of Mechanical Engineering, University of Glasgow, Glasgow G12 8QQ, Scotland. 184.

MACDONALD Alexander Barrett Hon, b. 21 Oct 1918, Vancouver, British Columbia, Canada. Adjunct Professor of Political Science; Politician. m. Dorothy Bower Lewis, 4 Nov 1944, 1 d. *Education:* BA, Univ BC; LLB, Osgoode Hall Law School; Called to Bar, BC. *Appointments:* Asst to C O Howe, Min Munitions and Supply, World War II; Parly Sec to Hon M J Caldwell, 1944-45; Elected to House of Commons for Vancouver-Kingsway; Mbr, Legis Assembly, BC, elected, 1960, re-elected, 1963, 1966, 1969, 1972, 1975, 1979, 1983; Opposition Critic on Intergovtl Rels, Nat Dem Party; Created QC, 1972; Atty Gen, BC, 1972-75; Min Ind Trade and Commerce, 1973; Adj Prof, Pol Sic, Simon Fraser Univ, 1987-; Regular Speaker, early ed, CBC Radio. *Publication:* My Dear Legs: Letters to Young Social Democrat, 1985. *Memberships:* UN Assn Can, Vancouver Br, Pres. *Honours:* Award of Merit, BC Centennial Celebrations, 1966, 1967; Hon Disting Citizen, State of WA, USA, 1973; Award from Profl Engrs, 1975; Hon Citizen, City of Victoria, 1985. *Hobbies:* Squash; Tennis; Badminton; Fishing; Classical music; Reading. *Address:* 3461 Point Grey Road, Vancouver, British Columbia, Canada V6R 1A6. 142.

MACDONALD Brian Scott, b. 6 June 1939, Sudbury, Canada. Specialist Consultant in Defence and International Relations. m. Margaret L Young, 11 Aug 1962, 2 s, 1 d. *Education:* BA (Hons), Royal Mil Coll Can, 1961; HS Specialist Cert, Ont Coll Educ, 1966; MBA w distinction, York Univ, 1982; PhD in progress,

Univ Toronto. *Appointments:* Off, Dept Nat Def, 1961-64; Served Mil Reserve: CO, Battery Cmdr, Lt-Col, 7rh (Toronto) Regt RCA, 1965-75, Off Commanding, Ctrl Mil Area Off Trng School, 1975-82, Dpty Cmdr, Cmdr, Sr Staff Off, Col, Toronto Militia Dist, 1982-86; Tchr, Asst Dept Hd, N York Bd Educ, 1966-80; Exec Dir, Can Inst Strategic Studies, 1982-89; Hon Gov, Can Corps Commissionaires, 1984-86; Hon ADC to Gov-Gen Can, 1984-86; Dir, Royal Can Mil Inst, 1986-88; Dir, 1986-89, Rsch Chmn, Dir, 1989-90, Sr VP, Dir, 1990, Atlantic Coun Can; Pres, Strategic Insight Planning and Communications, 1989-. *Publications:* The International Strategic Environment (co-author), 1983; Deterrence, 1988; The Verification Dilemma: Phenomena and Means, 1990. *Contributions to:* jrnls; Editor, 15 books on defence matters. *Memberships:* Conf Def Assns, Vice-Chmn 1977-78; Royal Can Artillery Assn, Pres 1976-77; Assn Pol Risk Analysts; Can Inst Strategic Studies; Can Operational Rsch Soc; Royal Can Mil Inst; Int Soc Planning and Strategic Mgmt; Toronto Bd Trade. *Honours:* Marsh and MacLennan Scholarship, York Univ; Nat Def Strategic Studies Scholarship, Univ Toronto; Mobile Command Achievement Award, Formation Level; Can Forces Decoration; Queen's Silver Jubilee Medal. *Hobbies:* Gardening; Reading. *Address:* 169 Newton Dr, Willowdale, Ontario, Canada M2M 2N6. 2, 142.

MACDONALD James Stewart, b. 11 Aug 1925, Mauritius. Retired Medical Practitioner; Deputy Chairman of Company. m. Catherine Wilton Drysdale, 19 Oct 1951, 2 s. *Education:* Sedbergh School; MB ChB, 1950, DMRD, 1956, Univ Edinburgh; FFR, 1960, FRCR, 1975, Royal Coll Radiologists; MRCP, 1973, FRCP, 1979, Royal Coll Physns, Edinburgh. *Appointments:* Served RAMC, 1951-53: Major 2 i/c 23 Parachute Field Ambulance, 1953; Asst Radiologist, St Thomas' Hosp, London, England, 1959-62; Cons Radiologist, Royal Marsden Hosp, London, 1962-85; Currently Dpty Chmn (Scotland), Timber Growers UK. *Publications:* Num contbns to sci jrnls and chapts on the radiology of cancer w esp ref to the lymphatic system. *Memberships:* Brit Med Assn; Royal Soc Med; Brit Inst Radiology; Coun Mbr, Royal Coll Radiologists, 1968-73; Royal Scottish Forestry Soc; RSA; Med Rsch Coun, several working parties; Inst Cancer Rsch, Mmgt Comm 1969-82; Royal Marsden Hosp, Bd Govs 1967-82, Vice-Chmn Bd 1975-82; European Assn Radiology, several comms, 1968-81, Sec-Gen, Symposium Ossium (London), 1968; Union Europeenne des Medicins Specialistes, UK Del for Diagnostic Radiology 1972-81; S Metrop Cancer Registry, Exec Comm 1971-82; Ludwig Inst Cancer Rsch, London Comm 1971- 84. *Hobbies:* Farming; Forestry; Field sports. *Address:* Darquhillan, Gleneagles, Auchterarder, Perthshire PH3 1NG, Scotland. 170.

MACDONALD John A(rthur), b. 26 Sept 1912, Toronto, Ontario, Canada. Public Servant (retired). m. Catherine Mary Hilder, 12 Dec 1939, (dec), 3 d, currently common law relationship with Hylda Kathlyn Bateman. *Education:* BA, Univ Toronto, 1935. *Appointments:* Served Royal Can Naval Vol Reserve, 1939-45; Served Govt Can, 1946-73, incl Asst Dpty Min, Hlth and Welfare; (Retired as Cmdr (S)); Some years int social and econ dev work for Govts of Can, UN, other countries incl: Special UN Rapporteur; Can Rep, UNICEF Exec Bd and Int Coun Social Dev; Active vol, several orgs. *Publications:* Darkly the River Flows, novel, 1945. *Memberships include:* Amnesty Int; Life Mbr, NAACP; MATCH Int; Temagami Wilderness Assn; Blisssymbolics. *Honours:* Winner, All-Can Competition for novel, 1945; Can Centennial Medal. *Hobbies include:* Writing; Conservation promotion; Amnesty International work; Support of movements concerned with improving level of government activities. *Address:* 130 Broadway Avenue, Ottawa, Ontario, Canada K1S 2V8. 142.

MACDONALD Karen Crane, b. 24 Feb 1955, Denville, New Jersey, USA. Registered Occupational Therapist; Geriatric Counsellor. *Education:* BS, Quinnipiac Coll, CT; MS, Univ Bridgeport, CT; Doct cand, NY Univ. *Appointments:* Occupational Therapist, 1977-87, Coord,

Special Care Unit, 1987-, Jewish Home, Fairfield, CT; Instr, NY Univ, NYC, 1983-89; Instr, Quinnipiac Coll, Hamden, CT, 1986-. *Publications:* Special Care Unit: A guide for families, 1985; Psychopathology of Aging, 1986; Roles and Functions of Occupational Therapy in Adult Day Care, 1986; Occupational Therapy and Music Therapies for Nursing Home patients with dementia, 1986; Occupational Therapy approaches to treatment of dementia patients, 1986; Specialized Means and Recipes to Enjoy, 1989. *Memberships:* World Fedn Occupational Therapy; Am Occupational Therapy Assn; CT Occupational Therapy Assn; Nat Coun Aging; Alzheimer's Disease Assn. *Honours:* Maddak Award, design of equipment, 1984; Scholar-in-Residence Award, Am Occupational Therapy Fedn, 1985; Elected to Int Platform Assn, 1987; Elected to NY Acad Scis, 1987; Serv Award, Am Occupational Therapy Assn, 1988. *Hobbies:* Antiques; Photography; Hiking; Poetry. *Address:* 2600 Park Avenue No 3Y, Bridgeport, CT 06604, USA. 5, 6, 52, 138.

MACDONALD Robbin Rieck, b. 14 Oct 1944, Martins Ferry, Ohio, USA. Clergyman. m. Roberta Price, 21 Dec 1967, 1 s. *Education:* BA, Philos, 1966; MDiv, 1970; DMin, 1972. *Appointments:* Terra Bella Presby Ch, 1973-78; Grandview Presby Ch, 1978-82; Pomona Presby Ch, 1982-89; Dexter Presby Ch, 1989-90; Community Presby Ch, Springerville, AZ, 1990-91; Shepherd of the Valley Presbyterian Church, 1991. *Publication:* A New Vision of Jesus. *Memberships:* VP, San Fran Theological Sem Alumni Coun, 1975; de Cristo Presbytery; Coronado Chapt, AZ Archaeological Soc; Assn Presby Interim Min Specialists. *Honours:* Nat Hon Soc Philos, 1966. *Hobbies:* Weight lifting; Jogging; Reading; Writing; Languages (Latin, Old Testament Hebrew, New Testament Greek, Spanish); Travel. *Address:* 3433 S Robinson Avenue, Thatcher, AZ 75552, USA.

MACDONALD William Atwood, b. 15 Dec 1927, Montreal, Canada. Lawyer. m. Molly Anne Patterson, 17 Nov 1951, 3 s, 1 d. *Education:* BA 1st class hons, Pol Sci, Econs, McGill Univ, 1948; LLB, Osgoode Hall Law School, 1951; Barrister-at-Law, 1951. *Appointments:* Joined 1951, currently Ptnr, McMillan Binch (mbr firm of McMillan Bull Casgrain), Toronto. *Publications:* Income Taxation in Canada (ed); Mobilizing the Resources - the Flow of Savings (w J W Popkin); Bill C-13: An Analysis of Central Issues (w J W Rowley); Disclosure of Corporate Information (w E K Weir); Overview of Competition Law Changes, 1986-Style; Contbns to Financial Post and Globe and Mail on taxation, competition law, other legal and econ policy subjects. *Memberships include:* Chmn, Fndng Dir, Exec Comm Mbr, Japan Soc in Canada; Canada Japan Bus Coop Comm; Brit N Am Comm; Former Gov, Can Tax Fndn; Former Off, former Nat Taxation Sect Chmn, Can Bar Assn; Dir, Comm Chmn, Mbr of Comms, Imperial Oil Ltd; Trustee, Investment Comm Mbr, Imperial Oil Employee Pension Plans; Dir, Comm Mbr, Marathon Realty Oil Ltd; Dir, Exec Comm Mbr: Nat Trust Co; Nat Victoria and Grey Trustco Ltd; Timmminco Ltd; Dir, Honda Canada Inc. *Hobbies:* Reading; Cross country skiing; Swimming; Fishing; Theatre; Movies; Porcelain; Food; Wine. *Address:* McMillan Binch, PO Box 38, Royal Bank Plaza, Toronto, Ontario, Canada M5J 2J7. 88, 142.

MACDONOGH Giles Malachy Maximilian, b. 6 Apr 1955, London, England. Author; Journalist. *Education:* Inst Cath, Paris, 1974; Balliol Coll, Oxford, 1975-78; BA Hons, Mod Hist; MA; Ecole Pratique des Hautes Etudes, Paris, 1980-83. *Appointments:* Tchr, Translator, Paris, 1978-83; Freelance Jrnlst, 1983-; Columnist, Food for Thought, Financial Times, 1989-. *Publications include:* A Palate in Revolution, 1987; A Good German, 1990. *Memberships:* Int PEN; Guild of Food Writers; Octagon Wine Writers. *Honours:* Short-listed for Andre Simon Prize, 1987; Glenfiddich Special Award, 1988. *Hobbies:* Music; Architecture. *Address:* c/o Curtis Brown, 121-126 Regent Street, London W1, England. 30.

MACDOUGALL Hugh Andrew, b. 9 Nov 1922, Nova Scotia, Canada. Adjunct Professor of History. m. Beverlee McIntosh, 6 Sept 1975, 1 s, 1 d. *Education:* BA, 1945; PhD (Cantab), Hist, 1960. *Appointments:* Assoc Prof, Hist, 1960-61, Dean, 1961-67, 1972-76, St Patrick's Coll, Ottawa; Vis Fellow, Cambridge Univ, England, 1970-71; Prof, 1976-89, Adj Prof, Hist, 1989-, Carleton Univ, Can. *Publications:* Acton-Newman Relations, 1962; Lord Acton on Papal Power, 1973; Racial Myth in English History, 1982. *Membership:* Can Histl Assn. *Hobbies:* Skating; Swimming; Classical music; Drama. *Address:* 691 Highland Avenue, Ottawa, Ontario, Canada K2A 2K5. 142.

MACDOWALL David William, b. 2 Apr 1930, West Derby, Liverpool, England. College Principal (retired). m. Mione Beryl Lashmar, 21 June 1962, 2 d. *Education:* Corpus Christi Coll, Oxford, 1947-51, 1953-55; BA, 1952, MA, 1954, DPhil, 1959, Oxford Univ; Brit School Rome, 1954. *Appointments:* 2nd Lt, Royal Signals, 1951-52; 2nd Lt, 1953, Lt, 1956, Territorial Army; Asst Keeper, Dept Coins, Brit Mus, London, 1956-60; Prin, 1960-70, Asst Sec, 1970-73, Mins Educ and Univ Grants Comm; Master, Univ Coll, Lectr, Classics, Ancient Hist, Oriental Studies, 1973-78, Durham; Asst Dir, 1979, Dir, 1980-85, Polytechnic N London. *Publications:* Coin Collections, Their Preservation, Classification and Presentation, 1978; The Western Coinages of Nero, 1979; Num papers on Roman and Indian numismatics. *Memberships:* Royal Numismatic Soc, Fellow 1958, Hon Treas 1966-73, Ed Bd; Royal Asiatic Soc, Fellow 1958, Coun Mbr; Soc Afghan Studies, Hon Sec 1972-82; Chmn, Soc S Asian Studies; Hon Treas, Brit Archaeological Assn. *Honours:* Barclay Head Prize for Ancient Numismatics, Oxford Univ, 1953, 1956; Medal, Asociacion Numismatica Espanola, 1964; Nelson Wright Medal, Numismatic Soc India, 1973; Corres Mbr, Istituto Italiano per Il Medio ed Estremo Oriente, 1986; Corres Mbr, am Numismatic Soc, 1991. *Hobbies:* Travel; Antiquities; Photography; Natural history; Genealogy. *Address:* Admont, Dancers End, Tring, Herts HP23 6JY, England. 1.

MACFARLAND Craig George, b. 17 July 1943, Great Falls, Montana, USA. Private International Consultant in Natural Resources Management. m. Marilyn Ann Swanson, 19 Mar 1988, 1 s, 4 d. *Education:* BA, Biology, Austin Coll, TX, 1965; MA, Ecology, Univ WI, 1969. *Appointments:* Dir, Charles Darwin Rsch Station, Galapagos, Ecuador, 1974-78; Hd, Wildlands and Wetlands Mgmt Unit, CATIE, Costa Rica, 1978-85; Pres, Charles Darwin Fndn for the Galapagos Isles, 1985-; Pvte Cons, 1985-. *Publications:* Portions of 4 books, 3 symposium papers, over 50 scholarly and profl papers. *Memberships:* Assoc Tropical Biology; Int Soc Tropical Foresters; Ecological Soc Am; World Wildlife Fund, USA; Commn Nat Pks and Protected Areas, Int Union Conservation of Natural Resources; Nature Conservancy, USA; Sigma Xi. *Honours:* DSc hc, Austin Coll, Sherman, TX, 1978; Int Conservation Medal, Zoological Soc San Diego; Order of the Golden Ark for int conservation work, presented by Prince Bernhard, Netherlands, 1982. *Hobbies:* Hiking; Cross-country skiing; Tennis; Camping; Nature photography; Archaeology; International travel to other cultures and natural areas. *Address:* 836 Mabelle, Moscow, ID 83843, USA. 2.

MACFARLANE Alan Donald James, b. 20 Dec 1941, Assam, India. Academic. m. (1) Gillian Ions, 1965, (2) Sarah Harrison, 1981, 1 d. *Education:* Sedbergh School; Worcester Coll, Oxford; London School Econs; School Oriental and African Studies, London Univ; MA (Oxon); PhD; DPhil. *Appointments:* Sr Rsch Fellow, Hist, 1971-75, Fell, 1981-, King's Coll, Cambridge; Lectr, Social Anthropology, 1975-81, Reader, Histl Anthropology, 1981-91, Prof, Anthropological Sci, 1991-, Cambridge Univ. *Publications:* Witchcraft in Tudor and Stuart England, 1970; Family Life of Ralph Josselin, 1970; The Diary of Ralph Josselin (ed), 1976; Resources and Population, 1976; The Origins of English Individualism, 1977; The Justice and the Mare's Ale, 1981; Marriage and Love in England, 1986; The Culture of Capitalism, 1987. *Membership:* Fellow, Brit Acad. *Honours:* Rivers Mem Medal, 1984. *Hobbies:* Gardening; Walking; Music. *Address:* 25 Lode Road, Lode, nr Cambridge CB5 9FR, England. 1, 34.

MACFARLANE Peter Wilson, b. 8 Nov 1942, Glasgow, Scotland. Professor in Medical Cardiology. m. Irene Grace Muir, 8 Oct 1971, 2 s. *Education:* BSc (Hons), 1964, PhD, 1970, Univ Glasgow. *Appointments:* Asst Lectr, Med Cardiology, 1967-70, Lectr, Med Cardiology, 1970-74, Sr Lectr, Med Cardiology, 1974-80, Reader, Med Cardiology, 1980-91, Prof, Med Cardiology, 1991- , Univ Glasgow. *Publications:* Computer Techniques in Clinical Medicine (ed), 1985; Comprehensive Electrocardiology (ed), 3 vols, 1988; Ed/author, 8 other books; Co-author, over 150 papers. *Memberships:* Mbr, Brit Cardiac Soc, 1974; Fellow, Brit Computer Soc, 1976; Fellow, Royal Soc of Edinburgh, 1992; Sec, Int Coun Electrocardiology. *Hobbies:* Running; Playing the violin. *Address:* University Dept of Medical Cardiology, Royal Infirmary, 10 Alexandra Parade, Glasgow G31 2ER, Scotland. 184.

MACGREGOR Graham Alexander, b. 1 Apr 1941, St Albans, England. Professor of Cardiovascular Medicine. m. Christiane Bourquin, 2 Nov 1968, 1 s, 2 d. *Education:* Marlborough Coll, 1955-60; Trinity Hall, Cambridge, 1960-64; BA, MA, Cambridge Univ; Middlesex Hosp, London, 1964-67; MB BChir; House jobs, Middlesex and Hammersmith Hosps, London, 1967-70; FRCP. *Appointments:* Registrar, St Thomas' Hosp, London, 1970-73; Sr Registrar, Sr Lectr, Charing Cross Hosp, London, 1973-89; Prof, St George's Hosp, 1989-. *Publications:* Salt Free Diet Book, 1986; Hypertension in Practise, 1987; Num sci papers on high blood pressure. *Memberships:* Brit Hypertension Soc, Past Treas. *Hobby:* Gardening. *Address:* Dells Farm, Cadmore End, Bucks HP14 3UR, England.

MACGREGOR-HASTIE Roy Alasdhair Niall, b. 28 Mar 1929. Historian; Writer; Administrator. m. diss, 2 s, 1 d. *Education:* BA, Univ Manchester, England, 1950; MFA, Univ IA, USA, 1972; Fellowship, PhD, Univ Hull, England, 1979. *Appointments:* Prof, Mod European Hist, Perugia, Italy, to 1980; Prof, San Jose State Univ, CA, USA, 1980-83; Dean, US Grad School Europe, 1983-86; Prof, Social Hist, Osaka Gakuin Univ, Japan, 1986-92; Dir Gen, East Asia Fndn, 1992-. *Publications:* Biog, hist: The Man from Nowhere, 1960; The Red Barbarians, 1961; Pope John XXIII, 1962; The Throne of Peter, UK Ed, 1966, US Ed, 1967; The Mechanics of Power, 1966; Pope Paul VI; The Day of the Lion, 1963, other eds; Never to be Taken Alive, 1985; Nell Gwyn, 1987; Short History of Western Civilisation, 1990; Travel, autobiog: The Compleat Migrant, 1962; Dont Send Me To Omsk, 1964; Signor Roy, 1967; Africa, 1968; Picasso's Women, 1988, 1989; Poetry, criticism: Poems Lyrical and Empirical, 1954; The Mirror to the Mind, 1956; A Case for Poetry, 1960; Interim Statement, 1962; Poems, 1980; Poeme, 1980; Translations; Contbns to anthologies. *Memberships:* Evr Comm Writers; Inst Jrnlsts; Brit Assn Romanian Studies, Pres, Sec; Int Assn Lit Translators; Sr Brit Collaborator, UNESCO; Japan Inst, VP. *Honours:* Victorian Poetry Prize, 1957; Lit Translation Prizes, 1961, 1968, 1972, 1990 (UNESCO Gen Conf Comm Vol 1989); Co-recipient, Lane Bryant Prize, 1963. *Hobbies:* Cooking; Calligraphy. *Address:* c/o Chelsea Arts Club, 143 Old Church St, London SW3, England. 32, 43, 52, 139.

MACHIN George Ian Thom, b. 3 July 1937, Liverpool, England. Professor of British History. m. Jane Margaret Pallot, 2 Apr 1964, 2 s. *Education:* Jesus Coll, Oxford, 1955-61; MA, DPhil, Oxford Univ. *Appointments:* Asst Lectr, Lectr, Hist, Univ Singapore, 1961-64; Lectr, Sr Lectr, Reader, Mod Hist, 1964-89, Prof, Brit Hist, 1989- , Univ Dundee, Scotland. *Publications:* The Catholic Question in English Politics, 1820 to 1830, 1964; Politics and the Churches in Great Britain, 1832 to 1868, 1977; Politics and the Churches in Great Britain, 1869

to 1921, 1987; The Liberal Government, 1905-1991. *Memberships:* Fellow, Royal Histl Soc; Pres, Dundee Br, Histl Assn; Ecclesiastical Hist Soc. *Honours:* Wylie Prize, Oxford Univ, 1957. *Hobbies:* The arts; Hill-walking; Photographing historic signposts. *Address:* Dept of Modern History, The University, Dundee DD1 4HN, Scotland. 184.

MACHOWSKI Jozef Jan, b. 10 Mar 1930, Wierzchostawice, Poland. High School Professor in Electrical Engineering. m. Jadwiga Kowalik, 12 July 1958, 1 s, 1 d. *Education:* MSc, 1954, PhD, 1964, Prof, 1988, AGH, Univ Mining and Metall, Cracow. *Appointments:* Lectr, 1954-57, Sr Lectr, 1957-64, Asst Prof, 1964-88, Prof, 1988-, Univ Mining and Metall, Cracow. *Publications:* 5 sci books as co-author, 7 manuscripts, 60 papers as author or co-author, concerning haulage and driving. *Memberships:* Polish Soc Theoretical and Applied Elec Engrng, Hd, Cracow Br. *Honours:* Cross, Polonia Restituta. *Hobbies:* Photography; Painting. *Address:* University of Mining and Metallurgy, al Mickiewicza 30, Cracow, Poland.

MACHT Betsy Jean, b. 23 Feb 1957, Abington, Pennsylvania, USA. Environmental Engineer. m. Steven R Senderling, 20 June 1981, 1 s. *Education:* BS, Environmental Engrng, PA State Univ, 1979; Postgrad Bus courses: Univ PA, Wharton School; Fairleigh Dickenson Univ, NJ. *Appointments:* Product Engr, Baby Products Div, Johnson & Johnson, 1980-86; Mgr, Environmental Mgmt, Hart Environmental Mgmt Corp Inc, 1986-89; Sr Environmental Engr, Grp Ldr, Dames & Moore, 1990-91; Div Environmental Engr, Special Chem Div, Rhone-Poulenc Inc, Cranbury, NJ, 1991-. *Memberships:* Am Inst Chem Engrs; Soc Women Engrs; Altousa Int; US Chem Manufacturers Assn, Alkylphenol and Ethorylates Panel; DE Valley Profl Network, Fndr 1980, Steering Comm. *Hobbies:* Skiing; Reading; Sailboarding; Travel. *Address:* Rhone-Poulenc Inc, CN 7500, Cranbury, NJ 08512, USA. 5.

MACHWE Prabhakar, b. 26 Dec 1917, Gwalior (MP), India. Newspaper Editor; Author. m. Sharad Parnerkar, 7 Nov 1940, 1 s, 1 d. *Education:* BA, 1935, MA, Philos, 1937. MA, Engl Lit, 1943, PhD, Hindi, 1958, Agra Univ, Agra. *Appointments:* Sec, Nat Labour Union, Indore, 1937; Lectr, Philos, Ujjain, 1938-48; Prog Prod, All India Radio, Nagpur, Allahabad, 1948- 54; Asst Sec, Sahitya Akademi, New Delhi, 1954-75; Vis Prof, Indian Studies, Univs WI and CA, USA, 1959-61; Hindi Off, UPSC, 1964-66; Dir, Bharatriya Bhasha Parishad, Calcutta, 1979-85; Ed, Chautha Sansar (Hindi daily newspaper), Indore, 1989-. *Creative works include:* In Hindi: 4 poetry collections; 15 novels; 3 collections of light essays; 2 travelogues; Several translations from Hindi and Marathi into Engl and vice versa; Many books on lit criticism; Many paintings. *Memberships:* Hon Mbr, Hindi Sahitya Sannelan, Allahabad; Maharashtra Sahitya Parished, Pune; Indian PEN; Inst Histl Rsch; Vis Fellow, Inst Adv Study, Simla; Authors Guild India. *Honours:* Soviet Land Nehru Award, 1972; U P Hindi Sansthan Award, 1985; Sahitya Vachaspati hons degree, Hindi Sahitya Sannelan, 1986; Delhi Hindi Akademi Award, 1990. *Hobbies:* Painting; Learning languages; Travel. *Address:* E-180 Greater Kailash, Part II, New Delhi 110048, India.

MACINTYRE Alexander Cringan, b. 3 June 1931, Ogdensburg, New York, USA. Investor. m. Frances Marian Sheffield. *Education:* BA, Hobart Coll, 1953; MBA, Dartmouth, 1957; Postgrad: Univ The Americas, Mexico City, 1957-59, Univ Paris, 1969. *Appointments:* Served USNR, 1953-55; Pres, Dir, Am Hosp Supply Corp de Venezuela, Caracas, Venezuela, 1960-65; VP, Am Hosp Supply Corp de PR, San Juan, PR, 1965-68; Am Hosp Supply Export Corp, Evanston, IL and Miami, FL, USA, 1965-68; Currently engaged in real estate and investments. *Memberships:* YMCA; AIM; Sigma Chi; Miami Comm For Rels; Int Advsry Bd; Frederick Remington Art Mus; Coral Reef Yacht Club; Children's Home Soc; Alexander C MacIntyre Charitable Trusts I and II. *Address:* 1835 Bayshore Dr, Miami, FL 33133, USA.

MACK Alan Osborne, 24 July 1918, London, England. Emeritus Professor of Prosthetic Dentistry. m. Marjorie Westacott, 19 June 1943, 2 s, 1 d. *Education:* London Univ, 1939-42; LDSRCS, 1942; MDS (Dunelm), 1958; FDSRCS, England, 1971. *Appointments:* Served RAF Dental Br, 1943-47; House Surg, Lectr, Sr Lectr, Asst Dir, Royal Dental Hosp, Univ London, 1948- 56; Prof, Dental Prosthetics, Univ Newcastle-upon-Tyne, 1956-67; Cons, ENT Hosp, Examiner Royal Coll Surgs, 1956, Univ, Manchester, 1959, Leeds, 1961, Glasgow, 1961, Liverpool, 1965, London, 1965, Edinburgh, 1968, Lagos, Nigeria, 1970, Singapore and Khartoum, 1977, Benghazi, 1978; Prof, Dental Prosthetics, 1967-80, Emeritus Prof, 1980-, London Univ; Cons, RAF, 1978-88; P/T Cons Stoke Mandeville Hosp & John Radcliffe Hosp, 1976-81; Vis Prof: Singapore, 1981, Jordan, 1987. *Publications:* Full Dentures, 1971, Revised Reprint, 1978. *Contributions to:* profl jrnls. *Memberships:* Brit Dental Assn; Brit Soc Study Prosthetic Dentistry, Pres 1963; Am Acad Implant Dentures. *Honours:* Elected Fellow, Dental Surg, Royal Coll Surgs, without exam, 1971; Hon Mbr: Am Acad Implant Dentures, 1966; British Soc Study Prosthetic Dentistry, 1980. *Memberships:* Bowls; Pottery; Gardening. *Address:* Home Farm, London Road, Aston Clinton, Aylesbury, Bucks HP22 5HG, England. 1.

MACKAY Ian Munro, b. 14 Sept 1947, Brora, Scotland. Chartered Accountant. m. Maureen Mackay, 12 June 1970, 2 s, 1 d. *Appointment:* BCom, Univ Edinburgh, 1969; Chartered Acct trng, 1969-73, qualified, 1973. *Appointments:* Trng, 1969-74, Chartered Acct, 1974-76, Ernst & Young, Edinburgh; Mgr, Shair & Co, Pub Accts, Abu Dhabi and Dubai, 1976-79; Proprietor, own firm of Chartered Accts, Dornoch and Golspie, Scotland, 1979-. *Memberships:* Pres, Sutherland Curling Province; Royal Dornoch Golf Club; Dornoch Heritage Soc; Auditor, Treas, Sec, var local charities, clubs and others. *Honours:* Hon Sheriff, Dornoch Sheriff Ct, 1985-. *Hobbies:* Curling; Garden; Golf; Local history. *Address:* An Cala, 4 Sutherland Road, Dornoch, Sutherland. 184.

MACKIE Peter Howard, b. 13 Oct 1947, Oxford, England. Medical Practitioner (Consultant Haematologist). m. Joanna Jane McGhee, 14 July 1973, 4 d. *Education:* Cheltenham Coll, 1961-65; Hertford Coll, Oxford, 1966- 70; Middlesex Hosp Med School, London, 1970-72; MA, BM, BCh (Oxon), 1972; MRCP, 1978; MRCPath, 1981. *Appointments:* Sr House Off, Registrar, Bristol Royal Infirmary, 1974-76; Rsch Registrar, Queen Elizabeth Hosp, Birmingham, 1976-77;Lectr, Dept Immunology, Univ Birmingham, 1977-79; Sr Registrar, Haematology, John Radcliffe Hosp, Oxford, 1979-82; Cons Haematologist, E Berks Dist, 1982-. *Publications:* Several papers on haematology esp on detection of infection in leukaemia. *Memberships:* Chmn, Div Med, E Berks; Vice-Chmn, Hosp Med Advsry Comm, E Berks Hlth Auth; Coun Mbr, Windsor and Dist Organists Assn; Brit Med Assn, Sec 1985-91; Ancient Soc Coll Youths; Reg Rep, Brit Soc Haematology; Windsor Med Soc, Coun Mbr 1988-90. *Honours:* Music Scholar, Cheltenham Coll, 1961-65; Marcan Music Prize, 1962; Open Exhib, Hertford Coll, Oxford, 1966-70. *Hobbies:* Music; Bellringing; Gardening; Walking. *Address:* Westbury, Duffield Lane, Stoke Poges, Bucks SL2 4AH, England.

MACKINNON John (Jack), b. 6 Apr 1925, Vancouver, Canada. Economist; Association Executive. m. Leona Marie Mulligan, 8 May 1954, 2 s, 4 d. *Education:* BComm, 1950, BA, 1952, Univ BC; MA, Univ Toronto, 1954; Doct studies, Univ Ottawa, 1955-66. *Appointments:* Served Can Army, 1944-46; Off, Intelligence Div, Brit Control Commn Germany, 1946-48; Exec Trainee, Can Imperial Bank Commerce, 1951-53; Sales, Sales Promotion, Burroughs Bus Machines, 1953-56; Jr to Sr Economist, Govt Can, 1956-83; Capt, then Maj, Cameron Highlanders of Ottawa, 1961-64; Nat Pres, Economists, Sociologists and Statisticians

Assn Can, 1983-91. *Publications:* Several short papers on econ subjects related to Can fed govt matters. *Memberships:* Trustee, Past Chmn, Ottawa RC School Bd; Exec Sec, Can (Mil) Intelligence and Security Assn; Pres, Civil Liberties Assn, Nat Capital Reg; Former Pres, Fedn Cath PTA Ont. *Honours:* 2 scholarships, 1 bursary, Univ BC. *Hobbies:* Playing tennis; Playing bagpipes. *Address:* 2190 Tawney Road, Ottawa, Ontario, Canada K1G 1C5. 88.

MACLEAN OF DOCHGARROCH Allan Murray, The Very Rev, b. 22 Oct 1950. Provost. m. Anne Cameron Cavin, 29 Jan 1990, 1 stepson. 1 s, 1 d. *Education:* MA 1st class Hons, Scottish Hist, Univ Edinburgh; Cuddesdon Coll and Pusey House, Oxford. *Appointments:* Deacon, 1976; Priest, 1977; Chaplain, St Mary's Cathedral, Edinburgh, 1976-81; Rector, Holy Trinity, Dunoon, 1981-86; Exam Chaplain to Bishop of Argyll and The Isles, 1983-; Provost, St John's Cathedral, Oban from 1986. *Publications:* Telford's Highland Churches, 1987; Ed: Clan Maclean, 1975-85; Argyll and The Isles, 1984-. *Membership:* VP, Clan Maclean Assn; National Council: Architecture Heritage. Soc of Sirlaw *Hobbies:* Topography; History; Genealogy; Architecture. *Address:* The Rectory, Ardconnel Terrace, Oban, Argyll PA34 5DJ, Scotland. 1.

MACLEOD Allan Martin, b. 4 May 1931, Stornoway, Scotland. Crofter. m. Margaret MacLeod, 20 Jan 1956, 2 s. *Education:* Attainment Cert, Carloway Pub School. *Appointments:* Served RAF, 1949-51; Police Service, 1952-84, incl: Insp, Stornoway, Chief Insp, Kirkwall, Supt, Inverness; JP, Wn Isles Scotland. *Creative works:* Researching 19th century policing; Compiling list of Gaelic/English proverbs and fauna of the Outer Hebrides. *Memberships:* Pres, Rotary Club, Stornoway. *Honours:* Long Serv and Good Conduct Police Medal, 1974; Prizewinner, Queen's Police Gold Medal Essay Competition, 1974; Queen's Silver Jubilee Medal, 1977. *Hobbies:* Shooting; Fishing; Golfing; Curling; Bowling; Tweed design; Hill walking. *Address:* Glen House, Carloway, Isle of Lewis, Scotland.

MACLEOD Donald Macrae, b. 19 Oct 1956, Kyle of Lochalsh, Scotland. Consultant Anaesthetist. m. Moira Catherine Anderson, 19 Apr 1986, 1 s, 1 d. *Education:* Nicolson Inst, Stornoway, 1971-74; Univ Aberdeen, 1974-79; MB, ChB, Aberdeen, 1979; FFARCS, Ireland, 1984. *Appointments:* Registrar, Anaesthetics, Aberdeen Tchng Hosps, 1982-86; Lectr, Anaesthetics, London Hosp Med Coll, 1986-88; Vis Assoc, Anaesthesiology, Duke Univ, USA, 1988; Cons Anaesthetist, Aberdeen Royal Infirmary, 1989-. *Publications:* Several articles in med jrnls on subjects pertaining to practice of anaesthesia. *Memberships:* Brit Med Assn; Assn Anaesthetists GB and Ireland. *Hobbies:* Sailing (Banff Sailing Club); Gold (Royal Aberdeen Golf Club); Gardening. *Address:* Hansville, 44 Gilbert Road, Bucksburn, Aberdeen, Scotland AB2 9AN, Scotland.

MACLEOD Iris Jean, b. 18 May 1927, Calgary, Alberta, Canada. Musician; Poet; Artist. Div, 2 s. *Education:* BA, Eng, San Jose Univ, 1961; BA, Music, California State Univ, 1982; Western Bd of Music Piano VI, Theory IV, Honours, 1942. *Appointments:* Formerly Sec-Tech Ed; Currently Musician-Poet, Comps emphasis; Early trouvère perfms in pass-the-hat art fairs and Civic volntr perfms; TV and radio perfms assocd with coll and univs, inc choral, piano and chamber music emphasis, 1972-82; Continuation of comps and personal recording (Ye Olde Experimental Recording Studio). *Creative Works:* 65 trouvère compositions, beginning with The Marlows Variations and concluding with the Echoes, 1972-75; Selections from Alexander, 1975-; Pippa's Song, 1975; Chord of nonchord, for piano and speaking poet; Fugue in B Flat; Fugue in A Flat; Partite 1; L'Etudiante, prelude and Fugue, for piano; Autumn Leaves, for piano; Autumn Variations; Two-Part invention for Piano; Canon for poet voice and piano; Etudes for piano and for drums; Little Girl and Her Lace Valentine, canonic variations on 01826; The Tempest, for synthesizer, improvised and taped; Shadings for violin and clarinet, parts 1 and 2; Convergences for piano; Lullaby for Ben for soprano and piano; Melody in B for Barry, for piano; Song for Valentines, for Barry, Judy, Ben, Clay; A Masque for All Souls Eve, 1982; Piano Compositions; Chamber Music Compositions; Trouvère recorder duets; Recordings: Private recordings of most of the above compositions. *Memberships:*California State Univ Alumni; Astronomical Soc of the Pacific; World Poetry Soc Intercontnl. *Honours:* Include prizes for song lyrics, in poetry competitions; International Order of Merit in Music, 1990; Grant for Alexander TV Production from SM Arts Council, 1975. *Address:* 1332 Paloma Ave, Belmont, CA 94002, USA.

MACLEOD John Alasdair Johnston, b. 20 Jan 1935, Stornoway, Scotland. General Medical Practitioner. m. Lorna Jean Ferguson, 4 Nov 1972, 2 s, 1 d. *Education:* Glasgow Univ; MRCGP; MB, ChB; DCH; DRCOG. *Appointments:* Jr hosp posts, Glasgow and London, 1963-72; Gen Practitioner, Lochmaddy, Isle of N Uist, 1973-. *Publications:* Med articles on isolated prac; Chapt in Myocardial Medley and in Nervous Laughter; Photographs for The Curlew in the Foreground. *Memberships:* Brit Med Assn; Fellow, Royal Soc Med; Wn Isles LMC, Sec 1977-91, Vice-Chmn 1991-. *Honours:* Dpty Lt, Wn Isles, 1979-; Vis Prof, Univ NC, 1985-. *Hobbies:* Sea and loch fishing; Growing trees in a barren island; Time sharing; Promoting Western Isles; Director, Olscot Ltd. *Address:* Tigh- na-Hearradh, Lochmaddy, Isle of North Uist, Western Isles PA 82 5AE, Scotland. 194.

MACLEOD Murdo Allan, b. 5 Sept 1926, Isle of Skye, Scotland. Minister of Religion. m. Nancie Margaret Johnstone, 11 Sept 1954, 2 s, 2 d. *Education:* Inverness Royal Acad; MA, Edinburgh Univ, 1952; Free Ch Coll, Edinburgh, 1952-55; Ordained, 1955. *Appointments:* Min, Tarbert Free Ch Scotland, 1955-63; Min, London Free Ch Scotland, 1963-70; Dir, Christian Witness to Israel, 1970-92. *Contributions to:* Hold Fast Your Confession, 1962; International Bible Dictionary, 1962; International Bible Encyclopedia, 4 vols, 1979; Illustrated Bible Dictionary, 3 vols, 1980; Witness of Jews to God, 1982; 20th Century Encyclopedia of Religious Knowledge, 1991. *Honours:*Pres, Lausanne Cons on Jewish Evangelism, 1982-1990; Moderator, Gen Assembly, Free Ch Scotland, 1984. *Hobbies:* Antique furniture; Photography; Walking. *Address:* 11 St Martins Drive, Eynsford, Kent DA4 0EY, England.

MACMAHON Douglas Graham, b. 1 Jan 1951, London, England. Consultant Physician; Medical Director; General Manager. m. Pauline Angela Mitchell, 4 Jan 1974, 2 s. *Education:* King's Coll London, 1968-70; King's Coll Hosp, 1970-73; MB, BS, London; LRCP, MRCS; MRCP, 1976; FRCP, 1991. *Appointments:* Jr med posts, London, Portsmouth, Aylesbury; Sr Registrar, Oxford; Cons, Cornwall, 1980-; Med Dir, 1991-. *Publications:* Dpty Ed, Care of the Elderly, 1989-91; 26 publs in med jrnls on topics related to care of the elderly, Parkinson's disease and var med conditions of late life. *Memberships:* Brit Geriatrics Soc, Coun Mbr 1984-87, Exec Mbr 1987-90; Parkinson's Disease Soc, Pres Truro Br, Coun Mbr; Brit Diabetic Assn. *Hobbies:* Walking; Skiing; Fishing. *Address:* Barncoose Hospital, Redruth, Cornwall TR15 3ER, England.

MACMILLAN (John) Duncan, b. 7 Mar 1939, Beaconsfield, England. Reader in Fine Art; Gallery Curator. m. 5 June 1971, 2 d. *Education:* Gordonstoun School; MA, St Andrews Univ, 1961; Acad Dip, London Univ, 1964; PhD, Edinburgh Univ, 1972. *Appointments:* Lectr, 1964, currently Reader, Fine Art, and Curator, Talbot Rice Gall, Edinburgh Univ; Radio and TV appearances. *Publications:* Painting in Scotland: The Golden Age, 1986; Scottish Art 1460-1990, 1990; Num articles; Exhib catalogues. *Memberships:* Chmn, Scottish Soc Art Hist; Edinburgh Fest Coun. *Hobbies:* Art; Walking. *Address:* 20 Nelson St, Edinburgh EH3 6LJ, Scotland. 1984.

MACNEACAIL Aonghas, b. 7 June 1942, Isle of Skye, Scotland. Writer. m. Gerda Stevenson, 21 June 1980, 1 s. *Education:* Glasgow Univ. *Career:* Writer's Fellowships: Gaelic Coll, Sabmal Mor Ostaig, Skye, 1977-79; An Comunn Gaidhealach (The Gaelic Assn), 1979-81; Ross and Cromarty Dist Coun, 1988-90; Writer's Bursary, Scottish Arts Coun, 1983; Overseas recitals/lecture tours: Republic of Ireland, 1972, 1976, 1984; FRG, 1985; 7 univs, N Am, 1987; European Poetry Fest, Belgium, 1988; Poland, Japan, 1990. *Publications:* Poetry Quintet, 1976; Imaginary wounds, 1980; Sireadh Bradain Sicir/Seeking Wise Salmon, poem in Gaelic, parallel text, 1983; An Cathadh Mor/The Great Snowbattle, poem in Gaelic, parallel text, 1984; An Seachnadh/The Avoiding, poems in Gaelic, paralley text, 1986; Rock and Water, 1990; Work in: Pembroke Magazine, USA, 1976; Poetry Australia, 1977, 1985; International Poetry Review, USA, 1979; Tijd Voor Poezie, Belgium, 1984; 2 PLUS 2, Switzerland, 1986. *Memberships:* Nat Union Jrnlsts; Brit Actors Equity Assn. *Honours:* Grampian TV Poetry Award; Gaelic Books Coun Award; Diamond Jubilee Award, Scottish Assn for Speaking of Verse; Nat Mod Lit Prize, An Comunn Gaidhealach. *Hobbies:* Reading; Walking. *Address:* 1 Roseneath Terrace, Edinburgh EH9 1JS, Scotland. 11.

MACPHAIL Mary Jean, b. 8 Feb 1938, Sudbury, Ontario, Canada. Opera Singer; Music Professor. m. Eric Domville, 13 July 1987, 1 s, 2 d, 1 stepdaughter. *Education:* Assoc, Royal Conservatory Mus, 1959; Artist Dip, 1962, Mus Bac, 1975, MMus (incomplete), 1978, Univ Toronto. *Career:* Sang in operas: Madam Butterfly, 1962, Mikado, 1963, HMS Pinafore, 1964, Berlin to Broadway, 1974, Die Walkurie, 1976, Magic Flute, 1977, Die Fliegende Hollander, 1981, Electra, 1983, Faust, 1986, Suor Angelica, 1991; Recording, Loving (Murray Schafer); Recitals, Rome, Paris, London, Toronto, San Fran; Soloist w maj Can orchs incl Toronto Symph Orch, Arts Ctr Orch, Hamilton Phil, Kitchener Phil; Prof, Singing, Univ Toronto. *Memberships:* Actors Equity Union; ACTRA; Heleconian Club; Nat Assn Singing, Pres, Ont Chapt. *Honours:* Arts Grant, Can Coun, 1977; Arts Grant, Ont Arts Coun, 1982. *Hobbies:* Gardening; Swimming; Walking. *Address:* 342 Brunswick Ave, Toronto, Ontario, Canada M5R 2Y9.

MACPHERSON Andrew Hall, b. 2 June 1932, London, England. Author; Consultant. m. Elizabeth Menzer, 8 May 1957, 2 s, 1 d. *Education:* Bs Carleton Univ, Can, 1950; MSc, 1954, PhD, 1967, McGill Univ. *Appointments:* Asst Curator, Birds, Nat Mus Can, 1957-58; Rsch Biologist, 1958-63, Rsch Mgr, 1963-70, Reg Dir, 1970-75, Can Wildlife Serv; Dir-Gen, Dept Environment, 1975-85; Dir-Gen, No Affairs, 1985-89; Retired, 1989. *Publications:* Num papers on taxonomy, faunistics, ecology and zoogeog of Can Arctic animals; The Canadian Ice Angler's Guide, 1985. *Memberships:* Gov, Arctic Inst N Am; Cnslr, Soc Systematic Zoology; Bd Mbr, True N Strong and Free Inquiry Soc; Bd Mbr, Sustainable Population Soc; Nat Dir, Trout Unltd, Can. *Honour:* Centennial Medal, 1969. *Hobbies:* Fly fishing; Big game hunting; Conservation, environment and population; The Canadian Arctic. *Address:* 9619 96A Street, Edmonton, Alberta, Canada T6C 3Z8. 142, 143.

MACPHERSON Annie Mary Donaldson, b. 20 Aug 1917, Edinburgh, Scotland. Retired Headmistress. *Education:* MA (Hons), 1940, DipEd, 1940, Edin Univ; Moray House Coll Ed, 1940-42; London Guildhall Tchrs Dip, Speech, Drama, 1950s; LAMDA, 1950s. *Appointments:* Tchng, Edinburgh Educ Auth, 1942-44, 1945-69, incl 17 yrs Leith Acad; George Sq Girls School, Edinburgh, 1944-45; Hd, Hist, Aburi Girls School, Accra, Ghana, 1969-73; Hd, Tabeetha School Int Second Mixed School, Jaffa, Israel, 1973-79. *Publication:* Pamphlet on 1930s in N England. *Memberships:* Past Sec, Coun Christian and Jews; Univ Staff Club; Caledonian Club. *Hobbies:* Music; Drama; Drawing; Embroidery; Church work. *Address:* Cluny House, 13 Parkside Terrace, Edinburgh EH16 5BL, Scotland. 138.

MACPHERSON Archibald Ian Stewart, b. 10 Aug 1913, Newtonmore, Scotland. Retired Surgeon. *Education:* Open Scholar, Fettes Coll, 1927- 31; MC, ChB, Univ, 1936, ChM, 1952, Univ Edinburgh; FRCS Edinburgh, 1940. *Appointments:* Clin Tutor, 1940-42, Lectr, Clin Surg, 1952-54, Univ Edinburgh; Active Serv, Lt Col, RAMC, 1942-47; Cons Surg: Royal Hosp Edinburgh and Royal Edinburgh Hosp, 1954-78; Leith Hosp, 1961-68. *Publications:* The Spleen, book, 1975; Over 100 sci papers on surg of blood vessels, liver, spleen in med jrnls; Papers on Clan Macpherson and related subjects in Creag Dhubh and in Clan Chatnan. *Memberships:* Coun Mbr, Assn Surgs GB; Fndr Mbr, Vascular Surg Soc, Pres 1977; Hon Mbr, Surg Rsch Soc; Royal Coll Surgs Edinburgh, VP 1976-69; Univ Edinburgh Grads Assn, Pres 1972-75; Royal Celtic Soc, VP. *Honours:* Gunning Victoria Jubilee Prize, 1941; Rockefeller Rsch Fellowship, 1948-49; Honeyman Gillespie Lectr, 1952; Fellow, Royal Soc Edinburgh, 1960; Gordon Taylor Lectureship, 1978; Chief, Gaelic Soc Inverness, 1984; Chmn, VP, Clan Macpherson Assn. *Hobbies:* Outdoor sports esp cricket (Scottish International 1934-35); Golf; Fishing; Highland history. *Address:* 18 Grange Terrace, Edinburgh EH9 2LD, Scotland. 184.

MACPHERSON Gavin Kennedy, b. 15 Dec 1934, Leeds, England. Property Manager; Company Director. m. Jeane Mary Hartley, 23 Apr 1960, 1 s, 1 d. *Education:* Leeds Coll Technology, 1955-58. *Appointments:* Serv, RAF, 1953-55; Mgmt appts and dir'ships, Brit Textile Manufactury Ind, 1955-83; Conservative Party Parly Cand, Leeds S Constituency, 1970; Pres, Leeds Jr Chmbr of Comm, 1972-73; Nat VP, Brit Jr Chmbr of Comm, 1973; Mbr, Nat Air Transp Users Consultative Comm, Brit Civil Aviation Auth, 1973-79; Mbr, Advsry Comm on Brit Airports Policy, Dept Trade, 1978-79; Gov, Moorlands School, Leeds, 1979-; Chmn, Brit Inst Mgmt, Leeds and Ctrl Yorks, 1981-83; Mbr, Nat Coun, Brit Inst Mgmt, 1983-89; Coun Mbr, Leeds Chmbr of Comm and Ind, 1985-; Trustee, Leeds Schools Awards Project, 1986-; Reg Policy Spokesman, Brit Inst Mgmt, 1987-; Pres, European Senate of Int Jr Chmbrs of Comm, 1990- 91; Dpty Chmn, Leeds Wn Hlth Auth, 1990-91; Chmn, Mgmt Rsch Grps, Leeds Grp 10. *Memberships include:* Mgmt Rsch Grps; Rotary Club Leeds; Railway Travel and Correspondence Soc. *Honours:* Companion, Brit Inst Mgmt; Fellow, Inst Dirs. *Hobbies:* Industrial and professional management; European politics; Railways; Travel. *Address:* 4 Dyneley Hall, Bramhope, Leeds LS16 9BQ, England.

MACRORY Avril, b. 5 Apr 1956, Republic of Ireland. Commissioning Editor, Television. m. Val Griffin, 9 July 1983, 1 s. *Education:* BA Hons, Hist Art, Engl, Music, Univ Coll, Dublin, 1978. *Appointments:* Radio, Telefis Eireann, RTE (Irish Nat TV), 1978-86; Prod, Dir, 1986-88, Hd, Variety, Music, Commissioning Ed, Music, 1988-, Channel 4 TV, London, England. *Creative works:* TV progs: Drama, music, current affairs, children's progs. *Memberships:* Brit Acad Film and TV Arts; Royal TV Soc; Fndr Mbr, TV Prods Assn Ireland; Fndr Mbr, Ctr Performing Arts; Celtic Film and TV Assn; Bd Mbr, IMZ Int Music Prods. *Honours:* Best Dir Award, Theatre, Ireland, 1976, 1977. *Hobbies:* Music; Theatre; Cinema; Reading; Tennis; Watersports. *Address:* Channel 4 TV PLC, 60 Charlotte St, London W1P QA4, England.

MADALA Mani Kumari, b. 23 Sept 1951, Secunderabad, India. Consultant; Researcher; Trainer. *Education:* Postgrad Hons Dip, Personnel Mgmt and Indl Rels, Labour Rels Inst, India, 1973; MPhil, Jawaharlal Nehru Univ, New Delhi, 1979; PhD, Indian Inst Technology, New Delhi, 1983. *Appointments:* Cons, 1975-83, Sr Cons, Dpty Dir, 1983-, Nat Productivity Coun, New Delhi. *Publications include:* Motivating the Affluent Workers. The Challenge of Coming Years (co-author), 1979; Training Technology (co-author), 1979. *Memberships:* Int Indl Rels Assn, Geneva; Life Mbr: Indian Inst Pub Admin; Indian Acad Applied Psychology, Calcutta; Indian Inst Technology Delhi Alumni Assn. *Honours:* Award, Best Paper on Women's Dev, Indian

Comm Int Women's Yr, 1975; Allahabad Univ Award, Best Int Essay on Is Gandhi Relevant to Modern India, 1976; Shri Ram Award, Best Mgmt Article, 1981. *Hobbies:* Reading; Cooking; Interior decoration. *Address:* No 1 Wellingdon Road, Secunderabad, Andhra Pradesh, India.

MADARASZ Imre, b. 1 May 1962, Budapest, Hungary. University Professor. *Education:* MA, Hungarian and Italian Lang and Lit, Budapest Elte, 1988; Cand in Lit studies, 1992. *Appointments:* Tchr, Gymnasium, L.Nemeth, Budapest, 1987-91; Postgrad Scholaship, Hung Acad of Scis, Budapest, 1988-91; Asst Prof, Kossuth Lajos Univ, Debreceen, 1990-; Asst Prof, Eotvos Lorand Univ, Budapest, 1991-. *Publications:* Translations: Beccaria, 1989; Sade, 1989; Ungaretti Commentary on Dante's Inferno, 1992; Author of: Alfieri the Tyrannicide, 1990; Kolcey, Gotvos, Madach, 1989; Analyses of 18- 19th C Hungarian Poems, 1991; 370 publications inlcuding book chapters, articles and reviews in 5 languages. *Memberships:* Assn of Modern Philol, Budapest; Assn of Hungarian Lit Hist; Hungarian Assn of Polis Scis; Hungarian Assn of Philos. *Address:* Klauzal Ter 16, Budapest 1072, Hungary.

MADRZAK Henryk, b. 18 Dec 1929, Skalmierzyce Nowe, Poland. Professor of Law. m. 4 Oct 1969, 2 s. *Education:* LLM, 1955; Doct, 1963; Habilitation, 1978. *Appointments:* Asst, 1955-64; Adj, 1964-69; Asst Prof, 1969-91; Prof, Law, Inst Civil Law, Fac Law, Wroclaw, 1991-. *Publications:* Provisional Execution of Judgements in Civil Matters in Poland. The Responsibility of Married Partners for Each Others' Debts in the Community of Property According to Polish Law, monograph, 1977. *Membership:* Soc Scis and Letters Wroclaw. *Honours:* Sci prize, Min Nat Educ. *Hobbies:* Baroque music (Handel); Classical music (Mazart, Haydn, Beethoven). *Address:* ul Czarnieckiego 34 m 6, 53-651 Wroclaw, Poland.

MAEDA Yukio, b. 29 Mar 1922, Japan. Engineering Educator. m. Junko Minakata, 8 Dec 1961. *Education:* BEng, 1945, Postgrad, 1947, Hokkaido Univ, Sapporo; DEng, Univ Tokyo, 1966. *Appointments:* Lectr to Asst Prof, Civil Engrng, Hokkaido Univ, Sapporo, 1947-57; Tech Dir, Sakurada Iron Works Co, Tokyo, 1958-66; Asst Prof to Prof Emeritus, Civil Engrng, Osaka Univ, Suita, 1966-; Prof, Kinki Univ, Higashi-Osaka, 1985-89; Hd, Structural Rsch Ctr, Osaka, 1989-. *Publications:* Author or ed, 9 acad or profl books; Author or co-author, 310 acad or profl papers. *Memberships:* Dir, Hon Mbr, Japan Soc Civil Engrs; Int Assn Bridge and Structural Engrng, Chmn Tech Comm, Hon Mbr; Fellow, Am Soc Civil Engrs, Pres Kansai Br, Japan. *Honours:* Hiroi-Osamu Grant, Hokkaido Univ, 1945; Fulbright Grant, US Educl Comm, Tokyo, 1955; Tanaka Prize, published paper at 1979 Proceedings, Japan Soc Civil Engrs, 1981; Achievement Prize, Min Labour, Japanese Govt, 1988; Life Mbrship, Japan Welding Soc, 1989. *Hobby:* Photography. *Address:* 404 Iwazono 10-16, Ashiya, Hyogo 659, Japan. 52.

MAES-JELINEK Hena, b. 27 Dec 1929, Liege, Belgium. Professor of English and Commonwealth Literature. m. Rene Maes, 8 Jan 1955. *Education:* BA, BYU Univ, USA, 1951; Licence en Philologie Germanique, 1957; Tchrs Trng Dip, 1958, PhD, 1965, Univ Liege. *Appointments:* Tchr, Engl, coll educ, 1957-59; Tchng Asst, Lectr, 1959-77, Prof, Engl Lit, then Prof, Engl Lit, C'wlth Lit, 1977-, Univ Liege. *Publications:* Criticism of Society in the English Novel between the Wars, 1970; The Naked Design, A Reading of Palace of the Peacock, 1976; Wilson Harris, 1982, 2nd Ed in preparation; Heart of Darkness, a Critical Commentary; 51 articles on Engl lit and new lits in Engl esp Caribbean, Australian, S African; Ed or co-ed, var books; Gen Ed of series, Cross/ Cultures, Readings in the Post-Colonial Literatures in English. *Memberships:* Fdng Mbr, Past Sec, Assn C'wlth Lit and Lang Studies; V- Chmn, Soc d'Etudes pour le C'wlth, France; Fellow, Royal C'wlth Soc; C'wlth Trust; Vice-Chmn, Belgian Assn Anglicists in Higher Educ;

Vice-Chmn, Assn des Germanistes de l'Univ de Liege; CELATMA, Sorbonne Nouvelle. *Honours:* OBE; Prize, Criticism of Society in the English Novel between the Wars, Assn des Amis de l'Univ de Liege, 1971. *Hobbies:* Literature; History; Painting. *Address:* Residence Petit Paradis, 1 Quai de Rome (072), 4000 Liege, Belgium.

MAGAZOV Oleg Albertovich, b. 7 June 1966, Shucheay, Kurgan Region, USSR. Biologist; Group Head. m. Lubov Nickolaevna Magazova, 18 Aug 1987, 1 s. *Education:* Degree, Biology Dept, Perm Univ, 1990. *Grp Hd, Reg Station, Young Lovers of Nature, 1990-*. *Publication:* Article on biology in Student's Research Work collection. *Hobbies:* Theoretical biology; Aquarial fishes; History of ancient Russia; Basketball. *Address:* Komsomal prospect 24, Flat N13, Chalabinsk 454138, Russia.

MAGENTA Amelie, Duchess of, b. 2 July 1963, Pitfour, Scotland. m. Philippe Duke of Magenta, 4 May 1990. 1 d. *Education:* Heathfield, 1974-81; Dundee Col of Commerce, 1982-83; City of London Poly, 1983-85. *Hobbies:* Gardening; Winemaking. *Address:* Abbaye de Morgeot, Chassagne Montrachet, 21190 France.

MAGNUSDOTTIR Torunn, b. 12 Dec 1920, Iceland. Historical Researcher. m. (1) Bjorn Gudmundsson, 29 June 1940, (2) Helgi Jonsson, 24 Sept 1954, 4 s, 1 d. *Education:* Tchrs Cert, 1971, BEd, 1982, Kennaraskola Islands, 1971; BA, Hist, 1979, Cand mag, Hist, 1982, Haskola Islands. *Appointments:* Tchr, 1971-76; Hdmistress, 1976-86; Rsch in Women's Hist, 1983-. *Publications:* Lond og lydir, X. Ungverjaland og Rumenia, 1977; Sjosokn sunnlenskra kvenna 1697-1980, 1984; Sjokonur a Islandi 1891- 1981, 1988; Thórfin Knyr Upphaf Verkakvennah & Lyfingar a Islandi, 1991. *Memberships:* Comm, Conf Nordic Women's Rsch, 1983, 1986; Writer Assn Iceland; Assn Non-Fiction Writers Fedn Women's Rights; WIDF. *Hobbies:* Travel; Literature. *Address:* Hofsvallagata 17, 101 Reykjavik, Iceland. 3, 138, 152.

MAGNUSSON David, b. 5 Sept 1925, Nassjo, Sweden. Professor of Psychology. m. Anita Grotenfelt, 1 s, 2 d. *Education:* Dip, Erica Fndn, 1953; BA, 1955; Fil lic, 1957; PhD, 1959; Docent, Dept Psychology, Stockholm Univ, 1959. *Appointments:* Elem School Tchr, 1946-52; School Psychologist, 1954-55; Rsch Asst, 1955-58, Lectr, 1958-65, Asst Prof, Hd, Univ Applied Psychology, 1965-69, Olof Eneroth Prof, Psychology, 1965-, Chmn, Dept Psychology, 1969-77, 1980-84, Stockholm Univ. *Publications:* Test theory, 1961, translated into Engl, German, Spanish, Portuguese, Polish, other langs; Individual development and adjustment (w A Duner and G Zetterblom), 1975; Individual development from the interactional perspective, 1988; Data quality in longitudinal research (w L R Bergman), 1990; Pubertal maturation in female development (w H Stattin), 1990; Female life careers (w S Gustafson), 1991; Matching problems and methods in longitudinal research (w L R Bergman), in press; Articles in sci jrnls. *Memberships:* Swedish Psychological Assn, Sec 1957-59, VP 1959-60, Pres 1960-61; Swedish Assn Univ Tchrs, VP 1959-63; Swedish Assn Univ Profs, Pres 1970-78; Former Mbr, Swedish Rsch Coun Social Scis and Humanities, Vice-Chmn 1977-83, Chmn Exec Comm 1980-83; European Sci Fndn, Coun Mbr 1983-86, VP 1986-89; VP, Academia Europaea; Royal Swedish Acad Letters, Hist and Antiquities; VP, Royal Swedish Acad Scis; Royal Swedish Acad Engrng Scis. *Honours:* Kt, Order of Northern Star, 1973; Hon Dr, Univ Jyvaskyla, Finland, 1984; Speaker of Yr, Brit Soc Social Psychology, 1984; Royal Medal of Serafim, 1989; Speaker of Yr, Irish Psychological Assn, 1990. *Hobbies:* Music; Literature; Sports. *Address:* Department of Psychology, University of Stockholm, S-106 91 Stockholm, Sweden.

MAGOR Edward Walter Moyle, Major, b. 1 June 1911, Lamellen, St Tudy, Cornwall, England. Retired Government Servant. m. Daphne Davis Graham, 15 Aug 1939, dec. 1972, 2 d. *Education:* Magdalen Coll, Oxford

(Demy), 1929-32; Magdalene Coll, Cambridge, 1932-33; Staff Coll, Quetta, 1942; Imperial Def Coll, 1962. *Appointments:* The Poona Horse, Indian Army, 1934-37, 1939-43; Indian Pol Serv, 1937-39, 1943-47; Colonial Admnstv Serv, Keny, 1947-61, incl Ag Min Def, 1956, Sec to Cabinet, 1958; Home Civil Serv, Bd Trade, 1961-71. *Publications:* Ed, Royal Hort Soc's Rhododendron and Camelia Yearbook, 1974-82. *Memberships:* Pres, Cornwall Garden Soc, 1982-84; Pres, Royal Cornwall Agricl Assn, 1983; Chmn, St John Coun Cornwall, 1973-78. *Honours:* OBE, 1956; CMG, 1960; Medaille de la Belgique Reconnaissante, 1961; Dpty Lt, Cornwall, 1974; CStJ, 1978; High Sheriff, Cornwall, 1981; Veitch Mem Gold Medal, Royal Hort Soc, 1985. *Hobbies:* Horticulture; Plant ecology. *Address:* Lamellen, St Tudy, Bodmin, Cornwall PL30 3NR, England. 1, 41.

MAGUIRE Bassett, b. 4 Aug 1904, Alabama City, Alabama, USA, dec. 6 Feb 1991. Botanist. m. (1) Ruth Richards, 1926, 1 s, 1 d, (2) Celia Kramer, 25 Mar 1951. *Education:* Univ GA, 1926; Grad studies, Univ Pitts, 1926; PhD, Cornell Univ, 1938. *Appointments include:* Instr, Univ GA, Cornell Univ; Prof, UT State Univ, Columbia Univ, NYC, CUNY; Curator, Hd Curator, Coord of Tropical Rsch, Asst Dir/Dir, Bot, Nathaniel Lord Britton Disting Sr Curator, NY Botan Garden; Bd Mgrs, NY Botan Garden Corp; Advsry Comm, Cary Arboretum, Assessor, Dir of Bot, Jardin Botanico Nacional, Santo Domingo, Dominican Republic; Also var field activities, N and S Am, W Indies, Africa, Asia. *Publications:* Articles, treatises on Wn Am bot, neotropics vegetation, geog. *Memberships include:* Hon Mbr, Sociedad Venezolana de Ciencias Naturales; Life Corres Mbr, Royal Netherlands Botan Soc; Hon Life Mbr, Am Geogl Soc; Life Mbr, Newcomen Soc; Fellow, Fndr, Assn Tropical Biology; Fndg Mbr, Academia de Ciencias de la Republica Dominicana; Fndr, Councillor, Org Tropical Studies; Org Flora Neotropica. *Honours include:* Sarah Gildersleeve Fife Mem Medal, 1952; Discoverer, mountain complex, Sierra de la Neblina, 1953; David Livingstone Gold Centenary Medal, 1965; Num grants. 1, 2, 6, 52, 128, 139.

MAHAFFY Sarah Georgiana, b. 21 July 1952, England. Managing Director. m. William Baker, 16 Dec 1977, 1 s. *Education:* St Hugh's Coll, Oxford, 1971-74; BA Hons, Mod Hist, 1974. *Appointments:* Methuen Educl, 1974-75; Macmillan Educ, 1975-84; Ran own co, 1984-86; Mng Dir, Boxtree Ltd, 1986-. *Hobbies:* Theatre; Ballet; Food. *Address:* 28 Cassland Road, London E9 7AN, England.

MAHAFZAH Ali Mifleh, b. 15 Mar 1938, Kofr Jayez, Jordan. University President. m. Fawzieh Shago, 2 Oct 1968, 2 s, 2 d. *Education:* Licence, Hist, Dip, Educ, Damascus Univ, Syria, 1960; Doct, 3rd cycle, Islamic Studies, Hist, 1971, Doct d'Etat, Arts, Humanities, 1980, Sorbonne Univ, Paris. *Appointments include:* VP, Acting Pres, 1981-84, Prof, Hist, 1982-, Pres, 1984-89, Mutah Univ; Prof, Hist, 1982-, Pres, 1989-, Yarmouk Univ, Irbid. *Publications:* Jordanian British Relations; Attitudes of France, Germany and Italy towards Arab Unity; Political Thought in Palestine; Political Thought in Jordan, 2 vols; Contemporary History of Jordan, The Emirate; Arab Intellectual Trends in the Renaissance Period; German Palestinian Relations, 1841-1945; Intellectual Movement in Palestine and Transjordan, 1775-1925. *Memberships:* Int Assn Univs; Int Assn Univ Presidents; Assn of Arab Univs; Assn Arab Histns; Coun Educ; Jordanian Coun Higher Educ; Comm Hist of Bilad Al-Sham, Gtr Syria; Chmn, Union Jordanian Writers and Men of Letters; Royal Comm Mutah Univ, Jordan. *Honours:* Jordanian Independence Medal, 4th Order; Iron Cross, 3rd Order, FRG; Chevalier, Legion Hon Order, French Govt; Acad Palm Medal, French Govt; Jordanian Education Medal of the Highest Order; State Prize of Merit for Social Sciences. *Hobbies:* Swimming; Tennis; Hunting. *Address:* Yarmouk University, Irbid, Jordan.

MAHAN Danny Milton, b. 16 Oct 1963, Conway, Arkansas, USA. Engineer. m. Tamara Joan Mahan, 6 June 1987. *Education:* BS, Indl Engrng, 1986, MBA, 1987, Univ AR. *Appointments:* Indl Modernisation Prog, USAF/MSO/ENP, 1988-91; Mgr, AMRAAM MRL Mfg, USAF/ASO/YMEM, 1991; Hazardous Materials Engr, USAF/AFDTC/SES, 1991-. *Creative works:* Air Force System Command Papers, Prog Winner, 1989. *Memberships:* Tau Beta Pi, Recording Sec 1986, VP 1987; Alpha Pi Mu, Engrs Coun Rep 1986; Gamma Beta Phi; Cardinal Key; Golden Key; Blue Key; Shriners; Masons, 32nd degree; Inst Indl Engrs, Treas 1986; Soc Mfg Engrs. *Honours:* Outstanding Merit in Indl Engrng, 1983, 1984, 1985, 1986; Ray Belknap Ldrship Award, 1986, 1987.*Hobbies:* Computers; Water-skiing; Camping. *Address:* 121 Meadow Woods Lane, Niceville, FL 32578, USA. 7.

MAHENDRA Balram Kumar, b. 25 Aug 1927, Noormahal, Punjab, India. Company President. m. Prem Mahendra, 12 Feb 1959, 1 s, 1 d. *Education:* BSc (Met), Metall Engrng; MIIM; MMGI; FGMS; Indl Mgmt, USA; UN Fellow. *Appointments:* Self-employed Businessman; Fndr, Mng Ptnr, Chief Tech Expert, Mecanico Indl Engrs, 1949; Fndr, Ptnr, Mecanico Mgt Engrs, 1950; Fndr, Mecanico Magnetic Products, 1958; Currently Pres, Mahendra Grp, Profl Engrng Indl Mgmt. *Publications:* Var papers incl: Non-destructive Testing of Materals, Structures, Castings and Welds with Ultra-Violet Light, 1953; A Plan for Establishing Aluminium Industry in Central India, 1955; Vacuum Metallizing - A New Industry, 1955; High Tension Separation of Minerals, 1956; Surface Finishing by Vacuum Metallizing, 1958; Prospecting and Mining with Ultra- violet Light, 1958; Mineral Beneficiation and High Tension Separation, 1959; Development of Chemical Industries, 1959; Patent: MECANICO Swarf Crusher. *Memberships:* Delhi Gymkhana Club Ltd; Chmn, US Mgmt Assn; Hon Sec, Indian Inst Metals, Delhi Chapt, 1953-59; Hon Sec, Okhla Indl Estate Assn; Indian Econ Mission. *Honours:* Industrialist, having foudned several Metall and engrng firms, Indian Inst Metals; Award for Disting Servs Award as Fndr-Sec, Indian Inst Metals, Delhi Chapt, 1978. *Hobbies:* Painting; Poetry; Tennis; Writing. *Address:* C5 Chiragh Enclave, New Delhi 110048, India.

MAHER ALI Abd El Moneim, b. 9 Mar 1922, Dammanhour, Egypt. Emeritus Professor of Plant Protection; Company President. m. July 1948, 2 s. *Education:* BSc, Agricl, Fac Agric, Cairo Univ, 1943; PhD, Fac Sci, Univ Coll London, England, 1953. *Appointments:* Tutor, Fac Agric, Cairo Univ, to 1948; Dir, Ctrl Agricl Pesticides Lab, Min Agric, UNDP Project, 1948- 69; Chmn, Plant Protection, 1969-82; Prof Emeritus, Plant Protection, 1982-, Assiut Univ; Pres, Aradis Co. *Publications:* Textbook on pest control; Over 170 sci papers in sci periodicals; Chief Ed, Egyptian Journal of Natural Resources and Wildlife. *Memberships:* Fndr, Past Gen Sec, Egyptian Youth Hostel Assn; Gen Sec, Egyptian Zoological Soc; Gen Sec, Egyptian Assn for Conservation of Natural Resources. *Honours:* Award for Conservation Merit, World Wildlife Fund; Order of the Republic, 5th, 4th, 2nd Class; Order of Sci and Arts, 1st Class; State Prize, Sci and Arts, 1965. *Hobbies:* Travel; Archaeological studies. *Address:* 50 Wizaret Ziraa Street Dokki, Giza, Egypt. 97.

MAI Joachim, b. 14 Mar 1930, Berlin, Germany. University Teacher. m. Elizabeth Kapitza, 17 Aug 1963, 2 d. *Education:* Humboldt Univ, Berlin, 1949-53; Dr phil, 1957; Dr phil habil, 1969. *Appointments:* Asst, Chief Asst, 1957-70, Asst Prof, 1970-75, Prof Ordinary, 1975- , Univ Greifswald. *Publications:* Die preussisch-deutsche Polenpolitik 1885-1887, 1962; Das deutsche Kapital in Russland 1850-1894, 1970; 48 articles; Vom Narew bis an die Elbe. Erinnerungen sowietischer Kriegsteilnehmer der 2 Belorussischen Front (ed), 1965. *Memberships:* Verband der Osteuropahistoriker, Cologne; Heinrich-Schliemann-Gesellschaft, Ankershagen. *Hobbies:* Jogging; Travel. *Address:* Erwin-Haak-Weg 11, 2200 Greifswald, Germany.

MAIBAUM Matthew, b. 14 Aug 1946, Chicago, Illinois, USA. Psychologist; Writer. *Education:* Univ California, AB, 1969; UCLA; MPA, 1973; Calif Sch Prof Psychology, PhD, 1975; Claremont Grad Sch, PhD, Pol Sci, 1980. *Appointments:* Intern Pacific State Hosp, 1976-77; Metropolitan State Hosp, 1977-78; Private Practice, 1978-; Soc Sci Research & Writer, 1972-. *Publications:* Articles & Chapters. *Memberships:* Member Authors Guild of America; Dramatists Guild of America; Soc of Authors; Soc Advancement Field Theory. *Honours include:* Sigma Xi; Pi Gamma Mu. *Hobbies:* History; History of Technology; Theatre. *Address:* 826 Greentree Road, Pac Palisades, CA 90272, USA.

MAIER Franz Georg, b. 25 Oct 1926, Stuttgart, Germany. Historian. 3 d. *Education:* Army Service, 1944-45; Univ of Tubingen, Zurich, Rome, 1946-52; Dr Phil, Tubingen, 1951. *Appointments:* Research Fellow, Greece, 1952-56; Lectr Tubingen, 1957-63; Prof of Anc History, Frankfurt, 1963-66; Konstanz, 1966-72; Zurich, 1972-. *Publications include:* Paphos History & Archaeology. *Memberships include:* Hon Soc of Antiquar; Archaeological Inst; Alexander V Humboldt Foundation. *Honours:* Faculty Prize for PhD. *Hobbies:* Water Colour Painting. *Address:* Weinmanngasse 60, CH 8700 Kusnacht, Switzerland.52.

MAILVAGANAM Noel Paul, b. 20 June 1938, Sri Lanka. Snr Research Scientist. m. Moyra Nalini Ramanathan, 20 Nov 1964, 2 s. *Education:* BSc Univ of London, 1970; MSc, Council for Natl Acad Award, 1974; Chartered Chemist. *Appointments:* Research Tech, Poly of Central London, 1965-68; Res Chemist, Ashford, 1969-72; Res Chemist, Uxbridge, 1973-74; Vice Pres, R&D Sternson Ltd, Canada, 1975-87; Dir, R&D Master Builders, Canada, 1987-88; Hd Polymer Grp, Materials Sections Ins for Res in Construction, 1988-. *Publications include:* Ed, Repair Protection of Concrete Structures, CRC Res; Concrete Admixtures Handbook; Handbook of Grouts & Grouting; 20 Tech Papers. *Memberships include:* RILEM Cmtts T-IZY Repair of Concrete Structures, T-94; Hot Weather Concrete; CSA Committee; ACI Comm of Conc Admixtures; CSA Canadian Standards Assn; ACI; ASTM. *Honours:* CSA Reconition for Long Standing Chairmanship; Best Publ Award, IRC 1989. *Hobbies:* Reading; Gardening; Hiking. *Address:* 705 Cezanne Cr, Orleans, Ontario, K4A 2A7, Canada.5.88.

MAITLAND Militsa, b. 18 Nov 1946, London, England. Tchr. *Education:* BA, Univ of London, 1969; Dip ED, Moray House, 1972. *Hobbies:*Song and Dance. *Address:* 12 St Vincent Street, Edinburgh, EH3 6SH, Scotland.

MAJ Stanislaw Jozef, b. 28 Jan 1932, Staszow, Poland. Physician; Hematologist. m. Barbara Maria Drzewiecka, 8 May 1973, 2 s, 2 d. *Education:* Medical Acad, 1957; MD, 1965; DS, 1973; Prof of Medicine & Hematology, 1986. *Appointments:* Inst of Hematology, Warsaw, Research Asst, 1957-64; Asst Prof, 1965-73; Assoc Prof, 1974-85; Hd Dept Hematology, 1977-. *Publications:* Progress in Hematology; Polfa Drugs in the Treatment of Blood Diseases; Hematology; Normal Values in Internal Medicine; Atlas of Hematology. *Memberships:* Intl Soc of Hematlgy; Polish Soc of Hematology & Transfusiology; Polish Medical Assn. *Honours:* Outstanding Health Serv Worker; Gold Cross of Merits; Medal XL Years of Polish Republic. *Hobbies:* Reading; Clinical & Laboratory Hemotology. *Address:* Inst of Hematology, Chocimska 5, PL 00957 Warsaw, Poland. 50, 52, 139, 152, 158.

MAJCHROVICH Alfred Stepano, b. 2 June 1937, Minsk, USSR. Scientist; Philosophy. m. Sharafanovich Iness, 1 Apr 1961, 1 s. *Education:* Minsk Univ, 1959; Postgrad, 1964; DP, 1984. *Appointments:* Editor, Acad Ed, 1959-61; Scientist, Inst of Art in Acad of Sci, Minsk, 1964-69; Inst of Philosophy & Law, 1969-80; Chief of Dept, Inst of Philosophy, 1980-92. *Publications include:* J Kupala & J Kolas; Search on Truth Being & Men. *Memberships:* Byelorussian Philosophical Soc; Hunting

Soc; Scientific Councils. *Honours:* Medal of State Exhib; Byelorussian State Prem. *Hobbies:* Reading; Hunting; Sporting. *Address:* Gorny Zavulak 7 Kv 54, Minsk 220071, Respublica Byelorus.

MAJEWSKA Anna, b. 11 Nov 1927, Gorlice, Poland. Prof Dept of Conservation; Dentistry Medical Acad of Wroclaw. m. Janusz Majewski, 16 Oct 1952, 2 s. *Education:* Diploma, 1951; Doctor of Medicine, 1964; Habilitation, 1977; Prof, 1989. *Appointments:* Asst Dept of Conservative Dentistry, 1951; Lectr, 1964; Assoc Prof, 1978; Prof, 1990. *Publication include:* Researches in Oral Biology & Oral Pathobiology; Composition of Human Saliva & Dental Caries. *Memberships:* Polskie Towaezystwo Stomatologiczne. *Honours include:* Rectors Award. *Hobby:* Gardening. *Address:* Katedra Stomatologil Zachowawczej, ul Kuznicza 43/45, 50-138 Wroclaw, Poland.

MAJEWSKA Zofia, b. 25 Aug 1952, Jaszczów, Poland. Adjunct Lectr, Acad Tchr. m. Krzysztof, 8 May 1977, 2 d. *Education:* Polish Philology, 1971-76; Philosophy, Univ of Maria Sklodowska Curie, Lublin, 1974-76; Master of Polish Philology, 1976; Doc of Philosophy, 1988. *Appointments:* Asst, 1976-88; Adjunct Lectr, UMCS, Lublin, 1988. *Publications include:* Doctors Dissertation; Studies of Ingardens & Husserls Philosophy, Axiological Studies in Collective Editions. *Memberships:* Polish Philosophical Soc. *Hobbies:* Reading; Touring; Phenomehology; Axiology; Philosophy of Culture. *Address:* ul Paryska 7/14, 20 854 Lublin, Poland.

MAJOR John, b. 1943. m. 1 s, 1 d. *Appointments include:* Councilor, London Borough of Lambeth, 1968; Chmn, Accounts Committee, Housing Committee, 1969; Treasurer, Vice Chmn, Political Officer, Chmn, Brixton Young Conservatives, 1960-64; Chmn of brixton Conservative Assn, 1970-71; Joint Sec, Conservative Parliamentary Enviroment Committee, 1979; Parliamenary Private Sec, ministers of State, Home Office, 1981; Asst Government Whip, 1983; Lord Commissioner to the Treasury, 1984; Chief Sec to Treasury, 1987-89; Foreign Chancellor of Exchequer, 1989; Prime Minister, 1990-. *Memberships include:* Natl Union of Bank Employees. *Address:* Conservative Central Office, 32 Smith Square, London, England.

MAKANJUOLA Dorothy Ibifuro, b. 28 Aug 1946, Nigeria. Medical Practice, Radiologist. m. 29 Apr 1972, 2 s. *Education:* Univ of Lagos, 1965-66; Univ of Ibadan, 1966-71; Univ of Edinburgh, 1975; FRCR, London, 1977. *Appointments:* Internsjip UCH, Ibadan, 1971-72; Registrar, SnrRegistrar, Royal Inf Edinburgh, 1975-78; Lectr, Snr Lectr, Reader, Univ of Ife Nigeria, 1978-86; Prof of Radiol, Univ of Ife Nigeria, 1986; Vice Dean, Actg Dean, Faculty of Health Sc, Huniv ife. *Publications:* Over 30 Sci Publ. *Memberships:* Royal Coll of Radiology; Assn of Radiologist of West Africa; West African Coll of Surgeons; Zonta Intl. *Honours:* West African Coll of Surgeons, Fellow; Nigerian Post Grad Medical Coll, Fellow. *Hobby:* Swimming. *Address:* Dept of Radiology, Faculty of Health Sci, OA Univ, LE/FE Nigeria, West Africa.

MAKI Atsushi, b. 14 Jan 1948, Kanagawa, Japan. Prof of Economics, Keio Univ. m. Michie Yabu, 28 Feb 1975, 1 s, 1 d. *Education:* Keio Univ, Japan, BA, 1971; MA, 1973. *Appointments:* Asst Prof, Keio Univ, 1973-79; Assoc Prof, Keio Univ, 1979-87; Visiting Scholar, Harvard Univ, 1982-84; Prof, Keio Univ, 1987-; Visiting Prof, Osaka Univ, 1989-90; Visiting Fellow, Australian Natl Univ, 1990. *Publications:* A Theroy & Measurement of Demand; Articles to Profl Journals. *Memberships:* American Economic Assn; Japan Assn of Economic & Econometrics; Japan Assn of statistics; Japan Soc of Household Economics. *Honours:* Joe Walding Memorial Lectr at Massey Univ; Union of Natl Economic Assn in Japan, Japan Foundation Visiting Professorship. *Hobbies:* Reading; Tennis. *Address:* Keio Univ, Mita, Minato Ku, Tokyo 108, Japan.52.

MAKOGON Yuri Feodorovich, b. 15 May 1930, City of Kherson, USSR. Hydrocabons Recovery, Transport & Utillization Physical Chemical Processes. m. Makogon Inna, 17 Dec 1961, 1 s, 1 d. *Education include:* Asst Prof, Moscow Petroleum Inst, 1965; Doctor of Tech Sci, 1975; Prof, 1985; Full Member Russian Acad of Natural Sci, 1990. *Appointments include:* Shebelinka Gas Field, 1956-58; Post Grad Student, 1958-61; Asst, 1961-; Asst Prof, 1965-; Hd of Laboratory, Moscow Natl Gas Inst, 1974-88;Dir, Hydrocarbons & Environment Inst, 1991-. *Creative Works include:* 32 Patents; 170 Scientific Articles; 8 Monographs. *Memberships include:* US Soc of Petroleum Engrs; Russian Acad of Sci; USSR US Scientific Tech Collaboration on the Gas Hydrates Problem. *Honours include:* Ukraine Tech Comp Prize Winner; Gubkin State Prize Winner. *Hobbies:* Painting; Travel. *Address:* Leninsky Prosp, 63 Oil & Gas Research Inst, Moscow 117917, Russia.

MAKOSZA Mieczyslaw, b. 16 Nov 1934, Cieszewla, Poland. Scientist; Prof of Organic Chemistry. m. Anna Jaskowska, 8 Mar 1974, 1 s, 2 d. *Education:* Univ of Rostov D & Univ of Leningrad, MSc, 1951-55; Tech Univ, Warsaw, 1963. *Appointments:* Tech Univ, Warsaw, Asst, 1956; Docent, 1969; Prof, 1974; Inst of Organic Chemistry, Polish Acad of Sci, Prof, Dir, 1979. *Publications:* Scientific Publ in Field of Organic Chemistry over 230; Organic Synthesis. *Memberships:* Polish Acad of Sci; Natl Committee of Chemistry. *Honours include:* Jurzykowski Foundation Award. *Hobbies:* Reading; Skiing; Tennis. *Address:* ul siemiatycka 1 m 47, 01 312 Warsaw, Poland.

MALABANAN Ernesto Herella, b. 8 Aug 1919, Philippines. Physician. m. 29 Sept 1957, 4 s, 2 d. *Education include:* Univ of Philippines, AA, 1938; NY Believue Hosp, 1955-56; Cardiology, Western Reserve Unv, 1958. *Appointments:* WW 11 Veteran, 1944-46; Pres, Medical Dir, Batangas Doctors Hosp, 1959-82; Conslt, St Patricks Hosp, 1969-; Conslt, Golden Gate Hosp, 1970-; Conslt, Heart Centre, 1975-; dir, Malabanan Clinic, 1984-. *Publications:* Scientific Papers; Chronic Indolent Ulcers; Elctrolytes in Hypertension. *Memberships include:* Lions Intl; Intl Coll of Angiology; Philippine Coll of Cardiology; Philippine Acad of Family Physicians. *Honours include:* Diploma of Honor, Phil Medical Assn; Most Outstanding Fremason in the Phil, Field of Medicine. *Hobbies:* Sports, Basketball; Swimming; Baseball. *Address:* Hilltop, Batangas City 4201, Philippines.52.

MALASCHAK Dolores B, b. 19 Mar 1923, Illmo, Mo, USA. Retired Educator; Free Lance Writer. m. Anthony M Malaschak, 17 May 1941, 3 s, 2 d. *Education:* Missouri Grade Sch, 1966; Ba, Secondary Southern Illinois Univ. *Appointments:* Illinois Public Sch, 1971-78; Missouri Work Subbing, 1984-89; Belleville Area Coll, creative Writing, 1968-80. *Publications:* Run in the Morning Poetry; Rainbow in my Hand; the Prodigal; The Trilogy; Midnight in the Study. *Memberships include:* Natl League of American Pen Women; McKendree Writers Assn; Intl Belles Letters. *Honours include:* Diploma of Merit & Medal of Honor, Centro Studi E Scambi Intl. *Hobbies:* Oil Painting; Quilting; Music; Gardening & Flowers; Church Work; Puzzle books; Chickens; Children; GrandChildren; Friends. *Address:* RR 1 Box 96A, Gilman City, MO 64642, USA.5.8.11.

MALEEVA Alevtina, b. 16 May 1939, Moskow, Russia. Prof of Endocrinology, Hd of Steroid Hormone Lab, Inst of Nuclear Medicine, Medical Acad, Sofia. m. Christo Maleeva, 28 Jan 1961, 1 s, 1 d. *Education:* First Moscow Medical Inst, Internal Medicine, 1963-69; Asst Prof, 1969- 73; Snr Asst Prof, 1973-80; Assoc Prof, 1980; Full Prof, 1982. *Appointments:* Clinic of Intl Medicine, Jnr Asst Prof, 1963-73; Inst of Endocrinology, Medical Acad, Sofia, 1973-76; Inst of Nuclear Medicine, Snr Asst, Assoc Prof, Full Prof, 1976-91. *Creative Works include:* More than 200 Sci Papers; Clinicl Obstetric Gynecologic Endocrinology; Hormonotherapy. *Memberships include:* Bulgarian Soc of Nuclear

Medicine; European Assn of Nuclear Mediciene. *Honours include:* Jubilee Medal; Diploma Distinguished Medical Service. *Hobby:* Painting. *Address:* Radioimmunoassay Lab, Medical Acad, G Sofiisky Blvd 1, Sofia 1431, Bulgaria.

MALEY Alan, b. 20 July 1937, Southend On Sea, England. Dir Gen, Bell Educ Trust. m. Viva Patricia Hart, 24 Feb 1983, 1 s, 1 d. *Education:* BA, Cambridge, 1961; Cert Ed, Cambridge, 1962; Dip Tefl Univ of Leeds, 1963. *Appointments:* British Council Belgrade, 1963-66; ACCRA, 1966- 70; Milan, 1970-74; Paris, 1974-80; Peking, 1980-84; Madras, 1984-88; Bell Educational Trust, Cambridge, 1988-. *Publications include:* Guided English Conversations; Learning to Listen; Poem into Poem; Living Words, Living Worlds; The Mind's Eye. *Memberships:* Soc of Authors; Intl Assn of Tchrs of English as a Foreign Language. *Honour:* OBE. *Hobbies:* Food & Wine; Foreign Travel. *Address:* c/o Bell Educational Trust, Hillscross, Red Cross Lane, Cambridge, CB2 2QX, England.

MALHAN Prem Sheel, b. 15 Nov 1933, Panjab, India. Engr, Bhabha Atomic Research Centre. m. Karuna, 21 Nov 1983. *Education:* Physics & Mathematics, 1953; Electronics Engrng, 1957. *Appointments:* Apprentice Engr, Natl Physical Lab, 1957-58; Engr, Electronics Ltd, 1958-60; Engr Atomic Energy, 1962-68; Engr, 1968-76; Engr, Bhabha Atomic Energy Research Centre, 1976-. *Memberships:* Indian Nuclear Soc; Electron Microscope Soc of India; Cricket Club of India. *Honour:* Coll Colours. *Hobbies:* Swimming; Hiking; Rover Scout; Gardening; Reading. *Address:* 62 Vibha, 341 A Ramkrisna Paramhans Road, Opposite Cardinal Gragius Sch, Bandra, Bombay 400 051, India.52.

MALINAUSKAS Edvardas, b. 24 May 1937, Radviliskis. Free Artist. m. Neringa Jankauskaite, 24 Dec 1987, 3 s, 1 d. *Education:* Lithuania Inst of Art, 1963. *Appointments:* Klaipeda Pedagogical Sch, Tchr, 1963-65; Klaipeda Art Enterprize Artist, 1965-69; Klaipeda Sch of Art, Dir, 1969-79. *Creative Works include:* Oil Canvas; Marine Canvas. *Memberships:* The USSR Soc of Artists; The Soc of Artists of Lithuania; Klaipeda Yacht Club. *Honours:* City Award, The Best Summer Work; Honored Art Worker. *Hobbies:* Mountain Skiing; Yachting. *Address:* Misko Str 6, 5818 Klaipeda, Lithuania.

MALLAH Munawar Ali, b. 8 Jan 1966, Sakrand, Sindh. *Education:* Matriculation, 1982; Intermediate, 1985; Grad BBA (Honor), 1990; Masters MBA, 1991; MA, Sociology, 1992; Diploma Banking, 1992. *Publications include:* Articles; Books; Research reports. *Honours include:* Scholarship from primary Sch to Univ; Different Honors, Awards & Prizes. *Hobbies:* Reading; Travelling; Playing Cricket; Badminton; Music; Research. *Address:* c/o Moti Jewellers Sonara, Street Sakrand, Dist Nawabshah, Sindh, Pakistan.

MALLEK Janusz Marcin Michal, b. 24 May 1937, Dzlaldowo, Poland. Historian. m. Ewa Tybor, 17 July 1969, 1 d. *Education:* Magister Artium, 1960; Phil Dr, 1965; Habil, 1974; Assoc Prof, 1975; Prof Extraord, 1988; Full Prof, 1991. *Appointments:* Prof, Copernicus Univ Torun, Poland, 1990-91. *Publications include:* The Constitution of Ducal Prussia; M Kromer, Historyja Prawdziwa. *Memberships include:* Commission for the Hist of Representative a Parliam Institutions; Renaissance Soc of America. *Honours:* Ministry of Educ, Honor Ring from the Polish President. *Hobbies:* Vacation in Masuria; Reading; Politics. *Address:* ul Dobra 13, 87 100 Torun, Poland.

MALLETT Bernard Louis James, b. 23 Sept 1924, Bristol, England. Conslt Psychiatrist. m. (1) Vera Louise Pateman, 24 July 1948, 1 s, (2) Beryl Mary Ashworth, 1 Mar 1987, 2 s, 1 d. *Education:* Colstons Sch, Bristol, 1935-42; Guys Hosp Medical Sch, 1946-52; London Univ, 1957-60; MB. BS (Hons) 1952; MRCP, 1956; FRC

Psych, 1983. *Appointments:* RNVR Sub Lieut, HM Ships at Sea, 1942-46; House Surgeon, Phsyscian & Registrar, Guys Hosp, 1952- 57; Snr Reg, Profl Unit, Mandsley Hosp, 1957-60; Nuffield Research Fellow, Guys Hosp, 1960-63; Cons Psychiatrist, Fairfields Hosp, 1963-73; Snr Conslt Psychiatrist & Hd of Dept, Lister Hosp, 1973-89; Mental Health Tribunals, London & Oxford, 1973-. *Publications:* Sci Papers. *Memberships:* Royal Soc Med; Med Research Soc; Soc Pyschosomatic Research; Medico Legal Soc. *Honours include:* Colstons Sch, Foundation Scholar; NHS Distinction Awards. *Hobbies:* Fell Walking; Photography; Bridge. *Address:* The Tilehouse, 27 Tilehouse Street, Hitchin, Herts, SG5 2DY. England.

MALLOY Ruth Lor, b. 4 Aug 1932, Brockvilee, Ont, Canada. Freelance Travel Writer; Author; Editor. m. T Malloy, 5 June 1965, 2 s, 1 d. *Education:* Brockville Collegiate; Brockville Business Coll; Victoria Coll, BA, 1954; Sch of Social Work, BSW, 1960; Univ of Toronto. *Appointments include:* Sec, Canadian Friends Serv Committee; Sec, Canadian Mental Health Assn; Human Rights Researcher; Social Worker; Freelance Writer; Editor, Travel China Newsletter, 1986-. *Publications include:* Travel Guide to the Peoples Republic of China; Post Guide Hong Kong; Hong kong Gems & Jewelry. *Hobbies:* Travel; Photography; Collecting Handicrafts of Chinas Natl Minorities for Museums; Buying & Selling Silk, Antiques & Handicrafts from China. *Address:* c/o Writers Union of Canada, 24 Ryerson Avenue, Toronto, Ontario, Canada M5T 2P3.

MANAV Mahendra Kumar, b. 22 Mar 1921, Chhatarpur. Freedom Fighter; Writer; Politician; Translator; Publisher; Journalist. m. Vimla Agarkar, 6 June 1946, 1 s. *Education:* MA, 1945; Research Fellow, 1945-47; Sahitya Ratna, 1948; LLB, 1963. *Appointments:* Minister for Finance & Social Serv, 1952-56; Madhya Pradesh Leg Assembly, 1967-77. *Publications include:* Personal Essays; Translations; Travel; Reminiscences. *Memberships:* Lalik Kala Acad; Cooperative Bank Chhatarpur; MP Lekhak Sangh; Swani Pranava Hand Savaswati Literature Trust of India. *Honours include:* Best Journalist in the District. *Hobbies:* Reading; Writing; Travel. *Address:* 28 New Colony, Chhatarpur, Madhya Pradest, India.

MANAZIR ALI Syed, b. 11 Apr 1958, India. Teacher. m. 11 Jan 1987. *Education:* BSc Hons Chem, 1976; MBBS, 1982; Dipl in Child Hlth, 1985; MD, Paed, 1987. *Appointments:* Hs Phys, Paed, 1983-84; Registrar, 1987- 88; Lectr under PPP, 1988-. *Memberships:* Intl Col of Paed, 1985; Lif, Indian Acad of Paed, 1989; Nat Neonatol Forum, 1989; VP Chap, IAPS, 1992; Exec Mem, IAP, VP Chap, 1990; Insian Assn of Preventative and Soc Med, 1989; Nat Fac Mem on Neonatal Resus, 1992. *Honours:* Gold Medal, Gynae & Obs; Individual Res Grant, Chromosomal Analysis in Congenital defect. *Hobbies:* Music; Neonatology; Computer Medicine. *Address:* Dept of Paediatrics, Jawahar Lal Nehru Medical College. Aligarh Muslim Univ, Aligarh 202002, India.

MANCHEV Dimiter Todorov, b. 17 July 1934, Sofia. Bulgaria. Actor. m. Maria Pouchleva, 29 July 1965, 1 s, 1 d. *Education:* Natl Theatrical Acad, Sofia, 1954-59; Vidin Repertory Theatre, 1959-62. *Appointments:* Actor, Satirical Theatre, Sofi, 1962-. *Creative Works:* The best Person I Know; Nameless Band; The Grand Piano; TV & Radio Plays; Variety Show Performances. *Membership:* Union of the Bulgarian Actors. *Honours:* 2nd Degree State Award for Artists; 1300 Yrs Bulgarian Award. *Hobbies:* Cookery; Football. *Address:* 38B Gourko Street. Sofia 1000, Bulgaria.

MANDELL Sara Ross Sindel, b. 11 May 1938, New York, USA. Assoc Prof, Religious Studies. m. Leon Mandell, 23 Apr 1971, 2 Stepsons. *Education:* BA, Univ New York, 1964; MA, 1966; PhD, 1969. *Appointments:* Page Turner, Virgil Fox Organist, 1958-64; Asst Prof Classics, 1969-72; Asst Prof Classical, Univ of South

Florida, 1986-91; Assoc Prof, 1991; Assoc Prof Religious Studies, 1991-. *Publications include:* Articles; Harvard Theological Review; Ancient World; Classical Bulletin. *Memberships include:* Catholic Biblical Soc; American Acad o Religion; American Philosophical Assn. *Honours:* Honorable Mention, Westinghouse Sci Talent Search; Lute Award for Excellence in Undergraduate Tchrng. *Hobbies:* House Cats; Large Felines. *Address:* Dept of Religious Studies CPR 304, Univ of South Florida, 4202 Fowler Avenue, Tampa, FL 33620, USA.

MANDER John, b. 5 Aug 1924, Sheffield, England. Conslt Gynaecologist. m. Mary Josephine Clifford, 24 July 1957, 2 s, 2 d. *Education:* Dean Close Sch, 1937-42; Emmanuel Coll, Cambridge, 1942- 45; Univ Coll Hosp, Medical Sch, 1945-48. *Appointments:* House Officer, Registrar & Snr Reg, London Hospitals, 1948-60; Conslt Gynaecologist, York, 1960-. *Membership:* Royal Soc of Medicine. *Honours:* Natural Sci Tripos, 1st Class Hons; Volunteer Reserve Decoration. *Hobbies:* Sailing; Lawn Tennis; Walking; Crosswords; Music. *Address:* 99 Station Road, Upper Poppleton, York, England.

MANGUS Carl William, b. 20 Aug 1930, Broken Bow, Okla. USA, Conslt Tech, safety & Standards. m. Dortha Marie Wood, 10 Aug 1955, 2 s, 1 d. *Education:* BS, ME, Oklamhoma State Univ, 1955-58. *Appointments:* United States Air Force, 1951-55; Shell Oil Co & Shell Offshore Inc, 1958-86; Conslt Tech, Safety & Standards, 1986-91. *Publications include:* Standards Offshore Facilies; Standards Offshore Drilling Units; Personnel Safety. *Memberships include:* Reg Profl Engr; American Bureau of Shipping; American Petroleum Org; Natl Acad of Sci. *Honours:* Sc Holastic Honor Award, Oklahoma State Univ; American Petroleum Citation for Serv, New Orleans. *Hobbies:* Hunting; Fishing; Woodworking; Swimming; Boating; Travel. *Address:* PO Box 250, 59131 Cypress Bayou Lane, Lacombe, LA 70445, USA.7.

MANIWA Mitsuyuki, b. 15 Nov 1934, Japan. Sociology Researcher; Educator. m. 15 Apr 1970. *Education:* Kyoto Univ, 1960-65; MA, Kyoto Univ, 1962. *Appointments:* Toyama Univ, 1968-83; Shizuoka Univ, 1983-. *Publications:* The Sociology of Japanese Gemeinschaft; The Sociology of Crime; The Characteristics of Crime in Modern Japan; The Sociology of Japanese Group. *Membership:* Japanese Sociological Soc. *Hobbies:* Travel; Taking Pictures. *Address:* 3-3-1-152 Oshika, Shizuoka Shi 422, Japan. 52.

MANJURA Bonnie Doreen, b. 2 Mar 956, Duluth, Minnesota, USA. Partner. m. Daniel Charles Bood, 31 Jan 1984, 1 s. *Education:* Univ of Vienna, Univ of Munich, 1977-78; Univ of Oviedo, 1979; Notre Dame, Organ Mngt Inst, 1984. *Appointments:* State of Florida, Dept of Commerce Div of Tourism, 1979-80; State of Florida, Dept of Economic Devel, 1981-85; Greater Orlando Chamber of Commerce, 1980-85; Heathrow Land & Devel Corp, 1985-90; Jep & Assoc of Florida inc, 1988-90; The Centrra Group, 1985-; Gilbert Mktng & Advertising, 1991-. *Memberships include:* Florida Public Relations Assn; Leukemia Soc; Travel Ind Assn of America; PRSA. *Honours include:* Grand Patron, Tunon Intl Sch; AATG German Language Fluency Award. *Hobbies:* Tennis; Horticulture; Childrens Charities. *Address:* 1840 Wingfield Drive, Longwood, FL 32779, USA.7.132.

MANKA Malgorzata, b. 15 Jan 1951, Poznan, Poland. Scientific Worker; Univ Prof. *Education:* Agricl Univ, 1968-73; MSc Forestry, 1973; PhD Plant Pathology, 1979; Habilitation Pl Pathology, 1990. *Appointments:* Dept for Plant Pathology, Research Asst, 1973-80; Asst Prof, 1980; Dept for Forest Pathology, Assoc Prof, 1990; Univ of Agricl, Poznan. *Publications:* Over 40 Sci Papers. *Memberships:* Polish Phytopathological Soc (Secretary 1991-93); European Foundation for Plant Pathology (President 1992-94); Intl Soc for Plant Pathology. *Hobbies:* Gardening; Culture History; Gothic Art.

Address: Dept for Forest Pathology, Agriclt Univ, ul Wojska Polskiego 71c, 60-625 Poznan, Poland.

MANN Anthony Howard, b. 11 Dec 1940. Prof of Epidemiological Psychiatry. *Education:* Rugby Sch, Jesus Coll Cambridge, St Bartholomews Hosp. *Appointments:* Prof of Psychiatry, Royal Free Hosp Medical Sch, 1987; Prof of Epidemiological Psychiatry, Inst of Psychiatry, 1988; Vice Dean, Inst of Psychiatry, 1990. *Memberships:* Council of Section of Psychiatry; Royal Soc of Medicine; Royal Coll of Psychiatrists; Royal Coll of Physicians. *Honour:* Gaskell Gold Medal. *Address:* Inst of Psychiatry, De Crespigny Park, London SE5 8AF, England.

MANNERS Gerald, b. 7 Aug 1932, Durham, England. Prof of Geography. m. 11 Dec 1982, 1 s. *Education:* St Catharines Coll, MA, 1954. *Appointments:* Univ Coll of Swansea, 1957-67; Univ Coll of London, 1967-. *Publications include:* Geography in Energy; Coal in Britain; Office Policy in Britain. *Membership:* Sadlers Wells Foundation. *Hobby:* Theatre. *Address:* 105 Barnsbury Street, London N1 1EP, England.1.

MANNIKAINEN Osmo Tapio, b. 31 May 1944, Mantsala, Finland. Admin Dir; Mngt Conslt; Auditor. m. Ritva Helena Tiilikaiene, 27 June 1970, 1 s, 1 d. *Education:* LLM, 1967; MSc, 1972; Approved Accountant, 1988. *Appointments:* Mngng Dir, Mediekono Ltd, 1977-; Admin Dir, Mehilainen Group, 1984-. *Memberships:* Intl Hosp Federation Assn of Approved Accountants; Finnish Lawyers Assn; Finnish B SC Assn. *Hobbies:* Languages; Conditioning. *Address:* Elontie 95 E, 00660 Helsinki, Finland.52.

MANNING-WEBER Claudia Joy, b. 17 Mar 1950, Oak Park, IL. USA. Educator. *Education:* AAS, 1980; BA, Allied Health Educ & Mngt, 1986; MS, Adult Continuing Educ. *Appointments:* Adjunct Faculty: Prescott College, Prescott, AZ, 1991-; Clinical Co-ordinator, Phoenix Baptist Hospital, Phoenix, AZ, 1992-; South Suburban Coll, 1989- 91; Triton Coll, 1988-90; Coll of Dupage, 1987-91. *Publications:* Copyright, Feasibilty of Distance Delivered Educ in Nuclear Medicine Technology. *Membership:* Arizona State Soc of Radiologic Technologists. *Honours include:* Delta Kappa Gamme; Phi Beta Kappa; AAS Degree in Radiologic Tech; Eva Grace Long Scholarship. *Hobbies:* Reading; Writing, Stort Stories & Fiction; Bicycling; Hiking. *Address:* 10938 W Bermuda Drive, Pheonix, AZ 85039, USA. 138, 152.

MANNINGS David Michael, b. 19 Dec 1940, Guildford, Surrey, England. Univ Lectr. *Education:* Canterbury Coll of Art, 1957-60; Birkbeck Coll Univ of London, 1967-71; PhD, 1977. *Appointments:* Art Tchr, Manchester, 1961-63; northern Nigeria, 1963-66; Univ Lectr, 1971- . *Publications include:* Numerous Articles. *Memberships:* Walpole Soc; British Soc for 18th C Studies; Assn of Art Historians. *Hobbies;* Reading; Travel. *Address:* Dept of History of Art, Kings Coll, Univ of Aberdeen, Aberdeen AB9 2UB, Scotland.

MANOHAR Sujata, b. 28 Aug 1934, Bombay, India. Judge, Bombay High Court. m. 13 Mar 1959, 2 s, 1 d. *Education:* BA, Bombay; MA, Oxon; Barrister At Law. *Appointments:* Judge, Bombay High Court. *Publications:* Papers & Articles in Profl Journals. *Memberships:* Indian Federation of Women Lawyers; Disciplinary Committee; Bar Council; Standing Committee, Bombay Bar Assn. *Honours include:* F G Selby Memorial Scholarship; 2 Scholarships of Bombay Univ. *Hobbies:* Classical Music; Drama; Reading. *Address:* 16 Walke Shwar Road, Bombay 400 006, India.93.

MANOLACHE Laura, b. 11 May 1959, Bucuresti, Romania. Musicologist. m. Manolache Dan, 9 Nov 1954. *Education:* Acad of Music, Bucharest, 1978-82; Instl Seminary, Weimor, 1980-87; Ferienjurse fur neue

Musik in Darmstadt, 1990. *Appointments:* Broadcaster, Romanian Broadcasting, 1984-. *Publications:* George Enescu Interviews, Vol 1 & 11. *Memberships:* Union of Composer & Musicologists in Romania. *Honours:* Prize of the Union of Composers & Musicologists in Romania. *Hobbies:* Reading; Walking. *Address:* Str Pastorului 4 bl, 4 bis, SC A Et 4 Apt 16, 72306 Bucharesti 2, Romania.

MANOLOV Tihomir, b. 17 Sept 1959, Grudovo, BG. Fine Artist. m. Yavora Petrova, 14 Nov 1984, 1 s. *Education:* High Sch of Arts, Sofia, 1978; Acad of Fine Arts, Sofia, 1986. *Appointments:* Printings, Illustrations, Paintings & Drawings; One Man Show, Sofia, 1988; Exhibitions Abroad are Numerous. *Honours include:* 1st Prize Printing Tarcovisrite; 3rd Prize Illustrations, Nalt Illustration Comp. *Hobbies:* Eastern Fighting Techniques. *Address:* Zone B 18 Bl6 et 14 At 4, Sofia 1300, Bulgaria.

MANSFIELD Norman, b. 27 Apr 1916, Wilkes County, Rayle, Georgia. m. 3 Jan 1943, 2 s. *Education:* Univ of Georgia. *Appointments;* Railway Express Agency, 1941-. *Memberships include:* Shrine & Eastern Star; Lions Club President; Boy Scout Leader; Woodmen of the World; Mem, First Baptist Church, Washington, Georgia; Served 40 yrs as Usher, First Baptist Church, Washington; Deacon, 13 yrs, Sunday School Superintendent, Training Union Dir, Royal Ambassador Leader, Pres of Mens Brotherhood, First Baptist Church, Washington; 20 yrs; Pres of Mens Sunday School Class and Church Welcome Commitment. *Honours:* Little League Baseball Team Mgr; Football Official for 13 yrs; Baseball Official for 14 yrs. *Hobby:* Sport. *Address:* 209 Hudson Drive, Washington, GA 30673, USA.1.

MANSFIELD Roger, b. 18 Jan 1942, Iver, Bucks, England. Univ Prof. m. Helene Rica, 24 July 1969, 2 d. *Education:* Gonville & Caius Coll, Cambridge; Wolfson Coll, Cambridge. *Appointments include:* Student Apprentice, Stewart & Lloyds Ltd, Corby, 1960-65; Research Engr, 1965-66; Foundation for Mngt Educ Tchng Fellow, Univ of Cambridge, 1967-68; Visiting Lectr, Yale Univ, 1968-69; Snr Research Officer, London Business Sch, 1969-73; Prof of Business Admin, UWIST, 1976-; Dir, Centre for Grad Mngt Studies, UWIST, 1986-. *Publications include:* Research in Organisational behaviour; Managerial Roles in Industrial Relations; Frontiers of Management Research & Practice. *Memberships:* British Acad of Mngt; Inst of Welsh Affairs; South Glamorgan TEC. *Hobby:* Gardening. *Address:* 64 Bishops Road, Whitchurch, Cardiff, CF4 1LW, Wales.53.

MANSOUROV Vladimir, b. 22 Sept 1943, Frunze, USSR. Scientist; Physics of Rock; Fracture Mechanics. m. Elizabeth Bolshakova, 26 Aug 1973, 2 d. *Education:* BA, 1965; MS, 1975; PhD, 1991. *Appointments:* Scientist, 1966-91; Hd Intl Sci Centre, 1991-. *Publications:* Brittle Fracture of Rock; Predictions of the Failure of Rock. *Hobbies:* Skiing; Cycling; Reading. *Address:* Dushanbinskaya 6 a Ap 9, Bishkek 55, 720055 Republik of Kirgizstan.

MANTEL Hilary Mary, b. 6 July 1952, Derbyshire, England. Author. m. Gerald McEewen, 23 Sept 1972. *Education:* London Sch of Economics, Sheffield Univ. *Appointments:* Too Many to List. *Publications:* Novels. Every Day is Mother Day; Vacant Possession; Eight Months on Ghazzah Street; Fludd; A Place of Greater Safety. *Memberships:* Royal Soc of Literature. *Honours:* Shiva Naipaul Memorial Prize; Winifred Holtby Prize; Chelthamham Festival Prize; Southern Arts Literature Prize; Sunday Express, Book of The Year Award, 1992. *Hobby:* Cricket. *Address:* c/o AM Heath & Co, 79 St Martins Lane, London WC2N 4AA, England.

MANTELL Brian Stuart, b. 14 Jan 1935, London, England. Conslt; Radiotherapist; Oncologist. m. Janet Share, 15 Aug 1971, 1 s, 1 d. *Education:* London Hosp Medical College, Univ of London, 1953-58. *Appointments:* Conslt, Radiotherapy & Oncology, The Royal London Hosp, 1970-; The Royal Brompson & Natl Heart Hosp, 1971-. *Publications:* Numerous Papers & Chapters. *Memberships include:* British Medical Assn; Royal Soc of Medicine; British Inst of Radiology. *Honours include:* Northeast Thames Regional Post Graduate Adviser. *Hobbies:* Travel; Swimming; Music; Theatre. *Address:* 10 Ferrings, College Road, Dulwich, London SE4 7LW, England.

MAO Bangzhuo, b. 17 July 1936, Shanghai, China. Snr Geologist. m. Liu Yuzhen, 8 Aug 1964, 3 s. *Education:* China Univ of Geosciences, 1957. *Appointments:* Drilling Worker & Mason, 1957-62; Hydrogeologist, Coal Geologist, Stratigrapher, Gansu Inner Mongolia & Liaoning, 1962-79; Snr Geologist, Chief of Chief Engrs Office, China Natl Admin of Coal Geology, 1979-. *Publications include:* Cenozic Geology of Ju Ud Leage, Inner Mongolia; Regional Stratigraphic Timetable of Northeast China. *Memberships:* Geological Soc of China; Coal Soc of China. *Hobbies;* Read Chinese & Foreign Literary Works; Stamp Collecting; Learn Foreign Languages. *Address:* China Natl Admin of Coal Geology, Zhuozhou, Hebei, China.139.152.

MAPLESON William Wellesley, b. 2 Aug 1926, London, England. Prof Emeritus of the Physics of Anaesthesia. m. Gwladys Doreen Wood, 10 July 1954, 1 s, 1 d. *Education:* BSc, 1947; PhD, 1953; DSc, 1973. *Appointments:* RAF Flying Office, 1947-49; Univ of Wales Coll of Medicine, Lectr, 1952- 65; Snr Lectr, 1965-69; Reader, 1969-73; Prof, 1973-1991; Prof Emeritus, 1991-. *Publications:* Automatic Ventiliation of the Lungs; Over 100 Scientific Papers. *Memberships include:* Inst of Physics; Inst of Physical Sci in Medicine; Royal Soc of Medicine. *Honours include:* Faculty Medal of the Facults of Anaesthetics, Royal Coll of Surgeons. *Hobbies:* Work; Theatre; Walking. *Address:* Dept of Anaesthetics, Univ of Wales Coll of Medicine, Cardiff CF4 4XN, Wales.

MARA David Duncan, b. 3 Oct 1944, Bath, England. Prof of Civil Engrng, Univ of Leeds. m. Christine Margaret Ball, 3 Aug 1968, 1 s, 1 d. *Education:* BSc, Univ of St Andrews, 1963-67; PhD, Univ of Dundee, 1967-70. *Appointments:* Lectr, Univ of Nairobi, 1970-73; Snr Lect, Univ of Dundee, 1974-79; Prof, Univ of Leeds, 1979- ; Visiting Prof, Federal Univ of Paraiba, 1976-. *Publications include:* Bacteriology for Sanitary Engrs; Waste Stabilization Ponds. *Memberships:* Inst of Civil Engrs; Inst of Biology; Inst of Water & Enviromental Mngt. *Honours:* IAWPRC/Pergamon Publ Gold Medal. *Hobbies:* Reading; Walking. *Address:* 36 Moor Road, Leeds, LS6 4BJ, England.

MARACHKIN Alaksiej Antonavich, b. 10 Apr 1940, USSR. Artist; Dir of Painting Dept of Byelorussian Acad of Art. m. Marachkina Irina Siaregjewna, 24 May 1962, 1 s. *Education:* The Art Dept of Vitsebsk Pedagogical Inst, 1958-62; Army Serv, 1962-64; Painting Dept Byelorussian Acad of Art, 1966-72. *Appointments:* Tchr Painting, Middle Sch, 1964- 67; Artist Union of Byelorussia, 1977-; Chief Artist, Art Foundation of BSSR, 1982-86; Dir, Painting Dept, Byelorussian Acad of art, 1989-. *Creative Works include:* Painting. Granny Marilja; The Wakening. *Memberships:* Byelorussian Popular Frount; Painting Dept of Byelorussian Acad of Art; Byelorussian Artists Soc; Artists Union of Byelorussia. *Hobbies:* Travel; Poetry; Verses. *Address:* Zukouskaga Street 10-2, Fl 131, 220007 Minsk, Russia.

MARCINIAK Andrzej, b. 23 Sept 1952, Cleciulow, Poland. Lawyer; Univ Prof. m. Krystyna Porazka, 3 Dec 1977, 1 s. *Education:* MA, 1975; PhD, 1983; Habilitation in Law, 1991. *Appointments:* Assistantship, Dept of Civil Law Procidure, Univ of Lodz, 1975-83; Asst Prof, 1983-. *Publications:* Limitation of the Execution of a Court Judgement; The Basis for the Execution a Court Judgement/A Writ of Execution. *Honours:* Panstwo i Prawo Award for PhD Thesis; Rector of the Univ of Lodz for a Series of Papers. *Address:* ul Czernika 2 m.16, 92 543 Lodz, Poland.

MARCINIEC Bogdan Jozef, b. 4 Feb 1941, Secemin. Chemist; Prof. m. Barbara Kaminska, 15 May 1965, 1 d. *Education:* MCH, 1963; PhD, 1970; Post Doc Fel, Kansas, USA, 1970-71; DSC, 1975; Asst Prof, Poznan, 1976; Prof, 1986. *Appointments:* Hd of Dept of Phys Chem, 1977; Dept Organometal Chem, 1987; Dean Fac Chem, 1985-88; Rector, Pozn Univ, 1988-90. *Publications include:* Books; 80 Papers; Chapters; 40 Patents. *Memberships:* Applied Organometdlic Chem; Union of Pure & Applied Chemistry; Rotary Club Intern. *Honours:* 7 Awards of Ministry of High Educ; Poznan City Award. *Hobbies:* Music; Literature on Popular Sci; Sport; Dancing. *Address:* Wilkonvskich 13, 62 020 Swarzedsz, Poland.

MARCINKEVICIUS Justinas, b. 10 Mar 1930, Lithuania. Univ of Vilnius, Faculty of Literature & Languages; Writer. m. Genovaite Kalvaityte, 31 July 1955, 2 d. *Education:* Univ of Vilnius, 1954. *Appointments:* Editor, Magazin Genys, 1954-59; Vice Pres, Lithuania Writers Union, 1959-64; Profl Writer, 1964-. *Publications:* About 120 Books. *Memberships:* Lithuanian Writers Union; Lithuanian Acad of Sci; Lithuanian Sci Council; Lithuanian Council of Culture & Art. *Honours:* Rewards of State of Lithuania; Various Medal from Russia. *Hobbies:* Chess; Books. *Address:* Mildos 33-6, 2055 Vilnius, Lietuva, Lithuania.

MARCOVIC Vladimir, b. 28 Nov 1936, USSR. Professor. m. Ludmila Mamcova, 26 Mar 1959. *Education:* Grad, Kazakh Pedagog Inst, 1966; Candidates Deg, 1982, Dr Deg, Philog Sci, 1982. *Appointments:* Tchr, Kazakh Pedagog Inst, 1962; Sr Lectr, Leningrad Univ, 1972; Prof, St Petersburg Univ, 1984-. *Publications:* Chelovek v Romanah Turge-reva, Leningrad 1975; Turgenev i Russkii realisti-cheskvi roman, Leningrad 1982; Peterburgskiepovest Goglja, Leningrad, 1989. *Memberships:* Union of Writers of St Petersburg. *Hobby:* Travelling. *Address:* Chair of Russian Literature, University Embankment 11, St Petersburg 199164, Russia.

MARCUS Richard, b. 10 July 1951, Barquismeto, Venezuela. Sculptor; Designer. m. Rose Penzari, 14 Feb 1981, 2 d. *Education:* Self Taught Artist; Sculptor. *Appointments:* Mammoth Enterprises inc, 1986-. *Creative Works include:* New York Art Expo;Los Angeles Art Expo; Yokohama Yes 89, Japan; Jacobi Jewellers Special Presentation Stuttgart; Exhib, Rosenheim, West Germany. *Membership:* BC Sculptors Soc. *Honours include:* Canadian Whos Who, Univ of Toronto Press; Holt Renfrew, Toronto, Ont; Dallas Fashion Festival, Dallas, Texas; Burke Gallery, Tilburon, Cal. *Hobbies:* Bonsai; Reading; Writing. *Address:* 1286 Eigth Street, North Vancouver, BC, Canada V5Y 3T7.88.

MARDER Samuel, b. 11 Dec 1930, Czernowitz, Romania. Violinist; Recitalist; Tchr. m. 1959. *Education:* Coll Diploma, 1954; Bach of Music, 1955; Master of Music, 1956. *Appointments:* Concert Master, Russian Moxeseyen Dance Co, 1965; Concert Master, Natl Ballet of Wash, 1972- 75; Concert Master & Asst Conductor, Leonard Berstein Galaorch, 1972-75; Condr, String Ensemble, 1972-75; Internat Artist Ensemble, Tully Hall, NY, 1987. *Memberships:* Intl Artists Alliance; Riverside Music Soc. *Honours:* Award of the City; Full Scholarship, Manhattan Sch of Music; Masters Degree. *Hobbies:* Writing poetry; Study of Philosophy. *Address:* 3039 Johnson Avenue, Riverdale, NY 10463, USA.

MARGED Judith Michele, b. 27 Nov 1954, Philadelphia, Penna, USA. Educator. *Education:* Drexel Univ, Phila, penna, 1972-73; AA, Broward Community Coll, Fla, 1975; Florida Atlantic Univ, Boca Raton, BA, 1977; BA, 1980; MEd, 1984; Nova Univ, EdD, 1991. *Appointments:* Tchr, Coral Springs Middle Sch, 1979-80; Tchr, American Acad Wilton Manors, Fla, 1980-83; Ramblewood Middle Sch, Coral Springs, 1984-. *Publications include:* 2 Papers; Program to Increase the Knowledge of Middle Sch Students in Sexual Education & Substance Abuse Prevention; An Alternative Education Program to Create Successful Learning for Mid Sch Students at Risk. *Memberships:* Natl Sci Tchrs Assn; American Sch Counselor Assn; American Assn for Counseling & Devel; Assn for Supervison & Curriculum Devel, Nat Assn of Sch Psychologists; Fla Assn of Sci Tchrs; Fla Assn for Counseling & Devel. *Honours include:* Natl Honor Soc; Oustanding Improvment Projects; Deans list. *Hobbies:* Working with Adolescents; Sports; Music; Leathercrafting; Computer Programing; Travel. *Address:* 9107 NW 83rd Street, Tamarac, FL 33321, USA. 5, 7, 15.

MARINELLI Carlo, b. 13 Dec 1926, Rome Italy. Musicologist; Discographer. 1 s, 1 d. *Education:* Degree in Letters, Univ of Rome, 1948. *Appointments:* Prof, Storia Della Musica, Univ of L'Aquila, Italy, 1970-; Assoc, 1985; id, Storia della musica moderna e contemporanea, 1992-. *Publications include:* La Musica Strumentale de Camera di Goffredo Petrassi; Lettura di Messiaen; Le Cantate Profane di J S Bach; Opere in disco; Faust e Mefistofele Nelle Opere Teatrali e Sinfonico Vocali, Discografia; Le opere di Mozart su libretti di Da Ponte, discografia; Discografia ragionta delle opere Teatra di Mozart, 1, Singspiele. *Memberships:* IRTEM, President; AIASA, President; IASA; IMS; SidM; AuMS; SME; AMS; ARSC; Mem, Bd of IMZ, 1992-. *Address:* Via Francesco Tamagno 67, 00168 Rome, Italy.

MARINESCU Lucia Ana, b. 6 Sept 1935, Sibiu, Rumania. Archeologist; Dir of the History Museum of Rumania. m. Floricel Marinescu, 26 Dec 1970, 1 d. *Education:* The Faculty of History, 1956; Doctorate, 1977. *Appointments:* Univ of Cluj, The Faculty of History, 1969; The History Museum of Rumania, 1969-91. *Publications:* Fumerary Momuments from Dacia Superior & Dacia Porolissensis, Oxford, Bar; Studies on Roman Art in Dacia. *Memberships:* The Intl Committee for Limc; Rumanian Commitee ICOM. *Hobbies:* Reading; Travel. *Address:* Drumul Taberei 63, Bl TD46 , Ap 58, 77381 Bucharest, Rumania.

MARINOV Stefan, b. 1 Feb 1931, Sofia, Bulgaria. Physicist; Inventor. m. Elena Kriakova, 25 Oct 1955, 1 s. *Education:* Soviet Middle Sch, Prague, 1948; High Military Naval Sch, 1953; Univ of Sofia, 1960; Sofia Polytechnic, Radioengineering, 1970. *Appointments:* Research, Physical Inst of Bulgarian Acad of Sci, 1961-73; Hd, Lab for Fundament Physics, 1973-77; Inst of Fundamental Physics, 1981-. *Publications:* Eppur si muove; Economia Politica Teorica; Classical physics; The Thorny Way of Truth; Editor of Deutsche Physik. *Hobbies:* Poet; Satirical Writer; Tennis. *Address:* Morellenfeldgasse 16, A 8010 Graz, Austria.

MARINOVSKY Svetlomir, b. 11 Jan 1965, Gorna Oriahovitsa. Graphic Artist. *Education:* Special High Sch of Art, 1983; Acad of Fine Arts, Sofia, 1991. *Creative Works:* Graphic Works in Original Technique; Coloured Offset; Series of Drawing. *Hobbies:* History of Art; History & Theory of Culture. *Address:* J K Mladost 1, Bl 11, vh b, Apt 58, Sofia 1184, Bulgaria.

MARKARYAN Maro, b. 20 Dec 1915, Shulaver. m. Sarkis Bayandour, 1 s, 1 d. *Education:* Art Acad, Tiflis; State Univ of Yerevan, 1933- 38. *Appointments:* post Grad Fellow, Armenian Folklore, Acad of Sci, Inst of Literature, 1939-41; Jnr Scientist, 1941-44. *Publications include:* Intimacy; Poems; The Tree; From the Depth of my Days; Selected Poems. *Membership:* Mothers Foundation. *Honours:* American State Prize; Sign of Honor; Order of Peoples Friendship. *Hobby:* Painting. *Address:* Teryan Str 57, Apt 22, 375009 Yerevan, Armenia, Russia.

MARKHAM (Arthur) Geoffrey, b. 27 Sept 1927, Leeds, England. Solicitor. m. Patricia Holliday, 26 Sept 1959. 1 s, 1 d. *Education:* Giggleswick Sch; Leeds Univ. *Appointments:* Solicitor, 1949; Snr Partner, Raley & Pratt, Barnsley 1967-89; Conslt, 1990-; Chmn, Social Security Appeal Tribunal, 1981-. *Publications:* Woolley Hall, The Historical Development of a Country House; Various Papers. *Membership:* Law Soc. *Hobbies:* Reading; Writing; Historical Research; Music; Gardening.

MARKKANEN VAYRYNEN Lilli Kaarina Margareta, b. 9 May 1920, Lappeenranta. Make Up Artist. m. Kauko Varyrynen, 23 Dec 1955, 1 s. *Education:* Librarian Sch, 1948; Theatre Cources STKL, 1951-55; Make Up Studies, 1960-71. *Appointments:* Actress, Pori Theatre, 1947-48; Kuopio Theatre, 1948-50; Vaasa Theatre, 1950-51; Hameenlinna Theatre, 1951- 53; Dir, Actress. Kuopio Theatre, 1953-57; Tampere Theatre, 1957-59; Joensuu Theatre, 1959-60; Hd of Make Up, Finnish Broadcasting Co, 1960-85. *Memberships:* Finnish Assiciations of Stage Actors, Dir, & Make Up Artists; Finlands Culture Assn. *Honours:* Minna Statue; Finlands White Cross Order First Class Golden Cross; YLE Honors; Finnish Actors Assn Golden Award; Savonlinna Opera Festival Artist of the Year. *Hobbies:* Reading; Cooking; Theatre; Ballet. *Address:* Rauhankatu 2 C, SF 00170 Helsinki, Finland.

MARKO Szilard Szaniszlo, b. 13 May 1934, Budapest, Hungary. Electricl Engr; Scientific Conslt. m. Eva Kover, 4 Dec 1957, 1 s, 1 d. *Education:* Dipl Elec Engrng, Univ of Budapest, 1957; Tech Doctor Degree, Tech Univ, Budapest, 1978; Hungary Acad of Sci, 1978. *Appointments:* Sci Asst to Snr Scientist, Research Inst for Telecommunications, 1957-71; Hd of research Dept to Dir, 1972-91; Sci Conslt, 1991-. *Publications:* Microwave Handbook; Microwave Passive Circuits; articles to Profl Journals & Lectures. *Memberships:* Hungarian Soc for Telecomminications; Lorand Eotvos Physical Soc; Hungarian Fulbright Assn. *Honours:* State Prize, Hungarian Presdl Council. *Hobbies:* Listening to Music; Playing Bridge; Making Photos; Swimming. *Address:* Tusnadi u 47, 1125 Budapest, Hungary.52.

MARKOVA Aglika Yossifova, b. 8 July 1942, Sofia, Bulgaria. Journalist; Translator of English; Language Literature. *Education:* Dept of Linguistics, Univ of Sofia, 1967. *Appointments:* Bulgarian Trade Assn, 1964; Dental research Inst, 1966; Bulgarian News Agency, 1968; Sofia Monthly, 1982; Bulgarian Culture Att in London, 1991-. *Publications include:* Translations of Evelyn Naughs Decling & Fall; The War Trilogy; Brideshead Revisited. *Memberships:* Bulgarian Translators Assn; Intl Translators Federation. *Honours:* Local Literary Prizes. *Hobbies:* Swimming; Travel; Mountaineering; Music; Theatre; Visual Arts. *Address:* Dame Gruev 40, 1606 Sofia, Bulgaria.

MARKOWSKA Maria, b. 23 Jan 1923, Strzyzow, Poland. Artist; Printer. m. (1) 3 Aug 1974, (2) 1983. *Education:* Acad of Fine Arts, Cracow, 1955. *Appointments:* Tchr, Dept of Drawing & Sculpture, Inst of History of Archiecture & Conservation of Historical Monuments, cracow Univ of Tech, 1961-; Asst Prof, Docent, 1977-82. *Creative Works include:* One Man Shows of Paintings, Drawings; Youth Festival, Berlin; Exhib of Paintings of the Realists, Denmark, Berlin; Instl Exhib of Drawings, New Zealand. *Membership:* union of Polish Artists & Designers in Cracow. *Honours include:* Numerous Award & Honors for Paintings & Drawings; Gold Cross of Merit for Achievements in Didactic & Educ Work; Numerous Scholarships. *Hobby:* Psychology. *Address:* Karmelicka 35 m7. 31-131 Krakov, Poland.

MARKS Gerald Samuel, b. 13 Feb 1930. Educator. m. Marion Zoe, 1 s, 1 d. *Appointments include:* Task Force on Chemicals in the Environment & Human Reproductive Problems, New Brunswick, 1983-84; Visiting Prof, Sch of Pharmacy, Univ of Calif, 1984-85; Prof of Pharmacol, Queens Univ, 1988-. *Publications include:* Heme & Chlorophyll, Chemical, Biochemical & Medical Aspects; Book Chapters; Numerous Publ on Biosynthesis of Heme & Porphyrins; Canadian Journal of Physiology & Pharmacology. *Memberships include:* Canadian Heart & Stroke Foundation Grants Cttee; Intl Union of Pharmacology. *Honours include:* Aesculapian Soc Lectureship Award, Queens Univ; Alumni Award foe Excellence in Tchrng. *Hobbies:* Swimming; Squash; Tennis; Curling. *Address:* Dept of Pharmacology & Toxicology, Queens Univ, Kingston, Ont, Canada K7L 3N6.

MARKS Paul Alan, President, Memorial Sloan-Kettering Cancer Center. m. Joan H Rosen; 2 s, 1 d. *Education:* Columbia Coll, Columbia Univ, 1945; Coll of Physicians & Surgeons, Columbia Univ, 1949. *Appointments include:* Chmn, Dept of Human Generics & Devel, Columbia Univ, 1969-70; Vice Pres, Medical Affairs, Columbia Univ, 1970-73; Frode Jenson Prof of Medicine, Columbia Univ, 1974-80; Pres, Chief Exec Officer, Memorial Sloan Kettering Cancer Centre, 1980-; Adj Prof, Rockerfeller Univ, 1980-; Vis Physician, Rockefeller Univ Hospital, 1980-; Prof Of Medicine, Cornell Univ Medical Coll, 1982-; Prof, Cornell Univ Grad Sch of Medical Sci, 1983-. *Publications:* Over 350 Articles; 8 Books. *Memberships include:* American Acad of Arts & Sci; Nat Acad of Sci; Intl Soc of Devel Biologists; Third World acad of Sci; American Soc of Hematology. *Honours include:* Bicentennial Medal; Robert Wood Johnson Foundation Medal for Distinguished Serv; Pres, Nat Medal of Science (USA). *Address:* PO Box 1485, Washington, CT 06793, USA. 2, 15, 52.

MARLIN Brigid Nella, b. 16 Jan 1936, Washington DC, USA. Artist; Writer. m. Benjamin Oakley, 27 June 1957, div, 18 June 1987, 3 s, 1 dec. *Education:* Natl Coll of Art, Dublin, 1953; Atelier Andre L'Hote, Paris, 1954; Centre D'Art Sacre, Paris, 1954' Beaux Arts Montreal, 1955; Arts Students League, NY, 1956. *Appointments:* Art Tchr, West Herts Coll, 1961-91; Artist in Residence, Bezalil Coll, Jerusalem, Univ of California. *Publications include:* From East to West; Book Illustrations. King Oberons Forest; Celebration of Love; Paintings: J.G. Ballard in Natl Portrait Gallery; Official Portrait of the Dalai Lama, Queen Mother in Collection of Sir William Butlin. *Memberships:* PEN Club. *Honours include:* Intl appreciation Award; 1st Prize Sculpture Comp, London. *Hobbies:* Travel; Special Interest in Comparative Religions.

MARR Lindsay Grigor David, b. 14 Sept 1955, Cambridge, England. Solicitor; Partner in Fresfields. m. Susan Ann Scott, 23 Feb 1991. *Education:* Conville & Caius Coll, Cambridge, 1975-78; Reading Law, BA, 1978; MA, 1982. *Appointments:* Freshfields, Articled Clerk, 1979- 81; Asst Solicitor, 1981-87; Partner, 1987- . *Memberships:* The Law Soc; The City of London Solicitors Co; The Intl Bar Assn. *Honours include:* Coll Entrance Scholarship; Univ Tapp Law Scholarship. *Hobbies:* Reading; Music; golf; Squash.53.

MARSDEN William, b. 15 Sept 1940, Cambridge, England. Minister (Trade Policy) British Embassy, Washington, 1989-92. m. Kaia Collingham, 1 s, 1 d. *Education:* Winchester Coll, USA; Trinity Coll, Cambridge; London Univ, BSc. *Appointments:* Foreign Office, 3rd Sec UK Delegation to NATO, 1962-64, 1964-66; British Embassy, Rome, 1966-69; Asst to Gen, 1970; FO European Community Dept, 1971-76; First Sec, Cultural Attache, British Embassy, Moscow, 1976-79; Asst Hd, Eyropean Community Dept, 1979-81; Counsellor UK Representation to the EC, Brussels, 1981-85; Hd East African Dept, Commissioner British Indian Ocean Treasory, 1985-88; HM Ambassador to Costa Rica & Nicaragua. *Memberships:* Chmn, Diplomate Serv Assn. *Honour:* CMG. *Address:* c/o Foreign & Commonwealth Office, King Charles Street, London SW1A 2AH, England.1.

MARSH Gordon Victor, b. 14 May 1929, Williston, N Dakota, USA. Member, Police Complaints Authority. m. Millicent Rowsell, 13 June 1959, 1 s, 1 d. *Education:* Keble Coll, Oxford, 1949-52; BA, 1952; MA, 1957; Fellow, Inst Health Serv Admin, 1964; Sloan Business Sch, Cornell Univ, 1967. *Appointments:* NHS Admin, England & Wales, 1952-72; Admin, Bd of Governors, Univ Coll Hosp, 1972-74; Area Admin, Lambeth, Southwark & Lewisham Area Health Auth (Teaching), 1974-82; Dep Health Ser Commissioner, England, Scotland & Wales, 1982-89; Police Complaints Auth, 1989-. *Publications:* Articles in Profl Journals. *Memberships:* Inst of Health Serv Mngt; Assn of Chief Admin of Health Auth; Advisory Bd Coll of Occupational Therapists; Wndsman, St Pauls Cathedral. *Hobbies:* Music; Gardens; Bird Watching; Voluntary Work, St Pauls Cathedral, London. *Address:* Springwater, St Lucians Lane, Wallingford, Oxon, OX10 9ER. England.1.

MARSHALL (Ann) Innes (Elliot), b. 11 Jan 1924, Edinburgh, Scotland. Editor; Publisher. m. James Douglas Marshall, 7 Sept 1953. *Education:* Edinburgh Univ, 1939-41; Womens Auxilliary Air Force, 1941-46; Edinburgh Univ, 1946-50. *Appointments:* Script Writer, Campbell Harper Documentary Films, 1950-51; Researcher, Scottish Ancestry Research, 1951-53; Tchr, 1953-68; General Editor, Publ, Haile Selassie Addis Ababa Univ Press, 1968-. *Publications:* The Crows; Articles. *Memberships include:* Ethiopian Horticultural Soc; Intl Assn of Scholary Publ; The African Publng Record. *Hobbies:* Painting; Drawing; Horticulture; Conversation. *Address:* c/o Addis Ababa Univ Press, PO Box 1176, Addis Ababa, Ethiopia.1.52

MARSHALL Christopher James, b. 24 Sept 1959, London, England. Snr Music Producer, BBC. m. Wendy Jane Thompson, 30 Aug 1985, 2 s. *Education:* John Lyon Sch, Harrow, 1971-78; Reading Univ, 1978-81; Goldsmiths Coll, Univ of London, 1981-83. *Appointments:* BBC, 1981-; Producer, Radio 3 Music Dept, 1985; Producer, Proms, 1988-89; Snr Producer, R3 Music Dept, 1988; Snr Producer, R3 Midlands, 1990. *Hobbies:* Reading Contemporary Fiction; Cooking. *Address:* BBC, Broadcasting Centre, Pebble Mill Road, Birmingham B5 7QQ, England.139.

MARSHALL Enid Ann, b. 10 July 1932, Boyndie, Scotland. Non Practising Solicitor; Univ Reader. *Education:* Bell Baxter Sch, Cupar, 1950; MA, 1955; LLB, 1958; PhD, 1966; St Andrews Univ. *Appointments:* Law Apprentice, Cupar, Fife, 1956-59; Lectr in Law, Dundee Coll of Tech, 1959-72; Lectr in Business Law, 1972-74; Snr Lectr, 1974-77; Reader in Business Law, 1977. *Publications include:* General Principles of Scots Law; Scottish Cases on Agency; Scottish Cases on Partnerships & Companies; Charlesworth & Cain Company Law. *Memberships include:* Law Soc of Scotland; Royal Inst of Chartered Surveyors; Chartered Inst of Arbitrators; FRSA. *Honours:* Miller Prize for Faculty of Arts. *Hobbies:* Animal Welfare; Veganism. *Address:* 24 Easter Cornton Road, Stirling FK9 5ES, Scotland.184.

MARSHALL Geoffrey, b. 22 Apr 1929, Chesterfield, England. Univ Thr. m. 10 Aug 1957, 2 s. *Education:* Arnold Schh, Lancs, 1940-47; Manchester Univ, 1947-52; Glasgow Univ, 1956; Oxford Univ, 1957. *Appointments:* Research Fellow, Oxford, 1955-57; Fellow & Prac Lectr, Queens Coll, Oxford, 1957-; Univ Lectr, 1957-. *Publications include:* Constitutional Theory; Ministerial Resp. *Membership:* Political Studies Assn of the UK. *Honours include:* City Sheriff Oxford; Andrew Dixon White Prefessorship, Cornell Univ. *Hobbies:* Jurisprudence; American Football; Works of Stephen Leacock. *Address:* Queens Coll, Oxford, England.1.

MARSHALL Howard Lowen, b. 21 July 1931, Nokesville, VA, USA. Coll Prof. m. Doris Rosencranz, 14 July 1962. *Education:* BME, Music Educ, 1952; MM, Musicology, 1958; PhD, 1968. *Appointments include:*

United State Navy, 1952-57; Sycamore High Sch, Cincinnati, 1958-60; Chelternham High Sch, Pennsylvania, 1960-63; Asst Prof of Music, Lake Forest Coll, Illinois, 1968-73; Roberts Prof of Music, Mercer Univ, Geogia, 1984-87; Thompson Prof of Music, Mercer Univ, 1987-. *Creative Works include:* Book. The Four Voice Motets of Thomas Crecquillon; Papers. Scott Joplin & Treemonisha; Sources for the Motets of Georg Prenner. *Memberships:* American Musicological Soc; American Assn of Univ Profs; Phi Mu Alpha. *Honours:* Grad Fellowship, eastman Sch of Music; Pi Kappa Lambda. *Hobbies:* Photography; Languages. *Address:* 1324 Maplewood Drive, Macon, GA 31210, USA.4.7.

MARSHALL Hugh, *Education:* Tech Coll, Barking, 1950-53; Intermediate Arts & Crafts, 1951; Royal Coll of Art, 1953-56; ARCA, 1956; Travelling Scholarship, Germany, 1957. *Appointments include:* Freelance Illustrator & Design, 1960-90; Gave Lects at various Schs in London, Lincolnshire, 1977-79; Editor, Designer, Royal Coll of Art Sco Newsletter, 1986-90; Hd of Special Design Unit, Kingston Univ, 1990. *Creative Works include:* Exhibitions. Brno, Czechoslovakia; Jerusalem, Israel Museum. *Honours include:* IGI of America, Silver Medal for Drawings, Ranx Xerox; Merit Award x 2, for design, Wine Soc. *Address:* 36 Stanhope Gardens, London SW7 5QY, England.

MARSHALL Sally Rose, b. 2 Nov 1938, Lancashire, England. Chmn; m. 27 Aug 1961, 2 s, 1 d. *Education:* MA, Lady Margaret Hall, Oxfrd, 1957-60. *Memberships include:* ACC Community Services Committee; Wymondham Coll GMS; Borfolk County Council. *Hobbies:* Local Politics; Reading; Gardening; Embroidery. *Address:* Salle Place, Salle, Reepham, Norfolk NR10 5S7, England.

MARSZALEK Janusz, b. 3 July 1955, Oswiecim, Poland. Economist. m. Marta Baranska, 19 Aug 1978. *Education:* Higher Pedogogical Sch, 1975-76; Acad of Economy, Krakow, 1977-80; Master of Economy, 1083. *Appointments:* Private Economy & Mkt, 1975-; Cooperation with german Organisations SOS, Kinderdosf & Kolpingsfamilie, 1987-. *Memberships:* Fndr, Foundation ChildrenVillages MAJA. *Hobbies:* Music; Gardening. *Address:* ul Wyzwolenia 17, PL 32 600 Oswiecim, Poland.

MARTCHENKO Michael, b. 1 Aug 1942, Carcassone, France. Illustrator; Art Dir. m. Patricia Kerr, 28 May 1983, 3 d. *Education:* Glenview Park SS, 1962; Ontario Coll of Art, 1966. *Appointments:* Spitzer Mills & Bates, Art Dir, 1966-69; Needham Harper & Steeps, Art Dir, 1969-70; Art Assoc Designer, Illustrator, 1970-72; TDF Artist Ltd, Creative Dir, 1972-. *Creative Works include:* Illustrator. The Paper Bag Princess; The Boy in the Drawer;Horray for the Dorchester; Friends Meet; The Ruhr Express; McKnights Hattrick. *Memberships:* Art Directors of Toronto; American Soc of Aviation Artists; The Canadian Aircrew Assn; Ontario Aviation Historical Soc; The Canadian Airforce Assn. *Honours include:* AD Clubb of Toronto, 3 Awards of Merit; Silver Medal, Studio Mag Awards Show. *Hobbies:* Aviation Art; Collecting Aviation & Military Memorabilia. *Address:* c/o Annick Press, 15 Patricia Avenue, Willowdale, Ontario, Canada M2M 1H9.88.

MARTIN Alan Douglas, b. 4 Dec 1937, Bexleyheath, Kent, England. Prof of Theoretical Physics, Univ of Durham. m. Penelope Elizabeth Johnson, 4 Apr 1964, 1 s, 2 d. *Education:* Eltham Coll, 1948-55; Univ Coll London, 1955-61; BSc, 1958; PhD, 1962. *Appointments:* Research Asst, Univ Coll, London, 1961-62; Research Assoc, Univ of Illinois. 1962-63; Research Assc, Rutherford Lab, 1963-64; Lectr, 1964; Snr Lectr, 1971; Reader, 1975; Prof, Univ of Durham, 1978-, Hd of Dept, 1989-. *Publications include:* Books. Elementary Particle Theory; Quarks & Leptons; Hadron Interactions; Particle Physics & Cosmology. *Memberships:* Inst of Physics; American Physical Soc. *Hobbies:* Tennis;

Badminton; Gardening. *Address:* Dept of Physics, Univ of Durham, Durham DH1 3LE, England.

MARTIN David Alfred, b. 30 June 1929, Mortlake, SW14. England. Univ Prof, Emeritus, Retired. m. 30 June 1962, 2 s, 1 d. *Education:* Westminster Coll, Oxford, 1950-52; London Univ; LSE Post Grad. *Appointments:* Lectr, LSE, 1962-67; Reader, 1967-71; Prof, 1971-89; Emeritus, 1989-. *Publications include:* 20 Books. *Memberships:* London Soc for the Study of Religion; Intl Conference for the Soc of Religion. *Honour:* Select Preacher Univ of Cambridge. *Hobbies:* Piano Accompaniment. *Address:* Cripplegate Cottage, 174 St Johns Road, Woking, Surrey GU21 1PQ. England. 1.

MARTIN David McLeod, b. 30 Dec 1922, Glasgow, Scotland. Artist. 4 s. *Education:* Glasgow Sch of Art, 1940-42; RAF, 1943-46.1946-48; Jordan Hill Tchrs Training Coll, 1948-99. *Appointments:* Tchr & Principal Tchr, Glasgow Schs, 1949-73; Principal Tchr, Hamilton Grammar Sch, 1973-83; Full Time Painter, 1983-. *Creative Works:* Painter in Oils, Gouache & Pastels; Mainly Landscapes, Still Life, Portraiture. *Memberships include:* The Royal Scottish Soc of Painters in Watercolour; The Royal Glasgow Inst of the fine Arts; Soc of Scottish Artists. *Honours include:* Elected RSW; Elected R.G.I, Special award of Merit, R Colquhoun Memorial Art Prize; Prizewinner, Laing Exhib the Mall Gallery, London; E.I.S. Purchase Award, S.S.A., 1985; May Marshall Brown Award, R.S.W., 1984; Mabel Mackinley Award, R.G.I., 1990. *Hobbies:* Music; Gardening. *Address:* The Old Schoolhouse, 53 Gilmour Street, Eaglesham, Glasgow, G76 0LG, Scotland.19.

MARTIN Geoffrey Haward, b. 27 Sept 1928, Colchester, England. Prof of History, m. Janet Douglas Hamer, 12 Sept 1953, 3 s, 1 d. *Education:* Merton Coll, Oxford, 1947-51; BA, 1950; MA, 1954; D Phil, 1955; Univ of Manchester, 1951-52. *Appointments:* Lectr, Econ History, Univ of Leicester, 1952-66; Reader, Univ of Leicester, 1966-73; Prof of History, 1973-82; Keeper of Public Records, 1982-88; Snr Research Fellow, Merton Coll, Oxford, 1990-; Research Prof, Univ of Essex, 1990-. *Publications include:* The Town; Municipal History; Recognizance Rolls of Ipswich. *Memberships:* Royal Commission on Historical Monuments; Soc of Antiquaries; Royal Historical Soc. *Honours:* CBE; Besterman Medal, Library Assoc. *Hobbies:* Fell Walking; Gardening. *Address:* Flat 27, Woodside House, Woodside, Wimbledon, SW19 7QN, England.1.52.

MARTIN Holger, b. 3 Dec 1942, Achern, Germany. Prof of Thermal Process Engrng. m. Nana Reich, 15 May 1964, 1 s, 1 d. *Education:* Dipl Ing U Karlsruhe, 1969; Dr Lug, 1973; Dr Lug habil, 1980. *Appointments:* Research Asst, Inst Therui, U Karlsruhe, 1969-77; Oheriugeuieur, 1977-80; Prof Thermal Process Engrng, 1980-. *Publications include:* Warmeubertrager; Heat Exchangers; Numerous Articles. *Memberships include:* Scientific Dir, Instl Seminar for Research & Tchrng iu Chemical Engrng & Physical Chemistry; VDI. *Honours include:* Arnold Eucken Preis GVC-VDI. *Address:* Therm Verfahrenstechnik, U Karlsruhe, Postfach 6980, D 7500 Karlsruhe, Germany. 1, 52.

MARTIN John Governor, b. 4 Jan 1929, Aiken, South Carolina, USA. Pastor; Admin; Medica Researcher. m. Ruth, 5 Feb 1965, 1 s, 1 d. *Education:* BS, South Carolina State Coll, 1950; Engrng Drafting Cert, 1951; Grad Study, MS, PhD, Howard Univ, 1955-56; Christian Theological Seminary, 1955; M Div, 1972; Cultural Doc, Therapeutic Philosophy, 1988. *Appointments include:* Engrng Draftsman, 1950-51; Snr Medical Technologist, 1951-54; US Air Force, Garfield Hosp, 1954-58; Chief Chemist, Childrens Hosp, 1958-60; Medical Researcherm Washington Hosp Centre, 1959-60; Private Medical Research, 1960-; Founder & Pastor, Holy Comforter Baptist Church; Life Underwriter, Supreme Life Insurance Co. *Publications include:* Various Documents, Medical Research & Theology. *Memberships include:* Various Offices, Baptist Ministers

Conference, District of Columbia; Alpha Theta Nu Omega Theological Fraternity; Third World Political Party. *Honours include:* Staff Mngr of Year; Numerous Orders of Chivalry. *Address:* PO Box 29101, Washington, DC 10017 USA. 125, 130, 139, 145, 151, 152, 155, 156.

MARTIN Leland M 'Pappy', b. 8 Aug 1930, Patrick Co, Va, USA. Tchr; History Lect. m. Milred Greer, 12 May 1956, 2 d. *Education:* Berea Coll, 1953; Univ of Tenn, 1954; Air War Coll, 1978. *Appointments:* United states Air Force, 1954-86; Co-Chair w Sir Douglas Bader, International Air tattoo, RAF Greenham Common, 1976; Chmn, Air Fetes 80 and 81 RAF Mildenhall; Amer Airpower Heritage Fdn, Exec Dir, 1986-88; Univ of Texas, Pan American, 1988-. *Publications:* Co-Editor, History of United States Military Assistance Command/Vietnam. *Memberships include:* Air Force Assn; Britt Off Club Philadelphia; Rotary Intl. *Honours include:* 49 Military Awards; Amb Award Ct St James London. *Hobbies:* Clock Repair; Fishing; Golf. *Address:* 3001 Emerald Lake Drive, Harlingen, TX 78550, USA. 7, 176.

MARTIN Peter Robert, b. 6 Sept 1949, Budapest. Psychiatrist. m. Barbara Ruth Bradford, 23 Dec 1985, 1 s. *Education:* BSc, 1967-71; MD, CM, 1971-75; McGill Univ MSc, Univ of Toronto, 1976-79; Internal Medicine, 1975-78. *Appointments:* Chief, Section of Clinical Sci, Natl Inst of Alcohol Abuse & Alcoholism, 1983-86; Assoc Prof of Psychiatry & Pharmacology. *Memberships include:* Royal Coll of physicians; American Assn for the Advancement of Sci; The American Coll of Psychiatrists. *Honours include:* McGill Univ Entrance Scholarship; Medal of the Natl Inst for Nervous & Mental Disorders of Hungary. *Hobbies:* Sports; Reading; Cinema. *Address:* Dept of Psychiatry, Vanderbilt Univ Sch of Medicine, Room A-2215 Medical Centre North, Nashville, TN 37232, USA.7.

MARTIN-ALONSO Olga, b. 13 Nov 1959, Madrid, Spain. Registered Accounting Auditor. m. Angel Ogueta Fernandez, 15 Oct 1986. *Education:* M. Econs, Univ Autonoma, Madrid, 1981; M. Laws, Univ Complutense, Madrid, 1982; M. in Accounting & Auditing, Inae Madrid, 1983-86; m. in Maths, Univ Complutense, Madrid, 1983; M. in Fin Auditing, Gen Coun Econ Colls, Spain, 1988; CPA, 1988-; Cert Fin Auditor, 1988-; Auditor Censor jurado de Cuentas, 1988-; Reg Accounting Auditor, 1989-; Fin Auditor, 1989; Lectr, Auditing Standards, Madrid, 1991. *Appointments:* Cons Various Firms, Madrid, 1981-; Lawyer, Coll of Lawyers, Madrid, 1982-; Prof Public Economics, Univ Autonoma, Madrid, 1981-85; Economist, 1987-; Snr Auditor, Private Practice, Madrid, 1988-; Mathematician, 1988-. *Publications include:* Urban Development in Spain, 1982; State monopolies and Legality in the EEC, 1983; Spainish Public Firms in the EEC, 1984; EEC Laws & Public Firms, 1984. *Memberships include:* Coll, Economists of Madrid; Coll, Lawyers of Madrid; Coll, Mathematicians, Madrid; Registered Economists Auditors; Spanish Assn of Accounting & Fin Admin; Ins of Auditors; Inst of Contabilidad y Auditoria de Cuentas; Internat Accounting Standard Comm; Internat Fed Accts; European Union of Economics, Accounting & Fin Experts. *Honours include:* Recipient End of Career Award in Econs, Spainish Ministry of Edn, 1981; Idem in Law, 1982; Grantee Spainsh Ministry of Edn, 1981, 1982. *Hobbies:* Yatching; Golf; Tennis; Software & Computers. *Address:* C/Nuria 80, Mirasierra, 28034 Madrid, Spain. 52.102.132.

MARTIN-MOLERO Francisca, b. 10 Mar 1943, Granada, Spain. Prof, Univ Complulense of Madrid. *Education:* Univ of Granada, 1962; Tchrng Cert, 1965; Proficency in English, Univ of Cambridge, 1970; Degree Phil & Educ Sci, 1979; Doctorate on Educ, 1981. *Appointments:* High Sch Techr, 1965-66; Tchr of Spanish, 1968-70; Hd Mistress English Centre Sch, 1972-74; Dir, British Sch of Aragon, 1974-75; Asst Prof, 1978-82; Assoc Prof, 1982-86; Prof, 1986-. *Publications* *include:* More than 10 Books; Over 30 Articles; Numerous Papers. *Memberships include:* Assn for Tchrs in Europe; European Assn for Research on Learning & Instr; ASELE; AESLA. *Honours include:* Honors in Didactics, Psychopathology. *Hobbies:* Painting; Music; Reading; Sports; Theatre. *Address:* Dpto des Didáctica, Facultad de Educación, Las Moreras. Juan XXIII S/n, Universidad Complutense de Madrid, 28040 Spain. 152.

MARTINEK Karel, b. 20 July 1933, Dvur Kralove. Dir of the Inst of Org Chem & Biochem. 1 d. *Education:* Chem Textile Ind Sch, 1949-51; Moscow State Univ, 1953-58; DSc, 1972. *Appointments:* Scientist, Prof of Moscow State Univ, 1960-85; Dir, Inst Org Chem & Biochem, Prague, 1986-; Scientific Sec, Czech Acad of Sciences, 1987-90. *Publications include:* More than 200 Scientific Papers. *Memberships:* Acad Europaea; Royal Soc of Chem, London; Europ J of Biochemistry. *Honours:* State Prize of the USSR; Lenins Prize of the USSR; Medal of Honor of the Int Union of Biochem. *Hobby:* Tourism. *Address:* Dir, Inst of Org, Chem & Biochm, Fleming Sq 2, CS 166 10 Prague 6, Czechoslovakia.

MARTINET Andre, b. 12 Apr 1908, Saint Alban. Prof Emeritus. m. Jeanne Allard, 11 Apr 1947. *Education:* Doctor, Sorbonne, Paris, 1937. *Appointments:* Ecole des hautes etudes, Sorbonne, 1938-47; Columbia Univ, New York, Prof, 1947-55; Sorbonne Paris, Prof, 1955-77; Ecole des hautes eludes, 1956-. *Publications include:* 24 Books. *Memberships include:* Soc Linguistica Europaea & Soc de Linguistique de Paris. *Honours include:* Knight Legion of Honor; Doct. h.c. Louvain, Turku, Valparaiso, Liège, Freiburg, Bolbao; Mem, 6 Sc Academies. *Hobby:* Gardening. *Address:* 16 Rue Pierre Bonnard, F92260 Fontenay aux Roses, France.

MARTINEZ David Roger, b. 22 Jan 1954, Toledo, Ohio USA. Chemist. *Education:* Univ of Toledo, Bach of Sci, 1978. *Appointments:* Quality Control Tech, 1985-86; Research Asst, Chardonol Corp, 1987-91; Baylor Coll of Medicine, 1991-. *Publications:* Scientific Publ. Computer Calculations in the Quantitative Analysis Course. *Memberships:* American Chemical Soc; Intl Platform Assn; St Michaels Young Adult Club. *Hobbies:* Radio Electronics; Chess; Sci Fiction; Computers; Computer Programming. *Address:* Baylor Coll of Medicine, Dept of Medicine, Athevo & Lipo, Building ALKT, Room A654, Mail Station A601, One Baylor Plaza, Houston, TX 77030, USA.7.

MARTINEZ Robert Bob, b. 6 Sept 1943, Holly, Colorado, USA. State Senator. m. Frances K Martinez, 8 Nov 1984, 3 s. *Education:* Southern Colorado State Coll, 1968; Univ of Colorado, 1971. *Appointments:* Vice Chancellor, Acad Serv Metropolitan State Coll, 1974-78; Univ of Colorado, 1978-; Colordao House of Representatives, 1981-84; Colorado State Senate, 1985-92. *Memberships include:* Denver Boys Club; Denver Goodwill Inc; Natl Mexican American State Legislators Policy Inst. *Honours:* Humanitarian of the Yr Award. *Hobbies:* Reading; Fishing; Bowling; Politics. *Address:* 6462E 63rd Avenue, Commerce City, CO 80022, USA.

MARTINEZ SANCHEZ Luis Antonio, b. 21 Oct 1959, Madrid. Bank Exec. m. Robyn Cynthia, 23 June 1990. *Education:* Univ De Bruxelles, 1981. *Appointments:* Banco Central, SA, Brussels Branch, 1982-88; Banco Espanol De Credito, Brussels Branch, 1988-. *Publications:* Trends Tendances/Interviewu. *Membership:* Centre Interinstitutionnel European, Brussels. *Hobbies:* Tennis; Jogging; Informatics. *Address:* Klarissenbos 5, 1651 Beersel, Belgium.

MARTON Laszlo, b. 23 Apr 1959, Budapest. Writer; Trnaslator. *Education:* Faculty of Arts, Budapest, 1983; Hungarian & German Language & Literature, Sociology. *Creative Works include:* Terror in Great Budapest; Asylum; Butterflies on the Hat; Way Through the Glass.

Memberships: Assn of Hungarian Writers; Intl Pen Club. *Honours:* Fust Milan Prize; Dery Prize. *Hobbies:* History; Theatre. *Address:* Rath Gyorgy utca 21, H 1122 Budapest, Hungary.

MARTYN C Philip, b. 17 July 1948, London, England. Joint Gen Mngr, Legal Adviser of the Sumitomo Bank, London. *Education:* St Dunstan's Coll, London, 1959-66; Exeter Univ, 1966-69. *Appointments:* Solicitor, Coward Chance, 1970-77; Solicitor, Clifford Turner, 1977-79; Legal Advisor, Sumitomo Bank, 1979-. *Memberships:* Law Soc; Anthroposophical Soc. *Hobbies:* Gardening; Green Issues; Studying Rudolf Steiner's Works; Esoterics; Playing the Organ; Bach; Waldorf Education. *Address:* 39 Chester Road, London SW19 4TS, England.53.

MARTYNOV Victor Vladimirovich, b. 25 Jan 1924, Odessa. Linguist; Gen, Appled & Slavic Linguistics. m. Metelitskaya Elvira Mikhailovma, 18 Sept 1947, 1 s, 1 d. *Education:* Odessa State Univ, 1948; Lvov State Univ, 1951; Cad of Sci, 1951; Doc of Sci, 1968; Prof, 1971. *Appointments:* Hd of Dept, Foreign Languages, 1951-60; Hd of Dept, Gen & Slavic Linguistics, 1962-89. *Publications include:* Kategorii Yazyka; Over 260 Publ Works. *Memberships:* Languages of the World; Acad of Sci of USSR; Soviet Ann of Artificial Intelligence. *Honours:* Order of the Patriotic War; Supreme Council Dinloma of Honor; Merited Sci Worker. *Hobbies:* Labour of Letters. *Address:* Kulman Street 15, App 98, 220100 Minsk, Byelorussia.

MARWOOD Anthony Cheuallier, b. 6 July 1965, Blackheath, England. Violinist. *Education:* Royal Acad of Music, 1977-83; Guildhall Sch of Music, 1983-87. *Appointments:* Concerto Engagements, 1985-; Numerous Recital & Chamber Music Tours; Frequent Broadcasts on BBC Radio 3; Solo TV Appearances. *Honours include:* 1st Prize Shell Lso Scholarship; Dorothy Parkinson Award, Harrogate International Festival. *Hobbies:* Hill Walking; Tennis; Theatre. *Address:* Neil Chaffey Concert Promotions, 8 Laxton Gardens, Baldock, Herts SG7 6DA, England.

MARZA Ioan, b. 23 June 1930, Ghiolt, Romania. Prof. m. Monica, 1975, 2 d. *Education:* Pedagogical High Sch, 1951; Univ of Cluj, 1955; PhD, Budapest Univ, 1967. *Appointments:* Asst Prof, 1955-65; Asst Lectr, 1965-68; Lectr, 1968-90; Prof, 1990. *Publications include:* 130 Publ Scientific Papers. *Memberships:* Geological Soc of Romania; Assn of Hobbyist Mineralogists, Paleontologists & Gemologists of Romania. *Honours:* Romanian acad Award in Geology. *Hobbies:* Viticulture; Apiculture; Artistic Roots; Ping Pong. *Address:* Boul 1 Decembrie 1918, Nr 36, 3400 Cluj Napoca, Romania.152.162.

MASEFIELD John Thorold, b. 1 Oct 1939, Kampala, Uganda. Brit High Commnr to Tanzania. m. Jennifer Mary Trowell, 18 Aug 1962, 2 s, 2 d, 1 dec. *Education:* MA, St John's Coll, Cambridge, 1958-62. *Appointments:* Joined CRO 1962; Kuala Lumpur 1964-65; Warsaw 1966-67; Disarm Conf 1970-74; Planning Staff, FCO 1974-77; Islamabad 1979-82; Hd, Far Eastern Dept 1985-87; Assistant Under-Secretary of State for Southern Asia and the Pacific at the FCO, 1992-. *Publication:* Article in Int Affairs. *Membership:* C'wlth Trust. *Honour:* CWG, 1986. *Hobbies:* Fruit and Vegetables. *Address:* c/o Foreign and Commonwealth Office, King Charles St, London SW1A 2AH, England. 1.

MASEFIELD Patrick William Bussell, b. 17 Sept 1942, Kampala, Uganda. Arts & Disability Cons. m. (1) Andrea Jean Duncan, 29 Apr 1967, div 1974, (2) Marcia Cherie Kranz, 31 Dec 1976, div 1983, 1 d. *Education:* MA (Cantab). *Appointments:* Arts Admnstr, 1967-69; Theatre Dir, 1969-84; Arts Cons, 1974-86; Disability Advsr, 1988. *Publications:* 30 performed plays, adaptations and collaborations; 21 commissioned reports on theatre, arts and education. *Memberships:* Hon Life Mbr, Dirs Guild of GB; Hon Life Mbr, ASSITEJ, Brit Br; Coun, Vice Chmn, M E Assn; Chair of Mgmt Coun, Collar & TIE Co; Planning Bd Mbr, Arts Coun of GB; North East Soc of Playwrights. *Honour:* Welsh Nat Dramatists Prize for co-authorship of Play With Fire, 1971. *Hobbies:* Disability Issues; The Arts; Education; Marathon Running. *Address:* 68 The Hill Avenue, Worcester WR5 2AG, England.

MASINOVSKY Zinovij, b. 28 July 1949, Chmelnicki, Czech. Scientist. m. Eva Rezkova, 21 Dec 1972, 1 d. *Education:* Dip in Biophys 1966-71, Postgrad 1971-74, Moscow State Univ; PhD, Czech Acad of Scis, Prague, 1979. *Appointments:* Supervised Rsch, Moscow State Univ, 1971-74; Rsch Scientist, Inst of Microbiol, Czech Acad of Sci, 1975-85; Rsch Scientist, Lab of Evolutionary Biol, Czech Acad of Sci, 1985-. *Publications:* Evolutionary aspects of Photobiology (with B Vechet), 1986; Author of over 60 scientific papers in biophys, evolutionary biochem, evolutionary biol. *Memberships:* Cnslr, Int Soc for the Study of the Origin of Life; Comm on Space Rsch. *Hobbies:* Reading; Gardening; Sports. *Address:* Fibichova 5, Prague 3, Czechoslovakia.

MASON Harvey Christopher, b. 22 Dec 1932, Glasgow, Scotland. Brit Army; Dir. m. Rosemary Elizabeth Fisher, 27 Dec 1957, 2 s, 1 d. *Education:* MB, ChB, Glasgow, 1960; DTM & H, 1972; MRCGP, 1972; FRCGP, 1977. *Appointments:* Army, served in Korea, Cyprus and Germany; Dir of Army Gen Pract, 1988-91. *Memberships:* BMA; FRSM; FMS. *Honours:* Montefiore Medal, 1971; Knott Mem Prize, 1979; Off (Brother), Order of St John, 1987; Queen's Hon Surg, 1989. *Hobbies:* Opera; Food and wine; History; Cats. *Address:* Mytilus House, 75 Brown Street, Salisbury, Wiltshire SP1 2BA, England.

MASON Michael D, b. 27 Apr 1950, Grand Rapids, MI, USA. m. Donna L Hatfield Mason, July 1972, 1 s, 1 d. *Education:* BSL, Gt Lakes Bible Coll, 1972; MA, MI State Univ, 1981. *Appointments:* Assoc Libn, Dept of Educ, State of MI, Lancing, 1968-73; Assoc Min 1973-79, Min 1979-, First Ch of Christ, Jackson; Assoc Min, First Christian Ch, Angola. *Publications:* Articles in Key to Christian Education, 1985; Go For the Gold, 1987. *Membership:* Evangelical Tchr Trng Assn. *Honours:* Awded Honoured Min by Grand Commardery of MI with a Pilgrimage to Holy Land, 1987; Assoc of the Yr, LY Am Bus Women's Assn, 1990-91. *Interests:* Music - study and performance; Reading; Studying art. *Address:* 2395 West High Drive, Jackson, MI 49205, USA. 145.

MASSEY Alan, b. 28 Sept 1935, Bolton, Eng. Mng Dir. m. Merril Ann Upton, 4 Oct 1964, 1 s, 1 d. *Education:* BSc Tech, AMCST, Manchester Univ, 1955-60; D.Sc (Hon) South Bank University. *Appointments:* Holland & Hannen, Cubitts Ltd, 1960-68; Richard Costain Ltd, 1968-69; APCI Grp (PMI), 1969-; APCI (Grp), 1969-92; PMI, 1969-92; Arlingotn Securities, 1991-. *Publications:* Tech papers and articles. *Memberships:* Chartered Inst of Bldg, 1960, Pres 1990-91; FBIM; FRSA. *Honour:* UMIST Grad of the Yr Awd, 1991. *Hobbies:* Golf, Capt Huntercotmbe GC, 1989-90; Pres, Reading Cricket and Hockey Club; Pres, Berkshire Assn of Cricket Umpires and Scorers; Travel; Art; Gardening. *Address:* Tall Trees, Tanners Lane, Chalkhouse Green, Nr Reading, Berkshire RG4 9AD, England.

MASSIER Paul F, b. 22 July 1923, Pocatello, ID, USA. Engr. m. (1) Miriam Parks, 1 May 1948, dec 1975, (2) Dorothy Hedlund Wright, 12 Sept 1978, 2 d. *Education:* BS, Univ of CO, 1948; MS, MA Inst of Tech, 1949. *Appointments:* Engr, Constrn and Maintenance Dept, Pan Am Refining Corp, Texas City, 1948; Design Engr, Maytag Co, Newton, 1949-50; Rsch Engr, Boeing Co, Seattle, 1950-55; Sr Rsch Engr, Grp Supvsr, Mbr of Tech Staff, Task Mgr, Jet Propulsion Lab, CA Inst of Tech, Pasadena, 1955-88, ret'd 1989, but continued as a Mbr of the Tech Staff on call. *Publications:* Author

of 39 publs in journs and book series. *Memberships:* Assoc Fellow, AIAA; Aeoracoustics, Propellants and Combustion, Nuclear Propulsion; AAAS; Planetary Soc; Sigma Xi; Tau Beta Pi; Sigma Tau; Pi Tau Sigma; Interagency Comm for Planning Univ Transp Noise Symposia; Fellow, Int Biog Assn; Life Fellow, Am Biog Inst Rsch Assn. *Honours:* Mil Unit Cit Awd, 1946; Apollo Achmt Awd 1969, Basic Noise Rsch Awd 1980, NASA; Life Mbr Serv Awd, CA Parent Tchrs Assn, 1970; Layman of the Yr Awd, Arcadia Congl Ch, 1971; Sustained Serv Awd, AIAA, Los Angeles Sect, 1980-81. *Hobbies:* Travelog motion picture production; Sheet music and other collectibles; Antique phonographs. *Address:* 1000 No First Avenue, Arcadia, CA 91006, USA. 9, 59, 139, 143, 152, 155, 156, 164, 178.

MASUD Naiyer, b. 16 Nov 1936, Lucknow, India. Prof. m. Sabeeha Khatoon, 30 Sept 1971, 1 s, 3 d. *Education:* MA 1957; DPhil 1965; PhD 1966. *Appointments:* Lectr in Urdu & Persian, FRI Coll, Bareilly, 1965; Lectr in Persian 1965, Reader in Persian 1978, Prof in Persian 1990, Lucknow Univ. *Publications include:* Rajab Ali Beg Suroor, 1967; Kafk Ke Afsaney, 1978; Seemiya, 1984; Itr-e-Kafur, 1990; Marsiya Khwani K Fan, 1990. *Honours:* UP Urdu Akademic Awd for Tabeer-i-Ghalib 1973, Seemiya 1984, Itr-e-Kafur 1990. *Hobbies:* Painting; Gardening; Reading; Writing. *Address:* Adabistan, Din Dayai Road, Lucknow 226003, India.

MASUDA Sumiko, b. 11 Aug 1930, Nagoya, Japan. Prof Emeritus. m. Ken-ichi Masuda. *Education:* MA, Keio Univ Grad Sch of Letters, 1965. *Appointments:* Instr 1970-74, Assoc Prof 1974-82, Prof 1982-91, Prof Emeritus 1991-, Gifu Women's Univ. *Publications:* Book, Tsurezuregusa-no- kokoro, 1989; Author of 49 articles. *Memberships:* Soc of Japanese Lang and Lit; Soc of Japanese Lit in the Middle Ages; Soc of Arts. *Address:* 3-4-5 Ishiodai, Kasugai, Aichi Prefecture, 487 Japan. 52.

MATAGA Noboru, b. 20 May 1927, Japan. Prof Emeritus. m. Shizuyo Tsuno, 29 May 1958, 1 s. *Education:* BSc 1951, DSc 1959, Univ of Tokyo. *Appointments:* Rsch Assoc of Chem 1951, Lectr of Chem 1958, Assoc Prof of Chem 1962, Osaka City Univ; Prof of Chem 1964, Prof Emeritus 1991, Osaka Univ. *Publications:* Molecular Interacitons and Electronic Spectra, 1970; Electron Transfer in Inorg Org & Biol Systems (Ed), 1991; Author of: many articles in profl journs; Many review articles in multi-authored books. *Memberships:* Chem Soc of Japan; Am Soc for Photobiol; AAAS; Phys Soc of Japan. *Honours:* Sci & Tech Grantee, Toray Sci Fndn, 1976; Sci Rsch Grantee, Mitsubishi Fndn, 1977; Sci Rsch Grantee, Yamada Sci Fndn, 1982; Awd of the Chem Soc of Japan, 1986. *Hobbies:* Reading; Hiking; Playing with cat. *Address:* Daiwa Higashi 2-3-14, Kawanishi 666-01, Japan. 52, 154.

MATANO Tsuneo, b. 20 Jan 1924, Kyoto, Japan. Prof. m. 26 Nov 1951, 1 s, 1 d. *Education:* BS, Nagoya (Japan) Univ; Dr Sci, Ngoya Univ. *Appointments:* Rsch Assoc, Inst of Nuclear Study, Univ of Tokyo, 1956-67; Assoc Prof, Saitama Univ, 1967-68; Prof 1968-89, Prof Emeritus 1989-; Prof Fuki Institute of Technology (Japan), 1989-; Vis Prof, Tata Inst of Fundamental Rsch, India; Prof Emeritus, Univ Mayor de San Andres, Bolivia, 1989-. *Publication:* Radiation Detectors and its Applications, 1960. *Membership:* Phys Soc of Japan. *Hobby:* Cosmic Ray Physics. *Address:* Fukui Institute of Technology, 3-6-1 Gakuen, Fukui 910, Japan. 52.

MATAS David, b. 29 Aug 1943, Winnipeg, Can. Lawyer. *Education:* BA, Univ of Man, 1964; MA, Princeton Univ, 1965; BA 1967, BCL 1968, Oxford Univ. *Appointments:* Law Clerk, Chief Justice of the Supreme Ct of Can, 1968-69; Articling Student, Thompson, Dorfman, Sweatman, 1970-71; Assoc, Schwartz, McJannet, Weinberg, 1973-79; Sole Practitioner, 1979-. *Publications:* Canada Immigration Law, 1986; Justice Delayed: Nazi War Criminals in Canada, 1987; Closing the Doors: The Failure of Refugee Protection, 1989; The Sanctuary Trial, 1989. *Memberships:* Chmn, Constl & Int Law Sect, 1979-82, Chmn, Immigration Comm 1980-81, Can Bar Assn; Legal Coord, Amnesty Int, Can Sect (Eng Speaking), 1980-; Dir, Man Assn for Rights and Liberties, 1983-89; Sr Counsel, League for Human Rights, B'nai Brith Can, 1989-; Dir, Int Def and Aid Fund for S Africa, 1990-91. *Address:* 2nd Floor, 205 Edmonton Street, Winnipeg, Manitoba, Canada R3C 1R4. 142.

MATEV Ivan, b. 26 May 1925, Bourgas, Bulgaria. Hand Surg. m. Kate Matev, 21 July 1952, 2 s. *Education:* Fellow WHO, UK, 1966; Silicon Implant Rsch Prog, Grand Rapids, 1969; Prof, Orthopaedic Surg, 1971; DSc, 1978. *Publications include:* Rehabilitation der Hand, 1982; Reconstructive Surgery of the Thumb, 1983; The Hand (Co-author), 1985; Plastic Surgery, 1986; Diseases of the Hand, 1990; Plastic Surgery (Co-author), 1990. *Memberships:* Pres, Bulgarian Soc for Hand Surg, 1985-; Pres, Union of Scientists in Bulgaria, 1990-; Brit, German, Italian, French Socs for Surg of the Hand; Corr Ed: The J Hand Surg, London; Rev Espanola Circugia Mano, Zaragozza; Acta Chir Plast Prag. *Honours:* Gt Awd of the Union of Scientists, Bulgaria, 1972; Hon Mbr of: Aust 1979, Am 1988, S African 1991 Socs for Surg of the Hand; Hon Mbr, Hungarian Traumatologic Assn, 1978. *Hobbies:* Music; Tennis. *Address:* The Union of Scientists, Oborishte tr 35, Sofia, Bulgaria.

MATHAUSER Zdenek, b. 3 June 1920, Rudolfov. Prof. m. Svetla Bartosova, 26 Mar 1949, 1 d. *Appointments:* Asst of Russian Dept 1949-, Assoc Prof 1956-, Prof 167-, Charles Univ, Prague; Rschr, Czech Acad of Scis, 1960-; Dir, Inst for World Lits, 1969-70; Rschr, Inst for Theory and Hist of Arts, 1971-. *Publications include:* The Art of Poetry, 1961; The Spiral of Poetry, 1965; Unwelcome Studies, 1969; Literature and Anticipation, 1982; Methodological Meditations, or the Mystery of Symbol, 1989; Author of over 600 articles in various lit and aesth journs. *Memberships:* L'Assn Int de Litterature Comparee; Lit Assn of Czech Acad of Sci; Aesthetic Assn of Czech Acad of Sci; Czech Comm of Slavists. *Honours:* Prize of the Czech Writer Pubing Hse, 1964; Prize Awded by the Capital of Prague, 1967. *Hobbies:* Aesthetics; Philosophy; mainly Husserl's Phenomenology; Film; Festival. *Address:* Vrsovicka 81, 100 00 Prague 10, Czechoslovakia. 1.

MATHAUSEROVA Svetla, b. 7 Mar 1924, Antalovce. Prof. m. Zdenek Mathauser, 26 Mar 1949, 1 d. *Education:* PhD, 1949; CSc, 1959; DSc, 1990. *Appointments:* Asst, Sch of Educ, Ceske Budejovice, 1949-53; Asst of Russian Dept of Philosl Fac 1953-, Assoc Prof of Art 1962-, Univ Prof 1990- , Charles Univ, Prague. *Publications:* Russian Tradition of Monological Narratives, 1961; Old Russian Theories of Literary Arts, 1979; On Vasilij the Golden-haired, the Czech Prince, 1982; Ways of Centuries, 1988; Author of over 170 rsch articles in various journs. *Memberships:* Lit Assn of Czech Acad of Sci; Medieval Assn of Czech Acad of Scis. *Honours:* Prize for the best acad book of 1980, awded by Czech Lit Fund for the book, Old Russian Theories of Literary Arts; Medaled by Charles Univ, 1989. *Hobbies:* Medieval Literature and Arts; Gardening. *Address:* Philosophical Faculty of Charles University, Nam J Palacha 2, 110 00 Prague 1, Czechoslovakia.

MATHESON John Ross, b. 14 Nov 1917, Arundel, PQ, Can. m. 4 Aug 1945, 4 s, 2 d. *Education:* BA (Hon), Queen's Univ, 1940; Barrister at Law, Osgoode Hall, 1948; LLB, York Univ; LLM, Univ of Western Ont, 1954; MA, Mt Allison Univ, 1975. *Appointments:* Called to Bar of Ont, 1948; Created QC 1967; MP for Leeds in 24th, 25th, 26th, 27th Parliaments of Can; Parliamentary Sec to PM of Can, 1966-68; Appointed Judge, 1968; Retired, Justice of the Ont Ct of Justice, 1992. *Publications:* Canada's Flag: A Search for a Country; Sinews of the Heart. *Memberships:* Hon Pres, United Empire Loyalists Assn of Can; Heraldry Soc of

Canada; Genealogist, Priory of Can, Order of St John; Hon Sec, Can Amateur Boxing Assn; Life Gov: Can Bible Soc, Can Corps of Commissionaires; Life Mbr: Royal Can Artillery Assn; Royal Can Legion; Can Econ(s) Assn; Can Bar Assn; Can Inst for the Admin of Justices; Hon Life Mbr, Can Olympic Assn. *Honours:* K St J; CD; KCLJ; OMLJ; Fellow: Royal Econ Soc, FSA of Scotland, FHS of Can, Int Biographical Assn, Paul Harris Fellow of Rotary Int, 1991; Awded Montreal Medal for serv to Queen's Univ Chancellor's Award, LL.D Honoris Causa; William Mercer Wilson Medal for serv to freemasonry. *Hobbies:* Heraldry; Heritage. *Address:* Box 43, Ridean Ferry, Ontario, Canada K0G 1W0. 88, 142.

MATHIAS Richard Gordon, b. 22 July 1944, Agassiz, BC, Can. Assoc Prof; Dir. 2 s, 1 d. *Education:* MD, Univ of Alta, 1964-68; LMCC, 1968; FRCPC, 1975. *Appointments:* Field Epidemiologist, Hlth & Welfare, Can, 1975-77; Clin Assoc Med, Mem Univ NFLD, 1976-77; MHO, Yorkton/Melville, 1977- 80; Clin Lectr, Univ of Sask, Regina, 1977-80; Dir, Prof Epidemiologist, Sask Hlth Regina, 1978-80; Cons Phys Epidemiologist, Min of Hlth, BC, 1980-83. *Publications:* Can Consultant on AIDS: What Young Adults Should Know; What Young Adults Should Know - Accompanying Vol - Teacher Guide. *Memberships:* Alta Coll of Physns & Surg; Am Soc of Microbiol; BC Med Assn Infection Disease Comm; Ed Bd, Can Journ of Pub Hlth; Advsry Bd, Envir Hlth BCIT; Can Infectious Diseases Soc. *Hobbies:* Exec, Richmond Summer Swim Assn, 1984-86; Mgr 1986-88, Coach 1986-88, Ctrl Raiders Soccer Club; Official, BC Summer Swim Assn, 1986-. *Address:* Health Care and Epidemiology, University of British Columbia, Faculty of Medicine, 5804 Fairview Crescent, James Mather Building, Vancouver, Canada V6T 1Z3. 142.

MATIJEVIC Egon, b. 27 Apr 1922, Otocac, Croatia. Disting Univ Prof. m. Bozica Matijevic, 27 Feb 1947. *Education:* PhD 1948, Dr Habil 1952, Univ of Zagreb; Dr Sci (Hon), Lehigh Univ, Bethlehem, USA, 1977; Dr Sci (Hon), Maria Curie-Sklodowska Univ, Lublin, Poland, 1990; Dp. Sci (Hon), Clarkson Univ, Potsdam, NY, 1992. *Appointments include:* Rsch Fellow, Cambridge Univ, Eng, 1956-57; Rsch Assc 1957-59, Assoc Prof of Chem 1960-62, Prof of Chem 1962-86, Assoc Dir 1966-68, Dir 1968- 81, Inst of Colloid and Surface Sci, Chmn, Dept of Chem 1981-87, Disting Univ Prof 1986-, Clarkson Coll of Tech, Potsdam (changed to Clarkson Univ 1984). *Publications:* Author of 450 scientific papers, books. *Memberships include:* Am Assn for Crystal Growth; Am Ceramic Soc (Hon); ACS; Int Assn of Colloid and Interface Scientists; Materials Rsch Soc; Sigma Xi; Chem Soc of Japan, Div of Colloid Chem, Tokyo (Hon); Croatian, Acad of Scis & Arts; Academy of Ceramics, Italy. *Honours include:* Disting Tchng Awd, Clarkson Coll of Tech, 1975; Langmuir Disting Lectr Awd, Div of Colloid and Surface Chem, ACS, 1985; Thomas Graham Prize, Kolloid-Ges, Berlin, 1985; Kendall Award, AM Chem Soc, 1972; Iler Award, Amer Chem Soc, 1993; Bozo Tezak Medal, Croatian Chem Soc, Zagreb, 1991. *Hobby:* Art collection. *Address:* Clarkson University, Centre for Advanced Materials Processing, Box 5814, Potsdam, NY 13699, USA.

MATILLON Yves, b. 26 Sept 1948, Lyon, France. m. Nicole Bermond, 6 Sept 1976, 3 s, 1 d. *Education:* MD, 1978; DEA, 1979; Dip in Hlth Econ(s), 1983. *Appointments:* Hopitaux de Lyon, 1976-; Claude Bernard Univ, 1980; Dir, Nat Agcy for the Dev of Med Evaluation, 1989. *Memberships:* Int Assn for the Study of Pain, 1986; Int Soc for Quality Assurance, 1987; Int Soc of Epidemiology, 1988; Am Soc of Decision Making, 1990. *Honours:* Bourie Fondalion Jacques Cartier, 1987; Prix du Haut Comite Medical de la Securite Sociale, 1987. *Hobbies:* Tennis; Skiing; Gardening. *Address:* AN DEM, 5 bio Rue Perignon, 75015 Paris, France.

MATIS Elena Yakovlevna, b. 24 Oct 1953, Vorkuta, Russia. Biogeochemist. m. V P Rudenko, 7 Jan 1978, 1 s, 1 d. *Education:* Dr of Chem Sci, 1989. *Appointments:* Assistant, 1973-77, Ingenier, 1978-88, Reschr, Inst of

Petroleym Chem, 1989-. *Publications:* The Structure and Functions of Carotenoids in Hyper Saline Lakes, 1988; Carotenoid pigments found in sedimentary rocks of Eastern Siberia, 1989. *Memberships:* Mendeleev Chem Assn; Biological Assn. *Hobbies:* Music; Aerobics; Tourism. *Address:* Institute of Petroleum Chemistry, 3 Akademichesky, Tomsk 634055, Russia.

MATIUSHKIN Alexei, b. 20 Dec 1927, Russia. Psychologist. m. Makazova Jamaza, 18 Feb 1967, 2 d. *Education:* Moscow Univ, 1948-53; Postgrad student, 1953-57; Candidate of Psychol Sci, 1961; Dr of Psychol Sci, 1974; Prof, 1982. *Appointments:* Inspector of Educ, Moscow Univ, 1957- 61; Sci Worker, Inst Psychol, 1961-79; Chief, Lab Psychol Higher Educ, 1974- 80; Chief Labor Psychol Thinking, 1980-83; Dir Inst Gen and Educ Psychol, 1983-91; Chief, Ctr of Creative Giftedness, 1990. *Publications:* Chief Ed, Vopzosi Psychology, 1980; Problem situations in thinking and education, 1972; Psychological basis of problem education, 1973; The current status of child and educ psychology, 1984; The conception of creative giftedness, 1990. *Memberships:* Pres, Soviet Pshcyol Assn, 1983-84; Acad, Acad of Pedagog Sci, Russia, 1990. *Honours:* Hon Prof, Intl Assn into Psychol, Italy, 1990. *Hobbies:* Bicycling; Skiing; Tourism. *Address:* Prospect Marxa 20 Bldg V, Inst of General and Educational Psychology, Moscow 103009, Russia.

MATLOFF Gregory Lee, b. 3 Feb 1945, NYC, NY, USA. Adj Phys Prof; Sci Writer. m. 7 Aug 1986. *Education:* BA, Queens Coll, NY, 1961-65; OMS 1966-69, PhD 1972-76, NY Univ. *Appointments:* Aerospace Engr, 1965- 69; Astronomer, Weslayan Univ, 1970; Asst Ed, Phyics Today, 1971-72; Post Doct Scholar, NY Univ, 1976-78; Admnstr, Tchr, Prof, Cons, 1978-. *Publications:* The Starflight Handbook (co-author); 1989; The Urban Astronomer, 1991; Author of about 50 articles in Applied Optics, JBIS, Spaceflight, Icarus, ATAAJ, J Energy, JGR, Acra Astronautica, J Astronaut Sci. *Memberships:* FBIS; AAAS; OSA; NY Acad of Sci; Planetary Soc; World Space Fndn; Space Studies Inst. *Honours:* Mbr, Sigma Xi, 1970; Awded NSF, Univ Challenge Grant, 1976; Dubbed a Kt of Malta, 1986. *Hobbies:* Amateur Astronomy; Reading Science Fiction; Swimming; Fitness. *Address:* 417 Greene Avenue, Brooklyn, NY 11216, USA. 6, 52, 139.

MATSUHISA Hiroshi, b. 5 Aug 1947, Osaka, Japan. Prof. m. Reiko, 3 May 1976, 1 s, 2 d. *Education:* BS, Engrng Dept 1970, Dr of Engrng 1982, Kyoto Univ; MS, IE Dept, GA Inst of Tech, 1972. *Appointments:* Assoc Prof of Precision Engrng Dept, Kyoto Univ, 1976-. *Publications:* Author of papers on Mechanical Vibration and Sound. *Membership:* Japan Soc of Mech Engrs. *Hobby:* Tennis. *Address:* 1-22-27 Hieidaira, Otsu, Japan.

MATSUMOTO Hiroshi, b. 11 Mar 1948, Akashi, Japan. Mech Engr. m. 7 Aug 1973, 1 s, 1 d. *Education:* BE, Akashi Tech Coll, 1963-68. *Appointments:* Dev Engr, NEC, 1968-80; Dev Engr, Olympus, 1980-81; Chief Engr, Seiko-sha, 1981-83; Chief Engr, DEC, Japan, 1983-91. *Membership:* The Laser Soc of Japan, 1983-. *Honours:* Commendation on patents, NRC, 1980; Commendation of Mgmt Course, Japan Exec Contabulation Ctr, 1986. *Hobbies:* Reading; Music; Swimming; Moutain climbing; Travelling; Psychology; Ecology; Cosmology; Jexology. *Address:* 4-15-5-402 Motogou, Kawaguchi 332, Japan. 52.

MATSUMOTO Kiyoshi, b. 23 Sept 1922, Hokkaido, Japan. Standing Auditor. m. 21 May 1954, 2 d. *Education:* BSc, Hokkaido Univ, 1946. *Appointments:* Dir 1973, Mng Dir 1978, Toyota Motor Co Ltd; Sr Mng Dir 1982, Exec VP 1984, Toyota Motor Corp; Chief Exec Off, Toyota CRDL Inc, 1988; Standing Auditor, Toyota CRDL Inc, 1992. *Creative works:* Author of many articles in various journs of academic societies; Contributed to about 8000 patents. *Memberships:* Fellow, S of Automotive Engr; Chmn of Pub Nuisance Subcomm, Safety and Pub Nuisance Comm, Japan Automobile

Mfrs Assn Inc; Chmn, Tokai Br, The Japan Soc of Mech Engrs; Dir, Ind Property Coop Ctr. *Honour:* Nat Medal of Hon w Blue Ribbon, 1986; 3rd Class Order of the Rising Sun, 1992. *Hobbies:* Golf; Skiing; Gardening. *Address:* 41-1, Aza-Yokomichi, Oaza-Nagakute, Nagakute-cho, Aichi-gun, Aichi pref 480-11, Japan.

MATSUMOTO Yuko, b. 17 June 1963, Shimane Pref, Japan. Novelist; Essayist. *Education:* Bach of Sociology, Tsukuba Univ, 1987. *Appointments:* TV News Reporter, Asahi TV, 1985-88; Novelist & Essayist 1987-; Freelance Announcer, 1988. *Publications include:* The Anguish of an Overeater, 1987; Androgynous Love, 1988; The Fake Marilyn Monroe, 1990; The Aesthetics of Parting, 1991; The Reading Hour: A Collection of Book Reviews, 1991. *Memberships:* Japan Writers Assn; Japan Chapt, Int PEN Club. *Honour:* Subaru Lit Awd, 1987. *Hobbies:* Overseas travel; Swimming; Movies. *Address:* c/o 10th Editorial Department, Shueisha, 1-5-14 Sarugaku-cho, Chiyoda ward, Tokyo 110, Japan.

MATSUNO Ryuichi, b. 24 May 1939, Osaka, Japan. Prof. m. 6 Dec 1964, 2 d. *Education:* BE 1962, ME 1964, DE 1968, Kyoto Univ. *Appointments:* Instr 1967, Assoc Prof 1970, Prof 1984, Kyoto Univ; Assoc Prof, Okayama Univ, 1968. *Publications include:* Ion-Exchange Chromatography of Proteins, 1988; Author of over 90 papers in the field of fluidized bed, enzyme engineering, bioseparation, biochemical engineering & food engineering. *Memberships:* ACS; Chem Soc of Japan; Japan Soc of Biosci, Biotech & Agrochem; Soc of Chem Engrs, Japan; Soc of Fermentation & Bioengineering, Japan. *Hobbies:* Watching sports; Track & field games; Reading books. *Address:* Department of Food Science and Technology, Faculty of Agriculture, Kyoto University, Sakyo-ku, Kyoto 606-01, Japan.

MATSUSHITA Masaaki, b. 5 Nov 1937, Nagasaki, Japan. Prof. m. 20 Oct 1962, 2 s, 2 d. *Education:* BM 1968, DM 1986, Fac of Med, Univ of Tokyo. *Appointments:* Matsuzawa Metrop Mental Hosp, 1966-73; Psych Rsch Inst of Tokyo, 1973-86; Yokohama City Univ Sch of Med, 1987-90; Prof, Dept of Psych, Univ of Tokyo, 1990-. *Publications:* Author of many articles on neuropathology of aged brains, 1965-92. *Memberships:* Int Soc of Neuropathology; Int Psychogeriatrics Assn; Japanese Soc of Psych and Neurology; Societas Neurologica Japonica. *Hobbies:* Golf; History of Medicine, especially Psychiatry and Neurology. *Address:* Department of Psychiatry, Faculty of Medicine, University of Tokyo, 7-3-1 Hongo, Bunkyo-ku, Tokyo, Japan.

MATSUZAKI Isao, b. 6 Jan 1930, Hakodate, Japan. Chem Prof. m. Yukiko Sato, 10 Jan 1957, 1 d. *Education:* BS 1952, PhD 1960, Hokkaido Univ; Postdoct Rsch, Northwestern Univ, 1960-62; Postdoct Rsch, TX A&M Univ, 1969-71. *Appointments:* Rschr, Hitachi Wks, 1952-57; Prof, Shinshu Univ, 1961-; Asst Prof 1964-66, Assoc Prof 1966-71, Hokkaido Univ. *Publications:* 5W3H - Random Basic English, 1978; 5W3H - Chemical English, 1981; How To Improve Eyesight, 1992. *Memberships:* Eng Reviser 1981-, Japan Chem Soc; Catalysis Soc, Japan. *Hobbies:* Logical Science; Logical Linguistics. *Address:* Tanbajima 3-818-2, Nagano 381-22, Japan. 52.

MATTHEWS Geoffrey Vernon Townsend, b. 16 June 1923, Norwich, Eng. Rsch Dir, Ret'd. m. (1) 1 s, 1 d, (2) Mary Elizabeth Evans, 26 Jan 1980, 1 s, 1 d. *Education:* MA, PhD, Christ's Coll, Cambridge. *Appointments:* Operational Rsch, RAF, 1943-46; Postdoct Rsch, Cambridge, 1950-55; Dir of Rsch, Wildfowl Trust, Slimbridge, 1955-88. *Publications:* Bird Navigation, 1st ed 1955, 2nd ed 1968; Author of about 100 papers on bird onientation x conservation. *Memberships:* Dir, Int Waterfowl Res Bur; Pres, Assn Study Animal Behaviour; VP, Brit Ornithologists' Union; FIBiol; Corr Fellow, Am Ornithological Union; Corr Fellow, Swiss Soc on Bird Study. *Honours:* Hon Prof, Univ of Cardiff; Union Medal, Brit Ornithologists' Union, 1980;

OBE, 1986; Off of the Dutch Order of the Golden Ark, 1987; Soc Medal, RSPB, 1989. *Hobbies:* Fossil hunting; Stamp collecting; House maintenance; Gardening; Reading. *Address:* 32 Tetbury Street, Minchinhampton, Stroud, Gloucestershire GL6 9JH, England.

MATTHEWS John Chester, b. 1 May 1920, Essex, Eng. Ret'd; Naval Surg; Dentist; Graphologist. m. 27 Feb 1954, 2 s, 1 d. *Education:* MRCS, LRCP, London; LMSSA, London; LDS RCS, Eng. *Appointments:* SMO, Princess Elizabeth Hosp; Eastbourne, 1945; Surg, M Navy, 1945-49; Dental Surg, Principal Bath, 1954-72; Cons Graphologist. *Memberships:* BMA; Brit Inst of Graphologists. *Hobbies:* Graphology; Painting & Drawing; Living in France; Humour; Handwriting. *Address:* c/o Midland Bank, Shaftesbury, Dorset, England.

MATTHEWS John Duncan, b. 19 Sept 1921, Rainhill, Lancs, Eng. Ret'd Cons Physn. m. Constance Margaret Moffat, 12 Oct 1945, 2 s. *Education:* BA, Cambridge Univ, 1940-42; MB ChB, Edinburgh Univ, 1942- 45; MRCPE 1951; FRCPE. 1958. *Appointments:* RAMC, Germany, 1946-48; Registrar, Sr Registrar 1950-56, Cons Physn 1956-86, Royal Infirmary, Edinburgh; Hon Sr Lectr, Edinburgh Univ. *Publications:* Author of articles on diabetes and heart disease; Col, RAMC, TA & TARO; Cons to Army in Scotland; Surg to High Constables and Guard of Hon, Palace of Holyrood Hse, 1961-91, Moderator, 1987-89; VP, RCPEd, 1982-85. *Honour:* CVO 1989. *Hobbies:* Gardening; Fishing; Golf; Played cricket for Scotland. *Address:* 3 Succoth Gardens, Edinburgh EH12 6BR, Scotland.

MATTSSON Jan Orvar, b. 8 Sept 1930, Malmo, Sweden. Prof; Hd of Dept of Phys Geogr. m. Elisabeth Bengtsson, 19 June 1959. *Education:* PhD, 1967. *Appointments:* Univ Lectr 1966-68, Docentshp 1969-75, Rsch Fellow 1975-82, Hd 1986-, Prof 1991, Univ of Lund, Sweden. *Publications:* Author of several scientific textbooks, about 150 scientific papers, about 300 reviews. *Memberships include:* Mbr of Bd, S Swedish Geogr Soc; Mbr of Bd, Swedish Soc for Anthropology & Geog; Swedish Nat Comm for Geog; Swedish Nat Comm for Geophys; Royal Physiographic Soc in Lund' Working Mbr, Royal Swedish Acad of Agric and Forestry; Working Mbr, Climatic Commn of the Int Geographic Union. *Hobbies:* Oil and gouache painting, 2 exhibitions in Malmo, Sweden, 1988, 1989. *Address:* Department of Physical Geography, University of Lund, Solvegatan 13, S- 22362 Lund, Sweden.

MATTSSON Nils G, b. 1 Oct 1938, Ostersund, Sweden. Prof of Law. m. Christina Rosen, 1 June 1963, 1 s, 1 d. *Education:* LLM, 1963; LLD, 1974. *Appointments:* Asst Dist Ct Judge, 1963-65; Co Lawyer, Tetra Pak Int, 1965-69; Sr Lectr, Lund Univ, 1970-75; Prof of Fiscal Law, Uppsala Univ, 1975-. *Publications include:* VAT, An introduction, 6 ed, -1990; Swedish Int Taxation, 10 ed, -1991; Taxation of Partnerships, 8 ed, -1991; Fiscal policy, An introduction, 3 ed, -1991. *Memberships:* Nordic Tax Rsch Coun; Mbr of Bd, Upsala Nya Tidning; Expert on several parliamentary comms on taxation. *Honours:* Vis Prof, Boston Coll Law Sch, 1980; Univ of MN Law Sch, 1987; Univ of Chicago Law Sch, 1989. *Hobby:* Books, especially old and rare books of legal interest. *Address:* Bergagatan 4, S-75238 Uppsala, Sweden.

MATULA Milos, b. 31 Aug 1919, Frenstat, Czech. Scientific Wkr. m. Eva Matulova, 21 Mar 1951, 1 s. *Education:* Magister in Maths, Charles Univ, Prague. *Appointments:* Scientific Wkr 1956-80, Dep Mgr 1981-86, Math Inst of Charles Univ. *Publications:* Modern Shorthand; Theory and Practice of Shorthand; Frequency of Words; Frequency of the Roots of Words; Mathematical analysis of the process of writing; High Speeds in Shorthand. *Membership:* Union of Czech Maths & Physicists. *Honours:* Speed record in shorthand (525 syllables per minute), 1957; Gabelsberger Medal, 1973. *Hobbies:* Mathematical

linguistics; Psychology; Tennis. *Address:* Mathematical Institute of Charles University, Sokolovska 83, 186 00 Prague 8, Czechoslovakia. 152, 156.

MATVIEVSKAYA Galina Pavlovna, b. 13 July 1930, Dnepropetrovsk, Ukraina. Scientist. m. Karim R Rahimov, 10 Jan 1957, 1 d. *Education:* Cand of Scis, 1959; DSc, 1968. *Appointments:* Jr Wkr, Inst of the Hist of Sci & Tech, Leningrad, 1958-59; Jr Wkr 1959-60, Sr Wkr 1960-85, Chief 1985-, Inst of Maths, Acad of Sci Uzbek SSR, Tashkent. *Publications include:* On the History of Mathematics of Central Asia, 1962; The Doctrine of Number in Medieval Near and Middle East, 1967; Descartes, 1976; Ramus, 1981; Albrecht Dürer-scientist, 1987; Essays on the History of Trigonometry, 1990. *Memberships:* Corr Mbr, Acad of Scis, Uzbek SSR, 1984; Corr Mbr, Int Acad of the Hist of Sci, 1991. *Honours:* Beruni Prize 1974, Meritorious Sci Wkr 1980, Uzbek SSR. *Hobby:* Painting. *Address:* Institute of Mathematics, Academy of Sciences Uzbek SSR, 29 F Khodjayev str, 700143 Tashkent, Uzbekistan.

MATVIYISHYN Yaroslav Oleksiyovych, b. 30 June 1941, Hai Nyjni, Drohobych. Mathn; Histn of Sci. m. Jeanne Matviyishyn, 6 Oct 1972, 1 s, 3 d. *Education:* Univ of Lviv, 1958-63. *Appointments:* Tchr of Maths, Sch of Lviv, 1960; Tchr of Math, Drawing, Phys, Astron, Schs in Lybohora & Jasinka, Dist of Turka, 1961; Army Serv, 1963; Engr, Inst of Math, 1969; Scientific Wkr, Inst of Maths, Ukrainian Acad of Sci, 1970-. *Publications include:* Yuri Z Drohobytcha, 1969; Martyn Z Jouzavytzi, 1969; Nevidomyi Matematychnyj Rukopys XVIII viku Z Kyyevo-Mohylyans'kono kolehiuma, 1981; La cultura e la scienza mei zapporti tza Italia e Uczaina, Padova, 1991, II ed, Roma, 1992. *Memberships:* Am Math Soc; SIAM; The Math Assn of Am; The Goethe-Geselschaft in Weimar; The Scientific Soc, T H Shevtchenko; Int Acad of Scis, San Marino, 1990-. *Hobbies:* Books; Cards; Stamps; Badges; Small calendars; Video cassettes. *Address:* Institute of Mathematics, Repin str 3, 252000 Kiev, Ucraina. 152.

MATWIEJUK Eulalia Henryka, b. 12 Apr 1944, Radom. Archt; Urbanist, Town & Country Planner. m. Jozef Matwiejuk, 22 June 1968, 2 s. *Education:* Master's degree, Gdansk Polytech, Fac of Arch, 1968; Postgrad Studies, Fac of Arch, Warsaw Polytech, 1969-71. *Appointments:* Gen Designer, Hd of a Planner Grp, Provincial Off of Phys Planning, Bialystok, 1968-; Designer, Teams of Designed Servs in Sejny, Hajnowka, Olecko, 1969-75; Hd of Off, Phys Planning Inst, 1986-. *Publications:* Physical Management Plans of about 40 Communees, 20 Towns & 5 Natural Turistic Areas; Prizes and Awards in 3 Town and Country Planning Competitions; Author of several papers and articles. *Memberships:* Soc of Polish Archts; Soc of Polish Town Planners; League for the Preservation of Nature; Polish Tourist Country Lovers' Assn. *Honours:* Meritorious for Bialystok Province, 1985; Silver Awd, Soc of Polish Town and Country Planners, 1986; Silver Cross of Merit, 1987. *Hobbies:* Jogging; Cycling; Solving cross-words; Learning English; Cooking. *Address:* ul Antoniukowska 12A m 84, 15-845 Bialystok, Poland.

MAURISSENS Marc, b. 29 June 1949, Brussels, Belgium. Mktng Communications Mgr. 1 d. *Education:* Univ of Brussels, 1972. *Appointments:* Product Mgr, UNILEVER, 1974-81; Account Dir, LINTAS, 1982-84; Strategic Planning Dir, EUROCOM, 1984-87. *Creative works:* Fishing Writer, Photographer; Painter (Acrylic), Exhib in Rhode, Belgium, 1991. *Honour:* Epica Awd for Best Pan-European Advt, 1990. *Hobbies:* Game fishing; Painting. *Address:* 37 Avenue des Erables, 1640 Rhode-Saint-Genese, Belgium.

MAVIGLIANO Darlene Carol Dargento-Chapetta, b. 23 Aug 1952, Chicago, Illinois, USA. Cardiology Technician; Telemarketing. s, 2 d. *Education:* Patrcia Stevens Prof Modeling, Finishing Sch. *Appointments:* Modeling Field, Photos, Catalog, Store Flyers; PR Work, Film; Educational Movie. *Creative Works:* 2 Patents,

Character; Utility. *Memberships:* Civil Air Patrol; Search & Rescue operations Missions, Airplane Exhibits, Model Displays; Say No to Drugs. *Honours:* Planetarium Coordinator; Safety Awards. *Hobbies include:* Swimming; Cooking; Sewing; Antiques; Music; Church Choir; Art Drama; Aerospace Educ. *Address:* 1203 Elsie, Melrose Park, IL 60160, USA.138

MAVROMMATIS Fragiskos, b. 17 Dec 1931, Athens, Greece. Assoc Prof. *Education:* Dip of Med, Univ of Athens, 1957; Doct in Med, Univ of Gottingen, Germany, 1960. *Appointments:* Hd, Cytology Lab, Univ of Lausanne, Switz, 1960-63; Hd, Cell Rsch Lab, Univ of Gottingen, Germany, 1963- 67; Bio-Phys Dept, King's Coll 1963-65, Lectr, Electron Microscopy 1968-69, Univ of London, Eng; Univ of Cambridge, 1965-67; Assoc Prof, Univ of Athens, 1971-79; Hd of Genetics Ctr, M Iliadi Maternity Hosp, Athens, 1975-80; Hd, Rsch Ctr 1979-86, Assoc Prof, Hosp Thorac Diseases of Athens; Rsch Collaborator or Rsch Fellow at several Rsch Labs incl: the Ctr for Electron Microscopy of Romande Switz; the Anticancer Inst of Romande Switz; the Nuclear Rsch Ctr Dimokritos, Athens, 1972-87; the Phys Dept, Nuclear & Particle Phys Sect, Univ of Athens, 1987-; Fdr of several Labs of Applied and Experimental Med. *Publications:* Unpublished Lectures, 1980; Selected Communications, 1984; Index of Scientific Publications, 1987; Author of over 60 articles in various scientific journs. *Memberships include:* FEBS; Hellenic Biophys Biochem Soc; IUB; Int Union of Pure and Applied Biophys; European Soc of Human Genetics. *Honours include:* D B Phys (Hon), 1986; DSc (Hon), 1987; Albert Einstein Int Acd Bronze Medal, 1988. *Address:* 6 Alimedontos Str, Kipseli, GR-113 63 Athens, Greece. 139, 151, 152, 156.

MAXWELL Jane Marilyn Davis Smith, b. 18 May 1949, LaPorte, IN, USA. Profl Writer. m. Donald Lee Smith, 15 Apr 1967, 2 s, 2 d. *Education:* Certified Dental Asst, Elkhart Univ of Med & Dental Technique, Elkhart; Inst of Chd's Lit, Redding Ridge, 1981; Nat Writers' Club Practical Mag Writer's Course, 1982; Fiction Course 1983, Non-Fiction Course 1984, Writers Digest Sch; Non-Fiction Course 1985, Fiction Course 1986, Rocky Mountain Writer's Inst, Denver. *Appointments:* Univ of Notre Dame; Clerk Typist, Fac Steno Pool; Clerk Typist, Grad Sch, 1966-71. *Publications:* No Easy Breathing, New York Daily News, 1988; Central Coast Parent, California, No Easy Breathing, 1991. *Memberships:* Int Platform Assn. *Honours:* 3rd place for Byline Mag Prose Essay Con, 1985; Medal of Hon 1990, Nominated Woman of the Yr 1990, 1991; Am Biog Inst. *Hobbies:* Writing; Dancing; Bowling. *Address:* 139 Timber Lane, South Bend, IN 46615, USA. 125, 138, 151, 152, 155, 156, 162, 178.

MAXWELL John Frederick Michael, b. 20 May 1943, Sidcup, Kent, Eng. Barrister. m. Jayne Elizabeth Hunter, 1 Sep 1986, 1 s, 1 d. *Education:* MA (Hon Jurisprudence), New Coll, Oxford, 1961-64. *Appointments:* Barrister, Inner Temple, 1965; Midland and Oxford Circuit; Dep Stipendiary Magistrate, Birmingham, 1978-90; Asst Recorder, 1991. *Memberships:* Chmn, Karma-Kagyu Trust (for promotion of Tibetan Buddhism); Chmn, Johnstone Hse Trust (Samye Ling Tibetan Ctr); Chmn, Birmingham Karma Ling Buddhist Ctr; Trustee, Rokpa Trust (for Tibetan Refugees); Royal Yachting Assn; Gravesend Sailing Club; Old Gaffers Assn. *Hobbies:* Music; Yachting. *Address:* Grey Walls, 1131 Warwick Road, Solihull, West Midlands B91 3HQ, England.

MAXWELL Kenneth Robert, b. 3 Feb 1941, England. Sr Fellow for Latin Am. *Education:* BA 1963, MA 1966, St Johns Coll, Cambridge Univ; MA 1966, PhD 1970, Princeton Univ. *Appointments:* Columbia Univ, 1976- ; Tinker Fndn, 1979-85; Coun on Foreign Rels, 1989- . *Publications:* Conflicts and Conspiracies: Brazil and Portugal, 1973; Portugal: Ancient Country, New Democracy (ed w Michael Haltzel), 1989; Spanish Foreign & Defense Policy (ed), 1991. *Memberships:* Am Histl Assn; Latin Am Studies Assn; ChmnComm on Brazilian Studies 1981-83, Chmn Comm on Int Scholarly Rels 1982- 85, Conf on Latin Am Hist; Int Conf Grp on Modern Portugal; VP, Bd of Dir, Am Portuguese Soc Inc; Sec, Nat Comm, Am Foreign Policy Inc; Coun on Foreign Rels. *Honours:* Univ of Madrid, 1963; Gulbenkian Scholar, Lisbon, 1964; Ford Reg Studies Fellow, Princeton Univ, 1964-65; Princeton Reg Studies, Fellow in Brazil, 1966-68; Newberry Lib Gulbenkian Fellow, 1968-69; Herodotus Fellow, 1971-72; John Simon Guggenheim Mem Fellowship, 1976-79; Loso-Am Fndn Fellow, 1986-87. *Address:* Council on Foreign Relations, 58 East 68th Street, New York, NY 10021, USA.

MAXWELL-IRVING Alastair Michael Tivey, b. 1 Oct 1935, Witham, Essex, Eng. Chartered Engr. m. Esther Mary Hamilton, 21 Sept 1983. *Education:* BSc, London Univ. *Appointments:* GEC, 1957-58; Allen West, 1958-59; Eng Elec, 1960-64; Annandale Estates, 1966-69; Econ Forestry, 1969-70; Weir Pumps Ltd 1970-91, Commercial Mgr 1990-91. *Publications:* The Irvings of Bonshaw, 1968; The Irvings of Dumfries, 1968; Early Firearms and Their Influence on the Military and Domestic Architecture of the Borders, 1974; Cramalt Tower, 1982; Borthwick Castle, 1982; Hoddom Castle, 1989; The Cadtles of Buittle, 1992. *Memberships:* FSA Scot, 1967; AMICE, 1970; MIEE, 1972; CEng, 1973; MBIM, 1974; Scottish Comm, Antiquarian Horological Soc; Logie Comm Coun, Treasurer. *Hobbies:* Architecture and history of the border towers of Scotland; Archaeology; Family history and genealogy; Art and architecture of Tuscany; Horology; Photography; Heraldry; Gardening. *Address:* Telford House, Blairlogie, Stirling FK9 5PX, Scotland. 20, 184.

MAXWELL-MAHON William Dundas, b. 12 Sept 1924, Sydney, NSW, Aust. Prof of Eng; Prof Emeritus; Prod & Indl Engr. *Education:* Elec Mech III, Sydney Tech Coll, Aust, 1940-42; BA 1956, BA Hons cum laude 1962, MA cum laude 1965, DLitt et Phil 1971, Univ of S Africa, Pretoria; Nat Dip, Mech Engrng 1961, Nat Dip, Prod Engrng 1963, S African Dept of Educ, Arts & Sci. *Appointments:* Asst Prod Engr, S Africa, 1956-64; Sr Lectr in Eng 1966- 75, Prof of Eng 1975-80, Univ of S Africa; Sr Tutor in Eng, Univ of Qld, Australia, 1981; Prof of Eng 1982-89, Prof Emeritus 1990-, Univ of Pretoria. *Publications:* Critical Texts: Plato to the Present Day; How to Read a Poem; Co-author of 12 textbooks on Eng composition and criticism. *Memberships:* Fndn Mbr, S African Inst for Prod Engrng; Fndn Companion, S African Inst of Indl Engrng; Fndn Mbr, Irish Assn of Pretoria; Pres, Aust Assn of S Africa; FRCSoc; Eng Acad of S Africa; Assoc Scientific & Tech Societies of S Africa; Hon Life Fellow, S African Inst for Prod Engrng; Comm, Caledonian Soc, Pretoria; Mbr, South African Society for Professional Engineers, 1990-; Mbr, Australian Committee of the South African Foundation, 1991-. *Honours:* MA Exhib, Univ of S Africa; DLitt et Phil Exhib, 1965; Sr Rsch Grant, Human Scis Rsch Coun, S Africa, 1984. *Hobbies:* Historical and theatre research; Reading and writing about literary theory and criticism; Book reviewing. *Address:* Department of English, University of Pretoria, Hillcrest 0083, South Africa. 151, 152, 154, 178.

MAY Stephen James, b. 10 Sept 1946, Toronto, Can. Novelist; Histn; Essayist; Short Story Writer; Edr. m. Caroline Casteel, 13 Oct 1973. *Education:* BA 1975, MA 1977, CA State Univ. *Appointments:* Prof of Eng, Pikes Peak Coll, CO Springs, 1978-91; Profl Writer & Artist, 1983-. *Publications:* Pilgrimage, 1987; A Land Observed, 1991; Fire From the Skies, 1991; Hunter From the Hill, 1992; Footloose on the Santa Fe Trail, 1992. *Memberships:* Hon Coun, Int Biog Ctr; Rsch Bd of Advsr, Am Biog Inst. *Honours:* Outstg Young Writer of Am, 1978; Denver Post Awd for Best 1st Non-Fiction Book, 1987. *Hobbies:* Travelling; Walking; Writing; Drawing. *Address:* 610 Country Drive, Monument, CO 80132, USA. 3, 30, 139, 156, 178.

MAY Walter, b. 22 Dec 1912, Brighton, Sussex, Eng. Design Artist; Design Engr; Primary Sch Tchr; Ed; Trans. m. Lyudmila Serostanova, 1 Mar 1973. *Education:* Cert, Brighton Coll of Art, 1926-30; Cert, Wolverhampton Tech Coll, 1940-44; Tchrs Dip 1952. *Appointments:* Design Artist, Brighton; Advt Artist, London; Tech Engrng Draughtsman, Wolverhampton; Primary Sch Tchr, Hove, Sussex; Ed, Moscow; Trans of Russian Classical and Soviet Poetry & Prose. *Publications include:* Translated works 1976-: 16 books of verse for children, 24 books of verse; Late Harvest, 1982. *Contributions to:* a number of journs. *Memberships:* Sec, Jt Fdr 1950-, Sussex Anglo-Russian Lit Soc, Mus of Art; Hon Mbr, Hse of Lit, Moscow, 1968; Moscow Univ Eng Lit Club, 1984. *Honours:* Hon Badge Disting Man of Letters, Moscow Press Comm, 1967; Poetry Prize, Union of Writers of USSR, 1968; Dip, Minsk for Anthology, Fair Land of Byelorussia, 1978; Dips on 70th birthday from many republics of USSR. *Address:* Block 53/55, Flat 82, Bolshaya Pirogovskaya St, Moscow 119435, Russia.

MAYDEN Richard Lee, b. 16 Dec 1955, East St Louis, IL, USA. Assoc Prof of Biol. m. Michelle Joy Burr, 27 Nov 1987, 1 s. *Education:* BS, Univ of IL, 1978; MA, Southern IL Univ, Carbondale, 1980; PhD w Hons, Univ of KS, 1985. *Appointments:* Rsch Asst, Curatorial Asst, Univ of IL & IL Natural Hist Survey, 1976-78; Rsch Asst, Curatorial Asst, Southern IL Univ, Carbondale, 1978-80; Rsch Asst, Curatorial Asst 1980-85, Rsch Assoc in Ichthyology, Mus of Natural Hist 1986-, Univ of KS; Rsch Assoc in Ichthyology, Div of Fishes, Los Angeles Co Mus of Natural Hist, 1985-; Postdoct Rschr, Collections Mgr, Dept of Biol, UCLA, 1985-87; Ed, Bulletin AL Mus of Natural Hist, Univ of AL; Asst Prof, Curator of Ichthyology, Dept of Biological Scis & Mus of Natural Hist, Univ of AL, Tuscaloosa, 1987-. *Publications include:* Speciose and depauperate phylads and tests of punctuated and gradual evolution: Fact of artifact?, 1986; Faunal exchange between the Niobrara and White river systems of the Great Plains of North America, 1987; Systematics and biogeography of Notropis lutipinnis and N chlorocephalus (w R M Wood), 1992; Phylogeny and biodiversity: Conserving our evolutionary legacy (w D R Brooks, D A McLennan). *Memberships include:* Assn of Ecosystems Rsch Ctrs; Biological Soc of WA; Nat Geographic Rsch Soc; Soc of Systematic Zoology. *Honours:* Assoc Mbrship 1979, Full Mbrship 1986, Sigma Xi; Phi Kappa Phi Hon Soc, 1980; Stoye Awd (Hon Mention), ASIH Meetings Knoxville, 1985. *Hobbies:* Fishing; Scuba diving; Bird watching; Boating; Leather craft. *Address:* Department of Biological Sciences, University of Alabama, Tuscaloosa, AL 35487, USA.

MAYER Eric Anton, b. 11 Apr 1930, Vienna, Austria. Co Dir. m. Wendy Mildred Sara Wright, 1 Mar 1969, 2 d. *Appointments:* Nat Mut Life Assn of A'asia Ltd, Melbourne 1949-90, Mng Dir 1983, Grp Mng Dir, Chief Exec Off 1988-90; Bd of Dirs: Nat Mut, Melbourne; McPherson's Ltd, Melbourne; Walter & Eliza Hall Inst of Med Rsch, Melbourne; Chair, Bus/Higher Educ Round Table, Melbourne; Aust Tax Rsch Fndn, Sydney; VP, Comm for Econ Dev of Aust; Chair, Docklands Auth, Melbourne; Committee for Melbourne; Optus Pty Ltd (Group); Chmn, Life Ins Fedn of Aust, 1986-87; Mbr, Aust Govt's Econ Planning and Advsry Comm, 1988-91. *Memberships:* Fellow, Aust Computer Soc; Aust Inst of Mgmt; Cnslr, Inst of Pub Affairs; Aust Club of Melbourne; Melbourne Savage Club; Melbourne Cricket Club; Am Nat Club of Sydney. *Hobbies:* Farming; Cooking; Home computers; Tennis. *Address:* GPO Box 60A, Melbourne, Victoria 3001, Australia. 23, 174.

MAYHEW Elza Lovitt, b. 19 Jan 1916, Victoria, BC, Can. Sculptor. m. Charles Alan Mayhew, 10 Sept 1938, dec 1943, 1 s, 1 d. *Education:* BA, Univ of BC; Studied w Jan Zach, Victoria, 1955-58; MFA, Univ of Ore, 1963. *Appointments:* Dir, Intl Sculpture Ctr, KS, 1958-79; Cons, BC Comte on Art, 1974-76. *Creative works:* Solo Exhibs incl: The Point Gall, Victoria 1960, 1962; Art Gall of Greater Victoria 1961, 1964, 1971; Fine Arts Gall, Univ

of BC, 1961; Lucien Campbell Plaza, Univ of Ore, 1963; Venice Biennale Candn Pavilion, 1964; Dorothy Cameron Gall, Toronto, 1965; EXPO 67, Montreal (two sculptures); The Backroom Gall, Victoria, 1978; Burnaby (BC) Art Gall, 1979; Equinox Gall, Vancouver, 1980; Albert White Gall, Toronto, 1980; Wallack Gall, Ottawa, 1981; EXPO 86, Vanvouver, ZONG I and Supplicant, both bronze; Port Angeles Fine Art Ctr, 1988; rep in nat and int group exhibs; rep in various perm colls incl Nat Gall, Can; Nat Capital Comm, Meditation Piece, Rideau Canal, Ottawa. Commns incl: BC Archives and Mus, Victoria, 1967; Expo 67, 2 sculptures, 1967; Bank of Can, Vancouver, bronze mural, 1968; Confed Ctr, Charlottetown, Column of the Sea, Centennial Proj, 1973; Univ of Victoria Bronze Priestess, 1988. *Membership:* Acquisitions Comte, Art Gall of Greater Victoria, 1983-85. *Honours:* Sir Otto Beit Medal, Royal Soc Brit Sculptors, 1962; BC Centennial Sculpture Exhib Purchase Awd, 1967. *Address:* 698 Beaver Lake Rd, Victoria, British Columbia, Canada V8Z 5N8. 142.

MAYNARD Alan Keith, b. 15 Dec 1944, Merseyside, Eng. Prof of Econ(s). m. 24 June 1968, 2 s, 2 d. *Education:* BA (Hons), Class 1, Univ of Newcastle-upon-Tyne, 1963-67; B Phil, Univ of York, 1967-68. *Appointments:* Asst Lectr, Lectr in Econ(s), Univ of Exeter, 1968-71; Lectr 1971-77, Sr Lectr 1978-81, Reader 1982-83, Prof of Econ(s), Dir of the Ctr for Hlth Econ(s) 1983-, Univ of York. *Publications:* Author of over 200 publs in the form of books, book chapts, journ articles, reports. *Memberships:* MRSM; Royal Econ Soc; Soc for the Study of Addiction; Royal C'wlth Soc; Econ & Social Rsch Coun, 1985-88; Hlth Servs Rsch Comm, Med Rsch Coun, 1986-92; Trials Comm, VKCCCR, 1990-; Chmn, Evaluation Comm, Fourth Med and Hlth Rsch Prog of the European Commn, 1990. *Honour:* Hon Mbr, Fac of Pub Hlth Med. *Hobbies:* Walking; Cricket; Football; History. *Address:* Centre for Health Economics, University of York, Heslington, York YO1 5DD, England.

MAYO Joseph M, b. 13 June 1932, Hope, AR, USA. Printer; Tchr; Acct; Maintenance Supt; Author. 2 s, 1 d. *Education:* AA, Coll of the Redwoods, 1968; BA, Humboldt State, A br of Univ of CA, 1970. *Appointments:* US Navy Ship, Curtiss AV-4; Ship's Printing Mgr, Ed of Curtiss Courier; Printer, Heritage Printing Co, N Lt Rock; News Release Drafter and Thermographic Printer; Hd of Maths Dept, Southern AR. *Publication:* World Peace through Law (co-author w Neva Talley Morris), 1987. *Memberships:* Nat Bus Educ Assn, 1970-76; CA Tchr's Assn, 1970-72; AR Educ Assn, 1975-76; Nat Educ Assn, 1975-76; Am Assn of Retired Persons, 1986-87. *Honours:* Ball Club Coach & Mgr, Ch League; Bd Mbr, Deacon and Trustee, various chs, Hope, AR; Sunday Sch Tchr, Acatia. *Address:* 1013 West Markham Street, Little Rock, AR 72201, USA.

MAZUR Aneta Judyta, b. 26 Dec 1961, Opole, Poland. *Education:* Cand for a Dr's degree. *Appointment:* Tchr, Pedagogical HS, Opole, 1985-. *Publications:* The Suicides and the Dreamers Among Poets of Non- poetic Period (co-author); Author of 24 reviews of books, 13 essays and articles. *Membership:* Adam Mickiewicz's Lit Assn. *Hobbies:* Swimming; Walks; Touring; Gardening; History of Art. *Address:* ul Grunwaldzka 2 m 6, 45-054 Opole, Poland.

MAZURIN German Alexeevitch, b. 10 Aug 1932, Penza, USSR. Artist; Illustrator; Prof. m. Galina Kalashnikova, 27 Jan 1962, 1 d. *Education:* Dip, Sch of Art, Penza, 1952; Dip, Surikov Arts Inst, Moscow, 1958. *Appointments:* Artist, Illustrator, Children Literary, 1955; Prof, Surikov Arts Inst, 1974. *Creative works:* Illustrator of books: OLd Hottabitch; Uncle Stena; Elefamt; Kashtanka; Tom Soyer; Oblomov. *Memberships:* Journalists Union of USSR, 1960; Artists Union of USSR, 1961; Commn on Aestetic Educ. *Honours:* Dip of Goscomizdat for the illustration of the book, Dostorvsky for Children, 1971; Medal for Conscientious Labour, 1983; Honoured Artist, 1988.

Hobbies: Tennis; Slalom. *Address:* Mishin st 23-19, Moscow 125083, Russia.

MCARTHUR Thomas Burns, b. 23 Aug 1938, Author; Lecturer; Language Consultant. m. Fereshteh Mottahedin, 1963, 1 s, 2 d. *Education:* MA Glasgow Univ, 1958; MLitt, 1970, PhD, 1978, Edinburgh Univ. *Appointments:* Ofr, Instr, RAEC, 1959-61; Asst Master, Riland Bedford Sch, Warwicks, 1961-63; Hd of Eng, Cathedral and John Cannon Sch, Bombay, 1965-67; Vis Prof, Rajendra Prasad Col of Mass Comm, Univ of Bombay, 1965-67; Dir of Extra Mural Eng Lang Courses, Univ of Edinburgh, 1972-79; Assoc Prof of Eng, Univ of Quebec, Can, 1979-83; Co-fdr, Intl Lexicography Crs, Univ of Exeter, 1987-; Conslt, Min of Educ, Quebec, 1980-81. *Publications:* BBC Radio series, The Story of English, 1987; Patterns of English, 1972-74; English for Students of Economics, 1973; Collins Dict of Eng Pharasal Verbs, jt ed, 1974; Languages of Scotland, 1979; A foundation course for Language Teachers, 1983; Worlds of Reference, 1986; Yoga and the Bhagavad-Gita, 1986; Understanding Yoga, 1986; The English Language as used in Quebec: a Survey, 1989. *Memberships:* Soc for the Promotion of Teaching Eng as a second language, Quebec, 1980- 83; Henson Intl TV, 1985-86; Dictionary Res Ctr, Exeter Univ, 1987- ; Ed Bd, Intl Jour of Lexicography, 1988-. *Hobbies:* Reading; Television; Walking; Cycling; Travel. *Address:* 22-23 Ventress Farm Court, Cherry Hinton Road, Cambs CB1 4HD, England.

MCAVITY John, b. 30 Oct 1950, St John, NB. Exec Dir. *Education:* BA, Univ of NB, 1972; CAE, 1981. *Appointments:* Kings Landing Histl Settlement, 1972-73; NB Mus, 1973-76; Ont Mus Assn, 1976-81; Can Mus Assn, 1981-. *Memberships:* Bd of Dir: Tourism Ind Assn of Can; Assn of Cultural Exec; Copyright Consumers Soc of Can; Can Soc of Assoc Exec, Ottawa Chapt. *Honours:* Hon Life Mbr, Quaco Histl and Lib Soc; Life Mbr, Heritage Can. *Address:* 306 Metcalfe Street, Ottawa, Ontario K2P 1S2, Canada. 2, 88.

MCAVOY Helen Margaret, b. 20 Oct 1949, Campbeltown, Scotland. Hd of Documentary Rsch Serv. m. Robert Francis McAvoy, 8 Aug 1973, 2 d. *Education:* MA Hons, Glasgow Univ, 1967-72; Mgmt Dev Cert, Dundee Coll of Tech, 1977; Masters degree, Brussels UNI, 1991-92. *Appointments:* Off, EC Commn, 1973-76; Proj Mgmt, Glasgow Marine Tech Ctr, 1977-79; Off, European Parliament, 1979-82; Hd of Press Assessment Serv, European Parliament, 1982-85; Hd of Documentary Rsch Serv, Directorate-Gen for Rsch, European Parliament, Brussels, 1985-. *Memberships:* BIM; Inst of Info Scientists; Inst of Petroleum; Soc for Underwater Tech; European Parliament's Equal Opportunities Comm. *Hobbies:* Celtic folk music; International affairs; Guitar; Bohdran; Swimming; Walking. *Address:* 12 Rue Du Bemel, 1150 Brussels, Belgium. 43.

MCBRIEN William, b. 20 Nov 1930, Huntington, NY, USA. Univ Prof; Ed; Author. *Education:* BA 1952; MA 1954; PhD 1959. *Appointments:* St John's Univ, 1958-65; CCNY, 1966; Hofstra Univ, 1966-; Ed, Twentieth Century Literature, 1974-. *Publications:* Me Again: Uncollected Writings of Stevie Smith, 1981; Stevie: A Biography of Stevie Smith, 1985; Stevie Smith A Bibliography (co-author, ed), 1987. *Memberships:* MLA; PEN. *Honours:* NEH Fellowship; Mac Dowell Coleny Fellowship; Am Coun of Learned Societies Fellowship. *Hobby:* Piano playing. *Address:* Department of English, Hofstra University, Hempstead, NY 11550, USA.

MCCAFFER Ronald, 8 Dec 1943, Glasgow, Scotland. Prof, Hd of Dept of Civil Engrng; Dean of Engineering. m. Margaret Elizabeth Warner, 13 Aug 1966, 1 s. *Education:* BSc, Univ of Strathclyde, 1961-65; PhD, Loughborough Univ of Tech, 1976. *Appointments:* Design Engr, Babtie, Shaw & Morton, 1965-67; Site Engr, The Nuclear Power Grp Ltd, 1967-69; Site Engr, Taylor Woodrow Const Ltd, 1969-70; Lectr 1970-78,

Sr Lectr 1978-83, Reader 1983-86, Prof 1986-, Loughborough Univ. *Publications include:* Worked Examplesin Construction Management, 1984; Modern Construction Management, 3rd ed 1989; Estimating & Tendering for Civil Engineering, 1991; Managing Construction Equipment, 1991. *Memberships:* FICE; FCIoB; MBIM; Fellow, Royal Acad of Engineering. *Hobbies:* Golf. *Address:* Department of Civil Engineering, Loughborough Univerity of Technology, Loughborough, Leicestershire LE11 3TU, England.

MCCALLA Cecil Eugene, b. 4 Apr 1941, Wichita, KS, USA. Self-Employed. m. 1 June 1968, 2 s, 1 d. *Education:* Emporia State Univ, 1963-65; Prairie Bible Inst, 1986-87; Liberty Univ, 1987-91; Trinity Coll & Sem, 1991-. *Appointments:* McCalla Ins, Wenatchee, WR, 1969-74; Washington Hlth Servs, Bellevue, 1974-76; McCalla Enterprises, Missoula, 1976-89. *Publications:* Socialistic Tendencies of the United States, 1959; Syllabus for Studies in Systematic Theology, 1989; Syllabus for Studies in New Testament Survey, 1990. *Memberships:* Commnr 1971-72, Dist V Chmn 1972-74, Boy Scouts of Am; PTF Pres 1984-85, Valley Christian Sch; Adult Educ Tchr of Theology, 1989-91, Christian and Missionary Alliance Ch; Trinity Alumni Assn. *Honours:* Meritorious Promotion 1961, Hon Discharge 1966, US Marine Corps; Cert of Appreciation, Boy Scouts of Am, 1974. *Hobbies:* Theology; Philosophy; History; Music; Bicycling; Flyfishing; Gardening; Writing. *Address:* 4022 S Avenue West 45, Missoula, MT 59801, USA. 139, 152.

MCCALLUM John (Ian), b. 13 Oct 1920, Glasgow, Scotland. Cons Naval Archt. m. Christine Peggy Sowden, 19 June 1948, dec 1989, 2 s. *Education:* BSc w First Class Hons, Univ of Glasgow, 1939-43. *Appointments:* Asst Lectr, Naval Arch & Marine Engrng, Glasgow Univ, 1943-44; Ship Surveyor, Sr Ship Surveyor 1944-61, Chief Ship Surveyor 1970-81, Lloyd's Register of Shipping, Newcastle, Glasgow & London; Chief Naval Arch, Tech Dir, John Brown Shipbuilders Ltd, Clydebank, 1961-70; Cons Naval Archt, 1981-. *Creative works include:* Chief Designer of QE2, Kungsholm (now Sea Princess). *Memberships:* Fellow, The Fellowship of Engrng, 1977-, Royal Acad of Engng, from 1992; VP, FRINA; FICE; Fellow, The Soc of Naval Archs & Marine Engrs, NY; MIES; Liveryman, Worshipful Co of Shipwrights; Freeman, City of London; Smeatonian Soc of Civil Engrs, 1979-; Technical Comm, Lloyd's Register of Shipping, 1982-. *Honours:* Reid Birrell & George Harvey prizes, Glasgow Univ, 1942, 1943; Title of Eur Ing, Conferred Paris, 1992; 35 papers presented and or published in UK and abroad, many containing original work, 1948-; Medalist, Assn Maritime et Aeronautique, Paris, 1978. *Hobbies:* Piano; Pastel painting; Applications of mathematics and logic to archaeology; Travel Documentaries: Oriental Safari; Occidental Safari. *Address:* Dala, Garvock Drive, Kippington, Sevenoaks, Kent TN13 2LT, England. 1, 26, 139, 149.

MCCALLUM Robert Ian, b. 14 Sept 1920, Largs. Med Cons. m. Jean K B Learmonth, 28 June 1952, 2 s, 2 d. *Education:* MD 1946; FRCP (Lond) 1970; DSc 1971; FRCP (E) 1985. *Appointments:* Prof, Hd of Dept of Occupational Hlth & Hygiene, Univ of Newcastle-upon-Tyne, 1981-85; Hon Cons, Inst of Occupational Med, Edinburgh, 1985. *Publications:* Author of papers in med journs. *Memberships:* Pres 1979-80, SOM; Pres 1983-84, Brit Occupational Hygiene Soc; Dean 1984-86, Fac of Occupational Med. *Honours:* Rocke Feller Travelling Fellowship, MRC, 1953-54; Sydenham Lecture, Soc of Apothecaries, 1983; Stanley Melville Mem Lecture, Coll of Radiographers, 1983; CBE 1987; Ernestine Henry Lecture, RCP London, 1987. *Hobbies:* Gardening; Oriental art. *Address:* Institute of Occupational Medicine, Roxburgh Place, Edinburgh EH8 9SU, Scotland. 1.

MCCARL Henry Newton, b. 24 Jan 1941, Baltimore, MD, USA. Prof. m. (2) Mary Frederica Rhinelander, 31 Jan 1987, 3 stepdaughter. *Education:* SB, MIT, 1962;

MS 1964, PhD 1969, Penn State Univ. *Appointments:* Vulcan Materials Co, Birmingham, 1967-69; Dept of Econ(s), Sch of Bus, Univ of AL at Birmingham, 1969-. *Publications:* Energy Policy (co- author), 1986; Introduction to Energy Conservation Economics (co-author), 1987. *Memberships:* Bd of Dir 1979-81, Soc of Mining Engrs of AIME; Sect Pres 1982-84, Am Inst of Profl Geologists; Bd 1990-92, Mineral Econ(s) & Mgmt Soc. *Honours:* Fulbright Sr Lectr, Acad of Econ Studies, Bucharest, Romania, 1977-78; Irex Grant, Ford Fndn, Bucharest, 1978; Vis Fellow, Dept of Econ(s), Grad Sch of Arts & Scis, Harvard Univ, 1987. *Hobbies:* Collecting obsolete paper currency and scriptophily; Investments; Computers and data analysis; Collecting art. *Address:* Department of Economics, School of Business, The University of Alabama at Birmingham, Birmingham, AL 35294, USA. 7, 26, 125, 132, 153.

MCCARRELL Richard John, b. 1 Feb 1954, Oak Park, IL, USA. Sr Min. m. Susan Jean Burlingame, 14 June 1975, 1 s, 1 d. *Education:* Dip, Grand Rapids of the Bible and Music, 1977; Cert, Christian Counselling Educl Fndn 1988, 1990. *Appointments:* Min of Youth, Hudsonville Bapt Ch, Hudsonville, 1976-78; Asst Pastor, Westchester Bible Ch, Westchester, 1978-80; Sr Pastor, Factoryville Bible Ch, Athens, Admnstr, Factoryville Christian Sch & Camp Elvin, 1980-87; Sr Min, Grace Chapel, 1987-. *Publications:* Child Evangelism Fellowship Magazine, 1986; Moody Monthly, 1986, 1988; The Biblical Evangelist, 1988; The Quiet Hour, 33 devotionals, 1989-91. *Memberships:* VP, Bd of Dir, Spanish World Gospel Mission; Bd of Dir, Fellowship of Indep Missions; Bd of Dir, Bible Evangelism Inc; Bd of Dir, UFM Int; Bd of Ref, EICM; Indep Fundamental Chs of Am-liaison, Coun of Reg Pres, Nat Exec Comm. *Honours:* Ordained, 1981; Sec of Alumni Bd, Grand Rapids Sch of the Bible/Music, 1982-85; Sec of Exec Bd, RBM Ministeries, 1984-87; Nat Youth Comm, Indep Fundamental Chs of Am, 1985; Mbr of Pres's Advsry Coun, Philadelphia Coll of Bible, 1989. *Hobbies include:* Bible Conf Min, Nat Youth Convention, IFCA; Moody Pastor's Conf; Bryan Coll Pastor's Conf. *Address:* Grace Chapel Church, 1 West Eagle Road, Havertown, PA 19083, USA.

MCCARTER Keith Ian, b. 15 Mar 1936, Scotland. Sculptor. m. 5 Jan 1963, 1 s, 1 d. *Education:* DAEd, Edinburgh Coll of Art, 1956-60. *Appointments:* Staff Designer, Steuben Glass, NY, 1961-62; Self employed Sculptor, 1964-. *Creative Works:* Exhibited: Royal Acad, Monaco; Alwyn Gall, Berkeley; Square Gall. Commns incl: Brit Embassy, Lagos, Nigeria; Midland Bank, London Docklands; Dept of Environment HQ, London; Park Road, London; Guys Hosp, London; Thames Park, Marlow; Bath Street, Glasgow. *Memberships:* FSIAD; FRSA; ARBS. *Honour:* Andrew Grant Scholarship, Edinburgh Coll of Art, 1960. *Hobbies:* Music; Literature; Travel; Gardening. *Address:* Ottermead, Church Road, Great Plumstead, Norfolk NR13 5AB, England. 19, 34.

MCCAULEY Janie Caves, b. 18 Oct 1946, Chattanooga, TN, USA. Prof; Arts Critic. m. William Erwin McCauley, 20 Jan 1968, 2 d. *Education:* BA, TN Temple Univ, 1968; MA, Clemson Univ, 1971; PhD, Miami Univ, 1978. *Appointments:* Prof, Tchng Asst, Chattanooga Pub Schs, 1968; Bob Jones Univ, 1968-69; Clemson Univ, 1969-71; Miami Univ, 1971-74; Bob Jones Univ, 1974-. *Publications:* Articles in Lit Publs; Ed, Macbeth, 1984; Romeo and Juliet, 1989; The Greenville News, 1989-; A Midsummer Nights Dream, 1990; Shakespeare Criticism, The Shakespeare Bulletin, 1990-; The Greenville Piedmont, 1991-. *Memberships:* Shakespeare Assn of Am; Int Shakespeare Assn; Carolinas Symposium on Brit Studies; Southeastern Renaisance Conf; South Atlantic Modern Lang Assn; Reach to Recovery Vol for Am Cancer Soc. *Honours:* Nat Endowment for the Humanities Fellowship, Princeton Univ, 1989, 1990. *Hobbies:* Writing; Travelling. *Address:* 108 Oxford Street, Greenville, SC 29607, USA. 7, 13, 15.

MCCLEARY Benjamin Ward, b. 9 July 1944, Washington, DC, USA. Investment Banker. m. Jean Luce Muchmore, 15 Oct 1983, 1 s, 1 d. *Education:* AB, Princeton Univ, 1962-66. *Appointments:* VP, Chem Bank, 1975-81; Sr VP, Lehman Bros, 1981-84; Mng Dir, Shearson Lehman Bros, 1984-89; Ptnr, McFarland Deweg & Co, 1989-; Dir, Detrex Corp, 1990-. *Hobby:* Skiing. *Address:* 230 Park Avenue, Suite 1450, New York, NY 10169, USA.

MCCLELLAN Anthony, b. 12 Apr 1925, Liverpool, England. Barrister. m. Marie-Jose Alberte Joriaux, 14 Jan 1958, 1 s, 1 d. *Education:* Clare Coll, Cambridge, 1943-44, 1947-48; Called to Bar, 1958. *Appointments:* HM Forces, 1943-47; HM Colonial Serv, 1948-57; Gen Counsel in Ind, 1959- 74; Legal Serv, Commn of the European Communities, 1974-90; Pvte Pract, 1990-. *Publications:* Author of various articles in specialist legal journs. *Memberships:* Bar of Eng and Wales; Bar Assn for Commerce Fin & Ind; ACIArb; London Ct of Int Arbitration European Coun. *Honour:* CBE 1991. *Hobbies include:* Reading; Music; Art. *Address:* European Law Chambers, Ground Floor, 5 Paper Buildings, Temple EC4 7HB, England.

MCCLELLAN Barbara Helene Elizabeth Vogl, b. 24 May 1945, Bronxville, NY, USA. World Civilization Tcher; Dept Hd Social Studies. m. Richard Allen McClellan, 29 June 1968, 2 d. *Education:* BS, State Univ of New Paltz, NY, 1966; Univ CO, 1967; NS Fndn Inst, 1972. *Appointments:* Tazzan Zee HS, Orangeburg, NY, 1967-68; Ctrl Cath HS, Abilene, TX, 1968-69; McMurry Coll, 1968-70; Abilene, TX, T C Williams HS and F C Hammond, 1970-, Alexandria, VA; Sent by Armonk Inst, NY, to Germany to study Post World War Germany and School System. *Publications:* Arizona and the West, 1971; 2 reviews, 1972; Co-author, A Child's Introduction to Historic Alex. *Memberships:* AAUW, VP; Alpha Delta Kappa; NFS Inst; NEA; Project Links-All. *Honour:* 8th Congressional District Coordinator for the National Bicentennial Commission. *Hobbies:* International Ballroom Dancing, Travelling, Piano. *Address:* 8189 Ships Curve Lane, Springfield, VA 22153, USA. 7, 15.

MCCLURE Robert Baird, b. 23 Nov 1900, Portland, OR, USA. Ret'd Missionary, Surg. m. Amy Louise Hislop, 5 Oct 1926, 1 s, 3 d. *Education:* MB, Univ Toronto Meds, 1917-22; FRCS (Edin), 1931; Hon LLD; Hon DD; FRCP&S (Can), 1991. *Appointments:* Surg, Hwaiking Hosp, N China, 1924-27, 1931-37; Surg, McKay Hosp, Taipei, 1927-30; Red Cross Field Dir, Sino-Jap War Intern, 1937-41; Cmdr, Friends Ambulance Unit, 1941-48; Surg, Union Hosp, Hoankow, 1948; Pvte Pract, 1949; Chief Surg, Gaza Hosp, Cairo, 1952-56; Chief Surg, Ratlam Hosp of United Ch, 1954; Elected First Lay Moderator, United Ch of Can, 1968; Companion, Order of Can, Ottawa, 1971; Surg, Kapit Christ Hosp, Sarawak, 1971-74; Vol Surg, Hosp Amazonico, Jungle of Peru, 1975; Vol Surg, Caribbean Isl of St Vincent, 1976; Vol Dr, Home Mission Hosp, Port Simpson, BC, 1978. *Memberships:* Christian Med Assn, China, 1924-48; Christian Med Assn, India, 1954-67, VP 1958-64; Rotary Club Ratlam, India, 1954-67; Rotary Club Toronto-Eglington, 1967-91; Moderator, United Ch of Can, 1968-71; Hon Mbr, Toronto Acad of Med, 1982. *Honours:* Companion Order of Can, 1971; Mbr of Order of Ont, 1989. *Hobbies:* Research on small plant electric generators from coal; Tribal customs of Tropical Primitives; Amateur Private Pilot, -1977. *Address:* Leaside Gate, Apt 105, 955 Millwood Road, Toronto, Ontario, Canada M4G 4E3.

MCCORMICK Laurel Anne, b. 20 Dec 1973, Macon, GA, USA. Student; Newspaper Co-Ed; Writer. *Education:* Grace Bapt Acad, Chattanooga; Currently, Graphic Design, Chattanooga State Technical Community College. *Appointments:* Red Cross Vol, Life Care Nursing Home, Collegedale, 1987; Sales Assoc, One Price Clothing Store, Chattanooga, 1990-91. *Publications:* Poetry published in: The Writing Class, Wide Open, Chimera, TACS Literary Magazine; and num anthologies. *Membership:* Secretary, CSTCC Chapter of College Republicans. *Honours:* Hon Mention, Gt Free Int Poetry Contest, 1990; Chosen as a Golden Poet, World of Poetry, 1991; 1st Place, Grace Freshman Poetry Contest; 2nd Place, TN Assn of Christian Sch's Dist Poetry Competition, 1991. *Hobbies:* Writing and marketing poetry, songs and YA fiction; Rollerskating; Collecting books, art and antiques; Interior decorating; Architecture; desktop publishing; Clothing design; Soccer; Track; Reading. *Address:* 239 Carrol Drive, Route 8, Ringgold, GA 30736, USA.

MCCROSKEY Lenora Estelle, b. 18 July 1943, Wilmington, NC, USA. Musician. *Education:* BA, BMus, Stetson Univ, 1966; AM, Harvard Univ, 1969; DMA, Eastman Conservatory of the Univ of Rochester, 1982. *Appointments:* Vis Instr, Stetson Univ, 1970-71; Asst Organist, Choirmaster in the Mem Ch, Harvard Univ, 1971-78; Instr, Eastman, 1979-82; Assoc Prof in Music, Univ of N Texas, 1982-. *Creative works:* Recitals, Workshops throughout the USA (Specialist in Baroque Keyboard Lit) incl convention of the Am Guild of Organists. *Memberships:* Dean 1987-89, Am Guild of Organist, Dallas Chapt; Organ Histl Soc; Southeast Histl Keyboard Soc. *Honours:* Wesley Weyman Fndn, 1969, 1974; John Anson Kittredge Fund, 1988; Mary Ingraham Bunting Fellow, 1990-91. *Hobbies:* Mystery books; Cats; Cooking gadgets. *Address:* University of North Texas, College of Music, Denton, TX 76203, USA. 7.

MCCULLOUGH John, b. 23 Mar 1949, Glasgow, Scotland. Consulting Engr; Co Dir. m. Geraldine Gardner, 25 Mar 1971, 1 s, 2 d. *Education:* MSc 1976; PhD 1979. *Appointments:* Various Appts in N Ireland, Eng, Scotland; Ptnr, Hancox & Ptnrs, 1982-88; Dir, Rendel Hancox, 1988-91; Dir, Rendel Palmer & Tritton, Scotland, 1991-; Several Appts as Forensic Engr and Expert Witness for Litigation, Accident Investigation and Pub Inquiry Scotland, Eng, Holland. *Publications:* Author of several scientific, engineering papers in int journs and at int confs. *Memberships:* Chartered Engr; FIMechE; Fellow, Inst of Energy; Eur Ing Dip, FEANI, Paris; Chmn, Scottish Reg, Inst of Energy, 1984-85. *Hobbies:* Music; Swimming; Walking; Forestry. *Address:* Kinnoul, Kilmacolm, Renfrewshire PA13 4DZ, Scotland.

MCCULLOUGH Kimberly Anne, b. 17 Feb 1956, Winona, MN, USA. Owner, Pres. *Education:* BA cum laude, Winona State Univ, 1977; MS, Case Western Reserve Univ, 1978. *Appointments:* Petrophys Field Engr, Prod Unit Engr, Sr Geol Engr, Shell Oil Co, 1978-83; Sr Dev Geologist, Dist Exploration Supvr, Mark Producing Inc, Houston, 1983-89; Owner, Pres, PetroVal Inc, 1989-. *Creative works:* Author of 4 articles to Shell's Tech Journs; Instructional Guitar Book; Introductory Petroleum Asset Valuations Workshop, Course Manual; Copyrighted num songs. *Memberships:* Am Inst of Profl Geologists; Am Assn of Petroleum Geologists; Houston Geological Soc; Soc of Exploration Geophysicists. *Honours:* AFS Foreign Exchange Student to Peru, 1972; Nat Hon Soc Scholar, 1973-74; HEW Fellowship and Rsch Asstship to Case Western, 1977; Deleg to The Hague to present a paper to the Royal Dutch Gp, 1982; Disting Young Alumni Awd, Winona State Univ, 1991. *Hobbies:* Golf; Softball; Scuba diving; Photography; Travel; Guitar. *Address:* 3427 Ashfield Drive, Houston, TX 77082, USA. 7.

MCDANIEL Asher William, b. 8 Oct 1946, Wabash, IN, USA. United Meth Min. m. Diane Collins, 23 July 1978, 3 d. *Education:* AB, Taylor Univ, 1968; MTh, Perkins Sch of Theology, 1972. *Appointments:* Pastor, United Chapel Meth, 1966-68; Prosect UMC, 1968; Travis Park UMC, San Antonio, 1970-71; Port Lavaca, TX UMC, Presby Youth Min, summer 1971; Assoc Pastor, Broadway UMC, 1972-74; Green City Charge UMC, 1974-78; Tipton Charge UMC, 1978-82; Pastor, Tarkio-Westboro UMC 1982-85; Pastor, 1st UMC, Warsaw, 1985-92; Pastor, 1st UMC, Excelsior Springs, MO, 1992-. *Honour:* Outstg Young Men of Am, 1977.

Hobbies: Water skiing; Snow skiing; Golf; Coin collecting; Football; Basketball; Tennis. *Address:* PO Box 368, 947 Red Bud, Warsaw, MO 65355, USA.

MCDANIEL Henry Curtis Jr, b. 5 Dec 1959, Richmond, VA, USA. Min. m. 2 July 1983, 1 s, 2 d. *Education:* DMin, Fuller Theological Sem; Master of Divinity, Covenant Theological Sem; BA, Columbia Bible Coll. *Appointments:* Min of Outreach, Trinity Presby Ch, Montgomery, 1985-; New Covenant Presby Ch, Bartlesville. *Publication:* Dissertation, Contemporary Evangelism. *Memberships:* Montgomery Lions Club Int; Montgomery STEP Fndn; Jimmy Hitchcock Mem Awd; Birmingham Theological Sem; AL Dept of Youth Servs; Blue-Grey All Star Football Classic; Billy Graham Assn. *Hobbies:* Flower, vegetable, rose & greenhouse gardening; Collecting; Fishing; Reading. *Address:* 551 Larkin Lane, Montgomery, AL 36109, USA. 117.

MCDONALD Angus Wheeler, b. 21 Apr 1927, Washington DC, WA, USA. Farmer. m. Mary Joan Montgomery, 8 May 1952, 1 s, 1 d. *Education:* BA, Columbia Union Coll, 1974. *Appointments:* US Army, 1946-67; Owner, Operator of Farm, 1967-. *Memberships:* Jefferson Co Farm Bur; AARP; WV State Horticultural Soc; Northern WV Automobile Club. *Hobbies:* Travel; Photography; Attending historial events. *Address:* Pleasant View Farm, Route 3, Charles Town, WV 25414, USA.

MCENERY John Hartnett, b. 5 Sept 1925, Coatbridge, Scotland. Former Under-Sec, Dept of Ind; Author; Cons; Conceptual Analyst. m. Lilian Wendy Gibbons, 24 Sept 1977. *Education:* MA, hons, Glasgow Univ, 1949. *Publications:* Manufacturing Two Nations, 1981; Towards a New Concept of Conflict Evaluation, 1985; Epilogue in Burma 1945-48, 1990. *Contributions to:* Economic Affairs; CHEC Journal; Daily Telegraph; Financial Times; Yorkshire Post. *Address:* 56 Lillian Road, London SW13 9JF, England. 1, 3.

MCFARLAND Kevin John, b. 18 Mar 1958, Mt Clemens, MI, USA. Pres. m. Betty Bolton, 26 Nov 1976, 1 s, 2 d. *Education:* BS, Abilene Christian Univ, 1980; MS, TX Tech Univ, 1981. *Appointments:* Abilene State Sch, 1976-78; Landscape Design, 1978-80; Rsch Assoc, TX Tech Univ, 1981; Min of Youth and Family, Redwood City Ch of Christ, 1981-83; Pres, Manna Int, 1984-. *Memberships:* Am Assn of Marriage and Family Therapists; Nat Coun on Family Rels; Soc for Non-Profit Orgs; Soc for Int Dev Interaction; Inst for Cultural Affairs; Acad of Polit Sci; Dir, Inst for Coop in Int Dev. *Honour:* Alpha Chi, 1980. *Hobbies:* Musical composition; International development; Travel; Reading. *Address:* 227 E Street, Redwood City, CA 94063, USA. 2, 9, 52, 59, 117.

MCFARLAND Violet Sweet Haven, b. 26 Feb 1908, Seattle, WA, USA. Author; Tchr. *Education:* BA, WA State Univ, 1928; MA, Columbia Univ, NYC, 1933. *Appointments:* Tchr, Hawaiian Isl, 1928-30; Tchr, Am Sch, Tokyo, Japan, 1930-31; Soc Ed, Japan Times, 1930-31; Ed Asst, Dept of Justice, WA, Dist of Columbia, 1934-43; Soc Ed, Hong Kong Telegraph, Hong Kong, 1940; Curator, Oriental Art and Lit. *Publications:* As Violet Sweet Haven: Hong Kong for the Weekend, 1939; Many Ports of Call, 1940; Gentlemen of Japan, 1944. *Contributions to:* Profl Journs. *Memberships:* Delta Zeta; Nat Bd of Realtors; Past Mbr, Pen & Brush, NYC. *Honours:* Num int lit awds; Fellow, Int Inst of Arts and Letters, Geneva & Zurich, 1965; Life Mbr, Nat Pres Club, Washington DC, 1986. *Hobbies:* World travel; Curator of oriental art. *Address:* PO Box 872, Lake Elsinore, CA 92330, USA.

MCFARLANE Ian Sir, b. 25 Dec 1923, Sydney, Aust. Co Chmn. m. Ann Shaw, 10 Nov 1956, 1 s, 2 d. *Education:* BSc 1944, BE 1946, Sydney Univ; MS, MIT, USA, 1950. *Appointments:* RANVR, 1939-45; Assoc, Morgan Stanley & Co, 1949-59; Mbr, Sydney Stock

Exchange, 1959-64; Dir, Trans City Discount Ltd, 1960-64; Dir, Consolidated Rutile Ltd, 1964-68; Ptnr, Ord, Minnett, T J Thompson & Ptnrs; Dep Chmn, Magellan Petroleum Aust Ltd, 1964-70; Chmn, Trans Pacific Consolidated Ltd, 1964-; Dir, Int Pacific Corp, 1967-73; Dir, Aust Gen Ins Co Ltd, 1968-74; Chmn, Mng Dir, Southern Pacific Petroleum NL, Ctrl Pacific Minerals NL, 1968-; Dir, Mercantile Mutual Ins Co Ltd, 1969-74; Dir, Concrete Constrns Pty Ltd, 1972-74; Int Pacific Aust Investments Pty Ltd, 1972-73; Dir, Morgan Stanley & Co Int, 1976-80. *Memberships include:* Fdr, Sir Ian McFarlane Travelling Professorship in Urology, 1980; Life Gov, Royal Prince Alfred Hosp, Sydney, 1982; Fndg Gov, St Luke's Hosp Fndn, 1982; Chmn, Royal Brisbane Hosp Fndn, 1985; Cnslr, Imperial Soc of Kts Bach, 1985; Fellow Commonr, Christ's Coll, Cambridge, Eng, 1987. *Honour:* Kt Bach, Created, 1984; Hon Colonel, Kentucky, 1984. *Hobbies:* Swimming; Tennis. *Address:* 40 Wentworth Road, Vaucluse, NSW 2030, Australia. 1, 23, 157.

MCFETRICH Charles Alan, b. 15 Dec 1940, Lachine, Quebec, Can. Chartered Acct. m. (2)Janet Elizabeth Henkel Munro, 3 Aug 1990, 2 s 1 d. *Eduction:* MA Magdalene Coll, Cambridge, 1961-64. *Appointments:* Trainee Acct, Graham Proom & Smith, 1959-61, 1964-66; Qualified Acct 1966- 68, Cons 1968-73, Consultancy Ptnr 1973-80, Consultancy Ptnr on secondment to the Dept of Ind as Under Sec (Dep Dir Indl Dev Unit) 1981-82, UK Operations Ptnr 1983-84, UK Mng Ptnr 1985-89, Deloitte Haskins & Sells; UK Mng Ptnr, Coopers & Lybrand Deloitte, 1990-1992; Exec Partner, Coopers & Lybrabd, 1992-. *Memberships:* FICA; Fellow, Royl Soc for Encouragement of Arts, Manufacture and Commerce. *Hobbies:* Gardening; Theatre. *Address:* Coopers & Lybrand, 1 Embankment Place, London WC2N 6NN, England.

MCGILL Stuart Michael, b. 24 July 1957, Richmond Hill, Ont, Can. Assoc Prof. m. Kathryn A Barr, 11 Aug 1990. *Education:* BPHE, 1980; MSc, 1982; PhD, 1986. *Appointments:* Hd of S M McGill & Assoc, 1985-; Prof of Biomech, Univ of Waterloo, 1986-. *Publications:* Author of over 45 scientific papers dealing with low back mechs. *Memberships:* Int Soc for Biomechs; Can soc for Biomechs; Human Factors Assn of Can. *Honours:* Alumni Awd, Univ of Toronto, 1978; Julian Christensen Awd, top grad student paper of Human Factors Assn meeting, Vancouver, 1986; Alumni Gold Medal, top PhD in Univ of Waterloo, 1986; Volvo Bioengrng Awd for low back pain rsch, 1986. *Hobby:* Fishing. *Address:* RR2, Elora, Ontario, Canada N0B 1S0. 142.

MCGLOWN David John, b. 5 Sept 1938, Darwen, Lancs, Eng. Clin Dir. m. Winifred McNicholas, 3 June 1961, 3 s, 1 d. *Education:* MSRR Dip, Blackburn Royal Infirmary & Manchester Sch of Radiography, 1960; Tchng Cert, Hon BEd, Univ of Lancaster, 1968-72; PhD, 1987. *Appointments:* Radiographer (Diagnostic), Blackburn & Dist Hosps, 1958-60; Hd of Biological Rsch, Rsch Labs, Crown Paint Co, Darwen, 1960-68; Tchr, Christ the King Sch, Southport, 1972-73; Hd of Biol Dept, John Rigby Sch, Blackburn, 1973-75; Co-fdr, The Inst for Neuro-Physiological Psychology, Chester, 1975-82; Clin Dir, The BIRD Ctr, 1982-. *Publications:* An Organic Basis for Neuroses and Educational Difficulties (co-author), 1979; Developmental Reflexive Rehabilitation, 1990. *Membership:* Nat Coun of Psychotherapists. *Hobbies:* Reading; Writing; Gardening; DIY Activities. *Address:* The Centre for Brain Injury Rehabilitation and Development, 131 Main Road, Broughton, Chester CH4 0NR, England.

MCGOWAN Bruce Henry, b. 27 June 1924, Birmingham, Eng. Ret'd Hdmaster. m. Beryl McKenzie Liggitt, 26 July 1947, 1 s, 3 d. *Education:* BA 1947, MA 1949, Cert Ed 1949, Jesus Coll, Cambridge. *Appointments:* Royal Artillery, India & Burma, 1943-46; Asst Master, Kings Sch, Rochester, 1949-53; Sr Hist Master, Wallasey Grammar Sch, Cheshire, 1953-57; Hdmaster, DeAston Sch, Market Rasen, 1957-64;

Hdmaster, Solihull Sch, 1964-73; Hdmaster, Haberdashers Askes Sch, Elstree, 1973-87; Chmn, Ch Schs Co, 1987-92. *Memberships:* Ch Assembly (C of E), 1963-70; Chmn, Boarding Schs Assn, 1967-69; Pub Schs Commn, 1968-79; FRSA; Chmn, Hdmasters Conf, 1985. *Honour:* Page Scholar of Eng-Speaking Union, 1961. *Hobbies:* Walking; Swimming; Foreign travel; Music; Theatre. *Address:* The Bell House, 29 Union Street, Woodstock, Oxon, OX20 1JF, England. 1.

MCGOWAN Mabel, b. 28 Mar 1921, Brighouse. Ret'd Tutor, Cnslr. m. Daniel McGowan, 1 Apr 1947, 3 s, 2 d. *Education:* Cert in Educ 1941, Acad Dip in Geog 1942, BA Hons 1946, Univ of London; MA, Univ of York, 1978. *Appointments include:* Brighouse Girls' Grammar Sch, 1956-67; Tng Mature Students as Primary Sch Tchrs, Castleford Mature Students' Annexe to Lady Mabel Coll of Wentworth & Bretton Hall Coll of Wakefield, 1967-81; Tutor, Cnslr, Open Univ, 1971-86; Tchr Tng, BA Studies, Bretton Hall Main Coll of Higher Educ, 1981-86. *Creative works:* Price of Freedom, 1978; Testament to a Life (Poetry/Music Tape), 1987; Tapes of Poetry Broadcasts to Second Schs; Lifelong Learning - Counselling Sect, 1987; UK Sect of the Hebrew Univ of Jerusalem's Publ on Continuing Educ Worldwide, 1989; Testament to a life and Fight the Good Fight, 1990; Wastage Amongst Mature Students (Rsch Study); Rsch in progress to produce two books: Women Amongst the Ancient Hebrews; Comparative Study of Impact of Christianity and Islam Upon the Same Hebrew Tribes in Relation to Women. *Memberships include:* Nat Comm, Assn for Recurrent Educ; Bradford Samaritans, 1975-85; Comm Mbr from Inception 1979, Sec 1989-91, N East Adult Educ Conf; Chaired Fndn Steering Grp 1981-82, Nat Assn for Educl Guidance for Adults. *Hobbies:* Reading; Writing; Research; Mountain walking and climbing; International folk dancing and sacred dance; Public poetry reading. *Address:* 5 Lane Hackings Green, Lower Cumberworth, Nr Huddlesfield HD8 8PW, England.

MCGURN Barrett, b. 6 Aug 1914, New York, NY, USA. Writer. m. Janice Ann McLaughlin, 19 June 1962, 5 s, 1 d. *Education:* AB 1935, Litt D Hon 1958, Fordham Univ. *Appointments:* Reporter, Foreign Corres, NY Herald Tribune, 1935-66; US Foreign Serv, 1966-73; Asst Press Spokesman, US Dept of State, 1969-72; Press Spokesman, US Supreme Ct, 1973-82; Communications Dir, Publr, Archdiocese of Washington, 1984-91. *Publications:* The Best from YANK (Co-author), 1945; Decade in Europe, 1958; Reporter Looks at Vatican, 1962; I Can Tell it Now (Co-author), 1964; Reporter Looks at American Catholicism, 1967; Heroes for Our Times (Co- author), 1968; Saints for All Seasons (Co-author), 1978; The Courage to Grow Old (Co-author), 1989; Close to Glory, co-author, 1992. *Memberships:* Treas 1955, Anglo-Am Press in Paris, France; Pres 1961, 1962, Assn of Foreign Press in Italy; Pres 1963-65, Overseas Press Club of Am; Nat Press Club, Washington DC; Cosmos Club, Washington DC; Kenwood Club, Washington DC. *Honours:* Purple Heart, 1944; Hon Doct of Letters, Fordham Univ, 1958; Polk Awd for best foreign corres, Long Isl Univ, 1956; Overseas Press Club Awd for best foreign correp, 1956; Grand Kt, Italian Govt, OM, 1962; Vietnam Govt Psychological Warfare medal, 1st class, 1969; US State Dept Meritorious Hon Awd, 1972. *Hobbies:* Water colour painting; Reading; Travel; Swimming. *Address:* 5229 Duvall Drive, Westmoreland Hills, MD 20816, USA. 2, 6, 7, 29, 49, 52, 128, 155, 162.

MCHUGH John Laurence, 24 Nov 1911, Vancouver, BC, Can. Prof Emeritus. m. Sophie Kleban, 30 Mar 1979, 1 s, 2 d. *Education:* MA, Univ of BC, 1938; PhD, Univ of CA and Scripps Instn of Oceanography, 1950. *Appointments include:* Chief 1959-63, Asst Dir 1963-66, Dep Dir of Bur 1966-68, Bur of Commercial Fisheries, Dept of Interior, Washington DC, Div of Biological Rsch; Acting Dir, Off of Marine Resources, Dept of the Interior, 1968-70; Hd, Off for the Int Decade of Ocean Exploration NSF, Washington DC, 1970; Prof of Marine Resources 1970-82, Prof Emeritus 1982-,

Marine Scis Rsch Ctr, SUNY at Stony Brook. *Publications:* Fishery Management; Author of 180 scientific papers. *Memberships:* Hon Mbr, Am Fisheries Soc; Hon Mbr, Nat Shellfisheries Assn; Emeritus Int Oceanographic Fndn; Hon Mbr, Whaling Mus Soc, Cold Spring Harbour. *Honours include:* Disting Tchng Awd, Assoc of the Marine Scis Rsch Ctr, 1977; Cit for exceptional serv, Nat Shellfisheries Assn, 1984; Awd of Excellence and an inscribed medal, Am Fisheries Soc, 1984; NY Bight Restoration Plan, 1988. *Address:* Marine Sciences Research Centre, State University of New York, Stony Brook, NY 11794, USA. 2, 14, 88.

MCHUGHEN Alan G, b. 13 Apr 1954, Ottawa, Can. Rsch Scist; Edr. m. P Jane Billinghurst, 12 July 1980, dec 1992, 2 d. *Education:* BSc Hons, Dalhousie Univ, 1972-76; D Phil, Magdalen Coll, Oxford Univ, 1976-79; MIBiol, 1981; CBiol, 1985. *Appointments:* Lectr, Yale Univ, 1979-82; Rsch Scist, Univ of Saskatchewan, 1982-; Genetic Engineering; Biotechnology and Environmental Regulatory Issues; Application of Genetic Engineering to Crop Improvement. *Publications:* Author of over 75 scientific works. *Memberships:* Inst of Biol; Genetics Soc of Can; Can Soc for Plant Molecular Biol; Int Soc for Plant Molecular Biol; Int Assn for Plant Tissue Culture. *Honours:* Rsch Fellow, Royal Commn or the Exhib of 1851, 1979; NATO Rsch Fellow, 1981; Robert B Anderson Fellow in Biochem, 1982. *Hobbies:* Sports; Outdoor Activities; Community Volunteer Services. *Address:* Crop Development Centre, University of Saskatchewan, Saskatoon, Sask, Canada S7N 0W0. 88.

MCILWRAITH George Robert, b. 15 July 1941, Southport, Lancs, Eng. Cons Physn. m. Isabel Margaret Manwaring, 24 July 1982, 1 s. *Education:* MB ChB, 1966; MRCP, 1972; FRCP, 1988. *Appointments:* Hosp training appts in UK, 1966-78; Asst Prof of Internal Med (Pulmonary), Univ of MI Med Sch, Ann Arbor, 1979-80; Cons Physn, Maidstone Dist Hosps, Kent 1981-. *Publications:* Author of articles, papers, chapts on Cardiological & Respiratory, Medical matters. *Memberships:* BMA; Brit Thoracic Soc; Brit Geriatric Soc; FRCP. *Hobbies:* Travel; Medieval Architecture; Rifle shooting. *Address:* Noah's Ark Farmhouse, East Sutton Road, Headcorn, Ashford, Kent TN27 9PS, England.

MCINNES Edward, b. 5 July 1935, Maybole, Ayrshire, Scotland. Prof of German. m. Jean Kilgour, 4 July 1964, 1 s, 3 d. *Education:* BA 1958, MA 1961, King's Coll, Univ of London; PhD, Univ of Edinburgh, 1974. *Appointments:* Lectr in German, King's Coll, London, 1961-62; Lectr in German 1962-73, Reader 1973, Univ of Edinburgh; Prof of German, Univ of Strathclyde, 1974-79; Prof of German, Univ of Hull, 1979-. *Publications:* German Today (w A J Harper), 1967; German Social Drama 1840-1900; From Hebbel to Hauptmann, 1976; Die Soldaten, 1977; Das deutsche Drama des 19. Jahrhunderts, 1983; Ein ungeheures Theater, The Drama of the Sturm and Drang, 1987; German in Society (ed), 1989; Hansers Sozialgeschichte der Deutschen Literatur (w G Plumpe), 1991; JMR Lenz: Der Hofmeister, 1991; Georg Büchner: Woyzeck, 1992; The Critical Reception of Dickens in Germany, 1837-1870, 1992. *Hobbies:* Reading Theology; Walking the dog; Supporting Hull City. *Address:* Department of German, The University, Hull HU6 7RX, England. 34.

MCINNIS Robert Francis Michael, b. 11 Mar 1942, Saint John, NB, Canada. Artist; Painter. 1 s. *Education:* Dip in Fine and Applied Arts, Saint John Vocational Sch, 1961. *Appointments:* News Reporter and Photographer, Telegraph Journ and Evening Times Globe, Saint John, 1960-62; Photographer, RCAF, 1962-66; Artist in Residence, Hd of Art Dept, Prince George Coll, Prince George, 1968-71. *Publications:* Toronto We Love You, The Brunswick House, 1974; The Renegrades Lament, 1974; Steel and Steam, 1985. *Creative works:* Paintings are incl in many major pvt and pub collections throughout Can and the World. *Memberships:* Branchline Railway Soc, Ottawa; Upper-Can Railway Soc, Toronto; Alberta Pioneer Railway Assn, Edmonton; Histl Comm, Mural Comm, Chmn, Old Strathcona Histl Soc, Edmonton. *Honours:* Can Armed Forces Art Awds, 1964, 1965, 1966. *Hobbies:* Model Railway; Railway Locomotive Photography; Artical Writing; Canadian Railway Historical Research; Canadian History; Painting Train Paintings. *Address:* 9928-83 Avenue, Edmonton, Alberta, Canada T6E 2C1. 142.

MCINTOSH David Angus, b. 10 Mar 1944, Frome, Somerset, Eng. Sr Ptnr, Solicitor. m. Jennifer Mary Dixon, 14 Sept 1968, 2 d. *Appointments:* Clerk, Ames Kent & Rathwell, Frome, 1961-63; Articled Clerk, Ptnr, Sr Ptnr, Davies Arnold Cooper, 1979-. *Publications include:* Preparing for the Worst, 1989; Defendants' Tactics, Defendants' Negotiations and Tactics in Mass Tort Litigation, 1989; The Immediate Aftermath of a Disaster - Responding on Behalf of Defendants, 1989; Deep Pockets of Liability, 1990; Contingency Planning and Crisis Management - The Legal Framework, 1990; Asbestosis, The Superfund Clean-up and Now The S & L Collapse: Implications for the London Insurance Market (co-author), 1990; Product Liability Trends in Europe and the United Kingdom, 1991. *Memberships:* Jt Working Comm, Senate of the Bar and Law Soc; Law Soc's Working Party; Sec of Comm S on Consumer Affairs, Advt, Unfair Competition and Prods Liability, Chmn of the Disaster Litigation Worldwide Prog, Strasbourg 1989, IBA; Int Assoc Mbr, Am Bar Assn; Soc of Eng and Am Lawyers; Assoc, Chartered Inst of Arbitrators; US Int Assn of Def Coun; Def Rsch and Trial Lawyers Assn of Am. *Hobbies:* Golf; Keet fit; Reading; Travel. *Address:* 6-8 Bouverie Street, London EC4Y 8DD, England.

MCINTYRE Michael Edgeworth, b. 28 July 1941. m. Ruth Hecht, 1968, 2 stepsons, 1 stepdaughter. *Education:* Sr Sci Scholar, BSc, Univ of Otago, NZ; PhD, Trinity Coll, Cambridge. *Appointments:* Asst Lectr in Maths, Univ of Otago, NZ, 1963; Postdoct Fell Woods Hole Oceanographic Inst, 1967; Postdoct Rsch Assoc, Dept of Meteorology, MIT, 1967-69; Rsch Fellow, St John's Coll, Cambridge, 1968-71; Asst Dir of Rsch in Dynamical Meteorology 1969-72, Lectr 1972-87, Reader in Atmospheric Dynamics 1987-, Dept of Applied Maths and Theoretical Phys, Univ of Cambridge; Sr Vis Fellow, Japan Soc for the Promotion of Sci, 1984; Sr Cons Sci & Tech Corp, Hampton, VA, 1987-; Jt Prin Investigator 1987-; Mbr Sci Steering Gp 1990-, UK Univs' Global Atmospheric Modelling Prog; Sr Cons, Jet Propulsion Lab, Pasadena, CA, 1991-. *Publications:* Author of num papers in profl journs incl Journ of Fluid Mech, Journ of the Atmospheric Sci. *Memberships:* Ed Bd, Journ of Fluid Mech, 1969-80; FRMets, 1970; New Violin Family Steering Comm, Royal Coll of Music, 1976-80; VP, Catgut Acoustical Soc, 1978-83; Int Commn for Meteorology of the Upper Atmosphere, 1979-; IUTAM/WMO, Working Group on Tropical Cyclone Disasters, 1990-91; Strateole Sci Steering Comm, 1992-; Atmospheric Sci Comm, NERC, 1989-. *Honours:* Academia Europea, 1989; FRS, 1990; Fellow, Am Meteorological Soc, 1991; Adams Prize, Univ of Cambridge, 1981; Robert Jack Prize, Univ of Otago; NZ Inst of Chem Prize; Carl-Gustaf Rossby Rsch Medal opf the AM Meteorological Soc, 1987. *Hobbies:* Music; Gliding. *Address:* 98 Windsor Road, Cambridge CB4 3JN, England.

MCINTYRE Robert Douglas, b. 15 Dec 1913, Motherwell. Ret'd Med Cons. m. Lila Sarah MacLeod, 11 Sept 1954, 1 s. *Education:* MB ChB, Edinburgh Univ, 1938; DPh, Glasgow Univ, 1942; DUniv Hon, Univ of Stirling. *Appointment:* Cons in Tuberculosis and Diseases of the Chest, 1951-75. *Publications:* Some Principle of Scottish Reconstruction; Author of articles chiefly in the Scots Independent & The Perthshire Advertiser. *Memberships include:* MP - Motherwell, 1945; Chmn, Pres 1958-80, SNP; Provost, Freeman 1967-75, Royal Burgh of Stirling. *Honours:* Fellow, Scottish Coun; JP. *Hobbies:* Sailing; Conversation. *Address:* 8 Gladstone Place, Stirling FK8 2NN, Scotland. 1.

MCIVER Norman Keith Ian, b. 20 Aug 1940, Northampton, Northants, Eng. Med Practitioner; Dir. m. Rita Elvertine Dyke Calver, 31 Oct 1964, 2 s, 1 d. *Education:* MBBS (Lond), 1965; LRCP; MRCS, 1965; AFOM, 1982. *Appointments:* RAMC SSC, 1966-71; Prin in Gen Pract, 1972-; Dir, Mbr of Permanent Staff, N Sea Med Ctr, 1974-; Tutor to Biomed Sems, 1987-. *Publications:* Offshore Medicine (Chapt), 1982; Treatment of Compressed-Air Decompression Accidents, 1989; Author of over 100 papers on Occupational & Diving Medicine, 1974-91. *Memberships:* BMA, 1965-, Pres of Gt Yarmouth Div, 1991; SOM, 1975-; Diving Med Advsy Comm, 1975-; FRSM, 1977-; Sec Exec Comm 1979-82, European Undersea Biomed Soc, 1975-; Int Affairs Comm 1980-85, Workshop Comm, 1980-82, Ed Bd 1983-86, Undersea & Hyperbaric Med Soc, USA, 1987-. *Honours:* Craig Hoffman Mem Awd (USA) for contribution to Diving Safety, 1981; Mbrship of Fac of Occupational Med, RCP through distn, 1988; Officer, Ord of St John of Jerusalem, 1991. *Hobbies:* Reading; Squash; Windsurfing. *Address:* North Sea Medical Centre, 3 Lowestoft Road, Gorlston-on-Sea, Great Yarmouth, Norfolk NR31 6SG, England.

MCIVER Susan Bertha, b. 6 Nov 1940, Hutchinson, KS, USA. Writer; Edr. *Education:* BA, Univ of CA, 1962; MSc 1964, PhD 1967, Washington State Univ. *Appointments include:* Asst Prof, Dept of Parasitology, Fac of Med 1967-71, Assoc Prof, Dept of Microbiol & Parasitology 1971-80, Dept of Zoology 1980-84, Prof 1984-90, Univ of Toronto. *Publications:* Author of over 100 original scientific rsch papers; several major scientific review articles; several short stories (fiction). *Memberships:* Dir 1975-78, Pres 1984-85, Entomological Soc of Can; Pres 1980-81, Entomological Soc of Ontario; Chair, Med Sect 1982-83, Entomological Soc of Am; Pres, Guelph Chapt 1986-87, Sigma Xi Rsch Hon Soc.*Honours:* InterAm Fellowship in Tropical Med, 1973; Travel Awd, Med Rsch Coun, 1978-79; Gordon Hewitt Awd, Entomological Soc of Can, 1978; Fellow, Entomological Soc of Can, 1981; von Hofsten Mem Lectr, Univ of Uppsala, Sweden, 1983. *Hobbies:* Literature; Hiking; Cooking; Chair, Bd of Dir, Women in Crisis, 1988-89. *Address:* C 95 Reynolds Road, RR 1, Fulford Harbour, British Columbia, Canada V0S 1C0. 5, 142, 143.

MCKANE Christopher Hugh, b. 13 July 1946, Reading, Eng. Journalist. m. Anna Rosemary Henshell, 31 Oct 1970, 3 d. *Education:* MA Oxon. *Appointments:* The Oxford Times, 1968-71; The Birmingham Post, 1971-74; The Times, 1974-86; The Independent, 1986-. *Hobbies:* Bonsai; Wine; Running. *Address:* The Independent, 40 City Road, London EC1Y 2DB, England.

MCKEE Francis John, b. 31 Aug 1943, Brooklyn, NY, USA. Hlth Care Cons; Atty. m. Antoinette Mary Sancis, 8 Aug 1970, 3 s, 1 d. *Education:* BA, Stonehill Coll, N Easton, 1965; JD, St John's Univ Law Sch, Brooklyn, 1970. *Appointments:* Assoc, Finch & Finch, Esq, Long Isl City, 1970-72; Staff Atty, Med Soc of the State of NY, Lake Success, 1972-77; Exec Dir: Suffolk Physns Review Org, East Islip, 1977-81; NY State Soc of Surgs, Orthopaedic Surgs, Upstate NY Chapt, Am Coll of Surgs, 1981-; NY State Ophthalmological Soc, 1984; NY State Soc of Ob-Gyn, 1984-; Nat Commn for Preservation of Ortho Prac, 1981-. *Memberships:* NY State Bar Assn, 1970-; Oneida Co Bar Assn, 1981-; Am Assn of Med Soc Execs, 1981-; Am Soc of Assn Execs, 1981-. *Hobbies:* Golf; Baseball; Football; Computers; Reading. *Address:* 40 Chenango Avenue, Box 308, Clinton, NY 13323, USA. 6, 52, 132, 163.

MCKENNA John Dennis, b. 1 Apr 1940, NYC, NY, USA. Engr. m. Christel Klages, 26 Dec 1964, 1 s, 1 d. *Education:* BS, Manhattan Coll, 1961; MS, Newark Coll of Engrng, 1968; MBA, Rider Coll, 1974; PhD, Walden Univ, 1991. *Appointments:* Tech Asst, Pres, Eldib Eng & Res, Inc, Newark, 1964-67; Proj Ldr, Princeton Chem Res, Princeton, 1967-68; Proj Dir, Rsch-

Cottrell-Bound Brook, NJ, 1968-72; VP, Enviro-Systems & Res, 1978-; Pres, ETS Inc, Roanoke, 1979-. *Publication:* Fabric Filter - Baghouses I (Co- author), 1989. *Memberships:* Bd Mbr of VA State Advsry Bd, Air & Waste Mgmt Tech Coun; Treas, Ctrl VA Chapt, AIChe; Ctrl VA Sect Chmn 1980-81, AIChe. *Honours:* Scientific Reviewer for EPA Publs, 1977-78; EPA Fabric Filter Workshop Lectr, 1978-79; NSF Cons for the Coll Fac Workshop Prog Grant, 1978- 79. *Hobbies:* Tennis; Skiing; Piano; Gardening. *Address:* 4118 Chaparral Drive SW, Roanoke, VA 24018, USA. 26, 52, 132.

MCKENZIE Joyce Peters, b. 2 Jan 1939, St Vincent. Creative Writer. m. W McKenzie, 26 Oct 1968, 1 s. *Education:* BA Hons Hist, UCWI/London, 1962; Cert Mgmt Studies, UWI, 1976. *Appointments:* Hg Sch Tchr, 1963-70; Civil Servant, 1970-76; Univ Adminr, 1976-84. *Publications:* Short poems and book reviews published in The New Voices magazine and the Caribbean Writer. *Memberships:* Sec, Univ Guild of Grads, St Vincent, 1965-66; Sec, Bus and Profl Women's Club, St Vinvent, 1973-74; Treas, UWI Womens CLub, 1979-80. *Honours:* Lit Awds: Taleisa Prize, 1987, The New Voices Prize, 1988. *Hobbies:* Reading; Attending the Theatre; Travel. *Address:* Petersville Residence, Kingstown Park, St Vincent, West Indies.

MCKEOWN Martin, b. 28 Sept 1943, Glasgow, Scotland. Mfg Exec. m. Anne Campbell, 30 Dec 1967. *Education:* HNC (dist) Mech Eng, Stow Coll, Glasgow, 1964; BSc Hons, Mech Eng, Univ of Strathclyde, Glasgow, 1966. *Appointments:* Apprentice, Rolls Royce, Glasgow, 1960-66; Methods Engr, N Elec, Toronto, Can, 1966-67; Mfg Engr, Nuclear Fuel Div 1968-72, Tool Specialist, Steam Turbine Div 1972-79, Mgr Mfg Dev, Elevator Div 1979-83, Westinghouse; Mfg Tech Mgr, Transp Div 1983, Prod Line Mgr1983-91, 1991-, Transp Systems, AEG-Westinghouse; Mfg Cons, AEG-Westinghouse, Berlin, Germany 1989-91. *Memberships:* Assoc Mbr, Inst of Prod Engrs; Sr Mbr, Soc of Mfg Engrs; Sr Mbr, Robotics Int; Certified Mfg Engr. *Hobbies:* Golf; Photography; Reading. *Address:* AEG-Westinghouse Transportation Systems, 1501 Lebanon Church Road, Pittsburgh, PA 15236, USA. 6, 132, 139.

MCKERNAN John Joseph, b. 11 May 1942, Omaha, NB, USA. Prof of Eng. m. 7 Aug 1967, 1 d. *Education:* BA, Univ of NB, 1965; MA, Univ of AR, 1967; MFA, Columbia Univ, 1971; PhD, Boston Univ, 1981. *Appointment:* Prof of Eng, Marshall Univ, 1967-. *Publications:* Walking Along The Missouri River, 1977; Erasing the Blackboard, 1978; Writers Handbook, 1987. *Memberships:* NWP; MLA; SAMLA; WVACET; WVELAC; NCTE; CCC. *Honours:* Fellowships from: Boston Univ, Nat Endowment for Humanities, Nat Endowment for Arts, WV Humanities Coun. *Hobby:* Poetry. *Address:* Marshall University, English Department, Huntington, WV 25701, USA.

MCKILLOP James Hugh, b. 20 June 1948, Glasgow, Scotland. Muirhead Prof of Med, Univ of Glasgow; Hon Cons Physn, Gtr Glasgow Hlth Bd. m. Caroline Annis Oakley, 17 Aug 1973, 2 d. *Education:* Univ of Glasgow, BSc 1970, MB ChB 1972, PhD 1979; FRCP Glasgow 1987; FRCP Edinburgh 1990; FRCP London, 1992. *Appointments:* Harkness Fellow, Stanford Univ, CA, USA, 1979-80; Sr Lectr, Univ Glasgow, 1982-89. *Publications:* Co-author Imaging in Clinical Practice, 1988; Scientific papers on nuclear med and thyroid diseases. *Memberships:* Brit Nuclear Med Soc, Hon Sec 1988-90, Pres 1990-92; Scottish Soc for Expmtl Med, Treas 1982-87; Assn of Physns of GB and Ireland. *Honours:* Watson Prize Lectureship, Royal College of Physicians anmd Surgeons of Glasgow, 1979; Robert Reid Newall Award, Stanford University Medical Center, 1980. *Hobbies:* Music; Cricket; Reading. *Address:* University Department of Medicine, Royal Infirmary, 10 Alexandra Parade, Glasgow G31 2ER, Scotland.

MCKINNEY Frank Kenneth, b. 13 Apr 1943, AL, USA. Prof of Geology, Palaeontologist. m. Marjorie Ann Jackson, 1 Sept 1964, 2 s, 2 d. *Education:* Birmingham Southern Coll, 1961-63; BS, Old Dominion Coll, 1964; MS, PhD 1970, Univ of NC. *Appointments:* Instr 1968-70, Asst Prof 1970, Assoc Prof, Prof, Appalachian State Univ. *Publications:* Bryozoan Evolution, co-author, 1989; Exercise in Ivertebrate Paleontology, 1991; Over 70 monographs and jrnl articles. *Memberships:* Paleontological Soc, Cnslr; Int Bryozoology Assn, Cnslr; Soc Econ Paleontologists and Mineralogists; AAAS; NC Acad of Science; American Mus of Zoologists; Linnean Soc of London. *Honours:* Smithsonian Postdoct Fellow, 1972-73; Rsch Assoc, Field Mus of Natural Hist, 1980-; Rsch Assoc, American Mus of Natural Hist, 1991-; Vis Fellow, Wolfson Coll, Cambridge, 1992-93. *Hobby:* Choral Music, esp Tudor and 20th century Anglican Liturgical Music. *Address:* Dept of Geology, Appalachian State University, Boone, NC 28608, USA. 143.

MCKINNEY William Douthitt Jr, b. 2 Sept 1955, Memphis, TN, USA. Pres, McKinney Assocs. *Education:* BBA, Mktng, Univ MS, 1978; CLU, 1979. *Appointments:* Br Mgr, Metrop Life Ins Co, 1978-79; Br Mgr, Carloss Well Supply, 1980-82; Pres, McKinney & Assocs (Mfrs Rep), 1981-; Sales Engr Mgr, Bryan Custom Plastics. *Memberships:* Mfrs Agts Nat Assn; United Assn of Mfrs Reps; American Mktng Assn; American Inst Chemical Engrs; Soc of Plastic Engrs; American Water Skii Assn; Phi Beta Lambda; Delta Sigma Pi. *Honours:* Eagle Scout and Scout of the Year, 1969; Member, The University of Mississippi Football Team, 1974-78; Charter Member, State of Liberty Ellis Island Commission, 1984; Member US Water Ski Team, 1984-85; Member of Water Ski Hall of Fame, 1985; A Thousand Points of Light Award by United States President George Bush, 1989. *Hobbies:* Antiques, Football, Basketball, the Arts, Golf, Water Skiing, Hunting. *Address:* 684 Tealwood Lane, Cordova, TN 38018, USA. 1, 7, 132.

MCLAWS Derek James, b. 19 Aug 1928, London, England. Can Forces (Ret'd); NATO Exec. m. Margaret, 7 July 1951, 2 s, 1 d. *Education:* RCAF Command and Staff Coll, 1960-61; Laval Univ, 1972-73; Adv Mil Trng Courses. *Appointments:* RCAF, 1950; w Maritime Patrol Aviation, to 1966; Dpty Dir, Cadets, NDHQ Ottawa, 1969-73; Dpty Dir-Gen, Bilingualism and Biculturalism, 1973-76; Dir, Can Forces Exchange System, 1976-78; Base Cmdr, St Jean, Quebec, 1978-80; Dir-Gen Recruiting, Educ and Trng, NDHQ, Ottawa, 1981-84; Project Mgr, Mil Lang Trng Improvement Prog, 1984-; Ret'd 1984; Chief of Personnel and Admin, NATO Underseas Rsch Ctr, 1984-. *Memberships:* Former Mbr, Bd Trustees Riverside Hosp, Ottawa; Peoples Warden, Ch of St Thomas Apostle, Ottawa; Garrison Club, Quebec City; Circolo San Giorgio, La Spezia, Italy. *Honours:* Centennial Medal, 1967; Queen's Jubilee Medal, 1977; Can Forces Decoration (2 clasps). *Hobbies:* Jogging, Bridge. *Address:* Via Poggi, 28, 19032 Lerici (SP) Italy.

MCLEOD William Richard, b. 28 Mar 1933, Melbourne, Australia. Psych. m. Margaret Frances Stuckey, 10 Oct 1960, 1 s, 3 d. *Education:* BA, Med Surg 1963, Dip Psychological Med 1968, MD 1970, Univ of Melbourne. *Appointments:* Assoc Prof, Psych 1971-77, Chmn of Dept 1975-77, Univ of Auckland, NZ; Censor-in-Chief, Chmn Bd of Examiners, Royal Aust and NZ Coll of Psychs, 1978-84. *Publications:* Many works in jrnls in UK, USA, Sweden and Australasia on naturally occurring hallucionogens; coronary risk factors; alcohol and drug abuse; philosophy and epistemology. *Memberships:* Fellow, Royal Coll Psychs; Royal Asian Coll Physns; Aust and NZ Coll Psychs; American Psych Assn; Collegium Internationale Neuropsychopharmacologicum; American Grp Therapy Assn; Sec, Int Postgrad Psych Educ Grp, USA, Can, UK, Aust and NZ; Treas, World Psych Assn Comm Educ in Psych; Fellow, Academia, Medicina & Psychiatria Foundation, 1992. *Honours:* Medical Research Foundation Grants, 1971; Wolfson Travelling Fellow for

N Z Post Graduate Federation for 1974; Squibb Academic Lecturer for ANZCP Congress in Singapore, 1978; Mental Health Donations Trust Fund, Victoria, 1978-79. *Hobbies:* Computers and Cybernetics, Altered States of Consciousness, Hallucinogens, Hypnotic, Meditative and Ecstatic States; Mythology, Comparative Religion, Opera, Expmtl approaches to treatment of mental illness arising from childhood trauma. *Address:* 18 Waratah Street, Ascot Vale, Victoria, Australia 3032. 52, 139, 149.

MCLYNN Francis James, b. 29 Aug 1941, Redhill, Surrey, England. Author. *Education:* MA, Wadham College, Oxford; MA, PhD, Univ Coll, London. *Appointments:* Brit Coun, Bogota, Colombia, 1969-71; Alistair Horne Fellow, St Antony's Coll, Oxford, 1987-88. *Publications:* Charles Edward Stuart, 1988; Stanley, 1989-91; Burton Snow Upon the Desert, 1990. *Memberships:* Fellow, Royal Histl Soc; FRGS; Soc of Authors. *Honour:* Cheltenham Prize for Literature 1985 for book The Jacobite Army in England. *Hobbies:* Music, Travel, Films. *Address:* c/o Andrew Lownie, 15-17 Heddon Street, London W1, England.

MCMURDO Margaret Anne, b. 30 Aug 1954, Brisbane, Aust. Judge of Dist Cts. m. Philip Donald McMurdo, 23 Jan 1976, 2 s, 1 d. *Education:* ASDA (AMEB), 1972; LLB, Qld, 1973; Admitted to Bar of Supreme Ct of Qld, 1976. *Appointments:* Clerk to His Honour Judge Denack, 1975-76; Asst Pub Defender, 1976-89; Barrister in pvte prac, Brisbane, Qld, 1969-91; Appointed Judge of Dist Cts (the first female judge in Qld), 19 Jan 1991. *Memberships:* Women Lawyers Assn of Qld, Pres 1980-81; Zonta Club of Brisbane. *Hobbies:* Child education, a beagle, Swimming, Walking, Gardening, Theatre, Reading. *Address:* District Court Building, George Street, Brisbane, Queensland 40000, Australia.bblank

MCNABB Frances Perle Cody, b. 17 Mar 1913, Cooke County, TN, USA. Supvsr of Educ. m. H Royce McNabb, 4 Oct 1940, 1 s, 1 d. *Education:* BS, summa cum laude, Milligan Coll, 1933; MA, Duke Univ, 1938; Graduate Study, Admin and Supervision, Univ TN, 1964-65. *Appointments:* Instr, Math, Biology, Chem, Cocke Co HS, TN, 1933-49, 1951-64; Instr Math, Engl, Cosby HS, 1950-51; Duke Univ Grantee in Zoology Rsch, summers 1938-39; Supvsr of Instrn, Cocke Co Schls, 1964-72; Instr, Contemporary Math, Univ TN Ext, 1967-68; Supvsr, Adult Educ, Cooke Co, 1965- 77; Cons in Tchr Trng in E TN, 1970. *Publications:* Thesis: Changes in the Central Nervous System of Passalus Cornutus Fabricius, Jrnl of Morphology, May 1938. *Memberships:* NEA; TEA; RTEA; CCEA; NCSM; NAPCAE; TAPCAE ASCD; Newport Music Club; TFMC State Chmn Comm on Composition; Delta Kappa Gamma; Alpha Omega. *Honours:* Valedictorian, Milligan Coll, 1933; First Lady of Newport, TN, 1972. *Hobbies:* Travelling, Reading, Cooking, Golf, Grandchildren. *Address:* 271 Cherokee Dr, Newport, TN 37821, USA. 7, 140.

MCNEILL John, b. 15 Sept 1933, Edinburgh, Scotland. Botan; Mus Admnstr. m. (1) Bridget M Winterton, 28 July 1961, 2 s, (2) Marilyn L James, 6 Apr 1990. *Education:* George Heriot's, Edinburgh, 1940-51; Univ Edinburgh, 1951-57; BSc (1st Class Hons. Bot), 1955; PhD 1960. *Appointments:* Lectr, Univs of Reading and Liverpool, 1957-69; Rsch Scientist, Plant Rsch Inst Agric, Canada, 1969-77; Sr Rsch Scientist, Biosystematics Rsch Inst, Agric, Canada, 1977-81; Prof and Chmn, Dept Biology, Univ Ottawa, 1981-87; Regius Keeper, Royal Botan Gdn, Edinburgh, 1987-89; Assoc Dir, Curatorial, Royal Ont Mus, Toronto, 1989-90, Acting Dir, 1990-1991, Dir, 1991-. *Publications:* Over 100 papers in scientific and tech publs; 10 chapts in books; over 30 abstracts and book reviews; sev books. *Memberships:* Biological Coun of Can, Pres, 1986-87;Can Coun of Univ Biology Chmn, Pres, 1984-85; Int Union of Biological Sciences; Int Assn for Plant Taxonomy, Coun Mbr, 1981-87, Admin Finances, 1987-; Int Org of Plant Biosystematists, Coun Mbr, 1989-1992. Ed Comm, Int Code of Botan Nomenclature, Sec, 1987-

; Int Botan Congress, Berlin, July 1987, V-Rapporteur, 1982; Int Botan Congress, Tokyo, Aug 1993, V-Rapporteur 1988; Am Soc Plant Taxonomists; Botan Soc of Edinburgh; Fellow, Linnean Soc of London. *Honour:* Vans Dunlop Scholar, University of Edinburgh, 1955. *Hobby:* Botan nomenclature. *Address:* Royal Ontario Museum, 100 Queen's Park, Toronto Ontario, Canada M5S 1C6. 1. 142. 143.

MCREE John Browning, b. 9 Dec 1950, Anderson, SC, USA. Physn. m. Melody Jennings, 29 May 1976, 2 d. *Education:* BS, Presby Coll, 1969- 73; MD, Med Univ of SC, 1973-77. *Appointment:* Family Prac Assocs, 1980-. *Membership:* American Acad of Family Physns, Fellow. *Hobbies:* Tennis, Shortwave Radio, Rock Collecting. *Address:* 201 Oakhurst Drive, North Augusta, SC 29841, USA. 7.

MCSHERRY James Andrew, b. 20 May 1942, Comrie, Scotland. Physn. m. Helen Margaret Weetch, 3 Feb 1968, 2 s, 1 d. *Education:* MB ChB, Glasgow, 1965; DObstRCOG, 1967; MRCGP, 1972; FRCGP, 1982; CCFP, 1976; FCFP, 1985; FRSH, 1980; FAAFP, 1982; FABMP, 1989. *Appointment:* Prof of Family Med and Psychology and Dir, Student Hlth Serv, Queen's Univ, Kingston, Can. *Publications:* Num publs on primary med care topics esp eating disorders, med and Scottish hist, humour. *Memberships:* Dir, Ont Coll of Family Physns; Pres, Kingston Regl Chapt, Coll of Family Physns of Can; Pres, John Austin Soc of Queen's Univ; Sometime Maj, RAMC(V); Fellow, Soc of Antiquaries of Scotland. *Honours:* Territorial Decoration, 1973; Canada Volunteer Award and Medal of Honour, 1986; Officer, Most Venerable Order of St John of Jerusalem, 1989. *Hobbies:* Choral Singing, Scottish Country Dancing. *Address:* 8 Casterton Avenue, Kingston, Canada K7M 1R5.

MCTAVISH Myron Alexander, b. 30 July 1911, Blenheim, Ontario, Canada. Ecclesiastical Musician, Organist. m. Ethel Luella Duego, 26 Sept 1938, 1 s. *Education:* Mus.B, Toronto, 1937; Lic, Royal Conservatory of Music, Toronto, 1933; Fellowship, Royal Can Coll of Organists, 1937; Fellowship, American Guild of Organists, 1944; Choirmaster, American Guild of Organists, 1948. *Appointments:* Organist, Holy Trinity, Blenheim, Ont, 1924-29, Danforth Baptist, 1933-36, 1st Ch of Christ Scientist, Ottawa, 1936- 53, St John's Cathedral, Spokane, WA, 1957-61, St Paul's Episc, Salinas, CA, 1961-76; Music Master, Elmwood Schl, 1939-56; Lectr in Music, Carleton Coll, 1945-50; Organist, Can Broadcasting Corp, 1950-53; Conductor, Ottawa Choral Union, 1953; Hartnell Coll, Salinas, CA, 1962-76; Music Master, St George's Episc Schl, 1957-60. *Creative Works:* Music for The Nativity Wallace B Shute MD; Orchestration (on Syntheciser) of Music by Leslie Belrose for play Christus by Wallace B Shute MD. *Honour:* Paul Harris Fellowship (honoris causa) Rotary, 1990. *Hobbies:* Calligraphy, Short Wave Radio. *Address:* 222 Katherine Avenue, Salinas, CA 93901, USA.

MEAD Richard Barwick, b. 18 Aug 1947, Shanghai, China. Chartered Acct. m Sheelagh Margaret Thom, 25 June 1971, 2 s. *Education:* Marlborough Coll, 1960-65; MA, Pembroke Coll, Cambridge, 1969. *Appointments:* Arthur Young McLelland Moores, 1969-73; Wm Brandts Sons & Co Ltd, 1973-75; Dir, Antony Gibbs & Sons Ltd, 1975-83; Dir, Credit Suisse First Boston Ltd, 1983-85; Ptnr and Nat Dir of Corporate Fin, Ernst & Young, 1985-. *Membership:* Fellow, Inst Chartered Accts in England and Wales. *Hobbies:* Family, Gardening, Hist, Walking. *Address:* Shambles, Watts Cross, Hildenborough, Tonbridge, Kent TN11 9NR, England. 53.

MEADER Darrell Lee, b. 21 Oct 1941, Covington, Kentucky, USA. Psychologist, RN, Cons, Disaster Specialist, American Red Cross. m. 22 June 1965, 2 s. *Education:* Holmes & Dixie HS; US Army, Nuclear Theory courses; Graduated Psychgology; AD, Nursing. *Appointments:* US Army, 1958; Staff, St Elizabeth Hosp,

1968; Staff, Children's Hosp, 1979; Charge Nurse, Critical Care Nurse, Cons. *Publications:* sev papers on Philos, Psychology and Med. *Memberships:* Nat Red Cross, Disaster Specialist; Reserve Offs Assn, Col Life; American Def Preparedness Assn; Disabled Veterans of America, Life; Vietnam Veterans Assn, Life; Blue Grass Swim Club; Meader Assn; Special Forces Assn; Critical Care Assn; American Legion; American Amateur Karate Fedn; Mil Intelligence Assn. *Honours:* 12 Mil Awards, USA; French Special Forces Wings; Mental Health (Charles Baron) Award, 1974; sev Red Cross awards for nat work. *Hobbies:* Karate, 3rd degree Black Belt, Snorkling, Reading, Climbing, Ch, Outdoors, Genealogy, Rsch, Flying, Mil, Photography, Community Serv, Swimming, Chow-Chow Dogs and Peacocks, Cats, Family, Grandson. *Address:* 800 Kyles Lane, Fort Wright, KY 41017, USA. 7.

MEAGHER Douglas Raymond, b. 10 Feb 1941, Melbourne, Australia. QC. m. Rosemary Ann Batt, 21 Mar 1970, 1 s, 2 d. *Education:* LLB (Hons) Melbourne. *Appointments:* Barrister-at-Law, Vic, 1963-84; QC, Vic, Aust Capital Territory, NSW, S Aust, WA, Tas, 1984-; Sr Counsel Assisting the Royal Commn into the Federated Ships Painters and Dockers of Aust, 1980-84. *Publications:* Papers: Organised Crime, 1983; Computer Use by the Costigan Commission, 1985; Commercial Crime Trials, 1988; Computerisation of Courts, 1989; Evidentiary Problems of Computers, 1989; Administering Complex Trials, 1990; Computerisation and the Courts, Appointments to the Judiciary, 1990. *Memberships:* Exec Comm for Computerisation of Vic Cts, 1987-; Coun of Aust Inst of Judicial Admin, 1990-. *Honours:* ED, 1973; QC, 1984. *Hobbies:* Computer Science, Hist. *Address:* 11 St Ninians Road, Brighton, Victoria, Australia 3186. 23, 157.

MEARS Patrick Michael, b. 19 Jan 1958, London, England. Solicitor. m. 27 Aug 1983, (dec 5 Sept 1987), 1 d. *Education:* LLB London Schl of Econs, 1979; Solicitor of the Supreme Ct, 1982. *Appointments:* Allen & Overy, Solicitors, 1980-; Corporate Tax Ptnr, 1988-; Corporate Tax Lectr. *Memberships:* Law Soc; City of London Solicitors Co, Mbr Revenue Sub-Comm; Gov, Tax Rsch Unit, Kings Coll, London Univ. *Hobbies:* Theatre, Bridge, Squash, Parenthood. *Address:* c/o Allen & Overy, 9 Cheapside, London EC2V 6AD, England. 53.

MEDEIROS DE MENEZES Lena, b. 23 July 1945, Rio de Janeiro, Brazil. Hist Tchr. m. Antonio Carlos Paes, 25 Sept 1970, 1 s, 1 d. *Education:* Lic in Hist, Univ do Estado do Rio de Janeiro, 1969; MA, Univ Fed Fluminense, 1986; PhD studies, Social Hist, Univ Sao Paulo. *Appointments:* Tchr, Pub Schls, 1964-78; Assoc Prof, Univ Estado do Rio de Janeiro, 1976, Hd, Hist Dept, 1984-86, Hd, Trng Coll, 1986; Hd, Instituto Superior de Estudos Brasileiros e Relacoes Internacionais, UERJ, 1987. *Publications:* Modernizacao e Imigracao no Brasil Imperial, 1986; Os Efeitos da escra vidao na adocao do trabalho livre no Brasil, 1987; modernizacao e Criminalidade: o exemplo do Rio de Janeiro Imperial, 1988; trabalho e liberdade no Brasil: ensaio sobre a questao das permanencias, 1989; A Prioncesa adormecida, 1990; O trafico internacional de mulheres e a modernizacao do Rio de Janeiro, 1991. *Memberships:* Sociedade Brasileira de Pesquisa Historica; Associacao dos Professores Universitarios de Historia; Instituto Historico de Petropolis. *Hobbies:* Dancing, Drawing, Writing Poetry, Gardening. *Address:* Rua Sao Francisco Xavier, 524, History Department, Rio de Janeiro, Brazil 20550.

MEDER Cornel, b. 23 Sept 1938, Esch-Alzette, Luxembourg. Dir, Nat Archives Luxembourg. m. Nicole Wagner, 10 Apr 1965, 1 s, 1 d. *Education:* Leuven, 1959-60; Bonn, 1960-61; Paris, 1961-62; Tuebingen, 1962-63; PhD, 1963. *Appointments:* Tchr, Lycee de Garcons, Esch/Alzette, 1964-69; Hdmaster, Lycee Mathias Adam Petange, 1969-87; Dir, Nat Archives Luxembourg, 1987-. *Publications:* Loewener Schriften, 1960; Renzo

Pontevias Briefe, 1962; Der Aufstand, 1970; Lesebuchlein, 1972; Schumann, 1976; In kleinen Dosen, 1980; Stadtschreiber, 1988; Remi F Engelmann, 1990. *Memberships:* Institut Grand-Ducal, Sect de Linguistique, Pres, 1978-91; Ctr Cultural Differdange, Pres, 1968-; Conseil d'Etat. *Honour:* Commandeur dans l'Ordre de la Couronne de Chene, 1989. *Hobby:* Lecturing (Lit, Hist). *Address:* 69 Prinzenberg, L-4650 Niederkorn, Luxembourg. 52.

MEDLEY Donald Bruce, b. 20 Sept 1932, Monroe, Michigan, United States of America. Educl Admnstr. m. Louise Lee Spencer, 1 Sept 1956, 2 s, 1 d. *Education:* Dip Accounting, Int Correspondence School, Scranton, PA, 1967; BVE, Cal State Coll, Los Angeles, 1971; MA, Cal State Univ, Los Angeles, 1972; EdD, Brigham Young Univ, 1976. *Appointments:* USAF, 1952-56; var positions in OH and CA, 1956-68; Moorpark Coll, CA, 1968-82; US Dept Agric, Beltsville, MD, 1980-81; CA State Polytechnic Univ, Pomona, 1981-89; Ventura Co Community Coll Dist, CA, 1989-. *Publications:* Co-author: Programming Principles with Cobol II, 1985; Advanced Office Systems, 1986; Management Information Systems: Planning and Decision Making, 1987; Information Resource Management, 1987; Computer Center Operations, 1988. *Memberships:* Assn of CA Community Coll Admnstrs; Assn for Computer Educators; Data Processing Mgmt Assn; Assn for Computing Machinery; IEEE Computer Soc. *Honours:* Outstanding Educator, California Polytechnic SBA, 1984; Selected Outstanding Educator of the Year 1985 by The Society of Data Educators. *Hobbies:* Reading, Golf, Travelling. *Address:* 110 Flora Vista Avenue, Camarillo, CA 93012, USA. 9, 52, 59. 132, 155, 179.

MEEL Raul, b. 2 Mar 1941, Jalase Village, Raikyla Dist, Estonia. Painter, Graphic Artist, Concrete Poet. m. Mari Saat, 14 Mar 1975, 1 s (dec), 2 d. *Education:* Elec Engrng, Tallinn Technic Univ, 1959-64. *Appointments:* Electn, Tallinn Trust Elektromontaaz, 1959-61; Constructor, Graduator, Inst of Design and Technology of Estonian Min of Local Ind, 1962-87; Soviet Army, 1964-67; Mgr, Expmtl Graphic Workshop by Estonian Art Fund, 1987-90; Profl Artist, 1990-. *Creative Works:* More than 2000 art works; Under the Heavens, 1973 (serigraphy); Windows and Landscapes, 1985 (serigraphy); Spell and Spirit, 1988 (acrylic on canvas). *Membership:* Estonian Union of Artists. *Honours:* 3rd Laureate Prize at Copernicus Competition, Cracow, Poland, 1971; 4th Laureate Prize at Cracow Graphic Art Biennale, Poland, 1972; Laureate Prize at Frechen Graphic Art Biennale, Germany, 1974; Art Critics Award at the New Talents and Ideas of the World Art Exhibition, Boston, USA, 1979; Kristjan Raud's Annual Art Award, Tallinn, 1989; Eduard Viiralt's Graphic Prize at Tallinn Graphic Art Triennale, Tallinn, 1989. *Hobbies:* Bee-keeping, Gardening, Hunting, Shooting. *Address:* Estonian Union of Artists, Vabaduse Square 6, EE0105 Tallinn, Estonia.

MEHTA B S, b. 25 May 1921, Jaunpur, India. Pathologist. m. 26 Feb 1948, 2 s. *Education:* BSc, 1942, DB BS, 1947, DCP, 1956, Lucknow Univ; Visharad, Hind, 1942. *Appointment:* Pvte Clin Pathologist, 1948-. *Publications:* Books on Health (in Hindi); Books on Drama (in Hindi); Poetry, Humour, Essays, Letters, Benares, Ramlile, Children, Family Welfare,Travelogues, Transls. *Memberships:* Indian Med Assn; Naqu Natak Mandali; Sangeet Parishad; Thalue Chule. *Honours:* Dr B C Roy Nat Award, Med Coun of India; UNESCO Prize for Neo-Literato Book, 1984; UP Govt Prize for Books, 1986; UP Govt Prize for transl from Gujrati. *Hobbies:* Writing, Drama, Music (compere), Social Work, Med Assn; Hist of Med, Banares Ramlila. *Address:* B 37-67 Manidweep, Birdopur, Varanasi (UP), India 221010.

MEIER Heinrich, b. 8 Apr 1953, Freiburg i Br, Germany. Dir, Carl Friedrich von Siemens Fndn. m. Wiebke Neupert, 21 Oct 1983. *Education:* PhD, Philos, Pol Science, Sociology, Univ of Freiburg, 1985. *Appointment:* Dir, Carl Friedrich von Siemens Fndn, 1985-. *Publications:* Author, Ed, transl: Diskurs ueber

die Ungleichheit: Discours sur l'inegalite, 1984, 2nd Ed, revised and enlarged 1990; Author: Carl Schmitt, Leo Strauss und Der Begriff des Politischen, 1988, French transl 1990, Japanese transl 1993; Die Lehre Carl Schmitts, 1993; Ed, Contributing Author: Die Herausforderung der Evolutionsbiologie, 1988; Zur Diagnose der Moderne, 1990. *Honour:* Studienstiftung des deutschen Volkes Fellow, 1973-83. *Address:* Carl Friedrich von Siemens Stiftung, Suedliches Schlossrondell 23, D-8000 Munich 19, Germany. 1, 52.

MEISEL John, b. 23 Oct 1923, Vienna, Austria. Sir Edward Peacock Prof of Pol Science at Queen's Univ, Can. m. Murie Augusta Kelly 6 Aug 1949, dec. *Education:* BA, 1948, MA, 1950, Univ of Toronto; PhD, Econ, London, 1960. *Appointments:* Instr, Asst, Assoc, Full Prof, Hardy Prof of Pol Science, Queen's Univ, Kingston, Ontario, Can, 1949-79; Chmn, Can Radio-TV and Telecommunication Commn, 1980-83; Sir Edward Peacock Prof of Pol Science, Queen's Univ, 1983-. *Publications:* Books: Ethnic Relations in Canadian Voluntary Associations, co-author, 1972; Working Papers on Canadian Politics, 1972, 73, 75; Cleavages, Parties and Values in Canada, 1974; Articles and Chapts in Books; Videotapes. *Memberships:* Int Pol Science Assn, co-Ed of Review; Can Pol Science Assn, former Pres; Social Science Rsch Coun of Can, former Pres. *Honours:* Killam Award, Canada Council, 1960s; Fellow of the Royal Society of Canada, 1974; Officer, Order of Canada, 1990; International Canadian Studies Award of Excellence, 1991. *Hobbies:* Music, The Arts, Photography, Indoor Gardening, Skiing, Swimming. *Address:* Colimaison, Tichborne, Ontario, Canada K0H 2V0. 2, 88.

MELE Alfred Remen, b. 22 May 1951, Detroit, Michigan, USA. Prof of Philos. m. Constance Pfister, 20 July 1970, 2 s, 1 d. *Education:* BA, Wayne State Univ, 1973; PhD, Univ of MI, 1979. *Appointments:* Asst Prof of Philos, 1979-85, Assoc Prof of Philos, 1985-91, Prof of Philos, 1991-, Davidson Coll. *Publications:* Irrationality, 1987; Springs of Action, 1992; many jrnl articles. *Memberships:* American Philos Soc; Southern Soc for Philos and Psychology; NC Philos Soc, Sec 1985-87, Pres 1987-89. *Honours:* National Endowment of the Humanities, Year- long Fellowship, 1985-86; National Endowment of the Humanities, summer Fellowship, 1989. *Hobbies:* Racquetball, Tennis. *Address:* Dept of Philosophy, Davidson College, Davidson, NC 28036, USA.

MELKOWSKI Stefan, b. 21 May 1931, Torun, Poland. Writer, Author, Univ Lectr. m. Krystyna, 16 Aug 1972. *Education:* Univ of Torun, 1950- 53; MA special hons in Polish Lit, Univ of Warsaw, 1955; PhD, Univ of Warsaw, 1962. *Appointments:* Lit debut, 1955-; Libn, Nat Lib, Warsaw, 1955-65; Lectr, Univ Torun, 1965-; Mbr, Lit Criticism Sect in wkly Literature, Warsaw, 1976-79; Ed, monthly Poezja, Warsaw, 1973-81. *Publications:* Rozne st rony, travel book, 1983; Domena prozy, lit criticism, 1984; Wojciech Zukrowski, critical portrait, 1985; Wyznania zawieszonego, essays, 1987 and 8 others books; over 600 studies, essays, critiques, criticism reviews, articles, travel stories published in var publs. Some translated into English, German, Bulgarian and Russian. *Memberships:* Polish Writers Assn, Pres Torun Sect; Scientific Soc in Torun; Adam Mickiewier Lit Soc, Warsaw; Societe Europeenne de Culture (SEC), Venezia; Rotary Intr, Torun Br. *Honour:* Cavalier Cross, Polonia Restituta, 1990. *Hobbies:* Reading, Theatre, Travel, Gardening. *Address:* ul Mita 9, 87-100 Torun, Poland.

MELLIS David Barclay Nairne, b. 13 June 1915, North Berwick, E Lothian, Scotland. Ret'd RN (Capt). m. 13 Apr 1940, 1 s, 2 d. *Education:* Cargilfield Schl, Edinburgh, 1925-28; RN Coll Dartmouth, 1929-32; RN Coll Greenwich, 1935-36. *Appointments:* RN, Jan 1929-Aug 1967; Comptroller, Dart Castle, 1967-68; Warship Trials Master, 1969-79; Navigation Specialist 1938. *Memberships:* Elder of the Ch of Scotland; Royal

Highland Yacht Club, Trustee; Trinity House, Younger Brother; RN Pipers Soc, Jt Fndr, Sec, Chmn; RN Club, Argyll, Jt Fndr; RN Sailing Assn, Life Mbr. *Honours:* Dunkirk Evacuation 1940 Mentioned in Despatches; Distinguished Service Cross, June 1941. *Hobbies:* Reading Hist and Biog, Sailing, Bridge, Pol, Fly Fishing. *Address:* High Water, Aros, Isle of Mull, Argyll PA72 6JG, Scotland.

MELSEN Birte, b. 9 June 1939, Fredericia, Denmark. Prof, Dr Orthodontics, Hd of Dept of Orthodontics. m. Flemming, 5 Apr 1963, 2 s. *Education:* DDS, Royal Dental Coll, 1964; Specialist, 1971; Dr Odont, 1974. *Appointments:* Royal Dental Coll, Aarhus, Denmark: Asst Tchr, Inst of Cardiology, 1964-65; Rsch Assoc, Inst of Orthodontics, 1965-67; Asst Prof, 1967-72; Acting Hd of Inst, 1971; Assoc Prof, 1972-75; Prof and Hd of Inst, 1975-; Pt-time Pvte Prac, 1980; Vis Prof, Univ of Padova, Italy, 1981- 84; Contract Prof, Univ of Napoli, Italy, 1990-. *Publications:* More than 150 pubns on Growth and Development studied on human autopsy material; Bone biology; Implant studies; Malocclusion; Epidemiology; Adult orthodontics. *Memberships:* Scandinavian Orthodontic Soc, Pres, 1976; Danish Orthodontic Soc, Pres, 1988-91; Pres, 3rd Int Symposium on Feeding and Dentofacial Dev, 16-17 June 1990, Aarhus; European Orthodontic Soc, Copenhagen, VP; Hon Mem, Finnish Orthodontic Soc, 1992; Receiver of the Zendium, price, 1991; Hon Mem, Italian Orthodontic Soc, 1991. *Honours:* Knight of Dannebrog, Ridder of Dannebrog, 1987; Honorary Member: Austrian Dental Society, 1982, Deutsche Kieferorthopadische Gesellschaft, 1987, Egyptian Orthodontic Society, 1989; Receiver of Robert Strang Award of Orthodontics, 1984; Receiver of Marie Longaard Award for Female Researchers, 1986. *Hobbies:* Opera, Active mbr of Youth for Christ. *Address:* Elsdyrvej 28, DK-8270 Hoejbjerg, Denmark. 52.

MELWANI Manohar Narain, b. 4 Jan 1948, Karachi, W Pakistan. Profl Bespoke Tailor. m 28 Dec 1975, 1 s, 2 d. *Education:* HS; Engl Schl, Hong Kong. *Appointments:* Profl Bespoke Tailor since 1975; w Sam's Tailor, Hong Kong. *Memberships:* Hong Kong Royal Jockey Club; Rotary Int; Kowloon Cricket Club; Brit Inst of Dirs, 1991. *Honour:* Hon PhD for wildlife conservation and ecology from The International Academy of Leadership an affiliate of the University of San Toma, Philippines, 13 Nov 1991. *Hobbies:* Swimming, Cricket, Horse racing, Tennis, Travelling. *Address:* 94 Nathan Road, 12th Floor B-4, Burlington House, Kowloon, Hong Kong.

MENDEL Renee, b, 22 Sept 1908, Elmshorn. Sculptor. *Education:* Matriculation, Hamburg Univ, Frankfurt, 1933; Paris, 1934; Studied Sculpture w Pablo Garzula; Exhib Salon d'Automme, 1934. *Creative Works:* Sculpture Exhibs Peter Jones Gall, Lord Halifax, N Chamberlain, 1940; Royal Acad, 1942; Lord Beaverbrook, London Art Centre, 1967; The Beatles sold at Sothebys; Idi Amin, Royal Exchange, 1977; James Joyce Nat Portrait Gall, 1987; Bronze Portrait Bust of Dr Winsley Stolz GP, 1989. *Address:* 27 Onslow Gardens, Muswell Hill, London N10 3JT, England.

MENSER George Warren, I, b. 31 Mar 1917, Hooversville, PA, USA. Ret'd Band-Choral Dir, Composer. m. (1) 1939-50, (2) 1951-81, dec, (3) 1984- , 5 s, 1 d. *Education:* Pvte studies Piano w Miss Richards and Mrs Ethelyn Wagner; MD Music, Frostburg State Coll, MD, 1946; BS Music, IN Univ of PA, 1950; Studied choral work w Fred Waring Chorale, Penn State; Adv Band and Instrumental, Penn State Univ, 1963. *Appointments:* Pianist and Arranger for dance bands; Dir and Accompanist for MD Folk Singers of Frostburg Coll; Band and Chorus: Fort Hill HS, Cumberland, MD, Cambridge Springs, PA HS, Coalport, PA, HS, Randolph East Mead HS; Chorus and Gen Music, Maplewood School. *Creartive Works:* Nature Suite: Flowers in My Garden, Ode to a Pine Tree, To a Winter's Eve, Orange Blossoms; The London Cycle, piano trilogy; Chalene

Piano Concerto in D; Music for Young Moderns; Processional in F Maj for organ; Quebec Suite; Piano pieces, songs, 5 Christmas Carols. *Honours:* At Fort Hill HS Cumberland, Maryland State awarded Artist Teacher; Plaque Misslemen Band commemorating playing of first concert at Oneida Tower, Niagara Falls, Ontario, 1964; 1967 Appt from Gov Shafer of PA: Misselmen Band appointed as goodwill Ambassadors and my personal envoys to the 1967 World's Fair in Montreal. *Hobbies:* Model Railroading, Reading, Writing Music, Family, Ch. *Address:* P O Box 234, Cambridge Springs, PA 16403, USA.

MENYHART Laszlo, b. 14 June 1949, God, Hungary. Jrnlst, Histn. *Education:* Tech Coll, Budapest, 1971; Acad of Jrnlsm, Budapest, 1975; Course of Aesthetics, Budapest, 1978; Dips: Mech Engrng, Jrnlst, Critic. *Appointments:* Auto-Motor wkly, 1974-75; Muveszet, Art Mag, 1975-90; Panorama of God, local monthly, 1990; Heti Magyarorszag, pol wkly, 1991-. *Publications:* Books: Mihaly Schemer, 1981; Endre Szasz, painters, 1983; Film Scenery, 1981; Koller Gallery, 1987; Ed-Reporter, TV Prog, Ceramic Art, 1988; Horoscope, 1990-91. *Membership:* Nat Assn of Hungarian Jrnlsts. *Honours:* The Best Art Book of the Year, 1981; Honoured Journalist of the Cabinet, 1984; Professional Level Prize of the Pallas Publishing House, 1984, 86. *Hobbies:* Tennis, Reading, Gardening, Travelling. *Address:* Heti Magyarorszag, Budapest Pf 634 1396 Hungary. 52.

MEPHAM Derek John Amoore, b. 26 Mar 1954, Inverell, Australia. Primary Producer, Bus Investor. *Education:* BEc, Univ of New England, Armidale, 1979. *Appointments:* Wayland and Wayland, Chartered Accts, Sydney, 1978; Own bus, 1980-; Studying for MBA. *Memberships:* United Graziers Assn; Grain QGGA Assn. *Hobbies:* Snow Skiing, Flying, Tennis, Golf, Politics, Reading. *Address:* P O Box 344, Hyland Downs, Clermont, Queensland 4721, Australia. 52.

MERCER Terence, b. 4 Sept 1931, Hull, Yorkshire, England. Advt Agcy Chmn. m. Frances Karene, 21 Nov 1959, 2 s. *Education:* Leeds Coll of Commerce. *Appointments:* Commissioned Brit Army, 2 yrs Middle East Land Force, 1953-55; Army Emergency Res, 1956-59; Jt Mng Dir, 1961-71, Chmn and Jt Mng Dir, 1971-83, Chmn, 1983-, Tattersall Advg Ltd, Harrogate, N Yorkshire. *Memberships:* Life Fellow, RSA; Inst of Practitioners in Advg; Fellow, Zoological Soc, London; Yorkshire Retriever Field Trial Soc; Inst of Adv Motorists; Noise Abatement Soc; Ripon Diocesan Synod, 1970-73; Coun Mbr, Ripon Cathedral Trust Appeal; Yorkshire N Conserv European Constituency Coun, 1981-83; Mbr, ROSPA; Mbr, ABC Council; Fndr Benefactor, The Mercer Gallery, Harrogate. *Honours:* Honorary Publicity Adviser Save The Children Fund; Created Honorary Life Member for contribution to the Arts, The Friends of Harrogate District Museums. *Hobbies:* Field Sports, Charity Work, Sketching, Pol. *Address:* Low Bridge House, Markington, Harrogate, North Yorkshire HG3 3PQ, England.

MERCIECA Charles, b. 3 Feb 1933, Malta. Prof of Philos and Pol Science. m. 28 May 1970, 1 s, 1 d. *Education:* BA, Aloisianum Coll, Italy, 1958; MS, KS State Univ, USA, 1964; PhD, Univ KS, 1966. *Appointments:* Prof, 1967-, Dir, Inst for Int Rels, AL A & M Univ; Exec VP, Int Assn of Educators for World Peace; Vstng Prof, Tver State Univ, Russia, 1992-92; Dir, Peace Educ Pilot Schools Project, 1978-. *Publications:* Mismanagement in Higher Education; Education for Peace: What It Entails; Role of Buddhist Education in the Decade of the Nineties. *Memberships:* Int Assn of Educators for World Peace, Exec VP; World Constitution and Parl Assn, Cabinet Mbr; NEA; Philos of Educ Soc; AAUP. *Honours:* Doctor of Divinity, University of Remo, Nigeria, 1973; Chief of Idarne, Nigeria, 1974; Cultural Doctorate in World Education, World University, 1975; Honorary Secretary of State, Kentucky, 1983; Kentucky Colonel, 1983 . *Hobbies:* Swimming, Cycling, Tennis, Boating, Travelling, Lecturing, For Langs. *Address:* P O Box 3282, Mastin

Lake Station, Huntsville, AL 35810, USA. 129, 139, 152, 162.

MERKLEIN Helmut, b. 17 Sept 1940, Aub, Germany. Univ Prof. *Education:* Theol. Abschlussexamen 1964 Phil-Theol. Hochschule Bamberg; ThD, 1972, ThD Habil, 1976, Univ Würzburg. *Appointments:* Kaplan, Rehau, Diözese Bamberg, 1965-68; Wissenschaftlicher Asst, Kath-Theol. Fakultät, Univ Würzburg, 1972-77; Privatdozent, Würzburg, 1977; o. Prof, Gesamthochschule Wuppertal,1977-80; Kath-Theol. Fakultat, Univ Bonn, 1980-. *Publications:* Das kirchliche Amt nach dem Epheserbrief, 1973; Christus und die Kirche, 1973; Die Gottesherrschaft als Handlungsprinzip, 1978, 84; Jesu Botschaft von der Gottesherrschaft, 1983, 89; Studien zu Jesus und Paulus, 1987. *Membership:* Studiorum Novi Testamenti Societas, Mbr Comm, 1987-90. *Address:* Neutestamentliches Seminar der Kath.-Theol Fakultat der Universitat Bonn, Regina-Pacis-Weg 1A, D-5300 Bonn 1, Germany.

MERRIL Judith, b. 21 Jan 1923, New York City, USA. Writer, Perf. m. 3 times, 2 d. *Education:* CCNY. 1939-40; BA, 21st Century Mythology, Rochdale Coll, Toronto, Can, 1971. *Appointment:* Writer-in-Res, Univ of Toronto, 1991-92. *Publications:* Novels: Shadow on the Hearth, 1950; Gunner Cade, co-author, 1952; Outpost Mars, co-author, 1952; The Tomorrow People, 1960; The Testaments (in work); Collections: The Best of Judith Merril, 1976; Survival Ship, 1977; Daughters of Earth and Other Stories, 1985; Novellas; Short Stories; Critical Writings; Non-fiction. *Memberships:* PEN, Can Ctr; Writers Union of Can; Assn of Can TV and Radio Artists; SF Can; World SF; Stafford Beer Fndn, Dir; Inst for Twenty-First Century Studies, Ed Bd; Hydra North, Fndr. *Honours:* Grants from Canada Council and Ontario Arts Council; Fourth Annual Canadian Science Fiction and Fantasy Award, 1983; Casper Award , English Canada, 1985 for Lifetime Achievement in Editing; The 1990 Milford Award for Lifetime Achievement in Science Fiction and Fantasy Editing. *Hobbies:* Conversation, Reading, Jazz, Reggae, Dancing, Water Sports, Grandchildren, Great Grandchildren. *Address:* c/o The Merril Collection of Science Fiction, Speculation and Fantasy, Toronto Public Library, 40 St George Street, Toronto, Ontario, Canada M5S 2E4. 3, 48, 138, 142, 177.

MERRISON Maureen Michele, b. 29 Oct 1938, Grantham, England. Co Dir. m. Alexander Walter Merrison, 23 May 1970, 1 s, 1 d, 2 stepsons. *Education:* Bedford Coll, Univ of London, 1957-62; BA Hons Hist, 1960; Rsch Fellow, Inst of Histl Rsch, 1962-63. *Appointments:* Tutorial Rsch Fellow, Bedford Coll, Univ of London, 1963-64; Lectr in Hist, Univ of Bristol, 1964-90; Dir: HTV, 1978-, Bristol and W Bldg Soc, 1990-, Western Provident Assn, 1990-. *Membership:* Histl Assn. *Honours:* University of London Paul Philip Reitlinger Essay Prize, 1959; Bedford College Clay Scholar, 1960-61. *Hobbies:* Hill-walking, Tennis, Skiing. *Address:* The Manor, Hinton Blewett, Temple Cloud, Bristol BS18 5AN, England.

MERTENS-FONCK Paule Anne Marie, b. 13 Oct 1925, Morlanwelz, Belgium. Ret'd Prof, Medieval Engl (Lang and Lit) Univ Liege. m. Paul Ghislain Mertens, 21 Mar 1951, 1 s, 1 d. *Education:* Lic, Germanic Philology (Engl-Dutch), Univ Liege, 1947; Cert, Univ Groningen, 1948; PhD. Univ Liege, 1955. *Appointments:* Second Schl Tchr, Lycee Warocque Morlanwelz, 1949- 50; Asst Lectr, Univ Liege, 1950-70; Prof, Univ Liege, 1970-90. *Publications:* A Glossary of the Vespasian Psalter and Hymns, 1960; contbr of articles to num profl jrnls. *Memberships:* Pres, Contact Grp for Medieval Philology, Nat Fund for Scientific Rsch; Former Pres, Univ of Liege Ctr for Medieval Philology; Corresp Mbr, Acad of Messina; New Chaucer Soc; ISAS; Arthurian Soc. *Hobbies:* Music, Cooking, Gardening. *Address:* Boulevard Frere-Orban, 35A, bte 091, B-4000 Liege, Belgium. 52, 154.

MESKIN Kinl Petrov, b. 23 May 1943, Asenovo, Pleven, Bulgaria. Sculptor. m. Maria Dimitrova Koeva, 28 Jan 1968, 2 d. *Education:* Graduate Gymnasium, 1961; Fine Arts, Univ Velico Turnovo, 1965-70; Speciality Sculpture. *Appointments:* Expert of Culture Sect of Town of Pleven, 1971-75; Curator at Ilia Beshcou Art Gall in Pleven, Sculpture Sect, 1975-84; Mgr, Pleven Art Gall-Collect Gift by Prof Ruseu. *Creative Works:* Works mainly in stone in the field of portret, figured, monumental- decorative and small plastic art. Homage, coloured marble, 1986; Mystery, Head in coloured marble, 1987; Ecology, torso of man, coloured marble, 1988; The Truth, head in coloured marble, 1989; Survival, coloured marble, Sofia, Bulgaria, 1990; A Head III, coloured marble, Essen, Germany, 1990; Torso of a Woman, coloured marble, Belgium, 1991. *Membership:* Bulgarian Artists Union. *Honours:* In Regional and National Exhibitions in Bulgaria, 1971-92; Representative Exhibitions of Bulgarian Art in foreign parts; International Symposia of Sculpture: Germany 1981, Bulgaria 1983, Czechoslovakia 1988. *Hobby:* Travel. *Address:* Storgozia 60-A- 15, Pleven 5802, Bulgaria.

MESSENGER Michael, b. 30 Dec 1936, Hove, England. Co Libn and Arts Off, Hereford and Worcester Co Coun. m. Inge Nicholson, 16 July 1960. *Education:* Brighton Grammar Schl; Fellowship of Lib Assn, 1965. *Appointments:* Borough Libn and Curator, Shrewsbury, 1965-74; Asst Co Libn, Shropshire, 1974-76; Dpty Co Libn, Glos Co Coun, 1976-84. *Creative Works:* 6 plays; 2 maj ceramic catalogues; num articles on ceramics, music and libs. *Memberships:* Lib Assn; Soc of Co Libns, Hon Sec; Fellow RSA; Lib Info Servs Coun. *Hobbies:* Music, particularly Opera, Writing, Engl Ceramics, Pvte Press Books. *Address:* County Hall, Spetchley Road, Worcester, WR5, England.

METDEPENNINGHEN Carlos Maurits Walter, b. 13 May 1935, Ghent, Belgium. MD, Radiologist. m. Claudine Vanderheyde, 30 July 1960, 2 s, 3 d. *Education:* MD, State Univ, Ghent, 1961; Postgrad: Inst Tropical Med, Antwerp, 1962; Radiology, State Univ, Ghent, 1963-66. *Appointments:* Off, Army Med Serv, 1954-75 in Belgium and Germany; Lt Col, Army; Radiologist, St Camillus Clin, Antwerp, 1969-; Chmn, Med Bd of Fusion- Hosp St Augustinus-St Bavo-St Camillus. *Contributions to :* articles to profl radiological jrnls; Book: Genealogie metten Penninghen, 1987; Articles in Genealogical jrnls. *Memberships:* Royal Belgian Soc for Radiology; Profl Union of Radiologists; Admission Bd for Radiologists of Min of Hlth. *Honours:* Named Officer of the Crown Order, 1980; Named Officer of the Leopold Order, 1983. *Hobbies:* Genealogy, Family Hist. *Address:* Magdalena Vermeeschlaan 19, B-2540 Hove, Belgium. 52.

METZLER Paul Raymond, b. 19 Sept 1949, St Louis, Missouri, USA. Cons, Constrn Quality Control. m. (1) Barbara Mary Dolan, 18 May 1974, div 1985, (2) Roxy Susan Clark, 20 Dec 1987, 1 s, 2 d. *Education:* BS Elec Engrng, Univ MO at Rolla, 1973. *Appointments:* Sr Elec Engr, N L Inds, Titanium Pigment Div, 1974-76; Sr Elec Engr, Kennecott Corp, Carborundum Environmental Systems Div, 1976-81; Instrument and Control Engr, Chem Separation Corp, 1981-82; Cons Engr, 1982-84; Cons, 1989-, PM Engrng Assocs; Sr Elec Engr, Reynolds Elec & Engrng Co, 1983-88; Quality Control Engr, C R Fedrick Inc, 1988-89; Vice-Pres, Pacific Rim Consulting Inspection Corp, 1991-92. *Memberships:* Illuminating Engrng Soc of N America; Instrument Soc of America; Nat Soc Profl Engrs; Hawaii Soc Profl Engrs; Silver State Computer Users Grp, VP 1984-86, Libn 1986-88; Life Membr Brotherhood of St Andrew, Inc; IBA Life Fellow. *Honours:* Profl Engrng Registration, State of TN, 1982; Elec Engr; Profl Engrng Registration, State of NV, 1988; Elec Engr-Power. *Hobbies:* Automobiles, Off-rd Driving, Home Computers, Railroads. *Address:* 7215 SW Oxford Avenue, Lawton, OK 73505-7434, USA. 9.

MEWES Dieter, b. 18 Dec 1940, Berlin, Germany. Prof at Univ of Hannover, Germany. m. Hannelore, 21 July 1969, 1 s, 2 d. *Education:* Dip Engr 1966, Dr Ing 1970, Habil 1972, Inst of Process Engrng, Tech Univ of Berlin. *Appointments:* Degussa AG, Frankfurt, 1973-82; Degussa Antwerp, Belgium, 1978; VP, Engrng, Degussa, Mobile, AL, USA. 1979-81; Dir, Engrng Rsch, Degussa, Frankfurt, 1981-82; Prof, Process Engrng, Univ Hannover, 1982-. *Publications:* 2 books, more than 80 publs. *Memberships:* VDI; Dechema; AIChE; German Rheological Soc. *Honour:* Studienstiftung des Deutschen Volkes, 1963. *Hobbies:* Rowing (German Championship, Double Twin 1965), Skiing. *Address:* Brennenhorst 1, D-3012 Langenhagen, Germany.

MEWS Douglas Kelson, b. 22 Sept 1918, St Johns, Newfoundland. Composer. m. Constantia Radius, 27 Aug 1947, 2 s, 1 d. *Education:* United Ch Coll, 1926-34, Mem Univ, 1934-36, St Johns, Nfld; B.Mus London, 1939; D.Mus London, 1961; FRCO, 1938; FTCL, 1956. *Appointments:* Prof and Examniner, TCL, UK, 1946-63; Lectr, Colchester Tech Coll, 1963-68; Sr Lectr, Assoc Prof, Univ of Auckland, NZ, 1969-84; Dir of Music, St Patrick's Cathedral, Auckland, 1970-82. *Creative Works:* Choral: Ghosts, Fire, Water; The May Magnificat; The Circle of a Girl's Arm; Melodies of Passion and Dispassion, cello; Tangi Pohutu, flute; Concerto (T S Eliot) for two pianos and orch; Suite Aotea, accordian; Japan Physical, song cycle soprano; The Kiss, Passover opera; The Cloud on the Mountain, oratorio; Introduction to Harmony, textbook; Liturgical Music. *Honours:* Missa Brevis International Competitions, 1975, 76; Papal Knighthood of St Gregory, 1990. *Hobbies:* Model Railways, Meccano. *Address:* 5 Remuera Gardens, Auckland 5, New Zealand. 4.

MEYER Fritjof, b. 21 May 1932, Magdeburg, Germany. Sr Ed Der Spiegel. m. Brigitte Meyer-Schmildan, 1 Oct 1966. *Education:* Matr.Dom- und Kloster Gymnasium Magdeburg, 1949; Dip, Deutsche Hochschule fur Politik, Berlin, 1955; Dip, Osteuropa Institut, Berlin, 1964; Dip, Otto-Suhr-Institut, Berlin, 1966; Dip, Verwaltung Akademie, 1966. *Appointments:* Factory Worker, 1950-55; Referee Senate Berlin, 1955-62; Asst, Freie Universitat Berlin, 1964-66; Ed, Der Spiegel, Hamburg, 1966-. *Publications:* China- Aufstieg und Fall der Vererbande, 1981; Weltmacht im Abstiel- Der Nie - der Gang der Sowjetunion, 1984; Nach Dem Sturm Erhebt Sich Der Gebeugte Bambus: China im Umbruch, 1987; Die Katastrophe des Kohmunismus Von Marx bis Gorbatschow, 1991; Interviews w Gromyko, Gorbatschow, Jelzin, Krawtschuk, Walesa, Ceausescu, Hua Guo-Feng, Sihanouk, Lukacz, Brandt; about 100 cover stories in der Spiegel. *Hobbies:* Travelling, Reading, Collecting. *Address:* Grosshansdorf, Never Achterkamp 48, Germany.

MEYER Hans Henrik Hoven, b. 13 Mar 1950, Skibet, Denmark. Cons. m. Karin, 12 May 1977, 2 s, 1 d. *Education:* MSc, Chem Engrng, Technological Univ of Denmark, 1974. *Appointments:* Dev Engr, Danish Sugar Corp, 1975-78; Mgr, Polyester Yarn Dev, Div Hoechst A G, 1978-84; Mgr, Protein Prods, Grindsted A/S, 1984-91; Cons, Biotechnological Inst, 1991-. *Creative Works:* Patents: Flexible Dye Spring, Water Binding Pork Protein, Injectable Water Binding Pork Protein. *Hobbies:* Music, Pol, Science. *Address:* Farravej 31, DK-8464 Galten, Denmark. 52.

MEYER Harvey Kessler, b. 6 Feb 1914, Carlisle, Pennsylvania, USA. Ret'd Acad Admnstr. m. Jessie Hamm, 22 Feb 1935, 2 s, 1 d. *Education:* BA, Berea Coll, KY, 1936; MA, Eastern KY Univ, 1942; EdD, Univ FL, 1951. *Appointments:* USNR, 1943-46; Tchr, Prin, Schls in FL; Assoc Prof, Univ FL, Gainesville, 1948-65; Dir, IAVE, Repub Nicaragua, 1955-57; Assoc Dean, Acad Affairs, FL Atlantic Univ, 1965-68; Prof, FL Atlantic Univ, 1968-73. *Publications:* Technical Education in Nicaragua, 1957; Historical Dictionary of Nicaragua, 1972; Historical Dictionary of Honduras, 1976, 92. *Memberships:* Rotary Club, Richmond, KY; FL Dist

Moravian Ch, Pres, 1970-73; Melrose Lib Assn, FL, Pres, 1983-89; Phi Kappa Phi; Phi Delta Kappa; Off Club, Jacksonville, Fl. *Honours:* Laureate Member and Trustee, Epsilon Pi Tau, 1950s; Distinguished Alumnus, Berea College, 1986. *Hobbies:* Boating, Arch, Pistol Shooting, Furniture Design, Bldg. *Address:* 8146 Alderman Road, Melrose, FL 32666, USA. 13, 15, 81, 176.

MEYER Richard Jules, b. 15 June 1942, Sierentz, France. Psych. m. Veronique Fischer, 2 s, 3 d. *Education:* MD Psych, 1975; PhD Sociology and Ethnology, 1978. *Appointments:* Interne CHU Strasbourg, 1971-75; Asst in Med, Univ Lausanne, 1973; Psych Liberal, 1975-. *Publications:* Le Corps Aussi, 1982; Portrait de Groupe avec Psychiatre, 1984; Les Therapies Corporelles, 1986; La Somatologie, 1991; Chief Ed, Somatotherapies, French and Engl issues; Chmn 1st and 3rd Int Congress on Somatotherapy. *Memberships:* Pres, Fondateur de l'innovation Psychiatrique; Pres, Fondateur de l'association Internationale de Somatotherapie. *Address:* 20 Place des Halles, Tour Europe, 67000 Strasbourg, France. 52.

MEYER Zygmunt, b. 9 May 1944, Swornegacie, Poland. Prof of Civ Engrng. m. Maria Telega, 12 Aug 1967, 1 s. *Education:* MSc, Civ Engrng, 1968, PhD 1974, Tech Univ Szczecin; Dr Habil, Tech Univ Gdansk, 1983; Scientific Title of State Prof, Conferred by Pres of Poland. *Appointments:* Tech Univ of Szczecin, Jr Asst 1968, Lectr, Sr Lectr, 1969-84; Univ of London, Imperial Coll, 1976-77; Prof of Civ Engrng, 1990-. *Publications:* Vertical Circulation Reservoir Due to Selective Withdrawal, 1981; Introduction to Sediment Transport, 1982; Encyclopedia of Fluid Mechanics, Vol.2 Chapt 23, 1986; Momentum and Mass Exchange in Stratfield Flows, proceddings of The Polish Academy of Science, Warsaw, 1991. *Memberships:* Int Assn for Hydraulic Rsch, Delff, The Netherlands; Polish Acad of Science, Sect of Soil Mechs and Fundaments; Szczecin Scientific Soc. *Honour:* Polonia Restituta, Bachelor Class. *Hobby:* Mod Hist. *Address:* Bartnicza St 26/4, 71-487 Szczecin, Poland.

MEZNARIC Sulvija, b. 22 May 1939, Zagreb, Yugoslavia. Sr Rsch Fellow. *Education:* BA, I Gymnasium, Zagreb, 1958; MA, Fac of Law, Zagreb, 1964; PhD, Fac of Pol Sciences and Sociology, Ljubljana, 1984. *Appointments:* Inst for Soc Rsch, Zagreb, 1965-68; Conf for Women, 1969-72; Univ of Ljubljana, FSPN, 1973-81; Trade Unions of Slovenia, 1981-83; Unemployed, 1983-86; Univ Zagreb, 1987-. *Publications:* Slovenia as an Immigrant Society, 1982; Bosnians, Where do Slovenes Go On Sundays, 1986; Space Instead of Time: Migration in Yugoslavia, 1991. *Memberships:* Int Sociological Assn; Wilson Ctr Alumni; Dem Oppositional Forum, Zagreb, Coord. *Hobbies:* Sports, Pets, Rock Music, Blues. *Address:* Mestni TRG 17, Ljubljana, Slovenia 61000, Yugoslavia. 52.

MGBAJAH Francis Onwubiko, b. 21 July 1939, Umunachi Obowu, Nigeria. Educl Admnstr (Registrar). m. 14 June 1975, 2 s, 2 d. *Education:* BSc (Hons), Sociology, Anthropology, Univ of Nigeria, Nsukka. *Appointments:* Tchr, Second Schls, 1978-79; Supvsr of Schls at Schl Bd, 1979; Sr Asst Registrar, Coll of Educ, Dpty Registrar, Coll of Educ, 1980-88; Registrar, 1988-. *Publication:* Chmn of Obowu Hist Comm that produced the book: Obowu--The Igbo Heartland People, 1983-86. *Memberships:* Assoc Mbr, Nigerian Inst of Mgmt; Chmn, Obowu Dev Assn (Federated) Caretaker Comm, 1986-87; Chmn, Ehunachi Second Schl Bd of Govs, 1984-86. *Honour:* Given Honorary Chieftaincy Title by the Ehume Umunachi Autonomous Community, Obowu on 29 December 1990. *Hobbies:* Choral Singing, Chess Playing, Reading. *Address:* Michael Okpara College of Agriculture, Umuagwo Ohaji, PMB 1472, Owerri, Nigeria.

MI Jiarong, b. 13 Aug 1930, Tianjin, People's Republic of China. Prof, Stratigraphy, Palaeontology, Paleobotany and Paleogeography. m. Wen Mingzhu, 30 Sept 1963, 2 d. *Education:* Nankai Univ; Qinghua Univ, 1949-52. *Appointments:* Changchun Univ of Earth Science, 1952-. Worked in Albania to rsch into the stratigraphy of the ophiolite suite, 1971-74. *Publications:* Late Triassic Stratigraphy, Paleontology and Paleography of the Northern Part of the Circum-Pacific belt, China; Early Carboniferous Fossil Plants from Benxi, Liaoning. *Memberships:* Mbr of Coun, Chinese Inst of Palaeontology; V-Chmn of Coun, Chinese Br of Paleobotany. *Hobbies:* Music appreciation, Dancing. *Address:* Dept of Geology, Changchun University of Earth Science, Changchun, 130061, Jilin, China.

MICHAEL Milad Ishak, b. 15 Jan 1930, Luxor, Egypt. Emeritus Prof of Embryology, Dept Zoology, Fac of Science, Alexandria Univ, Egypt. m. Hilda Maurice Hanna, 20 Sept 1964, 1 s, 1 d. *Education:* BSc, Hons, Univ Cairo, 1949; MSc, Embryology, 1953, PhD, Embryology, 1956, Univ of Alexandria. *Appointments:* Demonstrator of Zoology, 1949, Lectr of Zoology, 1958, Asst Prof of Zoology, 1965, Prof of Zoology, 1972, Alexandria Univ; Hd, Dept of Zoology, 1975-81; V-Dean for Grad Studies and Rsch, 1981-83, 1986-90. *Publications:* author or co-author of 60 profl publs in jrnls of over 10 countries. *Memberships:* Zoology Soc of Egypt; Int Soc for Developmental Biologists; European Developmental Biology Org, Bd Mbr 1976-; American Soc for Zoologists; AAAS; Herpetological Soc of OH; Societe Batrachologique de France; Chmn, Gen Promotion Comm for Profs of Zoology in Egyptian Univs; Mng Ed, Bulletin of Fac of Science, Alexandria Univ, 1981-83, 1986-90; Mbr, Ed Bd, Jrnl of Egyptian German Soc of Zoology, 1989-. *Honours:* Honour of Contribution in XXI Colloquium Science Faculty, Medical University Carolinae, Prague, 1976; Certificate of Honour, Faculty of Science, Alexandria University, 1988; Honorary Member Marcus Singer Society, 1982-. *Hobbies:* Reading, Walking, Photography, Visiting Museums. *Address:* 24 Dr Abdul Hameed Badawy Street, Sooter, Alexandria, Egypt. 152.

MICHAELIS Walfried, b. 8 Mar 1931, Medebach-Brilon, Germany. Prof Univ Hamburg; Dir, Inst of Phys GKSS Rsch Ctr. m. Christina, 6 Apr 1990, 1 d. *Education:* Univ Heidelberg, 1951-55; Univ Gottingen, 1955-58; Dip, Max-Planck Inst, 1958; PhD, Univ Karlsruhe Nuclear Rsch Ctr, 1962; Habil, Univ Frankfurt, 1974. *Appointments:* Grp Ldr, Nuclear Rsch Ctr, Karlsruhe, 1958; Inst of Neutron Phys and Reactor Techn; Dpty Dir, Inst of Applied Nuclear Phys, 1963; Dir, Inst of Phys, GKSS Rsch Ctr, 1973. *Publications:* Over 220 scientific publs in fission phys, nuclear spectroscopy, nuclear safeguards, electronics, laser phys, laser remote sensing, trace analytical chem, rsch on aquatic and forest ecosystems; Book: Estuarine Water Quality Management. *Memberships:* Exec Bd, Sonderforschungsbereich 327, Hamburg; Ed Bd, Nuclear Geophys; mbr sev expert and cons comms. *Hobbies:* Painting, Classical Music. *Address:* Elbring 14, D-2105 Seevetal- Bullenhausen 2, Germany. 1

MICHAELS Leslie, b. 24 July 1925, London, England. Prof of Pathology. m. Edith Waldstein, 21 Sept 1951, 2 d. *Education:* Westminster Med Schl, London, MB, BS, 1949; MD, 1960; FRCPath. *Appointments:* Trng in Pathology, London, Bristol, Manchester, 1950-59; NY, 1959-61; N Ont, Can, 1961-70; Prof of Pathology, ENT, London, 1970-90; Emeritus Prof, Univ of London. *Publications:* Pathology of the Larynx, 1984; Ear, Nose and Throat Histopathology, 1987; sev books and chapts. *Hobbies:* Walking, Music. *Address:* Romany Ridge, Hillbrow Road, Bromley, Kent BR1 4JL, England. 1.

MICHAILOVA Albena, b, 9 July 1959, Plovdiv, Bulgaria. Artist. m. 17 Aug 1988, 1 d. *Education:* Graphics, Schl of Fine Arts, Plovdiv, 1974-78; Graphics Maj, Acad of Fine Art, Sofia, 1978-84. *Appointments:* Lectr: Schl of Fine Arts, Plovdiv, 1985; Second Schls in Plovdid, 1986-87; The Acraboff Gall Art Schl, 1990-91. *Creative Works:* 11 Individual Exhibs iin Plovdiv,

Sofia, Tunis, Leipzig; Biennals in Gabrovo, Tuzla, Liubliana, N Bistritsa, Rodom, Hungary, Spain and Varna, 1987-91. *Memberships:* The Edge Art Grp; Art in Action Assn; The Young Artists Club; Bulgarian Artists Union. *Honours:* Varna Biennal, 1989, 91; Group Exhibition of Bulgarian Young Artists, 1991. *Hobbies:* Yachting, Trips, Antique Collecting. *Address:* 21 Trakia Str, 4000 Plovdiv, Bulgaria.

MICHALSKA Anna, b. 3 June 1940, Warsaw, Poland. Prof of Int Law. *Education:* LLM 1962, LLD 1967, Assoc Prof 1974, Prof of Law 1986, Fac of Law, Poznan Univ. *Appointments:* Dept of the Theory of Law, 1962-80; Dept of Int Law, 1980-92. *Publications:* International Covenants on Human Rights and the Fundamental Human Rights in the National Legal Order, 1975; Human Rights in the International Law, 1982 (both in Polish). *Membership:* Polish Helsinki Comm. *Hobbies:* Reading; Tourism. *Address:* Ogrodowa 13/4, 61-821 Poznan, Poland. 151.

MICHEL-MICHOT Paulette Georgette, b. 22 Apr 1932, Vierset-Barse, Belgium. Prof of Engl Lit, Univ of Liege, Belgium. m. Henri Michel 28 Apr 1962, dec 1976, 1 s. *Education:* Licence en philologie germanique, Univ Liege; Univ of Groningen, 1956; Univ of Nottingham, England, 1960-61; PhD, Univ Liege, 1968. *Appointments:* Grammar Schl Tchr of Engl: Spa 1956-57, Malmedy 1957-60; Asst 1961-70, Chef de travaux 1970-77, Lectr 1977-80, Prof of Engl Lit 1988-, Univ Liege. *Publications:* William Sansom: A Critical Assessment, 1971; articles on 19th and 20th century novel and short fiction. *Contributions to:* Annual Bibliography of English Language and Literature, 1968-87, Continental Ed, Studies in Short Fiction. *Memberships:* Assn Britannique, Sec 1961-71; Belgian Assn of Anglicists in Higher Educ; ESSE; European Assn for Commonwealth Lit; Societe des anglicistes de l'Enseignement Superieur; Modern Humanities Rsch Assn, GB. *Hobbies:* Music, Gardening, Sports (swimming, tennis), Cinema, Painting. *Address:* 113 Rue de la Charrette, B 4130 Tilff, Belgium.

MICHELBERGER Pal, b. 4 Feb 1930, Vecses, Hungary. Prof Rector of Tech Univ of Budapest. m. Ilona Torma, 21 Sept 1957, 1 s, 1 d. *Education:* MSc, Mech Engrng, Tech Univ of Budapest, 1952; PhD 1960, DSc 1970. *Appointments:* Design Engr, Chief Design, Tech Dir, 1956-68, Ikarus Bus and Coach Factory; Prof, Tech Univ of Budapest, 1968, Rector 1990-92. *Publications:* Over 200 publs; over 100 confs. *Memberships:* Corresp Mbr, Hungarian Acad of Science, 1982; Mbr Hungarian Acad of Science, 1990. *Honour:* FISITA Medal 1978. *Hobbies:* Lit, Hist. *Address:* Muegyetem rkp. 3, H-1111 Budapest, Hungary.

MICHELMANN Hans J, b. 22 Feb 1944, Osterburg, Germany. Prof of Pol Studies, Hd of Dept of Pol Studies. m. Martha Johanna S, 25 Nov 1967. *Education:* BA, Univ Alta, 1970; PhD, IN Univ, 1975. *Appointments:* Univ of MO, St Louis, 1975-77; Univ of Sask, 1977-. *Publications:* Organizational Effectiveness in a Multinational Bureaucracy, 1978; Co-Ed and Co-author: Doing Business with Europe, 1989; Federalism and International Relations, 1990; The Political Economy of Agricultural Trade and Policy, 1990. *Memberships:* Dir Gen, Can Coun for European Affairs; Co-Ed, Jrnl of European Integration; Mbr sev profl and pol science assns. *Honours:* Woodrow Wilson Fellow, 1970-71; Can Coun Fellow, 1971-75; 5 Social Science and Humanities Rsch Coun of Can Rsch Grants. *Hobbies:* Underwater Photography, Scuba Diving, Photography, Reading. *Address:* Department of Political Studies, University of Saskatchewan, Saskatoon, Saskatchewan, Canada S7N OWO. 142.

MICHIE Donald, b. 11 Nov 1923, Rangoon, Burma, Scientific Worker. m. (1) Zena Margaret Davis, 1948, 1s, (2) Anne McLaren, 1952, 1s. 1d. (3) Jean Elizabeth Hayes, 1 Mar 1971. *Education:* Rugby Schl, 1937-42; Balliol Coll (Schl), Oxford, 1945-52, MA, Anatomy and

Physiology; DPhil, Genetics; DSc (Oxon) in Biological Sciences, 1971. *Appointments:* Rsch Assoc, Univ London, 1952-58; Sr Lectr, Rdr in Surg Science, 1958-65, Dir, Expmtl Programming Unit, 1965-73, Personal Chair of Machine Intelligence, 1967-84, Dir, Machine Intelligence Rsch Unit, 1973-84, Prof Emeritus of Machine Intelligence, 1984-, Univ of Edinburgh; Fndr and First Exec Dir, 1983-84, Dir of Rsch, 1984-86, Chief Scientist, 1986-, Turing Inst. *Publications:* On Machine Intelligence; Machine Intelligence and Related Topics; The Creative Computer; Ed-in-Chief, Machine Intelligence, 1967-. *Memberships:* Scientific Fellow, London Zoological Soc; Fellow, Royal Soc of Edinburgh; Fellow, Brit Computer Soc; Fellow, American Assn for Artificial Intelligence. *Honours:* Pioneer Award, with A McLaren, of the International Embryo Transfer Society; Hon DSc, Council for National Academic Awards for contributions to Artificial Intelligence, 1991; Hon DSc, Salford University, for contributions to Artificial Intelligence, 1992. *Hobbies:* Chess, Travel. *Address:* 6 Inveralmond Grove, Edinburgh, EH4 6RA, Scotland. 1, 52.

MICHIELSEN Jean-Pierre, b. 29 Jan 1933, Antwerp, Belgium. Urologist. m. Margareta Muls, 17 July 1957, 2 d. *Education:* KUL MD, Institut de Medecine Tropicale, Antwerp, 1957; Nymegen, Netherlands, Doct Thesis, 1968. *Appointments:* Physn, Compagnie BCK, Lubumbashi, 1957-60; Specialist in Urology at Antwerp, Roermond's Gravenhage and Nymegen, 1960-66; Serv Chief, St Camille and St Augustin Hosp, Antwerp, 1966- *Contributions to:* profl jrnls; Co-author, Uncommon case report: Primary actinomycosis of the urinary bladder (in publ); co-author: The use of warmen cold glycine during transurethal prostatic surgery (in publ). *Memberships:* Rotary Club Antwerpen-Park, Past Pres; Belgische Vereniging voor Urologie, Past Pres; Nederlandse Vereniging voor Urologie, Societe Belge d'Urologie and administrator, Collegium Chirurgicum Belgium. *Hobbies:* Hunting, Photography, Walking. *Address:* Bosmmanslei, 19a, 2018 Antwerp, Belgium. 43, 52.

MICHNA Leon, b. 2 July 1954, Iwonicz Zorój, Poland. Artist, Easel and Wall Painting. m. Ewa Sokołowska, 28 Aug 1976, 1 s, 1 d. *Education:* Acad of Fine Arts, Warsaw, 1978-83; MA, Painting, Classes Prof Tadeusz Dominik, Prof Ryszard Wojciechowski. *Appointment:* Tchr, Acad in Warsaw, 1988-. *Creative Works:* Individual Exhibs in Warsaw, Jaslo, Stalowa Wola, Krosno, Tarnów, Biała Podlaska, Siedlce, Ciechanów, Przemyśl, Stichting de Voorst Eefde Holand, 1984-92; Grp Exhibs in Poland from 1984 to the present. *Honours:* Schlrship Min of Art Culture, 1984-85; Awards in Competition II Religion Art Exhibition, 1990. *Hobbies:* Touring, Preserving Objects of Art. *Address:* 6 Kenara Street, 38-440 Iwonicz Zdrój, Poland.

MICHNIEWICZ Marian, b. 5 Dec 1922, Wilno, Poland. Prof of Plant Physiology. m. Zofia Stankiewicz, 31 Aug 1946, 1 s, 1 d. *Education:* Univ M Curie Skesdowska, MSc, Bot, 1948, PhD, Natural Science, 1951, PhD, Biol, 1956. *Appointments:* Asst, Univ M Curie Skesdowska, 1946-53; Asst Prof 1955-64, Full Prof 1964-, Univ N Copernicus; Dean of Fac of Biol, 1958- 61; Dir, Biol Inst, 1969-78. *Publications:* Over 100 papers on hormonal regulation of plant growth and dev; Co-author: Outline of Physiology of Scots Pine, 1969; Plant Physiology, 1977, 85. *Memberships:* Polish Botan Soc; Polish Copernicus Soc of Naturalists; Scientific Soc of Torun; Polish Soc of Biochem; Polish Acad. *Hobby:* Hist of 19th and 20th centuries, espec Polish-Lithuanian. *Address:* Copernicus University, Institute of Biology, Gagavina 9, 87-100 Torun, Poland. 52.

MICKIEWICZ Grazyna Anna, b. 21 Sept 1950, Poland. Scientific Worker. div. *Education:* Pharm Fac of Med Acad, Warsaw, 1973; Doct, Acad of Phys Educ, Warsaw, 1986; Postdoct studies, Inst of Environmental Stress, Univ of CA, Santa Barbara, USA, 1987. *Appointments:* Inst of Sports Med in Warsaw, Dept Clin Analysis, Dept

Antidoping Control, 1973-80; Inst of Sport, Dept Physiology, 1980-88; Hd, Dept of Ergonomics, Main Schl of Fire Fighting in Warsaw, 1988-91; Dept of Physiology, Inst of Sport, Warsaw, 1991-. *Publications:* Co-author, Limiting Factors of Physical Performance, 1976; The Physiological Aspects of Fatigue and Recovery in Training and Contest, 1982; Tests for Physiological Evaluation of Work Capacity of Judo Competitors, 1986. *Honours:* Bronze Cross of Awards, 1987. *Hobbies:* Hunting, Gardening. *Address:* Institute of Sport, ul Trylogii 2/16. 01-892 Warsaw, Poland.

MIDDLETON Stanley, b. 1 Aug 1919, Bulwell, Nottingham, England. Writer. m. 22 Dec 1951, 2 d. *Education:* Univ of Nottingham, BA Hons Engl, 1940, M.Ed, 1952. *Appointments:* Hd of Engl, High Pavement Coll, Nottingham, 1938-81; Judith E Wilson Vis Fellow, Emmanuel Coll, Cambridge, 1982-83. *Publications:* 31 novels: Harris's Requiem, 1960; A Serious Woman, 1961; Him They Compelled, 1964; The Golden Evening, 1968; Wages of Virtue, 1969; Cold Gradations, 1972; Holiday, 1974; Two Brothers, 1978; In a Strange Land, 1980; Blind Understanding, 1982; Entry Into Jerusalem, 1983; Valley of Decisions, 1985; An After Dinners Sleep, 1986; Recovery, 1988; Changes and Chances, 1990; Beginning to End, 1991; A Place to Stand, 1992. *Membership:* Fellow, PEN. *Honours:* Booker Prize with Nadine Gordimer, 1974; Hon MA, Nottingham University, 1975. *Hobbies:* Walking, Music, Watercolour Painting. *Address:* 42 Caledon Road, Sherwood, Nottingham NG5 2NG, England. 1.

MIDHA Kamal K, b. 26 Oct 1941, India. Prof of Pharm. 1 s, 1 d. *Education:* B.Pharm 1964, M.Pharm 1966, Univ of Saugar, India; PhD, Univ Alta, Can, 1969; DSc, Univ Sask, 1985. *Appointments:* Instr, Fac of Pharm, 1969-71; Lectr, Dept Pharmacology, 1970-71, Univ of Alta; Rsch Scientist, Hlth Protection Br, Ottawa, 1973-79; Prof of Pharm, Univ Sask, 1979-; Adjunct Prof, Dept Psych, Univ Sask, 1985-; Co-Chief Psychopharmacology Unit, UCLA, 1986-; Vis Rsch Pharmacologist, UCLA, 1986-. *Memberships:* Chmn Bd, Pharm Sciences of Int Pharm Fedn, 1988-; Chmn, Pharm Sciences Comm for Med Rsch Coun of Can, 1984-88; Fellow. American Assn Pharm Scientists; Fellow, Chem Inst of Can; Fellow, Can Coll of Neuropsychopharmacology; Fellow, American Pharm Assn Acad of Pharm Rsch and Sciences. *Honours:* McNeil Research Award AFPC, 1984; Kolthoff Gold Medal Award in Analytical Chemistry, AAPS, 1989. *Address:* College of Pharmacy, University of Saskatchewan, Saskatoon, Saskatchewan S7N OWO, Canada.

MIELE Angelo, b. 21 Aug 1922, Formia, Italy. Educator, Researcher, Cons, Author. *Education:* D.Civ Engrng, Univ Rome, Italy, 1944; D.Aero Engrng, 1946. *Appointments:* Asst Prof, Poly Inst Bklyn, 1952-55; Prof, Purdue Univ, 1955-59; Dir, Astrodynamics, Boeing Scientific Rsch Labs, 1959-64; Prof, Aerospace Sciences, Math Sciences, Rice Univ, Houston, 1964-88; Foyt Family Prof Engrng, 1988-; Cons, Douglas Aircraft Co, 1956-58, Allison Div Gen Motors Corp, 1956-58, US Aviation Underwriters, 1987, Boeing Commercial Airplane Co, 1989. *Publications:* Flight Mechanics, 1962; Ed, Theory of Optimum Aerodynamic Shapes, 1965; Math Concepts and Methods in Science and Engineering, 1974-; Ed-in-Chief, Journal Optimization Theory and Applications, 1966-; Assoc Ed, Journal Astronautical Sciences, 1964; Applied Math and Computation, 1975-; Optimal Control Applications and Methods, 1979-; num rsch papers in aerospace engrng, windshear problems, hypervelocity flight, math programming, optimal control theory and computing methods. *Memberships:* Ed Bd, RAIRO Operations Rsch, 1990-; Mbr Advsry Bd, AIAA Educ Series, 1991-94; Pres, Italy in America Assn, 1966-68; Fellow AIAA, American Astronautical Soc, Franklin Inst; Int Acad Astronautics; Corresponding Member, Acad Sciences, Turin. *Honours:* Decorated Knight Commander Order of Merit, Italy, 1972; Levy Medal Franklin Institute of Philadelphia, 1974; Brouwer Award AAS, 1980; Schuck Award American Automatic Control Council, 1988;

AIAA Pendray Award, 1982; Mechanics anmd Control of Flight Award, 1982; Honorary Doctor of Science, Technicion - Israel Institute of Technology, 1992. *Address:* 3106 Kettering Drive, Houston, TX 77027, USA.

MIHALACHE Adrian Nicolae, b. 22 Oct 1948, Bucharest, Romania. Assoc Prof. m. Susanu Roxana, 2 Nov 1987, 1 d. *Education:* MSc, Electronics, 1971, PhD Reliability, 1979, Polytechnical Inst of Bucharest. *Appointments:* Asst Prof 1971-80, Lectr 1980-90, Assoc Prof 1990-, Polytechnical Inst of Bucharest, Dept of Electronics. *Publications:* Theoretical Reliability, 1983; Reliability Fundamentals, 1989; over 50 scientific papers and cultural essays. *Memberships:* IEEE Reliability Soc; Romanian Reliability Soc, VP 1990-; Romanian Scientists Assn. *Hobbies:* Art, Lit. *Address:* Bd m Kogalniceanu 61, Bucharest, Romania.

MIKALOW Alfred Alexander, Captain, b. 19 Jan 1921, New York City, USA. Marine Surveyor and Licensed Ships Master. m. Janice Mary, 1 Aug 1961, 2 s. *Education:* Rutgers Univ, NJ; MS, Univ CA, Berkeley, 1948; Lic Merchant Marine Capt; Cert Marine Insp. *Appointments:* Capt, Merchant Marine Off, Lt Cmdr, Salvage Off, WWII; Marine Surveyor; Dir, Coastal Schl of Deep Sea Diving, Oakland, CA; Marine Diving Contractor; Licensed Master of Vessels, Coastal Rschr; Designer of Diving Equipment inclng Mixed Gas Diving. *Creative Works:* Designer: One-Atmosphere Diving Suit, Remote Observation Vehicle, Semi-Dry Wet Submarine. Author: Fell's Guide to Sunken Treasure Shops of the World; The Knight from Maine; The Sea and I; Salvage. *Memberships:* Pres, Diver's Assn of America; Former Dir, Advsry Bd Mbr, Medic Alert Fndn; Res Offs Assn; Navy League; Assn of Diving Contractors; Diving Accident Network; Marine Technol Soc; CA Assn of Pvte Educators; Submarine Veterans of WWII; Pres, CA Assn of Marine Surveyors; Tail Hook Assn. *Honours:* Selected by People-to-People Citizens Ambassador Program to go to Russia with a diving and HBO Therapy-Technical Group as a diving technician, lecturing in Moscow, Minsk, Baku and Leningrad; Received 2 Purple Hearts and Silver Star, Combat, WWII. *Address:* 320-29th Avenue, Oakland, CA 94601, USA. 9, 22, 120, 129, 130, 139, 151, 179.

MIKESHIN Michael, b. 10 Dec 1955, Leningrad, USSR. Rschr in Philos and Hist of Science and Culture. m. Tatiana V Artem'eva, 29 Dec 1982, 2 s. *Education:* Dept of Phys, Leningrad Univ, 1973-79; PhD, USSR Cand of Philos Degree, 1986. *Appointments:* Rschr in Oceanography, 1979-85; Prof in Philos, 1985-89; Rschr, Inst for Hist of Science and Technol, S Petersburg, Russia, 1988-92. *Publication:* Mikhail Vorontsov, 1992. *Hobbies:* Cycling, Travelling, Toy Models. *Address:* 22-1-56 Prosveshchenia Prospect, S Petersburg 194358, Russia.

MIKHELSON Viktor Mikhailovich, b. 27 Jan 1935, Leningrad, USSR. Pres, V-Chief of Radiation Lab of Inst Cytology Acad Science, Leningrad. m. Irina Ivanovna Chizhevskaya, 4 Sept 1956, 2 s. *Education:* 1st Leningrad Med Inst, MS Med 1953-59, PhD Biology 1965, DS Biology 1981. *Appointments:* Chief of Hosp, Karelia, 1959-61; Graduate, Inst Cytology, Leningrad, 1961-66; Chief, Cytological Lab of Nat Ctr of Science, Havana, Cuba, 1966-68. *Publications:* Books in Russian: Radiation and Life, 1965; Magadan Baby-Mammoth, Ed, 1981; Hereditary Defects of DNA Repair in Human, 1981; DNA Repair Diseases, 1983; Oncogenetic Syndromes, 1989. *Memberships:* VP, Leningrad Soc of Radiation Biology; Mbr of Admin, Soviet Soc of Radiation Biology; Mbr of Admin, Soviet Soc of Radiation Biology; Mbr of Admin, Nat Coun of Radiation Biology of Acad of Science, USSR; Mbr Elefant Interest Grp, Detroit, USA. *Hobbies:* Zoological Collects (esp sea shells), Stamp Collections, Ancient Hist. *Address:* Fontanka Embankment 64, ap 4, Leningrad 191002, Russia.

MIKULAS Radek, b. 9 Jan 1964, Prague, Czechoslovakia. Geologist and Paleontologist. m. A Pospichalova, 13 June 1991. *Education:* RNDr, Geology, Charles Univ, Prague, 1987; Mil Serv, 1987-88; CSc, PhD. Inst of Geology, Czechoslovak Acad of Science, 1991. *Appointment:* Entrance at Inst of Geology as Specialist in Palaeontology. *Contributions to:* profl jrnls of over 17 publs. *Membership:* The Soc of Friends of the Nat Mus, Prague. *Hobbies:* Alpinism, Visit of Caucasus in 1987. *Address:* Jeseniova Street 93, 130 00 Praha 3. Czechoslovakia.

MILADINOVIC Dusan, b. 20 Feb 1924, Subotica, Yugoslavia. Conductor. m. Milica Miladinovic, 6 July 1947, 1 s. *Education:* BA, Opera and Concert Singing, Music Acad, Univ of Belgrade, 1948; Depts for Conducting and Composing, 1953. *Appointments:* Rehearser, 1943, Conductor, 1949-, Leading Conductor, 1964-84, Hd of Belgrade Opera House, 1969-73; Prof, Music Acad in Belgrade, 1957-62; Hd of Opera House in Novi Sad, 1965-68. *Creative Works:* A symph for a large orch, ballet Deserted, theatre music, pieces for choir and solo singers. *Memberships:* Serbian Assn of Music Artists; Pres, Serbian Assn of Music Artists, 1983-89. *Honours:* Medal for Working Merits with Gold Wreath, 1969; Gold Lyra Great Award of Music Artists Association of Yugoslavia, 1980; Great Medallion of National Theatre in Belgrade for Outstanding Artist, 1984; 7 Annual Awards of National Theatre, Gold Medallion of Serbian Amateur Organization, 1985; Order of St Sava, first class Serbian Orthodox Church, 1991. *Hobbies:* Cynology, Hunting. *Address:* Georgio Dimitrova 39, 11000 Belgrade, Serbia, Yugoslavia.

MILBURN Anthony, b. 3 Aug 1942, Halifax, England. Exec Dir. m. Julia Margaret Weeden, 6 June 1983, 1 s, 1 d. *Education:* B.Tech, Hons, Civ Engrng, Univ Bradford, 1968; MSc, Civ Engrng, Univ Birmingham, 1972. *Appointments:* Articled Pupil, Boro of Brighouse, 1958-62; Asst Engr, City of Leeds, 1962-64; Undergraduate, Univ Bradford, 1964-68; Asst Engr, Wye River Auth, 1968-70; Rsch Assoc, Univ Birmingham, 1970-72; Trng Mgr, Nat Water Coun, 1972-80; Exec Dir, Int Assn on Water Quality, 1981-. *Publication:* Ed, Water Pollution Research and Control, 1982. *Memberships:* Instn of Civ Engrs; Instn of Water and Environmental Mgmt; Inst of Dirs; Mbr and Asst to Court of Guild of Water Conservators; Governor, St Matthews School, Surbiton; Mbr, Nominating Cttee for Stockholm Water Prize; VP, COWAR. *Hobbies:* Sailing, Modern Jazz, Pols, Philos. *Address:* 34 Church Meadow, Long Ditton, Surrey KT6 5EW, England.

MILEVA Jeni, b. 18 Sept 1935, Sofia, Bulgaria. Physn. m. Shinkov Dimiter, 17 Sept 1961, 1 s. *Education:* Med, Fac of Med, Sofia, 1953- 59; Graduated Hons, 1959; Specialist in Internal Med (Internal Diseases), 1965; Specialist in Clin Biochem, 1970; PhD, 1970; MD, 1988, Specialist in Clin Allergology, 1990. *Appointments:* GP 1960-64; Med Fac, Sofia, 1964-66; Rsch Assoc, Allergology, Med Acad, 1966-80; Asst Prof and Hd of Clin of Allergy, Med Acad, Sofia, 1980-90; Prof and Hd of Chair of Allergology, Med Acad, 1990. *Publications:* On Some Problems of the Histamine Metabolism in Patients with Asthma, 1970. *Contributions to:* profl jrnls; some 150 rsch works. *Memberships:* Mbr and VP Med Scientific Soc of Internal Diseases, Bulgaria; Mbr and Hd of Scientific Soc of Allergology, Bulgaria; USB. *Hobbies:* Collection of decorative plates from all over the world, Theatre, Lit. *Address:* Chair of Allergology, Medical Academy, G. Sofiiskie 1, 1431 Sofia, Bulgaria.

MILJAN Toivo, b. 14 Nov 1938, Tallinn, Estonia. Prof of Pol Science. m. Aina Anna, 30 Oct 1962, 2 s. *Education:* BA, Hons 1962, MA 1963, Univ Toronto; PhD, Univ London, 1976. *Appointments:* Prof, Wilfrid Laurier Univ, 1980-; Joined WLU, 1963; Rsch Off, Royal Commn on Bilingualism and Biculturalism, 1965-67; Co-Dir, Ctr on For Policy and Federalism; Vis Prof, Helsinki, 1977, 87; Adjunct Prof, Pol Science, Swedish

Schl of Bus and Econ, Helsinki, 1988-; Cons, UN Inst on Trng and Rsch; Ctr des Estudos Econ y Soc del Tercer Mundo, Mexico, 1979-81; Chmn of Bd, FRC Composites Ltd; Tapecrete Ltd; Dir, Tartu Inst; Fndng Dir, K-B Br, CIIA; Waterloo Br UNAC. *Publications:* Bilingualism in Finland, Vol 1 1966, Vol II 1967; The Reluctant Europeans, 1977; Food and Agriculture in Global Perspective, 1980, Ed: Culure and Legitimacy, 1982; Energy in the Eighties, 1984; L'Energie et les annes 80, 1985; The Political Economy of North-South Relations, 1987; co-ed, Unity in Diversity, 1980. *Memberships:* Can Assn Univ Tchrs; Can Pol Science Assn; Assn for Advancement of Baltic Studies; Deutscher Gesellschaft f Kan Stud; Korp ! Club; Rotalio, Toronto, NY, Stockholm, Sydney. *Hobbies:* Swimming, Hunting. *Address:* 46 Combermere Crescent, Waterloo, Ontario, Canada N2L 5B1. 142.

MILLAN Bruce, b. 5 Oct 1927, Dundee, Scotland. Politician. m. Gwendoline May Fairey, 22 Aug 1953, 1 s, 1 d. *Appointments:* Chartered Acct, 1950-59; MP, Glasgow Craigton, 1959-83, Glasgow Goven, 1983-88; Under- Sec of State for Def for the RAF, 1964-66; Jt Party Under-Sec of State for Scotland, 1966-70; Min of State for Scotland, 1974-76; Sec of State for Scotland, 1976-79; Privy Councillor, 1975; Opposition Spokesman on Scotland, 1979-83; European Commissioner, 1989- . *Membership:* Inst of Chartered Accts (Scotland). *Honours:* Hon.LLD. University of Dundee, 1989; Hon Fellow, Paisley University, 1991; Hon. D.Litt, Heriot-Watt University, 1991. *Address:* Commission of the European Communities, Rue de la Loi 200, B- 1049 Brussels, Belgium.

MILLER Bonnie Sewell, b. 24 July 1932, Kentucky, United States of America. Mktng Dir. m. (1) William G Tournado Jr, 5 Nov 1950 (2) Bruce G Miller, 15 Nov 1983, 1 s, 2 d. *Education:* BA Engl Educ, 1968, MA Engl Educ, 1973, Univ of S FL. *Appointments:* Engl Tchr, 1968-80; Chairperson, Tampa Cath HS Engl Dept, 1973-77; Prod Mgr, Tech Publs, Paradyne Corp, Largo, FL, 1980-83; Corp Communications Mgr, Porta-Printer Systems Inc, Largo, FL, 1984-87; Writer, Niydorf Computer Corp, Tampa, 1988-89; Mktng Dir, Suncoast Schls Fed Credit Union, Tampa, 1989-. *Publications:* Var articles in Nat Trade Jrnls. *Memberships:* Int Assn of Bus Cos; Nat Assn of Female Executives; Credit Union Exec Soc; Fin Inst Mktng Assn; Kappa Delta Pi. *Honour:* Outstanding Secondary Educator, 1973. *Hobbies:* Writing, Reading, Sewing, Gardening, Travelling. *Address:* 4014 Hudson Terrace, Tampa, FL 33624, USA. 5, 132.

MILLER Francis Edward, b. 20 Jan 1940, London, England. Cons Conciliator and Arbitrator specializing in the resolution of disputes in bldg, civ engrng and process inds. m. Valerie Read, 28 Nov 1964, div 1987, 2 s. *Education:* Brixton Schl of Bldg; Univ of Westminster. *Appointments:* Jr Quantity Surveyor, 1956; Later Surveyor and Mgr of bldg and civ engrng projects, commenced in prac in 1972 specializing in the resolution of disputes. *Publications:* Arbitration: Recommendations and Survey, 1988; Building and Civil Engineering: Cost Value Comparison, 1992. *Memberships:* FRICS; FCIArb; Assoc, Inst of Patentees and Inventors; Arbitration Panel of RICS and CIArb; Ed, Arbitration - News & Views; Liveryman of the Worshipful Co of Arbitrators, 1981. *Hobbies:* Watercolour Painting, Writing, Walking, Talking. *Address:* Candida, Harlequin Lane, Crowborough, East Sussex TN6 1HU, England.

MILLER Geoffrey Peter, b. 9 June 1942, Western Australia. Barrister. m. Sandra Dale, 13 Mar 1943, 2 s, 1 d. *Education:* LLB (first class hons), Univ of WA, 1963; Admitted to Bar, WA, 1965. *Appointments:* Godfrey Virtue & Co, Solicitors, 1965-74; Barrister & Solicitor on own account, 1974-80; Barrister, 1980-. *Memberships:* Pres, Law Soc of WA, 1980-81; VP, WA Bar Assn, 1989, 91; Mbr Legal Aid Commn of WA. 1978-80; Mbr Barristers Bd of WA. 1980-; Comm, WA Turf Club, 1983-. *Honours:* LLB, first class honours, 1963;

Athletics Blue, Univ Western Australia, 1963; Queen's Counsel for Western Australia. 1980; Queen's Counsel for Victoria, 1990. *Hobbies:* Thoroughbred Horse Racing, Motorsport. *Address:* Floor 16, Allendale Square, 77 St George's Tce, Perth. 23.

MILLER Helena Agnes, b. 25 Apr 1913, Ohio, United States of America. Ret'd Prof. *Education:* BA 1935, BSc 1935, MSc, 1938, OH State Univ; Harvard Univ and Radcliffe Coll, PhD, 1945. *Appointments:* Tchng Fellow, Bot and Biology, Harvard Univ, 1943-44; Instr, Bot: CT Coll for Women 1944-45, Wellesly Coll 1945-48; Assoc Prof 1948-49, Prof, Biology 1952, Asst to Dean of Coll of Arts and Sciences, 1966-78, Duquesne Univ. *Publications:* Teaching and Research, The Proper Balance, 1963. *Contributions to:* profl jrnls; Poem, Psychic Observer, 1969. *Memberships:* Life Fellow, Int Biog Assn; Phi Epsilon; Sigma Delta Epsilon; Sigma Xi; Phi Beta Kappa. *Honours:* Valedictorian of Senior Class in Liberty Township High School, 1931; Scholarship of Fellowship from Radcliffe or Harvard, yearly 1942-45; Woman of the Year for Pittsburgh area, Sigma Lambda Phi, 1959; First Lady of the Day., Radio Station WRYT, Pittsburgh, 1962. *Hobbies:* Gardening and Greenhouse Work, Reading current publs, Currently working on a publ implementing and extending Montessori's perspective anmd methods. *Address:* 523 Highview Road, Pittsburgh, PA 15234, USA. 152.

MILLER Jacques Francis Albert Pierre, b. 2 Apr 1931, Nice, France. Med Rschr. m. Margaret Denise Houen, 17 Mar 1956. *Education:* BSc Med 1953, MB BS 1955, Univ Sydney; PhD 1960, DSc 1965, Univ London; BA 1985, Univ Melbourne. *Appointments:* Royal Prince Alfred Hosp, Sydney, 1956-57; Chester Beatty Rsch Inst, London, 1960-65; Hd of Expmtl Pathology and Thymys Biology Unit, Walter and Eliza Hall Inst of Med Rsch, 1966-; Prof, Expmtl Immunology, Univ Melbourne, 1990. *Publications:* Over 330 publs in scientific jrnls on immunology and cancer. *Honours:* Esther Langer Bertha Teplitz Memorial Prize for Cancer Research, 1965; Encyclopaedia Britannica Austral Award, 1966; Intern Gairdner Award, 1966; FAA, 1970; FRS, 1970; Burnet Medal, 1971; Paul Ehrlich Prize, 1974; Rabbi Shai Shacknai Memorial Prize, 1978; Officer of the Order of Australia, 1981; International St Vincent Prize for Medical Science, 1983; For Assoc US National Academy of Science, 1982; Inaugural Medawar Prize of the Transplantation Society, 1990; First Sandoz Prize for Immunology, 1990. *Hobbies:* Art, Music, Photograohy, Lit. *Address:* The Walter and Eliza Hall Institute of Medical Research, Post Office Royal Melbourne Hospital, Victoria 3050, Australia. 1, 23, 34, 52, 128, 129, 139, 149.

MILLER John Albert Peter, b. 30 July 1931, London, England. Painter. *Education:* Schl of Arch, London, 1951-56. *Appointments:* Nat Serv Commn, RASC, 1949-51; Prin Asst, Milner's Craze, Achts, London, 1956-58; Full-time Painter, 1958-. *Creative Works:* Paintings: Cornubia, Land of the Saints; Truro Cathedral; Pub Collects: Victoria & Albert Museum, London: Avon County Council; Cornwall County Council; Autobiog: Leave Tomorrow Behind; Collects: TRH Prince and Princess of Wales; TRH Prince and Princess Michael of Kent. *Memberships:* Newlyn Soc of Artists, former Chmn; FRSA, 1964. *Hobbies:* Books, Gardens, Travel. *Address:* Sancreed House, Sancreed, Penzance, Cornwall TR20 8QS, England.

MILLER Joseph Edward Jr, b. 4 Jan 1945, Seattle, Washington, USA. Writer Prod, Motion Pictures and TV. *Education:* AA, Montgomery Coll, 1974; BS, Motion Picture Prod, Psychology, 1976, MA, Radio TV and Film Prod Psychology, 1978, Univ of MD. *Creative Works:* Prod-Rsch: Missing Reward, 1989; Space Research, 1975; Research from the Air, 1975; Prod-Writer: Chess: A Game of Life, 1972; Prod-Mgmt: Men of the Forest, 1973; All Systems Go, 1972; Problems of Separation, 1972; Prod-Cameraman: Aortic Bypass, 1979; The Perfect Projectionist, 1971; Prod-Editing: Industrial

Hygiene Surveying: Equipment and Techniques, Part 1, 1979, Part 2, 1979; The Occupational Therapy Patient on the Nursing Unit, 1978; Prod-Dir: Karate, 1975; Home Shopping, 1975; Meet the Carpeteria People, 1975; Prod-Multiple Function:: The Stellar Thread, 1981; Maxillofacial War Wounds, 1981; Dermis Fat Graft, 1980; Epiguard Transplants, 1980; Cold: The Bitter Enemy, 1980; TV Series: TV Movie, Remember Me, 1991; Author num articles in profl jrnls and mags; Novel: The House on Thayer Hill, 1988. *Membership:* Co-chair, Organizing and Sponsoring Comm, 101st Airborne Div Assn participation in Salute II, second dedication of Vietnam Veterans Memorial 1982. *Honours:* United Way Gold Award, 1984, 85; President's Certificate of Appreciation, 101st Airborne Division Association, 1981, 85. *Hobbies:* Pols, Photography, Parachuting. *Address:* Laurel Canyon Boulevard, Unit 306, Studio City, CA 91604, USA. 9.

MILLER Madelyn Sue Jensky, b. 4 Mar 1947, Chicago, Illinois, USA. Pres, CEO, Madelyn Miller Agcy Inc. m. Howard Miller, 26 May 1968, 1 s, 1 d. *Education:* BA, Jrnlsm, Univ MI, Ann Arbor, 1968. *Appointments:* Creative Assrt, Campbell-Ewald Co Inc, detroit, 1967; Creative Asst, Young and Rubicam Inc, detroit, 1968; Copywriter, Burton Soghigian Inc, detroit, 1969; Copywriter, Yaffe Stone August Inc, Detroit, 1969-70; Copywriter, Neiman Marcus, Dallas, TX, 1976; Sr Copywriter, Tracy-Locke-BBDO, Dllas, 1976-82; Pres, CEO, The Madelyn Miller Agcy, dallas, 1982-. *Contributions to:* popular mags. *Memberships:* Southqwestern Assn Advt Agcys, Advsry Bd Mbr; Dallas Ad league; TZ PR Assn; PR Soc of America; Chmn: Women in Communications; Women in ezxec Ldrship; American Film inst; TX Film-Tape Profls; Dallas Soc Visual Communications; American Women in Radio and TV; Dallas Chmbr of Comm. *Honours:* Entrepreneur of the Year Semi-finalist, Inc Magazine, 1985; The Biographical Roll of Honor, 1985; head Judge, 1983 IABC printed Communications; Judge, 1983 CLIO Competition. *Hobbies:* Travelling, Sewing, Reading, Shopping. *Address:* 8140 Walnut Tree Lane, Suite 411, Dallas, TX 75231, USA. 7, 132,138, 152.

MILLER Philip Vernon, b. 16 Nov 1948, Albuquerque, New Mexico, USA. Clergyman. m Paula Colker, 29 May 1971, 2 d. *Education:* BA, TX Christian Univ, Ft Worth, 1970; M.Th 1973, D.Min 1974, Southern Meth Univ, Dallas. *Appointments:* Assoc Min, First Christian Ch, Abilene,TX, 1974- 78; Sr Min, Madison Ave Christian Ch, Covington, KY,,1978-85; Sr Min, First Christian Ch, Paducah, KY, 1985-. *Publications:* Poetry, Sermons and Articles. *Memberships:* Gen Bd, Christian Ch, Disciples of Christ; Bd, Rotary Club, Paducah, KY; Chair, Ecumenical Concerns Comm, Christian Ch in KY; Pres, Paducah Area Mins Fellowship; AF Assn; Reserve Offs Assn; Assn of Disciples Pastors for Theological Discussion. *Honours:* C S Lewis Award for Religious Literature from Texas Christian University, 1970; Chaplain of the Year from Air Reserve Personnel Center, 1989; Air Force Commendation Medal, 1991. *Hobbies:* Reserve Chaplain, USAF, Admissions Liaison Off, USAF Acad, Music, Golf, Bicycling. *Address:* PO Box 7372, Paducah, KY 42002, USA. 145.

MILLER Richard Elroy, b. 1 Oct 1931, New Haven, Connecticut, USA. Lib Mgr-Rschr. m. Eugenia Knox Randal-Clayton, 26 Feb 1960, 1 s. *Education:* BS, Southern CT State Univ; MS, Univ Southern CA; PhD, Royal Univ, Phnom Penh, Cambodia; Studies in German, Pasadena, CA Community Coll. *Appointments:* Port Angeles Pub Lib, Washington, 1966-70; Arcadia Pub Lib, CA, 1970-78; Oshkosh Pub Lib, WI, 1978-82; Dallas Pub Lib, TX, 1982- 91. *Publications:* Biog of Lucky Baldwin; Gone But Not Forgotten - Epitaphs. *Memberships:* Rotary Int, Ed Newsletter; Kiwanis, Past Pres; CA Lib Assn, Pres, 1975; American Field Serv, Pres. *Honours:* Commendation, Los Angeles County Commissioners; Life Memberships, California Parent-Teacher Association, Honorary; Award of Excellence, Dallas Public Library, Texas, Staff Association. *Hobbies:* Reading, Writing, Arts, Genealogy, Photography, Dogs.

Address: 2417 Redbrook Court, Arlington, TX 76014, USA. 7.

MILLER Roger Simon, b. 16 Feb 1938, Seaford, Sussex, England. Schlmaster. m. Sara Elisabeth Battersby Atkins, 16 June 1962, diss, 2 d. *Education:* Harrow Schl, 1951-56; BA (Hons), Trinity Coll, Oxford. *Appointments:* Subaltern. HM Forces, 3rd Greenjackets; Mgr, Imperial Grp, 1966-78; Prop, Appleby and McGrath, Booksellers, 1978-82; Schlmaster, Sunnindale Schl, 1981-. *Publication:* Influential Dates in British History, 1989. *Memberships:* Liberal Party, Parliamentary Cand for Horncastle, 1970-74 and Weston-super-Mare 1974; Area Commnr, St John Ambulance, 1975-80; Freedom of City of London and Liveryman of Carpenters Company. *Hobbies:* Horses (own and ride one ret'd racehorse), Cricket (former mbr of Sussex and Dorset Co Clubs), Bridge, Walking. *Address:* 23 Netherton Road, St Margarets, Twickenham, Middlesex TW1 ILZ, England.

MILLINGTON Alan Fred, b. Stourport, England. Prof of Land Econ, Dean of Fac of Bus and Land Econ, Univ of Western Sydney, NSW. m Joyce Imogen Edwards, 7 Aug 1963, 2 s. *Education:* Coll of Estate Mgmt, Univ of London, 1962-65; BSc, Estate Mgmt, Urban, 1965; BSc, Estate Mgmt, Rural, 1967. *Appointments:* Surveyor w Edwards Son and Bigwood, Birmingham, UK, 1965-67; Lectr, Coll of Estate Mgmt, Univ of London, 1967-72; Lectr, Univ Reading, 1972-78; Prof, Land Econs, Paisley Coll,1978-84; Superintending Estates Surveyor, Dept of Hlth and Social Security, London. 1984; Prof, Land Econs, Paisley Coll, 1985-86; Dean of Fac of Bus and Land Econ, Univ Western Sydney, Australia, 1986. *Publications:* An Introduction to Property Valuation, 1975, 82, 88; 5 other impressions; Malaysian Ed 1987, Chinese Ed 1990. *Memberships:* Fellow, Royal Instn of Chartered Surveyors; Fellow, Brit Inst of Mgmt; Fellow, Aust Inst of Valuers and Land Economists (Val and Econ); Fellow, Soc of Land Econs; Inst of Revenues, Rating and Valuation; BSc Estate Mgmt Club, Pres 1983-84, VP 1982-83. *Hobbies:* Sports (soccer, rugby league, hockey, swimming, tennis, motor-sport, motorcycling), Photography, Reading, Music. *Address:* Dean of Faculty of Business and Land Economy, University of Western Sydney, Hawkesbury, Richmond, NSW 2753, Australia. 139.

MILLS Cynthia Marceil Spraker, b. 11 June 1962, Williamsburg, Virginia, USA. Asst Exec Dir, NACAS (Assn Mgmt). m. John Edwards Mills, 18 Oct 1986. *Education:* BA, summa cum laude, Queens Coll, 1984; MA, Univ of York, England, 1986. *Appointments:* Fin Aid Off, American Motor Inst, 1987-88; Assoc Dir, Programming and Systems Inc, 1988-90; Asst Exec Dir, Nat Assn of Coll Aux Servs, 1990-. *Memberships:* Nat Assn Female Execs; American Soc of Assn Execs. *Honours:* National Dean's List, 1980-84; Presidential Scholarship, 1980-84; Valedictorian, 1980; School Board Award, 1980; Outstanding Senior in Social Sciences, 1984; Outstanding Senior in Humanities, Orb and Sceptre Society, 1984; Zetetic Society. 1984; Mortar Board, 1987; Rotary Foundation International Scholarship, 1984; Outstanding Young Woman in America, 1984, 86; Algernon Sydney Sullivan Award, 1987. *Hobbies:* Reading, Stained Glass and Cathedrals, Spanish, Needlework, European Studies, Clogging. *Address:* 237 Sycamore Street, Staunton, VA 24401, USA. 46, 138.

MILLS Rollin William, b. 17 Feb 1944, Dayton, Ohio, USA. Coord of Educl Assessments. m. Sharon Polk, 18 June 1966, 2 s. *Education:* BS, Bob Jones Univ, 1966; M.Ed, W Carolina Univ, 1969; Ed.S 1976, PhD 1988, Univ of SC. *Appointments:* Tchr, Greenville Jr HS, 1966-69; Asst Prin, Slater Marietta HS, Greenville, SC, 1969-70; Asst Prin, Dent Jr HS, Columbia, SC, 1970-71; Prin, Harbor Christian, W Columbia, 1971-72; Prin, Lexington Intermediate, Lexington, SC, 1972-87; Coord Educl Assessments, 1987-. *Publications:* A Study in Procedures and Problems in Recruiting, Selecting

Teachers in South Carolina Public Schools, 1971; Teacher Evaluations and Student Achievement in High Average Classes, 1988. *Memberships:* Assn of Supervision Curric Dev; Univ of SC Alumni; Nat Assn Schl Admnstrs; SC Assn of Schl Admnstrs; SC HS League; SC Assn of Indep Schl Athletic Assn; Lions Int. *Honours:* Dean's List, Bob Jones Univ, 8 semesters, 1962-66; Magna cum laude graduation Professor, 1974-88. *Hobbies:* Sports officiating, Reading, Travel, Walking, Watching mystery movies, Pols, Hist, Relig, Tchr evaluation rsch. *Address:* 1417 Whippoorwill Drive, W Columbia, SC 29169, USA. 7, 125.

MIŁOBĘDZKI Jerzy Adam, b. 17 July 1924, Warsaw, Poland. Prof, Univ of Warsaw. m. 1 s, 2 d. *Education:* M.Arch 1948, Dr.Tech.Sc in Arch 1952, Politechnika Warsaw. *Appointments:* Asst, Dept Arch, AG Krakow, 1946; Asst, Dept Arch 1949, Docent, Dept Arch 1952, Politechnika, Warsaw; Docent, Dept Hist, 1971, Asst Prof 1974, Full Prof 1982, Univ Warsaw. *Publications:* About 120 publs inclng 5 books on hist of art, arch and culture. *Membership:* Comite International d'Histoire de L'Art, 1989, Pres Polish Nat Comm, 1990. *Honours:* Hon FSA, 1991; Polish State Award 1st Class. *Address:* ul Schroegera 27 m.2, PL 01-822 Warsaw, Poland.

MILOVANOV Victor, b. 22 Jan 1904, Moscow, USSR. Scientific Worker. m. Iren Sokolovskaya, 22 Feb 1924, 1 s. *Education:* Moscow Zootechnical Institut, 1921-23; Dr of Biological Science, 1936; Prof, Dr, 1945; Acad, 1956. *Appointments:* Asst, State Univ, 1924-28; Asst, Inst Expmtl Vet, 1929-30; Hd Scientific Worker, Institut of Animal Husbandry, Moscow, 1931-34; Hd of Lab of Artificial Insemination, Institut of Hybridization and Acclimatization, Asksnia Nova, Herson Province, 1935-36; Hd, Scientific Worker, All-Union Institut of Animal Husbandry, Moscow, 1937-40; Hd of Lab of Artificial Insemination in All-Union Institut of Animal Husbandry,. Moscow, 1941-56; Asst Dir for Science, 1957-67; Hd of Scientific Dept, Biology Reproduction and Artificial Insemination in same Institut, 1968-. *Publications:* Artificial Insemination of Cattle, 1932; Stock Breeding and Artificial Insemination, 1943; Immunology Reproduction of Animals, co- author, 1981; Discovery of the Possibility to Receive the Offspring from Frozen Mammals Semen, 1947. *Memberships:* For Mbr, Italian Societe of Zootechnical Progress; For Mbr, Japan Soc for Investigation of Reproduction. *Honours:* Order of Lenin, 1936; Order of Red Banner of Labour, 1946, 49, 50, 74; Badge of Honour, 1966; Order of October Revolution, 1971; Order of People's Friendship, 1984; Honorary Title of Laureat of State Prize, 1951; Member of Science Academie, 1956. *Hobby:* Discovering the mysteries of interrelation between different biological systems in organism at reproduction. *Address:* P O Strelkovo, Moscow Province, Podolsk District Settlement Bykovo n.30, Russia. 1.

MILSTED David, b. 5 Jan 1954, Sussex, England. Author. m. (2) 1 Dec 1984, 4 s. *Education:* B.Ed (Hons), Univ of Newcastle-upon-Tyne, 1976. *Appointments:* Tchr, Stromness Acad, Orkney, 1978-85; Full-time Author, 1985-. *Publications:* Novels: The Chronicles of Craigfieth, 1988; Market Forces, 1989; Telling Stories, 1992; Others: Bluff Your Way in Weather Forecasting; The Green Bluffer's Guide; The Bluffer's Guide to World Affairs; Bluff Your Way in Whisky. *Memberships:* Soc of Authors; Educl Inst of Scotland. *Hobbies:* Hill Walking, Reading, Mending Clocks. *Address:* c/o Harper Collins, 77-85 Fulham Palace Road, Hammersmith, London W 6, England.

MIN En-Ze, b. 4 Feb 1924, Chengdu, China. Chem Engr. m. Lu Wanzhen, 14 June 1950, 1 d. *Education:* BS, Nat Ctrl Univ, 1946; MS 1948, PhD 1951, OH State Univ, USA. *Appointments:* Assoc and Sr Chem Engr, Nat Aluminate Corp (now Nalco Chem Co), 1951-55; Dept Dir, Chief Engr, Petroleum Rsch Inst, 1955-83; VP, Chief Engr, Rsch Inst of Petroleum Processing, 1983-. *Creative Works:* Development of Petroleum

Refining Catalysts; Research of New Catalytic Materials. *Memberships:* Academia Sinica; VP, Chinese Petroleum Soc; Dir, Standing Comm, Chinese Chem Soc; Corres Mbr, Scientific Comm, 14th World Petroleum Congress. *Honours:* Significant Contributor to the Development of China's Science and Technology by National Science Conference, 1978; Distinguished Alumnus, The Ohio State University, 1989; National Advanced Worker, State Council, 1989. *Hobbies:* Reading, Music. *Address:* 18 Xue Yuan Road, Beijing 100083, China.

MINC Henryk, b. 12 Nov 1919, Lodz, Poland. Prof Emeritus, Maths. m. Catherine T Duncan 16 Apr 1943, 3 s. *Education:* MA (Hons) Maths and Nat Philos, 1955, PhD Maths, 1959, Univ of Edinburgh; Scottish Tchng Cert, 1956. *Appointments:* Asst Prof, Univ of BC, 1958-60; Assoc Prof, Univ of FL, 1960-63; Prof, Maths, Univ CA, Santa Barbara, 1963-90; Vis Prof, Technion, Israel Inst of Technol, Haifa, 1969-80. *Publications:* A Survey of Matrix Theory and Matrix Inequalities, 1964; Permanents, Encyclopedia of Mathematics and Its Applications Vol 6, 1978; Nonnegative Matrices, 1988; Textbooks in Maths; Rsch Papers; Mimeographed Math Books and 3 Articles; Rsch Papers in Ancient Numismatics. *Memberships:* American Math Soc; Inst for Antiquity and Christianity, Claremont Grad Schl, Advsry Bd; Scottish Soc of Santa Barbara, Pres. *Honours:* US Air Force Office of Scientific Research, Contract, 1960; US Air Force Office of Scientific Research Grants, 1962-83; Ford Award, Math Association of America, 1966; Lady Davis Fellowships, 1975, 78; Office of Naval Research, Research Contract, 1985-89. *Hobbies:* Piobaireachd (Piping), Scottish Poetry, Lit and Hist, Scots Lang, Numismatics and Archaeology of Ancient Middle East, Semitic Langs and Scripts, Swimming. *Address:* 4076 Naranjo Drive, Santa Barbara, CA 93110, USA. 1, 2, 9, 54.

MINEEV Vladimir Petrovich, b. 9 Oct 1945, Moscow, USSR. Physicist. m. Olga Brazovskaja, 28 Feb 1976, 1 s, 2 d. *Education:* Moscow Fizico Tech Inst, 1963-69; Dip Ingener, 1969; PhD, 1974; Dr of Physics, 1983. *Appointments:* Inst for Solid State Physics, 1972-80; Landau Inst for Theoretical Physics, 1980-, Dpty Dir, 1990-. *Publications:* Over 50 articles in scientific jrnls. *Memberships:* Prof of Moscow Physico-Tech Inst, 1991, Chmn of Chair of Problems of Theoretical Physics in Moscow Physico-Tech Inst, 1991. *Hobbies:* Reading, Hiking, Kayaking. *Address:* 99 Leninsky Avenue, Apt 457, Moscow 117421, Russia.

MING Nai-Ben, b. 9 Aug 1935, Jiangsu, China. Professor of Physics; Deputy Director. m. Chuan-Zhen Ge, 31 Oct, 1961, 1 s, 1 d. *Education:* Dipl, Phys, Nanjing Univ, 1959; DSc Hons, Tohoku Univ, Japan, 1986. *Appointments:* Tchg Asst, 1959-63, Lectr, 1963-78, Assoc Prof of Phys, 1978-82, Nanjing Univ; Vis Assoc Prof, Univ of Utah, USA, 1982-84; Vis Prof, Tohoku Univ, Japan, 1986-87; Prof of Phys, nanjing Univ, 1984-86; Prof of Phys, Dir of Inst of Mats Sci, Dpty Dir of Nat Lab of Solid State Microstructures, Nanjing Univ, 1987-. *Publications:* Physical Fundamentals of Crystal Growth, 1982; Author of 72 papers published in professional journals and magazines. *Memberships include:* Chinese Phys Soc; Exec Com, Chinese Space Sci Soc; Chm, Phys Gp, Nat Sci Foun of China; V-Chm, Phys Gp, Sci and Tech Com, Nat Educ Com of China; Chm of Synthetic Crystal Gp, Nat Hg Tech Com of China; Chinese Academy of Sciences, 1991-. *Honours:* Second Degree Awds, 1964, 1982; Hercules Awd, Univ of Utah and Hercules Inc, USA, 1983; Chinese Sci Publications awd, 1983; Sci Progress Awd, Chinese Nat Educ Com, 1986. *Hobbies:* Drinking tea; Smoking; Travel; Reading novels. *Address:* National Laboratory of Solid State Microstructures, Nanjing University, 22 Hankou Road, Nanjing 210008, China.

MINOGUE Kenneth Robert, b. 11 Sept 1930, Palmerston North, New Zealand. Professor of Political Science. m. Valerie Pearson Hallett, 16 June 1954, 1 s, 1 d. *Education:* BA, Sydney Univ, 1949; BSc Econ,

London Sch of Econ, 1955. *Appointments:* Asst Lectr, Univ Col, Exeter, 1955-56; Asst Lectr, London Sch of Econ, 1956; Sen Lectr, 1964, Reader, Prof, 1984. *Publications:* The Liberal Mind, 1961; Nationalism 1967; The Concept of a University, 1974; Alien Powers: The Pure Theory of Ideology, 1985. *Memberships:* Dir, Governmental Opposition; Dir, Ctr for Policy Studies; TV Presenter, The New Enlightenment, 1986. *Hobbies:* Wine; Women; Song; Tennis. *Address:* 43 Perrymead Street, London SW6 3SN, England. 1.

MINTZ Jack Maurice, b. 6 Mar 1951, Edmonton, Canada. Economist. m. Eleanor Janice Schwartz, 31 Aug 1975, 1 s, 1 d. *Education:* BA Hons, Univ of Alberta, 1971; MA Econ Queens Univ, Canada, 1973; PhD, Univ of Erick, 1980. *Appointments:* Asst Prof, 1978-84, Assoc Prof, 1984-89, Queens Univ; Prof of Econ and Bus Econ, Univ of Toronto, 1989-. *Publications:* Measure Canadian Banking, 1979; Taxation of Capital Income in Canada, 1987; Economic of Tax Reform, 1989. *Memberships:* Canadian and Am Econ Assns; Dir, John Devtich Inst, 1986-89, Hsg Coun, 1984-; Assoc, Inst of Policy Analysis, 1989-. *Honours:* Arther Andersen Prof of Taxation. *Hobby:* Squash. *Address:* 59 Robingrove Road, Willodale, Ontario, Canada M2R 3A1. 88.

MIRA GALIANA Jaime Jose Juan, b. 23 May 1950, Alicante-Spain. Economist; Consultant in organization and logistics systems. m. Juana Camara Saez, 5 May 1974. 2 s. *Education:* Deg, Econ; Dipl: Indust Mgmt, Computer IBM, Multimodal Transport; Educ Dynamic Gp. *Appointments:* Unitransa, 1972-76; Frigosa, 1977-84; Henkel Iberica, 1984-85; Tecnicas Logisticas, 1985-86; Creditoy Docks de Barcelona, 1986-87; Electrolux Holding SA, 1987-90; Conslt, own company, 1990-. *Publications:* Logistics articles in professional magazines and journals. *Memberships:* Inst of Catalan of Logistics; Spanish Ctr of Logistics. *Hobbies:* Computers; Books; Tennis; Swimming. *Address:* P Juan Carlos I T9 2-2, 0832 Masnou, Barcelona, Spain. 52.

MIRONOVICH Lyubov Ivanovna, b. 31 Jan 1948. Associate Professor of Composite Materials Department. div. *Education:* Student, Perm Polytech Inst, 1966-72; Masters Deg, 1972; Dr Deg, Continuous Media Mech Inst, 1980. *Appointments:* Engr, Sr Res Worker, Inst of Continuous Media Mechanics, Ural Branch, USSR Acad of Scis, 1972-80; Dr, Assoc Prof of Composite Materials, Dept of Perm Polytech Inst, 1980-. *Publications:* 17 printed articles on the topic of mathematic modelling of behaviour of composite materials. *Hobbies:* Growing flowers; Books; Music; Travelling; Sport. *Address:* Mira 90 fl 34, 614036 Perm, Russia.

MIRZAI Mohammed, b. 24 Feb 1945, Iran. 1 s. 1 d. *Education:* AA, Hartnell Col, Calif, 1970; BS, Calif State Univ, 1972; Postgrad, 1973- 74. *Appointments:* Prodn Worker, 1970-72, Chemist, 1972-76, Lab Mgr, 1976-77, Quality Assurance Mgr, 1977-78, Campell Co, Sacramento; Instr, Calif State Univ, 1972-73; Asst Prodn Mgr, 1982-83; Company Quality Assurance Mgr, 1983-87, Ragu Foods Inc; Hd, Food and Drinks Application Unit, Unilever Res Lab, The Netherlands, 1987-. *Memberships:* Pres, Intl Student Org, Salinas, 1968-69; Sec, Sacremento, 1970-71; Inst Food Technologists; Nat Food Processors Assn; Calif League of Food Processors; Intl Assn Quaity Circs; Am Soc for Quality Control. *Hobbies:* Golf; Running; Walking; Travel. *Address:* Unilever Research Laboratory, Olivier van Noortlaan 120, 3133 AT Vlaardingen, The Netherlands. 132, 52.

MISHRA Jayamanta, b. 15 Oct 1925, Haripur, Bihar. Retired Vice Chancellor and University Professor. m. Sushila Devi, July 1946, 1 s, 4 d. *Education:* BA Hons, 1950; MA 1952. *Appointments:* Lectr in Sanskrit, Bihar Univ; Asst Prof, 1950; Prof, Indian Coop Mission, Govt of India, 1963-69; Prof of Skt, 1972-75; V-Ch, KS & Samskrit, Univ of Darbhanga, 1980-. *Publications:* Kavyatma Mimansa; Nibandha Kusumansali; Alankara Prakasa; Abhilekh- Gita Mala; Sanskrita-Vyakara Nodaya; Mithilinatakapara; More than 150 research papers; Editre more than 20 works. *Memberships:* VP, All India Oriental Conf; Exec mem, AIOC; World Sanskrit Conf; Adv Bd, Sahitya Acad, New Delhi; Pres, All India Maithili Sahityaparisad Darlihanga. *Honours:* Recipient: President's Awd, 1986; Sanskrait-Ratnam, 1988; Kalidsa Awd, 1986; Cert of Hon, 1983. *Hobbies:* Reading; Writing. *Address:* Hanumanganj, Mishratula, Darbhanga, Bihar, India. 93.

MISRA Durgamadhab, b. 7 Oct 1958, Nayagarh, India. Assistant Professor. m. Aparajita 18 Jan 1987, 1 d. *Education:* PhE Elec Eng, 1988, MS 85, Univ of Waterloo; MTech, Indian Inst of Tech, New Delhi, 1983. *Appointments:* Asst Prof, New Jersey Inst of Tech, Elect & Comp Engrg, 1988-; Res Assoc, Univ of Waterloo, 1985-88; Res Conslt, DSRC, Princeton, NJ, 1990. *Publications:* Seven papers on Damage due to plasma etching; Three papers on Magnetic Sensors. *Memberships:* IEEE; Electrochem Soc; Sigma Xi. *Honours:* Canadian Govt Commonwealth Scholarship, 1983-88. *Hobbies:* Photography; Travelling. *Address:* Electrical & Computer Engineering Department, New Jersey Institute of Technology, University Heights, Newark NJ 07102, USA.

MITAMA Masataka, b. 22 May 1944, Shizuoka. Electric Company Executive. m. Yasuko Seo, 5 May 1978. *Education:* MEng, Univ of Tokyo, 1971. *Appointments:* Nippon Elec Corp; Kawasaki, Japan, 1971-80; Supvr, Nippon Elec Corp, 1980-86; Mgr, Nippon Elec Corp, 1986-. *Publications:* Author: An improved computational method for noise parameter measurement; IEEE Transaction on Microwave Theory and Techniques; UHF low noise GaAs MESFET amplifier for colour TV broadcasting translator, Electronic Letters, 1978. *Memberships:* IEEE; Inst of Elec Info and Communication Engrs of Japan. *Hobbies:* Driving. *Address:* 2-2-23 Tachibanadai, Midori- ku, Yokohama 227, Japan.

MITCHARD Shirley Anne, b. 15 Feb 1953, Somerset, England. Chartered Accountant. *Education:* BA Hons, Social Admin, 1975; Assoc of ICAEW, 1978. *Appointments:* KPMG Peat Marwick, 1975-81; Arthur Andersen, 1981-84; Clark Whitehill, 1985-; Partner, Corp Tax Specialist, 1987. *Publication:* Booklet, The Investor's Guide to the Business Expansion Scheme. *Memberships:* ICAEW; IOD. *Hobbies:* Interior decorating; Gardening; Antiques; Watercolours; Tennis. *Address:* 25 New Street Square, London EC4A 3LN, England. 53, 52.

MITCHELL Ann Katharine, b. 19 Nov 1922, Oxford, England. Retired Research Sociologist. m. Angus Mitchell, 13 Dec 1948, 2 s, 2 d. *Education:* BA 1943, MA 1947, Lady Margaret Hall, Oxford. MPhil, Univ of Edinburgh, 1980. *Appointments:* Foreign Ofc, Govt Code and Cypher Sch, 1943-45; Hon Sec, Edinburgh Marriage Guidance Counc, 1966-74; Res Asst, Univ of Edinburgh Dept of Social Admin, 1980-84. *Publications:* Someone To Turn To, 1981; Children in the Middle, 1985; When Parents Split up, 1986; Coping with Separation and Divorce, 1986; Families, 1987; Divorce, 1990. *Hobbies:* Family history; Local history; Grandchildren. *Address:* 20 Regent Terrace, Edinburgh EH7 5BS, Scotland.

MITCHELL Jeremy George Swale Hamilton, b. 25 May 1929, Manchester, England. Consumer Policy Adviser. m. (1) Margaret Mary Ayres, 28 July 1956, div 1988, 3 s 1 d; (2) Janet Rosemary Powney, 16 Mar 1989. *Education:* Ampleforth Col, York, 1942-47; MA Brasenose & Nuffield Col, Oxford Univ, 1949-53. *Appointments:* Consumers Assn, 1968-65; Nat Ec Devel Ofc, 1965-66; Res Social Sci Res Coun, 1966-74; Dir of Consumer Affairs, office of Fair Trading, 1974-77; Dir, UK Nat Consumer Coun, 1977-86. *Publications:* Betting; Electronic Banking and Consumer, 1988; Bankers Racket or Consumer Benefit, 1991. *Memberships:* Dpty Chm, Voice of the Listener; NAt

Coun of Gambling, Dpty Chm; Dir Mail Sers Standards Bd; Ind Com for the Supervision of Telephone Info Sers; Life Assurance and Unit Trust Regulatory Org Monitoring Com. *Hobbies:* Swinburne. *Address:* 214 Evering Road, London E5 8AJ, England. 1.

MITCHELL John Marvin, b. 10 July 1948, Toronto, Canada. Financial Services Executive. m. Bernadette, 13 Nov 1971, 1 s, 2 d. *Education:* Bus Admin Dipl, Ryerson, 1969; Profl Bus Progs, part-time, Harvard, 1971- 86; MBA, 1987, PhD, 1988, Pacific Western Univ. *Appointments:* Chm, Dir, Beneficial Canada Inc, 1986- 88; Sr VP and GM, Bentax, IG Tax Sers, Investors Gp, 1988-90; Pres, CEO, Canadian Fin Investments, 1991. *Creative works:* Co-author: Professional Selling Prog, 1977; Soctia Leasing Plan, 1980; Author: Fathers of Motivation, 1988, How to design Effective management Training Programmes, 1988. *Memberships:* OSTD, 1973-75; PAT, 1974-76; Bd of Trade, Toronto, 1981- 91; Assoc Con Fin Corp, Legal and Legislative mem, 1987-88; Con Coun, Better Bus Bureaus; Dir, Disciplinary and Ethics Comm, 1989-91. *Hobies:* Golf; Tennis; Baseball; Gardening; Hockey; Travel. *Address:* 41 Humber College Blvd, Etobicoke, Ontario, Canada M9V 1P2. 142.

MITCHELL John Wallace, b. 31 May 1931, Hove, Sussex, England. Management Consultant. m. Dheirdre Margaret Jessett Brown, 23 Sept 1989, 1 d. *Education:* Telecom Engr (Radar), Reme Radar Sch, 1950; FCA, 1957; FInst, 1962; FBCS, 1958; FVRS, 1972; FMS, 1964; FIMC, 1965; MIWPA, 1980; MIAM, 1985; EurolE, 1989; ACI Arb, 1992; RSCDS, Tchrs Cert, 1976. *Appointments:* Richard Knight & Co, 1951-57; Remington Univac, 1957-60; Rank Org, 1960-63; Harold Whithead and Ptnrs, 1963-67; Thornton Baker, 1967-77; Stoy Horwath, 1977-82; Wallace Mitchell & Co, 1982-93. *Publications:* Whetherly Books of Scottish Country Dances, Nos 1-24; Scottish Country Dancing - A recommended course of instruction. *Memberships include:* Hove Conservative Assn; Carlton Club; Royal Automobile Club; City Livery Club; City of London Branch of the Royal Soc of St George; United Wards Club of the City of London; Honourable Artillery Company. *Honours:* Knight of the Military and Hospitaller Order of St Lazarus of Jerusalem, 1990; OMLJ, 1989; KSJ, 1990; Fellow, Soc of Antiquaries of Scotland, 1981. *Hobbies:* Motor sport; Scottish dancing; Charity work; Reading; Music - especially Opera; Politics. *Address:* Whetherly House, 52 Shirley Drive, Hove, Sussex BN3 6UF, England.

MITCHELL Richard Charles, b. 22 Aug 1927, Witley, Surrey, England. Retired Part Time Lecturer. m. Doreen Lilian Mitchell Gregory, 27 May 1950, 1 s, 1 d. *Education:* BSc Econ Hons, 1951, Southampton Univ, 1948-52; Postgrad Cert in Educ, 1952. *Appointments:* Tchr, 1953-66, Dpty Hd, 1964-66, Bartley Co Sec Sch; MP Southampton Test, 1966-70; MP Southampton Itchen, 1971-83; MEP, 1975-79; Mem, Speakers Panel of Com Chm, 1979-83; Lectr in Public Admin, 1984- 89. *Publication:* Jt author, Public Administration - A Case Study Approach. *Memberships:* Southampton City Coun, 1955-67; Past Pres, Totton and Dist; Tchr's Assn (NUT); Labour party, 1945-81; SDP, 1981-90. *Hobbies:* Correspondence chess; Reading; Watching Southampton Football Club. *Address:* 49 Devonshire Road, Southampton SO1 2GL, England. 1, 43.

MITCHELL Richard George Bruce, b. 2 Nov 1923, Rugby, England. Retired Consultant. m. Sheila Moorhouse Dean, 10 June 1950, 1 s. *Education:* Marlborough Col, 1937-42; Gonville and Caius, Cambs, 1942-43. *Appointments:* Sales Dev Engr, Bakelite Ltd, 1944-63; Mktg Exec, BXL Plastics Ltd, 1963-73; Mkt Dev Mgr, BIP Ltd, 1973-80; Fed Sec, Glass & Glazine Fed, 1981-88. *Publications:* Plastics in the Building Industry, 1968; Glass Reinforced Plastics, 1970; Developments in Plastic Technology, 1982; Numerous technical articles in trade journals and national newspapers. *Memberships:* Fellow of the Plastics and Rubber Inst, Chm, London Section, 1963-64; Mem of Coun, 1963-68; Chm of Papers Com, 1964-68; Liveryman Worshipful Co of Horners, 1977; Freeman, City of London, 1977. *Honours:* FPRI, 1966. *Hobbies:* Freelance journalism; Golf; Travel. *Address:* Danes Way House, 3 Danes Way, Oxshott, Leatherhead, Surrey KT22 OLU, England.

MITEK Eugeniusz, b. 17 May 1935, Sambor. Academic Teacher; Priest. *Education:* Master of Phil Psycho, 1964, Dr of Pedagogics, 1970, Lublin KUL; Asst Prof of Theol, 1986, Krakow PAT. *Appointments:* Wroclaw PFT, 1970- . *Publications:* Kandydat Naministranta, 1985; Ministrant Swiatla, 19893; Ministrant Oetarza, 1986; Postawy Religinje Mlodziezy Pracujacej, 1970. *Hobbies:* Christ; Pedagogics. *Address:* Macedonska 19/4, 51-113 Wroclaw, Poland.

MITKOWSKI Wojciech, b. 5 Oct 1946, Krakow, Poland. Professor of Automatics. m. Maria, 24 Apr 1980, 2 s. *Education:* MSc Elec Engrg, 1970; Dr of Tech Scis, 1974; Dr hab Tech Scis, (Automatics), 1984; Prof of Tech Scis, 1992. *Appointments:* Inst of Automatics, Univ of Mining and Metallurgy, Krakow, 1970-. *Publications:* Algorithms and control programms, 1980; Co-author, The LQ problem of optimal control, 1983; Stabilization of Dynamical systems, 1991. *Memberships:* Comm of Elec and Automatics Acad of Sci, Poland, 1988-. *Honours:* Minister of Sci and Educ Awd, 1975. *Hobbies:* Mountain tourism; Cycling; Swimming; History of Krakow. *Address:* ul Michalowskiego 5/6, 31-126 Krakow, Poland.

MITROFANOVA Olga Danilovna, b. 25 Aug 1930, Russian Federation. Frist Pro Rector. m. Mitrofanov Valentin Dmitrievioh, 26 Jan 1957, 2 s. *Education:* MA, Moscow State Pedagogical Inst, 1953; Asst Prof, 1965; Dr Philology, 1975; Prof, 1978. *Appointments:* Hd of Dept, Peoples Friendship Univ, 1960-67; Hd of Dept, Dpty Dir, First Pro-Rector, Inst of Russian Lang, 1967- . *Publications:* 19 textbooks and about 200 articles. *Memberships:* Intl Assn of Tchrs of Russian Lang and Lit; Assoc Mem, Pedagogical Acad of the USSR: Acad Coun: Inst of Problems of Bilingualism and Inst of Russian Lang. *Honours:* Badge of Hon, 1980; Hon Dr, Univ of Brno, 1982; Medal, Ministry of Culture, Hungary, 1986; Hon Title, Soc of Friendship of the USSR, 1990; Hon titles from Poland, Germany and Mongolia. *Hobbies:* Theatre; Drama; Ballet; Swimming; Skiing. *Address:* ul Ivana Babushkina, 117292 Moscow, Russia.

MITROPOULOU Elpis, b. 21 Feb 1935, Tsagarada, Greece. Research Archaeologist. div. 1 d. *Education:* BA Greek and Eng Lit, 1958; BA, Ancient Hist and Archaeol, 1962, Athens Univ; Dipl, Univ of Piraeus, 1962; Ancient Hist and Classical Archaeol, (Sculpture), Univ Col London, 1962-64; PhD Archaeol, 1st clas Hons, Univ of Oxford, 1968. *Appointments:* Tutor, Modern Green, Dept of Extramural Studies, Univ of Birmingham, 1969- 71; Res Fellow, 1970-73, Tutor, Classical Archaeol, 1970-71. *Creative works:* Books include: Deities and Heroes in the Form of Snakes, 1975; Kneeling Worshippers in Greek and Oriental Literature and Art, 1975; Afrodite auf der Ziege, 1975; Attic Votive Reliefs of the 6th and 5th Centuries BC, 1978; Votive Reliefs, Coins, Gems and Amulets, 1978. *Memberships:* Socs for the Rights of Women and the Promotion of Hellenistic Studies; Cultural Com of the Intellectual Central of Demos of Athens, 1981-83; Bd of Admnrs, Philip Soc of Scists; Pres, Tsagarada's People living in Attica, 1984-; Women's Dining Club, Univ Col of London; Convocation of the Univ of London. *Honours include:* Res Fellow, Univ of Birmingham, 1970-73; Recipient of 10 scholarships from Greece, England and Germany; Work displayed in two individual and eighteen group exhibitions. *Hobbies:* Painting. *Address:* Agathoupoleos 11, 112 52 Athens, Greece. 152.

MITSAKIS Kariofilis, b. 12 May 1932, Thessaloniki, Greece. University Professor. m. 14 Aug 1966, 2 s. *Education:* BA, 1956, PhD, 1963, Univ Thessaloniki; MA,

1968, DPhil, 1965, Univ of Oxford. *Appointments:* Univ of Maryland, 1966-68, Oxford, 1968-72, Thessaloniki, 1972-75, Athens, 1977-93; Inst of Balkan Studies, 1972-80. *Publications:* March through time, 1982; The Living Water, 1983; Byzantine Hymnography, 1985; The Language of Romanos the Melodist, 1967; Points of Reference, 1987; The Boston Essays, 1993. *Memberships:* Modern Greek Studies Assn, USA: Nat Guild of Greek Writers; Greek Soc of Translators of Literature; Soc of British Univs Grads; Soc of Fullbright Scholars; Griechischer Humboldt Club. *Honours:* Ofr of the Ecumenical Patriarchale, 1968. *Hobbies:* Music; Painting; Travelling. *Address:* 25 Troados Str, 15342 Aghia Poraskevi, Athens, Greece.1, 2, 43, 156.

MITSUO Kodama, b. 15 May 1927, Tokyo, Japan. Director of Kodama Research Institute. m. Toshiko Kodama, 15 Nov 1963. *Education:* Grad, Nagoya Univ Sch of Med; MD, PhD, 1958. *Appointments:* Reschr, Nagoya Univ Med, 1953-59; Reschr, Roswell Pk Meml Inst, 1959-63; Reschr, Aichi Cancer Ctr Res Inst, Nagoya, 1965-88; Dir, Kodama Res Inst of Preventative Med, Nagoya, 1988-. *Publications:* Articles in professional journals and magazines. *Memberships:* Corres Mem, Am Assn of Cancer Res; NYAS: Intl Soc for Prev Oncol; Japanese Cancer Assn. *Honours:* Princes Takamatsu Cancer Fund, 1981. *Hobbies:* Reading; Hearing Classic Music; Cultivation of Roses. *Address:* Kodama Research Institute of Preventative Medicine, 50-5 Chiyogaoka, Chikusaku, Nagoya 464 Japan.

MIYACHI Iwao, b. 27 Sept 1916, Kochi, Japan. Professor. m. Kazuko Nagano 3 Apr 1943, 2 d. *Education:* BEng, 1940; DEng, 1953, Univ of Tokyo. *Appointments:* Lectr, Assoc Prof, prof, Nagoya Univ, 1940-80; Pres, Soc Franco-Japanaise de Nagoya, 1971-74; Pres, IEE, Japan, 1977; Prof, Aichi Inst of Tech, 1980-. *Publications:* Power Transmission and Distribution, 1958; Fundamentals on Electric Power Engrg, 1965; Electric Power Generation, 1988. *Memberships:* Hon mem, IEE, Japan; CIGRE, France; SEE, France. *Honours:* Oficier des Palmes Academiques, 1975; Merit for Dist Sers, IEE, Japan, 1980; 2nd Order of Nat Merit, Japan, 1990. *Hobbies:* Historical sightseeing; Driving; Skiing. *Address:* 3-6-5 Nishizaki-cho, Chikusa, Nagoya 464, Japan. 52.

MIYAKADO Masakazu, b. 22 Feb 1947, Osaka, Japan. Chemist; Biochemist. m. Yoshiko Imahori, 25 Feb 1973, 2 s, 1 d. *Education:* BA 1970, MA, 1972, Kyoto Univ; Doctorate, Nagoya Univ, Japan, 1980. *Appointments:* Agric Scis Res Lab, Sumitomo Chem Co Ltd, 1972-84, 1986-; Dept of Chem, Acad Fac, Cornell Univ, NY, USA, 1984-86. *Creative works:* Books: Natural Product Chemistry, 1983; Pesticides of Plant Origin, 1989; Developments of Agrochemicals, 1991. *Memberships:* Intl Soc of Chem Ecol; The Am Assn for the Advancement of Sci; Pesticide Sci Soc, PSS, Japan; The Japan Soc of Biosci, Biotech & Agrochem; Kinki Chem Soc Japan. *Honours:* Awd for Encouragement, PSS, Japan, 1986. *Hobbies:* Building musical instruments; Wood Block Printing; Mountain lodge Building. *Address:* 51 Arakusacho, Kamigamo, Kita, Kyoto 603, Japan. 52.

MIYAKE Akio, b. 29 June 1931, Kyoto, Japan. University Professor of Biology. m. Terue Harumoto, 30 Dec 1988, 1 s, 2 d. *Education:* BSc, 1953, DSc, 1959, Koyoto Univ, Japan. *Appointments:* Asst, Osaka City Univ, 1953-63; Lectr, Kyoto Univ, 1963-70; Gp Leader, Max Planck Inst, Molecular Genetics, Berlin, 1970-74; Prof, Univ Camerino, Italy, 1983-. *Publications:* Articles on sexual reproduction in microorganisms on professional journals and books; Discovery of chemical induction of conjugation in Paramecium; Formulation of the Gamone-receptor theory of conjugation in ciliates. *Memberships:* AAAS; Soc of Protozoologists; Zoological Soc of Japan; Zoological Union of Italy; Genetics Soc of Japan; Italian Soc of Protozoology. *Honours:* Zoological Soc of Japan Prize, 1981. *Hobbies:* Italian Opera Music; Evolution of Life. *Address:* Department of Molecular Cellullar & Animal Biology, University of

Camerino, Via F Camerini 2, 62032 Camerino (MC), Italy. 52.

MIYAZAWA Tatsuo, b. 21 Sept 1927, Kyoto, Japan. Research Director, Protein Engng Rsch Inst, 1991. m. Reiko Ishiwata, 26 May 1956, 2 s. *Education:* BSc, Chem, 1950, DSc, Univ of Tokyo, 1956. *Appointments:* Prof: Osaka Univ, 1964, Univ of Tokyo, 1974; Prof Emeritus, Univ of Tokyo, 1988; Prof, Yokohama Nat Univ, 1988. *Memberships:* Chem, Biochem, Biophys and Spectoscopical Socs of Japan; Polymer Soc. *Honours:* Prize, Chem Soc of Japan, 80. *Hobby:* Tennis. *Address:* Protein Engineering Research Institute, 6-2-3 Furuedai Suita, Osaka Japan.

MIZE Claiborne Jackson, b. 21 May 1958, Haleyville, Alabama, USA. Insurance and Financial Services. *Education:* Univ of Alabama, 1976-77; BS Fin, 1980, MBA, 1990, Univ of N Alabama. *Appointments:* Nat Sales Mgr, Tidwell Industries, 1980-82; VP, Sales, Energy Resource Measurement Inc, Houston, TX, 1982-84; pres, Mize and Assocs, 1984-87; Pres, Mize Waller & Assocs, 1987-. *Memberships:* IMA; Life Underwriters Assn; Dir Health Underwriters Assn; Nat Assn of Securities Dealers. *Honours:* Pres Citation Prog for Pvt Sector Initiatives Awd, 1989; Omicron Delta Epsilon. *Hobbies:* Tennis; Boating. *Address:* 920 North Wood Ave, Florence, AL 35630, USA.

MIZUSHIMA Keiichi, b. 3 Aug 1928, Tokyo, Japan. Professor of Psychology. m. 21 May 1955, 4 d. *Education:* BA, Univ of Tokyo, 1948- 51; PhD, Waseda Univ, 1965. *Appointments:* Clin Psychol: Yokohama Juvenile Classification Home, 1951-55; Tokyo Child Guidance Ctr, 1955-63, Serigayaen Mental Hosp, 1963-66; Prof, Rissho Womens Univ, 1966-76, Prof, Bunkyo Univ1976-. *Publications:* Collective Works in Humanistic Psycholology, 10 Vols; Introduction to Counselling; Personality; Delinquency; Ed, 7 vols of Clinical Psychology and 4 vols of Image Psychology. *Memberships:* Japan Assns of Clin Psychol, Humanistic Psychol, Educ Psychol Counselling Sci; Jap Psychol Assn; Japan Union of Psychomed Assn; Tokyo inst of Clin Psychol. *Hobbies:* Suibokuga - Japanese water-ink painting. *Address:* 2-10-6 Tamagawa Denenchotu, Setagaya, Tokyo, Japan.

MLECZKO Andrzej, b. 5 Jan 1949, Tarnobrzeg, Poland. Draughtsman; Graphic Artist. div. 1 d. *Education:* Dept of Arch, Politech Krakow, 1967-75; Inst of Tech, Krakow. *Appointments:* Artistic Conslt, Jaracz Theatre, Lodz, 1979-, Kochanowski Theatre, Opole, 1975-79; Owner, Galeria Autorska, Krakow, 1983-. *Publications:* 10,000 drawings published in Polish, European and American magazines; Books include: Obrask, 1975; Anormalka, 1977; Jak Zyc, 1979; Seks Dla Niezamoznych, 1980; Zycie Codzienne W Polsce, 1983; Rozmowki Polsko Polskie, 1984. *Memberships:* The Polish Artists Assn. *Hobbies:* Walking in his studio. *Address:* ul Grodzka 15/10, 31-005 Krakow, Poland.

MLYNARCZYK Katarzyna Barbara, b. 4 Dec 1952, Myslowice, Poland. Art Director. *Education:* Master of Hist of Art, Jagiellonian Univ, Cracow, 1982. *Appointments:* Literary Advr: Puppet Theatre, Bedzin, 1982-87; Actors and Puppets Theatre, Katowice, 1987-90. *Publications:* Poems: It was me, 1980; Venus of Willendorf, 1982; It's difficult to tell about happy love, 1987; Pairs of Lovers, 1989; I Love the City at Night, 1990. *Honours:* A Prize for Poetical works in Silesia, 1988. *Hobbies:* Films, especially old French films. *Address:* ul Sowinskiego 15/26, 40-032 Katowice, Poland.

MOAT Frank Robert, b. 10 Aug 1948, Tynemouth, England. Barrister. *Education:* Giggleswick Sch, 1962-66; LLB Hons: Leeds Col of Commerce, 1966-68; Col of Law, London, 1968-69. *Appointments:* Called to the Bar, Lincoln's Inn, November 1970; In Practice at the Bar, 1972-. *Memberships:* Bar Coun, 1989-90, Western

Circuit Jr Rep. *Hobbies:* Theatre; Opera; Architecture; Cinema. *Address:* 5 Prior Bolton St, Canonbury, London N1 2NX, England.

MOCHIZUKI Shigeru, b. 5 Feb 1931, Mishimi, Shizuoka, Japan. Professor; Architectural Engineer. m. 17 Apr 1961. 1 d. *Education:* BEng, 1954, MEng, 1956, DEng, 1967, Waseda Univ, Tokyo. *Appointments:* Asst, 1956-58, Lectr, 1958-62, Assoc Prof, 1962-71, Prof, 1972-, Musashi Inst Tech, Tikyo. *Publications:* Author: Today's Structural Designers in the World, 1979; Translator: Structure in Architecture, 1968; Structural Design in Architecture, 1969. *Memberships:* Arch Inst of Japan, Gen Dir, 1982-83; Japan Concrete Inst, Educ Dir, 1983-84, 1987-88; Coun on Tall Bldgs and Urban Habitats, V-Chm, 1992. *Hobbies:* Reading; Walking; Art Appreciation. *Address:* 1076-11 Ichigao Midori-ku, Yokahama 225, Japan. 1, 52.

MOCK Harmon Roy, b. 6 Jan 1938, Kansas City, Missouri, USA. Transit Analyst. *Education:* BArch, Univ of Kansas, 1963; Grad Study, Urban Planning, Morgan State Univ, Baltimore, 1974-77. *Appointments:* Jr Planner, City of Kansas, Planning Dept, Missouri, 1962-67; Jr Planner, Metropolitan Area Planning Comm, Wichita (Kansas)-Sedgwick County, 1967- 72; Planner II, Mid Ohio Reg Planning Comm, Columbus, 1972-73; Sr Planner, Maryland-Nat Capital Pk and Planning Comm, Riverdale, 1973; Transit Analyst, Mass Transit Admin, Baltimore, 1977-. *Publications:* MTA State of the System, 1977, 1978, 1979. *Memberships:* Am Planning Assn; Univ of Kansas Alumni Assn; Delta Sigma Phi; Alpha Phi Omega. *Honours:* Eagle Scout, Boy Scouts of Am, 1952; Recipient, Letter of Commendation, Gov of Maryland, 1982. *Hobbies:* Classical music; Plants; Yard work. *Address:* 4 East 39th Street, Baltimore, MD 21218, USA. 6.

MOERK Alice Anne, b. 1 Mar 1936, Philadelphia, Pennsylvania, USA. Musician; Teacher; Writer. *Education:* BMus, Dipls Piano, Organ, Carthage Col, 1957; MFA, Ohio Univ, 1959; PhD W.Virginia Univ, 1971. *Appointments:* Hd Mus Dept, Marion Col, VA, 1959-63; Prof of Music, Vardell Hall, Red Springs, NC, 1964-65; Dir of Musicl Lees Col, Jackson, KY, 1967-69; Prof of Music, Fairmont State Col, WV, 1969-. *Publications:* Texts: Pattes of Sound, 1989; Perspectives, 1979; Perception and music, 1981; A Short History of Popular music, 1975; Sonic Insights, 1991; Numerous choral, organ, instrumental works and electronic compositions. *Memberships:* AMS; Sigma Alpha Iota; Popular Culture Soc; Music Tchrs Nat Assn. *Honours:* SAI Sword of HOn, 1957; Rose of Hon, 1971; Outstanding Tchr, Fairmont State Col, 1972; Res Grants, 1972, 1989, FSC: Fac Recognition, 1989; WV Humanities Awd, 1990. *Hobbies:* Organ; Synthesizers; Reading. *Address:* 1616 Fairfield Road, Fairmont, WV 26554, USA.

MOFFAT Anthony Frederick John, b. 30 Jan 1943, Toronto, Canada. Professor. m. Ruth Ann Huntley, 10 Sept 1966, 1 s, 1 d. *Education:* BSc 1965, MSc, 1966, Univ of Toronto; Dr rer nat, 1970, Dr habil, 1976, Ruhr Univ, Germany. *Appointments:* Wiss Hilfskraft, Univ Bonn,1967-69; Wis Asst, Ruhr Univ, 1970-76; Prof agrege, 1977-80, porf Tutilaire, 1981-, Univ of Montreal. *Publications:* Author of over 150 refereed scientific publications and over 100 other articles on astronomy, objects of high luminosity and the structure of our galaxy. *Memberships:* Royal Astro Soc of Canada, 1977-, Bd, 1985-90, VP, 1988-90, Montreal Ctr); Canadian Astronom oc, 1977-, Coun, 1981-83; Am and German Astronom Socs; Intl Astronom Union, 1973-. *Honours:* Silver medal, Phys and Maths, Victoria Col, Univ Toronto, 1965; Royal Astronom Soc of Canada Gold Medal, 1965; NCR Canada Bursary, 1965-66; Imperial Oil Fellow, 1966-69; Alexander von Humboldt Fellow, 1982-83, 1989. *Hobbies:* Music; Philately; Canoeing; Tennis; Travel. *Address:* Department of Physics, University of Montreal, CD 6128 Succ A, Montreal, Quebec, Canada H3C 3J7. 1, 142.

MOFFAT Robin John Russell, b. 18 Oct 1927, London, England. Medical Practitioner; Forensic Medical Examiner. m. Beryl Longmoor, 18 Nov 1980, 2 s, 1 d. *Education:* Whitgift, Guys Hosp; MRCS: LRCP (Lond), 1954; DRCOG, 1958; FRCGP, 1991. *Appointments:* Royal Navy, 1946-48; Hosp Residencies, 1954-57; NHS Principal GP, 1959-89; Med ADvr, Whitgift Foun, TB Bank. *Contributions to:* School health, medico-legal subjects in text books, medical and national press, radio and television, and book reviews. *Memberships:* Pas Pres: Med Ofrs Schs Assn and Croydon Med Soc; FRSM; Pres, Clin Forensic Section; Assn of Police Surgs; Medico-Legal Soc; Brit Acad Foren Scis. *Honours:* RSM, Carlton and Anglo-American Sporting CLubs; Liveryman Soc of Apothecaries; Vis Lectr, St George's Hosp, London. *Hobbies:* Collecting first editions; Horse racing; Boxing; Writing to the press; Lecturing abroad; Politics. *Address:* 8 Arundel Terrace, Kemp Town, Brighton, E.Sussex BN2 1GA, England. 170.

MOFTAH Mounir Amin, b. 22 Nov 1922, Cairo, Egypt. Engineer. m. Marcelle El Mahmoudy, 6 Aug 1950, 2 s, 2 d. *Education:* BMechEng, Hons, Cairo Univ, 1948; CEng, London, 1970; Eur Ing (FEANI), Paris, 1988. Came to Australia 1968, Naturalised 1972. *Appointments include:* Workshop/Maintenance Engr, Kaliobia Gov, 1949-53; Field Engr, Ministry of Municipal and Rural Affairs, Egypt, 1953-54; Workshops Engr, Ministry of Hsg. and Utilities (MHU), 1954-56; Engr in Charge, Support Sers, Mech and Elec Power Admin, MHU, 1956-60; Asst Dir, Dir, Mech Fleet Admin, 1960-66; Mgr, Transp and Workshops, Utd Distribution Co, Egypt, 1966-67; Dir, Mech Fleet Sector Planning Dept, Min of Hsg and Public Utilities, 1967-68; Engr, Mech and Elec Design, Water Auth of W. Australia, 1969-86; Dpty Mgr, KESCON JV Egypt, 1986-88; Water and Wastewater Specialist, Engrg Conslts Gp, (ECG), Cairo, Egypt, 1986-. *Publications:* An Investigation into the factors governing the yield of artesian water bores in egypt, 1956; Gas Turbine performance under varying ambient temperature, ASME paper, 1979; Pump Stations Design Manual, Western Australia, 1986; Water and Wastewater Treatment Design Manuals, 1989; Contributor to various professional articles and lectures. *Hobbies:* Music; Reading; Chess; Walking; Tennis. *Address:* 8 Gameat e Dowal El Arabia Street, Apt 27, ElMohandseen 12411, Cairo, Egypt, and 11 Syrinx Place, Mullaloo, W. Australia 6025.1.

MOGENSEN Finn, b. 19 Sept 1934, Frederikshavn. Chief Physician. m. Jane Voss Frank, 2 Apr 1960, 2 s, 1 d. *Education:* Acad Col, Copenhagen, 1960; Med Grad, Arhus Univ, Denmark, 1969; ENT Specialist, Arhus Hosp, 1976; Audiol, Odense Hosp, 1978; Sr Resident, Kalundborg Hosp, 1969-70; Hobro Hosp, 1970-71; Randers Hosp, 1971-72; Arhus Hosp, 1972-74; Vejle Hosp, 1974-76; Odense Hosp, 1976-78; Holstebro Hosp, 1979-; Chief Phys, ENT Dept and Audiol Clinic, Holsteboro, 1981-; Constl in Audiol, Greenland, 1978, 1980, 1981, 1984. *Publications:* Evaluation of low-cost hearing aids in support of people with hearing disability in: WHO report, 1991. *Memberships:* The Assn for Better Hearing, Scandinavia, 1985; Chm, Scandinavian Expert Panel, Risk of Damage at Different Levels of Noise, 1987; Intl Conslt, The Assn for Better Hearing, Denmark, 1977-, VP, 1988-; Tech Audiol Lab, Bd, European Coop of Sci and Tech Res, Holstebro Golf. *Address:* Centralsygehuset, Laegardsvej 12, 7500 Holstebro, Denmark. 52.

MOHAMMED Abdel Hamid Ibrahim, b. 25 Apr 1935, Egypt. m. Zeinab Amer, 18 Mar 1940, 2 s. *Education:* BA Arabic Lang and Islamic Studies, Dar Al-ulum, Cairo, 1962; MA, Classical Arabic Lit, 1965; PhD Modern Arabic Lit, 1969. *Appointments include:* Lectr, 1972-75; Reader, 1979-80, Fac of Arts, Minya, Egypt, 1972-75; Reader, Sanaas Univ, Yemen, 1975-79; Vis Prof, Sch of Oriental and African Studies, Univ of London, 1980-82; Prof, Egyptian and Arab Univs, 1983; Hd of Dept of Arab Lang, Fac of Arts, Al Minia, 1984-86; Dean of Arab Studies, 1986-. *Publications:* More than 30 books on modern and classical Arabic literature and

Islamic studies and over 100 articles published in professional magazines. *Memberships include:* Writer's Union, Cairo; Senate, Minia Univ; High Coun for Egyptian Univs; Com for Improving Texts of Arabic Lang, Ministry of Educ; Ed in Chief of: The Southerner, and Arabic Studies. *Honours:* Recipient of honours from: Union of Modern Literature; Sanaa Univ; Ministry of Culture, Egypt; Fac of Educ in Domiat; Nat Biog of Famous Egyptian Personages.

MOHAN Devendra, b. 1 Apr 1932, Meerut, India. Homeopathic Physician. m. Surrinder Kaur, 11 Dec 1954, 1 s, 2 d. *Education:* DMS, 1954. *Publications:* Papers presented at the Proceeding of Homeopathic Congress, Rotterdam, 1975, Moscow, 1990. Radio talk on immunology, 1966. *Memberships:* Int Homeopathic League; Sr Active Rotary Intl; Worshipful Master, Lodge Yadvindra 141 GLI India; Treas, Ramakrishna Mission, Chandigarth, India; Whole Health Inst, USA. *Honours:* Physician to His Excellency the Gov of Punjab State, 1979-85; Paul Harris Sustaining Mem, Rotary Foun of Rotary Intl, USA *Hobbies:* Photography; Gardening; Reading; Inspiring sick patients. *Address:* House 1561, Sector 18D, Chandigarh 160018, India.

MOHNS Grace Updegraff Bergen, b. 20 Nov 1907, Dubuque, Iowa, USA. Composer; Pianist; Teacher; Poet. m. Edward A Mohns, 28 June 1932, 1 s, 1 d. *Education:* BA Univ of Minnesota, 1930; Composition fellowship, Julliard Sch, 1930; Postgrad study, S.Methodist Univ; Studied privately, piano with L Godowsky and composition. *Appointments:* Tchr of Piano, composition and theory, 1930-80; Music Tchr, Pvte and Pub Schs, 1930-32; Piano recitals of original piano and song concerts, nationally, 1930-; Bible Teacher at Churches, Lect recitals on Am Indians, nationally, 1949-; Composer, 1930-. *Publications include:* Thine is the Power, used as theme hymn by Presbyterian Women; In God we Trust; Nocturne; Love is God's gift, wedding song; Christ is Risen; Music Everywhere; L'Armistice; Intermezzo and numerous others. *Memberships:* Oregon Symph Assn; Delta Gamma; Sigma Alpha Iota; Beta Sigma Phi; Oregon Music Tchrs Assn; Nat Music Tchrs Assn; Oregon Composers Soc; Am Assn of Univ Women. *Honours:* 1st Prize, Piano Composition, Minnesota Hg Schs, 1922, 1925; Fellowship in Composition, Julliard Sch of Music, NY, 1930-; Intl Hon Mem, Beta Sigma Phi. *Hobbies:* Piano improvisation; Reading; Swimming. *Address:* Welcome Retreat, 12705 SE River Rd Apt 405-S, Portland, OR 97222, USA. 4, 5, 7, 9, 120, 138.

MOISIUK Jan G., b. 28 Mar 1960, Moscow, Russia. Transplant Surgeon. m. Aleshkevich Galina, 2 Apr 1988, 1 s, 1 d. *Education:* Med Inst, Moscow, 1977-83; Liver Transplant Training Crse, Pittsburgh Univ, USA, 1989; MD, 1987; PhD, 1992. *Appointments:* Transplant Surg, 1983-89; Hd, Kidney and Liver Transplant Dept, Res Inst of Transplantol and Artificial Organs, Moscow, 1989-92. *Publications:* Over 60 published scientific papers on surgery, kidney, heart and liver transplantation, 1980-92. *Honours:* Best student research work prize, Med Scis Acad, 1981. *Hobbies:* Fishing; Travelling. *Address:* Research Institute of Transplantology & Artificial Organs, Schukinskaya St 1, Moscow 123436, Russia.

MOK Jacqueline Yek Quen, b. 1 Feb 1951, Kuala Lumpar, Malaysia. Consultant Paediatrician and Part-Time Senior Lecturer. m. Charles Court- Brown, 6 July 1974, 1 s, 1 d. *Education:* DCH, Glasgow Univ, 1976; MBChB 1974, MD 1983, FRCP 1989, Edinburgh Univ; MRCP, 1977. *Appointments:* Conslt Paed, Reg Infectious Diseases Unit, City Hosp, Edinburgh and Dept of Community Child Hlth, Lothian Hlth Bd; Pt-time Sr Lectr, Child Life and Health Dept, Edinburgh Univ. *Publications:* Several articles on mother to child transmission of human immunodeficiency virus and on the care and management of paediatric AIDS. *Memberships:* Brit Paed Respiratory Gp; European Paed Respiratory Soc; Paed Res Soc; Scottish Paed Soc; Brit

Paed Assn. *Honours:* Ettles Scholar and Leslie Gold Medallist, Edinburgh Univ Med Sch, 1969-74; Prize, Scottish Assn for Med Edn of Women; Dist and Class Medal in Child Life and Health; Lawson Gifford prize for Obs and Gynae and Dist in Gen Surgery. *Hobbies:* Skiing; Swimming; Running around after the family. *Address:* Craigesk House, Dalkeith EH22 4TP, Scotland.

MOL Pieter Laurens, b. 26 Oct 1946, Breda, The Netherlands. Visual Artist. m. Ludmila Danon, 1978, 2 s. *Education:* Art Acad, St Joost, Breda, Holland. *Publications include:* Solo Exhibs: Stedelijk Van Abbemuseum, Eindhoven, 1975; Galerie Seriaal, Amsterdam, Deux Artistes de la Bienale (with Paul van Dijk), Inst Stedelijk Museum, Amsterdam, 1977; Galerie Helen van der Meij, Amsterdam, 1978; Galerie Helen van der Meij, Amsterdam, Wurttembergischer Kunstverein, Stuttgart, 1980, Ikon Gallery, Birmingham, Kunsthalle, Basel, Galerie Toni Gerber, Bern, 1981; Galerie Helen van der Meij, Amsterdam, 1982; Galerie Helen van der Meij/Paul Th. Andriesse, Amsterdam, 1983; Kunstverein in Hamburg, Hamburg, Le Museeé de Valence, Valence, Galerie Nikki Diana Marquardt, Paris, 1988; Galleria Mikkola and Rislakki, Helsinki, Louver Gallery, New York, Galerie Cintrik, Antwerp, 1990; Galleria Sperone, Rome, 1991; La Charge Utile, Centre dArt Contemporain, Geneva, Stedelijk Van Abbemuseum, Eindhoven, Ferro Fever, Institute of Contemporary Art/Amsterdam, Amsterdam, 1992. Group Exhibs include: Nachtregels/Nightlines: Words without Thoughts Never to Heaven Go, Centraal Museum, various sites in the city, Utrecht, 1991; Strata, Tampere Art Museum, Tampere, Joy and Pain, Instutute of Contemporary Art/Amsterdam, Poiesis, Fruitmarket Gallery, Edinburgh, 1992. *Address:* Zandpad 75, 3621 Ng Breukelen, Holland.

MOLES Abraham, b. 19 June 1920, France. University Professor. *Education:* Elec Engr, 1942; PhD Sci, 1952; PhD Phil, 1956. *Appointments:* Engr, Lab for Testing Materials, 1946; Sci Dir, Kister Pub, Res Fellow, French CNRS, 1946-54; Prof, Organisation Sch, 1956-60; Univ Prof, Hochschule Gestaltung, 1961-68; Prof, Strasbourg Univ, 1968-86; Invited Prof, Univ Firenze, Italy, 1984-85. *Publications:* 25 books: Theory of Information and Perception; Musiques Experimentales; Psicologie del Espacio; Kunst und Computer; Micropsicologia; Sociodinamica Della Cultura; Teoria de Actos Science de L'Imprecis; Creation Scientifique Theorie Communication. *Memberships:* Assn of Phys; Soc Gens de Lettre; Int Assn of Micropsychol; Soc D'Acoustique; Soc Ecrvains Sci France; Intl Assn of Psychol; Soc Francaise de Psychol; Intl Assn of Sociol. *Honours:* Grant, Rockefeller Foun, Columbia Univ, NY. *Hobbies:* Graphic Art; Sketching; Mexican Culture. *Address:* 5 Impasse Des Pierres, 6700 Strasbourg, France.

MOLLARD John Douglas, b. 3 Jan 1924, Regina, Saskatchewan, Canada. Consulting Engineer and Geologist. m. Mary Jean Lynn, 18 Sept 1952, 1 s, 2 d. *Education:* BE Civil Engrg, Univ of Saskatchewan, 1945; MSCE, Purdue Univ, 1947; PhD, Engrg Geol, Cornell Univ, 1952. *Appointments:* Conslt Engr, Sask Highway Dept, 1945; Res Engr, Cornell Univ, 1950-52; Chief, Engrg Geol Div, PFRA, Can Agric, 1953-56; Tech Advr, Aerial Resource Sur, Govts of Pakistan and Ceylon, 1955; Pres, JD Mollard & Assocs Ltd, 1956-. *Publications:* Author and co-author of over 100 publications in scientific and technical journals and two books. *Memberships:* Fellow, Geol Assn Canada; Geol Soc Am; Am Soc Civil Engrs; Am Soc Photogramm Remote Sensing; Intl Explorers Club, NYC: Eng Inst Can; Assoc Conslt Engrs, Can; Can Geotech Soc; Can Soc Petrol Geol; Sask Geol Soc; Regina Geotechs Soc. *Honours include:* Dist Lectr, Can Geotech Soc, 1969; Recognition for pioneering photointerpretation in engineering and geology, Am Soc of Philogramm, 1979; Thomas Roy Awd, 1989; Vis Lectr, Univs in Can and Am, 1952-91; R F Legget Award, Can Geotech Soc, 1992. *Hobbies:* Arctic exploration; Collecting unusual rock specimens; Nature Study; Hiking; Bibliophily; Sport.

Address: 2960 Retallack Street, Regina, Sasketchewan, Canada S4S 1S9. 2, 14, 52.

MOLLER Annemarie Ewald, b. 20 Mar 1951, Copenhagen. Opera Singer; m. Ivar Munk, 25 Nov 1977, 1 s. *Education:* Royal Acad of Music, Copenhagen, 1977; Royal Opera Acad, 1980. *Appointments:* Royal Opera, Copenhagen; Debut, Mercedes Carmen, 1980. *Creative works include:* Ludmila & Tiger, Animalen, 1981; Meg Page, Falstaff, 1982; Cherubino, Figaro, 1983; Flora, La Traviata, 1983; Olga, Eugen Onegin, 1984; David, Saul, 1985; 3rd Boy and 3rd Lady, Magic Flute, 1985; Lola, Cavalleria, 1985; Flosshilde, Rhinegold, 1986; Page, Salome, 1986; Tara, Siddharta, 1987; Messaggiera, Orfeo, 1982; Fjodor, Boris, 1986; Grimgerde, The Valkyrie, 1987; Dorabella, Cosi, 1988; Suzuki, Butterfly, 1989; Parsifal, 1989; Sorceress, Dido, 1989; Alisa, Lucia, 1989; Margaret, Wozzeck, 1985; Emilia, Otello, 1989; Mother, Hoffman, 1990; Sonetka, Lady Macbeth, 1991; Marcellina, Figaro, 1991; St Mathew Passion, 1985-86; First Maid, Elektra, 1986; Verdi Requiem, 1986; B-minor Mass, 1990. *Address:* Bog Ehoj 37, DK-2900, Hellerup, Denmark.

MOLLOVA Milena, b. 19 Feb 1940, Razgrad. Piano Professor. div. 1 s, 2 d. *Education:* Dipl, Piano Performance, Bulgarian Music Acad; Studied with: Mrs Pavla Gekova, Prof Dimiter Nenov and Prof Panka Pelishek in Bulgaria; Prof Emil Gillels in Moscow. *Appointments:* Deubt, aged 6; Recitals and concertos in Bulgaria, Japan, Germany, Belgium, Hungary, Poland, Czech, Cuba, Italy, Yugoslavia; Prof in Bulgarian Music Acad. *Creative works:* Concert performance, 1987-88; 32 sonnatas, Beethoven in 9 concerts; Recordings include works by Tchaikovsky, Beethoven, ozart, Chopn, Liszt, Vladigeroff, Dimiter Hristov, Kjurkchiyski. *Memberships:* Unions of Bulgarian Compositors, and Bulgarian Musicians. *Honours:* Special 1st Prize, Bulgarian Competition, 1949; 1st prize, 6th World Festival, Moscow, 1957; 5th Prize, Tchiakovsky Competition, Moscow, 1958; 3rd Prize, Long- Thibaud, Paris, 1959; 3rd prize, Intl Competition, Munich, 1962; 4th Prize, Intl Beethoven Competition, Vienna, 1969. *Hobbies:* Reading; Grandaughter. *Address:* Hypodruma 24-5, Sofia 1612, Bulgaria.

MOMOZAWA Chikara, b. 30 May 1918, Tokyo, Japan. Professor Emeritus of English. m. Yuko Nakamura, 1 s. *Education:* Tokyo Col of Foreign Studies, 1938-41; Postgrad, Univ of Michigan, 1951-52; Res Fellow, Cornell Univ. *Appointments:* Asst Prof, Oita Col, Japan, 1946-48; Asst Prof, Prof, Prof Emeritus, Chuo Univ, Tokyo. *Publications:* An outline Syntax of English, 1959; On Jespersen, 1962; On Prepositions, 1966; Modern English Syntax, 1971; How to Write English, 1974; English Teaching and learning. *Memberships:* Japan Assn of Current English, VP, 1980-85; Japan Assn of Col Eng Tchrs, Counsellor, 1985-88; Soc of Testing Eng Proficiency, Counsellor, 1969-; Soc of Eng Philol and Educ, Hon Pres, 1989-. *Honours:* Dist Acad Awd for Achievement, Univ of Michigan, USA, 1952. *Hobbies:* Gardening; Shakuhachi, (Japanese Flute); Go; Shogi (chess).*Address:* 5-13-4 Yoyogi, Shibuya-ku, Tokyo 151, Japan. 52.

MONDY Nell I, b. 27 Oct 1921. Professor. *Education:* BA, MA, summa cum laude, Ouachita Univ, 1943; MA Biochem, Texas Univ, 1945; PhD Biochem, Cornell Univ, 1953. *Appointments include:* Conslt; The RT French Co. Rochester, NY, Inst Food and Nutrition, Ctr for Hlth, Univ Wisconsin, 1981; Proctor & Gamble, Cincinnati, 1985; Frito-Lay, Rhinelander, Wisconsin, 1988; Vis Scist, Intl Inst of Tropcl Argric, Ibadan, Nigeria, 1983-84; Vis Scholar, Inter Univ Ctr, Food Sci & Tech, Gadjah Mada Univ, Indonesia, 1989; Asst Prof, 1953-57, Assoc Porf, 1957-61, Prof, 1981-, Food and Nutrition, Cornell Univ. *Publications:* Author of reports and articles in professional journals and magazines; Papers presented at conferences and seminars. *Memberships include:* ACS; AAUP; Fellow, Am Inst of Chemists; Fellow, AAAS; Fellow, Inst of Food Technologists; Soc of Environ Toxicol

and Chem; NYAS. *Honours include:* Charter Mem, Phi Tau Sigma; Sigma Xi; Pi Lambda Theta; Sr Dir, 1990, Nat Hon Mem, 1986, Pres, 1983-84, Grad Women in Sci, 1990; Centennial Achievement Awd, Ouachita Univ, 1986; Hon Life Mem, Potato Assn of Am, 1983. *Hobbies:* Gardening; Photography. *Address:* 126 Honness Lane, Ithaca , NY 14850, USA. 2, 5, 6, 15, 28, 152, 132, 130, 162, 154, 125, 156, 155, 129.

MONKS John Christopher, b. 21 Jan 1954, Manchester, England. Artist. m. Susan Phyllis Herbert. 1 s, 1 d. *Education:* BA Painting, Sch of Art, Liverpool Poly, 1972-75; MA Painting, Royal Col of Art, London, 1977-80. *Appointments:* Brit Coun Rep, Strumica Univ, Yugoslavia, 1987; Artist in Residence, Brit Inst, Madrid, Spain, 1990. *Publications:* Collection, Metropolitan Mus of Art, NY, 1985; Car Door: Collection Lord Palumbo, London, 1986; Collection: Centre for British Art, Yale University, New Haven, USA, 1992. *Honours:* John Moores Scholarship, Liverpool, 1975-76; New Contemporaries Prize Winner, ICA, London, 1976. *Hobbies:* Reading; Natural history; Cycling. *Address:* Paton Gallery, 2 Langley Court, London WC2, England.

MONRO Jean Anne, b. 31 May 1936, India. Medical Director of Environmental and Allergy Hosp. 2 s. *Appointments:* Res Asst, Nat Hosp for Nervous Diseases, 1974-82; Conslt, Clin Allergist, Humana Hosp, St Johns Wood, 1982-84; Med Dir, Allergy and Environmental, 1984-. *Publications include:* Some Dietary Approaches to Disease Management, 1974; Co-author, Chemical children, 1987. *Memberships:* Principal Med Advr to EMF; Med Advr to Sanity, Coeliac Assn; Henry Doubleday Res Assn; Fellow, Am Acad for Environ Med; Diplomate, Int Bd of Environ Med; Brit Soc for Allergy & Environ Med; Brit Soc of Immunol; Am Coll Occup Environ Med. *Hobbies:* Tennis; Badmington. *Address:* Breakspear Hospital for Diagnostic Medicine, Allergy and Environmental Medicine, 1 High Street, Abbots Langley, Herts WD3 OPU, England.

MONRO Jean, b. 25 June 1916, London, England. Interior Designer. *Education:* Sch Cert, Miss Ironside, Queens Gate, London; Matric, Francis Holland Graham St; Mrs L'Estrange Florence; Art & Hist of Art, Italy. *Appointments:* Army Ser, 1942-46; Mrs Monro Ltd, 1946. *Publication:* 11 Montpolier St. *Memberships:* FRSA; Fellow, Interior Decorators and Designers Assn; Exec Com, Georgian Gp; V-Chm, Leche Trust; Bath Preservation Trust. *Hobbies:* Painting; Gardening; Conservation; Reading; Travel. *Address:* Flat 8, 46 Elm Park Gardens, London SW10 9PA, England.

MONTGOMERY Alan Everard, b. 11 Mar 1938, England. HM Diplomatic Service. m. Janet Barton, 16 July 1960, 1 s, 1 d. *Education:* RGS Guildford, 1949-54; Cert of Educ, County of Stafford Tchrs Training Col, 1961; BA Hons, PhD, Birbeck Col, Univ of London, 1962-69. *Appointments:* Tchr, Staffs and ILEA, 1961-65; Lectr, Univ of Birmingham, 1969-72; FCO, 1972, First Sec, 1972-83, Counsellor, 1983-92, HM Ambassador, Manila, 1992-. *Contributions to:* collection of essays, Lloyd George, 1971, The Historical Journal, 1972. *Hobbies:* Gardening; Theatre; Writing Pantomimes; Jazz. *Address:* c/o FCO, King Carles Street, London SW1A 2AH, England. 1.

MONTIJO Ralph Elias Jr., b. 26 Oct 1928, Tucson, Arizona, USA. Chief Executive Officer, Omniplan Corp. m. Guillermina Paredes, 26 Dec 1947, 1 s, 2 d. *Education:* BS, Elec Engrg, Univ of Arizona, 1952. *Appointments include:* Computer Systems Division, PRC: Dir, Advanced Systems Planning, 1967-68, Dpty Div Mgr for Eastern and Europe Ops, 1968, Depty Div Mgr for Advances Systems Planning, and Mgr, Reservations Systems, 1968-69; VP and Gen Mgr, Intl Reservations Corp, (IRC) 1969-70; Pres and Dir, IRC Intl Devel Corp, 1971-; VP, Systems Sci Devel Corp, 1972-. *Publications:* Author: The Proposed System of Computer-Communications Network for California's Dept of Motor Vehicles, 1965; Preliminary Cost-

Effectiveness Models, 1968; Technology and the Human Spirit... People in Tomorrow's World, 1968; Minority Business Enterprise in American Public Transit, 1976; Computerizing California's Past: Ways and Means, 1976. *Memberships:* IEEE; AMA; Assn for Computing Machinery; Nat Soc Prfl Engrs. *Honours:* Scabbard and Blade, 1949; Alumni Achievement Awd, 1984, Centennial Medallion Awd, 1989, Univ Arizona. *Hobbies:* Snow Skiing; Scuba Diving; Music; Arts; Travel. *Address:* Omniplan Corporation, 17041 El Camino Real, Houston, TX 77058, USA. 2, 7, 57, 59, 132.

MONTINOLA Lourdes Reyes, b. 25 Nov 1927, Manila, Philippines. Chairman, Bd of Trustees, Far Eastern University. *Education:* BA cum laude, Marymount Col, NY, 1948; Inst of Ed Mgmt, Grad Sch of Educ, Harvard Univ, 1985; MA, Cultural Hist, Asean Grad Inst of Afts, 1991. *Appointments:* FEU: Fac Mem, Inst of Educ, 1948-51; Soc Coor, 1949-51; Asst to the Treas, 1951-52; Corp Sec, 1957-89; V-Chm, Bd of Trustees, 1983-89; Chm, Bd of Trustees, 1989-. *Publications:* Poetry: Green Poem, Bravo 2; Articles: Value of Elegance, 1986; An Elegy for Things Past, 1988; Pina in Peril, 1988; Pina Queen of Philippine Textiles, 1988; Delicate Tales of Kerchiefs, 1989; Pina, 1991. *Memberships:* Hd, Cultural Com, Bd of Dirs, 1987-89, Pres, Alliance Francaise de Manille, 1989-91; Concerned Citizens for the National Mus; Oriental Ceramic Soc; Friends, Cultural Ctr of the Philippines. *Honours:* Curian Hon Soc, Marymount Col; Cert of Recognition, Barangay Forbes Pk, Makati, 1968; Sr Writing Fellow, Univ of Philippines; Creative Writing Ctr, 10th Nat Writers Summer Workshop, 1982. *Hobbies:* Reading; Tennis; Collecting paintings; Antique porcelain; and Artifacts. *Address:* 11 Molave, Forbes Park, Makati, Metro Manila, Philippines.

MOODY Anthony David, b. 21 Jan 1932, New Zealand. University Teacher. *Education:* BA 1951, MA Hons, 1952, Canterbury Col, Univ of New Zealand; BA Hons, 1955 MA, 1962, Oxford Univ. *Appointments:* UNHCR, Geneva, 1957-58; Lectr, Sr Lectr in Eng, Univ of Melbourne, 1958-65; Lectr, Dept of Eng and Related Lit, Univ of York, 1966-; Currently, Prof of Eng and Am Lit. *Publications:* Virginia Woolf, 1963; The Merchant of Venice, 1964; T S Eliot: Poet, 1979; At the Antipodes, 1972; News Odes: THe El Salvador Sequence, 1984. *Memberships:* Assn of Univ Tchrs; Nat Poetry Foun; T S Eliot Soc; Assn of Little Presses. *Honours:* Univ of New Zealand Shirtcliffe Fellow, 1953-55; Nuffield Foun Travelling Fellow, 1965; Brit Acad/Leverhulme Vis Prof, 1988; Vis Prof, Univ of Toledo, Ohio, 1988. *Hobbies:* Walking; Looking; Listening; Publishing poetry; Tennis. *Address:* Dept of English & Related Literature, University of York, York YO1 5DD, England. 57.

MOOR Philip Drury, b. 15 July 1959, Bridport, Dorset, England. Barrister. m. Gillian ELizabeth Stark, 18 July 1987. *Education:* Canford Sch, 1972-77; Pembroke Col Oxford, MA Jurisprudence. *Appointments:* Called to the Bar, Inner Temple, 1982; Practice in family law, 1983-. *Contributions to:* The magazine, Family Law. *Memberships:* Gen Coun of the Bar, 1987-89; Coun of Legal Educ, 1988-; Com of Family Law Bar Assn, 1987-. *Hobbies:* Cricket; Association Football. *Address:* 1 Mitre Court Buildings, Temple, London EC4Y 7BS, England.

MOORE Basil Herbert, b. 22 Dec 1910, London, England. Retited Civil Servant and Lang Agent. m. Frances Foster Kay, 6 d. *Education:* Royal Agric Col, 1928-31; Dipl, Est Mgmt, MRAC; Fellow, Chartered land Agents Soc; FRICS.Articled to: Sir Anchor Simmonds & Sons, Henley, 1931-32 Sir George Langley-Taylor, Archts, 1932-33. *Appointments:* Lectr, Est Mgmt, Royal Agric Col, 1933-34; Asst Lang Agent, Norfolk C.C, 1934-36; County Land Agent, Lindsey, Lincs, CC, 1936-45; Asst Land Commr, MAFF, 1940; Lands Ofr, W.Riding Wav AEC, 1941-43; Rural Land Utilisation Ofr, Yorks, MAFF, 1943-45; Land Commr: Lancs & Cheshire, 1945-55, Licolnshire, 1955-72. *Memberships:* Diploma in Estate Mangement; Fellow of Chartered Land Agents

Soc; Fellow of Royal Ins of Chartered Surveyors. *Honours:* Fdr, Aberystwyth Mental Health Charity; ASH in Mid Wales; Chm, Mid Wales and Lincoln Conservative Socs; Chm, Brit Humanist Assn. *Hobbies:* Reading; Gardening; Swimming. *Address:* Y Fielin Penpompren, Tal y Bont, Dyfed, Wales SY24 5HH.

MOORE David Austin, b. 8 May 1935, Phoenix, Arizona, USA. Teacher; Oner, Nutrition and Medical Research. m. (1) 2 s, 1 d, (2) Emily Jane McConnell, 26 Jan 1991. *Education:* Music and Voice, with Joseph Lazzarini, 1953-54, 1957-64. Italy, 1955-56. *Appointments:* Salesman, 1960; Salesman, Enzyme Process Co, 1963; Fdr, David A Moore Inc, 1969; Fdr, Biological Labs Ltd, 1969-71. *Publications:* Articles on hair analysis, 1987; Inventor, First computerized hair analysis interpretation with recommendations, 1976; Introduced Di Calcium Phosphate Free Concept and 100% label disclosure, 1975-79. *Memberships:* Am Soc of Elemental Testing Labs, 1980-83. *Honours:* Speaking Awd Plaque, Arizona State Soc for Med Tech, 1982. *Hobbies:* Teaching operatic singing; Opera and Classical Music; Researching various subjects of interest; Visiting Historical sites; History study. *Address:* Nutrition and Medical Research, PO Box 98, Barnesboro, PA 15714, USA. 57, 9, 132, 155.

MOORE Harry Russell, b. 28 Dec 1921, Cumberland, Ohio, USA. Lawyer. m. Marcella Virginia Williams, 12 Jan 1946. *Education:* Naval War Col, 1962-63; AB, 1964, AM, 1965, Int Affairs, George Washington Univ; JD Intl Sch of Law, 1977; JD Confirmed George Mason Univ, 1982. *Appointments:* US Navy, 1942-72, incl Combat Serv, S.Pacific, 1943-44, Vietnam 1969; Commd Ensign, 1945, Advanced to Capt, 1967, Sea Commands Atlantic, USS Hawk, (AMS-17), 1948-49; Mine Div, 85, 1960-62, USS Hugh Purvis, (DD-709), 1965- 67; US Naval Attache and Naval Attache for Air Karachi, Pakistan, 1967-68; Sea Commd in Pacific, Mine Flotilla Three, 1968-69; Prof, Nav Sci Col of Holy Cross, Mass, 1970-72; Pvt Practice Law, Moneta, VA, 1977-92; Pvt Atty, Legal Aid Soc, Roanoke Valley, 1983-92; Gen Practice, Real Property and Legal Aid to elderly and poor. *Publications:* A Nagivation Compedium. *Memberships:* Bars: VA, 1977, US Dist Ct, West Dist, VA, 1980, US Ct of Appeals, 4th Cir, 1982, US Supreme Ct, 1990; Bedford Co VA Bar Assn; Re'td Ofrs Assn, Roanoke Valley, Am Legion, Post 54. *Honours:* Legion of Merit, 1972; Various campaign medals and ribbons including battle stars for Guadalcanal and Consolidation of Southern Solomons. *Hobby:* Beekeeping. *Address:* Honeymede, Route 4 Box 760, Moneta, VA 24121, USA. 7, 52, 163.

MOORE Howard Ernest, b. 12 Oct 1947, Roswell, New Mexico, USA. Psychologist. m. Lynn S Kuttnauer, 18 Aug 1984, 1 d. *Education:* BA Wayne State Univ, 1971; PhD Clin Psychol, Univ of Detroit, 1980; Internships: Ypsilante State Hosp, 1976-77, Henry Ford Hosp, 1977-78. *Appointments:* Botsford Gen Hosp, 1984-; Mt Carmel Hosp, 1979-85; Van Dyke Family Conselling Ctr, 1986-89; Univ of Detroit, 1985-; Dir, Behavioural Med, Providence Hosp, 1984-. *Publication:* Ego Strength, Defense Mechanisms and the Sense of Humour, 1980. *Memberships:* Am Psychol Assn; Michigan Psychol Assn; Am Assn of Marital and Family Therapists; Am Orthopsychi Assn; Michigan Soc for Psychoanalytic Psycho; Assn for the Advancement of Psychoanalysis; Soc of Tchrs of Family Med; Michigan Psychoanalytic Coun. *Honours:* Foun Scholar, 1965-67; Tchg Fellow, 1973-75; Fellow, Am Col of Psycho, 1984; Fellow, Am Orthopsychi Assn, 1985; Diplomate and Fellow, Am Bd of Med Psycho, 1987; Dip, Am Bd of Psycho (Child Psycho), 1987. *Hobbies:* Gardening; Golf; Cycling; Wines. *Address:* 32255 Northwestern Highway, Suite 250, Farmington Hills, MI 48334, USA.

MOORE James Russell, b. 19 Nov 1962, Traverse City, Michigan, USA. Director of Christian Education. m. Kimberly Joy McCann, 7 June 1986, 1 s. *Education:* BA, Hist and Biblical Lit, Indiana Wesleyan Univ, 1985;

MA Ministerial Educ, 1986; Grad work, Trinity Evangelical Div Sch, Huntington Col. *Appointments:* Asst Pastor, Wesleyan Ch, Oak Pk, IL, 1986-87; Dir of Christian Educ, Moeller Rd Wesleyan Ch, Ft Wayne, IN, 1987-. *Publications:* The Call to Ministry, 1986; Numerous articles. *Memberships:* Wesleyan Theol Soc; Profl Assn for Christian Educrs; Sec; Treas, Three Rivers Sunday Sch Assn; Pi Gamma Mu. *Hobbies:* Biblical Research; Coin collecting; Reading; Writing. *Address:* 4822 Hessen Cassel Road, Ft Wayne, IN 46806, USA. 2.

MOORE John Royston, b. 2 May 1921, Manchester, England. Retired Principal, Bradford and Ilkley College. m. 28 Mar 1947, 2 s. *Education:* BSc, Univ of Manchester; Hon MPhil, Chartered Chemist, Univ of Bradford. *Appointments:* Chemist-in-Charge, JNJ Mfg Plants; Grammar Sch Tchr; Principal, N Manchester Col; Principal, Bradford & Ikley Community Col. *Memberships:* FRSC; Leader, W.Yorks Metropolitan Coun, 1977-81; Opposition Leader, W.Yorks County Coun, 1981-86; Dir, Yorks Enterprise Bd, 1982-90. *Honours:* CBE, 1983; Hon MPhil, Univ of Bradford. *Hobbies:* Bridge; Cricket. *Address:* Bicknor 33 Station Rd, Baildon, Shipley, W Yorks BD17 6HS, England.

MOORE Sonia, b. 4 Dec 1902, Russia. Artistic Director. m. Leon Moore, 11 May 1926, 1 d. *Education:* Reale Acad Philarmonica, Italy, 1939; Reale Conservatorio di Musica, Santa Cecelia, Italy, 1939; Inst Interuniv, Italy, 1937; Alliance Francaise, France, 1927; The Moscow Art Theatre, 1920-23. *Appointments:* Artistic Dic, Am Stanislavski Theatre, 1970-; Fdr and Pres, the Am Ctr for Stanislavski Theatre Are, 1964-; Artistic Dir, Sonia Moore Studio, 1961-. *Publications:* Stanislavski Revealed, 1991; Training an Actor, 1968, Revised 1979; Videotape: Renowned Actress Julie Harris Inreviews S.M. on Stanislavski's final technique: solution to spontaneity on stage with demonstration; The Stanislavski System, 1965, Revised 1974 and 1984; The Stanislavski Method, 1960. *Memberships:* J F Kennedy Library Fdn, Hon Fellow; Charter Mem, Battle of Normandy Fdn; Fdg Mem, Nat Mus of Women in the Arts; Assoc of Theatre in Higher Educ; Smithsonian Inst; Am Library Assn; Authors Guild; Soc of Stage Dirs and Choreographers. *Honours:* NFK Library for Minorities Ser to the Community Awd, 1974; Am Heritage Awd; Katherine Engel Community Ser Awd; Hon Mem, Res Bd of Advrs of the ABI; George Freedley Awd nomination. *Hobbies:* Art; Music. *Address:* 485 Park Avenue, 6-A, New York, NY 10022, USA. 2, 5, 6, 138, 156, 155.

MOORE Sophia Evelin, b. 30 Sept 1924, Ghana. Teacher. m. 15 May 1953, 2 s, 1 d. *Education:* Tchr Training, 1942; Dipl, Home Econ, 1946; Dipl, Com Dev, 1965. *Appointments:* Tchr, 1943-45; Home Econ Tchr, 1948-70; Educ Ofr, 1971-80; Principal, Voc Inst, 1981. *Publications:* Women's Fell Handbooks; Women's Fell Manuals' Women's Fell Constitution; Cookery Book; Song Book. *Memberships:* ODD Dist Chm, 1986; WF Dist Sec, 1968-80, CONN Pres, 1980, Sec, 1981-89; VP, Meth Ch, 1989-92; Class Leader, 1952; Local Preacher, 1949. *Hobbies:* Sewing; Needle Craft; Dress making; Vegetable gardening; Writing. *Address:* Mancell Girl's Voc Institute, PO Box 498, Kumasi, Ashanti, Ghana, West Africa.

MOORE William David, b. 2 June 1949, Andalusia, Alabama, USA. Pastor; President. m. Rebecca Harper, 1 Jan 1972, 2 d. *Education:* BA cum laude, Stamford Univ, 1970; MDiv, S.Western Bap Theol Sem, 1972; PhD, Baylor Univ, 1978. *Appointments:* Grad Tchg Asst, Baylor Univ, 1973-74; Pastor, Deer Pk Bapt Ch, 1975-81; Pastor, Southside Bapt Ch, 1981-87; Pastor, Immanuel Bapt Ch, Bine Pluff, AR, Pres of TV-65, 1987-. *Publications:* The Orgin of Porneia Reflected in I Corinthians 5-6. *Memberships:* AAR; SBL; ACTS Nat Affiliates. *Hobbies:* Computers; Golf; Boating; Drama; Music; Amateur Radio. *Address:* PO Box 2374, Pine Bluff, AR 71603, USA. 145.

MOORE-SMITH Bryan, b. 6 Nov 1930, London, England. Consultant in Geriatric Medicine. m. Elizabeth Jean Dale, 26 May 1962, 1 s, 1 d. *Education:* Ampleforth Col, York, 1944-49; Oriel Col, Oxford, 1949-53; St Thomas's Hosp, London, 1953-55; MA BM BCh, Oxon; FRCP, London. *Appointments:* Conslt, Geriatric Med, 1968-. *Publications:* Papers and chapters in books on illness in elderly people. *Memberships include:* Brit Geriatrics Soc; Sch of Jesus and Mary Educ Trust Ltd, Chm, Bd of Govs, 1975-82; Sec, Geriatrics Com, RCP, 1971-90; Chm, 1990-, Bd of Examiners, RCP, London, 1984-; Occupational Therapists Bd of CPSM, 1986-; E.Suffolk Hlth Auth, 1987-90. *Hobbies:* Gardening, especially growing roses; Travel; Reading; Listening to music. *Address:* Wolmers, Stonham Aspal, Stowmarket, Suffolk IP14 6AS.

MOOSA Ismail, b. 17 July 1945, Male, Maldives. m. Shameema, 13 Nov 1964, 3 s, 3 d. *Education:* Ameer Ahmed Sch, 1953-58; Majeediyya Sch, 1958-63. *Appointments:* Clerk: Min of Justice, 1970-71, Min of Exeternal Affairs, 1971; English Clerk, Min of External Affairs, 1971-72; Sec: Ministry of Justice, 1972-76; Sec, 1976-79, Sr Sec, 1979-80, Asst Mgr, 1980, Mgr, 1980-81, Asst Dir, 1981-82, Dpty Dir, 1982-84, Dir, 1984-, State Trading Org; Dir, Silverline Garments Maldives Ltd, 1984-; Bd of Dirs: Maldives Ports Auth, 1991; Maldives Transp & Contracting Co Ltd, 1991; Bank of Maldives Ltd, 1982-91. *Memberships:* Atolls Devel Advy Bd, 1991; Advy Bd for Labour, 1987; Bd for Pharmaceuticals, 1989. *Hobby:* Photography. *Address:* State Trading Organization, 7 Haveeree Higun, Male 20-01, Maldives.

MORAIS Cesar, b. 3 Jan 1918, Vila Nova de Gaia, Portugal. Composer; m; Olga Cananho, 25 Sept 1948, 2 d. *Education:* MEduc, Hons, Composition, Piano and Mus Hist, Porto Superior Music Conservatoire; Conducting Courses, A Pitamic and Pierre Kelin. *Appointments:* Prof of Composition, Porto Music Conservatoire, 1968-88. *Publications:* Author of many symphonic and choral works mainly: Masses; Te Deums; Cantetas; Symphonic Poems: April Symphony; Autumn Poem; Mare-Cheia; Lusiadas; Mensagem; Life of Jesus, Oratoria; Piano, violin and cello concertos. *Memberships:* Portuguest Union of Composers. *Hobbies:* Reading; Playing cards. *Address:* Rua Fernao Mendes Pinto 327, 4400 Vila Nova de Gaia, Portugal.

MORAIS Maria Jose, b. 30 July 1953, Porto, Portugal. Concert Pianist. m. Vladimir Stoyanov, 19 Mar 1983, 2 d. *Education:* Superior Dipl, Piano, Nat Conservatoire of Porto, 1967; Masters Deg, Sofia Sup Conservatoire, 1983; Bacharel in Eng Lang, Univ Coimbra, 1970. *Appointments:* Intl Concert Pianist performing over 70 concerts a year in France, Belgium, Germany, Portugal, Spain, Italy, USSR, Poland, Austria, England, Asia and USA. Over 100 engagements to perform with distinguished orchestras incuding: London Mozart Players; RTBF, Antwerpen, Baden-Baden, Leningrad. *Publications:* Several records: Chopin Piano Music; Schumann Piano Concerto; M J Morais in Recital. *Memberships:* Lisbon Music Conservatoire. *Honours:* Prize Carlos Seixas, 1962; Prize Gulbenkian, First Prize of the Portuguese National Conservatoire, 1967; Special Awd, Viotti Piano Competition, 1972; Special Awd, Portuguese Press, 1985. *Hobbies:* Reading; Writing; Driving. *Address:* Av Eng Arantes e Oliveira 34 8 Esq, 1900 Lisboa, Portugal.

MORAN Thomas Francis, b. 11 Dec 1936, Manchester, New Hampshire, USA. m. Joan Elinor Belliveau, 5 June 1960, 1 s, 3 d. *Education:* BA Chem, St Anselm's Col, NH, 1958; PhD Chem, Univ Notre Dame, IN, 1962; Postdoc Fellow, Brookhaven Nat Lab, NY, 1962-64. *Appointments:* Postdoc Fellow, Brookhaven Natl Lab, 1962-64; Scist, 1964-66; Asst Prof, Prof of Chem, Georgia Inst of Tech, 1966-. *Publications:* Over 120 publications in refereed scientific literature in the are of gaseous ion chemistry and mass spectrometry as well as a number of patents. *Memberships:* ACS: APS:

Am Soc for Mass Spectrometry; AAAS. *Honours:* Danforth fellow, MA, Ferst Awd for Res Contributions at Georgia Tech; Conslt to US Dept of Energy. *Hobbies:* Gardening; Music. *Address:* Chemistry Department, Georgia Inst of Technology, Atlanta, GA 30332, USA. 7, 15, 125, 155, 162, 164.

MORAWSKI Stefan Tadeusz, b. 20 Oct 1921, Krakow, Poland. Reasearch Professor. m. (1) 1 d, (2) Helena Opoczynska, 1 July 1957. *Education:* BA, Eng Lit, Lang, 1947, Sheffield, England; PhD Philos, 1948, Univ Warsaw, Poland; MA, 1948, Univ of Krakow. *Appointments:* Tchr, Jangiellonian Univ, 1946-47, 1948-51; Res Work, Inst of Art, Warsaw, 1951-54; Prof, Univ of Warsaw, 1954-68; Res Prof, Inst of Art Hist and Theory, presently Emeritus within the same Inst; Retn'd Univ of Warsaw, 1988, taught until 1992. *Publications:* 7 books translated into foreign languages icluding: Absolute and Form, 1971, 1972; On Marxism and Esthetics, 1973; Inquiries into the Fundamentals of Aesthetics, 1977. *Memberships:* Polish and Greek Philos Socs; Polish Semiotic Soc; Bd, Jour of Aesthetics and Art Criticism; Praxis Intl; Knizevna Kritika, Belgrade; Chief Ed, Studia Estetyczne, 1965-68; Polish Art Studies, 1978-. *Honours:* Brit Coun Scholarship, 1946-47; Ford Foun Scholarship, 1962; Sr Fellowships at Princeton, 1973; Milwaukee, 1977; Brit Acad, 1984; Chapel Hill, 1985. *Hobbies:* Walking; Chess; Swimming; Film Criticism. *Address:* ul Waszyngtona 20 m 21, 03910 Warsaw, Poland.

MORDLER John Michael, b. 8 Nov 1938, London, England. *Education:* Merchant Taylor's Sch, 1952-58; MA, St Andrews Univ, 1959- 61; Acad Commerciale HEC Paris, 1958-59. *Appointments:* Producer, Decca Record Co, 1963-73; Sr Producer, EMI Records, 1973-83; Gen Dir, Monte-Carlo Opera, 1984-. *Memberships:* Bd, Ctr Nat D'Insertion Prof D'Art Lirique, France; Jury Mem: Toti Dal Monte, Italy; Belvedere, Vienna; Madame Butterfly, Tokyo; Prand Prix Lyrique, Monte Carlo; Artistic Conslt, Orquestra do Porto, Portugal. *Hobbies:* Squash; Skiing. *Address:* Opera de Monte Carlo, Place du Casino, Monte Carlo, Monaco. 57.

MORE David John, b. 11 Sept 1947, Aberdeen, Scotland. Artist. m. Yvette Brideau, 7 Apr 1984. *Education:* Dipl Painting, Alberta Col of Art, Calgary, 1972. *Appointments:* Med Graphics Artist, Univ of Calgary, 1973-74; Inst, Drawing and Design, Alberta Col of Art, 1975-78; Instr, Design, Red Deer Col, 1984-90. *Publications:* Co author, illustrator, Joy of Hockey, 1978; Joy of football, 1980; Golf, the Agony and the Ecstasy, 1982; Tennis, it Serves you right, 1984; The US or us - What's the Difference, eh?, 1986. *Honours:* Can Coun Arts Grant in Painting, 1974; Mayors Citizenship Recognition Awd for Nat Touring Exhib of Paintings, Forest - Fade to Silent, City of Red Deer, 1991. *Hobbies:* Music; Architecture; History; Ecology. *Address:* 5708-47A Avenue, Red Deer , Alberta, Canada T4N 6M2. 142.

MORETON (Cecil) Peter, b. 25 July 1927, Wellingborough, England. Consultant Surveyor; Broadcaster; Author. m. Eileen Frost, 6 Apr 1953, 1 s, 1 d. *Education:* Wellingborough Sch, 1941-44; Col of Est Mgmt, 1948-53. *Appointments:* W & H Peacock, Bedford, 1944-52; H P Barnsley, Hereford, 1952-53; Stimpson Lock & Vince, Watford, 1953-59; Anglia Bldg Soc, 1959-87; Chief Surveyor, 1977-87; RICS Insurance Sers Ltd, 1987-. *Publications:* Exec Ed, The Surveyors Factbook. *Contributions to:* The Estate Agents Factbook; Ser Ed, Surveyors Insurance News Ser; Chartered Surveyor Weekly; Producer; Presenter, It Ought to be Band, BBC Northampton. *Memberships:* RICS, Residential Valuation and Survey Com, Past Branch Chm; Inc Soc of Valuers and Auctioneers (ISVA); Chartered Bldg Socs Inst, (CBSI), Past Branch Chm; The Charter Soc; Rotary Intl, Dist Gov 1991-92. *Honours:* Paul Harris Fellow, 1985; FRICS, 1965; FSVA, 1988; FCBSI, 1985. *Hobbies:* Sport; Music; Author; Lecturer;

Writer; Freelance Broadcaster. *Address:* 86 Church Way, Weston Pavell, Northampton NN3 3BY, England.

MORGAN Daryle Whitney, b. 4 Nov 1929, Liberty, Idaho, USA. University Professor. m. Ima Joan Sandrus, 27 Nov 1951, 4 s. *Education:* BS, Utah State Univ, 1963; MEd, 1966, EdD, 1968, Univ of Missouri. *Appointments:* USAF 1951-55; Utah State Univ Inst, 1963-65; Asst Prof, 1968-71, Assoc Prof, 1971-76, Prof, 1976-, Texas A&M Univ. *Publications:* The Weldability of Steels and its Relationship to mechanical Properties, 1991; Metallurgy, weldability and inspection of Ferrous Metals, 1985; Welding metallurgy and Fabrication, 1982. *Memberships:* Am Welding Soc, Houston Ed Dir, 1976-81, 2984-87; Am Soc for Nondestructive Testing, Nat NDT Educ Opportunities Com, 1974-79; Am Soc for Metals; Texas Assn of Col Tchrs. *Honours:* Outstanding Fac Awd, 1989, 1991, Dist Tchg Awd, 1982, Texas A & M Univ; Dist Mem Awd, 1989, Dist Meritorious Cert Awd, 1987, Am Welding Soc; Outstanding Fac Awd for Tchg, Col of Engrg, TAMU, 1977. *Hobbies:* Camping; Hunting; Gardening; Landscaping. *Address:* Engineering Technology Department, Texas A & M University, Col Station, TX 77843, USA. 1, 7, 141.

MORGAN Myfanwy Ann. Senior Lecturer in Medical Sociology. *Education:* BA Hons Sociol, London, 1968; MA Sociol, Massachussets, 1972. *Appointments:* Res Ofr, Dept of Health, London, 1972-73; Res Fellow, Univ of Kent, 1974-79; Lectr, St Thomas Hosp, 1980-86; Sr Lectr, Utd Med and Dental Schls, St Thomas Hosp, 1987-. *Publications:* Over 35 articles on social aspects of health and illness and the organisation and provision of health care; Chapters in 6 books including Sociological Approaches to health and Medicine, 1985. *Memberships:* Brit Sociol Assn; Intl Epidemiol Assn; Soc for Social Med. *Honours:* Fellowship, Univ of Massachussets, 1970-72; Hon Mem, Fac of Public Health Med, (MFPHM), 1991. *Hobbies:* Reading; Travel; Theatre. *Address:* Department of Public Health Medicine, St Thomas Hospital, Lambeth Palace Rd, London, SE1 7EH, England.

MORGAN Rodney Emrys, b. 16 Feb 1942, England. Academic. m. Karin Birgitta Lang, 19 Aug 1966, 3 s. *Education:* Paston Sch, N.Walsham, 1952-60; Southampton Univ, 1964-68. *Appointments:* Res Fellow, Univ of Southampton, 1968-72; Lectr, Univ of Bath, 1972-89; Prof of Criminal Justice, Univ of Bristol, 1989-91; Dean of Law, Univ of Bristol, 1992-. *Publications:* A Taste of Prison, 1976; The Future of the Prison, 1980; Prisons and Accountability, 1985; Coming to terms with Policing, 1989. *Memberships:* Brit Soc of Criminology; Howard League; Amnesty Intl; NACRO: Socio Legal Studies Assn. *Honours:* Expert adviser to Coun of Europe, Home Office and Amnesty Intl. *Hobbies:* Sailing; Gardening; Theatre. *Address:* Faculty of Law Univ of Bristol, Wills Memorial Bldg, Queens Rd, Bristol BS8 1RJ, England.

MORI Hiroko, b. 5 May 1942, Hakkaido, Japan. m. 27 Dec 1974. *Education:* Womens Col of Fine Arts, Tokyo, 1960-63. *Appointments:* Prof of Sapporo Graphic Workshop, 1975-. *Publications:* Scrawl Series, 1983-84. *Memberships:* Hokkaido Fine Artist Assn. *Honours:* Chiji prize at Zendoten, 1992; Hokkaido Modern Mus Prize, at Zendoten, 1973; Kaiyu Prize at Zendoten, 1975; Second Prize at Hanga Grand Prix, 1976; Second Prize at Image Water Exhib, 1985. *Hobbies:* Cooking; Gardening. *Address:* 1-16-33 Midori Otaru, 047 Japan.

MORI Toshio, b. 27 Jan 1946, Aichi, Japan. Research Director and General Manager, The Japan Research Institute Limited. *Education:* Ba Econ, Keio Univ, Tokyo, 1968; MBA Prod Mgmt, Michigan State Univ, USA, 1969. *Appointments:* Sr Mgmt Conslt, Nomura Res Inst, Japan, 1970-82; Principal Conslt and Dir, Svc Industries Conslt Prog, SRI Intl, 1982-90; Res Dir and Gen Mgr, The Japan Res Inst Ltd, 1990-. *Publication:* Co-author of book, Think Tank Business, 1988. *Memberships:* Dir,

Assn of Tourism, Tokyo; Dir, Tokyo Mita Club; Pres, California Wine CLub Co Ltd; Pres, Mori Assocs Co Ltd; Japan Assn of Info Securities Mgmt. *Hobbies:* Golf; Yatching; Fishing. *Address:* 774-1 Isshiki, Hayama-machi, Miura-gun, Kanagawa Pre, Japan. 1.

MORIARTY James Joseph Patrick, b. 17 Mar 1938, Ireland. Psychologist. m. Joan Kowalski, 29 Oct 1971, 1 s. *Education:* Theol and Philos, St patrick's Col, Carlow, Ireland, 1959-61; MA, 1969, PhD, 1974, Clin Psycho, Univ of Detroit, Michigan. *Appointments:* Archdiocese of Miami, 1961-67; Psycho, Univ of Detroit, 1967-69; Dir, Family Coun Ctr of Broward County, Fla, and, Instr, Barry Univ, Fla, 1969-70; D G Clinic, Seaway Hosp, Trenton, Mich, 1972-74; Hutzel Hosp-Wayne State Univ Schl of Med, 1974-78; Pvt Prac, 1975-. *Publications:* Collage Group Therapy with Female Chronic Schizophrenic inpatients, 1973; Combining Activities and Group Psychotherapy in the treatment of chronic Schizophrenics, 1976. *Memberships:* Menninger Foun; APA; Am Assn for Marriage and Family Therapy; AAAS; NYAS: Employee Asst Profls Assn of N.Am; Am Soc for Applied Psychophysiol and Biofeedback; Am Soc of Clin Hypnosis. *Hobbies:* Painting; Gardening; Music; Nature; Physical fitness; Golf; Tennis; Travel; Celtic culture. *Address:* 55 W Maple, Birmingham, MI 48009, USA.

MORIMOTO Iwataro, b. 5 June 1928, Japan. Professor of Anatomy. m. 28 Oct 1928, 3 d. *Education:* MD, Shinshu Univ, 1955; Med License, Japan, 1956; DMSci, Shinshu Univ, 1962. *Appointments:* Instructor, 1956, Asst Prof, 1961, Shinshu Univ; Assoc Prof, Niigata Univ, 1963; Prof of Anatomy, Marianna Univ, 1972-. *Memberships:* Japanese Assn of Anatomists, Coun, 1972-; Anthropol So of Nippon, Coun, 1973-; Japan Association for Nile-Ethiopian Studies, Coun, 1992-; Japan National Comm for Anthropological Sciences of Science Councl of Japan. *Address:* Dept of Anatomy, St Marianna University School of Medicine, 2-16-1 Sugao, Miyamae-ku, Kawasaki 213, Japan. 52.

MORIN Sylvia Smith Crane, b.24 Oct 1922, Los Angeles, California, USA. Retired Neuropsychiatrist. m. Georges laurent Morin, 30 Mar 1948, 2 s, 1 d. *Education:* BA, Univ California, 1944; MD, Fac de Med de Bordeaux, France, 1961; Dipl of Neurol and Psychi, Fac de Med de Paris, 1968. *Appointments:* Pvt Prac, Neuropsychiatry and Electroencephalography, St Brieuc, France, 1962-91; Co-Fdr, Pvt Psychi Hosp in Yffiniac, France, 1964, Res Psychia, 1964-85; Attachee of Electroencephalography at Hosp de la Salpetriere, paris, 1972-74. *Publications:* Articles to professional magazines and journals and papers presented at national and international conferences. *Memberships:* Titulam Mem, French Speaking Soc of Clin Neurophysiol; French and Intl Leagues Against Epilepsy; Bd of Dirs and Sec, Franco-Am Inst, Rennes; French Soc of Psychi Epidemiol. *Honours:* Hon for MD Thesis which was sent to French medical schools and the medical library in Paris. *Hobbies:* Swimming; Sailing; Computer Research; Voluntary liaison work for Intl League Against Epilepsy. *Address:* Clinique du Val Josselin, 22120 Yffiniac, France. 52.

MORLAND Richard Boyd, b. 27 June 1919, Huntsville, Alabama, USA. Retired Educator. m. Jessie May Parrish, 17 Mar 1947, 1 d. *Education:* AB, Birmingham S. Col, 1940; MEd, Springfield Col, MA, 1947; PhD, NY Univ, 1958. *Appointments:* Phy Dir, YMCA, Frankfort, KY, 1940-41; USNR, Lieut, 1941-45; Dir, Athletics, Hd Basketball Coach, Fl S.Col, 1947-50; Lectr in Educ, NY Univ, 1950-51; Chm, Dept of Phy Educ, 1952-60; Assoc Prof, 1958- 63, Prof, 1963-90, J Ollie Edmunds Prof, 1982-83, Chm, grad Div, 1962-69, Chm, Educ Dept, 1969-75, Stetson Univ, DeLand, FL. *Publication:* The Five Flghting Lexingtons of the US Navy, 1776-1991. *Memberships:* Fla Coun Deans and Dirs, Tchr Educ, Pres, 1974-75; Phi Educ Soc, Regional Pres, 1963- 64; Phi Delta Kappa, Regional Pres, 1977-78, Ed Bd, 1978-82; Kappa Delta Pi; Omicron Delta Kappa; Kappa Alpha;

Am Educl Res Assn. *Honours:* McEnery Awd for Excellence in Tchg, 1983; Stetson Univ Sports Hall of Fame, 1981; Educr of the Yr, Phi Delta Kappa, 1991; Richard B Morland Dist Alumni Awd named in his honour, 1988. *Address:* 524 N McDonald Avenue, DeLand, FL 32724, USA. 7, 13, 141,

MOROUX Anthony Drexel, b. 29 Aug 1948, Houston, Texas, USA. Attorney. m. Julia Martha Domengeaux, 4 Aug 1973, 2 s 1 d. *Education:* BA, USL, 1974; JD, LSU Law Ctr, 1977. *Appointments:* Law Clerk, USDC, Judge W Eugene Davis, 1976-78; Partner, Domengeaux & Wright law Firm specialising in trial practice, 1978; Sr Partner, Moroux, Domengeaux & Davis, 1988-. *Memberships:* Am Trial Lawyers Assn; Louisiana Trial Lawyers Assn; Fed Bar Inst; ABA; Louisiana State Bar Assn. *Address:* 107 Stonehenge, POB 3787, Lafayette, LA 70502, USA. 7, 52, 163.

MORRICE Philip, b. 31 Dec 1943, Aberdeen, Scotland. Counsellor, HM Diplomatic Service. m. Margaret Clare Bower, 1 Apr 1989, 1 s, 1 d. *Education:* Robert Gordon's Col, Aberdeen, Scotland. *Appointments:* HM Diplomatic Ser, 1963-: Kuala Lumpur, 1964-69, Caracus, 1969-72, Paris, 1973-75, Brussels, 1975-78, Rome, 1981-85, Lagos, 1986-88, Brasilia, 1988-91. *Publications:* The Schweppes Guide to Scotch, 1983; The Distilleries of Scotland and Ireland, 1987; Numerous articles. *Memberships:* Royal Overseas League; The RAC Club. *Hobbies:* Tennis; Golf; Writing; Travel. *Address:* c/o FCO Brasilia, King Charles Street, London SW1A 2AH, England. 1.

MORRIS Edwin David, b. 31 July 1928, Swansea, Wales. Consultant Obstetrician Gynaecologist. m. Barbara May Evans, 21 Aug 1954, 1 s, 1 d. *Education:* Welsh Nat Sch of Med, 1945; MBBCh, 1950; RCOG, 1951; FRCS ENg, 1958; MRCOG, 1960; F, 1972; MD, 1969. *Appointments:* HS Prof Surg Unit and Prof Obs & Gynae, Cardiff, 1950-51; Active Ser, Malaya RAMC, 1951-53; Lectr Anat, Cardiff, 1953-55; Registrar Posts and Dulwich Hosp and Cardiff, 1955-60; Sen Lectr, Charing Cross, 1960-62; Reschr, Queen Charlottes Hosp, 1962-66; Conslt, Swansea. 1966; Conslt, Guys and Queen Charlottes Hosp, 1967-; Hon Civ Conslt Advr to Army, 1989-; Regional Assessor, Mat Mortality, 1977-. *Publications:* Articles in appropriate professional journals. *Memberships:* Coun, RCOG, 1983-86; Coun, Sec, Obs and Gynae Sect of RSM, 1969-76, Pres, 1987; BMA. *Honours:* Distinctions in Anatomy and Obs and Gynae at MB; Hopburn Med and McLean Prize at Med Sch. *Hobbies:* Music; Reading; Glass blowing; Playing with grandson. *Address:* 22 Sheen Common Drive, Richmond, Surrey TW10 5BN, England.

MORRIS James Matthew, b. 13 July 1935, Reed City, Michigan, USA. Professor of History. m. Nancy Christina Becker, 23 Aug 1958, 4 s, 2 d. *Education:* BA, Aquinas Col, 1957; MA Central Michigan Univ, 1962; PhD Hist, Univ of Cincinnati, 1969. *Appointments:* Hg Sch Tchr, 1957-62; Instr, Col of Stuebenville, 1962-64; Asst Prof, Providence Col, 1967-71; Asst Prof, Assoc Prof, Prof, Christopher Newport Univ, 1971-. *Publications:* America's Maritime Legacy, 1979, research ed; Author: Our Maritime Heritage, 1979; History of the US Navy, 1984; History of the US Army, 1986; America's Armed Forces, 1991. *Memberships:* USNI; N.Am Soc for Oceanic Hist; Nat Assn of Scholars; Am Military Inst. *Honours:* Cert of Appreciation, US Dept of Educ, 1985; First Honoree, Alpha Chi, Virginia Zeta Chapter, Dist Prof Awd, 1985. *Address:* Department of History, Christopher Newport University, 50 Shoe Lane, Newport News, VA 23606, USA. 7, 13, 15, 30, 154.

MORRIS Joseph, b. 14 June 1913, Ince, Lancs, England. Consultant. m. Margaret Cameron, 30 July 1913, 3 s, 1 d. *Education:* INCE Central Sch; Canadian Army, Ofrs Training Sch; Commd, 1944. *Appointments:* Trade Union Ofr, local, regional, national and international, 1946-78; ILO, 1966-80; Mem of GB and Chm of Gov Body, 1977-78. *Publications:* Manifesto for

Canadian labour, 1976; Alcoholism and drugs at the workplace, 1965; Many papers on corporate statism and politics in Canada. *Memberships:* St Johns Masonic Lodge, BC; E.Gate Masonic Lodge; AFAM North Burnaby, BC. *Honours:* Off Order of Canada, 1979; Companion of the Order of Canada, 1984; Hon LLD, Univ of Victoria, 1984. *Hobbies:* Music and sports; Nat and international affairs. *Address:* 4257 Thornhill Crescent, Victoria, BC, Canada V8N 3G6. 142,

MORRIS Lynda Hiawatha Mitchum, b. 18 Sept 1950, New Orleans, USA. Systems Consultant. div. 1 s. *Education:* Currently attending Loyola Univ, New Orleans. *Appointments:* AT&T Communications Conslt, 1976-. *Memberships:* IPA; Bd, Sales Mktg Execs; Alpha Sigma Lambda; Past Dist Gov, Toastmasters Intl. *Honours:* Top productivity Awd, New Orleans, 1986-88, PR Awd, 1989, Achievers Club, 1988, 1989, AT&T; Distinguished Sales Awd, SME, 1989; Cert of Merit, New Orleans City Coun, 1991. *Hobbies:* Public Speaking; Reading; Biking; Volunteer, Utd Way, Greater New Orleans. *Address:* 1013 Race Street, New Orleans, LA 70130, USA. 1, 7.

MORRISH Jack (John Edwin), b. 23 Sept 1915, London, England. Education Consultant; School Governor; Gen Sec, Assoc Northants Sch Gov Bodies. m. (1) Norah Purser Luke, 1937, diss, 1943; (2) Violet Saunders, 1944, diss, 1977; (3) Betty Lupton Wear, 1984, dec, 1990. 1 s, 2 d. *Education:* Univ Col Sch, Hampstead, 1926- 32; Northampton Poly, London, 1933-35; MA, Leics Univ, 1990-91. *Appointments:* Telecom Engr, GPO, 1932-54; Coalminer, 1943-45; Asst Sec, Civil Ser Union, 1954-72; Gen Sec, Customs and Excise Gp, 1972-76; Asst Gen Sec, Soc of Civil Servants, 1974-76; chm, Nottingham Child Poverty Action Gp, 1979-81; Admr, Northants Rural Comm Coun, 1980-81. *Memberships:* Dpty Leader, Labour Councillor, Northants CC; Ch of Educ Com, 1981-85; Ch of Govs, Nene Col, 1981-85; Assn fo Co Couns, 1981-85; Councillor, LB Hounslow, 1986-90, V-Chm, Educ Com; Assn for Met Auths, 1986-90. *Honours:* Masters degree, 1991. *Hobbies:* Current affairs; Thinking; Pursuit of justice; Continuing learning; Music; Opera; Theatre; Friendship and human relationships. *Address:* The Old Bakehouse, 1 Church Street, Broughton, Kettering, Northants NN14 1LU, England. 1.

MORRISON Bryce, b. 27 Nov 1938, Leeds, Yorkshire, England. Teacher; Pianist; Critic; Lecturer. *Education:* MA (Oxon), 1963; MA (Dalhousie), 1964; MMus (SMU), 1970; Music Scholar, The Kings Sch, Canterbury, 1952; Studies with Ronald SMith, Kings Sch; Iso Elinson, Guildhall Sch of Music; Alexander Uninsky, S. Methodist Univ, TX, USA. *Career:* Lectured and given masterclasses in Australia, Poland, USA and England; Held the Corinna Frada Pick Professorship of advanced piano studies at the 1988 Ravinia Festival in Chicago; Holds a professorship at the RAM, London. *Publications:* Published extensively in The Times, The Times Literary Supplement, Observer, Gramaphone etc., also in USA and Australia; Has published interviews with virtually every pianist of world class including Horowitz, Rubinstein, Sir Clifford Curzon. *Contributions to:* The Phaidon Book of the Piano; Two BBC talks; Short Biography of Liszt; Biography of Jorge Bolet; Short study of the Piano music of Gabriel Faure; Author of over 200 annotations for Decca, EMI, Philips and Sony including: In Memory of Terrence Judd, for Chandos; Artistic Dir and compilor of album, The Art of Eileen Joyce. Broadcasts extensively for BBC, ABC, CBC and in Poland, USA and New Zealand. *Memberships include:* Elected Mem, Critics Circle; FRSA; Jury member of national and international piano competitions including Naumburg, New York; Chm, First Terrance Judd Intl Awd, 1982. *Honours:* Invitation to tour China and Japan and to Lecture and Perform at Symposium at Ravinia Festival, Chicago, 1988. *Address:* 19 Hinde House, 11 Hinde Street, London W1M 5AQ, England. 7, 132.

MORRISON Joseph Young, b. 4 Jan 1951, Flushing, NY, USA. VP, Transportation. *Education:* AS, Montreat Anderson Col, 1971; BA, Oglethorpe Univ, 1989. *Appointments:* Uniform Patrol, Atlanta Police Dept, 1979-80; Special Agent, US Dept of Transp, ATlanta, 1980-82; Gp Dir, Western Express, Atlanta, 1982-85; VP, Safety & Risk Mgmt, Burlington Morto Carriers, Hurst, TX, 1985-. *Publications:* Co-author: Hazardous Materials. *Memberships:* Am Trucking Assn; Safety Mgmt Coun; Injury Control Com, Chm; Hazardous Materials Com; Nat Safety Coun; Risk and Insurance Mgmt Soc Inc. *Hobbies:* Tennis; Golf; Remodelling and restoring old MGs. *Address:* 4210 Oak Springs Drive, Arlington, TX 76016, USA. 7, 132.

MORRISON William Robert, b. 26 Jan 1942, Hamilton, Ontario, Canada. Professor of History; Dean. m. Linda Deacon, 1 May 1976, 1 s, 3 d. *Education:* BA 1963, MA 1964, McMaster Univ; PhD, Univ of W.Ontario, 1973. *Appointments:* Brandon Univ, 1969-89; Lakehead Univ, 1989-1992; Univ of Northn British Columbia, 1992-. *Publications:* Showing the Flag: The Mounted Police and Canadian Sovereignty in the North, 1894-1925, 1985; Co-author: Land of the Midnight Sun: A History of the Yukon, 1988; The Sinking of the Princess Sophia: Taking the North Down with her, 1990; Interpreting Canada's North: Selected Readings, 1989; For Purposes of Dominion: Essays in Honour of Morris Zaslow, 1989; My Dear Maggie: Letters from a Western Manitobia Pioneer, 1991, The Forgotten North, 1992; The Alaska Highway in World War II, 1992. *Hobbies:* Music; Gardening. *Address:* U.N.B.C. PO Box 1950, Prince George, B.C; Canada, V2L 5P2. 142.

MORRISS Nicholas Anson, b. 17 Sept 1950, Kent, England. Chartered Accountant; Financial Adviser. m. Suzette, 29 June 1974, 1 s, 1 d. *Education:* Radley col, 1964-68; BA Econ, York Univ, 1969-72. *Appointments:* Mgr, Price Waterhouse London, 1972-79; Asst Dir, Barclays De Zoete Wedd, 1979-86; Ptnr, Coopers and Lybrand Deloitte, 1986-. *Publication:* Author of Financing Growth, 1990, and numerous articles. *Memberships:* ICA (Fellow). *Hobbies:* Golf; Skiing; Theatre; Travel. *Address:* 3 Akehurst Street, London SW15 5DR, England. 53.

MORROW Herbert Stanley, b. 21 Feb 1915, Willington. Public Relations and Fundraising Consultant. m. Marjorie Davison, 6 July 1942. *Education:* BCom, Dunelm, 1937. *Appointments:* Dir, Appeals and PR, Nat Coun of YMCAs England, Ireland and Wales, 1969-80; Independent Fund raising and PR Conslt, 1980-. *Memberships:* Durham Univ Soc, VP and Chm, Fin Com; Methodist Scramental Fellowship, VP: Inst of Public Relations. *Hobbies:* Gardening; Reading; Travel. *Address:* Dunelm , 27 Maes Y Cnwce, Newport, Dyfed, SA42 ORS, Wales.

MORSE Barry Herbert, b. 10 June 1918, London, England. Actor; Director; Writer. m. Sydney Sturgess, 26 Mar 1939, 1 s, 1 d. *Education:* Royal Acad of Dramatic Art, 1935-36. *Career:* Appearances on radio and television for CBC Canada, BBC and ITV in England, CBS, NBC and ABC in the US as well as many film and stage production in all three countries as actor and director; to date has played over 2,000 rolls in various media; Dir of Staircase, Broadway, 1968; Devised and presented one-man stage show, Merely Players, 1983, 1987-88; TV series include: The Fugitive, 1963-67; The Adventurer, 1973; Space 1999, 1975-76; The Winds of War, 1981; Host of Strange but True, 1983; Master of the Game, 1984; War and Remembrance, 1986-87; Feature films and films for TV include: Power Play, 1977; The Changeling, 1978; Klondike Fever, 1979; A Tale of Two Cities, 1980; Mark Twain's Innocents Abroad, 1982; A Woman of Substance, 1984; Fight for Life, 1987; Hoover vs the Kennedys, 1987; Glory Glory, 1988; Artistic Dir, Shaw Festival Niagara on the Lake, Ont, 1966; Adjunc Prof, 1968; Drama Dept, Yale Univ; VP, Shaw Soc of UK, 1976; Fdg Artistic Dir, Gobe Playhouse, Victoria, BC, 1980; Pres, Planet Productions Ltd, Ontario.

Honours: Five times winner of Best Actor Awd in Canadian Television, 1954-61. *Address:* Apt 506, 71 Charles St East, Toronto, Ontario M4Y 2T3, Canada. 18, 142, 173.

MORSE Leon William, b. 13 Nov 1912, New York City, USA. Distribution Management Executive. m. Goldie Kohn, 30 Mar 1941, 2 s. *Education:* BS, NYU, 1935; Grad, Acad of Adv Traffic, 1937; DBA, Columbia Pacif Univ. *Appointments:* Gen Traffic Mgr, Food Fair Stores Inc, 1940-43; Served to Capt, Transp Corp, US Army, WWII; Individual freight traffic management business, Philadelphia, 1950-58; Gen Traffic Mgr, William H Rorer Inc, 1958-77; Ret'd; Adj Prof, Ogontz Campus, Penn State Univ, 1960-83; Owner, Morse Assocs, to 1992; Sr Assoc, Dollar Gp Inc, Texas; Seminar Leader, Freight Traffic Mgmt. *Publications:* 6th and 7th eds of Practical Handbook of Industrial Traffic Management, 1980, 1988; Training manuals in traffic management, transportation contract negotiations and freight claims. *Memberships:* Traffic Clubs of Phila and Norristown; Traffic and Transp Club of Phila; Delta Nu Alpha; Am Soc of Transp & Logistics; Coun of Logistics Mgmt; Trans Res Forum; Am Soc of Intl Execs, Past Pres and Sec; Drug and Toilet Preparations Traffic Conf, Ret'd Pres and Ch of Bd, 1973-77. *Honours:* Delaware Valley Traffic Mgr of the Yr, 1963; Registered Practitioner, US Interstate Commerce Comm and the U.S. Fed Maritime Comm. *Address:* 2505 Manchester Dr, Springfield, IL 62704, USA. 6, 52, 132.

MORTLEY Raoul John, b. 25 Sept 1944, Sydney, Australia, Vice Chancellor, Univ of Newcastle. m. 16 Nov 1983, 1 s, 2 d. *Education:* BA Hons, Latin, Greek and Philos, Univ of Sydney, 1966; MA, Ancient Philos, Monash Univ, 1968; Doctorat 3rd Cycle, 1971, Doctorat ès Lettres, 1981, History of Religions, Univ of Strasbourg. *Appointments:* Tutor in Classics, Monash Univ, Sydney, 1966-67; Asst Prof of Theol, Strasbourg Univ, France, 1971-73; Lectr, Assoc Prof in Hist, Macquarie Univ, Sydney, 1973-86; Dir of Res Philos, Ctr Nat de la Recherche Sci, Paris, 1986; Dean, Sch of Humanities and Soc Scis an Prof of Philos, 1989-90, Acting V- Chancellor, 1990-, Bond Univ, Queensland, Australia. *Publications:* Connaissance religieuse et herméneutique chez Clémeny d'Alexandrie, (Brill 1973; Womanhood: The Idea of the Feminine in Ancient Religions, 1981; From Word to Silence: Vol 1, The Rise and Fall of Logos, 1986, Vol II, The Way of Negation, Christian and Greek, 1986; Désir ed Différence, 1988; French Philosophers in Conversation, 1991. *Memberships:* Fellow, Acad of the Humanities of Australia, 1986-. *Hobbies:* Applied economics. *Address:* University of Newcastle, Newcastle 2308, Australia. 23.

MORTON Brian (James Weir), b. 17 June 1954, Paisley, Scotland. Writer; Broadcaster. m. Pamela Anne Collins, 1 d. *Education:* MA Hons, Univ of Edinburgh; Univ of E.Anglia, 1976-81. *Appointments:* Lectr, Univ of E.Anglia, 1977-79; Lectr, Univ of Tronso, Norway, 1979; Features Ed, Lit Ed, Times Higher Educn Supplement, 1981-91; Currently Freelance Writer and Broadcaster. *Creative Works:* Books: Contemporary Composers, 1991; Sax, 1992; Scherzo, 1992; Penguin Guide to Jazz on Record, 1992; Music: A Book of Words, 1993; Women in Music, 1993; Translator of The Seer, 1990; presenter, Impressions, BBC Radio 3; Saxophonist with: Phlogiston, Things we Like, The Golden Horde (UK) and the Colin Smith Quintet. *Hobbies:* Jazz; New music; Collecting pictures. *Address:* 39 Darrell Road, London SE22 9NJ, England.

MORTON Colin, b. 26 July 1948, Toronto, Canada. Writer. m. Mary Lee Bragg, 30 Aug 1969. 1 s. *Education:* BA, 1970; Profl Tchg Cert, 1975, Univ of Calgary; MA, Univ of Alberta, 1979. *Appointments:* Tchr, County of Red Deer, 1975-77; Scriptwriter, ACCESS TV, 1979-80; Writer-Ed, Govt of Canada, 1982-; Lectr, Univ of Ottawa, 1987-89. *Publications:* Poetry: In Transit, 1981; This Won't Last Forever, 1985; The Merzbook: Kurt

Schwitters Poems, 1987; How to Be Born Again, 1992; Film: Primiti Too Taa, 1986; Collaborations: The Scream, 1984; North/South, 1987. *Memberships:* League of Canadian Poets. *Honours:* CBC Lit Awds, 1984; Archibald Lampman Poetry Awd, 1986; Best Soundtrack, ASIFA East Film Festival, 1987; Bronze Apple, Nat Educ Film and Video Festival, 1987. *Hobbies:* Fiction. *Address:* 40 Grove Avenue, Ottawa Ontario, Canada K1S 3A6. 142.

MORTON Harry Stafford, b. 18 Aug 1905, Port Giville, NS. Obstetrician and Gynaecologist. m. 15 July 1937. *Education:* BA, 1925; MSC, 1927; MRCS LRCP, 1929; MBBS, London, 1932; FRCS, Eng, 1935; FRCSC, 1935; MRCOG, 1936; FRCOG, 1958; FACS, 1945. *Appointments:* Lectr, Surg and Anat, McGill, 1937-79; RCNVR, 1939-45; Asst, Assoc Prof Surg, McGill, 1945-70; Surg, RVH Montreal, 1945-70; Chief Surg, QMRH, Montreal, 1960-69. *Publications:* Text of Surgery, H F Moseler, 1952, 1955, 1959; Appendix Colon Rectum and Anus. *Memberships:* Sec and Pres, Local Chapt, Phi Rho Sigma; FRSM, London; Centrl Surg Assn; DMDSAB rep, CMA East; Chm, Past Pres of the Bd, RVH; Quebec Med Assn. *Honours:* OBE, 1946; CO, 1950; Mt Allison Univ, 1976; Life of Canada, 1955-84; Hunterian Prof, RCS, 1954. *Hobbies:* Dialing and construction of sun dials especially equatorial; Photography; Teaching sailing. *Address:* RRI Lunenburg, Nova Scotia, Canada BOI 2CO. 142, 32.

MORTVEDT John Jacob, b. 25 Jan 1932, Dell Rapids, South Dakota, USA. Senior Scientist. m. Marlene Fodness, 23 Jan 1955, 3 d. *Education:* BS, 1953, MS 1959, Soil Sci, SD State Univ; PhD Soil Chem, Univ of Wisconsin, 1962. *Appointments:* Soil Chem, 1962-87, Sr Scist, 1987-, Tennessee Valley Auth, AL. *Publications:* Ed, Micronutrients in Agriculture, 1972, 1991; 68 technical journal papers and 31 non technical papers. *Memberships:* Soil Sci of Am, Pres, 1989; Am Soc of Agronomy; AAAS; Intl Soc of Soil Sci; Soc for Environ Geochem and Health. *Honours:* Fellow: AAAS, 1989; ASA, 1979; SSSA, 1979; Hon Mem, Colombian Soc of Soil Sci, 1989; Soil Sci Soc of Am Profl Ser Awd, 1991. *Hobbies:* Golf; Photography. *Address:* Agricultural Research Department, National Fertilizer & Environmental Research Centre, Tennessee Valley Authority, Muscle Shoals, AL 35660, USA. 2, 7.

MOSER Anton Alfred Richard, b. 22 Mar 1939, Graz, Austria. University Professor. m. Marianne Rannberg, 29 Nov 1975, 1 s, 1 d. *Education:* Dipl Ing, 1966, Dr Tech, Biotech, 1970, Univ Docent, Biotech, 1977, TU, Graz. *Appointments:* Asst, Inst of Biotech, 1969-77; Docent, TU Graz, 1977-83; Vis Prof: UWO Canada, 1980, ULB Belgium, 1981, TU Delft, Netherlands, 1986; Assoc Prof, TU Graz. *Publications:* Bioprozesstechnik, 1981; Bioprocess technology, 1988; Ecologic Process Engng the new technology Paradigm, 1992; Chapters in Biotechnology, 2nd ed, 1992. *Memberships:* Chm, Austrian Assn Bioprocess, Technol Chm, Task Gp Ecol Bioprocessing; EFB Mem Sci Adv Comm Europe; Fed of Biotechnol; Europ Rep Intern Organ Biotech and Bioengrg. *Hobbies:* Holistic thinking; Mountain climbing; Folk dancing; Ecology and nature. *Address:* Inst of Biotechnology , TU Graz, Petersgasse 12, A-8010 Graz, Austria. 1.

MOSES Don V, b. 21 Dec 1936, Garden City, KS, USA. Director, Univ of Illinois Sch of Music; Conductor. m. Anne Swedish, 26 Jan 1973, 1 s, 1 d. *Education:* BMusEd, Ft Hays State Univ, 1959; MMus, 1962, DMus Arts, 1968, Indiana Univ, Bloomington. *Appointments:* Choral Tchr, Hays Hg Sch, 1959-61; Asst Prof, Indiana Univ, 1964-73; Dir, Choral Activities, Univ of Iowa, 1973-86; Dir of Choral Activities, Univ of Illinois, Urbana, 1986-. *Publications:* Face to Face with an orchestra, 1986; Historical Approach to conducting, 1991; Recording: Harmoniemesse, 1982. *Memberships:* Am Choral Dirs Assn; Nat Assn of Music Execs. *Honours:* Guest Conductor: Taipei Phil Orches, 1988; Gyor Phil Orch, Hungary, 1983; Conductor, Intl Choral Festival,

Lincoln Ctr, NY, 1972. *Hobby:* Golf. *Address:* 3050 Music Bldg, 1114 W Nevada Street, Univ of Illinois, Urbana, IL 61801, USA.

MOSES Elbert Raymond Jr, b. 31 Mar, 1908, New Concord, Ohio, USA. Emeritus Professor of Education. m. (1) Mary M Sterrett, 21 Sept 1933, dec 1984, 1 son, dec 1981; (2) Caroline M Chambers, 19 June 1985. *Education:* AB Univ of Pittsburgh, 1932; MSC, PhD, Univ of Michigan, 1936. *Appointments:* Univ of N.Carolina Women's Col, 1936-38; Ohio State Univ, 1938-46; State Univ of Illinois, Charleston, 1946-56; Michigan State Univ, 1956-59; Clarion Univ, Penn, 1959-71; US Army Signal Corps, 1942-46, 1952-53, ret'd as Lt Col. *Publications:* Guide to Effective Speaking, 1956, 1957; Phonetics: History and Interpretation, 1964: 3 Attributes of God, 1983; Adventure in Reasoning, 1988: Beating the Odds, 1992. *Contribution to:* Jour of Am Speech and Hearing Mag, Jour of AM Speech; Speech Monographs; Veterans Voices. *Memberships include:* Life, Am Speech & Hearing Assn; Past Pres, Am Overseas Educrs Assn; Past Dist Gov, Rotary Intl; Lions Intl, (past Tres, Yvapai Lions Club); Rosicrucian Order; Assn of Former Intelligencs Ofrs; Ret'd Ofrs Assn; Pasc Comdr, Am Legion; Veterans of Foreign Wars. *Honours include:* Phi Delta Kappa Ser Key, 1978; Cert for Sers in Educ, 1981; Chevalier, Order of Holy Cross, Jerusalem; Order, St John of Jerusalem; The NIADH NASK, NN Mem, 1989; Marshal of Kilbonane, 1990; Chevalier, Ordre Souverain et Militaire de la Milice du St Sepulcre, 1991; Mem, Grand Coun World Parliament, Confed of Chivalry, 1991; Hon Mem, Adv Coun, IBC. *Hobbies:* Ham radio; Writing. *Address:* 2001 Rocky Dells Dr, Prescott, AZ 86303, USA. 2, 3, 6, 11, 13, 15, 22, 30, 52, 70, 116, 126, 129, 130, 145, 152, 156.

MOSES John Henry, b. 12 Jan 1938, London, England. Provost of Chelmsford. m. Susan Elizabeth Wainwright, 25 July 1964, 1 s, 2 d. *Education:* Ealing Grammar Sch; Nottingham Univ - Gladstone Memorial Prize 1958, BA 1959, PhD 1965; Trinity Hall Dept Educ, Cambridge; Lincoln Theol Col; Visiting Fellow Wolfson College, Cambridge, 1987. *Appointments:* Asst Curate, St Andrew, Bedford, 1964-70; Rector, Coventry E. Team Ministry, 1970-77; Examining Chaplain, Bishop of Coventry, 1972-77; Rural Dean Coventry East, 1973-77; Archdeacon of Southend, 1977-82; Provost of Chelmsford, 1982-; General Synod, 1985-; Church Commissioner, 1988-. *Publications:* The Sacrifice of God, 1992; Club Athenaeum. *Address:* The Provosts Hse, 3 Harlings Grove, Waterloo Lane, Chelmsford CM1 1YQ, England.1.

MOSKVINA Marina, b. 15 June 1954, Moscow, Russia. Writer. m. Tishkov Leonid, 20 Nov 1976. 1 s. *Education:* Journ Fac, Moscow Univ, 1971-77. *Appointments:* Newspaper Corres, 1975-82; Over 30 author's radio progs, Marina Moskvina, 1988-92; Author of plays for animated films, 1983-90. *Publications:* Children's books, Seven Flying Passengers, 1989; Glass for Large, 1991; My Dog Likes jazz, 1992. *Memberships:* Russian Assn for Children's Writers. *Honours:* Interanimated Festival, honour prize for play, What Happened to the Crocodile, Varna, Bulgaria, 1985. *Hobbies:* Walking; Observing. *Address:* Orekhoviy bul 47/33-223, Moscow 115580, Russia.

MOSS Trevor Simpson, b. 28 Jan 1921, Buglawton, Cheshire, England. Scientific Editor. m. Audrey Nelson, 6 Mar 1948. *Education:* BA 1941, PhD 1950, DSc 1986, Cambs. *Appointments:* Scist, Royal Aircraft Estab, 1941-42, 1954-78; Royal Signals and Radar Estab, 1942-54, 1978-80; Dpty Dir, 1978-81. *Publications:* Ed, Infared Physics' Photoconductivity in the Elements, 1952; Optical Properties of Semiconductors, 1959; Semiconductor Opto-Electronics, 1973; Handbook on Semiconductors, 1980-; Over 100 papers in international scientific journals. *Memberships:* FIPhy; European Phys Soc. *Honours:* Max Born Medal, UK and German Phys Socs, 1978; Denis Gabor Awd of the Intl Soc for Optical Engrs, 1988. *Hobbies:* Woodworking;

Classical Music. *Address:* Shelsley Meadow, Colwall, Malvern, Worcs WR13 6PX, England. 1, 52.

MOTOKI Ken, b. 31 Mar 1930, Tokyo, Japan. University Professor. m Sumie Mizusaki, 17 Feb 1955, 1 s, 1 d. *Education:* BEd, 1953, MEd, 1955, Tokyo Univ. *Appointments:* Reschr, Nat Inst of Educ Res, 1955; Assoc Prof, 1967, Prof, 1974, Osaka Univ. *Publications:* Methodology of Technical Education, 1963; Social Studies as a Study of Humans, 1966; Human Rights and Education, 1989; Technology and Human Formation, 1990. *Memberships:* Ed Adv Com, Intl Coun for Adult Educ; Am Assn of Adult and Continuing Educ; Dir Japanese Soc for Study of Adult and Community Educ; Conslt, Osaka City Inst of Educ Res. *Hobbies:* Fine arts appreciation; Travelling. *Address:* Higashi-ashiya-cho 17-23-206, Ashiya-shi, Hyogo- ken 659, Japan. 1, 52.

MOTTLEY Wendell A, b. 2 July 1941, Trinidad, West Indies. Government Minister. m. 6 June 1964, 2 d. *Education:* BA Hons Econ, Yale Univ; MLitt Econ, Cambs Univ. *Appointments:* Company Dir, Steel processing and Floriculture; Min of Hsg, 1981-85; Min of Trade and Indust, 1985-86. *Honours:* Silver Medal, Tokyo Olympics, 400m, 1964; Gold Medal, Commonwealth Games, 440 yds, 4x400 yds relay, Kingston, 1966. *Hobbies:* Floriculture; Sport, especially athletics and tennis. *Address:* Saddle Rd, Upper South Cruz, Trinidad, West Indies.

MOUNT Paul Morrow, b. 8 June 1922, Newton Abbot, England. Sculptor. m. (1) 1 s, 1 d, (2) June Miles, 22 Oct 1978. *Education:* Newton Abbot Grammar Sch, 1933; Royal Col of Art, 1940, ARCA, 1948. *Appointments:* Lectr, Winchester Sch of Arts, 1948; I/C Art Dept, Yaba Tech Inst, Lagos, Nigeria, 1955; Freelancer, 1962-. *Creative works:* Sculpture commissions: Private collections in EEC, USA, Canada, Swiss Embassy, Lagos, Chase Manhattan, Bank Lagos, Cabinet Offices, Accra, Cocoa House, Ibadan, York House Bristol, Fibreglass HQ, St Helens, BSC London, Govt House Lagos, CRS Redruth. *Memberships:* RWA: Penwith Soc. *Hobbies:* Music; Photography; Poetry. *Address:* Nanaherrow Studio, St Just, Penzance, Cornwall TR19 7LA, England. 19.

MOURÉ Erin, b. 17 Apr 1955, Calgary, Canada. Writer; Poet. *Education:* Arts: Univ of Calgary, Univ of Brit Columbia, 1972-75. *Appointments:* Via Rail Canada, Customer Services, various positions, 1976-. *Publications:* Empire, York Street, 1979; Whisky Vigil, 1981; Wanted Alive, 1983; Domestic Fuel, 1985; Furious, 1988; WSW, 1989; sheepish Beauty, Civilian Love, 1992. *Memberships:* League of Canadian Poets; Writers Union of Canada. *Honours:* Gov Gen's Awd for Poetry, 1988; Pat Lowther Meml Awd, 1985. *Hobbies:* Weight lifting; Cycling; Reading; Translation. *Address:* c/o League of Canadian Poets, 24 Ryerson Avenue, Toronto, Ontario, Canada M5T 2P3. 142

MOWAT Alexander Parker, b. 5 Apr 1935, Scotland. Professor of Paediatric Hepatology. m. Mary Ann Shanks-Hunter, 23 Sept 1961, 2 s. *Education:* Fordyce Acad, Aberdeen Univ, 1952-58; MBChB, 1958; DRCOG, 1962; DCH, 1963; MRCP, 1964; FRCP, 1975. *Appointments:* Conslt Paed, King's Col Hosp, London, 1970-; Clin Tchr, Univ of London, 1970-90; Prof of Paed Hepatol, Kings Col Hosp, 1990-. *Publications:* Textbook: Liver Disorders in Infancy, 1979, 1987; Over 100 original articles on aspects of paediatric liver disease; Over 50 review articles on paediatric liver disease. *Memberships:* Brit Paed Assn; European Soc for Paed, Gastroenterol and Nutrition; British, European and American Assn for Study on Liver; Brit Soc of Gastroenterol. *Honours:* Fellowships: Wellcome Trust, 1968, Gail Zukermann, 1969; Charles West Lectr, RCP, 1982; Prof of Paed Hepatol, Univ of London, 1990; Datta Meml Lectr, Chandigarh India, 1991. *Hobbies:* Golf; Sailing; Gardening. *Address:* Variety Club Children's

Hospital, King College Hospital, Denmark Hill, London SE5 8RX, England.

MOWRY Philip Stephen, b. 22 Dec 1953, Pittsburgh, PA, USA. Geophysical Consultant. m. Janet Kay Miller 3 May 1980, 2 d. *Education:* BSc cum laude, Phys, Univ of Miami, 1974; Completed coursework for MS Geophys, Univ of Houston, 1980. *Appointments:* Shell Oil Co, 1975-76; Cities Ser Intl, 1977-80; Eenneco Oil E & P, 1980-84; Union Pacific Resources, 1984-86; Mowry Geophys Conslt, 1986-. *Memberships:* Am Inst of Prof Geols (AIPG); Soc of Exploration Geophys; Am Assn of Petroleum Geols. *Honours:* Cert Profl Geologist, AIPG. *Hobbies:* Music; Bible study; History; Biking; Wright lifting. *Address:* Mowry Geophysical Consulting, 25 Cascade Springs Place, The Woodlands, TX 77381, USA. 7.

MOYLS Benjamin Nelson, b. 1 May 1919, Vancouver, BC, Canada. Retired Professor of Mathematics. m. (1) Ina Elizabeth Barbour, 7 Nov 1942, dec 1974; (2) Toby Claire Buller, 7 May 1976, 2 s. *Education:* BA, 1940, MA 1941, Univ of Brit Columbia; AM, 1942, PhD 1947, Harvard Univ. *Appointments:* Univ of Brit Columbia: Lectr in Maths, 1947-48; Asst Prof, 1948-54; Assoc Prof, 1954-59; Prof, 1959-84; Emeritus Prof Maths, 1984-; Asst Dean, Grad Studies, 1967-76; Dir of Ceremonies, 1977-84. *Publication:* Research in Linear Algebra. *Memberships:* Am and Can Math Socs; Math Assn of Am; Soc for Indust and Applied Math. *Hobbies:* Music (organist); Gardening. *Address:* 2016 Western Parkway, Vancouver, BC, Canada V6T 1V5.

MOZNY Ivo, b. 31 Aug 1932, Prostejov, Czechoslovakia. Professor of Sociology. m Lenka Kasalova, 3 Nov 1956, 2 s. *Education:* Brostejov Bus Sch, 1947-50; Fac of Arts, Brno Univ, 1951-56; PhD, Sociol, Brno Univ, 1966; CSc, Charles Univ, Prague, 1989. *Appointments:* Laborer, Iron Mill, Ostrava, 1950-51; Radio Reporter and Ed, Ostrava, Brno, 1956-64; Asst Prof, 1964-68, Res Fellow, 1969-79; Marraige Coun, 1976-86, Assoc Prof, 1986- 92, Prof of Sociol, 1992-. *Publications:* Over 80 papers published in journals and three books: Family of University Educaded couples, 1983; The Modern Family, 1990; Why so easy: Some family resons for the Velvet Revolution, 1991. *Memberships:* Czech Acad of Sci, Philos and Sociol Bd; V-Chm, Masaryk Sociol Assn; Hd Ed Bd, Sociologicky Casopis. *Hobbies:* Skiing; Swimming; Outdoor activities; Bricklaying. *Address:* Fillova 9, 638 00 Brno, Czechoslovakia.

MRACEK Ann Michelle, b. 13 Nov 1956, St Louis, Missouri, USA. Musician; Composer. 1 d. *Education:* BMus, 1978, MMus, 1979, Composition, Univ of Kansas. *Appointments:* Piano, voice, composition, orchestration and music theory, Ann Mracek Studio, St Louis, MO, 1979-91; Piano, voice, music theory, music pre-school, Patzius Performing Arts, St Louis, MO, 1986-90; Vocal Soloist and Dancer, Palace Show, Six FLags Over Mid America, Eureka Mo, 1975; Vocal Soloist, Al Molos Band, St Louis, 1981; Band Vocal Soloist, Patzius Studio Performers, St Louis, 1987. *Creative works:* Poetry published in: The Young Citizen, Nat Essay Press and Nat Hg Sch Poetry Press, 1972. Numerous orchestral, chamber, piano and vocal compositions. *Memberships:* Am Women Composers, 1980-91; Friends of the Gifted FOG, 1983-86; Exec Bd Mem, FOG, 1985; Sec, Midwest Dance Theatre, 1989. *Honours:* Piano Finalist, 1971, Vocal Performance Winner, 1973, Fontbonne Col Mus Festival; Kansas State Tchrs Assn Awd, 1977; Composition performed at the Symp of Contemporary Music, Univ of Kansas, 1979. *Hobbies:* Painting; Gardening. *Address:* 22 Morwood Lane, St Louis, MO 63141, USA.

MUELLER Werner August, b. 14 Apr 1947, Klesberg. Director. *Education:* Dipl, JW Goethe Univ, Frankfurt, 1975; DPolit Sci, Univ Regensburg, 1980. *Appointments:* Asst Prof, Univ Regensburg, 1975-80: Reschr, European Univ Inst, Florence, Italy, 1980-81;

Exec Econs Ed, Springer Verlag, Heidelberg, 1982-; Dir, Springer-Verlag, 1988-; Chief Exec Ofr, Physia-Verlag, Heidelberg, 1985-. *Publications:* Bankenaufsicht und Glaeubigerschutz, 1980; Ed book series: Contributions to Economics, 1987-; Contributions to Management Science, 1990-, Wirtschaftswissenschaftlicke Beitraege, 1987-, Umwelt uns Ockonomie, 1990-. *Contributions to:* articles to various publications. *Memberships:* Verein Sociolpolitik, European Univ Alumni Assn. *Honours:* Grantee, Walter Kolb Stiftung, 1968-70; Studienstiftung des Deutsche Volkes, 1971-75, Deutscher Akademischer Auslandsdienst, 1980-81. *Address:* Springer Verlag, Tiergarten Strasse 17, D-6900 Heidelberg, Germany.

MUENDER Peter Rudolph, b. 9 Nov 1941, Neustadt, Wpr, Germany. Journalist. m. Regine Reim, 31 Mar 1988, 1 s, 1 d. *Education:* Magee Univ Col, Londonderry, N.Ireland, 1961-62; Freie Univ Berlin and Univ Hamburg, 1962-74; Eng, German, PHilos, PhD Hamburg Univ, 1974. *Appointments:* Freelane author and critic, 1974-77; Assoc Prof, Germal Lit, Chulalongkorn Univ, Bandgok, 1977-81; Theater Ed, Szene Hamburg, Chief Reporter Winners Mag, 1982-88. *Publications:* H Pinter unde die Problematik des absurden Theatres, 1974; JS Salinger, 1977; U Plenzdorf, 1979; S Beckett, 1980; B Brecht, 1976. *Memberships:* MLA, New York; AMTV Chess Club, Hamburg. *Honours:* Grovers Co Scholarship, Londonderry, N.Ireland. *Hobbies:* Chess; Theatre; Long distance running; Table Tennis. *Address:* Fensenfeldstr 8, 2000 Hamburg 73, Germany. 52.

MUHSIN Abu Ubaid Muhammad, b. 19 Dec 1953, Rajshahi, Bangladesh. Asst Prof of Pathology. *Education:* SSC, 1970, HSC, 1972, MBBS, 1977; MPhil Path, 1986; Postgrad Training in Kidney Path, UK, 1987-88. *Appointments:* Lectr, Path, Raj Med Col, 1981-86; Asst Registrar, Haemtol, IPGMR, 1986-87; Higher Training, New Castle Varsity, 1987-88; Asst Prof, Path, IPGMR, 1988-. *Publications include:* Articles and papers in various professional journals and magazines; Books: Health care of the Hajj-pilgrims, Srijan Prakashani, 1990; Breast feeding: Why and How, Srijan Prakashani, 1989; If you want to live disease free, (Bengali Juvenile Literature on Health); Bichita Shayastha Chinta (a book on various health related subjects in Bengal. *Memberships include:* Gen Sec, Bangladesh Soc of Path; Jt Sec, Third Congress, Asia Pacific Assn of Socs of Paths; Exec Com, Bangladesh Students Soc in New Castle UK, 1987-88; Fdr Gen Sec, Sci Club, Rajshahi Med Col, 1978-79; Bangladesh Delegation to the 2nd Intl Conf of Pakistan Assn of Paths, Karachi, 1986. *Honours include:* Gold Medal, Inter-Col Nat Sci Speech Competition, Nat Coun for Sci and Tech, 1979; Inter-Col National Sci Speech Competition Winner, Min of Info, Bangladesh, 1974; Highest points, Annual Lit and Cultural competition, Central Students Union of Rajshahi Univ, 1974; A popular presenter (condctr) in Natnl TV (for Health Progrms), already presented 7 episodes in eight months till Dec 1992. *Hobbies include:* Reading; Badminton; Watching Historical, educational, scientific and cultural subjects on TV and Video. *Address:* C-85 Sepoypara, Upazilla, Boalia District, Rajshahi, Bangladesh.

MUKAWA Akio, b. 10 June 1928, Kanazawa, Japan. Professor of Pathology. m. Hiroko Matsuo, 5 May 1968, 2 s. *Education:* MD, 1954, PhD, 1959, Univ of Kanazawd Med Sch, Japan; Dipl, Am Bd of Path, 1963. *Appointments:* Resident, Path, Queens Hosp Ctr, NYC, 1959-63; Neuropath Fellow, Albert Einstein Col of Med, NYC, 1966-67; Prof of Path, kanazawe Med Univ, Uchinada, Japan, 1972-. *Publications:* Autopsy Technique, 1988. *Memberships:* Japanese Path Soc, Trustee, 1971-; Am Soc of Clin Paths, foreign fellow, 1989-. *Hobbies:* Gardening; Cameras; Reading. *Address:* Taiseidai 55, Uchinada, Ishikawa 920-02, Japan. 52.

MUKHAMEDOV Valeriy Ashirovitch, b. 7 Apr 1950, Moscow, Russia. m. Kerbabaeva Ailaz, 2 Feb 1980, 1

d. *Education:* Moscow State Univ, 1972; Doc Dissertation on Molecular Acoustics, 1979. *Appointments:* Programist, 1972-74; Engr, Acoustics, 1974-78. *Publications:* 70 papers on molecular physics, acoustics, earthquake prediction and seismoacoustics, geophysics. *Hobbies:* Detective stories and animal novels; Medical statistics. *Address:* Physio-technical Institute Acad of Science of Tuzkmenistan, 74400 Ashkhabad, Gogd Street, 15, Tuzkmenistan, Russia.

MULCAHY Sean, b. 5 Sept 1930, Bantry, Republic of Ireland. Actor; Director; Writer. *Education:* St Mary's of the Pole, Cork; The North Monastry, Cork; The Sch of Art, Cork; BA Univ of Bristol. *Appointments:* Artistic Dir: The Shaw Theatre, 1963-65; The Citadel Theatre, 1968-73; The Gryphon Theatre, 1974-78; The Press Theatre, 1978-83; The Stephenwills Festival, 1988-90. *Publications:* Starred in hundreds of stage plays, and TV plays, 2,000 radio plays; Dir, The Picture of Dorian Gray, Canada, for Columbia Pictures TV, 1977. *Memberships:* Canadian Actors Equity, Coun, 1970-; Alliance of Canadian Cinema, TV and Radio Artists, Pres, 1978-89; Fraternal Benefit Soc, V-Chm and Gov, 1990-; Performing Arts Lodges, Gov, 1990-. *Honours:* Queens Silver Jubilee Medal, 1977; The ACTRA Awd, 1986. *Hobbies:* Rowing; Travel; Talking. *Address:* 391(A) Palmerston Boulevard, Toronto, Canada M6G 2NS. 142.

MULDER Martin Jan, b. 25 Dec 1923, Ter Aaz, Netherlands. Emeritus Professor of Theology. m. Andringa Jitske, 9 Dec 1949, 3 s, 6 d. *Education:* DTheol, VU, Amsterdam, 1962; Drs Lit Sem, RU, Leiden, 1969. *Appointments:* Clergyman, Neth Reform Ch, 1949-64; Asst Prof Semitic Langs, VU, Amsterdam, 1964-70; Prof, 1970-79, VU; Prof Old Testament, 1979-89, Leiden (State Univ). *Publications:* Many books and articles on Old Testament and North West Semitic topics since 1962; Book reviews in scientific quarterlies. *Memberships:* Chm, Bible Mus, Amsterdam, 1974-; Advr, Reformed Church, 1975-; Soc of Old Testament Studies, Netherlands, 1970-, CHm, 1978-81; Dean Fac of Theol, RU Leiden, 1982-84. *Hobbies:* Heraldry; Playing checks; Travelling; Cycling. *Address:* Amperestraat 48, 1171 BV Badhoevedorp, Netherlands. 52.

MULDOON Robert David, Sir, b. 25 Sept 1921, Auckland, New Zealand. Member of Parliament. m. 17 Mar 1951, 1 s, 2 d. *Education:* FCMA FANZ FCIS. *Appointments:* Chartered Acct in Practice, 1947-60; MP, 1960-91; Min of Fin, 1967-72, 1975-84; Prime Minister, 1975-84. *Publications:* The Rise and Fall of Young Turk, 1974; Muldoon, 1977; My Way, 1980; The NZ Economy: A Personal View, 1989; NO 38, 1986. *Memberships:* NZ Gov IMF and World bank, 1967-72, 1975-86; NZ Delegate Ministerial Coun, 1975-84, Chm, 1982; NY Gov Asian Devel bank, 1969- 72, 1975-84; S.Pacific Forum, 1975-84; Chmn, Global Economic Action Inst, 1988-1992. *Honours:* Rawlines Scholar, 1932; Maxwell Awd, NZICA, 1949; Leverhulme Prize, ICMA, 1947; Companion of Hon, 1976; GGMG 1983. *Hobbies:* Horticulture, (liliums); Patron, Auckland Horticultural Coun; NZ Tree Soc. *Address:* 7 Homewood Place, Birkenhead, Auckland, New Zealand.

MULHERON Linda Marion, b. 6 May 1951, London, England. Librarian. m. Donel Patrick Mulheron, 4 June 1972, dec 1992. 1 d. *Education:* Lib Cert, 1973; BA 1978, Dip Bus Studies, 1983; MEduc Admin, 1991. *Appointments:* State Library of NSW, 1970-75; Nepean Col of Advanced Educ, 1975-80; Cumberland Col of Health Scis, 1980-86; Westmead Hosp Lib, 1986-. *Publications include:* Annotated Bibliography of Works of Banjo Patterson, 1972; Health Librarians coping with imposed change, Paper presented at Health Libraries Seminar, 1st Biennial Conference of ALIA, Perth: ALIA), 1990; Bibliographic Instruction in Australian Hospital Libraries, (M. Ed. Admin Thesis), 1991; Achieving Excellence: Proceedings of the 4th Asian Pacific Special and Law Librarians' conference with 9th biennial Health Librarians, Canberra: ALIA, 1991. *Memberships:* Assoc

Aust Lib and Info Assn, 1973-; NSW Pres Health Libs, 1988-92; Nat Pres Health Lib, 1990-91, Branch Coun, NSW, 1988-89. *Honours:* Public Ser Bd Scholarship, 1972; Anne Harrison Awd, 1987. *Hobbies:* Reading; Swimming; Self education. *Address:* 29 Clarke Pl, Castle Hill, NSW 2154, Australia.

MULLER Gert Heinz, b. 29 May 1923, Troppau. Professor Emeritus, Univ Heidelberg. *Education:* PhD, Philos, Univ Graz, Austria, 1947; PhD Maths, Univ Heidelberg, Germany, 1962. *Appointments include:* Docent, 1963-65, Assoc Prof, 1965-74, Prof, 1973-90, Prof Emeritus, 1990-, Maths, Univ Heidelberg, Germany. *Publications:* Das Philosophische Werk Franz Kroners, 1962; Ed: Omega-Bibliography of Mathematical Logic, 1987; Articles in various professional journals and magazines. *Memberships:* Intl Soc Study of Time; German Soc Math Logic and Founs of Math; Am Math Soc; Assn Symbolic logic; Acad Intern de Philos des Scis, Brussels; Sonnblick Verein, Austria. *Honours:* Grantees and Guest professorships include: Sophia Univ, Tokyo, 1980; Greece, 1983; Nat Univ Canberra, Australia, 1984; Math Inst Acad of Sci, Prague, 1986; Math Inst Univ Nanjing, 1987; Computer Sci Ctr, Acad of Sci, Moscow, 1988, 1990. *Hobbies:* Studies in metaphysics and history of Central and East Asia. *Address:* Maths Institute, University of Heidelberg, Im Neuenheimer Feld 288, D-W-6900 Heidelberg, Germany. 1, 2, 43, 92.

MULLICK Ramendranath, b. 16 Jan 1933, Calcutta, West Bengal, India. Editor. m. Hembrova Mullick, 11 Nov 1962. *Education:* MA BEngali, Calcutta Univ. *Appointments:* Sub Ed, Viswabharati Univ Pub Dept; Sec to V-Chancellor, Rabindrabharati Univ; Sec, Pub Bd of RU; Ed, Rabindrabharati patrika; Sc, Ed Bd, Rabindra Gharati Jour. Mistiman Akas- Piposa Salit Sabanya Juddha Jignasa Suvadna O Mini, RamanayanMahabharut Oaj, Salmali, Protham Phalgen Sandhyar JyotenaSakales Rod, Dwitio Diganto, Sudhui Chanehal Enealiptas, JibaniSubar-nanekha, Ek Paloker Pakhi Swadesh Sahitya O Momonsilata, Banga Sahitya Bonohul, Ouponnyasik Upendraneth, Adhunik Kavita O Sudhin dra-Kavimanas Rabindre Monongiter Alobe Rammuhan. *Memberships:* Sec, Sahityatirtha. *Honours:* Raleibasar, Diamont Jubilee Yr, 1987; Sarbojanin Durgotsav, Silver Jubilee, 1991; Kavyaleharati from Jasone Sahitya Sangha, 1951. *Hobbies:* Writing; Good companionship. *Address:* Sahityatirtha Jadulal Mullick Hse, 67 Pathuriaghat Street, Calcutta 700006, WB India.

MULUNDIKA Mundwe Godfrey, Capt, b. 11 May 1948, Kabwe, Zambia. Company Director; Airline Pilot. m. Rhoda Banda, 22 Nov 1980, 3 s, 2 d. *Education:* RAF, S.Cerney, UK, 1967; Scuola Aeronautica Militare, LECCE, Italy, 1970-71. *Appointments:* Zambia Air Force, 1967-73; Zambia Airways, 1973-90; IAPCO, UK Ltd, 1991-. *Memberships:* Exec Com, Intl Air Transp Assn; Exec Com, African Airlines Assn; Pres, African Airlines Assn. *Honours:* Special Awd, Commercial Aviation Assn of S.Africa, 1988; Special Citation, Africa Travel Assn of Am, 1989. *Hobbies:* Flying; Golf; Squash. *Address:* IAPCO UK Ltd, Grantley House, 9 Park Lane, Cranford, Middlesex TW5 9RW, England.

MULZER Johann Hermann, b. 5 Aug 1944, Prien. Professor of Chemistry. m. Juge, 21 Sept 1974, 2 s, 1 d. *Education:* PhD, 1974; Habilitation, 1980. *Appointments:* Univ Munich, 1976-82; Univ Dusseldorf, 1982-83; Free Univ, Berlin, 1984-. *Contributions to:* scientific various international journals. *Memberships:* Gasellschaft Deutscher Chemiker; Am Chem Soc. *Hobbies:* Piano playing; Languages; History. *Address:* Organic Chemistry Institute, Free University of Berlin, Takustr 3, W-1000 Berlin 33, Germany. 1.

MUNEKATA Shizu, b. 11 Nov 1957, Sasebo. Business Consultant. *Education:* BS Linguistics, cum laude, 1980; MA, US-Japan Relations, Stanford Univ, 1983. *Appointments:* Sr Assoc, Tech Analysis Grp, Washington DP, 1983-84; Dir of Public Affairs, Nippon

Telegraph & Telephone, 1984-85; Japan Specialist, Mktg, Itel Corp, California, 1985-88; Asst to the Chm, Sony Corp, Tokyo, 1988-. *Publications:* Some special insights into the Japanese market and customer, 1984; Software Development and the Japanese Customer; Tokyo, the Bid Mikan, short story. *Memberships:* Am Elec Assn; Japan Soc; Asia Foun; Foreign Corres Club; Am and French Chambers of Commerce. *Honours:* Scholarship at Georgetown; Licensed to teach the art of Kimono. *Hobbies:* Oil and water colour painting; Squash; Cooking; Jazz; Classical music. *Address:* 535 Middlefield Rd, Suite 150, Menlo Park, CA 94025, USA.

MUNGER James G, b. 8 Sept 1951, Elyria, Ohio, USA. Fire Protection Consultant. m. Karen Johnson, 2 Oct 1971, 1 d. *Education:* Assoc Deg, Applied Sci Fire Sci, Wallace State Com Col, Alabama, 1979; Cert in Fire Prevention Tech, Memphis State Univ, 1988; Univ of Alabama, 1979-80; US Fire Admin Nat Fire Acad, Maryland, 1980-87; Alabama Fire Fighters Personnel Standards and Traiming Comm, Alabama, 1978, 1984, 1985. *Appointments:* Pres, James G Munger and Assocs, 1985-; Dpty State Fire Marshall for State of Alabama, 1980-85; Adjunct Fac, Nat Fire Acad, 1984-. *Publications:* Articles: The Red Flag Syndrome, 1987; The Effects of Fire on Concrete, 1988; Developer of course for Nat Fire Acad: Come Management - A Systems Approach, 1988. *Memberships include:* Soc of Fire Protection Engrs; Intl Assn of Arson Investigators; Alabama Assn of Arson Investigators; Nat Fire Protection Assn; Intl Assn of Elec Inspectors; Soc of Nat Fir Acad Instrs; Cullman City Councl- Fire Commissioner, 1992. *Honours:* Certified: Fire Protection Specialist, Fire Prevention Ofr III, Fire Investigation Ofr III, Fire Investigator; Soc of Fire Protection Engrs-tech; Dean's List, Memphis State Univ. *Hobbies:* Tropical fish. *Address:* PO Box 1773, Cullman, AL 35056, USA.

MUNS Joaquim Albuixech, b. 25 June 1935, Barcelona, Spain. University Professor. m. Gloria Rubiol, 1967, 1 s. *Education:* BLL, Univ 1958, BSc Econ, 1959; PhD Econ, Univ Barcelona; Res Student, LSE, 1959-61. *Appointments:* Econ, OECD, Paris, 1962-63; Econ, IMF, 1965-68; Exec Dir, IMF, 1978-80; Exec Dir, World Bank, 1980-82. *Publications:* various books and articles on international economic relations. *Memberships:* Am Econ Assn; Catalan Econ Assn, Pres. *Honours:* Cross of St George of Catalan Govt, 1984. *Hobbies:* Travel; Music. *Address:* C Muntaner 268, 08021 Barcelona, Spain. 52,

MURCHISON Duncan George, b. 13 Jan 1928, Glasgow, Scotland. University Professor; Pro Vice Chancellor. m. (1) Dorothy Jean Charlton, 23 July 1953, (2) Gail Adrienne Hermon, 27 July 1982, 3 s, 3 d. *Education:* BSc 1952, PhD 1957, Dunelm. *Appointments:* Geol, Royal Dutch Shell, 1958; Lectr, Sr Lectr, Rdr in Geochem, 1964-76; Prof of Organis Petrol, 1976-; Dean of Fac of Sci, 1980-83; Hd, Dept Geol, 1982-86; Pro V-Chancellor, 1986-; Acting V-Chancellor, 1991. *Publications:* Numerous articles in learned journals in the field of reflected light microscopy, organic petrology and organic geochemistry. *Memberships:* Royal Microscopical Soc, VP, 1975, 1979; Pres, 1976-78; Intl Com for Coal Petrol, Pres, 1979-83; Geol Soc of London; Edinburgh Geol Soc. *Honours:* FRSE, 1973; Hon FRMS, 1979; Thiessen Medal, 1987. *Hobbies:* Philately; Fishing. *Address:* Vice Chancellor's Office, 6 Kensington Terrace, Univ of Newcastle upon Tyne, NE1 7RU, England.

MURDOCH Robert Whitten, b. 21 Mar 1937, Pittsburg, PA, USA. Attorney at Law. m. Eleanore L Uram, 23 Sept 1967, 1 s. *Education:* BA, Pittsburgh Univ, 1960; Pvt Law Study, Duquesne Univ Sch of Law. *Appointments:* Ptnr, Jones Gregg Creehan & Gerace, 1967-85; Ptnr, Grogan, Graffam, McGinley & Lucchino, PC, 1985-. *Publications:* Pfeifer: The Supreme Ct and LHWCA and Inflation; The Economic Expert in Litigation, 1984. *Memberships:* US Supreme Ct; Supreme Ct of PA; Acad of Trial Lawyers of Allegheny Co; Am Soc

of Law and Med; Sons of Am Revolution; Descendants of Colonial Clergy; Sons of Union Veterans of Civil War; Natl Soc Sons of Colonial New England. *Hobbies:* Music (tenor soloist); Golf; Geneology. *Address:* 920 Prospect Road, Pittsburgh, PA 15227, USA. 6, 52, 132, 163.

MURIO Jay, b. Louisiana, USA. Concert Soprano. *Education:* BA, Arkansas Col; MMus, Am Conservatory of Music, Chicago, 1934; MA, Univ of Chicago, 1933. *Appointments include:* Concert soprano: Merrie England Century of Progress Chicago, 1934; Texas Centennial, 1936; Concerts, Mexico, 1937-42; Nat Opera of Mexico, Chicago Civic Opera, 1943-46; Throughout the USA and Latin Am. *Publications:* Feature stories, editorials, treatise. *Memberships:* Pres, Charter mem, Psi Chap, Chicago Chap, Illinois Opera Guild Assoc, Lyric Opera; Utd Daughters of Confederacy; Daughters of Am Revolution. *Honours:* 1st prize, college essay; Past pres, every organisation, club or sorority has belonged to, including: L'Etoile Lit Soc, Delta Omicron, NSAL, College and conservatory orchestra musical programme productions. *Hobby:* Animals, including pet deer, dogs, cats. *Address:* Box 678, Oak Park, IL 60303, USA.

MURPHY Eugenie Victorine Ullmann, b. 10 Jan 1913, Brooklyn, NY, USA. Retired Teacher. m. (1) William Clarke, 1931; (2) Harry Muelhauser, 1956; (3) Martin Murphy, 1970, 2 s, 1 d. *Education:* Grad, Washington Irving Hg Sch, majored in Art; Studied Oil painting with Paul Pusisias. *Appointments:* Tchr, oil classes, Nat Art Leauge, NY, 1956- 58; Tchr, oil painting, Women's Club in Great Neck, 1956-58; Tchr, Watercolours, porcelain painting, Own Studio, NY, 1956-88; Specialise in florals, landscapes, seascapes, still life and portraits and figure paintings. *Memberships:* Nat Art League, Sec, NY; Am Artist Prof League; Wospo Douglaston Art league, NY; Wet paints Art League, NY. *Honours:* Awd: Washington Sq Outdoor Art Exhib, 1962; Winning watercolour shown in Huntington Hartfords Gal of Modern Art; Water Colour awd from Mayor Lindsay of NY, 1967; Chosen to show at the NY World's Fair, 1964; Water colour shown at Nat Arts Show, Hudson Valley Art Assn, NY; Winner, Travel Exhib; Watercolour pictures held in private collections nationally and internationally. *Hobbies:* Travelling; Swimming; Visiting museums; Designing. *Address:* 7188 Crown Oaks Drive, Spring Hill, FL 34606, USA. 37.

MURPHY Stuart John, b. 7 Feb 1933, London, England. Chartered Architect and Town Planning Consultant. m. Jane Elizabeth Tinkler, 2 Dec 1966, 1 s, 1 d. *Education:* City of London Sch, Poly of Central London, Dip Arch (Dist), Dip Town Planning. *Appointments:* Arch Dept, LCC, 1956-63; Llewellyn Davies & Weeks, Sen Arch, 1963-65; Gp Arch, City of Westminister Arch & TP Dept, 1965-68; London Borough of Harrow, 1968-76; Dpty Borough Arch and Planning Ofr, 1968-71; Controller of Arch, Borough Arch, 1971-76; Corp of London, Dpty, 1978-79, City Arch and Planning Ofr, 1979-86. *Memberships:* VP, Hon Treas, RIBA, Fellow, 1970; FRTPI, 1973; FRSA, 1977; FBIM, 1978; Brit Acad of Experts, 1987; Sr VP, SCALA, 1984-85; Pres, CLAWSA, 1984-86; Freeman, City of London, 1954; Master, Worshipful Co of Chartered Archs; Liveryman, Worshipful Co of Merchant Taylros; Parish Clerk, Ch of St Lawrence Jewry next Guildhall; Worshipful Co of Parish Clerks. *Hobbies:* Theatre; Musichall History; Gardening. *Address:* 6 Coval Lane, London SW14 7DS, England.

MURRAY Athol Laverick, b. Tynemouth, Northumberland, England. Archivist. m. Irene Joyce Cairs, 11 Oct 1958, 1 s, 1 d. *Education:* BA 1952, MA 1958, Jesus Col, Cambs; LLB, 1957, PhD, 1961, Edinburgh Univ. *Appointments:* Res Asst, Foreign Ofc, 1953; Asst Keeper, Scottish Record Ofc, 1953-83; Dpty Keeper, 1983-84, Keeper of Records of Scotland, 1984-90; Conslt, Jersey Archives Steering Gp, 1991-92. *Publications:* The Royal Grammar School Lancaster: A History, 1951; The Lag Charters, 1958; Articles on Scottish history. *Memberships:* Soc of Antiquaries of

Scotland, VP, 1989-92; Scottish Record Soc, Sec, 1957-76, Chm of Coun, 1981-90; Business Comm of General Councl, Edinburgh Univ, 1992-; Fellow, Royal Hist Soc, 1971. *Honours:* David Anderson Berry Prize, RHS, 1971. *Hobbies:* Bowls; Reading; Walking. *Address:* 33 Inverleith Gardens, Edinburgh EH3 5PR, Scotland. 1, 184.

MURRAY Douglas Millar, b. 25 Sept 1946, Edinburgh, Scotland. Lecturer in Church History, Univ of Glasgow. m. Freya M Smith, 16 Sept 1983. *Education:* MA 1968, BD, 1971, Univ of Edinburgh; PhD, Fitzwilliam Col, Cambs, 1976. *Appointments:* Minister, Ch of Scotland at St Bride's Ch, Callander, 1976-80, at Polwarth, Edinburgh, 1980-89; Lectr, 1989-. *Publications:* Jt Ed, Studies in the History of Worship in Scotland, 1984; Assoc Ed, Scottish Jour of Theol, 1981-87; Ed, Liturgical Review, 1977-81. *Memberships:* Convener of Panel of Doctrine of the General Assembly of the Ch of Scotland, 1986-90; Coun of Scottish Ch Hist Soc, 1990-; Eccles Hist Soc. *Honours:* Chalmers Lectr, New Col Univ of Edinburgh and St Mary's Col, St Andrews, 1991. *Hobbies:* Scottish country dancing; Walking; Golf; Cross-country skiing. *Address:* Department of Theology and Church History, University of Glasgow, Glasgow G12 8QQ, Scotland.

MURRAY Ewan Skinner, b. 18 Sept 1931, Glasgow, Scotland. Insurance Official. *Education:* Hyland School, Glasgow. *Appointments:* Insurance Official, Iron Trades Insurance Gp, 1960-91; Ret'd 1991. *Memberships:* European Athletic Assn, Coun, 1987; Brit Amateur Athletic Bd, Hon Life VP, 1987; Commonwealth Games Coun for Scotland, Coun, 1973-83; Brit Olympic Assn, Coun, 1984-89; Scottish Amateur Athletic Assn, Life VP, 1981; Scottish Cross Country Union, Life VP, 1979; Garscube Harriers Club, Hon Sec, 1952-62. *Honours:* OBE, 1984; O.St.J., 1989. *Address:* 25 Bearsden Road, Glasgow G13 1YL, Scotland.

MURRELL Janice Marie, Dame, b. 29 Nov 1937, St Louis,Missouri, USA. Concert Opera Artiste. *Education:* Deg, Krocgen Sch of Music, 1971; Deg, Julliard Sch of Music, 1979; Citation, Washington Univ, 1971. *Appointments:* St Louis Public Sch System, Vocal Instr, 1968-90; Concert Opera Presenter. *Creative works:* World distributed poetic anthologies; Writer of lyrics to songs; Short stories and published manuscripts internationally. *Memberships:* St Louis Symph Assn; Womans Div, Young Artiste; Metropolitan Opera Guild Assn; Platform Assn; Intl Writers Assn; Friends of Placido Domingo Assn. *Honours:* Knighted Dame of Honour, Washington, 1989; Intl Musicians Mus of Hon, 1989; London St Louis Bd of Educ Hon Review, 1989-90. *Hobbies:* Writing; Painting; Sculpture; Sketching; Designing. *Address:* 5556 Riverview Blvd, St Louis, MO 63120, USA. 5.

MUSA Maryam Talatu, b. 7 Sept 1969, Kaduna, Nigeria. Clerical Officer, Chief Magistrate Court. *Education:* Crowther Meml Col, Lokoja, Kwara State, 1981-86; OND Textile Tech, Kaduna Poly, 1987-89. *Appointments:* Clerical Officer, Chief Magistrate Court, High Court of Justice, Kaduna State. *Honours:* Best Student in Islamic Religion, Crowther Meml Col, 1986. *Hobbies:* Reading; Dancing; Praying; Watching films; Handball; Volleyball; Travelling. *Address:* c/o Victoria Emmanuel, Public Relation Dept, Kaduna Textile Ltd, PO Box 168, Kaduna State, Nigeria.

MUSCUTARIU Ioan, b. 11 June 1939, Arini jud Brasov, Romania. Pyhsicist; University Professor. m. Elena Rosiuta, 5 July 1968, 1 s, 1 d. *Education:* Fac of Phys, Univ of Cluj, 1958-63; PhD, Univ of Timisoara, 1972. *Appointments:* Asst Lectr, Polytech Inst, Romania, 1963-67; Asst Lectr, 1967-70, Asst Prof, 1970-74, Assoc Prof, 1975-90, Prof, 1990-, Univ of Timisoara, Romania. *Publications include:* Cristale lichide si aplicatii, 1981; Introducere in fizica cristaleler lichide, 1984; Electricitate si magnetism, vol I, 1974; Structura si simetria monocristaleler de alfa-SiO2, 1986; Fizica

corpului solid si a semiconductorilor, 1987, 1991. *Memberships:* Am, European and Romanian Phys Socs; NYAS, 1988. *Honour:* Northwestern Univ, USA, 1974-75. *Hobby:* Hunting. *Address:* str Popa Laurentiu 7 sc A Apt 5, 1900 Timisoara, Romania. 152.

MUSTAPIC Zvonko, b. 13 Sept 1914, Lovrec, Crotia. Entrepreneur; Teacher. m. Stephany Valencic 12 Jan 1940, 2 s, 1 d. *Education:* Hg Sch, Split, Croatia, 1928-36; Hg Sch Tchg Qual, Fac of Maths, Univ of Zagreb, 1936-40. *Appointments:* Hg Sch Tchr, 1943; Auxiliary Ser; Tchr, Auxiliary Acad, 1944-45; Entrepreneur, 1948-. *Memberships:* Pres, Univ Choir; Sec Org of the Croatian Peasant Party for the County of Imotski; Pres, Croatian Peasant Party, South Am. *Hobbies:* Sociology; Politics, especially the historical development and social and political problems of the peasantry in east European countries. *Address:* Andonaegoi 2059, Buenos Aires, Argentina.

MUSTONEN Aki Kaarlo, b. 20 June 1948, Oulu, Finland. Head, Dept of Clinical Genetics, Kuopio University Hospital. m. Anna-Liisa Hakulin, 30 Aug 1973, 4 s. *Education:* MD, 1973; Dr (thesis), 1984; Specialist in Paediatrics, 1982; Specialist in Med Genet, 1990. *Appointments:* Pres in Paed, Oulu Univ Hosp, 1975-79; Pvt Practice, Oulu, 1975-; Chief Paed Reg Hosp, Oulainen, 1982-85; Chief Med ofr, Clin Genet, Kuopio Univ Hosp, 1990-. *Publication* Islet-cell antibodies and HLA antigens in children with insulin-dependent diabetes mellitus. *Memberships:* Finnish Med Assn; Finnish Assn of Paed; Finnish Assn of Med Genetics. *Hobbies:* History; Reading; Chess; Languages. *Address:* Dept of Clin Genetics, Kuopio University Hospital, SF-70210 Kuopio, Finland. 52.

MUTAGI Ramachandra, b. 26 Mar 1948, Belgium. Head, Baseband processing Division. m. Vijaya, 20 Aug 1976, 1 s, 1 d. *Education:* BE Telecoms, 1971; DIISc, Elec Design Tech, 1976. *Appointments:* Lectr om PES, Col of Eng, Mandya, 1971-72; R & D Engr, Space Appl Ctr, ISRO, 1972-85; Hd, Speech Proc Sec, 1985-91, Hde, Baseband Proc Div, 1991-, SAC Ahmadabad. *Publications:* Developed equipment for satellite communications. *Memberships:* Fellow, Inst of Elec & Telecom Engrs, India. *Hobbies:* Cricket; Reading; Movies. *Address:* A-163 Ashok Nagar, SM Road, Ahmedabad 380015, India. 52,

MUTO Takasuke, b. 18 Feb 1930, Sociologist; Educator. m. Masako Nagashima, 23 June 1958, 1 s, 1 d. *Education:* MEd, Tokyo Univ of Educ, 1955. *Appointments:* Reschr, Res Inst of Ed, Shinano Ed Assn, 1958-66; Lectr, Fac of Educ, 1966-67, Assoc Prof, 1967-78, Prof, 1978, Shinshu University, Nagano. *Publications:* The Development of Pupils' Value-Judgements and Valuation Process in the Classroom, 1969; Group Guidance in the Classroom, 1976; Moral Education in the Life World, 1978; Translator of sociology books. *Memberships:* Japan Soc of Educ Sociol, Bd of Dirs. *Hobbies:* Skiing; Go. *Address:* Faculty of Eduation, Shinshu University, 6 Nishinagand, Nagano 380, Japan. 52.

MWALUKO Gabriel M P, b. 3 Aug 1942, Dodoma, Tanzania. m. Bibiana Daudi Manyilika, 23 June 1973, 1 s, 1 d. *Education:* MBChB, E.Africa/Makerere Univ Col Med Sch, Kampala, Uganda, 1969; MSc, 1973, PhD, 1975, Victoria Univ, Manchester England; Registered Med Practitioner; Tanganyika Med Coun, 1970-, Gen Med Coun of GB, overseas list, 1979-. *Appointments include:* WHO Fellow, 1972-75; Lectr, Clin Pharmacol, Univ of Dar es Salaam, 1975-77; Sr Lectr, 1977-83, Assoc Prof, 1983-; Vis Prof, Godfrey Huggings Sch of Med, Harare, Zimbabwe, 1986-87; Sec Gen, Assn of Med Schls of Africa, 1990-94. *Publications:* Numerous articles in professional journals and magazines as well as the following books: Health and Diseases in Tanzania; Snake Venom Poisoning and Management. *Memberships:* Med Assn of Tanzania; Brit Pharmacol Soc; BMA; Tanzania Public Health Assn; Task Force on

Med Educ in Africa, 1989-91; Pres, African Drug Utilisation Res Gp, 1988-90; Pres, Soc of Clin and Experimental Pharmacol, 1990-95. *Honours:* Dar es Salaam Unin Coun Mem; External Examiner: PhD Thesis, Univs of Nairobi and Makerere, MSc Thesis, Univ of Zimbabwe; WHO Advr: Expert Gp on non-communicable diseases, 1989, Methodology on Res in Hypertension in Devel Countries, 1988. *Hobbies:* Gardening; Badmington. *Address:* P O Box 65024, Dar es Salaam, Tanzania.

MYERS Edward David, b. 15 July 1925, Harare, Zimbabwe. Consultant Psychiatrist. m. Sybil Brearley Chatfield, 14 Jan 1966, 2 s. *Education:* MBChB, Univ of Capetown, 1948; DTM & H, England, 1950; MRCP, Edinburgh, 1954; DPM England, 1959; FRCP, Edinburgh, 1971; MRCPsych, 1972; FRCPsych, 1986. *Appointments include:* RMO, Gen Hosp, Harare, 1949; Hse Phys, Hg Wycombe War Meml and Romford Old Ch Hosps, 1950-52; Med Registrar, Royal Infirmary, Preston, Lancs, 1952-53; Psychi Registrar, Banstead and Charing Cross Hosps, London, 1956-59; Conslt Psychi: in Pvte Practice and sessional Consultant at Harare Ctl Hosp, 1960-62; Sr Psychi Registrar, St Edwards and City Gen Hosps, Stoke-on-Trent, 1963-65; Conslt Psychi, N.Staffs Health Dist, 1965-91; Ret'd, 1991; Sr Res Fellow, Psychi, 1980-90, Hon Res Fellow, 1991-, Univ Keele. *Publications:* Papers on compliance with treatment group therapy, attempted suicide and psychoedoncrinology. *Memberships:* North Staffs Med Inst, Treas, 1977-80; Hosp Conslts and Specialists Assn; Brit Assn of Psychopharmcol; Osler Club of London. *Hobbies:* Fly-fishing; Bowls; Theatre; Psychiatric and medical history. *Address:* St Davids, 96 Lancaster Rd, Newcastle , Staffs ST5 1DS, England.

MYERS John Annesley, b. 1 May 1915, Bradford, Yorkshire, England. Retired Pharmaceutical Chemist. m. Jean D Falconer, 13 Apr 1950, 2 s, 2 d. *Education:* MPS, 1937; DPA Leeds, 1952; FRPharm.S, 1954; LLB, Leeds, 1955; MInst Pkg, 1963; Minst PS, 1967; ACIS, 1970; MCPP, 1985. *Appointments include:* Pharm, Leeds, Bradford & Leics Royal Infirmaries, 1933-42; Pharm, Royal Naval Hosp, Haslar, 1942-44; Pharm, RNA Hosp, Diyatalawa, Snr Pharm, RN Med Depot, Trincomalee, Ceylon, 1944-46; Grp Chief Pharm, Bradford Royal Infirmary & 'A' Gp Hosps, 1946- 58; Gp Chief Pharm, Royal Infirmary, Edinburgh & Assoc Hosps, 1958-72; Reg Pharm, SE Reg Hosp Bd, Edinburgh, 1972-74; Chief Admin Pharm Ofr, Lothian Health Bd, 1974-80. *Publications:* Over 50 papers on pharmaceutical subjects in various books and journals on the effects of surgical dressings on wound healing, practical pharmaceutics and geriatric medicine. *Memberships:* Numerous advisory bodies, committees, professional associations including Brit Standards Inst Tech Cttees. *Honours:* 1st place prize exam, Pharmaceutical Soc of GB, 1940; Pereira Medal, 1940; Frank Edward Harrison Prize, 1940; Hill's Prize, 1940; Evans Gold Medal, 1978; *Hobbies:* Reading Biographies; Walking; Gardening; Chmn and various offices, Edinburgh and Lothians Branch, NHS Retirement Fellowship. *Address:* 5 Dalhousie Terrace, Morningside, Edinburgh EH10 5NE, Scotland.

MYERS Philip Jacob, b. 22 Aug 1944, Philadelphia, PA, USA. College Professor; Writer. m. Kathryn Zeman, 20 Dec 1968, 5 s, 4 d. *Education:* BA, Taylor Univ, 1966; ThB, Florida Bible Col, 1973; MA Dallas Theol Sem, 1985; DMin, S.Western Bapt Theol Sem, 1992. *Appointments:* Family Seminar Lectr, 1974-91; Dallas Theol Sem Lay Inst, 1983-84; Prof Christian Educ, Florida Bible Col, 1971-77; Prof, Christian Educ, Miami Christian Col, 1985-91. *Publications:* Articles: Choosing your successor; Blue Collar Father; Jesus was a children's Worker; Why I'm sold on Bible Colleges; Am I going to Heaven? At the moment of Birth. *Memberships:* Nat Assn of Profs of Christian Educ; Assn of Christian Ser Personnel; Grace Evangelical Soc. *Honours:* Runner up, Indiana State Intercollegiate Wrestling, 1966. *Hobbies:* Cycling; Jigsaw puzzles; Preaching; Teaching Sunday School. *Address:* UFM

International, 306 Bala Avenue, Bala Cynwyd, PA 19004, USA.

N

NAARDEN Lucien John, b. 27 Dec 1955, Paramaribo Suriname. m. Walcott Anita Bernadetta, 20 Mar 1981. *Education:* Psychol, 1976-81, Tchr of Econ deg, 1980-81, Univ of Leiden, The Netherlands; Postgrad, Hogeschool van Amsterdam, 1991. *Appointments:* Hd, Dept for Forengical Psychol,1981-85, Hd, Dept Delinquent Care, 1985-89, Policy Advr, 1989, Min of Justice; Sec Gen, Chamber of Commerce and Indust, 1989-. *Publications:* How does Surinamese in The Netherlands score on the Dutch Wechler Adult Intelligence Scale, 1981; Needs Assessment for training among deliquents, 1983; Criminal statistics for the UN, 1984-87. *Memberships:* VP, Lion's Club North; Chm, Assn of Psychols; Chm, Nat Drug Abuse Control Coun, 1986-89; Govt Controller of Pvt Mgmt Insts. *Hobbies:* Football; Basketball; Fishing; Music; Socialising. *Address:* 10 Leo Heinemanstraat, Paramaribo, Suriname.

NAERGER Maurice John, b. 4 Mar 1931, Weymouth, Dorset. Company Director. m. Brenda Mary Cross, 7 Apr 1956, 1 s, 1 d. *Education:* Weymouth Grammar Sch. *Appointments:* Retail Mgr, 1957-73; Retail Ops Mgr, 1973-75; Dir, W H Smith Hldgs, 1975-81; Conslt BR, 1982-83; Chm, Helping Hand Charity Shops Ltd, 1982-91; Chm, CSC Appeals Ltd, 1982-91. *Memberships:* MBIM, 1971; FIPM, 1972. *Hobbies:* Sailing; Bowling; Music; Current Affairs. *Address:* Trenton House, Eversley Road, Bexhill on Sea, E.Sussex TN40 1HE, England.

NAETS Guido, b. 25 Nov 1934, Antwerp, Belgium. Press Spokesman, European Parliament. m. 11 Oct 1958, 2 d. *Education:* Philos, 1955, Econ, 1961, LLD, 1958, Louvain. *Appointments:* Sec Cepess, 1958-62; Freelance journalist for European affairs, 1962-80; Dir of Info, European Parl, 1980-. *Publication:* Europe - Dream, Adventure, Reality, 1987. *Memberships:* Chm, Alumni Louanienses; Chm, Hon Senate, Movement for the US of Europe. *Honours:* European Press Awd, 1966, 1967. *Hobby:* Golf. *Address:* Tramlaan 444, B-1933 Sterrebeek, Belgium. 185.

NAGAI Tsuneji, b. 10 June 1933, Gumma, Japan. Professor of Pharmaceutics. m. Kiyoko Usui, 5 May 1964. *Education:* BA 1956, MS 1958, PhD, 1961, Univ of Tokyo; Postdoc Fellow, Columbia Univ, NY, 1965-66, Univ of Michigan, 1966-67. *Appointments:* Res and Tchg Assoc, Dept of Pharmaceutics, Univ Tokyo, 1961-71; Prof, Hoshi Univ, Tokyo, 1971-. *Publications:* 340 refereed research papers, 300 reviews and other scientific articles, 70 books. *Memberships:* Japan Pharm Assn, Dir; Pharm Soc of Japan, Dir; Acad of Pharm Scis & Tech, Japan, Fdr Pres; Intl Pharm Fed, VP; Japan Soc of Drug Delivery System, Pres. *Honours:* Hoest Madsen Medal, 1986; Japan Nat Invention Prize, 1984; Most Encouraged Res Prize, 1972, Pharm Tech Wed, 1982, Most Prestigious Acad Prize, 1988, Pharm Soc of Japan. *Hobbies:* Kabuki (Japanese Opera): Classical Music. *Address:* 1-23-10 No 103, Hon-Komagome, Bunkyo-ku, Tokyo 113, Japan. 1.

NAGATA Takao, b. 17 Jan 1943, Osaka, Japan. Director of Tokyo Dome Corporation. m. 13 May 1971, 1 d. *Education:* BA Law, Keio Univ, 1966; MBA, Claremont Grad Sch, USA, 1982. *Appointments:* Chief Mgr, Mktg Dept, 1985-86, Chief Mgr of Planning & Control Dept, 1989-91, Korakuen Co; Dir, Strategic Planning, Tokyo Dome Corp, 1991-; Lectr on Sports Mgmt, Nippon Col of Phys Educ. *Membership:* Takene Country Club. *Hobby:* Golf. *Address:* 2-12-1 Jyosuishinmachi, Kodaira, Tokyo 187, Japan. 52.

NAGESWARA RAO Guttikonda, b. 1 July 1938, Pamidimukkala, India. Prof Eng; Dean Fac Arts. m. Vijayalakshmi, 14 Feb 1966, 3 s. 1 d. *Education:* BA Eng Lang & Lit 1959, MA Eng Lang & Lit 1961; PhD

Elizabethan Drama 1964; PGCTE 1972. *Appointments:* Lectr in Eng 1966- 76; Reader in Eng 1976-82; Prof Eng 1982-; Dean, Sch of Humanities, & Dean Fac Extn Stds 1988-91, Arts 1991-. *Publications:* The Peace which passeth understanding, 1976; The Epic of the Soul, 1977; The Domestic Drama, 1978; Encounter with Nothing, 1979; Hidden Eternity, 1986. *Memberships:* PEN Intl; Milton Soc Am; All India Eng Tchrs' Assn; Indian Comparative Lit Assn; Intl Poets Acad. *Honour:* Awd'd Univ Grants Comm Post Doctoral Fellowship 1964-66, for working on The Influence of Indian Thought on T S Eliot. *Hobbies:* Painting; Dance; Gardening; Birdwatching. *Address:* Faculty of Arts, S V University, Tirupati 517 502, AP, India. 93.

NAGL Ludwig, b. 27 Apr 1944, Voecklabruck, Austria. m. Herta U Docekal, 10 Apr 1970. *Education:* Dr Phil, Univ Vienna, Austria, 1969; Habil (Univ Doz), Univ Vienna, Austria, 1981. *Appointments:* Asst Prof, Millersville State Univ, Lancaster, PA, USA, 1970-71; Asst, Univ Klagenfurt, Austria, 1971-77, Univ Vienna, 1977-81; Docent, Univ Vienna, 1981-89; tit Ao Univ Prof, Univ Vienna, 1991-; Vis Scholar, Dept Phil, Harvard Univ, 1987. *Publications:* Author: Gesellschaft und Autonomie, 1983; Charles Sanders peirce, 1992; Ed, Wo Steht die Analytische Philosophie heute?, 1986; Nach der Philosophie; Essays von Stanley Cavell, 1987; Die Philosophen und Freud, 1988; Philosophie und Psychoanalyse; Symposium der Wiener Festwochen, 1990; Philosophie und Semiotik, 1992. *Memberships:* Am Phil Assn; Austrian Phil Soc, Bd Dirs, 1987-88, 1992-1993; Sigmund Freud Soc, Vienna; N Am Kant Soc; Charles S Peirce Soc. *Honours:* Grantee, Fulbright Foun, 1987. *Hobby:* Films. *Address:* Weimarerstr 82/ 2/7, A-1190 Vienna, Austria. 52.

NAGL-DOCEKAL Herta Ursula, b. 29 May 1944, Wels, Upper Austria. University Professor. m. Ludwig Nagl, 10 Apr 1970. *Education:* PhD, sub auspiciis praesidentis, 1967; Habilitation in Philos, 1981, Univ Vienna. *Appointments:* Asst Prof, 1968-85, Prof, 1985-, Dept of Phil, Univ Vienna. *Publications:* Books: Erns von Lasaulx. Ein Beitrag zur Kritik des organischen Geschichtsbegriffs, 1970; Die Objektivitat der Geschichtswissenschaft, 1982; Tod des Subjekts?, 1987; Feminstische Philosophie, 1990; Denken der Geschlechterdifferenz, 1990; Postboloniales Philosophiereu: Afrika, 1992; Numerous articles in the fields of philsophy of history, theory of the historical sciences, ethics, and feminist theory. *Memberships:* Intl Assn of Women Phils; Soc for Women Phil; Allgemeine Gesellschaft fur Phil in Deutschland; Intl Hegel-Vereinigung; Soc for Asian and Comparative Phil. *Honours:* Forderungspreis der Stadt Wien fur Wissenschaft, 1984. *Address:* Dept of Philosophy, University of Vienna, Universitatsstr 7, A-1010 Vienna, Austria.

NAGOVITSIN Vyahcheslav, b. 21 Dec 1939, Magnitogorsk, USSR. Composer; Violinist; Pianist. 1 s. *Education:* Musorgsky Music Col, Violin, St Petersburg, 1954-58; Vionon and Composition, Rimsky-Kozsdkov Conservatoire, St Petersburg, 1958-63; Postgrad, Consevatoire Dept of Composition, with Prof D Shostakovich, 1963-66. *Appointments:* Music Mgr, Leningrad Acad Comedy Theatre, 1968-70; Ed, Music Pubing Hse, Soviet Composer, 1970-73; Lectr, Ch of Composition and Theory of Music, St Petersburg State Conservatoire, 1971-. *Creative works:* Symph, Concerto for a violin with orchestra; Sonata for flute and piano; Three sonatas for piano; Dramatic capriccio for flute and piano; Toccata in the form of a fugue for piano; two quartets; Orchestration of the unfinished opers of Musorgsky, Salambo, and The Marriage, for Mazyinsky opera-house, Kizov Theatre, St Petersburg. *Memberships:* Union of Soviet Composers; Docent, St Petersburg State Conservatoire, Rimsky-Korsakov; Bd, Union of Composers of St Petersburg. *Honours:* 2nd Prize, Composition for Performance, Intl Tchaikovsky Competition, Moscow, 1966; 1st prize, Composers Competition, Leningrad, 1976. *Hobbies:* Photography;

Painting. *Address:* Energetikov Str 60-220, St Petersburg 195253, Russia.

NAGY Karoly, b. 24 May 1934, Nyiregyhaza, Hungary. Professor of Sociology. m. 26 Nov 1988, Katalin Toth, 2 d. *Education:* Tchg Dipl, Hungary, 1955; BA Rutgers Univ, NJ, USA, 1962; MA, 1966, PhD 1970, New Sch for Social Res, NY, USA. *Appointments:* Tchr, Hungary, 1954-56; Rehab Counsellor, State of NJ, 1962-68; Lectr, Dept of Sociol, Rutgers Univ, 1966-; Assoc Prof, Prof, Middlesex Co Col, 1968-. *Publications:* 90 articles and chapters in USA and European publications; three books Ed: Istvan Bibo: Democracy, Revolution, Self-determination, 1991. *Memberships:* Am Sociol Assn; Intl PEN; Am Assn for the Study of Hungarian Hist; Intl Assn of Hungarian Studies; Hungarian Alumni Assn; Anyanyelvi Konferencia. *Honours:* Lajos Kassak Awd of Magyar Muhely, Paris, 1976; Geza Barczi Awd of Anyanyelvi Konferencia, Pecs, 1981. *Address:* 25 Redbud Rd, Piscataway, NJ 08854, USA. 2, 6, 122, 130, 140,

NAGY Peter, b. 12 Oct 1920, Budapest, Hungary. Research Professor of Literary History. m. Eva Zombory, 19 Jan 1966, 1 d. *Education:* Minta Gimn, Budapest, 1930-38; Eotvos Col, Budapest, 1938-42; PhD, Pazmany Univ, 1942; Univ de Geneve, 1943-45. *Appointments:* Min Foreign Affairs, 1945-49; Hung Acad Sci Admin, 1950-53; Lit Dir, Ed Hse, 1953-56; Hung Acad Sci Lit Inst, 1957-63; Corvina Ed Lit Dir, 1963-65; Prof, Pazmany Univ. *Publications:* 18 books on literary history, comparative lit, criticism, theatre. Main works: Moricz Zsigmond, 1953; Szabo Dezso, 1964; Libertinage et Révolution, 1975; Dramai arcelek, 1978. *Memberships:* Hungarian Writers Assn; ILCA; ICLA; Hung Pen, VP. *Honours:* Jozsef Attila Prize, 1953, 1954; Palmes Academiques Officier, France. *Hobbies:* Gardening; Swimming. *Address:* Pasareti ut 117/a, H-1026 Budapest, Hungary. 43, 52.

NAIMARK Arnold, b. 24 Aug 1933, Winnipeg, Canada. President and Vice Chancellor. m. Barbara Jean Alder, 28 Feb 1960, 1 s. 1 d. *Education:* DMed, 1957; BSc Med, 1957; MSc, 1959. *Appointments:* Asst Prof, Univ Manitoba, Assoc Dir, Cardio Resp Unit, Winnipeg Gen Hosp, 1963-64; Staff Phys, Winnipeg Gen Hosp, 1964-65; Conslt, Deer Lodge Veterans Hosp, Winnipeg, 1964-71; Assoc Prof, Physiol, 1965-66, Hd of Dept Physiol, 1966-71, Dean, Fac of Med, 1971-81, Pres and V-Chancellor, 1981-, Univ Manitoba; Conslt Phys, Health Scis Ctr, St Boniface Gen Hosp, 1971-. *Publications:* Presentations at conferences and symposia; numerous research papers and articles published including: Clinical implications of research on lung cells, 1976; The capacity of Canada's universities to educate higly qualified scientists and engineers, 1989; Transfer and transformation of medical ideas and institutions in the Commonwealth: A Canadian perspective, 1990. *Memberships:* Can Med Assn; Can and Am Physiol Socs; Can Soc for Clin Investigation; Med Res Soc of GB; Fellow, AAAS; Can Lung and Diabetic Assns; The Royal Soc of Canada; Coun on Respiratory Dis, Am Heart Assn. *Honours include:* Queen Elizabeth Silver Jubilee Medal, 1977; Hon Mem, Can Soc for Ortho Res; Dist Serv Awd, Ben-Gurion Univ of the Negev; Designation, Arnold Naimark Wing, Health Scis Library, Ben Gurion Univ; Hon LLD, Mt Allison Univ; Fellow, Royal Soc of Can; Ofr, Order of Canada. *Hobbies:* Racquet sport. *Address:* The University of Manitoba, Winnipeg, Mannitoba, Canada R3T 2N2. 2, 32, 142, 154.

NAIR P K Ramachandran, b. 12 Mar 1942, Kerala, India. Prof of Agroforestry. m. Vimala Devi, 29 Aug 1973, 3 s. *Education:* BSc Agric, 1961, MSc Agric, 1968, Kerala, India; PhD Agronomy, Pantnagar, India, 1971; Dr Sci Agric, Gottingen, Germany, 1978. *Appointments:* Agronomist, ICAR, Kasaragod, India, 1972-78; Principal Scist, ICRAF Nairobi Kenya, 1978-87; Prof of Agroforestry, Univ of Florida, USA, 1987-. *Publications:* Over six dozen scientific publications, author, ed and joint ed of 5 books. *Memberships:* Life Mem: Intl Soc

of Soil Sci, Intl Soc of Tropical Foresters; Am Soc of Agronomy; Soi Sci Soc of Am. *Honours:* Jr 1966-68, Sr Res Fellow, 1968-71, Indian Coun of Agric; Commonwealth Res Fellow, England, 1971-72; Alexander von Humboldt Sr Fellow, 1976-78; Vis Pros, East- West Ctr, Hawaii, USA, 1984. *Hobbies:* Gardening; Reading. *Address:* 3625 NW 31st Terrace, Gainesville, FL 32605, USA. 7.

NAIRN John Graham, b. 23 Aug 1928, Toronto, Canada. m. 2 Aug 1954, 1 s, 3 d. *Education:* BSc Pharm, Univ of Torontoy, 1952; PhD Org Chem, State Univ of NY, 1959. *Appointments:* Practising Pharm, Toronto, 1952-54; Tchg Asst, Buffalo, 1954-58; Asst Prof, 1958-65, Assoc Prof, 1965-73, Prof, 1973-, Univ of Toronto. *Publications:* Solutions, emulsions, suspensions and extracts, 1990; Disperse Systems, 1991; Numerous research papers on microencapsulation, drug stability and topical preparations, in professional journals. *Memberships:* Univ of Toronto Senate, 1968-72; Assn of Facs of Pharm of Canada; Can Pharm Assn Coun of Delegates, 1972- 77; Univ of Toronto Fac Coun; Ontario Col of Pharm, 1952-; Drug Quality and Therapeutic Com, Ministry of Health, 1982-91. *Honours:* Alumni Awd, 1976, Undgrad Tchg Awd, 1987, Alumni Ser Awd, 1989, Univ of Toronto. *Hobbies:* Camping; Canoeing; Skiing; Woodworking. *Address:* Faculty of Pharmacy, University of Toronto, 19 Russell St, Ontario, Canada M5S 2S2. 142.

NAISMITH Robert James, b. 4 Mar 1916, Edinburgh, Scotland. Author and Planning Consultant. *Education:* Heriot Watt Col; Edinburgh Col of Art; Dip Art in Arch; Dip TP, 1941, 1942. *Appointments:* Archt: 1945, engaged in post-war plans for Greenock after blitz; Future plans for coalfirlds in Lothians; Jt Sr Ptnr, Sr Frank Mears and Ptnrs, 1952-85; Burgh Arch, Penicuik, 1945-75; Do Dalkeith, 1950-75; Planning Conslt, Perth, Scotland, 1950-75. *Publications:* Exhib Arch watercolours, RA, RSA, Glasgow, RHA: Author: Buildings of the Scottish countryside; The Story of Scotland's towns. *Memberships:* FRIBA; FRIAS; FRTP, ret'd; FSHS; FSAS. *Honours:* Civic Trust Awd,; Do Do Commendation for Conservation; Bronze Medal for Adv Engrg, Heriot Watt Col, 1941; RIBA Archibald Dawnay Scholarship, 1939-41; RIAS Rutland Prize, 1939. *Hobbies:* Writing for newspapers, journals and books; Drawing and watercolours; Travel; Photography; Research in Art. *Address:* 14 Ramsay Garden, Royal Mile, Edinburgh EH1 2NA, Scotland.

NAKAJIMA Hiroshi, b. 16 May 1928, Chiba-shi, Japan. Director General, World Health Organization. m. (1) Andree Mary Josette Guillien, dec. 1981; (2) Hatha Ann Dewitt, 30 Mar 1984, 2 s. *Education:* MD, Tokyo MEd Co, 1950-55; Neuropsychi and Pharmacol, Fac of Med, Univ of Paris, 1956- 58; PhD Med Scis, Tokyo Med Col, 1960. *Appointments:* Reschr, Inst of health and Med Res, Paris, 1958-67; Dir of Res and Admin, Nippon Roche Res Ctr, Tokyo, 1967-73; Scist, 1973-76, Chief, Drug Policies and Mgmt, 1976-79, Dir, Reg Ofc for W.Pacific, Manila, 1979-88, WHO, Geneva; Dir Gen, WHO, 1988-. *Publications:* 60 scientific articles and reviews published in Japanese, French and English. Directed seminars and expert committees of WHO in Africa, S.E.Asia and W.Pacific regions. *Memberships:* Corres, l'Academie de Pharmacie, Paris, 1988; Fellow, Col of Phys and Surgs of Pakistan, 1990; Hon Mem, Acad de Med de Belgique, 1991; Hon mem, Japanese Pharmacol Soc, 1990. *Honours:* Kojimi Prize for achievement in public health, Japan, 1984; Okamoto Awd, 1989; Order of Merit, Republic of Poland; Medaille de Vermeil de la Ville de Paris, 1990; Chevalier de la Legion d'Honneur, 1991; Vis Prof, Univ of Tokyo; World Rehab Fund Dist Ser Awd in Intl Rehab, USA. *Address:* Director General, WHO, CH 1211, Geneva 27, Switzerland. 43, 52.

NAKANO Takeo, b. 7 June 1926, Kanazawa, Japan. m. Ryoko Tsuruta, 23 Apr 1959, 1 s, 1 d. *Education:* BS, 1948, ScD, 1967, Tokyo Univ. *Appointments:* Lectr,

1954-59, Asst Prof, 1959-65, Utsnomiya Univ; Asst Prof, 1965-68, Prof, 1968-92, Rikkyo Univ. *Contributions to:* articles to professional journals. *Membership:* Math Soc of Japan. *Hobby:* Gardening. *Address:* Suginamiku, Minami-Ogikubo, 1-4-15 Tokyo 167, Japan. 52.

NAKASHIMA Toshio, b. 6 Sept 1920, Japan. Hokkaido University Emeritus Professor. m. Sumiko Asakura, 7 June 1950, 1 s, 1 d. *Education:* Dr Agric, Hokkaido Univ, 1952; Univ Massachussets, 1959-60. *Appointments:* Asst Fac of Agric, Hokkaido Univ, 1950; Lectr, 1959; Asst Prof, 1961; Prof, 1972, Univ Senate, 1977-79, Ret'd, 1984; Emeritus Prof, Hokkaido Univ, 1984-; Prof of Hokkaido Musashi Women's Jr Col, 1984-93. *Publications:* More than 50 scientific papers and books on ecology of Scarabaeidae and Ambrosia Beetles; Textbook: New Applied Entomology. *Memberships:* Japanese Soc of Applied Entomol and Zoology; Entomol Soc of Japan; Japanese Soc of Sericultural Sci; V-Chm, Com of the Environ Impact Assesment on: the Otarunai Dam, 1975-78; Dvlp of the Tokachi River, 1979-81, Drainage Canal of the Chitose River, 1983-. *Honours:* Emeritus Prof, Hokkaido Univ, 1984. *Hobbies:* Gardening; Photography. *Address:* 1-16 South 11, West 12, Chuo-Ku, Sapporo 064, Japan. 162.

NAKAZAWA Hiromu, b. 25 May 1938, Tokyo, Japan. University Professor of Michiko Minakata, 29 Apr 1968, 1 s, 1 d. *Education:* BEng, 1961, MEng, 1970, DEng, 1980, Waseda Univ, Tokyo. *Appointments:* Engr, Mitsubishi Heavy Indust, Mihara, 1961-68; Asst Prof, 1977-82, Prof, 1982-, Waseda Univ, Tokyo; Vis Reschr, MIT, USA, 1980-81. *Publications:* 34 papers, Author: Information Integration Method, 1987; New Technology of Machine Tools, 1988; Easy Precision Engineering, 1991. *Memberships:* Japan Soc of Mech Engrg; Japan soc of Precision Engrg; Soc of Instrument and Control Engrg. *Hobbies:* Photography; Listening to classical music. *Address:* Matsugaoka 1-50-7, Tokorozawa, Saitama 359, Japan. 1.

NALIN Chakra Dhar, b. 19 July 1939, Raebareli, India. m. Gomti Nalin, 10 May 1960. 1 s. 1 d. *Education:* Sahitya Ratna, 1957; MA Eng, 1962; LLB, 1964. *Appointments:* Advocacy, 1964-65. *Publucations:* Dhire Bahti Nadi, 1980; Phool Khile Gandhauri, 1985; Kabyakash, 1984; Tyagwant, 1980; Lai and Dhyani, 1990; Srjan Swar, 1990; Shashwat Agit, 1991; Agni Shikha, 1980; Children's poetry, stories and drama, Prose and translations. *Memberships:* Pres, Rachnatmak Sangh Raebare Nautanki Kala Kendra; Sec, Kisan Higher Secondary Sch, Ataura Buzurg, Raebareli; VP, Manas Vichar Manch; Ed, Mahavani Yearly. *Honours:* Bal Sahitya Sri; Hon Kavya Sri from Kanhaiya Lal Prayag Daj Smarak Samiti Lucknow, 1989; Special Hon from Bal Sahitya Sansthan and Prurskar, 1990; Saraswati Samman Hon from Nagrik Bal Sahitya Sanstahn Balia, 1990, Pune, 1990. *Hobbies:* Studying literature and creative writing. *Address:* Prabhu Town, Raebareli UP 229 001, India.

NANJI Amin Akbarali, b. 21 Feb 1954, Mombasa, Kenya. Physician; Professor. m. Zenobia S B Jaffer, 10 June 1978. 2 d. *Education:* MBChB, 1977, Univ of Nairobi; FRCPC, Univ of Brit Columbia, 1982. *Appointments:* Chem Path, Vancouver Gen Hosp, 1981-84; Hd, Clin Biochem, Ottawa Gen Hosp and Univ of Ottawa, 1984-88; Chief Clin Biochem, Assoc Prof, Harvard Med Sch, New England Deaconess Hosp, 1988-. *Publications:* over 150 profl articles and book chapters. *Memberships:* Fellow, Royal Col of Phys and Surgs of Can; RCPath, UK: AAAS; Am Fed of Clin Res; Am Assn for Clin Chem; Can Assn for Paths. *Honours:* Young Investigators Awd, Acad of Lab Phys and Scists, 1982; NATO Travel Awd, 1986; Wild Lietz Awd, Can Assn of Paths, 1989; US Patent, for Method of Drug Detection. *Hobbies:* Hiking; Walking; Travel. *Address:* Department of Pathology, New England Deaconess Hospital, Harvard Medical School, 185 Pilgrim Road, Boston, MA 02215, USA. 142.

NANOPOULOS Dimitri, b. 13 Sept 1948, Athens, Greece. Professor of Physics. m. Myrto Vassiliou, 27 July 1972. *Education:* BSc, Univof Athens, 1971; PhD Theoretical Phys, Sussex Univ, Brighton. *Appointments:* Fellow, CERN, 1973-75; Culle Fellow, ENS, Poris Switzerland, 1975-76; Fellow, Harvard Univ, 1977-79; Staff, CERN, Switzerland, 1974-86; Prof, Univ of Wisconsin, 1986-89; Prof, TA&M Univ, USA, 1989-. *Publications:* 330 papers on high energy physics and cosmology; Books: Supersymmetry Confronts experiment, 1983; The Road to no scale supergravity, 1987; Grand Unification with and without supersymmetry, 1984. *Memberships:* FAPS; Fellow, Houston Advanced Res Ctr. *Hobbies:* Films; Reading. *Address:* 10600 Six Pines Dr Apt 732, The Woodlands, TX 77380, USA.

NANUCK Hassenally, b. 22 Aug 1949, Triolet, Mauritius. Auto Body Mechanic. m. Hawah Bibi, 15 May 1977, 1 s, 1 d. *Education:* Apprenticeship Cert, Welding, 1964, Welders and Fabricators Course, 8 years, 1972, Long Mountain, Mauritius; Practitioners Cert, Municipality, 1979. *Appointments:* Mng Dir, Asuna Panel Beaters Pty Ltd, Gaborone, 1988-; Mng Dir, Al Sadiq Pty Ltd, 1988-; Sr Tech Ofr, Central Transp Org, Govt of Botswana, 1981-88; Mng Dir, Aristos, Triolet, Mauritius, 1979-81; Supervisor, Bhugello, Mauritius, 1974-79. *Publications:* Designer and proj coor of state security vehicle in Botswana used for visits of Pope Paul II and Nelson Mandela, 1988; Designer and developer of Austin pick-up in Mauritius, 1977. *Memberships:* Trustee, Botswana Muslim Assn; Asst Treas, Botswana Muslin Assn Interim Com; Bosstana Motor Traders Assn, Gaborone; Botswana Confed of Commerce, Industry and Manpower, Gaborone and Botswana. *Honours:* Nominee, 1st Intl Leading Co Awd, Madrid, 1991; 3rd Intl Europe Awd, Paris 1989; 10th Intl Africa Awd, Paris, 1989; 14th Intl Awd for the best trade name, 1989, Trade Leaders' Club, Spain. *Hobbies:* Photography; Sightseeing; Gardening; Video production; Friendship and community development. *Address:* PO Box 40346, Gaborone, Botswana, S.Africa.

NAPIONTEK Marek Maksymilian, b. 6 January 1955, Poznan, Poland; Orthopaedic Surgeon; Lecturer. m. Emilia Szuminska, 1 June 1985, 2 d. *Education:* Dipl and MD, 1974-80, K Marcinkowski Univ of Med Scis of Poznan; Phd, 1988. *Appointments:* Dept of Ortho, K Marcinkowski Univ of Med Scis of Poznan, 1980-89; Dept of Paed Ortho, Poznan, 1989-. *Publications:* The value of peritalar reduction in treatment of congenital vertical talus, pes plano-valgus talofexus congenitus (doctor's thesis) and other in Chir Narz Ruchu Ortop Pol, Röfö, Can Ass Radiol Y, Y Bone Joint Surg, Y Neurol Orthop Med Surg. *Memberships:* Polish Soc for Ortho Surg and Traumatol; Intl Assn of Lions Clubs. *Honours:* Polish Minister of Health Awd, 1990. *Hobbies:* Coins; Ancient objects d'art. *Address:* Department of Paediatric Orthopaedics, Institute of Orthopaedics and Rehabilitation, ul 28 Czerwca 1956 nr 135/147, 61-545 Poznan, Poland.

NAPUTI Matilda Maria, b. 2 Dec 1973, San Diego, California, USA. Student; Writer. *Education:* Computer Sch: Pacific Inst, Maite, Guam, 1987, Pacific Basin Educ Ctr, Agana, Guam, 1985; COI Prep Sch, Notre Dame Hg Sch, 1987-91; Col Univ of Guam, 1991, summer. *Appointments:* Islandwide Sci Fair, 1990; Nat Bible Essay Contest, 1989-90; Tribute and presentation of poem, Bank of Guam, 1991; Poetry contest semifinalist The Nat Library of Poetry, The Poetry Ctr; Pegasus Press; Creaive Arts of Sci Enterprises; Poets Corner, Am Poetry Assn. *Publications:* Teenager Pros and Cons, 1990; How your attitude can help you, 1991; Reporter for the Guam Tribune, 1991-92. *Memberships include:* Students Agains Drunk Driving; Athletic Com; Spirit Com; House of grounds Com, Notre Dame HS, 1987-91; Jr Achievement PIC Gp, Guam, 1989. *Honours include:* Ed Choice Awd, Nat Library of Peotry, 1990; Gov Art Awd, 1990; Young Citizens Awd, Soroptimist Intl, Guam, 1990; Legislative Cert of Recognition, Guam Coun on the Arts and Humanities Agency, 1991; A &

B Hon Rolls. *Hobbies:* Poetry; Reading; Collecting coins and stamps. *Address:* Matilda M Naputi, PO Box 24097, GMF, Guam 96921.

NARAIN Hari, b. 21 Sept 1922, Mainpuri up India. Emeritus Scientist. m. Saroj Srivastava, 20 Dec 1953, 1 s, 1 d. *Education:* BSc Hons, 1942; MSc Phys, 1943, DPhil, 1950, Allahabad Univ; PhD, Sydney Univ, 1954. *Appointments:* UNDP Chief Proj Coor, NGRI, 1983-86; Dir, NGRI Hyderabad, 1964-78, 1981-83; Surveyor Gen of India, 1972-76; V-Chancellor, Banaras Hindu Univ, 1978-81. *Publications:* A number of original and review papers in scientific journals in India and abroad on geopysics and geosciences. *Memberships:* Fellow, Nat Acad of Scis, Pres, 1979-80; Fellow, Indian Nat Sci Acad; Hon Prof, Indian Inst of Geomagnetism, Bombay; Nat Com on Sci and Tech, 1971-77. *Honours:* Padma Shree, Govt of India, 1974; Hon DSc: Indian Sch of Mines, 1978, Kakatiya Univ Andhra Pradeh, 1981. *Hobbies:* Reading; Writing; Photograpy; Gardening. *Address:* 44/ 2 Vasant Vihar, Road 8, Habsignda, Hyderabad 500007, India.

NARAYANAN Ram Mohan, b. 25 Sept 1955, Tambaram, India. Asst Prof of Electrical Engineering. Vijayalakshmi Lakshminarayanan, 21 June 1987. 2 d. *Education:* BTech, IIT, Madras, 1971-76; PhD, Univ of Massachusetts, Amherst, USA, 1983-88. *Appointments:* Dpty Engr, 1976-80, Sr Engr, 1980-83, Bel, India; Res Asst, Univ Mass, 1983-88; Asst Prof, Univ Nebraska, USA, 1988. *Publications:* Over 11 technical papers and 26 conference presentations in the are of electromagnetics and optics. *Memberships:* IEEE; Am Geophys Union; Am Soc for Photogrammetry and Remote Sensing; Intl Union of Radio Sci Comm F. *Honours:* Grad, Fac Fellow, 1989, Fac Tchg Awd, 1991, Univ of Nebraska; Fellow, Ctr for Great Plains Studies, 1990; Outstanding Fac Awd, IEEE Student Section, 1991. *Hobbies:* Reading; Sightseeing. *Address:* 5610 Coyote Circle, Lincoln, NE 68516, USA.

NARBUTT Jerzy, b. 12 Oct 1925, Warsaw, Poland. Writer. *Education:* Aesthetics Fac, Warsaw Univ, 1958-62. *Publications:* Debut, 1965; November will blossom again, 1972; Wedding in the City, 1973; A letter not sent by post, 1975; Salt of the earth, 1980; This day is ours, 1981; Last face of the portrait, 1981; Other face of the portrait, 1982; From Poland and From Italy, 1983; In press: Benefits; A Few Verses. *Memberships:* Assn of Polish Writers; Intl PEN Club. *Honours:* Awd, Kosciuszko Foun, USA, 1972. *Hobbies:* Journalism; Political writing. *Address:* Association of Polish Writers, ul Krakowskie Przedm 87/89, 00-079 Warsaw, Poland.

NARSKI Igor S, b. 18 Nov 1920 Morshansk, Russia. Professor of History of Philosophy. m. Helen P Popova, 24 Sept 1946, 2 s, 1 d. *Education:* Dr Phil Sci, Moscow Univ, 1961; Asst Prof of Phil, 1953; Prof in ordinary 1963-. *Appointments:* Tchr, Hist of Philos, Moscow Univ, 1951-71; Tchr Hist of Phil, Acad of Soc Scis, Moscow, 1971-. *Publications:* 14 books, 350 article, and 14 books including: West European Philosophy of the XVIII Century, 1973; W-European Philosophy of the XIX Century, 1976; The Philosophy of David Hume, 1967; The Pathos of Reason, 1991; Contemporary Positivism, 1961; Alienation and labour, 1982. *Memberships:* Assoc Mem, Logical Soc in Bologna (Italy); Ed Bd, Philosophical Sciences mag; Sci Worker of Inst of Philos, Acad of Scis of USSR, 1951-80. *Honours:* Hon Scist of Russia, 1981. *Hobbies:* Chess; Tourism; Hiking; Boating. *Address:* Olympic Village 15, Apt 116, 117602 Moscow, Russia.

NARUSE Teruo, b. 25 Feb 1931, Tokyo, Japan. President, Tokyo Engineering Co Ltd. m. 22 Oct 1963, 1 s, 1 d. *Education:* Grad, Fac of Civil Eng, 1953; DEng, 1977, Waseda Univ. *Appointments:* Ishikawajima Harima Heavy Industries Co Ltd, Steel Structures Div. *Publications:* Book, Design of Steel Structures; Papers include: IABSE; Der Stahlban. *Memberships:* Japan Socs of Civil Engineers and Steel Construction; Intl Assn

for Br and Structural Engrg. *Hobbies:* Japanese Classical Ballads; Mountaineering; Gardening. *Address:* Tokyo Engineering Co Ltd, 4-12-4 Chuo-ku Hacho-bori, Tokyo 104, Japan.

NASH Timothy Paul, b. 13 Aug 1946, Fareham, Hants, England. Consultant in Anaesthetics and Pain Relief. m. Bridget Eleanor Harrison, 18 Oct 1969, 1 s, 3 d. *Education:* Andover Grammar Sch, 1960-64; MBBS, 1969, London; DRCOG, 1971; FFARCS, 1974. *Appointments:* Conslt in Anaes and Pain Relief, 1976-, Basingstoke and N.Hants Health Auth; Sr Registrar, E.Anglia and Cambs Health Auths, 1974-76. *Contributions to:* Pain, Chronic Non-Cancer pain, The Pain Clinic; British Medical Jour, Brit Jour of Hosp Med, Med Intl. *Memberships:* Asst Ed, The Pain Clinic, 1989-; Ed, Frontiers of Pain, 1988-; President Elect, The Pain Soc, Foun Ed IPS forum, 1981-85, Sec, 1985-88. *Hobbies:* Music; Walking; Reading. *Address:* Pain Relief Clinic, Basingstoke District Hospital, Park Prewett, Basingstoke, Hants RG24 9NA, England.

NASON Ian Geoffrey, b. 11 Nov 1936, Guernsey, Channel Islands. Army Officer. m. Anne Mary McKergow, 31 Dec 1960, 2 s, 2 d. *Education:* Wellington Col, Berks, 1950-54; RMA, Sandhurst, 1955-56; Army Staff Col, Can, 1966-67; Nat Defence Col, 1976-77; Nigerian Staff Col, 1979-81. *Appointments:* Comm, Seaforth Highlanders, 1956; Cmdr, Queens Own Highlanders, 1977-79; Chief of Staff Brit Forces Falkland Islands, 1983; Col Cmdr, RMA Sandhurst, 1984-86; Defence Advr, Brit Hg Comm, Lagos, 1987-91. *Publications:* Enjoy Nigeria, 1990, a tourist guide. *Honours:* Nigerian Chief AKU TWBA of Bakana, Rivers State Nigeria, 1990. *Hobbies:* Golf; Bird photography; Travel. *Address:* c/o Midland Bank, PO Box 31, Guernsey, Channel Islands

NASTA Kris, b. 28 Aug 1943, India. Vice President, Teradyne Inc. m. Ann Beatrice Clifton, 5 July 1969. 1 s, 1 d. *Education:* BS Hons, Econ and Sociol, Univ of Salford, 1967; Postgrad, GEC Ltd, 1967-69; Postgrad Dipl, Mfg Tech, E.Warwick Col of Further Educ, 1968. *Appointments:* Mktg Mgr, ITT bus Systems, 1971-73; Mktg Exec, 1973-77, Home Sales Exec, 1977-79, Plessey Telecoms Ltd; Gen Mgr, Europe Teradyne Telecoms, 1979-88; VP, Teradyne Inc, 1988-91. *Hobbies:* Contract duplicate Bridge; Reading; Music; Racquet Sports. *Address:* 7 Hilgay Close, Guildford, Surrey GU1 2EN, England.

NASU Yukio, b. 24 Jan 1946, Nagoya, Japan. *Education:* BA 1968; MS 1970; Dr Prog, 1970-75, Keio Univ, Tokyo. *Appointments:* Res Assoc, 1971-75, Staff Reschr, 1976-82, Sr Staff Reschr, 1983-, Mitsubishi Res Inst; Prof, Sch of Bus and Econ, Nippon Bunri Univ, 1988-. *Publications:* Articles in international professional journals: Commercial Message and Regulations, 1979; Analysis of Management Concept, 1986; R&D On Office Automation in USA, 1988; Strategic Info System and Networing, 1990; The Direction of Marketing Study in the Era of Corporate Charm, 1989. *Memberships:* Japan Inst of Mktg Sci; Am Mktg Assn; Japan Soc of Study of Bus Admin; Acad of Mgmt Philos; Am Soc of Info Sci; Acad Assn for Org Sci; Japan Soc of Commercial Sci; Kyushu Assn of Econ Sci; Japan Soc for Mgmt Informatics. *Hobbies:* Computer telecommunications; Reading; History. *Address:* 271-8 Aza Takajou, Oaza Senzai, Oita-shi, Oita-ken 870-01, Japan.

NAU Heinz, b. 10 May 1943, Feldkirchen, Austria. University Professor. m. Nina Ness, 31 Aug 1974, 1 s. *Education:* PhD, Chem, Univ Insbruck, 1961-70. *Publications:* 230 in scientific journals, several books. *Memberships:* Am Chem Soc; AAAS; Gesellschaft Deutscher Chem; NYAS; Deutsche Ges; Pharmakol und Toxitologie; European Teratology Soc. *Honours:* Hon Doctorate, Univ Uppsala, Dept Pharm Scis, 1990. *Address:* Institute of Toxicology, Free University of

Berlin, Garystr 5, D-1000 Berlin 33, Germany. 2, 52, 92.

NAWARA James Edward, b. 25 Jan 1945, Chicago, Illinois, USA. Lucille Procter, 14 Dec 1969, 1 s, 1 d. *Education:* BFA, Sch of Art, Inst of Chicago, 1967; MFA, Univ of Illinois, Champaign, 1969. *Appointments:* Prof, (drawing and painting), Dept of Art and Art Hist, Wayne State Univ, Detroit, Michigan. *Publications:* Collections: Detroit Inst of Arts; Boston Mus of Fine Arts; Cleveland Mus of Art; Nat Air and Space Mus; Bradford City Art Gal, England; Jagiellonian Univ, Poland; Nat Mus of Warsaw, Poland. *Memberships:* Col Art Assn of Am; Am Assn of Univ Profs; M Fillmore Inst of Manual Dexterity. *Honours:* Fac Res Grants from Wayne State Univ; Three, Michigan for the Arts Creative Artist Grants; Wayne State Univ Bd of Govs Fac Recognition Awd, 1981. *Hobbies:* Travelling; Beer Tasting; Gardening; Fishing. *Address:* 150 Art Bldg, Dept of Art and Art History, Wayne State University, Detroit, MI 48202, USA. 37.

NAWARA Lucille Procter, b. 26 June 1941, Oklahoma City, USA. Artist; Art Instructor. m. James E Nawara, 14 Dec 1968, 2 s, 1 d. *Education:* BA, Smith Col, Mass, 1962; MFA, Univ Illinois, 1969; BFA equiv, Boston Univ, 1968. *Appointments:* Asst Prof, Wayne State Univ, 1969-; Artist in Residence, Henry Ford Community Col; MCA Grant, Fraser Pub Schls, MI; Dir, Nawara Gal, Walled Lake, MI; Instr, Nacomb Community Col. *Creative works:* Oil mural, Broken Symmetries, 1985; 21 colour screenprint, Bash Bish Falls, 1989; Oil/lin, Pixley Falls, 1989; lil/lin, Buttermilk falls, 1991. *Memberships:* pres of Bd, Detroit Focus Gal; Michigan Watercolour Soc; Chm, Fdr, Percent For Art in Detroit Com; Co-chm, Fdr, Proj Retree, Detroit. *Honours include:* Arts Foun of Mich Awd, 1991; Cash Awd, Mich Watercolour Soc 43rd Exhib, 1989; Artist in the Schools Residency Grant, Mich Coun Arts, 1983-86; Individual Grants, Mich Coun for the Arts, 1981, 1983; A Commemorative Resolution, Mich Hse of Reps, 1978. *Hobbies:* Violin; Piano; Gardening. *Address:* 13343 Kingston Ave, Huntington Woods, MI 48070, USA. 37, 138.

NAWROCKI Stanislaw, b. 20 Nov 1927, Stara Wies. Proressor. m. Janina Nawrocka, 28 June 1950, 2 s, 1 d. *Education:* Agric Dept, UMCS, Lublina, 1947-51; Dr Deg, Timiriazev Agric Acad, Moscow, 1952-56. *Appointments:* Adjunct Prof, Agric Fac, UMCS, Lublin, 1956-64; Asst Prof, Agric Fac, UMCS, 1964-68; Dir, Inst of Soi Sci and Cult of Plants, Pulawy, 1968-91. *Publications:* General Tillage of Soil and Plants, 1970-81; The Deep amelioration of sandy soils by using special kinds of plough, 1964; The Agrotechn Recommendations, 1974, 1981; Works of Soil Tillage. *Memberships:* Polish Sol Sci Soc; Lublins Sci Soc; Intern, Sil Tillage Res Org; Polish Acad of Sci; Province Counsellor of Province; Lublin Mem, Polish Soc for Soil; Foreign Mem of Agric, Acad of Sci at Moscow. *Honours:* Hons Insignis of Lublins Agric Acad, 1975; Hons Insignia of Olsztyn Agric, Tech Acad, 1976; Insignif of 1000 years of the Polish State; Medal of XXX Years Anniv of Polish People Rep, 1974; Silver Cross of Merit, 1968; Bachelors Cross of the Polish Renaisance, 1973; Dr Hon Cause, Agri Acad, Olsztyn, 1990. *Hobby:* Hunting. *Address:* Zulinki 17, 24-100 Pulawy, Poland. 156, 52,

NAYLOR Albert Edward, b. 12 Oct 1925, Bootle, England. Consulting Engineer. m. Mildred Gillies, 10 Sept 1949, 1 s, 3 d. *Education:* MEng, Dip Town Planning, Univ of Liverpool, 1943-45. *Appointments:* Asst Borough Engr, Bootle, 1956-64; Dpty Asst Borough Engr, Luton, 1964-69; City Engr, Leeds, 1970-74; Exec Dir, W.Yorks Met County, 1974-79; County Engr, Greater Manchester Met County, Engr to Manchester Airport, 1979-86. *Publications:* Papers on traffic, transportation, waste and disposal and airports and management. *Memberships:* FEng; FICE: FIHT; FRSA: Past Pres, Assn of Municipal Engrs. *Hobbies:* Family history; Gardening; Theatre; Travel; Rotary. *Address:*

Greenhill, Greenhill Common, Lower Whitley nr Warrington, Cheshire WA4 4JD, England. 186, 149.

NAYLOR Bryan, b. 2 Aug 1949, Oldham, England. Manufacturing Executive. m. Krystyna Anna 20 May 1972, 1 d. *Education:* Cert Gen Acct (CGA). *Appointments:* Pres and Dir, Columbus McKinnon Ltd. *Memberships:* Cert Gen Accts; Assn of Ontario; Conf Bd of Can; Coun for Econ Relations Between Can and USA; Standards Coun of Can, Chm, ISO/TCIII; Presidents Assn of Am; Dir, Jr Achievement, Cobourg, Ontario, 1984-86; Dist Chamber of Commerce. *Address:* 828 Lavis Street, Oshawa, Ontario, Canada. 142.

NAZIR AHMED Vellore Sharif, b. 27 Oct 1929, Melmattai. Retired Chief Librarian. m. Razia Sultana, 25 May 1958, 2 s, 4 d. *Education:* BA 1959; LLB, 1954; Dip Lib Sci, 1955; Prof in French, 1958. *Appointments:* Librarian, Railway Res Ctr, Lucknow, 1955-59; Librarian, Heavy Elec India Ltd, Bhopal, 1959-65; UNESCO Expert, Sudan, 1976-78; Librarian, Intian Inst of Tech, Madras, 1965-89. *Publications:* Handbook of Library Administration; Union Catalogue of Periodicals. *Memberships:* Bd of Studies, Calicut, Madurai and Madras Univs; Exec Mem, Indian Assn of Special Libraries and Info Ctrs; Examiner, Indian Nat Sci Documentation Ctr, New Delhi; Assoc Mem, IEEE, New York. *Honours:* IATUL Tchg Fellowship, 1973; UNESCO Fellowship, 1975; Netherlands Fellow, 1967; DAAD Fellowship, West Germany, 1967. *Hobbies:* Reading; Gardening; Trecking. *Address:* 16 12th Cross Street, Indiranagar, Madras 600036, India. 57, 156,

NDUKA Amagh, b. 12 Oct 1942, Nigeria. Vice Chancellor. m. Elizabeth Nwaku, 15 June 1976. 2 s, 4 d. *Education:* BSc, Univ of Calif, Kerleley, 1965; MSc Stanford Univ, 1967; PhD Univ of Chicago, 1971. *Appointments:* Lectr, Maths, Univ of Illinois, 1971-74; Sr Lectr, OAU, Nigeria, 1976-81; PRof, Futo, 1981-; V-Chancellor, Futo, 1987-94. *Publications:* Over 50 in learned journals and society proceedings and several key note addresses. *Memberships:* APS; AMS; Smithsonian Assocs; Nigerian Math Soc; Nigerian Inst of Phys; Computer Assn of Nigeria. *Honours:* Scholarships for secondary and university education, 1955-71; Sr Trevelling Fellow, Assn of Commonwealth Univs; Vis Scist, IAEA, ICTP, Trieste Italy; Oxford; Cambridge. *Hobbies:* Writing; Reading; Sports; Games. *Address:* Federal University of Technology, Owerri, Imo State, Nigera.

NDUKWE Tobechi, Chief, b. 26 Nov 1946, Ozuitem, Nigeria. Journalist; Public Relations Consultant. m. Obioma Tohechi-Ndukwe & Eva Tobechi-Ndukwe, 22 Apr 1973, 2 s, 6 d. *Education:* Meth Col Pract Sch UZ, 1960; Delta Comm Col, 1960-64; London Sch of Jour, 1972. *Appointments:* Columnist, Eastern Star, 1963-65; Biafra Commando Ofr, 1967-69; Info Ofr, 1975; Radio Commentator, 1970-75; Sr Edit TV News, 1975-80. *Publications:* Producer and presenter of many TV programmes including the following: View Point; Face the Press; Behind the News; From the Editorials; News Highlights. *Memberships:* NUJ; IOJ; NIM: NIPR: ABE. *Honours:* NUJ Hons Awd, 1990; NUJ Awd, 1989; Chieftaincy Title, 1982; Fellow, ABE, USA, 1987; Merit Awd, Aba Community, 1989. *Hobbies:* Reading; Travelling; Dancing; Sports. *Address:* 47 Hospital Road, PO Box 238, Aba, Nigeria.

NDZENYUIY Francis Wirnsungnin, b. 1 Jan 1944, Kitiwam, NSO, Cameroon. Teacher; School Principal. m. Esther Sujla Ndzenyuiy, 24 Dec 1965, 3 s 3 d. *Education:* BMC and TTC, Batibo, B'oa, 1958, 1961-62, 1964-65, Tchr Training; BA, Fourah Bay Col, Univ of Sierra Leone, 1978-81. *Appointments:* Tchr: BMS Kishong, 1959; BMS Mbande, 1960; BMS Nsoh, 1961; BMS Nkambe, 1965-67; PS Kishong, 1968-73; PS Mbam-nkum, 1974; PS Kumbo, 1975-77 (Headmaster); PSS Batibo, 1977-78 (Tutor); PRRC Mbengwi, 1981-82; PSS Kumba 1983-84; PSS Besoneabang Mamfe, 1985-87 (Principal); PSS Mankon, Bamenda, 1987-91,

(Principal). *Publications:* Yearly reports on college administration; Paper on Cameroonian Youth and Culture. *Memberships:* Camerron Unino of Tchrs, Treas; Nat Union of CameroonStudents, FBS Branch Pres; FBC Union of Students; Presbyterian Secondary Schls, Principal, Treas; Presbyterian Ch in Cameroon, Synod; Presbyterian Educ Auth. *Honours:* Profl Tchrs Certs, 1962, 1965; BA Deg, Fourah Bay Col, Univ of Sierra Leone, 1981. *Hobbies:* Football; Gardening; Music. *Address:* Principal, PSS Mankon, PO Box 191 Bamenda, Republic of Cameroon.

NE'EMAN Yuval, b. 15 May 1925, Tel Aviv, Israel. Theoretical Physicist; Gov Scientist; Defense Specialist; Political Leader. m. Dvora Rubinstein-Schiff, 1951, 2 ch. *Education:* BSME, 1945, Dipl, Mech Engrng, 1946, Israel Inst of Tech, Haifa; PhD, London Univ, 1962. *Appointments:* Served to Col, Israel Def Forces, 1948-60; Scient Director, Israel AEC Soreq Rsch, 1961-63; Asst Prof, 1962, Prof, Phys, 1965, Pollak Chair Phys, 1969-76, Pres, 1971-75, Wolfson Chair Extraordinary, Theoretical Phys, 1977-, Dir, Sackler Inst Adv Studies, 1979-, Tel Aviv Univ; Rsch Fellow, 1963-64, Vis Prof, 1964-65, CA Poly Inst Technology, USA; Mbr, 1965-82, Acting Chmn, 1982-84, Israel AEC; Def Chief Scientist, 1974-76, Prof, Phys, Dir, Ctr Particle Theory, Univ TX, Austin, USA, 1968-91; Chmn, Hatehiya Pty, 1979-92; Mbr, Knesset, Jerusalem, 1981-90: Min Sci and Dev, 1982-84, 1990-92, Min, Energy and Infrastructure, 1990-92, Israeli Cabinet; Chmn, Israeli Space Agcy, 1982-; Discovered (simultaneously with and independently of M Gell-Manns) 'Eightfold Way' classification of Elementary Particles, 1961, and Quark Structure of Matter, 1962-63, other important results in Particle and Nuclear Physio and Astrophysics, also Philosophy of Science. *Publications:* The Eightfold Way, 1964; Algebraic Theory of Particle Physics, 1964; The Past Decade of Particle Physics, 1973; Symmetries, Jauges et varietes de Groupes, 1979; Group Theoretical Methods in Physics, 1980; To Fulfill a Vision, 1981; The Particle Hunters, 1986; Dynamical Groups and Spectrum Generating Algebras (w Barut and Bohm), 1989; Other lecture series; Over 300 articles in profl jrnls; Reviews. *Memberships:* Nat Assn Children w Mental Deficiencies, Pres 1969-75; Pub Comm USSR Jewry, Chmn, Scientists Comm USSR Jewry, 1971-82; Israel Phys Soc; Israel Nat Acad Scis and Humanities; Int Astronom Union; Bd Govs, Israel Coun For Rels; For Hon Mbr, AAAS; For Assoc, US Nat Acad Scis; Hon Life Mbr, NY Acad Scis: Fellow: Am Phys Soc; Inst Phys. *Honours include:* Hon DSc: Israel Inst Technology, 1966; Yeshiva Univ, 1972; Clausthal Tech Univ, 1990; Rothschild Prize, 1968; Albert Einstein Medal, 1970; Wigner Medal, 1982. *Address:* Tel Aviv University, Sackler Institute of Advanced Studies, Ramat Aviv, Tel Aviv 69978, Israel.

NEAL Alan Christopher, b. 9 Jan 1950, Bath, England. Professor of Law. m. Alessandra Tadini, 30 July 1981, 1 s, 1 d. *Education:* LLB, Univ Warwick, 1973; LLM, London School Econs, 1974; Called to the Bar, Gray's Inn, 1975; DGLS, Univ Stockholm, Sweden, 1976. *Appointments:* Lectr, Law, 1976-86, Sr Lectr, Law, 1986-88, Prof, Law, 1988-, Univ Leciester; Dir, Int Ctr Mgmt, Law and Indl Rels. *Publications:* Law and the Weaker Party (ed), 5 vols, 1981-90; A Perspective of Labour Law, 1982; Collective Agreements and Collective Bargaining, 1984. *Memberships:* Barrister, Gray's Inn, London; Int Soc Labour Law and Social Security; Int Indl Rels Assn. *Honours:* State Scholarship, Dept Educ and Sci, 1974; Wolfson Fellowship, 1982; Parsons Scholar, Univ Sydney, Australia. *Hobbies:* Hockey (formerly played for Somerset and Warwickshire); Skiing; Squash; Music. *Address:* High Trees House, Hall Wood, Hallaton, Leicestershire LE16 8UH, England.

NEAME Basil Desmond, b. 14 Oct 1921, London, England. Farmer. m. Stella Roe, 3 Apr 1948, dec., 2 s, 2 d. *Education:* Higher School Cert, Cheltenham Coll. *Appointments:* Mil Serv, Royal Engrs, 1941-46; Self-employed Farmer. *Memberships:* Nat Farmers Union, Nat Coun 1960-66; Agricl Trng Bd, Chmn 1966-70;

Apple and Pear Rsch Coun, Vice-Chmn 1989-; Vice-Chmn, E Malling Rsch Assn. *Honours:* CBE, 1970. *Hobby:* Bird watching. *Address:* Macknade Manor, Faversham, Kent ME13 8XE, England.

NEBHRAJANI Vir Tirathdas, b. 1 Sept 1931, Karachi, India. Consultant Ear, Nose and Throat Surgeon. m. Jayantee Chanda, 9 Aug 1991, 2 d. *Education:* MB, BS, 1957, Resident Surg, ENT, Gen Surg, Assam Med Coll, India, 1957; DLA, England, 1961; FRCS, Edinburgh, 1969. *Appointments:* Var jr appts, ENT Surg, London, Birmingham, Glasgow, UK, 1960-72; Currently: Cons Otologist, John Scott Audiology Clin City and Hackney Family Hlth Serv Auth, London; Cons ENT Surg, Manor House Hosp, London and BUPA Roding Hosp, Redbridge, Essex. *Memberships:* Brit Med Assn; Patron, Bengali Cultural Assn, UK; Vice-Chmn, Anandam UK; Exec Fndr Mbr, Drs Assn Med Aid (working for India); Mbr, Rotary Club, Redbridge, Past Chmn Intl. *Hobbies: ssa 00*Cultural activities; Fund raising for charities; Photography; Reading. *Address:* 22 Harley Street, London W1N 1AA, England.

NECHIFOR Mihai, b. 2 Sept 1951, Dorohoi. University Professor. m. Ana-Maria, 25 Oct 1975, 2 d. *Education:* Grad, Fac of Med, Univ of Med and Pharm, (UMP), Iasi, 1976. *Appointments:* Surgeon, 1976-78, Asst, Dept of Pharm, 1979-86, Lectr, 1986, Asst Prof, 1986-92, Prof, 1992, UMP, Iasi. *Publications:* Prostaglandins in pathology and therapeutics, 1982; Drug friend and enemy, 1983; The metabolism of the active biological lipids, 1984; Guide of Toxicological data, 1985; The Medical treatment of the smooth muscle, 1985; Leukotrienes biomedical implications, 1988; Beta-lactam antibiotics, 1988. Numerous articles in professional journals. *Memberships:* Soc of Phys and Naturalists, Iasi, 1975; Nat Soc of Cellular Biol and Path, Bucharest, 1982; l'Union Med Balkanique, Bucharest, 1988; Union Therapeutique Intl, Paris, 1989; Intl Sov for Study on Xenobiotics, USA, 1990; Worldwide Hung Med Acad, Boston, 1991. *Hobbies:* Literature; Pictures; Basketball. *Address:* Dept of Pharmacology, Univ of Medicine and Pharmacy, Str Universitatii nr 16, Iasi 6600, Romania.

NEERGAARD Ole Henry, b 5 Apr 1952, Fredrikstad, Norway. Financial Director. m. Grethe A Valen, 13 Sept 1990. *Education:* MSB, 1976. *Appointments:* Cons, Min Industry, Norway, 1977-78; Planner, Analyst, A/S Norske Esso, 1978-80; Controller, 1980-83, Treas, 1983-87, Norsk Elektrisk & Brown Boveri; Fin Dir, 1987-92, Mbr, Bd Dirs, 1990-, 3M Norge A/S, Fin Dir, 1992, 3M Nordic Region, 1987-; Mbr, Bd Dirs: Sigma Elektroteknisk A/S, 1984-89; A/S ISMA, 1986-87; Haaland A/S, 1987-. *Membership:* Norwegian Assn Masters Svc in Bus, Oslo. *Hobbies:* Sailing; Jogging; Fishing; Reading. *Address:* Borgenv 27B, 0373 Oslo 3, Norway. 52.

NEERMANN Carolyn G, b. 6 May 1933, Jenera, Ohio, USA. Registered Nurse. m. 2 s, 1 d. *Education:* RN, Luth Coll Hlth Profns, IN, 1954; Cert Psych Mental Hlth Nurse, Am Nursing Assn, 1990; Currently: registration, TX, LA. *Appointments:* Hd Nurse, Instr, El Paso Gen Hosp, TX, 1954-55; Staff Nurse, Community Mem Hosp, La Grznge, IL, 1957-63; Staff Nurse, Shallowford Community Hosp, Atlanta, GA, 1974-78; Relief Supvsr, Silsbee Dr's Hosp, Silsbee, TX, 1978-81; Nurse Mgr, Adolescent Psych, CPC Brentwood Hosp, Shreveport, LA, 1984-91. *Memberships:* Am Nurses Assn; LA Nurses Assn; Shreveport Nurses Assn; Altar Guild; Red River Equestrian Assn. *Honours:* Nursing Excellence, Humana Hosp, Brentwood, 1985; Nurse of Yr, Shreveport Nursing Assn, 1988. *Hobbies:* Antiques; Thoroughbred horses; Therpeutic riding for handicapped; Arts and crafts. *Address:* Behavioral Medicine, 2600 Greenwood Road, Shreveport, LA 71101, USA. 7.

NEGOSANU Petronela, b. 17 June 1913, Copacel, Rumania. Writer. m. 28 June 1965. *Education:* Bach

Langs; LLD, Cluj Univ, 1937. *Appointments:* Barrister, Cluj, 1938-40; Reviewer, Propaganda Min, 1940-44; Pol Sect, For Off, 1944-47; Freelance Writer. *Publications:* Am Ucis Albatorsul, short stories, 1943; Destinul unui Artist, lit biog, 1973; Radio plays: Rubens and the Gallery of Maria de Medicis, 1974; Rembrandt and Saskia, 1975; Var translations, incl poetry w Virgil Teodorescu. *Memberships:* Rumanian Writers Union; Writers Assn, Bucharest. *Honours:* Lit Award, Tinerimea Romana, 1930. *Address:* Str Poiana Narciselor Nr 5, 70718 Bucharest, Rumania.bblank

NEKRASOV Andrei Borisovich, b. 14 May 1940, Moscow, USSR. Architect. m. Iren Osipian, 13 Sept 1977, 1 s. *Education:* Student, 1957-61, 1962-63, Dip Arch, 1963, Aspirantura, 1968-71, PhD, Arch, 1971, Moscow Inst Arch; Student, 1961-62, Dip Arch, 1962, Engrng Bldg Inst Sofia, Bulgaria; Prof, Markhi, 1990. *Career:* Archt, Project Inst Moscow, 1963-66; Asst Prof, 1966-68, Sr Tchr, 1971-88, Prof, 1988, Moscow Inst Arch; Exhibs: Architectural Education in USSR, Paris, 1974, Ferrara, 1975; Architecture and Urbanism in USSR, Residence and Clubs sect, Paris, 1978, Austria, 1980; Vkhutemas-Markhi, Moscow, 1980, DRG, 1984, Paris, 1985; The City for a Man, Germany, 1981; The 50th Anniversary of Markhi, Moscow, 1983; Uses of Traditions in Russian and Soviet Architecture, London, 1989; The Moscow Institute of Architecture, USA, 1989-90; Art of Architecture USSR, Venice, 1991; Markhi, 1991. *Creative works:* Books: Andrei Nekrasov-Cartoons, 1980; Cartoons, 1984; Vkhutemas-Markhi 1920-1980, 1980; Moscow Institute of Architecture, 1989; The Socially Responsible Environment: USA/USSR 1980-1990, 1990; Institute of Architecture Moscow, 1991; Moscow, Architectural Guide, 1991; Projects: The City Ring Rail Road, 1980; New City Space, 1981; Theatre for Travelling Troupes, 1981; House for Today, 1985; Centre of Bakuriani (Georgia), 1986; Playhouse in Amsterdam, 1987; Realised reconstruction of V Maiakovski Theatre, Moscow 1984-90. *Memberships:* Union Archts USSR; Int Ski Club of Archts, VP 1985. *Honours:* Grand Prix, Cartoons, Int Biennale, Gabrovo, Bulgaria; Silver Medal, New City Space, Int Biennale, Sofia, 1981; 1st Prize, Theatre for Travelling Troupes, Int Competition, Sweden, 1981; 1st Prize, House Bakuriani, Int Competition, Georgia, 1985; Venice Prize, 1991. *Hobbies:* Cartoons; Mountain skiing. *Address:* Botanicheskij Pereulok Dom 12 KV 97, Moscow 129010, Russia.

NELSON Alan David, b. 6 June 1954, Bristol, England. Art Dealer; Country Gentleman. m. Margaret Pauline Kennefick, 13 Sept 1985. *Education:* Prince of Wales Coll, Dover. *Appointments:* Brit Petroleum, 1970- 74; Lane Fine Art Ltd, Fine Art Dealers, 1974-. *Publications:* Books: Sporting Paintings, 1985, 1991; Paris Portrayed, 1988. *Memberships:* BADA; LAPADA; E Cork Golf Club. *Hobbies:* Sailing; Golf; Shooting. *Address:* 13 Halkin Mews, Belgravia, London SW1, England.

NELSON Ronald Roy, b. 11 Nov 1941, Sioux Falls, South Dakota, USA. Representative of the US Secretary of Defense. *Education:* BA, Univ SD, 1963; MA, 1965, PhD, 1967, Duke Univ. *Appointments:* 1st Lt, Capt, 1967-69, Capt, 1973-77 incl 3rd Armoured Div, Frankfurt, FRG, 1974-77, Maj, Mil Intelligence, assigned Int Negotiations Div, Def Intelligence Agcy, 1977-81; US Army; Asst Prof, Hist, Wn Carolina Univ, 1969-73; Col, US Army Reserves, 1980-; Profl Staff, Senate For Rels Comm, 1981-82; Dpty US Rep to Mutual and Balanced Force Reduction Talks, Vienna, 1982-83; Cons, Bus Mgmt, Exporting, 1983-85; Exec VP, 1983-85, Exec Dir, 1989-90, Am For Policy Coun; Vis Prof, Bus Adm, Pacific Luth Univ, Jan 1984; Rep of Sec Def, Conf on Disarmament, 1985-89, 1990-; Vis Scholar/Lectr, Wn Carolina Univ, 1988; Chem Weapons Issues Cons, var businesses, 1989-90; Rep of Sec Def, UN 1st Comm, 1990-. *Publications:* The Home Office, 1782-1801, 1969; Soviet Concepts of Peace, Peaceful Coexistence, and Detente (co-author), 1988; A New Soviet Military. The Next Generation (co-author), 1989; Soviet Military in Midst of Its Own Revolution (co-

author), 1989; Soviet Reductions Signal Revolution in Military Affairs (co-author), 1989; Soviet Cuts Do Little Damage to Military Capacity, 1989; Russia's 19th Century Gorbachev, 1989; Editorials, New York Times, others. *Memberships:* Conf Brit Studies; Nat Audubon Soc; Nat Wildlife Fedn; Nature Conservancy; Reserve Offs Assn; Soc Histns of Am For Rels; World Wildlife Fund. *Honours:* Hon socs incl Phi Beta Kappa; Fellow, 1963, Dissertation Fellow, 1966, Woodrow Wilson; Combat Infantry Badge, 1968; Army Commendation Medal, 1968, Purple Heart, 1969; Bronze Star, 1969; Meritorious Serv Medal, 1977; Def Meritorious Serv Medal, 1981, other Army awards; Sec Def Medal, Meritorious Civilian Serv, 1989. *Hobbies:* Hunting; Fishing; Birdwatching; Jogging; Travel. *Address:* 4500 S Four Mile Run Dr No 1034, Arlington, VA 22204, USA. 7.

NELSON-JONES Rodney Michael, b. 11 Feb 1947, England. Solicitor. m. Kusum Dhorajiwala, 21 Sept 1988. *Education:* Repton School; Hertford Coll, Oxford; MA (Oxon), 1970; Admitted as Solicitor, 1975. *Appointments:* Prothero & Prothero, 1973-77; L Bingham & Co, 1977-83; Field Fisher Waterhouse, London, 1983-. *Publications:* Product Liability: The New Law under the Consumer Protection Act 1987, 1987; Medical Negligence Case Law, 1990; Nelson-Jones and Nuttally Tax and Interest Tables, 1988, 1989, 1990, 1991. *Membership:* Campden Hill LTC. *Honours:* Hubert Ruse Prize, 1974. *Hobbies:* Cinema; Tennis; Travel. *Address:* 69 Warrington Crescent, London W9 1EH, England. 53.

NEMA Suresh Kumar, b. 13 Jan 1944, Narsinghpur, M P, India. Research Centre Director. m. Shashi Prabha Nema, 11 June 1971, 1 s, 2 d. *Education:* MSc (Applied), 1967. *Appointments:* Jr Scientist, Sr Scientist, 1967-81, Hd, Polymer Div, 1982-88, Vikram Sarabhai Space Centre, Trivandrum; Dir, Macromolecular Rsch Ctr, R D Univ, Jabalpur, 1988-. *Memberships:* Am Inst Aeronautics and Astronautics; Int Assn Hydrogen Energy; Indian Aeronautical Soc; Soc High Energy Materials India. *Honours:* Republic Day Award, indigenous dev of propellant systems, Nat Rsch Dev Corp, Delhi, 1986; FIE Fndn Award, furtherance sci and technology in India, 1990. *Hobbies:* Gardening; Music. *Address:* Macromolecular Research Centre, R D University, Jabalpur, India 482 001.

NEMESCU Octavian, b. 29 Mar 1940, Pascani, Rumania. Music Educator; Composer. m. Erica Rottner, 20 July 1974, 1 s. *Education:* Grad, Acad Music, Bucharest, 1963; Dr, Musicology, 1978. *Appointments:* Prof, Schools of Music, 1963-70; Asst, Lectr, Fac Music, Brasov, 1971-78; Prof, Lyceum of Music, Bucharest, 1978-90; Reader, Acad Music, Bucharest, 1990-. *Creative works:* Compositions incl: Four Dimensions in Time, for orch; Suggestions, for mixed grp; Concentric, for mixed grp; Will you be able by yourself, imaginary music; Natural-Cultural, electroacoustic music; Metabizantinirikon, for 1 instrument and magnetic tape; Finaleph, for orch; Non Symphony V, for orch. *Memberships:* Union Rumanian Composers; SACEM. *Honours:* Prize for composition Aaron Copeland, USA, 1970; Prize, Int Electronic Music Contest, Borges, France, 1980, 1982; Prize, Rumanian Acad, 1981; Prize, Confedn Int de Musique Electroacoustique. *Address:* Masina de piine Nr 16, app 32, sect 2, COD 72216 Bucharest, Rumania. 4, 43.

NEOPTOLEMOS John Phiyoyiannis, b. 30 June 1951, Cyprus. Reader in Surgery; Consultant Surgeon. m. Linda Joan Blaylock, 2 Feb 1974, 1 s, 1 d. *Education:* BA (Cantab), 1973; Guy's Hosp, London, 1973-76; MB, BChir (Cantab), MA (Cantab), 1977; FRCS (England), 1981; Rsch Fellow, Univ CA, San Diego, 1984-85; MD (Leicester), 1985. *Appointments:* House Surg, Guy's Hosp, 1976; Sr House Off, Registrar, Sr Registrar, Leicester, 1977-87; Cons, Dudley Rd Hosp, Birmingham, 1987-; Reader, Univ Birmingham, 1990-. *Publications:* Num sci publs on aetiology and treatment of pancreatobiliary disease and colorectal cancer. *Memberships:* Colorectal Cancer Comm, Med Rsch Coun; Chmn, UK Pancreatic Cancer Trials Comm; Jt Sec, European Grp for Study of Pancreatic Cancer. *Honours:* Rodney Smith Prize, Pancreatic Soc, 1987; Hunterian Prof, Royal Coll Surgeons England, 1987-88; Moynihan Travelling Fellow, Assn Surgs, 1988; Travelling Prof, Royal Soc Med, 1989. *Hobby:* Squash (Member, Edgbaston Priory Club, Birmingham). *Address:* Department of Surgery, Dudley Road Hospital, Birmingham B18 7QH, England.

NEPIL Frantisek, b. 10 Feb 1929, Hyskov, Czechoslovakia. Writer. m. Zdenka Kocova, 25 Aug 1951, 1 d. *Education:* Commercial Acad, Prague, 1948. *Appointments:* Advt Cons, Prague, 1948; Advt Text Writer, Prague, 1954-68; Ed, Czechoslav Broadcasting Corp, Prague, 1969-71; TV Narrator. *Creative works:* Books incl: How to build a Cottage, 1968; The Little Poppyman, 1976; Me, Baryk a Dog, 1977; Paint My Beak Red, 1979; The Small Purposers, 1981; The Shoes of Bast, 1982; Wandering Through Prague, 1982; Good and Still Better Morning, 1983; The Lime Avenue, 1985; The Night and The Rock, 1988; The Robbers from The Toothed-Auntie-Inn, 1988; The Apocryphs of Aether, 1990; The Ring of a Princess, 1990; The Little Atlas of My Heart, 1991; The Anatomy for The Young Generation, 1991; Good and Still Better Sunday, 1992; The Little Fairy Lamp, 1992; 200 articles and 100 fairy tales for Czech Broadcasting; 50 gramphone records; texts for Hurvinek and Spejbi Theatre; Theatre and puppet theatre plays. *Memberships:* PEN Club, Prague; Int Bd Books for Young People, Prague; Czech Writers Assn, Prague; Masaryk's Dem Movement, Prague. *Honours:* Czechoslovak Broadcasting Corp Award, 1979; For Dist'd Achmt in Emotional Education of Czech Chd Award, 1977. *Hobbies:* Gardening; Tourism; Photography. *Address:* Jeremenkova 52, Prague 4-147 00, Czech Republic.

NEROZNAK Vladimir Petrovich, b. 17 Nov 1939, Bozhedarovka village, Omsk region, USSR. Scientist; Philologist. m. 21 Mar 1969, 1 s. *Education:* Univ Leningrad, 1958-63; Postgrad, Inst Linguistics, 1963-66; Cand degree, 1970; Doct, 1979; Prof, 1989. *Appointments:* Inst Linguistics, Leningrad (now St Petersburg), 1966-68; Inst Linguistics, Moscow, 1970-85; Sci Worker, Dept Lit and Lang, USSR Acad Scis, 1985-; Hd, Dept Philology, Moscow Linguistic Univ. *Publications:* Palaeobalkanian languages, 1978; Names of the Old Russian Cities, 1983; Phrygian (in Engl), 1985; Monuments of the most ancient Greek script, 1988; Soviet New Speak on the Geographical Map, 1991. *Memberships:* Geogl Soc, USSR; Histl Linguistic Soc; Presidium, Soviet Cultural Fndn, 1988; EURALEX; Union Soviet Jrnlsts; Pres, Soviet Assn Ellinistes, 1989. *Honours:* Hon Scientist of Russia, 1989. *Hobby:* Travel. *Address:* Department of Literature and Language, USSR Academy of Sciences, Leninsky prospekt 32 A, Moscow, Russia.

NESKOW Elizabeth, b. 14 Nov 1948, Chicago, Illinois, USA. Manager of Programme Evaluation. *Education:* BA, Engl, NWn Univ, 1970; BM hons, Theory, Composition, Am Conservatory Music, 1972; Certs Completion and Excellence, French, Sorbonne, Paris, 1973; MBA hons, Mgmt, Roosevelt Univ, 1983; Cert Auditor. *Appointments:* Sr Tech Ed, Mktng Mgr, Corp Mgr Quality Assurance, Dames & Moore, 1973-87; Mgr Quality Assurance, Mgr Prog Evaluation, Waste Mgmt Inc, Oak Brook, IL, 1987-. *Publications:* Quality Assurance: Beyond the Laboratory, 1988; Quality Assurance in the Waste Industry (w Patricia A McIsaac), 1988. *Memberships:* Am Soc Quality Control; Chairperson Subcomm Quality Control; Nat Assn Female Execs; Sigma Alpha Iota; Bd Dirs, Grace Welsh Int Endowment Fund. *Honours:* 1st Place, Gold Medal, Piano Competition, 1963. *Hobbies:* Reading; Director, Serbian Singing Society Branko Radicevich, 1973-, touring USA and holding concerts; Responds to Sunday liturgy in Holy Resurrection Serbian Orthodox Cathedral, Chicago. *Address:* 634 N Merrill Avenue, Park Ridge, IL 60068, USA.

NEUBERGER Julia Babette Sarah, b. 27 Feb 1950, London, England. Rabbi; Academic. m. Anthony John Neuberger, 17 Sept 1973, 1 s, 1 d. *Education:* Newnham Coll, Cambridge, 1969-73; BA Hons, 1973; MA, 1975; Leo Baeck Coll, 1973-77; Rabbinic Ordination, 1977. *Appointments:* Rabbi, S London Liberal Synagogue, 1977-89; Vis Fellow, King's Fund Inst, 1989-91; Harkness Fellow, Harvard Univ, USA, 1991-92. *Publications:* Caring for Dying People of Different Faiths, 1987; Whatever's Happening to Women, 1991; A Necessary End, 1991; Ethics in Healthcare: Research Ethics Committees in the UK, 1992. *Memberships:* Patients Assn, Chair 1988-91; Trustee, Runnymede Trust; Human Fertilisation and Embryology Auth; Coun Mbr, St George's House, Windsor; Coun Mbr, St George's Hosp Med School; Chmn Des, Camden & Islington Comm Servs NHS Trust; Chair, UK Clearing House on Health Questions. *Honours:* Hon VP, Royal Coll Nursing; Hon Doc, Univ of Humberside. *Hobbies:* Irish life; Opera; Setting up the Old Girls Network. *Address:* 36 Orlando Road, London SW4 0LF, England. 1, 138.

NEUMAN Frantisek, b. 28 May 1937, Brno, Czechoslovakia. Chief Research Fellow; Mathematician. m. Olga Rackova, 26 Aug 1961, 2 d. *Education:* MS, 1960, RNDr, 1965, PhD, 1965, Univ Brno; DrSc, Acad Sci and Charles Univ, Prague, 1980. *Appointments:* Asst Prof, 1960-65, Assoc Prof, 1965-74, Prof, 1991-, Univ Brno; Sr Rsch Fellow, 1974-80, Chief Rsch Fellow, 1980-, Math Inst, Acad Brno Br. *Publications:* 80 sci publs in int math jrnls; Global Properties of Linear Ordinary Differential Equations, monograph, 1991. *Memberships:* Hd, Brno Br, Math Inst Acad; Ed Bd, Mathematica Bohemica; Ed Bd, Archivum Mathematicum; Sci Coun, Math Inst Acad; Sci Coun, Masaryk Univ, Brno; Sci Coun, Fac Natural Sci, Brno. *Honours:* Dip w hons, Univ Brno, 1960; Award for Young Rsch Mathns, Union Czechoslovak Mathns and Physicists, 1965; Award, Math Coun, Czechoslovak Acad Scis, 1977, 1982; Invited plenary lectr, several int confs and num univs, USA, Can, UK, others. *Address:* Mathematical Institute of Academy, Brno branch, Mendelovo nam 1, 66282 Brno, Czechoslovakia.

NEUVO Yrjo Aunus Olavi, b. 21 July 1943, Turku, Finland. Research Professor. m. Tuula Halsas, 3 Feb 1968, 2 s, 1 d. *Education:* Dip Engr, 1968; Lic Technology, 1971; PhD, 1974. *Appointments:* Acting Prof, Helsinki Univ Technology, 1975-76; Prof, Tampere Univ Technology, 1976-; Sr Rsch Fellow, 1979-80, Rsch Prof, 1984-94, Acad Finland; Vis Prof, Univ CA, USA, 1981-82. *Publications:* Over 300 articles. *Memberships:* Bd Mbr, Finnish Acad Tech Scis; Phi Kappa Phi; EURASIP; Acadamiae Europaeae; Royal Swedish Acad of Engrng Scis; Nordisk Industrifond; EC Comm Dev Sci and Technology. *Honours:* Fellow, IEEE; Hon Doc of Med, Univ of Tampere; Annual Prize, Finnish Elec and Electronic Ind Assn; Annual Prize, Nokia Corp; Tekniikka ja Talous Prize; ASLA-Fulbright Grant; Disting Lectr, IEEE Circuits and Systems Soc; Planet 1938 DN named Neuvo in his hon. *Address:* Tampere University of Technology, Signal Processing Laboratory, PO Box 553, SF-33101 Tampere, Finland. 34, 52.

NEVO Eviatar, b. 2 Feb 1929, Tel-Aviv, Israel. Professor of Biology. *Education:* MSc w special distinction, Biology, 1958, PhD summa cum laude, Biology, 1964, Hebrew Univ, Jerusalem. *Appointments:* Lectr, Biology, Oranim Tchrs State Coll, 1956-63; Vis Prof, Zoology, Univ TX, USA, 1964-65; Fellow in Biology, Harvard Univ, 1965-66; Rsch Assoc, 1967-68, Lectr, Genetics, 1968-70, Sr Lectr, Genetics, 1970-71, Hebrew Univ, Jerusalem, Israel; Rsch Assoc, Mus Vertebrate Zoology, Univ CA, Berkeley, Snr Postdoct Rsch Fellow, Dept Biol, Univ Chgo, IL, USA, 1972-73; Assoc Prof, Biology, 1973-75, Prof of Biology, 1975-, Dir, Inst Evolution, 1977-, Chair, Evolutionary Biology, 1984-, Univ Haifa, Israel; Incumbent Chair of Evolutionary Biology, 1984-. *Publications:* Population Genetics and Ecology (w S Karlin), 1976; The evolutionary significance of genetic diversity: Ecological, demographic and life history correlates (w A Beiles and R Ben-Shlomo), 1984; Evolutionary Processes and Theory (w S Karlin), 1986; Cosmic, biological and human evolution: Past, present, future - Problems, patterns, processes, hypotheses and thoughts, 1989; Evolutionary theory and processes of active speciation and adaptive radiation in subterranean mole rats, Spalax ehrenbergi superspecies in Israel, 1991; Evolution of Subterranean Mammals at the Organismal and Molecular Levels (ed w O A Reig), 1990; 390 papers in var fields of evolutionary biology. *Memberships:* Soc for the Study of Evolution; Am Assoc for the Adv of Sci; Am Soc of Naturalists; Genetics Soc of Am; Genetical Soc of Israel; Zoological Soc of Israel; Geo Soc of Israel. *Honours:* Fulbright Fellow, 1964; VP, Soc of Study of Evol, 1978-; Guggenheim Fndn Fellow, 1978-80; Fellow, Explorers Club, 1980-; Fellow, Am Assoc of the Advt of Sci, 1985-; Fellow, The Linnean Soc of Lon, 1989-; Mbr, NY Acad of Scis, 1989-; Foreign Mbr, Linnean Soc of Lon, 1990-; Hon Cultural Doct, World Univ Roundtable, 1990-; Inaugural Mbr, Charles Darwin Assoc of the NY Acad of Scis, 1992-; vars ed bds. *Address:* Institute of Evolution, Haifa University, Haifa 31905, Israel.

NEWBERRY Raymond Scudamore, b. 8 Feb 1935, Bristol, England. British Council Officer. m. Angelina Nance, 26 Aug 1967, 1 s, 1 d. *Education:* Selwyn Coll, Cmabridge, 1955-58; BA (Cantab), 1958; Dip Engl as Second Lang, Univ Leeds, 1963; Dip Educ, Univ Bristol, 1975. *Appointments:* Nat Serv, 1953-55; Lectr, Coll Arts, Baghdad Univ, Iraq, 1959-62; British Coun, 1962-: Lectr, Teheran, Iran, 1963-64; Educ Off, Calcutta, India, 1964-66; Hd, Engl Dept, Adv Tchr Trng Coll, Winneba, Ghana, 1966-70; Advsr on Engl Lang, Min Educ, Singapore, 1970-74; Rep, Colombia, 1975-80; Dir, N and Latin Am Dept, 1980-82; Dir, Am and Pacific Dept, 1982-84; Rep, Australia, 1984-89; Dir, Brazil, 1990-. *Publication:* Between You and Me (w A Maley), 1974. *Honour:* OBE, 1989. *Hobbies:* Bookbinding; Golf. *Address:* c/o The British Council, 10 Spring Gardens, London SW1A 2BN, England. 1.

NEWBON Gary, b. 15 Mar 1945, Cambridge, England. Television Executive. m. Katherine Janet While, 26 Oct 1973, 2 s, 1 d. *Education:* Culford School, Bury St Edmunds, Suffolk, 1954-64. *Appointments:* Jeacocks News Agcy, 1964-67; Hayters Sports Agcy, 1967-68; Westward ITV, 1968-71; ATV Network ITV, 1971-81; Ctrl Indep TV, Birmingham, 1982-. *Publications:* Over the Sticks; Under Starter's Orders. *Memberships:* Midland Soccer Writers, former Chmn, former Sec; Variety Club GB; Lord's Taverners. *Hobbies:* Jazz; Drinking champagne. *Address:* Central Independent Television, Broad Street, Birmingham B1 2JP, England.

NEWBORN Jud, b. 8 Nov 1952, New York City, New York, USA. Cultural Anthropologist; Museum Historian; Writer. *Education:* BA magna cum laude, NY Univ, 1974; Grad study, Clare Hall, Cambridge, England, 1974-75; MA, 1977, Grad study, 1977-; PhD, 1993, Univ Chgo. *Career:* Mus Tech, Asst Crew Chief, Nassau Co Mus Natural Hist, Garvies Point Mus, Glen Cove, NY, 1971-72; Archaeological Researcher, Pololu Valley, HA, 1973; Trade Copywriter, Publicist, Oxford Univ Press, NYC, 1975-76; Fellow, Clare Hall, Cambridge, England, 1978; Anthropological Researcher on Nazi Germany, Munich, FRG, 1978-79, 1980-83; Freelance Writer, 1983-86; Museum Historian, Snr Researcher, Writer, Design Team Mbr, NY Holocaust Mem Commn, Mus Jewish Heritage, NYC, USA, 1986-; Lectr, Freelance Writer, Translator, Cons. *Publications:* Shattering the German Night: The Story of the White Rose (w Annette E Dumbach), 1986; Work Makes Free: The Hidden Cultural Meaning of the Holocaust, in progress; Articles and book reviews in Journal of Asian Studies, Journal of Modern History, Newsday, New York Times, Philadelphia Inquirer; Poetry and fiction in Little Magazine, and Nation. *Memberships:* Am Anthropological Assn; Am Hist Assn; Authors Guild; Phi Beta Kappa. *Honours:* Fellowship, Mem Fndn Jewish Culture, 1978-79; Fulbright Fellowship, 1980-82; Grant, Wenner-Gren Fndn Anthropological Research, 1984; Newcombe

Fellowship, Woodrow Wilson Nat Fellowship Fndn, 1984-85. *Address:* 12 Mitchell Ave, Plainview, NY 11803, USA.1, 37, 152.

NEWBURY Anthony Charles, b. 19 Jan 1940, Australia. Dental Surgeon. m. Brigitte Stevenson, 4 Oct 1986, 1 s, 1 d. *Education:* LDS, Victoria, 1963; BDSc, 1964, MDSc, 1969, Melbourne Univ. *Appointments:* Gen Dental Practice, Melbourne, 1963-64; Pt-time Sr Lectr, Dept Anatomy, Sr Clin Demonstrator, Dept Restorative Dentistry, Univ Melbourne, 1964-69; Specialist Orthodontic Practice, Melbourne, 1965-70; Private Practice, Harley St, London, England, 1972-. *Contributions to:* Mercury and Other Toxic Metals in Humans, 1989; Art restoration for colleagues. *Memberships:* Metrop Br, Brit Dental Assn, Pres 1983, Sec 1975-81; Brit Dental Assn, Rep Bd Mbr 1975-81; Royal Soc Med; Pierre Fauchard Acad; Int Coll Dentists; European Orthodontic Soc; Brit Soc Study of Orthodontics. *Hobbies:* Tennis; Golf; Reading; Wine; Water sports; Health and healing. *Address:* 72 Harley Street, London W1N 1AE, England.

NEWHAUSER Richard Gordan, b. 24 Nov 1947, USA. Associate Professor. m. Andrea Ilona Nemeth, 24 July 1975, 2 s. *Education:* BA, Univ Cinn, 1970; MA, Univ Chgo, 1972; PhD, Univ PA, 1986. *Appointments:* Instr, Univ Cinn, OH, 1971; Tutor, 1975-76, Fac Assoc, 1980-86, Asst Prof, Mediaeval Philology, 1986-90, Univ Tubingen, FRG; Tchng Fellow, Univ PA, Phila, USA, 1976-79; Instr, Rutgers Univ, Camden, NJ, 1977-79; Instr, Univ Augsburg, FRG, 1979-80; Assoc Prof, Mediaeval Lit, Trinity Univ, San Antonio, TX, USA, 1990-. *Creative works:* Essays, articles, reviews in profl jrnls; Librettist, The Tinder Box (H C Andersen), 1980. *Memberships:* MLA; Medieval Acad Am; New Chaucer Soc; Soc Arthurienne; Wolfram von Eschenbach Gesellschaft. *Honours:* 1st Prize, Univ Cinn Poetry Contest, 1970; 3rd Prize, Univ Chgo Poetry Contest, 1972; Fulbright Grant to Germany, 1973-74; 3rd Prize, H C Andersen Music Competition, 1980; Rsch Travel Grants, DFG, Germany, 1986-87, 1989-90. *Address:* Department of English, Trinity University, 715 Stadium Dr, San Antonio, TX 78212, USA. 52.

NEWITT John Garwood Jr, b. 9 Apr 1941, Charlotte, North Carolina, USA. Lawyer. m. Catherine Elizabeth Huggard, 28 Aug 1965, 2 d. *Education:* AB, 1963, JD, 1965, Wake Forest Univ; Postgrad studies, Univ VA, 1966-68. *Appointments:* Capt, Lectr, The Judge Advocate Gens School, 1965-68; Ptnr, Newitt & Newitt, 1968-73; Sr Ptnr, Newitt & Bruny, 1973-91. *Publications:* Income Averaging: 1964 Tax Relief for the Copyright Artist, 1965. *Memberships:* Lectr, United Way Vol Ldrship Dev Prog, 1986-91; Chmn, Bd Zoning Adjustment, 1971-77; NC Acad Trial Lawyers; Pres, Selwyn Men's Fellowship, 1988-89; Goodfellows; Int Platform Assn. *Honours:* Nathan Burkan ASCAP Award, 1965; Cert Competency, NC Coll Advocacy, 1984. *Hobbies:* Jogging; Golf; Reading; Tennis. *Address:* 3216 Ferncliff Road, Charlotte, NC 28211, USA. 7, 52, 132, 163.

NEWLANDS George McLeod, b. 12 July 1941, Perth, Scotland. University Teacher. m. Mary Elizabeth Wallace, 1 Sept 1967, 3 s. *Education:* Univs Edinburgh, Heidelberg, Cambridge, 1959-68. *Appointments:* Asst Min, Muirhouse, Edinburgh, 1969-70; Lectr, Divinity, 1969-73, Prof, Divinity, 1986-, Dean, Fac Divinity, 1988, Univ Glasgow; Univ Lectr, Divinity, Cambridge, England, 1973-86; Fellow, Wolfson Coll, Cambridge, 1975; Fellow, Dean, Trinity Hall, Cambridge, 1982; Prin, Trinity Coll, Glasgow, 1991. *Publications:* Books: Hilary of Poitiers, 1978; Theology of the Love of God, 1980; The Church of God, 1984; Making Christian Decisions, 1985. *Address:* Faculty of Divinity, The University, Glasgow G12 8QQ, Scotland. 184.

NEWLIN Beverly Jane Agnew, b. 16 June 1947, Greenwood, South Carolina, USA. Registered Nurse. m. Kimrey Dayton Newlin, 9 Mar 1968, 1 s, 2 d. *Education:*

Dip Nursing, Greenville Gen Hosp School Nursing, 1968. *Appointments:* Registered Nurse: Texarkana Hosp, 1968-69; Kenner Army Hosp, 1970-78; Miami Children's Hosp, FL, 1979-. *Memberships:* Active: PTA; Presby Ch; Repub Contbr. *Hobbies:* Campaign Staff of Bruce Hoffmann for House of Representatives, District 114, Florida, 1986, 1988, 1990; Assisted husband in Charles Dussain Campaign for County Commissioner, Dade County, 1988; Assisted son in Mike Hill Campaign, Trustee, Key Biscayne Village. *Address:* 755 Allendale Road, Key Biscayne, FL 33149, USA. 76.

NEWTON Christopher, b. 11 June 1936, Deal, Kent, England. Artistic Director. *Education:* BA Hons, Univ Leeds; MA, Univ IL, USA. *Appointments:* Fndng Dir, Theatre Calgary, Can; Artistic Dir, Vancouver Playhouse; Artistic Dir, Shaw Fest. *Creative works:* Plays: You Two Stay Here The Rest Come With Me; Trip; The Sound of Distant Thunder; Slow Train to Saint Ives; Others. *Honours:* LLD, Brock Univ, 1986; LLD, Univ Guelph, 1988. *Hobbies:* Music; Landscape architecture. *Address:* PO Box 774, Niagara-on-the-Lake, Ontario, Canada L0S 1J0. 88.

NEWTON Roger Surtees, b. 7 Aug 1928, Croydon, Surrey, England. Managing Director. m. Else-Grete Skov, 5 Apr 1980, 1 s, 1 d. *Education:* Glyn Grammar School, Epsom. *Appointments:* S H Benson, Advt Agcy, 1950-51; ICI Pharmaceuticals, 1951-53; Ciba-Geigy, Manchester, 1953-63; Glaxo Labs Ltd, 1963-68; Warner Lambert UK Ltd, 1968-83; Mng Dir, Newton Communications Ltd, 1983-; Chmn, Gwent Hlth Auth, 1990-. *Memberships:* Fellow, Inst Dirs; Chartered Inst Mktng. *Hobbies:* Music; Tennis; Theatre. *Address:* Forester's Lodge, Itton, Chepstow, Gwent NP6 6BZ, Wales.

NGO Khai Doan The, b. 30 Apr 1957, Vinh Long, Vietnam. Professor. m. Kieu-Hanh Tran Ngo, 13 July 1991. *Education:* BS summa cum laude, Elec Engrng, CA State Polytechnic Univ, 1979; MS, Elec Engrng, 1980, PhD, Elec Engrng, 1984, CA Inst Technology. *Appointments:* Mbr, Tech Staff, Gen Elec Corp Rsch and Dev Ctr, 1984-88; Prof, Univ FL, 1988-. *Memberships:* IEEE; AAAS; Am Soc Engrng Educ; Instrument Soc Am. *Honours:* President's Hon Lists, 1975-79; Ker-McGee Scholarship, 1978; Outstanding Tchr, Elec Engrng Core Course, Univ FL, 1989; Presidential Young Investigator, 1989; Sigma Xi; Phi Kappa Phi; Tau Beta Pi; Eta Kappa Nu. *Hobbies:* Music, classical and jazz; Sports; Books. *Address:* ssa 00University of Florida, Larsen 334B, Gainesville, FL 32611, USA. 6, 7, 15, 52, 139, 155.

NGOBESING SUH Romanus, b. 20 Sept 1956, Mforya Bafut, Cameroon. Journalist. m. Emilia Siri Chungong, 15 Mar 1989, 2 s, 2 d. *Education:* Dip, Fundamental Studies, 1977; BA Hons, Engl and French Langs and Lit, 1979, BA, Jrnlsm, 1981, Univ Yaounde and Int School Jrnlsm, Yaounde. *Appointments:* Pt-time tchng, 1975-79; Jrnlst, 1981-; Hd, Progs Serv, Radio Bagoussam, 1983-86; Hd, Progs Serv, 1986-87, Dpty Ed-in-Chief, 1987-89, Radio Yaounde; Hd, Progs and Info, Cameroon Radio TV, Bamenda, 1989-. *Publications:* Several books for primary schools; Fndr, Something Useful book series of educl material; Short stories and plays incl: Intoxication; What a Man; Beware of Bad Friends; Achievement thro' Struggle; Over 20 radio plays. *Memberships:* Pres, Cameroon Radio TV Bomenda Social Fund; Sec-Gen, NW Artists Assn; Sec-Gen, other local assns; Exec Comm Culture, NW Province, Cameroon. *Honours:* Winner, Lit Award, Excellent Poetry, Cameroon, 1982. *Hobbies:* Writing plays, short stories, inspirational material; Reading inspirational books and articles in Readers' Digest; Listening to inspirational talks. *Address:* Cameroon Radio Television, Bamenda, Cameroon.

NI Bo, b. 1 Jan 1936, He County, Anhui Province, China. Professor of Library and Information Science. m. Caoying Lu, Aug 1963, 3 s. *Education:* Bach, Dept Lib Sci, Beijing Univ, 1960. *Appointments:* Jilin Normal Univ, 1960-63; Joined, 1963, Assoc Prof, 1986, Prof, 1988-, Nanjing Univ; 1st Convener, Lib and Info Sci Grp, Acad Comm, State Coun, 1990. *Publications:* Over 40 books and 200 articles in fields of lib and info sci, lit, hist of sci and technology, editing, publng, other topics. *Memberships:* Acad Comm, Chinese Inst Libs, Dpty Dir, Lit Retrieved Br; Standing Comm, Jiangsu Inst Libs, Dir Editing and Publng Comm; Dpty Chief Ed, Jiangsu Lib Jrnl; Evaluation Grp, Sys Sci, Lib and Info Sci, Acad Comm, State Coun, mbr of evaluation grp, scifc rsrch items of 'the English Five-Year plan' of lib and info sci, arch sci, State Educ Comm, 1992. *Honours:* Nat Articles and Works of Excellence Award, 4 books, 1 article, incl series of 8 books, 1989, 1 book, 1990. *Hobbies:* Textual research; Reading; Running; Swimming; Climbing. *Address:* Department of Documentation and Information Science, Nanjing University, Nanjing, Jiangsu 210008, China.

NIBLETT Keith Ivor, b. 8 June 1947, Lowestoft, England. Director of Business Planning; Management Lecturer. m. Jayne Lizabeth Niblett, 4 Aug 1967, 3 s, 1 d. *Education:* LRAM, Acad Music, 1964; BA, Univ Bath, 1968; Cert Inst Mgmt, Norwich City Coll, 1973; DMS, Norwich City Coll, 1979. *Appointments:* Mgr, Thetford and Watton Times, 1972-74; Grp Mgr, Norwich Mercury series of newspapers, 1975-78; Videotex Mgr, Prestel, 1978-79; Sr Exec, En Cos Newspapers, 1979; Gen Mgr, Adprint Mag Publrs, 1986-88; Dir, Bus Planning, Pyramid Dev Servs (Europe) Ltd, Barnham Brook Ctr, Barnham Broom, Norfolk, 1988-; Vis Lectr, Norwich City Coll, 1989-. *Publication:* Viewdata in Action, book, 1978. *Memberships:* Chmn, Norwich Round Table No 1, 1984; Chmn, Norfolk Area Round Table, 1987; NT Councillor, Round Table, 1985-88; Comm Mbr, Waveney Conservative Assn; Publicity Advsr, Norwich Fest. *Hobbies:* Squash; Music; Writing; Reading; Politics. *Address:* Hillside House, Hillside Road West, Bungay, Suffolk NR35 1PJ, England.

NICA Anca Rodica, b. 16 June 1946, Braila, Rumania. Dentist. m. 31 Jan 1970, 1 s, 1 d. *Education:* School Dentistry, 1964-70. *Appointments:* Viziru Hlth Ctr, 1970-71; Gaesti Hlth Ctr, 1971-75; Dragodana Hlth Ctr, 1975-87. *Publications:* The incidence of munps antibodies in the population of Bucharest, 1970; Removable and non- removable provisory prosthetics. *Memberships:* USSM Rumania. *Hobbies:* Music; Reading; Fine arts. *Address:* 3848 W 226th Street No 123, Torrance, CA 90505, USA.

NICHEV Ivan, b. 31 July 1940, Kazanlak, Bulgaria. Film Director. m. Tatiana Granitova, 2 d. *Education:* MA, Polish Film School, Lodz; Studied w Andrzej Wajda. *Appointments:* Film Dir, Boyana Film Studios, Sofia, 1970-; Sr Lectr, Acad Film and Theatre Arts, Sofia, 1975-. *Creative works:* Full-length feature films: Memory, 1975; Stars in the Hair - Tears in the Eyes, 1977; Boomerang, 1978; Play for the King, 1980; The Lonely People's Ball, 1981; The Black Swan, 1984; Ivan and Alexandra, 1988; The Last Somersault; Short feature films: The Human Heart; Theatre Night; Teenager; TV: Three Hours before the Flight; Family Chronicle; Baj Ganiu series, 1991; Documentaries: The Letters of Chopin; A Town; The School of the Future; Ballad for Two and a Guitar; Sofia in Green; Peasant Chronicle; Human Fetes; Behind the Scenes; Circus; London-Paris Super Triathlon; 6 concerts; La Traviata. *Membership:* Pres, Union Bulgarian Film Dirs Sect, Union Bulgarian Film Makers. *Honours:* Decorated St Cyril and Methodius Award for Culture; Order of Cultural Merit, Poland; His films selected for num film fests; Locarno Film Fest Jury Prize, 1975; Silver Orange Prize, Antalya Film Fest, 1977; Grant Prix The Golden Rose, Varna Film Fest, 1988; Gold Plaque, Chgo Film Fest, 1989; Special Prize, Montecatini Film Fest, 1989; Official selection, Priz-Italia, 1991. *Hobbies:* Music; Ballet; Good beer. *Address:* 8 Liuben Karavelov str, Sofia, Bulgaria.

NICHOL Donald Wingate, b. 4 Aug 1952, Canada. Associate Professor. m. Susan Gwyneth Aitken, 5 Jan 1985, 1 s, 2 d. *Education:* BA (Hons), 1976, MA, 1978, Carleton Univ; PhD, Edinburgh Univ, Scotland, 1984. *Appointments:* Tutor, Concordia, Mem, Edinburgh and Open Univs, Canada and UK, 1976-84; Asst Prof, 1984-90, Assoc Prof, 1990-, Mem Univ, St John's, Newfoundland. *Publications:* Pope's Literary Legacy, 1992; Short stories, articles, reviews in Canadian Fiction Magazine, Globe and Mail (Toronto), Times Higher Education Supplement (Thes), London; Contributing Ed, Books in Canada, 1982-. *Memberships:* Can Soc 18th-Century Studies, Pres 1991-92, Reg VP 1987-93; Am Soc 18th-Century Studies; Brit Soc 18th-Century Studies; Int Soc 18th-Century Studies; Can Assn Scottish Studies; 18th Century Scottish Studies Soc. *Honours:* Rsch Grant, Writing, Editing and Publishing in the 18th Century, Social Sciences and Humanities Rsch Coun Can, 1990-93. *Hobbies:* Songwriting; Creative writing (fiction); Reviewing books, TV, arts; Desktop publishing (Macintosh); Book browsing. *Address:* Dept of English, Memorial University, St John's, Newfoundland, Canada A1C 5S7. 142.

NICHOLAS Herbert George, b. 8 June 1911, Treharris, Wales. Retired. *Education:* Mill Hill School, 1925-30; New Coll, Oxford, 1930-35; Yale Univ, 1935-37. *Appointments:* Fellow, Exeter Coll, Oxford, 1946-51; Am Div, Min Info and H M Embassy, Wash DC, USA, 1941-46; Fellow, New Coll, Oxford, 1951-; Nuffield Reader, 1956-69, Prof, Am Hist and Instns, 1969-78, Oxford Univ. *Publications:* The British General Election of 1950, 1951; The United Nations as a Political Institution, 1959; Britain and the United States, 1963; The Nature of American Politics, 1980; Washington Despatches, 1951-45 (ed), 1981. *Memberships:* Fellow, Brit Acad, VO 1975-76; Hon Fellow, New Coll, Oxford, 1980; Brit Assn Am Studies, Chmn 1960-62. *Honours:* Hon DCL, Univ Pitts, 1968; Fellow, Brit Acad (FBA), 1969. *Hobbies:* Gardening; Music. *Address:* 2 Quarry Hollow, Old Headington, Oxford OX3 8NX, England.

NICHOLS Ralph Galen, b. 1 Mar 1907, Oxford, Nebraska, USA. Retired Professor. m. E Lucile Smith, 28 Dec 1933, 2 s. *Education:* BA, Univ No IA, 1929; MA, 1934, PhD, 1948, State Univ IA. *Appointments:* Instr, Speech, Engl, Elkader HS and Jr Coll, IA, 1929-31; Instr, Speech, Engl, Fort Dodge, IA, 1931-37; Instr to Prof, 1937-44, Hd, Dept Rhetoric, 1944-72, Univ MN. *Publications:* Over 100 articles in popular mags and profl jrnls; Author or co-author, 24 books, several reprinted in at least 4 different langs. *Memberships:* Fndng Mbr, Nat Soc Study of Communication, 1949; Int Communication Assn, Pres 1951; Speech Assn Am, Pres 1961; Fndng Mbr, Int Listening Assn, 1980. *Honours:* Outstanding Tchr Award, Univ MN, 1958. *Hobbies:* Achieving learning economy through teaching of Perceptive Listening; Emphasising the role of listening in business management; Emphasising the role of listening in the resolution of conflict. *Address:* Essex House, Unit 214, 2437 Harbor Boulevard, Port Charlotte, FL 33952, USA. 8, 13, 114, 15.

NICKLESS Christopher John, b. 17 Sept 1947, Bexley, Kent, England. Headmaster of Preparatory School. m. Mairi Nickless, 11 Apr 1987. *Education:* BA Hons, Univ Birmingham, 1968. *Appointments:* Asst Master, King's School, Rochester, 1968-; Hdmaster, King's Preparatory School, 1991-. *Memberships:* City Coun, Rochester-upon-Medway; Gov, Royal Nat Lifeboat Instn; Steward, Cathedral Ch Rochester. *Hobbies:* Cricket; Music; Gardening; Walking. *Address:* The Hawthorns, 121 Maidstone Road, Chatham, Kent ME4 6JA, England.

NICOL Dominik, b. 25 Sep 1930, Oltenia, Rumania. Writer; Photographer. *Education:* Baccalaureat Diploma, Lyceum Rm Val, 1949; Diploma in Chemistry and Antibiotic Techniques, Technical School of Antibiotics, Bucharest, 1954. *Appointments:* Photo-Reporter, Agerpress, Bucharest, 1950-51; Medical Photographer, Cantacuzino Hospital, Bucharest, 1955-68; Freelance Photographer, New York, USA, 1969-. *Creative works:* Original icons painted in oils on canvas, exhibited Trinity Church, New York City, 1975; Books (published); Self Encounter, 1979; Vacuum (Colocviu de abis), play, 1979; Ten oneiric sketches, 1980; Rendez-Vous sau intalnire cu mine insumi, 1987; Vacuum-Void, play, Bilingual Edition, 1988; Poetry, essays, sketches. *Hobbies:* Painting; Ancient history. *Address:* PO Box 411, Times Square Sta, New York, NY 10108, USA. 6.

NICOLL Walter Lyon Gordon, b. 25 Mar 1925, Cheshire, England. Ret 1978. m. Willa Ellen Mary Clay, 2 Aug 1951, 1 s, 3 d. *Education:* Glenalmond; Leys School, Cambridge; Radio and Elec Engrng, Bolton. *Appointments:* Served RAF, 1943-48; Experience in Mgmt and Sales, 1949-58; Fndr, Harford Pumps, 1959-62; Cons to Merchant Bank; S Dir Gen Mgr, Rotherham Grp, Coventry; Fndr, Scarab Engrng; Mng Dir, Humber Grp; Fndr, Nocorrode Grp of Steel. *Publication:* Centenary of the Oldest Old Boys Rugby Football Club - The OLFC. *Memberships:* Life Fellow, Inst Patentees and Inventors; Life Fellow, Inst Domestic Heating; Fellow, Inst Dirs; Centenary Pres, OLFC; Pres, London Br, OLU; SMMT Mission to USA. *Hobbies:* Inventing (23 worldwide patents); Cars; Travel. *Address:* 57 Hurlingham Court, London SW6 3UP, England. 32, 41.

NICOLSON OF TARANSAY Aeofric Lachlan Bryan, Kt, b. 27 Aug 1945, New Silksworth, England. Writer; Historian; Armorist. *Education:* Ruskin Coll, Oxford; The Coll of Piping; Dr Kenneth MacKay's School of Piping. *Appointments:* Dir, Most Hon Co Armigers, 1991. *Publications:* Clan Nicolson Annals; Frederick II Hohenstaufen; Northern Genealogies; The Barons of Hylton, their Heraldry and Genealogy. *Memberships:* Heraldry Soc, London; Heraldry Soc Scotland; White Lion Soc; Heraldisch-Genealogische Gesellschaft Adler, Vienna; Augustan Soc, USA; Int Chivalric Inst; Surtees Soc; Bookplate Soc; Brit Falconers Club. *Honours:* Fndr, Armiger Prin, Most Hon Co of Armigers, 1987; Chevalier of Justice and Grace, Order of Constantine the Gt, 1990; Kt, Noble Co of the Rose, 1991; Mbr, Hereditary Order of Augustans, 1991; Knight of The Imperial Order of St Eugene of Trebizond, KETr, 1991. *Hobbies:* History; Heraldry; Genealogy; Literature; Music; Restoration of Castellated and crenellated buildings; Golf; Fishing; Falconry; Piobaireachd; Castellated architecture; Castles and their history; Collector of the armorial bookplate; Collector of Clan Nicolson - heraldry and its septs; Ancient and rare coins; Highland bagpipe. *Address:* 49 Avebury Drive, Washington Village, District 9, Tyne-Wear NE38 7BY, England.

NIELSEN Jorn, b. 11 Aug 1947, Tinglev, Denmark. Chief Surgeon. m. Ruth Nielsen, 19 June 1971, 1 s, 1 d. *Education:* Degree, Med, 1975, Specialist, Gen Surg, 1985, Aarhus Univ. *Appointments:* Army Serv, Copenhagen and Tonder, 1967-68; Registrar: Dept Med, Skene Hosp, Sweden, 1976- 77; Dept Anaesthesiology, Sickeborg Hosp, Denmark, 1977-78; Dept Surg, 1978-80, 1982-84, Dept Orthopaedics, 1980-82, Aarhus Co Hosp; Dept Gastroenterology, Aarhus Univ Hosp, 1982; Sr Registrar: Dept Surg, Viborg Hosp, 1984-87; Randers Hosp, 1987-89; Dept Gastroenterology, Aalborg Hosp, 1989-90; Lectureship, Aarhus Univ, 1987-89; Chief Surg, Viborg Hosp, 1990-. *Hobbies:* Tennis; Golf; Skiing. *Address:* Vibevei 16, 8870 Langa, Denmark. 52.

NIELSEN Kirsten, b. 12 Oct 1943, Svendborg, Denmark. Associate Professor of Old Testament. m. Leif Nielsen, 29 July 1967. *Education:* BA, French; MA, Religious Studies, 1970; Dip Tchng, 1970; PhD, 1976; Dr theol, 1985; Ordained, 1989. *Appointments:* Asst Prof, 1971; Assoc Prof, 1976; Fac Dean, 1984-89. *Publications include:* Yahweh as Prosecutor and Judge, 1978; There is Hope for a Tree, 1989; Satan - den fortabte son, 1991. *Memberships:* Bd Mbr, Danish Bible soc; Danish Rsch Coun Humanities; Det laerde selskab. *Hobbies:* Family; Literature; Art. *Address:* Vagogade 5, DK-8200 Aarhus N, Denmark.

NIELSEN Knud, b. 19 Jan 1930, Silkeborg, Denmark. Professor of Veterinary Medicine. m. Ragnhild Nielsen, 27 Feb 1957, 1 s. *Education:* DVM, 1955; DVetSc, 1967; Prof, Internal Med, 1967. *Appointments:* Gen Prac, 1956-59; Lectr, Sr Lectr, Prof, Royal Veterinary and Agricl Univ, Frederiksberg, 1959-. *Publications:* Gastrointestinal Protein Loss in Cattle, thesis, 1967; About 100 papers on large animal med; Textbooks in large animal med. *Memberships:* World Assn for Adv'ment Vet Parasitology; Int Pig Vet Soc; Int Soc Bujatrics. *Honours:* Abildgaard Gold Medal, 250th anniversary of Fndr, Danish Vet School, 1990. *Hobbies:* Watercolour painting; Playing the flute; History esp Danish history (Viking age, late 18th century); Fly fishing. *Address:* Clinical Institute, Division of Internal Medicine, Royal Veterinary and Agricultural University, 13 Bulowsvej, DK 1870 Frederiksberg C, Denmark.

NIELSEN Palle, b. 8 Aug 1920, Copenhagen, Denmark. Graphical Artist; Professor. m. Elsa Bendixsen, 31 Apr 1946, 1 s, 1 d. *Education:* Art and Craft School, 1937-39; Royal Acad Fine Arts, 1945-47. *Career:* Freelance Artist; Prof, Graphical Dept, Royal Acad Fine Art, 1967-73; *Exhibs:* Smithsonian Fndn; Venice, Sao Paulo, Tokyo and Ljubljana Biennales; Danish State Mus Fine Arts, Copenhagen. *Creative works:* Usually interprets contemporary problems in epic series; Books on some series (graphics or drawings): Passion, 1949; The great world bunker, 1951; The soldier and the child, 1954; Orpheus and Eurydice, 1955-59; Isola, 1959-70; Nekropolis, 1970; Catalogue, 1983; Pictures of the day, 1990; Represented: Print Room, Danish State Mus Art; Several museums, Scandinavia; Victoria and Albert Museum, London; Printroom, Brit Mus. *Memberships:* Hon Mbr, Danish Acad Fine Arts, 1980; For Mbr, Swedish Acad Fine Arts. *Honours:* Premio Agenzia Giornalistica, Italy, 1958; Thorvaldsen Medal, 1963; Prince Eugen Medal, 1963; Henrik Steffen Prize, 1984; Award, 51th Triennale, New Delhi, 1986. *Address:* Caroline Amalievej 50, 2800 Lyngby, Denmark.

NIELSEN Peter Vilhelm, b. 4 Apr 1942, Hobro, Denmark. Professor of Indoor Environmental Technology. 2 s, 1 d. *Education:* MSc, Mech Engrng, 1967, PhD, 1974, Tech Univ Denmark; Imperial Coll, London, 1976-77. *Appointments:* Engr, 1967-76, 1977-85, Chief Engr, 1985-86, Ctrl Rsch Dept, Danfoss A/S; Prof, Aalborg Univ, 1986-. *Publications:* Flow in Air Conditioned Rooms, thesis, 1975; 80 papers, articles and chapts in tech books on air movement in rooms, energy flow in bldgs and control equipment. *Memberships:* Int Inst Refrigeration, Commn E1; Danish Tech Rsch Coun, Commn B; Danish Bldg Rsch Inst, Mng Bd; Danish Acad Tech Scis. *Honours:* Rockwool Prize, Dev Acoustic and Thermal Environment in Bldgs, Denmark, 1990. *Hobby:* Art. *Address:* Aalborg University, Sohngaardsholmsvej 57, DK-9000 Aalborg, Denmark.

NIEMAN Cornelis, b. 2 Mar 1924, Amsterdam, Netherlands. Biochemist. m. Greta Catharina Oosterloo, 27 Aug 1947, 2 s. *Education:* MA, Univ Amsterdam; PhD, Univ Amsterdam, 1954. *Appointments:* Asst Lab Biochem, Dept Hd, Dutch Inst Nutrition, 1949-54; Dir, Ctrl Inst Liquorice Processing Ind, Cnslr, Dutch Assn Confectionery Ind, 1955-69; Cnslr, Dutch Food Ind and Assn Glucose Mfrs, 1970-89. *Publications:* Trail leads to Paris (co-author), detective novel; Nutritive value of butter, etc, thesis; Several sci publs in Dutch, German, UK and US jrnls. *Memberships:* Royal Dutch Chem Assn; Emeritus Mbr, Inst Food Technologists. *Honours:* Grant for thesis, Nat Dairy Bd, 1954. *Hobbies:* History; Sailing. *Address:* Johannes Verhulst straat 172, 1075 HC Amsterdam, Netherlands. 43, 52.

NIEMI Mikko Ilmari, b. 13 Sept 1929, Turku, Finland. Professor of Anatomy. m. Irmeli Kuusisto, 14 Apr 1953, 1 s, 2 d. *Education:* MD, 1955; PhD, 1958. *Appointments:* Prof, Anatomy, Univ Turku, 1965-; Dir Gen, Higher Educ and Sci, Min Educ, 1973-79. *Publications:* Cell and Molecular Biology, 1989; Mors Gaudet Succurrere Vitae, 1990. *Honours:* Dr Med hc, Univs Tampere and Oulu; Dr Hlth Care hc, Univ Kuopio. *Hobbies:* Sheep keeping; Farming. *Address:* SF-21570 Sauvo, Finland.

NIENBURG George Frank, b. 14 Feb 1938, New York City, New York, USA. Nurses Aide; Photographer. *Education:* Grad, Gen Off Work, Evander Childs HS, 1956; Grad, Germain School Photography, 1989. *Appointments:* Am Soc for Prevention Cruelty to Animals, 1971-82; Ctrl Nat Investigation Agcy, 1983-88. *Memberships:* Nominating Bd Mbr, Am Biog Inst, 1988; Life Mbr, Repub Presidential Task Force, 1988; Repub Nat Comm, 1986; President's Congressional Task Force, 1990. *Honours:* Pres Ronald Reagan's Task Force Hon Roll, 1988; Pres George Bush's Hon Roll, 1989; Man of Yr Award, 1990; Nominated for Inclusion in Pres Election Registry, 1992; Com Hon Roll Comtng 10th Anniv of Repub Presdl Task Force and Regan - Bush Era, Regan - Bush Admin. *Hobbies:* Music; Photography; Bowling; Swimming; Gardening; Night clubbing; Singing; Partying; Attending meetings and lectures. *Address:* 22 Edgewood Park, Po Box 511, New Rochelle, NY 10802, USA. 6, 52, 132, 139, 152, 156.

NIEZABITOWSKI Aleksander, b. 26 July 1936, Cracow, Poland. Physician. m. Lucyna Mastor, 26 June 1962, 1 s. *Education:* Med FAc, Cracow, 1954-59; MD, Med Fac; Assoc Prof, Ctr Oncology, Warsaw, 1981. *Appointments:* Inst Pathology, Med Fac, Cracow, 1961-73; Rsch Dept, German Acad Sci, Berlin Buch, 1973-77; Hd, Pathology Dept, Ctr Oncology, Cracow, 1978-. *Publications:* Over 100 papers on tumour pathology and expmtl cancer rsch in multilingual jrnls. *Memberships:* European Assn Pathology; European Assn Cancer Rsch; Polish Soc Oncology, Pres, Cracow Br; Polish Soc Pathology. *Honours:* Polish Min Hlth Award, 1987. *Hobby:* Classical music. *Address:* Centre of Oncology, Garncarska 11, 31- 115 Cracow, Poland.

NIGAM Shyam Behart Lal, b. 7 Apr 1924, India. Retired UN Official and Consultant. m. Prem Kumari Nigam, 22 June 1946, 2 s. *Education:* MA Econ, India, 1944; MCom, 1946; PhD Econ, London Sch of Econ, London, UK, 1949. *Appointments include:* Lectr, Econ, Agra Univ, India, 1945-47; Res Scholar, London Sch of Econ, 1947-49; Lectr, Econ, Lucknow Univ, India, 1950; Hd of Dept, Univ od Sagar, India, 1951; Asst Ins Commr, Min of Labour, Govt of India, 1951-54; Asst Econ Advr, 1954-56, Dpty Econ Advr, 1957, Min of Food and Agric, New Delhi; Jd Dir, Indian Econ Ser, 1958-63. Dir, 1964, Govt of India; Intl Labour Ofc, Govt of Somalia, 1963-84. *Publications:* Papers, articles and reports to professional journals and magazines and presentations to conferences and seminars as well as Government and UN reports including: Human Resource Development and Utilisation in Sabah and Sarawak; Human resource-led growth and action plan in Malaysia. *Memberships include:* Sec, Wkg Gp on Unemployment Insurance in India, 1954; Sec, Indian Jute Enquiry Com, 1956; Adv, Land Reforms Comm, Govt of Somalia, 1956; Com of Higher Educ in Somalia, 1968; UN Task Force Mission on Rural Devel in Somalia, 1977. *Honours:* Book published by ILO/JASPA in honour, The Challenge of Employment and Basic Needs in Africa, 1986. *Address:* K-118 Hauz Khas Enclave, New Delhi 110016, India.

NIGGELING Nora, b. 12 Dec 1964, Frankfurt am Main, Germany. Musician. *Education:* Began Violin, 1975, Viola, 1978; Studies w Jrg Heyerin, Frankfurt Conservatoire, 1984; Studies w Wolfram Christm solo-violist, Berlin Phil Orch, 1987; Exam w distinction, 1990; Currently solo dip studies w Thomas Riebl, Mozarteum, Salzburg. *Career:* Mbr: Bundesjugendorch; Landesjugendorch Hessen; Mbr, Soloist, Schwanheimer Kammerorch; Mbr, Antonio String Quartet, 1981-87; Substitute, Berlin Phil Orch; Mbr, Mandelring-Quartett, 1989-, participating int competitions, disc, radio and TV recordings, tours, SE Asia, Israel, many European countries. *Honours:* Several prizes, Jugend musiziert competition, 1982-84;

Scholarship, Studienstiftung des deutschen Volkes, 1986-90; 2nd Prize w Mandelring Quartett, String Quartet Int Competition, Evian, France, and ARD Competition, Munich, 1991. *Hobbies:* Reading; Learning languages; Israeli and South American folk music. *Address:* Katernberger str 4, 5600 Wuppertal 1, Germany. 139.

NIGHTINGALE Richard Mervyn, b. 9 July 1954, Kenya. Architect. *Education:* Rugby School; Emmanuel Coll, Cambridge; BA, MA, Dip Arch, Cambridge Univ. *Appointments:* Dalgliesh Marshall, Nairobi, 1977; Var work, UK, Hong Kong, Can, 1978-81; Colin St John Wilson and Ptnrs, 1981-85; Cullum & Nightingale Archts, 1985-. *Creative work:* Exhibited and published archl work incl: House in Hampstead, 1988; New Brit High Commn, Nairobi, 1990-91. *Memberships:* Royal Inst Brit Archts. *Hobbies:* Tennis; Polo; Travel; Old cars. *Address:* 30A Parkhill Road, London NW3 2YP, England.

NIKIFOROV Ivan Nikolov, b. 14 Aug 1934, Marjan, Bulgaria. Faculty Dean; Architect; Town Planner. m. Rositza Jordanova Nikiforova, 9 July 1966, 2 d. *Education:* MArch, 1958, PhD, 1967, DSc, 1979, Univ Civil Engrng and Arch, Sofia; Postgrad, Univ Arch, Civil Engrng and Geodesy, Sofia, 1961-64. *Appointments:* Town Planning Designer, Design Bur, Plovdiv, 1958-61; Jr Rsch Assoc, Rsch Sci Inst Trade and Catering Estab, 1964-67; Asst Prof, 1967- 73, Assoc Prof, 1973-83, Hd, Dept Town Planning, 1979-, Prof, 1979-, Dean, Fac Arch, 1986-, Univ Arch, Civil Engrng and Geodesy, Sofia; Participant, 86 nat and 5 int archtl competitions. *Creative works:* Books, articles: Shops- Design and Equipment, 1971; Supermarkets-Design and Equipment, 1974; Catering Establishments, 1976; Shopping Centers, 1979; Town Planning, 1982; Renovation of Old Shopping and Residential Streets and Quarters in Town Centers, 1982; Art Synthesis in Urban Environment, 1985; Renovation of Town Centers, 1988; Over 80 articles on design, dev planning, town planning and educ in Bulgarian mags; Projects: Plans, over 30 Bulgarian towns, town ctrs, sts, pedestrian sts and sqs, shopping and residential complexes, monuments; Currently Caninda New Town, Angola. *Memberships:* Union Archts Bulgaria; Int Union Archts; Union Scis Bulgaria. *Honours:* 3rd Prize, Arch, Bulgaria, 1969; 2nd Prize, Koljo Ficheto Silver Medal, 1971; 2nd Prize, Int Competition, Town Ctr Karlsruhe, Germany, 1972; 3rd Nat Prize, Creative Works, 1976; National Award, Archtl Book, 1978; Urbanism Award, World Biennale Arch, Sofia, 1985; 1st Nat Prize, Urbanism, Best Project, 1989. *Hobbies:* Painting; Drawing; Skiing. *Address:* Milevska planina 16, Sofia 1407, Bulgaria.

NIKIFOROVA Diljana Ivanova, b. 10 Mar 1973, Sofia, Bulgaria. Ballet Dancer. *Education:* Student of Prima Ballerina K A Koldamova, grad, State Choreographic School, Sofia Nat Opera, 1983-91; Dip, studied w T Dalberg, B Felixdal, H Vogl, Int Summer Ballet Acad, 1991. *Career:* Danced: Variations, in Pachita, Florina, Lilac Fairy in The Sleeping Beauty, 1988; Aurora in The Sleeping Beauty, 1989-91; Pas-de-deux in Don Quichote Act 4, Festival of the Flowers in Genzano, Peasant, Pas-de-deux, Pas- de-deux of Giselle and Albert Act 2 in The Waves of Valencia, The Leaves are Fading, Pas-de-deux Odile in Swan Lake, 1990; Variation in Esmeralda, Sylphida in Sylphida Act 2, 1991; Appeared as Guest Artist, Austria, Cyprus, France, Yugoslavia, Japan. *Honours:* Token Award, 3rd Creative Meeting of Young Ballet Dancers, 1988, 1st Prize, 4th Creative Meeting Young Ballet Dancers, 1989, Tolbuchin, Bulgaria; Youth Prize, Classical Choreography Perf, Meeting of Young Dancers, La Baule, France, 1989; 3rd Class Distinction, Jrs, 14th Int Ballet Competition, Varna, 1990; Silver Medal, NY Int Ballet Competition, 1990; Finalist, 4th Eurovision Competition for Young Dancers, Helsinki, 1991. *Hobbies:* Architecture; Literature; Skiing; Swimming. *Address:* Milevska Planina Str 16, Sofia 1407, Bulgaria.

NIKKEL Ronald Wilbert, b. 8 June 1946, Canada. Chief Operative Officer (President). m. Celeste Friesen, 11 June 1970. *Education:* BA, Univ Winnipeg, 1970; Univ Lethbridge, 1971-73; York Univ, 1976-77; MPS, Loyola Univ, USA, 1983. *Appointments:* Researcher, Psychology, Univ Lethbridge, 1972-73; Youth Guidance, YFC, 1973-82; Prison Fellowship Int, 1982-. *Publications:* Self Help Employment Projects (ed), 1980; Volunteer Mobilization, 1981; Child Abuse and Neglect, 1982; Guidelines for Justice Volunteerism (ed), 1986. *Memberships:* Int Assn Justice Volunteerism, VO 1983-85; NGO Alliance Criminal Justice, UN, NY, Chmn 1987-. *Hobbies:* Mountain hiking; Canoeing; Gardening; Reading; Writing; Collecting old books (religion, theology). *Address:* PO Box 17434, Washington, DC 20041, USA.

NIKOLOVA Milka, b. 4 Nov 1933, Sofia, Bulgaria. Professor of Pharmacology. m. Tihomir Vasilev Katzarov, 7 Nov 1970, 1 d. *Education:* Higher Med School, Sofia, 1951-57; MD, 1958; Neuropsychopharmacology specialisation w Prof P B Bradley, Birmingham, England, 1965; PhD, 1967; DSc, 1982; Rsch Prof, 1983. *Appointments:* Pharmacologist, Chem Pharm Factory, 1958-60; Sci Rsch Worker, 1960-, Chief, Medico-Biological Dept, 1973- 88, VP Sci, 1989-, Chem-Pharm Rsch Inst, Sofia; Sci Advsr for PhD and postgrad courses. *Publications:* Over 380 sci publs; Co-author, 7 monographs; 27 reviews; Over 50 reports at int sci forums; Monographs incl pharmacology of cerebral blood flow and of pain. *Memberships:* Bulgarian Soc Pharmacology; Int Brain Rsch Org; Collegium Int Neuro-psycho-pharmacology; European Brain Behaviour Soc; Cerebral Blood Flow and Metabolism; Ed Bd, jrnls: Drugs of Today, Drugs of the Future, Methods and Findings, Medical Archives, Medical Biological Information. *Honours:* Gold Medal of Labour, 1981. *Hobbies:* Tourism esp climbing mountains; Music; theatre. *Address:* Chemical Pharmaceutical Research Institute, Sofia, Bulgaria.

NIKULA Henrik Viking, b. 6 May 1942, Abo, Finland. Associate Professor of Germanic Philology. m. Kristina Birgitta Norrholm, 29 July 1967. *Education:* MA, Abo Akademi, 1969; Dr phil, Univ Uppsala, Sweden, 1976. *Appointments:* Tchr, Swedish, Uppsala, Sweden, 1970-73; Acting Assoc Prof, German, Univ Vaasa, Finland, 1976-77; Acting Full Prof, German, Abo Akademi, 1977-78; Rsch Asst, Acad Finland, 1978-79; Assoc Prof, Germanic Philology, Univ Turku, 1979-92; Full Prof of the German Lang, Univ Vassa. *Publications:* Verbvalenz, 1976; Kontextuell und lexikalisch bedingte Ellipse, 1978; Dependensgrammatik, 1986; Warum sind literarische Texte linguistisch interessant, 1990. *Hobbies:* Photography; Literature. *Address:* University of Vassa, Institute for German Language and Literature, PO Box 297, SF-65101 Vassa, Finland.

NILSSON Bo Ingvar, b. 15 Sept 1947, Sweden. Medical Doctor; Director Medical Affairs; Oncology. m. Elsa S V Warkander, 20 Aug 1971, 1 s, 2 d. *Education:* MD, 1973, ECFMG, 1975, PhD, 1985, Univ Lund; Bd Certification: Internal Med, 1978, Haematology, 1980. *Appointments:* Var positions, 1972-76; Dept Internal Med, Univ Hosp, Lund, 1976-83; Dept Int Med, Helsingborg, 1983-86; Med Dir, Oncology, 1986-88, Rsch Dir, Oncology, 1989-91, Kabi Pharmacia, Helsingborg; Director, Medical Affairs, 1992-. *Publications:* Num articles and sci presentations in haematology and oncology: regulation of proliferation and differentiation, differentiation induction, chemotherapy, immunomodulation. *Memberships:* European Soc Med Oncology; Swedish Soc Oncology; Swedish Soc Haematology; NY Acad Scis; Am Assn Adv Scis; Swedish Soc Pharm Physns. *Hobbies:* Family life; Reading. *Address:* Kabi Pharmacia Therapeutics, Box 941, S-25109 Helsingborg, Sweden. 52.

NIMBKAR Nandini, b. 30 June 1954, Tucson, Arizona, USA. Agricultural Scientist. m. Anil Kumar Rajvanshi, 12 Dec 1976, 2 d. *Education:* BSc, Bot, Univ Poona,

Pune, India, 1974; MS, Agronomy, 1978, PhD, Agronomy, 1981, Univ FL, USA. *Appointments:* Rsch Scientist, 1981-84, Dir, 1984-90, Pres, 1990-, Nimbkar Agricl Rsch Inst, India. *Memberships:* Indian Soc Agronomy; Am Soc Agronomy; Am Soc Hort Scis; Nitrogen Fixing Tree Assn. *Honours:* Invited Expert to Prosopis germ plasm workshop, Mendoza, Argentina, sponsored by Int Dev Rsch Ctr, Can, 1991. *Hobbies:* Reading; Music; Gardening; Travel. *Address:* PO Box 44, Phaltan 415523, Maharashtra, India.

NIMMO Derek Robert, b. 19 Sept 1932, London, England. Actor; Producer; Author. m. Patricia Sybil Ann Brown, 9 Apr 1955, 2 s, 1 d. *Career:* 1st appearance, Ensign Blades in Quality Street, Bolton Hippodrome, 1952; Stage appearances incl: Waltz of The Toreadors, Criterion, 1957; Duel of Angels, Apollo, 1958; The Amorous Prawn, Savill, 1959; See How They Run, Vaudeville, 1964; Charlie Girl, Appolo, 1965-71, overseas, 1975; Why Not Stay for Breakfast, Apollo, 1973, overseas, 1975; See How They Run, A Friend Indeed, Shaftesbury, 1984; The Cabinet Minister, Albany, 1991-92; TV series incl: All Gas and Gaiters, Oh Brother, Oh Father, Sorry I'm Single, The Bed Sit Girl, My Honourable Mrs, The World of Wooster, Blandings Castle, Life Begins at Forty, Third Time Lucky, Hell's Bells, If It's Saturday It Must Be Nimmo, Just a Nimmo; Films incl: Casino Royale, The Amorous Prawn, The Bargee, Joey Boy, A Talent for Loving, The Liquidator, Tamahine, One of our Dinosaurs is Missing; Radio: Just a Minute, 1967-93; Produced and appeared in num prods, touring worldwide for Intercontinental Entertainments. *Publications:* Books: Derek Nimmo's Drinking Companion, 1979; Shaken and Stirred, 1984; Oh Come All Ye Faithful, 1986; Not In Front Of The Servants, 1987; Up Mount Everest Without A Paddle, 1988; As The Actress Said To The Bishop, 1989; Table Talk, 1990; Memorable Dinners, 1991. *Memberships:* Clubs: Garrick; Athenaeum, Liverpool; Lords Taveners; Beafsteak. *Hobbies:* Sailing; Travel; Horse racing. *Address:* Field House, Easton Maudit, Northamptonshire, England. 1.

NISH Ian Hill, b. 3 June 1926, Edinburgh, Scotland. Professor of International History. m. Rona Margaret Speirs, 29 Dec 1965, 2 d. *Education:* MA, Univ Edinburgh; MA, PhD, School Oriental and African Studies, Univ London. *Appointments:* Army Serv, 1944-48; Univ Sydney, NSW, Australia, 1958-62; London School Econs, England, 1962-. *Publications:* Anglo-Japanese Alliance, 1964; Alliance in Decline, 1972; Anglo-Japanese Alienation, 1978; Origins of Russo-Japanese War, 1984; European Studies on Japan, 1987. *Memberships:* Brit Assn Japanese Studies, Pres 1979-80; European Assn Japanese Studies, Pres 1985-88. *Honours:* CBE, 1990; Order of the Rising Sun, 1991. *Hobbies:* Golf; Music; Tennis. *Address:* Oakdene, Charlwood Drive, Oxshott, Surrey KT22 OHB, England.

NISHIKAWA Jun, b. 22 Sept 1936, Taipeh, Formosa. Professor of Economics. 2 s. *Education:* MA, Grad School Econs, Waseda Univ; Dip, Ecole Pratique des Hautes Etudes, Paris. *Appointments:* Prof, Waseda Univ, Tokyo, 1977-; Rsch Fellow, UN Inst Trng and Rsch, 1981-83; Vis Prof, Univ Paris I, France, 1989. *Publications:* ASEAN and the United Nations System, 1984; Challenge of Asian Developing Countries (co-author), 1989. *Memberships:* Dir, Peace Studies Assn; Dir, Japanese Assn Int Economy; Dir, Japan Soc Int Dev; Exec Dir, CIRIEC, Japanese Sect. *Honours:* Chevalier, Ordre des Palmes Academique, France, 1990. *Hobbies:* Gardening; Tennis; Swimming; Travel. *Address:* 4-5-4 Asagaya-Kita, Suginami-ku, Tokyo 166, Japan.

NISHIMOTO Nobushige, b. 19 Oct 1929, Osaka, Japan. University Professor. m. Itsuyo Iwakiri, 28 Dec 1959, 2 s. *Education:* Dr Pharm Sci, Tohuku Univ, Sendai, 1968. *Appointments:* Asst Researcher, Osaka Univ, 1951-58; Nat Inst Hygienic Sci, 1958-63; Rohto Pharm Co Ltd, 1963-83; Prof, Tokushima Bunri Univ, Tokushima, 1983-. *Creative works:* Articles in profl jrnls;

1st in world to isolate insect moulting hormones from plant kingdom, 1966. *Hobbies:* Mountain walking; Reading; Gardening. *Address:* 5-7-209 Shinkanaoka-cho, Sakai, Osaka, Japan.

NJEMOGA-KOLAR Ana, b. 5 July 1951, Padina, Yugoslavia. Senior Television Journalist. m. Samo Kolar, 5 Apr 1980. *Education:* Grad, Slovak Lang and Lit, Fac Philos, Univ Novi Sad, 1975. *Appointments:* Jr Jrnlst, Radio Novi Sad, 1976-81; Sr Jrnlst, TV Novi Sad, 1981-. *Creative works:* Children's radio and mag short stories incl: Olivera; The New Theatre Lovers; Radio plays incl: The Departure of Mr Toma; An Unsuccessful Experiment; Children's radio plays incl: The Inverted Case; Love; TV and theatre plays incl: Silentsmallcreaturethatlikestodream. *Memberships:* Vojvodina Assn Jrnslts; Vojvodina Assn Writers. *Honours:* 2nd Prize, Best Yugoslav Children's Radio Play, The Street of Pearly Glow, Radio Sarajevo, 1987; 2nd Prize: Best Children's Radio Story, Olivera, 1988, Children's Radio Story, At My Desk, 1989, Radio Novi Sad; 2nd Prize, Best Children's Story, The Story with Happy End, Children's Mag Pioneers, 1989; 1st Prize, Children's Theatre Creation, Silentsmallcreaturethatlikestodream, Serbian Children's Theatre Creation Fest, 1990. *Hobbies:* Reading; Guitar playing; Spending time with friends. *Address:* Vojvode Misica 32, 21000 Novi Sad, Yugoslavia.

NKOGO ONDO Eugenio, b. 18 Oct 1944, Bibas, Rio Muni, E G, Spain. Professor in Philosophy; Investigator; Writer. m. Isolina Robles Diez, 3 Dec 1977, 2 d. *Education:* MPhil, 1973, DPhil, 1975, Complutense Univ Madrid; Postdoct rsch, Univ Paris-Sorbonne, 1976. *Appointments:* Lectr, Univ Ghana, Accra, Legon, 1978-80; Private Rsch, Univ of Delaware, Newark and Georgetown, Wash DC, USA, 1980-81; Lectr, Univ Coll, León, 1981-82; Prof, Philos, Instit of Baccalaureate, 1983-, Leon, Spain. *Publications:* El problema humano, 1985; Sobre las ruinas de la republica de Ghana, 1988; La encerrona, 1991; La aldea encontrada, 1992; Rsch books: El especto etico y social del existencialismo, 1982; El metodo filosofico en Jean-Paul Sartre, 1983; La trascendencia en la noche oscura, 1989. *Hobbies:* Reading; Travel. *Address:* San Guillermo 34 6o C, 24006 Leon, Spain.

NMOR Isusu Edwin, b. 25 Oct 1955, Ogume, Nigeria. Architect. m. Mabel Nmor, 13 Apr 1984, 2 d. *Education:* St George's Coll, Obinomba, 1971-75; Univ Nigeria, Nsukka, 1977-83. *Appointments:* Tutor, Ogume Grammar School, Ogume, 1975-76; Youth Corper Ldr, Inst Mgmt and Technology, Enugu, Sept 1983; Youth Corper Arch, Fed Min Works and Housing HQ, Lagos, 1983-84; Arch, Min Works and Transport, Benin City, 1986-. *Creative works:* Uwelu Youth Centre, Benin City; Monumental gate for specialist hosp, Irrua, Edo State; Tourist Centre, Ossoso, Edo State. *Membership:* Nigerian Inst Archts. *Honours:* Govt Scholarship, 1973-75; 6th Place Prize, Sea-Mole Design Presentation, Nat Assn Arch Students Competition, 1981-82. *Hobbies:* Sports; football, boxing, swimming; Reading spiritual books and scientific magazines; Travel and sightseeing. *Address:* PMB 3670, Benin City, Edo State, Nigeria.

NOBRE Fernando Jose de la Vieter Ribeiro, b. 16 Dec 1951, Luanda, Angola. Medical Doctor; General Surgeon; Urologist. m. Daniele Focquet, 3 Sept 1977, 1 s, 1 d. *Education:* MD, 1978, Gen Surg, 1983, Urologist, 1986, Brussels. *Appointments:* Univ Hosps, Brussels, Belgium, 1978-86; Asst Prof, Anatomy and Human Embryology, Fac Med, Brussels, 1980-86; Adminstr, Medecins sans Frontieres, Brussels, 1980-84; Fndr, Pres, Int Med Assistance Fndn, Lisbon, Portugal, 1982-92; Med Specialist, pvte Med, Portugal. *Memberships:* European Assn Urology; Soc Royale Belge de Cirurgie; Portuguese Assn Urology; Portguese Non-Govtl Deleg, EEC. *Honours:* Prize, European Assn Urology, 1984; Hon Mbr, Lions Club, 1989; Grande Oficial, Ordem Nacional do Merito, Portugal, 1991;

Refused Pax Mundi Prize and Dag Hammarskjold Medal for Humanitarian Work in favour of Medecins sans Frontieres, France, 1983. *Hobbies:* Tennis; History; Reading; Karate; Special interest in humanitarian assistance: medical help missions, Iran, Lebanon, Chad, India, Zaire, Rumania, Jordan, Angola, Mozambique, Guinea, S Tome, Principe, Cabo-Verde, Ecuador. *Address:* Largo D Joao II no 3, 8500 Portimao, Portugal. 52.

NOBRE Marlos, b. 18 Feb 1939, Recife, Brazil. Composer; Pianist; Conductor. m. Maria Luiza Corker-Nobre, 1 July 1982. *Education:* Grad, Piano, Theory, Music Conservatory, Pernambuco, 1955; Grad, Harmony, Counterpoint, Ernani Braga Inst, 1959; Composition w H J Koellreuter and Camrago Guarnieri, 1960-61, w Messiaen and Ginastera, 1963-64; Berkshire Music Ctr, Tanglewood, 1969; Electronic Music, Columbia-Princeton Electronic Music Ctr, 1969. *Career:* Musical Dir, Radio MEC, 1961; Conductor, Nat Symph Orch, Brazil, 1963-76; 1st Dir, Nat Inst Music, 1976-79; Pres, Brazilian Music Comm, 1975-; Composer-in-Residence: Brahms-Haus, Baden-Baden, FRG, 1980-81; Berlin, FRG, 1982-83; NYC, 1985-86; Vis Prof, Yale Univ, USA, 1992-; Participant, num Int Fests, France, England, Finland, Austria, Netherlands, Spain, Switzerland, FRG, Poland, USA, Venezuela, PR, Cuba, Mexico; Pianist, Conductor, var orchs; Mbr, Int Jury, var int competitions. *Creative works:* Num compositions incl: Convergencias for orch, 1968; Ludus Instrumentalis for chamber orch, 1969; Concerto breve for piano and orch, 1969; Biosfera for string orch, 1970; In Memoriam for orch, 1973; Concerto for string orch II, 1981; Cantata do Chimbarazo for soloist, choir and orch, 1982; Christopher Columbus, cantata; Instrumental and chamber works. *Memberships:* Int Music Coun, UNESCO, Pres 1986-87; Brazilian Acad Music, Pres 1985-. *Honours include:* Music and Musicians Brazil Award, 1960; Broadcasting Music Inc Award, NYC, 1961; Jeunesses Musicales Int Prize, 1962; Rockefeller Fndn Scholarship, 1963; Nat Composers Contest, Brazil, 1963; IMC/UNESCO TIC Prize, 1974; Oliveira Lima Gold Medal of Cultural Merit, Pernambuco, 1978; TIMALCA Prize, 1979; Grand Off, Brasilia Order of Merit, 1988; Off, Rio Branco Order, 1989; Off, Guarapes Order of Merit, Pernambuco. *Hobbies:* Fishing; Theatre; Swimming. *Address:* Rua Pres Carlos de Campos 115 B1 02, apt 902, ZC 22231 Rio de Janeiro, RJ, Brazil. 21, 52.

NOCOL Dominik, b. 25 Sept 1930, Oltenia, Rumania. Writer; Photographer. *Education:* Baccalaureat Dip, Lyceum Rm Valcea, 1949; Dip, Chem, Antibiotic Techniques, Tech School Antibiotics, Bucharest, 1954. *Appointments:* Photo-Reporter, Agerpress, Bucharest, 1950-51; Med Photographer, Cantacuzino Hosp, Bucharest, 1955-68; Freelance Photographer, NYC, USA, 1969-. *Creative works include:* Original icons painted in oils on canvas, exhibited Trinity Ch, NYC, 1975; Books: Self encounter, 1979; Vacuum (Colucviu de abis), play, 1979; Ten oneiric sketches, 1980; Rendez-Vous sau Intalnire cu mine insumi, 1987; VacuumVoid, play, Bilingual Ed, 1988; Poetry, essays, sketches. *Hobbies:* Painting; Ancient history. *Address:* PO Box 411, Times Square Sta, New York, NY 10108, USA.

NODEL Roman, b. 10 Feb 1942, Tchusovoj, USSR. Music Professor; Violinist. m. Vera Kramarova, 31 Mar 1965, 1 s, 1 d. *Education:* Studied w A Tushmalov, Music School, Dnepropetrovsk, Ukraine, 1948-56; Studied w D Tsyganov: Ctrl Special Music School, Tchaikovsky Conservatory, Moscow, 1956-60, Tchaikovsky Conservatory, Moscow, 1960-67. *Career:* Concert Soloist and Tchr, State Conservatory, Minsk, 1967-80; Emigrated to FRG, 1980; 1st Concertmaster, State Orch, Lower Saxony, 1980-88; Prof, Musikhochschule, Heidelberg-Mannheim, 1989-; Concert series: The History of Violin Concertos (18 concertos), 1973-75; All Mozart's Violin Concertos, 1978; All Beethoven's Violin Sonatas w Prof Michael Voskressensky, 1980. *Honours:* 1st Prize, Gold Medal, Int Competition, VIIIth Youth Fest,

Helsinki, 1962; 4th Prize, Jacques Thibaud Competition, Paris, 1963; Prize, 1st Violin Competition, Montreal, Can, 1966; 4th Prize, Silver Medal, Queen Elisabeth Competition, Brussels, Belgium, 1967; Harriet Cohen Medal, 1967. *Address:* Musikhochschule Heidelberg-Mannheim N 7, 18, 6800 Mannheim, Germany.

NOEL Emile Ernest, b. 17 Nov 1922, Istanbul, Turkey. President of the European University Institute. m. Lise Durand, 1946, dec. 1985, 2 d. *Education:* Ecole Normale Superieure, Paris, 1941-45; Degrees, Sci and Maths, Univ Paris, 1943. *Appointments:* Sec, Gen Affairs Comm, 1949-52; Chief of Cabinet to Pres, 1954-56; Consultative Assembly, Coun Europe; Dir, Constitutional Commn, Assembly for European Pol Community, 1952-54; Dpty Dir, Cabinet to Pres, Coun Mins, Paris, 1956-57; Exec Sec, Commn European Econ Community, Brussels, 1958-67; Sec-Gen, Commn European Communities, Brussels, 1968-87; Pres, European Univ Inst, Florence, Italy, 1987-. *Publications:* Le Comite des Representants permanents, 1966; Working together, 1975; Les Rouages de l'Europe, 1976; The Single European Act (Government and Opposition - London), 1988. *Honours:* Dr hc: Ireland, 1981; Edinburgh, 1982; Urbino, 1987; Marmara, Turkey, 1988; Ritsumeikan-Kyoto, Japan, 1989; Braga, Portugal, 1990; Georgetown, Wash DC, 1991; Hon Sec Gen, Commn European Communities, 1987; Hon Prof: Fudan and Sichuan Univs, 1988; Free Univ Brussels, 1990. *Address:* European University Institute, Badia Fiesolana, Via dei Roccettini 5, I-50016 Sam Domenico di Fiesole, Italy. 34, 52, 91.

NOGUCHI Shun, b. 28 Jan 1930, Tokyo, Japan. Professor of Chemistry. m. Etsuko Sahashi, 16 Nov 1956, 3 d. *Education:* BS, 1952, Doct, 1961, Univ Tokyo. *Appointments:* Rsch Worker, Mitsuwa Soap Co, 1952-65; Asst Univ Tokyo, 1965-70; Lectr, Tokyo Univ Agric, 1968-70, 1988-; Asst Prof, 1970-74, Prof, 1974-, Kyoritsu Women's Univ, Tokyo. *Publications:* Water Behavior on Cooking, 1978; Food Science in Relation to Water, 1992; Contbr, articles to profl jrnls on soap, fats and oils, water in foods, 1957-. *Memberships:* Chem Soc Japan; Japan Soc Biosci, Biotechnology and Agrochem; Japan Sc Home Econs, Dir 1978-79, 1980-84, 1986-90, 1992-; Japan Soc Sci of Cookery. *Honours:* Prize for Excellent Treatises, Japan Assn Fats and Oils Ind, 1964; Prize for Excellent Treatises, Japan Soc Home Econs, 1989. *Hobbies:* Tennis; Music; Gardening. *Address:* Kyoritsu Women's University, 1- 710 Motohachioji, Hachioji, Tokyo 193, Japan. 52.

NOLTE Ernst Hermann, b. 11 Jan 1923, Witten, Germany. Professor. Professor Emeritus. m. Annedore Mortier, 4 Mar 1956, 1 s, 1 d. *Education:* Dr phil, Univ Freiburg, 1952; Prof, Univ Marburg, 1965. *Appointments:* Prof, Mod Hist, Univ Marburg; Prof, Mod Hist, Free Univ Berlin. *Publications:* Der Faschismus in seiner Epoche, 1963, Engl Ed, Three Faces of Fascism, 1965, translations into Italian, French, Spanish, Serbian; Deutschland und der Kalte Krieg, 1974; Marxismus und industrielle Revolution, 1983; Der europeische Burgerkrieg, 1917-1945, 1987, translation into Italian; Geschichtsdenken im 20 Jahrhundred, 1991. *Memberships:* Berliner Wissenschaftliche Gesellschaft; Chmn, Dept Hist, Free Univ Berlin, 1976-78; Historische Kommission; PEN Zentrum. *Honours:* Hanns Martin Schleyer Prize, 1986. *Address:* Bambergerstr 32, 1000 Berlin 30, Germany. 2, 52, 92.

NONUS Maurice Joseph Antoine, b. 7 Jan 1954, France. Engineer; Researcher. *Education:* MSc, 1976; PhD, 1982. *Appointments:* Adour-Spechim, 1978-82; Compiegne Univ, 1982-88; Rhone-Poulenc, 1988-91. *Publications:* Sci publs in biotechnology field. *Memberships:* Societe de Genie Chimique, France; Societe de Microbiologie, France. *Honours:* French Distillers Soc, 1985; UNGDA. *Hobbies:* Archery; Books; Cycling; Diving. *Address:* Domaine de Rimberlieu, 9 Voie d' Offement, 60150 Villers sur Coudun, France.

NOOTENBOOM Pieter, b. 20 July 1947, Driebergen, Netherlands. Managing Partner of Jewellery Shop. m. Winnie Lee-Bing Tao, 25 Aug 1973, 1 stepson, 1 stepdaughter. *Education:* Ctrl School Arts and Crafts, London. *Appointments:* Tech Dir, Cartier Hong Kong, 1970-71; Mng Ptnr, Chaumont Hong Kong, 1971-. *Memberships:* FRSA; Fellow, Inst Dirs; Fellow, Brit Inst Mgmt; Fndg Comm Mbr, Past Hon Sec, Past Jrnl Ed, Gemmological Assn Hong Kong; Elected Rep, Jewellery Shops Owners Comm Retailers, Hong Kong Tourist Assn; Heraldry Soc; Bookplate Soc; Hong Kong Rifle Assn; Manorial Soc; Sub-Comm Mbr, Hallmarking Order Sub-Comm, Hong Kong Customs and Excise Dept; City Livery Club. *Honours:* Freeman, Worshipful Co Clockmakers, 1989; Freeman, Worshipful Co Goldsmiths; Freeman, City of London, 1990. *Hobbies:* Reading, Gardening, Heraldry, Music, Shooting, Sculpting. *Address:* Lion Villa, Lot 951 in DD 369, Pak Tam Chung, Sai Kung Country Park, NT, Hong Kong. 191.

NORDENSTAM Tore Sigvard, b. 2 Dec 1934, Nykoping, Sweden. Professor of Philosophy. m. Ruth Milde, 20 Oct 1989, 1 s, 2 d. *Education:* BA, 1956, MA, 1961, PhD, 1961, Univ Gothenburg; PhD, Univ Khartoum, 1965. *Appointments:* Lectr, Univ Khartoum, Sudan, 1961-66; Lectr, Univ Umea, Sweden, 1966-68; Prof, Philosophy, Univ Bergen, Norway, 1968-; Vis Prof, Theory of Arch, Royal Tech Inst, Stockholm, Sweden, 1990-93. *Publications:* Sudanese Ethics, 1968; From Art to Science, 1987; Other books; Contbr, articles to profl jrnls. *Honours:* Alexander von Humboldt Rsch Fellow, FRG, 1973, 1975, 1980. *Hobbies:* Art; Music; Swimming; Skiing; Cycling. *Address:* Dept of Philosophy, University of Bergen, Sydnesplass 9, N-5007 Bergen, Norway. 52, 162.

NORDSTROM Carl-Otto, b. 20 Mar 1916, Stockholm, Sweden. Professor. m. Harriet Holmqvist, 4 Sept 1948. *Education:* MTh, 1945; DPhil, 1953. *Appointments:* Assoc Prof, Hist of Arts, 1953; Prof hc, 1978. *Publications:* Ravennastudien, 1953; The Duke of Alba's Castilian Bible, 1967. *Honours:* Imagines Medievales, Festschrift Nordstrom. *Address:* Torsgatan 8B, S-75315 Uppsala, Sweden.

NORFOLK Jeremy Paul, b. 7 Mar 1948, Oxford, England. Banker. m. Rosemary Frances Raffan, 20 July 1972, 1 s, 1 d. *Education:* MA, Aberdeen Univ, 1972. *Appointments:* Bell Lawrie Robertson & Co, 1973-75; Citibank, 1975-83; Co-Fndr, 1983-91, Mng Dir, 1988-91, Adam & Co. *Hobbies:* Gardening; Golf; Tennis. *Address:* 8 Henderland Road, Edinburgh EH12 6BB, Scotland. 53.

NORMAN Herbert John La French (John), b. 15 Jan 1932, Hornsey, Middlesex, London. Consultant. m. Jill Frances Sharp, 11 Aug 1956, 1 s, 2 d. *Education:* Imperial Coll, London Univ, 1950-53; BSc (Hons), Phys, 1953; Assoc, Royal Coll Sci, 1953. *Appointments:* Wm Hill & Son and Norman & Beard Ltd, 1953-74, incl Dir, 1961-74, Mng Dir, 1970-74; Responsible for work on organs in cathedrals, Gloucester, Norwich, Lichfield, Chelmsford, Brisbane, also instruments, Bath Abbey, Southwell Minster, Royal Coll Organists; IBM UK Ltd, 1974-90; Organ Cons, 1974-, incl: Harrow School, Lancing Coll, Mill Hill School, Sherborne Abbey, Stratford-on-Avon Parish Ch, Liberal Jewish Synagogue, St John's Wood; Cons, Skillbase Ltd, 1991-. *Publications:* The Organ Today, 1966, Revised Ed, 1980; The Organs of Britain, 1984; Sandboard column in The Organist's Review, 1980-; Ed: Music Instrument Technology, 1969-; The Organbuilder, 1983-. *Memberships:* Fellow, Past Pres, Coun Mbr, Inst Musical Instrument Technology; Fellow, Inc Soc Organbuilders; London Guildhall Univ Music Technology Consultative Comm; Coun for Care of Chs, Organs Advsry Comm; London Diocesan Advsry Comm; Cathedrals Fabric Commn England; Freeman, City of London; Liveryman, Worshipful Co Musicians. *Hobbies:* Writing about Organs, Listening to Music. *Address:* 15 Baxendale, London N20 0EG, England.

NORN Mogens Stig, b. 25 Feb 1925, Aarhus, Denmark. Ophthalmologist; Professor of Ophthalmology. m. Inger Gelius, 27 Jan 1951, 1 s, 1 d. *Education:* Grad, Med, 1951, Specialist Ophthalmology, 1958, MD, 1960, Univ Copenhagen. *Appointments:* Chief Surg, Eye Dept, Copenhagen Municipal Hosp, 1966-89; Asst Prof, 1971-75, Prof, Ophthalmology, 1975-89, Univ Copenhagen; Chief Ed, Acta Ophthalmologica, 1975-88. *Publications:* Cytology of conjunctiva, thesis, 1960; External Eye, Scriptor, 2nd Ed 1983; Several books; 250 sci papers. *Memberships:* Danish Ophthalmological Soc; Med Histl Museum, Univ Copenhagen. *Honours:* Hans Rasmussen, Falkenberg Prize, 1964; KKK Lundsgaard Prize and Gold Medal, 1973; Victor Larsen Prize, 1981. *Hobbies:* Greenland (Ophthalmic Surgeon, 10 periods, 1975-91); Ophthalmic history (Adviser, Medical Historical Museum, University of Copenhagen). *Address:* Klovervej 15, DK 3600 Frederikssund, Denmark.

NORRIE William, b. 21 Jan 1929, St Boniface, Manitoba, Canada. Mayor of City of Winnipeg. m. Helen Isobel Scurfield, 20 Aug 1955, 3 s. *Education:* BA, United Coll Univ Man, 1950; Queen's Coll, Oxford, England, 1953; LLB, Univ Man Law School, 1955. *Appointments:* Articled, Sir Charles Tupper, 1950; Joined, 1955, Ptnr, 1961, Tupper Adams & ADams, 1955; Mortgage Investment Mgr, Monarcvh Life Assurance Co, 1963; Ptnr, Richardson, Richardson, Huband, Wright & Norrie, 1964; Sr Ptnr, Richardson & Co; Appted Dpty Sec, Law Soc Man, 1975; QC, 1977; Dpty Mayor, 1977, Mayor, 1979-, City of Winnipeg. *Memberships:* Trustee, Sir William Stephenson Scholarship Trust, Univ Winnipeg; Former Mbr, Past Chmn, Winnipeg School Bd; Man Rhodes Scholarship Selection Comm; United Ch Can; Former Mbr, Nat Commn on Ch Union; Past Chmn, Bd of Regents, Univ Winnipeg; Dir, Past Pres, Winnipeg Conven Ctr Corp; Life Mbr, Past Pres, Man Assn School Trustees. *Honours:* Legion Hon Degree, Can Order of Demolay; Hon Mbr, Carpenters Union; Rhodes Scholar, Man; Friendship Medal, Repub of Philippines; Overseas Friendship Medal, Repub of China; B.nai B'rith Humanitarian Award; Shevchenko Medal, Ukrainian Can Comm; Hon LLD, Univ Winnipeg, 1981; Citizen of Yr Award, Winnipeg Chinese Community, 1991. *Hobbies:* Swimming; Camping. *Address:* 212 Waverley Street, Winnipeg, Manitoba, Canada R3M 3L2. 142.

NORTHMORE-BALL Martin Dacre, b. 14 Feb 1943, Plymouth, England. Consultant Orthopaedic Surgeon. m. Averina Constance Frances Knowles, 26 July 1969, 2 s, 1 d. *Education:* Scholar, Clifton Coll; King's Coll, Cambridge; BA, 1965, MA, 1968, Cambridge Univ; MB, BChir, St Thomas's Hosp Med School, 1968; FRCS; CIMechE. *Appointments:* Jr posts, Nat Hlth Serv; Orthopaedic Registrar, Charing Cross and King's Coll Hosps, London, 1973-76; Orthopaedic Registrar, 1976-78, Sr Registrar, 1978-79, 1979-81, Addenbrooke's Hosp, Cambridge; Clin Fellow, Orthopaedics, Univ Toronto, Can, 1978-79; Currently Cons Orthopaedic Surg, Dir, Unit for Joint Reconstruction, Robert Jones and Agnes Hunt Orthopaedic Hosp, Oswestry, and Cons Orthopaedic Surg, Leighton Hosp, Crewe, Cheshire. *Contributions to:* profl jrnls mainly on surg of the adult hip and knee. *Memberships:* Brit Med Assn; Fellow, Brit Orthpaedic Assn; Fndr Mbr, Brit Hip Soc. *Honours:* Exhib in Maths, Kings Coll, Cambridge, 1961; Zimmer Travelling Fellowship, 1985. *Hobbies:* Study of antiquities; Mechanics; Books; Travel. *Address:* Higher Grange, Ellesmere, Shropshire SY12 9DH, England.

NORTON Rita Faye, b. 29 July 1949, Miami, Florida, USA. Attorney. m. Scott Frederic Rosenberg, 3 Aug 1988. *Education:* BEd, 1971, JD, 1974, Univ Miami, Coral Gables; Admitted FL Bar. *Appointments:* Law Clerk, Am Agronomics, Miami, FL, 1974; Attorney, Law Offices of Henry Norton, Miami, 1974-. *Publications:* Articles in Am Bar Assn's Family Law Newsletter and

Univ Miami School of Law's Barrister mag. *Memberships:* Dade Co Bar Assn, Probate and Real Property Comms; Phi Delta Phi, Past Histn Bryan Inn Chapt; Heritage Soc Am, Comm Shaare Zedek Hosp; Heritage Soc Miami Jewish Home and Hosp for Aged; Gtr Miami Jeiwsh Fedn; Ctr for Fine Arts; Histl Assn So FL; Holocaust Documentation and Educ Ctr. *Honours:* Soc of Bar and GAvel, 1974. *Hobbies:* Travel; Sports; Reading. *Address:* 19 West Flagler Street, Suite 1201, Biscayne Building, Miami, FL 33130, USA. 76, 138, 163.

NOSSE Tetsuya, b. 24 Mar 1927, University President. m. Kobayashi Nobuko, 25 Mar 1950, 1 d. *Education:* BA, Kobe Univ, 1949; DPhil, Oxford Univ, 1965. *Appointments:* Jr Rsch Fellow, Kobe Univ, 1950-53; Assoc Prof, 1955, Prof, 1964, Hd Economic Rsch, 1969-86, currently Pres, Kobe Univ Commerce. *Publications:* A Quasi-macro-economic Analysis of the Effective Incidence of Personal Taxes, thesis; The Working of Econometric Models (w M Morishima), 1972; The Econometric Analysis of Public Finance, 1982. *Memberships:* Int Inst Pub Fin; Auditor, Japanese Assn Pub Fin; Japanese Assn Theory and Econometrics. *Honours:* Advsry Ed, Public Finance. *Hobbies:* Painting; Croquet; Housing design. *Address:* 7-16-32 Seiryodai, Tarumi, Kobe 655, Japan. 190.

NOTHMANN Rudolf S, b. 4 Feb 1907, Hamburg, Germany. United States Citizen, 1943-. Legal Researcher. *Education:* Univ Hamburg Law School, 1925-31; Referendar trng (law clerk), Hamburg Law Cts, 1929-31, 1932-33; Referendar (LLB), 1929, PhD, Law, 1932. *Appointments include:* US Army, Europe, 1943-45; Asst Prof, Bus Law, Ins Contracts, For Trade, 1950-52, Vis Assoc Prof, 1951, UCLA; Contract work, USN, USAF, Los Angeles, CA, 1953-59; Contract Negotiator, Space Projects, w ind, Space and Missile Systems Org, USAF, Los Angeles, 1959-77; Rsch, Int Commercial Law, 1977-; Pres, Hanseatic Dev Corp, 1989. *Publications:* The Insurance Certificate in International Ocean Marine Insurance and Foreign Trade (Das Versicherungs Zertifikat), 1932; The Oldest Corporation in the World: 600 Years of Economic Evolution (Pacific Coast Economic Association), 1949. *Honours:* Exchange Scholarship, Univ Liverpool Law School, England, 1931-32; Gold Tape Award, script and narration, Samso Procurement Series TV legal prog, USAF Systems Command, 1970. *Hobbies:* Photography; Travel; Walking. *Address:* PO Box 32, Pacific Palisades, CA 90272, USA. 9, 132, 143.

NOULTON John David, b. 5 Jan 1939, London, England. Director. m. Anne Elizabeth Byrne, 7 Oct 1961, 3 s, 1 d. *Education:* Clapham Coll. *Appointments include:* Asst Prin, 1970, Prin, 1972, Min Transport; Asst Sec, 1978, Under-Sec, 1985-89, Depts Environment and Transport; Dir, Transmanche-Link, 1989; Dir, Eurotunnel, 1992; Fellowship, Royal Soc of Arts. *Membership:* Chartered Inst Transport. *Hobbies:* Riding; Writing for fun; Walking; Boats. *Address:* 12 Ladderstile Ride, Kingston Hill, Coombe, Surrey KT2 7LP, England. 1.

NOURSE Christopher Stuart, b. 13 Aug 1946, Salisbury, Wiltshire. Arts Administrator. *Education:* Hurstpierpoint Coll, Sussex, 1960-65; LLB, Univ of Edinburgh, 1968; Hon Soc Mid Temple, 1968-70. *Appointments:* Legal Exec, Life Offices Assn, 1970-72; Var managerial positions: Royal Opera House, Engl Opera Grp, Royal Ballet New Grp, 1972-76; Gen Mgr, Admnstr, Sadler's Wells Royal Ballet and Admin Dir, The Birmingham Royal Ballet, 1976-91; currently Asst to the Gen Dir, Royal Opera House. *Hobbies:* The performing and visual arts; the Orient; the countryside. *Address:* Royal Opera House, Covent Garden, London WC2E 9DD, England.

NOVAK Slobodan, b. 3 Nov 1924, Split, Yugoslavia. Writer. m. Nada Novak, 29 Sept 1947, 2 s. *Education:* Dips, Philos Fac, Zagreb, 1953; Yugoslav Langs and Lit, Slavistic Dept. *Appointments:* Mladost publng firm,

1947; Naprijed newpapers, 1948; V jesnik newspapers 1953-55; Dir Drama, Croatiana Nat Theatre, 1955-56 Ed, Cultural Page, Slobodna Dalmacija newspaper 1956-58; Ed, Lykos publng firm, 1958-61; Ed, Radic Zagreb, 1961-64; Ed, Zora publng firm, 1964-77; Mair Ed, Naprijed publng firm, 1977-83; Ed, 5 lit jrnls: Izvor 1948-51; Krugovi, 1952-55; Mogucnosti, 1956-58 Knjizevnik, 1961; Forum, 1984-88. *Publications include* Glasnice u oluji, poems, 1950; Iza lukobrana, poems 1953; Izgubljeni zavicaj, novel, 1955; The Stray Bullet novel, 1959; Trofej, play, 1960; Tvrdi grad, stories, 1961 Gold, Frankincense and Myrrh, novel, 1968; Off-Ship Log, novel, 1976. *Memberships:* Assn Croatian Writers PEN Club Croatia; Matica Hrvatska; Croatian Acad Sc and Art. *Honours include:* Awards for novel and stories City of Zagreb, 1955, 1961; Int Award for radio-play Prague, 1966; Matica of Croatia Award for novel, 1968 Critics Award, NIN Belgrade, 1969; Nazor Vladimir fo novel, 1969, for life work, 1990; Many minor awards *Hobbies:* Roses; Gardening. *Address:* Nova Ves 45/1 41000 Zagreb, Croatia.

NOWAK Leopold Rene, b. 2 Jan 1934, Cologne Germany. Producer; Director; Publisher; Actor; Publicist m. 1 Sept 1977, 1 s, 1 d. *Education:* Jangiellonian Univ Hist of Art, 1954-58; Psychol, 1958-60. *Career:* Owner of private film studio, Galicia, in Cracow. First private full-length feature film in east Europe, Eye of the Storm Full length documentary, Diaspora - History of Polish Jews. *Honours:* Awards: Paris Festival, 1951; Specia Awd, Festival of Socio-Polit Films, Lodz, 1986 Nominations: Margaret Mead Film Festival, NY, 1987 Leipzig Festival, 1987, Festival of Films about Art Zakopane, Short Films Festival, Cracow, 1989, 1990 *Hobbies:* Work; Sport; Cars. *Address:* Oficyna Filmowa Galicja, 31-511 Krakow , ul Rakowicka 11, Poland.

NOWAK Zygmunt Marian, b. 14 Apr 1941, Krzykawka Poland. Journalist; Reporter. m. 16 Mar 1968, 1 d *Education:* Master's degree, Jagiellonian Univ, Cracow 1967. *Appointments:* Trybuna Opolska newspaper 1974; Dir, Culture Club, Kozle, 1984; Nowiny Oploskie bi-weekly newspaper, 1989; Trybuna Opolska, 1990 Contbns to Gazeta Opolska, 1992. *Publications include* Trojkat Bermudzki, articles, 1983; Obywatele Europy article, 1990; Rozmowki Slasko-Niemieckie, report 1992; Przedbiegi, report, 1992; Na Wschod, article 1992. *Memberships:* Polish Assn Jrnlsts; Polish Ecological Club. *Hobbies:* Ecology; Travel; Reading Holocaust. *Address:* ul Paderewskiego 10, 47-22C Kedzierzyn-Kozle, Poland.

NOWAKOWSKA Zofia Helena, b. 6 Sept 1931, Lwow Poland. Architect. m. Wieslaw Nowakowski, 15 June 1956, 1 d. *Education:* MArch, Fac Arch, PhD, 1968 DSc, 1988, Cracow Univ Technology. *Career:* Prof Archtl Designer, 1958-, incl Designer, Engr Coop Desigr Studio, 1958-64; Asst Prof, 1964-68, Assoc Prof, 1968-1992, Prof, 1992-, Housing Chair, Fac Arch, Cracow Univ Technology; Chief, Polish Experts Sci Grp fo Housing Standards, Gen Housing Prog, Iraq, 1976 1978; Juror, Int Archtl Biennale, Cracow, 1985 Participant, archtl projects exhibs, Poland, NYC, Buenos Aires, Leipzig. *Creative works:* Over 60 archtl projects 1959-91; Interior designs incl: Students Campus Cracow, 1965-80; Globus bookstore, Cracow, 1976 Chapel, Skotniki, 1987; Conservatoire Club, Cracow 1987; Polish Archtl Assn Club, Cracow (w Wieslaw Nowakowksi), 1988; Archtl designs incl: Multi-family houses, Cracow (w Janusz Gawor), 1965, (w Wieslaw Nowakowski), 1986; 1-family houses, 1965-91 Horizontal Hotel, Cracow (w Wieslaw Nowakowski) 1988; Tenement house, City of Cracow, 1990 Orphanage house, Children's Village, Rajsko-Oswiecim 1991; Reconstruction and interior design, grp of olc bldgs, Przegorzaly, 1975-90; Sci publs in housing sci Books incl: Method of determining housing standards on the example of Iraq, 1987. *Memberships:* Archtl anc Urban Commn, Polish Acad Scis; Housing Sect, Archt and Urban Commn, Polish Acad Scis, Sec 1970-88 Polish Archtl Assn; Jurors Tea, SARP. *Honours:* Polish Govt Awards: Students Campus interiors, 1965, 1970

1972, creative participation in Gen Housing Prog, Iraq, 1981; Vicemaster, City of Cracow, 1972; Awards, Polish Archtl Assns competitions incl 1st Prize for Hotel, Cracow, 1988. *Hobby:* Protection of wronged animals. *Address:* Cicha Street 7a, 30-129 Cracow, Poland.

NOWICKI Andrzej Ruslaw, b. 27 May 1919, Warsaw, Poland. Professor of Philosophy of Culture. m. Zenobia Skrzek, 26 Dec 1942, 2 s, 1 d. *Education:* PhD, 1948; Docent, 1962; Prof, 1971. *Appointments:* Univ Warsaw, 1952-62; Univ Wroclaw, 1963-73; Univ Lublin, 1973-91. *Publications:* 40 books and over 1200 articles; Works incl: Giordano Bruno, 1962, 1979; Vanini, 1970, 1975, 1987; Man in His Works, 1974; Portraits of Philosophers in Poetry, Painting and Music, 1978; My Teachers, 1981; Meetings in Things, 1991. *Memberships:* Hon Pres, Polish Soc for Study of Religs, Pres 1973-1989; For Assoc, Accademia di Scienze Morali e Politiche, Naples. *Honours:* Hon Citizen of Taurisano, for studies about Vanini, 1967; Hon Citizen of Nola, for studies about Giordano Bruno; Many others. *Hobbies:* Chinese calligraphy; Collecting portraits of philosophers and composers. *Address:* ul Dantego 7 m 330, 01914 Warsaw, Poland.

NOWICKI Janusz, b. 3 Feb 1937, Zasule, Poland. Scientist. m. Anna Nowicki, 21 Apr 1960, 1 s. *Education:* Master's degree, Agronomy, 1960; Doct, Agronomy, 1969; Asst Prof, 1983. *Appointments:* Asst, 1960-69, Adj, 1969-83, Asst Prof, 1983-91, Prof, 1983, Hd Soil Tillage and Grassland Husbandry, 1987-, Agricl and Technological Univ, Olsztyn. *Publications:* Basic problems of agriculture in North-East part of Poland (co-author); Co-author, 13 books on subject of agric in Zulawy Region; Author or co-author, over 100 papers in Polish and for periodicals. *Memberships:* Hd, Div Plant Husbandry, Polish Acad Scis, Warsaw; Polish Soc Agrotechnology Scis, Warsaw; Int Soil Tillage Rsch Org, Wageningen, Netherlands. *Honours:* Award, Min Educ, 1986; 17 prizes, fields of scis and educ, Rector of Agricl and Technological Univ, Olsztyn. *Hobbies:* Hunting; Classical music; Reading. *Address:* ul Warszawska 66/38, 10-084 Olsztyn, Poland.

NOWICKI Piotr, b. 25 July 1951, Warsaw, Poland. Art Dealer; Art Historian. *Education:* MA, Inst Art Hist, Warsaw Univ, 1975. *Appointments:* Dept Applied Arts, Nat Mus, Warsaw, 1974-76; Currently Art Dealer, Galeria PN, Warsaw. *Creative works:* Authorship and layout, 28 exhibs of individual artists incl: Leszek Rozga, 1983; Krzysztof Witold Skorczewski, 1984; Marian Czapla, 1985; Stefan Gierowski, 1986; Jonasz Stern, 1987; Barbara Falender, 1988; Henryk Musialowicz, 1989; Jaroslaw Wojcik, 1989; Maksim Vardanian, 1989; Eduard Gorokhovski, 1991; Authorship and layout, collective exhibs: Masters of Contemporary Art in Poland: Herbert F Johnson Mus Art, Cornell Univ, USA, 1986, Munson-Williams-Proctor, Utica, USA, 1988; Contemporary Polish Masters Works, Edith Barrett Art Gall, Utica Coll, Syracuse Univ, 1988; In the Circle of the Acad Fine Arts in Warsaw, Warsaw, 1988; Furmanny Lane, Warsaw, 1989, Martigny, Switzerland, 1990; Russian Art Sect, Kunstlerische Konfrontationen exhib, Torun, 1991; Organised 40 from Israel exhib, Warsaw, 1990. *Memberships:* Assn Art Histns, Warsaw; Pres, Polish Mod Art Fndn, Warsaw; Soc Friends of Nat Mus in Warsa, Bd Mbr 1991. *Hobbies:* Collecting Polish and Russian contemporary art; Old Oriental carpets. *Address:* Villa Pallas Athenae, 32 Piasta str, 05-510 Konstancin, Poland.

NOWIK Henry Ian Alexander, b. 3 Feb 1917. University Lecturer. Consultant. m. Evelyn Phyllis Barnard, 17 Sept 1949. *Education:* Dr, Sci Pol, Ecole de Droit, Beirut; Filiale, Fac de Droit, Lyon, France, 1947. *Appointments:* Advsr, External Students, Fac Econs, Univ London, England, 1948-52; Export Mktng Exec, Parke Davis Ltd, London, 1952-54; Mgr, Mkt Rsch, Mather and Crowther Ltd, London, 1954-56; New Products Mgr, Hoover Ltd, London, 1956-58; Mgr, Mkt Rsch Dept, Petfoods Ltd, Melton Mowbray, 1958-64; VP Mktng and Sales, 1964-

68, Gen Mgr, 1968-69, Uncle Ben's Of Australia Pty Ltd, Wodonga, Vic, and Mng Dir, Effem Pty Ltd, Matraville, NSW, Australia, 1969-78, VP Mktng, 1979-80, Grp Pres, 1980-84, Worldwide Mars Inc, McLean, VA, USA (all pt of Mars Inc); Cnslr to Landegger Prog, 1984-88; Disting Prof, Int Mktng and Pub Diplomacy, School For Serv, Georgetown Univ, Wash DC, 1985-; Cons to number of US cos incl Mars Inc. *Publications:* Author, num articles to profl jrnls and confs. *Memberships include:* Fellow, Royal Statistical Soc; Int Law Assn; Fellow, Brit Inst Mktng; Mkt Rsch Soc, UK; Inst Mktng and Sales Mgmt; Fellow, Australian Inst Mgmt. *Honours include:* OBE, 1975; Off, Order of Australia, 1982; Kt Cmdr of Justice, Kts of Malta, 1985. *Hobbies:* Numismatics: XIXth century Australian first editions. *Address:* School of Foreign Service, Georgetown University, Washington, DC 20057, USA.

NOWOTNY Edgar, b. 26 Sept 1929, Potosi, Bolivia. Univ Full Prof. m. 4 Oct 1959, 1 s, 2 d. *Education:* Pharmaceutical, 1953; Biochemistry, 1956; PhD, 1963; Full Prof, 1966-. *Appointments:* Faculty of Chemical Sci, Natl Univ of Cordoba, 1959-. *Publications include:* 29 Sci Studies & Publ. *Memberships:* Alexander von Humboldt Stiftung; Sociedad Argentina de Investigaciones Biologieas; Sociedad de Biologia de Cordoba. *Honours include:* Teresa Mora de Roel Award. *Hobbies:* Table Tennis; Postage Stamp & Coins Collecting. *Address:* Faculted de Ciencias Quimicas UNC, Suc 16 CC 61, 5016 Cordoba, Argentina.

NÖTH Winfried Maximilian, b. 12 Sept 1944, Gerolzhofen, Bavaria, Germany. Professor of Semiotics and Linguistics. m. Ursula Hartlich, 5 July 1969, 1 s. 2 d. *Education:* Dr phil, 1971, Habilitation, 1976, Univ Bochum. *Appointments:* Rsch Asst, Univ Bochum, 1969-76; Acting Prof, 1977-78, Univ Aachen, 1977-78; Univ Prof, 1978-, Dean, Fac Mod Langs, 1981-82, Univ Kassel; Vis Prof, Univ WI, USA, 1985-86. *Publications:* Books: Strukturen des Happenings, 1972; Dynamik semiotischer Systeme, 1978; Literatursemiotische Analysen, 1980; Handbuch der Semiotik, 1985; Handbook of Semiotics, 1990. *Memberships:* Anglistentag; Deutsche Gesellschaft fur Semiotik; Int Semiotic Assn; Int Assn Visual Semiotics. *Honour:* Hon Mbr, Int Assn Visual Semiotics, 1990. *Address:* Auf der Bunte 1, 3500 Kassel, Germany. 52.

NTIRI Isaac Kofi, b. 15 Nov 1968, Prestea, Ghana. Student; Civil Engrng. *Education:* City Guilds of London Inst, 1987-89; Diploma in Civil Engeng, Univ of Sci & Tech, 1989-91. *Appointments:* Tutor, Technical Drawing, Woodwork, General Sci & Mathematics, Brentu Secondary Tech Sch, 1989; Field Training, ABP Conslt Engrs, Accra, Ghana, 1991. *Creative Works:* Woodworking Decorative Works. *Memberships:* Ghana Inst of Engrs. *Honours include:* Best Student in Building Drawing & Woodwork; Best Student in Civil Engrng & Building Const. *Hobbies:* Corespondence; Reading; Gardening; Woodworking; Tennis; Soccer; Swimming. *Address:* Post Office Box 100, Enchi, Ghana West Africa.

NUFFIELD Edward Wilfrid, b. 13 Apr 1914, Gretna, Man, Canada. Prof Emeritus Geology, Univ Toronto. m. Islay Marion Sturdy, 25 Feb 1939, 1 s, 2 d. *Education:* BA, Univ of British Columbia, 1940; PhD, Univ of Toronto, 1944. *Appointments:* Univ of Toronto, Prof, 1943-79; Assoc Dean, arts & Sci, 1962-64; Chmn, Dept of Geology, 1964-72; Ontario Dept Mines, Field Chief, 1949-51. *Publications:* X Ray Difraction Methods; With The West in Her Eyes; The Pacific Northwest. *Memberships:* Royal Soc of Canada; Mineral Assn Canada; Miner Soc America; American Crystallographic Assn. *Honours include:* Royal Soc Canada, Snr Award. *Hobby:* Canadian History. *Address:* 1603 1835 Morton Avenue, Vancouver BC, Canada V6G 1V3.2.142.143.

NUNN Marie Louise Downs, b. 23 May 1905. Writer; Poet; Editor; Photographer. m. (1) L H Dahlgren, 5 May 1956, dec, 1 s. *Education:* AB in Eng, San Jose State Univ; Grad of Healds Business Coll; MA, San Francisco

State Univ; Grad Work Univ of Calif; Temple Buell Coll; Univ of Kentucky; Briar Cliff Coll; Brigham Univ. *Appointments include:* Sec, US Civil Serv, Air Corps; Editor Airy Views; Sec in Adult Educ; Writer of Radion Script for Garden Chatters; Chancellor, WPSI; American Editor & Book Review Editor, Mag Poet. *Publications include:* Rumbling Wagon Wheels; Adventures on the Trail; Articles; Stories; Poems. *Memberships include:* World Poetry Soc; The Natl Historical Soc; The Natl Geographic Soc. *Hobbies:* Oil Painting; Flower Arranging; Music; Travel. *Address:* 2490 erced Street, Napa, CA 94558, USA.9.

NURIEV Ziyatin, b. 8 May 1955, Kirdjali, Bulgaria. Sculptor. m. Vicdan Kenanova, 9 Oct 1983, 1 s, 1 d. *Education:* Art Coll, Kazanlak, 1974; Art Acad of Sofia, 1982. *Appointments:* Sculptor. *Creative Works:* Dream, Basalt; Whisper, Marble; Mother, Marble; Over 100 Works in Marble & Basalt. *Memberships:* Union of Bulgarian Artists. *Honours include:* Grand Prix at the Intl Symposium of Sculpture; 1st Prize General Art Exhib, Pirin. *Address:* Blok Roza, Ap 1, Kardjli, Bulgaria.

NUTT Niven Robert Jr, b. 6 Dec 1929, Delhi, LA, USA. Chmn of Bd, Gladstone Farms Ltd. m. Marion McNally, 1954, 4 s, 2 d. *Education:* Henderson State Univ, Ba, 1951. *Appointments:* 1st Lt, USAF, 1951- 55; Pres, Orange Hill Farms, 1955-57; Gladstone Farms, 1957-80; Chmn of Bd, Gladstone Farms, 1980-. *Publications:* The Williams Family; The Nutt Family in the Bahamas; The Nutt Family; The Niven Family. *Memberships:* Bahamas Hist Soc; New England Hist Soc; Bahamas Chamber of Commerce; Delta Phi Fraternity; Methodist. *Honours:* World Food Medal; Bahamas c of C, Citizen Award. *Hobbies:* Hiking; Fishing; Research. *Address:* 13324 SW 111 Terrace, Miami, FL 33186, USA.7.52.

NUTTALL Christopher Guy, b. 16 Aug 1957, Knutsford, England. Journalist. *Education:* Sir John Deanes Grammer Sch, 1968-75; Univ Coll London, 1975-78. *Appointments:* Reporter, Warrington Guardian Series, 1978-81; BBC Radio, 1982-; BBC Srilanca Correpondent, 1988-90; BBC World Serv Washington Correspondent, 1991-. *Hobbies:* Cinema; Computers; Travel. *Address:* 2030 M Street NW, Suite 607, Washington DC 20036, USA.

NUTTALL Grant, b. 20 Nov 1932, Toronto, Canada. Vice Pres, Exec Devel & Organ, Imperial Oil Ltd. m. 20 Feb 1981, 1 s, 2 d. *Education:* Michigan Tech Univ, 1959. *Appointments:* Imperial Oil Ltd, Toronto, Canada, 1959-91. *Memberships include:* Advisory Committee, Inst for Mngt Studies; Human Resources Advisory group; Federal Governments Exec Exchange Program Organizing Committee. *Honour:* Phi Kappa Phi. *Hobbies:* Horology; Travel; Golf; Cranite Club, Toronto. *Address:* c/o Imperial Oil Ltd, 111 St Clair Avenue W, Toronto, Ontario, Canada M5W 1K3.142.

NUTTGENS Patrick John, b. 2 Mar 1930, Buckinghamshire, England. Hon Prof; Writer; Broadcaster. m. Bridget Ann Badenoch, 21 Aug 1954, 5 s, 3 d. *Education:* MA, Edinburgh, 1954; Dip Arch, Edin, 1954; PhD, Edin, 1959. *Appointments:* Lectr, Univ of Edinburgh, 1955-62; Reader, Prof, Univ of York, 1962-69; Dir, Leeds Poly, 1970-85; Hon Prof, Univ of York, 1986-. *Publications include:* York the Continuing City; The Home Front; What Should We Teach. *Memberships:* ARIBA; FRSA; ARIAS. *Honours include:* CBE; Litt D. *Hobbies:* Painting; Drawing; Theatre; Thinking. *Address:* Roselea Cottage, Terrington, York, YO6 4PP, England.1.

NUTTING Jack, b. 8 June 1924, Mirfield, York, England. Emeritus Prof; Conslt Metallurcist. m. Thelma Kippax, 2 Sept 1950, 1 s, 2 d. *Education:* BSc, Leeds Univ, 1945; PhD, Leeds Univ, 1948; ScD, Cambridge Univ, 1967. *Appointments:* British Iron & Steel Research Assn, 1948-49; Demonstrator, Lectr, Metallurgy, Cambridge Univ, 1949-60; Prof, Leeds univ, 1960-89. *Publications:* Microstructure of Metals; 100 Sci Papers.

Memberships: Metals Soc; Inst of Metaalurgists; Historical Metallurgy Soc; Inst of Metals. *Honours include:* Fellowship of Engrng; Hadfield Medal; Inst of Metals Platinum Medal. *Hobbies:* Foreign Travel; Mountain Walking; Cooking. *Address:* 57 Weetwood Lane, Leeds, LS16 5ND, England. 1

NWEKE Florence Chunwe, b. 22 May 1964, Enugu. m. Lawrence D Nweke, 31 Dec 1988, 1 s, 1 d. *Education:* St John of God Secondary Sch; Tchr Training Coll, 1985; Anambra State Coll of educ, 1988; Univ of Nigeria, BSc, 1990. *Appointments:* Tchrng Practice, Tchr Training Coll, 1985; Tchrng Practice, Comprehensive Secondary Sch, 1989; Primary Sch Mngt Bd, 1991. *Publications:* The Incidence of Helmuth Paraciter in Human Population of Part of Old Njikoka L G A of Anambra State; Iniation into O 20 Title in Awka; From Begining, this is Awka. *Memberships include:* Awka Devel Union; Anambra State Coll of Educ Awka. *Honours include:* Sch of Educ Proze; Dept of Interigated Sci Prize. *Hobbies:* Reading; Games. *Address:* Awka Devel Union, PO Box 3, Federal Capital Territory, Abuja, Nigeria.

NWOKE Mba Anaga, b. 11 Sept 1954, Nigeria. Argricultural Economist. *Education:* St Stephens, 1966; West African Sch, Nigeria, 1972; Gen Agricl, Univ of life Nigeria, 1978; BSc, Univ of Ibadas, 1984. *Appointments:* Research Asst, 1973-85; Production Economist, 1985-86; Project Dir, 1986-91; Agricl Econs Conslt, 1989-90; Mgr, 1990-91. *Publications include:* Holistoc Production of Small Ruminanl; Designing/ Production of 1st Successfull Millet/Sorghum Thresher in West Africa. *Memberships:* Assn Intl des Etudient Sci Economoques et Commerciales; Jaycees; Natl Council of Nigerian Farmers. *Hobbies:* Broadcasting; Woodworking; Reading. *Address:* Puppa Farms Intl West African Ltd, 15 Awolowo Way, Ikeja, Nigeria.

NWUFO Martin Ike Chukwu, b. 5 Apr 1952, Ibada, Nigeria. Lectr. m. Regina Chinyere, 22 Aug 1981, 1 s, 2 d. *Education:* BSc, 1977; MSc, 1980; PhD, 1984. *Appointments:* Snr Research Officer, Natl Rout Crop Research Inst, 1978-84; Lectr ii, 1984-85; Lectr i, 1987-89; Snr Lectr, 1989- *Publications:* About 20 Articles. *Memberships include:* Nigerian Soc for Plant Protection; Botanical Soc of Nigeria; Intl Biodeterioration Soc, Nigeria. *Honours:* Federal Government of Nigeria Scholarship Award. *Hobbies:* Football; Gardening; Reading. *Address:* Dept of Crop Production, Federal Univ of Tech, PM B1526, Owerri, Nigeria.

NYPELS Eduardus Hermannes Theresia Maria, b. 1 Apr 1950, Den Helder, Netherlands. Mayor of Breda. m. J M Pieters, 8 July 1983, 2 s. *Education:* State Univ of Utrecht, 1976. *Appointments:* Dutch Lower House, 1978-86, 1989-90; Chmn Dutch Parliamentary Liberal Party, 1982- 86; Minister of Public Housing, Physical Planning & Environmental Affiars, 1986-89. *Memberships include:* Dutch Royal Military Acad; World Wildlife Fund Netherlands; Commissioner of Flakt Nederland. *Honours:* Companion of the Order of the Dutch Lion; Eimer Sinoo Award. *Hobbies:* Collect Miniature Trains; Antique Cards & Prints. *Address:* Burgemeester de Manlaan go, 4036 Ap Breda, The Netherlands.

NYVLT Jaroslav, b. 20 Mar 1932, Bratislava, Czechoslovakia. Scientist. m. Eva Muchova, 27 Dec 1957, 1 d. *Education:* Ing, TU Chem Tech, Prague, 1956; PhD, 1960; Dr Sc, 1967. *Appointments:* Res Inst Inorg Chem, 1959-78; Inst Inorg Chem Czech Acad Sci, 1978- . *Publications:* 315 Sci Papers; 28 Books. *Memberships:* Czechoslovak Chem Soc; Czechoslovak Soc Chem Eng; working Party on Crystallization in European Federation of Chem Engr; Verein Deutscher Ingenieure. *Honours include:* The Moulton Medal; Prize of the Czech Acad Sci. *Hobbies:* Music; Photography; Reading; Gardening. *Address:* Inst Inorg Chem Czech Acad Sci, Pelleova 24, 160 00 Praha 6, Czech Republic. 1.

O

O'BRIEN Denis Patrick, b. 24 May 1939, Knebworth, Herts, England. Univ Tchr. m. Eileen Patricia O'Brien, dec, 5 Aug 1961, 1 s, 2 d. *Education:* Douih Sch, 1952-57; Univ Coll of London, 1957-60; BSc (Econ), 1960; PhD, Queens Univ, Belfast, 1969. *Appointments:* Asst Lectr; Lectr; Reader, Queens Univ, Belfast, 1963-72; Prof of Economics, Durham Univ, 1972-. *Publications:* J R McCulloch; The Correspondance of Lord Overstone; The Classical Economists; Lionel Robbins. *Honour:* Fellow of British Acad. *Hobby:* Violin. *Address:* Dept of Economics, Univ of Durham, 23-26 Old Elvet, Durham, DH1 3HY, England. 1, 52.

O'BRIEN Margaret Mary, b. 3 Sept 1950, Leamington Spa, England. Ursuline Sister of Tildonk; Dir of Young Adult Ministry, Diocese of Rockville Centre, NY. *Education:* BA, St Johns Univ, NY, 1972; MA, St Bonaventure Univ, 1984; Centre for Spirituality & Justice, Bronx, NY, 1985; DMin (Cand) Graduate Theological Foundation, Indiana, 1992. *Appointments:* Sch Tchr, 1972-84; Dir, Formation for Ursuline Sisters, 1984-90; Spiritual Dir, 1984-; Dir, Young Adult Ministry, 1987-. *Publication:* Discovering Your Light: Common Journeys of Young Adults. *Memberships:* New York State Representative on Bd of Natl Catholic Young Adult Ministry Assn. *Hobbies:* Reading; Travel; Walking; Devel of a United States Spirituality. *Address:* Diocese of Rockville Centre, 50 North Park Avenue, Rockville Centre, NY 11570, USA.

O'BRIEN Robert Neville, b. 14 June 1921, Nanamo, BC, Canada. Prof Emeritus of Chemistry. m. Helen Ireva Bryan, 28 June 1952, 4 s, 1 d. *Education:* Bach of Sci, UBC, 1951; MA, 1952; PhD, 1955. *Appointments:* Post Doctoral NRC Canada, 1955-57; Asst, Assoc Prof, Chemical Dept, Univ of Alberta, Edmonton, 1957-66; Assoc, Full Prof, Univ of Victoria, 1966-86; Prof Emeritus, Adjunct Prof, 1986-. *Publications:* 2 Lab Manuals; 2 Chapters; 120 Articles; 5 Patents. *Memberships include:* Royal Soc of Arts; Electrochemical Soc; Intl Electrachem Soc; American Assn Advance Sci. *Honour:* Fellow of the Chemical Inst of Canada. *Hobbies:* Flying; Boating; Gardening; Squash; Badminton. *Address:* 2614 Dullnswood Dr, Victoria, BC, Canada V8N 1X5. 2, 142.

O'BRIENT David Warren, b. 2 Oct 1927, Toledo, Ohio, USA. Sales Exec; Conslt. m. Enid Jo Wynne, 21 Feb 1962, div, 1 s. *Education:* BS, Univ of Texas, 1949. *Appointments:* Smith Engrng, Sales Engr, 1949-53; Dunham Bush Inc, District Sales Mgr, 1953-60; W L Lashleys Assoc, Sales Mgr, 1960-67; O J & C CO, Pres, Owner, 1967-78; Exec VP, 1980-83; O'Brient Eng Co, Pres, Owner, 1983-. *Memberships include:* ASAE; ASHVE; ASRE; ASHRAE; 1st Meth Church, Houston. *Honours:* Phi Eta Sigma; Tau Sigma Delta; Tau Beta Pi. *Hobbies:* Sports; Music; Reading. *Address:* 9550 Ella Lee Lane 811, Houston, TX 77063, USA. 7, 125.

O'CHESTER Harold Eugene, b. 19 Aug 1927, Brooklynn, New York. Minister. m. Barbara J Hostetter, 9 Aug 1957, 3 d. *Education:* BA, Miss Coll, 1954; ThM, New Orleans Seminary, 1958; DD, 1981. *Appointments:* FBCH Purvis, 1959-64; Popular Sp, 1964-69; Great Hills Baptist Church, 1969-91. *Publications:* Why Me Lord; Divorce, Biblical Perspective; 5 Ways to Shape A Childs Life; How to Give The Master Change; Man Shall Not Live By Bed Alone. *Membership:* Lions Lub. *Honours include:* Dist Serv Award. *Hobbies:* Golf; Hunting; Travel. *Address:* 10500 Jollyville Road, Austin, TX 78759, USA. 7.

O'CONNELL David Henry Anthony, b. 26 Feb 1955, Cork, Ireland. Family Doctor. *Education:* Ed, Presentation Brothers COll; Univ Coll, Cork; MB BCh, BAO, 1978; DRCOG, 1982; MICGP, 1985. *Appointments:* House Surgeon, House Physician, Royal Hosp, Wolverhampton,

1978-79; GP Trainee St Bartholomews & Hackney Hosp, 1979-82; Chmn, District Jnr Exec, City & Hackney District, 1980-81; Medical Adviser, St Wilfreds Chelsea, 1985; Memb, Exec Cttee, Chmn Insurance Cttee; Sec Audit Cttee, independant Doctors Forum; Audit Sub Committee of the Independent Doctors Forum, 1990. *Publications:* Various Contributions to Popular Medical Press. *Memberships:* BMA; Royal Soc Medicine; Med Soc London; Chelsea Clinical Soc; Worshipful Soc of Apothecaries; RSA; Cross of Merit; GMUR Scholarship (pianoforte). *Hobbies:* Wine; Travel. *Address:* 25 Sloane Court West, London SW3 4TD, England.

O'DONOGHUE Daniel Francis, b. 27 Mar 1947, Manchester, England. Advertising. m. 1 Apr 1972, 3 s, 1 d. *Education:* St Bedes Coll, Manchester, 1958-65; Sheffield Univ, 1966-68. *Appointments:* Trainee Gus, 1968-69; Mktng Research Mgr, Rowntree, 1973-76; Mktng Officer Shepherd Building, 1976-77; Account Planner, 1977-79; Planning Dir, 1979-82; Planning Dir, McCormicks, 1982-87; Dept Chmn Publics, 1989-; Joint Chief Exec Publics UK, 1991. *Memberships:* Mktng Committee IPA; IPA Council; MRS. *Hobbies:* Fine Art Collecting; Football; Ancient History. *Address:* Woodcroft Castle, Marholm, Peterborough, Cambs, PE6 7HW, England.

O'GORMAN Margaret Elizabeth Nelson, b. 20 July 1938, Glasgow, Scotland. Conslt, Child & Adolescent Psychiatry. *Education:* MB ChB, Glasgow, 1963; DPM, Scottish, 1966; MRc Psych, 1971. *Appointments:* Registar Psychiatry, Southern Gen Hosp, Glasgow, 1966-68; Snr Reg, Child Psychiatry, Royal Hosp for Sick Children, 1968-71; Conslt, Child & Adolescent Psychiatry, 1971-; Visiting Lectr, Dept Sociology, Univ of Stirling, 1974. *Hobbies:* Gardening; Sailing; Quilting. *Address:* Royal Infirmary, Stirling, FK8 2AU, Scotland.

O'KEEFE Lynn Marie Miller, b. 12 Apr 1955, Chicago, IL, USA. Surgical Tchnologist. m. Michael E O'Keefe, 12 Aug 1983, 1 s, 1 d. *Education:* Il Morane Valley Comm Co, 1973-74, 1976-78; Rockford Memorial Sch of Nursing, 1974-76; Rock Valley Comm Coll, 1974-76; Santa Fe Comm Coll. *Appointments:* Christ Hosp OA/L Lawn Il, 1976; McNeal Memorial Hosp, 1976-77; Palos Comm Hosp, 1978-86; North Fla Regional, 1986; Lake Butler Hand Centre, 1986-89; Shands Ganesville, Fla, 1989-. *Creative Works:* Artist Oil in Canvas. *Membership:* Assn of Surgical Technologists. *Honours include:* Neurosurgical Team Shands Hosp. *Hobbies:* Profl Artist, Realistic Oil on Canvas; Antique Dealer. *Address:* PO Box 721, High Springs, FL 32643, USA. 7.

O'KEHIE Collins Emeka, b. 4 Apr 1952. Layer; Interl Legal Conslt. m. Justina Amuche Mnadi, 6 Aug 1983, 2 s, 1 d. *Education:* Assoc in Bus, Ellsworth Coll, 1977; BS, Univ of Texas, 1979; MBA, N Texas State Univ, 1981; JD, Tharbood Marshall Sch of Law, 1984. *Appointments:* Shell Oil Com, Corporate Lawyer, 1984-85; Gregg O'Kehie & Cashin, Houston, 1985-90; Partners, O'Kehie & Assoc, Houston, 1990-. *Memberships:* State Bar of Texas; ABA; Texas Bar Assn; Assn Trial Lawyers; MBA; Chartered Ins Instl; Intl Bar Assn; intl Platform Assn; Texas Trial Lawyers. *Honours include:* Phi Delta Phi. *Hobbies:* Tennis; Jogging; Soccer. *Address:* O'Kehie & Assoc, 1300 Main Building, Suite 1930, Houston, TX 77002, USA. 7, 52, 163.

O'MEARA Gary David, b. 13 Feb 1955, Quebec City, Canada. Headmaster. m. Suzanne Barbara Tevlin, 16 June 1979. *Education:* Princeton Univ, 1972-76. *Appointments include:* Dir of Studies, St George's Coll, 1983-85; Head of Upper Sch, St George's Coll, 1985-88; Founding Headmaster, Lycee, Cambridge, 1988-. *Publications:* Beyond the Courts & Constitution; Snr Economics Guidelines for Ontario Ministry of Education. *Memberships:* Princeton Alumni Schools Committee of the UK; Princeton Club of G Britain; Royal Overseas League; British Assn for Canadian Studies; Canada Club; Canada UK Chamber of Commerce; Alliance Francaise of Cambridge. *Hobbies:* Reading; Music; Theatre; Tennis; Skiing; Travel. *Address:* Manor Cottage, Church Road, Toft, Cambs, CB3 7RH, England.

O'NEILL Paul, b. 26 Oct 1928, St Johns, Newfoundland, Canada. Writer; Actor; Radio & Tv Producer. *Education:* St Bonaventures Coll, 1947; Natl Acad of Theatre Arts, New York, 1949; Georgetown Univ, Washington, 1962. *Appointments:* Freelance Actor, USA & England, 1949-53; CBC Regional Supervisor, 1955-70; CBC Tadio & Tv Exec Producer, 1970-86; Lectr, Actor, Writer, 1986-. *Creative Works include:* Radio, Stage Plays; Tv, Film Scripts; Numerous Contributions to Newspapers & Mag Journals; Books. The Oldest City, a Seaport Legacy, Upon This Rock, Others. *Memberships include:* Newfoundland & Labrador Arts Countil; Folk Arts Council of Canada; Natl Youth Orchestra; Canadian Writers Union. *Honours include:* Numerous Medal & Awards in Arts & Letters; LLD Memorial Univ, Nfld Arts Hall of Fame Order of Canada. *Hobbies:* Gardening; History; Travel; Music; Literature. *Address:* 115 Rennies Mill Road, St Johns, Newfoundland, Canada A1B 2P2. 3.

O'SIADHAIL Micheal, b. 12 Jan 1947, Dublin, Ireland. Poet. m. Brid Carroll, 2 July 1970. *Education:* BA, M Litt, Trinity Coll, Dublin, 1964-68; Univ of Oslo, 1968-69. *Appointments:* Lectr, Trinity Coll, Dublin, 1969-73; Prof, Dublin Inst for Advanced Studies, 1974-87; Guest Lectr, Univ of Iceland, 1981; currently Full time Writer. *Publications:* Poetry: An Baliain Bhisigh, 1978; Runga, 1980; Springwight, 1983; The Image Wheel, 1985; The Chosen Garden, 1990. Linguistics: Coras Funimeanna Na Gaeilge, 1975; Tearmai Togala Agus Tis As Inis Meain, 1978; Learning Irish, 1988; Modern Irish, 1989. *Memberships:* Arts Coun, Repub of Ireland; Cultural Rels Advsry Comm, Repub of Ireland; ADSDANA, Acad of Disting Irish Artists; Bd Mbr, Dublin Int Writers' Conf. *Honour:* Irish Am Cultural Inst Awd for Lit, 1982. *Hobbies:* Music; Reading; Swimming. *Address:* 5 Trimleston Avenue, Booterstown, County Dublin, Ireland.

O'SULLIVAN Bernard Anthony, b. 23 Nov 1948, S Africa. Barrister. *Education:* MA Cantab. *Appointments:* Called to Bar, Inner Temple, 1971; Barrister, Pvt Pract, 1971-. *Hobbies:* Travel; Theatre; Skiing. *Address:* 27 Bonnington Square, London SW8 1TF, England.

OAKES Helen Miller, b. 17 June 1932, Teague, TX. Post Master. m. Wayland Oakes, 18 Aug 1961, 4 d. *Education:* Baylor Univ, 1960; McLennan Community Coll, Waco, 1983. *Appointments:* Tchr, Teague, 1961-64; Tchr, Houston TX, 1960-61; Tchr, Remedial Baylor Reading, Groesbeck Isd, 1964-74; Tchr, Teague Isd, 1974-76; Tchr, Leon Isd, 1977-78; Postmaster, US Postal Serv, 1980-. *Creative Works include:* Operation Head Start. *Memberships include:* Groesbeck Study Club; First Baptist Church; Order of Eastern Star. *Honours include:* Postal Review Bd; Postmaster Trainer. *Hobbies:* Reading; Walking; Community Involvement; Travel; Family & Activities. *Address:* Rt 1, Box 61, Donie, TX 75838, USA. 7, 15.

OBERHAUSEN Joyce Ann Wynn, b. 12 Nov 1941, Shreveport, LA, USA. Aircraft Company Exec; Artist. m. James J Oberhausen, 15 Oct 1966, 1 s, 2 d. *Education:* Ayers Business Coll, Shreveport; Univ of Huntsvilee, Alabama, USA. *Appointments:* Stenographer, Sec, Lincoln Natl Life Co, Louisiana, 1964-65; Sec, Baifield Indu, 1965-66; Intl Art Tchr, 1974-; Vice Pres, Co Owner, Precision Specialty Corp, 1966-; Military Aircraft Sales, 1979-; Wynnson Enterprices, 1984-; Owner, artist, Designer of Wynnson Galleries Flowers & Art, 1987-; Owner, North Alabama Wholesale Flowers, 1987-; Owner, Wynnson Enterprises Military Packaging Co, 1988-. *Publications:* Intl Biographical Book of Dedications. *Memberships include:* Natl Museum Women in Arts; Natl Assn Female Exec; Intl Porcelain Guild; People to People. *Hobbies:* Oil Painting; Antiques; Handcrafts; Gourmet Cooking; Horseback Riding;

Swimming; Water & Snow Skiing; Tennis. *Address:* 150 Wells Road, PO Box 440, Meridianville, AL 35759, USA. 5, 132, 138, 152.

OBI Keiichiro, b. 22 May 1927, Toyko, Japan. Prof of Economics, Keio Univ. m. Fusa Kamiya, 10 July 1962, 1 d. *Education:* BA, Keio Univ, 1950; PhD, Keio Univ, 1966; Rockefellow Fellow, Harvard Univ, 1963-64. *Appointments:* Asst Prof, Keio Univ, 1950-57; Assoc Prof, 1957-66; Prof, 1966-; Snr Research Officer, Economic Planning Agency Govt, 1961-63. *Publications:* Observations vs Theory of Household Labor Supply; Introduction to Econometrics; Labor Market in Japa. *Memberships include:* Statistics Council, Govt of Japan; Japan Statistical Soc; Japan Assn of Economics & Econometrics; Intl Input, Output Assn. *Honours:* Rockefellow Foundation; Japan Securities Scholarship Foundation; Japanese Ministry of Educ Research Grant. *Hobbies:* Painting; Estronomy. *Address:* 2-15-45 Mita, Minato Ku, 108 Tokyo, Japan. 52.

OBIEFUNA Julius Chiedozie, b. 4 June 1948, Agulu. Lectr; Agronomist. m. Obiefuna Caralyn Adaku Needure, 18 Mar 1978, 2 s, 3 d. *Education:* BA, 1973; PhD, 1980. *Appointments:* Master ii, Egigie Coll, Abudu, 1974-76; Research Officer, Nihort Ibadan, Nigeria, 1976-83; Gen Mgr, Chi Ltd, Lagos, 1987; Lectr, Futo, 1983-. *Publications:* Over 45 Scholary Intl Journal Articles; Over 20 Conference Papers. *Memberships:* Agric Soc of Nigeria; Assn of Nigeria; Hort Soc of Nigeria; WARCROP/INIBAP. *Hobbies:* Singing; Drama; Sports; Athletics; Cultural Dancing. *Address:* Dept of Crop Production, Sch of Agric & Agricl Tech, Federal Univ of tech, PMB 1526, Owerri, Nigeria. 1.

OBOLENSKY Nicholas Prince, b. 7 June 1956, Toronto, Canada. Develp Dir. m. Charlotte Isabella Sharpe, 28 Nov 1987, 1 s. *Education:* Harrow, 1970-74; RMA Sandhurst, 1975-76; BA Hons Durham Univ, 1978-81; MBA Imede, Lausanne, 1988. *Appointments:* Commissioned 17/21 Lancers, 1976, Troop Leader BAOR, Army Scholarship Univ, Captain, 1981, Major, 1986, Retired, 1988; Conslt, 1989, Snr Conslt, 1990, Ernst & Young; Mgng Conslt, 1991, Retail Change Prog Exec, 1991, Launch Dir, 1992, Develop Dir, 1993, Gateway Foodmarkets Ltd. *Hobbies:* Mountaineering; Climbing; Skiing; Flying; Marathon. *Address:* c/o Natl Westminster Bank, 92 High Street, Harrow on Hill, Middlesex, England.

OCHIAI Shinya, b. 6 June 1935, Kofu City, Japan. Engr. m. Hisako Ozawa, 6 May 1966, 1 d. *Education:* BSME, Waseda Univ, 1960; MSME, Rice Univ, 1962; PhD, Purdue Univ, 1966. *Appointments:* Instrumentation Devel Engr, Celanese Fibers Co, 1965-68; Snr Ptocess Cystem Engr, 1968-74; Engrng Assoc, 1974-90; Snr Engrng Assoc, Hoechst Celanese, 1990-. *Publications:* 16 Publ on Automatic Controls in Profl Journals; 3 US Patents. *Memberships include:* Fellow, Instrument Soc of America; Soc Instrument & Control Engrs, Japan; Sigma Xi. *Hobby:* Tennis. *Address:* Hoechst Celanese, PO Box 9077, Corpus Christi, TX 78469, USA. 7, 143.

ODAGESCU Irina, b. 23 May 1937, Bucharest, Romania. Composer; Assoc Prof of Music. m. Teodor Tutuianu, 17 July 1968. *Education:* Bucharest Conservatory, 1957-63. *Appointments:* Assoc Prof, Score Reading, Bucharest Music Acad, 1967-. *Compositions include:* Peaks, Symphonic Poem; Music for Two Pianos & Percussion; Choral Music. *Membership:* Union of Romanian Composers & Musicologists. *Honours include:* Silver Medal, Intl Contest of Polyphonic Music, Ibague, Colombia; Prizes of the Union of Romanian Composers. *Address:* Str Gheorghe Manea 6, 74314 Bucharest, Romania. 138, 139.

ODDY William Andrew, b. 6 Jan 1942, Bradford, England. Keeper of Conservation, The British Museum.

m. Patricia Anne Whitaker, 4 Aug 1965, 1 s, 1 d. *Education:* New Coll, Oxford, 1961-65; BA, 1964; BSc, 1965; MA, 1969. *Appointments:* The British Museum, 1966-, as Keeper of Conservation, 1985-. *Publications:* More than 150 Papers; Reviews; Articles. *Memberships:* Intl Inst for Conservation; Soc of Antiquaries of London; Freeman of the Worshipful Co of Goldsmiths. *Hobbies:* Archaeology; History; Travel. *Address:* c/o Dept of Conservation, The British Museum, London WC1B 3DG, England. 1.

ODERSKY Walter, b. 17 July 1931, Neustadt, OS. Prasident des Bundesgerichtshofes. m. Renate Pustet, 25 May 1957, 2 s, 3 d. *Education:* Gymnasium in Breslau; Jura; Pisa; Doc Juris, 1954. *Appointments:* Public Prosecutor & Judge, Munich, 1957-83; Offical, State Ministry of Justice, 1983-87; Pres of the Bayer, Oberstes Landesgesicht, 1988; Pres of the Bundesgerichtshof; Hon Prof Jurst, Fac Univ Munich. *Memberships include:* Bar of the Court of Ministry Appeals in Washington. *Honours include:* Bayer Verdieusfordem; Österreich, Gropes Ehrenzeiden in Gold. *Hobbies:* Tennis; Tours in the High Mountains; Music. *Address:* Herrenstr 45a, 75 Karlsruhe, Germany.

ODESCALCHI Edmond Pery, Prince, b. 11 Oct 1928, Budapest, Hungary. Intl Financial Conslt. m. Esther de Kando, 30 Sept 1961, 2 s. *Education:* Cornell Univ, 1951; Univ of Pennsylvania, 1956-57; St Andrews Univ, 1959. *Appointments:* Admin Asst, French Govenment, Baden, Germany, 1948-50; Proj Mgr, Devel Mgr, IBM Corp, 1952-75; Pres, Global Tech Inc, 1975-91. *Publications:* The Global Arena; Faces of Reality; Numerous Articles. *Memberships include:* Business Conslts Assn; Acad of Political Sci; Pan-European Corp. *Address:* 6 Freedom Road, Pleasant Valley, NY 12569, USA. 52, 132.

ODMANN Jan Christer, b. 10 Apr 1920, Stockholm, Sweden. Novelist; Publicist. m. (1) 2 s, 2 d, (2) Birgitta Margareta Lonnegardh, 21 Oct 1962. *Education:* Master of Laws, Univ of Stockholm, 1945. *Appointments:* Assessor District Judge,Kristinehamn, 1946-48; Magistrates Court, Kristinehamn, 1948; Officer Royal Bd of Civil Aviation, Stockholm, 1949-56; 1st Asst Sec, Swedish Ministry of Home Affairs, 1956-62; Principal Asst Sec, Swedish Ministry of Soc Affairs, 1962-71; Resigned, 1971. *Creative works include:* Munk i Neutralien; Den inbillade rike; Doktorns Pojke; Short Stories; Poems; Articles. *Memberships:* Sallskapet; New Sporting CLub. *Hobbies:* Tennis; Painting. *Address:* 1068 Les Vertes Campagnes, F 01170 GEX, France. 52.

ODROWAZ-PIENIAZEK Janusz, b. 2 July 1931, Opatowice. Writer; Historian of Literature; Curator of Museum. m. Izabella Romanowska, 26 Aug 1965, 1 s. *Education:* Warsaw Univ, Polish Philology, 1949-52; Russian Philology, 1953-54, grad 1960; Montreal Univ, 1968-69. *Appointments:* Sec Editorial Com Anniversary Edition of Mickiewicz Collected Works, 1954-55; Asst Searcher, Literary Inst Lite Research, 1956-72; Dir, Adam Mickiewicz Museum of Literature, 1972-; Chief Editor, 1981-. *Publications include:* Paris Stories; The Theory of the Wawes; Coctail Party chez la Princess Gyeorigjev. *Memberships include:* Assoc of Polish Writers; PEN; Canadian Inter American Research Inst. *Honours:* Prix du Merite Cultural; Cr Or du Merite; Ch c Polonia restituta; Prix de la Ville de Varsovie. *Hobbies:* Travel; Bibliophily. *Address:* ul Uniwersytecka 1 m 2, 02-036 Warsaw, Poland. 3, 43.

ODUM Jeffery Neal, b. 11 Sept 1956, Bristol, TN, USA. Edngng Mngr. m. Stacy Elaine Ferrell, 18 Mar 1989, 1 s. *Education:* BS, 1978; MBA, 1979; MS, 1983. *Appointments:* Stone Webster Engrng Corp, Snr Project Engr, 1978-84; E I Dupont De Nemours, Division Engr, 1984-89; Fluor Daniel Wc, Engrng Mngr, 1989-. *Publications include* Articles Contributed to Pharmaceutical Engrng. *Memberships:* Intl Soc of Pharmaceutical Engrs; Soc of Manufacturing Engrs; Presidents Club, Univ of Te Wessee. *Honours:* Order

of the Engr; E I Dupont Engrng Achievements Award. *Hobbies:* Cooking; Biking; Physical Fitness. *Address:* PO Box 205, Beech Island, SC 29842, USA. 7.

OEI Tat le, b. 4 Aug 1921, Mediun, Indonesia. Physician, Gen Practice. m. Marie Thio, 5 Oct 1945, 2 s, 1 d. *Education:* Univ of Indonesia, Sch of Medicine, 1950; Rotating Internship, Middlesex Gen Hosp, New Brunswick, 1968-69. *Appointments:* Private Practice, 1950-59; District Health Officer, Brebes County, 1959-77; Private Practice, 1977-; Medical Dir, Santa Maria Hosp, 1980-. *Memberships:* Indonesian Medical Assn; Rotary Club of Tegal. *Hobbies:* Reading; Correspondence; Dogs. *Address:* 18 Jalan dr Soetomo, Tegal 52113, Java, Indonesia. 52.

OERIPAN Soegiharto, b. 25 May 1963, Surabaya, Indonesia. President Dinecton. *Education:* Computer & Accounting Morced Coll, California, USA, 1982-85; Business Admin Area of Specialty; Mngt & Mktng, Kennedy Weston Univ; Bachs Masters & Doctorate Major. *Appointments:* Bank Official Bank Central Asia Surabaya, 1986-89; pres Dir, Wina Plastic, 1989-; Finance Wina Plastic, 1987-; Pres Dir, Swastha Artha Praunathana, 1991- ; Pres Dir, PT Buana, 1991-. *Membership:* Atlas Clarck Hatch Sports Club. *Honours include:* Cert of Panticipation, Intl Advertising Seminars/Workshop Indonexia. *Hobbies:* Reading; Tennis; Sightseeing; Hiking. *Address:* Kenjerais 139 141, Surabaya 60134, Indonesia. 52, 132.

OERIPAN Toha, b. 17 Feb 1941, Banchung. Gen Mgr. m. 9 Sept 1961, 2 s. *Education:* Yanion High Sch, Petna, 1954-56; Snr High Sch, Petna, 1957-59. *Appointments:* Gen Mgr, Wina Plastic, 1970-. *Hobbies:* Swimming; Hiking. *Address:* Kenjeran 139 141, Surabaya 60134, Indonesia.

OFUNGUO Aloyse Bunguo Chanatra, b. 11 Nov 1948. Prinicap Tutor. m. Phillipinna, 12 May 1979, 2 s, 2 d. *Education:* BA, 1874; MA, 1977; RDPM, Birmingham, 1986; PGD CDP, 1989; PhD, 1991. *Appointments:* Educ Officer, IIB Secondary Sch Tchr, 1974; Asst Resident Tutor, Morogoro Based Centre for Expatriate Workers, 1977; Asst Lectr, Snr Lectr, IDM Mzumbe Tanzduia, 1978-87; Prinicpal Tutor, Moshi Cooperative Coll, 1988- . *Publications include:* Labour on the Muadui Diamond Mine; Matti Party Systems Versus Single Party Systems. *Memberships:* Tanzania Historical Assn; Anto Aids Club of Kilimanjaro; Youth Employment; IBC. *Honours:* East African Award for best Student in Educ; Appointed Councillor for Moshi Municipality, Tanzduia.

OGATA Hiromaru, b. 17 Jan 1931, Tokyo, Japan. Prof, Chmn. m. 28 May 1964, 1 s, 1 d. *Education:* Kumamoto Univ, Doc of Medicine, 1957. *Appointments:* Intern Nat Toyko 2d Hosp, 1957-58; Resident in Anesthsia Univ, Toyko, 1958-63; DMS, Univ Toyko, 1964; Lectr, Sch Med Nihou Univ, Toyko, 1964-65; Assoc Prof, 197-72; Research Fellow, Albert Einstein Coll Med, Bronx, 1966-67; Prof Sch Medicine Juntendo Univ, Toyko, 1975-78; Prof, Chmn Sch Medicine Dokkyo, 1979-. *Publications:* Anesthesia and Resuscitation; Emergency Drugs ABC; Anesthesia Handbook; How to Manage Anesthesia. *Memberships include:* Japan Soc Anesthesiologists; Japan Resuscitation Soc. *Hobby:* Tennis. *Address:* Dokkyo Univ Sch Medicine, 1st Dept Anesthesiology, 880 Kitakobayashi, Mibu, Tochigi, Japan 321 02.

OGBONNAYA Chukwuemeka, b. 30 June 1953, Akoli Imenyi, Nigeria. Prof. m. Joycelynn Ogbonnaya, 30 Mar 1985, 3 d. *Education:* Univ of Nebraska, BS, 1979; Northwest Missouri State Univ, MS, 1981; Univ of Nebraska, PhD, 1985. *Appointments:* sst Prof, Mountain Empire Coll, 1985-90; Assoc Prof, 1990-; Visiting Prof, Penn State univ, 1990. *Publications include:* Lab Studies in Environmental Sci. *Memberships:* Amer Soc of Agronomy; Entomological Soc of America; Soc of Young American Profl; Virginia Acad of Sci. *Honours include:*

Chancellors C.Wealth Prof Award; Phi Beta Kappa. *Hobbies:* Tennis; Exercise; Soccer; Photography; Travel. *Address:* PO Box 957, Bigstone Gap, VA 24219, USA. 7, 15.

OGG Wilson Reid, b. 26 Feb 1928, Alhambra, Calif, USA. Poet; Graphic Artist; Curator in Residence, pinebrook; Retired Lawyer & Admin Law Judge. *Education:* AA, Univ of California, 1947; BA, 1949; LLB, JD, Boalt Hall Sch of Law, Univ of California, 1952. *Appointments:* Instr, Taegue English Language Inst, Korea, 1954; Psychology Instr, 25th Station Hosp Taegue, 1954; Snr Editor, Continuing Educ of the Bar, Univ of California, 1958-63; Arbitrator, American Arbitration Assn, 1963-; Curator in Residence, Pinebrook, 1964-; Certified as Instr of Law, Soc Sci & Real Est, California Community Coll, 1976; Dir of Admissions, ISPE, 1981-84; Attorney at Law, Private Practice, 1955-78. *Publications include:* Various Law Handbooks; Poetry. *Memberships include:* American Mensa Ltd; Triple Nine Soc; ISPE; Instl Soc of Unified Sci; Press Club of San Francisco; City Commons Club of Berkeley. *Honours:* Cultural Doctorate, Philosophy of Law; Commendation Ribbon with Medal Pendant, US Army. *Hobbies:* Landscape Designing; Gardening; Reading; Philosophy. *Address:* Pinebrook, Bret Harte Way, 1104 Keith Avenue, Berkeley, CA 94708, USA. 9, 16, 22, 52, 57, 59, 74, 128, 129, 130, 132, 133, 139, 163.

OGILVIE Kelvin Kenneth, b. 6 Nov 1942, Windsor, NS, Canada. Acad Admin & Prof of Cehmistry. m. E Roleen Lockhart, 7 May 1964, 1 s, 1 d. *Education:* BSc, Acadia Univ, 1963; BSc in Chemistry, 1964; PhD, Northwestern Univ, 1968. *Appointments:* Asst Prof, Chemistry, Univ of Manitoba, 1968-72; Assoc Prof, 1972-74; Assoc Prof, McGill Univ, 1974-78; Prof of Chemistry, mcGill Univ, 1978-87; Canadian Pacific Prof of Biotechnology, 1984-87; Prof of Chem, Vice Pres, Acadia Univ, 1987-; Dir, Office of Biotechnology, McGill, 1984-87. *Publications include:* 150 Refered Sci Publ; 12 Primary Patents; 31 Derivative Patents; 90 Conference Papers; 115 Lectrs; 72 Biotechnology Presentations. *Memberships:* American Chemical Soc; Chemical Inst of Canada; Ordre des Chimistes du Qubec; American Assn for the Advancement of Sci. *Honours include:* DSc Honoris Cause, Univ of New Brunswick & Acadia Univ; Buck Whitney Medal of the American Chemical Soc; Steacie Fellow; Mbr of the Order of Canada; Knight of Malta; Manning Principal Award; Fellowship of the Chemical Inst of Canada; Upjohn Fellow. *Hobbies:* Curling; Philately; Wood Working; Skating; Dog Sled Racing. *Address:* Acadia Univ, Wolfville, Nova Scotia, Canada BOP 1XO. 2, 142, 143.

OGIMI Kaoru, b. 6 Aug 1929, Spain. Dir; President, Kaic Corporation. m. Kikuko Nishikawa, 19 Mar 1962, 1 s. *Education:* Sophia Univ, 1949-50; Reed Coll Oregon, USA, 1950-54. *Appointments:* Asst Editor, Charles E Tuttle Co, 1955; Publicity Dir, 20th Century Fox Film, 1964; Pres, Readers Digest, Japan, 1975; Mngng Dir, Seiyu Dir, Seibu Dept Stores, 1983. *Publications include:* Nakiri Daio no Boken; Comeback. *Memberships include:* Nippon Ocean Racing Club; Sail Training Assn; Offshore Racing Council; Chamber of Commerce in Japan. *Honours:* Asahi Sports Award; Japan Yachting Assn Award; Minister of Transportation Citation. *Hobbies:* Yachting; Calligraphy; pottery; Environmental Issues; Philosophy. *Address:* 45 Yamanishi, Ninomiya-machi, Naka-gun, Kanagawa Prefecture 259-01, Japan.

OGUNNIYI Isaac Folorunso Oladosu, b. 5 Sept 1943, Ilesa, Nigeria. Barrister. m. Abigael Olanike, 26 Sept 1968, 2 s, 4 d. *Education:* ACIS, Assoc Inst of Chartered Sec, 1969; LLB, 1984; BL, 1985. *Appointments:* Admin Asst, Nigeria Tobacco Co, 1969-71; Personnel Officer, Co Sec, Wellcome Nigeria Ltd, 1971-73; Trebor Nigeria Plc, 1973-74; Rank Xerox Nigeria, 1974-80; Legal Pactitioner, Hd of Chamber. *Publications include:* Preparing for A Job Interview; Nigerian Labour & Employment Law in Perspective. *Memberships:* Assoc

Chartered Inst of Sec; British Inst of Personnel Mgmt; Nigerian Inst of Personnel Mgmt; Inst of Mgmt Conslts; Nigerian Bar Assn. *Hobbies:* Reading; Biographies of Achievers the World Over; Debating on Current Affairs. *Address:* Oladosu Ogunniyi & Co, PO Box 4015, Ikeja, Nigeria.

OGUNREMI Olakayode Olatunde, b. 13 Feb 1938, Lagos, Nigeria. Professor of Psychiatry and Consultant Psychiatrist. m. 29 Dec 1966, 2 s, 2 d. *Education:* MBBS London, 1966; MB, London, 1975; DPM, Edin, 1970; FMCPsych, 1976; FWACP, 1976. *Appointments:* Lectr, Psychi, 1972-75; Sr Lectr, Conslt, 1975-78; Prof, 1978-; Dean of MEd, 84; Chief Med Dir, 1984. *Memberships:* Assn for Psychophysiol Study of Sleep, 1972; Assn of Psychi, Nigeria; African Psychi Assn. *Honours:* Fulbright Hays Fellow, 1981; German Acad Fellowship, 1985; Sr C'wlth Univs Fellowship, 1986; Third World Acad of Scis Fellow,1989; WHO Expert Panel on Drug Dependence, 1981-. *Hobbies:* Table Tennis; Travelling; Collecting coins. *Address:* Department of Behavioural Sciences, University of Ilorin, PMB 1515, Ikorin, Nigeria.

OH Taeho, b. 18 Jan 1958, Korea. Dir, Hosp Pharmacy; Asst Prof, Univ. m. Evangeline Pena, 10 July 1987, 2 d. *Education:* BS, Juniata Coll, 1980; BS, Ohio State Univ, 1983; MS, 1986. *Appointments:* Asst Dir Pharmacy, St Francis Hosp, 1986-88; Asst Dir Pharmacy, Mt Sinai Med Crentre, FL, 1989-90; Clinical Asst Prof, Univ of Florida, 1989-; Asst prof, SECOPS, 1989-; Dir Pharmacy, Mercy Hosp, Miami, 1990-. *Publications:* Several Articles. *Memberships:* Soc of Hosp Pharmacists; Florida Soc Hosp Pharmacist. *Honours:* Ohio Sec of Hosp Pharmacist Research Award; Fl Soc of Hosp Pharmacist Publ Award. *Hobbies:* Golf; Hunting; Research; Reading. *Address:* 12685 Maple Road, North Miami, FL 33181, USA. 7.

OHASHI Kiyohide, b. 5 May 1924, Osaka, Japan. Literary Educ, Vice Pres. m. Kyoko Nishikawa, 30 June 1974, 2 s, 1 d. *Education:* BA, Ritsumeikan Univ, Kyoto, 1948. *Appointments:* Lectr, Osaka Inst Tech, 1954-62; Asst Prof, 1962-68; Asst Prof Tezukayama Gakuin Univ, Osaka, 1968-71; Prof Japanese Lit, 1971-; Chief Libr, 1985-91; Vice Pres, 1991-. *Publications include:* Izumi Shikibu Nikki no Kenkyu, A Study of the Diary of Izumi Shikibu; A Text Critic of Diary of Izumi Shikibu, Japanese Literature. *Hobbies:* Music; Photography. *Address:* 2-19-4 Machikuzuha, Hirakata, Osaka 573, Japan. 52.

OHNAMI Masateru, b. 6 Apr 1931, Kyoto. Pres; Prof. m. Hiroko Nakajima, 10 Oct 1959, 1 s. *Education:* BE, Ritsumeikan Univ, 1954; DrEngrng, Kyoto Univ, 1960. *Appointments:* Asst, Kyoto Univ, 1955-61; Assoc Prof, Ritsumeikan Univ, 1961-67; Res Fellow, Columbia Univ, 1963-64; Prof, Ritsumeikan Univ, 1967; Pres, 1991. *Publications include:* Strength & Frcture of Polycrystalline Bodies; Fracture & Society. *Memberships include:* Soc Mater Sci, Japan; Honorary mem, DVM; Res Liason Com; Jap Sci Counc. *Honour:* JSMS Award. *Hobbies:* Oil Painting. *Address:* 8-10 Hyugacho Takatsuki City, Osaka Prefecture, Japan 569.

OHNISHI Shun-ichi, b. 9 Jan 1930, Osaka, Japan. Pro. m. Yoko, 25 Oct 1959, 2 s, 1 d. *Education:* Osaka Univ, Faculty of Sci, BS, 1961. *Appointments:* Osaka Univ, Asst Prof, 1953-57; Japanese Assn for Radiation Research on Polymers, 1957-63; Kyoto Univ, Assoc Prof, 1963-68; Stanford Univ, Research Assoc, 1964-66; Kyoto Univ, Prof, 1968-. *Publications:* Dynamic Structure of Biological Membranes. *Memberships:* The Biophysical Soc of Japan; The Biochemical Soc of Japan; Japan Soc for Cell Biology; The Soc of Japanese Virologysts. *Honours:* Prize for Young Chemist, Chemical Soc of Japan; The Naito Prize for Sci. *Address:* 2-6-123 Myojyo cho, Uji, Kyoto 611, Japan.

OHNUMA Masahiko, b. 5 Aug 1932, Iwate Prefecture, Japan. Linguist. m. Tazuko Nishimura, 18 Apr 1965, 1 s, 2 d. *Education:* Toyko Univ of Education, BA, 1955;

MA, 1957. *Appointments:* Instr English Linguistics, Kobe City Univ of Foreign Languages, 1961-63; Asst Prof, 1963-69; Fulbright Research Scholar, 1963-64; Assoc Prof, Osaka City Univ, 1969-78; Prof of English Linguistics, 1978-89; Prof, Nara Women's Univ, 1989- ; Visiting Prof of Various Univs. *Publications include:* Studies in English Expressions of Quality, State & Comparison; Writer's Guide to English Usage, Second Edition (co-author); Numerous Articles. *Memberships:* Linguistic Soc of America; Kwansai Linguistic Circle; English Linguistic Soc of Japan; English Literary Soc of Japan. *Hobby:* Gardening. *Address:* 12-10 Ohnodai 5 chome, Osaka- Sayama 589, Japan. 1, 52.

OHTA Hiroshi, b. 2 Oct 1940, Hamamatsu, Japan. Prof of Economics. m. Yuko Narita, 3 June 1966, 2 s. *Education:* MA, Aoyama Gakuin Univ, 1966; PhD, Texas A&M Univ, 1971; Dr Econ, Aoyama Gakuin Univ, 1978. *Appointments:* Lectr, Aoyama Gakuin Univ, 1971-73; Assoc Prof, 1973-82; Prof, 1982-; Adjunct Prof, Univ of Houston, 1980-. *Publications include:* Theory of Spatial Pricing & Market Areas (Co-authored); Spatial Price Theory of Imperfect Competition. *Memberships include:* Regional Sci Assn; American Econ Assn; Applied Regional Sci Conference. *Honour:* Best 1977 Article, Western Econ Assn. *Hobby:* Fishing. *Address:* 4-19-10 Kugayama, Suginami ku, Toyko, 168 Japan. 52.

OHTA Tomoko, b. 7 Sept 1933, Aichi ken, Japan. m. Yasuo Ohta, 19 Mar 1960, div, 1 d. *Education:* Univ of Toyko, 1952-56; North Carolina State Univ, 1962-66; PhD, 1967; DSc, 1972. *Appointments:* Kihara Inst of Biological Sci, 1958-62; Natl Inst of Genetics, 1967- . *Publications:* Evolution & Variation of Multigene Families. *Memberships:* American Acad of Arts & Sci; Jour of Mol Evol; Jour of Theor Biol; Trends in Ecol & Evol; IMA J of Math Appl in Med & Biol. *Honours include:* First Saruhashi Prize; Weldon Memorial Prize. *Hobbies:* Reading. *Address:* 20 20 Hatsunedai, Mishima shi, Shizuoka ken, 411 Japan. 52.

OIDE Kyoji, b. 23 July 1940, Japan. Univ Prof. m. Reiko Yuza, 27 Apr 1969, 1 s. *Education:* BA, Tohoku Univ, 1964; MA, 1966. *Appointments:* Lectr, Yamagata Univ, Japan, 1969-72; Assoc Prof, 1972-75; Assoc Prof, Tohoku Univ, 1975-89; Prof, 1989-; Hd of Dept of English, Coll of Gen Educ, 1991-92; Chmn, Educ Affs Cttee, Coll of Gen Educ, 1992-. *Publications:* Articles on Shakespeare to Profl Journals. *Memberships:* The English Literary Soc of Japan; The Shakespeare Soc of Japan; The Renaissance Inst. *Hobbies:* Gardening; Sports. *Address:* 10-21 Yagiyama Kasumi-cho, Taihaku-ku, Sendai 982, Japan. 52.

OIKAWA Atsushi, b. 27 Jan 1929, Toyko, Japan. Prof Emeritus, Tohoku Univ. m. Masako, 4 Oct 1960, 3 s. *Education:* BSc Univ of Toyko, 1953; PhD, Osaka Univ, 1960. *Appointments:* Asst, Osaka Univ, Sch of Medicine, 1957; Lectr, 1961; Research Assoc, Natl Cancer Centre Research Inst, 1962; Section Hd, 1962; Prof, Tohoku Univ, 1974. *Publications:* Pigment Cell; Cancer; Scientific Papers. *Memberships:* NY Acad of Scis; Japanese Soc for Pigment Cell Research; Japanese Biochemical Soc; Japanese Cancer Assn. *Honours:* Seiji Memorial Award. *Hobbies:* Observing of Nature; Music; History of Universe; Earth & Human Beings. *Address:* Rm 405 Bld 2, Asahi Plaza, 49-12 Kuzuokashita, Goroku, Aobaku, Sendai 989-31, Japan. 52.

OIZERMAN Theodor liych, b. 14 May 1914, Petroverovka by Odessa, USSR. Scholar, Philosophy, History of Philosophy. m. Kasavina H, 11 Oct 1938, 2 s, 1 d. *Education:* Mosc Inst Hist, Philos Literature Philosophical Faculty, 1938; PhD, 1941; Habilitation, 1951. *Appointments:* Ind Worker, 1930-33; Army Serv, 1941-46; Asst prof, Moscow State Univ, 1946-53; Prof, Chair Dept Hist of Philosophy, 1953-68; YHd of Dept, 1986. *Publications include:* Die Philosophie Hegels. Dietz Verlag, Berlin; The Making of the Marxist Philosophy; The Main Trends in Philosophy.

Memberships: Ac SC USSR; Intl Inst of Philosophy; Jena Univ, Germany; Intl Soc of Dialectical Philosophy; Intl Soc of Feuerbach; Schelling Soc. *Honours include:* Red Star Order; Plekhanov Prize; Stte Prize. *Hobby:* Walking. *Address:* Inst of Philosophy, Acad of Sci, Volkhonka 14, Moscow, 119842, Russia. 1, 139.

OJOKO Sydney Simeon, b. 30 Nov 1940, Nembe. Snr Lectr, Agricl & Extension Educ. m. Janet Ngozi Nwankwo, 2 Sept 1967, 2 s, 4 d. *Education:* Umudike Sch, Nigeria, 1963; Diploma Gen Agricl, 1967; BSc, 1977; Masters Degree Agricl Educ, 1978; Tuskegee Inst; PhD, Penn State Univ, USA, 1979. *Appointments:* Boarding Clerk, Port Harcourt, 1961; Agricl Reporter, Ministry of Agric, Enugu, 1963-65; Asst Agricl Superintendent, 1968-69; Agricl Superintendent, Acting Higher Agricl Super, Rivers State Ministry of Agric, Fisheries & Natl Resources in Port Harcout, 1970-74; Natl Publicity Sec, Nigerian Audo Visual Assn, 1972-73; Commissioned Salesman, 1975-76;Exec Dir, Agricl Devel Agency in River State, 1979-83; Editor in Chief, Nigerian Audio Visual Journal, 1981-82;Interministerial Committee, Rivers Agricl Deve Project, 1982-83; Poject Mgr, Aborted Rivers Agricl Devel Project, 1982- 83; Dir, Centre for Continuing Educ, 1985-; Exec Editor, Nigerian Journal of Agricl Tchr Educ. *Publications include:* More than 300 Newspaper Articles; Youth Employment Scheme: A Case Study of Rivers State Sch to Land Agricl Programme. *Memberships include:* Phi Delta Kappa; Kappa Delta Pi; Gamma Sigma Delta. *Honours include:* River State Scholarship Award. *Hobbies:* Writing; Photography; Travel. *Address:* PO Box 4241, Port Harcourt, Nigeria. 139, 169.

OKA Masa Aki, b. 31 Dec 1926, China. Banker. m. Emiko Masaki, 14 Dec 1955. *Education:* Toyko Univ, LLA, 1949-52; Yale Law Sch, LLM, 1952-53. *Appointments:* Bank of Toyko, 1953-68; Snr Vice Pres, Bank of Toyko Trust Co, 1969-75; General Mgr, Toyko, 1975-77; Snr Mgmt Mgng Dir, Bank of Toyko Intl, 1978-85; NBD Bank, Vice Pres & General Mgr, Toyko, 1985- *Memberships:* City Club of Toyko; American Club, Univ Club; Yale Club of NYC and Japan; Ashigara Shinrin Country Club; Pymble Golf Club; American Chamber of Commerce. *Honour:* Fullbright Scholarship. *Hobbies:* Gardening; Golf; Reading; Travel. *Address:* 3 24 15 401 Tsurumaki, Setagaya ku, Toyko 154, Japan.

OKABAYASHI Ichizo, b. 29 Aug 1926, Kyoto, Japan. Prof, Niigata Coll of Pharmacy. m. Kyoko Yutani, 21 May 1960, 1 d. *Education:* Bach of Pharmacy, Kyoto Univ, 1952; Doc of Pharmacy, 1960. *Appointments:* Asst, Osaka College of Pharmacy (now Osaka Univ of Pharmaceutical Science), 1952-58; Asst Prof, 1958-62; Assoc Prof, 1962-65; Prof, 1965-72; Chief Research Worker, Morishita Pharmaceutical Inc, 1972-75; Hokuto Pharmaceutical Inst, 1975-77; prof, Niigata Coll of Pharmacy, 1977-. *Publications include:* Pharmaceutical Synthetic Chemistry. *Memberships:* The Pharmaceutical Soc of Japan; The Chemical Soc of Japan; The Soc of Synthetic Organic Chemistry, Japan. *Hobbies:* Playing Piano; Appreciation of Classical Music & Paintings. *Address:* 5 1 904 Sasaguchi 3 Chome, Niigata 950, Japan. 52.

OKAFOR Fabian Chinemelu, b. 24 July 1948, Igbo Ukwu, Nigeria. Lectr. m. Victoria Nwamaka Madueke, 22 May 1982, 3 s, 3 d. *Education:* BSc, 1977; MSc, 1980; PhD, 1985. *Appointments:* Univ Ibadan, 1978-88; Graduate Asst, 1978-81; Asst Lectr, 1981-85; Lectr ii, 1985-88; Lectr i, 1988-90; Snr Lectr, 1990. *Publications include:* The Theory & Application of Sampling Over Two Occasions for the Estimation of Current Population Ratio. *Memberships:* Nigerian Statistical Assn. *Honours:* British Council Staff Devel Scholarship. *Hobbies:* Football; Organising Club for Boys. *Address:* Dept of Statistics, Univ of Nigeria, Nsukka, Nigeria.

OKECKA BROMKOWA Maryna, b. 26 June 1922, Uscilug na Wolyniu. Journalist; Writer. m. Bohdan

Bromek, div. *Education:* Secondary Monastic Sch. *Appointments:* Polish Broadcasting station, olsztyn; 1 Hr Monthly Broadcasting Cyclic Serv, Through the Pepople And Songs Traces. *Creative Works include:* The Archive of Foklore Collected by Maryna okecka. *Memberships:* Polish Journalist Assn; Polish Writers Assn. *Honours:* Gol Microphone. *Hobbies:* Country House Near the Lake Bioenergytherapentic. *Address:* ul Niedzialkowskiego 17/7, 10-347 Olsztyn, Poland.

OKEH Peter Igbonekwu, b. 12 Sept 1939, Ebe Enu Gu, Nigeria. Unit Techng & Research. m. Lucie Desrochers, 15 Aug 1968, 1 s, 2 d. *Education:* St Charles Coll, Nigeria, 1955-58; Univ of London, 1959-62; Univ of Nigeria, 1962-64; Laval Univ, Quebec, Canada, 1964-67, 1968-72. *Appointments:* St Charles Coll, Nigeria, Tutor, 1960-62; Univ of Moncton, Canada, Asst Prof, 1969-73; Assoc Prof, 1973-77; Prof, 1977-79; Univ of Benin, Nigeria, Assoc Prof, 1979-86; Prof, 1986-92. *Publications include:* Numerous Essays; Fiction. Stories for our Fathers; Racism in a Mixed Marriage; Men in our Folktales; Five Igbo Myths & Legends. *Memberships include:* Canadian Assn of African Studies; Intl Federation of French Tchrs; Intl Assn of Semiotics. *Honours:* Scholarship Award; Canadian Intl Devel Agency. *Hobbies:* Farming; Tennis; Christian Fellowship. *Address:* Deans Office, Faculty of Arts, Univ of Benin, Benin City, Edu State, Nigeria.

OKUBO Hiroshi, b. 3 Mar 1929, Aichi Ken, Japan. Prof of Hosei Univ. m. Setsuko Horii, 22 Mar 1961, 1 s, 1 d. *Education:* Hosei Univ, BA, 1951. *Appointments:* Research Asst, English Dept, Hosei Univ, 1951-54; Instr, 1954-56; Lectr, 1956-60; Asst Prof, 1960-68; Prof, 1968-. *Publications include:* Translations, Mark Twains Letters from Hawaii. *Memberships:* Modern Language Assn, Japan; PEN; Mark Twain Circle of America. *Address:* Seki 1-22-1-526, Tama Ku, Kawasaki Shi, Kanagawa Ken 214, Japan.

OKUDA Hiroaki, b. 25 Jan 1950, Chiba, Japan. Medical Doctor. m. Kaoru Okuda, 19 Apr 1981. *Education:* Faculty of Medicine, Hirosaki, Univ Sch of Medicine, 1969-75; MD, 1975; PhD, 1985. *Appointments:* Inst of Gastroenterology, Toyko Womens Medical Coll, 1975-81; Clinical Asst, 1981-87; Asst Prof, 1987-90; Assoc Prof, 1990-. *Publications include:* Various Publ. *Memberships:* Intl Assn for the Study of the Liver; American Assn for the Study of Liver Diseases; Japanese Assn for the Study of the Liver; Japanese Soc of Gastroenterology. *Honours:* Japanese Assn for the Study of Liver, Award. *Hobby:* Tennis. Address: 13-34-305 Yocho Cho, Shinjuku Ku, Toyko 162, Japan. 139.

OKUI Kazumitsu, b. 8 July 1933, Gumma, Japan. Kitasato Univ Prof. m. Aoki Mizue Okui, 6 May 1961, 1 s, 1 d. *Education:* Toyko Univ of Agric, BA, 1962; MA, 1964; PhD, 1967. *Appointments:* Lectr, Kitasato Univ, 1970-72; Asst Prof, 1972-82; Prof, 1982-. *Publications include:* Entomolgy; General Zoology; human Sci. *Memberships:* Sec of Intl Wild Silkmothes; Intl Wild Silkmoth Research Centre. *Hobbies:* Collection of any Living Things; Travel. *Address:* Sch of Liberal Arts & Sci, Kitasato Univ, 1 15 1 Kitasato, Sagamihara, Kanagawa 228, Japan. 2.

OKUTSU Fumio, b. 26 Jan 1935, Toyko, Japan. Univ Prof. m. Yoshiko Miyasaka, 21 Apr 1963, 2 s. *Education:* Tokyo Gakugei Univ, 1954-58; Intl Christian Univ, 1960-64; Univ of Texas, 1964-65. *Appointments:* Prof, Wayo Womens Univ, 1981-; Chmn, Dept of Eng Lit, Wayo Womens Univ, 1982-89; Dean of Students, 1990-. *Publications include:* Eng & Japanese Proverbs: A Comparative Study. *Memberships:* Japan Assn of Coll Eng Tchrs; Kanto Koshinetsu Assn of Tchrs of Eng. *Honours:* Jacet Prize. *Hobbies:* Tennis; Shogi. *Address:* 5-17-24 Sakai, Musashino-Shi, Toyko 180, Japan. 1, 52.

OKWUOWULU Philip Asomba, b. 31 Dec 1941, Nnewi, Nigeria. Research Sci. m. Maria, 5 Mar 1970, 3 s, 3 d. *Education:* Agricl Sch Umudike, 1962-63, 1966-67. *Appointments:* Agric Asst, 1963-65, 1968- 72; Tech Officer, 1972-76; Research Officer, 1979-80; Snr Research Officer, 1980-83; Principal Research Officer, 1983-88; Asst Chief Sci Officer, 1988-. *Publications:* Compiled Vol, 1 - 111 of the Book of Abstracts. *Memberships:* Agricl Soc of Nigeria; Bio Tech Soc of Nigeria; Genetics Soc of Nigeria. *Hobbies:* Gardening; Backyard Poultry Keeping. *Address:* Nat Root Crops Research Inst, Umudike, PMB 7006, Umuahia, Imo State, Nigeria.

OLEKOV Peter, b. 29 May 1940, Sofia. Architect. m. Rumjana Genova, 3 July 1966, 2 s. *Education:* Higher inst for Civil Engrng & Arch, 1966. *Appointments:* Research Inst for Urban Planning, 1966-73; Designers Firm, 1973-77; Work Abroad, Algeria, 1977-79; Hd of Dept for Urban Planning, 1980-90; Private Bureau for Urban Planning, Arch Projects, 1990-. *Publications include:* Regional Planning for Resorts' Spots. *Membership:* Assn of the Architects. *Honours include:* Natl Exhibition of Bulgarian Arch. *Hobbies:* Fishing; Literature; Classical music. *Address:* Str Dospat 20, Sofia 1606, Bulgaria.

OLES Laura Treadgold, b. 21 June 1956, Seattle, WA, USA. Lawyer. m. Douglas Stuart Oles, 18 Dec 1979. *Education:* Stanford Univ, 1978; JD, Univ Washington, 1981; Bar, Wash, 1981; US District Ct, Wash, 1981. *Appointments:* Assoc, Bogle & Gates, Seattle, 1981-83; Weinrich & Gilmore, seattle, 1983-87; Counsel, Davies Wright & Jones, 1988-89; Prtnr, Davies Wright Tremaine, Seattle, 1990-; Natl Bd Dir, MIT Enterprize Forum, 1990-; Bd Dir MIT Enterprize Forum of Northwest, 1985-; Chmn, 1989-90; Assoc Editor, WAsh Law Rev, 1980-81. *Memberships:* ABA; BAr Assn; Seattle King County Bar Assn; Japanese Am Soc for Legal Studies; Phi Beta Kappa; Episcopalian Securities. *Honour:* Kenndy Ctr Award. *Address:* Davis Wright Tremaine 1501, 4th Avenue, Seattle, WA 98101, USA.

OLESZKIEWICZ Jerzy, b. 12 Feb 1926, Baranowicze, Poland. Physician. m. Jadwiga, 3 Aug 1976, 2 s, 2 d. *Education:* Medical Academy Warsaw, 1952; Doctors Degree, Medical Acad Krakow, 1963. *Appointments:* Lectr, Univ of Warsaw, 1980-81; General Dir, state Childrens Hosp, Warsaw, 1981-91; Hd of Psychosomatic Clinic, State Childrens Hosp, Warsaw, 1981-. *Publications include:* The Role of Magnesium Deficit in Psychosomatical Diseases and Disturbances in Childrens Age. *Memberships:* Polish Medical Soc; Polish Pediatric Soc; Polish Soc for Research on Magnesium; Deutsche Januz Korczak Gesellschaft, Giessen. *Honours include:* A Number of Prizes pof Polish Medical Authorities. *Hobbies:* Hunting; Reading; Music. *Address:* Sienkiewicza 49, 05-080 Izabelin, Poland.

OLIE Jean Pierre, b. 17 Apr 1945, Aubin, France. Psychiatrist. m. Prades D'Aubrac, 10 Aug 1968, 2 s, 1 d. *Education:* Doc in Medicine, Paris, 1975; Conslt High Court of Justice of Paris, 1988. *Appointments:* Prof Medical Univ of Paris; Pschiatrist, Str Anne Hosp, Paris. *Publications include:* Many Papers; 3 Books. *Memberships include:* French Biological Pyduatric Anouackin. *Honours:* Joulyn Chedoudi. *Hobbies:* Politics; Soccer. *Address:* Sainte Anne Hosp, 1 Rue Cabaris, 75014 Paris, France.

OLIVA Karel, b. 26 Nov 1958, Louny, Czechoslovakia. Computational Linguistics. *Education:* Charles Univ, Prague, 1978-83; Degree Doc of Natural Sci, 1986. *Appointments:* Dept of Mathematical Linguistics, CU Prague, 1983-88; Bulgarian Acad of Sci, Sofia, 1989-90; Univ of Saarland, 1990-. *Publications include:* A Number of Articles. *Membership:* Assn for Computational Linguistics. *Hobbies:* Classical Music; Travel; Foreign Languages; Sports. *Address:* Waldwiese 9 11, W 66 00 Saarbrueken, Germany.

OLIVA Pavel, b. 23 Nov 1923, Prague. Prof of Ancient History; Hd Researcher at Inst of Classical Studies. m. Vera Pavova, 23 June 1949, 1 s, 1 d. *Education:* Charles Univ, 1945-49; PhD, 1951; Czech Acad of Sci, 1961. *Appointments:* Political & Economic Univ, Asst Prof, 1949- 51; Charles Univ, Asst Prof, 1951-52; Czech Acad of Sci, Vice Dir, Inst of History, Hd Researcher, Inst of Classical Studies, 1952-; Visiting Prof, Oxford, 1981. *Publications include:* The Early Greek Tyranny; REcko mezi Makedonif a Rimen. *Memberships include:* Czech Acad of Sci; Austrian Archaeological Inst; Hungarian Soc of Classical Studies. *Honours:* F Palacky Medal in Humanities. *Hobby:* Reading. *Address:* Na Micance 18, Prague 6, 160 00 Czechoslovakia.

OLIVOVA Vera, b. 13 Nov 1926, Prague, Czechoslovakia. Prof of History. m. Pavel Oliva, 23 June 1949, 1 s, 1 d. *Education:* Charles Univ, Prague, 1945-59; PhD, 1951; CSc, 1957; Dr Sc, 1991. *Appointments:* Asst Prof, Charles Univ, Prague, 1951-63; Assoc Prof, 1964-70; Political Reasons out of job in Modern History, 1970-89; Prof in History, Charles Univ, 1990-. Publications: Czech Soviet Relations; The Doomed Democracy; Men & Games; Sports & Games in the Ancient World; Czech History. *Memberhips:* Edvard Benes Soc; Historical Soc; Ethnographical Soc; Intern Soc for Hist of Sport; HISPA; ISHPES; Czech History Confernce. *Hobbies:* History; History of Ary; History of Literature. *Address:* Na Micance 18, Praha 6, 160 00, Czechoslovakia.

OLLOR Walter G, b. 20 Dec 1950, Eleme, Nigeria. Economist. m. Helen Yorowa Osarolior, 3 Jan 1978, 2 s, 1 d. *Education:* BSc, Univ of Lfe, 1975; PhD, Low State Univ, USA, 1980. *Appointments:* Grad Asst, 1976-77; Lectr, 1980-85; Snr Lectr, 1985-; Univ of Port Harcourt; Research Asst, Lowa State Univ, 1977-80; Bd Chmn, Intl Merchant Cank. *Publications include:* A Review of Lance Taylors Macro Models for Devel Countries. *Memberships:* American Economic Assn; Econometric Soc; Nigerian Economic Soc; Jaycees Intl Port Harcourt Lom; Eleme Social Club; Academic Staff Union of Univ. *Honours include:* Staff Devel Award. *Hobbies:* Lawn Tennis; Music. *Address:* Intl Merchant Bank Ltd, 1 Akin Adesola Street, Victoria Island, PMB 12028, Lagos, Nigeria. 52.

OLSON Holvar Edwin, b. 4 Jan 1948, Frankfurt Am Mein, Germany. Psychotherapist. m. 8 Jan 1992. *Education:* BA, Salem Coll, West Virginia; BS; MA, Chapman Coll, California; Currently, PhD in Clinical Psychology, Kensington Univ, Los Angeles, CA. *Appointments:* Boy Scout Exec, 1970; Psy Asst, Central State Mental Hosp, 1970-72; Regl Rec Therapist, 1972-78; Dir Vol Sus, 1978-83; Snr Psychotherapist, 1983-. *Publications include:* Numerous Papers. *Memberships include:* Acad of Psychology; American Assn for Psysiological Psy; American Assn for Hypnotherapists. *Honours include:* Outstanding Young Men of America. Eagle Scout Award. *Hobbies:* Rebuild Antique Watches & Clocks; Sailing; Reading; Clinical Hypnosis; Enjoying Cottage at Lake Gaston. *Address:* Tri City Counseling Serv, 1585 Berkeley Avenue, Petersburg, VA 23805, USA. 2, 117.

OLSZEWSKA Maria Joanna, b. 21 Apr 1929, Dabrowka Polska Sanok. Prof of Plant Cytology & Cytochemistry. m. Waclaw Olszewski, 27 Oct 1948, 1 d. *Education:* Engr Sch Agricl, Lodz, 1949; MSc, 1950; Dr Biol Univ Lodz, 1956; Docent Habilitation, 1960; Assoc Prof, 1969; Full Prof, 1978. *Appointments:* Asst Sch Agricl, Lodz, 1949-50; Asst Pedagogical Coll, 1950-53; Staff Univ, 1953-; Snr Asst Prof, Hd Lab, Cytochemistry, 1961-71; Hd Dept Plant Cytology & Cytochemistry, 1971-. *Publications include:* About 100 Publ. *Memberships:* Polish Acad of Sci; New York Ac Aci; Soc Sci Lublinensis; Polish Hist & Cytochemical Soc; Polish Botanical Soc; Copernicus Soc. *Honours include:* Polonia Restitute Cross 11 & 111. *Hobbies:* Cats; Mushrooms; Recr; Reading Books. *Address:*

Wierzbowa 38 m 43, 90 245 Lodz, Poland. 2, 52, 138, 162.

OLSZEWSKI Andrzej K, b. 21 Oct 1931, Warsaw. Art Historian. m. (1) Krystyna Romaszewska, 5 Jan 1954, (2) Irena Grzesiuk, 21 Jan 1978, 1 s, 1 d. *Education:* MA, Dept of History of Art, Warsaw Univ, 1955; Phil Dr, 1965; Dr Habilitatus, 1985; Prof Acad of Catholic Theology, 1990. *Appointments:* Inst of History of Art, Polish Acad of Sci, Asst, 1955-75; Acad of Catholic Theology, Hd of studies, 1977; Hd of Modern Art Studes, Acad of Catholic Theology, 1992; Hd of Modern Art Studies, Catholic Univ in Lublin, 1992. *Creative Works include:* Art Course Concerned with Study of Art; Three Books; 135 Monographic Studies; Papers; Articles. *Memberships:* Research Council in the Inst of Art; polish Acad of Sci; Assn of Art Critics; AICA; Polish Section of Docomomo; Documentation & Conservation of Buildings, Sites & Neighbourhood of the Modern Movement. *Honours include:* Awards of the Assoc of Art Historians, 1958, 1966; Polish Acad of Scis, 1973, 1989; Diplome d'Honneur of the Friends of Warsaw Soc, 1987; Gold Medal for The Proteccion of Monuments, 1979; Golden Cross of Merit, 1981. *Hobbies:* Classicl Music; Pets. *Address:* Kartaginy 1 m 369, 02 762 Warsaw, Poland. 139.

OLUDIMU Olufemi Ladipo, b. 1 Mar 1951, Lagos, Nigeria. Educator; Agricl Economist. m. Adeyinka Adedyin Ogunbanjo, 2 s, 3 d. *Education:* BSc, Univ of Ibadan, 1971-74; MSc, Univ of Oxford, 1975-76; Natl Youth Serv, 1974-75; Leed Poly, 1977-78; Obafemi Awolowo Univ, MBA, 1981-83; PhD, 1984-87. *Appointments:* Lectr, Obafemi Awolowo Univ, 1980-84; Snr Lectr, 1984-; Contl, Natl & Intl Organ, Obafemi Awolowo Univ, 1984-. *Publications include* 2 Monographs; Book Chapters; Articles. *Memberships:* Intl Farm Mngt Assn; West African Assn of Agricl Economists; Nigerian Economics Soc; Nigerian Agricl Economics Assn; Gideons Intl Ife Comp; Red Cross Soc of Nigeria. *Honours include:* T e Elias Prize for Scholarship; Western State Government Scholar. *Hobbies:* Travel; Reading; Table Tennis. *Address:* House 8, 0 Close, 3rd Avenue, Festac Town, Lagos, Nigeria. 52.

OLUFOKUNBI Banwo, b. 14 May 1946, Nigeria. Univ Tchr; Researcher. m. Karen Denise Cowan, 14 May 1977, 4 s. *Education:* BSc, 1969; MS, 1973; PhD, 1977. *Appointments:* Univ of 1LE 1FE, Asst, 1971- 73; Oregon State Univ, Grad/Research Asst; Univ of Hawatt, 1974-77; Obafemi Awolowo Univ, 1977-. *Memberships:* Nigeria Economic Soc; Nigerian Agricl Economists Assn; American Agricl Economists Assn; Int of Mktng London; Inst of Mktng India. *Honours:* Phi Kappa Phi. *Hobbies:* Film Watching; Acting; Music; Literature. *Address:* Dept of Agricl Economics, OBafemi Awolowo Univ, ILE IFE, Nigeria.

OMER El Fadil El Obeid, b. 1 Jan 1944, Sudan. Prof of Medical Microbiology. m. Zeinab Saeed Hijazi, 31 July 1970, 1 s, 5 d. *Education:* MBBS, 1969; Dp Bact, 1975; Dip Ven, 1976; MD, 1984; MRC Path, 1985; FICTM, 1985; AIMLS, 1990; MRCP, 1991. *Appointments:* Med Officer Ministry of Health, Khartoum, 1969-73; Research Asst, 1973-76; Lectr, 1976-82; Assoc Prof, 1982-88; Cons Pathologist, 1988-91; Prof Microbiology, 1991-. *Publications include:* Numerous Research Papers; Review Articles; Books; Patents. *Memberships include:* British Soc Microbiology; Am Assn Venereal Diseases; Union Against Venereal Diseases; Internat Soc of Andrology. *Hobbies:* Scientific Research Work; Watching Football Matches. *Address:* Saudia Medical Serv, PO Box 167, Jeddah 21231, Saudi Arabia. 52.

OMOLE Gabriel Gbolabo, b. 15 Mar 1940, Akungba Akoko. Intl Investor. 1 s, 2 d. *Education:* United Sch, Akungba Akoko; Salvation Army Sec Modern Sch, Supare Akoko. *Appointments:* Chmn, Gay Omole Investments, London, Brunel, New York, Lagos, Singapore; Chmn, Brunei Resources; Brunei Intl

Investors Ltd, Lagos, London; Combined Billionaires Network; Combined Intl Investors. *Memberships:* US Chamber of Commerce; New York Chamber of Commerce; Nigerian American Chamber of Commerce; New York Acad of Sci. *Honours:* Deputy Governor, American Biographical Inst Research Assn; Intl Biographical Assn. *Hobbies:* Business Travel. *Address:* PO Box 74447, Victoria Island, Lagos, Nigeria. 52, 132, 152, 162.

ONDEK Violet C Hughes, b. 29 Dec 1913, Philadelphia, PA, USA. Retired. m. Steve M Ondek, 29 July 1963, 1 s, 1 d. *Education:* Colwyn & Darby, Pa, Public Schs; Numerous Courses & Seminars. *Appointments:* Corr Evening Bulletin, phila, Pa, Corr upper Darby News, 1948-51; Adv Dept, Gettysburg Times, 1951-53; Residential Contractor, 1953-72; Built Hundreds of Homes in 6 Countries; Founder Sec Treas, Corporate Investment Co, 1970-84; Founder, Sec Treas, Corporate Life Ins, 1972-84; Retired, 1984. *Memberships include:* Adams County Home Builders; Hist Soc Ch Natl Apple Museum; Thronsburgs Small Business Council; Womens Republican Club. *Honours include:* Distinguished Merit Adams County Republican Club. *Hobbies:* Oil Painting; Politics; Antiques; Government; Community; Travel. *Address:* Biglerville, PA 17307, USA. 6, 52, 132, 138, 152, 162.

ONO Syu, b. 5 Sept 1918, Fukuoka, Japan. Prof Emeritus. m. Choyo Ono, 5 Mar 1944, 1 d. *Education:* Grad 3 Yr Course, Toyko Coll of Sci, 1940; BSc, 1942; Completed 2 yr Course, 1945; Kyushu Imperial Univ, DSc, 1951. *Appointments:* Sub Asst, Faculty of Engrng, 1942-43; Assoc Prof, 1945-54; Assoc prof, 1954-79; Prof Emeritus, 1979-; Pres, Gunma Univ, 1981- 85. *Publications include:* Molecular Theory of Surface Tension in Liquids; Thermodynamics. *Memberships:* Physical Soc of Japan; Sci Council of Japan. *Honours:* Commission of Thermodynamics & Statistical Mechanics, Intl Union for Pure & Applied Physics; Organizing Committee, Intl Conference of Statistical Mechanics. *Hobbies:* Gardening; Travel. *Address:* 6 30 13 Minamirikan, Yamatoshi, Kanagawa 242, Japan.

ONO Yasokichi, b. 5 Apr 1933, Nagano Ken, Japan. German & German Literature Educ. m. 20 Sept 1964, 1 s, 1 d. *Education:* BA, Nagoya Univ, 1958. *Appointments:* Guest Researcher, Freie Univ, Berlin, 1965- 67; Lectr, Nagoya Hokeneisei Univ, 1968-72; Shinshu Univ, Matsumoto, 1974-; Prof, Matsumoto Dental Coll, 1972-. *Publications include:* The Structure of the Japanese Mind, Kokoro; Easy German Grammar for Students. *Memberships:* The Philosophical Assn of Japan, Tokyo. *Address:* Matsumoto Dental Coll, 1780 Gobara Hirooka, 399 07 Shiojiri, Japan. 2, 52.

OPACKI Ireneusz Maria, b. 5 Aug 1933, Tochortkow, Poland. Prof of Theory & Polish Literature. m. Anna Chruszczewska, 8 Apr 1958, 3 d. *Education:* Ma, Catholic Univ of Lublin, 1958; PhD, Jagiellonian Univ, Cracow, 1966; Polish Acad of Sci, Warsaw, 1972; Prof, 1977. *Appointments:* Asst, Adjunct, Catholic Univ, Lublin, 1959-73; Assoc Prof, Prof, Univ of Silesia, Katowice, 1973-; Dept Hed of Theory of Literature, 1974-; Dir, Inst of Polish Literature, Univ of Silesia, 1977-87, 1990-; Dean of Film Sch Univ of Silesia, 1987-90; Vice Chancelers Deputy/Prorector, 1980-82. *Creative Works include:* Evolution of Ballad Narration; The Movement of Convention. *Memberships:* Scientific Soc of Catholic Univ, Lublin; Lublin Scientific Soc; Polish Literary Sci; Polish acad of Sci; Literary Soc of Adam Mickiewicz; Soc of Zofia Kossak; History of Polish Literature; Polish Acad of Sci, Katowice Branch. *Honours include:* Minister of Educ Prizes; Prize of Silesian Politechnic Rector. *Hobbies:* Sports; Painting; Film. *Address:* ul Brzozowa 23, 41 200 Sosnowiec, Poland. 152.

OPPENHEIMER Michael Anthony, His Hon Judge, b. 22 Sept 1946, London, England. Circuit Judge. m. Nicola Anne Brotherton, 14 Apr 1973, 1 s, 1 d.

Education: Westminster Sch, 1960-65; London Sch of Economics, 1966-68; Middle Temple, 1969-. *Appointments:* Called to the Bar, 1970; Asst Recorder, 1985; Recorder, 1989; Circuit Judge, 1991. *Hobbies:* Theatre; Cinema; Books; Performing & Listening to Music. *Address:* Athenaeum, 107 Pall Mall, London SW1Y 5ER, England.

OPPENHEIMER Tamar Mariamne, b. 20 Nov 1925, London, England. Co Dir; Bd Member. m. Hanz Herman Oppenheimer, 22 Oct 1949, dec. *Education:* MA, Columbia Univ, 1933; BA, McGill Univ, Montreal, 1946. *Appointments:* United Nations Sec, Asst Sec General, 1946-87; Dir UN div Narcotic Drugs, 1982-86; Sec Gen, UN Int Conference, Drug Abuse, 1985-87. *Publications include:* Numerous Articles. *Memberships:* Alliance for Drug Free Canada; Foundation for Responsible Computing; Natl Council Canadian Human Rights Foundation. *Honour:* Officer, Order of Canada. *Hobbies:* Music; Decorative Arts; Reading. *Address:* Foundation for Responsible Computing, One First Canadian Place, Suite 6300, PO Box 50, Toronto, Ontario, Canada M5X 1B8. 52.

ORCHARD Dennis Frank, b. 21 May 1912, Portsmouth, England. Emeritus Prof, Univ of New South Wales. m. Joyce Clyde Stewart, 14 Oct 1965. *Education:* Bradfield Coll, Berkshire, 1926-29; Imperial Coll, London Univ, 1933-37. *Appointments:* Ministry of Works, UK, 1939-46; Road Research Lab, UK, 1946-50; Harlow Devel Corporation, 1950-54; Acting Engr, Chief Firm of Conslt Engrs to Ghana Government, 1954-57; Foundation Prof of Highway Engrng Univ, NSW, 1959-77; Conslt to United Nations, 1966-67. *Publications include:* Concrete Technology, Properties of Materials; Factors Influencing The Wear of Coarse Aggregates in the Los Angeles Test. Many Papers. *Memberships:* Inst of Civil Engrs; Inst of Engrs of Australia; Standards Inst of Australia; Road Pavements Committee of Australian Road Research Bd. *Honours include:* Telford Prize; Miller Prize; James Forest Medal. *Hobbies:* Giving of Expert Evidence in Court on Road Accidents; Swimming; Gardening. *Address:* 1 Jenkins St, Chatswood, NSW 2067, Australia.

ORD-HUME Arthur W J G, b. 20 May 1932. m. (1) Brenda, June 1952, div, (2) Judith Rose, 1968, div, 2 s, 1 d. *Education:* Wellington, Harow, Univ of London, BSC. *Appointments:* Royal Air Force, 1949-55; Post War Pioneer in Home Built Light Aircraft Movement; Historian & Restorer, Mechanical Musical Instruments; Writer on Mechanical Music; Chief of Design; Agricl Aviation Co, Mngr Southern Aircraft Co; Dir, Britten Norman Ltd; European Rep of the Experimental Aircraft Assn; Mgrng Dir, Phoenix Aircraft Ltd; Prof of History of Instruments of Music; Editor, Music & Antomata. *Publications include:* Light Aircraft Design & Construction; Clockwork Music - An Illustrated History; Joseph Haydn and the Mechanical Organ. *Honours:* EAA Trophy, Distinguished Serv to Aviation Educ; Q David Bowers Literary Awd for Musical Educ Advancement in Am. *Hobbies:* Music; Flying; Writing. *Address:* Plestor House, Farnham Road, West Liss, Hampshire, GU33 6JQ, England.

OREL Ahmet, b. 27 Nov 1952, Paris, France. Vice Pres, Legal & Corporate Sec. m. Ilhan, 22 June 1984, 1 s, 1 d. *Education:* Grad Ankara Univ, Faculty of Law, 1976; The Fletcher Sch of Law & Diplomacy, Tufts Univ, 1981. *Appointments:* Military Serv, Turkish Naval Hdquarters, 1978-79; Attorney at Law, 1981-83; Corporate Lawyer, 1983-88; Corporate SEc, Legal Counsel, 1988-. *Memberships:* Ankara Bar Assn; Turkish Basketball Coaches Assn; Ankara Coll Alumni Assn; Ankara Coll Sports Club; Fletcher Sch Alumni Assn; Tufts Univ Alumni Assn. *Hobbies:* Photography; Gardening; Sports; Fishing; Sailing. *Address:* Netas Northern Electric Telekomunikasyon AS, Alemdag Caddesi, Umraniye 81244, Istanbul, Turkey.

ORGAD Ben-zion b. 21 Aug 1926, Germany. Retired Musician. 2 s. *Education:* Composition, Jerusalem Acad with Josef Tal and NY with Aaron Copland, 1940-49; Supervisor of Mus Educ, Israel Min of Educ and Culture, 1975-; Master of Fine Arts Deg, Musicol, Brandeis Univ, 1961. *Publications:* Poetry: Disqualified witness, 1984; Visible to an eye, 1985; Open Martins, 1986; Prose: Lingerings and studying, an interim report, 1986; Dissension, 1988; Translations of selected poems, 1987; Compositions: Symph in two movements for baritone and orchestra, 1949; Biblical Cantata for mixed choir and orchestra, 1951; Quintet for mezzo soprano, 1956; Monologue for viola solo, 1957; Mizmorim for sooists and chamber orchestra, 1966-68; passion in five testimonies for soloists, two mixed choirs and chamber orchestra, 1970; ballad for symphony orchestra, 1971; Permissions for piano, 1978; Concertante for clarinet and chamber orchestra, 1981; Eight songs or choir a cappella, 1981; Hymn for mezzo-soprano, boritone and hcmber orchestra, 1989; Filigrees for clarinet and string quartet, 1989-90, and for oboe and string quartet, 1992; Three rain song Songs for two choirs, English horn and French horn, 1991.

ORIORDAN Timothy, b. 21 Feb 1942, Edinburgh. Prof of Environmental Sci. m. Ann Morison, 18 May 1968, 2 d. *Education:* MA, Univ of Edinburgh, 1963; MS, 1965; PhD, 1967. *Appointments:* Asst Prof, Geography Simon Fraser Univ, 1967-72; Assoc Prof, 1972-74; Reader, Univ of East Anglia, 1974-80; Prof, 1980-. *Honour:* Gill Memorial Award. *Hobbies:* Classical Double Bass Playing. *Address:* Sch of Environmental Sci, Univ of East Anglia, Norwich NR4 7 TJ, England. 1.

OROVEANU T Mihai, b. 24 Oct 1916, Caracal, Romania. Lawyer; Prof of Law. m. Aglaia Lulu, dec, 1 d. *Education:* Bucharest Faculty of Law, 1938; Doc of Law, 1942. *Appointments:* Barrister, Bucharest, 1938-47; Asst Lect, 1942-47; Prof of Admin Law, 1939-47, 1972-75, 1990-. Snr Researcher, 1968-91. *Publications include:* 13 books and Over 60 Studies on Law & Articles Publ. *Memberships:* Romanian Assn of Men of Sci; Nominated Correspondent of the Romanian Acad, Juridical Section. *Hobby:* Music. *Address:* Aleea Barajul Uzului 2, BL Y 16, Ap 28, 74664 Bucharest, Romania.

OSEMLAK Jerzy Michal, b. 20 Apr 1940, Tarnow. Doc of Medicine. m. 29 Sept 1963, 1 s, 1 d. *Education:* Fac of Medicine, Lublin, Poland; Diploma of Physician, 1963; MD, 1970; DSc, 1975; Prof, 1987. *Appointments:* Faculty of Medicine, Sch of Medicine, Lublin, Asst, 1964; Snr Asst, 1966; Adjunct, 1970; Asst Prof, 1977; Assoc Prof, 1987; Hd of the Tchrng Dept, 1976-. *Publications include:* 112 Treatises, Anatomical Atlas of Human Body. *Memberships:* Polish Anatom Assn; Polish Med Assn; Polish Assn of Ped Surg; World Feder of pediatr Surg; Assn Polish Plastic Surg Assn. *Honours:* Scientific Prize, Minister of Health & Welfare. *Hobbies:* Skiing; Yachting. *Address:* Balladyny 18/21, 20-601 Lublin, Poland.

OSERS Ewald, b. 13 May 1917, Prague. Translator. m. Mary Harman, 3 June 1942, 1 s, 1 d. *Education:* Univ in Prague & London. *Appointments:* BBC Monitoring Serv, 1939-77; Freelance Translator, 1945-77, Part Time; 1977-, Full Time. *Publications include:* Over 110 Translated Books; 1 Vol of Poetry. *Memberships include:* Translators Assn; Inst of Translation and Interpreting; English Centre of International PEN. *Honours include:* Schlegel Tieck Prize; Gold Medal or Czech Socfor Intl Relations; Austrian Translation Prize; Officers Cross of the Order of Merit, Federal Republic of Germany. *Hobbies:* Music; Travel; Skiing. *Address:* 33 Reader Lane, Sonning Common, Reading, Berks, RG4 9LL, England. 52, 139.

OSIEK Carolyn Ann, b. 11 June 1940, USA. Prof of New Testament. *Education:* BA, Fontbonne Coll, 1962; MAT, Manhattanville Coll, 1966; ThD, Harvard Univ, 1978. *Appointments:* HS Tchng, 1966-69; Instr Rel St, Maryville Coll, 1974-75; Asst Prof, Assoc Prof, Prof, Cath Theological Union, Chicago, 1977-. *Publications:* 15 books and tapes, 80 articles. *Memberships:* Soc of Biblical Lit, 1972-; Cath Biblical Assn, 1973-; Chicago Soc for Biblical Rsch; Societas Novi Testamenti Studiorum. *Honours:* Assn of Theological Schs Rsch Grant, 1984-85; Nat Endowment for the Humanities Summer Sem, 1991. *Hobbies:* Gardening; Horseback riding. *Address:* Catholic Theological Union 5401 S Cornell Avenue, Chicago, IL 60615, USA.

OSINSKI Jerzy Kazimierz, b. 18 Dec 1951, Warsaw, Poland. Acad Tchr; Prof. m. Anna Grazyna, 26 July 1976, 2 s, 1 d. *Education:* MSc, Warsaw Univ of Tech, 1974; PhD, 1949; Habilitate Dr, 1990. *Appointments:* Inst of Machine Design Fundamentals, Warsaw Univ of Tech, 1974-91. *Honours:* Prizes from the Min of Educ, Poland, 1980, 1986, 1990. *Address:* St Puszczyka 18a m 25, 02-777 Warsaw, Poland.

OSMAN Mahomed Hussen, b. 5 Mar 1947, Mozambique. Fin Advsr. m. Dina Maria Conceicao Cardinal, 17 June 1972, 1 s, 1 d. *Education:* Univ of Oporto, 1967-71. *Appointments:* Gen Mgr, Banco de Mozambique, 1977- 85; Dep Dir, Uniao de Bancos Portugueses, 1986-88. *Hobby:* Reading. *Address:* Rua De Ceuta, 118-4 S/27, 4000 Porto, Portugal. 52.

OSTER Walter, b. 17 May 1939, Toronto, Can. m. Mary Elizabeth Bobyk, 30 Sept 1961, 2 s. *Appointments:* Blueprint Boy, Draftsman, 1956; Constrn Ind, 1967; Restauranteur, 1973, 1991; Hotelier, 1987. *Memberships:* Pres, Hidden Lake Golf & CC; Advsry Bd, Foodservs & Hospitality Mag; Bd, Nautical Ctr; Chmn, Tor Seaquarium; Fdr, Whaler's Charities for Chd Fndn; Dir, MTCC; Past Chmn, MTCVA, CRFA; Coun of Metro Tor Bd of Trade; Dir, Can Nat Sportsmen Show; Dir, Can Hospitality Fndn; Variety Club. *Honour:* Hon Dr of Comm Sci, Pacific Western Univ, Los Angeles, 1988. *Hobbies:* Boating; Fishing; Hunting; Golf; Car racing; Antique cars; Collecting wines and antiques. *Address:* PH 1, Admiralty Point, 251 Queen's Quay West, Toronto, Ontario, Canada M5J 2N6. 142.

OSTERMAN Eurydice Valenis, b. 5 Apr 1950, Atlanta, GA, USA. Assoc Prof. *Education:* Bach of Music 1972, Master of Music 1975, Andrews Univ; Dr of Musical Arts, The Univ of AL, 1988. *Appointments:* Mt Vernon Acad, Mt Vernon, 1972; Berean SDA Elem Sch, Baton Rouge, 1976; Oakwood Coll, Huntsville, 1978. *Creative works:* Composer of: Songs; Choral works; Instrumental works; Orchl works; Piano works; Organ works. Published in: The new 7th day Adventist Hymnal; Westminster Presby Hymn Suppliment Book; Oakwood Coll Journ; Roger Dean Music Pub. *Memberships:* Am Guild of Organists; Am Soc of Composers, Arrangers, Publrs; Am Choral Dirs Assn; Kappa Phi Lambda; Int Adventist Musicians Assn. *Honours:* b. Composition Awd, Andrews Univ, 1983; Outstg Tchr Awd, Oakwood Coll, 1984; Outstg Young Edr, Huntsville Jaycees, 1984; Appreciation Awds, Oakwood Coll, 1987-91; Music City Song Fest Awd, 1989; Zapara Excellence in Tchng Awd, 1990. *Hobbies:* Walking; Cooking healthfully; Crocheting; Sewing; Composing and arranging music. *Address:* 3610 Williamsburg Drive NW, Huntsville, AL 35810, USA. 76.

OSTLEITNER Elena, b. 15 June 1947, Caracus, Venezuela. Asst Prof. 1 s. *Education:* Piano, Acad of Music, Vienna, 1957-67; Sociology, Univ of Vienna, 1970-74. *Appointments:* Tchng and Rsch, Hochschule fur Musik, Inst of Sociology in Music, Vienna, 1975-. *Publications include:* Musicsociography in Austria, 1980; Massenmedien, Musikpolitik und Musike erziehung (ed), 1987; Ist die Musik mäunlich (w U Simek), 1991. *Memberships:* Bd Mbr, Latin Am Inst, Vienna; Govt Advsry Comm, Min of Educ & Culture, Min of Women's Affair. *Hobbies:* Listening to music; Reading. *Address:* Skraupstr 24/23, A-1210 Vienna, Austria.

OTANI Yoshihiko, b. 10 Jan 1938, Japan. Prof. m. Junko Amaike, 22 Oct 1969, 2 s. *Education:* BA, Kobe Univ, 1960; PhD, Univ of MN, 1969. *Appointments:* Asst Prof, Univ of MN, 1969-70; Asst Prof 1970-74, Assoc Prof 1974-76, Purdue Univ; Assoc Prof 1976-81, Prof 1981-82, Univ of KS; Prof, Univ of Tsukuba, 1981-. *Publication:* Microeconomic Theory, 1987. *Honour:* Woodraw Wilson Fellowship, 1968-69. *Hobby:* Jogging. *Address:* Institute of Socio-Economic Planning, University of Tsukuba, Tsukuba, Ibaraki 305, Japan. 52, 156.

OTUDEKO Ayoola Oba, b. 18 Aug 1943, Odogbolu, Nigeria. Companies' Dir. m. Adebisi Aderonke Otudeko, 25 Nov 1972, 2 s, 5 d. *Education:* FCIB, 1964; FCCA Hons, 1968; FCIS (Hons), 1968; FCA, 1970. *Appointments:* Accounts Clerk, Acctng Asst 1960-64, Acct 1965-66, Overseas Trainee, Attachee 1966-68, Sr Acct 1969-72, Chief Acct 1972-77, Dep Gen Mgr: Admin, Sec to the Bd 1977-83, Coop Bank Ltd, Ibadan. *Publications:* Public Relations in Banking, 1980; The Banking Industry in Nigeria and its Service, 1983; Youth in National Development, 1983; Graduate Unemployment in Nigeria, 1983; A Disciplined Youth: A Better and Greater Leader, 1985; An Overview of The Management of Our Reserves, 1985; Some Reflections on the Nigerian Economy and The Role of The Universities, 1985; Credit Guidelines, Commerce and Banking, 1985. *Memberships include:* Chmn of Bd of Dirs: Honeywell Enterprise Ltd, Lagos; Pivot Engrng Co Ltd, Lagos; Coral prods Ltd, Odogbolu; Quality Printing & Paper Co Ltd, Lagos. Dir: Ideal Flour Mills Ltd, Kaduna; Sheraton Hotel Plc, Ikeja; Forum Advt Co Ltd, Lagos; Franco-Nigerian C of C and Ind. *Honours:* Mayor of Leeds for Best Final Acctcy Student, 1967; 3rd Prize ACCA Final Acctcy Student (Hon), 1967; London Best Final Student, CIS, 1968. *Hobbies:* Squash racquets; Jogging; Classical music. *Address:* Honeywell Group, PO Box 1504, GPO, Dugbe, Ibadan, Nigeria.

OU Ming, b. 5 Dec 1925, Hong Kong. Medical Professor. m. 16 Feb 1950, 3 s, 1 d. *Education:* MD, Lignan Univ, China, 1948. *Appointments:* Phys, Army Ser, 1949-51; Attending Phys,1952-58, Dept Hd, 1959-72, Prof, 1973, Guangzhou. *Publications:* Concise TCM Dictionary; Chinese-English Dictionary of TCM; Regular Chinese Medicine Handbook; Chinese Medicinal Prescription Handbook; Practice of Acupuncture and Moxibustion. *Memberships:* Chinese Med Assn; Chinese Assn of Integration of Trad and Western Med. *Honours:* Sci Awds, Guangdong Prov, 1980, 1982, 1987, 191, 1992. *Hobbies:* Classical music. *Address:* Guangzhou College of Traditional Chinese Medicine, San Yuan Li, Guangzhou 510407, China.

OUDET Xavier, b. 6 June 1936, Saintes, France. Rschr. m. 27 Feb 1960, 1 s, 2 d. *Education:* Degrees: Maths, Phys & Chem 1957, Gen Phys 1968, Math Techs of Phys 1959, Tech Methods of Phys 1959, Systematical Chem 1959; Dr 3rd Cycle, Paris Univ, Orsay. *Appointments:* Asst, Fac of Scis, Paris Univ, Orsay, concurrently Rschr, Lab of Metallurgy, Ctr d'Etudes Nucleaires, 1960-63; Engr, IBM, Corbell-Essonnes, France, 1964; Attache de Recherche, CNRS, Lab des Terres Rares, Bellevue, 1964-73; Charge of Recherche, CNRS, Lab de Magnetisme et Materiaux Magnetiques, Meudon Cedex, 1974-. *Publications include:* Conductivity and Superconductivity, 1989; The Statistical Distribution of the Thermal Energy; Valence Competition in High-Tc Superconductors, 1990; Corpuscular aspect of electrons and valence notion in metallic oxides, 1992. *Membership:* Fndn Louis de Broglie. *Hobbies:* Psychanalysis; Reading; History; Music. *Address:* Laboratoire de Magnetisme et Materiaux Magnetiques, CNRS, 1 Place Aristide Briand, 92195 Meudon Cedex, France.

OUELLET Henri, b. 29 Jan 1938, Quebec, Can. Ornithologist. m. Yvette Testuz, 12 Sept 1964, 1 s. *Education:* BesL, 1958; BA 1962; MSc, 1967; PhD, 1977. *Appointments:* Assoc Curator, Vert Zoology,

Redpath Mus McGill Univ 1967-70; Asst Curator 1970-76, Curator 1977-1991; Res Ornithologist, 1991-; Ornithology, Chief, Vertebrate Zoology 1977-86, Canadian Museum of Nature, Ottawa. *Publications:* Les Oiseaux des Collines Montérégiennes et de la région de Montréal, 1974; Proceedings XIX Congressus Internationalis Ornithologicus (ed), 1988. *Memberships:* Fellow, Am Ornithologists' Union; Corr Fellow, Deutsche Ornithologen Gesellschaft; Past Sec Gen, XIX Congressus Int Ornithologicus; Exec Comm Mbr, Int Ornithological Comm. *Honour:* Best Nature Film, Le Grand Héron, Nature Film Fest in France, 1978. *Hobbies:* Cross-country skiing; Photography; Fine woodworking. *Address:* 3820 Autumnwood Street, Gloucester, Ontario, Canada K1T 2G8. 143.

OUSPENSKI Georgi Leonidovitch, b. 6 Dec 1942, Pugachov, USSR. Asst Prof. m. Tatiana Dmitrievna Kitchkareux, 11 July 1982, 2 s. *Education:* Dip, Piano, Musical Coll, Simteropol, 1958-64; Piano composition under Prof A Goldenweiscz, 1959; Piano under Prof J Zak, 1964; Piano, Prof L Giusburg, A V Nezdanova State Conservatory, Odessa, 1964-67; Composition, Prof Kzosotov, 1978-82. *Appointments:* Free Composer, Moscow Reg Musical Coll, 1968-71, 1971-78; Asst Prof, Class of Composition, Class of Composition, A V Nejdanova State Conservatory, Odessa, 1982-. *Creative works include:* Compositions: Concert for piano and chamber orch, 1982; Double concert for clarinet, piano and chamber orch, Sleeplessness - vocal cycle for mezzo-soprano and piano, 1984; Cantus magnificat - oratorio for soloists' piano, mixed chorus and symphony orch, 1988; Lyric songs - choral concert for 4 soloists, mixed chorus a capella, 1990. Author of a number of articles. *Memberships:* USSR Composers' Soc; Bd, Vice Chmn of Odessa Br, Ukrainian Composers' Soc. *Honour:* Dip, Ukrainian Repub Pianists' Competition. *Hobbies:* Tourism; Reading. *Address:* 4 30 L Tolstoy str, Odessa 270020, Ukraine.

OUTERBRIDGE William Robert, b. 10 Aug 1926, Kobe, Japan. Criminologist. m. Frances A Wardle, 7 Aug 1953, 3 s, 1 d. *Education:* BA, McMaster Univ, 1948; BSw 1950, MSW 1961, Univ of Toronto; MCrim, Univ of CA at Berkeley, 1966. *Appointments:* Supervising Probation Off, 1952-62; Juvenile Ct Judge, 1954; Mbr 1969-72, Chmn 1974-86, Nat Parole Bd; Prof of Criminology, Univ of Ottawa, 1972-74; Adj Rsch Prof, Carleton Univ, Ottawa, 1983-91. *Publications:* Author of various reports, articles in profl journs; Frequent Pub Lectr. *Memberships:* Bd Mbr, Can Corrections Assn; Exec 1974-86, Assn of Paroling Auths Int; Fndng Chmn, Can Assn of Paroling Auths, 1978-86; Fndng Bd Mbr, Coun of Admin Tribunals; Soc for the Reform of Crim Law; Bd of Advsrs, The Int Ctr for Crim Law Reform and Crim Justice Policy, 1991. *Honours:* Queen's Silver Jubilee Medal, 1977; Int Awd, Assn of Paroling Auths, 1986. *Hobbies:* Musician (Flugelhorn, Violin); Various sports. *Address:* 534 Golden Avenue, Ottawa, Ontario, Canada K2A 2E7. 142.

OUZIEL Jacky, b. 15 Aug 1948, Neuilly, France. Strategy Cons. m. Michele de Botton, 17 Oct 1975, 1 s, 1 d. *Education:* Lic en Droit 1971, diplôme d'etudes supéméures eu Print des Apprines en Droit des Affaires 1972, MBA 1972, Univ de Paris. *Appointments:* Rothschild Bank, France, 1973-76; Chn of the Bd, EGO SA, 1977-. *Creative works:* Author of several articles in Fin Reviews; Several chronicles on TV and Radio. *Memberships:* French Assn of Corporate and Fin Cons & Experts. *Hobbies:* Painting; Sculpture; Stamp collecting; Movies; Music; Trips; Gardens. *Address:* 130 Av Charles de Gaulle, 92200 Neuilly, France. 52.

OVENDEN Juliet Ann, b. 9 Nov 1959, Hitchin, Herts, Eng. Tchr of Ballet. *Education:* Various Ballet Tchrs, incl Dame Merle Park, 1977- 78; Student 1979-82, Dip, London Coll of Dance and Drama; City Lit Inst, London, 1982-85. *Appointments:* Asst Ballet Tchr, Gdn Hse Preparatory Sch & The Hampshire Sch, London, 1982-83; Tchr of Fitness & Dance, YWCA, Bloomsbury, 1983;

Ballet Tchr, Holy Cross Convent, 1983-85; Tchr of Movement & Dance, London Acad of Performing Arts, 1986; Artistic Dir, Link-up Dance Co (for deaf and hearing performers), 1986-87; Tchr of Dance & Ballet, Founder of Ballet Dept, Queen's Coll, Harley Street, London, 1986-89; Ballet Tchr, Founder of Ballet Dept, Cavendish Sch, London, 1988-90; Prin, The Marylebone Ballet Sch, 1990-. *Memberships:* ISTD; The Sacred Music-Drama Soc. *Honours:* Cello Grade 5 Merit 1975, Piano Grade 8 Merit 1977, Associated Bd, Royal Sch of Music; Bronze Medal for Acting, London Acad of Music & Dramatic Art, 1976; Gold Medal and Woman of the Year, ABI, 1991. *Hobbies:* Classical singing; Music; Drama; Reading. *Address:* Flat 1A, 16 Maresfield Gardens, London NW3 5SU, England. 138.

OVERTON Nerina, b. 12 Nov 1953, S Africa. Prof; Hd. *Education:* D Litt et Phil in Communication Sci, Rand Afrikaans Univ. *Appointments:* Prof, Hd, Dept of Communication, Rand Afrikaans Univ. *Publications:* Author of about 35 publs; Num paper and mag articles, features and columns written. *Memberships:* Coun, Exec Comm, US S Africa Ldrship Exchange Prog; Int Advt Assn; Assoc, SA Akademie Vir Netenskap En Kuns. *Hobbies:* Music; Reading. *Address:* Department of Communication, Rand Afrikaans University, PO Box 524, Johannesburg 2000, South Africa. 39, 52.

OVNATANOVA Nonna S, b. 14 Nov 1936, Baku, USSR. Micropaleontologist. m. Romen A Terteryan, 25 Dec 1934, 2 s. *Education:* PhD, 1972. *Appointments:* Engr, All-Union Sci Rsch Inst of Gas, 1959-60; Micropaleontologist of Geological Fuel Exploitation Inst, 1960-64; Scientific Wkr, All-Union Rsch Geological Oil Prospecting Inst, 1964-. *Publications:* Author of about 100 publs of different problems of Paleozoic Stratigraphy incl: On a large stratigraphic unconformity in the Prekaspian depression marginal zone internal part (w VA Goroschkova, TK Zamilatskaya), 1989; Reworked conodonts of Upper Paleoizoic deposits of Prekaspian syneclise (w LN Klenina), 1990. *Memberships:* Chief of Devonian Subcommn, Ctrl and S Regs, Russian Platforms, Indept of Stratigraphic Comm of the USSR; Moscow Soc of Naturalists (Geol); Pander Soc (IN Geological Survey). *Hobbies:* Reading; Domestic economy. *Address:* All- Union Research Geological Oil Prospecting Institute, 36 Shosse Entusiastov, Moscow 105819, Russia.

OWEN William John, b. 14 Mar 1914, Acton, London, Eng. Actor; Playwright; Lyricist; Autobiographer. m. Kathleen O'Donoghue, 3 Mar 1977, 1 s, 1 step daughter. *Appointments:* Entertainer, Dover Ct Holiday Camp, 1938-39; Actor, Playwright, Dir, Unity Theatre, 1938-56; Numerous stage plays incl: As You Like It, 1949-50; The Threepenny Opera, 1955; The Mikado, 1962; appearances at the Royal Nat Theatre, 1978-90. Films: Num films incl: When the Bough Breaks; Rainbow Jacket; In Celebration; Laughterhouse, 1986. TV: Num plays incl: Middle Watch, 1949; The Adding Machine, 1956; Three Piece Suite, 1964; Time Passing, 1972; current role as Compo in Last of the Summer Wine; Host to various TV game shows. *Creative works include:* Plays; Musicals; Film - Published, Performed; Ragged Trousered Philanthropist; Breakout; Lysette; Fringe of Light; In the Palm of Her Hand; Romance With a Double Bass; Num short plays written for Youth Theatre; Num lyrics to Brit & Int popular songs incl: Matt Monroe, Sacha Distel, Al Martino, Cliff Richard. *Memberships include:* Chair, Arts for Labour; Chair, Arts for Labour Trust; Chair, Unity Theatre Trust; Kirklees Theatre Trust; Chair, Nat Assn Bopys Clubs Perf Arts Panel; Exec Comm, Drama, London Fed Boys Clubs; Pres, ATC, Holmfirth Squad. *Honours:* MBE, 1977; This Is Your Life, TV Presentation, 1980; Assn Mbrship, Yorkshire Soc, 1989; Brit Acad Composers, Authors, Songwriters Gold Badge of Merit, 1990. *Hobbies:* Working with boys clubs; Politics. *Address:* Richard Stone Association, 25 Whitehall, London SW1A 2BS, England. 18.

OWEN-JONES David Roderic, b. 16 Mar 1949, N Wales. Barrister-at-Law. *Education:* LLB, 1970; LLM, 1971; Called to the Bar, Temple, 1972. *Career:* Contested several Elections as a Liberal, Carmathen 1974, Rugby 1983, Kenilworth 1987; Mbr Lord Chancellor's Advsry Comm on the appt of JP's for Inner London, 1985-90; Acting Metrop Shipendiary Magistrate, 1991. *Membership:* Chmn, Nat Liberal Club, 1988-91. *Address:* 3 Temple Gardens, Temple, London EC4, England.

OWENS Joseph, b. 17 Apr 1908, St John, NB. *Education:* MSD, Pontifical Inst of Mediaeval Studies, Toronto, 1951. *Appointments:* Mbr Ed Bd, The Monist; Parish Asst, St Joseph's, Moose Jaw, 1934-35; St Patricks, Toronto, 1935-36; Lectr in Philos, St Alphonsus Sem, Woodstock, 1936-40, 1948-51, 1953; Missionary, Dawson Creek, 1940-44; Lectr, Accademia Alfonsiana, Rome, Italy, 1952-53; Vis Lectr, Assumption Univ, Windsor, 1954; Staff Mbr, Pontigical Inst of Mediaeval Studies, Toronto, 1954-; Asst Prof, Assoc Prof 1954-61, Prof, Sch of Grad Studies 1961, Univ of Toronto. *Publications:* St Thomas and the Future of Metaphysics, 1957; A History of Ancient Western Philosophy, 1959; An Elementary Christian Metaphysics, 1963; An Interpretation of Existence, 1968; The Wisdom and Ideas of St Thomas Aquinas (w E Freeman), 1968; The Doctrine of Being in the Aristotelian Metaphysics, 3rd ed 1978; The Philosophical Tradition of St Michael's College, Toronto, 1979; St Thomas Aquinas on the Existence of God, 1980; Human Destiny, 1985; Towards a Christian Philosophy, 1990; Critical reviews in various learned journs. *Memberships:* Pres 1965-66, Am Cath Philos Assn; Pres 1971-72, Metaphys Soc of Am; Pres 1971-73, Soc for Ancient Greek Philos; Pres 1981-82, Can Philos Assn; Am Philos Assn. *Honours:* Hon DLitt, Mt Allison, 1975; DHumLitt, Cath Univ, 1984; Hon LLD, St Francis Xavier, 1988. *Hobby:* Swimming. *Address:* St Patrick's Rectory, 141 McCaul Street, Toronto, Ontario, Canada M5T 1W3. 142.

OXLADE Roy, b. 13 Jan 1929, London, Eng. Painter. m. Rose Forrest Wylie, 10 Aug 1957, 1 s, 2 d. *Education:* Bromley Coll of Art, 1950-55; Attended David Bomberg's Classes, Borough Polytech, 1951-53. *Creative works:* One Man Exhibs: Vancouver Art Gall, Can, 1963; Ian Clarkson Gall, Edinburgh, 1968; Midland Grp Gall, Nottingham, 1975; New Metropole Gall, Folkestone, 1983; AIR Gall, 1983; Odette Gilbert Gall, 1985, 1987, 1988; Gardner Ctr, Univ of Sussex, 1990. Group Exhibs: Young Contemporaries, 1952- 54; Borough Bottega Grp - Heffer Gall, Cambridge 1954; Walker's Gall, London 1955; Winnipeg Biennale, 1960; John Moores Liverpool Exhib, 1964; London Grp, 1965, 1967-68; Midland Grp, Nottingham, 1966, 1968; The Nude, Morley Gall, 1975; The Hayward Annual, 1982; Odette Gilbert Gall, 1984-90; Getler/Pall/Saper, New York, 1984; Royal Acad Summer Exhib, 1984, 1985, 1989, 1990; Rocks and Flesh, Exhib of drawing selected by Peter Fuller, Olympia Art Fair, 1986; Chicago Art Fair, 1987; Los Angeles Art Fair, 1987; Waddington Schiel Gall, Toronto, 1987; Jan Turner Gall, Los Angeles, 1988; Cleveland Int Drawing Biennial, 1989; Tribute to Peter Fuller, Beaux Arts Gall, Bath, 1990; David Bomberg, Some Students & Current Influences Towner Gall, 1991; RA Summer Exhibs, 1992; John Moores Liverpool Exhib, 1991/1992. *Publication:* David Bomberg, 1981. *Honour:* 1st prize drawing, Winnipeg Biennale, 1960. *Address:* Odette Gilbert Gallery, 5 Cork Street, London W1, England. 19.

OYELAKIN Lawrence Olufolahan Oladejo, b. 13 June 1936, Nigeria. Dipl. m. Elizabeth A Ablaba Oyelakin, 21 Jan 1970, 4 s, 5 d. *Education:* GCE Ordinary Level 1961, Advanced Level 1961; ACCS Final, 1962; Dip, Tchngr Eng as Foreign Lang, SIU, USA, 1965; ACIS 1970; Fellow, Soc of Commercial Tchrs, 1975. *Appointments:* Confidential Sec, Nigerian Railways, 1956-64; Exec Off, Western Nigeria Govt, 1964-67; Min of External Affairs, Lagos, 1968-; Diplomatic positions incl: 2nd/1st Sec, Lome, Togo 1970-72; 1st Sec (Econ & Consular), Bonn 1972-74; 1st Sec, Cnslr, Hd of

Chancery, Nairobi, Kenya 1975-79; Sec, Foreign Serv Review Panel 1980-81; Min, Dep Hd of Mission, Dublin, Ireland 1981-84, Bonn, Germany, 1984-85; Dep Dir, Acting Dir, Hon Min's Off, Lagos 1986-87; Amb, Nigeria to Congo, Brassaville, 1987-; Amb, Min of External Affairs, Abuja, Nigeria. *Publications include:* Nigerian Foreign Service Administration; Various unpublished fiction & non-fiction. *Memberships:* Assoc: Corporate of Secs; CIS; Fellow, Soc of Commercial Tchrs, London. *Hobbies:* Writing; Walking; Photography. *Address:* PO Box 261, Yaba, Lagos, Nigeria.

OZARA Nino Albert, b. 18 May 1960, Elele, Uzairue. Lecturing. m. Mary B Idanwekhai, 2 Jan 1988, 2 s. *Education:* BSc 1977-81, MSc 1982- 83, Univ of Ibadan; PhD, Silsoe Coll, 1986-89. *Appointment:* Fed Univ of Tech, Owerri, 1984-. *Publication:* Ed, Management and Control of Erosion in Agricultural Practice. *Memberships:* Soil Sci Soc of Nigeria; Brit Soil Sci Soc; Subtheme Ldr, Erosion Rsch Ctr, FUT, Owerri. *Honours:* Fed Merit Awd, Undergrad, 1978-81; Cocoa Mktng Bd Scholarship, 1978-81; Fac Prize, 1981; Nupemeco Prize, 1981; Bawac Prize, 1981; C'wlth Scholarship, 1986-89; Jr Associateship, Int Ctr for Theoretical Phys, 1990-93. *Hobbies:* Reading; Squash; Soccer. *Address:* Department of Crop Production, School of Agriculture and Agricultural Technology, Federal University of Technology, PMB 1526, Owerri, Nigeria.

OZAWA Keiya, b. 23 Feb 1953, Nagano, Japan. Hematologist. m. Masami Inokuchi, 16 Oct 1983, 1 s, 1 d. *Education:* MD, 1977; PhD (DMSci), 1984. *Appointments:* Resident in Med, Tokyo Univ Hosp, 1977-79; Rsch Fellow 1979-84, Staff Fellow 1984-87, Asst Prof 1987-90, Assoc Prof 1990-, Univ of Tokyo; Fogarty Fellow, NIH, USA, 1985-87. *Memberships:* NY Acad of Scis; AAAS; Am Soc of Hematology; Am Fedn for Clin Rsch; Japanese Soc of Hematology; Japanese Soc of Internal Med; Japanese Cancer Assn. *Address:* 1-2-12-302 Yushima, Bunkyo-ku, Tokyo 113, Japan. 52.

OZIM Igor, b. 9 May 1931, Ljubljana, Yugoslavia. Prof of Violin. m. Dr Breda Volovsek, 1963, 1 s, 1 d. *Education:* Akademija za glasbo, Ljubljana, 1945-49; RCM, London, 1949; Studies with Max Rostal, 1949-51. *Appointments:* Prof of Violin, Akad za glasbo, Ljubljana, 1960-63; Staatliche Hochschule fur Musik, Cologne, 1963-; Berne Conservatoire, 1985-. *Creative works:* Num recordings; Ed of classical and contemporary works. *Membership:* Fndng Mbr, ESTA. *Honours:* 1st prize, Int Carl-Flesch Competition, London, 1951; 1st prize, ARD Int Competition, Munich, 1953. *Address:* Breibergstr 6, D-5000 Cologne 41, Germany. 34.

OZKAN Suha, b. 14 June 1945, Ankara, Turkey. Sec Gen; Prof. m. Zulal Menderes, 17 Aug 1968, 1 s. *Education:* BArch 1967, MArch 1969, PhD 1980, Middle East Tech Univ, Ankara, Turkey; AA, Archt Assn, London, 1971. *Appointments:* Vis Prof, Columbia Univ, New York, Pennsylvania State Univ, 1975; Assoc Dean, Fac of Arch 1977-79, VP 1979-82, VP of Fac Club 1979- 82, Middle East Tech Univ, Ankara; Dep Sec Gen 1982, Sec Gen 1989, The Aga Khan Awd for Arch, Geneva. *Publications:* Summer Practices, 1975; A Village in the Year 2000, 1984; Sedad Eldem-Architect in Turkey (w S Bozdogan, E Yenal), 1986; An Approach to Theory of Architecture, 1992; Author of over 70 articles on hist, theory and pract of arch and various aspects of archtl rsch. *Creative works:* Art Shows: Sculptures, 1965; Closely (Photographs), 1982, 1984; Form and Context (Paintings), 1990. *Memberships:* IUA, Ankara-Paris, 1967; Archtl Assn, London, 1970-; Salzburg Sem Alumni Assn, 1973-. *Honours:* Godrey Design Awd, 1965; Summer Rsch Awd, 1966; Brit Coun Scholar, Govt of UK, 1970; Salzburg Sem in Am Studies Fellowship 1973. *Hobbies:* Painting; Photography; Travel. *Address:* The Aga Khan Award for Architecture, 32 Crets de Pregny, 1218 Grand Saconnex, Geneva, Switzerland. 52, 104.

OZOLINS Janis Alfreds, b. 29 Sept 1919, Riga, Latvia. Conductor. m. Adine Uggla, 15 May 1951, 3 chd. *Education:* Grad, Latvia Conservatory Music, 1944; Student Composition, Royal Acad of Music, Stockholm, 1946-49; Exam in Musicology, Univ of Uppsala, Sweden, 1962; studied cello under Erico Mainardi, Rome, song under Jolanda di Maria Petris, Helsinki, Finland. *Career:* Violincellist, Latvian Nat Opera, Rigas, 1938-44; Solo recitals, soloist with symph orchs in Latvia, Sweden, London; Performances on Radio, Sweden, Denmark, Switzerland, 1938-51; Condr, Landskrona Symph Orch, 1957-64; Dir of Music 1964-83, Condr 1968-81, Vaxjo (Sweden) Symph Orch; Condr, Opera and Ballet, also bass soloist in Verdi's Requiem, Beethoven's 9th Symph, oratories and lieder recitals. *Honours:* Nat Prize of Latvia, 1944; Culture Prize, Vaxjo Lions Club, 1976; Royal Gold Medal, Swedish Orchs Nat Fedn, 1977. *Address:* Via Sicilia 1, 63039 San Benedetto del Tronto, Italy.

OZOLS Vilis, b. 3 May 1929, Naukseni, Latvia. Painter; Prof. m. Austra Ozola, 4 Jan 1958. *Education:* Latvian Acad of Arts, 1952-58. *Appointments:* Painter; Prof, Latvian Acd of Arts. *Creative works:* One Man Shows: Dole Mus; Riga; Cesis. Grp Shows: Riga; Moscow; Leningrad; Vilnius; Poland; Hungary; Italy; Romania; Cuba; Bulgaria; Japan; Finland; France. Selected Collections: The Latvian Mus of Art, Riga; Moscow; Lvov. *Hobbies:* Fishing; Cookery. *Address:* Gailezera iela 6 - 32, Riga, Latvia.

P

PABEL Janusz Grzegorz, b. 21 Aug 1940, Ostrowiec, Swietokrzyoki. Painter. m. Malgorzata Raczkowska, 23 June 1979, 2 d. *Education:* MA, Acad of Fine Arts, Warsaw, 1965. *Appointments:* Lectr 1971, Asst Prof 1978, Prof of Painting Dept, Graphics Fac 1991, Acad of Fine Arts, Warsaw. *Creative works:* Portraits Period, Tempera, 1965-70; Registrations, Acryl, 1970-73; Astories Period, 1973-75; Infinity Cases, 1975-85; Poetic Registration of the Space, 1980-; Participated in many polish and Int Painting Exhibs, 1985-. *Memberships:* VP 1980-83, Artistic Advsry for Painting of Main Bd, Pres 1990, Warsaw Sect, Assn of Polish Visual Arts Creators; Artistic Advsry attched to the Pres of Warsaw, 1991. *Hobby:* Carpentry. *Address:* Al Jerozolimskie 147/13, 02-326 Warsaw, Poland.

PACHOLSKI Zdzislaw Stanislaw, b. 3 May 1947, Osieki. Artistic Photographer. m. Janina Wojcikowska, 6 Aug 1977, 2 s, 1 d. *Career:* Exam 1977, Mbr of Arts Coun 1989-, Polish Union of Art Photographers. *Creative works:* Individual Exhibs: Sociological photography, Norderstadt, Germany; Attributes-Requisites, Gothenborg Sweden; Feeling is believing, Rheine, Germany, 1981. *Honours:* II prize, Competition, Polish Family, 1979; I prize, Competition, Professional Photography, 1985; Work of Yr, 1987. *Hobby:* Video. *Address:* ul Fijalkowskiego 6, 75-016 Koszalin, Poland.

PADLUZHNY Alexandr, b. 16 Aug 1935, v Zalesje, Mogiljov reg, RB. Scientific Wkr; Linguist. m. Valentina Moisejenko, 3 Oct 1961, 1 s,1 d. *Education:* Bielorussian State Univ, 1959; Post-grad Studentship, 1964; Cand of Scis, 1967; DSc, 1982. *Appointments:* Tchr of Belorussian, 1959-61; Jr Rsch Wkr 1964-69, Chief, Dept of Experimental Phonetics 1969-, Asst Dir 1983-89, Dir 1989-, Inst of Linguistics, Acad of Scis of Bielarusj. *Publications:* Author and co-author of a number of publs. *Membership:* Corres Mbr, Acad of Scis, Bielarusj. *Honours:* Hon Dip, Supreme Soviet of the USSR, 1983; Badge of Hon, 1986. *Hobby:* Walks in the forest. *Address:* Institute of Linguistics, Academy of Sciences of Bielarusj, F Scorina st 25, 220072 Minsk, Russia.

PADMADINATA Tjetje Hidajat, b. 22 June 1935, Bandung, Indonesia. Mbr of Parliament. m. Marlina Nenden, 15 Jan 1975, 3 s, 1 d. *Education:* LLB, Pajajaran Univ, Bandung, 1964. *Career:* Free-lance Columnist. *Publications:* Struggle Contemplation, 1988; Author of num articles on politics and cultures in several newspapers in Indonesia. *Membership:* First Gen Chmn, Siliwangi Younger Generation, 1966-76. *Honours:* Recipient of uncountable hons and awds mostly given by univ students, younger generations, press orgs in Indonesia. *Hobbies:* Reading; Writing; Football; Listening to classical music. *Address:* Jl Sagittarius No 1, Bandung 40275, Indonesia.

PAGE Patricia Kathleen, b. 23 Nov 1916, Eng. m. W Arthur Irwin, 16 Dec 1950, 1 step son, 2 step daughters. *Publications include:* The Sun and the Moon; As Ten as Twenty; The Metal and the Flower; Cry Ararat!; Poems Selected and New; Evening Dance of the Grey Flies; The Glass Air; A Flask of Sea Water; Brazilian Journal; The Travelling Musicians. *Memberships:* League of Can Poets; Writers Union of Can; PEN. *Honours:* Oscar Blumenthal Awd, Poetry, Chicago; Gov Gen's Awd for Poetry; Can Authors' Assoc Lit Awd for Poetry; Nat Mags Awd; OC; Hon Degrees from Univs of: Victoria, Guelph, Calgary, Simon Fraser; Order of Canada. *Hobbies:* Drawing: Works in National Gallery of Canada; The Art Gallery of Ontario. Group and One Woman Shows in Mexico and Canada. *Address:* 3260 Exeter Road, Victoria, British Columbia, Canada V8R 6H6. 30, 142.

PAICE Elisabeth Willemien, b. 23 Apr 1945, Washington DC, WA, USA. Cons Rheumatologist. m. Clifford Paice, 6 July 1968, 1 s, 2 d. *Education:* BA; MB; BCh; BAO. *Appointments:* Hse Off, St Stephen's Hosp, Westminster Hosp, London, 1970-71; Registrar, Stoke Mandeville Hosp, 1971-79; Sr Registrar, Univ Coll Hosp, 1979-82; Cons Rheumatologist, Whittington Hosp, 1982-. *Memberships:* Brit Soc for Rheumatology; FRSM; FRCP; Nat Assn of Clin Tutors. *Honours:* Daniel J Cunningham Medal & Prize, 1967; Irish Med Students Assn Gold Medal, 1967; Non-fndn Scholar, TCD, 1967; Handcock Prize, RCS, 1970. *Hobbies:* Theatre; Medical journalism. *Address:* Department of Rheumatology, Whittington Hospital, Highgate Hill, London N19 5NF, England.

PAICE Robert Tasker, b. 2 July 1921, London, Eng. Ret'd. m. Rosemary Alison Foster, 8 Oct 1955, 2 s, 1 d. *Education:* MA. *Appointments:* War Serv, Russian Convoys, Mediterranean Invasion of Sicily, Pacific, 1941-46; Mng Dir, Ryders Discount Co, 1949; Dep hmn, Cater Ryder & Co Ltd. *Memberships:* FIB; Inst of Dirs; Royal Brit Legion; Coun, RNVR Off Assn. *Hobbies:* Sailing; Tennis; Music; Painting. *Address:* Andreds Bourne, Mayfield, East Sussex TN20 6UN, England. 43.

PAKENHAM-WALSH Mabel, b. 2 Sept 1937, Lancaster, England. Wood-carver. *Education:* NDD Sculpture, 1959. NATKI Mbr in Pinewood & Shepperton Film Studios, 1960-61; Tchng & Workshops in Carving, Self-employed. *Creative works:* Painted woodcarvings in Craft Coun Collection; Ulster Mus; Grizedale Sculpture Park, Cumbria; Ceredigion Museum, Aberystwyth. *Membership:* Contemporary Applied Arts. *Hobbies:* Planting trees; Bird wrecking; Colour; Swimming; Public transport. *Address:* Arch Noa, 7 Tanyfynwent, Llanbadarn Fawr, Aberystwyth SY23 3RA, Wales.

PAKHOMOVA Nenell Nellei Nena, b. 26 July 1931, Veadimer. Physicist; Prof; Scientist; Ldr. m. Pakhomov, 19 July 1951, dec 1986, 1 d. *Education:* Dip w hons, 1953; Post-grad course of sub-fac Phys, MIIT, 1961-64; Bach of Phys, Mat Scis, 1964; Doct Phys, 1984. *Appointments:* Asst 1953-61, 1964-65, Docent 1966-85, Scientific Ldr of Ferrites Lab 1977-, Prof 1986, MIIT, sub-fac phys. *Publications include:* Employment of statistical models to ferrosp, 1977; Effect of substitutions on magnetic anisotropy and exchange interaction in ferrites, 1981; Piculiarity on magnetic anisotropy and magnetostriction in Mn-conteining ferrites materials, 1987; Effect of the synthesis conditions of Mn-Zn ferrites on formation their physics-chemicals properties, 1989; Linear and volume magnetostriction of Mn- Zn ferrites, 1990. *Memberships:* Chmn of Commn on Thermodynamics and Tech Ferrites, Scientific Coun on Inorganic Chem, Acad of Sci, USSR; Learned Coun of MIIT; Learned Coun of Tech Kybernetic Fac. *Honours:* State Hon for many years Standing and Conscientious Work, 1985; Hon of Merit in Reg of High Educ, 1987; for Active Participation in Progressof Railway, 1987. *Hobbies:* Vesification; Reading; Skiing; Collection of paintings, graphic arts and work of art. *Address:* Udalcova st 10-104, SU 117415, Moscow, Russia.

PALDIEL Mordecai, b. 10 Mar 1937, Antwerp, Belgium. Dir. m. Rachel Mizrahi, 15 Aug 1966, 1 s, 2 d. *Education:* BA, 1968; MA, 1979; PhD, 1982. *Appointments:* Dir, Dept for the Righteous Among the Nations, Yad Vashem, Jerusalem, 1982-. *Publications:* Author of various profl books and articles. *Honours:* H Schulwells Humanitarian Awd, 1991; Ida King Disting Vis Scholar, 1991. *Hobbies:* Rowing; Hiking. *Address:* Yad Vashem, POB 3477, Jerusalem, Israel.

PALEY Maureen, b. 17 Sept 1956, New York, USA. Art dealer. *Education:* BA, Brown Univ, Providence, 1975; MA, RCA, London, 1980. *Appointments:* Fdr, Dir, Interim Art Gall, East End of London, 1984; moved Gall to West-End of London, 1990; Resumed Gall in East End, 1992. *Creative works:* Over 80 exhibs incl: Hannah Collins, 1984; Window Wall Ceiling Floorshow, 1985;

Antidotes to Madness, 1986; Fischli & Weiss, 1987; Jenny Holzer, 1988; Sarah Charlesworth, 1989; Jessica Diamond/Mike Kelley, 1990; Langlands & Bell, 1991. *Membership:* Arts Coun Panel, 1990-. *Honours:* Gall recipient of grants, Greater London Arts, 1984-90; London Arts Bd Project Grant, 1992. *Hobbies:* Reading; Travelling; Music. *Address:* 21 Beck Road, London E8 4RE, England.

PALIA Satnam Singh, b. 5 Oct 1952, Punjab, India. Cons Psych. m. Valwinder Kaur Karir, 21 Aug 1976, 3 d. *Education:* MBBS, 1976; DPM, 1980; MRCPsych, 1981. *Appointments:* Registrar, 1981-83; Sr Registrar, 1983-85; Cons Psych, 1986-. *Publications:* Water Intoxication in Psychiatric Patients; Mood Disorders in Epileptic Patients; Psychopharmacology. *Memberships:* Chmn, Sikh Assn of S Wales, 1988; Treas, Welsh Psych Soc, 1991-. *Honours:* FRSH; Hon Postgrad Organiser in Psych, Clin Tchr & Clin Tutor in Psych, 1986-92. *Hobbies:* Badminton; Reading; Music. *Address:* 35 Herbert March Close, Raydr Vale, Cardiff, S Glamorgan CF5 2TD, Wales.

PALINKAS Jozsef, b. 18 Sept 1952, Galvacs. Physicist. m. Eva Berenyi, 14 Feb 1976, 2 s, 1 d. *Education:* Dip in Phys, Jozsef Ahila Univ, 1977; PhD in Phys, Kossuth Univ, 1981; Dr of Phys Sci, Hungarian Acad of Scis, Budapest, 1989. *Appointments:* Inst of Nuclear Rsch, ATOMKI, Debrecen, 1977-83, 1985-, Dir 1991-; Post Doct, Cyclotran Inst, TX A&M Univ, 1983-85. *Publications:* Author of rsch papers on Ion-atom collisions. *Membership:* Roalnd Eotvos Phys Soc. *Honour:* of the Hungarian Acad of Scis, 1985. *Hobbies:* Tennis; Reading. *Address:* Institute of Nuclear Research, Hungarian Academy of Sciences (ATOMKI), Debrecen PP 51, H-4001 Hungary.

PALJETAK Luko, b. 19 Aug 1943, Dubrovnik, Yugoslavia. Writer. m. (1)Mirjana Vujanic, 27 Mar 1970, 1 s, (2)Anamarija Kobal, 30 Apr 1979. *Education:* MA, Fac of Philos, Univ of Zagreb, 1991. *Appointments:* Actor, Stage Mgr, Puppet Theatre of Zadar, 1969-73; Asst, Fac of Philos, Zadar, 1973-78; Ed Staff, Lit Review, Dubrovnik, 1979-91. *Creative works include:* Books: Mice & Cats, 1973, 1975, 1976, 1983, 1985, 1987; Arrival of the Little Mistresses, 1984; Poems in the Ragusian Mode, 1984, 1991; Sandosten Forte, 1987; At the Edge of the Body, Selected Poems, 1987; Stork on the Mother's Way, 1988; Small Room Stories, 1989; Insights into Older and Newer Croatian Literature, 1990; Puppet Theatre, from either sides, 1990; Singer in the Frog Chorus, 1991. Maps: Clown's Songs, 1989; Hands, 1990. Plays: Three Leaps of a Lizard; Knee-strap; Shoemaker and the Devil; Man who was Mad; The Last Flower of the Summer; Fairy tale about the Magical Instrument; Ghoasts from the Planet Strahurn. *Memberships include:* Croatian Lit Trans Union; Croatian Theatre Artist Union; Croatian Lit Soc. *Honours include:* Lit Awd, Ivana Brlic-Mazuranic for the childrens book, Mice and Cats Topsyturvy, 1973; Lit Awd, A B Simic for the first poetry book, Devil of the Rose; Annual Awd of the Croatian Writers Union for the poetry book, The Lowered Door, 1990. *Hobbies:* Painting; Book-collecting. *Address:* Gorica Sv Vlaha 155, 50000 Dubrovnik, Croatia, Yugoslavia.

PALLAS Christopher William, b. 27 Mar 1956, Chattanooga, TN, USA. Physn; Clin Rschr. *Education:* BA, Univ of TN, 1978; MD, Bowman Gray Sch of Med, Wake Forest Univ, 1982; Cardiology Fellowship, 1986-89. *Appointments:* Attending Physn 1989-, Asst Prof of Med 1989-, Med Coll of GA 1989-. *Memberships:* AMA; FACC; FACCP. *Honour:* Outstg Clin Fellow, Med Coll of GA, 1987. *Hobbies:* Golfing; Antiques. *Address:* Medical College of Georgia Hospital & Clinics, Veterans Administration Medical Centre, 1 Freedom Way, Augusta, GA 30910, USA. 2, 7.

PALLOTTI Giovanni, b. 25 Feb 1934. Prof. m. Gabriella Foschini, 26 Dec 1970, 2 s, 2 d. *Education:* DME 1959, Dr of Phys 1962, Univ of Bologna; DIC, Imperial Coll

of Sci & Tech, Univ of Londn, Eng, 1964. *Appointments:* Asst Prof 1959-, Prof of Phys, Fac of Veterinary Med, 1969-77, Prof of Biophys 1976-77, Prof of Phys 1976-79, Prof of Med Phys 1979-88, Prof of Biomaths, Prof in Postgrad Schs, Fac of Med and Surg, Univ of Bologna. *Publications:* Author of over 200 publs in Med and Biological Mech, Phys & Engrng. *Memberships include:* Fellow, CNR - NATO, 1968; Unione Matematica Italiana (Life); Imperial Coll Union, London (Life); Biological Engrng Soc of UK; Nat Grp for Mathl Phys, C N R, Italy; Advsry Bd, Int Off for the Confs on Mech in Med and Biol; Scientific Bd, 2nd Int Conf on Bio-Impedance, Lyon, France, 1975; Chmn, Session of 4th Int Conf on Med Phys, Ottawa, Can, 1975; Chmn, European Mechs Colloquium 170, Caserta, Italy, 1983; Accademia dei Lincei - Royal Soc, 1983. *Hobbies:* Architecture; Art; History. *Address:* Chair of Biomathematics, Department of Physics, Faculty of Medicine and Surgery, University of Bologna, Via Irnerio 46, 40126 Bologna, Italy.

PALMER Adrian Bailie Nottage, The Lord, b. 8 Oct 1951, Reading, Eng. Farmer; Impressario. m. Cornelia Wadham, 7 May 1977, 2 s, 1 d. *Education:* Eton; Edinburgh Univ. *Appointment:* Huntley & Palmers Ltd, 1970-77. *Memberships:* Coun of HHA, 1980; Coun of SLF, 1986-; Scottish Rep to Euro Landowning Org, 1986-. *Hobbies:* Gardening; Shooting. *Address:* Manderston, Duns, Berwickshire, Scotland.

PALMER Philip Stuart, b. 2 July 1906, London, Eng. Ret'd. m. Sybil Madeline Conway Cox, 10 July 1931, 2 s. *Education:* Cheltenham Coll, 1920-25; Brighton Tech Coll, 1925-28. *Appointments:* Pupil, Brighton Wks 1925-28, Asst to Wks Mgr, Lancing Wks 1928-31, Southern Railway Co; Asst Mech Engr 1931-37, Dept Mech Engr 1937-47, Acting Chief Mech Engr 1945-46, Ceylon Govt Railway; Cons Engr, Freeman Fox & Ptnrs, London, 1947-72. *Memberships:* Coun 1958-76, Jt Hon Sec 1969-75, Hon Mbr, CGLI; Coun 1962-70, 1980-88, Hon Sec 1984-88, VP, Soc of Sussex Downsmen; Liveryman of the Mercers Co. *Hobbies:* Classical music; Opera; Theatre; Photography; Gardening. *Address:* 46 Berriedale Avenue, Hove, East Sussex BN3 4JJ, England.

PALMER Robert Leslie, b. 15 Mar 1944, Exeter, Eng. Psych; Sr Lectr in Psych. m. Mary Carter, 19 July 1969, 1 d. *Education:* MB BS (London); MRCPsych, 1972; FRCPsych, 1984. *Appointments:* Lectr in Psych, Univ of London, St Georges Hosp MS 1971-73, St Mary's Hosp MS 1974-75; Sr Lectr, Hon Cons, Univ of Leicester, 1975-. *Publications:* Anorexia Nervosa: A Guide for the Sufferers and Their Families, 1980, revised 1989; Author of over 40 papers on eating disorders, ECT and other psychiatric topics. *Hobbies:* Reading; Bird watching. *Address:* 61 Central Road, Leicester LE3 5EJ, England.

PALOUS Radim, b. 6 Nov 1924, Prague, Czechoslovakia. m. Anna Strausova, 29 Jan 1949, 2 s. *Education:* Phd Philos, 1948, Charles Univ, 1948; PhD Pedagogics, Fac of Natural Scis, Pedagog Univ, 1966; Asst Prof, Philos, 1967, Prof, 1990. *Appointments:* Lectr, Analyt Chem, Fac of Natural Scis, 1957-59; Inst of Univ Studies of Tech Univ of Prague, 1960; Asst Prof of Fac of Pedagog, UK, 1961-77; Chm, Educ Techniques Dept, Fac of Pedagog, Charles Univ, Prague, 1968-69; Rector, 1990-. *Memberships:* Chem Soc of Czech Acad of Scis; Pedagog Soc of Czech Acad of Scis; Independent Czech Helsinki Com; Movement for Civic Freedom. *Honours:* Hon Doctorates: Univ Pittsburg, 1990; Univ of Nebraska, 1990, Intl Acad for Philos, Furstentum Liechtenstein, 1991, Pontifikalni Teologicka Acad Krakov, 1991, Moravian Col, Bethlehem, Pennsylvania, USA, 1991. *Address:* Charles University, Ovocny Trh 5, 11636 Prague 1, Czechoslovakia.

PALSSON Einar, b. 10 Nov 1925, Reykjavik, Iceland. Researcher; Cultural Historian; Writer; Educator. m. Birgitte Laxdal, 24 Dec 1948, 2 s, 1 d. *Education:* Cand Phil, Univ of Iceland, 1946; Cert of Merit, Royal Acad of Dramatic Art, 1948; BA Danish and Eng Lit, Univ of Iceland, 1957. *Appointments:* Chm, Reykjavik City Theatre, Drama Gp, 1950-53; Owner, Dir, Mimis Lang Sch, 1954-84; Dir of Nordic Soc, 1966-69; Freelance Play Production. *Publications:* The Roots of Icelandic Culture, 10 vols, 1969-91. *Memberships:* The Reykjevik Drama Soc, Chm, 1950-53; The Nordic Soc, Dir, 1966-69; The Icel Lit Soc. *Honours:* Prize, Icel Cultural Coun for one-act play, Trillan, 1962. *Hobbies:* Flying (when young, Hon Mem, AOPA); Classical Music; Reading; Surveying of ancient cultural sites. *Address:* Solvallagata 28, 101 Reykjavik, Iceland.

PALTE Lambertus, b. 12 May 1953, Bergen-op-Zoom, Holland. Repair Co Exec. *Education:* BSc 1978, MSc 1981, Twente Univ, Enschede. *Appointments:* Rschr, Televerkets Centralforvaltning, Farsta, Sweden, 1979; Rschr, Holec Control Systems, Hattem, Holland, 1980-81; Mng Dir, Vortex Balanceer-techniek, Soest, 1981-. *Memberships:* Pres, Scintilla Electrotechnische Studievereniging, 1974-75; Pres, Experimentele Telecom Groep Drienerlo, 1974-78; Bd Dir, Scholengemeenschap Eemland, 1982-; Bd Dir, Kort Middelbaar Beroeps Onderwijs, 1986-; Bd Dir, Streekschool Beroeps Begeleidend Onderwijs; Royal Engrng Soc, KIVI. *Hobbies:* Learning foreign languages; Travelling; Historic cars. *Address:* Roggeveld 25, 3764 ZB Soest, Holland. 52.

PALUSZAK Naoko Omura, b. 25 Nov 1957, Japan. Artist. m. Stephen Paul Paluszak, 27 June 1982. *Education:* Grad, Japan Designer Inst, Tokyo, 1979. *Appointments:* Comml Artist, Ad Pro Co, Okihawa, Japan, 1979-81; Freelance Artist, Ft Myers, 1985-. *Creative works:* Group show, Lancaster Mus/Art Gall, CA, 1988; Two person show, BIG Art, Sanibel, 1989; Group show, Parkshore Gall, 1990; One person show, Fine Arts Risk Mgmt, Inc, 1991. *Honours:* Cert of Excellence in Painting, Int Art Competition, Art Horizons, New York, 1988; Cert of Excellence in Painting, Int Art Competition Artitudes, New York, 1989; Grand Prize, Int Art Competition, Ariel Gall, New York, 1990. *Hobbies:* Reading mysteries; Watching vintge TV comedies. *Address:* 12924 Meadowood Ct, Fort Myers, FL 33919, USA. 1, 7.

PAMDETH Narayanan Menon, b. 15 June 1929, Irinjalakuda, India. Leading Metallurgist & Materials Technologist; Materials Engr. m. Else Jensen, 2 s. *Education:* BSc, 1949; MSc, 1953; Welding Tech, Cranfield Inst of Tech, 1962. *Appointments:* Special Insp, Supvsr, Tata Locomotive & Engrng Co, 1953-60; Hd, Materials & Welding R&D, Harvey Fabrications Ltd, UK, 1964-68; Sr Engr, Chief Metallurgist, BOC-AIRCO Cryoplants Int, UK, 1968-73; Sr Metallurgical Engr, Burmeister & Wain Motor, Copenhagen, 1973-75; Quality Mgr 1975-81, Leading Metallurgist, Materials Technologist 1989-, Burmeister & Wain Energy, Denmark; Prin Surveyor, Det Worske Veritas, Copenhagen, 1981-86; Ldr Materials Tech, Safety & Quality Technologies A/S, Denmark, 1986-89. *Memberships include:* The Welding Inst, UK; Fellow, Int Inst of Welding; The Inst of Welding, UK; Corporate Mbr, Engrng Coun, UK. *Honours:* Fellowship Awd, The Welding Inst, Cambridge; Scholarship, Brit Oxygen Co, UK, 1961-62; Rschr Awd, Cranfield Inst of Tech, UK, 1962-64. *Hobbies:* Badminton; Tennis; Gardening; Walking; Music; Dancing; Travelling for professional updates and pleasure; Attending international seminars and conferences in multi diciplined scientific spheres. *Address:* Vestervang 45, Bloustrod, DK 3450 Allerod, Denmark. 52.

PAN Guo-Zong, b. 6 Aug 1930, Shanghai, China. Chief; Prof of Med. m. Wei-Ming Liu, 6 Aug 1976, 1 d. *Education:* BS, Dept of Biol, Yenching Univ, 1949-52; MD, PUMC, 1952-57; Rsch Fellow, Peking M Coll & PUMC, 1962-65. *Appointments:* Resident Physn 1957-61, Chief Resident 1961-62, Attng Physn 1964-80, Assoc Prof of Med, Chief, Div of Gastroenterology 1983-86, Prof 1987-, Peking Union Med Coll Hosp.

Publications: Author of over 80 papers; Participated in the publ of 10 books. *Memberships include:* VP, Chinese Soc of Gastroenterology; Chn, Chinese Soc of Gastrointestical Hormones, Chinese Med Assn; Nat Comm of Drug Evaluation; Ed Bd, Chinese Med J. *Honours:* 2 Acad Awds, Chinese Acad of Med Scis for contributions in rsch works on Chinese herbal medicine and gastrointestinal hormones, 1985, 1989. *Hobbies:* Taking photos; Watching athletic games. *Address:* Department of Medicine, Peking Union Medical College Hospital, Chinese Academy of Medical Sciences, Beijing 100730, China. 152.

PAN Jiahua, b. 31 Mar 1930, Suzhou City, Jiangsu Province, P R China. m. Guanqing Chen, 1 Jan 1957, 1 s. *Education:* Grad, Beiyong Univ, 1952. *Appointments:* Asst, Lectr, Qinghwa Univ, Beijing Petroleum Coll, 1952-55; Asst Prof, Dept Vice Chmn, Beijing Petroleum Coll, 1956-62; Engr, Oil Refining Design Inst, 1962-70; Engr, Pipeline Design Inst, 1970-78; Chief Engr, Sr Engr, Pipeline Bur, Min of Petroleum Ind, 1978-. *Publications include:* The design of storage tank; Application of fracture analysis on pipe line; Strength of storage tank & pipeline; Strength of buried pipeline; Author of over 70 compositions. *Memberships include:* Standing Dir, Pres, Transportation & Storage Inst, China Petroleum Soc; Cons, China Petroleum Equipment Soc, Dir, Petroleum Software Inst, Computer Software Soc. *Honours:* Excellent Lectr; High-qualified Designer; Design of storage tank was awded Outstng Scientific Book of China; First Awd for outstng commandingness in the oil storage fire putting activity, 1990. *Hobbies:* Poetry composing; Music; Singing. *Address:* Pipeline Bureau of China National Petroleum Corp, Jinguang Road, Langfang City, Hebei Province, China.

PANAYI Gabriel Stavros, b. 9 Nov 1940. Prof of Rheumatology. m. Alexandra, 11 Mar 1973, 2 s. *Education:* BA Hons 1962, MB 1965, MD 1971, ScD 1991, Cambridge Univ; MRCP, 1972; FRCP, 1981. *Appointments:* Arthritis and Rheumatism Coun Sr Lectr, Cons in Rheumatology 1976-80, Prof, Arthritis and Rheumatism Coun Chair of Rheumatology 1980-, Guys Hosp, London. *Memberships:* BSR; RSM; AAI; BSI Am Coll of Rheumatology. *Honours:* Max-Bonn Prize, Gold Medal in Pathology, St Mary's Med Sch, 1964; Sir Lionel Whitby Medal, Univ of Cambridge for most meritorious MD Thesis for the Acad Yr 1970-71, 1971; Margaret Holroyde Prize, Heberden Soc, 1975; Phillip Ellman Lectr, RSM, 1978; Allesandro Robecci Prize, European League against Rheumatism, 1979; Ballabio Prize, Italian Soc of Rheumatology, 1986; Metro Ogryzlo Lectr, Can Arthritis Soc, 1990; Heberden Orator, Brit Soc for Rheumatology, 1992; Kave Berglund Lectr, Univ of Lund, Sweden. *Hobbies:* Photography; Painting; Reading. *Address:* Rheumatology Unit, Division of Medicine, United Medical and Dental Schools of Guys and St Thomas Hospitals, Guys Hospital, St Thomas Street, London SE1 9RT, England.

PANDIT Hirday Nath, b. 26 Jan 1938, Kashmir. Educ Sector Planner. m. Chand Rani Pandit, 10 June 1962, 2 s, 2 d. *Education:* PhD. *Appointments:* UNESCO, 1977-83; Univ of Jos, 1984-88; Cambridge Educ Cons Ltd, 1988-. *Publications:* Author of books & articles on Educational Planning in India, Nigeria, Ghana. *Hobby:* Reading. *Address:* UNDP, PO Box 1423, Accra, Ghana.

PANEK Emil, b. 9 Feb 1948, Poland. University Professor. m. Irena Mazur, 4 Apr 1970, 2 s. *Education:* Grad, Moscow Univ, 1970; Phd, Poznan Univ of Econ, 1974; Asst Prof, 1986, Prof, 1991. *Appointments:* Lectr, Tech Univ Zielona Gera Informatic Ctr, 1974-75; V-Dir, Inst of Econ Cybernetics, Poznan Univ of Econ, 1982-86; V-Dean, Fac of Planning and Mgmt, 1987-90, Hd of Dept of Math Econ, 1991-, V-Rector, 1991-. *Publications:* Modelling and Planning of the National Economy, 1982; Optimal Trajectories of Growth in the Aggregate Economic Models, 1986; Economic Growth Processes and Optimum Control Theory, 1989;

Turnpikes in the Input-Output Systems, 1992. *Honours:* Min of Educ Prizes, 1984, 1987, 1990. *Hobbies:* Choral singing; Cooking. *Address:* University of Economics, Department of Mathematical Economics, Al Niepodleglosci 10, 60-967 Poznan, Poland.

PANEVOVA Jarmila, b. 8 Apr 1938, Prague, Czech. Linguist. m. Petr Panev, 8 Nov 1960, 1 d. *Education:* Bach 1956-61, PhD 1968, Fac of Philos, Charles Univ. *Appointments:* Rschr 1961-85, Assoc Prof 1985-89, Rsch Prof 1990-, Fac of Maths & Phys, Computer Ctr, Sect of Linguistics, Charles Univ, Prague. *Publications:* Tense and Modality in Czech (jtly w E Benesova, P Sgall), 1971; From Tectogrammatics to Morphemics, Vol IV, 1979; Forms and Functions in the Structure of the Czech Sentence, 1980; The Meaning of the Sentence in Its Semantic and Pragmatic Aspects (jtly w P Sgall, E Hajicova), 1986; Author of over 150 papers and studies regarding Czech, Slavonic, Gen and Computational Linguistics. *Memberships:* Scientific Sec 1984, Chairperson 1990-, Linguistic Assn of the Czecho-Slovak Acad of Scis; Societas Linguistica Europaea; Int Sect for Grammical Structure of the Intern Comm of Slavists. *Hobbies:* Literature; Contemporary art. *Address:* Faculty of Mathematics and Physics, Institute of Formal and Applied Linguistics, Charles University, Malostranske n 25, CS-118 00 Praha 1, Czechoslovakia.

PANG Zhi-Yuan, b. 31 Oct 1938, Sichuan, P R China. Prof. m. Ru-Ping Wan, 18 May 1967, 2 d. *Appointments:* Dept of Maths & Mech, Peking Univ, 1960-61; Dept of Maths, Guizhou Univ, 1961-85; Dept of Maths, Guizhou Normal Univ, 1985-. *Publications:* The Finite Element Method and its Theoretical Fundamentals, 1980; The Semi-Linear Diffusion Equations with Right-Hand Side Containing Dirac's Measure and a Related Optimal Control Problem, 1981; On the Basis Function in Tetrahedral Element with 16 and 20 Degrees of Freedom, 1983; Exact Solution for the Problem of Crossflow in a Bounded Two-Aquifer System with an Aquitard, 1986; Error Estimates for Mixed FEMs, 1986; Natural Frequency of Vibration of Contactor and Convergence of the Approximation by FEM, 1987; The Method of Thinking for Solving Mathematical Problems Most in Use, 1988. *Memberships:* Standing Comm of Guizhou Br, Mathl Inst of China; Bridge Assn of China. *Honours:* Prize in scientific meetings of China, 1978; Prize in Scientific Meeting of Guizhou Province, 1978; Third class prize 1981, 1990, Second class prize 1987 for progress in sci & tech in Guizhou Province; First class prize for excellent teaching material, Nat Educl Comm, 1987; Nat Prize for excellent achievement in teaching, 1989; Outstanding Contrb in Guizhou Province, 1990; Spec Allow, State Coun, 1991. *Hobbies:* Exercising; Playing Bridge and Chess. *Address:* Department of Mathematics, Guizhou Normal University, Guiyang 550001, China.

PANHUYSEN Paul Benedictus Maria, b. 21 Aug 1934, Borgharen, Holland. Visual Artist; Dir. m. Helene Hulshof, 3 Dec 1968, 1 s, 1 d. *Education:* Studied Monumental Art and Painting, Jan van Eyck Ac, Maastricht, 1954-59 and Sociology of Art, State Univ of Utrecht, 1957-61. *Appointments:* Artist, 1959-; Dir, Art Acad Vredeman de Vries, Leeuwarden, 1962-65; Curator, Municipal Mus, The Hague, 1966; Curator, Van Abbemuseum Eindhoven, 1966-68; Artist Advsr in Urban Planning Teams, Zoetermeer, Nieuweschans, s-Hertogenbosch, 1974-83; Fdr, Dir, Het Apollohuis, Eindhoven, 1980-. *Creative works include:* Catalogues: Ars Electronica, Linz, Austria, 1987, 1988; Klang und Raum, Darmstadt, Germany, 1989; L'Europe des Createurs, Utopies 1989, Paris, France, 1989; Installations, PSI Museum, NY, 1991; Death, Love, War, Montbeliard, France, 1990; Paul Panhuysen Solo, Arti et Amicitiae, Amsterdam, 1991. Monographies: Paul Panhuysen: Van Abbe Museum, 1978; Long String Installations, 1986. *Memberships include:* Trustee of the Bd: Dutch Artists Assn 1969-73, Fndn of Art and Ind 1971-84, Dutch Social Fund for Artists 1976-86, Fedn of Dutch Artists Assn 1981-84; Co-fdr, Trustee of the Bd, Assn of Environment Artists, 1977-79; Chmn,

Consultative Comm for State Grants to Visual Artists, 1982-85; the Jury for Royal Awds to Painters, 1983-89. *Address:* Tongelresestraat 81, 5613 DB Eindhoven, Holland.

PAO China Shan, b. 28 Apr 1918, Peking, China. Prof. m. Feng-Mi Yao, 23 Dec 1953, 3 s. *Education:* BS, Yenking Univ, 1940; MS 1941, PhD 1943, Washington Univ. *Appointments:* Staff Mbr, MIT Red Lab, 1943-45; Proj Engr, Sperry Co LINY, 1945-46; Prof, 1946-49, 1949-53 Nankai Univ; Prof, Shanghai Univ of Sci & Tech, 1983-. *Publications include:* Principle of Microwaves, 1st ed 1965, 2nd ed 1985; Microwave Antennas, Microwave Ferrites and Devices; Microwave Superconductivity. *Memberships:* Fellow, Chmn, Superconducting Elecs, Dep Chmn of MTT Comm 1962-83, Chinese Inst of Elec. *Honours:* the superconducting elecs rsch group of Nanjing Univ won the Scientific and Tech Advancement Prize, Nat Educl Comm, 1987; Principles of Microwaves won the prize of excellent textbook, Nat Educl Comm, 1988. *Address:* 15/489 Taku Road, Shanghai 200041, China.

PAPACOSTEA Serban, b. 25 June 1928, Bucharest, Romania. Histn. *Education:* Dr in Hist, Inst for Hist, Romanian Acad of Scis, 1968. *Appointments:* Scientific Rschr, Inst for Hist, 1951-52, 1957-89; Libn, Ctrl Lib of Univ, 1954-57; Dir, Nicolae Iorgs Inst, Romanian Acad, 1990-. *Publications include:* Wittenberg und Byzanz: die Moldau im Zeitalter der Reformation, 1970; Little Wallachia under Austrian Rule, 1971; Stephen the Great Prince of Moldavia (1457-1504), 1975; Die politischen Voraussetzungen fur die wirtschaftliche Vorherrschaft des Osmanischen Reiches im Schwarzmeergebiet (1453-1484), 1978; Quod non iretur ad Tanam, 1979; La Mer Noire: du monopole byzantin a la domination des Latins aux Detroits, 1988; Gênes, Venise et la Mer Noire a la fin du XIII-e siecle, 1990. *Memberships:* Corr Mbr, Rumanian Acad; Ed Bd, Revue Roumaine d'Histoire, Studii si materiale de istorie medie, Revista istorica. *Honour:* Prize of the Rumanian Acad of Scis, 1972. *Address:* Caragea Voda 19, Bucuresti 71149, Romania. 34.

PAPANDREOU Constantine, b. 28 Aug 1939, Messolongi, Greece. Teleinformatics Scientist; Prof. m. Antonia Tsafoulia, 22 Mar 1971. *Education:* ME 1965, MPhil 1972, Tech Univ of Munich; PhD, Ludwig Maximilian's Univ of Munich, 1984. *Appointments:* Hd of Ops Rsch Dept, Ctr for Nat Def, Athens, 1968-70; EDP Specialist, Tech Dist Mgr, Greek Telecom Org, 1970-; Asst Prof of Informatics, Athens Univ of Econ(s) and Bus, 1986-; Bd Mbr, EDP Ctr of Social Servs in Greece, 1990-; Mbr, Tech Bd of Informatics, Greek Govt, 1990-; Nat Rep of the progs, Value and Telematique of the EEC, 1991-. *Publications:* Electronic Computers and Information Systems, 1973; The Development of New Forms of Telecommunications, 1984; Teleinformatics (Scientific Ed), 1989. *Contribution to:* Over 40 articles and conf papers on telecommunications and informatics. *Memberships include:* Bd Mbr 1973-76, Ops Rsch Soc of Greece; Bd Mbr 1985-89, Soc of the Greek Engrng Economists; VP 1990-, Greek Computer Soc; Union of German Engrs; Engrng Chamber of Greece. *Honours:* Grantee, Govt of Bavaria, 1972; Prize for the best contribution of the 23rd Conf, Fedn of Telecommunications Engr of the EEC, Rome, 1984; Kt, Int Order of St Constantive the Great, 1990; Pres of Parliament of the Int Order of St Constantine the Great, 1991; Recognition Dip, City of Messolongi, 1991. *Hobbies:* Reading; Photography; Fishing; Swimming; Boating. *Address:* Kalliga str 17, GR-11473 Athens, Greece. 52.

PAPP A'rpa'd, b. 19 Mar 1934, Somogyaszalo. Lectr; Hdmaster. m. Maddalena Koch, 24 July 1959, 2 s. *Education:* BA, L Eotvos Univ, Budapest, 1959; Univ of Athens, 1982, 1987. *Appointments:* Tancsics Second Grammar Sch, Kaposvar, 1959-89; L Eotvos Univ Coll, Budapest, 1990-. *Publications:* Points of Intersection, 1976; Thousand Faces Behind a Masque, 1987; Points of Intersection, 1988. *Memberships:* Encyclopedia of World Lit, 1970-91; Fedn of the Hungarian Writers; Int PEN Club; Antigruppo Siciliano; Mnione Europea Scrittoried Artisti, Roma. *Honours:* Prize for the best first work, 1976; Golden prize for poem, Argonauts by the Parnossos, Lit Soc of Athens, 1982; The best transl of the Yr, Greece, 1990. *Hobby:* Gardening. *Address:* Menesi UT 11-13, 1118 Budapest XI, Hungary.

PAPPAJOHN George John Peter, b. 15 Aug 1939, Vancouver, BC, Can. Tourism Cons. m. 25 July 1978, 3 s, 1 d. *Education:* Univ of BC, 1956. *Appointments:* Realtor, 1965-71; Restauranteur, 1971-76, 1987-; Owner, Constrn Co, BC & Ont, 1971-. *Creative works:* Ekistical Study-Rural Canada, 1991-93; Rural Tourism Study-South WIstluw-Ontario Canada, 1992-93. *Membership:* Chmn, Rural Ekistics Rsch and Development. *Hobbies:* Cooking; Philately; Ekistics; Building Renovation Architectural Preservation; Toy soldiers; Travel; Landscaping. *Address:* PO Box 25, Sombra Village, Ontario, Canada N0P 2H0. 142.

PAPPAS Panagiotis, b. 30 May 1947, Athens, Greece. Prof. m. Dimitra Kavvada, 9 Nov 1985, 2 s. *Education:* Maths degree 1971, PhD w distn, 1984, Univ of Athens. *Appointments:* Prof of Phys, Prof of Maths, Technological Educl Inst of Pireous, Athens. *Publications:* Author of num publs and pioneer rsch for the Electrodynamic Force of Ampare, Electromagetism Spce-Time. *Memberships include:* Greek Math Soc; Greek Phys Soc; FRG Soc; Int Tesla Soc. *Honours:* Scholar of Greek State of Scholarships, 1973-76; Scholar of Fulbright Fndn, 1988. *Hobbies:* Search for natural knowledge; Deep sea diver. *Address:* 26 Marcopulioti Street, Athens 11744, Greece.

PAQUIN Wilfrid Arthur, (Charles Lorenzo), b. 28 Aug 1919, Montreal, Can. Prof Reader. *Education:* BA, Lic in Pedagogy, MA, Univ of Montreal; PhD, Univ of Ottawa, 1959. *Career:* Tchr of French for 30 yrs; Ed, Proof-reader, Editions FIC of La Prairie. *Publications:* under pen name of Charles Lorenzo: 10 vols of poems, Reflets, Chatoiements, Rutilances, Diaprures, Moires, Parhelies, Coruscations, Spasmes, Palpitations, Agonies; 10 vols of Contes et Recites; Initiation a la poesie; Short plays in classical verse; novels; essays on Quebec authors; Books of spirituality. *Honours:* Mention du Merite scolaire after 30 yrs of serv, The Min of Educ; 2nd prize, the 38th poetry contest, Societe des poetes canadiens-francais, 1963; Silver medal for Fascination, 8th Floral Games of Quebec, Arts et lettres du Quebec, 1984; Bronze medal for his work, Contes et Recites. *Hobbies:* Reading; Composition. *Address:* 870 Chemin De St Jean, La Praire, Canada J5R 2L5.

PARADOWSKI Leszek Ireneusz, b. 27 Jan 1946, Leszno. Physn. m. Barbara Zoll, 28 Apr 1973, 1 d. *Education:* Physn Dip, 1970; Dr's degree, 1978; Dr hab, 1990. *Appointments:* Asst 1970-78, Asst Prof 1978-90, Assoc Prof 1990-, Dept & Clin of Gastroenterology Med Acad, Wroclaw. *Publications:* Author of 95 publs on gastroenterology. *Memberships:* Polish Internist's Soc; Polish Med Soc; Polish Assn of Physiology; Sec, Polish Assn of Gastroenterology. *Honour:* Scientific Awd, Polish Min of Hlth and Social Welfare, 1991. *Hobby:* History. *Address:* Department of Clinic and Gastroenterology, Medical Academy, ul Poniatowskiego 2, 50-326 Wroclaw, Poland.

PARASCA Pavel, b. 8 July 1939, Brinzenii Vechi, Repub of Moldova. Assoc Prof, Chair Hd. m. Victoria Sucleian, 1 July 1975, 2 s. *Education:* Grad, Moldavian State Univ, 1967; Cand Sci, 1981. *Appointments:* Rschr, Moldavian Acad of Scis, 1967-85; Assoc Prof 1985-89, Hd, Chair for the Hist of the Romanians 1990-, Moldavian State Univ. *Publications:* The Golden Horde and the formation of the Moldavian feudal state, 1972; The policy of the Hungarian Kingdom in Eastern Subcarpathian and the formation of the Moldavian feudal state, 1979; Territorial consolidation of the Moldavian feuda state in the second half of the 14th

century, 1980; Foreign- political conditions of forming the Moldavian feudal state, 1981; The problems of the study of historical sources on Moldo-Lithuanian relations in the second half of the 14th - 15th centuries, 1983; Foreign-political history of the Moldavian Principality (last third of the 14th - early 19th centuries), (co- author), 1987; Istoria RSS Moldovenesti, vol I 1987-88. *Membership:* Chmn, Assn of the Histns of Moldova, 1990-. *Hobbies:* Crosswords; Puzzles. *Address:* 37/1 Sarmizegetusa St, Apt 78, Chisinau 277032, Republic of Moldova.

PARK Phocion Samuel Jr, b. 7 Oct 1944, Baltimore, MD, USA. Family Therapist; Chem Dependency Cnslr; Pvt Pract, Individual, Marital & Family Therapy. m. Cheryl Antoinette Seethaler, 17 Dec 1983, 2 s. *Education:* BA, cum laude, Univ of St Thomas, Houston, 1967; MA, Am Hist, Univ of Houston, 1971; MDiv, Univ of St Michael's Coll, Toronto, 1973; MASci, Human Rels & Counselling Studies, Univ of Waterloo, Waterloo, 1975; Post-profl studies, Clin Behavioral Scis, McMaster Univ, Hamilton, 1979-82. *Appointments:* Social Wkr, Family Servs Dept, Children's Aid Soc, Guelph, Ont, 1974-79; Team Ldr, Family Counselling Unit, Cath Social Servs, Hamilton, 1979-82; Family Cnslr, Theology, Hist Tchr, Diocese of Galveston- Houston, Houston, 1982-85; Individual, Marital & Family Therapist, Houston Ctrs for Christian Counselling, 1986-87; Family Therapist & Chem Dependency Cnslr, Christian Psych Unit, Ralpha Inc; Pvt Pract, Individual, Marital & Family Therapy, Houston. *Publications:* Brickmaking In & Around Early Austin, 1977; Creative Rosary Meditations (w Mary B Reinhard), 1979; Anointing with Blessed Oil, 1979; Christianity & the Occult Today, 1980; How a Christian Family Can Cope with a Family Crisis, 1981. *Memberships:* Profl Mbr, Assn of Christian Therapists, 1979-; Clin Mbr, Am Assn of Marriage & Family Therapists, 1980-. *Honours:* Recipient of num scholarships & fellowships incl: 2nd place in TX Jr Histn Writing Contest, 1962. *Hobbies:* Operation rescue; Religious & country singer; Swimmer. *Address:* 8114 Trail Side Drive, Houston, TX 77040, USA. 7, 130.

PARK Roberta J, b. 15 July 1931, Oakland, CA, USA. Prof; Chair. *Education:* AB 1953, PhD 1971, Univ of CA, Berkeley; MA, The Ohio State Univ, 1955. *Appointments:* Instr, The Ohio State Univ, 1954-56; Tchr, Oakland Pub Schs, 1956-59; Supvsr 1959-76, Assoc Prof 1976-80, Prof 1980-, Dept Chair 1982-, Univ of CA, Berkeley. *Publications include:* From Fair Sex to Feminism: Sport and the Socialization of Women (w J A Morgan), 1987; Sport and Exercise Science: Essays in the History of Sports Medicine (w J Berryman), 1992. *Memberships:* VP 1989-, Int Assn for the Hist of Sport and Phys Educ; Pres 1990-91, Am Acad of Phys Educ; N Am Soc for Sport Hist; Am Alliance for Hlth, Phys Educ, Recreation & Dance. *Honours include:* Fellow, Danforth Fndn; Fellow, Rsch Consortium, Am Alliand for Hlth, Phys Educ, Recreation & Dance; Fellow, Am cad of Phys Educ; Fellow, Brit Soc for Sports Hist; Seward Staley Address, N Am Soc for Sport Hist, 1979; Amy Morris Homans, Lectr, Nat Assn of Phys Educ in Higher Educ; C H McCloy Rsch Lectr, Am Acad of Phys Educ, 1988-89. *Hobbies:* Hiking; Opera; Cooking; Painting; Carpentry. *Address:* 200 Hearst Gymnasium, University of California, Berkeley, CA 94720, USA.

PARK Sei-Young, b. 27 Jan 1940, Mil Yang Eup Mil Yang Kun, Kydong Sang Nam Do, S Korea. Chmn; Enterpriser. m. Sook-Hee Kim, 8 Mar 1969, 1 s, 2 d. *Education:* BA, Coll of Commerce, Seoul Nat Univ, 1964; Finished AMP course, Sch of Bus Admin, Harvard Univ, USA, 1982. *Appointments:* Pres, Dae Woo Corp, 1969-82; Chmn, Korea-Tunisia Econ Coop Comm, 1980; Chmn, Korea- India Econ Coop Comm, 1981; Chmn, Korea-Argentina Econ Comm, 1981; Hon Consul- Gen, Kingdom of Lesotho, 1981; Chief Exec Off, Bus Affairs Div, Seoul Olympic Org Comm, 1982-85; Chmn, Hanjoo Grp, Seoul, 1985. *Honours:* Awded Silver Tower of Indl Serv Merit, Tax Day, 1988; Awded Tower of US Million Dollars Export, Korea Export Day, 1988. *Hobby:* Golf.

Address: Hanjoo Group, Dong-A B/D 88, Da-Dong Jung-Gu, Seoul, Korea.

PARKER Charles George Archibald, b. 30 Jan 1924, Zomba, Malawi. Publr. m. Shirley Follett Holt, 3 Nov 1958, 1 d. *Education:* MA, New Coll, Oxford, 1946-48. *Appointments:* Capt, Rifle Brigade, 1942-46, served France, POW, Germany; The Times, 1949-56; Charringtons, 1956-61; BMA Publs, 1961-76; Chmn, Ct & Judicial Publ Co, 1976-. *Memberships:* Coun 1956-66, FRGS; Pres, ALPSP; Chmn, Tower Hill Improvement Trust; Chmn of Coun, Order of St John, Oxon; Freeman of London; FRSA; Gov, Manchester Coll, Oxford. *Honours:* JP 1978-; High Sheriff of Oxon, 1989-90; O St J, 1990; DL (Oxon), 1992. *Address:* The White House, Nuffield, Oxon RE9 5SR, England.

PARKER Constance Anne, b. 19 Oct 1921, London, Eng. Ret'd; Sculptor. *Education:* ATD, RA Schs Dip. *Appointments:* Asst Libn 1958-74, Libn 1974-86, Royal Acad of Arts; Lectr, RA, NADFAS. *Publications:* Mr Stubbs the Horse Painter, 1971; RA Cookbook, 1976; Art Animals and Anatomy, 1984. *Membership:* Fellow, Royal Soc of Brit Sculptors. *Honours:* 4 silver & 2 bronze medals, RA Schs; Landseer, Leverhulme & David Marray Scholarships. *Address:* 1 Melrose Road, Barnes, London SW13 9LG, England. 19.

PARKER Diana Jean, b. 7 June 1932, Eng. Co Dir. m. Dudley Frost Parker, June 1960 (dec 1971), 1 s, 1 d. *Education:* BComm, Birmingham Univ, 1951-54. *Appointments:* Non-exec Dir: Vacu-Lug Traction Tyres Ltd 1957-, Ctrl Indep TV plc 1982-, Lincs Ambulance & Hlth Transp Trust 1991-92; Mbr, Nat Westminster Bank, Eastern Advsry Bd, 1985-92. *Membership:* CBIM, 1986. *Honour:* CBE, 1989. *Hobbies:* Reading fiction; Church architecture. *Address:* 93 Manthorpe Road, Grantham, Lincolnshire NG31 8DE, England. 1.

PARKER Elinor Sheila Halling, b. 21 Sept 1940, London, Eng. Dental Surg. m. David Parker, 24 Sept 1966, 1 s, 1 d. *Education:* BDS, Sheffield Univ, 1961-66. *Appointments:* Hse Off, Charles Clifford Dental Hosp, Sheffield, 1966-67; Asst Lectr, Oral Pathology, Sheffield Univ, 1967-68; Gen Dental Pract: Kuala Lumpur, Malaysia, 1969-74; Surrey, 1975-. *Publications:* Dental Journalism. *Memberships:* WID News, Ed 1986-, Chair 1989-90, Women in Dentistry; Gen Dental Practitioners Assn; Behavioural Scis in Dentistry Grp; Brit Soc for Restorative Dentistry; Bd Mbr, The Probe. *Hobbies:* Sec, New Malden Geriatric Badminton Club;Past Chair of Govs, Tiffin Girls Sch, Kingston; Fdr Mbr, Kingston Feminists; Kingston Boro Coun Women's Comm Mbr; Mgmt Comm Mbr, Kingston Womens Ctr; Mbr, various choirs. *Address:* 16 Alric Avenue, New Malden, Surrey KT3 4JN, England.

PARKER James Mavin (Jim), b. 18 Dec 1934, Hartlepool, Eng. Composer; Conductor. 2 d. *Education:* Guildhall Sch of Music & Drama; AGSM (silver medal); LGSM; LRAM. *Career:* Oboist, City of Birmingham Orch; Mbr of Barrow Poets; Freelance Composer & Conductor. *Creative works:* Concert works: Banana Blush (w J Betjeman); Mayhew's London (w C Herbert); La Comedie Humaine (w C Herbert). Operas & Musicals: The Burning Bush (w T Stanier); The Shepherd King (w T Stanier); Blast Off (w T Stanier); All Aboard (w T Stanier); Babylon Times (w T Stanier, C Ellis); Follow The Star (w W K Daly); Captain Beaky (w J Lloyd); Make Me A World (w W K Daly); Heaven's Up (w J Lloyd). Instrumental: A Londoner in New York (Brass Ensemble); Mississippi Five (Wind Quintet); English Towns (Flute & Piano). Films: The Blot; Girl Shy (H Lloyd); Late Flowerin Love (w J Betseman). TV work incls: Mapp & Lucia (Ch 4); House of Cards (BBC); Parnell & The Englishwoman (BBC); House of Eliott (BBC); Soldier, Soldier (ITV); approximately 100 Documentaries and Plays. *Honour:* Hon GSM. *Hobbies:* Literature; 20th Century Art. *Address:* 19 Laurel Road, Barnes, London SW13 OEE, England. 1, 4.

PARKER Kenneth Michael, b. 15 Oct 1945, Oklahoma, USA. Clin Biochem; Assoc Prof. m. Sandra Letz, 20 Aug 1965, 2 d. *Education:* BS magna cum laude, Abilene Christian Univ, 1968; PhD, Univ of TX at Austin, 1972. *Appointments:* Asst Prof of Pathology, Univ of Mo, Hlth Sci Ctr, 1976-81; Assoc Prof of Pathology, Dir of Toxicology Lab, Univ of OK, Hlth Sci Ctr, 1981-. *Publications:* 3 books, chapts; 54 scientific articles, abstracts. *Memberships:* Deleg to Hse of Delegs, Am Assn for Clin Chem; Fellow, Nat Acad of Clin Biochem; Fellow, Assn of Clin Scientist; Sigma Xi; Acad of Clin Lab Physns & Scientists. *Honours:* Dipl, Am Bd of Clin Chem; Outstng Clin Chem Awd, TX Sect, Am Assn for Clin Chem, 1988. *Hobbies:* Woodworking; Furniture restoration; Photography; Biblical studies. *Address:* Oklahoma Medical Centre, Toxicology Laboratory, PO Box 26307, Oklahoma City, OK 73126, USA.

PARKER Lynda Christine Rylander, b. 21 Apr 1949, Bremerton, WA, USA. Tchr. m. Joseph Hiram Parker, 7 Feb 1987, 1 s. *Education:* BA 1971, MA 1981, Prin's Credential 1982, Pacific Lutheran Univ, Tacoma. *Appointments:* Tchr, Lang Arts, Ctrl Kitsap Schs, Silverdale, 1971-74; Tchr, Cnslr, Okanagan Schs, Kelouna, BC, Can, Tchr, Coll Preparatory Classes, Eng & Lit, 1974-78; Tchr, Lang Arts, Hons, Fed Way Schs, Fed Way, 1978- 86; Tchr, Remedial Reading Lang Arts, Gifted Humanities, Bethel Schs, Spanaway, 1986-. *Publication:* How to Be a Smart Student. *Memberships:* WA Educ Assn; Nat Educ Assn; Assn for Supervision & Curric Dev; Bethel Educ Assn; WA Assn of Second Sch Prins. *Honours:* Favourite Tchr of the Yr, Kilo Jr High, Fed Way Schs, Fed Way, 1983-86; Outstng Tchr of Yr, Christa McAnlitte Awd for excellence in educ, WA State, 1988; Superstar Staff for excellence and dedication to educ, Cedarest Jr High, Bethel Schs, Spanaway, 1990. *Hobbies:* Piano; Bodybuilding; Snow skiing. *Address:* Phyallup, WA, USA. 15, 138.

PARKER Robert Stewart, b. 13 Jan 1949, Collar Hse, Prestbury, Cheshire, Eng. Parly Counsel. *Education:* Trinity Coll, Oxford; Open Major Scholarship in Classics 1966; First in Mods 1969; BA (Hons) 1971; MA 1974; Called to Bar Middle Temple, 1975; MBIM 1984; MIMgt, 1992. *Appointments:* Classics Master, Brentwood Sch, 1971-74; In Pract at Bar, 1975-80; Asst Parly Counsel, 1980-85; At Law Commn, 1985-87; Dep Parly Counsel, 1987-92; Parly Counsel, 1992. *Publication:* Cases and Statutes on General Principles of Law (w C R Newton), 1980. *Memberships:* Middle Temple, 1970; Lincoln's Inn, Ad Eundem, 1977; Athenaeum, 1981; Liveryman, Worshipful Co of Wheelwrights, 1984; Freeman, City of London, 1984. *Honours:* Harmsworth Exhib, Middle Temple, 1970; Astbury Sr Law Scholarship, 1975. *Hobbies:* The Livery; Cricket; Bridge; Books; Music. *Address:* Office of the Parliamentary Counsel, 36 Whitehall, London SW1, England. 1.

PARKIN Andrew Terence Leonard, b. 30 June 1937, Birmingham, Eng. Prof; Poet; Critic. m. (1)Christine Patricia George, 14 June 1961, (2)Francoise Alice Marguerite Lentsch, 28 Apr 1990, 1 s. *Education:* Ba 1958-61, MA 1965, Pembroke Coll, Cambridge; PhD, Bristol Univ, 1969. *Appointments:* Cambs HS for Boys, 1961-63; St George's Sch, Kowloon, Hong Kong, 1963-66; Coll of St Matthais, 1967-69; Univ of BC, 1970-90; Chinese Univ of Hong Kong, 1991-. *Publications:* Stage One: A Canadian Scenebook; The Dramatic Imagination of W B Yeats; Shaw's Caesar and Cleopatra; Dancers in a Web; Dion Boucicault: Selected Plays; Yeats's The Herne's Egg; Yokohama Days, Kyoto Nights; Ed, Can Journ of Irish Studies, 1975-89. *Memberships:* Hon Life Mbr: Can Assn for Irish Studies, Can Celtic Assn; Can Writers' Union; Int Assn for Study of Angl-Irish Lit; MLA; Int Assn of Univ Profs of Eng; Fellow, Shaw Coll, Chinese Univ of Hong Kong. *Honours:* Open Exhib in Eng, Pembroke Coll, Cambridge, 1956; Cert of Merit, Master Tchr, Univ of BC, 1976; Winner, Salmon Arm Sonnet Competition, 1985; Vis Fellow, Humanities Rsch Ctr, Canberra, 1987; Most Disting Retiring Ed Awd, Coun of Eds of Learned Journs, Washington DC, 1989. *Hobbies:* Travel; Tennis; Theatre. *Address:* English

Department, The Chinese University of Hong Kong, Shatin, New Territories, Hong Kong. 52, 142.

PARKIN Sara Lamb, b. 9 Apr 1946, Aberdeen, Scotland. Environmental Campaigner. m. Donald Maxwell Parkin, 30 June 1969, 2 s. *Education:* RGN, Edinburgh Royal Infirmary, 1967-70; Biochem Course, Univ of MI, 1979-80; Post-grad Nursing Course, Leeds Polytech, 1980-81. *Appointments:* Staff Nurse, Ward Sister, Edinburgh Royal Infirmary, 1970-74; Nursing Rsch Asst, Univ of Edinburgh, 1972-73; Coun Mbr, sex-educ, Brook Advsry Ctr, 1974-76; Self-employed (sex educ), Family Planning Nurse, Leeds Area Hlth Auth, 1976-80; Newsletter Ed, Press Off, Yorks & Humbs Green Party, 1978-80; Coun Mbr 1980-81, Int Liaison Sec 1983-90, Speaker (European Elections) 1989, Speaker (Int Affairs) 1990-91, Chair Exec, 1992, Green Party; Co-sec 1985-90, Newsletter Ed 1986- 89, European Greens. *Publications include:* General Election Manifesto, Green Party (co-author), 1987; Green Parties: An International Guide, 1989; Green Politics: An International Perspective, 1990; Green Light on Europe, 1991; Green Futures: An Agenda For The 21st Century. *Memberships:* Green Party; New Econ(s) Fndn; Charter 88; Friends of the Earth; Scottish Green Party; 300 Grp; Islay Mus Trust; Finlaggan Trust. *Hobbies:* Walking; Camping; Gardening; DIY; Reading; Cooking; Theatre; Opera. *Address:* 18 Boulevard Pinel, 69003 Lyon, France. 1, 138.

PARKINSON Ewart West, b. 9 July 1926, Leicester, England. Chartered Engineer; Chartered Team Member; Dev Advsr, specialising in urban generation. m. Patricia Joan Wood, 21 Aug 1948, 2 s, 1 d. *Education:* BSc (Hons), Coll of Tech, Leicester; Dip, Pub Admin. *Appointments:* Engrng Learner, Leicester, 1942-48; Engr, Wakefield, 1948-49; Sr Engr, Bristol, 1949-54; Chief Engr, Dover, 1954-57; Dpty Borough Surveyor, Chelmsford, 1957-60; Dpty City Surveyor, Plymouth, 1960-64; City Planning Off, Cardiff, 1964-74; Dir of Environment, S Glamorgan, 1974-85. *Memberships:* FICE; FRTPI; Pres Royal Town Planning Inst; Hon Life Mbr, Intl Fedn of Housing & Planning; Vis Lectr, China Acad of Urban Planning and Design. *Honours include:* Miller Prize, ICE, 1953; Jubilee Silver Medal, Nat Housing and Town Planning Coun, 1979; O St J; Many design awards. *Hobbies:* Being with family; Chmn of several charities. *Address:* 42 South Rise, Cardiff CF4 5RH, Wales. 1.

PARKINSON Ronald Dennis, b. 27 Apr 1945, Rochester, Kent, Eng. Mus Curator. *Education:* MA Hons, Clare Coll, Cambridge, 1964-72. *Appointments:* Educ Dept 1972-74, Asst Keeper 1978-, Victoria & Albert Mus; Asst Keeper, Tate Gall, 1974-78. *Creative works:* Richard Redgrave, exhib catalogue, 1988; Catalogue of British Oil Paintings 1820-1860, 1990. *Membership:* Assn of Am Histns; Walpole Soc. *Hobbies:* Reading; Shopping. *Address:* Victoria and Albert Museum, London SW7 2RL, England. 1.

PARKINSON Thomas I Jr, b. 1914, USA. Co Pres. m. Geralda E Moore, 1937, 2 s, 1 d. *Education:* BA, Harvard Coll; LLB, Univ of PA. *Apointments include:* Assoc, Ptnr 1946-56, Milbank, Tweed, Hope & Hadley, Lawyers; Bd Chmn, Breecom Corp, 1980-. *Memberships:* Pilgrims of USA; ABA; City of NY Bar Assn; State Comms Aid Assn; Brit War Relief Soc, NYC; Various Clubs. *Address:* 780 Third Avenue, 25th Floor, New York, NY 10017, USA.

PARKYN Brian, b. 28 Apr 1923, Essex, Eng. Ret'd. m. Janet Stormer, 17 Mar 1951, 1 s, 1 d. *Appointments:* Plastics Chem 1947-53, Dir 1953-83, Scott Bader Co Ltd; Mbr of Parl, Bedford, 1966-70; Chmn, Parly Enquiry on Carbon Fibres, 1969-70; Dir, Halmatic Ltd, 1979-87; Gen Mgr Trng, British Caledonian Airway Ltd, 1981-88. *Publications:* Polyester Handbook, 1953; Polyester Resins, 1967; Glass Reinforced Plastics, 1970; Democracy, Accountability and Participation, 1979. *Memberships:* Chmn, Reinforced Plastics Sect, Brit

Plastics Fedn, 1961-63; FPRI, 1969; Mbr of Coun, Cranfield Inst of Tech, 1970- ; Hon Treas 1978-83, FRSA. *Honours:* Plastics Lecture, Worshipful Co of Horners, 1967; Gold Medal, Int Reinforced Plastics Conf, 1974. *Hobbies:* Industrial Democracy; Reinforced Plastics. *Address:* 9 Clarendon Square, Leamington Spa, Warwickshire CV32 5QJ, England. 1.

PARLETT Michael Harold James, b. 16 Nov 1940, Beijing, China. Investment Mgr. m. Elizabeth Ann Gusterson, 2 Sept 1967, 2 d. *Education:* BSc Hons, St Andrews Univ, 1961-65. *Appointments:* Shell Int Petroleum Co, 1965-68; Shell Sekiyu KK, 1968-73; Stewart Fund Mgrs, 1973-74; Murray Johnstone, 1974- . *Honours:* Dir, Murray Johnstone Ltd, -83; Dir, Kemper Murray Johnstone Int Inc, 1983-89; Mng Dir, Murray Johnstone Int Ltd, 1989-. *Hobbies:* Hillwalking; Skiing; Golf; Japan. *Address:* Glebe House, Manse Road, Linlithgow EH49 6QP, Scotland.

PAROLEK Radegast, b. 1 Dec 1920, Prague, Czechoslovakia. University Professor. m. Olga Oktabcova, 4 July 1955, 3 d. *Education:* Philos Fac, 1945-47, Philog Fac, 1947-51, Charles Univ; PhD, Charles Univ, 1952. *Appointments:* Prof, Charles Univ, Prague, 1952-86; Re'td, 1986, but still teaching Baltoslavic Philol there. *Publications:* Translations from Latvian and Lithuanian Literature as well as many articles. *Memberships:* Czech Writers and Czech Translators Assns. *Honours:* Doc Hon Causa, Rigas Univ, 1991; Winner, Intl Congress of Baltic Lit Translators, Riga, 1985; Prize Winner, Intl Baltic Conf, Riga, 1988. *Hobbies:* Translation of poetry; Reading. *Address:* Praha 10, Tolsfeho 18, Praha 10, Czechoslovakia.

PARRY Victor Thomas Henry, b. 20 Nov 1927, Newport, Monmouthshire. Ret'd Libn. m. Mavis Russull, 16 May 1959, 2 s, 1 d. *Education:* BA, MA, St Edmund Hall, Oxford Univ, 1945-48; Postgrad Dip in Libnship & Archives, Univ Coll London, 1951-52. *Appointments:* Libn, Sch of Oriental & African Studies, Univ of London, 1978-83; Dir, Ctrl Lib Servs Goldsmiths' Libn, Univ of London, 1983-88; Cons, 1989. *Memberships:* FLA; FRSA; FRAS. *Hobbies:* Reading; Ball games; Railways; Bridge. *Address:* 69 Redway Drive, Twickenham TW2 7NN, England. 1.

PARSAMIAN Elma, b. 23 Dec 1929, Erevan, Armenia. Leading Astronomer. m. Juri Schachbrazian, 5 Jan 1952, 1 d. *Education:* PhD, 1963; Dr of Phys & Math, 1983. *Appointments:* Scientific Wkr 1954-67, Sr Scientific Wkr 1967-83, Leading Scientific Wkr 1983- , Byurakan Astrophys Observatory, Armenia. *Publications:* Author of 110 printed scientific articles. *Membership:* IAU, 1976. *Hobby:* Archeoastronomy. *Address:* Byurakan Astrophysical Observatory, Republic of Armenia.

PARTINGTON Alan, b. 23 Sept 1930, Oldham, Lancs. Eng. Chartered Acct. m. Marian Smith, 12 Sept 1953, 1 s, 1 d. *Appointments:* Wm Wrigley & Son, 1948-54; H L & H L Holden, 1956-60; Ptnr, Alan Partington & Co, 1960-92; Dir, Lancastrian B S, 1969-92; Dir, Northern Reg Bd, Northern Rock B S, 1992-; Dir, Bank Hall Fin Mgmt Ltd, 1992-. *Memberships:* ICA; CBSI. *Hobbies:* Cricket; Football; Bowls; Food; Wine; Reading; Travel. *Address:* Wood Mount, 2 Woodland Park, Royton, Oldham, Lancashire OL2 5UY, England.

PASHUNKOVA Chrysanthema Ivanova, b. 5 Apr 1954, Ruse, Bulgaria. Concert Violinist; Rsch Fellow in Residence. *Education:* BA, Sofia State Conservatory, 1976; MM 1980, DMus 1981, Moscow State Conservatory. *Appointments:* Trainee under Prof Leonid Kogan 1976-77, Tchng Asst 1980-81, Moscow State Conservatory; Lectr, Sofia Music Sch, 1981-83; Rsch Fellow in Residence, Bulgarian Acad of Scis, 1983-; Lectr, Plovdiv Music Inst, 1989-90; Concert Violinist under own Mgmt, 1989-. *Contributions to:* Bulgarian Newspapers; Bulgarian Music; Musicalni Horizonti;

Bulgarsko Musicosnanie. *Memberships:* SPNM, London; ISCM, Isralei Section. *Hobbies:* Psychology of music interpretation and creativity; Concert performances of 20th Century Music.

PASSY Sophia Isaac, b. 20 Feb 1964, Sofia, Bulgaria. Biologist. *Education:* Dip of Higher Educ, MSc, Fac of Biol, Sofia Univ, St Kliment Ohridski, 1986. *Appointment:* Asst Prof of Bot, Dept of Bot, Fac of Biol, Sofia Univ, 1988-. *Publications:* Author of scientific publs in the field of palaeocology, ecology and taxonomy of algae. *Membership:* Bulgarian Boton Soc, 1988. *Honour:* Annual Awd for scientific and tech dev, Fac of Biol, Sofia Univ, 1986. *Hobbies:* Reading; Sport. *Address:* Boul P Evitimi 20, Sofia 1000, Bulgaria.

PASZKIEWICZ Joanna Jagers, b. 7 Dec 1941, Warsaw, Poland. Journalist; Art Critic; Artist. m. Jan Jagers, 21 Nov 1986, 1 d. *Education:* Fac of Sociology, Univ of Warsaw, 1966. *Appointments:* Sociologue, City Planning Off, Warsaw, 1969-73; Journalist, Art Critic in: Biuletyn Prasowo-wydawniczy, Prasa Polska, Radar, Sztuka, 1973-87; Free-lance Journalist, 1987-. *Publications include:* My Programme for 24 hours; A book collection of short prosa; A Woman with a Suitcase, 1991. *Membership:* Polish Journalists Assn, 1977-. *Honours:* Prize, Polilsh Anti- Alcohol Comm, 1985; OM for the Polish Culture, Min of Culture and Art, Polish Govt, 1985. *Hobbies:* Contemporary Art. *Address:* Brugstraat 20, 9844 PC Pieterzijl, Holland.

PATAKI-SCHWEIZER Kerry Josef, b. 1 Nov 1935, Peekskill, NY, USA. Behavioural Scientist; Med Anthropologist. m. Lalitha Shirin Harben, 16 Nov 1973, 2 s, 1 d. *Education:* SB, Univ of Chicago, 1960; MA 1965, PhD 1968, Univ of WA. *Appointments:* Reed Coll, 1967-69; Univ of CO, 1970; Univ of CA, San Fran, 1971-73; Univ of Papua New Guinea, 1974-. *Publications:* A New Guinea Landscape: Community Space & Time in the Eastern Highlands, 1980; The Ethics of Development: Justice and the Distribution of Health Care, 1987. *Memberships:* Fellow, Royal Anthropological Soc; Fellow, World Assn for Social Psych; Fellow, Am Anthropological Assn; Fellow, Int Coll of Psychosomatic Med; Malaysian Soc of Parasitology & Tropical Med; Papua New Guinea Med Soc; Assn of Acad Psych; Soc for Med Anthropology. *Honours:* French Govt Awd, Transl, Univ of Chicago, 1958; Woodrow Wilson Fellowship, 1960-61; Predoct Rsch Fellowship, Nat Inst of Mental Hlth, 1965-66; Vis Scholar, Univ of WA, 1977-78; Vis Prof, Max-Planck Inst, 1987-88. *Hobbies:* Aviation; Photography; Mountaineering; Literature. *Address:* PO Box 5623, Boroko, Papua New Guinea. 52, 149.

PATE J'Nell LaVerne, b. 31 July 1938, Jacksboro, TX, USA. Prof. m. Kenneth D Pate, 3 June 1960. *Education:* BA 1960, MA 1964, TX Christian Univ; PhD, Univ of N TX, 1982. *Appointments:* Ft Worth Indep Sch Dist, 1960-67; Tarrant Co Jr Coll Dist, 1972-. *Publications:* Livestock Legacy The Fort Worth Stockyards 1887-1987; Document Sets for Texas and the Southwest in US History (edited). *Memberships:* Ed Bd of Western Histl Quarterly, Western Hist Assn; TX State Histl Assn; Bd, W TX Histl Assn; Bd, Westerners Int. *Honours:* Outstng Grad Student Awd for Hist Univ of N TX, 1977-78; Coral H Tullis Awd for the most outstng book in the field of TX hist, 1988; Joseph J Ballard Jr Heritage Awd, N Ft Worth Histl Soc. *Hobbies:* Reading; Knitting; Travel. *Address:* Tarrant County Junior College, NE Campus, 828 Harwood Road, Hurst, TX 76054, USA. 7.

PATEJUK Mikolaj, b. 19 Dec 1934, Lozice. Geog; Town Planner. m. 17 July 1962. *Education:* Master's degree, Fac of Geog, Lublin Univ, 1959. *Appointments:* Cartographer, Dept of Agric & Forestry, Voivodship, Bialystok, 1959-60; Gen Designer, Hd of a Planning Grp, Provincial Off of Phys Planning, Bialystok, 1960-. *Creative works:* Phys mgmt plans of 52 communes, 20 towns, 6 natural-touristic area, natural model and conception of the spatial structure of Bialystok; Town

Planning Competitions: Grajewo 1971, Koszalin 1974, Wodzislaw 1975. *Memberships:* Soc of Polish Town-Planners; League for the Preservation of Nature; Polish Tourist Country-Lovers Assn. *Honours:* 2 prizes, Min's of Phys Mgmt and Environmental Protection for the great creative achievements in phys planning, 1973, 1981; Prizes & Awds in 3 Town Planning Competitions; Silver and Gold Awds. *Address:* ul Legionowa 11/28, 15-099 Bialystok, Poland.

PATEL Atulkumar B, b. 24 Feb 1958, India. Reg Dir. m. 21 Feb 1981. *Education:* BA Hons, Univ of Sussex, 1976-79. *Appointments:* Youth Wkr, Self help Neighbourhood Proj, 1979-81; Dir, ASRA Hon Assn, 1982-88; Area Mgr 1988-90, Reg Dir 1991-, Housing Corp. *Memberships include:* MBIM; ASRA Greater London Housing Assn, 1984-; Ramakarishna Vedanta Ctr, 1985-; Trustee, Housing Assns Charitable Trust, 1986-1991; Anchor Housing Assn, 1986-; Guardian Housing Assn, 1986-; Fedn of Black Housing Orgs, 1988-; ASRA Housing Assn, 1988-. *Hobby:* Indian music. *Address:* Surbahar, 5 Chrisett Close, Leicester LE5 6RD, England.

PATEL Dipak K. A, b. 12 July 1953, Lusaka, Zambia. Deputy Minister, Ministry of Trade, Commerce and Industry. m. 6 July 1975, 1 s, 1 d. *Education:* Quantock Sch, Bridgewater, Somerset, UK. *Appointments:* MD, Palatine Holdings Ltz, Zambia, 1970; Nat Trustee, Campaign Mgr, Movement of Multi-Party Dem, current ruling party in Zambia, 1990-; Dpty Min, Govt of the Rep of Zambia, Min of Trade, Commerce and Industry, 1991. *Hobbies:* Squash; Speed boating; Water Skiing; Parasailing; Wind Surfing. *Address:* PO Box 31079, Lusaka, Zambia.

PATEL Hasmukh, b. 1 Jan 1945, Kampala, Uganda. Cons Paediatrician; Reg Postgrad SubDean. m. Mrudula Patel, 16 July 1969, 1 s, 1 d. *Education:* MBBS 1967; MRCS 1967; DCH 1970; MRCP 1972. *Appointments:* Cons Paediatrician, Dartford, 1976; Clin Tutor 1981-91, Reg Postgrad SubDean 1991-, Univ of London. *Memberships:* BPA; BMA; Brit Paediatric Gastroenterology Soc. *Honours:* FRCPEd, 1985; FRCP, 1986. *Hobbies:* Photography; Travel; Wine tasting. *Address:* 9 Irene Road, Orpington, Kent BR6 0HA, England.

PATENAUDE Pierre, b. 5 May 1942, Montreal, Can. Prof; Barrister. m. Lise McManiman, 25 Jan 1969, 1 s, 2 d. *Education:* Lic en Oroit, 1966; BA, 1966; Master degree, 1968. *Appointments:* Univ of Sherbrooke, 1969-91; Dean of Law Sch, Univ of Moncton, 1978-80. *Publications:* La Protection des Conversations, 1976; La Preuve, Les Techniques Modernes et le Respect des Valeurs Fondamentales (Ed), 1991. *Membership:* Barreau du Quebec. *Honour:* Kt of Magistral Grace of the Sovereign and Mil Order of Malta, 1983. *Address:* Law School, Universite de Sherbrooke, Sherbrooke, P Quebec, Canada J1K 2R1.

PATRICOLA James, b. 25 Mar 1935, Buffalo, NY, USA. World Ldr. m. Becky M Patchet, 2 Nov 1984, 1 s, 2 d. *Education:* Schs, NY & CA; Various other accredited educl insts, 1958-91; PhD, 1978. *Appointments:* USN, hon discharged in 1953; VAU 2-931 Functional Logistics Oct 24; Status earned, Dir of Philos; Pres Dr Patricola is an Inventor Scientist, Intl Wld Advsr; Dip Serv, Polit Govt Intiatives and of Constnl Philsphs, all levels, all issues. *Creative works include:* Master plans, grand proportional logistics & high functional degree systems of efficiency, at the apex level of all the nine major fields being: Garment and Apparel; Agriculture; Education; Architecture; Communications; Entertainment; Transportation; Defence and Health and Metaphysics. *Memberships:* Municipal Mbr of Beverly Hills, CA. *Honours:* Copyrights, countries worldwide. *Hobbies:* Fine arts and crafts; Physical, industrial, economical, environmental, structural, universological progress & spiritual unfoldment. *Address:* PO Box 5239, Maple Annex, Beverly Hills, CA 90209, USA.

PATTERSON James Hardy, b. 12 Oct 1935, Kingston, GA, USA. Asst Prof; Profl Musician. m. Lois G, 24 May 1958, 2 d. *Education:* AB, Clark Coll, 1957; MM, Univ of MI, 1965. *Appointments:* Profl Musician, early 1950's-; Music Tchr, Dept Chair, Fulton Co Bd of Educ, 1957-84; Clark Atlanta Univ, 1962-. *Creative works include:* Compositions: Song for Mr HP; Reminiscence. Author: Jazz and the Young Black Audience. Asst Proj Dir, Film, In Search of Improvisation, The Essence of Virtuosity in Jazz. *Memberships:* AAUP; ASCAP; Nat Educ Comm, Bd of Govs, Nat Acad of Rec Arts & Scis; Nat Flute Assn; Int Assn of Jazz Edrs; N Am Saxophone Am Fedn; Alliance World Saxophone Cong; Bd of Dirs, Atlanta Fedn of Musicians; Int Double Reed Soc; Int Clarient Soc; Duke Ellington Soc; Optimists; YMCA; Alpha Phi Alpha. *Honour:* Bronze Jubilee Awd, Sta WETV, 1983. *Hobbies:* Tennis; Research; Composition. *Address:* 413 Fielding Lane, SW, Atlanta, GA 30311, USA. 4, 7, 52, 117, 125.

PATTERSON James Willis, b. 29 Dec 1946, Takoma Pk, MD, USA. Physn; Med Edr. m. Julie Wyatt, 30 Dec 1989. *Education:* BA, Johns Hopkins Univ, 1968; MD, Med Coll of VA, 1972. *Appointments:* Dermatologist, Dir of Med Educ, US Mil Acad, W Point, 1976-79; Dermatologist, Fitzsimons Army Med Ctr, Denver, 1980-82; Prof of Pathology & Dermatology, Med Coll of VA, 1982-. *Publications:* Dermatology, A Concise Textbook, 1987; Author of over 100 articles and abstracts in Dermatology and Pathology. *Memberships:* FACP; Fellow, Am Acad of Dermatology; Fellow, Am Soc of Dermatopathology; Col, USAR; Pres 1989-90, VA Dermatological Soc; Asst Ed, Journ of Cutaneous Pathology, 1989-. *Honours:* Army Commendation Medal, 1979, 1982; Stuart McEwen Awd, Assn of Mil Dermatologists, 1980, 1983; Army Achmt Medal, 1985. *Hobbies:* Golf; History and Biography; Collecting political memorabilia. *Address:* Medical College of Virginia, 11th and Marshall Streets, Box 407, Richmond, VA 23298, USA. 7, 15, 17.

PATTERSON Neil Michael, b. 22 Mar 1951, Aberdeen, Scotland. Co Partner; Copywriter. m. Doris Karen Bell, 23 July 1983, 1 s. *Education:* Shirley House, Watford, 1959-63; Trinity Coll, Glenalmond, 1964-68; Watford Sh of Art. *Appointments:* Hall Advertising, 1971-73; Saatchi & Saatchi, Copy Writer, 1972-73; TBWA, Creative Dir, 1973-85; Y&R, 1985-89; Mitchell Patterson Aldred Mitchell, Creative Partner, 1990-. *Publications include:* Columist, Trout Fisherman; Books: The Complete Fly Fisher; The One That Got Away: The Art of the Trout Fly. *Memberships:* D & AD; Creative Cirle; Fly Dressers Guild. *Honours include:* Lego, Land Rover Nursing Recruitment; First Aids Ad to Apear on British TV. *Hobbies:* Fly Fishing; Fly Tying; Writing; Cooking; Drawing; Guitar. *Address:* Wilderness Lodge, Little Wawcott, Elcot Turn, Bath Road, Newbury, Berks, R6l6 8NH, England.

PAUL Donald William, b. 11 Apr 1947, Pawtucket, Rhode Island, USA. Audiologist. m. Leslie Christine Berry, 8 June 1968, 2 s. *Education:* BS, 1973; MS, 1975; Boston Univ. *Appointments:* Audiologist, 1974- 77; Dir, Audiology, 1977-; Conslt in Audiology, 1980-; Instr, Northeastern Univ, Boston, 1978-82; Instr, Bridgewater State Coll, Bridgewater, 1980-82. *Publications:* Hearing Conservation Report; Trends in Audiology. *Memberships:* Ameican Speech Language Hearing Assn; Natl Hearing Conservation Assn; Council For Accreditation in Occupational Hearing Conservation; Eastern Lions Club. *Honour:* Cert of Clinical Competence. *Hobby:* Sailing. *Address:* PO Box 312, 44 Baltic Avenue, North Easton, MA 02356, USA.

PAUL Fritz Werner, b. 4 Apr 1942, Nesselwang. Prof of Germanic, Especially Scandinavian Philology. m. Brigitta Mathilde Breitschadel, 22 Nov 1968, 1 d. *Education:* Dr Phil, Univ of Munich, 1968; Habilitation, 1972. *Appointments:* Asst, Univ of Munich, 1968-72; Prof, Univ of Bochum, 1972-79; Full Prof, 1979-; Dir Dep, Dean Faculty, 1983-84, Univ of Goettingen.

Publications include: Henrik Ibsen; Swedish Literature in German Translation, 7 Vols. *Memberships:* Soc of Philos; Faculties Brueder Grimm Soc; Royal Swedish Acad of Letters, History & Antiquities. *Honour:* Deutsche Forschungsgemeinschaft Scholar. *Hobbies:* Opera; Theatre. *Address:* Klosterweg 6a, D 3400 Goettingen, Germany. 43, 52.

PAUL William, b. 31 Mar 1926, Deskford, Banffshire, Scotland. Physicist; Professor of Physics. m. Barbara Anderson Forbes, 28 Mar 1952, 1 s. *Education:* MA Hons, 1946, PhD 1951, Aberdeen Univ; MA HOn, Harvard Univ, 1960. *Appointments:* Lectr, Aberdeen, 1946-52; Asst Prof, 1956-60, Assoc Prof, 1960-63; Havard; Gordon Mckay Prof, 1963-, Mallinckrodt Prof, 1991, Harvard. *Publications:* 350 published scientific papers; Ed of 5 books. *Memberships:* FAPS; FBIPhys; NYAS; RSEdin; Assoc Clare Hall, Camba; Chartered Physicist, UK. *Honours:* Carnegie Fellow, 1952; Guggenheim Fellow, 1969; Prof Associe, Univ of Paris, 1966; Ripon Prof, Calcutta, 1983; Humboldt Awardee, 1990. *Hobbies:* Travel; Reading; Gardening. *Address:* 229 Pierce Hall, Harvard University, Cambridge, MA 02138. USA. 2.

PAULIN Pierre, b. 9 July 1927, Paris, France. Dessinateur. m. Maia Wodzislawska, 15 May 1982, 2 s, 1 d. *Education:* Lycei de Laon; Ecode Camonder. *Appointments:* Stone Cutter, 1947-48; Ceramist, 1950; Design Furniture Garcoin Soc Creating Forms, 1951; Created ADSA, Pierre Paulin Soc, 1979. *Creative Works include:* Contracts with French Ministry of Cultural Affairs. *Honours include:* Design Award; Ressources Council Award; Natl Design Award. *Address:* 74 Rue du Faubourg, St Antoine, 75012 Paris, France. 91.

PAUSON Peter Ludwig, b. 30 July 1925, Bamberg, Germany. Emeritus Prof of Chemistry. m. Lai ngau Wong, 7 June 1952, 1 s, 1 d. *Education:* Univ of Glasgow, 1942-46; Univ of Sheffield, 1946-49. *Appointments:* Temp Asst Lectr, Sheffield Univ, 1949; Asst Prof, Duquesne Univ, 1949-51; Post Doc Research Fellow, Univ Chicago, 1951-52; Harvard Univ, 1952-53; Lectr, Univ of Sheffield, 1953-59; Freeland Prof of Chemistry, Royal Coll of Sci & Tech, 1959-; Univ of Strathclyde, 1964-90; Visiting Prof, Univ of AZ, 1966-67. *Publications:* Organometallic Chemistry; 200 Original Articles & Reviews. *Memberships include:* Royal Soc of Edinburgh; Royal Soc of Chemisty; Deutsche Abademilder Naturforscher, Leopoedina. *Honours include:* Tilden Lectureship of the Chemical Soc; Makdougall Brisbane Prize of the RSE. *Hobbies:* Skiing; Hill Walking; Gardening; Music. *Address:* 40A Station Road, Bearsden, Glasgow G61 4AL, Scotland. 47, 161, 184.

PAVELIC Kresimir, b. 19 July 1952, Slavonski Brod, Croatia. Medical Doctor. m. Jasminka Pavelic Matakovic, 4 Dec 1976, 1 s. *Education:* MD, 1975, MSc, 1977, PhD, 1979, Fac of Med, Univ of Zagreb. *Appointments:* Res Asst, Ruder Boskovic Inst, Zagreb, 1975-79; Vis Prof, Roswell Pk Meml Inst, Buffalo, NY, 1978, 1984-86; Prof and Atom and Physiol, Univ of Zagreb, 1987-89; Vis Prof, Univ of Hamburg, 1985; Vis Prof, Univ of Cincinnati, OH, USA, 1990; Prof of Molec Biol, Univ Zagreb, 1990-. *Publications:* 90 scientific papers on basic science, biology, biomedicine, oncology and 3 books. *Memberships:* Euro Assn for Cancer Res; Croatian Socs of Immunol, Cancer, Genetics and Physiol. *Honours:* Prize, Univ of Zagreb, 1972, 1973; Drago Perovic Prize, Zagreb Med Sch, 1973; Fed Prize for Young Scis, 1978; Vuk Urhovac Prize for Res in Diabetol, Crotian Med Assn, 1982; Roswell Pk Meml Inst Fellowship, 1984, 1986; Fulbright Fellowship, US Govt, 1990, 1991. *Hobby:* Gardening. *Address:* Ruder Boskovic Institute, Molecular Oncology Laboratory, Bijenika 54, PO Box 1016, Zagreb 41001, Croatia.

PAVKOVIC Aleksandar, b. 19 May 1950, Belgrade, Yugoslavia. Snr Lectr. m. Mirjana Djukic, 27 Dec 1979, 2 s. *Education:* BA, MA, Yale Univ, 1972; B Phil, Univ of Oxford, 1974; Dr Sci, Belgrade Univ, 1983; G Dipp App Sci, Univ of Tech, Sydney, 1990. *Appointments:* Asst, Belgrade Univ, 1976-84; Docent, Belgrade Univ, 1984-87; Research Fellow, Melbourne Univ, 1985-87; Hd Slavonic Studies, Macquarie Univ, 1987-90; Snr Lectr, 1990- *Publications include:* Mind & Knowledge; Reasons for Doubt. *Memberships:* American Philosophical Assn; Philosophy Soc of Serbia. *Honour:* Phi Beta Kappa. *Hobbies:* Jogging; Classical Music. *Address:* Slavonic Studies, Macquarie Univ, NSW 2109, Australia.

PAVLOV Dimcho, b. 29 Dec 1944, Plovdiv. Artist. m. 7 Oct 1968, 1 s, 1 d. *Education:* Acad of Fine Arts, 1971. *Appointments:* 17 One Man Shows; Many Group Exhib. *Creative Works include:* Simpoziums; Lindabrun; Brianson; Nisa. *Memberships:* Union of Fine Arts. *Honours include:* Plovdiv, Prize for Fine Arts; Prize from Simpozium Teulada. *Address:* Bvd Svoboda 34 VHG, 4000 Plovdiv, Bulgaria.

PAWLAK Ryszard Jerzy, b. 3 Apr 1952, Lodz, Poland. Mathematician. m. Helena Nonas, 28 Apr 1979, 1 s. Education: Master, 1975; Doctor, 1979; Doctor Habilited, 1986; Prof, 1990. *Appointments:* Hd of Dept of the Methods of Tchng Mathematics; Asst Prof, Lodz Unit; Prof Lodz Univ. *Publications include:* Przeksztalcenia Darboux; 40 Articles. *Memberships:* Polish Mathematical Soc; American Mathematical Soc. *Honours include:* Medal of the Glorious Studies; Reward of the Union of the Rectors of the Higher Schs of Lodz. *Hobbies:* Sport; Music. *Address:* Lokietka 6 m 40, 93 335 Lodz, Poland.

PAWLEY G Stuart, b. 22 June 1937, Ilford, Essex, England. Prof of Computational Physics. m. Anthea Jean Miller, 29 July 1961, 2 s, 1 d. *Education:* Bolton Sch, 1956; Cambridge, Corpus Christi Coll, MA, 1959; PhD, 1962. *Appointments:* Research Asst, Harvard, 1962-64; Lectr, 1964; Reader, 1970; Prof, 1985; Edinburgh Univ; Guest Prof, Arhus, Denmark, 1969-70. *Publications include:* Over 200 Scientific Papers; 2 Books, Co Author. *Membership:* Fellow of Royal Soc of Edinburgh. *Hobbies:* Music & Choral Singing; Mountain Walking. *Address:* 35 Grange Loan, Edinburgh EH9 2ER, Scotland.

PAWLOWSKA Elzbieta, b. 28 June 1956, Warsaw, Poland. Painting; drawing; Graphic; Set Designing. *Education:* Acad of Fine Arts, warsaw, Faculty of Graphic Arts, 1976-81; Diploma AFA, 1982. *Appointments:* Theatre Studio, Center of Contemporary Art, Warsaw, Poland, 1982-83. *Creative Works include:* Die Verfolgung und Ermordung Jean Paul Marats; An Individual Exhib of Drawing, The Medical Acad Gallery, Warsaw; 2nd Annual Intl Exhib of Miniature Art in Toronto. *Memberships:* Union of Polish Artists & Designers; ARCO, ARTE, Contemporaneo. *Honours include:* The Grant for Young Artists, Polish Ministry of Culture & Art; Artists Grant from Bundes Ministerium fur Unterricat und Kunst in Wien. *Hobbies:* Theatre; Writes; Poetry. *Address:* Chmielna 2 m 29, 00 022 Warsaw, Poland.

PAXMAN Jeremy Dickson, b. 11 May 1950, Leeds, England. Journalist. *Education:* Malvern Coll; St Catharines Coll, Cambridge. *Appointments:* Reporter, Northern Ireland, 1973077; BBC TV Reporter, 1977-85; Presenter, Breakfast Time, Newsnight, 1989-. *Publications:* A Higher Form of Killing; Through the Volcanoes; Friends in High Places. *Honours:* Royal TV Soc Intl Cultural Affairs Award. *Hobby:* Fly Fishing. *Address:* c/o Simpson Fox Assoc, 52 Shaftesbury Avenue, London W1V 7DE, England. 1

PAYNE R Gordon, b. 25 Oct 1940, England. Intl Port Conslt. m. (1) Patricia D Michael, (2) Victoria Chodachek, 2 s. *Education:* Arethusa Training Ship, 1954-56; King Edward Nautical Coll, 1957; Faculty of Commerce & Business Admin, Univ of BC, 1984. *Appointments:* Deck Officer MN, 1958-63; President & CEO Empire

Stevedoring Co Ltd, 1963-88; Ports & Harbours, Int Port Conslt, 1990; Founder, Pres, CEO Meridian Stevedoring, 1988-90. *Memberships:* Terminal City Club; Navel Officers Assn of Canada. *Hobbies:* Tennis; Gardening. *Address:* 13470 26 Avenue, Ocean Park, Surrey, BC, Canada V4A 6E6. 142.

PEACOCK Graham John, b. 21 Dec 1944, St Albans, Herts, England. Pension Admin. m. 23 Mar 1985, 3 s, 1 d, 1 Stepson. *Education:* Sedgehill Sch, Kent. *Appointments:* Trainee Estimator, 1962-63; Trainee Surveyor, 1963-64; Police Officer, 1964-90; Pension Admin, 1990-. *Memberships:* Freeman of City of London; Liveryman Worshipfull Co of Loriners; Royal Soc of St George; Farringdon Ward City Livery Club; United Wards Club; Brothers in Law Lunchtime Club. *Honour:* Police Long Serv & Good Conduct Medal. *Hobbies:* Reading; Rugby; Shooting; Camping. *Address:* 80 Chapel Green, Reedham Drive, Purley, Surrey CR8 4DS, England.

PEACOCK Jospeh Henry, b. 22 Oct 1918, London, England. Retired Emuritus Prof of Surgical Sci. m. Gillian Frances Pinchney, 24 June 1950, 1 s, 1 d. *Education:* Univ of Birmingham, 1935-41; MBCHB, 1941; MRCSLRLP, 1944; FRCS, 1949; CHM, 1957; MD, 1963. *Appointments:* R & MC, 1942-47; Surgical & Athopaedic Spec, Univ of bristol, Lectr, 1953; Reader, 1965; Prof of Surg Sci, 1969; Conslt Surgeon, United Bristol Hosp, 1955-84; SW Reg Hosp, 1960-84. *Publications include:* Numerous Publi. *Memberships include:* European Soc of Surgical Research; Assn of Surgeons of Gr Britain & Ireland; BMA; GMC. *Honours include:* Royal Coll of Surgeons of England; RockeFellow Fellow in Surgery. *Hobbies:* Short Wave Radio; Gardening; Travel. *Address:* The Old Manor, Ubley, Nr Bristol BS18 6PJ, England. 1.

PEACOCK Oliver L, Brigadier General, b. 12 June 1940, West Palm Beach, Florida, USA. Civilian, Exec; Military, Chief of Staff SCSG. div, 1 d. *Education:* Sewanee Military Acad, 1958; Florida Atlantic Univ, BA, 1965; US Army Infantry Sch, 1964; US Army Natl Defence Univ, 1989. *Appointments:* Active Duty US Army, 1963-68; Peacock Fruit & Cattle, VP, 1968-70; Army Reserve & State Guard, 1968-91; 27 US Foreign decs, Knight Grand Cross, Order of St Stanislas; Florida Indian Affairs Commnr, 1969-70; Florida Game & Fresh Water Fish Commn, 1971-1974; Dir, Nat Wildlife Fed, 1974-1976; Peacock Fruit & Cattle, Pres & General Mngr, 1990-. *Memberships include:* Florida Historical Soc; South Carolina Historical Soc; Reserve Officers Assn; The Company of Military Historians. *Honours include:* US Army Infantry Hall of Fame. *Address:* 2180 Park Avenue, North Suite 320, Winter Park, FL 32789, USA.

PEARCE Petra, b. 17 July 1967, California, USA. Educator. *Education:* Bach of Arts, Intl Relations, 1989; United State Intl Univ. *Appointments:* Admissions & Financial Aid Counselor, United States Intl Univ, 1989-91. *Hobbies:* Horseback Riding; Reading; Intetcultural Exchange; Intl Travel; Ethnic Cuisine; Dancing; Swimming; Yachting. *Address:* PO Box 1572, Santa Ynez, CA 93460, USA. 152.

PEARCE GROTSKY Lisa Anne, b. 30 May 1957, Columbus, Ohio. Designer; Musician; Advertiser; Marketer; Producer. m. Allen Grotsky, 1 Mar 1991. *Education:* Johnstown Monroe, 1975; Dale Carnegie Grad Course. *Appointments:* Coronet Recording Co, 1985-; Footprints, Inc, 1990-; Musician; Composer; Dancer; Designer; Marketing; Advertising. *Creative Works include:* Anestimi Nephesh, 4 Part Flute Composition; Psalm 6, 12 Works. *Memberships:* USO; womens Music Club; NAFE; Footprints. *Honours:* In The Know; USO Winner; Dale Carnegie Winner; Desginier of the Year, Ovation Mag. *Hobbies:* Embroidery; Finance. *Address:* LA Music & Assoc, PO Box 141534, Cols, OH 43214, USA.

PEARCEY Leonard Charles, b. 6 June 1938, Westminster, England. Writer; Broadcaster; Presenter; Singer; Producer. *Education:* Christs Hosp, 1948-57; Corpus Christi Coll, Cambridge, 1959-62. *Appointments:* Dir Studies, Rapid Results Coll, 1962-63; Tchr, Wimbledon, 1964-65; Arts Admin, Harold Holt Ltd, 1965-66; Music Dir, Guildhall Sch of Music & Drama, 1966-70; Compn, Sec Int Violin Compn, 1966-70; Dir, Merton Festival, 1972-76; Adviser, BBC Radio and TV Drama Awards, 1972-90. *Creative Works include:* Numerous Major Arts & Religious Progs; Own Series Singer & Guitarist; Presenter, BBC Radio 2 Young Musicians' series; Director, 'Forte Music at Leisure'. *Memberships:* Polruan Carnival Regatta & Childrens Sports; Actors Equity. *Hobby:* Travel. *Address:* 53 Queens Road, Wimbledon, London SW19 8NP, England.

PEARLMAN Joseph Joshua, b. 26 Apr 1933, Redcar, England. Solicitor. m. Bernice, 18 June 1961, 2 d. *Education:* LLB, 1954; Solicitor, 1956. *Appointments:* Pearlman Grazin & Co, 1958-91; Godlove Pearlman, 1991-. *Publications include:* Numerous Articles. *Memberships include:* Leeds Law Soc; Ramblers Assn. *Hobbies:* Rambling; Travel; Food; Drink. *Address:* 10 Lakeland Crescent, Leeds, LS17 7PR, England.

PEARSON Alfred Charles, b. 20 Feb 1914, Perth, Western Australia. Lieutenant Commander RANVR, Retired. m. Betty Helen Chinner, 28 Nov 1952, 1 s, 2 d. *Appointments include:* Clerk, 1930-38; Distribution Officer, BP Australia Ltd, 1938-41; Royal Australian Naval Volunteer Reserve, Seconded to Royal Navy, 1941; Returned to RAN, 1945; Mktng Div, BP Australia Ltd, 1946-73; Public Relations Mngr, Mount Newman Mining Co Ltd, 1973-79; Mktng Mngr, West Trade Centre, Perth, 1979. *Memberships include:* Naval Officers Assn; Naval, Military & Air Forces Club; United Service Inst; Australian Sea Cadet Corps. *Honour:* Volunteer Reserve Decoration, VRD. *Hobbies:* Philately; Numismatics; Assistance to Ex Service Personnel & Dependants. *Address:* 52 Glenelg Street, Applecross, WA 6153, Australia.

PEARSON Barclay Andrew, b. 13 Jan 1912, Dorset, England. Retired Army Officer. m. Heather Campell Gray, 5 Apr 1944, 1 d. *Education:* West Downs, Winchester, 1921-25; Sherborne Sch, 1925-29; Brasenose Coll, Oxford, 1931-35; BA, 1935. *Appointments include:* Commissioned Argyle & Sutherland Highlanders, 1934; Capt, 1939; Adjutant, 1940-42; ME Staff Coll, 1942; AA & QMG HQ 51 Div, 1945-46; HQ Scot Comd Edinborgh, 1950-51; Comd 154 Highland Brigade, 1957-60; Retired, 1960; Stirling Clark & Kimross, 1960-68; Chmn, Museum Com Stirling Castle, 1975-89. *Honours include:* DSO; Silver Acom; Mention in Despatches. *Hobbies:* Country Pursuits; Gardening; Croquet; Travel. *Address:* Spinneyturn, Rumbling Bridge, Kinross shire KY13 7PY, Scotland.

PEARSON C Andrew, b. 10 Dec 1921, China. Retired Medical Practitioner. m. Jeam M Frost, 30 Nov 1948, 3 s, 1 d. *Education:* Liverpool Univ: MBChB, 1944, DTM, 1946, FRCGP, Nigeria, 1970, FWACP, (GP), 1987. *Appointments:* Union Hosp, Wuhan, China, 1949-51; Med Supt, Wesley Guild Hosp, Nigeria, 1952-75; Col of Med, Ibadan, Nigeria, 1975-83; Dir of Training, Fac of Gen Med Prac, Nigeria, 1983-85. *Publications:* Training for General Medical Practice in Nigeria, 1981; Medical Administration for Frontline Doctors, 1990. *Memberships:* Christian Health Assn of Nigeria, Exec Mem, 1975; Action Intl Med, Exec Mem and Conslt. *Honours:* OBE, 1974; Chieftaincy Titles in Nigeria, 1984, 1985, 1987. *Hobbies:* DIY; Music (violin). *Address:* 2 Springfield Road, Bury St Edmunds, Suffolk IP33 3AN, England.

PEART Tony Christopher, b. 23 June 1951, Ambleside, England. Painter; Writer. m. 4 Apr 1978, 2 s, 2 d. *Education:* Oundle Sch, 1962- 69; Univ of Leeds, BA, 1969-72; Univ of Newcastle, MA, 1972-74.

Appointment: Self Employed since Graduation. *Creative Works:* One Man Exhibs; Book, Trouble at the Edge; The History of the Frame. *Memberships:* RSA; TSB; ROI; NWA; RSWA. *Hobbies:* Water Diving; Brick Laying; Icelandic Cooking. *Address:* The Piccadilly Gallery, Cork Street, London W1, England.

PEASE Rendel Sebastian, b. 2 Nov 1922, Cambridge, England. Conslt Physicist. m. Susan Spickerwell, 9 Aug 1959, 2 s, 3 d. *Education:* Natl Sci, Cambridge Univ, BA, 1942; Ma, 1949; ScD, 1964. *Appointments:* Operational Research for min Aircraft Prod, 1942-46; Experimented Physics Research, Harnell, 1947-64; Dir, Culham Lab, 1967-81. *Publications include:* Numerous Scientific Papers. *Memberships:* Inst of Physics; Royal Soc; Inst of Elect Engrng; American Inst of Physics; British Pugwash. *Honours include:* Keloin Premium IEE; Europe Nuclear Energy Soc. *Hobby:* Music. *Address:* The Poplars, W Ilsley, Newbury, Berks, RG16 0AW, England. 1, 52.

PECHERNIKAVA Irina, b. 2 Feb 1945, Grozny, Russia. Cinema & Theatre Actress. m. div. *Education:* High Artistic Sch of Moscow Art Theatre, 1962-66. *Appointments:* Participation in more than 30 Films; 40 Plays. *Memberships:* Artists union; Film Artists Union; Artistic Guild. *Honour:* Honoured Art Worker. *Hobbies:* Painting; Travel. *Address:* Tverskaja Street 9, App 41, Moscow, Russia.

PEĆINA Marko, b. 23 Mar 1940, Oborovo. Orthopaedic Surgeon; Prof of Univ. m. Ana Hrncevic, 5 Mar 1966, 1 s, 1 d. *Education:* Zagreb Univ, 1964; MSc, 1968; PhD, 1970; Orthopaedic Surgery, 1973. *Appointments:* Asst Lectr, 1965-70; Asst Lectr, Dept of Othop Sur, Sch of Medicine, Zagreb, 1971-76; Snr Lectr, 1977; Asst Prof, 1979; Assoc Prof, 1980; Prof, 1984; Chmn Orthopaedic Surgery, Univ of Zagreb, 1986-. *Publications include:* More than 300 Expert & Sci papers; Book. Pecina et al Tunnel Syndromes; Book: Pecina M, Bojanic J, Overuse Injuries of Musculoskeletal System. *Memberships:* Croatia Medical & Orthop Assn; European Spinal Deformities Soc; Intl Knee Soc; European Knee Soc; French Orthop Traumat Soc; Italian Knee Soc; Coll Europ Traum Sport; Soc Intl Chirurgie Orthop Traumat; Mem, Croatian Olympic Cttee, Pres of Medical Commission; Mem, Int Assoc of Olympic Medical Officers; Mem, Fondateur Mediterranean Tricontinental Medical Assoc. *Honours include:* Balkan Medical Union Award for Sci Achivement; Associated Mamber Croatian acad of Arts & Sci. *Hobbies:* Walking Tour; Skiing; Reading. *Address:* Marticeva 21, 41000 Zagreb, Croatia.

PECZENIK Aleksander, b. 16 Nov 1937, Krakow, Poland. Prof. m. Irena Nowak, 7 Apr 1960, 1 s. *Education:* LLM, 1960; LLD, 1963; LL Candidate, 1975; PhD, 1983. *Appointments:* Asst, Snr Asst, 1960-66; Assoc Prof of Law, 1966-69; Asst Prof of Law, 1970-76; Prof, Lund Univ, 1977-. *Publications include:* Essays in Legal Theory; The Basis of Legal Hustification; On Law and Reason. *Memberships:* Acad of Finland; Swedish Assn for Philosophy of Law; Lunds Acad of Sci. *Honours:* LLD; HC. *Hobbies:* Marathon Running; Chess; Politics. *Address:* Kallarekroken 34, 22647 Lund, Sweden. 52.

PEDDIE Peter Charles, b. 20 Mar 1932, Somerset, England. Solicitor. m. Charlotte Elizabeth Ryan, 2 s, 2 d. *Education:* Canford Sch, Dorset, 1945-50; St Johns Coll, Cambridge, BA, 1954; Law Soc Honours, 1957. *Appointments:* Articled Clerk Freshfields, London, 1954-57; Asst Solicitor, Freshfields, 1957-60; Partner, Freshfields, 1960-92; Consultant, Freshfields, 1992; Adviser to Governor, Bank of England, 1992-. *Memberships:* Law Soc; City of London Solicitors Co; Gov, Canford Sch. *Honour:* CBE. *Hobbies:* Gardening; Foreign Travel. *Address:* c/o Bank of England, Threadneedle Street, London EC2R 8AH, England. 53.

PEDRO Nicholas J, b. 8 Apr 1949, St Paul, Minn, USA. Dir, Cobb Adult Community Education & After Sch Programs. m. Jane Ellen Pedro, 31 Dec 1971, 1 s. *Education:* Stetson Univ, Deland, Fl, 1969-72; West Ga Coll, Carrollton, Ga, 1973-75. *Appointments include:* Abbott Sea Walls & Constr, Constr Asst, 1971; Atlanta Braves Camp Rabun, 1972; John McEchern High Sch, Physical Educ Tchr, 1973; Tapp Community Schs, Community Sch Dir, 1977- 78; Cobb County Bd of Educ, Admin Asst, 1978-81; Cobb County Bd of Educ, 1982- *Publications include:* Journal of Instructional Media; Extended Day Care Serves Children, Community. *Memberships include:* ASCD; GAVA; NAPR; NCEA. *Honours include:* Outstanding Young Community Educ for the State of Georgia. *Address:* 1050 Windmill Lane, Marietta, GA 30064, USA.

PEHL Erich Ludwig, b. 13 Mar 1939, Montabour, FRG. *Education:* Reifeprufung, 1958; Univ Darmstadt, 1965. *Appointments:* Devel Engr on Communication Theory & Navigation, Stuttgart & Munchen, 1965-72; Tchr Mathematics & Physics, High Sch, Munchen, 1972-74; Prof Electrical Engrng, Tech Coll, Osnabruck, 1974-; Course Leader, Mathematics & Physics, High Sch, Osnabruck, 1975-. *Publications include:* Author & Chmn on Various Microwave Conferences; Books. Mikrowellentechuick Vol 1 & 2. *Hobbies:* Classical Languages; Reading; Radio Amateur. *Address:* Fachhochschule Osnabruck, 4500 Osnabruck, Germany.52.

PEITCHINIS Stephen G, b. 12 Oct 1925, Greece. Prof. m. Jacquelyn, 13 Sept 1952. *Education:* Univ of Sofia, Bulgaria, 1946-49; Univ of Western Ontario, London, Canada, BA, 1954; MA, 1955; London Sch of Econs, PhD, 1960. *Appointments:* Western Ontario, Canada, 1955-68; Univ of Calgary, Canada, 1968-; Univ Dean, 1972-75; Univ Hd, 1984-91. *Publications include:* Employment & Wages in Canada; Computer Technology and Employment; Women at Work. *Memberships include:* Canadian Econ Assn; American Econ Assn. *Hobbies:* Reading; Travel; Golf. *Address:* 13, 1901 Varsity Estates Drive NW, Calgary, Canada. 141.

PEITERSEN Erik, b. 8 June 1931, Herlufsholm, Denmark. Chief Surgeon; Assoc Prof. m. Birgit, 6 May 1961, 1 s, 1 d. *Education:* Univ of Copenhagen, Denmark, 1959; Doctorate, 1965; Ear, Nose, Throat Specalist, Danish Natl Bd of Health, Denmark, 1968. *Appointments:* Univ State Hosp, Copenhagen, 1959-65; Snr Resident, 1965-68; Conslt, Municipal Hosp, Copenhagen, 1968-72; Chief Surgeon, 1972-78; Chief Surgeon, Copenhagen City Hosp, 1978-; Assoc Prof, Univ of Copenhagen, 1972-. *Publications:* Thesis, Vestibulor Spinal Reflexes; Cholesteatoma & Mastoid Surgery; World Congress of O to Rhino Laryngology; Natl History of Bells Palsy. *Memberships:* Danish Oto Laryngological Soc; Medical Faculty IV, Copenhagen City, Univ of Copenhagen; Barany Soc. *Honours include:* Dr Valdemar Klein & Dr Ms Johanne Klein, Award. *Hobbies:* Golf; Hunting. *Address:* Enighedsvej 49C, DK-2920 Charlottenlund, Denmark. 1.

PEITSO Martti Samuli, b. 24 Aug 1924, Raahe, Finland. Sculptor; Educator. m. Saga Valborg Hollsten, 22 June 1951, 1 d. *Education:* Helsinki Arts & Crafts Inst, 1947-50; Studies with Wäinö Alltonen, 1950- 54. *Appointments:* Prof Sculpting Helsinki Univ of Tech, 1955-86. *Creative Works include:* Fountains; Public Sculptures; Finland, Sweden. *Honours include:* Recipient Prize in Monument Comp; Finnish Trade Union, 1957; Jean Sibelius, 1962; Nat Epic Kalevala, 1968. *Hobby:* Music. *Address:* 3 Kaivokatu, 10600 Tammisaari, Finland. 43, 52, 90.

PELL Marian Priscilla, b. 5 July 1952, England. Solicitor. m. Gordon F Pell, 4 Aug 1973, 2 s, 1 d. *Education:* Southampton Univ, 1970-73. *Appointments:* Herbert Smith, 1974-. *Membership:* Law Soc. *Hobbies:* Music; Walking; Tennis. *Address:* Exchange House, Primrose Street, London, EC2A 2HS, England. 53.

PELLETIER Marcel Raymond, b. 2 Sept 1936, Canada, Quebec. Lawyer. m. Pierrette Leduc, 14 July 1990, 1 s, 1 d. *Education:* Univ of Ottawa, BA, B Ph, 1960; Pol Sc, Law, 1963; Law & Admin, 1964; Hague acad of Intl Law, 1965. *Appointments:* Foreign Serv Officer, Geneva at UN, 1965-66; Research Officer, Parliament of Canada, 1966-69; Clerk Asst, House of Commons, 1969-83; Parliamentary Counsel, 1983-91; Lawyer & Prof, 1991-. *Publications include:* Articles on Parliamentary Law. *Memberships:* Canadian Bar Assn; Quebec Bar Assn; Clerk at the Table Canada; Editorial Bd of Parliamenary Gorernment; Assn of Clerk at Table in Commonwealth Parliament; Canadian Assoc of Law Teachers. *Honours:* Queens Counsel; Knight of L'Orde de la Pleiade. *Hobbies:* Reading; Music; Opera; Skiing; Skating; Gardening. *Address:* Poltimore, Quebec, Canada. 142.

PELTON Virginia Lue Keng, b. 15 Apr 1928, Utica, Kansas, USA. Small Business Owner. m. Harold M Pelton, 11 July 1970, 2 d. *Education:* Kansas Univ, 1946-47; Washington Univ, 1950-51; Patricia Stevens Finishinf, 1948. *Appointments:* Couture Model, Berforf Goodman, 1951- 53; Fashion Conslting Titches Dallas, 1955; Charles Galley, 1975-79; Buyer/Mngr Slavicks Gewelry, 1980-83; Owner, PJ Secretarial, 1983-; Co Owner, HP Financial, 1982-. *Publications:* Author/Editor, Profl Network Newsletter. *Memberships include:* Profl Network; Leukemia Soc; Republician Womens Club; Los Angeles Museum. *Honours:* Valedictorian Snr Class; Home Economics Scholarship Grant; Complete Costume Design Award; Rivera Cruise; Bahamas Fantasy Cruise. *Hobbies:* Gourmet Cooking; Art; Travel. *Address:* 24942 Georgia Sue Drive, Laguna Hills, CA 92653, USA. 5, 9, 132, 138.

PENDLE Karin, b. 1 Oct 1939, Minneappolis, MN, USA. Prof of Musicology. m. Frank E Pendle, 17 Dec 1966. *Education:* BA, Univ of Minnesota, 1961; MA, Univ of Illinois, 1964; PhD, 1970. *Appointments:* Oberlin Coll, 1964-69; Univ of Western Ontario, Asst, Assoc Prof, 1970-76; Univ of Cincinnati, Prof of Miscology, 1976-. *Publications include:* Eugene Scribe & Fench Opera of the Ninteenth Century; Women and Music. *Memberships include:* American Musicological Soc; American Assn of Univ Profs; American Handel Soc; American Assn of Univ Women. *Honours include:* Phi Beta Kappa; Phi Kappa Phi; Research Grants of Various Types. *Hobby:* Singing. *Address:* Coll Conservatory of Music, Univ of Cincinnati, Cincinnati, OH 45221, USA. 138.

PENLEY John Francis, b. 22 Dec 1948, Bristol, England. Solicitor and Notary Public. m. Caroline Anne Myfanwy James, 1 s, 1 d. *Education:* Marlbourough Coll, 1962-67; Coll of Law, 1972; Staff Coll, 1988. *Appointments:* Solicitor, Clifford Turner, 1973-78; Penleys, 1978-; Partner, Co Royal Wessex Yeomary, 1989-91. *Publication:* Co Author, Tempered by Reality. *Memberships:* Law Soc; Notaries Soc; CLA Glos; Bow Group. *Honours:* OBE; TD. *Hobbies:* TA; Riding; Gardening.

PENN Christopher Robert Howard, b. 24 Aug 1939, Southend On Sea, England. Conslt in Clinical Oncology. m. Elizabeth Griffin, 27 May 1967, 3 d. *Education:* Trinity Hall, Cambridge; The London Hosp; BA, 1961; MA MB B Chir, 1965; DMRT, 1969; FRCR, 1972. *Appointments:* House Physician, House Surgeon, The London Hosp, 1965-66; Snr House Officer, Lincoln & Grimsby, 1966-67; Sho, Registrar, Snr Reg, The London Hosp, 1967-73; Conslt in Clinical Oncology, 1973-; Snr Conslt, 1982-. *Publications:* Multiple Papers in Medical Journals; Chapters in Radiotherapy in Modern Clinical Practice. *Memberships:* Royal Coll of Radiologists; British Inst of Radiology; British Oncological Assn. *Hobbies:* Sailing; Martime History; Sailing for the Disabled; Jubilee Sailing Trust. *Address:* 1 Holcombe Road, Teignmouth, Devon, TG14 8UP, England.

PENNIE John Anthony, b. 18 Feb 1955, Oxford, England. Solicitor. m. 12 Feb 1983, 1 s, 1 d. *Education:* Marlborough Coll, 1971-74; Cambridge Univ, 1974-77; Univ Libre de Bruxelles, 1978. *Appointments:* Solicitor, Partner, Messrs Dickinson Dees, 1985-. *Memberships:* Law Soc; Sandhoe Parish Council; Tynedale Environmental Group; Solicitors European Group. *Honour:* Licensed Insolvency Practitioner. *Hobbies:* Local History; Gardening; Rare Breeds. *Address:* Beaufront Hill Head, Hexham, Northumberland, NE46 4NB, England.

PENNINGER Antal, b. 18 Nov 1943, Budapest, Hungary. Department Head. m. Zsuzsanna Kovats, 30 Aug 1973, 1 d. *Education:* Adv Level, 1988, Dr Techn, 1978, MSc, 1967. *Appointments:* Supvr, Powerplant Maintenance Co, 1967-69; Asst, 196978, Lectr, 1979-88, Techn Univ, 1989-. *Publications:* Cumbustion Instabilities in Industrial furnaces, 1988; Chapter in, Combustion Noise, 1986; The Steam Turbine, co-author, 1983; Chapter in, The Gas Turbine, 1975; The Steam Turbine, co-author, 1975, transl from German. *Memberships:* Sci Soc of Meas and Autom; Hungarian Acad of Engrg; Presidum, Treas, Dir, Intl Ctr for Engrg Progs, Honours: Awd for Outstanding Work, 1989. *Hobbies:* Music; Opera; Tourism; Nature; Philosophy. *Address:* Technical University of Budapest, Department of Head Engines, Muegyetem rkp 3-9, Budapest 1521, Hungary.

PENNINGTON Beverly Melcher, b. 8 Feb 1931, Vermillion. Small Business Owner. m. Glen D, 1 Sept 1965, dec, 1 d. *Education:* BS, Univ SD, Vermillion, 1952. *Appointments include:* Sec Budget Dept, BIA Aberdeen, 1952-53; Admin, Asst US Pub Health Serv, Anchorage, 1955-58; Grant Admin, Dental Pub Health, 1961-65; Co Owner, Pennington Tax Serv, Platte, 1974-86; Enrolled Agt, Intl Revenue Serv, 1987-. *Publications include:* Numerous Articles to Profl Journals. *Memberships include:* Plattes Womens Club; NAFE. *Hobbies:* Collecting Jewelry; Reading; Designing; Gourmet Cooking. *Address:* 420 Main, Platte, SD 57369, USA.

PENTELEICIUC Dragos, b. 11 Apr 1931, Horodnic, Romania. Stomatological Doctor. m. Dana Carmen, 27 Oct 1955, 1 s. *Education:* Fac of Stomatol, 1956; Spec in Protetics, 1965; MD, 1972. *Appointments:* Stomatol since 1956 in Sighisoara, Bucharest; Lectr, Dir of Stomatol Polyclin, Bucharest; Specialist in Dental Surg. *Publications:* 12 certs of inventions in stomatol; 50 Articles in papers and scientific reports; Book: Dento-Alveolobone grafts and transplants. *Memberships:* Nat Union of Romanian Scists; The World Fed of Dentists; Union of Med Scis Socs. *Honours:* Romanian Acad Awd for the book, Bone Grafts and Transplants. *Hobbies:* Fishing and Hunting. *Address:* Str Stefan Furtuna 173, Bucharest, Romania.

PEPIN KEYS Madeleine, b. 4 Aug 1943, USA. Asst Prof of Philosophy. m. David W Keys, 6 May 1969, 1 s, 1 d. *Education:* Portland State Univ, BS, 1970; Univ of Idaho, MA, 1974, 1978; Univ of Texas, Austin, PhD, 1990. *Appointments:* Univ of Idaho, IA, 1972-77; Boise State Univ, Instr, 1979-80, 1983-85; Univ of Texas, AI, 1980-82, 1986-87; Our Lady of the Lake Univ, Asst Prof, 1987-91. *Publications:* South Augustine, Synthesis of Faith & Reaseon; The Idea of Feminism in Western Political Thought; Sextus Empircus & Ancient Scepticism. *Memberships:* Medical Acad of America; American Philosophical Soc; Soc for Ancient Greek Philosophy; Medieval & Renaissance Philosophy Soc; Intl Soc of NeoPlatonic Studies. *Honours include:* Phi Kaap Phi. *Hobbies:* Reading; Natural History. *Address:* Our Lady of the Lake Univ, 411 SW 24th, San Antonio, TX 78207, USA.

PERCIVAL John, b. 11 July 1937, Great Tey, Essex, England. Prof of Ancient History; Hd of Sch of History & Archaeology. m. (1) Carole Ann Labrum, 11 Aug 1962, dec, 2 d, (2) Jacqueline Anne Gibson, 10 Sept 1988. *Education:* Hertford Coll, Oxford, BA, 1956-61; Merton Coll, Oxford, MA, 1963; D Phil, 1967. *Appointments:* Univ Coll, Cardiff, 1972-; Asst Lectr, 1962; Lectr,1964; Snr Lectr, 1972; Reader, 1979; Prof, 1985. *Publications include:* The Roma Villa. *Memberships:* The Soc of Antiquaries; Classical Assoc. *Hobbies:* Music; Gardening. *Address:* 26 Church Road, Whitchurch, Cardiff, CF4 2EA, Wales. 1.

PERCY John Pitkeathly, b. 16 Jan 1942, Southport, England. Chartered Accountant. m. Sheila Isobel Horn, 26 June 1965, 2 d. *Education:* The Edinburgh Acad, 1953-60; Edinburgh Univ, 1963-64. *Appointments:* Graham Smart & Annan CA, 1962-68; Martin Currie & Scott, 1968-71; Grant Thornton, 1971-; Mgrng Partner London, 1980-88; Snr Partners, Scotland, 1991-. *Memberships:* Inst o Chartered Accountants of Scotland; Prof of Accounting Aberdden Univ; Royal Soc of Arts; British Acad of Experts. *Honours include:* Freemen City of London; Livery Worshipful Coy of Painter Stainers. *Hobbies:* Golf; Fishing; Gardening. *Address:* 30 Midmar Drive, Edinburgh, EH10 6BU, Scotland. 1.

PEREIRA Teresinka, b. 1 Nov, Brazil. Writer; Prof. Div, 2 s, 2 d. *Education:* Univ of New Mexico, PhD. *Appointments:* Tulane Univ, 1964-68; Stanford Univ, 1968; Georgetown Univ, 1973; Univ of Colorado, 1975-88; Moorhead State Univ, 1988; Bluffton Coll, 1991. *Publications:* Alien; Writers Poetry; A Cow on the Sad Plains; La Literature Antillana. *Memberships:* Intl Writers & Artists Assn; World Poetry Bd of Research of American Biographical Inst. *Honours include:* Natl Prize for Theatre, Brazil; Nominated for the Gold Crown World Poets. *Address:* Box 775, Bluffton Coll, Bluffton, OH 45817, USA. 138.

PERES Asher, b. 30 Jan 1934, Beaulieu, France. Prof of Physics. m. Aviva Grunspan, 24 Aug 1958, 2 d. *Education:* BSc, Israel Inst Tech, 1956; Inst Saclay, France, 1957; DSc, Technion, 1959. *Appointments:* Technion Faculty, 1959-; Visiting Prof, Univ of Maryland, 1967-68; Drexel Univ, 1975-76. *Publications:* About 200 articles in Profl Journals & Books. *Memberships include:* Physical Soc of Israel; American Physical Soc; American Assn for Advancement of Sci. *Address:* Dept of Physics, Technion, Israel Inst of Technology, 32 000 Haifa, Israel.

PEREZ DE CUELLAR Javier, b. 19 Jan 1920, Lima, Peru. Lawyer; Intl Diplomat. m. Marcela Temple. *Appointments include:* Peruvian Ministry of Foreign Affairs, 1940; Duir of Legal Dept, Dir of Admin, Dir of Protocol, Dir of Political Affairs, 1961-66; Sec General Foreign Affairs, Ambassador of Peru to Switzerland, 1981-; Sec General, United Nations, 1981-. *Publications:* Manual of Diplomatic Law. *Honours include:* Honorary Doctorates, Univ Worldwide; Prince of Asturis Prize. *Address:* Exec Office of the Secretary General, United Nations, New York 10017, USA.

PERHAM Richard Nelson, b. 27 Apr 1937, London, England. Prof of Structural Biochemistry. m. Nancy Jane Lane, 22 Dec 1969, 1 s, 1 d. *Education:* St Johns Coll, Cambridge, BA, 1961; MA, 1965; PhD, 1965; ScD, 1976; FRS, 1984; FRSA, 1988. *Appointments:* Univ Dummstator,Cambridge, 1964-69; Lectr, 1969-77; Reader, 1977-89; Prof, 1989-. *Publications include:* Instrumentation in Amino Acid Sequence Analysis; Numerous Papers; Articles; Reviews. *Memberships:* Royal Soc of London; Royal Soc of Arts; Biochemical Soc; European Molecular Biology Organ; Royal Inst of Gt Britian; St Johns Coll, Cambridge; Member, Academia Europaea, 1992. *Honours include:* Slater Studentship and Henry Humphreys Prize, St John Coll. *Hobbies:* Gardening; Rowing; Theatre; Antique Shops. *Address:* Dept of Biochemistry, Univ of Cambridge, Tennis Court Road, Cambridge CB2 1QW, England. 1.

PERL Jeffrey Michael, b. 30 May 1952, Minneapolis, Minn, USA. Prof; Journal Editor; Writer. *Education:* Stanford Univ, AB, 1974; Univ of Oxford, B Phil, 1976; Princeton Univ, MA, 1979; PhD, 1980. *Appointments:* Asst Prof, Columbia Univ, 1980-87; Assoc Prof, 1987-89; Prof, Univ of Texas, 1989-; Founding Editor, Common Knowledge. *Publications include:* Skepticism & Modern Enmity; The Tradition of Return. *Memberships:* Oxford Centre for Postgraduate Hebrew Studies; Modern Language Assn of America; American Comparative Literature Assn. T S Eliot Soc of St Louis. *Honours include:* Guggenheim Fellowship; Rockfeller Fellowship; Natl Endowment for the Humanities; Visiting Fellowship, Mansfield Coll, Oxford Univ. *Address:* Common Knowledge, JO 31 Univ of Texas, Box 830688, Richardson, TX 75083, USA. 7.

PEROSA Sergio, *Education include:* Princeton Univ; Indiana Univ Sch of Letters. *Appointments include:* Chmn, English Dept, Univ of Venixe; 1966-83; Prof of Anglo American Literature, 1968-. *Publications include:* Annali di Ca Foscari; L'arte di F S Fitzgerald; Dimore Adam; Le isole Aran, Figure Letterarie Inglesi. *Contributions to:* English Literature Corriere Della Sera, 1969-. *Memberships include:* Italian Assn of American Studies; European Assn for American Studies; Intl Snn Univ; IAUPE; EAAS. *Honours include:* Fulbright Fellow, Princeton Univ. *Address:* Universita Di Venezia, Dorsoduro 3246, 30100 Venezia, Italy. 43, 95.

PERRAULT Georges Gabriel, b. 31 July 1934, Vincennes, France. Research Scientist; Engeniet. *Education:* Baccalaureat, Lemans; Eng Dipp, Strasbourg; Dr 3e Cycle; Dr Es Sciences. *Appointments:* Research Sci, 1958-; Natl Centre Scientific Research, France; Duke Univ, Durham; CNRS, France. *Publications include:* Chapters in Books; 31 Papers; 94 Tapes. *Memberships include:* NY Acad of Sci; Electrochemical Soc; Nouvelie Rev Ent Paris. *Hobbies:* Astronomy; Travel; Camping; Photography. *Address:* BP 21, 92292 Chatenay Malabry Cedex, France. 1.

PERRIAM Wendy Angela, b. 23 Feb 1940, London, England. Author. m. (1) 22 Aug 1964, 1 d, (2) John Alan Perriam, 29 July 1974. *Education:* St Annes Coll, Oxford, BA, 1961; MA, 1972; London Sch of Economics, 1963-64. *Appointments:* Advertising Copy Writer, Colman, Prentis & Varley; Notley & Pritchard Wood; Full Time Author. *Publications:* Absinthe for Elevenses; Cuckoo; After Purple; Born of Woman; The Stillness The Dancing; Sin City; Devils, For A Change; Fifty-Minute Hour; Bird Inside; Michael, Michael. *Memberships:* Soc of Authors; PEN; British Actors Equity Assn. *Address:* Curtis Brown & John Farquharson, 162-168 Regent Street, London W1R 5TB. England. 3, 138.

PERRY Jacqueline Anne, b. 7 Mar 1952, London, England. Barrister; Broadcaster. m. Victor Levene, 17 Feb 1980, 1 s. *Education:* Lady Margaret Hall, Oxford, BA, 1973; MA, 1977; Coll of Law, Barrister, 1975. *Appointments:* Barrister at Various Addresses; Pupillage, Temple; Broadcaster on Legal Topics, Temple. *Publications:* Legal Columnist, Prima Mag; Co Author. *Membership:* Grays Inn. *Hobbies:* Reading; Cinema; Travel; Art. *Address:* Lamb Building, Temple, London EC4, England.

PERSSON (Nils) Bertil (Alexander), b. 10 Nov 1941, Trelleborg, Sweden. Priest; Prof; Headmaster; Sch Book Producer. m. Maud Gunnel Maria, 1966, 1 s, 1 d. *Education:* MA, 1965; LittB, 1970; EdM, 1972; DD, 1974; DDSc, 1982; DTh, 1989. *Appointments include:* Tchr, Religion & Literature, 1964-83; Priest, Moravian Church, 1965-71; Church of Sweden, 1965-79; Editor in Chief, Religion Och Kultur, 1972-80; Dir, St Ephrems Inst, 1974-; Fellow, Royal Soc of Arts, England, 1982-; Headmaster, Enskilda Gymnasiet/Carissons Hogstadieskol, Stockholm, 1983-90; Dep Hdmaster, Storvretskolan, Tumba, 1990-; Prof, Geneva Theological Coll, 1989-; Chaplain, Order of the Holy Cross of Jerusalem, The Melkite Greek Catholic Church, 1987;

Philippine Ind Ch, Europe, 1988-; Igreja Catolica Apostolica Brasileira, Scandinavia, 1988-; Western Orthodox Catholic Church, America, 1989-; Iglesia Orthodoxa Catholica Apostolica Mexicana, 1991-; Pontife, Ordo Supremas Militaris Hierosolymitant, German Priorate, 1991-; Sec, Sigvard & Marianne Bernadotte Rsch Fndn for Children Eye Care, 1989-. *Publications include:* Kulter Sekter Samfund; Fran Jesu eget Sprak; Religionsboken; Independent Bishops, An International Directory; An Apostolic Episcopal Ministry. *Contributions to:* Numerous Periodicals Encyclopaedias. *Memberships include:* Odd Fellow Order; Syriac Acad; Vilatte Guild; World Literay Acad; Intl Parliment for Safety & World Peace. *Honours include:* Europe Pace Progresso; Grand Cross, Imperial Constantinan Military Orde of St George; Gold Cross, Polonia Restituta, Pres Rep, Poland in Exile; Ehrenzeichen für Wissenschaft und Kinst, Albert-Schweitzer-Gesellschaft; Croix, St Antoine du Dessert, Coptic Orthodox Church. *Address:* PO Box 7048, S171 07 Solna, Sweden.

PERSSON Eskil, b. 10 Feb 1930, Helsingborg. Chmn Bd of Appeal, European Patent Office. m. Margaretha Jonsson, 23 Oct 1972, 1 s. *Education:* Univ of Uppsala, LLB, 1954. *Appointments:* Royal Swedish Navy, 1954-55; Court Practice & Legal Advisor, 1956-67; Deputy Hd of Legal Dept, EFTA, 1968-72; Judge, District Court, 1973-77; Judge, Court of Appeal, 1978-80; Judge, Pres of Court of Patents Appeal, Stockholm, 1981-86; Legal Bd of Appeal, EPO, 1987-; Chmn, Technical Bd of Appeal, EPO, 1990-. *Hobbies:* History; Tennis; Sailing. *Address:* European Patent Office, D8000 Munchen 2, Germany. 43.

PERUMAL I R, b. 25 July 1952, Madras, India. Joint Dir, Food & Civil Supplies Government of Karnataka, Bangalore. m. Lalitha, 13 Sept 1978, 1 s, 1 d. *Education:* Master of Arts, 1974. *Appointments:* Indian Postal Serv, 1979; IAS, 1982. *Publications include:* More than 200 Poems; Book. Hasivina Loka; Kanneer Kanasu. *Memberships:* IAS Officers Assn; Century Club; Diners Club, Madras; Intl Poets Acad, Madras. *Honours:* Intl Poets Acad, Diploma. *Hobbies:* Writing Poems; Reading Books; Chess; Shuttle; Helping the Poor. *Address:* 6 Madras Bank Road, Bangalore 560001, India.

PETAR Sasa, b. 24 Mar 1962, Samobor. m. Vlatka Kovacic, 23 Mar 1991. *Education:* BSc 1981-85, MSc 1987-89, Univ of Econ, Zagreb. *Appointments:* Dept Mgr, Org for Scientific and Rsch Work, 1983-85; Rsch Cons 1985-89; Dept Mgr, Rade Koncar Engrng Co, 1989-90; Dpty Prin, The Zagreb Bus Sch, 1990-91; Gen Mgr, Bus Club, Zagreb, 1991-. *Honour:* Citizenship Awd, Mayor of Zagreb, 1987. *Hobbies:* Reading; Tennis; Golf; Urban Economics. *Address:* Rade Koncara 248, 41000 Zagreb, Croatia. 52.

PETECEL Despina Viorica, b. 5 May 1949, Craiova. Musicologist. m. 20 Mar 1992. *Education:* Acad of Mus, Bucharest, 1970-73. *Publications:* Cycles: Our musicians confess themselves, 1975-87; Tradition and modernism in Romanian Music, 1990; Music collision's sphere. *Contributions to:* different printed works including the Dictionary of Musical Terms, 1984; Researches in Musicology, 1987; Julia J Ropea vol with musical chronicles, 1882-1904, 1987; Our Musicians Confess themselves, vol I, 1990; A translation from French to Romanian; As well as publications of studies, musical chronicles, reviews, and introductions to symphonic performances. *Honours:* Composers and Mucols Union, 1983-; Mus Criticism Prize, 1990. *Hobbies:* Foreign languages; Linguistics; Philosophy; Arts History. *Address:* Str Emile Zola m 4 cod 71272, Bucharest 7000, Romania. 138.

PETER Mihaly, b. 8 Nov 1928, Budapest. Prof of Russian Philology. m. Ilona Boros, 15 Aug 1962, 2 d. *Education:* St Peterburg, Leningrad, 1949-54; PhD, 1959; CSc, 1965; DrSC, 1988. *Appointments:* Dept of Russian Philology, Eotvos Lorand Univ, Budapest, 1988-91. *Publications include:* Historical Grammer of the

Russian Language; Means & Devices of The Expression of Emotions In Language. *Memberships:* Slavic Stylistics & Poetics in the Interm; Slavic Sec of the Hung Linguistics Soc; Linguistic Commitee of the Hung Acad of Sci. *Honours:* Award of the Publishing House, Hung Acad of Sci. *Hobbies:* Travel; Photography. *Address:* Budai Laszlo u 7, H-1024 Budapest, Hungary.

PETEROS John Basil, b. 3 Nov 1952, Vancouver, Canada. m. Lisa Marie Snow, 22 Apr 1989. *Education:* Dipl Tech, Elec & Elect, Hons, BC inst of Tech, 1973; BASc, Hons, Elec Engrg, 1977, PhD, Elec Engrg, Univ of BC, Vancouver, Can. *Appointments:* Lectr, Reschr, Dept of Elect Engrg, Univ of BC, 1977-; Satellite Receiver R&D, Earth Station Rech Inc, Richmond, BC, 1978-80; Channel One Video Corp, VHF/UHF TV Transmitter R&D, Vancouver, 1979-81; RMS Indust Controls Inc, UHF Digital Mobile Radio R&D, 1980-82; Co- Fdr, Chm and CEO, Nexus Engrg Corp, Burnaby, BC, 1982-. *Publications include:* SMATV Sys Design, 1986; Processing distant and strong local off- air signals, 1984; How to eliminate interference in off-air signal processing, 1984. *Memberships:* Young Pres Org; Assn of Profl Engrs or BC; IEEE Inc. *Honours include:* BC Sci and Engrg Gold Medal, 1988; BC Export Devel Awd, 1987; Best Bus Achievement Awd, BC Chamber of Commerce, 1986; Awd of Excellence, Elect Mfgr Assn of BC, 1988. *Hobby:* Running. *Address:* 7000 Lougheed Hwy, Burnaby, BC, Canada V5A 4K4.

PETERS Douglas Dennison, b. 3 Mar 1930, Brandon. Man. Canada. Snr Vice Pres, Chief Economist, Economist & Banker, Toronto Dominion Bank. m. Audrey Catherine Clark, 26 June 1954, 1 s, 1 d. *Education:* Queens Univ, Kingston, Ontario, 1963; PhD, Univ of Pennsylvania. *Appointments:* Chief Economist, Toronto Dominion Bank, 1966; Vice Pres & Chief Economist, 1972; Snr Vice Pres, 1981. *Publications include:* The Monetarist Counter Revolution, A Critique of Canadian Monetary Policy; Numerous Articles. *Memberships include:* Toronto Assn of Business Economists; Canadian Economics assn; American Economic Assn; Royal Economic Soc. *Hobby:* Tennis. *Address:* Toronto Dominion Bank, Dept of Economic Research, PO Box 1, Toronto Dominion Centre, Toronto, Ontario, Canada M5K 1A2. 142.

PETERS Mercedes, b. New York, USA. Psychoanalyst. *Education:* BS, Columbia Long Island Univs, 1945; MS Soc Work, Univ of CT, 1953; Cert Psychoan, Postgrad Ctr for Mental Hlth, 1976; PhD, Psychoan, Union Inst, 1989. *Appointments:* Various social agencies as Case Worker and Supvr, 1953- 63; Pvte Practice Psychotherapy and Pshcyo, 1974-76; Staff. Affiliate, PCMH. *Publications:* Psychosocial determinants of depression among Blacks; Analyst as Real Person; Analytic Neutrality; Culture as an Object. *Memberships:* NASW; Soc of Clin Soc Workers; NAAP, Legislative Com. *Honours:* Intl Woman of the Yr, 1991-92. *Hobbies:* Needlepoint; Embroidery; Friends. *Address:* 142 Joralemon Street, Billyn , NY 11201, USA. 6, 52, 162.

PETERSEN Bruce Lee, b. 18 Nov 1942, Brainerd Minnesota. Minister; Snr Pastor. m. Jacquelyn Stone, 18 Dec 1965, 1 s, 1 d. *Education:* BA, Olivet Nazarene Univ, 1965; M DIV, Nazarene Theological Seminary, 1971; D MW, Trinity Euangelical Divinity Sch, 1982. *Appointments:* Assoc Pastor, Coll Church of the Nazarene, 1967-71; Pastor, 1st Church, Nazarene, Mich, 1971-79; Pastor, Springfield, Ohio, 1979-87; Pastor, Coll Church of the Mazarene, Nampa, 1987- . *Publications include:* I Peter, Worship & Preaching Helps; Conributor, Preachers Mag. *Memberships include:* Saginaw County Evangelica Ministers; Nazarene Denominational Commission on the Calling of the Pastor; Northwest Nazarene Coll. *Hobbies:* Music; Golf; Back Packing. *Address:* 1015 South Canyon, Nampa, ID 83686, USA. 145, 176.

PETERSMANN Hubert, b. 20 Aug 1940, Klagnenfurt, Germany. University Professor. m. Astrid Mahr, 11 July

1969. *Education:* MA 1964, PhD 1965, Habil (Univ Doz), 1976, Univ of Vienna. *Appointments:* MA 1964, PhD 1965, Habilitation, 1976, Univ of Vienna. *Publications:* Plautus Stichus, 1973; Petrons Urbane Prosa, 1977; Rom Lit, 1992; Ed of Periodical and books. *Memberships:* Memmsen Gesselschaft, 1984-; Goerres Gesellschaft, 1984-; V-Dean, Fakultat fur Oriental u Altertumswiss, Univ Heidelberg, 1983-84. *Hobbies:* Reading; Travelling; Sport; Theatre. *Address:* Seminar fur Kassische Philologie Universitat, Heidelberg, Marshtallhof 4, D-6900 Heidelberg, Germany.

PETERSON Barbara Ann, b. 6 Sept 1942, Portland, USA. Prof of History. m. Frank Lynn Peterson, 1 July 1967. *Education:* BA, BS, Oregon State Univ; MA, Stanford Univ; phD, Univ of Hawaii. *Appointments:* Professor, Univ of Hawaii, 1967-93; Chapman Coll, 1974; Univ of Colorado, 1978; Wuhan Univ, China, 1988-89. *Publications include:* Notable Women of Hawaii; America in British Eyes; The Pacific Region; A Women's Place Is In The History Books. *Memberships:* AHA; OAH; ASA; Hawaian History Soc; Council of Bishop Museum; American Biographical Research Inst; IBS; Hawaii State Comm on the Statues of Women. *Honours include:* Outstanding Snr Women; Tchr of the Year; Phi Kappa Phi; Fulbright Scholar to Japan and China; Hon PhD, London Inst of Applied Rsch. *Hobbies:* Tennis; Cooking; Skiing; Lectrng. *Address:* 1341 Laukahi Street, Honolulu, HI 96821, USA. 5, 15, 52, 138.

PETERSON Jimmy L, b. 16 Aug 1947, Rutherford, Alabama. Coll Administrator. m. Hazel, 10 Mar 1975, 1 s, 2 d. *Education:* PhD, Univ of Michigan; MS, Univ of Wisconsin; BS, Alabama State Univ. *Appointments:* Voorhess Coll, Prof of Sociology, 1976-77; Milw Area Tech Coll, Instr/Suprv, 1977-83; Edison Community Coll, Dean of Soc Sci, 1983-. *Publications:* Thesis. Growth of Black Political Participation; Dissertation. The Changes in the Educational System in Three Blackbelt Counties. *Memberships:* Nalt Council on Intructional Admin; Phi Delta Kappa; Natl Alliance of Black Sch Educators; Fla Assn of Community Coll. *Honours:* Horace H Rackham Outstanding Dissertation Award; Outstanding Young Men of America. *Hobbies:* Reading; Fishing; Gardening. *Address:* 3006 SW 6th Place, Cape Coral, FL 33914, USA. 7, 15.

PETERSON Leslie Raymond, b. 6 Oct 1923, Viking, Alberta. Barrister; Solicitor. m. Agnes Rose, 6 June 1950, 1 s, 1 d. *Education:* Camrose Lutheran Coll; McGill Univ, Montreal; London Univ, England; Univ of British Columbia. *Appointments:* Law Firm, Peterson & Anderson, 1949-51; Minister of Educ, 1956-68; Minister of Labour, 1960-71; Attorney General of BC, 1968-72; Boughton & Com, 1972-88; Snr Partner, Boughton Peterson Yang Anderson, 1988-. *Memberships:* Univ of British Columbia; Terminal City Club; Central Capital Corp; Gov Downtown Van Assn; Inst of Corp Dir in Canada. *Honours include:* Doc of Laws; Distinguished Alumnus Award. *Hobbies:* Skiing; Tennis; Boating; Hunting. *Address:* 2500 Four Bentall Centre, 1055 Dunsmuir Street, PO Box 49290, Vancouver, BC, Canada V7X 1S8. 88, 52, 142.

PETERSON Sally, b. 23 July 1942, Waukegan, Illinois, USA. Evangelist; TV Ministry; Ordained Minster. *Education:* Governors State Univ, 1983. *Appointments include:* Grand Chapter of the Eastern Star, state of illinois, 1969-90;Dir of Bd, Cable TV, CABAC; Recording Sec, 1983; Vice Pres, 1984; Pres, 1985, 1988-91. *Creative Works include:* Plays 15 Instruments; Sung with Choirs at the Gurnee Comm Church. *Memberships include:* Lake Forest Hosp Womens Aux;American Business Womens Assn; American Harp Soc. *Honours:* Best Lake County video Comp. *Hobbies:* Cartooning; Acrylic Painting; TV Producing & Directing; Tchrng 6 Instruments; Playing 45 Instruments. *Address:* 33712 No 1 Plaine Road, Gurnee, IL 60031, USA. 5, 152.

PETFIELD Ross Matthew, b. 1 July 1944, Brisbane, Australia. Stockbroker. m. Elaine Margaret Butcher, 3

Sept 1966, 1 s, 2 d. *Education:* The Scots Col, Queensland Inst of Tech. *Appointments:* Charterd Acct, Hutton & McFarlane, 1963-64; Hastings Deering, 1964-68; Frederick A Neilson, 1968-70; Elected Mem, Aust Stock Exchange, 1970-. *Memberships:* Fellow, Securities Inst of Aust, Red Pres, 1991-; Aust Inst of Co Dirs, Fellow; Soc of Sr Executives, Fellow; Aust Stock Exchange Ltd. *Hobbies:* Tennis; Gardening; Fishing. *Address:* Ambleside, Gold Creek Road, Brookfield, Queensland, Australia. 23.

PETHERBRIDGE Stephen, b. 3 Oct 1942, Bournemouth, England. Newspaper Editor. m. Heather Linda Mallick, 7 June 1990, 2 d. *Appointments:* Reporter, Bideford Gaz, 1958-61; Reporter, Harmsworth Newspapers, 1961-65; Sud Editor, Melbourne Herals, 1965-68; Asst Featurers Ed, Melbourne Age, 1968-69; Snr Editor, Newsday, 1969-70; Sub Editor, London, 1970-71; Chief SUb Editor, London, 1972-76; Mgrng Editor, Toronto Star, 1982-87; Exec Editor, The Financial post, 1988-. *Hobbies:* Reading; Cooking; Travel; Gardening. *Address:* 333 King Street E, Toronto, Ontario, Canada M5A 4N2. 142.

PETHYBRIDGE Roger William, b. 28 Mar 1934, Skipton, England. Univ Prof. *Education:* MA, Oxford, 1955-58; Geneva Inst for Intl Studies, D Phil, 1959-62. *Appointments:* Lectr, Univ Coll, Swansea, 1962; Dir, A Centre for Russian & East European Studies, 1972. *Publications include:* A History of Post War Russia. *Memberships include:* SSRC; Natl Assn for Slavonic and East European Studies. *Honours include:* Visiting Profl Fellow, Australian Natl Univ; Visiting Fellow, Washington, DC; Dc Carle Lecturer, Univ of Otago. *Hobbies:* Music; Painting. *Address:* 113 Dunvant Road, Swansea, Wales.

PETITTO Laura Ann, b. 18 May 1954, New York City, USA. Research Scientist and University Professor. m. Kevin N Dunbar, 28 Oct 1989, 1 d. *Education:* BS, Ramapo State Col, NJ, 1975; Masters Deg, NY Univ, 1978; Masters Deg, 1981, Doctorate, 1984, Harvard Univ. *Appointments:* Tchg Experience: Instr, NY Soc for the Dear, 1979; Tchg Fellow, Dept of Psychol and Soc Relations, Harvard, 1980; Instr, Am Sign Lang I & II, Harvard Univ, 1981- 82; Psychol Tutor, Harvard, 1981-83; Assoc Prof, Dept of Psychol, McGill Univ, 1983-. *Publications:* Primary Tchr and Res Coor, Proj Nim Chimpsky, the sign language acquisition and developmental study of an infant chimpanzee. *Memberships:* NYAS; AM and Can Psychol Assns; Am Psychol Soc; Ling Soc of Am; Ling Assn of Quebec; Soc for Res in Child Devel; Intl Aswn for the Study of Child Lang; Nat Assn of the Deaf. *Honours:* Fellowship, Ctr for Adv Study in Behav Scis, Stanford, CA, 1991-92; Young Scist Awd, 1988, Young Psychol Awd, 1988, Am Psychol Assn. *Hobbies:* Architecture. *Address:* Department of Psychology, McGill University, 1205 Dr Penfield Avenue, Montreal, Quebec H3A 1B1, Canada.

PETKUS Viktoras, b. 22 Oct 1930, Lithuania. University Lecturer. *Education:* Secondary Sch, 1940-45. *Appointments:* Exiled to Siberia, 1947-53, 1957-65, 1977-88; Worked as a miner and wook-cutter in Taiga. *Publications:* Christian Democracy in the world and Lithuania, 1992; History of the Basilica of Vilnius Archcathedral; Ed and Publisher of mag, Lithuanian Guard and paper, Independent Lithuania. *Memberships:* Signatory, Kith Helsinki Gp; Chm, Lith Christian Dem Union; Chm, Lith Indep Union; Lith Polit Prisoners Presidium; Hon Chm, Lith Assn for the Protec of Human Rights; Bd, Lith Soc for Prisoners Wardship. *Honours:* Candidate for the Nobel Peace Prize, 1978, 1979, 1981. *Address:* Akmenu 1-17, Vilnius 2009, Lithuania.

PETRA BASACOPOL Carmen, b. 5 Sept 1926, Sibiu, Romania. Composer Musicologist. m. Alexandru Basacopol, 1 s. *Education:* Acad of Music; Doc of Musical Sci, Paris Sorbonne Univ. *Appointments:* Prof, Acad of Music, Bucharest 1962-; Prof, Consltng for Doctors

Degree in Music, 1981. *Creative Works include:* Chamber Music; Vocal Music; Symphonic Music; Opera; Ballet. *Memberships:* Composers Union, Bucharest, Romania; SACEM. *Honours include:* Prize of Romanian Acad; Bucharest; Intl Composition Contest; Mannheime Ludwigshafen. *Hobby:* Travel. *Address:* Blv Eroilor Sanitari m 14, Bucharest 5, Romania. 138.

PETRENCU Anatol, b. 22 May 1954, Causeni, Rep of Moldova. Univ Prof of Historica. m. Lidia, 1 Sept 1976, 2 d. *Education:* Army Serv, 1972-74; Univ of Moldova, 1974-80; Master of Philosophi, 1980; Doc of Philosophi, 1986. *Appointments:* Univ of Moldova, Asst, 1980; Post grad, Studies, 1982-85; Docent, Ad Interim, 1985-91; Full Docent, 1991-. *Creative Works include:* The Tchrng of History in Romania; Chisinau Publishing House, Stiinta. *Memberships:* Patrimoniu; Istoria Moldovei; Univ Senate; History Sch, Senate. *Hobbies:* Athletics; Italian Culture; Minorities Style of Life in Bessarabia. *Address:* Str Bernardazzi 57 Ap 2, 277061 Chisinau, Rep of Moldova.

PETROSYANTS Maija A, b. 11 Sept 1931, Sverdlovsk, USSR. Palynologist. m. Gololobov Yuri G, 11 Dec 1953, 1 s. *Education:* Moscow Univ, 1954; Phd, 1971. *Appointments:* Palynologist, 1954-71; Scientific Worker, VNIGNI, 1971-. *Publications include:* Ship on the Next Topics; Typical & Correlative Texons Gymnosperms' Pollen. *Memberships:* Palynological Commission, USSR; Paleontological Soc of the USSR. *Hobbies:* Domestic Economy; Cycling. *Address:* Dept Stratigraphy, All Union Sci Research, Inst of Petrol & Geol Exploration, Shosse Entuziastov, 105819 Moscow, Russia.

PETROV Rem Viktorovitch, b.22 Mar 1930, Volgograd, USSR. Vice pres, Acad of Sci, USSR; Immunologist. m. Emez Natalla, 8 Apr 1978, 1 s, 2 d. *Education:* Medical Faculty, Voronez, 1947-53; Physician, Doc of Sci, 1962; Prof, 1967; Academician, 1984. *Appointments:* Scientific Worker, 1953-62; Chief of Lab, 1962-83; Dir of Immunology Inst, 1983-88. *Publications include:* Immunology of Acute Radiation Injury; Artificial Antigens & CAccines; Me or Not Me. *Memberships:* Allunion Immunology Soc; World Acad of Art Sci; Acad of Sci of the USSR; Bar lean Univ. *Honours:* Metchnikov Gold Medal; Hero of Socialist Labor. *Hobbies:* Fishing; Hunting; Wooden Handwork. *Address:* USSR Acad of Sci, Leninsky Prospect 14, Moscow B-71, Russia. 1.

PETROVEKAYA Ira Fedorosna, b. 22 Oct 1919, Russia. Historian. *Education:* State Historical Archives Inst, Moscow, 1947; Historical Sci, 1956; Doc of Art History, 1978. *Appointments:* The Central State Historical Archives of the USSR, 1937; Leningrad State Inst of Theatre, Music & Cinema, 1958; Russian Research Inst. *Publications include:* Numerous. *Membership:* Russia Theatre Union. *Honour:* Medal for Leningrad Defence. *Hobbies:* Reading; Poetry; Floriculture. *Address:* Russian Research Inst of Arts, Isaakievskaga Pl 4, St Petersburg 190000, Russia.

PETROVIC Vojislav, b. 2 Jan 1925. University Professor. m. Dusica Glavaski, 8 July 1952, 1 s, 1 d. *Education:* Fac Sci Biol, Univ Beograd; PhD, 1959. *Appointments:* Hg Sch Tchr, 1953, Asst Dept Biol, Univ Beograd, 1956; Asst Prof, 1960, Assoc Prof, 1968, Prof, 1974, Dean of Fac of Sci, 1971, Hd, Dept Biol, 1973, V-Rector, 1977, Rector, 1981, Hd Dept Comp ENvir Physiol, 1971, Univ Beograd. *Publications include:* The Effect of cold and ACTH on RNA, DNA and proteins in adrenals and liver in rats and Squirrel, 1969; Comp study of calculation of NOR, 1973; Adren. control of MAO activ, 1974; Effects of cold on endocrine system, 1976; Increase in SOD activity induced by throid hor. in the brain of neonate and adult rats, 1982; Ade depend. resist. to Pq-rel to SOD activ, 1986; Hormones and antioxidat. defense, 1991; Textbook of Comparative Physiology, 1991. *Memberships:* CRE, Geneva, 1984; Pres, Nat Coun for Educ Beograd, 1988; French Soc Biol Physiol, 1964; Hiber Exch Infor, USA, 1967.

Hobbies: Gardening; Piano playing; Reading. *Address:* Ohridska Str 9, 11000 Beograd, Yugoslavia. 1.

PETRY Alice Hall, b. 8 July 1951, Hartford, Connecticut. Coll Prof; Scholar; Writer. *Education:* PhD, Brown Univ, 1979; MA, Connecticut Coll, 1976; BS, Univ of Connecticut, 1973. *Appointments:* Full Prof, Assoc Prof, Asst Prof, Instr of English, Rhode Island Sch of Design, 1979–; Visiting Prof, Univ of Colorado, 1987. *Publications include:* A Genius in His Way: The Art Of Cables Old Creole Days; Critical Essays on Anne Tyler; Understanding Anne Tyler; Fitzgerald's Craft and Short Fiction: The Collected Stories, 1920-1935. *Memberships include:* Modern Language Assn; Natl Womens Studies Assn; F Scott Fitzerald Soc. *Honours:* Snr Post Doc Fellow, American Council of Learned Societies; Fulbright Scholar, Brazil; United States Information Agency Lectr in Japan. *Hobby:* Travel. *Address:* Dept of English, Liberal Arts Division, Rhode Island Sch of Design, Providence, RI 02903, USA.

PETTERSSON Rosemary Winifred, b. 23 May 1939, England. Conslt Physician. m. Michael Petterson, 9 May 1964, 2 d. *Education:* Royal Tree Hosp Sch of Medicine, 1959-64. *Appointments:* Medical Officer, Stirling County Council, 1972-73; Deputy Medical Officer of Health, Stirling Burgh, 1973-74; Assoc Specialist Stirling Royal Infirmary, 1978-81. *Memberships:* Medical Womens Federation; British Soc of Medical & Dental Hypnosis. *Honours:* Scholarship for Medicine, Sir Owen Roberts; Honorary State Scholarship. *Hobbies:* Reading; Travel; Cooking; Gardening; Walking, Cats. *Address:* Greenrig, Hawksland, Lesmahagow, Lanark ML11 9QB, England.

PFEIFFER David Graham, b. 13 May 1934, Dallas, Texas. Univ Prof. m. Barbara Glennon, 5 Apr 1986, 1 s, 2 d. *Education:* MA, 1963, Univ of Texas, Austin; PhD, Univ of Rochester, 1975. *Appointments:* Keuka Coll, 1964-68; Univ of Rochester, 1969-70; Northeastern Univ, 1970-74; Suffolk Univ, 1975-. *Publications include:* The Infuence of the Socio Economic Characteristics of Disbabled People on Their Employment Status & Income. *Memberships:* Soc for Disability Studies; Policy Studies Assn; American Political Sci Assn; Assn for Public Policy Analysis & Management. *Honours:* Pi Alpha Alpha; Pi Sigma Alpha; Pi Gamma Mu; Whitney Carnegie Award. *Address:* Dept of Public Mgmt, Sch of Mgmt, Suffolk Univ, Boston, MA 02108, USA. 143.

PFISTER Edward Joseph, b. 9 Apr 1934, NYC. Univ Admin. m. Kathryn M Luchsinger, 18 June 1960, 2 s, 1 d. *Education:* BA, St Peters Coll, 1957; Ma, Seton Hall Univ, 1965. *Appointments include:* Mgr, Info Svcs Natl Ednl, 1960-55; Dir, Info Svcs, Agy for Instructional TV, 1965-70; Dir, Pub Relations, Natl Assn Ednl Broadcasters, 1970-72; Dir, Chmns Coordinating Com, 1972-73; Exec Asst, Pub Broadcasting Svc, 1973-76; Pres, Chief Exec Officer Corp for Pub Broadcasting, 1981-85; Dean Sch communication, U Miami, Coral Gables, Fla, 1985-86. *Publications:* The Peoples Business; A Review of Public TV; The Financial Status of Public Broadcasting Stations in the US; Also articles. *Memberships:* Ednl Communications Assn; Natl Assn Ednl Broadcasters, Assn Pub Broadcasting; Assn for Communication Admin; NATAS; Natl Press Club. *Address:* U Miami Sch Communication, 120 Merrick Bldg Coral Gables, FL 33124, USA.

PFISTER Karstin Ann Dutch, b. 26 Apr 1955, Philadelphia, PA. Dir. m. William Howard, 10 July 1977, 1 d. *Education:* EdD, Virginia Poly & State Univ, 1990; CAGS, 1986; MEd, George Mason Univ, 1983; BA, Cornell Coll, Psychology, 1977. *Appointments:* Instr, Natl Meterological Inst, 1977-78; Instr, Kabul Univ, Afghanistan, 1978-79; Program Coordinator, Pepperdine Univ, 1989-81; Counselor, Family Serv Centre, 1981-87; Acting Dir & Program Coordinator, 1987-88; Dir, Family Serv Centre, US Government HQMC, 1988-. *Publications include:* The Impact of the PACE Treatment Program on Five Physically Abusive Military Men; Counseling the Military Family *Memberships:* Phi Delta Kappa; American Assn for Counseling & Devel; Virginia Counseling Assn; Northern Virginia Counselors Assn; Northern Virginia Chapter of Clinical Counselors. *Honours include:* 2,000 Notable American Women; Cert of Appreciation from the US Ambassador to Afghanistan. *Address:* 13805 Cynthia Court, Manassas, VA 22111, USA. 5, 76, 138, 155, 156.

PHAN-TAN Tai, b. 7 July 1939, Kien Giang, Scientist; Researcher. m. Do Thanh Van, 8 Nov 1968, 1 s, 2 d. *Education:* Tech Coll, Engr, Aachen, FRG, 1966; French Inst, Paris, 1966-68; D of Engrng, Univ of Hanover, 1982. *Appointments:* Researcher, Univ of Hanover, 1976; Hd of Sect, Materical Research Inst, Univ of Hanover, 1984-86. *Memberships:* Verein Deutscher Eisenhuttenleute; Verein Deutscher Korrosion Fachleute. *Hobby:* Gardening. *Address:* Inst fur Werkstoffkunde, Univ Hanover, Appelstrasse 11A, 3000 Hannover 1, Germany. 52.

PHELPS Richard Wintour, b. 26 July 1925, Bath, England. Retired, Conslt in Planning, Housing & Urban Devel. m. Pamelr Marie Lawson, 12 Feb 1955, 2 d. *Education:* Merton Coll, Oxford, 1946-49; Ma, 1953. *Appointments:* Indian Army, 1944-46; HM Overseas Civil serv, Nigeria, 1948-57, 1959-61; HM Treasury, 1957-59, 1961-65; General Mgr, New Town Devel Corp, 1967-86; Conslt, Housing & Planning, 1986-. *Memberships:* Royal Commonwealth Soc. *Honour:* CBE. *Hobbies:* Travel; Reading; Changing the World. *Address:* Fell Foot House, Newby Bridge, Ulverston, Cumbria LA12 8NL, England. 1.

PHILIPP Christiane Elsa, b. 8 Nov 1959, Kiel, Germany. Snr Research Asst. *Education:* Law, Univ Kiel; Munich Univ; Doctoral Degree, Univ Kiel. *Appointments:* Jnr Research Asst, 1989-90; Snr Research Asst, Inst of Intl Law, Kiel, 1990-. *Publications include:* The Judicial Committee of the Privy Council and Its Jurisdiction for the Commonwealth of Nations. *Hobbies:* Reading; Sport; Paintings. *Address:* Inst of Intl Law, Olshausenstr 40-60, 2300 Kiel, Germany.

PHILIPS Justin Robin Drew, b. 18 July 1948, London, England. Metropolitan Stipendiary Magistrate. *Education:* John Lyon Sch, Harrow Coll of Law, London. *Appointments:* Barrister in Criminal Law Chambers, 1970-89; Appointed Metropolitan Stipendiary Magistrate, 1989. *Memberships:* Mensa; British Acad of Forensic Sci; Hendon Reform Synagogue. *Hobbies:* Music; Travel; Reading. *Address:* Camberwell Green Magistrates Court, 15 Deynsford Road, London SE5 7UP, England. 1.

PHILIPSON John, b. 2 Jan 1910, Newcastle Upon Tyne, England. Retired. m. Mary E Richardson, 2 Apr 1937, 2 s, 3 d. *Education:* St Catharines Coll, Cambridge, 1928-31, BA, 1931; MA. *Appointments:* Dir, Philipson & Son, Newcastle, 1933-; Dir, E & J Richardson, 1950-69; Chmn, 1965-69; Dir, Hislop & Day Ltd, Edinburgh, 1960-. *Publications include:* Northumberland Natl Park Guide; The Library. *Memberships:* Soc of Antiquaries of London; Soc of Antiquaries of Newcastle; Literary & Philosophical Soc of Newcastle; Federation of Master Process Engravers; Northumberland Natl Park Committee. *Honours:* Honorary MA. *Hobbies:* Fell Walking; Local History; Bibliography; Book Binding. *Address:* Hernspeth House, Harbottle, Morpeth, Northumberland NE65 7DQ, England.

PHILLIPS Benjamin Ademoyegun, b. 18 Nov 1947, Ile Ife, Nigeria. Protroleum Dealer; Insurance. 3 s, 1 d. *Education:* West African Sch Cert, 1966; Diploma in Insurance, 1978. *Appointments:* Sales Clerk, Scoa motors, 1966-69; Resident Inspector, 1972; Area Mgr, 1988; Petroleum Dealership, 1990. *Memberships:* Intl Insurance Salemen with American Life Insurace;

Recreation Club, Ile Ife. *Honours:* Contest of the Best Salesmen in Personel Accident. *Hobbies:* Football; Table Tennis; Reading; Films. *Address:* 25 Mbabi Nbayo Layout, PO Box 1156, Ile Ife, Nigeria.

PHILLIPS Celia Mary, b. 16 Dec 1942, Lougton, Stffs, England. Univ Tchr. m. Ronald Frederick Swan, 23 June 1973, 1 s, 1 d. *Education:* London Sch of Economics, 1961-67; BSc; PhD. *Appointments:* Asst Lectr, LSE, 1967-70; Lectr, LSE, 1970-. *Publications include:* Changes in Subject Choice at School & University; Violence at Work. *Memberships:* ILEA Education Committee; St Catherines Cuckoland Lodge; Dean of Undergraduate Studies LSE; FRSS. *Honours:* Bonley Prize; Honorary Citizen of Tralee. *Hobbies:* Choral Singing; Walking; Reading. *Address:* Statistic Dept, London Sch of Economics, Houghton Street, Aldwych, London WC2A 2AG, England.

PHILLIPS David, b. 3 Dec 1939, Kendal, Cumbria. Prof. m. Lucy Caroline Scoble, 21 Dec 1970, 1 d. *Education:* BSc, Univ of Birmingham, 1961; PhD, 1964. *Appointments:* Post Doctoral Fellow, Univ Texas, USA, 1964-66; Visiting Scientist, Acad Sci, USSR, Moscow, 1966-67; Lectr, 1967-73; Snr Lectr, 1973-76; Reader, Univ of Southampton, 1986-80; Wolfson Prof, 1980-89; Acting dir, 1986; Deputy Dir, Royal Inst of Gt Britain, 1986-89; Prof, IC, 1989-; Hd of Dept, 1992-. *Publications:* Time Correlated Single Photon Counting; Over 400 Scientific Papers. *Memberships:* Royal Soc of Chemistry; Faraday Div; Royal Inst of GB; British Assn for Advancement of Sci; Athenaeum, London. *Honours:* Fulbright Fellow, Univ Texas; JWT Spinks Lectureship; Wilsmore Fellowship of Univ of Melbourne. *Hobbies:* Popularisation of Sci; Music; Opera; Theatre; Travel. *Address:* 195 Barnett Wood Lane, Ashtead, Surrey KT21 2LP, England. 1.

PHILLIPS Dewi Zephaniah, b. 24 Nov 1934, Wales. Professor of Philosophy. m. 2 Sept 1959, 3 s. *Education:* BA, 1956, MA, 1958, Univ Col at Swansea; BLitt, Univ of Oxford, 1961. *Appointments:* Lectr in Philos, Queens Col, Dundee, 1961-63; Univ Col of N.Wales, Bangor, 1963-65; Univ of Swansea, 1965; Prof of Philos, 1971-. *Publications:* Books: The Concept of Prayer, 1969; Faith and Philosophical Enquiry, 1970; Death and Immortality, 1970; Moral Practices, 1970; Sense and Delusion, 1971; Athronyddu am Grefydd, 1974; Religion without explanation, 1976; Through a darkening Glass, 1982; Dramau Gwenlyn Parry, 1982; Belief Change and Forms of Life, 1986; RS Thomas: Poet of the Hidden God, 1986; Faith After Foundationalism, 1988; From Fantasy to Faith, 1991; Interventions in Ethics, 1991. *Memberships:* Aristotelian Soc; Welsh Philos Soc. *Hobbies:* Lawn tennis; Supporting Swansea City AFC. *Address:* HS Queens Road, Sketty, Swansea SA2 OSB, Wales.

PHILLIPS Douglas Alan, b. 10 July 1949, Volga, SD, USA. Education Admin & Conslt; Author. m. Marlene Rydberg Phillips, 3 Oct 1970, 2 s, 1 d. *Education:* BS, Northern State COll, 1971; MS, 1975; Admin Cert, Univ of Alaska, 1987. *Appointments:* Community Action Program, Community Organizer, 1971-72; Tchr, Gettysburg, SD Public Sch, 1973-75; Tchr, LRE Coordinator, Brookings, SD Sch, 1975-80; Social studies Specialist, SD Div of Elementary & Secondary Educ, 1978-81; Social Studies Program Coordinator, Anchorage, Alaska Sch District, 1981-91. *Publications include:* The Pacific Rin Region: Energing Giant. *Memberships:* Sen Vice-Pres, Curriculum and Instruction, Natl Council for Geographic Education, 1992-; VIP Program for the Natl Council for the Social Studies; South Dakota Council for the Social Studies; Alaska Council for the Social studies; Alaska Federation of Tchrs; Vice-Pres, Alaska Coun for Econ Educ, 1992-1993; Pres, Nat Coun for Geographic Educ, 1993. *Honours include:* Distinguished Tchrng Achievement Award; Outstanding Service Awd, nat Coun for Social Studies, 1992. *Hobbies:* Travel; Friends; Writing.

Address: 2310 Paxson, Anchorage, AK 99504, USA. 9, 15.

PHILLIPS Estelle, b. 17 Mar, London, England. Psychologist. div. 3 s. *Education:* BSc Hons, Brunel Univ, 1976; PhD, Univ Col, London, 1976-80. *Appointments:* The Open Univ, Milton Keynes, 1980-84; Independent Conslt, 1984-87; Birbeck Col, London Univ, 1987-91. *Publications:* Co-author: How to get a PhD, 1987; Numerous papers in learned journals and chapters in books on the PhD, women and work, equal opportunities in organizations. *Memberships:* Assoc Fellow, Brit Psycho Soc; Chm, Standing Com on Equal Opps, 1986-91; Asst Ed, The Psychologist, 1991-92; Assn of Learned Socs in Soc Sci. *Hobbies:* Films; Relationships; Reading; Writing; Conversation; Listening to music. *Address:* BPS, St Andrew's House, 48 Princess Road East, Leicester LE1 7DR, England.

PHILLIPS Geneva Ficker, b. 1 Aug 1920, Staunton, Illinois, USA. Mgrng Editor. m. James Emerson Phillips, 6 June 1955, dec. *Education:* BS, Journalism, Univ of Illinois, 1942; MA, Eng Lit, Univ of CA, 1953. *Appointments:* Copydesk, Chicago Journal of Commerce, 1942-43; Editorial Asst, Patent Disclosures, Radio Research Lab Harvard Univ, 1943-45; Asst Editor, Univ of Illinois, 1946-47; Editorial Asst, Quarterly Film, Radio & TV, UCLA, 1952-53; Mgrng Editor, The Works of John Dryden, Dept of English, UCLA, 1964-. *Memberships:* Bd of Dirs, Univ Religious Conference, Los Angeles; Assn of Academic Women, UCLA; Friends of Huntington Library; Friends of UCLA Library; Renaissance Soc of Southern California; Samuel Johnson Soc; Assoc of the Univ of California Press Conference of Christianity & Literture; Soc of Mayflower Descendants. *Honours:* UCLA Tchng Fellow; UCLA Graduate Fellow. *Address:* 213 First Anita Drive, Los Angeles, CA 90049, USA. 5, 9, 52, 138, 189.

PHILLIPS Ian, b. 10 Apr 1936, Rochdale, England. Medical Microbiology. *Education:* St John Coll, Cambridge, 1955-58; St Thomas Hosp Medical Sch, 1958-61. *Appointments:* Lectr, STHMS, 1965-66; Lectr, Makerere Univ, Uganda, 1966-69; Snr Lectr, 1969-72; Reader, 1972-74; Prof, STHMS, 1974-; Honorary Conslt, St Thomas Hosp, 1969-. *Publications include:* Over 400 Publ; Books; Chapters. *Memberships:* MRCpath; MRCP; FRC Path; FRCP; R C Pathologists; British Soc for Antimicrobial Chemotherpy; Assn of Medical Microbiologists; Hospital Infestion Soc. *Honours:* Rolleston Scholarship; British Prize Foord Caiger Prize. *Hobbies:* Botany; Music. *Address:* Dept of Microbiology, United Medical & Dental Schs of Guys & Sy Thomas Hosp, St Thomas Campus, Lambeth Palance Road, London SE1 7EH, England. 170.

PHILLIPS Kevin G, b. 22 Apr 1960, Middletown, NY. Coll Prof; Chmn of Christian Education Dept. m. Sarah Collingwood Prescott Philliyis, 28 May 1983. *Education:* Wheaton Coll, BA, MA, 1978-83; Syracnse Univ, MBA, 1991; Columbia Univ, Tchrs Coll, EdD, 1991. *Appointments:* Wheaton Coll, 1978-83; First United Methodist Church, Dir of Christian Educ & Youth, 1983-89; Lakewood United Methodist, Youth Dir, 1985-86; Nyack Coll, 1988-. *Publications include:* Human Tendancies Versus Gods Will; Developing Leadership Skills in the Church. *Memberships:* Natl Assn of Professors of Christian Educ; Religious Educ Assn; Religios Researchers Assn; Natl Assn of Church Business Admin; Phi Delta Kappa; Council for Adult & Experiontial Lerning. *Honours include:* Leadership Research Grant. *Hobbies:* Stamp & Coin Collecting; Camping; Boy Scout Leader & Trainer. *Address:* Nyack Coll, Nyack NY 10960, USA. 176.

PHILLIPS Leslie Samuel, b. 20 Apr 1924, Tottenham, England. Theatrical Actor; Dir; Producer. m. Angela Scoular, 31 July 1982, 3 s, 2 d. *Education:* Chingford Sch; Italia Conti Stage Sch; Army, DL Infantry. *Appointments include:* Acting, 1937; Army, 1942; Invalided Out, 1945; Adult Career in Theatre, Films,

Radio, TV. *Creative Works include:* Theatre. Peter Pan; Daddy Long Legs; The Whole Truth; The Deadly Game; TV. The Suit; Life After Life; Thacker; The Oz Trial; Radio. The Navy Lark; Drop Me Here Darling. *Memberships:* Royal Theatrical Fund; Theatre of Comedy; DLI; Lloyds. *Hobbies:* Photography; Racing; Antiques; Restoring Houses; Gardening; Travel; Poker; Weaving; Chess; Cats; Football. *Address:* c/o Julian Belfrage & Assoc, 68 St James Street, London SW1, England. 1.

PHILLIPS Michael Lynn, b. 18 June 1952, Erwin, TN, USA. Business Executive. m. Gloria Jean Schwermann, 4 June 1983, 1 d. *Education:* Tenn Tech Univ, 1976; MA, 1978. *Appointments:* Night Clk, Clinchfield YMCA, Erwin, 1970; Machine operator, Cyrstal Ice Coal & Laundry, 1970; Engrng Dept, Union Carbide Corp, Oak Ridge, 1971-72, 1973-74; Salesman Southwestern Co, Nashville, 1975; Report & Instrns Manual Writer Citizens Bank, Cookville, Tenn, 1977-78; Team Mgr, Buckeye Cellulose Corp, Memphis, 1978-80; Team Mgr, Huntsville, Ala, 1980; Contract Mfg Mgr, 1980-83; Sales Rep, Procter & Gamble, Dallas, 1983-84; Tech Mgr, Procter & Gamble Crush Internat, 1984-86; Duncan Hines, Cookie Nat Dist Dept Mgr, 1986-87; Svc Ops Dept Mgr, 1987-89; Info Systems Dept Mgr, 1989-91; Phillips and Assoc Inc, President and Founder, 1992-. *Publications:* Rapid Computer Solution of Imlicit Thermodynamic Functions, Developing A Planned Capacity Model, A Research Report. *Memberships include:* Salvation Army; NSPE: ASME. *Honours include:* Named one of Outstanding Young Men of Am; Phi Kappa Phi. *Hobbies:* Classic Antique Atomobile Restoration; Racquet Ball; Inspirational Reading. *Address:* 97 Thornfield Drive, Bells, TN 38006, USA. 7, 52, 176.

PHILLIPS Robert Sneddon, b. 15 Sept 1932, Edinburgh, England. Orthopaedic Surgeon. m. Isabella Forrest, 2 Oct 1957, 1 s, 1 d. *Education:* George Meriots Sch, Edinburgh, 1944-50; Edinburgh Univ, 1950-56; FRCSE, 1959; FRCS, 1991. *Appointments:* Conslt Orthopaedic Surgeon, North Manchester Health Auth, 1967-; Regional Advisor, Orthopaedic Surgery, 1990-. *Publications include:* Numerous Articles; Papers. *Memberships:* British Orthopaedic Assn; MCC; Forty Club. *Hobbies:* Cricket; Golf; Bridge. *Address:* 3 Milverton Drive, Bramhall, Stockport, SK7 1EY, England.

PHILPS Frank Richard, b. 9 Mar 1914, Potters Bar. Retired Clinical Pathologist. m. Emma Lilla Schmidt, 26 Apr 1941, 2 s, 1 d. *Education:* Christ's Hosp, Sussex; Univ Coll Hosp. *Appointments:* House Surgeon, UCH, 1940; Royal Air Force, 1940-46; Conslt, Pathologist, Eastbourne Group of Hospitals, 1954-64; Conslt Cytologist, UCH, 1964-73; Dir, Royal Free & UCH Combined Cytology Dept, 1970-73. *Publications include:* A Short Manual of Respiratory Cytology; Water Colour Paintings, exhibited Royal Inst of Painters in Watercolour. *Memberships:* Assn of British Medical Assn; Royal Photographic Soc. *Honours include:* MBE; Council For Nature Film Prize. *Hobbies:* Painting; Photography; Video; Woodwork; Watching Wildlife. *Address:* Woodlands, Sydenham Wood, Lewdown, Okehampton, Devon EX20 4PP, England. 1, 170.

PHRINLEY Byams Pa, b. 15 June 1962, Llasa, Tibet. Deputy Dir, Public Health Bureau of Tibet; Dir of Traditional Tibetan Hosp of Tibet. m. Oct 1948, 3 s, 2 d. *Education:* Inst Llasa for Medicine & Astrology. *Appointments:* Principal, Traditional Medical Coll; Pres, Traditional Tibetan Hosp; Deputy Dir, Tibet Health Bureau; Vice Chmn, Chinese Sci Assn. *Publications include:* Texese for Traditional Medicine Coll; Translation for Tebitan Medicine. *Memberships:* Chinese Sci Assn; Traditional Chinese & Traditional Tibetan Medicine Soc; Scientific Assn of Autonomous Region, Tibet, China. *Honours:* State Level Expert on Traditional Tibetan Medicine & Anthrology; Exemplary Hosp Pres of All China. *Hobbies:* Picnic in Summer; Enjoy Tibetan Classical Music. *Address:* Traditional Tibetan Medical Hosp of the Tibet Autonomous Region, Menzi Kang Road, Llasa Tibet, China.

PIBERNIK France, b. 2 Sept 1928, Komeda, Slovenia. Professor. m. Jolanda, 13 Aug 1960, 1 s, 2 d. *Education:* Classical Col, Kranj, 1949; Lit and Philol, Univ at Ljubljana, 1955. *Appointments:* Tchr, Secondary Sch, Dobrovo, 1955; Classical Col, Kranj, 1989-90. *Publications:* Poetry: Hills and Streets, 1960; The Plain, 1968; September, 1974; The Resonance, 1979; Essay Treatiese: Between Tradition and Modernisme, 1978; Between Modernism and Avantgarde, 1981; The Gloomy Gulf of France Balantic, 1989. *Memberships:* Sci Inst, Univ of Ljubljana. *Hobbies:* Cycling; Mountaineering. *Address:* Kidriceva 47a, 6400 Kranj, Slovenia.

PICCINI Assis Pedro Perin, b. 29 June 1948, Soledade, RS, Brazil. Chemist. m. Carmen Da Silveira Piccini, 22 Feb 1975, 2 s. *Education:* Univ Catolica Do Rio Grande do Sul; Master of Metallurgical Engrng, Porto Alegre. *Appointments:* Lectr, Sch of Public Health, 1972-77; Dir, Environmental Lab of the Governmental Health Agency, 1977-83; Mgr, Pollution Sources Control, 1983-84; Dir, Biological Research Inst, 1987-89; Dir, Ind Pharmaceutical Lab, 1989-91. *Memberships:* Brazilian Assn of Chemistry. *Hobbies:* Piano; Classic Guitar. *Address:* Trujillo Street, 40 Ap 201, 91 050 Porto Alegre RS, Brazil. 52.

PICHON Michel Maurice, b. 28 Apr 1940. Deputy Dir, Australian Inst of Marine Sci. m. Janice Ivy Morrissey, 20 Aug 1983, 3 s. *Education:* Oceanogr Marseille, 1961; Orston, Oceanographic, Paris, 1962; Doctorat, 1963; Doctorat es Sci, 1973. *Appointments:* Research Scientist, Orstom, Paris, 1963-67; Lectr, Univ of Aix Marseille, 1967-74; Assoc Prof, James Cook Univ, Townsville, 1974-87; Deputy Dir, Australian Inst Marine Sci, 1987-. *Memberships:* Marine Sci Assn; Australian Coral Reef Soc; Intl Soc Reef Studies; Intl Assn Biol Oceangraph; Pacific Soc Assn; Inst Biology, UK. *Honours:* Acad d Agriculture de France, Prix Tisserand; Medaille Inst Natl Agronomique. *Hobbies:* Reading; Music; Photography; Swimming; Scuba Diving; Gardening. *Address:* 11 Maple Court, Kirwan, Townsville 4817, Australia.

PICKERING Donald Ellis, b. 15 Nov 1933, Newcastle Upon Tyne, England. Actor. *Education:* Private; Trained Old Vic Theatre Sch. *Appointments include:* Old Vic Paper Jury, 1952; Bristol Old Vic, 1957-59; Glasgow Citizens, 1967; West End, Case in Question, 1974; *Appearances,* 1981; Hay Fever, 1984; TV Appearances; Doctor Who'60; Sherlock Holmes; Yes Prime Minister. *Honours:* Nominated Tony Award, Best Supporting Actor; Best Supporting Circle, NY Drama Critics. *Hobbies:* Gardening; Riding; Croquet. *Address:* Manor Farm House, Eastbeach, Glos GL7 3NQ, England.

PICKETT David Franklin Jr, b. 3 May 1936, Littlefield, TX, USA. Aerospace Exec. m. B Christine Klop, 21 Aug 1971. *Education:* AA, Del Mar Coll, TX, 1960; BS, Univ of Texas, Austin, 1962; MA, 1965; PhD, 1970. *Appointments:* Research Chemist, Amer Magnesium Co, 1970; Chemist, Chem Engr, USAF Aeropropulsion Lab, 1970-78; Sect Hd, El Segundo, CA, 1978-84; Asst Dept Mgr, Hughes Aircraft, 1984-89; Product Line Mgr, 1990-91; Program Mgr, 1991-. *Publications include:* Over 30 Publ. *Memberships:* Phi Lambda Upsilon; American chemical Soc; American Inst of Aeronautics & Astronautics; Electro Chemical Soc; Nevada Section. *Honours include:* S D Heron Award, USAF Aeropropulsion Lab; Elected to Phi Lambda Upsilon. *Hobbies:* Travel; Golf; Big Game Fishing. *Address:* 4 Hill Top Circle, Rancho Palos Verdes, CA 90274, USA. 8, 9.

PICKFORD John Aston, b. 28 Dec 1924, London, England. Prof. m. Daphne Annie Ransom, 27 Sept 1947, 3 s, 1 d. *Education:* Imperial Coll of Sci & Tech, BSc. *Appointments:* Army Serv, REME, 1943-47; Local Government, UK, 1943-54; Town Engr, Sekondi Takoradi, Ghana, 1954-60; Lectr, Snr Lectr, Prof, Loughborough Univ of Tech. *Publications include:*

Analysis of Surge; Developing World Water; More than 80 Papers. *Memberships:* Instn of Civil Engrsg; Instn of Water & Environmental Management. *Honours:* Honorary Doctor of Tech, Loughborough Univ of Tech; OBE; Paul Harris Award. *Hobbies:* Water Supply & Sanitation for Developing Countries; Indian History; African Culture; Travel. *Address:* Water Engrng & Devel Centre, Loughborough Univ of Tech, Leicestershire, LE11 3TU, England.

PICKWOAD Michael Mervyn, b. 11 July 1945, Windsor. England, Film Production Designer. m. Vanessa Orriss, 27 Oct 1973, 3 d. *Education:* Charterhouse, Godalming, 1959-63; Southampton Univ, 1964-67. *Appointments:* Prod Designer, Comrades, 1985; Withnail & I, 1986; The Lonely Passion of Judith Hearne, 1987; How to Get Ahead in Advertising, 1988; The Krays, 1989; Let him Have It, 1990; Ex, Murder Most Horrid, 1991; Running Late, Century, 1992. *Creative Works include:* Architectural prints for Hugh Evelyn; Arch Model Kits for Natl Trust; Exhibition Design for Treasures of the Mind, Trinity College, Dublin, 1992. *Memberships:* ACTT; Feorgian Group; Rolls Royce Enthusiast Club. *Hobbies:* Arch History; Painting; Drawing; Photography; History of Transport; Sailing; Windsurfing; Carpentry. *Address:* 3 Warnborough Road, Oxford, OX2 6HZ, England.

PIERCE Catherine Maynard, b. 11 Oct 1918, York County, Ripon Hall, Virginia. Educator, American History & Researcher. m. Frank Marion Pierce Jr, 4 Oct 1940, 2 s. *Education:* Longwood Coll, Farmville, 1935-39; Coll of William & Mary, Williamsburg. *Appointments:* Collegiate Profl Certification, Tchr, VA Public Schs, 1939-45; Instr, Chesapeake, VA Public Sch, 1946-49, 1957-74; Conslt Volunteer Serv, 1975-. *Publications include:* Author-Audio-Visual Historical Narratives Peraining to American History. *Memberships include:* Pilot Club Intl of Williamsburg, Virginia; Daughters of the American Revolution; Assn for Preservation of Virginia Antiquities. *Honours:* Virginia Tchr Chosen 1969 by Virginia State Bar Assn to Attend Graduate Seminar at Freedons Foundation. *Hobbies:* Collector of Antiques; Historic Research; Genealogy. *Address:* 4 Bray Wood Kingsmill on the James, Williamsburg, VA 23185, USA. 7, 15.

PIERSON Anne Bingham, b. 9 June 1929, New York City, New York, USA. Physician; Watercolourist; Housewife. m. (1) Richard Norris Pierson Jr, 10 July 1954, div. 1974, 1 s, 3 d, (2) Richard Taliaferro Wright, 25 Nov 1978. *Education:* BA, Vassar Coll, 1951; MD, Columbia Univ Coll Physns and Surgs, 1955; Substitute Internship, AUH, Beirut, 1955; Intern, Lenox Hill Hosp, NYC, 1955-56; MPH coursework, Columbia Univ School Pub Hlth, and Univ CA Berkely School Pub Hlth, 1969-72. *Appointments include:* Gen Prac, Outpatient Clin, 7th Day Adventist Hosp, Taipei, Taiwan, 1957; Clin Physn, Bd Mbr, Med Dir, Planned Parenthood, Bergen Co, Hackensack, NJ, USA, 1960-74; Asst Clin Prof, Dept Obst and Gynaecology, Columbia Univ Coll Physns and Surgs, and Int Inst for Study Human Reproduction, 1972-74; Med Dir, Memphis Assn Planned Parenthood Inc, 1974-75; Pvte Pract, Gynaecology, Family Planning, 1976-77; Med Dir, Planned Parenthood Assn, Hudson Co, NJ. 1976-79; Staff Physn, NY Telephone Co, 1976-87; Co Physn, Sonalysts, Waterford, CT, 1988-. *Publications:* The Doctor and Sex Education (w George Langmyhr), 1968; Regular contbns to Bride's Mag, 1966-71. *Memberships include:* Nat Med Advsry Comm, Planned Parenthood-World Population, 1966-69; Exec Comm, Am Assn Planned Parenthood Physns, 1969-71; Am Med Assn; Am Coll Preventive Med; Am Occupational Med Assn; Occupation Med Assn CT; Am Pub Hlth Assn; Jr League; Pres, No NJ Vassar Club, 1964-66; Life Mbr, Nat Soc Colonial Dames in State of CT; Artist Mbr, Clinton Art Soc. *Honours:* Physns Recognition Award, Am Med Assn, 1973-93. *Hobbies:* Watercolour painting; Tennis; Jogging; Needlework; Reading. *Address:* PO Box 132, Old Lyme, CT 06371, USA.

PIGOT Thomas Herbert, b. 19 May 1921, London, England. Retired Circuit Judge. m. Zena Marguerite Wall, 19 Aug 1950, 3 d. *Education:* Somerset Scholar, Brasenose Coll, Oxford; BA 1st class hons, Jurisprudence, 1941; MA, 1946; BCL, 1947; Called to the Bar, Inner Temple, 1947. *Appointments:* 2nd Lt, Welsh Regt, 1941, Lincs Regt, 1942; Served N Africa; Barrister, 1947; QC, 1967; Dpty Sr Judge, 1971-84, Sr Judge (now resident), 1984-90, Sovereign Base area, Cyprus; Circuit Judge, No Circuit, 1972-; Common Serjeant, City of London, 1984-90; Bencher, 1985-. *Publication:* Chmn, Home Office Report of the Advisory Group on Video Evidence, 1989. *Memberships:* Worshipful Co of Cutlers; Vincent's, Oxford. *Address:* c/o Central Criminal Court, London EC4M 7EH, England. 1.

PIGOTT Hugh Sefton, b. 21 Dec 1929, Cheadle Hulme, Cheshire, England. Solicitor. m. (1) Venetia Caroline Mary Stopford Adams, 31 Aug 1957, diss. 1984, 4 s, (2) Fiona Margaret Miller, 1 Nov 1986. *Education:* Oundle School; King's Coll, Cambridge; BA, MA, Cambridge Univ. *Appointments:* Articled Clerk, 1952-55, Asst Solicitor, 1955-60, Ptnr, 1960-92, Clifford Chance (formerly Coward Chance). *Memberships:* Law Soc, Standing Comm on Company Law, 1972-85; Advsry Working Party on Europe, 1976-79; Hon Legal Advsr to Acctng Standards Comm, 1986-90; Top Salaries Review Body, 1988-; Member Joint Disciplinary Scheme of the UK Accountancy Profession, 1992-; Liveryman, Worshipful Co Solicitors. *Hobbies:* Poetry; The visual arts; Piano playing; Cooking. *Address:* 28 Marlborough Road, Richmond, Surrey TW10 6JR, England. 53.

PILGRIM Constance Maude Eva, b. 3 Dec 1911, London, England. Textile designer. m. (1) Paul Smither, dec. 1943, 1 s, 1 d, (2) Richard Wrenford Pilgrim, 1957, dec. 1979. *Education:* Art school, 3 yrs; Textile Designer, City of London; Trng, writing Egyptian Hieroglyphs, Prof Battiscombe Gunn, Queen's College, Oxford, for book publications. 1940's: Eng Litt. Oxford Univ, External Dept and WEA 3 yr crse, 1952-56. *Appointments:* Textile Designer, London; Tutor; Writer. *Publications:* Dear Jane, biog study, Jane Austen, 1971, Reprint, 1991; This is Illyria, Lady, life, rambles, friends of Jane Austen, 1991. Research now, 3rd book on Jane Austen; Jane Austen and her Christian Faith. *Memberships:* Soc Authors; W Country Writers Assn; Genealogical Soc; Somerset Archaeological and Natural Hist Soc. *Hobbies:* Study of English Literature; Writing; Biographical research; Drawing and Painting. *Address:* 24 Withington Court, Abingdon, Oxfordshire OX14 3QB, England, 152.

PILKINGTON Roger Windle, b. 17 Jan 1915, St Helens, England. Author. m. (1) Miriam Jaboor, 27 July 1937, (2) Ingrid Geijer, 23 Oct 1973, 1 s, 1 d. *Education:* Rugby School, 1928-33; Magdalene Coll, Cambridge, 1933-37; MA (Cantab); PhD. *Career:* Rsch, Genetics, 1937-43; Full-time Author, 1943-. *Publications:* Over 50 books; Small Boat series, 1959-89, incl: Small Boat down the Years, 1988; Small Boat in the Midi, 1989; Children's books incl: The Ormering Tide, 1974; Sci philos and Christianity, notably: World Without End, 1960; Heavens Alive, 1962; Books on inland waterways; I Sailed on the Mayflower, 1990; One Foot in France, 1992; Recent contbns to Sunday Telegraph. *Membership:* Master, Glass Sellers Co, 1968. *Honours:* Chevalier, Confrerie du Minervois, 1988. *Hobbies:* Viticulture; Walking; Water-colour painting. *Address:* La Maison du Coti, St Aubin, Jersey, Channel Islands. 1, 3.

PINDER John Humphrey Murray, b. 20 June 1924, London, England. Economist. m. Pauline Hawtayne Lewin, 2 Apr 1964. *Education:* Marlborough Coll, 1938-42; King's Coll, Cambridge, 1942-43, 1947-49; MA, Econs. *Appointments:* Served Royal Artillery, 1943-47, incl Lt, seconded to W African Artillery; Int Dir, Economist Intelligence Unit, 1952- 64; Dir, Policy Studies Inst (formerly Pol and Econ Planning), 1964-

85; Currently Vis Prof, Coll Europe, Bruges, Belgium. *Publications:* Britain and the Common Market, 1961; Europe against De Gaulle, 1963; Federal Union: The Pioneers (w Richard Mayne), 1990; European Community: The Building of a Union, 1991; The European Community and Eastern Europe, 1991. *Memberships:* Pres, Union European Federalists, 1984-90; VP, European Movement, Int; Vice-Chmn, European Movement, UK; Chmn Fed Trust; Coun Mbr, Overseas Dev Inst; Bd Mbr, Inst European Environmental Policy. *Honour:* OBE, 1973. *Hobbies:* Special interest in European unification; European languages and literature; Walking; Bach and Mozart. *Address:* 26 Bloomfield Terrace, London SW1W 8PQ, England. 1.

PINSON William Meredith Jr, b. 3 Aug 1934, Fort Worth, Texas, USA. Executive Director, Baptist General Convention of Texas. m. Bobbie Ruth Judd, 4 June 1955, 2 d. *Education:* BA, Univ N TX, 1955; BD, 1959, ThD, 1963, SWn Bapt Theological Sem. *Appointments:* Prof, SWn Bapt Theological Sem, 1963-75; Pastor, 1st Bapt Ch, Wichita Falls, TX, 1975-77; Pres, Golden Gate Sem, 1977-82; Exec Dir, Bapt Gen Conven TX, 1982-. *Publications:* Applying the Gospel, 1975; Families with Purpose, 1978; Word Topical Bible, 1981; The Biblical View of the Family, 1981; Ready to Minister, 1984. *Memberships:* Stewardship Commn, So Bapt Conven; State Missions Commn, Bapt Gen Conven TX. *Honours:* Disting Alumni Award, Univ N TX; Disting Alumni Award, SWn Bapt Sem; Disting Serv Award, Christian Ethics, Christian Life Commn, So Bapt Conven; LHD, CA Bapt Coll; DD, Univ Mary Hardin Baylor; LHD, Howard Payne Univ; LLD, Dallas Bapt Univ. *Hobbies:* Travel; Writing; Grandchildren. *Address:* 333 North Washington, Dallas, TX 75246, USA. 1, 3, 13, 52, 145.

PIONTEK Eugeniusz Ignacy Innocenty, b. 17 June 1935, Warsaw, Poland. Professor of International and Comparative Law; Legal Consultant. m. Danuta Goclawska, 29 Jan 1978, 2 s. *Education:* LLM, 1956, PhD, 1966, LLD, 1976, SJD (Prof), 1987, Fac Law, Univ Warsaw. *Appointments:* Lectr, 1956-60; Sr Lectr, 1960-66; Reader, 1966-76, Prof, 1976, Fac Law, Univ Warsaw; Pres, Uni-Expert Ltd, 1988-. *Publications:* UN Peace Force, 1973; Socialist Countries in GATT, 1974; Legal Instruments of External Economic Policy of the EEC, 1979; EEC Competition Law, 1984; GATT Rules on Subsidies, 1986. *Memberships:* Rotary Int, Rotary Club Warsaw Old Town, Pres 1991-92; Int Law Assn, Polish Br, Bd Mbr 1988-90; Polish Lawyers Assn; Assoc Bd, Exec Bd, Ctr European Law, King's Coll, London; Assoc Bd, Exec Bd, Soviet and East European Business Law Bulletin. *Honours:* Golden Cross of Merit, 1976; Cross, Polonia Restituta, 1984; Gold Distinction, Polish Lawyers Assn, 1984; Commn Nat Educ Medal, 1989. *Hobbies:* Fine music; Sailing. *Address:* 9A H Wieniawskiego St, 01-572 Warsaw, Poland.

PIPER Priscilla Joan, b. 7 Jan 1939, Watford, Hertfordshire, England. Professor of Pharmacology. m. John Piper, 27 Apr 1963, 1 s. *Education:* BSc, Physiology, 1962, PhD, Pharmacology, 1969, Univ London. *Appointments:* Boots Pure Drug Co, 1963; Parke Davis & Co, 1964-69; Joined, 1969, Reader, 1978, Prof, 1984, Vandervell Prof, Pharmacology, 1990-, Royal Coll Surgs, London. *Publications:* SRS-A and leukotrienes (ed), 1981; Leukotrienes and other lipoxygenase products (ed), 1983; The Leukotrienes: their biological significance (ed), 1986; Advances in the Understanding and treatment of asthma (ed w R D Krell), 1991; Hon Sr Lectr, Dept Thoracic Med, King's Coll Hosp, London. *Memberships:* Fellow, Royal Soc Med; Soc Apothecaries, Sec Respiratory Sect; Brit Pharmacological Soc, Ed Bd 1980-86; Physiological Soc; Brit Soc Immunology; Ed Bds: Prostaglandins; Pulmonary Pharmacology; Systems Bd A, Med Rsch Coun; Soc Drug Rsch; Brit Inflammation Rsch Assn. *Honours:* Vis Prof, Royal Postgrad Med School, 1982; Hon MRCP (London), 19085; Vis Prof, Univ Kuwait, 1987; Royal Soc Med Vis Prof, USA, 1989. *Hobbies:* Cooking; Gardening; Reading; Listening to music. *Address:* Department of Pharmacology, Hunterian Institute, Royal College of Surgeons, Lincoln's Inn Fields, London WC2A 3PN, England.

PIRAMAL Dilip Gopikishan, b. 2 Nov 1949, Bombay, India. Chief Executive. m. Gita Piramal, 20 May 1972, 2 d. *Education:* BCom (Hons). *Appointments:* Dir, 1970, Mng Dir, 1975-80, Morajee Mills, Bombay, 1970; Chmn, Mng Dir, 1973, Dir, 1975-80, Blow Plast Ltd, Bombay; Bd Dirs, 1980-, currently Chief Exec, Universal Luggage Mfg Co Ltd; Bd Dirs, 1980-: VIP Inds Ltd, Morris Electronics Ltd, Alkyl Amines Chems Ltd, Zenith Ltd, Furn Plastics Inds Ltd, Stellar Plastics Inds Ltd, Kiddy Plast Pvt Ltd, Mattel Toys (India) Ltd, Quality Plastics Ltd. *Memberships:* All India Plastics Mfrs Assn, Pres 1980-81; Rotary Club Bombay Midtown, Pres 1981-82; Org Plastic Processors India, Pres 1991; Mng Comm, Associated Chmbrs of Comm and Ind, India. *Honours:* Named Industrialist of Yr, Jaycees, 1983. *Hobbies:* Reading; Music; Swimming. *Address:* Piramal House, 61 Pochkhanawala Road, Worli, Bombay 400 025, India. 52.

PIRIE David Tarbat, b. 4 Dec 1946, Dundee, Scotland. Writer. m. 21 June 1983, 1 s, 1 d. *Education:* Univ York; BA (Hons) Univ London. *Appointments:* Film Ed, Time Out mag, 1970-83; Freelance Writer for The Times, Sunday Times, others; Tutor, Screenwriters Studio, Dartington Hall (annual sponsored ind course). *Creative works:* Mystery Story, novel, 1980; Films: Rainy Day Women, 1984; Wild Things, 1987; TV serials: Never Come Back, 1989; Ashenden, 1990; Natural Lies, 1992. *Honours:* Prizewinner, NY Film Fest, 1984; Prizewinner, Best Network TV Series, Chgo Film Fest, 1991. *Hobbies:* Walking; Running. *Address:* c/o Stephen Durbridge, Lemon, Unna & Durbridge, 24 Pottery Lane, London W11, England. 3.

PISHTIALOVA-ADAMU Bogdanka Kirilova, b. 15 Mar 1958, Plovidv, Bulgaria. Lecturer; Teacher. m. Abdullahi Adamu, 1 Apr 1983, 3 d. *Education:* BA Philol, Russian Lang and Lit, 1976-80. *Appointments:* Lectr, Russian Lang and Lit, Min of Educ, Smolivan, Bulgaria, 1980-83; Lectr in Eng Lang, Fed Poly Nasarawa, Plateau State, Nigeria, 1985-90; Lectr in Eng, Min of Fed Capt Territory, Nigeria, 1990-. *Publications:* The War Literature of Urii Bonda Riyev (Comparative Analysis of Burning Snow and Banks). *Hobbies:* Reading; Travelling; Writing poetry and short stories. *Address:* 12 Zlatna Panega Str All6, Plovdiv Town 4003, Bulgaria.

PITA Dan, b. 11 Oct 1938, Romania. Film Director. m. Carmen Galin-Pita, 11 July 1978. *Education:* High Cinema School, Film Direction. *Appointments:* Film Director and Stage Director at the Bucuresti Film Studio. *Memberships:* Union of Film Makers. *Honours:* Chevalier des Arts ed des Lettres, French Min of Culture. *Address:* Str Hristo Botev 8, Bucharest 3, Romania.

PITCHUGIN Nickolaj J, b. 24 Dec 1961, Vladimir. Chemical Engineer. m. Larisa M Pitchugina, 27 Apr 1985, 1 d. *Education:* Vladimir Polytech Inst, 1983-89. *Appointments:* Vladimir Chem Plant, 1978-92. *Hobbies:* Collecting insects; Hiking.

PITFIELD Michael, b. 22 May 1945, Durham City, England. Director of Corporate Affairs. *Education:* BSc, Univ London; MA, Univ Reading; DPM, Slough Coll. *Appointments:* Asst Dir, Inst Personnel Mgmt, 1978-89; Dir, Thames Valley Bus School, 1989-90; Dir, Corp Mktng, Henley Mgmt Coll, Henley-on-Thames, 1990-. *Publications include:* How To Take Exams, 1980; Many jrnl articles. *Memberships:* Inst Personnel Mgmt, Fellow 1980, Educ Comm Mbr; Royal Soc of Arb, Fellow, 1992. *Hobbies:* Genealogy; History; Swimming; Travel. *Address:* Henley Management College, Greenlands, Henley-on-Thames, Oxon RG9 3AU, England.

PITFIELD Thomas Baron, b. 5 Apr 1903, Bolton, Lancs, England. Composer; Writer; Artist; Craftsman. m. Alice

Maud, 26 Dec 1934. *Education:* Bolton Municipal Sch; Bolton Tech Col; Royal Manchester Col of Mus; Bolton Sch of Art. *Appointments:* Millwright Draughtsman, 1917- 24, Tchr, Wolverhampton Coun of Soc Serv, 1934-36; Pt and supply Tchr, Art and Mus, Tettenhall Col, 1935-47; 26 yrs freelance designer and composer and Prof of Composition, Royal Northern and Manchester Col of Music, 19347-73; Br Mus Heritage, 26 songs; Exhibited in Royal Acad of Art, numerous one-man exhibs in municipal and other Galls. *Publications:* The Poetry of Treses, 1945; Words without songs, Musiciansip for Guitarists, Art Teaching Course, No Song No Supper, autobiog Vol 1, A Song after Supper, autobiog vol 2; A Cotton Town Boyhood, autobiog; My Words, (poems); Limusics; From a Wayfarer's Sketchbook. *Hobbies:* Nuture study; Woodcarving; Ornithology. *Address:* Lesser Thorns, 21 East Downs Road, Bowdon, Altrincham, Cheshire WA14 2LG, England.

PITT Barrie (William Edward), b. 7 July 1918, Galway, Ireland. Author and Editor of Military Histories. m. (1) Phyllis Kate Edwards, 1943, 1 s (dec.), (2) Sonia Deirdre Hoskins, 1953, diss, 1971, (3) Frances Mary Moore, 1983. *Education:* Portsmouth So Grammar School. *Appointments:* Bank Clerk, 1935; Served Army, 1939-45; Surveyor, 1946; Writer, 1954-; Info Off, Atomic Energy Auth, 1961; Histl Cons to BBC series, The Great War, 1963; Ed, Purnell's History of the Second World War, 1964; Ed-in-Chief: Ballantine's Illustrated History of World War 2, US Book Series, 1967; Ballantine's Illustrated History of the Violent Century, 1971; Ed: Purnell's History of the First World War, 1969; British History Illustrated, 1974-78. *Publications:* The Edge of Battle, 1958; Zeebrugge, St George's Day 1918, 1958; Coronel and Falkland, 1960; 1918 The Last Act, 1962; The Battle of the Atlantic, 1977; The Crucible of War: Western Desert 1941, 1980; Churchill and the Generals, 1981; The Crucible of War: Year of Alamein 1942, 1982; Special Boat Squadron, 1983; The Chronological Atlas of World War II (w Frances Pitt). *Contributions to:* Encyclopaedia Britannica; The Sunday Times. *Hobby:* Golf. *Address:* 10 Wellington Road, Taunton, Somerset TA1 4EG, England. 1.

PITT Desmond Gordon, b. 27 Dec 1922, Croydon, Surrey, England. Retired. m. 14 Sept 1946, 1 s, 2 d. *Education:* Bournemouth Grammar School. *Appointments:* HM Customs and Excise, 1947-83; Retired as Under-Sec and HM Commnr Customs and Excise, 1983. *Memberships:* Fellow, Chartered Inst Cert Accts; Assoc, Chartered Inst Co Secs; Assoc, Inst Bankers. *Hobbies:* Sailing; Historical research. *Address:* 4 Ken Road, Southbourne, Bournemouth, Dorset BH6 3ER, England. 1.

PITT-KETHLEY Helen Fiona, b. 21 Nov 1954, Middlesex, England. Poet; Novelist; Travel Writer; Journalist. *Education:* BA Hons, Fine Art, Chelsea School of Art, 1976. *Career:* Freelance Writer, articles for newspapers incl: Independent, Times, Guardian, London Review of Books, Forum, New Statesman, GQ, Elle, Woman's Journal; Full-time Poet, 1978-. *Publications:* Poetry books: London, 1984; Rome, 1985; The Tower of Glass, 1985; Sky Ray Lolly, 1986; Gesta, 1986; Private Parts, 1987; The Perfect Man, 1989; Journeys to the Underworld, travel book, 1988; The Misfortunes of Nigel (novel), 1991; The Literary Companion to Sex, 1992; Literary Companion to Sex, 1992; Too Hot To Handle, 1992; The Maiden's Progress, 1992. *Memberships:* Chelsea Arts Club; Soc Sussex Authors; Film Artistes Assn; The London Lib. *Hobbies:* Opera; Weight-training; Herbalism; Sex; Revenge. *Address:* c/o Sheil Land Associates, 43 Doughty Street, London WC1N 2LF, England. 3, 138.

PITTAWAY David Michael, b. 29 June 1955, Edgebaston, England. Barrister. m. Jill Suzanne Newsam, 26 Mar 1983, 2 s. *Education:* Uppingham School; Exhibitioner, Sidney Sussex Coll, Cambridge; MA (Cantab). *Appointments:* Practising Barrister, 1977-

; Fellow, Chartered Inst of Arbs, 1990. *Hobbies:* Country Life; Travelling. *Address:* No 1 Serjeants' Inn, London EC4 1LL, England.

PITTILLO Jack Daniel, b. 25 Oct 1938, Hendersonville, North Carolina, USA. Professor of Biology. m. Jean H Farr, 28 Aug 1966, 1 s, 1 d. *Education:* AB, Berea Coll, 1961; MS, Univ KY, 1963; PhD, Univ GA, 1966. *Appointments:* Asst Prof, 1966-71, Assoc Prof, 1971-77, Prof, 1977-, Wn Carolina Univ, Cullowhee, NC. *Publications:* National Natural Landmarks of the Southern Blue Ridge Province, 1976; Manual of Important Habitats of the Blue Ridge Parkway, 2 vols, 1978, 1987. *Memberships:* So Appalachian Botan Club, Pres 1977-78, Ecology Ed 1983-86, Newsletter Ed 1993-; NC Acad Sci, Bd Dirs 1983-86; Sigma Xi, W Carolina Univ Sec-Treas 1981-83; Ecological Soc Am; Assn SE Biology; Botan Soc Am. *Honours:* Co-recip, Rsch Award, Assn SE Biology, 1985; O Max Gardner Nominee, 1986; NC Trails Award, NC Trails Comm, 1987; Esther B Cunningham Award, W NC Alliance, 1989; Paul A Reid Distinguished Service Awd, 1991-92; Govs Awd for Excellence, 1992. *Hobbies:* Hiking; Photography. *Address:* Department of Biology, Western Carolina University, Cullowhee, NC 28723, USA. 7, 125, 139.

PITTMAN Jacquelyn, b. 22 Dec 1932, Pensacola, Florida, USA. Professor of Nursing. *Education:* EdD, 1974, MA, 1959, Tchrs Col, Columbia Univ; BSNE, Florida State Univ, 1958. *Appointments:* Instr, Pensacola Jr Col, 1959-63; Dept Chm, Gulf Coast Community Col, 1963-66; Asst Prof, 1970-72, Assoc Prof, 1972-80, Univ of Texas at Austin; Prof, Lousiana State Univ Med Ctr, 1980-. *Memberships:* Am Nurses Assn; Nat League for Nsg; Ctr for the Study of the Presidency; NYAS; Nsg Archives Assocs; Nat Trust for Hist Preservation; Sigma Theta Tau; Acad of Polit Scis; Wilson Ctr Assocs. *Honours:* Women's Inner Circle Achievement of N.Am, 1991; Profl of the Yr in Educ, 1991; Kappa Delta Pi, 1959; Pi Lambda Theta, 1959; Sigma Theta Tau, 1971. *Hobbies:* Swimming; Golf; Travel; Louisiana history; Reading. *Address:* Louisiana State University Medical Centre, School of Nursing, Graduate Programme, 1900 Graviek Street, New Orleans, LA 70112, USA. 5, 7, 52, 138, 152, 155.

PLASECKI Ryszard, b. 2 Oct 1951, Lodz, Poland. Prof of Economics. m. 20 Sept 1979, 2 s. *Education:* Univ of Lodz, 1970-73; Univ of Nancy 11, France, 1974-75; PhD, Univ of Lodz, 1977; Habilitation, 1989; Prof, 1990. *Appointments:* Univ of Lodz, 1973-91; Vice Dean, Univ of Lubumbash, Rep of Zaire, 1981-88. *Publications include:* Marshall Plan-Phase Two; Over 50 Publ; 2 Books. *Memberships include:* CIFE; European Movement; Conslt of Appropriate Technology Intl. *Honours include:* Individual Award for Scientific Achievements. *Hobbies:* Travel; Reading; Film & Theatre. *Address:* 32/34 M.17, Kraszewskiees Str, 93161 Lodz, Poland.

PLATIKANOV Dimo, b. 2 Feb 1936, Sofia, Bulgaria. Professor in Physical Chemistry. m. Dotchi Exerowa, 22 Apr 1962, 1 d. *Education:* Dip, Chem, 1958, PhD, 1969, Univ Sofia; DrSc, Bulgarian Acad Scis, 1989. *Appointments:* Lectr, 1958, Sr Lectr, 1964, Assoc Prof, 1970, Prof, Dept Hd, 1989-, Dept Phys Chem, Fac Chem, Univ Sofia. *Publications:* Over 80 sci papers in jnrls such as J Colloid and Interface Sci, Colloids and Surfaces, Colloid and Polymer Sci, Langmuir, Colloid J USSR. *Memberships:* Int Union Pure and Applied Chem, Assoc Mbr Commn Colloid Chem, Mbr Subcomm Thin Films; Int Assn Colloid Interface Scientists; Kolloid-Gesellschaft, Germany. *Honours:* Order of Cyrill and Methodius, 3rd degree, 1981, 2nd degree, 1986; Medal, 100 Yrs Anniversary, Univ Sofia, 1988. *Hobbies:* Mountaineering; Reading. *Address:* University of Sofia, Department of Physical Chemistry, Boul James Bourchier 1, 1126 Sofia, Bulgaria.

PLATO Sharyll Adelle (Brunner), b. 22 June 1935, St Joseph, Ohio, USA. College/University Instructor. m. Leonard John Plato, 18 Sept 1954, dec. 13 Oct 1954. *Education:* BS, Mankato State Univ, Mankato, MN, 1963; MEd, Univ VA, Charlottesville, 1969; MSA, Oklahoma City Univ, OK, 1982. *Appointments:* Mil serv: USAF, 1955-57; USNR, 1958-62; Served to Maj, US Marine Corps, 1962-72; Instr, Acctng, Univ Ctrl OK, Edmond, 1982-. *Publications:* Teaching Transparencies, Accounting Principles I and II, 1990; Sunset Hills Community Country Club, Accounting Principles Practice Set, 1991; Var comparison accounting books reviews, 1983-. *Memberships:* Assoc, Am Inst CPAs; Am Acctng Assn; Woman Marine Assn; VFW, Post 18SZ. *Honours:* Navy Achievement, US Marine Corps, 1968; Outstanding Grad, Oklahoma City Univ, 1982. *Hobbies:* Writing poetry; Golf; Music. *Address:* 1610 NW 42nd Street, Oklahoma City, OK 73118, USA. 15, 76.

PLATT David Wallace, b. 13 Sept 1964, Ulster, Northern Ireland. Barrister. *Education:* Campbell Coll; Cambridge Univ, 1983-86; MA (Cantab). *Appointments:* Barrister; Pt-time TV Presenter; Pol Aide. *Memberships:* Vice-Chmn, Westminster Conservatives; Chmn, Cambridge Univ Conservative Assn. *Honours:* Scholarships to Campbell Coll and Cambridge Univ. *Hobbies:* Architecture; Skiing; Politics. *Address:* 44 Denbigh St, London SW1, England.

PLATT Denise, b. 21 Feb 1945, England. Director of Social Services. *Education:* BSc Econ, Univ Coll, Cardiff, 1967; Assoc, Inst Med Social Work, 1968. *Appointments:* Asst Tchr, Stoke-on-Trent, 1963- 64; Social Worker, then Sr Social Worker, Middlesex Hosp, London, 1968-73; Team Ldr, Guys Hosp, London, 1973-76; Southwark Social Servs, 1976-78; Prin, Social Work, Hammersmith Hosp, 1978-83; Asst Dir, Social Servs Dept, 1986, Dir, Social Servs, 1986-, Hammersmith and Fulham. *Memberships:* Trustee, Nat AIDS Trust; Assn Dirs Social Serv, Exec Coun Mbr, Chair London Br. *Hobbies:* Music; Watercolour painting; Walking. *Address:* Social Services Department, 145 Kings Street, Hammersmith, London W6 9XY, England.

PLAYFAIR Hugh George Lyon, b. 5 Dec 1935, St Andrews, Scotland. Schoolmaster. m. Bridget Ingledew Jane Garland, 22 Aug 1970, 2 s, 1 d. *Education:* Oundle School, 1949-54; King's Coll, Cambridge, 1954-57; New Coll, Oxford, 1959-60; MA (Cantab) Hist; Dip Ed (Oxon). *Appointments:* Army Serv, Somaliland Scouts, 1958-59; Marlborough Coll, Wilts, 1960-68; Cranbrook School, Sydney, NSW, Australia, 1969-73; Canford School, Wimborne, Dorset, England, 1974-; OC, Canford School Combined Cadet Force, 1974-. *Publication:* The Playfair Family, 1984. *Memberships:* Royal and Ancient Golf Club; Sherborne Golf Club; Fndg Mbr, Sec, Canford School Golf Club; Lay Reader, Diocese Bath and Wells, 1987. *Honours:* OBE (Mil), 1989. *Hobbies:* Gardening; Walking; Golf; Tennis; Stamp collecting. *Address:* Canford School, Wimborne, Dorset BH21 3AD, England.

PLEWES John Lawrence, b. 5 Sept 1940, Luton, England. Orthopaedic Surgeon. m. Jenna Rose Glassborow, 12 Feb 1966. *Education:* Marlborough Coll, 1953-57; Christ Church, Oxford, 1958-62; MA (Oxon), 1964; Middlesex Hosp, 1962-64; BM BCh, 1964, FRCS, London, 1970. *Appointments:* Orthopaedic Surg, Bathurst, NB, Can, 1975-80; Orthopaedic Surg, Sr Lectr, Univ Birmingham, England, 1982-. *Honours:* Orthopaedic Fellowship, Toronto, Can, 1973-74. *Hobbies:* Sailing; Oenology. *Address:* Selvas Cottage, Withybed Green, Alvechurch, Worcestershire B48 7PR, England.

PLICHTA Zdzislaw Edmund, b. 21 Nov 1942, Lapy, Poland. Architect; Director of Regional Planning Office. m. 4 Jan 1969. *Education:* MArch, Fac Arch, Polytechnic Warsaw, 1967; Postgrad studies, Fac Arch and Village Planning, 1969-71. *Appointments:* City Planner, Dist Planning Corp, Bialystok, 1967-68; Mgr, 1968-75, City Planner, 1975-, Dir, 1984-, Reg Planning Off, Bialystok.

Creative works: City planning: Town ctrs of Tykocin, 1968, Lapy, 1977, Gizycko, 1986, Suwalki, 1989, Bialystok, 1990; Towns of Suprasl, 1977, Lipsk on the Biebrz, 1977, Kadzidlo, 1987; Communes of Wasilkow, 1986, Suprasl, 1988, Choroszcz, 1988. *Memberships:* Polish Archts Soc, Bialystok; Polish City Planning Soc. *Honours:* Polish Nat City Planning Soc competition awards: 2nd Prize, Grajewo; 3rd Prize, Sieradz; 2nd Prize, Wodzislaw; 2nd Prize, Kalinowice; 1st Prize, Gizycko; Department awards: 3rd Prize for Town Planning of Town Centres, Tykocin, 1968, Suwalki, 1989, Bialystok, 1991. *Hobbies:* Fishing; Literature; Films. *Address:* Ukosna 7 m 13, 15-836 Bialystok, Poland.

PLINT Dennis Arthur, b. 9 Mar 1924, Cape Town, South Africa. Retired. m. 16 Dec 1950, 2 s. *Education:* BDS, Witwatersrand Univ, 1950; FDSRCS, DOrth, Royal Coll Surgs, England, 1956. *Appointments:* Orlando Clin, Soweto, 1951-52; House Surg, St Thomas' Hosp, London, England, 1952-54; Registrar, Gt Ormond St Hosp, 1955-56; Sr Registrar, Lectr, Royal Dental Hosp, London, 1957; Pvte Prac, Durban, S Africa, 1958-60; Sr Lectr, Royal Dental Hosp, London, England, 1960-61; Cons, Orthodontics, Hastings, Eastbourne, Tunbridge Wells, 1961-67; Cons Dental Surg, Orthodontics, Children's Dentistry: Royal Dental Hosp, 1967-86, Gt Ormond St Hosp, 1967-89, Univ Coll Hosp Dental School, 1986-89; Locum, Gt Ormond St Hosp and Univ Coll Hosp Dental School, 1989-. *Publications:* Chapt in Walther's Orthodontic Notes; Chapt in Scott Brown's ENT. *Memberships:* Brit Soc Study Orthodontics; European Orthodontic Soc; Fndr Mbr, Trustee, Cleft Lip and Palate Assn. *Honours:* Brit Empire Medal, 1945; Floyd Mem Medal, 1950. *Hobbies:* Gardening; Travel; Reading; Crosswords. *Address:* Tillingham, Beckley Furnace, Nr Brede, Rye, East Sussex TN31 6ET, England.

PLONKA Andrzej, b. 3 Nov 1936, Lodz, Poland. Professor of Chemistry. m. Ewa Wilczynska, 30 May 1970, 1 s. *Education:* MSc, Chem, 1959, PhD, 1964, DSc, 1969, Prof, 1983, Tech Univ Lodz. *Appointments:* Mil Acad Med, Lodz, 1960-64; Tech Univ Lodz, 1964-; Fellowships: Wayne State Univ, USA, 1975-76; Max Planck Inst, Mulheim/Ruhr, Germany, 1980; Univ Houston, TX, USA, 1983-84. *Publications:* 140 sci papers on radiochem and radiation chem; Time-Dependent Reactivity of Species in Condensed Media, monograph, 1986. *Memberships:* Int Assn Radiation Rsch, Councillor 1983-87; Polish Assn Radiation Rsch, Pres local br. *Honours:* Awards: Polish Chem Soc, 1967; Min High Educ, 1977, 1980, 1987, 1990; Polish Atomic Energy Agcy, 1985; Polish Assn Radiation Rsch, 1986, 1989. *Hobbies:* Hiking; Cycling. *Address:* Piekna 51/53 m 61, 93-558 Lodz, Poland.

PLOTNIKOV Pavel, b. 4 Nov 1947, Dushanbe, Tadjikistan. Mathematician. m. Nina Tarasova, 14 Nov 1968, 1 s, 1 d. *Education:* Novosibirsk State Univ, 1965-70; Cand PhD, 1972; DSc, 1986; Corres Mbr, USSR Acad Scis, 1990. *Appointments:* Jr Researcher, 1970-76, Sr Researcher, 1076-86, Leading Researcher, 1986-90, Lab Chief, 1990-, Lavrentyev Inst Hydrodynamics, Novosibirsk. *Publications:* 40 sci articles incl: Solvability of the problem of spatial gravitational waves on a liquid surface, 1980; Foundation of the Stores conjecture in the theory of water waves, 1983; Existence of infinitely many periodical solutions of the problem of forced oscillation for weakly nonlinear hyperbolic equations, 1988; Bifurcation of the critical points of the smooth functionals and non-uniqueness of solitary water waves, 1991. *Membership:* Acad Scis Russia. *Hobby:* Gardening. *Address:* Lavrentyev Institute of Hydrodynamics, Lavrentyev pr 15, Novosibirsk 630090, Russia.

POCOCK Thomas Allcot Guy (Tom), b. 18 Aug 1925, London, England. Writer. m. Penelope Casson, 26 Apr 1969, 2 d. *Education:* Cheltenham Coll, 1940-43. *Appointments:* Staff Jrnlst: Hulton Press, 1944-48; Daily

Mail, 1948-52; The Times, 1952-55; Daily Express, 1955-57; Evening Standard, 1959-88. *Publications:* 12 books incl: Horatio Nelson, 1987; Alan Moorehead, 1990; Sailor King, 1991. *Membership:* Garrick Club; Chelsea Soc, Hon Ed. *Hobbies: Travel; Naval history. Address:* 22 Lawrence Street, London SW3 5NF, England.

PODBIELSKI Henryk, b. 27 May 1939, Szumowo, Lomza District, Poland. Professor of Classical Philology. m. Jadwiga Skibinska, 17 July 1966, 1 s, 1 d. *Education:* Classical Philology studies, Cath Univ Lublin, 1958-63; PhD, 1969, Dr habilitatus, 1974, Univ Warsaw. *Appointments:* Asst, 1963-69, Adj, 1969-74, Docent, Holder Chair of Greek Lit, 1975-84, Prof, 1985-, Cath Univ Lublin. *Publications:* Books: La structure de l'Hymne hom, a Aphrodite, 1971; Mit Kosmogomczny w Teogonui Heijoda, 1978; Transl and commentary: Arystoteles, Poetyka, 1983, 2nd Ed, 1989; Arystoteles, Retoryha-Poctzha, 1989; Pausanias, Description of Greece, vols VIII-XIm 1989. *Memberships:* Sci Soc, Cath Univ Lublin; Sci Soc Lublin; Polish Philological Soc, Pres Lublin; Comm Ancient Culture Sci, Polish Acad Scis; Philological Commn, Polish Acad Scis, Cracow. *Honours:* Best Student, Classics Paper Award, 1963; Cath Univ Rector's Awards, doct thesis publ, 1971, habilitation thesis publ, 1978; Co-recip, IInd Class Award, monograph About Drama: From Aristotle to Goethe, Polish Min Educ, 1990. *Hobbies:* Gardening; Touring. *Address:* Classical Philology Department, Catholic University of Lublin, PL 20-950 Lublin, Poland.

PODESTA LE POITTEVIN Giulia Eugenia, b. 18 June 1941, Milan, Italy. Council of Europe Administrator. m. Yanic Le Poittevin, 11 Feb 1989. *Education:* Cambridge Cert Proficiency Engl, 1958; Fac Pol Scis, Univ Pavia, 1960-64; Italian Doct maxima cum laude, Pol Sci, w pub Int Law thesis, 1964; Studies incl Pub, Pvte and Int Law, Pol Sci, Philos Law, Mod Hist, Hist and Instns of Afro-Asian Countries, Pol Econ, Pol and Econ Geog, Stats, Langs. *Appointments:* Collaborator, weekly mag, Istituto per gli Studi di Politica Internazionale, Milan, Sept-Nov 1964; Asst, Int Law, Univ Pavia, Nov 1964; Rsch Asst, Eurofinance, Paris, France, Dec 1964-Apr 1965; Coun Europe, Strasbourg, France, 1965-: Admnstv Off, 1965-72, Prin Admnstv Off, 1974-78, Directorate Econ and Social Affairs; Admnstv Off, Pol Directorate, 1982-74; Prin Admnstv Off, 1978-85, Advsr, Dpty to Dir, 1985-86, Pvte Off of Sec Gen and Dpty Sec Gen, 1978-85; Hd, School Educ Div, 1986-90, Hd, Ctrl Div, 1990-, Directorate Education, Culture and Sport. *Publications:* La Corte di Giustizia delle Comunita Europee e la liberta giudiziale, 1964; Treatises: L'evoluzione giuridica e constituzionale della Nigeria, 1964; Montesquieu e lo storicismo romantico, 1964; Il concetto di 'Rule of Law' nel pensiero di Dicey e di Hayek. 1964. *Honours:* 3rd Prize, Concours European de Langue Francaise, Alliance Francaise, 1956. *Hobbies:* Reading; Swimming; Walking in the mountains. *Address:* Conseil de l'Europe, BP 431 R6, F- 67006 Strasbourg Cedex, France.

PODHAJSKI Marek, b. 7 Apr 1938, Nowogrodek, Poland. Music Theorist; Musicologist. m. (1) Anna Wisniewska, 1959, (2) Anna Bubak, 31 Dec 1977, 4 d. *Education:* MA, Music Theory, 1961, MA, Composition, 1966, Acad Music, Gansk; Doct, Music Theory, Acad Music, Warsaw, 1972; Prof, State Coun Poland, 1982. *Appointments:* Tchng, Acad Music, Gdansk, 1961-90, positions incl: Asst, 1961, Dean, Fac Music Educ, 1972-75, Hd, Chair Composition and Theory of Music, 1972-78, Dean, Fac Theory of Music and Composition, 1975-78, Dir, Fndr, Inst Music Theory, 1978-82, 1987-90, Pro- Rector, 1981-90; Prof, Akureyri Music School, Akureyri, Iceland, 1990-; Organiser, Sci Mgr: Int sci confs, Poland; 1st Fest Icelandic Piano Music, Akureyri, 1992; Lectures, Poland, Australia, Bulgaria, Czechoslovakia, Germany, Iceland, Russia. *Publications:* 4 books incl: Interpretacja matematyczno-logiczna elementarnych pojec harmonii funkcyjnej, 1974; Formy muzyczne, 1991; Nowy system muzyki, Jana Jarmusiewicza w perspektywie polskich prac z

harmonii XIX wieku, 1992; About 80 papers. *Memberships:* Polish Composers Union; Int Musicological Soc. *Honours:* Awards, Min Culture, Poland, 1973, 1977, 1982; Nominated Int Man of Yr, Int Biog Ctr, Cambridge, 1991-92; Silver Shield of Valor, Am Biog Inst, 1992. *Hobbies:* Methodology; Teaching methods of musical theory in different countries; Hindu music; Contemporary Polish history, Travel; Photography. *Address:* ul Komandorska 6, 80-299 Gdansk, Poland. 4, 152.

PODILUK Walter, b. 4 Mar 1927, Saskatchewan, Canada. Hospital President and Chief Executive Officer. m. Sonia Trotzuk, 12 Aug 1947, 3 s, 3 d. *Education:* BEd, BA, Univ Sask. *Appointments:* Hlth Educ Off, 1951-55; School Prin, 1955-63; Asst Dir Educ, 1963-67; Dir Educ, 1967-82; Dpty Min Social Servs, 1982-84; Dpty Min Hlth, 1984-88; Dpty Chmn, Commn on Dirs in Hlth Care, 1988-90; Pres, CEO, St Paul's Hosp (Grey Nuns) Saskatoon, 1990-. *Publications:* Directions and Targets - A Development Strategy on Saskatoon Catholic Schools; Future Directions for Health Care in Saskatchewan; Tomorrow's Schools for Tomorrow's Children. *Memberships:* Med Labs Licensing Bd; Ctr Agricl Med; Dev Coun; Hlth Servs Execs. *Honours:* Papal Medal, Pro Ecclesia et Pontifice; Disting Serv Award; Can Assn School Admin; Hon Life Mbrship, Can Educ Assn; Fndrs Award, Coll Ed, Univ Sask; Hon Mbrship, Sask Registered Nurses Assn; LLD (Hon), Univ Sask. *Hobbies:* Outdoors; Reading; Travel; Geography; History. *Address:* St Paul's Hospital (Grey Nuns) of Saskatoon, 1702 20th Street West, Saskatoon, Saskatchewan, Canada S7M 0Z9.

POEHLMANN Gerhard Manfred, b. 28 Nov 1924, Gotha, Germany. Cartographer; Geographer; Engineer; Professor of Cartography (retired). m. Ilse I D Schmidt, 2 Dec 1945, 2 d. *Education:* Cartography w Prof Dr H Haack, Perthes, Gotha, 1945-47; Engrng degree, Acad f Arch, W Berlin, 1952; Postgrad, Eidgenossische Technische Hochschule and Univ Zurich, Switzerland, 1956-59; Doct, SCL, Free Univ Berlin, 1974. *Appointments:* Lt, German Army, France, Russia, 1942-45; Map Ed, Prod Mgr, Perthes, Gotha, GDR and Darmstadt, FRG, 1947-56; Asst, Eidgenossische Technische Hochschule, Switzerland, 1956-59; Ed-in-Chief, Mairs Geogl Publng House, Stuttgart, FRG, 1959-62; Lectr, Prof, 1962-88, Fac Dean, 1981-84, TFH, Berlin. *Publications:* Num maps, lit, reviews and lectures on cartography, Germany, Austria, Switzerland, India, China, Yugoslavia, Egypt, Nigeria, 1949-90; Ed, Berl Geowiss ABH, 1980-88; New Mapping of Egypt 1:500,000, 1981-88. *Memberships:* Deutsche Gesellschaft fur Kartographie; Geographische Gesellschaft Zurich; Gesellschaft fur Erdkunde zu Berlin; Schweizerische Kartographische. *Address:* Cimberstrasse 11/i, D-1000 Berlin 38 Germany. 52.

POJMANSKA Teresa, b. 19 Apr 1929, Godziesze, Poland. Professor of Natural Sciences. m. Henryk Pojmanski, 28 June 1954, 2 s. *Education:* 1st degree, Univ Studies, Univ Lodz, 1952; MSc, Zoology, 1956, PhD, Natural Scis, 1961, Dr Hab, Parasitology, 1969, Univ Warsaw; Prof, Natural Scis, Coun State, Poland, 1980. *Appointments:* Mus Zoology, Polish Acad Scis, Lodz, 1950-54; W Stefanski Inst Parasitology, Polish Acad Scis, Warsaw, 1954-; Nat Inst Biology, Tlemcen, Algeria, 1976-78; Rsch Assoc, Postdoct Fellow, Univ Lethbridge, Alta, Can, 1991. *Publications:* The parasites of Fish in Poland. I. Tapeworms; General Parasitology (w K Niewiadomska, B Grabda-Kazubska, B Machnicka); Over 90 papers in scholarly jrnls dealing w parasitology, on parasites of small mammals, morphology, biology and systematics of the trematodes esp family Leucochloridiidae, influence of temperature on fish parasites, population biology of some trematodes, cestodes and crustaceans. *Memberships:* Polish Parasitological Soc, Pres Warsaw Div, Gen Sec, 2 terms; Sci Soc Warsaw; Sci Coun, W Stefanski Inst Parasitology, Pres 1 term, Vice-Director; Comm Parasitology, Polish Acad Scis, Gen Sec 2 terms. *Honours:* 3 Sci Awards, Sec, Polish Acad Scis, for rsch on Biology and life cycles of some Digenea as a basis for the recognition of their phylogenetic affinities, 1972, The structure of the parasite fauna of fish from the lake Goplo and heated lakes of Konin region, 1974, Analysis of the seasonality of the incidence and maturation of some fish parasites, with regard to thermal factor, 1983. *Hobbies:* Flower cultivating; Hiking in mountains; Knitting. *Address:* W Stefanski Institute of Parasitology, Polish Academy of Sciences, Pasteur str 3, PO Box 153, 00-973 Warsaw, Poland.

POLACK Gillian Sarah, b. 25 Apr 1961, Melbourne, Victoria, Australia. Public Servant. *Education:* BA, Univ Melbourne, 1983; MA, Ctr Medieval Studies, Univ Toronto, 1984; PhD, Univ Sydney, 1990; Dip superieur francais des affaires, 1991. *Appointments:* Pt-time positions, mainly tchng cross-cultural orientation and trng courses in communication studies, pre-1988; Admnstv Trainee Scheme, Pub Serv Commn, 1988; Off Structures Implementation Taskforce, Dept Indl Rels, 1989; Crops Div, Dept Primary Inds and Energy, 1989-1991; Assistant Dir, Management Skills, Dept of Employment, Education and Training, 1991. *Publications:* 7 pieces of fiction, mostly short stories. *Memberships:* Nat Coun Jewish Women, Australia, Pres Canberra Sect, Nat Bd Mbr, Chmn Status of Women; Life Charter Mbr, World Fndn Successful Women; Assoc, Fellowship Australian Writers, Vic; Alliance francaise, Australia. *Honours:* Felix Raab Prize, European Hist, 1981; Margaret Kiddle Prize, final Hons thesis, 1982; Can C'wlth Scholarship, C'wlth and Fellowship Plan, 1983-84; C'wlth Postgrad Rsch Award, 1083-87; Frazer Travelling Scholarship, 1985. *Hobbies:* Writing; Reading; Folk cultures esp European and Asian; Languages. *Address:* Unit 37, Melrose Mews, Chifley, ACT 2606, Australia.

POLAN Nancy Moore, b. USA. Artist. m. 28 Mar 1934, 2 s. *Education:* BA, Marshall Univ, 1936; Studies w several artists incl Fletcher Martin, Paul Puzinas, Robert Freimark, Hilton Leech, Al Schmidt. *Creative works include:* Magazine covers: Revue Moderne, Paris, France, 1961-66; WV Hillbilly, 1973; Int Platform Assn Talent, 1947; Catalogue covers, travelling exhibs: Joan Miro Graphics, Barcelona, Spain, 1970-71; Framed Am Watercolour show, 1972-73. *Memberships include:* Nat Arts Club, NYC; Pen and Brush Inc, USA; Centro Studi e Scambi Internazionale, Italy; Accademia Italia; Hon VP, Accademia Leonardo da Vinci; Art and Antiques. *Honours:* Awards incl: Nat Arts Club, 1962, 1963, 1968; Pen and Brush, Grumbacher, 1978, Hors Concours, 1975; Gold Medal, Accademia Italia, 1979, 1984, 1986. *Hobbies:* Collecting snuff bottles and paintings. *Address:* 2 Prospect Drive, Huntington, WV 25701, USA. 2, 5, 6, 7, 37, 52, 57, 133, 138, 178.

POLANSKA-NIEDZIELOWA Irena Anna, b. 8 Aug 1959, Tarnow, Poland. Teacher of English. m. Roman Niedziela, 11 Feb 1982, 1 d. *Education:* MA, Engl Philology Dept, Jagiellonian Univ, Cracow, 1984. *Appointments:* Inst Hist, Polish Acad Scis, 1982-83; HS Tchr, Engl, 4th Second School, 1983-84; Dept For Lang Tchng, Jagiellonian Univ, Cracow, 1984-. *Publication:* Headlines in American Press. *Membership:* Univ Tchrs Assn. *Hobbies:* Sociolinguistics; Music; Dancing; Reading. *Address:* Uniwerstytet Jagiellonski, Studiuk Praktycznej Nauki Jsrykow Obcych, ul Sw Anny 6, Cracow, Poland.

POLDROOS Enn, b. 21 May 1933, Tallinn, Estonia. Artist (Painter). Member of Supreme Council of the Republic of Estonia. m. Meeli Poldroos, 5 May 1973, 1 s, 3 d. *Education:* Estonian Art Inst, 1952-58. *Memberships:* Exec Bd, Estonian Popular Front; Speaker, Exec Bd, Estonian Artists Assn; Former Mbr, Artists Union USSR. *Honours:* Grand Prix, Baltic Painting Triennal, Vilnius, 1969, 1975; Estonian Kr Raud Art Prizes, 1972, 1982, 1985; USSR State Prize, 1987. *Address:* Ranniku tee 29-9, 200021 Tallinn, Estonia. 139, 152.

POLIKAROV Azarya, b. 9 Oct 1921, Sofia, Bulgaria. Professor of Philosophy of Science. m. Margarita Zajcharov, 2 Mar 1970, 2 s, 1 d. *Education:* Grad, Phys Fac, Moscow State Univ, 1951; PhD, Inst Philos, USSR Acad Scis, Moscow, 1964. *Appointments:* Asst, Asst Prof, Prof, Inst Philos, 1952-72, Dir, Sci Info Ctr, 1972-, Bulgarian Acad Scis; Vis Prof, Univs Leipzig and Berlin, 1956-62; Expert, UNESCO, Paris, 1967-70. *Publications include:* Relativity and Quanta, 1963, Russian Ed, 1966; Science and Philosophy, 1973; Problems of Scientific Knowledge, 1977; Methodological Problems of Science, 1983; Orientation in the Methodology of Science, 1987. *Memberships:* Int Inst Philos, Paris; Int Acad Philos Sci, Brussels; Int Coun Sci Dev, Munich; European Acad Art, Sci and Humanities, Paris. *Honours:* Nat Prize, Sci, 1974; Prize, Union Scientists Bulgaria, 1989. *Hobbies:* History of science; Science policy; Humour. *Address:* Bulgarian Academy of Sciences, 1040 Sofia, Bulgaria.

POLITEYAN Ronald Chrysostom, b. 29 Apr 1908, Manchester, England. Retired Solicitor. m. Beryl Marguerite Richards, 5 Nov 1941, 1 stepson. *Education:* Queens' Coll, Cambridge, 1928-31; BA (Cantab), 1931; MA (Cantab). *Appointments:* Asst Solicitor, Pringle and Co, Redhill, 1936-37; Asst Solicitor, Edward Mackie and Co, 1937-40, 1946, Prin, Sr Solicitor, 1946-72, Ealing, London; Alderman, Councillor, 1947-72, Mayor, 1962-63, Ealing. *Memberships:* Past Pres, Middlesex Co Assn; Past Pres, Ctrl and S Middlesex Law Soc. *Honours:* School Capt, Radnor House, Redhill, 1921; Snr House Prefect, St Lawrence Coll, Ramsgate, 1926. *Hobbies:* Press reporting incl Primrose League and bowls; Primrose League (Ruling Comm, Ealing Br and Chmn, W Sussex Br). *Address:* 6 Marechal, 101 Elmer Road, Elmer, Bognor Regis, West Sussex PO22 6LH, England.

POLKINGHORNE John Charlton, b. 16 Oct 1930, Weston-super-Mare, England. College President. m. Ruth Isobel Martin, 26 Mar 1955, 2 s, 1 d. *Education:* Perse School, Cambridge, 1945-48; Trinity Coll, Cambridge, 1949-55; PhD, 1955, MA, 1956, ScD, 1974, Univ Cambridge; Westcott House, 1979- 81; Ordained: Deacon, 1981, Priest, 1982. *Appointments:* Fellow, Trinity Coll, Cambridge, 1954-86; Lectr, Univ Edinburgh, Scotland, 1956-58; Lectr, 1958-65, Reader, 1965-68, Prof, Math Physics, 1968-79, Univ Cambridge; Parochial Clergyman: Curate, Cambridge and Bristol, 1961-84; Vicar, Blean, Kent, 1984-86; Fellow, Dean, Chaplain, Trinity Hall, Cambridge, 1986-89; Pres, Queens' College, Cambridge, 1989-. *Publications:* The Analytic S-Matrix (co-author), 1966; Models of High Energy Processes, 1980; The Way the World Is, 1984; The Quantum World, 1984; One World, 1986; Science and Creation, 1988; Science and Providence, 1989; Rochester Roundabout, 1989; Reason and Reality, 1991. *Memberships:* FRS; Science Rsch Coun, 1975-79, Chmn Nuclear Physics Bd 1978-79; Chmn, Comm to Review Guidance on Rsch Use of Fetuses and Fetal Material, 1988-89; Ch of England Doctrine Commn; Gen Synod, Ch of England. *Honours:* Hon Prof, Theoretical Phys, Univ Kent, 1984-; Hon Fellow, Trinity Hall, 1989. *Hobby:* Gardening. *Address:* The President's Lodge, Queens' College, Cambridge CB3 9ET, England. 1, 34.

POLL David Ian Alistair, b. 1 Oct 1950, Mirfield, West Yorkshire, England. Professor of Aeronautical Engineering. m. Elizabeth Mary Read, 31 May 1975, 2 s, 1 d. *Education:* 1st class hons, Aeronautical Engrng, Imperial Coll Sci and Technology, 1972; College Aeronautics, Cranfield Inst Technology, 1975-78; PhD, 1979; Chartered Engr. *Appointments:* Future Projects Grp, Hawker Siddeley Aviation, Kingston-upon-Thames, 1972-75; Lectr, 1978-85, Sr Lectr, 1985-87, Hd, Dept Engrng, Hd, School Aeronautical Engrng, Dir, Goldstein Rsch Lab, Univ Manchester; Mng Dir, Flow Sci Ltd. *Publications:* Over 100 papers and reports on aerodynamics, fluid mechanics and aeronautical engineering. *Memberships:* Royal Aeronautical Soc, Fellow 1987, Coun Mbr 1987-88; Am Inst Aeronautics and Astronautics; NATO Advsry Grp Aeronautical Rsch and Dev Fluid Dynamics Panel; Manchester Lit and Philosl Soc. *Honours:* Brit Belting and Asbestos Outward

Bound Scholarship, 1969; Univ Prize, Royal Aeronautical Soc, 1972; Fletcher Trophy, London Univ Air Squadron, 1972; Assoc, City and Guilds Inst London, 1972. *Hobbies:* Fell walking; DIY; Political debate; Swimming. *Address:* Department of Engineering, Simon Building, University of Manchester, Oxford Road, Manchester M13 9PL, England.

POLLARD Nicholas Anthony (formerly Nicolas Antonio de la Roca), b. 22 Mar 1924, Bacalar, Mexico. Teacher; Lecturer. m. Eleanor Elizabeth Hoffmann, 9 Feb 1948, 6 s, 1 dec, 6 d, 1 dec. *Education:* 1st Place, straight A's, Second School; 1st Place, Cambridge Overseas School Cert w Exemption from London Matriculation Exam. *Appointments:* Chem Asst, Sugar Factory, Belize, 1942; Organising Chmn, Bd Dirs, Holy Redeemer Credit Union Ltd, 1944-50; Pol-Trade Union Ldr, 1948-69; Fndr, Pres, Mercantile Clerks Union, 1948-50; Organiser, Pres or Gen Sec, several Trade Unions, 1950- 69; Jt Exec Sec, Latin-Am Confedn Christian Trade Unions, HQs, Santiago, Chile and Caracas, Venezuela, 1961-68; Fndr, Ed, The Beuze Times, 1956-58; Radio News Ed, 1970-71; Tchr-Lectr, 1982-91; Host, radio talk show, 1991-92. *Publications:* Var essays, short stories, poems. *Honours:* Var Gold Medals and Monetary Prizes for poems, essays, short stories, 1937-75; 4 Gold Medals for highest marks, 1938-41; Gold Medal, Oratory, 1941; 3 Gold Medals for special acad subjects; Offered 1st Open Univ Scholarship, Govt, 1942. *Hobbies:* Acting; Singing; Yoga; Writing letters to the Editor, incl 2 in Times Magazine. *Address:* 12 6th St, King's Park, Belize City, Central America. 52.

POLLOCK David Raymond John, b. 22 Oct 1949, London, England. Association Director. m. Barbara Ann Chambre, 30 June 1975, 1 s, 1 d. *Education:* Dulwich Coll, 1961-68; BA Jt Hons 1st class, Chem, Econs, Univ Keele, 1972. *Appointments:* Min Def, UK, 1968-86; Stock Exchange, London, 1986-91; Dir Designate, Newspaper Publrs Assn, 1991-. *Creative works:* Articles on def and securities mkt matters; Var paintings and drawings. *Memberships:* Brit Inst Mgmt, City of London Comm, Reg Councillor; Royal Instn GB, Fin Comm. *Hobbies:* Arts; Architecture; Painting; Squash; Conviviality. *Address:* 46 Dacres Rd, Forest Hill, London SE23 2NR, England.

POLLOCK Griselda Frances Sinclair, b. 11 Mar 1949, South Africa. Professor of Social and Critical Histories of Art. m. Antony Bryant, 30 Oct 1981, 1 s, 1 d. *Education:* Lady Margaret Hall, Oxford; BA(Oxon), 1970; MA, distinction, 1972, PhD, 1980, Courtauld Inst Art, London Univ. *Appointments:* Pt-time Lectr, Hist Art, Canterbury Coll Art, 1972-74; Pt-time Lectr, Hist Art, Reading Univ, 1972-74; Lectr, Hist Art, Manchester Univ, 1974-77; Lectr, 1977-85, Sr Lectr, 1985-90, Dpty Dir, Ctr Cultural Studies, 1985-87, Dir, Ctr Cultural Studies, 1987-, Prof, Social and Critical Hists Art, 1990-, Leeds Univ; Exhib Curator: Purity and Danger in Victorian Painting, Univ Leeds, 1978; Vincent van Gogh and His Dutch Years, Rijksmuseum Vincent van Gogh, Amsterdam, 1978-80; Northern Young Contemporaries, Manchester Univ, 1981. *Publications:* Millet, 1977; Mary Cassatt, 1980; Vincent van Gogh en zijn Hollandse Jaaren, 1980; Old Mistresses, Women, Art & Ideology (w R Parker), 1981; A Feminist Guide to the Manchester City Art Gallery, 1987; Framing Feminism (w R Parker), 1987; Vision and Difference Feminism, Femininity and the Histories of Art, 1988; Avant-Garde Gambits: Gender & the Colon of Art History, 1992; Dealing with Degas (w R Kendal), 1992; Co-author, several other books. *Contributions to:* books, refereed and other jrnls. *Memberships include:* Yorkshire Arts Assn, BFI Nominee on Exec and Coun; Advsr, Visual Arts Panel, Yorkshire Arts; Advsry Comm, Tate Gall, Liverpool; Humanities Bd, Subcomm on Rsch, Coun Nat Acad Awards; Bd, Var Ed Bds. *Address:* Dept of Fine Art, University of Leeds, Leeds LS2 9JT, England.

POLLOCK John Charles, The Rev, b. 9 Oct 1923, London, England. Author; Clergyman. m. Anne Barrett-Lennard, 4 May 1949. *Education:* Charterhouse, 1937-41; Trinity Coll, Cambridge, 1942, 1945-46; BA, 1946, MA, 1948; Ridley Hall, Cambridge, 1949-51. *Appointments:* Commissioned in Coldstream Guards, 1943; Capt on Lord Mountbatten's Staff, SE Asia, 1945; Asst Master, Wellington Coll, 1947-49; Ordained Deacon, Ch of England, 1951, Priest, 1952; Rector, Horsington, Somerset, 1953-58; Full-time Author, 1958-; Chaplain to High Sheriff, Devon, 1990-91. *Publications:* Candidate for Truth, 1950; A Cambridge Movement, 1953; The Cambridge Seven, 1955, New Ed, 1985; Shadows Fall Apart (History of Zenana Mission), 1957; Way to Glory (Havelock of Lucknow), 1957; The Good Seed, 1958; Earth's Remotest End, 1960; Hudson Taylor and Maria, 1962; Moody without Sankey, 1963; The Keswick Story, 1964; The Christians from Siberia, 1964; Billy Graham: The Authorized Biographies, 1966, 1979, 1984; The Apostle (St Paul), 1969; A Foreign Devil in China, 1972, rev ed 1988; Victims of the Long March, 1972; George Whitfield and the Great Awakening, 1973; Wilberforce, 1977; The Siberian Seven, 1979; Billy Graham, Evangelist to the World, 1979; Amazing Grace: John Newton's Story, 1981; The Master: A Life of Jesus, 1983; Billy Graham, Highlights of the Story, 1984, US Ed, To All the Nations; Shaftesbury: The Poorman's East, 1985; A Fistful of Heroes, 1988; John Wesley, 1989; On Fire for God: Missionary Pioneers, 1990; Fear No Foe: A Brothers Story, 1992; Some books translated into other langs. *Hobbies:* Tennis; Mountain and moorland walking. *Address:* Rose Ash House, South Molton, Devonshire EX36 4RB, England. 3.

PONS Xavier Jean-Paul, b. 10 May 1948, Rodez, France. Professor of English. m. Geraldine Ribot, 24 May 1980, 2 d. *Education:* Licence-es-Lettres, 1968; Maitrise-es-Lettres, 1969; Agregation, 1970; Doctorat-es-Lettres, 1978. *Appointments:* Lectr, Engl, 1970-83, Prof, Engl, 1983-, Univ Toulouse-Le Mirail; Vis Prof, Engl: Univ Newcastle, Australia, 1987, Univ NSW, Australia, 1990. *Publications:* Henry Lawson, l'Homme et l'oeuvre, 1982; L'Australia et ses population, 1983; Out of Eden, 1984; Colonisations, 1985; Le Geant du Pacifique, 1988. *Memberships:* VP, Assn Culturelle Franco-Australienne; VP, Soc Francaise d'Etudes des Pays du C'wlth. *Hobbies:* Tennis; Spearfishing. Address: 3 rue Richet, 31130 Balma, France.

POOL Lea, b. 8 Sept 1950, Geneva, Switzerland. Freelance Filmmaker. *Education:* Bac Lit, 1969, Bac Pedagogy, 1971, Switzerland; Bac Communications, Univ Quebec, Montreal, Can, 1978. *Career includes:* Dir, Writer, Num videograms, short and feature films, TV progs, 1978-; Tchr, Film and Video courses, Univ Quebec, Montreal, 1978-83; Dir, 9 progs, Radio Quebec, 1980-81; Participant, fests, Montreal, Toronto, Quebec, Halifax, Chgo, Denver, Los Angeles, Paris, Namur, Berlin, Troia (Portugal), Venice, Salso Majore Fest (Italy), Edinborgh, Brussels, Budapest, Cuba, Jerusalem, Tokyo, Melbourne, Sydney; Jury Mbr, int fests, Chgo, Locarno, Taormina. *Creative works include:* La Femme de l'hotel (co-writer, dir), 1983-84; Anne Trister (writer, dir), 1985-86; A Corps Perdu, 1987-88; La Demoiselle sauvage, 1991. *Membership:* Assn des realisateurs et realisatrices de film du Quebec. *Honours include:* Prize for Excellence in Can Film, Fest of Fests, Toronto, 1984; Int Press Prize, Montreal World Film Fest, 1984; PrixL E Ouimet-Molson, Assn quebecoise des critiques de cinema, 1985; Prix du public, Festival de femmes de Creteil, Paris, 1985, 1986; Critic's Prize, Troia Fest, 1986; Prize for Excellence, Atlantic Film Fest, Halifax, 1988; 1st Prize, Premiere mag, 1988. *Hobbies:* Travel; Music. *Address:* 33 rue des Perdrix, Bromont, Quebec, Canada J0E 1Z0.

POOLE Matthew David, b. 6 Feb 1969, Leicester, England. Business Systems Sales Executive. *Education:* Roundhill Coll and Laurel's Acad to age 17. *Appointments:* Office Interiors and Bus System's Sales in fam bus, 1986-. *Honours:* England Rugby Rep, Colts under-19s level, 3 caps (Italy, Wales, France), under 21s, 3 caps (Rumania, Netherlands, France); Mbr, full England Sr Team, 3 games Argentina tour; Australian season for club champions Randwick of Sydney. *Hobbies:* All water sports; Crewing and racing yachts; Music; Driving. *Address:* The Cottage, Main St, Leyham, Leicester, England.

POOLE Millicent Eleanore, b. 29 Jan 1940, Ingham, Queensland, Australia. University Pro-Vice-Chancellor. *Education:* Cert ED, Kelvin Grove Tchrs, 1960; BA, 1963, BEd, 1967, Univ Qld; MA hons, 1st class, Univ New England, 1970; PhD, La Trobe Univ, 1973. *Appointments:* HS Tchr: Hughenden State High Top School, 1960; Ingham State HS, 1961-63; Te Awamutu Coll, NZ, 1964-65; Writer, Rsch Off, Pt-time Lectr, Qld Hlth Educ Coun, 1966-67; Rsch Asst, Pt-time Tutor, Student Counselling Unit, Univ New England, 1967-69; Sr Tutor, 1970, Lectr, 1971-72, Sr Lectr, 1973-76, Ctr Urban Educ, La Trobe Univ, Vic; Assoc Prof, School Educ, 1977-81, Interschool Fellow, 1981, Assoc Prof, School Educ, 1982-86, Macquarie Univ, NSW; Prof, Fac Educ, Monash Univ, Vic, 1987-91; Pro-Vice-Chancellor, Rsch and Dev, Qld Univ Technology, Brisbane, 1991-. *Publications:* Num books, book chapts and jrnl contbns in field of education on areas of life span development (culture, context and life possibilities), language and cognition (class and cultural factors), policy research, general education. *Memberships:* Australian Rsch Coun, Humanities and Social Sci; Chr, Soc Sci, 1992; Australian Rsch Coun, 15 Yr Forward Strategy (Educ); Australian Coun Educl Rsch; Pro-Vice-Chancellor (Rsch) Nat Comm; Australian and NZ AAS; Australian Assn Rsch Educ; Australian Psychological Soc. *Honours:* Mackenzie Travelling Lectr'ship, NZ Coun EduclRsch, 1982; Affiliate Fac Mbr, Ctr Youth Dev and Rsch, Univ MN, USA, 1987; Fellowship, Australian Coll Educ, 1988; Fellow, Academy of Social Sciences, 1992. *Hobbies:* Theatre; Films; Art; Music; Bush walking; Beach walking; Swimming. *Address:* Queensland University of Technology, GPO Box 2434, Brisbane 4001, Australia.

POPE Nicholas, b. 1949, Sydney, New South Wales, Australia. Sculptor. *Education:* Bath Acad Art, England, 1970-73; Private study visit, Makonde Plateau, Tanzania, 1981. *Career:* Brit Coun Cultural Vis: Rumania, 1976, Zimbabwe, 1981; Brit Rep, C'wlth Games Symposium, Edmonton, CA, 1978; Australian Coun Cultural Vis, Australia, 1979; Arts Coun Selector, sculpture, Hayward Annual, 1979; Brit Rep, Brit Pavilion, Venice Biennale, 1980; Vis Lecturer, Art Colls and Univs, GB, Europe, N Am, Australia; 1-man exhibs: Garage Gall Ltd, London, 1976; City Portsmouth Mus and Art Gall, 1976; Anthony Stokes Gall Ltd, London, 1979; Art and Project, Amsterdam, 1979, 1981, 1984, 1985; Gall A, Sydney, 1979; Ray Hughes Gall, Brisbane, 1980; Rijksmus Kroller Muller, Netherlands, 1981; John Hansard Gall, Southampton, 1982; Galerij S65, Belgium, 1982, 1984, 1986; Waddington Galls, London, 1984, 1986; Participant, var grp exhibs, London and provinces, FRG, Italy, Netherlands, USA. *Creative works include:* Pub commns: The Large Arch, Portsmouth Mus and Art Gall, 1974; A Thin Water Sculpture, Shepshed Hindleys Coll, Leics, 1977; Four Odd Woods, Peter Simmonds Coll, Winchester, 1978; Three Wilderness Stones, Southampton Univ, 1980; Sun Life Stones, Sun Life Assurance Co, Bristol, 1980; Big Balls, Peterborough Dev Corp, 1982; Sculpture for Int Garden Fest, Liverpool, 1984; 5th Henry Moore Grand Prize Exhib, Japan, 1987; Works in var pub collections, England and abroad. *Honours:* Bursary, So Art Assn, 1974; Exchange Scholarship, Rumanian Govt, 1974-75. *Address:* Avenue Cottage, Much Marcle, Ledbury, Hertfordshire HR8 2NU, England.

POPIELA Tadeusz, b. 23 May 1933, Nowy Sacz, Poland. Professor of Medicine. m. Mieczyslawa Werner, 28 Oct 1955, 1 s, 1 d. *Education:* Med School, Cracow, 1950-55; Dip Physn; MD, 1961; Assoc Prof, 1965; Prof Med, 1972. *Appointments:* Rsch Asst, Dept Surg, 1955-65, Asst Prof, 1965-71, Hd, Surg Unit, Gastroenterology, III Dept and Clin, Gen Surg, Med School, Cracow; Hd,

I Dept, Gen and GI Surg, Med School, Cracow, 1976-. *Publications:* Books: Clinical Chemistry, 1982; Internal Diseases, 1983; Clinical and Operative Surgery, 1983; Clinical Gastroenterology, 1987; Gastric Cancer, 1987. *Memberships:* Polish Surg Assn; Polish Assn Gastroenterology; Am Gastroenterology Assn; CIOD; SIC; Int Acad Sci; NY Acad Scis; W German Assn Endoscopy; World Assn HPB; Int Gastro-Surg Club; EAGE. *Honours:* Hon Citizen, City of Minneapolis, MN, 1973; Hon Dip, Disting Achievement Award, Polish Med Alliance USA, 1976; Hon Citizen, City of Ft Worth, TX, 1979; Hon Mbr, Cybernetics Assn Poland, 1982. *Hobbies:* Travel. *Address:* ul Zulawskiego 5/8, 31-145 Cracow, Poland. 34, 52, 139, 158.

POPITZ Heinrich, b. 14 May 1925, Berlin, Germany. Professor of Sociology. m. Maria von Handel, 28 Aug 1958. *Education:* Dr phil, Univ Basel, 1949; Habilitation, Univ Freiburg, 1957. *Appointments:* Univ Tchr, 1957, o Prof, 1964-, Univ Freiburg; o Prof, Univ Basel, Switzerland, 1959; Theodor Heuss Prof, New School Social Rsch, NYC, NY. USA, 1971-72. *Publications:* Der entfremdete Mensch Zeitkritik und Gesch phil d jungen Marx, 1953, 1968, 1973, 1980, in Spanish, 1971, in Japanese, 1978; Das Gesellschaftsbild d Arbeiters, 1957, 1971, in Italian, 1960, in Engl, 1969; Technik und Industriearbeit, 1957, 1976; Die Ungleichheit d Chancen, 1964, 1965; Prozesse d Machtbildung, 1968, 1973; Der Begriff der sozialen Rolle, 1969, 1975, in Engl, 1972, in Japanese, 1987; Die normative Konstruktion von Gesellschaft, 1980; Phanomene der Macht, 1989, in Italian, 1991. *Membership:* Deutsche Gesellschaft fur Soziologie. *Hobbies:* Painting; Gardening. *Address:* Sonnhalde 117, D-7800 Freiburg, Germany. 34, 92.

POPKOV Yury Andronovich, b. 18 Nov 1937, USSR. Physicist; Professor. m. Zoya Ivanovna Shkurpila, 6 Sept 1963, 1 s. *Education:* MSc, Phys Dept, Kharkov Univ, 1959; Postgrad, Phys Tech Inst Low Temperatures, 1961-64; Cand Sci (equiv PhD), 1966; DSc, Calculus, 1978. *Appointments:* Rsch Fellow, Phys Tech Inst Low Temperatures, 1964-80; Prof, Kharkov State Univ, 1980-. *Publications:* Sci articles in magneto-optics of antiferromagnets, phase transitions in magnetics, ferroelectrics, ferroeleastics, magnetic properties of spin glass systems. *Memberships:* A few assns of Solid State Phys, Magnetism and Optics, USSR. *Hobbies:* Sport; Tourism; Gardening; Numismatics. *Address:* Lenin Ave 63, Apt 36, Kharkov 310164, Ukraine.

POPLAWSKI Aleksander, b. 4 Jan 1937, Bialystok, Poland. Physician; Professor of Nephrology. m. Tamara Fiedoruk, 25 June 1963, 1 s. *Education:* Med School, 1955-61; MD, 1963; Internal Med Specialisation I, 1964, II, 1969; Asst Prof, 1981; Nephrology Specialisation, 1987; Prof, 1992. *Appointments:* Biochem Dept, 1961-71, Dialysis Ctr, 1971-81, Nephrology Dept, 1981-, Med School, Bialystok. *Publications:* Influence of plasmin on the clotting and anticlearing activities of platelets (w S Niewarowski and J Prokopowicz), 1963; Inhibition of dog fibrinolytic system in experimental tubular necrosis in kidney (w S Niewiarowski, J Prokopowicz, K Worowski), 1964; Neutralization of antithrombin VI (fibrogen breakdown products) with platelet antiheparin factor (platelet factor 4) (w S Niewiarowski and R Farbiszewski), 1965; Purification and separation on platelet factor 2 (fibrinogen activating factor) and of platelet factor 4 (antiheparin factor) (w K Farbiszewski and S Niewiarowski), 1966; Thrombotoc disease in gynaecology and obstetrics (w J Bar-Pratkowska and S Niewiarowski), 1967; The release of platelet factor 4 during platelet aggregation and the possible significance of this reaction in hemostasis (w S Niewiarowski, B Lipinski, R Farbiszewski), 1968; The effect of angiotensin II on the platelet aggregation induced by adenosine-diphosphate, epinephrine and thrombin, 1970; The effect of vitamin C on heparin activitiy, 1973; The effect of heparin on fibrinolysis in chronically haemodialyzed uraemic patients (w J Chmielewska), 1976; The effect on fibrinolytic activity of chromatographic fractions of blood ultrafiltrates of uraemic patients (w M Mysliwiec and J Soszka), 1990. *Memberships:* Polish Soc Physns; Polish Nephrological Soc. *Honours:* IIIrd Award (individual), 1964, IInd (collective), 1976, Ist, 1968, 1991, Polish Min Hlth and Welfare; Golden Cross of Merit; Excellent Work in Hlth Serv Award; Meritorious Award, Bialystok, Lomza and Suwalki Provinces. *Hobby:* Tourism. *Address:* Rysia 1, 15-540 Bialystok, Poland.

POPNEDELEV Vihroni, b. 1 Mar 1953, Plovdiv, Bulgaria. Artist. m. Adelina Popnedeleva, 14 Apr 1976, 2 d. *Education:* School Arts, 1967-71; Nat Acad Arts, 1972-78. *Career:* Tchr, School Arts, 1979, 1988; Lectr, 1989-90, Sr Lectr, 1991, Nat Acad Arts; 1-man shows, paintings: Bulgaria, 1981, 1984, 1985, 1987, 1989, 1990; Poland, 1984; Participant, gen art shows: France, 1987; Nottingham, London, England, 1990; Iserlohn, Haltern, Germany, 1991. *Membership:* Bulgarian Assn Artists. *Honours:* Nat Prize for Young Artists, 1979; Nat Prize, 1979; 1st Prize, Spring Exhib, Bulgaria, 1984; 1st Prize, Painting, Artists Union Exhib, 1985. *Hobbies:* Gardening; Cooking. *Address:* ssa 00Blok No 2, Zone B5, Vhod B, 1303 Sofia, Bulgaria.

POPOV Alexander, b. 13 Mar 1957, St Petersburg, Russia. Composer; Doctor. m. Polina Mograchova, 26 July 1986. *Education:* Dips: Dr, Med Inst, 1980; Composer, St Petersburg Conservatory, 1984. *Career includes:* Represented: Int Fests Young Composers Music, St Petersburg, 1989, 1991; Musical Spring 92 Int Fest, St Petersburg, Apr 1992. *Creative works include:* 4 piano sonatas, 1974-79; Sonata for cello solo, 1983; Passion, concerto for French horn, organ and percussion, 1983; The Top, cantata for chorus, 2 pianos and percussion, 1984; The Landshaft, for 6 instruments, 1984; Concerto for Flute and Orchestra, 1985; Symphony, 1986; Piano Quintet, 1987; ARBOR I for 6 French horns, 1988; ARBOR II for 10 instruments, 1988; Musical Frescoes, About Life and Death, for soprano and orchestra, 1988; Requiem, 1989. *Membership:* Composers Union. *Honours:* 1st Prize, Competition for Best Polyphonic Work, St Petersburg, 1987. *Hobbies:* Drawing; House-plant growing; Reading. *Address:* ul Pravdy 4-3, 191126 St Petersburg, Russia.

POPOV Chavdar, b. 26 Apr 1950, Sofia, Bulgaria. Art Historian; Art Critic. m. Snejana Popova, 16 Aug 1980, 2 s. *Education:* Grad, Hist and Theory of Fine Arts, Dept Hist Art, Moscow Univ, 1974; PhD, Art Hist, 1988. *Appointments:* Curator, Chief, Dept Mod Art, Nat Art Gall, 1976- 80; Rsch Assoc, 1981-92, Sr Rsch Assoc, 1992-, Inst Art Studies, Bulgarian Acad Scis. *Publications:* Contemporary Bulgarian Painting in the National Art Gallery, 1980; Bulgarian Painting 1878-1978, 1981. *Memberships:* Union Bulgarian Artists; AICA, Paris; Soc Europeenne de Culture, Venice. *Hobbies:* Classical music; Tourism. *Address:* 16 Janko Sakazov Blvd, 1504 Sofia, Bulgaria.

POPOV Theodor, b. 11 Dec 1955, Sofia, Bulgaria. Dance Critic; Journalist; Dance Manager; Interpreter. m. Antonia Zaharieva, 1 Oct 1989. *Education:* Licencie, Linguistics, Alger Univ, 1977. Dipl phil, Germany Philology, St Kliment Ohridski, Sofia Univ, 1981; Dipl ped, Music, St N Rilski Blagoevgrad Univ, 1985. *Appointments:* Ed: Sofiiska pravda newspaper, 1982-83; Kostinbrodska zvezda newspaper, 1984-85; Chief Ed: Srednogorska iskra newspaper, 1986-87; Ustram newspaper, 1988-89; Mladezhko zemedelsko zname newspaper, 1990-; Corresp, Das Tanzerchiv ballet jrnl, Sofia. *Publications:* Meetings-interviews with dance and ballet workers, 1987; From Kitri to Juliet and Esmeralda, 1990; Articles in Ballet Encyclopaedia of USSR, 1981- . *Membership:* Union Bulgarian Jrnlsts. *Hobbies:* Opera; World political life; Religion; Loving dogs and having 2. *Address:* Tzar Assen Str 7, Sofia, Bulgaria.

POPPER Karl (Raimund), Sir, b. 28 July 1902, Vienna, Austria. Author; Emeritus Professor. *Education:* PhD, Univ Vienna, 1928; MA, Univ NZ, 1937; DLit, Univ

London, 1947. *Appointments:* Sr Lectr, Philos, Univ NZ, 1937-45; Reader, Logic, Sci Method, 1945-50, Prof, Logic, Sci Method, 1949-69, Emeritus Prof, 1969-, Univ London, England. *Publications include:* Logik der Forschung, 1934; The Open Society and Its Enemies, 1945, 15th Impr, 1986; The Poverty of Historicism, 1957, 12th Impr, 1987; Conjectures and Refutations, 1963, 10th Impr, 1989; Objective Knowledge, 1963, 10th Impr, 1986. *Memberships include:* FRS; Fellow, Brit Acad; Inst de France; Assoc Mbr, Acad Royale de Belgique; Socio Straniero, Accademia Nazionale dei Lincei; For Hon Mbr, Am Acad Arts and Scis; For Assoc, Nat Acad Scis USA; Hon Mbr, Austrian Acad Scis. *Honours include:* Knighthood; Companion of Hon; Gold Medal, disting servs to sci, Am Mus Natural Hist, NYC; Sonning Prize, merit in work furthering European Civilisation, Univ Copenhagen; 1st Catalonia Prize; Gorsses Verdienstkreuz mit Stern under Schulterband, FRG; Order of Merit, FRG; 16 hon docts, univs UK, USA, Austria, Germany, NZ, Can. *Hobby:* c/o The London School of Economics, University of London, Houghton Street, Aldwych, London WC2A, England.

POPPLE Richard Thomas, b. 26 Jan 1931, Boston, Lincolnshire, England. Consultant; Chairman and Managing Director. m. Audrey Rosalyn Swift, 24 Aug 1950, 2 s, 2 d. *Education:* RAF Staff Coll; Assoc, 1975, Choirmaster Dip, 1978, Royal Coll Organists. *Appointments:* RAF Off, 1952-78; Served UK and Middle East; Wing Cmdr, 1976; Sr Personnel appts: W Midlands Co Coun, 1978, W Midlands Passenger Transport Exec, 1979-85; Mgmt Cons, 1986-; Currently Chmn, Mng Dir, Fulcrum Mgmt Cons Ltd. *Publications:* Regular contbr and Mng Ed, Organists Review. *Memberships:* Inc Assn Organists, Hon Gen Treas 1982-89, Hon Gen Sec 1988- ; Royal School Ch Music, Chmn Birmingham Area; Fellow, Inst Personnel Mgmt, 1984, Vice-Chmn Hereford and Worcester Br 1990-92, Chmn, Hereford and Worcester Br, 1992-94; Fellow, Inst Dirs; Inst Mgmt Cons, Treas, Midlands Reg, 1991-. *Honours:* MBE, New Yr Hons, 1976. *Hobby:* Church and organ music. *Address:* 24 Hither Green, Abbey Park, Redditch, Worcestershire B98 9BW, England.

PORNBACHER Johann Nep Karl Victor, b. 2 May 1929, Schongau, Lech, Germany. Professor Emeritus. m. Irmtraud Lumpp, 2 May 1959, 1 s, 1 d. *Education:* Staatsexamen, Munich, 1957; PhD, Frankfurt/Main, 1963. *Appointments:* Asst, Univ Frankfurt, 1961; Full Prof, Cath Univ, Nijmegen, Netherlands, 1967. *Publications:* Bayer Bibliothek, vols I- III, 1978-90; Literatur in Bayer Schwaben, 1979; Spielmannsepik I, 1984. *Membership:* Bayer Benediktinerakademie. *Honours:* Oberbayer Kulturpreis. *Hobbies:* History of art; Theology. *Address:* Holz 3, D-8121 Wildsteig (Bavaria), Germany. 43, 52.

PORTEOUS Christopher Selwyn, b. 11 Nov 1935, London, England. Solicitor. m. Brenda Jacqueline Wallis, 27 Feb 1960, 4 d. *Education:* Law Soc School Law, 1955-59; Admitted as Solicitor, Supreme Ct, 1960. *Appointments:* London Co Coun, 1960-62; Legal Asst, 1962-68, Sr Legal Asst, 1968-76, Asst Solicitor, 1976-87, Solicitor to Commnr of Police of the Metropolis, 1987-, New Scotland Yard, London. *Publications:* Articles in legal mags; Hymns in mod hymn books; Seeing and Serving Christ, local hist; Sing Me A Song, children's book. *Memberships:* Law Soc; Former Mbr, Rochester Diocesan Pastoral Comm; Anglican Reader, 1959-. *Hobbies:* Writing; Gardening; Poetry; Listening to classical music. *Address:* c/o The Solicitor, New Scotland Yard, Broadway, London SW1H 0BG, England. 1.

PORTER Arthur, b. 8 Dec 1910, Ulverston, Cumbria, England. Professor Emeritus. m. P Patricia Dixon, 26 July 1941, 1 s. *Education:* BSc (Hons), 1933, MSc, 1934, PhD, 1936, Univ Manchester; C'wealth Fund Fellow, MIT, USA, 1937-39. *Appointments:* Sci Off, Admiralty, 1939-45; Prof, Inst Technology, Royal Mil Coll Sci, 1946; Dir Rsch, Ferranti Ltd, 1949; Prof, Elec Engrng, Imperial

Coll, London, 1955; Dean, Engrng, Univ Sask, Can, 1958; Prof, Indl Engrng, 1961, currently Prof Emeritus, Univ Toronto; Chmn, Royal Commn on Elec Power Planning, 1975. *Publications:* Introduction to Servomechanisms, 1949; Cybernetics Simplified, 1962; Towards a Community University, 1971. *Memberships:* Fellow, Instn Elec Engrs; Pres, Can Operational Rsch Soc. *Honours:* Fellow, Royal Soc Can, 1970; Off, Order Can, 1983; Fndr Fellow, Can Acad Engrng, 1988. *Hobbies:* Tennis; Travel; Reading. *Address:* 78 Green Briar Rd, Alliston, Ontario, Canada L0M 1A0. 1, 2, 88.

PORTER Joshua Roy, b. 7 May 1921, Godley, Cheshire, England. Professor of Theology Emeritus. *Education:* BA Mod Hist, Class 1, Merton Coll, Oxford, 1942; BA Theology, Class I, St Stephen's House, Oxford, 1944; MA, Univ Oxford, 1948. *Appointments:* Curate, St Mary's, Portsea, 1945-47; Resident Chaplain to Bishop of Chichester, 1947-49; Fellow, Chaplain, Tutor, Univ Lectr, Oriel Coll, Oxford, 1949-62; Prof, Hd, Dept Theology, Univ Exeter, 1962-86; Lectr, Old Testament Studies, Holyrood Sem, NYC, USA, 1987-. *Publications:* World in the Heart, 1944; Moses and Monarchy, 1963; The Extended Family in the Old Testament, 1967; Proclamation and Presence, 1970, Revised Ed, 1983; The Non-Juring Bishops, 1973; Leviticus, 1976, Japanese Ed, 1984; Animals in Folklore, 1978; The Crown and the Church, 1978; Translator, The Living Psalms (C Westermann), 1989. *Contributions to:* Num learned jrnls and dictionaries. *Memberships:* Proctor in Canterbury Convocation and Mbr, Gen Synod, 1964-90, Panel of Chmn, 1984-86; Hon Mbr, Folklore Soc, Pres 1976-79, Vice-Chmn 1987-90; Soc Old Testament Study, Pres 1983; Pres, Anglican Assn; Vice-Chmn, Prayer Book Soc; Fellow, Ancient Monuments Soc; World Congress Jewish Studies. *Honours:* Liddon Student, 1942; Kennicott Hebrew Fellow, 1955; Sr Denyer and Johnson Scholar, 1958; Canon and Prebendary of Wightring and Theological Lectr, 1965-88, Wiccamical Canon and Prebendary of Exceit, 1988-, Chichester Cathedral; Vis Prof, SEn Sem, NC, USA, 1967; Dean, Arts, Exeter Univ, 1968-71; Ethel M Wood Lectr, 1979; Michael Harrah Wood Lectr, 1984; Examining Chaplain to Bishop of London, 1981-91, to Bishop of Gibraltar in Europe, 1989-. *Hobbies:* Theatre; Opera; Book-collecting; Travel. *Address:* 36 Theberton Street, Barnsbury, London N1 0QX, England. 1, 3, 43, 118.

PORTFORS Sven Hakan, b. 29 May 1931, Vasa, Finland. Actor. m. Solveig Retti, 28 Apr 1962, 1 s, 1 d. *Education:* Theatre School, The Swedish Theatre, Helsingfors, 1948-50; Studies in Pars, London, Berlin. *Career:* Lilla Teatern, Helsingfors, 1950-52; Wasa Teater, Vasa, 1952- 53; Svenska Teatern, Helsingfors, 1953-; Has appeared in over 150 plays incl: My Fair Lady, 1958; How to Succeed in Business, 1964; Im weissen Rossel, 1967; Anatol, 1972; Ah, Wilderness, 1975; The Little Foxes, 1982; Played Fagin, in Oliver; Radio and TV roles; Producer, 5 musical shows, 1975-90. *Membership:* Odd Fellows. *Honours:* Scholarship, State of Finland, 1968; Honoured by Ctrl Assn, The Finnish Theatre Orgs, 1976, 1990; Honoured by The Swedish Theatre, Helsingfors, 1990. *Hobby:* Piano playing. *Address:* Norra Jarnvagsgatan 17 B 17, 00100 Helsingfors, Finland.

PORTSMOUTH Owen Henry Donald, b. 24 May 1929, Swansea, Wales. Consultant Physician. m. (1) Moira Heloise Sinclair, 18 Sept 1954, dec. 1979, (2) Glennis Cook, 3 Jan 1981, 3 s, 1 d, 1 stepdaughter. *Education:* St Thomas's Hosp Med School, 1947-53; MB, BS, London, 1953; FRCP, London; FRCP, Edinburgh; DTM and H. *Appointments:* Med Specialist, Kenya med Serv, 1956-66; Cons Physn, Geriatric Med, E Birmingham Hosp, England, 1966-; Sr Clin Lectr, Univ Birmingham, 1969-; Dir W Midland Inst Geriatric Med, 1975-; Vice-Chmn, Solihull Hlth Auth, 1984-90. *Publications:* Articles in med jrnls. *Honours:* Erle K Dawson Mem Lectr, Queen's Univ, Kingston, Ontario, Can, 1984. *Hobbies:* Medical ethics; Heraldry; History; Architecture;

Foreign travel. *Address:* East Birmingham Hospital, Yardley Green Road, Birmingham B9 5PX, England. 170.

PORUMB Marius, b. 9 Oct 1943, Grozesti, Rumania. Art Historian. m. Zoe Vida Porumb, 3 Aug 1974. *Education:* Grad, Fac Hist, 1966, Dr Hist Art, 1973, Univ Cluj. *Appointments:* Inst Hist and Archaeology, Cluj-Napoca, 1966-; Dpty Dir, Inst Archaeology and Hist Art, Cluj-Napoca. *Publications:* Bisericile din Feleac si Vad doua ctitorii Moldovenesti din Transilvania, 1968; Icoane din Maramures - Ikonen aud der Maramures, 1975; Pictura Romaneasca din Transilvania - Die rumanische Malerei in Siebenburgen, vol I, 1981; Studii de istorie a artei (co-author), 1982; Monumente istorice si de arta religioasa din Arhiepiscopia Vadului, Feleacului si Clujului, 1982; 56 studies and articles; Reviews, essays, dissertations. *Memberships:* VP, Commn Histl Monuments Transylvania; Exec Comm, Histns Assn, Transylvania; Exec Comm, Histns Assn, Banat; Nat Comm Museums; Magna Grecia Inst Hist, Taranto, Italy; Exec Comm, Eurocerc, Italy-Rumania; Chief Ed, Ars Transilvaniae. *Hobbies:* Art collecting; Listening to sacred songs; Reading; Travel. *Address:* Str Padis No 3, sc 2, ap 22, 3400 Cluj-Napoca, Romania.

POSADAS Martin, b. 11 Nov 1921, San Carlos, Pangasin, Philippines. Physician; Educator. m. Rosalina Quebral-Posadas, 14 Feb 1950, 1 d. *Education:* BA, Univ Philippines, 1942; MD, Univ Santa Tomas, 1949; Postgrad trng, Pangasin Provincial Med Ctr, 1950; St Luke's Med Ctr, 1953; Quezon Inst, 1958; Dev Acad Philippines, 1975; Mgmt, Career Tract Int. *Appointments:* Started Posadas Medico-Dental Clin, 1952; Pres, Fndr: Virgon Milagrosa Educl Instn; No Philippines Inst Med Fndn; Plaza View Hotel and Restaurant; San Carlos Press and Publrs; Palaris Radio Broadcasting Station Inc; Chmbr of Comm and Ind. *Creative works:* Textbooks for midwives; Textbooks on pharmacology and micro-biology for nurses; English-Pangasinan Dialect Dictionary; Art works: Anatomical models and phys structure models. *Memberships:* Past Pres, Pangasinan Med Soc; Past Pres, Philippine Hosp Assn; Sr Exec, Past Pres, Jaycees; Faithful Navigator, Past Grand Kt, Past Dist Dpty, Kts of Columbus; Pres, Chmbr Comm and Ind; Pes, Histl and Cultural Fdnd. *Honours:* Outstanding Jaycee, 1965; Outstanding Physn of Philippines, 1966; Papal Awardee, 1970; Outstanding Educator, 1978; JCI Senator, 1979; Mbr, NY Acad Scis, 1985; Outstanding Citizen in the Rural Areas; Diners Book Award. *Hobbies:* Inventions; Sciences. *Address:* Virgen Milagrosa Educational Institutions Inc, Taloy District, San Carlos City, Pangasinan, Philippines 2420. 52, 139, 191.

POSER Hans August Louis, b. 13 Mar 1907, Hanover, Germany. Professor Emeritus; Geography Educator. m. 29 July 1933, Johanna von Stiepel, 3 s. *Education:* Geog, Geology, Ethnology, Hist; Dr phil, 1930, Dr phil habil, 1935, Univ Gottingen. *Appointments:* Asst, Lectr, 1930-41, Prof, Dir, 1962-71, Prof Emeritus, 1971-, Geog Inst, Univ Gottingen; Lectr, Asst Prof, Hd, Geog Inst, 1941-55, Mbr, Senate, 1954-55, Tech Univ Brunswick; Prof, Dir, Geog Inst, 1955-62, Dean, Fac Natural Sci and Humanities, 1957-68, Mbr, Senate, 1957-62, Tech Univ Hanover. *Publications:* Untersuchungen zur Morphologie Ost Gronlands, 1932; Morphologische Studien aus dem Meissner-Gebiet, 1933; Geographische Studien uber den Fremdenverkehr im Riesengebirger, 1939; Briefwechsel zwischen G F Gauss und E A W von Zimmermann, 1987; Num publs on geomorphology, climatology of ice age, human geography, regional geography (Central Europe, Mediterranean region, Arctic, Madagascar), 1930-; Ed and co-ed, 48 geog books. *Memberships:* German Acad Scis Leopoldina; Acad Scis, Gottingen; Corres Mbr: Acad Area Rsch and Planning; Geogl Soc Hanover, Pres 1955-62; Austrian Geogl Soc; Geogl Soc Finland; Geological Soc Belgium; Hon Mbr: Geogl Soc Hamburg; Geogr Soc Brunswick; C F Gauss Soc. *Honours:* Bronze Medal, Univ Liege, 1958; Carl Ritter Silver Medal, Gesellschaft fur Erdkunde, Berlin, 1963; Bronze Medal, Univ Helsinki, 1964, 1968; Ferdinand von Richthofen Gold Medal,

1972; Gustav Heinrich Kirchenhauer Silver Medal, Geogl Soc Hamburg, 1972; Albrecht Penck Medal German Soc Quarternaary Rsch, 1992; Hans-Poser Festschrift in his hon, 1972; Cross of Merit w band, Germany, 1982; Dr rer nat hc, Tech Univ Brunswick, 1986. *Hobbies:* Research; Reading; Collecting graphic art. *Address:* Charlottenburger Str 19, D-3400 Gottingen, Germany. 52, 92, 139.

POSER Wolfgang Edgar, b. 28 Feb 1941, Stolberg/ Harz. Associate Professor of Clinical Pharmacology. m. Sigrid Wahl, 28 Feb 1970, 1 s, 1 d. *Education:* Study of Med, 1960-66; MD, 1967; Physn, 1968; Habilitation, 1974; Prof, Pharmacology, 1978. *Appointments:* Army Serv, 1967; Clin Pharmacology Specialist, Addictions, Psych Univ Hosp, Gottingen. *Publications:* Num on all forms of addiction (prescription drugs, alcoholism, illegal drugs). *Address:* Psychiatric University Hospital of Gottingen, V Sieboldt str 5, D-3400 Gottingen, Germany.

POSINOVEC Jasminka, b. 8 Mar 1926, Zemunik-Zadar, Croatia. Retired Professor. m. Vladimir Posinovec, 13 Sept 1949, 1 s. *Education:* Grad, Med Fac, Zagreb, 1954; Scholarship, Nat Ctr Sci Rsch, Genoa, 1st Anatomia umania normale, 1963; French For Off Scholarship, Nat Ctr Sci Rsch INRA, Nouzilly and Necker Hosp, Paris, 1976. *Appointments:* Asst, 1955-65, Asst Prof, 1965-69, Assoc Prof, 1969-75, Hd, 1972-79, Full Prof, 1975-90, Inst Histology and Embryology, Med Fac, Zagreb; Vice-Dean, Tchng, Med Fac Zagreb, 1978-80; Retired, 1991. *Publications:* Textbooks; Bibliographies; Chaps in books; Num Sci works, papers, congresses, sympoosia. *Memberships:* Anatomical Assn, Yugoslavia; Croatian Med Acad, Mbr Presidency 1980-83; Croatian Med Assn, 1st Pres Sect Normal Morphology to 1977; Edit Bd, Lijecnicki vjesnik . *Honours:* Several dips, Med Fac, Zagreb, 1968, 1975, 1976, 1985, 1987; Dip, European Sterility Congress Org, 1969; Medal, City of Zagreb, 1970; Pavao Culumovic Award, 1974; Order of Work w Golden Wreath, Pres Yugoslavia, 1978. *Hobbies:* Music; Sculpture; Reading. *Address:* Goljak 46, 41000 Zagreb, Croatia. 52, 138, 152.

POTAMITIS Demetrios, b. 18 Mar 1944, Cyprus. Actor; Director; Writer. *Education:* Dip, Theatrical Studies, Dramatic School, Nat Theatre Greece, 1965; Philology, Univ Athens. *Career:* Debut, Eumylus in Alkestes (Euripides), Epidaurus theatre, Nat Theatre Greece; Num important roles, plays by Rattigan, Strindberg, mod Greek writers; Leading actor, Proscenium Theatre, 1967-70; Appearances incl As If Five Year Past (Lorca), The Bed Bug (Mayakofsky), Malade Imaginaire (Moliere), Thesmofotiazouses (Aristophanes), The Good Fellow of Setzuan (Brecht), Oh, Dad, Poor Dad, Mama's Hung You in the Closet and I'm Feeling So Sad (Kopit), Fndr, Rsch Theatre Athens (expmtl w co for adults, co for children), Ano Ilissia, 1973; Star and Dir, over 40 plays incl Equus (Shaffer), The Elephant Man (Pomerange), Scapen (Moliere), The Portrait of Dorian Gray (Wilde), Metamorphosis (Kafka), The Clockwork Orange (Burgess), Lents (Bychner), Torch Song Trilogy (Ferstein), 1973-; Dir, var plays incl: Collage, based on 7 ancient tragedies of Aeschylus, Sophocles and Euripides, 1979; My Fair Lady; Cabaret; Gone with the Wind; Played main role in Orestes (Euripides) in Epidaurus ancient theatre, 1989. *Creative works include:* Collections of poems: Symposium; The Migration of Angels; The Ancient Saxophone; A tree which thinks it's a bird; The Alter Demetrios; The Core Poems; 6 plays: The gobbling of the little Red Riding Hood; The last adventures of Adam and Eve; The leash of Socrates; The upside down Tales; The Alibi; Tales of Grandar Aristophanes; Tranls, Engl and Am plays. *Memberships:* Greek Soc Writers; Int Org Children's Theatre; Int Ctr Theatre. *Honours:* Kozjou Award, Best Actor of Yr, 1984; Hon Award, contbn to Greek theatre, Mayor of Zograjou. *Hobbies:* Gardening; Swimming. *Address:* Pontou 18, Athens 11528, Greece.

POTAPOV Vsevolod, b. 11 Mar 1964, Bucharest, Rumania. Linguist. *Education:* Student, 1981-86, Postgrad student, 1986-89, Moscow State Lomonosov Univ, Moscow; Thesis, 1990. *Appointments:* Sci Researcher, Moscow State Lonomosov Univ, Russia, 1986-90; Sci Researcher, Inst Linguistics, Russian Acad Scis, 1990-. *Publications:* 55 articles; Rhythm of Prose in Slavonic Languages, in press. *Hobby:* Art (painting). *Address:* Leningradskoje sosse, d 112/1, korp 3, kw 609, 125445 Moscow, Russia.

POTTER J(effrey) Stewart, b. 8 July 1943, Fort Worth, Texas, USA. General Manager, Property Management. m. 31 Dec 1970, 1 s. *Education:* AA, San Diego Mesa Coll, 1967; San Diego State Coll; Cand Certification Property Supvsr, Stewart NAA Deck, 1962; Cert Apt Mgr, NAA, 1988; Merchant Marine Z Card Eng. *Appointments:* Scripps Inst Oceanography, 1961-63; Advt Mgr, Student Instr, Advt Dept, Mesa Coll, CA, 1964-67; Advt Mgr, Disc Jockey, Radio Station KJLM, La Jolla, CA, 1965-67; Cost Acct, Zellerback Paper Co, 1966-67; Mgr, Inflight Catering, Host Int, San Diego, CA, 1967-69; Lead Aircraft Refueller, Lockheed Co, San Diego, 1969-70; Mgr, Property, Int Dev and Fin Corp, La Jolla, 1970-72; Mgr, Bus Property, BWY Constrn CoSan Diego, 1972-73; Mgr, Residents, Coldwell Banker, San Diego, 1973-74; Mgr, Grove Investments, Carlsbad, CA, 1974-76; Mgr, Villa Granada, Villa Seville Properties Ltd, Don Cohn, Chula Vista, CA, 1976-83; Gen Mrg, AFL-DIO Bldg Trades Corp, National City, CA, 1983-. *Memberships:* Nat City Chmbr of Comm; Toastmasters; Fndng Families San Diego Histl Soc (6th Generation San Diego); Lajolla Monday Night Club, Treas 1984-89. *Hobbies:* Golf; Tennis; Cards (gin, cribbage); Backgammon; Motor boating; Skiing; Reading. *Address:* 4616 Granger Street, San Diego, CA 92107, USA. 2, 9.

POTURLJAN Artin Bedros, b. 4 May 1943, Kharmanli, Bulgaria. Composer; Teacher of Polyphony. m. Anahid Aram Akopjan, 28 June 1974, 2 s. *Education:* Grad, Musical Pedagogy speciality, Theoretical Fac, State Acad Music, Sofia, 1967; Composition speciality, Yerevan State Conswervatoire Komitas, 1974. *Career:* Tchr, Polyphony, State Musical Acad, Sofia; 1st perfs of compositions, Yerevan, Moscow, Tbilisi, 1970-74; Perfs, Symphs Nos 1 and 2, Sofia, 1976, 1978; Regular appearances in New Bulgarian Music, 1980-91; Own recitals of chmbr compositions, Yerevan, Armenia, 1987, Sofia, 1991. *Creative works:* Compositions incl: Concerto for Violin and Symph Orch; Music for 3 flutes, 2 pianos, tam-tam and strings; Klavier-Quintet; Sonata for Violin and Piano; 4 spiritual songs on Themes by Nerses Shanorhali, for organ; Fantasia, Worlds for 2 pianos. *Membership:* Bulgarian Composers Union. *Honours:* Prize for Arabesques, 1983, for Violin Concerto, 1989, Bulgarian Composers Union; 1st Prize for Music in memory of Evariste Galois for small symph orch, Pazardjik Composition Competition, 1985. *Hobbies:* Chess; Bulgarian Composers Union and Bulgarian Section of ISCM. *Address:* Iztok, Bl 4, vch B, 1113 Sofia, Bulgaria. 4.

POTVON Jean-Albert, b. 8 Mar 1915, St Boniface, Manitoba, Canada. Priest. *Education:* Ottawa; Scis, Institut Catholique, Paris, Philos, Theology, Rome, 4 yrs; Dips, Philos, Theology; Ordained Priest, Ottawa, 1937. *Appointments:* Taught Sci, Apologetics, Philosophical Dissertation, other subjects, Seminaire St Joseph de Mont-Laurier, 10 yrs; Curate, 3 or 4 parishes incl Ste Anne du Lac, Nominingue, Lac des Seize Iles, Lac Marois; Almoner, Accueil Vert, Pre d'Huberdeau; Currently retired, also tchng, Commn Scolaire des Laurentides, St Jovite, Val David, Ste-Agathe and St Donat; Guide, Advsr, several youth grps and adult educ, incl field trips studying nature, esp fungi. *Contributions to:* num sci mags incl Le Naturaliste (Cercle des Jeunes Naturalistes), Le Mycologue, Trail and Landscape. *Memberships incl:* Past Pres, Montreal Mycological Soc; Past Dir, Quebec Young Naturalists Club; Fndng Mbr, Can Nature Fedn; Fndng Mbr, Quebec 4H Clubs; Fndng Mbr, Les Amis du Jardin Botanique de Montreal; Club

Ornithologique des Hautes; Ldr, nature groups incl bird watchers and mycologists; Past Dir, Soc d'Histoire des Pays d'en Haut; Past Dir, Soc Genealogique des Laurentides; Nat Wildlife Soc; Interprovincial Conservation Club; Ottawa Field-Naturalists Club. *Honours:* Hon Mbr, Montreal Mycological Soc. *Address:* POB 149, Huberdeau, Prov Quebec, Canada J0T 1G0.

POUNDER Derrick John, b. 25 Feb 1949, Rhondda, Wales. Professor of Forensic Medicine. m. Georgina Kelly, 28 Nov 1975, 1 s, 2 d. *Education:* MB, ChB, Birmingham, 1973; FRCPA, 1980; FFPathRCPI, 1984; FCAP, 1985; MRCPath, 1986. *Appointments:* Clin Sr Lectr, Univ Adelaide and Specialist Pathologist, Inst Med and Vet Sci, S Australia, 1980-85; Dpty Chief Med Examiner, Edmonton and Associate Prof, Univs Alta and Calgary, Can, 1985- 87; Prof, Forensic Med, Dundee, Scotland, 1987-. *Memberships:* Physns for Human Rights, Chmn 1990-; Life Gov, Royal Nat Lifeboat Inst; Life Mbr, Nat Trust Scotland. *Honours:* Freeman, Llantrisant. *Hobbies:* Photography; Medieval architecture; Almost-lost causes. *Address:* 12 Hill Street, Broughty Ferry, Dundee DD5 2JL, Scotland.

POWELL David Beynon, b. 9 Feb 1934, Loughor, Wales. Legal Director. div. *Education:* Christ's Coll, Cambridge; BA, 1957, LLB, 1958, MA, 1961, Cambridge Univ; Grad Fellow, LLM, Yale Law School, 1963; SMP 18, Harvard Bus School, 1982. *Appointments:* Nat Serv, Flying Off, RAF, 1952-54; Dpty Legal Advsr, BLMC Ltd, 1970-73; Dir, Legal Servs, BL plc (Brit Leyland), 1974-83; Grp Legal Dir, Midland Bank plc, 1984-91; Dir of Grp Legal Services, Guiness plc, 1992-. *Membership:* Law Soc England and Wales; Friend of Templeton College, Oxford. *Address:* 20c Randolph Crescent, London W9 1DR, England. 53.

POWELL Jane, b. 19 Jan 1957, Sheffield, England. Head of Physical Education; Teacher; International Hockey and Cricket Player. *Education:* BEd (Hons), Chelsea Coll Phys Educ, 1979; Adv Cricket Coach, 1989; Adv Hockey Coach, 1991. *Appointments:* The City School, Sheffield, 1979-84; The Chase HS, Malvern, Worcs, 1985-. *Memberships:* Christians in Sport; Assoc, Inst Leisure and Amenity Mgmt; Capt, Women's Cricket Assn, World Cup Organising Comm Mbr 1993; All-England Women's Hockey Assn. *Hobbies:* Cricket and Hockey: Mbr, 1979-, Capt, 1988-, England Women's Cricket Squad, Mbr, England under 23/Sr Hockey, 1976-80, Hockey Coach, Midlands under 21, Asst Coach, England under 21, England univs. *Address:* 24 Alicante Close, Malvern, Worcestershire WR14 2SH, England.

POWELL Neil Ashton, b. 11 Feb 1948, London, England. Writer; Editor. *Education:* BA II:1, Engl and Am Lit, 1969, MPhil, Engl Lit, 1971, Univ Warwick. *Appointments:* Engl Tchr, Kimbolton School, Huntingdon, 1971-74; Engl Tchr, 1974-78, Hd, Engl, 1978-86, St Christopher School, Letchworth; Bookshop Owner, Baldock Bookshop, 1986-90; Freelance Writer and Ed, 1990-. *Publications:* Suffolk Poems, 1975; At the Edge, 1977; Out of Time, 1979; Carpenters of Light, 1979; A Season of Calm Weather, 1982; Selected Poems of Fulke Greville (ed), 1990; True Colours: New and Selected Poems, 1991; Unreal City, 1992. *Memberships:* En Arts Assn; Poetry Soc; Soc Authors. *Honours:* Gregory Award, Soc Authors, 1969. *Address:* c/o Carcanet Press Limited, 208-212 Corn Exchange Buildings, Manchester M4 3BQ, England.

POWELL Trevor John David, b, 3 Feb 1948, Hamilton, Ontario, Canada. Archivist. m. Marian Jean McKillop, 1 May 1976. *Education:* BA, 1971, MA, 1980, Univ Sask, Regina. *Appointments:* Archivist, 1971-, Registrar, 1979-, Diocese of Qu'Appelle; Staff Archivist, 1973-80, Dir, 1980-86, Asst Provincial Archivist, 1986-87, Provincial Archivist, 1988-, Sask Archives Bd, Univ Regina, Regina; Archivist, Ecclesiastical Province of Rupert's Land, 1988-. *Publications:* Living faith: A Pictorial History of the Diocese of Qu'Appelle, 1884-

1984 (co-author), 1984; Var scholarly articles and book reviews relating to Sask hist and Anglican Ch hist. *Memberships:* Assn Can Archivists, Dir without Portfolio 1979-81; Sask Coun Archives, Sec 1987-88, 1990-; Soc Am Archivists; Can Histl Assn; C'wlth Archivists Assn; Advsry Coun, Sask Order of Merit. *Hobbies:* Reading; Music; Walking; Gardening. *Address:* 241 Orchard Crescent, Regina, Saskatchewan, Canada S4S 5B9. 142.

POWELL-SMITH Vincent, b. 28 Apr 1939, Westerham, Kent, England. m. (1) 2 children, (2) Martha Marilyn Du Barry, 4 Apr 1989. *Education:* LLB Hons, 1962, DipCom, 1963, LLM, 1968, Univ Birmingham; Int Fac Comp Law, Luxembourg; Int Islamic Univ Malaysia; Inns of Ct, 1962-64; Admitted Hon Soc Gray's Inn, 1963; FPhS, 1969; DLitt, 1971; FCIArb, 1977; MBAE, 1988; AIArba, 1992; Dip Sh LP, 1993. *Appointments include:* Law Lectr, De Montfort Univ, 1961-63; Lectr, Law, Univ Aston, 1968-75; Cons, 1968-85, incl: Sec, Steeplejacks Ind Trng Grp Assn, Sec, Nat Fedn Master Steeplejacks & Lightning Conductor Engrs, Registrar, Steeplejacks Registration Coun, 1969-79; Sec, Nat Fedn Demolition Contractors Ltd, Jt Sec, Demolition Ind Conciliation Bd, 1970-78; Sec, Norwich Union Grp Staff Assn, 1972-73; Jt Registrar, Demolition & Dismantling Ind Register, 1974-78; Fndr Sec, Inst Explosives Engrs, 1974-79; Vis Prof, Constrn Law, Technological Univ Malaysia, 1987-91; Prof, of Law, Univ Malaya, 1991-; Dir, Ctr Asian-Pacific Constrn Law, 1991-. *Publications include:* Horse and Stable Management, 1984; Building Contract Dictionary, 2nd Ed, 1985; Construction Law Reports, 29 vols, 1985-; Determination and Suspension of Construction Contracts, 1985; A Contractor's Guide to The JCT Standard Form of Building Contract (JCT 80), 2nd Ed, Building Contract Claims, 3rd Ed, The JCT Management Contract: A Practical Guide, 1988; Civil Engineering Contract Claims, The Building Regulations Explained and Illustrated, 8th Ed 1992, Construction Arbitrations-a Practicel Guide, A Building Contract Casebook, 2nd Ed, Building Contracts Compared and Tabulated, 2nd Ed, Engineering Contract Dictionary, 1989; Corres, Contract Jrnl, 1974-; Ed, Annual Surv Malaysian Law, 1991-; Gen Ed, Federated Statutes of Malaysia, 1992-. *Memberships include:* Former Deleg, European Demolition Assn; Past Vice-Chancellor, Order of Crown of Stuart; Coun, Chartered Inst Arbitrators, 1980-83; Freeman, City of London; Liveryman, Worshipful Co of Paviors. *Honours:* Gold Cross of Merit, Repub of Poland; Many chivalric orders. *Hobbies:* Portugal and the Portuguese; Heraldry; Field sports; Golf. *Address:* Faculty of Law, University of Malaya, 59100 Kuala Lumpur, Malaysia. 43, 52, 139, 151, 154.

POWER Michael Charles, b. 31 Dec 1935, Lamberhurst, Kent, England. Market Research Consultant. m. (1) Margaret Katharine Dene, 6 Oct 1962, div. 1974, (2) Ann Genevieve Just, 1 July 1976, 1 s, 2 d. *Education:* Lincoln Coll, Oxford, 1956-59; BA 2nd Class Hons, Mod Hist, 1959; MA (Oxon). *Appointments:* Advt, J Walter Thompson Co Ltd, London, 1959-63; Tobacco Mktng, W D & H O Wills, Bristol, 1964-68; Engrng Mkt Rsch, Stothert & Pitt, Bath, 1969-71; Dir, Power Rsch Assocs, 1971-. *Publications:* Annual Statistical Studies of UK Franchising, 1984-. *Memberships:* Inst Dirs; Mkt Rsch Soc; Mktng Soc; Hon Soc of Inner Temple. *Honours:* Hutchins Scholar, Hist, Lincoln Coll, Oxford, 1953. *Hobbies:* Art; Music; Literature; Travel; Gardening; History; Philosophy and religion. *Address:* Lizard Farm Cottage, Foulsham, Dereham, Norfolk NR20 5RN, England. 146.

POZDEEVA Irina, b. 1 Feb 1934, t Volokolamsk, Russia. Historian of Russian Culture, Church and Books. m. V G Kisunko, 4 Apr 1964, 1 s. *Education:* Student, 1950-55, Postgrad, 1955-87, Dr Hist, 1962, Sr Rsch Worker, 1977, Fac Hist, Moscow State Univ. *Appointments:* Main Libb, Dept Rare Books and Manuscripts, 1957-71, Chief, Archaeographical Rsch, 1966-, Sr Rsch Worker, 1971-91, Chief, Archaeographical Lab, 1991-, Moscow State Univ. *Publications:* Author or co-author, 8 books, many articles and booklets. *Memberships:* Soc Protection

Mems of Hist and Culture; Archaeographical Commn USSR; Soc Knowledge; Soc Book, formerly VDK); Russian Libns Assn; Russian Soc Archivists. *Honours:* Medal, Methods of Book Description, Exhib Econ Achievement, Hon Awards, VDK, 1984; Veteran of Labour Medal, 1986; Book Prize, VDK, 1986-88; Hon Awards, Soc Protection Mems of Hist and Culture, 1990. *Hobbies:* Sailing; Mountaineering; Travel; Their family library. *Address:* Vernadskogo 119 no 73, 117571 Moscow, Russia.

POZZO Jorge, b. 11 Jan 1926, Buenos Aires, Argentina. Engineer. m. Maria Angelica Conca, 30 Dec 1958. *Education:* HS Grad, Colegio Nacional, Buenos Aires, 1944; Off Argentinian Army, Nat Mil Coll, 1948; Mil Engr, Higher Tech School, Univ of Army, 1960. *Appointments include:* Dept Hd, 1966-69, Nat Security Coun, 1966-69; Army Gen Staff, 1969-71; Mil Attache, Argentinian Embassy, France, 1973-75; Asst Dir, Higher Tech School, 1976; Dept Hd, Legis Advsry Commn, 1976; Dir, Fabricaciones Militares, 1976-80; Pres, Fiat Materfer, 1981-83; Pres, Alto Parana SA, 1981-84; Asst Pres, Consulbaires SA, 1981-90; Dir, Banco Mercantil Argentino, 1984-92; Pres, Macpetrol, 1989-91; Pres, Tech Commn, Asociacion Argentina para el Uso Racional de la Energia, 1991-93. *Creative works:* Lectures: Role of the executive in period of recession with inflation, Latin Am Mktng Conven, Peru, 1983; Technical Investigation of Military Production and its part in Economic Development, Univ MA, Amherst, USA, 1985. *Memberships:* Asociacion Dirigentes de Empresa, VP 1983-87, Dir 1991-93; Pres, UN Conf On Tech Coop between Developing Countries, 1978. *Honours:* Ordre Nat du Merite, Pres of France, 1976; Brig Gen, Argentine Army, 1976-80. *Hobbies:* Music (Asociacion Wagneriana de Buenos Aires, Festivales Musicales, Harmonia); Pena El Ombu (VP 1987-91); Military Club. *Address:* Banco Mercantil Argentino, Corrientes 629, 13th floor, Buenos Aires, Argentina. 52.

PRAIN Philip James Murray, b. 14 Nov 1936, Dundee, Scotland. Merchant Banker. m. Susan Ferrier Marr, 28 Sept 1972, 1 d. *Education:* Oppidan Scholar, Eton Coll, 1950-55; Clare Coll, Cambridge, 1957-60; MA (Cantab); Called to the Bar, Inner Temple, 1963. *Appointments:* 2nd Lt, The Black Watch, 1955-57, later Lt, Territorial Army Reserve Offs; Kleinwort Benson Ltd, 1962-, incl currently Asst Dir; Dir, Kleinwort Benson Hong Kong Ltd, 1979-83. *Memberships:* Queen's Bodyguard for Scotland, Royal Co Archers; Chmn, Manor Gdns Enterprise Ctr, Islington; Vice-Chmn, Westminster Amalgamated Charity; Coun, Nat Canine Def League; Cncl, United World Coll of the Atlantic; Fin Cttee, British Red Cross; Trustee, St Clement Danes Holborn Estate Charity; Trustee, All Saints Fdnd, Margaret St; Freeman, City of London, 1978; Liveryman, Worshipful Co Fndrs, 1978. *Hobbies:* Travel; Photography. *Address:* 73 Woodsford Square, London W14 8DS, England.

PRASAD Rajnish, b. 21 Feb 1962, Patna, India. Electronics Engineer. *Education:* BS, Elec Engrng, BS, Computer Sci, Univ KS, USA, 1987; MS, Elec Engrng, Univ VA, 1992; Accepted, LLB studies, Univ London, MBA studies, Univ Durham, England, 1991, for completion, 1995. *Appointments:* Electronics Engr, Ctr for Night Vision and Electro-Optics, Ft Belvoir, VA, USA, 1987-. *Creative works:* Dev and testing of night vision components and systems; Oil paintings. *Memberships:* People-to-People Int; IEEE; Engrng Soc Detroit. *Hobbies:* Tennis; Music; Guitar; Jaguar automobiles; Small business; Dance; Fine and performing arts; Drums; Oil painting. *Address:* 13904 Stonefield Lane, Clifton, VA 22024, USA.

PRATER John L, b. 28 Feb 1939, Granite City, Illinois, USA. Chaplain; Counsellor; Educator. m. Eloise Grace Crum, 6 Apr 1963, 2 s. *Education:* BA, Los Angeles Pacific Coll, 1963; MDiv, Asbury Theological Sem, 1967. *Appointments:* Min, Missionary, Licensed Psychological Counsellor, Free Meth Ch, 1959-74; Min, Educator, Pentecostal Ch of God, 1974-75; Min, Counsellor,

Educator, Assemblies of God, 1976-; Chaplain, Dept of Veterans Affairs, 1987-. *Creative works:* Curriculum for mentally dysfunctional students; Curriculum and guidelines for addictive personalities; Programs for diagnosis of spiritual and religious dysfunctions; Counselling guidelines for spiritual and religious dysfunctions. *Memberships:* Nat Assn Veterans Affairs Chaplains; Mil Chaplains Assn; Soc Preservation and Encouragement of Barbershop Quartet Singing in America, Chapter Pres, Area Counselor; NW AZ Chap, Am Red Cross, Hlth Servs Instr; Caseworker, Serv to Mil Families. *Honours:* Certs of Appreciation: City of Duarte, CA; City of Barstow, CA, 1974; Bullhead City, AZ, 1983; Dept of Army, Chief Army Reserve, 1991; Office of Asst Sec Def (Reserve Affairs), 1991; Special Contbn Award, Outstanding Perf Award, Dept VA, 1991-1992. *Hobbies:* Aviation; Electronics; Computers; Photography; Travel. *Address:* 1840 Iron Springs Rd (A4J), Prescott, AZ 86301, USA. 9, 145.

PRATHNADI Pongsiri, b. 5 Sept 1934, Thailand. Doctor of Medicine. m. Nantgana Prathnadi, 2 s, 1 d. *Education:* Cert, Bd Gen Surg and Thoracic Surg; FCCP, 1970; FACS, 1970; FRCS, 1980; FICS, 1981. *Appointments include:* Dept Surg, Fac Med, Chiangmai Univ, Chiangmai. *Memberships:* Royal Coll Surgs Thailand; Int Coll Surgs Thailand; Assn Thoracic Surgs Thailand; Int Assn Disease of the Oesophagus. *Honours:* Red Cross Medal, recognition of Red Cross med serv, HM Queen of Thailand, 1983; 1st Class, Order of the White Elephant, HM King of Thailand, 1987; Hon FICS, Japan, 1989. *Hobbies:* Golf; Reading; Walking. *Address:* Department of Surgery, Faculty of Medicine, Chiangmai University, Chiangmai 50000, Thailand.

PRATSCHLER Leslie Ann (Polnaszek), b. 28 Aug 1946, Minneapolis, Minnesota, USA. Educator. m. Theodore W Pratschler, 21 May 1973. *Education:* BA, Ctrl WA State Univ, 1969; MEd, Mercer Univ, 1972; Further study, various colls and univs. *Appointments:* Libn, Robins Elem School, Robins AFB, GA, 1969-70; 5th Grade Tchr, Maths, Sci, 1970-71, 2nd Grade Tchr, 1971-72, Linwood Elem School, Robins AFB; Libn, 1972-73, Var aid positions, 1973-76, Soesterberg Am School, Soesterberg, Netherlands; Adult Basic Educ, Bus Mgmt, City Coll Chgo, Soesterberg, 1973-76; Instr, Adult Basic Educ, En NM Univ, Clovis, USA, 1976-78; HS School Libn, Algebra, Basic Maths, Farwell HS, Farwell, TX, 1978-79; 6th Grade Tchr, Lang Arts, Intermediate School, Neosho, MO, 1979-81; 4th Grade Tchr, S Elem, Neosho, 1981-84; 5th Grade Tchr, 1985, 1st Grade Tchr, Grade Level Chair, Vice-Chair, School Advsry Coun, 1985-86, 3rd Grade Tchr, 1986-91, Kaiserslautern Elem School, Kaiserslautern, Germany; 3rd Grade Tchr, East Clayton Elem, Jonesburg, GA, USA, 1991-. *Membership:* Beta Sigma Phi, Pres Coord Coun twice, Chpat Pres twice, Chapt VP 3 times. *Honours:* Chapt Woman of Yr, Chapt Sweetheart of Yr, Coun Woman of Yr, Beta Sigma Phi. *Hobbies:* Travel; Reading; Cross-stitching. *Address:* 7614 Mt Zion Blvd, Jonesboro, GA 30236, USA.

PRECLIK Mojmir, b. 9 Feb 1931, Dlouha Ves, Czechoslovakia. Sculptor; Restorer. Free loyality partnership, 1980, 1 d. *Education:* Middle Profl School Ceramics, Teplice, 1946-49; Studies w Prof Jan Kavan, 1949-54, grad, 1954, HS Applied Art, Prague. *Career:* Freelance Sculptor and Restorer, 1957-; Specialist in stone, stucco, backed clay, 1964-; 2-person exhibs: Gall Czechoslovak Writers, Prague, 1964; U Recickych Gall, Prague, 1980; Dist Mus, Turnov, 1985; Reg Gall, Jicin, 1986; Stare Hrady Castle, 1989; Atrium, Prague, 1991; Participant, exhibs: Salon, Prague, 1958; Group M57, Prague, 1959, 1960, 1962, 1965, 1969, Liberec, 1960, Cheb, 1961, Mlada Boleslaw, 1962, Bratislava, 1970; Youth Biennale, Paris, 1962; Exhib Mod Art, Rychnov nad Kneznou, 1963; Exhib Ornamental Sculptures, Liberec, 1967; Sculpture and Town, Liberec, 1968; Artists of River Jizera REg, Mala Skala, 1979; Exhib, 40th Celebration of Liberation, Prague, 1985; Manes, Prague, 1989; Represented in collections: Nat Gall, Prague; Gall of the Capital, Prague; Reg galls, Louny,

Roudnice, Pardubice, Hradec Kralove, Olomouc; Num pvte collections, Czechoslovakia and abroad. *Creative works:* Sculptures and statues in stone and backed clay. *Memberships:* Union Czech Sculptors; Union of Czech Restorers; Grp M57, 1959-70; Former Mbr, Soc Czech Artists. *Hobbies:* Music (flute player); Photography; Filming (video). *Address:* Rasinovo Nabrezi 46, 12800 Prague 2, Czechoslovakia.

PREEDY Victor Ralph, b. 28 Oct 1952, Hong Kong. Lecturer; Research Scientist. m. Joann Pinney, 16 June 1986, 2 d. *Education:* BSc Hons, Univ Aston, England, 1974; PhD, Nutrition, Metabolism, Univ London, 1981. *Appointments:* Rsch Fellow, School Hygiene and Tropical Med, 1981-83; Postdoct Asst, Lectr, 1983-86, Univ London; Rsch Scientist, Med Rsch Coun Clin Rsch Ctr, Harrow, 1986-88; Lectr, King's Coll, Univ London, 1988-. *Creative works:* Internationally recognised expertise in field of alcoholism and protein turnover; Chapts in 4 books; Over 160 rsch publs, reviews, others. *Memberships:* Med Rsch Soc; Bone and Tooth Soc; Mbr, Edtrl Bd of Alcohol and Alcoholism. *Hobby:* Being with his family. *Address:* Dept of Clinical Biochemistry, Kings College School of Medicine and Dentistry, Bessemer Rd, London SE5 9PJ, England.

PREGIEL Ryszard Piotr, b. 14 Mar 1935, Vilna, Lithuania. Electronics and Computer Scientist; Educator. m. Barbara Miecznikowska- Pregiel, 2 July 1959, 1 s. *Education:* Wroclaw Tech Univ, 1956-60; Acad Social Scis, Warsaw, 1969; DTech Sc, 1969; D habil, 1979; Prof, 1990. *Appointments:* Asst, Wroclaw Tech Univ, Poland, 1960-61; Dir, Telecommunication Dists, 1961-70; Mng Dir, Inst Control Systems, Katowice, 1970-85; Undersec State, Sci and Technology, 1985-90; Prof, Inst Control Systems, Katowice, 1990-. *Publications:* 43 monographs and books incl: Mathematical Theory of Connecting Networks, 1977; Optimal Control Problems, 1979; A Generalization of the Wald Principle, 1984. *Memberships:* Polish Cybernetic Soc, Chmn Katowice Br; Polish Electricians Assn; Polish Comm Sci and Technology. *Honours:* Awards, Polish Comm Sci and Technology, 1963, 1969; Kts Cross, 1976, Offs Cross, 1986, Order of Polonia Restituta. *Hobbies:* Tennis; Mountaineering. *Address:* ul Wiktorii Wiedenskiej 5 m 10, 02-957 Warsaw, Poland.

PREISSLER Peter M, b. 22 Mar 1943, Vienna, Austria. Theatre Director. m. Sussan Winter, 17 Dec 1986, 1 s, 1 d. *Univ Vienna, 1961-71; Music, Drama, Acting School, Vienna, 1963-65; Trumpet study, Acad Music.* *Appointments:* Burgtheater, Vienna, 1965-70; Staatstheater, Hannover, FRG, 1971-74; Bayerischer Rundfunk, 1974-81; Volkstheater, Vienna, 1981-87. *Creative works:* Author, TV series and theatre play. *Honours:* Kainz Medal; Skraut Prize; Austrian Audience's Prize. *Hobbies:* Sports; Music. *Address:* Westermuhlstrasse 31, D-8000 Munich 5, Germany.

PREMANAND Raya, b. 25 Nov 1947, Madanapalle, Andra Pradesh, India. Medical Doctor. m. R Madhavi, 21 Nov 1971, 1 s, 1 d. *Education:* MBBS, 1970; MD, 1982; FCCP, 1986. *Appointments:* Tutor, Microbiology, Govt India, 1971-73; Self-employed Rural Med Practitioner, 1973- 76; Rural Hlth Serv, Andra Pradesh State Govt, 1976-78; Tutor, Asst Prof, TB, Chest Diseases, 1978-82, Prof, TB, Chest Diseases, 1982-, S V Med Coll, Tirupati; Postgrad Examiner, TB, Chest Diseases; Mbr, Selection Comm Specialists, Govt India. *Publications:* Control of Tuberculosis: Repeat sputum microscopy in case finding at a peripheral Health Institute, 1987; Bronchial Asthma: Ipratropium Bromide and Salbutamol in Asthma and Chronic Bronchitis, 1989, *Memberships:* Hon Sec, Indian Med Assn, Tirupati Br; Indian Chest Soc; Working Comm, Tuberculoses Assn Andhra Pradesh State; Fine Arts Acad, Tirupati; Hon Sec, Acad Med Scis, S V Med Coll, Tirupati; Hon Sec, Civil Surgs Assn, S V Med Coll, Tirupati. *Honours:* Best Paper Award, TB Assn Andhra Pradesh State; Best Sec Award, Andhra Pradesh Indian Med Assn. *Hobbies:* Social service to improve the health of the poor; Reading.

Address: Buddha Dhamma Vandana, 1228 Sreenivasa Nagar, K T Road, Tirupati 517507, India.

PRESCOD Margaret, b. 11 Aug 1948, Barbados, West Indies. Community Activist. 1 d. *Education:* BA, Ll Univ, USA, 1970. *Appointments:* Tchr, Ocean Hill Brownsville, Brooklyn, NY, USA, 1969-73; Staff Mbr, SEEK (Search for Educ, Elevation and Knowledge), Queens Coll, CUNY, 1973-80; Currently Spokeswoman, Coord, Int Wages for Housework Campaign and Int Black Women for Wages for Housework. *Publication:* Black Women: Bringing It All Back Home, 1984. *Memberships:* Co-Fndr, Co-Coord, Int Black Women for Wages for Housework, Nat Coord US Network; Community Outreach Coord, Pay Equity Community Outreach Project, 1991; Save Out Servs Coalition; Mgmt Comm, Legal Action for Women; Fndr, Coord, Black Coalition Fighting Back Serial Murders; Steering Comm, Huntington Lib Women's Sem; Rep, Housewives in Dialogue; Co-Coord, Every Mother Is a Working Mother Coalition; Co-Coord, Nat Women Count Network; Coord, Women Count Implementation Comm; Coord Bd, Coalition Against Discrimination in Nursing; Fndg Mbr, Coalition Grassroots Women, 1976-77; Co-Fndr, Friends of the Islanders, 1963-65. *Honours:* Honoured by: B'nai B'rith Women, Ctrl Pacific and Pacific SW Regs; CA Legislative Assembly; City Councilwoman Joy Picus; City of Los Angeles Human Rels Commn; Freemont-Newhart Community Coll Dist; Los Angeles Commn on Assaults Against Women; Los Angeles Mayor Tom Bradley; Nat Women's Pol Caucus, San Fernando Valley; US Congressional Record. *Hobbies:* Aboriginal cultures; Music; Alternative health and healing practices. *Address:* PO Box 86681, Los Angeles, CA 90086, USA.

PRESCOTT THOMAS John Desmond, b. 28 May 1942, Prestatyn, Wales. Mng Dir, Westcountry TV. m. Bridget Margaret Somerset-Ward, 7 Oct 1967, 2 d. *Education:* Mod Langs, Jesus Coll, Oxford, 1960-63; BA, MA, Oxford Univ. *Appointments:* BBC Gen Trainee, 1963-65, Asst Producer, School TV, 1965-68, Producer, School TV, 1968-76, Sr Producer, Mod Langs and European Studies, 1976-81, Hd, School Broadcasting TV, 1981-84, Hd, Bristol Network Prod Ctr, 1984-86, Hd, Broadcasting, S and W, 1986-91; Mng Dir, Westcountry TV, 1991-. *Creative works:* Over 16 TV series; Adapted and produced The Black Lamp (Peter Carter) for TV; Author: Encounter: France; Dès le Début; Alles Klar; Dicho y Hecho; Who's That Out There?, Bolland Lecture, Bristol Polytechnic, 1984; Articles in educl and lang jrnls. *Memberships:* SW Arts Bd; Cncl of Mgmt; Trustees, Bath Int Fest; Gov, Univ of West of England, Bristol; Trustee: St George's Music Trust, The Exploratory, Bristol Cathedral Trust; Formerly: Trustee, TV Trust for the Environment; VP, Bristol-Oporto Assn; Mgmt Comm, SW Arts; Friends Comm, Arnolfini Gall; Publicity Comm, Royal Bath and W Show; Communications Grp, Diocese of Bath and Wells; Policy Advsry Comm, Univ Bristol Vet School. *Honours:* 4 award nominations for TV series. *Hobbies:* Languages; Sailing; Photography; Industrial archaeology; Model engineering; Heraldry; Playing the alto saxophone. *Address:* Earl's Pool, Ladymead Lane, Lower Langford, Avon BS18 7EQ, England.

PRESLEY David Buckley, b. 18 Feb 1959, Tampa, Florida, USA. Preacher. m. Brenda Kay Dixon, 8 Dec 1977, 1 s, 2 d. *Education:* BS, Roanoke Bible Coll, Elizabeth City, NC, 1984; Ordained Min, Christian Ch, 1984; MEd, Coll of William and Mary, Williamsburg, VA, 1988; Post-Master's studies, Johns Hopkins Univ, 1990; MA, Johnson Bible Coll, Knoxville, TN, 1992; Doctoral Studies, Howard Univ, Wash DC, 1992. *Appointments:* Smithfield Ch of Christ, Smithfield, VA, 1984-88; Fruitland Christian Ch, Fruitland, MD, 1988-. *Publications:* Articles in The Restoration Herald and The Journal of Psychology and Theology. *Hobbies:* Swimming; Surfing; Water skiing. *Address:* PO Box 566/305 E Main St, Fruitland, MD 21826, USA.

PRESTON Michael Richard, b. 15 Oct 1927, England. Design Consultant and Teacher. m. (1) Anne Gillespie Smith, 13 Aug 1955, (2) Judith Gaye James, 22 Aug 1980. *Education:* Sutton & Cheam School Art, 1948-52; Nat Dip, Design, Guildford School Art, 1953; Art Tchrs Dip, Goldsmiths' Coll, 1954, Dip, Humanities, 1961, Univ London. *Appointments:* Career: Served: Brit Army, 1944-48, Territorial Army, 1948-61; Drawing Master, Dulwich Coll, 1955-64; Hd, Design, Sci Mus, London, 1964-87; Keeper, Dept Mus Servs, 1987; Design Advsr: Wellcome Fndn, 1986-; Nat Gall, London Ext, 1986; Canterbury Cathedral, 1987-; Design Expo '89, Japan, 1988-89; Tricycle Theatre, 1989-; Mus Far E Antiquities, Bath, 1989-; Royal Nat Theatre, 1989-90; Accademia Italiana, London, 1990-; Int Cons, 1987-; Vis Prof, Nat Inst Design, India, 1989-; Official Advsr, mus projects: Royal Mint, 1974-75; Iran 1976-79; Spain, 1977-80; FRG, 1979-79; Can, 1979-82; Trinidad, 1982-83; Expo '86, Vancouver, BC, 1984-86; Turkey, 1984-90; Hong Kong, 1985. *Creative works:* Mus exhibs incl: Centenary of Charles Babbage, 1971; A Word to the Mermaids, 1973; Copernicus Quincentenary, 1973; Tower Bridge Observed, 1974; The Breath of Life, 1974; Science & Technology of Islam, 1976; Stanley Spencer in the Shipyard, 1979; Science & Technology of India, 1982; The Great Cover-up Show, 1982; Beads of Glass, 1983; Louis Pasteur & Rabies, 1985; Many permanent galls incl: Sci Mus, 1964-86; Nat Railway Mus, York, 1971-75; Wellcome Mus Hist Med, 1975-80; Nat Mus Photography, Film and TV, Bradford, 1977-83. *Memberships:* Fellow, Chartered Soc Designers, Hon Treas 1974-75, VP, 1976, 1979-81, Mbrship Bd Chmn 1976-79, Design Mgmt Panel Chmn 1976-80; Nat Soc Art Educ, 1952-69; FRSA, 1955-68; Greenwich Soc, Chmn 1961-64; Int Coun Museums; Hon Fellow, Pres, Guild Glass Engravers; Mus Advsry Panel Tubitak, Turkey, 1984-90; Bd, Com Int d'Arch et Techniques des Musees; Trustee, Vivat Trust. *Hobbies:* Looking at buildings; Jazz; Travel; Conversation; Food. *Address:* 37 Walham Grove, London SW6 1QR, England. 1.

PRETTYMAN Elijah Barrett, b. 1 June 1925, Washington, District of Columbia, USA. Attorney. div., 1 s, 1 d. *Education:* BA, Yale Univ, 1949; LLB, Univ VA Law School, 1953. *Appointments:* AUS, 1943-45; Law Clerk to Supreme Ct Justices Jackson, Frankfurter and Harlan, 1953-55; Assoc, 1955-63, Ptnr, Hogan & Harton law firm, Wash, DC; Special Asst to US Atty Gen, 1963, White House, 1963-64; President's Rep to Interagcy Comm Transport Mergers; Special Cons, US Senate Judiciary Comm, Vietnam, 1967-68; Outside Cons, Subcomm, House of Reps Comm Internal and For Commrce, 1978; Special Cons, Comm Standards of Official Conduct, US House of Reps, 1980-81. *Publications:* Articles in profl jrnls; The Supreme Court in the American System of Government (ed w William E Jackson), 1955. *Memberships:* Trustee Emeritus, Past Mbr Exec Comm, Am Univ, Wash DC; Trustee, Mbr Exec Comm, Wash Jrnlsm Ctr; Bd Dirs, Nat Coun Crime and Delinquency; Advsry Comm, Media Law Reporter; Past Corp Mbr, Salvation Army; Advsry Comm, Procedures of Judicial Coun, DC; Advsry Bd, Inst Communications Law Studies, Cath Univ; Past Chmn, Bd Govs, St Albans School; Past Mbr, Nat Advsry Comm, Nat Inst Citizen Educ in Law; Pres, PEN/Faulkner Award Fndn; VP, Chmn, Prog Comm, Exec Comm, Supreme Ct Histl Soc; Fellow, Am Bar Assn; Am Coll Trial Lawyers; Judicial Conf DC Circuit; Past Pres, DC Bar Fndn; Metro Wash Bd Trade; DC Bar, 1st Pres 1972-73, Bd Govs 1973-74; Am Jusdicature Soc, Exec Comm; Am Acad Appellate Lawyers. *Hobbies:* Collector of inscribed books. *Address:* Hogan & Hartson, 55S 13th St NW, Washington, DC 20004, USA. 2, 163.

PREVOST Winthrop Warren, b. 10 June 1917, Lowell, Massachusetts, USA. Record Company Executive; Artist, Painter of Fine Art. m. Josephine Darois, 1 July 1939. *Education:* Jrnlsm, World Lit, 1945; Grad, Commercial Art, Illustration, Design, Famous Artists School, Westport, CT, 1971. *Career:* Commenced painting, early 1920s; Exhibs, oil paintings: Jordan Marsh, Boston and Pub Lib, Lowell, 1942; Maintenance,

Catherine La Boure School Nursing, Lowell, 1958-71; Songwriter, 1963-65; Talent Scout, Chas Wright Agcy, 1970-74; Sales Rep, March Music and Rutland Records, Chesterfield, England, 1975; Talent Rep, Nashville RCA Records, Warner Bros Records, EMI Am Records, 1985-87. *Creative works:* Songs: Loneliness, 1942; I'll Love You at Starlight, 1954; Moon Over Hampton, 1954; I Love Jimmy, 1963; I'll Love You in the Autumn; Created emblem Nashville Music seal, 1966; Paintings incl commns for Mrs Jimmy Durante, several entertainers, Coe Mus. *Memberships:* Lowell Art Assn; Lifetime Mbr, Acad Country Music. *Address:* Archie Kenefick Manor, Apt 302, 50 Stackpole St, Lowell, MA 01852, USA. 191.

PRÉVOST Philippe Guy, b. 16 July 1942, Paris, France. Vice-President, Finance. m. Marie-Laure Réchaussat, 9 July 1969; 2 s, 1 d. *Education:* Ecole Supérieure de Comm et d'Admin des Entreprises, Amiens, 1965; Commissaire aux Comptes, Statutory Auditor, Paris, 1977; Expert Comptable, Pub Acct, Paris, 1978. *Appointments:* Mgr, Gen Acctng, 1974-75, Mgr, Sales Admin, 1975-77, Eli Lilly France; Fin Dir, Elizabeth Arden France, Paris, 1977-80; Dir, Acctng, Distbn, Lilly France SA, Paris, 1980-85; VP, Fin, IN2 Groupe Intertechnique, 1989, Siemens, 1989-, Plaisir, France, 1985-90; Rep, Mem Bd of Dirs, Léanord, 1987-89; Ferma, 1988-89; CEFI, 1988-90; Prés of CMC-IN2, Portugal, 1988-90; Gen Mgr, Finance, Valmende, Paris, 1990-91; Vice-President, Fin, Intertechnique, Plaisir, 1991-; Mem of Bd, Valmonde, 1990-; Parsec, 1992-. *Memberships:* Assn Nat des Directeurs Financiers et Controleurs de Gestion, 1976; Nat Assoc of Accnts, France, 1986-; Elected Rep, Assn des Parents d'Eleves, Versailles, 1979-91; Admnstr, Prés, Syndicat des Copropriétaires, 1978-88; Admnstr, Assn Inst Serviam, Paris, 19811-; Admnstr, Assn Gen des Familles de Versailles et des Environs, 1983-; Admnstr, Assn Sauvegarde du Quartier Notre-Dame-Ermitage, Versailles, 1983-91. *Honours:* Promoted to Capt, French Army Reserve, 1984. *Hobbies:* Swimming; Photography. *Address:* 24 Rue Molière, 78150 Le Chesnay, France. 139.

PRICE Barry David Keith, b. 28 June 1933, Lydbrook, Forest of Dean, England. Drugs Intelligence Unit Coordinator; Former Chief Constable. m. Evelyne Jean Horlick, 4 July 1953, 3 d. *Education:* Southall Grammar School. *Appointments:* Constable, uniformed and CID, through ranks to Detective Chief Supt, Metrop Police, London, 1954-75; Asst Chief Constable, Northumbria Police, 1975-78; Dpty Chief Constable, Essex Police, 1978-80; Chief Constable, Cumbria Constabulary, 1980-87; Coord, Nat Drugs Intelligence Unit, New Scotland Yard, London, 1987-. *Publications:* Var articles in law enforcement and med publs. *Memberships:* Co Dir, St John Ambulance Assn, 1981-87; Advsry Coun on Misuse of Drugs, 1982-87; Pres, Engl Police Golf Assn; Drugs Intelligence Steering Grp; Advsr to ACPO Crime Commn on drugs matters, Past Chmn, Past Sec; Fellow, Brit Inst Mgmt, 1975. *Honours:* Police Long Serv and Good Conduct Medal, 1976; Queen's Police Medal, 1981; CBE, 1990. *Hobbies:* Golf; Painting; Gardening. *Address:* National Drugs Intelligence Unit, New Scotland Yard, Broadway, London SW1H 0BG, England. 1.

PRICE Margaret Morgan Samuel, b. 9 Feb 1947, Cleveland, Ohio, USA. Artist. m. John F Price, 23 Feb 1985, dec. 14 Oct 1990, 2 s, 1 d. *Education:* Ringling School Art, Sarasota, FL. *Career:* Illustrator, Hallmark Cards, 1969; Art Dir, Lake Co New Herald Art, 1970-72; Opened own studio, taught, exhibited, show juror, Ardmore, OK, 1972-81; Workshops, Europe, AK, BC, USA; Opened present studio and gall, 1989. *Creative works:* Oils, pastels, watercolours; Published, American Artists Magazine, 1991. *Memberships:* Knickerbocker Artists NY, VP; Copley Soc Boston; Pastel Soc Am; Am Artists Profl League; Assn pour la Promotion du Patrimoine Artistique Francais LOI 1901. *Honours:* Winsor Newton Award, Oil, 1988, Joseph Hartley Mem Award, Oil, 1990, Anthony Cirino Award, Pastel, 1991, Salmagundi Club, NY; Watercolour Award, Brevard Cultural Alliance, 1989; 1st in Oil, Copley Soc, Boston,

1991; Nat Park Acad for the Arts, Jackson Hole, Wyoming Awd for Excellence, Top 100 Paintings, Painting, The Interior, Chosen for Nat Park Calendar, 1994; The Artists Mag, New York, Hon Mention Painting Comp, 1992; Napa Valley Art Comp, Hon Mention Painting Comp, 1992; Allied Artists of America, Nat Arts Club, New York Leon Stacks Memorial for Southern Artist Award. *Hobbies:* Skiing; Golf; Reading; Children's issues - mental health. *Address:* 490 Tina Place, Merritt Island, FL 32952, USA.

PRIEDE Anna, b. 11 May 1920, St Petersburg, USSR. Prima Ballerina. *Education:* Pvte ballet school of H Tangiyeva and A Fyodorova, w Harry Plucis and An Viltsak, 1929-32; State Ballet School, 1932-37; Pvte studies w O Preobrazhenska, Paris, summer 1937. *Career:* Prima Ballerina, Latvian Nat Opera, 1937-62; Leading roles: Les Sylphides (Chopin), 1934, 1958; Vienna Waltz (Strauss), 1935; Coppelia (Delibes), 1936; Swan Lake (Tchaikovsky), 1937, 1939, 1941, Odette-Odile, 1951; Citrie, in Don Quixote (Minkus), 1941; Habanera (Dostale), 1943; Skaidrite, in Staburags (Kalninsh), 1944; Le Spectre de la Rose (Weber), 1944; Mary, in The Fountain of Bakhchisarai (Asafyev), 1946; Laima (Liepinsh), 1947; Sleeping Beauty (Tschaikovsky), 1948; Laurensie (Carne), 1949; Lena, in Youth (Chulaki), 1950; Lelde, in Sakta of Freedom (Skulte), 1950; Esmeralda (Pugni), 1951; Masha, in Flower of Alenka (Kochmarev), 1952; Syoumbike, in Shurale (Yarulin), 1952; Romeo and Juliet (Prokofiev), 1953; Raimonda (Glazunov), 1954; Cendrillon (Prokofiev), 1955; Medora, in Corsair (Adam), 1956; Gisele, 1956; Anele, in an der schonen blauen Donau (Strauss), 1957; Frigie, in Spartak (Khachaturian), 1960; Symphonic Dances (Rachmaninoff), 1961; Theatre and Life, Riga, Almanach, 1961. *Honour:* Winner, USSR State Prize, 1951. *Hobby:* Giving ballet lessons at a private studio, 1942-80. *Address:* Ritupes str 34, Flat 9, 226019 Riga, Latvia.

PRIEST Margaret Diane, b. 15 Feb 1944, Tyringham, Buckinghamshire, England. Artist; Educator. m. Tony Scherman, 1 Sept 1972, 1 s, 2 d. *Education:* SW Essex Tech Coll, 1963; Dip, Art, Design, Maidstone Coll Art, 1967; MA, Royal Coll Art, London, 1970. *Career:* Lectr: Harrow School Art, 1970-74; St Martins School Art, London, 1972-76; School Arch, Univ Waterloo, Can, 1982-83; School Arch, Univ Toronto, 1983; Vis Critic, Schools Art and Arch, England, Can; Assoc Prof, Fine Art, Dept Fine Art, Univ Guelph, Guelph, Ont, 1983-; Solo exhibs: Arnolfini Gall, Bristol Garage Art Ltd, London, 1974; Felicity Samuel Gall, London, 1976; Theo Waddington Gall, London, 1976, 1980; Theo Waddington Galls, Toronto, 1981, 1982; Theo Waddington and Co Inc, NYC, 1982; Theo Waddinton Inc, Montreal, 1983; Marianne Friedland Gall, Toronto, 1985, 1987; Albemarle Gall, London, 1989; Num grp exhibs, England, Yugoslavia, Switzerland, Belgium, Germany, USA, Can, Italy, 1969-. *Creative works include:* Works in num pub and pvte collections, Can and abroad. *Memberships:* Univ Art Assn Can; Bd, Gershon Iskowitz Fndn. *Honours:* Arts Coun GB Award, 1969; Silver Medal, Royal Coll Art, 1970; John Minton Scholarship, 1970; Drawing Award, Ont Arts Coun, 1981; Artist w winning team, Bay/Adelaide Pk Competition, 1990. *Hobby:* Gardening. *Address:* 38 Dunvegan Road, Toronto, Ontario, Canada M4V 2P6. 142.

PRIJATELJ Niko, b. 31 Jan 1922, Ljubljana, Slovenia. Professor of Mathematics. m. Ivana Prijatelj, 22 Aug 1945, 2 d. *Education:* Dip, Maths, Philos, 1946, PhD, Maths, 1961, Univ Ljubljana. *Appointments:* Asst, 1957, Asst Prof, 1961, Assoc Prof, 1972, Prof, 1978-, Univ Ljubljana. *Publications:* Introduction to Mathematical Logic, 1960; Mathematical Structures, Vol I, 1964, Vol II, 1967, Vol III, 1972; Elements of Mathematical Logic, Vol I, 1982, Vol II, 1992. *Memberships:* Inst Maths, Phys and Mech, Ljubljana, Past Dir; Slovenian Soc Mathns, Physicists and Astronomers, Ljubljana, Past Pres. *Honours:* Medal of Work w Golden Wreath, 1974; Several prizes, 1974, 1978, 1979, 1990. *Hobbies:* History; Literature; Travel. *Address:* Jadranska 19, 61000 Ljubljana, Slovenia.

PRIMAROLO Dawn, b. 2 May 1954, London, England. Member of Parliament. m. (1) Oct 1972, div., 1 s, (2) Thomas Ian Ducat, 29 Nov 1990. *Education:* BA (Hons), Bristol Polytechnic, 1984; PhD postgrad rsch student, Univ Bristol, 1984-87. *Appointments include:* Legal Sec, Law Ctr; MP, House of Commons, 1987-. *Address:* House of Commons, Westminster, London SW1A 0AA, England. 1, 138, 185.

PRIMES Gary Louis, b. 17 Mar 1959, Los Angeles, California, USA. Service Merchandising Company Operations Professional. *Education:* BSArch, 1980, Profl BArch, 1981, Cal Polytechnic State Univ, San Luis Obispo. *Appointments:* Data Processing Mgr, 1981-85, Hd Buyer, 1982-85, VP, Ops, 1985-88, Merchandising Unltd, San Diego, CA and Phoenix, AZ Divs; VP, Ops, M U Div, 1988-90, Project Mgr, Cons, Wn Div, 1990, Asst Dist Ctr Mgr, Wn Div, 1991, Tash Inc. *Membership:* Advsry Bd, Nat Back-to-School Merchandise Show, 1987-90. *Honours:* Passed Nat Coun Archtl Registration Bds Licensing Exams, 1981. *Hobbies:* Computer software and games; Golf; Automotive technology and things technological; Extensive reading. *Address:* 7903 Elm Ave No 271, Rancho Cucamonga, CA 91730, USA. 9.

PRIMROSE Robert William, b. 3 July 1921, Teddington, Middlesex, England. Retired. m. Elizabeth Katherine Maud Wong, 28 Dec 1948. *Education:* Matriculation, Co School for Boys, Gillingham, Kent; FCIS. *Appointments:* Civil Serv, Admiralty, 1938-44; Lt, RNVR: Brit Assault Area, Normandy, 1944, Brit Pacific Fleet, 1945, Hong Kong, 1945-47; Hong Kong Civil Serv, 1947-77; Colonial Admnstv Serv, incl: Clerk, Exec Coun; Clerk, Legis Coun; 1st Admnstv Sec, UMELCO Off; Hong Kong Ptnrship Sec, Johnson Stokes and Master, Solicitors, 1977-88. *Honours:* MBE, 1970; Imperial Serv Order, 1977. *Hobbies:* Music; Philately; Reading. *Address:* 52 Beechwood Avenue, Kew Gardens, Surrey TW9 4DE, England.

PRINCE Anna Lou, b. 28 May 1935, Isabella, Tennessee, USA. Television Producer and Host. 3 d. *Education:* Dip, Carolina School Broadcasting, 1966; Dip, SWn Tech Inst, 1970; Dip, Israel Bible Coll, Jerusalem, 1974; Cert, Licensed Bible Tchr, United Christian Mins, 1973. *Career:* Songwriter, Hank Locklin Music Co, Nashville, TN, 1963-70; Guest, Grand Ole Opry, Nashville, 1970; Owner, Operator, Prince Wholesale Bait Co, Canton, NC, 1976-82; Owner, Ptnr: Grad Bldrs, Canton, 1982-86, Prince Music Publng, 1982-, Prince TV Co, 1986-; Entertainer, 17 perfs, World's Fair, 1982; Producer, Dir, Community Access TV; Publr, Writer, Broadcast Music Inc. *Creative works:* Songs include 2 No 1 hits, England (RCA): I Feel A Cry Coming On, 1965; The Best Part of Loving You, 1966; Over 20 int songs; TV prods: Songwriting and Stuff (producer, host), 1987; Spirits, Dreams and Visions (producer, host), 1990; Current int musical w Australia: Down Home Down Under. *Memberships:* Country Music Assn; Moderator, Tchr, Nashville Songwriters Assn Int; VP, Macon Co Taxpayers Assn; Fraternal Order Police; Educ Dir, Head Start; Chmbr of Comm. *Honours:* Nominated Disting Woman of NC, NC Coun on Status of Women, 1984; Jefferson Award, WVFF TV and Am Inst Pub Serv, 1984; Outstanding Small Bus Woman, Small Bus Assn, 1984. *Hobbies:* Gourmet cooking; Landscape painting; Guitar. *Address:* 3703 Dickerson Rd No 41, Nashville, TN 37207, USA. 5, 7, 52, 125, 138, 151, 152, 155, 156, 191.

PRINCE Frances Anne, b. 20 Dec 1923, Toledo, Iowa, USA. Editor; Civic Worker. m. Richard Edward Prince Jr, 17 Aug 1951, 1 s (dec.), 1 d. *Education:* Univ Louisville, 1947-49; AB, Berea Coll, 1951; Kent School Social Work, 1952; Creighton Univ, 1969; MPA, Univ NE, 1973. *Appointments:* Instr, Flower Arranging, Wn WY Jr Coll, 1965, 1966; Ed, NE Garden News, 1983-

Memberships: Int Platform Assn; Active, past and present offs, num community and charitable orgs incl: Girl Scouts; Community Improvement; WY Fedn Women's Clubs State Lib Servs; US Constitution Bicentennial Commn, NE; Omaha Commn on Bicentennial; Nat Subcomm, Commn on Bicentennial; WY State Advsry Bd on Lib Inter-Coop; Sweetwater Co Lib System; Am Lib Assn; School Bd Advsry Coun; Opera Angels; NE Forestry Advsry Bd; NE Tree Planting Commn; New Neighbours League; Ikebana Int; Omaha Coun Garden Clubs. *Honours:* Awards: Girl Scouts, 1967; Sweetwater Co Lib, 1968; US Forestry Serv, for conservation, 1981; Plant 2 Trees, 1981; Nat Arbor Day, 1982; Joyce Kilmer Award, 1990; Nat Coun State Garden clubs, 1986, 1987, 1989; President's Award, 1986, 1987, 1989; Nat Bicentennial Ldrship Award, Advancement of Citizenchip, 1989; Conservation Medal, DAR, 1991. *Hobbies:* Trees and environment; Classical and folk music; Travel; Art; Writing prose and poetry; Gardening; Botany; Reading; Philosophy; Historic commemoration work; Psychology; Flower arranging. *Address:* 8909 Broadmoor Drive, Omaha, NE 68114, USA. 5, 52, 129, 138, 152.

PRINCZ Daniel, b. 1 July 1953, Venezuela. Educational Administration Executive. *Education:* BS, Biology, Univ PR, 1977; MSc, PhD, Oceanology, Univ de Bretagne Occidentale, France, 1986. *Appointments:* Rsch, Educ, Fubndacion La Salle, Venezuela, 1977-81, 1983-85; VP, Politechnical Inst FL, Miami, FL, USA, 1987-. *Publications:* Author or co-author, 28 rsch publs. *Membership:* Am Assn Counseling and Dev. *Honours:* Cofradia del Alba, Spain, 1982. *Hobbies:* Reading; Music; Canoeing. *Address:* Politechnical Institute of Florida, 11865 (H3) Coral Way, Miami, FL 33175, USA.

PRITCHARD Robert Hugh, b. 25 Jan 1930, London, Eng. Ldr, Liberal Democrats, Leicester County Coun. m. Susan Beth Rosenberg, 4 Nov 1973, 2 s, 1 d. *Education:* BSc, London; PhD, Glasgow. *Appointments:* Lectr in Genetics, Glasgow, 1956-59; Scientific Staff, MRC, 1959-64; Prof of Genetics, Leicester Univ, 1964-85; Ldr, Liberal Democrats, Leicester City Coun, 1985-90; Ldr, LibDem, Leicestershire County Council. *Publication:* Basic Cloning Techniques, 1985. *Memberships:* Genetic Soc; Soc Microbiol; Am Soc for Microbiol. *Honour:* Carter Prize, King's Coll, London Univ, 1951. *Hobbies:* Politics; Gardening. *Address:* 8 Knighton Grange Road, Leicester LE2 2LE, England.

PRITCHARD Sparky, b. 24 May 1950, Richmond, VA, USA. Pastor. m. Kathy Sue Neslon, 5 Aug 1972, 3 d. *Education:* BA 1972, MA 1974, Bob Jones Univ. *Appointments:* Greek Prof, Bob Jones Univ, 1974-76; Assoc Pastor, S Sheridan Bapt, 1976-89; Sr Pastor, Immanuel Bapt Ch, 1989-. *Publications:* Rubbing Elbows with Royalty, 1983; Columnist, Pro Basketball Fellowship Newsletter, 1984-89. *Memberships:* GOP Committeman, 1976-83; Biblical Archaeological Soc, 1978-; Area Coord, Inst in Basic Life Prins, 1980-89; Dev Comm, The Wilds - Rockies, 1984-85; Team Chap, NBA Denver Nuggets, 1984-89; Pro Basketball Fellowship, 1984-89. *Honours:* Golden Pyramid Competition Awd of Merit, 1979; Yrbook Dedication, Silver State Bapt Sch, 1985. *Hobbies:* Golf; Biking; Flying; Photography; Reading. *Address:* 10906 Branberry Lane, Richmond, VA 23233, USA. 117, 176.

PROCHAZKA Anton, b. 15 Sept 1948, Vienna, Austria. Author; Tchr; Tchr Trainer. m. 6 Feb 1976, 4 s, 1 d. *Education:* Grad Degree, Universität f Bildungswissenschaften, Klagenfurt, 1983. *Appointments:* Tchng Eng at primary, second gen schs, pre-vocational and comprehensive schs, 1967-88; Tchr, Tchr Trainer, VHS - adult sch, 1971-75; Lectr, Pedagogical Inst, Vienna, 1975-; Tchr Trainer, 1975-; Hd, Ctr for Info on Foreign Lang Tchng and In-Serv Trng, Vienna, 1988-; Organizer, Proj Mgr, yearly schs' prog, EXPO-LINGUA, Vienna, 1989-; Organizer, 1st Int Symposium Eng Lang Tchng Across the Borders, 1990; Sems and workshops held in all parts of Austria and

abroad. *Publications:* Look Listen and Learn (co-author), 4 vols in 2 eds, 1973-78; Doodie, 1982-84; Bridges, 1989-92; Various articles in int tchr's mags. *Memberships:* Brit Coun, Vienna; IATEFL, Whitstable; FMF, Berlin; TEA, Vienna. *Honours:* by the Vienna Bd of Educ, 1973, 1985. *Hobbies:* Jogging; Hiking; Reading; Travelling. *Address:* Centre for Information on Foreign Language Teaching and In-Service Training, Pädagogisches Institut d Bundes, Grenzackerstrasse 18, A-1100 Vienna, Austria.

PROCTER (Mary) Norma, b. 15 Feb 1928, Cleethorpes, Eng. *Career include:* Int Concert Singer (Contralto), now ret'd; Vocal studies w Roy Henderson; Musicianship w Alec Redshaw, Lieder w Hans Oppenheim & Paul Hamburger; London debut at Southwark Cath, 1948; Specialist in concert works, oratario & recitals; appeared w all major fests in UK & Europe; Operatic debut as Lucretia in Britten's, Rape of Lucretia, Aldeburgh Fest, 1954, 1958; Covent Gdn debut in Gluck's Orpheus, 1960; Performed in Germany, France, Spain, Portugal, Norway, Sweden, Denmark, Holland, Belgium, Austria, Israel, Luxembourg, S Am; Recordings incl, Messiah, Elijah, Samson, Mahlers; 2nd, 3rd, 8th Symphonies, Das Klagende Lied; Hartmann 1st Symph; Julius Caeser Jones-Williamson; Nicholas Maws Scenes & Arias; BBC, Last Night of the Proms; Prelude recording Brahms, Mahler, Ballads; Conductors incl: Bruno Walter, Bernstein, Rafael Kubelik, Karl Richter, Pablo Casals, Sirs: Malcolm Sargent, Charles Graves, David Willcocks; Alexander Gibson, Charles Mackerras, Norman del Mar. *Membership:* Pres, Grimsby Phil Soc. *Honour:* Hon RAM, 1974. *Hobbies:* Sketching; Painting; Tapestry; TV. *Address:* 194 Clee Road, Grimsby DN32 8NG, England. 1, 34.

PRODANOVA Kina-Velichka Stephanova, b. 24 Apr 1938, Gabrovo. Sr Lectr; Musicologist; Piano Tchr. m. Dinko Kunev, 30 Jan 1966, 3 d. *Education:* BA, State Musical Acad, 1957-61; PhD, State Moscow Conservatoire, 1965-69. *Appointments:* Lectr 1957-61, Sr Lectr 1970- 91, Musical Acad, Sofia; The Special Musical Sch, Rousse, 1961-64; Aspirant, Moscow Conservatoire, 1968-69. *Publications:* Principles of formation in Shubert's early chamber and symphonic works, 1975; Relationship of dramaturgy and thematic processors in a Symphony-cantata called He Has Not Died by Al Raitchev, 1978; The Musical History of the Town of Gabrovo (co- author w S Prodanov), 1982; B Britten, War Requiem, 1984. *Memberships:* Union of Bulgarian Composers and Musicologists; Union of Musical Pedagogist in Bulgaria; Schubert Soc; Esperanto Soc. *Honours:* granted by the Union of Bulgarian Composers and Musicologists for the work The Musical History of the Town of Gabrovo, 1986; Gold Badge for Pedagogical Activities granted by Union of Musical Wkr of Bulgaria. *Hobbies:* Bringing up children; Bird and animal watching; Gardening; Mountain hiking; Drawing pictures; Singing Bulgarian folk songs. *Address:* Block 37, Entr 2, Apt 30, Todor Atanasov Str, Sofia 1408, Bulgaria.

PRODANOVA-DRAGANOVA Bojana Ivanova, b. 2 May 1917, Gabuovo. m. Stefan Christov Prodanov. *Appointments:* Sec, Tchrs Coun, 1951-73. *Publications:* Chronicle of the Stenography in Gabuovo Dist; History of Esperanto in Gabuovo Dist; Articles in various newspapers and mags. *Memberships:* Tchr's Assn; Culture Club; Pres, Stenography & Typewriters Club; Esperanto Red Cross; UWCA; UEA. *Honours include:* 2 Esperanto Golden Piins, 1968, 1985; Silver Order Saints Cyril and Methodius, 1973; Golden Pin and Honorous Dip in connection w 100 Yrs of Esperanto in Bulgaria, 1979. *Hobbies include:* Nature; Tourism; People; Poetry; Music. *Address:* 6 Jury Venelin Street, 5800 Gabrovo, Bulgaria.

PRODHON Francoise Claire, b. 30 Dec 1961, Courbevoie, France. Art Critic; Pvt Curator. *Education:* Hist of Art, Ecole du Louvre, 1980-84; Ancien Eleve, 1983; Museologie, 1984. *Appointments:* Critic, Flash

Art Int, Milano, 1983-; Critic, ETC Mag, Montreal, Can, 1987-. *Creative works:* Exhibs: D'Une Lose L'Autre, Opera de Paris, 1985; Vivae Imagines, Frankfurt, Germany, 1989; 90 2 5 0, Avves sur Oise, 1990; L'Objet de la Sculpture, Milano, Italy, 1991. Num Missions for: French Ministere de la Culture, 1985, 1990, 1991; French Foreign Off AFAA, 1989, 1990-91; Cartier Fndn for Contemporary Art, 1988-89; World Gold Coun, 1991. *Hobbies:* Reading; Fashion; Music; Cinema; Advertising concept; Theatre; Contemporary life in general. *Address:* 1 Allee Marie Laurent, 75020 Paris, France.

PROKOPENKO Joseph, b. 3 Apr 1939, Ukraine, Lugansk. Hd, Rsch & Prog Dev in Mgmt and Entrepreneurship. m. Nelly Glotova, 18 Mar 1961, 1 s. *Education:* MD in Aviation Engrng, 1956-62; MA in Econ(s), 1963-67; PhD in Econ(s) & Mgmt, 1965-71. *Appointments:* Aviation Designer, Mgr of Youth Dev Progs, Sr Rschr, Acad of Scis, USSR, -75; Sr Rschr & Cons, Mgmt Dev Br 1975-81, Sr & Cons, Mgmt Dev Br 1985-89, Hd, R & Prog Dev, Entrepreneurship & Mgmt Dev Br 1989-, ILO, Geneva; Mgmt of Rsch & Dev, Acad of Sci, Ukranian SSR, Inst of Econ(s), Kiev 1981-85. *Publications include:* Modular Programme for Supervisory Development, 1981; Productivity Management: A Practical Handbook, 1987; Diagnosis of Managment Development and Training Needs, 1989; Entrepreneurship in Public Enterprise, 1991; Human Resource Management in Economics in Transition: The East European Case, 1992. *Membership:* Int Mgmt Inst Alumni. *Hobbies:* Skiing; Tennis; Photography; Training; Publications. *Address:* International Labour Office, CH-1211 Geneve 22, Switzerland. 52.

PROMIENSKA Halina Marianna, b. 21 Dec 1935, Bydgoszcz, Poland. Prof. m. 24 Nov 1962, 1 s. *Education:* Doct, Univ of Silesia, 1968; Habil, Univ of Warsaw, 1981. *Appointments:* Univ of Wroclaw, 1960-65; Prof of Philos and Ethics, Univ of Silesia, 1968-. *Publications:* The Human Knowledge and Moral Values, 1980; The Principle of Tolerance in Science and in Ethics, 1987; Lasting and Change of Moral Values, 1991. *Membership:* Dept of Silesia, Polish Soc of Philos. *Honours:* Min of Nat Educ, 1982, 1988. *Hobbies:* Reading; Playing the piano; Mountain-climbing. *Address:* Institut of Philosophy, University of Silesia, ul Bankowa 11, 40 007 Katowice, Poland.

PRONKO Leonard Cabell, b. 3 Oct 1927, Cebu, Philippines. Tchr; Writer; Lectr. *Education:* BA, Drury Coll, 1947; MA, WA Univ, 1950; PhD, Tulane Univ, 1957. *Appointments:* Instr, French, Spanish, Lake Erie Coll, Painesville, 1954-56; French, Spanish, Pomona Coll, 1957-84; Theatre, 1984-; Chair, Theatre Dept, 1984-91. *Publications:* World of Jean Anouilh, 1961; Avant-Garde, 1962; Theatre East and West, 1967; Guide to Japanese Drama, 1973; Labiche and Feydeau, 1982; Trans of Alfonso Sastre; Dir of 15 Kabuki prods in Eng, 1965-91. *Memberships:* Assn Theatre in Higher Educ; Assn for Asian Performance. *Honours:* Los Angeles Drama Critic's Circle Awd for Kabuki, 1972; Am Coll Theatre Fest Awd of Excellence for Kabuki performed at Kennedy Ctr, WA, 1974; Phi Beta Kappa Vis Scholar, 1981; Order of the Sacred Treasure, 3rd Degree, Japanese Cultural Prize. *Hobbies:* Travel; Music; Opera; Gourmet food: pastry; Ceramics; Prints. *Address:* 1543 Bates Place, Claremont, CA 91711, USA. 13, 30.

PROSSER David John, b. 16 Mar 1953, Aberdeen, Scotland. Newspaper Ed. m. Barbara Mae Dunn, 20 May 1978. *Education:* Scottish Cert of Educ, Inverurie Acad, 1965-71; MA Hons, Aberdeen Univ, 1971-75; MA, Queen's Univ at Kingston, 1975-77; Non-Credit Fellowship, Univ of Toronto, 1991-92. *Appointments:* Announcer, Grampian TV, 1975; Actor, Theatre 5, 1978; Journalist, currently Assoc Ed, Kingston Whig-Standard, 1978-. *Publication:* Out of Afghanistan, 1987. *Memberships:* Can Assn of Journalists; Pres 1989-91, Can Theatre Critics Assn; Int Assn of Theatre Critics. *Honours:* Nathan Cohen Awd for excellence in theatre criticism, 1985, 1986, 1987; Ctr for Investigative

Journalism Awd, 1987; Nat Newspaper Awd, 1988, 1989, 1991. *Hobbies:* Bicycling; Amateur theatre; Sailboarding. *Address:* 427 Tanglewood Drive, Kingston, Ontario, Canada K7M 7V8. 142.

PROSSER Robert John Marie Vianney, b. 23 Sept 1951, Tredegar. Schmaster. *Education:* BEd Hons; Cert Ed; ACP, 1978; MRIPHH, 1980; MCollP, 1982; FRSH, 1986; MIHE, 1988. *Appointments:* Asst Master of Biol 1975-88, Hd of Biol Dept 1976-88, Fairfield HS, Widnes; Asst Master, Eng Dept, The Heath Sch, Runcorn, 1988-. *Memberships:* The Brit Soc for the Hist of Pharm; The Poetry Soc; Coll of Preceptors Eng Assn. *Hobbies:* History of Pharmacy; Horology; Philosophy. *Address:* 13 Allerton Road, Widnes, Cheshire WA8 6HP, England.

PROTASOWICKI Mikolaj, b. 20 Jan 1947, Jozefin, Poland. Professor of Ecotoxicology. m. Anna Rutkowska, 9 June 1973, 2 s. *Education:* Acad Agric, Olsztyn, 1964-68; MSc, Acad Agric, 1969; PhD, 1978; Dr hab, 1987. *Appointments:* Jr position, Commercial Insp, 1969-70; Asst Lectr, 1970- 88, Assoc Prof, Dept Hd, 1989-, Toxicology Dept, Acad Agric, Szczecin. *Publications:* 2 books; Over 100 sci papers and/or reports concerning food toxicology and aquatic ecotoxicology. *Memberships:* Polish Hydrobiological Soc; Polish Magneziological Soc; Polish Ecological Club; Comm Analytical Atomic Spectrometry, Polish Acad Scis; Working Grp Biological Effects of Contamination, Int Coun Exploration of the Sea. *Honours:* Min Educ Awards, Poland, 1982, 1989. *Hobbies:* Gardening; Diving; History. *Address:* ul Wiosny Ludow 13/9, 71-471 Szczecin, Poland.

PROTHEROE David Trevelyan, b. 22 Feb 1937, Sheffield, Eng. Cons Anaesthetist. m. Margaret Catherine Cooke, 22 Oct 1963, 2 s. *Education:* BA, Oxford; MA, BM, BCH, Oxford, 1963; FFARCS, England, 1968. *Appointments:* Sr Registrar, Bristol, 1968-72; Cons Anaesthetist, Bath, 1972-. *Memberships include:* BMA; Brit Assn of Anaesthetists, 1966; Linkman for Bath RCS, 1968; Intensive Care Soc, 1974; RSM, 1985. *Hobbies:* Golf; Gardening. *Address:* Long Barn, Charlton, Kilmersdon, Somerset BA3 5TN, England.

PROUDFOOT (Vincent) Bruce, b. 24 Sept 1930, Belfast, N Ireland. Prof. m. Edwina Valmai Windram Field, 16 Dec 1961, 2 s. *Education:* BA 1951, PhD 1957, Queen's Univ, Belfast. *Appointments:* Rsch Off, Lectr, Queen's Univ, 1954-58-59; Durham Univ, 1959-67; Vis Fellow, Univ of Auckland, 1966; Assoc Prof, Prof, Univ of Alberta, 1967-70-74; Prof, Univ of St Andrews, 1974-; Trustee, Nat Mus of Antiquities of Scotland, 1982-85. *Publications:* The Downpatrick Gold Find, 1955; Frontier Settlement Studies (ed w R G Ironside et al), 1974; Site, Environment and Economy ed 1983; Num articles in geogl, archaeological and soils journs. *Memberships:* Convenor, Publs Comm 1978-, Vice Chmn 1980-81, RSGS; FRSE 1979, Coun 1982-85, 1990-91, VP 1985-88, Convenor, Grants Comm 1988-9, Gen Sec, 1991-; Chmn 1979-83, Soc for Landscape Studies; VP 1982-85, Soc Antiquaries of Scotland; Pres, Sect H 1985, BAAS. *Honours:* FSA, 1963; FRSE, 1979; Lectures: Lister, BAAS 1964, Annual Soc for Landscape Studies 1983, Evans Queen's Univ Belfast 1985; Hon Pres, Scottish Assn Geog Tchrs, 1982-84; FRSGS, 1991. *Hobby:* Gardening. *Address:* Westgate, 12 Wardlaw Gardens, St Andrews, Fife KY16 9DW, Scotland. 1, 52, 184.

PROUDFOOT Edwina Valmai Windram, b. 9 Mar 1935, Dover, Kent, Eng. Archaeological Cons. m. Vincent Bruce Proudfoot, 16 Dec 1961, 2 s. *Education:* MA 1953-56, Dip Ed 1957, Edinburgh Univ; Tchr's Gen Cert, Miray Hse Trng Coll, 1957. *Appointments:* Sch Tchng, Edinburgh, Durham, 1957-61; Adult Educ: Lectr, Edinburgh 1957-61, Durham 1961-66, Edmonton 1969- 74, St Andrews 1977-; Temp Lectr in Archaeology, Durham Univ, 1963-66; Pt-time Lectr in Archaeology 1977-81, Dir, Fife Archaeological Index 1977-, Hon Rsch Fellow in Archaeology 1981-, Univ of St Andrews; Dir, St Andrews Heritage Servs, 1988-; Dir, num excavations, Scotland and Eng. *Creative works:* Discovery & Excavation in Scotland (Ed), 1977-; The Edmondsham Barrow, 1983; Ancient Monuments, Historic Buildings and Planning (Conf Organiser, Ed of Proceedings), 1983; Our Vanishing Heritage, (Conf Organiser 1987, Ed of Proceedings 1989); The Wilsford Shaft, 1990; Author, Ed of num mag, journ articles. *Memberships include:* Fdr, Chmn, Tayside and Fife Archaeological Comm, 1978; Coun Mbr, Soc of Antiquaries of Scotland, 1979-82; Pres 1981-89, Hon VP 1989-, Coun for Scottish Archaeology; Coun Mbr, Nat Trust for Scotland, 1985-90; Mbr, Ancient Monuments Bd for Scotland, 1986-; Chmn 1987-, St Andrews Preservation Trust; Countryside Commn for Scotland, Popular Mountain Areas Panel, 1989-90. *Hobbies:* Gardening; Music; Photography; Travel; Vernacular buildings. *Address:* Westgate, 12 Wardlaw Gardens, St Andrews, Fife KY16 9DW, Scotland.

PRUNARIU Dumitru-Dorin, b. 27 Sept 1952, Brasov. Dipl Eng Cosmonaut. m. Crina-Rodica Prunariu, 17 Aug 1974, 2 s. *Education:* Cosmonauts Trng Course, Star City, USSR, 1978-81; Doctorand, Pol Inst; Trng Inst, Montreal, Can, 1991. *Appointments:* Aircraft Engr, 1976-78; Cand in Cosmonautics, 1978-81; Space Mission, Soyuz 40-Saliut 6, 1981; Flight Chief Insp, 1981-90; Chief of the Civil Aviation Dept, Under-State Sec, 1990-91. *Publications:* 5 Minutes After Coming From the Outer Space, 1981; The Outer Space: Laboratory and Plant For the Future of Mankind, 1984; Psychic Dimensions of the Airspace Flight, 1985; 5 scientific papers at the Romanian Acad; about 20 articles on space tech. *Memberships:* Int Aviation Fedn; Astronautical Soc, Hermann Oberth-Wernher von Braun, Germany; Fndn Mbr, Assn of Space Explorers; Corresp Mbr, Int Astronautical Acad, 1992; Pres, Romanian Aeronautical Fedn. *Honours include:* Hero of Romania, Hero of USSR, 1981; Y Gagarin Medal, 1981; Gold Medal, Hermann Oberth, 1986. *Hobbies:* Photography; Computers. *Address:* Sector 2, Cod 70231, Sfintul Spiridon Str 12, Bucharest, Romania.

PRUSINKIEWICZ Zbigniew Andrzej, b. 18 Nov 1923, Poznan, Poland. Hd of Dept; Prof. m. Regina Gabriela Wendlandt, 8 Mar 1951, 1 s, 1 d. *Education:* MSc, Fac of Forestry 1950, PhD 1957, Dr habil 1962, Adam Mickiewicz Univ, Poznan. *Appointments:* Jr Asst, Adam Mickiewicz Univ, 1950-52; Sr Asst, Adj, Agricl Acad, Poznan, 1952-63; Mbr Fac of Biol and Earth Sci, Hd of Dept of Soil Sci 1963-, N Copernicus Univ, Torun; Docent, 1963-69; Assoc Prof, 1969-77; Full Prof, 1977-. *Publications include:* Forest and pedological problems in coastal dunes region of Swina gateway, 1961; Biological aspects of soil fertility, 1963; Pedological studies in the Biatowieza National Park, 1964. *Memberships:* Int Soil Sci Soc; VP, Polish Soc Soil Sci; Int Soc Plant Geog and Ecology; Polish Soc Forest Sci; Polish Bot Soc; Societas Scientiarum Torunensis. *Honours:* Gold Medal, Polish Soc Soil Sci, 1961; Polonia Restituta Cross, 1973; Oozapowski 1st prize, Polish Acad of Sci, 1977, 1989. *Hobbies:* Serious music; Contact with nature; Computers. *Address:* 30 Sienkiewicza, Torun, PL-87-100, Poland. 52.

PRUZANSKI Waldemar, b. 23 Oct 1928, Warsaw, Poland. Physn; Scientist. m. Vera Hochfelsen, 29 Oct 1963, 1 s, 1 d. *Education:* MD, Hebrew Univ, Hadassah Med Sch, Israel, 1956; FRCPC, 1968; FACP, 1972; FACR, 1986. *Appointments:* Rsch Fellow, Dept of Immunochem, Weizmann Inst of Sci, Israel, 1964; Dpty Chief of Med, Asat Harofe Hosp, Tel-Aviv Univ, Israel, 1964-65; Rsch Assoc, Columbia Univ Inst of Cancer Rsch, New York, 1965-66; Fellow, Can Arthritis & Rheumatism Soc 1967, Sr Physn 1968-, Cross-Appt, Rheumatic Disease Unit 1968-, Hd, Div of Immunology 1973-, The Wellesley Hosp, Toronto; Asst Prof of Med 1968-71, Assoc Prof of Med 1972-77, Mbr, Inst of Med Scis 1972-, Dir, Immunology Diagnostic & Rsch Ctr 1973-, Mbr, Inst of Immunology 1975-85, Prof of Med 1977-, Mbr, Royal Coll Specialty Comm for Clin Immunology 1982-, Dir, Dv of Clin Immunology and

Allergy, Fac of Med, 1984-, Mbr, Dept of Immunology 1985-, Dir, Inflammation Rsch Grp 1989-, Univ of Toronto. *Publications:* Author or co-author of over 340 papers, 22 book chapts; Ed, 2 books; Assoc Ed, J Rheumatology. *Memberships include:* Can Soc of Clin Investigation; CMA; Can Arthritis and Rheumatism Soc; Am Fedn for Clin Rsch; Am Coll of Rheumatology. *Honours:* Invited Speaker, NIH Conf on PLA2, 1989; Co-owner of 2 patents related to phospholipase A2. *Hobbies:* Theatre; Music; Travel. *Address:* The Wellesley Hospital, 160 Wellesley Street East, Room 104, The Jones Building, Toronto, Ontario, Canada M4Y 1J3. 6, 88, 139, 143.

PRYDZ Svein II, (Also known as Svein Dunker Prydz), Knight Baron, b. 3 Feb 1932, Oslo-Akershus, Norway. Scientist; Philos; Politician; Socio & Systems Analyst. *Education:* Cand Mag 1957, Cand Real 1961, Dr Philos 1972, Oslo Univ. *Appointments:* Rsch Asst 1960-61, Amanuensis 1961-63, 1st Amanuensis 1968-78, Phys Dept, Oslo Univ; Rsch Fellow, Royal Norway Coun for Sci & Indl Rsch, Keele Univ, Staffs, Eng, 1967-68; Annual Assoc, Int Advsr, ABI Rsch Assn; IBC Rsch Employment. *Creative works:* 10,000 logical sketches, an example on a first-stage production of a basis for models relating to forcasting computation on socio-econ or political modification in systems or sociaties, 1970-80; Doctoral Thesis I, ESR Spectroscopy detection of Free radicals in Dry Amino Acids upon X-ray Irradiatiron, Oslo Univ, 1961; Doctoral Thesis II (incl 10 printed sci journ papers), Some Detection methods in Radiochromatogetc, Universitetsforlaget, 1971; 60 sci papers, popular sci articles, newspaper articles, 250 poems (not published). *Memberships:* Optical Soc of Am; Nordic Soc for Radiation Protection; Phys Soc of Norway; European Phys Soc; NY Acd of Scis; LPIBA; DDG; IOM; Hon Mbr, IBC Advsry Coun; Assembly Dpty Mbr, Int Parl for Safety and Peace; Inaugural Mem, Charles Darwin Assoc, NY Acad Scis, 1992. *Honours:* Bronze Medal, Silver Medals, Gold Medals, AEIAF, Alfred Medal for Peace (AEANM), 3rd Class, 1991; Dr Sci, Hon causa, MGSIUF, 1988; Int Biog Roll of Hon, for disting serv to the Transcendance of the Human Culture, Am Biog Inst, 1983; Dr polit Sci, Hon Causa, AEIAF, 1991. *Hobbies:* Listening to classical music; Clarinet; Theatre; Teaching sound politics to politicians. *Address:* Kvernfaret 10, o-Ullern, Oslo, Norway. 43, 52, 78, 129, 134, 139, 152, 156, 162.

PRZYBYLSKI Henryk Jerzy, b. 16 July 1938, Lodz, Poland. Prof; Scientist. m. Maria Zdzienicka, 23 Sept 1961, 2 s. *Education:* MD, 1968; Dr hab, 1977. *Appointments:* Hist Mus, Lodz, 1961-64; Study Dr, 1964-67; Inst of Social Scis, Silesian Polytech, Gliwice, 1967-79; Inst of Social Scis, Acad of Econ(s), Katowice, 1979-. *Publications include:* Front Morges, 1972; The Christian Demokracy and National Workers Party in 1926-1937 Years, 1979; The Christian Demokracy and the National Workers Party, 1980; The Political Ideas of Wojciech Korfanty, 1986; The Political Crisis in Poland 1956-1981, 1986; Ignacy Jan paderewski, 1956-1981. *Memberships:* Sec 1968-71, Vice Chmn 1971-75, 1981-, Chmn 1975-81, Polish Assn of Pol Scis, Katowice; Vice Dir 1972-79, Dept of Social Scis, Silesian Polytech, Gliwice; Dir 1979-, Dept of Social Scis, Acad of Econ(s), Katowice; Chmn of Social Scis Assn, 1989; Lion's Club. *Honours:* Prizes of the Min of Educ, 1973, 1978, 1980; Mbr of Pol Scis Comm 1974-81, Mbr, Hist Comm 1978, Polish Acad of Scis, 1974-81; The Cross of Scauting Achmt, 1978; Gold Cross of Achmt, 1979; The Kt Cross of Achmt, 1987; Prize, Cath Univ, Lublin, 1990; Prize of W Korfanty, Katowice, 1991. *Hobbies:* Archology; Prehistory of North Africa; Music of Paderewski and Chopin. *Address:* ul Piastow 11 m 37, Katowice, Poland.

PSACHAROPOULOS George, b. 6 Aug 1937, Athens, Greece. Sr Human Resources Advsr. m. Helen Typaldou, 28 Aug 1965, 1 s, 1 d. *Education:* BA, Athens Sch of Bus and Econ(s), 1960; MA 1966, PhD 1969, Univ of Chicago. *Appointments include:* Tchng: Lectr in Econ(s), London Sch of Econ(s), 1971-81; Vis Lectr, Sch of Educ,

Univ of Chicago, 1974; External Examiner, Open Univ, 1976-82. Rsch: Chief, Educ Rsch Div 1981-87, Dir, Comparative Study on Poverty, Equity and Growth 1987-89, The World Bank; Chief, Human Resources Div, Latin Am Tech Dept, 1987-91. Consultancies: OECD, Dev Ctr and Directorate for Scientific Affairs, 1970-81; Unesco, Int Inst for Educl Planning and Div for Educl Policy and Planning, 1974-81; Educ Dept, World Bank, 1979-81. Journ Ed: Assoc Ed, The Econ(s) of Educ Review, 1981-; Guest Ed, The Int Review of Educ, 1988; Guest Ed, Higher Educ, Holland, 1991. *Publications include:* Diversified Secondary Education and Development: Evidence from Colombia and Tanzania (w W Loxley), 1985; The Financing of Education in Developing Countries: Exploration of Policy Options (w J P Tan and E Jimenez), 1986; Recovering Growth with Equity, 1989; Studies on Implementation of African Educational Policies (ed), 1990; The Economic Impact of Education: Lessons for Policy Makers, 1991; Essays on Poverty, Equity and Growth (ed), 1991. Author of chapts in edited works; Encyclopedia entries; Guest Ed, Journ special issues; Journal articles; TV Prods. *Hobbies:* Photography; Oil painting; Stamp collecting; Piano playing. *Address:* 6711 Melody Lane, Bethesda, MD 20817, USA.

PUCEK Zdzislaw Kazimierz, b. 2 Apr 1930, Radzyn Podlaski. Zoologist; Mammalogist. m. Michalina Swatek, 26 Dec 1955, 1 s. *Eucation:* Master degree, Warsaw Univ, 1954; PhD, M Curie-Sklodowska Univ, Lublin, 1961; Dr habil, Jagiellonian Univ, 1966. *Appointments:* Jr Sci Wkr 1954-66, Dir 1962-, Sr Sci Wkr 1966-, Mammal Rsch Inst, Polish Acad of Sci; Asst Ed 1958, Ed in Chief 1963, ACTA Theriologica. *Publications:* Ed, Co-ed, Author of 5 books; Author of about 150 journ papers and articles. *Memberships:* Polish Zoological Soc 1954-, Theriological Sect, Chmn, Vice Chmn 1969-82; N Copernicus Soc of Naturalists, 1955-; Deutsche Geselschaft fur Saugetierkunde e V, 1963-; Rep of P1 1974-85, Intern Theriological Coun; Chmn 1985-, Bison Specialist Grp, SSC/IUCN. *Honours:* Hon Mbr, Am Soc of Mammalogists, 1982; Hon Mbr, Theriological Soc, Russian Acad of Sci, 1990. *Hobby:* Classical music. *Address:* Mammal Research Institute, Polish Academy of Sciences, 17-230 Bialowieza, Poland. 52, 139, 162.

PUCHALSKI Jacek, b. 21 Nov 1964, Warsaw, Poland. Academic Teacher. m. Katarzyna Puchalska (Krol), 14 July 1990. *Education:* MLS and Info, Dept Hist, Inst Libnship and Info Sci, Univ Warsaw, 1989. *Appointments:* Lib, Warsaw Univ, 1989-91; Dept Hist, Inst Libnship and Info Sci, Univ Warsaw, 1991-. *Publications:* Articles: Political literature in seventeenth-century residential collections in Kingdom of Poland and the publishing output 1501-1732; Seventeenth-century gentry in Kingdom of Poland as owners and users of political literature. *Membership:* Polish Bibliological Soc. *Hobbies:* Photography; Film. *Address:* ul Janinowka 11 m 18, 03-562 Warsaw, Poland.

PUCKETT Laura Treadgold, b. 21 June 1956, Seattle, WA, USA. Lawyer. m. Allen Weare Puckett, 10 Jul 1992. *Education:* Stanford Univ, 1978; JD, Univ Washington, 1981; Bar, Wash, 1981; US District Ct, Wash, 1981. *Appointments:* Assoc, Bogle & Gates, Seattle, 1981-83; Weinrich & Gilmore, seattle, 1983-87; Counsel, Davis Wright & Jones, 1988-89; Ptnr, Davis Wright Tremaine, Seattle, 1990-; Natl Bd Dir, MIT Enterprize Forum, 1990-; Bd Dir MIT Enterprize Forum of Northwest, 1985-; Chmn, 1989-90; Assoc Editor, Wash Law Rev, 1980-81. *Memberships:* ABA; Bar Assn; Seattle King County Bar Assn; Japanese Am Soc for Legal Studies; Phi Beta Kappa; Episcopalian Securities. *Honour:* Kenndy Ctr Award. *Address:* Davis Wright Tremaine 1501, 4th Avenue, Seattle, WA 98101, USA.

PUDLIK Wieslaw Wladyslaw, b. 26 Aug 1930, Gdynia, Poland. Prof. m. Alicja Wojtczuk, 23 Mar 1961, 1 s. *Education:* BSc 1950-54, MSc 1954-56, Politechnika Gdanska; PhD 1966, PhD habil 1973, Tech Univ of Gdansk. *Appointments:* Energy Insp, State Dredging Co,

Gdansk, 1950-54; Rschr, Inst of Fluid Flow Machines, Polish Acad of Scis, 1955-65; Lectr, Prof, Politechnika Gdanska, 1966-. *Publications:* Original publs on investigations into fuel conversion in MHD power plants, 1975-83; Heat Transfer and Heat Exchangers, 1976, 1980, 1988; Thermal Measurements (ed, co-author), 1986; Testing of Thermal Equipment (ed, co-author), 1991. *Memberships:* Mbr of Bd, Polish Soc of Theoretical and Applied Mechs; Comm of Thermodynamics and Combusstion, Polish Acad of Scis. *Honours:* Prizes of the Min of Educ: for achmts in rsch 1974, 1979, 1984; in educ 1980, 1987. *Hobbies:* Sailing; Cross-country skiing; Swimming; Classical music. *Address:* ul Biata 6 m 30, 80-435 Gdansk, Poland.

PULLIAINEN Erkki Ossi Olavi, b. 23 June 1938, Varkaus, Finland. Prof. m. Riitta Haaranen, 2 Feb 1974, 2 s, 3 d. *Education:* BSc 1960, MSc 1964, Lic Sc 1964, Dissertation 1965, PhD 1966, MSc 1968, Univ of Helsinki. *Appointments:* Rsch Asst 1962, Admnstr 1962-65, Scientist 1964-74, Dir of Varrio Subarctic Rsch Sta 1967-, Docent of Wildlife Biol 1968-, Univ of Helsinki; Sr Scientist, Acad of Finland, 1975; Full Prof of Zoology 1975-, Hd of the Zool Dept and Perameri Rsch Sta 1978-, Dean of Fac of Natural Scis 1980-, Univ of Oulu, 1975-. *Publications:* Finnish Great Predators, 1974; Trade Union Policy of Civil Servants, 1975; Rearing of Game Birds in Captivity, 1975; Behavior and Character of Dogs, 1980; Finland in the year 2000, 1982; Predators and Man, 1984; Author of about 350 articles. *Memberships include:* PP, Mammal Soc of Finland, 1977-; NY Acad of Scis, 1981-; VP, Third Int Theriol Cong held in Helsinki, 1982; City Govt and City Coun of Oulu, 1985; Mbr of Parliament, 1987-, C Parliament Grp, 1989-91; ABIRA. *Honours:* Silver Badge of Merit, Finnish Nature Fedn, 1968; Order of Kthood of Finnish Lion, 1st class order, 1975; Hon Pres, Univ of Tchrs and Employees Union, 1978; Gold Badge of Merit, State Offs' Union, 1980; Commemorative Medal of Hon, ABIRA, 1986. *Hobbies:* Philately; Forwarding of green policy in the world. *Address:* Rantakalliontie 6, 90800 Oulu, Finland. 52, 90, 156.

PULMAN Michael Barraclough, b. 20 Apr 1933, Liverpool, Eng. Unit Prof. *Education:* AB, Princeton Univ 1960; MA 1961, PhD 1964, Univ of CA at Berkeley. *Appointments:* Asst Prof of Hist, FL State Univ, 1964-71; Assoc Prof of Hist, Univ of Denver, 1971-. *Publications:* The Elizabethan Privy Council in the 1570s, 1971; Articles & Reviews in The Journ of Lib Hist, The Journ of Pol, Albion, The Am Histl Review. *Memberships:* FRHistS; The Historic Soc of Lancs & Cheshire. *Hobbies:* Gardening; Travelling; Reading; Dog breeding (Norwegian Elkhounds); Carpentry; Writing. *Address:* History Department, University of Denver, Denver, CO 80208, USA. 9, 30.

PUNDHIR Pramod, b. 1 July 1956, Etah, U P, India. Associate Professor of Plant Breeding. m. Ranjana Pundhir, 19 June 1987. *Education:* BSc (Hons), Agric, Animal Husbandry, 1975; MSc Agric, Plant Breeding, 1977; PhD, Plant Breeding, 1983. *Appointments:* Rsch Assoc, Pant Univ, 1982; Asst Prof, Sukhadia Univ, 1983; Assoc Prof, Rajasthan Agric Univ, 1991. *Memberships:* Ed Bd, Ganganegar Kheti agric mag; Indian Soc Genetics and Plant Breeding; Indian Soc Oilseed Rsch. *Honours:* Sr Fellowship, Indian Coun Agric Rsch, 1977; Inservice Fellowship, Int Crops Rsch Inst Semi Arid Tropics, Patencheru, India, 1986; Fellow, Indian Soc Genetics and Plant Breeding, 1989. *Hobbies:* Studying the culture of other states and countries; Studying socio-economic conditions of farmers. *Address:* Agriculture Research Station, Rajasthan Agriculture University, Sri Ganganegar 335001, India.

PUNGOR Erno, b. 30 Oct 1923, Vasszecseny. Chem; Hd of Rsch Grp. m. Dr Tunde Horvath, 8 Sept 1984, 2 s, 1 d. *Education:* PhD, 1949; Cand of Chem Sci, 1952; DSc, 1956; Corr Mbr, 1967. *Appointments:* Asst Prof 1948-53, Assoc Prof 1953-62, Prof 1962-70, Eotvos L Univ Budapest; Inst Dir, Chem Univ, Veszprem, 1962-

70; Dir, Inst for Gen and Anal Chem Techn, Univ of Budapest, 1970-90; Hd of Rsch Grp for Techn Chem Anal, Hungarian Sci Acad. *Publications:* Author of books and over 300 papers on modern analytical. *Memberships:* Hd, Anal Grp, Hungarian Acad of Sci, 1970-; Int Fedn of the Scientific Eds Assn, 1981; Chmn, Anal Div, Hungarian Chem Soc, -89; Pres, Nat Comm for Tech Dev, 1990-; Min without Portfolio, 1991. *Honours include:* Gold Medal for Excellent Inventors, 1976, 1979; Redwood Lectr, 1979; Gold Medal for Merit in the Serv of the Fatherland, 1980; Pro Natura, 1986; Robert Boyle Gold Medal; Talanta Gold Medal, 1987; Hungarian Acad of Sci Gold Medal, 1988; Gold Medal, Tech Univ of Wien, 1988. *Hobby:* Recorded history. *Address:* Research Group for Technical Analytical Chemistry, Hungarian Academic Sciences, Institute for General and Analytical Chemistry, Technical University of Budapest, Gellert ter 4, 1111-Budapest, Hungary.

PURDY Martin Terence, b. 22 Feb 1939, Oakham. Archt. *Education:* Dip Arch 1961; Dip TP 1969; PhD 1984; MA 1986. *Appointments:* Rsch Fellow, Lectr, Birmingham Sch of Arch and Univ of Aston, 1964-82; Ptnr, APEC, 1969-. *Publications:* Housing on Sloping Site (co-author w Barry Simpson), 1984; Churches and Chapels, 1991. *Creative works:* Archt of num ch bldgs; Archt to Sheffield Cath, 1989-. *Memberships:* RIBA, 1962-; Registered Archt of UK, 1962-. *Hobbies:* Fell walking; Music, Opera. *Address:* 72 Stephenson Tower, Station Street, Birmingham B5 4DR, England.

PURDY Quentin Alexander, b. 23 Aug 1960, Leicester, Eng. Barrister. m. Elizabeth Hazelwood, 3 Sep 1988. *Education:* BA Hons, Leicester Poly, 1982; Called to Bar, Gray's Inn, 1983; LLM (Lond), 1985. *Appointment:* Barrister, 1983-. *Membership:* Criminal Bar Assn. *Honour:* Band Trust Awd, Gray's Inn, 1983. *Hobbies:* Walking; Sailing; Foreign travel; Reading. *Address:* 14 Gray's Inn Square, Gray's Inn, London WC1R 5JP, England.

PURNELL John Howard, b. 17 Aug 1925, Rhondda, Wales. Prof. m. Elizabeth Mary Edwards, 24 Aug 1954, 1 s, 1 d. *Education:* BSc, U C Cardiff, 1943-46; PhD, Univ of Wales, 1953; MA 1954, PhD 1955, ScD 1968, Univ of Cambridge. *Appointments:* Lectr, U C Cardiff, 1947-52; Univ Demonstrator, Cambridge, 1955-60; Lectr, Univ of Cambridge, 1960-65; Prof, U C Swansea, 1965-. *Publications:* About 200 rsch papers in learned journs on gas kinetics, photochem, heterogeneous catalysis, chromatography. *Memberships:* Hon Treas 1985-90, FRSC. *Honours:* Beilby Gold Medal, 1970; Tswett Int Medal, 1977; Evans Medal, 1979; Commemorative Medal, Acad of Scis, USSR, 1979; Separation Sci Medal, RSC, 1983; Redwood Lectr, RSC, 1990; OBE, 1992. *Hobbies:* Rugby football; Gardening; Music. *Address:* 1 Bishopston Road, Bishopston, Swansea SA3 3EH, Wales.

PUSTILNIKOV Leonid Moiseyevich, b. 17 April 1941, Kiev, Ukraine. Researcher; Scientific and Mathematical Programme Specialist. *Education:* Grad w highest hons, Phys, Al-Pharabi Kazakh Univ, 1964; Cand, Phys-Maths, 1968; Sr Lectr, Fac ADv Maths, 1976; Dr Tech Sc, 1981. *Appointments:* Acting Prof, then Hd, Dept Applied Maths, Mil School ADv Engrng, Vladivostok, then St Petersburg, 1973-88; Currently: Chief of Sci, Dept Math Modelling Sci and Rsch Projects, Institute Halurgy, St Petersburg and Prof, St Petersburg Sci-Mfg Org School, Mgr Systems; Sci Cons, firms, Moscow, St Petersburg, Vladivostok and Kazakhstan. *Creative works:* Series inventions; Several collections, computer software programmes; 150 publications incl co-author, books: Heating slope cylinder mobile source, 1971; The Theory of Mobile Control of Systems with Distributed Parameters, 1980; Various Approaches to the Problem of Interpolation of Physical Fields, 1983; The End of Integral Transformations and their Application to Research in Distributed Parameter Systems, 1986; Mobile Control of Distributed Parameter Systems, 1987; Przeksztatcenia Calkowe Skouczone, 1990;

Characteristics of Distributed Parameter, 1992; Modelling and Control in Underground Salt Solutions in Strata, 1992; . *Memberships:* Special Coun Def of Dissertations, Inst Hydrogeology and Hydrophys, Kazakhstan Acad Scis. *Honours:* Gold Medal, HS graduation, Alma-Ata, Kazakhstan, 1958. *Address:* Narodnoye Opolcheniye Prospectus 221, app 124, 198334 St Petersburg, Russia.

PUXLEY Herbert Lavallin, b. 6 Nov 1907, Goring, Eng. Ret'd. m. Mary Sedgewick, 18 June 1932, 2 s, 1 d. *Education:* BA Hons, 1929; MA Yale, 1931; MA, Oxford, 1934. *Appointments:* Prof of Econ(s), Univ of AGRA, 1932-40; Chmn, Rsch Sect, VP, Bd of Higher Educ, AGRA; Inaugurated Rural Dev Prog in Agra Dist; Indian Army, ret'd as Lt Col, 1940-46. *Publications:* A Critique of the Gold Standard, 1934; Agricultural Marketing in Agra District, 1936; Christian Land Settlement, 1940. *Honours:* Hon DD, Univ of King's Coll, 1963; Hon DD, Trinity Coll, Toronto, 1964; Hon DCL, Acadia Univ, 1966; Hon D Litt, St Mary's Univ, 1967; Hon DD, Wycliffe Coll, Toronto, 1968. *Hobbies:* Critical bible study; Philately. *Address:* 45 Dahlia Street, Dartmouth, Nova Scotia, Canada B3A 2S1. 88.

PYPER George Earl, b. 5 June 1927, Toronto, Can. Columnist & Critic in Arts, Entertainment, Theatre; Concert Violinist; Instr. *Education:* Violin & Theory, Toronto Conservatory of Music w J Montague, Godfrey Ridout, Dr Healey Willan, 1940-48; Licentiate Concert, Exams w Hons, Violin Studies, Alexander Brott, McGill Conservatorium, Montreal, 1945; Alexander Chuhaldin, Advanced Studies, 1949; Drawing & Painting, Ont Coll of Art; Acting, Burton James, Banff, 1950. *Appointments:* CBC Soloist on Tomorrow's Concert Stars, 1945-47; Concertmaster, Royal Alexandra Theatre, Toronto, 1948-55; Full Performing Mbr, London Symph Orch, Eng, 1956-57; Toronto Symph Orch, Can, 1958-63; Orquesta Sinfonica da Chihuahua, Mexico, 1963; Nat Ballet Orch Tours, Instr of Violin, 1970-74; Lakefield Coll Sch, Ont, Concertmaster & String Coach, Peterborough Symph Orch, 1970-76; Fdr, Conductor, Peterborough Symph Orch Youth Orch, 1973-76; Instr, Violin, Viola, Cello, Nanaimo, BC, 1978-87; Music Critic, Nanaimo Times, 1985-88; Columnist, Violin Soloist; Weekly Columnist, Campbell River Mirror, 1988-91. *Memberships:* Am Fedn of Musicians; FCA. *Honours:* Silver Medal, Toronto Conservatory of Music, 1942; Election to full performing mbrship, London Symph Orch, 1956; Medal, World Decoration of Excellence, Am Biog Inst, 1989; Awded Cert of Commendation, Coun of Dist of Campbell River: in Recog of Outstng Community Serv 1990, Exemplary Citizenship, 1991; Nominated by Community Arts Coun for Promoting Dev of the Arts; Dep Gov (Lifetime), Am Biog Inst Rsch Assn; IBC Music Silver Medal. *Hobbies:* Painting; Drawing; Playing concerts; Writing. *Address:* c/o Toronto Musicians' Association, Local 149, AFM, 101 Thorncliffe Park Drive, Toronto, Ontario, Canada M4H 1M2. 4.

Q

QADEER Saad Abdul, b. 4 Sept 1962, Karachi, Pakistan. Dir. m. Farah Qadeer, 25 Dec 1987, 1 s. *Education:* BBA, 1987. *Appointment:* Muhamad Amin Bros Ltd. *Memberships:* Pakistan Jute Mills Assn; Karachi Gymkhana Club. *Address:* 4-A 7 Central Lane, Defence Housing Society, Karachi, Pakistan.

QI Shaomei, b. 17 Aug 1932, Feicheng. Econ Geology. m. Langsheng Liu, 23 Apr 1962, 2 d. *Education:* Bethune Med Coll, Jinan, 1951; BSc, Changchun Geology Coll, Jilin, 1960. *Appointments:* Pharmacist, Hlth Hosp of Women and Children, Jinan, 1951-56; Assoc Prof, Inst of Mineral Deposits, Chinese Acad of Geological Sci, 1960-. *Publications:* Author of a number of publs. *Memberships:* Geological Soc of China; China Assn for Sci & Tech. *Honours:* Decoration by Chinese Sci Conf, 1978; 1st class prize, Sichuan Sci Comm, 1979; 1st class prize, Geology and Resource Min of China, 1983; 4th class prize, CAGS. *Hobbies include:* Biogeochemistry; Biochemistry; Pharmacology; Swimming; Touring. *Address:* Institute of Mineral Deposits, Chinese Academy of Geological Science, 26 Baiwanzhuang Road, Beijing 100037, China.

QI Shiyu, b. 20 June 1936, Changchun City, Jilin Province, P R China. Spring Wheat Breeder. m. Xiulan Wu, 8 Mar 1961, 1 s, 1 d. *Education:* Harbin Foreign Lang Coll, 1954-57; Northeast Agricl Coll, 1957-62. *Appointments:* Asst, Foreign Lang Off, Northeast Agricl Coll, 1960-61; Techn 1962-78, Asst Rsch Prof 1978-85, Assoc Rsch Prof 1985-88, Full Rsch Prof 1988-, Crop Breeding Inst, Heilongjiang Acad of Agricl Sci. *Publications:* Chinese Wheat Varieties and Pedigree, 1983; Spring Wheat Ecological Breeding, 1988. *Memberships:* Expert Grp, Chinese Sci and Tech Comm; Chinese Crop Assn; Chiense Seed Assn; Chinee Genetics Assn. *Honours:* 1st degree Awd 1985, 3rd degree Awd 1986, Min of Agric of China; 2nd degree Awd, Chinese Sci & Tech Comm, 1987; 1st degree Awd, Govt of Heilongjiang Province, 1987. *Hobbies:* Tabletennis; Literature. *Address:* Crop Breeding Institute, Heilongjiang Academy of Agricultural Sciences, Harbin, China.

QIAN Jiazheng, b. 8 June 1935, Huzhou, Zhejiang Province, China. Chief Senior Engineer, CTV Design and CAD. m. Xu Shu Qing, 1 Jan 1963, 2 s, 2 d. *Education:* Grad, Shanghai Jiao Tong Univ, 1955; Acad Chin Inst Phys, 1955; Study, Rsch, CAD, Japan, Dec 1988. *Appointments:* Tech, Shanghai Instrument Inst, 1957-68; Dir, Missiles and Rockets, 1959-64; TV Rsch Inst, Shanghai Broadcast Equipment Factory, 1965-91. *Publication:* Colour Television, book, 1985. *Memberships:* China Electronics Assn; Shanghai Electronics Assn; Shanghai Communications Assn. *Honours:* Excellent Mbr, Sci and Technology, 1991. *Hobbies:* Tennis; Touristic visits. *Address:* The Educational Department, Shanghai Broadcast Equipment Factory, ADD 1319 Yanan West Road, Shanghai, China.

QIAN Jing-ren, b. 23 July 1935, Jiangsu Province, China. Prof. m. Wang Chung, 1 Jan 1960, 1 s, 1 d. *Education:* Nanjing Inst of Tech, 1956. *Appointments:* Inst of Electronics, Chinese Acad of Scis, 1956- 65; Inst of Electronics, Chengdu, 1965; Xian Radio Tech Inst, 1968; joined Univ 1978, Prof 1985-, Univ of Scis and Tech of China. *Publications:* Over 40 profl articles and two patents. *Memberships:* Fellow, Chinese Inst of Electronics; Soc of Microwaves; Assoc Ed, Journ of Univ of Sci & Tech of China. *Hobbies:* Skating; Dancing. *Address:* Department of Radio and Electronics, University of Science and Technology of China, Hefei, Anhui 230026, China.

QIAN Xin, b. 5 Feb 1932, Liao-ning. Prof. m. Chui Ying Zhang, 1956, 2 s, 2 d. *Education:* North-East Inst of Tech, 1953; Grad Sch, Zhang Nan Indl Univ, 1956. *Appointments:* Hd, Ore Dressing Technique Grp, 1974-78; Vice Dir, Nat Resource Dev Dept, 1978-84; Dir, Educ Mgmt Off, 1984-85; Dean, Grad Sch, 1985-92; Advsr of Doct Student, appointed by Degree Comm, 1990. *Publications:* On the Concentration of Copper, 1982; The Study of the Flotation Reagents, 1988; Process Monitoring Techniques, 1991. *Memberships:* Ore Dressing Technique Commn, Ore Indl Acad Assn of China; Noble Metal Commn, Metal Acad Assn of China. *Honours:* Hon Tchr 1974, Advanced Labour 1978, Kunming Inst of Tech; Cert of Hon for work over 30 yrs, Gen Non-ferrous Metal Ind Co of China, 1991. *Hobbies:* Music; Chess. *Address:* Natural Resource Developing Department, Kunming Institute of Technology, Yun Nan 650093, China.

QIN Zenghao, b. 21 July 1933, Ningbo, China. Prof. m. Xuejun Feng, 27 Jan 1962, 2 s. *Education:* Dept of Meteorology, Nanjing Univ, Nanjing, 1952-56. *Appointments:* Asst, Dept of Meteorology, Nanjing Univ, Nanjing, 1956- 57; Asst, Dept of Oceanography, Univ of Shandong, Qingdao, 1958-62; Lectr 1962-77, Assoc Prof, Vice Chmn 1978-82, Dept of Phys Oceanography and Marine Meteorology, Prof, Dpty Dir, 1983-85, Inst of Phys Oceanography, Shandong Coll of Oceanology, Qingdao; Sr Rsch Scientist 1986-, Shanghai Typhoon Inst; concurrent Prof, Ocean Univ of Qingdao, Qingdao; Disciplinary Judge, Academic Deg Cttee of State Coun of China, 1991-. *Publications:* Ocean Circulation Dynamics; Author of 73 papers on dynamics of atmosphere and ocean, ocean-atmosphere interaction, storm surge, marine meteorology. *Memberships include:* Chmn, Comm on Marine Meteorology, Chinese Metorological Soc, 1986-; Shanghai Meteorological Soc, 1989-; Vice Chmn, Chinese Soc of Storm Surgs and Tsunami, 1983-; Exec Mbr, Chinese Soc of Oceanography, 1985-; Chinese Oceanological and Limnological Soc, 1992-; Mem, Comm for Natural Marine Hazards, Int Assoc of Physical Scis of Ocean, 1988-; Mem, State Antartic Scientific Expedition Cttee of China, 1991-; Ed Comm, Acta Oceanlogica Sinica, 1980-; Acta Meterologica Sinica, 1987-; Antarctic Res, 1990-; Acta Geophysica Sinica, 1989-; Oceanologia et Limnologia, 1990-; Ed-in-Chief, Atmospheric Scis Rsch and Application, 1990-. *Honours include:* Chief Winner, Nat Natural Scis 3rd prize, 1982; Chief Winner of 2nd prize of Sci & Tech, Nat Comm for Educ, 1987; Chief Winner of 1st prize of Sci & Tech, Shandong Provincial Comm for Educ, 1989. *Hobbies:* Sports; Music. *Address:* Ocean University of Qingdao, PO Box 90, Qingdao 266003, China. 139, 152.

QIU Changqiang, b. 12 July 1934, Calcutta, India. Prof. m. Yuanbing Liu, 1 Jan 1961, 3 s. *Education:* Dept of Chem, Wuhan Univ, 1952-56. *Appointments:* Began working at the Inst of Hydrobiol, Academia Sinica 1956, Asst Prof 1963, Assoc Prof 1979, Prof 1986-. *Publications:* Investigation of Qinhai Lake, 1977; Studies and Examples of the Background Values of Water Environment, 1990; Author of over 40 papers in mags and journs in Chinese. *Memberships:* Acd Comm, Inst of Hydrobiol; Chinese Assn of Aquatic Environment; Ed Bd: Acta of Hydrobiol Sinica, Journ of Chinese Environmental Monitoring. *Honours include:* Awds on the 2nd level scientific progress, Scientific Comm of Hunan Province, 1986; Awds on the 3rd level scientific progress, 1986; Awds on the 2nd level scientific progress 1987, 1991, 3rd level scientific progress 1988, Chinese Acad of Sci, 1987. *Hobbies:* Scientific researchment. *Address:* Institute of Hydrobiology, Academia Sinica, Wuhan 430072, China.

QIU Shihua, b. 5 July 1932, Rugao, Jiangsu, China. Prof; Dir. m. Lianzhen Cai, 15 Feb 1956, 1 d. *Education:* Dept of Phys, Zhejiang Univ, 1951-52; Grad, Dept of Phys, Fudan Univ, 1952-55. *Appointments:* Inst of Phys, CAS, 1955-59; Rsch on Counters, Inst of Archaeology, CASS, 1959-; initiating a first 14C dating lab in China, 1965; setting-up Chinese 14C reference standard, 1981. *Publications:* Radio-carbon dating in chinese archaeology, 1965-81; ed in chief, 14C chronological research in China, 1990. *Memberships:* Hd of Radiocarbon Dating Soc, Chinese Quaternary Rsch Assn; Dpty Dir of Coun, Chinese Soc of Archaeometry; Chinese Archaeology Soc. *Honours:* 1st class prize for 14C dating, Chinese Acad of Social Scis, 1988; Nat 3rd class prize for The Chinese Sucrose Charcoal Standard, 1989. *Address:* The Institute of Archaeology, CASS, 27 Wangfujing Dajie, Beijing, China.

QU Xian He, b. 20 Sept 1944. Hd. m. Jun Ying Zhang, 23 Mar 1967, 1 s, 1 d. *Education:* Bach's degree, China Ctrl Drama Inst, 1965. *Appointments:* Actor, Minority Nationality Art Ensemble, 1965-73; Actor 1973, Ldr 1984, China Coal-Mine Art Ensemble. *Creative works:* Declaim in The Chorus - The Yellow River; Recorded over 1000 famous lit works for the ctrl and local broadcasting sta; The host in the atrical performance for the ctrl and local TV broadcasting sta; Dubbing for a number of foreign films; Plays incl: The Midsummer Night Dream; The Mousetrap; Plot & Love. Chinese Classical Drama: Picking Up Jade Bracelet; King Wu Ling of Zhao. Film: The Last Eight Men; Announcer, Dubbing, Reciting Poems with expression on stage. *Memberships:* Coun, China Dramatist Assn; Comm Mbr, Art Comm; Standing Comm, China Nation Youth Union; Conduct Comm, China Nation Returned Overseas Chinese Union; Coun, China Arts and Lang Rsch Party; China TV Artist Assn. *Honours:* Awded 1 of the 10 outstng announcers in China, Ctrl People's Broadcasting Sta, 1986; Prominent Actor of China, 1988; Pyong Yeng Fest Art Dipl, 13th World Youth Fest & the Metal of Int rt Fest, 1989. *Hobbies:* Collecting stamps; Riding a horse; Bowling. *Address:* He Ping Xi Jie, China Coal-Mine Art Ensemble, Beijing 100013, China.

QUAN Heng, b. 5 May 1938, Yan Ji, P r China. m. Xiangshu Han, 14 Feb 1964, 2 s. *Education:* Bach degree, Changchun Coll of Geology, 1959-64. *Appointments:* Asst Engr of Geology Explortion, 1964-66; Engr of Geological Exploration, 1966-85; Assoc Rsch Fellow, 1985-91. *Publications:* Author of 15 papers and reports of rsch work incl: regional geology, volcanics rock, mineral deposits; The Features and prospecting of mineral-genetics of polymetal, gold and silver in Yan-Liao District (Monograph). *Memberships:* Chinese Inst of Geology; Chinese Inst of Geochem and Mineralogy. *Honours:* 3rd prize, Iron ore deposit in Huanggang, 1980; 4th prize, Stability of the Dan dong electric plant, 1987; 4th prize, Volcanics in Da Xinganling, 1989; 3rd prize, Polymetal genetics in Yan Liao District, 1991. *Hobbies:* Music; Football; Skating. *Address:* Geological Books Publishing House, East City Hepingli, Beijing 100013, China.

QUANJER Johan Henri, b. 23 May 1934, Sourabaia, Java, Indonesia. Publr; Ed; Lectr. *Education:* HBS, The Hague, Holland, 1946-52; Agricultural Coll, 1952-53. *Appointments:* Fdr of Pneumatocratic, Social, Philosophical and Political Princs, 1973; Publr, Ed of the New Humanity Journal, 1975- ; Lectr on: Philos, Psychology, Hist, Humanities. *Publications:* One World One Truth, 1964; Author of num papers. *Hobbies:* Collecting antique books; Gardening; Classical music. *Address:* 51A York Mansions, Prince of Wales Drive, London SW11 4BP, England.

QUASTEL Anthony Stephen, b. 14 Nov 1955, London, Eng. Dr of Med. *Education:* Middlesex Hosp Med Sch, Univ of London, 1974-79. *Appointments:* Sr Hse Off in Psych, Middlesex Hosp, 1982; Gen Pract Prin, 1984; Fdr of Diet and Medicare, 1986; Prin of 4 Pvt Hlthcare Practs covering SE Eng. *Honours:* Charles Bell Prize, St Dunstons Coll, Eng, 1974; Dip, Royal Coll of Obstetricians for Family Planning, 1984. *Hobbies:* Gardening; Politics; Talking; Golf. *Address:* Hightrees House, Highclere Close, Kenley, Surrey CR8 5JU, England.

QUE Duan-Lin, b. 19 May 1928, Fuzhou, China. Prof. m. Zai-Liang Yang, July 1960, 1 s, 1 d. *Education:* Grad, Elec Engrng Dept, Xia-Men Univ, China, 1951.

Appointments: Asst, Xia-Men Univ, 1951-53; Asst 1953-54, Lectr 1954-78, Assoc Prof 1978-80, Full Prof 1981-, Zhejiang Univ. *Creative works:* Holds five Chinese (invention) patents for the techniques for CZ-silicon crystalgrown at Nitrogen with reduced pressure. *Membership:* Chienese Electronics Inst. *Honours:* Chinese Nat Invention Prize, 1988, 1989; Gold Medal, World Fair for invention rsch and indl innovation, Brussels, 1988. *Address:* Zhejiang University, Hangchow, China.

QUICK Roy Dixon Jr, b. 27 June 1951, Washington, USA. Exec Off. m. Anette B Lai, 23 Apr 1988, 1 d. *Education:* BS 1969-73, MA 1973-75, VA State Univ; Dip, Basic AMEDD Offs Course, 1975; MA, Webster Univ, 1976-78; Dip, Advance AMEDD Offs Course, 1981; Dip, Command and Gen Staff Coll, 1986. *Appointments:* Commissioned 2nd Lt, US Army 1973-, entered active duty 1975-; Field Med Asst, 32nd Med Depot 1975-76, Platoon Ldr, 429th Med Co 1976- 77, Med Off, 12th Avn Grp 1977-78, Ft Bragg, NC; Co Cmdr 1978-80, Exec Off 1991-, Walter Reed Army Med Ctr; Co Cmdr, 2nd Med Bn, Korea, 1982; Career Plans Asg Off, USAMEDPERSA, Washington DC, 1983-88; Hlth Care Admin Off, Brooke Army Med Ctr, San Antonio, 1988-90; Resident US Army Command & Gen Staff Coll, Ft Leavenworth, 1990-91. *Memberships:* US Mil Surg Assn, 1977; Biomed Instrumentation Mgt Assn, 1980; Am Security Coun Ed Found, 1982; Am Assn of Indiv Investor, 1982; Am Entrepreneur Assn, 1983; Am Mgmt Assn, 1988; Assn of US Army, 1988. *Honours:* Nat Def Serv Medal, 1975; Army Commendation Medal, 1978; Meritorious Serv Medal, 1981; US Congressional Cert of Recognition, 1981; Meritorious Serv Medal 1st OLC 1982, 2nd OLC 1988; Army Achmt Medal, 1982. *Hobbies:* Chess; Tennis; Racquetball; Skating; Baseball; Sailing; Travelling. *Address:* PO Box 1802, Wheaton, MD 60902, USA. 6, 7, 52, 117.

QUILLIAN Warren Wilson II, b. 21 Jan 1936, Miami, FL, USA. Physn. m. Sallie Creel, 26 July 1958, 1 s, 3 d. *Education:* MD, Emory Univ Sch of Med, 1961; Intern, Vanderbilt, 1961-62; Resident, Children's Hosp, Boston, 1962-63; Chief Resident, Grady Mem Hosp, 1963-64. *Appointments:* US Army Med Corps, 1964-66; Pvt Pract, Coral Gablu, 1966-; Clin Prof of Pediatrics, Univ of Miami; SA Attng Pediatric, Miami Children's Hosp. *Publications:* Author of various articles in med journs. *Memberships:* Dipl, certified 1966-80-87, Pres, VP, Treas, Am Bd of Pediatrics; Bd of Gov, Emory Univ; Bd of Dir, Miami Childrens Hosp; Dir, Bank of Coral Gablu; Dir, Am Pediatric Fndn; AMA; FMA; YMCA; AAP; Pres, Greater Miami Pediatric Soc. *Honours:* Cit of Merit, Emory Univ, 1980; Commendation, Miami Childrens Hosp, 1983. *Hobbies:* Fishing; Football. *Address:* 305 Granello Avenue, Coral Gables, FL 33146, USA. 7.

QUINN Phillip David Roger, b. 18 Sept 1946, Bromley, Kent, Eng. Hypnotherapist; Cnslr. *Education:* Grimsby Tech Coll, S Humberside, 1963-65; Therapy Trng Colls, 1976-79. *Appointments:* Acctcy Trainee, 1963-65; Police Off, 1965-79; Hypnotherapist, Cnslr, 1979-. *Creative works:* The Therapeutic Value of Hypnotherapy Interventions in Non-Medical or Unexplained Infertility; Hypnotherapists Trng Manuals; Therapy Progs; Num Articles. *Memberships:* Dir, The Assn for Applied Hypnosis; Pres, The Fedn of Hypnotherapists; Cons Lectr, UK Trng Coll of Hypnosis and Counselling; Psychological Oncology Grp, Kings Coll Hosp; Brit Infertility Counselling Assn. *Honour:* Appointed Pres, Fedn of Hypnotherapists, 1989. *Hobbies:* Family; The spiritual and psychosomatic implications of matters relating to Quantum Mechanics and Evolution History. *Address:* 33 Abbey Park Road, Grimsby, Sth Humberside DN32 0HS, England.

QUINN-MUSGROVE Sandra Lavern Nowland, b. 30 Oct 1935, Grand Rapids, MI, USA. Assoc Prof. m. Freddy G Musgove, 24 Oct 1986, 1 s, 4 d. *Education:* BA 1975, MA 1976, UNLV; PhD, Claremont Grad Sch, 1978.

Appointments: Chair, Dept of PO SC, EC, SJC/S, Houston, 1981-88; UH/CL, PO, HS, 1984-88; Chair, Dept of SS, Assoc Prof, OLLU/SA, 1988-. *Publications include:* How to Pass Essay Exams; How to Pass Objective Exams; America's Royalty: All the Pres Children; On Education, weekley newspaper colm. *Memberships:* APSA; SWPSA; SWSSA; AWRT; ABWA; L of W Voters. *Hobbies:* Fishing; Painting; Sewing; Reading; Writing; Poetry; Gardening. *Address:* 411 SW 24th Street, OLLU, San Antonio, TX 78207, USA. 7.

QUIRCE BALMA Carlos Manuel, b. 15 June 1942, San Jose, Costa Rica. *Education:* BS 1965, MA 1968, Fordham Univ; PhD, IN Univ, 1974. *Appointments:* NSF Student Rsch Fellowship, 1964-65; Rowe Fund Grantee, 1964-68; OAS Fellowship, 1967-68; Student Grad Asst, IN Univ, 1968-71; NIMH Student Rsch, 1972; Prof, Rschr, Univ of Costa Rica, 1973-86. *Creative works:* Experimental and theoretical work on stres; Experimentation on rats and nutritional biogenic amine precursors that impeded development of sustained aftermath stress states of functioning. *Memberships:* ALAMOC, 1976-83; Colegio de Psicologos, Costa Rica, 1977-; Fulbright Fellowship Assn, 1990; Life Fellow, Am Biog Assn. *Honours include:* Am Chem Rubber Co Awd, 1961-62; Merck Index Awd, 1963-64; Affiliate Assoc Prof, Dept of Pharmacology & Toxicology, Sch of Pharm, 1978-84; Fulbright Fellowship Awd, 1982-83; Cert of Merit, IBC, 1987; Dip de Reconocimiento, Colegio de Psicologos, 1988; Dip de Reconocimiento, Universidad de Costa Rica, 1989; Various times Deans List: Fordham Univ, Purdue Univ. *Hobbies:* Fishing; Hunting; Collecting precolumbian objects, amulets, fetishes, coins; Meditational techniques. *Address:* Apartado (Box) 1431-1000, San Jose, Costa Rica, America Central. 52, 139, 152, 155.

QUIRICI Daniel, b. 8 June 1948, Chelles, France. Chief Exec. m. Margaret Mann, 1 Sept 1972, 2 s, 1 d. *Education:* MA, Sorbonne, Paris, 1970; MBA, Ecole des Hautes Etudes Commerciales, 1970; PhD, Stanford Univ, USA, 1974. *Appointments:* Assoc, Arthur D Little, 1976-82; VP, Credit Commercial de France, 1982-85; MD, CCF, Laurence Prust Ltd, 1986-91; CEO, Deloitte Ross Tohmatsu Corporate Fin Europe Ltd, 1991-; Chmn, Reverie Antiques Ltd; Ptnr, Touche Ross (GB). *Memberships:* Traffic Comm 1988-, Knightsbridge Assn; RAC, London; Hurlingham Club, London. *Hobbies:* Tennis; Golf; Antiques; Music. *Address:* 8 Montpelier Square, London SW7 1JU, England. 53.

QUIRK Randolph, b. 12 July 1920, Isle of Man. Cons. *Education:* DLitt, Univ of London, 1961. *Appointments:* Prof of Eng, Univ of Durham, 1954-60; Prof of Eng 1960-81, Vice Chancellor 1981-85, Univ of London. *Publications:* Comprehensive Grammar of the English Language, 1985; English in Use, 1990. *Membership:* Pres 1985-89, Brit Acad. *Honours:* CBE 1975; Kt 1985; Hon Docts from 21 Univs in 9 Countries. *Address:* University College London, Gower Street, London WC1E 6BT, England. 1.

QUIROZ Antonio Castro, b. 27 Jan 1933, Apalit, Pampanga, Philippines. Physn; Assoc Prof. m. Estenela R Rovillos, 7 June 1961, 1 s, 3 d. *Education:* AA, 1950; DM, 1955. *Appointments:* Asst Prof of Med, Univ del Valle, Cali, Colombia, 1960-64; Asst Prof of Med 1964-70, Asoc Prof of Med 1978-, Tulane Med Sch, New Orleans; Dir of Cardiology, East Jefferson Gen Hosp, 1971-78. *Publications:* Author of over 40 publs in scientific journs. *Contributions to:* a chapt to a book. *Memberships:* FACP; FACC; Fellow, Am Heart Assn; Pres, Louisiana & Gulf Coast, Assn of Philippine Physns in Am. *Honours:* Luis Guerrero Mem Lectr, Santo Tomas Univ, Manila, 1980; Outstng Filipino Physn in Am, Assoc of Philippine Physns in Am, 1988. *Hobbies:* Tennis; Fishing; Chess. *Address:* Cardiovascular Research Laboratory, Tulane University School of Medicine, 1430 Tulane Avenue, New Orleans, LA 70112, USA. 7, 28.

QURESHI Abdul-Saleem, b. 15 Jan 1938, Hyderabad, India. Barrister. m. Sajida Khadeerunnissa, 6 Jan 1980, 1 s, 2 d. *Education:* BA, Punjab Univ, 1961; LLB, Karachi Univ, 1964; Called to the Bar, Middle Temple, 1972. *Appointments:* Asst Ed, Weekly, Satluj, 1955-57; Sub Ed, Daily, Rehbar, 1959; Mary Claco Sch for Boys and Girls, Karachi, 1961-62; Pub Sch, Karachi Cantonment, 1962, 1964; Tchr, Govt Sch, Bahawalpur, Pakistan, 1964; Practising Mbr of the Eng Bar, SE Circuit, 1973. *Publications:* Ed, Nationalism & Internationalism, Bahawalpur, Pakistan, 1957; Author of Law articles and lectures on Muslim Family Law, 1983. *Contributions to:* Govt Publ, Hum Log, Lahore, Pakistan, 1959. *Memberships:* Sec, Pub Speaking Union, SM Law Coll, Karachi, 1963-64; Hon Legal Advsr, UK-Pakistan Cultural Fndn; Fdr, Sec Gen, MA Jinnah Soc, London; Fdr Mbr, World Assn of Muslim Jurists, 1978; Chmn, Police Monitoring Grp, Waltham Forest, 1982-83. *Hobbies:* Swimming; Lawn tennis; Badminton; Participation in poetic symposia. *Address:* 12 Old Square, Lincoln's Inn, London WC2 3TX, England.

R

RAAD Virginia, b. 13 Aug 1925, Salem, WV, USA. Concert Pianist; Musicologist. *Education:* BA, Wellesley Coll, 1947; Piano w David Barnett, New Eng Conservatory, 1948-49; Dip, Ecole Normale de Musique, 1950; Doct, With Hons, Univ of Paris, 1955. *Career:* Artist in Residence, Salem Coll, 1957-70; Musician in Residence, NC Arts Coun & Comm Colls, 1971-72; Concerts, Lectures, Master Classes throughout USA & Abroad; Adjudicator-Grant Reviewer: National Endowment, The Humanities and the American Soc for Aesthetics; West Virginia Teachers Assoc, West Virginia Fed Music Clubs, National Guild of Piano Tchrs. Various Representative Engagements Including, Concerts, Lectures, Master Classes in: Kentucky Wesleyan Coll, Kentucky; Trinity College, Washington, D.C; University of Notre Dame, Notre Dame, Indiana; Mount de Chantal Acad, Wheeling, West Virginia; The Phillips Gallery, Washington, D.C; Curry College, Milton, Massachusetts; Mount Union College, Alliance, Ohio; Berea College, Berea, Kentucky. *Publications include:* Sketches of Claude Debussy, Pianist, 1971; Notes of a Musician-in-Residence, 1973; Claude Debussy's Sarabande, 1981; The Cathedrals of Monet and Debussy, 1986; Claude Debussy's Neverland, 1986. *Memberships:* Am Musicological Soc; Int Musicological Soc; Societe Francaise de Musicologie; Coll Music Soc; Am Soc for Aesthetics; Musicology Prog Chmn 1983-87, Music Tchrs Nat Assn; Amnesty Int; Urgent Action Network. *Honours:* 2 Grants, French Govt; Travel Grant, Am Coun of Learned Socs, 1962; Outstng WV Woman Edr, Delta Kappa Gamma. *Hobbies:* Gardening; Birding. *Address:* 60 Terrace Avenue, Salem, WV 26426, USA. 2, 4, 138.

RAATZ Sherry Louise Swett, b. 20 Sept 1933, Seattle, Washington, USA. Regent, Rainier Chapter, NSDAR. m. Charles Frederick Raatz Jr, 27 Jan 1961, 1 s, 3 d. *Education:* BS, Gen Studies, maj Creative Dramatics and Drama, Univ WA, 1955. *Career includes:* Singer on Radio KJR, Seattle, WA; Appeared Vaudeville Palomer (Pantages), Orpheum and Paramount Theatres, Seattle; Entertained the Forces, World War II; Joined, 1979, 1st Vice-Regent, 1985, Regent, 1985-, Rainier Chapt, NSDAR, Seattle. *Creative works:* Illustrator for article Piracy in Iceland, 1961; Author: The NSDAR March, 1982; The Freedoms Foundation Song, 1982; Oh, My Country, My America, 1983. *Memberships:* Exec VP, Past Pres, Sea King Co Chapt, Freedoms Fndn; Recording Sec, WA Capts, Daughters of Fndrs and Patriots of Am; State Chmn, Am Heritage for WA State Soc, NSDAR; Am Guild Variety Artists and Actors Equity; WA Alpha Chapt, Phi Beta Kappa; United Chapts, Phi Beta Kappa; Int Platform Assn; Presidents' Forum; US Capitol Histl Soc; WA Gens. *Honours:* Var Certs of Merit, Appreciation and Thanks; Gold Locket w Wings from Men of Flying Fortress Wing, Seattle; Voted Most Accomplished Woman of 1985, ABI. *Hobbies:* Writing; Music and lyrics; Poetry; Sketching; Collecting antique jewellery; Genealogy. *Address:* 7500 27th NE, Seattle, WA 98115, USA.

RABBANI Habib, b. 23 July 1932, Iran. Prof; Clin & Med Psychologist; Cons. m. Ghodsyeh, 3 Sept 1958, 2 s, 1 d. *Education:* Dip in Natural Sci, Tehran, 1951; Dip in Scis of Psychology 1955, Dip & Lic es Lettres 1956, Univ of Tehran; Doct in Psychology, Sorbonne, 1963. *Appointments:* Prof, Dir, HS, Iran, 1956-60; Expert, Rschr, Tehran, 1964-67; Asst, Assoc Prof, Iran, 1967-77; Prof, Clin Psychologist, 1977-; Vstng Prof and Res Univ of IL, USA, 1979; Prof, Rschr, Cons Psychogeriatrist, 1983-. *Creative works:* Psych of Intelligence and Ability; Medical and Clinical Psychology; Mental Tests in Psych and Ed; Psychopathology and Abnor Psych; Develop Psychology. *Memberships:* Int Assn of Ap Psychology; World Assn for Psychological Rehab; Int Psychogeriat Assn; Int Assn of Sch Psychologists; Iranian Psychology Assn; Societe Francaise de Psychologie. *Honours:* World Forensic Psychology and Psychiatry Assn, 1987; World Hlth Org, 1988; Int Acad for Mental Hlth, 1988; World Psych Org,

1989. *Hobbies:* Theatre; Music; Cinema; Sport; Travelling over the world; Participating in Confs and Congresses; Writing; Reading. *Address:* c/o Dr N Bendersky, 2 Rue Lacharriere, 75011 Paris, France.

RACZKOWSKI Jozef Wojciech, b. 10 Sept 1930. Dir. m. Olga Sarna, 28 Apr 1957, 1 d. *Education:* MSc, 1955; DSc, 1963. *Appointments:* Asst, Dpty Dir, Inst Dir, Dept of Drilling and Petroleum, Mining and Metallurgy Acad, 1951-75; Designer, Oil Ind Projs, 1957-58; Sup Engr, Drilling Dept, Geological Works, 1959-62; Dir, Petroleum & Gas Inst, 1976-. *Publications:* Author of 7 books, 136 articles to profl journs. *Memberships:* Mbr of Bd, VP, Soc of Petroleum and Gas Engrs & Techns, 1958; Mining Comm 1976, Energetics Comm 1979, Polish Acad of Scis; Soc of Mining Engrs & Techns, 1984; Int Energy Fndn, 1991. *Honours:* Prize, Main Tech Org for outstng achmts in engrng, 1972, 1979, 1982, 1985; Mbr of Orgl Comm, Int Conf Petrolgeochem, 1976-91; Prize, Min of Sci Higher Schooling andTechnics for rsch work, 1977, 1978, 1979; Prize, Min-Hd of Tech Prog Off for devs in engrng, 1987; Lukasiewicz Prize, 1987. *Hobby:* Tourism. *Address:* ul 18 Stycznia 47 m 12, 30-040 Krakow, Poland. 162.

RADAMPOLA Jayasena, b. 3 Mar 1932, Sri Lanka. Town Planner; Land Surveyor. m. Daya Abeywickrema Gunasekera, 30 May 1960, 1 s, 2 d. *Education:* Surveyors' Final, Survey Trng Sch, Diyatalawa, 1954; Exam in Advanced Surveying, Univ of Cambridge, Eng, 1967; MSc, Univ of Sri Lanka, 1977. *Appointments:* Land Surveyor 1954-67, Asst Supt of Surveys 1967-80, Supt of Surveys 1980-88, Dpty Surveyor Gen 1989-92, Cons Surveyor, Town Planner 1992-retirement, Sri Lanka Survey Dept. *Publications:* Proposals for an Electoral District Development Programme in Sri Lanka, 1979; Graphic Survey - Answer to accelerated land alienatiron programme in Sri Lanka, 1980; Land Development Planning - Technical Manual, 1989. *Memberships:* Hon Treas 1986-87, Fellow, Surveyors' Inst of Sri Lanka; Fdr Mbr, Inst of Town Planners, Sri Lanka. *Honour:* 1st Prize, Sri Lanka Surveyor Gen's Prize, 1954. *Hobbies:* Gardening; Reading; Listening to music; Social studies. *Address:* 10 Dillenia Road, Colombo - 08, Sri Lanka.

RADCLIFFE Neville Browne, b. 21 Aug 1932, Nelson, Lancs, Eng. Solicitor. m. Mabel, 5 Apr 1958, 2 d. *Education:* LLB Hons, Manchester Univ; Solicitor (Hons) admitted Oct 1957. *Appointments:* Asst Solicitor 1957-61, Ptnr 1961-, Sr Litigation Ptnr 1976-, Sr Ptnr 1990-, Messrs Browne Jacobson. *Memberships:* Past Pres, Notts Law Soc, 1988-89; Past Pres, Nottingham Medico-Legal, 1988-89; Former Area Chmn, No 10 East Midlands Legal Aid; Former Vis Lectr in Law, Former Mbr, Law Advsry Coun, Nottingham Univ; Law Advsry Coun, Nottingham Polytech; Solicitors Assistance Scheme; Chmn of Ethics Comm, Univ Hosp, Queens Med Ctr, Gen Hosp, Highbury Hosp; Nottingham & Notts United Servs Club; Nottingham Rugby Football Club. *Hobbies:* Fell walking; Rugby football; Cricket; Soccer; Gardening; Travel; Music. *Address:* 44 Castle Gate, Nottingham, Nottinghamshire NG1 6EA, England.

RADINSKA Valentina Dimitrova, b. 11 Sept 1951, Sliven, Bulgaria. Poet; Transl. m. Krikor Stepan Azarjan, 4 Feb 1987, 1 s. *Education:* Lit Inst, Maksim Gorki, Moskow, 1971-76. *Appointments:* Ed, Friendship, 1977-78; Reporter, Narodna Mladezh, 1978-79; Ed, Sofia Cinema Ctr, 1979-91. *Publications:* A man is coming up to me, 1977; Night Book, 1983; No, 1988. Transl: Marina Tsvetaeva - poetry and prose; Ana Ahmatova - poetry; Valery Osipov, The Forerunner; Boris Zolotaryov, The Quiet Emma. *Membership:* The League of Bulgarian Writers. *Honour:* Prize winner for poetry, Tzvetan Zangov. *Hobby:* House plants. *Address:* Experimental Complex, Vitosha Bl 4, A 4, ZK Emil Markov, 1404 Sofia, Bulgaria.

RADOEV Boryan, b. 2 Sept 1941, Sofia, Bulgaria. Assoc Prof. m. Lina Atanassova, 4 Nov 1971. *Education:*

PhD, Univ of Sofia, 1971. *Appointments:* Asst, Dept of Phys Chem 1966, Sr Asst 1971, Assoc Prof 1981, Univ of Sofia. *Publications:* Author of over 60 papers on colloid and interface sci: hydrodynamics, fluctuations, stability of liquid surfaces, thin liquid films and three phase contacts. *Membership:* Hd of Sect, Ctrl Lab of Mineral Processing, Bulgarian Acad of Sci, 1987. *Hobbies:* Bridge; Music. *Address:* Department of Physical Chemistry, Faculty of Chemistry, University of Sofia, 1126 Sofia, Bulgaria.

RADOSLAVOVA Anna, b. 27 Nov 1937, Sofia, Bulgaria. Ed. *Education:* Dip, Theorectical Dept, Bulgarian Acad of Music, 1962. *Appointments:* Ed of Musical Sect 1963-73, Ed of Cultural Sect of Info Dept 1973-79, Bulgarian TV; Musical Sect, Bulgarian Radio, 1979-. *Creative works:* Organiser of TV films for Bulgarian composers, conductors, performers, musical grps; Initiator of TV heading, musical review, existing for over 20 yrs; Accumulated a large quantity of material for the musical life in Bulgaria; Author of num articles on Bulgarian musicians for newspapers and mags in Bulgaria and abroad. *Memberships:* FIPRECI; Assn of Bulgarian Journalists, Sofia. *Hobbies:* Literature; Cinema. *Address:* 24 Zanko Zerkovski Street, 1421 Sofia, Bulgaria.

RADULESCU Mihai Sorin, b. 13 Nov 1966, Bucharest, Rumania. Historian; Genealogist; Research Fellow. *Education:* Grad, Hist Fac, Univ Bucharest, 1991; Doctorandd, Institut Nat des Langues et Civilisations Orientales, Paris, France, 1991-92. *Appointments:* Rsch Fellow, Social Hist, Genealogy, Prosopography, Nicolae Iorga Hist Inst, Bucharest, 1991-. *Publications:* Studies and articles about hist and genealogy of Rumanian noble families, about genealogy of Rumanian personalities, about prosopography of Rumanian pol parties in the mod age. *Memberships:* Nat Rumanian Commn Genealogy, Heraldry and Sigillography, Sec 1990; Athenaeum Soc, Bucharest; Soc Hist of Right and Instns, Bucharest. *Honours:* Promotion Chief, Germany Lyceum, Bucharest, 1985; Promotion Chief, Hist Fac, Bucharest, 1991. *Hobbies:* Classical music; Reading. *Address:* str Levanticai 32, sect 3, 74328 Bucharest, Rumania.

RAE Elizabeth, b. 9 Aug 1953, Gosport, Hants, Eng. Ballet Dancer; Tchr; Choreographer. m. Paul D Figler, 23 June 1981, 2 s. *Education:* Arts Educl Trust Sch, Tring, 1964-66; Braybrook's Acad, Bradford, 1966-70; Dip, Choreographic Dip, The Royal Ballet Sch, London, 1973; Assoc Dip (Advanced), Royal Acad of Dancing, 1973. *Career include:* Ballet Tchr, Urdang Sch of Ballet, London, 1977-79; Soloist, London Theatre Ballet, 1977-78; Soloist, Compania Balletto Classico, Italy, 1978-79; Soloist, ostgota Ballet, Sweden, 1979-80; .Soloist, Stadtische Buhnen, Frankfurt-am-Main, 1980- 84; Soloist, Staatstheater Oldenburg, Germany, 1984-85; Ballet, Dance Tchr, Ballettschule Kroke, Oldenburg, 1986-88; Guest Ballet Mistress, Stadttheater, Oberhausen, Germany, 1987; Ballet, Dance Tchr, Ballettschule Steigerwald, Oldenburg, 1988-90; Guest Ballet Tchr, The Northern Sch of Contemporary Dance, Leeds, 1991. *Creative works include:* Choreographic Works: Genesis, Breathing 1972, Pulcinella, Silence 1973, Ophelia, Text 1973, The Place, London; Primum Mobile, Bodman Rae 1975, House of Life, V Williams 1976, Polish Solo, Chopin 1976, San Fran Dance Theatre; None but the Lions, Kabuki, Stadtische Buhnen, Frankfurt, 1982; Coppelia Pas de Deux, Delibes, Staatstheater, Oldenburg, 1987. *Memberships:* Equity; ARAD; Assoc 1973, Imperial Soc of Tchrs of Dancing, Nat Dance Br, Ballet Br, Cecchett Br. *Honour:* Scholarship, West Ridding Co Coun to the Royal Ballet Sch, 1970-73. *Hobbies:* History; Gardening; World Affairs. *Address:* 30 Chelwood Avenue, Round Hay, Leeds, West Yorkshire LS8 2AZ, England.

RAE John Malcolm, b. 20 Mar 1931, London, Eng. Dir. m. Daphne Simpson, 31 Dec 1955, 2 s, 4 d. *Education:* MA, Cambridge Univ, 1951- 55; PhD, Dept

of War Studies, London Univ, 1963-65. *Appointments:* Asst Master, Harrow Sch, 1955-66; Hdmaster, Taunton Sch, 1966-70; Hdmaster, Westminster Sch, 1970-86; Dir, Laura Ashley Fndn, 1986-89; Dir, Portman Grp, 1989-. *Publications:* The Custard Boys, 1960 (filmed as Reach for Glory, 1961); Conscience and Politics, 1970; The Public School Revolution, 1981; Letters from School, 1987; Too Little, Too Late?, 1989; Delusions of Grandeur, 1993, 5 books for children. *Memberships:* Chmn 1977, Hdmasters Conf; Dir, Observer Newspaper Ltd. *Honours:* UN Awd, Jt Author of Film, Reach for Glory, 1961; Hon Fellow, Coll of Preceptors. *Address:* 101 Millbank Court, 24 John Islip Street, London SW1P 4LG, England. 1.

RAEBURN John Alexander, b. 25 June 1941, Adlington. Prof. m. (1)div, (2) Arlene Rose Conway, 17 May 1980, 1 s, 2 stepson, 2 d. *Education:* MB ChB; PhD, Edinburgh Univ. *Appointments:* Lectr in Therapeutics 1969-73, Sr Lectr in Human Genetics 1973-89, Edinburgh Univ; Prof of Clin Genetics, Nottingham Univ, 1990-. *Publications:* Author of more than 100 papers in med journs. *Membership:* MRCP (Edin), 1968. *Honours:* TD, 1976; FRCP (Edin), 1976. *Hobbies:* Reading; Gardening; Fishing. *Address:* Tighlagan, Grove Farm, Lambley Road, Lowdham, Notts, NG14 7AY.184.

RAFFA Jean Alyda Benedict, b. 23 Apr 1943, Lansing, MI, USA. Educl Cons; Writer. m. Frederick Anthony Raffa, 15 June 1964, 1 s, 1 d. *Education:* BS Elem Educ 1964, MS,Elem Educ 1968, FL State Univ; EdD, Curric and Instrn, Univ of FL, 1982. *Appointments:* Elem Sch Tchr, 1964-69; Adj Instr of Elem Educ 1977-85, Educ Cons, Tchr Educ Ctr 1980-, Univ of Ctrl FL; Coord of Children's Programming, WFTV TV Sta, 1978-80; Vis Asst Prof, Stetson Univ, 1988-89. *Publications include:* On the Go (Children's TV Show), 1979-80; Television: The Newest Moral Educator?, 1983; Television and Values: Implications for Education, 1985; Television Conveys Authority Images, 1988; Introductionto television literacy, 1989. *Contributions to:* Elementary Social Studies: Knowing, Doing and Caring. *Memberships:* Kappa Delta Pi, Nat Educ Hon; Phi Delta Kappa; Assn for Supervision and Curric Dev; FL Assn for Supervision & Curric Dev; Soc for the Scientific Study of Relig. *Honours:* Recip, FL State Tchr's Scholarship, 1961; ACT Awd for Children's TV Show, On The Go, 1980; Nominee, Kimball Wiles Awd for Best Dissertation, Coll of Educ, Univ of FL, 1982. *Hobbies:* Reading psychology, philosophy and religion; Collecting antiques; Rose gardening. *Address:* 45 Eastwind Lane, Maitland, FL 32751, USA. 15, 76.

RAGETLY Paul Rene, b. 23 Jan 1944, 51-Fere, France. Dir. m. Florence Huas, 31 Dec 1977, 1 s, 1 d. *Education:* Grad Engr, ENSA (Aeronautics), Paris; MSc, Univ of CA, Berkeley. *Appointments:* Loan Off, World Bank (IBRD), Washignton DC, 1970-74; Loan Off, IDI (Paris) Investment Bank, 1974-76; Dir of Int Dept, Lazard Freres et Cie, 1976-. *Hobbies:* Flying; Skiing; Horses. *Address:* 8 Rue De Levis, 75017 Paris, France.

RAGHAVAN Bahukutumbi Srinivasa, b. 29 Aug 1927, Sirkali, Tamil Nadu, India. Int Mgmt Cons; Advsr. m. 15 May 1952, 1 s, 1 d. *Education:* BSc Hons. *Appointments:* Mbr, Indian Admnstv Serv, 1952-85; Cons, Policy Advsr to UN (FAO), 1978-84. *Publications include:* The Principles and Practice of Public Administration; An Indian Theory of Management; The Jitters of the Junior Scale; Emergency is for Laughs or One Man's Emergency; The Heart of the Hoomans; A variety of articles on public administration, food and energy issues, security, wild life. *Memberships:* Fellow, Madras Sci Fndn; US Congressional Fellow, 1966; Madras Mgmt Assn. *Hobbies:* Grass Roots Leadership Development Management Education; Public Administration; Writing; Communicating and Broadcasting. *Address:* 4 Second Main Road, Nehru Nagar, Adyar, Madras 600 020, India. 93.

RAGUOTIENE-TEVELYTE Genovaite, b. 27 June 1931, Lauciskiai village, Sakiai district, Lithuania. Librarian; University Lecturer. m. Bronius Raguotis, 16 Sept 1951, 1 s, 1 d. *Education:* Vilnius Univ, 1950-55; Dr, Pedagogics, 1965. *Appointments:* Asst Lectr, 1955-69, Vice-Dean, Histl Fac, 1968-71, 1976-81, Docent, 1970-, Hd, Libnship Chair, 1981-, Vilnius Univ, Vilnius. *Publications:* Books: One Hundred Riddles about a Book, 1974, 1981; ABC Book of Reading (White Plains, Black Sheep), 1983; Theoretical Fundamentals of Librarianship (compiler, co-author), monograph, 1990. *Memberships:* Lithuanian Libn Assn; Lithuanian Pedagogues Assn; IBBY, Lithuanian Sect. *Hobbies:* Reading; Knitting. *Address:* Svyturio 22-16, 2040 Vilnius, Lithuania.

RAHMAN Kaleel, b. 12 June 1944, Colombo, Sri Lanka. Chmn. m. Nazeera Ahmed, 24 June 1972, 3 s, 1 d. *Education:* Bach in Commerce, Loyola Coll, Madras, 1968. *Appointments:* Chmn, K Darwin & Co Ltd, Colombo, 1968; Cargo Boat Co Ltd, Colombo, 1968; Capitol Communication Systems Ltd, Colombo, 1979; Capitol Paper Converters (Pte) Ltd, Colombo, 1983; Capitol Air Express Int (Pte) Ltd, Colombo, 1983; Capitol Overseas Courier Serv (Pte) Ltd, Colombo, 1983; Kara Property Dev Co Ltd, Colombo, 1983. *Memberships:* FBIM; FAIM; Profl Mgr, Can Inst of Mgmt; Pres 1981-82, Lions Club; JP. *Hobbies:* Reading; Music. *Address:* 38 Siripa Road, Colombo - 5, Sri Lanka. 1.

RAHMAN Muhammad Mujibur. *Address:* Binodpur Bazar, PO Code No 6206, Rajshahi, Bangladesh.

RAI Jaswant, b. 18 Mar 1943, Jullundur, India. Med Scientist; Prof. m. Latika, 4 Dec 1973, 1 s, 3 d. *Education:* MBBBS, Govt Med Coll, Amritsar, 1969; MS, PGI, Chamdigarh, 1972. *Appointments:* Lectr 1977-78, Asst Prof 1978-86, Assoc Prof 1986-89, Additional Prof 1989-90, Prof 1990-, Dept of Orthopaedics, PGI, Chamdigarh. *Creative works:* Published about 50 scientific papers in nat and int journs; Invented Indigenous Instrument for Total Knee Replacement Report in Science, 1988. *Memberships:* Assn of Surgs of India; Indian Med Assn; Indian Orthopaedic Assn; Exec Mbr, N Zone, Chapt IOA; VP, Youth Tech Trng Soc; Rotary Club, Past. *Honours:* Honoured by: Chandigarh Med Practitioners Soc; Rotary Club of Chandigarh; Mid Town Rotary Club; Assn of Surgs of India (N Chapt). *Hobbies:* Gardening; Photography; Badminton. *Address:* Department of Orthopaedics, Post Graduate Institute of Medical Education and Research, Chandigarh, India.

RAI Satvinder Singh, b. 20 Oct 1943, Dar-Es-Salaam, Tanzania. Lectr; Writer. m. Gabriele Antonie Wagner, 10 June 1988. *Education:* BSc, London Sch of Econ(s), 1971; MA, Univ of Lancaster, 1972; DPhil, Univ of York, 1987. *Appointments:* Brit Civil Serv: Min of Power, Min of Tech, Dept of Trade & Ind, 1967-70; Benedict Sch, Essen, 1977-91; Zentrum Wissenschaftliche Weiterbildung, Univ of Essen, 1991-; Freelance Appts. *Publications:* Red Star & The Lotus: The Political Dynamics of Indo- Soviet Relations, 1990; Articles in Acad Journs on South Asian Affairs and Politics. *Membership:* Brit Assn of S Asian Studies. *Honour:* Post-Grad Quota Awd, Social Sci Rsch Coun of GB, 1973-76. *Hobbies:* Reading; Travelling; Jogging; Squash; Skiing; Surfing; Photography; Modern ballet; Cinema. *Address:* Oskarstrasse 4, W-4300 Essen 1, Germany. 52.

RAJAH Nagalingam Thurai, b. 29 Apr 1928, Ipoh, Malaysia. Lawyer. m. Gnanambigai, 12 June 1960, 1 s, 2 d. *Education:* Sr Cambridge Cert, 1948; Mbr, Royal Soc of Hlth, 1955; Barrister-at-Law, Gray's Inn, London. *Appointments:* Hlth Insp, Town Coun, Ipoh, 1949-55; Legal Asst, KC Cha Jr & Co, 1959; Legal Asst 1960-62, Ptnr 1962-, Maxwell, Kenion, Cowdy & Jones. *Memberships:* Com Mbr, Pres, Jaycees Ipoh; VP, Pres 1966-78, Bar Assn of Perak; Visitor to Detainees, Batu Gajah Detention Camp, 1970-78; Fdr Mbr, Pres 1980-91, Rotary Club of Ipoh-Kinta; Pres, VP, Dir 1975-91, Malayan Ceylonese Educ Fndn; VP 1982-91, Ipoh Soc for Prevention of Cruelty to Animals. *Hobbies:* Mbr of ACS Players 1949-70; Football; Hockey; Cricket; Rugby; Badminton; Swimming; Riding; Polo; Golf; Gardening; Reading. *Address:* No 3 Laluan Harimau, 31400 Ipoh, Perak, Malaysia. 98.

RAJAN Periasamy Karivaratha, b. 20 Sept 1942, Karur, Tamil Nadu, India. Prof; Chairperson. m. Visalakshi, 31 Jan 1971, 1 s. *Education:* BE, Coll of Engrng, Guindy, 1966; MTech 1969, PhD 1975, IIT, Madras. *Appointments:* Lectr, Reg Engrng Coll, Trichy, India, 1969-70; Assoc Lectr, IIT, Madras, 1970-75; Lectr 1975-77, Asst Prof 1978-80, SUNY Coll, Buffalo, USA; Assoc Prof, ND State Univ, Fargo, USA, 1980-83; Assoc Prof 1983-85, Prof 1985-, Interim Chairperson 1991-, Chairperson 1992-, TN Tech Univ, Cookeville, TN. *Publications:* Num articles to profl journs; A chapt in a book on Multidimensional Systems. *Memberships:* Sr Mbr, Assoc Ed 1985-87, IEEE; Am Soc of Engrng Educ; Sigma Xi; TN Acad of Sci. *Honours:* Caplemor Rsch Awd, TN Tech, 1990; Most Appreciated Tchr Awd, Most Challenging Prof Awd, 1990. *Hobbies:* Reading; Politics; Volleyball. *Address:* 852 Lone Oak Drive, Cookeville, TN 38501, USA. 7, 143.

RAJCA Brunon, b. 4 Aug 1933, Rokitno, Poland. Journalist. m. Izabella Lipka, 9 Oct 1976, 2 d. *Education:* Masters degree, Krakow Univ, 1954. *Career:* Polish Daily; News Weekly; TV, Krakow; Dir, Mashkaron. *Publications:* Don't Be a Simpleton, 1980; Steal and Kil, 1982; Cheers Folles, 1984; Got You Devil, 1984; You Were Not a Parrot, 1987. Plays: UFO - They?, 1978; I Have Lived Three Thousand Litres of Vodka, 1990. *Memberships:* Union of Polish Journalists; Soc of Polish Authors. *Honours:* Merit for Krakow Town Awd, 1974; Golden Cross of Merit, 1979; Polonia Restituta Cross, 1985; Merit for Polish Culture Awd, 1989. *Hobby:* Talking to wife. *Address:* ul F Kona (BKP) Bandurskiego 12A m 1, 31-515 Krakow, Poland.

RAKOWSKI Andrzej, b. 16 June 1931, Warsaw, Poland. Acustician; Musicologist; Prof. m. Magdalena Jakobczyk, 30 Dec 1972, 1 s, 2 d. *Education:* MSc 1957, PhD 1963, Tech Univ, Warsaw; MA, State Coll of Music, Warsaw, 1958; Dr habil, Warsaw Univ, 1977. *Appointments:* Sound Engr 1952-53, Asst, Assoc, Full Prof 1953-, Sound Prod 1955-58, Pres 1981-87, Chopin Acad of Music, Warsaw; Prof of Musicology, Warsaw Univ, 1987-. *Publications:* Selected Topics on Acoustics, 1959; Categorical Perception of Pitch in Music, 1978; Author of over 100 articles. *Contributions to:* Archives of Acoustics Acustica, Muzyka, Journ of the Acousatical Soc of Am, Folia Phoniatr, Psychology of Music, Musique en Pologne. *Memberships:* VP, Comm of Acoustics, Polish Acad of Scis; VP, Polish Music Coun; Pres 1981, Solidarity Union at Chopin Acad of Music. *Honours:* Individual Awds, Min of Culture and Arts in Poland, 1966, 1968, 1982, 1987; Polish State Awd Cross of Merits, Silver 1971, Golden 1973; Bach's Cross, Order of the Revival of Poland, 1983. *Hobbies:* History; Touring; Skiing. *Address:* Pogonowskiego 20, 01 564, Warsaw, Poland. 4.

RALPH Colin John, b. 16 June 1951. Registrar; Chief Exec. *Education:* RGN, Royal West Sussex Hosp; DN, RCN, Univ of London; MPhil, Brunel Univ. *Appointments:* Staff Nurse, Student, Nat Heart Hosp, 1974; Charge Nurse, Royal Free Hosp, 1974-77; Nursing Off, London Hosp, 1978-83; Dir of Nursing: Westminster Hosp, Westminster Children's Hosp, 1983- 86; Chief Nursing Advsr, Gloucester Hlth Auth, 1986-87; Registrar, Chief Exec, UK Ctrl Coun for Nursing, Midwifery & Hlth Visiting, 1987-. *Contributions to:* Nursing Profession Journs and Books. *Memberships:* Nat Exec Comm 1974-76, Nursing Advsr 1975-, BRCS; Florence Nightingale Scholar 1981, Nat Florence Mem Comm; Coun of Mgmt, 1983-; Standing Nursing and Midwifery Advsry Comm, 1986-; Profl Servs Comm, RCN, 1986-87; EC Advsry Comm on Trng in Nursing, 1990-. *Hobbies:* Friends; The

Arts; Travel. *Address:* 23 Portland Place, London W1N 3AF, England. 1.

RALSTON Timothy John, b. 2 Apr 1956, Toronto, Can. Acad (Sem Prof). m. Carol Anne Bigelow, 5 May 1979, 1 d. *Education:* BSc, Univ of Waterloo, Can, 1978; ThM 1983, ThD 1992, Dallas Theological Sem, USA. *Appointments:* Pastor, Can, 1983-87; Instr, Ctrl Bapt Sem, Toronto, 1987; Assnt Prof, Dallas Theological Sem, 1988-93. *Memberships:* Evangelical Theological Soc; Soc of Biblical Lit. *Honour:* Henry C Theissen Awd, New Testament Studies, Dallas Theological Sem, 1983. *Hobbies:* Sailing; Skiing; Scuba diving. *Address:* 1525 Bosque Drive, Garland, TX 75040, USA.

RAMAGE James Alfred, b. 6 May 1940, McCracken Co, KY, USA. Prof. m. Ann Winstead, 6 June 1964, 1 d. *Education:* BS 1965, MA 1968, Murray State Univ; PhD, Univ of Kentucky, 1972. *Appointments:* Hist Tchr, Mehlville HS, St Louis, 1965-67; Asst to the Pres, Asst Prof of Hist 1972-75, Prof of Hist 1976-, Northern KY Univ. *Publications:* John Wesley Hunt: Pioneer Merchant, Manufacturer and Financier, 1974; Rebel Raider: The Life of General John Hunt Morgan, 1986. *Memberships:* Fac Advsr, Alpha Beta Phi Chapt, Phi Alpha Theta; Exec Comm, KY Histl Soc; Exec Comm, KY Assn of Tchrs of Hist. *Honours:* KY Gov's Vol Activist Awd, 1978; Douglas Southall Freeman Awd for the most outstng work in Southern Hist 1986, 1987, KY Gov's Awd for outstng book in KY Hist for 4 yrs 1987, for the book, Rebel Raider; Outstng Prof of the Yr Awd, Northern KY Univ, 1988. *Hobbies:* Reading; Sports; Exercise. *Address:* Department of History and Geography, Northern Kentucky University, Highland Heights, KY 41076, USA. 7, 30, 117, 139.

RAMLJAK Olga, b. 29 Oct 1948, Split. Journalist; Ed. m. Josip Ramljak, 13 Aug 1973, 2 s, 1 d. *Education:* Fac of Philos, Zagreb, 1973. *Appointments:* Tchng, First Gymnasium, Zagreb, 1974; Journalist for the Daily Newspaper, Slobodna Dalmacija, Split, 1974; Corres, Slobodna Dalmacija, Zagreb, 1975-; Special Reporter, Croatian Parl, 1976-; Chief Ed, Zagreb Bur of Slobodna Dalmacija, 1989-. *Membership:* Fedn of Croatian Profl Journalists. *Honour:* from the Comm for Info, Repub of Croatia, 1988. *Hobbies:* Sailing; Animals. *Address:* Albinijeva 4, 41020 Zagreb, Croatia.

RAMOS-BLUE Hazel, b. 2 Sept 1936, Davao City, Philippines. Food Serv Mgr; Culinary Instr. m. (1) William H Snyder, 21 Mar 1964, div 1981, (2) Alan Blue, 30 May 1986, div 1989, 1 s, 1 d. *Education:* Bach degree, Univ of the Philippines, 1958; Master's degree, PA State Univ, 1963. *Appointments:* Dir of Comm Arts Workshop, Silliman Univ, 1958-59; Peace Corps Trng Staff, PA State Univ, 1961-63; Sociology Instr, Albright Coll, 1964-65; Rsch Asst, Meth Ch, 1965-66; Exec Dir, Halifax Ct Child Care and Family Svcs Ctr, 1973-79; Tchr, Learning Together Inc, Raleigh, 1982-83; Mortgage Specialist, Raleigh Fed Savings Bank, Raleigh, 1983-84; Entrepreneur, Chef, Mgr, Hazel's On Hargett (restaurant), 1985-86; Cooking Instr, Wake Tech Community Colls, 1986-; Social Wkr, Admissions Coord 1986-88, Food Serv Dir, Social Wkr 1988-89, Brian Ctr Nursing Home, Raleigh; Reg Dir, La Petite Acad (Nat Child Care Corp), 1989-90; Asst Food Servs Mgr, Granville Towers, Chapel Hill, 1990-. *Creative works:* Evaluation of some Variables, An Approach to Evaluate the Peace Corps Training Programme for the Philippine Project at PA State Univ (MA Thesis), 1963; Dev of 7 Cooking Courses for the Wake Tech Community Colls, 1986-. *Memberships:* Pres's Team, Bd of Dir, Nominating Comm, Vol Recruitment Comm, Serv Area Mgr, Troop Ldr, Pines of Carolina, Girl Scout Coun; Int Fest of Raleigh; Cooking Demonstration Coord Phil-Am Assn, Liaison and Pub Rels Off; Nat Assn of Coll & Univ Food Servs. *Honours:* Juliette Low Girl Scout Int Awd, 1963; Ramon Magsaysay Presidential Awd, 1957; Rockefeller Grant, 1959; Gov of NC Cert of Appreciation, 1990; Mayor of Raleigh Cert of Appreciation, 1990. *Hobbies include:* Music; Creative and modern dance;

Theatre; Children's books. *Address:* 108 Cromwell Court, Cary, NC 27513, USA. 7.

RAMOVS Primoz, b. 20 Mar 1921, Ljubljana, Slovenia. Composer. m. Stefanija Schubert, 17 Jan 1955, 2 s, 1 d. *Education:* Music Acad with Dip, 1941; Acad Musicale Chigiana, Siena. *Appointments:* Libn 1945-52, Libn-in-Chief 1952-87, Slovene Acad in Scis & Arts; Prof Conservatory, 1948- 52, 1955-64. *Creative works:* Books and pamphlets on libnship; 5 symphonies, 12 symphonic poems, 28 concertos for various instruments with orch, chamber & instrumental music. *Memberships:* Slovene Acad of Scis & Arts; Sec 1953-65, VP 1969-73, Assn of Slovene Composers; Assn of Slovene Libns; Slovene Lit Soc; Slovene Alpine Soc; Mbr of Hon, Slove Philharmony; Life Fellow, Int Biog Assn; Life Fellow, Am Biog Inst; Life Fellow, World Inst of Achmt; Doct Mbr, World Univ Roundtable; Life Mbrship of Merit, Confedn of Chivalry; Yugoslav Acad of Scis & Arts. *Honours include:* Order of Work w Golden Wreath, 1982; Cultural Doct in Philos of Music, 1982; Preseren's Prize, 1983; Commemorative Medal of Hon, 1986; Dr of Music Honoris Causa, 1988; World Decoration of Excellence, 1989; Order of the White Cross Int, 1990; Order of the Lyre Bird in the Class of Gold, 1990. *Hobby:* Mountaineering. *Address:* Kardeljeva 18, 61000 Ljubljana, Slovenia. 52, 139, 151, 152, 156.

RAMPLING Roy Peter, b. 13 Sept 1946, Malta. Physn. m. 27 Dec 1976, 2 s, 1 d. *Education:* BSc 1965-68, PhD 1968-71, Imperial Coll, London; MBBS, Univ Coll, 1974-79; FRCR; FRCP. *Appointments:* Hammersmith Hosp, London, 1981-84; Churchill Hosp, Oxford, 1984-87; Physn, Beatson Oncology Ctr, Glasgow, 1987-. *Publications:* in Radiotherapy & Neuro-Oncology. *Membership:* Inst of Phys. *Address:* Beatson Oncology Centre, Western Infirmary, Glasgow G11 6NS, Scotland.

RAMSON William Stanley, b. 4 Dec 1933, New Zealand. Lexicographer. *Education:* BA (NZ), 1953; MA (NZ), 1954; PhD (Sydney), 1963. *Appointments:* Lectr in Eng, Aust Nat Univ, 1960; Hd, Aust Nat Dictionary Ctr, 1988-. *Publication:* The Australian National Dictionary, a dictionary of Australianisms and historical principles, 1988. *Membership:* Fellow, Aust Acad of the Humanities. *Address:* Australia National Dictionary Centre, PO Box 4, Canberra, Australia 2601.

RAMSOUR James Larry, b. 6 July 1936, Brownwood, TX, USA. Christian Min; Evangelist. m. Valetta Allene Stripling, 29 May 1956, 2 d. *Education:* BA, Baylor Univ, Waco, 1957; Master of Divinity, Southwestern Bapt Theological Sem, Ft Worth, 1961. *Appointments:* Pastor, Navarro Mills Bapt Ch, Purdon, 1956-61; Pastor, Beall Chapel Bapt Ch, Jacksonville, 1961-64; Pastor, First Bapt Ch, Troup, 1964-66; Pastor, First Bapt, Farmerville, 1966-71; Pastor, Trinity Bapt, Lake Charles, 1971-78; World-wide Evangelist w indigenous mission work in Nepal, 1979-. *Publication:* Ed, The Encourager. *Memberships:* Pres, Troup Rotary Club, 1966; Trustee, LA Bapt Children's Home, 1972-78; VP, LA Bapt Exec Bd, 1977; Conf of TX Bapt Evangelists, 1979-; Conf of Southern Bapt Evangelists, 1979-. *Honour:* Jaycee Disting Serv Awd as Outstng Young Man of Farmerville, 1969. *Hobbies:* Photography; Art; Computer applications. *Address:* 211 Church Street, Winnsboro, TX 75494, USA. 145.

RANCK John Stevens, b. 14 Sept 1945, Warren, OH, USA. Cons; Pres. m. Bibbie-Ann Ranck, 25 Dec 1975, 2 s. *Education:* BS, USAF Acad, 1971; MS, Human Resources Mgmt 1979, MBA 1984, Gonzaga Univ. *Appointments:* Mil Serv, USAF 1966-80 resigned as Capt; Personnel Mgr, United Paint Mfg Co Inc, Spokane, 1981-82; Personnel Dir, Sheraton Spokane Hotel, Spokane, 1982-83; Pres, Owner, The Personnel Dept, Spokane, 1983-86; Personnel Mgr, Students Book Corp, WA State Univ, Pullman, 1984-87; Personnel Analyst, Spokane Co, 1988-90; Human Resources Cons, Pres, Top Ranck Mgmt, 1990-. *Memberships:* Spokane Area

C of C, 1979-86; Spokane Valley C of C, 1980-86; Spokane Co Repub Party, 1980-; Spokane Chapt PNPMA SHRM, Pacific Northwest Personnel Mgmt Assn, Soc for Human Resource Mgmt 1981, Chapt Advsr, WA State Univ Student Chapt 1984-87, Chair, Coll Rels Comm 1989, VP Progs 1990, Legis Liaison 1991-; Int Personnel Mgmt Assn, 1987-; Rotarian. *Honours:* Masonic: Kt of York Cross of Hon, Kt of York Grand Cross of Hon, Kt Cmdr Ct of Hon, Order of the Purple Cross; Certified Adminstv Mgr, Admnstv Mgmt Soc, 1983; Sr Profl in Human Resources, Soc for Human Resource Mgmt 1990. *Hobbies:* Racquetball; Outdoor activities; Photography; Personal computers; Reading. *Address:* E16004 Rich Avenue, Spokane, WA 99216, USA. 9.

RANIVILLE Frank Fritz Francis, b. 19 Oct 1920, Grand Rapids, Michigan, USA. Retired. *Education:* Grad, Todd HS, 1939; Albion Coll, 1 yr; Self-taught, Poetry Forms. *Career:* Var positions, Factory, Lab Products, Advt Store Servicing Trad, Maintenance, 2nd VP, F Raniville Co, 1938-78; Special Conversion, 1942; Special Calling, 1943. *Creative works:* Rel and creative poetry incl publs: Ranivilla; Revilo; Poems in anthologies. *Memberships:* Vol, Past VP, Poet Laureate, Kent Community Hosp Men's Club; Bards of Grand Rapids, MI, Treas 8 yrs, Chaplain 8 yrs; US President's Comm. *Honours:* About 7 awards, Grand Rapids; William Bible Haiku Award for Early Spring, Bards of Grand Rapids, MI, 1968; UN Day Award of Hon for Bible Hymns, UPLI, 1969; Magna cum laude Award for hymn Lord Of All Nations Hear Out Prayer, World Poetry Soc Int, 1970; 2 Gold Medals for Sonnet, Hollywood, CA, 1971, Rome, Italy, 1975; World Belletrist Award for poem form Raniville, 1974, Revilo, 1981; Award from Pres George Bush; Cert Appreciation, 1992. *Hobbies:* Writing poetry; Landscapes and still life oil paintings; Bible Word studies; Bible Phrase studies; Numerology, science of numbers and how numbers vibrate on one's life. *Address:* 2350 4 Mile Rd NE, Grand Rapids, MI 49505, USA.

RANKINE Jean Morag, b. 5 Sept 1941, England, Dpty Dir. *Education:* BA 1963; MPhil 1967; Fellow 1990. *Appointments:* RA, Dept of Printed Books 1967-73, AK, Dir's Off 1973-78, Hd of Pub Servs 1978-83, Dpty Dir 1983-, Brit Mus. *Hobbies:* Skiing; Opera. *Address:* British Museum, London WC1B 3DG, England. 1.

RANNEY Maurice William, b. 13 Jan 1934, Buffalo, NY, USA. VP; Int; Mgmt. m. Elisa Ramirez, 21 Dec 1974, 2 s, 3 d. *Education:* BS, Chem 1957, MS, Organic Chem 1959, Niagara Univ, PhD, Phys Organic Chem, Fordham Univ, 1967. *Appointments:* Grp Ldr, Tech Mgr, Union Carbide Corp, Tarrytown, 1957-75; Gen Mgr, Union Carbide Japan KK, Rep Dir, Union Carbide Servs Eastern Ltd, Dir, Nippon Unicar Co Ltd, 1976-80; Ex VP, Showa Union Gosei Co Ltd, Dir, Showa Unox KK, 1976-80; Pres, Union Carbide Formosa Co Ltd, Pres, Union Indl Gas Corp, Rep Dir, Oriental Union Chem Corp, 1980-82; Bus Dir, Union Carbide Eastern Inc, Tokyo, Asian Pacific Reg, Mng Dir, Nippon Unicar Co Ltd, 1982-85; Pres, Rep Dir, Union Carbide Japan KK, Vice Chmn, Nippon Unicar Co Ltd, Dir, Union Showa KK, VP, Int, Union Carbide Chems and Plastics Co, 1986. *Publications:* Flame Retardment Textiles, 1970; Powder Coatings, 1971; Synthetic Lubricants, 1972; New Curing Techniques; Fuel Additives; Durable Press Fabrics, 1976; Silicones, Vols I, II, 1977; Reinforced Plastics and Elastmers, 1978; Offshore Oil Technology, 1979; Oil Shale and Tar Sands, 1980; Primary Electrochemical Cell Technology, 1981. *Memberships:* Yomiuri Int Econ Soc, Japan; Am C of C, Japan; Press Club, Tokyo; Am C of C, Taiwan; Taipei Int Bus Club; Am Univ Club, Taiwan; AAAS; Phi Lambda Upsilon; Sigma Xi Soc of the Plastics Ind; Japan Mgmt Assn; Trustee, Am Sch in Japan. *Honours:* Union Carbide Fellowship, Mellon Inst of Indl Rsch, 1958-60; Num Lectures, Tech Publs and Patents in USA, Japan, France, Germany, Sweden, Russia. *Hobbies:* International Travel; Cross-Cultural Studies; Golf. *Address:* Homat Governor 402, 5-17

Roppongi I-chome, Minato-ku, Tokyo, Japan 106. 6, 14, 139.

RANSCHER Elizabeth Ann, b. 18 Mar 1945, Oakland, CA, USA. Nuclear & Astrophysicist, div. 1 s. *Education:* BS 1964, MS 1966, PhD 1979, Univ of CA, Berkeley. *Appointments:* Lawrence Berkeley Lab, Univ of CA, Berkeley, 1964-79; Navy Grant, 1970-74; SRI Int, 1974-79; Stanford Linear Accelerator Center, 1971-72; Univ of CA, Berkeley teaching, 1971-74; Nuclear & Astrophysicist, Magtek 1978-; Pres, Tecnic Rsch Labs, 1979-90; Adjunct Physis Prof, Univ of Nevada, 1991-1993. *Publications:* The Philosophy of Science, 1971; A Unifying Theory of Fundamental Processes, 1971; Theory of Quentin Measurement, 1992. Patents: Pulsed magnetic field external cardiac pacemaker, 1988; Non-super conducting magnetic and electro-magnetic field detector, 1988; Pazn reduction system utaizing pulsed magnetic fields, 1990. Published 185 papers, books, abstracts, talks; TV, Radio and Public Lectures. *Memberships:* Am Phys Soc; Am Math Soc; Am Nuclear Soc; IEEE; SIAM. *Honours:* Delta Delta Delta Scholarship, Iota Sigma Pi Fellow, 1962; Deleg to the UN, 1979, 1989; USPA Person of the Yr, 1990. *Hobbies include:* Poetry writing; Ink sketches; Skin and scuba diving; Under water photography; Flying. *Address:* Magtek Laboratories Inc, 7685 Hughes Drive, Golden Valley, Reno, NV 89506, USA. 59.

RAO Man-Ren, b. 17 Sep 1930, Fujian Province, China. Prof. m. 4 May 1954, 1 s, 1 d. *Education:* MD, Fujian Med Coll, 1946-52; Rsch Fellow, Dept of Pharmacology, Shanghai 1st Med Univ 1954-55, Nanjing Traditional Chinese Med Coll 1958-61. *Appointments:* Asst 1953, Instr 1958, Culture Revolution 1966-76, Assoc Prof 1980, Prof of Pharmacology 1985, Chmn, Prof of Dept of Cardiovascular Pharmacology 1986, Nanjing Med Coll; Ed Bd of: Acta Pharmaceutica Sinica 1982, Chinese Cardiovasc Pharmacol Bulletin 1982, Chinese Pharmacol Bulletin 1985, Information of Chinese Pharmacol Bulletin 1986; Vis Prof: Inst of Biochem Pharmacology, Univ of Innsbruck, Austria 1988-89, Dept of Physiology, Univ of Alberta, Can 1990. *Publications include:* Co-ed of: Methods in Pharmacology, 1982; Cardiovascular Pharmacology, 1989. *Contributions to:* Eur J Pharmacol, J Mol Cell Cardiol, Chinese Medical J, Acta Pharmacol Sinica, Acta Pharmaceutica Sinica. *Memberships:* Coun Mbr of Jiangsu Br 1979-, Chinese Pharmacological Soc; Dpty Sec Gen 1980-91, Chinese Cardiovascular Pharmacological Soc; Int Soc for Heart Rsch, 1987; Int Union of Pharmacology; Chinese Pharmaceutical Soc. *Honours include:* Achmt Awd of Scientific Rsch of Women, CST of Jiangsu Govt, 1986; CYCLOVIVOBUXINED, a new drug for angina pectoris Invent Award by National Committee of Science and Technique, 1992; Conf Organizer: Mat Meeting of Cardiovascular Pharmacology in Yellow Mountain 1991, Shengyang 1991. *Hobbies:* Arts: folk literature, folk dancing. *Address:* Department of Cardiovascular Pharmacology, Nanjing Medical College 210029, Han Zhong Road 140, Nanjing, China. 152.

RAO Pengzi, b. 26 Feb 1935, Chaozhou, China. VP; Prof. m. Chaohuai Wu, 24 Jan 1959, 2 d. *Education:* BA, Zhongshan Univ, 1953-57. *Appointments:* Tchr of Chinese Lit, Zhongshan Univ, Jinan Univ, 1957- 81; Vice Prof of Lit, Dean of Chinese Lit & Langs 1981, Prof of Lit 1985, VP 1987, Jinan Univ. *Publications include:* Ed-in-chief, author of: A course in the Comparative Study of Chinese and Western Dramas; Elementary Literature; Traditional Literature and Consciousness of the Contemporary Era; Literature Crticism ad Comparative Literature. *Memberships:* VP of Guangdong Br, Coun of Chinese Writers; Vice Chmn, Social-Sci Fedn, Guangdong; Dir of Standing Comm, China's Comparative Lit Assn; Dir, China's Assn of the Theoretical Study of Lit and Art. *Honours:* Guangdong highest prize for the excellent works on critical lit, 1978-85; 2nd prize for excellent works on comparative lit, 1979-80; Highest prize in Guangdong for excellent achmt in educ, 1989. *Hobbies:* Study of comparative literature, especially the comparative study of Chinese and Western dramas and novels; Promotion of the Oversea Chinese Literature. *Address:* Room 202, Building 21, Shuzhou Garden, Jinan University, Guangzhou 510632, China. 152.

RAO T R, b. 4 June 1926, Vadakunte, India. Pres. m. Saroja Rao, 16 Feb 1956, 2 s, 2 d. *Education:* BA, Banaras Hindu Univ, 1952; MA 1955, LLB 1957, PhD 1963, Lucknow Univ. *Appointments:* Pool Off, Coun of Scientific & Indl Rsch, New Delhi, 1965-68; Lectr in Psychology 1968-84, Reader in Psychology 1984-86, Univ of Hysore; Fdr, Pres, Inst of Psychological Rsch, 1986-. *Publications include:* General Psychology; Correlates of learning in albino rats; Effects of Curcuma Longa on BMR, Emotionality and Learning; Indian Methods of Character Analysis with a Special Reference to Occupational Life; Sports Psychology; Ed of: Indian Journ of Behaviour; Applied Psychology. *Memberships:* Sec, Sri Geeta Satsang Kailas Kshetra, Naini Tal, 1950-56; Int Assn of Applied Psychology, 1968-72; Trustee, Keladi Mus & Histl Rsch Bur, Keladi, 1978-. *Honour:* Sahitya Acad Awd, 1969. *Hobbies:* Reading literature on Indian Psychology; Indian philosophy; Yoga. *Address:* Institute of Psychological Research, 780 I Cross Road, Mahalakshwi Layout, Bangalore 560086, India.

RAPER Peter Edmund, b. 17 Dec 1939, Springs, S Africa. Hd; Dir. m. Margaret Gwendoline Hooper, 30 Nov 1963, dec 1989, 1 s, 1 d. *Education:* BA 1961, BA (Hons) 1965, PhD 1971, Witwatersrand Univ; TTHD, Johannesburg Coll of Educ, 1961. *Appointments:* Tchr in Second Sch, 1962-69; Hd, Onomastic Rsch Ctr, Human Scis Rsch Coun, Pretoria, 1970-. *Publications:* Author of 75 articles 11 books incl: Dictionary of Southern Africa Place Names, 1989; Robert Jacob Gordon Cape Travels 1777-1786 (w M Boucher), 2 vols. *Memberships:* S African Nat Place Names Comm, 1972-; Int Comm of Onomastic Scis, 1981-; Am Name Soc, 1983-; S African Acad of Arts & Scis, 1983-; (UN Group of Experts, 1984-; Chrmn. 1991), Chmn 1991-, UN Grp of Experts on Geogl Names; Pres, Names Soc of Southern Africa. *Honours include:* Gold Medal for Afrikaans Folk Culture, 1977; P M Robbertse Medal for outstng merit in Onomastics, 1983; Presented papers at seven int congresses. *Hobbies:* Classical music; Collecting Africana books; Reading; Travelling. *Address:* 40 Junction Road, Bramley, 2090 Johannesburg, South Africa.

RAPIN Charles Rene Jules, b. 10 Jan 1935, Lausanne, Switz. Prof of Computer Sci. *Education:* Baccalaureat-es-Lettres, 1954; Diplome d'Ingenieur-Physicien, 1959; Dr ès Sciences Techniques (PhD), Ecole Polytechnique, Univ of Lausanne, 1964. *Appointments:* Asst 1959-64, Chef de Travaux 1964-67, Ecole Polytechnique, Univ of Lausanne; Vis Asst Prof, Univ of KY, USA, 1967-68; Scientific Collaborator 1969-72, Prof of Computer Sci 1972-, Ecole Polytechnique Federale, Lausanne. *Publications:* The Newton Language' Sigplan Notices (ACM), 1981; Several internal publs for tchng purposes. *Memberships:* ACM; Societe Mathematique Suisse; Societe Suisse des Informaticiens. *Hobbies:* Public transport (trams, trains, trolleybuses); Reading novels. *Address:* Laboratoire de Compilation, Department d'Informatique Ecublens (IN), Ecole Polytechnique Federale de Lausanne, CH-1015 Lausanne, Switzerland. 151, 152, 154.

RASCHKE Krystyna Oleszczuk, b. 1 Jan 1939, Lida, Poland. Doctor of Medicine; Paediatric Radiologist. m. Julian Raschke, 16 Dec 1961, 1 s. *Education:* Physns Dip, 1963, Specialisation, Radiology, I, 1969, II, 1973; DrMedSc, 1974, Szczecin, Poland; DAAD Fellowship, Univ Klinik Eppendorf, Hamburg, FRG, 1976; Specialisation, Paediatric Radiology, Heidelberg, Germany, 1991. *Appointments:* Inst Radiology, Pomeranian Med ACad, Szczecin, 1966-83; Paediatric Radiologist, Radiology Dept, Univ Cape Town, S Africa, 1985-88; Paeidatric Radiologist, Dept Paediatric Radiology, Univ Heidelberg, Germany, 1988-92. *Publications:* Co-author: Clinical Radiology, set of

teaching aids, 1981; Radiologia, textbook, 1984; Nierensonographie, textbook, 1992. *Memberships:* Polish Radiological Soc, Former Mbr Radiological Methodology Comm; Soc Paediatric Radiology, German-speaking countries. *Honours:* Rector's Awards, Acad and Tchng Achievements, Pomeranian Med Acad, Szczecin, 1978, 1980, 1982. *Hobbies:* Music; Reading; Languages; Travel. *Address:* Monchhofstr 32, 6900 Heidelberg, Germany.

RASHKOV Dimitar, b. 30 Nov 1954. Sculptor. m. Lilyana Nicolova Rashkova, 1 Apr 1979, 1 s, 1 d. *Education:* Acad for Fine Arts, Sofia, 1975-81. *Appointments:* Tchr in Arts, 1981-85; Chief Artist of a Dist, 1985-88; Chief of Gall, 1988-. *Creative works:* Nat Exhibs in Bulgaria, Greece, England, Kuwait, Portugal, China. *Membership:* Coun, Bulgarian Union of Artists. *Hobbies:* Sport; Tourism; Art; Music; Literature. *Address:* 6 Panayot Volov str, 4300 Karlovo, Bulgaria.

RASMUSSEN Folke, b. 11 June 1930, Holbaek, Denmark. Prof. m. Marie Jensen, 22 Sept 1956, 1 s. *Education:* Dr med vet 1955, Dr, Lc 1966; Dr med vet hc, 1985. *Appointments:* Assoc Prof 1966, Dean for Vet Fac 1974-77, Rector (Vice Chancellor) 1981-87, Prof 1987, Dept of Pharmacology and Toxicology, Royal Vet & Agric Univ, Copenhagen. *Creative works include:* Guest Lectures: Drug residues in meat and milk, Inst fur Lebensmittel Hygiene, Berlin, 1977; Veterinary medicine as a must in modern livestock production, Sokoine Univ of Agric, Morogoro, 1986. *Memberships include:* Danish Agricl and Vet Rsch Coun, 1979-87; Jt Comm, Royal Vet and Agricl Univ, Danish Int Dev Agcy for scientific coop with developing countries, 1981-; Ad hoc working grp on Ethical aspects in biotechnology, animal production and use of laboratory animals, NKVet, 1989-91. *Honours:* Gen J F Classens Awd, The Royal Danish Scientific Soc Silver Medal, 1976; Ulrik Brinch and Marie Brinch Awd, 1977; Danish order Rpp, 1983; Icelandic order I F 3, 1984; Dr Sc hc, 1985; The Lloyd E Davis award, The Am Acad of Veterinary Pharmacology, Canada, 1992; Hon Mem, Finnish Veterinary Assoc, 1992. *Address:* Katrinedalsvej 27, 2720 Vanlose, Copenhagen, Denmark.

RASNIC Carol, b. 2 July 1941, Norton, VA, USA. Atty; Univ Prof. m. (1) Joe McDaniel Duncan, 12 Feb 1965, div 1976, (2) R Jackson Rasnic, 30 Dec 1980, 2 s. *Education:* BA, Univ of KY, 1962; JD, Vanderbilt Univ Sch of Law, 1965. *Appointments:* Atty, Metrop Nashville Legal Dept, 1965-66; Atty, Burch, Porter & Johnson, Memphis, 1966-68; Asst Prof of Bus Law, Memphis State Univ, 1972-76; VA Employment Comms, 1977-78; Hse Coun, Westmorland Coal Co, 1978-80; Assoc Prof of Labour Law, VA C'wlth Univ, 1980-. *Contributions to:* Employee Relations Law Journ; Labour Law Journ; FL State Law Review; St Louis Univ Law Journ; Duquesne Law Review; Creighton Law Review; Am Bar Assn Journ. *Memberships:* Am Bus Law Assn; VA Bar Assn; VA State Bar; Richmond (VA) Bar Assn; Metrop Richmond Women's Bar Assn; VA Women Attys Assn; TN Bar Assn; Memphis-Shelby Co (TN) Bar Assn; Am Bus Law Assn; Am Trial Lawyers' Assn. *Honours:* Best Paper Awd, 1987; Hon Mbr, Delta Sigma Pi Int Bus Frat, 1987; Hon Mbr, Beta Gamma Sigma Bus Frat, 1989; Best Article Awd, 1990. *Hobbies:* Piano; Swimming; Professional baseball. *Address:* 907 Bevridge Road, Richmond, VA 23226, USA.

RASOR Garry Girard, b. 3 Apr 1943, Houston, TX, USA. Telecommuications Mgr; Engr. 2 d. *Education:* Assoc of Applied Sci, Jefferson Community Coll, 1974-75; BSc, Univ of Louisville. *Appointments:* Telecommunications Test Engr, Southwestern Bell Telephone, Houston, 1964- 67; Communications Engr, Philco/Ford Corp, Johnson Space Ctr, Mission Control, NASA, Clear Lake, 1967-72; Self employed Carpenter, Louisville, 1972-73; Communications Analyst, First Nat Bank, Louisville, 1978-81; Telecommunication Mgr, Engr, Greenville, TX, Div E Systems Inc, 1981-. *Creative* *works:* Many landscape, animal and portrait art work; Sem Participant, Assn Dta Comm Users, 1985; N TX Telecomm Assn, 1986; Southern Univ of Baton Rouge, 1990, 1991. *Contributions to:* Communications News, 1980, 1988; Computer World, 1980; Greenville Harold Banner, 1982; Information Networking, 1986; Voice/Data Trng Course for IBM Mgmt, 1986; Source Book, 1990. *Memberships:* Reg Dir 1979-80, Bd of Dir 1989-90, Assn of Data Communications Users; Pres 1983-84, Bd of Dir 1983-87, VP 1984-85, Parliamentarian 1985-87, N TX Telecomm Assn; Local Pub/Pvt Schs 1989, 1991, Telecomm Presentations. *Honours:* Reg Dir of the Yr, Assn of Data Communications, 1980; Reg of th Yr, 1980; Honorable Presiential Plaque, N TX Telecommunications Assn, 1983-84. *Hobbies include:* Gardening; Reading; Wood working; Camping; Community volunteer work; Volunteer carpenter for Visiting Nurces Assn, 1981-82. *Address:* PO Box 813, Greenville, TX 75403, USA. 7.

RASTEGAR Farzad A, b. 25 June 1956, Teheran. Investment Banker. m. Neda Modjtabai, 20 Oct 1990. *Education:* BSc Hons, Imperial Coll, London Univ, 1977; MBA, Columbia Univ, 1982. *Appointments:* 2 dLt, Imperial Iranian Army, 1977-79; Asst VP, Phoenix Earth Resources Corp, San Fran, 1982-83; VP, Capital Properties Inc, New York, 1984-85; Exec VP, Asian Oceanic Real Estate Corp, New York, 1986-87; Investment Banker, Wellsford Grp Inc, New York, 1988-; Dir: Filofax Grp plc, London; Renafa Inc, Atlanta; Capital Properties, New York. *Creative work:* Specialised art research work. *Memberships:* MIMM; Engrng Coun; ARSM; Nat Alumni Assn, Columbia Bus Sch Bd of Dir, 1984-88. *Hobbies:* Skiing; Theatre; Carpentry; Gardening. *Address:* Wellsford Group Inc, 375 Park Avenue, Suite 307, New York, NY 10152, USA. 6, 52, 132.

RASTEGAR Nader E, b. 12 May 1953, Tehran, Iran. Industrialist; Real Estate Developer. m. Soheila Gharaii, 6 Apr 1979, 3 d. *Education:* BSc, Univ of WI, 1976; MBA, Iran Ctr for Mgmt Studies, 1979. *Appointments:* Pres, Shahgard Indl Co, Teheran, 1977; Foreign Serv Desk Ed, Kayhan Newspaper, Teheran, 1979; Pres, Renafa Inc, 1984; Bd of Dir of num firms. *Publications:* Author of several articles and papers. *Memberships:* Royal Philatelic Soc; Collectors Club; RAS; Soc of Iranian Profls; Urban Land Inst; Nat Home Builders Assn. *Hobbies:* Reading; Chess; Philatelics; Historical research; Social works; Environmental issues. *Address:* PO Box 725048, Atlanta, GA 30339, USA. 7, 132.

RATAJCZAK Jozef Grzegorz, b. 29 Feb 1932, Poznan, Poland. Writer; Poet; Transl. m. Dobrochna Dunin Michalowska, 10 Aug 1965, 2 s. *Education:* Univ of Warsaw, 1953; Univ of Poznan, 1956; Doct, 1960. *Appointments:* Redactor Broadcasting, 1960; TV, 1965; Lit Mgr of Theatre, Poznan, 1970. *Publications:* Poems incl: Bad Weather, 1956; Closing of the Landscape, 1958; The Positions and the Acts, 1960; Beggarly Ballads, 1962; The Removal on Atlandid, 1970; View Hours, 1985; Light Out of the Ash, 1987; Marriage Lyrics, 1988; David's Little Stones, 1991. Prose incl: The Dreams in the Sun, 1962; The Nest on the Clouds, 1965; Night after Nighet, 1970; With the Coffin in the Procession, 1979; The Day of Your Mother, 1984. Essays: The Final of the Daybreak of the Epoch, 1979; Scream and Ecstasy, 1980; Lessons by K Illakowicz, 1986; The Don Juan of Poznan, 1987; Romantics lowers, 1989; Poems and Prose for Children. *Honours:* S Pietak Awd, 1972; Reymonts Awd, 1978; Pres of the Mins Counsel, 1980; J Kasprowicz Awd, 1984. *Hobby:* Digging garden plot. *Address:* ul Rycerska 12 m 13, 60 347 Poznan, Poland.

RATH Sura Prasad, b. 11 July 1950, Balugaon. University Professor and Administrator. m. Manju Rajaguru 12 May 1974, 2 s. *Education:* BA Ravenshaw Col, 1972; MA Utkal Univ, 1972; MA Tulane, Univ, 1982; PhD Texas A&M Univ, 1985. *Appointments:* Nat Coun for Ed Res and Training, New Delhi, 1974-75; Buxi

Jagabandhu Bidyadhar Col, 1974-75; Loyola Univ, 1979-81; Tulane Univ, 1976-81; Texas & A M Univ, 1982-85; Louisiana State Univ, Shreveport, 1985-. *Publications:* Research articles magazines and professional journals. *Memberships:* Modern Lang Assn; S.Central MLA; Phi Kappa Phi, Chapt Sec, 1988-90, Pres Elect, 1991, Pres, 1992. *Honours:* Outstanding Fac Achievement Awd, LSU-S, 1988. *Hobbies:* Travel; Reading; Writing. *Address:* Office of Academic Affairs LSVS, 1 University Place, Shreveport, LA 71115, USA. 1, 7.

RATI Robert Dean, b. 8 Jan 1939, Pittsburg, Kansas, USA. Data Processing Executive. m. Margaret Fort Henry, 7 June 1969, 1 s, 1 d. *Education:* BA, Maths, Univ Kansas, 1961; MA Econ, N.Eastern Univ, 1970; MBA, Mgmt and Personnel, Columbia Univ, 1973. *Appointments:* Sys Engr, IBM Corp, Boston, 1965-72; Mgr, Mgmt Sers, Arthur Young & Co, NYC, 1973- 75; Mgr, Client Sys, Touche Ross & Co, NYC, 1975-76; Mgr, Sys and Prog, Walker Mfg Div, Tenneco Inc, Wisconsin, 1976-78; DP Mgr, Schwitzer Div, Household Intl, Indianapolis, 1979-87; MIS Mgr, Nat Machinery Co, Ohio, 1988-90; Pres, Dunhill Profl Search, Indiana, 1990-; MIS Mgr, ABB Power TED Co, Indiana, 1991-. *Publications:* Articles for fraternal organizations; Newsletters. *Memberships:* Pi Mu Epsilon; Illinois Soc Sons of the Revolution, Pres, 1980-82; Chm, Awds Com, Gen Soc Sons of the Revolution, 1982-90; Huguenot Soc of Indiana, Pres, 1985-89; Soc of Indiana Pioneers, Bd of Govs, 1985-91; V-Chm, Swimming Pool Comm, Ramsey, NJ, 1972-74; Admin Bd, Utd Methodist Ch, Carmel, IN, 1987-90. *Honours:* IBM Reg Mgr Awd, 1967. *Hobbies:* Home computing; Genealogy. *Address:* 4919 Regency Place, Carmel, IN 46033, USA. 8, 57, 132, 155.

RATOSI Erno, b. 4 Oct 1931, Zalagyomoro, Hungary. Chairman and Director of the Board. m. Anna Kerekes, 14 Aug 1961, 3 d. *Education:* Chem Engr, 1956-60; Postgrad studies in Chem Engrg 19071-73; Doctorate, 1981. *Appointments:* Plant Mgr, Cspel Refinery, 1960-63; Engr, Danube Refinery, 1963-68; Chief Engr, Min of Heavy Indust, 1968-69; Chief Technol, 1969-73, Dep Dir, 1973-74, Gen Dir, 1975-91, Danube Refinery; Asst Prof of Chem Engrg, Veszprem Univ. *Publications:* Co-author of 16 patents on crude oil processing technologies. *Memberships:* Techno-Chem Com of Hungarian Acad of Scis; Techno Sci Com of Hungarian Chem Soc; Hungarian Chem Indust Assn, V-Chm. *Honours:* Medal of Labour in Gold; Eotvos Lorand Awd; Pfeiffer Ignac Awd. *Hobby:* Gardening. *Address:* Bocskai 21, Budapest, H-1114, Hungary.

RATZABY Yehuda, b. 11 May 1916, Yemen, Israel. Retired Pensioner. m. 1953, 3 d. *Education:* MA, Jerusalem Univ, 1963. *Appointments:* Hagana Ser, 1939-48; Defence Min, 1949-63; Bar Iban Univ; Hebrew Univ; Tel Aviv Univ, 1964-85. *Publications:* 21 books; 513 articles; Bibliography printed in, Studies in Hebrew Literature and Yemenite Culture, 1991. *Memberships:* Hebrew Land Acad; Mkise Nirdamim. *Honours:* Histadruth Prize, 1962; Bialik Prize, 1966, 1979; Ben Zuri Prize, 1987; Jerusalem Prize, 1988; Holon Prize, 1989; Rubbe Kook Prize, 1990; Notable of Tel Aviv. *Address:* 10 Oliphant Str, Tel Aviv, Israel.

RAUSCHER Elizabeth Anne Bloomfied, b. 18 Mar 1945, Oakland, California, USA. div. 1 s. *Education:* BS Phys, 1964, MS Nuclear Engrg, 1968, PhD Nuclear Sci, 1979, UC Berkeley, CA. *Appointments:* Lawrence Berkeley Lab, 1964-74; SRI Intl, 1974-79; Stanford Linear Accelerator, 1971- 72; US Naval Contract, 1970-74; Pres, Technic Res Labs, 1979-91; VP Magtek, 1988-91. *Publications:* Three patents; 4 books: The Philosophy of Science, 1971; The Unifying Theory of Fundamental Processes, 1971; Theory of Quantum Measurement, 1990; The Iceland papers, 1979. *Memberships:* APS; AMS; IEEE; IAM; ANS; Pres, N.West Ctr for the Study of Non Ionizing Radiation. *Honours:* UN delegate, 1979, 1989; Fellow, Iota Sigma Pi, 1962; Delta Delta Delta

Scholarship, 1960; UUPA Person of the Yr Awd, 1990; USA Sci Awd, 1991. *Hobbies:* Poetry; Art; Scuba Diving and Instruction; Photography; Flying. *Address:* Magtex Laboratories Inc, 7685 Hughes Dr, Golden Valley, Reno NV 89506, USA. 50, 59,

RAVA Paolo Antonio, b. 7 Nov 1950, Torino, Italy. Physicist. *Education:* BSc Elec Engrg, Poly Torino, Italy, 1975; MSc Solid State Phys, Univ London, 1976; PhD Phys, Mass Inst of Tech, USA, 1981. *Appointments:* Reschr, Heliosil, Italy, 1981-83; R & D Mgr, Elettrorava, Torino, 1983-1991; Dir, Rothchild Asst Mngmnt, Isle of Man, Ltd, 1987-1991; Dir. *Publications:* About 50 articles in professional journals, conference proceedings. *Memberships:* Am Vacuum Soc; IEEE; Materials Res Soc. *Hobbies:* Mountaineering; Skiing; Yoga; Trekking; Sailing. *Address:* Via Talucchi 23, 10143 Torino, Italy.

RAWCLIFFE Roger Capron, b. 2 Aug 1934, Lancaster, England. Chartered Accountant. m. Mary Elizabeth White, 18 June 1960, 1 s. *Education:* Rossall Sch, 1942-52; Trinity Col Cambs, Exhibitioner, Classical Tripos, (1st Pt I). *Appointments:* Articled Price Waterhouse, 1957-60; Master, House Master, Stowe Sch, Hd Dept, Cmdr, CCF, 1960-80; Ptnr, Pannell Kerr & Foster, Isle of Man, 1980-1991; Dir Rothschild Asst Mngmnt, Isle of Man, 1987-1991; Dir, Singer and Friedlander, Isle of Man, 1992-; Dir, Isle of Man Breweries Ltd, 1992-; Governor Rossall Sch 1982-; Trustee and Governor, King's William's Coll, 1986-; Trustee Manx Nat Heritage, 1991-. *Publications:* Numerous occasional articles published on antiquity and taxation; Guest lecturer, Swan Hellenic; Occasional Lectr, Univ of Liverpool. *Memberships:* FICA, Eng and Wales; Nat Ser and TA, Grenadier Guards; E.Lancs Rgt and HAC Major Stowe CCF; Hon Col, Isle of Man ACF. *Honours:* Gregg Bury Prize for Greek Verse; Henry Arthur Thomas Travelling Scholarship; Cadet Forces Medal and Bar. *Hobbies:* Antiquities; Architecture; History. *Address:* The Malt House, Bridge Street, Castletown, Isle of Man.

RAWI Ousama, b. 3 May 1939, Baghdad, Iraq. Film Director. m. Rita Tushingham, 27 Aug 1981, 1 s, 2 d. *Education:* Edinburgh Acad, Scotland; London Univ. *Appointments:* Photographer, 1965-67; TV industry, 1968-69. *Creative Works:* TV and cinema commercials and CFF Feature, The Oxbone Buccaneers, 1970-71; TV: Philby, A Ruthless Journey and commercials, 1971-72; Once upon a time is now - The story of Princess Grace, 1978-; Exec Producer, Lancaster and Miller, TV mini-series, 1985; Producer, TV series, War of the Worlds, Friday' Curse, 1989. Films: Pulp; The 14, 1972-73; Black Windmill Gold, 1974; Rachel's Man, Alfie Darling, 1975; The Human Factor, Sky Riders, 1977; Power Play, Bovver Boots; Girl in Blue Velvet, Zulu Dawn, 1978; Charlie Muffin, 1979; Producing and directing in Can, 1980; Assoc Producer, Flying, 1986; Director, A Judgement in Stone, 1987-88; Flying, 1986. *Memberships:* Can Indep Commercial Producers Assn, Chm; Can Ctr for Adv Film Studies, Foun Com; Acad of Can Cinema; Dirs Guild of Am; BAFTA: Brit Soc of Cinematographers. *Honours:* Brit Cameraman of the Yr, 1971; London Intl Ad Awd; Cannes Ad Film Festival; Ad Club of NY; Houston Intl Film and TV Festival of NY: Mondial Awd, Paris; Clio Awds, 1972-. *Hobbies:* Photography; Computing. *Address:* 567 Queen Street West, Toronto, Ontario, Canada M5V 2B6. 142.

RAY Brian Daniel, b. 30 Oct 1954, Vancouver, WA, USA. Researcher; Educator. m. Betsy Anne Brigs, 2 Sept 1978, 1 s, 3 d. *Education:* Bs Biol, Univ of Puget Sound, 1976; MS Zoology, Ohio Univ, 1979; PhD Sci Educ, Oregon State Univ, 1988. *Appointments:* Res and Tchg Asst, Oregon State Univ, 1983-88; Asst Prof, Seattle Pacific Univ, 1988-90; Ed, Home Sch Reschr, 1985-; Pres, Nat Home Educ Res Inst, 1990-. *Publications:* The academic achievement and effective development of home schooled children, 1991; Determinants of grades 3 to 8 students' intentions to engage in laboratory and non-laboratory science, 1991; Social capital value consistency and the achievement outcomes of home education, 1990. *Memberships:* Am Educ Res Assn; Nat Assn for Res in Sci and Tech; Nat Sci Tchrs Assn; Oregon Acad of Sci. *Honours:* US Dept of Educ Grant, 1990-91; Nat Ctr for Home Educ Res contract, Seattle Pacific Univ Res Grants, 1988-90. *Hobbies:* Organic gardening; Woodworking; Running; Reading. *Address:* National Home Education Research Institute, 25 West Cremona Street, Seattle, WA 98119, USA. 7, 9.

RAYBURN Alan, b. 15 Nov 1932, Ontario, Canada. Toponymist; Geographer; Writer; Columnist. m. Mary Teresa Fox, 7 Sept 1960, 3 s. *Education:* BA Univ W.Ontario, 1956; MA, Univ of Kentucky, 1957; DesL, (Courses only), Univ Laval, 1971. *Appointments:* Dept of Energy, Mines and Resources, Ottawa, 1957-87; Exec Sec of Can Perm Com on Geog Names, 1973-87. *Publications:* Geographical names of Renfrew County, Ontario, 1967, reprint, 1989, 1990; Geographical names of Prince Edward island, 1973; Geographical names of New Brunswick, 1975. *Memberships:* Pres, Am Name Soc, 1985; Pres, Can Soc for the Study of Names, 1979-82; Rapporteur, UN Gp of Experts on Geographical Names, 1977-87; Fellow, 1974-, Dir, 1986-, Royal Can Geog Soc. *Hobbies:* Local history and geography; Writing and Publishing; Genealogy and Family history. *Address:* 5 Solva Drive, Nepean, Ontario, Canada K2H 5R4.

RAYMOND Diana Joan, b. 25 Apr 1916, London, England. Novelist. m. 20 Aug 1940, 1 s. *Education:* Cheltenham Ladies College, 1921-32. *Appointments:* Personal Assistant, Com of Imperial Defence and Cabinet Ofrs, 1936-40. *Publications:* Novels include: The Small Rain, 1954; Between the Stirrupand the Ground, 1956; Guest of Honour, 1960; The Climb, 1962; People in the House, 1964; The Noonday Sword, 1965; Incident on a Summer's Day, 1974; The Dark Journey; Emma Pride, 1981; House of the Dolphin, 1985; Lily's Daughter, 1988. *Honours:* Book Society Choice for, The Small Rain, 1954. *Hobbies:* Reading; Travel; Theatre. *Address:* 22 The Pryors, East Heath Road, London NW3 1BS, England.

RAZZELL Mary Catherine, b. 20 Feb 1930, Calgary, Alberta, Canada. Writer. m. Eric Patrick Nicol, 11 Feb 1986, 2 s, 1 d. *Education:* St Pauls, Sch of Nsg, Vancouver, 1951; Refresher Course in Nsg, 1980; First year, fine Arts, Univ of BC, 1981; Childbirth Educr, 1989. *Appointments:* Registered Nurse: Medical, Surgical, Private, 1951-56; Childbirth Educr, Gynaecology, 1980-90. *Publications:* Snow Apples, 1984; The Secret Code of DNA, 1986; Salmonberry Wine, 1987; Night Fires, 1990. *Memberships:* Children's Literature Rountable; CANSCAIP. *Honours:* Univ Alumni Short Story Contest Awd, 1979; Shortlisted: Gov Gen Awd, Children's Lit, 1984; Geoffrey Bilson Awd for historical fiction, 1987, Sheila A Egoff Children's Prize, 1987, Best Children's information book, 1986; First Prize, Poetry knowledge Network, TV, 1991. *Hobbies:* Swimming; Weight lifting; Reading. *Address:* 3993 West 36th Avenue, Vancouver, BC, Canada V6N 2S7.

READ Allan Alexander, b. 19 Sept 1923, Toronto, Canada. Retd Bishop of Ontario. m. Mary Beverly Sophie Roberts, 28 Sept 1949, 2 s, 2 d. *Education:* BA, LTh, DD, Trinity Col, DD, Wycliffe Col, Univ of Toronto; STD, Thornloe Col, Ontario. *Appointments:* Parish of Mono, 7 Chs, Diocese of Toronto, 1947-54; Trinity Ch, Rector of Barrie, 1954-71; Fndr, Barrie East End Mission (Parish of St Giles) 1954; Dir, Diocesan Town and Country Ch Comm, 1952-62; Canon, St James Cathedral, Toronto, 1957; Archdeacon, Simcoe, 1961; Chmm, Provincial Synod Rural Ch Unit, 1955-65; Chaplain, Simcoe County Gaol, 1955-71; Biship, Suffragan, Toronto, 1972-81; Diocesan Bishop, Diocese, Ontario, 1981-91; St Patrick's Cathedral, Trim, Diocese, Meath and Kildare, Ireland, 1992. *Publications:* Unto the Hills; Shepherds in Green Pastures. *Memberships:* Rural Workers Fellowship, America, Canadian Hon Pres; Gen Synod, The Anglican Ch, Canada, 1959-89; Provincial Synod,

1955-91; The Anglican World Widee Lambeth Conference, 1978, 1988. *Honours:* Rural Ministry Award, 1952; Barrie Citizen of the year, 1966; Region Conservation Authority, 1977; Govnmt, Ontario Citizenship Awards. *Hobbies:* Music; Reading; Stamps; Gardening; Hymnology. *Address:* 39 Riverside Drive, RR I Kingston, Ontario K7L 4V1, Canada.

READ Paul Eugene, b. 13 July 1937, New York, USA. Professor and Head of Department. m. Christine Streed, 13 Aug 1989, 1 s, 2 d. *Education:* BS 1959, MS 1964, Cornell Univ; PhD, Univ of Delaware, 1967. *Appointments:* Co Extension Agent, Fulton Co, NY, 1959-62; Asst Prof, 1967-72, Assoc Prof, 1972-78, Prof, 1978-87, Univ of Minnesota; Prof and Hd, Univ of Nebraska, 1987-. *Publications:* Plant propagation lab manual; 6 book chapters, over 100 scientific journal articles. *Memberships:* Bd, Am Soc Hort Sci, 1972, 1985-87; VP, Educ Div, 1986-87; Plant Growth Reg Soc Am, Ed, 1975-87, VP, 1990-91; Am Chestnut Foun, VP, 1991-; Intl Assn Plant Tissue Cult, US Rep,; Tissue Cult Assn; Intl Plant Prop Soci Intl Soc Hort Sci; Bot Soc Am. *Honours:* Fellow, Am Soc Horticultural Science, 1987-. *Hobbies:* Gardening; Racquetball; Public speaking; Wine Collecting; Cooking; International travel and consulting. *Address:* Dept of Horticulture, University of Nebraska, Lincoln, NE 68583, USA. 50.

REAL Francisco X, b. 9 Dec 1957, Barcelona, Spain. Physician, Medical Research. *Education:* MS 1980, PhD, 1986, Specialist, Med Oncol, 1985. *Appointments:* Asst Att Phys, Meml Hosp, NY, 1986-88; Hd, Dept of Immunol, Inst Mun Inv Med, Barceolona, Spain, 1988- . *Publications:* Multiple publications in medical journals. *Memberships:* Am Assn of Cancer Res; Am Soc Clin Oncol; AAAS. *Honours:* Conslt, WHO, for China Med Univ, 1989. *Hobbies:* Reading; Music. *Address:* Dept of Immunology, Inst Mun Invest Med, P Maritim 25, 08003-Barcelona, Spain. 57.

RECH Peter Wilhelm, b. 21 May 1943, Werdohl, Germany. Professor. m. Notburga de Byl, 9 Apr 1969, 1 s. *Education:* Tchg Dipl, Tchr Col, 1969-70; Educ Dipl, 1972; DEd, 1974; Habilitation, 1978. *Appointments:* Tchr, Art Therapy, 1971; Asst Instr, Art Educ, Univ Munster, 1972-79; Prof, Art Educ, Univ Cologne, 1979- ; Headmaster, Cologne Sch of Art Therapy, 1987-. *Publications:* Author of art education books, and art therapy; Solo and group painting exhibitions. *Memberships:* German Soc for Art Therapy and Therapy with Creative Media, Fdr, MD, 1984-; Intl Assn for Art Creativity and Therapy, Wider Directorium, 1990. *Address:* Durener Str 217/219, 5000 Koln 41, Germany. 57.

REDDAWAY George Frank Norman, b. 2 May 1918, Cambridge, England. Retired from HM Foreign Service. m. Jean Brett OBE, 19 Feb 1944, 2 s, 3 d. *Education:* Kings Col Choir Sch, 1925-31; Oundle Sch, 1931-35; Ba, Kings Col, Cambs, 1936-39; PSC, Camberley, 1944; Imperial Def Col, 1960. *Appointments:* Army Ser, 1939-46, UK, France, Belgium, North Africa, Italy; France, Belgium, Germany, 1945-46; FO, 1946-49; Rome, 1949-52, Ottawa, 1952-55; FO, 1955-59; IDC, 1960; Beirut, 1961-65; Singapore, 1965-66, Khartoum, 1967-69; FCO, 1970-74; Warsaw, 1974-78; Bus Conslt, 1978-; Chm, Intl House, 1978-; Trustee, Thomson Foun, 1978-. *Memberships:* Anglo Arab Assn; Anglo German Assn; GB-China Assn; GB-USSR Assn; British Assn for Central & East Europe. *Honours:* MBE, 1946; CBE, 1965; Polish Order of Merit, 1985. *Hobbies:* International affairs; Family history; Gardening. *Address:* 51 Carlton Hill, London NW8 OEL, England. 1.

REDDAWAY William Brian, b. 8 Jan 1913, Cambridge, England. Professor Emeritus of Economics. m. Barbara Agusta Bennett, 17 Sept 1938, 3 s, 1 d. *Education:* Kings Col Sch, 1920-23; Ludgate Hse, Hunstanton, 1924-26; Oundle Sch, 1926-31; Kings Col, Cambs, 1931-34; BA, 1934, MA 1938. *Appointments:* Asst, Bank of England, 1934-35; Research fellow, Univ of

Melbourne, 1936-37; Fellow, Clare Col, Cambs, 1938- ; Univ of Cambs, 1939-80, Lectr, 1955, Dir, Dept of Applied Econ, 1970, Professor 1979. *Publications:* Russian Financial System, 1935; Econs of a Declining Population, 1938; Measurement of Production Movements, 1948; Development of the Indian Economy, 1962; Effects of UK direct investment overseas, 1967-68; Effects of selective employment tax, 1970-73; Some key features of the development of PNG Economy, 1986. *Memberships:* Fellow, Royal Econ Soc, 1936; Fellow, Brit Acad, 1967; Edit, Economic Jour, 1971-76. *Honours:* Adam Smith Prize, Cambs, 1934. CBE, 1971. *Hobbies:* Current affairs; Portfolio management; Walking; Skating. *Address:* 12 Manor Court, Grange Road, Cambridge CB3 9BE, England. 1.

REDDOCH Mildred Lucas, b. 1 Mar 1916, Texarkana, Texas, USA. Feeelance Writer, Poet; Retired Educator. m. Elbert D Reddoch, 1 s, 1 d. *Education:* Texarkana Col, 1934-36; BS, Houston State College, 1963- 64, MA, 1972. *Appointments:* Tchr, Ind Schls: Houston, 1943-64; Cypress Fairbanks, 1964-67; Texarkana, 1967-72; Houston, 1974-75. *Publications:* Poems, anthologies, essays, and novel, So White the Lilies, 1982; Sold many pieces of art. *Memberships:* NES; Nat League of Am Pen Women, Houston Pres, Nat Librarian; World Inst of Achievement, Life; Woman of the Year, 1990-91. *Honours:* Outstanding Tchr of Ark, 1969; Life Mem, Rep Pres Task Force, 1990; Medal of Merit, presented by George Bush, 1990; Golden Poet Awd, World of Poetry, 5th consecutive yr, 1990; Republican Presidential International Legion of Merit, Membership accepted, 1992; International Honors Cap, 1992. *Hobbies:* Reading; Writing; Solving word puzzles; Watching TV. *Address:* Tara Oaks, Apt 127, 3800 Sherwood Lane, TX 77092, USA. 2.

REDGROVE Peter William, b. 2 Jan 1932. m. (1) 1 d, 2 s, (2)Penelope Shuttle. *Education:* Taunton Sch; Queens Col, Cambs. *Appointments:* Sci journalist and copywriter, 1954-6 Vis Poet, Buffalo Univ, NY, 1961-62; Gregory Fellow in Poetry, Leeds Univ, 1962-65; Study with John Layard, 1968-69; Prof of Lit, Colgate Univ, NY, 1974-75; Emeritus Fellow, 1985-87. *Publications include:* Poetry: The Apple Barodcast, 1981; The Working of Water, 1984; The Man Named East, 1985; The Mudlark Poems and Grand Buveur, 1986; the First Earthquake, 1989; Dressed as for a Tarot pack, 1990; Prose Fictions: The Sleep of the Grat Hypnotist, 1979; The God of Glass, 1979; The Beekeepers, 1980; The Facilitators, 1982; The One Who Set out to Study Fear, 1989; The Cyclopean Mistress, 1993; Plays: Radio: The God of Glass, 1977; Martyr of the Hive,s 1980; Florent and the Tuxedo Millions, Prix Italia, 1982; Six Tales from Grimm, 1987; TV Plays: The Sermon, 1963; Jack be Nimble, 1980. Non Fiction: The Wise Wound, 1978; The Black Goddess and the Sixth Sense, 1987. *Honours:* Writer at Large, N Cornwall Arts, 1988; George Rylands Verse- speaking Prize, 1954; Fulbright Awd, 1961; Poetry Book Soc Choices, 1961, 1966, 1979, 1981; Arts Coun Awds, 1969, 1970, 1973, 1975, 1977, 1982; Guardian Fiction Prize, 1973; Prudence Farmer Poetry Awd, 1977; Cholmondeley Awd, 1985; FRSL, 1982. *Hobbies:* Work; Photography; Judo (1st Kyu Judo: Otani and Brit Judo Assn); Yoga. *Address:* c/o David Higham Assocs, 5-8 Lower John Street, Golden Square, London W1R 4HA, England.

REDMOND Robert Spencer, b. 10 Sept 1919, Wallasey, England. Writer. m. Majorie Helen Heyes, 19 May 1949, 1 s. *Education:* Liverpool Col. *Appointments:* Army, 1939-46; Conservative Constituency Agent, 1947-56; MD, Heyes and Co Ltd, Wigan Elec Engrs, 1956-66; Ashley Assocs Ltd, 1966-72, Commercial Mgr, 1966-69, MD, 1969-70, Commercial Dir, 1970-72; MP for Bolton West, 1970-74; Executive Selection Conslt, 1972-76; Dir and Chief Exec, Nat Fed of Clay Indust, 1976-84. *Publication:* How to Recruit Good Managers. *Memberships:* V-Chm, Employment Com; V-Chm, All Party Anglo- Irish Gp; Select com, Nationalised Industries. *Honour:* TD, 1951. *Hobbies:* Gardening.

Address: 194 Grove Park. Knutsford, Cheshire WA16 8QE, England. 1.

REED James Anthony, b. 12 June 1939, Marion, Ohio, USA. Hotel and Resort Executive and Consultant. *Education:* Florida State Univ, 1957- 59; Univ o Hawaii, 1967-69; Ctr for Constructive Change, 1978. *Appointments:* Mgr, Mauna Kea Beach Hotel, 1963-71; VP, C Brewer & CO Ltd, 1971-77; VP, Dunfey Hotels, 1977-80; VP, Marriott Hotels, 1980-90; Pres, The Reed Gp, 1990-. *Publication:* Hotel and Motel management, 1967. *Memberships:* Appaloosa Horse Lcub; Sch of Am Res; California Thoroughbred Breeders Assn; California Hotel and Motel Assn. *Honours:* Gen Mgr of the Yr, Marriott Hotels, 1982; Citation of Merit, Univ of Hawaii, 1968; Outstanding Young Men of Am, 1969. *Hobbies:* Painting; Horse Breeding. *Address:* 603 Old Taos Hwy, Santa Fe, NM 87501, USA. 1, 117, 156, 130.

REED John Thompson, b. 27 Dec 1946, Little Rock, Arkansas, USA. Minister. m. Toni Denise Powers, 18 June 1971. *Education:* AB, Ch Music, S.Nazarene Univ, 1964-69; Nazarene Theol Sem, 1969-74. *Appointments:* Natioch Ch of the Nazarene, KS, 1969-74; Richardson, TX First Navzrene, 1974-76; Garden City KS First Nazarene, 1976-77; Williams Meml Nazarene, Bethany, OK, 1977-78; Clovis, NM First Nazarene, 1987-91; Clovis Nazarene Sch Admr, NM, 1987-90; Clovis Nazarene Sch Music Tchr, 1990-91. *Memberships:* Dallas Dist Nazarene Young People Soc, Young adult representation and Dir, 1974; Dallas Sist NYPS Teen Dir, 1975-76; Delegate, Gen NYPS Convention, 1976; NW OK Nazarene Youth Intl Campus, Career Dir, 1978; NWO NYI Teen Dir, 1979-80, VP, 1981-85, Pres, 1985-87; Delegate, Gen NYI Convention, 1980, 1985; South Central Regional NYI Talent Dir, 1985-87. *Hobbies:* Photography; Crafts; Drama; Music, vocal and instrumental; Swimming; Waterskiing; Racketball. *Address:* 1505 Kingston Avenue, Clovis, NM 88101, USA.

REED Maximillian Glenn, b. 25 Dec 1955, Cinderford, Glos, England. Barrister at Law. m. Deborah Lyn Reed, 31 July 1985. *Education:* Henbury Sch; LLB Hons, Univ of Southampton, 1981. *Appointments:* A Practising Barrister in the field of general common law, 1983- . *Memberships:* Hon Soc of The Inner Temple, London; Com, Commercial Rooms, Bristol. *Honours:* Duke of Edinburgh Scholar of the Inner Temple, 1981. *Hobbies:* Oriental Cooking; Ancient History; Bonsai; Reading; Gardening; Theatre. *Address:* Greycroft, 25 Lake Road, Henleaze, Bristol BS10 5HY, England.

REED Renee, b. 22 May 1951, St Louis, MO, USA. Psychologist; College Professor. *Education:* BA 1972, MA 1976, St Louis Univ; EdD, Texas Tech Univ, 1981. *Appointments:* Psychol, N.Arizona Univ, 1982-86; Dir, Grad Counselling Progs, St Francis Col, 1986-. *Publications:* Various articles published in journals. *Memberships:* Royal Soc of Health (RSH); Am Bd of Med Psychotherapists (ABMP); N.Ctl Assn of Counselling and Supervision; Foun for Shamanic Studies. *Honours:* Fellow, RHS, London; Fellow and Diplomate, ABMP; Jones Leadership Fellow in Educ, Texas Tech Univ, 1978-79. *Address:* 3318 Vesey Avenue, Ft Wayne, IN 46809, USA.

REEDAY Thomas Geoffrey, b. 20 July 1924, Wakefield, Yorks, England. Retired. *Education:* Queen Eliz Grammar Sch, Wakefield, 1935- 41; LLB, Univ of London, 1949-51. *Appointments:* Army, 1943-47; Clerk; Lloyds Bank Ltd, 1941-43, 1947-55; Barrister, London, 1955-57; Legal Asst, Heller & Partners Ltd, 1957-64; Holborn Col, Poly of Ctrl London, 1964-85, Law Lectr, 1970, Ret'd as Hd of Dept, Fac of Law. *Publications:* Law Relating to banking, 1985; Co-Ed, Legal Decisions Affecting bankers, Vols 9 & 10, and Vol II. *Memberships:* Cert AIB, 1943; FIB, 1982; ACIS, 1949; FICS, 1978; Called to the bar, Lincoln's Inn, 1954; Liveryman, Worshipful Co of Chartered Secs and Admnrs, 1978. *Honours:* Hon Fellow, CIB, 1989. *Hobbies:* Railway

preservation. *Address:* 66 Lamorna Grove, Stanmore, Middlesex HA7 1PG, England.

REES Brinley Roderick, b. 27 Dec 1919, Tondu, Wales. Retired. m. Zena Muriel Stella Mayall, 23 Aug 1951, 2 s. *Education:* MA, Oxon, 1945; PhD, Wales, 1956. *Appointments:* Lectr in Classics, UCW Aberystwyth, 1948-56; Sr Lectr in Greek, Manchester Univ, 1956-58; Prof of Greek: UC Cardiff, 1958-7C, Birmingham Univ, 1970-75; Principal, SDUC, Lampeter, 1975-80. *Publications:* The Merton Papyri, Vol 2, 1959; Papyri from Hermopolis, 1964; Lampas, 1970; Classics for intending Students, 1970; Pelagius: A Reluctant Heretic, 1988; Letters of Pelagius and his Followers, 1991. *Memberships:* Classical Assn, Hon Sec, 1963-69, VP, 1969-, Pres, 1978-79, Life Mem. *Honours:* Hon LLD, Univ of Wales, 1981; VP, UC Cardiff, 1987-89. *Hobby:* Theology. *Address:* 31 Stephenson Court, Wordsworth Avenue, Cardiff CF2 1AX, Wales. 1.

REES Robin Lodowick Douglas, b. 25 Sept 1946, Clevedon, England. m. Ceridwen J L Bailey, 12 July 1986. *Education:* Westminster Sch, 1959-64; Bedford Col, Univ of London, 1965-73; BSc, 1968, MPhil, 1973; Univ of Sheffield, 1986-91; PhD, 1991; Archbishop of Canterbury's Cert in Ch Music, 1981. *Appointments:* Various appointments in computing; Documentation Ofr at Oxford Univ Computing Ser, 1984. *Creative works:* The role of music and musicians in current English parish church worship. *Memberships:* MInstP, 1973; CPhys, 1985. *Hobbies:* Singer and choral conductor, especially in church music; Fdr, and Chief Admnr, The St Hugh Singers; Academic dress; Riding in trains. *Address:* 1 Little Howe Close, Radley, Abingdon, Oxfordshire OX14 3AJ, England. 161.

REES William Hurst, b. 12 Apr 1917. m. Elizabeth Mary Wight, 1941, 2 s, 1 d. *Education:* BSc Est Mgmt, Col of Est Mgmt, Univ of London; FRICS. *Appointments:* War Ser, RA and RE (SO2), 1940-46; Liaison Ofr, Belgiam Army Engrs, Hd of Valuation Dept, Col of Est Mgmt, 1948- 51; Principal in Pvt Practice as Chartered Surveyor; City of London, Richard Ellis & Son, 1951-61; E.Grinstead, SX Turner, Rudge and Turner, 1961-70; Mem of London Tribunal, 1973-89; Chm, Bd of Studies in Est Mgmt, Univ of London, 1970-74; Chm, Surveying Bd, CNAA, 1976-77. *Memberships:* Hon Mem, Rating Surveyors Assn, Pres, BSc Est Mgmt Club, 1961-62; Chm Exams Bd, Incorp Soc of Valuers and Autioneers, 1984-; Hon FSVA, 1987. *Publications include:* Modern Methods of Valuation, 1943-1971; Valuations: Principles into Practice, ed, 1992, 4th Edn. *Hobbies:* Music; Mainly Opera. *Address:* Brendon, Carlton Road, S.Godstone, Surrey RH9 8LD, England.

REESE Virginia Margaret Pearson, b. 11 Nov 1929, Atlanta, Georgia, USA. Organizational Development Consultant. m. John Renowden Reese, 15 Sept 1951, 4 s, 1 d. *Education:* BS Gp Psycho, 1982; MA Org Behaviour, Univ Houston, 1985. *Appointments:* Catering Trainee, Petroleum club of Houston, 1979-80; Mgmt Trainee, Sunbelt Hotels, 1980-81; Personnel Dept, Warwick Post Oak Hotel, 1981; Creative Catalyst Hotel Conslt and Convention Planner, 1981-88; Pres, C G Jung Educ Ctr, 1988-91. *Creative Works:* Org Devel Network; Org Devel Inst; Asia Soc; Intl Transactional Analysis Assn; Singapore Training & Devel Assn. *Honours:* Charter, Alumni of UH-CL, 1983; Galveston Family Inst, 1988; Am Soc of Training and Devel; Houston Community Col Sys in Hosp Mgmt, 1984; Cert for Div of Continuing Educ, Houston Bapt Univ, 1980; C J Jung Educ Ctr Confs, 4, 1984- 89. *Hobbies:* Snow Skiing; Swimming; Reading; Going to the Beach. *Address:* 12631 Pebblebrook Drive, Houston, TX 77024, USA. 7.

REEVE Michael Arthur Ferard, b. 7 Jan 1937, London, England. Company Director. m. 30 Dec 1970, 2 s. *Education:* Eton Col; Univ Col, Oxford; MA Jurisprudence; FCA. *Appointments:* Arthur Andersen & CO, 1959-63; M Samuel & CO, 1963-65; Charterhouse

Bank, 1965-74; Copleys Bank, 1974-80; Rea Bros, 1977-80; Greyhound bank, 1981-87. Directorships include: Collins Collins & Rawlence, 1982-85; The Elliott Gp of Peterborough, 1969-83; Finsbury Trust, 1990- ; Finsbury Growth Trust, Chm, 1991-. *Memberships:* Chartered Accts; IOD; Royal Inst of Intl Affairs. *Hobbies:* Horses; Gardening; Reading. *Address:* 138 Oakwood Court, London W14 8JL, England.

REGAN Michael James, b. 18 Jan 1947, Ruislip, Middlesex, England. Composer; Teacher. m. Sonia Jong, 1 Aug 1987. *Education:* Gunnersbury Catholic Grammar Sch; Guildhall Sch of Music; LGSM; BMus (Durham); Hon FLCM. *Creative Works:* Christmas Preludes, (org); Malaysian Folksongs, (pf); Caribbean Dances, (pf duet); Divertimento (cl or pf); Mood Impressions, (fl and pf); Quartet for flutes, guitar pieces, etc. Unpublished: Violin Concerto, Mass, 1989; Songs, choral work and piano pieces. *Hobbies:* Reading; Countryside; Ancient and modern history. *Address:* 85 Northwood Way, Northwood, Middlesex HA6 1RT, England.

REGO Gilbert Blaize, b. 3 Sept 1921, Bombay, India. Bishop of the Shimla-Chandigarh Diocese. *Education:* Sr Cambs, 1940; Inter Sci, 1944; ordained Priest, 1953; Leadership Coady Dipl, 1965; Masters in Social Wk, Washington DC, 1967. *Appointments:* Asst Dir, Caritas, India, 1967; Exec Dir, 1968-71; Consecrated Bishop, 1971. *Publications:* Build the Chandigarh Cathedral according to own design; Photograph published of Cathedral Monument. *Memberships:* Pres, Youth Tech Training Soc; Governing Body of Caritas India; Indo German Soc; Ser Soc Devel; Justice and Peach Comm of the Cath Bishops' Confed, India. *Hobbies:* Creative craft Art; Wildlife; Nature; Camping; mechanics; Photography; Gadgets and inventions; People, especially the rural poor; Soccer; Hockey; Tennis; Hunting; Classical music; Gardening. *Address:* Bishops House PO Box 709. Sector 19-A, Chandigarh 160019, India.

REID Addie Lois, b. 20 June 1915, Mississippi, USA. Housewife; Retired Arch-Designer. m. Boland A Reid, 2 July 1932, 1 d. *Education:* Engrg trainee, Tulane Univ, 1943, related courses, 1944-58; Hg Sch Dipl, Miss, 1958; Univ of Alabama, 1959; Jefferson State Com Col, AL, 1980. *Appointments:* Draftsman, S.Ctrl Bell, New Orleans, 1943-45; Dpty Tax Collector, Greenville, MS, 1951-54; Hall and Norwood Arch & Engrs, Greenville, 1954-58; Draftsman and Designer, Rust Engr Co, Birmingham, AL; Redstone Arsenal AL, 1959-64, Civil Service, Logistics, 1966; Family business, 1967-87. *Publications:* BPW Candid camera movie, 1963; Book, Golden Anniversary yearbook. *Memberships include:* Birmingham Bus Profl Womens Club (BBPWC), 1965, Pres; Birmingham Genealogy Soc; Arlington His Assn; Capt Truss Chap; Utd Daughters of Confed, Fdr, Charter Pres, 1977. *Honours include:* Awd, BBPWC, 1965; Elected Alabama Delegate for Conf on Small Business, 1979; Appreciation Cert from Pres Carter, 1980. *Hobbies:* Gardening; Sewing; Drawing; Arts and crafts; Travelling; Genealogy; Research; Church related benevolent work. *Address:* 3277 Queenstown Road, Trussville, AL 35173, USA.

REID John Kelman Sutherland b. 31 Mar 1910, Leith, Scotland. Retired Professor of Theology. m. Margaret Winifred Brookes, 3 Jan 1950. *Education:* George Watson's Boy's Col, 1919-25; MA, BD, Univ of Edinburgh, 1928-38; Heidelberg, 1933; Basel 1938-39; Marburg, Strasburg, 1939. *Appointments:* Minister, Craigmillar Pk, Edin, 1938-50; Cpl, RAC, parachute Rgmt, 1942-46, TA, 1946-62; Prof of Theol: Univ of Leeds, 1950-61, Univ of Aberdeen, 1961-76. *Publications:* The authority of scripture, 1957; Presbyterians and Unity, 1962; Life in Christ, 1963; Christian Aplogetics, 1969; Calvins Concerning Eternal Predestination; Oscar Cullmann: Baptism in NT. *Memberships:* HCC, F & O Comm, 1961-82; BCC, 1961-68; Soc for Study of Theol; Ch Ser Soc; Scottish Ch Soc. *Honours:* DD Edin, 1957; CBE, 1970; TD, 1961. *Hobbies:* Theol Study6; General reading. *Address:* 8

Abbotsford Ct, 18 Colinton Road, Edinburgh EH10 5EH, Scotland.

REID Kathaleen, b. 6 Mar 1953, Jackson, Mississippi, USA. Associate Professor. *Education:* BA of Maryland, 1976; MA 1980, PhD, 1984, Univ of Denver. *Appointments:* Asst Res Prof, Univ of Denver, 1984-85; Vis Asst Prof, Colorato State Univ, 1985-86; Assoc Prof, Lee Col, Clevelant, TN, 1986-; Conslt Eng Lang Inst, 1990-91; Conslt, Bureau of Justice Asst Grant to Univ of Wisconsin. *Memberships:* Intl Communication Assn; Assn of Educ in Jour and Mass Communication; Speech Communication Assn; Midwest Assn of Public Opinion Reschrs; Bd: Rennovation of Cratgmile Hse, Public Lib, Cleveland, 1989-91; Geel Ministries, Philadelphia, 1988-. *Honours:* Fac Res Awd, Lee Col, 1980. *Hobbies:* Travel; Hiking; Choral and classical music; Art and architectural history. *Address:* 920 Oak Street NW, Cleveland, TN 37311, USA.

REID Milton Reginald, b. 18 Jan 1943, Norris Point, Canada. Judge. m. Marina Ford, 17 Apr 1965, 1 d. *Education:* BA, Meml Univ, 1968-70, 1970-71; LLB, BSW Dalhousie Univ, 1980-83; French Lang Training, CAE, 1985. *Appointments:* Sch Tchr, 1960-63; Social Wkr, 1965-72; Parole Ofr, 1972-75; Magistrate, 1975-80; Prov Ct Judge, 1983-. *Publications:* Numerous published legal decisions: Ed-in-Chief, Provincial Judges Jour, Ed pg, 1987-. *Memberships:* Nfld Prov Judges Assn, VP, 1978-80, Pres, 1983-85; Can Assn Prov Ct Judges, Rep for Nfld, 1983-87. *Honours:* Notary Public, 1976; Commr of the Supreme Ct, 1977. *Hobbies:* Reading; Hiking; Fishing; Amateur Photography; Curling. *Address:* 41 Baker Street, St John's, NF, Canada A1A 5C3. 142.

REIERSOL Olav, b. 28 June 1908, Krodsherad, Norway. Professor Emeritus. m. (1) Signy Altern, 5 July 1950; (2) Margrete Landmark, 1971, 3 s. *Education:* Bsc Phys, Chem and Botany, 1932; MSc 1935, PhD, 1945, Maths and Stats. *Appointments:* Maths Prof, Univ of Oslo, 1950-61; Math Stats Prof, Univ of Oslo, 1961-75; Vis Prof, Cornell Univ, USA, 1964-65. *Publications:* Probability, statistical inference, confluence analysis, identifiability, population genetics, mathematical and statistical terminology in Esperanto, Esperanto grammar. *Memberships:* FIMS; Fellow, Econometric Soc; Intl Statis Inst; Norwegian Acad of Scis. *Hobbies:* Esperanto and interlinguistics. *Address:* Torodveien 109, N-3135 Torod, Norway. 1, 152.

REIFF Theodore Curtis, Ted, b. 6 Aug 1942, Cleveland, OH, USA. Investment Banker. m. Theresa Dolores Van Lengen, 30 Oct 1982. *Education:* Staunton Military Acad Grad, 1961; BS Bus, Ohio State Univ. *Appointments:* Pres; Dir, Creative Bus Strategies, San Diego, 1986- ; Ptnr, Greenstone & Keiff, San Diego, 1982-86; Pres, Cartunes Corp, San Diego, 1987-79; Mgr, Raytheon Ser Co, Burlington, MA, 1979-82. *Publications:* Intl Fin Column in international newsletter, 1987-89. *Memberships:* Exec Com, San Diego Coun of the Am Elec Assn; Chm, Small Bus and Fin Com, 1988-. *Honours:* Outstanding Ser, Bus Adv Com, San Diego State Univ, 1983; Outstanding Businessman, Columbus, OH, 1975. *Hobbies:* Skiing; Tennis. *Address:* Creative Business Strategie, 9868 Scranton Road 410, San Diego, CA 92121, USA. 9, 132.

REILLY Bruce, b. 10 Nov 1933, Toronto, Canada. President. m. Carole Curtis, 1 Aug 1968, 1 s, 1 d. *Education:* Vaughan Rd Col, 1949; NY Inst of Photography. *Appointments:* RCAF, 1950-60; Self employed, 1960, Pres, The Piper Studio Ltd. *Memberships:* Profl Photos of Ontario and Can; Royal Photo Soc; Weyford masonic Temple; Scotish Right; York Ctl Hosp; Bayview Golf and Co Club. *Honours:* Winner of 20 ribbons through professional photographers of Ontario, Can. *Hobbies:* Sailing and golf. *Address:* 391 Woodland Acres CR, RR 2, Maple, Ontario, Canada L6A 1G2. 142.

REILLY Robert Quentin, b. 13 Aug 1945, Adelaide, Australia. m. 13 Nov 1976, 1 s, 2 d. *Education:* MBBS, Adelaide, 1969; DPH, 1974, MPH, 1983, Sydney; FRACMA; FAFPHM. *Appointments:* Prov Hlth Ofr, Mawus, 1972-74; Madang 1975-78, Decentrilisation Prof, Port Moresby, 1978-79, Asst Sec Health, W.New Brit, 1979-82; Sec of Health, Port Moresby, 1982-91. *Publications:* Decentrilisation of health Services, monography; More power to the People; Achieving health for all by year 2000. *Memberships:* Coun of PNG Inst of Med Res; Coun of St John; Med Bd of PNG; Med Soc of PNG; Exec Bd of WHO. *Honours:* Queens Awd of Imperial Ser Order, 1987. *Hobbies:* Chin Sun Kung Fu; Vipassana Meditation; Fruit tree growing; Acupuncture. *Address:* Box 3041 Boroko, National Capital District, Papua New Guinea.

REIMERS David Dean, b. 28 Nov 1943, Laredo, Texas, USA. Micropaleontologist. m. Denise Daigre, 16 Oct 1982, 1 d. *Education:* BS, Lamar Univ, 1967; MS, Texas A&M Univ, 1972; PhD,Tulane Univ, 1976. *Appointments:* Micropaleontol, Tenneca Oil Co, 1975-80; Asst Prof, Univ S.Western Louisiana, 1980-82; Micropaleontol, ARCO Exploration, 1982-85; Owner, Reimers Res, 1985-. *Memberships:* Intl Nanoplankton Assn; Am Assn Petroleum Geols; Soc Sedimentary Geols. *Hobbies:* Raising Orchids; Canoeing; Rafting. *Address:* 120 Rue Beauvregard, Suite 201, Lafayette, LA 70508, USA. 7, 50.

REINER Zeljko, b. 28 May 1953, Zagreb, Croatia. Physician; Endocrinologist; University Professor. m. Eugenia Tedeschi Reiner, 22 Oct 1983. 1 s. *Education:* MD, 1976, PhD, 1982, Univ of Zagreb. *Appointments:* Conslt Specialist, Dept of Endocrinol, Univ Hosp, Zagreb, 1983-86; Hd, Dept of Clin Res, Inst of Pathophysiol, Univ Hosp Rebro, 1986-; Assoc Prof of Pathophysiol, 1986-88, Prof, 1987-, VP, Med Fac Coun, 1987-90, Univ of Zagreb; Fdr, Pres, Cro-Slov Lipid Com, 1992; V-Dean, Intl Relations, Med Fac, Univ Zagreb; Acad of Sci and Arts, Croatia. *Publications:* Book of poetry, 1984; Patrhophysiology Textbook, 1989; Internal Med Textbook, 1991. *Memberships:* Nat Health Coun, VP, 1991; Univ of Zagreb Hosps Coun, Pres, 1991. *Honours:* Univ Awd for Sci. *Hobbies:* Reading and writing poetry. *Address:* Ilica 218, 41000 Zagreb, Croatia.

REINITZER Sigrid Friedrun, b. 11 Feb 1941, Graz, Austria. Director of University Library. *Education:* PhD, 1968; Chemotechnol, 1970-72, Library and Inf Sci, 1972-74. *Appointments:* Univ Lib of Graz, 1971-73; Info Specialist, 1974-77; Leader of EDP Dept, 1978-88; Dpty Librarian, 1985-88; Lib Dir, 1989-. *Memberships:* Lingue des Bibliotheques Europeennes de Recherche; European Lib Autom Gp; Verein Deutscher Bibliothekare; Dt Gesellsch fur Dokumentation; Vereinigung Osterr Bibliothekare; Alps Adria Libary Wkg Gp. *Honours:* Pro Meritis Medaill, Univ Graz, 1985; Dr Josef Bick Ehrenmedaille of the VOB, 1980; Goldene Ehren zeichen fur Verdienste um die Republik Osterreich, 1986. *Hobbies:* Music; Theatre; Sport. *Address:* Universitatsbibliothek Graz, Universitatsplatz 3, A-8010 Graz, Austria. 1.

REINL Harry Charles, b. 13 Nov 1932, Germany. Economist. *Education:* BS Fordham univ, 1953; Cert, US Dept of Agric Grad Sch, 1966; AM, George Washington Univ, 1968; Mass Inst of Tech, 1972. *Appointments:* US Army Ordnance Corps to 1st Lt; Hon Discharge, 1st Lt ORDC, 1962; Jr Observer, Sperry Rend Corp, USA, 1958-62; Lab Econ, Manpower Adm, US Dept Labour, 1962-68; US CSC Ofc of Pers Mgmt, Washington DC, 1968-. *Publications:* Articles include: Phoenix Programme, Alcoholic and Drug Abuse 1988-89; VAMC Washington DC Heurology Testing, 1989- . *Memberships include:* Life, RNC; Res Bd of Advrs, ABI; Res Assoc, IBC; Lifetime Achievement, ABI, 1991. *Honours:* Medal of Hon, CBI, 1991; Res Advr of the Yr, 1991; Man of the Year, ABI, 1991; Selected Intl Man of the year, 1991- 92; Lifetime Achievement Acad Golden Acad Awd, 1991; Statue of Victory, Personality

of the Yr, 1984; World Culture Prize, Acad Italia; Medal of Hon, Great Eagles of Am Soc, 1984. *Address:* 2425 Mt Vernon Avenue, Alexandria, VA 22301, USA. 6, 125, 156, 155, 152, 162, 178.

REIS A do Carmo, b. 17 Jan 1942, Modivas, Portugal. Teacher. m. Maria da Conceicao M A Carmo Reis, 2 Sept 1970, 3 s. *Education:* Army Ser, Angola, 1968-70; Deg of Licenciate, 1972, MHist, 1987, Univ Oporto. *Appointments:* Tchr in Hg Sch of Povoa de Varzim, 1970-75, Famalicao, 1975-77, Vila do Conde, 1977-91. *Publications:* New History of Portugal; Chronical of Discoveries; History of Portuguese Ships; The Liberalism in Portugal and Catholic Church. *Memberships:* Portuguese Writers Assn; Jours and Writers Oporto Assn; Commercial Athenaeum of Oporto. *Honours:* Concourse, Portuguese Navigators, Ministry of Youth and National Ctr of Culture, 1988. *Address:* R Bernardino Jose Alves 178, Fajozes, 4480 Vila do Conde, Portugal. 1.

REISS Stephen Charles, b. 7 Aug 1918, Bookham, Surrey, England. Art Consultant. m. Elizabeth Ruth Gladden, 17 Jan 1942, 1 s, 1 d. *Education:* Gresham's Sch, Holt, 1928-36; Balliol Col, Oxford, 1937-38; Chelsea Sch of Art, 1938-39 and 1947-49. *Appointments:* Capt, Beds and Herts Regt, 1939-45; Gen Mgr, Aldeburgh Festival of Music and Art, 1955-71; Dir, Fanfare for Europe, 1972-73; Admnr, London Symph Orch, 1974-75; MD, Curwen Prints, 1975-80; Fdr and MD, Bus Art Galls; MD, Stephen Reiss Fine Art, 1985-. *Publications include:* Aelbert Cuyp, 1975; The Child Art of Peggy Somerville, 1990; Arranged, Aelbert Cuyp in British Collections, at the Nat Gall, 1973. *Honour:* OBE, 1973. *Hobbies:* Study of 17th Century Dutch Painting. *Address:* 5 Westgate, Thorpness, Leiston, Suffolk IP16 4NE, England.

REISS Timothy James, b. 14 May 1942, Stanmore, Middlesex, England. Professor; Author. m. Patricia J Penn Hilden, 7 Aug 1988, 2 s, 1 d. *Education:* BA Hons, Manchester Univ, 1964; MA 1965, PhD, 1968, Univ of Illinois. *Appointments:* French Instr, Univ Illinois, 1967-68; Instr, Asst Prof, Yale Univ, 1968-73; Assoc Prof, Prof, Comp Lit, Univ Montreal, 1973-84; Dir, Comp Lit, 1976-81; Prof, Comp Lit, French and Philos, Emory Univ, Atlanta, 1983-87; Prof, Chm, Comp Lit, NYU, 1987-; Vis Professorships, 1976-89. *Publications:* Toward Dramatic Illusion, 1971; Tragedy and Truch, 1980; Discourse of Modernism, 1982, 1985; Uncertainty of Analysis, 1988; Meaning of Lit, 1992; 100 articles. *Memberships:* MLS; CCLA, VP, 1981-83; ICLA; ACLA: Renaissance Soc of Am; C S Peirce Soc; Can Semiotics Soc; FRSC. *Honours:* Fellowships: Paris, 1971-72, Univ Montreal, 1979, 1980, Emory Univ, 1986-87, Am Coun of Learned Socs, 1986-87; Jeuven, 1989, Cambs, 1990-91; Can Coun Sr Fellow, Oxford, 1977-78; Soc Scis and Humanities Res Coun of Canada, Sr Fellow, Oxford, 1983-84. *Address:* Department of Comparative Literature, New York University, 19 Univ Pl 4th Fl, New York, NY 10003, USA. 1, 2, 13, 15, 30, 142, 149.

REITAN Elling, b. 20 July 1949, Trondheim, Norway. Painter. m. Mairs, 1 s. *Education:* BA Eng, BA German; Studies with Norwegian Painter, OFF Nerdrum, 1982-87. *Creative works:* Numerous solo shows in Norway; 4 solo exhibitions in New York and Philadelphia; Summer 1992, Art Equity Services, PA; Noho Gall, NY, 1991; Morin-Miller Galls, NY, 1989; Ariel Gall, NY, 1987. *Hobbies:* Painting; Arts. *Address:* Viktor Baumanns V 19B, 7020 Trondheim, Norway.

REJONY Michel, b. 22 July 1953, Roanne, France. Managing Director. div. 2s. *Education:* Deg, Eng Dept, Univ of Human Scis, St Etienne; Pvte Pilots License. *Appointments:* MD, Helijet, 1978; MD, SAR, 1979-; Pres, Groupment des Professionnels; VP, D Syndicat L'Aviation Des Compagnies Aeriennes Regionales et d'Affaires; MD Air Executive Services. *Publications:* La grande aventure de 'laviatin Rhone Alpes des Origines a nos jours. *Memberships:* Pres, Argile Genas; Conseiller Municipal, Ville de Genas; Pres of Syndicat D' Initiative, Plaine De Lyon. *Hobbies:* Aviation; Tourism. *Address:* Boite Postale 100, 69744 Genas Cedex, France. 1, 52.

REKETTYE Gabor, b. 12 July 1944, Villany, Hungary. Professor of Marketing. m. 10 Aug 1968, 2 s. *Education:* Budapest Univ of Econ, 1967; PhD, 1972; Econ Sci Cand, Hungarian Acad of Scis, 1984. *Appointments:* Mgr, Hunor Glove Factoryl 1967-73; Asst Prof, Pecs Univ, 1973-78; VP, Tannimpex Co, 1978-84; Commercial Counsellor, Tokyo Embassy of Hungary, 1984-89; Prof of Mktg, Janus Pannonius Univ, Pecs, 1989-. *Publications:* Economics of Foreign Trade, 1975; Marketing Policy of Producing Enterprises, 1977; 50 articles on international marketing. *Memberships:* Mktg Com, Hungarian Acad Scis; Pres, Hungary-Japan Econ Club. *Honours:* Acad awd for book, Marketing Policy of Producing Enterprises, 1977; Commended for excellence in work, Min of Trade, Hungary. *Hobbies:* Tennis; Reading. *Address:* Hunyadi Ju 28, H-7625 Pecs, Hungary. 1, 52.

RELPH Michael Leighton George, b. Broadstone, Dorset, England. Film Producer; Writer; Designer; Director. m. (1) Doris Gosden, 1939; 1 s, (2) Maria Barry, 1950. 1 d. *Education:* Bembridge Sch, 1924-31. *Appointments:* Gaumont Brit, 1932-35; Warner Bros, 1935-38; MGM, 1938- 39; Ealing Studios, 1942-57; Rank Org, 1957-; Allied Film makers, 1959-; Utd Artists, 1963-67; Brit Film and TV Prod Assn, 1972-76; Boyd's Co, 1978-88; Relph Dearden Prod Ltd, 1984-. *Memberships:* Brit Film & TV Prod Assn, Chm, 1971-76; Brit Film Inst: Gov, 1972-77; Chm Prod Bd, 1972-77; Cinematograpy Film Coun, 1972-76. *Honours:* Nominated Hollywood Oscar, Colour Design for Saraband for Dead Lovers; Brit Film Acad Best Brit Film, Prod: The Blue Lamp, and, Sapphire. *Address:* The Lodge, Primrose Hill Studios, Fitzroy Road, London NW1, England. 1.

REMER Claus Jochen Theodor, b. 4 Jan 1931, Strelitz Alt, Neustrelitz, Germany. Historian. m. Dr Gertrude Remer, 6 Oct 1970, 1 d. *Education:* Abitur, 1950; Dipl Hist, 1955; Dissertation, 1960; Habil, 1984, Dozent, 1970, 1986. *Appointments:* Karl-Marx-Univ, Leipzig: Aspirant, Assistent, Oberassistent, Wahrn-Dozent, 1955-64; Friedrich-Schiller Univ Jena: Wahrn-Dozent, 1955-64; Friedrich-Schiller-Univ, Jena: Wahrn-Dozent, Oberass, Lektor, Dozent, 1965-90. *Publications:* Deutsche Arbeiterdelegation in der Sowjetunion, Berlin 1963; Zur Ukrainepolitik des dt. Imperialismus, 1969; Zur Geschichte der BSSR, Jena 1981; Konservatismus-Forschung, Heft 5-12, Jena 1985-1990. *Memberships:* Jahrbuch, ab Band 3, Berlin. *Address:* Binswangerstr 22, 0-6902, Jena-Lobeda, Germany.

REN Feng Renee, b. 1 Oct 1953, Kunming, China. Medical Pathologist. m. Fu Shen, 10 June 1979, 1 s. *Education:* MD, 1976, MSc, 1989, 4th Mil Med Univ, Xian; PhD, Univ Hong Kong, 1992. *Appointments:* Asst Lectr, Pathology, 1976-86, Lectr, Pathologist, 1986-90, 4th Med Univ, Xian. *Publications:* Monoclonal antibody HAb5 to human hepatoma, 1990; Monoclonal antibody prepared against hman primary hepatoma and immunohistochemical localization of its associated antigen, 1991; production and assessment of monoclonal antibodies specific for rat retinal ganglion neuronotrophic factor, 1991. *Memberships:* Assn Rsch Vision and Ophthalmology, USA; Hong Kong Soc Neuroscis; Int Brain Rsch Org; Asian-Pacific Org Cell Biology. *Honours:* Prize, Excell in Tchng Pathology, 4 Mil Med Univ, 1991; Excell in Rsch Award, Electron Microscopic Soc, NW China, 1989. *Hobbies:* Reading; Dancing; Singing; Drummer; Plays; Scientific research; Teaching. *Address:* Department of Anatomy, University of Hong Kong, 5 Sassoon Road, Pokfulam, Hong Kong.

REN Jiyu, b. 15 Apr 1916, Shandong, China. Director, National Library of China. m. Feng Zhongyun, 15 Sept

1946, 1 s. 1d. *Education:* S.West Utd Univ, Kunming, 1938; Lit Inst of Beijing Univ Acad, 1942. *Appointments:* Asst Prof, Dept of Philos, S.West Utd Univ, 1942-46; Assnt Prof, 1946-49; Lectr, Dept of Philos, Beijing Univ, 1946-49; Assoc Prof, 1949-56, Prof, 1956- 64; Dir, 1964-87, Hon Dir, Inst of Res on World Religs, 1987- ; Dir, Nat Library of China, 1987-. *Publications:* Buddhist Ideas of Han-Tang Dynasties, 1963; On History of Chinese Philosophy, 1981; A Developing History of Chinese Philosophy, 1983, 1985, 1988; A History of Chinese Buddhism, 1981, 1985, 1988; A Dictionary of Religions, 1981. *Memberships:* Chm: Chinese Soc of Relig Study, Assn of Chinese Philos, Chinse Soc of Lib Sci. *Hobbies:* Calligraphy; Music and Arts Appreciation; Sport (Ping Pong or Table Tennis). *Address:* National Library of China, 39 Baishiqiao Road, Beijing 100081, China. 52.

RENDALL Peter Godfrey, b. 25 Apr 1909, Bushey Heath, Herts, England. Retired schoolmaster. m. Ann McKnight Kauffer, 7 Feb 1944. 2 s, 1 d. *Education:* Rugby Sch, 1922-27; Corpus Christi Col, Oxford, 1927-31; Hon Moderations, Class I, 1929 ; Lit Humanities, Class II, 1931, BA 1931, MA 1936. *Appointments:* Felsted Sch, 1931-34, 1935-43; Upper Canada Col, Toronto, 1934-35; RAF Intelligence, Fl Lt, 1943-46; St Bees Sch, Cumberland, 1946-48; Hd Master, Achimota Sch, Goldcoast, Ghana, 1948-53; Lanling Col, Sussex, 1954-59; Hd Master, Bembridge Sch, Isle of Wight, 1959-74; Burford Town Clerk, 1977-85. *Memberships:* Oxford Union Soc; Royal Empire Soc; UN Org; Hd Master's Conf. *Honours:* Coronation Medal, 1953. *Hobbies:* Reading; Woodwork; Gardening. *Address:* Chippings, 155 The Hill, Burford, Oxon OX18 4RE, England. 1.

RENNIE Archibald Louden, b. 4 June 1924, Guardbridge, Fife, Scotland. Retired Civil Servant. m. Kathleen Harkess, 14 Sept 1950, 4 s. *Education:* Madras Col; BSc, St Andrews Univ, 1945. *Appointments:* Experimental Ofr, Admty, 1944-47; Scottish Ofs, 1947-84: Pvt Sec to the Sec of State for Scotland, 1962-63, Seconded as Registrar Gen for Scotland, 1969-73, Sec, Scottish Home and Health Dept, 1977-84. *Memberships:* Assessor, St Andrews Univ Ct, 1984-89; Scottish Records Adv Coun, 1985-; V-Chm, Adv Com on Dist Awds, 1985-; Coun on Tribunals, 1987-88; Chm, Disciplined Sers Pay Review Com, Hong Kong, 1988; Lockerbie Air Disaster Trust, 1988-91. *Honours:* CB, 1980; LLD, St Andrews, 1990. *Hobbies:* Sailing; Sea fishing; Walking; Bird watching. *Address:* St Rules, South Street, Elie, Fife, Scotland. 1, 184.

REVEL Ricky Joe, b. 19 Oct 1956, Paris, Tennessee, USA. Producer; Director; Singer; Songwriter. m. Jenniffer Dianne Scott, 17 Sept 1983, 1 d. *Education:* Grad, Henry Co Hg Sch, 1974. *Appointments:* Entertainment Mgr, Loretta Lynns Ranch, 1977-80; Owner: Campfire/Jen Ric Studios 1977-, CNC Productions, Son of the South Music, 1980-. *Publications:* Albums: Campfire Special, 1977; Some of Theirs, Some of Ours, 1978; Magical Campfire Show, 1979; Eagle Creek Country, 1980; Ballads of America, 1989; Screenplay: Follow me Boy's, 1991. *Memberships:* Nashville Entertainment Assn; Country Music Assn; Intl Songwriters Assn; Am Fed of Musicians; S.Europeal Soc of Authors and Composers. *Honours:* Outstanding Young man of the Year, 1983; Top 25 Music City Song Festival Profl Div. *Hobbies:* Blackpowder shooting; Horse riding. *Address:* Rt 3 Box 204C, Paris, TN 38242, USA.

REYNOLDS Graham, b. 10 Jan 1914, London, England. Writer. m. Daphne Dent, 6 Feb 1943. *Education:* Highgate Sch; BA Hons, Queens' Col, Cambs, 1932-35. *Appointments:* Asst Keeper, 1937-39, 1945-46, Keeper, 1959-74, Dept of Prints, Drawings and Paintings, Victoria and Albert Mus,; Asst Principal, Principal, Ministry of Home Security, 1939-45; Dpty Keeper, Dept of Paintings, Victoria and Albert Mus, 1946. *Publications:* The Engravings of S W Hayter, 1967; The Etchings of Anthony Gross, 1968; Nicholas Hilliard and Isaac Oliver, 1971; Painters of the Victorian Scene, 1953; Catalogue of the Constable Collection V&A Mus, 1973; Constable the Natural Painter, 1965; English Watercolours, 1988; English Portrait Miniatures, 1988; The Later Paintings and Drawings of John Constable, 1984. *Memberships:* Chm, Gainsborough's Hse Soc, Sudbury, 1977-79; Reviewing Com on Export of Works of Art, 1984-90. *Honours:* Leverhulme Emeritus Fellowship, 1980-81; OBE, 1984; The Mitchell Prize for Later paintings and Drawings of John Constable, 1984. *Address:* The Old Manse, Bradfield St George, Bury St Edmunds, Suffolk IP30 OAZ, England. 1, 19,

REYNOLDS Marius Lawrence, b. 15 May 1931, Windhoek, Namibia. Architect. m. Leonie Lancie de Villiers, 12 Sept 1959, 1 s, 1 d. *Education:* BArch, Univ of Capt Town, 1954; MArch, 1958, MCP, 1959, Univ of Pennsylvania. *Appointments:* Ptnr, Cowper Poole Reynolds and Towns, London, 1960-86; Tutor: Arch Assn, 1959-67; Bartlett Sch, Univ Col London, 1965-69, Columbia Univ, 1967, Harvard Univ, 1969; Vis Prof, Washington Univ, 1977-1982, 1991-. Co-ordinating Arch, Corp of London, 1986-91. *Publications:* Buildings designed at Rothamsted and Brooms Barn, W.Suffolk; Designed proposals for the refurbishment of Smithfields Mkt, London. *Memberships:* ARCUK; RIBA; FRSA, Past Chm, Highgate Soc. *Honours:* Work exhibited at RIBA, the AA, Royal Acad, and Barbican. Haringey Conservation Awd, 1983. *Hobbies:* Gardening; Squash; Music; Philately and Postal History. *Address:* 2 Shepherds CLose, Highgate, London N6 5AG, England.

REYNOLDS William Derek, b. 19 Nov 1947, Toronto, Canada. Freelance Author, Artist and Photographer. m. Margaret Alice Elizabeth Fleming, 17 May 1975. *Education:* BA, Wilfred Laurier Univ, Waterloo, Ont, 1974. *Career:* Career: Num 1-man exhibs incl: Recent Graphics, The Wells Gall, Ottawa, Ont, 1977; Works on Paper, Waterloo, 1978; Num art works incl: Sir Sanford Fleming Coll Invitational, Peterborough, Ont, 1973; Recent Works (w Karen Fletcher), Sir Sanford Fleming Coll, 1974; Eight from Town, Univ Waterloo, 1975; Works on Paper (w Paul Fournier), Thielsen Gall, Kitchener, Ont, 1976; Vis Instr, Fine Arts, Univ Guelph, Guelph, Ont, 1977; Instr, Fine Arts (Intersession), Wilfred Laurier Univ, Waterloo, 1978, 1981; Dssigner, Sculptor, original bronze awards, Can Advt and Sales Assn; Represented in maj corp pub and pvte collects, Can, USA, incl: Bell Canada Collect, Mercantile & Gen Reins, Dow Chem, IBM Corp, Toronto-Dominion Bank Collect, Wilfrid Laurier Univ, Guelph Univ, Victor Technologies, Mutual Life Collect, Can Photoctr Lib. *Publications:* Books: Point Pelee, 1981; Algonquin, 1983; Wildflowers of Canada, 1987; Wildflowers of America, 1987; Seasons of Light: Images of Ontario, 1988; Photographs in NY Times, Reader's Digest, Nature Canada, Landmarks Mag, others. *Honours:* Ont Arts Coun Grants, 1974, 1975, 1976, 1977, 1978. *Hobbies:* Golf; Snowshoeing; Birdwatching. *Address:* PO Box 331, Kingston, Ontario, Canada K7L 4W2. 142.

RHEW David Thompson, b. 31 July 1941. Corpus Christi, Texas, USA. Asst Professor; Director. *Education:* BA Univ Corpus Christi, 1962; MLS, N.Texas State Univ, 1965; MDiv, Southwestern Bap Theol Sem, 1971; DMin, Luther Rice Sem, 1985. *Appointments:* Lib, Grand Canyon Col, Phoenix, 1971-82; Asst Prof, Dir of Lib, Luther Rice Sem, Atlanta, GA, 1982-. *Memberships:* Am Theol Libr Assn; Assn of Christian Libs. *Hobbies:* Reading; Biography; Travel. *Address:* 3100 Topawa Pl, Lithonia, GA 30038, USA.

RHOADS David Michael, b. 17 Nov 1941. Professor of New Testament. m. Sandra Roberts, 12 Sept 1964, 2 d. *Education:* BA, Gettysburg Coll, 1963; MA, Oxford Univ, 1965; BD, Luth Sem, Gettysburg, 1966; PhD, Duke Univ, 1973. *Appointments:* Pastor, St John Luth, Asheboro, NC, 1968-70; Carthage Coll, Kenosha, WI, 1973-88; Luth School Theology, Chgo, IL, 1988-. *Publications:* Israel in Revolution: 6 to 74 CE, 1976; Mark as Story, 1982. *Memberships:* Soc Biblical Lit; Cath Biblical Assn; Soc New Testament Studies; Chgo Soc Biblical Rsch. *Address:* Lutheran School of Theology, 1100 E 55th St, Chicago, IL 60615, USA.

RHODAS Virginia, b. Rhodas, Greece. Journalist; Freelance Writer; Translator. *Education:* Lit, 1968; Jrnlsm, 1969; Human and Pub Rels, 1970; E and W Philos, 1979; Comp Rels Rels, 1988; Living Langs, continuously. *Career:* Jrnlst, 1969; Sec, Ed Bd, several jrnls, 1972; Freelance Writer and Jrnlst, 1975; Dir, Int Poetry Letter (Carta Internacionale de Poesia), 1978- . *Creative works:* Poetry books: Blossoms; There Will Come A Day...and Other Poems; Brother Century XXI; Listen To Me, Humanity; Open Letter To Humanity; Short stories, essays, theatre plays, written and performed by her; In progress: From the Root of Greece; To Your Heart. *Memberships:* Christian Argentine Comm, World Day of Prayer, affiliated to World Movement, Greek Orthodox Ch; Lit and cultural assns; Latin-Am Regenmt, Perigramma, Greece; World Poetry Soc Intercontinental, India. *Honours:* Poetry, Essay, Buenos Aires, 1968; World Poetry Soc, 1970; Acad Arts and Culture, 1975; Dr hc, Lit, World Univ, NY, 1981; Medallion, Poetry Day, Australia, 1991-92. *Hobbies:* Translating poetry from Spanish into English, English into Spanish, Greek into Spanish and so on, for publication in International Poetry Letter; Christendom, giving forth spiritual items and lectures about the Cosmic Wisdom, God's Eternal Son, Our Lord Jesus Christ, His immortal teaching in every language, with humility and love. *Address:* Rivadavia 2284, PB J, 1034 Buenos Aires, Argentina.

RHODES Gary, b. 22 Apr 1960, Dulwich, London, England. Head Chef. m. Yolanda Jennifer Adkins, 7 Jan 1989, 2 s. *Education:* Thanet Tech Col, City and Guilds Adv Chefs Dipl. *Appointments:* Commis de Cuisine, Chef de Partie, Amsterdam Hilton Hotel, 1979-81; Solis Chef, Reform Club, 1982-83; Hd Chef, Winstons Eating Hse, 1983; Sr Sous Chef, Capital Hotel Knightsbridge, 1983-85; Hd Chef, Whitehall, 1985-86; Castle Hotel Taunton, 1986-90; Greenhouse Rest, Mayfair, 1990-. *Publications:* TV Series, BSB, 1990. *Memberships:* Acad Culinaire de France; Cercle des Ambassadeurs de L'Excellence, (Fdr). *Honours:* Mumm Champagne, Chef of Tomorrow, runner up, 1978; Finalist, Meilleur Ouvrier de Grande Bretagne, 1987; Caterer, 30 under 30 Acorn Awd, 1988; Michelin Star, 1986, 1990; GB Rep, Festival of Food Singapore Hilton Hotel, 1987. *Hobbies:* Dining Out; Cooking; Football; Golf. *Address:* The Greenhouse Restaurant, 27a Hays Mews, Mayfair, London, England.

RHODES James Devers, b. 28 Apr 1955, Midland, Texas, USA. Therapist. m. Moira S J Elmore, June 1986. *Education:* BS Urban Studies, Texan Christian Univ, 1978; MEduc, Univ of N.Texas, 1991; Licensed Chemical Dependency Counsellor, 1987. *Appointments include:* Sr Counsellor, CPC, Millwood Hosp, Arlington, 1986-89; Family Therapist, Parkside Lodge, Denton, 1989-90; Co-Dependence Therapist, Dir, Parkside Outpatients Sers, Ft Worth, 1990-91; Therapist, Behavioural Health Unit, La Hacienda Treatment Ctr, Hunt, 1991-; Pvte Practice, Kerrville, TX, 1991-. *Publication:* Adult Recovery Handbook, 1988. *Memberships include:* Evaluator, TX Bd of Alcoholism and Drug Abuse Counsellors; TX and Nat Assns of Alcoholism and Drug Abuse Counsellors; Nat Consortium Addiction Profls; TX Assn for Counselling and Devel. *Honours:* IPA, 1991-92. *Hobbies:* ·Coil Collecting; Beatlemania; Music; Politics. *Address:* Revine 1, Ingram, TX 78025, USA. 7.

RHODES James Richard, b. 28 Nov 1945, Omaha, Nebraska, USA. Professor of Economics. m. Kimie Hyoto, 27 Dec 1980, 1 s, 1 d. *Education:* BA 1969, MA 1973, PhD 1980, Univ Washington, Seattle. *Appointments:* Tchg Assoc, Univ Washington, 1974-76, 1977-79; Asst Prof: W.Washington Univ, 1976-77, Washington State Univ, 1979-80, Kansas State Univ, 1980-88; Vis Prof, Intl Univ of Japan, 1987-88; Pres, Prof, Saitama Univ, 1988-. *Publications:* Articles in books and professional journals; News media articles; Two books in progress.

Memberships: Alpha Sigma Nu; Beta Gamma Sigma; Civil Affairs Assn; Am Econ Assn; Phi Alpha Theta; Reserve Ofrs Assn; Far East Econometrics Assn; Assn for Asian Studies; Bd, Children's Res Ctr. *Honours:* US Army Decorations: Bronze Star (3 awards), Meritorious Ser Medal, Army Commendation medal (2 awards), Combat Infantryman Badge, Parachutist Badge; F. Leyroy Hill Fellowship; Grants. *Hobbies:* Swimming; Jogging; Literature; Languages. *Address:* Graduate School of Policy Science, Saitama University, Urawa, Saitama 338, Japan. 1.

RHODES John Guy, b. 16 Feb 1945, England. Lawyer. m. Christine Joan Batt, 11 June 1977, 2 s. *Education:* MA Law, Jesus Col, Cambs, 1964-67. *Appointments:* Trainee, 1968-70, Asst Solicitor, 1970-71, Macfarlanes; Seconded, White & Case, NYC, 1971-1972; Asst Solicitor, 1972-75, Ptner, 1975-, Macfarlanes. *Hobbies:* Tennis; Skiing; Woodlands. *Address:* Macfarlanes, 10 Norwich Street, London EC4A 1BD, England.

RHODES Philip b. 2 May 1922, Sheffield, England. Retired Dean of Medicine. m. Mary Elizabeth Worley, 26 Oct 1946, 3 s, 2 d. *Education:* Clare Col, Cambs, 1940-43; St Thomas' Hosp Med Sch, 1943-46; MB, 1946, FRCS Eng, 1953, FRCOG, 1964, FRACMA, 1976, FRSA, 1989, FFOM, 1990. *Appointments:* Prof of Obs and Gynae, St Thomas's, 1964-74; Dean, St Thomas's Hosp Med Sch, 1968-72; Dean, Fac Med, Univ of Adelaide, 1974-77; PG Dean, Univ Newcastle upon Tyne, 1977-80; PG Dean, Univ Southampton, 1980-87. *Publications:* An outline history of medicine, 1985; The value of medicine, 1976; Dr John Leake's Hospital, 1977; Letters to a young Doctor, 1983; Reproductive Physiology, 1969. *Memberships:* GMC, 1979-89; Coun, King Edward's Hosp Fund for London. *Honours:* Bronte Soc Prize, 1974. *Hobbies:* Reading; Writing; Photography. *Address:* 1 Wakerley Court, Wakerley, Oakham, Leics LE15 8PA, England. 1.

RHODES Richard David Walton, b. 20 Apr 1942, Blackpool, England. Headmaster. m. Stephanie Heyes, 11 Aug, 1966, 2 d. *Education:* Rossall School, 1951-66; BA, St Johns Col, Durham, 1960-62; DipEd, Hertford Col, Oxford, 1963-64. *Appointments:* Asst, St John's Sch, Leatherhead, 1964- 75; Dpty Hdmaster, 1975-79, Hdmaster, 1979-87, Arnold Sch, Blackpool; Hdmaster, Rossall Sch, 1987-. *Memberships:* HMC; SHA. *Honours:* JP, 1978. *Hobbies:* Motoring; Gardening; Travel; Photography. *Address:* The Hall, Rossall School, Fleetwood, Lancs FY7 8JW, England. 1.

RHODES Roderick Arthur William, b. 15 Aug 1944, Bradford, Yorkshire, England. Professor of Politics. m. Cynthia Margaret Marshall, 1 Dec 1978, 1 s, 1 d. *Education:* BSc Hons, Bus & Admin, 1967; BLitt, Oxon, 1975; PhD, Essex, 1985. *Appointments:* Univ Lectr: Birmingham, 1970-76, Stratclyde, 1976-79; Lecturer and Reader, Univ of Essex, 1979-89; Prof, Univ of York, 1989-. *Publications:* Public administration and policy analysis, 1979; Control and Power in central local government relationships, 1981; The national world of local government, 1986; Beyond Westminster and Whitehall, 1988. *Memberships:* Polit Studies Assn of the UK; Hon Ed, Public Administration. *Hobbies:* Genre fiction; Popular fiction; Cricket; Rugby league. *Address:* Dept of Politics, Univ of York, Heslington, York YO6 1AG, England.

RHYS William Joseph St Ervyl-Glyndwr, b. 6 July 1924, Newport, Gwent, Wales. Retired Consultant Physician; m. Dr Ann Rees, 29 Apr 1961, 1 s, 6 d. *Education:* BSc, 1945, DPH, 1966, Univ of Wales; MB, BS, Guy's Hosp, London Univ, 1948; MA St John's Col, Cambs Univ, 1950; MRCOG, 1961; MFCM, RCP, UK, 1974. *Appointments:* Squad Ldr, RAF Inst of Aviation Med, Univ Demonstrator, Cambs, 1949-54; Hs Surg, Registrar, Sr Registrar, Conslt, Obs & Gynae, including Royal Postgrad Med Sch, London; Welsh Nat Sch of Med, Cardiff, Welsh Hosp Bd, 1954-63; Asst MOH, Glamorgan, 1964-66; MOH, Cardiganshire, 1966-74;

Conslt Phys in Community Med, Dyfed, 1974-82. *Publications:* Papers include: High Altitude Flying, 1952; Meig's Syndrome - Commentary, 1957; Theses: Management of Pregnancy associated with Hodgkin's Sarcoma, 1958; parapartum Mental Illness, 1966. *Memberships:* Cambs Univ Rep, Coun of Univ Col Wales, 1979-86; Chm, Trustees, St John's Col, Dyfed; Commr, St John's Ambulance, Ceredigion; Pres, Scout Assn, Ceredigion; Chm, Hospitallers Club, Dyfed; Chm, Govs Ceredigion Schls; Trustee, The Two Red Dragons Educ Trust, Wales and Japan; Exec Com, Assn of Friends of Nat Lib of Wales; RAF Club; Shrievalty Assn; Intl Soc for the Hist of Med. *Honours:* Lord of the Barony of Llawhaden, Lord of the Manor of Llanfynydd (Celtic, Pre-Norman); High Sheriff County of Dyfed, 1979; Hon Mem, White Robe, Gorsedd of Bards of Wales, 1986; Cmdr, Most Venerable Order of St John of Jerusalem, 1987; Freeman, City of London, 1987; Liveryman, Worshipful Soc of Apothecaries, 1990. *Hobbies:* Swimming; Celtic history; Poetry; Musing in churchyards. *Address:* Plas Bronmeurig, Ystrad Meurig, Dyfed, Wales. 170.

RIAL Juan, b. 18 Sept 1943, Montevideo, Uruguay. Political Scientist. m. Carina Perelli, 21 Jan 1987, 3 d. *Education:* MHist, Montevideo, 1974. *Appointments:* Reschr, Peitho Polit Annalysis Soc, 1986-; Prof, Polit Sci, Univ of Montevideo, 1985-. *Publications:* The Military and Democracy, 1990; Transidious in Latin America on the threshold of the 1990's, Ed. *Memberships:* Intl Polit Sci Assn; Intl Sociol Assn; Latin Am Study Assn. *Honours:* Social Sci Res Coun, NY Awd, 1981; Fulbright Comm, Scholarship, 1986; Kellog Inst Univ of Notre Dame USA Awd, 1987; Woodrow William Ctr for Scholars Awd, 1991. *Address:* Peitho, Coronel Alegre 1162 bis, Montevideo 11300, Uruguay.

RICE Argyll Pryor, b. Virginia, USA. Professor of Hispanic Studies. *Education:* BA Smith Col, 1952; MA, 1956, PhD, 1961, Yale Univ. *Appointments:* Spanish Instructor, Yale Univ, 1959-60, 1961-63; Asst Prof, Spanish, Connecticut Col, 1964-67; Assoc Prof, 1967-72; Prof, 1972- ; Chm, Dept, 1971-74, 1977-84. *Publications:* Emilio Ballagas: poeta o poesia, 1967; Emilio Ballagas, Latin American Writers, III ed, 1989. *Memberships:* MLA; Am Assn of Tchrs of Spanish and Portuguese; New England Coun on Latin Am Studies. *Honours:* Phi Beta Kappa. *Hobbies:* Music; Tennis. *Address:* 133 Cliffmore Road, West Hartfort, CT 06107, USA. 6, 5.

RICE Ferill Jeane, b. 4 July 1926, Hemingford, Nebraska, USA. Writer. m. Otis Laverne Rice, 7 Mar 1946, 1 s, 1 d. *Education:* Grad, Alliance Nebraska Hg, 1943; Continued education credits: Univ of Omaha, 1960, Univ of Wisconsin, 1975. *Appointments:* Clk, Stenographer, Fed Pub Hsg Auth, 1943-45; Civilian Clk-Stenographer, US Army, 1945; Alliance Theatre, 1945; Self employed co-owner, Rice Electrical Wiring, 1951-65; Machine Op, Gen Tire, 1967; Mgr, Jewellery and Hoisery, K Mart, 1967-69; Tchr, Adventure in Antiques, Fox Valley Tech Col, 1969-76; Dir of Social Sers, Peabody Manor Nsg Hm, 1975; Co-Owner, Rice and Rice Inc, 1976-. *Publications:* Ed, Yesteryear Mag, 1972-74; Ed, newsletter, Butterfly Net, 1977-; Ed, Publr, Descendants of Lewis and Asenath Moffat; Numerous articles on glass in magazines. *Memberships:* Co-Fdr, Past Sec, Past VP, Fenton Art Glass Collectors of Am Inc; Matron, Order of the Eastern Star, 1956, 1964; Fdr, Jr Auxiliary, Tabor, Iowa; Co-Fdr, Nishna Valley Chap, Order of DeMolay for Boys; 1st Pres, Mothers Club; Past Co Educ Chm, Am Cancer Soc; Former Co Chm, Educ Chm, Gen Fed of Women's Clubs; Past Pres, Tabor Women's Club, GFWC; Leader, Dir of Ed, Adult Coor, Girls Scouts, 1963-65. *Hobbies:* Collecting antique glass; Genealogy and family history. *Address:* Kaukauna, WI 54130, USA. 5.

RICHARD Joseph Jacob III, b. 2 Mar 1957, Chicago, Illinois, USA. pastor, United Methodist. m. Linda Annne Phillips Richard, 14 Aug 1982. *Education:* BSc Botany,

Univ of Illinois, 1979; MDiv, The Garrett Evangelical Theol Sem, Evanston, IL, 1982. *Appointments:* Pastor, Fairview and Providence Chapel Utd Methodist Chs, 1982-84; Assoc Pastor, Wesley Utd Methodist Ch in Canton, 1984-88; Co-Pastor, Annawan-Fairview and Annawan-Community Utd Methodist Chs, 1988-; Dir, Youth Leadership Camp, Ctl Illinois Conf. *Memberships:* Sec, Treas, Graham Hosp; Chaplain, Say Assn in Canton, IL; Pres, Annawan Area Min Assn; Peoria Dist Evangelism and Youth Coor. *Hobbies:* Playing the piano; Singing; Youth ministry and preaching. *Address:* RRI Box 59, Sheffield, IL 61361, USA.

RICHARDS Jeffrey Michael, b. 5 Nov 1945, Birmingham, England. Professor of Cultural History. *Education:* BA, 1967, MA, 1972, Cambridge Univ. *Appointments:* Lectr, Hist, 1969-81, Sr Lectr, 1981-87, Reader, Hist, 1987-90, Prof, Cultural Hist, 1990-, Lancaster Univ. *Publications:* Visions of Yesterday, 1973; Swordsmen of the Screen, 1977; The Popes and the Papacy in the Early Middle Ages, 1979; Consul of God, 1980; Age of the Dream Palace, 1984; The Railway Station, 1986; Britain Can Take It, 1986; Thorold Dickinson, 1986; Mass-Observation at the Movies (ed), 1987; Happiest Days, 1988; Imperialism and Juvenile Literature (ed), 1989; Sex, Dissidence and Damnation, 1991. *Hobbies:* Cinema; Theatre; Railways; Football. *Address:* Department of History, Lancaster University, Lancaster LA1 4YG, England.

RICHARDSON David, b. 24 Apr 1928, London, Engalnd. International Civil Servant. m. Frances Joan Pring, 24 Feb 1951, 3 s, 1 d. *Education:* BA Hons, 1st class, London. *Appointments:* HM Inspector of Taxes, 1952-56; Dept of Employment, 1956-62; Under Sec, Indust Relations, 1972; Dir, Adv Consiliatory and Arbitration Ser, 1977. *Memberships:* FIPM; Gov Body, Brit Inst of Human Rights. *Hobbies:* Music; Landscape gardening; Walking. *Address:* 183 Banstead Road, Carshalton, Surrey SM5 4DP, England. 1.

RICHARDSON James John, b. 28 Mar 1941, Exeter, England. Executive Director. m. Janet Rosemary Welstand, 30 July 1966, 2 s, 1 d. *Education:* BA, Hull Univ, 1960-63; DipEd, Sheffield Univ, 1963-64; Cuddesdom Col, Oxford, 1966-69; FRSA, 1991. *Appointments:* Asst Master, Westfield Comp Sch, Sheffield, 1964-66; Asst Curate, St Peters Col Ch, Wolverhampton, 1969- 72; Priest-in-Charge, All Saints, Hanley, 1972-75; Rector of Nantwich, 1975- 82; Vicar or Leeds, Hon Can of Ripon Cathedral, 982-88; Exec Dir, CCJ, 1988-. *Creative works:* Articles on Jewish Christian dialogue. *Contributions to:* Saturday Sermon column, Yorkshire Post, to 1990; Four Score years, book. *Honours:* Ashworth Theol Prize, 1970. *Hobbies:* ·Study tours and pilgrimages to Israel; Biographies; Church restoration; Working holidays. *Address:* Council of Christians and Jews, 1 Dennington Park Road, London NW6 1AX, England. 1.

RICHARDSON Joanna, b. London, England. Biographer. *Education:* The Downs Sch, Seaford, Sussex; MA St Anne's Col, Oxford. *Publications include:* Fanny Brawne, 1951; Rachel, 1956; Théophile Gautier: His Life and Times, 1958; Sarah Bernhardt, 1959; The Everlasting Spell: A study of Keats and his friends, 1963; Edward Lear, 1965; George IV: A Portrait, 1966; Creevey and Greville, 1967; Princess Mathilde, 1969; Verlaine, 1971; Stendhal: A critical biography, 1974; Victor Hugo, 1976; Zola, 1978; Colette, 1983; Judith Gautier, 1987. *Contributions to:* BBC, Times Lit Supplement, Sunday Times, Spectator, New Statesman, Modern Language Reivew, French Studies, French Studies Bulletin, New York Times Book Review, Washington Post. *Memberships:* Fellow, RSL, Coun, 1961-86. *Honours:* Chevalier de l'Ordre des Arts et des Lettres, 1987; Prix Goncourt de la biographie, 1989, first time to non-French author. *Address:* c/o Curtis Brown Group, 162-168 Regent Street, London W1R 5TB, England. 1.

RICHARDSON John Stuart, b. 4 Feb 1946, Ilkley, Yorkshire, England. Professor of Classics. m. Patricia Helen Robotham, 12 Apr 1969, 2 s. *Education:* MA, DPhil, Trinity Col, Oxford, 1964-68; Ordained Deacon 1979, Priest, 1980, Scottish Epis Ch. *Appointments:* Lectr in Ancient Hist, Exeter Col, 1969-72; Lectr in Ancient Hist, St Andrews Univ, 1972-87; Prof of Classics, Univ of Edinburgh, 1987-. *Publications:* Roman Provincial Administration, 1976; Hispaniae, 1986; papers on ancient history and Roman law n learned journals. *Memberships:* Jt Assn of Classical Tchrs, Hon Treas, 1983-77; Roman Soc, Coun, 1976-8, 1989-. *Hobbies:* Choral singing. *Address:* 29 Merchiston Avenue, Edinburgh EH10 4PH, Scotland. 184.

RICHARDSON William Winfree III, b. 12 Aug 1939, Williamsburg, VA, USA. Attorney at law. m. Constance Diane Niver, 21 June 1969, div, 19 July 1985, 1 s, 1 d. *Education:* BA, Col of William and Mary, 1963; Bachelor Civil Law, 1966; JD, 1967. *Appointments:* Admitted to Virginia State Bar, 1968; Atty, Correctional Univ, 1968-91; Atty at Law, 1968-; Commr of Accts, New Kent Co Circuit, CT, 1968-; Asst Commr of Accts, Charles City Co Circuit, CT, 1970-. *Memberships:* Bar Assns of Am and Williamsburg; Virginia Trial Lawyers Assn; Am Judicature Soc; Phi Alpha Delta; Sigma Pi; IPA. *Honours:* Intl Order Kings Daughters and Sons Scholarship, 1957. *Hobbies:* Historical restoration; Collecting antiques. *Address:* Chelsea Plantation, West Point, VA 23181, USA. 7, 163.

RICHTER Dieter M, b. 19 Mar 1930, Bonn, Germany. Professor of Geology. m. Claire Schembecker, 11 Aug 1958, 2 d. *Education:* Univs Marburg and Berlin, 1950-54; Doctorate, Univ Berlin, 1959; Habilitation, Univ Frankfurt, 1960. *Appointments:* Asst Lectr, Univ Munster, 1955-57; Sci Co-worker, Univ Aachen, 1958-64; Sr Vis Fellow, Univ Exeter, England, 1964-65; Prof of Geol, Fachhochschule, Aachen, 1965-. *Publications:* Geologischer Fuhrer Aachen und Umgebung, 1975, 1985; Grundriss der Geologie der Alpen, 1974; Geologischer Fuhrer Allgau, 1984; Allgemeine Geologie, 1976, 1980, 1986, 1992; Ingenieur und Hydrogeologie, 1989; 128 Scientific geol publications. *Memberships:* Deutsche Geol Gesellschaft, (DGG); Geol Vereinigung. *Honours:* Hermann Credner Awd, DGG. *Hobbies:* Numismatics; Super 8 sound films. *Address:* Sandweg 14, D-5100 Aachen, Germany. 57, 43, 92.

RICKAYZEN Gerald, b. 16 Oct 1929, London, England. University Professor. m. Gillian Thelma Lewin, 20 Dec 1953, 3 s, 1 d. *Education:* BSc London, 1951; PhD, Cambs, 1954. *Appointments:* Res Fellow, Admiralty, 1954-57; Res Assoc, Univ of Illinois, 1957-59; Lectr, Univ of Liverpool, 1959-65; Reader, 1965-66; Prof, Univ of Kent, 1965-; Pro V- Chancellor, 1981-90, Dep V-Chancellor, 1984-90. *Publications:* Theory of superconductivity, 1965; Green's Functions and condensed matter, 1980; Many research papers on superconductivity and liquid state theory. *Memberships:* FInstP, CPhys; Am Inst of Phys. *Hobbies:* Playing the Cello; Tennis. *Address:* The Physics Laboratory, The University, Canterbury, Kent CT2 7NR, England.

RICKERBY David George, b. 8 Apr 1952, Chorley, Lancs, England. Physicist. m. Elisabetta Maria Emma Golin, 16 Sept 1978, 2 s. *Education:* BSc, Leicester Univ, 1970-73; PhD, Cambs Univ, 1973-76; CPhys, Inst of Phys, 1986. *Appointments:* Res Asst, Cavendish Lab, Camb, 1977; Res Assoc, Penn State Univ, 1977-80; Vis Scist, Jr Res Ctr, Ispra, 1980-81; Sci Ofr, 1982-. *Publications:* Author of articles in scientific journals and book chapters; patent holder on semiconductor backscattered electron detector. *Memberships:* FRMS; Cambs Philos Soc (CPS); Inst Phys; European Phys Soc; Italian Soc of Elec Microscopy; Am Soc for Metals; Corpus Assn; Oxford and Cambs Soc of N.Italy. *Honours:* Res Scholarship, CPS, 1976; Sci and Tech Grant, European Comm, 1980; Invited Lectr, Penn State Univ 1985; Competition Medal, Intl Metallographic Soc, 1989. *Hobbies:* Skiing; Gardening. *Address:* Institute of

Advanced Materials, Jt Research Centre TP 750, 21020 Ispra, Varese, Italy. 52.

RICKETT Raymond Mildmay Wilson, b. 17 Mar 1927. Chmn, Mid Kent Health Care Trust. m. Naomi Nishida, 1958, 1 s, 2 d. *Education:* BSc, London; PhD, Illinois Inst of Tech, 1946-68; CChem; FRSC. *Appointments include:* Plymouth Col of Tech, 1959; Lectr, Liverpool Col of Tech, 1960-62; Sr Lectr, Principal Lectr, West Ham Col of Tech, 1962-64; Hd, Dept of Wolverhampton Col of Teh, 1965-66; V-Principal, St JOhn Cass Col, 1967-69; Vice-Provost, City of London Poly, 1969-72; Dir, Middlesex Poly, 1972-1991; Chm, Coun for National Academic Awds, (CNNA), 1991-93; Com of Dirs of Polys, 1980-82, 1986-88; UK Nat Comm for UNESCO Educn Adv Com, 1983-85; IUPC, 1988-91; Com for Intl Coop in Higher Educ, 1988-91; UK Erasmus Students Grants Coun, 1988-. *Publications:* Experiments in Physical Chemistry, 1962, 1968; Chapters in The Use of the Chemical Literature, 1962, 1969; Articles on polytechnics in the national press. *Contributions to:* learned jouranls. *Memberships include:* Oakes Com, 1977-78; Higher Educ Review Gp for NI, 1978-82; NAB Bd, 1981-88; Open Univ Coun, 1983-; Coun for Indust & Higher Educ, 1985-91; Brit Coun, Bd, 1988-92; Erasmus EEC Adv Com, 1988-91; Gov, Yehudi Menuhin Live Music Now Scheme, 1977-. *Honours:* Ofrs Cross of Merit, FRG, 1988; Kt, 1990; CBE, 1984. *Hobbies:* Cricket; Theatre and Opera. *Address:* c/o Mid Kent Health Care Trust, The Maidstone Hospital, Hermitage Lane, Maidstone, Kent ME16 9QQ, England. 1.

RICKS David Trulock, b. 28 June 1936, London, England. Director, British Council France and Cultural Counsellor, British Embassy Paris. *Education:* BA, Philos Polit Econ, Merton ol, Oxford, 1955-58; MA, London Univ Inst of Educ, 1959-60; Licence et Lett, Univ of Lille, 1964-67; MA, Applied Lings, Univ of Essex, 1970-71. *Appointments:* Tchr, Lycee Francais de Londres, 1962-67; Brit Coun, 1967: Rabat, 1967-70, Jaipur, 1971- 74, New Delhi, 1974, Dar Es Salaam, 1974-76, Tehran, 1976-80, London, 1980-85, Rome, 1985-90. *Publications:* Penguin French Reader, 1967; New Penguin French Reader, 1992. *Memberships:* FRSA. *Honours:* OBE, 1981. *Hobbies:* Music; Playing the piano; Skiing. *Address:* The British Council, 9 Rue de Constantine, 75007 Paris, France. 1, 91.

RIDEOUT Roger William, b. 9 Jan 1935, Bedford, England. m. (1) Majorie Olive Roberts, 30 June 1960; (2) Gillian Margaret Lynch, 24 Aug 1977, 1 d. *Education:* Bedford Sch, 1946-53; Univ Col London, 1953-58; LLB, 1956, PhD, 1958, Bar Finals, 1964, Barrister, Grays Inn. *Appointments:* Lectr in Law: Univ Sheffield, 1960-63, Univ Bristol, 1963-64; Univ Col London, 1964-: Sr Lectr, 1964-65, Rdr, 1965-73, Prof of Labour Law, 1973-, Dean of Fac of Laws, 1975-77. *Publications:* Principles of Labour Law, 1972, 1989; Right to membership of trade union, 1963; Trade Unions and the Law, 1973; Industrial Tribunal Law, 1980; Ed, Current Legal Problems, Federation News, Longmans Law Series. *Memberships:* Bar, Grays Inn, 1964; Zoological Soc; Indust Law Soc, Chm, 1977-80, VP, 1984-; Chm, p-t, Indust Tribunals; Dpty Chm, Ctl Arbitration Com. *Honours:* Postgrad studentship, Univ of London, 1956-58. *Hobbies:* Local history; Gardening. *Address:* 255 Chipstead Way, Woodmansterne, Surrey SM7 3JW, England.

RIDGEON Jonathan Peter, b. 14 Feb, 1967, Bury St Edmunds, Suffolk, England. Sportsman. *Education:* BA Geog, Magdalene Col Cambs, 1986-89. *Career:* World Student Games and European Jr Champion; World Jr and World Sr Runner-up at 110m hurdles; World Bronze medalist and European Silver medalist at 60m indoor hurdles. *Memberships:* The Hawks Club; Achilles Club; Belgrave Harriers Athletics Club. *Honours:* Brit Sportswriter's Male Athlete of the Year, 1987. *Hobbies:* Sports; Media and Sketching. *Address:* Battersea, London SW11, England.

RIDGEWAY Thomas Graeme, b. 29 Dec 1918, London, England. Retired Naval officer. m. Jane Clinton-baker, 17 July 1957, 1 s. *Education:* RN Col, Dartmouth, various staff and technical courses, 1932-36. *Appointments:* Navy Ser, 1936, Submarines, 1940-47, NMS Templar in Command, 1944-46; Admiralty, 1957, Ret'd, 1959. *Memberships:* Contemporary Art Soc; The Nautical Inst; Submarine Old Comarades Assn; Royal Naval Sailing Assn; Royal Utd Sers Inst; Brit Field Sports Soc. *Hobbies:* Hunting; Fishing; Shooting; Sailing. *Address:* Higher Hill, Hittesleigh, Exeter EX6 6LQ, England. 7, 117.

RIDGWAY Paul Campbell, b. 21 Apr 1951, Brookfield, Missouri, USA. m. 29 July 1973, 3 s. *Education:* BA, 1973, MM, 1974, N. Western Univ; DMA, Peabody Inst, 1981; Hochschulefur Musik, Munich, 1974-75. *Appointments:* Carson Newman Col, 1975-; P-t Music Dir, First Bapt Ch, Gatlinburg, TN, 1987-92. *Publications:* Articles in: Am Music Tchr; Contemporary Lit for the Intermediate and, Advanced Student; I've got Rhythm - Or do I?, 1987; Musicality can be taught, 1989. *Memberships:* Pi Kappa Lambda, Pres, Gamma Alpha Chap; Nat Guild of Piano Tchrs; Knoxville, and Tennessee Mus Tchrs Assns; Music Tchrs Nat Assn. *Honours: include:* Winner. Soc of Am Mus Young Artists Comp, 1971; SAM Talman Awd, 1972; SAM Allied Arts Awe, 1976; Debut Recital, Orch Hall Chicago, 1977; Northshore Musicians CLub, 1970; Illinois Music Tchrs Assn, 1973; Rotary Foun Scholarshp, 1974-75; Soloist with Memphis and Knoxville Symphs. *Hobbies:* Gardening; Hiking; Bridge. *Address:* 1506 Rayburn Drive, Morristown, TN 37814, USA.

RIDLEY William Patrick, b. 22 Mar 1935, London, England. Stockbroker. m. Elizabeth Marie, 26 Mar 1986, 2 d. *Education:* Law Deg, Oxford, 1955-58; LSE, (ext); 1965; BSc, Econ; Archaeol, UCL; 1989-92. *Appointments:* Black Geogehan & Till, 1958-62; Bank of London, S. America, 1962-65; C'wlth Devel Corp, 1965-68; Mierrett Cyriax Asst, Man Conslts, 1968-73; Wood Mackenzie & Co, 1973-89; Hill Samuel, 1986-87; of Nat West, 1988-89. *Publications* Book, Making use of Economic statistics; Sundry articles in Management of Interest Rates; Company Handbook Admin. *Memberships:* ICA: Assoc, 1962, Fellow, 1973; Stock Exchange, 1974. *Honours:* AMEX Bank Review Essay Competition Awd, 1987. *Hobbies:* Archaeology; Travel. *Address:* 15 John Spencer Square, London N1 2LZ, England.

RIEDERER Josef, b. 29 Dec 1939, Munchen, Germany. Research Laboratory Director. m. Christel Heel, 26 Aug 1967, 2 d. *Education:* Univ, 1958-63; Dr rer nat, 1964; Prof of Archaeometry, 1987. *Appointments:* Univ of Munich, 1964-67; Bayerische Staats gemaelde, Munich, 1967-74; Rathgen-forschungslaber der Staatichen Museen zu Berlin, 74-. *Publications:* Kunst und Chemie, 1977; Kunstwerke Chemisch betrachtet, 1987; Archaelogie und Chemie, 1987; Restaurieren, Konservieren, 1989, translations in English, French, Portuguese, Spanish, Romanian, Sinhalese. *Memberships:* Coor, ICOM Com for Conservation; Corresp Mem, German Archaeol Inst. *Hobbies:* Underwater archaeology. *Address:* Rathgen-Forschungslabor, Schloss-Str 1a, D-1000 Berlin 19, Germany.

RIGBY Alfred, b. 18 June 1934, Lytham, Lancs, England. Architect. m. Ann Patricia Flynn, 4 Sept 1958, 1 s, 1 d. *Education:* BA Arch, Class I Hons, MA, 1958, London Univ, Manchester Univ; Dipl Town Planning, 1966. *Appointments:* Personal Asst, Basil Spence, 1958-60; Prixde Rome Scholar Br Acad Rome, 1960-64; Dpty Reg Archt, NWMRHB, 1963-73; City Arch of Westminster, 1973-79; Dir Arch, Camden, 1979-; John R Hams partnership. *Contributions to:* Sir Banister Fletcher, A History of Architecture on the Comparative Methods; Various paintings. *Memberships:* FRIBA; FBIM; FRSA; Athenaeum; MCC; lancs CCC: Pres, Corsham RFC. *Honours:* Prix de Rome in Arch, 1958;

4 Civic Trust Awds and numerous Commendations, 1958-81. *Hobbies:* Painting; Music; Sport; Theatre. *Address:* Meadlands, 3 Pickwick, Corsham, Wilts SN13 0JD, England.

RIGBY George Reginald, b. 15 July 1908, Stoke on Trent, England. Retired. m. Ada Mavis Allen, 28 Dec 1933. 1 d. *Education:* N.Staffs Tech Col, 1924-28; Imperial Col, Royal Col of Sci, 1928-32; ARCS; BSc, London, 1930, both 1st class hons; DIC Phys Chem, 1932; PhD, London, 1962; DSc, London, 1957. *Appointments:* Brit Refractories Ceramic Res Assn, 1932- 56; Dir, Res Can Refractories Ltd, 1957-68; Sr Res Fellow, Leeds Univ, 1968- 71; Sr Lectr, Univ of Cape Town, 1971-73; Vis Assoc Prof, Univ of Penang, 1975-77. *Publications:* Author: 112 sci papers in Brit, Am and European Ceramic, jour. *Contributions to:* The Victoria County History, Can Geographical J; N.Staffs Field Club; Author: Thin section minerology ceramic materials, 1948. *Memberships:* Fdr Fellow and Mem, Inst of Ceramics; FRChS; Ex Conslt: Hindustan Sanitary Ware, Delhi, Cullinan Holdings, S.A, English China Clays; Extra Mural Lectr, Oxford Univ, 1950-56; Special Lectr, Can Inst of Chem, 1964. *Honours:* Beilby Meml Awd, Inst of Chem, 1948; Lynan Prizeman, N.Staffs Field Club, 1949; John Jeppson Awd, Am Ceramic Soc, 1966; Mellor Meml Lectr, Inst of Ceramics, 1966. *Hobbies:* Medieval church architecture; Gardening. *Address:* 1 Oakfield CLose, Garforth, Leeds, LS25 1HW, England.

RIGBY John Thomas, b. 9 Dec 1922, Brisbane, Australia. Artist. m. Margaret Shaw Auld, 14 Apr 1954, 2 s, 1 d. *Education:* Central Tech Col, Brisbane, 1937-38; Dipl in Fine Art, E.Sydney Tech COl, 1948-51. *Appointments:* Australian Military Forces, 1942-46; Commercial Artist; Cartoonist, 1946-48; Painting, Graphic Arts, 1952-72; Education in Arts, 1973-84; Painting, 1984-. *Creative works:* 80 One man exhibs, Brisbane, Sydney, Melbourne, 1954-91; Mixed exhibs, Am, Australia; Printmaking and Drawing Exhibs. *Memberships:* Sr Instr, Ofr in Charge, Sch of Fine Art, Queensland Col of Art, 1974-84; Trustee, Queensland Art, Gall, Brisbane, 1969- 87. *Honours:* Italian Travelling Scholarship, 1956; Womens Weekly Portrait Prize, NSW Art Gall, 1958; Sulman Prize, Sydney NSW, 1962; Melrose Prize, SA, 1963; David Jones Prize, Queensland, 1965, 1967; Gold Coast Prize, 1971, 1973; H C Richards Prize, 1960; Naracorte Purchase Prize, 1972. *Hobbies:* Gardening; Fishing; Travelling. *Address:* 2678 Moggill Road, Pinjarra Hills, Brisbane, Queensland 4069, Australia.

RIGGS David Lynn, b. 9 Oct 1943, Tulsa, Oklahoma, USA. General Manager and Vice President. *Education:* AA, N.Eastern A & M, 1964; BS, N.Eastern Univ, 1966; Grad, Borcher Aviation Sch, 1966; Cert in Design Tech, 1964. *Appointments:* Wm L Riggs Co Inc, 1966-. *Memberships:* Trustee, Tulsa Bible Sch; Cherokee Nation of Oklahoma; Phi Theta Kappa; SAR: Sons of Union Vets; Soc War 1812; SCV; Soc Mil Order Stars and Bars. *Hobbies:* Art; Reading; Fishing. *Address:* 565 SO 127 E Ave, Tulsa, OK 74128, USA. 7, 132.

RIGGS Lawrence Wilson, b. 25 Aug 1943, Wilmington, Del, USA. Director, Customer Service Operations. m. Ann Rae Holbert, 12 Aug 1978, 1 s, 2 d. *Education:* Univ of Arizona, 1965-67; Cert in Engrg, Heathkit Continuing Educ, 1977. *Appointments:* Asst Mgr, Panafax Corp, CA, 1978- 80; Diagnostic Supr, NEC Am Inv, 1980-83; Reg Ser Mgr, CA, 1983-85; NEC Am Atlanta GA, 1985-87; Natl Ser Mrg, Savin Corp, 1987-90; Dir, CUST Ser Ops, Audiofax Inc, Marietta, GA, 1990-; VP, Tele-Enterprises, Atlanta, 1988-90. *Publications:* Inventor: Tele-Cube, 1988; Image Roll, 1988. *Memberships:* Assoc for Sers Mgmt Intl. *Hobbies:* Fishing; Golf; Computers; Facsimile technology. *Address:* 225 Farm Court, Roswell, GA 30075, USA. 7.

RIGO Michael Maurice, b. 24 Nov 1956, Royal Oak, Michigan, USA. Police Lieutenant. m. Marion L Bennett,

20 May 1983, 2 s, 1 d. *Education:* PhD, Columbia Pacific Univ, 1991-; MS, 1989, BS, 1988, Georgia State Univ, AA, Floyd Jr Col, 1982; FBI Nat Acad, 1991. *Appointments:* Lt, Marietta Police Dept, 1981-91; Ofr: US Army Police, 1975-78, Atlanta Police Dept, 1980. *Publications:* Field survey of Georgia's Police Chiefs on a Bill of Rights for Georgia Police Officers. *Memberships:* Intl Assn of Chiefs of Police; Nat Assn of Black Law Enforcement Execs; Am Bus Women's Assn; Kiwanis Intl; Peace Ofrs Assn of Georgia; Fraternal Order of Police. *Honours:* Phil Peters Scholarship for outstanding academic merit in criminal justice, 1988; Phi Kappa Phi Hon Soc, 1988; Golden Key Hon Soc, 1988; Outstanding Col Students of Am, 1989. *Hobbies:* Diving; Running; Sailing; Basketball; Antiques. *Address:* 67 Oakmont Drive, Marietta, GA 30064, USA.

RILEY Alan John, b. 16 July 1943, Denton, Oxon, England. Specialist in Sexual Medicine and Pharmaceutical Physician. m. 11 Dec 1976, 3 s, 1 d. *Education:* MB, BS, Univ of London, 1967; MSc, Univ of Manchester, 1976. MRCS, Eng, 1967; LRCP, London, 1967, DObst, RCOG, 1969; MFPM, 1987. *Appointments:* GP, 1970- 75; Sr Res Phys, 1977-90; Specialist in Sexual Med, 1970-. *Publications:* Ed, Brit J Sex Med, 1983-1990; Ed, Sexual and Marital Therapy, 1985-; Direcor, MAP Publishers Ltd. *Contributions to:* The Literature on Sexual Medicine and Sexual Physiology. *Memberships:* RSM; Assn, Sexual and Marital Therapists; Soc for Endocrinol; World Congress for Sexol; BMA: Fellow, Royal Zoological Soc. *Honours:* Ofr of the Order of St John, 1983. *Hobbies:* Photography; Natural History; Writing; Cooking; Woodwork. *Address:* Field Place, Dunsmore nr Wendover, Bucks HP22 6QH, England. 170.

RILEY Gerald Patrick, b. 6 Sept 1941, Oklahoma, USA. Professor of Art. m. Jonita Riley, 4 June 1976, 5 s, 2 d. *Education:* BFA, 1964, MA Educ 1971, Univ of Oklahoma; Currently, EED emphasis Art Educ, 1990-. *Appointments:* Oklahoma City Pub Schls, 1964-91; S.Western Oklahoma STate Univ, Weatherford, 1991-. *Creative works:* Masks designer; performer - craft objects of art sculpture, Family Unity, commd by S.Community Hosp, Oklahoma City. *Memberships:* Nat Art Educ Assn; Okla Art Ed Assn, Bd; Okla Alliance for Arts Ed, Sec; Okla Visual Arts Coalition. *Honours:* Tchr Fellowship, John F Kennedy Ctr for the Performing Arts, 1986. *Hobbies:* Yoga; Meditation; Psychology; Physical medicine. *Address:* 1616 Markwell Ave, Oklahoma City, OK 73127, USA. 37.

RILEY John Price, b. 6 July 1922, Southport, England. Emeritus Professor. m. Denise M Hayes, 26 Nov 1985, 1 d. *Education:* Dean CLose Sch, Cheltenham, 1936-40; BSc, 1940-43, PhD, 1946, DSC, 1959, Liverpool Univ. *Appointments:* Asst Lectr in Chem, 1947-50, Lectr in Oceanography, 1950-59, Rdr, 1960-72, Personal Chair, 1972-89, Hd of Dept, 1983-89, Univ of Liverpool. *Publications:* Introduction to Marine Chemistry, 1972; Ed, Chemical Oceanography, 2 VOls, 1965, 10 vols, 1975-90. *Memberships:* FRSChem: Estmarine and Brackish Water Sci Assn, Trustee. *Hobbies:* Gardening; Riding. *Address:* Woodside Tivington, Minehead, Somerset, TA24 8ST, England.

RITCHIE Anthony Elliot, b. 30 Mar 1915, Edinburgh, Scotland. Retired. m. Elizabeth Lambie Knox, 28 June 1941, 1 s, 3 d. *Education:* Edinburgh Acad, 1922-30; MA, 1930-36, BSc, 1933, Univ of Aberdeen; MBChB, 1040, MD, 1945, Univ of Edinburgh. *Appointments:* Carnegie Scholar, 1940-41; Lectr in Physiol, Edin Univ, 1941-48; Prof of Physiol, St Andrews Univ, 1948-69; Sec and Treas, Carnegie Trust for Univs of Scotland, 1969-86. *Publications:* Scientific and medical papers on clinical electromyography. *Memberships:* BMA; Royal Soc of Edinburgh: Fellow, 1951; Coun, 1957-60; Gen Sec, 1966-76; Trustee, Nat Lib of Scotland, 1976-. *Honours:* Hon FCSP, 1970; Hon DSC, St Andrews, 1972; Hon LLD, Strathclyde, 1985; Hon FRCPE, 1986; CBE, 1978. *Hobbies:* Reading; Hill- walking; Motorcars; DIY.

Address: 12 Ravelston Park, Edinburgh EH4 3DX, Scotland. 1.

RITCHIE Marguerite Elizabeth, b. 20 May 1919, Edmonton, Canada. Lawyer; Pres, Human Rights Institute of Canada. *Education:* BA, 1944; LLB,, 1944, Univ ALberta; LLM, McGill Univ, 1958; LLD, Univ Alberta, 1975. *Appointments:* Law student, Lawyer, Edmonton, 1944-45; Chief, Report on War Labour Bd, 1946; Counsel, Dept of Justice, Govt of Can, 1946-72; V- Chairperson, Anti-dumping Tribunal, 1972-79. *Publications:* Articles dealing with women, human rights, international law, natural justice; Numerous briefs for Human Rights Inst of Can on Women, Aboriginal peoples in Can, Middle East and Can's Policies, Can's Constitution, Kurds. *Memberships:* Can Bar Assn; Alberta Law Soc; Human Rights Inst of Can; Intl Comm of Jurists; Can Fed of Univ Women, Pres, Ottawa Club, 1958-60; Intl Law Assn; Hon Mem, Indian Rights for Indian Women, Ontario. *Honours:* First woman appointed to Queen's Counsel by Govt of Can; LLD, honoris causa, for work in the cause of Human Rights, 1975; Special Necklace conferred by Indian Rights for Indian Women, 1973; Outstanding Woman Awd, Province of Ontario, 1975. *Hobbies:* Research; Travel; Walking; Swimming; Foods. *Address:* President, Human Rights Institute of Canada, 244 Queen Street, Suite 303, Ottawa, Ontario, Canada K1P 5E4. 142.

RITTERSPORN Gabor Tamas, b. 14 Jan 1948, Budapest, Hungary. Historian. m. Yuri Okamoto, 19 Jan 1972, 1 s. *Education:* MA, Univ of Szeged & Leningrad,, 1967-72; Tokyo Univ, 1973-76; PhD, Hist, Sorbonne, 1972- 76. *Appointments:* Ctr Nat de la Recherche Sci, 1977-; Vis Prof: Univs of Calif, 1984, and Helsinki, 1991. *Publications:* Stalinist Simplifications and Soviet Complications, 1991, revised version. *Memberships:* Ed Assoc Telos, NY; Am Assn for the Adv of Slavic Studies. *Honours:* Guest Scholar, The Wilson Ctr, Washington DC, 1985; Humboldt Scholarshp, 1987-88. *Address:* CNRS/IMESCO, 9 Rue Michelet, Paris 75006, France.

RIXSON Denis Fenn, b. 12 Dec 1918, London, England. Retired RAF Officer. *Education:* Christ's Hosp, Horsham, 1930-36. *Appointments:* Advisor, Trustee, Consultant to Service and Medical and Disabled Charites; Gen Duties, Ofr, RAF, 1937-70. *Memberships:* Trustee: Dev Trust for Young Disabled; Compaid Trust; Dev Trust Chalk Pits; Heritage Mus; VP: Throgmorton European Med Gp; RAF Ben Fund, Sussex Rep. *Hobbies:* Cricket; Swimming; Gardens. *Address:* Hesworth, Close Walks Wood, Midhurst, W Sussex GU29 OET, England.

RIZNIC Jovica Radomir, b. 17 Jan 1951, Zemun, Serbia, Yugoslavia. Senior Research Engineer. m. Natalija Vasilija Vasikic, 29 Oct 1987, 1 s, 1 d. *Education:* Dipl Inz, Mech Engrg, 1976; MSC, 1983, DSc, 1989. *Appointments:* Boris Kidric Inst of Nucl Scis, Belgrade, 1976-83, 1985- ; Argonne Nat Lab, Illinois, USA, 1983-85. *Publications:* Nuclear Energies - Arguments, 1989; Phase Interface Phenomena in Multiphase Flow. *Memberships:* ASMEng; Intl Ctr for Heat and Mass Transfer, Org Sec; Yugoslav Soc of Thermal Scis, Sec Gen. *Honours:* ASME Corres, 1990; Ed, Thermotehnika, jour, 1985-. *Hobbies:* Reading; History and science of technology. *Address:* Dzona Kenedija 31, 11070 Novi Beograd, Serbia. 52.

ROACH Gary Francis, b. 8 Oct 1933, Penpedairheol, Wales. Professor of Mathematics. m. Isabella Grace Willins Nicol, 3 Sept 1960. *Education:* BSc, Univ Col Cardiff, 1955; MSc Birbeck Col, London, 1961; PhD 1964, DSc, 1991, Univ of Manchester. *Appointments:* Res Math, Brit Petroleum, London, 1958-61; Lectr, Univ Manchester, 1961-66; Vis Prof, Univ of BC, Canada, 1966-67; Lectr, Univ Strathclyde, Glasgow, 1967-79; Sr Lectr, 1970-71; Rdr, 1971-79; Prof, 1979-, Dean Sch of Sci, 1982-. *Publication:* Green's Function. *Memberships:* FIMA; FRAstroS; FRSA; FRSEdin; Edinburgh Math Soc, Pres, 1982-83. *Hobbies:* Music; Photography; Philately; Mountaineering. *Address:* 11 Menzies Avenue, Fintry, Glasgow G63 OYE, Scotland. 1,50, 52, 184.

ROACHE Gordon, b. 26 Dec 1937, Halifax, Nova Scotia, Canada. Artist. m. Jovanna Isaac, 21 July 1978, 1 s. *Education:* Art Dept, St Mary's Univ, 1962-66. *Career:* Painting career began in 1960, with first one-man exhibition in 1967, followed by 31 other exhibitions across Canada, in Guelph, Halifax, Hamilton, Trenton, Toronto, Charlottetown, Edmunston, St John, algary, Moncton, Montreal, to 1980; Annual exhibs in Halifax, 1981-91; A 30 year Retrospective at Art Gall, NS, 1990. Collections included in: Corporate, Government and private collections in N.Am, Europe and Japan, NS Centennial Col, 1967, Art Gal of NS, permanent collection, 1973, NS Art Bank, 1975, and City Hall, Hakadate, Japan, 1989. Featured in CBC film, Portraits of the Maritimes, 1982; Paintings in The National Book, Canadian Childhoods, 1989 and author of book, A Halifax ABC, 1987, (best picture book selection by the Can Lib Assn). *Honours:* Choice Bk Awd, Can Childrens Bk Ctr, Toronto, 1988-89; First Place Awd, 42nd Annual Maritime Art Assn Exhib, 1978; Canadian Forces Exhib Awd, Ottawa, 1966. *Hobbies:* Swimming; Music; Art history. *Address:* 6038 Cedar Street, Halifax, Nova Scotia, Canada B3H 2J3. 142.

ROBBINS-WILF Marcia, b. 22 Mar 1949. Educator. m. 1 child. *Education:* BA Elem Educ, George Washington Univ, 1969-71; MA Educ Psychol, NYU, 1973-75; MS, with spec in Reading, 1981, DEduc, 1986. *Appointments:* Tchr; Dir; Owner, Wee Folk Nursery Sch, 1978-82; Adj Prof, Seton Hall Univ, 1987; Foun Bd Mem, Stern Col for Women, 1987; Co- Chairperson, Jewith Bk Festival, 1987; Adj Prof, Middlesex Co Col, 1987; Vis p-t Lectr, Rutgers Univ, New Brunswick, 1988; Educ Conslt, Cranford Hg Sch, 1988; Asst Adj Prof, Long Island Univ, 1988; Asst Adj Prof, Pace Univ, 1988. *Publications:* A Status Report of Private New Jersey Reading Service Ctrs, 1986; Community Resourece File, 1979; Presenter and Chairperson of numerous workshops. *Memberships:* Life, NYAS: Nat and NJ Couns of Tchrs of Eng; Am Educ Res Assn; Life, Col Reading Assn; Life, Phi Delta Kappa; Assoc, Child Devel Ctr, NYC. *Honours:* Profl Certs in Attendance: In- Ser Workshops for The Star Ledger's Newspaper in Educ Prog, 1985, 1986; Profl Improvement Awds, Seton-Essex, Reading Coun, 1985-86, 1984-85. *Address:* 242 Hartshorn Drive, Short Hills, NJ 07078, USA. 6, 15, 156, 191.

ROBERTS Anthony John, b. 26 Aug 1944, Hawarden, N Wales. Managing Director, Post office Counters Ltd. m. Diana June Lamdin, 3 Oct 1970, 2 s. *Education:* Hampton School, 1956-67; BA Hons, Univ of Exeter, 1964-67. *Appointments:* Post Office Corp: Dir, Chm's Ofc, 1978-80; Sec of The Post Office, 1980-81; Dir, Counter Sers, 1981-85, MD, 1985-. *Memberships:* Companion, Brit Inst of Mgmt; Liveryman, Worshipful Company of Gardeners. *Honour:* CBE, 1991. *Hobbies:* Opera; Gardening; Cricket; Rugby; Golf; Squash. *Address:* Drury House, 1-16 Blackfriars Road, London SE1 9UA, England. 1.

ROBERTS Bryon Edward, b. 17 Feb 1933, Leeds, England. Consultant Haematologist. m. Audrey Jeanette Knee, 17 Aug 1957, 1 s. *Education:* Rothwell Grammer Sch, 1943-51; Leeds Univ, 1951-57: MBChB, 1957, MD, 1971. *Appointments:* Hs Ofr, 1957-58, Registrat in path, 1958-62, Leeds Gen Infirm; Registrar, Haematol, Royal Postgrad Med Sch, 1962-63; Lectr in Path, Univ of Leeds, 1963-70; Conslt, Haematol, Leeds Gen Inf, 1970- . *Publications:* Standard Haematology Practice; Blackwell Scientific Publications, 1991. *Memberships:* Assoc Clin Paths; FRCPath, Reg Advr; Brit Soc for Haematol, Sec. *Hobbies:* Gardening; Running; Walking; Football; Reading; Listening to music. *Address:* 9 Ladywood Mead, Leeds LS8 2LZ, England.

ROBERTS David Gwilym Morris, b. 24 July 1925, Harlech, England Engineering Consultant. m. (1)

Rosemary E E Giles, 22 Oct 1960, dec 1973, 1 s, 1 d; (2) Wendy A Moore, 14 Oct 1978. *Education:* Merchant Taylors's Sch, Crosby, merseyside, 1935-43; MA, Sydney Sussex Col, Cambs, 1943-45. *Appointments:* Royal navy, 1945-47; Sr Ptnr, John Taylor & Sons, 1981- 88; Chm, Acer Gp Ltd, 1988-82; Vis Prof, Loughborough Univ of Tech, 1991-. *Memberships:* FICE, Pres, 1986-87; FIMechE; Fellow, Fellowship of Engrg; Hon Fellow, Inst of Water and Environ Mgmt. *Honours:* ICE: George Stephenson Medal, 1986; Overseas Premium, 1978; Halceow Premium, 1985; IWEM: Silver, 1974, and Gold 1987 medals. *Hobbies:* Tennis; Walking; Engineering Archaeology of Middle East. *Address:* North America Farm, Westmeston, Hassocks, Sussex BN6 8SH, England. 1.

ROBERTS Dorothy Elizabeth Lee, m. William Glen-Doepel, 1 s. *Education:* Methodist Ladies Col, Sydney; Sydney Conservatorium. AMusA, 1945; LMus, 1947. *Appointments:* Broadcasting for 13 years on Australian Radio; Solo recitals in Sydney; Accompanied Dame Joan Sutherland in recital; Farewell Recital in Beecroft Sch of Arts also with Dame Joan Sutherlane, 1950; London, 1952, Royal Overseas League, Balliol Col Oxford, 1953; Royal Albert Hall, 1955; Strolling Players, 1956; London Bach Orch, 1957; Halle Orch 1961; Northern Sinfonia Orch, 1965; Numerous recitals in London and the provinces; Lincoln Cathedral, 1965; Usher Gall, 1983, 1987, 1990. Recital Schloss Leitheim Concerts, Germany, 1971; Known as performer of the Clara Schumann tradition; Protegee of Sir John Barbirolli, St Malcolm Sargent, Sir Eugene Goossens and Adelina de Lara, OBE. Exhibited and sold own paintings in London, NY, and provincial galleries; Paintings in private collections in England, Can, Am, Australia, Japan and France. *Address:* Alveley House, 17 Lindum Road, Lincs LN2 1NS, England.

ROBERTS Jeffrey David, b. 30 June 1943, Liverpool, England. Investment Advisor. m. Marie-Christine Livingstone, 1 June 1974, 1 s, 1 d. *Education:* BA Geol, MA, New Col; PhD, Geol, Univ of Wales. *Appointments:* Cambs Univ Press, 1966-67; Univ of Wales, Cardiff, 1967- 71; Conoco Europe N.Sea, 1971-72; Wood Gundy Lte, 1973-79; Rowe & Pitman, 1979-083; CRM Vermogensb, 1983-85; Schroder Securities, 1985-88; Union Bk of Finland, 1989-91. *Publications:* Articles in various papers including: What if? Liberals Ran Hackney, 1985; Finland Review, 1990. *Memberships:* Fellow, Geol Soc of London; DVFA; Nat Liberal Club. *Honours:* Liberal Candidate in Gen Elections, 1979, 1983, 1987; Liberal Councillor, Shoreditch, 1980-87. *Hobbies:* Outdoor (Hills and the Sea); Piano. *Address:* 30 Countess Road, Kentish Town, London NW5 2XJ, England. 52.

ROBERTS Norman Stafford, b. 15 Feb 1926, Liverpool, England. Eduational Consultant. m. Beatrice Best, 5 Apr 1965, 1 s, 2 d. *Education:* Quarry Hg Sch, Liverpool, 1934-43; Hertford Col, Oxford, 1943-44, 1947-51. *Appointments:* Lt, 6th Field Rgt, Royal Artillery Palestine and Egypt, 1944-47. *Memberships:* HMC Chm So and SW Div, 1980; Chm of Govs, Staudries Sch; Gov of King Edward Sch, Witley; Gov of Wycliffe Col; Trustee, SFIA Educ Trust. *Honours:* Open Hist Exhibition: Hertford Col, Oxford, 1943; Walter Hines Page Eng Speaking Union Scholarship to USA, 1958, 1980; School Master Fellow, Merton Col, Oxford, 1964; Hon Maj, 1965. *Hobbies:* Sport; Bridge; Travel. *Address:* Chestnut House, 23 Mount Street, Taunton, Somerset TA1 3QF, England. 1.

ROBERTS Ray Crouse, b. 8 Jan 1929, Burlington, NC, USA. Professof or Economics. m. 24 June 1952, 3 s, 1 d. *Education:* BA Econ, Duke Univ, 1950; MS Indust Relations, 1957, PhD Econ, 1961, Univ of N.Carolina. *Appointments:* Asst through to full Prof, Old Dominion Univ, 1956-67; Vis Assoc Prof, Duke Univ, 1964-65; Dean, Sch of Bus Admin, Winthrop Col, 1967-69; Frederick W Symmons Prof of Econ, Furman Univ. *Publications:* Several articles in professional journals

and contributor to newspaper editorials; monographs. *Memberships:* S.Econ Assn; Indust Relations Res Assn; Piedmont (SC) Econ Club, Sec, Treas. *Honours:* Fellowship, S. Fellowship Foun, 1959-60; Dist Professorship, Furman Univ. *Hobbies:* Jogging; Reading. *Address:* 102 Oundee Lake, Greenville, SC 29609, USA. 2, 7.

ROBERTS Thomas Ian, b. 8 Nov 1956, Yorkshire, England. Solicitor. *Education:* Giggleswick Sch, 1969-74; BA, Modern Hist, 1978; MA 1982. *Appointments:* Solicitor, qualified, 1982; Booth and Co, 1982-91, Partner, 1988-. *Publication:* A Walk Round Stackhouse. *Memberships:* The Law Soc; Manchester Raquets and Tennis Club; Yorks Archaeol Soc; Nat Trust; Yorks Young Solicitor's Gp, Treas, 1987-88; Yorks Glass Mfr Assn, Sec, 1983-88. *Hobbies:* Geneaology; Local history; Long case clocks; Numismatics; Fires. *Address:* Booth & Co, PO Box 8, Sovereign Hse, S.Parade, Leeds LS1 1HQ, England. 53.

ROBERTS Trevor John, b. 22 Apr 1940, Coven, W.Midlands, England. Managing Director; Company owner. m. Judith Wiggin, 30 Mar 1970, 1 s 1 d. *Education:* King Edward Grammar Sch, Stafford; Wolverhampton Poly: CEng, 1988; FIProdE, 1988; FBIM, 1987; FIIM, 1987. *Appointments:* Charles Richards and Sons Ltd, Mgr, Mfg Depts, 1969-74; Charles Richards Fasteners Ltd, Prodn Mgr, 1974-78; Tech Mktg Mgr, 1978-80; Doran Eng Co Ltd, Mfg Dir, 1980-82; Jt Owner and MD, Doran Engrg Holdings Ltd and Village Engrg Co Ltd, 1983-; Dir, Petrospec Bolting Ltd, 1990-. *Memberships:* Inst of Ind Mgrs, Former Nat Coun, Nat Membership Exec, Chm and Pres, Wolverhampton Branch; Pres, Willenhall Rotary Club; Mgmt Com, Inst for the Blind Workshops, Wolverhampton. *Hobbies:* Reading; Swimming; Photography; Gardening; DIY. *Address:* Doran Engineering Co Ltd, Planetary Road, Willenhall, W.Midlands WV13 3XW, England.

ROBERTSON Anderson Bain, b. 22 Oct 1929, Bristol, England. Retired Teacher. m. Mary Margaret Moffat Christie, 13 July 1955, 2 s. *Education:* Gray's Sch of Art, Aberdeen, 1951-52; Glasgow Sch of Art, 1952-55; Aberdeen Col of Educ, 1955-56; Glasgow Sch of Art, 1981-82; Dipl of Art, 1955, ATC 1956, BA Hons, 1982. *Appointments:* Hd of Art Dept, Nicholson Inst, Sternoway, 1967-69; Gov of Aberdeen Col of Educ, 1974-78; Convener, Ctl Adv Com on Art, 1977-81, Assessor, Cert of Sixth Yr Studies in Art and Design, 1977-89. *Creative Works:* Exhibs at RSA, Royal Glasgow Inst of Fine Arts; Royal Soc Soc of Painters in water Colours, Royal Soc of Portrait Painters, Soc of Scottish Artists and Soc of Scottish Artist of Craftsman Exhibs. *Memberships:* Glasgow Art Club. *Hobbies:* Sailing; Fishing; Politics. *Address:* The Coppice, 2 College Park, Barassie, Troon, Ayrshire KA10 6UH, Scotland. 19.

ROBERTSON John Trevelyan, b. 15 Sept 1926, Charlton, England. Company Director; Marketing Consultant; m. Katherine Elizabeth Scott, 8 Sept 1951, 2 s, 1 d. *Education:* Haileybury and Imperial Ser Col, 1940-44; Univ of Edinburgh, 1944; MA Econ, Univ of Cambs, 1948-80. *Appointments:* Dist Sales Mgr, Brit Oxygen Co Ltd, 1951-56; Dir and Gen Mgr, Oxhycarbon Co Ltd, 1959-60; Asst MD, Kompass Register Ltd, 1960-64; Sales Dir, John G Stien & Co, 1964-73; Dir, John Robertson Sales Ltd, 1973. *Memberships:* Magnesite and Chrome Brickmakers Assn, Chm, 1972; Inst of Refractories Engrs, 1964. *Hobbies:* Sailing; Gardening. *Address:* The Old Smithy, Cuthill, Dornoch, Sutherland IV25 3RW, England.

ROBERTSON Lawrence Marshall Jr, b. 4 Feb 1932, Denver, Colorado, USA. Neurosurgeon. m. (1) Joan T White, 13 May 1958, div, 1973, 1 s, 2 d; (2) Lee Ann Crawford, 24 Sept 1982, 1 s. *Education:* BA, Univ Colorado, 1953; MD Univ of Colorado Med Sch (UCMS), 1957; Intern, Kings Co Hosp, Brooklyn, 1957-58; Residencies: Gen Surg, St Joseph Hosp, Denver, 1958-59; Neurol, UCMS, 1959-60; Neurosurg, Boston City

Hosp, 1960-64; Fellowship, Neurosurg, Lahey Clin Boston, 1963; Univ of Denver Col of Law, 1981-85. *Appointments:* Assoc Neurosurg, Drs C G Freed & H R Boyd, Denver, 1964- 68; Solo Practice, Denver, 1968-71; Sole Owner, Colorado Neurosurg PC, Denver, 1971-; Arbitrator, Am Arb Assn, 1983; US Reserve Med Corps, Lt, 1957; Lt Cmdr, 1975, Capt, 1977-. *Publications:* An analysis of professional malpractice, 1983; Reduced malpractice and augmented competence: A Proposal, 1983. *Memberships:* Colorado and Interurban Neurosurg Socs; Rocky Mt Traumatologic Soc; Phi Alpha Delta; Colorado and Denver Bar Assns; NYAS; ATLA; Nat Railway Hist Soc; Assn of Military Surgs of the US; Naval Reserve Assn; Reserve Ofrs Assn; US Naval Inst; AAAS. *Honours:* Fellow, Am Acad of Neurol and Ortho Surgs, Cert; Dipl of Am Bd of Med-Legal Analysis in Med and Surg; Continuing Educ Certs, Jt Com on Educ, Am Assn of Neurol Surgs and Congress of Neurol Surgs, 1976, 1983; Phys Recognition Awds, Am Med Assn, 1976-79, 1980-83, 1984-87, 1987-90. *Address:* Colorado Neurosurgery PC, 1635 Gilpin Street, Denver CO 80218, USA. 3, 6, 30.

ROBINSON Ann Elisabeth, b. 9 Apr 1933, Ilford, Essex, England. Science Policy Adviser. m. (1) Richard George Lingard, 17 Dec 1960, dec; (2) Francis Edward Camps, 22 Feb 1972, dec. *Education:* Queen Ann's Sch, Caversham; BPharm Hons, Chelsea Col, 1955; PhD, 1958; CChem, FRSC, (UK); CCHEM, FCIC. *Appointments:* Asst Lectr, Lectr, Pharm Chem, 1957-64; Lectr, Sr Lectr, London Hosp Med Col, 1964-77; Ontario Ministry of Labour: Chief Occup Health Lab & Conslt in Toxicol, 1978-80, Asst Dept Min, Occp Health Safety, 1980-87. *Publications:* Many in scientific litarature; Co Ed, Gradwohls Legal Med, 1976. *Memberships:* RSChem; CHemIC: RIGB; Am Acad of Forensic Scis. *Honours:* Adjunct Prof, Univ of Toronto, 1978-. *Hobbies:* Soroptimist Intl, Toronto, Pres, 1985-87. *Address:* 80 Quebec Avenue Apt 601, Toronto, Ontario M6P 4B7, Canada. 142, 138.

ROBINSON Berol, b. 25 June 1924, Michigan, USA. Retired Physicist. m. Shirley Richie, 27 June 1948, 1 s, 2 d. *Education:* AB, Harvard Col, 1948; The Johns Hopkins Univ, 1953. *Appointments:* Asst Prof of Phys: Univ of Arkansas, 1952-56, Western and Case Western Reserv Univs, 1956-69; Staff Scist: Mass Inst of Tech, 1969-71, UNESCO, 1971-84; Vis Scist: Soreq Res Estab, Isarel, 1961-62, Oak Ridge Nat Lab, 1964-68; Vis Prof of Phys, Rensselaer Poly Inst, 1965. *Publications:* Over forty articles describing the result of research in physics and in physics education; Sector report of the US Metric Study - Education. *Memberships:* European and Am Phys Socs; AAUP; AAPT; AAAS. *Honours:* Various scholarships; Phi Beta Kappa, 1953; Sigma Xi, 1950; Phys Tchg Equipment Prize, 1965. *Hobbies:* Science; Reading; Travel in France. *Address:* 1 Rue du General Gouraud, F-92190 Meudon, France. 52,

ROBINSON Christopher John, b. 20 Apr 1936, Peterborough, England. Organist; Director of Music. m. Shirley Ann Churchman, 6 Aug 1962, 1 s, 1 d. *Education:* Rugby Sch, 1949-54; Christ Ch Oxford, 1954-58; FRCO, 1954; BA, 1957: MA 1962; BMus, 1958; Hon RAM, 1982; Hon MMus, Birmingham, 1987; Hon Fellow, Birmingham Poly, 1990. *Appointments:* Mus Master, Oundel Sch, 1959-62; Asst Organist, 1962-63, Organist, 1963-74; Worcester Cathedral; Organist, St George's Chapel, Windsor, 1975-91; Conductor: City of Birmingham Choir, 1963-, Oxford Bach Choir, 1977. *Memberships:* Pres Royal Col of Organists, 1982-84; Chm, Elgar Soc, 1988-. *Honours:* LVO, 1986. *Hobbies:* Watching cricket. *Address:* St John's College, Cambridge, CB2 1TP, England. 1.

ROBINSON Colin, b. 7 Sept 1932, Stretford, England. Professor of Economics. m. (2) 18 June 1983, 4 s, 2 d. *Education:* Stretford Grammar Sch, 1942-49; Univ of Manchester, 1954-57; BA Econ, 1st class hons; Gladstone Meml Prize. *Appointments:* Procter and Gamble, Newcastle, 1957-60; Esso Petroleum Co, London, 1960-66; Esso Europe Inc, London, 1966-68; Prof of Economics, Univ of Surrey, 1968-. *Publications:* Bus Forecasting, 1971; North Sea Oil in the Future, 1971; Can Coal be Saved?, 1985; The Economics of Energy Self-Sufficiency, 1984. *Memberships:* Soc of Bus Econs, Hon Sec, 1961-63; Adv Coun: Inst of Econ Affairs, Ctr for Policy Studies; Intl Assn of Energy Econs; FIPet; Fellow, Royal Stats Soc. *Honours:* Gladstone Meml Prize, 1957. *Hobbies:* Walking; Gardening; Listening to music. *Address:* Dept of Economics, University of Surrey, Guildford, Surrey GU2 5XH, England.

ROBINSON David B, b. 14 Apr 1937, Richmond, Virginia, USA. Poet and Writer. *Education:* AA, 1970; BA, 1973; BS, 1959; MSc, 1961; PhD, 1979. *Publications:* Characteristics of Cesium; Collected Poems; Praise the Wilderness. *Memberships:* Am and Mexican Phys Socs; ACS; NYAS; Florida Acad of Scis; Acad of Am Poets. *Honours:* Phi Theta Kappa, 1979, Sigma Xi, 1986; USA Pres Medal of Merit, 1982; World of Poetry Golden Poet Awd Trophy, 1987; World of Poetry Plaque Golden Poet, 1985; Pres Sports Awd Bicycling, 1976. *Hobbies:* Chess; Amateur Paleontology. *Address:* 215 NE 117th Street Apt 1, North Miami, FL 33161, USA. 7,

ROBINSON David Foster, b. 29 May 1936, Macclesfield, Cheshire, England. Corporate Consultant. m. Hannah Watson, 5 Nov 1966, 2 s, 1 d. *Education:* Kings' Sch, Macclesfield, 1944-53; BA Com, Manchester Univ, 1953-56; Chartered Acct, 1959. *Appointments:* Dir Consultancy Co, 1969, Ptnr, 1974, Spicer and Oppenheim; Corp Consult, 1990; New Exec Dir, Finlay Packaging Plc, Whitton Gp Plc, MM&K Ltd. *Publications:* Finance and Accounting, 1980; MAnaging People, 1979; Getting the best out of people, 1988; The Naked entrepreneur, 1990. *Memberships:* FICA; FIMC; FIOD. *Hobbies:* Walking; Gardening; Enjoying the countryside. *Address:* Luards, Langford, Maldon, Essex CM9 6QB, England.

ROBINSON Donald Sewart, b. 3 Oct 1927, Whittington, England. m. Majorie Agnes Adamson, 6 Aug 1953, 2 s. *Education:* BA Cantab, 1948; PhD Cantab, 1951; MA, Oxon, 1962. *Appointments:* Extended Staff, Med Res Coun, at Sir William Dunn Sch of Poth and Dept of Biochem, Univ of Oxford, 1952-71; Prof of Biochem, Univ of Leeds, 1971-90; Hd, Dept of Biochem, Univ of Leeds, 1975-85. *Publications:* Many articles in scientific texts and biochemical research journals. *Memberships:* Biochem Soc: Past Com and Dpty Chm of Ed Bd of Biochem Jour, 1968-73; FIBiol; Atherosclerosis Discussion Gp: Past Sec and sunsequently Chm. *Honours:* Alan Johnston, Lawrence and Moseley Royal Soc Res Fellow, 1954. *Hobbies:* Gardening; Mountain Walking. *Address:* The Cottage, Main St, Saxton, Tadcaster, N.Yorks LS24 9PY, England.

ROBINSON John Martin, b. 10 Sept 1948, Lancashire, England. Historian. *Education:* Ft Agustus Abbey Sch; St Andrews Univ; Oriel Col, Oxford, MA, DPhil, FSA. *Appointments:* Historian: Ptnr, in Hist Bldg Conslts; Lib to the Duke of Norfolk. *Publications:* The Wyatts, 1980; Royal Residences 1981; Georgian Model Farms, 1982; Dukes of Norfolk, 1983; Latest Country Houses, 1984; Cardinal Consalvi, 1987; Oxford Guide to Heraldry, 1988; Country HOoses of the North West, 1990. *Memberships:* Coun, Sof of Antiquaries; Exec Com, Georgian Gp, Pres, N.West Branch; Sec, Roxburghe Club. *Address:* Beckside House, Barbon via Carnforth, Lancs, England.

ROBINSON Kenneth Paul, b. 5 Feb 1925, Skegness, England. Managing Director. m. Helen Elizabeth McKissock, 30 June 1951, 5 s. *Education:* Skegness Grammar Sch, 1936-41; BSc Hons, Phys, Durham Univ, 1943, 1947-50. *Appointments:* RAF, 1943-47; GEC Applied Labs, 1950-64; GEC Road Signals, 1964-66; Plessey Co, 1966-72; Marconi Co, 1973-. *Memberships:*

FIEE; FIP; IOD. *Honour:* CBE, 1991. *Hobby:* Golf; Gardening; Swimming. *Address:* Frenchmans, High Street, Odinam, Hants RG25 1LE, England.

ROBINSON Marie J, b. 21 Jan 1915, Monaca, Pennsylvania, USA. Retired Professor. *Education:* BLI Hons, Emerson Col, Boston, 1935; MA Hons, Michigan State Univ, 1944; PhD, N.Western Univ, Illinois, 1960. *Appointments:* Tchr, Lockport Sr Hg, NY, 1935-43; H, Dept of Speech and Drama, State Tchrs Col, Bemidji, Minnesota, 1944-45; Instr, Sch of Speech, Syracuse Univ, NY, 1944-45; Prof of Speech, Hd, Dept of Speech, 1953-74. *Publications:* Lectures and articles including: Lecture: Mark Twain; Book Chapter: The Influence of the Arts,, 1965; Speech, the Future of..., 1967; Speech, the Multifaced Prism, 1970; Lecture, Speech, the Magnificent Gift, 1967. *Memberships:* Life Emeritus: Speech Comm Assn, 1980, Illinois Speech and Theatre Assn, Life Emeritus, 1980, VP, 1961-62, Pres, 1962-63; Am Theatre Assn; Am Forensic Assn, Life Emeritus, 1980. Ctl States Speech Assn, Adv Comm, 1961-63. *Honours include:* Tchr of the Yr Awd, Illinois Wesleyan Univ, 1966-67; Community Leader of AM Awd, 1969; Vis Artist, Carthage Col, Wisconsin, 1966-68, Vis Lectr, Interpretation Contest, Ottawa, 1969; Alpha Epsilon Rho; Alpha Lambda Delta; Phi Kappa Phi, Life Emeritus; Phi Kappa Delta; Theta Alpha Phi. *Hobbies:* Reading; Bridge; Swimming; Travel; Shopping; Crocheting; Presenting oral programmes of poetry, drama and prose. *Address:* 2205 Lamon Drive, Bloomington, IL 61704, USA. 2, 5, 8, 13, 14, 126, 130, 138, 152, 155, 156, 162.

ROBINSON Michael Hill, b. 7 Jan 1929, Preston, Lancs, England, Zoo Director. m. Barbara Cragg, 19 May 1955. *Education:* Cert in Educ, Univ of Liverpool, 1953; BSc summa cum laude, Univ of Wales, 1963; DPhil, Oxford Univ, 1966. *Appointments:* Rdr, Biol, New Univ of Ulster, N.Ireland, 1971; Biol, 1971-84, Asst Dir, 1980, Actg Dir, 1980-81, Dpty Dir, 1981-84, Smithsonian Tropical Res Inst; Dir Nat Zoological Pk, Wash DC, 1984-. *Publications:* Over 100 published articles including: The Evolution and function of Behaviour, 1975; The ecology and biogeography of spiders in Papua New Guines, 1982; Arachnologia neotropical: Aspectos historicos, ecologicos y evolutivos, 1983; Man and Beast Revisited, co ed, 1991. *Memberships:* Sci Fellow, Zoological Soc of London; Fellow, Linnean Soc; FRES; IBiol; Am and Brit Arachnol Socs; Intl Soc for Tropical Ecols; Soc for Study of Animal Behaviour. *Honours:* Environmental Achiever Awd, 1989; Scholar in Residence, Univ of Dayton, OH, 1991; Mass Media Letter of Recognition, 1991. *Hobbies:* Theatre, especially Shakespeare; Reading European history; Evolution theory. *Address:* National Zoological Park, 3000 Block of Connecticut Ave NW, Washington DC 20008, USA. 2, 6.

ROBINSON Thomas Lloyd, b. 21 Dec 1912, Swansea, Wales. Retired. m. 6 Sept 1939, 1 s, 2 d. *Education:* Wycliffe Col, 1925-30; Staff Col, Camberley. *Appointments:* E S & A Robinson Ltd, 1931-66; Dlr, 1952, MD, 1958, V-Chm, 1963; Dir, DRG, 1966-77; MD, 1966, Chm, 1974-77; Legal and Gen, Dir, 1970-83, V-Chm, 1978-83; Brit Waterworks Ltd, Dir, 1978-84; Vanheer Gp, Holland, Dir, 1977-81; Legal and Gen, S & Western Adv Bd, Chm, 1972-84; Chm, Com of Govs, Wycliffe Col, 1970-83; Mem com Bristol Inv, 1977-83, Pro Chancellor, 1983-; Soc of Merchant, 1977-78; Hg Sheriff, Avon, 1979-80. *Memberships:* Pres, Pres CCC, 1980-83; Pres, Warminster Co Cricket Assn, 1989; Royal and Ancient Golf Club of St Andrews; FBIM; FRSA. *Honours:* TD, 1945; LLD, Bristol Univ, 1985. *Hobbies:* Music; Golf; Cricket; Literature. *Address:* Lechlade, 23 David Stoke Avenue, Bristol BS9 1DB, England. 1,

ROBSON Peter (Gordon), b. 5 Nov 1937, Scarborough, Yorks, England. Publisher. *Education:* Scarborough Hg Sch for Bous, 1949-57. *Appointments:* Asst Master, Marton Hall Sch, Bridlington, 1962-70; Hd of Maths, Cundall Manor, Helperby, York, 1971-90, Sr Master,

1973-76; Fdr, Newby Book Publishers, 1990. *Publications:* Between the Laughing Fields, Poems, 1966; Maths Dictionary, 1979; Maths for Practice and Revision, 5 vols, 1982-90; Fountains Abbey, A Cistercian Monastery, 1983; The Fishing Robsons, 1991. *Hobbies:* Music; Genealogy; Photography. *Address:* P Box 40, Scarborough, N.Yorks YO12 5TW, England.

ROBSON Reginald Arthur Henry, b. 11 Apr 1921, London, England. Professor Emeritus. m. Monica Agnes Welch, 12 Apr 1947, 1 s, 2 d. *Education:* BSc Econ, Univ of London, 1949; MA, 1951, PhD, 1952, Univ of Minnesota. *Appointments:* Instr, Univ of Minnesota, 1949-52; Asst, Prof, Assoc Prof, Univ of Nebraska, 1958; Asst Prof, Prof, Univ of Brit Columbia, 1958-86. *Publications:* Ethnic Conflicts in Vancouver, 1985; Formal Theory of Experimental Sociology, 1971; Effects of different sex compositions on support rates and coalition formation, 1971; Comparison of men's and women's salaries in the academic profession, 1969. *Memberships:* Am Sociol Assn; Can Sociol Anthropol Assn; BS Civil Liberties Assn, Dir; Can Rights and Liberties Fed, Dir; Friends of London Sch of Econ and Polit Sci; Pacific Sociol Assn. *Honours:* Law and Behavioural Scis Fellowship, 1957-58; Assoc of Univs and Cols of Canada Study Leave Fellowship, 1963-64; Canada Coun Study Leave Fellowship, 1970-71, 1977-78. *Hobbies:* Hiking; Gardening; Skating. *Address:* Po Box 37, Garry Oaks, RR2, Nanoose Bay, BC, Canada VOR 2RU.

ROCHE-GORDON Delphine Mary, b. 2 Apr 1945, Poole, Dorset, England. Television. Costume Designer. m. 28 Oct 1972, 2 s, 1 d. *Education:* Ealing of Art, 1963-66; Art and Design Dipl with Dist; City and Guilds Dress Mfg with Dist. *Appointments:* Plays and films include: Dad's Army Royal Variety Special Secret Servant, 1984; All Creatures Great and Small, 1985; Tuti Fruitti, 1986; The Dark Room, 1987; Justice Game, 1988-89; Wreck on the Highway, 1989; Separation, 1990; The Black Velvet Gown, 1990. *Memberships:* Greenpeace; Flora and Fauna Nat Trust; RSPB; Friends of the Earth, Scotland; Princess of Wales Hospice; World Wildlife Fund. *Honours:* Nominated for BAFTA costume design award for Tutti Fruitti. *Hobbies:* Riding; Gardening; Cinema; Reading; Animals. *Address:* Drummit House, Gartmore, Stirling FK8 3RY, Scotland.

ROCHETTE Louis, b. 19 Feb 1923, Quebec, Canada. Vice Chairman and President. m. Nicole Barbeau 12 Oct 1968, 1 s, 2 d. *Education:* Master of Commerce, Laval Univ, Quebec, 1948. *Appointments:* Pilor, Royal Can Air Force, 1943-45. Pres, 1982-86, V-Chm,1986-, Socanav Inc; Chm and Pres, David Shipbuilding Inc, 1976-82; Exec VP, Marine Industries Ltd, 1966-76. *Publication:* Le Reve Separatiste, 1969. *Memberships:* ICA; Can Corp of Mgmt Accts; Lloyds Register of Shipping, Can Com, former Chm. *Honours:* Hon Col, 6th Field Artillery Rgt, Levis, Canada; Gov: Chamber of Commerce, Province of Quebec, Quebec Opera Foun, Laval Univ; Gov and former Pres, Coun for Can Unity. *Hobbies:* Sailing; Deep Sea Fishing; Reading. *Address:* 1080 des Braves Avenue, Quebec G1S 3C8, Canada. 2, 142.

RODRIGUEZ Raymond A, b. 5 Apr 1947, Corpus Christi, Texas, USA. Investment Advisor. m. Bertha Idalia Abrego, 16 Nov 1991. *Education:* AA, Del Mar Col, 1967; BA, St Mary's Univ, 1969; Grad Sch of Urban Studies, Trinity Univ, 1970. *Appointments:* Tex Ofs of Minority Bus Enterprise, 1971-73; VP, Merrill Lynch, 1973-89; VP, Dean Witter Reynolds, 1989-91; Dir, Intl Dept, Arneson Kerchville Ehrenberg, 1991-. *Memberships:* Bd of Trustees, Del Mar Foun; Fdr, McAllen 1000. *Honours:* Equestrian Order of the HOld Sepulchre, 1988; Rising Star of Texas, Texas Bus Mag, 1983; Texas Gov's Task Force on Pvt Sector Initiatives. *Hobbies:* Reading; Jogging. *Address:* 5409 N New Braunfels, San Antonio, TX 78209, USA.

ROE Betty Joyce, b. 16 Oct 1944, Tullahoma, Tennessee, USA. University Professor. m. Michael H Roe, 26 Aug 1967. *Education:* BS, 1966, MS, 1967, EdD, 1969, Univ of Tennessee. *Appointments:* Tchr, Oak Ridge City Sch, 1969-70; Asst Prof, 1970-74, Assoc Prof, 1974-79, Prof, 1979-, Tennessee Tech Univ. *Publications:* 23 books including: Teaching Reading in Today's Elementary Schools, 1992; Secondary School Reading Instruction, 1991; An Introduction to Teaching the Language arts, 1990; Developing power in reading, 1990; Informal Reading Inventory, 1989; Student Teaching and Field Experience Handbook, 1987; The Case of Basic Skills programmes in Higher Education, 1986. *Memberships include:* Intl Reading Assn; TN Reading Assn, Past Pres, Dir of Membership Devel; TX Tech Reading Coun, Past Pres, Advr; Nat Coun of Tchrs of Eng; Nat Assn for the Preservation and Perpetuation of Story Telling. *Honours:* Lit Awd, Intl Reading Assn, 1990; TN Reading Assn Dist Prof Awd, 1989-90; Pres Club of the Intl Reading Assn, 1987-88; Phi Delta Kappa Outstanding Univ Tchr Awd, 1985- 86; Awds for outstanding Contributions to reading, 1974, 1977; Betty Dunn- Minnie Perl Cert of Merit, 1974. *Hobbies:* Water skiing; Travel; Reading. *Address:* Department of Curriculum and Instruction, Tennessee Technological University, Cookeville, TN 38505, USA. 5, 7, 15, 125, 138, 141.

ROE Peter Frank, b. 17 Jan 1931, Cairo, Egypt. Medical Practitioner. m. Margaret Sapp, 1 s, 1 d. *Education:* MA, St John's Col, Cambs, 1949-52; Edin Univ, 1952-55, MB, ChB, 1955, MD,1 1969: Royal Col of Phys and Surg of Glasgow, MRCP, 1962, FRCP, 1981. *Appointments:* Registrar, Addenbrooks Hosp, 1960-62; Sr Registrar, Adelaide Hosp and Clin Tutor, Trinity Col, Dublin, 1963-65; Conslt Phys, Uganda Govt, 1966-67; COnslt Geriatrician, Somerset, 1970-; Clin Dir for Community Sers, W.Somerset, 1991. *Publications:* various medical journals in general and geriatric medicine. *Memberships:* Med Branch, RAF, 1956-59; Brit Geriatric Soc; Dir, Somerset Care Ltd. *Hobbies:* Choral singing; Heraldic painting; Church of England Reader. *Address:* Kirkmead, Stadlegrove, Taunton, Somerset TA2 6AP, England.

ROEBUCK John Athey, b. 22 June 1920, Barnsley, S.Yorks, England. Author; Lecturer; Executive; Advisor and Consultant Industrial Psychologist to Industry. m. Dorothy Elsa McLeod, 21 Nov 1949, 2 s. *Education:* PhD, Psychol, 1951. *Appointments:* RAF, Trans-Can Ferry Cmd and UK Coastal Cmd, 1939-45; Eng Admin, Nationalised Industry, 1946-64; Hd of Gp, Intl Personnel Sers, Bridon Plc, 1964-85; GGGG Grandson of Dr John Roebuck, Fdr of Carron Co, 1718-1794; GG Nephew of Rt Hon John A Roebuck, PC, QC, MP, 1802-1879; GG Nephew of Miss Florence Nightingale, OM, 1820-1910. *Publications:* Philosophy of Everyman, 1948; Life Mind Man, 1948; E Tenebris Lux, 1951; Accepted Principles of Planned Maintenance, 1956; The Roebuck Story, (with Senator the Hon A W Roebuck QC), 1963. *Memberships:* FBIM; FIPM; FRSA; Inland Waterways Assn; Waterways Recovery Gp; Barnsley Canal Gp. Soc; Social Security and Med Appeals Tribunal, 1985-; Indust Mem, Geog Com Schls Exam and Assessment Coun, 1985-90. *Honours:* Intl Awd of Hon 1st Intl Congress of Doctors, 1969. *Hobbies:* Organs; Playing and listening; Inland waterways. *Address:* Inglewood, Back Lane, Campsall, Doncanster, N. Yorks DN6 9AH, England. 3, 11, 30, 43, 52.

ROEGIEST Eugeen Herman Joseph, b. 31 Oct 1946, Deurne, Belgium. University Professor. m. Agnes Detollenaere, 28 June 1976, 1 s, 1 d. *Education:* MA 1968, PhD, 1976, Univ Ghent, Belgium. *Appointments:* Asst Prof, 1969-83, Lectr, 1983-85, Prof, 1985-, Dir, Dept of Romance Langs, 1985-, Univ of Ghent; Dir, Postgrad Bus Communication and Applied Langs, 1987-; Conslt Mem, Fac Conseil, 1985-; Prof, Economical Spanish, Sch of Interpreters, 1978-85; Prof, Spanish Lings, Univ of Brussels, 1986-. *Publications:* 40 articles in international reviews: Books: Les prepositions 'a' et 'd' en espagnol comtemporain: Valeurs contextuelles

et signification generale, 1980; Verbe et phrase dans les langues romanes, 1983. *Hobbies:* Gardening; Photography; Cultural Tourism. *Address:* Goed ten Pauw 17, B-9080, Lochristi, Belgium. 1.

ROGAN-ILIOPOULOU Theodora, b. 29 May 1944, Athens, Greece. Art Critic; Professor of History of Art. m. A Rogan, 25 Sept 1965, div 1977, 1 d. *Education:* Licence d'Histoire de L'Art, Sorbonne, Univ of Paris, 1967; Doctorat en Histoire de L'Art, Univ of Paris, 1970; Dipl, Ecole Pratique des Hautes Etudes, Paris, 1971. *Appointments:* Art Critic, Kathimerini Newspaper, 1974-90, and Living Mag, 1991-; Prof of Hist of Art: Deg Col Greece, 1979-; Nat Sch of Dramatic Art, 1945-89. *Publications:* Man History and Monuments, 1974; Ghikas Paraccels, 1980; K Karas and Retrospective of his paintings, 1984; 11 other books on art. *Memberships:* Intl and Greek Assns of Art Critics; Intl Assn of Esthetica; Art and Environ Gp. *Honours:* Chavalier des Arts et des Lettres, 1986. *Hobbies:* Music; Reading; Swimming. *Address:* 4 Sekeri Street, Athens 10674, Greece. 1.

ROGERS Leonard John, b. 30 Oct 1931, Croydon, Surrey, England. Managing Director. m. Avery Janet Morgan, 16 July 1955, 4 s. *Education:* Stadtisches Und Staatliches Gymnasium, Neuss am Rhein, 1950; Trinity Col, Cambs, 1952-55; BA, 1955; MA, 1959. *Appointments:* Asst Sec, Brit Aeroplace Plastics Ltd, 1960-62; Mgr, Export Contracts, Brit Aircraft Corp, 1973-76; Bus Dir, BAC Civil Aircraft Div, 1976-77; Mktg Dir, Brit Aerospace, Weybridge, 1978-79; Conslt, Roconslt AG, Zug, Zchweiz, 1980-84; Dir, AIM Gp Plc, 1984-. *Memberships:* FID; ARAS; Liveryman, Worshipful Co of Coachmakers and Coach Harness Makers. *Honours:* OBE, 1979. *Hobbies:* European languages; Roses; Opera; Travel; Biographies; History of the theologist church.. *Address:* Willow Pool, Effingham, Surrey KT24 5JG, England. 1, 132.

ROGERSON Michael Anthony, b. 19 Feb 1941, Winchester, England. Chartered Accountant. m. Margaret Jane Blake, 27 Sept 1969. 1 s, 1 d. *Education:* Harrow. *Appointments:* Spicer and Pegler, 1959-64; Hancock and Woodward, 1964-66; Ernst & Young, 1966-73; Grant Thornton, 1973-. *Memberships:* FICA; FBIM; CBI, Coun, Regional Coun, Immediate past Chm, London Region. *Hobbies:* Golf; Bridge; Gardening; Racing. *Address:* Millcroft, Mill Lane, Pirbright Surrey GU24 0BN, England. 53.

ROHATGI Pradip Krishna, b. 10 Nov 1939, Calcutta, India. Chartered Accountant. m. Pauline Mary, 13 July 1974. *Education:* BCom, Univ of Calcutta, 1960; Univ of London: BSc Econ, 1964; FCA (E&W), 1969; ATII, 1967; MBCS, 1976; FCA, India, 1980. *Appointments:* Sr Econ & Stats, 1963-66; Articled, Mann Judd & CO, 1966-69; Arthur Andersen & Co, London, 1970, Mgr, 1973, Ptnr, 1980, Dubai Ofc, 1980-84; Man Ptnr, India, 1982-89, Sr Ptnr, London, 1989-. *Publications:* Various written articles and speaker on various business and professional issues; Specialist on business in India, its regulations and business strategies for international companies. *Memberships:* Direct and Indirect Com, Assn of Chamber of Commerce in India, 1986-89; Chm, Econ Affairs Com, Indo-Am Chamber of Commerce, 1986-89; Appeals Com, Asian Piazza Appeal, (Shakespeare Globe Theatre), 1990-; Gov, Intl Students House, London; Exec Com, Bombay Mgmt Assn, 1987-89; Oriental Club, Durbar Club; Rotary Club of London. *Hobbies:* Classical guitar; Music; Fine Arts; Travel; Golf; Sailing; Wine tasting; French. *Address:* 43 Great Brownings, College Road, London SE21 7HP, England.

ROLLIN Henry Rapoport, b. 17 Nov 1911, Glasgow, Scotland. Consultant Psychiatrist. m. Anna-Maria Tihanyi, 27 July 1973, 1 s, 1 d. *Education:* MB, CHb, 1935, MD, 1949, Leeds Univ; Hon FRCPsych, 1989; FRCPsych, 1971; MRCP,1975; DPM, 1940. *Appointments:* Wing-Cmdr, RAFVR, 1942-47; Conslt Psychi, 1945-; Mental Heath Review Tribunal, 1960-

83, Parole Bd, 1970-73. *Publications:* The mentally abnormal offender and the Law, 1969; Coping with Schizophrenia, 1980; Festina Lente: A Psychiatric Odyssey, 1990. *Memberships:* RCPsych, Hon Lib, 1975-85; Osler Club of London, Pres, 1974-76; RSM, Pres, Hist of Med Section, 1990-91. *Honours:* Fulbright fellow, Temple Univ Hosp, Philadelphia, USA, 1953-54; Gwilyn Gibbon Res Fellow, Nuffield Col, Oxford, 1963-64; Hon FRCPsych, 1989. *Hobbies:* Music; Theatre; History of medicine. *Address:* 101 College Road, Epsom, Surrey KT17 4HY, England.

ROMENSKA Monika, b. 5 Dec 1958, Plovdiv, Bulgaria. Artist. m. Prodan Dimov, 1 May 1985. *Education:* Graphics, Acad of Fine Arts, Sofia, 1977-83; Russian Lang Sch, Plovdiv, 1972-76. *Appointments:* Individual exhibs: Plovdiv, 1985, Plevdiv, 1987; Sofia; Leipzig, Plovdiv, 1988; Nat Chamber Exhibs, Plovdiv and selected Group exhibs, 1990; Symbols and Signs, 1989; Great Photography, 1991; Graphics Bienalle Spain, Bulgaria, 1991; Jugoslavia. 1988; Bulgaria, 1983, 1987, 1989; Work in private collection in Europe, USA and Asia. *Publications:* Cycles; Try to Fly; My Town; Shadows in the Dreams; Sunrises; The woods and the time; Interval; For dogs and Men; Doors. *Memberships:* Young Artists Club, 1983; Union of Bulgarian Artists, 1989; Rub Edge Rup, 1989. *Hobbies:* Travelling; Swimming; Reading; Writing; Poetry. *Address:* 20 G Vaygand Str, 4000 Plovdiv, Bulgaria.

RONALDSHAY Robin Lawrence, The Earl of, b. 5 May 1965, Windsor, England. *Education:* Harrow School; Royal Agric Col, Cirencester. *Appointments:* Dir, Catterick Racecourse Ltd; Dir, Redcar Racecourse Ltd; Ptnr, Zetland Estates; Ptnr, Zetland Stud. *Hobbies:* Golf; Shooting. *Address:* 7 Hasker Street, London SE3 2LE, England. 1.

RONDEAU Edmond P, b. 7 Dec 1945, Brockton, MA, USA. Corp Facility and Real Estate Consultant. m. Sarah D Rondeau, 15 Apr 1982. *Education:* Army Ser, 1969-71; BArch, GA Inst of Tech, 1969; MBA Real Est, GA State Univ, 1981. *Appointments:* Staff Archt, 1977-80; Constrn Mgr, Coca Cola Co, 1980-83; VP, Constrn and Design, 1984-85; Nat Bk of GA, VP of Property Mgmt, 1985-86; Mgr, Corp Real Est, Contel Corp, 1987-88; Principal, Rondeau & Assocs, 1990-. *Publications:* Principles of corporate real estate, Handbook; Co-author, Facility Managment Software: Facility Kit. *Memberships:* Am Inst of Archs; Construction Specifications; Intl Intl Fac Mgmg Assn, Sec, 1988-84, VP, 1985-87, Pres, 1988. *Honours:* Achievement Awd, Dist Mem Awd, Dist Author Awd, Intl Fac Mgmt Assn. *Hobbies:* Golf; Racketball. *Address:* 3293 Breton Circle NE, Atlanta, GA 30319, USA.

RONG Zhenhua, b. 25 Feb 1940, Shanghai, England. Associate Professor, Chairman of Department. *Education:* BS Shanchai, 1963; PhD, Karlsruhe, Germany, 1982. *Appointments:* Univ Lectr and Reschr, 1963-. *Publications:* Ein Krafteplazierungsverfahren, 1983; A layout Methodology, 1985; Selected works of Ludwig Feuerbach, 1983. *Memberships:* China Assn of Computer Sci; Specialized Com for CAD and Graphics, Coun; Shanghai Assn of Railway Tech, Coun. *Hobbies:* History of Philosophy and Logics; Theory of Music; Piano. *Address:* Chang Ning Road, Lane 712 No 15, Shanghai 200042, China.

RONNBERG Sten O, b.7 July 1931, Kalix, Sweden. Professor of Social Work. m. 4 Sept 1972, 1 s, 1 d. *Education:* PhD, 1978; Asst Prof, 1982; Prof, 1982; Psychol, 1965.*Appointments:* Psychol, Nat Bd of Educ, 1966-67; Lectr, Preschool Tchr Col, 1967-68; Lectr, Dept of Ed, Stockholm, Univ, 1969-87; Prof Sch of Social Wk, 1987-. *Publications:* Introduction to Behaviour Therapy, 1969; Behaviour Analysis, 1978; Seven Steps to Decreased Alcohol Dependence, 1988. *Memberships:* Pres, Swedish Assn for Alcohol and Drug Res, 1985-88; Fdr, Pres, Swedish Assn of Behaviour Therapy.

Hobby: Health Promotion. *Address:* School of Social Work, Univ of Stockholm, S-106 91 Stockholm, Sweden.

RONNEL Jacob, b. 1 Nov 1956, Istanbul, Turkey. Industrial Company Executive. m. Cornelia, 14 Feb 1983, 1 d. *Education:* Dipl, (Hons), Hotel Admin, Lusanne Hotel Sch, Switz, 1981. *Appointments:* Reservations Mgr, Asst Front Ofc Mgr, Quality Inn, Knoxville, TN, 1981-82; Sales Mgr, Sheraton Hotel, Israel, 1983-84; Gen Mgr, Manpeta (Indust Co) Natanya, Israel, 1984-; Dir, A Gafni (Constrn and Investment), Erez, Israel, 1990-. *Publications:* Inventor of board, card and educational games. *Memberships:* Bd of Trustees, Salti Scholarship Foun; Bnei Brit Org. *Honour:* Hons Grad, Lausanne Hotel Sch, Switzerland, 1981. *Hobbies:* Photography; Inventing games; Business publications. *Address:* 1 Rekananti Str, Tel Aviv 69494, Israel. 52.

ROSE Anna Elizabeth Guillemard, b. 28 May 1924, Croy, Inverness, Scotland. *Appointments:* Served in the WRNS, 1944-46; Sec, 3rd Intl Gerontol Congress; Sec to Solicitors, Grays Inn; Sec to Headmaster of Lockers Park Prep Sch; Sec, Principal Tutor, Middlesex Hosp Nsg Sch; Running Kilravok Castle as a Christian Guest Hse, 1967-. *Memberships:* VP, The Christian Alliance. *Hobbies:* Oil painting; Dress making; Travelling to Australia, Am and Can. *Address:* Kilravok Castle, Croy, Inverness IV1 2PJ, Scotland.

ROSE Christopher Dudley Roger, b. 10 Feb 1937, Hyde. High Court Judge. m. 5 Aug 1964, 1 s, 1 d. *Education:* Morecambe Grammar Sch, 1947-50; Repton, 1950-54; LLB, Leeds Univ, 1954-57; BCL, Wadham Col, Oxford, 1957-59. *Appointments:* Lectr in Law, Wadham Col, Oxford, 1959-60; Bigelow Tchg Fellow, Univ of Chicago, 1960-61; Barrister, 1961-85; QC, 1974; Judge, 1985-. *Memberships:* Middle Temple: Barrister, 1960, Bencher, 1983. *Honours:* Hughes Prize, Leeds Univ, 1957; Eldon Scholar, Oxford Univ, 1959; Harmsworth Scholar, Middle Temple, 1961. *Hobbies:* Music; Travel; Golf; Gardening. *Address:* Royal Courts of Justice, Stand, London WC2A 2LL, England. 1.

ROSE Stephen John, b. 20 Mar 1951, London, England. Consultant Paediatrician. m. Beatriz Alessandra Miranda Oyursun, 29 Jan 1987, 2 d. *Education:* Sidney Sussex Col, Cambs, BA 1972, MA 1976, MBBChir 1975; MRCP 1979, MD 1987, Guy's Hosp Med Sch. *Appointments:* Res Lectr, Westminster Hosp, 1980-83; Lectr, Univ of Aberdeen, 1983-87; Sr Clin Lectr, Conslt Paed, Univ Birmingham, 1987. *Publications:* Scientific papers on new born psychology, nutrition; Medical author. *Memberships:* Cambs Union: Brit Paed Assn; Dir, Hlpkins and Netherwood Ltd. *Address:* 92 Dovehouse Lane, Solihull, W.Midlands B91 2EG, England.

ROSE-INNES Alistair Christopher, b. 4 Dec 1926, London, England. Sculptor. m. Barbara Ellen Nicholls, 2 s, 2 d. *Education:* MA 1951, DPhi, 1954, Merton Col, Oxford Univ; DSC, Manchester, 1970; Chartered Engr. *Appointments:* P/O Radar Instr, RNVR, 1944-47; RN Sci Ser, 1954-64; Prof of Phys and Elec Engrg, UMIST, 1967-89. *Publications:* Books: Semiconducting III-V Compounds; Low Temperature Techniques; Introduction to superconductivity; Papers: in scientific journals; paintings, drawings and sculptures in exhibitions and private collections. *Memberships:* FIPhys. *Honours:* Harkness Fellow of the C'wlth Fund, 1960-61; Sculpture Prize, Manchester Poly, 1990. *Hobbies:* The visual arts; Growing Cacti. *Address:* c/o UMIST PO Box 88, Sackville St, Manchester M60 1QD, England.

ROSEN Daniel, b. 15 Sept 1952, Chicago, IL, USA. Professor of Law. m. Sheri Rosen, 22 May 1976, 1 s. 1 d. *Education:* BA Trinity Univ, 1975, MA Univ of Texas at Austin, 1976; JD, S.Methodist Univ, 1982; LLM, 1983, JSD, 1986, Yale Univ. *Appointments:* News Reporter, KTRK TV, Houston, 1976-79; News Reporter, WFAA TV, Dallas, 1980-82; Law Clk to Chief Judge

US Ct of Appeals, 9th Circuit, 1983-84; Fulbright Lectr, Kobe and Osaka Univs, Japan, 1987-88; Prof, Loyola Univ Sch of Law, 1984-. *Memberships:* Order of the Coif; Order of Barristers; Phi Kappa Phi; Fulbright Alumni Assn; Soc of Profl Jours. *Honours:* Fulbright Lectr in Japan, 1987-88; Ed in Chief, Southwestern Law Jour, 1981-82; Elected to the Order of the Coif, 1982. *Hobbies:* Japanese Language; Aikido; Yoga. *Address:* Loyala University School of Law, 7214 St Charles Avenue, New Orleans, LA 70118, USA.

ROSENBERG Terry, b. 6 Feb 1954, Hartford, CT, USA. Artist. *Education:* New York State Col of Ceramics; MFA, Alfred Univ, 1978; BFA, Univ of Miami, 1976; AA, Miami Dade Com Col, 1974. *Appointments:* Self employed artist. *Creative Works:* Solo Exhibs include: Benis Foun, Omaha, NE, 1987, Jon Oulman Gall, Minneapolis, MM, 1988, Sharpe Gal, NY, 1989; Gp Exhibs include: Art Against AIDS, Bette Stoler Gall, NY, 1987; Summer Gp Exhib, Sharpe Gall, NY, 1988; Sculpture from the Bemis Foun, Contemporary ARt Ctr, Kansas CIty, 1989; Public Collections: Albright Knox Art Gall, Buffalo, NY; Brooklyn Mus; Smart Gall, Univ of Chicago; Walker Art Ctr, Minneapolis; Virginia Mus of Fine Arts, Richmond; Vis Artist and Lectr at: Louisiana State Univ, Cranbrook Acad of Art, Univ Miami, Ohio State Univ, Paul Mellon Arts Ctr, CT, Chicago Art Inst; Jamaica Arts Ctr, NY, Univ of Nebraska, *Honours:* NY Foun for the Arts, 1989; Bemis Foun, 1986-87. *Hobbies:* Sport; Swimming; Tennis; Piano. *Address:* PO Box 1192 Canal Street Station, NY 10013, USA. 37, 152.

ROSENBUSCH Jurg Peter, b. 24 May 1938, Zurich, Switzerland. Biochemist; Molecular Biologist. m. Brigitte M Silberschmidt, 11 Dec 1964, 1 s. 1 d. *Education:* MD, Univ Zurich, 1963; MA, 1963; PhD Biochem and Molec Biol, 1971, Harvard Univ, USA. *Appointments:* Clin Med, Switz, 1964; Postdoc Fellow: Harvard Med Sch, Boston, 1965-66, Harvard Univ, Camb, MS, 1971-72; Asst Prof, 1972-77, Assoc Prof, 1978-82, Univ of Basel, Switzerland; Sr Scist, European Molec Biol Lab, Heidelberg, 1982-85; Univ of Basel, (Forschungsgruppenleiter), 1985-. *Publications:* about 100 scientific papers in international journals; Co-Ed, Annales de L'Institut Pasteur (Mircobiol), Pasteur, Paris. *Memberships:* European Molec Biol Org; Swiz Socs for Biochem and Cell Biol. *Honours:* Friedrich Miescher Awd for Biochem, 1975. *Hobby:* Literature. *Address:* Rhiensprung 17, CH-4051 Basel, Switzerland. 52.

ROSENSTEIN Henri, b. 3 June 1941, Paris, France. Cardiologist. m. Adida Marie Laure, 5 Dec 1969, 2 d. *Education:* Baccalaureat, 1959; Fac Des Scis, 1960; Fac de Med de Paris, 1961-67; Externe Des Hopitaux de Paris, 1963-67. *Appointments:* Interne Des Hopitaux de Paris, 1968-72; S.Reanaud's Lab Inst de Cardiol de Montreal, 1972; Chief de Clin Asst, Des Hopitaux de Paris, 1973-77; Attache des Hopitaux Hopital Jean Verdier (Bondy), 1977-. *Address:* 45 Rue Jean-Jaures, 94500 Champigny, France. 57.

ROSIKON Janusz, b. 8 Jan 1942, Choron, Polon. Photographer. m. Grazyna Kasprzycka, 19 Apr 1980, 2 s. *Education:* Grad, Electronics, Warsaw Poly, 1966. *Appointments:* ITD - Photoreportages, 1963; The Polish Review, 1968; Polish Photographic Agy, 1970; Dir, Gall of Assn of Photographers, 1975; Freelance work for: Newsweek, Time Mag, East Light. *Creative Works:* Albums: Shrine of Black Madonna; Jewish Cooking; Polish Madonnas; Solo exhibs in: Warsaw, The Papal Visit and Pilgrimage, 1980- 83, 1977-; London, Barbican Ctr, Poland a Nation of Paradox, 1988; Oxford, People of Poland, 1990. *Memberships:* Assns of Polish Photographers and Journalists and, Authors and Composers. *Honours:* Warsaw, Landscapes of the World, 1987; 150 Anniversary of Photography, Warsaw, 1989. *Hobbies:* Photography; Classical music. *Address:* Al Debow 4, 05-080 Izabelin, Warsaw, Poland.

ROSKOV Yuri, b. 16 Mar 1964, Leningrad, USSR. Scientist; Botanist; Systematist. m. Sokolova Trina, 25

Feb 1989, 1 s. *Education:* Biol Dipl, Univ Leningrad, 1981-86; Postgrad, Botanical Inst, Leningrad, 1986-89. *Appointments:* PhD Candidate in Biol Scis, Botanical Inst, St Petersburg. *Publications:* Thesis: Revision of the genus Grifolium in the flora of the USSRA and over 20 papers in scientific journals on systematic evolution of higher plants. *Memberships:* Intl Legume Database and Info Ser Proj, Southampton Univ, UK; Section Sec, Botanical Coor Coun of USSR Acad of Scis, St Petersburg. *Hobbies:* Art Photography; Painting; Cycling. *Address:* Herbarium Botanical Institute, 2 Prof Popov St, 197367 St Petersburg, Russia.

ROSOCHA Wieslaw, b. 16 Sept 1945, Sokolow, Podlaski, Poland. Graphic Artist. m. Ulrike Herbst, 27 Oct 1984. *Education:* Fac of Graphics, Acad of Fine Arts, Warsaw, 1969-74; Dipl, Poster-Workshop, Prof Henryk Tomaszewiski, 1974. *Appointments:* Tchg Asst, Painting-Workshop, Prof Teresa Pagowska, Acad of Fine Arts, Warsaw, 1975-78; Freelance Graphic Artist publishing work as posters and postcards. *Creative works include:* Typography and illustrations in fiction books include: Abelard and Heloise, 1978; The Secrets of Words, 1981; The Painted Bird, 1988; Ball at the Opera, 1989; Opera and theatre posters for Hamlet, Amadigi, And Wozzeck, 1982- 84; Exhibs include: Participation in poster biennials in Warsaw, Finland and Japan and in a series of ecumenical exhibs in Warsaw churches, 1978-89. *Membership:* ZPAP, 1978-. *Honours include:* Best Fiction Book of the year, Poland, 1990; Awd, Intl Exhib of Book Art, Germany, 1982; Best Children's Book of the Year, Poland, 1985; Gold Medal, Poster Biennial, Finland, 1985; Bronze Medal, Poster Triannial, Japan, 1991. *Hobbies:* Photography; Film; Literature; Hiking. *Address:* Waleska 2/89, PL 04-019 Warsaw, Poland.

ROSS Euan M, b. 13 Dec 1937, England. m. Jean Mary Palmer, 11 June 1966, 2 s. *Education:* MBChB, Bristol, 1962; DCH, Glasgow, 1965; MRCP, UK, 1971; MD, Bristol, 1975; FRCP, London, 1980; MFPHM, Hon, 1991. *Appointments include:* Clin Lectr, Child Health, Res Asst, Paed Epidemiol, 1969-, Hon Sr Paed Registrar, 1971-74, Univ Bristol. Sr Lectr and Hon Conslt Paed, St Mary's Hosp and Med Sch, London, 1971-74; Sr Lectr, Child Health and Community Med, Middlesex Hosp Med Sch, Conslt Paed, Brent Hlth Dist, 1974-84; Conslt Community Paed, Riverside HA, Hon Sr Lect, Paed, Charing Cross and Westminster Med Sch, 1984-89; Prof of Community Paed, Kings Col, Univ of London, Hon Conslt Paed, Camberwell HA, 1989-. *Publications:* 70 articles, reviews, book chapters on child development, handicap, epilepsy, immunisation and social problems in childhood. *Memberships include:* Chm, Nat Child Health Computing Com; Nat Child Health Computing Mgmt Exec; Gov Coun, King's Col Sch of Med and Dentistry, 1991; Coun, Univ of Bristol; Brit Paed Assn and Communicable Dis Surveillance Ctr Jt Res Com. *Hobbies:* Design; Current affairs; Photography. *Address:* Linklater House, Mt Park Road, Harrow HA1 2JZ, England.

ROSS Randy K, b. 14 July 1959, W.Hamlin, WV, USA. Assistant Professor of Mathematics. 1 d. *Education:* BA, 1977-80, MA, 1980-82, Marshall Univ; Univ of Tennessee, Knoxville, 1982-85. *Appointments:* Instr in Maths, Marshall Univ, 1985-86; Asst Prof of Maths, Morehead State Univ, 1986. *Memberships:* Am Maths Soc; Math Assn of Am; Kentycky COun Tchrs of Maths; Kentucky Assn of Col Maths Educrs; Kentucky Section, MAA. *Hobbies:* Basketball; Softball; Baseball; Tennis; Reading. *Address:* 1429 Chestnut Lane, Morehead, KY 40351, USA. 7.

ROSS MARTYN John Greaves, b. 23 Jan 1944, Stockport, Lancs, England. Barrister. m. Pauline Jennings, 4 Aug 1973, 1 s, 1 d. *Education:* Ryleys Sch, Cheshire, 1950-57; Repton Sch, Derbyshire, 1957-66; BA, LLM, Cambs Univ, 1962-66. *Appointments:* Asst Lectr, Birmingham Col of Commerce, 1966-68; Practice as Barrister, 1970-; Asst Reschr, 1988-. *Publications:*

Family Provision: Law and Practice, 1985; Jt Ed, Mortimer and Sunnucks, 1982; Jt Ed, Theobald. *Memberships:* Chancery Bar Assn; Subscriber, Bar Coun. *Hobbies:* Gardening; Skiing. *Address:* 5 New Square, Lincoln's Inn, London WC2A 3RJ, England.

ROSSIER Jean, b. 18 June 1944, Brussels, Belgium. Neuropharmacologist. 14 Apr 1972, 1 s, 1 d. *Education:* MD, U Brissels, 1969; DSC, Univ Paris, 1975. *Appointments:* Intern, City Hosp, Brussels, 1966-69; Res Asst, Coll de France, Paris, 1969-75; Asst Prof, Tufts Univ Med Sch, Boston, 1975-76; Roches Inst, Nutley, NJ, 1979; Dir Neurophysiol, Ctr Nat de la Rec Sci, Gif sur Yvette, 1980; Dir Res, Inst Nat Sante et Rec Med, Paris, 1971-. *Publications:* Ed: Neurochem Intl, 1987- ; Neuropeptides, 1987-. *Memberships:* FISN; Intl Brain Res Org; Soc Francaise Neuroendocrinol Experimentale; Coll Intl Neuropsychopharmacol. *Honours:* Laureat de l'Academie des Scis, 1983, 1990. *Hobbies:* Skiing; Sailing. *Address:* Laboratoire de Physiologie Nerveuse du CNRS, 91198 Gif sur Yvette, Cedex, France. 1.

ROSSITER-THORNTON John Francis, b. 4 Oct 47, Dublin, Ireland. Doctor; Psychiatrist; Professor; Educator. m. Maria G Manning, 6 Sept 1972, 1 s, 2 d. *Education:* MBBCh, BAO, Univ Col, Dublin, 1972; FRCPC Psych, Univ Toronto, 1977. *Appointments:* Med Internship, St Vincent Hosp, Dublin, 1973; Psych Training, St Brendans Hosp, Dublin, 1973, Univ Toronto, 1974, Toronto Addiction Res Foun, 1974-78; Clark Inst of Psychi, Toronto, 1978-80, Prog for Schizophrenia, 1980-, Seminar Leader, 1991-. *Publications:* Living and working with Schizophrenia, 1982, 1990; Many booklets and research articles on schizophrenia and other topics; Co-author and Ed, Schizophrenia Simplified, 1991; Author and developer of, Dreamweaving Seminars. *Memberships:* Can Psychi Assn; Ontatio Med Assn; Clarke Inst Med Staff Assn, past Pres; Assn in Psychi Clarke Inst, past VP; Ontario Psychi Assn, past Chm of Local Arrangements. *Honours:* Significant Achievement Awd, APA, 1981; Letter of Commendation, Can Friends of Schizophrenics, 1986; Special Leadership Awd, Friends of Schizophrenics Prog, 1990. *Hobbies:* Travel; Reading; Swimmer: Student Games Vienna, 1965, Iris Intl Swimming Team, 1966. *Address:* PO Box 1165 POSTNQ, Toronto, Ontario, Canada M4T 2P4. 142.

ROSTROPOWICZ Joanna Eleonora, b. 12 Jan 1943, Zdzieszowice, Upper Silesia. m. Tadeusz Rostropowicz, 11 Apr 1966, 2 s, 2 d. *Education:* MA 1966, PhD, 1976, Habilitation Schrift, 1987, Professorship, 1990. *Appointments:* Tchr of Latin, 1968-69, 1970-77, Prof of Ancient Hist, 1987-, Pedagogical Univ Opole, Asst, Inst of Class Studies, Wroclaw, 1969-70. *Publications:* The Reflection of the Political, Social and Economic Reality in the Alexandrian Poetry, 1983; Argonautica of Apollonios of Rhodes, 1988; 40 articles. *Memberships:* Upper Silesian Unino, VP, Polish Philol Soc; Bd, Silesian Inst Soc; Opole Soc of Sci; Club of Catholic Inteligentsia. *Hobby* Gardening. *Address:* ul Akacjowa 29, 45- 434 Opole, Poland.

ROTH Klaus Friedrich, b. 29 Oct 1925, Breslau. Mathematician. m. Melek Khairy, 29 July 1955. *Education:* BA, Peterhouse, Cambs, 1943-45; MSc, 1948, PhD, 1950, Univ Col London. *Appointments:* Asst Master, Gordonston Schl, 1945-46; Dept of Maths, Univ Col of London, 1948-66, Rdr, 1956-61, Prof, 1961; Prof of Pure Maths, Imperial Col, London, 1966-88; Vis Prof of Pure Maths, Imperial Col, London, 1988-; Vis Lectr, 1956-57, Vis Prof, 1965-66, Mass Inst of Tech, USA. *Publications:* Articles, papers and reports in professional journals. *Memberships:* London and Am Math Socs. *Honours:* Fields Medal Awd, Intl Cong of Mathns, 1958; FRS, 1960; Foreign Hon Mem, AAAS, 1966-; De Morgan Medal, London Math Soc, 1983; Fellow, Univ Col London, 1979; Hon Fellow, Peterhouse Cambs, 1989; Prof Emeritus, Univ of London, 1989; Royal Soc Sylvester Medal, 1991. *Hobbies:* Chess; Cinema;

Ballroom Dancing. *Address:* 24 Burnsall Street, London SW3 3ST, England. 1, 52.

ROTHENBERG Robert Michael, b. 10 Aug 1950, London, England. Chartered Accountant. Chartered Accountant. m. Philippa Jane White, 10 July 1981, 1 s, 2 d. *Education:* Highgate Sch, 1963-68; BA combined hons, Univ Exeter, 1969-72. *Appointments:* Deloitte Haskins & Sells, 1972-77; Blick Rothenberg, Chartered Accts, 1977-. *Publications:* Jt author, Understanding Company Accounts, 1987, 1991; Mastering Business Information Technology, 1989. *Memberships:* FICA, Eng and Wales; ATTI; Brit Acad of Experts. *Hobbies:* Theatre; Opera; Skiing; Family. *Address:* 12 York Gate, London NW1 4QS, England.

ROTHMAN Julius L, b. 22 Sept 1920, NYC, NY, USA. Professor Emeritus of English. m. Stella Lambert 23 June 1948. *Education:* BSS, City Col of NY, 1941; MA, 1947, PhD, 1954, Columbia Univ. *Appointments:* Lectr: Hunter Col, 1947-50, Rutgers Univ, 1950-53; Prof, Nassau Com Col, NY, 1962-86, Prof Emer, 1986-. *Publications:* Articles on folklore in Dictionary of Folklore Mythology and Legend, 1950; Articles on Am Lit in Cabellian, 1968-72. *Memberships:* Res Advr, ABA, 1980-; Lif, RPEA, 986- ; NCPSSM, Washington DC, 1982-; Nat Wildlife Fed, 1989-. *Honours:* Fellow, ABI, 1968; Advr, Sr Citizen Affairs, 9th Senatorial Dist of NY State, 1984-88. *Hobbies:* Ping Pong; Pool; Music, classical and popular; Driving; Art appreciation; Being a home owner. *Address:* 19819 Stardust Blvd, Sun City West, AZ 85375, USA. 6, 9, 15, 57.

ROTHNEY Gordon Oliver, b. 15 Mar 1912, Richmond, Quebec, Canada. Retired University Professor. m. Alice Ross, 31 July 1943, 2 s, 1 d (dec). *Education:* BA Hist, 1st class hons, Bishops Univ, Quebec, 1932; MA Dist, 1934, PhD, 1939, Univ of London, England. *Appointments:* Prof of Hist, Sir Geo Williams Col, Montreal, 1941-52; Prof and Hd Hist Dept, Meml Univ, Nfld, 1952-63; Dean of Arts and Prof, Takehead Univ, Ontario, 1963-68; Vis Prof of Hist, Univ of W.Ontario, 1969-70; Prof of Hist, Univ of Manitoba, 1970-79. *Publications:* Newfoundland: A History; Canada in One World; Articles and reviews for academic and professional publications. *Memberships:* Charter Mem, Com of Dirs, Inst d'Hist de l'Amerique Francaise, Montreal, 1947-71; Coun, Can Hist Assn, 1948-51; Chm, Humanities Res Coun of Canada, 1963-64; Royal Hist Soc, London; St Andrews Soc, Winnipeg. *Honours:* Gov Gen Medal, Bishops Univ, 1932; Scholarship, Prov of Quebec, 1932-34; Can Coun Sers Res Fellowship, 1959-60; Hon Fellow, St Johns Col, Univ Manitoba, 1983; LLD, Hon, Meml Un, Nfld, 1987. *Hobby:* Canadian history. *Address:* 904-333 Vaughan St, Winnipeg, Man, Canada R3B 3J9. 142.

ROUDYBUSH Franklin. *Educator. Education:* MA, PhD, Univ of Strasburg; Counsellor, Academie, Vienna; Univs of Vienna, Paris, Madrid; Harvard Bus Sch, USA; Cordon Bleu Cooking Sch, Paris, 1960-70. *Appointments include:* Dean, Roudybush Foreign Ser Sch, 1931-; Ed of Affairs, Pan Am Inst, 1938-42; Prof Intl Econ Relations, Washington DC, Foreign Ser Inst; Dept of State; Coun of Europe, Strasbourg; Am Embassy, Dublin, Ireland; Roudybush For Ser Sch, France, 1953-; Also: Econ Div, Dept of State, Censor of Dipl Pouch, WWII. *Publications:* Several books, French and English, including: Analysis of Educational Background and Experience of 828 US Foreign Service Officers; Why the Tragic Collapse of the British Empire; Evaluative Criteria for Foreign Service Schools and graining for Foreign Service (in French); XX Century Diplomacy; Economic Geography; Diplomacy and Art; Also: 120 years exhibitions, oil painting. *Memberships:* Am Soc of Intl Law; Brit Soc of Intl Comp Law; Assn des Amis du Salon d'Automne, Paris; Salon des Independants, Paris; Nat Press Club, Washington DC; AFSA. *Honour:* Prix Julien, Paris. *Hobbies:* Golf; Cooking. *Address:* Sauveterre de Rouerque, 12800 Areyron, France.

ROUHANI Shahrokh, b. 28 Mar 1956, Tehran, Iran. University Professor. m. Firouzeh Yekta, 18 Aug 1983, 2 s. *Education:* BS CEng, 1978, BA Econ, 1978, Univ California, Berkeley; SM, Engrg, 1980 PhD, Environ Scis, 1983, Harvard Univ. *Appointments include:* Tchg Fellow, 1978-83, Res Asst, 1979-83, Harvard Univ; Chm, Task Com, Am Soc of Civil Engrs, (ASCE), 1987-89; Asst Prof, Georgia Inst of Tech (GIT), 1983-90; Chm, Nat Ground Water Hydrol Com, ASCE, 1991-92; Assof Prof, Sch of Civ Engrg, GIT, 1990-. *Contributions to:* Geostatistical schemes for groundwater quality management in Southwest Georgia, 1987; Landfill Site Selection, 1989; Also articles and reports in professional journals and conference papers. *Memberships:* ASCE, Assoc Mem, 1983-87, Mem, 1987-, various posts; Am Geophys Union; Intl and Am Water Resources Assns; N.Am Coun on Geostats; Water Aid Intl: Treas, Bd of Dirs, 1987-89; Intl Geostats Assn. *Honours:* Tau Beta Pi; Chi Epsilon; Phi Beta Kappa; Sigma Chi; Watson Awd, Applied Scis Div, Harvard Univ, 1979-82; ASCE Task Com Excellence Awd, Hydraulics Div, 1991. *Hobbies:* History; Politics; Philosophy; Arts. *Address:* School of Civil Engineering, Georgia Institute of Technology, Atlanta GA 30332, USA.

ROULSTON John Frank Clement, b. 12 Aug 1941, Brisbane, Australia. Moderator, Queensland Synod; Director, Education and Communication Dept. m. Lynette Catherine Burgess, 4 Jan 1964, 1 s, 1 d. *Education:* BEd, Univ of Queensland, Aust, 1967; BLitt, 1972, MEd Admin, 1974, MLitt, 1988, Univ of New England, Aust; PhD, Univ of Idaho, USA, 1976. *Appointments:* Tchr, 1961-67, Eng Subj Master, 1968-69, Dpty Principal, 1969-71, Principal, 1972- 73, Dept of Educ; Principal, Cromwell Col, Univ of Queensland, 1973-75; Sr Lectr in Educ Admin, Brisbane Col of Adv Educ, 1977-78; Dir, Dept for Educ and Communication, 1984, Moderator, 1990-91, Uniting Ch in Australia, *Contributions to:* numerous articles to referenced journals and contributing Ed to, Ministry Magazine. *Memberships:* Queensland Inst for Educ Admin, (QIEA), Pres, 1980-86; Aust and C'wlth Couns for Educ Admin; Aust Col of Educ; Phi Delta Kappa; World Methodist Coun; Queensland Assn of Massage Therapists. *Honours:* Fellow, QIEA, 1986; Fellow, Aust Coun for Educ Admin, 1989; Nat Travel Scholar in Educ Admin, 1988. *Hobbies:* Public speaking; Writing; Acupuncture; Massage Therapy. *Address:* 44 Bulcock Avenue, Mt Nebo, Queensland 4520, Australia. 57.

ROUNDS Philard Leaon, b. 9 Jan 1928, Des Moines, Iowa, USA. Minister. m. Shirley Anne Newberg, 12 Sept 1946, 1 s. *Education:* East Hg Sch, 1946; Open Bible Col, 1950-57; BA, Florida S.Col, 1955; Grad Sch, Wheaton Col, 1961. Speaks fluent Japanese. *Appointments:* Pastor Open Bible Ch, Jefferson, IA, 1949-50; Missionary to Japan Open Bible Chs, Des Moines, 1950-87; Oral Roberts Univ, 1967-87; Presently, First Utd Meth Ch. *Publications:* Books: Yutakanaru Seikatsu; Seirei Ni Okeru Seikatsu. *Memberships:* Nat Planned Giving Inst, 1988; Nat Soc of Fund Raising Execs, 1988; Fl Acad of Scis, 1955-; Pi Gamma Mu, 1955-. *Hobbies:* Writing books and for other publications. *Address:* 6443 S. Sandusky Avenue, Tulsa, OK 74136, USA.

ROUSSAKI Peter E, b. 16 Oct 1946, Bridgeport, CT, USA. Clergyman. m. Phyllis Berkshire, 31 Oct 1970, 2 s. *Education:* BS 1968, MS 1973, S.Connecticut State Univ; MCM, 1973, S.Bapt Theol Sem; DMin, Austin Presb Theol Sem, 1986; STM, Boston Univ, 1991. *Appointments:* Adj Prof of Ch Music, Ashland Theol Sem, 1974-80; Assoc Pastor, First Utd Meth Ch, Shelby, OH, 1977-80; Asst Prof of Music, S.Western Univ, Georgtown, TX, 1980-86; Pastor and Music Dir, Community Ch, Atton, NH, 1989-. *Publications:* Hyms, O God of Hope; O Savior Lead Us; Conductor of major sacred choral works; Lectr in Hymnology; Articles: Using Analogical Imagination: Interpreting Another's Hymn, 1983; Foundations of Bretheren Hymnology, 1973. *Memberships:* Hymn Soc of US and Can; N.Am Acad of Liturgy. *Honours:* Guest Lectr in Ch Music, Asland

Theol Sem; Cum Laud Grad, Boston Univ, 1991. *Hobbies:* Collecting old hymnals and church music texts. *Address:* PO Box 338, Alton, NH 03809, USA.

ROUSSEAU Alain P, b. 10 Mar 1929, Paris, France. MD; Ophthalmologist; Professor. m. Madeleine Leduc, 29 Sept 1958, 2 d. *Education:* BA 1951, MD, 1956, Laval Univ; LMCC, 1956; Opthalmol Specialization, Havard Univ, 1958, Univ of Toronto, 1958-61; FRCS (C), 1963. *Appointments:* Asst Prof, 1966, Assoc Prof, 1968, Prof, 1975, Laval Univ; Hd of Dept, Hosp d'Enfant Jesus, 1963-70; Hd of Dept, Univ Hosp, 1970- 90. *Publications:* 32 Research publications and 101 communications on cancer of the eye and other diseases of the retina vitreous. *Memberships:* Club Jules Gonin; Retina Soc, Foun Mem, VP, 1987-89, Pres, 1989-; Can Sof of Ophthalmol, Coun and Pres, 1984-85; Am Acad of Ophthalmol; French Soc of Ophthalmol; Royal Col of Can; ARVO; Schepens Intl Soc. *Honours:* Order of Can. *Hobbies:* Alpine Skiing; Tennis; Horse riding; Cycling; Photography; Music. *Address:* 2790 Mont Royal, Ste Foy, Quebec, Canada G1W 2E2. 142.

ROUSSEV Ivan, b. 1 July 1954, Sofia, Bulgaria. Art Gallery Curator. m. Marijana Rousseva, 3 July 1977, 2 d. *Education:* Grad, Sculpture, Acad of Fine Arts, Sofia, 1979. *Appointments:* Tchr, Sch of Decorative Arts, 1979-84; Pres, Union of Young Bulgarian Artists, 1982-88; Curator, Art Gall, 1985-. *Publications:* Stone sculptures in galleries and private collections including: Peter Ludwig's Collection in Germany, Esslingen Collection in France and Spa Collection in S.Korea. *Memberships:* Bulgarian Artistic Union; Bulgarian Artistic Gp; Coun, Intl Foun, SS Cyril & Methodius. *Honours:* Prizes for sculpture: 4th Nat Exhib, Bulgaria, 1982; Gen Art Exhib, Sofia, 1983; Arterri Prize; Grand Prize for Open-air Sculpture, Varna, Bulgaria. *Hobbies:* Collecting works of art; Coins; stamps; Gardening; Culinary art; Windsurfing. *Address:* 37 Latinka Street, Sofia 1113, Bulgaria.

ROWAT Donald C, b. 1921, Somerset, Manitoba, Canada. m. 2 children. *Education:* BA Toronto, 1943; MA columbia, 1946; PhD, Columbia, 1950. *Appointments include:* Lectr, Polit Sci, N.Texas State Tchr's Col, 1947; Lectr, Dalhousie Univ, 1947-49; Lectr, Univ of Brit Columbia, 1949-50; Asst Prof, Polit Sci, Carleton Col, Ottawa, 1950-53; Assoc Prof, 1953-58; Acting Dir, Sch of Public Admin, Carleton Univ, 1957-58, Prof of Polit Sci, 1958-. Can Coun Sr Fellow in W.Europe, 1960-61; Chm, 1962-65, Supervisor, Grad Studies, 1965-66, Dept of Polit Sci; Exec Com, Can Assn of Univ Tchrs, 1965-67; Chm, Policy Com, Parliamentary Internship Prog, 1971-76; Coun and Exec Com, Soc Sci Res Coun of Can, 1974-78, VP, 1978-79, Chm, Com on the freedom of Communication of Social Scists, 1980-82; Appraisals Com, Ontario Coun Grad Studies, 1977-80, 1983-86. *Publications include:* The Ombudsman in Finland, 1973; The Provincial Political System, 1976; Political Corruption in Canada, 1976; Administrative Secrecy in Developed Countries; Intl Handbook on Local Government Reorganisation, 1980; Public Administration in Developed Democracies. Also edited 13 books of graduate student essays. *Memberships include:* Ed Bd, Internat Rev of Admin Scis, 1983-; Chm, Acad Adv Bd of Ombudsman Forum, Intl Bar Assn, 1984-.

ROWBOTHAM David Harold, b. 27 Aug 1924, Toowoomba, Queensland, Australia. Author and Journalist. m. Ethel Jessie Matthews, 14 Jan 1952, 2 d. *Education:* BA Univ Queensland, 1965; MA (QUAL), 1969. *Appointments:* Hon Vis Prof, Univ of California, Berkeley, 1972; Guest Lectr, Japan-Aust Cultural Ctr, Tokyo; Cultural Vis, Italy, 1976; Aust Del, World Cong of Poets, 1981; Cultural Vis, USA Lib of Congress, 1988; C'wlth Lit Fund Lectr in Aust Lit, 1956, 1961, 1964; nat Book Reviewing Panel, Aust Broadcasting Comm, 1954-563; Lit Ed, Brisbane Courier-Mail, 1980-87. *Publications:* Poems: Ploughman and Poet, 1954; Inland, 1956; All the Room, 1964; Hungalow and Hurricane,

1967; The makers of the Ark, 1970; The Pen of Feathers, 1971; Mighty Like a Harp, 1974; Selected Poems, 1975; Maydays, 1980; Novel: The Man in the Jungle, 1964; Stories: Town and City, 1956. *Memberships:* Pres, State Branch, Fellowship of Aust Writers, 1982; Fdg State VP, 1963-72, and Nat Councillor, 1963-, Aust Soc of Authors; Reserve Mem, Australian Jour Assn. *Honours include:* Pacific Star, WWII, 1945; Emeritus Fellow, Aust Lit, Aust Coun, 1989; Poetry awards: 2nd Prize, NSW Capt Cook Bi-Centenary Celebrations Lit Comp, 1970; Grace Elven Prize, 1964; 3rd Prize, Sydney Morning Herald Comp, 1949; Univ of Sydney Henry Lawson Prize, 1949; Univ of Queensland, Ford Meml Medal; Order of Aust, 1991. *Address:* 28 Percival Terrace, Holland Park, Brisbane, Queensland 4121, Australia.

ROWE Heather, b. 16 Oct 1957, Welwyn Garden City, England. Solicitor. *Education:* LLB, Manchester Univ. *Appointments:* Solicitor: Wilde Sapte, 1979-82; S J Berwin & CO, 1982-84; Durrant Piesse, 1984-88; Ptnr, Lovell White Durrant, 1988-. *Memberships:* Intl bar Assn; Law Soc; Chartered Inst of Arbitrators. *Honours:* Hons Law Soc Finals and John Mackrell Prize, 1979. *Hobbies:* Fishing; Reading; Birdwatching; Music. *Address:* 65 Holborn Viaduct, London EC1, England. 53.

ROWELL ALfred Gordon, b. 2 June 1913, Sydney, Australia. Retired Prosthodontist. m. Jeanne Rundle, 9 May 1942, 2 s, 1 d. *Education:* BDS Hons, 1934, MDS, 1947, Univ Sydney; DDS, N.Western Univ, USA, 1936; FRACDS, 1965; FDS, RCS, England, 1968; FACD, 1956; FICD, 1962; MICD, 1980; FADI, 1980; FPFA, 1975. *Appointments:* Tchg Staff, UDH and Univ Sydney, 1934-35; Pvt Practice, 1936-39; War Ser, AIF, 1939-47; P-time Sr Lectr in Pros Dent, Univ Sydney, 1988-; P-t Lectr, Post Grad Com in Dental Sci, Univ of Sydney, 1947-84; P-t Admin Duties, RAADC, 1960-81. *Publications:* Lectured in all states of the C'wealth and overseas; local and international journals. *Memberships:* Pres, NSW Branch, ADA, 1954-55; Fed Pres, 1960-62, VP, 1954-60; Pres, Aust Sec, Intl Col of Dents, 1971-78; Intl Pres, ICD, 1977-78; Pres, Asian Sec, Pierre Fauchard Acad, 1981-88; Life, Fed Dentaire Intl; Inaugural and First Pres, Royal Australasian Col of Dent Surgs, 1965-68. *Honours include:* Prof A J Arnott's Prize, 1934; N.Western Univ Scholarship, 1935-36; Fairfax Reading Meml Prize, 1966; Elmer S Best Meml Prize, 1985; Bronze Plaque Awd, PFA, 1990; Merit Awd, Alumni Soc, N.Western Univ, 1989; Ottofy Okamura Prize, 1991; OOA, 1978; CBE, 1970; ED, 1972. *Hobbies:* Travel; Photography; Swimming; Woodworking. *Address:* 120 Bellevue Road, Bellevue Hill, NSW 2023, Australia. 23, 149,

ROWLAND Jan R, b. 3 June 1944, Texas, USA. Consulting Inventor. m. G Hannelore, 28 Jan 1969. *Education:* PhD, Univ of Hard-Knocks, 1966-81. *Appointments:* Factory Mgr, VP of Berkshire Organ Co, MA, 1969-73; Co-Fdr, XVP of Visser-Rowland Asson Inc, Organbuilders, Houston, TX, 1973-81; Self-employed, 1981-. *Publications:* Several trivial advancements in the field of piep-organbuilding not individually important enough to note tbat are now 'industry standard'. Currently the 'infamous' maker of some small pipe-organ parts nation-wide (few to Europe, as well). *Memberships:* Charter, Am Inst of Organbuilders (AIO); Intl Soc of Organbuilders, (ISA) Am Ed of publication, Information, 1980-91. *Honours:* Master Organbuilder Exam, AIO, 1979; Co-hosted ISO Congress in Houston and Mexico, 1980; Hosted AIO Convention in Houston, 1976. *Hobbies:* Digital electronics; light machining (metalworking); Designing and building custom- machines for organbuilding-specific tasks. *Address:* 15310 Cypress Garden Drive, Houston, TX 77069, USA.

ROWLAND John, b. 17 Jan 1952, England. Barrister. m. Juliet Hathaway, 8 Dec 1979, 3 s. *Education:* BEcon, W Australia, 1983; MEcon, UCLA, 1974; LLB, London, 1978. *Appointments:* Barrister, 1980-; Lectr, Univ of W.Australia, 1974. *Memberships:* COMBAR; Middle

Temple. *Hobbies:* Cricket; Walking; Skiing; Wing. *Address:* 4 Pump Court, Temple, London EC4Y 7AN, England.

ROWLAND PAYNE Christopher Melville Edwin, b. 19 May 1955, Aldershot. Conslt Dermatologist; Landowner. *Education:* Clifton, 1965-72; St Bartholomews Hosp, London Univ, 1972-77. *Appointments:* House Surgeon, St Bartholomews Hosp, 1978; House Physician, Med Prof Unit Royal Infirmary, Edinburgh, 1978; Royal Marsden Hosp, 1979; Dermatological Reg, St Thomass Hosp, London, 1980-83; Westminster Hosp, 1983-89; Prof Univ Faculté de Medecine de Paris, 1985-86; Conslt Dermatologist, Kent & Canterbury Hosp, William Harvey Hosp, Thanet Hosp, Chaucer Hosp, St Saviours Hosp, Cromwell Hosp, 1990-; Clinical Prof of Dermatology, Ros Univ, NY, 1990-. *Publications include:* British Medical Journal; Journal Royal Soc Med. *Memberships:* British Assn Dermatologists; Soc Francaise de Dermatologie; Intl Soc for Dermatologic Surgery. *Honours include:* Roxburgh Prize; Dowling Club Prizes. *Hobbies:* Shooting; Cycling; Military History. *Address:* High Street, Elham, Nr Canterbury, Kent, England.

ROWLEY Frank Selby Jr, b. 2 Aug 1913, New York City, USA. Painter. m. Dorothy Folger, 30 June 1942. *Education:* Art Students League, NY, 1934; Nassau Inst of Art,- Hempstead, NY, 1934-38; Univ of Richmond, VA, 1952. *Appointments:* Designer, Illustrator, Greeting Card Industry, 1938-41; US Army, 1941-45; Designer, Muralist, 1946-49; Tchr, John Marhsall Hg Sch, Richmond, VA, 1949-57; Self-employed Portrait Painter, 1957-. *Creative works:* Lectr, Art Orgs, 1957-; Judge, Art Exhib, 1957; Ex Portraits Inc, NY, 1959-87; Represented in permanent collections in VA Mus of Fine Arts; Richmond Meml Hosp; VA Fed of Womens Clubs; Numerous private collections USA, England. *Memberships:* Lions Intl, 1957-87; Richmond Band Assn, Chm of Bd, 1977-; Fdr of Richmond Concert Band, 1970, Music Dir, Conductor, Richmond Pops Band, 1977-.*Honours:* Intl Pres Awd, Lions Intl, 1967-68. *Hobbies:* Musician; Volunteer Teacher, The Virginia Home. *Address:* Richmond, Virginia, USA. 7.

ROXBURGH Ian Walter, b. 31 Aug 1939, Sheffield, England. m. Diana Patricia Dunn, 20 Aug 1960, 2 s, 1 d. *Education:* BSc 1st class hons, Maths, Nottingham Univ, 1960; PhD, Cambs, 1962. *Appointments:* Asst Lectr, 1963-64, Lectr, 1964-66, Maths, King Col, London; Rdr, Astronomy, Univ of Sussex, 1966-67; Prof of Applied Maths, Queen Mary Col (QMC), London Univ, 1967-87; Prof of Math and Astronomy, Queen Mary & Westerfield Colls (QMC&W), Univ of London, 1987-; Hd Dept of Applied Maths, QMC, 1978-84; Hd, Sch of Math Sci, 1984-; Dir, Astronomy Unit, 1983-, QMC&W. *Publications:* 150 articles in professional journals and magazines. *Memberships:* Intl Astronomical Union, Pres Comm, 1949, 1982-85; FRAstroS; FIPhys; FRSA; Brit Soc Philos Sci; London Maths Soc; European Phys Soc. *Honours:* Kelvin Lectr, Brit Assn, 1968. *Hobbies:* Politics; Philosophy; Economics. *Address:* Astronomy University, School of Math Sciences, Queen Mary & Westfield Col, Mile End Rd, London E1 4NS, England.

ROXBURGH James William, b. 5 July 1921, Leeds, England. Assistant Bishop of Liverpool. m. Marjorie Winifred Hipkiss, 22 Jan 1949, 1 s, 1 d. *Education:* Whitgift Sch, Croydon, 1933-39; BA, 1942, MA, 1946, St Catharines Col, Cambs; Wycliffe Hall, Oxford, 1942-44. *Appointments:* Ordained Deacon, 1944, Priest, 1945, Bishop, 1983. Curate Christ Ch, and Holy Trinity, Folkeston, 1944-47; Handsworth, Birmingham, 1947-50; Vicar, St Matthew, Bootle, 1950-56, Drypool, Hull, 1956-65, Barking, 1965-77; Archdeacon of Barking, 1983-90; Ret'd Oct 1990; Asst Pisbop of Liverpool, Jan 1991-. *Memberships:* Rotary, Past Pres of Barking, 1976-77; C'wlth Trust. *Honours:* Hon Freeman of Barking and Dagenham, 1990. *Hobbies:* Philately;

Travel. *Address:* 53 Preston Rd, Southport, Merseyside PR9 9EE, England.

ROY James Henry Barstow, b. 17 July 1922, London, England. Retired Agricultural Scientist. m. Irene Ann Turner, 11 Aug 1956, 1 s, 2 d. *Education:* Sidney Sussex Col, Cambs, 1940-41, 1946-49, BA, MA, Dip Agric (Cantab), 1949; Univ of Reading: PhD, 1956, DSc, 1973, FIBiol, CBiol, 1984. *Appointments:* Royal Artillery Rgt, 1942, Capt, 1944, Adjutant, 1945-46; Nat Inst for Res in Diarying, 1949-85, Sci Ofr, 1949, Sr Principal Sci Ofr, 1985, Hd of Dept of Feeding and Metabolism. *Publications:* Author of over 140 publications, including over 100 articles in scientific journals and over 20 review articles, together with chapters in books, and contributions to encyclopaedias. *Memberships include:* Nutrition Soc; Ed Bd, Brit Jour Nutr, 1968-74; Brit Soc of Animal Prod, Ed Bd, 1980-86; Vet Res Club; Brit Cattle Vet Assn; Inst of Biol. *Honours:* C-in-C's Cert, BLA, 1946; Kellog Foun Fellowship, 1954-55; US and Can Res Awd in Animal Nutr, Assn of Eng Mfgs, 1959; Res Medal, Royal Agric Soc of England, 1971; Hon Fellow, Univ of Reading, 1985. *Hobbies:* Squash; Tennis; Henley Sailing Club, Gardening; Music (Woodley String Orch, Newbury Symph Orch, Pangbourne Col Choral Socs). *Address:* Bruncketts, The Street, Mortimer, Reading, Berks, RG7 3PE, England.

ROYLE Edward, b. 29 Mar 1944, Huddersfield, England. Reader in History. m. Jennifer du Plessis, 2 Aug 1968, 1 d. *Education:* King James Grammar Sch, Almondbury, 1955-62; BA, 1965, Christ's Col, Cambs, 1962-68; MA, PhD, Selwyn Col, 1968. *Appointments:* Fellow, Selwyn Col, Cambs, 1968-72; Lectr in Hist, Univ of York, 1972; Sr Lectr, 1982, Rdr, 1989. *Publications:* Victorian Infidels, 1974; Radicals, Secularists and Republicans, 1980. *Membership:* FRHS. *Hobbies:* Local Preacher, Methodist church. *Address:* Department of History, University of York, Heslington, York YO1 5DD, England.

ROZANOV Alexei Yu, b. 18 June 1936, Moscow, Russia. Stratigraphist and Paleontologist. m. Rozanova Natalia Ye, 23 Feb 1982, 1 s, 2 d. *Education:* Moscow Geol Prospecting Inst, 1958: PhD, 1966, Dr of Scis, 1971, Prof, 1983. *Appointments:* Sci worker, Geol Inst, USSR, AS, 1948-77; Dpty Dir, Hd of Lab of Ancient Skeletal Organisms, PIN, USSRAS, 1977-; Prof, Moscow State Univ, 1989-. *Publications:* Over 200 works papers and 20 monographs on Paleontology, Stratigraphy and Paleogeography, including: Tommotian Stage, 1969; Regularities of Morphological Evolution, 1973; Regular Archaeocyaths, 1990. *Memberships:* VP, VPO (USSR Paleontol Soc: V-Chm, USSR Stratigraphical Comm; Chm, Cambrian Subcomm of the Intl Comm on Stratigraphy, 1984-92. *Honour:* Prize, Moscow Soc of Naturalists, 1974. *Hobbies:* Literature on history and geography. *Address:* Profsoyuznaya 123, 117868 TCM-7, Moscow B321, Russia.

ROZENTALE Ira, b. 17 Apr 1959, Svitene, Latvia. Painter. *Education:* Svitene 8-Year Sch, 1966-74; Arts Deg, Riga Applied Arts Sch, 1974-79; Deg, Artist, Painter, Tchr, Dipl cum laude, Latvian Acad of Arts, 1981-88; Postgrad Student, USSR Acad of Arst, with Prof Boriss Berzins, 1990-. *Appointments:* Art Tchr, Ikskile Eight-Year Sch, 1979-81; Tutor, painting and Drawing, Riga Applied Arts Sch, 1986-91; Tutor, Painting, Latvian Acad of Arts, Riga, 1989. *Creative works:* More than 200 oil paintings, 1988-91; Selected collections with: The Latvian Art Foun, Mus of Art, Riga; USSR Acad of Arts, Moscow; Pvt Collections in Latvia, France, Belgium, Sweden, Germany, USA; Paintings: The Portrait of Father, 1989; Midsummer Night, 1989; Dedication to Exupery, 1989; Dedication to Rauschenberg, 1990; Portrait of Leonids Vigners, 1990; Game, 1990; Chinon, 1991; Nocturne of Paris, 1991; Composition. *Memberships:* Union of Latvian Artists. *Honours:* Gold Medal, USSR Min of Culture, 1989. *Hobbies:* Travelling and visiting arts and culture centres

of the workd. *Address:* Bauskas Rajons, Lielsvitene Grundini, Latvia, Russia.

RUAN Zhonghua, (Jean-Jacques Juin), b. 4 Jan 1946, Yangzhou, Jiangsu, China. Artist; Art Researcher. m. 26 Jan 1973, 1 d. *Education:* Univ study, Paris and Rennes, France, 1964-68; Postgrad, 1986-89, Master, Art (Art Hist), 1989, Peking Univ; Postgrad, 1987-89, Master Mod Art (Art Environment in Europe and China), 1989, Univ Paris III. *Appointments:* Transl, Interpreter (Amateur Artist), State Bur of Sea, China, 1979-86; Art Rsch, Ctrl Acad Applied Art, Peking, 1986-89; Rsch Dir, Acad Chinese Painter, Peking, 1989-. *Publications:* On the History of Development of Chinese Sigillary Art on Two Roads; Le Langage des Sceaux Chinois et ses Valeurs de Communication Esthetique, 1st article in a Western language systematically discussing Chinese sigillary art; Echo from Ancient Greece, Herald of Ancient Rome - On the historic status of the Etruscan art, 1st text on Etruscan art in China; Co-compiler: The History of World Art; Dictionary of Modern Art; Dictionary of World Famous Works; Li Keran on Art. *Memberships:* China Assn Fine Art; China Assn Calligraphers; Seals Inst, Xiling; China Assn Transls and Interpreters; Assn Sino-French Culture; China Assn Ex Libris. *Honours:* Prize, Calligraphy and Zhuanke (litterati seals) Contest, Peking, 1984; Prize, Peking Artists, Peking, 1985; Hiroyama Prize, Ctrl Acad Applied Art, Peking, 1989. *Hobbies:* Painting; Calligraphy; Seal-cutting; Swimming; Tourism; Chinese flute. *Address:* Academy of Chinese Painting, No 54 Xisanhuan Beilu, Beijing 100044, China.

RUBENS Robert David, b. 11 June 1943, Woking, Surrey, England. Professor of Clinical Oncology. m. Margaret Chamberlin, 30 Oct 1970, 2 d. *Education:* BSc Kings Col, 1964; MBBS, St George's Hosp, 1967; MRCP (UK), 1969; MD, Univ of London, 1974; FRCP, 1984. *Appointments:* Hse and Registrar posts 1968-72 at St George's, Brampton, Hammersmith and Royal Marsden Hosps; Res Fellow, Imperial Cancer Res Fund, 1972-74; Conslt PHys, Guy's Hosp, 1975-. *Publications:* Author and editor of books and papers on experimental and clinical cancer therapy and other medical subjects. *Memberships:* Brit and AM Assns for Cancer Res; Brit Breast Gp; Am Soc of CLin Oncol; Sociedad Brasileira De Mastologia; Brit Oncolog Assn; Assurance Med Soc, Coun; Soc of Apothecaries, Liveryman; Trollope Soc; European Soc of Mastology. *Hobbies:* Golf; Anthony Trollope. *Address:* Guys Hospital, London SE1 9RT. England. 52.

RUBINSTEIN Hilary Harold, b. 24 Apr 1926, London, England. Literary Agent. m. Helge Kitzinge, 6 Aug 1955, 3 s, 1 d. *Education:* Cheltenham Col, 1940-44; Merton Col, Oxford, 1948-50. *Appointments:* Ed Lectr Victor Gollancz, 1952-63; Special Features Ed, Observer, 1963-64; Dpty Ed, Observer Magazine, 1964-65; Ptnr, Dir, MD, AP Watt Ltd, Literary, 1965-. *Publications:* The Good Hotel Guide, published annually since 1978; The complete insomniac, 1974; Hotels & Inns, 1984. *Memberships:* Coun, Inst of Contemporary Arts; Treas, Open Col of the Arts. *Hobbies:* Finding new writers; Hotel watching. *Address:* 61 Clarendon Road, London W11 4JE, England. 1.

RUCHARDT Christoph Johannes, b. 10 Aug 1929, Munich, Germany. Professor of Chemistry. m. Kate Bartels, 2 Aug 1957, 1 s, 2 d. *Education:* Vordiplom, Chem, 1951, Diplomchemiker, 1955, Dr rer nat, 1956, Univ Munich, Habilitation, 1963; MSc, Univ GA, Athens, USA, 1952; Postdoct Fellow: Harvard Univ, 1957-58, CA Inst Technology, 1958-58, USA. *Appointments:* Asst, Akademischen Rat, Univ Munich, 1959-68; Full Prof, Univ Munster, Westphalia, 1968-72; Full Prof 1972-, Dean, Chem, 1976-77, Prorector, RScyh, 1977-81, Rector, 1987-91, Univ Freiburg. *Publications:* Over 200 publs or patents in sci lit. *Memberships:* Gesellschaft Deutscher Chemiker; Am Chem Soc; Selection Comm, Alexander v Humboldt Fndn; Ed Bd, New Jrnl Chem, 1976; Ed Bd, Angewandte Chemie; Chmn, Comm

Organic Chem, Deutsche Forschungsgemeinsschaft, 1975-84; Heidelberger Akademie; Deutsche Akademie der Naturforscher Leopoldina, Halle. *Honours:* Fellowship, Fonds der Chemischen Industrie, 1962; Adolf von Bayaer Commemorative Medal, Gesellschaft Deutscher Chemiker, 1983. *Address:* Institut fur Organishce Chemie und Biochemie der Albert-Ludwigs-Universitat, Albertstrasse 21, D. 7800 Freiburg, Germany.

RUDDER Kenneth Wayne, b. 16 Aug 1949, Texas, USA. Sr Production Technician. m. Anna L Aycock, 16 Aug 1974, 3 d. *Education:* Lee Jr Col, 1990; Currently at Univ of Houston, Clear Lake. *Appointments:* Plant Supervisor, ARCO Environmental Coor Texas Petrochem Co; Med Spt, USAF Vietnam. *Publications:* Critique of The Thirteenth Valley, 1989. *Memberships:* Nat Rifle Assn, Life; Pres and Fdr, Eagles Underground, 1985. *Hobbies:* Camping; Fishing; Hunting; Gardening; Hiking; Environmental awareness. *Address:* PO Box 693, Baytown, TX 77527, USA.

RUDIN Stephen G, b. 29 July 1938, Boston, MA, USA. Psychologist. m. Marsha H Goldman, 16 Oct 1986, 2 s, 1 d. *Education:* AB, Brandeis Univ, 1960; EdM, N.Eastern Univ, 1962; EdD, Univ of Illinois, 1971. *Appointments:* Dir, Behavioural Med Assocs, specialising in stress, pain and headache management; Vis Prof, Bridgewater State Col; Master Lectr, Boston Univ, 1991-. *Publication:* Bioinstrumentation, 1971. *Memberships:* Am Psycho Assn; Fellow, Am Orthopsychi Assn; Fellow, Mass Pshcyo Assn; Am Soc of Clin Hypnosis. *Honours:* Diplomate, Fellow, Am Bd of Med Psychos. *Hobbies:* Amateur Radio; Music. *Address:* Behavioural Medical Assocs, 312 Bedford St, Whitman Medical Centre, Whitman MA 02382, USA. 6.

RUDKIN James David, b. 29 June 1936, England. Dramatist; Screenwriter. m. Alexandra M Thompson, 3 May 1967. 2 s, 2 d. *Education:* King Edwards Sch, Birmingham, 1947-55; MA, St Catherines, Oxford, 1957-61. *Appointments:* Schoolmaster, Bromgrove County Hg Sch, Worcs, 1961-64; Freelance Author, 1964-. *Creative works:* Stage plays: Afore Night Come, 1960; The Sons of Light, 1965, revised, 1975; Ashes, 1972; the Triumph of Death, 1976; The Saxon Shore, 1983; Radio play: Cries from Casement as His Bones are Brought to Dublin, 1972; White Lady, 1985; Screenplays inc: Testimony, 1985; December Bride, 1988. *Honours:* Evening Standard most promising Dramatist Awd, 1962; John Whiting Awd for contribution to Brit Theatre, 1974; Broadway Awd for Stage Play, Ashes, New York, 1977; NY Film Festival Gold Medal for Screen Play Testimony, 1987; European Film Festival Special Jury Awd for film, December Bride,1990. *Hobbies:* Languages; Anthropology; Piano; Bridge. *Address:* c/o M Ramsay Ltd, 14a Goodwins Ct, St Martins Lane, London WC2N 4LL, England. 52.

RUDNIK Stefan, b. 15 Oct 1935, Grudziadz, Poland. Scholar of Pedagogical University. m. 18 Aug 1962, 2 s. *Education:* Master's degree, Hist, Warsaw Univ, 1962; Dr Pol Sci, Poznan Univ, 1973; Dr habil, Acad Social Scis, 1984. *Appointments:* Tchr, Elem School, 1953-56; Army serv, 1956-58; Tchr, HS, Kwidzyn, 1962-70; Pedagogical Univ, Slupsk, 1973-91; Szczecin Univ, 1986-89. *Publications:* Stosunki polsko-wloskie w I 1945-1975, 1979; Badania nad pokojem w Fep Red Niemiec, 1984; Ruchy pokojowe w Rep Fed Niemiec, 1990. *Memberships:* Polish Soc Pol Sci; Instytut Zachodni, Poznan; Assn Polish Authors. *Hobbies:* Gardening; Touring; Reading. *Address:* ul Herbsta 10 m 13, 76-200 Slupsk, Poland.

RUDOWSKI Witold J, b. 17 Aug 1918, Piotrkow, Poland. Emeritus Professor of Surgery. m. 2 s, 1 d. *Education:* Entered Med School, 1936, MD, 1947, Univ Warsaw; MB, Clandestine Med School, Warsaw, 1943; Postgrad trng, Hammersmith Hosp, London, England,

1956-57. *Apointments:* Asst and Assoc to Prof, Dept Surg, Warsaw Univ Med School, 1945-54; Cons Surg, Rsch Worker, Mme Curie Cancer Inst, 1947-64; Dir, Dept Surg Hd, Inst Haematology and Blood Transfusion, Warsaw, 1964-88; Mbr, Polish Acad Scis, 1973-; Cons, Inst Biocybernetics and Biomed Engrng. *Memberships:* Hon Fellow: Am Coll Surgs; Colls Surgs, Edinburgh, England, Can, Australia, Ireland, S Africa; Corres Mbr, Swedish, Dutch, Swiss, German Assns Surgs; Hon Mbr, Italian, Czechoslovak, Hungarian, Polish Assns Surgs. *Honours:* State Award Class II, Sci, Poland, 1972, 1978; Hon MD, Med Schools: Poznan, 1975, Warsaw, 1978, Lodz, 1979, Wroclaw, 1980, Cracow, 1989, Bialystok, 1990; Hon MD, Univ Edinburgh, 1983; Prize, Int Surg Soc, Toronto, 1989. *Hobbies:* Classical music; Literature; Photography. *Address:* Aleja Armii Ludowej 17-1, 00-832 Warsaw, Poland. 34, 139, 152.

RUDOWSKI Witold Janusz, b. 17 Aug 1918, Piotrkow, Poland. Emeritus Professor of Surgery; Consultant. widower, 2 s, 1 d. *Education:* Med Fac, 1936-39, MB, Clandestine Med School, 1943, MD, 1947, 1947, Univ Warsaw; Postgrad Med School, Univ London, 1956-57. *Appointments:* Med Off, Home Army, Poland, 1940-44; Asst, Dept Surg, Clandestine Med School, Warsaw Univ, 1943-44; Assoc Prof, Dept Surg, Warsaw Med School, 1945-54; Cons Surg, Mme Curie Cancer Inst, Warsaw, 1948-64; Dir, Hd, 1964-88, Emeritus Prof, 1988-, Dept Surg, Warsaw Med School, 1988-; Currently Cons, Inst Biomed Engrng, Warsaw. *Publications:* Books: Burn Therapy and Research, 1976; Disorders of Hemostasis in Surgery, 1977; Surgery of the Spleen, 1987; Over 500 papers in Polish and int jrnls. *Honours:* Hon MD, Med Schools: Univs Poznan, 1975, Warsaw, 1978, Lodz, 1979, Wroclaw, 1982, Cracow, 1989, Bialystok, 1990; Hon MD, Univ Edinburgh, 1983; Hon Fellowship, Colls Surgs: Am, 1971, Edinburgh, 1972, England, 1973, W Africa, 1975, Irish, 1978, Italian; Hon Fellowship: N Pacific Coll Surgs, 1974, Indian Surg Soc, 1976, Royal Australian Coll Surgs, 1979. *Hobbies:* Classical music; Photography; Literature. *Address:* Aleja Armii Ludowej 17-1, 00-632 Warsaw, Poland. 43, 52, 139.

RUETHER Rosemary Radford, b. 2 Nov 1936, St Paul, Minnesota, USA. Professor of Applied Theology. m. Herman J Ruether, 1 s, 2 d. *Education:* BA, Relig, Philos, 1960, PhD, Classics, Patristics, 1965, Claremont Grad School. *Appointments:* Lectr, var instns; Assoc Prof, Histl Theology, Howard Univ School Relig, 1966-76; Georgia Harkness Prof, Applied Theology, Garrett- Evangelical Theological Sem, and Grad Fac, NWn Univ, Evanston, IL, 1976-; Columnist, Nat Cath Reporter; Contributing Ed: Christianity and Crisis; The Ecumenist; The Journal of Religion and Intellectual Life; Theology Today; Women of Power; Sojourners. *Publications:* Author or co-author, 23 books incl: The Church Against Itself, 1976; The Radical Kingdom: The Western Experience of Messianic Hope, 1970, Spanish Ed, 1971; Faith and Fratricide: The Image of the Jews in Early Christianity, 1964, German Transl, 1978; Women and Religion in America: The 19th Century, A Documentary History (w Rosemary Keller), 1981; Disputed Questions: On Being a Christian, 1982, New Ed, 1989; Contemporary Roman Catholicism: Crisis and Challenges, 1987; Beyond Occupation: American Jewish, Christian and Palestinian Voices of Peace (w Marc Ellic), 1990; Abt 400 articles, 1963-90. *Memberships:* Bd Mbr: Chgo Clergy and Laity Concerned; Mary's Pence; Caths for Free Choice; Palestine Human Rights Campaign; Dem Socialists Am; Ctr Oecumenique de Liaisons Int; Grail Inst Feminism and Relig. *Honours:* Hon DHL: Denison Coll, Granville, OH, Emmanuel Coll, Boston, 1982; Wittenberg Univ, Springfield, OH, Xavier Univ, Chgo, Hamilton Coll, Clinton, NY, 1983; St Olaf's Coll, Northfield, MN, Walsh Coll, Canton, OH, 1984; DePauw Univ, 1986. *Hobbies:* Art; Philosophy. *Address:* Garrett-Evangelical Theological Seminary, 2121 Sheridan Road, Evanston, IL 60201, USA.

RUGGLES Charles Mervyn, b. 25 June 1912, London, England. Consultant; Fine Art Conservator and Restorer.

m. Winnifred M Hughes, 4 Nov 1943, 1 s, 2 d. *Education:* BSc, Univ Ottawa, Can. *Appointments:* Restorer, Conservator, Sci Authentication of Fine Art Works: Internship, Art Restoration, Nat Gall Can, 1938-42; Chief Sci Rsch Conservator, 1960-70; Chief, Restoration and Conserv Lab, Nat Gall Can; Prof, School Grad Studies, Queen's Univ, Kingston, 1977-80; Bilingual Cons, Montreal Mus Fine Arts, 1980- 84; Cons, Lectr, Nat Lab Conserv, Lucknow, India, 1981. *Publications:* Num articles relating to art restoration and conserv incl: A Resurrected Portrait and its Case History; The Care of Prints and Drawings; A Reynolds Revived; The Interpretation of Double Paintings; A History of Art Conservation in Canada: Developments to the Early 1970's; Practical Application of Deacidification Treatment of Works of Art on Paper; An Exercise in Authentication; Stereomicrography Using the Binocular Microscope; An Art Fraud Case. *Memberships:* Fellow, Int Inst Conserv, London; Fellow, Am Inst Conserv, Wash DC; Fndr, 1st Chmn, Can Assn Profl Art Conservators, Ottawa; 1st Hon Mbr and Councillor, Inst Conserv Can Grp. *Honours:* Mbr, Order Can, 1978; Queen's Silver Jubilee Medal. *Hobbies:* Pilot and aircraft owner, flying light aircraft, Mbr, Can Owners and Pilots Assn and Ottawa Flying Club; Swimming. *Address:* 15 Letchworth Road, Ottawa, Ontario, Canada K1S 0J3. 142.

RUMINS John Sandford, b. 16 Dec 1934, Isleworth, Middlesex, England. Chartered Accountant. m. (Margaret) Ruth Clarke, 13 Sept 1960, 1 s, 2 d. *Education:* BA, Univ Bristol, 1956; FCA, 1959. *Appointments:* Served RAF, 1959-62: Pilot Off, 1959-61; Flying Off, 1961-62; Chartered Acct: Qualified w Tansley Witt, 1959; Cooper Brothers & Co, 1962-72; Bank of England, London, 1972-, incl currently Hd, Fin and Resource Planning Div. *Hobby:* Tennis. *Address:* 3 Lyle Park, Sevenoaks, Kent TN13 3JX, England.

RUNGTA Ajay Kumar, b. 27 May 1939, India. Director of Companies. *Education:* LLB, MCom, Calcutta Univ; Assoc, Brit Trng Inst, London; Dip, Bus Mgmt; Special Dip, Pub Speaking. *Appointments include:* Dir: Hind Wire Inds Ltd; Zenith Alloys and Steels Ltd; Pearl Inds Ltd; Jayshree Chems Ltd; Orient Steel and Inds Ltd; W Bengal Time Ltd; Aaekay Investment Ctr Ltd; Bharat Rubber Regenerating Co Ltd; Zenith Fibres Ltd; Sunrise Products Ltd. *Memberships include:* Comm Mbr, Past Pres, All India Org Employers; Past Pres: Bharat Chmbr of Comm, Calcutta; Fedn Indian Mineral Inds; Steel Wire Mfrs Assn India; Chmn, Ind Standing Comm, FICCI; Comm Mbr, Fedn Indian Chmbrs of Comm and Ind; Indian Nat Comm, Int Chmbr of Comm; Indian Nat Comm, World Energy Conf; W Bengal Bus Conven; Former Comm Mbr, Assn Indian Engrng Ind; Hon Mbr, Int Panel Arbiters, Am Arbitration Assn; Hon Mbr, Indian Steering Comm, Int Exposition Rural Dev; Advsry Coun Trade, Mineral Ores Export Advsry Comm, Consultative Comm Iron Ore, Consultative Comm Manganese Ore, Min Commerce; Nat Railway Users Consultative Coun, Min Railways; Steel Consumers Coun, Min Advsry Bd, Min Mines and Steel; Rd Transp Advsry Comm, Min Shipping and Transp; Calcutta Telephones Advsry Comm, Min Communication; Ctrl Coun Hlth and Family Welfare, Min Hlth and Family Welfare; Sports Auth India; Tustee, Calcutta Improvement Trust; Gov, Indian Inst Social Welfare and Bus Mgmt; Dir, W Bengal Indl Infrastructure Dev Corp; Calcutta Electric Supply Consultative Comm; Indl Liaison Bd; State Tourism Dev Bd; State Employment Advsry Comm; State Labour Advsry Bd; Calcutta Art Soc; Pres, Vividh Kala Vihar; VP, Marwari Relief Soc; Comm Mbr, Light, House for Blind; Past Dir, Rotary Club, Calcutta: Kiwanis Club, Calcutta; Past Vice Chmn, Indian Red Cross Soc, W Bengal. *Address:* 1/A Gurusaday Road, Calcutta 700019, India.

RUNKEL Claus Dieter, b. 28 Mar 1958, Bonn, Federal Republic of Germany. *Education:* Christie's Fine Arts Course, London, 1980-81. *Appointments:* Hd, Dept Art Books and Graphics, Gustav Weiland Inc, Lubeck, 1980; Freelance Art Cons and Curator, 1981-86; Claus Runkel Fine Art, 1986-88, 1992; Runkel-Hue-Williams Ltd,

London, 1988-1991. *Publication:* Will Maclean - Sculptures and Wood Constructions, 1987. *Membership:* Patrons New Art, Tate Gall. *Hobbies:* Opera; Modern litarature in 1st editions; Travel. *Address:* 97 Cambridge Street, London SW1, England.

RUPE Meredith, b. 31 Aug 1941, Noblesville, Indiana, USA. Campus Minister; Adjunct Professor. m. Pauline Esther Wirt, 16 Mar 1963, 2 s, 1 d. *Education:* BS, Ball State Univ, 1963; MDiv, Drew Univ, 1966; Univ Notre Dame Grad School, 1968-71; DMin, McCormick Theological Sem, 1973. *Appointments:* Pastor, Hillcrest United Meth Ch, Elkhart, IN, 1966-68; Pastor, Keeler/Silver Creek United Meth Parish, 1968-70; Pastor, Three Oaks United Meth Ch, Three Oaks, MI, 1970-75; Sr Chaplain, Marquette Br Prison, Marquette, MI, 1975-79; Campus Min, Wesley Fndn, 1979-, Adj Prof, 1979-, Ferris State Univ, Big Rapids, MI. *Memberships:* Int Transactional Analysis Assn; Relig Rsch Assn; Soc Sci Study Relig; Nat Campus Mins Assn; PSR. *Honours:* Fndrs Award, Big Rapids Intermediate School Advocates. *Hobbies:* Drama; Indianapolis 500; Gardening. *Address:* 628 S Warren Ave, Big Rapids, MI 49307, USA. 117, 145.

RUSANOV Anatoly Ivanovich, b. 20 Apr 1932, St Petersburg, Russia. Scientist. m. Vera Chekh, 14 July 1963, 1 s, 1 d. *Education:* Phys and Chem Facs, St Petersburg State Univ, 1949-55; PhD, 1958; DSc, 1963; Prof, Phjys Chem, 1966. *Appointments:* Jr Rsch Worker, 1955-61, Sr Rsch Worker, 1961-67, Lab Hd, 1967-87, Hd, Dept Colloid Chem, 1987-, St Petersburg State Univ. *Publications:* Thermodynamics of Surface Phenomena, 1960; Phasengleichgewichte und Grenzflachenerscheinungen, 1978; Surface Separation of Substances, 1980; Micellization in Surfactant Solutions, 1992. *Memberships:* Hd, St Petersburg Div, Mendeleev Chem Soc; Int Assn Colloid and Interface Scientists. *Honours:* USSR State Prize, 1981; Corres Mbr, USSR Acad Scis, 1990; Academician, Russian Acad Scis, 1991. *Hobbies:* Philately in chemistry. *Address:* Mendeleev Center, St Petersburg 199034, Russia.

RUSH Michael David, b. 29 Oct 1937, Kingston-upon-Thames, England. University Lecturer. m. Jean Margaret Telford, 25 July 1964, 2 s. *Education:* Univ Sheffield, 1959-64; BS (Hons), Mod Hist, Govt, 1962; PhD, Pol, 1966. *Appointments:* Lectr, Pol, 1964-81, Sr Lect, 1981-90, Reader, Parly Govt, 1990-, Univ Exeter; Vis Lectr, Univ Wn Ont, Can, 1967-68; Rsch Fellow, Carleton Univ, Ottawa, 1975 & 1992; Vis Prof, Acadia Univ, Nova Scotia, 1980. *Publications:* The Selection of Parliamentary Candidates, 1969; Parliament and the Public, 1976, 2nd Ed, 1986; Parliamentary Government in Britain, 1981; The Cabinet and Policy Formation, 1984; Politics and Society, 1992; Co-author: The MP and His Information, 1970; An Introduction of Political Sociology, 1971; Ed or co- ed: The House of Commons: Services and Facilities, 1974; The House of Commons: Services and Facilities, 1972-82, 1984; Parliament and Pressure Politics, 1990; Num articles on Brit and Can pol. *Memberships:* Pol Studies Assn; Former Acad Sec and Chmn, Study Parliament Grp; Can Study Parliament Grp. *Honours:* Gilbert Campion Award for PhD thesis, 1965-66; FRSA, 1992. *Hobbies:* Classical music; Theatre; Travel. *Address:* Department of Politics, University of Exeter, Exeter, Devon EX4 4RJ, England.

RUSHMAN Geoffrey Boswall, b. 20 Aug 1939, Northampton, England. Consultant Anaesthetist. m. Gillian Mary Rogers, 12 Oct 1963, 3 d. *Education:* St Bartholomew's Hosp, 1957-62. *Appointments:* Jr Lectr, Physiology, 1965-67, Anaesthetist, 1969-73, St Bartholomew's Hosp, London; Cons Anaesthetist, Southend Hospital, Southend-on-Sea, 1974-; Examiner, Royal Coll Anaesthetists. *Publications:* Synopsis of Anaesthesia, 8th, 9th, 10th, 11th eds w Spanish, Polish, Greek, Italian German Transls. *Memberships:* Royal Soc Med, Sect Anaesthetics, Coun Mbr, Hon Sec; Brit Med Assn; Fellow, Royal Coll Anaesthetists; Assn

Anaesthestists, Linkman; Intensive Care Soc. *Honours:* Hichens Prize, St Bartholomew's Hosp, 1962; Police Award for Bravery, 1969; Prize for Contbns to Anaesthesia, Assn Anaesthetists, 1971. *Hobbies:* Skiing; Mountaineering; Lay readership. *Address:* Dept of Anaesthesia, Southend Hospital, Prittlewell Chase, Southend-on- Sea, Essex SSO ORY, England.

RUSHTON David Nigel, b. 21 Dec 1944, London, England. Neurologist. m. 30 Mar 1968, 1 s, 2 d. *Education:* BA (Cantab), Class I, 1966; MB BChir (Cantab); MRCP (UK); MD (Cantab), 1978; FRCP, 1989. *Appointments:* Sci Staff, Med Rsch Coun Neurological Prosthesis Unit, 1970-; Neurologist, King's Coll and Maudsley Hosps, 1970-. *Publications:* Sci papers and book chapts on neurology, neurological prostheses, neurophysiology and psychophy. *Memberships:* Assn Brit Neurologists; Shoreham Soc; Nat Traction Engine Club. *Honours:* Open Maj Scholarship, 1963, Sr Scholarship, 1966, Trinity Coll, Cambridge; Ralph Noble Prize, Cambridge, 1978. *Hobbies:* Repairing, restoring and running steam road vehicles; Repairing and restoring a mediaeval timber-Frame hall house. *Address:* Holly Place, High Street, Shoreham, Kent TN14 7TD, England.

RUSSELL Carol Ann, b. 14 Dec 1943, Detroit, Michigan, USA. Personnel Service Owner. m. Victor Rojas, div. *Education:* Hunter Coll, 1961-64; Univ Phoenix, AZ, 1991-. *Appointments:* Var Personnel Servs, 1964-74; Wollborg-Michelson, 1974-82; Pres, Russell Personnel Servs Inc, CA, 1983-; Media Guest; Speaker and Workship Ltd. *Contributions to:* profl publs. *Memberships:* No CA Human Resource Assn, Comm Chair; Bay Area Personnel Assn Chapt, Int Assn Personnel Women, Past Pres; Golden Gate Chapt, CA Assn Personnel Consultants, Pres 1984-85; Int Platform Assn. *Honours:* Named to Inc 500 list of Am's Fastest-Growing Pvte Cos, 1989, 1990. *Hobbies:* Reading; Biblical commentary collector. *Address:* Russell Personnel Services Inc, California, USA. 5, 52, 132.

RUSSELL Helen Durham, b. 21 Oct 1931, Chapel Hill, North Carolina, USA. Pastor; Director. m. George Lewis Russell Sr, 31 Dec 1950, 1 s, 1 d. *Education:* A&T State Univ; Baltimore School of Bible, 1969; Nat Inst Practical Nursing; Francis Scott Key Med Ctr. *Appointments:* Nurse, 1956-; Pastor, Fndr, Baltimore St Ch of God, Baltimore, MD, 1973- 91; Fndr Ellicott City Ch of God, 1989-. *Publications:* The Cutting Edge of Racism, manuscript; Poetry books: Voices on the Wind, 1989; Fireside Meanderings, 1989; Poems: Little Sparrow; Lean on Jesus. *Memberships:* Bd Dirs, Nat Assn W Middlesex, PA, Sec 1981-90; Sec, Exec Coun Bus Comm, Anderson, IN. *Honours:* 1st Black Woman Pastor's to open Prayer to US Congress, 1984; Citations, Mayor of Baltimore, 1985-86; Afro-American Awards, mid-1980s; Prison Min Awards. *Hobbies:* Travel; Dining out; Piano; Assisting the less fortunate and helping those who cannot help themselves. *Address:* 2 South Mt Olivet Lane, PO Box 3045, Baltimore, MD 21229, USA.

RUSSELL Oris Stanley, b. 26 Apr 1922, Nassau, Bahamas. Government Official; Agricultural Consultant. m. (1) Dorothea Elodie Malone, Dec 1963, dec. May 1976, (2) m. Gloria Rowena Claridge, 13 May 1978. *Education:* BAgric w high hons, 1950, MAgric, 1951, Univ FL, USA. *Appointments:* Clerk, 1940-44, Chief Clerk, 1944-47, Colonial Sec Off, Nassau; Sr Agricl Off, Bd Agric and Fisheries, Nassau, 1951-54; Dir. Agric and Fisheries Dept. Agric and Fisheries, Nassau, 1954-65; Permanent Sec: Min Agric and Fisheries, Nassau, 1965-73, Min External Affairs, 1973-83; Mbr. C'wlth Sci Coun, England, 1973-83; Bahamas Deleg to UN, 1973-83. *Publications:* A Preliminary Report on the Flora of the Exuma Cays, 1959; Those Min-named Pine-Barrens, Bahamas Handbook, 1980; Articles in profl jrnls. *Memberships:* Hon Rep, Royal C'wlth Soc, Bahamas; Bahamas Nat Trust, Nassau, Pres 1966- 67, 1972-73; Coun Mbr, Coll of Bahamas, Nassau, 1975-

76; Chmn, Advsry Coun Pub Records, Nassau; Police Serv Commn; Int Soc Hort Sci; AAAS; NY Acad Scis; Am Soc Econ Bot; Rotary Club; St Andrew Soc; FRGS. *Honours:* OBE, 1971; Silver Jubilee Medal, London, 1977; Companion, Order of St Michael and St George, London, 1983. *Hobbies:* Gardening; Yachting: Mbr Royal Nassau Sailing Club and Nassau Yacht Club. *Address:* PO Box N-561, 21 Woodland Road, Nassau, Bahamas. 52, 109, 149.

RUSSELL Peggy Sue, b 19 Oct 1969, Richmond, Virginia, USA. College Student, Accounting. m. Paul Ray Deel, 9 Sept 1989. *Education:* AA and S, summa cum laude, Bus Admin, Danville Community Coll, 1989; Acctng studies, Averett Coll, in progress. *Membership:* Phi Theta Kappa. *Honours:* Who's Who Among Am HS Students, 1985-86, 1986-87; Valedictorian, HS Graduation, Southall Christian School, 1987; Nat Dean's List, 1987-88; Who's Who Among Students in Am Jr Colls, 1988-89. *Hobbies:* Playing the piano; Writing short stories; Volleyball; Basketball. *Address:* 753 Arlington Road, Danville, VA 24541, USA.

RUTTER Allen Edward Henry (Claude), b. 24 Dec 1928, Bromley, Kent, England. Clerk in Holy Orders. m. Elizabeth Jane Leonard, 26 Apr 1960, 2 s, 2 d. *Education:* Queens' Coll, Cambridge, 1949-53; MA, DipAgric (Cantab); St John's Coll, Durham; DipTh (Dun). *Appointments:* Sci Liaison Off, E Malling Rsch Station, Kent, 1953-56; Curate: Bath Abbey, 1959- 60, E Dereham, Norfolk, 1960-64; Rector, Cawston Grp and Chaplain, Cawston Coll, Norfolk, 1964-69; Rector, Gingindhlovu, Zululand, 1969-73; Rector, Queen Thorne, Dorset, 1973-; Rural Dean, Sherborne, Dorset, 1976-; Chmn, 1984-, Rural Link Off, 1987-, Lay Educ Comm; Canon, Prebendary, Salisbury Cathedral, 1986-; Advsr, Archbishops' Commn on Rural Areas, 1989-. *Creative works:* Sports career: Played cricket for Cambridge Univ, 1953, Wilts Co Cricket Club, 1948-55, Norfolk Co Cricket Club, 1961-65; Hockey for Cambridge Univ Wanderers and Maidstone; Clergy Golf Champion, 1977. *Memberships:* Hawks Club, Cambridge; Marylebone Cricket Club. *Hobbies:* Cricket; Hockey; Golf; Farming; Gardening; Picture framing. *Address:* Trent Rectory, Sherborne, Dorset DT9 4SL, England.

RUTTER Michael Llewellyn, Sir, b. 15 Aug 1933, England. Professor of Child Psychiatry. *Education:* MRCS (Eng), LRCP (London), 1955; MB, ChB, distinction Pharmacology and Therapeutics, 1955, MD Hons, 1963, Birmingham; MRCP (London), 1958; Acad DPM, distinction, London, 1961; FRCPsych, 1971; FRCP, 1972. *Appointments include:* Registrar, Sr Registrar, 1958-61, Mbr, Sci Staff, Med Rsch Coun Social Psych Rsch Unit, 1962-65, Maudsley Hosp, London, 1958-61; Nuffield Med Travelling Fellow, Paediatrics, Albert Einstein Coll Med, NYC, 1961-62; Belding Travelling Scholar, Assn for Aid of Crippled Children, 1963; Hon Cons Psych, Jt Bethlem and Maudsley Hosps, London, 1963-; Sr Lectr, Reader, 1965-73, Prof, Child Psych, 1973-, Inst Psych, Univ London; Hon Cons Psych, Soc School Autistic Children, London, to 1980; Hon Dir, Med Rsch Coun Unit Child Psych, 1984-; Var vis positions incl: Vis Prof, Princess Margaret Hosp Childrn, Perth, Wn Australia and Royal Alexandra Hosp Children, Sydney, NSW, 1983; Culpepper Vis Prof, Boston City Hosp, Boston Univ School Med, MA, USA, 1985; Roerig Vis Prof, Psych, Univ SC, USA, 1990. *Publications:* Diagnosis and Prognosis in Autism, film, 1970; Author or co-author, 12 books incl: Children of Sick Parents: An Environmental and Psychiatric Study, 1966; Changing Youth in a Changing Society, 1980; A Measure of Our Values: Goals and Dilemmas in the Upbringing of Children, 1983; Treatment of Autistic Children, 1987; Ed or co-ed, 17 books. *Memberships:* Num comms and ed bds; Coun, Policy Studies Inst; Ctrl Acad Coun, Brit Postgrad Med Fedn; Trustee Grp, Autistic Care and Trng Dev Trust; Coun, Med RSch Coun; VP, Young Minds; Corres Mbr, Germany Soc Child and Adolescent Psych; Temporary Advsr, WHO; Hon Mbr: Am Acad Child Psych, 1981; Royal Soc Med, Sect Psych,

1983; Am Psychopathological Assn, 1984; Finnish Soc Child Psych, 1986; Am Coll Psychs, 1991; Hon Fellow: Brit Psychological Soc, 1978; Am Acad Pediatrics, 1981. *Honours include:* CBE, 1985; FRS, 1987; Kt, 1992; 5 hon docts. *Address:* Institute of Psychiatry, De Crespigny Park, Denmark Hill, London SE5 8AF, England.

RVACHEV Michael, b. 24 Sept 1948, Lvov, USSR. High School Teacher, Mathematical Mechanics. m. Bubusara Nosinova, 10 Jan 1970, 3 s. *Education:* Moscow State Univ, 1966-74; DSc, 1975; DSc, 1991. *Appointments:* Scientist, Kirghiz Academy, 1975-79; Tchr, Vinnitza Polytech Inst, 1979-; Full Prof, Vinnitza Polytech Inst. *Publications:* Over 50 articles incl: Solutions of S Ulam's problem on a cut motion and G Mounge's problem on mass motion; Computer modelling of influenza epidemics; Construction of possible variations for Castiliano's functional; Methods of visioplasticity. *Hobbies:* Reading; Gardening; Hunting. *Address:* Polytechnical Institute, Ukraine, Vinnitza.

RYABUKHIN Alexander Sergeevich, b. 8 Nov 1955, Khabarovsk, Russia. Entomologist. m. Marina Vladimirovna Ryabukhina, 28 Aug 1982, 1 d. *Education:* Far East State Univ, Vladivostock, 1972-77; Dip Zoology. *Appointments:* Engr-Geobotan, Dalgiprozem Rsch Inst, Khabarovsk, 1977- 80; Rsch Fellow, Inst Biological Problems of the North, Russian Acad Scis, Magadan, 1981-; Army Serv, 1982-84. *Publications:* 15 sci publs in entomology (Beetles: Order Coleoptera, families Styphylinidae, Micropeplidae, Silphidae. *Membership:* Entomological Soc, USSR. *Hobbies:* Gardening; Aquarium fishes; Reading; Music. *Address:* Koltsevaya Str 50-32, Magadan 685027, Russia.

RYAN David Stuart, b. 22 Oct 1943, Kingston-upon-Thames, England. Advertiser; Publisher. m. Jacqueline Wills, 16 June 1971, 1 d. *Education:* BA, Ancient Hist, King's Coll, London, 1964. *Appointments:* Ogilvy and Mather, 1965-70; Grant's Overseas, 1971-74; Benton and Bowles, 1976-78; Time-Life, 1979-86; KDM, 1987- *Publications:* The Affair is All, 1976; John Lennon's Secret, 1982; Looking for Kathmandu, 1982; India. A Guide to the Experience, 1983; America. A Guide to the Experience, 1986; The Lost Journal of Robyn Hood, 1989. *Memberships:* Poetry Sc; BDMA; IPG. *Honours:* Winner, All Nations Poetry Contest, 1974; 23 Advertising Awards, UK and USA, 1970-90. *Hobbies:* ssa 00Poetry; Travel; Photography; Writing. *Address:* 83 Gloucester Place, London W1H 3PG, England.

RYAN Suzanne I, b. 13 Mar 1939, Yonkers, New York, USA. Professor of Nursing. *Education:* BA, Physiology, Mt St Agnes Coll; BSN, Nursing, Columbia Univ; MA, Nursing Serv Admin; MEd, Nursing Educ; EdD, Nursing Educ, ABD. *Appointments:* Hd Nuse, Intensive Care Unit, So Nassau Community Hosp, 1968-70; Prof, Nursing, Admnstr, Molloy Coll, Rockville Ctr, NY, 1970-; Pres, CEO, SIR Enterprises Inc PC. *Creative works:* Writer, plays, poems; Painter; Profl photography, postcards, area pix books of San Fran, Carmel, Big Sur, Monterey, New England, NH. *Memberships include:* Sigma Theta Tau; Am Assn Univ Profs; Sierra Club; Nature Conservancy; Gtr Yellowstone Coalition; Natural Hist; NY State AIDS Coun; NY State Drugs and Alcohol Assn; Audobon Soc; Smithsonian Soc; NY State Nurses Assn; NY State Fedn Hlth Educators; Intermat Congress Cancer Nurses; Malverne Environmental Assn; Williamsburg Restoration Soc; Presidents Clubs, Malloy Coll and Loyola MD; Nat Assn Female Executives. *Honours:* Coll Athlete of Yr, Mt St Agnes Coll, 1958-62; US Pub Hlth Fellow, Univ MD Med School, 1962; Chairperson, Night of Song, Molloy Coll, 1970-; Nat Cancer Inst Fellow, Stanford Univ, CA, 1981; Sigma Theta Tau Rsch Fellow, 1985; Caritas Medal, Molloy Coll, 1991. *Hobbies:* Photography; Oil painting; Writing prose and poetry; Research; Athletics; Tennis; Golf; Skiing; Gardening. *Address:* 16 Walker St, Malverne, NY 11565, USA. 6, 34, 152.

RYDBERG Sven, b. 25 Mar 1933, Stockholm, Sweden. Psychology Consultant; Educator. m. Mariann Fall, 30 May 1959, 1 s, 1 d. *Education:* MA, 1956, PhD, 1964; Univ Stockholm. *Appointments:* Educ Dept, 1959-69, Psychology Dept, 1970-, Univ Stockholm; UCLA, USA, 1964-66; Univ CA, Berkeley, 1973-74; Prof tf, Abo Acad, Finland, 1969-70, 1977. *Publications:* Bias in Prediction, 1963; Articles in educ and psychological sci jrnls on psychometrics, learning, attention, memory, dev, cognitive and behaviour change, personnel selection, documentation. *Memberships:* Life Mbr, AAAS; Swedish Union Univ Profs, minor off; Chmn, Inst Applied Social Scis. *Honours:* Fulbright Scholar, USA, 1964- 66; Rsch Assoc, Inst Human Learning, Berkeley, CA, USA, 1973-74. *Hobbies:* Reading; Hiking; All-seasons outdoor swimming; Travel; Languages; Philosophy; Archaeology. *Address:* Palmbladsvagen 2, S-112 58 Stockholm, Sweden. 52.

RYNELL Elisabeth Ingrid Marianne, b. 17 May 1954, Stockholm, Sweden. Writer. 1 s, 1 d. *Education:* A-level Evening Classes, 2 yrs. *Publications:* Books: Lyrsvit, poetry (debut), 1975; Veta Hut, novel, 1979; Onda Dikter, poetry, 1980; Humanismens Seger, essay, 1982; Sorgvingesang, poetry, 1985; Sjuk Fagel, poetry, 1988; En Berattelse om Loka, novel, 1990; Nattliga Samtal, poetry, 1990. *Membership:* Swedish Writers Union. *Honours* Dan Andersson Prize, 1987; Var grants. *Address:* Sweden.

S

SAAT Mari, b. 27 Sept 1947, Tallinn, Estonia. Writer. m. Raul Meel, 14 Mar 1975, 3 s (1 dec.), 2 d. *Education:* Economist, Tallinn Polytechnic Inst, 1970; Scholar, Educl Prognosis, Inst Econs, ESSR Acad Scis, 1972-75; Dr Phil, 1977. *Appointments:* Economist, Inst Econs, 1970-72, Sci Rsch Worker, 1975-82, ESSR Acad Scis; Profl Writer, 1982-. *Publications include:* Buds of Rose-Tree, collection of short stories, 1975; Hazel-Grouse, novel, 1980; Apple by Light and by Shade, novel, 1985; I Myself, collection of short stories for children, 1988; Spell and Spirit, novel, 1991. *Memberships:* Estonian Writers Union. *Honours:* Fr Tuglas Lit Prize for Short Stories, 1973, 1986. *Hobby:* Biodynamical gardening. *Address:* Mari Saat, Harju 1-1, Tallinn EE0001, Estonia.

SABADOS Marina Ileana, b. 25 Aug 1952, Ploiesti, Rumania. Researcher in Rumanian Mediaeval Art. *Education:* Grad, Hist and Theory Art Sect, Inst Fine Arts, Bucharest, 1975; Doct in progress, 1990-93. *Appointments:* Art Histn, Suceava Co Hist Mus, 1975-80; Art Histn, Neamt Co Hist Muse, 1980-90; Researcher, Inst Art Hist, Rumanian Acad, Bucharest, 1990-. *Publications:* The Diocesan Cathedral of Roman, 1990. *Contributions to:* sci sessions and articles in hist and art hist reviews, concerning Rumanian mediaeval art such as icons, wood carving, silverware, embroidery, incl: O valoroasa piesa de sculptura medievala moldoveneasca din orasul Suceava, 1978; O ferecatura de carte necunoscuta din Moldova, secolul al XVI-lea, 1979; Schita de studiu asupra iconostaselor de secol XVIII din judetul Suceava, 1979-80; O noua contributie la cunoasterea picturii de sevalet din Moldova secolului al XVI-lea, 1984; Contributii la studiul sculpturii decorative in lemn din Moldova, in prima jumatate a sec al XVII-lea: doua iconostase mai putin cunoscute din judetul Neamt, 1985; Zugravi moldoveni din secolul al XVIII-lea. Pictura pe lemn din judetul Neamt, 1986; Un document cu portretul voievodului Miron Barnovschi si citeva observatii privind arta miniaturii in actele emise de cancelaria moldoveneasca in prima jumatate a secolului al XVII-lea, 1986; Ursul - un zugrav moldovean de la inceputul sec. al XVIII-lea, 1987; Une icone moldave inconnue du commencement du XVIe siecle, 1991. *Hobbies:* Playing the piano; Cinema. *Address:* Soseaua Viilor 92, bl 4B, sc 8, ap 1, sector 5, 75241 Bucharest, Rumania. 152.

SABATELLA Elizabeth M, b. 9 Nov 1940, Mineola, New York, USA. Psychiatric Social Worker; Writer. 1 s. *Education:* BS, 1961, MA, 1971, MSW, 1983, SUNY, Stony Brook, NY; Cert Social Worker, State of NY, 1984. *Appointments:* Tchr, NY, 1961-63; Tchr, Hlth, Phys Educ, mentally and emotionally Handicapped, NY, 1964-67; Grp Ldr, Brookhaven Narcotic Guidance Coun, NY, 1973-79; Tchr, Hlth, Phys Educ, NY, 1968-73; Therapist, NY, 1973-84; Educator, NY, 1984-90; Writer, poetry, children's books, 1984-; Therapist, Albuquerque, NM, 1990-. *Creative works include:* Design and cutting of woven fabric, art works, var art shows and shops throughout NY, 1971-78; The Health Delivery System of Costa Rica, 1983; Poetry in: Poetic Voices of America; On The Threshold of a Dream, 1988; The American Poetry Anthology, Am Poetry Assn, 1988; Meta Scoop, 1988; Boundary, 1989. *Memberships:* Int Platform Assn, USA; Nat Writers Club, CO; ESP, NY; NY Tchrs Assn. *Honours:* Funded Grant, NYS Div of Substance Abuse, 1980-84; Ed's Choice Award for poem Smile Not, Nat Lib Poetry, USA, 1988; Best New Poets, Am Poetry Assn, 1988; Awards of Poetic Excellence, Honorable Mention, His Soul Remained, 1992, What Would Your Friends Think; Honorable Mention, His Soul Remained, 1992. *Hobbies:* Therapeutic tough; Biofeedback; Meditation; Dance; Acting; Target shooting; Cycling; Travel; New York. *Address:* 5801 Eubank NE, Apt 207, Albuquerque, NM 87111, USA. 5, 156, 191.

SABATINI Lawrence John, b. 5 Dec 1919, Bushey, Hertfordshire, England. Retired. Patricia Dyson, 19 July 1947, 1 s, 1 d. *Education:* Jt Servs Staff Coll, 1955. *Appointments:* HM Off Works, 1938-39; Army Serv, 1940-46: Commissioned 5RTR, served NW Europe; Asst Prin, 1947, Asst Pvte Sec to Min, 1948-49, Min Works, London; Joined, 1955, Prin Pvte Sec to Min, 1958-60, Asst Under-Sec State, 1972-79, Min Def, London; Def Cnslr, UK Delegation to NATO, 1963-67. *Memberships:* Marylebone Cricket Club; Royal Zoological Soc; Rpyal Hort Soc. *Hobbies:* Gardening; Photography; Travel. *Address:* 44A Batchworth Lane, Northwood, Middlesex HA6 3DT, England. 1.

SABISTON David Coston Jr, b. 4 Oct 1924, Onslow County, North Carolina, USA. Educator; Surgeon. m. Agnes Foy Barden, 24 Sept 1955, 3 d. *Education:* BS, Univ NC, 1943; MD, Johns Hopkins Univ School Med, 1947. *Appointments:* Intern, 1947-48, Asst Resident, 1948-49, 1950-52, Chief Resident, 1952-53, Surg, Johns Hopkins Hosp; Asst, Surg, 1948-49, 1950-52, Harvey Cushing Fellow, Surg, 1949-50, Instr, Surg, 1952-53, Asst Prof, Surg, 1955-59; Assoc Prof, Surg, 1959, Nat Insts Hlth Researcher, 1962-64, Prof, Surg, 1964, Johns Hopkins Univ School Med; Capt, US Army Med Corps, 1953-55; Investigator, Howard Hughes Med Inst, Johns Hopkins Univ, 1955-61; Fulbright Rsch Scholar, Nuffield Dept Surg, Univ Oxford, England, 1960-61; Rsch Assoc, Nuffield Professorial Unit, Univ London and Gt Ormond St Hosp, London, 1961; Cons, Surg; Prof, Chmn, Dept Surg, 1964, James Buchanan Duke Prof, Surg, Chmn, Dept Surg, 1971, Duke Univ Med Ctr, Durham, NC. *Publications:* Textbook of Surgery: The Biological Basis of Modern Surgical Practice (ed); Essentials of Surgery (ed); Surgery of the Chest (co-ed). *Memberships include:* Am Coll Surgs, Past Pres, num offr offrs; Am Surg Assn, Past Pres; Inst Med, Nat Acad Scis; Am Assn Thoracic Surg, Past VP, Past Pres; Soc Univ Surgs, Past Pres; Soc Clin Surg, Past Chmn; So Surg Assn, Past Sec, Past Pres; Soc Surg Chmn, Past Sec-Treas, Past VP, Past Pres; Int Soc Cardiovascular Surg; Soc Vascular Surg, Past VP; Soc Thoracic Surgs GB and Ireland; Int Surg Grp; Soc Surg Alimentary Tract; Soc Thoracic Surgs; Am Coll Cardiology; Soc Int de Chirurgie; Hon Mbr, num for Colls Surgs. *Honours include:* Phi Beta Kappa, 1944; Alpha Omega, 1947; Golden Apple Award, Best Clin Tchr, Duke Med Students, 1966, 1977; Hunterian Lectr, Royal Coll Surgs, London, 1984; Coll Medallist, Am Coll Chest Physns, 1987. *Address:* Department of Surgery, Duke University Medical Center, Durham, NC 27710, USA. 2, 34, 52.

SACHS John Raymond, b. 3 May 1957, London, England. Writer; Presenter; Producer. m. Lisa Jayne Miles, 29 July 1985, 2 d. *Appointments:* Radio Presenter: Radio 1, 1978; Swansea Sound, 1978; Capital Radio, 1979- 91; TV Presenter, BC 1, 1979-91; TV Pres, ITV, Brian Conley Show; TV Pres, BBC1, Four Square; Commentator ITV, Gladiators; Radio Presenter, BBC Radio 2, Much More Music in Concert, 4, in Concert. *Publications:* Private Files, 1991; Babylon, 1991; Column for Sunday Mag; Secretlives, 1991. *Memberships:* Mossimans; Tramp; Limelight Study; VP, Variety Club GB; Cliveden. *Honours:* Radio Personality of Yr, Variety Club, 1988; NY Silver Award, World Radio Personality of Yr, 1988. *Hobbies:* Shooting; Water-skiing; Golf. *Address:* Kimberley House, 79 Christchurch Ave, London NW6 7NT, England.

SACHSSE Rolf, b. 28 Apr 1949, Bonn, Federal Republic of Germany. Author; Artist. m. Roswitha Sachsse-Schadt, 24 Oct 1975, 1 s. *Education:* Apprenticeship as Photographer, 1967-70; Studies, Art Hist, Communication Rsch, German Lit, 1971-78; Preservation Campaign, 1978-79; PhD, Univ Bonn, 1983. *Career:* Freelance Advt Photographer, 1970-71; Landeskonservator, Rheinland, 1978-79; Freelance Artist and Author; 1979-85; Prof, Photography, New Media, Dept Design, Uefeld Polytechnic, 1985-; 15 individual exhibs, over 50 grp shows as artist, 1975-89. *Publications:* Monographs on photographers: Hugo Schmolz, 1982; Lucia Moholy, 1985; Peter Keetman, 1987; August Sander, 1988; Over 400 articles on photography hist. *Memberships:* European Soc Hist Photography; Int Kunster Grenium; Formerly: Artist Placement Grp, London; Deutsche Gesellschaft fur Photographie; Gesellschaft Deutscher Lichtbildauer. *Address:* c/o FB 02 Design FHN, Frankenring 20, D-4150 Krefeld 1, Germany.

SACKIN Claire, b. 1 Oct 1925, New York City, New York, USA. Professor and Director of Social Work Programme. m. Milton Sackin, 4 Feb 1955, 3 s. *Education:* BA, Hunter Col, 1946; MEd, 1968, MSW, 1972, PhD, 1976, Univ Pitts. *Appointments:* Tenured Tchr, Jr HS, Bronx, NY, 1947-57; Rsch Asst, Model Cities and School Educ, 1973, Instr, Dept Urban Mgmt, 1974, Rsch Assoc, School Social work, 1975-76, Prof, Social Work, Dir, Social Work Prog, 1976-, Univ Pitts, PA; Rsch Assoc, Hlth and Welfare Planning Assn, 1974. *Publications:* An Analysis of a Systems Approach to the Treatment of Alcoholism: Response to Planned Intervention, dissertation, 1977; Deinstitutionalization: Articles: Spreading the Word through Continuing Education in Social Work, 1977; Aged and Youthful Drinkers: Some Policy Implications, 1980. *Memberships:* Coun Social Work Educ; Nat Assn Social Workers; PA State Chapt, Nat Assn Social Workers, Social Action Comm 1983-85, elected to House Delegs 1984, En Reg Coalition Liaison to Bd 1984; PA State Chapt, Assn Baccalaureate Social Work Prog Dirs, 1983-85. *Honours:* Mbr, Nat Advsry Bd, Alpha Delta Mu, 1977-; United Mental Hlth Rsch Grant, 1979-80; Mbr, Comm Alcohol Educ, 1981, Appt to Prevention Comm, 1982, Registered Trainer, 1983, PA Gov's Coun Drug and Alcoholism Abuse; Mbr, Nat Assn Substance Abuse Trainers and Educators, 1987-; Mbr, several comms, St Francis Coll incl Off, Grad Studies Comm. *Hobbies:* Travel; Reading; Opera; Gardening; Crossword puzzles. *Address:* 531 Sandrae Drive, Pittsburgh, PA 15243, USA. 138, 151, 152, 155, 156, 189, 191.

SADA Eizo, b. 28 Nov 1930, Nagoya, Japan. Professor of Chemical Engineering. m. 3 Nov 1958, 2 s. *Education:* BEng, Nagoya Univ, 1953; MEng, 1955, DEng, 1958, Nagoya Univ Grad School. *Appointments:* Asst Prof, 1959-60, Assoc Prof, 1960-69, Prof, 1969-77, Nagoya Univ; Prof, Dept Chem Engrng, Fac Engrng, Kyoto Univ, 1977-. *Publications:* 16 books and 230 rsch reports on chem engrng and biochem engrng. *Memberships:* Soc Chem Engrs, Japan; Chem Soc Japan. *Honours:* Award, Soc Chem Engrs, Japan, 1991. *Hobbies:* Stamp collecting; Reading novels and mystery stories. *Address:* 3-29-301 Higashibiraki 1-23, Sakyo, Kyoto, Japan 606.

SADAVOY Joel, b. 5 Feb 1945. Psychiatrist. m. 20 Nov 1977, 2 s, 2 d. *Education:* MD, 1968, DPsych, 1972, FRCP Can, 1973, Toronto. *Appointments include:* Psych-in-Chief, Baycrest Ctr Geriatric Care, 1980-91; Assoc Prof, 1986-, Hd, Div Geriatric Psych, 1991, Univ Toronto; Dir, Geriatric Psychiatry, Mount Sinai Hosp, Toronto, 1991-. *Publications:* Books: Treating the Elderly with Psychotherapy, 1987; Psychiatric Consequences of Brain Disease in the Elderly, 1990; Comprehensive Review of Geriatric Psychiatry, 1991; 38 other profl publs. *Memberships:* Founding Pres, Can Acad of Geriatric Psych, 1991-; Am Assn Geriatric Psych, Bd Dirs 1987-91; Coun on Aging, Am Psych Assn, Cons 1989-91; Profl Advsry Bd, Can Psych Rsch Fndn; Bd Dirs, Sr Care and Jewish Family and Child Serv, Toronto, 1985-90; Ed Bd, Jrnl Geriatric Psych; Assoc Ed, Am Jrnl of Geriatric Psych; Cons, Baycrest Ctr Geriatric Care; Bd Advsrs, Int Newsletter on Elder Abuse; Exec, Psychotherapy Sect, Ont Psych Assn. *Hobbies:* Travel; Raquetball; Reading. *Address:* Mount Sinai Hospital, 600 University Ave, Toronto, Ontario, Canada M5G 1X5. 142.

SADYRKHANOV Ruslan, b. 5 Sept 1947, Baku, USSR. Mathematician; Chief Research Officer. m. Mariam Shabanbekova, 8 Apr 1975, 1 s, 1 d. *Education:* MS, Dept Maths, Univ Azerbaijan, 1970; PhD, Inst Cybernetics, Acad Scis Azerbaijan, 1974; DSc, Maths, Kiev Inst Maths, Acad Scis, 1989. *Appointments:* Jr Rsch

Off, Sr Rsch Off, Inst Cybernetics, Baku, 1973-79; Researcher, Doctorand, Gen Maths Chair, Moscow State Univ, 1979-84; Sr Rsch Off, Chief Rsch Off, Inst Matha and Mech, Baku, 1984-. *Publications:* Over 30 articles on nonlinear analysis in math jrnls, USSR and USA; Selected Questions of Nonlinear Functional Analysis, monograph, 1990. *Memberships* Azerbaijan Math Soc; Radical Assn Azerbaijan; USSR Knowledge Soc. *Hobbies:* Music; Philosophy; Ideology, Travel. *Address:* K Izmailov Street 5-58, Baku 1, Russia.

SAEKI Shoichi, b. 26 Apr 1922, Tokyo, Japan. Literary Critic. m. Apr 1948, 2 s. *Education:* BA, Am Lit, Tokyo Univ, 1943. *Appointments:* Navy Serv, 1943-45; Asst Prof, Toyama Univ, 1945-53; Asst Prof, Tokyo Motrop Univ, 1953-67; Prof, Tokyo Univ, 1968-83; Prof, Chuo Univ, 1983-. *Publications:* Problems in the Contemporary American Novel, 1956; Literary America - Possibilities of Multi-Ethnic Society, 1967; Japanese Literature from Without and Within, 1969; Yukio Mishima - A Critical Biography, 1978; Narrative Art in Modern Japan, 1979; Autobiography in Modern Japan, 1981; Literature in the Context of US-Japan Relationship, 1984; The Autobiographical Century, 1985; Shintoist Vision, 1989; Eros in Biography, 1990. *Memberships:* Japan Acad Art and Lit; Dir, Japan Assn Lit Writers; Dir, Congress Japanese Culture. *Honours:* Yomiuri Lit Prize, 1979; Prize for Translation, 1979; Prize, Min Educ, 1985. *Hobbies* Swimming; Travel; Book-collecting. *Address:* 6-38-23 Todoroki, Setagaya-ku, Tokyo, Japan.

SAEV Stoyan Konstantinov, b. 20 Sept 1928, Sofia, Bulgaria. Physician; Professor in Anaesthesiology. m. Milka Lubenova Mincheva, 12 July 1953, 1 d. *Education:* Higher Med Inst, Sofia, 1952; Postgrad Med Inst, Sofia, 1959; Anaesthesiology Ctr, WHO, Copenhagen, 1959, 1965; Dip Anaesthesiology, 1949; MSc, 1963; Asst Prof, 1964; DMSc, 1973; Prof, 1974. *Appointments:* Med Dr, 1952; Univ Asst, Anaesthesiology, 1960; Hd, Tchng Grp, 1963; Hd, Chair Anaesthesiology, Postgrad Med Inst, Sofia, 1965; Hd, Chair Anaesthesiology, Med Fac, Sofia, 1990. *Publications:* 350 books. *Contributions to:* publs, congress papers. *Memberships:* Bulgarian Soc Anaesthesiology, Past Pres; Academician, European Acad Anaesthesiology; Mainz WAEDM Club; Pres, Bulgarian Red Cross Water Life Saving; Int Fedn Water Life Saving, Comm Direction Mbr. *Honours:* Elected Fellow, Royal Soc Anaesthesiologists, England; Hon Mbr: Bulgarian Red Cross; Socs Anaesthesiology, Poland, Rumania, Yugoslavia, USSR, Vietnam. *Hobbies:* Reading; Music; Gardening. *Address:* Chair of Anaesthesiology and Intensive Medicine, Medical Faculty of Sofia, Bd G Sofiiski 1, Sofia, 1431 Bulgaria.

SAGAR Derrick Alan, b. 3 Aug 1950, Lancaster, England. Consultant Anaesthetist, 29 Aug 1981, 1 s, 1 d. *Education:* Med School, Leeds Univ, 1970-76. *Appointments:* Med Rsch Coun Researcher, Dept Anaesthesia, Leeds Univ, 1981-83; Sr Registrar, Yorks Reg Hlth Auth, 1984-87; Cons Anaesthetist, S Lincs Hlth Auth, 1987-. *Memberships:* Assn Anaesthetists; Coll Anaesthetists; Brit Med Assn, Hon Sec Holland Div; Lives Lincs Integrated Voluntary Emergency Serv. *Hobbies:* Paramed Training; Chmn, Lincs Ambulance Advsry Panel; Environment and wildlife; Charity work. *Address:* Keys Toft House, Boston Road, Wainfleet, Lincolnshire PE24 4EX, England.

SAHOO Prasanna, b. 10 Mar 1951, Rampella, India. University Professor. *Education:* MSc, Univ Regina, Regina, Sask, Can, 1979; PhD, Univ Waterloo, Waterloo, Can, 1986. *Appointments:* Rsch Asst, Univ Regina, 1979-80; Post Doctoral Fellow, univ Waterloo, Can, 1986-87; Asst Prof, Univ Louisville, KY, USA, 1987-. *Publications:* Over 35 scholarly papers in leading jrnls in maths and computer scis. *Memberships:* Am Math Soc; Math Assn Am; Can Applied Math Soc; IEEE Computer Soc; Assn Computing Machinery; Pi Mu Epsilon. *Honours:* Recip, President's Young Investigator Award, Univ Louisville, 1990. *Address:* Department of

Mathematics, University of Louisville, Louisville, KY 40292, USA. 7.

SAIDI Samira Miriam, b. 8 July 1961, Manchester, England. Ballet Dancer. m. Alain J Dubreuil, 28 Feb 1988. *Education:* Royal Ballet School, 1977-79. *Career:* Sadler's Wells Royal Ballet, London, 1979-90; Currently 1st Soloist, Birmingham Royal Ballet; Created roles incl: Title role in David Bintley's The Snow Queen; Sybil Vane in The Picture of Dorian Gray; Dances most prin roles incl: Giselle, Les Sylphides, Valse Nobles, Hobson's Choice. *Membership:* Equity. *Honours:* Adeline Genee Silver Medal, 1978; Awarded Solo Seal, 1979. *Hobbies:* Theatre; Interior design; Antiques; Acting; Gardening. *Address:* The Royal Opera House, Covent Garden, London WC2, England.

SAINT-JACQUES Bernard, b. 26 Apr 1928, Canada. Professor of Linguistics. m. Marguerite Fauquenoy, 3 Apr 1967. *Education:* BA, 1949, MA, 1954, Montreal Univ; MA, Sophia Univ, 1962; MS, Georgetown Univ, USA, 1964; PhD, 1964, Doct-es-Lettres, 1975, Univ Paris. *Appointments:* Var positions, 1966-89, Prof Emeritus, 1989-, Univ BC, Vancouver; Prof, Linguistics, Aichi Shukutoku Univ, Aichi, Japan, 1990-. *Publications:* Books: Analyse structurale du japonais moderne; Structural Analysis of Modern Japanese; Aspects sociolinguistiques du bilinguisme canadien; Language and Ethnic Relations. *Memberships:* Linguistic Soc Am; Assn Tchrs Japanese; Review Ed, Bulletin de la Soc de linguistique de Paris; Fndg Mbr, BC Soc Transls and Interpreters; Cons, Inter Pacific Club. *Honours:* Mbr, Royal Soc Can; Grants: Ford Fndn; Can Coun; Leon and Thea Koerner Fndn; The Japan Fndn; Japan Soc Promotion Sci. *Address:* Department of Linguistics, University of British Columbia, Vancouver, BC, Canada V6T 1W5. 2, 9, 88.

SAITO George (Joji), b. 26 Aug 1917, Tokyo, Japan. Literary Critic. m. Hideko Oshima, 10 Mar 1946, 2 d. *Education:* MA, Dept Linguistics, Kyoto Imperial Univ, 1943; Ford Fndn Rsch Scholar, 1963; Fulbright Rsch Scholar, 1971-72. *Appointments:* Cultural Advsr, US Embassy, Tokyo, 1952-71; Vis Prof, Dartmouth Coll, England, 1963, 1971-72; Prof, Engl, 1971-82, Pres, 2 yrs, Ibaraki Christian Coll, Japan; Prof, Engl, Rissho Univ, Tokyo, 1982-88. *Publications:* Nihon no Kokoro wo Eigo de; Soseki and Salinger (w Philip Williams). *Memberships:* Japan PEN Club; Life Mbr, Thoreau Soc Inc; Past Pres, Thoreau Soc Japan; Am Lit Soc Japan. *Honours:* Ford Fellowship, 1963; Fulbright Fellowship, 1971-72. *Hobbies:* Photography; Music (a long-time church organist); Book- binding; Archery. *Address:* 2-19-13 Wakabayashi, Setagaya-ku, Tokyo, Japan 154. 166.

SAKA Ibrahim Abdulkadir, b. 1 Apr 1961, Accra, Nigeria. Civil Servant; Catering Officer. m. Funmilayo Sikirat, 27 Dec 1986, 3 s. *Education:* Tchrs Grade II Cert, 1979; Nat Dip, 1983; Higher Nat Dip, 1986. *Appointments:* Tchng, 1979-81, 1983-84; Asst Social Mobilisation Off, 1989; Catering Off, Fed Govt Coll, Maiduguri, Borno State, 1990-. *Publications:* The Significance of Communication in Hotel and Catering Management, 1986; Palm Wine: Making Process and its Economic Importance, 1986. *Memberships:* Nigerian Hotel and Catering Inst; Chm, Non-Acad Staff Union, Fed Govt Coll Maiduguri Br. *Honours:* Best Student, Phys and Hlth Educ, 1979. *Hobbies:* Reading novels; Playing indoor games such as chess and monopoly; Football; Table tennis. *Address:* 24 Omodada Street, Okekere Quarters, Ilorin, Kwara State, Nigeria.

SAKAI Toshihiko, b. 17 July 1943, Nagoya, Japan. Senior Researcher. m. (1) 7 Oct 1943, (2) 25 Nov 1989, 2 s, 1 d. *Education:* BSc, Nagoya Inst Technology, 1967; MSc, GA Inst Technology, USA, 1969; PhD, Univ Manchester Inst Sci and Technology, England, 1974. *Appointments:* Joined, 1967, Assoc Engr, 1967-73, Researcher, 1975-84, Staff for CEO, 1982-, Sr Researcher, 1984-, Toyota Ctrl R&D Labs Inc, Nagakute,

Aichi. *Publications:* Author or co-author, 19 tech articles. *Memberships:* Submissions Referee, Textile Machinery Soc Japan; Soc Fibre Sci and Technology, Japan; Soc Automotive Engrs, USA; Nagoya Jr Chmbr, Exec VP 1982. *Honours:* 51 domestic and for patents awarded or pending; Fellow, Textile Inst, UK, 1986. *Hobbies:* Travel; Driving; Playing golf. *Address:* City Corp B1003, Ueda 3-1501, Tempaku, Nagoya, 468 Japan. 52.

SAKATA Shogo, b. 12 Apr 1957, Japan. Assistant Professor. m. 12 Mar 1988. *Education:* Bach Arts and Scis, 1981, MSc, 1983, ME, 1990, Hiroshima Univ. *Appointments:* Rsch Asst, Physiology, 1983-87, Instr, Psychology, 1987-91, Asst Prof, 1991-, Hiroshima Univ. *Publications:* Var rsch papers incl: Adrenomedullary origin of the hindquarter vasodilation during the transposition response of the rat, 1988. *Memberships:* Japanese Soc Physiological Psychology and Psychophysiology; Off, Hiroshima Univ. *Hobbies:* Jogging; Baseball; Tennis. *Address:* 12-23-301 6 chome, Rakurakuen, Saeki-ku, Hiroshima 731-51, Japan.

SAKOWSKI Edward Lech, b. 8 Sept 1952, Wroclaw, Poland. Art Historian; Fine Art Conservator. m. Ludmila Sakowska, 29 Nov 1977, 1 s, 1 d. *Education:* Dip Graphic Designer, Fine Art Lyceum, 1973; MA, Hist (Cultural Property Conserv), Fac Hist, Univ Wroclaw, 1977. *Appointments:* Bur Study and Documentation of Cultural Property, 1977-79; Chief, Off of Conservator of Silesia Dist and Wroclaw City, 1979-81; Internship, Auckland City Art Art Gall, Auckland, NZ, 1990-. *Creative works:* Num poems and theatre perfs, 1970-75. *Memberships:* Polish Assn Art Histns, 1977-81; NZ Profl Conservator Grp, Reg Rep for Otago and Dunedin 1990-91. *Honours:* 1st Prize for play Efeb, Theatre Ochota, Warsaw, 1975. *Hobbies:* Paintings; Photography; Writing poetry. *Address:* 56 Peter St, Dunedin 9001, New Zealand.

SAKURAI Kunitomo, b. 27 May 1933, Saitama, Japan. Professor of Physics. m. Nobuko Ueda, 6 Dec 1964, 1 d. *Education:* BS, Univ Kyoto, 1956; MS, 1958, PhD, 1961, Kyoto Univ Grad School. *Appointments:* Rsch Assoc, 1961, Assoc Prof, 1964, Kyoto Univ; Sr Assoc, NASA, GSFC, USA, 1968; Prof, Univ MD, IFDAM, 1975; Prof, Kanagawa Univ, Japan, 1976-. *Publications:* Books: Physics of Solar Cosmic Rays, 1974; Cosmic Ray Astrophysics, 1988; SETI Pioneers, 1990; Neutrinos in Cosmic Ray Physics and Astrophysics, 1990. *Memberships:* Int Astronomical Union; Int Assn Geomagnetism and Aeronomy; Am Astronomical Soc; Phys Soc Japan; Astronomical Soc Japan; AAAS. *Honours:* Tanakadato Prize, Soc Terrestial Magnetism and Electricity Japan, 1967; Honorary Citizen, Huntsvill, Arabama, USA, 1988; Sci Merit Award, Japan Soc Univ Alumni, 1989. *Hobbies:* Study of the vegetation in Japan; Classical music; Writing, over 40 books written about various topics. *Address:* 2617-144 Imajuku- cho, Asahi-ku, Yokohama 241, Japan. 52.

SALAM Abdus, b. 2 Mar 1955, Rajshahi, Bangladesh. University Educator. m. Bilkis Ara Parvin, 3 Aug 1984, 2 s, 1 d. *Education:* BA, Hons Arabic, 1979; MA, Arabic, 1980; PhD, 1989. *Appointments:* Lectr, 1984-87, Asst Prof, 1987-91, Assoc Prof, 1991-, Rajshahi Univ. *Publications:* 5 articles in Encyclopaedia of Islam (in Bengali); 1 article in Qulam; PhD thesis in Hadith. *Hobby:* Research. *Address:* Dept of Arabic and Islamic Studies, Rajshahi University, Rajshahi, Bangladesh.

SALE Thomas Arthur, b. 12 June 1916, Liverpool, England. Surgeon (retired). m. Victoria Bruce Hunter Tomlinson, 22 Apr 1944, 2 d. *Education:* MB ChB Hons, Univ Liverpool, 1940; FRCS Edinburgh, 1949; AM (Singapore), 1957; FRACS, 1964; FRACMA, 1967; FACRM, 1986. *Appointments:* Resident Med Off, 1940-41, Resident Surg Off, 1946-47, Liverpool Stanley Hosp; Surg Lt, RNVR, 1941-46; Sr Surg Registrar, Tutor, Royal Liverpool Children's Hosp, 1949-52; Gen prac, 1952-53; Sr Surg Registrar: Broaadgreen Gen Hosp, 1953;

Clatterbridge Gen Hosp, 1953-54; Surg, Singapore Gen Hosp, 1954-59; Surg Lt-Cmdr, Prin Med Off, Malayan RNVR, 1955-59; Surg Lt-Cmdr, RANVR, 1957; Med Supt, Sr Surg, Rockhampton Base Hosp, 1959-72; Ldr, Qld Surg Team, Bien Hoa, S Vietnam, 1967-68; Gen Supt, CEO, Canberra Hosp, ACT, Australia, 1972-76; Surg Lt Cmdr, RANR, 1973; Med Off i/c, Community Hlth Ctrs, Qld Govt, 1976-82; Sr Specialist, Rehab: Repatriation Hosp, Rosemount, 1976-82; Repatriation Gen Hosp, Greenslopes, Brisbane, 1976-90. *Creative works:* Performed 1st heart op, mitral valvotomy, 1955. *Contributions:* 14 to med jrnls; Accidents to Patients - a Review of 850 instances, in preparation. *Memberships:* Australian Med Assn, NSW Br and ACT, Pres Rockhampton Br 1964; Brit Med Assn; C'wlth Profl Offs Assn; Royal Inst Pub Admnstrs, ACT; Australian Hosps Assn; ACT Med Offs Assn; Councillor, ACT Br Chmn, Australian Coll Med Admnstrs; Patron, Yeppoon Old Age Pensioners Assn; Coun Mbr, European Civil Serv Assn Singapore, 1956-59; Exec Comm, Blue Nursing Serv, Rockhampton, 1962- 67; Div Surg, St John's Ambulance Brigade, Rockhampton. *Honours:* OBE, serv in Vietnam, 1969; Campaign medals; Med Medal 1st Class, S Vietnam Govt. *Hobbies:* Reading; Carpentry; Unpaid attendant, Cardiac Rehabilitation Unit, St Andrew's War Memorial Hospital. *Address:* 47 Pennant Street, Jamboree Heights, Brisbane, Queensland 4074, Australia.

SALLES Maurice Auguste Robert, b. 23 Dec 1943, Briouze, France. Professor of Economics. m. Annie-Claude Buthon, 5 July 1966, 1 s, 1 d. *Education:* Licence en Scis Econ, 1967; Doctorat d'Etat, Scis Econ, 1974; Agregation, Scis Econ, 1979. *Appointments:* Lectr, 1974-79, Prof, 1982-, Univ Caen; Prof, Univ Nantes, 1979-82. *Publications:* Social Choice and Welfare (co-ed), book, 1983; Social Choice and Welfare (coord ed), journal, 1984-. *Memberships:* Econometric Soc; Aristotelian Soc; Mind Assn; Assn Symbolic Logic; Soc Math de France; Am Math Soc; Soc Social Choice and Welfare, Sec-Treas. *Hobbies:* Classical music and jazz; Reading; Walking. *Address:* 1 Allee du Bucquet, 14111 Louvigny, France. 52.

SALMON Mark Emmet, b. 1 May 1949, Summit, New Jersey, USA. Presbyterian Minister. m. Dee Salmon, 13 July 1974,, 1 d. *Education:* BA, Pol Sci, Univ SC, 1973; MDiv, Austin Presby Theological Sem, 1982; DMin, 1984, DTh, 1987, Trinity Theological Sem. *Appointments:* Min, 1st Presby Ch, Belton, TX; Adj Fac, Trinity Theological Sem; Host, Shalom from Texas weekly int radio prog, Radio Paradise-Caribbean. *Memberships:* Pres, Bluebonnet Red Cross; Pres, Creative Therapies Inc. *Hobbies:* Golf; Ham radio; Camping; Archaeology and travels to Middle East. *Address:* First Presbyterian Church, Church , St at Greenbriar, PO Box 571, Belton, TX 76513, USA.

SALO Jarmo Antero, b. 11 Feb 1947, Oulu, Finland. Surgeon; Associate Professor. m. 1 June 1973, 1 s, 1 d. *Education:* MD, Univ Basel, Switzerland, 1974; DMSc, Univ Helsinki, 1983. *Appointments:* Specialist, Surg, 1980; Subspecialist, Gastroenterology, 1983; Subspecialist, Thoracic and Cardiovascular Surg, 1986; Docent, Surg, Univ Helsinki, 1988. *Memberships:* Scandinavian Surg Assn; Int Soc Diseases of the Esophagus. *Hobbies:* Outdoor activities. *Address:* Airoparintie 5-7 F 34, SF-00980 Helsinki, Finland. 52.

SALO Timothy Mark, b. 24 July 1960, Detroit, Michigan, USA. Minister. m. Kareena K Campau, 16 Oct 1982, 1 s, 1 d. *Education:* Ctl MI Univ, 1978-80; BS magna cum laude, Pastoral Mins, United Wesleyan Coll, 1982. *Appointments:* Min: Hopewell Wesleyan Ch, VA, 1982-83; Madisonville Wesleyan Ch, OH, 1983-89; Burt Ave Wesleyan Ch, Coshocton, OH, 1989-. *Memberships:* Bd Mbr, Sec-Treas, Cinn Wesleyan Pastors Assn; Bd Mbr: Cinn Meth Heritage Assn; Tri-State Christian Holiness Assn; Cinn Christian Action Coun; Madisonville Emergency Assistance Ctr. *Honours include:* Alpha Lambda Delta, 1978-80; Phi Eta Sigma,

1978-80; United Wesleyan Coll Hon Soc, 1980-82, Nat Dean's List, 1980-82. *Hobbies:* Collecting books, coins, stamps; Athletics; Camping; Gardening. *Address:* 212 Burt Avenue, Coshocton, OH 43812, USA.

SALONGA Ma Lea Carmen, b. 22 Feb 1971, Manila, Philippines. Actress. *Education:* Pre-med, Biology, Ateneo de Manila Univ, 1988-89. *Career:* Appearances in plays and musicals: Princess Ying Yao Lac in The King and I, 1978; Cat on a Hot Tin Roof, 1978; Fiddler on the Roof, 1978; The Rose Tattoo, 1980; Title role in Annie, 1980, 1984; Brigitta in The Sound of Music, 1980; Rhoda in The Bad Seed, 1981; Lucy in The Goodbye Girl, 1982; Addie in Paper Moon, 1983; Luisa in The Fantasticks, 1988; Kim in Miss Saigon, London, 1989-90, Broadway, 1991-; Host, num TV shows, Philippines; Supporting roles, films: Tropang Bulilit, 1985; Like Father, Like Son, 1986; Ninja Kids, 1986; Female Lead, films: Captain Barbell, 1986; Pik Pak Boom, 1988; Dear Diary, 1989; Appeared, several concerts. *Creative Works:* 5 record albums incl: Small Voice, 1981; Miss Saigon, 1990. *Honours include:* Aliw Award, Best Child Performer, 1981, 1982, 1983; Gold Discs, 1982, 1990; Tinig Award, Outstanding Singer, 1983, 1984, 1990; Cecil Award, Best Recording by a Child, 1984; Laurence Olivier Award, Best Perf by an Actress in a Musical, 1990; Theatre World Award, Outstanding Debut, 1991; Best Lead Actress in a Musical: Outer Critics Circle Award, Drama Desk Award, Tony Award, 1991; 10 Outstanding Young Men Award for Arts, 1991. *Hobbies:* Music; Reading; Jigsaw puzzles; Needlepoint. *Address:* c/o Alan Wasser Associates, General Management, 1650 Broadway, Suite 800, New York, NY 10019, USA.

SALT Julia, b. 4 May 1955, Cottingham, England. Solicitor. m. David Sidney Salt, 29 Mar 1980, 1 s, 1 d. *Education:* St Hilda's Coll, Oxford, 1973-77; BA, Mod Langs; Chester Coll Law, 1977-78. *Appointments:* Articled,, 1978-80, Asst Solicitor, 1980-85, Ptnr, 1985, Allen & Overy, London. *Memberships:* Law Soc; London Solicitors Co. *Hobbies:* Sailing; Birdwatching; Opera; Languages; Travel. *Address:* 9 Cheapside, London EC2V 6AD, England. 53.

SALTER John Rotherham, b. 2 May 1932, London, England. Solicitor; International Business Lawyer. m. Cynthia Brewer, 3 June 1961, 1 s, 2 d. *Education:* Ashridge Coll, 1950-51; Lincoln Coll, Oxford, 1953-56; King's Coll, London, 1958-59; MA (Oxon); Solicitor (Hons), 1959. *Appointments:* Lt, Royal Artillery, 1951-53; Articled, 1956, Ptnr, 1961-, Denton Hall Burgin & Warrens, London; Expert in TV series, The Law is Yours, 1964; Management Comm, Lindsey Oil Refinery, 1965-68; Burmah-Total Refineries Trust, 1971-81; EMI Ltd, 1975-79; Chair, North Sea Gas Gathering Consortium, 1979-80. *Publications:* Planning Law for Industry (jt ed), 1981; UK Oil and Gas Law, Land Use Planning and Environment, 1984; Halsbury's Laws of England on Environment, 1986; UK Onshore Oil and Gas Law, 1986; Law of European Communities, Environment, 1986; Vaughan, Law of European Communities Service, 1990; Environment and Planning Law, North Sea, 1991; Corporate Enviromental Responsibility, Law and Practice, 1992; Directors' Guide to Environmetal Issues, 1992. *Memberships:* Fellow, Brit Inst Mgmt; FRSA; FRGS; Assoc, Chartered Inst Arbitrators; Law SAoc Planning Panel, 1991-; Legal Assoc, the Royal Town Planning Inst, 1992-; Int Bar Assn, Vice-Chmn Comm Energy and Natural Resources Law and Comm Int Environmental Law, Chmn Sect Bus Law; Am Bar Assn, Vice-Chmn, Comm Comp Govt Law and Comm Int Law; Treas, Bd Govs Mbr, Anglo-Am Real Property Inst; Cons, UNIDO, Chmn Comm Oil and Gas Constrn Law; Pres, Oxford Univ Law Soc. *Honours:* Law Soc Hons, 1959; Hon Mbr, Bar of Madrid; Mem, Senior Common Room, Lincoln Coll, Oxford, 1991-; Hon Fellow Centre, Petroleum and Mineral Law and Policy, Univ of Dundee; Freeman of the City of London and of City of Glasgow. *Hobbies:* The arts; Archaeology; Sailing. *Address:* Five Chancery Lane, Cliffords Inn, London EC4 1BU, England. 34.

SAMAIN Bryan, b. 14 Jan 1925, Chelmsford, England. Public Relations Consultant; Writer. m. Helen Pauline Maddison, 1 May 1948, 2 s. *Education:* Royal Masonic School, 1933-40. *Appointments:* Nat newspaper jrnlsm, 1940-42; War Serv incl Royal Marines Commando Off, Europe, Far East, 1942-46; Press Corres, Hong Kong, 1950; PR Exec, steel ind, 1950-58; Subsequent appts, 1958-70, incl: Hd, PR, Ford Motor Co, UK; Hd, Info Servs, Brit Steel Corp, S Wales; Hd, PR, Richard Costain Ltd; Dir, PR, EMI Grp Cos, 1970-80; Communications Cons, 1980-. *Publications:* Commando Men, book, 1948, 1976, 1988; Num articles on Commando ops, WW2, and UK ind and mgmt. *Memberships:* Former Chmn, Publicity Comm, Save The Children Fund; Former PR Advsr, Duke of Edinburgh's Award Scheme; Former Chmn, PR Comm, Brit Assn Indl Eds. *Hobbies:* Theatre; Swimming; Walking. *Address:* 33 Warwick Gardens, Worthing, Sussex, England.

SAMARAS Zoe, b. 30 July 1935, Karpathos, Greece. Professor of French Literature. m. Nicholas Samaras, 25 Dec 1960, dec. 15 Sept 1981, 1 s, 1 d dec. *Education:* BS, 1959, MA, 1960, PhD, 1967, Columbia Univ, NYC. *Appointments:* Lectr, French, Columbia Univ, NYC, USA, 1960-65; Lectr, 1965-68, Asst Prof, French, 1968-73, CUNY; Assoc Prof, 1978-80, Prof, French Lit, 1980-, Aristotle Univ, Greece; Vis Prof, Theory of Lit, Univ Athens, 1987. *Publications:* The Comic Element of Montaigne's Style, 1970; Le Regne de Cronos, 1983; Text Perspectives (in Greek), 1987; For Maria (in Greek), poetry, 1991; L'Enfant du Taygete, transl of poetry, 1974; Articles in profl jrnls. *Memberships:* MLA; Am Assn Tchrs of French; Soc Francaise des Seizi mistes; Soc des Amis de Montaigne; Greek Soc Comp Lit. *Honours:* Scholarships, Columbia Univ, 1958-62; Phi Beta Kappa, 1959; Silver Medal, City of Paris, 1988; Nat Order of Merit, French Govt, 1988. *Hobbies:* Main interests in scholarly research and education; Translation of contemporary literature. *Address:* Vassilikou 10, 54636 Thessaloniki, Greece. 52.

SAMERSOV Vilor Fridmanovich, b. 24 July 1937, Vologda Region, USSR. Plant Protection Researcher; Entomologist. m. Valentina Alexandrovna Zacharevich, 14 June 1960, 1 s, 2 d. *Education:* Grad, Plant Protection Fac, St Petersburg Agricl Univ, 1960; Postgrad, Byelorussian Acad Scis, 1963- 66. *Appointments:* Slavgorod Plant Breeding Expmtl Station, Altai Krai, Slvagorod, 1960-61; Minsk Expmtl Station, All-Union Inst Plant Protection, Minsk, p Priluki, 1961-63; Zoological and Parasitological Inst, Byelorussian Acad Scis, 1963-78; Dept Hd, Dpty Dir, Dir, Byelorussian Sci Rsch Inst Plant Protection, Minsk, Priluki, 1978-. *Publications:* 252 publs incl: About the mechanism of Mineral Fertilizers Influence on Insects (w S L Gorovaya), 1973; Pests and Diseases of Cereals and Methods of their Control (w S F Buga), 1978; Intensive Technologies of Plant Protection, 1986; Scientific Basis for Agricultural Crops Protection under the Intensive Crop Growing, 1988; The Integrated Ssystem of Cereals Protection against Pests, 1989; Useful Insects of Orchard and Garden (w V I Sidlyarevich and V V Bolotnikova), 1990; Ecologic Aspects in Using Means for Plant Protection, 1990. *Memberships:* All- Union Entomological Soc; Ecologic Comm, Byelorussian Acad Scis; Lenin All- Union Acad Agricl Scis, Dept Plant Protection; Sci Priorities Co of Soviet Sci, Byelorussia. *Honours:* Prof, Corres Mbr Mbr, All-Union Acad Agricl Scis; 2 Gold Medals, Exhib Nat Econ Achievement, 1978, 1990; Order of Badge of Hon, USSR. *Hobbies:* Swimming; Skiing; Great interest in history of Russia. *Address:* Uritskogo 4, flat 112, 220050 Minsk, Byelorussia.

SAMLOT Frank, b. 21 July 1916, Budapest, Hungary, (Nationality Czech). Chem Engr; Forensic Science Technologist. m. Rose Puldova, 20 Sept 1941. *Education:* Indust cheml engrng, Prague, Czechoslovakia, 1953; Dip, cheml engrng, Univ of Chem & Cheml Tech, Prague, 1961; PhD, cheml engrng, American Nat Univ, 1983. *Appointments include:* Res chem, Inst of Res & Utilisation of Solid & Liquid Fuels,

Prague, 1955-66; Emigration to France, 1966, USA, 1967; Res chem, leather finishing, Wilmington Chemicals Corp, Delaware, USA, 1970-72; Consulting cheml eng, Polyurethane Finishes, 1974-76; Chief chem, vice pres, Blue Hen Finishing Com, Wilmington, 1972-74; Toxicology res chem, Forensic Sci Laboratory, Office of Chief Medical Examiner, Delaware, 1977-. *Creative works:* Res, effectiveness of machines (Kalander) for cutting textiles & rubber, 1958-59; PhD dissertation, Method of Finishing Leather & Resulting Product, 1983. *Memberships:* Czechoslovak Soc of Arts and Sciences; Am Soc for Testing & Materials; Am Leather Chemists Assoc. *Honours:* Active mem, Comite Nat Tchecoslovque en France, 1940-45; Life charter mem, Republican Presidential Task Force, USA, 1985; Sustaining mem, Republican Nat Cttee, Washington DC, 1986; Proclamation of Decoration: Outstanding Serv in Chem Tech; Outstanding Contrib to Forensic Tech; Distinguished Service to the Community; World Decoration of Excellence Medallion. *Hobbies:* Scientific research literature; Opera; Arts. *Address:* 2669 Gorda Bella Avenue, St Augustine, Florida 32086, USA.

SAMORODOV Victor Nickolayevich, b. 5 Aug 1951, USSR. Biologist; Teacher of Botany and Ecology. *Education:* Grad w hons, then postgrad course, Poltava Agricl Inst. *Appointments:* Farm Agronomist, Chernigov area, Ukraine; Army Serv, 1974-75; Sr Tchr, Bot, Ecology, Poltava Agricl Inst, 1975-. *Publications:* Over 100 publs in Botanical Journal, USSR, Ukranian Botanical Journal, Citology and Genetics, USSR, Agricultural Science Report, topics incl rsch in plant pollination and fertilisation, pear fruit and seed formation, regulation of those processes, hormone stimulated apomyxes and parthenocarpia, problems of plant lectins role in life of plants and soil; Articles on hist of sci. *Memberships:* Chmn, Poltava Br, Ukrainian Botan Soc, Presidium Mbr; Ukrainian Soc Genetics and Selection; Vavilov Commemoration Commn, USSR Acad Scis; Ukrainian Br, Soviet Cultural Fund. *Honours:* Vavilov Medal, USSR Acad Scis; Medals, Ukrainian Exhib Nat Achievements; Dips, var Soviet sci and cultural instns; 18 invention certs. *Hobbies:* Postcard collection (roses and still life with flowers and fruit); Organisatin of Poltava Agricultural Institute Museum; Cultivation of unique plants. *Address:* Shevchenko 5, flat 24, Poltava 314019, Ukraine.

SAMSOVA Galina, b. 17 Mar 1937, USSR. Artistic Director of Scottish Ballet. *Education:* State Ballet School, Kiev, 1950-56. *Appointments:* Soloist, Kiev Opera House, 1956-60; Prin Dancer, Nat Ballet Can, 1961-64; Prima Ballerina, London Fest Ballet, England, 1964-73; Co-Dir, Prin Dancer, New London Ballet, 1973-78; Prin Ballerina, Sadlers Wells Royal Ballet, London, 1980-90; Artistic Dir, Socttish Ballet, Glasgow, 1991-. *Honours:* Best Female Dancer, 1st Int Ballet Fest, 1963. *Hobbies:* Cats; Dogs; Gardening; Reading; Classical music; Opera; Theatre. *Address:* The Scottish Ballet, 261 West Princes St, Glasgow G4 9EE, Scotland. 138.

SAMUEL John Thenganamannil, b. Kerala, India. Economist. m. Aleyamma P Mathew, 29 Dec 1960, 3 s. *Education:* MA, Econs, Univ Kerala, 1958; PhD, Econs, Univ Toronto, Can, 1965. *Appointments include:* Adj Prof, Carelton Univ, 1985-; Dir, Race Rels, Sec of State, Govt Can, 1989; Acting Exec Dir, 1990, Sr Dir, 1991- , Employment and Immigration Advsry Coun. *Publications:* Over 50 scholarly papers in jrnls, books and so on. *Memberships:* Elected to Int Union Sci Study Population; Can Population Soc; Population Assn Am. *Honours:* 3 Gold Medals: Lepper Mem, A V George, M R V Nair, Univ Kerala, 1957; C'wlth Scholar, Can, 1961-65. *Hobbies:* Badminton; Collector of 19th century books. *Address:* 2060 Chalmers Rd, Ottawa, Ontario, Canada K1H 6K5. 88.

SAMUELS John Richard, b. 13 Sept 1952, Gravesend, Kent, England. Archaeologist; Publisher. m. Harriet Annabel Rickard, 7 Sept 1986, 1 s, 1 d. *Education:* BA

Hons, Univ Coll, Cardiff, 1974; PhD, Univ Nottingham, 1983. *Appointments:* Archaeologist to M180 Comm, 1975-76; Rsch Asst, Univ Nottingham, 1976-80; Asst Dir, Liverpool Univ Rescue Archaeology Unit, 1980-81; Lectr, Archaeology, Local Hist, Nottingham, 1981-90; Archaeological Cons, Publr, 1990-. *Publications:* Figure Brasses in West Lincolnshire, 1976; 18th and 19th Century Aslockton and Whatton, 1981; Lydiate Hall, Merseyside, 1982; History Around Us, 1989; 39 acad articles in jrnls. *Memberships:* Prehistoric Soc; Soc Mediaeval Archaeology; Vernacular Arch Grp; Exec Comm, Trust for Lincs Archaeology; Exec Comm, Trent and Peak Archaeological Trust; Chmn, Newark Castle Trust. *Honours:* Mbr, Inst Field Archaeologists, 1983. *Hobbies:* Archaeology; Local history; Dog walking. *Address:* 6 Old North Rd, Cromwell, Newark, Notts NG23 6JE, England.

SAMUT-TAGLIAFERRO John, b. 26 Mar 1946, Malta. Consultant Radiologist. m. Mary Cremona-Barbaro di San Giorgio, 15 Mar 1980. *Education:* MD, Royal Univ Malta, 1973; Dip, Med Radiodiagnosis, London, 1977; Fellow, Royal Coll Radiologists, UK, 1979; BA, Hist At, Univ Malta, in progress. *Appointments:* St Luke's Hosp, Malta, 1973-75; Registrar, King's Coll Hosp, London, England, 1975-78; Sr Registrar, St Thomas; Hosp, London, 1978-80; Cons, 1980-91, Dept Hd, 1982, Dr Daniel den Hoed Cancer Ctr and Rotterdam Radiotherapy Inst, Netherlands. *Publications:* Articles in med jrnls. *Memberships:* Radiological Soc N Am; Malta Study Circle, UK; The Casino (1852). *Honours:* Holder, Malta Open Nat Record for Javelin Throw, 1967; C'wlth Postgrad Med Scholarship, 1975. *Hobbies:* Books; Tennis; Painting. *Address:* 5/3 G Muscat Azzopardi St, Sliema, Malta. 99.

SAMWELL Stanley David, b. 12 June 1927, London, England. Chartered Accountant. m. Diana Mary Windsor, 23 Aug 1974. *Education:* Harrow Co Grammar School, 1938-43. *Appointments:* Gane Jackson Jefferies and Freeman, Chartered Accts, 1943-46, 1948-54; Served RAF, 1946-48; Am Express Co, 1955-63; Layton-Bennett, Billingham & Co (later Arthur Young), Chartered Accts, 1963-83; Dept Trade Insp, affairs of: Kuehne & Nagel Ltd, 1974-75, Peachey Property Corp, 1977-78. *Publication:* Corporate Receiverships, textbook, 2nd Ed, 1988. *Memberships:* Insolvency Practitioners Assn, Pres 1980-81; Inst Chartered Accts England and Wales. *Hobbies:* Skiing; Travel; Theatre; Photography. *Address:* ssa 005 Old Manor Yard, London SW5 9AB, England.

SAMYSHEV Ernest Zainullinovich, b. 28 Oct 1937, Pukhovichi, USSR. Hydrobiologist; Head of Department. m. Valentina Davydovna Tretyakova, 15 Nov 1991, 1 s, 1 d. *Education:* Technological Inst Fisheries and Fish Econs, Kaliningrad, 1958-63; MSc, 1970; DSc, 1987. *Appointments:* Asst, 1963-69, Sr Scientist, 1967-70, Hd, Environment Dept, 1970-74, Hd, Dept Hydrobiology, 1974-88, Dpty Dir, Hd, Dept Functioning of Marine Ecosystems, 1991-, Inst Biology of the So Seas, Sevastopol. *Publications:* Biochemical composition and calorific value of Guinean plankton, 1971; Nutrition of some dominant copepod species in Guinean Gulf, 1971; Antarctic krill and structure of plankton community in its areal, 1991. *Membrships:* Ichthyological Comm, Min Fisheries, 1974-89; Cons Coun Mariculture, State Comm Sci Technology, 1988-90; All-Union Hydrobiological Soc, USSR Acad Scis, 1965-90. *Hobbies:* Sports; Music; Fishing. *Address:* Institute of Biology of the Southern Seas, 2 Nakhimov Avenue, Sevastopol 335000, Ukraine.

SANDBACH Richard Stainton Edward, b. 13 June 1915, Sale, Cheshire, England. Retired Solicitor. m. Brenda Mary Cleminson, 10 Sept 1949, 2 s. *Education:* Fndn Scholar, St John's Coll, Cambridge, 1934-38; BA, 1937; LLB, 1938; MA, 1943; LLM. *Appointments:* Solicitor: Aylesbury, 1947-50, Peterborough, 1950-79; Ptnr, 1951-79, Sr Ptnr, 1970-79, Greenwoods. *Publications:* Priest and Freemasons, book, 1988;

Understanding the Royal Arch, book, 1992; Papers: George Oliver, 1985; Robert Thomas Crucefix, 1991; Il Compito dell'Arco Reale, 1991; The Freemasons Quarterly Review, 1834-1840; Peterborough Booklets 1-5, 1990-91. *Memberships:* Law Soc; United Oxford and Cambridge Univ Club; Past Provincial Grand Master, Northants and Hunts, Free and Accepted Masons of England; Master, Quatuor Coronate Lodge, Premier Lodge of Masonic Res, 1992; Chmn, Peterborough Diocesan Bd Fin, 1974- 84. *Honour:* McMahon Law Student, 1939. *Hobbies:* Hill walking; Photography; Historic research; Freemasonry. *Address:* 91 Lincoln Rd, Peterborough PE1 2SH, England.

SANDBERG Hans Torbjorn, b. 4 June 1946, Uppsala, Sweden. President of Seed Company. m. Britt Inger Olsson, 19 June 1971, 2 s, 1 d. *Education:* MSc, Agronomy, Univ Lund, 1973; MSc, Econs, Univ Uppsala, 1974. *Appointments:* Planning Mgr, AB Juvel, Stockholm, 1975; Farm Mgr, Baretofta-Christinelund, Tomelilla, 1976-79; Area Mgr, AB Fors Engstrom, Kalmar, 1979-81; Prod Mgr, 1982-83, Pres, 1984-, W Weibull AB seed co, Landskrona. *Hobby:* Veteran automobiles. *Address:* W Weibull AB, Box 520, S-261 24 Landskrona, Sweden. 32, 52.

SANDERS Carol, b. 31 Dec 1944, Cambridge, England. University Professor. m. Peter M E Figueroa, 27 July 1978, 1 s, 1 d. *Education:* New Hall, Cambridge, 1963-66; PGCE, Inst Educ, Univ London, 1968; MA (Cantab); Univ Toulouse, France; Doct Univ, Paris. *Appointments:* Lectr, French, Univ Reading, 1969-72; Lectr, French, Univ W Indies, 1972- 76; Lectr, 1977-84, Dir, Lang Ctr, 1980-83, Univ Sussex, England; Reader, then Prof, French, Australian Nat Univ, 1984-88; Prof, French, Univ Surrey, Guildford, England, 1988-. *Publications:* Saussure: Cours de Linguistique Generale, 1979; Beyond A-level in Teaching of French (ed), 1981; Cours de francais contemporain (w M M Gervais), 1986; Lire le Pacifique (w K Muller), 1989; Franc Exchange (w J Gladkow), 1990; French Today (ed), 1992; Transls: Odile (R Queneau); Armoires Vides (A Ernaux). *Memberships:* Assn French Lang Studies, Fndn Pres 1982-84; Soc French Studies; MLA, USA; Ed, Journal for French Language Studies. *Honours:* Chevalier des Palmes Academiques; Fellow, Inst Linguists. *Hobbies:* Travel; Reading. *Address:* Dept of Linguistic and International Studies, University of Surrey, Guildford GU2 5XH, England. 52.

SANDERS Roy, b. 20 Aug 1937, Hoddesdon, England. Consultant Plastic Surgeon. *Education:* BSc Hons, Anatomy, 1959, MB BS, 1962, Univ London; FRCS England, 1967. *Appointments:* Cons Plastic Surg: The Middlesex, Royal Nat Orthopaedic and Mt Vernon Hosps; Hon Sr Lectr, Univ London. *Publications:* Sundry chapts and sci articles in books and jrnls. *Memberships:* Co of Pikeman and Musketeers; Honourable Artillery Co; Brit Assn Plastic Surgs, VP 1992, Pres 1993; Pres, Plastic Surg Sect, Royal Soc Med London. *Hobbies:* Equestrian sports; Painting in watercolour; Writing comic verse. *Address:* Suite 1, 82 Portland Place, London W1N 3DH, England.

SANDFORD Cedric Thomas, b. 21 Nov 1924, Basingstoke, England. Emeritus Professor; Consultant; Publisher. m. (1) Evelyn Belch, 1 Dec 1945, 1 s, 1 d, (2) Christina Katarin Privett, 21 July 1984, 1 d. *Education:* BA Hons, Econ, 1948, MA, 1949, Univ Manchester; BA, Hist, Univ London, 1955. *Appointments:* War serv, RAF, 1943-46; Asst Lectr, Lectr, Barnley Municipal Coll, 1948-58; Sr Lectr, then Hd, Dept, Bristol Coll Sci and Technology, 1959-65; Prof, Pol Economy, 1965-87, Emeritus Prof, 1987-, Univ Bath; Var overseas vis prof'ships. *Publications:* 17 rsch books and monographs incl: Taxing Personal Wealth, 1971; Hidden Costs of Taxation, 1973; An Accessions Tax (w J R M Willis and D J Ironside), 1975; Costs and Benefits of VAT (w M Godwin, P Hardwick, I Butterworth), 1981; Tax Policy-Making in the United Kingdom (w Ann Robinson), 1983; The Irish Wealth Tax: A Study in

Ecnomics and Politics (w Oliver Morrissey), 1985; Administrative and Compliance Costs of Taxation (w Michael Godwin and Peter Hardwick), 1989; Va gen textbooks; Many contbns to other books; Many articles in learned jrnls. *Memberships:* Pres, Econs Assn, 1983-86; SW Elec Consultative Coun, 1981-90; Bath Dist Hlth Auth, 1984-90; Chmn, Bath Cancer Unit Appeal. *Honours:* Grad Fellow, Manchester Univ, 1948-49; Downing Fellow in Social Econs, Univ Melbourne, Australia, 1990; Leverhulme Emeritus Fellow, 1991-92. *Hobbies:* Fishing; Gardening; Walking. *Address:* Old Coach House, Fersfield, Perrymead, Bath BA2 5AR, England. 1.

SANDILANDS James Sebastian, b. 15 Oct 1944, Cambridge, England. Stockbroker. m. Gabriele Mellich, 1 July 1972, 1 s. *Education:* Eton Coll, 1957-62. *Appointments:* William T Hart, 1965-67; Ptnr, Sheppards, 1967-77; Ptnr, Buckmaster and Moore, 1977-90; Dpty Mng Dir, Quilter Goodison Co Ltd, London, 1990-; Mngng Dir, 1992-. *Memberships:* London Stock Exchange; Soc Investment Analysts. *Hobbies:* Skiing; Walking; Reading; Opera; Theatre. *Address:* c/o Quilter Goodison Company Limited, St Helens, 1 Undershaft, London EC3A 8BB, England.

SANDORFY Camille, b. 9 Dec 1920, Budapest, Hungary. Professor Emeritus. m. Rolande Cayla, 24 Aug 1971. *Education:* PhD, Univ Szeged, Hungary, 1946; DSc, Chem, Sorbonne, Paris, 1949; Postdoct Fellow, Ottawa, Can, 1951-53. *Appointments:* Rsch Worker, Tech Univ, Budapest, 1946-47; Charge de Recherches, Ctr Nat des Recherches Scientifiques, Paris, France, 1947-51; Prof, Univ Montreal, Can, 1954-. *Publications:* Les spectres electrniques en chimie theorique, 1959; Electronic Spectra and Quantum Chemistry, 1964; Semi-Empirical Wave Mechanical Calculations (w R Daudel), 1971; 240 rsch publs. *Memberships:* Royal Soc Can; Int Acad Quantum Molecular Sci; European Acad Arts, Sci and Lit. *Honours:* Killam Mem Scholarship, 1978; Herzberg Medal, 1980; Prix Marie-Victorin of quebec, 1982; Med, Chem Inst Can, 1983; Med, World Assn Theoretical Organic Chems, 1990. *Address:* Departement de Chimie, Universite de Montreal, Montreal, Quebec, Canada H3C 3J7. 34, 142.

SANDYK Reuven, b. 11 Mar 1951, Haifa, Israel. Professor of Neurological Sciences. m. Lea Dann, 25 June 1987, 1 d. *Education:* MD, Univ Bonn, FRG, 1979; Resident, Neurology, 1980-83; Postdoct, Neuropharmacology, 1983-84, MSc, 1984, Univ Johannesburg, S Africa; Rsch Fellow, Neurology, 1984-87; Rsch Fellow, Albert Einstein Coll Med, USA, 1989-91. *Appointments:* Vis Prof, Rutgers Univ, NJ, USA, 1986-; Vis Prof, Neurology, Juntendo Univ, Tokyo, Japan, 1987-88. *Memberships:* Am Acad Neurology; Am Coll Nutrition; NY Acad Scis. *Honours include:* Friedrich Ebert Stiftung, Bonn, 1973-79. *Hobbies:* Classical music; Greek Philosophy; Reading biographies. *Address:* PO Box 203 Bedford Hills, NY 10507, USA. 117.

SANGUINETTI Eduardo Felipe, b. 30 Dec 1951, Buenos Aires, Argentina. Artist. div., 1 s, 2 d. *Education:* BA, 1970; PhD, 1974; Theatre Workshop, 1977-80. *Creative works:* Books: Alter Ego, 1984; Morbi Dei, 1985; Per Se, 1987, edited and translated into 5 langs; Perfs: Solum, 1979; Solum 11, 1982; Solum (Imagen y sonido de la nueva tierra), 1982; Solum 111, 1984; Solum 1 plus 1, Berlin, 1987; Rekiem, 1988; The Last Tarzan, 1989; Art in the Pampas: Luminata Alterna - Solum X, 1991; Films: Bis, 16 mm, 1983; Border Line, 35 mm, 1988; Luninata Alterna, video, 1991. *Membership:* Wrld Lit Acad, Cambridge, England. *Honours:* Biographee of Yr Award, 1st Presidential Eds, Histl Preservation Am, 1986. *Hobby:* Gardening. *Address:* Jose Hernandez 2536 - 2B, CP 1426, Buenos Aires, Argentina. 52, 139, 151, 152, 156, 178.

SANKAR R S, b. 17 Jan 1947, Marathoni, Tamilnadu, India. Research Chemist. m. Parvathy Sankar, 2 May

1975, 1 s, 1 d. *Education:* BSc, Chem, 1967, MSc, Analytical and Inorganic Chem, 1968, Madras Univ; Doct, Cultural level, Agricl Sci, Univ Tucson, AZ, USA, 1984; PHd, Applied Scis, Field Agricl Chem, Univ FL, 1988. *Appointments:* Apprentice, Mfg Chem, 1970-71, Jr Lab Chem, 1971-74, Lab Chem, 1974-80, Chem, Rsch and Dev, 1980-, Sakthi Sugars Ltd, Sakthinagar, Tamilnadu. *Publications:* Level of Juice Potash in Sugarcane; Effect of Glyphosphine on Sugarcane Juice Quality; Papers presented at Sci Club Meetings. *Membership:* Assoc Mbr, Sugar Technologists Assn. *Honours:* Winner, Chess Tournament, 1984; Runner-up, Bridge Tournament, 1985; Winner, Basketball Throw, 1989, 1990; Prizes in Ring Throw. *Hobbies:* Chess; Bridge; Cricket. *Address:* s/o R S Subramanian, 11nd Floor, 84 Spur Tank Road, Chetput, Madras-600 031, India. 152.

SANTOS-MARTINEZ Jesus, b. 5 Mar 1924, Vieques, Puerto Rico, USA. Physiologist; Pharmacologist. m. Maria F de Jesus Santos-Martinez, 2 Jan 1955, 3 s, 1 d. *Education:* BS, Univ PR, 1946; MS, Univ IL, 1948; PhD, Purdue Univ, 1954; Postdoct trng, IN Univ School Med, 1966-67. *Appointments:* School Pharm, 1946-54, Sch med, 1954-79, Univ PR; Univ Ctrl del Caribe, 1979-. *Publications:* Original rsch articles in J Amer Soc Physiol, Biochem, Pharmacol, Archive Internat, Pharmacodyn et Therap, Proc Exper Biol Med, Rev Farm PR. *Memberships:* Am Physiological Soc; Am Soc Nephrology; Int Soc Nephrology; Soc Expmtl Biol and Med; AAAS; Rho Chi; Sigma Xi; Phi Lambda Upsilon; Hon Mbr, PR Med Soc. *Honours:* Vieques Favourite Son, 1947; Travel Award, Am Physiological Soc, 1968; Travel Award, Int Soc Nephrology, 1969. *Hobbies:* Music; Gardening. *Address:* Verona 1184, San Juan, PR 00924, USA. 7.

SANTOSO Budi, b. 16 Aug 1946, Yogyakarta, Indonesia. Atomic Physicist. m. Kusaladewi Hamengkubuwono IX, 27 Feb 1982, 2 s. *Education:* Doctorandus, Phys, Gajah Mada, 1970; MSc, Phys, 1971, PhD, Theoretical Phys, 1973, Essex Univ, England. *Appointments:* Currently Di, Nuclear Technology Assessment Ctr, Jakarta. *Publications:* Over 40 in atomic phys, nuclear and reactor phys, lasers, nuclear med and biology. *Memberships:* Indonesian Phys Soc; Indonesian Nuclear Med Soc; Am Phys Soc, 1979; Assoc Mbr, Int Ctr Theoretical Phys, UNDP, Trieste, Italy, 1983-89. *Honours:* Award for highest rank in Sr HS Exam, Indonesian Inst Sic; Award for Phys tchng, Indonesian Mil Acad; Brit Coun Colombo Plan Award for PhD scholarship, 1970-73. *Hobbies:* Old Javanese arts such as keris, spear; Chess. *Address:* Atomic Energy Agency of Indonesia, PO Box 85 Kby, Jakarta 12710, Indonesia.

SAPONOV Mikhail Aleksandrovich, b. 2 Apr 1946, Shcholkovo, nr Moscow, Russia. Musicologist; Professor. *Education:* Gnessiny Music Coll, Moscow, 1964-68; Student, 1968-73, Postgrad doct studies, 1973-66, Tchaikovsky Conservatory, Moscow; DA, Musicology, 1978; Dr habilitatus, arts, 1992. *Appointments:* Lectr, then Prof, 1976-, Dept Hd, 1990-, Dept Wn Music Hist, Tchaikovsky Conservatory, Moscow; Prof, Musicology, Mirkovic Acad Music, Lovran, near Rieka, Croatia, 1991-. *Publications:* The Art of Improvisation: Extempore Performing in Western Medieval and Renaissance Music, 1982; Oral Culture as Material for Medieval Studies, 1989; Minstrels, 1993. *Membership:* Union Composers Russia. *Hobbies:* Travel; Languages; Jogging; Art museums. *Address:* Garnizon 15-56, 140003 Lubertsy 3, Moscow, Russia.

SARAN Deo, b. 19 Feb 1955, Labasa, Fiji. Manager of Finance and Planning; Company Secretary. *Education:* BA, Univ of S Pacific, 1976. *Appointments:* Asst Acct, CIG (Fiji) Ltd, 1977-79; Asst Acct, 1979-80, Mgmt Acct, 1986-87, Fin Mgr, 1987-90, Fiji Pine Commn; Audit Sr, Price Waterhouse, 1980-86; Mgr, Fin and Planning, Co Sec, Fiji Pine Ltd, Lautoka, 1991-. *Memberships:* Fiji Inst Accts; Inst of Management

Accountants, USA; Australian Inst Mgmt. *Hobbies:* Motor sports; Soccer. *Address:* 2 Adams St, Tauakubu, Lautoka, Fiji. 52, 132.

SARCHET-WALLER Paul Robert, b. 13 Jan 1947, Barnsley, Yorkshire, England. Missionary; Minister. m. Diane Winifred Sarchet, 19 Dec 1970, 1 s, 2 d. *Education:* DPhEd, Welsh Nat Coll, Cardiff, 1969; Chinese Dip, Hong Kong Chinese Univ, 1980; BTh, Shiloh Bible Coll, Oakland, CA, USA, 1980. *Appointments:* Team Mbr, 1967-68, Capt, 1968-69, Welsh Nat Colls Swimming Team; Tchr, Barnsley Educ Auth, England, 1969-72; Tchr, Munro Coll, Jamaica, 1972-74; Tchr, Missionary, Diocesan Boys School, Hong Kong, 1974-78; Fndr, Sr Pastor, Elim Full Gospel Ch, Hong Kong, 1982-; Fndr, Chmn, Elim Full Gospel Publs, Hong Kong, 1985-; Fndr, Prin, Elim Discipleship Trng School, Hong Kong, 1985-; Fndr, Elim Asia Missions, 1987-; Fndr, discipleship trng schools, SE Asia, Malaysia, Philippines, India; Conf speaker, NZ, England, USA, Malaysia, Philippines, Egypt. *Publications:* Books: The Holy Spirit, 1985; Principles of Ministry, 1985; Foundation Doctrine, 1987; Principles of Discipleship, 1987; Praise and Worship, 1988; Principles of Missions, 1988; Equipped to Serve, 1990; Life Style Evangelism, 1991; Abundant Life, in Chinese, 1991.; Articles in profl jrnls; Vocalist, In Praise of Jesus, album, 1981. *Honours:* Hon DD, So CA Coll, 1991. *Address:* PO Box 68, Shatin, Hong Kong. 52, 139, 145.

SARGENT John Richard, b. 22 Mar 1925, Birmingham, England. Economist. m. (1) Anne Elizabeth Haigh, 1 s, 2 d, (2) Hester Mary Campbell, 18 Oct 1980, 3 stepsons. *Education:* Christ Church, Oxford Univ, 1946-48; BA, MA, Oxford. *Appointments:* Fellow, Lectr, Econs, Worcester Coll, Oxford, 1951-62; Prof, Econs, Univ Warwick, 1965-73; Grp Econ Advsr, Midland Bank, London, 1974-84. *Publications:* Num articles in learned jrnls concerning econ matters. *Memberships:* Royal Econ Soc; Am Econ Assn; Gov, Nat Inst Econ and Social Rsch; Coun Mbr, Soc Univ Europeenne de Recherche Financiers, Pres 1985-88. *Hobbies:* Gardening; Voluntary work for local hospital. *Address:* Trentham House, Fulbrook, Burford, Oxfordshire OX18 4BL, England. 1.

SAROOP Narindar, b. 14 Aug 1929, India. Management Consultant. m. (1) Ravi Gill, Oct 1952, diss. 1967, 1 s 2 d, (2) Stephanie Denise Cronopulo, Feb 1968. *Education:* Aitchison Coll for Punjab Chiefs, Labore; Indian Mil Acad, Dehra Dun. *Appointments:* Served 2 Royal Lancers (Gardner's Horse), Queen Victoria's Own The Poona Horse: Squadron Off, Regimental Signals Off, Regimental Gunnery Off, Acting Squadron Ldr; Mgmt Trainee, Yule Catto and Co Ltd, England, 1954-55; Snr Exec, Andrew Yule and Co Ltd, 1955-61; Subsidiary Bd Dir: Davy Ashmore Grp, 1961-64, Turner and Newall Grp, 1965-71; Mgmt Consultancy, 1972-76; Councillor, Royal Borough Kensington and Chelsea, 1974-82; Dev Advsr, H Clarkson Grp, 1976-87; Parly Cand (1st Asian Conserv Party cand this century), Greenwich Gen Election, 1979; Cons, Banque Belge, 1987-91. *Publications:* Books: In Defence of Freedom (co-author), 1978; A Squire of Hindoostan, 1985. *Memberships:* India Welfare Soc, Past Pres; Former Coun Mbr, Freedom Assn; Coun Mbr, IOD; Former Mbr, BBC Advsry Panel; Charity Review Royal Borough Kensington and Chelsea; Vice-Chmn, Conserv Party Int Off; Fndr, Past Chmn, Anglo-Asian Conserv Soc; Fndr, Chmn, The Durbar Club. *Honours:* CBE, 1982. *Address:* 25 de Vere Gardens, London W8, England. 1, 34.

SARTORI Eva Maria, b. Subotica, Yugoslavia. Author. *Publications:* Pierre, mon amour, 1967; Wie eine Palme im Wind, 1968; Oh, diese Erbschaft, 1969; Karriere ist Silber, Heiraten Gold, 1977; Die Rheinhagens, 1980; Spuren, die kein Wind verweht, 1981; Damals in Dahlem, 1982; Konigin Luise, 1983; Der Sunder und die Heilige, 1984; Streite nicht mit dem Wind, 1985; Venedig sehen und sterben, 1986; Das Geheimnis der

roten Rose, 1987; Das Schicksal stellte die Weiche, 1987; Im Banne des weissen Drachen, 1988; Bittere Vergangenheit, 1989; Ein Herz sucht eine Heimat, 1990; Wir wissen weder den Tag noch die Stunde, 1991. *Contributions to:* num illustrated mags incl: Neue Welt; Sieben Tage; Frau mit Herz; Die Aktuelle; Das Neue Blatt; Frau aktuell; Romanwocher. *Memberships:* Freier Deutscher Autorenverband. *Honours:* Doct Mbrship, Lit, World Univ Roundtable. *Hobbies:* Social work; Music; Arts; Travel; Languages; Gardening; Collecting stamps. *Address:* Kirchenstrasse 32, D-8261 Stammham, Germany. 3, 92, 138, 152, 189, 191.

SASAKI Ryuji, b. 5 July 1935, Shiga, Japan. Professor of History. m. Michiko Yoshiwara, 17 Dec 1961, 2 s, 1 d. *Education:* BA, 1958, MA, Grad Inst, 1960, Kyoto Univ; PhD, 1991. *Appointments:* Hagoromo Jr Coll, 1964-68; Shizuok Univ, 1968-72; Tokyo Metrop Univ, 1972-. *Publications:* In Japanese: A History of the Japanese Capitalism (w Goto and Fuji), 1979; Asia and Japan in World Politics, 1988; The Peace Settlement in San Francisco, 1988; Origins and Functions of the Contemporary Tenno System, 1990. *Memberships include:* Japanese Histl Coun; Assn Japanese Hist; Histl Sci Soc Japan. *Hobbies:* Violin and viola playing; Reading; Cycling. *Address:* 2-18-13 Sakura, Setagaya-ku, Tokyo 156, Japan.

SASIADEK Eugeniusz, b. 17 Feb 1929, Zyrawa, Poland. Artist- Musician (Singer); Professor. m. Helena Zupok, 29 Sept 1951, 1 s , 2 d. *Education:* Grad, Fac Maths, Univ Wroclaw, 1952; Grad, Fac Singing, Acad Music, Wroclaw, 1956; Corse di Perfezionamento, Singing, San Cecilia Conservatorio, Rome, 1967-68. *Career:* Prof, 1960-, REctor, 1987-90, Acad Music, Wroclaw; Soloist Singer: Philharmonic Hall, Bydgoszcz, 1962-68; Cappelle Cracoviensis, 1969-82; Complesso di musica antica, Wroclaw, 1969-; Dir, Opera House, Wroclaw, 1982-84; Soloist (Tenor) Num concerts, Poland, En and Wn Europe, Australia, Can, Scandinavia, GB; TV and radio concerts; Pres, 35 sci confs, 1970-; Dir, master courses for singers, 1976-. *Publications:* 17 records: Series of articles on ancient music in Zeszyty Naukowe; Ed, 20 issues, Zeszyty Naukowe, 1975-91. *Memberships:* Pres, Polish Assn Tchrs Singing; V-Pres, Assn Polish Artist Musicians, 1992-; Pres, Inst Singing, Acad Music, Wroclow. *Honours:* prize, Min Culture and Arts, 1970, 1977, 1982, 1990; Gold Order of Merit, 1971; Medal, Commn Nat Educ, 1978; Cavalier Cross, Order of Polonia Restituta, 1979; Tchr of Merit, Poland, 1988. *Hobbies:* Theatre; Tourism; Swimming. *Address:* al Wiazowa 64, 53-119 Wroclaw, Poland. 4.

SATO Hisayoshi, b. 11 July 1933, Japan. Director General of Mechanical Engineering Laboratory. m. 3 Oct 1963, 2 s, 1 d. *Education:* BEng, Mech Engrng, 1958, DrEng, Mech Engrng, 1963, Univ Tokyo. *Appointments:* Assoc Prof, Mech Engrng, 1963, Prof, Mech Engrng, 1976, Inst Indl Sci, Univ Tokyo; Rsch Assoc, MIT, Boston, MA, USA, 1966-67; Dir Gen, Mech Engrng Lab, AIST, MITI, Japan. *Publications:* Development of Methodology for Aseismic Design of Mechanical Structures; Evaluation for Correlation of Stiffness of Machine Tool with Machining Accuracy. *Memberships:* Japan Soc Mech Engrs; Am Soc Mech Engrs; Japan Soc Profl Engrs; Engrng Assn Japan; CIRP; Assoc Mbr, Belgian Royal Acad. *Honours:* Award for Good Paper, Japan Soc Mech Engrs, 1969, 1978, 1987; Award for Good Paper, Technology Promotion for Machine Tools, 1982, 1983, 1984, 1988, 1990. *Address:* 1-2 Namiki, Tsukuba, Ibaraki 305, Japan.

SATO Masachiyo, b. 18 Feb 1926, Kanazawa, Ishikawa, Japan. Honorary Professor. m. Mie Saito, 18 Oct 1956. *Education:* BSc, 1947, DrSc, 1962, Univ Tokyo. *Appointments:* Asst, Inst Indl Sci, Univ Tokyo, 1947; Assoc Prof, Fac Engrng, 1964, Prof, Fac Engrng, 1967, Hon Prof, 1990, Yokohama Nat Univ; Prof, 1990, Yokohama Sohei Junior Coll. *Publications:* Rsch articles and papers in int jrnls in field of theoretical phys, nuclear phys and applied maths. *Memberships:* Phys Soc Japan;

Info Processing Soc Japan; Soc Franco-Japonais des Scis Pures et Appliquees; Soc des Anciens Boursiers Techniques du Gouvernement Francais. *Hobby:* Wine tasting. *Address:* 12-18 Tana-cho, Midori-ku, 227 Yokohama, Japan. 52.

SATO Masuko, b. 4 Nov 1938, Osaka, Japan. Professor; Doctor of Medicine. m. Yoshinobu Sato, 28 May 1963, 2 d. *Education:* Degree, 1963, Grad degree, 1957, Kyoto Prefecture Med School. *Appointments:* Japan Bapt Hosp, 1967; Assoc Prof, 1972-82, Prof, 1982, Kyoto Women's Univ. *Publications:* Recent Child Health, 1983; Encyclopaedia of Infant Development (contbr, ed), 1985; Practice in Child Health (author, ed), 1988. *Memberships:* Dir, Yukawa Social Gathering of World Federalists, Kyoto; Councilor, Japan Soc Child Health. *Hobbies:* Music; Sports. *Address:* 8 Shimogamo-Maehagicho, Sakyoku, Kyoto, Japan 606. 52.

SATO Yoshinobu, b. 16 Dec 1934, Kyoto, Japan. Otorhinolaryngologist; Educator; Consultant. m. Masuko Yoshida, 28 May 1963, 2 d. *Education:* Grad, Kyoto Prefectural Univ Med, 1961; MD, 1962; Postgrad Med courses, 1963-67; PhD, Biochem Studies on Acid Mucopolysaccharides in Paranasal Mucous Membranes in Chronic Sinusitis, 1967. *Appointments:* Invited Guest Investigator, Tchng Asst, Dept Otorhinolaryngology, NY Univ Med Ctr, USA, 1867-68; Asst Prof, Dept Otorhinolaryngology, Kyoto Prefectural Univ Med, Japan, 1970-75; Prof, Clin Pathology, Dept Med Technology, Kobe Tokiwa Coll, Kobe, 1979-; Cons, Biomed and Environmental Consultants Inc, Richland, WA, USA, 1989-. *Publications:* Clinical Pathology (ed, author), 1988; Aerosol Inhalation Therapy (ed, author), 1989; Heisei Job's Story of the Bible, 1989; Author or co-author, 205 sci publs. *Memberships:* Oto-Rhino-Laryngological Soc Japan; Japan Rhinologic Soc; Exec Bd, Japan Soc Aerosols in Med; Exec Bd, Int Soc Aerosols in Med; Japan Soc Phys Educ. *Honours:* Chmn, Comm Educl Affairs, 1983-85, Ed-in-Chief, Bulletin, 1985-90, Kobe Tokima Coll; Mbr, Exec Bd, 1985-, VP, 1991-, Japan Assn Aerosol Sci and Technology; Ed, Journal of Aerosol Medicine, Stony Brook, NY, USA, 1988-. *Hobbies include:* Japanese classical swimming. *Address:* 8 Shimogamo-Maehagicho, Sakyoku, Kyoto 606, Japan. 166.

SATTERWHITE Ronald Dean Sr, b. 4 Dec 1953, Tallahassee, Florida, USA. Senior Pastor. m. Melody Pye, 1 July 1978, 1 s, 2 d. *Education:* Dip, T R Robinson High, 1971; BA, FL Bible Coll, 1975. *Appointments:* City Missionary, Calvary Community Ch, Tampa, FL, 1976-78; Min Educ and Activities, Calvary Bapt Ch, Spartanburg, SC, 1979-80; Pastor, Stafford, Furman, Steep Bottom Bapt Chs, Furman, SC, 1981-84; Pastor, Rocky Grove Bapt Ch, Salley, SC, 1984; Pastor, 1985-, currently Sr Pastor, 1st Bapt Ch, Port Tampa, Tampa, FL; Min Youth and Music, Pine Grove Bapt Ch, Clover, SC, 1988. *Memberships:* Hampton Co Ministerial Assn, Pres 1983; Gen Bd, SC Bapt Conven, 1984; Tampa Bay Bapt Mins Conf, 2nd VP 1987, 1st VP 1988, Pres 1989. *Honours:* 5 Awards for Sunday School Growth, FL Bapt Sunday School Conven, Orlandom FL, 1985-90, 1991; Eagle Award, Outstanding Sunday School Growth, 1989; 3 New Work Awards, Home Mission Bd, S Bapt Ch. *Hobbies:* Church growth; Fishing; Family activities. *Address:* 6907 S Sparkman St, Tampa, FL 33616, USA.

SATTLER Rolf, b. 8 Mar 1936, Goppingen, Germany. Professor of Biology and Biophilosophy. m. Liv Hamann, 1 May 1963, div, 1985. *Education:* Dr rer nat, Univ Munich, 1961. *Appointments:* NATO Fellow: Univ Alta, Can, 1962-63, Univ CA, USA, 1963-64; Asst Prof, 1964-69, Assoc Prof, 1969-77, Full Prof, 1977-, McGill Univ, Montreal, Can. *Publications:* Organogenesis of Flowers, 1973; Biophilosophy, 1986; Over 60 articles in profl jrnls; Ed: Theoretical Plant Morphology, 1978; Axioms and Principles of Plant Morphology, 1982. *Memberships include:* Botan Soc Am; Can Botan Assn; Sigma Xi; Int Soc for Study of Hist, Philos and Social Studies of Biology. *Honours:* Lawson Medal, Can Botan Assn,

1974; Fellow, Royal Soc Can; Fellow, Linnean Soc London; Awards for book Organogenesis of Flowers, AAUP and Am Inst Graphic Arts. *Hobbies:* Music; Swimming; Tai Chi; Hiking. *Address:* Biology Department, McGill University, 1205 Dr Penfield Ave, Montreal, Quebec, Canada H3A 1B1. 2, 52, 142, 143.

SAUDEK Jan, b. 13 May 1935, Prague, Czechoslovakia. Photographer. m. (1) Marie Saudek (no 1), 24 Feb 1958, (2) Marie Saudek (no 2), 21 Oct 1977, 3 s, 3 d. *Education:* Apprenticeship, Photography, School for Sergeants, Army, 1954-56. *Career:* Ordinary Workman, 1950-83; Freelance Photographer, 1983-. *Publications:* Books: Il teatro de la vita, 1980; The World of Jan Saudek, 1984; Love, Life, Death and other studies, 1991; Divadlo zivota, 1991. *Honours:* Chevalier des Arts et Lettres, FRance, 1990; Higishawa Prize, Japan, 1991. *Hobbies:* Women; Gymnastics; Long- distance running. *Address:* Konevova 142, 130 00 Praha 3, Czech Republic.

SAULLE Maria Rita, b. 3 Dec 1935, Caserta, Italy. Full Professor of Internation Law and European Economic Community Law. m. Francesco Durante, 7 Dec 1964, 1 s, 1 d. *Education:* Piano, Conservatory, 1940-56; LLD, Univ Rome, 1958; Acad Int Law, 1960, 1962. *Appointments:* Vol Asst, 1958-64; Ordinary Asst, 1964-80; I/c courses, 1969-80; Full Prof, Fac Pol Scis, La Sapienza Univ, Rome, 1980-. *Publications:* Divulgation about law to newspapers Il Tempo and Italia Oggi; Many books on int law; Abt 100 articles. *Memberships include:* Pres, Comm for Communication, Nat Commn, UNESCO; Nat Commn Equality; Interministerial Comm Human Rights; Nat Coun Refugees. *Honours:* Prize, Presidence, Coun Mins, 1988, 1991. *Hobbies:* Reading; Concerts; Visiting museums. *Address:* Faculty of Political Sciences, University La Sapienza, Piazza Aldo Moro No 5, Roma, Italy. 52.

SAUNIER Jacques, b. 13 July 1948, Bienne, Berne, Switzerland. Orthopaedic Surgeon. m. Bernadette Moery, 29 Jan 1952, 2 s, 1 d. *Education:* Dip Physn, Geneva, 1975; Resident, Surg, 1975-76, Orthopaedic Surg, 1977-80, Geneva; MD, Univ Geneva, 1978; FMH, Orthopaedic Surg, 1984. *Appointments:* Paediatric Orthopaedic Surg, Montpellier, France, 1980-81; Chief Resident, Orthopaedic Surg, Geneva, 1982-85; Orthopaedic Surg, Geneva. *Publications:* Med publs in orthopaedic and sport med. *Memberships:* Soc suisse d'orthopedie; Soc suisse med du sport; European Soc Knee Arthroscopy; Fedn int med du sport; Soc francaise de pathologie traumatique du sport. *Hobbies:* Tennis; Football. *Address:* 12 Ch Beau Soleil, CH 1206 Geneva, Switzerland.

SAVAGE Peter Edmund Annesley, b. 25 Nov 1935, Long Marston, England. Consultant Surgeon. 3 s, 1 d. *Education:* MB, BS, 1960, MS, 1972, London; FRCS, England, 1964. *Appointments:* Cons Surg, Queen Mary's Hosp, Sidcup, 1974; Assoc Dean, Postgrad Med, Univ London, 1991. *Publications:* Books: Disasters - Hospital Planning, 1979; Problems in Peripheral Vascular Disease, 1983; Papers on disaster planning. *Memberships:* Brit Med Assn; Royal Soc Med; Royal Soc Hlth; World Assn Emergency and Disaster Med. *Hobby:* Hill walking. *Address:* 52 Grosvenor Rd, Orpington, Kent BR5 1QU, England.

SAVAGE Richard Mark, b. 8 Feb 1950, Rockville Centre, New York, USA. Staff Administrator. m. Jean Ann Hively, 19 Sept 1970, 2 s. *Education:* Cert (hons), Bus Mid-Mgmt, Wilbur Wright Coll, 1975; AAS, Communications Processing Mgmt, Community Coll Air Force, 1979; Assoc Tech, Telecommunications, 1987, Assoc Mgmt, Bus Mgmt, 1991, GTE Telephone Ops; var tech courses. *Appointments:* Greeter Driver, Boyd Funeral Homes, Babylon, NY, 1969; Served USAF, 1969-79: Radio Communications Analyst, Iraklion AS, Crete, Greece, 1970-72, RAF Chicksands, England, 1972-77; Radio Communications Tech, Goodfellow AFB, TX, USA, 1977-79; Personnel/Sales Recruiter, Interglobal Tech Servs, Austin, TX. 1979-80; Switching

Servs Maintenance Asst, GTESW, Baytown, TX, 1981-82; Switching Servs Budget Analyst, 1983-85, Switching Servs Systems Analyst, 1985-87, Admnstv Results Supvsr, 1987-89, GTESW, San Angelo, TX; Sr Admnstr, Maintenance Admin, 1989-90, Staff Admnstr, CO Maintenance Support, 1990-, Irving, TX; Owner, Savage Innovations, computer cons and software design. *Memberships:* DeWitt Perry PTA Exec Bd; Past PTA Pres, McGill Elem School; Past Mbr, Effective Educ Comm, San Angelo ISD; Past Cubmaster, Past Comm Chmn, Pack 12; Past Unit Commnr, Boy Scouts Am; Past Mbr, Fiesta del Concho Talent Show Comm. *Honours include:* Brit Commendation, Communications Analysis, GCHQ, 1971, 1976; Good Conduct Medal, 1972, 1975, 1978, Commendation Medal, Meritorious Serv, 1977, 1980, USAF; 2 Awards, 1974, Award, 1975, NASA. *Hobbies:* Computer programming; Tole Painting; Auto mechanics; Theatre; Golf. *Address:* GTE Telops/ HQW03G41, PO Box 152092, Irving, TX 75015, USA. 2, 7, 52, 117, 132, 155, 191.

SAVARD Jean-Guy, b. 7 Aug 1931, Quebec, Canada. Professor of Linguistics. Administrator m. Rejeanne Marcotte, 25 Aug 1956, 2 s, 2 d. *Education:* Lic Pedagogy, 1963, Lic Lettres, 1965, Dip, Adv Studies in Linguistics, 1966, Univ Laval. *Appointments:* Prof, 1966, Dir, Dept Linguistics, 1970-71, Dir, Ctr Rsch on Bilingualism, 1972-78, Pres, Rsch Comm, 1978-84, Dpty Rector, 1984-87, Sec Ctr Rsch on Info Org, 1987-89. Vice-Dean, Fac Arts, 1988-, Univ Laval. *Publications:* Bibliographie analytique de tests de langues, 1969; La valence lexicale, 1970; Les indices d'utilite du vocabulaire..., 1970; Le vocabulaire disponible du francais, 1971; Test Laval, A, B, C (co-author). *Memberships:* Can Assn Applied Linguistics; Can Assn Linguists; Association canadienne-francaise de linguistique appliquee; Killam Arts Scholarships Selection Comm, Coun Can, 1987-90. *Honours:* Award, Achievement in Tchng, Min Educ, Quebec, 1961; Scholarships, Min Educ, 1963-66; Pres, Can Assn Applied Linguistics, 1977-79. *Hobbies:* Swimming; Reading; Music; Travel. *Address:* Bureau 5630, Pavillon Louis-Jacques-Casault, Universite Laval, Sainte-Foy (Qc), Canada G1K 7P4. 142, 149.

SAVICKY Andrew, b. 30 Jan 1950, Berngen, Belgium. Psychologist. m. Irene Madej, 10 July 1971, 2 s. *Education:* BA, Montclair Coll, NJ, USA, 1972; MA, Seton Hall Univ, NJ, 1974; MS, 1978, PhD, 1980, Univ PA; Psychology Lic, PA and NJ, 1978-. *Appointments:* Asst Dir, Psychology, Woodbine Development Ctr, 1985-88; Psychology Dir, So State Correctional Facility, Delmont, NJ, 1988-; Capt, NJ Air Nat Guard, 1988-; Num pub speaking engagement on psychology. *Publication:* A World without Tears, The Charles Rotherberg Story (co-author), 1990. *Memberships:* Phi Delta Kappa; Pi Lambda Theta; Am Psychological Assn; NJ Psychological Assn; Assn Med Surgs USA; Am Legion; Am Nat Guard Assn; NJ Nat Guard Assn; Mil Order of World Wars; Forensic Soc Am. *Honours:* Air Force Achievement Medal, 1990; Nt Def Medal, 1991; NJ Desert Storm Medal; Air Force Commendation Medal, 1990. *Hobbies:* Coaching and playing soccer, baseball and judo; Avid race walker and winner, 3 best race awards, NJ State Sports Challenge; Fluent in Russian and Ukrainian. *Address:* 27 Princeton Road, Glassboro, NJ 08028, USA. 117.

SAVITHRI Kappagantula, b. 6 Aug 1932, Repalle, Guntur District, India. Editor. *Education:* MA, Presidency Coll, Madras, 1953; MS, PhD, Univ Baroda, 1958-61; Univ CO, Boulder, USA, 1962-63; Postdoctoral Fellow, Univ NH, 1967-68. *Career:* Def Sci Labs, C'wlth Coun Sci and Indl Rsch, Delhi, 1964-66; Instr, Univ NH, USA, 1967-68; Asst Prof, Univ Puerto Rico, Mayaguez, 1968-70; Var activities incl Tutor, Handicapped Tchr, work w pvte funds for schools, programming sales, 1970-76; Women's Coll Courtrallum, 1977- 78; Worked w assistance from H F Consultants, Madras, India, 1978-80; Emerald Heights Coll, Ootacumund, Tamil Nadu, 1980-82; Lectr, Nava Bharat Ferro Alloys, 1982-83; H F Consultants, Sciencus Publs, 1984-86; Set up

Sciencus off, Ed, USA, 1986-, currently based Columbia, SC; Ed, ASIAN, student newspaper; House Parent, Epworth Children's Home, 2 months, 1991. *Publications:* Thesis on Quadratic Forms; Computational Methods in Number Theory; The Pell Equation for Algebraic Numbe Fields, 1963; The Class Number Porblem, 1966; Units of Certain-Quadratic Forms, 1969; Number Theory Seven, 1986; The Goldbach Conjecture, 1990; Research Problems in Applied Mathematics, books for children's educ, to appear; Sciencus Publs, student employment, in progress. *Memberships:* Indian Math Soc; Am Math Soc; Math Assn Am; Soc Indl and Applied Maths, USA; AWM; YWCA; Indian Statistical Soc. *Honours:* Jr Red Cross Prize, 1946; Mrs Drysdale Prize, 1947; Sir P S S Iyer Gold Medal and Prize, 1947; Kalyani Prize, 1949; Stuart Gold Medal, 1951; Fulbright Scholarship, 1962-63; NSF Fellowship, 1967-68. *Hobbies:* Writing; Arts; Religion; Gardening; Music; Reading; Community activities. *Address:* PO Box 2802, Columbia, SC 29202, USA. 2.

SAVITZ Lily, b. 11 Apr 1933, Cape Town, South Africa. Musician (Pianist); College Lecturer. m. Morris Berman, 17 June 1958, 2 s. *Education:* Matriculated w distinction in Music (Tchr Marjorie Hill), 1949; Studied w Doris Lardner for PLRSM, TLRSM, UTLM, UPLM; Further study, under Vivian Langrish and Lois Phillips, LRAM, Royal Acad Music, London, 1954; Studied w Sona Whiteman and Elizabeth Kemp, Coll Music, Univ Cape Town, 1961, w Peter Feuchtwanger, London, 1980, Peter Feuchtwanger's master classes, Switzerland, 1984. *Career include:* Debut w Cape Town Municipal Orch, conductor Enrique Jorda, 1952; Recitalist, Soloist, Cape Town Symp Orch and Nat Orch, S African Broadcasting Corp; Appearances w conductors incl Cosma, Tintner Boler, Edgar Cree, David Tidboald; Frequent broadcasts incl 1st S African perf of 2 of Kadosa's works, S African Broadcasting Corp; Gave 1 S African perf of Gyorgy Kurtag's Jatekok; Pt-time Lectr, Piano, Coll Music, Univ Cape Town, 1977-; Examiner, Univ S Africa, 1986-. *Publications:* Musicus. *Memberships:* European Piano Tchrs Assn; S African Soc Music Tchrs. *Hobbies:* Drawing; Reading; Antiques. *Address:* College of Music, Rondebosch 7700, Cape Town, South Africa. 4, 138, 154.

SAVVAITOVA Ksenia Alexandrovna, b. 7 Nov 1931, Moscow, USSR. Biologist (Ichthyology, Population Biology, Microevolution and Speciation in Fishes). m. Boris Mikhailovitch Mednikov, 13 Nov 1959, 1 d. *Education:* Student, Biological Fac, 1954, Postgrad Student, 1959-62, Cand Biological Scis (PhD), 1962, DSc, 1983, Moscow Univ. *Appointments:* Tech Asst, 1954-58, Jr Sci Assoc, 1962-68, Sr Sci Assoc, 1968-86, Leading Scientist, 1986-90, Chief, Lab Fish Systematics and Ecology, Biological Fac, Moscow Univ. *Publications:* The noble trout of Lamchatka (w V A Maksimov, M V Mibna et al), 1973; Arctic charr (structure of population systems), 1989; The trout of the Sevan lake (w E Dorofeeva et al), 1989. *Memberships:* Int Soc Arctic Charr Fanatics; Drottningholm Inst Freshwater Rsch, Sweden. *Hobbies:* Travel; Reading. Address: Department of Ichthyology, Faculty of Biology, Moscow State University, 119899 Moscow, Russia.

SAWCHUK Oryst Harry, b. 23 Feb 1928, Winnipeg, Manitoba, Canada. Architect; Planner. 1 s. *Education:* BArch, 1954, MArch (Community Planning), 1955, Univ Manitoba, Winnipeg. *Career:* Louis Fabbro Arch, 1955-57; Planning Advsr to Sudbury Area Planning Comm, 1955-59; Ptnr, Sawchuk & Peach Archts-Planners (now Sawchuk Peach Assocs), Sudbury, 1957-; Solo exhibs: Sculpture, painting, graphics, Sudbury, 1972: Graphics, Sudbury, paintings and graphics, Sudbury, 1973; Scukpture, Sudbury, ink drawings, Toronto, 1974; Toronto, 1986; Participant, various group shows. *Creative works include:* Housing projects; Community plans and studies; Thornhill-Vaughan Community Plan, Vaughan, Reg Municipality of York, Ontario; Nickel Basin Planning Study, Sudbury, Ontario; Several lectures; Contbn to Art Mag, 1972. *Memberships:* Royal Archtl

Inst Can; Ont Assn Archts; Can Inst Planners; Ont Profl Planners Inst; Soc Canadian Artists; No Ont Art Assn; Past Pes, Sudbury and Dist Chmbr of Comm; Provincial No Dev Coun; Mem Nvb, Nat Shevchenko Musical Ensemble Guild of Can. *Honours:* Fellowship, Community Planning, Central Mortgage and Housing Corp, 1954; Award for Serv to Profl Planning Org in Province of Ont, Ont Profl Planners Inst, 1986; Several awards and hon mention, juried shows. *Hobby:* Music. *Address:* 198 Oak St, Sudbury, Ontario, Canada P3C 1M7. 142.

SAWCZUK Basil, b. 22 May 1954, Bradford-upon-Avon, England. Chartered Architect and Arbitrator. m. Sonia Elizabeth Sawczuk, 19 May 1979, 1 s. *Education:* Dip Arch, Leicester Polytechnic, 1979; Dip Mgmt, Open Univ, 1990. *Appointments:* Project Archt, Harper Fairley Ptnrship, 1979-80; Assoc, Malcolm Payne and Assocs, 1980-83; Assoc, 1983-86, Dir, 1986- 91, DGI Int plc. *Publication:* Safe as Houses, article, 1991. *Memberships:* Royal Inst Brit Archts; Fellow, Chartered Inst Arbitrators; Brit Acad Experts. *Hobbies:* Reading; Writing; Gardening; Photography. *Address:* Woodlands Cottage, West Side, North Littleton, Evesham, WR11 5QP, England. 1.

SAWITSKY Orest, b. 14 Feb 1934, Wakaw-Cudworth, Saskatchewan, Canada. Company President; Welder; Farmer; Musician. m. Laura Bodnar, 20 Jan 1973, 1 s , 2 d. *Education:* Hon average, Chgo Voc Coll, USA, 1949; Hon Dip, 1957. *Career includes:* Orchestra, 1945-50; Farming, 1950-51; Oil rig drilling, 1951-52; Foreman, constrn work, 1952-53; Road bldg and Owner, grocery store, 1956-58; Electn, 1958-68; Owner, auto-electric bus, Saskatoon; Farming; Assistance, tchng music to children. *Creative works:* Pre- school, tool settings; Invention, plate-press test, cast welding, others. *Memberships include:* Saskatoon Bd of Trade, 1960-86; UCT; Telemircle; Saskatoon Coun for Crippled Children, 1985-88; Profession for Community Work Educ. *Honours include:* UCT, 1979; Saskatoon Coun for Crippled Children, 1985-88. *Hobbies include:* Private wildlife sanctuary; Photography; Video-filming; Making things incl learning equipment for pre- school children and music. *Address:* 2021 Alberta Ave, Saskatoon, Saskatchewan, Canada S7K 1S2.

SAWYER Michael Evan, b. 8 June 1953, Martinez, California, USA. Director; Librarian. *Education:* BA, Columbia CII, MO, 1974; MLS, 1976, Cert Adv Studies, 1978, Univ Pitts, PA. *Appointments:* Libn, So OH Correctional Inst, Lucasville, 1977-84; Admnstv Asst, Finlay-Hancock City Pub Lib, OH, 1984; Libn, Chillicothe Correctional Inst, OH, 1985-89; Dir, Auglaize City Pub Lib, OH, 1989-1992; Dir, Clinton Public Library, IA, 1993-. *Publications:* A Bibliographical Index of Five English Mystics, 1978; The Photocopying Machine: How Did It Begin, 1979; Inmates Evaluation of a Maximum Security Prison Library at SOCF, 1980; Classic Journal (co-ed), 1983-87; History of the Ohio Jaycees, 1986-89; Albert Lewis Kanter and the Classics: The Man Behind the Gilberton Company, 1987; Automation Goes to Prison, 1989; Inmates Do Ask Questions: Automation and Reference Service in a Correctional Setting, 1989; I Know What's Best For You: Censorship in Prison, 1991. *Memberships:* Fraternal Order of Eagles; Benevolent and Protective Order of Elks; Auglaize Co Histl Soc; OH Lib Assn; Bd Mbr, Big Brothers/Big Sisters, Anglaize-Mercer City; Wapakoneta Jaycees; OH Jr Chmbr Int Senate, var offs incl Pres 1988-89; OH Jr Chmbr Int Senate Fndn, Chmn 1991-92. *Honours:* Delta Phi Alpha, 1973; Jaycee of Yr, 1980, 1981; Outstanding Programming VP, 1982, Outstanding Area VP, 1986, Statesman Award, 1987, OH Jaycees; Jaycees Int Senatorship Award, 1984; Bill Barnhart Mem Award, Chillicothe Jaycees, 1987; Bill Butler Mem Award, US Jaycees, 1987; 1 of 5 Outstanding Ohioans, 1988; Al Maresh Mem Award, Correctional Educ Assn, 1988; ASCLA Exceptional Serv Award, Am Lib Assn, 1989; Commendation, OH Senate, 1989; Outstanding State Jr Chmbr Int Pres, US Jr Chmbr Int Senate, 1989. *Hobbies:* Travel; Bowling; Collecting comic books.

Address: 2604 North 4th St, Apt 237B, Clinton, Iowa 52732, USA. 8, 117.

SAXBY Graham, b. 4 Nov 1925, Redcar, England. Holography Company Director; Lecturer. m. Christine Mary Smalley, 23 May 1953, 1 stepdaughter. *Education:* Univ Coll of SW (now Exeter Univ), 1943-45; BSc (London); Bolton Coll Educ (Tech), 1966; PGCE, distinction, Univ Manchester; BA Hons Class I, Open Univ 1979, 1990. *Appointments:* Joined as Photographer, RAF, 1947; Served Singapore, Hong Kong, FRG, Bahrain, final rank Chief Techn; Commissioned Educ Off (Tech), 1966; OC Photographic Sci Flt, Jt School Photography, to 1974; Ret'd as Squadron Ldr, 1974; Lectr, Educl Technology, 1974-90, estab Holography Unit, 1986, Hon Rsch Fellow, Holography, 1990-, Wolverhampton Univ. *Publications:* The Focaluide to Slides, 1979; Holograms: How to Make and Display Them, 1980; Newnes Book of Photography (contbr), 1983; Practical Holography, 1988; Manual of Practical Holography, 1991; Num articles in profl jrnls. *Memberships:* Fellow, Brit Inst Profl Photography; Havergal Brian Soc; Mensa. *Honours:* City and Guilds Insignia Award, Photographic Technology, 1970; Tech Writers Award, Specialist Div, 1981; 2nd Prize, Dip de la Musee de la Photographie (Prix Louis-Philippe Clerc), 1983; Nominee, King Feisal Award, Sci Writing, 1988; Hon Fellow, Royal Photographic Soc, 1988. *Hobbies:* Photography; Music; Vegetable gardening. *Address:* 3 Honor Avenue, Goldthorn Park, Wolverhampton WV4 5HF, England.

SAXON David Harold, b. 27 Oct 1945, Stockport, England. Kelvin Prof of Physics. m. Margaret Flitcroft, 13 July 1968, 1 s, 1 d. *Education:* Manchester, GS, 1956-63; Balliol Coll, Oxford, 1963-68; Jesus Coll, Oxford, 1968-70; D phil, 1970; DSc, 1989. *Appointments:* Jnr Research Fellow, Jesus Coll, Oxford, 1968-70; Research Officer, Nuclear Physics Dept, 1969-80; Research Assoc, Columbia Univ, New Yrk, 1970-73; Rutherford Appleton Lab, Research Asst, 1974-75; Snr Sci Officer, 1975- 76; Principal, 1976-89; Grade 6, Individual Merit, 1989-90; Glasgow Univ, Kelvin Prof, 1990-. *Memberships:* C Phys; F Inst P. *Honours:* Brackenbury Scholar, Balliol Coll; Scott Prize for physics, Oxford Univ. *Address:* ssa 00Dept of Physics & Astronomy, Glasgow Univ, Glasgow, G12 8QQ, Scotland.

SAXON George Edward, b. 17 July 1932, Pittsburgh, Pennsylvania, USA. Business Man; Engr. m. Frances Jane Bartosiewicz, 30 June 1956, 3 s, 1 d. *Education:* BS, Univ of Pittsburg, 1955; Manufacutirn Engrng Programme, General Electric Co, Schenectady, NY, 1957-60. *Appointments:* US Army, 1955-57; General Electric Co, 1955-63; Engr, Westinghouse Electric Co, 1963-66; Mgr, Badcock & Wilcox Co, 1967-70; General Mgr, Univ Lunricating Systems Inc, 1970-71; Presm Chmn, Conco Systems Inc, 1971-. *Creative Works include:* Tube Cleaning Tool, Patented; Author. Tchnical Articles. *Memberships include:* American Soc of Mech Engrs; Small Business Advisory Council; ASME; Assoc of Energy Engrs; Seven Oaks Country Club. *Honours:* SVA, Small Businessman of the Year; Governors Export Award; SBA, Exporter of the year. *Hobbies:* Extensive Study, Military History; Reading; Golf; Walking; Activist; Small Business/Free Enterprize System. *Address:* 665 Nonth Street, Oakmont, PA 15139, USA.6.

SAXTON Patrick Vincent, b. 6 Sept 1929, Woolwich, England, European Conslt. m. Vera Margaret Temple, 19 July 1960. *Education:* High Oakham Sch, Mansfield. *Appointments:* Willis Faber & Dumas, 1950-53; Caledonian Insce Copy, 1953-63; Chartered Insce Inst, 1964-90; Dir General, 1983-90. *Publications:* Allured to Adventure; Insurance Personnel & Training Handbook. *Memberships include:* British Inst Mgmt; FBIM; British Insurance Law Assn; All Saints Educational Trust. *Honours:* Assoc Member, Inst of Insce Sci; Hon Fellow, FICO Inst of Careers Officers. *Hobbies:* Cricket; Music; Photography; Travel; Gold & Silver Wyre

Srawers; Insurers; Member Cripplegate Ward Club. *Address:* 24 Lakeside, Wickham Road, Beckenham, Kent BR3 2LY, England.

SAYER Stephen Thomas, b. 8 July 1945, Manchester, England. Solicitor; Partner-Competition Law. m. Aileen Wegener, 1 s, 1 d. *Education:* Framlingham Coll, 1958-63. *Appointments:* Gush, Phillips, Walters & Williams, 1964; Sliffe Sweet & Co, 1965-67; Richards Butler, 1968-. *Publications:* Agency & Distribution in Longmans Commercial Precedents; English Law Section on Joint Ventures with Intl Partners. *Memberships:* Law Soc; Intl Bar Assn; The Lawyers Club; UK Assn of European Law; Ordre Francais Des Avocats Du Barreau De Bruxelles; The Soc of English & American Lawyers; Reform Club; City of London Club; Queens Club. *Hobbies:* Golf; Tennis; Theatre; Reading. *Address:* Beaufort House, 15 St Botolph London EC3A 7EE, England.53.

SCALON Larisa, b. 29 May 1949, Vladivostok, USSR. Musician; Philologist; Magazine Editor. m. Nicolay Scalon, 29 June 1975, 2 d. *Education:* Violin study, Alma-Ata Music Coll, 1964-68; Philological Dept, Kazakh State Univ, 1968-75. *Appointments:* Violinist, Opera and Ballet Theatre N Abay, 1967-69; Music Ed, Kazakh Republic TV, Alma-Ata, 1969- 72; Kazakhtelefilm cinema studio, 1972-78; Oner publng house, 1978-85; Educator, Children's Theatre, 1985-90; Ed, Sahna-Szena (Stage), 1990. *Hobbies:* Reading; Music, playing and listening; Theatre; Ancient and modern history; History of religion. *Address:* 6 Microrayon 23 app 8, 780113 Alma-Ata, Kazakhstan.

SCATENA Lorraine Borba, b. 18 Feb 1924, San Rafael, California, USA, Ranching; Womens Rights Advocate. m. Louis Giovanni Scatena, 14 Feb 1960, 1 s, 1 d. *Education:* BA, Dominican Coll, 1945; Elementary Tchrs Diploma, 1946; California Sch of Fine Arts, San Francisco, 1948; Univ of California, Berkeley, 1956-57; State of California Elementary Tchrs Credential, 1946. *Appointments include:* Tchr of Spanish, Dominican Coll, San Rafael, 1946; Tchr, Mentally Handicapped Public Sch, California, 1946; Tchr, Fairfax Public Elementary Sch, California, 1946-53; Tchr, Librarian, US Dependent Schs, Federal Republic of Germany, 1953-56; Translator, Portugal Travel Tours, 1954; Bonding Sec, America Fore Insurance Group, San Francisco, 1958-60; Ranching, Farming, Louis G Scatena Ranch, Nevada, 1960-. *Memberships include:* American Ass of Univ Women, Nevada State Pres, 1981-83; Eleanor Roosevelt Fund for Women & Girls; Italian Catholic Federation. *Honours include:* American Assn of Univ Women, Natl, Future Fund Award; Outstanding Serv Award, Nevada State Retired Tchrs Assn; Recipient Soroptimist Int Women Helping Women Award, 1983. *Hobbies:* Writing; Reading; Quilting; Weaving; Photography. *Address:* 1275 Highway 208, Yerington, NV 89447, USA.

SCHAFER Hans Wilhelm, b. 18 Dec 1935, Kassel, Germany. Dir of Studies. m. Hildegard Bahr, 1 Mar 1963, 3 s, 1 d. *Education:* Univ of Frankfurt, Freiburg, Marburg, 1956-63. *Appointments:* Prof Itesm, Monterry, Mex, 1963-66; Dir of Goethe Inst, Chili, Peru, 1967-74; Dir, G J Zaire, 1979-81. *Publications:* Indipohdi Und Der Weisse Heiland; Kelch Und Stein Ffm, Bern; Worte Vonmeer, San Jose; Buscando Al Dios Perdido, Monterrey. *Memberships:* Intl Vereinigung Fur Germanische Sprach - Und Literaturwissenschaft; Intl Deutsch Lehrervereinigung. *Honour:* Dr Phil, Univ of Prague. *Hobbies:* Blue Water Sailing; Hunting; Motoring. *Address:* Am Burghardsberg 7, 3549 Twistetal 1, Germany.

SCHALEKAMP Jacob Cornelis, b. 16 June 1942, The Hague, The Netherlands. Foundation Admin, Dep Dir Gen, Caregie Foundation. *Education:* Univ Amsterdam, 1965; LLB, 1968; LLM, Vrye Univ, 1973. *Appointments:* Project Mgr, Gruener Publ, BV Amsterdam, 1968-75; Dep Sec Gen, Ogem Holding, NV, Rotterdam, 1976-

78; Dir, Schalekamp, Kuenzi & Co, 1978-80; Dir, Peace Palace Library, Carnegie Found,1980-; Dep Dir Gen, Carnegie Found, 1988-. *Publications include:* Numerous Articles; Co Editor, Spica Mag. *Memberships:* NVB 75 Found;Dutch League Law Librarians; Intl Fedn Library Assns; League Sci. *Hobbies:* History; Art; Metaphysics. *Address:* Celebesstraat 61, NL 2585, TE The Hague, The Netherlands.52.100.

SCHALEKAMP Maarten, b. 14 Dec 1930, Gaiserwald, GS, Switzerland. General Mgr, Water Supply Zurich. m. Maria Johanna Paulina Sytske Baron, 5 Nov 1956, 3 s, 2 dec, 1 d. *Education:* Civil Engr Diploma, 1954. *Appointments:* Engr, Private Ind, 1955-59; Vice Dir,City Workd of St Gallen, 1960-64; Dir, 1964-69; General Mgr, Water Supply. City of Zurich, 1969-. *Publications:* Approx 340 Publ on Water Technology; Painting, Figurative Exhib in Zurich. *Memberships include:* Intl Ozone Assn; Intl Committee for Water Supply Assn; Swiss Gas & Water Assn; Austrian Gas & Water Ind Assn. *Honours:* Outstanding Paper Houston; Outstanding Paper Los Angeles; Maarten Schalekamp Award. *Address:* Chalet, Marco Franco, CH 9641 Ennetbuhl SG, Switzerland.

SCHEIN John Edward, b. 26 Feb 1911, Oshkosh, Wisconsin, USA. Semi Retired Fastener Conslt; Quality Control. m. Germaine Anne Ziebell, 25 Nov 1932, 1 s, 1 d. *Education:* Univ of Wisconsin, 1932; Oshkosh Business Coll,1933. *Appointments:* Self Employed, Sales, 1933-48; Oshkosh Bd of Educ, 1948-60; Fastener Sales Rep, 1960-70; Fastener Mgr, 1970-73; Semi Retired, Fastener Conslt. *Publications:* , Guides to Tipping; The Art of Tipping. *Memberships:* Encyclopedia Of Assns. *Honors:* TV & Radio Talk Shows. *Hobbies include:* Flying; Boating. *Address:* Tippers Intl Ltd, PO Box 2351, Oshkosh, WI 54903, USA.

SCHELUDKO Alexei, b. 18 May 1920, Halle Germany. Prof, Physical Chemistry Of Surfaces Dept, Sofia Univ. *Education:* Sofia Univ, 1949. *Appointments:* Hd of the Physical Chemistry Dept, Sofia Univ, 1970-90. *Publications:* Colloid Chemistry; Over 100 Scientific Works. *Memberships:* Bulgarian Acad of Sci; German acad of Sci Leopoldina; Acad of Sci, New York. *Honours:* German Acad of Sci Leopoldina; Acad of Sci, New York, Member. *Hobbies:* Classical Music; Politics; Human Rights. *Address:* Sofia Univ, Sofia, Bulgaria.139.

SCHERZER Suzana, b. 8 Sept 1931, Timisoara, Romania. Mgr; Library Patents & Documentation. m. Julius Scherzer, 26 Mar 1955, div, 1 s. *Education:* Univ of Bucharest, 1950-54; Inst of Tech, Israel, 1967-68; DSc, 1968. *Appointments:* Asst Physical Chemistry, Poly Inst, Bucharest, 1954-57; Eng & Snr Eng, State Office Bucharest, 1947-63; Researcher, Technion R & D Found, 1963-69; Res Eng, IMI Inst for R&D Haiga, 1969-72; Mgr, Library Patents & Documentation, 1972-. *Publications:* Translation of 2 books; 1 Patents. *Memberships:* Israel Soc Special Libraries & Information Centres; Israel Assn Univ Women Haifa; Assn Engrs. *Hobbies:* Travel; Hiking; Swimming; Classical Music; Photography. *Address:* 18 Peretz Markish St, Haifa 32805, Israel.52.

SCHIDLOWSKI Manfred Oskar Gerhard, b. 13 Nov 1933, Stettin, Germany. Snr Research Geochemist; Earth Sci Educator. m. Ingrid Piegler, 3 Oct 1964, 3 d. *Education:* Free Univ, Berlin, Diploma Cert Geologist, 1960, Dr rer nat, 1960; Habilitation Univ Heidelberg, 1968. *Appointments:* Mining Geologist, Anglo Transvaal Cons Inv Co, Johannesburg, S Africa, 1961-63; Research Asst, Univ Gottingen & Heidelberg, 1963-68; Privat Dozent, Univ Heidelberg, 1968-69; Snr Research Geochemist, Paleoenvironental Research Group; Adj Prof, Univ Heidelberg, 1976-. *Publications include:* 132 Publ, Earth Sci, incl monographs and book editions in field. *Memberships include:* Geochemical Soc; European Union of Geosciences; Deutsche Geologische Gesellschaft; American Chemical Soc; Geological Soc of India. *Honours:* Honorary Research Fellow, Dept Geol

Sci, Harvard Univ, 1972-73; Medaille d'Hommage, Univ Libre de Bruxelles, 1981; Fellow, Geological Soc of South Africa, 1986; Honorary Fellow, Geological Soc of India, 1987. *Hobbies:* History; Poetry. *Address:* Max Planck Inst fur Chemie, Saarstrasse 23, Postfach 3060, D-6500 Mainz, Germany.52.92.156.

SCHIELE Paul Ellsworth, b. 20 Nov 1924, Philadelphia, Pennsylvania, USA. Sci Curriculum Conslt. m. Sarah Knauss, 20 Aug 1946, 3 d. *Education:* BA, La Verne Univ, 1955; MA, Claremont Grad Sch, 1961; PhD, US Intl Univ, California, 1970. *Appointments:* Tchr, Lincoln High Sch, Philadelphia, 1956-57; Tchr, Lincoln Sch, Ontario, 1957-65; Conslt, Hacienda La Puente Unified Sh District, 1965-75; Dir, ESSA Tile III, Project Mile Program, 1974-75; Conslt for Program, 1985-80; Asst Prof, California State Univ, 1975-83; Owner, Pres, Creative Learning Environment & Resources, 1983; Sci Curriculum Constl, 1983-. *Creative Works include:* Sci Curriculum Articles; 4 Filmstrips on Processes of Sci; Primary Sci, Sci Text, Tchrs Manual; Model set of Activities foer ESEA, Title III Project; Twenty One Sci & Math Activity Books. *Memberships:* California Inter SciCouncil; California Sci Tchrs Assn; Phi Delta Kappa; Elementary Sch Sci Assn;California Elementary Educ Assn. *Honours:* on Life Member, Natl Parents & Tchrs Assn; Appointed, Advisory Committee Sci & Humanities Symposium; State Sci Collecting Permit Review Committee. *Hobbies:* Collecting Etchings; Art Collecting; Fencing; Theatre; Travel. *Address:* 231 North Catherine Park Drive, Glendora, CA 91740, USA.9.

SCHILLER Gertrud, b. 7 Jan 1905, Beerbach, B Nurnberg. History of Art. *Education:* Univ of Hamburg. *Appointments:* Activity in Social Facilities, 1926-28; Occupation in the Church of Hamburg, 1929-69; The Art in the Churches of Hamburg, 1946-69; Adult Educ in art. *Publications include:* Bilder Zur Bibel; Die Boten Gottes; Hamburgs Nene Kirchen. *Memberships:* Deutsches Verein Fur Kunstwissenschaft; Service Club Zonta; Ausschnss Fur Kirchen; Bar dor Evangelischen Kirdein. *Honour:* D Yheol HC. *Hobby:* Iconographie. *Address:* Guttersloher Verlagshals, Gerd Mohn, 4830 Outersloh, Germany.

SCHLESINGER Helmut, b. 4 Sept 1924, Penzberg, Germany. Pres of the Deutsche Baundesbank. m. Carola Schlesinger, 1949, 1 s, 3 d. *Education:* Univ of Munich, 1951; Univ of Admin Sci Speyer. *Appointments:* Ifo Inst of Economic Research, 1949-52; Research Stat Dept, Bank Deutscher Lander, 1951-57; Deutsche Bundesbank, 1957-64; Hd of Research & Stat Dept, 1964-72; Bd of the Bundesbank, 1972-79; Vice Pres, 1980- 91; Pres, 1991-. *Memberships:* Extended Bd of the Gesellschaft Fur Wirtschafts und Sozialwissenschaften; Freiherr Vom Stein Gesellschaft; Univ of Frankfurt & Gottingen. *Honours include:* Ludwig Erhard Proze for Economic Journalism; Knight Commanders Cross of the Royal Order of the Polar Star. *Hobbies:* Social Activitoes; Art; Music; Mountaineering. *Address:* Pres of the Deutsche Bundesbank, Postfach 10 06 02, 6000 Frankfurt am Main 1, Germany.

SCHLOTTERBACK Edward Earl, b. 11 Feb 1952, Garrett, Indiana. Manufacturing Engr. m. 26 Sept 1982, 1 s, 2 d, 1 Stepdaughter. *Education:* Assoc of Sci Degree, LA Com Coll, Major-Air Conditioning/Refridgeration, Grad 1979; Assoc of Sci Deg, State Tech Inst at Memphis, Major Vocational Tech Educ, Grad, 1979; BSc, Southern Illinois Univ, Major Technology Grad, 1984; Hn Doc Deg in Philosophy, London, Inst of Applied Res, 1992; Hon Doc Deg in Philosophy, Australian Inst for Co-ordinated Res, 1992. *Appointments:* Assoc Electrical Engr, King Seeley Thermos Co, 1979-82; Snr Instrument Lab, Tech Magnavoc Co, 1982-87; Tech Foreman, Magnavox Co, 1987-88; Manufacturing Engr, Magnavox Co, 1988-91; Manufacturing Engr, Philips Ind Electronics Co, 1991; Pres, Schlotterback & Assoc, 1990-; Manufac Engr, Philips Technologies, 1992-. *Memberships include:* Life Mem, Nat Rifle Assoc; Life Mem, Int Freelance Photographers Org; Repub Nat

Cttee; Sen Mem, Soc of Mfrng Engrs; Am Legion; Lagrange Historial Soc; Smithsonian Nat Assoc; Surface Mount Technology Assoc; Assoc Mem, Nat Wildlife Fed; Nat Threshers Assoc; Northeast Indiana Steam & Gas Assoc; Maumee Valley Steam & Gas Assoc; Tri-State Gas Engine & Tractor Assoc; Int Inventors Club. *Honours:* Commemorative Medal of Honor. *Hobbies:* Constructing & Collecting Electronic & Mechanical Gadgets. *Address:* 9812 N 1000E, Kendallville, IN 46755. USA.

SCHLUETER Linda Boston, b. 12 May 1947, Los Angeles, Cal, USA. Attorney; Law Prof. m. David A Schlueter, 22 Apr 1972, 1 s, 1 d. *Education:* BA, Univ of Southern California, 1969; JD Baylor Univ, Sch of Law, 1971. *Appointments:* Government Relations Specialist, Postal Serv Hdgrs, Washington, 1973-75; Staff Attorney, The Research Group, Charlottesville, 1979-81; Private Practice, Washington, 1981-83; Asst Prof, St Marys Univ, Sch of Law, 1983-87; Assoc Prof, 1987-90; Prof of Law, 1990-. *Publications include:* Annual Supplements to, Punitive Damages; Punitive Damages 2d ed., 2 vols, and annual supplements; Legal Research Guide: Patterns and Practice, 1st and 2nd ed; Assoc Editor, Modern Legal Systems Cyclopedia, 20 vols, 1990-; Editor, Community Property Journal, 1986-88, Community Property Alert, 1989-90. *Memberships:* District of Columbia Bar; US Supreme Court Bar; US Court of Military Appeals; Dir Inst for Comparative & Intl Legal Research; Phi Alpha Delta. *Honours:* Order of Barristers; Texas Women Scholars Program. *Hobby:* Writing. *Address:* St Marys Univ Sch of Law, One Camino Santa Maria, San Antonio, TX 78228, USA.7.15.52.163.

SCHMALTZ Larry G, b. 11 Feb 1957, USA. Business Owner; Conslt. *Education:* Bach of Sci, Civil Engrng, 1979; MBA, Currently pursuing. *Appointments:* Skidmary Owings & Merrill, 1979-82; Civilian, US Air Force, 1982-84; Gen Partner, LJS properties, 1984-90; Coordinator & Adjunct Faculty Univ of North Florida, 1989-; Pres, CE Systems Inc, 1989-. *Publications:* Copyright Computer Estimating Program; Underground Storage Tank Removed. *Memberships:* Natl Soc of profl Engrs; Florida Engrng Soc; Florida Environmontal Auditors Assn. *Honours:* Letter of Commendation US Air Force; MVP Basketball. *Hobbies:* Running; Reading; Public Speaking. *Address:* 13014 N Dale Mabry, Suite 334, Tampa, FL 33618, USA.7.132.

SCHMÄHL Winfried A, b. 31 May 1942, Liegnitz. Full Prof of Economics. m. Johanna Nicolai, 31 May 1963. *Education:* Study of Economics, 1962-67; Dr rer Pol, 1972; Habilitation, 1976. *Appointments:* Asst Prof of Econ, Frankfurt, 1973-76; Full prof, Free Univ Berlin, 1976-89; Centre for Social Policy Research Hd of Economics, Univ of Bremen, 1989-. *Publications include:* Several Books on Economic Problems of Social Security. *Memberships include:* European Soc of Population Economics. *Honours:* First Prize Woelfgang Ritter Foundation; Chmn Advisory Bd of the German Government on Pension Policy; Mem, Enquete Comm German Parliament Ondemographic Changes. *Hobbies:* Classical Music; Literature. *Address:* Osterdeich 133, D2800 Bremen 1, Germany.52.92.

SCHMIDT-NIELSEN Knut, b. 24 Sept 1915, Trondheim, Norway. Emeritus Professor. *Education:* Univ Oslo, 1933-37; Mag Sci, 1941, Dr Phil, 1946, Univ Copenhagen, Denmark. *Appointments:* Rsch Assoc, Swarthmore Coll, USA, 1946-48; Rsch Assoc, Stanford Univ, CA, 1948-49; Docent, Univ Oslo, Norway, 1947-49; Asst Prof, Coll Med, Univ Cinn, OH, USA, 1949-52; Prof, Physiology, 1952-63, James B Duke Prof, Physiology, 1963-85, Emeritus Prof, 1985-, Dept Zoology, Duke Univ; Prof, Physiology, 1980-85, Emeritus Prof, 1985-, Dept Physiology, Duke Med Ctr; Brody Mem Lectr, Univ MO, 1962; Harvey Soc Lectr, 1962; Regents Lectr, Univ CA, Davis, 1963; Hans Gadow Lectr, Univ Cambridge, 1971; Vis Agassiz Prof, Harvard Univ, 1972; Vis Prof, Univ Nairobi, Kenya, 1977; Chief Ed, 1985-

88, Cons Ed, 1988-; News in Physiological Sciences; Wellcome Vis Prof, Univ SD, 1988. *Memberships:* Fellow, AAAS; Nat Acad Scis; Am Acad Arts and Scis; Fellow, NY Acad Scis; Royal Norwegian Acad Arts and Scis; Royal Danish Acad; For Assoc, Academie des Scis, France; Norwegian Acad Sci; Assoc Mbr, Physiological Soc, UK; For Mbr, Royal Soc, London; Hon Chmn, Past Chmn, Int Confs Comparative Physiology; Past Pres, Int Union Physiological Scis; Several Ed Bds. *Honours:* Rsch Fellowship, Carlsberg Lab, Copenhagen, 1941-44; Rsch Fellowship, Univ Copenhagen, 1944-46; Univ Fellowship, Univ Oslo, 1945-47; Guggenheim Fellowship, Algeria, 1953-54; Hon MD, Univ Lund, Sweden, 1985; Hon Mbr, Deutsche Ornithologen-Gesellschaft, 1988; Hon Fellow, Zoological Soc London, 1990; Hon Mbr, Am Soc Zoologists, 1990.

SCHNARR Arthur Willard, b. 18 Feb 1952, Biloxi, Mississippi, USA. Minister of New Church of New Jerusalem. m. Gretchen Lee Williams, 16 June 1973, 1 s, 3 d. *Education:* BS, 1974; M Div, 1981. *Appointments:* Carpenter, Habitate For Humanity in America, Georgia, 1979-80; Paster, Church of the Open Door, 1979-80; Asst Pastor, Toronto, Canada, 1981-82; Evangelization Minister of Gen Church in Canada, 1982-91; Dir of Maple Leaf Acad, 1981-91. *Creative Works include:* Editor, ISI News; Chapter in, Spirit of Toronot; Lectr Tour, Life After Death The Details. *Memberships:* Information Swedenborg Inc; Evangelization General Church of New Jerusalem in Canada; Spires Mag; Swedenborg Foundation; Maple Leaf Acad; Adult Children of Alcoholics, Lakeshore Group. *Hobbies:* Coach Little League Baseball; Swedenborg Study Group; 60's Music; Auto Racing; Sports Spectator. *Address:* 279 Burnhamthorpe Road, Etobicoke, Ontario, Canada M9B 1Z6.

SCHNEEMANN Rudoplh Jan CM, b.5 July 1919, Ubbergen, The Netherlands. Retired. m. Sheelagh Hunter, 28 May 1949, 2 s, 2 d. *Education:* Canisius Coll, Nymegen, 1937; Univ of Utrecht, 1945. *Appointments:* Military Serv, 1938-40; Full Time Resistance, Amsterdam, 1942-45; District Officer, Netherlands East Indies Admin, 1945- 47; Asst Trade Commissioner, Netherlands Consulate General Singapore, 1947- 50; First Sec, Commercial: Indonesian Embassy, Australia, 1950-53; Australian Embassy, Bonn, 1954-57; Hong Kong, 1958-59; Australian Trade Commissioner/Commercial Counsellor, Hong Kong, 1959-60; Bangkok, 1960-64; Vienna, Moscow, Belgrade, 1964-71; Consut General/Snr Trade Commissioner, Sao Paulo 1973-77; Ambassador, Brasilia, 1978-82; Retired, 1982. *Memberships:* Australian Club; Commonwealth Club; Royal Sydney Glof Club; Federal Golf Club. *Honours:* Netherland Resistance Remembrance Cross. *Hobbies:* Music; Sailing; Downhill Skiing; Tennis; Golf; Chess. *Address:* PO Box 44, Batemans Bay, NSW 2536, Australia.

SCHNEIDER Bertrand Jules Alfred, b. 11 Mar 1929, Grenoble. Sec Gen of the Club of Rome; Pres, Sycor. m. Ghislaine Depoutre, 13 Apr 1970, 3 s, 3 d. *Education:* Economy; Sociology; Political Sci. *Appointments:* Pres, Sycor, Conslts, Intl Strategy, 1979-; Sec, Club of Rome, 1984-. *Publications:* The Barefoot Revolution; The First Global Revolution. *Membership:* The World Acad of Art & Sci. *Hobbies:* Reading; Travel; Sport; Cooking; Modern Art. *Address:* 5 Square Lamartine, 75116 Paris, France.

SCHOBINGER Juan, b. 18 Feb 1928, Lausanne, Switzerland. Univ Prof. m. (1) Daisy Gugelmeier, 1954, (2) Liliana Schickendantz, 1980, 1 s, 1 d. *Education:* Univ, Buenos Aires, 1947-51; Dr Phil, 1954. *Appointments:* Prof, Facultad de Filosofia y Letras, Univ Nacional de Cuyo, 1956-. *Publications include:* La Momia Del Cerro El Toro; Prehistoria de Sudamerica. *Memberships include:* Intl Union of Prehistoric & Protohistoric Sci; ICOMOS. *Honours include:* Tercer Premio Nacional a la Produccion Cientifica; Educacion y Cultura de la Argentina. *Hobbies:* Music; History of

Religions; Philosophical Anthropology. *Address:* Videla Castillo 1968, 5500 Mendoza, Argentina.52.152.

SCHOELL Konrad Otto, b. 6 July 1938, Freudenstadt, Germany. Univ Prof. m. Roswitha Dombrowsky, 2 d. *Education:* Abitur, 1957; Staatsexamen Univ Freiburg, 1962; De Phil, 1966; Habilitation, Univ Erlangen, 1973. *Appointments:* Asst Tchr, Univ Berlin, 1966-69; Asst Univ Erlangen, 1969-73; Prof, Univ Kassel, 1973-. *Publications include:* Die Franz Komodie; Other Books; 50 Articles. *Memberships:* modern Language Assn of America; Deutscher Romanistenverband; Soc Intl Pour l'Etude du Theatre Medieval. *Address:* Fachbereich Anglistik, Romanistik, Univ Kassel, Georg Forster Str 3, D 3500 Kassel, Germany.92.

SCHOFIELD John Norman McMichael, b. 11 Apr 1926. Otolaryngologist. m. Arlette Marie Elvire Van Calck, 3 June 1952, 2 s, 1 d. *Education:* St Georges Sch, Harpenden; Middlesex Hosp Medical Sch, 1950; Royal Navy. *Appointments:* House Surgeon & Casualty Officer, 1950-52; Snr Reg, Middlesex Hosp, 1959-62; Conslt Ent Surgeon, Warwick Hosp, 1962-90. *Publications:* Papers on Otorhinological Subjects; Rhinology Examiner to Royal Coll of Surgeons. *Memberships:* British Acad Conference in Otolaryngogy; Royal Soc of Medicine; British Medical Assn; Assn of Otolaryngologist; Coll of Surgeons, England & Edinburgh. *Hobbies:* Golf; Tennis; Opera; Music; Reading; Travel. *Address:* Brookhampton Farm, Kineton, Warwick, CV35 0NR, England.

SCHOLES Alwyn Denton, b. 16 Dec 1910, Bournemouth, England. m. Juliet Angel Ieme Pyne , 16 Dec 1939, 1 s, 4 d. *Education:* Cheltenham Coll; Selwyn Coll, Cambridge; Called to the Bar, 1934. *Appointments include:* Practice English Bar, 1934-38; Afftd District Magistrate, Gold Coast, 1938; Acting Crown Council, Solicitor Gen, 1941; Appld Supreme Court Judge, Hong Kong, 1958; Afftd Magistrate, Hong Kong, 1948; First Magistrate, 1949; Hong Kong, 1949; Afftd District Judge, 1953; Supreme Court of State of Brimni, 1964-67, 1968-71; Pres/Mem, Hong Kong Full Court of Appeal on Occasions, 1949-71; Acting Chief Justice, Hong Kong, 1970; Retired, 1971. *Memberships:* Royal Commonwealth Soc; Sedmouth Parish Church Council, 1972-82; Govenor of St Nicholas, 1984-89. *Honour:* Queens Medal. *Hobbies:* Gardening; Walking. *Address:* West Hayes, Convent Rod, Sidmouth, Devon EX10 8RL, England.1.

SCHOUVALOFF Alexander, b. 4 May 1934, London, England. Writer. m. (1) Gillian Baker, 1 s, (2) Daria Chorley, 18 Nov 1971. *Education:* Jesus Coll, Oxford, 1953- 56. *Appointments:* Asst Dir, Edinburgh Festival, 1965-67; Dir, North West Arts Assn, 1967-74; Curator Theatre Museum, 1974-89. *Publications:* Stravinsky on Stage; Catalogue of Thyssen-Bornemisza Collection of Set and Costume designs; Theatre Museum; Theatre on Paper; Leon Bakst, The Theatre Art; Summer of the Bullshine Boys; London Archives of the Dance. *Honour:* Polonia Restituta. *Hobby:* Motoring Holidays. *Address:* 10 Avondale Park Gardens, London W11 4PR, England.1.

SCHRAMM Ryszard Wiktor, b. 8 June 1920, Poznan, Poland. Univ Prof; Biochemist. m. Halina Irena Rutkowska, 3 Aug 1946, 1 s, 1 d. *Education:* Mgr Sci Chem, Poznan Univ, 1947; Mgr Sci Biol, 1951; phD, 1949. *Appointments:* Asst Poznan Univ, 1946-50; Adjunct, 1951-56; Assoc Prof, A Mickiewicz Univ, 1956-74; Prof, 1974-. *Publications:* Over 90 Scientific Papers; Over 170 Articles; Chapters in Books. *Memberships:* The Explorers Club, New York; Polish Polar Club; Polish Alpine Feder; Polish Tatra Soc. *Hobbies:* Exploration; Mountaineering; Alpimism; Polaristic. *Address:* Orzeszkowej 4 m 1, 60 778 Poznan, Poland.

SCHRAMM Tomasz, b. 22 Nov 1949, Poznan, Poland. Historian. *Education:* Univ Poznan, MA, 1971; PhD,

1977; Habilitation, 1988. *Appointments:* Asst, 1972-77; Asst Prof, 1977-89; A Mic Senate, 1983- 85, 1989-90; Assoc Prof, 1989-; Deputy Dir, Inst of History, 1984-87; Vice Dean, faculty of History, 1990-. *Publications include:* Books, French Histoorians on the Causes of the World War 1; French Military Missions in Central Europe; To Win Poland. *Memberships:* Assn of Intl d'Histiore Contemporaine de l'Europe; Polar Club of the Polish Geographical Soc; polish Historical Soc; Polish Learned Soc for the Earth Sci. *Hobbies:* Pola Exploration; Operatic Music. *Address:* ul Podlaska 8 m 2a, 60-623 Poznan, Poland.

SCHRAMM Werner, b. 28 Apr 1926, Hohenlockstedt, Germany. Author; Painter. *Education:* Teaching Training Inst, Langemarck Studies. *Publications:* Stefan Zweig, 1961; Im Malstrom der Zeit: Eine Darstellung des dichterisches Lebenswerkes von Lee van Dovski, 1976; Hugo Wolfgang Philipp im Spiegel der Nachwelt: Philipp als Romancier, 1979; Das antike Drama Die Bacchantinnen in der Neugestaltung durch H. Wolfgang Philipp, 1980; Hugo Wolfgang Philipps Tragikomodie Der Clown Gottes, 1983; Moderner deutscher Roman, 1983; Stefan Zweig: Bildnis eines genialen Charakters, 1984. *Memberships:* ABI Research Assn; Intl Biographical Assn; Intl Order of Merit; IBC Advisory Council. *Honours include:* Intl Biographical Roll of Honor; Medal of Honor; Bronze Medal, One-in-a-Million; Grand Ambassador of Achievement Intl. *Hobbies:* History; Philosophy; Psychology; Literature; Phonetics; Low German Language. *Address:* Eckenerweg 8, D-221 Itzehoe, Germany.

SCHROCKE Helmut Heinrich, b. 18 June 1922, Zwickau, Sachsen, Germany. Univ Educator. m. 22 Dec 1952, 2 s, 2 d. *Education:* Real Gymnasium, 1932-39; Studium Von Geologie und Mineralogie, 1946-51; Diplomgeologe, Dr Rer Nat. *Appointments:* Asst, Univ Heidelberg, Karlsruhe, Munchen, Habilitation Univ, Heidelberg, 1958; Prof, Univ Munich, 1967-. *Publications:* Grundlagen der Magmatogenen Lagerstattenbildung; Die Entstehung der Endogenen Erzlagerstatten; Siebenburgen, Menschen, Stadte Kirchenburgen; Sclavi, Slawen, Ostgermanen; Naturwiss Tafelwerke Mineralien; Naturwiss Tafelwerke Mineraux; Mineralogie ein Lehrbuch auf Systematischer Grundlage. *Honour:* Recipient Winklermedaille Berkademie Freiberg. *Address:* Am Hohen Weg 22, D-8081 Kottgelsering, Germany.52.92.

SCHRODER Josef, b. 7 Mar 1937, Fortuna, Germany. Contemporary History Educator. m. Inge Arnolds, 27 Mar 1990. *Education:* Doct, 1968, Univ Lectr, 1975, Univ Bonn. *Appoointments:* Sci Asst, History, 1969- 71, Asst Prof, Hist, 1971-77, Extraordinary Prof, Hist, 1977-79, Prof, Hist, 1980-90, Univ Bonn; Prof, Hist, Univ Cologne, 1990-. *Publications:* Italiens Kriegsaustritt, 1943, 1969; Italien im Zweiten Weltkrieg-Eine Bibliographie, 1978; Bestrebungen zur Eliminierung der Ostfront 1941-43, 1980; Renzo Die Deutungen des Faschismus (ed), 1980; Co-ed: Dienst fur die Geschichte fur Walther Hubatsch, 1985; Aspekte der Geschichte fur Peter Gerrit Thielen, 1990. *Membership:* Dir, Seminar fur Geschichte. *Honours:* Recip, Richard Franck-Preis, 1978. *Hobby:* Christmas crib. *Address:* Metzstrasse 24, Postfact 4112, D-5010 Bergheim-Niederaussem, Germany. 52, 92.

SCHROLL Marianne, b. 1 Apr 1942, Rudkobing, Denmark. Conslt Dept of Geriatrics; prof of Geriatrics, Copenhagen Univ. m. Gustav Schroll, 7 Aug 1965, 1 s, 3 d. *Education:* MD, 1968; Specialization in Intl Medicine, 1977; Geriatrics, 1981; DM Sc, 1982. *Appointments:* Conslt Dept of Geriatrics Roskilde County Hosp, 1982-91; Const, Dept of Geriatrics Copenhagen City Hosp, Copenhagen Univ, 1991. *Publications include:* Thesis, A Ten Year Prospective Study of Cardiovascular Risk Factors in Men & Women from the Glostrup Population, Born in 1914; Studies of the Future Aged. *Honours include:* Medit Prize for Preventive Efforts against Cardiovascular Diseases; The Hagedorn Prize. *Hobbies:* Gerontology; Epidemiology; Nutrition;

Hiking; Music; Arts. *Address:* Dept of Geriatrics, HL, Kommunehospitalet, Oster Farimagsgade 5, DK 1399 Kobenhavn K, Germany.

SCHUESSLER Stephen Mark, b. 29 July 1962, Somers Point, New Jersey, USA. Clergyman; Snr Pastor of a Church, Sparta Assembly of God. *Education:* Thomas A Edison, 1980; Biblical Studies, Central Bible Coll, 1983; BA Christian Educ, 1985. *Appointments:* Assoc Pastor, Ozark Assembly of God, 1985-86; Assoc Pastor, Berea Temple Assn of God, 1986-88; Snr Pastor, Sparto Assembly of Gold. *Publications include:* Numerous Articles. *Memberships:* Southern Missouri District Council of the Assemblies of God; Univ Christian Fellowship; Committee for A Drug Free Sch; Southern Mo District Council. *Honours include:* Deans List Central Bible Coll; Invited to be Guest Lectr at Central Bible COll. *Hobbies:* Collecting Antiques; Nostelgic Sports Memorabilia; Tennis; Softball; Basketball; Travel; Writing. *Address:* PO Box 239, Sparta, MO 65753, USA.46.

SCHUFF Karen Elizabeth, b. 1 June 1937, Highland Park, MI, USA. Poet; Writer. m. Henry Clifton Schuff, 7 Sept 1955, 1 s, 1 d. *Creative Works:* Of June 1 Sing, 1979; Green As April, 1987. *Memberships:* Soc for the Study of Mid Western Literature; Poetry Soc of Michigan; Poets & Playwrights; Intl Platform Assn. *Honours:* First Prize for a Poetry Manuscript from Poetry Forum of America. *Hobbies:* Reading; Gardening; Watercolour Painting; Keyboards; Rock Collecting. *Address:* 15310 Windemere Avenue, Southgate, MI 48195, USA.2.3.8.

SCHULTE Josephine, b. 9 May 1929, Foley, Alabama, USA. Prof of History. *Education:* PhD, Loyola Univ, Chicago; MA, Trinity Univ, San Antonio; MA, Univ of Southern Mississippi; BS, Spring Hill Mobil Ala; AA, Sacred Heart, Jr Coll Cullman Ala. *Appointments:* Steamship Agent, Gulf PS Agency, 1949-58; Southern Inst of Mgmt, Research Assoc, 1959-60; Prichard Jr High Mobil, 1962; Special Lectr, Brodkley AFB, 1951-62; Special Lectr, Spring Hill Coll, 1960-62; Tchrng Fellow, Loyola Univ, Chicago, 1962- 66; Prof of History, 1970; Asst Prof, Univ of the Americas, 1967-70. *Publications include:* Translation of Two of Leopoldo Zeas Books and articles in scholarly journals. *Memberships include:* Southwestern Conference of Latin American Studies; Phi Alpha Theta Honors Soc. *Honours include:* 500 Yrs Collogug Univ of Lima, Peru; OAS, Fullbright, and Spanish government Grants. *Hobbies:* Needlework; Genealogy; Photography; Postcard Collecting; Natl Costume; Collecting Intl Cooking; Travel. *Address:* Mission Hills Apt 605, 1415 Babcock Road, San Antonio, TX 78201, USA.5.7.13.138.152.

SCHULTHEIS Michael James, b. 9 May 1932, USA. Jesuit Priest; Dir, Jesuit Refugee Service in Africa. *Education:* MA, Econ, Spokane, 1963; MA, Phil, Gonzaga, Spokane, 1959; MA, Theology, Rejis Coll, 1966; PhD, Cornell Univ, 1976. *Appointments:* Research Assoc, MISR, 1970-73; Visiting Prof, Mailerere Univ, 1971-73; Assoc Prof, Univ of Dar es Salaam, 1976-82; Staff Assoc, Center of Coreen, 1981-84; Assoc Dir, Jesuit REfugee Serv, 1985-88; Dir, Jesuit Refugee Serv, 1988-92. *Publications include:* Catholic Social Tchrng, our Best Kept Secret; Several Articles. *Memberships:* American Econ Assoc; African Studies Assn; Assn Concerned Afric; US Catholic Mission Assn. *Hobbies:* Bird Watching; Kite Flying; Gardening. *Address:* Dir, Jesuit Refugee Service in Africa, PO Box 14877, Nairobi, Kenya.52.

SCHULZ Robert Adolph, b. 20 Aug 1943, Long Branch, USA. Mgmt Prof; Conslt. *Education:* BA, St Vincents Coll, 1965; BSME, Univ of Notre Dame, 1966; MBA, Univ of Pittsburgh, 1967; PhD, Ohio State, 1971. *Appointments:* Asst Pres, Kerry Fab Ins, Pittsburgh, 1967; Research Asst, Ohio State Univ, 1968; Tchrng Asst, Mktng Dept, Ohio Stte Univ, 1969; Snr Conslt

Assoc, Columbus, Ohio, 1969-70; Mgmt Horizons Data Systems Inc, Olumbia, Computer Conversion Coordinator, 1970; Dir of Tech Educ, 1971; Dir of Educ, 1972-73; Univ of Calgary, Assoc prof, 1973-87; Prof, 1988-; Academic Dir, 1983-; Coordinator, 198-. *Memberships include:* Silver Springs Golf & Country Club; Calgary Sponsor Refugee Soc; Alberta Catholic Sch Trustees Assn Blueprints Committee. *Honours include:* Deans List, Univ of Notre Dame; 6 Outstanding Tchrng Awards; Beta Gamma Sigma. *Hobbies:* Golf; Jogging; Basketball. *Address:* Faculty of Management, The Univ of Calgary, 438 Scurfield Hall, 2500 Univ Drive NW, Calgary, Alberta, Canada T2N 1N4.8.142.

SCHUMANN OLSEN Per Erik, b. 6 Sept 1950, Bergen, Norway. Vice Pres. *Education:* Ex Artium, 1971; NHHK, 1972-75. *Appointments:* Shipbroker, J G Reig, 1975-88; Vice Pres, Star Shipping A?S, 1988-. *Hobbies:* Gardening; Fresh Water Fishing; Skiing; Mountain Hiking. *Address:* 2 10 10 Hiroo, Shibuya Ku, Toyko, 150, Japan.

SCHUNCKE Michael Gottfried, b. 8 May 1929, Dresden. Tchr; Conslt; Author. m. Dorothea Czibulinski Dressler, 22 Dec 1956, 2 d. *Education:* Cymnasium, 1939-49; 4 yrs with Prof Otto Schaefer, Baden (musicology); 2 yrs with Prof Lysinski, Mannnhein (advertising). *Appointments:* Chief Copywriter, 1963-68; Bd of Dir, Werbefachverband Niedersachsen, 1966-70; Tchr, 1966-; Chief Copywriter, Conslt, 1971-82. *Creative Works include:* Wanderer Zwischen 2 Welten; Many articles and 2 books for Advertising and Music-history. *Memberships:* Robert Schumann Gesellschaft; Mendelsohn Gesellschaft; Gesellschaft Fuerdeutsche Sprache. *Honours include:* Honor Kavalier der Strasse; Golden Hans Buchholz Medaille. *Hobbies include:* Special Problems in Language; Research in Literature; Organ; To Wander. *Address:* Heschmattweg 11, D-7570 Baden Baden, Germany.

SCHUPP Ronald Irving, b. 10 Dec 1951, Syracuse, New York, USA. Baptist Clergyman & Missionary. *Appointments:* Ordained to Ministry, The Old Country Church, 1972; Missionary & Asst Pastor, 1972-76; Ordained to Baptist Ministry, 1976; Missionary, Solid Rock Baptist Church, 1976-89; Missionary, Marble Rock Missionary Baptist Church, 1990-. *Memberships include:* Nalt Coalition for the Homeless; Chicago Coalition for the Homeless; Chicago Pledge of Resistance; American Civil Liberties Union. *Honours include:* Letter of Commendation, Chicago Fire DEpt; Proclamation, Mayor Richard M Daley. *Hobbies:* Bicycle Riding; Writing Poetry. *Address:* 6412 N Hoyne Avenue, Chicago, IL 60645, USA.8.52.152.

SCHUYLER Daniel Merrick, b. 26 July 1912, Oconomowoc, Wisconsin, USA. Attorney; Educator. m. Claribel Seaman, 15 June 1935, 1 s, 1 d. *Education:* BA, Dartmouth Coll, 1934; JD Northwestern Univ, Sch of Law, 1937. *Appointments include:* Tchr, Constituional History, Chicago Latin Sch, 1935-37; Treasurer, Sec & Controller, B W Supercharges, 1942-46; Lectr, Strusts, Real Property & Future Interests, 1946-50; Assoc Prof, 1950- 52; Prof of Law, 1952-80; Prof Emeritus, 1980-. *Publications include:* Illinois Law of Future Interest; Illinois Will & Trust Manual. *Memberships include:* American, Illinois, Chicago Bar Assn; Chicago Estate Planning Council; American Coll of Probate Counsel. *Honours:* Phi Belta Kappa; Distinguished Serv Award. *Hobbies:* Growing Bonsai. *Address:* One Prudential Plaza, Suite 3800, 130 East Randolph Street, Chicago, IL 60601, USA.2.52.163.

SCHWAB George D, b. 25 Nov 1931. Prof of History; Author. m. Eleonora Storch, 27 Feb 1965, 3 s. *Education:* MA, Columbia Univ, 1955; PhD, Columbia Univ, 1968. *Appointments:* Prof of History, City Univ of New York, 1980-. *Publication:* The Challenge of the Exception. *Memberships:* National Comm on American Foreign Policy. *Honours:* Earhart Foundation Grant; City Univ Research Grants. *Hobbies:* Collecting Art. *Address:* The

Graduate Centre, Cuny, 33 West 42nd Street, New York, NY 10036, USA.2.6.

SCHWAGER George, b. 8 Aug 1911, Cincinati, Ohio, USA. Retired Profl Engr. m. Virginia R Carnan, 4 Apr 1937. *Education:* Univ of Cincinati, 1935; Radiological Engr, Kelley, Koett Mfg, 1935-42; Jnr Office Anti Aircraft Artillers Bd, 1942-44. *Appointments:* Radiological Engr, Design Radiological Equip, 1935-42; Instr, Anti Aircraft Sch, 1944; Medical Equip Officer, 1946; Bio Medical Engr, Veterans Admin, US Army, State Dept to Aid Government of India, Venezuela, Columbia with Hosp Equip, 1959-69; Electrical Safety, Hosp OR & Intensive Care Area. *Memberships:* IEEE; Profl Engr for VA & US Army Medical Dept. *Honours:* Distinguished Career Award; Veterans Administration. *Hobbies:* Photography; Engrng; Sci. *Address:* 4504 Lake Vista Drive, Sasasota, FL 34233, USA.7.132.

SCHWARTZ Alexander Lvovitch, b. 19 Feb 1945, Moscow, USSR. Free Profl Artist. m. Elena Danliiovna Scwartz, 1 Mar 1975, 1 d. *Education:* Moscow Arts Acad Theatre Stage Operator, 1963-64; Moscow Arts Acad Theatre Workshop, Staging & Decorative Dept, 1964-69; Master of Arts. *Appointments:* Moscow Central Childrens Theatre, Decorative Design, 1969; Moscow Gorky, Film Studio, Sequence Decorative Designer, 1970-72; Spys Mistake, 1970; Pipe All Hands on Deock, 1971; The Land to be Called For, 1972; Free Profl Artist, 1973-. *Publications:* 4 Book Illustrations; 200 Oil Paintings; Monumental Paintings; 1000 pices of Balck & White, Colour Graphics. *Memberships:* Moscow Graphic Artists Union; Intl federation of Artists; UNESCO; IFA. *Honours:* Participant Group Art Shows; One Man Shows. *Hobbies include:* Music; Reading; Travel. *Address:* Ogariov Str 13, Apartment 63, Moscow 103009, Russia.

SCHWARZ Elena Daniilovna, b. 17 Feb 1955, Moscow, USSR. Hd of the English Language Dept; Asst Prof Polytechnical Inst, Moscow. m. Alexander Lvovitch Schwarz, 1 Mar 1975, 1 d. *Education:* Moscow Pedagogical Coll, 1972-77; Ma, 1977; Postgraduate Course, 1980-83; phD, 1984. *Appointments:* Tchr English, Moscow Secondary English Sch, 1977-79; Tchr, Moscow Pedagogical Coll, 1978-84; Snr Tchr, Moscow Textile Inst, 1984-85; Hd of English Language Dept, Asst Prof, Poly Inst, Moscow, 1985-92. *Publications:* Text forming Function of a Semantic Unit Transformation; 24 Articles; 3 Text Books. *Memberships:* Moscow Politechnical Inst Methodological centre. *Hobbies:* Reading; Collecting Books; Music; Collecting CD's, Records; Swimming; Travel; Fine Arts. *Address:* Ogariov Str 13, Apartment 63, Moscow 103009, Russia.

SCHWARZ Kurt Karl, b. 24 May 1926. Conslt; Visiting Ind Prof, Univ of Southampton. m. Brenda Patrica Pilling, 6 Aug 1949, 1 s, 2 d. *Education:* Univ of Cambridge, 1944-47; BA, 1947; MA, 1950. *Appointments:* Laurence Scott & Electromotors Ltd, 1947-86, Tech Dir, 1965-86, Dir, 1968-86. *Creative Works:* Design & Wealth Creation; Design of Industrial Electric Motors Drives; 30 Engrng Inst Papers; Articles. *Memberships:* Inst of Electrical Engineers Institution of Mechanical Engineers; Inst of Measurement & Control; Inst of Materials; British Nuclear Energy Soc. *Hobbies:* Music; Walking; Swimming; Gardening. *Address:* Threshfield, Bullockshed Lane, Bramerton, Norwich, NR1A 7HG, England.

SCHWARZ Wolfgang Karl, b. 21 Apr 1934, Selb, Germany. Full Prof of Mathematics. m. Doris Schwarz, 19 Oct 1963, 1 s, 2 d. *Education:* Univ Erlangen, 1951-56; Promotion, 1959; Univ Freiburg, Habilitation, 1964; Asst Math, Univ Erlangen, 1956-60; Univ Freiburg, 1960-64; Asst Prof Math, 1964-69. *Appointments:* Full prof, Univ Frankfurt, 1969-. *Publications:* About 80 Articles; Books inc. Prime Numbers; Sieve Methods; Introduction to Number Theory; Basic Programmes. *Memberships include:* Scientific Soc, Univ Frankfurt;

German Mathematical Soc; Pres, German Math Soc, 1986-1987; Sprecher Kunferent Math Fachberache, 1991-1993. *Hobbies:* Chess; Mountaineering; Music; Composition. *Address:* Dept of Mathematics, Univ of Frankfurt, Robert Mayer Straße 10, D-6000 Frankfurt, Germany.1.

SCHWARZKOPF H Norman, General, b. 22 Aug 1934, Trenton, New Jersey, USA. General, US Army. m. Brenda Holsinger, 1 s, 2 d. *Education:* Valley Forge Military Acad; United States Military Acad, West Point, New York; Advanced Infantry Officer Traingin, Fort Benning, Georgia; Command & General Staff Coll, Fort Leavenworth, Kansas; Army War Coll, Carlisle Barracks, Pennsylvania; Univ of Southern california. *Appointments include:* Task Force Advisor, Vietnamese Airbourne Div; Battalion Commander 1st Battalion 6th Infantry, 23rd Infantry Div; Commander of 2 Infantry Brigades, Fort Lewis, Washington; Asst Div Commander, 8th Infantry Div, United States Army Europe; Commander 24th Infantry Div, Fort Stewart, Georgia; Deputy Commander, Joint Task Force, US Forces; Deputy Dir, Military Plans & Policy, United States Pacific Command, Camp Smith, Hawaii; Dir, Military Personnel Mgrmt, Asst Deputy Chief of Staff for Personnel, Headquarters Dept; Army Operations Deputy, Joint Chiefs of Staff; Commander of Operations Desert Shield, Desert Storm. *Publications:* It Doesent Take a Hero. *Honours include:* DIB; Defense Distinguished Serv Medal; Most Honorable Order of Bath; Bahrain Decoration of the First Degree; Honorary Private First Class, French Foreign Legion.

SCHWEITZER Mori Aaron, b. 27 Apr 1932, New York City, NY, USA. Investment Banker. m. Suzanne Barbara Rose, 21 Aug 1958, div, 2 s, 1 d. *Education:* Army Serv, 1955-56; Brooklyn Coll, 1949-51; Brooklyn Law Sch, 1951-56. *Appointments:* Private Practice of Law, 1956-58; Pres Int Escrow Cop, 1958-64; Partner, Radnor General, 1964-67; Merr & Llynich, Pierce Fennes Smith, 1967-69; Chmn, Westhouse Minerals, 1969-71; Atlantic & Pacific Bank, 1971-74; Advisory Bd, Bank of Los Angeles, Chmn, Biometrics, 1978; Traduy Corp, 1989-81; Jaguar Capital, 1989-91. *Memberships:* Single Sailors; oca Museum; Gulf Breeze Radio Network. *Hobbies:* Ocean Sailing; Tennis; Golf; Reading; Poker. *Address:* c/o Captains & Crew, Rt 5 11 Longbay, St Thomne, WI 00802, USA.

SCICLUNA William Leslie, b. 10 Nov 1921, Malta. Chmn, Natl Employment Auth; Port Conslt. m. Miriam Gouder, 29 Apr 1945, 1 s, 4 d. *Education:* Inst of Transport, London, 1956-59. *Appointments include:* Clerk Navel Sea Transport Dept, Ministry of War Transport, 1941- 45; Mgr, Port Workers, 1946-57; Snr Mgr, Port Work Scheme, 1957-65; Port Mgr Malta, 1965-71; Dir, Ports Malta, 1971-82; Lectr, Univ of Malta, 1987; Independent Port Conslt, 1982-; Chmn, Natl Employments Auth, 1990-. *Memberships:* Chartered Inst of Transport; Intl Materials Managment; The Maritime Assn, Malta. *Hobbies:* Golf; Swimming; Sailing; Reading. *Address:* 1 Spencer Flats, Blata 1 Bajda, Malta.52

SCIONTI Isabel Laughlin, Concert Pianist; Tchr. m. (1) Silvio Scionti, dec, (2) William R Hicks, Deceased. *Education:* Bach of Music, Baylor Univ, Waco, 1932; Master of Music, Chicago Musical Coll, 1934; Doc of Music, Baylor Univ, 1945. *Appointments:* Faculty Chicago Musicial Coll, 1934-36; Artist Tchr of Many Profl Piantist. *Creative Works include:* Debut in Carnegie Hall, NY, 1938; Composed & Orchestrated a Piano Concerto. *Memberships:* Music Tchrs Natl Assn; NITNA; Teas Music Tchrs Assn; Texas Girls Choir. *Honours include:* Texas Music Tchrs Assn, Tchr of the Year Award; Community Recognition Award for Outstanding Contribution to Arts & Cultureal Life of the City of Denton. *Hobby:* Travel. *Address:* 1111 Emerson Lane, Denton, TX 76201, USA.4.5.7.15.138.

SCOTLAND Leslie Hubert, b. 18 July 1943, Trimdad, WI. General Mgr. m. Jocelyn Hyland, 27 Dec 1964, 2 s, 1 d. *Education:* BA, Sir George Williams Univ, Canada, 1965-69; MA, Univ of Mindsor, Canada, 1969-71. *Appointments:* Minstry of Finance, Clerk, 1962-65; Royal Bank of T7T, Corporate Mgr, 1972-87; Ind Denlor Corp, General Mgr, 1988-89. *Publications include:* Economic Profile of T & T; Articles. *Memberships:* American Economic Assn. *Hobbies:* Computing; Photography; Reading; Travel. *Address:* 50 Luke Road, Blue Range, Diego Martin, Trindad Tobago, West Indies.142.

SCOTT Ainsworth David, b. 27 Jan 1912, Kingston, Jamacia. m. (1) 2 children, (2) Verity Wills, 4 Children. *Education:* Kingston Coll; BSc, McGill Univ. *Appointments include:* Instr of Surveying, McGill Univ, Canada; Snr Asst Engr, Royal Canadian Aire Force; Engr in Charge, Aerodrome Const, Canadian Government; Group Leder Engr, Canadair Ltd; Engr in Charge of Const, Univ Coll of West Indies; Helped to Construct Palisadoes Airport, Jamacia, 1961; Headed Consortium, Natl Stadium; Main Contractor, North American Building; Counsellor, Jamacian Tourist Bd, 1981; Chmn, Dosco Ind Ltd; Contemporary Jamaican Artists Assn; Jamacia Lawn Tennis Assn Intl Circuit. *Creative Works include:* Exhit Own Paintings; Sculpture; One Man Shows. *Memberships include:* Government Educ Bd; Natl Gallery; United Nations Assn of Jamacia. *Honours include:* State of Victory as Personality of the Year; Knght of St John of Jerusalem; Silver Musgrave Medal; Jamaican Order of Distinction; Inst of Jamaica Centenary Medal; Jamaica Weight Lifting Champion; Canadian Intercollegiate Wrestling Champion. *Hobbies:* Music; Sport; Travel. *Address:* Olympic Intl Art Centre Apartments, 202 Old Hope Road, Kingston 6, Jamacia, West Indies.

SCOTT Donald Fletcher, b. 29 Nov 1930, Norfolk, England. Retired; Conslt Medical Practitioner. m. 2 Sept 1967, 1 s, 1 d. *Education:* Edinburgh Univ, 1951-57; London Univ, 1965; Royal Coll of Physicians, London, 1979. *Appointments:* Snr Reg, Maudsley Hosp, London, 1963-65; Research Asst, Mayo Clinic, USA, 1965-66; Conslt in Charge, Clinical Neurophysiology, 1967-. *Publications include:* About Epilepsy; Understanding EEG; Beating Job Burnout; About 150 Articles in Journals. *Memberships:* EEG Soc; Assn of British Clinical Neurophysiology; Assn of british Neurologists; The Soc of Authors, London. *Hobbies:* Writingl Reading; Gardening. *Address:* 25 Park Gate, Blackheath, London, SE3, England.

SCOTT John Andrew Ross, b. 6 May 1951, Hawick, Scotland. Journalist; Councillor. m. 5 May 1979, 2 s. *Education:* Higher Educ, night classes, Northumberland Agricl Coll. *Appointments:* Shepherd, Newton Farm, Hawick, 1966-74; Works Mgr, Kibbutz Baram, Israel, 1974-76; Jrnlst: Hawick News, 1977-78; Hawick Express, 1978-79; Kelso Chronicle and Jedburgh Gazette, 1979-86; Chief Reporter, Southern Reporter, 1986-; Mbr, 1980-85, Chmn, Licensing Bd, Roxburgh Dist Coun; JP, Roxburgh, 1984-; Mbr, 1985-, Chmn, Planning and Dev, 1987-90, Borders Reg Coun. *Publications:* Journalistic works, as John Ross Scott; Novel and local book planned. *Memberships:* Borders Social Dem Party, 1st Chmn 1981-84; Roxburgh and Berwickshire Liberal Dems, 1st Sec 1988-89. *Honours:* Achieved top local govt posts; Achieved top majority in each election (contested 3, twice unopposed). *Hobbies:* Broadcasting; Writing; Tennis; Music, collecting 1960's music. *Address:* 8 Union Street, Hawick, Roxburghshire, Borders TD9 9LF, Scotland. 139, 184.

SCOTT Maurice FitzGerald, b. 6 Dec 1924, Dublin, Ireland. Economist. m. Eleanor Warren Dawson, 30 Mar 1953, dec. 1989, 3 d. *Education:* Wadham Coll, Oxford, 1946-48; Nuffield Coll, Oxford, 1948-49. *Appointments:* OEEC, Paris, 1949-51; Lord Cherwells Office, London, 1951-53; NIESR, 1953-57; Christ Church, Oxford, 1957-

68; Offical Fellow, Nuffield Coll, 1968-92; Emeritus Fellow, 1992-. *Publications include:* New View of Economic Growth; Industry & Trade in some Developing Countries; Other Books; Articles. *Memberships:* British Acad; Royal Economic Soc. *Hobby:* Walking. *Address:* 11 Blandford Avenue, Oxford OX2 8EA, England.1.52.

SCOTT-MANDERSON Marcus Charles William, b. 10 Feb 1956, England. Barrister. *Education:* Christ Church, Oxford, 1974-79; The Hague Acad of Intl Law, The Netherland, 1980; Univ of Glasgow, Scotland, 1981. *Appointments:* Called to the Bar, Lincolns Inn, 1980; Sec, Family Law Bar Assn Conciliation Bd. *Memberships:* British Acad of Forensic Sci; Forensisch Medisch Genootschap, The Netherlands. *Honours include:* Ver Heyden de Lancey Prize in Forensic; Postgraduate Scholarship, Univ of Glasgow. *Hobbies:* Ancient History; Archaeology; Fencing; Travel. *Address:* 4 Paper Buildings, Temple, London EC4 7EX, England.

SCOTT-MANDERSON William, b. 28 Aug 1925, England. Medical Practitioner. m. Pamela Maud Welch, 1 s. *Education:* Univ of Glasgow, 1948; Royal Coll of General Practitioners. *Appointments:* Medical Practitioner. *Publications:* Labetalol, A Study of a New Anto Hypertensive in General Practice; The Practitioner. *Hobbies:* Antiquarian Books, Collecting & Admiration. *Address:* Park House, The Strand, Ashton-In-Makerfield, Nr Wigan, Lancashire, WN4 8 LD, England.

SCRUGGS Jan Craig, b. 11 Mar 1950, Washington, DC, USA. Lectr; Attorney; Author. m. 23 June 1974. *Education:* American Univ, BA, 1975; M Ed, 1976; Univ of Meryland, JD, 1990. *Appointments:* US army, 1968-70; Pres, Vietnam Veterans Memorial of Washington DC, 1979-91. *Publication:* To Heal A Nation. *Memberships:* American Bar Assn; Natl Speakers Assn. *Honors:* VFW American award; Jefferson Award; Purple Heart. *Hobbies:* (F)Shooting; Golf; Skiing; Reading. *Address:* c/o VVMF, 1360 Beverly Drive 300, McLean, VA 22101, USA.

SCUDDER Lance Alan, b. 16 Mar 1965, Oklahoma, USA. Applications Engr, Epitaxial Silicon Lab, Applied Materials. *Education:* BS, Engrng Physics, Univ of Oklahoma, 1989. *Appointments:* Tchrng Asst, Univ of Oklahoma, 1987; Phys Sci Aide, Natl Sevale Storms Lab, 1985-89; Super Conductivity Research, Design Staff, 1989-91; EPI Applications Engr, Applied Materials, 1990-. *Memberships:* Intl Solar Energy Soc; Greenpeace; Tau Beta Pi; Golden Key. *Honors include:* McAlestor Scottish Rite Fellowship; Employee of the Quarter, AMAT. *Hobbies:* Volleyball; Biking; Scuba Diving; Sailing; Mechanical Design; table Tennis. *Address:* 2709 N Donald, Oklahoma City, Ok 73127, USA.117.

SCURLOCK Ralph Geoffrey, b. 21 Aug 1931, Southampton, England. Boc Prof of Cryogenic Engrng. m. Maureen Mary Oliver, 7 Aug 1956, 4 s. *Education:* St Johns Coll, Oxford, BA, 1954; D Phil, 1957. *Appointments:* Lectr, Univ of Southampton, 1959-66; Snr Lectr, 1966-68; Reader, 1968-85; Prof, 1985-. *Publications include:* Low Temperature Behaviour of Sofids, History and Origins of Cryogenics; Over 150 Papers in Scientific Journals. *Memberships:* Inst of Physics; Inst of Mechanical Engrng. *Address:* 22 Brookvale Road, Southampton, SO2 1QP, England.

SEAMAN Gerald Roberts, b. 2 Feb 1934, Leamington Spa, England. Musicologist. m. Lorna Viven Johnston, 21 Dec 1964, 2 d. *Education:* Birmingham School of Music, 1951-52; Keble Coll, Oxford, 19540-62; MA, DPhil, Oxford; Leningrad Conservatory, 1960-61. *Career include:* 1st broadcast, age 15; Regular Broadcaster, UK, then Australia and NZ; Currently Assoc Prof, School of Music, Univ Auckland, NZ. *Publications:* History of Russian Music, 1968; Orchestral Scores: A Finding List, 1984; Rimsky- Korsakov, A Bibliographical Research Guide, 1988; The Letters of Borodin, article, 1984.

Membership: Int Assn Music Lib, NZ Br, Pres 1981-82. *Honours:* Sr Assoc Mbr, St Antony's Coll, Oxford, 1972-. *Hobbies:* Languages; Travel. *Address:* Department of Music, University of Auckland, Private Bag, Auckland, New Zealand. 3, 52, 139.

SEDELNIKOV Gleb Serafimovich, b. 6 Aug 1944, Moscow, Russia. Composer; Poet. m. Olga Sedelnikova, 17 June 1966, 1 s. *Education:* Theory of Music, 1966-71, Musical Composition, 1974, Postgrad, 1975-79, Moscow Conservatoire. *Creative works:* Num compositions incl 3 operas: Poor People (on F Dostoevsky), 1972-73; The Bear (on A Chekhov), 1976; The Land of Electricity (on A Platonov); As poet Valentin Zagoryansky: Over 40,000 poems; Short-term rain, book of poetry, 1990. *Memberships:* Union of Russian Composers. *Honours:* 1st Prize, Int Contest of Composers, Prague, 1976. *Hobbies:* Reading; Chess; Collecting LP records; Tourism. *Address:* Sadovo-Triumphalnaya 14/12 ap 2, Moscow 103006, Russia.

SEDLAK Valerie Frances, b. 11 Mar 1934, Baltimore, Maryland, USA. Educator, Univ Admin. *Education:* BA, Coll of Notre Dame, Maryland, 1955; MA, Univ of Hawaii, 1962; Ph.D Univ of Pennsylvania, 1992. *Appointments include:* Tchr, Sacred Heart Sch, Florida, 1955-56; Tchrng Fellow, Univ of Hawaii, Admin Asst, Korean Councul General, Honolulu, 1959-60; Tchr, Boyertown Snr High Sch, Pennsylvania, 1961-63; Asst Prof, English, Univ of Baltimore, 1963-69; Morgan State Univ, Baltimore, 1970-; Communications Officer, Morgan State Univ, 1989-90; Dir, Writing for Television Program, 1990-. *Publications include:* Articles; Book Chapters; Poetry; Various Anthologies & Journals. *Memberships:* Modern Language Assn; College Language Assn; Coll Eng Assn; Middle-Atlantic Writers Assn, Founding Mem, 1982-; Coll Eng Assn, Middle Atlantic Group, VP, 1986-89; Pres, 1990-92; Women's Caucus for the Modern Languages; Maryland Poery and Literary Soc; Sth Atlantic Mod Lang Assoc; Maryland Council of Teachers of English. *Honours:* Fac Res Scholar, Morgan State Univ, 1983, 1993; Nat Endowment for the Humanities Fellow, 1984; Outstanding Teaching Prof in English, Morgan State Univ, 1986-87; Delta Epsilon Sigma, Nat'l Scholastic Honor Soc, 1988, VP, 1992-. *Address:* 102 Gorsuch Road, Lutherville- Timonium, MD 21093, USA.

SEELEY Roderick Eli. b. 21 Jan 1946, Los Angeles, California, USA. Cruise Travel Exec. m. June Carol Frei, 17 Aug 1972, 1 s, 1 d. *Education:* Business Admin & Mktg, Santa Barbara City Coll, 1965-67, 1971; Mitchell Coll, New London, Connecticut, 1969-71; Profl Training Travel & Cruise Ind, 1980-81. *Appointments:* US Navy, 1967-70; Advertising Production Specialist, JC Penney Co, 1971-72; Advertising Prod Mgr, Assoc Valley Publi, 1972-73; Vice Pres, Creative Dir, Abonnir Advertising Northridge, 1973-76; Santa Barbara, 1976-78; Vice Pres, Operations, Barlin Publi, Encino, 1978-80; Dir, Mktng Experwolrd & ExperCruise Van Nuys, 1980-83; Pres, Chief Exec Officer, Cruise Pro Inc, 1983-; Dir Mktng Advisory Bd, Norwegian Cruise Line, 1985-; Dir, Cruise Advisory Bd, Sunset Mag, 1987-. *Publications:* Articles; Travel Trade Mag. *Memberships include:* Santa Barbara Advertising Federation; American Advertising Federation; Natl Assn of cruise Agencies. *Honours:* Profl Awards; Santa Barbara Advertising Federation; Mag Publishers Assn; Travel Trade Publi; Military Cilations. *Address:* Cruise Pro Inc, 99 Long Court, Suite 200, Thousand Oaks, CA 91360, USA.59.130.139.

SEFANOV Valentin, b. 16 Feb 1959, Sofia, Bulgaria. Artist. m. Kovacheva Nina, 14 Apr 1985, 1 d. *Education:* BA, acad of Fine Arts, Sofia, 1985. *Appointments:* Freelance Artist. *Creative Works include:* Solo Exhibitions inc. Prints & Drawing in Hemus Gallery, Sofia; Selected Intl Exhibitions & Biennials; Representativa Exhibitions of Bulgarian Art. *Memberships:* Union of Bulgarian Artist Assn. *Honours:* First Prize, 5th Intl Print Bienale Varna; First Prize, Autumn Salon 90, Sofia. *Hobbies:* Travel; Different

Cultures; Yachting; Appreciating Jazz Music. *Address:* str Dimitar Stoianov, Bl 65 A, Sofia 1407, Bulgaria.

SEGALL James Arnold, b. 19 Aug 1956, Columbus, Ohio, USA. Lawyer. m. Janice Faye Wiesen, 14 Mar 1981, 1 s, 2 d. *Education:* Coll of William & Mary, Williamsburg, 1978; Washington & Lee Univ, Sch of Law, 1981. *Appointments:* Assoc, Phelps & King PC Newport News Va, 1981-84; Buxton & Lasris, PC, Yorktown Va, 1984-85; Sole Practice, Newport News, Va, 1985-89; Pres, James A Segall & Assoc, 1990- . *Memberships include:* Va State Bar; American Bar Assn; Assn of Trial Lawyers of America; City of Newport News Cable TV Advisory Commission. *Honours include:* Lectr, Hampton Roads Regl Acad of Criminal Justice; Lectr, Volunteer Program, 7th District Court Serv Unit. *Hobbies:* Weightlifting; Basketball; History; Philosophy. *Address:* James A Segall & Assoc, 525 Oyster Point Road, Suite G, Newport News, VA 23602, USA.7.132.

SEGEL Karen Lynn Joseph, b. 15 Jan 1947, Youngstown, Ohio, USA. Cert Tax Profl; Attorney. m. Alvin Gerald Segel, 9 June 1968, 1 s. *Education:* Bach of Arts, Boston Univ, 1968; Doct of Jurisprudence Southwestern Univ, Sch of Law, 1975. *Appointments:* Adminstrv Asst, Olds Brunel & Co, NYC, 1968- 69; US Banknote Corp, NYC, 1969-70; Tax Acct, SN Chilkov & Co, CPAs, beverly Hills, 1971-74; Tax Snr Oppenheim, Appel & Dixon Los Angeles, 1977-78; Fox, Westheimer & Co, LA, 1978; Zebrak Levine & Mepos, LA, 1978-79; Indep Cons Acct, Taxation Specialist, Beverly Hills, 1980-; Dir, World Wild Motion Picture Corp. *Memberships:* Natl Assn of Tax Profls; World Wild Motion Picture Corp. *Honours include:* Woman of The Year; Womens Inner Circle of Achievement; Int'l Directory of Distinguished Leadership; Community Leaders of America. *Hobbies:* Collector of Seashells; breeding Lhasa Apso Dogs; Art; Music; Literature; Needlework. *Address:* 223 South Willaman Drive, Beverly Hills, CA 90211, USA.2.59.138.152.

SEGERMANN Krista, b. 24 Oct 1941, Krefeld. Asst Prof. *Education:* Dortmund Univ, PHD, 1969; Habilitation, 1992. *Appointments:* Asst Prof, Dept of Romance Languages, Univ of Bochum; Managing Dir, Foreign Language Centre, Univ of Dortmund. *Publications include:* Das Motto in der Lyrik, München 1977, Typologie des fremdsprachlichen Ubens, Bochum 1992; Various articles on Foreign Language Didactics; Co-Editor of Zeitschrift für Frendsprachenforschung. *Hobbies:* Sports; Music. *Address:* FB 15 Sprachenzentrum, Univ Dortmnud, Emil-Figge-Str 50, D 4600 Dortmnud 50, Germany.

SEHOVIC Enver, b. 22 Sept 1938, Zagreb, Yugoslavia. Univ Profl. m. Djurdjica Petras, 30 Dec 1966, 1 s, 1 d. *Education:* BSc, Univ of Zagreb, 1962; MSc, 1966; PhD, 1970. *Appointments:* Asst, Assoc Prof, Full Prof, Univ of Zagreb, 1963-; Conslt, Telecommunications Ind & PTT's. *Publications:* 2 Books; 120 Papers. *Memberships:* Assembly of the Univ of Zagreb; Inter Univ Centre for Postgraduate Studies, Dubrovnik; EC Research Project. *Honours:* Nikola Tesla Award for Achievements in Digital Telecommunications. *Hobby:* Sailing. *Address:* Elektrotehnicki Fakultet, Unska 3, 41000 Zagreb, Croatia.52.

SEIDERER Franz Rolf, b. 29 July 1933, Landsberg, Germany. Treaseurer of the European Space Agency. m. Annegret Ullrich, 18 Dec 1981, 1 s, 1 d. *Education:* MBA, Univ of Munich; Law, Univ of Munich. *Appointments:* Dresdner Bank, 1965-72; Bayer Vereinsbank, 1972-77; European Space Agency, 1977- . *Membership:* L'Etrier, Paris. *Hobbies:* Horse Riding & Breeding; Collecting Modern Paintings & Sculptures. *Address:* Chateau de Rochefort, 1 Rue Guy le Rouge, 78730 Rochefort, France.52.

SEITZ Victoria Ann, b. 7 Aug 1956, Riode Oaneiro, Brazil. Prof. *Education:* BS, Kansas State Univ, 1978;

MS, Oklahoma State univ, 1984; PhD, 1987. *Appointments include:* Apprentic Designer, Carol Gown,s Chicago, 1977; Asst, Acting Dept Mgr, Saks Fifth Avenue, Arizona, 1980- 81; Dept Mgr, 1981-82; Graduate Tchrng Asst, Clothing, Textiles & Merch Dept, OSU, 1983-85; Graduate Tchrng & Research Assoc, 1986-87; Asst Prof, Sch of Human Resource Mgmt, UNT, 1988-91; Assoc Prof, Dept of Mktng, CSU, 1991- . *Publication include:* Power Dressing; The Art of Packaging Yourself. *Memberships:* American Mktng Assn; Southwest Mktng Assn; American Colleciate Retailing Assn; Intl Textile & Apparel Assn; Acad of Mktng Sci; Direct Mktng Assn of North Texas. *Honours:* Voted One of Oustanding Young Women of America; Spark Plug Award. *Hobbies:* Writing; Travel; Exercise. *Address:* 1601 Barton Rd, Apt 3904, Redlands, CA 92373, USA.

SELBY Philip, b. 6 Feb 1948, England. Composer. m. Rosanna Burrai, 21 Dec 1974, 1 s. *Education:* Royal Manchester Coll of Music; Composition Studies. *Debut:* As Composer with 1st Performance, From the Fountain of Youth , Royal Spa Centre, Leamington, 1975. *Appointments:* Appearances as Guitar Soloist, Town Hall Birmingham, 1966; Royal Albert Hall, London, 1970; All India Radio & TV; Pakistani TV; Youth Palace, Tehran, Iran; Istanbul Univ, Turkey. *Creative Works include:* Compositions. Suite for Guitar; Symphonic Dance for Orchestra; A Nature Meditation for Violin & Small Orchestra; Branch Touches Branch, Pastorale; Compositions: Guitar Concerto; Isa Upanishad (Canatata Sacra) for Double Chorus & Orchestra; Siddhartha (Dance Symphony); Symphony of Sacred Images, for Soprano & Bass Soli, Double Chorus Orchestra; Various Songs. *Memberships:* Composers Guild of gt Britain; Performing Right Soc. *Honours:* Chevalier Commandeur Ordre Souverain et Militaire de la Milice du Saint Sepulchre. *Hobbies:* Reading; Travel. *Address:* Hill Cottage, Via Maggio 93, 00068 Rignano Flaminio, Rome, Italy.139.191.

SELIGSON Esther, b. 25 Oct 1941, Mexico City, Mexico. Writer; Teacher. m. Alfredo Joskewicz, 23 Oct 1960, div, 2 s. *Education:* Degrees: Spanish Lit, UNAM; French Lit, IFAL-UNAM; Hist Art, Instituto de Cultura Superior SEP; Studies: Judaism, Ctr Univ d'Etudes Juifs, Paris; Talmud, Mahon Pardes, Jerusalem, 1981-82; Nahuatl, Museo de El Carmen, Mexico DF, 1987-88. *Appointments:* Tchr, Hist of Theatre, var state educl ctrs, 1964-; Transl; Critic; Essayist. *Publications:* Tras la ventana un arbol, 1969; Otros son los suenos, 1973; Transito del cuerpo, 1977; Luz de dos, 1978; De suenos, presagios y otras voces, 1978; Dialogos con el cuerpo, 1981; La morada en el tiempo, 1981; Sed de mar, 1987; La fugacidad-come metodo de escritura, 1988; Indicios y Quimeras, 1989; El teatro festin efimero, 1990; Isomorfismos, 1991. *Contributions to:* jrnls incl El Heraldo Cultural Supplement, Revista Plural, Revista UNAM, Revista de Bellas Artes, Suplemento Cultural Diorama, Revista Dialogos, Revista Vuelta. *Memberships:* Gen Soc Writers Mexico; Assn Writers Mexico; Int Union Writers; PEN; Asociacion Int de Escritores Judios en Lengua Hispana y Portuguesa, Jerusalem. *Honours:* Fellowship, Centro Mexicana de Escritores, 1969-70; Xavier Villaurrutia Prize, 1973; Magda Donato Prize, Lit, 1979. *Hobbies:* Myths and comparative religions; Healing; Acupuncture; Crystals and human energy; Hiking. *Address:* Ave Mexico 19 No 1101, Col Hipodrome-Condesa, Mexico DF 06170, Mexico. 3.

SELIM Mahmoud, b. 16 Oct 1964, Cairo, Egypt. Architect. m. Mona Zaki, 7 Oct 1988, 1 d. *Education:* Cairo Univ, 1986; China LAC, Beijing, 1988; Army Serv, Cairo, 1988. *Appointments:* Lee Borrero Arch, New York, 1984; RS & D, New York, 1985; Al Guezira, Constr & Arch Bureau, Founder & Managing Dir, 1987-91. *Creative Works include:* Designer, Al Essra; Al Thawra. *Membership:* Gezira Sporting Club. *Hobbies:* Painting; Photography; Chess. *Address:* 5 Mahmoud Sidki Str, Zamalek, Cairo, Egypt.

SELWYN John Jasper, b. 11 Aug 1918, Repton, Derby. Retired Army Officer; Barrister. m. (1) Margaret Evelyn Whittingham, 25 Sept 1943, dec, 2 s, 1 d. (2) Mary Mitchell Radcliffe, 16 Mar 1983. *Education:* Eton Coll, 1935; Trinity Cambridge, 1936-39; Army Staff Coll, 1948. *Appointments:* Regular Army Officer, 1939-59; War Serv NW Europe; Barrister, 1963; Deputy Circuit Judge, 1974-78. *Memberships:* Cavalry & Guards Club; 13/18 Hussars Assn; RUSI; Royal British Legion; Lincolns Inn; County Counsellor, Berkshire. *Honour:* Military Cross, Dieppe. *Hobbies:* Field Sports; Sailing; Rowing; Genealogy. *Address:* The Orchards, Pinkets Green, Maidenhead, Berks SL6 6PA.

SELWYN Sydney, b. 7 July 1934, Leeds, England. Prof of Medical Microbiology; Snr Conslt Microbiologist. m. Flora Dagmar Schmerling. *Education:* Univ of Edinburgh, BSc, 1958; MB, ChB, 1959; MD, 1966; MRCPath, 1967; FRCPath, 1979; FIBiol, 1979; DHMSA, 1970. *Appointments:* Resident Physician, Edinburgh City Hsop, 1959; Carnegie Trust Scholar, 1960; Polio Research Fellow, 1961; Lectr, Unib of Edinburgh, 1962; Snr Lectr, 1966; Reader, Univ of London, Westminster Medical Sch, 1967-78; Prof, Univ of London, 1979-; Conslt, Westminster Hosp, 1967-; Prof, Charing cross Hosp Medical Sch, 1983-84; Prof, 1984-. *Publications include:* The Beta Lactam Antibiotics - Penicillins & Cephalosporins in Perspective; Numerous Chapters; Over 250 Papers. *Memberships:* Faculty of History & Philosophy of Medicine & Pharmacy; Medical Sci Historical Soc; Osler Club of London; Royal Soc of Medicine; Pathology Sec; Harveian Soc; Royal Coll of Pathologists. *Honours include:* State Scholarship; Wellcome Medal & Prize; Peel Medical Research Award. *Hobbies:* Exotic Travel; photography; History of Medicine & Art; Music. *Address:* Dept of Medical Microbiology, Charing Cross Hospital, Fulham Palace Road, London W6 8RF, England.52.

SEMENOVKER Boris Ar'evich, b. 21 Oct 1935, Moscow, Russia. Researcher in Bibliographical Science. *Education:* Grad, Engl Fac, Moscow Inst For Langs; Cand Pedagogical Scis (Lib and Bibliog Sci); Dr Pedagogical Scis (Lib and Bibliog Sci), 1990. *Appointments:* Tchr, Engl, second school; Lib, Bibliographer, Rschr, Acquisition Dept, USSR State Lenin Lib, 1963; Rschr, All-Union State Lib For Lit, 1968-75; Dept Chief, Theory Nat Bibliog, Leading Rschr, All-Union Book Chamber, 1975-. *Publications:* Over 120 monographs, ref books, bibliographical indexes and jrnl articles in Russian incl: Monograph on computer production of union catalogues, 1970; Monograph on computer formats for machine-readable cataloguing, 1972; Monograph on history of national bibliography in Latin America, 1974; Var articles on Universal Bibliographical Control; The USSR Retrospective National Bibliography, ref book, 1990; History of Bibliography in Byzantium, unpublished dissertation, 1990. *Address:* B Cherkizovskaya 4-4-25, Moscow 107061, Russia.

SEMMENCE Adrian Murdoch, b. 5 Apr 1926, Scotland. Conslt in Occupational Medicine. m. Joan Wood, 24 Sept 1949, 4 s, 1 d. *Education:* MB, Univ Aberdeen, 1953; MD, 1957; MSc, Univ London, 1972; FRCGP, 1972; FFOMRCP, 1983. *Appointments:* House Officer, Aberdeen Royal Infirmary, Aberdeen Maternity Hosp, 1953-54; Principal in Central Practice E Yorks, 1954-60; Berkshire and Oxfordshire, 1961-76. *Memberships:* Royal Soc of Medicine; Oxford Medical Soc. *Honour:* Companion of the Bath. *Hobbies:* Gardening; Golf; Reading. *Address:* Stone Cottage, 13 High Street, Steventon, Abingdon, Oxon OX13 6RZ.1.

SEMPLE James Henry, b. 23 Aug 1931, Tifton, Georgia, USA. Director, Baptist Missions Commission. m. Betty Bennett, 2 s, 4 d. *Education:* BA, John B Stetson Univ, Deland, FL, 1953; BD, 1957, ThD, 1962, SoWn Bapt Theological Sem, Ft Worth, TX. *Appointments:* Student Pastorates, FL and TX, 1951-62; Pastor, 1st Bapt Ch, Plano, 1962-63; Pastor, 1st Bapt Ch, Paris,

TX, 1963-88; Dir, State Missions Commn, Bapt Gen Conven TX, Dallas, 1989-. *Publications:* On Wings of Eagles, book, 1968; Contbr to the Holman Discipleship Bible; Articles in Home Life, The Adult Teacher, Home Missions Magazine, Baptist Standard, Florida Baptist Witness, Christian Life, Christianity Today, The Baptist Program, others. *Memberships:* Chmn of Bd, Bapt Gen Conven TX Ch Loan Corp; Chmn, Constitutional Review Comm, Resolutions Comm, Credentials Comm, Bapt Gen Conven TX; Parliamentarian, So Bapt Conven, 1983-84. *Honours:* Award as Outstanding Evangelistic Pastor of Multi-Staff Ch, So Bapt Conven Home Missions Bd, 1987; Alumni of Yr Award, SoWn Bapt Theological Sem, TX, 1988. *Address:* State Missions Commission, Baptist General Convention of Texas, 333 N Washington, Dallas, TX 75246, USA. 7, 145.

SEMPLE William David Crowe, b. 11 June 1933, Grangemouth, Scotland. Dir of Educ. m. Margaret Bain Donald, 9 July 1958, 1 s, 1 d. *Edcation:* Glasgow Univ, 1957; Jordanhill Coll, 1958; London Univ, 1970. *Appointments:* Educ Officer, Northern Rhodesia, 1958-64; Deputy Chief, 1964-66; Chief, Zambia, 1966-67; Act Dir of Tech, Ed, 1967-68; Depute Dite of Ed, Edinburgh, 1968-74. *Publications:* Various Journals. *Memberships:* Assn of Directors of Educ in Scotland; General Sec Rotary. *Honour:* Commander of the British Empire, CBE. *Hobbies:* Gardening; Walking; Reading. *Address:* 15 Essex Park, Edinburgh, EH4 6LH. Scotland.1.

SENATOR Ronald Paul, b. 17 Apr 1926, London, England. Composer; Author. m. Miriam Brickuan, 17 Oct 1988. *Education:* City of London Sch; Marlborough Coll, Oxford; London Univ. *Appointments:* Dir, Counterpoint Publi; Lectr, Goldsmiths Coll; Snr Lectr, Columa; Dir SSRC Programme, London Univ; Prof, Guildhall Sch. *Creative Works include:* Five Operas inc. Wolf of Gubbio; Holocast Reqiqm; Mobiles; Spring Changes; Books. General Grammer of Music; The Kaddish Letters. *Memberships:* Montserrat Assn of Composers; PRS; ASCAP; Composers Guild. *Honour:* Pulitzer. *Hobby:* Travel. *Address:* 81 Hillcrost Avenue, Park Hill, NY 10705, USA.

SENGUPTA Jati D Kumar, b. 4 Jan 1934, Pampurhat, West Bengel, India. Prof of Economics & Operations Research. m. Kristna Senguptal, 5 June 1965. *Education:* MA, Calcutta Univ, 1955; PhD, Iowa State Univ, 1962. *Appointments:* Prof of Economics & Statistics, 1963-69; Prof, Dir of Indian Inst of Mgmt, Calcuta, 1970-76; Prof of Economics & Operations Research, Santa Barbara, California, 1976-. *Publications:* Over 200 Research publi; 9 Books. *Memberships:* Econometric Soc; TIMS; Intl Journal of Systems Sci; Journal of Economics. *Honours include:* Univ Gold Medal; Centennial Scholar. *Hobbies:* Reading; Classical Music; Swimming; Hiking. *Address:* Prof of Economics & Operations Research, Univ of California, Santa Barbara, CA 93106, USA.

SEPCIC Juraj, b. 28 Oct 1935, Cres. Neurologist; Full Prof. m. Kopac Snezna, 20 Dec 1969, 1 d. *Education:* Medical Faculty, Univ Zagreb, 1960; Spec Training Neurology Psychiatry, Zagreb, 1967; Magister in Sci, Rijeka, 1973; Doc in Sci, 1979. *Appointments:* Hd Demyelinating Diseases Univ, Dept Neurology, Univ Med Centre Rijeka, 1972-; Asst Prof, 1980; Full prof, 1985; Hd of the Chair of Neurology, Univ of Rijeka, 1988. *Publications include:* 120 Sci & Profl Papers; Sci Monographs & Textbooks. *Memberships include:* IMAB of IFSS; Acta Facultatis Medicae Fluminensis, Rijeka. *Honours:* Yugoslav Union of Multiple Sclerosis Assn Award; Yugoslav Union of Medical Snns Award; Rijeka Town Prize. *Hobbies:* Bibliophily; Collecting Paintings; Underwater Fishing. *Address:* Dubrovacka 2, 51000 Rijeka, Croatia.

SEPHTON Peter Stanley, b. 24 June 1957, Chicago. Prof of Economics. m. Susan Elizabeth Pettet, 25 June 1983, 1 s, 1 d. *Education:* Hillfield, Strathallan Coll,

1966-76; McMaster Univ, BA, 1980; Queens Univ, MA, 1981; PhD, 1984. *Appointments:* Asst Prof, Univ of Regina, 1984-86; Univ of Brunswick, 1986-. *Publications:* Various Journal Articles. *Memberships:* Canadian Economic Assn; American Finance Assn. *Honours:* MacKenzie Memorial Prize in Development Economics; Merit Award. *Hobbies:* Swimming; Sailing. *Address:* 279 Woodlawn Lane, Frederiction, New Brunswick, Canada E3C 1JY.

SEPPINEN Jukka Tadani, b. 24 Oct 1945, Henslinki, Finland. Sec General. m. Tuisa Herja, 2 Nov 1985. *Education:* LLM, 1969; MPolit, 1975, Univ of Helsinki; Diploma ENA, Paris. *Appointments:* Ministry Foreign Affairs, 1970-87; Sec General Project Rvotsinsalmi, Fineland. *Creative Works:* Columnist Paper Etela Svomi; Paper Kymen Sanomat. *Memberships:* DDG of IBC; ABIRA; Club of Kitka. *Honour:* Knight 1st Class Order of Lion. *Hobbies:* Painting; Literature. *Address:* Laavaksoki, 48750 Nikeli, Finland.52.139.152.191.

SEREBROV Alexander, b. 15 Feb 1944, Moscow. Flight Engr; Physicist. m. 4 Dec 1965, 1 s. *Education:* Moscow Inst of Physics & Tech, 1961-67; Doc Degree, Gas & Termodynamics. *Appointments:* Bach Degree, 1967; Prof, 1970-76; Snr Researcher, 1976-78; Test Pilot, 1978-. *Publications:* Few Dozen Articles. *Memberships:* Russian Acad of Engrng; All Union Aerospace Soc. *Honours include:* Hero of the Soviet Union; Bulgarian Republic Oder; Liague de Honneur Oficer. *Hobbies:* Hunting; Scooba Diving; Tennis; Aplic Skiing; Non Government Educ Programs; Reading; Photography; TV Movie; Car Designing. *Address:* Hovanskya St 3, App 23, 129515 Moscow, Russia.

SERGEJEVA Tatjana, b. 28 Nov 1951, Kalinin, USSR. Composer; Pianist; Organist. m. Ivan Vikharev, 14 May 1982. *Education:* Central Musical Spec Sh, Moscow, 1959-70; Moscow Conservatoize, 1970-75; Composer Degree, 1977-79; Post Grad Composer Degree, 1979-81. *Appointments:* Pianist, Moscow Conservatoire, 1975-88; Composer, Concert Pianist, Organist, 1988-. *Creative Works include:* Arias; Trombone Concerto; Concerto for Violin & Keyboard Instruments; Variations of Theme by Tatiania L Tolstaja for Violin, Organ, Tromba, Saxofone; Two Piano Concertos; Two Cello Sonatas. *Memberships:* USSR Composers Union. *Honour:* Prize of the Composers Union. *Hobbies:* Painting in Oil; Poetry. *Address:* Noropestchanaya St 19/10 165, 125252 Moscow, Russia.

SERWANSKI Maciej, b. 5 Nov 1946, Poznan, Poland. Prof of History; Historian. m. Widower, 1 s. *Education:* MA, Adam Mickiewicz Univ, Poznan, 1969; PhD, 1974; Habilitation, 1985; Prof, 1991. *Appointments:* Adam Mickiewicz Univ, 1969-; Asst, 1969-72; Asst Lectr, 1972-74; Tutor, 1974-88; Asst Prof, 1988-91; Prof, 1991-. *Publications include:* Henryk 111 Walezy w Polsce, Stosunki Polsko-Francuskie w Latach, 1566-1576; France & Poland during Thirty Years War, 1618-1648. *Membership:* Polish Historical Assn. *Honours:* Acad Award of the Ministry of Educ, Poland, 1977 & 1988. *Hobbies:* Travel; Foreign Languages. *Address:* Wichrowe Wzgorze 21 m 73, 61 677 Poznan, Poland.

SESTAK Zdenek, b. 10 July 1925, Citoliby, Czechoslovakia. Composituer. m. Marie Zatecka, 2 Apr 1950, 1 s, 1 d. *Education:* Gymnasium, 1944; Conservatorium, 1950; Univ Charles, Prague, 1950. *Appointments:* Prof de la Musique, 1953-57; Freelance Composer de, 1957-91; Dans le Temps, 1968-70; Le Drama Turque Central de la Musique Dans le Radio Prague. *Creative Works include:* Symponies II-V; Concerto for String Orchestra; II Concerto for Violin; String Quartet III; Quintet Puor Les String. *Membership:* Assn Des Artists Musicaux Teheques. *Hobby:* Cycliing. *Address:* Pracska 2594, 10600 Prague 10, Czechoslovakia.52.

SETH Bernie, b. 5 Apr 1957, Bonbay, India. Business Devel Mgr. m. Nancy Claire Mills, 23 Apr 1983. *Education:* Bach of Engrng, Monash Univ, 1979; Master of Engrng, Univ of NSW, 1982; Master of Business Admin, Univ of Tech Sydney, 1989. *Appointments:* OTC, Australias Overseas Telecommunications Co, 1979-. *Publications include:* Polarization Performance Measurement of Earth Station Antennas. *Memberships:* Inst of Engrs; Australian Inst of Management; Inst of Radio & Electonics Engrs; Telecommunications Soc of Au; Inst of Electrical & Electronic Engrs. *Honours:* Top of MBA; Schroder Darling Grauate Award. *Hobbies:* Cricket; Tennis; Music; Movies; Aerobics. *Address:* 13 Moonah Road, Alfords Point, NSW 2234, Australia.

SETHURAMAN Salem Venkataraman, b. 23 May 1935, Madras. Senior Economist ILO. m. Rajam 29 Apr 1963, 1 s, 1 d. *Education:* PHD, Univ Chicago; MA, Delih Univ; BSC, Univ Mysore; BSC (Hons), Univ Mysore; Diploma French Univ of Mysore. *Appointments:* Economist, Natl Council of App Eco Research, 1958-64; Research Economist, US Agency for Intl Devel, 1969-72; Snr Fellow, Eastwest Center, 1972-73; ILO, Geneva, 1973-. *Publications include:* Urban Development and Employment, Jakarta; Rural Small Scale Industries & Employment in Asia & Africa; The Urban Informal Sector in developing Countries; Technological Capatility in the Informal Sector; The Urban Informal Sector in Asia: An annotated bibliography. *Honour:* Fulbright Scholar. *Hobbies:* Gardening; Di It Yourself; Classical Music. *Address:* 64 Route Du Vallon, 1224 Chene Bougeries, Switzerland.

SEVEN Marilyn, b. 22 Mar 1947, Boston, Massachusetts, USA. Playwright. m. Richard B Shull, 7 July 1989. *Education:* BA magna cum laude, Vassar Coll, 1969. *Appointments:* Playwright-in-Resid, The Playwrights Ctr, Minneapolis, MN, 1983-84; Playwright, Sci Mus MN, St Paul, 1983-87; Lectr, Dramaturgy: Nat Arts Club, NYC. 1984, Engl Speaking Union, NYC, 1985; A Playwright, Mus Sci, Boston, MA, 1985-; Playwright-in-Res, Actors Theatre, St Paul, MN, 1987-88; Lectr, Dramaturgy: Vassar Coll, 1987, Young Playwrights Fest, 1988. *Creative works:* Plays, staged: Life upon the Wicked Stage, 1976; Double Dutch, 1982; Listen to the Robe, 1983; Charles and Mrs Darwin, 1984; The Ladies Who Lunch, 1985; The Barber-Surgeon Had a Wife, 1985; Coming of Nuclear Age, 1986; N'Yawk N'Yawk...Who's There, 1987; American Express, 1987; The Goose Sings Low, 1988; The Grotto of Purity, 1988; No Easy Answers, 1989; Einstein's Little Finger, 1990; Mother's Little Helper, 1991; Shall We Dance, 1991; Circle in the Square, 1991; Children's plays: Bring Back My Sweet Pea to Me; The Many and Wondrous Adventures of Splish and Splash; At Seventeen I Climbed a Cherry Tree, 1990. *Memberships:* Playwrights Ctr, Minneapolis, Former Playwrights Rep to Bd Dirs, Former Artistic Comm Mbr; Nat Arts Club, NYC; New England Soc, City of NY; Vassar Club, Intermedia Arts; Women in Film; Dramatists Guild; Phi Beta Kappa. *Honours:* Edward Albee Fndn Artistic Residencies for Millay Colony for the Arts, Tyrone Guthrie Ctr, William Flanagan Mem Creative Persons Ctr, 1983-87; Jerome Fellowship, Playwrighting, 1983; PEN Am Grant, 1984; Twin Cities Mayors Pub Art Award, The Ladies Who Lunch, 1985; Composer/Librettist Workshop Fellowship, MN Opera, 1987; Travel and Study Grant, Dayton Hudson/Jerome Fndn, 1988; 2 Jones Commns for 6th Day, Playwrights Ctr, 1988, 1989. *Hobbies:* Animals; Birds. *Address:* 400 West 43rd St, No 33A, New York, NY 10036, USA. 34, 189.

SEVERIN Adrian, b 28 Mar 1954, Bucharest, Romania. m. Pineta Emilia Maria, 23 July 1978. *Education:* Univ of Bucharest, 1978; Doc in Law, 1984. *Appointments include:* Snr Lectr, Acad of Social & Political studies, 1986-89; Natl Sch for Policital & Admin Sci, 1989-; Sec of state, Romanian Government, 1990; Deputy Prime Minister, Romania, 1990-91; Pres, Natl Agency for Privatization & Medicon Sized Business Devel, 1991-. *Publications include:* Intl Scale of Goods Amoung East European Countries. *Memberships include:* Law Section of the Romanian Assn for Intl Law & Intl Relation; Romanian Consltng Inst. *Hobbies:* Symphonic Music; Tourism. *Address:* 24 Kiseleff Av, Bucharest, Romania.

SEWPERSHAD Lionel, b. 2 Sept 1940, Guyana. Asst Principal. m. Marta Cecilia Orta, 31 Dec 1985, 2 d. *Education:* BA, IAU, 1967; MA, 1981; Post Grad, Suny Bingaamton, 1967-68; Lim Miami, 1987. *Appointments:* Elementary Sch Tchr, Guyana, 1958-60; Civil Service Clerk, ministry of Home Affairs, 1960-64; Lectr, Inter American Univ, 1968-70; Sociologist, Planning Sec, Ministry of Econ Dev, George Town, 1972-74; Social Worker, 1974- 76; Tchr, Jnr High Sch, 1976-86; Asst Principal, Elementary Sch, 1986-; Lectr, Univ of the Virgin Islands, 1983-. *Memberships include:* Community Action Agency; Frederiksted Lions Club; Phi Delta Kappa; Caribbean Light Lodge. *Honours include:* Intl Scholarship; Dept of Sociology Award , IAU. Dept of Sociology Fellowship. *Hobbies:* Cricket; Baseball; World Government; World Peace. *Address:* Box 2814, Frederiksted St Croix, Virgin Islands 00840.7.15.

SEYERSTED Finn, b. 29 Dec 1915, Oslo, Norway. Prof of Intl Law. m. Sölvi Gierlöff, 23 Dec 1957. 2 d. *Education:* Oslo Univ, 1941; Paris Univ, 1950-51; Defence Acad, 1965-66; dr of Law, 1966. *Appointments:* Deputy Judge, Altz, Lapland, 1942-43; Intl Law Officer, 1944-45; Deputy Permanent Repr to UN, 1946-49; Mission for UNESCO, 1953-54; Chief Of Div, Min for Affairs, 1955-60; Dir, Legal Div, Intl Atomic Energy Agency, 1960-65; Ambassador, Buenos Aries, 1968-73. *Memberships:* Norwegion Assn of Intl Law; Norwegion World Federalists. *Honours:* War Medal; St Olsv, Norway; Szn Martin, Argentina. Hobby: Languages. *Address:* Jerpefaret 28, 0393 Oslo, Norway. 3.

SEYHOUN Houshang, b. 22 Aug 1920, Tehran, Iran. Artist. m. Noushine Massoumeh, 11 May 1953, div, 1 s, 1 d. *Education:* Tehran Univ, 1944; Ecole Natl Superieure Des Beaux Arts, Paris, 1948. *Appointments:* Prof, Faculty of Fine Arts, Tehran Univ, 1949; Dean of Faculty of Fine Arts, 1962-69; Active Member of City Council, Tehran, 1967-71. *Creative Works include:* Moumental Building in Memories of, Avicenna at Hamadan; Worldwide Exhibs; Publi. Regards Sur L'Iran; At The Passage of the Desert. *Memberships:* Editorial Bd of L'Architecture Francaise; Archeological Council Iran; Iran Univ Council; Iran Urban Council; ICOMOS Related to UNESCO. *Honours include:* Recipient of many Awards, Medalions & Prizes. *Hobbies:* Reading; Listening to Classical Music; Walking. *Address:* 2066 Marine Drive, West Vancouver, BC, Canada V7V 1J9.52.

SEYMOUR Harry Taylor, b. 19 May 1936, Hamilton, Ontario, Canada. Managing Partner, Waterston group of Companies. m. Lillian stanley, 24 Apr 1964, 2 d. *Education:* Univ of Toronot, BSA, 1961; BASc, 1962; Univ of Western Ontario, MBA, 1966. *Appointments:* Vice Pres & Dir, Dominion Securities Inc, 1974-88; Pres, Dir, Dominion Sec Investment Management, 1984- 88; Pres, Dir, Waterston Financial Ins, 1988-; Pres, Dir, Bay Port Midland Holdings, 1990-; Pres, Chief Exec Officer, Dir, Pathfinder Learning Systems Cooporation, 1991-. *Publiction:* Royal Commission On Corporate Concentration Ergus Corporation. *Memberships include:* The Empire Club of Canada; Art Gallery of Ontario Foundation; Youth Employment Skills Canada; Assn of Profl Engrs of Ontario. *Hobbies:* Tennis; Skiing; Golf. *Address:* Suite 200, 90 Adelaide Street West, Toronto, Ontario, Canada M5H 1P6.88.142.

SGALL Petr, b. 27 May 1926, C Budejovice. Prof. m. (2) Kveta Sgallova, 6 Jan 1958, 2 s, 1 d. *Education:* Charles Univ, Prague, 1949; Cand of Sci, 1955; Docent, 1959; Doc of Sci, 1966; Prof, 1990. *Appointments:* Charles Univ, Asst, 1949; Docent, 1959; Research Collaborator, 1962; Hd of Labor of Algebraic Linguistics, 1968-72; Research Prof, 1967; Hd of Inst of Theoretical & Computational Linguistics, 1990. *Publications include:* Infinitive in Rigveda; Meaning of Sentence;

Other Linguistic Publi. *Memberships:* Intl Committee of Computational Linguistics; European Chapter of Computational Linguistics; Soc Linguistica Europaea; Czechoslovak Assn of Linguists, Mathematicians, Cybernetics, Computer Sci. *Honour:* Alexander Von Humboldt Prize. *Address:* Ortenovo m 24, 17000 Prague 7, Czechoslovakia.52.

SHADIX Daniel Alan, b. 15 Aug 1955, Birmingham, Alabama. Pastor. m. Carolyn Jones, 26 Mar 1983, 2 d. *Education:* Samford Univ, Birmingham, 1976; The Southern Baptist Theological Seminary, 1980; Drew Univ; Doc of Ministry, 1986. *Appointments:* Mission Pastor, First Baptist Church De Ridder, 1980-85; Pastor, Eutaw Baptist Church, Alabama, 1985-90; Pastor, Southside Baptist Church, 1991-. *Publications include:* Booklet, In Time of Need; Parson's Porch Swing. *Memberships:* Eutaw Ministerial Assn; Samford Univ Band; Instr, Samford Univ Extension Div. *Hobbies:* Writing; Golf; Collecting Books. *Address:* 4455 Narrow Lane Road, Montgomery, AL 36116, USA.

SHAFFER Richard Paul, b. 12 Oct 1949, Fort Worth, Texas, USA. Owner Company Benefits. *Education:* AA, Coll of the Mainland, Texas, 1975; BBA, Houston State Univ, 1975; MBA, 1976. *Appointments:* Personnel Supervisor, Texas Air Natl Guard, Ellington Air Force BAse, Texas, 1967-87; Personnel Tech, 1968-75; Personnel Recruiter, The Univ of texas, 1976-79; Accounting Tax Auditor, The state of Texas, 1979-82; Owner, Conslt, Company Benefits, 1982-. *Hobbies:* Flying; Fishing. *Address:* 743 Marlin, Bayou Vista, Hitchcoch, TX 77563, USA.7.132.

SHAFFER Sherwood, b. 15 Nov 1934, Bee Co, Texas, USA. Composer; Tchr. *Education:* HS, Tyler, Texas, 1953; BM, Curtis Inst of Music, 1960; MM, Manhattan Sch of Music, NYC, 1962. *Appointments:* Neupaur Conservatory, Phil PA Tchr of 20th Cent Harmony & Fugue, 1959-60; Manhattan Sch of Music, Tchr, 1962-65; North Carolina Sch of the Arts, 1965-. *Creative Works include:* Sonata for D Bass/Piano; A Feast of Music for St Cecilias Day; Concerto for Orch. Plus 140 Other Musical Works. *Memberships:* BMI; American Music Center; NC Composers Alliance; Southeastern Composers Alliance; Winston Salem Symphony; ECKANKAR, Intl Co Director of Music. *Honours include:* Outstanding Educ of Americ Awards; Commission Awards. *Hobbies:* Pinting; Attending Arts Events/ Theatre/Concerts/Museums. *Address:* c/o The North Carolina Sch of the Arts, PO Box 12189, Winston Salem, NC 27117, USA.

SHAH Ajendra, b. 2 Nov 1941, Bombay, India. Medical. m. 10 Oct 1970, 1 s, 1 d. *Education:* MBBS, 1965; MD, 1969; FCCP, 1982. *Appointments:* Internal Medicine, Bombay, 1970; Asst Prof, 1976-; Visiting Asst Phy, LTMG Hosp, LTMM Coll, 1976-; Pioneer Worker, Pulmonary Medicine, 1976-; Hd of Respiratory Care Serv, dept of Respiratory Diseases, LTMG Hosp, Bombay. *Creative Works include:* 80 Papers on Asthma, Bronchitis, Emphysema, Allergy, Tetanus; Booklet, Common Poisoning; Book. Mara Videshna Sansmarno. *Memberships:* Ghatkopar Jaycees; Assn of Physicians of India; American Chest Assn; Indian Occupation Health; SMTA LTMG Hosp; Indian Chest Soc; Indian Medical Assn; Staff & Research Soc of LTMG Hosp. *Honours include:* Prizes in Physiology; Gold Medal in Surgery; Minifellowshio in Pulmonary Medicine. *Hobbies:* Gardening; Reading; Research; Tchrng; Photography; Writing; Organising; Mountaineering; Visiting Historic Places. *Address:* 4 Golwala House, Hingwala Lane, P O Box 7294, Ghatkopar (East), Bombay 400 077, India.139.156.162.

SHAH Maya, b. 18 July 1942, Surat, India. Univ Tchr. m. 30 May 1963, 2 d. *Education:* BA, Univ Baroda, 1962; MA, MS Univ, 1965; PhD, MS Univ Baroda, 1978. *Appointments:* Asst Lectr, Econ Dept MS Univ; LEctr; Reader; Prof. *Publications include:* Growth, Productivity & Technical Progress in Electricity in India.

Memberships: American Economic Assn; Royal Economic Soc; Gujarat Economic Assn. *Honours:* Commonwealth Fellowship; Shastri Indo Canadaian Fellowship. *Hobby:* Reading. *Address:* Purva, Old Padra Road, Baroda 390015, India.

SHAH Shoaib Akhter, b. 11 Aug 1960, Hyderabad, Sindh, Pakistan. Airlines District Manager. m. 8 Oct 1982, 1 s, 3 d. *Education:* BA (Hons), Econs; LLB; MBA, Mktng; Dip Pub Admin; Dip Banking. *Appointments:* Lectr, Inst Bus Studies, Univ Sindh; Off, Tariffs, curently Dist Mgr, Pakistan Int Airlines, Nawab Shah, Sindh. *Creative works:* Dev of package in Pakistan Int Airlines computer (REPAK) to feed world wide fares. *Memberships:* Hyderabad Gymkhana Club; Nawab Shah Gymkhana Club; Rotary Club, Nawab Shah; YMCA, Hyderabad; Sindh Grads Assn. *Honours:* Gold Medal for 1st position in 1st class, BA (Hons) Econs and MBA, Univ Sindh. *Hobbies:* Developing new tour packages; Developing agricultural forms; Introducing mechanised agricultural farming; Visiting countryside villages. *Address:* Muhalla Baqar Pota, Post Office Matiari, District Hyderabad, Sindh, Pakistan.

SHAHIN Majdi Musa, b. 5 Dec 1936, Jerusalem. Dir, Dept of Chem Protection and Photochem Rsch in Vitro, L'Oreal Adv Rsch Ctr, Aulnay-sous- Bois, France. m. Anneliese Edith Heun, 8 Mar 1962, 1 d. *Education:* Predip Biology, Fac of Maths and Natural Sciences, Free Univ Berlin, 1962; Dip in Biology, 1965. *Appointments:* Postdoct Fellow, Atomic Energy of Can Ltd, Chalk River, Ont, 1970-73; Vis Fellow, Nat Inst Environmental Hlth and Science Rsch, Triangle Pk, NC, USA, 1973-74; Rsch Assoc, Dept Genetics, Univ Alta, Edmonton, 1974-78; Dir, Dept Mutagenesis L'Oreal Rsch Labs, Aulnay-sous-Bois, France, 1978-90; Dir, Dept Chem Protection and Photobiological Rsch in Vitro, L'Oreal Adv Rsch Ctr, Aulnay- sous-Bois, 1991-. *Publications:* Articles in profl jrnls, chapts in books, Ed, Special issue Mutation Research on Structure Activity Relationships in Chem Mutagenesis. *Memberships:* AAAS; American Soc Microbiology; European Environmental Mutagen Soc; The Genetic Soc Canada; American Soc for Radiation Rsch; Environmental Mutagen Soc, USA; NY Acad of Science. *Hobby:* Art Collector. *Address:* L'Oreal Research Laboratories, 1 Avenue Eugene Schueller, 93601 Aulnay-sous-Bois, France. 52.

SHAIR Salem A, b. 4 Sept 1937, Jerusalem, Palestine. Professor of Microbiology; Faculty Dean. m. Samira Thaher, 2 Sept 1969, 1 s, 2 d. *Education:* BSc, 1957, MSc, 1959, Roosevelt Univ, USA; MSc, Univ Chgo, 1961; PhD, Union Grad School (The Union Inst), 1977. *Appointments:* Microbiologist, W R Gracve and Co, USA, 1964-66; Grp Ldr, Rsch Microbiology, Dearborn Chem, W R Grace, 1966-74; Sr Rsch Ldr, 1974-77, Dir, Environmental and Reg Affairs, 1977-78, Dearborn Chem; Asst Prof, Microbiology, 1978-84, Assoc Prof, 1984-91, United Arab Emirates Univ; Prof, Dean, Fac Sci, Applied Sci Univ, Jordan, 1991-. *Publications:* Man and Nutrition; Man, Health and Disease; Man and the Environment; Num articles on microbiological matters. *Memberships:* Am Soc Microbiology; Am Acad Microbiology; Am Soc Indl Microbiology; IL Soc Microbiology; Am Inst Biological Socs; Am Soc Clin Pathology; Am Pub Hlth Assn; Am Chem Soc; AAAS; ASTM; Nat Hist Mus; NY Acad Scis. *Honours:* Int Scholarship, Univ TX, 1954; Int Scholarship, Roosevelt Univ, 1956; Union Inst, 1976; Dearborn Chem President's Award, Outstanding Rsch, 1966, 1967, 1969, 1971, 1973, 1975; Cert Ldrship and Recognition, United Arab Emirates Univ, 1986, 1987, 1988, 1989, 1990, 1991. *Hobbies:* Reading; Classical music; Tennis; Swimming; Hunting; The outdoors. *Address:* 530 Surryse Rd, Lake Zurich, IL 60047, USA. 8.

SHAKUN Lew, b. 14 Sept 1926, Minsk, Byelorussia. Linguist; Lectr. m. Koktish Helena, 24 Feb 1959, 1 s. *Education:* Byelorussian State Lenin Univ, 1950; MD, 1953; DS, 1966. *Appointments:* Lect, Byelorussian State Lenin Univ, 1953-; Asst Prof, 1959-; Chief of the Chair,

Byelorussian Language, 1967. *Publications include:* Essays of the History of the Byel Liter Language, Minsk; The Byel Language Morphemic Dictionary Minsk. *Membership:* The Intl Assn of Byelorusists. *Honours:* The Byelorussian State Prize; F Skorina Medal. *Hobby:* Theatre. *Address:* Odoyevski Street 81, App 50, 220015 Minsk, Byelorussia.

SHALIT Jonathan Sigmund, b. 17 Apr 1962, London, England. Chmn, Sigmund Shalit and Assoc. *Education:* Eastbourne Coll, 1975-78; City of London, 1978-80. *Appointments:* CT Bowring, 1981-83; Saatchi And Saatchi, 1983-87; Sigmund Shalit and Assoc, 1987- . *Memberships include:* The Princes Trust; Cancer Research Campaign; Freeman City of London. *Hobbies:* Triathlon; Sailing; Skiing. *Address:* 2 Charleville Mansions, Charleville Road, London W14 9JB, England.

SHAMTALLY Bhye Mahmood (Danny), b. 7 June 1951, Curepipe, Mauritius. Proprietor, Nursing and Residential Care Homes (Pioneering Work in Pvte Mental Hlth Care for the Elderly). m Carmelita Paat Panaligan, 19 Sept 1973, 1 s, 1 d. *Education:* Registered Mental Nurse, 1974; Registered Welfare Off, 1983. *Appointments:* Psych Nursing, 1970-75; Off i/c, Mental Illness, London Borough of Sutton, 1975-83; Prin, Owner, Pvte Homes for the Elderly (Psych). *Memberships:* Fellow, Inst of Welfare Offs; Fellow, Royal Soc of Hlth; Mbr of Royal Inst of Pub Hlth and Hygiene. *Hobbies:* Gardening, Collecting Cars, Antiques, Countryv Walks, Reading. *Address:* Standish, Rockshaw Road, Merstham, Surrey RH1 3BZ, England.

SHANBHAG Sanjay, b. 11 Apr 1963, Karwar. Chartered Accountant; Lectr. *Education:* Karnatak Univ. *Appointments:* Chartered Accoutant; Part Time Lectr, Accounts & Audit, Bkt Coll, Ulhasnagar. *Publication:* A Born Artist. *Memberships:* Forum of Free Enterprise; Consumer Guidance Soc of India; Bombay All India Bank Depositors Assn; Inst of Chartered Accountants of India. *Honours:* Best Actor, State Level Drama Comp; Writing Letters to the Editors of Varioys Newspapers. *Hobbies:* Writing; Drawing; Acting. *Address:* Sanjay Sadan & Shanbhag, B-206 Laxmi Malhar, Second Floor, Agarkar Road, Dombivli (East), 421201 India.

SHAND John Alexander, b. 5 Dec 1956, Manchester, England. Univ Lectr; Course Tutor. m. Judith Spencer, 30 Mar 1985. *Education:* Univ of Manchester, BA, 1977-80; kings Coll, Univ of Cambridge, 1980-87. *Appointments:* Philosophy Supervisor, Kings Coll Cambridge, 1981-83; Course Tutor, Open Univ, 1987- ; Tutor/Counsellor, Open Univ, 1989-90. *Publications:* Philosophy & Philosophers: An Introduction to Western Philosophy. *Memberships:* Alexander Soc, Univ of Manchester; Moral Sci Club, Univ of Cambridge; The Mind Assn; Royal Inst of Philosophy. *Honours include:* Wegner Prize; Polany Prize. *Hobbies:* Walking; Music; Carpentry. *Address:* 69 Cromwell Road, Stretford, Manchester M32 8QJ, England.

SHANG Dengxi, b. 22 Mar 1940, Shandong, People's Republic of China. Rsch Prof. m. Peihua Ding, 1 May 1967, 2 d. *Education:* Degree in Elec Engrng, Shandong Indl Univ, 1959. *Appointments:* Engr of Elec Engrng, 1978-87; Rsch Prof, 1987-. *Publication:* Concepts and Applications of Gas Chromatograph, 1989. *Memberships:* Bd Mbr, China Instrument Soc; Bd Mbr, Shandong Analysis and Test Soc; Dir, Technique Ctr for Dev of Chromatograph; Dir, No.1 Dept of Shandong Chem Inst. *Honours:* Provincial Award for Outstanding Research Work, 1978; Award from Chemistry Industrial Administration for Outstanding Achievement in Research, 1985; National Award for Outstanding Achievement in Research, 1991. *Hobbies:* Music, Fine Arts. *Address:* Shandong Chemistry Institute, Jinan, China.

SHANKAR R S, b. 17 Jan 1947, Marathoni, Tamilnadu, India. Off Rsch and Dev; Chem. m. Parvathy, 2 children.

Education: BSc, Chem, Presidency Coll, 1967; MSc, Analytical and Inorganic Chem, A C Coll of Tech, Madras Univ; PhD, Agricl Chem, InterAmerican Univ, FL, USA, 1988. *Appointments:* w Sakthi Sugars Ltd, Sakthinagar, Tamilnadu, India, Apprentice, 1970-71, Jr Lab Chem, 1971-74, Lab Chem, 1974-80, Rsch and Dev Chem, 1980-91; Off, Rsch and Dev, 1991-. *Publications:* Articles on Level of Juice Potash in Sugarcane and Effect of Glyphosine on Sugarcane Juice Quality, presenting them at mtgs of Science Club organized by Sugarcane Breeding Inst. Has guided three MSc cands for their project work and assisted for PhD study of VP of Cane, Sakthi Sugars Ltd. *Membership:* Sugar Technologists Assn, India. *Honour:* Awarded a doctorate at cultural level in Agricultural Science by University of Tucson, Arizona, USA, 1984. *Address:* Sakthi Sugars Ltd, Sakthinagar 638 315, Tamilnadu, India. 152.

SHANN Mary Halligan, b. 23 Aug 1945, New York City, New York, USA. Professor of Education; Researcher. m. Robert Allen Shann, 28 Dec 1968; 2 s. *Education:* BS, 1966, MEd, Prog Evaluation, 1967, PhD, Educl Psychology and Rsch, 1969, Boston Coll. *Appointments:* Asst Prof, 1969-75, Assoc Prof, 1969-75, Assoc Dean, 1980-85, Prof, 1985-, Boston Univ School Educ, Boston, MA; Project Dir, Prog Evaluations, Nat Sci Fndn, 1973-77; Dir, Cairo Univ Fac Dev, World Bank-IDA, Egypt Educ Project, 1981-89. *Publications:* Num tech reports, monographs, jrnl articles on prog evaluation, profl dev and complex problem solving, incl: Preparing Teachers for the Challenge of Interdisciplinary Science Instruction, 1989; Making Schools More Effective, 1990; The Reform of Higher Education in Egypt, 1992; Visual and Interactive Modes of Learning Science and Mathematics with Advanced Technology, computer software, 1989. *Memberships include:* Am Educl Rsch Assn, Int Comm 1988-91, Govt and Profl Liaison Comm 1984-87; Am Evaluation Assn; Am Psychological Assn; AAAS; Assn Supervision and Curric Dev; Int Assn Applied Psychology; Phi Delta Kappa; Fulbright Alumni Assn. *Honours:* ESEA Title IV Doctoral Fellow, 1967-69; Boston Univ Disting Fac Lecture, 1979; Designer, Fac Dev Prog for Portuguese ESE's, 1981; Boston Coll Alumni Award of Excellence, 1981; Hon Fellow, John F Kennedy Lib, 1985; Fulbright-Hays Sr Rsch Scholar, Brazil, 1986; Inducted Phi Beta Delta Int Hon Soc, 1987. *Hobbies:* Golf; Tennis; International travel; Main interests: Role of universities in educational, economic and social development; Teaching and learning with advanced technologies. *Address:* Boston University, School of Education, 605 Commonwealth Avenue, Boston, MA 02215, USA. 5, 6, 76.

SHAO Chen Ming, b. 13 Aug 1914, Guangdon Daipu, People's Republic of China. Prof VP, Beijing Polytechnic Univ. m. 1 Jan 1938, 1 s, 1 d. *Education:* BSc, Tsing Hua Univ, 1936. *Appointments:* Lectr, Assoc Prof, Northwest Agricl Univ, 1939-42; Prof, N E Univ, China, 1942-48; Prof, Peking Univ, 1948-53; Currently Prof, VP, Beijing Polytechnic Univ. *Publications:* Engineering Fluid Mechanics, textbook, 1979; Mechanism of Gas Solid Separation, 1981; Impact of Energy on Environment, 1983; Traditional Culture of China, series compositions, 1988-91. *Memberships:* Comm Mbr, CPPC, 1983-; V-Chmn, Sept 3rd Party, 1988-; Dpty Chmn, Standing Comm, Beijing People's Congress, 1982-; V-Chmn, Beijing Soc for Science and Technology, 1983-91; Chmn, Beijing Energy Soc; Chmn Computer Use in CSCE 1981- *Honours:* Honourable Certification of Chinese Society of Civil Engineers, 1981; Honourable Certification of China Society of Architecture, 1987; Certificate of Merit for GB 3100, 3102-86, 1989; Honourable Committee Member of Beijing Society of Science and Technology, 1991. *Hobbies:* Do Taijiquan (a kind of traditional Chinese shadow boxing), Reading. *Address:* Beijing Polytechcnic University, Beijing, China.

SHAO Dazhen, b. 18 Nov 1934, Jiangsu Province, China. Prof; Art Critic. m. Xi Jingzhi, 24 Sept 1935, 1 d. *Education:* Dept Lit, Suzhou Univ, 1952-53; BA, Art Hist, Leningrad Inst of Fine Arts, 1960.

Appointments: Lectr and Prof of Ctrl Inst of Fine Arts, Beijing, 1960- 91; Chief Ed, World Art, 1979-85; Chief Ed, Art, 1985-90. *Publications:* On Modernism, 1983; Traditions and Modernism, 1984; Oil Painting History in Europe, 1985; The Modern Arts Thought of West-Ward, 1990. *Memberships:* Mbr Standing Comm, Chinese Artists Assn; Mbr and Chmn, China Art Critic Comm. *Hobbies:* Chinese Water-Ink Painting, Swimming. *Address:* Department of Art History, Central Academy of Fine Art, Beijing, China, 100730.

SHAO Yanxiang, b. 10 June 1933, Beijing, The People's Republic of China. Writer. m. Xie Wenxiu, 27 Jan 1957, 1 s, 1 d. *Education:* Studied, L'Universite Franci-Chinoise, 1948-49. *Appointments:* Ed Reporter, Ctrl People's Broadcasting Stn, 1949-54; Exiled to Huanghua State Farm, 1958-59; Clerk, Date Editing, CPBS, 1960-66; Labourer, Beijing and Huaiyang, 1966-77; Play Writer, Ctrl Broadcasting and Video casting Troupe, 1977-78; Ed, Poetry Periodical Slri Kan, 1978-84; Profl Writer, 1985-. *Publications:* Singing of the City of Beijing, 1951; Going to the Far Away Place, 1955; To My Comrades, 1956; The Campfire in August, 1956; A Reed Pipe, 1957; Love Songs to the History, 1980; Making Farewell Smilingly to the Seventies, 1981; At the Far Away Place, 1981; Bearing Witness to Youth, 1982; In Full Blossom Lake Flowers, 1983; Time and Wine, 1985; Collection of Long Lyrics by Shao Yanxiang, 1985; There's Joy, There's Sorrow, 1988; other works: To an 18-year-old Poet, 1984; Honies and Thorns, 1986; Essays Written at Mornings and Evenings, 1986; 100 Articles with Sorrow and Joys, 1986; Green Light, 1987. *Memberships:* PEN; Presidium Chinese Writers Assn. *Honours:* At the Far Away Place, National New Poetry Competition, 1983; Flower Late in Blossom, National New Poetry Competition, 1986; 100 Articles with Sorrows and Joys, National Essays Competition, 1989. *Hobbies:* Reading, Enjoying Music. *Address:* No A 15-3-401, Hufang Road, Beijing 100052, China. 3, 152.

SHAPIRO Isadore, b. 4 Apr 1916, Minneapolis, Minnesota, United States of America. Material Scientist. m. Mae Hirsch, 4 Sept 1938, 2 s. BCHemE, high distinction, 1938, PhD, Phys Chem, 1944, Postdoct Rsch Fellowship, 1944-45, Univ MN. *Appointments:* Chem, E I duPont, Phila, PA, 1946; Lab Dir, Naval Ordnance Test Stn, Pasadena, CA, 1947-52; Dir, Pascal Lab, Olin Mathieson Chem Corp, Pasadena, 1952-59; Dir, Chem Lab, Hughes Tool Co Aircraft Div, CA, 1959-62; Aerospace Chem Lab, 1962-66; Dir, Contract Rsch HITCO, Gardena, 1966-67; Prin Scientist, McDonnell Douglas Astronautics Co, CA, 1967-70; Sr Scientist, Mgmt, Garrett Airsch Mfg Co, CA, 1971-82; Pres, Universal Chem Systems Inc, 1982-. *Creative Works:* Discovered Carborane series of Compounds, 1953, originated name Carborane, 1956; Developed process for high modulus carbon fibres from coal tar pitch; Equation relating compaction of powders named Shapiro Equation in textbooks of prominent powder metallurgists; 20 patents; over 150 publs and presentations, profl jrnls and scientific mtgs. *Memberships:* American Chem Soc; American Phys Soc; American Ceramic Soc; Nat Inst Ceramic Engrs; Fellow, American Inst of Chems; Assoc Fellow, American Inst of Aeronautics and Astronautics; Soc for Advancement of Materials and Process Engrng; Int Plansee Soc for Powder and Metallurgy; Soc of Rheology; American Def Preparedness Assn; Reg Profl Engr CA; Sigma Xi; Tau Beta Pi; Phi Lambda Upsilon. *Honours:* Inaugurated by American Biographical Institute Research Association as a Deputy Governor, 1988 and in 1989 as Deputy Director General of International Biographical Centre; Selected by ABI as Man of the Year, 1990. *Address:* 5624 West 62nd Street, Los Angeles, CA 90056, USA. 9, 12, 14, 16, 28, 52, 59, 120, 128, 130, 132, 139, 151, 155.

SHARIF Khalid, b. 2 May 1936, Lahore, Pakistan. Finance Company Director. m. Farhat Sharif, 20 Sept 1970, 3 s. *Appointments include:* Currently Dir, London Finance Co Ltd, England. *Memberships:* Chmn, School Bd Govs; Social Security Appeal Tribunals; Valuation and Community Charge Tribunals; Bd Visitors, Prison Serv; Parole Bd, HM Wandsworth Prison; SOVA, vol serv w offenders, ex-offenders and their families; Police Consultative Grp; Fndr, Luncheon Club for Sr Citizens in London. *Hobbies:* Reading; Travel. *Address:* 11 High Street, Penge, London SE20 7HJ, England.

SHARLAND Desmond Edward, b. 13 Apr 1929. London, England. Cons Physn; Pt-time Sr Lectr in Aanatomy. m. Dulcie Newboult, 12 Apr 1986. *Education:* BSc (Hons) Anatomy 1950, MB BS 1953, London Hosp; MD, Univ of London, 1967; FRCP 1975, Royal Coll of Physns, London. *Appointments:* Cons Physn, Geriatric Med, Whittington Hosp, London, 1966-; Sr Lectr, Pt-time, in Anatomy, Royal Free Hosp, 1970-. *Publication:* Jt author, Whittington Hospital, Postgraduate Medicine. *Membership:* Royal Soc of Med. *Hobbies:* Cruising, Ballroom Dancing. *Address:* Fircroft, St Andrews Close, London N12 8BA, England.

SHARMA Arjun D, b. 2 June 1953, Bombay, India. Physn; Cardiologist. m. Carolyn D Burleigh, 9 May 1981, 2 s, 1 d. *Education:* BSc, Univ Waterloo, Ont, Can, 1972; MD, Univ Toronto, 1976; FRCPS, Can, 1981. *Appointments:* Asst Prof, Med 1983-88, Asst Prof, Pharmacology and Toxicology, 1987-89; Assoc Prof, Med 1988-89, Univ of Western Ont; Rsch Assoc, Washington Univ, St Louis, MO, 1981-83; Assoc Prof, Univ CA, Davis, 1990-; Dir, Interventional Electrophysiology, 1990-. *Publications:* Author and Co-author 120 scientific publs and 130 scientific abstracts. *Memberships:* Can Med Assn; Fellow, American Coll of Cardiology; Fellow, American Coll of Physns; Can Cardiovascular Soc; NY Acad Sciences; American Fedn for Clin Rsch; CA Med Assn; N American Soc for Pacing and Electrophysiology. *Honours:* John Melady Award, 1972; Dr C S Wainwright Schlrship, 1973-75; Toronto Gen Hosp Rsch Award, 1980-81; Ont Min of Hlth Career Scientist Award, 1983-89; Can Heart Fndn Operating Grants, 1983-89. *Hobbies:* Tennis, Philately, Skiing, Photography, Sailing. *Address:* Diagnostic and Interventional Cardiology, 3941 J Street, Suite 260, Sacramento, CA 95819, USA. 9, 142.

SHARON Nathan, b. 4 Nov 1925, Brisk, Poland. Biochemist. m. Rachel Itzikson, 1948, 2 d. *Education:* MSc, Biochem 1950, PhD, Biochem 1953, Hebrew Univ, Jerusalem. *Appointments:* Rsch Asst 1954, Rsch Assoc 1957, Sr Scientist 1960, Assoc Prof 1965, Prof 1968, Hd Dept Biophys 1973-83, 1987-90, Dean Fac of Biophys-Biochem 1976-77, 1980-83, 1984-86, Chmn, Scientific Coun 1972-74, 1988-90, The Weizmann Inst of Science, Dept of Biophys, Rehovot; Vis Prof var Univs USA, England and France. *Publications:* Over 400 scientific publs; 3 books on popular science. *Memberships:* American Chem Soc; The Biochem Soc, UK; European Molecular Biology Org; Int Science Writers Assn; Israel Biochem Soc, Pres 1969-70; Soc for Complex Carbohydrates; Fedn European Biochem Socs, Chmn 1980- 81; Int Glycoconjugate Org, Pres 1989-91. *Honours:* Landau Prize, Mifal Hapayis, 1973; Weismann Prize in Exact Science, City of Tel Aviv, 1977; Honorary Member, American Society Biological Chemistry, 1980; Datta Lectureship Award, Federation of European Biochemical Societies, 1987; Olitzki Prize, Israel Society for Microbiology, 1989; Bijvoet Medal, Ultrecht University, 1989; Docteur Honoris Causa, University Rene Descartes, Paris, 1990. *Hobbies:* Swimming, Stamp Collecting. *Address:* The Weizmann Institute of Science, Department of Membrane Research and Biophysics, Rehovot 76100, Israel.

SHARP John Frederick, b. 11 July 1954, Dallas, Texas, United States of America. Sr Petroleum Engr; Cons. m. Diana Raye Jones, 26 June 1983, 1 s. *Education:* BSc, Petroleum Engrng, Univ Tulsa, 1976. *Appointments:* Shell Oil Co, Midland, TX, 1976-78; Amerada-Hess, Tulsa, OK, 1978-81; ARAMCO, Saudi Arabia, 1981-82; Lee Keeling & Assoc, Tulsa, OK, 1982-91. *Membership:* Soc Petroleum Engrs. *Hobbies:* Electronics, Computers, Camping. *Address:* c/o Lee Keeling & Associates Inc,

3500 First Tower, 15 E 5th Street, Tulsa, OK 74103, USA. 7.

SHASTRI Vastoshpati, b. 9 Aug 1968, Varanasi, UP, India. Asst Prof. *Education:* BSc, Hons, Stats, 1988; MSc (Gold Medalist) in Stats, 1990; French Dip, 1989. *Appointment:* Asst Prof, Univ of Sagar (MP), 1991-. *Publication:* Composition on Vedic Mathematics in book Vangmay Manthnam. *Membership:* Sec, Yogic Voice Consciousness Inst, Varanasi, 1988-90. *Honour:* Gold Medal in Masters Degree from Banaras Hindu University. *Hobbies:* Music, espec instrumental, Cricket, Math Computation of difficult problem. *Address:* B3-131A, Shiwala, Varanasi (UP) 221001, India.

SHATSILLO Kornely Fyodorovich, b. 11 Apr 1924, Tashkent, Uzbekiston Region, USSR. Univ Prof. m. July 1979, 2 s. *Education:* Graduate, Pacific Navy Coll, Vladivostok, 1946; Graduated 1955, PhD 1958, Moscow State Univ; DSc, Acad of Sciences, Moscow, 1968. *Appointments:* CO, USSR Navy, 1946-50; Assoc Prof, 1958-68, Full Prof, 1968-, Inst of Hist of USSR. *Publications:* Russian Imperialism and Navy Development, 1968; Russia Before World War I, 1974; 1905, 1980; Russian Liberalism, 1985; The First Revolution in Russia, 1985. *Honours:* Medal for Victory over Japan, 1945; Order of the Patriotic War, 1985. *Hobbies:* Walking, Reading. *Address:* ul Profsoyznayag 97, Apt 20, Moscow 117279, Russia. 1

SHAW Dorothy Mary, b. 26 Apr 1919, Sydney, Australia. Ret'd. Div. 2 s. *Education:* Leaving Cert, NSW, 1936. *Appbintments:* Sec, Bank, 1938-47; Sec, Stockbroker, 1948-57; Prop, Coffee Lounge, 1960-66; Sec, Univ, 1968-84. *Publications:* Poetry in Muse and The Poetry of Canberra. *Membership:* Fellow, Aust Writers, Canberra Br. *Honours:* Highly Commended 1985, 1st Prize 1987, 1st Prize 1990, Banto Patterson Poetry Competition; Commended, Canberra FAW Local Literary Competition, 1990. *Hobbies:* Reading, Writing, Writing Workshops, Gardening. *Address:* 62 Arndell Street, Macquarie ACT 2614, Australia.

SHAW George Gavin, b. 18 June 1957, London, England. Co Dir; Advt and PR Cons. *Education:* BA (Hons) Pol, Bristol Univ, 1979. *Appointments:* Co Dir, Joslin Shaw Adv, 1984-; Co Dir, Shaw PR, 1988-. *Publication:* Women I Have Had, 1986. *Hobbies:* Assn Football, Skiing, Cricket, Hunting, Fishing, Gardening. *Address:* 241 Upper Street, Canonbury, Islington, London N1 1RV, England.

SHAW Josephine, b. 15 Aug 1930, Coventry, England. Chmn and Mng Dir. *Education:* Birmingham Secretarial Coll, 1946-47. *Appointments:* Educ Mgr, Speedwruiting Ltd, 1963-65; ILO Advsr, Sierra Leone and Ghana, 1965-75; Mng Dir 1976-88, Chmn and Mng Dir 1988-, Teaching Aids Ltd. *Publications:* Teach Yourself Office Practice, 1972; Retail Distribution for the Junior Certificates, 1970; Essential Secretarial Studies, 1974; Secretarial Work Experience, 1978; Secretarial Management: Guide to the Effective Use of Staff, 1977; Office Organisation for Managers, 1978; West African Office Practice, 1978; Analysis of Standard Clerical and Secretarial Tasks for the Development of Occupational Skills and Competence, 1978; Revision of Office Management by J C Denyer, 1980; Administration in Business, 1981; Training Packages, 1981; Caribbean Office Procedures, 1984; Training Techniques for Word Processing and Computer Trainers, 1988; Business Administration, 1991; Administrative Management (Chapt) Management Services Handbook, 1991. *Memberships:* Fellow Inst of Dirs; Fellow, Brit Inst Mgmt; Inst of Personnel Mgmt; Inst of Admnstv Mgmt. *Honour:* Serving Sister of The Order of St John of Jerusalem, 1960. *Hobbies:* Photography, Classical Music, Needlework. *Address:* Teaching Aids Limited, Denestead House, Station Road, New Milton, Hampshire BH25 6LD, England.

SHCHEMELEV Leonid, b. 5 Feb 1923, Vitebsk, USSR. Artist. m. Svetlana Siniakevich, 10 Dec 1968, 1 s, 3 d. *Education:* Minsk Art School, 1947-52; Byelorussian Inst Theatrical and Fine Arts (now Acad Arts), 1953-59. *Career:* War Veteran, World War II, 1941-43; Army Serv, USSR, 1943-47; Tchr, Drawing, Fine Arts, Composition, Minsk Art School, 1959-66; Repub Specialised School Music and Fine Arts, Minsk, 1967-74; Dpty Chmn, 1977- 79, Sec, 1979-81, 1982-84, Byelorussian Union Artists Bd, Minsk, 1977-79. *Creative works:* Paintings include: Hard Years, 1964; My Birth, 1967; Portrait of a Teacher, 1969; Portrait of Artist Chepik, 1970; Sunday, 1974; Riders, 1974; Svetlana, 1975; Leaves Blowing, 1977; Flax in Ivenets, 1977; B Savinkov's Arrest in Minsk, 1978; Saturday in Novoye Pole, 1979; Spring on the Dvina, 1979; Winter in Our Street, 1980; Vesnianka Flax, 1981; Wedding Party in Novoye Pole, 1982; Portrait of Ynka Kupala, Byelorussian National Poet, 1982; Portrait of the Son, 1982; Winter in Rakov, 1982; Trees of My Youth, 1982; Lesya Ukrainka, 1983; First Day of Peace, 1983; Unforgettable Memory, 1984; Vitebsk Province Fields, 1985; Saturday Evening on the Berezine, 1986. *Memberships:* Byelorussian Culture Fund Bd, Minsk; Former Mbr: USSR Union Artists Bd, Moscow; Presidium, Repub Coun War and Labour Veterans, Minsk. *Honours:* 2 Great Patriotic War Medals; Several medals for participation, World War II; Nat Econ Achievements Exhib, Bronze Medal, 1969, Silver Medal, 1975; Honoured Artist, 1977, People's Artist, 1983, Repub Belarus; Repub State Prize for Leaves Blowing, Thunderstorm June 22, Summer, Flax in Ivenets, 1982. *Hobbies:* Reading; Cinematography. *Address:* Surganova St 42 Ap 56, Minsk 220013, Belarus.

SHEARER Anthony Patrick, b. 24 Oct 1948, London, England. Fin Dir Mr G Group, Mng Dir Mr G Securities. m. Jennifer Dixon, 1 Dec 1972, 2 d. *Education:* Rugby Schl, 1962-66. *Appointments:* Fin Dir, Mr G Group; Mng Dir, Mr G Securities. *Membership:* Fellow, Inst of Chartered Accts. *Hobbies:* Skiing, Tennis, Family, Rock 'n Roll. *Address:* Quarter, By Denny, Near Stirling, Scotland.

SHEARER Carolyn Juanita, b. 20 May 1944, Heber Springs, Arkansas, USA. Reading Cons Educ. *Education:* BS 1966, MA 1972, Univ of CO. *Appointments:* Primary Grades Tchr, 1966-72; Intermediate Grades Teacher, 1972-83; Reading Resource Tchr, Cons, Middle Schl, 1983- (all posts with Aurora Pub Schls, CO). *Publications:* Writing for a Reason, Grade 5; Computer Literacy, Grades 3-5; Middle School Child Abuse Training Module; Middle School Reading Handbook; A Writing Sampler: Using Language Patterns; Enriching Curriculum with Folktales. *Memberships:* Nat, State and Local Educ Assns; Bd Dirs, Local, Int, State and Local Reading Assns, State Conf Comm; Assn for Supervision and Curric Dev; Pi Lambda Theta; Parent-Tchr Assn. *Honours:* University of Colorado Regents Scholarship, 1968-72; Aurora Public Schools Teachers Scholarships, 1967, 82, 84; Gesell Institute Scholarship, 1967; Star Grant (CCIRA), 1989; Director Right to Read Federal Grant, 1978-80. *Hobbies:* Painting, Needlework, Writing novels and poetry, Storytelling, Computers, Owning Boston terriers. *Address:* 205 South Tucson Circle, Aurora, CO 80012, USA. 15.

SHEARER Jonathan Turbitt, b. 4 Dec 1945, West Reading, Pennsylvania, USA. Lawyer; Barrister. *Education:* BA Econ, Columbia Univ, 1966; JD, Fordham Univ, 1971. *Appointments:* Asst Corp Counsel, NYC, 1971-72; First Judicial Dept, NY State, 1972-74; Self-employed Atty, NYC, 1974-82; US Dept of Treasury, Dallas, TX, 1983-84; Jones, Day, Reavis and Pogue, Dallas, 1984-85; Self-employed Atty, 1986-. *Memberships:* State Bar of TX; PA Bar Assn, Comm on Alcohol and Drug Addiction; Bar of State of NY; Bar of Supreme Court of the US; Lawyers Concerned for Lawyers; Children of the American Revolution. *Honours:* Mil: NDSM, 1967; VSM and VCM, 1968, Republic of Vietnam. *Hobbies:* Reading, Shortwave Radio, Genealogy, Hist, Astronomy, Hiking, Fishing, Hunting.

Address: Shearers' Road, Vinemont, PA 17569, USA. 7, 163.

SHEBAN Andrej, b. 23 June 1962, Bratislava, Czechoslovakia. Musician. Composer, Arranger. m. Dagmar Skarupova, 2 Dec 1989, 1 d. *Education:* Jan Komensky Univ, Bratislava, Music Science, Music Theory; 10 yrs pvte lessons Composition. *Appointments:* as a Studio Musician,. Guitarist and Keyboard Player. *Creative Works:* Music for Movies and Theatre; Songs for different singers; Jazz compositions; 25 LP's. *Membership:* Slovak Jazz Soc. *Hobbies:* Swimming, Skiing, Reading, Cooking, Eating. *Address:* Lehotskeho 2, 81105 Bratislava, Czechoslovakia.

SHEIKH Atique Zafar, b. 15 Nov 1940, Lucknow, India. Archivist. m. Rukhsana Aneela Atique, 15 Oct 1967, 2 s, 1 d. *Education:* MA, Hist, Punjab Univ, Lahore, 1962; Cert, Nat Inst of Pub Admin, Lahore, 1970; Postgrad Dip, Archives Admin, Univ Coll, London, 1976; Cert, Pub Sector Admin, Royal Inst Pub Admin, London, 1986. *Appointments:* Lectr, Govt Coll, D G Khan and Sahiwal, Pakistan, 1963-65; Sect Off, Min of Educ, Pakistan, 1965-72; Dpty Dir, Prime Minister's Inspection Team, Islamabad, 1972-73; Chief Conservator, Quaid-i-Azam Papers Cell, Min of Educ, 1973; Dpty Dir, Nat Archives of Pakistan, Islamabad, 1973-74; Dir, 1975-86; Dir Gen, 1987-. *Publications:* Quaid-i-Azam and the Muslim World: Selected Documents 1937-48, 1978, 90; Developmenmt of the Central Secretariat in British India 1919-35, 1980; National Archives of Pakistan, 1981; 30 articles and rsch papers in jrnls and mags. *Memberships:* Bd of Govs and Exec Comm, Quaid-i-Azam Acad, Karachi, 1982-; State Enterprise Officers Cooperative Housing Soc, Lahore, 1982-; Staff Welfare Org, Islamabad, 1974-; Exec Comm, Int Coun on Archives, Paris, 1987-89. *Honours:* Medal for participation in International Congress on Quaid-i-Azam Mohammad Ali Jinnah, 1976; Medal for participation in International Round Table Conference on Archives in Italy, 1987. *Hobbies:* Gardening, Photography, Reading, Rsch. *Address:* House No.24-G, Street No. 1, G 6/3, Islamabad, Pakistan. 52.

SHEIKH Muhammad Mubbashshir Mukram, b. 22 Feb 1950. Kasur, Pakistan. Govt Official, PR Specialist, Mktng Exec. m. (1) Musarrat, 24 Sept 1972, dec 1975, (2) Zainib, 6 June 1976, 4 s, 1 d. *Education:* BA, Econs and Stats, Govt Coll, Lahore, 1969; MA Hist 1972, MA Pol Science 1973, MA Econs 1982, Punjab Univ, Lahore; PhD, Bus Admin, Int Inst for Adv Studies, MO, USA, 1986. *Appointments:* Govt Official, PR Specialist asnd Mktng Exec; Chief Trade Off, assigned as Chief of Info and PR, Publs and Publicity, Trade and Investment Info Serv, Min of Commerce and Ind, Repub of Botswana, Southern Africa, 1982. *Publications:* Directory, Botswana Trade Directory 1st Edition, 1982; Botswana Manufacturing Directory 1st Edition, 1985; Rsch Report, Import Procurement Operation and Techniques, 1982; series of papers on statistical briefs on foreign trade, 1981-82. *Memberships:* Sec, Bazmi-E-Adab-O-Amal, 1970-72; Pres, Anjman Farogh-e-Quran, 1973-74; Registrar, Rover Leader, Pak Pioneers Boy Scout Grp, 1974-75; Chmn, Pak Pioneers Youth League, 1976-80; Fellow, Inst Commerce, Brit Soc of Commerce; Inst of Sales and Mkt Mgmt, Brit Inst of Mgmt; Int Inst of Social Econs; Inst of Mktng; Assn of MBA Execs; Botswana Jrnlsts Assn. *Honours:* Badges of Merit Civil Defence, Rover Scouts and Ambulance from Government College, Lahore, 1970; PhD, Marketing and Economics, honoris causa, International Institute for Advanced Studies, Missouri, USA, 1984. *Hobbies:* Badminton, Creative Writing, Social Services, Gardening. *Address:* P O Box 1974, Gaborone, Botswana, Southern Africa. 139, 151.

SHELTON Jacquelyn James, b. 6 Nov 1950, Darlington, South Carolina, USA. Dir, Off of Investigations, Off of Fair Housing and Equal Opportunity, US Dept Housing and Urban Dev. div. 1 d. *Education:* BSc, magna cum laude, SC State Coll, Orangeburg, 1972; Brookings Inst Conf for Fed Execs,

1991. *Appointments:* Asst Reg Dir, Region 3, US Fed Labor Rels Auth, 1979-83; Dpty to Asst Gen Counsel, US Nat Labor Rels Bd, 1983-85; Policy Specialist, Off of Prog Ops, US EEOC, 1985-87; Dir, Field Mgmt Progs-West, US Equal Employment Opp Commn, 1987-90; Dir, Off of Fair Housing Enforcement and Sect 3 Compliance, US HUD, 1990-91. *Memberships:* Nat Assn Female Execs; Exec Women in Govt; NAACP, Life Mbr. *Honours:* Certificate of Award for Outstanding Service as Staff Support for US EEOC National Investigator Training Session, 1987; Special Commendation for Outstandiong Performance in the US Senior Executive Service, 1988, 90, 91; US EEOC Nominee for Arthur Fleming Award recognising Outstanding Federal Government Managers and Supervisors, 1990. *Hobbies:* Gardening, Music, Reading. *Address:* 1304 Ava Road, Severn, MD 21144, USA. 46, 152.

SHEMSHUCHENKO Yury Sergeyevich, b. 14 Dec 1935, Glukhov, USSR. Lawyer, Dir, Inst of State and Law. m. Inna, 13 Dec 1959, 2 s. *Education:* Law Fac, Kiev Univ, 1957-62; Degree of Cand of Law, 1970; LLD, 1979; Prof, 1983. *Appointments:* Pub Prosecutor, Sumi Reg, 1962-66; Scientific Rschr, Kiev, 1966-88; Dir, Inst of State and Law, 1988-. *Publications:* More than 200 scientific works; Books: Responsibility in the Field of Environment, 1978; Law on the Protection of Nature, 1981; Legal Problems of Ecology, 1989. *Memberships:* Corres Mbr, Acad of Sciences, Ukraine; Pres, Union of Lawyers of Ukraine; Pres, Ukrainian Politological Assn; Reg Gov, Int Coun of Environmental Law. *Honour:* Award of the Ukrainian Academy of Sciences for books in the field of Environmental Law. *Hobbies:* Hist of Ukraine, Painting, Sport, Travelling. *Address:* Turgenevskaya St 29, Apt 14, Kiev 25205 4, Ukraine.

SHEN Dao-Xiu, b. 6 Mar 1926, Shanghai, China. Prof of Pharmacology. m. Zhang Xiao-Wen, 24 Dec 1954, 1 d. *Education:* Shanghai German Med Acad, 1944-45; Graduated Med Coll of Tongji Univ, Shanghai, 1951. *Appointments:* Study of Pharmacology, Dept of Pharmacology, Shanghai Med Coll, 1951-53; Teaching of Pharmacology and Toxicology, Dept Pharmacology, Shanghai Second Med Coll, 1958-79; Pharmacological teaching and rsch of clin pharmacology and traditional Chinese drugs (TCD) in Shanghai Coll of Traditional Chinese Med (TCM), 1980-; Dir of Rsch, Dept of TCD, Shanghai Coll of TCM. *Publications:* More than 40 theses. *Memberships:* Chinese Pharmacological Soc; Chinese Pharm Assn; Chinese Assn of The Integration of Traditional and Western Med; Chinese-German Med Assn. *Honour:* Second Award of Scientific Technological Achievement given by the Health Ministry of the People's Republic of China, 1982. *Hobby:* Music. *Address:* 381 He Fei Road, Room 602, Shanghai 200025, China.

SHEN Guang-Yu, b. 25 Apr 1932, Shanghai, The People's Republic of China. Prof of Maths. *Education:* Graduated Peking Univ, 1956; Postgrad student, Peking Univ, 1957-59. *Appointments:* Assoc Prof 1982-86, Prof 1986-, East China Normal Univ. *Publications:* Over 20 rsch articles in var math and scientific jrnls. *Memberships:* Math Soc of People's Republic of China; American Math Soc; Shanghai Soc of Molecular Science. *Honour:* 1990 Prize for the Advance of Science and Technology awarded by the National Education Committee of People's Republic of China. *Hobby:* Reading. *Address:* Department of Mathematics, East China Normal University, Shanghai 200062, China. 139, 152.

SHEN Jiamo, b. Aug 1944, Kunshan County, Jiangsu Province, China. Dir and Prof Jiangsu Provincial Information Research Centre. *Education:* Graduate, Nanjing Univ. *Appointments:* Prof: East China Normal Univ, Wuhan Univ and Suzhou Univ together with other Colls and Univs in China; He has given acad reports and lectures in Beijing Univ, Nanjing Univ, Yunnan Univ and Hebei Normal Coll and many orgs and assns in over 20 cities and provinces. He is currently Dir and

Prof, Jiangsu Provincial Informatuion Research Centre in Nanjing. *Publications:* Special contbr to the Informatics of Chinese Encyclopaedia; Ed of Information Journal and 3 other periodicals and concurrrently Special Corres of Informatics and 9 other newspapers and periodicals. Written and compiled 15 books and over 120 articles. Books: An Introduction to Psychoinformatics; A Survey of Governmental Information Researches; A Survey of Informatics on Town-owned Enterprises. *Memberships:* Chinese Sociological Info Coun; Chinese Sociological Info Acad Comm; Comm Mbr, China Assn of Talents; Coun Mbr, Jiangsu Provincial Assn; Comm Mbr, China Assn of Pub Rels; Life Fellow, IBA and ABIA. *Honours:* Awarded one of the outstanding young and middle- aged scholars and specialists by Jiangsu Provincial Government, 1990. *Address:* Jiangsu Provincial Information Research Centre, 12 North Huju Road, Nanjing 210013, China.

SHEN Qi Peng, b. 13 Dec 1946, Nantong, Jiangsu, China. Painter. m. Zhou Ming Jian, 1 May 1974, 1 d. *Education:* Nantong Middle School, 1961-66; Beijing Traditional Chinese Painting Inst, 1987-88. *Career:* Peasant, Rudong Co, 1968-75; Worker, Nantong City, 1975-79; Painter, Traditional Chinese Painting, Nantong City, 1979-; Currently Dir, Calligraphy and Traditional Chinese Painting Inst, Nantong; Num works published, displayed or collected by provincial and nat level orgs; Many works displayed abroad incl Japan, USA, France, Can, Hong Kong; Personal show, Japan. *Publications:* Special Album of Paintings from life in Yunnan, 1991; Album of Paintings by Shen Qi Peng, 1992. *Memberships:* China Artists Assn; Chmn, Nantong Artists Assn; Vice-Chmn, Nantong Youth Fedn; Coun Mbr, Nantong For Friendship Assn. *Honours:* 3 works cited nationally, 1973; 2nd Prize, provincial level, for Coming the Fishing season, 1985; Excellent Works Prize, provincial level, for Sentiments and Charms on Plateau, 1986; Excellent Works Prize for The Mounting Spring, Beijing Int Wash Paintings Exhib, 1988; 1st Prize, provincial level, for Iron Flow. *Hobbies:* Reading; Calligraphy. *Address:* 2 Wenfeng Road, Nantong City, Jiangsu Province, China.

SHEN Tsuin, b. 12 July, 1913, Wujiang, Jiangsu, China. Prof. m. Kao Pei-lan, 5 Apr 1940, 2 s. *Education:* BS 1934, Univ Nanking, China; PhD 1940, Cornell Univ, Ithaca, NY, USA. *Appointments:* Prof, Univ Nanking. Changdu, Sichuan, 1941-44; Sr Horticulturist, Nat Bureau of Agri Res, Chongqing, Nanking, Peiping, 1944-47; Prof, Tsing-hua Univ, Beijing, 1947-49; Prof Beijing Agri Univ, Beijing, 1949-. *Publications:* Studies on iron-deficiency chlorosis, 1948; Pears in china, 1980; Dipterax as a fruit thinning agent for apples, 1985. *Memberships:* Chinese Soc Hort Sci, VP, Pres & Hon Pres 1956-; Chinese Assn Agric Sci Soc, VP, Mem Exec Com 1978-; Nat Com, Chinese Assn Sci Tech 1980-86; Am Soc Hort Sci, 1940-49. *Honours:* Awds: Nat Sci Cong for the breeding of cold-breeding wine grapes, 1978; Beijing Municipality, Min Agri, 1982; Nat Sci Tech Com, 1985 for chemical thinning of apples. *Hobbies:* Photography; Reading novels and history; Music. *Address:* Department of Horticulture, Beijing Agriculture University, Beijing 100094, China.

SHEN Xiu-zhi, b. 3 May 1933, Wenling, Zhejiang Province, The People's Republic of China. Prof of Geology. m. Zhouhui, Feb 1961. *Education:* Earth Science Dept, Science Coll of Zhejiang Univ, 1951; Graduated, Geology Dept, Nanjing Univ, 1955. *Appointments:* Assoc Lectr, Geology Dept, Nanjing Univ, 1955-78; Studied for Assoc Dr's Degree of Structural Geology, 1956-58; Promoted to Lectr, Earth Sciences Dept, Nanjing Univ, 1978, Assoc Prof, 1985 and Prof, 1992-. *Publications:* Ed or one of the Eds of seven geological textbooks: Structural Geology; Geomechanics; Principles of Structural Geology; Petroleum Structural Geology; Introduction to the Earth Structure; Remote Sensing Technique and its Geological Application; Guidebook of Geological Fieldwork in Nanjing; Zhengjiang and Hangzhou Areas. More than 50 articles in provincial, countrywide and for publs.

Honours: Research achievements have been given several rewards by provinces and the country. *Address:* Department of Earth Sciences, Nanjing University, Nanjing 2100078, China.

SHEN Xuechu, b. 15 Apr 1938, Jiangsu, The People's Republic of China. Prof of Phys; Dir of Nat Lab for Infrared Phys. m. 1 Feb 1963. 1 s, 1 d. *Education:* BS, Phys Dept, Fudan Univ, 1958; Degree similar to PhD Academia Sinica, 1964. *Appointments:* Grp Ldr, 1964-78; Vis Scientist, Stuttgart, 1978-80; Dir of Dept, 1981-85; Dir of Lab. 1985-90; Advsr for PhD Degree, 1983-; Prof of Phys, 1986-; Dir of Nat Lab, 1990-. *Publications:* Optical Properties of Semiconductors, 1991; More than 100 scientific articles in field of Spectroscopies of semiconductors and their microstructures. *Memberships:* Chinese Phys Soc; Chinese Optical Soc; V-Chmn, Phys Soc of Shanghai; American Phys Soc. *Honours:* National Awards seven times; First Class Awards of Chinese Academy of Sciences twice in 1987 and 1990 respectively; National Awards for Natural Sciences in 1988; National Excellent Scientist with Middleage, 1988. *Address:* National Laboratory for Infrared Physics, Chinese Academy of Sciences, 420 Zhong Shan Bei Yi Road, Shanghai 200083, China.

SHEN Yongzhi, b. 16 June 1940, Jilin Province,. The People's Republic of China. Geologist; Dir Liaoning Mineral Resources and Geology Inst. m. 10 Apr 1966, 2 s. *Educationm:* Graduated from Changchun Geological Univ, 1964. *Appointments:* Geologist in Geological Team, 1964-74; Dir, Isotope Geology in Inst, 1975-82; Study of early praterozoie stratigraphic time in Eastern Liaoning Province, 1983-86; Study of minerogenetic conditions of inner Mongolia and Western Liaoning, 1987-92. *Publications:* On discussion of Isotope age in Liashe and Anshan Group, 1980; On K-Ar age Contour and Geology of Liashe Group in Central Liaoning, 1986; Minerogenetic model and exploratory mark of Sn-polymetallic ore deposits in Dajingzhi, 1989. *Memberships:* Geological Soc of China; Non-ferrous Metal Soc of China; Mineral Rocks Geochemical Soc of China; Isotope Age Compilation Group of China. *Honours:* First Prize for Scientific Works in Yanbian Youngsters Works Exhibition in 1956; Activist for Socialist Construction in Chang Chun Geological University in 1959; Excellent Geologist of Liaoning Exploration Company, 1978; Encouragement Prize in Staff and Workers paintings Exhibition of Shenyang Branch of China Nonferrous Metal Company, 1983. *Hobbies:* Photography, Art, Sports, (more than 70 photographs and paintings published in sev publs). *Address:* Liaoning Mineral Resources and Geology Institute, Central Road, Xinchengzhi District, Shenyang, China.

SHEPHERD David, b. 25 Apr 1931. Artist. m. Avril Gaywood, 4 d. *Education:* Studied Art under Robin Goodwin, 1950-53. *Appointments:* Started career as aviation artist, founder member of Guild of Aviation Artists; many worldwide trips for aviation and mil paintings for Servs; began specializing in African wildlife subjects, 1960. *Creative Works:* Exhibs; RA, RP; one-man exhibs in London, Johannesburg, NY; Work in Permanent Collects: 15ft reredos of Christ for Army Garrison Ch, Bordon, Hants, 1964; Portraits: H E Dr Kenneth Kaunda, Pres of Zambia, 1967; H M The Queen Mother, 1969; H E Sheikh Zaid of Abu Dhabi, 1970; Life st RA, RP; one-man exhibs in London, Johannesburg, NY; Work in Permanent Collects: 15ft reredos of Christ for Army Garrison Ch, Bordon, Hants, 1964; Portraits: H E Dr Kenneth Kaunda, Pres of Zambia, 1967; H M The Queen Mother, 1969; H E Sheikh Zaid of Abu Dhabi, 1970; Life story subject of BBC TV documentary, The Man Who Loves Giants, 1971; Harlech TV documentary Elephants and Engines. Auctioned five wildlife paintings in USA in 1971 and raised funds for Bell Jet Ranger Helicopter for anti-poachinundeThe East Somerset Railway. Publications: Artist in Africa, 1967, A Brush With Steam, 1983. Videos: The Man Who Loves Giants; The Most Dangerous Animal. *Honours:* Hon DFA, Pratt Inst, NY,

1971; Order of Golden Ark, The Netherlands, 1973; Mbr of Honour, World Wildlife Fund, 1979; OBE, 1979; FRSA, 1986; FRGS, 1988; Hon Doctor of Science, Hatfield Polytechnic, 1990. *Hobbies:* Driving Steam Locomotives, Raising Money for Wildlife. *Address:* Winkworth Farm, Hascombe, Godalming, Surrey GU8 4JW, England. 19.

SHEPHERD Warren Keith, b. 17 May 1953, Steubenville, Ohio, USA. Min. m. 27 Feb 1976, 2 d. *Education:* BA, Harding Univ, 1976; MAR, Harding Graduate Schl, 1980; Ohio Valley Coll, 4 yrs, then transferred to a 4- yr schl. *Appointments:* Douglass Ch of Christ; Turrell Ch of Christ; summers 1974,75, worked for Chs of Christ in Russia, Czechoslovakia, Poland, Yugoslavia, Austria, Germany. *Honours:* Sophomore Class Pres, Coll Ohio Valley, 1972; Outstanding Young Men of America, 1981, 83. *Hobbies:* Fishing, Hunting. *Address:* 515 South Taylor, P O Box 369, Douglass, KS 67039, USA.

SHEPHERD William, b. 20 Oct 1928, Nottingham, England. Pro V- Chancellor and Prof of Elec Power Applications, Univ of Bradford. m. Elisabeth Mary Gahan, 28 July 1956, 3 s. *Education:* BSc, Elec Engrng, London, 1955; MASc, Elec Engrng, Toronto, 1958; PhD, Elec Engrng, London, 1966; DSc, Engrng, London, 1975. *Appointments:* Qualified School Tchr, Univ of Leeds Inst of Educ, 1951; Chartered Engr, 1958; Pro-V-Chancellor and Prof of Elec Power Applications, Univ of Bradford. *Publications:* Thyristor Control of AC Circuits; Energy Flow and Power Factor in Nonsinusoidal Circuits; Power Electronics and Motor Control. *Memberships:* IEEE, NY, Fellow; IEE, Fellow; IEEE Yorks Ctr Comm, 1970-80; IEE Coun, 1977-80, var comms. *Hobbies:* Christianity, active mbr of local parish ch, Music, espec choral, Sport, Reading, Gardening. *Address:* Department of Electrical Engineering, University of Bradford, Bradford BD7 1DP, West Yorkshire, England.

SHERBORN Derek Ronald, b. 7 May 1924, Streathan, London, England. Ret'd. *Education:* Streatham Grammar Schl; Streatham Hill Coll. *Appointments:* Investigator of Historic Bldgs, Min of Town and Country Planning; Ret'd as Prin Insp, Historic Bldgs Coun for England. *Publications:* The Sherborns of Bedfont 1386-1983; Articles in Country Life, Architectural Review; Family Tree. *Memberships:* Fellow, Soc of Antiquaries; Comm, Regency Soc of Brighton and Hove; Comm, Friends of Brighton Pavilion; V-Chmn, Conservation Areas Advsry Grp of Brighton B C; Pres, Kingscliffe Soc; Sr Trustee, Robert McKenzie Charitable Trust. *Hobbies:* Country Houses and their Contents, Parks and Gardens, Theatres, Cinemas, Music Halls, Historic Towns, Family Hist, Historic Photographs. *Address:* Bedfont House, 161 Marine Parade, Brighton, Sussex, England.

SHERIFF D Sultan, b. 6 July 1947, Tiruchi, India. Prof of Biochem. m. H Fathima Sultan, 12 Sept 1974, 1 s. *Education:* BSc, Chem, 1968; MSc, Clin Biochem, 1971; PhD, Biochem, 1977. *Appointments:* Lectr; Rsch Coord; Asst Prof and Assoc Prof, Libya; Prof, India. *Publications:* Poems, Essays, Scientific Articles, Eds in Nat and Int Jrnls. *Memberships:* Fellow, Nat Acad of Clinical Biochem, USA; Inst of Sex Educl Parenthood, USA; Acad of Zoology; United Writers Assn of India. *Honours:* Best Expatriate Teacher; Citizen Ambassador. *Hobbies:* Cricket, Chess, Rotary and Round Table, Debates, Lectures, Writing. *Address:* 84C Thubal Ahmed Street, Salem 636001, India.

SHESTALOV Ivan Nikolaevich, b. 22 June 1937, Komratka, Tiumen, USSR. Writer; Ed. m. Ivanova Elizaveta Vladimirovna, 6 Nov 1959, 1 s, 1 d. *Education:* Leningrad State Pedagogical Inst, Fac of the Peoples of Northern part of USSR. *Appointments:* Writer; Ed, first mansi lang mag founded by himself, 1958-; Worked in Komsomol Dist Comm, Tumen, 1963-64; Ed in Chief of mag Sterh and a newspaper White Crane, 1989-. *Publications:* Breathing of the Earth (in mansi lang), 1959; Sing, My Stars (Russian), 1959; Misne (Mansi,

Russian), 1961; Blue Wind of Kaslanie (Russian), 1964; The Pagan Poem, 1967; When the Sun was Swinging Me. 1970; First There Was a Fairy Tale, 1981; Songs of Nature, schl textbook in Mansi lang; The Fire of Healing, 1988; The Cry of a Crane, 1988. *Memberships:* Dir, Creativity Club of the Peoples of the Northern Part of USSR, founded by himself; Sec, Leningrad Dist Union of the Soviet Writers; Soviet Writers Union; Finnish Literary Soc; Int Assn of Ugrian Philology; Bd of Dirs, Russian Writers Union; Coord Comm of Saving the Ugara. *Honours:* Order of the Friendship of Peoples, 1984; Order of the Red Banner of Labour, 1987; The Gorky Award of the RSFSR (Russia). *Hobbies:* Hunting, Fishing. *Address:* Mokhovaia St. 28, Apt 76, 191028, Leningrad, Russia.

SHEVCHENKO Arkady N, b. 11 Oct 1930, Gorlovka, Ukraine. Writer; Lectr; Prof, American Univ, Washington DC, USA. Widower, 1 s, 1 d. *Education:* PhD, Int Law, Moscow State Inst of Int Rels, 1962. *Appointments:* USSR For Min, 1956-63; Soviet Mission to UN, 1963-70; USSR For Min, 1970-73; UN Under Sec-Gen, 1973-78; Pres, A & E Assocs Inc, 1984-90; Prof, American Univ, Washington D C, 1989-. *Publications:* Breaking with Moscow, 1985; sev books in Russian. *Membership: (F1The Jamestown Fndn, Mbr Bd Advsrs. *Honours:* Citation Award, Council for Defense of Freedom, Washington, DC, 1982; The Jamestown Foundation, Educational Achievement Award, 1988; Sev Soviet Decorations and Medals. *Hobbies:* Reading, Gardening, Books, Collecting. *Address:* 4941 Tilden Street NW, Washington, DC 20016, USA. 30, 34.

SHEVCHENKO-VESELAGO Kirill Alexandrovich, b. 7 May 1962, St Petersburg, Russia. Writer; Music Critic. m. Elena N Prokina, 6 Mar 1992. *Education:* Classical Guitar, Special Music School, 1983; Study w Prof K Plugnikov, Vocal Dept, St Petersburg State Conservatory, 1989. *Appointments:* Ed, TASS, 1988; Corres, Russian Music Newspaper, 1990; Music Observer for Smena, Evening Petersburg, Today, The Capital newspaper and mag. *Creative works:* Fit in War Time, book, 1989; Essays, book, 1990; Sketches of the Classics, film script, 1992. *Memberships:* Jrnlsts Union Russia; New Critical Soc; VP, Hanin Music Soc. *Hobbies:* Playing classical guitar; Yachting; Family. *Address:* Mayorova prospectus 37, apt 42, 190000 St Petersburg, Russia.

SHEW Edmund Jeffrey, b. 23 Dec 1936, Bosbury, England. Chartered Acct. m. Vivien Dawn Jones, 21 Nov 1987. *Education:* Rossall Schl, Fleetwood. *Appointments:* Articled Clerk, 1954-59; Nat Serv RAF, 1960- 62; Ptnr, Stanley Marsh & Co, St Helens, 1962-66; Prin, Edmund Shew & Co, 1966-. *Memberships:* Fellow, Inst of Chartered Accts in England and Wales; Fellow, Chartered Assn of Cert Accts; Fellow, Brit Inst of Mgmt; Inst of Taxation. *Honours:* Member of Council, Institute of Chartered Accountants in England and Wales; Member of Guild of Freemen of The City of London. *Hobbies:* Classical Music, Gardening, Art, Theatre, Agriculture. *Address:* 35 Westfield Street, St Helens, Merseyside WA10 1QD, England.

SHEWBRIDGE Deborah Kay, b. 3 June 1963, Roanoke, Virginia, USA. Music Dept Chair, Instr, Acad Advsr. *Education:* Assoc of Science in Music, Tomlinson Coll, 1983; B.Mus Educ, Lee Coll, 1985; MSc Music Educ, Radford Univ, 1986. *Appointments:* Choral Dir, Wm Fleming HS, 1987; Guitar Tchr, Woodrow Wilson Jr HS, 1987; Music Tchr, Breckinridge Jr HS, 1987; Music Tchr, Tomlinson Coll, 1987- (all in Roanoke, VA); Music Instr, Acad Advsr, Music Dept Chair, Tomlinson Coll, 1987-. *Memberships:* Music Educators Nat Conf; Orff-Schulwerk Cert Level I; Phi Theta Kappa; Alpha Chi; Phi Kappa Phi. *Honours:* Valedictorian Scholarship to Tomlinson College, 1981; Academic Honours Scholarship to Lee College, 1983; Graduate Fellowship (liaison between Communications and Music Dept) at Radford University, 1985. *Hobbies:* Travel, Crossword

Puzzles, Sewing. *Address:* Tomlinson College, PO Box 3030, Cleveland, TN 37320, USA. 2, 7, 15.

SHI Yu-Quan, b. 18 June 1919, Shanghai, China. Hon Dir, Inst of Neurology, Shanghai Med Univ; Neurosurg. m. Wen Jun Liu, 3 June 1950, 2 s, 1 d. *Education:* Nat Med Coll of Shanghai, 1938-44. *Appointments:* Res Surg, Municipal Hosp of Chung Qing, 1944-46; Res Surg, Zhongshan Hosp, Shanghai, 1946-49; Neurosurg, Huashan Hosp, Shanghai, 1951-80; Dir, Inst of Neurology, Shanghai Med Univ, 1981-85. *Publications:* Practical Neurology, 1st and 2nd Eds, 1978, 91; Sect in Neurosurgery, Chinese Medical Encyclopedia, 1983. *Memberships:* Chinese Med Assn; Int Brain Rsch Org; Academia Neurochiragia Eurasian. *Hobbies:* Stamp Collection, Photography. *Address:* 1360 Fuxing Zhong Road 4/5, 200031, Shanghai, China.

SHI Zhengqing, b. 7 May 1945, Henan, China. Ed of Shanghai Transl Publng House. m. 20 Jan 1984, 1 s. *Education:* Zhejing Fine Arts Coll, 1963; Shanghai 2nd Ind Univ, 1978. *Appointments:* Ed, Labor Daily, 1982-84; Indl Art Designer of China and Schindler Elevator Co Ltd, 1984-85; Ed, Shanghai Transl Publng House, 1985-92. *Creative Works:* About 200 cartoons; about 1,000 illustrations; since 1963 cartoons, oil paintings, prints, Chinese paintings exhibited in China, Japan, India and Pakistan. *Memberships:* China Artists Assn, Shanghai Br; China Animation Drawing Soc; China and Abroad Contemporary Artists Assn;; Mbr of Jury on Law and Morality, Cartoon Competition of China. *Honours:* Art Prize of Shanghai Art Works Exhibition, 1978; Third Prize of Shanghai Life Cartoon Competition, 1985; Excellent Prize of First China Cartoon Exhibition, 1988; Exhibition Prize of 7th China National Art Exhibition, 1989; Exhibition Prize of Arts Exhibition of The XI Asian Games, 1990. *Hobbies:* Swimming; Fishing; Chess. *Address:* Shanghai Translation Publishing House, Yan An Zhong Lu Lane 955, Room 14, Shanghai, China.

SHIBATA Akikazu, b. 25 Feb 1935, Sendai, Japan. Electronic Engr. m. Saeko Margaret Kurakake, 6 Nov 1960, 1 s, 1 d. *Education:* BA, Int Christian Univ, 1957; MS, Cornell Univ, 1959; Dr.Engrng, Nagoya Univ, 1967. *Appointments:* Rsch Asst, Cornell Univ, 1957-59; Rsch Scientist, Semiconductors, 1959-72, 1982-87, Rsch Admin, 1973-81, Sony Corp; Gen Mgr, Engrng, Sony Trading Corp, 1979-82; Sony Corp Int Standardization, 1987-. *Publications:* Over 50 papers published and/or presented in var scientific periodicals and mtgs; over 20 papers in tech jrnls; over 15 patents issued and/or filed mainly in field of semiconductor technology. *Memberships:* IEEE, Sr Mbr; Materials Rsch Soc; Soc for Info Display, Japan; Soc of Applied Phys; SPIE. *Hobbies:* Reading, Listening to Music. *Address:* 914 Serizawa, Chigasaki 253, Japan. 52.

SHIDEHARA Francesco Eichi, b. 8 May 1935, Kobe, Hyogo, Japan. Prof of Musicology, Fac of Educ, Hiroshima Univ. m. Naoka Takagawa, 20 Nov 1967, 2 d. *Education:* B in Econs, Osaka Univ, 1958; BA 1964, MA 1967, Tokyo Univ. *Appointments:* Lectr, Musashino Academia Musicae, 1967-69; Assoc Prof 1969-84, Prof, 1984-, Hiroshima Univ. *Publications:* Co- author Bigakushi Ronso, 1983; (id) Ongaku Kyoikugaku, 1990. *Memberships:* Japanese Soc of Aesthetics; Musicological Soc of Japan; Int Musicological Soc; Japanese Soc for 18th Century Studies. *Hobby:* Violin Playing. *Address:* 1565 Kishimoto, Mikage, Higashinada-ku, Kobe 658, Japan. 52.

SHIELDS Paul Keith, b. 3 Jan 1949, Tulsa, Oklahoma, USA. Psychotherapist; Cons. m. 10 Apr 1983, 1 s, 1 d. *Education:* MA, Guidance and Counseling, 1976, BS, Psychology, 1975, EdD, Counseling Psychology, 1984, Tulsa Univ. *Appointments:* Clinical Prog Dir, Countryview Psych Hosp, 1984-86; Clinical Prog Dir, Green Country Counseling Ctr, 1986-88; Pvte Prac in Psychotherapy, 1989-. *Publications:* Articles in profl jrnls. *Memberships:* American Assn for Marriage and Family Therapy, Clinical Mbr; American Psych Assn;

American Grp Psych Assn; Nat Bd of Cert Counselors; OK Assn of Drug and Alcohol Counselors; Nat Assn of Alcohol and Drug Abuse. *Hobbies:* Travel, Tennis, Skeet Shooting, Swimming, Movies. *Address:* 7666 E 61st Street, Suite 253, Tulsa, Ok 74133, USA. 7.

SHIELDS Robert, b. 8 Nov 1930, Paisley, Scotland. Prof of Surg, Univ of Liverpool and Hon Cons Surg, Royal Liverpool and Broadgreen Hosps. m. Marianne Swinburn, 19 Jan 1957, 1 s, 2 d. *Education:* MB BS 1953, MD (Hons) 1965, Univ of Glasgow; Western Infirmary, Glasgow, FRCSEd, 1959; FRCS, England, 1966. *Appointments:* Capt, Argyll and Sutherland Highlanders, 1953-56; House Off Posts, Western Infirmary, Glasgow, 1953-55; Lectr, Univ Glasgow, 1960-62; Mayo Fndn Fellow, 1959-60; Sr Lectr, Rdr in Surg, Welsh Nat Schl of Med, Cardiff, 1963-69; Currently Prof of Surg Univ of Liverpool and Hon Cons Surg, Royal Liverpool and Broadgreen Hosps. *Publications:* Books and num articles in med press on surg and gastroenterology. *Memberships:* Pres, Brit Soc of Gastroenterology; Med Rsch Coun and Its Strategyu Comm; Coun of Royal Coll of Surgs of Edinburgh; Gen Med Coun and its Educ Comm Pres's Advsry Comm; V-Chmn, Brit Jrnl of Surgery. *Honours:* Moynihan Medal, Association of Surgeons of Great Britain and Ireland, 1966; Fellow (Hon) American College of Surgeons, 1990; DSc (Hon) University of Wales, 1990; Fellow of the College of Surgeons of South Africa, 1991. *Hobbies:* Sailing, Walking. *Address:* Strathmore, 81 Meols Drive, West Kirby, Wirral L48 5DF, England. 1, 52.

SHIH Chung-Hsiang, b. 10 June 1937, Tainan, Taiwan, The People's Republic of China. Mbr of Control, Yuan. m. Mei-Chi Lin, 1964, 2 s, 2 d. *Education:* Jien Kung Cml HS. *Appointments:* Mbr, Kaohsiung Municipal Coun, 1973-77; Mbr of Control, Yuan, 1981-86. *Membership:* Taiwan Provincial Assn, 1977-81. *Hobbies:* Reading, Handwriting, Sports. *Address:* No 2, Section 1, Chung Hsiao East Road, Taipei, Taiwan, China.

SHIMIZU Keiichi, b. 14 Apr 1936, Tokyo, Japan. Exec of Meitetsu World Travel Inc; Tourism Instr. m. Noriko Hakata, 4 June 1967. *Education:* BA, Aoyama Gakuin Univ, 1960. *Appointments:* Staff, Meitetsu World Travel, Inc, 1960-84, Gen Mgr 1984-87, Exec 1987-; Sr Instr of Engl for Tourism, Japan Assn of Travel Agts, 1982-; Special Instr of Engl for Tourism, Yokohama Commerce Coll, 1987-. *Publications:* What Should We Be Offering the Japanese Travellers, Services, their Range and Quality; English and Etiquette for Japanese Travellers. *Membership:* The American-Japan Soc Inc, Tokyo. *Honour:* The Second Prize, The 13th Annual Intercollegiate English Oratorical Contest for the English Mainichi Trophy, 4 July 1959. *Hobbies:* Classical Music, Opera, Drama, Cinema, Golf, Tennis. *Address:* The Australia-Japan Economic Institute, Suite 902, Australia Square, Sydney, NSW 2000, Australia. 52.

SHIMIZU Michiyuki, b. 25 Nov 1917, Kyoto City, Japan. Physn; Prof Emeritus. m. Yasuko Kobayakawa, 3 Apr 1946, 1 s, 1 d. *Education:* MD, 1942, PhD 1950, Tokyo Univ; Dept of Med, Tokyo Univ Hosp, 1943-53; Dept of Pathology, Univ of NC, USA, 1954-56. *Appointments:* Prof, Med, Showa Univ, Tokyo, 1956-83; Hosp Dir, Showa Univ Hosp, 1976-82, Prof Emeritus 1983-; Dir, Setagaya Hlth Serv Ctr, 1983-. *Publications:* Hematology, 1982; Nutritional Anemia, 1982; Papers: Different Peroxidase of Eosinophil and Neutrophil Leucocytes, 1954; Ceruloplasmin, 1959; Ursodeoxycholic Acid, 1959; Chloroma, 1960. *Memberships:* NY Acad of Sciences; American Biog Inst Rsch Assn. *Honours:* Fulbright Scholarship to University of North Carolina, USA, 1954-56; The Third Order of Merit in Japan, 3 November 1990. *Hobbies:* Reading, Golf. *Address:* Department of Medicine, Showa University Medical School, 1-5-8 Hatanoda, Shinagawa-ku, Tokyo 142, Japan. 52.

SHIMMEL Stephen Miller, b. 22 Nov 1952, Kansas City, Missouri, United States of America. Instr. m. Shirley Fumiye Nishino, 30 Oct 1981. *Education:* BS Zoology 1974, MS Bot 1979, PhD Bot 1984, Univ of GA. *Appointments:* Rsch Techn II, Univ of GA, Marine Inst, Sapelo Island, GA, 1977-79; Tchng Asst, Univ GA, Athens, 1979-84; Instr, Univ GA Athens, 1984-85; Instr, Chipola Jr Coll, Marianna, FL 1985-. *Contributions to:* profl jrnls. *Memberships:* Int Assn of Meiobenthologists; Ecological Soc of America; Phycological Soc of America; Assn of Southern Biols; FL Acad of Science, participant in vis scientist prog, 1988-90. *Honour:* Teacher of the Year, Student Government Association, Chipola Junior College, 1986-87. *Hobbies:* Running, Hiking, Canoeing, Dancing, Bicycling. *Address:* Chipola Junior College, 1200 College Street, Marianna, FL 32446, USA. 7, 15, 164.

SHIMODA Takeso, b, 4 Apr 1907, Tokyo, Japan. Pres, Int Law Assn of Japan; Judge. m. Mitsue Suzuki, 19 May 1938, 1 s, 2 d. *Education:* Graduated, Fac of Law, Tokyo Imperial Univ, 1931. *Appointments:* Entered Japanese Diplomatic Serv, 1931; Amb to Belgium, 1960; Amb to USSR, 1963; V-Min of For Affairs, 1965; Amb to USA, 1967; Justice of the Supreme Ct, 1971-77; Judge of Permanent Ct of Arbitration, 1972-; Pres, Honda Fndn, 1978- 91; Pres, Int Law Assn, 1991-. *Publication:* Japanese Diplomacy after World War II, 1984, 85. *Memberships:* Pres, Tokyo Club; Japan Club, Metrop Club of Washington DC; Hodogaya Country Club; Chiba Country Club; Tokyo Rotary Club. *Honours:* Grand Crosses of Order of Rising Sun, Japan, Order of Merit, Belgium, Order of Merit, Luxembourg, Order of Southern Cross, Brazil, Order of Merit, Argentine, Commandeur de la Legion d'Honneur, France. *Hobbies:* Golf, Travelling, Reading. *Address:* 1-4-16 Nishikata, Bunkyo-ku, Tokyo 113, Japan. 2, 52.

SHINER Brendan Elias John, b. 23 June 1928, Essex, England. Barrister-at-Law. m. 27 May 1954, 3 s, 1 d. *Education:* Stonyhurst; MA, Pembroke Coll, Oxford. *Appointments:* Barrister-at-Law; Called to the Bar Middle Temple 1955. *Hobbies:* Farming, Racing, Cricket. *Address:* The Culver House, Culver Hill, Amberley, Gloucestershire GL5 5BA, England.

SHINKARUK Vladimir Illarionovich, b. 22 Apr 1928, Gaivoron, Kiev, USSR. Dir of Inst of Philos, Ukrainian Acad of Sciences; Scientist; Philos. m. 23 June 1948, 1 s, 1 d. *Education:* Kiev State Univ, 1945-50; PhD 1964; Prof 1966. *Appointments:* Tchr, Hist of Philos, 1951-65; Hd of Dept, Dean of Philos Fac, 1965-68, Kiev Univ; Dir, Inst of Philos of Ukrainian Acad of Sciences, 1968-91. *Publications:* Over 300 scientific publ; Hegel's Dialectics, Logic and Theory of Knowledge, 1964; Kant's Theory of Knowledge, Logic and Dialectics, 1974; Unity of Dialectics, Logic and Theory of Knowledge, 1977. *Memberships:* Ukrainian Acad of Sciences; Assoc Mbr, Acad of Sciences of USSR; People's Dpty of Supreme Soviet of USSR; Soviet Union and Ukraine Philos Soc; Soc Knowledge of Ukraine and USSR; Presidium of Ukraine Peace Def Comm. *Honours:* Medal for Labour Valour, 1970; Order of Red Banner of Labour, 1971; Badge of Honour, 1976; Manuilski Prize Laureate of Ukraine Academy of Sciences, 1977; Diploma of Presidium of Supreme Soviet of Ukraine SSR, 1978; Order of Lenin, 1982; State Prize Laureate on Science and Technics of Ukraine SSR, 1982. *Hobbies:* Fishing; Mushrooming. *Address:* Geroev Revolutsii Street 4, Kiev 252601 GSP 1, Russia.

SHIPLEY Ronald Eugene, b. 2 Nov 1947, Youngstown, Ohio, United States of America. Min; Pres, Fundamental Bapt Theol Sem. m. 3 Sept 1967, 1 s, 2 d. *Education:* BA, Bible, TN Temple Schls, 1969; ThM 1980, ThD 1982, Citadel Bapt; DDiv, Faith Bapt Coll, 1986. *Appointments:* Pastorate: Gospel Bapt, Poland, OH, 1969-72; First Bapt, Altamount, IL, 1972-74, First Bapt, Pk Forest, IL, 1975-76, Emanuel Bapt, Salem, IL, 1974-75, Whiteville Ind Bapt, Whiteville, NC, 1976-85, Mill Creek Bapt, Youngstown, OH, 1985-. *Publications:* How To Pastor

Smaller Church; Curric, S S & New Members Class. *Membership:* Pres, Fundamental Bapt Theol Sem, 1982- *Honour:* Honorary Doctor of Divinity, Faith Baptist College. *Hobby:* Chess. *Address:* 248 S Schenley, Youngstown, OH 44509, USA. 15.

SHIRLEY-BEAVAN Mary Sevasty, b. 19 Oct 1917, Plymouth, England. Artist. m. Michael Shirley-Beavan, 17 June 1950, 4 s, 2 d. *Education:* North Foreland Lodge, Kent; Chelsea Polytechnic; Hammersmith Schl of Art. *Appointments:* WRNS, 1940-46; JP, Hertford, 1959-84. *Creative Works:* Paintings sold worldwide; currently exhibited at The Osborne Gall, London; painting under maiden name of Mary Hamilton. *Honour:* Diploma of Art, 1949. *Hobbies:* Hunting, Racing, Grandchildren. *Address:* Gardener's Cottage, North Moor, Dulverton, Somerset TA22 9QG, England.

SHISHIDO Koichi, b. 30 Sept 1936, Japan. Dir, Int Acct Servs. m. Setsuko Komori, 7 July 1966, 1 d. *Education:* BA, Gakushuin Univ,. Tokyo, 1966; MBA, OR State Univ, USA, 1970. *Appointments:* Ted Bates, NY, 1970; Franklin Mint, Japan, 1974; Gillette, Japan, 1976; Kyodo Advg Co, 1985-. *Publications:* Audio Use of Transmitting Tube; Reg contbr to M J Mag. *Memberships:* Japan Advg Agencies Assn; Japan Mktng Assn; Int Advg Assn. *Honour:* Marketing Man of the Year, 1973, Japan Marketing Association. *Hobbies:* Audio, Music, Golf, Tennis. *Address:* Higashi 3 Chome 21-6, Yachiyodai, Yachiyoshi, Chiba 276, Japan. 1.

SHIU Shan-chun, b. 19 Aug 1928, China. Dir, Secretariat of Nat Assembly, Repub of China. m. Yen-fen Wang, 15 Sept 1956, 1 s, 1 d. *Education:* BA, Law, Fu-hsing-kang Coll. *Appointments:* Supvsr, Sun Yat-sun Instn on Policy R&D, 1955-69; Gen Whip, KMT Pty Div of Legis Yuan, 1969-77; Dept Chief, Min of Personnel, 1977-87; Dir, Nat Assembly, 1987-. *Publications:* Dr Sun Yat-sen's Thoughts; Introduction of Chinese Culture; Problems in Chinese Rural Area; Outlines of Modern Chinese History. *Honours:* For ROC Governmental Officials: Best Performance Award; Superior Personnel Award; Practice Award (twice); First Service Award; Second Service Award; Third Service Award. *Hobbies:* Reading; Gardening. *Address:* 1st 4th F, No.76 Wen-chou Street, Taipei, Taiwan, China.

SHNEIDMAN Noah Norman, b. 24 Sept 1924, Wilno, Poland. Prof. 2 d. *Education:* MPHE, Minsk (USSR), Warsaw (Poland), 1954; Dip Russian E Eur.St, 1966, MA Slavic, 1966, PhD Russian Lit, 1971, Univ of Toronto. *Appointments:* Asst Prof 1971-75, Assoc Prof 1975-79, Prof 1979-, Dept of Slavic Lang and Lit, Univ of Toronto. *Publications:* Literature and Ideology in Soviet Education, 1973; The Soviet Road to Olympus, 1978, 79; Soviet Literature in the 1970s, 1979; Dostoevsky and Suicide, 1984; Soviet Literature in the 1980s, 1989. *Memberships:* American Assn for the Advancement of Slavic Studies; American Assn of Tchrs of Slavic and E European Lang; Can Assn of Slavists. *Honours:* Distinguished Visiting Professor, McMaster University, Hamilton, Ontario, Canada; Research Grants awarded by The Canada Council, The Social Sciences and Humanities Research Council of Canada, The Canadian Federation for the Humanities. *Hobbies:* Sports, Stamps (postal). *Address:* Department of Slavic Languages and Literatures, University of Toronto, Toronto, Ontario, Canada M5S 1A1. 52.

SHOENFELT Catherine Ruth, b. 9 Dec 1954, Dallas, Texas, USA. Med Sales Exec. *Education:* Univ TX Austin, 1973-75; Univ TX, San Antonio, 1975-80; BMus Educ, magna cum laude. *Appointments:* Music Tchr, Viva Musica, 1980-81; Music Tchr, Northside ISD, 1981-84; Mktng Mgr, Austin Pathology Assocs, 1984-86; Dir Mktng, Nat Lab Servs, 1987; Sales, Roche Biomed Labs, 1987-88; Med Sales, Milex Soutern, 1989-. *Memberships:* Chmbr Chorale Symph, San Antonio, 1982; Symph Designer Showplace, Austin, 1986; Nat Assn Female Execs; American Choral Dirs Assn; TX Music Educators Assn; Music Educators Nat Conf, Pres;

Keyboard Club, UTSA; Mu Phi Epsilon. *Honours:* National Honor Society, 1973; National Latin Honor Society President, 1973; Honor Seminar University of Texas, Austin, 1974; Best Pledge, Mu Phi Epsilon, 1974. *Hobbies:* Music, Tennis, Jazzercize, Crewel, Needlepoint, Swimming, Reading, Cooking, Travelling, Skiing, Genealogy. *Address:* 1822 Barker-Cypress Road No. 2502, Houston, TX 77084, USA. 2, 5, 132, 176.

SHOJI Sadao, b. 17 Nov 1931, Sendai, Japan. Prof of Soil Science. m. 28 May 1963, 3 d. *Education:* Fac of Agric, Tohoku Univ, Japan, 1951-54; MSc, Coll of Agric, MI State Univ, USA, 1958; Doctor of Agric, Fac of Agric, Tohoku Univ, 1966. *Appointments:* Rschr, Hokkaido Nat Agricl Expmtl Stn, 1954-62; Rsch Asst 1963-73, Asst Prof 1973-75, Prof, 1975-, Fac of Agric, Tohoku Univ. *Publications:* Many scientific papers on volcanic ash soils (Andisols). *Memberships:* Japanese Soc Soil Science and Plant Nutrition; Japanese Soc Crop Science; Clay Science Soc, Japan; Japanese Assn Quat Rsch; American Soc Agronomy; Soil Science Soc of America. *Honour:* Award of Japanese Society Soil Science and Plant Nutrition, 1973. *Hobbies:* Fishing, Gardening. *Address:* 5-13-27, Nishitaga, Taihaku-ku, Sendai 982, Japan. 52.

SHORE Jacques Jean Meor, b. 13 Sept 1956, Montreal, Canada. Atty. m. Donna A Cohen, 19 Mar 1978, 3 d. *Education:* LL.L, Universite de Montreal, 1978; LL.B, McGill Univ, 1980; Dip Int Law, City of London Polytechnic, England, 1977. *Appointments:* Criminal Justice Policy Analyst, Solicitor Gen, Can, 1981-83; Rsch Prog Admnstr and Exec Asst to Dir of Rsch, Legal and Constitutional Rsch, Royal Commn on the Econ Union and Dev Prospects for Can (MacDonald Commn), 1983-85; Dir of Rsch, Security Intelligence Review Comm, 1985-87; Assoc, Heenan Blaikie, 1987-90; Sr Cons and Coun of The Fairfax Grp, 1990-. *Publications:* Matthew's First Sunset (children's book); var published articles on law, pub policy, med ethics. *Memberships:* Law Soc of Upper Can; The Can Bar Assn; Former Permanent Mbr and Legal Advsr to Med Rsch Ethics Comm, Montreal Gen Hosp; Former Dir and Co-founder of Quebec Soc of Med and Law; Former Exec Mbr and Co-founder of The Bar Admission Advsry Comm, Law Soc of Upper Can; Past Pres, New Edinburgh Community Assn; Dir, The Lord Reading Law Soc; Former Mbr of Univ Club of Montreal. *Honour:* Diploma in International Law, City of London, England, Polytechynic, Summer Programme (with Distinction). *Hobbies:* Writing, Painting, Skiing, Waterskiing, Squash. *Address:* 25 Cowichan Way, Ottawa, Ontario, Canada K2H 7E6. 142.

SHRIMPLIN Roger Clifford, b. 9 Sept 1948, Luton, England. Chartered Archt and Chartered Town Planner. m. Catalina Maria Eugenia Alomar, 21 Sept 1974, 3 s. *Education:* Jesus Coll, Cambridge Univ; MA (Cantab) 1970; Dip Arch (Cantab) 1973. *Appointment:* Ptnr and Prin, Clifford W and R C Shrimplin, Chartered Archts and Chartered Town Planners, 1975-. *Memberships:* RIBA; FRTPI; FCIArb; Arquitecto Colegiado, Baleares, Spain; Coun Mbr ARCUK; var comms RIBA and ARCUK; External Examiner Bartlett, London Univ, Schl of Arch; Liveryman (1974) Worshipful Co of Glaziers and Painters of Glass, Steward 1990; Hon Keeper, London Stained Glass Repository, 1990. *Honour:* Lord of the Manor of Shimpling, Norfolk. *Address:* 11 Cardiff Road, Luton, Bedfordshire LU1 1PP, England.

SHTEINBERG Valentine, b. 4 Apr 1918, Odessa Dist, Latvia. Scientist; Philos. m. Maha Strawme, 3 Mar 1990, 1 s. *Education:* Dip, The Higer Pol Schl, 1945-47; Hist, Pedagogical Inst, 1948, Cand of Historical Sciences, 1952; PhD, 1961; Prof, 1963. *Appointments:* Railway Worker, Russia, 1933-45; Lectr, Latvian State Univ, Pedagogical Inst, Politechnical Inst, 1945-70; Rektor, Latvian State Univ, 1963-70; Latvian Acad of Sciences: Dir of Inst of Hist, 1970-80, Dir of Inst of Philos and Law, 1980-87. *Publications:* The Philosophical Life in Latvia at the Beginning of the XXth Century, 1966;

Charles Skott from Latvia, 1981; Gentlemen in Latvia, 1983; Charles Skott, His Friends and Enemies, 1983; Looking at Sernika Pikassa, 1985; According to the Law of Conscience TV Script for actors and documentary film, 1987; Jakob Peters, 1989; more than 200 works in scientific and popular publs. *Honours:* Medal of Valiant Work in World War II, Red Banner Order, 1961, 75; The October Revolution Order, 1985; The Silver Medal at the Exhibition in Moscow, 1986. *Hobbies:* Photography, Volleyball, Reading. *Address:* Tarbatas Street, 46-7. 226011 Riga, Latvia.

SHUBA Pavel Pavlovitch, b. 15 Jan 1926, Village of Tonezhytchy, Slutsk Reg, Belarus, USSR. Prof of Russian and Byelorussian Linguistics. m. Raisa Sergeevna Rhyvotkevitch, 1 s, 1 d. *Education:* Minsk Pedagogical Inst, Tchr, 1951; PGT in Byelo Linguistics, Cand of Philology, 1955; PhD, 1971; Prof of Russian Linguistics, 1973. *Appointments:* Prof of Byelorussian Linguistics, Grodno, 1954-55; Scientific Asst, Byelorussian Acad of Sciences, 1955-61; Bylorussian Univ, 1961-91. *Publications:* Adverb in Byelorussian Language, 1962; Verb in Byelorussian Language, 1968; Proverb in Byelorussian Language, 1971; Modern Byelorussian Language, 1987. *Membership:* Assoc Mbr of Int Assn of Tchrs of the Russian Lang and Lit, Mapryal. *Honour:* Honorable Scientific Worker of Byelorussia, 1982. *Hobbies:* Photography, Fairy Tales for Children, Verses for School Textbooks, Gardening. *Address:* Voronianski Street 3, Apt No. 88, Belarus, 220039 Minsk 39, Russia.

SHUI Ji-Sheng, b. 16 Feb 1928, SuoZhou, Shanxi, The People's Republic of China. Artist. m. Han Zheng, 22 Nov 1963, 3 s. *Education:* Graduated from normal schl; Self-taught artist. *Appointments:* Before retirement: Sr Ceramic Engr; Chief Engr of Science and Technology Sect, Shanxi Dept of Light Ind; Chief Engr, Shanxi Inst of Glass and Ceramics Science; After retirement: Mbr of Shanxi Advsry Comm of Chinese People's Consultative Conf; Mbr of Shanxi Advsry Comm of Science and Technology Policy- making. *Creative Works:* The History of Shanxi Ceramics; A Preliminary Study on Ancient Kiln Setters and Setting Methods in Shanxi Province; A Study on the Traditional Kilns In Shanxi; Characteristic Firing Schedule for Coal- fired ManTou Kilns; Humble Opinion on the Origin of Porcelain; A Study on Ancient Decorative Technique of Ceramics and its Application in Shanxi; A Brief Study on the Northern Technology of Porcelain-making in Tang Dynasty in the Light of the Ancient Kiln Sites in Shanxi; Black Glazing Porcelains with Decorative Pattern Discovered in Ancient Kiln Sites in Shanxi; The Painted Pottery and Porcelain in Shanxi; The Hare's Fur and Oil Spot Discovered in Ancient Kiln Site in Shanxi. *Memberships:* Dir and Mbr of many profl assns. *Honours:* More than 70 calligraphy works in pvte collects. *Hobbies:* Study of ceramics, calligraphy and seal cutting. *Address:* 15 Dian ShanSuo, Taiyuan, Shanxi, China.

SHUI Tian Zhong, b. 3 Jan 1935, Lanzhou, Gansu, China. Art Historian. m. Li Zhihe, 9 Aug 1959, 2 d. *Education:* Grad, Art Coll Xian, 1955; Studied Hist Chinese Art, 1979-81, MA, 1981, Grad School, China Acad Arts. *Appointments:* Painter, Art Ed, Cultural Bur Studio, Gansu, 1955-58; Art Tchr, Chinese Tchr, Gansu Province, 1959-79; Assoc Rsch Fellow, Dir, Fine Arts Rsch Inst, China Acad Arts, Beijing, 1987-; Ed-in-Chief: Fine Arts in China; History and Theory of Fine Arts quarterly. *Publications include:* Li Gonglin and His Age, 1982; Reviewing the ARgments about the Innovation of Traditional Chinese Painting, 1983-84; A Concise History of Chinese Oil Painting, 1988; The Dictionary of Appreciating Traditional Chinese Calligraphy and Painting, 1989; The Theory and Review of Modern of Modern Chinese Painting, 1990. *Membership:* Vice-Dir, Art Theory Comm, Chinese Artists Assn. *Honours:* 1st Award for Oil Painting, Gansu Province Art Exhib, 1956. *Hobbies:* Classical music; Travel. *Address:* Fine Arts Research Institute, China Academy of Arts, 17 Qianhai Xijie, Beijing 100009, China.

SHULER Samuel Peter, III, b. 2 Mar 1943, Carmel, California, USA. Lawyer; Gen Counsel for Arab Banking Corp. m. Pakinee Amarapitak, Aug 1984. *Education:* AB (Hons) Hist, IN Univ, 1965; JD, MBA, Schls of Law and Bus, Columbia Univ, NY, 1970. *Appointments:* Atty, Fed Reserve Bank of NY, 1970-73; Counsel, Int Banking American Express Co, London and NY, 1973- 80; Legal Counsel, Arab Banking Corp (BSC), 1981-. *Publication:* Bahrain: No Brass Plates Please, 1986. *Memberships:* American Men's Assn of Bahrain, Pres, 1988-Bd of Govs, Chmn, Constitution and Picnic Comms; Int Bar Assn; American Bar Assn; Assn of the Bar of the City of NY; Columbia Law Schl Alumni Assn. *Hobbies:* Squash, Photography. *Address:* House 169, Road 2905, Al Markh 529, State of Bahrain.

SHULTZ Susan Kent Fried, b. 25 Mar 1943, New York City, New York, USA. President, Executive Search Group. m. 28 Nov 1968, div. 1980. *Education:* BA, Govt, Econs, Univ AZ, 1964; All core grad work, Int Affairs, Int Econs, George Washington Univ, Wash, DC, 1964-67. *Appointments:* Legis Asst for Rep William E Brock, Wash, DC, 1964-69; Owner, SSA Pol and Mktng consultancy, Phoenix, AZ, 1969-81; Jrnlst, Phoenix Mag, others, Phoenix, 1974-86; Pres, SSA Exec Search, Phoenix, 1981-; Pres, SSA Int, Phoenix, 1986-. *Publications include:* Books: Beverly Hills Diet, 1981; Beverly Hills Lifetime Diet, 1983; Adopt the Baby You Want, 1990; Building a Society, article, 1991. *Memberships:* Chair, Trade Promotion Comm, AZ Dist Export Coun; Exec Comm, Phoenix Comm For Rels; Small Bus Dev Ctr Advsry Bd, Small Bus Assn; Advsry Coun, AZ State Univ School Agribus and Environmental Resources; Charter Mbr, Valley Ldrship; Charter Mbr, Phoenix Econ Club; Charter Mbr, Charter 100; Fndng Dir, Phoenix City Club; Assn Corp Growth; Chair, Int Trade Comm, AZ Small Bus United; Chair, Nat Assn Women Bus Owners; Chamber Aviation Comm; Camelback E Village Planning Comm; Var couns on for rels. *Honours:* US Ptnr, Morgan and Ptnrs Grp, Europe 11 Countries, 1985-; Cons, cnducted mktng and hiring sem, Poznan, Poland, 1991. *Address:* 6001 E Cactus Wren Road, Paradise Valley, AZ 85253, USA. 52.

SHUM Stephen, b. 18 Nov 1956, Hong Kong. President of Institute Satellite Office. m. Wendy Leung, 17 Jan 1986, 1 s. *Education includes:* PhD, Mgmt, City Univ Los Angeles and School of Law, USA. Dip, Chartered Inst Mktng, UK. *Appointments:* Currently Pres, Hong Kong Satellite Off, Can Inst Mgmt, Kowloon. *Memberships:* Dir, Rotary Club, Tsuen Wan; VO, Lions Club, N Kowloon. Can Inst Mgmt; Chartered Inst Mktng, UK; Fellow, Inst Commercial Mgmt, UK; Fellow, Cyprus Inst Mktng; Fellow, Assn Practising Accts, Australia; FRGS; Fellow, Royal Statistical Soc, UK. *Hobbies:* Thinking; Writing. *Address:* 5/F Bangkok Bank Building, 490-492 Nathan Road, Kowloon, Hong Kong.

SHUPE Terry William, b. 4 Mar 1942, Vancouver, British Columbia, Canada. Provincial Court Judge. m. Yolanda, 29 Sept 1973, 2 s, 1 d. *Education:* Univ of BC, B.Comm 1966, LL.B 1967. *Appointments:* Called to Bar, 1968; Judge of Provincial Court of BC, 1976-; Admin Judge, Kamloops Reg, 1982; Educ Comm, Chmn, Provincial Court of BC, 1984-, Founding Chmn, Hon Life Chmn, 1980-. *Memberships:* Pres, Kamloops Bar Assn, 1973, 74; Bd of Trustees, W Can Theatre Co; Adv Trustee, Big Brothers, Kamloops; Mbr United Ch; Scout Ldr, 1st Cherry Creek Scout Troop, 1987-. *Hobbies:* Fishing, Woodworking, Flying, Skiing, Horseback Riding. *Address:* SS No. 2 Cherry Creek, Kamloops, British Columbia, Canada V2C 6C3, Canada. 142.

SHUR Chaim, b. 6 Apr 1926, Grodno, Poland. Ed-in-Chief, New Outlook, Middle East Monthly. m. Shulamit Gutelevesky, 2 June 1946, 4 s (1 dec). *Education:* Self-educated; HS; A few yrs of higher learning, no degrees, Tel Aviv Univ, Israel; Givat Haviva Educ Ctr, Israel; Johns Hopkins Univ, Schl of Adv Int Studies, Washington, DC, USA. *Appointments:* Instr, Middle East and Jewish

Studies, Regl Kibbutz HS, The Negev, Israel, 1969-83; Dpty Ed-in-Chief, Al-Hamishmar, Tel Aviv, 1970-74; Ed-in-Chief, Al- Hamishmar Daily, Tel Aviv, 1974-80; Ed-in-Chief, New Outlook, Middle East Monthly, 1982-. *Publications:* American Scenes, 1976; 4 anthologies of essays; hundreds of articles published in periodicals such as New Outlook, Al Hamishmar, Davar, Yediot Achronot, The New York Times. *Memberships:* Emissary, United Workers' Party, Mapam and Hashomer Hatzair, 1949-50; Sec- Gen, Young Guard, Ha-Kibbutz Ha-Artzi Fedn, Israel, 1956-57; Sec-Gen, Hashomer Hatzair Socialist Zionist Youth Movement, Israel, 1959-62; Sec-Gen, Ha-Kibbutz Ha-Artzi Fedn, 1964-69; Chmn, Dept Int Affairs, United Workers' Party, Mapam, 1981-82; Chmn, Dept Educ and Info, Mapam, 1981-82; Bur of Secretariat, Ctrl Comm, Mapam, 1970-. *Hobbies:* Music, Book Reading, Cinema, Theatre. *Address:* Kibbutz Shoval, MP Negev, Israel. 52. 94.

SHURMAN Laurance Paul Lyons, b. 25 Nov 1930, Gosforth, Northumberland, England. Banking Ombudsman. m. Mary Seamans McMullan, 22 Nov 1963, 2 s, 1 d. *Education:* Newcastle-upon-Tyne Grammar Schl; MA Magdalen Coll, Oxford. *Appointments:* Asst Solicitor: Haswell Croft, Newcastle, 1957-58; Hall Brydon, London, 1958-60; Kaufman Siegal, London, 1960-61; Ptnr, Shurman and Bindman Solicitors, London, 1961-64; Shurman and Company, London, 1964-67; Kingsley Napley, 1967-89, Mng Ptnr 1975-89; Banking Ombudsman, 1989-. *Publications:* The Practical Skills of the Solicitor, 1981, 85. *Contributions to:* On Mental Hlth Tribunals in Vol.26, Atkins Encyclopaedia of Court Forms, 2nd Ed 1985. *Memberships:* Pres, City of Westminster Law Soc, 1980-81; Mbr Coun of Justice, 1973-; Gov (V-Chmn), Channing Schl, 1985-; Gov, Newcastle-upon-Tyne Royal Grammar Schl, 1991-. *Hobbies:* Fell Walking, Swimming, Law Reform, Theatre. *Address:* Citadel House, 5-11 Fetter Lane, London EC4A 1BR, England. 1

SIAME Musalilwa Stanley, b. 4 Aug 1939, Mbala, Zambia. Bus Exec. m. 5 July 1969, 2 s, 3 d. *Education:* BSc, Econ (Hons), London, 1965; Postgrad Dip, Bus Mgmt Science, Holland, 1966. *Appointments:* Investment Projects Analyst, 1965-67; Exec Asst to Exec Chmn, 1967; Off i/c, Br Mgmt, 1968; Dpty Chief Exec Off, 1969-71; resigned 1971 to found own Int Grp Mutende Int Ltd. *Creative Works:* Created large bus grp from one purchased small ailing co into one of Zambia's biggest locally owned grp of diverse cos with subsidiaries and assoc cos in UK Europe and almost every Southern African Country. *Membership:* Inst of Dirs, UK. *Hobbies:* Reading of biogs or autobiogs of successful men and women in bus, Success stories in bus, Cultivation and implementation of measures and methods to make own Grp grow both locally in Africa and overseas, Efforts directed toward creation of wealth as a means of alleviating human hardship. *Address:* PO Box 33741, Lusaka, Zambia.

SIBLEY Richard Edmonde Miles Phillippe, b. 23 May 1949, Hornchurch, Essex, England. Chief Exec of Charitable Housing Trust. m. Hannelore Njammasch, 5 June 1976, 1 s. *Education:* Clark's Coll, London; Anglian Reg Coll, Dept of Environment. *Appointments:* Co Sec, Calderwood Housing Assn, 1970-75; Chief Exec, Ogilby Housing Soc Ltd, 1987-; Dir, Sibley Property Co Ltd, Libra Fin Co Ltd. *Memberships:* London NE Valuation and Community Charge Tribunal, Chmn, 1981-; Freeman City of London, 1980; Liveryman Worshipful Co of Coopers, 1980; Rotarian, Jr VP, 1991. *Hobbies:* Engl Vineyard Owner, Painting, Pols, Vol Housing Movement (Calderwood Housing Assn Comm Mbr). *Address:* Ogilby Housing Society Limited, Estate Office, Greenways Court, Butts Green Road, Hornchurch, Essex RM11 2JL, England.

SICHEWSKI Vernon Roger, b. 10 Dec 1942, Winnipeg, Manitoba, Canada. Med Dr. *Education:* BSc, Univ Man, 1960-63; Cairo Univ, Fac of Med, Egypt, 1974-79, MD;

Residency, Charity Hosp of LA, New Orleans, LA and Bellevue Hosp, NYC, 1980-83. *Appointments:* Pvte Prac, Broward Gen Med Ctr, Ft Lauderdale, FL, 1983-86; Trauma Care Assocs, N Miami, FL, 1986-; Flight Physn, Nat Jets, Ft Lauderdale, FL, 1986-; Attending Physn, Surg, Trauma Unit, Jackson Mem Med Ctr, Univ Miami, FL, 1989-; Jet Fighter Pilot, RCAF, 1963-74. *Memberships:* Fellow, American Coll of Emergency Physns; Dipl, American Bd of Emergency Med; American Coll of Emergency Physns; AMA; Southern Med Assn. *Hobbies:* Antiques, Stamp Collecting. *Address:* 1108-2841 North Ocean Boulevard, Ft Lauderdale, FL 33308, USA. 7.

SIDEK Supki H J, b. 24 Dec 1946, Singapore. Specialist Insp, Malay Lang. m. Absah Bte Mohamad, 19 Nov 1972, 2 s, 1 d. *Education:* Cert Educ, 1967; BA Hons (London), 1979; Masters in Educ, Malaya, 1985. *Appointments:* Primary Schl Tchr, 1964-65; Second Schl Tchr, 1966-79; Specialist Insp, 1984-. *Contributions to:* essays, poems, artworks and articles on Malay lang and lit, arts and educ to reg publs. *Memberships:* Malay Lang Tchrs Assn, VP; Malaysian Linguistic Assn; Int Reading Assn. *Honours:* Top Student in Malay language from Institute of Education, Singapore, 1967; Awarded a Singapore Government Scholarship to do a Master's Degree in Language Education at the University of Malaya in 1982. *Hobbies:* Reading, Painting, Travelling, Badminton, Music. *Address:* Apartment Block 332, UBI Avenue 1, 03-755 Singapore 1440, Republic of Singapore.

SIDIMUS Joysanne, b. 21 June 1938, New York City, USA. Exec Dir, Dancer Transition Ctr. separated, 1 d. *Education:* Adelphi Acad, 1946- 55; Barnard Coll, 1955-57. *Appointments:* NYC Ballet, 1958-63; London Festival Ballet, Soloist, 1963; Nat Ballet of Can, Prin Dancer, 1963-68; PA Ballet, Prin Dancer, 1968-70; Num concert appearances, TV and Off Broadway, 1956-73; Ballet Mistress: Grand Ballet de Geneve, Switz, 1971-72; Ballet Repertory Co, 1972-75, Currently Nat Ballet of Can whenever performing a Balanchine work; Tchr: Dance Theatre of Harlem; American Ballet Theatre Schl; Nat Ballet Schl, Toronto; Briansky Saratoga Ballet Ctr; York Univ, Toronto; George Brown Coll, Toronto; Fac Mbr, NC Schl of Arts, 1975-82; Staged Balanchine Ballets for PA Ballet, Grand Ballet de Geneve, Nat Ballet of Can and Nat Ballet Schl; Fndr and Exec Dir, Dancer Transition Ctr, 1985-. *Publication:* Exchanges: Life After Dance, 1987. *Memberships:* Exec Mbr, Actors Equity, 1964-68; NC Schl of Arts; Bd Dirs Dancer Transition Ctr, Dance Ont, Performing Arts Lodges; Can Advsry Comm, Status of the Artist; Ont Status of the Artist Coalition. *Honours:* Canadian Olympic Association Certificate of Appreciation, 1988; Dance Ontario Award, 1989. *Hobbies:* Classical Music, Antiques, Knitting, Lit. *Address:* Dancer Transition Centre, 66 Charles Street East, Toronto, Ontario, Canada M4Y 2R3. 2, 142, 177.

SIEGERT Barbara Marie, b. 22 May 1935, Boston, Massachusetts, USA. Human Servs; Community Mental Hlth. m. Herbert C Siegert, 1958, dec. 1974, 1 s, 1 d. *Education:* Dip, Newton-Wellesley Hosp Schl of Nursing, MA, 1956; Courses at North Shore Community Coll, Beverly, MA, 1978-79; M.Ed, Antioch Univ, OH, 1980. *Appointments:* Operating Room Staff Nurse, Night Supvsr, Pvte Duty Nursing, Crisis Screening, 1956-73; Nursing Supvsr, Hogan Reg Ctr, Hathorne, MA, 1974-78; Community Mental Hlth Nursing Advsr, Dept Mental Hlth, Cape Ann Area, Beverly, MA 1978-79; Dir of Case Mgmt, 1979- 88; Dir of Case Mgmt, Dept of Mental Hlth, Gtr North Shore Area Off, Beverly, MA, 1988-91; Dir, Case Mgmt, North Shore Area, Lynn Site, MA, 1991-. *Memberships:* American Nurses Assn; MA Nurses Assn. *Honours:* Special Recognition Award, Lexington Public Schools, 1973; Peter Torci Award for community service, Lexington, Massachusetts, 1974; Citation for Outstanding Performance, State of Massachusetts Performance Recognition Programme, 1984; Vanguard Award Nominee, as an outstanding woman leader on North Shore of Massachusetts, sponsored by Project Rap and Newburyport YWCA, 1988. *Hobbies:* Reading, Travelling, Cultural activities,

Metaphysics. *Address:* 63 Willow Road, Boxford, MA 01921, USA. 2, 5, 6, 52, 132, 151, 152, 155, 162.

SIKORA Wlodzimierz Janusz, b. 22 May 1928, Cieszyn, Poland. Researcher; Professor of Mining Engineering. m. Krystyna Gerwin, 21 May 1960, 1 d. *Education:* MSc, Mining Engrng, 1951; PhD, 1960; Prof, 1969. *Appointments:* Chief, Mechanization Dept, Sosnica Coal Mine, 1951; Rsch Worker, 1953-, Dpty Dir, Rsch Projects, 1970-, Main Inst Mining, Katowice; Prof, Mining Engrng, 1979-, Hd, Mining Dept, 1981-82, Vice-Rector, 1990-, Silesian Tech Univ, Gliwice. *Publications:* Co-author, books: Exploitation systems in Coal Mining (co-author), 1966; Development of Coal Mining Mechanization in Poland, 1967; Handbook of Mining Engineer, Vol 2, 1976; 150 papers in mining and sci mags. *Memberships:* Bd Mbr, Mining Comm, Polish Acad Sci; Int Bur Strata Mech; Soc Theoretical and Applied Mech; Nat Sect, Int Mining Congress; Bd Mbr, Soc Mining Engrs and Techns. *Honours:* Main Nat Award, 1966; Awards, Min High Educ, Sci and Engrng, 1972, 1974, 1975, 1976; Awards, Min Educ, 1989, 1990. *Hobbies:* Yachting; Skiing; Hiking; Classical music. *Address:* ul Osikowa 74, 40-181 Katowice, Poland. 139.

SIL Narasingha Prosad, b. 11 Dec 1937, Calcutta, India. Assoc Prof. m. Sati Makhija, 12 Aug 1965, 1 d. *Education:* BA Hist (Hons) 1958, MA Mod Hist 1961, Univ of Calcutta; MA Eng Hist 1973, M.Ed Curric and Instrn 1974, PhD Eng Hist 1978, Univ of OR, USA. *Aoppointments:* Lectr, Vidyasagar Coll, Univ Calcutta, 1962-63; Chadernagore Govt Coll, Burdwan Univ, W Bengal, 1963-64; Rep, Ave Co of India (Pvt) Ltd, Calcutta, 1964-675; Tractel Tirfor India (Pvt) Ltd; Tchr, Imperial Ethiopian Min of Educ, 1967-71; Tchng Fellow, 1971-75, 1977-78, Adjunct Instr, 1978-79, Asst Prof 1979-80, Vis Prof, Summer 1986, Univ of OR; Prin Educ Off, Min of Educ, Nigeria, 1975-77; Pt- time Asst Prof, OR State Univ, Winter 1980; Assoc Prof, Univ Benin, 1980-86; Asst Prof 1987-89, Assoc Prof 1990-, Western OR State Coll. *Publications:* William Lord Herbert of Pembroke 1507-1570; Politique and Patriot, 1988, Kautilya's Arthasastra: A Comparative Study, 1989; Ramakrishna Pramahansa: A Psychological Profile, 1991; Articles on European and Eng Hist in jrnls worldwide. *Memberships:* Americanm Histl Assn; N American Conf on Brit Studies; Renaissance Soc of America; Inst of Histl Studies, Calcutta; Histl Soc of Nigeria; Phi Kappa Phi. *Honours:* Honours Scholarship, Director of Public Instructions, West Bengal, 1959; British Council Summer Programme Grant, University of Benin, 1981; National Endowment for the Humanities Summer Seminar Grant, 1989; various research grants from, University of Benin and Western Oregon State College. *Hobbies:* Badminton, Reader of Histl and Relig Books; Writer; Biographer, Beer and Bonhomie. *Address:* Department of History, Western Oregon State College, Monmouth, OR 97361, USA. 9. 15. 162.

SILANI Vincenzo, b. 24 Apr 1952, Brescia, Italy. Neurology and Neuroscience Educator. m. Sabine M Pabisch, 23 Apr 1991. *Education:* Classic Lyceum 1971; MD 1977; Neurologist 1981; Neurosurg 1989; ECFMG USA, 1980; Postdoctoral Fellow in Neurobiology, Baylor Neurology, Houston, USA, 1979-80; Rsch in Molecular Genetics, Inst Sieroterapico Milanese, Milan, 1987- 90. *Appointments:* Med Internship, Inst Neurology, Univ Milan, 1977- 79; Postdoctoral Fellow, Neurology, Baylor, Houston, USA, 1979-80; Asst Prof, Inst Neurology Univ, Milan Med Schl, 1980-89; Vis Prof, Neurology, Baylor, Houston, USA, 1989; Assoc Prof, Inst Neurology Univ Milan and Dino Ferrari Ctr, 1990-. *Publications:* More than 60 papers, sev chapts in books, over 100 int communications; Co-author First Neurotransplant of Adrenal after Pre-cavity in Parkinsonian Patients; Inventor Human Neuronal and Adrenal Freezing; Adult Neuron Cultured; NGF Gene Sequence and Expression in the Human Central Nervous System. *Memberships:* European Neuroscience Assn; Soc for Neuroscience USA; NYAC; NECTAR, Sec 1991; AAAS; Italian Neuropathology Assn, Fndr, Cnslr 1985-87; Italian Neuroscience Assn; Italian Neurology Assn. *Honours:*

Grant University of Milan for Research Neurobiology in USA, 1979-80; MD with honours; Neurology Residency with honours, 1981; American Parkinson's Diseases Association and Maggiore Hospital Grants for Neurotransplantation, 1987-90; Neurosurgery Residency with honours, 1989. *Hobbies:* Tennis, Skiing, Reading, Riding, Classical Music, Bridge. *Address:* Corso Indipendenza 35. I 20129 Milan, Italy. 52

SILBERSTON (Zangwill) Aubrey, b. 26 Jan 1922, London, England. Prof Emeritus and Sr Rsch Fellow. m. Michele Ledic, 23 May 1985. *Education:* Jesus Coll, Cambridge, 1940-41, 1945-46; MA (Cantab); MA (Oxon). *Appointments:* Economist, Courtaulds Ltd, 1946-50; Rsch Fellow, St Catharine's Coll, Cambridge, 1950-53; Lectr in Econs, Univ of Cambridge, 1953-71; Fellow, St John's Coll, Cambridge, 1958-71; Fellow, Nuffield Coll, Oxford, 1971-78; Prof of Econs, Imperial Coll, London, 1978-87; Sr Rsch Fellow, Mgmt Schl, Imperial Coll, 1987-. *Publications:* The Future of the Multi-Fibre Arrangement, 1989; sev books and articles. *Membership:* Royal Econ Soc, Sec-Gen. *Honour:* CBE 1987. *Hobbies:* Opera, Ballet. *Address:* 53 Prince's Gate, London SW7 2PG, England. 1, 43.

SILIN Andrejs Roberts, b. 12 Oct 1940, Riga, Latvia. Institute Director; Physicist. m. Elga Janis Balta, 14 Aug 1965, 1 s, 2 d. *Education:* Dip Phys (MS Phys), Moscow State Univ, 1966; Cand Phys and Maths (PhD), Univ Latvia, Riga, 1971; Dr hab phys, Riga, 1983. *Appointments:* Asst Prof, Phys, Phys and Maths Fac, Univ Latvia, Riga, 1966; Jr Scientist, 1966-67, Aspirant, 1967-70, Div Hd, 1971-78, Vice-Dir, Sci, 1978-84, Dir, 1984-, Inst Solid State Phys, Univ Latvia. *Publications:* Point Defects and Elementary Excitations in Crystalline and Glassy SiO2, book, 1985; Over 120 articles in sci jrnls. *Memberships:* Fellow, Sci Union Latvia; Am Phys Soc; Full Mbr, Latvian Acad Scis; Chmn, Latvian Coun Sci. *Honours:* Award of Hon, achievement in trng young scientists, Parly Presidium, Repub Latvia, 1989; Medal, achievements in people's educ, Educ Min, Repub Latvia, 1990. *Hobbies:* Sports esp volleyball; Gardening; Child education; Apiculture. *Address:* Institute of Solid State Physics, University of Latvia, 8 Kengaraga St, 226063 Riga, Latvia. 52, 139, 152.

SILVER Carole Greta, b. 6 June 1937, New York, USA. Prof of Engl Lit. m Norman Levy, 26 Feb 1990. *Education:* HS of Music and Art, 1954; BA, Alfred Univ, 1958; MA, Univ MI, 1959; PhD, Columbia Univ, 1967. *Appointment:* Prof of Engl Lit anmd Chairperson, Div of Humanities, Yeshiva Univ. *Publications:* Kind Words: A Thesaurus of Euphemisms; The Romance of William Morris; Ed, The Golden Chain: Essays on William Morris and Pre-Raphaelitism; Ed, Socialism and the Literary Artistry of William Morris. *Memberships:* William Morris Soc of North America, Exec Comm, 1970-88; Northeast Victorian Studies Assn, VP, 1978-82; MLA. *Honours:* Woodrow Wilson National Fellow, 1958-59; Woodbridge Honorary Fellow, Columbia University, 1967; President's Fellow, Columbia University, 1966; Presidential Award, Yeshiva University, Senior Professor Award, 1976; National Endowment for the Humanities Fellow, 1986. *Hobbies:* Film, Travel, Music. *Address:* Stern College for Women, Yeshiva University, 245 Lexington Avenue, New York, NY 10016, USA.

SILVERSTEIN Sasha, b. 6 Mar 1953, Trenton, New Jersey, USA. Artist; Art Tchr. *Education:* BA, Sarah Lawrence Coll, 1971; MA Sculpture, Parsons Schl of Design, 1984; NY Studio Schl; Educl Alliance; Art Students League. *Appointments:* Sculpture Tchr, Great Neck Adult Educ, 1989; Painting Tchr, Educl Alliance, 1990; Sculpture Tchr, Greenwich House, 1991-; Pvte Students. *Creative Works:* Paintings; Sculptures. *Membership:* Sculptors Alliance. *Honours:* Scholarship Grant for Parsons School of Design, 1983-84; Educational Alliance Outstanding Sculpture, 1986, 88. *Hobbies:* Jazz and Ethnic Dance; Yoga, Nature, Music. *Address:* 235 Lincoln Place, Brooklyn, NY 11217, USA.

SIM Ah-Tee, b. 6 July 1944, Singapore. Co Dir. m. Alice- Elizabeth. 26 June 1965, 2 s, 1 d. *Education:* AEB 'O' Level, Queenstown Tech Second Schl, 1957-60. *Appointments:* Supvsr, Gen Insulation, 1968-70; Mgr, Sun Yew Engrng Works, 1970-82; Co Dir, Sun Indl Coatings Pte Ltd, 1982-. *Creative Works:* Inventor, patentee: Drag Solder Plating, DIL Carrier, Drag Solder Dip, Quad Pad Carrier, SOIC Carrier. *Memberships:* Singapore Mfrs Assn, Comm; Assn Electronic Inds of Singapore; Semicodnuctor Equipment and Materials Int. *Hobby:* Keeping Tropical Fishes. *Address:* 19 Toh Crescent, Singapore 1750. 52.

SIMAAN Marwan, b. 23 July 1946. Prof of Elec Engrng. m. Rita. *Education:* PhD Elec Engrng, Univ of IL at Urbana-Champaign, 1972. *Appointments:* Rsch Engr, Shell Dev Co, Houston, TX, 1974-75; Prof of Elec Engrng, Univ of Pittsburgh, 1976-. *Publications:* Over 150 rsch papers and 4 edited books: Vertical Seismic Profiles, 1984; Two-Dimensional Transforms, 1985; AI and Expert Systems in Petroleum, 1989; Expert Systems in Exploration, 1991. *Memberships:* Fellow, IEEE; SEG; Eta Kappa Nu; Electromagnetics Acad. *Honours:* Two Best Papers Awards, 1985, 88; University of Pittsburgh Board of Visitors Award, 1985; Elected Fellow of IEEE, 1988; Beitle-Veltri Memorial Award for Teaching, 1990. *Hobbies:* Music, Tennis. *Address:* Department of Electrical Engineering, 348 Benedum Hall, University of Pittsburgh, Pittsburgh, PA 15261, USA.

SIMAKOV Kirill Vladimirovich, b. 1 Feb 1935, Leningrad, USSR. Scientist; Dr of Geology. m. Shevchenko Valentina Mikhailovna, 20 Oct 1959, 1 s, 1 d. *Education:* Leningrad State Univ, Geologic Dept, Honours Degree, Prospecting Geologist, 1952-57. *Appointments:* Chief of Field Team, 1957-64; Chief, 1965-66; Sr Geologist of Seimchan Exploration Team, Magadan Reg, 1967-70; Scientific Worker, 1970-79; Head of Lab, 1980-84; Sr Scientist, Ne Interdiscipl. Rsch Inst, 1985-91; V-Chmn Ne Rsch Ctr, 1991-. *Publications:* About 190 papers inclng 14 monographs: Concerning the General Theory of Time, 1981; Philosophy and Concepts of Geochronology, 1984. *Memberships:* Mbr 1976-83, V-Chmn 1984-91, Int D/C Working Grp; USSR Interdepartmental Stratigraphic Comm; Chmn, USSR NE Reg Interdepartmental Stratigraphic Comm, 1985-91; Acad Sciences Presidium Stratigraphic Scientific Coun, 1985; Acad Sciences Presidium Geology Scientific Coun, 1988; USSR Acad Sciences, Corres Mbr; Corres Mbr, Int Subcommn on Carboniferous and Devonian Stratigraphy. *Honours:* Prize of Academician Karpinsky, USSR Academy of Sciences, 1988; Honoured Scientist of Russia, 1991. *Hobbies:* Skiing, Reading Histl and Detective Stories. *Address:* 16 Portovaya SVKNII, 685000 Magadan, Russia.

SIMEK Ursula, b. 24 May 1961, Vienna, Austria. Theatre Scientist. *Education:* Theatre Science, Hist, Univ of Vienna, 1979-86. *Appointments:* Mgr, Frauen Kammer Orchester von Osterreich, 1987-88; Collaborator of Gesellschaft fur Max Reinhardt-Forschung, Vienna, 1987-89; Since 1989 Rdr; Lectr. Female Opera Composers, Univ of Vienna, 1990-. *Creative Works:* Dir, Alfred Bernau, Rudolf Beer in 100 Jahre Volkstheater Theater, Zeit, Geschichte, Vienna, 1989; Ostleitner, E Simek: 1st Die Musik Mannlich, Vienna, 1991; Simek: Das Berufs: Theater in Innsbruck im 18 Jahr Hundert, Vienna, 1991. *Membership:* Imagkunst (Interministerielle Arbeits Gruppe) of the Fedl Women's Dept, Vienna. *Hobbies:* Skiing, Tennis, Mountaineering. *Address:* Schuttaustr 4-10/6/6, A-1220 Vienna, Austria.

SIMIONESCU Cristofor, b. 17 July 1920, Dumbraveni, Suiceava, Romania. Prof of Organic and Macromolecular Chem. m. Natalia Voitenco, 22 June 1947, 2 s. *Education:* MSc (magna cum laude), 1944; PhD, 1948; Prof Organic Macromolecular Chem, Hd of Dept, 1951; Full Mbr, Romanian Acad, 1963. *Appointments:* Rector, Polytechnic Inst of Jassy, 1953-

76; Dir, P Poni Inst Chem, 1970-; VP, Romanian Acad, 1974-89; Pres, Jassy Br Acad, 1963-74. *Publications:* 25 books, 700 scientific studies, 1000 essays on hist, philos, science, 60 patents. *Memberships:* IAWSS; IUPAC; ACS; Soc Chimique France; Soc Chimie Ind. Paris; NY Acad of Sciences, Nobel Prize Comm. *Honours:* Honorary Member of German Academy of Sciences, 1982; Honorary Member of Hungarian Academy of Sciences, 1987; Doctor honoris causa of Higher Technico-chemical Institute of Sofia, 1986; Golden Medal of ACS at its Centennial, 1976. *Hobby:* Ornithology (canaries and other exotic birds). *Address:* Palade Street, 11- RO-6600 Iasi, Romania.

SIMKINS John Anthony Benjamin, b. 12 Dec 1944, Bombay, India. Chmn and Chief Exec; Master Mariner. m. Linda-Kay Brown, 30 Sept 1972, 2 s, 3 d. *Education:* HMS Conway, 1959-62; 1st Class Passing Out Cert, Southampton Univ Schl of Navigation, Master Mariner's Cert of Competency, 1970. *Appointments:* Navigating Apprentice, Brit India Steam Navigation Co Ltd, 1962-64; Navigating Off, BISN Co Ltd, 1964-70; Hovercraft Pilot, Int Hoverservices Ltd, Ocean Inchcape, 1970-72; Master Offshore Supply Vessels, 1972-74; Ops Mgr Ocean Inchcape Ltd (OIL), 1974-78; Hd, Marine OIL, 1978-79; Mgr, Mexico and Ctrl America OIL, 1979-81; Dir and Gen Mgr, OIL (Asia) Ltd, 1981-84; Dir and Gen Mgr, Mansal Offshore Ltd, 1984-86; Self-employed Cons, 1986-87; Chmn and CEO BT (Marine) Ltd, 1987-. *Publications:* Paper to Newcastle Univ, The Operation of Offshore Supply Vessels, 1976; Paper to Marintec China, Shanghai, 1982, Offshore Supply Vessels Their Operation and Development. *Memberships:* Inst of Dirs; Inst of Underwater Technology; Royal Inst of Navigation; Honourable Co of Master Mariners. *Hobbies:* Sailing, Flying, Squash, Reading Science Fiction. *Address:* 40 Whartons Lane, Ashurst, Southampton SO4 2EF, Hampshire, England.

SIMMERMAN Orin Miller Jr, b. 21 Oct 1926, Wilmore, Kentucky, USA. Dist Suptd of United Meth Ch. m. Mary Ella Ball, 19 Mar 1947, 2 s, 2 d. *Education:* AB Asbury Coll, 1949; M.Div, Asbury Theological Sem, 1956; DD, Asbury Coll, 1982. *Appointments:* Sr Pastor: Greenup Meth Ch, 1956- 58; Liberty Meth Ch, 1958-62; Founding Pastor, Aldersgate Meth Ch, 1962-69; South Ashland United Meth Ch, 1969-75; Versailles United Meth Ch, 1975-79; Advance United Meth Ch, Flatwoods, KY, 1983-89; Frankfort Dist Suptd, 1989-. *Memberships:* Chair of KY Conf Hlth and Welfare, 1972-80; Chair of Equitable Salaries Comm, 1980-89; Chair of SEJ Fellowship of Conf Leadership, Hlth and Welfare, 1978-79; Mbr Bd Trustees, Meth Home of KY, 1969-83. *Honour:* Rural Minister of the Year, Kentucky Conference 1961. *Hobbies:* Reading, Touring and Taking Tours. *Address:* 129 Tanglewood Drive, Frankfort, KY 40601, USA. 116.

SIMMONDS David Anthony Kenward, b. 8 Sept 1939, Lewes, Sussex, England. Chartered Surveyor. m. Valerie Barsley, 27 Mar 1975, 2 s, 2 d. *Education:* BSc, Estate Mgmt, London Univ, 1958-61; Fellow, Royal Instn of Chartered Surveyors, 1972. *Appointments:* Howell & Brooks, London, EC4, 1961-63; Simmonds and Ptnrs, 1963-, Ptnr 1967-. *Memberships:* Fellow, Royal Instn of Chartered Surveyors, 1972; JP, 1980, Barnet and S Mimms Bench, Dpty Chmn Juvenile Panel, 1989-; Chmn, Licensing Comm, 1990-; MCC; Liveryman, Tallow Chandlers Co, 1963. *Hobbies:* Travel, Wine, Gardening, Philately, Indl Archaeology. *Address:* Little Orchard, Barnet Lane, Elstree, Hertfordshire WD6 3QX, England.

SIMMONS Peter Hamilton, b. 2 Sept 1926, Teddington, England. Med Practitioner; Cons Anaesthetist. m. Elizabeth Coralie Houghton, 29 Sept 1956, 2 s (1 dec), 2 d. *Education:* St Bartholomew's Hosp Med Coll, 1944-50; MB BS, London; Dip. Anaes, 1952; Fellow, Fac Anaes, 1954. *Appointments:* Cons Anaesthetist, The North Middlesex Hosp, 1959-91; The Royal Northern Hosp, 1960-91; The Royal Free Hosp,

1985-91. *Publication:* Anaesthesia for Nurses, 1966. *Memberships:* Assn of Anaesthetists of GB and Ireland; Hist of Anaesthesia Soc; Assn of Dental Anaesthetists. *Honours:* Prizes: Westminster School and St Bartholomew's Hospital; Scholarship St Bartholomew's Hospital. *Hobbies:* Gardening, Upholstery, New Testament Greek. *Address:* Garden House, 3 Queens Road, Barnet, Hertfordshire EN5 4DH, England. 170.

SIMMS Alan John Gordon, b. 3 Apr 1954, Liverpool, England. Barrister. m. Julia Jane Ferguson, 2 Aug 1980. *Education:* LL.B, Univ of London, 1975; Called to Bar Lincoln's Inn, 1976. *Appointment:* Mbr of Northern Circuit 1980, Practising at the Criminal Bar. *Memberships:* Brit Acad of Forensic Science; Inst of Adv Motorists; Rospa Adv Drivers Assn Nat Rd Safety Comm; Brit Automobile Racing Club. *Honours:* Rospa Class One Advanced Driving Certificate, 1986; Diploma in Advanced Driving Instruction, 1986. *Hobbies:* Reading, Motor Racing, Motor Racing Marshalling Road Safety, Blues and Jazz Music, Guitar Playing, Forensic Science, Crime (theory only). *Address:* Chavasse Court Chambers, 2nd Floor Chavasse Court, 24 Lord Street, Liverpool 2, England.

SIMO Dennis Rafael, b. 19 Nov 1943, Santo Domingo, Dominican Republic. Economist. m. Julia Alvarez Sorrentino, 23 Jan 1966, 3 s, 1 d. *Education:* BA, Bus Admin; BA, Econs; MS, Banking. *Appointments:* Chief Fin Off, Industria Licores Int, SA, Santiago, 1979-80; Econ Advsr to Pres, Dominican Repub Santo Domingo, 1980-82; Chief Exec Off, Dominicana Airlines, Santo Domingo, 1987-88; Chief Fin Off, Delta Grp, Santo Domingo, 1982-; Creditos y Co Branzas, SA Chmn Pres CEO Dominicana Airlines, 1983-; Treas, Consorcio Agroin. Delta, SA, Santo Domingo, 1985-, Acumuladores nacionales, SA, 1984-, Data Sistema, SA, 1984-; Pres, Consorcio de Consultoria y De Sarrollo, 1987-; Advsr, Min Fin, Dominican Repub, 1988-89; Min, Ind and Commerce, 1988-90. *Publications:* Samana, 1983; Credit Manual, 1985; Tu, Yo y el Silencio, 1989. *Memberships:* VP, Centro de Estudios Monetarios, 1975-; VP, Fundacion Dominicana de Historia y Cultuura Inc, 1980-; Pres, Centro Apec de Educacion a Distancia, 1987-91; Pres, Fundacion Cultural Compromisso, Inc, 1990-. *Honours:* Cum Laudem Pontificia Universidad Catolica, 1967; Magna Cum Laudem, Universidad Pedro Henriquez Urena, 1975; Distinguished Alumnae, Universidad Pedro Henriquez Urena, 1989. *Hobbies:* Reading, Hist, Educ. *Address:* Delta Comercial, CXA P O Box 1376, Avenue J F Kennedy Esq, Gracita Alvarez de Tejera, Santo Domingo, Republica Dominica. 152.

SIMON Rose Anne, b. 23 June 1947, Westfield, New York, USA. Lib Dir. m. Sheridan A Simon, 19 July 1970. *Education:* A3, Univ Rochester, 1969; MA, Univ VA, 1970; PhD, Univ Rochester, 1977; MS in LS, Univ NC at Chapel Hill, 1978. *Appointments:* Guilford Coll, 1974-79; Salem Coll, 1979-. *Memberships:* ALA; NC Lib Assn, Assoc Ed, NC Libs, 1976-80, 1984-, Exec Bd, 1985-87; SOLINET, Bd Dirs, 1984-87, Sec, 1986-87; Phi Beta Kappa; Beta Phi Mu. *Hobby:* Nature Photography. *Address:* 5723-A Bramblegate Road, Greensboro, NC 27409, USA. 15.

SIMON Sheridan Alan, b. 20 Apr 1947, Buffalo, New York, USA. Prof of Phys; Writer. M. Rose Anne Schrader, 19 July 1970. *Education:* BS cum laude, Astrophys, 1969, MA, Phys, 1971, PhD, Phys and Astronomy, 1978, Univ of Rochester. *Appointment:* Prof of Phys, Guilford Coll, 1974-. *Publications:* Unlocking the Universe, 1991; The Biology Disk; The Physics Disk; The Astronomy Disk; Unprintable Physics. *Memberships:* Sigma Xi; American Astronomical Soc; American Phys Soc; American Assn of Phys Tchrs; Planetary Soc. *Honours:* Stoddard Prize in Physics, 1969; Excellence in Teaching Award of Guilford College, 1974, 87; Bronze Medalist Professor of the Year Programme of Council for Advancement and Support of Education, 1988. *Hobbies:* Computer Programming, Planetary Design, Writing Science Fiction, Writing Textbooks, Computer Art, Photography,

Travelling. *Address:* Physics Department, Guilford College, Greensboro, NC 27410, USA.

SIMONSEN Jorn, b. 28 Aug 1933, Denmark. Prof of Forensic Pathology. m. Inger Olsen, 29 Jan 1956, 1 s, 2 d. *Education:* Graduated from Copenhagen Univ Med Schl, 1959; Doctor by Thesis, 1966; Specialty in Anatomic Pathology and Histology, 1967; Exam Pub Hlth Off, 1964; ECFMG Cert, 1968. *Appointments:* Sr Lectr in Forensic Med, Copenhagen, 1962-69; Sr Lectr, Forensic Med, New York, 1969-70; Prof in Forensic Med, Univ of Odense, 1971-89; Prof of Forensic Pathology, Univ of Copenhagen, 1990-. *Publications:* Subarachnoid Haemorrhage due to Minor Head Injuries, 1966; Textbook of Forensic Medicine, 1989 (in Danish); Medical Law (in Danish), 1991. *Memberships:* Fellow, American Acad of Forensic Sciences; Overseas Mbr, Brit Assn of Forensic Med; Mbr, Praesidium, of Int Acad of Forensic and Social Med; sev Danish Scientific Socs. *Honour:* University of Copenhagen's Gold Medal for a Prize Essay concerning Head Injuries, 1961. *Hobbies:* Travelling; Hist, Biogs. *Address:* Christiansholmsvej 24, DK-2930 Klampenborg, Denmark.

SIMPSON Bernard Roy, b. 20 Nov 1922, Newport, Gwent, Wales. Retired Anaesthetist. m. Ann Stewart, 1 Nov 1951, 2 s. 1 d. *Education:* London Hosp Med Coll, 1943-49; LRCP; MRCS; FFARCS, 1958; DPhil (Oxon), 1965; MD, Univ TX, 1975. *Appointments:* Prof, Anaesthetics, London Hosp, 1967-75; Hon Cons, Royal Prince Alfred Hosp, Sydney, NWS, Australia, 1972-; Chief, Dept Anaesthesiology, Baylor Univ Med Ctr, TX, USA, 1975-89; Prof, Univ TX SW Med School, 1985-89. *Publications:* Over 100 incl: Effects of Anaesthesia and Elective Surgery on Old People (co-author), 1961; Extradural Analgesia and the Prevention of Post-Operative Respiratory Complications (co-author), 1962; Lactate Metabolism (co-author), 1975. *Memberships:* Examiner, Primary FFARCS, 1969-75; Chmn, Sub-Comm, Anaesthetics Bd Surg Studies, London Univ, 1971-75; Bd Mbr, Fac Anaesthetists, 1972-75; Comm Panels and Sci Papers, Am Soc Anesthesiologists, 1976, 1983. *Honours:* Inaugural Ellis Gillespie Lectr, Fac Anaesthetists of Australia, Singapore, 1973; Jobson Vis Prof, Univ Sydney, Australia, 1973; Prize for Rsch, Assn Anaesthetists, 1973; Prize for film Patent Airway, Brit Life Assurance Trust, 1973; Eliasburg Mem Lectr, Mt Sinai Hosp, NYC, 1974. *Hobbies:* Rugby football; Cricket; Athletics; Squash; Tennis; Golf. *Address:* Dynevor Mews, Rectory Lane, Ampthill, Beds MK45 2EL, England.

SIMPSON Clare Suzanne, b. 1 Jan 1958, Dunedin, New Zealand. Univ Lectr. *Education:* BA, Educ and Sociology, 1980; MA (Hons) Sociology, 1984; Dip of Tchng, 1984; ATCL Piano Perf. *Appointments:* Lectr, Lincoln Univ, 1985-, Tchng Social Theory, Human Dev, Commun Dev, Women and Recreation. *Publications:* Her Story Diary, 1989; 20 Years of Feminism in New Zealand and sev articles. *Memberships:* NZ Women's Studies Assn; NZ Sociological Assn; NZ Recreation Assn; World Leisure and Recreation Assn; Assn of Univ Tchrs; Status of Women Comm of Aust, 1989-91. *Honours:* Dux of School, 1975; Best All Round Girl, 1975; Rotary Youth Leadership Award, 1976; Operation Raleigh Selector, 1987. *Hobbies:* Playing Piano and Flute, Yoga, Chamber Music, Gardening, Cycling, Watching Old Films, Early TV, Drawing, Walking in Hills, Surfing, Reading, Learning French, Public Speaking, Getting asked to Talk on issues affecting Women, Making People Laugh. *Address:* c/o Department of Parks, Recreation and Tourism, P O Box 84, Lincoln University, New Zealand.

SIMPSON David Martin Wynn, b. 31 Jan 1938, London, England. Solicitor. m. Susan Katharine, 6 Dec 1968, 4 d. *Education:* Queens Coll, Taunton; Christs Coll, Cambridge, Law Tripos 1961, MA, 1966. *Appointments:* Solicitor admitted 1965; Licenced Insolvency Practitioner. *Memberships:* Bristol Law Soc, Pres, 1989-90; Gen Commnr of Taxes Chmn Wrington Div; Chmn, Area Comm, Legal Aid Bd. *Honours:* Fellow of Institute of Directors; Member Chartered Institute of Arbitrators. *Hobbies:* Flying, Gardening, Skiing, Travelling. *Address:* 34 St Nicholas Street, Bristol BS1 1TS, England.

SIMPSON Graham, b. 5 Sept 1951, Orsett, Essex, England. Chartered Archt. m. Elaine Emily Darby, 16 Aug 1980, 1 s, 1 d. *Education:* Archtl Assn, London, 1972-75; Univ of Southern CA, 1974; Archtl Assn, 1978-80; AA Dip; Polytechnic of Ctrl London, Schl of Environment, 1984-85; TIBA Pt.3. *Appointments:* The Halpern Ptnrship, Conversion of Grade II Listed Bldgs in Hyde Pk Sq, 1984-86; Czwg Archts, mixed use dev within the Tower Bridge Conservation Area, 1987-90. *Publication:* Currently writing book on Georgian, Victorian and Edwardian Public Buildings and Public Open Space with two offers of publ. *Memberships:* Reg Archt (Archts Registration Coun of The U K); Corporate Mbr of The Royal Inst of Brit Archts. *Honour:* The Neff Award for Residential Building Design, 1980. *Hobbies:* Cricket (Mbr of Middlesex Co Cricket Club), Skiing, Tennis. *Address:* 45 Anstice Close, Chiswick, London W4 2RL, England.

SIMPSON John Rowton, b. 19 Sept 1926, Leicester, England. Ret'd Solicitor. m. 8 Oct 1959, 2 s, 1 d. *Education:* Rugby Schl; Magdalene Coll, Cambridge, MA, LLM. *Appointments:* Solicitor, 1953; Sr Ptnr, 1978-91. *Memberships:* Leicestershire Rugby Union, Hon Sec, 1959-68, Pres, 1987; Rugby Football Union Comm, 1968, Pres, 1988; Capt, Leicestershire Golf Club, 1972. *Honours:* Lieutenant Colonel, RE (TA), 1968; TD; DL. *Hobbies:* Rugby Football, Golf. *Address:* 16 Knighton Grange Road, Leicester LE2 2LE, England.

SIMPSON Matthew William, b. 13 May 1936, Bootle, Lancashire, England. Educator. m. Monika Ingrid Weydert, 13 Dec 1962, 1 s, 1 d. *Education:* MA (Cantab), 1958; Cert Ed, Liverpool, 1959. *Appointments:* Wirral Grammar School for Boys, 1959-61; Studio School Engl, Cambridge, 1961-64; Millbank Coll Commerce, Liverpool, 1964-66; Liverpool Inst Higher Educ, 1966-. *Publications:* Poems, articles, reviews in wide variety of mags and jrnls; Collections of poetry: Letters to Berlin, 1971; A Skye Sequence, 1972; Watercolour from an Approved School, 1975; Uneasy Vespers, 1977; Making Arrangements, 1982; See You on the Christmas Tree, 1984; Dead Baiting, 1989; An Elegy for the Galosherman - New and Selected Poems, 1990. *Membership:* Chmn, Trustees of Window Project. *Hobbies:* Listening to Classical Music; Angling; Reading. *Address:* 29 Boundary Drive, Liverpool L25 0QB, England. 139.

SIMS Herman Christie, b. 3 Dec 1960, Fairmont, West Virginia, USA. Safety Specialist. m. Stephanie L Graham, 27 May 1989. *Education:* BS, Mining Engrng Technology, 1984; AS, Mech Engrng Technology, 1987; MS, Safety Mgmt, 1989. *Appointments:* Safety Specialist, WV Univ; APT Cons, Mining Engrng Techn. *Publication:* Evaluating a Wood Densification System for Producing Fuelwood Logs in Forest Products Journal, Nov/Dec 1990. *Memberships:* V-Chmn, Nat Safety Coun, Forest Inds; Nat Inst for Farm Safety; Phi Delta Kappa. *Hobbies:* Reading, Hiking, Weight Lifting. *Address:* Route 8, Box 212, Lot 127, Morgantown, WV 26505, USA. 7, 15.

SIMS Paul Edward, b. 20 Jan 1961, Toronto, Can. Hlth Admstr; Edr. *Education:* RN Dip, Senela Coll, Can, 1982; EMCA Dip, Centennial Coll, Can, 1983; EdD Honoris Causas, London Inst of Applied Rsch, 1991; DSc Honoris Causa, Collegium Sancti Spiritus, USA, 1992; D.Sc (Honoris Causa), Collegium Sancti Spiritus, California, USA; Ed.D (Honroris Causa), London Inst of Applied Res, London, UK, 1991. *Appointments:* Assoc Fac Mbr, Seneca Coll, 1981-; Shift Team Ldr 1982-84, Staff Nurse 1984-85, N York Gen Hosp; Bus & Clin Coord in Oral and Maxillofacial Surg Off, 1985-; Assoc Fac Mbr, Hamber Coll, 1990-; Certified Aireomedical Attendant, 1992. *Creative works:* Conducting of Clin Rsch for

several Pharmacological Studies. *Memberships:* Pres, Student Admnstv Coun, Seneca Coll; Corps Supt, St John Ambulance; Phi Delta Kappa, Univ of Toronto Chapt; RN Assn of Ont; Can Nurses Assn; Mem, Phi Delta Kappa, Univ of Toronto Chapter, 1992. *Honours:* Grand Prior's Awd, presented by Lt Gen of Ont, 1978; Duke of Edinburgh's Gold Awd, awded by HRH Prince Phillip, 1983; Priory Vote of Thanks 1984, Bassett Awd 1989, 1990, St Johns Ambulance; Serv Medal of the Venerable Order of St John, presented by the Gov Gen of Can, 1985; Off of the Venerable Order of St John, granted by Her Majesty The Queen of Eng, 1991. *Hobbies:* Cross country skiing; Baseball; Squash; Golf; Camping; Fishing; Photography; Woodworking. *Address:* 48 Graham Crescent, Markham, Ontario, Canada L3P 4M1.

SINDEN Marc, b. 9 May 1954, London, Eng. Actor. m. Joanne Lesley Gilbert, 20 Aug 1977, 1 s, 1 d. *Education:* Bristol Old Vic Theatre Sch, 1971-73. *Appointments:* Jeweller, H Knowles-Brown Ltd, Hampstead, 1973-78; Entered Theatre; Repertory Work; Whitby Weekly Repertory Co, 1978; Folkstone Weekly Repertory Co, 1978; New Shakespeare Co, 1979; Salisbury Playhouse Repertory Co, 1979-80; West End Prods: Enjoy, 1980; Chorus Girls, 1981; Her Royal Highness?, 1981-82; Underground (incl Can tour), 1983; School for Scandal (incl European tour), 1984; Two Into One, 1985; Ross (incl Can tour), 1986; John Bull's Other Island, Dublin, 1987; Major Barbara, Chichester Fest Theatre, 1988; Over My Dead Body, London, 1989. TV: Dick Turpin; If You Go Down to the Woods Today; Home Front; Bergerac; Strange But True; Crossroads; Magnum PI; All at No 20; Never the Twain; Wolf in the Slaughter; Rumpole of the Bailey; Fiddlers Green; The Country Boy. Films: Clash of Loyalties; Wicked Lady; White Nights; Manges d'Hommes. *Publications:* Researcher, Everyman Book of Theatrical Anecdotes. *Memberships:* Garrick Club; Liveryman, Worshipful Co of Inholders. *Honours:* Freedom, City of London, 1978; Fellow, Zoological Soc of London, 1982. *Hobbies:* Zoology; Ethology; Theatrical history; Hitory of stunt work; Cricket; Motor racing. *Address:* c/o CCA Personal Management Ltd, 4 Court Lodge, 48 Sloane Square, London SW1, England.

SINGH Hazara, b. 30 Nov 1922, Pakistan. Ret'd Univ Tchr. m. Phool Kaur, 13 Mar 1949, 2 s, 2 d. *Education:* BA, Punjab Univ, Lahore, 1945; MA 1950,LLB 1955, Panjab Univ, Chandigarh. *Appointments:* Lectr in Eng, Khalsa Coll, Amritsar, 1950-53; Asst Prof of Eng 1954-66, Assoc Prof 1966-77, Hd, Dept of Journalism, Langs & Culture 1977-84, Punjab Agricl Coll, Ludhiana; Sec to Vice Chancellor, Guru Nanak Dev Univ, Amritsar, 1985-88. *Publications:* Sikkhism and Its Impact on Indian Soc; An Arc of Beauty; On the Use of Library; Style in Writing Technical Papers and Theses; Aspirations; Yearnings. *Memberships:* Fellow, Punjab Univ, Chandigarh, 1956-62; All India Eng Tchrs' Conf, 1968-84; All India Journalism Tchrs' Assn, 1979-82; Life, Punjabi Sahitya Acad, Punjabi Bhawan, Ludhuiana; Indian Soc of Authors, 1989-; World Poetry Soc Int, 1990-. *Honours:* Gold Medal for standing first in BA, 1945; Tamra Patra, Govt of India, for participation in Freedom Struggle, 1973. *Hobbies:* Gardening; Story telling to children; Free legal aid to the poor. *Address:* 3-C Udham Singh Nagar, Ludhiana 141001, India.

SIPINEN Seppo Antero, b. 11 Aug 1946, Helsinki, Finland. Commd Cmdr. m. Taru Katriina Pohjavuori, 19 Oct 1968, 1 s, 1 d. *Education:* MD, Univ of Freiburg, Germany, 1971; Dr of Med Sci, Univ of Helsinki, 1981. *Appointments:* Resident in Ob-Gyn and Surg 1973-80, Sr Phys in Ob-Gyn 1981-83, Univ of Helsinki, State Maternity Hosp, Helsinki; Surg Gen 1983-, Commd Cmdr 1990, Finnish Navy Med Corps; Hd, Naval Dept, Rsch Inst of Mil Med, Helsinki, 1983-. *Contributions to:* Articles to profl journs. *Memberships:* Pres, The Finnish Soc of Divig & Hyperbaric Med; Undersea and Hyperbaric Med Soc; European Undersea Biomed Soc; European Comm, Hyperbaric Med Soc; Divers Alert Network Europe; Finnish Soc of Ob-Gyn; Finnish Med

Assn. *Honours:* Silver Medal for promotion of sport diving in Finland, 1986; Medal for Mil Merit, 1988; Diver of the Yr, The Finnish Sportdivers Fedn, 1989. *Hobbies:* Diving and diving medicine; Boating; Down-hill skiing; Gymnastics coaching. *Address:* Finnish Naval Headquarters, Pohjoiskaari 36, 00200 Helsinki, Finland. 52.

SIRJATSKY Victor, b. 3 Feb 1946, Kharkov, USSR. Prof. m. Tatjana Mitjashkina, 12 Oct 1990. *Education:* Dip of a pianist & composer; Cert of a pianist, composer & musicologist. *Appointments:* Asst Prof of Piano 1971-82,Prof of Piano Playing 1982-, Kharkov Inst of Arts. *Creative works:* Three Interpretations of Pictures, 1976; New Interpretation of Expressive Possibilities of the Piano, 1981. *Membership:* Composers Union of the USSR & Ukraine. *Honour:* Hon Dr, Weber Hochschule, Dresden, 1974. *Hobby:* Cooking. *Address:* Bozowaya 4/kv 1, 31 00 11 Kharkov, Russia.

SISSOM Denny Leighton, b. 6 July 1961, Manchester, TN, USA. Elec Engrng. m. Cynthia Kay Gilbert Sisson, 27 Aug 1983, 2 s. *Education:* BSc 1984, MSc 1985, TN Technological Univ. *Appointment:* Guidance and Control Systems Analyst, Coleman Rsch Corp, 1986-. *Publications:* Are SPACs Effective?, 1984; Interactive Creation and Automatic Conversion of N-S charts to FORTRAN-77 Source Code, 1985; Seeker and Data-Processing Modeling for the Strategic Defense Initiative, 1991. *Memberships:* Br Vice Chmn 1983-84, IEEE; Chapt Pres 1984-85, Eta Kappa Nu; Omicron Delta Kappa. *Hobbies:* Reading; Computers; Ping pong. *Address:* 294 Carter's Gin Road, Toney, AL 35773, USA. 176.

SIXTO Ramiro Ares, b. 25 Mar 1935, V de Oro, Lugo, Spain. Automotive Exec. m. Ercilia Martens Ares Sixto, 11 May 1963, 3 s. *Education:* BEc, Cath Univ of Pernambuco, Brazil, 1970; FECAP, Brazil, 1983. *Appointments:* Sr Auditor, Arthur Andersen & Co, Sao Paulo, 1962- 67; Controller, N E Ops Ford Brazil, Pernambuco, 1967-73; Controller, Klabin Embalagens SA, Sao Paulo, 1973-84; Fin, Control & Planning Dir, Aymore Produtos Alimenticios SA, Contagem, 1984-89; Fin & Admnstv Mgr, Industria de Autopecas Eluma Ltda, Contagem, 1989. *Memberships:* Ex VP, Jaboatao Rotary Club, Pernambuco; Fin Exec Inst, Brazil-Belo Horizonte; Minas Tennis Club, Belo Horizonte. *Honour:* Disting Mbrship Plate, Am C of C for Brazil, 1972. *Address:* Rua Tomas Gonzaga, 685 apt 901, 30 180 Belo Horizonte, MG, Brazil. 52.

SJUKUR Slamet Abdul, b. 30 June 1935, Surabaya. Composer. (1) Siti Soeharsini,1960, div 1968, (2) Francoise Mazurek, 1978, dis 1986, 1 s, 1 d. *Education:* Lice D'Enseignement de Piano, Lice de Composition, Ecole Normale de Musique de Paris, France. *Appointments:* Fdr, Chief, PMS Music Fndn, Surabaya, 1957; Lectr, Jakarta Inst of Arts, 1976-87; Hd of Music Comm, Jakarta Arts Coun, 1977-81; Fdr, Chief, Yayasan Musik Laras Fndn, 1985; Fdr, Forum Musik Jakarta (Indonesian Soc for Contemporary Music, Music Info Ctr & Sch of Music Awareness), 1991. *Creative works include:* Parentheses I-VII (Multi Media Music Composed), 1972-85; Jakarta 450 TH (Environmental sound of the whole city to celebrate its 450 yrs); Author of a number of articles on music published in journs and mags. *Membership:* Societe des Auteurs, Compositeurs et Editeurs de Musique, Paris. *Honours:* Bronze Medal, Fest de Jeux d'Automne de Dijon, France, 1974; Golden Record, Acad Charles Cros, France, 1975; Medaille Commemorative, Zoltan Kodaly, Hungary, 1983. *Hobbies:* Chess; Astronomy; Mathematics. *Address:* Kompl Diskum AD (i/3), Jl Media-Massa, Cipinang-Muara, Jakarta 13420, Indonesia.

SKADHAUGE Erik, b. 31 May 1935, Copenhagen, Denmark. Prof. m. Edda Anette Bloch, 30 May 1962, 1 s, 1 d. *Education:* MD 1961, Dr of Med Sci 1973, Copenhagen. *Appointments:* Assoc Prof of Physiology, Univ of CPH, 1968-83; Prof of Physiology, Royal Vet

& Agricl Univ, Copenhagen, 1983-. *Publication:* Osmoregulation in Birds, 1981. *Memberships:* Co-fdr, The European Soc for Comparative Physiology and Biochem, 1978. *Hobbies:* Running; Badminton. *Address:* 30 Solvaenget, DK-2960 Rungsted Kyst, Denmark.

SKARD Sigmund, b. 31 July 1903, Kristiansand, Norway. Poet; Scholar. m. Aase Gruda Koht, 5 Jan 1933, 2 s, 3 d. *Education:* Magister Artium, Univ of Oslo, 1931; PhD, 1938; Hon degrees, Univ of PA; Free Univ of W Berlin. *Appointments:* Libn 1922-33, Prof of Am Lit 1946-73, Univ of Oslo; Asst Prof of Gen Lit, 1933-38; Libn, Royal Acad, Trondheim, 1938-46; on leave as Cons, Libr of Congress, Washington 1941-43, as Chief Reg Specialist. US OWI, 1943-45; Fdr, Dir, Am Inst 1948-73, Pres Int Summer Sch 1958-68; Pres, Det Norske Samlaget, 1949-72. *Publications include:* Sola gaar mot vest, 1948; Amerikanske problem, 1949; Til Marcus Thranes idehistorie, 1949; American Studies in Europe: Their Development and Present Organisation, 2 vols, 1958; The American Myth and the European Mind, 1961; Dad og dikt, 1963; Haustraun, 1966; Americana Norvegica: Norwegian Contributions to American Studies, vols 1-3, 1966-71; American Civilization: An Introduction (w ANJ den Hollander), 1968; Poppel ved flyplass, 1970; The American Image in the World (w M Saito), 1972; Det levande ordet, 1972; Auga og hjarta, 1973; Dikt i utval, 1973; Ein arv til a goyma, 1974; Andlet til andlet, 1974; Ord mot morkret, 1976; The United States in Norwegian History, 1976; Trans-Atlantic: Memoirs of a Norwegian Americanist, 1978; Skymingssong, 1979; Classical Tradition in Norway, 1980; Solregn, 1980; Mennesket Halvdan Koht, 1982; AG Skard Bibliografi 1915-83, 1983; Blomster og brod, 1983; Vandringar, 1983; Menneske bi motte (w AG Skard), 1985; Atterklang, 1987; Karen Grude Koht, 1987; Norsk utefront i USA 1940-1945, 1987; Alders aar, 1989. *Contributions to:* Articles to profl journs. *Membership:* MLA Hon, Acads of Gothenburg, Oslo, Trondheim. *Address:* Fjellvegen 2, Lysaker, Norway.

SKET-JANKOVIC Neva, b. 7 Mar 1931, Ilir, Bistrica. Med Biochem. m. Mojmir Jankovic, 20 Dec 1952, 1 s. *Education:* Degree, Univ of Zagreb, Fac of Pharm & Biochem, 1957; Post-grad study, Clin Lab Diagnostics, Med Fac, 1970; Specialisation Med Biochem, 1978. *Appoointments:* Hd of Lab Diagnostical Serv, Policlin Ctr, Novi, 1958-67; Rsch Dept 1968-71, Hd, Lab of Allergy and Clin Immunology 1972-91, Gen Hosp Dr J Kajfes, Zagreb. *Publications:* Author of over 100 scientific and profl publs, monographs & parts of med books, 1968-91. *Memberships:* Sect of Hematology 1961-, Sect of Allergy and Clin Immunology 1968-, Med Assn of Croatia; European Acad of Allergy and Clin Immunology, 1987-. *Honours:* Charter Aw, Yugoslav Med Assn for Allergy and Clin Immunology, 1984; Med Assn Chart Awd, Croatia Assn, 1990. *Hobbies:* Tennis; Skiing; Music. *Address:* Szabova 21/V, 41000 Zagreb, Croatia.

SKIPP Allan, b. 20 Dec 1943, Ashford, Middlesex, Eng. Dir of Coaching. m. Audrey Farndon, 12 Apr 1969, 2 s. *Education:* Nat Cert in Engrng, 1963. *Appointments:* Completed Trng at W E Sykes Machine Tool Co, 1965; Crown Pumps & Engrng Co, 1965-76; Atlanta Pump Co, 1976-78; Profl Fencing Coach, Eton Coll, Oxon Univ, 1978-89; Dir of Coaching, Assoc, Amateur Fencing,1989-. *Publications:* Teachers Handbook of Foil Fencing; Club Coaches Handbook. *Memberships:* Chmn, AFA Coaches Club; Sr Mbr, Brit Inst of Sports Coaches. *Hobbies:* Squash; Tennis; DIY. *Address:* Amateur Fencing Association, 1 Barons Gate, 33-35 Rothschild Road, Chiswick, London W4 5HT, England.

SKJAERSTAD Ragnar, b. 15 Mar 1944, Oslo, Norway. Ops Mgr. m. Toril Elisabeth Nyquist, 24 June 1967, 1 s, 1 d. *Education:* Bus Admin, Oslo, 1974; Indl Admin, 1976; European Engr (Feani), Paris, 1987. *Appointments:* Electronic Test-Engr 1969, Proj Mgr 1970, Prod Mgr 1971, Mfg Mgr 1978, STK/ITT; Quality

Mgr, Alcatel STK, 1984; Mng Dir, Alcatel Lintron, 1987; Ops Mgr, Alcatel Telecom Norway, 1990-. *Memberships:* Norwegian Quality Coun; Norwegian Polytech Coun. *Honour:* Hon Mbr, Norwegian Engr Org, 1981. *Hobbies:* Photography; Video filming; Old cars; Sailing; Politics. *Address:* Alcatel Telecom Norway AS, Box 310 Oekern, 0511 Oslo, Norway. 132.

SKLYAROV Eugene Victorovich, b. 19 Oct 1954, Omsk, USSR. Chief of Lab. m. Olga A Sklyarova, 24 Feb 1982, 1 d. *Education:* Dip, Novosibirsk Univ, 1971-76; DSc, Inst of Geology & Geophys, Novosibirsk, 1983. *Appointments:* Engr, Inst of Geology & Geophys, Univ of Novosibirsk, 1976-79; Rsch Fellow 1979-88, Chief of Lab 1988-, Buryatian Geological Inst, Ulan-Ude. *Publications include:* Nataliite NaVSi206-new pyroxene from Sludyanka, 1985; Riphean-Paleozoic ophiolites of North Eurasia, 1985; Geology and metamorphism of the East Sayan, 1988; Ecligites and 1987. *Hobbies:* Basketball; Guitar; Amateur theatre. *Address:* Kluchevskaya st 58-50, 670012 Ulan-Ude, Russia. 139.

SKOCH Jiri, b. 24 Apr 1938, Pisek. Fotograf; Sociolog. m. Aja Skochova, 23 May 1970, 2 s, 1 d. *Education:* Dip, Philos Fac, Charles Univ. *Career:* Czech Acad of Sci; Photographic Sch, Prague; Czech TV. *Creative works:* Peva, 23 May 1970, 2 s, 1 d. *Education:* Dip, Philos Fac, Charles Univ. *Career:* Czech Acad of Sci; Photographic Sch, Prague; Czech TV. *Creative works:* Personal exhibs: Pisek 1962, 1989, Most 1964, Brno 1965, Paris 1967, Praha 1971, 1972, 1975, 1990, Berlin 1976, Budapest 1984, Enschede 1991. *Memberships:* Union of Czech Artists; Assn of Photographers - Photohse of Prague - Activ of Free Photography. *Hobbies:* Music; Literature; Painting. *Address:* Armensta 14, 101 00 Praha 10, Czechoslovakia.

SKOLD Hans E, b. 23 June 1918, Stockholm, Sweden. Ret'd Dipl; Writer. m. Ann Edman, 23 Oct 1953. *Education:* LLB, Univ of Stockholm, 1947; Further studies, France, Canada, Sweden. *Appointments include:* Min of Foreign Affairs, Stockholm, 1943-46; Swedish Embassies: Washington DC, USA 1947-49, Ottawa 1949-50; Stockholm 1950-52, 1956-60; Peking, China 1952-54; Wellington, New Zealand 1954-55; Tokyo, Japan 1955-56; Consul, London, Eng 1960-63; Hd, Consul Dept, Min of Foreign Affairs 1963-68; Amb, Monrovia, Abidjan, Conakry & Freetown 1969-72; Consul-Gen, San Fran, USA 1972- 76; Amb, Bogota, Panama & Quito 1976-79; Bucharest, Romania 1979-82. *Publications:* (in Eng) Ships' Command Ordinance, 1958; Statute Book for Swedish Missions Abroad, 1959; Various articles, newspapers, mags & profl lit in Swedish, Eng, Spanish, Romanian; Transl into Swedish, books & articles, various langs. *Memberships include:* Offices, various parly & other comms, 1949-68; Past Pres, Union of Swedish Dipls; Assn of Swedish Authors. *Honours:* Grand Cross: Order of San Carlos, Colombia; Humane Order of African Redemption, Liberia; Tudor Vladimirescu, Romania; Grand Off, Nat OM, Ivory Coast; Kt Cmdr: Royal Order of the Northern Star, Sweden; Royal Order of the Dannebrog, Denmark; Off, Imperial Order of the Crown, Iran; Kt, Papal Order of St Gregory the Gt. *Hobbies:* Golf; Rotary; Genealogy. *Address:* Ardennergatan 36 G, S-271 37 Ystad, Sweden. 12, 52, 139, 151, 152, 156, 162.

SKOLYSZEWSKI Jan, b. 27 Jan 1935, Krakow, Poland. Prof. m. Romana Machowska, 28 Apr 1959, 1 d. *Education:* Dip in Med, Med Sch, Krakow, 1958; MD, 1964; Dip in Radiation Oncology, 1966. *Appointments:* Clin Asst 1962-64, Hd of Radiation Oncology Dept 1974-, Dir of M Sklodowska-Curie Mem Inst 1981-, Prof of Med Scis 1984-, Ctr of Oncology, Krakow. *Publications:* Author of over 100 papers on radiation oncology in Polish & Int Journs; 3 manuals on radiotherapy of head and neck, neurological and urological tumours. *Memberships:* Polish Soc of Oncology; Mbrship Comm 1983-85, European Soc for Therapeutic Radiology and Oncology; 51 Radiotherapy Club, UK. *Honours:* Prize, Polish Min of Hlth for achmts in radiotherapy of head

and neck cancer, 1965; Prize, Mayor of Krakow City for achmts in radiotherapy, 1980. *Hobbies:* Walking; Reading. *Address:* Kochanowskiego 10/7, 31-127 Krakow, Poland.

SKOULA-PERIFERAKI M, b. Athens, Greece. Author; Poet. 1 d. *Education:* Grad, Lyceum. *Publications:* East Number One, poems, 1981; Recital of Self-Sacrifice, short stories, 1982; At the Twelfth Hour of Love, poems, 1983; Twentieth Century, poems, 1985; New Suns, poems, 1987; The History of the Greek Astronautical Society, 1989; Uranography and Greek Mythology, sci study, 1990; In Fancy's Shadow, poems, 1990. *Memberships:* Sec, Greek Authors Assn; Sec, Greek Soc Civilisation, Lit and Arts; Club des Intellectuels Francais; World Acad Arts and Letters, USA; House of Europe; Greek Press Assn; Hon Mbr, Centro Cultural de Felgueiras, Portugal; Deleg for Greece, Academie Internationale de Lutece. *Honours:* Gold Medal, Academie International de Lutece, Paris, 1984; Silver Medal, Societe Francaise d'encouragement L'Elite, 1989; Hon DLit, World Acad Arts and Culture, USA, 1990. *Address:* 100 Thiras ST, GR 104 46 Athens, Greece.

SKUPIEN Zdzislaw, b. 27 Nov 1938, Swilcza, Poland. Mathematician. 2 d, 2 s. *Education:* MSc, 1961, PhD, 1965, Jagiellonian Univ, Cracow; Habilitation, Tech Univ Warsaw, 1982; Titles: Assoc Prof, 1987; Prof, 1990. *Appointments:* Tchng, Rsch, 1961-78, 1982-, Asst Prof, 1971-68, 1982- 87, Assoc Prof, 1987-90, Prof, 1990-, Acad Mining and Metall, Cracow; Asst Prof, 1979-81, Full Prof, 1981-82, Kuwait Univ; Assoc Prof, Computer Sci Dept, Jagiellonian Univ, Cracow, 1988-. *Publications:* Author or co-author, about 70 reviews in Zentralblatt Math, about 70 sci items incl about 60 rsch articles and 8 items w 9 sci problems; About 30 items frequently cited incl: Locally Hamiltonian Graphs and Kuratowski Theorem, 1965; Locally Hamiltonian and Planar Graphs, 1966; Characterizing Line Graphs of Genaral Graphs (w A Marczyk), 1974; On Highly Hamiltonian Graphs (w A P Wojda), 1974; Hamiltonian Circuits and Path Coverings of Vertices in Graphs, 1974; Stirling Numbers and Colouring of q-Trees, 1977; On Homogenously Traceable Nonhamiltonian Digraphs and Oriented Graphs, 1981; On the Smallest Nonhamilton Locally Hamiltonian Graph (w C M Pareek), 1983; Homogeneously Traceable and Hamiltonian Connected Graphs, 1984; Sharp Sufficient Conditions for Hamiltonian Cycles in Tough Graphs, 1989; Co-transl, book in Russian by B P Demidovic, 1972; Co-ed, 6 math vols, 1976-92. *Memberships:* Polish Math Soc; Am Math Soc, 1983-87. *Hobbies:* Listening to music; Hiking; Participating in scientific conferences and numerous short scientific stays including talks or lectures, USA, Australia, Czechoslovakia, Hungary, USSR, FRG, UK, Finland, Netherlands, GDR. *Address:* Institute of Mathematics, AGH, Mickiewicza 30, 30-059 Cracow, Poland.

SKURIHIN Vitaly, b. 9 Jan 1959. Hd of Sect; Geotech Engr. m. Tatyana Tronoba, 25 Mar 1979, 1 d. *Education:* Mocow State Univ, 1976- 81. *Appointments:* Engr 1981-83, Scientific Collaborator 1983-85, Dpty Dir 1985-90, Hd of Sect 1990-, Sakhalin Oil & Gas Inst. *Publications:* Author of over 10 papers on soil investigations on Sakhalin Offshore. *Membership:* Charter, Int Soc of Offshore and Polar Engrs. *Hobbies:* Basketball; Music; Reading. *Address:* 18 K Mark St, Okha, Sakhalin 694460, Russia.

SKURNIK Mikael, b. 26 July 1952, Raahe, Finland. Hd of Lab; Scientist. m. Anna-Leena Miesmaa, 30 July 1977, 4 s, 1 d. *Education:* MSc 1977, PhLic 1981, BMed 1983, PhD 1985, Univ of Oulu. *Appointments:* Asst for rsch & tchng 1977-84, Hd of Lab 1984-85, Univ of Oulu; Post-doct Scientist, Nat Def Rsch Inst, Umea, Sweden, 1985-86; Post-doct Scientist, Univ of Umea, Sweden, 1986-87; Hd of Lab 1987-91, Asst Prof (Docent) 1988-91, Turku Univ. *Publications:* Author of over 30 scientific original articles. *Memberships:* Societas Biophysica

Biochemica et Microbiologica Fenniae, Helsinki; Am Soc for Microbiol, Washington DC; Finnish Immunological Soc, Helsinki. *Hobbies:* Fine Woodworking; Reading; Cross-country skiing; Jogging. *Address:* Turku University, Department of Medical Microbiology, Kiinamyllynkatu 13, SF-20520 Turku, Finland.

SLABAKOV Krasimir Petrov, b. 24 Nov 1955, Razgrad, Bulgaria. Artist; Wood-Carver. m. Maria Todorova Slabakova, 22 June 1977, 1 s, 1 d. *Education:* Speciality, Furniture, Wood-Carving, HS Arts and Crafts, Kotel, 1969-73; High Profl School Artistic and Spatial Arrangement, Sofia, 1975-77; Basic courses, Hist Fine Arts, Design, Drawing and Painting, Composition, Architecture, Wood-Carving, Acad Fine Arts, Sofia, 1977-82. *Career:* Tchr, Drawing, Painting, Karavelov HS, Burgas, 1982-83; Tchr, Composition, Wood-Carving, HS Arts and Crafts, Sliven, 1983-86; Artist-Designer, Decorator, incl artistic arrangement of firm stores, window dressing, Svezest Co, Sofia, 1986-; Participant, 7 Nat Exhibs; 1-man exhib wood-carving, Garden Plastics, Sofia, 1992. *Creative works include:* Wood-carving, desk and chair, Ritual Hall, Roza, 1984; Wood-carving, Interhotels, Vinarna Debelt, Burgas, 1986; Overal artistic arrangement, Ritual Hall Wood-carving, ceiling, desk, chairs, doors, panels, Michurin, 1987; Woodcarving, panel, Ritual Hall, Burgas, 1991. *Membership:* Bulgarian Union Artists. *Hobbies:* Ecology; Sea environment; Yachting. *Address:* Suha Reka, Block 22A, entr A, fl 12, ap 70, 1517 Sofia, Bulgaria.

SLACK Richard Charles Bewick, b. 4 Mar 1944, Adlington, Cheshire, Eng. Cons. m. Patricia Mary Cheshire, 10 May 1969, 2 s, 2 d. *Education:* BA (Cantab), 1965; MA, 1969; MBBChir, 1968; DRCOG, 1970; MRCPath, 1977. *Appointments:* Hse Surg, St Mary's Hosp, London, 1969; Lectr of Pathology, Middlesex Hosp Med Sch, 1971-73; Lectr of Microbiol, Univ of Nairobi, Kenya, 1973-77; Sr Lectr, Univ of Nottingham, 1978-90. *Publications:* Antimicrobial Chemotherapy (ed w D Greenwood), 7 chapts; Medical Microbiology (w D Greenwood, J Peutherer). *Memberships:* Comm, Pathological Soc; Coun, Brit Soc Antimirobial Chemotherapy; Comm, Assn of Med Microb; Examr, RCPath; Coun, Nottm Medico-Chirugical Soc. *Hobbies:* Tennis; Fell walking. *Address:* Nottingham Health Authority, Forest House, Nottingham NG3 5AF, England.

SLADE Edward Colin, b. 24 Mar 1935, Stockport, Eng. Cons. m. Beverly A Stafford, 20 Jan 1962, 1 s, 1 d. *Education:* BS 1950, BSME 1955, Stockport, Eng; Univ of TN, 1977-80. *Appointments:* Designer, Draftsman, Machine Shop Apprentice of Indl Furnaces, Dowson & Mason Ltd, Manchester, Eng, 1950-57; Design Engr, Hydro Elec Power Commn of Ont, Toronto, 1957-60; Design Engr, Standard Steel, Los Angeles, 1960; Design Engr, James M Montgomery, Los Angeles, 1960-61; Design Engr, Carnation Co, Los Angeles, 1961-66; Design Engr, Stone & Webter, Los Angeles, 1966-67; Design Engr, Donald R Warren, Los Angeles, 1967-68; Sr Design Engr 1968-69, 1972-76, Stearns Roger Corp, Denver, 1968-69; Sr Engr, QA Engr, Holmes & Narver, Dept of Def, Dept of Energy, Las Vegas, 1969-71; Staff Engr, Bechtel, San Fran, 1972; Sr Design Engr, Dravo Corp, Denver, 1976-77; Engr, Martin Marietta Energy Systems Inc, Oak Ridge, 1977-86; Cons, 1986-. *Publications:* Author of: 6 publs in Valves; 1 book; Peer Reviewer, Nat Eng Standards; 1 patent. *Creative works:* Exhibited Geneva, Switz 1980, Paris, France 1983, Main Lobby Oak Ridge Nat Lab 1983. *Memberships:* AAAS; Sec, Bd of Human Resources, Oak Ridge, 1980-83. *Honours include:* Awded Silver Medal, New Invention, Geneva, Switz, 1980; Registered Inventor, US Commnr Trades and Patents; Cited in ORNL Book of Disting Scientists and Engrs; Rolex Awd for Enterprise, 1984-85. *Address:* 203 Tusculum Drive, Oak Ridge, TN 37830, USA.

SLATER Keith, b. 20 Dec 1935, Oldham, Eng. Prof. m. Rosalind Hampson, 4 July 1959, 3 d. *Education:* BSc 1956; MSc 1958; PhD 1965; CTexr, FTI, 1971.

Appointments: Lectr, Wakefield Coll of Tech; Lectr, Leeds Coll of Tech; Asst Master, Leeds CHS, 1966-69; Assoc Prof 1969-75, Prof 1975-, Univ of Guelph. *Publications:* Directing Amateur Theatre; Human Comfort; Textile Mechanics; Comfort Props of Textiles; Thermal Behaviour of Textiles; Yarn Evenness; Textile Degradation; Physical Testing of Textiles; Chemical Testing of Textiles; 6 One-Act Plays; About 30 short stories; 1 TV Series. *Memberships:* VP, Textile Inst; Pres, Inst of Textile Sci; Pres, Textile Fedn of Can; Chmn, Textile Inst, Can Sect. *Honours:* Vis Fellow, Gonville & Caius Coll, Cambridge, 1983-84; Vis Fellow, Clare Hall, Cambridge, 1990-91. *Hobbies:* Theatre, Acting, Directing, Writing; Walking; Swimming; Cardiovascular Prevention; Travel; Languages. *Address:* School of Engineering, University of Guelph, Ontario, Canada N1G 2W1. 6.

SLATER S Donald, b. 8 Apr 1927, NYC, NY, USA. Corp Exec. 1 s, 1 d. *Education:* BA cum laude, Syracuse Univ; MA, Columbia Univ. *Appointments:* Investment Banker, Shields & Co, Eastman Dillon, E F Hutton, NYC, 1955-64; Chmn, Pres, Good Roads Machinery Corp, Canton, 1964-68; Pres, Amadon Corp, Boston, 1964-; Chmn, Richardson Polymer Corp, Madison, 1982-87. *Publication:* The Strategy of Cash: A Liquidity Approach to Maximising the Company's Profits, 1974. *Memberships:* Bd of Dir in Boston: World Affairs Coun, Eng Speaking Union, Alliance Francaise, Columbia Univ Club of New Eng, Nichols Hse Mus. *Honours:* Pi Sigma Rho; Pi Gamma Mu; Theta Beta Phi. *Address:* McCormack Station, Box 3421, Boston, MA 02101, USA. 52, 132.

SLAVKIN Vladimir Semenovich, b. 29 May 1950, Sayarskof, Irkutsk region. Engr; Geophysicist. m. Slavkina, 7 Sept 1973, 2 d. *Education:* Dip 1972, Post-grad Course 1975, Moscow Inst of Oil and Gas; Dr of Geol Miner Sc, 1975. *Appointments:* Prin, Chief Geologist, Special Expedition of Centregeophysics, 1975; Hd of Dept, VNIGNI, 1978. *Publications:* 64 articles; 1 patent. *Memberships:* Scientific Tech Soc of Oil and Gas; Scientist Tech Soc Geologist. *Honours:* Gold Medal for Sch, 2 Bronze, 1 Silver Medal, All Union Exhib; Medal of the Soviet Govt for Achmts in Labour; Min of Geology Competition Laureate. *Hobbies:* Actor-amateur of Drama Theatre; Classic music; Karate. *Address:* Novolesnaya 7/11 kv 11, 103 055 Moscow, Russia.

SLAVOV Yordan Nikolov, b. 8 July 1943, Sofia, Bulgaria. Med Dr. m. Galina Ivanova Stancheva, 15 June 1983, 2 s. *Education:* Mil Sch for Offs of Reserve, 1962; MD, Med Univ of Sofia, 1970; MD, Univ of Messiva, Italy, 1989. *Appointments:* Med Dr, Dist of Pernik, Bulgaria, 1970-73; Asst Prof, Univ for Phys Educ, Sofia, 1973-79; Ed, Nat Network, 1979-85; Rehab of Children's Cerebral Paralysis in Reggio Calabria, Italy, 1986-. *Hobby:* Antiquary - icons. *Address:* 6A Rumen Voivoda Street, Sofia 1505, Bulgaria.

SLIPMAN (Samuel) Ronald, b. 24 Aug 1939, New Orleans, LA, USA. Mgmt Cons. m. (1) Carole Marie Green, 1 July 1961, div 1982, 1 s 1 d; (2) Marily Morals, 5 Feb 1983, dec 1985; (3) Lolia Ruth Foster, 12 Jan 1986, 2 s. *Education:* BSc, Tulane Univ, 1961. *Appointments include:* Retail, Owner Mgr, Baton Rouge, 1984-86; Govt Exec Asst III, DHHR - Off of Hosps, Farl K Long Mem Hosp, Baton Rouge, 1984-85, 1985-86; Retail, Owner Mgr, Audubon Antiques, New Orleans, 1986-87; Govt Mgmt Analyst, Veterans Affairs Med Ctr, 1987-88, 1989-90; Self employed, Mgmt Cons, 1991-. *Memberships:* Admin Bd, First United Meth Ch; LA Soc Hosp Pharmacists; VP Bd of Dir 1990-91, Pres Bd of Dir 1991-, Southwest LA Bridge Assn. *Hobbies:* Duplicate bridge; Tennis; Horseback riding. *Address:* 105 Foxfire Lane, Kt 2, Alexandria, LA 71302, USA. 7, 132.

SLOCUM Rosemarie Raccard, b. 19 Dec 1948, Port Arthur, TX, USA. Physn; Pract Mgmt Search Cons. 1

s. *Education:* BS, La State Univ, Baton Rouge, 1971; Cert, Tchr, La Educ Specialist, La Dept Occupational Standards, Baton Rouge, 1971-74. *Appointments:* Account Exec, Uarco Inc, Baton Rouge, 1974-77; Owner, Broker Rosemarie Slocum Real Estate, Baton Rouge, 1977-; Physn Recruiter, MSI, New Orleans, 1985-86; Assoc Dir, Physn Recruitment, Physn Search Inc, Fairfax, 1986-88; Spl Cons, Caswell/Winters Physn Search Cons, Milwaukee, 1988-89; VP, US Med Search Inc, subs of Caswell/Winters, 1988-89; Dir, Physn Recruitment, Mktg, East Range Clins Ltd, Virginia, 1989- . *Hobbies:* Healthcare research; Anthropology; Historical preservation; Ballet. *Address:* 805 5th Avenue S, Virginia, MN 55792, USA. 5, 138, 152.

SMALL Rebecca Elaine, b. 5 Apr 1946, Meridian, TX, USA. Certified Pub Acct. 1 s, 1 d. *Education:* GED Exam, 1968; BS magna cum laude 1977, MA summa cum laude 1989, Ctrl State Univ, 1977; CPA Cert, 1978. *Appointments:* Staff Acct, Lowder & Co, 1975-80; Fdr, Mng Ptnr, Pres, Rebecca E Small, 1981-. *Publications:* Poems: Deep Feelings, 1983; Moel, 1983; Reach for the Stars, 1984; Best Friends, 1985; I Am; Girl Golden, 1988. *Memberships:* Am Psychological Soc; Southwestern Psychological Assn; AICPA; Am Women's Soc of Certified Pub Accts; OK State Bd of Certified Pub Accts; OK Soc of Certified Pub Accts. *Honours include:* Hon Mbrship and Scholarship, Bus and Profl Women's Club, Edmond Chapt, 1976; Bronze Key 1976-77, Psi Chi, Nat Hon Soc in Psychology 1987, Rsch Awd, Psychology Dept 1988, Ctrl State Univ. *Hobbies:* Neuroscience; Neurochemistry; Physics; Psychology; Writing poetry; Bicycle riding. *Address:* 6488 Avondale Drive - 309, Oklahoma City, OK 73116, USA. 5, 7, 123, 132, 138, 152, 176.

SMALLMAN Timothy Gilpin, b. 6 Nov 1938, Bournemouth, Eng. Co Chmn. m. Jane Holloway, 18 Apr 1964, 2 s. *Appointments:* Chmn: Smallman Lubricants (Hereford) Ltd, 1972; W F Smallman & Son Ltd, 1978; Smallman Lubricants Ltd, 1978; Coronet Oil Refineries Ltd, 1979; Needwood Oils & Solvents Ltd, 1986. *Memberships:* Nat Pres, Brit Lubricants Fedn, 1983- 85; FInst D; FInstPet; MInst D. *Hobbies:* Golf; Ornithology; Nature and environment conservation. *Address:* Luddington Manor, Stratford-upon- Avon, Warwickshire CV37 9SJ, England.

SMARANDACHE Florentin, b. 10 Dec 1954, Balcesti, Vilcea, Romania. Software Engr. m. Eleonora Niculescu, 28 May 1977, 2 s. *Education:* MD, Dept of Maths & Computer Sci 1975-79, Tchr Cert, Dept of Educ 1977- 79, Univ of Craiova; PhD studnet, AZ State Univ, Dept of Maths. *Appointments:* Tchr of Maths, several Romanian schs & colls, Craiova, 1981-82, 1984-88; Prof cooperant de mathematiques, Lycee Sidi El Hassan Lyoussi, Sefrou, Morocco, 1982-84; Pvt Tutor of French, Instanbul, Ankara, Turkey, 1988-90; Software Engr, Honeywell, Phoenix, 1990-. *Publications include:* Formule pentru spirit, 1981; Culegere de exercitii poetice, 1982; Sentimente fabricate in laborator, 1982; Problemes avec et sans ... problems!, 1983; Out in the left side, 1990; Inventario del general malo, 1991; America - paradisul diavolului, 1992. *Contributions to:* Many journs with proposed problems of maths and computer sci, solutions, generalizations of problems. *Memberships include:* Int Poets Acad, Madras, India; Les Amis de la Poesie, Bergerac, France; Societatea Romana de Haiku, Bucharest; Acad of Am Poets, NY; Int Writers and Artists Assn; Math Assn of Am. *Honours include:* Premiul Special la proza, Concursul Nat, Marin Predaso, Alexandria, 1982; Prix Special Etranger, IX-eme Grand Prix de la ville de Bergerac, France, 1990; Int Eminent Poet, Madras, India, 1991. *Hobbies:* Literary Avant-Garde; Chess; Soccer; Travelling; Reading. *Address:* PO Box 42561, Phoneix, AZ 85080, USA. 9, 139, 143, 152.

SMART Arthur David Gerald, b. 19 Mar 1925, Seaton, Devon. Emeritus Prof. m. Anne Patience Baxter, 18 June 1955, 2 d. *Education:* MA, Kings Coll, Cambridge, 1947-

50; Dip TP, Regent St Polytech, 1950-53. *Appointments:* Appts in local govt (planning), London, Midlands, North, 1950-63; Co Planning Off, Hants Co Coun, 1963-75; Prof of Urban Planning, Univ of London, 1975-85. *Publications:* Reviews of Area of Outstanding Natural Beauty, 1990; Author of many papers & reports for profl journs, confs, govt depts; Chapts in books. *Memberships:* ARICS; FRTPI; FRSA. *Honour:* CBE, 1991. *Hobbies:* Ornithology, Mbr of Coun, RSPB, 1985-90; Music; Walking; Sailing. *Address:* 10 Harewood Green, Keyhaven, Lymington, Hants SO41 0TZ, England. 1.

SMEDLEY (Roscoe Relph) George (Boleyne), b. 3 Sept 1919, Surbiton, Surrey, Eng. HM Diplomatic Serv (ret'd). m. (1) Muriel Hallaway Murray, 27 Sept 1947, dec 1975, (2) Margaret Gerrard Gourlay Hallaway, 11 July 1979, dec 1991, 1 s. *Education:* LLB, King's Coll, London, 1958-61; Barrister, Inner Temple, 1965. *Appointments:* Foreign Off, 1937-39; Pvt, Cutists Rifles 1939, Lt, South Lancs Regt 1940, Capt, Indian Army 1942; Foreign Off, 1946, 1958; Rangoon, 1947; Maymys, 1950; Brussels, 1952; Baghdad, 1954; Beirut, 1963; Kuwait, 1965; Foreign & C'wlth Off, 1969; Lubumbaslin, 1974; Brit Mil Govt, Berlin, 1974; FCO, 1976; Ret'd as Cnslr, Hd of Nationality and Treaty Dept, 1979; Various tribunals and inquiries, 1979-90; Chwarden. *Address:* Garden House, Whorlton, Bamand Castle, Co Durham DL12 8XQ, England. 1, 34.

SMELIK Klaas Antonius Donato, b. 21 June 1950, Hilversum, Holland. Prof. m. Elisabeth Mik, 8 Jan 1988, 1 s, 2 d. *Education:* Master degree in Divinity, 1974; DD, 1977; BA, 1984. *Appointments:* Asst Prof, Old Testament, Utrecht, 1982-90; Ordinary Prof, Old Testament & Hebrew, Brussels, 1990-. *Publications include:* Early Writing Edinburgh, 1991; Converting the Past, 1991. *Membership:* Dutch Soc for Old Testament Studies. *Hobby:* Stamp collecting. *Address:* Wagenweg 55, 2012 NC Haarlem, Holland.

SMIRNITSKAYA Olga Alexandrovna, b. 14 Dec 1938, Moscow, Russia. Linguist. m. Volf Solomonovich Pevzner, 8 Aug 1967, 1 s, 1 d. *Education:* Kandidat Nauk 1965, Doktor Nauk 1988, Univ of Moscow. *Appointment:* Lectr of Germanic Philology, Dept of Germanic Linguistics, Univ of Moscow, 1965-. *Publications:* The verse and the language of Germipoetry; Transl from Old Icelandic: The Prosaic Edda, 1970; Family Sagas, 1973, 1976; Skaldic Poetry, 1980; Author of over 60 papers on various subjs. *Membership:* Viking Soc for Northern Rsch. *Hobbies:* Drawing; Cooking. *Address:* 26 Bakinskikh, Komissarov str 3-3-256, 117571 Moscow, Russia.

SMITH Albert James, b. 5 Nov 1924, Cardiff, Wales. Ret'd. m. Gwyneth Margaret Lane, 10 Apr 1950, 1 s. *Education:* 1st class hons in English, Univ Coll of Wales, 1951; MA, Oriel Coll, Oxford, 1954; Univ of Florence, 1955-56. *Appointments:* RAFVR (Aircrew), 1943-47; East Barnett Grammar Sch, 1954-55; The Manchester Grammar Sch, 1956-59; Univ Coll of Swansea, 1959-71; Prof of Eng, Univ of Keele, 1971-74; Prof of Eng, Univ of Southampton, 1974-90. *Publications:* Short Story Study, 1960; John Donne: the Songs & Sonnets, 1964; John Donne: the Complete English Poems, 1971; John Donne: the Critical Heritage, 1974; Literary Love, 1983; The Metaphysics of Love, 1985; Metaphysical Win, 1991. *Honours:* Leverhulme European Fellow, 1955-56; Leverhulme Sr Fellow, 1966-67; Eng Speaking Union Disting Fellow, Brit Acad, 1974; D Litt, Southampton, 1991. *Hobbies:* Music; Theatre, Theatre Management; Walking; Drinking. *Address:* Department of English, University of Southampton, Highfield, Southampton SO9 5NH, England.

SMITH Cyril William, b. 7 Jan 1930, London, Eng. Cons; Ret'd Sr Lectr. m. Eileen Dorothy Jackson, 14 June 1958, 3 s. *Education:* BSc, Exeter Univ, 1953-55; BSc Hons, London (External), 1953-55; DIC, PhD, Imperial Coll, London Univ, 1956-59. *Appointments:* Asst Exp Off, TRE Gt Malvern, 1947-56; Rsch Fellow, Imperial

Coll London, 1956-59; Phys Master, Downside Sch, 1959-64; Lectr 1964-73, Sr Lectr 1973-89, Salford Univ; Cons, 1989-. *Publications:* Electromagnetic Man (w Simon Best), 1989; Author of over 100 rsch publs. *Memberships:* C Eng; FIEE; M Inst P; C Phys; SMIEEE; MBES; Sec, Dielectrics Soc, 1972-83. *Honours:* Book of the Yr Awd, Lamberts & Journ of Alternative & Compementary Med, 1989. *Hobbies:* Hill walking; Gardening; Music; Travel; International cooking.

SMITH David Chadwick, b. 12 Aug 1931, India. Prin, Vice Chancellor. m. Mary Hilda Taylor, 25 June 1955, 1 s, 1 d. *Education:* BA, McMaster Univ, 1953; BA 1955, MA 1959, Balliol Coll, Oxford Univ; PhD, Harvard Univ, 1959. *Appointments:* Asst Prof, Univ of CA, Berkeley, 1958-60; Asst Prof, Assoc Prof, Prof 1960-, Hd Dept of Econ(s) 1968-81, Prin, Vice Chancellor 1984-, Queen's Univ. *Honours:* FRS(Can); LLD honoris causa, McMaster Univ, 1991; LLD honoris causa, Queen's Univ of Belfast, 1991. *Address:* Queen's University, Kingston, Ontario, Canada K7L 3N6.

SMITH Dolores Maxine (Plunk), b. 22 Dec 1926, Webster City, IA, USA. Prof. m. Floyd E Smith, 13 July 1985, 2 s, 1 d. *Education:* BSEd, Black Hills Tchrs Coll, 1961; MA 1964, PhD 1974, TX Women's Univ. *Appointments:* One Rm Schs, Todd & Mellette Co, 1945-49; Sch of Dance, SD, 1952-57, 1960-61; St Francis Indian Day Sch, SD, 1957-59; Converse Co High, Douglas, 1961-62; GA TX Women's Univ, 1962-64; Sam Houston State Univ, 1964-65; Ctrl MO State Univ, 1965-. *Creative works include:* Ed, Am Dance Theory Assn Proceedings, 1972; Movement and Creativity - A Way to Learn, 1972; Dance inEd, 1975; Reflection of Temporal Expressions, 1977; The Role of the Univ in Promoting Multi-Cultural Ed Through Dance (speech), 1987, 1991; Cognition in Dance, 1990; Dance and the Child, 1990. *Memberships:* VP Dance Ed 1991-93, Heritage Comm & Luncheon, Ruth Whitney Dance Loan Fund, Special Services, Nat Dance Assn; AAHPERD; Chair - Dance Performance, Dance Div, VP Dance, Coll Div, CAAHP ERD; Pres, Dance Chair, MO AHPERD; Dance Rep, Presider, Int Cong HPER; Dance and the Child Int; Mid Am Dance Network; Int Assn Phys Ed, Sports for Girls & Women; VP, Ctrl Assn Phys Ed Higher Ed. *Honours:* Hons Awd, Ctrl Assn for Hlth, Phys Ed, Red & Dance, 1976; Serv Awd, MO Assn for Hlth, Phys Ed, Rec & Dance, 1977; Plaque, Student Recognition of Dance Prog, 1986; Advsr of the Yr, 1989. *Hobbies:* Raise and show Belgiums; Cake decorating; Stained glass; Gardening; Baking, Cooking. *Address:* Rt 1, Box 518, Warrensburg, MO 64093, USA. 8, 138, 140.

SMITH Doris Corinne Kemp, b. 22 Nov 1919, Bogalusa, LA, USA. Registered Nurse. m. Joseph Wm Smith, 13 Oct 1940. *Education:* RN Dip, City Hosp Sch of Nursing, Mobile, 1940; BS w hons 1957, MS, Nursing Admin 1958, Univ of CO. *Appointments:* Hd Nurse, Chicago Nridge Iron Co, 1941-45; Hd Nurse, Med Floor, Shannon Hosp, San Angelo, 1945-50; Dir, Inserv Ed, St Anthony Hosp, Denver, 1960-66; Coord, Sch of Nursing, Kiamichi Vo-Tech, Poteau; Hlth Care Sup, Lubbock State Sch, TX, 1978-85. *Publications:* Survey of Functions; Co-ed, Curriculum Materials and Bulletin, TNA; Hospital Journs. *Memberships:* Life, AAAS; Life, Am Assn of Univ Women; Treas, Alpha Roo Chapt, Pi Lambda Theta Hon Soc; TX & Nat Leagues Nursing; TX State & DNA No 18; Am Nurses Assn. *Honours:* Dean's Hon List, Univ of CO; Cert of Merit, Ctrl State Univ, Edmond; Former Mbr, Steering Comm, Western Interstate Commn for Higher Educ for Nurses; Former Mbr, Conf to Plan Nursing for the Future, Oklahoma City. *Hobbies:* Gardening, vegetables; Travelling; Fishing; Swimming; Nurse recruitment; Nursing; Science. *Address:* 2103 55th Street Lubbock, TX 79412, USA. 5, 28.

SMITH Earl Pearson, b. 30 Sept 1931, Detroit, MI, USA. Prof. m. Violet A, 6 Sept 1952, 3 s. *Education:* BA 1953, MA 1957, MI State Univ; PhD, Syracuse Univ, 1970. *Appointments:* Southfield Schs, MI, 1957-68; Dept of Curr and Instrn, Univ of VA, 1969-75; Auburn Univ,

1975-84; Prof of Art & Educ, Troy State Univ, 1985-. *Contributions to:* Art Educ; Educl Communications and Tech Journ; Educl Broadcast Journ; Journ of Experimental Ed. *Memberships:* Ed Bd, Art Educ Mag, Nat Art Ed Assn; Higher Ed Rep to Exec Bd, AL Art Ed Assn; African Studies Assn; Sec, TSU Ed Assn. *Honours:* Experienced Tchr Fellowship, USDE, 1966-67; Fulbright Lectr, Ghana, W Africa, 1987-88; Art Edr of the Yr, Higher Educ, AL, 1987. *Hobbies:* Water colour painting, Historic homes; Photography; Hiking; Rehabilitating old homes. *Address:* 205 West College Street, Troy, AL 36081, USA. 7.

SMITH Edward Richard, b. 19 Mar 1936, Finchley, Eng. Bus Cons; Co Dir; Antiquarian Bookdealer. m. Pamela Margaret Mundy, 10 Sept 1960, 2 s. *Appointments:* Martins Bank Ltd, 1953-68; Hill Samuel Bank Ltd, 1968- 90; Non Exec Dir, Gross Hill Properties Ltd; Control Securities Plc; Waterglade Int Holdings Plc; Sydney & London Properties Ltd. *Memberships:* FCIB; Freeman, City of London; Liveryman of Worshipful Co of Patten Makers; EIC; RAC; MCC. *Hobbies:* Gardening (vegetables); Secondhand books; Travel. *Address:* Sevenoaks, Kent, England.

SMITH Elizabeth Jean, b. 15 Aug 1936, Ajmer, India. Controller. m. 26 Feb 1960, 1 s, 1 d. *Education:* MA Hons, Univ of Edinburgh. *Appointments:* Prod, BBC Radio News, 1961-70; Dep Ed, Consumer Affairs, BBC Radio 4, 1970-78; Hd, Current Affairs 1984-88, Controller, Eng Servs 1988- , BBC World Serv. *Publications:* Columnist, Consumer Viewpoint, The Listener, 1975-78; Healing Herbs (Co-author), 1978; Sambo Sahib, 1981. *Memberships:* Radio Acad; RIIA; Royal C'wlth Soc. *Honour:* C'wlth Fellowship to study the impact of satellite tv in India, 1984. *Hobbies:* Children's books; Sailing; Gardening. *Address:* 12 Highbury Terrace, London N5 1UP, England.

SMITH Eric Morgan, b. 13 Feb 1953, Lafayette, IN, USA. Scientist. m. Janice K Smith, 26 May 1979, 1 s. *Education:* BS cum laude, Syracuse Univ, 1975; PhD, Baylor Coll of Med, 1980. *Appointments:* Postdoct Fellow 1979-81, Asst Prof 1982-85, Assoc Prof 1985-90, Prof 1990-, Univ of TX Med Br. *Publications:* Author of over 100 publs to profl journs; Fndng Co-ed, Avances in Neuroimmunology; Ed Bd, Progress in NeuroEndocrin Immunology. *Memberships:* Am Soc for Microbiol; Am Assn of Immunologists; Sigma Xi; Soc for Neurosci; Co-fndng Pres, Assn of Immuno- Neurobiologists; Charter, Int Soc for Neuroimmunomodulation; Int Soc for Immunopharmacology. *Honours:* NY State Regents Scholarship, 1971; James W McLaughlin Awd for Excellence in Infraction and Immunity Rsch, 1981; Nat Rsch Coun Travel Awd, 1989. *Address:* Department of Psychiatry, University of Texas Medical Branch, Galveston, TX 77550, USA. 7.

SMITH F Margaret, b. 30 May 1934, Niagara Falls, NY, USA. Ed. m. Clarence Smith, 1 s, 3 d. *Education:* Journalism Cert, Algonguin Coll, Ottawa, Can. *Appointments:* Pub Rels Off, Ed, Coll newspapers, Algonguin Coll, 1969-71; Ed, Canada: a Portrait, 1972- ; Ed, Canada, 1987-. *Creative works:* Canada: a Portrait covers life in Can in photos, text and tables, 1930s- ; Canada Yr Book, approximately 808 pages of text & tables covering a wide range of subjs relating to Can, 1867-. *Hobbies:* Reading; Writing; Travel; Needle crafts. *Address:* 1209 Firestone Crescent, Ottawa, Ontario, Canada K2C 3E4.

SMITH Gina Morton, b. 5 Feb 1966, Asheboro, North Carolina, USA. Legal Asst. *Education:* BA Eng, 1989, Univ of North Carolina, Greensboro. *Appointments:* Eng Tchr, 1990; Office Asst, 1991-92; Legal Asst, 1992-. *Creative Works:* Short story: Sarah's A, 1990. *Memberships:* NAFE; Asheboro Business and Professional Women's Club. *Honours:* Jr Scholar, 1987, Dean's List, 1985-89, Univ N. Carolina; Feere Grant Recipient, 1985; Asheboro Chamber of Commerce Short Story Contest Winner, 1990. *Hobbies:* Cross stich;

Collecting and reading classical literature; Writing short stories and poetry; Researching family genealogy. *Address:* 588 Revelle Trail, Asheboro, NC 27203, USA. 138.

SMITH Guy Thornton, b. 21 July 1923, London, Eng. Indep Aviation Cons. m. (1) Gwynneth Fishlock, 26 May 1962, (2) Charmain Whitby, 17 Dec 1988, 3 d. *Education:* BSc, 1st class hons, 1944; AKC. *Appointments:* Bristol Aeroplane Co Engine Div, 1945-60; Sales Mgr, Bristol Siddeley, 1960-66; Chief Engr Future Proj 1966-69, Mktng Dir 1969-74, European Dir 1974- 81, Pub Affairs Dir 1981-83, Rolls Royce. *Publications:* Papers in Aviation publs. *Membership:* FRAeS. *Hobbies:* Music; Gardening. *Address:* Chinnock House, Middle Chinnock, Crewkerne, Somerset TA18 7PN, England. 43, 91.

SMITH Hamilton, b. 27 Apr 1934, Stirling, Scotland. Prof. m. Jacqueline Ann Spittal, 14 May 1962. *Education:* BSc 1952-56, PhD 1956- 60, Glasgow Univ. *Appointments:* Rsch Asst, Greater Glasgow Hlth Bd, 1956-60; MRC Rsch Fellow 1960-63, Special Rsch Fellow 1963-64, Lectr, Sr Lectr 1964-84, Reader 1984-87, Titular Prof 1987-, Glasgow Univ. *Publications:* Author of over 100 articles, chapts, reviews. *Memberships:* FRSC; FRCPath; FRSE; Brit Acad of Forensic Scis; The Medico-Legal Soc; The Forensic Sci Soc; The Brit Toxicology Soc; Provisional, Am Acad of Forensic Scis. *Hobbies:* Gardening, Greenhouse; Model railway; Stamps; Golf. *Address:* Department of Forensic Medicine & Science, Glasgow University, Glasgow G12 8QQ, Scotland.

SMITH Henry Sidney, b. 14 June 1928, London, Eng. Prof. m. Hazel Flory Leeper, 18 May 1961, dec 1991. *Education:* BA 1949-53, MA 1953, Fellow 1955-63, Christ's Coll, Cambridge; DLitt, Univ of London. *Appointments:* Asst Lectr in Egyptology 1954-59, Lectr 1959-63, Cambridge Univ; Reader in Egyptian Archaeology 1963-70, Edwards Prof of Egyptology 1970-86, Emeritus 1986-, Univ Coll London. *Publications:* EES Archaeological Survey of NUBIA, 1961; A Visit to Ancient Egypt, 1974; The Fortress of Buhen, vol I 1976, vol II 1979; Saqqara Demotic Papyri, vol I (w W J Tait), 1985; The Anubieion at Saqqara, vol I (w D G Jeffreys), 1989. *Membership:* Field Dir 1971-88, Egypt Exploration Soc. *Honours:* FBA, 1985; Corres Mbr, Deutsches Archaologischei Inst. *Address:* Ailwyn House, High Street, Upwood, Huntingdon, Cambs PE17 1QE, England. 1, 43.

SMITH Ivo, b. 31 May 1931, Lincoln, Lincs, Eng. Cons Surg. m. Janet Twyman, 17 Feb 1962, 2 s, 1 d. *Education:* BA 1954, MA 1960; FRCS 1960; MChir 1965. *Appointments:* Cons Surg, Lowesham & N Southwark Hlth Auth, 1969; Surg Tutor, Guy's Hosp, London; Tchr in Surg, Univ of London. *Publications:* Author of lectures & papers on Diseases of the Breast and the Breast in Art. *Memberships:* FRSM; Fellow, Hunterian Soc; Fellow, Assn of Surgs of GB and Ireland. *Hobbies:* Family; Fishing; Agriculture. *Address:* 100 Harley Street, London W1N 1AF, England.

SMITH Jeffrey Alan, b. 25 Jan 1958, Valparaiso, IN, USA. Lectr. *Education:* BA w High Distinction, Valparaiso Univ, 1980; MA, Univ of Chicago, 1981; MFA, UCLA. *Appointments:* Lectr, Univ of IL, Chicago, 1981-82; Cons, News Election Serv & CBS-TV, 1982-84; Writer, Dir, Canal Cafe Prods, London, 1985-87; Instr, Bowling Green State Univ, 1986-87; Lectr, UCLA, 1987-. *Creative works:* Dir, Newsrevue, 1985; Writer, Dir, But NOOOOO! - The John Belushi Musical, 1986; Unthinking the Unthinkable: Nucler Weapons & Western Culture (author), 1989; Measure for Measure, Lysistrata, Othello (contemporary adaptations), 1990. *Memberships:* Am Fedn of Tchrs; Brit Actors Equity. *Honours:* Just Fndn Journalism Scholarship, 1976; Danforth Grad Fellowship, Honourable Mention, 1980; Patricia Erdoss Maxwell Fellowship, Univ of Chicago, 1980; Fulbright Fellowship to the UK, 1984. *Hobbies:*

Baseball; Softball; Cartooning; Graphic design. *Address:* UCLA Writing Programmes, 371 Kinsey Hall, 405 Hilgard Avenue, Los Angeles, CA 90024, USA. 30.

SMITH Noel Leslie, b. 22 Dec 1929, Otautau, Southland, New Zealand. Retired Secondary School Principal. m. Patricia Louise Stroud, 1958, dec. 1970, 3 d. *Education:* Dip Tchng, Dunedin Tchrs Coll; BA, Educ, Otago Univ; MA (Hons), Geog, Dip Ed, Vic Univ, Wellington. *Appointments:* Asst Tchr, Riverton Dist HS (now Aparima Coll), 1948; Asst Tchr, Rotorua HS; Asst Tchr, Dept Hd, Hutt Valley HS, 1950-67; NZ Army Cadet Force (rtd/rank Maj),1950-69; Dpty Prin, Prin, Freyberg HS, Palmerston N, 1968-91. *Publications:* Stokes Valley 1840-1965: The Change from Rural to Urban; The Benefits of Second Year Study on NZ School Certificate Students. *Memberships include:* Postprimary Tchrs Assn; Nat Prins Advsry Comm; Inst Educl Rsch; Palmerston N Tchrs Coll Coun; Rotary Int; Pres, Lower Hutt Athletic Club; Sec, Hutt Rugby Club; Pres, Patron, Freyberg Old Boys Rugby Club; Pres, Manawata Rugby Union, 1970, 1981; NZ Second Schools Rugby Coun. *Honours:* Efficiency Decoration, 1972; Queen's NZ Commemoration Medal, 1990. *Hobbies include:* Sport; Sports administration. *Address:* 373 Albert St, Palmerston North, New Zealand. 139, 151.

SMITH Philip Henry, b. 24 Nov 1946, Leicester, Leics, Eng. Dir of Treasury. m. Sonia Ioena Moody, 28 Dec 1968, 2 s, 1 d. *Education:* CIPFA, Leicester Reg Coll of Tech; CIPFA, Nottingham Polytech; Fellow, Chartered Inst of Mgmt Accts; Fellow, Assn of Corporate Treasurers; Assoc, Chartered Inst of Pub Fin and Acctcy; FBIM. *Appointments:* Audit Asst, Leics Co Coun, 1964-69; Sr Auditor, Lusaka City Coun, 1969-72; Area Acct, Zambia Dairy Produce Bd, 1972-74; Div Dir, Dorada Holdings Grp Plc, 1974-81; Div Dir, Brooke Tool Engrng Holdings Plc, 1981-83; Grp Treas, ASDA Grp Plc, 1983-91; Dir of Treasury, Nat Power Plc, 1991-. *Memberships:* Prog Comm, ACT; Chmn, Padbury United Football Club; VP, Padbury Cricket Club. *Hobbies:* ssa 00Wine; Gardening; Sports; Travel. *Address:* National Power Plc, Sudbury House, 15 Newgate Street, London EC1A 7AU, England.

SMITH Ray William, b. 1 Mar 1952, Kirksville, MO, USA. Exec Dir. m. Kathryn Diane Marshall Siegrist, 28 Dec 1974, 2 s, 1 d. *Education:* BS, Ctrl MO State Univ, Warrensburg, 1974; MDiv, DMin, Austin Presby Theol Sem, 1978; EdD, Memphis State Univ, 1985. *Appointments:* Pastor, Grace Presby Ch, San Antonio, 1978-81; Pastor, Shaovgrove Presb Ch, Memphis, 1981- 85; Assoc Pastor, First Presby Ch, Spokane, 1986-90; Exec Dir, Christian Counselling Ctr, 1988-; Area Repr, Active Parenting, 1990. *Publications:* Civil Religion in Texas, 1977; prayers in Pulpit Digest, 1983; book reviews in Leadership Mag, 1984; Liturgical Prayers in The Clergy Journ Planning Issues, 1988, 1989, 1990; introduction in Eating Disorders, 1991. *Memberships:* Am Assn for Counselling & Development; Assn for Relig & Value Issues in Counselling; Christian Assn for Psychological Studies; Mental Hlth Clergy; Toastmasters Int; Family Counselling Assn; Hospice of Spokane; Assn of Christian Cnslrs; Chap, Sales and Mktng Execs of Memphis. *Honours:* I Dare You Awd, Danforth Fndn, 1970; Best Boy Scout, Speech Contest to Meet Pres, Boy Scouts of Am, 1971; Kappa Delta Pi, Hon Soc in Am, 1983; Outstng Young Man in Am, Jr C of C, 1984. *Hobbies:* Writing; Reading; Snow skiing; Swimming; Mountain bike riding; Travelling; Conducting tours; Public speaking; Starting a foundation to provide pastoral counselling to those without insurance or funds for therapy; Using personal computers; Training parents. *Address:* Christian Counselling Centre, East 510 Francis Avenue, Spokane, WA 99207, USA. 2, 7, 52, 125, 176.

SMITH Robert Weldon, b. 8 Dec 1912, Boundary Creek, NB, Can. Chmn of the Bd. m. Florence Manuel, 28 July 1940, 2 s, 2 d. *Education:* BSc, Univ of NB, 1934. *Appointments:* Lineman & Substa Operator, Northern Quebec Power Co, 1937-39; Asst Chief Electn, Sladen

Malartic Mines Ltd, Quebec, 1940-42; Royal Can Engrs, 1943-45; Fac Mbr, Dept of Elec Engrng, Univ of NB, 1946-48; Operating Supt, Newfoundland Light & Power Co Ltd, 1949; Design Engr 1949-56, Sr Supvsr, Elec Sect 1956-62, Montreal Engrng Co Ltd;Proj Mgr, Shawmont Ltd, Can Int Dev Agcy Proj, Nigeria, 1971; Gen Mgr 1963-, Dir 1970, VP 1974, Pres 1978-83, Chmn of Bd 1984-, Maritime Elec Co Ltd. *Memberships include:* Assn of Profl Engrs of Prince Edward Isl; Life, IEEE; Life, Past Pres, Charlotteville C of C; Dist Gov, Rotary Int, 1985-86. *Hobbies:* Reading; Music; Woodworking. *Address:* 135 Queen Elizabeth Drive, Charlotteville, PEI, Canada C1A 3B2. 142.

SMITH Roland Hedley, b. 11 Apr 1943, Sheffield, Eng. Mbr of Brit Diplomatic Serv. m. Katherine Jane Lawrence, 27 Feb 1971, 2 d. *Education:* BA 1st class hons, 1965; MA, 1981. *Appointments:* Mbr of Diplomatic Serv 1967-: 3rd Sec, Foreign Off 1967; 2nd Sec, Moscow, 1969; 2nd, 1st Sec, UKDEL NATO, Brussels, 1971; 1st Sec FCO, 1974; 1st Sec, Cultural Attache, Moscow, 1978; FCO, 1980; Attached to Int Inst for Strategic Studies, 1983; Pol Advsr, Hd of Chancery, Brit Mil Govt, Berlin, 1984; Dep Hd of Sci, Energy & Nuclear Dept, FCO, 1988; Hd of Non-Proliferation & Def Dept, FCO, 1990. *Publication:* Soviet Policy Toward West Germany, 1985. *Hobby:* Music. *Address:* c/o Foreign & Commonwealth Office, London SW1A 2AN, England. 1.

SMITH Stuart Henry Byers, b. 29 Aug 1945, Montreal, Quebec, Can. Bus Exec. m. Wendy Patricia Burk, 27 June 1968, 1 s, 2 d. *Education:* BA, Univ of Ont, 1969; CA, Univ of Toronto, 1972. *Appointments:* Pres, Shipp Corp Ltd, Mississauga, 1972-89; Exec VP, Ops & Dev, Oxford Dev Grp Inc, Pres, Oxford Properties Inc, 1989-. *Memberships:* Dir: Appleby Coll; Halton Conserv Assn; Jr Achmt of Can; Past Chmn, Mississauga Hosp; Past Chmn, Urban Dev Inst of Ont & Can; Advsr, Sheridan Coll Nursing; Can Inst of Chartered Accts; Acad Acctng Assn; Urban Land Inst (US). *Honour:* Mississauga Young Citizen of the Yr. *Hobbies:* Skiing; Boating; Golf. *Address:* Oxford Development Group Inc, 120 Adelaide Street West, Suite 1700, Toronto, Ontario, Canada M5H 1T1. 142.

SMITH William Finch, b. 6 Apr 1916, Croydon, Eng. Ret'd Cons Engr. m. Theresa Edith Charlwood, 30 June 1941, 2 s. *Education:* Borough Polytech, 1937-38; Croydon Polytech, 1945-52. *Appointments:* Foxboro Yoxal Indl Instruments Mfr, 1938; Made a Structural Engr by F L Samuely: Hatfield Tech Coll & Sch, 1948; St Clements Danes & Burlington Sch, 1953; 6 No 18 storey Blocks of Flats, Southwark, London, 1955; Ptnr 1956; Biochem Bldg, Cambridge Univ, 1957; Univ Coll Lib, Dublin, 1961; Tivoli Flat, Birmingham, 1962; Shopping Precinct, Manders Paints, Wolverhampton, 1964; 16 storey Brick Bldg for the Army at Beaconsfield, 1968; 150 foot span Entrance Bridge, Office Block & Factory for WD & HO Wills, Hartcliffe, Bristol, 1969; Albany Hotel, Glasgow, 1970; Eldon Sq Shopping Precinct, Newcastle, 1970; Banks at Jeddah, Damman & Ryad for Sama Suade Arabia, 1974; Shopping Precinct, Harlow, 1978; Housing in Kuwait, 1978; Wakefield Shopping Precinct, 1980. *Publications:* Load Bearing Brickwork, 1968; Cores, Cubes & Specified Strength of Concrete, 1974; The Hartcliffe Project (jt paper), 1976. *Memberships:* MIStructE, 1959; F Welding Inst, 1959; FIStructE, 1964; MICE, 1969; FICE, 1972. *Hobbies:* Music; Pets; Gardening; Photography. *Address:* Beech House, Stonestile Lane, Westfield, Hastings, East Sussex TN35 4PE, England.

SMITH Wycliffe Dalton, b. 30 Sept 1947, Jamaica, W Indies. Graphic Designer. m. Yasmin, 22 Mar 1975, 1 s, 2 d. *Education: (1)George Brown Coll, 1973; Ryerson Polytech Inst, 1974. Appointments:* Retail Drug Co, 1973-74; Maclean Hunter Pubing,1975-81; Holt Rinehart & Winston, 1981-84; The Young Naturalist Fndn, 1984-89; Wycliffe Smith Design Off, 1989-. *Creative works:* Designed many books incl Educl and

Trade/Mass Market Books for adult and childrens market. *Memberships:* The Art Dirs Club of Toronto; Waterfront Racquet and Tennis Club; Wychwood Tennis Club. *Honours:* K R Wilson Awd for Bus Malazorts,1979; 10 Merit Awds 1980- 89, Silver Awd (Book Design) 1989, Art Dirs Club of Toronto; 6 Awds for Excellence in Design, Educl Press Assn of Am, 1984-89; 2 Merit Awds, Book Design Alcium Citations, 1989. *Hobbies:* Tennis; Architecture and furniture design; Reading. *Address:* 56 The Esplanade, Suite 301, Toronto, Ontario, Canada M5E 1AV. 142.

SMITH-CARINGTON John Hanbury (Wg Cmdr), b. 26 Oct 1921, Manchester, Eng. Ret'd Eing Cmdr; Ret'd Red Cross Dir. m. Noreen O'Hagan-Ward, 27 Sept 1951, 1 d. *Education:* Oriel Coll, Oxon, 1939-41; RAF Staff Coll, 1956. *Appointments:* RAF Pilot, 1941-72; OC No 98 Squadron, RAF 1953-56; Asst Air Attache, Poland, 1957-59; Mil & Air Attache, Denmark, 1965- 68; Insp of Serv Attache, 1970-72; Dir, Leics Red Cross, 1972-87. *Publications:* Various publs on local hist. *Memberships include:* Chmn of Trustees, Lord Carington Charity, 1946-; VP, Lecs Wildfowlers Asn, 1952-; Chmn, Gaddesby Parish Coun, 1972-; Leics Country Landowners Comm 1973-, Ctrl Coun Mbr 1985-; RAF Selected Mbr, Leics Territorial Assn, 1975-; Chmn, East Midlands Heraldry Soc, 1980-; Trustee, Tobias Rustat's Charity, 1982-. *Honours:* Mention in Dispatches, 1945; Queens Commendation for Valuable Serv in Air, 1952; Air Force Class, 1953; Dpty Lt of Leics, 1972-; High Sheriff of Leics, 1982-83; Red Cross Badge of Hon for Disting Serv, 1986. *Hobbies:* Country pursuits; Local history; Heraldry; Photography. *Address:* Ashby Folville Lodge, Nr Melton Mowbray, Leicestershire LE14 2TE, England. 41, 43.

SMITHERS Alan George, b. 20 May 1938, London, Eng. Prof. m. Angela Grace Wykes, 27 Aug 1962, 2 d. *Education:* BSc 1st class hons, London, 1959; PhD, London, 1966; MSc, Bradford, 1973; PhD, Bradford, 1974; MEd, Manchester, 1981; Chartered Psychologist, 1988. *Appointments:* Lectr in Biology, Coll of S Mark and S John, 1962-64; Lectr in Bot, Birkbeck Coll, Unif of London, 1964-67; Rsch Fellow in Educ 1967-69, Sr Lectr in Educ 1969-76, Univ of Bradford; Prof of Educ 1976-, Hd of Dept 1977-80, 1983-85, Univ of Manchester. *Publications include:* Sandwich Courses: An Integrated Education?, 1976; The Progress of Mature Students (w A Griffin), 1986; The Growth of Mixed A Levels (w P Robinson), 1988; The Shortage of Malthematics and Physics Teachers (w P Robinson), 1988; Increasing Participation in Higher Education (w P Robinson), 1989; Graduates in the Police Service (w S Hill, G Silvester), 1990; Teacher Provision in the Sciences (w P Robinson), 1990; Trends in Science and Technology Manpower Demands and Mobilities (w P Robinson), 1990; Gender Primary Schools and the National Curriculum (w P Zientek), 1991; The Vocational Route into Higher Education, 1991. *Memberships:* BPsS; SRHE. *Honours:* FSRHE, 1986; FRSA, 1991; Prof in Ind, BP, 1991. *Hobbies:* Theatre; Walking. *Address:* School of Education, University of Manchester, Manchester M13 9PL, England.

SMITHSON Peter Denham, b. 18 Sept 1923, Stockton on Tees, Eng. Archt. m. Alison Margaret Gill, 18 Aug 1949, 1 s, 2 d. *Education:* Dip Arch (Dist), Dublin. *Appointments:* TTA, London Co Coun, 1949; Archt in Pvt Pract, 1950-. *Creative works:* Buildings; Books; Publs; Paintings. *Address:* Cato Lodge, 24 Gilston Road, London SW10 9SR, England.

SMRCKA Antonin Klement Josef, b. 17 June 1931, Humpolec, Czech. Int Educl Cons; Admnstr; Mgr. m. Solanges Madeleine Gabrielle Domerson, 28 June 1958, 1 d. *Education:* BS 1957, BA 1967, Concordia Univ, Montreal, Can; Dip in Educ, McGill Univ, Montreal, 1971; PhD 1978, Cert of Educl Special Admin 1985, Univ of NM, USA; Certified Tchr, Certified Admnstr, NM, Quebec. *Appointments:* St Mktng Analyst, Allied Chem Co, Montreal, Can, 1953- 58; Owner, Profl Mgmt Srvs,

Quebec, 1963-; Natural Scis Coord, Tchr, Vaudreuil HS, Quebec, 1968-73; Tchr, Social Scis Supvsr, Plus X HS, Albuquerque, NM, USA, 1973-75; Instr, Educl Fndn, Univ of NM, Albuquerque, 1975-78; Asst to Pres, Planning and Grants Admnstr, Asst Prof, Univ of Albuquerque, 1978-84; Cons, PMS, Albuquerque, 1981-; VP, Bus Affairs, Coll of Santa Fe, NM, 1984-86; Exec VP 1985-89, Pres 1989-, AULC, Washington DC. *Publications:* Weekend column, Czechoslovak Daily Herald, Chicago, USA. *Memberships:* VP, Bd of Trustees, Dorion Gdn Community Coun, Quebec, 1961; Pres, Bd of Dir, Southwest Maternity Ctr Inc, Albuquerque, 1975; Sec, Treas, Bd of Trustees, Am Univ of Les Cayes, Haiti, 1983-89; Ed Staff, Czech Daily Herald; Hon Mbr, Ecole des Hautes Commerciales et Industrie, Port-au-Prince, Haiti; Chem Inst of Can; Can Soc for Chem Engrs; Emeritus Mbr, Am Assn of Univ Profs; Assn for Curric Dev; Phi Delta Kappa. *Hobbies:* History, strategy and creativity; Developmental process in human endeavours. *Address:* 1234 Massachusetts Avenue NW, Suite 823, Washington DC, WA 20005, USA. 9.

SNAYDON Roy William, b. 14 Apr 1933, East Coker. Univ Reader. m. Rita Anne, 3 Apr 1956, 2 s, 1 d. *Education:* BSc 1951-55, PhD 1957-60, Univ Coll of N Wales. *Appointments:* Lectr 1960-78, Reader 1978-, Reading Univ; Rsch Scientist, CSIRO, Aust, 1964-67. *Publication:* Managed Grasslands, 1987. *Membership:* Hon Treas 1969-73, Brit Ecological Soc. *Hobbies:* Choral singing; Walking. *Address:* Agricultural Botany Department, University of Reading, Reading RG6 2AS, England.

SNEADE Barbara Herbert, b. 15 Nov 1947, Altoona, PA, USA. Dir. m. Edward J Sneade, 18 Jan 1969, 2 d. *Education:* BA, Bridgewater Coll, 1969; MBA, Nova Univ, 1985. *Appointments:* Rsch Assoc, Am Tobacco Co, 1969-71; Tchr, Envir Coord, Lee Co Schs, 1971-73, 1977-80; Fdr, Dir, Lee Co Forensic Lab, 1973-77; Dir, Rsch & Dev, HF Scientific Inc, 1980-. *Publications:* Various tech papers in chem. *Memberships:* ACS; Am Assn of Clin Chem; Am Soc for Quality Control; Chairperson 1988-90, Lee Co Schs Advsry Comm. *Honour:* Nat Dean's List, 1984, 1985. *Hobbies:* Reading; Swimming; Skating; Cycling; Hiking. *Address:* H F Scientific Inc, 3170 Metro Parkway, Fort Myers, FL 33916, USA. 7.

SNEATH Christopher George, b. 27 June 1933, London, Eng. Chartered Acct. m. Patricia Lesley Spinks, 12 May 1962, 1 s, 1 d. *Appointments:* Joined 1958, Appointed Ptnr 1971-, Nd Mbr 1978-, KPMG Peat Marwick; Dpty Sec-Gen, Peat Marwick Int, 1978-80. *Publication:* Acquisitions in the US (co-author), 1989. *Memberships:* Receiver- Gen, Order of St John; Bd Mbr, Chmn of UK Comm, Brit-Am C of C; Gov, Queenswood Sch; Hon Treas, Saracens Rugby Club; Ethics Comm, ICA. *Hobbies:* KStJ. *Hobbies:* Cricket; Rugby; Motor cars (Lotus's). *Address:* 109 High Street, London N14 6BP, England.

SNOOK Paul Robert, b. 6 Apr 1954, Sheffield, Eng. Insolvency Practitioner. m. Victoria Marie Sadler, 8 Oct 1988, 1 d. *Education:* LLB Hons, London Sch of Econ(s) & Pol Sci, 1972-75. *Appointments:* Keeble Hawsons (Solicitors), 1980-84; Sr Mgr, Cork Gulby, 1984-87; Prin, Touche Ross, 1987-. *Publication:* Credition Rights in Insolvency, 1988. *Membership:* MICM. *Hobbies:* Reading; Shooting; Fishing; Golf. *Address:* Touche Ross, Friary Court, Crutched Friary, London EC3N 2NP, England.

SNOW Helen Foster, b. 21 Sept 1907, USA. Author; Rschr. *Education:* Hon DLitt, 1981. *Appointments:* Corres Scripps, Canfield League, Seattle, 1931; Freelance Journalist for Articles; Peking Corres, China Weekly Review, Shanghai, 1935-37; Book Reviewed for Saturday Review of Lit, 1941-46; Self-Publr, Bookmark Press Ltd. *Publications include:* Fables and Parables, 1952; Ancestor Hunting, 1954; The Christopher Foster Family History; The Land Beyond The Kuttawoo: The

Madison Story, 1974; The Saybrook Story, from 1619 in England, 1978; My China Years, 1984; Author of 7 trade books of travel and history. *Memberships include:* Fdr w E Snow & R Alley, Chinese Indl Coop Movement, Shanghai, 1938; Soc of Women Geogs, 1939-; Vice Chmn, Nat Am Comm in Aid of Chinese Indl Coops; Initiated Am Comm for Indl Coops for third world, 1981. *Honours include:* Lived and worked in China and the East with E Snow, 1931-40; Nominated for the Nobel Prize for Peace, 1981; 6 Hon Mentions, World of Poetry Contests, 1989-90. *Hobby:* Wildlife preservation. *Address:* 148 Mungertown Road, Madison, CT 06443, USA. 5, 6, 30, 51, 62.

SNOW Peter John, b. 20 Apr 1938, Dublin. TV Presenter; Reporter. m. (1) 24 Sept 1964, (2) 15 May 1976, 2 s, 3 d. *Education:* Balliol Coll, Oxon, 1958-62. *Appointments:* Newcaster, Reporter, Diplomatic & Def Corres, Election Presenter, Indep TV News, 1962-79; Newsnight Presenter, BBC Elections Presenter, BBC TV, 1979-. *Publications:* Leila's Hijack War, 1970; Hussein, 1972. *Hobbies:* Sailing; Skiing; Model railways. *Address:* c/o BBC TV, Wood Lane, London W12 7RJ, England. 1.

SNOWDEN Alan, b. 14 Dec 1920, London, Eng. Cons Ed. m. Kathleen Baxter, 18 July 1943, 1 s, 1 d. *Education:* Silver Medal, Acad of Music & Dramatic Arts, London, 1970. *Appointments:* RAF Signal Security Press, 1939-46; The Daily Sketch, 1947-61; The Daily Telegraph, 1961-86; Ed, The Magic Circular Mag, 1972-90. *Contributions to:* Brit & Am Mags. *Memberships:* Chmn, S Area Assn of Brit Motor Clubs; Sec, The Nat Press Automobile Assn; Assoc Comm & Gen Coun, RAC; Life, The United Wards Club of The City of London; Press Off, The League of Safe Drivers. *Honours:* Burma Star 1939-45; Def Medal; Victory Medal; Fellow, World Lit Acad, 1985; Commissioned Col in the State of KY, USA, 1988; Hon VP, Magic Circle, 1990-. *Hobbies:* Travel; Conjuring; Photography; Automobilia. *Address:* 5 Folkington Corner, Woodside Park, Finchley, London N12 7BH, England. 3, 182.

SNOWDON Graham Richard, b. 8 Feb 1944, Doncaster, Eng. Journalist. m. Peta Dawn Rawlings, 5 Aug 1967, 1 s, 1 d. *Appointments:* Jr Reporter, Barnsley Chronicle 1960-61, Yorkshire Evening News 1961-63; Family Sports Agcy, Doncaster, 1963-64; Competitions Press Off, RAC Motor Sport Div, London, 1964-66; Northern Press Off, RAC Manchester, 1966-70; Freelance Sports Journalist, 1970- (Cycling Corres, The Guardian and Press Assn, Contbr to Daily Telegraph as Graham Richards); Ptnr w Peta Snowdon, Snowdon Sports Ed, 1970-; Cons, Guinness Book of Records, 1971-. *Membership:* Hon Pro, Rotary Club of Hallam, Sheffield. *Honour:* Mary Daraux Prize for French, Doncaster GS, 1958. *Hobbies:* Food and Drink; Walking; Travelling; Motoring; Autonumerology. *Address:* Snowdon Sports Editorial, PO Box 154, Sheffield S10 4BW, England.

SNOWMAN (Michael) Nicholas, b. 18 Mar 1944. Gen Dir. m. Margo Michelle Rouard, 1983, 1 s. *Education:* BA Hons, Magdalene Coll, Cambridge. *Appointments:* Asst to Hd of Music Staff, Glyndebourne Fest, 1967-69; Co-Fdr, Gen Mgr, London Sinfonietta, 1968-72; Admnstr, Music Th Ensemble, 1968-71; Artistic Dir, IRCAM, Ctr d'Art et de Culture Georges Pompidou, 1972-86; Co-Fdr, Artistic Advsr, Ensemble InterContemporain, 1975-; Mbr, Music Comm, Venice Biennale, 1979-86; Artistic Dir, Projs in:Stravinsky 1980, Webern 1981, Boulez 1983, Fest d'Automne de Paris; Prog Cons, Cite de la Musique, La Villette, Paris, 1991-. *Publications:* The Best of Granta (ed), 1967; The Contemporary Composers(series ed), 1982-; Papers and articles on music, opera, cultural policy. *Honours:* Off, l'Ordre des Arts et Lettres, 1990 (Chevalier 1985); Polish Order of Cultural Merit, 1990. *Hobbies:* Films; Eating; Spy novels. *Address:* South Bank Centre, Royal Festival Hall, London SE1 8XX, England.

SNOWMAN Daniel, b. 4 Nov 1938, London, Eng. 2 children. *Education:* Double First Class Hons, Cambridge Univ, 1958-61; MA, Cornell Univ, USA, 1961-63. *Appointments:* Lectr in Hist & Am Studies, Univ of Sussex, 1963-67; BBC Prodr 1967-, currently Chief Prodr, BBC Radio Features; Vis Prof of Hist, CA State Coll, 1972-73. *Creative works:* Major BBC prods incl: Black Power, 1968; What Is News?, 1970; Whatever Happened to Equality?, 1974; New York & Chicago: Two Bicentennial Portraits, 1976; Forty Years On: How Young Europeans see World War II, 1979; Morality, 1981; Enjoying Opera, Conversations with Domingo, 1983; Castro's Cuba, Paco Pena in Cordoba, The Making of a Quartet, 1986; Hallelujah - The Chorus!, Songs My Mother Taught Me, Travel Sickness, Maps of the Mind, 1990; Pastime With Good Company, 1991. *Publications incl:* Eleanor Roosevelt, 1970; Kissing Cousins: An Interpretation of British and American Culture 1945-75, 1977, published in USA as Britain and America: An Interpretation of Their Culture, 1977; Beyond the Tunnel of History, 1989; Frozen Futures, 1993. Chapts in: The British General Election of 1966, 1966; Since 1945: Aspect of Contemporary World History (ed), 1966, 1971; The American Destiny: An Illustrated Bicentennial History of the United States (ed), 1976; Introduction to American Studies (ed), 1981. *Contributions to:* US newspapers and journs and Brit papers. *Membership:* London Phil Choir, 1967-, former Chmn. *Address:* 47 Wood Lane, Highgate, London N6 5UD, England.

SNUGGS Olive, b. 26 Nov 1924, Coventry, Eng. Poet; Freelance Writer. m. Frederick Eric Smuggs, 29 Jan 1944, 1 s, 4 d. *Appointments:* Keep Fit Instr incl Dance (Creative) with Disabled, 1972-85; Creative Writing W/Shops, 1985-. *Publications:* Ollie's Overtures, vols 1 & 2, 1985; Reflections in Cameo, 1986; I Came a Migrant, 1990. *Memberships:* Melbourne Poetry Soc; Fellowship, Aust Writers, SA; Aust Writers Profl Servs; SA Writers Ctr; World Poetry Soc; VP, Comm Mbr, 1972-85, SA Keep Fit Assn; Univ Third Age. Inclusion in: Anthology Aust Poetry 1987, SAFAW Sunlight & Shadows 1987-88, Beneath Sth Cross Book 1 & 2 1988, New Directions 1990, Sawsbury Speaks 1991, Social Images 1891-1991; 7th Poetry Aust Medallion, 1988; World Poetry Soc, 1988-91; Lib Comps for Poetry 1st, 1989-90; 1st Decade Poetry Day Medallion, 1991. *Hobbies:* Bush walking; Reading; Writing all forms; Poetry; S stories; Plays; Patchwork. *Address:* 6 Jacaranda Drive, Salisbury East, SA 5109, Australia.

SOBUTAY Yasar, b. 11 Apr 1947, Antalya, Turkey. Owner; Pres. m. 2 Dec 1979, 1 s. *Appointments:* Tourism Trng in Local Travel Agcy, 1959- 64; Estab Pamfilya Travel Agcy, pioneered first full-scale tourism org on Turkish Med-coast with world-wide connections. *Publications:* Many interviews with trade mags and newspapers. *Memberships:* Pres,Kaleici Rotary Club; VP, Skal Club. *Honours:* for highest foreign currency turnover in the travel ind, 1984, 1985, 1986, 1988, 1989. *Hobby:* Football. *Address:* Pamfilya Travel Agency, 30 Agustos Cad No 57, PO Box 117, 07100 Antalya, Turkey. 104.

SOCHOS Demetre Basile, b. 1 Jan 1921, Athens, Greece. Ret'd. *Education:* Degree, Archtl Engrng, Athens Polytech,Greece, 1950; Matric exam Hermods, NKI Inst Sch of Mech Engrng, 1969; Intermediate Proficiency in Eng, Univ of Cambridge, Eng,. 1975. *Appointments:* Asst Archt, Bank of Greece, Tech Servs, 1951-53; Asst Archtl Draughtsman, Swedish Archts in Sweden, 1954-57, 1959-66; Bur of Town Planning, Rhodes, Greece, 1957-58; Workshop Employee, Sweden, 1966-85. *Memberships:* Assn of Wkrs in the Ind of Metals, Sweden; Svensk Grekiska Sallskapet; Svenska Ateninstitutets Vanner; Fellow, Int Bio Assn, Cambridge; Hemvarnsveteran, Sweden. *Honours:* Simframjandet Simborgarmarket; Golden Medal, Roslagsmarschen, Sweden; Golden Serv Medal, Veteran Serv Medal, Hemvarnet, Swedish Army. *Hobbies:* Walking tours; Photography; Reading scientific literature; Swimming.

Address: Vattugatan 9 3rd Stair, S-17234 Sundbyberg 1, Sweden. 1, 52.

SOCOLOV Boris, b. 30 Dec 1930, Moscow, Russia. Geologist. m. Yulia Socolova, 30 Mar 1957, 1 s, 1 d. *Education:* Geology Dept, Moscow State Univ, 1949-54; Dr, 1978. *Appointments include:* Hd, Oil and Gas Dev project, Pakistan, 1963-65; Sr Scientist, 1966, Assoc Prof, 1967, Prof, 1980, Geology Dept, Moscow State Univ. *Publications:* Oil and Gas- Bearing Basins of the World, 1965; Geology Review of Pakistan, 1971; Regional Oil and Gas Generating Basis, 1977; 500 other papers and books. *Memberships:* Sci Couns, Moscow Geologists Union, VNIGNI and Acad Scis; Assn Oil Geology Educ; Edit Coun, Izvestia of the Academy of Sciences; Academician, Acad Natural Scis. *Honours:* Medals: For Labour Merit; For Courageous Labour; Veteran of Labour. *Hobby:* Travel. *Address:* Leninski pr 123/1, Fl 592, 117513 Moscow, Russia.

SODING Paul H, b. 20 Feb 1933, Dresden, Germany. Physicist. m. Regine Soding, 19 May 1961, 3 s, 1 d. *Education:* Dip Phys, 1960; PhD, Phys 1964. *Appointments:* Univ of Hamburg, 1960-66; Lawrence Berkeley Lab, 1966-68; Deutsches Elektronen-synchrotron DESY, 1969-, Dir, Rsch Div 1982-; Prof of Experimental Phys, Univ of Hamburg, 1974-. *Publications:* Ali and Soding, High Energy Electron Position Physics, 1988; Author of 100 publns in Phys letters, Phys Rev letters, Nucl Phys, Phys Rev. *Memberships:* German Phys Soc; Fellow, Am Phys Soc; Asst Ed, Zeitschrift f physik C; Asst Ed, Nuclear Phys B; Asst Ed, Reports on Progress in Phys. *Address:* Deutsches Elektronen-synchrotron DESY, Notkestrasse 85, D-2000 Hamburg 52, Germany.

SODNOM Namsrain, b. 25 May 1923, Mongolia. Scientist; Nuclear Physicist; Edr. m. Genden Tserendulam, 1 Aug 1945, 2 s, 3 d. *Education:* PhD, Moscow Univ, 1953. *Appointments:* Prof 1946-48, 1953- 56, Rector 1959-67, 1973-82, Mongolia State Univ, Ulan Bator; Rschr 1956-59, Vice Dir 1967-73, Jt Inst for Nuclear Rsch, Dubna; Chmn, State Comm of Higher Educ of Mongolia, 1980-82; Rschr, 1982-86; Pres, Acad of Scis of Mongolia, 1987-91; Team Ldr in Applied Phys, Inst of Phys & Tech, Acad of Scis, 1991. *Publications:* Author of over 100 papers on nuclear spectroscopy & activation anlaysis, higher educl problems; Univ textbooks on mechs and optics; Popular scientific articles. *Memberships:* Acad of Scis, Mongolia Peoples' Repub; Chmn, Mongol-Japanese Friendship Soc. *Honours:* Red Banner of Labour; Order of the Pole Star; Order of the Friendship of Nations; Various Govt and Educl State Awds. *Hobbies:* Mongolian Language Studies; Foreign Language Studies; Fishing; Reading. *Address:* Institute of Physics and Technology, Ulan Bator, Mongolia. 52.

SOETANTO Kawan, b. 10 Mar 1951, Surabaya. Assoc Prof. m. Jennie Herman, 31 July 1976, 1 s, 2 d. *Education:* BEng 1980, MEng 1982, Tokyo Univ of A & T; Dr Eng, TIT, 1985; Dr Med, Tohoku Univ, 1987. *Appointments:* Rsch Scientist, Toshiba Corp, Japan, 1985-87; Assoc Prof of Biomed, Drexel Univ, 1987-; Adj Prof, Dept of Radiology, TJU, 1989-; Vis Prof, TIT Tokyo, 1989, 1990. *Publications:* 96 journ articles and proceedings, 3 book chapts about Biomed Engrng, Imaging & Measurement. *Memberships:* Sr Mbr, IEEE; Sr Mbr, Am of Ultrasound in Med; Acoustical Soc of Am. *Honours:* Best Rsch Awd, NEC, Computer & Communication Fndn, 1986, 1987; Rsch Awd, Toshiba Corp, Japan, 1986-88; Medal, Asian Fedn of Societies of Ultrasound in Med & Biol, 1987; Outstng Achmt Awds in Med & Academia, Pan Asian Assn of Greater Philadelphia, 1990. *Hobbies:* Table tennis; Badminton; Reading. *Address:* 28 Berkeley Road, Broomall, PA 19008, USA.

SOFIANIDOV Dora Piliopovlov, b. 18 Nov 1922, Chios. Beautician. m. Panteis, 18 Jan 1948, 2 s. *Education:* Dip, Univ of Beauty, Paris; Dip, Green Sch of Beauty,

Athens. *Career:* Freelance Journalist, 1962-. *Publications:* My Songs, 1976; Fallen Leaves, 1990. *Contributions to:* Proodos; Chiaui Filologiki Epitheorisi; Chiayi Foni; Eleftheros; Eleftheri Ora; Amarinthiaka Nea. *Memberships:* Korais; Friends of Dromokaitio; Ebat; Lit Soc Panellinia Enosi Logotechnon. *Honours:* Prize of Poetic Games Delfi, Praise of Cultural Agcy Johanesburg; Dip of Intellectual Ctr of Athens, Praise of Newspaper Dimosiografik. *Hobby:* Writing. *Address:* Velissariou str 6, Agios Dimitrios, 173 42 Athens, Greece.

SOFRONITSKAIA Viviana, b. 13 Jan 1960, Moscow, Russia. Organ & Harpsichord Performer. m. Sergei Istomin Khoklov, 22 Nov 1987, 1 d. *Education:* MM 1979-85, DMA 1987-89, Moscow Conservatory. *Career:* Soloist, organ & harpsichord, Belorussian Philharmonic, 1983-89; Freelance organist, harpsichordist, Toronto, 1990-92; Artistic Dir, Acad Concert Series, Toronto. *Creative works:* Radio and TV Performances, Recordings; Fdr, Toronto Baroque Trio; Solo and Chamber Music Performances in Russia, Europe, USA, Can. *Memberships:* Soviet Organist Assn, Moscow; RCO, Can; Early Music Soc, Toronto. *Hobbies:* Reading; Waterskiing. *Address:* 583 Crawford Str, Toronto, Ontario, Canada M6G 3K1.

SOFTIC Nijaz, b. 11 Aug 1920, Prijedor. Prof. m. Muhedinovic Zekija, 15 Aug 1942, 1 d. *Education:* MD, Med Sch, Univ of Belgrade, 1948; DSc, Univ of Zagreb, 1961. *Appointments:* Univ Hosp, Balgrad, 1948-50; Univ Hosp, Sarajevo, 1950-54; Sarengradska Hosp, 1954-58; Dr Jospip Kajfez Hosp, 1958-62; Sch of Pharm and Biochem, 1962. *Publications:* Platelets and Haemostasis-Disorders of Haemostasis, 1986; Haematlogical Methods, 1st ed 1988; General Haematology, 2nd ed 1989. *Membership:* Haematological Soc of Germany, France, Yugoslavia. *Hobbies:* Fishing; Mountaineering. *Address:* Zagreb University, School of Pharmacy and Biochemistry, Institut of Haematology, Ante Kovacica 1/11, Zagreb, Croatia.

SOKOL Ronald Jay, b. 18 July 1950, Chicago, IL, USA. Physn. m. Lori Lubman Sokol, 20 Aug 1989, 1 s. *Education:* BS, Univ of IL, Urbana, 1972; MD, Prtizker Sch of Med, Univ of Chicago, 1976; Pedatric Residency, Univ of CO Med Ctr, 1976-80; Fellowship, Children's Hosp Rsch Fndn, Cincinnati, 1980-83. *Appointments:* Asst Prof of Pediatrics 1983-87, Assoc Prof of Pediatrics 1987-, Univ of CO Sch of Med. *Publications:* 71 med journ articles; 21 book chapts & review articles. *Memberships:* Exec Coun, N Am Soc for Pediatric Gastroenterology and Nutrition; Am Gastroenterological Assn; Soc for Pediatric Rsch; Am Assn for Study of Liver Disease; FAAP; Am Inst of Nutrition; Am Soc for Clin Nutrition; Am Soc for Parenteral and Enteral Nutrition. *Honours:* Phi Beta Kappa, 1969; Phi Kappa Phi, 1971; Alpha Omega Alpha, 1976; FIRST Grant Awd, Nat Inst of Hlth, 1987-92; Mead Johnson Awd for Nutrition Rsch, Am Inst of Nutrition, 1990. *Hobbies:* Hiking; Camping; Skiing; Windsurfing; Basketball; Baseball; Nature literature. *Address:* Department of Pediatric Gastroenterology and Nutrition, Box B290, Chidren's Hospital, 1056 E 19th Avenue, Denver, CO 80218, USA.

SOKOLEWICZ Wojciech Waclaw, b. 27 Mar 1931, Warsaw, Poland. Legal Scholar. m. Wanda Slusarczyk, 20 Dec 1975, 2 s, 1 d. *Education:* LLD 1964, JSD 1968. *Appointments:* Rschr 1963-, Asst 1963, Dpty Dir 1969-74, Hd of Dept 1969, Prof 1974, Inst of Law, Polish Acad of Scis. *Publications include:* Cabinet and Local Govts, 1964; Representation and Administration in Local Govt, 1968; Polish Constitution as Amended in 1976, 1978. *Memberships:* Int Assn of Const Law; Int Assn of Pol Sci. *Honours:* Cross of Merit, 1956; Acad Awd, Polish Acad of Sci, 1971, 1976, 1978; Order, Polonia Restituta, 1977, 1985. *Hobbies:* Reading; Swimming; Walking the dog. *Address:* Krolowej Marysienki 19/106, 02-954 Warsaw, Poland.

SOKOLNICKI Julius Nowina, Count, b. 16 Dec 1920, Pinsk, Poland. Politician. m. 2 s, 3 d. (3) Margaret Throburn, 29 July 1983. *Education:* Hist, Warsaw Univ, 1937-39; Dr of Pols in Arts, Gt China World Univ, 1978; PhD, Acad Int Americana, Mexico, 1979; Docent of Hist, Int Schwabische Univ Friedrich II, 1979. *Appointments include:* Fdr, Polish Nat Revival Movement, 1954; Coun Mbr 1954-71, Coun Vice Chmn 1967-70, Ed Rzeczpospolita 1967-71, Min of Info 1967-70, Min of Home Affairs 1970-71, Presidential Successor 1971, Pres 1972, Repub of Poland in Exile. *Publications include:* Articles in Polish, Eng & French; One of the Fdrs of Ctrl European Coun in NY which incls govts in exile of Albania, Bulgaria, Croatia, Czech, Estonia, Poland and Romania. *Memberships:* Grand Prior for Poland, Sovereign Mil Order of the Temple of Jerusalem, 1978; Advsry Bd, Am Security Coun, 1979; Del of Inst of Heraldique et Genealogieue de France, 1979; VP, London Appreciation Soc, 1981; Fellow, Can Guild of Authors, 1988. *Honours include:* Total of 153 decorations incl: Cross of Valour, 1944; Silver Cross of Virtuti Militari, 1945; Grand Croix de la Victoire, 1948; Grand Cordon of the Order of Polonia Restituta, 1972; Cmdr Merito Commercial Mexico, 1979; Kt of Justice Grand Cross of Sovereign Mil & Hospitalier Order of St John of Jerusalem, 1980; Etoile Civique Medaille d'Or, 1980; Cmdr of the Order of St Sava, 1981; Grand Croix Encouragement Pub, 1982; Hon Citizen of the States of NB, TX & the City of Minneapolis, 1982; Hon Citizen, Baltimore, 1984; Fdr, Ctrl European Coun NY 1986; recognised 18 Feb 1986 by 5 Polish Pol parties in the Underground in Poland as rightful Pres; Order of Besa, 1988; Order of Masaryk, 1987; Grand Master Sovereign Order of St Stanislas. *Address:* Oak Lodge, 42 Cornflower Close, Colchester, Essex CO3 5SE, England.

SOKOLOVSKAJA Zinaida K, b. 5 Nov 1927, USSR. Histn. m. (1) I M Sokolovski, 26 Dec 1963, dec 1982, (2) A A Shakhov, 28 June 1991, 2 stepsons, 1 stepdaughter. *Education:* First Sci Degree, 1953-56; Dr Hist Scis, 1991. *Appointments:* Sci Wkr 1956-61, Lerner Sec 1961-64, Sr Sci Wkr, Lerner Sec of Ed Bd of Acad Book Series Sci-Biograph Literature 1964-, Inst of Hist, Sci & Tech. *Publications include:* Sci Biography of W Struve, 1964; 400 Biographies of Scientists, 1988; Dictionary of Sci Biography (ed). *Memberships include:* Soviet Nat Assn for Hist, Sci & Tech; Consult Mbr, Int Astron Union - Kommission 41, Hist Astron; Sci Coun, Archives of USSR Aad of Scis; Moscow Scis Club. *Honours include:* Medal for Valiant Labour, 1970; Medal, Mikolaj Kopernik, 1974; Medal for Veteran of Labour, 1984; Honoured Cultural Wkr of RSFSR, 1989. *Hobbies:* Travelling; Collecting biographical books about scientists; Knitting; Sewing; Cooking. *Address:* Fl 57, Stroiteley str 9, Moscow 117311, Russia. 138, 152.

SOLAKOV Nedko Mitev, b. 28 Dec 1957, Tcherven Briag, Bulgaria. Artist. m. Svetloslava Nakovska, 23 Sept 1985, 1 s, 1 d. *Education:* Acad of Fine Arts, Sofia, 1975-81; Nat Hoger Inst voor Schone Kunsten, Antwerpen, 1985-86. *Career:* Free-lance Artist 1981-, One Man Shows: Sofia, 1982, 1988; Plovdiv, 1983, 1988; Esslingen, Germany, 1987; Bourgas, 1990. *Creative works:* Selected Group Exhibs: Cagnes Sur Meir, 1984; Sammlung Ludwig, Wien, 1984; Bulgarian Artists of Today, Amsterdam, 1984; Young Bulgarian Artists, Wien, 1985; Kunst im Schloss, Germany, 1986; 5 5, USA, 1986; The City?, Sofia, 1988; Visages, Creahm, Belgium, 1988; The Tower of Babylon, City Group Action, 1989; The Chameleon, The City Grp Action, 1990; The City Utopia, Bonington Gal, Nottingham, 1990; Expressions, Third Eye Ctr, Glasgow, 1990; Budapest Art Expo, 1991; Europe Unknown, Poland, 1991. *Memberships:* Indep Artists Grp, The City Grp, 1986-; New Bulgarian Univ Assn, Sofia, 1990-. *Honours:* Dip, VIth and VIIth Biennial of Humour and Satire in the Arts, Gabrovo, Bulgaria; Dip, III Int Competition for Young Painters, Sofia, 1984; Grand Prix, IV Int Competition for Young Painters, Sofia, 1989. *Hobby:* Reading. *Address:* Mladost I, Bl 91-B, A apt 8, 1797 Sofia, Bulgaria.

SOLANO Carl A, b. 26 Mar 1951, Pittston, PA, USA. Lawyer. m. Nancy M Solano, 28 Nov 1989. *Education:* BS magna cum laude, Pol Sci, Univ of Scranton, 1973; JD cum laude, Villanova Univ Sch of Law, 1976. *Appointments:* Law Clerk to Hon Alfred L Luongo, US Dist Ct, Eastern Dist, PA, 1976-78; Assoc 1978-84, Ptnr 1985-, Schnader, Harrison, Segal & Lewis, Philadelphia. *Memberships:* Am & PA Bar Assns; Justinian Soc; St Thomas More Soc; Pi Gamma Mu. *Honour:* Order of Coif. *Address:* Suite 3600, 1600 Market Street, Philadelphia, PA 19103, USA. 2, 6, 163.

SOLCH Werner Anton, b. 11 July 1938, Karlsbad. Engr; Archt. m. Kyriaki Koutsodonti, 10 May 1964, 1 s, 1 d. *Education:* Dip, Tech Univ, Munchen, 1957-63. *Appointments:* Bayerische Staatsbauverwaltung, Bauamt Tech Univ, Munchen; Landbauamt, Munchen, 1977-. *Creative works:* Author: Orient-Express, 1974, 1980, 1983; Jule Verne's Express, Die legendare Indian Mail Route nach Sudostasien, 1980; Orient Express in Bild, 1986; Kap-Kairo, 1986; Expresszuge im Vorderen Orient, 1989; Transsibirien und Ost-West-Express, 1993; Nord-Sud-Expresszuge - von Skandinavien bis Chile; Europa-Amerika-Australien; World Passenger Airlines of the Prop Age/of the Jet Age. *Membership:* The Community of Interests in Civil Air Transport (Coincat), Hamburg. *Hobbies:* Philosophy; Architecture; History of railways and airlines. *Address:* Leonrodstrasse 31, D-8000 Munchen 19, Germany.

SOLE-ROMEO Luis Alberto, b. 31 Aug 1934, Uruguay. Amb of Uruguay. m. 3 d. (2) Monica Assumpcao de Sole-Ramoe. *Education:* Dr in Law & Social Sci, Univ of Oriental, Repub of Uruguay. *Appointments:* Pres, Nat Assn of Broadcasters, 1971-75; Atty Cnslr of the Govt Exchequer, 1973-84; Dir, Correo de los Viernes, Montevideo, 1981-85; Co-Dir, El Dia, Montevideo, 1985-86; Dir, Maritime and Fluvial Matters Off 1985-87, Legal Diplomatic Counsel 1985, Min of Foreign Affairs; Amb for Uruguay. *Publications:* Basis for an Educational Policy for Private Broadcasting in America, 1971, USA 1976; Uruguayan Laws and Regulations on Broadcasting, 2 vols, 1974; Prevented Control of the Exchequer, 1976; Freedom, Essential for a Cultural Broadcasting, 1977; The Sex of the Angels: Sketches of Freedom, 1978; Articles and essays in newspapers and journs. *Membership:* Exec Comm, World Press Freedom Comm, Washington DC, 1978. *Honour:* Gold Medal, Ethics and Permanent Comm, IAAB for profl ethics and def of freedom of expression, 1975-77. *Hobbies:* Reading; Travelling; Music; Gardening. *Address:* 1 Campden Hill, London W8, England. 1.

SOLENDER Elizabeth Ellen, b. 30 May 1951, Dallas, Texas, USA. Commercial Real Estate Executive. m. Gary L Scott, 25 Nov 1977. *Education:* BA, Emerson Coll, 1973; MA, Purdue Univ, 1975; Licensed TX Real Estate Broker. *Appointments:* Exec Search Cons, Hayman and Hardison, 1976; Mgmt Cons, LWFW Inc, 1977-78; Sr Lectr, Univ Texas, Dallas, 1977-91; Human Resources Cons, Sunoco Energy Dev Co, 1978-80; Manager, Org, Human Resource Dev, Sunmark Exploration Co, 1980-82; Mgr, Employee Rels and Dev, Sur Exploration Co, 1982; Mgr, Human Resources, Domestic Exploration Div, Sun Co, 1983-87; VP, Robert L Solender Inc, 1987-; Pres, Solender/Hall Inc Inc, 1991-. *Publications:* Minimizing the Effect of the Unattractive Client on the Jury (w Ellen K Solender), 1976, reprinted, 1977; How to Give and Receive Feedback (w S H Clayton), 1981; Inquiries and Discoveries: Managing Interviewing Situations, 1984. *Memberships:* Pres, Bd Trustees, Dallas Mus Natural Hist; Pres, Mental Hlth Assn Gtr Dallas; Pres, The Family Place; Co-Chair, Steering Comm, President's Rsch Coun, SWn med School; Chair, Advsry Bd, Lifespan; Bd Dirs, Mental Hlth Assn TX; Co-Chair, Ramses the Gt Exhibit; Prog Comm Chair, Commercial Real Estate Women Dallas; Dallas Assembly. *Honours:* Disting Serv Award, Dallas Jaycees, 1990; Outstanding Young Texan, TX Jaycees, 1990; Extra Mile Award, Dallas Bus and Profl Women's Assn. *Hobbies:* Reading; Walking; Films; Needlepoint.

Address: Solender/Hall Inc, 8300 Douglas Ave, Suite 800, Dallas, TX 75225, USA.

SOLIMAN John Iskandar, b. 24 Sept 1926, Egypt. Int Cons. 1 s, 1 d. *Education:* BSc 1948, MSc 1950, Alexandria Univ; PhD, Univ of London, 1955. *Appointments:* Lectr, Alexandria Univ, Egypt, 1948-61; Sr Sci Off, Brit Iron & Steel Rsch Assn, London, 1961-62; Lectr, Queen Mary Coll, Univ of London, 1962-89; Chn, Int Comms, Europe; Organiser, Int Confs, Europe; Prof, Univ of Rome, 1981-; Vis Prof, Univs in USA, Europe; Cons to Multinat Corps incl: United Technologies, Allen Grp; Dir, Automotive Automation Ltd. *Contribution to:* Articles to many profl journs. *Publications:* Written many papers for presentation at intl conf. *Memberships:* MIMechE; SAE; Annabel's Club. *Address:* 42 Lloyd Park Avenue, Croydon CR0 5SB, England. 52.

SOLINA Franc, b. 31 July 1955, Celje. Univ Prof. *Education:* BS 1979, MS 1982, Univ of Ljubljana; PhD, Univ of PA, 1987. *Appointments:* Post Doc, GRAP Lab, Univ of PA, 1988; Asst Prof of Computer Sci, Univ of Ljubljana, 1988-. *Publications:* Scientific journs and conf proceedings. *Memberships:* IEEE; AAAI. *Honour:* Morris and Dorothy Rubinoff Awd for best PhD dissertation in computer sci, Univ of PA, 1987. *Hobbies:* Skiing; Sailing; Tennis; Photography. *Address:* Vurnikova 3, 61113 Ljubljana, Slovenia.

SOLJAN Antun, b. 1 Dec 1932, Belgrade. Author. m. Nada Mrakovcic, 6 Mar 1955, 2 d. *Education:* Univ of Zagreb. *Career:* Novelist; Playwright; Poet; Transl. *Creative works:* Novels: The Traitors, 1961; A Short Outing, 1965; The Port, 1974; Other People on the Moon, 1978. Short- story collections: Special Envoys, 1957; Ten Short-Stories for my Generation, 1966; Family Dinner, 1975; Croatian Joyce and Other Games, 1989. Plays: The Face, 1963; The Hill, 1964; Galileo's Ascension, 1966; Diocletian's Palace, 1969; Mototor & Tarampesta, 1972; The Romance of Three Loves, 1976; The Man Who Saved the Netherlands, 1983; The Bard, 1985. Poems: The Stone Thrower, 1985. Transl of the Eng & Am Lit. *Membership:* Croatian Acad of Arts and Scis, Zagreb. *Honour:* Prix Futura, Berlin for radio-play, 1985. *Hobby:* Sailing. *Address:* Draskoviceva 12, 41000 Zagreb, Croatia.

SOLOMON Irvin D, b. 20 July 1946, USA. Coll Prof. BS 1971, MA 1973, Edinboro Univ of PA; PhD, Univ of Akron, 1984. *Appointments include:* Adj Instr, African-Am Hist, US Hist, Univ of Ctrl FL, Orlando, 1984-87; Instr, Edison Community Coll, Ft Myers, 1988-; Adj Instr, African-Am Hist, Univ of S FL, 1990-. *Publications include:* Feminism and Black Activism in Contemporary America: An Ideological Assessment, 1989; Is Upward Mobility Possible Without Standard English? (w B L Winsboro), 1990; Standard English vs The American Dream (w B L Winsboro), 1990; Shared Spheres: The Public Policy of Contemporary Feminism and Civil Rights 1991; Black English in the Classroom: The Implications of Rhetoric vs Reality (w B L Winsboro), 1991. *Memberships:* Organisation of Am Histns; Am Histl Assn; Assn for the Study of Afro-Am Life and Hist; Former Pres, Phi Alpha Theta; Phi Delta Kappa. *Honours include:* Cits for Excellence in Writing, The Orlando Sentinel, 1985, 1986, 1987; Edr of the Yr Awd, Columbia Coll, Orlando Naval Trng Ctr, 1985; Co-sponser, Organiser, FL Coll Tchrs of Hist 27th Annual Conf, Ft Myers, 1989. *Hobby:* Travelling. *Address:* Edison Community College, Div of Social Sciences, Ft Myers, FL 33906, USA. 15.

SOLOMON John William, b. 22 Nov 1931, London, Eng. Tobacco Importer. m. (1) Anne Lewis, 25 July 1953, (2) Barbara Clamp, 5 Dec 1972, 3 s. *Appointments:* William P Solomon Ltd (Tobacco Importers) 1951-83, MD 1957-83; Freeman 1960, Liveryman 1962, Ct 1974, Master 1989-90, Worshipful Co of Tobacco Pipe Makers and Tobacco Blenders; Chmn 1962-64, VP 1975-83, Pres 1983-, The Croquet Assn; MD, John Solomon Inc

Ltd, 1983-. *Publication:* Croquet, 1966, 1983, 1989. *Memberships:* Tobacco Trade Benevolent Assn 1957-80, Hon Treas 1970-76, Vice Chmn 1976-82, VP 1980-, Chmn 1982-86; Chmn 1976-80, 1980-84, 1990-, Imported Tobacco Prods Advsry Coun. *Honours:* Croquet: 10 GB Open Champs; 10 GB Mens Champs; 10 GB Open Double Champs; 1 GB Mixed Double Champs; 9 Pres's Cup Winners; 2 NZ Open Singles Champs; 2 NZ Open Doubles Champs; 4 times Champion of Champions. *Hobbies:* Music; Acting; Croquet; Golf. *Address:* Pipersfield, Rusper Road, Newdigate, Dorking RH5 5BX, England.

SOLOMON Robert Douglas, b. 28 Aug 1917, Delaran, WI, USA. Physn; Scientist. m. 4 Apr 1943, 2 s, 2 d. *Education:* BS, Univ of Chicago, 1936-38; MD, Johns Hopkins, 1938-42. *Appointments:* Assoc Dir, Terre Haute Med Lab, 1950-54; Assoc Dir, Med Lab, Sindi Hosp, Balto, 1954-60; Dir, Pothol Res City of Hope, 1960-67; Lab Dir, Dr's Hosp, 1967-75; Dir, Med Lab, Edgewater Hosp, 1976; Prof of Path, Univ of MO, 1976-77; Prof of Path, SUNY, 1978-88. *Publications:* Author of 45 scientific articles dealing with nutrition in cancer. *Memberships:* FACP; FRSM; Am Soc of Clin Pathologists; Int Acad of Pathologists; ACS; Am Assn of Clin Scientists. *Honours:* Phi Beta Kappa, 1938; Sigma Xi, 1955. *Hobbies:* Biography in Science; Boating; Fishing; Astronomy. *Address:* 113 S Belvedere Drive, Hampstead, NC 28443, USA. 7, 15, 143.

SOLTYSIK Andrzej Karol, b. 21 May 1945, Dombrowa Gornicza, Poland. Film Production Manager. m. Alina Janina Wozniakowska, 1 Aug 1970, 2 s. *Education:* MEcon, HS Planning and Stats, Warsaw, 1968; MA, HS Film, TV and Theatre, 1969. *Appointments:* Film Prod Mgr, Polish Film Prods Corp, 1969-. *Creative works:* Films: Vabank (dir J Machulski), Pt I, 1980, Pt II, 1985; That was Jazz (dir F Falk), 1981; Sexmission, (dir J Machulski), 1983; Escape from Liberty cinema (dir W Marczewski), 1991; Tsynga (dir: L Wosiewicz), 1992. *Membership:* Rotary Club Int. *Honours:* Metronom for Best Music Video Clips, 1985. *Hobbies:* Reading; Basketball; Gardening; Tennis. *Address:* ssa 00Film Studio, Lakowa Street 29, 90-950 Lodz, Poland.

SOMMER Vladimir, b. 28 Feb 1921, Dolni Jiretin. Composer. m. Dana Hlupa, 12 Feb 1983, 1 s, 1 d. *Education:* BA, HS, 1932-40; Grad Sch of Art & Music, Prague, 1946-50. *Appointments:* Postgrad Studies, 1950-52; Radio Asst, 1952-53; Sec, Czech Union of Composers, 1953-56; Asst Prof, Grad Sch of Art & Music, 1953-56; Prof, Dept of the Theory of Music, Charles Univ, 1956-87. *Creative works:* Three Women Chorus, 1948; Sonata for two violins, 1948; Concerto for a violin, orch, 1950; Sonata for violin and viola, 1956; Overture to the Sophocles Tragedy Antighone, 1956; Vocal - Symph No 1 for the Mezzosopran, Solo, Speaker, Chorus, Orch, 1963; String Quartet, No 1 1957, No 2 1987; Concerto for a violincello, orch, 1979; Seven Songs for Mezzosoprano and the Piano, 1986; Three Women Chorus, 1986; Three Mixed Chorus, 1987; Symph for the piano, percussions, string orch, 1989; VocalSymph No 2 for three soloists, chorus, orch, 1990; Music for several Movie Pictures. *Memberships:* Comm, Union of the Czech Music Composers; Comm, Prague Spring Int Fest; Comm, Assn of the Czech Musicians. *Honours:* Czech Govt Awd, 1960, 1965; Nat Awd of Czech Musical Fndn, 1986; Special Awd, FANTON Pubing Hse, 1989. *Address:* Knezeveska 6, 16100 Praha 6, Czechoslovakia.

SONDASHI Ludwig Sanday, b. 13 Jan 1942, Zambia. Lawyer; Lecturer in Law; Government Minister. m. Virginia Sondashi, Oct 1971, 6 s, 1 d. *Education:* Fellow, Inst Local Govt Admnstrs, 1969; LLB, 1987; LLM, 1985; PhD, Law, 1990. *Appointments:* Town Clerk, Kafire Coun, 1968-74; Dist Gov, 1974-78; Min State, Solicitor-Gen, 1978-85; Mbr, Ctrl Comm, 1985-90; Min Labour and Social Security, 1991-. *Publication:* Marriage is not for weaklings, book. *Memberships:* Num incl: Legal Affairs Comm Chmn, MMD Party; Law Assn Zambia;

Amnesty Int; Focus for Democracy. *Hobbies:* Jogging; Sauna; Reading; Hunting. *Address:* PO Box 50987, Lusaka, Zambia.

SONDERGAARD Jorgen, b. 20 Aug 1937, Alborg, Denmark. Prof. *Education:* ECFMG, 1964; PhD 1973; Dip, Danish Bd of Dermatology & Venereology, 1974. *Appointments:* Univ of Newcastle, Eng, 1969; Univ of Stanford, USA, 1970; Univ of Copenhagen, Denmark, 1970-91. *Publications:* Textbook: Dermatology & Venereology; Warning Signs in Dermatology; Skin Signs in AIDS. *Memberships:* Danish Dermatological Soc; Danish Med Soc; BMA; Am Acad of Dermatology; World Acad of Population Hlth Serv; oc Bioengrng of the Skin; Scandinavian Dermatological Soc; World Fedn Contraception. *Honours:* Int Awd of AIDS Rsch, 1988; Kt of the Order of Dannebrog, 1991; Queen's Awd for Export Achmt, 1991; Med of Hon, Univ of Indonesia, 1991. *Hobbies:* Tennis; Golf. *Address:* Department of Dermatology, Bispebjerg Hospital, Bispebjerg Bakke 23, DK 2400 Copenhagen NV, Denmark.

SONE Toshio, b. 14 May 1935, Miyagi, Japan. Prof. m. Noriko Tanaka, 5 Sept 1964, 3 s. *Education:* BE 1958, ME 1960, DE 1963, Tohoku Univ. *Appointments:* Rsch Assoc 1963-64, Assoc Prof 1964-79, Prof 1979- 81, Fac of Engrng, Prof, Rsch Inst of Elec Communication 1981-, Tohuku Univ. *Publications:* Electroacoustic Engineering, 1963; Practice in Electromagnetics, 1973; Foundations of Acoustics, 1990; Life and Sound, 1991. *Memberships:* Fellow, Acoustical Soc of Am; VP, Acoustical Soc of Japan; VP, Inst of Noise Control Engrng, Japan, USA; Electronics Info and Communications Engrs; IEE, Japan; Japan Soc of Mech Engrs; Japan Audiological Soc. *Honours:* INCE/JAPAN Cons; Rch Grantee: Kajima Sci Promotion Fndn, Tokyo, 1984; Sound Tech Promotion Fndn, Tokyo, 1987; Hoso-Bunka Fndn,Tokyo, 1991. *Hobby:* Calligraphy. *Address:* 4-9-5 Midorigaoka, Taihaku- ku, Sendai, 982 Japan. 52.

SONG Jian, b. 29 Dec 1931, Shandong, China. Cnslr; Chmn; Prof. m. Yusheng Wang, 1 July 1961, 1 s, 1 d. *Education:* Degree in Engrng 1958, Cand of Sci 1960, MBTY, Moscow; DSc, Moscow Nat Tech Univ, 1990. *Appointments:* Hd, Lab of Cybernetics, Inst of Maths, Academia Sinica, 1960-70; Hd, Space Sci Div 1971-78, VP, Acad of Space Tech 1978-81, 7th Min of Machine Bldg Ind; Vice Min, Min of Astronautics, 1981-84; Chmn, State Sci & Tech Commn, 1985-; State Cnslr of the State Coun, 1986; Chmn, Environmental Protection Commn, State Coun, 1988-; Disting Vis Prof without Tenure Washington Univ, St Louis, USA. *Publications:* Reference Frames in Space Flight, 1963; Engineering Cybernetics, 1980; China's Population: Problems and Prospects, 1981; Population Projections and Control, 1981; Recent Development in Control Theory & Its Applications, 1984; Population Control Theory, 1985; Populatiton Control in China, Theory & Applications, 1985; Strategy of Population Control, 1985; Population System Control, 1988; Science & Technology and Social System, 1990; Over 100 profl articles. *Memberships include:* VP, China Systems Engrng Soc; Standing Comm, China Assn for Sci & Tech; Coun, Int Fedn of Automatic Control. *Honours:* Disting Contribution Awd, Beijing Sci & Tech Conf, 1977; Awd of Nat Sci Conf, 1978; Awds for Disting Contribution to Nat Def Sci & Tech, 1979; Min of Astronautics Hon & Awd for Disting Contribution to Space Sci & Tech, 1980; Nat Prize & Awd for Accomplishments in Natural Sci, 1982; A Einstein Awd of Int Assn for Maths Modelling, 1987. *Hobby:* Swimming. *Address:* The State Science and Technology Commission, 54 Sanlihe Road, Beijing 100862, China. 139.

SONG Ruyao, b. 16 Nov 1914, Liaoning, China. Prof. m. Chiao-Chag Wang, 3 July 1940, 2 s, 1 d. *Education:* DDS 1932-39, MD 1948-51, Dental Coll, W China Union Univ; DSc, Grad Sch of Med, Philadelphia, USA, 1943-48. *Appointments:* Asst Instr 1939-41, Sr Instr 1941-43, Prof of Plastic Surg 1948-51, W China Union Univ; Prof of Plastic Surg, Chinese Acad of Med Scis, 1952-

91. *Publications:* Repair of the Cleft Lip and Palate, 1959; Plastic Surgery Treatment of the Hand Injuries, 1963; One Stage Reconstruct, 1982; WB Saunders Aesthetic Plastic Surg, 1990. *Memberships:* Chinese Med Assn; Chinese Plastic Surg Soc; Am Soc of Plastic Surg; Am Soc of Aesthetic Plastic Surg; Am Acad of Facial Plastic Surg. *Honours:* Grade A Merit (Mil Awd) for excellent Plastic Surg Serv during Korean War, 1951; Golden Saw Awd, Am Acad of Facial Plastic Surg, 1983; Awd of Excellence, Am Soc of Aesthetic Plastic Surg, 1988. *Hobby:* Painting. *Address:* Plastic Surgery Hospital, Ba-Da-Chu, Beijing 100041, China.

SONG Shuhua, b. 19 June 1923, Chengdu, China. Prof. m. Huang Pu, 9 Dec 1949, 2 d. *Education:* BA, Yeching Univ, 1946; MA, Univ of Sydney, 1949. *Appointments:* Lectr, Assoc Prof, Prof, Central Inst o Nationalities, Beijing, China, 1952-; Member, CERD, United Nations, 1984-; Vice Chmn, China Latin American Fiendship Assn, 1984-. *Publications:* Lo Problems de las Nacionalidades de China; Ancient Bei Yue; The History of Primitive Soc; Over 50 Articles. *Memberships:* Chinese Ethnological Soc; Chinese Assn for Global Ethnic Studies; Royal Anthropological Inst of Great Britain & Ireland. *Honours include:* 1st Prize, State Commission for Nationalities Affairs. *Hobbies:* Jogging; Enjoyin Classical Music. *Address:* Central Inst for Nationalities, 27 Baishiqiao Road, Beijing, China.

SONG Suk Man, b. 19 Dec 1945, Dae Jun, Korea. Mgrng Dir, Overseas Div, Sung Corp. m. 8 Apr 1977, 1 s, 1 d. *Education:* BSc, Yon Sei Univ, Seoul, Korea, 1969. *Appointments:* Economist, Bank of Korea, 1970-76; Procurement Mgr, Hyundai Group, 1976-80; Procurement Mgr, Mktgng Mgr, GMINM East, MO Overseas, 1980-. *Publications include:* Some Economic Articles. *Memberships:* Korean Soc; Assn in Saudi Arabia. *Honours:* Export Promotion Award; Appreciation Award, Ministe of Defence of Korea, President of Korea, US Air Force. *Hobbies:* Golf; Swimming; Music. *Address:* 104-902 Family Apt, Munjung Dong, Songpa Ku, Seoul, Korea.

SONG Tao, b. 8 Apr 1955, Fuzhow, China. Dir of Univ Offices. m. Guo Jian Li, 30 Jan 1981, 1 d. *Education:* Graduated Fujian Forestry Inst, 1978; Post Grad Course, Zhejiang Univ, 1979-81; Monash Univ, Australia, 1988-89. *Appointments:* Tutor, Fujian Forestry Inst, 1981-88; Lectr, 1985-88; Visiting Scholar, Monash Univ, Australia, 1988-89. *Publications include:* Finger Joint & Manufacture; A study to Reduce Noise from Chipper. *Memberships:* Chinese Forestry Soc; Timber Engrng Tech Soc, New Zealand. *Hobbies:* Reading; Play Violin. *Address:* Fujian Forestry Inst, Nanping 353001, Fujian, China.

SONG Zhen Yu, b. 22 May 1915, Auguo, Hobei, China. Prof of Pharmacology. m. Qinn Su, 25 July 1945, 1 s, 3 d. *Education:* BS, Yenching Univ, Peiping, 1941; MS, George Washington Univ, Washington DC, 1949; PhD, Univ of California, San Francisco, 1952. *Appointments:* Asst, Yenching Univ, 1941; Lect, Coll of Pharmacy, Peking Univ, 1946-48; Post Doc, UCSF, USA; Asst Prof, Tufts Medical Coll, Boston, 1953-54; Asst Prof, Inst of Materia Medica, Chinese Acad of Medical Sci, Beijing, 1954-63; Prof, 1963-. *Publications include:* Co Discoverer, DDB, Used for Treatment of Chromic Hepatitis; Drug Metabolism Research, Significance, Methodology and Applications; 120 Research Papers & Reviews. *Memberships include:* Chinese Pharmac Assn; Instl Soc for Study of Xenobiotics; IUPHAR Section of Drug Metabolism. *Hobbies:* Classical Music. *Address:* Inst of Materia Medica, Chinese Acad of Medical Sci, 1 Xian Nong Tan Street, Beijing 100050, China.

SONOGASHIRA Kenkichi, b. 25 Oct 1931, Kagoshima, Japan. Prof; Chemistry Educ. m. Seiko Oka, 31 May 1962, 2 d. *Education:* Bach of Sci, Osaka Univ, 1956; Master of Sci, 1958; Doc of Sci, 1961. *Appointments:* Research Assoc, Inst of Sci & Ind

Research, Osaka Univ, 1961-68; Assoc Prof, 1968-81; Prof, Research Inst for Atomic Energy, Osaka City Univ, 1981-87; Dir, 1987-89; Prof, Faculty of Engrng, 1989-. *Publications include:* 60 Articles on Organometallic Chemistry; 10 Patents. *Memberships:* The American Chemical Soc; The Chemical Soc of Japan; Catalysis Soc of Japan; The Soc of Polymer Sci, Japan; Kinki Chemical Soc, Japan; The Soc of Synthetic Organic Chemistry, Japan. *Honour:* Alexander Von Humboldt Fellow. *Hobbies:* Gardening; Reading. *Address:* Ao Matani, Higashi 6 12 9, Minou, Osaka 562, Japan. 52.

SONPAR Prem, b. 17 Feb 1935, Shikarpur, Sind, India. m. Sundri Sonpar, 19 May 1963, 2 s, 1 d. *Education:* Diploma Mech Engrng, Poona Engrng Coll, Poona, India, 1957. *Appointments:* Exec Dir, Seven Seas Enterprises, 1957-81; Sonpar Td, 1965-81; Sonpar Singapore Pte Ltd, 1965-81; Mgrng Dir, Canwell Enterprises Ltd, Canwell Travel Suervices, 1982-. *Memberships:* Royal Hong kong Jockey Club; Rotary Club, Victoria Chapter. *Hobbies:* Travelling; Nature Walks. *Address:* Baguio Villas, Block 32, 12/Fl, 550 Victoria Road, Hong Kong. 1.

SOOSAAR Enn, b. 13 Feb 1937, Tallinn, Estonia. Freelance Translator; Essayist; Literary Critic. *Education:* Tartu Univ, Jartu, 1964. *Appointments:* Free lance Translator of American & English Literature into Estonian, Estonian Publi Houses, 1964-; Free lance Essayist & Literary Critic, Various Estonian Periodicals, 1970-. *Publications include:* Estonian Translations; Essyas; Articles; Introductions; Forewords; Book Reviews. *Memberships:* Estonian Writers Union; Intl PEN. *Honours:* Literary Mag LOOMING Annual Award; Estonian Writers Union annual Award; Merited Literator of the Estonian SSR. *Address:* Vilde Tee 66-9, Tallinn 34, Estonia. 3, 52.

SORDYLOWA Barbara Lucja, b. 8 Oct 1934, Cracow, Poland. Librarian, Bibliologist. m. Wladyslaw Sordyl, 31 Dec 1960, 1 d. *Education:* Master of Philoslogy, The Jagiellonian Univ, 1956; Doc of Arts, The Univ of Lodz, 1969; Asst Prof, The Univ of Wroclaw, 1987. *Appointments:* Librarian, The Jagiellonian Library, 1957-66; Dipl Libr, Custodian, Snr Cust, 1966-76; Deputy Mgr, 1974-76; Deputy Mgr, Library of Polish Acad of Sci, Warsaw, 1976-81; Dir, 1981-. *Publications include:* Over 50 Articles; The Dictionary of Polish Scientific Assn. *Memberships:* Library Council of Poland; Intl Assn Futuribles, Paris; Working Group on Information & Popluariazation of Sci at Committee of Sci Research, Warsaw. *Honours:* Award of ministry of Educ; Award of Assn of Editors; Gold Cross of Merit; Cross of Polonia Restituta. *Hobbies:* Reading; Theatre. *Address:* Biblioteka Polskiej Akademii Nauk w Warszawie, PKiN VIP, 00 901 Warsaw, Poland. 1, 52.

SORENSEN Bent, b. 8 Mar 1924, Denmark. Prof. m. (1) Kirsten Ammentorp, 1949, dec 1989, 2 s; (2) Inge Genefke, 1991. *Education:* MD, 1949; DM Sc, 1958; Spec in General Surgwery, 1960; Plastic Surgery, 1964; Chief of Staff, Kobenhavns Kommunes Hvidovre Hosp, Univ of Copenhagen, 1965-90; Full Prof, Univ Copenhagen, 1971. *Appointments include:* Vice Chmn, Chmn of the Advisory Bd on Health Educ, Minister of Educ, 1975-81; Danish Medical Research Council, 1976-84; Chmn, Co Founder, Danish Organ of Plastic Surgeons, 1983-88; Vice Chmn, Bd of Intl Rehabilitation Council for Torture Victims, 1990; Vice Pres, European Councils Committee for the Prevention of Torture, 1991-93. *Publications include:* Numerous Papers; Thesis; Reviews. *Memberships include:* The danish Medical Assn; Action Committee on Nurses Training; European Burns Assn. *Honours include:* Red Cross Prize; General Consul Ernst Carlsens Prize; Barfed Pedersens Honorary Prize. *Address:* 14 Hoje Skodsborgvej, DK 2942 Skodsborg, Denmark.

SOROKINA Elena, b. 6 Apr 1940, Moscow, USSR. Musicologist; Pianist. m. Alexander Bakhehiev, 28 Nov 1962, 1 d. *Education:* Moscow Central Music Sch, 1948-

58; Moscow State Conservatoire, 1958-63; Aspizaut of Moscow Conservatoire, 1963-65. *Appointments:* Moscow Central Music Sch, 1960-69; Moscow Conservatoire, 1965-; Prof, Doc of Arts, Pianist, Commentator. *Publictions include:* Piano Duet, History of Genze; Many Articles; More than 20 Disks. *Memberships:* Composers Union of USSR; Piano Duet Assn of USSR; Intl Piano Duet Assn. *Hobbies:* Autiquary; Organ of Interior. *Address:* 4-32 Koshkin Street, Moscow 115 409, Russia.

SOROKINA Tatiana Sergeyevna, b. 10 Apr 1942, Moscow, Russia. Professor of History of Medicine. m. Vladimir Variukhin, 14 Dec 1963, div. 1966, 1 s. *Education:* MD, 1966, PhD, Physiology, 1970, DSc, Hist Med, 1988, Prof, 1989, Med Fac, Russian People's Friendship Univ, Moscow. *Appointments:* Sr Tchr, Dept Physiology, 1970-74, Sr Tchr, Dept Hist Med, 1974-66, Asst Prof, Dept Hist Med, 1976-89, Prof, Hd, Dept Hist Med, 1989-, Med Fac, Russian People's Friendship Univ, Moscow. *Publications:* Over 70 sci publs; Main books incl: Ancient Mediterranean Medicine, 1978; Atlas of History of Medicine: Primitive Society, Ancient World, 1981, 1987; Atlas of History of Medicine: Middle World, 1983; Atlas of History of Medicine: Modern Times, 1987; University Programme for History of Medicine, 1987; A short course of History of Medicine, 1988; History of Medicine, textbook, 1991. *Memberships:* Presidium, All-Union Sci Soc Hist Med; Sci Coun awarding PhD and DSc in Field of Hist Med, Med Mus, Russian Acad Med Scis. *Honours:* 2 Prizes (for scenarios, compere, dancing), World Fests of Youth and Students, Xth Fest, Berlin, 1973, Xlth Fest, Havana, 1978; 2 Govt Medals for Work Success: For Fruitful Work, 1985, For Long Fruitful Work (Veteran of Labour), 1988; Bronze Medal, All-Union Exhib Econ Achievements, 1985. *Hobbies:* University drama and dancing groups, 1960-78; Writing poetry and scenarios; Compere; Producer; Swimming; Dress-designing; Theatre. *Address:* Miklukho-Maklaya Str 18-1032, Moscow 117437, Russia. 138, 152.

SOUTER David Cowley, b. 13 Apr 1917, Tynemouth, England. Retired Shipowner. m. Joan Margaret Wear, 25 Nov 1939, 3 s, 1 d. *Education:* Newcastle Preparatary Sch, 1926-30; Fettes Coll, Edinburgh, 1930-34. *Appointments:* Clerk, Wm Duckinson & Co, Ltd, 1934-39; Royal Navy, 1939-45; Royal Naval Volunteer Reserve, 1936-51; Retired Lient. Commander, RNVR; Dir, MD, Chmn, W A Sonter & Co, Ltd, 1945-83; Sherf Steam Shipping Co Ltd, Hetburn SS Co Ltd, Bamburgh Shipping Co Ltd, Atlantic Drilling Co Ltd. *Memberships include:* British Shipping Federation; Missions to Seamen, South Shields; Sea Cadet Corps; Northumberland Lawn Tennis Assn. *Honours:* Volunteer Reserve Decoration; Fellow, Inst of Chartered Shipbrokers; Fellow, North East Coast Inst of Engrs & Shipbuilding. *Hobbies:* Forestry; Gardening; Real tennis; Bee Keeping. *Address:* Chatsworth, Moor Crescent, Gosforth, Newcastle Upon Tyne, N3 4AQ, England.

SOUTH Raymond, b. 15 June 1907, Wadhurst, England. Retired. m. Marjorie Hirst, 30 July 1937, 2 d. *Education:* Wadhurst Natl Sch, 1912- 18; Skinners Sch, Tunbridge Wells, 1918-21; Maidstone Grammer Sch, 1921-26; Univ Coll, Oxford, 1926-30; BA, 1929; Educ Dip, 1930; MA, 1933. *Appointments:* Snr History Master, 1930-68; Deputy Headmaster, 1966-69. *Publications:* The Book of Windsor; Crown Coll & Railways; Royal Castle, Rebel Town; Royal; Lake; Heights & Depths; Numerous Articles. *Memberships:* Windsor Borough Council; Windsor & Eton Soc; Windsor & Eton Branch of Historical Assn; Middle Thames Natl History Soc. *Honours:* Labour Party Cert of Merit. *Hobbies:* Natl History; Politics; Literature; Music & Art. *Address:* 5 St Andrews Avenue, Windsor, Berks, SL4 4EH, England.

SOUTHALL Derek William, b. 5 June 1930, Coventry, England. Artist. m. Jenniffer Anne Wilson, 2 d. *Education:* Coventry Coll of art, 1947-49; Camberwell

Sch of art, 1949-51; Univ of London Goldsmiths Coll, 1952-53; Hochschosle fur Bildende Kunste, Berlin, 1954; Sen Fellow, Fine Art, Cardiff, 1980-83. *Appointments:* Lectr, Birmingham Coll of Art, 1962- 64; Hd of Fine art, Oxford Sch of Art, 1964-67; Dir, Post Grad Painting, Birmingham Coll of art, 1967-72; Artist, Yale Univ & Univ of South Carolina, 1972-75; Artist, Natl Art Sch, Sydney, Australia, 1984. *Creative Works include:* Mural for Main Entrance of DHSS, Newcastle Upon Tyne; Films. BBC2 Film on Work Directed by Barrie Gavin; BBC2 Participated with Dr Dannie Abse & Alfred Bvendei in Poetry and ... *Hobbies:* Walking; Visiting Churches. *Address:* The Chapel, Heatherton Park, Bradford on Tone, Somerset, TA4 1EU, England. 19, 133.

SOUTHWOOD William Frederick Walter, b. 8 June 1925, London, England. Conslt Sureon. m. Margaret Holderness, 1 May 1965, 2 s. *Education:* Charterhouse, Trinity Coll, Cambridge, MB, B Chir, 1948; FRCS, 1954; M Chir, 1956; MD, 1964. *Appointments:* Snr Asst Resident, New York Hosp, 1956-57; Resident Surgeon Officer, St Marks Hosp, 1959-60; Snr Reg, United Bristol Hosp, 1960-66; Const Surgeon, bath Health District, 1966- 90. *Publications:* Articles in Surgical Textbooks & Journals. *Memberships:* Master of Worshipful Soc of Apothecaries of London; Profl & Linguistic Assesment Bd. *Honours:* Hunterian Prof, Royal Coll of Surgeons; Visiting Prof of Surgery, Univ of Cape Town. *Hobbies:* Fishing; Shooting; Snooker. *Address:* Upton House, Bathwick Hill, Bath BA2 6EX, England. 1.

SOUTTER William Patrick, b. 12 Jan 1944, Canada. Gynaecologist. m. Winfred Christine Soutter, 30 June 1973, 2 d. *Education:* Univ of Glasgow, MB, ChB, 1961-67; Univ of Strathehyde, MSc, 1972-73; Royal Coll of Obstetricans & Gynaecologists, 1975-88; MD, Univ of Glasgow, 1979. *Appointments:* Lectr, Dept of Obstetrics & Gynaecology, Univ of Glasgow, 1978-81; Snr Lectr, Univ of Sheffield, 1981-85; Reader, Gynaecoligst Oncology, Royal Post Grad Medical Sch, 1985-. *Publications:* Over 70 Sci Papers; Co Editor, Gynaecology. *Memberships:* British Medical Assn; British Gynaecological Cancer Soc; Gynaecological Sub Committee of the United Kingdon Coordinating Committee for Cancer Research. *Hobbies:* Fishing; Golf; Computing; Music. *Address:* 135 The Fairway, North Wembly, Middlx, HAO 3TQ, England.

SOYAK Yusuf Edip, b. 8 Aug 1951, Zonguldak, Turkey. RDO Iberotel Turkey General Mgr, Iberotel Art Kemer. m. Janet Soyak, 8 Oct 1976, 1 s, 1 d. *Education:* Hotel Sch, Dipl, 1965-68; Cornel Univ Summer Sch, 1979. *Appointments:* Trainee, steigenberger Hotels, Germany, 1969-71; Military Serv, Istanbul, 1971-73; Cost Contr, Forum Hotel Wiesbaden Ger, 1973- 76; Accountants, Intercontinental Inst, Tr, 1976-78; Asst Mge, Intercontinential Amman Sordan, 1978-79; Asst Sales Mgr, Intercontinential Hannover, Germany, 1980-84; Front Officer Mgr,1985-87; Gm Iberotel Reina Paguera, Mallorca, Splain, 1987-88; GM Ibeerotel Side Palace, Antalya, Turkey, 1988-90; GM Iberotel Art Kemer, Antalya, 1990-. *Memberships:* Skal Club, Antalya. b2Hobbies: Squash; Fashion; Fine Arts; Tennis. *Address:* Iberotel Art Kemer, Kiziltepe Mevkii, Kemer, Antalya, Turkey. 52.

SPADY Callie Jeanetta, b. 24 Aug 1938, Townseand, Virginia. Caseworker; Support Enforcement Officer. *Education:* BA, Music Educ, Allen Univ, Columbia, South Carolina, 1961. *Appointments:* Tchr, English, Marion County Sch Bd, Ocala, Florida, 1961-62; Childrens Counselor, NYC, Human Resources Admin Bureau of Child Welfare, 1962-76; Asst Tchr, Sun Shine Nursery Sch, Bronx, NY, 1968-72; Cert Sivil Servant Investigator, Office of Child Support Enforcement Agency, 1976-88; Asstto IRS Coordinator, Office of Child Support Enforcement Agency, 1980-84. *Memberships include:* Inc's Inst for Absolute Ethnics; The Acad of Political Sci; League of Women Voters of the United States; Intl Federation Business & Profl Women;

Republican Capital Hill Club; Human Resources Admin Womens Advisors Committee. *Honours include:* The Womens Inner Circle of Achievement, ABI Inc; Music Scholarship, Allen Univ, Columbia. *Hobbies:* Walking; Reading; Coin Collecting; Political & Religious Activities; Arts. *Address:* Washbridge Station, PO Box 211, New York, NY 10033, USA. 5, 162.

SPALTON David John, b. 2 Mar 1947, Derby, England. Ophthalmic Surgeon. m. Catherine Bompas, 1989, 2 s. *Education:* Westminster Medical Sch, 1965-70; FRCS, 1976; FC Ophthal, 1989; FRCP, 1990. *Appointments:* Conslt Ophthalmic Surgeon, St Thomas Hosp, London. *Publications:* Papers on Ophthalmology Atlas of Clinical Ophthalmology. *Memberships:* Ophthalmic Surgeon, Royal Hosp, Chelsea. *Honour:* Best Medical Texkbook of the Year Award, 1985. *Hobbies:* Fly Fishing; Gardening; Ophthalmology. *Address:* 59 Harley Street, London W1N 1DD, England. 1.

SPANG HANSSEN Henrick Stakemann, b. 31 Oct 1953, Copenhagen. Lawyer. *Education:* Bach of Law, Copenhagen Univ, 1980; Diploma Mercantile, Copenhagen, 1988; The Assoc Diploma Management, Mercantil Assoc, 1988. *Appointments:* Firm of Silicitors, Nykbing Spelland, 1980; Law Soc, 1983; Firm of Solicitors Copenhagen, 1985. *Publications:* Lawyers Fee. *Memberships:* The Danish Mercantile Assn; Bd of the Committee of Copenhagen Lawyers. *Hobbies:* Soccer; Golf. *Address:* Advokat ADM Merkonom i Revision, H C Andersens Boulevard 11 1553 V, Copenhagen, Denmark.

SPANNER John Hedley, b. 21 Feb 1945, Nottingham, England. Banker. m. Mary Marshall, 27 Oct 1989, 2 d. *Education:* Reading Sch, 1956-63. *Appointments:* Standard Chartered Bank, 1963-. *Memberships:* Member of City of London Court of Common Council; Governor of City of London Sch; City of London Tavra; Bd Street Ward Club; Liveryman of Worshipful Co of Glovers. *Honours:* TD; Freeman of City of London. *Hobbies:* Territorial Army; Gardening; Art; Architecture; Antiques. *Address:* Standard Chartered Bank, 1 Aldermanbury Square, London EC2V 7SB, England.

SPARROW Margaret June, b. 26 June 1935, Inglewood, New Zealand. Medical Practitioner. m. Peter Sparrow, 7 Jan 1956, 1 s, 1 d. *Education:* BSc, Victoria Univ, 1956; MB, ChB, Univ of Otago, 1963; Dip Ven, Univ of London, 1976; FAC Ven, 1990. *Appointments:* Medical Research, Univ of Otago, 1956; Health Dept, New Plymouth, 1965-69; Student Health, Victoria Univ, 1969-81; N2 Family Planning Assn, 1971-; Venereologist, Wellington Hosp, 1977-; Abortion Operator, Wellington Hosp, 1980-. *Publications:* Co Author. Consumer Guide to Birth Control; Choosing the Right Contraception, 1990. *Memberships:* N2 Family Planning Assn; Abortion Law Reforn Assn; Nz Venerelogical Soc; Medical Womens Assn. *Honour:* MBE. *Hobbies:* Lonta Intl Scottish Country Dancing. *Address:* 62 Raroa Road, Kelburn, Wellington 5, New Zealand.

SPECTOR Roy Geoffrey, b. 27 Aug 1931, Leeds, England. Emeritus Prof; Honorary Conslt Physician. m. Eva Freeman, 15 Mar 1960, div 1979, 2 s, 1 d. *Education:* MB, ChB, Leeds Medical Sch, 1956; MD, Leeds Univ, 1962; PhD, London Univ, 1964; FRCP, Edinburgh Royal Coll Physicians, 1971; FRCP, Glasgow Royal Coll of Physicians, 1972; FRC Patn, Royal Coll Pathologists, 1976. *Appointments:* Snr Lectr, Paediatric Research Unit, Guys Hosp, 1964-66; Reader, Prof, Applied Pharmacology, Guys Hosp, 1967-89; Emeritus Prof, Clinical Pharmacology Dentistry, 1989. *Publications include:* Mechanism n Pharmacology; A Clinical Pharmacology Catechism; The Nerve Cell; Psychiatry Common Drug Treatments. *Memberships:* Clinical Pharmacology, West China Medical Sch; London Univ, Dartford & Gravesham Health Auth. *Hobbies:* Walking; Music. *Address:* 60 Crescent Drive, Petts Wood, Orpington, Kent BR5 1BD, England. 1.

SPEED George Raymond, b. 15 Apr 1925, Long Eaton, England. Unemployed. m. Helena Christina Fallowfield, 15 May 1954, 1 s, 1 d. *Education:* London Univ. *Appointments:* Var positions, Midland Bank Grp, 1941-85, incl Supervisory Credit Controller, 1941-85; Territorial Army (REME), 1943-47; Dir: Richmond Fin Ltd, 1977-80; Tririding Fin Ltd, 1977- 80; Forward Trust Car Leasing Ltd, 1977-84; Roadmaster Fin Ltd, 1977-84; Underwriting Mbr, Lloyds. *Memberships:* Dist Mbr, Toc-H; Auditor, Exec Comm Mbr, Int Camellia Soc; Hon Divisional Sec, Soldiers, Sailors and Airmen's Families Assn; Chmn, Cyclamen Soc; Coun, Royal Nat Rose Soc; Royal Soc St George; Int Shakespeare Soc; Royal Hort Soc; Nat Trust Scotland; Econ Rsch Coun; CABE: Local Nat Trust; Local Royal Soc Protection Birds. *Honours:* MIL, 1945; FBSC, 1949; Fellow, Chartered Inst Bankers, 1965; Fellow, Brit Inst Mgmt, 1975; Freeman, City of London, 1977; Liveryman, Worshipful Co of Feltmakers, 1977; Fellow, Linnean Soc, 1984. *Hobbies:* Horticulture; Photography; Music. *Address:* High Trees, Oldhill Wood, Studham, Bedfordshire, England.

SPELLMAN John William, b. 17 Sept 1925, Cambridge, Ma, USA. Management Conslt. m. Elizabeth M Halbritter, 25 June 1949, 5 s, 1 d. *Education:* Us Army & 8th Air Force, 1943-45; Boston Coll, Bach of Sci Degree, 1949; Massachuesetts Inst of Tech, Management Sci Degree, 1974. *Appointments:* Dir of Mktng, New York Worlds Fair Corp, 1962-64; Pres, Schenley Research Co, 1964-69; Vice Pres, Equitable Life Assurance Soc of the US, 1969-90; Faculty of Columbia Univ Grad Sch of Business, 1973-77. *Creative Works:* Editor in Chief, Boston Coll, Stylus. *Memberships:* The Inst of Managment Sci. *Honours:* Bronze Star; Purple Hart; Combat Infantry Badge; Presidental Citations (2); Battle Stars (3). *Hobbies:* Powerboats; Automobiles; Computers. *Address:* 315 Plantation Drive, New Bern NC 28562, USA.

SPENCER Elvins Yuill, b. 28 Oct 1914, Edmonton, Alberta, Canada. Retired Research Chemist, Biochemist. m. Hanna Gischl, 11 July 1942, 1 s, 1 d. *Education:* BSc, Univ of Alberta, 1936; MSc, 1938; PhD, Univ of Toronto, 1941. *Appointments:* Fine Chemicals of Canada, 1941-42; Gelatin Prod, Windsor Detroit, 1942-43; Cons, Mining & Smelting Trail, 1943- 45; Prof of Chem, Univ of Sask, 1946-51; Cord, Res, Sask Research Council, 1949-51; Pricipal Chemist, Research Int, 1951-60; Dir, Res Inst Agric Can, 1960-78; Editor, Pesticide Biochem & Physiol, 1978-90. *Publications:* 53 Research Papers; General Articles; Book; Chapters. *Memberships include:* Chemical Inst of Canada; American Chemical Soc; Canadian Bioche Soc. bb2Honours: FCIC '50; Fellow of Agrochemical Div Am Chem Soc; Scholar Rockefellow Study Centre. *Hobbies:* World Affiars; Tennis; Photography. *Address:* 7 Westview Drive, London, Ontario, Canada N6A 2Y2. 6, 142, 143.

SPENCER Herbert, b. 22 June 1924, London, England. Painter; Graphic Designer. m. Marianne mols Dordrecht, 27 Sept 1954, 1 d. *Education:* Royal Coll of Art, RCA, 1970. *Appointments:* Snr Research Fellow, RCA, 1966-78; Member, Post Office Stamp Advis Committee, 1968-; Dir, Lund Humphries Publi, 1970-88; Conslt, WH Smith Ltd, 1973-; Prof of Graphic Arts, RCA, 1978-85. *Creative Works:* One Man Exhib of Paintings. Bleddfa Trust, 1986; Gallery 202, London, 1988-89, 1990; Exhib of Photographs. Zelda Cheatle Gall, London, 1991; Photographs in perm collection of V & A Museum; Editor. Typographica; Penrose Annual; Publi. Design in Business Printing; Londons Canal; Traces of Man; The Visible Word; Pioneers of Modern Typography; New Alphabets A-Z; The Book of Numbers. *Honour:* RD1, 1965. *Address:* 75 Deodar Road, Putney, London SW15 2NU. England.

SPENCER John Hall, b. 17 Apr 1928, Cambridge, England. Author; Managing Dir. m. Edite Pommes Barrere, 1 Dec 1953, div, 2 s, 1 d. *Education:* Royal Naval Coll, Greenwich, 1947; Harvard Business Sch, 1974. *Appointments:* Royal Marines, Regular Officer,

1945-51; Beaser Brook Newspapers, Conservation Central Office 1959 Election; J Walter Thompson Co, 1959-82; John Spencer Assoc, 1982-. *Publications:* The Business of Management; Battle for Crete; The Wall Is Strong; The Surgenor Campaign. *Memberships:* Intl Public Relations Assn; Inst of Practitioners in Advertising. *Hobbies:* Boys Club; Golf; Literature; Films; The London Stage. *Address:* 76 Mill Bank Court, John Islip Street, London SW1 P4LG, England.

SPENCER John Loraine, b. 19 Jan 1923, Woodford, Essex, England. Retired Headmaster. m. Brenda Elizabeth Loft, 3 Apr 1954, 2 s, 1 d. *Education:* Bancrofts Sch, essex, 1933-41; Gonville Caius Coll, Cambridge, 1941-45. *Appointments:* Asst Master, Haileybury Coll, Hertford, 1947-61; Headmaster, Royal Grammer Sch, Lancaster, 1961-72; Headmaster, Berkhamsted Sch, 1972-83. *Memberships:* Soc of Scholmasters; GAP. *Honours:* MA, Class 1 Honors; Second with Essex Regt in NW Europe. *Hobbies:* People; The Countryside; Travel. *Address:* Crofts Close, 7 Aston Road, Haddenham, Bucks, HP17 8AF, England. 1.

SPENCER John, b. 17 July 1933, Bedford, England. Surgeon. m. Gwyneth Ann Griffiths, 5 Dec 1958, 3 s, 2 d. *Education:* Charing Cross Hosp Medical Sch, 1952-57; MB, BS London, 1957; FRCS Eng, 1963; MS, 1974. *Appointments:* Medical Officer, Uganda Medical Serv, 1958-61; Research Fellow, UCLA Los Angeles, 1969-70; Surgeon, Hammersmith Hosp, 1970-. *Publications:* Books on Radiation Enteritis & Peptic Ulcer; Numerous Papers. *Memberships:* Royal Soc of Medicine; Surgical Research Soc; Assn of Surgeons. *Hobbies:* Church Activities; Bible Tchrng; Sailing; Ornithology. *Address:* 99 Brunswick Road, Ealing, London W5 1AQ, England.

SPENCER Shaun Michael, b. 4 Feb 1944, Leeds, England. Queens Counsel. m. 9 June 1971; 2 s, 2 d. *Education:* Univ of Durham, LLB, 1962-65. *Appointments:* Asst Lectr, Sheffield Univ, 1965-66; Lectr, Sheffield Univ, 1966-68; Practised at the Bar, 1969-; Crown Court Recorder, 1985-. *Publications:* Articles in Learned Journals. *Memberships:* Called to Bar, Lincoln Inn. *Honour:* Hardwicke & Mansfield Scholar. *Hobbies:* Reading; Cookery; Books; Singing. *Address:* 6 Park Square, Leeds, LS1 2LW, England. 1.

SPERBER Matthew A, b. 17 Dec 1938, New York, USA. Pres, Intl Direct Mktng. m. Jane Trautman, 7 Oct 1988, 1 s, 1 d. *Education:* BS, Architecture, City Univ of New York, 1961. *Appointments:* Mgr, IBM Computers, 1968-80; Dir, Wang Computers, 1981-83 Dir, Datapoint Computers, 1983-85; Pres, Harte Hanks Direct Mktng, 1985-88; Pres, Intl Direct Mktng, 1988-. *Memberships:* American Management Assn; Direct Mktng Assn. *Honour:* Best Direct Mail Award. *Hobbies:* Tennis; Reading; Republican. *Address:* Intl Direct Mktng, 8045 Antoine, Suite 109, Houston, TX 77088, USA. 2.

SPIEWLA Edward Jerzy, b. 1 Aug 1940, Pstragowa, Poland. Physicist; Academic Teacher. m. Elzbieta Krupa, 18 July 1965, 1 s, 3 d. *Education:* MSc, Phys, 1963, Dr Phys Sc, 1973, Univ Maria Curie- Sklodowska; Qualifying Thesis, Silesia Univ, 1984. *Appointments:* Staff, Phys Dept, 1963-, Hd, Phys Dept, 1984-, Rector, Educl Affairs, 1987-, Tech Univ, Lublin. *Publications:* Electrical properties of the septum between cells of Characeae algae, 1973; Electrophysiological aspects of effects of some environmental factors on plants, 1983; Perspective and hopes of biophysics, 1987. *Memberships:* Bd, Polish Phys Soc; Bd, Polish Biophys Soc; Bd, Lublin Sci Soc; Ecological Club. *Honours:* Award, Min Sci and Higher Educ; Award, Min Nat Educ. *Hobbies:* Physical work in the countryside; Painting; Good books. *Address:* Emancypantek 3.13, 20- 636 Lublin, Poland.

SPILLER John Anthony Walsh, b. 29 Dec 1942, Cheltenham, England. Advisor, PHAB. m. 1 Sept 1972, 1 s, 1 d. *Education:* North Devon Coll, 1955-59; Bideford

Art Coll, 1960. *Appointments:* Organiser Liberal Party, 1962-82; Sec General, Liberal Party, 1983-86; CharityVolunteer, 1987-89; Advisor, Devon PHAB, 1990-. *Publications:* Joint Author, Effective Constituency Political Organisation. *Memberships:* Natl Assn of Liberal Agents; Gladstone Fund. *Honour:* MBE. *Hobbies:* Golf; Holidays in Ireland; Boxing. *Address:* 5 Royston Road, Bideford, Devonshire EX39 3AN, England. 1.

SPINAR Zdeuck V, b. 4 Apr 1916, Caslav, Czechoslovakia. Prof. m. 29 June 1963, 4 d. *Education:* Charles Univ, Praha, RN Dr, 1945; Dr Sc, 1958. *Appointments:* Dept of Paleontology, Charles Univ, Praha, 1945- 81. *Publications:* 162 Sci Publi; 6 Books. *Memberships:* Geological Soc of Czechoslavakia; Zoological Soc of Czechoslovakia. *Honour:* State Prize for Sci. *Hobby:* Gardening. *Address:* Machoclovci 2546, Praha 4 14100, CSFR.

SPINELLI Luca, b. 13 June 1955, Genoa, Italy. Dir, Agenzia Marittima Cambiaso & Risso. m. Ilaria Gambaro, 16 June 1984, 1 d. *Education:* MSc, Naval Arch & Marine Engr, Naples Univ, 1979; Post grad, Naval Acad, Leghorn, 1980; Chartered Engr, Uk, Italy, 1980. *Appointments:* Trainee Surveyor, Ing G Andalo, Conslt, 1980; Lt Italian Navy, 1980-81; Tech Surveyor, American Bureau of Shipping, London, 1981-84; Tech Mgr, Ulysses Cruises Inc, Miami-USA, 1984-88; Tech Dir, Premier Cruise Lines, Cape Canaveral, Fl, USA, 1988-90. *Memberships:* Royal Inst Naval Arch; Soc Naval Arch, Marine Engrs; Ordine Ingegueri, Genoa, Italy; Yacht Club Italiano; UCID, Genoa, Italy. *Honours:* Italian Navy, Leghorn Avad; 63 deg Course, Leader. *Hobbies:* Tennis; Skiing; Reading; Cinema; Football. *Address:* Viale F Gambaro 16/2, 16146 Genoa, Italy. 7.

SPOONER Bernard Myrick, b. 15 Oct 1934, Pine Hill, Alabama, USA. Minister; State Baptist Program Admin. m. Patricia Ann Fowler, 8 June 1957, 2 d. *Education:* BS, Mississippi Coll, 1957; MA, Southwestern Baptist Theological Seminary, 1962; EdD, 1975. *Appointments:* Commissioned Officer, United States Marine Reserves, 1957-60; Minister of Educ, First Baptist Church, Ruston, LA, 1962-64; Immanuel Baptist Church, Tulsa, 1965-66; Travis Avenue Baptist Church, 1966-77; Prof of Admin, New Orleans Baptist Theological seminary, 1977-79; Adjunct Prof, Southwester Baptist Theological Seminary, 1974-77, 1990-91. *Publications:* Co Author, You Can Reach People Now; The People Challenge; Contributed Articles to Various Publi. *Memberships:* USMCR; Metro Baptist Religious Educ Assn; Southwestern Baptist Rel Educ Assn; Southern Baptist Rel Educ Assn; Sweetshop USA; Center Street Properties. *Honours include:* Valedictorian & Walker award; Geene Lectr, Religious Educ. *Hobbies:* Travel; Reading; Gardening. *Address:* 900 Glen Vista, Irving, TX 75061, USA. 7, 46.

SPOONER Frank Clyffurde, b. 5 Mar 1924, Cleveland, Australia. Emeritus Prof of Economic History. *Education:* Christs Coll, Cambridge, BA, 1947; MA, 1949; PhD, 1953; Litt D, 1985. *Appointments:* Charge de Recherches, Centre Natl de la Recherche Sci, Paris, 1949-50; Fellow, Christs Coll, Cambridge, 1951-57; Connomwealth Fund Fellow, 1955-57; Ecole Pratique de Hautes Etudes, Paris, 1957-63; Lectr, Advanced Studies, Oxford Univ, 1958-59; Visiting Lectr, Harvard Univ, 1961-62; Irving Fisher Prof, Yale Univ, 1962-63; Univ of Durham, Lectr, 1963; Reader, 1964; Resident Tutor, 1965-70; Prof, 1966; Dir, 1969-76; Emeritus Prof, 1985. *Creative Works include:* The Intl Economy & Monetary Movements in France. *Contributions to:* Journals. *Memberships include:* Economic History Soc; Economic History Assn; Royal Economic Soc; Friends of the Natl Libraries. *Honours:* Prix Limantour de l'Academie des Sci Morales et Politiques; Leverhulme Fund Fellow. *Hobbies:* Music; photography; Walking. *Address:* 31 Chatsworth Avenue, Bromley, Kent, BR1 5DP, England. 2, 52.

SPORT Bonnie Montrose, b. 28 Mar 1937, Kansas City, MO, USA. Elementary Tchr. m. 25 Dec 1960, 1 d. *Education:* Kansas Univ, Pittsburg, 1955-60; BS, ED, Central State Wilberforce, Ohio, 1957; Pasadera City, 1963; Los Angeles City, 1974; Fashion Inst, 1971. *Appointments:* Wade Park Elem, Cleveland Ohio, Edwards Elem, Edwards Air Force, 1960; Los Engeles City Schs, 1972-84; Lynwood Schs. *Creative Works include:* Dress Design; Knotts Landing; Wedding Dress Design on TV Show, Dynasty; *Memberships:* NEA; Delta Sigma; Thea Sorority; Belta Phi Leld Adv; CIACEA; ASCD; ECEA. *Honours include:* Kappa Alpja Psi; Delta Sigma Theta. *Hobbies:* Designing Clothes; Drawing; Modeling; Tennis; Dancing; Travel. *Address:* 2520 Park Avenue, Kansas City, MO 64127, USA.

SPRAKER Harold Stephen, b. 13 May 1929, Cedar Bluff, VA. USA, Univ Prof; Dept Chmn. m. Betty Conley, 2 Oct 1954, 2 s. *Education:* Roanoke Coll, BS, 1950; Univ of Virginia, ME, 1955; D Ed, 1960. *Appointments:* Math Tchr, Falls Church HS, 1950; US Army, 1951-53; Math Tchr Richlands HS, 1953-55; Asst Prin, 1955-57; Research Assoc, Extension Instr, Univ of Va, 1958-60; Asst Assoc, Prof, dept Chmn, Middle Tenn State Univ, 1960-. *Memberships:* Natl Council of Tchrs of Mathematics; Mathematical Assn of America; Tenn Math Tchrs Assn; Middle Tenn Math Tchrs. *Honours:* Outstanding Tchrs Award; NSF Acad Year Inst Recipient. *Hobbies:* Camping; Reading; Gardening; Travel. *Address:* 2148 Elam Road, Murfreesboro, TN 37130, USA. 7, 15.

SPRIGGE Timothy Lauro Squire, b. 14 Jan 1932, London, England. Univ Tchr. m. Giglia Gordin, 4 Apr 1959, 1 s, 2 d. *Education:* BA, 1955; MA, 1961; PhD, 1961. *Appointments:* Lectr, Univ of London, 1961- 63; Lectr, Univ of Sussex, 1963-70; Reader, 1970-78; Prof, Edinburgh, 1979-90; Prof, Emeritus & Endowment Fellow, 1990-. *Publications include:* Facts, Words & Beliefs; The Rational Foundation ot Ethnics. *Memberships:* Mind Assn; Aristotelian Soc; Soc for Applied Philosophy; Scots Philosophical Soc. *Hobby:* Backgammon. *Address:* Philosophy Dept, David Hume Tower, Univ of Edinburgh, George Square, Edinburgh, EH8 9 JX, Scotland. 1.

SPRINGMAN Sarah Marcella, b. 26 Dec 1956, London, Englnad. Univ Asst Lectr. *Education:* Wycombe Abbey Sch, 1968-74; Girton Coll, Cambridge, 1975-78; Engrng Sci Tripos, Univ Roscoe Priae for Soil Mech; M Phil in Soil Mech, St Catherines Coll 1984; PhD,Magdalene Coll, Cambridge, 1989. *Appointments:* Engr, Sir Alexander Gibb & Partner, 1979-83; Australia, UK & Dam Engr, Monaskvu, Fiji, 1983-84; Research Student, Cambridge, 1985-88; Research Asst, 1988-89; Research Assoc, Research Fellow, 1990; Univ Asst, Lect, Magdalene, 1990-; Governor, Marlborough Coll, 1990-. *Publications:* Tech Papers in Engrng Journals; Conference Proceedings; Numerous Articles. *Memberships:* Inst of Civil Engrs; Chartered Engr; Inst of Royal Engrs; Womens Engrng Soc; Intl Trithlon Union; Womens Commission ITU; British Trithlon Assn. *Honours:* Univ Blue; Fiji & South Pacific Squash Champ; British Triathlon Champ; European Triathlon Champ; 5 Individual Silver; 2 Bronze; 1 Team Silver; 2 Team Bronze; Bronze Medal Bicycle Time Trial Nationals; Cosmopolitan Women of Chievement Award. *Hobbies:* Trithlon; Multisports; Opera. *Address:* Magdalene College, Cambridge, CB3 0AG, England.

SPROUL Loretta Ann, b. 25 Oct 1938, Milwakee, Wis, USA. Tchr; Reading & Mathematics Specialist. m. Hugh Ball Sproul, 30 July 1966, 1 s, 1 d. *Education:* Mount Mary Coll, BS, 1960; Univ of Wisconsin, MS, 1966; James Madison Univ, MS, 1978. *Appointments:* Tchr, Milwaukee Public Sch, 1960-62, 1963-64, 1965-66, 1967-78; Dept of Def Overseas Schs, 1962-63; Okinawa, 1964-65; Muscogee County sch, 1966-67; Fort Bragg Dependant Schs; Facilitator. Summer Educational Experiences for Knowledge, 1989-; Reading Specialist. Staunton City Schs, 1976-; Chmn, Maths

Dept, Staunton City Sch, 1980-. *Memberships:* Mothers Against Drunk Drivers; Natl Council of Tchrs of Mathematics; Valley of Virginia Council of Tchrs of Maths; Alphe Delta Kappa; Shenandoah Reading Council; Natl Reading Assn. *Honours:* Outstanding Young Women of America; Excellence in Educ Award. *Hobbies:* Reading; Travel; Volunteer Work; Swimming. *Address:* 951 E Beverley St, Staunton, VA 24401, USA. 7, 15.

SRIVASTAVA Awdhesh Chandra, b. 12 Apr 1934, Raiberalli, India. Conslt Physician. m. Sandra Bayliss, 10 Apr 1976, 2 s, 2 d. *Education:* MBBS, 1961; MD, 1971; Dip Ven, 1977; FPA cert, 1977; PhD, 1983. *Appointments:* Medical Officer, Snr MO, 1961-72; Registrar in GU Medicine, England, 1972-74; Snr Registrar, GU Medicine, 1974-80; Conslt GU Medicine, 1980-. *Publications include:* Journal of Experimental Medicine; Journal of Medical Microbiology; Modern Medicine; Hospital Doctor. *Memberships include:* General Medical Council; Blackliners AIDS Helpline; British Assn of Medical Mngrs; British Soc of Colposcopy & Cervical Pathology. *Hobbies:* Travel; Cooking. *Address:* 12 Chainwalk Drive, Truro, Cornwall, TR1 3ST, England.

SROKA Stanislaw, b. 12 Sept 1941, Wola Malowana, Poland. Inz Zootechnik. m. Sroka Teresa, 17 Sept 1966, 2 s. *Education:* Lyceum Pedagogic Czestochowa, 1959; Zootechnic Faculty of the Agricl Coll of Wroclaw, 1966; Master Degree Eng Zootechnician, Doc Degree on the Acad of agricl, Wroclaw, 1988. *Appointments:* Tchr, primary Sch Slupiec, Nowa Ruda, 1959-60; Trainee, asst Mgr, State Farm, Clinka, 1966-67; Mgr, State Farm Chocieborowice, 1968-71; Group of the Agricl Sch, Grabonog, Tchr, 1971-74; Vice Headmaster, 1974-77; Headmaster, 1977-. *Publications include:* About 50 Articles. *Memberships:* Assn of Engrs & Tech of Agricl in Gostyn; Polish Tchrs Assn; Culture Soc in Gostyn; Assn the Earths Koscian Lovers; The Bounds of the Voluntary Firebrigades Guards; Peoples Provincial Council; Peoples Univ of Great Poland. *Honours include:* Ministry of Agriclt, First Degree; Marks od Distinction; Cross of the Single of the Revival Poland; God Medal for the Care of the Ancients & Other Regions Medals. *Hobbies:* Ethnografic & History of Arts & Regionalism; Collection for Edmund Bojanowskis Museum in Grabonog; Poetry; Writing. *Address:* Grabonog 62 A, woj Leszczynskie, 63 820 Piaski, Poland.

SSU MA Chung Yuan, b. 2 Feb 1933. Bd Chmn, Chinese Youth Writing Assn. m. 8 May 1953, 1 s. *Appointments:* Bd Chmn, Chinese Youth Writing Assn; Member ROC Pan Assn; Standing Dir, Chinese Leterature Assn; Standing Dir, Chinese Copyright Owners Assn; Judge, Natl Literature Award. *Publications:* More than 70 Works; Wilderness; Spiritual Words; Violent Winds & Sands; Green Willow Village; Camel Bell; Belated Spring. *Memberships:* ROC pen Assn; Asian Chinese Language Authors Assn; Chinese Literature Assn; Chinese Youth Writing Assn; Copyrigh Owners Assn. *Honours include:* 1st Literature Award for Youth Nationwide; Award for Special Contributions to United Daily News; Natl Literature Award. *Address:* 34 Alley 34, Lane 101, Hsinhai Road, Sec 4, Taipei, Taiwan, China.

STA MARIA Felixberto, b. 22 Aug 1922, Philippines. University President. m. Teresita Pronove Sta Maria, 7 June 1953, 3 d. *Education:* BSE cum laude, Univ Philippines, 1948; MA, Engl Lit, Stanford Univ, USA, 1952; PhD, Communication, MI Univ, 1962. *Appointments:* Chmn, Engl Dept, 1962-64, Dean, Coll Educ, 1967-70, Univ Philippines; Dir, Ateneo de Manila Univ Press, 1970-75; Pres, Far Eastern Univ, Manila, 1989-. *Publications:* Philippine Folk Songs and Ballads: Through a Changing Culture, 1960; Scholarly Publishing in the Philippines: A Review and Assessment, 1973; The Philippines in Song and Ballad, 1976. *Memberships:* Past Pres, Philippine Accrediting Assn Schools, Colls and Univs; Chief Cons, Senate Comm Educ, Arts and Culture, 1988-90; Phi Kappa Phi, Phil Chapt, VP 1958-

59; Past Pres, Fedn Accrediting Agcys Philippines. *Honours:* Univ Philippines Fellow, Stanford Univ, 1951-52; ICA-Univ Philippines Fellow, MI State Univ, 1959-62; Ford Fndn Grantee to visit sci tchng ctrs, USA, Europe, 1968. *Hobbies:* Painting; Writing. *Address:* Far Eastern University, Nicanor Reyes Sr Street, Manila, Philippines.

STABLE (Rondle) Owen (Charles), b. 28 Jan 1923, London, England. Snr Circuit Judge. m. Yvonne Brook Holliday, 6 Apr 1949, 2 d. *Education:* Winchester. *Appointments:* Rifle Brigade, 1940-46; Barrister Middle Temple, 1948; Queens Counsel, 1963; Deputy Chmn Herts, 1963-71; Rencher Middle Temple, 1969; Recorder Crown Court, 1972-79; Cir Judge, 1979; Snr Cir Judge, 1982. *Memberships:* Chancellor Diocese of Bangor. *Hobbies:* Shooting; Music. *Address:* The Crown Court, Snares Brook, Hollybush Hill, London E11 1QW, England.

STABLEFORTH David Edward, b. Exeter, Devon, England. Conslt Physician. m. 11 May 1968, 1 s, 2 d. *Education:* Trino Sch, Cornwall, 1954-60; St Catherines Coll, Cambridge, 1960-63; St Marys Hosp, London, 1963- 67. *Appointments:* Snr Medical, London, 1975-77; East Birmingham Hosp, 1977-. *Memberships:* Royal coll of Physicians. *Hobbies:* Sailing; Canoeing; Hill Walking; Conversation; Theatre. *Address:* East Birmingham Hosp, Beverly Green Road, Birmingham B9 5PS, England.

STACEY Norma Elaine, b. 13 Sept 1925, Roanoke, LA, USA. Civic & Youth Worker. m. (1) Louis Brwer, dec, (2) Truman Stacey, 2 Feb 1980, 2 s. *Education:* Bach of Arts, St Marys Dominion Coll, New Orleans, La, 1946. *Appointments:* Accountant, Cities Serv Refinery, 1946-49; Sec, La Tchrs Retirement System, 1950-51; Mge, Brewer Studios, 1951-78; Co Owner, Trahan Insurance Corp, 1964-72; Co Owner, Trahan Farms, Ravat Estate, Trahan Estate, 1969-. *Memberships include:* American Rose Soc; Lake Charles Rose Soc; Art Assoc of Lake Charles; Natl Catholic Committee of Scouting; St Patrick Hosp Auxiliary; Natl Trust for Historic Presevation. *Honours include:* Natl Honors, American Guild of Piano Comps; Scouting Scroll of Honor; 25 Yr Appreciation Award, Lake Charles Club. *Hobbies:* Flower Gardening; Interior Decorating; Music; Reading; Flower Arranging. *Address:* 1802 Second Avenue, Lake Charles, LA 70601, USA.

STACY John William, b 5 Feb 1942, Columbus, Ohio, USA. Minister of the Gospel. m. 6 Aug 1965, 1 s. *Education:* BA, Okla Christian Coll, 1966; MA Ala Christian Coll, 1981; D Ministry Internal Bible Inst & Sem, Orlando, 1982. *Appointments:* Ordained to Ministry Ch of Christ, 1962; Minister Ch of Chrsit Various Locatins, 1967-; Newbern Tenn, 1984-; Itinerant Missionary, Ch of Christ, Ghana, West Africa, India, Guyana, S Am, Caribbean, 1977-89; Pres, Adv Com Freed Hardeman Coll, Henderson Tenn, 1977-78. *Publications:* Author of 50 Religious Books; 1 Novel. *Membership:* Intl Platform Assn. *Hobbies:* Art; Reading; Writing; Poetry; Policits; Music. *Address:* 6769 Lanesferry Road, Newbern, TN 38059, USA. 7.

STADLER Peter, b. 19 Sept 1946, Copenhagen. Charging Dir. m. Karin, 24 Aug 1968, 2 s. *Education:* East Asiatic Com, A/S, 1966; Higher Commercial Diploma, Niels Brock Business Coll, 1968; Merkonom in Mktg, 1972; Works Management, 1973; Organ Devel, 1975; Personeel Management, 1976; Accounting, 1977; General Management, 1977; Financing, 1978. *Appointments:* Dansk Form A/S, Export Mgr, 1968-70; Cederroth A/S, Snr Product Mgr, 1970- 73; Kevi A/ S, Sales Mgr, 1973-76; Levi Strauss Scandinavia Aps, Country Mgr, 1976-80; Alkor Nordic K/S, Managing Dir, 1981-. *Memberships:* Dansk Merkonomforening; Verein Deutscher Marktforscher. *Address:* Skovvangen 5, 2920 Charlottenlund, Denmark.

STAFFORD Maurice Beverley, b. 13 Jan 1934, Northampton, England. Management Conslt. m. Victoria Jane Forbes, 4 Sept 1971, div, 1 s, 1 d. *Education:* Pembroke Coll, Cambridge, 1954-57; City Univ, London, MSc, 1971-72. *Appointments:* Natl Serv, RAEC, 1952-54; Trainee Accountant, Derbyshire County Council, 1957-62; principal Accountant, West Sussex CC, 1962-65; Chief Financial Officer, Sussex River Auth, 1965-71; Conslt, Mgr, KPHE Management Conslt, 1972-90; Independant Conslt, 1991-. *Memberships:* Chartered Inst of Public Finance & Accountancy; Chartered Assn of Certified Accountants; Inst of Management Conslts. *Hobbies:* Music; Lawn Tennis. *Address:* 12 Beaver Close, Crowborough, East Sussex, TN6 2NZ, England.

STAIKOV Zahari, b. 19 Dec 1927, Peshtera, Bulgaria. Sociologist. m. Lilia Petrova, 28 Feb 1953, 3 s. *Education:* Univ Degree Economics, 1948-53; PhD, 1960; Dr Habil, 1978. *Appointments:* Secondary Sch Tchr, 1946-48; Bulgarian News Agency, Editor, 1953; Higher Inst of Sports, Asst Prof, 1953-66; Inst of Labour, Assoc Prof, 1966-73; Res Inst for Trade Union Studies, Dir, 1974-76; Inst of Sociology, Prof, Hd of Dept, 1977-. *Publications:* More than 100 Sci Works. *Memberships:* Intl Assn of Time Research; Research Committee on Leisure; Intl Sociol Assn. *Hobbies:* Tourism; Bridge. *Address:* Inst of Sociology, 13A Moskovska Street, 1000 Sofia, Bulgaria.

STAINES David, b. 8 Aug 1946, Toronto, Canada. Prof. *Education:* St Michaels Coll Sch, Toronto, 1963; St Michaels Coll Univ of Toronto, BA, 1967; Harvard Univ, AM, 1968; PhD, 1973. *Appointments:* Tchrng Fellow, Harvard Univ, 1968-73; Asst Prof, 1973-78; Visiting Assoc Prof, Summers, 1980, 1982; Visiting Asst Prof, Univ of PEI, Summer, 1975; Hon Research Fellow Univ Coll London, 1977-78; Assoc Prof, Univ of Ottawa, 1978- 85; Prof, Univ of Ottawa, 1985-. *Creative Works include:* Translator. The Complete Tromances of Chretien de Troyes; Publi Various Articles & Reveiws. *Memberships:* Medieval Acad Am; Internat Arthurian Soc; Modern Lang Assn; Assn Canadn Univ Tchrs English. *Hobbies:* Theatre; Bridge. *Address:* 12 Galt Street, Ottawa, Ontario, Canada K1S 4R4.

STAMBUK Drage, b. 20 Sept 1950, Selca, Island of Brac, Croatia. Croatian Representative to Britain; Medical Doc. *Education:* Medical Faculty, Univ of Zagreb, 1969-74; Spec in Internal Medicine, Zagreb, 1977- 81; Gastroenterology & Hepatology, Zagreb, 1981-83. *Appointments:* Univ Hosp Zagreb, 1977-83; Royal Free Hosp, London, 1983-87; St Stephens Hosp, Westminster Hosp, 1987-90; St Bartholomews Hosp, 1990-91; Croatian Rep to Britain, 1991-. *Publications:* 7 Books of Poetry' 2 Anthologies of Croatian Poetry. *Memberships:* Croatian Medical Assn; Croatian Writers Assn; British Medical Assn; English PEN; Intl PEN; Croatian PEN. *Honours:* Literary Prize, Marko Marulie; Young Writers Award. *Address:* 4 Abbeville Road, London SW4 9NJ, England.

STAMNES Jakob Johan, b. 30 June 1943, Roset, Norway. Prof of Physics. m. Sigrid Kristin Stamnes, 28 Aug 1970, 2 d. *Education:* Msc, 1969; PhD, 1975. *Appointments:* Resercher, 1974-85; Research Mgr, 1985- 88; Managing Dir, 1988-; Prof, 1990-. *Publications:* 1 Book, Waves in Focal Regions; 50 Articles in Sci Journals. *Memberships:* European Optical Soc; Norwegion Physical Soc; Optical Soc of America. *Honour:* simrads Award for Achievements in Electro Optics. *Address:* Kvernkallo 12A, 0382 Oslo, Norway.

STAMP Gavin Mark, b. 15 Mar 1948, Bromley, Kent, England. Lectr; Architecture Historian. m. Alexandra Artley, 12 Feb 1982, 2 d. *Education:* Dulwich Coll, London; Gonville & Caius Coll, Cambridge; MA; PhD. *Appointemnts:* Lectr, Mackintosh Sch of Architecture in Glasgow, 1990-. *Publications include:* The Architects Calender; Temples of Power; The great Perspectivists; Erno Goldfinger; The English House, 1860-1914; Telephone Boxes. *Memberships:* Thirties Soc; Alexander

Thomson Soc. *Address:* 1 Moray Place, Strathbungo, Glasgow, G41 2AQ, Scotland. 1.

STANESBY Derek Malcolm, b. 28 Mar 1931, London, England. Canon of Windsor. m. Christine A Payne, 29 July 1958, 3 s, 1 d. *Education:* Leeds Univ, BA, 1956; Manchester Univ, MEd, 1975; Manchester Univ, PhD, 1984. *Appointments:* GPO Radio Research Station, Dollis Hill, London, 1947-51; RAF Navigator, 1951-53; Ordained Deacon, Norwich Cathedral, 1958; Curate, Norwich, 1958-61; Ordained Priest, Norwich Cathedral, 1959; Curate, Southwark, 1961-63; Vicar, St Mark Bury, 1963-67; Rector, St Chad Ladybarn Manchester, 1967-85; Canon of Coll of St George, Windsor Castle, 1985-. *Memberships:* Sci Reason & Religion; Soc of Ordained Scientists; Archbishops Commission on Christian Doctrine. *Hobbies:* Walking; Sailing; Woodwork. *Address:* 4 The Cloisters, Windsor Castle, Berks, SL4 1NJ, England. 1.

STANFORTH Anthony William, b. 27 July 1938, Ipswich, England. Univ Prof. m. Susan Margaret Vale, 2 Jan 1971, 2 s. *Education:* Univ of Durham, 1956-60; BA, 1960; MA, 1961; Heidelberg Univ, 1960-61; Marburg Univ, 1961-64; Dr Phil, 1966. *Appointments:* Carl Grey Memorial Fellow, 1962- 64; Univ Manchester, 1964-65; Newcastle Univ, 1965-81; Wisconsin Univ, 1970- 71; Heriot Watt Univ, 1981-. *Publications:* die Bezeichnuhgen fur Gross, Klein, Viel und Wenig Im Bereich Der Germania. *Membership:* Royal Soc of Arts. *Hobbies:* Opera; Photography; Travel. *Address:* Dept of Languages, Heriot Watt Univ, Riccarton, Edinburgh EH14 4AS, Scotland.

STANGERUP Henrik, b, 1 Sept 1937, Copenhagen, Denmark. Novelist; Filmmaker. m. Susanne Krage, 28 Aug 1982, 1 s. *Education:* Univ of Copenhagen, Theology, 1956-60; French Filmsch I;Idhec, 1964-65. *Appointments:* More tha 20 Books; 3 Films; Novels Translated into English; The Man Who Wanted to be Guilty; The Road to Lagoa Santa; The Suducer; Broth Jacob. *Memberships:* La Comite d'Honneur of Europe et Liberte, Paris; Libeirie European des Idees, Paris; he Danish Pen Club. *Honours:* The Danish Bookseller Prize; The Danish Critics Prize; The Amalienborg Prize; The danish Acad Big Prize. *Hobbies:* Gardening; Travel; Reading; Movies. *Address:* Jordberves 5, 4772 Langebaek, Denmark.

STANKEVICS Aleksandrs, b. 10 Dec 1932, Rezekne, Latvia. Painter; Interior Designer. m. Karin Steinberg, 12 May 1956, 1 s, 1 d. *Education:* Janis Rozentals Art School, 1946-50; Dept Painting, Latvian Acad Arts, 1950-56. *Career:* Sr Lectr, Graphic Art, Dept Interior Design, Graphic Art, 1962, Asst Prof, Graphic Art, 1972- , Hd, Graphic Dept, 1975, Prof, 1980-, Latvian Academy Arts; 1-man shows, Riga, 1971, 1986. *Creative works include:* Eaeel paintings: Scientists, 1971; Solstice, 1982; Monumental art: Interior design of Airport Riga. *Membership:* Latvian Artists Union. *Honours:* Dip and Medal for best creative achievements of yr, Latvian Artists Union, 1972. *Hobby:* Housekeeping. *Address:* Pales iela 7-1, Riga 226024, Latvia.

STANKIEWICZ Ludomir Stanislaw, b. 8 May 1934, Kality. Library Custodian. m. Zofia Marta Liberska, 18 July 1973, 1 s, 1 d. *Education:* MA, Polish Philology Univ, Wroclaw, 1960. *Appointments:* Zaklad Narodowyimienio Ossohinskch, Library Custodian, 1961-91. *Publications include:* Article Reviews; Diary; Periodicals. *Hobbies:* Hiking; Reading. *Address:* ul Bacciarellego 5 m 6, 51 649 Wroclaw, Poland.

STANLEY Helen Camille, b. 6 Apr 1930, Tampa, Florida, USA. Musician; Composer; Pianist. m. Widowed, 1 d. *Education:* Mus C Cincinnati Conservatory of Music, 1951; M Mus, Florida State Univ, 1954; BSc, Muskingum Coll, 1961. *Appointments:* Lectr, Jacksonville Univ, 1962-67; Instr, Communications Jones Coll, Jacksonville, 1965-66; Constl, Beaches Fine

Arts Series, Neptune beach, Florida, 1973-; Pianist, Composer, Florida Contemporary Ensemble, 1986-. *Creative Works:* Rhapsody for Electronic Tape & Orchestra; Allegro for Orchestra; Passacaglia for Orchestra; Sonate for Trombone & Pian; String Quartet; Overture for Brass & Timpani; Duo Sonata for Tape Recorder & Piano; Night Piece for Womens Chorus & Chamber Orchestra. *Memberships:* ASCAP; American Music Centre; Natl Soc of Arts & Letters; Pi Kappa Lambda Music Honorary; Soc of Mayflower Descendants; Piano Tchrs Congress of New York. *Honours include:* Pogner Music Comp Award; FSMTA MTNA Comp Commission Award; St Pauls by the Sea Commission Award. *Hobbies:* Art; Dancing; Walking. *Address:* 1768 Emory Circle S, Jacksonville, FL 32207, USA. 5.

STANLEY Peter, b. 20 Mar 1930, Derby, England. Prof of Mech Engrng. m. (1) Rennie Elizabeth Wilkinson, 31 July 1952, dec, 1 d, (2) Kathlenn Mary Evans, 5 July 1980, 1 s. *Education:* Natl Serv, 1949-51; Selwyn Coll, Cambridge Univ, 1951-54; BA, 1954; MA, 1958; Univ of Nottingham, PhD, 1963; Univ of Manchester, MSc, 1983. *Appointments:* Natl Serv, 1949-51; Tech Asst, Rolls Royce Ltd, Derby, 1954-57; Univ of Nottingham, Snr Research Asst, 1957-61; Lectr, 1961-71; Snr Lectr, 1971-75; Reader, 1975-78; Univ of Manchester, Prof of Mech Engrng, 1979-. *Publications include:* Edited Several Tech Books; Publ Many Papers in Tech Journals. *Memberships:* MI Mech E; FIMech E; C Eng; I Mech E; A Inst P; F Inst P; C Phys. *Hobbies:* Walking; Swimming; English Heritaging; Jonathan. *Address:* Engrng Dept, Simon Building, Univ of Manchester, Oxford Road, Manchester M13 9PL, England. 161.

STANTON Marietta Phyllis. b. 12 Sept 1948, Kingston, NY, USA. Assoc Prof; Dir of Continuing Educ. m. Gary W Stanton, 3 July 1982, 1 s, 1 d. *Education:* AAS, MTST Marys Coll, 1968; BSN, 1972; MA, New York Univ, 1977; PhD, Univ at Buffalo, 1982. *Appointments:* Assoc Prof, Dir Continuing Educ, Sch of Nursing, Univ At Buffalo, 1980-; Lieutenant Colonel United States Army Reserve, 1977-. *Publications:* Our Children Are Dying, What Can We Do About It; Nightingale & Hertimes; Co Editor. Extensive Journal Publi. *Memberships:* American Nurses Assn; New York State Nurses Assn; Profl Nurses Assn; Sigma Theta Tall; Reserve Officers Assn; Leadership Buffalo; Buffalo Ambassadors; Assn of Military Surgeons. *Honours include:* Sigma Theta Tau Gamma Kappa Chapter; MT St Marys Coll & American Legion Scholarship. *Hobbies:* Reading; Porcelain Doll Making; Sewing; Skiing. *Address:* 27 Cascade Drive, Amherst, NY 14228, USA. 5.

STAPENHURST Frederick (Rick) Charles, b. 19 July 1948, Capetown, Canada. Diplomat; Civil Servant. m. Cathryn Louise Cochrane, 24 June 1975, 1 s, 1 d. *Education:* Bach of Arts, 1970; Master of Arts, 1976; Master of Business Admin, 1983; Doc of Business Admin, 1988. *Appointments:* Counselloe, Consul Addmin Ababa, 1987-91; Civil Servant, Ottawa, 1984-87; Economist, Banker, 1970-84. *Publications:* The Canadian Women Guide to Money; Industrial Democracy Today, A New Rose For Labour; Political Risk Analysis Around The North Atlantic. *Memberships:* Council for Intl Business Risk Management; Natl Assn of Business Economist; Acad for Intl Business; Inst of Profl Studies. *Honours:* Award of Excellence. *Hobbies:* Development Studies; Philately; Writing. *Address:* 181 Stewart Street, Ottawa, Ontario, Canada.

STAPLE David, b. 30 Mar 1930, Chesham, Bucks. General Sec, Free Church Federal Council. m. Margaret Lilian Berrinton, 23 July 1955, 1 s, 3 d. *Education:* Christs Coll, Cambridge, MA, 1950-53; Regents Park Coll, Oxford, 1953-55; Wadham Coll, Oxford, MA, 1953-55; BD London, 1957. *Appointments:* Baptist Minister, West Hamm Central Mission, 1955-58; Llanishen, Cardiff, 1958-74; Coll Road, Harrow, 1974-86; General sec, Free Church Federal Council, 1986-. *Memberships:* Baptist Missionary Soc; Baptist Union Council. *Honour:*

Bishop Gells Hebrew Prize. *Hobbies:* Fell Walking; Music. *Address:* Free Church Federal Council, 27 Tavistock Square, London WC1H 9HH, England. 1.

STAPLETON Guy, b. 10 Nov 1935, Derby, England. Chief Exec, Intervention Board. *Education:* Malvern Coll, 1949-53. *Appointments:* Clerical Office, Ministry of Transport & Civil Aviation, 1954-58; Exec Officer, 1958; Transferred to Ministry of Aviation, 1959; Civil Aviation Asst, British Embassy, Rome, 1960-63; Private Sec to Controller of Natl Air Traffic Control Services, 1963-65; Asst Principal, MAFF, 1965; Private Sec to Jt Parly Sec, 1967-68; principal, 1968; Asst Sec, 1973; Dept of Prices & Consumer Sec, Cabinet Office, 1982-85; Dir of Establishments, MAFF, 1985-86. *Publications:* poets England, Gloucestershire; Somerset & Avon; Devon; Hertfordshire; Leicestershire & Rutland; Vale of Moreton Churches; Memories of Moreton. *Membership:* First Division Assn. *Hobbies:* History of North Cotswolds; Family History; Tolographical Verse. *Address:* c/o Intl Board, PO Box 69, Reading, RG1 7QW, England. 1.

STARK Stanley Leroy, b. 25 Mar 1941, Eureka, California, USA. Author; Sch Admin. m. Dorothy June Shoemaker, 27 Dec 1957, 6 s, 6 d. *Education:* BA, Elementary Educ, 1965; MA, Educ Admin, 1989; California State Univ, Arcata; Life Credetials; General Elementary Tchrng, 1965; Admin Serv, 1982. *Appointments:* Tchr, Cutten Elementary Sch District Eureka, 196-67; Sacramento City Schs, Sacramento California, 1967- 69; River Delta Sch District, Rio Vista, California, 1969-79; Superintendent, San Lucas Sch District, 1982-89; Owner, Real Estate Business Eureka, 1964-80; Proprieter Restaurant, Bait Shop, Boat Rental, Sacramento, 1971-77; Newspaper Distributor, 1979-80. *Publications include:* Books. Trijnitje Jonas; John Stark and the Donner Party; Bi Monthly Column on Education. *Memberships:* Church of Jesus Christ of Latter Day Saints; Sunday Sch Superintendent; Seminary Tchr; California State Univ Alumni Assn; Assn of California Sch admin; Desert Club of Arcata; Boy Scouts of America; Cub Scoutmaster. *Honours:* Special award, Migrant Office of Educ; Outstanding Leadership Award. *Hobbies:* Reading; writing; Wood & Cahinsaw Carving; Painting; Drawing; Photography; Running; Playing the Ukelele & French Horn; Genealogy & Studying Local Histories. *Address:* 106 Melrose Court, Vacaville, CA 95687, USA. 59.

STARR David, b. 10 Apr 1950, Los Angeles, USA. Makeup Artist; Photographer. *Education:* Honorary Degree, Stanford Univ, Medicine, 1966; UCLA, BPA, 1972. *Appointments:* Davin Stark Beauty Inc; Conslt, Motown, Chanel, Revlon. *Publications:* The David Starr Beauty Book; Several Paintings; Photo Shows. *Memberships:* Modern Art Council; Shaiti Project; Opera Guild. *Honours include:* Cable Car Award; Best Makeup Artist in SF; Vogue Best in SF. *Hobbies:* Painting; Music; Weight Training; Exercise. *Address:* 166 Geary Street, Penthouse, SFO, CA 94108, USA.

STASINOPOULOU Maro, b. 13 Nov 1961, Athens. Writer; Editor. *Education:* Law, Univ of Athens. *Appointments:* Editor, Mag, Delphic Writing Books, 1984-88; Editor, Newspaper, Contemporary Thought, 1990-; Occasional Broadcasting in the Radio. *Publications:* World 75; Annunciations; Days withou Frontiers; Revolution; The Light that Travels. *Memberships:* Natl Assn of Greek Writers; Acad Culturale de l'Europa in Rome. *Honours:* Special Prize at the Acad of Kalavria; Medal of Loczi; First Prize of Poetry of the Organization of Friendship Between Italy & Greece. *Hobbies:* Painting; Horseback Rising; Swimming. *Address:* 8 Zakynthou Street, GR 113 61 Athens, Greece.

STAVELEY Norman Stuart, b. 3 Dec 1928, Hull, England. Chartered Accountant. m. Gwendoline Leaper, 26 Dec 1959, 1 s. *Appointments:* Fawley Judge, Easton, 1944-54; Practice in Own Name, 1954-67; Partner, AJ Downs & Co, Downs Kidsons, Kidsons, Kidsons Impey.

Publications: Still Working n Biographical Dictionary of Hull Musicians from 1780. *Memberships:* ICAEW; Hull Literary Club; Various Musical, Charitable Bodies. *Hobbies:* Music; Local History; Profl Interest in Authors & Playwrights. *Address:* 23 Anlaby Park Road North, Hull, HU4 6XN, England.

STAYSHYN Walter Theodore, b. 14 Nov 1934, Hamilton, Ontario, Canada. Superior Court Justice; Law. m. Katherine Josephine Dubois, 17 June 1967, 1 s, 1 d. *Education:* McMaster Univ, BA, 1958; Osboode Hall Law Sch, LLB, 1961; Read Law with John L Agro QC, 1961-62; Ontario Bar Exam, 1962- 63; Called to the Intari Bar, 1963. *Appointments:* Assoc Agro Cooper, 1963-64; Founding Partner, Borkovich & Stayshyn, 1964-75; Chmn, Ham Went Legal Aid Area Comm, 1973; Dir; District Court Judge, 1975-90; Ont Court of Justice, 1990-. *Creative Works:* Speaker & Panelist at Educ Legal And Insurance Functions. *Memberships:* Mount Mary Acad; Hamilton Lawyers Club; Ham Went District Health Council & Aids Steering Committee; Ont District Court Judges Assn; St Jospehs Villa Foundation; Ont Superior Court Judges Assn; Canadian Judges Conference; McMaster Alumni Assn; McMasters Lettermans Assn. *Honour:* McMaster Univ Letter, Football & Basketball. *Hobbies:* Gardening; Sports Fan. *Address:* Court House, 50 Main St East, Hamilton, Ontario, Canada, L8N 1E9. 142.

STEARS Michael John, b. 25 Aug 1934. Special Effects Film Dir. m. Brenda Doreen Livy, 15 Sept 1960, 2 d. *Education:* Harrow Art Coll; Southall Tech Coll; Army Serv, RMP. *Appointments include:* Reach for the Sky, Miniature Planes, 1956; Sin The Bismarck, Miniature Guns, 1960; From Russia with Low, Specture Helicopter, The Destruction of the Spectre Flotilla by fire, 1963; Fiddler On The Roof, Effect of Thousands of Rats, 1972; The Martian Chronicles, 1979; Escape 2000, 1980; Sahara, Miniature of the Boat, Full Size Storm Sequence Effects, 1984; Navy Seal, 1989. *Memberships:* ACTT; BKSTS; BSFA; SMAE. *Honours:* Oscar Best Special Effects, Thumberball, Star Wars. *Hobbies:* Showing; Breeding; Judging, Borzos; Pres, British Sight Hound Field Assn; Model Aircraft; Vintage Motor Cycle Collecting; Paintings in Oil. *Address:* Welders House, Welders Lane, Chalfont St Peter, Buckinghamshire, SL9 8TT, England.

STEDALL Robert Henry, b. 6 Aug 1942, Woking, England. Finance Dir. m. Elizabeth Jane Clay, 24 June 1972, 1 s, 1 d. *Education:* Marlborough Coll, Wilshire; McGill Univ, Montreal, Bach of Commerce, 1964. *Appointments:* McClelland moores Co, Glasgow & London, CA, 1967; Bowater Corporation, 1968-82; Gartmore Jnv Management, 1984-88; Natl Employers Life Assurance Co, 1989-. *Memberships:* Inst of Chartered Accountants of Scotland; Stock Exchange Exams; Ironmongers Co Master; Dunsfold Parish Council. *Hobbies:* Gardening; Tennis; Golf; Bridge. *Address:* Knightons, Dunsfold, Godalming, Surrey GU8 4NU. 53.

STEDMAN Patricia Rosamund Kathleen, b. 17 Feb 1938, Durban, SA. Managing Dir, Patricia Stedman Investment Management. *Education:* St Marys, Bucks, 1949-55; Catherine Judsons, Secretarial Coll, London. *Appointments:* J A Brevin, Stockbrokers, London, 1957-66; Secretarial/Stock Broker, 1976-86; Mgr Exec Brewin Dulpain, Jersey; Managing Dir, Jersey Overseas Investment Managmnt, 1989; Founder, Patricia Stedman Investment Management. *Memberships:* Royal Channel Island Yacht Club; Jersy Race Club. *Hobbies:* Sailing; Motor Cruising; Horse Racing; Travel; Politics; Humanitarian; Riding; Ecological; Literature. *Address:* The Stable Flat, North Dale, St Ouen, Jersey JE3 2DU, Channel Island, England. 138.

STEELE Stuart James, b. 13 Jan 1930. Medicine. m. Jill Westgate Smith, 23 Oct 1965, 2 s. *Education:* Westminster Sch, 1946-48; Trinity Coll, Cambridge, 1950-53; Middlesex Hosp Medical Sch. *Appointments:*

Gunner, 2lt RA, 1948-50; Snr Lectr, Middlesex Hosp Medical Sch, 1969-73; Hon Conslt, Middlesex Hosp, 1969-; Reader, 1973-87; Univ Coll, London, 1987-; Dir, Middlesex Hosp Medical Sch, 1973-87; Assoc Dir, Univ Coll & Hosp, 1987-. *Publications:* Gynaecology Obstetrics & The Neonate; Numerous papers. *Contributions to:* Books. *Memberships:* The Royal Soc of Medicine; The British Medical Assn; The Blair Bell Research Soc; British Fertility Soc. *Honour:* Who Fellowship. *Hobbies:* Gardening; Theatre; Opera; Ballet. *Address:* The Middlesex Hospital, Mortimer Street, London W1N 8AA, England. 170.

STEFANOV Tsenko Jelev, b. 17 June 1958, Sofia, Bulgaria. Photo Reporter. m. Raina Dimitrova Stefanova, 7 Feb 1986, 1 s. *Education:* Coll of Cinema Techics, 1980; Coll J Foutchik Soeciality phorgrapher, 1984. *Appointments:* Deputy Reporter, Newspaper, Sofia News, 1979-80; Asst Camerman, Bulgarian TV, 1980-82; Film Production Photographer, 1983; Photographer, Maguistrali, 1984-88; Natl Theatre, 1990-91; Newspaper Cultura, 1990-91. *Memberships:* Union of Bulgarian Journalists. *Honour:* Big Prize of the Cocours Organisied b the Newspaper Trasporten Glas. *Hobbies:* Theatre; Sports; Automobilism; Ballet. *Address:* 28 3rd April Street, Sofia 1003, Bulgaria.

STEFANOVIC Pera, b. 21 June 1927, Pristina, Yugoslavia. Publicist. m. Terezija Brus, 8 Nov 1948, 1 s, 1 d. *Education:* Law Sch, 1960-63. *Appointments:* profl Politican, 1946-52; Journalist, 1952-63; Dir, Natl Museum of Kosovo & Metohija, 1963-66. *Publications:* Tales; Short Stories; Books. *Memberships:* Writers Assn of Serbia; Redaction Edition Jedinstvo; Serbian Foundation Dragojlo Dudic; Folklor Assn of Kosovo & Metohia. *Honours include:* 4 War Awards & Decorations; Merited Citizen of Pristina; Award of Writers Assn of Kosovo, Book of the Year. *Hobbies:* Fishing; Walking; Reading. *Address:* Marsala Tita 24, 38000 Pristina, Yugoslavia.

STEICHEN Joanna, b. 22 Feb 1933, New York City, USA. Psychotherapist. m. Edward Steichen, 19 Mar 1960. *Education:* AB, Smith Coll, 1954; MSSW, Columbia Univ Sch of Social Work, 1973; Cert in Psychoanalytic Psychotherapy, 1976. *Appointments:* Young & Rubicam Inc, 1955-60; Mount Sinai Hosp, Social Worker, 1970-71; South Beach Psychiatric Centre, 1973-75; Private Practice of Psychotherapy, 1975-; New Hope Guild Centers, Dir of Group Therapy Training, 1981-88. *Publications:* Marrying Up; An American Dream, And Reality; Articles. *Memberships:* Center for the Advancement of Group Studies; American Group Psychotherapy Assn; American acad of Psychotherapists; Soc of Clinical Social Work Psychotherapists; Authors Guild. *Honour:* Art Directors Club, Distinctive Merit Award. *Hobbies:* Architectural Renovation; Healthy Uses of Religion; Folk Singing; Theatre. *Address:* 50 West 29th Street, New York, NY 10001, USA. 5, 6.

STEIN Ronald Max, b. 24 Nv 1927, London W1, England. Advertising, Design & Print Conslt. m. Rosalie Landau, 21 Sept 1958, 2 d. *Education:* Mary Lesbone Central Sch, 1935-39; City of London Sch, 1939; Marlborough Coll, 1939; Magdalen Coll, Brackley, 1940-42; Christs Coll, Finchley, 1942-44; St Martins Sch of Art, 1945-47. *Appointments:* Leon Goodman Displays, 1944; Royds Advertising Ltd, Asst to Mgrng Dir, 1945-55; Stowe & Bowden Ltd, Studio Mgr, 1955-59; Own Advertising Conslt, 1959-. *Publications:* Diabetic Cookery Book; Eve Assn Club Souvenir Brochure; St Lawrence Jewry Guid of Glass Engravers; Catalogue of Works by Fellows & Assoc Fellows. *Memberships:* Advertising Assn; Periodical Proprietors Assn; Publicity Club of London; Assn Member Inst of Directors; Creative Circle; Audit Bureau of Circulations; Guild of Glass Engravers. *Hobbies:* Photography; Opera; Classical Music; Current Affairs; History; Geography; Politics; Theatre; Cinema; Glass Engraving; drawing; Painting;

Industrial & Other Intelligence. *Address:* 11 Cleve Road, West Hampstead, London NW6 3RH, England. 52.

STEINER Robert Emil, b. 1 Feb 1918, Prague. Emeritus Prof of Diagnostic Radiology. m. Gertrude, 17 Mar 1945, 2 d. *Education:* Univ of Vienna, 1935-38; Univ Coll of Dublin, 1938-41; MB ChB BAO, 1940; FFR, 1948; MD, 1957; FRCP, 1965; FRCS, 1982. *Appointments:* Dupty Dir, Hammersmith Hosp, 1950-57; Lectr, Diag Radiol RPMS, 1950-57; Dir, Hammersmith Hosp, 1957-60; Prof, Univ of London, Dir, Hammersmith Hosp & Royal Post Graduate Medical Sch, 1960-83; Emeritus Prof, Univ of London Hammersmith Hosp, 1983-. *Memberships include:* Natl Radiological Protection Bd; Effects of Ionizing Radiation; Advisor in Radiology to The Dept of Health & Social Security. *Honours include:* Gold Medal of Royal Coll of Radiologists; CBE. bb2Hobbies: Gardening; Music; Walking; Skiing. *Address:* NMR Unit, Hammersmith Hospital, DuCane Road, London W12 0H3, England.

STEINKE Klaus Dieter Helmut, b. 27 Jan 1942, Mesertiz. Slavist Linguist; Prof. m. Marika Angelova, 6 Aug 1967, 2 d. *Education:* PhD, Univ Muchen, 1968; Habil, Univ Heidelberg, 1986. *Appointments:* Lectr, German Acad Exchange Serv, Rumania, 1969-73; Bucharest, 1973-77; Research Inst German Lang, Mannheim, 1977-78; Asst Prof, Univ Heidelberg, 1978-86; Prof, 1986. *Memberships:* Soc Linguistic Europaeae; Int Scholarly Ass of Researchers of Old Ritualism; Inst of Slavic Studies, Univ Erlangen, Germany. *Address:* Inst fur Slavistik, Friedrich Alexander Universitat, Erlangen Nurnberg, Bismarckstrasse 1, D-8520 Erlangen, Germany. 52.

STELL Christopher Fyson, b. 26 Jan 1929, Liverpool, England. Conslt. m. Dorothy Jean Mackay, 17 Aug 1957, 2 s. *Education:* Liverpool Coll; Univ of Liverpool, B Arch, 1955; MA, 1960. *Appointments:* Royal Commission on Historical Minuments, Investigator, 1955-89; Conslt, 1989. *Publications include:* Articles; Reviews; In Inventory of Nonconformist Chapels in South West England. *Memberships:* Royal Inst of British Architects; Soc of Antiquaries of London; Royal Archaeological Inst; Ancient Monuments Soc; The Chapels Soc; Cathederals & Churches Advisory Commitee of English Heritage. *Honour:* OBE. *Hobbies:* Book Binding; Photography. *Address:* Frognal, 25 Berks Hill, Chorleywood, Herts, WD3 5AG, England.

STELMASIAK Zbigniew, b. 18 Apr 1941, Lublin, Poland. Physician. m. Teresa Parzychowska, 11 July 1964, 2 d. *Education:* Faculty of Medicine, Sch of Medicine, Lublin, Poland, Diploma of Physician, 1964; MD, 1970; DSc, 1976; British Council Scholarship, Inst of Neurology, natl Hosp, London,1972-73. *Appointments:* Sch of Medicine, Faculty of Medicine, ept of Neurology, Asst, 1966; Snr Asst, 1968; Snr Lecyr, 1970; Asst Prof, 1977; Univ Dept of Neurology, Neurosrgery, Tridoli, Libya, 1989-; Snr Conslt Neurologist, 1982-89; Specialistic Hosp Lublin, 1989-. *Publications:* Original Papers in the Field of Patochemistry of CNS Diseases. *Memberships:* Polish Neurological Assn; Intl MS Soc; Intl Ligue Against Epilepsy; World Federation of Neurology. *Hobbies:* Lawn Tennis; Swimming; Chess. *Address:* Poli Gojawiczynskiej 80 Street, 20-827 Lublin, Poland.

STEN-KNUDSEN Nina Marie, b. 2 Dec 1957, Copenhagen, Denmark. Artist; Painter; Sculptor. m. 2 d. *Education:* Royal Acad of Art, Copenhagen, 1975-82. *Appointments:* Eight One Person Exhib, 1979-92; Over Forty Group Exhib, 1979-92. *Creative Works:* Axes; Horse; Yaibichai; Herrera; The River; The Art of the Alphabet; The Boat; The Fractal Painting; Lockaste; Nanoseconds. *Memberships:* The Soc of Artists; Tourisiana Museum of Art; Natl Gallery Copenhagen; Museum of Art n Aalborg. *Honours:* Endowment from the Danish State Art Foundation; Danish Natl Bank; The Memory of Kaastrup Olsens. *Hobbies:* Horseriding; Plyaing Drums; African Dancing; Shooting Bow &

Arrow. *Address:* Pile Alle 17 A itv, 2000 Fredericksberg, Denmark.

STENCLOVA Jitka, b. 10 Dec 1952, Opava, Czechoslovakia. Textile Artist. m. Cyril Hoschl, 21 Sept 1976, 2 s, 2 d. *Education:* Acad Applied Arts, Prague, 1968-72; Univ Applied Arts, Prague, 1972-77. *Career:* Indep Artist, 1977-; 2-person exhibs: Gall Centrum, Prague (w A Werner), 1979, (w A Hepnar), 1988; Gall Letna, Prague (w A Werner), 1981; Collection of tapestries, Mus Applied Art, Jindrichuv Hradec (w J Slamova), 1989; Participant, num exhibs: Jindrichuv Hradec, Prague, Opava; London, 1972; Leningrad, 1973; Annecy, Angers, 1978; Mulhouse, Calais, Mongolia, Moscow, 1979; Riga, Vilnius, Berlin, Munich, Vienna, 1980; Cuba, Copenhagen, 1983; Brussels, 1983, 1985, Erfurt, 1983, 1986; Vadstena, Gothenburg, Stockholm, Falun, 1989; Poperinge, Nordhalben, Chester, 1990; Frankfurt-am-Main, 1991. *Creative works include:* Four Seasons, bobbin lace, in Musee Royaux d'Art et Histoire, Brussels, 1975; Paradigm, tapestry, 1988; Four Appearances of Soul, tapestries, 1988-90; Works in other pub collections, Power House, Sydney, Mus Applied Arts, Prague, Arts and Crafts Ctr, Prague, N Bohemian Gall Art, Litomerice, Czech Fndn Arts, Lounovice, Jan Neruda Gymnasium, Prague, Gymnasium, Prague-Liben, Textile HS, Liberec; Works represented in Fiberarts Design Book Four, 1991. *Membership:* Czech Union Artists. *Honours:* Prize, Acad Applied Arts, Prague, 1976; 2nd Prize, 3rd Quadrennial Fine Art, Erfurt, Germany. *Hobbies:* Fibreart (weaving, bobbing, painting); Trees. *Address:* Rakovskeho 3143, 14300 Prague 4, Czechoslavakia.

STENLAKE John Bedford, b. 21 Oct 1919, Ealing, London, England. Honorary Prof. m. Anne Beatrice Holder, 14 July 1945, 5 s, 1 d. *Education:* Sch of Pharmacy, Univ of London, 1939-42; Birkbeck Coll, Univ of London, 1945-47. *Appointments:* Boots the Chemist, 1935-39; Sch of Pharmacy, Univ of London, 1939-42; Royal Air Force, Pilot, 1942-45; Demonstrator, Asst Lectr, Lect in Pharmaceutical Chemistry, Univ of London, 1945-52; Snr Lectr, Royal Coll of Sci & Tech, Glasgow, 1952-61; Prof, Univ of Strathclyde, 1961-82; Honorary Prof, 1982-. *Publications:* Over 100 Papers; Reviews; Articles. *Memberships:* British Pharmacopoeia Commission; European Pharacopoeia Commission; Medicines Commission; Lanarkshire Health Bd; British Pharmaceutical Conference. *Honours include:* Jacob Bell Memorial scholarship; Mullard Medal of the Royal Soc; Charter Gold Medal of the Royal Pharmaceutical Soc. *Hobbies:* Reading; Gardening. *Address:* Mark Corner, Twynholm, Kircudbright, DG6 4PR, England.

STEPANOV Yuri Sergueevich, b. 20 July 1930, Moscow, Russia. Researcher in Linguistics and History of Culture. m. Lilia Nicolaevna Pavlova, 19 June 1952, 1 s. *Education:* Dip, 1952, Postgrad studies, 1953-56, Moscow Univ; Ecole Superieure d'interpretes et de traducteurs, Sorbonne, Paris, 1957-58; Dr Philology (Cand), 1957, Dr, 2nd degree, 1966. *Appointments:* Lectr, French, German, Gen Linguistics, 1955-57, Hd, Chair Gen Linguistics, 1961-71, Moscow Univ; Russian-French Interpreter for Nikita S Khrushtchev, summits, 1960-61; Rschr, 1971-, Dept Hd, 1989-, Inst Linguistics, USSR (now Russian) Acad Scis, Moscow. *Publications:* Books in Russian: The French Stylistics, 1965; The Structure of French, 1965; Foundations of Linguistics, 1966; Semiotics, 1961, re-edited, Hungary, Japan, Bulgaria; Foundations of General Linguistics, 1975, re-edited, Viet-Nam; Methods and Principles of Contemporary Linguistics, 1985; Names, Predicates, Sentences (A Semiological Grammar), 1981; In the Three-Dimensional Space of Language (Semiotic Issues of Linguistics, Philosophy, and Art), 1985; The Indo-European Sentence (Reconstructed), 1989. *Memberships:* Societe de Linguistique, Paris, 1957-58; USSR (now Russian) Acad Sci, Corres Mbr 1984-; Academician 1990-. *Hobbies:* Theatre; Playwriting; Author of unpublished works incl: I am 20 this night, disguised biography of Russian poet Anna Akhmatova, 1977, Assemblee dans un parque, in Russian after novel

Les Liaisons dangereuses (Ch de Lacles), 1980. *Address:* Institute of Linguistics, Russian Academy of Sciences, ulitsa Semashko 1/12, Moscow 103 009, Russia.

STEPHEN (John) David, b. 3 Apr 1942, Luton, England. Dir. m. Susan Dorothy Harris, 28 Nov 1968, 3 s, 1 d. *Education:* Kings Coll, Cambridge, 1961-64; BA, 1964; MA, 1965; Univ of Essex, 1966-68; MA, 1968. *Appointments:* Runnymede Trust, 1970-75; Intl Univ Exchange Fund, 1975-77; Foreign & Commonwealth Office, 1977-79; Editor, Intl Affairs, 1980-84. *Memberships:* Royal Inst of Intl Affairs; Inst of Public Relations. *Address:* 123 Sundon Road, Harlington, Bedfordshire, LU5 6LW, England.1.

STEPHEN George Martin, b. 18 Jan 1949, England. Headmaster; Author. m. Jennifer Elaine Fisher, 21 July 1971, 3 s. *Education:* Uppingham Sch, Univ of Leeds, 1967-70; Univ of Sheffield, 1970-71; PhD, 1972-76. *Appointments:* Chil Supervisor, Various Remand Homes, 1966-72; Uppingham Sch, Tchr, 1971-72; Haileybury Coll Tchr, Housemaster, 1972-83; Sedbergh Sch, Second Master, 1983-87; Perse Chl, Head, 1987-. *Publications:* 14 Books inc. Warship Designs Since 1906. *Memberships:* Headmasters Conference Economic Research Council; Secondary Heads Assn; Assc Member of the Combination Room, Gonville & Caius Coll, Cambridge. *Hobbies:* Writing; Sailing; Theatre; Game Shooting; Fishing; My Family. *Address: b380 Glebe Road, Cambridge CB1 4S2, England. 1.*

STEPHENS Meic, b. 23 July 1938, Treforest, Pontypridd, Wales. Editor; Journalist; Conslt. m. Ruth Wynn Meredith, 14 Aug 1965, 1 s, 3 d. *Education:* Univ Coll of Wales, BA, 1961; Univ of Rennes, 1960; Univ of North Wales, 1962. *Appointments:* French Tchr, 1962-66; Journalist, 1966-67; Literature Dir, Welsh Arts Council, 1967-90; Visiting Prof, Birgham Young Univ, 1991. *Publications:* Poetry Wales; The Lilting House; Exiles All; Green Horse; A Book of Wales; The Gregynog Poets; The Bright Field; The Oxford Companion to the literature of Wales; The Oxford Illustrated Literary Guide to Great Britain & Ireland. *Memberships:* The Welsh Acad; The Gorsedd of Bards. *Honours:* St Davids Univ Coll, Honorary Fellow. *Address:* 10 Heol Don, Whitchurch, Cardiff, Wales.

STEPHENS Michael Dawson, b. 24 Sept 1936, St Agnes. Emeritus Prof. m. Margaret Heap, 2 Sept 1961, 1 s, 2 d. *Education:* MA, The Johns Hopkins Univ, 1962; phD, Edinburgh Univ, 1965; MEd Leicester Univ, 1970; Hon Prof, Shandong Univ, 1990. *Appointments:* Demonstrator, Edinburgh Univ, 1962-64; Lectr, Snr Lectr, Liverpool Univ, 1964-74; The Robert Deers Prof, Nottingham Univ, 1974-89. *Publications:* Various Books. *Memberships:* FRGS; FRSA. *Honours include:* Commonwealth Prestige Fellow; Fulbright Snr Scholar. *Hobbies:* Walking; Chinese & Japanese Art; Collecting Paintings. *Address:* 32 Thackerays Lane, Woodthorpe, Nottingham, NG5 4HQ, England.

STEPHENS William Peter, b. 16 May 1934, Penzance, England. Univ Prof; Methodist Minister. *Education:* Truri Sch, Cornwall, 1945-52; Univ of Cambridge, 1952-57; Univ of Lund, Sweden, 1957-81; Strasbourng, France, 1965-67; Muenster, Germany, 1966-67; MA, Cambridge, 1961; Docteures Sci Religieuses Strasbourg, 1967; BD, Cambridge, 1971. *Appointments:* Asst Turo, Hartley Victoria Coll, Manchester, 1958-61; Methodist Minister, Univ Chaplain, Nottingham, 1961-65; Methodist Minister, Croydon, 1967-71; Ranmoor Chair, Victoria Coll, Manchester, 1971-73; Randles Chair, Wesley Coll, Bristol, 1973-80; Research Fellow, The Queens Coll, Birmingham, 1980-81; Lectr, 1981-86; Prof, Univ of Aberdeen, 1986-; Dean of Faculty of Divinty, 1987-89; Provost of Faculty of Divinity, 1989-90. *Publications:* The Holy Spirit in the Theology of Martin Bucer; Faith & Love; Methodism in Europe; The Theology of Huldrych Zwinch; Huldrych Zwinch, An Introduction to His Thought. *Memberships include:* Soc for Study of Theology; World Methodist Council; British

Roman Catholic, Methodist Commission. *Honours include:* Fernley Hartley Lectr; British Acad Award. *Hobbies:* Tennis; Squash; Swimming; Skiing; Hill Walking; Theatre; Opera. *Address:* Faculty of Divinity, Kings College, Old Aberdeen, Scotland AB9 2UB. 43, 52, 139.

STEPONAVICIUS Algirdas-Eugenijus, b. 12 Jan 1927, Kaunas Ci, Lithuania. Artist. m. Zilyte Birute Janina Grasilda, 30 Sept 1950, 1 d. *Education:* Vilnius State Inst of Art, 1950. *Appointments:* Free Lance Artist. *Creative Works include:* Graphic Art; Mural Painting; Book Illustrations. *Memberships:* Lithuanian Artist Union. *Honours include:* Gold Medal, Intl Book Exhib; J K Yilcinskis Prize for the Best Book of the Year; Natl Prize 1990. *Hobbies:* Philosophy; Literature; Poetry; Music; Nature. *Address:* Pasvaistes 5-6, Vilnius 232021, Lithuania.

STERIO Alexandre Marius Baron Does de, b. Apr 1944, Koniqsberg. Univ Prof. *Education:* Paris, 1965- ; Diplomas de l'Scole Superieuro de Journalism, 1967; Diplome du l'Ecole Pratique Hautes Etudes, 1968; Doctorate, PhD Thesis, German Writer Wolfgang Borchert, 1977; Doctorate, Elat es Lettres of Sci Humanes, 1981. *Appointments:* Prof, CTU Univ, Strasbourg Heinrich Heins Univ, 1981-. *Publications:* Articles in different Sci Periodicals. *Memberships:* Natl Inst for Slavistic Studies; Soc Bibliology & Schematisation; Intl Wolfgang Borchert Assn; Vanous Humanist Assn. *Hobbies:* History; Sociology; Literature; Philosophy. *Address:* Centre de Tele Ensolgnement de l'Univ de Strasbourn 11, 1 Place de l'Univ, F-07000 Strasbourg, France.

STERN David Harold, b. 31 Oct 1935, Los Angeles, CA, USA. Writer; Publisher. m. Martha Frances Frankel, 21 Mar 1976, 1 d. *Education:* BA, UCLA, 1955; MA, Princeton Univ, 1957; PhD, 1960; MDiv, Fuller Theol Seminary Pasadena, Calif, 1975. *Appointments:* Lectr, in Bus Admin UCLA, 1960- 61; Asst Prof, Bus Admin, 1961-63; Lectr, San Diego State Univ, 1966; Instr, Fuller Theol Seminary, 1975-76; With Jews for Jesus, San Rafael, Calif, 1976- 77; Owner, Operator Back to Eden, LA, 1969-73; Freelance Writer, LA Jerusalem, 1973- ; Prin, Jewish New Testament Publi, 1988-; BD Dir, Netivyah Organ for Researching Scriptures, Jerusalem, 1984-. *Publications:* Messianic Jewish Manifesto; Restoring the Jewishness of the Gospel; Co Author, Surfing Guide to Southern California; Translator, Jewish NEw Testament. *Memberships:* Messianic Jewish Alliance of Israel; Am Econ Assn; Authors Guild; Sierra Club. *Hobbies:* Music; Mountain Climbing; Surfing. *Address:* 78 Manahat, 96901, Jerusalem, Israel. 52.

STEVEN Alasdair Robert Malcolm, b. 1 May 1942, Calcutta, India. Journalist. *Education:* Trinity Coll, Glen Almond; Univ de Grenoble. *Appointments:* City, 1963-75; Independent Producer, Theatre, 1975-; Journalist, 1979-. *Hobbies:* Food; Gardening; Opera; Ballet; Chatter. *Address:* Tomkins, Place de la Raive, In Court, France 62770.

STEVENS Carole Janette, b. 12 Jan 1938, Toronto, Canada. Bridal Conslt. m. Bruce Reilly, 1 Aug 1968, 1 s,1 d. *Education:* Shaw Coll, 1958; Vogue Intl Models, 1965-67; Degree Fashion Merchandising, High Fashion Modeling. *Appointments:* Dir, Louis Sch of Modelling, 1965-67; Di, Piper Studios, Sch of Modelling, 1967-69; Bridal Conslt, 1968-. *Publications:* Wedding Etiquette; Columnist, Markham Newspapers. *Memberships:* Piper Studios; Wedding Council of Ontario; Carol Stevens Bridal Conslt; Piper Studio Sch of Modelling. *Hobbies:* Floral Designing; Antiques; Egyptology; Minatures. *Address:* 391 Wood Lane, Acres Cr, RR2 Maple, Ontario, Canada L6A 1G2.

STEVENS Sharon Rebecca Ritenour, b. 24 Mar 1950, Winchester, Virginia, USA. Documentary Historian; Editor. m. Norman Scott Stevens, 25 June 1989.

Education: BA, Bridgewater VA Coll, 1972; MA, James Madison Univ, 1978. *Appointments:* History Tchr, Virginia Secondary Sch, 1973- 77; Librarian, 1978-79; Asst, Assoc Editor, The Papers of George Catlett Marshall, 1979-; George C Marshall Reserch Library. *Publications:* Co Editor, The Papers of George Catlett Marshall; The Soldierly Spirit; We Cannot Delay; The Right Man for the Job; Proceedings of the Rockbridge Historical Soc. *Memberships:* Documentary Editing; Assn for Documentary Editings Nominating Committee; Organ of American Historians; American Historical Assn; Phi Alpha Theta Honor Soc; Lambda Honor Soc. *Honours:* Lyman H Butterfield Award; Distinguished Service Award; Philip M Hammer Award; Award for Academic Achievement. *Address:* George C Marshall Research Library, PO Box 1600, Lexington, VA 24450, USA. 138.

STEVENS William Harris Jr, b. 6 Oct 1947, Ottawa, Canada. Filmmaker; Musician. m. Denise Madeline Cloutier, 10 Oct 1970, 1 s, 1 d. *Appointments:* Musician, 1965-; Crawley Films Ltd, 1967; Edited Sound Effects, Voice & Music Over 30 Films, 1968-74; Producer, 1970; Film Dir, 1971; Prod, Film Dir, Film Arts Ltd, 1974; Partner, Stevens & Kennedy Inc, 1979-; Pres, CEO, Crawley Films Ltd, 1982-; Stevens & Kennedy, 1989-91. *Creative Works include:* Numerous Films. *Memberships:* Country Club; Ottawa Hull Film & TV Assn; Canada Acad Recording Arts & Sci; Canada Acad Film & TV; SOCAN; ACTRA; Canada Film & TV Assn; Canada Film Ind Task Force; Adv Committee on Arts, Ottawa Bd of Edn; Orchard Estates Committee Assn. *Honours include:* United Way Presidents Award; Childresn Broadcast Inst Award; ACTRA Award; Gold Medal; Best Childrens Prog, US Home Video Awward. *Hobbies:* Motocycles; Fitness. *Address:* PO Box 11069, Station H, Nepean, Ontario, Canada K2H 7T8. 88, 142.

STEVENSON Dennis Elliott, b. 7 Apr 1943, Pontiag MI, USA. Assoc Prof, Computer Sci. m. Kathleen Mary Gardzinski, 10 Oct 1970, 1 s, 1 d. *Education:* AB, Mathematics, Eastern Michigan Univ, 1965; MS, Computor Sci, Rutgers, 1975; PhD, Mathematical Sci, Clemson, 1983. *Appointments:* US Army, Infantry Captain Viet Nam, 1965-69; Bill Tele Labs, 1969-80; Clemson Univ, Dept of Computor Sci, 1980-. *Publications:* Articles in Journals & Proceedings. *Memberships:* Assn for Computing Machinery; American Mathematical Soc; Soc of Instrial & Applied Mathematics; Assn for Symbolic Logic. *Hobbies:* Classical Music; Jazz; Reading; Gardening. *Address:* 442 Coll of Nursing Building, Clemson Univ, Clemson, SC 29634, USA.

STEVENSON Donald West, b. 11 Feb 1934, Stratford, Canada. Univ Lectr; Urban Affairs Conslt. m. Ana Tvrdisic, 25 Aug 1959, 2 d. *Education:* Univ of Toronto, BA, 1956. *Appointments:* Canadian Dept of External Affairs, 1956-59; Canadian Embassy Belgrade, 1957-59; Ontario Government, 1959-89; Deputy Minister of Intergovernmental Affairs, 1978-84; Deputy Minister Resources Devel, 1984-85; Ontario Representtive to Quebec & the Federal Government, 1985-89; Glendon Coll, York Univ, Assoc to the Principal, 1989-; Canadian Urban Inst, Conslt Assoc, 1989-. *Memberships:* Inst of Public Admin of Canada; Canadian Inst of Intl Affairs; Queens Inst of Intergovernmental Relations; Soc for Educ Visits & Exchanges. *Address:* 99 MacPherson Avenue, Toronto, Ontario, Canada M5R 1W7. 142.

STEVENSON Paul Timothy, b. 9 Mar 1940, Derby, England. Clerk to the Worshipful Co of Carpenters. m. Ann Douglas Drysdale, 26 June 1965, 1 s, 1 d. *Education:* Bloxham Sch, 1953-58. *Appointments:* Joiner Royal Marines, 1958; 41 Commando, 1960-62; 45 Commando, 1962-63; HMS Mohamc, 1965-68; 45 Commando, 1973-75; HMA Bulwark, 1975-76; Falklands Campain, SOI Plans, 1982; CO 42 Commando, 1983-84; Dir RM Personnel, 1987-88; Commander British Forces Falkland Islands, 1989-90; RETD, 1991; Modern Pentathlon British Team, 1962-69; Biathlon

British Team, 1965. *Membership:* FBIM. *Honours:* MBE; OBE; Major General. *Hobbies:* Hunting; Shooting; Fishing; Golf; Tennis; Skiin; Gardening. *Address:* c/o Lloyds Bank, 23 Long Street, Wotton Under Edge, Glos GL12 7DA, England.

STEVENSON Robert Wilfrid, b. 19 Apr 1947, Scotland, England. Dir, British Film Inst. m. (1) Jennie Erale Antonio, 1972, div, (2) Elizabeth Ann Minogue, 19 Apr 1991. *Education:* Univ Coll, BA, 1966-70; LACA, ALLA, 1986. *Appointments:* Research Officer, Edinburugh Univ Students Assn, 1970-74; Sec, Edinburgh, 1974-87; Deputy Dir, BFI, 1987-88. *Hobbies:* Cinema; Hill Walking; Bridge. *Address:* 21 Stephen Street, London W1P 1PL, England. 1.

STEVENSON Tracey Yvette Tamaline, b. 4 Dec 1963, Brooklyn, New York, USA. Business Manager/ Accounting and Computer Science. *Education:* Dip, Bus Mgmt, 1981; AAS, Bus Admin, Kingsborough Community Coll, 1985; Secretarial Cert, 1985; BS, Bus, Chadwick Univ, 1992. *Appointments:* Mortgage Loan Off, Bowery Savings Bank; Admnstv Asst, Merrill Lynch Life Ins Grp, 1989-91; Currently Acct, Heil Gotstal and Manges; Entrepreneur; Notary Pub; Pt-time Insp, Bd Election. *Memberships:* Coalition Concerned Citizens; NAACP; Grace McCollough Mag; Nat Assn Female Execs; Computer Sci Assn; NY Coun Homemakers of Am. *Honours:* Acctng, 1985; Outstanding Perf Award, 1989; Dedicated Person Award, 1990; Bookkeeping, Best Pres Award. *Hobbies:* Travel; Sewing; Coin collecting; Computers; Being creative; Decorating; Socialising; Music; Dancing; Acting; Singing; Choir member. *Address:* 2238 7th Ave, New York, NY 10027, USA.

STEVENTON Robert Wesley, b. 2 Nov 1948, Allentown, Pennsylvannia, USA. Maketing Exec. m. Deborah Damon Barrett, 29 Aug 1977, 2 s. *Education:* BA, Pennsylvania State Univ, 1970; MA, Univ of Minnesota, 1975; US Army Serv, West Germany, 1970-73; German Interpreter, US Army Defence Language Inst, 1971. *Appointments:* Mktng SPecialist, US Bureau of Census, 1975-77; Mktng Mgr, American Chemical Soc, 1978-83; Account Exec, Kreithlow & Assoc, 1983-84; Account Supervisor, Mktng General Inc, 1984-85; Vice Pres, 1985-88; Snr Vice Pres, 1988-. *Creative Works:* Public Speaker; American Soc of Assn Exec; Congress of Engrng & Sci Soc Exec; Direct Mktng Assn of Washington; Guest Lectr, American Univ. *Memberships:* Direct Mktng Assn of Washington; American Soc of Assn Exec; Greater Washington Bd of Trade; The English Speaking Union, Washington. *Honours:* Kappa Tan Alpha; Leadership Award. *Hobbies:* Alpine Skiing; Hiking; Tennis; Reading. *Address:* Snr Vice Pres, Mktng General Inc, 1613 Duke Street, Alexandria, VA 22314, USA. 7, 132.

STEWART David James, b. 15 May 1950, Ontario, Canada. Physician (Medical Oncology); Professor of Medicine and Pharmacology. m. Nancy Isobel Merab Hall, 26 July 1975, 2 s, 1 d. *Education:* MD, Queen's Univ, Kingston, 1974; Internship, Residency, Internal Med, McGill Univ, Royal Victoria Hosp, Montreal, 1974-76; Fellowship, Med Oncology, Univ TX, M D Anderson Hosp and Tumor Inst, Houston, 1976-78; FRCPC (Internal Med), 1978; Am Bd Internal Med (Med Oncology), 1979; FRCPC, Cert Med Oncology, 1985. *Appointments:* Fac Assoc, Instr, Dept Developmental Therapeutics, 1978- 79, Asst Internist, Asst Prof, 1979-80, Univ TX, M D Anderson Hosp and Tumor Inst, Houston, TX, USA; Med Oncologist, 1980-, Hd, Med Oncology, Civic Div, 1989-, OCTRF, Ottawa Reg Cancer Ctr, Ottawa, Can; Asst Prof, 1989-84, Assoc Prof, 1984-88, Prof, Med, Pharmacology, 1988-, Ottawa Univ Fac Med. *Publications:* Author or co-author, over 130 sci papers and book chapts and over 120 published abstracts on investigational chemotherapy treatments for cancer, natural hist of cancer, pharmacology and toxicology of anti-cancer drugs; Co-ed, book on nausea and emesis. *Memberships:* Am Soc Clin Oncology; Am

Assn Cancer Rsch; Can Soc Clin Investigation; Can Soc Clin Pharmacology; Can Assn Med Oncology; Can Oncology Soc; Can Med Assn; Can Urological Oncology Soc; Jt Sect on Tumours, AANS/CNS; Ont Med Assn. *Hobbies:* Skiing; Reading. *Address:* Ottawa Regional Cancer Centre, 190 Melrose Ave, Ottawa, Ontario, Canada K1Y 4K7. 142.

STEWART John Simon Watson, Bart, Sir, b. 5 July 1955, Glasgow, Scotland. Consultant in Clinical Oncology. m. Catherine Stewart Bond, 3 June 1978, 1 s, 1 d. *Education:* Charing Cross Hosp Med School; BSc, 1977; MB, BS, 1980; MRCP, 1983; FRCR, 1986; MD, 1990. *Appointments:* Cons, Clin Oncology, St Mary's Hosp, Paddington, London and Sr Lectr, Clin Oncology, Royal Postgrad Med School, London, 1989. *Memberships:* Oriental Club, London; Cavalhead Club, London. *Honours:* Roman William Medal, Royal Coll Radiologists, 1986. *Hobbies:* Skiing; Windsurfing. *Address:* 52 Gorsvenor Rd, London W4 4EG, England. 1.

STEWART John Stephen, b. 14 July 1922, Weston Underwood, England. m. Eileen Mary Stewart, 15 July 1954, 3 s, 1 d. *Education:* Scholar, Clifton College, Bristol; 1st MB, London Hosp Med School. *Career:* Royal Marines, 1941-56; Served Royal Marine Commandos, Europe; Wounded twice; Adjutant, RMB Chatham and Eastney; SRMO, HMS Implacable; 45RM Commando, Cyprus; Invalided w 80 percent disability; Farming, 1956-79; Dir, Nuffield Farming Trust, 1969-89. *Memberships:* Fellow, Royal Agricl Socs; Chmn, Gen Commnrs Income Tax, Milton Keynes. *Honours:* Freeman, City of London; OBE; Silver Medal, Int Wine and Food Soc. *Hobbies:* Gardening; Reading; Cooking; Food and wine; Caravanning; World travel; Running Wolsey Lodges Guest House. *Address:* The Mill House, Olney, Bucks MK46 4AD, England.

STEWART Shon Dwayne, b. 30 Sept 1973, Orange, Texas, USA. Student. *Education:* Grad, HS, 1993. *Career:* Hopes to become a Registered Nurse. *Publication:* I have a dream today by me, poem. *Memberships:* Pres, Orange Youth and Coll NAACP; Pres, Mt Zion Youth Choir; Dir, Mt Zion Jr Choir; Dir, Pastoral Choir. *Honours:* Winner, Mr NAACP, State of TX; 3rd runner-up, Nat Mr NAACP. *Hobbies:* Reading; Playing the piano; Singing and directing 2 choirs. *Address:* 2125 Lincoln Drive, Orange, TX 77630, USA.

STIEGLER Karl Drago, b. 24 Oct 1919, Zagreb, Yugoslavia. Mathematician. m. 23 Sept 1951, 1 d. *Education:* MS, Maths, Theoretical Phys, Univ Zagreb, 1946; PhD, Theoretical Phys, Tech Univ, Munich, 1963. *Career:* Prof, Maths, Engrng Coll, Zagreb, 1946-50; Rsch Mathn, constructed optical instruments, 1950-56, Hd, Dept Ophthalmologic Optics, 1957-59, Ghetalus, Zagreb; Constructed all sorts of eyeglasses (for myopia, hypermetropia, astigmatism, strabism), still produced at Ghetalus; Sci Cons, constructed optical instruments, AGFA-Camera-Work, Munich, FRG, 1960; Lectr in field, Tech Univ, Munich, 1964-84; Corresponded w Albert Einstein on axiomatic fndns of Special Theory of Relativity; UNESCO Rsch Fellow, Theoretical Phys, Inst Henri Poincare, Sorbonne, Paris, rsch w Nobel Prizewinner Louis de Broglie, active participant, Sem Nicolas Bourbaki, 1954-55; Joyce and Zlatko Balokovich Scholar, Sci Rsch, Harvard Univ, USA, 1961-63; Active, int congresses. *Creative works include:* Proved principle of constancy of velocity of light is not an indep axiom on the axiom of relativity, published, Comptes rendus, Acad des Scis, Paris, 1952, presented, Int Congress Maths, Nice, France, 1970, detailed publ, Int Jrnl Theoretical Phys, London-NY, 1972; Discovered law of anomalous (differential) rotation of spherical cosmic bodies w application to Sun, Jupiter, Saturn, presenting theory, Int Congress Maths, Nice, 1970, publng result, C R Acad des Scis, Paris, 1971-72; Over 50 original sci papers in relativity, quantum theory, cosmology, theory of grp representations, hist and philos of mathl scis (esp atomistic of Rogerius Boscovinv and calculus of Gottfried Wilhelm Leibniz). *Memberships:* Hon Fellow, Rsch Inst Hist Sci and Technics, Deutsches Mus, Munich; Fellow: Fac Maths, Tech Univ, Munich; Royal Astronom Soc, London; Nat Acad Scis, India; NY Acad Scis; Mbr: Soc Math de France; Int Math Union; Soc Astronom Italiana; Deutsche Gesell fur Angewandte Optik; Int Greenpeace Ecological Org. *Honours:* DSc hc, World Univ, USA, 1990. *Address:* Postfach 750 839, Munich 75, Germany. 52, 152, 156.

STIGLER Bedrich, b. 14 Mar 1960, Klatovy, Czechoslovakia. Maintenance Man; Photographer; Universal Artist. m. 28 Feb 1979-1986, 1 s, 1 d. *Education:* Inst Art Photography, 1985-89. *Appointments:* Motor Mechanic, 1975-78; Driver, 1978-79; Psychiatric Hosp, 1979-80; Freelance Photographer, 1980-91. *Publications:* Post, book, 1987; Er- Atelier Bazaar mag, 1990. *Memberships:* Union Czechoslovak Photographers; Gt Breclav Intelligence Ctr. *Honours:* Prizes, photographic exhibs. *Hobbies:* Snake-fancier; Lizard-fancier; Spider- fancier; Fashion designer. *Address:* Bratislavska 21, 69002 Breclav, Czechoslovakia.

STIJEPO Mijovic Kocan (Miovich Kitschan), b. 14 Apr 1940, Gjurinici, Dubrovnik, Croatia. Writer; Journalist; Professor; Film Director. m. 15 Feb 1964, 2 s. *Education:* Croatian Lang and Comp Lit, Fac Philos, Zagreb, 1069-66; BA, 1966; MA, 1984. *Appointments:* Primary School Tchr, Mala Subotica, 1965-68; HS Tchr, Zagreb, 1968-74; Ed, School Weekly, Zagreb, 1974-79; Freelance, 1979-; Prof, Jrnlsm, Zagreb, 1985-91. *Creative works:* Poetry books: The Confessional, 1969; I, from the Bottom, 1970; This Word, 1974; Straight into the Typewriter, 1981; Heptasound, 1981; Sonnet Sequence, 1982; Something Beyond, 1986; Tryptich about the Head, 1987; Konavle Embroidery, 1988; If Only I Could, for children, 1991; Essays and reviews: Chronicles, Critiques, Language, 1988; Konavle, monograph, 1984; LPs: Iliriae Lyra, anthology of lit and music of Croatian romanticism (choice, directing), 1981; Dubravka, according to Gundulic (adaptation, directing), 1987; Documentary films incl: Life, not Film, documentary TV series, 1985; The Last Limeburner, 1988;; Wounded Heart, 1988. TV films: Cross the River if You Can (screenplay), 1977; Grandmother the White (screenplay, directing), 1991. *Memberships include:* Matica Hrvatska, Zagreb; Croatian Writers Assn, Zagreb; PEN Croatian Ctr; Croatian Jrnlsts Assn; Film Artists Assn Croatia; Nouveaux Droits des Hommes, Paris. *Hobbies:* Theatre; Painting. *Address:* Drustvo Hrvatskih Knjizevnika, Trg Bana Jelecica 7/I, 41000 Zagreb, Croatia.

STILL Mary Jane, b. 14 Apr 1940, Kingsport, Tennessee, USA. Professor of Mathematics; Writer. m. 23 Feb 1962, div., 1 s, 1 d. *Education:* AB, Engl, Maths, Educl Psychology, Trevecca Nazarene Coll, Nashville, 1962; MEd, Maths (Stats), Auburn Univ, AL, 1969; Course work, Peabody, Univ TN, others. *Appointments:* FBI Clerk, Wash, DC, 1958; Statn, State of TN, 1962-64; HS Tchr, pub schools, AL GA, TN, FL, pvte school, FL, 1964-74; Prof, Maths, Palm Beach Community Coll, Lake Worth, FL, 1975-79; Prof, Maths, Palm Beach Community Coll, Palm Beach Gdns, FL, 1979-; Cons to FL Power & Light, 1989; Ed, Dellen Pub and Scott, Foresman Publrs. *Publications include:* Author, children's stories, math pamphlets and booklets, poetry, plays. *Memberships:* Lifetime Mbr, Palm Beach Animal Rescue League; Nat Educ Assn; TN Educ Assn; FL Educ Assn; FACC; SSA; Math Assn Am; Dreher Sci Mus; N Palm Beach Bus Women; Ch of the Nazarene. *Honours:* Athletic All-Star Citizenship, Ldrship, Sportsmanship Awards, Trevecca Nazarene Coll, 1960, 1961, 1962; Scholarship, 1967-69, Summer Fellow, NEn Univ, Boston, 1988, NSF; Shakespearean Soc Scholarship, Stratford-on-Avon, 1975; Special Speaker, Palm Beach Community Coll; Ed-in-Chief, coll yrbook and newspaper. *Hobbies:* Women's and co-ed softball, basketball, tennis, volleyball; Active in Little League and children's sports; Theatre; Music; Mountain hiking; TV; Reading. *Address:* Palm Beach Community College,

North Campus, 3160 PGA Blvd, Palm Beach Gardens, FL 33410, USA. 7, 15, 176.

STILLER Shale David, b. 23 Feb 1935, Rochester, New York, USA. Attorney. m. Ellen M Heller, 7 July 1984, 5 s. *Education:* AB, Hamilton Coll, 1954; LLB, Yale Law School, 1957; MLA, Johns Hopkins Univ, 1977. *Appointments:* Frank, Bernstein, Conaway & Goldman, 1959-; Adj Prof, Univ MD Law School, 1963-. *Publications:* Many books and articles on legal matters. *Memberships:* Am Law Inst; Am Coll Tax Counsel; Am Coll Trust and Estate Counsel; Am Bar Fndn; MD Bar Fndn. *Honours:* Order of the Coif. *Hobbies:* Chamber music; Foreign travel. *Address:* 300 E Lombard St, Baltimore, MD 21202, USA. 2, 6, 163.

STIRLING R Laird, b. 22 Aug 1938, Noranda, Quebec, Canada. Clergyman, United Church of Canada. m. Carolyn Ann Wilson, 16 Sept 1961, 1 s, 2 d. *Education:* BA, McMaster Unit, Hamilton, Ont, 1960; BD (MDiv), Pine Hill Divinity Hall, Halifax, NS, 1963; Ordained, United Ch Can, 1963. *Appointments:* Pastoral Clergyman, NS and Ont Pastorates, 1963-77; Hosp Chaplain, 1977-78; Elected, Mbr Legis Assembly (1st clergyman elected to NS Legislature), 1978, re-elected, 1981, 1984; Min responsible for coord Native Affairs, 1979-81; Min, Consumer Affairs, Min responsible for Residential Tenancies Act and Rent Review Act, 1979-80, 1981-87; Min, Consumer Affairs, NS, Chmn Social Dev Policy Bd, 1981-84; Min i/c Human Rights Act, 1981-87; Min, Environment, 1987; Min, Municipal Affairs, 1987-88; Interim Min (Pastoral): St James United, Dartmouth, NS, 1989, Stairs Mem United, Dartmouth, 1989-. *Memberships:* Past Pres, Ministerial Assn, Dartmouth and Yarmouth, NS; Past Chmn, Bd Dirs, Dartmouth Boys and Girls Club; Past Pres, Dartmouth Rotary Club; Past Pres, Metro Boys and Girls Club. *Honours:* Recip, Fndrs Pin, Credit Union Org, NS, 1966, Ont, 1969. Organised Scout, Guide, Cub and Brownie Grp, Carrot River Dist, N Sask, 1960; Deleg: World Coun Chs, Nairobi, 1967; Poverty Conf, Montreal, 1968; World Lay Congress, FRG, 1972; C'wlth Parly Assn, London, England, 1979; World Welfare Conf, Hong Kong, 1980; Mbr, Can Environmental Task Force, 1987. *Hobbies:* Theatre; Symphony; Swimming; Hiking; Reading; Boating; Travel. *Address:* 96 Chappell St, Dartmouth, Nova Scotia, Canada B3A 3P8. 142.

STIRLING OF FAIRBURN Roderick William Kenneth, b. 17 June 1932, Fairburn, Scotland. Landowner. m. Penelope Jane Wright, 26 Oct 1963, 4 d. *Education:* Special course, School Agric, Aberdeen Univ, 1953-54. *Appointments:* Nat Serv, 1950-52, commissioned, 1951, Scots Guards; Territorial Army: Seaforth Highlanders, Queen's Own Highlanders, 1953-69, retired as Capt, 1969; Mbr, Conan Dist Fishery Bd, 1966-; Appointed, Ross- shire Mainland Rep, 1968, Coun, 1971, Chmn, High Comm, Nat Playing Fields Assn; Owner, Mgr, Fairburn Estate; Trustee, Seaforth Sanatorium Trust, 1970-; Appointed Dpty Lt, Ross and Cromarty, 1971; Appointed JP, 1971; Dir, 1972-, Chmn, 1980-, Scottish Salnmon and White Fish Co Ltd; Mbr, 1972-, Chmn, 1982-, Highland Reg Valuation Appeal Panel; Dir, Moray Firth Salmon Fishing Co Ltd, 1973-; Gen Commnr Income Tax, 1975-, Chmn, 1988-, Inverness 2nd Dist; Mbr, Ross and Cromarty Dist Coun, 1984-; Appointed Lord Lt, Ross and Cromarty, Skye and Lochalsh, 1988. *Memberships:* Scottish Landowners Fedn Highland Comm, Chmn 1974-79; Brit Field Sports Soc, Stalking Comm 1966-89; Chmn, Mid Ross and Aird Pest Control Soc; Scottish Episcopal Ch, Ex Officio Mbr, Vestrey of St James the Gt, Dingwall, St Anne's, Strathpeffer; Rector's Warden; Ex Officio Trustee, Eden Ct Theatre; VP, Territorial and Army Vol Reserve; Supernumerary, Synod, Diocese Moray, Ross and Caithness; Scottish Accident Prevention Soc, Coun Rep, Home Safety Comm Mbr; COSLA Rural Affairs Comm, Coun Rep; New Club, Edinburgh; Num former mbrships incl: N Highland Comm, Agricl Exec; Highland Comm, Scottish Woodland Owners Assn; Highland Comm, Royal Scottish Forestry Soc; Red Deer Commn, Vice-Chmn 1975-89; Scottish Landowners Fedn, Deer Comm

Chmn 10 yrs. *Honours:* Territorial Decoration, 1965; Lord Lt's Cert, Territorial Army Serv, 1969; President's Cert, Nat Playing Field Assn. *Hobbies:* Gardening; Curling; Wildlife Mgmt. *Address:* Arcan, Muir of Ord, Ross-shire IV6 7UL, Scotland. 41, 146, 184.

STITT Iain Paul Anderson, b. 21 Dec 1939, Carlisle, England. Chartered Accountant. m. Barbara Mary George, 1 July 1961, 2 s, 3 d. *Education:* Royal Naval Coll, Dartmouth, 1958-60. *Appointments:* Served RN, 1958-66; Joined, 1966, Tax Ptnr, 1974, Mng Ptnr, Leeds, 1975- 81, Dir, Tax Competence, 1981-88, Mng Ptnr, EC Off, 1988-, Arthur Andersen & Co. *Publications:* Deferred Tax Accounting, 1986; Tax and the Single Market, 1991. *Memberships:* Inst Taxation, Assoc 1964, Fellow 1969, Coun 1969-89, Pres 1982-84; Inst Chartered Accts England and Wales, Assoc 1970, Fellow 1974, Tax Comm 1980-; Royal Inst Navigation. *Honours:* Queen's Telescope, RN, 1960; Inst Taxation Fellowship Prize, 1968; Inst Chartered Accts Tax Prize, 1970. *Hobbies:* Classical music; Skiing. *Address:* 2 Hereford Road, Harrogate HG1 2NP, England.

STLOUKAL Milan, b. 10 June 1931, Prague, Czechoslovakia. Museum Director; Scientific Worker. m. Marta Stloukalova-Brozova, 6 Dec 1957, 1 s, 1 d. *Education:* RNDr, Fac Natural Scis, 1957, Philos Fac, 1962, Charles Univ, Prague. *Appointments:* Scientific Worker, Inst Archaeology, Brno, 1957-69; Hd, Anthropological Dept, 1969-89, Dir, 1990-, Nat Mus, Prague. *Publications:* Over 400 sci publs in histl anthropology, mainly in phys anthropology of ancient slaves. *Memberships:* Pres, Czechoslovak Anthropological Soc; Var sci socs in field of anthropology, prehist, demography and palaeopathology. *Hobbies:* Music; Tourism. *Address:* Krizkovskeho 1, 130 00 Prague 3, Czechoslovakia.

STOCK Carl William, b. 5 May 1945, Oceanside, New York, USA. Professor of Geology. *Education:* BA, Biology, Hartwick Coll, Oneonta, NY, 1967; MA, Geology, SUNY, Binghamton, 1974; PhD, Geology, Univ NC, Chapel Hill, 1977. *Appointments:* Vis Instr, NC State Univ, 1075; Instr, 1965- 77, Asst Prof, 1977-84, Assoc Prof, 1984-90, Prof, 1990-, Dept Geology, Univ AL, Tuscaloosa. *Publications:* 6 articles in Journal of Paleontology, 1 each in Palaeontographica Americana, Alcheringa, and Geological Society Memoirs; 1 monograph in Bulletins of American Paleontology. *Memberships:* SEPM Soc Sedimentary Geology; Paleontological Soc; Paleontological Rsch Instn; Palaeontological Assn; Geological Soc Am; Sigma Xi, Chapt Pres 1986; Int Paleontological Assn. *Honours:* Mil: Army Serv, Vietnam, 1969-71. *Hobbies:* Gardening; Reading; Jogging; Swimming. *Address:* Department of Geology, University of Alabama, Tuscaloosa, AL 35487, USA. 7.

STODDARD Ellwyn R, b. 16 Feb 1927, Garland, Utah, USA. Professor of Sociology and Anthropology. m. Elaine Kirby Packham, 28 Aug 1964, 5 s, 4 d. *Education:* BS, Pol Sci, Econ, UT State Univ, 1952; MS, Sociology, Pol Sci, Brigham Young Univ, 1955; PhD, Sociology, Pol Sci, MI State Univ, 1961. *Appointments:* Asst Prof, 1959-64, Assoc Prof, 1964-65, Drake Univ; Assoc Prof, 1965-69, Prof, 1970-, Univ TX, El Paso. *Publications:* Over 125 books, articles, maj reports, profl papers and others incl: Conceptual Models of Human Behavior in Disaster, 1968; Mexican Americans, 1973; Borderlands Sourcebook (co-ed), 1983; Patterns of Poverty Along US-Mexico Border, 1987; Mauila, 1987. *Memberships:* Fndr, Pres, Assn Borderlands Scholars; Wn Social Sci Assn; SWn Social Sci Assn; 6 other profl assns; Life Mbr, Phi Kappa Phi; Life Mbr, Delta Tau Kappa. *Honours:* SW Book Award for Borederlands Sourcebook, Border Reg Lib Assn, 1984; Outstanding Scholarship and Serv to Assn Borderlands Scholars, El Paso, 1987; Disting Fac Achievement Award in Rsch, Univ TX El Paso Diamond Jubilee Award, Burlington Resources Fndn, 1990. *Hobbies:* Science fiction; Borders and borderlands around the world. *Address:* Department of Sociology,

University of Texas at El Paso, El Pas, TX 79968, USA. 3, 7, 15, 30, 130, 139, 140, 143.

STOILOV Stoimen, b. 18 Sept 1944, Varna, Bulgaria. Graphic Artist; Painter. m. Atanaska Stoilova-Nasil, 2 Nov 1969, 1 d. *Education:* Grad after specialising in Graphic Art under Alexander Poplilov, Acad Fine Arts, Sofia, 1972; Dip, Higher Educ. *Career includes:* Pver 20 1-man shows abroad, Europe, Can; Grp exhibs, Brazil, USA; Pres, Int Print Biennale, 1981-91. *Creative works:* Works in field of graphic art, book illustrations, drawings, paintings, murals. *Memberships:* Union Bulgarian Artists; AIAP, UNESCO. *Honours:* Prizes, City of Varna, 1974, 1975, 1976; Grand Prix, Biennale, Brno, Czechoslovakia, 1976; Silver Medal, Int Exhib, Leipzig, 1982; I Petrov Grand Prix, Mural Painting, Bulgaria, 1983; Gotfrid von Herder Prize, Univ Vienna, 1991; Prize for Graphic Art, 2nd Int Triennale, France, 1991. *Hobbies:* Books; Films; Boxing. *Address:* Bul Kniaz Boris I 109, Varna 9000, Bulgaria.

STOJANOV Tzvetanov Pencho, b. 9 Feb 1931, Sofia, Bulgaria. Composer. m. Elena Stojanova, 16 Sept 1967, 1 s. *Education:* Grad, Theoretical Dept, Bulgrian State Conservatory, 1951; Completed special course, Composition, 1955; Prof, Musical Analysis and Composition, 1972; Doct degree, 1981. *Appointments:* Lectr, 1956, Dpty Rector, 1968-70, Bulgarian State Conservatory; Dpty Rector, Bulgarian State Acad Music, 1989-. *Creative works:* 5 symphs; 3 symphonic poems; 2 overtures; Instrumental concertos; 2 string quartets; Clavier quintet; 3 sonatas for violin and piano; Over 350 children's songs; Music for movies. *Memberships:* Dpty Chm, Bulgarian Union Composers, Sec 1976-80; Anstalt zur Wahrung der Auffuhrungsrechte auf dem Gebiete der Musik, Germany. *Honours:* Prize for string quartet, Warsaw, 1955; Many prizes, nat competitions, 1975, 1982; Prominent Artist, 1976, 1982; Tribune Int des Compositeurs, 1978. *Hobbies:* Arts collector; Environmentalist. *Address:* 36 Oborishte str ent A, 1504 Sofia, Bulgaria.

STOKER Richard, b. 8 Nov 1938, Castleford, Yorkshire, England. Composer. m. Gillian Patricia Watson, 10 July 1986. *Education:* Music and Art Schools, Huddersfield, 1953-58; Studied w Lennox Berkeley, Royal Acad Music, 1959-62; Nadia Boulanger, Paris, 1962-63. *Appointments:* Prof, Composition, 1963-86, Tutor, 1969-74, Royal Acad Music; Ed, Composer mag, 1969-80; Mbr, Steering Comm, Treas, Lewisham Arts Fest, 1990. *Creative works include:* Open Window, Open Door, autobiog; Words without Music, poems; Portrait of a Town; Screened Take Five, play; Supermark, TV play; Strolling Players; Bennett in Baltimore, 1971; Num compositions incl: Feast of Fools, overture; Antic Hay, overture; Piano Concerto; Johnson Preserved, opera; Little Symphony; Sextet op 16; Polemics op 40; Trio Sonata; Concertino nos 1, 2; 3 Piano Trios; 3 String Quartets; Partita, organ; A Little Organ Book; Organ Symphony; Piano Sonata; A Poet's Notebook; 5 Nocturnes; 2 Jazz Preludes; Sonatina, guitar; Dance Movements; 4 Shakespeare Songs; Other vocal and chamber works; Films: The End of the Line; Portrait of a Town; Plays: Troilus and Cressida, Old Vic; Lysistrata; Macbeth; Ballets: Garden Party; My Friend-My Enemy; Songs: Can You Feel Love, Waiting for You; No Longer Cry-No Longer Sing; Recordings: 3 String Quartets; Aspects of Flight, Sonata and Concerto; Fine and Mellow, song album; Guitar Works; Many paintings and drawings. *Memberships:* Assn Profl Composers; Composers Guild, Former Exec Comm Mbr; Brit Acad Songwriters, Composers and Authors; MCPS; PRS; Royal Soc Music; RAM Guild; Blackheath Arts Soc. *Honours:* Mendelssohn Scholarship, 1962-63; ARCM, 1962; ARAM, 1967; FRAM, 1974; Dove and Corder Prizes, Manson Award, others, Royal Acad Music; 1st, Royal Amateur Orchl Soc Award; 1st, Eric Coates Award. *Hobbies:* Squash; Tennis; Skiing; Painting; Writing. *Address:* c/o Ricordi & Co Ltd, The Bury, Church Street, Chesham, Bucks HP5 1JG, England. 4, 21, 139.

STOLLMEYER Charles Victor Humphrey, b. 22 Dec 1947, Trinidad. Attorney-at-Law. m. Valerie Clare Jardim, 16 Dec 1977, 2 stepdaughters. *Education:* Coll Law, Surrey, England, 1969-70, 1973; Admitted to pract: Trinidad and Tobago, 1976; England and Wales, 1980. *Appointments:* Solicitors Articled Clerk, 1966-75, Assoc, 1975-77, Ptnr, 1978-, J D Sellier and Co, Port of Spain, Trinidad; Dir: Bermudez Containers Ltd; Caribbean Ispat Ltd; Caricom Chem Co Ltd; Colgate Palmolive (Trinidad) Ltd; Esmalan Ltd; E W Saybolt & Co (Trinidad and Tobago) Ltd; Gervette Ltd; Gordon, Grant Investments Ltd; H M B Investments Ltd; Kenwil Ltd; Kingsbay Estates Ltd; Mon Valmont Ltd; Pembroke Investments Ltd; Selco Ltd; Signal Hill Aggregates Ltd. *Publications:* Advertising by the Legal Profession: A Viewpoint (w K S P Sobion), 1985; Computerised Data and the Threat to Personal Privacy and Professional Privilege, 1986; The Commercial Laws of Trinidad and Tobago, 1987; The Trademark Laws and Practice of Trinidad and Tobago (w B A de Gannes), 1987; The Patent Laws and Practice of Trinidad and Tobago (w B A de Gannes), 1987. *Memberships:* Law Assn Trinidad and Tobago, Coun Mbr; Attys-at-Law Disciplinary Comm; Law Soc England and Wales; C'wlth Lawyers Assn; Assoc, Chartered Inst Arbitrators, London, England; Trinidad and Tobago Stock Exchange Panel on Takeovers and Mergers. *Hobbies:* Golf; Cricket. *Address:* J D Sellier & Co, 129/131 Abercromby Street, PO Box 116, Port of Spain, Trinidad. 52, 109.

STOLZ Stephanie Balog, b. 27 June 1938, USA. Psychologist. m. Yoshikazu Tomiyasu, 10 Mar 1985. *Education:* BA, Reed Coll, Portland, Oregon, 1959; MS, 1961, PhD, 1963, Univ WA, Seattle. *Appointments:* Instr to Asst Prof, Psychology, 1963-67, Dpty Chmn, Dept Psychology, 1965- 67, Beloit Coll, WI; Dir, Rsch, Jewish Fndn for Retarded Children, Wash, DC, 1967-70; Asst Prof, Behavioural Analysis, Dept Psych, Johns Hopkins Univ, Baltimore, MD, 1969-79; Chief, Small Grants Sect, Nat Inst Mental Hlth, Rockville, MD, 1970-77; Dir, Div Alcoholism, Drug Abuse and Mental Hlth Progs, US Pub Hlth Serv, Kansas City, MO, 1977-83; Adj Assoc Prof to Adj Prof, Human Dev and Family Life, Univ KS, Lawrence, 1977-85; Dir, Bur Family Hlth, KS State Dept Hlth and Environment, Topeka, 1983-84; Prof, Psychology, Temple Univ Japan, Tokyo, Japan, 1987-89. *Publications:* Ethical issues in behavior modification, 1978; Over 20 articles, chapts and monographcs in Engl in sci jrnls and books; 3 monographs in Japanese. *Memberships:* Fellow, Am Psychology Assn, Pres, Div for Expmtl Analysis of Behavior, 1985-88, Rep, Coun Reps, 1983-86; Soc for Expmtl Analysis of Behavior, VP, 1974-75, Chmn, Bd Dirs, Pres, 1975-77, Vice-Chmn, Bd Dirs, 1980-81; Fellow, Am Psychological Soc; Fellow, AAAS; Assn Behavior Analysis. *Honours:* Phi Beta Kappa, 1959; Sigma Xi, 1961. *Hobbies:* Photography; Sumi-e; Ikebana; Cooking. *Address:* c/o Tomiyasu, Cosmo Kanazawa Bunko 515, Kamariya-cho 750, Kanazawa-ku, Yokohama 236, Japan. 5, 52, 143.

STONE Marvin Jules, b. 3 Aug 1937, USA. Physician; Educator. m. Jill Feinstein, 29 June 1958, 1 s, 1 d. *Education:* MS, 1962, MD Hons, 1963, Univ Chgo; Diplomate: Nat Bd Med Examiners, 1964, Am Bds Internal Med, 1970, Haematology, 1972, Med Oncology, 1973. *Appointments include:* Fellow, Haematology-Oncology, 1969-70, Instr, 1970-71, Asst Prof, Internal Med, 1971-73, Assoc Prof, 1974-76, Clin Prof, Internal Med, 1976-, Chmn, Biomed Ethics Comm, 1979-81, Univ TX SWn Med School; Dir, Charles A Sammons Cancer Ctr, Dallas, TX. 1976-; Chief, Oncology, Dir, Immunology, Baylor Univ Med Ctr, Dallas, 1976-; Pres, Dallas Ctrl Unit, Am Cancer Soc, 1978-80. *Contributions to:* med textbooks and jrnls. *Memberships include:* Am Soc Hematology; Int Soc Haematology; Am Assn Immunology; Am Soc Clin Rsch; Am Fedn Clin Rsch; Am Soc Clin Oncology; FACP; Num offs, Leukaemia Soc Am and Am Med Soc; Var hon socs. *Honours include:* Established Investigator, Am Heart Assn, 1970-75. *Address:* Baylor University Medical Center, 3500 Gaston Avenue, Dallas, TX 75246, USA. 2, 7, 17, 125, 143.

STONE Raymond William, b. 22 June 1945, Detroit, Michigan, USA. Consulting Engineer. m. Martha G Stone, 17 Sept 1983, 1 s, 2 d. *Education:* BS, Engrng, 1978, Grad School, 1978-79, Univ William and Mary, Milwaukee; Profl Engr. *Appointments:* Project Engr: Allen Bradley Co, El Paso, TX, 1979-80; Phelps Dodge Copper Products, El Paso, 1980-82; RCA Serv Co, Ft Bliss, TX, 1983-85; Mfg Engr, Rockwell Int, El Paso, 1983; Cons Engr, Conde Inc, El Paso, 1985-88; Constrn Designer, Homeport Project, Corpus Christi, TX, 1988-90; Cons Engr, Govind and Assoc, Corpus Christi, 1990; Currently Cons Engr, BMW Engrng Ind, Corpus Christi. *Publications:* Particulate Removal at High Temperature and Pressure by Self Agglomeration in Hot Gas Cyclone (co-author), 1979. *Membership:* Am Soc Mech Engrs, Sec Corpus Christi Sect. *Honours:* Set Design, Int Thespian Soc, 1986. *Hobbies:* Sailing; Diving; Photography. *Address:* 3051 Quail Springs Rd, Corpus Christi, TX 78414, USA. 7.

STOOKE Philip John, b. 15 Mar 1952, Salisbury, England. Assistant Professor. m. Rosamund Kathryn Ells, 18 Aug 1973, 1 s, 1 d. *Education:* BSc, 1985, PhD, 1988, Univ Victoria, BC, Can. *Appointments:* Asst Prof, Univ Wn Ont, London, Ont, Can, 1988-. *Publications:* Landmarks and Legends of the North Island, book, 1978; 5 sci papers incl: Morphology of the Nucleus of Comet P/Halley, 1991. *Memberships:* Royal Astronomical Soc Can, VP Victoria Sect 1987-88; Planetary Soc; Can Cartographic Assn; Am Assn Geogs. *Honours:* 1984 Award in Cartography, Nat Geog Soc, 1984. *Hobbies:* Walking; Astronomy; Map collecting; Reading. *Address:* 723 Sevilla Park Place, London, Ontario, Canada N5Y 4H9. 88.

STOPPANI Andres Oscar Manuel, b. 19 Aug 1915, Buenos Aires, Argentina. Professor Emeritus; Research Centre Director. *Education:* Postgrad rsch, Physiology, Biochem, 1940-45; MD, 1941, DrChem, 1945, Univ Buenos Aires; Brit Coun Scholar, Enzyme Biochem, 1945-47, PhD, 1953, Univ Cambridge, England; Radioactivity, Lab Phys Nucleaire, Belgium, 1947; Phys Biochem, Nat Inst Med Rsch, Mill Hill, 1953; Photosynthesis, Univ CA, Berkeley, 1954. *Appointments:* Prof, Biochem, Univ La Plata, 1947-48; Prof, Biochem, 1949-81, Dir, Inst Biochem, 1955-81, Dir, Dept Physiological Scis, 1971-81, School Med, Univ Buenos Aires; Career Investigator, 1960-, Bd Dirs, 1963-66, 1981-83, Dir, Bioenergetics Rsch Ctr, 1980-, Nat Rsch Coun; Prof Emeritus, Univ Buenos Aires, 1981-. *Publications:* Spanish: Physiological and Pharmacological Studies on Amphibian Melanophores, 1941; Practical Biochemistry (w C T Rietti), 1962; Biological Chemistry (w A Marenzi and V Deulofeu), 1967; Biochemistry and Genetics of Yeasts. Pure and Applied Aspects (ed w M Bacila and B L Horecker), English, 1978; Over 300 rsch papers on biochem and related topics. *Memberships include:* Past VP, Argentine Chem Assn; Past Pres: Nat Acad Exact, Phys and Natural Scis; Argentine Assn Advancement Sci; Argentine Soc Biology; Argentine Soc Biochem Rsch; Argentine Soc Protozoologists; Hon Mbr, Argentine Soc Clin Rsch; Fellow, AAAS; Am Soc Biological Chems; Soc Expmtl Biology and Med, USA; Assoc, Royal Soc Chem, UK; Soc Gen Microbiol, UK; Soc Expmtl Biol, UK; Soc Chimie Biologique, France; Int Physns for Prevention Nuclear War; Int Cell Rsch Org, UNESCO; For acads incl NY Acad Scis. *Honours:* Num incl: Univ Gold Medal, 1951; Bunge-Born Prize, Chem, Bunge-Born Fndn, Argentina, 1980; Gold Medal, Fundacion Lillo, Argentina, 1980; Bernardo A Houssay Interam Sci Prize, Org Am States, Wash DC, 1989. *Hobbies:* Chess; History of science. *Address:* Centro de Investigaciones Bioenergeticas, Facultad de Medicina, Paraguay 2155, 1121 Buenos Aires, Argentina. 52, 139, 156.

STOREY Richard Alec, b. 2 June 1937, Hertford, England. Archivist. m. Jennifer Clare Storey, 14 Jan 1961, 2 s, 1 d. *Education:* Downing Coll, Cambridge, 1956-59; BA (Hons), Hist. *Appointments:* W Suffolk Co Coun, 1961-62; London Co Coun, 1962-63; Nat Register Archives, 1963-73; Mod Records Ctr, Univ Warwick Lib,

1973-. *Publications:* Primary Sources for Victorian Studies, 1977; Updating, 1987; Poems in Ambit and other jrnls; Num articles, reviews and others in profl jrnls; Ed, Business Archives, 1969-73, 1975-78. *Memberships:* Soc Archivists; Bus Archives Coun, Exec Comm, Past Ed; Hon Assoc Mbr, Veteran Car Club GB. *Hobbies:* Literature; Cinema; Local, business and road transport history; Ephemera; Industrial archaeology; Francophile; Local history publishing (Odibourne Press). *Address:* 32 High Street, Kenilworth, Warwicks CV8 1LZ, England.

STOTHER Ian G, b. 12 Feb 1945, Lytham, England. Orthopaedic Surgeon. m. Jacqueline Mott, 7 Apr 1969, 2 s. *Education:* King's Coll, Cambridge and St George's Hosp Med School, London, 1963-70. *Appointments include:* Cons Orthopaedic Surg, Glasgow, Scotland, 1978-; Hon Sr Lectr, Orthopaedic and Traumatic Surg, Univ Glasgow. *Publications:* Articles on knee surg and artificial jt fixation. *Memberships:* Fellow, Brit Orthopaedic Assn; Assn Surgs E Africa; Int Arthroscopy Assn. *Hobby:* Classic cars. *Address:* Orthopaedic Dept, Glasgow Royal Infirmary, Glasgow G4 0SF, Scotland. 184.

STOYANOV Toshko, b. 27 Apr 1955, Plovdiv, Bulgaria. Senior Research Scientist; Geophysicist-Seismologist. m. Valentina Stoyanova, 19 Dec 1982, 1 s. *Education:* Refrigeration Engrng and Technology, Tech Coll, Plovdiv, 1970-74; Rsch Off, Mil School, 1974-76; Atmosphere and Space Dept, Sofia Univ, 1976-81; MSc, Seismology, Seismic Energy, Seismicity, 1980-81; Engl Lang course, Feb-July 1983; PhD, Seismic Noise, Nonlinear Waves, 1991. *Appointments:* Seismological Dept, Geophys Inst, Bulgarian Acad Scis, 1981-81; Hd, Seismic Station, DIM, 1981-82; Rsch Scientist, Geophys Observatory, PLD, 1982-91; Rsch Assoc, IIIrd Class, 1984-87, IInd Class, 1987- 91; Dir Studies, Min Sci Educ, 1988-91. *Publications include:* The regime of small earthquakes, 1984; Depths and density of small earthquakes, 1984; Looking for seismological presursors, 1985; Velocity ratios, 1986; Non- linear effects in seismic wave, 1988; Seismic noise, 1990; Possibility for research on earth tides in Plovdiv, 1991. *Memberships:* Working Grp on Microseisms, European Seismological Commn, 1988-91; Working Grp Seismic Risk, IASPEI, 1991; Local Comm Natural Disaster, Plovdiv Coun, 1991. *Honours:* Gold Medal, Excellent Grades in Tech Coll, 1974; Silver Medal, Nat Volleyball Championship 2nd Div, 1978; Gold Medal, World Exhib Achievements of Young Inventors EXPO '91, 1991. *Hobbies:* Volleyball referee in National Division; Collecting sport badges; Playing the guitar; Modern music; Football. *Address:* Kolhida 12A, 4004 Plovdiv, Bulgaria.

STOYANOV Vladimir, b. 8 Apr 1953, Sofia, Bulgaria. Orchestra Conductor; Music Professor. m. Maria Jose Morais, 19 Mar 1983, 2 d. *Education:* Odessa Stoliarsky Musical School; Grad w highest hons, Clarinet, Conducting, Leningrad Superior Conservatoire, 1970; Master's degree, Sofia Superior Conservatoire, 1982. *Career:* Clarinetist, Mozart Clarinet Concerto K 622, Leningrad, 1974; 1st Solo Clarinetist, Bulgarian Radio Orch, 1979-83; Recorded for nat radios, USSR, Bulgaria, Italy, Spain, Portugal, BBC, others; Prof, Lisbon Music Conservatoire, Portugal, 1985-; Master Classes, Clarinet, Estoril Int Summer Courses, 1987; Clarinetist, Conductor, concerts throughout Europe, mainly Belgium, France, Italy, Spain, Portugal, USSR, England, Austria; Conducted orchs incl Sofia, Lisbon and RTBF Radio Orchs, London Mozart Players, Kirov Theatre Orch Leningrad, Polish Nat Orch, Virtuoses Hongrois; Sonata recitals in duo w Maria Jose Marais; Fndr, Music Dir, Lisbon Sinfonietta; Several records released, EMS-Belgium; Mbr, Jury, Brussels Int Clarinet Competition and others. *Hobbies:* Politics; Driving. *Address:* Av Eng Arantes e Oliveira 34 - 8 Esq, 1900 Lisbon, Portugal.

STRADLING Bernard, b. 18 Feb 1930, Woolwich, London, England. Retired. m. (1) Jean Hewinson, 30 Sept 1957, 1 s, 1 d, (2) Christine Young, 18 Dec 1981,

3 stepdaughters. *Education:* Manchester School Libnship, 1952-53. *Appointments:* Ctrl Lending Libn, Southend-on-Sea, 1959-67; Dpty Borough Libn, 1967-68, Borough Libn, 1968-72, Cheltenham, Glos; Co Libn (redesignated Co Lib Arts and Museums Off, 1987), Glos Co Coun, 1972-90. *Memberships:* Fellow, Lib Assn; Fellow, Royal Soc Encouragement of Arts, Manufactures and Commerce; VP, Workers Educl Assn, Cheltenham Br. *Honour:* MBE, 1987. *Hobbies:* Photography; Wine tasting; Travel. *Address:* Beechcroft, Kenelm Drive, Cheltenham, Gloucestershire GL53 0JR, England.

STRAIT C Neil, b. 10 Nov 1934, New Lexington, Ohio, USA. District Superintendent, Church of the Nazarene. m. Ina Niccum, 2 Sept 1958, 2 s, 1 d. *Education:* Jr Acctng, Meridith Bus Coll; AB, ThB, Olivet Nazarene Univ; BD, Nazarene Theological Sem. *Appointments:* Pastor: Rosewood Heights Ch of the Nazarene, E Alton, IL; Carmi Ch of the Nazarene, Carmi, IL; E Liberty Ch of the Nazarene, Akron, OH; Taylor Ave Ch of the Nazarene, Racine, WI; 1st Ch of the Nazarene, Lansing, MI; Currently Dist Supt, MI Dist Ch of the Nazarene. *Publications:* Words of Men at the Cross; Strait Lines; The Conquering Christ; New Dimensions in Life; Nehemiah (Bible Study); To Be Holy; Articles in over 100 publs incl The Upper Room, Quote, Pulpit Digest. *Membership:* Kiwanis Int. *Honours:* O Award, Outstanding Ministerial Alumni, Olivet Nazarene Univ; Hon Dr's degree, Oliver Nazarene Univ, 1990. *Hobbies:* Writing; Reading. *Address:* 2754 Barfield Drive SE, Grand Rapids, MI 49546, USA. 2.

STRAKER Timothy Derrick, b. 25 May 1955, London, England. Barrister. m. Ann Horton Baylis, 17 Apr 1982, 2 d. *Education:* Downing Coll, Cambridge Univ; MA (Cantab); Called to the Bar, Gray's Inn, 1977. *Appointments:* Practice at the Bar, 1978-. *Memberships:* Admnstv Law Bar Assn; Local Govt and Planning Bar Assn. *Honours:* Downing Coll Prize for Law, 1976; Sr Harris Scholar; Holt Scholar, Gray's Inn; Lord Justice Holker Sr Award. *Hobbies:* Cricket; Reading; Theatre. *Address:* 8 New Square, Lincoln's Inn, London WC2, England.

STRANGE John, b. 20 July 1934, Gentofte, Denmark. Theologian; University Pro-Rector. m. 31 May 1975, 3 s, 2 d. *Education:* Cand teol, Theology, 1962, Dr Theol, 1980, Univ Copenhagen; Archaeology studies: Univ Copenhagen, Hebrew Univ, Jerusalem, Israel, Brit School Archaeology, Jerusalem, Jordan, 1963-67. *Appointments:* Rsch Fellow, 1962-67, Asst Prof, 1967, Assoc Prof, 1972, Dean, Theology, 1985, Pro-Rector, 1991; Curate, Danish Ch, 1979-; Army Chaplain, Citadel, Copenhagen. *Publications:* Caphtor/Keftiu, dissertation, 1980; Bible Atlas, 1988; Num papers. *Membership:* Collegium Biblium. *Honours:* Gold Medal, Univ Copenhagen, 1960. *Hobbies:* Bird watching; Playing the piano and cello; Professionally: Old Testament, Near Eastern archaeology and geography. *Address:* Trondhjemsgade 5, DK-2100 Copenhagen O, Denmark. 145.

STRANRAER-MULL Gerald Hugh, b. 24 Nov 1942, Chester, England. Priest. m. Glynis Mary Kempe, 30 Dec 1967, 2 s, 1 d. *Education:* King's Coll, Univ London, 1966-69; AKC, 1969; St Augustine's Coll, Canterbury, 1969- 70. *Appointments:* Jrnlst, 1960-66; Curate, Hexham Abbey, 1970-72; Curate, Corbridge, 1972; Rector, Ellon and Cruden Bay, Aberdeenshire, Scotland, 1972-; Canpn, Aberdeen Cathedral, 1981-; Dean, Aberdeen and Orkney, 1988-. *Publications:* A Turbulent House, 1972; View of the Diocese, 1977; Ed: Aberdeen and Buchan Churchitan, 1976-84, 1990-. *Address:* The Rectory, Ellon, Aberdeenshire AB41 9NP, Scotland. 1, 118.

STRASSBURG Robert, b. USA. Teacher; Composer; Conductor; Musicologist; Poet. *Education:* Grad, New England Conservatory Music, Harvard; Grad, Univ Judaism; Studied w Igor Stravinsky. *Appointments:* Asst Dean, School Fine Arts, Univ Judaism, 1960-66; Prof,

Music; currently Prof Emeritus, CA State Univ, Los Angeles; Fndng Dir, Roy Harris Archives, CA State Univ, Los Angeles; Fndng Fac Mbr, Brandeis-Bardin Inst; Composer-in- Residencem Brandeis. *Creative works:* Bardin Inst, 1992; Co-Chmn, Walt Whitman Centennial, CA State Univ, 1992; Instrumental, solo and choral music for Walt Whitman's poems incl: Mother and Babe, soprano and piano, 1948; Beginning My Studies, soprano and piano; Beautiful Women, soprano and piano; Drum Taps - Memories of the Civil War; Tears for A Capella Choir w Soprano and Tenor solos; Reconciliation for Soprano, Alto, Tenor soloists and choir; Abraham Lincoln, Born February 12, 1809, An In Memoriam Ode for Mezzo-soprano, Flute and Piano, 1992; O Captain, My Captain; Leaves of Grass, choral symph; Var other compositions incl 2 Torah servs, many Psalm settings, folk opera Chelm; *Publications:* Ernest Bloch: Voice in the Wilderness, 1977; Fire and Fret. Volume of Love Poetry, 1977; Music, Art and You. Humanities Text, 2nd Ed, 1986; Walt Whitman's 'Leaves of the Grass'. An Introduction, 22nd Ed, 1992. *Memberships:* Jewish Music Commn, Valley Beth Shalom. *Honours:* Recip, Outstanding Prof Award, CA State Univ, Los Angeles. *Address:* 3394B Punta Alta, Laguna Hills, CA 92653, USA.

STRATFORD Neil Martin, b. 26 Apr 1938, London, England. Museum Keeper of Mediaeval and Later Antiquities. m. Anita Jennifer Lewis, 28 Sept 1966, 2 d. *Education:* Magdalene Coll, Cambridge, 1958-61; BA Hons, Engl Lit, Univ Cambridge, 1961; MA (Cantab); Courtauld Inst, 1963-66; BA Hons, Hist Art, London Univ, 1966. *Appointments:* Nat Serv, 2nd Lt, Coldstream Guards, 1956-58; Lectr, Westfield, London Univ, 1969-75; Keeper, Brit Mus, London, 1975-. *Publications:* La sculpture oubliee de Vezelay, 1984; Articles in Engl, French, German and Am periodicals on Romanesque and Gothic sculpture, arch and the minor arts. *Memberships:* Liveryman, Haberdashers Co; Hon Mbr, Acad de Dijon, France; FSA; Fellow, Soc Nat des Antiquaries de France. *Honours:* William Lincoln Shelley Fellow, London Univ, 1966-69; Leverhulme Sr Rsch Fellow, Brit Acad, 1991. *Hobbies:* Food and wine; Cricket; Football; Music esp opera. *Address:* 17 Church Row, London NW3 6UP, England. 1.

STRATIEV Stanislav, b. 9 Sept 1941, Sofia, Bulgaria. Writer; Playwright. m. Lilia Zheliazkova Ratcheva, 9 Sept 1966, 2 s. *Education:* Dip Higher Educ, Bulgarian Philology (MA equiv), Univ St Kliment Ohridski Univ, Sofia, 1968. *Appointments:* Reporter, Narodna Mladezh newspaper, 1964-68; Reporter, Starshei newspaper, 1968-76; Dramatist, 1976-, Mng Dir, 1983-89, Aleko Konstantinov State Satirical Theatre, Sofia. *Creative works:* Plays: Rimska Banya, 1973; Sako ot velour, 1975; Reis, 1980; Maksimalistat, 1983; Ragatse, 1984; Zhivotat Makar I Kratak, 1985; Zemyata Se Varti, 1986; Balkanski Sindrom, 1986; Mammoth, 1988; Books (fiction): Samotnite Vyatarni Melnitsi, 1966; Diva Patitsa Mezhdu Darvetata, 1970; Pateshestvie Bez Koufar, 1971; Podrobnosti ot Peyzazha, 1977; Zhivot v Neboto, 1983; Peyzazh s Koutche, 1985; Bulgarskiat Mdel, 1991; Posledno Kino, 1991; Film scripts: Pazachat na Krepostta, 1974; Garderob, 1975; Kratko Slantse, 1978; Slance Na Detstvoto, 1979; Orkestar Bez Ime, 1980; Ravnovesie, 1982. *Membership:* Union Bulgarian Actors, Vice-Chmn 1985-89. *Honours:* Dimitrov Award for Lit, Sofia Lit Award, 1969, 1976, 1986; Tchoudomir Award for Humour and Satire, 1978; Order of St Cyril and St Methodius, 1979; Silver Medal, Equilibrium (Ravnovesie), Moscow Film Fest, 1982; 1st Prize, Maubeuge European Plays Int Contest, France, 1990. *Hobbies:* Tennis; Swimming; Art. *Address:* Stanislav Stratiev, 33-A Nezabravka Street, Bl 315, Sofia 1113, Bulgaria.

STREET Brian Jeffrey, b. 8 May 1955, Hamilton, Ontario, Canada. Writer; Producer. m JoAnn Mallory, 1 s, 1 d. *Education:* McMaster Univ, Hamilton, 1976. *Appointments:* Tech Supvsr, Cinevision Can Ltd, 1973-74; Film Ed, Ross Briggs Ed Servs, 1974-75; Writer, Producer, Crawley Films, 1979-80; Sound Ed,

Animation City, Toronto and Tokyo, 1984-85; Hd Writer, Atkinson Film Acts, 1986; Writer, Assoc Producer, CBC, 1989-90; Writer, Producer, Royal Can Mounted Police, 1991-. *Creative works:* Books: The Parachute Ward: A Canadian Surgeon's Wartime Adventures in Yugoslavia, 1987; Champagne Navy: Canada's Small Boat Raiders of the Second World War (w Brian Nolan), 1991; Articles in Maclean's Magazine, Cinema Canada, Artmagazine, Entertainer Magazine, Ottawa Revue, Motion Magazine, 1973-79; Documentary films, 1975-91, over 100 film and TV credits incl: The Duel, 1975; Airplanes, Men and Memories, 1975; Next Stop: Cornwallis, 1977; A Different Adventure, 1979; We Need to Know, 1980; Energy Forever, 1980; After the Wars, 1981; The Adventures of Teddy Ruxpin, 6 half-hour episodes, 1986; Their Share of Glory: Dieppe 1942, 1987; The Parachute Ward, screenplay, 1988; We Shall Fight on the Beaches, 1990; Trouble in Khmer, 1991; Fortress North America, 1991. *Memberships:* Writers Union Can; Writers Guild (ACTRA). *Honours:* Visual Communications Award, Tech/Educ category, for It's Your Decision, 14-min documentary, US Aviation and Space Writers Assn, 1988. *Address:* c/o MGA Agency Inc, 10 St Mary Street, Suite 510, Toronto, Ontario, Canada M4Y 1P9. 142.

STREHLOW Kathleen Stuart, b. 10 Apr 1936, Northam, Western Australia, Australia. Research Director. m. T G H Strehlow, 1973, 2 s, 1 d. *Education:* Tchrs Cert, 1954; BA, 1968. *Appointments:* Var tchng posts, 1955-64; Researcher, aboriginal affairs in Ctrl Australia, Univ Adelaide, S Australia, 1964-75; Rsch Dir, The Strehlow Rsch Fndn, S Australia, 1975-. *Publications:* Symbolism in Aboriginal Art; Man and his Language in Central Australia; Aboriginals and Land in Central Australia; Aboriginal Central Australia; Aboriginal Women in Central Australia. *Memberships:* Fellow, Fellowship of Australian Writers; Fndn Mbr, Stockmen's Hall of Fame; Australian Soc Authors; The Strehlow Rsch Fndn. *Honours:* Tchrs Bursary; C'wlth Scholarship, 1954, 1968; PhD (hc), 1986. *Hobbies:* Tennis; Her family and work. *Address:* 30 Da Costa Avenue, Prospect, SA 5082, Australia. 3, 138, 152, 191.

STRIBRNY Zdenek, b. 1 Oct 1922, Bystrice p Host, Czechoslovakia. Professor Emeritus of English and American Literature. m. Mariana Pecirkova, 16 Aug 1952, 1 s. *Education:* MA, Engl, Russian, 1949, PhD, Engl Lit, 1951; CSc, 1957, DSc, 1965, Charles Univ, Prague. *Appointments:* Reader, Engl Lit, 1961, Prof, Engl Lit, 1965-70, Rsch Prof, Computing Ctr, 1970-88, reinstated, Engl Dept, 1990, Charles Univ, Prague. *Publications:* Shakespeare's History Plays, 1959; Shakespeare: A Portrait, 1964; Shakespeare's Predecessors, 1965; A History of English Literature, 2 vols, 1987; The Complete Works of W Shakespeare, 5 vols published in Czech (chief ed). *Memberships:* Int Shakespeare Assn; Int Assn Univ Profs Engl; Chmn, Circle Mod Philologists, Prague; Shakespeare Assn Am; Franz Kafka Soc. *Honours:* Awards, Czechoslovak Acad Scis and Arts, 1959, 1988; Medal for Outstanding Rsch, Fac Maths and Phys, Charles Univ, 1989; Hon Mbr, Deutsche Shakespeare-Gesellschaft, 1990; Hon DLitt, Univ Leicester, 1991. *Hobbies:* Walking; Theatre; Music; Sports; Weather reports on TV. *Address:* K Cervenemu vrchu 678, 160 00 Prague 6-Vokovice, Czechoslovakia. 139.

STRICKLER Howard Martin, b. 26 Oct 1950, New Haven, Connecticut, USA. Physician. m. Susan Hunter, 2 May 1982, 2 s. *Education:* BA, Berea Coll, 1975; MD, Univ Louisville, 1979; Residency in Family Prac, 1979-82; Fellowship, Addiction Med, Willingway Hosp, Statesboro, GA, 1985-86. *Appointments:* Physn, pvte pract (Family Pract and Addictive Diseases), Brimingham, AL, 1986-; Pres, Employers Drug Prog Mgmt Inc, 1990-. *Memberships:* Fellow, Am Acad Family Physns; Am Soc Addiction Med; Med Assn State of AL; Jefferson Co Med Soc; So Med Assn; 101st Airborne Div Assn. *Honours:* Bronze Star, Vietnam Campaign Medal, Vietnam Serv Medal w 2 Stars, Army Commendation medal, 1971; Phi Kappa Phi, 1975.

Hobbies: Tennis; Golf; Flying. *Address:* 9002-C Parkway East, Brimingham, AL 35206, USA. 7.

STRIEN Pieter Johannes van, b. 15 Oct 1928, Veere, Netherlands. Professor of Psychology. m. Renate Naujoks, Nov 1953, 1 s, 2 d. *Education:* Cand degree (BA), Psychology, 1950, Dr's degree (MA) cum laude, Psychology, 1953, Doct (PhD) cum laude, Social Scis, 1964, State Univ, Groningen. *Appointments:* Indl Psychologist, Inst Applied Psychology, Groningen, 1953-57; Joined, 1955, Prof, Work and Organisational Psychology, 1966-80, Prof, Introduction, Fndns and Hist Psychology, 1980-, State Univ, Groningen; Pt-time employment, var fields of psychology prac, 1960-67. *Publications:* Kennis en Communicatie in de Psychologische Praktijk, 1966; Om de kwalitet van het bestaan, 1978; Praktijk als wetenschap, 1987; Co- ed, co-aUthor: Grondvragen van de Psychologie, 1990; History and Theory, Annals Theor Psycho VIII, 1992. *Memberships:* Netherlands Inst Psychologists, Chief Ed of Jrnl 1968-72; Bd Appeals; Fellow, Netherlands Inst Adv Studies; Cheiron Europe (Hist Psychology); Int Soc Theoretical Psychology. *Hobbies:* Architecture; Carpentry; Reading; History. *Address:* Elsschotlaan 26, 9721 WN Groningen, Netherlands. 52.

STRIEN Tatjana Van, b. 12 Sept 1954, Groningen, The Netherlands. Psychologist. 1 s, 1 d. *Education:* Dipl, Willem Gym, 1972; DSc, PhD, Agric Univ, Wageningen, 1986. *Appointments:* Fac Mem: Psychol, Ryler Univ, Leiden, 1980-82; Human Nutri, Agric Univ, 1982-86; Univ of Lumberg, 1986-87; Dept of CLin Psycol and Women's Studies, Univ Nymegen, 1986-. *Publications:* Book: Eating Behaviour, personality traits and body mass; First author of Dutch Eating Behaviour Questionnaire; Various articles in national and international scientific jurnals and books on eathng disorders, slimness ideal, gender identity. *Memberships:* Ed Bd, De Psycholog, 1986-88; Sci Adv Bd, Dutch Obesity Assn, 1989-; Bd or Dirs, Dutch Foun of Women and Hlth Res. *Hobbies:* Music, playing the flute and traverso: Gardening; Reading; Swimming; Walking; Bringing up the children. *Address:* Psycological Laboratory, Department of Clinical Psychology and personality psychology, Postbus 9107, 6500 HE Ngmegen, Netherlands.

STRONG Julia Helen, b. 12 July 1954, York, Pennsylvania, USA. Psychotherapist. *Education:* BS, Univ VA, 1977; MSW, Univ GA, 1984. *Appointments:* Data Mgmt Dir, 1984-86, Mbrship Servs Dir, 1986-87, SE Network Youth and Family Servs; Sr Pub Hlth Educator, GA Dept Human Resources, 1987-89; Dir, Social Servs, AID Atlanta, GA, 1989-91; Pvte prac, 1991-; Fndr, AIDS Athens, 1987. *Memberships:* Nat Assn Social Workers, GA Chapt, Pres 1988-90; Acad Cert Social Workers; DeKalb Co AIDS Task Force; Bd Mbr, Out Common Welfare. *Honours:* Phi Kappa Phi; A105 Ethics Grp, Nat Ctr Social Policy and Prac, 1989; Nat Comm Lesbian and Gay Issues, Nat Assn Social Workers, 1990. *Hobbies:* Outdoors; Singing. *Address:* 1708 Peachtree Street NW, Suite 315, Atlanta, GA 30309, USA. 7.

STROVER Richard Guy, b. 3 July 1941, Lythan St Annes, England. Chartered Accountant. m. Collette Mary Watkins, 7 June 1968, 1 d. *Education:* FCA. *Appointments:* R F Frazer & Co, 1960-65, merged w Coopers & Lybrand Deloitte (via Harmod Bannek and Deloitte Haskings & Sells), 1965-91. *Publication:* Data Control Guidelines, booklet. *Memberships:* Brit Computer Soc; Inst Int Auditors. *Hobbies:* Bridge; Squash; Tennis; Sailing; Cooking. *Address:* 33 Ashley Gardens, London SW1P 1QE, England.

STRZEZEK Jerzy Ryszard, b. 25 June 1939, Kozminek, Poland. University Teacher. m. 3 Aug 1963, 2 s. *Education:* MSc, 1961, PhD, 1968, DSC, 1974, Full Prof, 1989, Univ Agric and Technology, Olsztyn. *Appointments:* Univ Tchr, 1963-, Pro-Dean, Fac Animal Husbandry, 1978- 81, Hd, Dept Animal Biochem, 1982-

, Vice-Rector, 1984-87, Rector, 1987-90, Univ Agric and Technology, Olsztyn. *Publications:* Over 200 sci publs in Polish and Engl in field of biochem and immunology of animal semen; 7 muniv books; 1 Patent, Poland. *Memberships:* Int Soc Immunology of Reproduction; Int Coord Comm Immunology of Reproduction; Comm Biology Animal Reproduction, Polish Acad Scis. *Honours:* Award, Min Nat Educ, 1968, 1975, 1983, 1987; Award, Min Agric, Forestry and Food Mgmt, 1985; Award, Dept Agric and Forestry Scis, Polish Acad Scis, 1987; Hon Medal, Bulgarian Acad Scis, 1987. *Hobbies:* Sport; Music; Gardening. *Address:* Department of Animal Biochemistry, University of Agriculture and Technology, 10-718 Olsztyn-Kortowo, Poland.

STUART-SMITH James, b. 13 Sept 1919, Brighton, England. Crown Court Recorder; Retired Judge Advocate General of the Forces. m. Jean Therese Young Groundsell, 25 Dec 1957, 1 s, 1 d. *Education:* London Hosp Med School, 1938; Law Soc Law School, 1939; Middle Temple, London; Barrister, 1948. *Appointments:* In prac as Barrister, London, 1948-55; Appointed Legal Asst, Off of Judge Advocate Gen, 1955; Dpty Judge Advocate, 1957; Asst Judge Advocate Gen, 1968; Vice Judge Advocate Gen, 1979; Judge Advocate Gen, 1984; Retired, 1991; Currently Crown Ct Recorder. *Publications:* Articles on mil law in Law Quarterly Review and other publs. *Membership:* Int Soc Mil Law and the Law of War, VO 1952, Pres 1985-91, Hon Pres 1991. *Honours:* CB, 1986; QC, 1988. *Hobbies:* Composing letters; Mowing lawns; Taking photographs. *Address:* The Firs, Copthorne, Sussex RH10 4HH, England. 1.

STUHL Oskar Paul, b. 23 Dec 1949, Wilhelmshaven, Germany. Industrial Chemist. Consultant. *Education:* Chem dip, 1976, PhD, 1978, Univ Dusseldorf. *Appointments include:* Inst Organic Chem, Dusseldorf Univ, 1976-79; Mgr, Product Dev, Drugofa GmbH, Cologne, 1980; Sci Rels Mgr, 1981-89, Sci Servs Mgr, 1989-, R J Reynolds Tobacco GmbH, Cologne. *Publications:* Var articles in sci jrnls; Ed Bd, Beitrage zur Tabakforschung International. *Memberships:* Gesellschaft Deutscher Chemiker; Gesellschaft Deutscher Naturforscher und Aerzte; Max-Planck Gesellschaft; Am Chem Soc; Am Pharm Soc; Acad Pharm Rsch and Scis; NY Acad Scis; Am Soc Pharmacognosy; Federation Internationale Pharmaceutique; AAAS; Royal Soc Chem, UK; Chem Soc Japan; Int Union Pure and Applied Chem; Duesseldorf Museumsverein; Metrop Mus Arts, NY; Verein der Freunde des Hetjens Museums; Verein Der Freunde und Foerderer des Universitaet Duesseldorf; Verein zur Foerderung Deutsch-Japanischer Beziehunger; Deutsche-Japanische Gesellschaft; Stadtmuseum Duesseldorf; Gesellschaft der Freunde der Kunstsammlung NRW; Foerderverein NRW-Stiftung; Zuercher Kunstgesellschaft; Kunstverein der Rheinlande und Westfalen; Christliche Demokratische Union; CDU Wirtschaftsvereinigung. *Hobbies:* Reading; Travel; Art collecting; Classical and contemporary music. *Address:* An der Thomaskirche 23, D- 4000 Duesseldorf 30, Germany. 52, 132, 139, 151, 152, 156.

STULOV Yurii Victorovich, b. 28 Jan 1945, Spassk-Ryazanski, Belarus. Lecturer in English and American Literature and in English; Literary Critic. m. Svetlana Alexeyevna Papkova, 2 June 1963, 2 d. *Education:* Dip w hons, Minsk State Tchr Trng Inst For Langs, 1966; Postgrad course, Moscow Pedagogical Univ, 1983-84; Cand Sci (doct), Philology, 1985; Assoc Prof, 1991. *Appointments:* Tchr, Engl, 1966-71, Sr Lectr, 1971-89, Asst Prof, 1989-91, VP, 1990-, Assoc Prof, 1991-, Minsk State Tchr Trng Inst For Langs. *Publications:* Lab Works in English Grammar, 1973; Conversational English, 1975, 2nd Ed, 1981, p 2, 1982; J Baldwin. Stories. With Preface Commentary by Yu Stulov, 1977; The Urban Themes in James Baldwin's Works, 1981; Peculiarities of James Baldwin's Prose of the 1950's- the mid-1970's (ideological and artistic evolution), 1984; New horizons of James Baldwin, 1985; In search for justice (Gore Vidal's novel 'Julian'), 1987; Documents, facts fiction: peculiarities of the novels by Gore Vidal, 1988; The novel 'Empire' in the context of Gore Vidal's 'The American Saga' 1989; Role plays in a class of English and American literature, 1990; A Guide to written English, 1990; The first step forward, 1990; The Fourth Power. Notes from the 1st Festival of mass media in Ldz, 1991; In continuation of traditions (Toni Morrison's novel 'Beloved'), 1990; Our own model, 1992. *Memberships:* Minsk Assn Tchrs Am Engl, Hd 1990; Minsk Film Club Assn, Hd 1989; LATEUM, Moscow Univ; Int Assn Rsch Am Culture and Lit. *Hobbies:* Theatre; Films and filming; Ballet; History of Russian culture and music. *Address:* Kazintsa Str 114/ 2, apt 15, 220064 Minsk, Belarus.

STURDEVANT Wayne Alan, b. 3 Apr 1946, Portland, Oregon, USA. Educator; Senior Systems Analyst. m. Helen Florence Radbury, 24 Sept 1976, 5 s. *Education:* AAS, Instructional Technology; AAS, Instructional Methodology; BS, Educ, 1980. *Appointments:* Served USAF, 1964-85; McDonnell Douglas Corp, 1985-88; SEn Computer Cons Inc, 1988-. *Publications:* Individual Training, 1983; Training: A Key to Readiness, 1984; Development of an Advanced On-the-job Training System, 1987; Training Innovations in the Work Place, 1988. *Memberships:* Past Pres, PTA; Bishop, Mbr Stake Presidency, Ch of Jesus Christ of Latter Day Sts; Commnr, Boy Scouts Am. *Honours:* Instr of Yr, 1976; Employee of Yr, 1979; Citation of Hon, nat award for developing an int prog, 1980; Meritorious Serv Medals, 4 times. *Hobbies:* Camping; Reading; Hiking; Actively involved in civic and community service. *Address:* 9214 Independence Loop, Austin, TX 78748, USA. 7, 132.

STUTTARD Arthur Rupert Davies, b. 16 July 1943. Barrister. m. Margaret Evelyn Sykes, 10 Aug 1972. *Education:* Christ Ch, Oxford; MA (Oxon); Barrister, Middle Temple, London. *Publications:* An English Law Notebook; Var articles on the Lancs Witchcraft Trials. *Honours:* Harmsworth Exhibitioner, 1965, Harmsworth Scholar, 1967, Middle Temple. *Hobbies:* Horses; Local history; Archaeology. *Address:* Acre House, Fence, Near Burnley, England.

STYLE Christopher John David, b. 13 Apr 1955, Godstone, England. Solicitor. m. Victoria Jane Miles, 7 Apr 1990, 1 s. *Education:* Trinity Hall, Cambridge, 1973-76l MA, Law. *Appointments:* Joined, 1977-, Ptnr, Litigation, 1985, Linklaters & Paines, London. *Publications:* Documentary Evidence, 3rd Ed, 1991. *Memberships:* Law Soc; City London Solicitors Co; London Solicitors Litigation Assn. *Hobbies:* Fell walking; Reading. *Address:* Barrington House, 59-67 Gresham St, London EC2V 7JA, England.

STYLES Ronald Arthur, b. 8 Nov 1917, Heanor, Derbyshire, England. Musician; Retired School Teacher. m. Celia Robertson, 3 Apr 1954, 1 d. *Education:* MA, Downing Coll, Cambridge, 1944; LRAM, 1944; ARCM, 1952; FRCO, 1961; FTCL, 1964. *Appointments:* Chem, Royal Ordnance Factory, 1940-45; Tchr, Christ's Hosp, 1945, 1948-51; Tchr, Felsted School, 1946-47; Chem, Rolls Royce Ltd, 1952-56; Tchr, Hymers Coll, Hull, 1956-82; Master of the Music, Holy Trinity, Hull, 1961-77; Organist, All Sts, Helmsley, 1978-; Music Tutor, Univ of 3rd Age, 1985-. *Contributions to:* Health, Medicine Science and the Law, Newsletter of the Brit Epilepsy Assn. *Memberships:* Fellow, Royal Soc Hlth; One-time Mbr, Brit Acad Forensic Scis. *Honours:* Exhib, 1936, Orchan Scholar, 1937, Downing Coll, Cambridge; DMus (hc), Ctrl School Relig, 1979; Hon FVCM, 1980. *Hobbies:* Motoring; Model railways; Relaxation as therapy; Piano playing (pupil of Frederic Lamond and Louis Kentner). *Address:* Flat 4, Wessex Court, Esplanade, Scarborough, North Yorkshire YO11 2AE, England. 4, 149.

SU Deying, b. 24 Dec 1934, Chengdu, Sichuan Province, China. Geologist; Researcher. m. Li Yougui, 4 Feb 1961, 1 s, 1 d. *Education:* Grad, Dept Geology, Chongqing Univ, 1956. *Appointments:* Rsch, Mesoxoic-Cenozoic Ostracoda, their stratigraphy and palaeo-

environmental application, 1956-91; Assoc Prof, 1982; Prof, 1991-. *Publications include:* The Cretaceous System of Chin, Stratigraphy of China No 12 (in Chinese), 1986; The non-marine Cretaceous Ostracoda from East China, 1987. *Memberships:* Chinese Micropalaeontological Soc, Permanent Mbr Coun 1984-88, Vice-Chmn Rsch Grp on Ostracoda 1984-88, Coun Mbr 1988-91; Chinese Palaeontological Soc, Coun Mbr 1988-91. *Honours:* Co-Winner, 1st Nat Nature and Scis Prize, for Daquing oilfield dev prog, 1982; 1st Sci and Tech Prize, as a chief author of Stratigraphy of China series of publs, Min Geological and Mineral Resources, 1985. *Hobbies:* Music; Dancing. *Address:* Institute of Geology, Chinese Academy of Geological Sciences, 26 Baiwanzhuang Road, Beijing 100037, China.

SU Zu-Fei, b. 23 Oct 1898, Shanghai, China. Paediatrician; Professor of Paediatrics. 1 adopted son. *Education:* BS, Shanghai Univ, 1928; MD, Peking Union Med Coll, 1932; Postgrad study, 1947-48, Dip, 1948, NY Univ, USA. *Appointments:* Assoc, Fndr, Paediatric Speciality, Hsing Ya Med Coll, 1934-37; Fndr, Chief Paediatrician, Vice-Supt, 1940-82, Hon Supt, Shanghai Children's Hosp (1st children's hosp in China); Prof, Paediatrics, Shanghai 2nd Med Univ, 1940-; Fndr, 1st Rsch Dept Paediatric Nutrition in China, 1978. *Creative works:* Textbook of Paediatric Nutrition, 1964, 2nd Ed, 1989; Over 40 sci papers in J Chinese Med Assn, J Chinese Paediatric Assn, Acta Nutrimenta Sinica, J Ped (USA), Nutrition Reports International (USA), other paediatric jrnls; 6 popular sci books in paediatric nutrition, 1933, 1954, 1982, 1989, 1991, 1992; 1st to cure children's TB meningitis in China, to introduce stronpathin to cure measles, 1958, to report result of chromosome analysis in case of mongolism, 1963; Only paediatrician to prevent and treat schistosomasis in children for 30 yrs; Nutritional rsch incl 1st to use fresh fish muscle to feed infants 1-6 months. *Memberships:* Dir, Chinese Med Assn, VP and Pres Shanghai Br; VP, Jrnl Ed, Chinese Paediatric Soc; VP, Shanghai Biochem Soc; Dir, Ed Advsr, Chinese Nutrition Soc; Bd Eds, Nutrition Reports International; Ed Advsr, other paediatric jrnls. *Honours include:* Nat Red Banner Award, 1978; Madame Sung's Prize, Maternal and Child Hlth Care Workers, 1985; Prize for Old People w High Aspirations, 1988. *Hobby:* Cultivating flowers. *Address:* Shanghai Children's Hospital, 2 Kang Ding Lu, Shanghai, China.

SUAREZ Xavier L, b. USA. Attorney; Mayor of Miami. *Education:* BME cum laude, Villanova Univ, 1971; MPP (Pub Policy), John F Kennedy School Govt, Harvard Univ, 1975; JD, Harvard Law School, 1975. *Appointments:* Atty, Shutts & Bowen law firm, Miami, FL, 1975; Currently Ptnr, Jorden, Schulte & Burchette, Miami; Elected Mayor, City of Miami, 1985, re-elected, 1987, 1989. *Publications:* Congressional Immunities - a criticism of existing distinctions and a proposal for a new definitional approach, article, 1974; Num articles in newspapers and mags incl Washington Post, USA Today, The Miami Herald, Baltimore Sun, Miami Today, The Miami Times, Miami News, The Orlando Sentinel, Diario Las Americas, The Voice, Sun Sentinel. *Memberships:* Bd Dirs, Legal Servs Corp; Metrop Planning Org; Chmn, Nat Subcomm Immigration Policy, Nominating Comm Mbr, US Conf Mayors; Nat League Cities Youth Task Force; Bd Trustees, Freedoms Fndn; Bd Regents, Cath Univ Am, 1987-88; Chmn, Downtown Dev Authority, City of Miami, 1985-88; Chmn, Little Havana Advsry Bd to Community Action Agcy, 1984; Bd Dirs, Hlth Systems Agcy, 1980-81; FL Consumer Fedn, 1979; Bd Dirs, Legal Servs Gtr Miami, 1979; Several others. *Honours:* LLD hc, Villanova Univ, 1988; Best Public Official, South Florida Mag, 1989, 1990, 1991; Best Local Politician, The New Times, 1990, 1991. *Address:* 701 Brickell Avenue, 24th Floor, Miami, FL 33131, USA. 2.

SUBRAMANIAN Venkateswarier, b. 24 Aug 1920, Tutigorin, India. Professor of Political Science. m. Jaya Subramanian, 26 Feb 1956, 1 s. *Education:* BSc (Hons), 1942, MA, Pol, 1954, Madras Univ; Doct studies, 1956-

59; PhD, Pol Sci, Australian Nat Univ, 1959. *Appointments:* Jrnlst, to 1956; Simon Sr Fellow, Manchester Univ, England, 1960-61; Sr Lectr, 1961-66, Univ Wn Australia; Prof, Indian Inst Pub Admin, India, 1967; Prof, Univ Zambia, 1968-74; Prof, Pol Sci, Carleton Univ, Ottawa, Can, 1974-. *Publications:* Transplanted Indo-British Administration, 1977; Cultural Integration in India, 1979; Sacred and the Secular in India's Performing Arts, 1980; Public Administration in the IIIrd World, 1990; Dance drama books: Panca Kanya Tarassgini; Veera Kanya Vahini; Kinkini Mala Dima Pancakam. *Memberships:* Int Sociological Assn, VP Rsch Comm 1937; Int Pol Sic Assn; Life Mbr, Indian Inst Pub Admin; S India Cultural Assn, Fndr Pres 1976- 79. *Honours:* Haldane Essay Prize, Royal Inst Pub Admin, 1956, 1957; Simon Sr Fellow, 1960-61; Sr Boursier, French Govt, 1970; Vis Prof, Heidelberg Univ and German Civil Serv Acad, 1977; Vis Fellow, Leningrad Univ, 1983. *Hobbies:* Internationally known composer of classical ballets (dance dramas) in Sanskrit on Buddhist themes; Classical music; Modern painting and sculpting. *Address:* 2044 Chalmers Road, Ottawa, Ontario, Canada K1H 6K5. 142.

SUCHANEK Lucjan Ludwik, b. 27 May 1937, Brzezinka, Oswiecim, Poland. Professor. m. 1 Sept 1961. *Education:* Jagiellonian Univ, Cracow, 1955-60; Dr, 1971; PhD, 1977. *Appointments:* Prof, Inst E Slavonic Philology, Cracow; Hd, Dept Russian Lit, 1982-84, 1990-, Inst E Slavonic Philology; Dir, Inst Russian Philology, Cracow, 1982-84; Dean, Fac Philology, 1984-91; Vice-Rector, Jagiellonian Univ, 1991-. *Publications:* Books: The Russian Romantic Ballad, 1974; Russian Poetry of the First Half of the Nineteenth Century. An Anthology, 1976; Lyrical Poetry of E Baratynski, 1977; The Old Russian Literature and Culture, 1980; The Russian Poetry of the First Half of the Nineteenth Century. Part II. A Pushkin, M Lermontov. An Anthology (w A Dudek), 1990; The Preromanticism in Russia, 1991; Ed: Turgenev in Memoirs, 1982; The Contemporary Russian Theory of Literature (w A Razny), 1982, 2nd Ed, 1985; A Chekhov, The Letters (w N Modzelweska), 1988; I Goncarov, Oblomov, 1990; The Contemporary Russian Theory of Literature. Part II. Tartu-Moscow School of Semiotics (w K Eimermacher), 1991; P Caadaev, The Letters, 1992. *Memberships:* VP, Commn Slavonic Studies, Polish Acad Scis, Warsaw; Commn Slavonic Studies, Polish Acad Scis, Cracow; Commn Hist of Lit, Polish Acad Scis, Sec 1982-86; Int Soc Dostoevsky; Ed-in-Chief, Slavia Orientalis; Ed Bd, Ruch Literacki. *Honours:* Award, Min Educ, 1975, 1978, 1983. *Hobby:* Travel. *Address:* ul I Fika 25/95, 31-214 Cracow, Poland.

SUCHODOLSKI Bogdan, b. 27 Dec 1903, Sosnowiec, Poland. Professor of Education. m. Maria Bartczak, 1946, 1 d. *Education:* Univ Cracow; Dr's degree, Warsaw Univ, 1925; Postgrad studies, Berlin, Paris. *Appointments:* Prof, Lvov Univ, 1938; Full Prof, Warsaw Univ, 1946-68; Mbr, 1952-, Mbr, Praesidium, 1960-80, Polish Acad Scis; Pres, Nat Coun Culture, 1983-90. *Publications include:* Books on education incl Theorie der sozialistischen Bildung, 1974, on anthropological philos and on Polish culture; Many translated into var langs; Ed: Great Universal Encyclopaedia, 13 vols, 1962-70; History of the Polish Science, 1970-. *Memberships:* Comp Educ Soc Europe, VP 1964-71; World Assn Educl Rsch, Pres 1969-73; Acad Int d'Hist des Scis, VO 1968-71; World Future Studies Fedn, VP 1977-90; Soc Europeenne de Culture. *Honours:* Banner of Labour; Builder of People's Poland; Award, Acad Int d'Hist des Scis; Dr hc: Silesian Univ: Warsaw Univ; High Pedagogical School, Opole; Univ Padua, Italy; Moscow Univ; Pedagogical Acad, Berlin. *Hobbies:* Cars; Travel; Dogs. *Address:* Smiala 63a, 01 526 Warsaw, Poland. 2, 34, 52, 139, 162.

SUCHY Jiri Jan, b. 6 Aug 1931, Plzen, Czechoslovakia. Forecaster; Philosopher; Sociologist. m. Dilbar Alijeva, 1 s. *Education includes:* PhD, Charles Univ, Prague, 1954; CSc, Moscow State Uni, 1964; Goethes Univ, Frankfurt am Main, FRG, 1968-69; Humboldt Stiftung.

Appointments: Docent, Philosl Fac, Comenius Univ, Bratislava, 1960-75; Prof, Social Scis, Cyril-Methodius Theological Fac, Bratislava, 1968-78; Inst Econs, 1980-83, Sr Researcher, Inst Forecasting, 1989-, Slovak Acad Scis, Bratislava; Rsch Inst Living Level, Bratislava. *Publications:* Youths in the Society, 1977; Youth and Society, 1980; Socialist way of life (w F Hronsky), 1979, Moscow, 1980; Socialization of youth in contemporary socialist society, 1989; About 200 articles in Czechoslovak, Russian and German jrnls. *Honours:* Collective Prize, Czechoslovak Broadcasting, 1968. *Hobbies:* Reading; Painting. *Address:* Mudronova 23, 821 00 Bratislava, Czech and Slovak Federal Republic. 52.

SUDARSONO Srihadi, b. 4 Dec 1931, Solo, Mid Java, Indonesia. Lecturer; Artist. m. Siti Farida, 23 Feb 1964, 1 s, 2 d. *Education:* MA, Tech Fac, Univ Indonesia, Bandung, 1959; MA, 1962, Fulbright-Hays Rsch Prog Art, 1980, OH State Univ, USA. *Career:* Lectr, Dept Art, 1959-, Chmn, Dept Art, 1971-73, Bandung Inst Technology; Lectr, 1970-88, Chmn, Dept Art, 1974-77, Jakarta Inst Arts; Chmn, ASEAN Symposium Painting and Photography, Jakarta, 1988; Exhibs: Galeria Palacyk, Warsaw, Poland, 1984; LB Bank, Braunschweig, FRG, 1985; Hankyu Art Gall, Osaka, Japan, 1987; Club Med Asian Arts Exhib, Malaysia, 1988; 8th Biennale, Jakarta, 1989; Art Expo, Jakarta, 1991; Mod Indonesian Art Exhib, Oakland, CA, USA, 1991; Indonesian Contemporary Art Exhib, Wash, DC, 1991. *Membership:* Int Artists Assn, Paris. *Honours:* Art Award, Republic Indonesia Govt, 1971; Cultural Award, Australian Govt, 1973; Cultural Grant, Netherlands Govt, 1977; Best Painting Prize, 3 Biennale, Jakarta, 1978; Silver Prize, Aquarelle, Seoul Int Art Competition, 1985; Best Painting Prize, 7th Biennale, Jakarta, 1987; Cultural Grant for travel in Japan, Japan Fndn, 1990. *Hobbies:* Music; Sport; Swimming. *Address:* Jalan Ciumbulleuit 173, Bandung 40142, Indonesia. 139.

SUDLENKOVA Olga, b. 10 Mar 1944, Brest, Belorussia. Teacher of English Language and Literature. div., 1 s, 1 d. *Education:* Grad, 1965, Dr Philology, 1985, Asst Prof, 1991; Minsk Inst For Langs; Summer Engl Lang Inst, Wash, DC, 1990. *Appointments:* Second School Tchr, Engl, 1965-68; lectr, Sr Lectr, 1968-91, Asst Prof, 1991-, Minsk Inst For Langs. *Publications:* English Literature, school textbook, 1974, 3rd Ed, 1991; Articles on English poetry-Wordsworth, G Byron, Th Campbell, J Keats. *Hobbies:* Gardening; Reading, esp literary borrowings and feminist problems in present-day English literature. *Address:* 52 Pritytski St, apt 108, Minsk 220121, Belorussia. 138.

SUELTENFUSS Elizabeth Anne, b. 14 Apr 1921, San Antonio, TX, USA. Univ Prof. *Education:* BA, Our Lady of the Lake Coll, 1944; MS 1961, PhD 1963, Univ of Notre Dame. *Appointments:* Pres, Our Lady of the Lake Univ; Admnstr, Congregation of Divine Providence; Coll Prof, Our Lady of the Lake Coll; HS Tchr. *Memberships:* Bd of Dir, Am Cancer Soc; San Antonio Avance; Mind Sci Fndn; YWCA; Sta KLRN Pub TV; SW Rsch Fndn; Bd of Visitors, Air Force Inst Tech; Indep Coll & Univ of TX; San Antonio Coun of Pres; Past Pres, Zonta; Vice Chmn, Grp San Antonio C of C. *Honours:* Ldrship Awd 1979, Community Serv Awd 1991, Univ of Notre Dame; Headliner Awd, Women in Communications, 1980; Good Neighbour Awd, NCCJ, 1982; Today's Woman Awd, San Antonio Light, 1982; Outstng Women Awd, San Antonio Express-News, 1983; named to San Antonio Women's Hall of Fame, 1985. *Hobbies:* Languages; Reading; Listening to music; Walking; Arts and crafts; Travelling. *Address:* 411 SW 24th Street, San Antonio, TX 78207, USA. 2, 5, 7, 15, 52, 132, 138, 145, 154.

SUGISAKI Mitsuyo Kawase, b. 19 Apr 1929, Yahata-higashiku, Kitakyushu, Japan. Educator; Professor of Civil Law. m. Tetsuo Sugisaki, 28 May 1958. *Education:* Seinan Jo Gakuin Jr Coll, 1946-49; Kyushu Int (Yahata)

Univ, 1951-53; LLM, Grad School, Kyushu Univ, 1961. *Appointments:* Seinan Jo Gakuin Jr Coll, 1958-67; Women's Jr Coll, Kinki Univ, 1967-79; Yahata Univ, Kitakyushu, 1978-89; Kyushu Int Univ (formerly Yahata Univ), 1989-. *Publications:* Co-author: Family Law and History, 1981; Current Problems of Family Law, 1990; Law of Relatives and Succession, 1991. *Memberships:* Kyushu Law Soc; Japan Assn Private Law; Japan Soc Socio- Legal Law on Family; Japan Assn Law of Fin. *Hobbies:* Music; Appreciation of fine arts. *Address:* Kyushu International University, 5-9-1 Edamitsu, Yahata-higashiku, Kitakyushu City, 805 Japan. 34, 52.

SUGIURA Masahisa, b. 8 Dec 1925, Tokyo, Japan. Professor. m. Keiko Adachi, 12 June 1962, 1 d. *Education:* MS, Univ Tokyo, 1949; PhD, Univ AK, USA, 1955. *Appointments:* Assoc Prof, 1957-62, Prof, 1962, Geophys Inst AK, USA; Sr Rsch Assn, NASA/Nat Rsch Coun, 1962-64; w NASA Goddard Space Flight, 1964-86; Prof, Kyoto Univ, Japan, 1985-89; Prof, Inst Rsch and Dev, Tokai Univ, Tokyo, 1989-. *Contributions to:* num articles to profl jrnls and books. *Memberships:* Fellow, Am Geophys Union; Soc Geomagnetism and Earth, Planetary and Space Sci; Exec Comm Mbr, Int Assn Geomagnetism and Aeronomy. *Honours:* Tanakadate prize, Soc Geomagnetism and Earth, Planetary and Space Sci, 1950; Exceptional Perf Award, Goddard Space Flight Ctr, 1982; Medal, Exceptional Sci Achievement, NASA, 1985. *Hobbies:* Music; Reading; Arts. *Address:* Institute of Research and Development, Tokai University, 2-28 Tomigaya, Shibuya-ku, Tokyo 151, Japan. 2, 52.

SUHARDIMAN Hendrik, b. 7 Oct 1955, Jakarta, Indonesia. Banker. m. Kwee Lie Pyng, 4 Jan 1982, 3 s. *Education includes:* Bach's degree, Banking, 1982; Bach, Indl Acad, 1983; Postgrad, Asian Inst Mgmt, Philippines, 1986. *Appointments:* Pres, Dir, PT Tamara Multi Steel Mfg Corp, 1979- 94; Mng Dir, PT Arta Tamarisca Ind, 1982-83; Fin Advsr, Success Enterprise Ltd, 1982-83; Dir, PT Arts Artamara Oil Seal Ind, 1983-84; Mbr, Credit Advsry Comm, PT Tamara Commercial Bank, 1983-85; Dir, PT Sapta Pragenta Utama, 1984; Dir, PT Anugerah Harta Leasing Int, 1984; Sr VP, Dir, PT Tamara Bank, Jakarta, 1985-; Mbr, Supervisory Bd: PT Duta Putra Tamara, 1986, PT Pantoru Mas, 1987, PT Senggigi Resort Hotel, PT Sri Tamaratu, others. *Publications:* Banking articles in newspapers and mags. *Memberships:* Indonesian Nat Pvte Bank Assn; Indonesian Bankers Club; Hilton Execs Club; Mercantile Club. *Hobbies:* Golf; Exotiç car collector. *Address:* 18th Floor, Tamara Centre, Jl Jendral Sudirman Kav, 24, Jakarta 12920, Indonesia. 34.

SUKORIANSKY Semion, b. 24 Dec 1947, USSR. Scientist; Lecturer. m. Tatiana Kurkina, 20 Mar 1970, 1 s, 1 d. *Education:* MSc, Maths, Mech, Moscow Univ, 1971; PhD w hons, Fluid Mech, Ben-Gurion Univ, Israel, 1987. *Appointments:* Mbr, Rsch Staff, Oil and Gas Inst, Moscow, 1971-81; Grp Hd, 1983-89, Lectr, 1991-, Ben-Gurion Univ, Beer-Sheva, Israel; Mbr, Rsch Staff, Princeton Univ, Princeton, NJ, USA, 1989-91. *Publications:* Over 50 papers in sci jrnls, collective vols and conf proceedings. *Memberships:* Am Phys Soc. *Honours:* Student Award, Am Nuclear Soc, 1988; Igal Alon Fellowship, Israel, 1990. *Hobbies:* Tourism; Reading. *Address:* Department of Mechanical Engineering, Ben-Gurion University of the Negev, PO Box 653, Beer-Sheva 84105, Israel.

SUMARIWALLA Adille Jehangir, b. 1 Jan 1958, Bombay, India. Service/Sports Consultant. m. Armaity Sam Rao, 5 Jan 1986, 1 d. *Education:* BCom, Fin Acctng and Auditing, 1983, MCom, Mgmt, 1985, Bombay Univ. *Appointments:* Tata Engrng and Locomotive Co Ltd Hd Off, Bombay, 1979-; Chmn, Profl Sports Servs sports promotion firm; Tech Cons to MONDO; Coach, Indian Team, Maharashtra State Team, Bombay Univ Athletics Team, 3 int athletes, others, school children's athletic camps; Press Corres, Asian Games, Beijing, China, 1990. *Memberships:* Hon Jt Sec, Selection Comm Mbr,

Fin Comm Mbr, Maharashtra Amateur Athletic Assn; Hon Jt Sec, Bombay City Dist Amateur Athletic Assn; Fin Coord, Amateur Athletic Fedn India; Bombay Univ Sports Comm; Organising Comm, 9th Asian Track and Field Championship, 1989; Sec, Athletics, Boxing, Cycling, Tata Sports Club; Pres, Secretariat Bombay Sports Assn; Former Gen Sec, Athletics Welfare Assn India; Athletics Comm, Cricket Club India; Bombay Gymkhana Ltd; Willingdom Cath Gymkhana; Athletic Comm, Bombay HSs Sports Assn. *Honours:* President's Award, Scouting, 1972; Shiv Chatrapati Award, Excellence in Sports, Maharashtra Govt, 1980; Arjuna Award, Excellence in Athletics, Pres of India, 1985; Maharashtra Gaurav Puraskar, Outstanding Perf in Sports, Maharashtra State, 1990; 6 Gold, 5 Silver, 6 Bronze Medals, int sprint and relay; 22 Gold, 13 Silver, 5 Bronze Medals, nat competitions; Indian Capt, World Univ Games, Mexico, and S Asian Fedn Games, Nepal; Represented India, Moscow Olympic Games, 1980; Champion: Nat 100 m Sprint, 11 times; Inter-State 100 m, 1979-85; Nat 200 m Sprint; All- India Univ 100 m, 1979, 1980, 200 m, 1980; Records: Inter-State Nat 100 m; All India Univ 100 m, 1980; 4 x 100 m relay teams. *Hobbies:* Scouting; Camping; Sports scribe and commentator. *Address:* c/18 Godrej Baug, off Nepeansea Road, Bombay 400 026, India.

SUMAROKOV Victor, b. 4 Mar 1954, Sympheropol, USSR. Composer. m. Elena Silshenco, 2 June 1977, 2 s, 1 d. *Education:* Grad, Aram Khachaturyan's Composition Class, Moscow Conservatory, 1978. *Appointments:* Ed, Ed Off for Chmbr and Instrumental Music, Soviet Composer publishing off, 1980-92. *Creative works:* Sonata de grotesco for Violin and Piano, 1976; 3 Pieces on Thema B-A-C-H for 2 Clarinets and Bass Clarinet, 1977; Divertimento for Symph Orch, 1978, pubd, 1982; The Poetry of Earth, chamber cantata on the poems of English Poets (Shelley, Blake, Keats), for Soprano,Bass and 5 Instruments, 1981-89; Quartet-capriccio for 4 Clarinets, 1982, pubd, 1984; Incrustations. 3 pieces for 4 Saxophones, 1983, pubd, 1985; Partita for Bassoon and Tape, 1984; Partita for Es, B and Bass Clarinet and Tape, 1984; Partita for 4 successive Saxophones (tenor, alto, baritone, soprano) and Tape, 1984; Concerto for Saxophone and String Orch, 1990; Parting. Composition for Violin and Tape, 1991; Christ Who speaks In Me. Quintet on the text from the Nash New Testament for Soprano and String Quartet, 1991. *Memberships:* USSR Composers Union; Bd Mbr, Eyrasia Ctr Spiritual Heritage; Assn Contemporary Music. *Hobbies:* Travel; Books; Collecting different recordings of contemporary and classical music. *Address:* Gospitalny Val 5, corp 7, apt 249, 105094 Moscow, Russia.

SUMITANI Satoshi, b. 3 Apr 1932, Tokyo, Japan. Professor. m. 29 May 1977, 1 s, 1 d. *Education:* Dip, Composition Class, Dept Music, Univ Tokyo Arts, 1954; Dip, Dept Music Educ, Ibaraki Univ. *Appointments:* Prof, Composition, Electroacoustic Music, High Technology Media, Univ Tokyo Gakaugei (State Univ) and Coll Toho Music, 1979. *Publications:* Books: Arrangement for Little Ensemble, 1970; HACAM for Piano, Oboe, Photographic Image and Graphic Score on the Electroacoustic Space, 1985; CD records: Fantasy in Super Future, 1984; The Illusive World in Super Future, 1986; Forest Marvelously, 1986; Monographs: SPACE-IDEA of electroacoustics, 1975; Expansion on the Sound Image, 1976; TRANSPARENT Sound and Negative Space, 1977; Mobile Sound Space at Acceleration, 1978; Topologic Sound Space with Electroacoustic, 1980. *Memberships:* Confederation Internationale de Musique Electroacoustique International; Int Soc Music Educ; Pres, Topologic Arts Tokyo Assn. *Honours:* Prize for Six Sketches, 23 Music Concours, NHK and Mainichi Press, 1954; Prize for Cluster of Nephrolepis Marshalles on 8-dimensional sound space, Int Soc Contemporary Music Reykjavik Music Days, 1973. *Hobbies include:* Hiking; Painting; Sculpture; Listening to birds; Motor cars and driving; Mechanic for TV display screen and audio system. *Address:* Department of Music, University of Tokyo Gakugei, Koganei-shi, Nukui-kita-machi 4-1-1, Tokyo, Japan 184.

SUMMERS Janie Irby, b. 22 July 1933, Spartanburg County, South Carolina, USA. Elementary School Principal. m. Johnnie W Summers Jr, 3 July 1958, 1 s, 1 d. *Education:* AB, Benedict Coll, 1954; MEd, SC State Coll, 1969; Univ Chgo; Univ NE; Univ SC; Appalachian State Univ. *Appointments:* Tchr, 1954-79; Tchr, Migrant Prog; Adult Educ Tchr; Educl Guidance Cnslr, 1979-83; Prin, O P Earle Elem, Landrum, SC, 1983-. *Memberships:* SC Assn Elem and Middle School Prins; Assn Supervision and Curric Dev; Kappa Delta Pi; Nat SC Educs Assn; Int Reading Assn. *Honours:* Dist I Tchr of Yr, 1971, 1972; Outstanding Elem Tchr Am, 1972; Hon Mention, Prin of Yr, Dist XII PTA, 1987, 1988, 1989; Dist I Admnstr of Yr, 1989; Lifetime Mbrship, SCPTA; Educ of Yr, Spartanburg Optimist Club, 1991-92. *Hobbies:* Church work; Gospel choir; Reading; Travel. *Address:* O P Earle Elementary, Landrum, SC 29356, USA. 15.

SUMMEY Steven Michael, b. 26 Jan 1946, Abingdon, Virginia, USA. Business Owner. m. Linda Lee Hoff, 28 July 1978, 3 s. *Education:* Wn Carolina Univ; Univ NC, Abingdon. *Appointments:* Pres, Summey Outdoor Advt Inc, 1967-. *Publications:* The Outdoor Advertising Package, computer software, 1986; num newspaper and periodical articles. *Memberships:* Fndr, Pres, Coun Indep Bus Owners Inc; Co-Fndr, Indep Advt Coun; NC Outdoor Advt Assn, Past Pres; Nat Speakers Assn, Past Pres; Int Platform Assn; Carolina Speakers Assn; NC Bd Realtors; Nat Assn Realtors; Asheville Bd Realtors; SC Outdoor Advt Assn; Dir, Outdoor Advt Assn Am; Buncombe Co Sheriff's Dept; Nat Sheriff's Assn; Aircraft Owners and Pilots Assn. *Honours:* Patent issued, Single Pole Outdoor Advt Sign, 1974. *Hobbies:* Hunting; Fishing; Golf; Bowling; Flying. *Address:* 95 Underwood Rd, Fletcher, NC 28732, USA. 7, 52, 132.

SUN Jinzhu, b. 14 Feb 1923, Beijing, China. Professor of Geography. m. Zhou Zhiming, 2 July 1956, 1 s, 2 d. *Education:* BSc, Geog Dept, Qing Hua Univ, 1948. *Appointments:* Dean, Studies, Tchr, Geog: Fen Dou Middle School, Beijing, 1948-50, Huhhot, 1950-53; Lectr, Assoc Prof, Full Prof, Vice-Dean, Geog Dept, Inner Mongolia Tchrs Univ, Huhhot, 1953-91. *Publications:* 3 monographs, 4 edited works, 10 jt works, 50 dissertations, China, abroad incl: The First Inquiry of Comprehensive Natural Divisions in Inner Mongolia, 1962; Natural Environment and the Reform of He Tao Plain, 1978; Agricultural Comprehensive Natural Divisions of Shelter- forest Areas in Three-north, 1982; About the Deterioration and Protection of the Steppe in Inner Mongolia, 1983; Environmental Protection and Reasonable Utilization of the Steppe in Inner Mongolia, 1986; China Geography, 1988, 1989; Environmental Management and Development in the Hulunbuir Steppe in Inner Mongolia, 1988; Livestock Husbandry Climate of the Steppe in Inner Mongolia, 1988; Strategies for Ecological Environmental Management in the Xi Liao River Basin, 1988; Lecturing China Geography on the TV-teaching Satellite, video tape, 1989; Strategies for Improving the Natural Environment on Ordos Plateau, 1990; Strategies for Agricultural Development and Ecological Environmental Management in He Tao Plain, 1990. *Memberships:* Phys Geog Comm, China Geog Inst; Hd, Coun, Geog Inst Inner Mongolia; Vice-Hd, Inst Territory Economy Inner Mongolia; Advsry Coun, Agricl Div, Inner Mongolia. *Honours:* 23 prizes and awards incl: Sci and Technology Progressive Collective Prize, 1st Class, Chinese Acad Scis, 1986, 1987; 3rd Class Prize, Excellent Social Sci Dissertation, Inner Mongolia, 1987; Top-grade Prize, Nat Excellent Tchng Achievements, 1989; Sci and Technology Progressive Prize, Nat Environmental Protection, 1990; Gold Medal, Brilliant Technology Achievements, 1990. *Hobby:* Peking Opera. *Address:* Geography Dept, Inner Mongolia Teachers University, Huhhot, China.

SUN Jun, b. 17 Sept 1926, Suchow, China. Professor. m. 2 Jan 1955, 2 s. *Education:* BS, Nat Jiao-tong Univ, Shanghai, 1949; Vis Scholar, NC State Univ, USA, 1980-81. *Appointments:* Asst, Jiao-tong Univ, Shanghai, 1949-52; Lectr, Assoc Prof, Full Prof, Hon Dean, Geotech Engrng Dept, Tong-ji Univ, Shanghai. *Creative works:* Designer: 1st underground shelter for airplanes in China; Largest prestressed concrete pneumatic caisson subway station in China; Books: Underground Structures, 1987; F E M for Underground Structures, 1988; Over 110 published papers. *Memberships:* Expert Grp, National Postdcot Mgmt Comm, People's Republic of China; Dir, China Civil Engrng Soc; Dir, China Rock Mech and Rock Engrng Soc; Dpty Pres, Shanghai Civil Engrng Soc; Int Soc Rock Mech; Acad Degree Conferment Comm, State Coun, People's Republic of China. *Honours:* 1st Prize, Sci and Technology Progress, Water Conservancy and Elec Power Min, China, 1987; 2nd Prize, Nat Sci and Technology Progress, China, 1987; 2nd Prize, Sci and Technology Progress, Nat Educ Comm, China, 1988, 1989; Gt Merit Record, Shanghai People's Govt, 1989. *Hobbies:* Touring; Drama; Gardening. *Address:* Department of Geotechnical Engineering, Tong-ji University, 200092 Shanghai, China.

SUN Keqin, b. 31 July 1955, Tieling City, Liaoning, China. Researcher in Palaeobotany. m. Zhang Fengying, 28 Apr 1981, 1 s, 1 d. *Education:* Grad, Geology, 1980, Doct degree, 1990, Changchun Univ Earth Scis; Master's degree, Palaeobotany, Lanzhou Univ, 1987. *Appointments:* Worker, 1971-76; Techn, 1980-85; Post-doct Rsch Worker, Palaeobotany, Changchun Univ Earth Scis, 1990-. *Publications:* Late Carboniferous and Early Permian Flra, Palaeoecology and Sedimentary Environment in Zibo Area, Shanddong, acad book, 1992; Over 20 acad papers, 1988-92. *Memberships:* Palaeontological Soc China; Palaeobotanical Soc China. *Honours:* Prize, Cert of Youth Geologist, Changchun Univ Earth Scis, 1991. *Hobbies:* Playing table tennis; Swimming; Painting. *Address:* Department of Geology, Changchun University of Earth Sciences, Changchun, 130061 Jilin, China.

SUN Naixiu, b. 12 Nov 1948, Qingdao City, China. Literary Critic; Comparative Literature Scholar. *Education:* BA, Chinese Lang and Lit Dept, 1981, MA, Grad School, 1984, Fudan Univ, Shanghai. *Appointments:* Lit Critic, Inst Lit, Chinese Acad Social Scis, Beijing, 1984-; Gen Ed, World Culture Master Series; Ed, Foreign Masters Series. *Publications:* Books: Turgenev and China: A Study of the Literary Relations between Sino- Foreign Countries in the 20th Century, 1988; A New Dictionary of Social Sciences (co-author), 1988; Selected Ts'u Poems of Li Qingzhao (1084-1155) with introduction and detailed interpretations, 1990; Selected Ts'u Poems of Xin Qiji (1140-1207) with introduction and detailed interpretations, 1991; Selected Ts'u Poems of Tang-Song Dynasties with interpretations, 1991; Dictionary of New Methods in Social Sciences (co-ed, co-author), 1992; A Contemporary Chinese Intellectual's Miserable Life in Pursuit of Truth: Biography of Jia Zhifeng, 1992; Var transls. *Memberships:* Fellow, Coun, Beijing Comp Lit Assn; China Comp Lit Assn. *Honours:* Best Book Prize, All China Com Lit Books (1978-90) for Turgenev and China, 1990. *Hobbies:* Music; Photography; Travel; Skating; Swimming; Snooker. *Address:* Institute of Literature, Chinese Academy of Social Sciences, 100732 Beijing, China. 139, 152, 190.

SUN Taidong, b. 13 Oct 1934, Longkou City, Sandong Province, China. Researcher and Developer of Optical Instruments. m. 20 Aug 1961, 2 d. *Education:* BS, Dept Mech Engrng, NWn Polytech Univ, 1958. *Appointments:* Tech, Shop Ldr, Wuzhong Material Testing Machine Factory, Ningxia Prov, 1958-63; Tech, 1963-79, Vice-Scientist (Vice-Prof), 1979-83, Vice-Ldr, Dept Precision Instruments, 1979-83, Sr Scientist (Prof), Dir, Dept Precision Instruments, 1988-91, Changchun Inst Optics and Fine Mech, Acad Sinica. *Publications:* Papers and reports in var jrnls incl: Multispectral Colour Image

Improvement and Enhancement, 1981; Research of Laser Typesetter; Technology of Laser Printer. *Memberships:* Nat Assn Space Sci; Nat Assn Instruments. *Honours:* 3rd Prize, Sci, 1980, 2nd Prize, Sci, Sanjiang Plain Nature Sources Resurvey, 1986, 2nd Prize, Sci, Laser Typesetter, 1986, 2nd Prize, JZJ-380 Laser Image Recorder, 1989, Acad Sinica; Nat Sci 1st Prize, Laser Typesetting System, 1987; Nat Sci 3rd Prize, Sanjian Plain Nature Sources Resurvey, 1988; Nat Five One Labour Medal, 1990. *Hobbies:* Basketball; Reading. *Address:* Changchun Institute of Optics and Fine Mechanics, Academia Sinica, Jilin, China.

SUN Xun, b. 29 Jan 1944, Jiangsu, China. Professor of Chinese Literature. m. Sun Juyuang, 1 Jan 1968, 1 s, 1 d. *Education:* BA, Chinese Lit, Jiangsu Normal Univ, 1965. *Appointments:* Asst, 1965-77, Lectr, 1978-85, Prof, 1986-, Dir, Rsch Inst Lit, 1986-90, Shanghai Tchrs Univ. *Publications:* A Preliminary Survey of the Zi Pin version of 'A Dream of Red Mansions'; Essays on A Dream of Red Mansions and Jin Pin Mei; Essays on the Novels of the Ming and Qing Dynasties; A Corpus of Aesthetic Date on the Chinese Classical Novels. *Memberships:* Chinese Writers Assn; Coun Chinese Writers; Vice-Chmn, Sec, Standing Coun Mbr, Shanghai Instn A Dream of Red Mansions; Vice-Chmn, Shanghai Instn Chinese Classical Lit. *Honours:* A Preliminary Survey of the Zi Pin version of 'A Dream of Red Mansions won: 2nd Prize for Outstanding Achievements in Field of Philos and Social Scis during Yrs 1976-82, Shanghai Instns Higher Educ; Works Prize during Yrs 1979- 85, Shanghai Philos and Social Scis. *Hobbies:* Collecting and appreciating Chinese paintings and calligraphic works; Enjoying feature films and Chinese classical music. *Address:* Research Institute of Literature, Shanghai Teachers University, 10 Guilin Road, Shanghai, China. 139.

SUN Yaxian, b. 27 Jan 1936, Jilin, China. University Teacher; Department Director. m. Cui Huaqing, 1 Jan 1963, 3 d. *Education:* Dept Econs Engrng, Baerbing Univ Technology, 1955-60. *Appointments:* Tchr, Zhejiang Univ, 1960-64; Tchr, later Dir, Indl Enterprise Mgmt Dept, Shanghai Univ Technology, 1964-. *Publications:* Textbook of Industrial Enterprise Management; 16 Kinds of Modern Management Methods; Production Management; Running Management; Mechanical Industry Enterprise Management. *Memberships:* Rsch Assn Tech Econ and Mgmt Modernisation; Shanghai Enterprise Mgmt Assn; VP, Sec-Gen, Shanghai Chief Engrs Friendship Liaison Assn; Dir, Mgmt Assn, Shanghai Mech and Elec Indl Bur. *Honours:* 2nd Grade Prize, Tchng Achievement, 1984-88, 3rd Grade Prize, Sci and Technology Improvement, 1985, Shanghai Univ Technology; 1st and 3rd Grade, Sci and Info, No 2 Light Ind Bur Shanghai, 1987, 1988. *Hobbies:* Dancing; Housework. *Address:* Department of Industry Management Engineering, Shanghai University of Technology, 313 Hengfeng Road, Shanghai 200070, China.

SUN Yichuang, b. 21 Apr 1960, Dalian, China. Teacher; Associate Professor. m. Xu Xiaohui, 1 Oct 1986, 1 s. *Education:* BSc, Elec Engrng, 1982, MSc, Elec Engrng, 1985, Dalian Maritime Univ. *Appointments:* Asst, 1985-88, Lectr, 1988-90, Assoc Prof, 1990-, Dalian Maritime Univ. *Publications:* 46 acad papers incl: Faulty-cut diagnosis in nonlinear circuits, 1990; Class-fault diagnosis theory and approach, 1990. *Memberships:* IEEE; Chinese Inst Electronics. *Honours:* Recip, 8 hons, prizes and awards incl: Excellent Tchr, Dalian Maritime Univ, 1987; Excellent Tchng Achievement Award, Liaoning Province, 1989; 1988-89 Model Worker, Dalian City, 1990; Youth Sci and Technology Award, Chinese Inst Navigation, 1991. *Hobby:* Reading. *Address:* Department of Electronic Engineering, Dalian Maritime University, Dalian 116024, China.

SUNAHARA Yoshifumi, b. 16 July 1927, Mie Prefecture, Japan. Professor. m. 10 Apr 1960, 1 s, 1 d. *Education:* BS, Engrng, Osaka Prefectural Univ, 1953;

MS, Engrng, 1955, PhD, Engrng, 1962, Kyoto Univ. *Appointments:* Rsch Asst, 1955-62, Assoc Prof, 1963-68, Kyoto Univ; Vis Asst Prof, Brown Univ, USA, 1966-67; Prof, Kyoto Inst Technology, 1968-91; Prof, Okayama Univ Sci, 1991-. *Publications:* Statistical Studies in Nonlinear Control Systems, 1962; Statistical Decision Theory in Adaptive Control Systems, 1967; Stochastic System Theory, I, 1979, II, 1981, III, 1982; Engineering Applications of Probability Theory, 1981. *Memberships:* NY Acad Scis; Soc Indl and Applied Maths; IEEE; Soc Instrument and Control Engrs, Japan; Japan Soc Mech Engrs. *Honours:* Emeritus Prof, Kyoto Inst Technology, 1991; Paper Awards: Japan Soc Mech Engrs, 1963; Soc Instrument and Control Engrs, Japan, 1982; Fellow: IEEE, USA, 1984; Soc Instrument and Control Engrs, Japan, 1988. *Hobby:* Painting. *Address:* Mita Press, Kyoto Annex, Asahi Karasuma Building 4F, 381 Shimizu-cho, Karasuma- East, Takeya, Nakagyo-ku, Kyoto 604, Japan. 34, 143.

SUNDHOLM Goran, b. 6 Aug 1936, Helsinki, Finland. Professor in Physical Chemistry. m. Franciska Diehl, 10 Sept 1960, 1 s, 1 d. *Education:* MSc, Engrng, 1959; Lic Technology, 1963; Dr Technology, 1969. *Appointments:* Rsch Asst, State Alcohol Monopoly Ltd (Alkoholiliike Oy), 1960-63; Tchng Asst, 1963-69, Assoc Prof, Phys Chem, 1971-76, Prof, Phys Chem, 1976-, Helsinki Univ Technology, Espoo. *Publications:* Doct thesis, 1969; About 100 sci publs in phys chem, esp electrochem; Quantum chemistry and spectroscopy (in Finnish), 1974; Electrochemistry (in Finnish), 1987. *Memberships:* Royal Soc Chem; Int Soc Electrochem; Suomalaisten Kemistien Seura; Tekniska Foreningen i Finland. *Honours:* Mbr, Swedish Acad Tech Scis Finland. *Hobbies:* Reading; History. *Address:* Kalevankatu 11, 00100 Helsinki, Finland. 90.

SUNNUCKS James Horace George, b. 20 Sept 1925, London, England. Barrister. m. Rosemary Ann Borradaile, 1 Oct 1955, 4 s. *Education:* Trinity Hall, Cambridge, 1946; MA (Cantab); Barrister, Lincoln's Inn, 1950. *Appointments:* War Serv, 1939; Barrister, Chancery Bar, London, 1950-; Bencher, Lincoln's Inn, London, 1980. *Publications:* Williams Mortimer and Sunnucks on Executors and Administrators; Halsbury's Laws (ed). *Memberships:* Local Parole Review Comm, 1970-82, Chmn 1981-82; Pres, Inst Conveyancers; Oxford and Cambridge Club; Garrick Club; Pres, En Area, Essex, Order of St John; Gardeners Co, 1986. *Honours:* Lic Reader, Chelmsford, 1954; Dpty Lt, Essex, 1990. *Hobbies:* Gardening; Local history; Sailing. *Address:* East Mersea Hall, Colchester, Essex CO5 8TJ, England.

SUOTMAA Juha Olavi, b. 22 Sept 1963, Turku, Finland. Bank Employee. m. Su Shu-Ming, 5 Sept 1986, 1 d. *Education:* Paasikivi Inst, 1983-84; BA, US Int Univ, San Diego, CA, 1988; London School Econs, 1989-90. *Appointments:* Serv Dept, May-Dec 1982, Dec 1983, July-Sept, 1984, Dec 1984, Int Dept, 1985-87 (summers), 1988-89 (summers), 1990-91, Okobank, Turku. *Publications:* The International Relations of Republic of China on Taiwan, master's thesis, 1990. *Memberships:* Order of St Lazarus; Order of St John; San Diego World Affairs Coun, 1986-88; Inst Europe, Turku; Nat Coalition Party Finland. *Honours:* Nat Deans List, USA, 1985, 1987; Dean's List, US Int Univ, fall 1985, fall 1986, winter 1987, fall 1987, winter 1988, spring 1988; Good Serv Award, Coast Artillery Finland, 1983; Half Colourr, London School Econs, 1990. *Hobby:* Table tennis: Turun Toverit ry, 1977-78, 1990-91, Turun Kaiku ry, 1978-90, Turun Poutatennisseura, 1990-, Pres, US Int Univ Table Club Pres, 1986-88, London School Econs Table Tennis Soc, 1989-90. *Address:* Taskulantie 2 C 51, SF-20300 Turku, Finland. 52.

SUPERANSKAYA Alexandra, b. 7 Oct 1929, Moscow, USSR. Linguist. m. Marc Averbukh, 8 Jan 1959, 1 s, 1 d. *Education:* Engl Fac, Moscow State Pedagogical Inst For Langs, 1947-52; Postgrad studies, Inst Linguistics, Acad Scis, Moscow, 1954-56; Cand Philological Scis, 1958; Dr Philological Scis, 1976; Prof,

1991. *Appointments:* Jr Researcher, Inst Sci Info, 1952-54, Jr Researcher, then Sr Researcher, Inst Linguistics, 1957-, Acad Scis, Moscow. *Publications:* The accentuation of proper names in Russian, 1966; The Structure of proper names, 1969; General Theory of proper names, 1973; Theoretical foundation of the applied transcription, 1978; General Theory of Terminology (co-author), 1989. *Memberships:* Geogl Soc USSR, Moscow Br; Int Comm Onomastic Scis, Leuven; State Terminological Comm, Moscow; State Comm Geogl Nomenclature; Onomastic Commn, Int Slavonic Comm, Prague. *Hobbies:* Skiing; Travel. *Address:* Institute of Linguistics RAN, 1/12 Semashko Street, Moscow 103009, Russia.

SUPERINA Riccardo Antonio, b. 30 July 1950, Trieste, Italy. Surgeon; Director of Liver Transplant Service. m. Diann Carton, 4 Aug 1973, 2 s, 2 d. *Education:* BSc, 1971, MD, CM, 1975, McGill Univ, Can. *Appointments:* Royal Victoria Hosp, Montreal, Can, 1975-81; Chief Resident, 1981-83, Dir, Transplantation, 1985-91, Hosp for Sick Children, Toronto; Rsch Fellow, John Radcliffe Hosp, Univ Oxford, England, 1983-85. *Memberships:* Royal Coll Physns and Surgs Can; Royal Soc Med; Transplantation Soc; Am Soc Transplant Surgs; Am Pediatric Surg Assn; Am Coll Surgs; Can Assn Pediatric Surgs. *Honours:* R Samuel McLaughlin Fellowship, 1983-85. *Hobbies:* Opera; Tennis. *Address:* 609 Avenue Road, Apt 201, Toronto, Ontario, Canada M8X 2M2. 142.

SUPRUN-BELEVICH Rostislav Adam Evgenyevich, b. 24 Oct 1928, Poltava, Ukraine. Professor of General and Slavic Linguistics. m. Anna Petrovna Klimenko, 14 June 1954, 1 s, 1 d. *Education:* Philological Fac, Kyrgyz Univ, Bishkek, 1952; Cand Philology, Moscow Univ, 1955; Dr Philology, Leningrad Univ, 1966; Univ Prof, Gen and Slavic Linguistics, 1967. *Appointments:* Asst Prof, 1955, Hd, Dept Russian, 1961, Kyrgyz Univ, Bishkek; Hd, Dept Gen (Theoretical) and Slavic Linguistics, Byelorussian Univ, Minsk, 1966. *Publications:* Over 50 books and 400 articles incl: Slavic Numerals, 1969; Parts of Speech in Russian, 1971; Frequency Dictionary of Byelorussian, 1976-90; Etymological Dictionary of Byelorussian, 1978-85; General Linguistics, 1983; Polabian Language, 1987; Introduction to Slavic Philology, 1989. *Memberships:* Linguistic Soc Paris, 1964; Commn Lexicology and Lexicography, Int Comm Slavists, 1973. *Honours:* Hon Scientist, Byelorussian SSR, 1990. *Hobby:* Photography. *Address:* Kozlov street 2, app 97, 220005 Minsk 5, Byelorussia.

SURKOV Yuri, b. 30 Mar 1926, USSR. Planetologist. m. 17 Sept 1953, 1 s. *Education:* Grad, Moscow Engrng Phys Inst, 1952; Cand's degree, Inst Chem Phys, 1958, Dr's degree, Phys, Maths, Inst Earth Phys, 1970, Prof, Vernadsky Inst, 1971, USSR Acad Scis; Full Mbr, Int Acad Aetronuatics, 1991. *Appointments:* Scientist, 1953-60, Dir, Planetary Exploration Lab, 1961-, Vernadsky Inst, Moscow. *Publications:* Gamma spectrometry in Space Exploration, 1977; Cosmochemical Study of Planets and Satellites, 1985; Chemical Composition of Venusian Rocks and Some Geochemical Implications (w Alexandr T Basilevsky), 1989; Exploration of Terrestial Planets from Spacecraft, 1990; Over 50 sci articles and reports on planetary exploration published USA. *Honours:* Lenin Prize, designing Venera 4, 5 and 6 spacecraft and sci study of Venus, 1970; USSR State Prize, sci achievements in planetary exploration, 1983; Korolev Medal, success achieved in space exploration, Gagarin Medal, 25th anniversary of 1st manflight in space, USSR Astronautic Fedn. *Address:* Vernadsky Institute, USSR Academy of Sciences, Moscow V-334, Russia.

SURLAKER Samir Manohar, b. 18 Feb 1953, Sanguem, Goa. Managing Director; Civil Engineer. m. Uma Gopalakrishnan, 9 Apr 1982, 2 s. *Education:* BE (Civil) 1st class, 1974, ME (Structures), 1st class, 1977, Bombay Univ; DMS (UK), Sales, Mgmt, 1983; Dip, Export Import Mgmt, IITC, 1984; Bach Bus Fin, 1991; Chartered Engr, India. *Appointments:* Asst Lectr, Victoria Jubilee Tech Inst, Matunga, India, 1976-77; Sr Engr, Shah Constrn Co Ltd, 1977-79; Engr, Trng, 1978-79, Asst Concrete Technologist, 1979, MC-Bauchemie Muller GmbH & Co, FRG; Resident Engr, MC-Bauchemie Muller GmbH & Co, Saudi Arabia, 1979-82; Tech Dir, MC-Bauchemie Muller GmbH & Co, Indian Liaison Off; Exec Dir, 1985-89, Mng Dir, 1989-, MC-Bauchemie (India) Pvte Ltd, Bombay. *Publications:* Analysis of Foundations by Finite Element Method, 1977; Comparison of DIN/ASTM/BS, 1978; Over 20 tech papers and lectures in concrete protection, 1980-91. *Memberships:* Instn Engrs India; Indian Concrete Inst; Indian Rd Congress; Am Concrete Inst; Am Soc Civil Engnrg; Fellow, Indian Inst Bridge Engrng; Indian Water Works Assn. *Honours:* Winner, Kamtekar Prize, for 1st rank, ME (Structures), 1977; Lok Shree Award, 1990; Udyog Shree Award, 1990; Udyog Rattan Award, Best Small Scale Industry in India, Inst Econ Studies, 1991. *Hobbies:* Philately; Coin collection; Swimming; Table tennis; Football; Badminton; Cricket; Hockey; Magic tricks; Hypnotism; Psychology. *Address:* 706 Sunder Towers, T J Road, Sewree, Bombay 400015, India. 34.

SURMAN Martyn C, b. 21 Nov 1944, Brighton, England. Chartered Building Surveyor. m. (1) 1 Oct 1966, diss, 1 s, 1 d, (2) 13 Mar 1976, diss, (3) Irene Florence Surman, 14 Sept 1990. *Education:* Brighton Coll Technology, 1964-68; Coll Estate Mgmt, Reading, 1969-75. *Appointments include:* Currently Dir, Bldg Surveying Servs, PSA Specialist Servs, Croydon, Surrey. *Publications:* Author and presenter, num profl and tech lectures and papers on bldg surveying and bldg constrn. *Memberships:* Royal Instn Chartered Surveyors, Gen Coun 1988-91, Bldg Surveyors Divisional Coun, Pres Bldg Surveyors Div 1990-91, Profl Assoc 1975, Fellowship 1986. *Hobbies:* Photography; Theatre; Dining out; Angling; Travel; Swimming; Tennis; Spectator of most sports; Philately. *Address:* Bramblehurst, Limes Lane, Potters Green, Buxted, East Sussex TN22 4PB, England. 139.

SURYAVANSHI O P Singh, b. 15 Oct 1961, India. Corporate Executive. *Education:* BA, 1983, MBA 1st class, IPM, 1987, LKO Univ; Dip, Profl Photographer, London School, 1985. *Appointments:* Chmn, Momco, India, 1988-; Freelance Jrnlsm and Photography; Bur Chief (UP), Off- the-Record, to present; Mng Dir, Omotel's India Ltd grp (Gonda, Barabanki and Lucknow), 1991-. *Creative works:* Author, freelance column; Journalistic editing w awarded photography; Mainly social serv involvement; Action Aid work; CARE initiation. *Memberships:* Lions; Fellow, Planetary Soc; MPA; PP Am; Ex Club; ABT; FBTC; Westn Ho; Am Mgmt Assn; Assocs Int Technology; NW Air Line; United Airline; China Air Line; One Pass; Survival Club. *Honours:* Membership Awards: Royal Overseas League; Minolta Club, UK; Canon Club, UK; Bronica Club, UK. *Hobbies:* Arts; Books; Culture; Driving; Dining out; Reading; Rare collections; Games; Gozals; Parties; Photography; Sport; Social activities; Travel nationwide and worldwide with writing. *Address:* Omotel's India Ltd, Civil Line, Gonda 271001, India. 34.

SURZHKO Sergej Vasiljevich, b. 18 Feb 1947, Vinnitsa, Ukraine. Mathematician. m. Liudmila Ziuzina Surzhko, 19 June 1976, 1 s, 1 d. *Education:* Master's degree, 1970, Dr's degree, 1979, Leningrad Univ; Postgrad, Leningrad Engrng-Econ Inst, 1976-79. *Appointments:* Instr, Sr Tchr, 1970-76, Assoc Prof, 1979-85, Lvov Univ; Lab Hd, Hd Mathn, Sci Rsch Inst Info and Control, 1987-90; Gen Dir, Information Systems Co. *Publications:* The Researching of General Linear Programming Problem in K-Space, dissertation, 1979; Over 60 sci publs in game theory, computer sci, methods of control, math modelling, 1970-91, incl: Theoretical Basics of Complex Economical Systems Design, book, 1981; Basics of Automatized Design of Information-Controlling Systems, book, 1985; Computation of Operators Values Preset by the Regular Circuits, article, 1989; Certain Classes of Algorithmic

Algebras, article, 1990; Modelling and Software Tools for Synthesis and Analysis of Enterprise Management System, 1990. *Honours:* Silver Medal, Exhib Nat Econ Achievement, 1989. *Hobbies:* Reading philosophical literature; Listening to classical music; Mushroom picking. *Address:* Apart 71, No 10 Mazepy Street, Lvov 290059, Ukraine.

SUSCHITZKY (John) Peter, b. 6 Apr 1940, London, England. Director of Photography (Films). m. 1964, 1 s, 2 d. *Education:* Inst des Hautes Etudes Cinematographiques, Paris. *Career:* Making documentary films, Latin Am, 1 yr; Photography, about 30 feature films incl: The Rocky Horror Picture Show; The Empire Strikes Back; Falling in Love; Leo the Last; Dead Ringers; Where the Heart is; Naked Lunch. *Membership:* Brit Soc Cinematographers. *Honours:* Nomination Best Photography, Valentino, Brit Acad Film and TV Arts, 1977; Best Photography, Valentino, Virgin Islands Film Fest, 1977; Nat Film Critics Award, USA, Where the Heart is, 1991. *Hobbies:* Literature; Art; Music incl performance (plays the transverse flute). *Address:* Sandra Marsh Management, Lee International Studios, PO Box 37, Studios Road, Shepperton, Middlesex TW17 0QD, England.

SUSKA-JANAKOWSKA Janina, b. 10 Sept 1923, Lodz, Poland. Retired Economist in Trade. m. Mieczyslaw Janakowski, 17 Apr 1954, 1 s. *Education:* Dip Econ, specialisation For Trade, HS Admin, 1951. *Appointments:* Wollwaren Fabrik Graudus und Jancke, Lodz, 1941-45; Exec, For Trade Off, 1945-50, Trade Dir, 1951-84, Norbelana wool factory. *Publications:* Reviews, surveys, reports on working conditions of women in textile factories incl: The Correlation between the Technical Progress, Women's Employment and Women's Work in the Textile Industry, report, 1977. *Memberships:* Pres, Polish Women's Assn, Lodz Sect; Polish Women's Assn Chief Bd; Participant, World's Women's Meeting, 1964. *Honours:* Hon Citizen, Lodz, 1972; Hon Citizen, Town of Slupsk, 1975; Kts Cross, 1978, Cmdr's Cross, 1986, Polonia Restituta. *Hobbies:* Welfare activity in the community with special reference to women's rights and improvement of their standard of living; Gardening; Driving; Theatre. *Address:* ul Mianowskiego 6 m 12, 91-812 Lodz, Poland.

SUTCH Andrew Lang, b. 10 July 1952, Bristol, England. Solicitor. m. Shirley Anne Teichmann, 22 May 1982, 2 s. *Education:* Oriel Coll, Oxford, 1970-74; Greats, Oxford Univ. *Appointments:* Grindlays Bank, 1974-76; Stephenson Harwood, London, 1977-. *Memberships:* Law Soc; City of London Solicitors Co. *Hobbies:* Lieutenant (rtd) in Territorial Army; Theatre; Running. *Address:* One St Paul's Cathedral, London EC4M 8SH, England. 53.

SUTCLIFF Rosemary, b. 14 Dec 1920, Surrey, England. Historical Writer. *Education:* Privately. *Career:* Histl Writer, chiefly for the young. *Publications:* The Eagle of the Ninth; The Lantern Bearers; Sword at Sunset; The Shining Company; Frontier Wolf; About 45 others. *Memberships:* Soc Authors; FRSL. *Honours:* Carnegie Medal, 1959; OBE, 1975; Phoenix Award. *Hobbies:* Dogs; Horses; Tapestry; Archaeology; Gazing into the middle distance. *Address:* Swallowshaw, Walberton, Arundel, Sussex BN18 0PQ, England. 1, 138.

SUTCLIFFE James Stocks, b. 9 Mar 1953, Louth, England. Chairman/Chief Executive, Shipping. m. Susan Diana Sutcliffe, 18 June 1988, 1 s. *Education:* Higher Nat Dip, Bus, Grimsby Tech Coll. *Appointments:* John Sutcliffe & Son, 1970; Anglo-S Am Agcies, to 1975; John Sutcliffe & Son Holding Ltd, Grimsby, 1976-. *Hobbies:* Motor racing; Flying; Anything fast. *Address:* Sutcliffe House, Market St, Grimsby DN31 1QT, England.

SUTHERLAND Ian Douglas, b. 23 Oct 1945, Colombo, Ceylon (now Sri Lanka). Chartered Surveyor. m. Kathryn

Lawrence, 11 Oct 1975, 1 s, 1 d. *Education:* St Bees School, Cumberland, 1959-64. *Appointments:* D M Hall & Son, Chartered Surveyors, Edinburgh, Scotland, 1965-. *Membrships:* FRICS; Co Merchants of the City of Edinburgh. *Hobby:* Classic cars. *Address:* 2 Ormidale Terrace, Edinburgh EH12 6EQ, Scotland.

SUTORIKHIN Nicolai Borisovitch, b. 8 Mar 1927, Harbin, China. Professor. m. Nina Petrik, 11 Aug 1950. *Education:* Grad, Harbin Inst Technology, 1950; Dr's degree, 1964, Dr sc techn, 1990, lst Telecommunications, Moscow. *Appointments:* Lectr, Harbin Inst Technology, 1950; Design Engr, New China Planning Inst, Beijing, 1951-54; Hd, Reg Bldg Admn Radio, Kazakhstan, USSR, 1954-58; Sr Engr, Radio Mgmt, Novosibirsk, 1958-60; Researcher, Dept Chief, Prof, 1960-, Hd, Rsch Lab of Dependability of Telecommunication Network Elements, 1976-, Novosibirsk Elec Inst Telecommunications (NEIS); Participant, Study Grp CCITT, 1979-; Sci Vis, India, Switzerland, China, Germany, Hungary, Bulgaria. *Publications:* Over 70 incl 5 books published in USSR and papers and articles published in var countries, all dealing w dependability and grade of serv under failure conditions. *Memberships:* A S Popov's All-Union Sci Tech Soc Radio Engrng Electronics and Telecommunications; Chmn, Coun, A S Popov's All Tech Soc Radio Engrng Electronics and Telecommunications Soc NEIS Br. *Honours:* Hon Radioman, USSR, 1966; Hon Fellow, Adv Level Telecommunication Trng Ctr, New Delhi, India, 1978; Several Medals, USSR Govt. *Address:* c/o NEIS, 86 Kirov str, Novosibirsk 630125, Russia.

SUTTON Andrew Jonathan, b. 7 Nov 1964, Frimley, Surrey, England. Computer Systems Engineer. m. Emma Clare Sutton, 18 May 1991. *Education:* BTech, Aeronautical Engrng, Loughborough Univ, 1987; MSc, Turbine Blade Rsch, Cambridge Univ, 1989. *Appointments:* Rsch Asst, NASA, Ames Rsch Ctr, Silicon Valley, CA, USA, 1986; Systems Engr, IMB (UK) Ltd, Nottingham, England, 1989-91. *Publication:* The Trailing Edge Loss of Subsonic Turbine Blades, book/ thesis. *Honours:* England B Rugby Int; Cambridge Blue, Rugby, *Hobbies:* Golf; Rugby; Photography. *Address:* 25 Gripps Common, Cotgrave, Nottingham NG12 3TF, England.

SUTTON Andrew William, b. 4 Oct 1939, Brentwood, England. Director, Foundation for Conductive Education; Psychologist. m. Kay Sutton, 13 July 1964, 1 s, 1 d. *Education:* BA, Psychology, Russian, 1962, Dip, Educl Psychology, 1966, Univ Birmingham; MPhil, Applied Psychology, Univ Aston, Birmingham, 1976. *Appointments:* Psychologist, Newport, Monmouthshire, Wales, 1965-67; Psychologist, Birmingham, England, 1968-84; Hon Lectr, Educl Psychology, 1970-84, Hon Rsch Fellow, Dept Psychology, 1984-, Univ Birmingham, 1970-84; Hon Assoc, Ctr Russian and East European Studies, 1980-; Dir, Fndn Conductive Educ, Birmingham, 1986-. *Publications:* Home, School and Leisure in the Soviet Union, 1980; Reconstructing Psychological Practice, 1981; Conductive Education, 1985. *Honours:* Peto Fellowship, Budapest, 1990. *Hobbies:* Flying; Garden railways; Gardening. *Address:* 78 Clarendon St, Leamington Spa, Warks CV32 4PE, England.

SUTTON Philip John, b. 20 Oct 1928, Poole, Dorset, England. Artist. m. 11 July 1991, 1 s, 3 d. *Education:* Slade School Fine Art, 1948-53. *Career:* Taught, Slade School Fine Art, London, 1954-88; Regular exhibs, Roland Browse and Delbanco, also Browse and Derby, Cork St, London, 1965-84; Retrospective exhibs: Leeds City Art Gall, 1960; Graves Art Gall, Sheffield, 1971; Royal Acad, London, 1977. *Membership:* Associate Royal Academician, 1977, Royal Academician, 1989. *Honours:* Scholarships to Spain, France, Italy, 1953. *Hobbies:* Running; Swimming. *Address:* 3 Morfa Terrace, Manorbier, Tenby, Dyfed SA70 7TH, Wales. 1, 34.

SUZUKI Jun-Ichi, b. 26 Apr 1929, Kanagawa Prefecture, Japan. Professor; Chairman, School of Medicine. m. Sachiko Suzuki, 1957, 2 s. *Education:* Fac Med, 1949-55, Postgrad Course, 1955-60, Univ Tokyo. *Appointments:* Asst Prof, Fac Med, Univ Tokyo, 1966-71, Prof, Chmn, School Med, Teikyo Univ, Tokyo, 1971-. *Publications:* Middle ear implant. Implantable hearing aids (ed), 1988; Complications of ear surgery. Immediate and delayed, 1988. *Memberships:* Reg Sec for Asia-Oceania, Int Fedn Otorhinolaryngological Socs; VP, Japan Soc Med Educ. *Hobbies:* Drawing; The fine arts. *Address:* Dept of Otolaryngology, Teikyo University School of Medicine, Kaga 2-11-1, Itabashiku, Tokyo 173, Japan.

SUZUKI Kei, b. 16 Dec 1920, Shizuokaken, Japan. Academician; Professor Emeritus; Museum Director. m. Teruko Kashiwagi, 15 June 1947, 2 s. *Education:* Bach, Tokyo Imperial Univ, 1944. *Appointments:* Govt Off, Tokyo Mus, 1947; Asst Prof, Tokyo Art Univ, 1960; Prof, 1967, Prof Emeritus, 1981-, Tokyo Univ; Dir, Shizuoka Prefectural Mus. *Publications:* Chinese Painting, vol 1-3; The Study of Cne School. *Membership:* Rep, Japan Art Hist Soc, Comm'man 1960-75. *Honours:* Purple Ribbon Prize, 1984; Japan Academy Prize, 1985; Tutor, Royal Ceremony of Lecture, 1988; Order of Merit, 2nd Order of the Sacred Treasure, 1991; Mbr, Japanese Acad, 1991. *Hobbies:* Walking; Classical music. *Address:* 13-3 Nakaochiai 3-chome, Shinjiku-ku, Tokyo 161, Japan.

SUZUKI Yoshihide, b. 26 Feb 1944, Kumamoto, Japan. Professor of Biblical and Ancient Near Eastern Studies. m. Setsuko Suzuki, 21 Mar 1970, 1 s, 1 d. *Education:* BA, Coll Liberal Arts, 1968, MA, Grad School Educ, 1972, Int Christian Univ; PhD, Claremont Grad School, 1982. *Appointments:* Lectr, 1982-84, Asst Prof, 1984-90, Prof, 1990-, Coll Gen Educ, Niigata Univ. *Publications:* The 'Numeruswechsel' in Deuteronomy, 1982; A Philological Study on Deuteronomy (in Japanese), 1986; Spiritual Background of the Torah and the Gospel (in Japanese), 1991; 53 articles on Old Testament studies. *Memberships:* Rsch Mbr, Japanese Biblical Inst; Exec Mbr, Japan Soc Old Testament Studies; Regular Mbr: Japan Soc Christian Studies; Soc Biblical Lit. *Honours:* Phi Bet Kappa, Claremont Grad School, 1979; Japan Acad Prize, 1990. *Hobbies:* Swimming; Playing baseball; Football; Listening to classical music. *Address:* 7492-62 Igarashi-Ninomachi No I-303, Niigata-shi, Niigata 950-21, Japan.

SVANCARA Josef, b. 2 Apr 1924, Bohunov, Czechoslovakia. Professor of Psychology. m, Lea Mullerova, 4 s, 1 d. *Education:* PhD, Psyshology, Masaryk Univ, 1950; Fellowship, Univ Montreal, Can, 1965-66. *Appointments:* Clin Psychologist, 1950-64; Rsch Psychologist, 1965-68, Assoc Prof, Psychology, 1969, Prof, Psychology, 1991-, Masaryk Univ, Brno. *Publications:* Diagnostics of Psychological Development (co-author), 1971, 3rd Ed, 1980, Russian Ed, 1978, Bulgarian Ed, 1988; Biological Determinants of Behavior, 1978. *Memberships:* Pres, Soc Talented Children, Prague; Czech Psychological Soc, Chmn Developmental Psychology Sect; Int Coun Psychologists; IBRO. *Honours:* Award, Purkyn Univ, 1984; Award, Gerontological Soc, 1991. *Hobbies:* Music (violoncello); Children's art; Travel. *Address:* Kounicova 51, 602 00 Brno, Czechoslovakia.

SWALES John Douglas, b. 19 Oct 1935, Leicester, England. Professor of Medicine. m. Kathleen Patricia Townsend, 7 Oct 1967, 1 s, 1 d. *Education:* Clare Coll, Cambridge, 1954-57; BA, 1957, MA, 1960, Cambridge; Westminster Med School, London, 1957-60; MB BChir, 1961; MD, 1971. *Appointments:* House Off, 1961-62, Registrar, 1964-68, Westminster Hosp, London; Sr Registrar, Royal Postgrad Med School, 1968-70; Sr Lectr, Manchester Univ, 1970-73; Prof, Med, Leicester Univ, 1974-. *Publications:* Sodium Metabolism in Disease, 1975; Clinical Hypertension, 1979; Platt versus Pickering, 1985; Hypertension Illustrated, 1991.

Memberships: Censor, Royal Coll Surgs, 1985-87; Chmn, Assn Clin Profs Med; Chmn, Fedn Assns Clin Profs; Former EdL Clinical Science; Journal of Hypertension. *Honours:* Passingham Prize, Univ Cambridge, 1957; Thomas Young Lectureship, St George's Hosp, 1981; Bradshaw Lectureship, 1987, Goulstonian Lectureship, 1991, Royal Coll Physns. *Hobby:* Bibliophile. *Address:* 21 Morland Avenue, Leicester LE2 2PF, England.

SWAMINATHAN Monkombu Sambasivan, b. 7 Aug 1925, Tamil Nadu, India. Agricultural Research Centre Director. *Education:* BSc, Travancore Coll, 1944; BSc, Agric, Coimbatore Agricl Coll, Madras Univ, 1947; Assoc, Genetics, Indian Agricl Rsch Inst, New Delhi, 1949; UNESCO Fellow, Genetics, Agricl Univ, Wageningen, Netherlands, 1949-50; PhD, School Agric, Univ Cambridge, England, 1952; Rsch Assoc, Genetics, Univ WI, USA, 1952-53. *Appointments:* Tchr, Researcher, Rsch Admnstr, Ctrl Rice Inst, Cuttack and Indian Agricl Rsch Inst, New Delhi, 1954-72; Dir-Gen, Indian Coun Agricl Rsch, Sec to Govt India: Dept Agricl Rsch and Educ, 1972-80, Min Agric and Irrigation, 1979-80; Acting Dpty Chmn, Planning Commn, Govt India, Apr-June 1980; Mbr, Agric, Rural Dev, Sci and Educ, Planning Commn, Govt Ind, 1980-82; Dir-Gen, Int Rice Rsch Inst, Los Banos, Philippines, 1982-88; Dir, Ctr Rsch on Sustainable Agricl and Rural Dev, Madras, India, 1989-; Andrew D White Prof- at-Large, Cornell Univ, USA. *Publications:* Num in basic and applied plant genetics and agricl rsch and dev. *Memberships:* C'wlth Chmn, Guyana Prog for Sustainable Tropical Forestry, 1990; Chmn, Govng Bd, C'wlth Agricl Bur Int; Global Bd Dirs, The Hunger Project; Past Pres, Int Bee Assn; Past Pres, Int Fedn Agricl Rsch Systems for Dev; Indep Chmn, FAO Coun, 1981- 85; Fellow, Indian Acad Scis; Fellow, Indian Nat Acad Scis; FRS, London; FRSA, London; Pres, Nat Acad Agricl Scis, India; Pres, Int Soc Mangrove Ecosystems; Past Pres, Int Union Conserv Nature and Natural Resources; Num others. *Honours:* Num incl: Albert Einstein World Sci Award, World Cultural Coun, 1986; 1st World Food Prize, Gen Foods Fund, 1986; Dr J C Bose Medal, Bose Inst, 1989; Tyler Prize, Environmental Achievement, 1991; 32 Hon DSc. *Address:* Centre for Research on Sustainable Agricultural and Rural Development, Madras, India.

SWAN Peter A, b. 17 Apr 1945, San Antonio, Texas, USA. Sr Systems Engr. m. Cathy Ann Wood, 5 July 1968. *Education:* BS, USMA, West Point, 1968; MS, Systems Mgmt, Univ Southern CA, 1977; PhD. Dynamics and Controls, Univ CA, Los Angeles, 1984. *Appointments:* USAF, Ret'd, Lt Col, Space Systems Expertise, Design, Dev and Ops, 1968-88; Mgr and Sr Systems Engr, Motorola, 1988-. *Publications:* Over 30 works: Dynamics and Control of Tethered Satellite Systems; Global Personal Communications-- This Decade with Iridium. *Memberships:* Fellow, Brit Interplanetary Soc; Assoc Fellow, American Inst of Aeronautics and Astronautics; AAS; TPS; SSI; ADPA. *Hobbies:* Golf, Tennis, Writing. *Address:* c/o Motorola, 1764 Old Meadow Lane, McLean, VA 22102, USA.

SWANER Paula Margetts, b. 23 Nov 1927, Salt Lake City, Utah, USA. Lic Clinical Psychologist. m. Leland Scowcroft Swaner, 22 May 1951, 2 s, 1 d. *Education:* BA, Eng Lit, 1949, MA Eng Lit 1972, MS Educ Psychology 1978, PhD Clin Psychology 1986, Univ of UT; Cand for Certification, Wash D C Schl of Psychiatry and Psychoanalysis, 1989. *Appointments:* Psychotherapist, Trng Off, Granite Community Hlth Ctr, Salt Lake City, Utah, 1978-80; Mental Hlth Unit 2nd Dist Juvenile Ct, Utah, 1984-87; Residency Pvte Prac, 1986-88; Pvte Prac, 1988-. *Publications:* Thesis: The Image of the Garden in Shakespeare's Plays; Thesis: Narcissism Vis a Vis; Dissertation: Self-Esteem and Expectancy Effects in an Adolescent Population. *Memberships:* American Psychological Assn; Utah Psychological Assn; Div 39 Psychologist-Psychoanalyst, APA; Norman S Anderson MD Award Fund Bd, Chmn, Prog Comm. *Hobbies:* Wasatch Mountain Club, Swimming, Hiking, Cross- country Skiing. *Address:*

1775 East 4500 South, Salt Lake City, UT 84124, USA. 9.

SWANSON Peggy Eubanks, b. 29 Dec 1936, Ivanhoe, Texas, USA. Prof of Fin. m. Kenneth A Swanson, 5 Sept 1964. *Education:* BBA 1957, MBE 1965, Univ of North TX; MA Econs 1967, PhD Econs 1978, Southern Meth Univ. *Appointments:* El Centro Coll, Dallas, TX, 1967-78, Bus Div Chmn, 1969- 71; Asst Prof 1978-84, Assoc Prof 1984-88, Chmn, Dept of Fin and Real Estate, 1986-88; Full Prof 1988-, Univ of TX Arlington. *Publications:* 22 refereed acad jrnl articles; 5 profl jrnl articles; 3 Proceedings; Presentations at Profl Mtgs 14; Acad Jrnl Reviewer for 14 jrnls. *Memberships:* Fin Execs Inst, Chair, Acad Rels Comm 1987-88, Prog Comm, 1987-88; Advsry Bd Mbr, Ryan-Reilly Ctr for Urban Land Utilization; American Fin Assn; American Econ Assn; Fin Mgmt Assn; Western Fin Assn; Southwestern Fin Assn; Int Trade Assn. *Honours:* W Paul Green Award for Excellence in Graduate Teaching, 1985-86; Honorary Faculty Member, Financial Management Association National Honor Society, 1985-86; Outstanding Graduate Teacher Award, College of Business Administration, University of Texas at Arlington, 1990-91, 1983-84. *Hobbies:* Tennis, Gardening. *Address:* Department of Finance and Real Estate, UTA Box 19449, College of Business Administration, University of Texas at Arlington, Arlington, TX 76019, USA. 7, 132.

SWARTZ Beth Ames, b. 1936, New York City, New York, USA. Artist. *Education:* BS, Cornell Univ, 1957; MA, NY Univ, 1960. *Career:* Num solo exhibs, many US States, 1970-, also Mexico City, 1971, Am Cultural Ctrs, Israel Revisited Travelling Mus Exhib, NYC, CA, AZ, TX, NM, and Tel Aviv and Jerusalem, Israel, 1981-83, Athens and Nafplion, Greece, 1989; Sitges, Spain, 1989; Participant, num invitational, touring and other grp exhibs, 1968-; Artist Rep, Rocky Mtn States Consultation on the Arts, Camp La Foret, 1975; Artist-in-Residence: Roosevelt School Dist, 1975; Volcano Art Ctr, HI, 1979; Sun Valley Ctr Arts and Humanities, 1980; Project Coord, Transformational Artist's Conf and Workshop, Rim Inst, Payson, AZ, Sept 1988. *Creative works include:* Num in many public collections, USA, incl: Nat Mus Am Art, Smithsonian Instn; San Francisco Mus Mod Art; Herbert F Johnson Mus Art, Cornell Univ; Univ AZ Mus Art, Tucson; Brooklyn Mus; Jewish Mus, NY; Mus Fine Arts, Santa Fe, NM; Nat Bank AZ, Scottsdale; IBM Corp; Subaru Corp; Mtn Bell Telephone Co, Denver, CO; Yuma Art Ctr, AZ; Prudential Life Ins Co, Newark, NJ; Am Repub Ins Co, Des Moines, IA. *Membership:* Fndr, Int Friends Tranformational Art. *Honours:* Education Grant, AZ Commn Arts and Humanities for Inquiry into Fire, 1977-78; Named Master Tchr, State Dept Pub Instruction, 1977-78; Gov Awards: Outstanding Women AZ and Women Who Create, 1985; Invited to present rsch study on Moving Point of Balance, MedArts Conf, 1992.

SWERDLOW Joel L, b. 8 June 1946, Washington, DC, USA. Writer; Lect. m. Marjorie L Share, 21 Aug 1981, 2 d. *Education:* BA, Syracuse Univ, 1968; MA 1971, PhD 1974, Cornell Univ. *Appointments:* Sr Fellow, The Annenberg Washington Programme; Northwestern Univ, 1984-90; Guest Schlr, Woodrow Wilson Ctr, Wash DC, 1990; Vis Prof, Georgetown Univ, 1991. *Publications:* Remote Control, 1979; Code Z, 1980; To Heal a Nation, 1985; Media Technology and the Vote, 1988; Presidential Debates, 1988. *Honour:* Work included in Best of the Washington Post, Popular Library, 1979. *Hobbies:* Crosscountry Skiing, Softball, Biking. *Address:* 3045 Albemarle Street, NW, Washington, DC 20008, USA.

SWIATECKA Grazyna Maria, b. 27 Nov 1933, Myszyniec, Poland. Professor of Cardiology. *Education:* MD, 1958, Postgrad, 1960-65, Gdansk Med School; DSc, Internal Disease, 1966; 2nd Specialisation, Internal Diseases, 1969; Cardiology trng, 1970-75. *Appointments:* Asst, Microbiology Dept, 1958-59, Asst, Internal Med Dept, 1960, Asst Prof, 1971, Assoc Prof,

Hd, Cardiology Dept, 1984, Prof, 1991-, Gdansk Med School; Reg Cons, Cardiology. *Publications:* Effect of Ipronal on chronic neurotropic stress, 1966; Suicidal attempts and suicide, 1980; ST seg, T wave ECG Changes of Spontaneous Sinus Beats after Cardiac Pacing, book, 1984; Transesophageal atrial pacing, 1988. *Memberships:* Polish Cardiological Soc; Polish Internal Med Assn; Polish Med Soc; Pres, Telephonic Emergency Serv Assn. *Honours:* Min Hlth Award, 1974. *Hobbies:* Theology; Skiing. *Address:* ul Krasickiego 10/6, 81-867 Sopot, Poland.

SWIDZINSKI Jan, b. 25 May 1923, Bydgoszcs, Poland. Multi Media. *Education:* Fine Art Sch, Warsaw. *Appointments:* Freelance Artist. *Creative Works:* Many One Man Shows; Paintings; Instalations; Performances, Intl Festivals; 4 Books. *Memberships:* Intl Alternative Art Assn. *Address:* Warynskiego 3 m. 50, Warsaw, Poland.

SWIETOCHOWSKA Urszula Anna, b. 9 Jan 1932, Biala, Poland. Acad Tchr. m. Jan Swietochowski, 30 July 1954, 1 d. *Education:* MA, Hist, 1957-62; Dr, 1967-79; Prof, 1980. *Appointments:* Second Schl, 1951-64; Tchrs Coll, Gdansk, 1964-70; Univ of Gdansk, 1970-. *Publications:* Modelling the extraschool educational system in the reformed system of national education, 1979; Selected elements of the present and future modelling of living conditions of the population, 1990. *Memberships:* IPSA; Politic Science Assn; Polish Pedagogic Assn. *Honours:* Rector's Academic Award, 1979; Rector's Award in Methodology, 1989. *Hobbies:* Gardening, Music of F Chopin, Cycling. *Address:* Wasowicza 1/12, Gdansk 80-318, Poland.

SWINBURNE Richard Granville, b. 26 Dec 1934. Prof of Philos. m. Monica Holmstrom, 1960, 2 d. *Education:* Exeter Coll, Oxford, 1952; BA, Philos, Pol, Econ, Oxford, 1957; B.Phil, Oxford, 1959; Fereday Fellow, St John's Coll, Oxford, 1958-61; Dip. Theol w Distinction, Oxford, 1960; Leverhulme Rsch Fellow in Hist and Philos of Science, Univ of Leeds, 1961-63. *Appointments:* Lectr 1963-69, Sr Lectr 1969-72, Univ of Hull; Vis Assoc Prof of Philos, Univ of MD, USA, 1969-72; Prof of Philos, Univ of Keele, 1972- 84; Vis Lectr Univs in England, Wales, Scotland, USA and Aust. *Publications:* 10 books inclng: The Evolution of the Soul, 1986; Responsibility and Atonement, 1989; Revelation, 1992. Books Edited: The Justification of Induction, 1974; Space, Time and Causality, 1983; Miracles, 1989. *Address:* Oriel College, Oriel Square, Oxford OX1 4EW, England.

SWIRE Hugo George William, b. 30 Nov 1959, London, England. Hd of Nat Gall Trust. *Education:* Eton Coll, 1972-77; Univ of St Andrew's. Fife. *Appointments:* Guard's Depot, Pirbright Royal Mil Acad, Sandhurst, 1980-81; Lt, First Bn. Grenadier Guards, 1981-84; Dir, Prospect Films, 1984-85; Acct Dir, Streets Fin Strategy, 1986-88; Hd, Trust Off, The Nat Gall, 1988-. *Memberships:* Clubs: Pratts; Beefsteak; 2 Brydges Place. *Hobbies:* The Arts, Pols, Field Sports, Skiing, Tennis. *Address:* 2 Holland Park Road, London W14, England.

SYMONS Martyn Christian Raymond, b. 12 Nov 1925, Ipswich, England. Prof. m. Janice Olive O'Connor, 12 Jan 1972, 1 s, 1 d. *Education:* BSc 1946, PhD 1953, Battersea Polytechnic, London; DSc, London Univ, 1960. *Appointments:* Army, Capt, 1946-48; Lectr in Chem, Battersea, 1948-53; Lectr in Chem, Southampton, 1953-60; Prof, Phys Chem, 1960-89, Rsch Prof, 1989-, Leicester Univ. *Publications:* 3 books, over 900 original papers. *Memberships:* Royal Soc; Royal Soc of Chem; American Chem Soc; RSA; Univ of Birmingham Court. *Honours:* Royal Soc of Chem: R A Robinson Lecturer, 1986; Bruker Lecturer, 1987. *Hobbies:* Watercolour Painting, Piano Playing. *Address:* 144 Victoria Park Road, Leicester LE 2 1XD, England. 1, 52.

SYMOTIUK Stefan Jerzy, b. 10 July 1943, Pawlow, Poland. Philos. *Education:* Fac of Pedagogy, UMCS,

Lublin, 1961-65; M.Ed, 1965; DHS, 1975; Asst Prof of Philos., 1988. *Appointments:* Asst 1965-75, Lectr 1975-88, State Univ, UMCS, Lublin; Hd of Dept of Philos and Culture, Hd of Fac of Philos and Sociology, UMCS, 1990-. *Publications:* Spatial Configurations of Social Mikrogroups and Types of Dialogical Thinking, 1985; The Concept and Patterns of Criticism in Polish Philosophical Controversies in the XXth Century, 1987; Seminar in Methodology of Teaching Philosophy, 1989. *Memberships:* Polish Philos Soc; Polish Soc of the Science of Rels; Lublin Science Assn; Nationwide Team for Rsch in Philos of Culture and Polish 20th Century Philos. *Honours:* Prize awarded by Ministry of Higher Education, 1975, 88; Golden Cross of Merit, 1988. *Hobbies:* Sailing, Alpinism. *Address:* ul Sowinskiego 7/10, 20- 040 Lublin, Poland.

SZABELSKI Kazimierz, b. 2 Apr 1937, Poland. Prof. m. Barbara Kosmala, 26 Dec 1960, 1 s, 1 d. *Education:* MSc, Warsaw Inst of Technology, 1960; Doctor's Degree of Technical Sciences, 1970; Asst Prof, 1973; Prof Title, 1984; Full Prof, 1991. *Appointments:* Car Factory in Lublin, 1960-67; High Engrng Coll, 1965; Lublin Inst of Technology; Scientific Trng at St Petersburg, 1972, Moscow, 1978; Prorector, 1973; Chief of Applied Mechanics Dept, 1981-. *Publications:* Over 120 scientific and technical papers concerning the theory of non-linear vibrations, the strength fatigue designs, fiberscopes mechanics, I C engines, cars and the helicopters vibrations. *Memberships:* Scientific Grps: Fatigue Materials and Design; Analytical Mechanics of the Polish Acad of Science; Chmn, Lublin Br, Theoretical and Applied Mechanics Science; Science and HSs State Bd Mbr, 1985- 90; Presidium Mbr of the Bd, 1985-88. *Honours:* Seven Ministerial Awards for Scientific, Didactic Works and the Applications in the Industry; Two State Honours. *Hobbies:* Reading, Music, Gardening. *Address:* ul. Langiewicza 3a/8, 20-032 Lublin, Poland.

SZABO E F Pal, b. 21 Sept 1919, Banlak, Hungary. Rschr in own Lab. m. Eva Apponyi, 4 Nov 1946, 2 d. *Education:* MD, Univs of Szeged and Budapest, Hungary, 1944; Specialist in Orthopaedics, 1948; Pulmonary Diseases, 1953; Surg, 1963. *Appointments:* Asst, Pharmacological Inst, Univ of Budapest; Asst, Orthopaedic Clin, Janos Hosp, Budapest and Univ Clinik of Surg, Budapest; Physn i/c, Budapest and Szobathely; Sr Surg, Rastpfunl Krankenhaus, Saarbrucken, FRG. *Publications:* Num publs on rsch work in field of vegetative nervous system (dev of the macromolecular hypothesis of the autonom system; isolation of the Neurovegetative substance, dimethylaminoacetoin, out of the adrenal gland and spleen) to profl jrnls and congresses. *Memberships:* ssa 00The Royal Soc of Med; The Royal Soc of Chem; The Int Union of Therapeutics; NYAS; Arpad Akademia; Soc of Endrocrinology; European Soc for Neurochem; European Soc Comparative Physiology and Biochem; Int Brain Rsch Org; European Brain and Behaviour Soc; Osterr. Biochem Gesellschaft; European Neuroscience Assn. *Honours:* Golden Plaque of Arpad Akademia (Hungarian Exile Academy); Doctor of Science (honoris causa) Marquis Giuseppe International University Foundation. *Address:* Mediator Forschungslaboratorium, Hof 7, A-4690 Schwanenstadt, Austria. 139, 158.

SZABO Magda, b, 5 Oct 1917, Debrecen, Hungary. Free-lance Writer. m. Tibor Szobotka, 5 June 1948. *Education:* Dr.Phil, Philology; Graduated Second Schl Tchr. *Appointments:* Tchr, 1940-45; Civ Servant in Min of Educ, 1950-58; Tchr, 1958-; Freelance writer currently. *Publications:* Books, poems, novels, plays: The Lamb, 1947; Back to the World, 1949; Poems Fresco, 1958; The Fawn, 1959; Tell Sally, 1959; The Night of the Pig-Killing, 1960; Pilate, 1963; The Danaide, 1953; Street Kathleen 1969; Old Well, 1970; The Onlookers, 1973; Abigail, 1973; Oldfashioned Story, 1978; He Has Not Changed His Name, 1983 novels: plays: The Bright Beautiful Day, 1973; The Meranian Trilogy, 1984; The Door, 1989; The Moment, 1991 novels; Outside of the Circle, 1980 essays. *Memberships:* Acad Europeenne

des Beaux Arts; Int Pen Club; Fellow, IA Univ, USA. *Honours:* Baumgarten Prize 1949 granted for 6 months by USA to spend half a year in the States; Jozsef Attila Prize, 1959, 72; Csokonai Prize, 1987; Kossuth Prize, 1978; Prize of the Town Budapest, 1981. *Hobbies:* Pets; Ancient Books, Collector of Latin and Greek Authors. *Address:* Julia u.3, Budapest 1026, Hungary.

SZABO Zoltan Gabor, b. 30 May 1908, Debrecen, Hungary. Prof Emeritus, Counsel at Acad. m. Stella Salome Almassy, 31 Mar 1947. *Education:* PhD, 1931, Privat Dozent, Habil, 1939, Univ Budapest. *Appointments:* Prof, Inorganic Chem, Univ Kolozsvar, 1940-44; Prof, Inorganic Chem, Univ Szeged, 1946-65; Prof, Inorganic Chem, Univ Budapest, 1965-79. *Publications:* Advances in the Kinetics of Homogeneous Gas Reaction; Inorganic Chemistry; Selected Chapters of Inorganic Chemistry, Structure and Reactivity. *Meberships:* Hungarian Acad of Sciences; For Mbr, Croatian Acad; Corres Mbr, Saxon Acad, Leipzig; Comprehensive Chem Kinetics Advsry Bd. *Honours:* Gold Medal of Hungarian Academy, 1989; State Prizes 1950, 57; Doctor honoris causa, Munich, 1967, Berlin Freie Univ, 1976, Wien T U, 1984, Szeged, 1982 and Budapest, 1985. *Hobbies:* Music, Gardening, Tourism in mountains. *Address:* Somloi ut 44, H-1118 Budapest, Hungary.

SZAFARCZYK Maciej, b. 7 Oct 1931, Wierbka, Poland. Prof. m Barbara Zychska, 26 Oct 1968, 2 s. *Education:* MSc 1956, PhD 1970, Warsaw Univ of Technology. *Appointments:* Asst 1956, Assoc Prof 1973, Prof 1983, Warsaw Univ of Technology. *Publications:* Books and papers on Automatic Supervision in Manufacturing. *Memberships:* CIRP; Int Instn of Prod Engrng Rsch, Coun Mbr; IGIP; Int Soc for Engrng Educ; SIMP; Polish Soc of Mech Engrs. *Hobbies:* Gardening, Collecting Pens and Pencils. *Address:* Asfaltowa 2 m 27, 02-527 Warsaw, Poland.

SZILARD Lena, b. 3 Apr 1933, Moscow, USSR. Prof of Russian Lit. m. Mihaly Szilard, 28 Feb 1962, 1 d. *Education:* Dip, The Moscow State Univ, 1955; postgrad student, 1955-58; HHD, 1972, Univ Budapest; Cand Philological Sciences, Hungarian Acad, 1977. *Appointments:* Lectr in Russian Lit, Moscow State Univ, USSR, 1958-62; Asst Prof, Univ Budapest, Elte, Hungary, 1962-77; Assoc Prof, Univ of Budapest Elte, 1977-. *Publications:* 7 books, 75 articles. *Memberships:* VP, Hungarian Comm of Slavonic- Romanic Comparative Studies, 1983-; Hungarian Dpty, Comparative Lits Sect of Int Comm of Slavists, 1988-; Co-fndr, Hungarian Soc of Russian Studies, 1990. *Honour:* Fulbright Fellowship, 1986-87. *Hobby:* Travelling. *Address:* Pala u. 9, 1011 Budapest I, Hungary. 138, 152, 162.

SZMIDT Boleslaw, b. 7 July 1908, Petersburg, Russia. Arch; Emeritus Prof. m. Stanislawa, 3 June 1933, 1 s. *Education:* Warsaw Polytech, 1933; Ford Foundation Granteecivic & Ind Architecture. *Appointments:* Private Practice, 1933-39; Snr Asst, Warsaw Faculty of Arch, 1942-47; Organizer, Polish Sch of Arch, Lectr, Dir, Prof, Liverpool Univ, 1952-78; Hd of Chair, Ind Arch, Wroclaw Polytech, Visiting Prof, 1960; UBS, Vancouver, 1963-65. *Publications include:* Granary in Gdynia; Savings Bank; Communal Savings Bank; Broadcasting Station in Raszyn; Several Office Blocks; Book. The Polish Sch of Architecture. *Honours include:* Status of a Creative Arch Award; Special Medal & Golden Distinction; Honorary Annual Prize by SARP; Outstanding Merits for Polish Archs. *Hobbies:* Classical Music; Naval Arch; Landscape Arch; Hatred for Slums. *Address:* ul Wiejska 9 m. 105, 00 480 Warsaw, Poland.

SZMITKOWSKI Maciej, b. 8 May 1946, Czeremcha, Poland. Prof, Hd of Dept of Biochem Diagnostics. m. Krystyna Siwicka, 6 July 1968, 2 d. *Education:* Physn, 1970; MD, 1973; Specialist in Lab Diagnostics, 1976, PhD, 1979, Prof, 1988, Med Fac, Med Schl, Bialystok. *Appointments:* Asst 1970-74, Sr Researcher 1974-79,

Asst Prof 1979-84, Dept of Clin Biochem; V-Dean 1984-87, Fac of Med Analytics; Hd 1985-, Dept of Biochem Diagnostics, Med Schl Bialystok. *Publications:* Author and Co-author of 70 scientific papers in Int and Polish Jrnls. *Memberships:* Int Fedn of Clin Chem, Polish Nat Rep 1987-90; Polish Soc of Lab Diagnostics, Exec Coun 1984-, VP 1987-90; Polish Biochem Soc; Polish Physns Soc. *Honours:* Awards of President (Rector) of Bialystok Medical School, 1972, 76, 77, 79, 81-89; DAAD Award one months stay in Institute of Hematology, Munich, 1974; Award of Polish Minister of Health and Social Welfare for Scientific Research, 1977, 78, 85; WHO Award for three months stay in Karolinska Institutet, Stockholm, 1978; British Council Award for three months stay in Paterson Institute, Manchester, 1990. *Hobbies:* Handiwork, Gardening. *Address:* Sw Wojciecha 4 17, 15-202 Bialystok, Poland.

SZOKE Gyorgy, b. 29 Mar 1935, Budapest, Hungary. Univ Prof. m. Eva Standeisky, 25 Aug 1971, 1 d. *Education:* Saratov Univ, 1953-55; BA, Moscow Univ, 1955-58; BA, Budapest Univ, 1957-60; PhD, Lit, 1967; MA, Psychology, 1985; D.Litt, 1991. *Appointments:* Second Coll, Budapest, 1958-60; Jozsef Attila Univ, Szeged, 1960-68; Asst Prof 1968-75, Assoc Prof, Chmn of Dept, 1975-, Prof, Budapest Univ. *Publications:* Lermontov, 1967; A Jozsef: Poetry and Psychopathology, 1985; Holocaust Survivors in Psychoanalytical Approach, 1990; A Jozsef: Modern Poetry in Psychoanalytical Approach, 1991. *Memberships:* Assn of the Hungarian Hist of Lit; Assn of the Hungarian Psychiatry. *Hobbies:* Listening to J S Bach;; Collecting CD. *Address:* Utca 14, Nyul, H-1026 Budapest, Hungary.

SZTULMAN Henri, b. 1 Oct 1939, Toulouse, France. Prof; Physician; Psychiatrist; Psychoanalyst. m. Laurence Lucas, 14 July 1989, 2 s, 3 d. *Education:* Doc in Medicine, Toulouse, 1966; Licence in Psychology, Toulouse, 1966; CBS Neuropsychiatry, Toulouse, 1968; Research Habilitation, 1987. *Appointments:* Prof, Univ Toulouse; Physician, Dept Hd, Psychiatrist Psychoanalyst; Dir, Collections of 3 Publi Houses. *Publications:* Oedipe et Psychanalyse d'Aujourd'hui; La Curiosite en Psychanalyse; Le Psychanalyste et son Patient; Les Fantasmes Originaires. *Memberships:* Intl Psychoanalytic Assn; Soc Medico Psycholog Paris; Assn Intl d' Histoire de la Psychoanalyse; Evolution Medico Psychologique, Paris; Soc Francaise de Psychologie, Paris. *Honours:* Chevalier Natl Order of Merit. *Hobbies:* Reading; Music; Theatre; Movies; Running. *Address:* Le Village, 31130 Pin Balma, France.

SZULCE Halina Maria, b. 1 Sept 1939, Poznan, Poland. Prof Dr of Econ-Mktng, V-Rector, Acad of Econs, Poznan, Poland; Dir, Institut of Mktng. m. Leszek, 5 Oct 1963, 1 d. *Education:* Graduate, Higher Schl of Econs in Poznan, 1964; Dip Dr Econs of Science, 1969; Dip Prof of Econ, 1983. *Appointments:* V-Rector, Acad of Econs, Poznan; Dir, Institut of Mktng. *Publications:* Over 150 articles, science reports and books. Economics of Consumption, 1984; Prices and Market, 1985; Trade in National Economy, 1989. *Honours:* Several Prizes including prominent result in economic science; Ministry of Education, 1971, 75, 82, 85 and 87. *Hobbies:* Gardening, Poetry. *Address:* ul Langiewicza 23 m 25, 61-502 Poznan, Poland.

SZULCZYNSKI Henryk, b. 3 Jan 1922, Ryzyn, Poland. Author; Poet. m. Wiktoria Mierzejewska, 7 Sept 1948, 1 s, 1 d. *Education:* Lyceum, Zakopane, 1960; Econ Studium by Jagellonian Univ, Cracow, 2 yrs; Hostellerie Studium, Zakopane, 2 yrs. *Appointments:* Before WWI worked on parents' land; Forced work by Germans, Tischler, 1939-42; In Concentration Camp Dachau, 1942-45; After War Trade Cooperative, Zakopane until 1977. *Publications:* Poetry in Poezja, Podtatrze, Zycie Literackie, Tygodnik Kulturalny, 1986- 88; Also on magnetophone in Tatra-Mus and Lyceums in Zakopane. Many confs in Zakopane, 1989-; 20 confs in var places. *Honour:* Second Prize, Jesien Tatrzanska (Tatra Autumn)

in Zakopane in 1989. *Hobbies:* Roots (Racine), Plastics. *Address:* ul Grunwaldzka 14 B, Zakopane, Poland.

SZULMAN Aron E, b. 3 May 1920, Poland. Physn. m. Irene Gulder, 1 s, 1 d. *Education:* MB, ChB, Univ of Birmingham, England, 1945. *Appointments:* Harvard Med Schl and affiliated hosps, Boston, MA, USA, 1951-64; Univ of Pittsburgh Schl of Med, 1964-. *Publications:* Co-ed, Gestational Trophoblastic Disease, 1987; Scientific papers and chapts in med books, approx 40. *Memberships:* Int Acad of Pathology; American Soc Human Genetics; Sociedad Latino-American de Patalogia; Fellow, Royal Coll of Pathology, London. *Honours:* NIH Fellowship, research; Visiting Associate Professor Universirty of California, Berkeley, 1969-70; Yoshida- Yamagiva Fellowship to study Trophoblastic Diseases in Hong Kong and Singapore, 1979; Visiting Scientist, University of Helsinki, Finland, Cambridge Univ. *Hobbies:* Hist, Lit, Music. *Address:* c/o Magee Women's Hospital, Pittsburgh, PA 15213, USA.

SZWAJCER, Piotr Jakub, b. 17 Aug 1959, Warsaw, Poland. Publr, Distributor, Wholesaler. m. Ewa Zagrzejewska, 20 July 1982. *Education:* Dept Psychology, Univ of Warsaw. *Appointments:* Niezalezna Oficina Wydawnicza Nowa, 1978-90; Inst of Philos and Sociology, Polish Acad Nauk, 1989-90; Don Ksiegarski Stowarzyszenmia Wolnego Stowa, 1990-. *Publications:* Collaborated w Konfrontacje, Krytyka; Ed-in-Chief, Przeglad Wydawniczy. *Memberships:* Polskie Towarzystwo Socsologiczne, 1988-; Stowarzyszenie Wydawcow Prywatnych Niezaleznich, Pres, 1989-90. *Hobby:* Sociology. *Address:* Narbutta 30 3, 02 5641 Warsaw, Poland.

T

TADROS Tharwat Fouad, b. 29 July 1937, Egypt. Sr Rsch Assoc. m. 25 July 1969, 2 s. *Education:* BSc, 1st class hon, 1956, MSc 1959, PhD 1959, Alexandria Univ. *Appointments:* Lectr, Phys Chem, Alexandria Univ, 1963; Rsch Assoc, 1978, Sr Rsch Assoc 1989, ICI. *Publications:* The Effects of Polymers on Dispersion Properties, Ed, 1982; Surfactants, Ed, 1984; Solid Liquid Dispersions, Ed, 1987; Polymer in Colloid Systems, Ed, 1988. *Memberships:* Royal Soc of Chem; Soc of Chem and Ind, previous Chmn; Int Assn of Colloid Scientists, Pres; Ed, Colloid and Surfaces; Ed, Advances in Colloid and Interface Science. *Honours:* Visiting Professor in Colloid Science, Bristol, 1983-84; Visiting Professor at Imperial College, 1988-92; Royal Society of Chemistry, Colloid and Surface Chemistry Award and Medal, 1989; Royal Society of Chemistry, Silver Medal Award and Industrial Lecturer, 1990. *Hobbies:* Chess, Reading, Int Pols, Debates. *Address:* ICI Agrochemicals, Jealotts Hill Research Station, Bracknell, Berkshire RG12 6EY, England.

TAFDRUP Pia, b. 29 May 1952, Copenhagen, Denmark. Poet; Playwright. m. Bohaken Jorgensen, 30 June 1978, 2 s, 2 d. *Education:* Univ of Copenhagen, 1978. *Appointments:* Poet, Playwright. *Publications:* When an Angel's Been Grazed, poems, 1981; The Innermost Zone, poems, 1983; Spring Tide, poems, 1985; White Fever, poems, 1986; The Bridge of Moments, poems, 1988; Walking Across the Water, Sketch for a poetic, 1991; Death in the Mountains, play, 1968. *Membership:* The Danish Acad. *Honours:* Three Year Scholarship for Authors from the Danish State Art Foundation, 1984; Holger Drachmann's Grant, 1986; Henrik Nathansen's Grant, 1987; Otto Rung's Grant, 1987; Tagea Brandt's Grant. 1989; Edith Rode's Grant, 1991; Einar Hansen's Grant, 1991. *Hobbies:* Reading, Travelling. *Address:* Rudmevej 110, DK-5750 Ringe, Denmark.

TAGER Romie, b. 19 July 1947, London, England. Barrister. m. Esther Marianne Sichel, 29 Aug 1971, 2 s. *Education:* LLB (hons, 1st class), Univ Coll, London, 1969; LLM, London Schl of Econs, 1970. *Appointments:* Barrister, specialising in commercial property law; Hd of Chambers at 13 Kings Bench Walk, Temple, 1987-91; Merged w and now practising from Chambers at Hardwicke Bldg, Lincoln's Inn, largest mixed common law set of barristers chmbrs. *Membership:* Int Bar Assn. *Honour:* Hurst Prize in English Law, University of London, 1968. *Hobbies:* Theatre, Travel, Opera. *Address:* 33 Ingram Avenue, Hampstead Garden Suburb, London NW11 6TG, England.

TAHZIB Nezamuddin, b. 1933, Suburbs of Khazni, Afghanistan. Senator of Kunduz in the Parliament. m. 1961, 4 s, 1 d. *Education:* Student, Abu Hanifa, Kabul, 1950-67; Fac of Islamic Law, Univ, Kabul, 1957-61. *Appointments:* Tchr, Habibia HS, Kabul, 1960; Staff Mbr, Ariona Ency, Kabul, 1962-74; Ed, State newspaper Kunduz Press, 1974; Expert in Lib, Kabul Pub Lib; Advocate Kunduz, 1978; Min of Boundaries Cabinet Coun, Kabul, 1978; Mbr, Educl Bd, Min of Educ, Kabul, 1979; Acting Min, Min of Culture, Kabul, 1979; Pres, Supreme Ct, Kabul, 1980-87; Chief Justice, 1987- 89; Sen of Kunduz in Parliament, Pres, Commn of Science and Culture of Senate. *Publications:* Ed, Kunduz newspaper, transl 3 books from Arabic to Pashto and Dari Zorooster, Buddah and Confucture. *Contributions to:* 197 articles in Ariana Ency to profl jrnls; Lectr Pol and Social subjects, Kabul, 1972. *Memberships:* Lawyers Assn, Repub of Afghanistan, Asst 1988-89; Jrnlsts Assn, Repub of Afghanistan. *Honour:* Prize award Ministry of Culture, Kabul, 1958. *Hobbies:* Listening to Music, Walking, Exercise. *Address:* Microryan 1st Block 55 No. 24, Kabul, Pashtoon, Afghanistan.

TAJIMA Yutaka, b. 30 Apr 1940, Aichi, Japan. Prof of Law. m. Hiroko, 13 Nov 1968, 1 s. *Education:* LLM,

Univ Tokyo, 1968, LLD, 1973; LLM, Univ CA, Berkeley, USA, 1969, JD, 1972; MLitt, Univ Cambridge, 1976. *Appointments:* Assoc Prof 1974-82, Prof Law 1982-90, Osaka City Univ, Japan; Prof Law, Tsukuba Univ, Tokyo, 1990-; Vis Prof, UCLA Schl of Law, 1978; Prof Law, Univ CA Schl Law, Berkeley, 1979-80; Vis Scholar, Fulbright Vis Prof, Harvard Law Schl, Cambridge, MA, 1986-87. *Publications:* Parliamentary Sovereignty and Rule of Law, 1979; Dicey's Law of the Constitution, 1983; Anglo-American Law, 1985; Ed: Anglo-American Law Dictionary, 1990; English Law, 1991. *Memberships:* Japanese American Soc Leg Studies, Cnslr, Ed, 1965-; Japan Soc Comparative Law. *Honours:* Fulbright Scholar, 1968-70; British Council Fellow, 1974-76; Fulbright Scholar, 1986-87. *Hobbies:* Hiking, Tennis. *Address:* No. 510, 5-10, Takara-cho 2-chome, Katsushika-ku, Tokyo, Japan 124. 1.

TAKACHI Jun'ichiro, b. 7 Mar 1939, Tokushima, Japan, Prof of Engl and American Lit. *Education:* BA, Engl 1962, MA Engl 1964, Hiroshima Univ; Vis Schlr, Univ of Cambridge, England, 1979-80. *Appointments:* Lectr in Engl, 1965-70, Asst Prof 1970-73, Assoc Prof in Engl 1973-84, Hirosaki Univ; Prof of Engl and American Lit, Obirin Univ, 1984-. *Publications:* The Piano in the Sky (poems), 1977; Spring and Fall in Cambridge (poems), 1982; King Arthur and the Grail (transl) Richard Cavendish, 1983; Agon: A Theory of Revisionism, (transl) Harold Bloom, 1986; The Garden of Orpheus (poems), 1986; The Mirror of Eros (poems), 1991. *Memberships:* Japan Modern Poets Assn; Japan PEN; Japan Int Comparative Lit Soc; VP, Japan Contemporary Anglo-American Poetry Soc; Ed, Poetry Tokyo. *Hobbies:* Travel, Dancing, Camera. *Address:* No. 10 Sakashito Corpo, 4-1361 Kogasaka, Machida, Tokyo 19400, Japan.

TAKAHASHI Yoshindo, b. 21 Apr 1931, Tokyo, Japan. Transp Co Dir. m. Noriko Masago, 7 Oct 1955, 1 s, 2 d. *Education:* BEcon, Aoyama Gakuin Univ, Tokyo, 1955. *Appointments:* Mgr, Overseas Ops, Hino Motors Ltd, 1961-77; Mng Dir, Hino Motors, Hellas SA, 1963-68; Dir, Thai Hino Motor Sales Ltd, 1970-71; Mng Dir, Okamoto Freighters Ltd, 1977-. *Hobbies:* Painting Pictures, Photography, Antique Collection, Listening to Classical Music, Swimming, Golf. *Address:* No. 3-15-4-816 Higashi-nogawa, Komae- shi, Tokyo 201, Japan. 52, 123, 152.

TAKAKI Ryuji, b. 7 Oct 1940, Hiroshima, Japan. Prof of Agric and Technology. m. Junko Naito, 5 June 1971, 2 s. *Education:* BSc 1963, MSc 1965, DSc 1969, The Univ of Tokyo. *Appointments:* Lectr, 1969-70, Assoc Prof, 1979-83, Prof, 1983-, Tokyo Univ of Agric and Technology. *Publications:* Investigation of Forms (in Japanese), 1969; Mechanics of Sports, 1983; Physics of Flows (in Japanese), 1988; Research of Pattern Formation, 1992; many other articles anmd monographs in scientific jrnls. *Memberships:* The Physical Soc of Japan; Japan Soc of Fluid Mechanics; Soc of Science on Form, Japan; Japanese Soc of Biorheology. *Hobbies:* Skiing, Swimming. *Address:* Tokyo University of Agriculture and Technology, Fuchu, Tokyo 183, Japan. 1, 52.

TAKAKUWA Yasuo, b. 21 Aug 1929, Nagoya, Japan. Univ Prof. m. Moeko Shinoda, 28 May 1961, 3 s. *Education:* BA, Univ of Tokyo, 1952. *Appointments:* Tchng Asst, Tokyo Inst of Technology, 1952-57; Asst Prof, Assoc Prof, Kokugakuin Univ, 1957-63; Asst Prof, Prof, Nagoya Univ, 1963-84; Prof, Sophia Univ, 1984-. *Publications:* Audiovisual Education in an Age of Innovation, 1976; Ed: Invitation to Media Education, 5 vols, 1987; Relationship of Teacher to Media, 1990. *Memberships:* Japanese Soc for Study of Audiovisual Educ, Bd Dirs 1964-, Pres 1988-; Japanese Soc for Study of Broadcasting Educ, Bd Dirs 1964; Japan Soc of Educl Technology, Bd Dirs 1989-. *Honour:* Honour of Leadership in Audiovisual Education, Japan Audiovisual Education Association, 1989. *Hobbies:*

Travel, Stamp Collection, Mozart. *Address:* 2-19-16 Shimomeguro, Meguro-ku 153. Tokyo. Japan. 52.

TAKASHIMA Hiroshi, b. 27 Feb 1912, Tokyo, Japan. Physn, Philos. m. Kimiko, 1953, 1 d. *Education:* MD, Nihon Univ, 1935; PhD, 1945; Trng as Asst in Internal Med, St Luke's Hosp, 5 yrs. *Appointments:* Lectr, Internal Med, Nihon Univ, 1940-48; Dir, Takashima Hosp and Hon Physn at Italian Embassy in Tokyo, 1938-45; Psychosomatologist, Hayashi Surg Hosp and Maruzen Clin, 1953-; Dipl and Fellow of Inst of Logotherapy, Berkeley, CA, USA and Dir, Cnslr and Trainer of the Inst; Guest Prof of Psychology, Tokyo Rissho Women's Coll, 1970-75. *Publications:* Author of 26 books in his field inclng Psychosomatic Medicine and Logotherapy, 1977; Humanistic Psychosomatic Medicine, 1984, transl into Hebrew and Japanese, 1990. *Memberships:* Chmn, Japan Soc of Humanistic Anthropology, New Age Anthropology; Japan Inst of Logotherapy, Tokyo; Mbr of Examining Jury for Doct d'Etat es-Lettres at the Sorbonne, Paris, 1983. *Honours:* Invited to give the Eighteenth Baron Pope Annual Lecture in South Australia, 1978; Awarded The Statue of Responsibility from The Institute of Logotherapy, 1982. *Address:* No. 103, 9-25, 2-chome, Minami-Aoyama, Minato-ku, Tokyo 107, Japan.

TAKATERA Sadao, b. 1 June 1929, Ibaraki, Japan. Prof of Accounting. m. 17 Nov 1956, 1 s, 1 d. *Education:* BA, Econs 1953, Dr Econs 1972, Kyoto Univ. *Appointments:* Lectr, Assoc Prof, Prof of Accounting, Kyoto Univ, 1958-; Dean of Fac of Econs, Kyoto Univ, 1979-80. *Publications:* General Theory of Bookkeeping; Historical Development of Accounting Policy and Bookkeeping; Studies in Depreciation Accounting of Meiji Era; Studies in Accounting History of Large Enterprises; A La Carte of Accounting. *Memberships:* Japanese Assn of Accounting Studies; Japanese Assn of Bus Hist; Japanese Assn of Accounting Hist; Acad of Accounting Histns. *Address:* 172-6 Uguisudai, Nagaokakyo, Kyoto, 617 Japan.

TAKEDA Mariko, b. 13 July 1948, Nagoya, Japan. Assoc Prof. *Education:* Kyoto Univ, 1968-72; Doct course in Grad Schl of Kyoto Univ, 1972-77; MA, 1974. *Appointments:* Kyoto Univ, 1977-80; Wakayama Univ, 1980-. *Publications:* Visual Imagery and Eye Movements: Effects of Projective Size of Image on Eye Movements (paper), 1977; Recording Eye Movements by Ultrasonic Method (paper), 1988. *Memberships:* Japanese Psychological Assn; Japanese Assn of Educl Psychology; Japanese Psychonomic Soc; Japanese Soc for Physiological Psychology and Psychophysiology; Japan Soc of Educl Technology. *Hobbies:* Classical Music, Sketching. *Address:* 59 Imaikawara-cho, Kamikamo, Kita-ku, Kyoto 603, Japan.bblank

TAKINO Masuichi, b. 14 Apr 1904, Hyogo, Japan. Physn in relation to allergy and parasympathetic system. m. Yoshi Aoyagi, 17 Nov 1930, 2 s, 2 d. *Education:* Graduated, Fac of Med, Univ Kyoto, 1929; Dept Physiology, 1927; Dept Pathology, 1928-35; Internal Med, Kyoto Univ, 1929-32; Inst for Internal Med, 1933-41; MD, 1934. *Appointments:* Lectr Internal Med, Kyoto Univ, 1939-41; Dir, Inst of Sengokuse Hosp of Pulmonary Tuberculosis, 1941-45; Dir, Dainippon Zoki Inst for Med Rsch, 1947-61; Dir, Nippon Zoki Inst for Constitutional Disease, 1962-80; Advsr, Nippon Zoki Pharm Co Ltd, 1968-80; Advsr, Nippon Inst for Constitutional Disease, 1980-. *Publications:* New Direction in the Asthma Treatment Based on Theory of the Movement of Tension in the Parasympathetic Nervous System, 1952; Allergy and Asthma (co² author), 1957; Pathogenesis and Therapy of Bronchial Asthma with Special Reference to Organ Vagotonial (co-author), 1976 and many other papers and books. *Memberships:* Japan Soc of Allergology, Exec Sec 1952-70; Int Acad of Chest Physns and Surgs, Fellow Emeritus 1984-; American Coll of Chest Physns; Japan Christian Med Assn; Cnslr, Japan Soc of Neurovegetative Rschrs; Former Cnslr, Japan Soc of Angiocardiology, 1944-64; Internal Med, 1948, Endocrinology, 1954-80,

Constitution, 1967-81. *Honour:* Prize of Allergology, 1970. *Hobbies:* Reading, Fishing. *Address:* Shinmido Blg 4-4-1, Minami-Kynhoji-cho, Chyu-oku, Osaka 541, Japan. 50, 52, 129, 139, 152, 162.

TALARD Philippe, b. 30 Jan 1956, Draguignan, Germany. Ballet Dir; Choreographer. m. Rosangela Calheiros, 10 Feb 1979, 1 s. *Education:* Educated by Erik Bruhn, Rosella Hightower, Sir Anton Dolin, Tatiana Leskova, Gabriel Popescu, Sonia Arova, Raymond Franchetti, Anne Wooliams and Jose Ferran. *Appointments:* Soloist Dancer, Ballet du XXe Siecle, 1976- 78; Ballet Nacional do Portugal, 1978-79; Ballet Municipal do Rio de Janeiro, 1979-80; Ballet Royal des Flandres, 1980-83; Tanz-Forum Koln, Ballet Dir, 1983-88; Ulm, Mannheim, 1988-91. *Creative Works:* Ballets created since 1979: Ballad for the Soldier's Wife, 1986; Der Puppe ward Gewalt getan, 1990; Romeo et Juliette, 1990-91. *Honours:* First Prize in Choreography, Festival de Lausanne, 1975; Presented by the Tanztheatertage Heilbronn, 1989, 90, 91.*Address:* c/o National Theater Mannheim, AM Goethe Platz, D-6800 Mannheim, Germany.

TALBOT KELLY Chloe Elizabeth, b. 15 July 1927, Hampstead, London, England. Artist, Illustrator, Picture Framer. m. Jeffrey G Smith, 10 Oct 1964, 1 s. *Education:* Private Tutor; St George's Schl for Girls; Convent of Sacred Heart; Co-Ed and Boys Prep Schl; Matric Schl Cert. *Appointment:* 1 July 1945 sent by Father to Bird Room, Brit Mus, Nat Hist, to paint birds until offered work. *Creative Works:* First work, 5 B & W drawings for David Lack's Darwin's Finches; many B & W drawings on Aust birds; 1947-71 worked on African Handbook of Birds; Exhibs: SWLA; UK Provincial Galls; Aust, Can; Oil Panel, Parts of Insect, Warwick Co Mus; Official orchid painter, Royal Hort Soc, 1953-54; Illustrations, Avicultural Soc Mag; Illustration, AUK American Ornithological Mag. *Memberships:* Brit Ornithologists Union; Fndr Mbr, Soc Wildlife Artists, 1964; Elected Mbr, Soc Indl Artists and Designers (now Soc Chartered Designers) on published work. *Hobbies:* Reading, Walking, Painting, Listening to Music, Chess, Bird Watching. *Address:* 22 St Philip's Road, Leicester LE5 5TQ, England. 19.

TALIAFERRO Elizabeth Ann, b. 9 Oct 1953, Missouri, USA. Pub Rels Cons. div. 1 s, 3 d. *Education:* BA, Quincy Coll, 1989; AA, Hannibal la Grange Coll, 1971. *Appointments:* Special Projects Coord, Heilbronn, W Germany, 1975-77; Special Projects Dir, Ft Carson, CO, 1984-86; Staff Writer, Quincy Herald-Whig, Quincy, IL, 1989-. *Contributions to:* profl jrnls, newspapers, mags. *Memberships:* Jaycees; Windstar Fndn; Nat Assn Female Execs; WGCA Christian Radio; WWQC Pub Radio; Vol work w Red Cross, Big Brothers-Big Sisters, Domestic Violence Prevention Shelter; var music grps. *Honours:* World Decoration of Excellence, 1989; Woman of the Year, American Biographical Institute, 1990; Women's Inner Circle of Achievement, 1990. *Hobbies:* Vol work, Reading, Music. *Address:* 815 Oak Street, Quincy, IL 62301, USA. 8, 132, 138, 151, 152, 155.

TALLMAN Johanna Eleonore, b. 18 Aug 1914, Lubeck, Germany. Lib Admnstr. m. Lloyd Anthony Tallman, 8 May 1954. *Education:* AB 1936, Cert in Librarianship 1937, Univ of CA, Berkeley, USA. *Appointments:* var positions, special and pub libs, 1937-44; Libn, Engrng and Math Sciences Lib, UCLA, 1945-73; Coord, Phys Sciences Libs, 1963-73; Dir of Libs, CA Inst of Technology, 1973-81; Lectr, Schl of Lib Serv, UCLA; Cons to var univs and corps. *Publications:* Check Out a Librarian, 1985; over 60 articles on lib science in profl jrnls, 1942-80. *Memberships:* Chmn, Southern Sect, CA Acad and Rsch Libs, CA Lib Assn; Chmn, Consultation Comm, Chmn, Science-Technology Div, Pres, Southern CA Chapt, Special Libs Assn; Pres, Libns Assn, Univ CA; Pres, UCLA Libns Assn; Chmn, Engrng Schl Libs Comm, American Soc for Engrng Educ; Subject Heading Comm, Div of Cataloguing and Classification, Coun Mbr, ALA; Chmn, Engrng Schl Libs Sect, Assn of Coll and

Ref Libs, ALA; Chmn, Los Angeles Reg Grp of Cataloguers; Bd Dirs, Pasadena Histl Soc. *Honours:* Walter Lowey Scholarship, University of California, Berkeley; Fulbright Grant, Brazil. *Address:* 4731 Daleridge Road, La Canada, CA 91011, USA 2, 5, 52, 59, 138.

TAMAS Attila, b. 17 June 1930, Budapest, Hungary. Univ Prof. m. Margit Markus, 10 Aug 1964, 2 d. *Education:* Univ, Tchr of Hungarian and German Lang and Lit, 1948-52; Cand of Lit Sciences, 1961; Dr of Lit Sciences, 1975. *Appointments:* Dramaturg of Hungarian Film Co, 1952-54; Educ, 1954-55; Mbr of Lit Review, 1955-56; Tchr, 1957-61; Lectr, Univ of Szeged, 1963-72; Lectr, Prof, Univ of Debrecen, 1972-76; Prof, Univ Wien, 1982-84. *Publications:* Koltoi mualkotasok fejlodese Arany Janostol Jozsef Attilaig, 1964; A koltoi mualkotas fo sajatsagai, 1972; Trodalomm es emberi teljesseg, 1973; Lira a XX szazadban, 1974; Weores Sandor, 1978; A nyelvi mualkotas jelentese, 1984; Illyes Gyula, 1990. *Memberships:* Int Assn of Hungarian Studies; Soc of Hungarian Authors. *Address:* Senyei Olah u. 39 v. 15, Debrecen, Hungary.

TAMM Mary, b. 22 Mar 1950, Dewsbury, England. Actress. m. Marcus Ringrose, 14 Jan 1978, 1 d. *Education:* RADA, Dip. *Appointments:* Theatre: Good Time Johnny, First Impressions, Birmingham Rep, 1971; Mother Earth, Roundhouse, London, 1971; Cards on the Table, Vaudeville, London, 1981; Good Morning Bill, Nat tour, 1985; Present Laughter, Theatre Royal, Windsor, 1989; Why's Here Everywhere Now?, Riverside Studios, 1991; TV BBC: Girls of Slender Means, 1974; Doctor Who, 1978; The Assassination Run, 1979; The Hello Goodbye Man, 1985; Guest Appearances: Bergerac, BBC, 1976; Jane Eyre, BBC, 1984; Poirot, London Weekend TV, 1990; Films: Witness Madness, Paramount, 1973; The Odessa File, Columbia, 1974; The Likely Lads, EMI, 1975; Rampage, Sri Lanka, 1977; Three Kinds of Heat, ABC, US TV movie, 1989. *Membership:* Assoc of RADA, Assocs Comm. *Honours:* Hannah Clarke Award; Emile Littler Award, RADA, 1971. *Hobbies:* Horse riding, Painting, Computer Scrabble, Walking, Opera, Crosswords, Cinema, Reading. *Address:* Barry Langford, Garden Studios, Betterton Street, London WC2H 9PB, England.

TAMURA Imao, b. 30 Sept 1923. Mgr Rsch Inst for Applied Sciences. m. Toshiko Otsuka, 28 Apr 1958, 1 s, 1 d. *Education:* BA, Metallurgy, Fac Engrng 1948, Graduate, Graduate Schl of Engrng in Metallurgy 1953, PhD 1958, Osaka Univ; Northwestern Univ, Evanston, IL, USA, 1958-59. *Appointments:* Asst, Dept Metallurgy, Fac Engrng, Osaka Univ, 1953-61; Assoc Prof, Osaka Univ Inst of Scientific and Indl Rsch, 1961-64; Assoc Prof, Fac Engrng 1964, Prof, Fac Engrng 1964-87, Kyoto Univ; Bd Dirs, Rsch Inst for Applied Sciences, 1971-; Prof Emeritus, Kyoto Univ, 1987-; Tech Advsr, Sumitomo Metal Ind Ltd, Osaka, 1987-90. *Publications:* 10 Papers and Books. *Memberships:* Fellow, ASM Int, USA; Hon Mbr, Japan Inst of Metals; VP, Int Fedn for Heat Treatment and Surface Engrng, 1990-; Pres, Japanese Soc for Heat Treatment; TMS AIME, USA; Iron and Steel Inst of Japan. *Honours:* Thermo.Tech. Award, Tanigawa Thermal Foundation, 1984; Hattori Pub. Service Award, Hattori Foundation, 1985; Murakami Memorial Award, Murakami Commemoration Foundation, 1989; var prizes and honours, Japan Institute for Metals, Iron and Steel Institute of Japan and Japan Society for Heat Treatment. *Address:* 142-16 Banjojiki, Fushimi-Ku, Kyoto 612, Japan.

TAMURA Kenji, b. 11 June 1933, Tokyo, Japan. Sr Coord, Coordination and Corp Planning Dept, Arabian Oil Co Ltd; Mng Dir, Int. m. Midori Yoshida, 28 Feb 1963, 1 s. *Education: B.Com, Waseda Univ, Tokyo, 1958. Appointments:* Dodwell & Co Ltd, Tokyo, 1958; Arabian Oil Co Ltd, Tokyo, 1960. *Memberships:* The Inst of Internal Auditors Inc, USA, 1984-. *Honour:* Received

Award Ohkuma Scholarship of Waseda University, 1955. *Hobbies:* Classical Music, Golf, Tennis. *Address:* 3-9-7 Nishikamakura, Kamakura City, Kanagawa Prefecture, 248, Japan. 52.

TAN Arjun, b. 6 Aug 1943, Santiniketan, Br India. Prof of Phys. *Education:* BSc (Hons), Phys, 1963, MSc, Phys, 1965, Univ of Calcutta; MS, Phys, Univ of FL, USA, 1974; PhD, Phys, Univ of AL Huntsville, 1979. *Appointments:* Instr, Visra Bharati Univ, 1966-67; Lectr, Krishnagar Women's Coll, 1967-71; Vis Instr, Newberry Coll, 1980-81; Asst Prof 1981-85, Assoc Prof 1985-88, Prof 1988-, AL A & M Univ. *Publications:* Over 80 papers in refereed jrnls. *Memberships:* American Phys Soc; American Geophys Union; American Assn of Phys Tchrs; Nat Coun of Teachers of Maths; The Mathl Assn of America; AL Acad of Science; Smithsonian Instn. *Honours:* Referee, American Journal of Physics, 1981, 85; Referee, Mathematics Teacher, 1986, 87, 88, 89, 90, 91; Research Grantee, National Science Foundation, 1983, 86; Research Grantee, NASA, 1987, 89; Merit Reviewer, NASA Proposal, 1991. *Address:* Department of Physics, Alabama A & M University, P O Box 447, Normal, AL 35762, USA. 7, 15, 143.

TAN Frederick Han-Chung, b. 1 Jan 1954, Taipei, Taiwan, The People's Republic of China. Film Dir, Film Critic, Ed. *Education:* Law Degree, Taiwan Univ, 1975; MFA, Motion Picture Prod, UCLA, 1984. *Appointments:* Hollywood Ed, China Times, Newspaper, Times-Weekly Mag; Film Critic Cinemart Mag, Hong Kong, 1975-90. *Creative Works:* Interviews with US and European Film Directors, Actors, Cinematographers and Producers, 3 vols, 1974, 76, 78; PBS Documentary: Taiwan R O C featured; Dir, Motion Picture, Rouge of the North, 1988 Officially accepted into Cannes Film Festival and Festivals in London, Edinburgh, New York, Los Angeles, Chicago, Asian, Montreal, Toronto, Denver, Houston, Dallas, Japan, Seattle, Hawaii, Cleveland, Santa Barbara, Boston, Baltimore, San Francisco, Figueria da Foz, Dunkerque, La Rochelle, France; Dir: Dark Night, 1985, Los Angeles and San Francisco Film Festivals; Writer, Dir, Split of the Spirit., 1986, Madrid Film Festival, Taiwan Film Archives, UCLA; Writer, Dir, Lovers, 1980, Medal at Festival of the Americas, Virgin Islands Int Film Festival, Frameline Film Festival. *Hobbies:* Travel in Europe, China, Japan, Mexico, Painting Watercolours of Nature, Miniature Set Designing, Published Photographer of Entertainment Figures, Nature, Arch, Travel, Nudes, Movie Stars. *Address:* 1134 North Ogden Drive, Los Angeles, CA 90046, USA.

TAN Hao Giang, b. Shanghai, China. m. Xiao Yun Zhang, 20 Mar 1963, 1 s, 1 d. *Education:* Tsinghua Univ, 1953-58. *Appointments:* Tsinghua Univ, Tchr, 1958-85; Asst Tchr, Asst Prof, Assoc Prof, Prof, Beijing Machinery & Electronics Coll, 1985-. *Publications:* 51 Works on Computer; Basic Computer Programming Language. *Memberships:* Research Assn of Fundamental Computer Educ; Educ & Training Council of Chinese Computer Federation. *Honours:* Merit for Post Secondary Tchrng; Prof with Outstanding Contribution; Popular Sci Writer with Exceptional Achievements. *Hobbies:* Classical Music; Travel. *Address:* 5 Huang Hao Men Street, Di An Men, Beijing, China 10009.

TAN Kim Leong, b. 30 Oct 1936, Malaysia. Prof of Paediatrics. m. Kwok Yee Leng, 15 June 1963, 1 s, 2 d. *Education:* MBBS, Univ of Singapore, 1962; MRCP 1966, FRCP 1977, Edinburgh, Scotland, 1962; DCH, Univ of London, 1967; FICP 1974, FRACP 1978. *Appointments:* Med Off, Min of Hlth, 1963-68; Lectr 1958-68, Sr Lectr 1971-75, Assoc Prof 1976-79, Prof 1980- , Univ of Singapore (now Nat Univ of Singapore); Examiner, Master of Pediatrics Examination-Postgrad Examination for Specialists. *Publications:* 170 papers; Co-Ed, Problems in Perinatology, 1979; Guest Ed, Paediatric Issue, 1975, General Paediatrics and Neonatology Issue 1985, Annals of the Acad of Med,

Singapore; Chapts in Books. *Memberships:* BMA; Singapore Med Assn; Acad of Med, Singapore; Singapore Paediatric Soc, Pres and VP; Hon Scientific Advsr, Int Ctr for Childhood Studies, Brit; Ed Bd, Jrnl of the American Med Assn, Southeast Asian Ed; Chmn, Expert Comm on Immunization Prog, Min of Hlth, Singapore; Chmn, Chapt of Paediatricians, Acad of Med, Singapore; NY Acad of Sciences; Nat Scientific Comm on Hepatitis and Related Disorders, Min of Hlth, Singapore; Expert Comm for Paediatrics, Schl of Postgrad Med Studies, Singapore; Exec Comm of Children's Aid Soc, Singapore. *Honours:* Sev lectures in his field. *Hobbies:* Reading, Photography. *Address:* Chief, Department of Neonatology, National University Hospital, 5 Lower Kent Ridge Road, Singapore 0511, Republic of Singapore.

TAN Peisheng, b. 4 May 1933, Jixian, Hebei, China. Prof of Drama. m. 15 Jan 1957, 1 s, 1 d. *Education:* Dept of Dramatic Lit, Ctrl Acad of Drama, 1952-56; Graduate Student, Dept of Lit, People's Univ. *Appointments:* Tchr, Dept of Dramatic Lit, Ctrl Acad of Drama, 1956-59; Prof, Chmn, Dept of Dramatic Lit, Ctrl Acad of Drama, 1962-. *Publications:* On Theatricality, 1981; Base of Film Aesthetics, 1984; Characteristics of Dramatic Art, 1985; Appreciating World-Famous Plays, 1985; Essentials of Dramatic Ontology, 1988. *Memberships:* Chinese Dramatic Assn; Chinese TV Playwrights Assn; Chinese World Film Assn. *Honour:* Conferred the title National Expert Making Outstanding Contributions to the State by Chinese Government, 1986. *Hobbies:* Fishing, Weiqi. *Address:* Central Academy of Drama, Beijing 100710, China.

TANAKA Motoharu, b. 11 Feb 1926, Ogaki, Gifu, Japan. Mbr of Science Coun of Japan, 1988-. m. Shigeko Hayashi, 15 Nov 1954, 1 s, 1 d. *Education:* BA, Univ of Tokyo, 1948; DrSc, Nagoya Univ, 1957. *Appointments:* Prof 1963-89, Vice Dean of Fac of Science, 1980-82, Dean of Fac of Science, 1983-85, Emeritus Prof 1989-, Nagoya Univ. *Publications:* Acids and Bases, 1971; Solvent Extraction Chemistry, 1977; Co-author; Reactions in Solution, 1977; Co-author and Co-ed, Complex Formation, 1974; Modern Chemistry, 17 vols, 1979-81; Chemistry Dictionary, 1989. *Memberships:* Japan Soc Analytical Chem;, VP 1979-80, Soc Award 1974; Chem Soc of Japan, VP 1989-90; American Chem Soc; Royal Soc of Chem; Science Coun of Japan, 1988-, VP 4th Grp Natural Sciences. *Honours:* Society Award of Japan Society of Analytical Chemistry, 1974; Kudo Science Foundation Award, 1979; Yamaji Science Foundation Award, 1979. *Hobby:* Golf. *Address:* Faculty of Science, Nagoya University, Chikusa, Nagoya 464-01, Japan. 52.

TANER Ruya, b. 17 Mar 1971, Germany. Presently Student, graduating July 1992 as a Concert Pianist. *Education:* Conservatoire of Music, Turkey, 1982-83; Jr Dept, Guildhall Schl of Music and Drama, London, 1983-88; Purcell Music Schl, London, 1985-87; Performer's Study, AGSM Course, Guildhall Schl of Music and Drama, London, 1988-92. *Honours:* Composition Prize, First, North London Music Festival, 1985; The Surrey Young Pianist of the Year Award, Second Prize, 1986; The Mozart Memorial Piano Competition, Second, 1987; Young Pianist of the Year Award, Second, 1988; Frank Britten Memorial Cup Award, First, 1990; Hatfield Music Festival, Mozart Prize, First, 1990; Oxford Music Festival, Recital Prize, Second, 1992. *Hobbies:* Swimming, Listening to Music, Going to Ballet, Watching Wimbledon, Going to Movies. *Address:* 11 Gunduz Tezel Street, Lefkosa, Mersin 10, Turkey.

TANG Zuo-Fan, b. 11 May 1927. Prof of Peking Univ. m. Jan 1943, 2 s, 1 d. *Education:* BA, Zhong Shan Univ, 1953. *Appointments:* Tutor, Zhong Shan Univ, 1953; Tutor 1954, Lectr 1960, Assoc Prof 1979, Prof 1985, Peking Univ. *Publications:* Phonetic Dictionary of Archaic Chinese, 1958; Lectures on Chinese Phonology, 1981; Ancient Chinese, 1981; The Phonetic History of

Mandarin, 1985; Study on Rhymes in Han Shan's Poetry, 1963; The Rhyming System of Zheng Yin Quan Yan, 1980. *Memberships:* Soc of Chinese Phonology, Chmn; Linguistics Society of Beijing, Exec Mbr; Linguistics Soc of China. *Honours:* First Award of Education Commission Distinguished Textbooks Prize; Second Award of Peking University Distinguished Publications Prize. *Address:* Department of Chinese Language and Literature, Peking University, Beijing 100871, China.

TANGUAY J Fernand, b. 30 Nov 1932, Sweetsburg, Quebec, Canada. Jurist, Diplomat and Publr. m. 1 Sept 1960, 1 d. *Education:* Coll Jean de Brebeuf, Montreal; BA, Univ of Ottawa, 1956; B.Phil, St Paul Univ, 1957; MA, Pol Science, 1960; LL.L, Civ Law, 1960; DESD. 1965; F U Berlin, 1959-60. *Appointments:* Joined Diplomatic Serv of Can, 1963; Posted to Moscow, 1966-68; Bonn, 1972-76; Dir of UN Affairs, 1978-82; Min and Dpty Perm Rep to UN, Geneva; Min at Can Embassy, Moscow, 1986-88; Dir Gen, Int Rels, Ottawa, 1988-90; Diplomat in Res and Guest Prof, Fac of Law, McGill Univ, 1990-91; Resigned from Diplomatic Serv to become Chmn of the Bd: Les Editions du Meridien, Montreal; Univ Lectr. *Publications:* Author of many articles. *Honours:* Scholarship, Austrian Government, 1958; Scholarship, German Government, 1959. *Hobbies:*)Art Collector, Skiing, Tennis, Swimming. *Address:* 475 Oakhill Road, Rockcliffe Park, Ottawa, Ontario, Canada K1M 1J5.

TANNER Roger Ian, b. 25 July 1933, Somerset, England. Prof of Mech Engrng. m. Elizabeth Bogen, 17 Sept 1957, 2 s, 3 d. *Education:* BSc, Univ Bristol, 1956; MS,. Univ CA, 1958; PhD. Univ Manchester, 1961. *Appointments:* Lectr, Univ Manchester, England, 1958-61; Rdr, Univ Sydney, Aust, 1961-66; Prof, Brown Univ, USA, 1966-75; Prof, Univ Sydney, Aust, 1975-. *Publication:* Engineering Rheology, 1988. *Memberships:* Fellow, Aust Acad Science; Fellow, Aust Acad of Technological Science and Engrng. *Hobby:* Tennis. *Address:* Marlowe, Sixth Mile Lane, Roseville 2069, Australia. 2, 23, 52.

TANT WRIGHT Julia, b. 3 Nov 1940, London, England. Painter; Writer. *Education:* BA, Central St Martins, 1985-90. *Appointments:* Shop Asst; Civil Servant. *Creative Works:* Paintings. Some Tesco Shoppers; Men in Drag Camping It Up; Work on Marilyn Monroe & Modonna; Publi. City Limits; Spare Rib; German/English Year Book. *Honours:* BA, Fine Art & Critical Studies. *Hobbies:* Disco; Womens Liberation Movement. *Address:* 3 Kestral Avenue, Herne Hill, London SE24 1ED, England.

TANTANASSIS Athanasios, b. 7 Sept 1914, Ano Porroia, Greece. Obst Gynecologist. m. Maria Kakaidis, 27 Apr 1950, 1 s, 1 d. *Education:* Univ of Athens, 6 yrs; MD, 1941; Dip of Obst and Gynecology, 1941; Dips of subspecialty on infertility from London, Geneva, Paris, 1957. *Appointments:* Dir, Pvte Clin in Thessaloniki; Co-Mayor of Thessaloniki, 1954-68. *Publications:* 4 books of poems; Participant in F World Congresses of UMEM. *Memberships:* UMEM (World Assn of Lit Drs); Greek Assn of Lit Doctors; participant in Les Poetes de France, Ed from 1966- 76. *Honours:* Silver Award of the Municipality of Thessaloniki, 1983; 4 Personal Painting Exhibitions. *Hobbies:* Painting, Writing, Sculpting. *Address:* Leoforos Nikis 21, 54623 Thessaloniki, Greece.

TAPIA Farzana Arastu, b. 3 Apr 1943, Hyderabad, India. Psychotherapist. m. Dr Moiez Ahmed Tapia, 19 Aug 1968. *Education:* BA, Women's Coll, Osmania Univ, Hyderabad, 1964; MA, Arts Coll, Osmania Univ, Hyderabad, 1966; BJ, Arts Coll, Hyderabad, 1968; MEd, Counseling, GA State Univ, Atlanta, USA, 1972. *Appointments:* For Student Cnslr, GA State Univ, 1972; Social Worker, Hampton, VA, Dept of Social Servs, 1973-74; Mental Hlth Cnslr, CHI Community Mental Hlth Ctr, Miami, FL, 1975-; Coord, Elderly Servs, Community Hlth Inc, Miami, FL, 1976-91. *Publications:*

Ed: Georgette Mag, Hyderabad, India, 1960; Vasudha Mag., Hyderabad, 1964; Inspirer, Miami, FL, 1976; Hyderabad Nama, Miami, FL, 1990; Hosted Radio Prog, Sound of Asia, Miami, FL, 1976; Articles in newspapers and mags; Advsr, Al- Husain Soc, 1968 and Ingra, Miami, FL, 1990. *Memberships:* American Assn of Counseling and Dev; HOME Fndn, Sec; Hyderabad Assn, Treas; Inst of Islamic Rsch and Educ, Bd Mbr; Bazme Qwateen, Sec. *Honour:* Best Guide of the Year 1960. *Hobbies:* Reading, Gardening, Painting, Eggery. *Address:* 5904 S W 64th Place, Miami, FL 33143, USA. 1.

TAPLEY Earl Mays, b. 8 Nov 1913, Marietta, GA, USA. Ret'd Dean Emeritus Schl of Grad Studies, Univ of Evansville, IN. m. Ruby Jewell Franklin, 5 June 1935, 1 s, 2 d. *Education:* Dip, Bible Trng Schl, 1935; AB, Vanderbilt Univ, 1945; MA, George Peabody Coll, 1946; PhD, Univ of Chgo, 1955. *Appointments:* Pastor, GA and TN, 1935-46; Prof, Dean, VP, Lee Coll, Cleveland, TN, 1946-53; Dir, Special Servs, Univ of Chattanooga, 1953-57; Dean, Univ of Evansville, 1957-65; Dean, Schl of Grad Studies, 1965- 79; Dir, Int Travel, 1965-79. *Publications:* General Education in the Junior College; The College Curriculum: General and Professional Components. *Memberships:* NEA; AAUP, Pres of Chapt; IN Assn of Grad Schls, Pres; Phi Kappa Phi, Local Pres; Phi Delta Kappa. *Honours:* Outstanding Contribution to Graduate Education in Indiana, 1979; Life Honorary Member of Phi Kappa Phi, 1981. *Hobbies:* Boating, Fishing, Watersports, Reading. *Address:* 1102 Burke Avenue, Dunedin, FL 34698, USA. 2, 7, 143, 154.

TARANOW Gerda, b. New York City, USA. Prof of Engl. *Education:* BA, 1952, MA, 1955, NY Univ; PhD, 1961, Post-Doctoral Fellow in Engl 1962-63, Yale Univ. *Appointments:* Instr and Asst Prof Engl, Univ of KY, 1963-66; Asst Prof Engl, Syracuse Univ, 1966-67; Asst Prof, Prof Engl, CT Coll, 1967-. *Publication:* Sarah Bernhardt: The Art Within the Legend, 1972. *Memberships:* American Soc for Theatre Rsch; Soc for Theatre Rsch, Engl; Societe d'Histoire du theatre; Int Fedn for Theatre Rsch; Assn of Recorded Sound Collects; MLA; Friends of Milton's Cottage; Restoration and 18th Century Theatre Rsch. *Honours:* Ford Foundation Grant, 1971, for completion of Sarah Bernhardt: The Art Within the Legend; National Endowment for the Humanities Research Fellowship, 1980-81, for research on The Bernhardt Hamlet (nearing completion). *Hobbies:* Theatre, Opera, Ballet. *Address:* Connecticut College, Box 5567, Department of English, New London, CT 06320, USA. 30, 138.

TARANTO Vernon Anthony Jr, b. 16 Nov 1946, New Orleans, LA, USA. Composer. *Education:* BMus, 1975; MMus, 1976; Doctor of Musical Arts, LA State Univ, 1983. *Appointments:* USAF Band, 1969-74; Prof, Music Theory and Composition, Nicholls State Univ, 1976-78; Grd Asst Instr, Theory and Orchestration, LA State Univ, 1979-83. *Creative Works:* Symphony, opera, ballet, chmbr music, choral works: Soliloquy for Strings, 1966; Sinfonia Orionis, 1974; Aeolus Liturgies, 1977; A Winter Canticle, 1981; Abendmusik, 1983; The Cistern (opera), 1986; Five Haiku Impressions, 1989; Capriccio and Fantasy Waltz, 1990; Sonata for Cello and Piano, 1991. *Memberships:* American Soc Composers, Authors and Publishers; The Tampa Bay Composers Forum, Pres; The Soc of Composers Inc. *Honours:* Louisiana Composer's Award, 1977; ASCAP Composer's Award, 1991. *Hobbies:* Gardening, Poetry, Lit. *Address:* P O Box 16251, St Petersburg, FL 33733, USA. 4, 125.

TARASIN Jan, b. 11 Sept 1926, Kalisz, Poland. Painter; Prof, Acad of Fine Arts, Warsaw. m, Natalia Maciwoda, 1966, 1 s. *Education:* Krakow Acad of Fine Arts, 1946-51; Dip, 1951. *Appointments:* Guest Lectr, Krakow Acad, 1963-67; Prof, Warsaw Acad, 1973; Pres, Warsaw Acad, 1987- 90. *Creative Works:* Cycles Graphics: The House, The Bank, 1953-55; Cycles Pictures; Objects; The Trifles, 1955-60; Objects Countes: Notations, 1960-

70; Situations; Collections, 1970-90; Notebooks; Opening, 1974-82. *Memberships:* Krakow Grp; Assn Polish Artists. *Honours:* Tokio- Yiomiuri Award, The 3rd International Young Artists Exhibition, Europe-Japan, 1965; San Marino X Biennale National Award, 1965; Warsaw Norwid Award, 1976; Warsaw Festival Award, 1978; Warsaw Cybis Award, 1984. *Hobby:* Walking in the Mountains. *Address:* ul Dolna 4 m 59, 00-774 Warsaw, Poland. 52.

TARKKANEN Ahti Helge Armas, b. 15 May 1930, Helsinki, Finland. Prof of Ophthalmology; Dir, Helsinki Univ Eye Hosp. m. Ulla Pirkko, 1959, 1 s, 2 d. *Education:* MD, 1955; Specialist in Ophthalmology, 1962; Docent in Ophthalmology, 1964; Prof in Ophthalmology, 1985. *Appointments:* Res in Ophthalmology 1958-62, Sr Ophthalmologist 1962-66, Asst Ophthalmologist-in-Chief 1966-68, Helsinki Univ Eye Hosp; Docent of Ophthalmology 1964-68, Full- time Assoc Prof of Ophthalmology 1968-85, Prof of Ophthalmology 1986-, Univ of Helsinki; Dir, Helsinki Univ Eye Hosp, 1986; Hd, Dept of Ophthalmology, 1986-; Mbr of Hosp Bd, Helsinki Univ Ctrl Hosp, 1990-; Med Fac Univ of Helsinki, Karolinska Institutet, Stockholm, Univ of Uppsala, Univ of Oslo, Univ of Cologne and Univ of Kuopio; sev Govt appointments. *Publications:* About 300 publs in Ophthalmology. *Memberships:* Finnish Med Soc; Finnish Ophthalmic Soc; European Ophthalmic Pathology Soc, Fndr; Int Coll of Surgs; Int Comm on Standardization of Tonometers; European Glaucoma Soc; Glaucoma Soc of Int Congress of Ophthalmology; Scandinavian Ophthalmological Comm; The Int Intro-Ocular Implant Club. *Hobbies:* Music; Sailing. *Address:* Department of Ophthalmology, University of Helsinki, Haartmaninkatu 4C. SF-00290. Helsinki, Finland.

TARNAS Kazimierz Antoni, b. 17 Oct 1942, Warsaw, Poland. Film Dir; Script Writer. m. Maria Siokowska, 8 June 1963, 1 s. *Education:* Tchrs Sem (Polish Philology), Warsaw, 1963; HS of Drama, Dept of Film Directing, Warsaw, expelled from schl for pol reasons in 1968. *Appointments:* The Nat Theatre, Warsaw, 1965-68; Rekonesans Theatre, Warsaw, 1968-70; TV Theatre, Warsaw, 1971-72; Film Realization Co Zespoly Filmowe, Warsaw, 1972-91; Agcy of Film Prod (former Film Realization Co Zespoly Filmowe, Warsaw 1990-91; Youth Acad of Film, estab and managed, Warsaw, 1990-. *Creative Works:* Directed and based on own scripts: TV Film: Strzal na Dancingu, 1981; TV Serial: Szalenstwa Panny Ewy, 1984; Feature Film: Szalenstwa Panny Ewy, 1985; Zlota Mahmudia, 1986; TV Feature-Document: W Cieniu Serca, 1987; TV Film: Dwie Wigilie, 1987; Feature Film: Pan Samochodzik i Praskie Tajemnice, 1988. *Membership:* Soc of Polish Film Makers. *Honours:* For Feature Film Szalenstwa Panny Ewy Grand Prix Crystal Fawns Festival of Films for Children and Youth, Poznan, 1985; Audience Award, Fotel Widza, Koszalin's Film Meetings, Koszalin, 1986; Distributors Award for the most popular film X Festival of Polish Films, Gdansk, 1986; For feature film Pan Samochodzik I Praskie Tajemnice: Children Jury Award, Marcinek, Poznan, 1989. *Hobbies:* Sailing, Skiing, Driving, Music, Paintings. *Address:* ul Pianistow 15, 02-403 Warsaw, Poland.

TARNOPOLSKY Alex, b. 17 Oct 1939, Buenos Aires, Argentina. Psychoanalyst. m. Alma Petchersky, 9 Nov 1968, 2 s. *Education:* Physn, Buenos Aires, 1962; MD, Buenos Aires, 1971; Psychoanalyst, London, England, 1978; MRC Psych, London, 1980; FRC Psych, London, 1985. *Appointments:* Prof, Dept of Psychiatry, McMaster Univ, Ont, Can, 1991; Dir, Psychotherapy Unit, Whitby Psychiatric Hosp, Ont, 1991; Cons Psychotherapist, Maudsley Hosp, London, England, 1981-; Sr Lectr, Inst of Psychiatry, London, 1981-. *Publications:* Scientific papers on epidemiology of mental disorders, treatment of personality disorders and tchng of psychotherapy. *Memberships:* Royal Coll of Psychiatrists, UK; Brit Psycho-Analytical Soc, UK; Royal Photographic Soc, UK. *Honours:* WHO Fellowship; ACTA Award for Psychiatric Research. *Hobbies:* Painting, Photography. *Address:* Department of Psychiatry, McMaster Medical Centre,

1200 Main Street, Hamilton, Ontario, Canada L8N 3Z5. 1.

TARRANT Eddie Faye (Battee), b, 8 Dec 1942, Dallas, TX, USA. Youth Worker; Family Cnslr. m. Kenneth Ray Tarrant, 27 Aug 1960, 2 s, 3 d. *Education:* Social Work, Univ of TX at Arlington, 1986-88; Drug and Alcohol Cnslr, Eastfield Coll, Mesquite, TX, 1987-88; Social Work Assoc Degree (Hons), Easfield Coll; var courses in Disfunctional Family Therapy, Off Mgmt and Tchrs Asst. *Appointments:* Client Advocate, Assn for Retarded Citizens; Bondwriter; PR Seagoville Correctional Prison; Cnslr, TX Coalition for Juvenile Justice; Casework Supvsr, Stars for Children; Youth Worker, Family Cnslr, Right Alternative for People, Dallas, TX, 1984, 86, 88; Cnslr, Shift Ldr, Casa de los Amigos, Dallas, 1985-86. *Creative Works:* Pub Speaker. *Memberships:* Int Platform Assn; N Garland HS Booster Club; PTA; Sponsor, Firefighters of Garland; Sponsor, AMVET; Sponsor, Oak Cliff Steelers Club; AID Interfaith Network Inc of N TX. *Honours:* Cert, The Business Womens Training Institute, 1988; Certificates, Alcohol/Drug Counselor Training, 1988; Certificates, Treating Survivors of Incest, 1988; Certificate, Suicidal Behaviour in Children and Adolescents; Certificate, Children and Youth at Risk. *Hobbies:* Reading, Meditation, Walking, Bowling, Art, Directing and instructing disfunctional family therapy sessions. *Address:* 2329 Glenbrook Meadows Drive, Garland, TX 75040, USA. 1.

TARRAS-WAHLBERG, Bo Casper Andreas, b. 23 May 1934, Stockholm, Sweden. Physn. m. Ellen Schmidt, 3 Nov 1972, 4 s, 2 d. *Education:* Med Trng, Karolinska Inst, completed 1963; Flying Trng, Air Force and Army Air Force, 1962-63. *Appointments:* Var Servs Surg and Orthopaedics, 1960- 62; Internal Med, Jonkoping, 1963-67; Dermatology at Karolinska Hosp, Stockholm, 1967-74; Hd, Dept of Dermatology, Nassjo Hosp, 1975- ; Flying Physn, Army Air Force, Rank Maj, 1963-75. *Memberships:* Swedish Med Assn; Swedish Soc of Med; Swedish Soc for Dermatology; Nordic Soc for Dermatology; Int Soc for Dermatologic Surg; The European Acad of Dermatology and Venereology; Rotary Int. *Hobbies:* Classical Music, Art, Antiques, Old Books, Hist, Birds, Philately, Jogging. *Address:* Skanegatan 15, S-571 40 Nassjo, Sweden.

TARRO Giulio Filippo Giacomo, b. 9 July 1938, Messina, Italy. div Chief of Virology. *Education:* MD, Naples Univ, 1962; State Bd Med Dipl, 1963; Nervous Diseases Dipl, Naples Univ, 1968; PhD, Virology, Rome Univ, 1971; Major, Navy, Leghorn, 1982-84. *Appointments:* Rsch Fellow, Rsch Chief, Nat Rsch Coun of Italy, 1966-76; Sr Scientist, Nat Cancer Inst, Frederick, MD, USA, 1973; Div Chief of Virology, Cotugno Hosp, Naples, 1975-. *Publications:* Oncological Virology, 1979; Aids Seen for Pictures, Mapograph, 1991; Inventor: Tumour Marker TAF Test, USA Patent, 1983; Tumour Associated Antigen TLP, European Patent, 1988; Discoverer RSV virus in Infant Deaths in Naples, 1979. *Memberships:* Pres De Beaumont Fndn For Cancer Rsch, 1978-; Pres, Italian Soc of Immuno-oncology, 1990-92. *Honours:* Recipient of International Prize of National Academy of Lindei, 1969; Golden Microscope Award, 1973; Gold Medal of Culture, 1975; Prime Minister Award, 1985; Decorated Knight of Malta, 1978; Commendatore National Order of Merit, 1991; Honorary degrees: Catholic University of Albany, New York, United States of America, 1989; St Theodora Academy, New York, 1991; Senate Mbr, Constantinian University, Providence, Rhode Island, USA, 1990. *Hobbies:* Soccer, Swimming, Good Food and Wines, Art Hist, Achievement of Science and Rsch for the Benefit of People, Abolition of Vivisection, Liberty of Vaccinations. *Address:* Via Posillipo 286, 80123 Naples, Italy. 52.

TATA Sam Bejan, b. 30 Sept 1911, Shanghai, China. Photographer. div. 1 d. *Education:* Univ of Hong Kong, 1931-32; Hon.LLD, Concordia Univ, Montreal, Can, 1982. *Appointment:* Freelance Photo-Jrnlst, Montreal, Can, 1956. *Contributions to:* Montrealer, Week-end

Mag, Star Wkly, Perspectives and Time Can; Montreal, 76 photos, text by Frank Lowe, 1963; A Certain Identity, 50 Portraits, 1983; Shanghai 1949, The End of an Era, 62 photos and text by Ian McLachlan, 1989. *Memberships:* Royal Photographic Soc, Bath; Royal Can Acad of Arts. *Honours:* Gold Plaque, Bombay, 1948; Silver Medal, Bombay, 1948; Prix Speciale du Jury, Fribourg, 1981; Life Time Achievement Award, The Canadian Association of Photographers and Illustrators in Communication, Toronto, 1990. *Hobbies:* Reading, Music. *Address:* 4361 Beaconsfield Avenue, Montreal, Quebec, Canada H4A 2H5. 37, 142.

TATE Dennis Randall, b. 26 Mar 1954, Hazard, KY, USA. Pastor. m. Patricia, 14 June 1975, 2 s. *Education:* BS, Cumberland Coll, Williamsburg, KY, 1976; Boyce Bible Schl, Columbus, OH, 1978; Ashland Theological Sem, OH, 1982; Eastern KY Univ, Richmond, 1985; Southern Sem, Louisville, KY, 1987. *Appointments:* Pastor: Cedar Hill Bapt Ch, Baxter, TN, 1976-77; Marion Bapt Ch, Marion, OH, 1977-80; Hanley Rd Bapt Ch, Mansfield, OH, 1980-83; Providence Bapt Ch, Winston, KY, 1983-88; First Bapt Ch, New Paris, OH, 1988-. *Publication:* Discipleship Is . . in Baptist Adult Discipleship Training Magazine. *Memberships:* Evangelism Dir, Estill Co Ministerial Assn, 1983-88, Sec 1985; Boone's Creek Bapt Assn, Evangelism Dir 1984-85; Chair, Sub-Comm on Ch Growth and Dev, 1984-85; Chmn, Fin Comm, 1987-88. *Hobbies:* Golf, Fishing. *Address:* 6751 St, Route 320, New Paris, OH 45347, USA.

TATE Donald McLean, b. 3 Sept 1943, Portage LaPrairie, Manitoba, Canada. Econ Geographer. m. Sharron Margaret Edey, 27 June 1970, 2 s. *Education:* BA, Univ of Toronto, 1965; MA, Univ of Western Ont, 1968; PhD, Univ of Ottawa, 1984. *Appointments:* Rsch Asst 1969-71, Econ 1971- 81, Sr Econ 1981-90, Environment Can; Hd, Water Resource Econs, Environment Can, 1990-. *Publications:* Over 80 articles, scientific papers and monographs on Can Water Mgmt. *Memberships:* Can Water Resource Assn; Assoc Ed, Can Water Resource Jrnl; Int Water Resource Assn; Assoc Ed, Water Int, 1985-90. *Hobbies:* Model Railroading, Jazz Music, Reading. *Address:* 74 Penfield Drive, Kanata, Ontario, Canada K2K 1M1. 142.

TATE Samantha Elizabeth, b. 30 Dec 1968, Derby, England. Self- employed Painter, Photographic Artist. *Appointments:* Worked for Wildsmith-Taile, 1986; Full Ptnr, Wildsmith-Taile, 1989. *Hobbies:* The Arts, Countryside, Walking, Animal Welfare. *Address:* St George's House, Bridge Street, Belper, Derbyshire DE5 1AZ, England.

TATSUMI Takayuki, b. 15 May 1955, Tokyo, Japan. Prof of Engl; Lit Critic. m. Mari Kotani, 4 Oct 1955. *Education:* BA Engl 1978, MA Engl 1980, Sophia Univ, Tokyo; PhD Engl, Cornell Univ, New York, USA, 1987. *Appointments:* Asst 1982-84, Lectr 1985-88, Assoc Prof 1989, Keioll, Tokyo; Pt-time Lectr, Univ of Tokyo and Tokyo Met Univ, 1988-. *Publications:* Cyberpunk America, 1988; Co-author, Young America in Literature -- Poe, Hawthorne and Melville, 1989. *Memberships:* MLA; American Lit Soc of Japan; Engl Lit Soc of Japan; Japan PEN Club. *Honours:* Prize for New Talent by English Literary Society, Japan, 1984; American Studies Book Prize by Japan-United States Friendship Commission for Cyberpunk America, 1989. *Hobbies:* Music, Science Fiction. *Address:* 9-11 Tanjogaoka, Hiratsuka 254, Japan. 52.

TATTERSALL John Hartley, b. 5 Apr 1952, Colwyn Bay, England. Chartered Acct. m. Madeleine Virginia Coles, 8 Sept 1984, 2 s, 1 d. *Education:* Shrewsbury Schl, 1965-69; MA, Christ's Coll, Univ of Cambridge, 1973; Univ of Besancon, France, 1975. *Appointments:* Kleinwort, Benson Ltd, 1973-75; Coopers & Lybrand Deloitte (formerly Coopers & Lybrand), 1975-, Ptnr, 1985-. *Publications:* Towards a Welfare World, Co-author, 1973; The Investment Business-Compliance with the Rules, 1990. *Memberships:* Fellow, Inst of Chartered Accts in England and Wales, 1989, Assoc, 1978-; Freenman, Worshipful Co of Horners, 1980; Churchwarden, St Jude's Ch, London SW5, 1984-; Dir, London City Ballet Trust Ltd, 1987-. *Hobbies:* Walking, Opera, Ballet. *Address:* 3 St Ann's Villas, Holland Pk, London W11 4RU, England. 53.

TATZ Golda, b. 1 May 1959, Vilnius, Lithuania. Pianist. m. Shmuel Tatz, 29 Mar 1981. *Education:* BMus, MMus, Tel Aviv Univ, Rubin Acad, Israel, 1977-83; Postgrad Dip, Juilliard Schl, NY, USA, 1984-86; Doctor of Musical Arts, Manhattan Schl of Music, NY, 1986-. *Appointments:* Piano Fac, Elaine Kaufman Cultural Center in NYC, 1986; Assoc Piano Fac, Manhattan Schl of Music, NYC, 1990. *Honours:* Winner of Claermont Competition, Israel, 1982, 83; Young Keyboard Artists International Piano Competition, Michigan, USA, 1986; American Music Scholarship Association International Piano Competition, Cincinnati, Ohio, 1987; Frina Averbuch International Piano Competition, New York, 1989. *Hobbies:* Reading, Computers, Electronics, Movies. *Address:* 23 West 73 Street, Apt 701, New York, NY 10023, USA.

TAYAR Rene Benedict, b. 3 Oct 1945, Malta. Cons Radiologist. m. Margaret Rose Tortell, 25 Jan 1971, 1 s. *Education:* St Aloysius Coll, Malta; MD, Royal Univ of Malta, 1969; FRCR London, 1980. *Appointments:* Registrar 1974-77, Sr Registrar in Radiology 1977-81, Bristol Royal Infirmary; Cons Radiologist, Merton and Sutton H A, 1981; Hon Sr Lectr, St George's Hosp Med Schl, 1988; Cons Radiologist, Parkside Hosp, Wimbledon. *Publications:* Xeroradiography, 1977; Transmission Electron Microscopy of Pertcutaneous Fine Needle Aspiration from Lung Thorax, 1987; Double Contrast C T Arthrography of the Shoulder, 1989; Video on Location: What GP's expect from their Radiology Department, 1990. *Memberships:* Fellow, Royal Coll of Radiologists, London; Bristol Radiology Club; Guildford Bone Tumour Registry; Fndr Mbr, Sir Harry Secombe C T Scanner Appeal completed 1985; Fndr Mbr Sir Harry Secombe M R Appeal. Appeal launched in May 1991. *Hobbies:* Tennis, Lit, Jazz Music, Gardening. *Address:* Elmstead, 45 Epsom Lane South, Tadworth, Surrey KT20 5TA, England.

TAYLOR Annita Saturnia, b. 21 Sept 1925, Mon Falcone, Italy. Co Dir. m. Alfred Oakley Taylor, 21 Oct 1946, 1 d. *Education:* Auviamento Proffessionale, Tecnico di Mon Falcone, Italy. *Appointments:* Abba D G Co Ltd, Mng Dir, 1978-90; Rosalia Mgmt Servs Co Ltd, Dir, 1988-90; Liglets Co Ltd, Dir, 1982-. *Memberships:* Guards Polo Club; Jockey Racehorse Owners Assn. *Hobbies:* Racing, Polo, Shooting, Pols. *Address:* Wadley Manor, Faringdon, Oxon, England.

TAYLOR Dennis Lee Sr, b. 21 Sept 1946, Weston, WV, USA. Licensed Profl Cnslr, Ordained Min. 1 s. *Education:* BA, Fairmont State Coll, WV, 1968; MDiv, Louisville Presby Theological Sem, KY, 1972; MA, Counselling, Univ AL Birmingham, 1985. *Appointments:* Parish Ministries, 1972-81; Mental Hlth Therapist, Satellite Off Coord, AL, 1981-83; Cnslr to Students, Univ AL Birmingham, 1986-89; Lic Profl Cnslr, 1988-. *Memberships:* American Assn for Counseling and Dev; AL Assn for Counseling and Dev; AL Assn for Psuchotherapists; Chaired, Student Affairs AIDS Task Force for Educ and Prevention, 1988-89, Univ AL at Birmingham; Chi Sigma Iota, Zeta Chapt. *Honour:* Honorary Member, Golden Key National Honor Society, University of Alabama at Birmingham Chapter. *Hobbies:* Running, Photography. *Address:* 1100 East Park Drive, Suite 224, Birmingham, AL 35235, USA. 1, 7.

TAYLOR Gladys Maime, b. 25 June 1917, Swan River, Manitoba, Canada. Author, Ed, Columnist, Publr. m. Lorne E Taylor, 27 Aug 1940, 3 s, 1 s dec, 1 d. *Education:* Bowsman HS; Swan River HS; Winnipeg Normal Schl. *Appointments:* Tchr, 1936-40; Can Women's Army Corp, 1943-45; Freelance Writer, 1950-; Ed, Book Page,

Sherbrooke Daily Record, 1955-65; TV Show Host, CHLT, Sherbrooke, 1958; Ed, Engl Sect, Thetford Mines Le Canadian, 1958-62; Ed, Can Author and Bookman, 1963-67; Columnist, Toronto Telegram, 1963-67; Past Columnist, United Ch Observer; Owner and Publr, Rocky View Five Village Wkly, Carstairs Courier, Wheel and Deal, 1975-; First and only woman to run in Canada's first Senate Election, Alberta, 1989 -- ran as Independent; Speaker to grps on writing, newspaper publng. *Publications:* Pine Roots, novel, 1955; The King Tree, novel, 1958; Alone in the Australian Outback, 1984; Alone in the Boardroom, 1987. *Memberships:* Nat Sec, Can Authors Assn, 1958- 62; Ed Advsry Bd, Quill and Quire, 1965-66; Jrnlsm Bd, Southern Alta Inst of Technology, 1973-76. *Honours:* Ryerson All-Can Fiction Award, 1955, 58; Calgary Businesswoman of the Year, 1983. *Hobby:* Travelling. *Address:* Box 40, Irricana, Alberta, Canada TOM 1BO. 142.

TAYLOR Glenn Donald Jr, b. 21 Aug 1948, Farmville, VA, USA. Mgmt Cons. m. Sally Joan Steele, 20 Mar 1971, 2 s. *Education:* BIE, GA Inst Technology, Atlanta, 1970; Cert Mgmt Cons. *Appointments:* Systems Analyst, Fulton Nat Bank, Atlanta, 1969-70; Indl Engr, Litton Ind, Florence, KY, 1970-72; Pres GlennCo Servs Inc, Ft Lauderdale, FL, 1972-; Bd Dirs, Glenn Properties Inc, Ft Lauderdale, 1976-; Bd Dirs, United Way, Broward Co, 1978-; Broward Employment and Trng Admin, 1982- . *Memberships:* Nat Assn Corp Dirs, Bd Dirs 1982-84; Inst Mgmt Cons, Bd Dirs, 1979-84; Nat Soc Profl Engrs; Rotary; Lauderdale Yacht Club; Ft Lauderdale Country Club; Meth Ch. *Hobbies:* Tennis, Golf, Skiing, Sailing, Reading. *Address:* GlennCo Services Inc, 509 N E 3rd Avenue, Fort Lauderdale, FL 33301, USA. 7, 117, 132, 139, 155.

TAYLOR John Rowland, b. 22 Feb 1929, London, England. Clerk in Holy Orders. m. Rosemary Weight, 13 Sept 1953, 1 s, 1 d. *Education:* Canton HS, Cardiff, 1940-44; Cardiff Tech Coll, 1944-47; St Michaels Theological Coll, Landaff; GCE 5 O Levels 1954; Gen Ordination Exam, 1958. *Appointments:* Asst Curate, Wales, 1958-61; Chap, The Missions to Seamen, 1961-73, Archdeacon of Diocese, 1961-73, Vicar Gen of Diocese, 1965- 73, Canon Emeritus of Diocese 1967-73, Dar-es-Salaam; Vicar of Christ Ch 1973- 81, Hon Chap, Brit Embassies, Fndr and Dir, Marriage Guidance Coun, 1974-81, Fndr and Dir, Samaritans of Thailand; Hon Chap, the Missions to Seamen 1978- 81, Bangkok; Chap, St Mary's Ch, Rotterdam, 1982-88; Sr Chap, Missions to Seamen, Rotterdam, The Netherlands; Gen Sec, The Missions to Seamen for the Netherlands; Vicar, St Margaret's, Warnham, 1988-. *Honour:* Officer of The British Empire for Services to Church and Community in Dar-es-Salaam, Tanzania, 1973. *Hobbies:* Philately, Golf. *Address:* The Vicarage, Warnham, Horsham, West Sussex RH12 3QW, England.

TAYLOR Kenneth MacDonald, b. 20 Oct 1947, Glasgow, Scotland. Prof of Cardiac Surg, Chief of Cardiac Surg. m. Christine Elizabeth Buchanan, 14 May 1971, 1 s, 1 d. *Education:* Univ of Glasgow, 1964-70; MB ChB 1970; FRCS Glasgow, 1974; MD, 1979; FRCS England, 1983. *Appointments:* Hall Fellow in Cardiac Surg 1971-73, Lectr in Cardiac Surg 1974-79, Sr Lectr in Cardiac Surg (Royal Infirmary Glasgow) 1980-83, Prof of Cardiac Surg, 1983-, Univ of Glasgow; Brit Heart Fndn Prof of Cardiac Surg, Univ of London; Chief of Cardiac Surg, Hammersmith Hosp, London. *Publications:* Handbook of Intensive Care, 1980; Cardiopulmonary Bypass, 1986; Pricniples of Surgical Research, 1990; Ed-in-Chief, International Journal Perfusion, 1986-. *Memberships:* Pres, Soc of Perfusionists, UK; Dir, UK Heart Valve Registry; Brit Cardiac Soc; Soc of Cardiothoracic Surgs; European Assn for Cardiothoracic Surgs; Soc of Thoracic Surgs of America; American Assn of Cardiothoric Surg; Bd Mbr, Annals of Thoracic Surg, USA. *Honours:* Gardner Medal, University of Glasgow, 1968; Cullen Medal, University of Glasgow, 1969; Patel Prize, Surgical Research Society, 1974; Watson Prize, Royal College of Surgeons, Glasgow, 1978; Fletcher Prize, Royal

College of Surgeons, Glasgow, 1980. *Hobbies:* Family, Ch, Music. *Address:* 129 Argyle Road, Ealing, London W13 ODB, England. 1, 52.

TAYLOR Kenneth, b. 26 Jan 1941, Gt Harwood, Lancashire, England. Expert Witness, Cons Engr, Magistrate. m. Jean Staff, 8 June 1962, 1 s, 1 d. *Education:* Accrington Tech Schl, 1952-56; ONC Bldg, Blackburn Coll, 1964; HNC Bldg, ONC Engl, Burnley Coll, 1968; IHVE Final, Burnley Coll, 1970. *Appointments:* Apprentice Plumber, 1956-62; Design Engr, Co Borough Burnley. 1963-71; Cons Engr, Ptnr, 1971-85; Chief Engr, Oldham MUC, 1985-88; Cons Engr, Mng Dir, 1988-. *Publications:* Co-author, Plant Engineers Reference Book; many articles in profl jrnls on legal aspects of Construction and Engrng. *Memberships:* C.Eng; FCIBSE, Comm Mbr; FI Plant E; FI Hosp E, FSE; FIOP; MASHRAE; FBIM; ACIArb; MCodsE. *Hobbies:* JP appointed to Family and Juvenile Panels and Selected as Chmn, Plays sev instruments. *Address:* 40 Wilkie Avenue, Glen View, Burnley, Lancashire BB11 3QE, England.

TAYLOR Linda Marianne, b. 13 Mar 1948, Woodruff, SC, USA. Admnstr. Coll and Pvte Cons. *Education:* BA Engl, magna cum laude, Limestone Coll, 1969; MA Engl, Clemson Univ, 1975; EdD Tech-Voc Educ, Clemson Univ, 1986. *Appointments:* Tchr, Woodruff, SC, 1970; Instr, Engl and Drama, N Greenville Coll, 1972-74; Instr, Engl and Speech, Tri-Co Tech Coll, 1974-88; Chair, Engl Dept, Tri-Co Tech Coll, 1988-; Educl Cons. *Publication:* Implementing Writing Across the Curriculum, 1985. *Memberships:* Phi Delta Kappa; Delta Kappa Gamma; SC Speech Communication Assn, VP Coll 1989-90; SC Tech Educ Assn; Nat Coun of Instructional Admnstrs; Southeastern Conf on Engl in Two-Yr Colls; Phi Theta Kappa. *Honours:* Presidential Medallion for Instructional Excellence, 1986; Fulbright Fellowship, 1986; Educator of the Year, 1986; Master Teacher, Adviser, 1987; Kentucky Colonel, 1986; Outstanding Tri-County Technical Woman, chosen by Anderson County Womans Club, 1989. *Hobbies:* Reading, Acting, Travelling. *Address:* 13 Oak Drive, Sandy Springs, SC 29677, USA. 7, 15.

TAYLOR Martin John, b. 18 Feb 1952, Leicester, England. Prof of Pure Maths. m. 1 Dec 1973, 2 s, 2 d. *Education:* MA, Pembroke Coll, Oxford, 1973; PhD, King's Coll, London, 1976. *Appointments:* Rsch Asst, King's Coll, London, 1976-77; Jr Lectr, Oxford, 1977-78; Lectr, QMC London, 1978-81; Fellow, Trinity Coll, Cambridge, 1981-85; Chair in Pure Maths, UMIST. 1986-. *Publications:* Rings of Integers in Elliptic Functions: Algebraic Number Theory; L-functions in Arithmetic. *Membership:* London Math Soc. *Honours:* Derbyshire Prize, 1971; Pembroke College Prize, 1973; Junior LMS Whitehead Prize, 1982; Adams Prize, 1983; Royal Society Leverhulme Senior Research Fellowship, 1991-92. *Hobbies:* Hill Walking, Fishing, French Lit. *Address:* Department of Mathematics, UMIST, P O Box 88, Manchester M60 1QD, England.

TAYLOR Merrick Wentworth, b. 7 June 1938, Birmingham, England. Chief Exec Off, Motor Panels Div of CH Indls PLC. m. Gisela Elli Kirsch, 20 Apr 1960, 2 d. *Education:* Birmingham Tech Coll, ONC, Mech.Eng. *Appointments:* Apprenticeship, Rover Co Ltd, 1954; Gen Mgr, Kieft Sports Car Co, 1957; Asst Works Mgr 1959, Works Dir 1961, Orton & Smith Ltd; Prod Mgr, Kenham Tools and Pressings Ltd, 1962; PA to Mng Dir 1966, Tech Dir 1968, Dpty Mgr 1972, Mng Dir 1973, Motor Panels (Coventry) Ltd; CEO, Motor Panels Div, 1989-; Directorships: CEO, Motor Panels Div of CH Indls PLC; Mng Dir, Motor Panels (Coventry) Ltd; Chmn, Motor Panels (Wigan) Ltd; Chmn, Motor Panels Inc USA; Chmn, Styling and Engrng Models Ltd; Dir, Park Sheet Metal Co Ltd; Chmn, MERGILA Ltd. *Publications:* Var articles on design. *Memberships:* Design Coun Advsry Comm, W Midlands; DTI W Midlands Indl Dev Bd; Dept Educ & Science Art Working Grp; Vis Comm to Royal Coll of Art; Brit Railways Bd Design Panel; Judging Panel,

RSA Design Bursaries Competition; SMMT Coun; Gov, Coventry Polytechnic; Fellowship of the Motor Ind; Coun Mbr, Ferrari Owners Club; Jaguar Drivers Club; Freeman City of London; Liveryman Worshipful Co of Coachmnakers and Coach Harness Makers. *Hobbies:* Design, Historic Motor Racing, Music, Travel. *Address:* Motor Panels (Coventry) Ltd, Holbrook Lane, Coventry CV6 4AW, England.

TAYLOR Pamela Jane, b. 23 Apr 1948, Blackpool, England. Med Practitioner. m. John Charles Gunn. *Education:* Merchant Taylors Girls Schl, Liverpool; Guy's and King's Coll Hosps, London; MB BS London; MRCP UK; FRCPsych. *Appointments:* Clin and Rsch postgrad trng posts in UK and USA, 1971-79; Sr Lectr, Inst of Psychiatry, London, 1980-89; Cons, Forensic Psychiatrist, Bethlem Royal and Maudsley Hosps, 1990-; Hd of Med Servs, Special Hosps Serv Auth, UK and Hon Sr Lectr IOP. *Publications:* Papers in acad jrnls on schizophrenia, violence and aspects of mental hlth law and forensic psychiatry servs. *Memberships:* American Psychiatric Assn; Royal Soc of Med, London. *Honour:* Gaskell Gold Medal in Psychiatry, 1976. *Hobbies:* 19th and 20th Century Lit and Painting, Opera. *Address:* Special Hospitals Service Authority, Charles House, 375 Kensington High Street, London W14 8QH, England.

TAYLOR Robert Murray Ross, b. 10 Dec 1932. Cons Surg. m. Margaret Cutland, 7 Jan 1959, 1 s, 3 d. *Education:* Univ of Glasgow, 1950-56; DRCOG, 1960; FRCS Edinburgh, 1964; FRCS England, 1965; ChM, Glasgow, 1968. *Appointments:* Registrar in Surg, Royal Victoria Infirmary, Newcastle- upon-Tyne, 1962-64; Rsch Assoc, Univ of Newcastle-upon-Tyne, 1964-65; Sr Registrar in Surg 1965-70, Cons Surg 1970-, Royal Victoria Infirmary, Newcastle-upon-Tyne; Hon Lectr in Transplantation Surg, Univ of Newcastle- upon-Tyne. *Memberships:* Fndr Mbr and Past Pres, Brit Transplantation Soc; Fndr Mbr, The Transplantation Soc; Mbr and Current Pres, N of England Surg Soc; Surg Rsch Soc; Chmn, Transplant Sports Assoc of GB; Trustee, Great North Run; Trustee and Chmn, Transplant Patient's Trust of GB. *Honours:* The McKeown Medal, Royal College of Surgeons of Edinburgh, 1990; Invited Lecturer at 10th Convocation of Newcastle University, 1990. *Hobbies:* Golf, Jogging, Fund raising for kidney transplantation (sometimes combined w jogging). *Address:* Ward One Office, Royal Victoria Infirmary, Queen Victoria Road, Newcastle-upon-Tyne NE1 4LP, England.

TAYLOR Stanley Thomas, b. 26 Sept 1923. Chief Exec, Sec to the Bd. m. Valerie May, 12 Feb 1955, 1 s, 1 d. *Education:* Archbishop Tenisons GS. *Appointments:* War Serv RAFVR; Admnstr, Herts Hlth Auth, until 1979; Chief Exec and Sec, Children's Film and Television Foundation Ltd, 1980-. *Memberships:* Freeman City of London; Fndr Mbr, Worshipful Co Chartered Secs and Admnstrs; FHSM 1968; FCIS 1970; RAF Club. *Hobbies:* Golf, Reading (biographies), Walking. *Address:* Children's Film and Television Foundation Ltd, Goldcrest Elstree Studios, Borehamwood, Hertfordshire WD6 1JG, England.

TAYLOR William Bernard, b. 13 Dec 1930, London, England. Pub Sector Cons, Specialist Advsr. m. Rachel May Davies, 26 Apr 1956, 1 s, 2 d. *Education:* MA, Univ of Kent, 1969. *Appointments:* Dist Audit Serv, 1951-61; Dpty Treas 1961-67, Treas 1967-70, Llwchwr UDC; Asst Educ Off, Manchester Corp, 1970-72; Asst Co Treas 1972-74, Dpty Co Treas 1974-80, Co Treas 1980-86, Kent; Specialist Advsr to Invesco MIM, Sedgwick James (Nat) Ltd, Lombard North Ctrl PLC. *Publications:* Terotechnology and the Pursuit of Life Cycle Costs, 1980; num articles for learned mags. *Memberships:* Chartered Inst of Pub Fin and Acctcy; RSA; Medway Hlth Auth; Chmn, Fin Comm, Kent Inst of Art-Design, 1989; Chmn, Fin Comm, Lloyds Underwriter, 1988. *Hobbies:* Public Speaking, Tennis, Cricket, Rugby, Golf. *Address:* Selby Shaw, Heath Road, Boughton Monchelsea, Maidstone, Kent, England. 1.

TAYLOR William Halstead, b. 26 Apr 1924, Wardle, Lancashire, England. Physn in Metabolic Med. m. June Helen Thorniley, 7 Sept 1950, 1 s, 3 d. *Education:* Christ Church, Univ of Oxford, 1942-47, MA, 1949; Radcliffe Infirmary, Univ of Oxford, 1944-48; BM BCh, 1948. *Appointments:* House Physn, Post-Grad Med Schl, Hammersmith Hosp and Radcliffe Infirmary, Oxford, 1948-49; Lectr, Sr Lectr, Clin Biochem, Univ of Oxford, 1949-59; Fellow and Tutor in Natural Science, St Peter's Coll, Univ of Oxford, 1957-59; Hd, Dept of Clin Pathology, United Liverpool Hosps and Liverpool Hlth Auth, 1959-89; Dir, Studies in Chem Pathology, Univ of Liverpool, 1962-74; Dir, Mersey Regl Metabolic Unit, 1965-89; Pt-time Asst in Metabolic Med, Halton Gen Hosp, Runcorn, 1989-. *Publication:* Fluid Therapy and Disorders of Electrolyte Balance, 1964, 2nd Eds 1970, 74, Italian Ed 1971, Spanish Eds 1967, 72. *Memberships:* Royal Coll of Physns, Fellow; Assn of Clin Biochems, Chmn NW Reg 1974-77; Assn Clin Pathologists; Med Rsch Soc; Ed Bd, Clinical Science 1962-67; BMA. *Honours:* Christopher Welch Scholar, University of Oxford, 1946; Emeritus Consultant, Liverpool Health Authority, 1989-. *Hobbies:* Music, Fly-fishing, Walking, Philately. *Address:* 16 Salisbury Road, Cressington Park, Liverpool L19 OPJ, England. 52.

TCHERNIAEV Gerard (Guy) Alexandrovitch, b. 12 July 1932, Istambul, Turkey. Ichthyologist, Embryologist, Ecophysiologist. m. Svetlana, 28 Mar 1980, 1 s. *Education:* Lomonossov Moscow Univ, Chair of Ichthyology, Fac of Biology, 1953-58; Cand Sc Biology, 1966; Dr Sc Biology, 1990. *Appointments:* Techn on Baikal Limnological St, 1958; Jr Rsch of Limnolodg Inst Baikal, 1966; Sr Rschr, Severtsov Inst of Animal Evolutionary Morphology and Ecology, 1971-91. *Publications:* The Development of the Omul: The Baikal Whitefish, monograph; The Breeding of the Omul-Baikal Whitefish, 1982. *Memberships:* Dpty Chmn, Salmon and Coregonid Subcommn of Ichthyological Commn of Min of Fishes; Expert, Baikal Kommission, Nat Comm of Nature Conservation, Russia. *Honours:* Gold Medal for the UNESCO Program Man and Biosphere, 1980 at National Exhibition of USSR Economic Achievements; Bronze Medal 1983 at the National Exhibition of USSR Economic Achievement for Development of Biotechnology for Breeding Whitefishes. *Hobbies:* Aquariumist, Frogmen, Horticulture. *Address:* Severtsov Institute of Animal Evolutionary Morphology and Ecology of Academy of Sciences of USSR, Prosp. Leninsky 33, Moscow 117071, Russia.

TCHHELEBIEVA Diana Guerguieva, b. 4 June 1952, Bourgas, Bulgaria. Actress. m. Dimitar Ganev, 13 May 1976, 1 s. *Education:* Acad of Theatre, Sofia, 1972-76; Theatre Sofia, 1979-90; Little City Theatre Off the Channel, Sofia, 1990. *Appointments:* TV Plays: Nymph; Blue and White Frost, 1983; Red and Brown, 1984; Films: The Peasant with the Bicycle, 1974; Advantage, 1977; King's Play, 1982; Stage Plays: Romeo and Juliet, 1975; Our City, 1975; My Fair Lady, 1976; Maneatress, 1979; The Butterflies Are Free, 1980; Birthday Party, 1981; Five Evenings, 1985; Oedipus Game, 1987; Ring, 1990; Igvana's Night, 1991. *Membership:* ITI. *Hobbies:* Reading, Fine Art. *Address:* Nadezda 1 Bl 139G AP72, Sofia 1220, Bulgaria.

TE Wei, b. 22 Aug 1915, Guang Dong, China. Pres, China Animation Film assn. m. Liao Rui Qun, 15 Aug 1945, 2 s, 1 d. *Appointments:* Profl Caricaturist, 1935037;North East Film Studio, 1949-50; Dir, Animation Dir, Shanghai Animation Film Studio, 1957-83. *Memberships:* China Artist Assn; Shanghai Artist Assn; Chinese Film Experts Assn; China Animation Film Assn; ASIFA. *Honours include:* Silver Prize of Locarno Intl Festival; 1st Prize of Zagreb Intl Animation Festival; The Best Short Film Prize of Montreal Intl Film Festival; Old Artist Prize, The First China Film Festival. *Hobbies:* Art; Music; Literature; Sports. *Address:* Shanghai Animation Film Studio, 618 Wan Hang Du Road, China.

TEASDALE Anthony Laurence, b. 4 June 1957, Old Windsor, England. Pol Cons on European Community Affairs. *Education:* Balliol Coll, Oxford, 1975-78; Nuffield Coll, Oxford, 1978-81; BA (Hons) First Class PPE; M.Phil, Pols, Oxford Univ. *Appointments:* Rsch Asst to Rt Hon Nigel Lawson, MP, 1978-79; Lectr in Pols, Corpus Christi and Magdalen Colls, Oxford, 1980-82; Policy Advsr, European Dem Grp in European Parl, 1982-86; Asst to Dir Gen (ECOFIN), EC Coun of Mins, 1986-88; Special Advsr to Rt Hon Sir Geoffrey Howe, QC, MP, as For Sec and Dpty PM, 1988-90. *Publications:* Var books and pamphlets. *Memberships:* Japan Soc; Carlton Club, 10D. *Hobbies:* Music, Reading, Travel. *Address:* 14 Buckingham Palace Road, London SW1, England.

TEED Eric Lawrence, b. 19 May 1926, Canada. Lawyer. m. Lois Anita Smith, 22 Aug 1949, 5 s. *Education:* BSc 1947, BCL 1949, BA 1971, Univ NB. *Appointments:* Teed & Teed, 1949-; Mayor of Saint John, 1960-64; Mbr, NB Legislative Assembly, 1970-74. *Publications:* Canada First City; Handbook for Commissioners of Oaths; Num articles in Canadian Bar Review; Ed, Univ NB Law Jrnl; Past Ed, Canadian Bar Review. *Memberships:* Can Citizenship Fedn, Nat Pres; Civil Liberties Assn, Saint John, Pres; Multicultural, Pres; Cancer Soc, Saint John, Pres; Human Rights Assn, Pres; NB Br UNA of Can, Pres; St Georges Soc, Pres. *Honours:* Canadian Forces Decoration, 1960; Queen's Jubilee Medal, 1977; Officer, Order of Canada, 1987; Knight of Dannebrog, 1990. *Hobbies:* Orgs, Camping, Fishing. *Address:* 1019 Seawood Lane, Saint John, New Brunswick Canada E2M 3G8. 142.

TELLING Arthur Edward, b. 22 Apr 1920, Newport, Gwent, Wales. Author. m. Diana Almond, 21 Mar 1959. *Education:* Jesus Coll, Oxford, 1938-41; MA; Barrister. *Appointments:* Rsch Asst, later Asst Sec, Bldg Inds Nat Coun, 1941-48; Asst Sec and Legal Advsr, Nat Fedn of Property Owners, 1949-52; Practising Barrister, 1953-91; Lectr in Law, Trent Polytechnic, Nottingham, 1964-82. *Publications:* Planning Applications Appeals and Inquiries (w Frank Layfield), 1953; Planning Law and Procedure, 1st Ed 1963 to 8th Ed 1990; Water Authorities, 1974. *Contributions to:* Halsbury's Laws of England, 3rd and 4th Eds. *Memberships:* United Reformed Ch; Rotary Club of Nottingham; UK Lawyers Ecology Assn; Pres, Hardwicke (Bar Debating) Soc, 1949-50; Chmn, N Dist London Congregational Union, 1958-60; Treas, Nottinghamshire Congregational Union, 1966-68; Rotary Fndn Off, Rotary Dist 122, 1974-76. *Hobbies:* Study of Ecology, Reading, Watching TV. *Address:* 43 Harrow Road, West Bridgford, Nottingham NG2 7DW, England.

TEMPLE-RICHARDS Susan Mary, b. 8 June 1932, Lewes, Sussex, England. Ed Asst (Pt-time) Geographical Journal. m. Peter Henry John Temple- Richards, 6 June 1964. *Education:* Cheltenham Ladies Coll, 1945-49; Badminton Schl, Bristol, 1949-51; London Univ, 1952-55; BA (Hons). *Appointments:* Min of Def, 1956-58, 1974-86; Duke of Edinburgh's Award, 1960-66; Self-employed Charitable Organiser, Fundraiser, 1966-74. *Publications:* Reviews: Painting, The Times; Books, Geographical Jrnl. *Memberships:* Brit Expedition Sec, Brit-Soviet Pamirs Expedition, 1962; Chmn, Newbury & Dist Duke of Edinburgh's Award Comm, 1977-80; Trust Mbr, Arts Educl Schls, 1976-; Coun Mbr, Brit Epilepsy Assn; Mbr, Ct of Assts, Cripplegate Ward Club, London EC2, 1989-. *Honours:* Fellow, Royal Geographical Society, 1963; Freeman, City of London, 1976. *Hobbies:* Gardening, Travelling, Opera. *Address:* 13 Colmstock Road, Battersea, London SW11 6LZ, England.

TENNANT Howard Edward, b. 15 May 1941, Lethbridge, Alberta, Canada. Univ Pres and Prof of Mgmt. m. Sharon Lea Buckley, 7 Sept 1963, 1 s, 2 d. *Education:* BBA 1963, MBA 1964, PhD 1970, P.Mgr 1977, Grade VI Piano, Royal Conservatory of Music, Univ of Toronto, Canada. *Appointments:* Asst Prof 1966-69, Assoc Prof 1969-72, Prof 1972, Univ Sask; Vis Schlr,

Univ of Washington, 1977-87: Assoc Dean, Acting Dean, Coll of Grad Studies and Rsch, Assoc VP and Dean of Coll of Grad Studies and Rsch, Univ Sask; Pres and V-Chancellor, Univ of Lethbridge, 1987-. *Memberships:* American Mktng Assn; Rotary Int; Assn of Univ and Colls of Can, Dir; Univs Coordinating Coun of Alta, Chmn; Admnstv Sciences Assn of Can; Alta Rsch Coun, Dir; Can Plains Rsch Ctr, Dir; Commonwealth Univ Pres's Assn; Beta Gamma Sigma. *Honours:* First Place, Calysmen Oratorial Contest, 1958; Delivered Hoechst Lecture, 1984; Delivered Evelyn Edwards Lecture, 1985; Adopted by Blood Indian Band and given name Young Eagle, 1987; Kainai Chief, Blood Indians of Can, 1991. *Hobbies:* Woodwork, Fishing, Gardening. *Address:* 61 Ridgewood Crescent West, Lethbridge, Alberta, Canada T1K 6C3. 142.

TEODOROWICZ-TODOROWSKI Tadeusz Ludwik, b. 25 June 1907, Lvov, Austria-Hungary. Archt, Town Planner, Educator, Artist. m. Anna Madurowicz, 26 Sept 1944, dec. *Education:* Engr Archt Degree, Lvov Tech Univ, 1931; Asst Lectr, 1931. *Appointments:* Staff, Lvov Tech Univ, 1931-45; Silesian Tech Univ, Gliwice, 1945-77; Organiser, Hd, Housing Estates Dept and Spatial Planning Team, 1945-77; Extraordinary Prof, 1950; Organiser, Hd, Arch Div, 1962-66; Co-organiser Arch Fac (exists since 1977); Ordinary Prof, 1970; Emeritus, 1977. *Creative Works:* Chs. in Lvov and Kolomyja (competition prizes), constrn stopped by War 1939; Six Villas, 1934-38; Poland's reconstrn and dev since WWII; Ch Design, Gdyniam competition prize, 1947; Gliwice: auditorium, 2 dept bldgs, tech hall, constrn lab, students picture theatre, 1949-73; Housing Estate Nowe Tychy, 1954-58; Soanowiec Dist Housing Estate, 1954-58. *Publications:* More than 30 papers in field of Arch and Town Planning; num reports, popular articles, reviews. *Memberships:* Assn Polish Archts; Soc Polish Town Planners; Polish Tchrs Assn; Chmn, Town Planning and Arch Commn, Pan Katowice Br, 1967-88; Int Acad of Sciences; Amnesty Int. *Honours:* Knight Polonia Restituta Order, 1957; Medal, Polish Architects Association, 1976; Creative Architect, 1980; Commander's Cross Polonia Restituta Order 1985; Medal of National Education Commission, 1985. *Hobbies:* Writing Poetry, Cycling, Cartoons, Applied Graphics, Motorcar Rally Racer, Aku-TA-TE-TO. *Address:* ul Karolinki 29, 44-121 Gliwice, Poland. 139, 162, 178.

TEODOSIO Roberto Aguon, b. 15 Nov 1955, Guam. Operations Mgr. div, 2 s, 2 d. *Education:* Los Angeles Harbor Community Coll, 1976; Calif State Univ, Bach of Sci, finance, 1979. *Appointments:* Intl Linen Supplt, 1979-85; The Guam Tribune, Reporter, 1985-87; Pacific Daily News, Asst City Editor, 1987-90; The Guam Tribune, Mgrng Editor, Operations Mgr, 1990-. *Memberships:* Soc of Profl Journalists. *Honours:* Guam Press Club, Best News Story; Best of Gannett, Gambling on Guam; Guam Press Club Gama Award; SPJ Profl Achievement Award. *Hobbies:* Martial Arts; Reading. *Address:* PO Box 930, Agana, Guam 96910.

TER-PETROSSIAN Levon, b. 9 Jan 1945, Aleppo, Syria. Pres, Parl of Repub of Armenia. m. Ludmila Pleskovskaya, 19 May 1970, 1 s. *Education:* Dept Oriental Studies, Erevan Univ, 1963-68; Doct Studies, Leningrad Oriental Inst, 1968-71; PhD in Phylology. *Appointments:* Rschr, Erevan Inst of Lit, 1972-78; Sr Rschr in Matenadaran, Inst of Ancient MSS, 1978-85. *Publications:* 6 books; more than 70 articles and book reviews on ancient hist of Near East. *Memberships:* Assn of Soviet Orientalists; Asia Soc, France. *Honours:* Honorary Doctor, University of La Verne, USA; Honorary Doctor, Mkhitarian Academy, Venice, Italy. *Hobbies:* Chess, Reading. *Address:* Supreme Council of Armenia, Baghramian Street 19, Armenia, Russia.

TERRINGTON Derek Humphrey, b. 25 Jan 1949, Cape Town, South Africa. Stockbroker. m. Jennifer Mary Jones, 15 July 1978, 1 d. *Education:* BA (Hons) Econs, 1972, MA Econs 1974, Univ of Cape Town.

Appointments: Grieveson Grant & Co, Assoc Ptnr, 1984; UBS Phillips & Drew, Exec Dir, 1991; Kleinwort Barsan Securities, Dir, 1991-. *Membership:* Assoc Mbr, Soc of Investment Analysts. *Hobbies:* Theatre, Music, Reading. *Address:* 16 St Winifred's Road, Teddington, Middlesex TW11 9JR, England.

TERRY Arthur Hubert, b. 17 Feb 1927, York, England. Univ Prof of Lit. m. 26 June 1955, 2 s, 1 d. *Education:* Trinity Hall, Cambridge Univ, 1944-47; BA 1947; MA 1950. *Appointments:* Lectr in Spanish, 1950- 63, Prof of Spanish 1963-72, Queen's Univ, Belfast; Prof of Lit, Univ of Essex, 1973-. *Publications:* La poesia de Joan Maragall, 1963; An Anthology of Spanish Poetry 1500-1700, 1965-68; Antonio Machado: Campos de Castilla, 1973; Selected Poems of Ausias March, 1976; Sobre poesia catalana contemporania, 1985. *Memberships:* Assn of Brit Hispanists; Int Catalan Studies Assn, Pres, 1982-88; Brit Comparative Lit Assn, Pres, 1986-. *Honours:* Bonay i carbo Prize of the Institute of Catalan Studies, 1966; Cross of St George, awarded by the Catalan Government, 1982. *Hobbies:* Local Hist, Playing the Piano. *Address:* 11 Braiswick, Colchester CO4 5AU, England.

TERRY William Hutchinson, b. 4 July 1951, New Orleans, USA. Marine Ins Underwriter. m. Victoria Rosich, 30 July 1984, 1 s, 2 d. *Education:* BA Polit Sci/ Psy, Tulane Univ, 1978. *Appointments:* Marine Off of Am Corp, 1978-79; Ina Marine & Aviation, 1979-82; VP, MY Brokers, 1972-88; Pres, Cygnus Ins Serv Ltd, 1989-; Ins Lectr, World Trade Club Nola; Dallas WTC; Tarranty Co JC. *Memberships:* Mariners Club, Dallas, Past Pres, 1979-82; Pres Round Table, 1991; N.O World Trade Ctr, 1989; Caribbean Shippers Assn, 1990. *Address:* 106 Park Place, Suite 301, Covington, LA 70433, USA.

TERVO Timo Martti Tapio, b. 9 Mar 1950, Helsinki, Finland. Chief Physn, Dept of Ophthalmology, Univ of Helsinki. m. Kaarina, 13 Aug 1977, 2 s. *Education:* B.Med, 1972; MD, 1975; PhD, 1977; Specialist Ophthalmology, 1983; Docent in Ophthalmology, 1986. *Appointments:* Asst, Dept Anatomy, Univ of Helsinki, 1972-79; Physn, Finnish Navy, 1979; Res, Dept Neurosurg 1980, Res, Dept Ophthalmology 1980-83, Asst Prof, Ophthalmology 1983-89, Chief Physn, Dept Ophthalmology 1989-, Univ of Helsinki. *Publications:* About 200 scientific publs on Ophthalmology, Anatomy and Naval Med. *Memberships:* Assn Rsch in Vision and Ophthalmology; Rsch in Vision and Ophthalmology; American Acad of Ophthalmology; Assn Finnish Mil Med. *Hobbies:* Singing, Music, Sailing, Cars, Boats, Cross country and Down hill Skiing. *Address:* Vanhavayla 19 B, 00830 Helsinki 83, Finland. 52.

TERZIAN Alicia, b. 1 July 1934, Cordoba, Argentina. Composer, Lectr, Conductor. 1 s, 1 d. *Education:* Dip, Nat Prof of Piano, Nat Conservatory of Music of Buenos Aires, 1954; Dip, Nat Prof of Composition, Nat Conservatory of Music, Buenos Aires, 1958; First Prize and Gold Medal, Nat Conservatory of Music, Buenos Aires, 1959. *Appointments:* Prof of Counterpoint, Orchestration, Hist and Esthetic of Music, Nat Conservatory of Music, 1960-91; Prof of Hist and Esthetic of Music, Nat Univ of La Plata, 1967--73; Prof of Hist of the Opera, Colon Theatre, 1967-91; Prof of Counterpoint, Municipal Conservatory of Music, 1975-891; Conductor, Chmbr Orchs in Italy; More than 2,500 lectures by Municipal and Nat Radios on XXth Century Music; TV broadcasts in Argentina; Official invitations by Govts of Holland, Denmark, Switzerland, France, Czechoslovakia, Spain, Armenia, UK, Italian-American Inst of Rome, Univ of Boulder, CO, USA, Fac of Music of Los Angeles, New Haven, Conservatory of San Francisco. *Creative Works:* Works commissioned by Gulbenkian Fndn of Lisbon, London Ice Festival, Friedrich Cerha at Colon Theatre, Biennial Festival of Zagreb, Aspekte Salzburg Festival, Group TMM Plus of France; Recordings and Cassettes. *Honours:* Prizes and Awards from Argentinian National Foundation for the

Arts; The Buenos Aires Municipal Prize for Orchl Music, 1964; The Gomidas International Prize, 1983. *Hobbies:* Cooking, Reading, Tennis, Swimming, Cinema, Theatre, Walking, Philately. *Address:* Santa Fe 3269 4B, 1425 Buenos Aires, Argentina.

TESU Ion-Constantin, b. 30 Oct 1957, Pipirig, Romania. Lectr, Electronic Engr. m. Anca Mihaela, 26 Apr 1979, 1 s. *Education:* MS Elec Engrng, Polytechnic Inst of Iasi, Poland, 1981. *Appointments:* Design Engr, IEA Aerafina Bucharest, 1981-83; Asst Prof 1983-91, Lectr 1991, Polytechnic Inst of Iasi. *Publications:* Optimal DC Spice Parameters Extraction for Bipolar Transistor Models, 1987; Spice Simulation of Thermistors and Thermistor Circuits, 1991. *Membership:* Romanian Soc of Fuzzy Systems. *Hobbies:* Classical Music, Tennis, Yoga, Computer Simulation of Electronic Circuits, Electron Device Modelling for CAD. *Address:* Str Prof Borcea NR5, Iasi 6600, Romania.

TETLIE Harold, b. 24 Aug 1926, Minnesota, USA. Parish Priest. *Education:* BA St Olaf Col, 1951; MBA, Univ of Denver, 1956; Doctoral Study, Cornell Univ, 1960-61; BSTheol, Luther Sem, 1965. *Appointments:* Military Ser, WW II, 1945-46; Tchr, Hg Sch, Montana, 1951-57; Instr, Bus Admin, Pacific Luth Univ, 1957-59; Parish Priest and Missionary Serving the Mexican People, 1965-. *Publications:* Brief Catechism, English and Spanish; Brief Mass, English and Spanish; Translation of Grieg's God's Son has Made me Free, to Spanish. *Memberships include:* Min Alliance; IPA; JACS Coor; Life, NEA; Thous and Trials; Family Motar Chach Assn; Dodge Chassis Chap; Am Legion Vets of Foreign Wars. *Honours:* Delta Pi Epsilon; Grad, cum laude, St Olaf Col, 1951; Pi Gamma Mu, 1956; WW II Victory Medal, Asiatic; Pacific Campaign Medal; Good Conduct Medal; Philippine Independence Medal; Ser to Mankind Awd. *Hobbies:* Computers; Organ; Photography; Archaeology; Auto mechanics; Gardening (roses); Anthropology; The Bible. *Address:* Box 1607, Alice, TX 78333, USA. 125, 155.

THAYER Carlyle Alan, b. 5 Nov 1945, USA. Associate Professor. m. Zubeida Bibi Abdulla, 11 July 1969. *Education:* MA S.East Asian Studies, Yale Univ, 1967, Polit Sci, Brown Univ; PhD, Intl Relations, 1977. *Appointments:* Lectr, Bendigo Col Adv Educ, 1975-78; Lectr, Sr Lectr, Royal Military Col, Duntroon, 1979-85; Sr Lectr, Assoc Prof, Austr Def Force Acad, 1986-. *Publications:* War by Other Means: National Liberation and Revolution in Vietnam, 1989; The Soviet Union as an Asian-Pacific Power, 1987. *Memberships:* Am and Intl Polit Sci Assns; Australasian Polit Studies Assn; Austr Inst of Intl Affairs; Assn for Asian Studies; Austr Assn for Asian Studies; Nat Soccer League of Austr, Match Official; Austr Soccer Referees Fed Inc, Nat Sec, Treas. *Honours include:* Res Scholarship, Austr Nat Univ, 1971-74; Austr Res Coun Grant, 1991-93; US Nat Defence Foreign Lang Fellowships, Yale and Cornell Univs, 1969-71. *Hobbies:* Soccer refereeing. *Address:* 11 Ambara Place, Aranda, ACT 2614, Australia. 52, 162.

THAYER Pamela Patricia, b. 9 Sept 1925, London, England. *Education:* MA, Girton Col, Cambs, 1945-48; Social Sci Cert, Bedford Col, London, 1948-49; Child Care Cert, London Sch of Econ, 1949-50. *Appointments:* Children's Dept, Inspectorate Home Ofc, 1954-70; Asst Chief Inspector, Social Servs Inspectorate, DMSS, 1970-85. *Publications:* Report; Forms of Child Care, 1988. *Memberships:* VP, Pre-Sch Playgroups Assn; Chm, Advy Gp, High/Scope UK: Hon Mem, Coun of NSPCC: Girton Roll Com. *Honour:* Imperial Ser Order, 1986. *Hobbies:* Politics; Writing; Theatre; Music; Motoring. *Address:* Great Wood Cottage, Ibstone Common, Buckinghamshire HP14 3XU, England.bblank

THEIN Edmund, b. 19 Jan 1934, Ebern, Germany. m. Marianne Krieger, 2 Apr 1959, 2 s, 1 d. *Education:* Bachelor of Econ Sci, Wurzburg Univ, 1957. *Appointments:* Acad Asst, Inst of Econ, Wurzburg Univ,

1958; Asst Econ, Brown Boveri & Co Mannheim, 1960-63; Govt Official, German Min of Def, Koblenz Ofc, 1963-. *Hobbies:* Jogging; Travel. *Address:* Kurfurstenstr 93, 5400 Koblenz, Germany. 52.

THEVOZ Michel, b. 15 July 1936, Lausanne, Switzerland. Professor; Curator. m. Emilienne Farny, 13 Feb 1973, 1 d. *Education:* Univ de Lausanne, 1954-58; Ecole du Louvre, 1961-64. *Appointments:* Musee Cantonal des Beaux-Arts: Curator Lausanne, 1968-74; Centre Intl de la Tapisserie, Lausanne, 1970-75; Curator Collection de l'art brut from 1975-. *Publications:* Louis Soutter ou l'ecriture du Desir, 1974; Art Brut, 1976; Catalogue Raisonne de l'oeuvre de Louis Soutter, 1976; Le Langage de la Rupture, 1978; L'Academisme et ses Fantasmes, 1980; The Painted Body, 1984; Art Folie LSD, Graffiti, 1985; Dubuffet, 1986; Jean Lecoultre, 1989; Detournement d'Ecriture, 1989; Le Theatre du Crime - Essai sur la peinture de David, 1989; Art Brut, Psychose et Mediumnite, 1990. *Hobby:* Jazz. *Address:* Collection de L'art Brut, 11 Ave des Bergieres, CH-1004 Lausanne, Switzerland.

THIBAULT de BOESINGHE Leopold Baron de, b. 4 Sept 1943, Gent, Belgium. Physician. m. 26 Mar 1981, 1 s, 1 d. *Education:* MD, Occup Hlth. *Appointments:* Dir, Dept of Occup Hlth, Univ Gent; Asst Hd, Dept of Radiotherapy and Nucl Med; Chief, Dept, Clinic ASZ of Aalst, Dept of Nucl Med. *Publications:* Several scientific articles published abroad and in Belgium. *Memberships:* Past Pres, Assn Europ de Thermol, ; Provincial Chamber of the Bd of Phys of Oost-Vlaanderen; Intl Col of Thermol; Belgian Assn of Radiation Protection, Pres; Ste Litt Club Gand, Ste des Redoutes, Univ Fdn, Assoc Foreign Sci. *Honours:* Hon mem, Am Acad of Thermol. *Hobbies:* Photography. *Address:* St Martensstraat 10, B-9000 Gent, Belgium.

THIEL Winfried, b. 29 June 1940, Cottbus. University Professor. m. Elfriede Schmidt, 17 Apr 1965, 2 d. *Education:* Dr Theol, Humboldt Univ, Berlin, 1970; DSc, Theol, 1977. *Appointments:* Asst, Old Testament, Humboldt Univ, 1970-78; Sr Asst, 1979-82; Prof, Univ Marburg, 1982-. *Publications:* Die deuteronomistische Rerdaktion von Jeremia, 1-25, 1973; Die deuteronomistische Redaktion von Jeremia, 26-45, 1981; Die soziale Entwicklung Israels in Vorstaatlicher Zeit, 1985; Biblische Zeittafeln, 1985; Altes Testament, 1989. *Hobbies:* Music; Reading. *Address:* Tilsiter Str 8, D-3550 Marburg 7, Germany. 52, 145,

THIRLWALL Anthony Philip, b. 21 Apr 1941, Workington, England. Professor of Applied Economics. m. Gianna Paoletti, 26 Mar 1966, 2 s, 1 d. *Education:* BA, Univ of Leeds, 1962; MA, Clark Univ, 1963; PhD, Leeds Univ, 1967. *Appointments:* Asst Lectr, Univ of Leeds, 1964-66; Lectr, Rdr, Prof, Univ of Kent, 1966-; Econ Advr, Dept of EMployment, 1968-70; Vis Prof in several overseas Univs. *Publications:* Growth and Development, 1989; Inflation, Saving and Growth, 1974; Regional Growth and Unemployment in the UK, 1975; Financing Economic Development, 1976; Balance of Payments Theory and the UK Experience, 1991; Nicholas Kaldor, 1987; Deindustrialisation, 1990; 6 edited vols of Keynes Seminars; Two edited vols of Kaldor's work. *Memberships:* Coun and Exec Comm Royal Econs Soc. *Hobbies:* Athletics and Tennis; Travel; Reading; Biography; Philately; Gardening. *Address:* 14 Moorfield, Canterbury, Kent, England. 52.

THOENI Mary Irene, b. 15 Jan 1950, Miami, Florida, USA. President, Business Solutions Etc, m. 8 Aug 1975, 1 s, 2 d. *Education:* BS, Hlth Scis, Charter Oak COl, 1989; MBA, Cardinal Stritch Col, 1991. *Appointments:* Pres; Fdr, Business Solutions Etc, 1988-91; US Veterans Admin, 1986-88; Charleston Naval Shipyard, 1981-86; US Forest Ser, 1978-81. *Memberships:* NAFE: Nat Org for Women; Math Assn of Am; Nat Assn of Resume Writers; Milwaukee Minority Chamber of Commerce. *Honours:* Chariol Foun Take Charge Awd, 1989. *Hobbies:* Computer programming; Water colour artist;

Poetry; Hunting; Fishing. *Address:* 6174 W. Spencer Place, Milwaukee, WI 53218, USA. 152.

THOMAS Berthold Ernst Friedrich, b. 1 June 1910, Berlin. Prof of Univ. m. Edith Franke, 29 July 1946, 1 s, 1 d. *Education:* Univ Berlin, 1929-35; Dr phil, 1936; Habilitation, tech Univ Berlin, 1962. *Appointments:* Asst, Vice Dir, Natl Inst for Cereal Processing, 1936- 45; Inst for Food Research, 1946-61; Food Rech, Tech Univ berlin, 1962-75. *Publications:* Die Nahr und Ballaststoffe der Getreidemehle; Ernahrung u Lebensmittellehre; Over 300 Articles. *Memberships include:* Dt Gesellschaft f Ernahrung; Dt Ges f Qualitatsforschung; Weltbund z Schutze des Lebens. *Honours:* Pelshenke Medal Deutsche; Medal of honor; Honorary Member, Verband Deutsch Lebensmitteltechniker. *Hobbies:* Music; Sport; Hiking; Gardening. *Address:* Rolandstrabe 12, D-1000 Berlin, Germany. 38.

THOMAS Edward John, b. 25 Nov 1937, Plymouth, Devon, England. Director of Continuing Education. m. Erica Jean Thomas, 12 Sept 1964, 1 s, 1 d. *Education:* MA Oxford, 1967; MSc London, 1964; PhD Manchester, 1968. *Appointments:* Res Scist, GEC plc, 1962-64; Lectr, Univ of Manchester, 1964-68; Staff Tutor, Univ of Bristol, 1968-80; Sr Lectr, 1980-81; Prof of Adult Educ, 1981-. *Publications:* Type II Superconductivity, 1969; From Quarus to Quasars, 1977. *Memberships:* Inst of Phys; FRSA; Univs Coun for Adult and Continuing Educ, Treas, 1987-. *Hobbies:* Reading; Writing; Eating; Drinking; Talking. *Address:* Department for Continuing Education, The University, Bristol BS8 1HR, England. 50, 52.

THOMAS Graham Stuart, b. 3 Apr 1909. *Education:* Botanic Garden Univ, Cambridge. *Appointments:* Foreman, Mgr, T Hilling & Co, 1931; Assoc Dir, Sunningdale Nurseries, Surrey, 1968-71; Gardens conslt, Natl Trust, 1974-; Vice Pres, Garden Distory Soc, 1990-; Vice Patron Royal Natl Rose Soc, 1966. *Publications:* The Old Shrub Roses; Colour in the Winter Garden; Shrub Roses of Today; Climbing Roses Old & New; Plants for Ground Cover; Perenial Garden Plants; Gardens of the Natl Trust; Three Gardens; Trees in Landscape; Recreating the Period Garden; A Garden of Roses; The Complete Paintings & Drawing of Graham Stuart Thomas; The Rock Garden and its Plants; An English Rose Garden. *Hobbies:* Music; Painting; Reading. *Address:* Briar Cottage, 21 Kettlewell Close, Horsell, Woking, Surrey, England.

THOMAS Ian Mitchell, b. 17 May 1933, Whitley Bay, England. Chairman and Managing Director, Culpeper Ltd. m. (1) Jeniter Diana Morris, 20 Aug 1960, 2 s, 2 d. (2) Diana Lesley Kathryn, 24 Oct 1977. *Education:* Liverpool Col; Selwyn Col, Cambs, 1951-57; BA 1957, MA 1987. *Appointments:* Salesman, Wrigley Prods Ltd, 1957-59; Asst MD, Hobson Bates & Ptnrs, 1959-65; Jt MD, Cavenham Foods Ltd, 1965-67; MD, Fabbri and Ptnrs, 1968-70; Chm, Culpepper Ltd, 1972-. *Publications:* Culpepper's Book of Birth, 1985; How to Grow Herbs, 1988; Culpepper Herbal Notebook, 1991. *Memberships:* Herb Soc, Coun, 1978-87, VP, 1988. *Hobbies:* Running; Skiing; Tennis; Gardening. *Address:* Floriston Hall, Wixoe, Halstead, Essex CO9 4AR, England.

THOMAS John David, b. 30 Mar 1951, Muncie, Indiana, USA. Composer; Musician; Photographer. m. Rosalie Faith Baldwin Thomas, 27 July 1974, div 1991, 1 s, 1 d. *Education:* BSc, Mus Theory and Comp, Ball State Univ, 1976; Elec Engrg and Maths, Purdue Univ, 1969-71. *Appointments:* Solo pianist, The Cascade Club, Washington, 1991; Solo Pianist at Arizona resorts including: Wrigley Mansion, 1988; Boulders Resort, 1987; Clarion Inn/McCormick's Ranch Resort, 1986; Keyboardist for Dee Dee Ryan, Longhorn Saloon, Apache Junction, 1984-86; Gulch Gang, Pinnacle Peak Pation, N.Scottsdale, 1984; Jetstream, Indiana, 1979-83. *Creative works:* Composed over 135 compositions including, instrumentals, songs, and themes; Christian

workship music, jazz-rock, movie theme music, theatre rock, gospel. *Memberships:* Am Soc of Composers, Authors and Publishers, 1974-; Pres, Quetico Records and Quetico Publishing Inc, 1974; ASCAP, 1973; MENSA: AM Contract Bridge League; Nat Hon Soc; US Chess Fed; Am Soc of Military Comptrollers, 1976-84. *Honours include:* General Motors Scolar, Purdue Univ, 1969-70; Palmer Meml Music Scholarship, Ball State Univ, 1971-74; Eagle Scout, BSA, Indianapolis, 1966; God and Country Awd, BSA, 1965; Outstanding Musician Awd, Purdue Univ Symph Orch, 1970; Hometown Hour Awd, WFBO-FM Radio, 1979. *Hobbies:* Listening to music; Music performance, composition,; Photography; Chess; Comtract Bridge; Euchre; Watching movies; Reading poetry and literature; Creative writing; Culinary cuisine; Dining Out; Tennis; Bowling. *Address:* 2704 Central Ct, Indianapolis, IN 46280, USA.

THOMAS Lindsey Kay, Jr, b. 16 Apr 1931, Salt Lake City, Utah, USA. Research Biologist; Educator; Consultant. m. Nancy Ruth Van Dyke, 24 Aug 1956, 2 s, 2 d. *Education:* BS Utah State Agric Col, 1953; MS Brigham Young Univ, 1958; PhD, Duke Univ, 1974. *Appointments:* Naturalist Nat Capaital Pks, 1957-62; Res Pk Naturalist, Washington Dc, 1963-66; Instr, Dept of Agric Grad Sch, 1964-66; Res Biol: Wash DC, 1966; N.Carolina, 1966-67, Maryland, 1967-74. *Publications:* Impact of three exotic plant species on a potomac Island; Ed, Management of Exotic Species in natural communities; Numerous articles in professional journals. *Memberships:* AAAS; Botanical Soc; Ecol Soc of Am; George Wright Soc; US Nature Conservancy; Soc for Early Hist Archaeol; Sigma Xi; Flora & Fauna Com, 1974-75; Washington Biols Field CLub. *Honours:* Incentive Awds, Safety Feature, Nat Park overlook, 1962, information on park service map, 1962; Res grants, Washington Biols Field Club, 1977, 1982. *Hobbies:* Camping; Hiking; Physical fitness. *Address:* 13854 Delaney Road, Woodbridge, VA 22193, USA. 7, 14, 52.

THOMAS Malayilmelathethil Koruthu, b. 26 Jan 1932, Vanmazhi, India. Professor of English; Priest. *Education:* BA Kerala Univ, 1952; GTh, Leonard Theol Col, 1956; BD, Serampore Univ, 1956; MTh, Princeton Theol Sem, 1960; MA, 1961; MA 1964; EdD, 1964. *Appointments:* Headmaster, ST George's Middle Sch, Kerala, India, 1952-53; Tchr, Calhohcate Hg Sch, 1956-59; Prof of Eng, Morehead State Univ, 1964-65; Assoc Prof, 1965-67, Prof, 1967-, Prof of Eng. *Memberships:* Modern Lang Assn; NCTE, Ky Philological Assn; Kappa Delta Phi; Phi Delta Kappa; Blue Key; Phi Kappa Phi. *Honours:* George Howell's Prize, Serampore Univ, 1956. *Hobbies:* Travelling; Fishing; Gardening. *Address:* 310 West Sun St, Morehead, KY 40351, USA.

THOMAS Michael Gavin Lynam, b. 14 Aug 1936, Rugby, England. Museum Director. m. Jane Allen, 11 Apr 1964, 1 s dec, 1 d. *Education:* Dragon Sch Oxford, 1945-50; Rugby Sch, 1950-55; MA Modern Hist, Trinity Col, Oxford, 1957-60. *Appointments:* Nat Ser Army, 1955-57; Bank of England, London, 1961-68; Dir, Avoncroft Mus of Bldgs, 1968-. *Memberships:* Nat Trust Coun and Exec Com; Chm, Severn Regional Com; Trustee, Landmark Trust; Chm, Worcs Cathedral Fabric Adv Com; Coun Assn Independent Mus; Bd, W. Midlands Area Mus Ser. *Hobbies:* Museums; Historic buildings; Music; Tennis. *Address:* 2 Stephenson Terrace, Worcester WR1 3EA, England.

THOMAS Norman, b. 1 June 1921, London, England. m. Rose Hensaw, 24 Dec 1944, 1 s, 1 d. *Education:* Latymer's Sch, Edmonton; Camden Training Col. *Appointments include:* Employment in commerce, industry and civil service, 1937-47; Tchr, London and Herts, 1948-56; Headteacher, Longmeadown JM Sch, Stevenage, 1956-61; Hm Inspector of Schs, 1962-81; Chair, Com of Enquiry into Primary Educ, in the ILEA, 1983-85; Advr, Hse of Commons Educ Sci and Arts Com, 1985-86; Vis Prof, NELP, 1985-87; Sec of State Task Gp on Assessment and Testing, 1987-88; Hon Prof of Educ, Univ of Warwick, 1986-; Evaluator of grant related in-service training, Bucks, 1987-77, Warwickshire, 1987-88; Educ Adv Ser in Warwickshire Review, 1988; Specialist Prof of Primary Educ, Univ of Notts, 1988-90; Chair, MELBAH Local CATE Com, 1990-91; Vis Prof in Educ, Hatfield Poly, 1991-. *Publications:* Paper, Age-related attainment in education: Objectives, benchmarks and milestones, 1987; Primary Education: From Plowden to the 1990's, 1990; Chapters in various books and articles in professional magazines and journals. *Memberships:* Nat Assn for Primary Educ; Col of Perceptors. *Honours:* Hon FCP, 1988; Life Mem, NAPE, 1990; CBE, 1980. *Hobbies:* Photography; Reading. *Address:* 19 Langley Way, Watford, Herts WD1 3EJ, England. 1.

THOMAS Patricia Anne, b. 3 Apr 1940. Local Government Ombudsman. m. Joseph Glyn Thomas, 20 July 1968, 1 s, 2 d. *Education:* LLB, 1961, LLM, 1962, Kings Col, London. *Appointments:* Lectr in Law, Leeds Univ, 1962-63, 1964-68; Tchg Fellow, Univ of Illinois, 1963-64; Sr Lectr, Principal Lectr, Hd, Sch of Law and Prof, Lancs Poly, 1973-85; Mem, Pres, Greater Manchester and Lancs Rent Assessment Pane, 1976-85; Chm, Blackpool Supplementary Benefit Appeal Trib, 1980-85; Commr for Local Admin in England, 1985-. *Hobbies:* Walking; Cooking; Travel. *Address:* Commission for Local Admin in England, Beverley House, 17 Shipton Road, York YO3 6FZ, England. 1.

THOMAS Richard Emery, b. 12 Dec 1929, Laconia, New Hampshire, USA. Environmental Consultant. m. Blythe Ann Jamieson, 14 June 1953, 2 s, 2 d. *Education:* BS 1952, MS 1954, Univ of New Hampshire; Postgrad studies at Univ of Maryland, 1954-56, Cornell Univ, 1961-63. *Appointments:* Res Scist, US Govt, 1957-70; Sr Res Scist, 1970-77, Sr Prog Scist, 1977-82; Prog Coor, 1983-86, Environ Protection Agy; Self-employed Environ Conslt, 1987-. *Publications:* Design manual, Land Treatment of Municipal Wastewater, 1977, revised, 1981, supplement, 1984; Chapter, Properties of Waste Waters, in Soils for Management of Organis Wastes and Wastewaters, 1977; Over 50 technicla papers in scientific journals. *Membeships:* Committees, Water Pollution Control Fed, Am Waterworks Assn, Irrigation Assn; Coun for Agric Sci and Tech; Soil Sc Soc of Am; Intl Comm for Irrigation and Drainage. *Honours:* Bronze Medal, 175, Dist Career Awd, 1986, Environ Protection Agy. *Hobbies:* Softball; Bowling; Hiking; Swimming; Fishing. *Address:* 4542 Airlie Way, Annandale, VA 22003, USA. 6.

THOMAS Richard James, b. 18 June 1949, Southend on Sea, Essex, England. Director of Consumer Affairs. m. Julia Delicia Clarke, 18 May 1974, 2 s, 1 d. *Education:* LLB Hons, Univ of Southampton, 1970; Col of Law, Guildford, 1971; Solicitor, 1973. *Appointments:* Freshfields, Solicitors, 1971-74; Greater London CAB, 1974-79; Nat Consumer Coun, 1979-86; Ofc of Fair Trading, 1986-. *Creative works:* Writen and broadcasted widely on legal and consumer issues. *Memberships:* Law Soc. *Hobbies:* Family; Maintenance of home and garden; Travel. *Address:* Office of Fair Trading, Field House, Bream's Building, London EC4A 1PR, England. 1.

THOMAS Trevor Anthony, b. 16 Mar 1939, Bristol, England. Consultant Anaesthetist. m. Yvonne Louise Mary Branch, 10 July 1965, 1 s. *Education:* MBChB, Univ of St Andrews, 1958-64; FFARCS, RCS, 1969; FCAnaes, Col of Anaes, 1989. *Appointments:* Conslt Anaes, Utd Bristol Hosps, 1972, Chm, Div of Anaes, 1977-80, Hon Clin Lectr, Univ of Bristol, 1980-, Chm, Hosp Med Staff Comm, 1988-90, Examiner for Part I FFARCS/FCAnaes, 1985-, Regional Assessor in Anaes for the Confidential Enquiries into Maternal Deaths, 1978-. *Publications include:* Author of chapters in Clinics of Obs Anaes, 1986, Problems of Obs Anaes, 1986; Cardiopulmonary Resuscitation, 1989; Controversies in Obs Anaes, 1990. *Memberships:* Assoc of Anaes of GB and Ireland; RSM; Hist of Anaes Soc;

Assn of Dental Anaes; Saudi Anaes Assn; Obs Anaes Assn, Hon Sec, 1981-85, Soc of Anaes of the SW Region, Hon Sec, 1985-88. *Hobbies:* Archery; Croquet; Music; Theatre. *Address:* 14 Cleeve Lawns, Downend, Bristol BS16 6HJ, England.

THOMAS William Ernest Ghinn, b. 13 Feb 1948, London, England. Consultant Surgeon. m. Grace Violet Samways, 30 June 1973, 2 s, 3 d. *Education:* King's Col, London Univ, 1966-69, St George's Hosp Med Sch, 1969-72; BSc, 1969; MBBS, 1972; FRCS, 1976; MS, 1980. *Appointments:* Surg Registrar, Cambs, 1975-77; Bernard Sunley Res Fellow, RCS, 1977-78; Surg Registrar, 1978-80, Sr Registrat, 1980-86, Bristol; Conslt Surg, Sheffield, 1986-. *Publications:* Preparation and Revision for the FRCS, 1986; Self Assessment Exercises in Surgery, 1986; Nuclear Medicine, - Applications to surgery, 1988; Over 130 scientific articles and book chapters; Ed of Current Practice in Surgery. *Memberships:* BMA, 1974; Brit Soc of Gastroenterol, 1980; Surg Res Soc, 1981; European Soc for Surg Res, 1981; Pancreatic Soc, 1981; Assn of Surgs, 1988; RSM, 1990; Ct of Exmrs of RCS, 1991. *Honours:* Hare Prize, 1969; Rabbeth Scholarship, 1969; Webb Prize, 1972; Kate Charles Prize, 1972; Royal Humane Soc Awd, 1974; Bernard Sunley Fellowship, 1977; Arris and Gale Lectr, 1981; Monynihan Fellowship, 1982; Doctor of the Year, 1985; Hunterian Prof, 1987. *Hobbies:* Photography; Oil painting; Skiing. *Address:* Ash Lodge, 65 Whirlow Park Road, Whirlow, Sheffield S11 9NN, England. 170.

THOMASEN Ole, b. 9 Feb 1934. m. 10 Apr 1965. *Education:* MEcon, 1934. *Appointments:* Asst Principal, Min of Commerce, 1961- 63; Asst Hd of Div, Jt Coun of Danish Commercial Banks, 1963; Hd, Dept, 1965-68; Asst Mgr, Amagerbanken A/S, 1969, Dpty Mgr, 1972, Mgr, 1975, MD, 1978-79; Bd of Govs, Danmarks Nat Bank, 1980-. *Memberships:* Danish Inter-bank Transfer Ctr, 1971-79; Reg Banks, 1974-79, Hsg Mortgage Fund, 1979; Fin Corp for Indust and Crafts, 1980-; Mortgage Fund for Danish Agric, 1981-; Ship Credit Fund for Denmark, Dpty Chm, 1982-; Danish Air Lines, 1986-; Laurits Andersen Foun, 1990-; Bombebossen Foun, 1990-. *Address:* Danmarks Nationalbank, Havnegade 5, DK-1093 Copenhagen K, Denmark.

THOMASON George Frederick, b. 27 Nov 1927, Hawkshead, Lancs, England. Management Consultant. m. Jean Elizabeth Horsley, 5 Sept 1953, 1 s, 1 d. *Education:* BA Univ of Sheffield, 1948-52; MA, Univ of Toronto, 1952-53, PhD, Univ of Wales, 1963. *Appointments:* Res Asst, 1953-54, Lectr, 1954-56, Res Assoc, 1956-69, Lectr, 1959-60, Dept of Indust Relations, Univ Col, Cardiff; Leverhulme Trust Bus Fellow, 1960-62; Lectr, 1962-63, Sr Lectr, 1963-69, Acting Hd of Dept, 1966-69, Rdr, 1969, Dept of Indust Relations; Montague Burton Prof and Hd of Dept of Indust Relations and Mgmt Studies, 1969-84; Dean, Fac of Econ and Social Studies, 1971-73; Dpty Prin for the Humanities, 1974-77; Mgmt Conslt, 1984-. *Publications include:* A Textbook of Human Resource Management; A Textbook of Industrial Relations Management; Job Evaluation: Objectives and Methods; The Management of Research and Development; Experiments in Participation; The Professional Approach to Community work. *Memberships:* IPM, VP; BIM, Coun; Chartered Inst of Transp. *Honours:* CBE, 1982; Fellow of Univ of Wales Col of Cardiff, 1980; Emeritus Prof, 1984. *Hobby:* Gardening. *Address:* 149 Lake Road West, Cardiff CF2 5PJ, Wales. 1, 43.

THOMPSON Alan Eric, b. 16 Sept 1924, University Professor. m. 3 Dec 1960, 3 s, 1 d. *Education:* Univ of Edinburgh: MA 1949, MA Econ, 1st class hons, 1951; PhD, 1953. *Appointments:* Emeritus Prof; Parliamentary Advr; Pharmaceutical Gen Coun, Scotland. *Publication:* Development of economic doctrine, 1980, jointly. *Membership:* FRSA. *Honours:* MP for Dunfermline Burghs, 1959-64; Formerly: Gov of the BBC; Royal Fine

Art Commr, Scotland; Chm, Newbattle Abbey Col. *Hobbies:* Bridge; Croquet; Writing children's stories and plays. *Address:* 11 Upper Gray Street, Edinburgh EH9 1SN, Scotland. 1.

THOMPSON David, b. 28 Oct 1944, Durham, England. Chartered Accountant. m. Glenys Collen, 24 Oct 1970, 2 s. *Education:* Kings Sch, Pontefract, 1956-61; Articled Clerk, Acty, 1961-65; Chartered Acct: Assoc, 1969, Fellow, 1979. *Appointments include:* Articled Clk, Mgr, John Gordon Walton, 1961-73; Mgr, Sr Ptnr, Buckle Barton, 1973-. *Memberships:* FICA; V-Chm, Bradford City Assn Football Club; Dpty Songster Leader, Castleford Corps of the Salvation Army. *Hobbies:* Music; Football and most other sports; Reading. *Address:* Stone Lea, Badsworth Ct, Badsworth, Pontefract, W.Yorks WF9 1NW, England.

THOMPSON Ernest Gerald, b. 22 Nov 1925, Goodmayes, Essex. Company Director. m. Janet Muriel Smith, 14 Sept 1968, 1 s. *Education:* Brentwood Sch, 1939-43; MA, Trinity Col, Cambs, 1947-50. *Appointments:* Flt Lt, RAF, 1943-47; Instrument Sales mgr, 1962-68; Baird & Tatlock Ltd, Dir, F C Dannatt, SA, Paris, 1968-86; MD, ChemLab Instruments Ltd, 1986-; Chm and MD, Chem Lab Scientific Products Ltd. *Memberships:* RIChem; IOD; Britain in Europe, Hon Sec, 1958-68; Conservative Gp for Europe, V-Chm; European Movement, Nat Coun; Union Europeenne des Federalistes, Int Com. *Honour:* OBE, 1973. *Hobbies:* Music; travel; Swimming; International Affairs. *Address:* Yew Tree House, 63 Morgan Crescent, Theydon Bois, Essex CM16 7DU, England.

THOMPSON Frank Robert, b. 1 Jan 1938, Newark, Notts. Labour Leader, Gloucestershire County Council. m. Janet Deirdre Skinner, 21 Dec, 1963. *Education:* BA Hons, Eng Lang and Lit, 1959; DEduc, 1960, Hull Univ. *Appointments:* Hd of Westbourne FE Ctr, 1971-72; Hd of Gen Studies Dept, Pontypool Col, 1975-89; Staunton Parish Coun, 1979-87, Chm, 1981-87; Glos Co Coun, 1981, Gp Leader, 1985-; Rep of Glos CC on ACC, 1985-; Parliamentary Candidate, 1964, 1970, 1974. *Publications:* Various newspaper articles on political subjects. *Memberships:* Nat Assn of Tchrs in Further and Higher Educ, Life; Pontypool Branch Chm, 1976-83, V-Chm, 1975-76 and 1983-84; Chm, Gwent Co Liasion Com, 1977-79. *Hobbies:* Long distance walking (completed the Downsman Hundred and the Across Wales Walk in 1975); Swimming; Chess; Listening to music. *Address:* Steep Meadow, Staunton, Coleford, Gloucestershire GL16 8PD, England.

THOMPSON Malcolm Keith, b. 30 June 1921, London. Author; Journalist. m. Jeanne Sophie Struys, 24 Oct 1953, 1 d. *Education:* Trinity Sch of John Whitgift, 1932-39; BA, ChB, Gold medal in Surg, Univ of St Andrews, 1947-52. *Appointments:* Hse Phys, Sir Ian Hill, 1952-53; Hse Surg Obs & Gynae, Wanstead, 1953; Trainee with Dr S Hamilton, 1954; Prin in Gen Prac, 1955-86; Lectr in UK and Hong Kong. *Publications:* Books: Geriatrics and General Practitioner Team, 1969; Health for Old Age, 1970; The Care of the Elderly in General Practice, 1984; Caring for an Elderly Relative, 1986; Commonsense Geriatrics, 1990; Med Corres for Yours Newspaper, 1974-. *Memberships:* FRSM: FRCGP, Provost S.London Fac: Brit Geriatrics Soc. *Honours:* Butterworth Gold Medal, 1967; Hunterian Soc Gold Medal, 1968; Nuffield Travelling Fellow, 1970; Med Gilliland Travelling Fellow, 1984; Ian Stokoe Meml Awd, 1986; Brit Geriatric Soc Awd, 1986; Balint Soc Prize, 1991. *Hobbies:* Music; Painting; Painting; Photography and microscopy; Swimming; Golf; Walking. *Address:* 28 Steep Hill, Stanhope Road, Croydon, Surrey CRO 5QS, England.

THOMPSON Ronald Paul, b. 14 Dec 1947, Toronto, Canada. University Professor and Senior University Administrator. m. Jennifer Christine McShane, 23 Dec 1971. 1 s, 2 d. *Education:* BA 70; MA 72; PhD 1979. *Appointments:* Asst Prof, 1979-83, Assoc Prof, 1983-

88, Prof, 1988-, Univ of Toronto; Principal and Dean, Scarborough Col, Univ of Toronto, 1989-. *Publications:* Books: The structure of biological theories, 1989; The Moral Question, 1981; Numerous scholarly articles in journals. *Memberships:* Philos of Sci Assn; Hist Philos and Social Studies of Biol Soc; Can Philos Assn; Can Assn for Hist and Philos of Sci. *Honours:* Social Science and Humanities Res Coun Postdoctor fellowship, 1981-82. *Hobbies:* Sailing; Canoeing; Woodworking; Winemaking. *Address:* Office of the Principal & Dean, Scarborough College, University of Toronto, 1265 Military Trail, Scarborough, Ontario M1C 1A4, Canada. 142.

THOMPSON Van Everett, b. 13 Dec 1940, Kilgore, Texas, USA. Project Leader, General Dynamics, NATO 155mm APGM. m. Maryka Hauet, 24 Mar 1978, 1 s, 3 d. *Education:* Master, Mgmt Sci, 1978; Bachelor Elec Engrg, 1963. *Appointments:* General Dynamics, Pomona, 1963-85; General Dynamics, Valley Systems, 1985-. *Memberships:* APDA; AUSA; AFA; NLUS; IEEE. *Hobbies:* Scuba diving; Camping; Aerospace/Defence. *Address:* 8557 Red Hill Country Club Drive, Rancho Cucamonga, CA 91730, USA. 2.

THOMSEN Dorn Ole Muff, b. 25 Nov 1944, Copenhagen. Chief Economist. m. Marie Louise Sorensen, 20 May 1967, 1 d. *Education:* Data Processing Deg, 1968; Econ Degs: Organisation, 1970, Gen Mgmt, 1975, Acct, 1975, Export Mktg, 1987. *Appointments:* Org Chief Gl Michaelsen, 1973- 74; Mgr, Nat Chemsearch, 1974-78; Conslt, Own Company, 1978-79; Fin Mgr, S-O DK, 1979-. *Memberships:* Bd of Dirs, K/S Fredholm. *Hobbies:* Tennis; Photography; Painting. *Address:* Bruhnsvej 6, 3600 Frederikssund, Denmark.

THOMSEN-REYNOLDS Dianna, b. 10 Nov 1963, Albany, CA, USA. Clinical Research Associate in immunodiagnostics. m. Seven E Reynolds, 24 Nov 1990. *Education:* BA, Vassar Col, 1985; MPH, Univ of Calif at Berkeley, Sch of Public Health, 1986. *Appointments:* Syntex pharmaceuticals, 1987-89; Parexel Intl, 1989-90; AAH Meditel, 1990-91; Metra Biosystems, Inc, 1992. *Memberships:* Beta Beta Beta; Regulatory Affairs Assocs; APHA. *Honours:* Hariet Gurnee van Allen Prize for Excellence in Biol, 1983; Pub Health Traineeship, 1985. *Hobbies:* Dancing; Gardening; Sailing. *Address:* 1158 Pembridge Drive, San Jose, CA 95118, USA.

THOMSON James Miln, b. 14 Mar 1921, Perth, W.Australia. Consultant Educator. m. Diana May Gregg, 19 Feb 1944, 2 s, 2 d. *Education:* BSc Hons, 1943, MSc, 1944, DSc, 1957, Univ of W.Austr. *Appointments:* Res Ofr, C'wlth Sci and Indust Res Org, 1945-65; Sci Dir, Marineland Oceanarium, 1963-65; Sr Lectr, 1965-66, Rdr, 1967, Prof, 1968, Hd Dept of Zoology, 1968-79, Dean of Sci, 1980-82, Pro V-Chancellor, 1983-86, Emeritus Prof, 1984, Univ of Queensland; Warden, Univ Col of the N.Territory, 1986-88; Dpty V-Chancellor, N.Territory Univ, 1989-90; Ret'd, Dec 1990. *Publications:* Author: Great Barrier Reef, 1967; Fish of Ocean and Shore, 1974; Guide to Fishes of Non-Tropical Australia, 1978. *Memberships:* Past Pres, Royal Soc of Queensland; Foun Sec, 1963-65, Past Pres, Austr Marine Scis Assn; Past Trustee, Queensland Mus; Coun, 1979-86, Austr Inst of Marine Sci; Com, 1980-86, Marine Sci and Tech Com. *Honours:* Hackett Res Scholar, Univ of W.Austr, 1943; CSIR Fellowship, 1944; FRIBiol, 1986; AIB, 1987; AIM, 1986; AM, 1989; Hon DSC, Univ of Queensland, 1990. *Hobbies:* Angling; Tennis; Reading. *Address:* 16 Marieville Esplanade, Sandy Bay, Hobart, Tasmania 7005, Australia.

THOMSON Pamela Ann, b. 27 Aug 1942, Canada. Provincial Court Judge. m. E G Hachborn, 5 May 1990, 2 s. *Education:* BA Queens Univ, 1963; LLB, Univ of Toronto, 1966; Called to the Bar: Ontario, 1968, Timmins High, 1960, Quebec, 1972. *Appointments:* Ptnr, Aubrey E Golden, 1968- 70, 1974-81; Dir, Ctr for Pub Interest Law, 1971-74; Prov Ct Judge, Ontario, 1981-.

Publications: Consumer Access to Justice, 1976; Role of Advertising and the cost of Food, 1975. *Memberships:* Can Assn of Prov Ct Judges: Civil Judges Educ Chm, Exec Dir, Sec, Tres; Intl Comm of Jurists; Assn des Juristes d'Expression Francaise; Jt Com on Ct Reform. *Hobby:* Amateur Theatre. *Address:* Judges' Chambers, 16th Fl 400 Univ Avenue, Toronto, Ontario, Canada M5G 1S8. 1.

THORN Jeremy Gordon, b. 23 Mar 1948, Lincoln, England. Managing Director and Author. m. Eilis Anne Coffey, 24 Mar 1971, 4 d. *Education:* BSc Hons Metallurgy, Leeds Univ, 1966; Dipl Mktg Res, European Col of Mktg, 1973; Ops Mgmt, Cranfield Inst of Tech, 1983. *Appointments:* Bus Dev, Foseco Minsep Plc, 1969-74; European Mgr, Astro-Metallurgical Corp, USA, 1975-78; Sales & Mktg Dir: Baugh & Weedon Ltd, 1978-81, Staveley Industries Plc, 1981-83; Spear & Jackson Plc, 1984-86; MD, Bridon Ropes Ltd, Bridon Plc, 1986-. *Publications:* How to negotiate better Deals, 1989; The First Time Sales Manger, 1990. *Memberships:* FBIM, Pres, Doncanster Branch, 1991; Chartered Engr, Inst of Metallurgists; Dpty Chm and Dir, Barnsley & Doncaster TEC: Chm, Fed of Wire Rope Mfr of GB; Exec, Brit Independent Steel Producers Assn. *Hobbies:* Fencing (past sabre champion); Music, (past member of Sheffield Phil Chorus). *Address:* c/o Bridon Ropes Ltd, Carr Hill, Doncaster, S.Yorks, DN4 8PG, England.

THORN Niels Anker. b. 1 Aug 1924, Horsens. Prof of Physiology. m. Ingrid Thorn, 7 Mar 1954, 2 s. *Education:* MD, Univ of Copenhagen, 1951; Dr Med Sci, 1960. *Appointments:* Fellow, Rockefellow Inst of Medical Research, NY, 1953-56; Asst Prof, Univ of Copenhagen, 1956; Assoc Prof, 1959; Prof, Chmn, Inst Med Physiol C, 1967; Conslt, Royal Danish Dental Sch, 1960-66. *Publications:* Advances Metabolic Disorders; Transport Mechanisms in Epothelia; Secretory Mechanisms of Exocrine Glands; Molecular Mechanisms in Secretion. *Memberships:* Scand Physiological Soc; Dan Med Res Council; EC Med Res Council; Dan Biol Soc; Harvey Soc; Soc for Exp Biol & Medicine; British Biol Soc; Intl soc of Neuroendocrinology; Intl Soc of Neurochemistry. *Honours:* The Alfred Benzon Prize; The Christian Bohr Prize; The Thorvald Madsen Prize; he Gaardon Prize. *Hobbies:* Skating; Sailing. *Address:* Institute of Medical Physiology C, Univ of Copenhagen, Blegdamsvej 3C, 2200 Copenhagen N, Denmark.

THORNHILL Richard John, b. 13 Nov 1954, England. Solicitor. m. Nicola Dyke, 30 Aug 1980, 1 s. *Education:* Malvern Co, 1968-72; St Johns Col, Oxford, MA Jurisprudence. *Appointments:* Slaughter and May, 1977-; Admitted, 1979; Ptnr, 1986; Sr Ptnr, Hong Kong, 1991. *Memberships:* Law Soc of England a Wales; Law Soc of Hong Kong. *Hobbies:* Modern Art; Opera; Gardening; Horse Racing. *Address:* 27th Fl, 2 Exchange Square, Hong Kong. 53.

THORSEN Nancy Dain, b. 23 June 1944, Alton, Illinois, USA. Real Estate Broker. m. Janes H Thorsen, 30 May 1980. 1 d. *Education:* BS Mktg, 1968, MS Bus Educ, 1975, S.Illinois Univ; Grad, Realtor Inst, Idaho, 1982. *Appointments:* Personnel Mgr, J H Little & Co, London, England, 1968-72; Bus Instr, Special Sch Dist, St Louis, MO, 1974-78; Mgr, Mktg and Ops, Isis Foods Inc, St Louis, 1978-80; Real Est Broker, Century 21 Sayer Realty Inc, 1981-89; RE/MAX Homestead Realty, 1989-. *Memberships:* CREA: Prog and Educ Coms, Chm of Legis Com, Idaho Falls Bd of Realtors; Pres, Idaho Million Dollar Club; Pres, Idaho Falls Civitan Club, 1989; SIUE Alumni Assn; Idaho Assn of Realtors Educ Com, 1990-93; Realtor Hon Soc, 1984- 90. *Honours:* Idaho Gov's Awd for Volunteerism, 1982; Mayor's Awd, 1982, 1987; Idaho Realtor Hon Soc, 1984-89; Civitan of Year, 1986, 1987; No 1 Century 21 Agent, Idaho, 1986-88; Century 21 Gold Assoc, 1987, 1988; '98 Re/MAX 100% Club, 1989; Guest Speaker: Century 21 Convention, Denver, 1988; RE/MAX Intl Convention, Orlando, 1990; Dist

Pres Awd, Civitan Intl, 1990; Realtor of the Yr, 1990; Cert Residential Specialist, CRS, 1990. Hobbies: Reading; Swimming; Water Skiing; Collecting bears and dolls. *Address:* 1270 First Street, Idaho Falls, ID 83401, USA. 5, 52, 132.

THURLIMANN Bruno, b. 6 Feb 1923, Gossau, Switzerland. Emeritus Professor of Structural Engineering. m. Susi Gimmel, 31 Mar 1953, 2 s, 1 d. *Education:* Dipl Cive Engrg, Swiss Fed Inst of Tech, 1946; PhD Civil Eng, Lehi Univ, PA, USA, 1951. *Appointments:* Res Assoc, Appl Math Brown Univ, Providence, USA, 1951-52; Prof, Struct Engrg, Lehigh Univ, 1953- 60; Prof of Struc Engrg, Swiss Fed Inst of Tech, Zurich, 1960-90. *Publications:* Multiple publications in scientific journals. *Memberships:* Intl Assn Bridge and Struct Engrg, Pres, 1977-85; US Acad of Engrg; Swiss Acad of Tech Scis; Am Concrete Inst, Hon mem; Am Soc of Civil Engrg, Fellow; Swiss Engrg and Archts Soc; German Engrs Assn; Serbian Acad of Scis. *Honours:* Am Soc of Civil Engrg Awds: Res Prize, 1960, Norman Medal, 1963, Moisseiff Awd, 1964, Howard Awd; Hon Doctor's Deg, Univ of Stuttgart, Germany, 1983; Ostenfeld Gold Medal, Tech Univ of Denmark, 1991. *Hobbies:* History; Hiking; Skiing. *Address:* Pfannenstiel-Strasse 56, 8132 Egg, Switzerland. 26, 43, 52.

THURLOW Alexander Cresswell, b. 13 Apr 1940, Ismailia, Egypt, Anaesthetist; Medical Practitioner. m. Jonna Woycicka, 29 June 1963, 2 d. *Education:* Brighton, Hove and E.Sussex Grammar Sch, 1951-58; MBBS, FCAnaes, St Mary's Hosp Med Sch, 1958-64. *Appointments:* Sr Registrar Anaes, St Thomas Hosp and Hosp for Sick Children, 1969-72; Conslt Anaes, St George's 1972-; Cons Anaes, Asst Prof, Stanford Univ, Calif, 1975-76. *Publications:* Book chapters in: Anaesthesia Review, 1982; Clinics in Anaesthesiology, 1983; Anaesthesia and Sedation in Dentistry, 1983; A Practise of Anaesthesia, 1984. *Memberships:* Assn of Anaes; Assn of Dental Anaes, Coun; BMA. *Honours:* Goldman Silver Medal, Inst of Dental Surg, 1988. *Hobbies:* Walking; Swimming; Opera; Theatre; Travel. *Address:* Dept of Anaesthesia, St Georges Hospital, Blackshaw Road, London SW17, England.

TIAGO DE OLIVEIRA Jose, b. 22 Dec 1928, Mozambique. Chair; Professor. m. Ermelinda, 28 May 1953, 1 s, 2 d. *Education:* Lic Maths, 1949, Geog Engr, 1950, Univ Porto; Dr Maths, 1957, Aggregation Applied Maths, 1965, Univ Lisboa. *Appointments include:* Res Asst, Marine Biol Inst, 1951-53; Asst, 1953-57, Asst Prof, 1957-65, Assoc Prof, 1965-67, Chair Prof, 1967-87, Coun Fac of Psychol, 1977-78, Univ of Lisboa, Fac of Scis; Ch Prof, New Univ of Lisboa, Fac of Scis and Tech, 1988-; Dir, Ctr for Applied Maths, 1969-75; Dir, Ctr for Stats and Appl, 1975-81; Res Dir, 1969; Pres, Applied Maths Gp, 1978-81; Pres Dept of Stats, Ops Res and Computing, 1981-85; Fac of Scis, Pres Dept of Maths, Fac of Scis and Tech, 1989-90, Dir Lib Fac of Scis and Tech, 1992-. *Publications:* 218 papers and 9 books. *Memberships:* Pres, Inst for Portuguese Actuaries, 1976-79; Fdr and Pres, Portuguese Soc for Stats and Ops Res, 1981-80; Fdr, Pres, Fulbright Alumni Assn, 1977-80 and of the Gen Assembly, 1980-82. *Honours:* Acad of Scis of Lisboa; Corres Mem, RAS MAdrid; Fellow Inst of Math Stats, 1974; Intl Stat Inst, 1966; Hon Fellow, Royal Stat Soc, 1987, Fellow, 1952-. *Hobbies:* Philosophy and History of Science. *Address:* Academia das Ciencias de Lisboa, 19 R da Academia das Ciencias, 1200 Lisboa, Portugal.

TIAN Niu, b. 8 Jan 1925, Heilongjiang, China. Professor and Doctor. m. Luo Yi, 17 Feb 1950, 2 s, 1 d. *Education:* MD, Med Univ of China, 1944-47; Postdoc Study, Beijing Union Med Univ, 1953-54; DMSci, Russian Acad of Military Scis, 1956-59. *Appointments:* Lectr, 1949; Assoc Prof, 1956, First Military Med Col; Assoc Prof, 1959, Prof, 1980, Acado PLA Military Med Scis; Prof, Dir of Microcirculation Lab, Chinese PLA Gen Hosp, 1986. *Publications:* Microcirculation 1st & 2nd edition; Microcirculation and Irradiation; Microcirculation disorders and related Diseases; Fundamental and Clinical microcirculation; Methodology in Microcirculation; Clinical Microcirculation. *Memberships:* Nat Com of Med Standards; Co-Chm, and Chm of Chinese Assn of Pathophysiol Microcirc Com and Microcirc Com of PLA; Ed: Chinese Jour of Radiol Med and Protection, Bulletin of Acad of Military Med Scis and Chinese Jour of Pathophysiol. *Honours:* 1st grade awd, Russian Acad of Military Med Sci, 1958; 1st grade awds of Achievement in Sci and Tech, PLA of China, 1963, 1984, 1988; 2nd grade awds of Achievement in Sci and Tech, Hlth Min of China, 1987, 1988; Highest Awd of Sci, Ctrl Govt of China, 1987; 1st grade awds of new books, Nat Com, 1986, 1988. *Hobbies:* Chinese Calligraphy; Beijing Opera; Reading. *Address:* 304 Bldg 4, 28 Fuxing Road, 100853 Beijing, China. 152.

TIAN Yuan, m. Daren Guo, 1 s. *Education:* Shanghai 2nd Medical Univ, 1963. *Appointments include:* Initiated, Book, Pediatric Intensive Care Unit, Its Organization & Techniques, 1982-89; Established Lab of Radioimmunology, Childrens Hosp, Assoc Chief, 1984-; Assoc Chief Physician, 1989-. *Memberships:* Acad of Endocrinology; Chinese Medical Assn; Conslt to chinese Assn of Nutrition & Health; China Bohai Bay Area Economic Information Constl Corp. *Honours:* Chinese Natl Award of Scientific Books of Excellence. *Address:* c/o Tianjin Childrens Hospital, Tainjin 300074, China. 139, 152.

TIBAZARWA Clemens Martin, b. 10 Nov 1933, Tanzania. Economic Expert. m. Amelia Remi Kagemulo, 30 Oct 1965, 3 s, 3 d. *Education:* BA Econ, Dillard Univ, 1962; MA Econ, Atlanta Univ, 1964; MA Econ, Claremont, 1970; PhD Econ, Claremont, 1974; GATT Dipl, Geneva, Switz, 1965. *Appointments:* Econ, 1964-67, Sr Econ, 1970-75, Dir of Planning, 1976- 77, Govt of Tanzania; Econ Expert, ACP Secretariat, Brussels, 1977-. *Publications:* PhD Dissertation: Economic Impact on Tanzania of the E.African Common Market; Economic Revolutions in Bahaya History; From Berlin to Brussels. *Memberships:* Royal Econ Soc; Soc for Hist of Tech. *Honours:* Fulbeight-Mundt Scholarship, 1960; UN Fellowship for GATT Course, 1965; African-Am Scholarhip, 1967-70, 1974. *Hobbies:* Gardening; Writing; Reading. *Address:* 9 Jezus Eiklaan, 3080 Tervuren, Belgium.

TIBBITS David Stanley, Captain Sir, b. 11 Apr 1911, Warwick, England. Retired Captain Royal Navy; Master Mariner. m. Mary Florence Butterfield, 3 Sept 1938, 2 d. *Education:* Royal Naval Col, Dartmouth, 1925-28. *Appointments:* Royal Navy, 1925; Navigation Spec, 1934; Navigating Ofr, HM Ships York, Norfolk, Devonshire, Anson, WWII; Radar Plotting Sch, 1943; Cmdr, 1946, Capt, 1953; Dir, Radio Equipment Dept, Admiralty, 1953-56; Cmdr, HM Ships Snipe, 1949-51, Manxman, 1956-57, Dryad and as Capt, HM Nagivation & Aircraft Derection Sch, 1957-59; 1st Capt, HMS Hermes, 1959-61; Ret'd, 1961; Elder Brother Trinity Hse, London, 1961-67 incl Chm, Lighthouse and Pilotage Coms, Nautical Assessor, Admiralty Cts; Elected Master's Dpty and Bd Chm, 1972; Anglo French Working party for Study of Shipping in Straits of Dover, Eng Channel, N.Sea, 1968-74; London Tribunal into ship's Loss, 1975-76; Pres, Marine Bds of Investigation, Bermuda, 1978, 1983, 1984. *Publications:* Artiles on navigation, weather, hurricanes in various publications. *Memberships:* Freeman, City of London, 1962; Liveryman, Ct, Worshipful Co of Shipwrights; Fdr Mem, Fellow, Nautical Inst; Com of Mgmt, Hon Treas, Intl Assn of Lighthouse Auths, 1972-76; Pilotage Com Ch, Bermuda Port Auth; Chm, Jt Pres, Bermuda Soc for the Blind; Past Pres, Bermuda Sea Cadet and Sail Training Assn; Lay VP, Missions to Seamen. *Honours:* Dist Serv Cross, Madagascar, 1942; KB, 1975. *Hobbies:* Sailing; Music; Photography. *Address:* Harting Hill, Point Shares, Pembroke HM05, Bermuda. 1.

TICHENOR Fred Cooper Jr., b. 20 Feb 1932, Kentucky, USA. Astrologist. m. Nancy Catherine Presco, 25 Aug 1956, div; 2 s, 1 d. *Education:* BA Philos, Univ Louisville, 1957; Postgrad, Dept of Psychi, Albert Einstein Col of Med, Bronx, NY, 1991. *Appointments:* US Army, 1951-53; Asst Mgr, Courier-Jour, Louisville, 1957-64; Asst VP, Grolier Pubs, Chicago, 1964-71; Bus & Personal Conslt, 1971-; Syndicated newspaper columnist, (Star Lore), Louisville, 1981-; Syndicated TV Jour, Inverness, FL, 1988-; Moonbow Astro Retreat Organizer, Cumberland Falls, KY, 1974-; Cradle of Civilization Tour Org, 1979-; Lectr, extensively in US as well as Italy, France and Soviet Union, 1980-. *Memberships:* Councilman, 1986-88, Chm, Planning and Zoning Comm, 1985-88, City of W.Point, KY; V-Chm, Salt River Area Coun for the Arts, 1983-88; Community Sch Bd, 1985-88; Community Messenger, Brandenburg, KY, 1985; Assn for Psychol Type, 1991-. *Address:* 937 Cherokee Road, Louisville, KY 40204, USA.

TICKELL James Nicolas, b. 1 June 1957, The Hague, Holland. Writer and Public Servant. m. Zita Beta Palkovits, 1 Oct 1991. *Education:* Ecole Paroissielle St HOnore, Paris, 1964; Moreton Hall, Suffolk, 1964-70; Westminster Sch, London, 1970-74; MA Arch, Trinity Col, Cambs, 1974-78. *Appointments:* Bowerbank Brett & Lacey, Archts, 1978-81; Special Hsg Coor, Community Hsg Assn, London, 1981-83; Dir of Hsg, Brit Refugee Coun, 1984-87; Registrar, Hsg Corp, London, 1987-. *Publications:* The American Express Guide to Mexico; Cusco Pery; Tikal, City of the Maya. *Memberships:* Sanctuary Hsg Assn. *Honours:* Scholarship to Westminister Sch, 1970; Samuaies Exhib to Trinity, Cambs, 1974; Harkness Fellowship of the C'wlth Fund, NY, 1990. *Hobbies:* Travel; Cycling; Walking. *Address:* 342 South Lambeth Road, London SW8, England.

TILDEN Lorraine H Frederick, b. 16 May 1912, Peoria, Illinois, USA. Writer; Educator; m. Wesley R Tilden, 20 June 1948. *Education:* AA, Illinois State Univ, 1931; BA, UCLA, 1948; MA Claremont Grad Sch, 1954; PhD Studies, Univ de Madrid, Spain, Univ de Guanajuato, Mexico; Tchg Fellow, UCLA, UC, Riverside, San Francisco State Univ. *Appointments:* Various Col Tchg posts, 1950-65; Assoc Prof, Hmanities, Spanish and Eng Lit, Upland Col, 1962-65; Tchr, World Lit, Glendora HS, Calif, 1967-77; Dir, Alumni Records Proj, Claremont Grad Sch, Calif, 1978-84; Foreign Firm Conslt, 1967-; Tchr, Eng Sch, Fac de Med, Univ de la Habana, Cuba, 1937-41. *Publications:* Numerous dramatic, music and literary reviews in magazines and newspapers. *Memberships:* State Arts Chm, AAUW; Nat Civic Com, People to People; Pres, Town Affiliation Assn of Claremont, Calif; Pres, Claremont Grad Sch Alumni Assn; Pres, Rembrandt Club; Pomona Col; Sigma Delta Pi; Pi Lambda Theta; Am Assn of Tchrs of Spanish and Portuguest; Vachel Lindsay Assn. *Honours include:* Recipient with husband, Best Single Proj Awd for Guanajuato Week and Best Overall Proj Awd, from Readers Digest, Nat League of Cities and People to People, 1964, 1965; Hon Citizen of Guanajuato, Mexico, 1963; Dist Serv Citations, Claremont City Coun, 1963-66 and Claremont Grad Sch, 1975; Rockfeller Grant, 1937-41. *Hobbies:* Foreign language study; Travel; Making travalogues; Swimming. *Address:* 351 Oakdale Drive, Claremont, CA 91711, USA. 2, 5, 9, 11, 13, 15, 59, 120, 130, 132, 138.

TILEV Georgi, b. 21 Sept 1943, Sofia, Bulgaria. Violinist. m. Anka Wladimirova, 25 Dec 1965, 2 s, 1 d. *Education:* MMus, Bulgarian Music Conservatory, 1971; Dipl in Chamber Mus, Moskow Conservatory, 1976; Master course with Prof Willmos Tatray and Ifrah Neeman, 1977-79. *Appointments:* Concertmaster and Soloist, Bulgarian Ratio and TV Symph Orch, 1966-73; Primarius of Bulgarian Radio String Quartet, 1973-84; First Concertmaster of Niederrheinische Sinfoniker in Germany, 1984. *Creative works:* Recordings with: Melodia Record Co, USSR, Balkanton, Bulgaria and Sound Products, Holland; Numerous works for string quartet and solo violin. *Honours:* Intl Bach Competition, Leipzig, 1968; Sibelius Intl Competition, Helsinki, 1970;

Paganini Competition Genua, 1972; String Quartet Competition, Colmar, 1978; Extra Prize for French works, Debussy,(string quartet), Evian, 1980. *Address:* Jungfernweg 31, 4150 Krefeld 1, Germany.

TILL James Edgar, b. 25 Aug 1931, Canada. Scientist; Professor. m. M Joyce Sinclair, 6 June 1959, 1 s, 2 d. *Education:* BA 1952, MA 1954, Univ of Sask; PhD, Yale Univ, 1957. *Appointments:* Postdoc Fellow, Connaught Med Res Labs, Toronto, 1956-57; Sr Sci Staff, 1957-, Hd, Div of Biol Res, 1969-82, Ontario Cancer Inst; Univ of Toronto: Asst Prof, Dept of Med Biophys, 1958-62, Mem, Grad Fac, 1958, Assoc Prof, 1962-65, Prof, 1965-, Grad Fac, Inst of Med Sci, 1968-, Assoc Dean, Life Scis, Sch of Grad Studies, 1981-84, Sr Fellow, 1989-90, Continuing, 1990-, Massey Col, Mem, Ctr for Bioethics, 1989-. *Publications:* Over 200 articles in scientific journals or chapters in scientific or medical books, mainly on various aspects of cancer research, both fundamental and applied. *Memberships:* Nat Cancer Inst of Can; Soc for Med Decision-Making; Soc for Judgement and Decision-Making; Can Bioethics Soc. *Honours:* Gairdner Foun Intl Awd, 1969; FRSC, 1969; Univ Prof, Toronto, 1984; Thomas W Eadie Medal, RSC, 1991. *Hobbies:* Reading; Microcomputers; Curling. *Address:* Ontario Cancer Institute, Princess Margaret Hospital, 500 Sherbourne St, Toronto, Ontario, Canada M4X 1K9. 2, 142.

TIMAR Tibor, b. 3 July 1953, Endrod, Hungary. m. Irena Nacsa, 27 Mar 1982, 1 s. *Education:* Deg in Chem with hons, Kossuth L Univ, Debrecen, Hungary, 1977; PhD, 1980; Postdoctoral Fellow, Dept Chem, Texas A & M Univ, USA. *Appointments:* Alkaloida Chem Co Tiszavasvari, Hungary: Chemist, 1977-78, Res Chemist, 1978-88, Hd of Res, 1988-. *Publication:* Inventions in Field. *Contributions to:* professional journals. *Honours:* Outstanding inventor in Hungary, 1985. *Hobbies:* Reading; Listening to music. Address: Kabay Janos 17, H 4440 Tiszavasvari, Hungary. 52.

TIMBERLAKE Charles E, b. 9 Sept 1935, South Shore, Kentucky, USA. University Professor. m. Patricia Perkins, 23 Dec 1958, 3 s. *Education:* BA Hist and Polit Sci, Berea Col, KY, 1957; Calif State Tchg Credential, 1958; MA Hist, Claremont Grad Sch, AL, 1962; PhD, Hist, Univ of Washington, Seattle, 1968. *Appointments:* Tchg Asst, Univ of Washington, 1962-64; Asst, Assoc Prof of Hist, Univ of Missouri, 1967; Vis Prof of Hist and Russian Studies, Univ of Manchester, 1987-88; Asst Dir Hons Col, Univ of Missouri, 1888-90. *Publications:* Numerous articles, papers and books including: The Middle Classes in Late Tsarist Russia, 1991; Ed, Religious and Secular Forces in late Tsarist Russia, 1991; Higher Learning the State, and the Professions in Russia, 1983; Detente: A Documentary Record, 1978; East Central and Southeastern Europe: A Handbook of library and archival resources in North America, 1976. *Memberships:* Am Assn for the Adv of Slavic Studies, 1961, Bd, 1980-82, 1984-86, Chm, Permanent Membership Com, 1981-84, Chm, Coun of Reg Affiliates, 1981-82, 1985-86; Am Hist Soc, 1958-; Conf on Slavic and E.European Hist, Exec Coun, Elected Rep of W.US, 1987-89; Ctrl Slavic Conf, 1967; Pres, 1969, 1977, 1984, 1989; Missouri Conf on Hist, 1967-, Pres, 1992. *Honours:* Hon Prof of Hist, Lanzhou Univ, China, 1991; Fac Awd, Univ of Missouri Alumni Assn, 1990; Ed Adv Bd, The Columbia Missourian, 1990; Res Fellowshp, Univ of Missouri Res Coun; Nat Endowment for the Humanities Grants; Am Coun of Learned Socs Fellowship. *Hobbies:* Travel; Running; Skiing. *Address:* History Department, University of Missouri, Columbia, MO 65211, USA. 2, 8, 13, 30, 117.

TIMMERMANN Leni, b. 5 Mar 1901, Witten, Ruhr, Germany. Retired. m. Franz Timmermann, 26 Feb 1931, 1 s, 1d. *Education:* Conservatoires of Recklinghausen and Essen, 1919-23; Final Exam as Mus Tchr, Westphalian Acad of Music, Muenster, 1923-27. *Appointments:* Self-employed Mus Tchr, 1923-66; Pianist, 1923-33 in Marl-Huels, Westphalia. *Creative*

works: Compositions: Numerous including Kleine Trommier, Luedenscheider, Wanderlied, Luedenscheider Heimatlied; Gehst du der Sonne Entgegen; Herrlicher Rhein; Memories of Yesteryear; Denk Daran (Schoen ist die Welt); Leise schwebend auf Engelshaenden (See descending from realms of glory); Christbaumlegende (The Christmas Tree Legend); Wunder von Bethlehem, (Miracle in Bethlehem); Numerous recordings. *Publications include:* Three German Carols, 1983; Lieder-Album von Leni Timmerman, 1984. *Memberships:* GEMA, Berlin; Intl Arbeitskreis Frau und Musik e V Dusseldorf. *Hobby:* The family. *Address:* c/o Dr Franz H Timmermann, Gerckensplatz 17, D-2000 Hamburg 63, Germany. 4, 151.

TIMOTHY Hamilton Baird, b. 13 Apr 1913, Irvine, Ayres, Scotland, Writer; Prof Eneritus. *Education:* MA, Glasgow, 1934; BD, London, 1941; BA, Edinburgh, 1943; PhD, Saskatchewan, 1958; PhD, Mental Testing & Child Psychology, Edinburgh, 1974; Tchrs Training Coll, 1946. *Appointments:* Exec Sec, United Christian Lit Soc, London, 1949-59; Asst Prof, Univ of Winnipeg, 1959-63; Asst Prof, Western Univ, 1963; Assoc Prof, 1966; Visiting Prof, Univ of Utrecht, 1971-72; Prof of Humanities, Assoc Dean, Dir of Relig Studies, Univ of Regina, 1973-80; Prof Emeritus, 1981. *Publications include:* The Early Christian Apologists & Greek Philosophy; Ukrainian Folk Stories by Marko Vovchov; Saskatoon, Saskatchewan. *Memberships:* Convocation, Univ of London; Writrs Union of Canada; Acad & Admin Pensioners Assn. *Honours include:* William Roxburgh Memorial Prize; Regina, Hon Title of Prof Emeritus. *Hobbies:* Drawing; Water Colour; Painting; Gardening. *Address:* 73 Louise Avenue, Sault Ste Marie, Ontario, Canada P6A 6A5.

TISHKOV Leonid, b. 4 May 1953, Vral, Russia. Artist; Poet; Cartoonist; Illustrator; Editor. m. Marina Moskvina, 20 Nov 1976, 1 s. *Education:* Medical Coll, Moscow, 1970-77. *Appointments:* Cartoonist, 1974-83; Illustrator, 1984-92; Participate Intl Exhib, 1987- 92. *Publications:* Living in the Trank; Gazely; The Simple actions of D; Drean of Fishman; Life of Smallman; Dabloides; Stomachs. *Honours:* Grand Prix, Intl World Cartoon SKOPIE; Grand Prix, Intl Book Art. *Hobby:* Dream. *Address:* Orekhoviy Bul 47/33-223, Moscow, 115580, Russia.

TITLOW Larry Wayne, b. 12 Oct 1945, Hearne, Texas, USA. Kinesiologist. *Education:* BS 1969, MEd, 1970, Univ of Houston; PhD, Texas A&M Univ, 1977. *Appointments:* Grad Asst, Univ Houston, 1969-70; Instr, Blinn Col, Breham, TX, 1970-72; Grad Asst, Texas A&M, Col Station, 1972-74, 1976-77; Tchr, Coach Pearland (TX) Ind Sch Dist, 1974-75; Tchr, Houston Ind Sch Dist, 1975-76; Asst Prof, N. Kentucky Univ, Highland Heights, 1977-82; Assoc Prof, Univ Cent Ark, Conway, 1982-89; Prof, 1989-; Fitness Conslt, Acxiom Conway, Ark, 1986-90; Res Conslt, Univ Ark, Fayetteville, 1983-. *Publications:* Joint author: A Resource manual for Workshops on Presenting the Educational Improvement Plan to the Community, 1980; Lifetime Fitness, 1981. *Contributions to:* articles to professional journals. *Memberships:* Instr, Lifesaving Am Red Cross, Conway, 1983-80; Speaker, Conslt, Ark Sch for the Deaf, Little Rock, 1985-88; Participant Conslt, Fairfield Bay Hlth Fair, 1986; Guest Speaker Kiwanis, Optimists, Conway 1982-. *Honours:* Res Grant, DaVinci Lab, Burlington, 1980; Ky Coun on Higher Educ, Lexington, 1980; Univ Ctrl Ark Res Coun, 1985-89; Am Alliance for Hlth Phys Educ Rec and Dance; Am Col Sports Med; Ark Assn Hlth Phys Educ Recreation and Dance. *Hobbies:* Travel; Hunting; Fishing. *Address:* University of Central Arkansas, PO Box 4991 UCA, Conway, AR 72032, USA. 7, 117.

TITOV Vladimir Mikhailovich, b. 19 Sept 1933, Leningrad. m. Titova Nina S, 28 Mar 1963, 1 s, 1 d. *Education:* Grad, Moscow Physico Tech Inst; Physicist-Engr, 1957; PhD, 1961; Dr of Phys and Maths, 1968;

Prof, 1971. *Appointments:* Jr Reschr, 1960-86; Sr Reschr, Hd of Lab; V-Dir of Lavrentyev Inst of Hydrodynamics, Dir, 1986-. *Publications:* Works on mechanics of cumulative processes high rate impact; Detonation physics discovery and investigation of UFD synthesis in detonation waves, 1968-90; Fisika goreniya i vzryva; Zhumal priclachji mekhaniki i technicheskoi fiziki; Proceedings of Intl Symposia on Detonation, USA. *Memberships:* Nat USSR Com on Theoretical and Applied Mechs, 1976; Corres, USSR Acad Sci, 1978, Academician, 1990. *Honours:* Four orders of the Soviet Union, 1967, 75, 8 86; Sci Prizes, Siberian Div of the USSR Acad of Scis. *Hobbies:* Trudgolick. *Address:* Lavrentyev Institute of Hydrodynamics, Siberian Div, USSR Acad of Science, Novosibirsk 630090, Russia.

TLALKA Jacek Stanislaw, b. 16 Dec 1937, Krosno, Poland. Professor of Mathematics. m. Alicia Tlalka, 30 Apr 1960, 1 s, 1 d. *Education:* MS Maths, Jagiellonian Univ, Cracow, 1960; PhD Mining and Metallurgy, Univ Cracow, Poland, 1971. *Appointments:* Asst Prof of Math, Mining and Metallurgy Univ, Cracow, 1963-77; Prof of Math, Dpty Chm, Livingstone Col, Salisbury, NC, USA, 1982-. *Publications:* 16 in Poland, 1967-78; 1 Student Textbook, 1978; 1 in the US, 1987. *Memberships:* AMS; MAA; NCTM. *Honours:* Special Awd, Sec of Higher Educ for PhD dissertation, 1978. *Hobbies:* Tennis; Skiing; Travel; Boating. *Address:* Rt 11 Box 524W, Salisbury, NC 28144, USA.

TODA Morikazu, b. 20 Oct 1917, Tokyo, Japan. Professor Emeritus. m. Kuniko, 29 Mar 1951. *Education:* Grad, Dept of Phys, Fac of Sci, Tokyo Univ, 1940. *Appointments:* Asst, Tokyo Univ, 1940, Prof, Tokyo Univ of Educ, 1952; Prof Yokohama Nat Univ, 1976; Prof, Univ of the Air, 1988. *Publications:* Statistical Physics, I, II; Theory of Nonlinear Lattices, 1988, 1991; Nonlinear Waves and Salitons, 1989. *Memberships:* Royal Norwegian Acad of Sci, 1981-. *Honours:* Fujihara Prize, Fujihara Sci Foun, Japan, 1981. *Hobbies:* Physics of mechanical toys; Water colour painting. *Address:* 5-29-8-108 Yoyogi, Shibuya-kun, Tokyo, Japan.

TODA Tadasumi, b. 15 Apr 1946, Morioka, Japan. Management Consultant. m. Shizue Yamaguchi, 10 May 1970, 3 s. *Education:* BA Commerce, Yokohama City Univ, 1969; NCB Computer Inst, 1988. *Appointments:* YS Line, 1969-88; Acct, 1969-72; Shipping Ofr, 1972-80; Nakhodka Rep, 1980-81, Forwarding Agent, 1981-86, System Analyst, 1986-88; Bus Conslt, 1988-. *Hobby:* Soccer. *Address:* 176 Karibacho, Hodogaya-Ku, Yokohama 240, Japan.

TODD Daphne Jane, b. 27 Mar 1947, York, England. Artist. m. 31 Aug 1984, 1 s. *Education:* Simon Langton Grammar Sch for Girls, Canterbury; Slade Sch of Fine Art, UCL: DFA, 1969, HDFA (London), 1971. *Appointments:* Dir of Studies, Heatherley Sch of Fine Art, 1980-86. *Creative Works:* Portrait Comm include: H R T THe Grand Duke of Luxemburg; Lord Adrian; Lord Pennock; Sir Austin Pearce; Sir Kirby Hardy Laing; Sir Edward Abraham; Dame Janet Baber; Neil Cossons Esq. *Memberships:* New English Art Club, 1984-; Royal Soc of Portrait Painters, 1985-, Hon Sec, 1990-; Gov Heatherley Sch of Fine Art, 1986-. *Honours:* 2nd Prize, John Player Portrait Awd, 1983; 1st Prize, Oil Painting of the Year, Hunting Gp Nat Art Prize Competition, 1984. *Hobby:* Gardening. *Address:* Salters Green Farm, Mayfield, E.Sussex TN20 6NP, England. 19.

TODERASCU Ion, b. 9 Sept 1938, Urechesti-Bacau. Professor of History. m. Nicoleta Toderascu, 20 Nov 1964. 1 d. *Education:* Fac of Hist, 1957-62; Dipl of Hist, Prof, 1962; Specialization, Univ of Gand, Belgium, 1974-75; Doctor of Hist, 1977. *Appointments:* The Univ Al J Cuza Jasi, Romania, Fac of Hist, Dept of Romanian Hist, 1962-. *Publications:* Volumes in collaboration: A D Xenopol Studies concerning his life and work, 1972; Petru Rares, , 1978; The History of Jasi University, 1985; History and Civilization, 1988. The Mediaeval Romanian Unity, 1988. *Honours:* The Nicolae Balcescu Prize,

Romanian Acad, 1984; Pres, Romanian Hist Dept, Univ of Jasi, 1991. *Hobbies:* Making long trips in the mountains; Volleyball; Reading. *Address:* Str Vascauteanu 12, 61 C1 et 4 Ap 13, 6600 Iasi, Romania.

TOLCHELNIKOVA-MURRI Svetlana Maria, b. 29 Nov 1936, Leningrad, USSR. Astronomer. m. Tolchelnikov Jury, 20 Dec 1973, 1 d. *Education:* Secondary Sch, Estonian Rep, 1944-54; Bachelor's Deg, Astronomy, Leningrad State Univ, 1959; Doctor's Deg in Phys and Math Sci, Main Astronomical Observatory, Leningrad, USSR, 1969. *Appointments:* Lab in Pulkuvo Observatory, 1959-; Jr Reschr, Reschr, Dept of Astrometry, 1963-, Demoted to Jr Reschr, 1987. *Publications:* Author of 41 papers in Russian, two in English on astrometry, the methods of positional observations, their reduction, reference frames and time and special relativity theory. *Honours:* Gold Medal, Secondary School Grad, 1954. *Hobbies:* Literature, especially poetry; Children's Education. *Address:* Pulkovo Observatory H 11 f2, 196140 St Petersburg, Russia.

TOLLEFSON Edwin Archer, b. 30 July 1933, Saskatchewan, Canada. Lawyer. m. Sheila Shaw, 24 May 1991, 2 s, 1 d. *Education:* BA 1954, LLB, 1956, Univ of Sask; BCL, 1958, DPhil, 1976, Oxford Univ. *Appointments:* Fac Mem, Col of Law, Univ of Sask, 1958-71; Fed Dept of Justice, Can, 1971-. *Publications:* Bitter Medicine, 1964; Cases and Comments on the law of Evidence, 1966, 1972; Ed: Report of the Federal/Provincial Task Force on Univorm Rules of Evidence, 1982. *Membership:* Sask Law Soc. *Honours:* IODE War Meml Scholarship, 1956, 1957; Can Coun Res Fellowship, 1968; Queen's Counsel, (Federal), 1980. *Hobbies:* Music; Bricolage; Crossword puzzles. *Address:* 3041 6th St SW, Calgary, Alta, Canada T25 2M1. 142.

TOLSTOJ Nikita, b. 15 Apr 1923. Philologist. m. Svetlana Tolstaja, 29 Sept 1964, 2 d. *Education:* Dr of Philol, Moscow State Univ, 1950; Dr Habil, Leningrad State Univ, 1972. *Appointments:* Res Fellow, Chief of Dept, Inst Slavjanovedenija, 1954-. *Publications:* Slavjanikja geograficeskaja terminologija, 1969; Istovija i struktura Slavjanstix Literaturnyx jazykov, 1988. *Memberships:* Acad of Scis, USSR: Prof, Moscow State Univ; Pres, Soviet Com of Slavists. *Honours:* Hon Mem of the following academies, Austrian, 1979, Macedonian, 1979, Serbian, 1985, Yugoslavian in Zagreb, 1988, Slovenian, 1987. *Address:* Opgomka. g 34/38 K6, 40, 109017 Mockba, Russia.

TOMCZAK Andrzej, b. 11 Nov 1941, Zerkow, Poland. Artist. m. Wieslawa Markiewicz, 3 May 1980. *Education:* MA Art Acad, Poznan, 1966. *Appointments:* Freelance artist, 1966-; Stenographer and Graphic Artist, TV Szczecin, 1966-73; Art Dir, Nat Editorial Agy, 1974-91. *Creative works:* Intl exhibs in Bulgaria, 1974, Riga, 1977, Cleveland, England, 1975, Poland, and Germany. Various art works 1966-91 including TV stage sets, posters, illustrations, book designs, graphic paintings, posters, illustrations. *Memberships:* Polish Artists Assn, 1966-; Pres, Szczecin area, 1977-80; VP, 1988-. *Honours:* Art competitions: Posters, 1st Prize, Poznan, 1964, Szczecin, 1971, 1974, 2nd Prizes, 1969, 1975, Szczecin, 3rd Prize, Warsaw, 1969. Open Air Performance 2nd Prize, Koszalin, 1987, 1989; The Golden Ex Libris Awd, Szczecin, 1987-89; The Autumn Art Salon, Drawing Awd, Szczecin, 1988. *Hobbies:* Travel; Skiing; Nature; Books; Wandering. *Address:* ul Szafera 72/40, 71-245 Szczecin, Poland.

TOMKINS James William, b. 28 July 1934, Sydney, Australia. Executive Chairman. m. 19 Mar 1958, 2 s, 1 d. *Education:* In Austr and USA. *Appointments:* Current Directorships: Exec Chm, Maracorp Fin Sers Ltd; Dpty Chm, Nat Mortgage Mkt Corp Ltd; Aspermont Ltd, Victorian Housing Bonds Ltd, Nat Mortgage Securities Ltd, Home Opportunity Loans, Ltd, Nat Mortgage Bonds Ltd, Wine & Food Soc of Austr Inc; JP, New S.Wales; Previous Directorships include: Interim Mortgage Fin

Ltd, Network Fin Ltd, 1986-87; Laser Lab Ltd, Financial Wisdom Ltd, Investors Life Ins Co of Austr Ltd, 1986-89; Darling Downs TV Ltd, Universal Telecasters (Qld) Ltd, 1987-89. *Memberships:* Austr Club, Malbourne; Austr Inst of Co Dirs; Austr Inst of Bankers; Soc of Sr Execs; Wine & Food Soc of Victoria Inc, Pres, 1984-86; Fed of Wine and Food Socs of Austr, Dir and VP; Nat Heart Foun of Austr. *Hobbies:* Soccer; Swimming; Orchestral music; Opera; Ballet; Food and Wine. *Address:* 42 Somers Avenue, Malvern, Victoria 3144, Australia. 23, 139, 156, 157.

TOMLINSON Rick, b. 18 Sept 1958, Bury, Lancs, England. Photographer. *Education:* King Williams Col, Isle of man, 1970-75. *Appointments:* Est Agy, 1976-81; Profl Yacht Racing Crew, 1981-86; Profl Marine Photographer, 1986. *Creative works:* Annual Calendar of own work, 1989-. *Contributions to:* international magazines and books. *Honours:* Bronze Medal for Bravery awarded by the Royal Nat Lifeboat Inst, 1991. *Hobbies:* Sailing; Photography. *Address:* Radleigh, Port St Mary, Isle of Man, England.

TOMLINSON Ruth Nourse, b. 18 July 1908. Artist; Portrait Painter. m. P D Wilson, dec. *Education:* BSc McGill Univ, Canada, 1930; Studies painting under A Sheriff Scott, Montreal, 1937-39; Dr Arthur Lismer 1954-55, City & Guild Art Sch, London, UK, 1956-58. *Appointments:* Bacteriologist and Chemist, Control Lab, Canadianwide E.Daries. *Creative works:* Numerous folk paintings including Exeter Morris Men, Masque; Uncle George & the Dragon; Hero of Waterloo's Waltz; Beaux of London City; Mon on a Bicycle; Court Dances; Also: Buttercups and Daisies, Embroidery; Several prints, etc; Portraits of members of the Dipl Ser, Church, Medical and Music professions in Can, UK and Holland. Music and art tour in Europe; Publications: The American Wedgewoodian, 1969; Folk in Kent, 1982, 1985; Numerous newspaper reproductions and reviews. Exhibitions include: One- woman shows: St Andrews East, 1959; Montreal Arts CLub, 1960; Edinburgh Festival, 1968; Broadstairs, 1969; Notelets, 1970, 1971, 1983; Permanent collections include: Baden Powell Hse Library, 1962; Gilwell Park; Wedgewood International Seminar; Private collections, various countries; Exhibition and lecture, 128 slides of own paintings, 1987; Second selection of slides of own paintings, Royal Overseas league, 1989; 2 paintings reproduced, Ridley catalogue, 1988. *Memberships include:* Chelsea Art Soc; Ridley Art Soc; Royal Overseas League; Life fellow, RSA; Life: Royal Overseas League, Monarchists League of Can. *Honours:* Chelsea Gardening Guild 3rd Prize for Balcony Cottage Garden, 1991. *Hobbies:* Nutrition; Swimming; Golf; Walking; Music. *Address:* c/o Royal Overseas League, Park Place, St James's Street, London SW1A 1LR, England.

TOMSIC Joseph Andrew Michael, b. 12 Aug 1949, Cleveland, Ohio, USA. Military Officer. m. Sylviane Madeleine Edelblut, 16 June 1989, 1 s. *Education:* BA Col of Artesia, New Mexico, 1970; MA Pepperdine Univ, Calif, 1981; MA, Salve Regina, 1987, MA, Naval War Col, 1990, Rhode Island. *Appointments:* Ofc Mgr, W.Union, Cleve, 1970-71; Enlisted USN, 1971 advanced through grades to Comdr, 1988; Interior Communications specialist, LPD-8 USN, San Diego, 1971; Dept Hd, Security/Nuclear Weapons Sect, Div Hd Bldg Ops, Maint Mgmt, USA, Bermuda, 1973-74; Engr Ofr, LPH-7, USN, Norfolk, VA, 1975-77; Dir Enlistment Recruit Area 5 USN Great Lakes, III, 1977-79; Dir Enlistment Prog, USN, Orlando, FL, 1979-81; Chief Engr, DDG-2USN, Mayport, Fla, 1982-83; Chief Engr, LPD-9 USN, Norfolk, 1983-85; Exec Asst Dir, CNO Strat, Study Gp USN, Newport, RI, 1986-87; Engr Ofr, LHA-4 USN, Norfolk, 1987- 88; Staff Ofr, Maritime Ops, Shape, USN, 1988-; Defence Lang Inst, Naval Security Gp Detachment Monterey, Calif, 1991-92. *Publications:* Today's Best Poems, 1980. *Memberships:* Assn Belgo-Ams; Am And Common Mkt Club; Am Club Brussels, Bd of Govs, 1991-; Bd, Am Overseas Meml Day Assn, Community Affairs, 1991-; SHAPE Ofrs Assn, 1990. *Hobbies:* Collecting art; Reading; Tennis; Classical

music. *Address:* Chemin de Neufvilles 127, 7060 Soignies, Belgium. 6, 57.

TONDL Ladislav, b. 28 Feb 1924, Znojmo. Professor and Director. m. Milica Tondlova, 14 Oct 1955, 2 d. *Education:* PhDr, Charles Univ, 1949; Ing, Econ Univ, 1949; PhD, 1955, Prof, 1968, Charles Univ. *Appointments:* Assoc Prof, 1955, Prof, 1968, Dir of Inst, 1968-89. *Publications:* Problems of Semantics, 1981; Scientific Procedures, 1973; Scientific Thought, 1973; Philosophy of Technology, 1990. *Memberships:* Intl Assn for Philos of Sci; Pres, Nat Com for Logic, Methodology and Philos of Sci. *Address:* Jilska 1, 110 00 Prague 1, Czechoslovakia. 156.

TONITZA-IORDACHE Michaela, b. 9 Nov 1942, Bucharest, Romania. Theatre Director. m. Stefan Iordache, 30 Apr 1970. *Education:* Grad, Univ of Bucharest, 1967; Foundationer, Univ ofVien, Austria; Dr of Theatre Sci, 1975; Foundationer, USA, 1984. *Appointments:* Rdr, Theatre Acad, 1967-79, 1990-; Head, Little Theatre, 1979-82; MD, Puppet Theatre, 1986-91. *Publications:* On the Art of the Theatre, 1975; On Acting, 1980; Eliza - A monography of a great Romanian actress, 1981. *Memberships:* Intl Coun of Union of Marionetists, Tokyo, Japan, 1988. *Hobbies:* The Art of the actor; Semiology; Cinema. *Address:* Intr Gr Cantilli 16, Bucharest 1, Romania 71137.

TOPOLSKI Jerzy, b. 20 Sept 1928, Poznan, Poland. Historian; University Professor. m. (1) Zofia Kulejewska, 21 Apr 1954, div, 1958; (2) Maria Barbara Antczak, 9 Sept 1962, div, 1978; (3) Maria Danuta Labedzka, 29 July 1978. *Education:* MPolit Econ, Univ of Poznan, 1950; PhD, Univ of Torun; Docent, 1956, Prof, 1961, Prof, 1968. *Appointments:* Asst, Univ of Poznan, 1951; Asst Prof, Acad of Scis Warsaw, Prof, Univ of Poznan, 1954- 56; V-Dir, Inst of Hist, 1968-81; Dir, 1981-87. *Publications:* 18 books including: Birth of Capitalism in Europe, 1965; Methodology of History, 1968; Thoery of Historical Knowledge, 1983; Outline History of Poland, 1976; Freedom and Coertion in History, 1990. *Memberships:* Polish Acad of Scis (PAS); Com, Intl Assn of Econ Hist; Pres, Com of Hist Scis, PAS; State Tribunal, 1981-89; Vis prof, Can, AM, France, Italy, Germany. *Honours include:* State Awds in the Humanities, 1969, 1971; Miesiecznik Literacki Montly Awd, 1975; ODRA Monthly Awd, 1983. *Hobby:* Travelling. *Address:* ul Bastionowa 45, 61-663 Poznan, Poland. 57.

TORII Shuko, b. 5 Apr 1930, Japan. Professor. m. Mochizuki Toshiko, 19 June 1975. *Education:* BA 1954, MA, 1956, PhD, 1964, Univ of Tokyo. *Appointments:* Res Asst, Univ of Tokyo, 1961-65; Res Assoc, Univ of Michigan, USA, 1966-68, Florida State Univ, 1968-69; Assoc Prof, 1970- 79, Prof, 1979-91, Univ of Tokyo; Prof, Univ of Sacred Heart, 1991-. *Publications:* The World of Vision, 1979; Psychology of Vision, 1982; Perception, 1983; Visual Perception in the Congenitally blinded after operation, in press. *Memberships:* Japanese Psychol Assn, ed, 1989-; Japanese Psychonomic Soc, Ed, 1989-; Optical Soc of Am, 1968-. *Hobby:* Art appreciation. *Address:* 2-17-26-204 Takada, Toshima-ku, Tokyo 171, Japan. 57.

TORIWAKI Jun-Ichiro, b. 20 July 1939, Japan. Professor. m. 21 Sept 1969, 1 s. *Education:* BEng, 1962, MEng, 1964, DEng, 1969, Elec Engrg, Nagoya Univ. *Appointments:* Res Assoc, 1970, Asst Prof, 1974, Assoc Prof, Compuational Ctr, 1974-77, Assoc Prof, Elec Engrg, 1977-80, Prof, 1983-85, Prof, Dept of Info Engrg, 1985-, Nagoya Univ; Prof, Toyohashi Univ of Tech, 1980-83. *Publications:* Digital Image Processing for Image Understanding; 200 research papers in leading academic journals in Japan and USA, as well as conference proceedings; Developed the programme package for image processing called SLIP. *Memberships:* IEEE, USA; Inst Elec Info and Comunication Engrs of Japan; Info Processing of of Japan; Japan Soc of Med Elec and Biol Engrg (JSMEBE); Japan Soc of Med Imaging Tech (JSMIT); Inst of TV

Engrs of Japan. *Honours:* Paper Awds: JSMEBE and JSMITO; Niwa- Takayanagi Awd, Best Book, Inst of TV Engs of Japan. *Hobbies:* Classical music; Reading. *Address:* 146 Meidai Yada-shukusha, 2-66 Yada-cho, Higashi-ku, Nagoya 464, Japan.

TOROK Istvan Vince, b. 1 Dec 1904, Tiszaeszlar, Hungary. Retired Professor of Theology. m. Etelka Ilona Pongracz, 4 Aug 1936, 3 s. *Education:* Debrecen Theol, 1923-26, Stipend Abroad, Berlin, 1926-28, Munster IW, 1928-29; Marburg AL, 1923; Debrecen Dipl Theol, 1929; Debrecen DTheol, 1931; Pvte Docent, Debrecen, 1936. *Appointments:* Tchr in Reformed Col, 1929-31; Prof of Theol, 1931-41; Prof of Theol Debrecen Univ, 1941-57, Pro of Theol, Debrecen Theol Acad, 1957-68; Enforced retirement, 1968. *Memberships:* Foun Mem, Societas Ethica, 1860-. *Honours:* Dr Hon Causa, Budapest Ref Theol Acad, 1989; Medal, Agriculture Worker of Excellence. *Hobby:* Pigeons. *Address:* Lugossy U 4, Debrecen H- 4028, Hungary.

TOROK Istvan, b. 22 Feb 1939, Hungary. Physicist. m. Anna Maria Palatinszky, 27 Jan 1972, div 1983, 2 s. *Education:* Fazekas M Gimnazium, Debrecen, Hungary, 1953-57; Kossuth L Tud Egy, Debrecen, Student, 1957-62, PhD, 1977. *Appointments:* Pyhsicist in Ctrl Res Inst for Phys, Budapest, Hungary, 1962-63; Atomiki Inst of Nuclear Res, 1963-. *Publications:* Over 50 scientific papers in professional journals and magazines; One book translation. *Memberships:* Eotvos R Phys Soc; J Neumann computer Sci Soc; Hungarian Friends of Minerals. *Hobbies:* Orienteering; Sport; Map reading; Minerals; Photography. *Address:* Atomki Institute of Nuclear Research, Bem-Ter 18/C pf 51, Debrecen H-4001, Hungary. 52.

TORRANCE Victor Brownlie, b. 24 Feb 1937, Glasgow, Scotland. University Professor of Building. m. (1) Mary McParland, 20 Sept 1964, div, 1981; (2) Inez Marjorie Ann Jack, 19 Oct 1982, 1 s, 2 d. *Education:* BSc, MSC, Heriot-Watt Univ, 1958-64; PhD, Univ of Edinburgh, 1964-66. *Appointments:* Sr Lectr, Singapore Poly, 1966-68; Assoc Prof, Univ of Singapore, 1968-72; Wm Watson Prof of Bldg, Heriot-Watt Univ, 1971-91; Pro fo Bldg, Loughborough Univ of Tech, 1991-. *Publications:* Research and conference papers. *Memberships:* Past Pres, Chartered Inst of Bldg; FBIM; FRSA; Hon Assoc, RICS. *Honours:* CBE, 1991. *Hobbies:* Music; Walking; Reading; Gardening; DIY. *Address:* Department of Civil Engineering, Loughborough University of Technology, Loughborough, Leics LE11 3TU, England. 184.

TOS Igor, b. 26 Mar 1943, Beograd, Croatia. Architect; Research. m. Ursic Neva, 11 May 1974. *Education:* Music Sch, Ljubljana, 1950-59; BSArch, Univ of Zagreb, 1961-67; Postgrad Study, Tech Univ of Hannover, 1972-73, and, Univ of Ljubljana, Slovenia, 1984-. *Appointments:* Experience in Town Planning, Lusanne, Switz, 1967; Arch Planning and Design, Zagreb, 1969-72; Postgrad study, Tech Univ of Hannover, Germany, 1972-73; Freelance Archt and Designer, 1973-74; Arch firm, Zabreg, 1974-80; Cofdr, Sistemprojekt, planning, design, consulting and engineering firm, 1980-, Gen Mgr, 1980-87, currently, R & D Mgr. *Creative works:* Arch projects, Graphical design solutions, theoretical work, computerised system for custom designed flexible flat bldg; Conception and presentaiton and staging of Croatian Nat Revival 1790-1848, exhibition at Mus of Applied Arts, Zagreb, 1986. *Memberships:* Croatian: Assn of Archts, Soc of Artists in Fine Arts/Applied Arts; Soc of Designers, Co Fdr; Assn of Engrs and Techs, Zagreb Salon, Jury Mem, 1974, Organising Com, 1975. *Honours:* Two Awds for Graphical Design, 1970; 1st Awd, Yugoslav Arch-Sculptural Competition, Monument Mus, 1971. *Hobbies:* Fine arts; Music; Theatre; Contemporary Dance; Film; Basketball; Mountain Hiking; Yoga. *Address:* Aleja Pomorara 11, 41020 Zagreb, Croatia.

TOSELAND Patrick Arthur, b. 8 Sept 1929, Kettering. Clinical Biochemist. m. Sheila Patricia Mawe, 4 June 1955, 3 d. *Education:* Sheffield Univ: BSc 1952, PhD 1955, MRCPath, 1982, FRC Path, 1983. *Appointments:* Forensic Sci, 1957-61; Indust Chem, J Bibby & Sons, 1961-64; NUS Sheffield, 1964-67; NUS Guys Hosp, 1967-. *Publications:* More than 120. *Contributions to:* 11 books. *Memberships:* Assn Clin Biochems; Inst Assn Forensic Toxicols; Brit Acad Forensic Sci, Pres, 1988-89. *Hobbies:* Rugby Union Referee, 1974; Photography. *Address:* Dept of Clinical Chemistry, Guy's Hospital, London SE1 9RT, England.

TOSHEV Borislav V, b. 1 Feb 1943, Beologradtchik. Associate Professor. m. Roumyana Vladova, 24 Sept 1967, 1 s, 1 d. *Education:* Army Ser, 1961-63; PhD, Sofia Univ, 1975; Postdoc Scholarship, Royal Inst of Tech, Stockholm, Sweden, 1976. *Appointments:* Lectr in Phys Chem, Sofia Univ, 1969; Asst Prof, 1976, Assoc Prof in Physico-Chem Thermodynamics, 1981, Sofia Univ; P-t Prof, Phys Chem, Colloid Chem, Univs of Shumen, 1976-86; Plovdiv, 1987-, Blagoevgrad, 1987-. *Creative works include:* Thermodynamics of Thin Films; Equilibrium and Stability Conditions in Capillary Systems; Capillary Theory of Flotation; barrier-less heterogeneous Phase Formation. *Memberships:* Bulgarian Chem Soc; Adv Bd, Langmuir; Am Chem Soc Jour of Surfaces and Colloids, 1990-. *Honours:* 1300 years Bulgaria Medal, 1981; 100 years Sofia Univ Medaly, 1988. *Hobbies:* Philately. *Address:* Department of Physical Chemistry, University of Sofia, 1126 Sofia, Bulgaria.

TOURE Tamaro, b. 31 Mar 1937, Segou, Senegal. Coordinator of SOS Children's Village. 1 s. *Education:* LLB, 1963; Admin Cert of ENA, 1967. *Appointments:* Factory Inspector, 1968; Advr to the Prime Minister, 1972; Advr to the Pres, 1981; Currently, Coordinator of SOS Villages. *Memberships:* ASBEF (IPPF); Red Cross; Senegal Lawyers Assn; SOS Kinderdorf Intl. *Honours:* Chevalier de L'Ordere Nat du Lion Senegal, 1980; Commandeur de L'Ordre du Merite Senegal, 1990. *Hobbies:* Reading; Arts. *Address:* Fann Residence, Rue C X 11, Dakar, Senegal.

TOVSTIC Vladimir Antonovich, b. 24 June 1949, Minsk. Painter; prof. m. Malik Lioubov Stepanovna, 3 Nov 1979, 2 d. *Education:* Belarus Acad of Art, 1972; USSR Arts Acad, 1976. *Appointments:* Belarus Arts Acad, Prof, Snr Prof, Hd of Chair, 1976-. *Creative Works:* Paintings; Canvas Oil; Portrait of Painter V Savich; Band is Playing in a City Garden; Spring of 1985; Eclipse; Triptych Inheritance; Alenas Way; Black Moon; Smaller Ark. *Memberships:* USSRs Artists Union. *Honour:* USSRs Honoured Arts Performer. *Hobbies:* Reading; Gardening. *Address:* Surganova St 42, Ap. 39, Minsk, Republic of Belarus 220013.

TOWNSLEY Justin L, b. 3 June 1950, Cincinnati, Ohio, USA. Real Estate Investment Banking. m. Phyllis M Gilpatrick 21 Apr 1973, 2 s. *Education:* BSEcon, USAF Acad, 1972; MA Econ, Univ of Pittsburgh, 1973; CFP, Col for Fin Planning, 1980. *Appointments:* USAF Capt, B! and F16 Aircraft Dev Progs; Fin Mgr, 1973-78; Conslt, 1978-86; La Salle Ptnrs, Real Est, 1986-. *Publications:* An Economic Development Plan for Petroleum Producing Native American Lands, 1985. *Memberships:* NACORE; ICFP. *Hobbies:* Venture development especially related to natural resources; Golf; Reading; Aviation. *Address:* 150 S 5th St No 3400, Minneapolis, MN 55402, USA.

TRACZYK Wladyslaw Zygmunt, b. 27 June 1928, Warsaw. Prof. m. Zdzislawa Andrysik, 7 Dec 1954, 1 s. *Education:* MS, Sch of Medicine, Warsaw, 1951; PhD, 1st Sch of Med, Moscow, 1955; D Med Sci, Sch of Med, Warsaw, 1962; Univ of California, Los Angeles, 1967. *Appointments:* Asst Hd, Polish Acad of Sci, 1956-62; Prof, Hd of Dept, Sch of Medicine, Lodz, 1963-; Dir, Inst of Physiology & Biochemistry, 1973-. *Publications:* Neurochormones; Outline of Human

Physiology; Human Physiology; Neuropeptides And Neural Transmission IBRO; About 90 Papers. *Memberships:* Intl Brain Research Organ; Intl Neuro Soc; Polish Physiological Soc; Polish Soc of EEG; Polish Endocrinological Soc. *Honours:* Chevalier Order Polonia Restituta; Officer Order Polonia Restituta; Order Educ of Merit; Ministry of Health Award. *Hobby:* Oil Painting. *Address:* Dept of Physiology, Inst of Physiology & Niochemistry, Medical Univ of Lodz, ul Lindleya 3, 90 131 Lodz, Poland. 52, 139.

TRAFFORD Ian Colton, b. 8 July 1928, Surrey, England. Retired. m. (1) Nella Georgara, 20 July 1949, dis 1964; (2) Jacqueline Carole Trenave, 10 Dec 1972, 1 d. *Education:* St Johns Oxford, 1948-51; Hons in Philos, Polits and Econs. *Appointments:* The Fin Times, 1951-58; UK Corres, Barrons Weekly, NY, 1954-60; Dir, Indust and Trade Fairs Holdings, 1958-71, MD, 1966-71; Dir, Brit Trade Fairs in: Peking, 1964, Moscow, 1966, Bucharest, 1968, Sao paolo, 1969, Buenos Aires, 1970, MD, The Economist Newspaper, 1971- 81; Chm, The Economist Intelligence Unit, 1971-79; Local Dir of W.London Bd, Commercial Union Assurance, 1974-83; Publisher, The Times Supplements, 1981- 88; Dpty Chm, Times Books, 1981-86; Ret'd, 1988. *Honour:* OBE, 1967. *Hobbies:* Gardening and books. *Address:* Grafton House, 128 Westhall Road, Warlingham, Surrey CR3 9HF, England. 1.

TRAJANOVA Bistra, b. 25 Mar 1961, Sofia, Bulgaria. Art Gallery Curator. m. Hristo Hristov, 6 July 1990. *Education:* Eng Lang Sch, Sofia, 1975-80; Hist of Art Dept, Univ of Leipsig, Germany, 1980-86; Postgrad Student, Alfried Krupp von Bohlen Foun, Germany, 1988-; Internship, Univ of Harare, Zimbabwe, 1989-. *Appointments:* Curator, Dept of African Art, Art Gall of S S Cyril & Methodius Foun, 1986-. *Publications:* African Art catalogue of the permanent collection of the art gallery; many articles in Bulgarian newspapers and magazines, 1989-. *Memberships:* Young Bulgarian Artistic Intelligence Club; Ed Bd, Bulgarian newspaer, Art & Exchange. *Hobbies:* Collecting contemporary Bulgarian paintings, sculptures and graphic works. *Address:* 45 Solunska Street, Sofia 1000, Bulgaria.

TRAJANOVA Iskra, b. 25 Mar 1961, Sofia, Bulgaria. Art Gallery Curator. *Education:* Eng Lang Sch, Sofia, 1975-80; Hist of Art Dept, Univ of Leipzig, Germany, 1980-86; Postgrad Student, Alfried Krupp von Bohlen Foun, Germany, 1990-; Internship, Univ of Harare, Zimbabwe, 1989-. *Appointments:* Curator, Dept of W.European Art, Art Gall of S S Cyril & Methodius Foun, 1986-. *Publications:* Painters of Poethic Reality, 1990; Catalogue of the permanent collection of the art gallery; many articles in Bulgarian newspapers and magazines, 1989-. *Memberships:* Young Bulgarian Artistic Intelligence Club; Ed Bd, Bulgarian newspaper, Art & Exchange. *Hobbies:* Collecting contemporary Bulgarian paintings, sculptures and graphic works. *Address:* 45 Solunska Street, Sofia 1000, Bulgaria.

TRAN Long Trieu, b. 10 Oct 1956, Saigon, Vietnam. Senior Quality Industrial Engineer. m. Khanh Thi-Hong Phan, 3 Aug 1988. *Education:* BS Hons, Mech Engrg, Univ of Kansas, 1976; MS Mech Engrg, Mass Inst of Tech, 1980; Manuf Mgmt Prog, 1982. *Appointments:* General Elec Co: Prod Prog Engr, 1980-81, Adv Manuf Engr, 1981-82, Quality Sys Engr, 1982-84, Quality Control Engr, 1984-86, Sr Quality Info Equip Engr, 1986-89, Sr Quality Indust Engr, 1990-. *Publications:* Aspects of force, temperature and work surface roughness in surface grinding, 1980. *Memberships:* Indust Computing Soc, Foun Mem; NYAS: ASMechE; ASQC; Computer And Automated Sys Assn; Robotics Intl; Soc of Mnfg Engrs; Instrument Soc of Am; AAAS; AMA. *Honours:* Pi Tau Sigma, 1975; Tau Beta Pi, 1975; Sigma Xi, 1978; Phi Kappa Phi, 1977; Outstanding Contributions Awds, 1980, 1982, 1988, 1990. *Hobbies:* Reading; Orchid growing; Gardening; Coin and Stamps collecting; Limited-Edition Plate collecting; Photography.

Address: 3410 Fountain Dr, Louisville, KY 40218, USA. 7, 132, 176.

TRAYLOR Joan S, b. 18 Dec 1943, Ohio, USA. Associate Professor of Interior Design. 1 s, 1 d. *Education:* Art, Univ of Kentucky, 1962-65; BS, 1981, MS, 1984, Interior Design, W.Kentucky Univ. *Appointments:* Interior Designer, Interiors by Biggers, KY, 1981-84; Instr, W.Kentucky Univ, 1985; Assoc Prof, Prog Coor, Interior Design, Univ of S.Mississippi, 1985-. *Publications:* Numerous presentations to international, national and regional meetings; Public Designers West, FIT Review; Prof Brit Housing and Interiors, London, 1989-91. *Memberships:* Interior Design Ed Coun; Am Soc Interior Desingers; Inst Bus Desigbers, VP, MS, LA and AR Chptrs, 1991; Ofr, Warren Co Arts Alliance, 1977-80; Nat Trust for Hist Preservation; Design Communication Assn. *Honours:* Phi Upsilon Omicron, Phi Delta Kappa; Delta Kappa Gamma; ASID Pres Citation, 1991. *Hobbies:* Drawing; Painting; Textile design; Travel. *Address:* SS Box 5035, The University of Southern Mississippi, Hattiesburg, MS 39406, USA. 7, 15.

TREACHER William Charles, (Bill) b. London, England. m. Katharine Kessey, 1 Dec 1971, 1 s, 1 d. *Education:* RAF; Webber Douglas Acad of Dramatic Art, 1955-57. *Career:* Repertory Theatre at Westcliff, Wimbledon, Worthing, Bromley and Watford; West End debut in Shout for Life, Vaudeville Theatre, 1963; Wide theatre experience includes: Brian Rix Theatre of Laughter Co, 1967-69; Uproar in the House; Stand by Your Bedouin; Let Sleeping Wives Lie; Garrick Theatre, London; An Italian Straw Hat; Theatre Royal, Stratford East, 1975; Reluctant Heroes; Greenwich Theatre, 1976; Murder at the Vicarage, Fortune Theatre, London, 1977-79; Simple Spyman, Oxford and Cambs Festivals, 1980; Stage Struck, Tour and then directed, Ten Little Indians, Harlow Playhouse, 1981; The Wizard of Oz, Ashcroft Theatre, Croydon, 1982; Also many pantomimes; Extensive television credits include: Dixon of Dock Green; Dick Emery Shows; Dad's Army; The Professionals; Softly Softly; Bless this House; Angels; Agatha Christie House; The Other 'Arf; Bergerac; Sweet Sixteen; The Bright Side (series); Who Sir? Me Sir? (series); Film, Pop Pirates, 1984; In 1985 created the character of Arthur Fowler in the BBC television series, EastEnders, and continues in this role. *Hobbies:* Reading; Gardening; Sailing. *Address:* c/o BBC Television, Elstree Centre, Borehamwood, Herts WD6 1JF, England. 173.

TREBACH Bertram Ira, b. 28 Sept 1936, New York City, USA. Licensed Real Estate Broker. m. Arlene S Berkowitz, 16 Nov 1957, 2 s, 1 d. *Education:* BBA, Bernard M Baruch Col, NYC, 1969. *Appointments:* Mktg Mgr, Sanitized Sales Co, NYC, 1967-75; Fdr, Trebach Realty Inv, 1972- , Pres, 1989-; Real Estate Appraiser, 1978-; Mortgage Broker, NY State, 1983-. *Memberships:* Bd of Dirs: Riverdale Sr Sers Inv, NY, 1984-89; Central Riverdale Bus Assn, NY, 1982-; Nat Assn of Fee Appraisers. *Hobbies:* Field sport; Handball; Gardening. *Address:* Trebach Realty Inc, 3801 Greystone Avenue, Riverdale, NY 10463, USA. 6.

TRIGGER Ian James Campbell, b. 16 Nov 1943, Ruthin. Barrister. m. Jennifer Ann Downs, 28 Aug 1971, 2 s. *Education:* Ruthin Sch, 1954-62; LLB, UCW Aberystwyth, 1962-65; MA, LLM, Downing Col, Cambs, 1965-67. *Appointments:* Lectr in Law Univ of Wales, 1967-70; Barrister at Law, 1970-; Crown Ct Recorder, 1990-; P-t Chm, Social Security Appeal Tribunal, 1983-; P-t Chm, Med Appeal Tribunal, 1989-. *Honours:* Major State Studentship, 1965-67; Duke of Edinburgh Entrance Scholarship, Inner Temple, 1966; Major Scholarship, Inner Temple, 1967. *Hobbies:* Keeping my wife, children, dog and Bank Manager happy; Attending Choral Evensong, especially when my sons are singing. *Address:* Oriel Chambers, 5 Covent Garden, Liverpool L2 8UD, England.

TRIPALO Ante Miko, b. 16 Nov 1926, Sing-Hrvatsua. Politician. m. Vinah Tomic-Tripalo, 1 s, 1 d. *Education:* Hg Sch of Polit Sci, Beograd, 1949; Fac of Law, Zabred and Beograd, 1961. *Appointments:* Fighter of Antifacist Movement; Pres of Yugoslav Youth Org, 1953-62; Assembly of the Spry, 1958-62; Pres of the Spry; Univ Prof, Cons Law. *Publications:* On the Battlefield, 1979; Croatia's Spring, 1991. *Memberships:* Presidency of Croatia People Party. *Hobbies:* Sport; Reading; Hunting. *Address:* Srotova 28, Zagreb, Croatia.

TRIPATHI Versha, b. 1 June 1963, Varanasi, Indian. Housewife. m. 20 Apr 1987, 1 d. *Education:* Hg Sch, 1980-; Intermediate Sch, 1982; BA, 1984; MA Psychol, 1987; Dipl, Fruit Preservation, Cooking and Baking. *Appointments:* Sec, Yogic Voice Conciousness Inst, Shiwala, Varanasi, India, 1989. *Memberships:* Vagyoga Chetana Peetham, 1988. *Hobbies:* Studying; Cooking; Decorating; Musical Instruments; Gardening; Languages. *Address:* B 31131 A Shiwala, Varanasi (UP) India.

TRIPURANENI Venkateswara Rao, b. 14 Dec 1929, Angaluru, Andhra Pradesh. Industrialist. m. Srimathi Vidyavathi, 18 Apr 1953, 1 s. *Education:* BSc, 1950. *Appointments:* Dir, Spartek Granites Ltd, madras; Wholetime Dir, Spartek Ceramics Inda Lit, Tirupathi, AP; Chm and MD, Neycer India Ltd. *Publications:* Tripuraneni Ramayana, 1991; Viswadabhirama Vinaravema 1981; Critique of Advaitha of Sankara, 1958; Science, Scientific Socialism and Dialect, 1983; Nagarjuna, 1975. *Memberships:* Fdg Sec, Andhra Pradesh Contractors Assn; Fdg Dir, Inst of Vemana Studies. *Honours:* Vardhamana Samajam Hon, Nellore, 1982; Cuddapah Writers Assn, Hon, 1984. *Hobbies:* Ancient Indian Geography; Puranic Dynasties. *Address:* House No 36-12-16 Mughalrajapuram, Vijayawada 520 010, Andhra Pradesh, India.

TRISTRAM Uvedale Francis Barrington, b. 20 Mar 1915, Wimbledon, England. Journalist. m. Elizabeth Eden-Pearson, 8 Sept 1939, 1 d. *Education:* St Georges Col, Weybridge. *Appointments:* Jour, Morning Post, Dpty Ed, Aeropilot, 1939; Army, 1940-47; Sr PR posts, Brit Petroleum, 19347-60; Mng Ed, Hulton Publications, 1960-61; Ed Mgr, Longacre Press, 1961-62; Dir of Info and Broadcasting, Govt, 1962-66; Dir of Info, UK Freedom from Hunger Campaign Com, Ed, World Hunger Voluntary, 1967-72; Press Advr Voluntary Com for Overseas Aid and Dev, 1972-75; Pres Advr, Catholic Fund for Overseas Dev, 1975-77; Freelance, 1977-. *Publications:* Adventre in Oil; John Fisher. *Memberships:* Master Guild of Catholic Jours; Inst of Jours. *Honours:* RICS Property Jour of the Yr, 1988; ISVA Provincial Property Jour of the Yr, 1990. *Hobbies:* Walking; Riding; Reading; Classical Music. *Address:* 19 Mallard's Reach, Weybridge, Surrey KT13 9HQ, England. 3.

TROCHIMIAK Jan Wladyslaw, b. 27 June 1944, Losice, Poland. Teacher; Senior Lecturer. m. Alina Wegiera, 19 Dec 1970, 2 d. *Education:* MA Hist and Russian Studies, 1968; PhD Humanities, Maria Curie Sktodowska Univ, Lublin, Poland. *Appointments:* Hd of Russian Lang Section, Dept of Foreign Langs, Med Acad Lublin, 1968 and Dept of Foreign Langs, Agric Acad, Lublin, 1970-79. *Publications:* Jwan Jurgieniew w pismiennictwie, polskim lat 1850-1914, 1982; Mikolaj Czernyszewskiw pismiennictwie polskim, 1983; Turgieniew 1985; Czernyszewski, 1988. *Memberships:* Prod of the Bd, Acad Circle of Polish Assn of Russian Studies in Lublin. *Honours:* Prizes, Mnn of Nat Educ and Min of Hlth, 1975, 1976, 1983, 1990, 1991. *Hobbies:* Music; Sport; Politics. *Address:* ul M Brzeskiej 4/13, 20-440 Lublin, Poland.

TROEGER Richard Walter, . 1 Sept 1953, Santa Barbara, Calif. Musician. m. Paulette Grundden, 12 Apr 1982. *Education:* B Mus, Indiana Univ, 1976; M Mus, 1982; D Mus, 1987. *Appointments:* Ind Univ, Assoc

Instr, 1976-81; The Kings Coll, Edmonton, Lectr, 1986-89; Univ of Alberta, Asst Prof, 1989-. *Publications:* Technique & Interpretation on the Harpsichord & Clavichord. *Memberships:* American Musicological Soc; Coll Music Soc; Midwestern Historical Keyboard Soc. *Honour:* Canada Research Fellow. *Hobbies:* Woodworking; Creative Writing; Book Collecting. *Address:* Dept of Music, 3-82 Fine Arts, Univ of Alberta, Edmonton, Alberta, Canada T6G 2C9. 4, 139.

TROTMAN-DICKENSON Aubrey Fiennes, b. 12 Feb 1926, Cheshire, England. Principal, University of Wales, Cardiff. *Education:* Oxford: BSc 1948, MA 1951; Manchester: PhD, 1952; Edinburgh: DSc, 1958. *Appointments:* NRC Ottawa, 1948-50; Manchester Univ, 1950-53; Edinburgh Univ, 1954-60; Prof of Chem, Aberystwyth, 1960-68; Prin, UWIST, 1968-88; Prin, UC Cardif, 1987-88. *Publications:* Gas Kinetics, 1955; Free Radicals, 1959; Tables of Biomolecular Gas Reactions, 1967; Comprehensive Inorganic Chemistry, 1974. *Contributions to:* 150 learned journals. *Honours:* Tilden Lectr, 1963; KB, 1989. *Address:* University of Wales Cardiff, PO Box 920, Cardiff CF1 3XP, Wales. 1, 3, 32, 43, 50, 52.

TROTTIER James, b. 10 Dec 1945, Valdior. Radiologist. *Education:* BA 1966, MD 1970, FRCP(C) CSPO, 1975; Admin, 1981. *Appointments:* Radiologist, Rouyn, 1975-81; Chief Radiol, CHRO, 1981-. *Creative works:* Colour Doppler; Integration of Imaging. *Memberships:* N.Am Assn of Radiols; Can Assn; Quebec Med Assn. *Honours:* First Satellite CT and MR images Transmission, (real time). *Hobbies:* Squash. *Address:* CP 768, Chelsea, Quebec, Canada J0X 1NO.

TRUBNIKOV Alexander, b. 5 June 1945, Parnu, Estonia. Sound Operator, Leningrad Film Company. m. Maya Zlot, 12 Jan 1988, 2 s. *Education:* Computer Programmer Grad, USA, 1983. *Appointments:* Soung Engr; Worked at the movie production studio for 15 years; Currently Sound Recordist working in movie productions, USA. *Publication:* A Biblical Poetic Retelling, 1991. *Memberships:* Friends of the GLobe Poetry; Russian Writer's Club, Columbia Univ. *Hobby:* Collecting. *Address:* 2730 West 33rd St No 11j, Brooklyn, NY 11224, USA. 11.

TRUCK Robert-Paul, Count, b. 3 May 1917, Calais, France. Writer; Poet; Historian; Lecturer. m. Jeanne Brogniart, 24 July 1942, 1 d. *Education:* Baccalaureat, 1935; French naval Sch, 1938. *Appointments:* Volunteer French Navy, 1938; Ofr, 1939, Treas of the Marines, Boulogne sur Mer, 1940-43; Severely wounded, 1943; Poet; Lectr, Historian. *Publications:* Pietry: Heures Folles, 1938; Au Bord de la Nuit, 1948; Intersignes, 1953; Vertiges, 1898; Bois des Iles, Marche des Rois Cicatrices (in process): Co-author: History: Medicins de la Honte, 1975 and, Mengele l'Ange de la Mort, 1976; Operation Euthanasie, Jean Bart, (in Process); Adventuriers de Ma Tribu (in preparation); Lit and Spiritualistic papers. *Memberships:* Acad Leonardo da Vinci; Intl Acad of Poets; World Lit Acad; Inst Acad de Paris; Soc des Poetes Francais. *Honours:* Master of the Intellectual Elite, Milan, 1953; Selection Dipl, Acad Inst of Paris, 1981; Dipl of Hon, La Gloire Intl Grat Prize, Rome, 1982; Gold Palms Leonardo da Vinci Intl Acad, 1984; Hon DLitt Marquis Giuseppe Scicluna, 1855-1907, Intl Univ Doun, USA, 1987; Commemorative Medal of Hon, ABI, 1987; Albert Einstein Acad Bronze Medal for Peace IIth Class with collar ribbon, USA, 1989. *Address:* Varouna 49 Rue de Lhomel, 62600 Berck-Plage, France. 139, 151, 152, 156.

TRUESDELL Clifford Ambrose III, b. 18 Feb 1919, Los Angeles, USA. Author; Editor. m. Beverly Poland, 18 Nov 1939, 1 s. *Education:* BS Math, Calif Inst Tech, 1941; BS Pyhs, 1941, MS, 1942; Cert in Mech, Brown Univ, 1942; PhD Math, Princeton Univ, 1943; Dott ing h.c olitechnico di Milano, 1965; DSc, Tulane Univ, 1976; FilD Hon, Uppsala Univ, 1979; Dr PHil, Hon, Basel Univ, 1979. *Appointments:* Asst in Hist, Debating and math,

Calif Inst Tech, Pasadena, 1940-42; Asst in Mech, Brown Univ, Providence, 1942; Instr Math, Princeton Univ, 1942-43, Univ Michigan, An Arbor, 1943-54; Staff Radiation Lab, MIT, Cambridge, 1944-46; Chief Theoretical Mech Subdiv, US Naval Ordnance Lab, MD, 1946-48; Hd, Theoretical Mech Sect, US Naval Res Lab, Washington, 1948-51; Prof Math, Ind Univ Bloomington, 1950-61; Prof, Rational Mechanics, Johns Hopkins Univ, 1961-89, Emeritus, 1989-. *Publications include:* Author or co-author of 25 books including: Introduction to Rational Elasticity, 1973; Rational Continuum Mechanics, 1977; Tragicomical History of Thermodynamics, 1980; An Idiot's Fugitive Essays on Science, 1984; Great Scientists of Old as Heretics in The Scientific Method, 1987. *Memberships include:* Fellow, AAAS, Boston, 1991; Soc for Natural Philos, Fdg Mem, Dir, 1963-85; Socio Onarario dell'Accademia Nazionale di Scienze, Letters ed Arti (Modena, Italy); Academie Intl d'Hist Des Scis; Inst Lombardo Accademia di Scienz e Lettere. *Honours include:* Birkhoff Prize, AMS, 1978; Ordine del Cherubino U Pisa, 1978; Guggenheim Fellow, 1957; NSF Sci Postdoctoral Fellow, 1960-61; Japan Soc Sci Fellow, 1981; US Sr Scist Awd Alexander von Humboldt Stiftung, Germany, 1986. *Address:* 4007 Greenway, Baltimore, MD 21218, USA. 2, 14.

TRUGLIA Lucia, b. 20 Jan 1949, Italy. Principal of English National Ballet School. *Education:* Segutana Commerciale. *Appointments:* Rome Opera, 1967; New London ballet, 1979; London Festival Ballet, 1979; Still dancing with the Festival Ballet, now called English National Ballet, 1989, promoted to Principal. *Hobbies:* Opera. *Address:* 75 Holland Road, London W14 8HL, England.

TRUSKOV Pavel, b. 10 June 1958. Engineer; Oceanologist. m. Kozlova Olga, 5 Aug 1978, 1 s, 1 d. *Education:* Far E.State Univ, Vladivostok, 1975-80; Doctor's Deg, Leningrad, 1989. *Appointments:* Engineer, 1980-87, Head of Lab, 1987-, Inst Sakhalin NIPI Morneft. *Publications:* More than 25 papers about sea ice investigations on Sakhalin Offshore. *Memberships:* Charter member, Intl Soc of Offshore and Polar Engrs. *Hobbies:* Collcting coins; Making wooden masks; Canoeing. *Address:* 18 K Marx St, Okha, Sakhalin 694460, Russia.

TRUSTED Jennifer Lesley, b. 28 Mar 1925, Cambridge, England. Author; Part-time University Lecturer. m. 5 Nov 1949, 1 s, 2 d. *Education:* BA Cantab, 1946; MA Cabtab, 1956; MA Exon, 1971; PhD Exon, 1973. *Appointments:* Lectr, Exeter Col of Furthe Ed, 1952-80; Tutor, p-t, Open Univ, 1974-; P-t Lectr, Univ of Exeter, 1975-. *Publications:* The logic of Scientific Inference, 1979; An introduction to the Philosophy of knowledge, 1981; Free Will and Responsibility, 1984; Explanation and Understanding Metaphysics 1987; Moral principles of social values, 1987; Physics and metaphysics, 1991. *Memberships:* Soc of Authors; Soc for Applied Philos; Murel Assn; Hon Treas, Northcott Theatre, Exeter; Chm, Eng Speaking Union, Exeter, Chm, SW Region. *Honours:* Exhibition Girton Col, Cambridge, 1944. *Hobbies:* Music, especially opera; Theatre; Visiting Art Galleries; Walking; Reading; Entertaining at home. *Address:* 15 Victoria Park Road, Exeter, Devon EX2 4NT, England.

TSAO Constance S, b. 27 July 1934, Hong Kong. Research Scientist. m. Donald S Tsao, 28 June 1975. *Education:* BS Chem, Texas Woman's Univ, 1962; PhD Chem, Cornell Univ; Postdoc Fellow, Brandeis Univ, 1967-69. *Appointments:* Res Fellow, Chem Path and Immunol, Harvard Med Sch, 1969-71; Res Scist, Electrochem and Phys Chem of fuel cells and batteries, Tyco Labs Inv, 1970-73; Res Scist, Electrochem and Membrane Phys Chem, Arthur D Little, 1973-75; Sr Res Scist, Dir, Dept of Pysiol Chem, Biochem and Nutrition, Linus Pauling Inst of Sci and Med, 1976-. *Memberships:* ACS; NYAS. *Hobbies:* Reading; Gardening; Hiking; Swimming. *Address:* Linus Pauling

Institute of Science and Medicine, 440 Page Mill Rd, Palo Alto, CA 94306, USA.

TSARUK Oles Volodymyr, b. 29 Jan 1962, Ukraine. m. Ieva Markevich, 29 Mar 1984, 1 s. *Education:* Artist Sch, 1977; Violin, 1979; Ukrainian Polygraphic Inst, 1981-85, 1987-89; Graphic Artist, 1990. *Appointments:* Mem Hutsulsky Song & Dance Ensemble, 1979-80; Artist, Designer, Ivano Frank Measurment Factory, 1980; Aestmetic Lab Artist, Oil & Gas Inst, 1981; Art Editor, Tribuna Newspaper, 1988-90; Dir, Art Studio Riga Ukrainian Sch, 1990-92. *Creative Works:* Cassette Recording Oles Oles; Calgary; One Man Show, Riga. *Memberships include:* Ukrainian Christian Dem Front; Ukrainian Support Group for Latvia Popular Front; Ukrainian Assn for Ind Artist of Creative Intelligence. *Honour:* Grad with Honors Acad of Arts. *Hobbies:* Poetry; Music; Numismatics; Old Paintings; Graphics; Post Cards; Photography; Writing. *Address:* 10 Teodora Zalkalna Str, Riga 226058, Latvia. 52.

TSE Tsun-Him, b. 2 Apr 1948, Hong Kong. Senior Lecturer in Computer Science. m. Tereas 15 Nov 1976, 1 s, 1 d. *Education:* BSc 1st class hons, Univ of Hong Kong, 1970; MSc and PhD, Info Sys, London Sch of Econ, Univ of London, 1979-88. *Appointments:* Sys Analyst/Programmer, Univ and Poly Computer Ctr, 1971-78; Lectr in Computer Sci,1979-90, Sr Lectr, 1990-, Univ of Hong Kong. *Publications:* 50 including The Cambridge Tracts in Theoretical Computer Science series. *Memberships include:* Vocational Training Coun; Dong Kong Phys Handicapped and Able Bodies Assn; Hon Coun Advr, Spastics Assn of Hong Kong; Exec Com, IEEE Tech Com on Software Engrg; Fellow, Brit Computer Soc; Fellowm Inst of Maths and its Applications; Sr Mem, IEEE; Chartered Engr, Engrg Coun. *Honours:* Ten Outstanding Young Persons Awd, 1981; MBE, 1982; Key of Success Awd, 1990; Disting Leadership Awd, 1990; SERC Vis Fellow, Oxford Univ, 1990. *Address:* Department of Computer Science, University of Hong Kong, Pokfulam Road, Hong Kong.

TSIRULNIKOV Efim Michailowitch, b. 19 Sept 1937, Leningrad, USSR. Doctor. m. Bunitch Stella Genrichovna, 17 Oct 1961. 1 s, 1 d. *Education:* Leningrad Med Inst, 1961; ORL Doctor, 1961-69, vestibular sensory physiol, 1958, hearing, 1966, romantical physiol, 1970; DMs, 1966; Sr Scist, 1982. *Appointments:* Spec Qual in ORL, 1961-63; Hospital worker, 1963-66; Scist, Leningrad, ORL Inst, 1966-69; Sechnov Inst of Evolutionary Physiol and Biochem, Acad of Sci, USSR, 1969; Sr Scist, 1980-. *Publications:* more than 150, 5 books in the area of ear and somatical sensory physiology, ultrasound in medicine and physiology. *Memberships:* ORL and Physiol Sci Socs in Leningrad; Com of Ultrasound in med and Biol; Untrasound Acad of Scis. *Honours:* Two medals for distinguished work, 1981, 1984; Hon Dipl for contributions to investigations into ultrasound in medicine, 1990. *Hobbies:* Acupuncture therapy. *Address:* Sechenov Institute of Evolutionary Physiology and Riochemistry, Academy of Sciences, Thorez pr 44, 192443 St Petersburg, Russia.

TSOK-NWOK Peter, b. 15 Sept 1960, Forom, Nigeria. m. Anyazi-Lydia Bitrus Wash, 25 Aug 1990, 1 s. *Education:* Dip, Univ de Tech, 1983; Baccalaureat de Technicien, 1981; W. African Sch Cert, 1977; Nigerian Sch Leaving Cert, 1972. *Appointments:* Clerk, Nat Electricity Power Auth, 1977; Survey Asst, JOS Metropolital Dev Bd, 1978; Sr Supervisor, Yankari Natural Water Co, 1984-90; Maintenance Engr, Boja Ind Ltd, 1991-. *Hobbies:* Walking; Cycling; Bible Reading and Gardening. *Address:* Kapwis Forom, PO Box 205, Bukuru, Plateau State, Nigeria.

TSONKOV Stoyan Michov, b. 24 Mar 1939, Debnevo, Bulgaria. Professor; Director. m. Lidia Tsonkova, 16 Feb 1964, 1 s, 1 d. *Education:* Grad, Automation, Sofia Tech Univ, 1966; PhD, 1972, DSc, 1984; Specialization, Int Sci Gp, Moscow, 1972-75. *Appointments:* Asst, 1967-

72, Assoc Prof, 1975-76, Hd of Dept and Dpty Chancellor of Univ, 1976-84, Process Automation Control Dept, Sofia Tech Univ; Prof BAS, Dir CLBA, 1984-. *Publications:* 20 books and textbooks on technological processes control and biotechnological processes control including: Elaboration of Variable Structures Systems; Complex Prod Systems Control; Biotechnological Processes Control. *Memberships:* Prof, Biotechnics Dept, TU, Sofia; Ed Ofc, Seicntific Instrumentation, Warsaw, and Biotechnology, Sofia magazines. *Honours:* BAS and Sofia Univ Awd for established scientists in the field of technical sciences. *Hobbies:* Reading; Meeting guests; Growing flowers; Gardening; Building own villa in the country. *Address:* Central Lab of Bioinstrumentation & Automation, Bulgarian Acad of Sciences, Acad G Bonchev Str B1 105, 1113 Sofia, Bulgaria.

TSUBOMURA Hiroshi, b. 12 Aug 1927, Nara, Japan. Professor Emeritus. m. Michi Tsuzuki, 12 May 1957, 3 s. *Education:* BSc Chem, 1950, DSc, 1957, Univ of Tokyo. *Appointments:* Res Assoc, Tokyo Inst of Tech, 1950-55; Res Assoc, 1955-60, Asst Prof, 196-62, Univ of Tokyo; Prof, Osaka Univ, 1962-91. *Publications:* Chemistry in the Excited States, 1967; Structural Physical Chemistry, 1971; Photoelectro-chemistry and energy conversion, 1980. *Memberships:* Chem Soc of Japan; Intl Solar Energy Soc; Japanese Solar Energy Soc, Kansai Branch chm; Japan Soc of Energy and Resources, VP; Electrochem Soc; Japanese Photochem Soc. *Honours:* Matsunaga Foun Awd, 1971; Chem Soc of Japan Awd, 1985. *Hobbies:* Travel; Golf; Gardening. *Address:* 8-19-38 Mino, Mino-shi, Osaka 562, Japan. 50, 152.

TSUKADA David Osamu, b. 31 Dec 1929, Niigata-Ken, Japan. Professor of Theology. m. Alice Gilgen, 2 Jan 1965, 1 s. *Education:* BA Rikkyo Univ, Tokyo, 1952; BD, Central Anglican Theol Col, Tokyo, 1957; DPhil Theol, Oxford Univ, 1959-62; Dipl with Dist, St Augustines Col, Canterbury, 1963. *Appointments:* Tutor, Ctl Theol Col, 1958-59; Asst Prof, 1963-67; Asst Prof, Rikkyo Univ, 1968-71, Prof, 1972-, Dean of Col of Arts, 1975-79, 1990-. *Publications:* Author of articles and books including: Modern Anglican Theology, 1967; The Christianity under the Emperor System, 1981; The Development and Problems of the Anglican Ch in Japan, 1978; The Emperor System and Christianity after World War II, 1990. *Memberships:* Priest of Nippon Seikokai (The Anglican Ch); Trustee, Rikkyo Univ, 1983-91; Trustee of japan Assn of Christian Studies, 1975-76, 1989-. *Hobbies:* Gardening; Walking; Tennis; Skiing. *Address:* Yoga 1-12-31, Setagaya-Ku, Tokyo 158, Japan. 1.

TSUNEYOSHI Ryoko Karo, b. 21 May 1961, USA. Assistant Professor of Sociology. m. 27 May 1989. *Education:* BA Hitotsubashi Univ, 1984; MA, 1986, PhD, 1990, Princeton Univ. *Appointments:* Asst Prof of Sociol, Bunkyo Women's Col, 1991-. *Publications:* The Hidden Curriculum, 1992; Equality and Quality in Japanese Education, 1986; Japanese women's subordination or domination?, 1989. *Memberships:* Japanese Sociol Soc, Assoc Ed; Japanese Assn of Intl Women's Rights, Ctl Ofr; Am Sociol Assn; Assn for Asian Studies. *Address:* Department of Management, Bunkyo Women's College, 1196 Kamekubo, Oimachi, , Iruma-gun, Saitama 354, Japan.

TSUSUE Akio, b. 24 Sept 1928, Tokyo, Japan. Professor and Dean Faculty of Science. m. 1 May 1957, 1 s, 2 d. *Education:* BS 1954, MS 1956, DSC, 1960, Univ of Tokyo. *Appointments:* Res Fellow, Univ of Tokyo, 1960-70; Postdoc Fellow, 1960-61, Res Assoc, 1961-62; Res Assoc, Princeton Univ, NJ, 1962-63, Assoc Prof of Econ Geol, 1970-73, Prof of Econ Geol, 1973-, Kumamoto Univ, Japan; Vis Prof, Penn State Univ, 1981; Prof and Trustee, 1983, 1988-; Prof and Dean of Fac of Sci, Kumamoto Univ, 1990-. Leader of overseas field research: Korean granitic rocks and associated ore deposits, 1979-81, 1982-84, 1985-87. *Memberships:*

Soc Econ Geolos; Soc Mining Geols Japan, Trustee, 1977-79, 1986-88; Geochem Soc of Japan; Geol Soc of Japan. *Hobbies:* Floriculture; Reading. *Address:* Shinyashiki 1-1-35, Kumamato 862, Japan. 1.

TSUTANI Motohiro, b. 22 Dec 1935, Aichi, Japan. Professor of Accounting. m. 1 Apr 1960, 2 d. *Education:* BA Nagoya Univ of Commerce, 1958; MA, Meijo Univ Grad Sch, 1960. *Appointments:* Admnr, Nagoya Univ of Com and Bus, 1960-. *Publications:* Structure of E Walb's Balance Sheet, 1963; Banking Accounting, 1972; Increase and Decrease Bookkeeping, 1985; Development of Chinese Acctg, 1988; Structure of Financial Acctg, 1991. *Memberships:* Japan and Am Acctg Assns; Japan Acctg Hist Assn; Japan Audiring Assn; Gen Assn of Japan Indust & Educ. *Hobbies:* Playing Golf. *Address:* 1707 Haranichome Tenpakuku, Nagoya 468, Japan.

TSYKHUN Henadz, b. 30 Oct 1936, Belarus. Philologist. m. Tyrtyshina Galina, 3 Apr 1969, 1 d. *Education:* St Petersburg Univ, 1953-58, Postgrad, St Petersburg and Sofia Univs, 1959-63; Master of Philol Sci, St Petersburg Univ, 1963; Dr of Philol Scis, 1982, all at Linguistics Inst of Acad of Scis of Buelorussia. *Publications include:* Author, coauthor and editor of books and papers, and articles in professional magazines and journals including: The pronoun clytics syntax in Southslav Languages; The problem of Shav contribution to Balkan linguistic area, 1983; Areal typology of Slav languages: Principles and trends of investigation, 1988. *Memberships:* Intl Assn of Byelorussists, Sci Sec; Soviet Com of Slavists; Byelorussian Com of Slavists, V-Chm; Assn of Byelorussian Lang, Bd; Assn of Belarus- Bulgaria, Chm. *Hobbies:* Gardening; Travelling. *Address:* Lingistics Inst, Academy of Sciences, 25 Skaryna Street, Minsk, Belarus 220072.

TSYPLAKOV Vladislav Vladimirovich, b. 7 May 1945, Odessa. m. 16 Jan 1968, 2 s. *Education:* Phys Fac, Moscow Univ, 1963; Dr of Phys Mat Scis, 1969. *Appointments:* Inst of Phys Measurements, 1971-78; Ints of Earth Phys, Scist, 1978-. *Publications:* Phenomenon of modulation high frequency seismic noises of the earth, 1984. *Memberships:* USSR Phys Soc. *Honours:* Mem, State Com on Causes of Discoveries and Inventions, 1983; Dipl for research work on the planets from JPE AS, 1979. *Hobbies:* Russian nature. *Address:* 10 B Gruzinskaja 123810, IPE AS, Moscow, Russia.

TU Houze, b. 25 Sept 1929, Zehjiang, China. Professor and Director of Institute of Exploration Techniques. m. 1 Jan 1957, 1 d. *Education:* Mechs Dept, Qing Hua Univ, 1948. *Appointments:* Lectr and Engr, 1956-59, V-Prof and Dean, 1960-79, Dir of Inst of Exploration Technique, 1979-92. *Publications:* The design principle on drilling equipment, 1980; Drilling Engineering, 1987; Rock Failure, 1991. *Memberships:* Chm, Course Indication Com of Exploration Engrg; V-Chm, Acad Deg Com of China Univ of Geoscis; V-Chief of Oil Geol, Mining & Chem Indust Section for Judgement Com of Inst of High Learning in Hubei. *Honours:* Nat Labor Model on Culture and Hygiene, 1960; Second Awd of Sci and Technique, Mid of Geol and Min Resources, 1984; First Awd, Basic Theory, Hubei Privince, 1985. *Hobbies:* Music and sport. *Address:* Dept of Exploration Engineering, China Univ of Geosciences, (Wuhan) Wuhan City 430074, Hubei Province, China.

TU Tran-viet, b. 26 Apr 1949, Hue, Vietnam. Surgeon. m. Le Thu- Huong, 23 July 1976, 2 s. *Education:* Med Sch of Tours, France, 1968- 73; Doctorat d'Etat de Med, 1974; Maitre du Conferences Agrege des Univs Paris, 1984. *Appointments:* Asst, Clinique du Val d'Or Saint Cloud, 1976-78; Asst, Hospital Laennec, Paris, 1978-83; Cardio Vascular and Thorac Surg, Hospital Claude Bernard, Metz, 1991. *Publications:* Tetralogie of Fallot,

1981; Communication Medicale, 1981-84; Extra Corporeal Circulation, video, 1984. *Memberships:* Soc de Chirurgie Thoracique et Cardiovas de Langue Francaise; Soc Europenne de Cardiol. *Honours:* Maitre es Scis Medicales, Paris, 1984; Laureat de l'Association de Cardiologie de L'ile de France, 1986. *Hobby:* Bonsai. *Address:* 12 Rue des Clercs, 57000 Metz, France. 52.

TUCK Donald Richard, b. 24 Apr 1935, Albany, NY, USA. Professor of Religious Studies and Philosophy. m. Ann Lee Livermon, 29 June 1957, 2 d. *Education:* BS, cum laude,Nyack Col, 1957; MA magna cum laude, Wheaton Grad Col, 1965; PhD, Univ of Iowa, 1970. *Appointments:* Minister: New Guinea, 1957-61, Utd Presbyterian Ch, 1963-65, Congregational Utd Ch of Christ, 1968-69; Asst, 197-, Assoc, 1972, Prof, 1978-, Univ of W.Kentucky. *Publications:* Buddhist Churches of America, 1987; The Concept of Maya, 1986; Book chapters: Radhakrishnan's Eternal Religion, 1992; Lacuna in Sankara Studies. *Memberships:* Am Acad of Religion; Assn for Asian Studies; Bengal Studies Conf; Religion in S.India. *Honours:* Pacific Cultural Foun Fellow, 1991; Nat Fac Role of Hon, CASE, Wash DC, 1985; Fac Excellence Awd, WKY, 1981, 1982; Tenney Awd, Wheaton Col, 1965; WKY Grants, six, 1983-90; NEH Seminar grants, three, 1977-81; Kentucky Humanities Coun Grants, 1990, 1992. *Hobbies:* Travel; Photography; Gardening; Wood work; Sport; Exercist. *Address:* Dept of Philosophy and Religion, W. Kentucky University, Bowling Green, KY 42101, USA. 145, 7, 15.

TUCKER Barbara Hartman, b. 19 July 1942, Hartford, Connecticut, USA, Chief Executive Officer, Concorde Enterprises Inc, m. William Quoos Tucker, 16 Dec 1967, 1 s, 1 d. *Education:* AA, Liberal Arts, Briarcliff Col, NY; BA, Educ and Polit Sci, Rollins Col, FL. *Appointments:* Chief Lobbyist and PR Conslt, Glass Constructors Inc, CT, 1974-75; Dir, CT Citizens Lobby, 1975-76; Exec Asst to the Senate Leadership, Hartford, CT, 1976-82; Chief of Staff, Senate Minority Ldr, CT, 1980-82; Mgr, CT State News Bureau, 1983-84; Exec DI, CT Safety Belt Coalition, 1985; Exec Asst to the Pres, Traffic Safety Now Inc, Detroit, MI, 1985-89; PRes, CEO, Concorde Enterprises Inc, CT, 1989-. *Publications:* Euroedge - interactive software on the European Community and E.Europa; articles and monthly column in Inbound Logistics. *Memberships:* Greater Htfd Chamber of Commerce; CT World Trade Assn. *Honours:* Multiple state awards in traffic safety; Cert of Recognition, Am Red Cross. *Hobbies:* Ballooning; Walking; Cruising. *Address:* Concorde Enterprises Inc, 56 Arbor Street, Hartford, CT 06106, USA. 5, 52, 162.

TUCKER Christopher Robey, b. 23 Mar 1941, Hertford, England. Creator of special make-up effects. *Education:* Eversley Sch, Southwold, Suffolk; Elizabeth Col, Guernsey, CH; Guildhall Sch of Music and Drama, London. *Appointments:* Films: Star Wars, 1976; Boys from Brazil, 1978; Elephant Man, 1979; Quest for Fire, 1980; Company of Wolves, 1983; High Spirits, 1988; Phantom of the Opera, 1986-; TV: I Claudius, 1975; War and Remembrance, 1986. *Contributions to:* The professional make-up artist, 1985. *Memberships:* BFI, BAFTA: AIP: Freeman: City of London, 1962, Worshipful Co of Haberdashers, 1962. *Honours:* Make Up Awds for, Quest for Fire: BAFTA Film 1982, Acad of Sci Fiction, USA, 1981. *Hobbies:* Local history; Archaeology; Natural history; Collecting antiquarian books; Opera; Antiquities. *Address:* Bere Court, Pangbourne, Berks RG8 8HT, England. 52.

TUCKER Edward Llewellyn, b. 19 Nov 1921, Crewe, Virginia, USA. Professor of English. *Education:* BA Roanoke Col, 1946; MA columbia Univ, 1947; PhD, Univ of Georgia, 1957. *Appointments:* Instr, Roanoke Col, 1949-53; Asst Prof, Univ of Richmond, 1957-60; Asst Prof, 1960-66, Assoc Prof, 1966-68, Prof, 1986-, Virginia Poly Inst and State Univ. *Publications:* Richard Henry Wilde: Life and Selected Poems, 1966; Vocaublary Power, 1968; The Shaping of Longfellow's, 1985. *Memberships:* MLA. SAMLA; Poetry Studies Assn; Soc for the Study of Southern Lit. *Hobbies:* Piano; Organ; Oil painting. *Address:* Department of English, Virginia Tech, Blacksburgh, VS 24061, USA. 13, 7.

TUCKER Ravenna Michele, b. 4 Jan 1962, Malaysia. Principal Ballet Dancer. *Education:* King George V Sch, Hong Kong. *Appointments:* Royal ballet, Covent Garden, 1979-90; Corps de Ballet, Soloist, 1983, principal Dancer; Joined Birmingham Royal Ballet (Former Sadlers Well Royal Ballet), 1990. *Creative works:* Leading roles in: Swan lake, Odette, Sleeping Beauty, Nutcracker, Giselle, Bayadere, Ondine, La Fille Mal Gardee, Romeo and Juliet, Les Biches, Rhapsody, L'Apres Midi d'un Faun, Scenes de Ballet. *Honours:* Gold Medal, Adeline Genee Competition, 1978; French Foun Prize, Prix de Lausanne, 1979. *Hobbies:* Tapestry; Sewing; Painting; Walking; Swimming; Reading; Travel. *Address:* The Birmingham Royal Ballet, Birmingham Hippodrome Theatre, Stage Door, Thorp Street, Birmingham B5 4AU, England.

TUDA Hideo, b. 15 June 1917, Osaka, Japan. m. 4 Apr 1951, dec 1991, 3d. *Education:* Tokyo Tchrs Col, 1937-40; Tokyo Bunri Course Univ, 1940-42; DLit, 1962. *Appointments:* Lectr, 1952; Asst Prof, 1953, Prof, 1974-78, Tokyo Educ Univ; Prof, Kansai Univ, 1989-90. *Publications:* Development of Hoyken Economical polity and market structure; A Study of the popular movement sin the modern period; A study of dissolve process in the Houken Society; A Study of the Rakumatu society. *Memberships:* Sci Coun of Japan; Rekisigaky Kenkyukais. *Honours:* Citizens of Osaka Cultural Merit Awd. *Address:* 1-6-23 Nanpeindai, Takatsuki City 569, Japan.

TUDOR-CRAIG Pamela Wynn, b. 26 June 1928, London, England. Art Historian. m. (1) Algernon James Riccarton Tudor-Craig, 27 July 1956; (2) Sir John Wedgwood 1 May 1982, 1 s. *Education:* BA 1st class Hons, 1949; PhD, 1952, Courtauld Inst of Art, Univ of London. *Appointments:* Reschr, Soc of Antiquaries, Nivholas Pevsner, Earls of Verulam and Salisbury, 1951-60; Organiser with husband of 7 exhibitions at Ickworth for Nat Trust, 1960-69; Tchg for Am Univs in England, 1969-. *Publications:* Numerous articles and chapters on English mediaeval topics for learned journals. *Creative Works to:* 14 exhibitions including: Age of Chivalry, at the Royal Acad, 1987, 1988; Books: Richard III, 1973; Secret Life of Paintings, 1986; Co-author, Bells Guide to Westminister Abbey. *Memberships:* Fellow, Soc of Antiquaries, Coun, 1989-92; Chm, Wal Paintings Com, Coun for Care of Chs, 1972-91; Cathedrals Adv Comm, 1975-90; Brit Archaeol Assn; Royal Archaeol Assn. *Honours:* Hon DHum, William Fewell Col, Liberty, Miss, 1983. *Hobbies:* All green issues; Preservation of wildlife; Abolition of nuclear bombs and reduction of armed forces; Survival of living globe; Walking the dogs; Music; Future of the arts. *Address:* Home Farm, Leighton Bromswold, near Huntingdon PE18 0SL, England.

TUERK Richard Carl, b. 10 July 1941, Baltimore, Maryland, USA. University Professor. m. Rosalind Paula Lerner, 24 June 1967, 1 s, 1 d. *Education:* AB, Col, Columbia Univ, 1963; MA, 1964, PhD, 1967, Johns Hopkins Univ. *Appointments:* Asst Prof of Eng, Univ of Cali,,f, 1967- 72; Assoc Prof 1972-77, Prof, 1977-, of Lit and Langs, E.Texas State Univ, (ETSU). *Publications:* Central Still: Circle and sphere in Thoreau's Prose, 1975; Annotated Teacher's Edition, Adventures in Appreciation, 1989. *Contributions to:* numerous scholarly books and periodicals. *Memberships:* Soc for the study of Multi-ethnic Lit of the US, Treas, 1976-79, Nat Chm, 1980-81; Modern Lang Assn; Col Eng Assn, Bd, 1986-87; Am Studies Assn; Am Studies Assn of Texas; Thoreau Soc. *Honours:* Cert of Appreciation, 1977; Special Awd, 1981; Hons Prof of the Yr, 1985, Dist Fac Tchg Awd, 1989-90; ETSU; Piper Prof, Minnie Stevens Piper Foun, 1991. *Hobbies:* Swimming; Dogs; Boy Scouting. *Address:* Dept of Literature and Languages, East Texas State University, Commerce, TX 75429, USA. 13, 7, 125.

TUKALLO Konstanty, b. 25 Sept 1929, Wilno, Poland. Professor of Surgery. m. Maria Chelkowska, 1 Aug 1956, 3 d. *Education:* BS 1953, MS 1961, Prof, 1990. *Appointments:* Assist, Surg Clin in Poznan, 1953-58; Tutor, 1959-74; Hdmaster, Dept of Surg, 1975-81, Prof of Surg, Med Acad, 1981-. *Publications:* Traumatology of the Chest and the abdomen, 1988; 70 other works of surgical science. *Memberships:* Assn of Polish Surgs; Polish Med Assn; Assn of Polish Orthopaedists. *Honours:* Polonia Restituta Medal. *Hobbies:* The history of eastern europe; Numismatics; Tourism. *Address:* Wojewodeki Szpital Zespolony, ul Juraszow 2-8 Poznan, Poland.

TUKE Peter Godfrey, b. 14 June 1944, Bournemouth, England. Architect. m. Susan Lawrence, 21 June 1975, 2 s. *Education:* Radley 1957-62; Keble Col Oxford, 1963-67; MA; Rowing Blue, PCL, 1971-74, 1975-77; Dip Arch. *Appointments:* Brit Petroleum, 1967-71; Corp Planning; Ptnr, Prior Manton Tuke Partnership, 1981-. *Memberships:* RIBA. *Hobbies:* Sailing; Rowing; Walking; Theatre. *Address:* 48 Brodrick Road, London SW17 7DY, England.

TULLIS William, b. 3 Feb 1953, Valdosta, GA. Broadcasting & Music. m. Martha Carlson, 19 Oct 1991. *Education:* BA, Georgia State Univ, 1974; MA, Emory Univ, 1982. *Appointments:* Audio & Music Dir, Turner Broadcasting Systems, 1975-. *Publications:* Various Custom Works. *Memberships:* IEEE; NAB; AES. *Honours:* Clio; Emmy. *Hobbies:* Music; Computer Sci; Structural Engrng. *Address:* c/o Turner Broadcasting System, 1050 Techwood Drive, NW, Atlanta, GA 30318, USA. 2, 7.

TUMPEL Christian Ludwig, b. 29 Mar 1937, Bielefeld, The Netherlands. Professor. m. Astrid Adeline Spengemann, 30 July 1965, 1 s. *Education:* Deg, Theol, 1963; PhD, 1968, 2nd Deg in Theol, 1970, all in Hamburg; Ordination as Lutherian Minister, 1970. *Appointments:* Vicar to Reverend, Luth Ch, Hamburg, 1969-84; Vis Asst Prof, Free Univ Berlin, 1978- 82; Prof, Univ Nijmagen, 1984; Chm, Inst Art Hlst, 1985-87, 1989-91. *Publications:* Rembrandg legt die Bibelaus, 1971; Rembrandt degroote Measters, 1975; Bilddokumenten, 1975; Rembrandt Mythos U Methode, 1986; Entartete beoldhouwkunzt, 1991; The old Testament in the Golden Age, 1991. *Memberships:* Res Proj of Cultures and Ideas; Assn German Art Hists; 52.Soc for Res in the 17th Century; Luth Soc; Ed Bd, Pantheon Intl Jour; Chm, Bd, Assn for Educ in Ch Hist and Art Hist, 1984-. *Honours:* Grant, Univ Hamburg, 1963-66; Wraburg Fellowship, Univ of London, 1968-69; Awd, Royal Dutch Acad of Sci, 1971; Grant, Deutsche Forschings Gemeinschaft, 1985. *Hobbies:* Drawing and painting; Reading. *Address:* Institute for Art History, Erasminplim 1, 6525 Nijmegen, The Netherlands.

TUPAN Maria-Ana, b. 19 Apr 1949, Buzau, Romania. Assistant, Bucharest University. m. Marius Tupan, 17 Jan 1976, 1 d. *Education:* Grad magna cum laude, Germanic Lang Dept, Bucharest Univ, 1972; PhD, 1990. *Appointments:* Ed, Romanian Books, 1972; Ed, Viata Romaneasca, lit review, 1989; PRof's Asst, Bucharest Univ, 1989-. *Publications:* Myths, Poetical structures, 1989; Translations from Am and Eng literature. *Memberships:* Romanian Writers Union. *Hobbies:* Travelling; Special interest in fine arts. *Address:* Apolodor 13-15, Ap 17, Bucharest 70661, Romania.

TUPAN Marius, b. 18 Apr 1945, Timma, Mehedinti, Romania. Editor in Cihef, Romanian Writers Union. m. Maria-Ana Ierdache, 17 Jan 1976, 1 d. *Education:* Grad, Romanian Lang and Lit Dept, Bucharest Univ, 1972. *Appointments:* Ed, Urzica magazine, 1974-89; Ed in chief, Lucifer, 1989-. *Publications:* Novels: Crisalide, 1977; Cereana Izabelei, 1982; Marmura Neagra, 1989; Three volumes of short stories. *Memberships:* Tje Romanian Writers Union; Assn of Romanian Profl Jours. *Honours:* Romanian Writers Union Awd for Cereana

Izabelei, 1982. *Hobbies:* Football; Sport; Travelling. *Address:* Apolodor 13-15, Ap 17, Bucharest 70661, Romania.

TURBERFIELD Alan Frank, b. 24 Sept 1930, Tipton, Staffs, Engalnd. m. Gilian Doris Markwell, 4 Aug 1956, 1 s, 1 d. *Education:* St John's Col, Oxford: Open Scholar, 1948-52; BA, Lit and Humanities, 1952; MA, 1955. *Appointments:* Staff Sgt, Royal Army Educ Corps, 1952-54; Asst Master at King Edward VII Sch, Sheffield, 1954-58; Birkenhead Sch, 1958-63; Sr Classics Master, Portsmouth GS, 1963-68; HM Inspector of Schs, 1968-90; Staff Inspector, Schs and Cols Awds, 1977-90; Dir, Royal Anniversary Trust, 190-91. *Publication:* Co-author, Voyage of Aencas, 1968. *Memberships:* Jt Assn of Classic Tchrs, 1965-; Classical Assn, Coun, 1979-82; Virgil Soc, 1965-; DES XX Club; Brit Sch in Athens; Assn of HM Inspectors of Schs; Oxford and Leics Methodist Dist - Dist Tutor. *Honours:* CBE; Open Scholarship in Classics, St John's Col, Oxford, 1948. *Hobbies:* Theatre; Theology; Travel in China and Classical Greece; Methodist Church. *Address:* 75 Hurst Rise Road, Gumnor Hill, Oxford OX3 9HF, England.

TURCANU Louis, b. 8 Dec 1919, Iassy, Romania. Professor of Paediatrics. *Education:* MD, Univ Iassy, 1944; PhD, Bucharest Sch of Med, 1957; Rdr, Paeds, Bucharest, 1972. *Appointments:* Asst Prof, Univ Iassy, 1946-60; Assoc Prof, Prof Paed, Timisoara Sch of Med, 1968-90; Hd, Children's Hosp, 1962-90. *Publications:* Paediatric Nephrology, 1975; Neonatology, 1982; Therapy guide in Paediatrics, 1981; Gastroenterology, 1988; Peadiatric haematology, 1988; 54 papers. *Memberships:* WHO Expert and Temporary Coun, 1974-77; VP, Nat Soc of Paeds; Pres, Union of Med Sci; Socs of Romania-Timisoara Sec; Balanic Union Med Sci. *Honours:* Order of Labour Awd; Awd for medical work; Prorector, Fac of Med, Univ of Timisoars, 1976-82. *Hobbies:* Symphonic Music; Public lectures. *Address:* 4 23 August St, Timisoara, Romania.

TURNBULL Christopher James, b. 15 Apr 1950, Southborough, Kent, England. Consultant Physician in Geriatric Medicine. m. Susan Mary Lovelock, 5 Jan 1974. 2 s, 1 d. *Education:* MA Cantab, 1971; MA BChir Cantab, 1974; MRCP, UK, 1977; DObs, RCOG, 1976; DCH, 1979; MRCGP, 1979. *Appointments:* Med Registrar, Wellington, NZ, 1979-80; Sr Registrar, Oxford and Liverpool, 1980-83; Conslt Geriatrician, Wirral, England, 1983-. *Publications:* Articles and chapters in book on Parkinson's Disease in the Elderly, diabetes in the elderly, glaucoma in the elderly and postural hypotension in the elderly. *Memberships:* Brit Geriatrics Soc, Merseyside Coun Rep and Policy Com Mem; Profl Adv Com, Brit Diabetic Assn and Chm Wkg Party on the Elderly; Chm, Wirral Assn for the Care of the Elderly and Wirral Planning Gp for the Elderly. *Honours:* Exhibitioner in Aileybury & ISC, 1963; Life Scholar Queens Col, Cambs, 1970; Sturges Prize in Med, 1973; Chadwick Prize in med, Surg and Path, 1974; Westminster Hosp,. *Hobbies:* Renaissance music; Gardening; Sailing; Caravaning.Renaissance music; Gardening; Sailing; Caravaning. *Address:* Arrowe Park Hospital, Upton, Wirral, Merseyside L49 5PE, England. 170.

TURNER Colin Francis, b. 11 Apr 1930, London, England. Retired. m. Josephine Alma Jones, 14 Apr 1951, 2 s, 1 d. *Education:* Beckenham Grammar Sch, 1944; Army Ser, 1949-51; LLB, Kings Col, London, 1952-55. *Appointments:* Civil Ser, 1949-; Dist Probate Registrar, York, 1965-68; Registrar of Principal Probate Registry, 1971-88; Sr Dist Judge, 1988-91; Ret'd, 1991. *Publications:* Ed, Rayden on Divorce, 9th, 11th 12th and 13th eds; Precedents in matrimonial causes and ancillary matters; Ed of the Annual Practice. *Memberships:* Brit Ornithols Union and Club; Brit Trust for Ornithol; RSPB; London Natural Hist Soc; Kent Ornithol Soc; The C'wlth Trust. *Hobbies:* Ornithology; Fishing. *Address:* Lakers, Church Road, St Johns, Redhill, Surrey RH1 6QA, England. 26, 125, 117.

TURNER Daniel Shelton, b. 9 Dec 1945, Montgomery, Alabama, USA. University Department Head and Researcher. m. 30 Dec 1978, 4 s. *Education:* BA 1968, MS 1970, Univ of Alabama; Phd, Civil Engrg, Texas A&M Univ. *Appointments:* Asst prof, GA S.Col, 1973-76; Asst Prof, Univ of Alabama, 1976-78; ASt Res Engr, Texas Trans. Inst, 1980; Act Dir of Engrg Tech Progs, 1981-83, Prof and Hd, Civil Engrg, 1984- Univ of Alabama. *Publications:* Over 40 res projs, 175 publications, 30 short courses written/conducted. *Memberships:* Inst of Trans Engrs, Ch, Nat Educrs Coun, Ec-Treas of S.Dist, past Pres, Alabama Sect; ASCE, Dist 14 Coun, Past Pres Alabama Sect; Transp Res Bd, Univ Rep; Nat Safety Coun; Capstone Engrg Soc. *Honours:* Engrg Tchr of the Yr,, 1984; Alabama Trans Engr of the Yr, 1990; Hensley Oustanding Acvitity Awd, 1991; Moody-Blackmon Awd; Dist Engrg Fellow, 1988; Univ Res Fellow, 1984. *Hobbies:* Church youth work; Canoeing; Golf; Photography. *Address:* Civil Engineering Department, University of Alabama, PO Box 870205, Tuscaloosa, AL 35487, USA.

TURNER Jonathan David Chattyn, b. 13 May 1958, Stourbridge, England. Barrister. m. Caroline Frances Esther Berman, 23 Nov 1986. 1 s, 1 d. *Education:* Rugby Sch, 1971-75; Corpus Christi Col, Cambs, MA Cantab, 1976-79; Lic Sp Dr Eur, Univ Libre de Bruxelles, 1980-81. *Appointments:* Barrister specialising in intellectual property and competition law, 1983- *Creative works:* Halsbury's Laws of England; Vaughan's Laws of the European communities; European Patent Office Reports; Association between Acute Glaucoma, the Weather and Sunspot Activity. *Memberships:* Gray's Inn, 1982-; Bar European Gp; Franco-Brit Lawyers Soc. *Honours:* Open Scholarship to Corpus Christi Col, Cambs, 1975; Lazard Awd, 1978; Avony Scholarship, 1979; Wiener Ampach Scholarship; Gray's Inn Jr Scholarhsip; Gray's Inn Entrance Awd. *Hobbies:* Walking; Theatre; Music; Gardening. *Address:* 3 Pump Court, Temple, London EC4Y 7AJ, England.

TURNER Lisa Phillips, b. 10 Apr 1951, Massachusetts, USA. Marketing Project Managment. m. Randolph Herbert Petren, 28 May 1988. *Education:* BA magna cum laude, Philos and Educ, Washington Col, 1974; AS Elec Tech, 1982, AA, Engrg, 1982, Palm Beach Com Col; MBA, 1986, DS Human Resource Mgmt, Nova Univ, FL, 1989; PhD, Bus, Kennedy W.Univ, CA, 1990. *Appointments:* Fdr, Owner, Turner's Bicycle Ser Inv, FL, 1975-80; Elec Engr, Audio Engrg & Video Arts, FL, 1980-81; Tech Writing Instr, Palm Beach Com Col, FL, 1981-82; Quality Engr, 1982-84; Training and Dev Specialist, 1984-86, Human Resources Specialist, 1986-88, Mitel Inc, FL; Mktg Communications Mgr, Modular Computer Sys, FL, 1988-90; US Mktg Proj Mgr, Mitel Inc, 1990-. *Publications:* SX-200A Power Supply Manual for Technicians, 1982; Steps to Succes, 1986; THe Influence of Operating structure on blue and white collar quality circle productivity in the Telecommunications Industry, 1989. *Memberships:* Acad of Mgmt; Am Soc for Training and Dev; Am Soc for Quality Control; Am Soc for Human Resource Mgmt; Am Soc for Quality and Participation. *Honours:* Sr Women's Hon Soc, 1972-74; Deans List; Fox Awd, Highest Freshman Average, 1970; Dist Acad Achievement, Nova Univ, 1986. *Hobbies:* Carpentry; Bicycling; Mechanics and electronics; Reading; Boating; Volunteer activities. *Address:* 2027 Southwest 12th Court, Delray Beach, FL 33445, USA.

TURNER Mark George, b. 27 Aug 1959, England. Barrister. m. Caroline Sophia Bullock, 23 Jan 1988, 2 d. *Education:* Sedbergh School, 1972-77; BA, Queen's Col, Oxford, 1977-80; Inns of Court Sch of Law, 1980-81. *Appointments:* Barrister at Deans Court Chambers, Manchester, 1981-. *Memberships:* Union Intl Des Advocates; Mastermind Club; Manchester & Dist Medico-Legal Soc. *Honours:* Uthwatt Scholarship, 1981. *Address:* Ogans Court Chambers, Cumberland House, Crown Square, Manchester, England.

TURNER Nancy Delane, b. 8 Nov 1956, Georgia, USA. *Education:* BS, 1978, MS, 1984, Pursuing PhD, Texas A&M Univ. *Appointments:* Student technician, 1980-84, Res Assoc, 1980-84, Texas A&M Univ; Freelance Con, Manuscript Ed, 1986-. *Publications:* 2 manuscripts, 17 abstracts and 13 short articles. *Memberships:* Am Assn Animal Sci; Am Assn of Cereal Chems; AAAS; Gamma Sigma Delta. *Honours:* Dan F Jones Meml Scholarship, 1990. *Hobbies:* Reading; Music; Gardening; Photography; Sport. *Address:* Texas A&M University, Dept of Animal Science, Rm 230 Kleberg Bldg, Col Station, TX 77843, USA. 7.

TURNER Wilfred, b. 10 Oct 1921, Littleborough, England. Retired Diplomat. m. June Gladys Tite, 26 Mar 1947, 2 s, 1 d. *Education:* Heywood Grammar Sch, 1932-38; BSc, London Univ, 1942. *Appointments:* Min of Labour, 1938-42; Brit Army, 1942-47; Min of Labour, 1947-75; Asst Labour Advr, Brit Hg Comm, New Delhi, 1955-59; Sr Wages Inspector, Midlands, 1959-60; Min of Hlth, Prin, 1960-66; Sec, Com on Safety of Drugs, 1963-66; Foreign and C'wlth Ofc, 1966-81: Kaduna, Nigeria, 1966-69; Kuala Lumpur, 1969- 73, Dpty Hg Commr, ACCRA, Ghana, 1973-77; Brit Hg Commr, Gaborone, Botswana, 1977-81; Dir, S.Africa Assn, 1983-88; Non Exec Dir, Transmark, 1987-90. *Memberships:* Royal Inst Intl Affairs; Royal C'wlth Soc, Coun; Royal Africa Soc; Hons: CMG, 1977, CVO, 1979. *Honours:* International affairs; Hill walking. *Hobbies:* International affairs; Hill walking. *Address:* 44 Tower Road, Twickenham, Middlesex TW1 4PF, England. 1.

TUSEO Norbert Joseph John, b. 9 Apr 1950, New York City, USA. *Education:* Grad: Bus and Hotel and Restaurant Mgmr, 1969, Mgmt, 1978, NYCC. *Appointments include:* Owner and Bus Mgmt, 1969-80; Dir of Sales, Mktg and Training, General Russell Ogan, Brig Gen, 1980-83; VP, Sales and Mktg, Treco/Sunstate, 1984-86; Pres, Sunstate Radon Conslts; Pres, Sunstate Mktg Inc; Publisher: The Real Estate Book, Jacksonville and St John's Co edits; Mortgage Broker, Sunstate Fin Sers; Real Est Broker, Interval Sunstate Mktg; Mgr, Sunstate Travel Agy, 1986-91. *Publications include:* Trade articles: Hypnosis saves low closers; Anticipate the problem then offer the solution; Manager must understand needs of individuals to motiate them; RX for cancellations; Anatomy of a Sellout. *Honours:* Nat 1991 Silver Awd for Mktg, Silver Awd for Sales and Silver Awd for Training, Am Resort and Residential Dev Assn; 1991 Capitol AWd, Nat Leadership Coun. *Address:* 101 LaQuinta Place, St Agustine, FL 32084, USA.

TUSHERSKI Vadim F, b. 17 Apr 1923, Kiev, USSR. Neurooncomorphologist. m. 6 Sept 1953, 2 s. *Education:* Med Inst, 1945- 50; Cand Med Sci, 1962; Doctor of Med Sci, 1978. *Appointments:* Gen Path; Neurooncomolphology. *Publications:* 1 book; 112 original articles. *Memberships:* Ukrainian Soc of Paths; Sci Grad Soviet; Ikrainian Soc of Electron Microscopists; Hd, Ctr of Electron Microscopy of Ukr SSR Min of Hlth. *Honours:* Dipl: All Union Histol Soc; Ukrainian Electron Microscopy Soc. *Hobby:* Cultivation of flowers. *Address:* Manuilsky St 32, Kiev-52, 252052, Russia.

TUTEN Robert Barry, b. 16 Mar 1959, Savannah, Georgia, USA. Attorney. m. Teresa Brown, 6 Mar 1978, 1 s, 1 d. *Education:* Fl Col, 1977-78; Univ of Alabama, 1978-83; BS, Athens State, 1984-85; JD, Jones Sch of law, 1985-88. *Appointments:* Instr, Hsv Police Acad, 1980-85; Instr, Faulkner Univ, 1985-88; Atty, Beasley Wilson Allen and Mendelsohn, 1987-88; Legal VP, Bomor Ser Electric, Atlanta; Atty, McDaniel and McDanie, 1988-89; Sole practitioner of Counsel McDaniel and McDanie, 1989. *Publication:* Divorce and Child Custody Remedies in Alabama, 1988. *Memberships:* Bars: Alabama State Bar and Am Bar Assn; ATLA: Nat Crim Def Lawyers Assn; US Dist Ct 11 Circuit Ct of Appeal; US Sup Ct; IPA. *Honours:* Meritorius Ser Awd, Huntsville Police Dept, 1983, 1984; Outstanding Law Student, Jones Sch of Law, 1988;

Midal of Hon, 1990. *Hobbies:* Sailing; Chess; Hockey. *Address:* 223 East Side Sq, Huntsville, AL 35801, USA. 117.

TUTT Leslie William Godfrey. Actuary and Mathematical Statistician. *Education:* Royal Military Col of Sci; MSc, PhD, London Univ. *Publications include:* Author, joint author: Private Pension Scheme Finance, 1970; Pension Schemes Investment Communications and Overseas Aspects, 1977; Pension Law and Taxation, 1981; Financial Aspects of Pension Business, 1985; Financial Aspects of Life Business, 1987; Financial Services Marketing and Investor Protection, 1988; Life Assurance, Pensions, 1988; Taxation and Trusts, 1989; Life Assurance and Other Investments, Personal Investment Planning, Corporate Investment Planning, 1991; Financial Aspects of Long Term Business, Pensions and Insurance Administration, 1991. Numerous research papers and technical articles to actuarial statistical and financial journals. *Memberships:* Fellow, Pensions Mgmt Inst, 1976; Exams Assessor, Charteret Ins Inst, 1980-; Exec Com, Pensions Res Accts Gp, 1976-85; Coun, Nat Assn of Pension Funds, 1979-83; Bd of Exmrs, 1980-90, Coun, 1975-78, Fac of Actuaries; Vp, 1987, Coun, 1968-74, 1975-81, V-Chm, 1981-84, Chm, 1984- 87, Inst of Statisticians. *Address:* 21 Sandilands, Croydon, Surrey CR0 5DF, England.

TUTT Sylvia Irene Maud. Chartered Secretary and Administrator. *Education:* Educated privately. *Publications:* Author and joint author: Private Pension Scheme Finance, 1970; Pensions and Employee Benefits, 1973; Pension Law and taxaton, 1981; Financial Aspects of Pension Business, 1985; Financial Aspects of Life Business, 1987; FInancial Aspects of Long Term Business, 1991; A Mastership of a Livery Company, 1988; Also numerous technical articles in professional and financial journals. *Memberships include:* FRSA; Liveryman, Worshipful Co of Scriveners, 1978-; Worshipful Co of Chartered Secs and Admrs, Liveryman, 1977, Master, 1983-84; Mng Trustee Charitable Trust, 1978-; Soroptimist Intl of Ctrl London, Pres, 1976-78; Sr Exmr, Chartered Ins Inst, 1975-; Inst of Chartered Secs and Admrs: Fellow, Coun, 1975-76, 1980-82, Pres Women's Sec, 1975-76, Chm, London Branch, 1984- 85; Benevolent Fund Mgmt Com, 1975-79, Educ Com, 1980-82, Publications and PR Com, 1980-82. *Address:* 21 Sandilands, Croydon, Surrey CR0 5DF, England.

TUTUNDZIC Sava, b. 2 Sept 1928, Belgrade, Yugoslavia. Associate Professor. m. Vera Mitrovic, 5 Sept 1971, 1 s. *Education:* Grad, Dept of Archaeol, Fac of Arts, Belgrade Univ, 1955; Postgrad Studies, Dept of Egyptology and Geography, Acad of Arts, Cairo Univ, 1959-60, 1960-61. *Appointments:* Jr Asst Lectr, 1957, Jr Lectr, 1958, Res Fellow, 1971, Asst Prof, 1980, Assoc Prof, 1987, Fac of Arts, Belgrade Univ. *Publications:* The group of Narrowing Necked Jars and One-loop hand lend Vessels at Maadi in Relation to the Palestinian Ceramic Wars, 1985. *Memberships:* Com of Serbian ARchaeol Soc, Pres, Near E.Archaeol Section, 1991-; Ed in chief, Recueil de travaux de la Fac de Philos, Belgarda, 1990; Vis Prof, Dept of Egyptol, Warsaw Univ, 1991; Mem, Int Assoc of Egyptologists, 1992-. *Honours:* Letter of thanks, Exec Bd, Assn of Libs of Belgrade Univ, 1985; Letter of Thanks and plaque, Fac of Arts, Belgrade Univ, 1988. *Hobbies:* Riding; Rowing; Sociology; Psychology. *Address:* University of Beograd, Fac of Arts Dept of Architecture, Cika Ljubina 18-20, 11000 Belgrade, Yugoslavia.

TWIVY Paul Christopher Barstow, b. 19 Oct 1958, Dunstable, England. Advertising and Freelance Writing. m. (2) 27 Oct 1991, 2 s. *Education:* MA Eng Lang and Lit, Magdalen Col, Oxford, 1977-80. *Appointments:* BD Dir, Hedger Mitchell Stark, 1982-83; MD, Price Court Twivy D'Souza, 1984-89; Dep Chm, Still Price: Lintas, 1989-. *Creative works:* Poems published in journals, comedy sketches for Chris Tarrant and BBC; A New Adam and Eve, 1992. *Memberships:* Steering Com,

Comic Relief; Coun, Inst of Practitioners of Advg; Mktg Soc; Exec Com, Healthcare Foun. *Hobbies:* Freelance comedy writer; Playwright; Poetry; Reading; Tennis; Guitar and Piano. *Address:* c/o Still Price Lintas, 84 Eccleston Square, London SW1V 1PX, England.

TWORKOWSKI Stefan, b. 17 July 1907, Ukraine. Retired Scientific Worker. m. 20 June 1938, 2 d. *Education:* Dipl Arch, 1933; Dr Tech Scis, 1964; Prof, 1972; Dean of Fac of Arch, Warsaw, 1964-66. *Appointments:* Workshop Designer, 1933; Projector in urbanism and arch for health-resort, Silesia, 1933-37; Own Workshop, Warsaw, 1937-39; Under- taking, Warsaw, 1940-44; Dir, Min of Rebuilding, 1945-48; State Workshop, 1961-. *Publications:* Architecture in the country. *Memberships:* Assn of Archs; Assn of Urbanists; Transformation of the Polish Landscape, 1944-80; My Experiences. *Honours:* 18 awards of distinction for various works from the State. *Hobbies:* Vagabondage in landscape. *Address:* Bagno 7-208, 00-112 Warsaw, Poland.

TYERS Anthony Gordon, b. 14 Sept 1944, Hampshire, England. Consultant Ophthalmic Surgeon. m. Renee Constance Barbara Dewaard, 7 Oct 1983, 2 s, 1 d. *Education:* Hampton Sch, 1959-63; Charing Cross Hosp Med Sch, 1963-70. *Appointments:* Registrar, Univ Col Hosp, London, 1973-76; Sr Registrar, Moorfields Eye Hosp, 1978-81; Fellow, Mass Eye and Ear Infirmary, Boston, 1981-82; Sr Registrar, Middlesex Hosp, Moorfields Eye Hosp, 1982-86; Conslt Ophthal Surg, Salisbury Gen Hosp. *Contributions to:* Bask Clinical Ophthalmology, 1984; Scientific papers on ophthalmic plastic surgery and other related subjects. *Memberships:* BMA; RSM: European Soc of Ophthal Plastic and Reconstructive Surg; FRCS, England and Edinburgh; Fellow, Col of Opthals; Sec, Wessex Reg Adv Com for Ophthal; Trustee, Salisbury Hosps Trust. *Honours:* Nuffield Travelling Scholarship, 1969; Keeler Award, 1982. *Hobbies:* Squash; Skiing; Walking; Clarinet; Campanology. *Address:* Eye Department, Odstock Hospital, Salisbury SP2 8BJ, England. 170.

TYLER Christopher, b. 9 July 1934, Dover, England. Resident Governor and Kepper of the Jewel House, HM Tower of London. m. Suzanne Whitcomb, 12 July 1958, 1 s, 3 d. *Education:* Beaumont Col, Old Windsor, 1946-52; RMA Sandhurst, 1953-54; Trinity Col, Cambs, 1955-58. *Appointments:* Commd Reme, 1954; Served in UK, Germany and Norway; Ret'd as Maj Gen, 1989. *Memberships:* CEng; FIMechE; FRAeS; FBIM. *Honours:* MA (Cantab), 1958; CB, 1989. *Hobbies:* Sport, especially rugby, football and tennis. *Address:* Queen's House, HM Tower of London, London EC3N 4AB, England. 1.

TYLER Peter Phillip, b. 31 Dec 1944, Warsaw, New York, USA. Executive Dir. m. Rosalind Giebel, 7 Jan 1967, 2 s, 1 d. *Education:* BS, Wayne State Univ, 1967; MA, E. Michigan Univ, 1970; Dipl, Atlanta Art Inst, 1977; Cert, Columbia Grad Sch of Bible and Missions, 1979; PhD, Century Univ, 1983. *Appointments:* Warren Woods Hg Sch, 1967-73; Easter Seal Soc, 1973-77; Bapt Med Ctr, 1977-80; Univ of S.Carolina, 1980-81; Am Assn of Osteo Specs, 1979-89; Clayton State Col, 1984-; Union Inst,1989-; Nat Bd of Anaesthesiol, 1989-; Am Bd of Sports Med, 1989-. *Memberships:* Past Pres, various offices, Gideons Intl; Am Assn of Med Soc Execs; Am Soc of Assn Execs; Rotary Intl. *Honours:* Trustee, 1972-74, Treas, 1974-76, Columbus Township; Chm, Bicentennial Observance Com, 1976; Ordained S.Bap Min, 1981. *Hobbies include:* Freelance photography, specialising in portraiture. *Address:* 6027 Fairfield Drive, Morrow, GA 30260, USA.

TYSON Helen Flynn, b. Wilmington, N.Carolina, USA. Retired. m. James Franklin Tyson, 25 Dec 1940, dec. *Education:* Guildird Col, N. Carolina; Am Univ, Wadhington DC; Numerous specialized courses and seminars in financial management and related fields. *Appointments:* US Govt Civil Ser, 1935-74; Supervisory Budget Ofr, HQ, MAC, 1955-57; Asst Budget and Acctg

Ofr, Pope AFB, NC, 1949-55; Chief Clerical Asst to Disbursing Ofr, 1941- 49; Auditor, AUS Disbursing Ofc, Ft Bragg, 1935-41. *Memberships:* ASMC; Am Inst of Parliamentarians; IFBPW; Altrusa Intl; Military Dist of Washington DC Ofrs Club; Nat Assn for Ret'd Fed Employees; NAFE. *Honours:* Outstanding Mem, Washington Chap, ASMC, 1988; Volunteer Activist Awd, Washington Metropolitan Area, 1981; Hon fellow, Anglo-Am Acad of England, 1980-; USA Engr Ctr, Ft Belvoir, VA, Civilian-Military ADv Coun Good Neighbour Awd, 1978; Woman of the Yr, Arlington Co, 1975. *Address:* 4900 N Old Dominion Dr, Arlington, VA 22207, USA. 2, 5, 7, 125, 129, 130, 138, 156, 162.

TZAFESTAS Spyros G, b. 3 Dec 1939. Professor of Robotics and Control. m. Niki Kalliamvakou, 4 Oct 1965, 1 s, 1 d. *Education:* Dipl Phys, 1963, Postgrad Dipl, Elec, 1965, Athens Univ; Dipl, Elec Engrg, Imperial Col, London, 1967; MEng, Auto Contr, London Univ, 1967; PhD, Elec Eng Contr Sys, Southampton Univ, 1969. *Appointments:* Dir of Computer Contr Sec, NRC Demokritos, Athens, 1969-73; Prof of Contr Sys, Dir of Sys and Control Lab, Elec Engrg Dept, Univ of Patras, Greece; Prof of Robotics and Contr, Dir of Intelligent Robotics and Contr Unit, IRCU, Nat Techn Univ of Athens. *Publications:* Ed and author of 20 books including; Multidimensional systems, 1986; System Fault Diagnosis Supervision and Control, 1989; Intelligent Robotic Systems, 1991; Microprocessors in Robotic and Manufacturing Systems, 1991; 150 publications in archival journals and 200 in international conference proceedings. *Memberships:* Fellow, IEEE, USA; Fellow IEEE, UK; ASME, USA; IMACS, VP, 1985-88, Coor of Tedin Coms, 1985-, Chm of TC on Control Sys and Robotics, 1985-. *Honours:* DSc, Southampton Univ, 1978; Hon DSc, Intl Univ Foun, 1989. *Address:* 91 E Venizelov Str, Halargos 15561, Athens, Greece.

TZALLAS Niove, b. 26 Jan 1938, Jannina, Greece. Painter. *Education:* Athens Sch of Beaux Arts, 1955-58; Atelier Andre Lhote, France, 1958-59; Ctrl Sch of Arts and Crafts, England, 1959-61. *Creative works include:* Numerous one-woman shows, France, Italy, Japan, Brazil, USA, UK, 1962-, most recent include: Gall Berheim-Jeune, Paris, 1982, Festival d'Art Graphique, Osaka, Japan, 1983, 1984, Salon d'Art, 1984, Sao Paulo, Brazil, BH Corner Gall, London, 1985, 1986, Everarts Gall, Paris, 1988, 1990; Group shows include: Floating exhibitions aboard SS Pegassos, Semiramis 1966; Olympia 1967, Salons des Independencs, Grand Palais des Champs Elysses, 1973-90; Gall Blaise St Maurice, Paris, 1974-77; Salon Populist, Paris, 1975; Maison de la Culture, Villneuve la Garenne, 1976-77; Ctr Culturel de Mussidan, Dordogne, 1977; Breakers Gall, Palm Beach, FL, 1978-78; Gall Haute-Feuille, Paris, 1988; Gall Quincampoix, Paris, 1989; Espace Delpha, Paris, 1989; Permanent collections at: Mus of Modern Art, Haifa, Israel; Nat Bank, Greece; Bibliotheque nat de France, Paris. *Address:* 15 Ekalis Street, 145 61 Kifissia. Attica, Greece. 52, 133.

TZANEV Stoian, b. 28 Feb 1946, Burgas, Bulgaria. Artist. m. Valentina Kostova, 8 Sept 1967, 2 d. *Education:* MA Graphics, Acad of Fine Arts, Warsaw. *Creative works:* About 40 one-man shows throughout Bulgaria and abroad including: Gall Wittgestein, Vienna, 1978; Gall Haut-Pauve Paris, 1979; Samuel Zax Gall, Toronto, 1981; Lalit Kala Acad Gall, New Delhi, 1981; Gall Ebla, Damascus, Syria, 1982; Gall Au Virage , Seprais, Switzerland, 1983, 1985, 1990; Gall Langegarden, Bergen, Norway, 1984; Gall 56-58, Dordrecht, Holland, 1984; Gall Vongreimissen, Oslo, 1986; Gall Pictor, Goteborg, 1987; Gall Nichido, Tokyo, 1988-91; Art Gall, Melbu, Norway, 1990; Bulgarian Cultural Info Ctr, Moscow, 1990; Art Gall, Sparkasse, Essen, Germany, 1991; Participation in over 50 international biennials since 1978; Works owned by almost all galleries in Bulgaria, and internationally. *Memberships:* Union of Bulgarian Artists. *Honours:* Over 20 national and international prizes of achievement.

Hobbies: Reading; Good wines. *Address:* Moskva 25, ap 21, 8000 Burgas, Bulgaria.

TZONIS Alexander, b. 8 Nov 1937, Athens, Greece. Prof; Chair Theory of Arch. m. Liane Lefaivre, 29 Oct 1973. *Education:* Yale Univ, 1963; Univ Tech, Athens, 1961. *Appointments:* Instr, Yale Univ, 1965-67; Asst, Harvard Univ, 1967-75; Assoc Prof, 1975-81; Prof, Univ Delft, 1981-. *Publications:* Architecture in Europe; Hemes and the Golden Machine; Classical Architecture; Towards a Non Opprenive Environment; Shape of Community; Garland Architecture Archives; Art Dir Film. *Memberships:* American Assn for Artificial Intelligence Royal Soc of Art. *Honours:* Research Grant, Dutch Government; Ministry of Culture, French Government. *Address:* 108 Oude Delft, 2611 CE, Delft, Netherlands. 52.

U

UDAL John Oliver, b. 2 May 1926, Folkestone, Kent, England. Retired JP and Trustee of Charities. m. (1) 2 s, 1 d, (2) Ann Marie Bridges Webb, 17 May 1979. *Education:* Winchester Col, 1939-44; MA, New Col, Oxford, 1948-49. *Appointments:* Irish Guards, Lieut, 1944-48; Sudan Polit Ser, 1950-55; Conservative Res Dept, 1955-66; Shipbroker and Shipping conslt, 1966-68; Economic League, 1984-89. *Publications:* Co-author, Paying for Schooling, 1975. *Memberships:* Principal, Baltic, Mercantile and Shipping Exchange, 1970-79; UNCTAD Roster of Intl Shipping Experts, 1983- 85. *Hobbies:* Historical Research. *Address:* 5 Soudan Road, London SW11 4HH, England.

UEDA Denemei, b. 14 Aug 1933, Ehime, Japan. University Professor. m. Kyoko Iwasa, 2 Jan 1957. *Education:* LLB, Okayama Univ, Japan, 1956; LLM, Nagoya Univ, 1966; LLD, Nagoya Univ, 1983. *Appointments:* Lectr, Niihama Tech Col 1966-69; Lectr, 1969-70, Asst Prof, 1970-76, Prof, 1976-, Shizuoko Univ. *Publications:* A historical study on the collapse of Indian Constitutions, 1974; Manifest Destiny and the US Constitution, 1988. *Memberships:* Comm on Folk Law and Legal Pluralism; Intl Union of Anthropol and Ethnol Scis; Jap Am Soc for Legal Studies. *Honours:* Grants: Oklahoma Hist Soc, 1969, Canada Govt, 1988; Honorarium, Utd Keetoowan Bank of Cherokee Nation, Oklahoma, 1977. *Hobbies:* Arts appreciation; Travel. *Address:* 2-10-20 Yokota- cho, Zhizuoka City, Japan 420. 1.

UEHARA Kazuma, b. 4 Jan 1916, Kasai City, Japan. Prof Emeritus. m. Saito Katsuko, 26 May 1943, 2 s, 1 d. *Education:* Toyko Imperial Univ, Bach of Arts, 1939. *Appointments:* Prof, Osaka Normal Sch, 1947-50; Asst Prof, 1950; Prof, 1960; Prof Emeritus, 1981-; Prof, Hyogo Kyoiku Univ, 1982-86; Sub Chmn of Belgium Flanders Exchange Centre, Osaka, 1984-. *Creative Works:* Cultural History of Music Educ in Japan; Formenlehre der Klaviermusik. *Memberships:* The Musicological Soc of Japan; Japan Acad Soc for Music Educ; The Japan Piano Tchrs Assn. *Honours:* Order of the Rising Sun. *Hobbies:* Play Piano; Driving Tour; Photography. *Address:* 1147 Kanaokacho, Sakai City, Osaka, 591 Japan. 52.

UEMATSU Minoru, b. 13 Nov 1920, Fuuoka, Japan. University Professor. m. Tatsuko Kitamura, 23 Sept 1949. *Education:* BM, 1944, DMSc, 1956, Keio-Gijuku Univ Sch of Med, Tokyo; Profl Cert: Med Dipl, 1944. *Appointments:* Phys: Nat Tokyo 1st Hosp, 1945-46, Nat Kurihama Hosp, 1946-49; Sch Hlth Ofr, Yokohama City Bd of Ed, 1949-56; Asst Prof of Hyg, Niigata Univ Sch of Med, 1956-61; Prof of Hyg and Pub Hlth, Iwate Med Univ Sch of Med, 1962-72; Prof of Pub Hlth: Kitasato Univ Sch of Med, 1972-83, Sagami Women's Univ, 1983-. *Publication:* Improved method of analysing mortality statistics, 1964. *Memberships:* Dir, Japanese Soc of Hlth and Human Ecol, 1962; Chief Ed, Japanes Jour of Hlth and Human Ecol, 1984-; Japanese Soc of Pub Hlth, 1962-; Coun, Japan Assn of Indust Hlth, 1972-; Intl Union for Hlth Educ, Paris, 1985-; Emeritus, The Japanese Soc for Hyg, 1991. *Address:* Sagami Women's University, 1-1 Bunkyo 2-Chome, Sagamihara- shi, Kanagawa 228, Japan. 52.

UGHAMADU Cyprian Ozo, b. 16 June 1956, Barakin Ladi, Nigeria. m. Martha Ughamadu, 11 Aug 1984, 2 s, 2 d. *Education:* BS Polit Sci, 1979; Postgrad Dipl, Bus Mgmt, 1990; Awaiting result of MBA Mgmt. *Appointments:* Lectr, Kano Poly, Nigeria, 1979-80; Principal Sec, Nat Party of Nigeria, 1980-83; Hon Mem of Parliament, 1983; Gen Mgr, Olympic Packers Ltd, 1983-. *Creative works:* Organization of African Unity in the Context of Cold War Politics, 1979. *Memberships:* Nigerian Jaycees, Inst of Mgmt, Inst of Secs and Admrs; Former Mem, Anambra Hse of Assembly, Nigeria; Lord Mayor, Nibton League. *Hobbies:* National and

international politics; Tennis. *Address:* Ughamadu Lodge, Umuanum, Nibo, Awka, Anambra State.

UJEVIC Danja, b. 28 Jan 1948, Split, Croatia. Journalist. m. Jure 4 May 1974, div, 1 s. *Education:* Natko Nodilo and Mus Grammar Schls, Split, 1956-65; Arts Fac, Zabreg Univ, 1966-72; BA Langs Lit and Comp Lit. *Appointments:* Ed, Exportdrvo, 1975-80; Journalist, Vecernji List, Zagreb, 1980-; Parliamentary Corres. *Memberships:* Assn of Croatia Jours. *Hobbies:* Music; Playing the piano; Literature. *Address:* Zelengorska Poltana 8, Zagreb, Croatia.

UJIIE Hiroshi, b. 16 Oct 1931, Tokyo, Japan. Professor. m. Toshiko Yoshikawa, 7 Nov 1963, 1 s, 1 d. *Education:* BSc, 1954, MSc, 1956, DSc, 1960, Tokyo Univ of Educ. *Appointments:* Sr Res Assoc, nat Sci Mus of Tokyo, 1962-70; Prof, Dept of Marine Scis, Univ Ryukyus, 1970- . *Publications:* Beneath the Rukyu Island Arc - Sedimentology and Geology, 1986; Topography and Geology of Okinawa, 1990. *Memberships:* Geol Soc of Japan, Cun; Palaeontol Soc of Japan; Ocenogr Soc of Japan; Geol Soc of Am; Am Geophys Union; Brit Micropalaeontol Soc; Geol Soc of Switzerland. *Honour:* Palaeontol Soc of Japan Awd, 1974. *Hobbies:* Reading; painting; Field trekking; Skin diving. *Address:* Department of Marine Sciences, University of the Ryukyus, Senbaru 1, Nishihara, Okinawa, Japan.

ULLAH Mohammed Rahmat, b. 4 Apr 1931, Comilla. Associate Professor. m. Iftekhar Khanam, 25 Aug 1953, 1 s, 4 d. *Education:* BSC Hons Chem, 1954, MSc, 1955, Dacca Univ, Bangladesh; Certs in Chem and Chem Engrg, Can, 1961, 1962; PhD, Univ of Glasgow, UK, 1965; Chartered Engr, UK. *Appointments:* Res Asst, Univ of Dacca, 1956, RCST, Glasgow, 1963-65; Vis Lectr, Bangladesh Univ of Engrg and Tech, 1971; Res Assoc, Heriot-Wayy Univ, Edinburgh, 19788-; Sr Lectr, Petroleum Engrg, Univ of W.Indies, 1980-; Vis Prof, Univ of Calgary Can, 1983; Assoc Prof, Sultan Quaboos Univ, Oman, 1990-; Also various industrial appointments in Pakistan, Bangladesh and Can, 1956-78. *Publications:* Numerous research papers, articles and government reports. *Memberships:* Fellow, Inst of Energy, London; Inst of Gas Engrs, London; Inst of Engrs, Bangladesh; Soc of Petroleum Engrs, USA. *Hobbies:* Reading; Writing; Travel; Gardening. *Address:* Department of Petroleum and Mining Engineering, Col of Engineering, Sultan Qaboos University, PO Box 32483, Al-Khod, Sultanate of Oman.

ULRICH Betty Garton, b. 28 Oct 1919, Indiana, USa. Writer; Editor. m. Louise E Ulrich Jr, 5 Jan 1946, 3 s, 2 d. *Education:* BS Educ, 1972. *Appointments:* Field Sec, Student Ser, Dept of Am Lutheran Conf, 1942-46; Instr, Avesburg Col, Minnsota, 1946-49; Hg Sch Latin Tchr, Grand Forks, N.Dakota, 1959-60; Sec, Lutheran Ch Lib Assn, 1975-80; Co-Fdr, and Co-Ed, The Inkling, writers journals, 1980-; Currently, Columnist, Sawyer County Record, Wisconsin. *Publications:* Away We go, 1970; Every Day with God, 1972; Rooted in the Sky, 1989; Many articles, short stories and poems in periodicals. *Memberships:* Wisconsin Reg Writers Assn; Christian Writers League of Am. *Hobbies:* Swimming; Reading; Canoeing; Fishing. *Address:* PO Box 265, Stone Lake, WI 54876, USA.

UMPLEBY Stuart Anspach, b. 5 Mar 1944, Tulsa, Oklahoma, USA. Professor. m. Gertraud Maria Zangl, 7 Mar 1986, 2 s. *Education:* BS Mech Engrg, 1967, AB 1967, AM 1969, Polit Sci, PhD Communications, 1975, Univ of Illinois at Urbana, Champaign. *Appointments:* Asst, Assoc, and full Prof, George Wash Univ, 1975-. *Publications:* A Science of Goal Formulation: American and Soviet Discussions of Cybernetics and Systems Theory, 1991; Cybernetics of National Development, 1991; Methods for making Social Organizations Adaptive, 1986; American and Soviet Discussions of the Foundations of Cybernetics and General Systems Theory, 1987; Strategies for regulating the global economy, 1989; The Science of Cybernetics and the Cybernetics of Science, 1990; A Preliminary inventory of theories available to guide the reform of Socialist Societies, 1991. *Memberships:* Am Soc for Cybernetics, Pres, 1980-82; Austrian Soc for Cybernetic Studies. Intl Soc for the Sys Scis. *Hobbies:* Gardening; Swimming; Playing with children. *Address:* Department of Management Science, George Washington University, Washington, DC 20052, USA.

UNDERWOOD Benjamin Hayes, b. 10 Mar 1942, Georgia, USA. Hospital Administrator. m. Sheri Vennell, 5 Dec 1984, 1 s, 1 d. *Education:* AA Georgia Military Col, 1962; BBA, Univ of Georgia, 1964; Cert, Adv Hlth Care Mgmt Prog, Yale Univ, 1983. *Appointments:* CEO, Metropolitan Psychi Ctr, 1966-82; CEO, Ridgeview Inst, 1976-83; Pres, Consltg and Healthcare, 1983-84; Pres, CEO, Anchor Hosp, 1985-, all in Atlanta, GA. *Memberships:* Am Col of Healthcare Execs; Am Col of Addiction Treatment Admrs; Assn of Mental Hlth Admirs; Nat Assn, and Am Col of Addiction Treatment Providers; GA Hosp Assn Coun for Psychi and SA Hosps. *Honours:* Boss of the Year, 1978; Quality Assurance Excellence, 1981; Gold Achievement Awd, 1981. *Hobbies:* Golf; Squash; Fishing. *Address:* Anchor Hospital, 5454 Yorktowne Drive, Atlanta GA 30349, USA. 152.

UNDERWOOD Richard Allan, b. 28 Mar 1933, Michigan, USA. Professor of English. m. Sandra Jane Hayes, 17 Nov 1962, 1 s. *Education:* BA Journalism, 1955; MA 1967, PhD 1970, English, Univ of Michigan. *Appointments:* Asst Prof, 1970-77, Assoc Prof, 1977-84, Prof, 1984-, Clemson Univ. *Publications:* A little bit of love, 1963, translated as En Smula Karlek, 1969, 1981; Phoenix with a Bayonet, 1971; Shakespeare's The Phoenix and Turtle: A Survey of Scholarship, 1974; Shakespeare on Love: The Poems and the Plays, 1985. *Memberships:* S.Atlantic Modern Lang Assn. *Honours:* Fellow, Bread Loaf Writer's Conf, Vermont, 1963; Vis Scholar, Rackham Sch of Grad Studies, Univ of Michigan, 1983-85, 1990-92. *Hobby:* Jazz piano. *Address:* Department of English, 809 Strode Tower, Clemson University, Clemson, SC 29631, USA. 7, 15, 13.

UNGUREANU Mihai-Razvan, b. 22 Sept 1968, Iasi, Romania. Student in History. *Education:* Admittance in Faculty, 1987; Now in Fourth Year of Study. *Appointments:* External Asst, Inst of History, Iasi, 1989; Editor,Tinerana Mag, 1990-; Editor in Chief, Dialog Mag, 1990-92. *Publications:* More Than 25 Sci Lectrs, Works, Conferences Publi; 2 Books; More than 50 Interviews. *Memberships:* Intl Student in History Assn; Young Historians Acad Soc. *Honours:* First of the Pupils Batch Promoted; First Classified in the Facultys Admittance Exam; Magna Cum Laude. *Hobbies:* Music; Old Documents; Basketball. *Address:* Str Costache Negri 62, Bl C2, SC A, Ft, 6, AP 22, Iasi-6600, Romania. 139.

UNNO Wasaburo, b. 2 Oct 1925, Urawa City, Japan. Professor Emeritus. m. Kikuko Nakamura, 20 May 1952, 2 d . *Education:* DSc, Astronomy, Univ of Tokyo, 1955. *Appointments:* Asst Prof, 1952-63, Prof, 1963-84, Prof Emeritus, 1984, Univ of Tokyo; Prof, Kinki Univ, 1984-. *Publications:* Heaven, Earth, Man, 1980; World of Stars and Galaxies, 1984; Non Radial Oscillations of Stars, 1979, 1989. *Memberships:* Astro Soc of Japan; Phys Soc of Japan; Intl Astro Union. *Hobbies:* Go; Fossil hunting; Visiting old Temple Art; Korean Language. *Address:* Research Institute of Science and Technology, Kinki University, Higashi-Osaka City 577, Japan.

URAGODA Christopher Gunapala, b. 22 Sept 1928, Hikkaduwa, Sri Lanka. Chest Physician. m. Padma Rambukpota, 26 Dec 1958, 2 s, 2 d. *Education:* MBBS, Ceylon, 1953; MRCP, Edin, 1961; MRCP, Glas, 1961; MD, Ceylon, 1963; Fellow, Am Col of Chest Phys, 1970; FRCP Edin, 1975; Fellow, Ceylon Col of Phys, 1982; MFOM, 1985; FRCP, Glasgow, 1991. *Appointments:* Phys, Chest Clin, Kandy, 1962-73; Phys in Charge, Ctrl Chest Clin, Colombo, 1973-88; Locum Conslt Chest

Phys, Tameside Gen Hosp, Lancs, 1977-78; Phys, chest Hosp, Welisera, 1988-. *Publications:* A history of medicine in Sri Lanka, 1987; Bibliography of Sri Lanka, 1811-1976, 1980; Bibliography on Health in Sri Lanka, 1977-80, 1983; A Bibliography of medical publications relating to Sri Lanka, 1981-88, 1991. *Memberships:* Pres, Royal Asiatic Soc of Sri Lanka; Chm, Ceylon Assn for the Prevention of Tuberculosis; Pres, Sri Lanka Med Assn, 1983-84; Ceylon Col of Phys, 1981-82; Ed, Ceylon Med Jour, 1979-. *Honours:* WHO: Expert Panel on Tuberculosis, Temporary Advr, Res Grants; Guiness Awd; Peter Pillai Awd. *Hobbies:* Camping in the jungle; Study of wildlife and archaeology of Sri Lanka; Collecting books. *Address:* 78/5 Old Road, Nawala, Rajagiriya, Sri Lanka. 52.

URBONAS Leonas, b. 19 Apr 1922, Lithuania. Artist. m. (1) Talva Tuldar, 1953, dec, (2) June Sutton, 1965, div, 2 s. *Education:* Acad of Fine Arts, 1946-48. *Appointments:* Self Employed, 1951-. *Creative Works:* Paintings; Essays; Guest Lectrs; Art Demonstrations; Seminars; Working Exhib. *Memberships:* CAS; Australian Natl Gallery Canberra; Lithuanian Natl Collection Vilnius; Ciurlionis Gallery Chicago USA. *Honours:* Nosman Prize Pastel; Miranda Fair, Watercolour; Hunters Hill, Oil; Australian Fashion Fabric Design, Gold Medallion; Ryde Calligraphic Art. *Address:* Aras Art Centre, Allambie Road, Mittagons, NSW 2575, Australia

URI Pierre Emmanuel, b. 20 Nov 1911, Paris, France. Economist. m. Monique Blanchtiere, 24 Oct 1939, 2 s, 2 d. *Education:* Ecole Normale Superieure, 1929; Agrege de Philos, 1933; DES Pub Law, Econ, 1941; Grad Fellowship, Princeton Univ, USA, 1934; Ctr de Perfectionnement aux Affaires, 1942. *Appointments include:* Prof of Philos, 1935-40; Econ Advr, French Planning Comm, 1947-52; Econ Dir, Coal and Steel Community, 1952-59; Advr, EEC, 1958-59; Prof, ENA, 1947-71, Paris IX, 1969-76. *Publications include:* La Reforme de 'Enseignement 1937; La Crise de la Zone de Libre Exchange, 1959; Dialogue des Continents, 1962; Une Politique Monetaire pour l'Amerique Latine 1965; Un Avenir pour l'Europe Agricole, 1971; L'Europe se gaspille 1973; Plan Quinquennal pour une Revolution, 1973; Aider le Tiers Monde a se nourrir lui-meme, 1981; Changer l'Impot Pour Changer la France, 1991. *Memberships:* French Econ and Soc Coun, 1974-79; Shadow Cabinet, 1966- 68, Pres, Univ et Entreprise; Hon Pres, Amis de Jean Monnet; Assn Franciase de Sci Econ; Soc d'Econ Polit; Soc de Stats. *Honours:* Criox de Guerre; Cmdr, Order of Leopold, Belgium, 1981; Legion of Hon, 1981; Grand Cmdr Cross, Nat Order of Merit, 1984; Robert Schuman Prize, 1981. *Hobbies:* Travel; Theatre. *Address:* 1 Avenue President Wilson, 75116 Paris, France. 34, 43, 52, 91, 139, 152, 178.

URIARTE REBAUDI Alfredo Arturo, b. 28 Feb 1928, Buenos Aires, Artentina. Economist. *Education:* Nat Pub Acct, 1958, Lec on Econ, 1968, Univ of Buenos Aires. *Appointments:* Judicial expert. *Publications:* Sociologia, marxismo y psicoanalisis, 1972; Sexo, drogas y alienacion, 1975; Bolsas y mercados de valores, 1984. *Memberships:* Assn ARgentina Descidientes de Guerreros del Paraguay; Bolsa de Comercio de Buenos Aires; Assn de Estudios Historicos San Nicolas, Pro Sec. *Honours:* Fundacion Bolsa de Comercio: Bolsas y mercados de valores, 1978; Fundacion Banco Mercantil Argentino: Inflacion, 1979; Chess, Empresa de Correos, 1951. *Hobbies:* Reading; Books. *Address:* Tucuman 1561, Buenos Aires 1050, R. Argentina. 52.

URIARTE REBAUDI Lia Neomi, b. 26 Mar 1925, Buenos Aires, Argentina. Educator; Writer. *Education:* Lit Scis Univ de Buenos Aires: Prof, 1949; Licentiate, 1972. *Appointments:* Asst Prof, Univ Catolica, Argentina, 1960-66; Assoc Prof, 1966-69, Prof, 1969-. *Publications:* Canto Elegiaco, 1986; Canto de Albanza, 1987, both poetry books; Articles on education and literature, 1960-; Writer of songs and music for piano,

1981- ; Painting works, 1982-87. *Memberships:* Asociacion Intl de Hispanistas; Modern Lang Assn. *Hobbies:* Music; Painting; Poetry. *Address:* Carabobo 250, 1406 Buenos Aires, Republic of Argentina.

URIARTE REBAUDI Roberto Ovidio, b. 27 Jan 1924, Buenos Aires, Argentina. Lawyer. *Education:* Lawyer, Univ de Buenos Aires, 1956. *Appointments:* Curator, Official of Incapables, to 1968. *Publication:* Poetry. *Memberships:* Patronato de liberados: Hon Sec; Col de Abogados; Asociacion Argentina Descendientes de Guerroros del Paraguay; Reviser of Bills; Argentina Assn of Intl Tourism, Assessor; Inst Moreniano; Asociacion Descendientes de Proceres de la Independencia. *Hobbies:* Reading; Walking. *Address:* Tucuman 1639, 1050 Buenos Aires, Republic of Argentina.

URSIC Srebrenka, b. 4 Mar 1947, Zagreb, Croatia. Microelectronics Research; Engineering Consultant. m. Damir Vuk, 20 Jan 1990. *Education:* BSEE, 1970, MSEE, 1973, Univ Zagreb. *Appointments:* Tchr, Fac of Elec Engrg, Univ Zagreb, 1983-85; Dev Specialst, 1970-80, Asst Gen Mgr, 1980- 82, IC Reschr, 1982-84, RIZ-Semiconductors; ASIC Design Gp Ldr, Rade Koncar Inst, 1984-90; Tech Conslt, Termoenergetika and Sistemprojekt, 1990-, all in Zagreb. *Publications:* Co-author, CAD in Microelectronics, 1971-90; Articles in professional journals and papers at conferences; Demiconductors Production and development management; ASIC Design Organizing; Co-author, Brac (Adriatic Island). *Memberships:* Yugoslav Soc of Microelectronics, 1972; IEE, 1977-; Croatian Nat Sci Com, 1982-84; UNESCO Wkg Gp for Microoelecs, 1984. *Honours:* Dist Distribution Awds, 1980, 1986; Best paper Awd, CTAN Conf, 1980. *Hobbies:* Music; Hatha Yoga; Ecology; Tennis and Sea Sports; Holistics. *Address:* Termoenergeitka Gundullceva 31, 41000 Zagreb, Croatia.

URSUL Arkadiy Dmitrievich, b. 28 July 1936, USSR. Institute Director. m. Ursul Tatiana Albertovna, 3 July 1985. 1 d. *Education:* Moscow Aviation Inst, 1953-59; Dr of Philos, 1969; Prof, 1971. *Appointments:* Engr, 1959-63; Lectr, 1964-70; Hd, Dept of Inst of Philos, 1970-84; VP, Acad of Scis, Moldova. *Publications:* Space Exploration, 1967; The Nature of Information, 1968; Information, 1971; Reflection and Information, 1973; The Information Problem in Contemporary Science, 1975; Mankind, Earth, Universe, 1977; Philosophy and integrative processes n the science, 1981; The perspectives of ecodevelopment, 1990; The informatization of the Society, 1990; Author of more than 500 scientific publications including 40 books. *Memberships:* Pres, Acad of Cosmonautics; Co Pres, Intern Inst for Noosphere; VP, Intern Assn Space and Philos; Dir, Inst for Noosphere; Directorate, Soc for Informatics and Computing. *Honours:* Full Mem, Acad of Sci of Moldova, 1984; Ecol Acad of Russia, 1991; Acad of Cosmonautics, 1991; Corres mem, Intl Acad of Astronautics, 1988; Hon Mem, Men and Space, 1975; Laureate, State Prize in Sci and Tech, 1987. *Hobbies:* Swimming; Yoga; Martial arts; Literature; Painting; Music.

USAREWICZ Maria. *Address:* ul Mariecka 34/36/9, 80-833 Gdańsk, Poland.

USPENSKY Boris, b. 1 Mar 1937, Moscow, Russia. University Professor. m. (1) Galina Korshunova, 19 July 1963, dec 1978; (2) Titiana Vladyshevskaja, 18 May 1985, 2 s. *Education:* PhD, 1963, DSc, 1972, Moscow Univ. *Appointments:* Res Fellow, Inst of African Studies, Acad of Scis, USSR, 1963-65; Sr Res Fellow, 1965-67, Prof, 1977-, Moscow Univ; Vis Porf, Vienna, 1988-89; Harvard, 1990-91. *Publications:* Structural Tupology of Languages, 1965; Poetics of Composition, 1970; The First Russian Grammar, 1975; The Semiotics of the Russian Incon, 1976; Philological Investigations in the field of Slavic Antiquities, 1980; The History of the Russian Literary Lang, 1987. *Memberships:* Foreign Mem, Austrian Acad of Scis; Acad Europae; Hon,

Slavonic and E.Europeal Mediaeval Studies Gp; Hon, Assn Intl de Semiologie de l'Image; Intl Assn for Semiotic Studies; Moscow Ling Soc. *Hobby:* Travelling. *Address:* Chasoraja ul 19/8 kv 20, Moscow 125315, Russia.

UTRIO-LINNILA Kaari Marjatta, b. 28 July 1942, Helsinki, Finland. Writer. m. Kai Linnila, 1974, 3 s. *Education:* MA, Helsinki Univ, 1967. *Creative works:* 25 books, mostly historical novels with a mediaeval Finnish theme. Main work: Daughters of Eve, a history of European women, 1984. *Memberships:* State Lit Com, 1980-86; Bd of Union of Finnish Writers, 1988- . *Honours:* State Lit Prize, 1973; Lit Prize of Trade Unions, 1984; Historischen Sachbuchpreis Schloss Burg, 1989. *Hobbies:* Amnesty Intl. *Address:* 31470 Somerniemi, Finland. 90.

UTTERBACK Will Hay Jr, b. 10 Mar 1947, Amarillo, Texas, USA. Labor Union Administrator. m. 31 Margaret Jane Smith, 31 July 1982. *Education:* Hon JD, 1981; Labor Law and Admin, 1988. *Appointments:* Conslt, Franklin D Roosevelt Lib, 1977-; Conslt, Smithsonian Inst, 1982- 83; Pres, Communications Workers of Am, 1988-; Conslt, Educ Video Gp, 1989-. *Publications:* An opinion on the nitrate file fire: Suitland, Maryland, 1978; A Report on the status of historical radio broadcasts in the US. *Memberships:* Nat Hist Soc; Am Hist Assn; Ctr for the Study of the Presidency; Independent Scholar's Network. *Hobbies:* Genealogy; Woodworking. *Address:* PO Box 150, Amarillo, TX 79105, USA. 7.

UY Paul, b. 30 July 1932, Brussels. Composer. m. Jacqueline Libon, 20 June 1956, 2 s. *Education:* Premiers Prix et Dipl Superieur, Conservatoire de Bruxelles. *Appointments:* Head of Productions, Ratio TV Belge (RTBF). *Publications:* Sarah, opera; Brel Rever in impossible Reve, oratorio; Smphonic Music, Concerti Chamber Music; Theme music for films. *Honours:* Prix du Millenaire de la Ville de Bruxelles; Prix de Composition Reine Marie-Jose, Geneve; Prix de L'Academic Charles Cros, Paris. *Hobbies:* Music. *Address:* 57 Avenue Des Campanules, Bruxelles 1170, Belgium.

UYEMOV Avenir, b. 4 Apr 1928, Russia. Logic Metodology & Philosophy of Sci. m. Fezentjeva Ledmila, 12 Oct 1984, 1 s. *Education:* Moscow Univ, 1949; Philosophical Sci, 1952; Doc of Philosophical Sci, 1964. *Appointments:* Pedagogocial Inst, Ivanovo, 1952-64; Odessa Univ, Chief of Dept Philosophy, 1964-73; Odessa Branch, Inst of Economics, 1973-. *Publications:* Dinge, Eigenschaffen und Relationan, Berlin; Analogy in Practice of Scientifical Research in Russ; Logical Foundations of the Model Method in Russ; System Approaches and The General Systems Theory. *Memberships:* Filosophical Soc of Ukraine; Pzaxeological Soc, Warsaw. *Hobbies:* Touring; Reading. *Address:* Perekopskoj Divisii 47 KV 14, 49 Odessa, Ukraine.

UYTTENBROECK Frans Joseph, b. 11 July 1921, Lier, Belgium. Gynaecologist; Oncologist. m. Elisabeth Switters, 24 Oct 1946, 5d. *Education:* MD, Univ of Louvain, 1946; PhD, Univ Amsterdam, 1952. *Appointments:* Prof Emeritus, Hd Dept, Obs and Gynae, Univ of Antwerp; Hon, Hd Dept, Obs and Gynae, St Camille St Agustine Clins, Antwerp. *Publications:* 17 medical books. *Contributions to:* articles to professional journals. *Memberships:* Intl Soc for Study Vulvar Dis; Intl Soc Gynae Oncol; Acad Europae; European Soc Gynae and Oncol; Belgian RAC, past Pres; Acad de Chirurgie Paris; Acad Nat Med Paris; Soc Pelvic Surgs. *Honours:* Decorated Cmdr Order of Leopold; Grand Ofr Crown Order; Grand Offr Leopold Order. *Hobbies:* Travel to many countries. *Address:* 12 Avenue Jan Van Rijswijck, 2018 Antwerp, Belgium. 1.

V

VACEK Jaroslav, b. 26 June 1943, Litostrov, Brno. University Associate Professor. m. Eva Manouskova, 19 Mar 1964, 1 s, 2 d. *Education:* MA, Fac of Arts, Charles Univ, 1965; PhD, 1973. *Appointments:* Asst, Dept of Asian and African Studies, Charles Univ, 1967; Sr Lectr, 1969; Assoc Prof, 1991. *Publications:* A Mongolian Mythological Text, 1983; The Tamil of the 17th Century ballad, 1970; The Sibilants in Old Indo- Aryan, 1976; Introducing Sagam Literature, 1989; Four textbooks on modern Mongolia, thirty papers and poetic translations. *Memberships:* Ed Bds: Archive Orientalina, Intl J of Dravidian Linguistics, PILC Jour of Dravidic Studies, Circle of Modern Philogists. *Hobbies:* Comparative linguistics; Music; Poetry; Gardening. *Address:* Dvorecke n 403/4, 147 OO Praha 4, Czechoslovakia.

VACHEK Josef, b. 1 Mar 1909, Prague, Czechoslovakia. Emeritus Professor of English. m. Paula, 28 Oct 1948, 1 s, 1 d. *Education:* PhD, Charles Univ, Prague, 1932; DSc, Czech Acad of Scis, 1962; PhD hon causa, Masary Univ, Brno, 1989. *Appointments:* Prof of Eng Lang, Masaryk Univ, 1947-62; Prof of Eng, Comenius Univ, Bratislavia; Sr Resr, Inst of Czech Langs, Prague, 1962-70; Prof of Eng, Leiden, Holland. *Publications:* Prof Karl Lolck and problems of Historical Phonology, 1935; Zum problem der Geschrifbenen Sprache, 1939; Prague School Reader in Linguistics, 1964; The Linguistic Sch of Prague, 1966; Selected writings in English and General Linguistics, 1976. *Memberships:* Hon, Ling Soc of Am; Hon Pres, Prague Ling Circle; Netherlands Acad of Scis; Corres Fellow Brit Acad. *Address:* Nam Jiriho Z Podebad 18, 130 00 Praha 3, Czechoslovakia.

VADAS Peter, b. 5 Aug 1953, Budapest, Hungary. Clinical Immunologist; Allergist. *Education:* BSc 1976, PhD, 1980; MD, 1983, FRCPC, 1990; FACP, 1991. *Appointments:* ASst Prof, Fac of Med, 1990; Asst Prof, Dept of Immunol, 1990, Univ of Toronto; Conslt, Immunol and Allergy, Wellesley Hosp, 1990. *Memberships:* Can Inflammatory Soc, Dpty Dir; Inflammation Res Gp, Dpty Dir; Shock Soc; Am Col of Rheumatol; Can Soc of Immunol; Ontario Allergy SOc. *Honours:* Med Scist Wed, Can Heart Foun, 1980-83; Fellowship, 1984-86, Scholarship, 1991-96, Med Res Coun of Can. *Address:* Division of Immunology, Department of Medicine, Wellesley Hospital, 160 Wellesley St East, Toronto, Ontario, Canada M4Y 1J3. 17.

VAHAMAKI Kurt Borje, b. 28 Mar 1944, Vasa, Finland. University of Professor. m. Varpu Lindstrom, 4 Mar 1990, 1 s, 1 d. *Education:* BA 1966, MA 1969, PhD, 1984, Docent, 1986, Abo Acad, Finland. *Appointments:* Instr, Univ of Oulu, 1973-75; Prof, Univ Stockholm, 1985-86; Asst Prof, Univ of Minnesota, 1975-83; Assoc Prof, Univ of Minnesota, 1983-91; Vis Prof, Univ of Toronto, 1989-. *Publications:* Spesieksenasema suomen kielen kuvauksessa, 1980; Existence and Identify, 1984; Minna Cathin Kielet, 1991. *Memberships:* Soc for the Adv of Scandianvian Studies, USA and Can; Finno-Ugric Studies Assn of Can, Bd; Can Friends of Finland, Bd; Finnish Lit Soc, Corres. *Honours:* Nat Dist Awd for best doctoral disseration, 1984. *Hobbies:* Lit; Sport; Baseball; Music; Languages. *Address:* 7 Bishop Avenue Suite 2303, Willowdale, Ontario, Canada M2M 4J4.

VALAGUSSA Roberto, b. 14 Nov 1952, Milano, Italy. Consultant. *Education:* Maturita Scientifica, 1971; Dottore Scienze Economiche, 1975. *Appointments:* Acct, Peat Marwick Mitchell, 1975; Standard Chartered Bank, 1976-78; Barcelona; Gen Mgr: Fabbri France, Paris, London and Hamburg, 1988; Bd Dirs, GE Ltd, London, 1988; Pres, Fabbri USA, NY, 1986; Ptnr, Helmut Neumann Intl, Paris, 190. *Honours:* Dottore Scienze Economische with hons, 1975. *Hobbies:* Sport; Travelling; Reading. *Address:* Via Borgospesso, 12

Milano, Italy, 9 Rue Charles V, 75004 Paris, France. 52.

VALAVANIS Kimon, b. 7 Mar 1957, Athens, Greece. Associate Professor of Computer Engineering. m. Areti A Marangaki, 1 d. *Education:* EE Dipl, Nat Tech Univ of Athens, Greece, 1981; MSc, 1984, PhD, 1986, RPI. *Appointments include:* Instr, Learning Ctrs, Athens, 1975-81; Res Assoc, Tchg Asst, Robotics and Automation Lab, Rensselaer Poly Inst, 1982-85; Instr, Nat Tech Univ, Boulder, CO, 1987-90; Asst Prof, Ch of Elec and Computer Engrg, Dir, Robotics Lab, N.Eastern Univ, 1986-90; Assoc Prof, Grad Fac of Engrg, Univ of S.W.Louisiana, 1991-. *Publications include:* Proceedings 4th IEEE Intl Symp on Intelligent Controls, Co-ed; Intelligent Robotic Systems: Theory, Design and Applications, 1991, co-author; Numerous book chapters, articles and papers to refereed journals. *Memberships:* IEEE: Control Sys Soc, Computer Sys Soc, Robotics and Automation Soc, Intelligent Controls Com; IFAC Educ Com; Sigma Xi, NYAS; Assoc Mem, ASME. *Address:* The Centre for Advanced Computer Studies, University of S.Western Louisiana, PO Box 44330 Lafayette, LA 70504, USA.

VALCAVI Umberto, b. 15 Sept 1928, Desenzano, Italy. University Professor. m. Ines Scrocca, 17 Sept 1960. 1 s, 1 d. *Education:* Grad, Indust Chem, Univ Milan, 1965; Libero Docente in Org Chem, 1965. *Appointments:* Reschr, Farmitalia Spa, Milan, 1955-59; Dir of Res, Inst, 1959-76, Sci Dir, 1977-80, Gen Mrg, 1981-86, Biochem Italiano Spa Milano; PRof, Organic Chem, Univ of Milan, 1964-. *Publications:* 2 books on organic chemistry, 90 scientific papers in international journals, 26 internal patents. *Memberships:* FNYAS; AAAS; ACS; Bd, Italian Soc of Pharm Scis; Sci Com, Loorenzini Foun; Rotary of Milano-Ovest. *Honours:* Grand Cross Knight, Italian Republic; Order of Merit, Cmdr Italian Republic. *Hobbies:* Archaeology; Prehistory; Biosciences. *Address:* viale Bianca Maria 21, 20122 Milano, Italy. 52, 95.

VALDES David Churchill, b. 12 Aug 1950, Los Angeles, CA. USA. Producer of Motion Pictures. m. Susan Margaret Jones, 14 Sept 1974, 2 d. *Education:* Assoc of Arts, AA, Orange Coast Coll, 1970; Bach of Arts, BA, Univ of California, Los Angeles, 1976. *Appointments:* Universal Studies, 1976-79; Warner Bros, 1979-86; Tri Star Pictures, 1986-87; Warner Bros, 1987-90; Disney, 1990-91; Warner Bros. *Creative Works:* Pale Rider; Gardens of Stone; Like Father Like Son; Bird; The Dead Pool; Pink Cadillac; White Hunter, Black Heart; The Rookie; Unforgiven. *Memberships:* Acad of Motion Picture Arts & Sci; Dir Guild of America; American Film Inst; British Columbia Motion Picture Assn. *Hobbies:* Computers; Cycling; Tennis; Reading. *Address:* 4000 Warner Boulevard, Building 81, Room 103, Burbank, CA 91522, USA. 2.

VALE Donald Mark James, b. 25 Apr 1941, London, England. Business Executive. m. Beverley Joan, 16 June 1967, 1 s, 2 d. *Education:* IAB, City of London Col, 1961-65; Univ of Toronto; Exec MBA, Univ of W.Bus Sch. *Appointments:* Chief Gen Mgr's Asst, Nat Westminister Bank UK, 1960-65; Mktg Trainee, Shell Canada, 1965-68; Dir, Corp Mktg Support, Philips Electronics Ltd, 1968-81; Pres, CO and Dir, Heritage Craftsman Inc, 1981-82; Intl Mktg Mgr, Rush-Hampton Industries, 1982-83; Gen Mgr, Matsushita Elec of Can Ltd, 1983-88; Exec VP and Chief Op Ofr, Nat Bus Systems Inc, 1988-90; VP and Gen Mrg, Sharp Electronics of Can Ltd, 1990-. *Creative works:* Played piano with Dave Clark; Composed music for commercial, Keep Our Lakes and Rivers Clean, Ontario Hydro. *Hobbies:* Classical, modern jazz and piano music; Reading; Sailing; Scuba diving. *Address:* 68 Carondale Crescent, Agincourt, Ontario, Canada M1W 2B1. 88, 32.

VALKOVIC Zvonimir, b. 23 Sept 1941, Malinska, Yugoslzvia. University Professor. m. Radmila, 17 June 1967, 2 d. *Education:* BEE, 1965; MSc 1970; DSc, 1975.

Appointments: Res Engr, 1964-70, Hd of R&D Dept on Transformers, 1970-, Inst Koncar; Prof, Univ of Zagreb, 1984-. *Memberships:* Intl Conf on Large High-Voltage Elec Sys, Paris. *Honours:* Nikola Testla Nat Awd for Sci Achievement, Zagreb, 1975. *Hobbies:* Reading. *Address:* Tijardoviceva 2, 41000 Zagreb, Croatia, Yugoslavia. 1.

VALLANCE Michael Wilson, b. 9 Sept 1933, Brentford, Middlesex, England. Headmaster. m. Mary Winifred Ann Garnett, 1 Apr 1970, 1 s, 2 d. *Education:* Brighton and St John's Cols, 1953-57; Cambs, 1953-57; MA Cantab, PGGE, Canteb. *Appointments:* Staff, Utd Steel Co Ltd, 1952-53; Abington Sch, 1957-61; Harrow Sch, 1961-72; Headmaster: Durham Sch, 1972-82, Bloxham Sch, 1982-91. *Memberships:* Headmaster's Conf, Chm, NE Div, 1981-82, Chm, Northern ISIS, 1976-78, ISIS Mgmt Com, 1977-79; Trustee, Bloxham Proj, 1986-. *Honours:* Host Prize, St John's Cambs, 1956. *Hobbies:* Sport, especially cricket; Books; The Sea; Gardens. *Address:* Bloxham School, Bloxham near Banbury, Oxon, OX15 4PE, England. 1.

VALLYATHAN Velayudhan, b. 14 Oct 1936, India. m. Usha, 7 Nov 1965, 1 s, 1 d. *Education:* BSc Hons, 1952-57, MSc, 1957-59; PhD, 1959- 63; Electron Microscopy, 1969; Scanning Elec Microscopy, 1976; Pulmonary Dis, 1980. *Appointments:* Asst Prof, 1964-68; Natl Res Coun, Post Doc Fellow, 1968-71; Res Assoc, 1971-74; Asst Prof, 1974-79; Res Pathol, 1979-83, Assoc Prof, 1983-90; Prof, 1991-. *Contributions to:* Occup Respiratory Diseases; Silica and Silica-induced diseases, co-ed; Published over 90 research works. *Memberships:* Soc of Animal Morphologists and Physiols; Univ of Baroda Inst for Muscle Dis; Univ of Guelph Univ of Vermont, W.Virginia Univ; Nat Inst for Occup Safety and Health. *Honours:* Coun of Sci and Indust Res Awd, 1959-63; Special Recognition Awd, Alice Hamilton Sci Awd for Occup Safety and Hlth, 1990; Employee Performance Awd, 1991. *Hobbies:* Photography; Collecting coins and stamps; Tennis; Travel. *Address:* National Institute for Occupational Safety & Health, 944 Chestnut Ridge Rd, Morgantown, WV 26505, USA.

VALNERE Rita, b. 21 Sept 1929, Latvia. Prof; Painter. m. Eduards Kalnins, 5 dec 1961, 1 d. *Education:* J Rozentals Art Sch, 1945-49; Latvian Acad of Arts, 1949-56. *Appointments:* Creative Works, 1956-67; Snr Tchr, 1967-78; Asst Prof, 1978-85; Prof of Painting, 1985-; Latvian Acad of Arts. *Creative Works:* Mothers Portrait; Mother & Child; Pnte Veccio; Talks on Painting; Dedication to the Poet; Responsibility; Intamacy. *Memberships:* Latvian Artists Union. *Honours:* Exhib Man in art, Order of Badge of Honors; Diploma & Medal, Best Creative Achievement of the Year. *Hobby:* Gardening. *Address:* Marijas iela 67-69 14A, Riga 226001, Latvia.

VAN AARDE Andries Gideon, b. 25 Apr 1951, Pretoria, South Africa. Prof; Chair of te Dept of New Testament Studies. m. Esther, 10 Nov 1973, 1 s, 1 d. *Education:* BA, 1971; BD, 1974; BA, 1977; MA, 1978; DD, 1982. *Appointments:* Lectr, Greek, Univ of Pretoria, 1978-80; Lectr, Biblical Studies, Univ of Pretoria, 1980-83; Assoc Prof, 1984-88; Full Prof, Chair New Testament Studies, 1989-. *Publications:* Narrative Point of View; The Seperation of Judaism & Christianity; Historical Criticism & Holism; Heresy in the Thessalonican Correspondence; Narrative Criticism; The Metaphor Temple. *Memberships:* SBL; Westar Inst; New Testament Soc of South Africa; The Contect Group. *Honours include:* Human Sci Research Council; Ad Hoc Research Grant; Inst for Ecumenical & Cultural Research, Resident Scholar. *Hobby:* Reading. *Address:* 529 Delphi Street, Waterkloof Glen, 0010 Pretoria, South Africa.

VAN APPLEDORN Mary Jeanne, b. 2 Oct 1927, Michigan, USA. *Education:* BM, Piano, 1948, MM, 1950, PhD, 1966, Eastman Sch of Music, Rochester, NY, USA; Postdoc, Mass Inst of Tech, 1982. *Appointments:* Paul Whitfield Horn Prof of Music, Texas Tech Univ Sch of Mus, Lubbock, 1950-. *Publications:* Set of Five, 1953; Concerto Brevis, 1954; A Choreographic Overture, 1957; Passacaglia and Chorale, 1973; Concerto for Trumpet 1960; Suite for Carillon, 1976; Cantata: Rising Night after Night, 1978; Cacophony, 1980; Lux Legend of Sankta Lucia, 1981; Set of Seven for NY City Ballet, 1988; AYRE, 1989; Terrestrial Music, 1992. *Memberships:* Am Soc of Composers, Authors and Publishers; Soc of Composers Inc. *Honours:* ASCAP Standard Panel Awd, 1980-91; Delta Kappa Gamma; Premiere Prix, World Carillon Fed, France, 1980; Virginia Col Band Dirs Nat Assn, 1981, 1982; Premio Ancona, Italy, Awd for Liquid Gold. *Hobby:* Travelling. *Address:* PO Box 1583, Lubbock, TX 79408, USA. 4, 138.

VAN BOSSTRAETEN Philip, b. 30 Jan 1939, St Kat. Waver, Belgium. Corporate Executive; Consultant Engineer; m. Yvonne Storms, 2 Apr 1960, 3 s, 1 d. *Education:* Grad, Hg Sch, Mechelen, Belgium, 1958; Registered Profl Engr, Belgium. *Appointments:* Purch Mgr, A Van Den Abeele Ltd, Bruges, 1960-62; Fdr, Co-Owner: PH Van Bosstraeten Ltd, Bruges, 1962-; Ovobel Ltd, Bastogne, 1972-, Belovo S C Bastogne, 1972-, Agroteco Belgasia Ltd, Lier, Belgium, 1982-, Belovo Engrg SC, 1986-, Kathmann Hong Kong Ltd, 1988-. Bd *Memberships:* Dirs, Poultry Union, Belgium, AGRIV, Belgium; Sec Gen, Egg Products Union, Belgium. *Honours:* Silver Star; Knight of the Crown, Belgium. *Hobby:* Tennis. *Address:* 93 Bilkske, 8000 Brugge, Belgium. 52.

VAN DEN BERG Petrus Maria, b. 11 Nov 1943, Rotterdam. Professor of Electromagnetic Theory. m. Cornelia van Ravesteyn, 30 May 1970, 2 s. *Education:* Polytech Sch, Rotterdam, 1961-64; MEE, 1968, DSc, 1971, Delft Univ of TEch, 1964-68. *Appointments:* Res Engr, Dutch Patent Ofc, 1967-68; Asst Prof, 1968-81, Prof of Electromagnetic Theory, 1981-, Delft Univ. *Publications:* About 100 papers in international scientific journals and conference proceedings. *Memberships:* Dutch Nat Com of URSI: Chm of Dutch Subcom, B.Fleld and Waves. *Honours:* Lund Sci Awd, 1987; NATO Collaboration Res Grants Prog Awd, 1988. *Hobbies:* Soccer; Tennis; Rally sport. *Address:* Delft University of Technology, Faculty of Electrical Engineering, PO Box 5031, 2600 GA Delft, The Netherlands.

VAN GOOL August Peter, b. 12 Feb 1939, Turnhout, Belgium. Professor. m. Emilienne M Van Cauwelaert de Wyels, 16 Apr 1971. 2 s. *Education:* BSc, 1960, MSc, 1962, Univ Louvain, Belgium; NIH, Postdoc Fellow, Univ Minn, Mpls, USA, 1966-68. *Appointments:* Asst Prof, Univ Louvain, 1969; Jr Rschr, Belgian Sci Foun, Univ Amsterdam, 1970-71; Reschr, Belgian Sci Foun, 1972-82, Assoc Prof, 1983-85, Prof Genetics, 1986-, Univ Louvain. *Publications:* Author of numerous research papers. *Memberships:* ASAS; Am Soc Microbiol; Am Soc of Geog; Belgian Soc for Cell Biol; Belgian Soc for Biochem; Nat Contact Com for Microb; Jean Brachet Foun. *Honour:* NIH Posdoc fellowship, 1966-68. *Hobbies:* Arts and Sci. *Address:* FA Janssens Meml Lab of Genetics, Willem de Croylaan 42, B 3001 Heverlee, Belgium. 1, 2.

VAN GORP Gary Wayne, b. 16 July 1953, Reasnor, Iowa, USA. m. Marietta Louise Burns, 29 Dec 1972, 2 s, 2 d. *Education:* Dipl, Pastoral Studies, Bible and Doctrine, 1975, MO; BS Degs, Pastoral Studies, Religious Educ, N.Ctl Bible Col, 1978; Dipl, Profl Ofc Mgmt, Alexandria Tech Sch, 1984. *Appointments:* Postor, Verndale Assem of God, 1979-82; Bookstore Mgr, Gospel Sttupply Ctr, 1981-82, Asst Mgr, Caretaker, Lake Geneva Bible Camp, 1982-83; Pastor, Elbow Lake Assem of GOd, 1983-84; Christian Educ & Outreach Postor, Alexandria Assem of God, 1983-84; Admin Asst Pastor, Allison Pk Assembly of God, PA, 1984-90. *Memberships:* Nat Assn of Ch Bus Admrs. *Honours:* Ordained in Ministry, Assem of God, 1981. *Hobbies:* Computers and Electronics; Hunting; Fishing; Motorcycles; Studying on Church Growth; Study on time

Management and Administration. *Address:* PO Box 75, Reasnor, IA 50232, USA.

VAN SWAAIJ W P M. *Education:* PhD. *Appointments:* Hd, Gasification Section, Shell; Sci Expert, EEC DG XII Energy for Biomass; Conslt, several large Dutch firms including Shell, DSM, Unilver; Conslt, Netherlands Min of Environ Protection. *Publications:* Over 150 orginal research papers in the area of chemical reaction engineering, process development, fuel and flue gas clean-up, thermochemical conversion processes, gasification, destruction of haloginated hydrocarbons. *Membership:* Royal Inst of Dutch Engrs; Royal Dutch Acad of Scis. *Honours:* Dow Chem Energy Prize, 1985; Austr European Fellowship Awd, 1987. *Address:* Twente University of Technology, Department of Chemical Technology, PO Box 217, 7500 AE Enschede, The Netherlands.

VANDENPLAS Paul Eugene Marie, b. 8 Dec 1931, Ixelles,Belgium. Professor. m. Denise Delcourt , 18 Dec 1954, 3 s. *Education:* Civil Eng, Ecole Royale Milit, 1954; Lic in Sci and Phys, 1958, Doctor Phys Sci, 1961, Univ Libre de Bruxelles, 1961. *Appointments:* Dir Assn, Euratom- Belgian State for controlled thermonuclear fusion, 1969-; Chm, Plasma Phys Div, European Phys Soc, 1973-76; Coun of Jt European Torus, Abingdon, UK, 1977-. *Publications:* Electron radio-frequency resonances in bounded plasmas, 1968; General radio-frequency properties of bounded plasma systems, 1974; Numerous other articles and papers in professional journals. *Memberships:* Assn Royale des Ingenieurs issus de l'Ecole d'Application de l'Artillerie et du genie; Belgian and European PHys Soc; FABI; SRBII. *Honours:* Triennal Prize, Assn of Engrs AIA, Brussels, 1962; Vanderlinden Prize, Royal Acad of Belgium, 1969. *Hobbies:* Classical paintings; Sport. *Address:* Lab Phys des Plasmas, Association Euratom- Etat Belge, Ecole Royale Militaire, Av de la Renaissance 30, B-1040 Brussels, Belgium. 52, 156.

VANDEWALLE Joos (Joseph) Pierre Lucien, b. 31 Aug 1948, Kortrijk, Belgium. Professor. m. Rita Dahiels, 9 Apr 1976, 2 s, 1 d. *Education:* Elec Engrg Deg, 1971, Doctoral Deg,, 1976, Special Doctors Deg, Katholieke Univ, Leuven, Belgium. *Appointments:* Asst, 1971-76, Asst Prof, 1979- 86, Prof, 1986-, Elec Engrg Dept, Katholieke Univ, Leuven; Postdoc Reschr, 1976-87, Vis Asst Prof, Univ Berkeley, 1978-79. *Publications:* More than 200 papers, in international journals; Co-ed of the proceedings of the Eurocrypt Conf, 1989; Co-author, book, The Total Lease Squares problem, 1991. *Memberships:* IEEE: Fellow, VP, CAS Soc; Intl Assn of Cryptol Res; European Assn of Sign Proc; Intl Neur Network Soc; Ed Bd, Jour of IEEE Transactions on Circ and Systems; Intl Jour of Circ Theor and Appl, Jour of Circ Systems and Comput. *Honours:* Best paper Awd, 1989; IEEE ICCD Conf, 1986; SWIFT Awd, 1985; 100 Yr Bell Telephone Awd, 1983. *Hobbies:* Gardening; Reading. *Address:* ESAT Electrical Engineering Department, Katholieke Univ Leuven, Kardinaal Mercierlaan 94, B-3001 Heverlee, Belgium.

VANNIER Marie Anne, b. 21 Feb 1957, France. Univ Lectr. *Education:* Philosophy, 1975-80; Doctorate, Theology, 1978-87; DEA DSTC & Pic English, 1979. *Appointments:* Tchrng Prof of Philosophy, 1980-90; Lectr, Univ of Strasbourg, 1990-; Univ of Fribourg, Switzerland, 1991. *Publications:* Creatio; Conversio; Formatio; Paradosis; Many Articles; Stories Broadcast on TV. *Memberships:* Assn Intl d'Etudes Patristiques; Assn d'Etudes Medievales; Assn des Prof de Philosophy. *Hobbies:* Sci; Audio Visual; Arts; Reading. *Address:* Palais Univ, 9 Place de l'Univ, F-67084 Strasbourg, Canada.

VARGA Zoltan Sandor, b. 23 July 1939, Debrecen, Hungary. Professor of Zoology. m. Julianna I Sipos, 14 Mar 1965, 2 d. *Education:* Biol Tchrs Dipl, 1962; Dr Sci Nat, Zoology, 1965; PhD, 1972; DSc, 1982. *Appointments:* Asst Lectr, 1962-66; Adj Prof, 1967-72;

Asst Prof, 1973- 82; Prof and Hd, Dir of Inst Biol, 1986-. *Publications:* 103 scientific papers on biogeography, entomology, Leipidopthera, evol research; 5 lecture notes for students; 1 text book of zoology. *Memberships:* Pres, Zool Com of Hung Acad Scis; Soc Europ Leipidopterology; Munchner Entomol Gesellschaft; Hung Soc Ornith & Nature Cons; IUCN Species Survival Gp; Hung Biological Soc. *Honours:* Frivaldszky prize for Entomol Res, 1973; For Human Environment, 1981; Herman Otto Priz, Hung Biol Soc, 1988. *Hobbies:* Aquarell painting; Travelling; Photography; Chess. *Address:* Department of Zoology and Evolution, University L Kossuth, Egyete-ter 1, H-4010 Debrecen, Hungary.

VARGO Mary Agnes (Leigh), b. 11 Sept 1934, Storrs, Connecticut, USA. Wellness and Fitness Specialist. m. Francis E Kapelewski, 11 Aug 1957, 1 d. *Education:* St Francis Med Ctr, Univ of Pittsburgh, 1955; Univ of Bridgeport, Univ of CT, Fairfield Univ, Pace Univ; Registered Nurse, MS, NP. *Appointments:* Dir of Nurses, Vis Nurses Assn, 1956-65; State Fed Regulations Inspector, 1947-76; Independent practice, Wellness/ Fitness, 1980-. *Publications:* Cultural changes in a changing world; Indo-Asian Boat People; Why did you choose Nursing? and Now? A pathway to Wellness is an extension to growth. *Memberships:* CT State Nurses Assn, Bd; Med Adv Bd on Nsg Homes; AM Nurses Assn; COHN: Concerned Nurses Assn. extension to growth. *Honours:* Guest speaker, Annual AM Nurses Assn Conf, 1981; State Awd, The Bloodmobile Sponser of the Year, 1986; Scholaship Awd; Organized first Expectant Fathers Classes; Introduced Health Educ, ADLS; Baby Sitting Courses for the Girl Scouts of Am. *Hobbies:* Telekenetics-long distance healing arts; Telepathic diagnoses; Adv figure skating; Equestrian; Pilor and and sea; Opera; Languages; Painting. *Address:* 140 Barncroft Road, Stamford, CT 06902, USA.

VARLAKI Peter, b. 23 Nov 1946, Budapest, Hungary. University Professor. m. Katalin Balajthy, 12 Oct 1976, 1 d. *Education:* MSc 1971, DEng, 1975, TUB, PHD, 1979; Inst of Control Scis, USSR Acad of Scis; DSC, Hungarian Acad of Scis, 1988. *Appointments:* Res Fellow, 1971-72, Lectr, 1971-76, Sr Lectr, 1976-82, Sr Res Fellow, 1983-88, Sci Conslt, 1989-, Prof, 1990, Tech Univ of Budapest. *Publications:* 3 books; 140 scientific and technical papers on control modelling and system identification; 3 textbooks. *Memberships:* Fellow, Hung IMechE; Sys Engrg Com of IFAC; Bd, COMNET; Fellow, Pres, Hung Acad of Engrg; Ed, Periodica Polytechnica, 1985-90. *Honours:* Tech Univ JUB Prize, 1983; Acad Priz, Hungarian Acad of Scis, 1987. *Hobbies:* Swimming; Classical music. *Address:* Technical University of Budapest, H-1521 Budapest, Hungary.

VARLEY Christopher John, b. 19 Sept 1950, Vancouver, BC. Canada, Art Historian; Private Dealer; Canadian Historical Art. m. (1) 1 s 1 d, (2) 18 Apr 1986. *Education:* BA, Simon Fraser Univ, 1972. *Appointments:* Asst Curate, Vancouver Art Gallery, 1974-77; Hd Curator, Curator, Canadian Art, Edmonton Art Gallery, 1979-83. *Creative Works:* The Contemporary Art Soc, Montreal; F H Varley, A Centennial Exhib; Winnipeg West, Painting & Sculpture in Western Canada. *Memberships:* Canadian Museums Assn; Research & Editorial Committee; Historical Resource Sub Committee; Alberta Assn of Arhitects; Private Art Dealers Assn. *Honours:* Publications Award, Western Canadian Art Assn. *Hobbies:* Hiking; Golf; Art Collecting. *Address:* 6 Kendal Avenue, Toronto, Ontario, Canada M5R 1L6. 142.

VARTANYAN Genrich, b. 16 Dec 1934, Tbilisi, Georgia. Geologist; Hydrogeologist; Dir, All Union Research Inst for Hydrogeol & Eng Geology. m. Elizabeth Vartanyan, 5 Feb 1959, 2 d. *Education:* Moscow State Univ, 1953-58; Candidate of Geological Mineralogical Sci, 1965; Doc of Geological Mineralogical Sci, 1974; Prof, 1978; Acad of Natural Sci of Russia, 1990. *Appointments:* Moscow state Univ, Jnr Reseacher,

1958-59; East Siberian Hydrogeological Field Exhib, 1959-63; Moscow State Univ, Post Grad, 1963-65; All Union Research Inst, 1965-68; Snr Researcher, 1968-72; Chief, Hydrogeology Lab, 1972-80; Deputy Dir for Research Work, 1980-83; Dir, 1983-. *Creative Works include:* Author of over 150 Scientific Publi; 12 Monographs. *Membeships:* J Razvedka i Okhrana Nedr; Intl Journ Applied Hydrogeology; Intl Assn of Hydrogeologists; Profl Member American Inst of Hydrology. *Honours:* Intl Prize, Diameks Intl. *Hobbies:* Music; Reading; Gardening. *Address:* All Union Research Inst for Hydrogeology & Engrng Geology, Moscow, Russia.

VARTORELLA William Frederick, b. 16 Jan 1949, Norwalk, Ohio, USA. Intl Mktng; Advertising; Fundraising. *Education:* Ohio Wesleyan Univ, Delaware, Ohio, BA, 1971; Ohio Univ, Athens, MS, 1974; PhD, 1979; Business Communications, 1982. *Appointments:* China Trade Post, Business Editor, 1980's; Mary Baldwin Coll, 1979-83; Sporting Classics Mag,Indigo Press, 1983-87; Craig, Vartorella Intl, 1987-. *Publications:* Spinx; Doing the Bright Thing with Your Company Logo. *Memberships:* Tarpon Unlimited; Egyptian Studies Assn; World fellowship of Egyptology; Overseas Press Club; One Club for Art & Copy; Intl Exec Serv Corps; American Research Centre in Egypt. *Honours include:* Numerous Grants & Fellowships; Phi Kappa Phi. *Hobbies:* Egypt; Near Eastern Archaelogical Site Protection; Hunting; Big Game Fishing; Cycling. *Address:* Craig Vartorella Inc, PO Box 1376, 277 Peckwoods Road, Camden, SC 29020, USA. 123.

VARTY E Kenneth C, b. 18 Aug 1927, Clark, Derbyshire, England. Retired Emeritus Prof of French. m. Hedwig H J Benninghof, 26 Sept 1958, 2 d. *Education:* BA, Univ of Nottingham, 1951; PhD, 1954; D Lih, Univ of Keele, 1987. *Appointments:* Asst Lectr, Keele, 1953; Hon Lectr, 1956; Lectr,Leicester, 1961; Snr Lectr, 1965; Stevenson Prof, Univ of Glasgow, 1968-91. *Publications:* Rewards & Punishments in Arthemen Romances. *Memberships include:* Int Reynard Soc; Clare Hall, Univ of Cambridge. *Honours:* Chevalier de l'Order des Polms Acad; Honorary Life Member, Phi Kappa Phi. *Hobbies:* Photography; Medieval Art & Architecture. *Address:* 4 Dundonald Road, Glasgow, Scotland, G12 9LJ.

VAS Istvan, b. 24 Sept 1910, Budapest, Hungary. Poet; writer. m. Piroska Szanto, 29 June 1951. *Appointments:* Publishers Reader, 1946- 56; Europa Koryohiak, 1956-71. *Publications include-* Autobiographical Novels; Poems. *Honours include:* Kossuth Prize; Order of Banner with Laurels. *Address:* Grora Petesrakpart 17, H-1015 Budapest, Hungary.

VASHOVSKY Anatoly, b. 13 Dec 1931, Opochka, Russia. Hd of Laboratory of Microwave Ferrites. m. Marina Gospodarskaya, 15 Nov 1963, 2 s. *Education:* Mosc Power Eng Inst, 1955; Cand Sci Degree, 1962; Doct Sci Degree, 1973; Diploma of Acas Sco Prof, 1982. *Appointments:* Researcher, 1955-63; Snr Researcher, 1963-68; Hd of Laboratory, IRE Acad Sci, 1968-. *Publications:* Many papers; articles. *Memberships:* Sci Council in Physical Electronics, USSR; Editorical Council of Radioengineering & Electronics. *Honour:* USSR state Prize in Sci. *Hobbies:* Reading; Skiing; Gardening. *Address:* Baikalskaya Str 23, Ap 37, Moscow 107207, Russia.

VASILICA Constantin, b. 5 Feb 1926, Tudora, Botosani, Romania. Prof. m. Margareta Savin, 17 Aug 1950. *Education:* Faculty of Agronomy, Iasi, 1947-51; doc in Agronomy, 1974. *Appointments:* Asst, 1951-60; Chief Asst, 1960-76; Lectr, 1976-82; Prof, 1982-. *Publications:* The Technology of Flax Cultivation; Plant Growing. *Memberships:* Soc of Plant Growing in Germany; Soc of Agricult Engrs from Romania. *Hobbies:* Collecting Medals, Stamps concerning Agriclt. *Address:* Str Pacurari 24, sc A Ap 4, Iasi 6600, Romania.

VASQUEZ William L, b. 9 Mar 1944, USA. Marketing. *Education:* AS, Accounting/Programming, 1972; BS, Management, 1983; MBA, Intl Business, 1985; Doctorate, Business Admin. *Appointments:* Control Data Corp, Texas, 1970-72; Data General Corp, Intl, 1972-80; Gould Inc, Florida, 1980-84; Tektronix Inc, Oregon, 1984-86; Marylhurst Coll, Oregon, 1986-88; Racal Milgo, Florida, 1988-90; Citibank NA, Asst Vice Pres, Latin America, Canada Div, Technology Office, 1991-. *Publications:* Chief Information Office Jornal; Business Communications Review. *Memberships:* Adjunct Faculty, Nova Univ; St Thomas Univ; Career Exchange Cert Manager; Intl of Cerified Profl Managers; Intl of Electrical & Electronic Engrs. *Honours:* ssa 00MBA; BS; Captains Commendation, US Navy; Bd of Dir, Nova Univ Alumni Assn. *Hobbies:* Freelance Author for Datapro; Physical Fitness; Fine Arts; Reading; Guitar. *Address:* 4090 NW 110 Avenue, Coral Springs, FL 33065, USA. 7. 15.

VASSILEV Vassil, b. 23 May 1952, Elhovo, Bulgaria. Designer. m. Polia Vassileva, 1 May 1976, 1 d. *Education:* Decorative Arts Sch, Sofia, 1970. *Appointments:* Natl Fashion Centre, Leading Designer; Field of Decorative Art. *Creative Works:* Panticipates in Personal & Collective Exhib; Works Owned by Lots of Galleries in USA & Europe. *Honours:* Natl Prize for Design; Special Reward for Literature & Art of the Bulgarian Youth Union. *Address:* 15 Elenag, Studio V-2, Sofia 1113, Bulgaria.

VASUDEVAN P A, b. 7 July 1947, Calicut, Kerala, India. Prof of Economics. m. M Rathi, 18 May 1988, 1 s, 1 d. *Education:* Diploma in Rural Serv, 1960; MA, Economics, 1968. *Appointments:* Joined Collegiate Education Serv, Lectr, 1969; Prof Economics, Post grad, Goverment Fictoria Coll. *Publications:* Book On Trade Uniones in India; Edited Malayalism Poetry; Saparya. *Memberships:* Natl Exam All India Peace & Solidarity Organ; Assoc with Major Literary Biological & Social Movements in the State. *Honour:* Dr G Roma Chandram Gold Medal. *Hobbies:* Reading; Writing. *Address:* Aksharam, Vidyut, Nagar, Palghat, Kerala State, India.

VAUGHAN Peter St George, b. 27 Nov 1930, Suffragan Bishop of Ramsbury Diocese of Salisbury. m. Elizabeth Fielding Parker, 2 Sept 1961, 1 s, 2 d. *Education:* Chaterhouse, 1944-49; Selwyn Coll, Cambridge, 1952-55; Ridley Hall, Theological Coll, 1955-57; MA, Oxon, 1963. *Appointments:* Asst Curate Birmingham Parish Church Chaplain, Oxford Pastorate, 1963-67; Vicar, Christ Church, Galle Face, Colombo 1967-72; CMS Rep Ceylon, 1968-72; Precentor Holy Trinity Cathedral, 1972-75; Principal, Crowther Hall Brimingham, 1975-83; Archdeacon, Westmorland & Furness, 1983-89; Bishop of Ramsbury, Commissary for Diocese of Colombo, Sri Lanka, 1989-. *Hobbies:* Walking; Gardening; Swimming. *Address:* Bishops House, High Street, Urchfont, Devizes, Wilts, SN10 4QH.

VAYO David Joseph, b. 28 Mar 1957, New Haven, CT, USA. Composer; Univ Prof. m. 16 May 1981, 1 s, 1 d. *Education:* Indiana Univ, 1980; M Mus In Composition, Indiana Univ, 1982; The Univ of Michigan, 1990. *Appointments:* Prof, Univ Natl de Costa Rica, 1982-84; Prof, Costa Rica Natl Symphony Youth Program, 1982-84; Asst Prof, Connecticut Coll, 1988-91; Asst Prof, Illinois Wesleyan Univ, 1991-. *Creative Works:* Symphony. Blossoms & Awakenings for Orchestra; Poem. for Flute, Claret, Violin, Cello, Piano; Time Elastic; Mother Goose Rhymes. *Memberships:* Soc of Composers; ASCAP; American Music Centre; Soc for Electro Acoustic Music in the United States; Natl Assn of Composers, USA. *Honours include:* ASCAP Standard Award; Scholarship, American Acad & Inst of Arts & Letters; Natl Assn of Composers, USA. *Hobbies:* Athletics; travel; Latin American Culture & Natural History. *Address:* Sch of Music, Illinois Wesleyan Univ, PO Box 2900, Bloomington, IL 61702, USA.

VAZ Keith, b. 26 Nov 1956, Aden, Saudi Arabia. MP. *Education:* Gonville & Caius Coll, Cambridge Univ, BA,

1979; MA, 1987; MCFI, 1988. *Appointments:* Solicitor, London Borough of Richmond Upon Thames, 1982; Snr Solicitor, London Borough of Islington, 1982-85; Solicitor, Highfields & Belgrave Law Centre, Leicester, 1985-87; MP Labour, for Leicester East, 1987. *Memberships:* Natl Union of Public Employeers; Labour Party; Labour Party Race Action Group;' Legal Services Campaign. *Address:* House of Commons, London SW1A 0AA, England.

VECERKA Radoslav, b. 18 Apr 1928, Brno, CSFR. Univ Prof. m. Jarmila Voracova, 5 July 1958, 2 d. *Education:* PhD, 1953; CSc, 1958; Habil, 1964; DrSc, 1987. *Appointments:* Asst, Univ Brno, 1950; Snr Asst, 1955; Assc Prof, 1964; Prof, 1990-. *Publications:* The Syntax of Active Participles in Old Church Slavonic; The Slavic Beginnings of the Czech Litterary Culture; Old Church Slavonic; Old Church Slavonic Syntax 1; Magnae Moraviae Fontes Historici; The Czech Slavonic Studies; The Introduction into Ethymology. *Memberships:* Intl Committee of Slavists; Intl Committee for Church Slavonic Dictionary. *Honours:* Czech Acad of Sci; Czech Litterary Foundation. *Hobbies:* Symphonic Music; Theatre; Up to Date Novels; Short Stories. *Address:* 1 Stredni Str, 60200 Brno, Czechoslovakia.

VEGA Steve, b. 13 Nov 1949, Manhattan, NY. USA. World Class Poet; Probation Officer. m. Veronica Gonzalez, 3 Jan 1971, 1 s, 1 d. *Education:* John Marshall Law Sch, 1977; Business Mgmt, Marion Business Coll, 1973; Loop Coll, 1986; APD, Wardogs Carbondale Wilderness Survival Team, 1987. *Publications include:* The Book of Golden Verse, Contributor; The World Treasury of Great Poems; Our Twentieth Centurys Greatest Poems; Todays Greatest Poems; Our Western Worlds Greatest Poems. *Memberships:* American Soc of Composers; ASCAP. *Honours include:* Knight Commander of the Order of St George, Outstanding Contributions to Mankind; Golden Poet Award; Silver Poet Award. *Address:* PO Box 18-096, Chicago, IL 60618, USA. 11, 139, 152.

VEKHOFF Dimitri, b. 18 Sept 1926, Paris. MD Research Engr, Inserm. m. Beal Madeleine, 24 Feb 1973, 2 s. *Education:* MD, 1956; Licence Es Sci, 1963; Ces Bichimie Bacteriologie Virologie Immunologie Hematologie, 1957-60. *Appointments:* Athenes Inst Phyiology Du Travail, 1958-62; Private Analysis Lab, 1962-65; Inserm, Lab Cell Biology Univ, Paris 7, 1965-. *Creative Works:* Expert Pres Les Tribunaux D'Appel de Paris, Cours de Cassation, Tribunal Administratif de Paris. *Address:* 123 Rue de Reuilly, Paris 75012, France.

VELIUS Norbertas, b. 1 Jan 1938, Gulbes, Lithuania. Researcher of Mythology & Folklore. m. Ramune Veliuviene, 6 Aug 1966, 1 s, 1 d. *Education:* Faculty of History & Philology, Vilnius Univ, 1962; Inst of Lithuania, 1966-69; Cand of Phillogy Degree, 1969; Doctoral Degree, 1989. *Appointments:* Jnr, 1962-66, 1969-85; Snr, 1985-89; Leading Research Assoc, Inst of Lithuanian Language & Literature, Lithuanian Acad of Sci, 1989; Prof, Padagogical Inst of Siauliai, 1975-79; Vilnius Univ, 1981-82; Lithuanian Conservatoire, 1989-90; Univ Vytauti Magni, Kaunas, 1990-91; Hd of the Dept, Anthropology, Univ Vytauti, Magni, 1991-. *Creative Works include:* Mythological Beings of Lithuanian Legends; The World Outlook of the Ancient Balts; A Wounded Wind: Lithuanin Mythological Legends; 250 Scientific Articles. *Memberships:* Soc of Lithuanina Ethnic Culture; Union of Lithuanian Scientists; Senate of Union Vytauti Magni; Scientific Council of the Inst of Lithuanian Literature & Folklore. *Honours:* Laureate of the Natl Prize in Sci of Lithuania; Winner of the M Slanciauskas Folklore Collectors Prize. *Hobbies:* Gardening; Tourism; Reading; Theatre. *Address:* Konarskio 21-23, Vilnius 232009, Lithuania.

VELLACOTT Elisabeth, b. 28 Jan 1905, Essex, England. Artist; Painter. *Education:* Willesdon Poly Tech, 1922-25; Royal Coll of Art, 1925-29. *Appointments:* Examiner in Art, Cambridge Univ, 1952-77. *Creative*

Works: Numerous Paintings & Drawings Exhib. *Memberships:* Cambridge Soc of Painters & Sculptors. *Honour:* Jubilee Award. *Address:* The New Art Centre, 41 Sloane Street, London, SW1, England.

VELLACOTT Philip Humphrey, b. 16 Jan 1907, Grays, Essex, England. Writer. m. Nancy Marion Agnew, 29 July 1939, 2 s, 2 d. *Education:* St Pauls Sch, 1922-25; Magdalene Coll, Cambridge, 1925-28; BA, 1928; MA, 1932; Westminster Theological Coll, Cambridge, 1928-31. *Appointments:* Ordained, England Prsbyterian Church, 1932; Resigned, 1936; Tchr Classics, 1937-67; Univ of Liverpool, Dungannon, NI, Stockport, Dulwich Coll, 1943-67. *Publications include:* Translator of 7 Vols, Penguin Classics. *Hobbies:* Music; Moutain Walking. *Address:* Tany Bryn, Franksbridge, Llandrindod Wells, Powys LD1 5SA, Wales.

VENKATARAMAN Rajamadam Subramaniam, b. 18 Jan 1935, Madras, India. Managing Dir. m. Saraswathi Natesan, 12 June 1960, 2 s. *Education:* Bach Degree, Mechanical Engrng, 1956; Diploma in Electrical Engrng & Metallurgy, 1958. *Appointments:* Tat Iron & Steel Co Ltd, 1958-69; M N Dastur & Co Ltd, 1964-69; Motor Industries Co Ltd, 1969-77; Camcraft Services Ltd, 1977-84; Enfield India Ltd, 1985-87; Shalimar Paints Ltd, 1988; Usha Siam Steel Industries Ltd, 1988-. *Creative Works:* Visiting Faculty at Asian Inst of Tech, Bangkok Thailand. *Memberships:* Inst of Engrs; Inst of Valuers; Inst of Metals. *Honours:* Excellent Exec Award, Bangkok, Thailand. *Hobbies:* Reading Management Books/Publi; Music. *Address:* Usha Siam steel Industries Ltd, 101-46 Navanakorn Ind Estate, Zone 1, Klongnuang, Klongluang, Pathumthani 12120, India.

VENKEN Raf Renaat Wies, b. 17 Mar 1958, Stokkem, Belgium. Mktng Mgr. m. Ann Borghoms, 20 Mar 1985, 1 s, 1 d. *Education:* Civil Engrng Degree, K U Leuven, Belgium, 1981. *Appointments:* Researcher, BIM, 1981-83; R & D Mgr BIM, 1984-88; Mktng Mgr, 1989-. *Publications:* More Than 60 Papers; Gandalf. *Memberships:* Assn for Logic Programming; American Assn for Artifical Intelligence; Belgium Assn for Artificial Intelligence. *Honours:* Guard Onerall European Artificial Intelligence Prize. *Hobbies:* Music; Soccer; Squash; Travel. *Address:* c/o BIM, Kwikstraat 4, 3078 Everberg, Belgium.52.

VENKOVA KOLEVA Milka, 23 Apr 1953, Elena, Bulgaria. Tchr of Special Piano. m. Vladimir Petrov Venkova, 23 July 1977, 1 s. *Education:* Musical Sch, Varna, 1966-72; Musical acad, Sofia, 1972-76; Master of Class, Prof, Panka Pelichek, Prof, Milena Mollova, 1976-78; Specialisation Moscow, Prof Micheal Voscressensky, 1983-84. *Appointments:* Varna Musical Sch, 1976-77; Sofia Central Musical Sch, 1977-. *Publications:* Problems of Memory Related to Musicians. *Memberships:* Bulgarian Soc of Musicians; Union of Tchrs Musicians. *Honours:* Intl Comp in Tchekoslovakia; Natl Comp Nenov; Award of her Pupils. *Hobbies:* Painting; Collector of Paintings of Contemporary Bulgarian Masters. *Address:* Todor Petrov, Str Block 94, Ent B, Sofia 1113, Bulgaria.

VENNING Philip Duncombe Riley, b. 24 Mar 1947, London, England. Sec. m. Elizabeth Frances Ann Powers, 4 Apr 1987. *Education:* Sherborne Sch, 1960-65; Principia Coll, USA, 1965-67; Trinity Hall, Cambridge, 1967-70. *Appointments:* Times Educational Eupplement, 1970-81; Freelance Writer, 1981-84; Spab Sec, 1984-. *Memberships:* Soc of Antiquaries; Royal Soc of Arts. *Hobbies:* Archaelogy; Book Collecting. *Address:* 17 Highgate High street, London N6 5JT, England.1.

VERBITSKY Taras, b. 21 June 1932, Ukraine. Geophysicist. m. Borachok Tetyana, 10 Feb 1958, 2 s. *Education:* Poly Tech Inst, 1951- 56; Lviv Branch of Inst Geophysics, 1963-68; Master of Geolog, 1978; Snr Research Worker. *Appointments:* Engr of Geophys,

Prospecting, 1956- 60; Engr Lviv Branch of Inst of Geophys, 1961-63; Jnr Research Worker, 1968- 70; Snr Research Worker, 1971-72; Snr Research, Inst of Appl Probl Math & Mech, 1973-81; Mgr, 1982-88; Hd of Dept, 1989-90. *Publications:* Co Author, Acoustic Method of Rock Investig in Wells; Mathematical Modeeling in Seismic Propspecting; 5 Articles. *Memberships:* Intern Council on Seismology & Seism; Modern Geodynamics & Earthquake Forecasting. *Honour:* Inventor of the USSR. *Hobbies:* Gardening; Inventing. *Address:* Carpathian Section of Inst of Geophysics Ukr, Acad Ukraine, Naukova St 3b, Lviv 290601, Russia.

VERE Raymond Andrew, b. 12 Jan 1924, London, England. Lectr. m. Joyce Morgan, 12 Apr 1952, 2 d. *Education:* Aberdeen Univ, 1948-51; BSc, 1951; Royal Artillery, 1942-47; Captain, France & Germany, 1944-47. *Appointments:* Schweppes Ltd, Control Chemist, 1947-48; Esso Petroleum Co Ltd, 1951-82; Fawley Refinery, 1951-64; Research Centre, Abingdon, 1964-82; Snr Staff Scientist, Aviation Fuels Specialist for Europe. *Publications include:* Aviation Fuels Chapter, Modern Petroleum Technology. *Memberships:* Inst of Petroleum; Modern Aviation Fuels Committee; Naflac Fire & Explosopn Hazards; NATO/AGARD UK Delegate Alternative Jet Engine Fuels; NATO/AGARD Conslt & UK Delegator Producibilty & Cost Studies of Aviation Kerosines. *Hobbies:* Photography; Swimming; Gardening. *Address:* 10 Farm Lane, Barton On Sea, New Milton, Hants BH25 7BR, England.

VEREKETI Constantin Kimon, b. 27 Oct 1908, Smytna, Turkey. Businessman. m. (1) Madeleine Paxino, 1931, (2) Smaragda Kalssounda, 1963. *Education:* Bucharest, Romania, 1922-30; Law Univ, Bucharest, 1937-47. *Appointments:* Various Leading positions, Concordia Petro Fine Group, Romania, 1958; Greek Oil Refinery, 1958-60; Mgrng Dir, Petrogaz, 1984-; Pres, Greek LPG Assn, 1962-84; Hon Pres, 1984; Vice Pres, Fina; Pres, Dragofina; Pres, Vice Pres of Several Affiliated Com. *Publications:* Marilena; Plays. Anna; Maria; Heloise; Short stories. Conference Speaker, Lectr. *Memberships:* Rotary Club of Athens; District Govenor. *Honours:* Numerous Prizes for Sporting Acheivements. *Hobbies:* Sports; Writing. *Address:* Semitelou Str no.7, 11528 Athens, Greece.

VERESCAGIN Eugene (Jevgenij Mihajlovic), b. 29 Oct 1939, Kazan. Research Worker; Linguist. m. Larissa Krasinec, 2 Oct 1984, 1 s, 1 d. *Education:* Leningrad State Univ, 1957-60; Moscow State Foreign Languages Inst, 1960-63; Research Scholarship, 1963-66; Degree of Cand of Sci, 1966; Degree of Doctor of Sci, 1973; Diploma of Univ Prof, 1982. *Appointments:* Jnr Research Worker, Scientific Sec, Hd of Language Oriented Regional Studies of the Russian Language Inst, 1966-86; Leading Research Worker, Main Research Worker, 1986-. *Publications include:* Over 150 Books; 300 Scientific Publi. *Honours:* Nadeshda Krupskaya Prize. *Hobbies:* Spiritual Choral Singing; Travel. *Address:* 18/2 Volhonka Street, Russian Language Inst, Academy of Sciences, 121019 Moscow, Russia.

VERESHCHAGUIN Igor Konstantinovich, b. 29 Oct 1924, Moscow, USSR. Physicist; Prof. m. Galina Zenkina, 29 Oct 1965, 2 d. *Education:* Army Serv, 1942-45; Stte Univ, Samarkand, 1946-51; Graduate Work, 1951-54; Theis for a Candidates, 1955; Doctors Degree, 1970. *Appointments:* State Univ, Chernovitsy, 1954-66; Inst of Energetics, Moscow, 1966-72; Inst of Railway Engrs, Moscow, 1973-92. *Publications:* 215 Sci Works; 3 Books. *Memberhips:* Acad Councils on Luminescence & Optoelectronics, Russian Physical Soc. *Honours:* Order of the Patriotic war & 10 Medals; Honored Scientist of Russia. *Hobbies:* Reading; Arts; Travel. *Address:* Komarova Street 1-70, 127276 Moscow, Russia.

VEREY Rosemary Isabel Baird, b. 21 Oct 1918, Chattham, Kent, England. Garden Designer; Author; Lectr; Owner. m. David Verey, 21 Oct 1939, dec, 2 s, 2 d. *Education:* Univ Coll, London. *Appointments:* Author; Lectr; Garden Designer, Owner of Garden Open to Public. *Publications include:* The Englishwomens Garden; The Englishmans Garden; Country Life; The Flower Arrangers Garden. *Membership:* RHS. *Address:* The Close, Barnsley, Cirencester, Glos, GL7 JEE, England.

VERMA Jatinder, b. 17 July 1954, Dar Es Salaam, Tanzania. Theatre Dir. m. Reikha Prashar, 14 Dec 1981. *Education:* BA, Univ of York, 1976; MA, Univ of Sussex, 1977. *Appointments:* Artistic Dir, Tara Arts Group, 1976-; Freelance Dir, Royal Natl Theatre, 1990-91. *Publications:* Written & Adapted over 40 Plays. *Contributions to:* Articles to Various Theatre Journals. *Membership:* Royal Soc of Arts. *Honours:* The out/01 for London Special Award; Asian City Club Drama Award. *Hobbies:* Gardening; Travel; Badminton. *Address:* 31 Revell Road, Kingston, Surrey KT1 3SL, England.

VESCOVI Ricardo, b. 11 July 1949, Montevideo. Economist. m. Maria A Schroth, 13 Feb 1981, 2 s, 2 d. *Education:* Licence in Economics, 1974; Master, 1975; Master in Development, 1976; Master in Promto Devel, 1979. *Appointments:* Docencie, Prof, Univ de la Republico, 1970-75; Economics Conslt, 1970-91. *Publications:* La Socialisation et la Planification en Vrss Mito Realidad; Euro Economia Para American Latina. *Address:* 11 Clos du Grand Feu, 1340 Ottignies, LLN, Belgium.

VESTLY Anne-Catharina, b. 15 Feb 1920, Rena, Norway. Author. m. 26 Apr 1946, 2 s. *Education:* Actress, Studioteatret, Oslo. *Appointments:* 5 Yrs, Actress, 1945-50; Cabaret Artist. *Publications include:* 37 Story Books for Children; 4 Plays. *Memberships:* Norwegian Authors Assn; Norwegian Children Book Authors Assn; Dramatists Soc. *Honours:* Language Prize; City of Oslo Artists Prize; Peer Gynt Prize; Dept of Culture Prize; Whole Authorship; Booksellers Prize; Save the Children Rainbow Prize; Oslo City Cultureprize; Paul Robeson Prize. *Hobbies:* Aquarell Paintings; Music; Theatre; Litterature. *Address:* Tiden Norsk Forlag, Storgt 23D, 0184 Oslo, Norway.

VETTESE Raymond John, b. 1 Nov 1950, Arbroath, Scotland. Tchr. m. Maureen Elizabeth Milne, 13 May 1972. *Education:* Montrose Acad; Dundee Coll of educ; Open Univ. *Appointments:* Montrose Review Editorial Staff, 1968-72; Student, 1972-75; Barman, Factory Worker, 1975-78; Librarian, 1978-85; Tchr, 1985-. *Publications:* 4 Scottish Poets; The Right Noise and Ither poems; Various Anthologies. *Memberships:* Scottish PEN; Advisory Council for the Arts in Scotland; Scottish Language Soc. *Honours:* Saltire Soc for Best First Book; William Soutar Writers Fellowship. *Hobbies:* Reading; Music; Chess; Food. *Address:* 9 Tayock Avenue, Montrose, Angus, Tayside, DD10 9AP, Scotland.

VETULANI Jerzy Adam, b. 21 Jan 1936, Krakow, Poland. Psychopharmacologist, Dept Hd. m. Maria Stanislawa Pajak, 8 July 1963, 2 s. *Education:* MSC, Jagiellonian Univ, 1957; MSC, Chemistry, 1963; PhD, PAN Wroclaw, 1966; DSc, 1976; Prof, 1983; Full Prof, 1989. *Appointments:* Inst of Pharmacology, Pol Ac Sci, Research Assoc, 1957067; Postdoc, Asst Prof, 1968-73; Vanderbilt Univ, Visiting Res assoc, 1973-74; Asst Prof, 1974-75; Inst of Parmacology Pol Ac Sci Asst Prof, 1975-77; Assoc Prof, 1977-83; Prof, 1983-89; Full Prof, 1989-. *Publications:* Editor in Chief of Wszechswiat; Assoc Editor of Polish Journal of Pharmacology & Pharmacy; Author of over 150 Research Papers; 70 Review Articles. *Memberships include:* Polish Acad of Sci & Letters; Polish Pharmacological Soc; CINP. *Honours include:* Award of the Sec of PAS; Award of the Medical Section of PAS; Gold Badge; The Copernicus Soc 110th Anniversary Diploma of Merit. *Hobbies:* Hiking; Skiing; Popularisation of Sci. *Address:* PL Inwalidow 4 M 7, 30-033 Krakow, Poland. 52, 162.

VI KHUÊ Tran Trinh-Thuan, b. 20 May 1934, Viet Nam. Sch Tchr; Writer; Editor; Journalist. m. Chu Ba Anh, 1955, 2 s, 2 d. *Education:* Bach of Art, Dalat Univ, 1970. *Appointments:* Principal, Van Khoa High Sch, Dalat City, 1970; Redactor in Chief, Vietnamese Youth Educ Assn, 1978; Novelist, Poet, Journalist, Writer for Many Vietnamese Language Mag, 1982; Editor in Chief, Tan Dien Mag, 1990. *Publications include:* Poems; Short Stories. *Memberships:* Vietnamese Youth Educational Assn; Vietnamese Writers Abroad PEN; Vietnamese Writers Abroad PEN Centre East Coast. *Address:* 5649 MT Barnside Way, Burke, VA 22015, USA.

VIDERMAN Linda Jean, b. 4 Dec 1957, Follansbee, WV, USA. Company Exec, Paralegal. m. David Gerald Viderman, 15 Mar 1974, 3 d. *Education:* AS Surgical Tech, 1983; West Virginia Northern Community Coll, 1980-83; Dynamark Inc, Charlottsville, VA, 1983. *Appointments:* Ward Clerk, Weirton Medical Centre, 1982-84; Owner, Sec Treasurer, Mountaineer Security Systems, 1983-86; Owner, The Button Booth Colliers, 1985-; Paralegal, Admin Attorney Dominic J Potts, 1987-; Partner, Company Exec Panhandle Homes, 1988-; Southern Career Inst Paralegal, Legal Asst Program, 1989-91. *Publications:* Numerous Articles; Poems. *Memberships:* La Leche League; Collier Primary PTA; PTA Colliers Primary Sch & Follansbee Middle Sch; Wellsburg Art Assn; West Virginia Writers Assn; Phi Theta Kappa. *Honours include:* West Virginia Northern Community Coll Cert of Award; Poetry Silver Poet Award. *Hobbies:* Family Camping; Home Computing; Reading; Christian Ministry. *Address:* Panhandle Homes, 3027 Pleasant Avenue, Wellsburg, WV 26070, USA. 7, 132, 138.

VIGMO Josef, b. 12 Nov 1922, Reykjavik, Iceland. Geriatrician, Retired. m. Soffia Axelsdottir, 24 Jan 1953, 1 s, 1 d. *Education:* MD, Univ Iceland, 1953; Postgrad, Univ Gothenburg, 1960. *Appointments:* Asst Med Officer, Sandtrasks Sanatorium, Sweden, 1953- 54; Resident, Pulmonary Diseases, 1956-57; Rotating Intern, White Meml Hosp, Clinic Loma Linda Univ, 1954-55; Resident, Intl Medicine Pitea County Hosp, 1958-59; Kalix & Skene County Hosps, Sweden, Norrkoping Gen County Hosp, 1961-65; Sub Chief Med Officer, Hultafors Health Centre, 1960; Sub Chief Med Officer, Geriatric Dept, Boras Gen County Hosp, 1966-77; Chief Med Officer, 1977-87; Conslt, Cardiologist, Boras Gen County Hosp, 1978; Lectr Sch Nursing, 1967-. *Memberships:* Swedish Med Assn; Swedish Geriatrics Assn; Swedish Assn Chief Medical Officers; South Alvsborg County Assn Chief Medical Officers. *Honour:* Recipient Gold Medal Alvsborg County Council. *Hobbies:* Linguistics; Genealogy. *Address:* Sjovagen 1, S-452 00 Stromstad, Sweden. 52.

VIJAYAKRISHNAN Oormila, b. 27 July 1977, Kottayam, Kerala, India. Student. *Education:* Std IX. Publications: Poetry Books, Flowers & Butterflies; Burning Candle; Many Paintings; Over 300 Peoms. *Memberhips:* World Poetry Soc; Acad of Arts & Culture, USA; Kuwait, For World Poetry Anthology; Intl Poets Acad, India. *Honours include:* Cert of Merit for Peom; Cert of Appreciation from World Congress of Poets. *Hobbies:* Poetry; Piano; Paintings; Drawings; Artistic Works; Cartoons. *Address:* Malikayil, ML Road, Kottayam 686 001, Kerala, India.

VINCZE Istvan, b. 26 Feb 1912, Szeged, Hungary. Mathematician. m. Maria Herman, 14 July 1948, 2 s, 1 d. *Education:* Tchrng Qual, Univ of Szeged, 1935; Cert Actuary, 1937; PhD, Univ of Budapest, 1946; Mathematical Sci, 1952; Dr Sc, 1971. *Appointments:* Actuary, 1st Hungarian Insurcance Com, 1935-45; Actuary, Statistician, Dept of Social Security, Ministry of Social Affairs, 1945-49; Hd Dept of Mathematical Statistics, 1949- 82; Asst Prof, Tech Univ of Budapest, 1949-52; Asst Prof, Prof, Roland Eotvos Univ, 1952-82; Prof Emeritus, Ibid & Sci Conslt, Mathematical Inst, HAS, 1982- ; Visiting Lectr. *Publications include:* Mathematical Statistik mit Industriellen Anwendungen;

Mathematical Methods of Statistical Quality Control; 70 Sci Articles. *Memberships:* Janos Bolyai Mathematical Soc; Soc for Popularisation of Knowledge; Quality Control Section; Sci Society for Machine Industry. *Honours:* State Award; Causs Medal; Order of Labour; Various Other Award & Recognitions. *Hobbies:* Music; Reading. *Address:* Mathematical Inst, Hungarian Academy of Sciences, Realtanodau 13/15, 1053 Budapest, Hungary.

VINGILIS Evelyn, b. 17 Dec 1949, Toronto, Ont, Canada. Snr Scientist; Hd of Drinking/Driving Research Program. m. Walter Wm Jaremko, 11 July 1980, 1 d. *Education:* BSc, McMaster Univ, 1971; MA, York Univ, 1973; PhD, 1978. *Appointments:* Addition Research Fnd, P/T Volunteer, 1971-72; York Univ Linicis, 1971-72; Hosp for Sick Children, Genetic Tech, 1972; York Univ, Research Asst, 1972-74; Dept of Psychiatry, Hosp for Sick Children, 1973-74; Clarke Inst of Psychiatry, 1974-76; York Univ, 1975-77; Ryerson Pol Inst Dept of Psychology, 1977-81; Addiction Research Fnd, Snr Scientist & Hd Drinking Driving Research Program. *Publications:* 44 Presentations; 53 Publi, Journals, Books. *Memberships:* Reg Psychologist in the Province of Ontario; Canadian Assn of Women in Sci; Canadian Road Safety Profl; Intl Committee on Alcohol, Drugs & Traffic Safety. *Honours:* Ontario Grad Fellowship; Editorial Bd of Accident & Prevention; Reseatch Advances in Alcohol & Drug Problems Series; PRIDE Award. *Hobbies:* Skiing; Tennis; Art; Music; Ballrom & Jazz Dancing. *Address:* Addiction Research Foundation, 33 Russell Street, Toronto, Ontario, Canada M5S 2S1. 138.

VIRTANEN Ilkka Tapio, b. 4 Jan 1944, Paimio, Finland. Prof of Operations, Research & Mngmt Sci. m. U'la Mielikainen, 31 Dec 1971, 2 s. *Education:* BA, Applied Mathematics, 1966; MA, 1968; PhD, Univ of Turku, 1977. *Appointments:* Asst, Turku Sch of Economics, 1968-78; Lectr, Lappeenranta Univ of Tech, 1978-81; Prof, 1981-; Vice Rector, 1984-87; Rector, 1987. *Publications:* Approx 80 Sci Works; Operations Research & Management Sci. *Memberships:* Inst of Mgmt Sci; Bernoulli Soc for Probability & Mathematical Statistics; Finnish Economic Soc; Finnish Operations Research Soc; Finnish Statistical Soc; Finnish Soc for Future Studies; Finnish Cultural Foundation; Foundation for Finnish Business Research. *Hobbies:* Literature; Cross Country Skiing; Travel. *Address:* Univ of Vaasa, PO Box 297, SF 65101 Vaasa, Finland.

VISANO Livy Anthony Bosna, b. 27 July 1949, Naples, Italy. Assoc Prof, York Univ. m. 1 s. *Education:* BA, Univ of Toronot, 1973; MA, 1974; PhD, 1986. *Appointments:* Ryerson Poly Tech Inst 1975-77; Centre of Criminology, Univ of Toronto, 1976-77, 1977-84; York Univ, 1984-. *Publications:* This Idle Trade; A Time For Action; Deviant Designations; Journal Articles; 65 Conference Papers. *Memberships include:* Prol Ethics, Can Assn of Sociology & Anthropology; Intl J of Comparative Sociology; J of Human Justice. *Honours include:* Deans Award for Outstanding Contributions in Tchrng; Distinction for Comprehensive Exam; Ontario Scholar. *Hobbies:* Chess; Photography; Travel; Community Work; Critical Pedagogy. *Address:* Room 428 South Ross, Dept of Sociology, York Univ, 4700 Keele St, North York, Ontario, Canada M3J 1P3. 142.

VISHINSKI Boris, b. 6 June 1929, Skopje, Yugoslavia. Journalist; Writer. m. Lucia Balabau, 24 Nov 1964, 2 d. *Education:* Belgrade Fac of Law, 1949-53. *Appointments:* Journalist, Nova Macedonia, 1952-59; Ed in Chief, Kulturen Zhivot, 1959-91; Gen Ed, Macedonian Review, 1971-91. *Creative Works include:* Plays; Short Storis; Historical Work; Novels. *Memberships:* Writers Union of Macedonia; Writers Union of Yugoslavia; Writers Assn of Europe; Roma PEN; Federation of Yugoslav Journalists. *Honours:* Kosta Ratsin; 4 Jul, Belgrade; Mario Giuseppe Restivo, Italy. *Hobby:* Philately. *Address:* Njegoseva 26, Macedonia, 91000 Skopje, Yugoslavia.

VISHNICK Martin Lawrence, b. 29 Sept 1952, Hackney, London, England. Musician. m. Lilian Susan Goldberg, 1 July 1990, 1 s, 1 d. *Education:* London Coll of Music, 1974-77. *Appointments:* Tutor, St Albans Boys Sch, 1989-; Tutor, Herts C.C, 1989-. *Creative Works include:* Evolation & Dance; The Vision for Choir & Stage. *Memberships:* Composers Guild of Gt Britian; British Assn of Songwriters & Anthems. *Honour:* Dr W S Lloyd Webber Performance Prize. *Hobbies:* Reading; Cricket; Walking; Squash. *Address:* 12 Watling St, St Albans, Herts AL1 2PX.4, England. 139.

VISSER Margaret Agar, b. 11 May 1940, South Africa. Writer; Lectr; Broadcaster. m. Colin Wills, 9 June 1962, 1 s, 1 d. *Education:* BA, Univ of Toronto, 1970; MA, 1973; PhD, 1980. *Appointments:* Newspaper Reporter, 1959-62; Mansfield, Notts, Tchr, 1962-64; Baghdad, Irac, Univ Lectr, 1973-87; York Univ, Toronto, 1987-. *Publications:* Much Depends on Dinner; The Rituals of Dinner; Saturday Night Magazine. *Membership:* American Assn of Wine & Food. *Honours:* Gold Medal, Classic, Univ of Toronto; Food Book of the Year; Glenfiddich Award. *Hobbies:* Reading; Fine Arts; Music. *Address:* MG Agency, 10 St Mary Street 510, Toronto, Ontario, Canada M4Y 1P9. 142.bblank

VITHOULKAS George, b. 25 July 1932, Athens, Greece. Intl Lectr in Homeopathy. m. Zissoula Antoniadou, 7 Feb 1970. *Education:* Civil Engrng Degree, Athens Univ,; Diploma in Homeopathy, N els Puddphat Sch, S Africa; Degree from Indian Inst of Homeopathy. *Creative Works:* Homepathy, Medicine of the New Man; The Sci of Homeopathy; A New Model for Health & Disease. *Memberships:* Athenian Sch of Homeoapthic Medicine for MDs only, Holland; Liga Medicorum Homeopathica Intl, Holland; Hahnemann Soc, England; Foundation for Homeopathy, USA; Hellenic Homeopathic Medcial Assn, Greece. *Honours:* Honoured for his Work, Washington DC; Guest of Honor, 10th All India Congress of Indian Inst of Hom Physicians, Hyderabed; Honoured for this Work, Seattle. *Hobbies:* Astrology; Chess; Gardening. *Address:* Athenian Sch of Homeopathic Medicine, 1 Periklous Street, 15122 Maroussi, Athens, Greece.

VITREY Daniele, b. 27 Aug 1940, France. Pathologist. m. Michel Vitrey, 16 Dec 1963, 1 s, 1 d. *Education:* Baccalaureat, 1960; PCB, Univ Lyon, 1961; MD, Univ Rouen, 1971; Cancer Inst Rouen. *Appointments:* Asst, Hosp Lyon, 1971-86; Asst, Master Univ Medicine, 1975-86; Conference, Master, 1986-; Hosp MD, 1986-. *Contributions to:* Articles; Varied Reviews. *Memberships:* Natl Concours of Piano; Anotomic Soc; Intl Acad of Pathology. *Hobbies:* Skiing; Music; Art. *Address:* Hosp de le Croix Rousse, Serv d'Anatomie Pathologioue, 69004 Lyon, France. 52.

VITYAZEV Andrey, b. 15 Jan 1945, Syktyvkar. Hd of Lab, Origin & Evolution of the Earth Physicist. m. Victoria A Vityazeva, 10 Apr 1971. *Education:* Moscow State Univ. *Appointments:* Sciectific Collaborator, Dept of Planetray Geophysics, Inst of Physics of the Earth Acad of Sci of USSR, 1971-91; Hd of Lab, 1989-. *Publications:* About 100 Sci Publi. *Memberships:* Russian Acad of Natl Sci. *Honours:* Award Medal O Y Schmidt for Investigation in Theory of Earth Origin & Evolution & Planetary Cosmogony. *Hobbies:* Travel; Reading. *Address:* Inst of Physics of the Earth, B Gruzinskaya 10, 123810 Moscow, Russia.

VLADEM Steven Allen, b. 24 July 1949, Chicago, Illinois, USA. Computer Specialist; Mathematician; Educator. *Education:* Bach of Arts, 1970; Master of Educ in Mathematics, 1973; Master of Arts in Educ Admin & Supervision, 1975. *Appointments:* High Sch Tchr, Chicago Cd of Educ, 1971-81; Statistician & Evaluator, Dept of Research & Evaluation, 1979; Supervisor of Program Serv, Chicago City Hall, 1981; Coordinator of Alternative Sch's Without Walls Program, 1982-87; Coordinator of Computer Assisted Instr, Chicago Metropolitan High Schs, 1987-. *Memberships include:*

Intl Biographical Assn; American Biographical Inst Research Assn; Intl Council for Computers in Educ; Intl Soc for Tech in Educ; Computer Learning Foundation; Illinois Council of Tchrs of Mathematics; Theatre Historical Soc of America. *Hobbies:* Computer Enthusiast; Backgammon; Chess; Reading; Travel; History & Arch; Cinema; Musical Theatre; Drama; Performing Arts; Classical Music; Opera; Symphony; Stamp & Coin Collecting. *Address:* 6237 North Hamlin Avenue, Chicago, IL 60659, USA. 139, 152, 155.

VLADIGUEROV Alexander Panchev, b. 4 Aug 1933, Sofia, Bulgaria. Conductor of the Bulgarian Radio Symphony Orchestra. m. Velichka Chobanova, 17 May 1970, 2 s, 1 d. *Education:* Coll of Music, 1959; Composer, Conductor, Pianist, Specialization in Moscow. *Appointments:* Conductor, Rousse Symphony Orchestra; Conductor, Bulgarian Radio Symphony Orch 1970-. *Creative Works:* Dilmano Dilbero; Toccata; Romantic Poem; Rondo Concertante; Little Red Riding Hood; The Wolf and the Seven Kids; The Bremen Musicians. *Membership:* The Union of Bulgarian Composer. *Honours include:* First Prize for Compisitions, Moscow; Special award for the Union of Bulgaraiin Composers; Honorary Citizen of Rousse. *Hobbies:* Ballet; Driving; Fishing. *Address:* 10 Jakubitza Str, Sofia 1126, Bulgaria.

VLADIMIROV Mladen Grigorov, b. 12 May 1937, Sofia, Bulgaria. Med Doctor. m. 1 Mar 1964, 1 s. *Education:* Medicine, 1961; Doc of Sci, 1985; Prof, 1988. *Appointments:* General Doc & Phisiotherapy, 1961-68; Internal Dis Training, 1968-71; Chief of Lab, Functional Diagnostics & Cardiology, 1971-81; Chief of Clinic of Functional Diagnostics & Cardiology, 1981-88; Chief of Centre of Cardiology, 1988-92. *Publications:* 210 Sci Reseach Papers. *Memberships:* Republic Cardiology Assn; Cardiology Sci Council. *Honour:* A Doctor of Sci. *Hobbies:* History; Literature. *Address:* Military Medical Academy, 3 G Sofiiski, 1000 Sofia, Bulgaria.

VLASIU Ioana Maria, b. 31 May 1943, Sibiu, Romania. Art Historian; Researcher. m. 1 s. *Education:* MA, Inst of Fine Arts, Bucarest, 1966. *Appointments:* Researcher, Inst of Art History of the Romanian Acad, 1966-; Deputy Dir, 1990; Asst Chief Editor, Journals of the Inst. *Creative Works:* Studies about Modern Romanian Art; Art Criticism, Journal ARTA. *Memberships:* Art Criticism Section, Union of Artists; Romanian Committee of CIHA; Commission of Museums & Collections of the Ministry of Culture, Bucarest. *Honour:* Prize for Art Criticism of the Union of the Artists. *Hobbies:* Literature; History. *Address:* 10 Brezoianu Str, Sc.A ap.9, 70624 Bucarest, Romania.

VO Van Thuong, b. 25 July 1940, Vietnam. Land Investment Realtor. separate, 2 d. *Education:* Bach of Sci, 1961; Natl Concervatory Inst of Republic of Vietnam, 1962. *Appointments:* Military Acad, 1963; Officer of Psychological Welfare Office, 1964; Officer Pacification & Devel, 1969-75. *Publications:* The Vietnamese Daily News; Musical Composer. *Memberships:* Vietnamese Musician Assn, California. *Honours:* First Prize in MANDOLIN Comp; First Prize Ping Pong Comp. *Hobbies:* Music; Sport. *Address:* 2221 W Knox St, Santa Ana, CA 92704, USA.

VODYANOY Vitaly Jacob, b. 2 June 1941, Kiev, Ukraine, USSR. Prof. m. Galina Rubin, 22 Apr 1967, 1 d. *Education:* MS, Moscow Physical Engrng Inst, 1964; PhD, Leningrad, UUSR, 1973. *Appointments:* Asst Prof, Inst of Semiconductors, Leningrad, 1965072; Assoc Prof, A I Ioffe Physico tech Univ, 1972-78; Snr Research Sci, New York Univ, 1979-82; Research Assoc, Univ of Calif, 1982-89; Assoc Prof, Auburn Univ, 1989-; Natl Sci Found, Washington, 1985-. *Publications include:* Physics of Solid State & Neutron Scattering; 52 Articles to Profl Journals. *Memberships:* AAAS; Am Assn Nutrititional Cons; The Am Physical Soc; The Biophysical Soc; Inst for Biol Detection Systems. *Honours:* Recipient Grants Natl Sci Found; US Army Research Officer.

Hobbies: Medical Herbs. *Address:* 541 Summertrees Dr, Auburn, AL 36830, USA. 7, 15.

VOGT Helmut Joachim, b. 6 Oct 1936, Berlin, Germany. Prof of Chemical Engrng. m. Renate Dogmar Scheffler, 5 Apr 1968, 1 s. *Education:* Grad in Chem Engrng, 1963; Doctor, 1977. *Appointments:* Chem Engr, Krebskosmo Berlin, 1964-73; Prof, Tech Fachhochschule, Berlin, 1972-. *Publications:* Ullmanns Encyklopadie; Comprehensive Treatise of Electrochemistry; Electrochemical Reactors. *Address:* Technische Fachhochschule Berlin, Fachbereich Verfahrens Und Umweittechnik, Luxemburger Str 10, D-1000 Berlin 65, Germany. 52.

VOLFENSOHN Sergey, b. 24 July 1903, Odessa. Composer; Pensioner. m. Natalya Polonskay, 5 Apr 1935. *Education:* Leningrad Musical Acad, 1927-31. *Appointments:* Musical Sch Tchr, 1927-32; Drama Theatre Pianist, 1932-37; Musical Acad Prof of Composition & Harmony, 1937-89. *Creative Works:* 2 Oratory Cantata; 2 Quators; Many Vocal & Instrumental Compositions. *Membership:* Sorietiques Composers Union. *Honours:* 7 Medals. *Hobbies:* History; Literature. *Address:* Ostrovsky Place 9-32 191011 St Petersburg, Russia.

VOLPIER CHEVALIER SYPNIEWSKI Ferdinand Josef, b. 15 Jan 1956, Wurzburg, Germany. *Education:* Int Sch Walterswi Baar; Coll Saint Michel Fribourg, Switzerland; Univ de Fribourg; Dartmouth Coll Hanover NH USA. *Appointments:* US Army Munich, 1977-81; Co Founder, Hanover Music Festival, Rollins Chapel Organ Recitals, Hanover, New Hampshire, USA, 1984-85; Dir Volpier Designs, 1985-89; Procurement & Contract Admin Coldman Sachs Int Ltd, 1980-. *Publications:* Whistling to the Tune; Glen Ellis; Les Arbres Chantent; La Gloire de Louis; Vierleeder. *Membership:* Hosp Order of St John. *Honour:* Pestalozzi Youth Prize.

VOLTES Pedro, b. 1 July 1926, Reus, Spain. Univ Prof; Writer. m. Maria Jose Buxo, 18 Apr 1963, 1 s, 2 d. *Education:* Ind Coll Armed Forces, Washington DC. *Appointments:* Prof, Univ of Barcelona, 1943- 91; Visiting Prof, Univ der Bundeswehr, Hamberg; Writer in History & Social & Economic. *Publications:* Some 125 titles on History, Economics, Law, Societry. *Memberships:* Assn Lawyers; Assn Press, Barcelona; Intl Soc System; Spanish Soc Systems; Royal Acad History & Economic Sc Spain. *Honours include:* Orders of Civil Military, Navel & Labour Merit of Spain; Commendatore Order of Merit, Italy. *Address:* Angli 2, Barcelona 08017, Spain.

VONCINA Nikola, b. 7 Oct 1934, Sibenik, Croatia, Yugoslavia. Editor in Chief, Drama Dept, Croatian TV, Zagreb. m. Leda Crbac, 5 Oct 1968, 2 s, 1 d. *Education:* Law Sch, Univ of Zagreb, 1957; Acad of Dramatic Arts, Zagreb; Doctoral Degree, 1986. *Appointments:* Dir, RAdio TV Zagreb, 1957-66; Artistic Mgr, Zagreb Youth Theatre, 1966-78; Editor Drama Dept, 1978-. *Publications:* Under Milk Wood; Radio Zagreb; Croatian Radio Drama to 1957; Theatre, Radio, TV. *Memberships:* PEN Club; Croatian Writers Assn Zagreb. *Honour:* Awarded City of Zagreb Proze. *Address:* Vocarsko Naselje 16, 41000 Zagreb, Croatia, Yugoslavia.

VORBRODT Christopher John, b. 27 Dec 1929, Vilnius, Poland. Pensioner. m. (1) Alexander Settich, 11 Jan 1958, div 1967, (2) Christine Brelewicz, 27 Feb 1968, div 1979. *Education:* Jagiellonical Univ, Cracow, 1950-56; Master of Biology, 1956; Doct of Biology, 1961. *Appointments:* Inst of Oncology, Poland, 1956-73; Inst of Metallurgy, 1973-76; Sthessian Tech Univ, 1977-90. *Creative Works:* About 200 Publi; 7 Individual Exhib. *Memberships:* Polish Historical Soc, Warsaw; Polish Oncology Soc, Warsaw; Photography Soc. *Hobbies:* Art Photography; Zoological Photography;

Painting; Reading; Poetry; Sci Fiction; Modern Literature. *Address:* ul Okrzei 10/1, Sliwice, Poland.

VOROS Jozsef, b. 18 May 1951, Szakmar, Hungary. Prof; Dean. m. Matild Kramm, 25 Aug 1973, 1 s, 1 d. *Education:* MSc, 1974; PhD, 1984. *Appointments:* Asst, 1979-81; Assoc Prof, 1981-84; Vice dean, 1986-89; Dean, 1989-. *Publications:* Production Management; Papers on European Journal of Operations Research. *Memberships:* Assn of Economic Modelling; Editor in Chief of Journal Szigma. *Hobby:* Bees. *Address:* 61 Bittner, Pecs, Hungary.

VRBA Karel, b. 1 Sept 1918, Krasovice, Czechoslavakia. Editor; Dir, Educational TV. m. Frauke Thiessen, 28 May 1976, 2 s, 1 d. *Education:* Natl Sci, Charles Univ, Prague, 1948. *Appointments:* Hd, Animated Educ Programmes, Technofilm, Teplice, 1945-49; Hd Educ Programmes, Prague CS State Film, 1949-68; Public Relations, Ciba Geigy, Basel, 1968-70; Dir, Educ Programmes, ZDF Mainz, Germany, 1970-. *Creative Works:* Approx 100 Films; Books; Instrukcni Film Ucebni Praxi. *Memberships:* Czachoslovak Soc of Arts & Sci; Friends of Czechoslovak Music. *Honours:* Film Prizes, Festivls at Karlovy, Vary & Olomouc. *Hobbies:* Music; Travel; Languages; Literature. *Address:* Richthofenstrasse 17, D 7800 Freiburg, Germany.

VUJAKLIJA STIPANOVIC Ksenija, b. 13 Apr 1939, Sisak, Yugoslavia. Hd of Blood Transfusion Inst; Physician. m. Zvonimir Stipanovic, 23 July 1966, 1 d. *Education:* Univ of Rijeka, MD, 1963; Conslt Physician, 1968; Primarius, 1980; PhD, 1989. *Appointments:* Clinical Hosp Centre, Rijeka Intern, 1963-64; Spec in Transfusion Medicine, 1964-68; Hd of Blood Transfusion Inst, 1968-. *Publications include:* Blood Transfusion in Kidney Transplantation; The Outcome of Pregnancy After Renal Transplantation; Pretreatment with Donor Specific Blood Transfusions in Related Kidney Graft Recipients. *Memberships:* Coation Medical Coll, Zagreb; Assn of Hematologists & Transfusiologist of Yugoslavia; Transufsiology of Croatia, Zagreb, Yugoslavia; Commision for Transfusiology of Yugoslavia. *Honours:* Award of the Town of Rijeka; Award of the Croation Medical Coll. *Hobbies:* Opera; Concerts; Theatre; Ballet; Reading; Arts; History; Walking in Nature. *Address:* Zdravka Kucica 29, YU- 51000 Rijeka, Yugoslavia.

VUK Damir, b. 24 Nov 1966, Novosfiec, Croatia. Reliability/Quality Control & Software Expert Mgr. m. Srebrenka Ursic, 20 Jan 1990. *Education:* Univ of Zagreb, 1980. *Appointments:* High Sch Tchr, 1981; Reliability Spec, RIZ Semiconduclors, Zagreb, 1981-85; Reliability Mgr, 1985-89; Reliability & Quality Control Mgr, 1988-89; Tech Mgr, 1989-91; Tech Conslt, Sistemprojeki, Zagreb, 1991-. *Publications include:* Semiconductors Failure Analyses Methods; Technical & Maketing Management for Small Enterprises. *Membership:* MIDEM, Yugoslav Soc on Micrelectronics. *Hobbies:* Chess; Hatha Yoga; Tennis; Sailing. *Address:* Sistemprojekt, Rakusina 4, 41000 Zagreb, Croatia.

VUKS Valery Janovich, b. 31 Jan 1954, Arkhangelsk, USSR. Geologist. *Education:* St Petersburg Univ, 1976. *Appointments:* All Union Geological Research Inst, 1978-91. *Publications:* 20 in Paper, Late Triassic Foraminifers From The Pebbles in the Dobridol formation, SW Bulgaria. *Contributions to:* 2 Books; The Jurassic Deposits of the South Part of the Transcaucasus. *Address:* All Union Geological Research Inst, 74 Sredny pr, St Petersburg, 199026, Russia.

VYSKOCIL Frantisek, b. 3 Sept 1941, Pelhrimov. Neurophysiologist. m. Emily Vondrakova, 10 Aug 1963, 1 s, 1 d. *Education:* Charles Univ, Prague, 1958-63; RNDr, 1963; PhD, 1968. *Appointments:* Research Asst, Dept Compar, Physiol, Faculty of Sci, Charles Univ, Prague, 1960-63; Post Doctoral Student, 1963-68; Research Scientist, 1969-89; Hd of Lab, Cellular

Neurophysiology Inst of Physiology, CAS, Prague, 1989-
. *Publications:* 150 Primary Scientific. *Memberships:* Inst
Physiol, Prague; Medical Soc J E Purkyne; American
Biophysical Soc; Collegium of Cel & Molec Biol CAS;
Physiological Research Editorial Bd. *Honours include:*
Purkyne Award of Czechoslovak Physiological Soc;
Award of Czechosl Acad Sci for Sci Achievement; Award
of CAS for Sci Popularization. *Hobbies:* Music; Essays;
Painting; Philosophy. *Address:* Inst of Physiology,
Czechoslovak Acad Sci, Videnska 1083, 142 20 Praha
4, CSFR. 139, 152.

W

WABLER Robert C, b. 14 Dec 1948, Dayton, Ohio, USA. m. Linda Adele Rayburn, 26 Mar 1976, 1 s. *Education:* Univ of Georgia, 1976; Univ of Dayton, 1971. *Appointments:* VP, Chief Financial Officer, Athlete Foot, 1989; Snr VP, World Bazaar, 1985-89; VP, Financial Analysis Munford Inc, 1983-85; VP, Controller Munford Inc, 1982-83; VP, Admin World Bazaar, 1980-82. *Publications:* Developed the Minimum Expenses Needed Technique; Auditing for Efficiency in the On Line System. *Memberships:* American Inst of CPA; Georgia Soc of CPA; Intl Platform Assn. *Honours:* Cert Public Accountant; Cert Systems Profl; Cert Information Systems Auditor; Cert Quality Analyst; Cert Intl Auditor. *Address:* 7171 Twin Branch Court, Atlanata, GA 30328, USA.

WADA Takao, b. 23 July 1930, Kawasaki, Japan. Prof; Physics Educ. m. Tomoko Wada, 23 Mar 1960, 2 s, 1 d. *Education:* BSEE, Ehime Univ, Japan, 1950-54; MS, Osaka Univ, 1959; Nagoya Univ, 1965. *Appointments:* Research Kobe, Kogyo Corp, 1954-59; Research Asst, Nagoya Univ, 1959-65; Lectr, 1965-66; Assoc Prof, 1966-70; Prof Mie Univ, Tsu, Japan, 1970-84; Nagoya Kogyo Univ, 1984-; Visiting Scholar Northwestern Univ, Evanston 111, 1974-75. *Publications include:* Articles to Profl Journals; Electron Beam Epitaxy of Alloy Semi Conductors. *Memberships:* Local Councillor, Japan Soc of Applied Physics; Inst of Electronics, Information & Communication Eng. *Honours:* Ministry of Educ Grantee; Sci Promotion Grant; Research Promotion Grant. *Hobby:* Painting. *Address:* Gokiso, Showa, Nagoya 466, Japan.52.

WADE Adrian Paul, b. 7 Apr 1960, Amersham, England. Asst Prof, Chemistry. m. Susan Nash, 22 May 1982, 3 s. *Education:* BSc, Univ of Southampton, 1981; PhD, Univ of Wales, 1985. *Appointments include:* Extra Mural Research Assoc, Univ Coll Swansea, British Petroleum Research Centre, 1984-85; Chemist/Computer Sci, 1985-87; Visiting Research Assoc, Research Centre Michigan State Univ, 1985-87. *Publications include:* A Versatile Automatic Development System of Flow Injection Analysis; Investigation of Temperature Effects on Dispersion in a Flow Injection Analyzer; Spectrophotometric Determination of Peroxydisulphate with o- Dianis dine by Flow Injection. *Memberships include:* Royal Soc of Chemistry; Chemical Inst of Canada; Canadian Soc for Chemistry; Canadian Pulp & paper Assn; The Assoc of Analytical Chemists. *Honours include:* Acad Ward & Distinctions; British Petroleum Research Studentship; Harry Hallam Memorial Prize for Distinguished Work in Physical/Inorganic Chemistry. *Hobbies:* Angling; Chess; Darts; Walking; Computers; Electronics. *Address:* Lab for Automated Chemical Analysis, Chemistry Dept, Univ of British Columbia, 2036 Main Mall, Vancouver, BC, Canada V6T 1Z1. 142, 143.

WADE David Anthony, b. 22 Dec 1925, Konigsberg, East Prussia. Barrister. m. (1) Nancy Stalker, dec, 3 d, (2) Amy Culley, 2 s, 1 d. *Education:* Stonyhurst Coll, Lancashire, 1939-43; Officers Training Sch, 1943-44; Council of Legal Educ, London, 1955-59; Called to Bar, London, 1959. *Appointments:* General Mgr, 1960-65; Managing Dir, 1966-69; MD, 1969-72; Chmn, 1974-. *Publication:* Disaster. *Memberships:* Chartered Inst of Arbritrators, London. *Hobbies:* Skiing; Sailing; Fishing; Writing. *Address:* 2 Mitre Count Buildings, Temple, London EC47 JB2, England.

WADE Thomas Edward, b. 14 Sept 1943, Jacksonville, Florida, USA. Univ Research Admin; Electrical Engr. m. Ann Elizabeth Chitty, 6 Aug 1966, 1 s, 2 d. *Education:* BSc, Electrical Engrng, 1966; MSc, Electrical Engrng, 1969; PhD, 1974, Univ of Florida. *Appointments:* Electrician & Circuit Designer, Allied Electric Co, 1964; Illumination Engr, Reynolds Smith & Hill Arch & Engr, 1965; Interim Asst Prof, Univ of Florida, 1974; VLSI Conslt, Natl Aeronautics & Space Adm, 1978; Prof of Electrical Engrng, dir of Microelectronics Research Lab, Mississippi State Univ, 1976-85; Solid Ckt Spec, Applied Mecro Circuits Corp, San Diego, California, 1981; Assoc Dean, Research, Univ of South Florida, 1985-. *Publications include:* Books. Polymides for LSI And VLSI Applications; Over 65 Journal Articles; Over 75 Papers. *Memberships include:* Sigma Xi; Florida Alpha; Eta Kappa Nu; Omicron Delta Kappa; American Soc for Engrng Educ. *Honours include:* Leadership Key; Outstanding Research Award; Oustandind Engrng Tchr Award. *Hobbies:* Collecting antiques; Restoring Old Cars; Travel; Sports Activities; Primarily Basketball. *Address:* Engrng Deans Office, Univ of South Florida, 4202 East Fowler Avenue, Tampa, FL 33620, USA.

WAETJEN Herman Charles, b. 16 June 1929, Bremen, Germany. Robert S Dollar prof of New Testament. m. Mary Suzanne Struyk, 15 July 1960, 2 s, 2 d. *Education:* BA, 1950; BD, 1953; Dr Theol, Univ of Tuebingen, 1958. *Appointments:* Instr, Concordia Seminary, 1957; Asst Prof, Univ of Southern California, 1959-62; Assoc Prof, San Francisci Seminary, 1962-72; Prof, 1972-. *Publications:* The Origin & Destiny of Humanness; An Interpretation of Matthews Gospel; A Reordering of Power; A Sociopolitical Reading of Marks Gospel. *Memberships:* Soc of Biblical Literature; Pacific Coast Theological Soc. *Honours:* Hebrew Univ Scholarship; Research Fellowship, American Assn of Theological Schs. *Hobbies:* Backpacking; Photography; Travel. *Address:* 83 Jordan Avenue, San Anselmo, CA 94960, USA. 2, 9.

WAGNER Donald R, b. 21 Sept 1926, Mpls, MN, USA. Realtor; Owner; Natl Speaker. m. Marjoire Lou Johnson, 21 Jan 1961, 2 d. *Education:* B.BA, Univ of Minnesota, 1948; CLU, Designation American Coll of Life Underwriters, 1974. *Appointments:* Natl Sales Promotion, Florida Developer, 1963-68; Publicity/Public Relations, 1984-87; Realtor/Broker/Owner, Royal Palm Beach Reality Inc, 1976-90; Owner, Wagco Co, 1985-. *Creative Works:* Organized, Instr Several Corp Sales Training programs; Presents, Billion Sales Rallies; Produces, Business Developement Workshops. *Memberships:* Intl Speakers Platform; Natl Speakers Assn; FAR Speakers Bureau; Natl Assn of Realtors; Publicity Chmn, W P B Bd of Realtors; FREC; Real Estate Broker, Florida. *Honours:* Realtor Assn of the Year; Natl Honorary pi Sigma Epsilon; Profl Fraternity of Mktng Sales & Mktng Exec Club, Educ Trophy. *Hobby:* Golf. *Address:* 5985 Del Lago Circle 121, Sunrise, Fl 33313, USA. 7, 132, 155.

WAGNER Donna Lee, b. 17 Sept 1939, Waukegan, IL USA. Poet; Writier; Shiatsu Practitioner. m. David M McCleskey, 4 June 1961, div, 1 d. *Education:* Univ of Texas, Auston, BA, 1962; Dialogue House, 1986; The Loft Writers Workshop, 1989; Bennington Writers Worshop, 1990. *Appointments:* ICA African Asia, Europe, Latin Amer Middle East, North Amer, 1972-86; Intl, ICA, 1986-90; Belgium, ICA, 1990-91. *Publications:* After There Are No More Fish to Catch; Silver Thread, Hearing Cries of the Earth; Imaginal Education. *Memberships:* Inst of Cultural Affairs; Poetry Soc of America. *Honours:* Commemorative Medal of Honor; BA Cum Laude Univ of Texas. *Hobbies:* Walking; Reading; Music; Friendships; Art; Anthropology; Archeology; Feminism; Symbols; World Cultures. *Address:* Rue Amedee Lynen 8, B-1030 Brussels, Belgium.

WAHAB Afsana, b. 9 Sept 1955, Dhaka, Bangladesh. Lawyer Conslt, Women in Developement Child Issues & Legal Afairs. m. Abdul Wahab, 24 Dec 1980, 2 s. *Education:* Masters in Law, Univ of Dhaka, 1984; Cert in Sales & Personnel Mgmt, UK, 1982; Inst of Mktng, UK, 1983. *Appointments:* Legal Adviser, MAWTS & MCC, 1987-; Conslt, SIDA, 1988; Dir, BCSU WID, 1989-90; Programme Officer, Radda Barnen, 1990-91. *Publications:* Exploited Children; Where Children are Adults. *Memberships:* Intl Law Assn; APWALD; Badda

Womens Self Help Centre; Bangladesh Womens Federation; Bangladesh Natl Womens Lawyers Assn; Ain O Shalish Kendra; Legal Adviser Peoples Welfare Organ. *Hobbies:* Reading; Travel; Music; Cooking. *Address:* Road no.15, House no.69, Block D, Banani Dhaka 1213, Bangladesh.

WAIDACHER Friedrich, b. 15 Sept 1934, Graz, Austria. Museum Dir. m. Christiane Felice, 13 Mar 1965, 1 s, 1 d. *Education:* Musical studies, Coll of M Graz, 1946-59; Dr Phil, Univ of Graz, 1964; Profl Training, 1974-79. *Appointments:* Several Appointments Acad of Music, 1954-87; Asst Curator, Applied Art, 1965-69; Sec of the Bd, Deputy Dir, 1969-76; dir, 1977-. *Creative Works:* About 40; Compositions for Jazz Band; Chamber Music Groups; Choirs. *Memberships:* Austrian Museusm Prize, Member of Jury; European Museum of the Year Award, Member of Committee; Austrian ICOM Natl Committee. *Honours:* Gropes Goldeues Ehoeuzeichen des Laudes; Eoske Preis der Historisden. *Hobbies:* Music; History; Philosophy. *Address:* Klosterwiesgasse 44, A-8010 Graz, Austria.

WAINWRIGHT Rupert Charles Purchas, b. 16 Oct 1913, Southsea, Hants, England. Retired Naval Officer. m. Patrica Mary Helen Blackwood, 28 Aug 1937, 2 s, 2 d. *Education:* Marlborough House, 1922-27; RAC Dartmouth, 1927-30. *Appointments:* Midshipman, 1931-33; Sub Lieutenant, Lieutenant, Lieutenant Commander, 1934-49; Commander, 1949-55; Captain, 1955- 65; Rear Admiral, 1965-67. *Memberships:* Naval Staff Coll; Joint Services Staff Coll. *Honours include:* Distinguished Service Corps; Order of Bath. *Hobbies:* Hockey; Swimming. *Address:* Regency Cottage, 30 Maidenhead Road, Stratford Upon Avon, Warwickshire, CV32 6XS, England. 1.

WAKAO Noriaki, b. 19 Aug 1930, Tokyo, Japan. Yokohama Natl Univ, Prof. m. Setsuko Shiga, 7 Feb 1964, 3 d. *Education:* Waseda Univ, BS, 1948-52; Toyko Inst of Tech, MS, 1953-55; Dr Eng, Univ of Toyko, 1955-58. *Appointments:* Assoc Prof, Univ of Toyko, 1964-65; Prof, Yokohama Natl Univ, 1965-. *Publications:* 130 Tech Research Papers on Chemical Engrng; Book. Heat & Mass Transfer in Packed Beds. *Memberships:* Japanese Soc of Chemical Engrs; Japan Petroleum Inst; Intl Advisory Bd of Canadian Journal of Chemical Engrng; Intl Advisory Bd of Latin American Applied Research. *Honours:* Research Paper Award from Japanese Soc of Chemical Engrs; Honorary Prof of Shenyang Inst of Chemical Tech. *Hobby:* Asian Archaeology. *Address:* 8-1-48 Hisagi, Zushi 249, Japan. 52.

WAKELEY John Halbert, b. 2 Nov 1932, Bucyrus, Ohio, USA. Vice Chancellor for Acad Affairs. m. Esther Shue Reed, 9 Sept 1956, 2 s, 2 d. *Education:* AB, Coll of Wooster, 1954; MS, NC State Coll, 1958; PhD, Michigan State Univ, 1961. *Appointments:* Research Assoc, Corning Glass Works, 1961-64; Asst Prof, Asst Dean, Assoc Prof, Prof, Chmn, Dept of Psychology, Michigan State Univ, 1964-80; Dean, Coll of Arts & Sci, Memphis State Univ, 1980-87; Vice Chancellor, Western Carolina Univ, 1987-. *Publications:* Co Author, Psychology of Ind Psychology; The Scanlon Plan; Author, Handbook of Organ Management. *Memberships:* American Psychological Assn; American Assn for Higher Educ; American Assn of Sci; Phi Kappa Phi; sigma Xi; Council of Coll of art & Sci. *Honours:* Tchrng Fellow; Cooperative Graduate Fellow; American Council on Educ Fellow. *Hobbies:* Reading; Walking; Racquetball. *Address:* Western Carolina Univ, Academic Affairs, Cullowhee, NC 28723, USA. 2, 7, 143.

WALCZAK Zbigniew Kazimierz, b. 27 Mar 1932, Gostyn, Poland. Chemist; Chemical Engr; Research Fellow. m. M Krystyna Szymusik Zygmuntowicz, 17 Sept 1976, 1 d. *Education:* Polytech of Lodz, Engr Chemist, 1954; Master Engrng Chemist, 1956. *Appointments:* Cooperative Chemical Ind, Lodz, 1956-59; Personer AB Ystad, Sweden, Chief Chemist, 1960-62; Abcasco, Stockholm, Sweden, 1962-63l Shawinigan Chemicals,

1963-64; E I duPnt De Nemours, Old Hickory Tenn, 1964-67; Phillips Petroleum Co, Bartlesville, Okla, 1967-70; M & T chemicals, Rahway, NJ, 1971-73; Inmont Corp, Clifton, NJ, 1973- 82; Kimberly Clark Corp, 1982-. *Publications:* Formation of Synthetic Fibres; Thermal Bonding of Fibres; Papers; Patents. *Memberships:* American Chem Soc. *Hobbies:* Philosophy; Music; Touring; Camping. *Address:* 1350 Witham Drive, Atlanta, GA 30338, USA. 7, 52.

WALDEN Joseph Lawrence, b. 2 Oct 1956, Padvcah, Kentucky, USA. Major, US Army. m. Julia Kay Johnson, 9 Oct 1982, 2 d. *Education:* BS, North Carolina State Univ, 1978; MBA, Florida Inst of tech, 1988; MS, 1989. *Appointments:* Asst Adjutant, 25th Supply & Transport Battalion, Schofield Barracks, Hawaii, 1978-79; Main Supply Platoon Leader, 25th Infantry Div, 1979-81; Supply Control Officer, 1981-82; Installation Supply Officer, Signal Sch, Ft Gordon, Georgia, 1982-83; Brigade Logistics Officer, 1983-84; Company Commander, 1984-86; Student, 1986-88; Logistics Plans Officer, 1988- 90; Materiel Div, Combat Developments, Ft Lee, Virginia, 1990-91; Student, US Army Coll, 1991-. *Publications:* 3 Articles; Co Author, US Army Strategic Logistics Concept. *Memberships:* Fellowship of Christian Athletes; Natl Strength & Conditioning Assn; Natural Athletes Strength Assn; United States Powerlifting Assn; Save the Manatee Club; American Sunbathing Assn; Florida Sherrifs Assn; Hopewell Virginia City Bd of Building Code Appeals; Delta Mu Delta. *Hobbies:* Powerlifting; Naturist. *Address:* 46 4th Artillery Road, Ft Leavenworth, KS 66027, USA. 7.

WALDENBORG Torsten, b. 9 June 1925, Orebro, Sweden. Economist; Dir. *Education:* BSc, Univ Gothenburg; Imede Lausanne, Switzerland. *Appointments:* Deputy Managing Dir, Intl Monthly continental Key Paris, 1959-61; General Mgr, Elof Hansson Bogota, Columbia, 1961-67; Mkt Mgr, Fagersta Bruk, Sweden, 1968-70; Area Mgr, Latin America Middle East & Southeast Asia, 1971-86; Dir, Business Activies, Outside Europe, 1987-88; Le Trading Ab Gothenburg, Sweden, 1989-. *Memberships:* The Centre of Interdisciplinary Sci; The Soc of Political Economy; Swedish Soc of Artificial Intelligence; Swedish Economist Assn; Imede Alumni Assn; Sociedad Sueco Hispano Americana; Travellers Club. *Hobbies:* International/Development Economics. *Address:* Landala Bergen 35,S- 41129 Gothenburg, Sweden.

WALKER Geoffrey Hurst, b. 7 Feb 1956, Forfar, Scotland. Company Finance Dir. *Education:* Bell Baxter HS, Cupar, Fife, 1968-74; Univ of Edinburgh, 1974-78. *Appointments:* Arthur Young, 1978-87; Cowells Plc, 1987-89; DPS Typecraft Ltd, 1989-. *Hobbies:* Philately; Sailing. *Address:* 2 Ransome Close, Sproughton, Ipswich, IP8 3DG, England.

WALKER Glen Dale, b. 22 Nov 1934, Maysville, Okla, USA. Prof, Electronics. m. Nita Ann Leadford, 5 Oct 1960, 1 s, 1 d. *Education:* Univ of Okla, BS, 1960; Univ of Texas, MA, 1976; East Texas State Univ, PhD, 1991. *Appointments:* Douglas Aircraft, 1960-62; Vard Inc, 1962-68; Texas Instruments, 1968-70; Farmers Branch S D, 1970-71; Richland Coll, 1972-. *Publications:* Statics; Moto Controls; Instrumentation Manual. *Memberships:* Inst of Electrical & Electronics Engr; Registered Profl Engrs, Texas. *Honours:* Prof Engr State of Texas; Extra Mile Award. *Hobbies:* Ranching; Reading; Travel; Electonics. *Address:* 14 Hillside Drive, Rockwall, TX 75087, USA. 7.

WALKER James Cornelius, b. 18 Feb 1953, Macon, GA, USA. Snr Staff Scientist. m. Dianne Louis Beidler, 15 June 1980, 1 s. *Education:* AA, Macon Jr Coll, 1972; BA, 1974; PhD, Florida State Univ, 1980. *Appointments:* Postdoctoral Fellow, Northwestern Univ, Evanston, IL, 1980-81; Research Assoc, Worcester Fdn for Expl Biol, Shrewsbury, MA, 1981-83; Asst Prof, C Davidson Coll, 1983-85; Snr Staff Scientist, 1985-. *Publications:* 11

Research Papers; 1 Books; 28 Presentations; 1 Patent. *Memberships:* Intl & American Assn for Dental Research Soc fro Neuroscience; Assn for Chemoreception Research; Sigma Xi. *Hobbies:* Canoeing; Woodworking; Camping; Political Philosophy. *Address:* BGTC 611-13W/104, R J Reynolds Tobacco Co, Winston Salem, NC, 27102, USA.

WALKER John Michael, b. 9 Apr 1942, New Orleans, USA. Conslt Hydrogeologist. m. Terry Ann Leff, 22 Aug 1969, 1 s, 2 d. *Education:* BS, Old Diminion Univ, 1973; Postgrad, Colorado State Univ, 1980. *Appointments:* Constr, Inspector, US Corps of Engrs, Arlington, Va, 1963-68; Sgt, US Army, Colo, Spgs, 1968-70; Geologist, Corps of Engrs, Norfolk, Va, 1970-73; Project Geologist, US Dept of Int Bureau of Reclamation, Denver, 1974-78; Project Design Geologist, US Corps of Engrs, Savannah, 1978- 81; Snr Conlt Engr, E I Du Pont de Hemours & Co, 1989-; Pres, SETI, Scientific Environmental Tng, Inc, 1989-. *Creative Works:* Writer & Producer, Educational Films in Geology; Planning Committee, Hazards & Solid Waste Inst, Univ of Texas. *Memberships:* Assn Engrng Geologists; Assn Ground Water Sci & Engrs; MENSA; Underground Injection Practices Council; Earthquake Engrng Research Inst; The Platform Soc. *Honours:* Telly Award for Training Film Excellence; Accomplishment Award; Bronze Award for Engrng Excellence; Safety Award, Dept of Interior. *Hobbies:* Mineral Collecting; Scuba Diving; Photography; Horticulture; Naturalist; Environmentalist. *Address:* 6795 Knollwood Drive, Beaumont, TX, 77706, USA. 7, 132.

WALKER Nigel David, b. 6 Aug 1917, Tientsin, China. Retired Univ Prof of Criminology. m. Sheila Margaret Johnston, 5 Dec 1939, 1 d. *Education:* Edinburgh Acad, 1927-35; Christ Church, Oxford, 1935-39; Edinburgh Univ, 1950-52. *Appointments:* Infantry Officer, Camerons, Lovat Scounts, Allied Forces HQ, 1940-45; Scottish Office, 1940-61; Reader, Criminology, Oxford, 1961-73; Prof, Cambridge, 1973-85. *Publications include:* Delphi; A Short History of Psychotherapy; Morale in the Civil Service; Crime & Insanity in England; Crimes, Courts & Figures; Public Attitudes to Sentencing; Why Punich?. *Memberships:* Howard League; Br Soc Criminology; Royal Coll of Psychiatrists; Royal Soc of Medicine; Br Psychological Soc; Kings Coll Cambridge. *Honours:* Chancellors Prize for Org Latin Poem; Honorary Scholar Christ Church; CBE; Honorary Fellow, Royal Coll of Psychiatrists. *Hobbies:* Chess; Mountains. *Address:* Kings College, Cambridge, England.

WALLACE Belle, b. 16 Sept 1935, Swansea, Wales. Snr Lectr; Educator; Psychology. 1 s. *Education:* Tchrs Cert of Educ, Coll of Educ, Swansea, 1957; Bach Educ, Univ London, 1970; Psychology Counselling, Univ London, 1972; Masters Degree, 1980. *Appointments:* Lectr, Theology, Coll of Educ Swansea, 1959-60; Adviser, Primary Sci, 1961-63; Hd of Sci Dept, Appleton Sch, Essex, 1966-70; Hd of Pastoral Care, 1966-70; Adviser, Conslt, Gifted Educ, 1970-84. *Publications:* Gifted Education Intl; Curriculum Extension Guides; Teaching The Very Able Child; Camoes; Worldwide Perspectives on Gifted Disadvantaged; Thimking Actively in a Social Contexy, TASC. *Memberships:* World Assn of Mentors; Educ Adviser, Leondido Trust; World Council for Gifted & Talented Children; Curriculum Developemtn Univ, Uni of Natal. *Honours:* Citation of Distinguished Serv. *Hobbies:* Writing Poetry; Art & Coll; Drama; Design of Educ Toys; Writing Childrens Stories; Interior Design. *Address:* Curriculum Develeopment Unit, Faculty of Education, Univ of Natal, Pietermaritzburg 3200, South Africa.

WALLACE Robert Ian, b. 31 Mar 1950, Canada. Author; Illustrator of Childrens Books. m. Debra Kay Olson, 2 July 1988. *Education:* Ontario Coll of Art, 1973-74. *Appointments:* Art Galler of Ontario, 1976-84; Kids can Press, 1974-76. *Publications:* Mr Kneebones New Digs; Morgan the Magnificent; The Sparrows Song; Chin Chiang and the Dragons Dance. *Memberships:* Writers Union of Canada; Childrens Book Centre, Canada. *Honours include:* Mr Christie Award; Elizabeth Cleaver Award; Lode Illustration Award. *Hobbies:* Movies; Theatre; Music; Walking. *Address:* 184 Major Street, Toronto, Ontario, Canada M5S 2L3. 142.

WALLACE Robin John Garfield, b. 28 Mar 1964, Bournemouth, England. Profl Skier. m. Jullian Mary Curry, 1 Sept 1990. *Education:* The Open Univ. *Appointments:* RWI Sports Promotions Choreographer, Volvo Ski Show Coach of British Ski Team. *Publication:* Corporate Philosophy 1990. *Membership:* British Acrobatic Soprts Club. *Honours:* 8 Times British Champion Freestyle Skiing; 8th Place Ski Ballet; European Cup Ski Champion; European Freestyle Ski Vice Champion. *Hobbies:* Global Economy; Politics; Trampolining; Water Skiing; Music; Computers; Chess; Finance; Mathematics; Art; Drama; Genetics; Astronomy. *Address:* 61 Inverness Terrace, London W2, England.bblank

WALLACE Shaun Patrick, b. 20 Nov 1961, Christchurch, England. Profl Racing Cyclist. *Education:* Nottingham Univ, BSc. *Honours:* 8 Natl Cycling Champs Gold Medals; Commonwealth Games Silver Medal 4000m; Olympic Games, Los Angeles; World Record, Flying Start Kilometre; World Champs Stuttgart, Silver Medal 5000m. *Hobbies:* Anything on Wheels. *Address:* 3 Forest Road, Chandlers Ford, Eastleigh, Hants SO5 1NA, England.

WALLACH Joelle, b. 29 June 1956, New York City, USA. Composer. m. 27 Mar 1988. *Education:* Bach of Arts, Sarah Lawrence Coll, Bronxville, 1967; Master of Arts, Columbia Univ, 1969; Doc of Musical Arts, Manhattan Sch of Music, 1984. *Appointments include:* Lectr, LaGuardia Community Coll, 1974; Lectr, John Jay Coll, 1976; Lectr, Bronx Community Coll, 1974-76; Fordham Univ, Asst Prof of Music, 1981-83; Preceptor, Evaluations Conslt, Empire State Coll, 1984-87; Lincoln Center Inst, Tchrng Artist, 1990-; New York Philharmonic Orchestra, Pre Concert Lectr, 1990-. *Creative Works include:* Orchestral Works; Dramatic/ Stage Works; Chamber Works; Choral Works; Solo Instrumental Works. *Memberships include:* Womansong Intl; American Soc if Univ Composers; New Jersey Guild of Composers; American Women Composers; New York Women Composers. *Honours include:* First Universalist Church New Music Compt; Natl League of American Pen Women; Inter American Music Awards. *Hobbies:* Reading; Swimming.

WALLER Valerie Lane Gaither, b. 26 Feb 1964, Roanoke Rapids, NC, USA. Title Abstractor. m. Charles Warren Waller, 23 Aug 1986. *Education:* Univ of Carolina, 1984; Halifax Community Coll, Business Admin, 1986. *Appointments:* Sec, South Shore Realty, 1974-86; Sec, Lake Gaston Supply Co, 1986; Sec, Longview Baptist Church, 1986-88; Housewife, 1988-89; Louisa Title Agency Inc, 1989-. *Creative Works:* Scale Models, Monticello; 1914 Church structure. *Memberships:* Halifax Community Coll, Phi Theta Kappa; Inter Varsity Christian Fellowship; ALumni Assn Member; Natl Right to Life Member. *Honours:* Soc of Distinguished American High Sch Students; John Motley Morehead Award; US Natl Leadership Merit Award; Deans List; Presidents List. *Hobbies:* Music; Drawing; Pencil Sketches; cartoons; Charcoal Drawing. *Address:* Route 3, Box 3620, Bumpass, VA 23024, USA.

WALLING William R, b. 27 Aug 1959, Union City, TN, USA. Product Mgr. *Education:* Bach of Sci, Univ of Tenn, 1982; MA, Mercer Univ, Atlanta, 1987. *Appointments:* Leasametric Inc, Gaithersburg, GA, Credit Mgr, 1982-84; Eczel Corp, Norcross, GA, Acct Conslt, 1984-85; BCS Insc, Norcross GA, Sales & Mktng Mgr, 1985-86; Wm Hobbs Ltd, Mktng Conslt, 1987-88; American Conslitng Corp, Project Mgr, 1988-89; American Conslt Corp, Zone Mgr, 1989-90; OKI Telecom, Suwanee, GA, Product Mgr, 1990-. *Memberships:* American Mktng

Assn; Mercer Univ Alumni Assoc; Tenn Alumni Assoc. *Honour:* Outstanding Young Men of America. *Hobbies:* Swimming; Basketball; Tennis; Reading; Travel; Collecting Olympic Pins. *Address:* 3400 Sweetwater Road 904, Lawrenceville, GA 30244, USA. 7, 46.

WALMSLEY Norma E, b. 12 Apr 1920, Winnipeg, Man, Canada. Retired Prof; Social Activist. *Education:* B Comm, McGill Univ, 1950; MA, 1954; LLD, Carleton Univ, 1983; LLD, Brandon Univ, 1988. *Appointments include:* Prof Political Sci, Brandon Coll, Manitoba, 1955-67; Dir, Univ Resources Study, Assoc of Univ & Coll of Canada, 1967-70; Founder, Pres, MATCH Intl Centre, 1975-80; Life Member of Bd of Dir. *Publications include:* Canada's Response to the Intl Problem of Displaced Persons; Some Aspects of Canada's Immigration Policy; Canadian Univ & Intl Development. *Memberships include:* Canadian Government Delegation; World Conference UN Decade for Women, Copenhagen; Intl Development Intl Council; Intl Centre for Human Rights & Democratic Development. *Honours:* Queens Silver Jubilee Medal; Persons Award; Lewis Perinbam Award for Intl Development. *Hobbies:* Reading; Golf; Photography; Travel. *Address:* Box 68, Wakefield, Quebec, Canada J0X 3G0. 142.

WALSH Bernard David James, b. 12 July 1923, London, England. Chmn of a Social Security appeal Tribunal. m. Gladys Angela Margot Lees, 28 Aug 1954, 3 d. *Education:* Eton, 1937-41; Trinity Hall, Cambridge, 1941-43. *Appointments:* Royal Artillery, 1943; TA Service, Essex Yeomanry, RA, 1947; Barrister, Inner Temple, 1948-56; Govt Legal Serv, 1952; Asst Registrar of Criminal Appeals, 1962; In General Practice, 1969-. *Publications:* The Stour Valley Railway; Various Articles. *Memberships:* Railway Club; Stour Valley Railway Preservation Soc; Great Eastern Railway Soc. *Honour:* TD. *Hobbies:* Railway History & Operating; Photography. *Address:* The Old Rectory, Burgate, Diss, Norfolk IP22 1QD, England.

WALSH Thomas Joseph, b. 18 Sept 1931, USA. Ophthalmologist. *Education:* BA, Fordham Coll, MD, 1958; Resident Ophthalmologist, 1961-64; Bowman Gray Sch of Medicine, Bascom Palmer Eye Inst, 1964-65. *Appointments:* Instr, Assoc Prof, 1956-79; Prof, 1979-; Ophthalmology & Neurology, Yale Sch of Medicine; Suregon General, US Army, Wahington, DC, 1972-; Silver Hill Foundation, Connecticut, 1966-; Advisory Bd, Retinitis Pigmentosa Foundation, 1972-. *Publications include:* Textbook on Neuro Ophthalmology. *Contributions to:* Numerous Medical Journals. *Memberships include:* American Acad of Ophthalmology & Otolaryngology;American Acad of Neurology; American Connecticut & Fairfield Country Medical Assn; Soc of Medical Conslts to Armed Forces; American Coll of Surgeons; Oxford Ophthalmology Congress; American Assn of Neurological Surgeons. *Honours:* Centennial Fellow, Johns Hopkins Univ; Knight of Malta; Distinguished Alumni, Bowman Gray Sch of Medicine. *Hobby:* Collecting Model Soldiers. *Address:* 1100 Bedford Street, Stamford, CT 06905, USA. 2, 6, 52.

WALTERS Rebecca Ellis, B. 10 June 1955, Alaska, USA. Trauma, Emergency Clinical Nurse Specialist. m. Fred N Walters, 2 Nov 1979. *Education:* BSN, Univ of South Alabama, 1977; MSN, George Mason Univ, 1990; Grad Cert, Nursing Educ, 1990. *Appointments:* Staff Nurse, CVICU/SICU, 1977-79; Staff Nurse, Asst Hd Nurse, Hd Nurse, ICU/PACU/ER Doctors Hosp, 1979-81; Staff Nurse, ICU West Alabama General Hosp, 1981-82; Staff Nurse, ICU Doctors Hosp, 1982-83; Staff Nurse, Asst Nursing Coordinator, 1983-90; Trauma, ED Clinical Nurse Specialist, Mary Washington Hosp, 1990-. *Memberships:* American Nurses Assn; American Assn of Critical Care Nurses; Emergency Nurses Assn. *Honour:* Sigma Theta Tau. *Hobbies:* Reading; Gardening; Sewing. *Address:* 10311 Campbell Drive, Fredericksburg, VA 22408, USA. 7.

WALTON Amanda Loretta, b. 16 Sept 1941, Georgia, USA. Tchr; Educational Conslt. m. Van L Walton, 3 June 1966, 1 s, 1 d. *Education:* Medical Aid Training Sch, 1968; AA, BMCC, 1975; BA, York Coll, 1980; MS, 1983; Advanced Cert in Supervision & Admin, 1985. *Appointments:* Auxilary Trainer, New York City Bd of Educ, 1974-81; Tchr, New York City Bd of Educ, 1981-; Developed Read to Reading Club, 1989-; Established John Paul Rutgers Memorial Award. *Publications:* Developed Cool Cats Don't Smoke. *Memberships:* Intl Reading Assn; Manhattan Reading Council; Legislative Advisory Committee; Natl Notary Assn; Natl Assn for Female Exec; Manpower Outreach Centre 2; The American Biographical Inst Research Bd of Advisors. *Honours:* Merit Award; Recognition for Accomplishment Millen News, Millen, Georgia; CSIP Grant; Impact 11 Developer Grant; American Cancer Soc; Women of the Year; Key of Success Award. *Hobbies:* Reading; Bowling; Travel. *Address:* 221-39 112th Avenue, Queens Village, New York, NY 11429, USA. 5, 15, 138, 156, 191.

WALTON Ernest Ward, b. 10 July 1926, Newcastle Upon Tyne, England. Conslt Pathologist; Chmn, Cleveland Medical Lab Ltd. m. Greta Elizabeth Wray, 11 Oct 1957, 3 s, 1 d. *Education:* Medical Sch; Durham Univ; MB, BS, 1949; MD, 1957; MRC Path, 1963. *Appointments:* Natl Service RAMC East Africa, 1950-52; Deomonstrator in Pathogy, Univ of Durham, 1952-57; Lectr, Univ of St Andrews, 1957-60; Conslt Pathologist, North Tees Health District, 1960-91; Chmn, Cleveland Medical Lab Ltd, 1981-. *Publications:* Articles in Various Sci Journals. *Memberships include:* British Medical Assn; British Acad of Forensic Sci; Intl Acad of Pathology; Pathological Soc. *Honours:* TD; BMA, Scientific Prize. *Hobbies:* Justice of the Peace; Rotary Club; Travel; Fell Walking; Cross Country Skiing. *Address:* Cleveland Medical Lab Ltd, Letch Lane, Carlton, Stockton On Tees, Cleveland TS21 1EE, England.

WANG An Hua, b. 21 Oct 1935, Changzhi, Shanxi, China. Dir, Gansu Natural Energy Research Inst; Prof. m. Gao Bao Ying, 1 Jan 1958, 1 s, 3 d. *Education:* Xian Jiaotong Univ, 1958; Colorado State Univ, USA, 1983. *Appointments:* Elec Engr, Human & Gansu Prov, Design & Mgmt, 1958-78; Gansu Natural Energy Inst, Proj Mgr, Deputy Dir, Dir, 1978-; Solar Heating & Cooling Deomstration Centre, Natl Project Dir, 1986-87; Dev of DV Systems in Western China, Natl Project Mgr, 1988-. *Creative Works:* Build 1st Solar Water Heater Test Equip in China; Invention of TRS 1 Anto Freeze Type Solar Water Heater. *Memberships:* China Solar Energy Soc; Photo Thermal Commission; Rural Enery Commission, China Energy Soc; Western China Solar Assn. *Honours:* Gansu Provincial Oustanding Achievement in Sci & Tech Award; Gansu Provincial Innovative Achievement in Sci & Tech Award; Gansu Xinglong Cup, Gold Prize for Invention. *Hobbies:* Reading; Music. *Address:* Gansu Natural Energy Research Inst, 77 South Dingxi Road, Lanzhou 73000, China.

WANG Bing Hua, b. 25 Nov 1935, China. Archaelogist. m. Wang Lu Li, 31 Dec 1967, 2 s. *Education:* Peking Univ, 1955-60. *Appointments:* Inst of Archaelogy, Xingjang Acad of Sci, 1960-71; Xinjiang Historical museum, Research Assoc, 1972-77; Inst of Archaeology, Xinjiang Acad of Soc Sci, 1978-85; Xinjiang Inst of Archaeology, Dir of the Inst, Prof, of Archaeology, 1986-. *Publications:* Wushun Studies; The Ancient Civilization of Turfan; Tianshan petroglyph, A Testimony of Fertility Worship. *Memberships:* Xinjiang Silk Road Research Assn; Dunhuang Turfan Research Assn; American Rock Art Research Assn. *Honours:* The Ancient Civilization at Turfan; Wushun Studies, Outstanding Works on Social Sci; Meritorious Scientific Worker. *Hobby:* Reading. *Address:* Xinjiang Inst of Archaeology, 4B South Beijing Road, Urumqi, Xinjiang 830011, China.

WANG Chao Cheng, b. 20 July 1938, China. m. 24 Aug 1963, 2 s. *Education:* BS, Natl Taiwan Univ, 1959; PhD, Johns Hopkins Univ, 1965; PE, 1991. *Appointments:* Asst Prof, Assoc Prof, Johns Hopkins Univ, 1966-68; Prof, Rice Univ, 1968-; Chmn, Math Sci Dept, Rice Univ, 1983- 89; Chmn, Mech Engrng & Mat Sci, Rice Univ, 1991-. *Publications:* Five Books; Over 70 Research Papers. *Memberships:* Am Acad Mechanics; Soc Natural Philosophy. *Honours:* Distinguished Young Sci; Noah Harding Chair. *Address:* Dept of Mech Engrng & Mat Sci, Rice Univ, PO Box 1892, Houston, TX 77251, USA. 2.

WANG Cheng Xu, b. 15 June 1912, Jiangyin. Educator. m. Duanying Zhao, 6 Aug 1939, 2 s. *Education:* BEd, Zhejiang Univ, 1936; Tchrs Diploma, Univ of London, 1940; MA, 1941. *Appointments:* Prof of Educ, Chmn of Dept of Educ, Zhejiang Univ, 1946-52; Prof Educ, Chmn of Dept of Educ, Deputy Dean, Zhejiang Tchrs Coll, 1952-57; Prof of Educ, Dept of Educ, Hangzhou Univ, 1958-. *Publications:* Postwar English Primary Education; Comparative Education; Readings in Western Educational Works; Postwar English Education. *Memberships:* Natl Comparative Educ Soc; Natl History of Educ Soc; Natl Higher Education Assn; Natl Tad Xing Zhi Soc; Zhejiang Provincial Higher Educ Assn; Zhejian Provincial Toa Xing Zhi Soc. *Honour:* Natl Educational Works Award. *Hobbies:* Mountain Climbing; Physical Exercise. *Address:* Dept of Education, Hangzhou Univ, Hangzhou 310028, China.

WANG Ching Yue, b. 26 Oct 1938, Hebei Province, China. Prof Laser Field. m. Junjuan Zhang, 1 Feb 1958, 3 s. *Education:* Physical Dept of Chinese Sci & Tech, Univ of China, 1963. *Appointments:* Asst Lectr, Lectr, Tainjin Univ, 1963-80; Visiting Scholar, Univ of Southern California, 1980-82; Lectr, Prof, Tianjin Univ, 1982. *Publications:* Introduction to Laser Physics; Modern Optical Experiments: 41 Papers in Optics Letters. *Memberships:* SPIE; Editorical Bd of Chinese Journal of Lasers; Chinese Journal of Quantum Electronics. *Honours:* Awards for Sci & Tech Progress from Natl Educ Council of China. *Hobbies:* Sports; Classical Music. *Address:* Dept of Precision Instrument Engrng, Tianjin Univ, Tianjin, China 300072.

WANG Dazhuang, b. 30 Nov 1936, Jinan, China. m. Shufen Wang, 1 s, 1 d. *Appointments:* Asst Art Editor, Heilongjiang TV Station, 1959-79; Editor, Heilongjiang TV Station Programming, 1980; Chief of Cultural Life, 1981-84; Editor, Synthesis Program Dept, 1985-86; Chief Editor, Foreign Affairs Dept, 1987-. *Publications:* Chinese Cartoon Art; Theoratical Essays on Cartoon; About 10 Papers; 1000 Cartoons Publi. *Memberships include:* Chinese Artist Assn; Chinese Broadcasting Studies; Cartoonist Federation of Provinces & Metropolitan Cities; Heilongjiang Press Art Soc; Heilongjiang Cartoonist Soc; Harbin Artist Assn. *Honours:* 1st Prize, Jinan City; 2nd Prize Shandong Youth Art Exhib8 1st Prize Satire & Humour Monthly; Prizes for TV Documentary Programs. *Address:* 5 Wenlin Street, Room 273, Harbin, Heilongjiang, China.

WANG De Bing, b. 11 Nov 1937, Henan, China. Doctor; Prof. m. 3 Aug 1963, 1 s, 1 d. *Education:* Medical Degree, Beijing Medical Univ, 1960. *Appointments:* Hysician, Chief Resident, Attending Doctor, Assoc Prof of Internal Medicine in Haematology, Peoples Hosp, 1960-81; Dir, Peoples Hosp, 1981-87; Prof, Vice Pres, 1987-; Visiting Assoc Prof, Einstein Medical Coll, USA, 1983-84; Intl Kellogg Medical Foundation Fellow in Health Programme, USA, 1986-89. *Publications include:* Acute Promyelocytic Leukemia; Allogeneic Bone Marrow Transplatation; Scanning Electron Microscopic Observation On Cells of Splastic Anemia & Paroxysmal Hemoglobinurea. *Memberships:* Chinese Medical Assn; Chinese Haematology; Chinese Oncology. *Honours:* Honorary Advisor, Beijing Hong Kong Acad Exchange Center. *Hobbies:* Music; Sport. *Address:* Beijing Medical Univ, 38 Xue Yuan Road, Beijing 100083, China.

WANG Dong Fang, b. 7 Mar 1937, Changchn, China. Tectonics & Structure on Geology. m. Yu Qin Lie, 20 Sept 1962, 2 s, 1 d. *Education:* Beijing Univ, 1961; Chinese Coll of Lawyer, 1987. *Appointments:* Snr Researcher, Shenyang Inst of Geology & Mineral Resources, CAGS, 1961-. *Publications:* 70 Papers in Journals. *Memberships:* Geol Assn of China; Assn of Geochemistry & Mineralogy of China. *Honours include:* 4 Prizes for Research, MGMR China; 2 Prizes for Excellent Papers from Sci & Tech Assn; Prize on the Discovery of a New Fauna of Early Cambrian Small Shelly Fossil. *Hobbies:* Sports; Touring. *Address:* Shenyang Inst of Geology & Mineral Resources, Beiling St No.25, 110032 Shenyang, China.

WANG Hong-Gang, b. 20 Dec 1929, Tianjin, China. Prof. m. July 1954, 1 d. *Education:* BA, Yunnan Univ, 1951; MS, Haerbin Univ, 1955. *Appointments:* Lectr, KIT, 1955-78; Assoc Prof, 1978-85; Prof, 1985-; Dean of Dept of Basic Sci, 1981-83; Vice Pres, 1983-88; Dir of Research Lab of Engrng Mech, 1985-. *Publications:* The Theory of Thermoelasticity; 36 Treatises on Thermoelasticity. *Memberships:* Mechanics Soc of China; Mechanics Soc of Yunnan Province; Applied Mathematics & Mechanics. *Honours:* Sci Research Achievement; Silver Medal of Intl Invention Exhib. *Hobbies:* Music; Art. *Address:* Dept Architectural Engineering & Mechanics, Kunming Institute of Technology, Kunming 650093, Yunnnan, China. 139, 151, 152.

WANG Hui, b. 10 Oct 1959, China. Assoc Prof. *Education:* Yangzhou Tchrs Coll, BA, 1978-82; MA, 1982-84; Chinese Acad of Social Sci, PhD, 1985-88. *Appointments:* Lectr, Inst of Literature, CASS, 1988-90; Assoc Prof, 1990-. *Publications:* A Revolt Against Desperation; Prediction & Crisis: The May 4th Enlightenment in Modern Chinese History; The destiny of Mr Sci in Modern China. *Memberships:* Inst of Literature of Chinese Acad of Social Sci. *Hobbies:* Swimming; Music; Reading. *Address:* Institute of Literature, Chinese Academy of Social Sci, Beijing 100732, China.

WANG Huning, b. 6 Oct 1955, Shanghai, China. Prof of Political Sci; Chmn. m. Zhou Qi, 7 Jan 1983. *Education:* BA, East China Normal Univ, 1977; MA, Fudan Univ, 1981. *Appointments:* Research Fellow, Shanghai Acad of Social Sci, 1977-78; Faculty Member, Dept of Intl politics, Fudan Univ, 1981-. *Publications:* Sovereignty of State; A Comparative Analysis of Politics; Ecological Analysis of Administration; Political Sci in Contemporary World; America Versus America; Counter Corruption. *Memberships include:* Chinese Assn of Political Sci; Shanghai Intl Studies Centre; Shanghai Social Sci Assn. *Honours:* Stein Pokian Memorial Award; Shanghai Prominent Young Tchrs award; Huo Yindong Award fpr Prominent Prof. *Hobbies:* Reading; Music. *Address:* Dept of International Politics, Fudan University, 220 Han Dan Road, Shanghai, China 200433.

WANG Ji Quan, b. 5 June 1932, Shaoxing, Zhejiang Province, P R China. Prof of Chinese Dept; Vice Dir, Modern Literature Research Section. m. Xia Shengyuan, 3 Mar 1956, 1 d. *Education:* Fudan Univ, 1956-61. *Appointments:* Huangpu District, Shanghai, 1951-56; Tchr, Chinese Dept, Fudan Univ, 1961-. *Publications:* History of Chinese Modern Literature; Dictionary of Chinese Modern Literature; Chronicle of Guo Moruos Life; Chinese Modern Novels. *Memberships:* Chinese Modern Literature Soc; Chinese Luxan Reserch Inst; Chinese Guo Moruo Research Inst; Soc of Historical Materical for Literature; Chinese Southern Soc. *Hobby:* Reading. *Address:* Chinese Dept, Fudan University, Shanghai, China.

WANG Ji Zu, b. 24 Oct 1922, China. Prof. m. Xi Ru Guo, Nov 1958, 1 s, 1 d. *Education:* BA, Natl Political Univ, Nanking, 1946; MA, Univ of Missouri, Columbia, 1951; PhD, Univ of Illinois, 1954. *Appointments:*

Research Assoc, Inst of Intl Relations, Acad of Sci of China, 1957-60; Research Assoc of Inst of Economics, Nankai Univ, 1962-81; Prof of Finance, 1982-. *Publications:* Economic Crises; Inflation & Principle of World Economy; More Than 30 Articles. *Memberships:* American Economic Assn; Finance Assn of Tianjin; Foreign Trade Assn of Tianjin; Intl Finance Assn of North China. *Honours include:* Award for Outstanding Tchrng. *Hobbies:* Reading; Table Tennis; Cinema. *Address:* Finance Dept, Nankai Univ, Weijin Road, Tianjin, China.

WANG Jia Long, b. 4 Sept 1935, Beijing, China. Assoc Prof. m. Jin Hsia Yu, 20 Jan 1966, 2 s. *Education:* Dept of Geophysics, Beijing Univ, 1962. *Appointments:* Asst Prof, Beijing Astronomical Observatory, Acad Sinica, 1977; Assoc Prof, 1986; Chief of Solar Acitivity Prediction Centre. *Publications:* 60 Papers; Book, Solar Flares; The Quiet Sun. *Memberships:* Intl Astronomical Union; Chinese Astronomical Union; Chinese Soc of Space Sci. *Honours:* Cert of Successful Contribution to Intern Sci Coop; 1st Class Prize, Solar Activity Prediction; 3rd Class Prize, Multi Wavelength Research of Solar Flares. *Hobbies:* Sport; Football; Table Tennis; Research, Solar Physics. *Address:* Centre of Solar Activity Prediction, Beijing Astronomical Observatory, Chinese Academy of Science, Beijing 100080, China.

WANG Kang-Le, b. 30 Oct 1907, Fenghua, Zhejiang. Chinese Painter. m. Huang Mulan, 1929, 3 s, 2 d. *Education:* Shushou Profl Art Coll, 1947. *Appointments:* Self Employed. *Creative Works:* Wang Kang Le's Paintings, Public Peoples Art Press. *Memberships:* Shanghais Assn of Zhang Daqians Pupils; Chinese Painting Soc for Old People; Shanghai Cultural History Inst; Shanhais Chinese Painting Assn. *Hobbies:* Music; Reading. *Address:* Rm 602, no.4, Lane 430, Xianxia Road, Shanghai, China 200335.

WANG Kangfu, b. 17 Oct 1928, Anqing, Anhui, China. Forestry, Dune Stablization, Desertification, Plant Acology. m. Jiang Jing, 8 Dec 1956, 1 s, 1 d. *Education:* Forestry Dept, Anhui Univ, 1949-53. *Appointments:* Dune Stablization, 1953-57; Dune Fixation & Railway Protection, 1958-69, 1977-82; Sand Control in Inner Mongolia, 1970-76, 1983- 91. *Publications:* Sand Hazard Control Along Railway; Desertification & Rehabilitation; Fixation of Mobile Dunes. *Memberships:* China Desert Soc; China Forestry Soc. *Honours:* 2nd Prize, Sci & Tech Advancement; Zhu Kezhens Proze; Top Prize of Natl Sci & Tech Advancement. *Hobbies:* PingPong Tennis; Chinese Chess; Gardening; Reading. *Address:* Institute of Desert Research, Academia, 174 Donggang West Road, Lanzhou 730000, Gansu, China,

WANG Li Ding, b. 2 Dec 1934, China. Fine Mech Prof. m. 20 Feb 1956, 2 s, 1 d. *Education:* Jilin Univ of Tech, 1960. *Appointments:* Chanchun Inst of Optics & Fine Mech, 1960-. *Publications:* Grinding Super Precise Gear by the Y7431 Gear grinding Machine; Grinding Teeth of High Precise Harmonic Transimission Ridig Wheel & Soft Wheel; Studing & Manufacture of Standard Gear with Modula Two; Method of Improve the Accurate of Gear Circular Pitch by a Gear Grinding Machine with a Dividing Plate. *Memberships:* Chinese Mech Engrng Soc; Chinese Fine Mech Engrng Soc. *Honours:* Natl Meeting of Sci; Researching Prize of China Acad of Sci; Natl Sci & Tech Program Prize; Honor of Talent Having Great Achievement of Sci Research; Researching Prize of Chinese Acad of Sci. *Hobby:* Football. *Address:* Changchun Institute of Optics & Fine Mechanics, China.

WANG Pelhua, b. 20 Dec 1935, Hebei, China. m. Zhang Junhua, 31 Dec 1961, 2 d. *Education:* Beijing Medical Univ, 1955-60. *Appointments:* Physical Exam to Donors, 1960-65; Donor Reg & Propaganda Work, 1965-70; Protein Fract, 1971-73; Deputy dir, Tech Work, 1973-84; Dir, All Work of Beijing Red Cross Blood Center, 1984-. *Publications:* Blood Component Therapy; Administration of Blood Center; Some Papers. *Memberships:* Beijing Red Cross Blood Center; Beijing Red Cross Blood Inst; Chinese Soc of Blood Transfusion;

Beijing Blood Transfusion. *Honours:* 2nd Award of Sci & Tech of Beijing Health Bureau; Sci & Tech of Imunicipality. *Hobbies:* Basketball; Table Tennis. *Address:* Beijing Red Cross Blood Center, No.1 Beihuan Xilu, Beijing, China 100088.

WANG Qianwei, b. 15 Jan 1940, China. Deputy Dir; Snr Engr. m. Liu Jingde, 25 June 1963, 2 d. *Education:* Tsinghua Univ, Beijing, 1958-64. *Appointments include:* The Step Design Method of the Bucket Energy Dissipators, Publi in Handbook of Hydraulic Calculations; 10 Results Obtained from my Researchs used in Practical Engrng. *Memberships:* Guangdong Provincial Soc of Hydroelectric Engrng; Guangdong Hong Kong Macao Promoting Assn of Economic Relations; Guangdong Provincial Quality Control Center of Water Conservatory & Hydropower. *Honours:* Guangdong Provincial Excellent Worker of Water Conservatory & Hydropower. *Hobbies:* Reading; Sports. *Address:* Guangdong Provincial Research Inst of Water Conservatory & Hydropower, Guangdong, China.

WANG Shou-ren, b. 8 Jan 1955, Shuzhou, China. Assoc Prof of English. m. You Lan Pan, 25 July 1983, 1 s. *Education:* BA, Nanjing Univ, 1983; MA, London Univ, 1985; PhD, 1988. *Appointments:* Lectr, Dept of Foreign Languages & Literature, Nanjing Univ, 1989-90; Assoc Prof, 1991-; Dir of English Faculty, 1991-. *Publications:* The Theatre of the Mind; Articles in Profl Journals. *Memberships:* American Literature Assn; Foreign Literature Assn. *Honours:* Social Sci Award; Man of Achievement. *Hobbies:* Calligraphy; Music; Reading. *Address:* Dept of Foreign Language & Literature, Nanjing Univ, Nanjing 210008, China.

WANG Shujin, b. 3 May 1956, China. Information Chief. m. Wan Yi, 1 Feb 1983, 1 s. *Education:* Amhui Agricl Coll, BS, 1982; Beijing Agricl Engrng Univ, MS, 1984. *Appointments:* Tchrng Asst, Nanjing Agricl Univ, 1985-86; Lectr, Researcher, 1987-91; Information Chief, Guangdong Jianlibao group Co Ltd, 1992-. *Publications:* Strategem & Skills for Private Business; How To Run The Sino Foreign Joint Venture. *Hobbies:* Reading; Chess; Table Tennis. *Address:* College of Agricl Econ & Trade, Nanjing Agricl Univ, Nanjing 210014, China.

WANG Shulin, b. 21 May 1932, Tianjin, China. Prof. m. Mei Duolun, 12 Feb 1961, 1 s, 1 d. *Education:* Peking Univ, 1955. *Appointments:* Inst of Math, Acad Sinica, 1955-56; Inst of Computing Technology, 1956-; Computing Centre, USSR Acad of Sci, 1957-58. *Publications include:* Over 50 Microprogramming & Its Applications; The Theory of Knowledge Representation; The Design Principles About Expert Systems. *Memberships include:* China Artificial Intelligence Assn; CIPSC; Chengdu Inst of Computer Application. *Hobbies:* Classical Music; Travel; Taichi. *Address:* Institue of Computing Technology, Academia Sinica, Beijing 100080, China.

WANG Tso Ren, b. 30 June 1943, Taiwan. Prof of Paediatrics. m. Yea Maei peng Wang, 8 Feb 1972, 1 s, 1 d. *Education:* MD, Taiwan Univ, 1970; Genetic Fellow, 1980-81; Rutgers Medical Sch. *Appointments:* Internship, 1960-70; Natl Taiwan Univ Hosp, 1976-82; Lectr, Coll of Medicine, 1982-85; Assoc Prof, 1985-; Prof. *Publications:* Clinical Pediatrics; Health & Diseases in Childhood; Glossary of Medical Genetics; Genetic Counselling; Medical Genetics. *Memberships include:* Am soc of Human Genetics; Chinese Taipei Paediatrics assn; Asian & Oceanian Assn of Child Nuerology. *Honours:* Best Paper Award; Best Research award. *Hobbies:* Football; Jogging. *Address:* No.8 Lane 20 Section 3, Jin Ai Road, Taipei, Taiwan, China. 52.

WANG Tze Ching, b. 26 Mar 1941, P R China. m. 14 Feb 1963, 1 d. *Education:* Nankai Univ, Tainjin, 1958-63. *Appointments:* Asst Research Fellow, Prof, Inst of

Zoology, Academia Sinica, 1963-. *Publications:* Handbook of Scale Insects; Economic Insect Fauna of China; The Scale Insects of Agricl Regions from china; Lac & Lac Cultivation. *Membership:* Entomological Soc of China. *Hobbies:* Swimming; Trumpet; Violin; Cultivating Flowers; Dogs. *Address:* Inst of Zoology, Academia Sinica, Beijing, China.

WANG Wang Caihua, b. 7 Nov 1936, China. Prof. m. 1 Oct 1969, 1 s, 1 d. *Education:* Bach of Engrng, Dept of Mech, Changging Univ, 1961. *Appointments:* Asst, Changgging Univ, 1961-78; Lectr, 1979-86; Assoc Prof, 1987-; Guest Prof, Guangzhou Univ, 1989-. *Publications include:* Fuzzy Theory Methodology; Fuzzy Comprehensive Evaluation of Engrng Design Parameters with Two Steps; Fuzzy Finite Element Method; Solutions of Structural Fuzzy Equilibrium Equations. *Honour:* Natl Natural Sci Foundation of China. *Hobby:* Gardening. *Address:* Dept of Engrng Mech, Changqing Univ, Changqing 630044, China.

WANG Xiao Ming, b. 15 Nov 1924, China. Prof of Phathophysiology. m. 1 May 1951, 1 s, 3 d. *Education:* Chinese Medical Univ, 1947; Sch of Moscow, 1st Medical Inst USSR, 1956-59. *Appointments:* Tchrng Asst, CMU, 1948; Instr, Harbin Medical Univ, 1951; Assoc Prof, 1962; Prof, Dean of Medical Basic SCi, HMU, 1978; Prof, Vice Pres, HMU, 1980; Prof, Chmn, 1985-. *Publications:* Text Book of Pathophysiology; Antigen Acts as Nervous System; Topics of Medical Basic Sci; Physiology of Endocrine Glands; Chinese Russian Dictionary; Text Book of Pathophysiology. *Memberships:* Chinese Pathophysiology Soc; Intl Soc for Heart Research; Heilingjiang Physiological Sci Soc; Harbin Sci & Tech Assn. *Honours:* Honorary Dir Heilongjiang Medical Basic Sci Inst; 1st Rate Prize for Sci Research; Heilongjiang Sci Advanced Prize. *Hobbies:* Foreign Language; Literature; Music; Sports. *Address:* Dept Pathophysiology, Harbin Medical Univ, Xuefu Road, Harbin, Heilongjiang, China.

WANG Xiao-feng Han cuan, b. 22 Nov 1951, China. Artist. m. Zhang Ye Qin, 13 May 1979, 1 s. *Education:* Lu Xun Art Inst, 1986; Guang Zhou arts Inst, 1990. *Appointments:* Art Designer, 1966-79; Chinese Painting Creator 1979-84; Artist, Qiqihar Painting & Calligraphy Coll, 1984-91. *Creative Works include:* Deep of Xing an Mountain; Bank of Heilongjiang River; The Living Early Spring; Life. *Memberships:* Heilongjiang Branch Chinese Artist Assn; Heilongjiang Chinese Painting Research Inst; Henan Yeng Bin Painting & Calligraphy Research Inst; Henan Shaolin Painting & Calligraphy Inst. *Honours:* 2nd Class Art Creative Award; Enrolled, Data Dictionary of Chinese Artists; Enrolled, Name Dictionary of Chinese Artists. *Hobbies:* Classical Poems & Music. *Address:* Qiqiahr Chinese Painting & Calligraphy Institute, Heilongjian Province, China.

WANG Xitong, b. 10 Nov 1933. Prof. m. Daiyao He, 10 Feb 1961, 2 s. *Education:* Dept of Agricl Economics, Southwest Agricl Univ, 1953; Peoples Univ of China, 1956. *Appointments:* Asst, Tianjin Tchrs Univ, 1956-57; Asst, Southwest Agricl Univ, 1957-63; Lectr, 1963-83; Assoc Prof, 1983-86; Prof, Dir. *Publications include:* Chinas Socialist Agricl Economics; Foreign Agricl Economics; Economics of Agricl Natural Resources; On Problems of Economics in Exploitation of Natural Resources. *Memberships include:* Assn of Agricl Economics of China;Assoc of Agricl Economics of Chongqing; Assn of Foreign Agricl Economics of China. *Honours include:* Excellent Tchr Award; Excellent Research Achievements of Social Sci of Sichuan Province. *Hobbies:* Poetry; Literature. *Address:* Dept of Agricl Economics, Southwest Agricl Univ, Beibei, Chongqing, China.

WANG Xueren, b. 13 Sept 1934, Yunnan, China. Prof. m. Yang Mingfang, 24 Aug 1960, 2 s. *Education:* Yunnan Univ, 1953057; Beijing Univ, 1958-60. *Appointments:* Lectr, Prof, Hd of Dept, Yunnan Univ, 1957-90; Prof, Hd of Dept, Coll YU, 1990-. *Publications include:*

Mathematical Geology; Applied probability & Mathematical Statistics; Applied Regression Analysis; Numerous Papers. *Honours include:* 1st Class Prize of Sci Conference of china; 2nd Class Prize of the Southwest Co of Geology Exploration; 1st Class Prize of Univ of Yunnan Province; 1st Class Prize of Academia Sinica of China. *Address:* Dept of Statistics, Yunnan Univ, Kunming 650091, Yunnan, China.

WANG Yi-He, b. 26 Mar 1935, Shanghai, China. Full Prof. m. Bai Zheng Jie, 1 Sept 1971, 1 s. *Education:* BSc, Jiaotong Univ, China, 1959. *Appointments:* Tchr, Lectr, Assoc Prof, Full Prof, 1959-; Deputy Dir, Computer Centre, 1981-88; Dir, Engrng Research Centre, 1988-. *Publications:* Principles of Digital Computers; Microcomputer Interfacing, Principles & Applications; Distributed Data Base Systems; System Design of Graphics Display; Design & Implementation of a Front End Computer; Design of Token Bus Protocols; Distributed Hotel System Based on PC & LAN. *Memberships:* IEEE; China Inst of Integrated Office Automation; Computer Users Assn; Xian Computer Inst; ELectronic Engrs Mag. *Honours:* Prize, Graphics Display Project, China Natl Sci Conference; Tech Papers, Natl Network & Applications Conference; 2nd Prize, State Council of China; 2nd Prize Promoting Sci & Tech Natl Comm of Educ; Honorary Dir, Suzhou Research Inst of Information Tech. *Address:* Engrng Research Centre of Information Systems, Xian Jiaotong Univ, Xian, Shaanxi Province, China.

WANG Yong, b. 27 July 1945, Beijing, China. Art Critic. m. Zhang Ying, 18 Sept 1971, 1 d. *Education:* Peking Univ, BA, 1962-67; Indian Arts & Aesthetics, 1978-81; Advanced study, Visvabharati Univ, India, 1987-88. *Appointments:* Asst Research Fellow, Chinese Acad of Social Sci, 1981-83; Assoc Research Fellow, Fine arts Research Inst, China Acad of arts, 1983-. *Publications include:* Indian Aesthetics; Indian Art; Greater Encyclopedia of China; Translated Works. *Memberships:* Fine Arts Research Inst; China Acad of arts; Artists Assn; South Asia Soc of China. *Hobbies:* Poetry; Calligraphy. *Address:* Fine Arts Research Institute, China acad of Arts, 17 Qianhai Xi Jie, Beijing 100009, China.

WANG Yongji, b. 11 Nov 1939, Liaoning, China. Research Prof. m. Xiaowei Xu, 1 Jan 1970, 2 d. *Education:* Beijing Univ, Bach Degree, 1959-65. *Appointments:* Research Asst, Inst Oceano, 1965-78; Research Assc, 1978-85; Research Prof, 1985-. *Publications:* Late Quaternary Sedimentation in the Yellow sea; The Algae & Sporor Pollen in the Sediments of the Yellow sea. *Memberships:* Intl Soc of Palynology; Intl Soc of Sedimentology; China Natl Assn of Oceanology; 1st Inst of Oceanography. *Hobbies:* Swimming; Fishing; Stamp Collecting; Music. *Address:* 1st Inst of Oceanography, State Oceanic Admin, PO Box 98, 13 Hongdao Road, Qingdao 266003, Shandong Province, China. 162.

WANG Yongquan, b. 5 Aug 1929, Shanghai, China. Univ Prof. m. Bao Xiaolou, 14 Feb 1953, 2 s. *Education:* BS, Tsinghua Univ, 1950. *Appointments:* Chmn, Peking Univ, 1958-76; Vice Pres, 1976-78; Dir, 1979-80; Dir, Inst of Higher Educ, Peking univ, 1980-; Provast, 1984-86. *Publications:* A Study of China Higher Educ Structure; The structure & Governance of Chinese Higher Educ; On the Rational structure of Univ Faculty in Reasearch in Economics of Educ. *Memberships include:* Chinas Assn for Higher Educ; Chinese Comparative Educ Assn; IAU. *Honours include:* Excellent Educational Research, 1st Prize; Excellent Research Paper Prize; Excellent Researches on Social Sci. *Hobby:* Basketball. *Address:* Inst of Higher Education, Peking Univ, Beijing 100871, China. 152.

WANG Yu-zhu, b. 29 Feb 1932, Hebei, China. Prof. m. Hui Juan He, 17 Mar 1961, 2 d. *Education:* Qing Hua Univ, 1955; phD, Academia USSR, 1960. *Appointments:* Asst Prof, Beijing Inst, 1961-64; Assoc Prof, Shanghai Inst, 1964-; Prof, Dir of Lab, SIOM, 1978-

. *Publications:* Laser Cooling of Gass Atoms Using Light Frequency Shift Effect; Test of Photon Statistics; Micro Spherical Laser Induced by Cavity QED Effect. *Memberships:* Intl Theoretical Physics; Center of Chinese High Tech & Sci; IQEC. *Honours:* Natl Prize of Sci & Tech Progress; Chinese Physical Soc; Natl Natural Sci Prize. *Hobbies:* Music; Travel. *Address:* Joint Lab for Quantum Optics, Shanghai Inst of Optics & Fine Mechanics, Academia Sincia & East China Normal Univ, PO Box 800-211, Shanghai, China.

WANG Yun Xi, b. 29 June 1926, Shanghai, China. Dir; Prof. m. Li Yang Die, 14 Oct 1962, 2 s. *Education:* BA, Fudan Univ, 1947-52; Lectr, 1952-60; Assoc Prof, 1960-78; Prof, 1978-; Dir, Chinese Language & Literature Inst, 1981-. *Publications:* Numerous Essays; Research in Wenxindlaolong. *Memberships:* China Tang Dynesty Literature Soc; China Ancient Literary Theory Soc; China Soc of Li Bai Studies; Chinese Ancient Literary Research Assn; Shanghai Authors Assn. *Honours:* Excellent Coll Tchrng Material Award; Award Outstanding Works on Humanities & Social Sci. *Address:* Dept of Chinese Language & Literature, Fudan Univ, Shanghai 200070, China. 139.

WANG Zhen-guo, b. 12 Aug 1954, Jilin, China. Chinese Trad Medical Researcher. m. 22 Feb 1979, 2 s. *Education:* Tong Hua Tchrs Coll, BA, 1982-85. *Appointments:* Janghua Baishan Pharmacology Works, 1977-83; Sec, Dept of Tanghua County 1983-84; Governmental Office, 1984-85; Governmental Office, Tonghua City, 1985-87; Jilin Anti cancer AZssn, 1988-. *Publications:* The Anti Cancer Treatment Observation & Experimental Research of Chinese Herbal Medicine Compound; Toyo Medicine. *Memberships:* Changbaishan Inst of Pharmacology; Intl Rehabilitation of Cancer Assn; China Anti Cancer Foundation; Jilin Provincial Assn. *Honours:* Premier Research Prize; 1 of 10 Outstanding Youth of China. *Hobbies:* Researching Anto Cancer; Literature; Swimming. *Address:* The Changbaishan Inst of Pharmacology, Jilin Province Anto Cancer Assn, China, 77- 1 Shengli Road, Tong Hua City, Jilin Province, China 134000. 152.

WANG Zhenduo, b. 6 July 1911, Hebei Province, China. Prof. m. Zhao Zhinan, July 1948, 2 d. *Education:* Yenching Univ, 1935. *Appointments:* Natl Central Museum, Nanjing, 1938-49; Prof of Museology, Beijing, 1950-73; Prof, Museum of Chinese History, 1973-. *Publications:* Papers in Tech Archaology. *Memberships:* Chinese Museum Assn; Natl Committee for Cultural Relics; China Soc Archaeology. *Honours:* Yang Quan Prize for the Humanities. *Hobby:* Calligraphy. *Address:* Museum of Chinese History, Beijing 100006, China.

WANG Zhibao, b. 30 Jan 1938, Tianjin, China. Prof. m. 23 Dec 1967, 1 s, 1 d. *Education:* Nankai Univ, 1964. *Appointments:* Asst, Nankai Univ, 1964-80; Lectr, 1980-83; Lectr, Dept of Computer & System Sci, 1984-86; Assoc Prof, 1986-90; Prof, 1990-. *Publications include:* Man Machine Interface Handling System on Expression in CADCS; Control System CAD Software System Design; design Control System CAD Software System. *Memberships:* Chinese Assn of System Simulation; Tianjin Assn of Computers; Tianjin Assn of Automation; Micro Minicomputer Development & Application. *Honours:* Excellent Paper Award; Advanced Member Award; Advanced Civector Award. *Hobbies:* Calligraphy; Biographies of Famour Persons; Book of Literature; Touring. *Address:* Dept of Computer & System Sci, Nankai Univ, Balitai, Tianjin, China.

WANG Zhijiang, b. 15 Oct 1930, Zhejiang, China. Prof; Dir. m. Gu Maihing, Sept 1955, 2 s, 1 d. *Education:* BS, Inst of Tech, 1952. *Appointments:* Changchun Inst of Optics, Researcher, 1952-64; Shanghai Inst Optics, Assoc Prof, 1964-78; Prof, Vice Dir, 1978-84; Prof, Dir, 1984-91. *Publications:* Fundamental of Optical Design Theory; Imaging Optics; Over 150 Papers. *Memberships:* Optical Soc of America; SPIE; Optical Soc of China.

Address: Shanghai Inst of Optics & Fine Mechanics, PO Box 8211, Shanghai, China 201800. 139.

WANG Zhixian, b. 1 July 1936, Wuhan, China. Prof; Deputy Dir. m. Shuqin Yin, 10 Feb 1965, 2 s. *Education:* Harbin Medical Univ, MD, 1950-56; Univ of California, 1984-86. *Appointments:* Asst, 1956-63; Research Assoc, 1963-77; Asst Prof, 1977-83; Assoc Prof, 1983-89; Deputy Dir, 1988-; Full Prof of Pathology, 1989-. *Publications:* Atlas of the Cochlea By Light & Electron Microscopy; 2 Books; 102 Papers. *Memberships:* Intl Commission on Occupational Health; Chinese Electron Microscopy Soc; Pathology, Chinese Medical Assn; Chinese Soc of Ind Hygiene & Occupational Disease. *Honours include:* 2nd Prize Scientific & Tech Progress. *Hobbies:* Music; photography; Table Tennis. *Address:* Institute of Hygiene & Environmental Medicine, 1 Da Li Dao, Tianjin 300050, China.

WANG Zhongde, b. 19 Mar 1937, Jiangsu Province, china. Prof. m. Manging He, 31 Jan 1965, 2 s. *Education:* Yunnan Univ, 1960. *Appointments:* Research Asst, Kunning Inst of Physics, 1960-78; Engr, 1978-80; visiting Scholar, Univ Arizona, USA, 1980-82; Research Assoc, 1982- 83; Assoc Research Prof, Kunming Inst of Phy, 1983-87; Assoc Prof, Beijing Univ, 1987-88; Prof, 1988-; Visiting Scientist, 1990-. *Publications:* Theory of Discrete & Continuous Fourier Analysis; Numerous Papers. *Memberships:* Chinese Inst of Electronics; IEEE; American Mathematical Soc; Chinese Inst of Telecommunications. *Honours include:* Natl Specialist with Outstanding Contribution; Advanced Science & Tech; Outstanding Paper. *Hobbies:* Weigi; Chinese Chess. *Address:* Box 93, Dept of Telecommunication Engrng, Beijing Univ of Posts & Telecommunications, Beijing 100088, China. 52.

WANG Zhongtang, b. 20 July 1929, Shaanxi, China. Coal Geologist. m. 30 Dec 1961, 1 s, 3 d. *Education:* Northwest Univ, 1948-52. *Appointments:* Office of Coalfied Geology of North China, Geology Engr, Chief Engr, 1952-64; Coal Line Construction Bureau, Chief Engr, 1965-73; Geological Bureau of China, Snr Engd Prof, 1973-90. *Publications:* Some Characterstic Structures of the Shansi Coal Bearing Regions; Coal Resources, Thier preospecting & Exploitation in China. *Memberships:* Geological Soc of China. *Hobby:* Song. *Address:* Coal Geological Bureau of China, Zuozhow, Hebei, China.

WANSBROUGH David James, b. 15 Apr 1948, Auckland, New Zealand. Artist; Poet. m. (1) 4 Children, (2) Roslyn Jones, 2 s. *Education:* Dip Tech Auckland Tchrs Coll, 1971; PhL Lic Theol, St Basil, Sydney, 1980. *Appointments include:* Exec Dir, Arupta Group of Finance, Property & Investment Companies; Exec Dir, Dir, New South Wales; Over 26 One Man Art Exhib. *Publications:* Poetry. On The Lip of the Pit; Seeing Through; Word Weaving; Poetry for a Human Centred Education; Pillar of Salt? *Memberships:* Miroma Rudolf Steiner Therapy Centre; Nordoff Robbins Music Therapy assn; China Educ Centre, Univ of Sydney; World Literary Acad; Intl Acad of Poets. *Honours:* Honorary Resurgent Prisoner; ABC, Australian Unsung Hero; Honorary DLitt Guiseppe Scicluna Intl Univ; Bronze Medal, Albert Einstein Intl Acad; Azias Alfred Nobel Medal. *Hobbies:* Collecting Rubble of Past Civilizations; Gardening; Attempting to form a Platonic Monistic World Conception. *Address:* PO Box C168, Clarence, Sydney, NSW 2000, Australia. 149, 152.

WARD David Edward Crosbie, b. 26 Feb 1941, Lyonshall, Herefordshire, England. Freelance Composer. m. Christine Christie, 3 Sept 1976. *Education:* Private Composition studies, Alexander Goehr, 1958- 62. *Creative Works include:* One Act Operas; Three Act opera, Jacks Engagement; Cello Concerto; Cello Variations; Cantata, Beyond the Far Haaf; String Quartets. *Membership:* Assn of Profl Composers. *Hobbies:* Fishing; Boats; Remote Places;

Haute Cuisine. *Address:* St Olaf, Sellafirth, Yell, Shetland ZE2 9PG, Scotland. 4.

WARD Graham Norman Charles, b. 9 May 1952, England. Chartered accountant. m. Ingrid Imogen Sylvia Baden Powell, 5 Apr 1975, div, 2 s. *Education:* Dulwich Coll, 1963-70; Jesus Coll, Oxford, 1970-74. *Appointments:* Price Waterhouse, Articles Cler, 1974; Qualified, 1977; Partner, 1986; Dir, Electricity Serv, Europe, 1990-. *Publications:* The Work of A Pension Scheme Actuary; Pensions: Your Way Through The Maze. *Memberships:* Inst of Chartered Accountants in England & Wales; ACA FCA; London Soc of Chartered Accountants. *Honours:* Oxford Boxing Prize; 2nd Place Final Exam of Icaew. *Hobbies:* Boxing; Rugby; Jazz; Classical Music. *Address:* Price Waterhouse, Southwalk Towers, 32 London Bridge Street, London SE1 9S4, England. 53.

WARD John Godsalve, b. 8 Jan 1940, St Ives, Cornwall, England. Secretary General. m. Martine Yvonne Dupuis, 25 May 1984, 1 Stepson. *Education:* Sherborne, 1953-58; Lausanne Hotel Sch, 1960-63; Cranfield, 1970-71. *Appointments:* Hotel Management, 1963-70; Thompson Holidays, 1971-74; Aevlingus, 1974-76; Organization of HH The Agakhan as Conslt, 1976-83; Alliance Intl de Tourisme, sec General, 1983-91. *Hobbies:* 4 Chenin du Pont Perrin, 1231 Villette Conches, Geneva, Switzerland.

WARD William Francis, b. 23 Aug 1928, Massachusetts, USA. Real Estate Investment Banker; Private Investor; Retired Major General US Army. m. Elaine Louise Wilson, 11 June 1950, 3 s, 2 d. *Education:* BS, United States Ministry Acad, 1950; MBA, Harvard Grad, 1956; LLB, Lasolle Univ, 1966. *Appointments:* US Army, 1950-55; El du Pont Investment Corp, 1956-58; Sect NY State Bridge Authority, 1958-60; GAP Corp, 1960-63; VP Grosset & Dunlop Inc, 1963-67; Pres, Dunt Bradstef Pus Corp, 1967-77; Eup American Cancer Soc, 1977-81; Pres, Grestam Inc, 1981-86; US Army, 1986-91. *Publications:* Army Magazine; Leadership for the 1990's Filed Artillery Journal. *Memberships:* West Point Soc of NY; NY City Univ Club; The Pilgrims; Financial Exec Inst; Reserve Officers Assn. *Honours:* Distinguished Service Medal; Legion of Merit; Meritorious Service Medal; Purple Heart; Army Commendation Medals. *Hobbies:* Golf; Reading. *Address:* 1 Bruce Court, Suffern, NY 10901, USA. 2, 6, 52, 132.

WARE Lancelot Lionel, b. 5 June 1915, England. Chancery Barrister. m. Joan Franc Sca Rae, 14 June 1980. *Education:* Royal Coll of Sci, 1934-38; Lincoln Coll, Oxford, 1945-48; Called to Bar, 1949. *Appointments:* Research Worker, Natl Inst for Medical Research, 1938- 39; Boots Chemist, 1940-41; St Thomas Hospital, 1941-45; Practising Barrister, 1949-. *Publications:* Founder of Mensa; Articles. *Memberships:* Intl Federation of Investors Anns; Royal Asiatic Soc; Inst of Patentees; Assn of Volunt Aided Secondary Sch. *Honours:* Royal Scholar at Imperial Coll of Sci & Tech; OE; Vice Pres, Eurotalent; Fons et Origo Mesae. *Hobbies:* Tennis; Field Sports; Chess; Music; Languages; Travel. *Address:* 11 Old Sqaure, Lincolns Inn, London WC2A 3TS, England.

WARE Tracy, b. 17 June 1956, Victoria, BC. Prof of English Literature. m. Brenda Reed, 22 Aug 1985. *Education:* MA, 1980; PhD, Univ of Western Ontario, 1984; BA, Univ of Victoria. *Appointments:* Asst Prof, English, Univ of Western Ontraio, 1984-85, 1986-87; Killam Postdoctoral Fellow, Dalhousie, 1985-86; Asst Prof, Bishops Univ, 1987-. *Publications:* Articles. *Memberships:* Assn of Canadian & Quebec Literatures; Assn of Canadian Univ Tchrs of English; Keats Shelley Assn; Poetry Studies Assn; Buron Soc. *Honours:* SSHRCC Doctoral Fellowship; Killam Postdoctoral Fellowship; SSHRCC Postdoctoral Fellowship. *Hobbies:* Golf; Travel. *Address:* 105 Oxford Crescent, Lennoxville, Quebec, Canada JIM 2G3. 142.

WARNER John Rudyerd, b. 22 Mar 1923, Thorpe, Surrey, England. Co Dir. m. Lesley Ann Collier, 30 Nov 1974, 4 d. *Education:* Pangbourne, 1937-41; Chelsea Coll, London Univ, BSc, 1963-66; Whitelands Coll, London Univ, PCE, 1966-67. *Appointments:* Indian Army, 1941- 47; Chemical Ind, 1951-62; Tutor of Sci & Maths, 1966-73; Co Dir, Republic Lands Ltd, 1973-; Chartered Chemist, 1992. *Publication:* The Medloc Route. *Memberships:* West India Committee; Mem, Royal Soc Chemistry. *Honours:* Private Polits Licence. *Hobbies:* Photography; Flying; Foreign Travel; Pottery. *Address:* 131 Wellington Close, Walton-On-Thames, Surrey KT12 1BG, England.

WARNER Lesley Rae, b. 21 July 1940, New Zealand. Tertiary Level Academic, Hd of Dept. m. (1) Roger Jospeh Smales, 21 Dec 1961, div 1981, (2) George Oliver Warner, 22 Dec 1981, 1 s, 1 d. *Education:* BHSc, New Zealand, 1961; BSc, Otago Univ, 1963; MSc, 1965; PhD, Adelaide Univ, 1976; Adelaide Coll of the Arts & Educ, 1981. *Appointments include:* Post Doctoral Visiting Scholar, Univ of Michigan, 1976-77; Lectr, Adelaide Coll of the Arts & Educ, 1979-80; Scientific Officer, 1981-82; Dean, Sch Scince, UCQ, 1988-90; Hd Biology Dept, Univ of Central Queensland, 1985-. *Publication:* Gippsland Flavours. *Memberships:* Royal Soc of South Australia; Australian Inst of Biology; Australian Soc for Parasitology; Wildlife Disease Assn. *Honours:* Snr Scholar in Sci; Archerfield Prize for Nutrition. *Hobbies:* Cooking; Reading. *Address:* 57 Canning Street, Rockhampton, Queensland 4700, Australia. 1.

WARNER Rullin Miles Jr, b. 25 Dec 1930, Evanston, Illinois, USA. *Education:* Tale, BA, 1953; Stanford, MBA, 1960. *Appointments:* Asst Dir, Stanford Univ, 1960-63; Tchr, Town Sch, History, 1963-70; Principal of Mt, Tamalpais Sch, Dir, Plant & Development, 1970-75; Dean of Students for Activities, Tchr Town Sch of Economics, Algebra, History, 1975- *Publications:* Free Enterprise at Work; Africa, Asia, Russia; Greece, Rome; America; Europe. *Memberships:* Inst of Certified Financial Planners; Real Estate Certificate Inst; California Real Estate Educ Assn; American Economic Assn; Intl Platform Assn; American Management Assn; Assn for Suporvision & Curriculum Developement. *Honours include:* Scouters Key; Sons of American Revolution Award; World Decoration of Excellence. *Hobbies:* Aquatic Sports; Book Collecting; Model Ship Building; Hiking. *Address:* 1690 Broadway 201, San Fransico, CA 94109, USA.

WARREN Jennifer Jayne, b. 4 Sept 1944, Braidwood, NSW. Retired Nursing Sister. m. Lionel Taylor, 12 Mar 1966, div 1980, 2 s. *Education:* General Nursing Cert; Cert in Profl Writing. *Appointments:* Nursing Ass, Braidwood Hosp, 1965; Cangerra Community Hosp, 1962-71; Act Red Cross Blood Transfusion Serv, 1973-89. *Publications:* Pulib Poet; Amateur Painter, Oils; Editor. Fellowship Aut Writers Newsletter; Co Author, A Necdotal History of Royal Canberra Hosp. *Memberships:* Fellowship of Australian Writers. *Honours:* Poetry Awards. *Hobbies:* Writing; Sketching; Painting. *Address:* 33 Kavel Street, Torrens, ACT 2607, Australia.

WARREN Michael Donald, b. 19 Dec 1923, Worthing, Sussex, England. Retired Emeritus Prof. m. Joan Lavina Peacock, 8 Mar 1946, 1 s, 2 d. *Education:* Guys Hosp Medical Sch, 1941-46; London Sch of Hygiene & Tropical Medicine, 1951-52. *Appointments:* RAF Medical Branch, 1947-51; Deputy Medical Officer of Health, Hampstead, 1952-54; Asst Principal MD, 1954-58; Snr Lectr, Royal Free Hosp Sch of Medicine, 1958-64; Reader in Public Health, London Sch of Hygiene & Tropical Medicine, 1964-71; Prof, Dir of Health service Research Univ, 1971-83. *Publications include:* Public Health & Social Services; Recalling the Medical Officer of Health; Health Service for People with Physical Disabilities. *Memberships:* FRCP; Soc of Social Medicine; Acad Registrar, Faculty of Public Health Medicine; British Journal of Preventive & Social

Medicine. *Honours include:* Assn of Ind Medical Officers Prize; Honorary Member, Soc of Social Medicine; Honorary Fellow, Faculty of Public Health Medicine, Royal Coll of Physicians. *Hobbies:* Genealogy; visiting Gardens; Reading; Music. *Address:* 2 Bridge Down, Canterbury, Kent CT4 5AZ, England. 1.

WARREN Patricia Nell, b. 15 June 1936, Helena, Mont. Writer; Artist. *Education:* Stephens Coll, assn Arts, 1955; Manhattanville Coll, BA, 1957. *Appointments:* Readers Digest, Book Editor, 1964-75; Condensed Book Editor, 1975-81. *Creative Works include:* The Last Centennial; The Beauty Queen; One is The Sun; 25 Paintings in Corp & Private Collections. *Memberships:* Authors Guild; Writers Guild of America; Intl Womens Writing Guild; American Assn of Zoological Parks & Aquariums. *Honours:* Atlantic Monthly Coll, Friction Prize; Walt Whitman Prize; Western Heritage Award. *Hobbies:* Farming; Wildlife; Womens History; Current Events. *Address:* 2222 Foothill Blvd, Suite E 155, LA Canada, CA 91011, USA.

WARSICK RINZIVILLO Mary Katrina, b. 3 Aug 1956, Tampa, FL, USA. Counselor; Educator; Licensed Mental Health Counselor. m. Ronald Carl Rinzivillo, 18 Nov 1990. *Education:* BA, English Educ, 1979; MA, 1984. *Appointments:* Mango Baptist Sch, Tchr, 1974-80; Eisenhower Jr High, Tchr, 1980-84; Dowdell Jr High, Guidance Chairperson, 1984-85; Lake Weir Middle, Counselor, 1985-87; Counselor, Guidance Dept Chairperson, 1987-. *Memberships:* American Assn of Counseling & Development; Hernando County assn of Counselors; Phi Kappa Phi; Phi Delta Kappa. *Honours:* Tchr of The Year; Counselor of The Year; Peer Leader of The Year. *Hobbies:* Reading; Biking; Sailing. *Address:* West Hernando Middle School, 9412 Fox Chapel Lane, Spring Hill, FL 34606, USA. 7.

WARZYWODA Witold, b. 15 Apr 1956, Lowicz, Poland. Graphic Acad Tchr. m. Denuta Wachowska, 9 Oct 1986, 1 s, 1 d. *Education:* MA, High Sch of Fine Arts, Lodz, 1981; DA, Graphic, 1992. *Appointments:* Employed as Academic Tchr, High Sch of Fine arts, Lodz, 1981-. *Publications:* Graphic seriers, Calander; Jewish Cementrary; Portraits; Cages; stones; Still Lives. *Memberships:* Union of Polish Artists of Fine Arts. *Honours:* 4th Award V Triennial of Presentations of Contemporary portraits; Grant for Creation Admitted by Pres Lodz. *Hobby:* Fishing. *Address:* ul Przedswit 6 m 7, 93 378 Lodz, Poland.

WASHINGTON Thomas Fredrick, b. 16 Nov 1950, Kansas City, Missouri, USA. Inspector; Supervisor. m. Janice C Clark, 8 Apr 1977, 1 s. *Education:* Cert Electronics, 1969; AAS, Penn Valley Jnr Coll, 1977; BA, Avila Coll of KCMO, 1987. *Appointments:* Xero, Tchr Rep, 1969; Western Electronic, Technician, 1970; US Navy, Electronics Tech, 1970; Allied Signal, Supervisor, 1976. *Publications:* Honorable Mention in a Photocontest for Kansas City. *Memberships:* Allied Signal Management Club. *Hobby:* Photography. *Address:* 11824 Bristol Avenue, Kansas City, MO 64134, USA.

WASS John Andrew Hall, b. 14 Aug 1947, London, England. Physician. m. Valerie Vincent, 4 Apr 1970, 1 s, 1 d. *Education:* Guys Hosp, Univ of london, 1966-71; Royal Coll of Physicians, 1973; Fellow, 1986; Univ of London, MD, 1980. *Appointments:* Registrar, KCH 1973-76; Guys Hosp, 1974-75; St Batholemus Hosp Medical Coll, Lectr, 1976-81; Snr Lectr, 1982-85; Reader, 1985-89; Sub Dean Medical Coll, Prof of Clinical Endocrimology, 1989-. *Publications:* Articles; Chapters; Books. *Memberships:* Royal Medical Benerdent Fund; Soc Endocrime Section of RSM; American Endocrime Soc. *Hobbies:* Music; Opera; Theatre; Wine. *Address:* Dept of Endocrinology, St Batholemus Hosp, London EC1A 7DE, England.

WATANABE Kazuyuki, b. 4 Apr 1932, Okayama, Japan. Prof. m. Hiromi, 8 July 1963, 1 s. *Education:* Okayama Univ, BA, 1956; Tchrs of Japanese, George Town Univ, 1966. *Appointments:* Mukogawa Womens Univ, 1968-79; Lectr, Prof, Shiga Univ, 1979-89; Prof, Kyoto Womens Univ, 1989-. *Publications:* Intenation of Contemporary English; Guide to English Rhythm; English phonetics for Cummunication; Listening to FEN and Satellite Broadcasts; FEN News. *Memberships:* Phonetic Soc of Japan; Japan Assn of Current English; Japan Assn of Coll English Tchrs. *Hobbies:* Listening to Overseas Broadcasts; British & American TV Dramas; Travel. *Address:* 8-15 Nango 2 Chome, Otsu, Japan 520. 52.

WATERFIELD John Percival, b. 5 Oct 1921, Dublin, Ireland. Retired. m. (1) Margaret Lee Thomas, 25 Feb 1950, dec, 2 s, 1 d. (2) Tilla Hevesi Vahanian, 2 Aug 1991. *Education:* Dragar Sch, Oxford, 1930-35; Charterhouse, 1935-40; Christ Church, Oxford. *Appointments:* Foreign & Commonwealth Office, 1946-70; Mgrng Dir, British Electrical & Mechanical Assn, 1970-73; Principal Finance & Establishment Office, North Ireland Office, 1973- 79; Dir, Intl Military Service, 1979-82; Chmn, Dir, Various Companies, 1982- 85. *Hobbies:* Fishing; Water Colour Painting; Gardening. *Address:* 5 North Street, Somerton, Somerset, TA11 7NY, England. 1, 12.

WATERHOUSE John Bruce, b. 5 Apr 1932, New Zealand. Conslt Geologist. m. Loris Vivienne Castle, 6 Jan 1962, 2 s, 2 d. *Education:* MSc, Univ of New Zealand, 1954; PhD, Univ of Cambridge, 1958. *Appointments:* Principal Sci Officer, NZ Geological Survey, 1954-67; Assc, Full Prof, Univ of Toronto, 1967-74; Dorothy Hill Prof of Stratigraphy & Palaeontology, Univ of Queensland, 1974-90. *Publications:* Some 300 Research Articles. *Memberships:* Geological Soc of Australia; Australian Inst of Mining & Metallurgy; paleontological Soc; Geological Soc of NZ. *Honour:* Royal Exhib Scholar. *Hobbies:* Mountaineering; Literature; Realforestation. *Address:* 274 Princes Drive, Nelson, New Zealand. 14.

WATERTON Betty Marie, b. 31 Aug 1923, Oshawa, Ontario, Canada. Childrens Author. m. Claude Waterton, 7 Apr 1942, 1 s, 2 d. *Publications:* 12 Books for Children. A Salmon For Simon; Quincy Rumpel; The Cat of Quinty; Starring Quincy Rumpel; Plain Noodles. *Memberships:* CANSCAIP; Federation of B C Writers. *Hobby:* Painting. *Address:* c/o Douglas & McIntyre Ltd, 1615 Venables Street, Vancouver, BC, Canada V5L 2H1.

WATES Jenifer, b. 17 Dec 1932, London, England. Artist; Charity Dir. m. Neil Wates, 17 Sept 1932, div 1984, 4 s, 1 d. *Education:* Somerville Coll, Oxford, 1951-55; MA, Oxon, 1960; MSc, Univ of Bristol, 1985. *Appointments:* Justice of the Peace, Inner London Juvenile Panel, 1964-75; Trustee, Commonwork Fund Trust, 1977-; Trustee, Scott Bader Commonwealth, 1986-. *Creative Works:* Many Paintings. *Hobbies:* Politics; Counselling & Psychotherapy. *Address:* 58 Upper Mall, Hammersmith, London W6 9TA.

WATKIN David, b. 23 Mar 1925, Margate, England. Cinematographer. *Education:* Still Going on. *Appointments:* Cinematographer, Documentaries, 1955-64; Features, 1964-. *Creative Works include:* The Knack; The Charge of the Light Brigade; Jesus of Nazareth; Out of Africa; Memphis Belle; The Cabinet of Dr Ramirez. *Honours:* New York Critics Circle; Acad of Motion Picture Arts; Bafta; Evening Standard. *Hobbies:* Reading; Music. *Address:* 6 Sussex Mews, Brighton, East Sussex BN2 1GZ, England.

WATKINS John William Nevill, b. 31 July 1924, Woking, Surrey, England. Prof. m. Millicent Joan Roe, 4 Apr 1952, 1 s, 3 d. *Education:* Royal Navel Coll, Dartmouth, 1938-41; London Sch of Economics, BSc, 1946- 49; Yale, MA, 1949-50. *Appointments:* Navel

Officer, 1941-46; Univ Tchr, London Sch of Economics, 195-89. *Publications:* Hobbies System of Ideas; Freiheit Und Entschedung; Science & Scepticism. *Memberships:* British Soc for the Philosophy of Sci; Mind Assn. *Honour:* Distinguished Service Cross. *Hobbies:* Chess; Digny Sailing. *Address:* 11 Erskine Hill, London NW11 6HA, England.

WATSON Alan John, b. 3 Feb 1941, England. Com Chmn; Broadcaster. m. Karen Lederer, 28 Dec 1965, 2 s. *Education:* Diocesan Coll, Cape Town, 1949-54; Kingswood Sch, Bath, 1954-58; Jesus Coll, cambridge, 1958-61. *Appointments:* Broadcaster, BBC TV, 1963-76; Hd of Div, EEC Commission, 1976-80; Chief Exec, Charles Barker City, 198-85; Dept Chmn, Sterling P R, 1985-87; Chmn City & Corp Counsel Ltd, 1987-. *Publications:* Monnett Father of Europe; Europe At Risk; Tou and 1992. *Memberships include:* Liberal Party; Govenors Westminster Coll; Royal TV Soc. *Honours:* History Scholar; Grand Prix Eyrodiaporama of the European Community; Commander of the British Empire; Visiting Fellow; Evasmus Visiting Prof. *Hobbies:* History; Writing; Theatre. *Address:* Cholmondeley House, 3 Cholmondeley Walk, Richmond, Surrey, England. 1.

WATSON Billy Jerrell, b. 4 Aug 1934, Texas, USA. Psychatherapist. m. Shirley Ann Ray, 27 Jan 1952, 2 s, 2 d. *Education:* Air Univ, 1955; Oklahoma Military Acad, 1959; Univ of Tulsa, BA, 1962; Harding Univ, MA, 1968- 76; Southwest Univ, PhD, 1991. *Appointments:* Pvt Practice, Memphis Count Centre; Gedarstone hosp, Little Rock; HCA Hosp, Jackson; Mid Sc Hosp; Northwest Count Centre; USAF. *Memberships include:* Am Assn of Murr & Fam Theapist; Chemical Abouse Counc; Am Assn of Profl Hyprotherapist. *Honours:* Alpha Kappa Delta; Lion of the Year. *Hobbies:* Golf; Black Belt, ATA Tackwondo Karate; Reading. *Address:* 45 Northland Drive, Jackson, TN 38301, USA. 125, 129.

WATSON Marilym Jane, b. 17 Sept 1952, England. Public Relations Conslt. 1 s. *Education:* St Marys Convent, Liverpool, 1963-69; Cambridge Coll of Arts & Tech, 1969-71. *Appointments:* Dir of MPR Leedex Group, 1986-89; Propietor, Watsons, 1989-. *Publications:* Numerous Corporate & Mktng Literature. *Membership:* Inst of Public Relations. *Hobbies:* Riding; Swimming; Gardening. *Address:* Watsons, Terrace Gardens, Barnes, London SW13 0HD, England. 138.

WATSON Sidney John, b. 31 Mar 1920, London, England. Land Owner; Admin of Church of Ireland. m. Diana Christine Isabella, 3 June 1950, 1 s, 1 d. *Education:* Eton Coll, 1933-34; Magdalen Coll, Oxford, 1939-40. *Appointments:* Enlisted British Army, 1940; Commissioned, 1941; Staff Coll, Camberley, 1949; United States Staff Coll, 1954-55; Military Attache, 1960-64; Retired, 1964. *Publications:* By Command of the Emperor; Between the Flags; Three Days Full; The Cottage Countess; A Dinner of Herbs; Furnished with Ability. *Memberships:* Dulverton Trust, London; Church of Ireland General Synod; Travellers Club, London. *Honours:* Mentioned in Despatches; MBE. *Hobbies:* Reading; Gardening. *Address:* Ballingarrane, Clonmel, County Tipperary, Ireland. 146.

WATTS Julie Chantal, b. 24 Aug 1974, TV, USA. Student; Writer. *Education:* Snr, Grace Acad, TN, USA. *Appointments:* Sales Assoc, Fabric Warehouse, 1990; Cashier, Red Food store, 1991. *Publications:* Poems Public. *Contributions to:* Chinera Poetry Mag. *Honours:* Golden Poet Award; Honourable Mention Great Free Intl Poetry Comp; Speed Reading Award; Sch Typing Award; Honourable Mention Design in Flight Comp. *Hobbies:* Writing; Cooking; Shooping; Reading. *Address:* 1707 Small Street, Chattanolga, TN 37412, USA.

WAUGAMAN Charles Allen, b. 5 Jan 1932, Lorain, Ohio, USA. Ordained Clergy. m. Judith Lee Clark, 27 July 1968, 4 s, 1 d. *Education:* Univ of the Arts, PA, 1954; Eastern Baptist Theological Seminary, 1957; Allegheny Coll, MEadville, 1967. *Appointments:* Edit, Dept Am Bapt Pub Soc, 1952-63; Vis Art Dept Head, Judson Coll, 1964-70; Pastor Churches, West Harpswell, 1970-76; Jewett City, 1976-79; Conneaut Lake, 1980-. *Publications:* Time of Singing; Cheyenne Artist; Patternsof Passing; Harvest of Willow; Fabric of Truth; Fruit by the Sea; Sweet Valley of Shadow; Moments in the Sun; Myrrh for my Birthday; First Quartet; 2 One Man Shows; Several Group Shows; 4 Book Illustrated. *Hobbies:* Antiques; Bird Watching; Book Illustration; Opera; Natural History; Reading; Travel; Collecting Stamps, Coins, Antique Postcards. *Address:* Time of Singing, PO Box 211, Cambridge Springs, PA 16403, USA.

WAXENBERGER Gabriele Maria, b. 12 June 1956, Muchldorf, Germany. Profs Asst. *Education:* Univ of Munich, MA, 1984; Doctoral Thesis, 1991. *Appointments include:* Substitute Tchr of English & German, W Germany, 1980; Asst to Prof of Historical Linguistics, Univ of Eichstatt, 1986-87; Adult Educ Programme, Hd of Dept English, 1988-; Tchr, Siemens AG Munich, 1991-; Special Reader, Dictionary of Old English, Toronto, Canada, 1991-. *Publications:* Doctoral Thesis on Old English Houn Types; Articles. *Memberships:* MLA; JSAS. *Hobbies:* Historical Linguistics; Foreign Language Tchrng; Dialectology; Lexicography. *Address:* 62 Stadtplate, 8260 Muehldorf, Germany. 52.

WAY James Leong, b. 21 Mar 1926, Watsonville, CA. Prof of Toxicology & Pharmacology. m. 1 July 1960, 1 s, 2 d. *Education:* Univ of CA Berkley, BA, 1951; George Washington Univ, PhD, 1955. *Appointments:* Prof, Pharmacol Washington State Univ, 1967-82; Visiting Prof, Pharmacol Taipei, Taiwan, ROC, 1981-82; Prof, Pharm & Toxicol Texas A&M Univ, 1982-. *Publications:* Over 200 Sci Works; Mechanism of Cyanide Intoxication & Its Antagonism; Encapsulation of Rhodanese by Mouse Carrier Erythrocytes. *Memberships:* American Soc of Pharmacology & Experimental Therapeutics; Soc of Toxicol; American Soc for Pharmacol & Experimental Therapeutics. *Honours:* Joseph H Shelton Endowed Chair; Natl Acad of Sci Scholar; Rockerfeller Resident Scholar. *Hobbies:* Suba Diving; Ballroom Dancing. *Address:* Dept of Medical Pharmacology & Toxicology, Texas A&M Univ, Medical Science Building, College Station, TX 77843, USA. 1, 129, 152, 164.

WAYMAN Morris, b. 19 Mar 1915, Canada. Prof of Chemical Engrng. m. Sara Gertrude Zadkin, 9 Jan 1937, 2 s. *Education:* PhD, MA, Univ of Toronto, 1937, 1941. *Appointments:* Research Chemist, Dye & Chemical Co Ltd, 1941-43; Ind Cellulose Research Ltd, 1943-52; Tech Dir, Columbia Cellulose Co Ltd, 1952-58; Research Dir, Sandwell Intl Ltd, 1958-63; Prof, Dept of Chemical Engrng & Applied Chemistry, Univ of Toronto, 1963-; Prof, Faculty of Forestry, 1973-. *Memberships:* Royal Soc of Canada; Am Assn for the Advancement of Sci; Chemical Inst of Canada Profl Engr; Innis Coll Sigma Xi; American Chemical Soc; Can Soc Microbiologists. *Hobbies:* Music; Hart House Chamber Winds. *Address:* 17 Noel Avenue, Toronto, Ontario, Canada M4G 1B2. 2.

WEALE Graham Alexander, b. 26 Aug 1953, Barnet, England. Energy Conslt. m. Anthea Crompton, 15 Mar 1978, 2 s. *Education:* Lincoln Coll, Oxford, MA, 1975; City Univ, MSc, 1977; Cranfield Sch Mngt, MBA, 1982. *Appointments:* Esso Petroleum Co, 1977-81; Touche Ross Mgt Consts, 1982-84; DRI Europe, 1984-86; The Wefa Group, 1987-. *Publications:* Europe Natural Gass Markets After Troll; Inter Fuel Comp in the European Electic Utilities. *Memberships:* Inst of Petroleum; Assoc Chartered Inst of Arbitrators; Worshipful Co Of Tinplate Workers; Freeman City of London. *Hobbies:* Playing Chamber Music; Travel. *Address:* 39 The Park, Ealing, London W5 5NP, England.

WEATHERHEAD Alexander Stewart, b. 3 Aug 1931, Edinburgh, Scotland. Solicitor. m. Harriett Foye, 22 Dec 1972, 2 d. *Education:* Glasgow Acad, 1942-49; Glasgow Univ, 1952-58; MA, 1955; LLB, 1958. *Appointments:* Partner, Tindale Darts, 1960-. *Memberships:* Law Soc of Scotland; Soc of Computers & Law; Lowland TAVRA. *Honours:* OBE; TD. *Hobbies:* Reading; Tennis; Sailing: *Address:* 52 Patrickhill Road, Glasgow, G11 5AB. Scotland. 1.

WEATHERS Philip, b. 4 Nov 1908, London, England. Actor, Theatre; Dir Playwright; Curator. *Education:* Cambridge Univ, 1927. *Appointments include:* Actor, 1929-37; Theatre Dir, 1937-40, 1946-57; Playwright, The Weary Heart, 1938; Arms and the Women, 1939; Murder insn't Cricket, 1959; Sometimes It Strikes, 1968; Three Shots in the Dark, 1970. *Memberships:* Sussex Playwrights Club; Crime Writers Assn; English Speaking Union. *Address:* Charterhouse, London, EC1M 6AN, England.

WEBB Clifford Frederick James, b. 8 Aug 1928, Brandon, Suffolk, England. Chartered Quantity Surveyor. m. Barbara Doreen Stringer, 20 Aug 1955, 1 d. *Education:* FRICS, 1956; FCI, ARB, 1964. *Appointments:* Articled Pupil Quantity Surveyor, Hewitt Bros, Grimsby, 1945-50; Private Practice, Ipswich, 1950-52; Courtaulds Ltd, Coventry, 1952-54; County Councils, Norfolk & Lindsey, 1954-60; Dir, Chief Quantity Surveyor, Two Major Contractors, 1960-65; Principal, Private Practice, 1965-. *Memberships include:* Inst of Quantity Surveyors; Freeman City of London; City Livery Club; St Stephens Constitution Club, London. *Hobbies:* Travel; Natural History; Rotary. *Address:* Matlock Bank House, Morton Terrace, Gainsborough, Lincolnshire, DN21 2RF, England. 139.

WEBB James Robert, b. 20 May 1954, Houston, Texas, USA. Mgmt Conslt. m. Karen A Hutson, 26 May 1984, 1 s, 1 d. *Education:* BS, US Military Acad of West Point, 1976; MBA, Univ of Dallas, 1984; MS, Pacific Western Univ, 1985. *Appointments:* Captain, Special Forces, 1976-81; Engrng Mgr, Texas Instruments, 1981-84; Project Mgr, Lockwood Greene, 1984- 85; Mgr, Price Waterhouse & Co, 1985-88; Snr Mgr, Deloitte & Touche, 1988-. *Publications:* Frequent Speaker & Author. *Memberships:* Inst of Mgmt Conslts; The Planning Forum. *Honours:* Dept of Defence Meritorious Service Medal; Presidental Medal of Merit; Cert Mgmt Conslt; Forth Degree Black Belt in Judo. *Hobbies:* Judo; Tennis; Running Marathons; Triathalons. *Address:* Deloitte & Touche, 2001 Bryan Tower, Suite 2400, Dallas, TX 75201, USA. 7, 132.

WEBB Robert Stopford, b. 4 Oct 1948, England. Barrister, Queens Counsel. m. Angela Mary Freshwater, 1 Apr 1975, 2 s. *Education:* Wycliffe Coll, 1958-67; Exeter Univ, 1967-70. *Appointments:* Called to the Bar, 1971; Inner Temple, QC, 1988. *Memberships:* Air Law Group; Royal Aeronautical Soc; Intl Bar assn; Intl Acad of Trial Lawyers. *Hobbies:* Golf; Fly Fishing. *Address:* 1 Harcourt Building, Temple, London EC4Y 9DA, England. 1.

WEBB PEPLOE Michael Murray, b. England. m. 2 children. *Education:* Trinity Coll, Cambridge; St Thomas Medical Sch Hosp, London. *Appointments include:* Conslt Physician, St Thomas Hosp, London; Honorary Civiliam Conslt Cardiologist to the Army; Conslt Cardiologist, Civil Service Commission; Conslt Cardiologist, Metropolitan Police Public Carriage Office. *Publications include:* Acute Transverse Myelitis as a Complication of Glandular Fever; Response of Large Hindlimb Veins of Dog to Changes in Temperature; The Cutaneous Venoconstrictor Response to Local Coolinf; Length of Left Main Coronary Artery; Assesment of Left Ventricular Function by Indices Derived From Aortic Flor Velocity; Enzymic Analysis of Endomyocardial Biopsy Specimens from Patients with Cardiomyopathies; Haemadyynamic & Metabolic Effects of atenolol in Patients with Angina Pectoris; The Effects of Oral

Digoxin Therapy in Primary Mitral Leaflet Prolapse; Cold Induced Pulmonary Oedema in Scuba Divers & Swimmers & Subsequent Development of Hypertension. *Memberships include:* Assn of Physicians of Great Britain & Ireland; Medical Research Soc; Mayo Alumni Assn. *Honours include:* Officer of the Order of the British Empire, OBE. *Address:* The Consulting Rooms, York House, 199 Westminster Bridge Road, London SE1 7UT, England.

WEDELL Eberhard Arthur Otto George, b. 4 Apr 1927. Prof of Communication Policy; Dir European Inst for the Media. m. Rosemarie Winckler, 1948, 3 s, 1 d. *Education:* Cranbrook; London Sch of Economics, BSc, 1947; Ministry of Educ, 1950-58. *Appointments include:* Sec Bd for Social Responsibility, Natl Assembly of Church of England, 1958-60; Dep Sec ITA, 1960-61; Prof, Adult Educ, Dir of Extra Mural Studies, Manchester Univ, 1964-75; Snr Official, European Commn, 1973-82; Greater Manchester Central, 1984; Vice Pres, Greater Manchester Liberal Party, 1984- *Publications:* The Use of TV in Education; Broadcasting & Public Policy; Tchrng At A Distance; Structure of broadcasting; Studyby Correspondance; Correspondence Educ in Europe; Tchrs & Educational development in Cyprus; Educ & The Developmentof Malawi; Broadcasting in the Third World; Mass Communications in Western Europe; Making broadcasting Useful. *Memberships:* Athenaeum; Foundation Univ, Brussels. *Honours include:* Natl Assn of Educational Broadcasters of USA Book Award. *Hobbies:* Gardening; Theatre; Reading. *Address:* 18 Cranmer Road, Manchester M20 0AW, England.

WEEKS Jane Sutherland, b. 22 Feb 1924, USA. Sociologist; Conslt; Writer; Lectr. m. 20 Mar 1948, 3 s, 1 d. *Education:* BA, 1950; MA, 1964. *Appointments:* Oak Ridge Natl Lab, 1950-56; Univ Tenn, 1956-70; Amer Univ, Cairo, Egypt, 1970-71; Carson Newmax Coll, 1972- 80; Univ Tennesse, 1980-81. *Publications include:* Journals; Newspapers; Periodicals. *Memberships:* Agape; Knoxville Womens Centre; Knoxville Urban Ministries; SE Womens Studies, Matrix. *Honours:* Selwyn Award; Mayors Award City of Knoxville. *Hobbies:* Writing; Travel; Gardening. *Address:* 2104 Tooles Bend, Knoxville, TN 37922, USA. 125, 156.

WEGELIN Arthur Willem, b. 5 Mar 1908, Nijmegen, Holland. Composer. m. (1) Bess Hiebendoal, 25 Apr 1935, 1 s, 1 d. (2) Wytske Johanna Zoetelief Tromp, 26 June 1950. *Education:* Muziek Lyceum, Amsterdam, 1930; Univ of South Africa, 1957-59; Trinity Coll Lord, 1960. *Appointments:* Violinist, Utrechtsch Sledelijk Orkest, 1933-41; Private Violin Tchr, 1930-44; Bazoque & Bach Ensembles, 1936-44; Chamber Music Player, Broadcasts & Recitals; Freelance Violinist, cape town, 1947-51; Violin Tchr, Lectr potchefstroom Univ, 1951-65; Founder, Hd Music Dept, Conservatoire, Univ of Port Elizabeth, 1965-70; Lectr, Univ of Pretoria, 1970-73; Snr Research Officer, Jr & Snr Musical Aptitude Sch Group Tests, Human Sci research Council, Pretoria, 1973-78; Private Composer, 1978-91. *Creative Works include:* Skoolmusiek Vir Suid Afrika; Prakiese Harmonieleer Van Die Diatoniek; Publi. Ses Liedere Op Afrikaanse Tekste; Several Sch Music Compositions Public. *Memberships include:* South African Soc of Music Tchrs; Musicological Soc of Southern Africa; Suid Africkaanse Akademie Vir Wetenskap en Kuns; Montagu Music Soc. *Honour:* Bothner Prize. *Hobbies:* Vegetable Garden; Philosophy; poem Writing. *Address:* Kzuinsingel 11, Montagu 6720, Republic of South Africa. 4.

WEGRZYN Jan Wladyslaw, b. 23 Nov 1923, Prof. m. Alicja Rubinowska, 5 June 1932, 1 s, 1 d. *Education:* BS, Acad of Mining Cracow, 1949; Doctorate, 1961; De Habilit, 1964; Assoc Prof, 1972; Full Prof, 1978. *Appointments:* Polish Welding Research Inst, Welding Engr, 1949; Head of the Welding Metallurgy Dept, 1951; Silesian Tech Univ, Deputy Rector, 1981-83; Hd of the Welding Dept, Silesian Tech Univ, 1981-91.

Publications: 175 Publi; 7 Books; 35 Patents. *Memberships:* General Council of the Polish welding Inst; Central Council of the Polish Inst of Metallurgy; Metallurgy Comm of the Polish acad of Sci. *Honours:* Natl Prize; Minstry's Prize; Rectors Prize; Natl Medals. *Hobbies:* Tennis; Skiing; Painting. *Address:* ul Czapli 41, 44 100 Gliwice, Poland.

WEI Hong Yun, b. 10 Feb 1925, Shaanxi, P R C. Prof. m. Wang Li, 2 s, 1 d. *Education:* Catholic Univ, Beijing, 1946-48; Nankai Univ, Tianjin, 1948-51. *Appointments:* Tchrng Asst, Nankai Univ, Tianjin, 1951-54; Lectr, 1954-78; Assoc Prof, 1978-80; Prof, 1980-; Chmn, 1973-85. *Publications include:* Biography of Shi Ke Fa; Selected Materials on History of Modern China; Anti Japanese War; The Course of Chinese Modern History; History in the jin Ji Lu Yu Border Region During The Anti Japanese War. *Memberships:* Commission of Degree Accreditation; Assn for Contemporary Chinese History; Tianjin Historical Soc. *Honours:* Fulbright Scholar; Moder Worker in Tianjin. *Hobby:* Shodow Boxing. *Address:* Dept of History, Nakai Univ, Weijin Road 94, Tianjin 300071, China. 152.

WEI Jinju, b. 29 July 1925, Jilin, China. Epidemiology; Microbiology. m. Tianni Zeng, 1 May 1952, 5 s. *Education:* Shenyang Medical Coll, 1947; Higher Tchr Training Classes, Acad of Military Medical Sci, 1955. *Appointments:* Doctor, 1947; Hd of Medical Inst of Zhejiang Military Command, China, 1955; Hd, Prof of Medical Spec Group, ZMC, 1984; Visiting Prof, Inst of Microbiology & Epdemiology, Acad of Military Medical Sci, 1986. *Creative Works include:* Engaged in Rickettsiological Study for more than 30 Yrs. *Memberships:* IEA; Chinese Medical Assn, Zhejiang Branch. *Honours:* Excellent Paper Award of Zhejiang Sci & Tech Comm; Scientific Progress Award. *Hobbies:* Gardening; Penmanship. *Address:* Medical research Unit, Zhejiang Military Command, 11 Shang Cong Qiao Road Hangzhou, China 310002.

WEI Xin Bang, b. 28 Aug 1927, Tong Liang County, China. Physician. m. Hua Xuan Chen, 9 Sept 1956, 2 s. *Education:* Jiangsu Medical Coll, MD, 1945-50; EENT Hosp, Shanghai Medical Univ, 1954-55; Guang Chi Hosp, 1957-58. *Appointments:* Resident, AT Changhai Hosp, second Military Medical Univ, 1951-59; Chief Physician, Changzheng Hosp, 1960-82; Assoc Prof, ENT, 1983-87; Prof, ENT, 1988-89; Prof Emiritus, 1989. *Publications include:* Abscesstonsillectomy; Ellis Operation; Experimental Study of Acute Trauma; Chapters in books. *Memberships:* ENT Assn; Medical Soc of China; Shanghai Natural Sci Soc. *Honours:* Third Awardsin; Acad & Research Writing Awards; Outstanding Achievement. *Hobbies:* Music; Reading. *Address:* Dept ENT, Chang Zheng Hosp, 415 Feng Yang Road, Shanghai 200003, China.

WEIGEL Richard David, b. 1 Feb 1945, Teaneck, New Jersey, USA. Prof. m. Leslie Anne Davis, 8 June 1968, 1 d. *Education:* Friends Sch, 1962; Dickinson Coll, BA, 1966; Univ of Delaware, MA, 1968; PhD, 1973. *Appointments:* Asst Prof, Univ of Phode Island, 1975; Asst Prof, Western Kentucky Univ, 1976-. *Publications:* Peace on the Ancient World; Lepidus; The Tarnished Triumph; Numerous Articles. *Memberships:* American Numesmatic Soc; Royal Numismatic Soc; Soc for the Promotion of Roman Studies; American Philological Assn; Assn of Ancient Historians; Classical Assn of the Middle West & South. *Honours:* NEH, Summer Seminars. *Hobbies:* Coins; Genealogy; Political Buttons. *Address:* 443 Ashmoor Drive, Bowling Green, KY 42101, USA.

WEIHS Daniel, b. 29 Oct 1942, Kweilin, China. Prof. m. Nira Zaretsky, 14 Feb 1967, 2 s, 1 d. *Education:* BSc, Aeronautical Engrng, 1964; MSc, 1968; PhD, 1971. *Appointments include:* Prof, Faculty of Aerospace Engrng; Dir, Samuel Neaman Inst for Advanced Studies in Sci & tech; Holder, Louis & Lyra Richmond Chair in Life Sci; Member, Ben Gurion Univ; Marine Sci

Center, Haifa Univ; Natl Committee for Space Research; Israel Space Agency. *Publications:* Fish Biomechanics; Over 90 Sci Publi. *Memberships:* Israel Soc of Aeronautics & Astronautics; American Soc of Zoologists; American physical Soc; Soc for Underwater Tech. *Honours:* Royal Soc Visiting Fellowship; Natl Research Council, Snr Research Fellowship. *Hobbies:* Stamp Collecting; Gardening. *Address:* Dept of Aerospace Engrng, Technion, Haifa 32000, Israel. 52.

WEINER Claire Muriel, b. 18 Dec 1951, Bronx, NY, USA. Freelance Writer. *Education:* BA, Univ of Miami, 1973; MA, Univ of Maryland, 1980. *Appointments:* Public Relations Spec, Recreation Div, City of Hialeah, Florida, 1974-77; Gov't Affairs Liaison, 1981-; Freelance Writer, 1981-. *Memberships:* Public Relations Soc of America; Natl Assn of Female Exec; Intl Platform Assn. *Honours:* Outstanding Young Women of America; Charter Member, B'nai British Women; Inclusion in Notable American Women. *Hobbies:* Travel; Reading; Museums; Classical & Folk Music. *Address:* 18828 Sky Blue Circle, Germantown, MD 20874, USA. 5, 6.

WEINER Richard Max, b. 6 Feb 1930, Czernowitz. Prof of Physics. m. Nina U Weiner, 19 Dec 1969, 1 d. *Education:* MS, 1953; PhD, 1958. *Appointments:* Research Assoc, 1953-69; European Centre for Nuclear Research, 1969-70; Visiting Prof, Indiana Univ, 1970-72; Imperial Coll, London, 1972-73; Prof of Physics, Marburg Univ, 1974-. *Publications:* Numerous Scientific Publi. *Membership:* Acad of Sci, New York. *Hobbies:* Literature; Art. *Address:* Univ of Marburg, Physics Dept, 3550 Marburg, Germany. 43, 52, 92.

WEIR Hugh William Lindsay, b. 29 Aug 1934. Writer; Correspondent; Publisher. m. Grania Rachel O'Brian, 17 July 1973. *Education:* Ireland; Great Britain; Hong Kong. *Appointments:* Grammer Sch Tchr, Cork & Dublin; Mgng Dir, Weir Machinery Ltd, 1964-; Ballinakella Press, 1982-; Dir, English Language Sch, Whitegate, 1962-70; Irish Heritage Historian, 1980-; Lectr, USA Canada, 1981. *Publications include:* Hall Craig, Words on an Irish House; Houses of Clare; O'Brian People & Places; Ireland, A Thousand Kings; Trapa, An Adventure in Spanish & English; Various Historical Journals. *Memberships:* General Synod; Church of Ireland; Clean Environment Group; Clare Young Environmentalists; Young Environmental Federation; Clare Arhaeological Soc; Clare Environment Council; Clare Community Radio. *Honour:* Ordhreacht Award. *Hobbies:* Writing; Drawing; Angling; Travel; Youth Work. *Address:* Ballinakella Lodge, Whitegate, County Clare, Ireland.

WEIR Thomas Edward, b. 6 Apr 1925, Washington, NC, USA. Ecclesiologist. m. Rebekah Kennedy Turner, 22 June 1946, 2 s, 2 d. *Education:* Univ of So, Carolina, BS, 1945; Emory Univ, BD, 1954; Univ of Edinburgh, PhD, 1961; Naval Sch, General Line, Dipl, 1949. *Appointments:* US Naval Officer, 1945-52; Campus Chaplin, Lexington, VA, 1957-64; US Naval Chaplin, 1964-75; Parish Minister, Lorton, VA, 1977-82; Dir, American Inst of Practical Theology, 1982-. *Publications:* The Role of the Chaplin in Military Corrections; Approx 40 Mag Articles; Pastor Parish, Games for United Methodists. *Memberships:* Boy Scouts of American; Soc of Antiquaries of Scotland; Masonic Order; Past Grand Chaplain of Virginia & Maryland; Grand Prelate Knights Templar; Ordained to Methodist Ministry, Lausanne, Switzerland; Past Natl Chaplain Soc. *Honours:* Ethredge Scholar; Hon Commissioner; Edinburgh Boy Scouts Silver Beaver. *Hobbies:* Model Railroading; Photography; Music. *Address:* PO Box 642, Riverdale, MD 20738, USA. 7.

WEISS Manfred, b. 1 June 1940, Tuttlingen, Germany. *Education:* Univ of Freiburg, Germany, 1964; California Univ, Berkeley, 1965-66; Asst Prof, J W Goethe Univ, Frankfurt, 1970-72; Assoc Prof, 1972-74; Full Prof, 1974. *Appointments include:* Constl, EEC Commission, 1986-; Faculty Member, Intl Seminar, Labour Law & Social Security, Szeged, Hungary, 1986-; Visiting Prof,

Law Schools of the Catholic Univ; Dean of the Law Sch, JW Goethe Univ, 1989-90; Member, German Law Assn, 1990-. *Publications include:* Labour Law & Industrial Relations in the Federal Republic of Germany; Industrial Relations in the Federal Republic of Germany; Legal And Contractual Limitations to Working Time in the FRG; Trade Union Democracy & Industrial Relations in FRG; Labour Law & Industrial Relations in Europe; Publi in German; Many Articles; Book Reviews.

WEISS Rhett Louis, b. 22 May 1961, Sasebo Naval Base, Kyushu, Japan. Banker; Attonery. m. Kristen Sue Krieger, 11 Oct 1987. *Education:* Coll of William & Mary, Marshall Wythe Sch of Law; Tulane Univ, AB, Freeman Sch of Business; Lord Fairfax Community Coll. *Appointments:* Court Admissions; Chicago Title Insurance Co; Ticor Title Insurance Co; Arthur Anderson & Sco, McLean, Virginia, 1986-87; Pentathlon Corp, Winchester, Virginia, 1988-; Anderson, Adamson, Crump Sharp & Weiss, Front Royal & Winchester, 1987-90; Rhett L Weiss, Esquire, Attoney, Consellor at Law, Front Royal, Virginia, 1990-; First Federal Savings Bank of Shenandoah Valley, 1990-. *Memberships:* Virginia State Bar; Virginia Bar assn; Virginia Trial Lawyers Assn; American Bar Assn; Assn of Trial Lawyers of America; Intl Platform Assn. *Honours include:* Natl Quality District Award; Eagle Scout. *Hobbies:* Cars; Sports; Music; Theatre. *Address:* First Federal Savings Bank of Shenandoah Valley, 1 South Royal Avenue, Front Royal, VA 22630, USA. 52, 132, 163.

WEITZ Wayne Paul, b. 16 July 1966, Brooklyn, NY, USA. Mergers & Acquisitions Profl. m. Marcy Heidi Bettinger, 8 July 1990. *Education:* MBA, Univ of Chicago, 1989; BA, Branders Univ, Waltham, 1987. *Appointments:* American Express, Fin Analyst, 1987; Entermanns Inc, Fin Analyst, 1988; Tax Assoc, 1989-90; Price Waterhouse, Atlanta, GA, Corp Finance Assc, 1990-. *Hobbies:* Squash; Reading; Ethnic Food. *Address:* 2565 North Arbor Trail, Marletta, GA 30066, USA. 7.

WEITZMAN Ronald, b. 26 Feb 1945, London, England. Writer on Music; Lectr; Editor. *Education:* Music Training, ir Meville Cardus, 1962-66; Dr H W Cassirer, 1963-79. *Appointments:* Contributor. The Guardian, 1963-66; The London Times, 1969; Financial Times, 1970; Daily Telegraph, 1970-75; Lectrs, USA, 1967; Broadcasts, Australia, 1988, 1990. *Publications include:* Heinz W Cassirers Later Works inc; Gods New Covenant; A New Testament Translation. *Contributions to:* Many Musical Journals; Programme of Royal Opera Covent Garden. *Honour:* Eleanor Roosevent Memorial Award. *Hobbies:* Exploring Jewish Roots of Christianity; Leading Bible Study Groups; Conversation; Reading. *Address:* 6 Frognal, Flat 6, London, NW3 6AJ, England. 4, 139.

WEJNERT Barbara Wilson, b. 3 Feb 1956, Sierakow, Poland. Asst Prof. m. James Wilson, 19 Nov 1988, 1 s. *Education:* Ba, MA, 1980; PhD, 1985. *Appointments:* Instr, Asst Prof, Dept of Sociology, Mickiewicz Univ, Poznan, 1984-86; Visiting Asst Prof, Univ of Florida, 1986- 87; Asst Prof, Georgia Southern Univ, 1987-. *Publications:* Polish Student Solidarity Movement on a Comparative Scale; Chapters in Books. *Memberships:* American Sciological Assn; Intl Sociological Assn; Georgia Sociological Assn; Georgia Southern Women Assn. *Honours:* Michiwicz Univ Award for Ma Thesis; Visiting Fellowship, Univ of Leiden; Award for Student Paper ; Profl Travel Award. *Hobbies:* Bicycling; Reading; Classical Music. *Address:* Dept of Sociology/Anthrop, Georgia Southern Univ, PO Box 8051, Statesboro, GA 30458, USA.

WELBANK John Michael, b. 2 Aug 1930, London, England. m. Alison Hopkins, 25 Aug 1956, 2 s, 1 d. *Education:* Natl Service Royal Artillery, 1948-50; Univ Coll, London, 1950-55. *Appointments:* Planning Officer, London County Council, 1957-59; Architect Ministry of Educ, 1959-62; Snr Arch, Ministry of Housing, Local Government, 1962-64; Shankland Cox, 1964-; Dir, 1968-. *Publications:* Many Papers. *Memberships:* RIBA;

MRTPI; FRSA. *Honours:* BA; Diploma Town Planning; Silver Medalist RIBA; Hounsfield Prize Man UCL; Hunt Bureau RIBA; Churchill Fellowship; Jnr warden Worshipful Co of Arch. *Hobbies:* Sailing; Walking; Reading; Painting. *Address:* 24 South Hill Park, London NW3 2SB, England.

WELCH Anthony Roy Clayton, b. 5 Sept 1942, Sleaford, Lincs. Arch, RIBA. m. Kathleen Margaret, 4 Feb 1967, 1 s, 1 d. *Education:* St Albans Abbey Sch, 1954-60; Poly of Central London, 1960-66. *Appointments:* London Partner, Mellich & Welch, Florida, 1970-74; Fndn Partner, Renton Welch Partnership, 1974-. *Creative Works:* 3D Structural Analysis of Space Frames; Rationalised Constructions; Longmans Press; Herts CC Educations Building. *Memberships:* RIBA; ARCUK; DES; Princes Trust; HM King Constantine of Hellenes; Cardinal Hume. *Honours:* RIBA, student of the Year Award; Soc of Carpenters Award; Civic Design Award; Education award; Environmental Design Award. *Hobbies:* Fund Raising; Voice Overs; Para Gliding; Reading; Gardening. *Address:* Renton Welch Partnership, 12 Stucley Place, London NW1 8NS, England.

WELCH O J, b. 25 Nov 1929, Tahlequah, OK. Oil & Real Estate Exec. m. 2 May 1959, 2 d. *Education:* BS, Sch of Mgtm & Engrng General Motors, 1951. *Appointments:* Owner, Operator, Welch Buick Co, Tahlequah, 1953-59; Pres, Chmn of the Bd, Welco Industries, 1958-62; Exec VP, Profl Investors Life Insurance Co, Tulsa, 1962-70; Vp Western Coach Mobile Homes, Tulsa, 1963-71; Liberty Loan Co, 1963-69; Pres, Welch Mgmt Corp, 1971- 72; CEO, Orenco Assc Inc, Tulsa, 1978-. *Publications:* Papers & Articles. *Memberships:* General Motors Public Relations Committee; Broker Securities Exchange Commission; Intl Platform Assn. *Hobbies:* Fishing; Golfing; Coin Collecting. *Address:* 1742 South Erie Avenue, Tulsa, OK 74112, USA. 7, 52, 132.

WELD FORESTER Anthony Edward, b. 24 Oct 1954, Marlborough, England. Auctioneer. m. 20 Oct 1979, 2 s, 2 d. *Education:* Harrow Sch, 1968-72; Magdalen Coll, Oxford, 1973-76. *Appointments:* Sotheleys, 1977-91; Regional Dir Sotheleys Glasgow. *Membership:* Brooks, Merchant House, Glasgow. *Honour:* Churchill Prize for Oratory. *Hobbies:* Tennis; Skiing. *Address:* Owl Manse, Gartmore, By Stirling, FK8 3RP, England.

WELFARE Jonathan William, b. 21 Oct 1944, Dunfermune, Scotland. Mgrng Dir. m. Deborah Louise Nesbit, 6 Sept 1969, 1 s, 3 d. *Education:* Bradfield Coll, Berkshire, 1958-62; Emmanuel Coll, Cambridge, BA, 1963- 66; MA, 1969. *Appointments:* Conslt, Drivers Jonas & Co, 1966-68; Conslt, Colin Buchanan & Partners, 1968-70; Corp Planning Mgr, Milton Keynes Development Corp, 1970-74; Chief Economist, Deputy Chief Exec, South Yorkshire County Council, 1974-84; Dir, The Landmark Trust, 1984-86; Dir, The Oxford Ventures Group, 1986-90; Dir, Venture Link Investors Ltd, 1990-. *Memberships:* The Northmoor Trust; The Oxford Trust; Company of Information Technologists; Friends of St Peters Church. *Hobbies:* Gardening; Tennis; Cricket. *Address:* Rooks Orchard, Little Wittenham, Abingdon, Oxfordshire, OX14 4Q7, England.

WELLBELOVED Alfred James, b. 29 July 1926, London, England. Dir General. m. Mavis Beryl Ratcliffe, 31 July 1948, 2 s, 1 d. *Education:* South East London Tech Coll, 1946-48; Royal Navy, 1942-46. *Appointments:* Commercial Conslt, 1951-65; Member of Parliament, 1965- 83; Dir General, The kidney Foundation, 1984-; Minister Defence, 1976-79. *Publication:* Local Government Text Book. *Memberships:* FBIM. *Hobbies:* Camping & Caravanning; Travel; Writing; Broadcasting. *Address:* Craigdon House, Lesney Park, Erith, Kent DA8 3DS, England. 1.

WELLER William Leslie, b. 23 Apr 1935, Horsham, West Sussex, England. Fine Art Auctioneer; Valuer. m. Brenda Olive Wilson, 1 s. *Education:* Cranleigh Sch, Collyers. *Appointments:* Newland Tompkins Taylor, 1951-55; King & Chasemore, 1955-57, 1959-78; SRAF, 1957-59; Sothebys, Sussex, MD, 1978-91; Sothebys, London, Dir, 1991-. *Memberships:* FRICS; FSVA; Naval Military club; Sussex Club; Chichester Cath Fabric Fund; Weald & Downland Mus; Council Sussex Archaeological Soc. *Hobbies:* Riding; Hunting; Gardening; Reading. *Address:* 35 New bond Street, London W1A 2AA, England.

WELLINGS Victor Gordon, b. 19 July 1919, London, England. Pres, Lands Tribunal. m. Helen Margaret Jill Lovell, 1 May 1948, 3 s. *Education:* Reading Sch, 1931-37; Exeter Coll, Oxford, MA, 1937-40; Called to Bar, 1949. *Appointments:* War Service, 1940-46; Practised at the Bar, 1949-73; Queens Counsel, 1973; Deputy Judge, High Court, 1975-. *Publications:* Woodfall on the Law of Landlord & Tenant; Other Legal Publs. *Memberships:* United Oxford & Cambridge Univ Club. *Hobbies:* Golf; Fishing; Photography. *Address:* Cherry Tree Cottage, Whitechurch Hill, Nr Reading, RG8 7PT, England. 1.

WELLS Carol Menthe, b. 3 July 1942, New York, USA. Co Dir, Corp Staff Training Div; Dir of research & Development Jobwatch Inc. m. Roger Wells, 2 s. *Education:* BS, Univ of Bridgeport, 1963; MA, Rutgers Univ, 1964; DP Ed, 1981; PhD, Univ of Connecticut, 1984. *Appointments:* Art Dir, The Boeing Co, 1965; Education Admin, Wadsworth Atheneum Museum, Enfield Public Schs, Windsor Public Schs, Chalmatte Public Schs, 1964-71; Paid Lectr, Staff Development Educ, Workshop Dir for Degreed Profls, 1969-78; Coll Level Curriculum Instruction & Supervision, 1965-68, 1977-79; Master Tchr, Independant Study Coll Programmes, Skidmore Coll, trinity Coll, 1977- 78; Accounts Dir, Public Relations, Windsor Communications, 1977-79; Mktng Sales Intangibles, Public Relations Ltd, US Express, 1979-80; Educational Admin, All Levels of Public Educ; Vice Pres, American Mgmt Inst, 1984-85; Arizona State Dept of Educ, 1985-86; Dir, Corp Image Conslt, 1981-86; Co Dir, Corp Staff Training Div, Jobwatch Inc, 1986; Dir Acad Assoc, 1986-91. *Creative Works:* Paintings & Sculptures, Museum Exhib Artist; Specific Accountability Instruments; Coprorate Prgrame Management Manuals. *Memberships:* American Mgmt Inst; Acad of Tucson. *Honours:* Dana Scholar. *Hobbies:* Creating Paintings; Sculpture. *Address:* Acad Assoc, Educationa, Corp Mgmt Conslt, POB 3854, Fullerton, CA 92634, USA.

WELLS Frances Jean, b. 28 Oct 1937, Washington, DC. Economist. *Education:* Wellesley Coll, BA, 1955-59; New York Univ, MBA, 1969-71. *Appointments:* Commerical Banking Dept, Bankers Trust con, NY, 1959-63; Program Dir, Development Fund, Wellesley Coll, 1963-67; Dir, Special Fund Programs, 1967-69; Analyst in Money & Banking, Economists Div, Congressional Research Serv, Washington DC, 1973-77; Specialist, 1977-88; Specialist in Economic Policy, 1988-. *Publications:* Numerous Publi, Articles & Reports; A Reference Guild to Banking & Finance. *Memberships:* American Economic Assn; American Finance Assn; Cosmos Club. *Address:* 1600 N Oak St, Arlington, VA 22209, USA. 52, 132.

WELLS Marrion, Music/Dance Recitalist. *Education:* Eastville Sch, Sheffield; Rossall Sch, fleetwood; Sheffield Univ. *Appointments:* Various Theatre Engagements; Founded Arion Presentations, 1957. *Creative Works:* Articles; Contributor, Drama in Therapy; Finale for a Piano Player. *Memberships:* Theatrical Mgmt Assn; Actors Equity. *Honours:* Dame Irene Vanbright Gold Medal; TVS Xharitable Trust Award; Singapore ABI Annual Assoc of the Year. *Hobbies:* Swimming; Photography; Anical Conservation. Welfare; cars; Music. *Address:* Arion Presentations, 27 Middle Road, Hastings, E Sussex, TN35 5DL, England. 152.

WELLS Robert Louis, b. 18 Mar 1939, Alexandria, LA, USA. Episcopal Priest. m. Carol Hunter, 3 Apr 1983, 3 s, 1 d. *Education:* BA, LSU, 1961; BD GGBTS, 1965; M Div GGBTS, 1971. *Appointments:* Pastor, Second Baptist Church, Lubbock, TX, 1966-78; Ex Dir, Contact Lubbock Inc, 1979-91; Asst Rector, St Pauls Episcopal Church, Waco, TX, 1991- ; Chaplin Baylor Univ, Canterbury Assn, 1991-. *Publication:* Nascod Journal. *Memberships:* Am Assn of Pastorial counselors; assn for Psychological Type Lambda Chi Alpha Fraternity; Natl Assn of eagle Scouts; Oliver Lodge. *Honours:* Parish Ministers Fellow; Citizen of the Year, Lubbock. *Hobbies:* Scuba Diving; Photography; Swimming; Travel. *Address:* St Pauls Episcopal Church, 515 Columbus Avenue, Waco, TX 76701, USA. 7, 145.

WELLS Stephen Earl, b. 20 Dec 1944, Patrick AFB, FL. USA. Engrng Co Exec. m. Linda Earle Fairley, 20 May 1983, 4 s, 1 d. *Education:* Honeywell Inc, Ft Washington, PA, 1971; Student, Univ of Alabama, 1974. *Appointments:* Field, Svr Rep, Honeywell Inc, Louisiana, 1974; Designer, Rust Engrng, Birmingha, Alabama, 1974-80; Cowan Intl, 1980-87; Control Sys Sen, Rust Intl Corp, 1987-. *Memberships:* Sunday Sch Tchr, High Sch Group, Baptist Church of the Covenant; Instrument Soc of America; Scottish Rite ACA. *Honours:* Recipient Servuce Medals. *Hobbies:* Writing; Fishing; Canoeing; Hiking; Reading; Painting; Carving. *Address:* 1549 Camden Avenue, Birmingham, AL 35226, USA. 7.

WELLS William Arthur Andrew, b. 14 June 1949, Glos, England. m. Tessa Gurney, 19 Oct 1974, 2 s, 1 d. *Education:* Eton Coll; Birmingham Univ; North London Polytech. *Appointments:* Publisher, 1970-81; Com Sec, minoies Holdings Ltd, 1981-91; Curator, Land agent, Leeds Castle, Kent, 1991-. *Publications:* Historical & Political Articles. *Memberships:* N Battersea Corr Assn; Tooting Corr Assn; Major Royal Green Jackets; RARO. *Honour:* TD. *Hobbies:* Country Pursuits; Architecural History. *Address:* Mere House Mereworth, Maidstone, Kent, ME18 5NB, England.

WEN Lipeng, b. 5 Oct 1937, Hubei Province, China. Prof. m. Zhang Tungxia, Feb 1952, 2 s. *Education:* Central Acad of Fine Arts, China, 1958, 1963. *Appointments:* Hd of Oil Painting Dept, Central Acad of Fine Arts, 1983-91. *Creative Works:* Oil Painting Works. Daughter of the Land; Ode to Red Candle; Fire; Moonlight; Blue Night; A Series of White Rock. *Memberships:* China Artist Assn; Oil Painting Art Council; China Artist Assn. *Honours:* Natl First Prize, Ode to Red Candle; Golden Prize, Natl Painting Show, Fire; Honorable Prize, 91 China Oil Painting Exhib. *Address:* No.3 Shuai Fuyuan Str, Wangfujing, Beijing, China 100005, China.

WEN Mingzhum, b. 1 Feb 1934, Hunan, China. Assoc Prof. m. Mi Jiarong, 30 Sept 1963, 2 d. *Education:* Huabei Univ, 1949-51; Changchun Coll of Geology, 1956-60. *Appointments:* Xinzhongguo Sugar Refinery, 1951-56; Changchun Univ of Earth Sci, 1960-91. *Publications:* Identification of Transparent Minerals; Petrological & Geochemical Characteristics of Gold Deposits in the Tuanjiegou Gold Mine of Heilongjiang, China. *Membership:* Chinese Inst of Geology. *Hobbies:* Music; Tourism. *Address:* Dept of Geology, Changchun Univ of Earth Sci, Changchun 130061, Jilin, China.

WERGER Marinus Johannes Antonius, b. 3 May 1944, Enschede, Netherlands. Full Prof. m. Karin Elke Klein, 26 Mar 1968, 1 d. *Education:* Univ of Utrecht & Groningen, MSc, 1968; Univ Nijmegen, PhD, 1973. *Appointments:* Scientific Officer, Botanical Research Inst, Pretoria, 1968-73; Lectr, Univ of Nijmegen, Netherlands, 1974-79; Full Profl, Plant Ecology, Utrecht Univ, 1979-. *Publications:* Biogeogr & Ecol Sthn Africa; Mans Impact on Vegetation; Plant Form & Vegtation Structure; Life Strategies of Desert Succulents. *Memberships:* Royal Netherlands Acad of Arts & Sci. *Honour:* Mid American State Univ Award. *Hobbies:* Exploration & Travel; History; Food & Cooking. *Address:*

Dept of Plant Ecology & Evol Biology, Utrecht Univ, PO Box 800 84, 3508 TB Utrecht, Netherlands. 34.

WERNER Dietrich, b. 10 June 1938, Greifswald. Prof. m. Traute Werner, 2 s, 2 d. *Education:* PhD, Univ of Gottingen, 1965; Dr of Sci, Habilitation, 1970. *Appointments:* Asst Prof, Univ of Marburg, 1966; Visiting Prof, Oregon State Univ, Corvallis, 1971; Visiting Prof, ANU, Canberra, 1982; Prof, Univ of Marburg, 1983. *Publications:* The Biology of Diatoms, Oxford; Biologische Versuchsobjekte, Stuttgart; Fast Growing & Nitrogen Fixing Trees, Stuttgart. *Memberships:* 12 Intl Biological & Biochemical Soc. *Address:* Fachbereich Biologie der Philipps Univ, Karl v Frischstr, D-3550 Marburg, Germany.

WERTH Albert Johannes, b. 15 Nov 1927, Bethlehem, OFS. Dir of Museums. m. Muriel, 22 Aug 1953, 1 d. *Education:* Matric, Grey Coll, Bloemfontien, 1944; PhD, Pretoria Univ, 1973. *Appointments:* Designer, SA Airways, Johannesburg, 1953-56; Lectr, Hd, Sch of Art, Prestoria Technikon, 1957-63; Dir, Pretoria Art Museum, Melrose House Museum, 1963-. *Creative Works:* 12 One Man Exhib of Paintings; Publ. Armando Baldinelli; Maud Sumner. *Memberships:* Fine Arts Commission; Foundation for Promotion of the Creative Arts; N Tvl Raad Vir Kultuurbevordering. *Honours:* Honorary Award for Art Promotion; Honorary Professorship; Hall in Pretoria Art Museum Named After me. *Hobbies:* Painting; Music. *Address:* 94 Van Wouw Street, Groenkloof, Pretoria 0181, South Africa. 39.

WESENER Gunter Ernst Helmuth, b. 3 June 1932, Graz, Austria. Professor of Roman Law. m. Carmen Lintner, 14 Mar 1959, 2 s, 1 d. *Education:* LLD, 1954, Dip Ed, Roman Law, Hist Pvte Law, 1957, Univ Graz. *Appointments:* Assoc Prof, Roman Law, 1959-63, Full Prof, 1963-, Dean, Fac Law, 1965-66, Dean, Fac Law, 1979-81, Univ Graz. *Publications:* Books: Geschichte des Erbrechtes in Osterreich seit der Rezeption, 1957; Das innerosterr Landschrannenverfahren im 16 u 17 Jh, 1963; Romisches Recht und Naturrecht an der Universitat Graz, 1978; Einflusse und Geltung des romischgemeinen Rechts in den altosterr Landern in der Neuzeit, 1989; Rewriting of G Wesenberg's Neuere Deutsche Privatrechtsgeschichte, 1969, 1976, 1985. *Hobbies:* Genealogy; Chess. *Address:* 21 Rosenberggurtel, A-8010 Graz, Austria. 43, 52, 86.

WESLAWSKI Jan Marcin, b. 11 Nov 1955, Gdansk, Poland. Marine Biologist. m. Maja Weslawska, 7 Oct 1978, 2 d. *Education:* Univ of Gdansk, 1979; Dr of Natl Sci, 1984. *Appointments:* Univ of Gdansk, Hel Marine Research Station, 1978-84; Polish Acad of Sci, 1984-85; Inst of Oceanology, Pol Acad Sci, 1985-. *Publications:* Atlas of Spitsbergen Marine Fauna. *Memberships:* Polar Club; Cordinative Committe on European Actic Ecological Research. *Hobbies:* History of Polar Exploration; Books. *Address:* Gdynia Orlowo 81 542, Orlowska 80/2, Poland.

WESLEY James Paul, b. 28 July 1921, St Louis, MO, USA. Physicist. m. (1) Margaret Ellen Martin, June 1943, 1 s. div 1952, (2) Dorothy Ree Casey, Aug 1952, 2 s, 1 d. div, (3) Michele Dudek, June 1963, 1 d, div 1967, (4) Gabriele Beate Modest, July 1975, 2 s, 1 d. *Education:* BA, Univ Minn, 1943; MA, UCLA, 1949; PhD, UCLA, 1952; Postdioc, Scripps Inst, Oceanography, La Jolla, Calif, 1952. *Appointments include:* Various Positions, 1943-50; Prof, Phsysics, Univ Idaho, Moscow, 1953-56; Research Geophysicist Newmont Exploration Ltd, 1955-56; Rsch Physicist Lawrence Radiation Lab, Univ Calif, 1956-61; Fellow, Ctr Advanced study Behavioral Sci, Stanford Calif, 1961-62; Rsch Physicist, Univ Denver, 1962-63; Melpar Inc, Falls Church, VA, 1963; Assoc Prof, Univ mo, Rolla, 1964-74; Lectr, Cons On Quantum Theory, Others Berlin & Blumberg Fed Republic Germany, 1974-. *Publications include:* Ecophysics; Casual Quantum Theory; advanced Fundamental Physics; Profl Journals. *Memberships:* APS; AAAS. *Hobbies:* Oil Painting; Piano; Stamp

Collecting; Hiking. *Address:* Weiherdammstrasse 24, 7712 Blumberg, Germany.

WEST Ronald Robert, b. 14 Nov 1935, USA. Prof. m. Dixie Pettit, 2 Aug 1982, 2 s. *Education:* BSc, 1958; MSc, 1962; PhD, 1970. *Appointments:* Stratigrapher, 1956-57; Micropalemtologist, 1958-59; Invatebrate Paleontologist, 1960-61; Palaeocologist, Humble Oil Co, 1962-67; Asst Prof, Kansas State univ, 1969-74; Assoc Prof, 1974-79; Full prof, 1970-; Ancillary Prof of Biology, 1974-; Univ Prof, Oxford, 1980; Geologist, Middle East, 1984, 1989. *Publications:* Structure & Classification of Paleocommunities; Over 60 Sci Papers. *Memberships:* Palemotological Soc; Intl Palaeontological Assn; Geological Soc of America; Ecological Soc of America; Maine Biological Assn. *Honours include:* ssa OOPhi Kaap Phi; Sigma Gamma Epsilon; Natl Sci Foundation; America Chemical Soc. *Hobbies:* Reading; Woodwork; Travel; Archaeology; Gardening. *Address:* Dept of Geology, Thompson Hall, Kansas State Univ, Manhattan, KS 66506, USA. 2, 143.

WESTBROOK Katherine Jane, Musician; Singer; Song Writer. m. (1) 1 s, 2 d. (2)Mike Westbrook, 23 Sept 1976. *Education:* Bath Acad of Art, Corsham; Reading Univ; London Univ. *Appointments:* Tchr, Part Time, Leeds Coll of Art, 1955-73; Mike Westbrook Band, 1974; London Symphony Orchestra; Matrixensemble NDR Band; Lindsay Cooper; Many Others. *Publications:* Compositions for Lgr Orchestras; 15 Albams; Radio; TV. *Membership:* Ronnie Scotts Club. *Hobby:* Painting. *Address:* Laurence Aston, 4 Ennerdale Road, Reading, RG2 7HH, England.

WESTBROOK Michael John David, b. 21 Mar 1936, High Wycombe, England. Composer; Musician. m. Katherine Jane, 23 Sept 1976, 1 s, 1 d, 1 Stepson, 2 Stepdaughters. *Education:* Kelly Coll, Tavistock, Plymouth Coll of art, 1958-61; Honorary sch of Art, 1965. *Appointments:* Art Tchr, 1966-68; First Band, 1958; Full time Musician, 1968-. *Creative Works include:* Celebration; Release; After Smiths Hotel; Revenge Suite; Quichotte; Goodbye Peter Lorre; Measure for Measure. *Memberships:* Musicians Union; Ronnie Scotts Club. *Honour:* OBE. *Hobby:* Walking. *Address:* c/o Laurence Aston, PO Box 354, Reading RG2 7JB, England. 1.

WESTERHEIDE William Joseph, b. 23 Oct 1945, Muskogee, Okhahoma, USA. Psychotherapist. m. Julianna Walsh, 4 June 1979, 1 s. *Appointments include:* Formerly Cons: Midwest Inst Gestalt Therapy, OK City; OK; Org Aplied Sci in Soc, Ann Arbor, MI; OK Div Rehab Servs, OK City; IL Dept Voc Rehab, Springfield; Reg Rehab Rsch Inst, Univ OK, Norman; Empire State Coll, Saratoga Springs, NY; Bd Educl Advsrs, Speech Co Corp, OK City; E Cntr State Univ, Ada, OK; Chem Abuse Unit, Fed Correctional Instn, El Reno, OK; OK State Dept Mental Hlth, OK City; Currently Psychotherapist, Prog Dir, Coord Outpatient Servs, Recovery Ctr, Edmond REg Med Ctr, Edmond, OK. *Publications:* Monographs: Case Difficulty and Client Change: A state of the art (w L Lenhart), 1974; Field Test of a Service Outcome Measurement Form: Case difficulty (w L Lenhart and M Clinton Miller III), 1974; Field Test of a Service Outcome Measurement Form: Client change (w L Lenhart and M Clinton Miller III), 1975; The CompetencyBased Degree Program: The program and the people it serves (w P Colyer, J White, R Krueger), 1977; Career Advising Workshop for College Faculty: Workshop Leaders Guide (w L Lenhart), 1977; Monographs I, II, III and IV on Telecommunications for Concerned Citizen Involvement (w P Bowerman, O Collins, C Hostetter), 1978; Co-author, several contbns to jrnls. *Address:* Recovery Center, Edmond Regional Medical Center, 1 S Bryant, Edmond, OK 73034, USA. 7.

WESTERINK Areno-Jan, b. 26 Oct 1933, Stad Delden, Netherlands. Secretary-General, International Road Transport Union. m. Irma Jonkman, 26 Oct 1991.

Education: Law studies, Univs Leiden and Utrecht. *Appointments:* Joined, Legal Dept, 1960, Dir, Legal Dept, 1965, Dir, 1986, Dutch Assn Int Road Transport, 1960; VP, Liaison Comm w EC Brussels for Profl Goods Transport by Road, 1986-89, Sec-Gen, 1990, Int Road Transport Union, Geneva, Switzerland. *Address:* IRU, 3 Rue de Varembe, BP 44, 1211 Geneva 20, Switzerland. 167.

WESTERMARK Torbjorn Erik Gunnar, b. 9 Apr 1923, Solleftea, Sweden. Professor Emeritus of Nuclear Chemistry. m. Ulla Hedquist, 22 July 1950, 1 s. *Education:* Civil Engr, Chem Engrng, 1946, Dr Technology, Phys Chem, 1961, Royal Inst Technology, Stockholm. *Appointments:* Rsch Asst, 1946-51, Lectr, Applied Nuclear Chem, 1952-62, Prof, Nuclear Chem, 1962- 88; Prof Emeritus, 1988-, Royal Inst Technology, Stockholm; Expert: Royal Commn Energy, Hlth and Environment, 1975-76; Com Safety and Environment, Govt Energy Commn, 1977-78; Mbr: Comm Energy Rsch, NE, 1975-76; Bd, Beijer Inst, Royal Acad Scis, 1977-83; Govt Reactor Safety Comm, 1979; Govt Comm Cancer Prevention, 1979-84; Govt Rsch Bd Energy, 1983-88; Bd, Swedish Coun Mgmt and Work Life Issues, 1986-89. *Publications:* Author or co-author, about 150 sci articles in jrnls and books incl article on mercury in fish (w A G Johnels), 1966. *Memberships:* Fellow: Royal Acad Engrng Scis, Stockholm; Royal Acad Scis, Stockholm; Norwegian Acad Natural Sci. *Honours:* Norblad-Ekstrand Gold Medal, Swedish Chem Soc, 1959; Co- recip, MIBIS Prize, Swedish Soc Water Hygiene, 1970; Edlund Award, 1975, King Carl XVI Gustaf Gold Medal Pro Mundo Habitabilis, 1989, Swedish Royal Acad Scis; John Erocson Gold Medal, Assn Swedish Engrs USA, 1978; Royal Inst Technology, 1986; Rosenberg Prize, Environmental Achievements, Rosenberg Fndn, 1987; Grand Gold Medal, Royal Swedish Acad Engrng Scis, 1989; Environmental Prize, Assoc of Swedish Chemical Engineers, 1991. *Hobbies:* Scandinavian floristics and ornithology; Environmental history and archives. *Address:* Division of Nuclear Chemistry, Royal Institute of Technology, S-10044 Stockholm, Sweden. 52, 139.

WESTFALL Una Elizabeth, b. 23 June 1943, Poplar, Montana, USA. Assistant Professor of Nursing. *Education:* BSN, Univ OR, 1965; MSN, Cath Univ Am, 1969; PhD, Nursing Sci, Univ WA, Seattle, 1990. *Appointments:* Staff Nurse, Univ OR Med School Hosp, Portland, 1965-67, 1970-71; Staff Nurse, Univ Hosp, Ann Arbor, MI, 1967-68; Instr, 1971-72, Asst Prof, 1972-74, School Nursing, Univ Tulsa; Asst Prof, Nursing, ID State Univ, 1974-76; Field Coord, Nursing Prac Standards, 1976-79; Prog Coord, Nursing Prac, 1979-80, Am Nurses Assn; Asst Prof, Fac Clinician, Dept Adult Hlth and Illness, School Nursing, 1983-85, Asst Prof, 1985-, OR Hlth Scis Univ; Fac Cons, Univ Hosp Nursing Serv, OR Hlth Scis Univ, 1985-; Rsch Asst, School Nursing, Univ WA, Seattle, 1988-90. *Publications include:* Book chapts: Accountability for clinical judgement and decision making. How can we assure quality, 1987; Measurement of new clinical forms: Testing for nursing strengths in a data base, 1989; GI physiology (w M Heitkemper), in press; Articles: Activating clinical inferences: A component of diagnostic reasoning in nursing (w C Tanner, D Putzier, K Padrick), 1986; Standards of practice: Nursing values made visible, 1987; Diagnostic reasoning strategies of nurses and nursing students (w K Padrick, U Westfall, D Putzier), 1987; Systemic responses to different enteral feeding schedules in rats (w M Heitkemper), in press. *Memberships:* Lifetime Mbr, Sigma Theta Tau, Beta Psi Chapt Archivist; Coun Nurse Researchers, Am Nurses Assn; OR Nurses Assn, Nursing Prac Comm; Am Soc Parenteral and Enteral Nutrition; Am Nursing Diagnosis Assn. *Honours:* Nat Rsch Serv Award, Nat Ctr Nursing Rsch, 1989-90; Sterling Drug Inc Scholar, Am Nurses Fndn, 1989. *Hobbies:* Swimming; Photography; Enjoying the outdoors. *Address:* 3150 SW Bertha Blvd No 7, Portland, OR 97201, USA. 76, 138, 152.

WETTENHALL Roger Llewellyn, b. 4 Feb 1931, Hobart, Tasmania, Australia. Professor of Public Administration. div., 1 s, 2 d. *Education:* BA, 1952, Dip Pub Admin, 1954, MA, 1956, Univ Tas; PhD, Australian Nat Univ, 1962. *Appointments:* Personnel Cadet Off, Australian C'wlth Pub Serv, 1948-59; Lectr to Reader, Univ Tas, 1962-71; Dept Hd, later Prof, Univ Canberra, ACT, 1971- . *Publications:* Bushfire Disaster: An Australian Community in Crisis, 1975; Organising Government: The Uses of Ministries and Departments, 1986; Public Enterprise and National Development, 1987; Jt Ed, Ed, Australian Journal of Public Administration, 1989-. *Memberships:* Nat Fellow, Jrnl Ed, Royal Inst Pub Admin, Australia; Hon Fellow, Australian Inst Municipal Admin; Reg VP, Project Dir, Int Assn Schools and Insts of Admin. *Honours:* Winner, Silver Medal, Haldane Essay Competition, 1965. *Hobbies:* Walking; Cycling; Gardening. *Address:* 12 Carmichael St, Deakin, ACT 2600, Australia. 3, 30, 52.

WETZEL Dave, b. 9 Oct 1942, Isleworth, Middlesex, England. Association Director. m. Heather Allman, 14 Feb 1973, 2 d. *Education:* Ordinary Nat Cert, Elec Engrng, Southall Teach Coll; Bus Studies, Ealing Coll; Econs, Henry George School Social Sci. *Appointments:* Student Engr, Wilkinson Sword, 1959-62; Bus Conductor, Bus Driver, Garage Insp, London Transport, 1962-69; Br Mgr, Initial Servs, 1969-70; Pilot Roster Off, Brit Airways, 1970-75; Pol Organiser, London Coop, 1975-81; Elected Mbr, Chmn, Transport, Gtr London Coun, 1981-86; Dpty Ldr, Chmn Planning, Ldr, Hounslow Coun, 1986-91; Dir, London Dial-a-Ride Users Assn, 1989-. *Publications:* Ed, Civil Aviation News, 1978-81. *Memberships:* Chmn, Labour Land Campaign; AMA Pub Transport Comm; Hounslow Campaign Nuclear Disarmament; Transport Studies Soc, pres 1991-92; Pres, W London Peace Coun; Pres, Reading Esperanto Grp. *Hobbies:* Socialist politics; Esperanto; Swimming; Sailboarding. *Address:* 28 Penderel Road, Hounslow, Middlesex TW3 3QR, England. 1.

WEXLER Michael, b. 24 Aug 1945, Pascani, Rumania. Quality Assurance Director. m. Mira Ariel, 4 Sept 1969, 1 s, 1 d. *Education:* BA, Stats, Sociology, Haifa Univ, 1973; BSME (Ed), 1978, MBA, 1987, Technion, Israeli Inst Technology, 1987; Cert Quality Engr, Am Soc Quality Control, 1985. *Appointments:* Min Def, Israel, 1968-71; Quality Control Supvsr, Soltam Ltd, 1971-73; Quality Lectr, Israeli Inst Productivity, 1973- 83; Dir, Quality Assurance, Elbit Computers, Haifa, 1983-. *Publications:* Basics for Calculating and Measurement of Tooted Wheels, 1970; Mathematical Formulae for Measuring Non-Symmetrical Forms, 1972. *Memberships:* Sr Mbr, Am Soc Quality Control; Israeli Soc Quality Assurance. *Hobbies:* Reading; Bridge; Tennis; Music. *Address:* 132 Moria St, Haifa, Israel. 34.

WHARTON Christopher Frederick Percy, b. 19 Feb 1937, Banbury, Oxfordshire, England. Consultant Physician. m. Pamela Mary Deane, 23 May 1980, 2 d. *Education:* Worcester Coll, Oxford, 1955-59; Guy's Hosp, 1959-62; MA (Oxon); DM (Oxon); FRCP. *Appointments:* House Off, Registrar, Guy's Hosp, London, 1963-72; Cons Physn, Cardiologist, Bromley Hlth Auth, Bromley, Kent, 1972-; Tchr, London Univ, 1986. *Publications:* Cardiological Problems in Practice, book, 1981; Management of Cardiological Diseases in Practice, book, 1986; Publs in echocardiology. *Memberships:* Brit Cardiac Soc; Brit Med Assn; Freeman, City of London; Liveryman, Worshipful Co Gunmakers; Athenaeum. *Hobbies:* Brit Heart Fndn Award, 1967. *Hobbies:* Shooting; Skiing; Tennis; Golf; Wine; Travel; Chelsea Football Club. *Address:* 24-26 High Street, Chipstead, Nr Sevenoaks, Kent TN13 2RP, England.

WHITBOURN Philip Robin, b. 10 Mar 1932, Coulsdon, Surrey, England. Architect. m. Anne Pearce Marks, 10 Jan 1959, 1 s, 1 d. *Education:* Dip Arch, 1955, Acad Dip, Town Planning, 1969, PhD, 1973, Univ London.

Appointments: Sir Edwin Cooper RA and Ptnrs, 1955-58; Stewart, Hendry and Smith, 1958-60; Fitzroy Robinson Ptnrship, 1960-66; Historic Bldgs Div, Gtr London Coun, 1966-86; London Divisional Arch, Engl Heritage, 1986-. *Memberships:* FRIBA; Chmn, Tunbridge Wells Br, RIBA, 1971; Fellow, Royal Town Planning Inst. *Honours:* Fellow, Soc Antiquaries. *Address:* English Heritage, London Region, Chesham House, 30 Warwick Street, London W1R 6AB, England.

WHITCOMB John Clement Jr, b. 22 June 1924, Washington, DC, USA. Lecturer; Author. m. Norma Aileen Pritchett, 1 Jan 1971, 5 s, 1 d. *Education:* AB, Princeton Univ, 1948; BD w high hons, 1951, ThM, 1953, ThD, 1957, Grace Theological Sem. *Appointments:* Served World War II, Europe, 1944-46; Prof, Theology, Old Testament, Grace Theological Sem, Winona Lake, IN, 1951-90; Lectured, USA, Can, Latin Am, Wn Europe, Ctrl African Republic, Far East; Extension Prog, Grace Sem, France, 1985-89. *Publications:* Darius the Mede, 1959; The Genesis Flood (w Henry M Morris), 1961; The Moon: Its Creation, Form and Significance (w Donald DeYoung), 1978; Esther; The Triumph of God's Sovereignty, 1979; Daniel, 1985; The Early Earth: An Introduction to Biblical Creationism, 1986; The World That Perished: An Introduction to Biblical Catastrophism, 1988; Israel: A Commentary on Joshua--2 Kings (w John Davis), 1989; Contbr to Wycliffe Bible Commentary; Charts on Old Testament chronology; 16 audio cassett albums; 12 video tapes. *Memberships:* Evangelical Theological Soc; Creation Rsch Soc; Spanish-World Gospel Mission, 1962-90; Conservative Grace Brethren Assn; Lakeland Child Evangelism. *Honours:* Alumnus of Yr, Grace Sem, 1970. *Hobby:* Photography. *Address:* PO Box 277, Winona Lake, IN 46590, USA. 3, 8, 15, 30.

WHITE Franklin Marshall Matthews, b. 7 June 1946, Perth, Western Australia, Australia. Director of Epidemiology Centre. m. Sharon Winifred Carlyle, 21 Nov 1970, 2 s, 1 d. *Education:* Univ Queensland, 1964-65; MD, CM, McGill Univ, Can, 1965-69; MSc, London School Hygiene and Tropical Med, England, 1973; FRCP Can, 1981. *Appointments:* Asst Prof, Epidemiology, Hlth, McGill Univ, Can, 1972-74; Chief, Communicable Disease Div, Hlth and Welfare Can, 1974-77; Dir, Communicable Disease Control, Alta, 1977-80; Dir, Epidemiology Div, Min Hlth, BC, 1980-82; Prof, Hd, Community Hlth and Epidemiology, Dalhousie Univ, 1982-89; Dir, Caribbean Epidemiology Ctr (PAHO/ WHO), Port-of-Spain, Trinidad, 1989-. *Publications:* Over 175 papers and reports in med and sci lit. *Memberships:* Can Pub Hlth Assn, Pres 1986-88; Chief Examiner, Community Med, Royal Coll Physns and Surgs Can, 1986-88. *Honours:* C'wlth (Australia) Scholarship, 1965; McGill Bursary, 1965-69; Breakthrough Award for Creativity, US Acad Educl Dev, 1989. *Hobbies:* Masters track and field (currently hold national titles, Canada, Trinidad and Tobago, in sprints and long jump); Sailing (offshore sea passages); Writing; Music (piano, voice, guitar). *Address:* Flat No 1, Box 164, Port-of-Spain, Trinidad, West Indies. 88.

WHITE Jerry Coleman, b. 25 May 1951, Spartanburg, SC, USA. Pastor of Baptist Church. m. Janet Scruggs, 9 June 1972, 2 s. *Education:* BA, Gardner-Webb Coll, 1974; Erskine Sem, 1975; Master's degree, 1978, DMin, 1980, Luther Rice Sem; SEn Sem, 1982. *Appointments:* Youth Min, Crestview Ch, 1969; Dir, YMCA, Chesnee, SC, 1970-71; Pastor: Goodes Creek Bapt Ch, 1972-75; Rock Creek Bapt Ch, 1975-76; Crestview Bapt Ch, 1976-78; Ebenezer Bapt Ch, 1978-84; Prof, Missions, Fruitland Bibla Inst, Hendersonville, NC, 1982-; Pastor, Chiquola Bapt Ch, 1984-. *Memberships:* SC Bapt Gen Bd, 1988-90; Tri-Co Bapt Conf, Pres 1987, 1990; Saluda Bapt Assn, Pres Pastors Conf 1986, Vice-Moderator 1990, Modrator 1991; SC Karate Assn; Pt-time Instr, Marty Knight Karate Assn. *Honours:* RA Serv-Aide Certs, 1966-70; Athletic Awards, Football, Basketball, Baseball, 1966-69; Fellowship Christian Athlete Award, 1969; Awards, Youth Sports Assn, 1970, 1979, 1980, 1990; Black Belt, Karate, 1985; 2nd Degree Balck Belt,

Karate, 1986; SC Black Belt State Champion, 1987. *Hobbies:* Fishing; Hunting; Golf; Karate. *Address:* 116 Murray Street, Honea Path, SC 29654, USA. 117.

WHITE Jillian Mary, b. 29 Jan 1942, Market Harborough, Leicestershire, England. Senior Music Producer. *Education:* Royal Acad Music, London, 1960-64; Acad Music and Drama, Vienna, 1966-67; ARAM, 1988. *Career:* Opera and Lieder Singer, to 1970; Prof, Music, Vienna, Austria, 1967-68; BBC Gramaphone Lib, England, 1970-71; Music Selector, BBC Sound Archive, 1971-75; Music Prod, BBC Pebble Mill, 1975-86; Sr Music Prod, BBC S and W, 1986-; LP/CD Prod, Coll Records, CRD, Toshiba EMI, Conifer Records; Vis Lectr, Fndr, Prod Techn course, Birmingham Conservatoire. *Memberships include:* Gov, Bath Coll Higher Educ Inc. *Honours:* Winner, Gramophone Award for Faure Requiem, 1985; Hon Mbr, Polish Composers Union, Warsaw, 1990; Hon Fellow, Birmingham Schools Music, 1990; Works dedicated to her, var composers incl Robert Simpson, Elis Pehkonen, Patrick Piggott, Marek Stachowski; Mbr, Fest Comms: Cheltenham Int Fest Music; Quarter, N London; Gt Elm Music Fest; S and W Concerts Bd; 1st woman Sr Music Prod in BBC regions. *Hobbies:* Music; Painting; Life drawing; Cooking; Cats esp recently cross-bred Abyssinian kittens. *Address:* BBC, Whitelands Road, Bristol BS8 2LR, England.

WHITE John Branum, b. 19 Mar 1952, North Kingstown, Rhode Island, USA. Senior Quality Control Engineer. m. Elaine Lenore Epps, 18 Aug 1973, 3 s, 3 d. *Education:* BS cum laude, Chem, Univ TX Dallas, Richardson, 1980. *Appointments:* Sr Rsch Asst, 1975-80, Quality Assurance Engr, 1980-83, Mbr, Tech Staff, Lab Mgr, 1983-87, Process Control Engr, 1987-89, Quality Circle Coord, 1988-89, TX Instr Inc, Dallas; Owner, Ptnr, Green Parrot Trading Co, Garland, TX, 1988-; Sales Dir, Univite Inc, Carlsbad, CA, 1989-; Engrng Cons, SW Semiconductor, Garland, 1988-89; Sr Quality Control Engr, Eveready Battery, Bennington, VT, 1990-. *Publication:* Instrumental Neutron Activation Analysis of Processal Silicon (co-author), 1985. *Memberships:* State Convention Deleg, Republican Party TX, 1986, 1990; Precinct Chmn, Local School Bd Cand, 1990; Work Grp Coord, United Way, Dallas Co, 1984; Awards Judge, 37th Int Sci and Engrng Fair, Ft Worth, TX, 1986; US Contact for La Combe, Biscarrose, Frnace, 1986-90; Am Soc Quality Control; Green Mountain Club; Past Mbr: Am Chem Soc; Micro Network Assn, Pres 1990; N TX Materials Characterization Soc. *Honours:* Quality Improvement Incentive Award, TX Instr Inc, 1981; Variability Reduction Team Project Award, Eveready Battery Co, Bennington, 1991. *Hobbies:* Christian church activities; International families and students host; Beekeeping; Teaching children in home school. *Address:* PO Box 4222, Bennington, VT 05201, USA.

WHITE Larry Thomas, b. 20 Mar 1948, Porterdale, Georgia, USA. School Administrator. m. Elizabeth Owen, 5 Oct 1969, 1 s, 1 d. *Education:* US Naval Communications School, 1966; Univ CA, 1966-67; AA, Psychology, Truett McConnell Coll, 1979; Calvary Bible Coll, 1987-88; BA, Christian Educ, Evangel Christian Univ and Sem, 1989. *Appointments:* E-5 Communication Tech, USN, 1965-68; Chem Analyst, Hercules Inc, 1969-71; Trainman, Norfolk So Railway, 1971-88; Sunday School Dir: Milstead Bapt, Milstead, GA, 1974-76; Ebenezer Bapt, Toccoa, GA, 1980-84; Youth Pastor, Tom's Creek Bapt, Martin, GA, 1985-86; Fndr, Sunday School Youth Dir, Admnstr, Ridge Road Christian School, Eastanollee, GA, 1986-; Pres, Word of Life, Carnesville, GA, 1986-; Fndr, Pres, Chosen Instruments of Faith Mins, 1986-. *Memberships:* Assn Evangel Gospel Assemblies; Stephens Co Ministerial Assn; Int Fellowship Christian School Admnstrs; Sec/ Treas, Word of Life Christian Ctr; Assn Christian Schools Int. *Honour:* Vietnam Serv Medal, USN. *Hobbies:* Camping; Fishing; Stamp collecting. *Address:* Route 1, Box 164, Ridge Road, Eastanollee, GA 30538, USA. 15.

WHITE Lonnie J, b. 12 Feb 1931, Haskell County, Texas, USA. Emeritus Professor of History. m. Nancy Louella Evans, 23 June 1951, 1 s, 1 d. *Education:* BA, W TX State Coll, 1950; MA, TX Tech Coll, 1955; PhD, Univ TX, Austin, 1961. *Appointments:* Admnstr Specialist, US Army, 1951-53; Tchng Asst, Univ TX, Austin, 1957-61; Mbr, Dept Hist, Memphis State Univ, TN, 1961-89. *Publications:* Books incl: Hostiles and Horse Soldiers Indian Battles and Campaigns in the West, 1972; Panthers to Arrowheads: The 36th (Texas-Oklahoma) Division in World War I, 1984; Over 40 articles and 90 book reviews. *Memberships include:* Am Mil Inst; Am Histl Assn; So Histl Assn; Edit Advsry Bd, Journal of the West, 1963-88. *Hobbies:* Multi-engine rated private pilot; Historical research and writing; Fishing. *Address:* 4858 Musgrave Trail, Abilene, TX 79606, USA. 7, 13, 30.

WHITE Stewart Dale, b. 23 July 1951, Sydney, New South Wales, Australia. Solicitor. m. 20 Sept 1980, 1 s, 1 d. *Education:* St Andrew's Coll, Univ Sydney: BA Hist Hons, 1972, LLB, 1975; Downing Coll, Univ Cambridge: LLM, Int Law Hons. *Appointments:* Sr Assoc, Allen Allen & Hemsley, Sydney, 1979-83; Ptnr, Blake Dawson Waldron, 1983-88; Ptnr, Denton Hall Burgin & Warrens, London, England, 1988-. *Memberships:* Int Bar Assn, Chmn Communications Law Comm; LawAsia, Chmn Media and Communications Law Comm; Chmn, Organising Comm Legal Symposium, Int Telecommunications Union Conf, 1989; Organising Comm Regulatory Symposium, Int Telecommunications Union Conf 1991; Cambridge C'wlth Trust, NSW Comm; Law Soc. *Hobbies:* Sailing (mbr, Royal Sydney Yacht Squadron, Bosham Sailing Club); Horse racing (mbr, Australian Jockey Club); Bridge; Music; Walking. *Address:* c/o Five Chancery Lane, London EC4A 1BU, England.

WHITEHEAD Frances, b. Lancashire, England. Editorial Director. *Education:* St Hilda's Coll, Oxford; BA (Oxon); MA (Oxon); MA, Univ Sheffield. *Appointments:* Lib, Lancs Co Libs, 1970-71; Ed, 1974, Dpty Ed Dir, 1985-87, Ed Dir, 1987-, Mills & Boon, Richmond; Freelance Author, Speaker, Broadcaster, all aspects of mass mkt fiction. *Publication:* And Then He Kissed Her...A Guide to writing fiction (co-author). *Memberships:* Soc Genealogists. *Hobbies:* Times crosswords; Sumo wrestling; Theatre; Travel off the beaten track. *Address:* c/o Mills and Boon, Eton House, Paradise Road, Richmond, Surrey, England.

WHITEHEAD John Michael Stannage, b. 19 Dec 1927, Leicester, England. Company Chairman. m. Alanda Joy Bentley, 28 Apr 1962, 1 s, 2 d. *Education:* Leicester Tech Coll (now Leicester Polytechnic). *Appointments:* 2nd Lt, Army Cadet Corps, 1945-48; Special Constabulary, 1950-68; Joined, 1945, Dir, 1948-74, G Stibbe and Co Ltd; Dir, J & H Hadden Ltd, 1954-63; Chmn, 1963-72, Mng Dir, 1963-74, Stibbe-Hadden Ltd; Chmn, John Whitehead Textiles Ltd, 1974-; Name, Lloyds London, 1979-; Chmn, H Harrison and Co Finishers Ltd, 1987-; Tax Commnr, 1966. *Memberships:* Former Vice-Chmn, Former Chmn, Govs Leicester Poly; Chmn Govs, Pro-Chancellor, Leicester Poly Higher Educ Corp; Var charities; Freeman, City of London; Freeman, City of Leicester; Liveryman, Worshipful Co of Merchant Taylors; Liveryman, Master, Worshipful Co of Framework Knitters. *Honours:* JP, 1968; FRSA, 1976; Dpty Lt, Leics, 1988; CBE, Birthday Hons, 1990. *Hobbies:* Watching Rugby football; Sailing; Gardening; Reading. *Address:* The Poplars, Main Street, Houghton on the Hill, Leicester LE7 9GD, England. 43.

WHITESELL Nolan Gary, b. 3 Dec 1953, Pittsburgh, Pennsylvania, USA. Canoe Designer and Manufacturer. m. Patricia Ann Harden, 25 Oct 1975, div. 1989, 1 d. *Education:* BA magna cum laude, Food Technology, Bus Mgmt, Univ GA, Athens, 1975. *Appointments:* Mgmt, Hyatt Corp, Atlanta, GA, 1975-78; Search Cons, Whitesell and Assocs, Atlanta, 1979-84; CEO, Whitesell Ltd, Atlanta, 1983-; CEO, Nantahala Riverside Inc,

Bryson City, NC, 1991-; Cons: Mohawk Canoe Co, Longwood, FL, 1983-89; Wn Canoeing, Vancouver, BC, Can, 1984-; Cons/Promoter, Save the Payette, Boise, ID, 1987-; Promoter, Whitewater Pre-Worlds Championships, Savage River, MD, 1988; Speaker, var orgs. *Creative works:* Articles in sports mags; Producer, 6 videos incl: Niagara Gorge; Canoe the Canyon. *Memberships:* Dir, GA Canoeing Assn; N Am Paddle Sports Assn; Am Canoe Assn; Nat Org River Sports; Piedmont Paddlers Assn; Atlanta Whitewater Club; Coastal Canoeists, Richmond, VA. *Honours:* Recordholder, Open Canoe Roll, Open Canoe Hands Roll, Guiness Book of World Records, 1986; 1st Place, Nat Champion, Am Canoe Assn: N Am Whitewater Rodeo, Ocoee River, TN, 1986, 1990, Open Canoe Wildwater, Ocoee River, 1987, 1990; Named Top Canoeist in US, Canoe Mag, 1987; Whitewater Legends, Video Review of Paddlers contributing most to the sport, 1987. *Hobbies:* Skiing; Swimming; Hiking; Weight training. *Address:* Whitesell Ltd, 2362 Dresden Dr NE, Atlanta, GA 30341, USA. 7, 132.

WHITESIDE Donald, b. 9 May 1931, Manhattan, New York, USA. Business Owner. m. Alvina Helen Adams, 11 Feb 1956, 4 s, 1 d. *Education:* BA, WI State Univ, 1958; MS, Univ WI, Madison, 1960; PhD, Stanford Univ, CA, 1967. *Appointments:* Combat Infantryman, US Army, Korean War, 1948- 54; Instr, NC State Univ, 1964-65; Asst Prof, Univ TN, Knoxville, 1965-67; Asst Prof, Univ Alta, Edmonton, Canada, 1967-90; Sociologist, Govt of Can, 1970-91; Owner, Donald Whiteside and Assoc Inc. *Publications:* Aboriginal people, 1973; A look into Indian history, 1983; 25 other articles. *Memberships:* Can Rights and Liberties Fedn, Pres 7 yrs; Alta Human Rights and Civil Liberties Assn, Pres 2 yrs; Civil Liberties Assn Nat Capital Reg, Pres 13 yrs; Pres, Ont Civil Liberties Assn. *Honours:* FSF Fellowship, summer 1963; Stanford Univ Fellow, 1963-64; Best Tchr Award, NC State Univ, 1964-65; Community Serv Award, 15 yrs, Govt Ont, 1984; Marion Keffer Award, Ont Genealogical Soc, 1990. *Hobbies:* Genealogy; History; Stamp collection. *Address:* 4 Newgale St, Nepean, Ontario, Canada K2H 5R2. 142, 143.

WHITLARK James Stuart, b. 2 Nov 1948, Detroit, Michigan, USA. English Educator. *Education:* BA, Engl, 1971, MA, Engl, 1973, Wayne State Univ; PhD, Engl, Univ Chgo, 1976. *Appointments:* Lectr, IL Inst Technology, 1977-78; Lectr, Loyola Univ, Chgo, IL, 1978-79; Asst Prof, 1979- 85, Assoc Prof, 1985-91, Prof, 1991-, TX Tech Univ, Lubbock. *Publications:* Illuminated Fantasy: From Blake's Visions to Recent Graphic Fiction, 1988; Behind the Great Wall: A Post Jungian Approach to Kafkaesque Literature, 1991; Chapts in : Aspects of Fantasy, 1986; Literature and Anthropology, 1989; The Shape of the Fantastic, 1990; Articles in profl jrnls. *Memberships:* MLA; Kafka Soc Am; Conf Christianity and Lit; Int Assn for the Fantastic in the Arts. *Honours:* New Prof, Excellence in Tchng Award, 1980, Dir Hons Award, 1985, TX Tech Univ. *Hobbies:* Anthropology; Philosophy; Psychology; Comparative religions. *Address:* Texas Tech University, English Dept, Lubbock, TX 79409, USA. 7.

WHITMAN Mara Aroen, b. 7 Oct 1964, New York City, New York, USA. Law Librarian. m. *Education:* BS, Bus, Skidmore Coll; MSLS, Simmons Coll; JD, Univ CT School Law, 1992. *Appointments:* Law Libn: Warner and Stackpole; New England School Law; Day, Berry and Howard; Atty Gen's Off, State of CT. *Memberships:* Law Libns New England; Am Assn Law Libns; Hanford Assn Law Libns; Delta Delta Delta; Elected Rep, Student Bar Assn; Pres, Jewish Law Students Assn. *Honours:* Mead Data Ctrl/A, Assn Law Libns Scholarshi; Scholarship Award, Law Libns New England; Baker and Taylor Grass Roots Grant; Starr Fellow, Univ CT School Law. *Hobbies:* Travel: Fishing; Swimming; Skiing; Dancing; Reading; Dogs; Aerobics; Theatre. *Address:* 86 Norwood Rd, West Hanford, CT 06117, USA.

WHITTLESEY Wellington Wheatcroft, b. 17 Mar 1920, Los Angeles, California, USA. Theologian; Seminary President. m. Nina Merle Brubaker, 28 Dec 1947. *Education:* AB, William Penn Coll, 1942; Trinity Sem, 1945; Earlham Coll, 1947; AM, Drake Univ, 1955; Univ IA, 1955-62; Univ S FL, 1967-; PhD, Northgate Grad School, 1984. *Appointments:* Ordained, consecrated (now Bishop, So Episc Ch), 1942, 1946, 1947; Wn Pilgrim Coll, 1942-44; Pastor, Lindsay Friends Ch, 1944-46; Kingswood Coll, 1946-47; Pastor: Indianopolis 2nd Friends, IN, 1947-49; Friends Chapel, 1949-52; IL Christian Endeavor, 1950-52; Liberty Friends Ch, 1952-55; Prof, Hist, Relig, 1955-62; Ottumwa HS, 1962-63; Tchr, Pinellas Co Bd Educ, 1963-83; Prof, 1983-, Pres, 1986-, St Petersburg Theological Sem, St Petersburg, FL. *Publication:* Program Guide for Christian Endeavor, 1951. *Memberships:* Youth Temperance Coun, Pres CA 1944-46; Int Christian Endeavor, Fac 1951 Conven, Pastor Cnslr, Field Sec 1950-52; Life Mbr, YMCA, Sponsor Jr Hi-Y, High Y, Y's Men's Mbr 1944-46. *Honours:* Prof's Week, Wash, 1958; Life Mbr, Young Republicans, 1962. *Hobbies:* Piano and organ, playing both for enjoyment; Listening to all classical music, also standard music; Reading; Walking; Swimming. *Address:* 4611 Duhme Road, Apt 1C, Madeira Beach, FL 33708, USA.

WHYBRA Julian Terence, b. 20 Sept 1952, Hampton Court, Middlesex, England. Advisory Teacher for Gifted Children. m. Patricia Elizabeth Turner, 25 Apr 1981, 1 s. *Education:* Dip, Swedish, Univ Uppsala, 1973; BA (Hons), Univ E Anglia, 1974; Fellow, 1974, Dip, Polish, 1975, Jagiellonian Univ, Cracow; Cert Ed, Cert A-V Aids, Chelmer Inst Higher Educ, 1978; Fellow, Girton Coll, Cambridge, 1984; PhD, Birkbeck Coll, 1993. *Appointments:* Transl, 1974; Rsch Asst, Jagiellonian Univ, Cracow, Poland, 1974-75; Tchr, England, 1975-77, 1978-84, 1984-85; Advsr, Gifted Children, Essex Co, 1985-. *Publications:* Jezyk Polski, 1976; Battle of Isandhlwana, 1984; A Lost English County, 1990; The Roll Call, 1990; The Defence of Rorke's Drift, 199o; The Charge of the Light Brigade, 1991. *Appointments:* Victorian Mil Soc; Authors Licensing and Collecting Soc; Nat Assn Curric Ext; Engl Corres, European Coun High Ability; Mayflower Morris Men, Squire 1981-84; Co-Dir, Gift Ptnrship. *Honours:* Polish Govt State Scholarship Award, Hist, 1974; Girton Coll Schoolmaster Fellowship, 1984; Browne Medal, Original Rsch in Hist, 1988. *Hobbies:* Reading; Walking; History; Languages. *Address:* 3 Coach Mews, Billericay, Essex, England.

WICKHAM Patricia Marie-Claire, b. 29 May 1951, Battle Creek, Michigan, USA. University Lecturer; Automotive Executive. div., 1 s. *Education:* Pre-Law studies, UCLA, 1969; BS, Fin, La Salle Univ, Chgo, 1975. *Appointments:* Cost Acct, 1975-79, MRP II Implementer, 1977-82, GTE Communications; Master Scheduler, GTE Network Systems, 1982-84; New Products Mgr, Cummins Engine Co, 1984-88; Materials Mgr, Johnson Controls, Europe, 1988-; Lectr, European Univ, Antwerp, Belgium, 1990-. *Memberships:* Memberships: Am Prod and Inventory Control Soc, Charter Mbr, Pres El Paso-Juarez Chapt 1979-81, Pres Rocky Mount Chapt 1984-85; Nat Assn Female Execs, Newsletter Ed; Assn Women of Europe; Advsr, Jr Achievement; Sponsor, Rocky Mount HS French Club; Am Mktng Assn. *Honours:* Jr and Sr Hon socs, 1963-69; Grad Top 10 percent, HS, 1969; 5-yr Award, Jr Achievement, 1982-87; Fundraiser Award, Sickle Cell Anemia, 1981, 1984; Logistics Process System featured in trade jrnls, Belgium. *Hobbies:* Camcording and video taping; Art; Music; History; Tennis; Fundraiser, charities incl Am Cancer Soc and Multiple Sclerosis. *Address:* 23A Marentak, 2970 's Gravenwezel, Belgium. 2, 5, 139, 152.

WICKWIRE Patricia Joanne Nellor, b. Sioux City, Iowa, USA. Consultant; Trainer; Lecturer; President, Wickwire and Associates. m. Robert James Wickwire, 7 Sept 1957, 1 s. *Education:* BA, Univ No IA, 1951; MA, Univ IA, 1959; PhD, Univ TX, Austin, 1971; Postgrad studies,

several univs and acads. *Appointments:* Tchr, Ricketts Indep Schools, IA; Tchr, Cnslr, Waverly-Shell Rock Indep Schools, IA; Reading Cons, Dormitory Hd, Univ IA; Tchr, School Psychologist, Coord Psychological Servs, Dist Admnstr (Dist Guidance, Student Servs, Special Educ), S Bay Union HS Dist, CA; Dir, Multi- Dist Consortium Special Educ, CA; Lectr, Loyola-Marymount Univ; Cons, State Dept Educ, CA; Indep Contractor, Cons, Trainer, Lectr; Currently Pres, Wickwire and Assocs, CA. *Publications:* The Academic Achievement and Language Development of American Children of Latin Heritage; Contbr, profl and popular jrnls, mags, newspapers. *Memberships:* Chair, Int Career Assn Network; Exec Bd, Pres, Am Assn Career Educ; Bd, Assn Measurement and Evaluation in Counseling and Dev; Network Dir, Nat Assn Female Execs; Am Psychological Assn; Exec Bd, Past Pres, CA Assn Couseling and Dev Fndn; CA Assn Measurement and Evaluation Guidance; Pres, Los Angeles Co Admnstrs Pupil Servs; Offs, many other bodies. *Honours:* Special Citation, Achievement in Educ, CA; S Bay Woman of Yr; Achievement awards. *Hobbies:* Reading; Writing; Walking; Gardening; Photography; Career and leadership development; Professional ethics; Equal opportunity. *Address:* 2900 Amby Place, Hermosa Beach, CA 90254, USA. 5, 9, 49, 52, 59, 138.

WIDDECOMBE (James) Murray, b. 7 Jan 1910, Saltash, Cornwall, England. Retired Admiralty Officer. m. Rita Noreen Plummer, 28 June 1936, 1 s, 1 d. *Appointments:* Entered Admiralty as Exec Off, 1928; Sr Armament Supply Off, Capt, RNVR, Staff of C-in-C Mediterranean, 1944-46; Prin Armament Supply Off, C-in-C Far East, 1953-56; Dpty Dir, Armament Supply, 1959-61, Dir, Victualling, 1961-66, Admiralty;Hd, RN Supply and Transport Serv, 1966-68, Dir, Gen Supplies and Transport, Naval, 1968-70, Special Duties Mgmt Servs, 1970-73, Min Def; Gen Sec, Civil Serv Retirement Fellowship, 1973-79. *Memberships:* Former Fellow, Brit Inst Mgmt; Former Fellow, Inst Purchasing and Supply; Pres, Navy Dept Golfing Soc. *Honours:* OBE, 1959; CB, 1968. *Hobbies:* Golf; Gardening; Amateur dramatics. *Address:* Keng Hua, 1 Manor Close, Haslemere, Surrey GU27 1PP, England. 1.

WIDJAJA Adidharma, b. 25 May 1930, Jakarta, Indonesia. Conductor; Violinist; Teacher. m. Tiara Sugiarto, 28 Sept 1960, 1 d. *Education:* Amsterdam Conservatory, 1951; Dip w highest distinction, College Musique de Belge, 1955; Juilliard School Music, NYC, 1962-63. *Appointments:* 1st Violinist, Utrecht Stedelyk Orkest, Netherlands, 1955-56; Concertmaster, Jakarta Radio Orch, Indonesia, 1957-60; Prin Conductor, Dir Music, Jakarta Symph Orch, 1961-86. *Creative works:* Composed music for films. *Memberships:* Jakarta Arts Coun, 1968-70; Jakarta Oratorio Soc. *Honours:* Australian Music Award, 1981; Adam Malik Award, 1988; Award, Min Culture and Tourism, Malaysia, 1990; Award, Min Educ and Culture, Indonesia, 1991. *Hobbies:* Outdoor sports; Swimming; Reading. *Address:* Taman Aries, Blok C1 No 3, Meruya Ilir, Jakarta 11620, Indonesia.

WIDJAYA Nani, b. 8 Sept 1942, Surabaya, Indonesia. Company Chairwoman. m. 9 Sept 1961, 2 s. *Education:* Sr HS, Petra, 1958-60. *Appointments:* Pres, Dir, 1970-87, Chairwoman, 1987-, Wina Plastic; Chairwoman, PT Swastha Artha Pramathana, Surabaya, 1991. *Hobbies:* Swimming; Travel. *Address:* Kenjeran 139-141, Surabaya 60134, Indonesia.

WIECEK-SRZEGANEK Brygida, b. 8 Aug 1936, Chorzow, Poland. University Professor. m. Jozef Wiecek, 7 Sept 1957, 1 s, 2 d. *Education:* MA, Archtl Engr, 1961; MBA, 1970; PhD, Econ, 1973; Expert Dip, Tech Scis, 1974; Asst Prof, Bus Admin, 1985; Prof, Bus Admin, Mktng, 1989; German Expert Dip, Mktng, Econ, 1991. *Appointments:* Jr Lectr, Silesian Polytechnic, 1961; Jr Lectr, Univ Vienna, Austria, 1963; Designer, Arch, Austrian Design Off, 1964; Mng Dir, PRE Bldg Co, 1965; Lectr, Warsaw Polytechnic, Poland, 1967; Lectr, Silesian Polytechnic, 1975; Prof, Bus Admin, Mktg, Univ Opole,

1979. *Publications:* Production programme model of the building enterprise in the system of awarding contracts by tender, 1982; Building production planning in risky and uncertain conditions, 1984; Building enterprise in the investment process, 1985; Application of selected organization techniques in the process of reviewing and attestation of work standards, 1987. *Memberships:* Polish Econ Soc; Chief Coun Mbr, Org and Mgmt Sci Soc; Polish Soc Bldng Engrs and Techns, Chmn Bd of Control; Int Mktg Fedn, Small Bus Advsry Comm Mbr. *Honours:* Award, Min High Educ, 1978; Golden Order of Merit, Profl Achievements, 1985. *Hobbies:* Sport; Classical Music. *Address:* ul H Sawickiej 16, Bytom 41-902, Poland.

WIESNER Dallas Charles, b. 19 Mar 1959, Brookings, South Dakota, USA. Research Immunologist. *Education:* BS w high hon, Microbiology, BS w high hon, Biology, SD State Univ, 1982. *Appointments:* HIV Tech Product Dev Techn, 1985-87, HIV Retrocell PHA Product Mgr, 1987-88, Sect Mgr, Infectious Diseases and Immunology Tech Product Dev, 1988-90, Dept Mgr, Sexually Transmitted Diseases Tech Product Dev, 1990-, Diagnostic Div, Abbott Labs, Abbott Pk, IL. *Creative works:* Retrocell HIV-1 Passive Hemagglutination Assay, article, 1990; Developer: Abbott Retrocell HIV PHA Assay for detection of AIDS Antibody; Abbott's Cytomegalovirus Total Antibody EIA Automation. *Memberships:* Am Soc Microbiology; Phi Kappa Phi; Int Platform Assn; Hope Luth Ch. *Honours:* Abbott Labs Presidential Awards: Dev contbr towards 1st AIDS Antibody Test, 1987; Dev and mkt entry achievements towards Abbott Retrocell HIV PHA AIDS Antibody Assay, 1989; Dev contbrs towards Automation of Abbott Cytomegalovirus Total Ab Assay, 1991. *Hobbies:* Fishing; Camping; Scuba diving; Amateur radio ham; Photography; Woodworking; Wine making and appreciation. *Address:* 2 Echo Ct No 2, Vernon Hills, IL 60061, USA. 8, 52, 139, 152.

WIGGINS Nancy Moore Bowen, b. 9 Oct 1946, Richmond, Virginia, USA. President of Market Research, Real Estate Brokerage and Appraisal Firm. m. (1) Stanley Spencer Saunders, 16 Aug 1969, (2) Edwin Lindsey Wiggins Jr, 16 Apr 1983, 2 s. *Education:* AA, St Mary's Coll, 1968; BA, US Int Univ, 1970; Special Scholar, Inst Social Rsch, 1974; MA, Univ TX, 1975; Postgrad, Tulane Univ, 1976. *Appointments:* Teller, Bank Am, 1971-72; Lectr, Univ TX, Arlington, 1974-76; Human Serv Planner, Ctrline CO6, 1978-80; Mkt Rsch Analyst, 1st Union N Bank, 1980-81; Mkt Rep, Burroughs Corp, 1981-83; Ptnr, George Seldon & Assoc, 1983-84; Pres, Mkt Rsch, Broker's Appraiser, The Bowen Wiggins Co, Charlotte, NC, 1984-; Adj Prof, Univ NC, Charlotte, 1984-92. *Publications include:* The Ideological Characteristics of Party Leaders: A Case of Texas; An Internal Service Level Inventory Process for DSS, 1979. *Memberships:* NS Assn Appraisers, Pres 1989-90; Mecklenburg Co Dem Women's Club, Pres 1990; Charlotte Sales and Mktng Assn; Vice-Chair, United Cerebral Palsy Coun, Charlotte, 1984; Charlotte Apt Assn; TPC Piper Glen Choir; Bd Dirs, Corriageltons Condominium, 1980-82; UNICEF; Mayor's Citizens Budget Advsry Comm, 1980-81. *Honours:* Pi Sigma Alpha, 1977. *Hobbies:* Politics; Reading; Golf; Tennis; Gardening; Travel; Community volunteer activities. *Address:* 6425 Felton Court, Charlotte, NC 28226, USA. 5, 132.

WIGGINTON Michael John, b. 26 Mar 1941, Nottingham, England. Architect. m. (1) Margaret Sheila Steven, 24 May 1969, div., 1 s, 1 d, (2) Jennifer Kay Bennett, 17 Dec 1988. *Education:* Gonville and Caius Coll, Cambridge Univ, 1959-64; MA (Cantab), 1964; DipArch, 1964. *Appointments:* Skidmore, Owings and Merrill, NYC, NY, USA, 1964-65; Associated Archts and Consultants, London, England, 1965-66; Yorke, Rosenberg and Mardall, Londojn, 1966-86; Dir, Richard Horden Assocs, London, 1987-. *Publications:* Glass Today, book, 1986; Articles: Window Design, 1968; Practice in the Netherlands, 1976; Offices, 1973; Into the Chromogenic Century, 1990; Architecture, Art and Glass, 1990; Light and Glass: Architecture and the

Photon, 1991; Can We have a Theory Please, 1991; Glass in Architecture, 1991. *Memberships:* RIBA; Assn Cons Archts; FRSA. *Honours:* Jt Winner (w R Horden), Stag Place Competition, London SW1, 1987; Architecture Prize, Royal Acad, London, 1988; Jr Winner (w R Horden), Epsom Clubstand Competition, 1989. *Hobbies:* Music; Reading; Tennis. *Address:* 41 Chiddingstone Street, London SW6 3TQ, England.

WIJESINGHE Somawera, b. 17 Sept 1924, Alawathuwala, Sri Lanka. Ambassador Extraordinary and Plenipotentiary. m. 22 Dec 1960, 3 s, 4 d. *Education:* Sr School Certs, Engl medium and Sinhalese medium. *Career:* Asst Supt, Yahalakale Estate, 1950; Elected Pres, Village Coun, Rambadagalla, 1958; Pres, Village Coun, Kohonaiyapattuwa, Matale, 1960; Entered Nat Pol, 1977; Dpty Min Reg Dev, 1981-83; Dpty Min, Highways, 1983; Dpty Min, Local Govt Housing and Constrn and Highways, 1984-88; Currently Ambassador Extraordinary and Plenipotentiary, Sri Lankan Embassy, Yangon, Myanmar. *Memberships:* Organizer, Kohansiyapathu Vol Assn Constrn; Chmn, Vol Assn Constrn Rambadagalla Village Coun; Organiser, Vol Rd Week Movement for Constrn Dev, 1983-88; Organiser, several religious activities; Off Holder, Religious Ldr (Buddhist), several religious socs. *Hobbies include:* Gardening; Reading; Photography; Construction. *Address:* Alawathuwala SPO, Via Kurunegala, Sri Lanka.

WILD David, b. 27 Jan 1930, Wardle, Lancashire, England. Practitioner of Public Health Medicine. m. Sheila Wightman, 19 June 1954, 1 s, 1 d. *Education:* MB ChB, Univ Manchester, 1953; DObstRCOG, 1957; Univ Liverpool, 1957-58; DPH; FFPHM, Dip Municipal Admin. *Appointments:* Hosp Appts; Mil Serv, Med Off, School Mil Engrng, Chatham, 1954-56; Dpty Co Med Off, 1962-74, Area Med Off, 1974-81, W Sussex; Reg Dir, Pub Hlth, 1981- 90; Dir, Info Support Unit, Jt Royal Colls, 1991-. *Memberships:* Jt Jrnl Ed, Fac Pub Hlth Med, 1976-82; Worthing Dist Hlth Auth. *Hobby:* Conversation. *Address:* 16 Brandy Hole Lane, Chichester, W Sussex PO19 4RY, England.

WILDSMITH-TOWLE Alan Geoffrey, b. 24 July 1939, Peterborogh, England. Photographic Artist. *Education:* Joseph Wright School of Art; Derby and Dist School of Art. *Appointments:* Family Pharm Bus, 1957-60; Photographer, RAF, 1960-63; Photographer, Rolls-Royce, 1964-68; Own Photographic Bus, Derbyshire, Huntingdonshire, Europe, Hong Kong, Singapore, Indonesia, S AFrica, 1968-. *Memberships:* Fellow, Brit Inst Profl Photography; Fellow, Royal Photographic Soc; Fellow, Master Photographers Assn; FRSA. *Honours:* Well over 100 int photographic awards for excellence and outstanding ability. *Hobbies:* Photography; Art; The countryside and conservation; Agriculture; Painting; Riding; Natural history. *Address:* St George's House, Bridge Street, Belper, Derbyshire DE5 1AZ, England.

WILENIUS Reijo Valfrid, b. 22 Apr 1930, Helsinki, Finland. Professor of Philosophy. m. Aijami Ant-Wuorinen, 5 June 1953, 3 s, 1 d. *Education:* MA, 1952, PhD, 1963, Univ Helsinki. *Appointments:* Ed, cultural review, 1957-68; Lectr, Univ Helsinki, 1966-72; Prof, Univ Jyvaskyla, 1973-. *Publications:* The Social and Political Philosophy of Francisco Suarez, 1963; Philosophy and Politics, 1967; Philosophy of Education, 1974; Towards a New Culture (in Finnish), 1990. *Memberships:* Philosl Soc Finland; Pres, Anthroposophical Soc Finland; Chmn, Finnish Rsch Coun for Humanities, 1975-79. *Honours:* State Prize for Publication of New Knowledge, 1977; Snellman Medaille, 1984. *Hobbies:* Literature; Skiing; Swimming. *Address:* Mantypaadentie 7C, SF-00830 Helsinki, Finland. 90.

WILHELMI Zdzislaw Ludwik, b. 20 Sept 1921, Lomza, Poland. University Professor; Nuclear Physicist. m. Hanna Szmit, 28 Oct 1970, 2 d. *Education:* MTechnSci, Tech Univ, Lodz, 1948; MSci, 1952, OhD, 1954,

Extraordinary Prof, 1962, Ordinary Prof, 1971, Warsaw Univ. *Appointments:* Participant, Polish Underground Movement, Armia Krajowa, 1939-45; Mbr, Fac, 1948-54, Prof, Nuclear Phys, Dept Chmn, 1954-, Warsaw Univ; Hd, Dept Nuclear Reaction, Inst Nuclear Rsch; Organiser, Dir, 20 int schools on Nuclear Physics, 1968-88; Dir, Div Nuclear Safety and Environmental Protection, Int Atomic Energy Agcy, Vienna, Austria, 1970-73. *Publications:* 130 sci articles, textbooks, monographs, on nuclear reactions and nuclear structure. bb2Memberships: European Phys Soc, Exec Comm 1975-78; Fellow, Am Phys Soc; Fellow, Inst Phys, UK; Polish Phys Soc, Pres 1974-81; Int Union Pure and Applied Phys, Nuclear Phys Comm 1975-81; NY Acad Scis; Polish Acad Scis, Phys Comm, Nuclear Phys Sect, Chmn 1982-90. *Honours:* Bronze Cross of Merit w Swords, 1943; Decoration, Polonia Restituta, 1964; Cross of Bravery, 1944; Copernicus Yr Award, 1954; State Coun Utilisation of Nuclear Energy Prizes, 1961, 1965, 1967; Prize, Min Higher Educ and Sci, 1977; Cross, Polish Home Army, 1983; Meritorious Tchr of Polish Republic, 1984. *Hobby:* Poetry. *Address:* ul Gornoslaska 16 m 7, 00-432 Warsaw, Poland. 52, 139.

WILKE Wolfgang Rudolf, b. 11 Mar 1934, Leipzig, Germany. Professor of Physics. m. Giselheid Wilke, 5 Apr 1962, 1 s, 2 d. *Education:* Dip, Phys, 1957; Dr rer nat, 1962; Habilitation, Crystallography, 1970; Inauguration, Phys, 1971. *Appointments:* Univ Asst, 1957-62; Rsch Asst, Fritz-Haber-Inst (Max-Planck-Gesellschaft), 1962-71; Co-Hd, Dept Expmtl Phys, Univ Ulm, 1971-. *Publications:* 70 sci papers in int jrnls. *Memberships:* German Phys Soc; German Mineralogical Soc; Comm Rsch Synchrotron Radiation. *Hobby:* Classical music. *Address:* Abt Exp Physik, Universitat Ulm, Albert-Einstein-Allee 11, DW 7900 Ulm, Germany.

WILKINSON Alan Bassindale, b. 26 Jan 1931, Cradley Heath, England. Priest; Writer. m. (1) 2 s, 1 d, (2) Fenella Ruth Holland, 29 Dec 1975. *Education:* St Catherine's Coll, Cambridge, 1951-57; MA, 1954, PhD, 1959, Cambridge; Coll of the Resurrection, Mirfield, 1957-59. *Appointments:* Curate, St Augustine's, Kilburn, 1959-61; Chaplain, St Catherine's Coll, Cambridge, 1961-67; Vicar, Barrow Gurney, Lectr, Coll of St Matthias, 1967-70; Prin, Chichester Theological Coll, 1970-74; Warden, Verulam House, 1974-75; Lectr, Crewe and Alsager Coll, 1975-78; Dir, Trng, Diocese of Ripon, 1978-84; Priest-i/c, Darley, Thornthwaite, 1984-88; Hon Priest, Portsmouth Cathedral, Tutor, Open Univ, 1988-. *Publications:* Books: The Church of England and the First World War, 1978; Would You Believe It, 1983; More Ready to Hear, 1983; Christian Choices, 1983; Dissent or Conform, 1986. *Memberships:* Gen Synod Bd Educ, 1982-86; Leeds Marriage Guidance Coun, 1980-84; Gov: Bishop Otter Coll, 1970-74; Ripon and York St John, 1984- 88; Soc Promoting Christian Knowledge, 1982-91. *Honours:* Select Preacher, Cambridge Univ, 1967; Hon Canon, Chichester Cathedral, 1970-; Select Preacher, Oxford Univ, 1982; Hon Canon, Ripon Cathedral, 1984-. *Hobbies:* Cinema; Gardening; Walking; Victorian architecture. *Address:* Hope Cottage, 27 Great Southsea Street, Portsmouth PO5 3BY, England. 1.

WILKINSON Jennifer Ruth, b. 29 Sept 1949, Lismore, Queensland, Australia. Performer and Teacher of Early Music. m. John Stinson, 8 May 1982, 1 s. *Education:* BMusEd (Hons), Univ Qld, 1971; Schola Cantorum Basiliensis, Basel, Switzerland, 1974-79. *Career:* Dir, Music, The Geelong Coll Preparatory School, 1972-74; Dir, Music, Eltham Coll, 1977-80; Tchr, Recorder, Melbourne Univ, 1978-; Dir, Music, St Michael's Grammar Jr School, Vic, 1990-; Mbr, La Romanesca, and Capella Corelli, early music ensembles; Recorded: Love Lyrics and Romances of Renaissance Spain; Medieval Monodies; For Ye Lovers and Masters of Music; Two Gentlemen of Verona. *Hobbies:* Marbled paper; Lace making. *Address:* 743 Drummond St, Nth Carlton, Victoria 3054, Australia.

WILKINSON Mark Lawrence, b. 19 May 1950, Watford, England. Senior Lecturer in Gastroenterology; Consultant Physician. m. Anna Maria Cassoni, 4 Jan 1975, 1 s, 1 d. *Education:* BSc, 1971, MB, BS, 1974, MD, 1985, Univ London; MRCP, Royal Coll Physns, 1977. *Appointments:* House Physn, 1975, Registrar, 1979-81, Middlesex Hosp, London; Rsch Fellow, later Lectr, Liver Unit, King's Coll Hosp, London, 1981-86; Sr Lectr, Gastroenterology, United Med and Dental School, London, Cons Physn, 1986-. *Publications:* Articles and chapts in sci and med jrnls, esp in fields of steroid biochem and gastrointestinal endoscopy. *Memberships:* Brit Soc Gastroenterology, Endoscopy Comm Mbr; Brit, European and Int Assns Study of the Liver; Med Rsch Soc; Brit Med Assn. *Hobbies:* Walking; Italy; Opera. *Address:* GI Unit, United Medical and Dental School, Guy's Campus, 18th Floor, Guy's Tower, St Thomas' Street, London SE1 9RT, England. 52, 170.

WILKINSON Tabert S, b. 28 Dec 1937, Wake Forest, N Canada. Plastic Suregon. m. Suzanne, 12 June 1982, 1 s, 3 d. *Education:* Wake Forest Univ, 1955-58; Duke Univ Medical Sch, 1958-62. *Appointments:* US Air Force Plastic Surgeon, 1969-71; Chmn, Div Plastic Surgery, Univ Texas Health Sci Centre, 1971-75; Dir, Inst for Aesthetic Plastic Surgery, 1973-. *Publications include:* Intestinal Volvulus Without Malrotation; Tissue Adhesives in Clinical Surgery; Symposium on Surgery of the Breast; Aesthetic Surgery; Clinics in Plastic Surgery; Numerous Equestrian Articles. *Memberships:* American Soc for Aethetic Plastic Surgery; Intl Soc for Aethetic Plastic Surgery; American Soc for Plastic & Reconstructive Surgeons; Texas Soc of Plastic Surgeons; Intl Soc of Clinical Plastic Surgeons; Southern Medical Assn; Bexar County Medical Soc; Texas Medical assn; San Antonio Surgical Soc. *Honours:* Phi Beta Kappa; Major Actor Award; Man of the Year; Emory Univ Resident Physician Research Forum; Missouri Chapter American Coll of Surgeons Research Forum; Plastic Surgery Residents Forum. *Hobbies:* Polo; Write & Edit Polo Mag. *Address:* 1901 Babcock road, San Antonio, TX 78229, USA.

WILLATTS Sheila Margaret, b. 6 June 1943, Cambridge, England. Consultant in Anaesthesia and Intensive Care. m. (1) David George Willatts, 16 July 1966, 1 s, 2 d, (2) Michael Crabtree, 25 Feb 1989. *Education:* MB BS, London, 1967; DRCOG, 1969; FCAnaes, 1973; FRCP, 1988. *Appointments:* Sr Registrar, King's Coll, London, 1975-78; Cons Anaesthetist, Frenchay Hosp, Bristol, 1978-85; Cons, Intensive Therapy, Bristol Royal Infirmary, 1985-. *Publications:* Lectures Notes in Fluid and Electrolyte Balance, 1982, 1987; Anaesthesia and Intensive Care for the Neurosurgical Patient, 1986. *Memberships:* Bd Examiners, Coun Mbr, Exams Comm Chmn, Coll Anaesthetists; Past Chmn, Sec, Intensive Care Soc; Anaesthetic Sect, Royal Soc Med. *Hobbies:* Skiing; Tandem cycling; Interior decoration. *Address:* 6, Westbury Park, Durdham Down, Bristol BS6 7JB, England.

WILLIAMS Alan, b. 19 June 1952, Montgomery, Alabama, USA. Minister. m. Terri C Sanchez, 16 Jan 1980, 3 d. *Education:* Univ TN, 1976-77; So Coll, SDA, 1980-82; BA summa cum laude, Theology, Oakwood Coll, Huntsville, AL, 1985. *Career:* Profl Percussionist, 1967-80; Nat tours, NY, 1970, HI, 1974, recording, Nashville, TN, 1976; Worked w Doobie Brothers, James Brown, Edgar Winter musical grps; Served US Army, 1973-74; Min, Pastor, 7th Day Adventist Ch: Gulf States Conf, Olive Br, MS, 1984-87; GA-Cumberland Conf, Baxley, GA, 1987-; Greeneville, TN; Guest Columnist: Baxley, GA News Banner, Alma, GA Stateman, 1987-89. *Memberships:* Appling Co Ministerial Assn, 1988; Baxley GA Unit, Am Cancer Soc, Pub Rels Off 1988; Int Platform Assn. *Honours:* Nat Dean's List, 1984, 1985. *Hobbies:* Hang-gliding; White water rafting; Croquet; Drumming; Swimming; Travel. *Address:* 1508 Sunvalley Drive, Greeneville, TN 37743, USA. 7.

WILLIAMS Carolyn Ruth Armstrong, b. 17 Feb 1944, Birmingham, Alabama, USA. Assistant Dean; Administrator; Educator. m. James Alvin Williams Jr, 16 Mar 1968. *Education:* BS, TN State Univ, 1966; Cert, HI Univ, 1970; MA, NWn Univ, 1972; MA, PhD, Connell Univ, 1978; Postdoct studies: Harvard Univ; Exeter Univ, England, 1985; MIT, 1990. *Appointments:* Assoc Dir, Cornell Univ Career Ctr, Ithaca, NY, 1976-82; Educ Cons, Le Moyne Coll Higher Educ Preparation Prog, 1977-83; Special Project Asst, US Senator Paul Tsongas, Boston, MA, 1983; Asst Vice-Chancellor, NC Ctrl Univ. Durham, 1983-87; Educ Cons, Youth Data, Ithaca, 1981-; Asst Dean, Assoc Prof, Venderbilt Univ Engrng School, Nashville, TN, 1987-; Cons, US Dept Educ Review Bd. *Contributions to:* several articles to profl jrnls; Ed, Nat Assn Minority Engrs Prog Admin Newsletter/Jrnl, 1990-. *Memberships:* So Policies Educ; Bd, 1983-87; Clean Commn System of Durham Bd, 1983-87; Rotary; Nat Assn Women Deans Admnstv Cnslrs, Exec Bd Mbr; Cornell Univ Women's Studies Prog, Exec Bd 1981-83; Nat Soc Women Engrs, Nat Tech Coord 1988-90, Coord Tech Paper Competition; WBGH TV, Boston TV, Bd Dirs, Pub TV Project Strike; Phi Delta Kappa, Harvard Chapt Exec Bd; Delta Sigma Theta Inc; Assn Women in Sci, Bd Dirs 1990-92; Nat Assn Minority Engrs, Pres Elect Reg B 1990, Prog Admnstr. *Honours:* Women of Achievement and Recognition Award, YWCA, 1984-87; Black Engrng Ldrship Award, Nat Soc Black Engrs, 1988; Affirmative Action Award, Vanderbilt Univ, 1989, 1990; Charles E Tunstall Award for Outstanding Minority Engrng Prog in US, Nat Soc Black Engrs Advsry Bd, 1990; Nat Soc Black Engrs Reg III Advsry Bd Award, 1991; Judge, B F Goodrich Coll Inventors Project, 1991. *Hobbies:* Bowling; Tennis; Cross-country skiing; Surfing; Playing violin, harp and piano. *Address:* 305 Summit Ridge Circle, Nashville, TN 37215, USA. 5.

WILLIAMS Charles Murray, b. 26 Dec 1931, Fort Bliss, Texas, USA. Professor of Computer Information Services. m. Stanley Bright, 31 Dec 1956, 1 s, 2 d. *Education:* BS, Phys, VA Mil Inst, 1953; MS, Computer Sci (1st to graduate under prog), Univ TX, Austin, 1967. *Appointments:* Physicist, USAF, 1954-58; Staff Mbr, Sandia Labs, 1958-62; Programmer Analyst, Control Data Corp, 1962-63; Mathn, Panoramic Rsch Inc, Mbr, Tech Staff, Thomas Bede Fndn, 1964-65; Rsch Scientist Assoc, Computer Sci, PA State Univ, 1967-72; Asst Prof, Computer Info Systems, VA Polytechnic Inst, 1972-75; Assoc Prof, Computer Info systems, 1975-83, Prof, Computer Info Systems, 1983- , GA State Univ; Cons: Visicon Inc, 1970-72; Broomall Inds, 1973-79; Bausch and Lomb, 1981; Bell-South Media Technologies, 1987-90; Mbr, Tech Staff, Bell Labs, 1979. *Publications:* Num articles in computer graphics and image processing publs. *Memberships:* State Dir (GA), Nat Computer Graphics Assn; Bd Dirs, Sec, GA Chapt Nat Computer Graphics Assn; Computer Graphics Pioneers. *Honours:* Graduated 1st in class, 1st in Maths, VA Mil Inst, 1953; Nat Hon Soc, 1953; Upsilon Pi Upsilon, 1970; Omicron Delta Kappa, 1983; Hon Mbr, Nat Computer Graphics Assn, 1985; Xerox Corp Grant, 1985. *Hobby:* Competitive road running (1st Place, 55059 Age Division, 1990-91 Running Journal Grand Prix for 12 Southern States). *Address:* 316 Argonne Drive NW, Atlanta, GA 30305, USA. 7, 143.

WILLIAMS Charlotte Bell (Bunny), b. 29 Mar 1944, Houston, Texas, USA. Sales and Marketing Executive. m. Edward Arthur Williams, 24 Oct 1980. *Education:* BA, Univ TX, Dallas, 1977. *Appointments:* Realtor, James M Brown Realtors, TX, 1978-79; Realtor, Broker, Hank Dickerson Realtors, Dallas, TX, 1980-81; Realtor, Broker, Merrill Lynch Realty, Plano, TX, 1981- 84; Dir, Mktng, KPT Inc, Dallas, 1984-88; Pres, Re:Source, Dallas, 1988-89; Chmn, Fndr, The Direct Source Inc, Carrollton, TX, 1989-; Chmn, CEO, VRMC, Dallas, 1990-. *Publications:* Articles in profl and popular jrnls. *Memberships:* Patron, Susan G Komen Fndn, Dallas; Sponsor, 500 Inc, Dallas; Dallas Women's Fndn; Dallas Histl Soc; Guild, Week-end to Wipe-Out Cancer, Dallas; Int Craniofacial Fndn Inc, Dallas; Co-Chmn, Rolex/

Corrigan's Cup Polo Ball, Dallas, 1989; Grad, Gtr Dallas Chmbr of Comm Opportunity Dallas, 1989; Ldrship Dallas Alumni; Doberman Pinscher Club Am, Deleg/ Chmn Nat Conven 1980; Am Soc Profl and Exec Women; AAUW; Past Mbr, N Dallas Fin Forum; Women in Communications; Doberman Pinscher Club Dallas, Pres 1978-80; Combined Specialties Dallas, Pres 1979; Data Processing Mgmt Assn, Bd Dirs 1985-86; Women's Direct Response Grp Inc; Direct Mktng Assn N TX, Sec 1988-89, Bd Dirs 1989-90; US Polo Assn; Gtr Dallas Bd Realtors. *Honours:* Distinguished Sales Award, Sales and Mktng Execs, 1986, 1987. *Hobbies:* Breeding and showing pure-bred dogs; Polo fancier and novice players. *Address:* The Direct Source Inc, 2019 McKenzie, Suite 150, Carrollton 24, TX 75006, USA. 2, 5, 7, 52.

WILLIAMS Desmond James, b. 7 July 1932, Manchester, England. Chartered Architect in Private Practice. m. (1) 3 s, 1 d, (2) Susan A Richardson, 30 Dec 1988. *Education:* Dip Arch; MRIBA; Univ Manchester, 1958-63. *Appointments:* Pvte prac, 1964-68; Ptnr, A Farebrother and Ptnrs; Fndr, Desmond Williams and Assts, 1968-75; Amalgamated into Ellis Williams Ptnrship, Cheadle, Cheshire, 1975-; Currently Sr Ptnr; Cons, World Bank and Brit Coun; External Examiner, Manchester Univ School Arch. *Creative works:* Design of educl estabs, offs, housing, incl New Ctr Ampleforth Coll, CTC Solihull, Standish HS Wigan. *Memberships:* Manchester Soc Arch, Pres 1988; RIBA NW Reg, Chmn 1989-92. *Honours:* Civic Trust Award, 1968; Educ Design Awards, 1970, 1978, 1980; OBE, 1988. *Hobbies:* Walking; Music - classical and opera; Art appreciation; Watercolourist; Reading; Visiting country houses; National Trust. *Address:* 2 Yew Tree Close, Wilmslow Park, Wilmslow, Cheshire SK9 2DW, England.

WILLIAMS Eric Charles, b. 14 Nov 1921, Bury St Edmunds, England. Retired Public Relations Consultant. m. 18 Aug 1947, 2 s, 3 d. *Education:* Wellingborough Grammar School. *Appointments:* Reporter, Chronicle and Echo, Northampton, 1938-41; Merchant Navy Serv, 1941-43; Sub-Lt, RNR, later Lt, RNVR, and Off Naval Reporter, 1943-46; Publicity Dir, Gainsborough Studios, 1947-49; PR Cons and Advt Agcy Dir, 1949-67; Chmn, Eric Williams and Ptnrs Ltd; Retired 1986. *Memberships:* Fellow, Inst PR; Int PR Assn; Chmn, Esher and Dist Christian Aid Comm. *Hobbies:* Fly fishing; Travel; Gardening; Boating; Conversation. *Address:* Fair Acre, 20 Meadway, Esher, Surrey KT10 9HF, England.

WILLIAMS Gareth Howel, b. 17 June 1925, Treherbert, Glamorgan, Wales. Retired Professor. m. Marie Jessie Thomson Mitchell, 2 Apr 1955, 1 s, 1 d. *Education:* BSc, PhD, Univ Coll, London, 1942-47; DSc (London); FRSC; CChem. *Appointments:* Asst Lectr, then Lectr, Chem, King's Coll, London, 1947-60; Reader, Organic Chem, Birkbeck Coll, London, 1960-67; Prof, Chem, Bedford Coll, London, 1967-84; Emeritus Prof, Univ London, 1984-; Vis Prof: Univ Ife, Nigeria, 1965; Univ Auckland, NZ, 1967; Rose Morgan Vis Prof, Univ KS, USA, 1969-70. *Publications:* Books: Homolytic Aromatic Substitution, 1960; Organic Chemistry: A Conceptual Approach, 1977; Advanced in Free-Radical Chemistry (ed)k, Vol 1, 1965, Vol 2, 1967, Vol 3, 1969, Vol 4, 1972, Vol 5, 1975, Vol 6, 1980; Num papers in Journal of the Chemical Society and elsewhere. *Memberships:* London Welsh Assn, Chmn 1987-90; Hon Soc Cymmrodorion; Athenaeum. *Honours:* JP, 1979-; Dpty Chmn, Brent PSA, 1989-. *Hobbies:* Music; Travel. *Address:* Hillside, 22 Watford Road, Northwood, Middlesex HA6 3NT, England. 1, 43, 52.

WILLIAMS Henry Pearlie Ronell, b. 1 Feb 1964, Jacksonville, Florida, USA. Minister; Senior Pastor. m. Gwendolyn Lorraine Hudson, 5 Sept 1981, 1 s, 2 d. *Education:* Ministerial Internship Prog, 1981; AA, 1982; BS, 1986; Ordination, Ch of God, 1990. *Appointments:* Budget Clerk, US Dept of Navy, 1979-81; Mgr, Computer Data Control, Fed Research Atlanta, GA, 1983-86; Sr Pastor, Victory Temple Ch of God, 1986-. *Publications:*

Man's Fatal Enemy - Man, book; Body Builders For Christ, books and tapes; Does Yesterday's Childhood Affect Today's Child, book. *Memberships:* S GA Med Ctr Chaplain Bd; Say No to Drugs Club Am; State of GA Christian Educ Bd; Gen Coun, Int Chs of God. *Honours:* Sci Award, GA So State Coll, 1980; Pastor of Yr, 1988. *Hobbies:* Constructing model cars and airplanes; Drawing cartoon characters; Reading; Weightlifting. *Address:* 331 Wallace Drive, Valdosta, GA 31602, USA. 117.

WILLIAMS James Royal, b. 24 Feb 1929, London, England. Chief Exec Officer; Dir & Pres. m. Marjorie Jill Wedge, 26 Mar 1955, 3 s. *Education:* City & Guild Of London, 1956. *Appointments:* Vice Pres, General Mgr, Elinca Communications, 1972-82; Pres, Jarowill, 1982-83; Pres, Itech, 1983-84; CAO, Pres, Mil Systems, 1971-; Dir, Commerical Mel DSL, 1984-87. *Publications:* Earl of March, A History; Flight Data Recorder Systems. *Memberships:* Canadian Aeronautics & Space Instl; Canadian Inst of Marine Engrs; Canadian Marine Industries Assn; Rideau Club. *Hobbies:* Reading; Golf; Alpine Skiing. *Address:* 12 Rutherford Crescent, Kanata, Ontario, Canada, K2K 1M9. 139.

WILLIAMS John Garrett Pascoe, b. 15 Sept 1932, London, England. Consultant in Rehabilitation Medicine. m. Sally Jennifer Handfield-Jones, 20 Sept 1958, 2 s, 1 d. *Education:* Gonville & Caius Coll, Cambridge, 1950-53; St Mary's Hosp Med School, 1953-56; FRCS Edinburgh, 1963; MSc, Salford, 1978; MD (Cantab), 1984; FRCP Edinburgh, 1986. *Appointments:* Cons Physn, Med, Mt Vernon and Harefield Hosp, 1965-76; Med Dir, Farnham Pk RC, 1965-89; Cons, Rehab Med, Wexham Pk Hosp, 1965-; Civil Cons, RN, 1981-. *Publications:* Sports Med (w P Sperryn), 2nd Ed, 1972; Atlas of Injury in Sport, 1980, 2nd Ed, 1990; Medical Aspects of Sport and Physical Fitness, 1965; Rowing-Scientific Approach (w Scott), 1967. *Memberships:* Former Hon Sec, Brit Assn Sports Med; Fellow, Former Sec-Gen, Int Fedn Sports Med; Brit Assn Experts, Comm Chmn, PSM 31, TCM 14/-/3, BSI; Comp Fellow, Brit Orthopaedic Assn; Med Advsr, Squash Rackets Assn. *Honours:* Bryant Trust Lectureship, 1973; Winston Churchill Fellowship, 1974; Philip Noel Baker Rsch Prize, UNESCO/ICSPE, 1974; Gold Medal, Int Fedn Sports Med, 1980. *Hobbies:* Flying; Model making; Real tennis. *Address:* Bon Secours Hospital, Candlemas Lane, Beaconsfield, Bucks HP9 1AG, England.

WILLIAMS John Gwynn, b. 19 June 1924, Llanfechain, Powys, Wales. Emeritus Professor. m. Beryl Thomas, 24 July 1954, 3 s. *Education:* BA, 1948, MA, 1952, Univ Coll N Wales, Bangor. *Appointments:* Staff Tutor, Dept Extra-Mural Studies, Liverpool Univ, 1951-54; Tchng, 1954-55; Lectr, 1955, Prof, Welsh Hist, 1963-83, Dean, Fac Arts, 1972-74, Vice-Prin, 1974-79, Univ Coll N Wales; Dir, Greynog Press, 1979-. *Publications:* The University College of North Wales: Foundations, 1985; Papers to learned jrnls. *Memberships:* Chmn, Past Coun Mbr, Univ Wales Press Bd; Cambrian Archaeological Assn, Pres 1987-88; Pres, Past VP, Nat Lib Wales; Royal Commn Ancient and Histl Monuments in Wales, 1967, 1977, 1987. *Honours:* Gladstone Mem Essay Prize, 1948; Hon Mbr, Gorsedd of Bards (White Robe), 1984; VP, Hon Soc of Cymmrodorion, 1988-. *Hobbies:* Travel; Walking. *Address:* Llywenan, Siliwen, Bangor, Gwynedd LL57 2BS, Wales.

WILLIAMS Leslie Sands, b. 12 Dec 1913, Shawnee, Oklahoma, USA. Retired Missionary Nurse. m. 13 Aug 1940, 2 s. *Education:* BA, OK Bapt Univ, 1935; MRE, SWn Bapt Theological Sem, 1937; RN, Baylor School Nursing, 1940. *Appointments:* Nursing Fac, Baylor School Nursing, TX, 1940-41; Nursing Fac, 1941-42, Bapt Student Dir, 1942-43, So Bapt School Nursing; Nursing Educ, Ognamoso Hosp, Nigeria, W Africa, 1944-64; Student Work, Bapt Mission, Nigeria, 1975-79. *Memberships:* Bapt Nursing Fellowship, Fndng Pres OK

1985-86, Nat Pres 1986-89, Ex Comm 1989-91, Rep to Nat Network Christian Nurses; Steering Comm, NCN, organising and executing 1st N Am Conf Nurses 1990, planning for 2nd Conf. *Honours:* Outstanding Alumni Achievement Award, OK Bapt Univ, 1959; Mortar Bd, Zeta Chi Chapt, Distinguished Serv Award, OK Bapt Univ, 1970; Sigma Theta Tau, Int Beta Delta Chapt, 1991. *Hobbies:* Reading history and historical novels; Listening to classical and semi-classical music. *Address:* 6304 NW 21st Drive, Bethany, OK 73008, USA.

WILLIAMS Maurice, b. 14 June 1942, Southampton, England. Consultant Neurosurgeon. m. 9 Sept 1968, 1 s, 3 d. *Education:* Pembroke Coll, Cambridge, 1961-64; 1st Class Hons, Natural Scis Tripos, Cambridge, 1964; St Thomas's Hosp Med School, 1964-67; MA (Cantab), 1967; MB Chir (Cantab), 1967; FRCS England, 1971; FRCP London, 1990. *Appointments:* Chief Asst, Neurosurg, St Bartholomew's Hosp, London, 1973-77; Cons Neurosurg, Brook Hosp, 1977-80; Sr Cons Neurosurg, Royal Free Hosp, London, 1980-. *Publications:* Articles in sci jrnls on surg and physiology of the brain and spinal cord; Spinal Degenerative Disease, 1981; Subarachnoid Haemorrhage, 1987; Ed, British Journal of Neurosurgery. *Memberships:* Athenaeum; Fellow, Hunterian Soc; Former Coun Mbr, Soc Brit Neurological Surgs. *Honours:* Open Scholarship, Natural Scis, Pembroke Coll, Cambridge, 1960; Cheselden Gold Medal, Surg, St Thomas's Hosp, 1967; Hallett Prize, Royal Coll Surgs, 1969. *Hobbies:* Walking; Country life. *Address:* c/o Regional Neurosurgical Unit, Royal Free Hospital, Pond St, London NW3 2QG, England.

WILLIAMS Michael, b. 24 June 1935, Swansea, Wales. Reader in Geography. m. Eleanore Williams, 25 June 1955, 2 s. *Education:* BA, 1951, PhD, 1960, DLitt, 1990, Swansea Univ Coll, Univ Wales; DipEd, St Catharine's Coll, Cambridge, 1960. *Appointments:* Dept Demonstrator, Swansea, 1957-60; Lectr, Sr Lectr, Reader, Univ Adelaide, S Australia, 1960- 77; Lectr, Geog, 1978-89, Reader, 1989-, Univ Oxford, England; Fellow, Oriel Coll, Oxford; Vis Prof: Univ Madison, USA, 1973-74, Univ Chgo, 1989. *Publications:* Draining of Somerset Levels, 1970; Making of South Australia Landscape, 1974; American and Their Forests, 1984; Wetlands: A Threatened Landscape, 1991; Planet Management, 1992. *Memberships:* Royal Geogl Soc, Ed Advsr; Progress in Human Geog, Ed; Inst Brit Geog, Ed Transactions 1983-88; Assn Am Geogs. *Honours:* Lit Prize, Adelaide Fest Arts, 1976; John Lewis Gold Medal, Royal Geogl Soc, S Australia, 1979; Hidy Award, 1987, Hon Fellow, 1989, N Am Forest Hist Soc; Fellow, Brit Acad, 1989. *Hobbies:* Walking; Music. *Address:* Westgates, Vernon Avenue, Harcourt Hill, Oxford OX2 9AU, England. 1, 30.

WILLIAMS Patricia J, b. 29 Sept 1942, St Louis, Missouri, USA. Business Owner, Financial Advisory Firm. *Education:* BA, Home Econs Educ, Fresno State Univ, CA, 1964; MA, Child Dev, San Jose State Univ, CA, 1968; EdD, Mgmt, Univ No CO, Greely, 1977; Registered Investment Advsr Assoc; Licensed Real Estate Agt; Licensed Ins Agt; Registered Rep, Nat Assn Securities Dealers; Cert Fin Planner. *Appointments:* Tchr, Supvsr, VP, E Side Union HS Dist, San Jose, CA, 1964-77; Ptnr, Ldrship Dev Inst, Colorado Springs, CO, 1978; Owner, The Fern Factory, Plant Store, Costa Mesa, CA, 1979; Trng Dir, Intel Corp, Santa Clara, CA, 1980; Ptnr, Dahl and Williams, Fin Planning, 1981-83; Ptnr, Pres, Delta Advisors Inc (dba The Delta Grp), Los Altos, CA, 1983-. *Publication:* Career Aspiratins of Selected Women Teachers, dissertation, 1977. *Memberships:* Quota Club Los Altos, 1984- 89, Pres 1986-87; Int Assn Fin Planning; Los Altos Chmbr of Comm; Los Altos Women in Bus, Bd Mbr 1987-88; City of Los Altos: Planning Commnr, Vice-Chair 1990, Chair 1991, Asst Chair, Loyola Corners-Specific Plan Comm 1989-90, Val Awards Comm 1988-89; Chair, Econ Sub-Comm, Gen Plan Review Comm, 1987; 2005 Comm, 1986. *Honours:* Soroptimist Woman of Achievement Award, Los Altos-Mountain View, 1987; Outstanding

Achievement, Pub Access TV, Access Los Altos CH 30, 1989. *Hobbies:* Gardening; Knitting; Weaving; Sewing and tailoring; Reading. *Address:* 167 So San Antonio Rd, Ste 7, Los Altos, CA 94022, USA. 5, 59, 189.

WILLIAMS Robert Charles Gooding, b. 28 Dec 1907, London, England. Chartered Electrical Engineer. m. Edith Emma (Molly) Morrow, 16 Dec 1937, 1 d. *Education:* BSc (Engrng), 1929, DIC, 1930, PhD, 1931, Imperial Coll Sci, Technology and Med. *Appointments:* Chief Engr, Murphy Radio Ltd, 1935-45; Exec Engr, N Am Philips Inc, 1946-47; Chief Engr, Philips Inds, 1948-69; Vis Prof, Electronics, Univ Surrey, 1969-74; Chmn, Prof and Sci Servs, 1974-. *Publications:* Num papers in Proc IEE, Journal of Society for Education in Film and Television, Royal TV Society Journal, Journal Royal Society of Arts, Trans IEEE; Feature articles in The Times, Financial Times and Guardian. *Memberships:* Life Fellow, Instn Elec Engrs, Mbr Coun 1962-65; Life Fellow, Instn Mech Engrs; Life Fellow, IEEE, Dir 1967-68; Royal TV Soc, Mbr Coun 1958-60, 1963-65; Athenaeum Club. *Honours:* Royal Scholar, 1926; Clothworkers Scholar, 1926; Henrici Medal, 1928; Siemens Mem Medal, 1928; Unwin Scholar, 1929; Freeman, City of London, 1946; Liveryman, Clothworkers Co, 1946; OBE, 1969. *Hobbies:* Theatre; Garden; Antique maps and atlases. *Address:* Field Plot, The Flower Walk, Guildford, Surrey, England GU2 5EP. 26.

WILLIAMS Veronica Ann, b. 8 Feb 1956, Washington, District of Columbia, USA. Senior Regional Manager. *Education:* BA, Brandeis Univ, 1977; MBA, NWn Univ, 1979. *Appointments:* Mktng Rep, Control Data, 1979-82; Product Mgr, AT&T, 1982-88; Dist Mgr, Unisoft Corp, 1988-89; Account Mgr, Lotus Dev Corp, 1989-90; Sr Reg Mgr, Software Corp Am, 1990-. *Memberships:* S Orange Planning Bd, 1985-87; S Orange Citizens Advsry Commm; Nat Black MBA Fin Chair, 1979-81. *Honours include:* Nat Black MBA Performance Award, 1981. *Hobbies:* Swimming; Scuba diving; Skiing; Music; Travel. *Address:* PO Box 978, South Orange, NJ 07079, USA. 6, 76, 132.

WILLIAMSON John Ramsden, b. 31 Oct 1929, Manchester, England. Music Teacher; Composer. m. (1) 2 s, (2) Valmai Roberts, 22 Apr 1976. *Education:* ARMCM, 1952; LRAM, 1961; BMus (Dunelm), 1973; FLCM, 1977. *Appointments:* School Music Tchr: Lancs, 1952-53; Manchester, 1953-59; Taunton, Somerset, 1959-64; Grays, Essex, 1964-70; Prestatyn, Clwyd, 1970-76; Notre Dame Coll Educ, Liverpool, 1976-80; St Mary's Coll, Colwyn Bay, 1980-; Pvte Music Tutor incl Piano. *Creative works:* Over 50 significant musical compositions: solo piano, piano, chamber music, songs, piano sonata, string quartet, works for trumpet, violin, viola, flute, clarinet, recorder, guitar and other instruments, cantata, mass, piano concerto. *Memberships:* Assoc Mbr, Composers Guild GB; Soc for Promotion of New Music. *Honours:* Barlow Trophy for Composition, Chester Competitive Music Fest, 1972, 1978, 1979, 1986, 1990, 1991. *Hobbies:* Cycling; DIY activities; Gardening; Reading. *Address:* 31A Aberconway Road, Prestatyn, Clwyd LL19 9HL, Wales. 4, 52, 139, 149, 152, 156.

WILLIAMSON Robert, b. 1 Aug 1930, Regina, Canada. Designer. m. Judith Bianche Ann Nichols, 25 Oct 1958, 2 s, 2 d. *Education:* Mining Geology, Univ Toronto, 1950-51; Assoc, Ont Coll Art, 1956. *Career:* Prospecting, Arctic, Quebec, Cuba, 1946-56; Sailed own boats, Can to Gulf of Mexico, 1950, Hamburg to Cannes, 1956; Mosaics for Picasso, France, 1956- 57; Mosaic studio, London, England, 1958-61; Freelance design, graphics, advt, London, 1961-62; Art Dir, Creative Dir, Alexander-Butterfield and Ayer, 1962- 69; Designer, Writer, 1970-; Clients incl Pyrex, Pirelli, Shell Chems, Rothmans, Lentheric; Danish Agricl Prods, Oxfam, Bowater-Scott, ICI Europa, Toyota, Esso; Photographer: Oxfam in India; Porjects, Canaries, Austria, UK; UN Cons, Cuba, Zimbabwe. *Publications:* Books: Cruise of the Schooner

Driftwood, 1962; Mosaics, 1964; Dogrib Dictionary, 1970; Project Calendar, 1971; How To Be A Doctor, cartoon book, 1988; Cartoons. *Memberships:* Soc Typographic Designers; Fellow, Soc Indl Artists and Designers; Assoc, Assn Typographique Internationale; Inst Packaging. *Hobbies:* Sailing; Skiing; Writing; Cartooning. *Address:* Robert Williamson Design, 95 Great Titchfield St, London W1F 7FP, England.

WILLIES Joan Millicent Anne, b. 23 Dec 1929, Bristol, England. Miniator (Miniaturist). m. Mark E Willies, 28 Aug 1949, 3 s. *Education:* Commercial Coll, Bristol; Pvte tuition, trng, Art, Music. *Career:* Exhibs, 1941-, incl: Bristol Mus, 1941; Dalhousie Univ, Can, 1967; Royal Miniature Soc, 1972; RI, 1973; SWA, 1975; Tiffanys, GA; Commissions: Num clients incl royalty (Lichtenstein), TV and stage personalities; Tchng: Pvte students, workshops, Eckerd Coll (USA), schools in Can, hosps; Interviewed for article in Victoria Mag, USA; Currently working on TV series. *Creative works:* Over 2000 miniature and large paintings, in watercolour, oils, alkyds and egg tempera; Captivating World of Miniature Painting, video; Children's painting book, 1961; Artists Workbook, 2 eds, 1988, 1989; Articles in Artists Mag, 1988, also Nutshell News, Miniature Collector, NAME Mag. *Memberships:* Elected Assoc, 1974, Full Mbr, 1976-, Royal Soc Miniature Painters, Sculptors and Gravers; Hon Mbr, Miniature Art Soc, FL; Hilliard Soc, England; Soc Limner, England; GA Miniature Art Soc; WA Soc Miniature Paintersx, Sculptors and Gravers; Hon Mbr, Dayton (OH) Miniature Soc. *Honours:* Num awards, exhibs, Miniature Art Socs, USA and UK, 1977-90; Runner-up, Hunting Grp Award, England; Hon Mention, Gold Mem Bowl, Royal Miniature Soc, 1989. *Hobbies:* Music, esp singing, guitar-playing; Teaching newly blind to play guitar; Teaching music, singing and theatre to underprivileged children and long-stay hospital patients esp those with emotional problems. *Address:* PO Box 7659, Clearwater, FL 34618, USA. 189.

WILLINGHAM Douglas Barton, b. 23 Feb 1954, Mobile, Alabama, USA. Dentist in Private General Practice; Dental Editor. m. Michele Joy Saunders, 21 Mar 1981, 1 d. *Education:* Hum Studies, Hist, TX Tech Univ, 1976; DDS, Baylor Coll Dentistry, 1980. *Appointments:* Self-employed Gen Dentist, pvte solo prac, Salado, TX, 1981-; Ed (elected), Texas Dental Journal, TX Dental Assn, 1986-. *Publications:* Articles and eds in Texas Dental Journal, Journal of Am Dental Assn, Bulletin of History of Dentistry, ADA News, Dental Student, The New Dentist, Dentistry 82, DDS News, Baylor Dental Journal, Quarterly, CTOS Newsletter. *Memberships:* Am Student Dental Assn, Ed, Bd Dirs, 1976-80; Xi Psi Phi, Ed Alpha Pi, Chmn Publs Comm; Am Acad Hist of Dentistry; Ctrl TX Dental Soc, Ed, Bd Dirs; Am Assn Dental Eds, Chmn Mbrship Comm; Baylor Dental Alumni Assn, Bd Trustees, Chmn Nominating Comm; Am Dental Assn; Pierre Fauchard Acad; Salado Histl Soc, Pres 1983; Railroad and Pioneer Mus, Pres 1985-86; Inst for Humanities Salado, TX, Coun Advsrs; Bell Co, TX, Histl Commn; Titanic Histl Soc; Phila Maritime Muse; Oceanic Navigation Rsch Soc; TX State Histl Assn; Sons of Republic of TX; SAR; Soc of War of 1812, State Surg. *Honours:* Omicron Delta Kappa, 1975; Dobro Slovo, Outstanding 2nd Yr Czech Lang Student, TX Tech Univ, 1975; Sigma Tau Delta, 1975; Phi Alpha Theta, 1975; M D K Bremner Award, histl writing, Am Acad Hist of Dentistry, 1978; Outstanding Ed Award, Xi Psi Phi, 1979; Golden Scroll Award, 1980, Golden Pen Hon Mention, 1981, Golden Scroll Hon Mention, 1988, Golden Pen Award, 1988, 1989, Special Citation, 1990, Int Coll Dentists in Jrnlsm Competition; Dentist of Yr, Ctrl TX Dental Soc, 1988; Nominee, TX Dentist of Yr, 1988. *Hobbies:* Maritime and Texas history; Genealogy. *Address:* Armstrong-Adams House, Salado, TX 76571, USA. 117, 139.

WILLIS Lloyd Allan, b. 29 Dec 1938, Merredin, Western Australia, Australia. College Professor; Religion Department Chairman. m. Edith May Bradbury, 28 Dec 1961, 1 s, 2 d. *Education:* BA, Relig, Avondale Coll,

NSW, 1961; MA, Relig, 1970, PhD, Relig, Archaeology, Old Testament, 1982, Andrews Univ, MI, USA. *Appointments:* Pastor, Evangelist, S Australia, 1961-63; Tchr, Boys' Dean, VHS, Mussoorie, India, 1964-69; Prof, Relig, Spicer Coll, India, 1970-89; Prof, Relig, SWn Adventist Coll, Keene, TX, USA, 1989-. *Publications:* Archaeology in Adventist Literature 1937-1980, book; The History of Archaeological Research in Transjordan (w L T Geraty), book article. *Memberships:* Biblical Archaeology Soc; Am Schools Oriental Rsch; Israel Exploration Soc. *Honours:* Graduation Class Pres, Avondale Coll, Australia, 1961. *Hobbies:* Archaeology; Stamp collecting; Insect collecting. *Address:* c/o Southwestern Adventist College, Keene, TX 76059, USA.

WILLIS Ralph Houston, b. 26 Dec 1942, McMinnville, Tennessee, USA. College Professor. m. Velma Inez Church, 10 Aug 1985, 1 stepdaughter. *Education:* BS, Maths, 1964, MA, Maths, 1966, Middle TN State Univ, 1964; Grad work, LA State Univ, 1964-65. *Appointments:* Army Serv: Lt, Air Def Artillery, 1966-68; Instr, Maths, 1968-73, Asst Prof, Maths, 1973-83, Assoc Prof, Maths, 1983-, Wn Carolina Univ. *Publications:* 24 articles in profl jrnls; Ed: Abelian Grapevine - Secondary Mathematics newsletter, 1970-88; The Child of Mathematics - Elementary/Middle Grade newsletter, 1972- 78. *Memberships:* Nat Coun Tchrs of Maths; NC Counc Tchrs of Maths; Kappa Mu Epsilon; Phi Kappa Phi. *Honours:* Paul A Reid Disting Serv Award for FAc, Wn Carolina Univ, 1990-91; Outstanding Local Site Contest Award, NC State Maths Contest Comm, 1990; Nominated, Gov's Award for Excellence, Chancellor of Wn Carolina Univ, 1990-91. *Hobbies:* Genealogy; Gardening; Military history; Model building; Carpentry. *Address:* Department of Mathematics and Computer Science, Western Carolina University, Cullowhee, NC 28723, USA. 7, 15.

WILLIS Timothy James Bethune, b. 12 Aug 1958, London, England. Currency Manager. m. Sara Elizabeth Hoyle, 11 Aug 1989. *Education:* Royal Artillery and Royal Mil Acad, Sandhurst, 1976-77. *Appointments:* Toy Salesman, Harrods, London, 1977; Bed Salesman, Oxford, 1978-79; Irving Trust and Bank of NY, 1980-91; Matuschka, Frankfurt, Germany, 1991-. *Memberships:* Econ Rsch Coun; MENSA; Greenpeace; Machrihanish GC, Argyll; GC Gut Neuhof, Frankfurt. *Hobbies:* Golf; The Economist; Malt whiskey. *Address:* Thorwaldsenplatz 1, 6-Frankfurt 70, Germany.

WILLMER John Honour, b. 11 Nov 1920, Friars Court, Clanfield, Oxfordshire, England. Farmer. m. Frances Irene Jackson, 8 Feb 1964, 1 s, 2 d dec. *Education:* Bradford Tech Coll, 1937-39. *Career:* Farming, environmentally sensitive, 1939-91; Started Caravan Club CCL, Caravan Rally Site, Boat Moorings, 1974; Started Nature Trail and Tearooms, 1988. *Memberships:* Young Farmers Club, Oxon Chmn 1959; Nat Farmers Union, Oxon Chmn 1965, Life Mbr Oxon Exec Comm; Country Landowners Assn, Oxon Exec Comm; Responsible for writer matters for Country Landowners Assn and Nat Farmers Union with Nat Rivers Auth and Thames Water; West Oxon Coll Gov; Westminster Tchr Trng Coll. *Honours:* OBE, 1989; Fellow, Royal Agricl Soc, 1989. *Hobby:* Conservation incl giving talks and lectures on all aspects - trees, fauna, flora, energy, insulation. *Address:* Friars Court, Clanfield, Oxford OX18 2SU, England.

WILLOCH Kaare Isaachsen, b. 3 Oct 1928, Oslo, Norway. County Governor. m. Anne-Marie Jorgensen, 30 Apr 1954, 1 s, 2 d. *Education:* Cand oecon (equiv MEcon), Univ Oslo, 1953. *Appointments:* Sec, Fedn Norwegian Shipowners, 1951-53; Cnslr, Fedn Norwegian Inds, 1954-63; MP, 1958- 89; Mbr, Nat Comm, 1961-89, Sec Gen, 1963-65, Chmn, 1970-74, Conservative Party; Min Trade and Shipping, 1963, 1965-70; Chmn, World Bank Grp, 1967; Chmn, Conservative Party Parly Grp, 1970-81; Mbr, 1970-81, Pres, 1973, Nordic Coun; Prime Min, 1981-86; Chmn,

For Affairs Comm Parliament, 1986-89; Co Gov, Oslo and Akershus, 1989-. *Publications:* Price Policy in Norway (w L B Bachke), 1958; Minner og meninger, memoirs, 1988; Statsminister, memoirs, 1990. *Honours:* Dr at Law (hc), St Olaf's Coll, MN, USA. *Hobby:* Cross-country skiing. *Address:* Blokkaveien 6B, 0280 Oslo, Norway. 52.

WILSON Barbara Gail, b. 20 Aug 1959, Ft Thomas, KY, USA. Coll Prof. *Education:* BA, Morehead State Univ, 1977-80; MA, Morehead State Univ, 1981-84; EdD, Univ of Pittsburgh, 1987-92. *Appointments:* Program Dir, WMKY FM. morehead, KY, 1981-86; Asst Prof, Indianada Univ of Pennsylvania. *Publication:* Signals Mag. *Memberships:* Natl Broadcasting Soc; Intl Radio TV Soc; Kappa Delta Soc; Natl Assn of Coll Broadcasters. *Honours:* Member of the Year; Advisor of the Year. *Hobbies:* Travel; Reading; Horse Back Riding; Watching Sports. *Address:* 4880 Lucerne Road, Indiana, PA 15701, USA.

WILSON Bryan Ronald, b. 25 June 1926. University Teacher. *Education:* BSc (Econ), London, 1952; PhD, London, 1955; MA (Oxon), 1962; DLitt (Oxon), 1984. *Appointments:* Lectr, Sociology, Univ Leeds, 1955-62; Reader, Sociology, Univ Oxford, 1962-. *Publications:* Sects and Society, 1961; Religion in Secular Society, 1966; Religious Sects, 1970; Rationality (ed), 1970; Magic and the Millenium, 1973; The Noble Savages, 1975; Religion in Sociological Perspective, 1982; Values (ed), 1988; Social Dimensions of Sectarianism, 1990. *Membership:* Conference internationale de Sociologie des Religions, Pres, 1971-75. *Honours:* Hon DLitt, Soka Univ, Japan, 1985. *Hobbies:* Claret; Gardens; Chinese porcelain. *Address:* All Souls College, Oxford OX1 4AL, England. 1.

WILSON David Geoffrey, b. 30 Apr 1933, Manchester, England. Health Authority Chairman; High Sheriff. m. Dianne Elizabeth Morgan, 10 Aug 1980. *Education:* Leeds Grammar School, Hulme Grammar School, Oldham, 1945-51. *Appointments:* Williams Deacon's Bank, 1951-70; Williams and Glyn's Bank, 1970-86; Nat Enterprise Bd, 1982-85; Brit Linen Bank, 1981-91; N Manchester Hlth Auth, 1991-. *Memberships:* Manchester Chmbr of Comm and Ind, Pres 1978-80; Manchester Luncheon Club, Pres 1980-81; Manchester Lit and Philosl Soc, 1981-83; Manchester Jr Chmbr of Comm, Pres 11967-68; Manchester Bankers Inst, Pres 1977-78. *Honours:* Hon MA, Univ Manchester, 1983; Dpty Lt, Greater Manchester, 1984; OBE, 1986; High Sheriff, Gtr Manchester, 1991-92. *Hobbies:* Music (Treasurer, Halle Concerts Society); Cricket (Mbr, Marylebone Cricket Club and Lancashire County Cricket Club). *Address:* Winton, 28 Macclesfield Road, Wilmslow, Cheshire SK9 2AF, England.

WILSON David Keith, b. 16 Jan 1947, England. Sculptor; Senior Lecturer in Sculpture. m. Alexis Wilson, 10 Jan 1985, 1 s, 1 d. *Education:* Dip Art, Sculpture, Nat Gall Art School, Melbourne, 1970; TTTC, Hawthorn Tchrs Coll, 1971; Study tour, Europe, UK, USA. *Career:* Tchng, var tech schools, Australia, 1971-73; Sessional Lectr, Sculpture, Hist, 1973-75, full- time Lectr, Sculpture, 1976-82, Prahran; Represented Australia, C'wlth Sculpture Symposium, Edmonton, Alta, Can, 1978; Pvte studio, London, England, 1981-82; Sr Lectr, Sculpture, Fac Art and Design, Vic Coll, Prahran, 1982-; Advsr: Victorian Min Arts and Melbourne Univ Gall, 1983-84; City of Colac, 1984-90; Pub Works Dept Archts, 1985; Curator, Sculpture at Riverside Quay exhib, Costain Australia Ltd and Comm 4th Australian Sculpture Triennial; 16 solo exhibs, sculpture, Melbourne, Sydney, Canberra, London, 1972-; Grp exhibs throughout Australia, Europe, N Am; Represented in all maj Australian galls, also galls, UK, Europe, N Am. *Memberships:* Var coll comms incl: BA (Fine Arts) Course Comm, Prahran, 1979-90; VCA/ Prahran Fine Art School Structure Working Party, 1990. *Honours:* Bernard Hall Award for Graduating Students, Nat Gall Vic Art School, 1970; Visual Arts Bd Grants,

Australia Coun, 1974, 1976, 1978, 1981; Commns, Australia, Can. *Hobbies:* Flying; Drawing; Gardening. *Address:* PO Box 44, Tyabb, Victoria 3913, Australia. 52.

WILSON Dudley Keith, b. 13 July 1936, Windermere, Cumbria, England. Educator; Administrator. m. Suzanne Haugland, div., 1 s. *Education:* King's Coll, Cambridge; BA (Hons), 1957; MA, 1960. *Career:* For Brit Coun: Lectr, Sr Lectr, Assoc Prof, Reader, Univs Zagreb (Yugoslavia), Teheran (Iran), Osmania, Hyderabad (India), 1957-67; Prin Lectr, Hd Liberal Studies, City of Salford, 1967-85; Fndng Hd, Dept Performing Arts and Media, Salford Coll Technology, Manchester, 1985-91; Fndng Dir, Ctr Performing Arts and Media, Salford, 1991-; Fndr: Europe's 1st BA (Hons) Band Musicianship, 1987, world's 1st BA (Hons) Popular Music and Recording, 1990, BA (Hons) TV and Radio, 1st Higher Nat Dips, Media Prod, Media Perf, Popular Music; Fndr, Salford Concert series, new music for brass, 1989-; Fndr Salford Coll Wind Band, Brass Band, Big Band, Salford Symphonic Wind Band; Dir: Aspects Prod Assocs, Aspects Theatre, Aspects Touring, Aspects TV and Video, Granada Film and Video Awards, L S Lowry Centenary Fest. *Creative works:* Feature articles, Daily Telegraph, Guardian, Scotsman, Times Educational Supplement, Times Higher; Contbr to BBC radio and TV, Granada TV, CBS, others. *Memberships:* Salford Univ Senate; Salford Coll Acad Bd; Fndr Mbr, Fedn Salford Coll and Salford Univ, Jt Acad Bd. *Honours:* Scholar Vis to Japan, GB-Sasakawa Fndn, 1990. *Hobbies:* Inner city renewal and the arts; Nordic lands and culture; Walking Cumbria's fells. *Address:* Centre for Performing Arts and Media, Salford College of Technology, College of Salford University, Adelphi, Peru St, Salford, Manchester M3 6EQ, England. 4, 139, 162.

WILSON James Noel, b. 25 Dec 1919, Coventry, England. Orthopaedic Surgeon (retired). m. 3 Sept 1945, 2 s, 2 d. *Education:* Univ Birmingham; MB, ChB, MRCS, LRCP, 1943; FRCS, 1948; ChM, 1949. *Appointments:* Res posts, Birmingham Gen Hosp, 1943; RMO, Army (Parachutist), 1943-46; Res Surg Off, Orthopaedic Hosp, Oswestry, 1949-52; Cons, Cardiff United Hosps, 1952-55; Cons, Royal Nat Orthopaedic Hosp, London, 1955-84; Cons Orthopaedic Surg, Hosp Nervous Diseases, Queen Sq, London, 1962- 84; Prof, Orthopaedics, Addis Ababa, Ethiopia, 1989. *Cobtributions to:* Various books and original papers; Ed: Watson-Jones Fractures and Joint Injuries, 5th Ed, 1976, 6th Ed, 1982. *Memberships:* Fellow, Brit Orthopaedic Assn; Fellow, Royal Soc Med; Late Pres, World Orthopaedic Concern; Egyptian Orthopaedic Assn; Bangladesh Orthopaedic Soc. *Honours:* Peter Thompson Prize, 1940; Sr Surg Prize, 1942; Arthur Foxwell Prize, 1943; Heaton Award, 1943; BOA Travelling Fellow to N Am, 1954. *Hobbies:* Golf; Photography; Old cars. *Address:* The Chequers, Waterdell, Nr Watford, Herts WD2 7LP, England. 1, 128, 139.

WILSON Janice Crabtree, b. 18 Jan 1932, WV, USA. Conslt; vice Pres. m. Arthur L Wilson, 28 May 1961, 2 d, div. *Education:* BA, Berea Coll, KY; MA, Miami Univ, Ohio; PhD, Univ of Cincinnati. *Appointments:* Public Sch Tchr, 1959-66; Wright State Univ, Ohio, Tchr, 1966-80; NCR Corp, Ohio, 1980-89; The Pacer Group, Oh, 1989-. *Publications include:* Numerous Articles & Papers. *Memberships:* Easter Seal Soc; Multiple Schlerois Soc. *Honours:* Phi Kappa Honor Soc; Recipient Charles Phelps Taft Graduate Fellowship. *Address:* 664 N Monroe Drive, Xenia, OH 45385, USA. 8.

WILSON Lois Miriam, b. 8 Apr 1927, Winnipeg, Manitoba, Canada. Minister of Religion. m. Roy F Wilson, 9 June 1950, 2 s, 2 d. *Education:* BA, 1947, BDiv, 1969, United Coll, Winnipeg; Ordained, United Ch Can, 1965; Cert TV Prod, Ryerson Tech Inst, 1974. *Appointments:* Min: 1st United Ch, Thunder Bay, 1965-69; 1st United Ch, Hamilton, 1969-78; Chalmers United Ch, Kingston, 1978-80; Moderator, United Ch Can, Kingston, 1980-82; Dir, Ecumenical Forum Can, Toronto, 1984-90;

McGeachy Sr Scholar, United Ch Can, 1990-92. *Publications:* Like a Mighty River, 1981; Turning the World Upside Down, 1989; Articles in profl publs. *Memberships include:* Bd, Amnesty Int, Can; Bd Dirs, VP, Civil Liberties Can; Chair, Urban Rural Mission; Pres, World Coun Chs, 1983-91; Can Inst Int Peace and Security, 1984- 89; Advsry Coun, Int Dev Studies, Univ Toronto; Can Assn Adult Educ, Bd Dirs 1986-90; Bd Dirs, Friends Can Broadcasting; Environment Assessment Panel Govt Can, Nuclear Waste Fuel Mgmt and Disposal Concept; Trustee, Nelson Mandela Fund. *Honours:* Pearson Peace Prize, UN-Can, 1984; Off, Order of Can, 1984; Order of Ont, 1991; Apptd Chancellor, Lakehead Univ, Thunder Bay, 1991; DDiv (hon): Victoria Univ, Toronto, 1978; United Theological Coll, Montreal, 1978; Wycliff Coll, 1983; Queens Univ, Kingston, 1984; Univ Winnipeg, 1986; Mt Allison Univ, 1988; LLD (Hon): Trent Univ, Peterborough, 1984; Dalhousie Univ, 1989; DCL (Hon), Acadia Univ, 1984; DHum (hon), Mt St Vincent, Halifax, 1984. *Hobbies:* Canoeing; Reading; Kayaking; Sailing. *Address:* 482 Markham St, Toronto, Ontario M6G 2L3, Canada. 145.

WILSON Randal D, b. 28 Feb 1950, Stephensburg, Kentucky, USA. Coordinator of Outward Bound; Counsellor. *Education:* BME, Voice, 1977; MS, Human Servs, 1979; Specialist, Coll Tchng, 1984. *Appointments:* KY Manpower Servs, 1979; Cnslr, 1979-86, Coord, 1986-, Outward Bound. *Memberships:* Comm Mbr, Chmn, Int Student Scholarship Comm, Murray State Univ, KY; Steering Comm, Ctr Int Progs, Murray State Univ; Past VP, Past Mbr-at-Large, Past Pres-Elect, Pres, KY Assn Educl Opportunity Prog Personnel; KY Rep to Bd Dirs, SE Assn Educl Opportunity Prog Personnel. *Honours:* USAF Commendation Medal, 1970-72; Jaycees Outstanding Young Men Am, 1981-83; Ky Col, Govs Off, 1989. *Hobbies:* Community theatre; Science fiction; Role play games; Music; Photography. *Address:* 1608 College Farm Rd No 5-E, Murray, KY 42071, USA. 7, 155.

WILSON Wanda, b. 15 May 1950, Pittsburgh, Pennsylvania, USA. Entertainment Promotions Professional. m. Kirby L Wilson Sr, 23 Apr 1976, 1 s, 1 d. *Education:* Connelly Tech School, Pitts, 1968; Allegheny Community Coll, Pitts, 1968-71; Univ Pitts, 1984-85. *Appointments:* Prod, Host, The Wanda Wilson Show, variety, Am Cablevision Co, Monroeville, PA, 1981-84; Warner Cable Co and Pitts Telecommunications Inc, 1984-87; Pres, W-W Prods, Entertainment Prods, 1984-; Mktng Mgr, Informer newspaper, 1984-87; Co-Host, Announcer, Int People's Radio, SAC, 1987; Sr Clerk, Chem Monitor, Gencorp Aerojet Tech Systems, SAC, CA, 1987-90; Studio Camera Operator, WPXITV-11, NBC Affiliate, 1990-; Promoter, Wanmar Prods; Prod, Host, Wanmar Info and Talent Showcase, 1991. *Creative works:* Love Traces on My Mind, poetry, 1972; The First Time I Saw You, song lyrics, 1982. *Memberships:* Pitts Models Assn; Pitts Media Fedn; AFTRA; Nat Assn Female Execs. *Hobbies include:* Interior decorating; Art; Swimming; Writing. *Address:* 924 California Ave, Pittsburgh, PA 15212, USA. 5, 9, 132, 152, 138, 189.

WILSON William Julius, b. 20 Dec 1935, Derry Township, Pennsylvania, USA. University Professor of Sociology and Public Policy. m. Beverly Ann Wilson, 31 July 1970, 1 s, 3 d. *Education:* BA, Wilberforce Univ, 1958; MA, Bowling Green State Univ, 1961; PhD, WA State Univ, 1966. *Appointments include:* Dir, Ctr Study of Urban Inequality, School Pub Policy, 1990-, Lucy Flower Univ Prof, Sociology, Pub Policy, 1990-, Univ Chgo, IL. *Publications:* The Declining Significance of Race: Blacks and Changing American Institutions, 1980; The Truly Disadvantaged: The Inner City, The Underclass, and Public Policy, 1987. *Memberships:* Bd Dirs, VP: Spencer Fndn; Russell Sage; Bd Dirs: Ctr Adv Study in Behavioral Scis; Nat Humanities Ctr; Ctr Budget and Policy Priorities; Bd Trustees, Spelman Coll. *Honours:* MacArthur Prize Fellowship, 1987-92; Am Acad Arts and Sci, 1988; Godkin Lectr, John F Kennedy School of Govt, Harvard Univ, 1988; AAAS, 1989; Am

Philosl Soc, 1990; Nat Acad Scis, 1991. *Hobbies:* Golf; Fishing; The symphony. *Address:* Department of Sociology, University of Chicago, 1126 E 59th Street, Chicago, IL 60637, USA. 2, 8, 143.

WILTROUT Ann Elizabeth, b. 3 Aug 1939, Elkhart, Indiana, USA. Professor of Foreign Languages. m. Joseph Alli, 25 Aug 1990. *Education:* BA, Hanover Coll, 1961; MA, 1964, PhD, 1968, IN Univ. *Appointments:* Vis Asst Prof, IN Univ, 1968-69; Asst Prof, 1969-71, Assoc Prof, 1971-87, Prof, For Langs, 1987-, MS State Univ. *Publications:* A Patron and a Playwright in Renaissance Spain, 1987; Num articles in scholarly jrnls, festschriften and actae. *Memberships include:* Asociacioa Internacional de Hispanistas; MLA; Am Assn Tchrs Spanish and Portuguese; AAUP; Cervantes Soc Am; Asociacion de Cervantistas. *Honours:* Dist Alumni Award, Hanover Coll, 1974; Cert Dist Serv, Inst Int Educ, 1986; Soc Scholars in Arts and Scis; Phi Kappa Phi; Sigma Delta Pi; Phi Sigma Iota; Alpha Phi Gamma. *Hobbies:* Shakespearean drama in performance; Spanish Golden Age drama; Travel; Reading fiction; Growing roses; Pets. *Address:* Department of Foreign Languages, Drawer FL, Mississippi State University, Mississippi State, MS 39762, USA. 5, 7, 13, 15.

WINCKEL Eddy A Van De, b. 25 Mar 1941, Belgium. Mgmt Conslt. m. Fe D Lozada, 3 d. *Education:* Master of Sci, Metropolitan Coll, Boston univ, MA, 1987; Commercial Airline Pilot, 1975-79; Flight Instr, 1980. *Appointments:* Conslt Strategic Proces Control & Logistics Computer Systems, 1982-; Air crew, Airline Opertion & Strategic Planning, 1977-80. *Publications:* Several Papers; Research on Artificial Intelligence & Learning Computers; Development of Own Knowledge Base Management System. *Memberships:* European Assc Conslt; Assn of Belgin Flight Instr. *Hobbies:* Computer Research; Corp Economics & Strategies; Sailing; Travel. *Address:* 21 Rue Marcq, B-1000 Brussels, Belgium.

WINDHAUSER John William, b. 30 Jan 1943, Rochester, New York, USA. Journalism Professor. m. Marlene Marie Most, 30 Aug 1975. *Education:* BS, Tri-State Univ, 1966; MA, Ball State Univ, 1967; PhD, OH Univ, 1975. *Appointments:* Reporter, Ed, var newspapers; PR, Advt; College Tchg: CO State Univ; Univ MS; Currently Manship School Jrnlsm, LA State Univ, Baton Rouge; Ed, College Press Review, 10 yrs. *Publications:* Over 75 rsch papers and articles; Editorial Process; The Media in the 1984 and 1988 Presidential Campaign. *Memberships:* Assn Educ in Jrnlsm; Exec Bd, Ed, Nat Coun Coll Publs Advsrs; Broadcast Educ Assn; Kappa Tau Alpha; Acad Criminal Justice Scis; So Speech Communication Assn. *Honours:* Life Mbrship Award, Nat Coun Coll Publs Advsrs. *Address:* Manship School of Journalism, Louisiana State University, Baton Rouge, LA, 70803, USA. 2, 7, 15, 155, 156.

WINGATE Robert Lee Jr, b. 28 May 1936, Columbia, South Carolina, USA. Medical Practitioner. div., 2 children. *Education:* BS, Univ SC, Columbia, 1957; MD, Med Coll SC, Charleston, 1961; Intern, 1961-62; Res, Internal Med, 1964-65; Cinn Gen Hosp, Univ Cinn; Res, Internal Med, Med Coll VA, Richmond, 1965-66; Res, Internal Med, 1966-67, Neurology, 1967-68, LSU Serv, Charity Hosp LA, New Orleans. *Appointments:* Served to Lt-Cmdr, USNR, 1958-66, active duty, 1962-64; Pvte Prac, Gen Internal Med, Columbia, SC, 1968-78; Staff: Richland Mem Hosp, Bapt Med Ctr and Providence Hosp, Columbia, 1968-78; Med Dir, Forest Hills Nursing Ctr, Columbia, 1970-78; Chief Med Cons, SC Commn for Blind, Columbia, 1970-78; Staff, York Co Hosp, Rock Hill, SC, 1978-80; Med Dir, M Lowenstein and Celanese Corps, Rock Hill, 1978- 80; Instr, School Nursing, Med Coll SC, Winthrop Coll Div, Rock Hill, 1978-80; Chief Physn, Med Dir, Nursing Home Care Unit, Dorn VA Hosp, Columbia, 1980-82; Instr, School Med, Univ SC, Columbia, 1980-82; Cons, SC Voc Rehab Disability Div, Columbia, 1983; Staff, Bapt Mem Hosps, Memphis, TN, 1983-85; Gen Internal Med, Hlth 1st Med Grp PC,

Memphis, 1983-85; Student Hlth Ctr, Univ SC, Columbia, 1985-86; Humana Medfirst Clin, W Columbia, and Rock Hill Urgent Care, 1986-87; Staff, Lexington Co Med Ctr, Lexington, SC, 1987-. *Publication:* We Are What We Eat, article, 1985. *Memberships:* AMA; Am Coll Physns; SC Med Assn; Am Soc Internal Med; Carolinas and Am Occupational Med Assn; Lexington Co Med Assn; Ruritans of Am, Pelion. *Honours include:* Hon Grad, US Naval Off Cand School, Newport, RI, 1962; AMA Physns Recognition Award, 1969, 1974, 1979, 1985-88. *Address:* 1225 Cedar Pine Rd, PO Box 480, Pelion, SC 29123, USA. 7.

WINGSTRAND Hans A, b. 20 Feb 1949, Gothenburg, Sweden. Associate Professor of Orthopaedics. m. Inga Bengtsson, 24 June 1974, 2 s, 1 d. *Education:* MD, 1974, PhD, 1986, Lectr, 1988, Univ Lund; Intern, Surg, Med, Psych, Co Hosp, Vastervik, 1974-75; Res: Surg, Anaesthesiology, Orthopaedics, Co Hosp, Helsingborg, 1975-79; Orthopaedics, Neurosurg, Univ Hosp, Lund, 1979-81, 1982-83; Hand and Plastic Surg, Univ Hosp, Malmo, 1981- 82; Bd Cert: Educl Commn For Med Grads, Boston, USA, 1977; Swedish Bd Orthopaedic Surg, 1983. *Appointments:* Sr Registrar, 1983-87, Rsch Fellowship, 1987-91, Assoc Prof, 1989-, Dept Orthopaedics, Univ Hosp, Lund; Co-Ed, Acta Orthopaedica Scandinavica, 1987-. *Memberships:* Swedish Med Assn; Swedish Soc Orthopaedic Surg; Scandinavian Assn Orthopaedic Surg; Swedish Soc Paediatric Orthopaedic Surg; European Orthopaedic Rsch Soc. *Honours:* Charnley Travel Grant, Swedish Soc Orthopaedic Surg, 1988. *Hobbies:* Yachting; Hunting; Skiing; Carpentry; History; Environmental protection. *Address:* Department of Orthopaedics, University Hospital, S-221 85 Lund, Sweden.

WINICK Myron, b. 4 May 1929, New York City, New York, USA. Physician; Medical School Administrator. m. Elaine L Lasky, 19 Sept 1964, 2 s. *Education:* AB, Columbia Univ, 1951; MS, Univ IL, 1952; MD, SUNY, 1956; Intern, Univ PA, Phila, 1956-57; Res, Paediatrics, Cornell Univ Med Coll, 1957-60. *Appointments:* Served USNR, 1960-62; Attng Paediatrician, Stanford Univ Hosp, CA, 1963-64; Asst Attng Paediatrician, NY Hosp, 1964-68, Assoc Attng Paediatrician, 1968-70, Attng Paediatrician, 1970-71; Asst Prof, Paediatrics, 1964-68, Assoc Prof, Paediatrics, Nutrition, 1968-70, Prof, 1970- 71, Cornell Univ Med Coll, NYC; Vis Prof, Univ Chile, Santiago, 1967; Attng Paediatrician, Presby Hosp, NYC, 1972-89; Prof, Paediatrics, 1972-89, Dir, 1972-89, R R Williams Prof, Nutrition, 1973-89, Inst Human Nutrition, Columbia Univ, NYC; Dir, Ctr Nutrition, Genetics and Human Dev, 1975-87; Pres, Univ Hlth Scis, Chgo Med School, N Chgo, IL, 1990-; Cons, Pan Am Hlth Org, 1966-. *Publications:* Malnutrition and Brain Development, 1976; Nutrition in Health and Disease, textbook, 1980; Growing Up Healthy: A Parent's Guide to Good Nutrition, 1982; For Mothers and Daughters: A Guide to Good Nutrition for Women, 1983; Your Personalized Health Profile: Choosing the Diet That's Right for You, 1985; Nutrition, Pregnancy and Early Infancy; Over 150 sci articles; Chapts in over 50 books; Ed, books. *Memberships include:* Fellow, Am Acad Paediatrics, Mbr Comm Nutrition; Fellow, Royal Soc Hlth; AAAS; Am Soc Cell Biology; Nat Acad Scis, Mbr Comm Maternal Nutrition; Food and Nutrition Bd, Nat Rsch Coun, 1982-88; NY Acad Scis; NY Acad Med; Int Soc Dev Neurosci; Num ed bds. *Honours include:* E Mead Johnson Award, Paediatric Rsch, 1970; Osborne and Mendel Award, Am Inst Nutrition, 1976; Agnes Higgins Award, March of Dimes Fndn, 1983. *Address:* University of Health Sciences, The Chicago Medical School, 3333 Green Bay Road, North Chicago, IL 60064, USA. 2.

WINKLER Cuno, b. 30 Sept 1919, Koenigsberg, Germany. Nuclear Medicine Educator; Professor of Radiology. *Education:* MD, Univ Hamburg, 1951; Rsch Fellow: Max Planck Inst Biophys, Frankfurt, FRG, 1954-55; Oak Ridge Inst Nuclear Studies, USA, 1956-57. *Appointments:* Asst Prof, Nuclear Med, 1966-72, Dir,

Inst Clin and Expmtl Med, 1972-87, Univ Bonn. *Publications:* Nuklearmedizin, Entwicklung, Methoden, Ergebniss, 1957; Nuklearmedizinische Tumordiagnostik, 1985; Nuclear Medicine in Clinical Oncology, 1987. *Memberships:* Deutsche Gesellschaft Nuklearmed; Soc Nuclear Med, USA; European Assn Nuclear Med, Erlangen, FRG; Gesellschaft deutscher Naturforscher und Arzte, Berlin. *Honours:* Recip; German Red Cross Award, 1960; PhD (hon), Univ Santo Tomas, Manila, 1978; Decorated Grand Cross, FRG, 1984; Medal, George V Hevesey Fndn, Switzerland, 1987. *Hobbies:* Philosophy; Cosmology; Playing viola in string quartet. *Address:* Trierer Str 55, 5300 Bonn 1, Germany. 34, 52.

WINTER Calvin A (Sonny) Jr, b. 25 Mar 1955, Selma, Alabama, USA. University County Extension Service Agent. m. Martha Elaine Poss, 14 Apr 1979, 2 s. *Education:* BS, Agricl Econs, Coll Agric, Univ GA, 1983. *Appointments:* Mgr, Herdsman, Beef Cattle Ctr, 1977-83, Co Ext Agt, Coop Ext Serv, 1983-, Coll Agric, Univ GA; Rsch Asst, Beef Cattle, USDA So Piedmont Conservation Rsch Ctr, 1981-83. *Memberships:* GA Aassn Co Agric Agts; Epsilon Sigma Phi; GA Cattlemen's Assn; Quitman Lions Club; Brooks Co Cattlemen's Assn; Quitman/Brooks Co Chmbr of Comm. *Honours:* Vol of Yr, Heart Assn, Bleckley Co, 1986, Brooks Co, 1989; Bronze Medallion, 1986, Silver Medallion, 1989, Am Heart Assn; Outstanding New Ext 4-H Agt, 1987; GA State Young Ext Profl of Yr, 1988. *Hobbies:* Purebred Angus cattle production; Junior livestock shows; Beef and dairy cattle artificial insemination; Football; Ch, Dawson Street Baptist, Thomasville, GA. *Address:* PO Box 97, Dixie, GA 31629, USA. 7, 15, 117.

WINTER Mark L, b. 7 Oct 1950, Joplin, Missouri, USA. Private Practitioner of Otolaryngology-Head and Neck Surgery. m. Debbie Wright, 11 Apr 1987, 1 s, 1 d. *Education:* BA cum laude, departmental distinction, Biology, Drury Coll, 1972; MD cum laude, School Med, Univ MS-Columbia, 1976; Intern, Gen Surg, 1977-78, Res, Otolaryngology, 1977-81, Univ TX Med Br. *Appointments:* Clin Asst Instr, 1981, Clin Asst Prof, 1983-, Dept Otolaryngology, Univ TX Med Br, Galveston; Pvte Prac, Otolaryngology-Hd and Neck Surg, 1983-; Clin Instr, Dept Surg, 1984-, Clin Asst Prof, Dept Med and Surg Neurology, 1987-, Adj Prof, Dept Speech and Hearing Scis, 1989-, TX Tech Univ Hlth Scis Ctr, Lubbock. *Publication:* Cervical node metastases from an unknown primary tumor (w B Leipzig and J Hokanson), 1981. *Memberships:* Lubbock-Crosby-Garza Med Soc; TX Med Assn; TX Otolaryngological Assn; Pan Am Allergy Soc; AMA; Am Acad Facial Plastic and Reconstrn Surg; Fellow, Am Acad Otolaryngology-Hd and Neck Surg; Am Acad Otolaryngic Allergy; Fellow, Am Neurotology Soc. *Honours:* Valedictorian, Diamond HS, 1968; Post Sophomore Fellowship, Pathology, Univ MS-Columbia School Med, 1974-75; Phi Eta Sigma, 1989; Phi Mu Alpha, 1989. *Hobbies:* Antique furniture; Clydesdale draft horse breeding and showing. *Address:* 2202 Slide Road, Lubbock, TX 79407, USA. 34.

WINTERS L Alan, b. 8 Apr 1950, Walthamstow, England. Professor of Economics. m. Margaret Elizabeth Winters, 3 Aug 1971, 2 d. *Education:* BSc, Bristol Univ, 1971; MA (Cantab), 1976; PhD (Cantab), 1978. *Appointments:* Rsch Off, Univ Cambridge, 1971-80; Lectr, Univ Bristol, 1980-86; Economist, World Bank, 1983-85; Prof, Univ Wales, Bangor, 1986-90; Prof, Univ Birmingham, 1990-. *Publications:* An Econometric Model of the Export Sector, 1981; International Economics, 1985, 1991; Europe's Domestic Market, 1988; 50 jrnl articles and chapts. *Memberships:* Brit Assn, VO Sect F; Coun Mbr, Royal Econ Soc; Prog Dir, Ctr Econ Policy Rsch. *Hobbies:* Cricket; Music. *Address:* Department of Economics, University of Birmingham, Edgbaston, Birmingham B15 2TT, England.

WIREMAN Billy Overton, b. 7 Oct 1932, Jackson, Kentucky, USA. College President. m. Kstie Marie Coomer, 3 Mar 1955, 1 s, 1 d. *Education:* BA,

Georgetown Coll, KY, 1954; MA, Univ KY, 1957; DEd, Peabody Coll, Vanderbilt Univ, 1960. *Appointments:* VP Dev, Dean of Men, Dir Tchr Educ, 1960-68, Pres, 1968-77, Eckerd Coll; Dean, Crummer School Fin and Bus Admin, Rollins Coll, 1977-78; Pres, Queens Coll, Charlotte, NC, 1978-. *Publications:* Getting It All Together: the New American Imperative (co-author), 1973; Extensive articles in var publs incl National Observer, Vital Speeches of the Day, Charlotte Observer, St Petersburg Times. *Memberships:* Advsr Adult Learning, The Coll Bd; Cons, United Bd Christian Higher Educ; Evaluator, Accrediting Agcy, So Assn Colls and Schools; Chmn, Charlotte-Mecklenburg Community Rels Comm. *Honours:* Algernon Sydney Sullivan Award, Peabody Coll, Vanderbilt Univ; Liberty Bell Award, St Petersburg Bar Assn, 1971; Newcomen Soc Award to Queens Coll, 1986; Univ Medal Hon, Han Nam Univ, Taejon, Korea, 1988; Dinner of Champions Hope Award, Multiple Sclerosis Soc, Charlotte, 1989. *Hobbies:* Pilot; Tennis player; Basketball fan; International traveller; Speaker; Author. *Address:* Queens College, 1900 Selwyn Avenue, Charlotte, NC 28274, USA. 2.

WISDOM John Oulton, b. 29 Dec 1908, Dublin, Ireland. Emeritus Professor. m. 5 June 1970, 2 s, 1 d. *Education:* BA, Maths, Philos, 1931, PhD, 1933, Trinity Coll, Dublin. *Appointments:* Misc tchng, 1934-39; Tchng, Downside School, 1939-43; Served as 2nd Lt, Home Guard, 1940-43; Alexandria Univ, Egypt, 1943-48; London School Econs, England, 1948-65; Disting Vis Prof, Univ So CA, USA, 1965-67; Univ Prof, SUNY, Fredonia, 1967-69; Univ Prof, York Univ, Toronto, Can, 1969-79. *Publications:* Books: The Metamorphosis of Philosophy, 1947; The Unconscious Origin of Berkeley's Philosophy, 1953; Philosophy and Its Place in Our Culture, 1975; Challengeability in Modern Science, 1987; Philosophy of the Social Sciences: A Metascientific Introduction, 1987; Philosophy of the Social Sciences: Schemata, 1987; Freud, Women, and Society, 1992. *Membership:* Hon Mbr, Former Pres, Soc Psychosomatic Med.

WISE Michael John, b. 17 Aug 1918, Stafford, England. Professor Emeritus of Geography. m. Barbara Mary Hodgetts, 4 May 1942, 1 s, 1 d. *Education:* BA, 1939, DipEd, 1940, PhD, 1951, Univ Birmingham. *Appointments:* War Serv, Royal Artillery and Northants Regt, 1941-46; Lectr, Univ Birmingham, 1946-51; Lectr, later Reader, Geog, 1951-, Prof, Geog, 1958-63, Pro-Dir, 1963-65, London School Econs and Pol Sci. *Publications:* Birmingham and its Regional Setting (hon ed), 1950; Pictorial Geography of the West Midlands, 1958; Cons Ed: Atlas of Earth Resources, 1979; Ordnance Survey Atlas of Great Britain, 1982; Others. *Memberships:* Royal Geogl Soc, Pres 1980-82; Geogl Assn, Pres 1976-77; Inst Brit Geogs, Pres 1974; Int Geogl Union, Pres 1976-80. *Honours:* Mil Cross, 1945; Fndr's Medal, Royal Geogl Soc, 1977; CBE, 1979; Alexander Korosi Csoma Medal, Hungary, 1980; Tokyo Geogl Soc Medal, 1981; Laureat d'Honneur, Int Geogl Union, 1984; Hon DUniv, Open Univ, 1978; Hon DSc, Birmingham Univ, 1982; Hon Fellow: London School Econs and Pol Sci, 1984; Birkbeck Coll, 1989; Landscape Inst, 1991; Hon Mbr, Geogl Socs, USSR, Poland, Mexico. *Hobbies:* Music; Gardening; Cricket. *Address:* c/o Dept of Geography, London School of Economics and Political Science, Houghton St, Aldwych, London WC2A 2AE, England. 1.

WISE Tammy Jean, b. 22 Nov 1965, Picayune, MS. USA. Univ Admin; Health Educator. *Education:* Bach, Psychology, 1987; Master Counseling, 1989; Doctoral, Adult Educ, Univ of Southern Mississippi, 1989-. *Appointments:* asst to Dir, Drug Educ & Prevention, Univ of Southern Mississippi, 1987-89; Dir Drug Educ & Prevention, 1989-. *Publications:* Numerous Articles. *Memberships:* American Assn of Counselling & Development; American Coll personnel Assn. *Honours:* Outstanding Young Mississippian; Outstanding Young Citizen of Hattiesburg; Outstanding Alumna; Kappa Delta Surority; Beta Signa Chapter; Hattiesburg Joycee of the Month; Golden Key Natl Honor Soc. *Hobbies:*

Collecting Antiques; Cooking; Travel; Gardening; Family. *Address:* Box 10031, Hattiesburg, MS 39406. USA. 176.

WISER Alice Louise, b. 22 Jan 1937, USA. University President. m. Bernhard George Nickel, 2 s, 1 d. *Education:* AA, Palomar Coll, 1969; BA, Goddard Coll, 1972; MA, Goddard Grad School, 1974; MEd, Harvard Univ, 1982; PhD, Univ London, 1990. *Appointments:* Co-Fndr, Organiser, Feminist Int for Peace and Food, 1983-89, providing Peace Tent, UN End of Decade of Women Forum, Nairobi, 1985, Women's Peace Caravans, 1985-89; Pres, Ovum Pacis, Women's Int Peace Univ, 1990-. *Publications:* Peace on Earth; A Six-Stage Developmental Theory of Peace Work, 1986; Women's Peace Caravans, 1989; Peace on Earth, Good Will Toward Women, in press; Num others. *Memberships:* Bd Dirs, Servas USA, 1986-88; Exec Comm, Friends Gen Conf, USA; Bd Mgrs, Friends Jrnl; Bd Dirs, Women for Meaningful Summits. *Honours:* Phi Delta Kappa, 1982; Isable Sanford Award, 1985. *Hobbies:* Travel; Writing; Reading; Walking her dog; Swimming; Public speaking; Visiting; Learning new things; Crochetting. *Address:* 100 Harris St, Guelph, Ontario, Canada N1E 5T1. 138.

WISZNIEWSKI Andrzej, b. 15 Feb 1935, Warsaw, Poland. Univ Prof; Electrical Engr. m. Eva Lutoslawski, 22 Nov 1958, 1 d. *Education:* MSc, 1957; PhD, 1961; DSc, 1966; Professorship, 1972. *Appointments:* The Tech Univ of Wroclaw, 1957; Hd, El Eng Dept Univ of Garyounis, Benghazi, 1976- 79; Pres, The Tech Univ of Wroclaw, 1990-. *Publications:* 132 Scientific & Tech Papers; 3 Books; 12 Patenets. *Memberships:* Polish Assn of Elect Engrs; Power System Control Committee; CIGRE; Polish Natl 34 Study Committee. *Honours:* Cross Polonia Restituta; Polsul Foundation Prize. *Hobbies:* Politics; Literature; Sport. *Address:* Krasickiego 18, 51 144 Wroclaw, Poland.

WITASEK Lisa, b. 8 Mar 1956, Salzburg, Austria. Author; Poetess. m. Hans-Jurgen Wormeck, 18 Nov 1991. *Education:* Studied German Lit, Linguistics, Philos, Univs Salzburg, Munich, Vienna; Music (Flute), Musikhochschule; Dr phil, 1981. *Appointments:* PR, Musikhochschule Mozarteum, Salzburg, 1981-86; PR, Musikhochschule, Vienna, 1986-. *Creative works:* Prose: Die Umarmung oder das weisse Zimmer, 1983; Friedas Freund, 1984; Many short stories, 1985-; Plays: Leibspeise, 1986; Fruher Vogel, 1989; Baum und Bank, 1990; Art (poetry and painting): Hochstand (w Hans Jurgen Wormeck); Many radio plays; Prose, verse and essays in anthologies, newspapers and for radio incl: Worte ohne Lieder, poem, 1985; Ecco, story, 1985; Inge, prose, 1986; Eli, der Mann ohne Schlussel, story, 1989; Die weissharige Fau, story, 1990; Pronto, story, 1990. *Membership:* Literar-Mechana. *Honours:* State Scholarships, Lit, Dramatic Art, 1984, 1990, 1991; Furtherance Prize, Theatre Workshop, Berlin, 1988; Scholarship, Literar- Mechana, 1990; Lit Prize, Hard, 1991. *Hobbies:* Music; Art; Dance; Writing letters; Design; Reading medical books. *Address:* c/o Publishers Hartmann and Stauffacher, Bismarckstrasse 36, D-5000 Koln 1, Germany.

WITMER John Albert, b. 29 Nov 1920, Lancaster, Pennsylvania, USA. Archivist (part-time); Retired Seminary Professor and Library Director. m. Doris May Ferry, 10 June 1943, 1 s, 2 d. *Education:* AB, 1942, Grad Fellow, 1942-44, MA, 1946, Wheaton Coll; THm, 1946, ThD, 1953, Dallas Theological Sem; MSLS, E TX State Univ, 1969; Cert Archival Mgmt, Univ TX, Arlington, 1988. *Appointments:* Mng Ed, Child Evangelism Mag, 1944-46; Instr, Child Evangelism Inst, 1945-47; Instr, 1947-54, Asst Prof, Systematic Theology, 1954-86, Dir, Lib, 1964-86, Assoc Prof, Systematic Theology, 1986- 87, Archivist, 1987-, Dallas Theological Sem, TX. *Publications:* Very many articles in relig mags and theological jrnls; Num essays in theological vols; Extensive Sunday School lesson materials. *Memberships:* Assn Christian Libs, Pres 1971-72; Soc Am Archivists; Evangelical Theological

Soc; Evangelical Philosl Soc; Soc SW Archivists. *Honours:* Jonathan B Cook Award in Oratory. *Hobbies:* Travel; Volunteer work; Reading; Writing. *Address:* 6630 Westlake Avenue, Dallas, TX 75214, USA. 2, 145.

WITMEYER Stanley H, b. 14 Feb 1913, Palmyra, Penn, USA. Prof Emeritus; Dir. m. (1) Marian Hebing, 22 June 1940, dec, (2) Helen Ickes, 31 Dec 1978, 3 s, 2 d. *Education:* Sch of Art, RIT, 1936; BS, Univ Coll Buffalo, 1939; MFA, Syracuse Univ, 1946; Univ Hawaii, 1945. *Appointments:* Freelance Designer, 1936-85; Rochester Gas, Elec Co, Rochester Telephone, Lapp Assoc, CUBA, Rochester Inst Tech. *Publications:* Articles; Journals; Exhibn Artist, Galleries & Private Collections. *Memberships:* Rochester Art Club; Torch Club of Rochester; RIT Alumni Assn; Arts Council Rochester; Genesee Com Coll; Rochester Stadium Club. *Honours:* Distinguished Alumni Award; Athlectic Hall Fame; NY state Art Tchrs Distinguished Service Award; Moore Coll of Art Award. *Hobbies:* Painting; Travel; Club Activity; Table Top Publisher. *Address:* 54 Clarkes Crossing, Fairport NY 14450, USA. 2, 6, 19.

WITTICH John Charles Bird, b. 18 Feb 1929, London, England. Freelance Author; Lectr; Guide Lectr. m. June Rose Taylor, 10 July 1954, 1 s, 1 d. *Education:* BA, 1950. *Appointments include:* Historical Assoc, 1946-47; Sch Oriental & African Studies, 1951-58; Automobile Assn, 1966-74; MEED, 1976-78; Elsom Pack & Roberts, 1979-86; Freelance, 1986-. *Publications include:* Off Beat Walks in London; London Street Names; London Parks & Squares; Catholic London; Guide to Bayswarer; Unknown London; Hyde Park & Kensington Gardens. *Memberships:* Royal Soc of St george; City Livery Club; Wig & Pen Club; Royal Photographic Soc; Minor Order of Readers of the Church of england; Worshipful Co of Parish Clerks; Worshipful Co of Woolemn; Freeman of the City of London. *Honour:* Fellow Royal Soc of Arts. *Hobbies:* Relaxing with family & Friends; Photography; Good Food & Wine. *Address:* 66 Saint Michaels Street, London W2 1QR, England.

WLADSLAW Malinowski, b. 28 June 1931, Sosnowiec, Poland. Musicologist; Music Critic. *Education:* Warsaw Univ, 1951-57; Warsaw High State Sch of Music, 1975. *Appointments:* Music Sritic, Polish Newspapers & Mag, 1956; Scientific Colleaborator of Inst of Arts, Polish Acad of Sci in Warsaw, 1957; Supernumerary Prof, Music Acad Poznan, 1984-86; Lodz, 1986; Vice Pres, Karol Szymanowski Musical Soc, Poland, 1983-86; Pres, 1986-89. *Publications:* Polifonia Mikolaja Zielenskiegol Many Musicological Papers. *Memberships:* Polish Composers Union; Intl Musicological Soc; Club Polonais Haute Montagne. *Hobbies:* Mountain Climbing; Skiing. *Address:* Lipska 40 m1, 03 908 Warsaw, Poland. 4.

WLODARCZYK Malgorzata Mariola, b. 6 Oct 1962, Krakow, Poland. Architect. m. Marcin Wledarczyk, 19 Dec 1987. *Education:* Tech Univ of Cracow, 1981-87; Intl Forum of Young Arch, Quebec, 1990; Avant Garde & Heritage, 1990; Profl Registration, 1991; Status of Arch, Creator, 1992. *Appointments:* Janusz Wlodarczyk Arch, 1986; Designing Office, Inwestprojek, cracow, 1987-89; Designing Office Zib, Cracow, 1988, 1989-90; Designing Studio, Wlodarczyk & Wlodarczyk Atch, 1987; Commissioner General, 4th Intl Biennial of Architecture, Cracow, 1991. *Creative Works include:* Sch in Wieprz n/Zywiec; First Polish American Bank in Swoszowice; One Family House; Small Hotel in Cracow. *Memberships:* Assn of Polish Arch; SARP. *Honours include:* The Park of Activities, St Quentin en Yvelin, 1st Prize; The centre of Japan Culture, 1st Prize; Sch in Pszczyna Stara Wies, Mention on Arch Review; Central Railway Station, Honored Mention. *Hobbies:* Tennis; Skiing; Sailing; Reading. *Address:* ul Imbramewska 1/15, 31 212 Krakow, Poland.

WLODARCZYK Marcia Jan, b. 5 June 1962, Krakow, Poland. Architect. m. Malgerzata Mariela Cudex, 19 Dec 1987. *Education:* MSc, Tech Univ, Krakow, 1981-87;

Pekka Salminen arch Office, Helsinki. *Appointments:* Inwestprejekt, Krakow, Designing Co, 1987-89; Sinax Polish Australian Desgning Office, 1989-90; Pekka Salminen Desgning Atelier, Helsinki, 1990-91; Wladarczyk & Wledarczyk Archs, 1990-. *Creative Works include:* Project of Small Hotel & Coffee Bar, Krakow; Tech Projects of the Interior & Furniture for 3 Primary Schs, Tychy; Bridge for Contemplation, Exhub Paris, France. *Memberships:* SARP; Assn of Polish Archs. *Honours:* Silesian Province Arch Review Mention; 1st Prize Plac Grunwaldzki, Warsaw; Souvenir form Krakow Comp. *Hobbies:* Drawing; Painting; Photography; Tennis; Skiing; Sailing. *Address:* ul Dunajewskiego 8/19, 31 133 Krakow, Poland.

WLODARSKI Josef, b. 30 June 1950, Bornice, Poland. Historian. m. Hedwig Wlodarska, 2 Dec 1980, 1 s, 2 d. *Education:* Dip, 1975, Dr, 1986, Univ Gdansk; Instr, Chinese Martial Arts, 1983. *Appointments:* Served Navy, 1976; Tchr, Coll, Paslek, Martial Arts Instr, Cosmos Club, Paslek, 1977-89; Adj, Hist, Inst HS Pedagogy, Olsztyn, 1990. *Publications:* Varmia in the Second Swedish War (1655-60), 1988; The Boxer Uprising and German Soldiers from East Prussia, 1990; China in the Polish Eyes (XIII-XVIII century), 1991; The History of Saint Bartholomaus Church in Paslek (1297-1990), 1991. *Membership:* Polish Soc Hist. *Hobbies:* Old books and weapons; Travel; Films. *Address:* ul Smolenska 2/6, 80-058 Gdansk, Poland.

WNUK-LIPINSKI Edmund, b. 4 May 1944, Sucha, Poland. Sociologist; Writer. m. Elzbieta Wnuk-Lipinska, 10 Apr 1966. *Education:* MA, Sociology, 1966, PhD, Humanities, 1972, Warsaw Univ; Habilitation, Polish Acad Scis, 1982; Assoc Prof, Sociology, 1988. *Appointments:* Statn to Hd Vital Stats Div, Ctrl Statistical Off, Warsaw, 1966-72; Hd, Leisure and Recreation Planning Div, Min Labour and Social Affairs, Warsaw, 1972-74; Hd, Sociology and Work Sect, Inst Labour and Social Affairs, Warsaw, 1974-77; Hd, Social Inequality Rsch Sect, Inst Philos and Sociology, Polish Acad Scis, Warsaw, 1977-90; Dir, Inst Pol Studies, Polish Acad Scis, Warsaw, 1990-; Mbr, Fac, Ctlr European Univ, Prague; Guest Lectr, var for univs. *Publications include:* Praca i wypoczynek w budzecie czasu, 1972; Czas wolny - wspolczesnosc i perspektywy, 1975; Budzet czasu - struktura spoleczna - polityka spoleczna, 1980; Equality and Inequality under Socialism - Poland and Hungary compared (ed w Tamar Kolosi, co-author), 1983; Non-Market Economics and Inequalities in Health (ed w Raymond Illsley, co-author), 1990; Novels: Whirlpool of Memory, 1979, 2nd Ed, 1989; Halflife, 1988; Founding Murder, 1989. *Memberships:* Exec Bd, Polish Sociological Assn; Int Sociological Assn; Fac, Ctrl European Univ; Solidarity Team to Round Table Talks, 1989; Fndg Father, Polish Assn Pol Studies, 1991; Ed-in-Chief, Sisyphus-Sociological Studies quarterly jrnl, Polish Acad Scis; Bd Mbr, Nat School Pub Admin, Warsaw. *Honours:* Mbr, rsch team Poles '81, awards by Polish Sociological Assn, 1982; POLCON Award '89 for Best Sci Fiction Writer in 1988; Sci-Fiction Writer of 1989, Soc-con (En Europe Congress Sci-Fiction Writers). *Hobbies:* Reading; Fishing; Golf. *Address:* ul Czerniakowska 159 m 75, 00-453 Warsaw, Poland.

WOCJAN Juliusz Marek, b. 14 May 1926, Warsaw, Poland. Neurosurgeon (Paediatric Neurosurgery). m. Halina Pawlowska, 1 Dec 1951, 1 s. *Education:* Dip, 1952, Dr med, 1960, Med Acad, Warsaw, 1952; Doc dr hab, 1972; Prof, Neurosurgery, 1984; Sci trng, visits: Cliniques Neurochirugique, Hopital des Enfants Malades, Paris, Hopital del la Timone, Marseille, Rennes, Louvain, Brussels, Neurochirurgische Univ Kliniks, Wurzburg, Hanover, Heidelberg, Frankfurt, Giessen, Hamburg, Vienna; Neuro surg clins: London, Lund, Gothenburg, Toronto, Chgo. *Appointments:* Hd, Organiser, 2 Dept Paediatric Surg incl: Neurosurg Ctr, Mem Hosp Children's Hlth Ctr, Warsaw; Ed, Neurological Sect, Neurologia i Neurochirurgia Polska. *Publications:* Pediatric Oncology (co-author), 1969; Neurosurgery, 1984, 1988; Epilepsy, 1992; Author or co-author, about 120 sci papers and articles in profl

jrnls in field of neurosurg and paediatric neurosurg. *Memberships:* Polskie Tow Neurochirurgow, Ed, Paediatric Sect Pres; European Soc Paediatric Neurology, VP 1988-90, Exec Bd; Int Soc Paediatric Neurosurg; Polish Acad Scis, Comm Neurological Scis; Exec Bd, Polish Soc Paediatric Neurology. *Honours:* Medaille pour la notre liberte et la votre, France, 1945; Publication prizes, EEG Changes in Brain Tumours in Children, Med Acad, Warsaw, 1968-69; Cross, Polonia Restituta, 1979; Croix d'Auschwitz, 1985; Prize, Trauma Project, Nat Inst Mother and Child, 1990. *Hobbies:* Photography; Auto touring; Reading. *Address:* Mieroslawskiego 24, 01-558 Warsaw, Poland.

WODEYAR Sadashiva Shivadeva, b. 7 Aug 1924, Karnatak, India. Retired Vice Chancellor. m. Sarvamangala, 20 June 1948, 1 s, 4 d. *Education:* BA, Bombay Univ, 1945; LLB, 1947; MA, 1948. *Appointments:* Lectr, Gujerat Coll, Ahmedabad, 1948; Lectr, Karnatak Coll, 1949; Asst Registrar, Karnatak Univ, 1950; Registrar, 1956-76; Educational Adviser, 1977; Vice Chancellor, 1978. *Publications include:* Rani Chennamma Biography in English; Rabindra Darshna in Kannada; Jeevana Kale, Essays in Kannada; Essays in English. *Memberships include:* Indian Pen Charter; American Book Club of India ; Natl Commission on Tchrs. *Honours:* Radindra Darshana State Sahitya Acad Award; Rani Chennamma, Award for Best Book of the Year. *Address:* Karnalak Univ, Sadamangala Bharatingor, Dharwad 580001, Karnatak, India.

WOJNAR Leszek, b. 4 Apr 1955, Cracow, Poland. Scientist; University Teacher. m. Grazyna Gabrys, 13 July 1985, 1 d. *Education:* MSc, Machine Technology, 1979, PhD, Materials Sci, 1985, Habilitation, Materials Sci, 1991, Cracow Univ Technology. *Appointments:* Jr Asst, 1978-79, Asst, 1979-86, Adj, 1986-91; Assoc Prof, 1991-, Cracow Univ Technology. *Publication:* Quantitative Fractography. Basic Principles and Computer Aided Research, book, 1990. *Memberships:* Int Soc Stereology; Sec, Polish Soc Stereology. *Honours:* Roman Wasilewski Scholarship, Clare Hall, Cambridge, July-Sept 1989. *Hobbies:* Skiing; Sailing; Photography. *Address:* ul Dukatwo 4, 31-431 Cracow, Poland.

WOJNECKI Stefan, b. 6 Apr 1929, Poznan, Poland. Artist Photographer; Lecturer. m. Barbara Malinowska, 5 Nov 1955, 1 s. *Education:* MSc, Phys, Poznan Univ, 1952; Artist Phographer, Mbr, Union Polish Artist-Photographers, 1971; Docent, 1987, Prof, 1991, Acad Fine Arts, Poznan. *Career:* Physicist in factory, Wroclaw, 1953-56; Tchr, Second, Poznan, 1956-75; Lectr, Acad Fine Arts, Poznan, 1976-; Exhibs: PTF Gall, Poznan, 1957, 1969, 1974; Wspolczesna Gall, Warsaw, 1971; Arsenal Gall, Poznan, 1978, 1986, 1988; Stilon Gall, Gorzow, 1981; Zacheta Gall, Warsaw, 1985, 1987; Mala Gall, Warsaw, 1987. *Publications:* Critical and theoretical articles in var periodicals. *Memberships:* Pres, Union Polish Artist-Photographers, Warsaw; Dean, Dept Painting, Graphics and Sculpture, Acad Fine Arts, Poznan. *Honours:* Artist, FIAP, 1972; Prize, Min Culture and Art, 1975, 1979, 1983; Gold Cross, 1986. *Hobbies:* His job; Philosophy of science and art. *Address:* Sw Marcin 29/34, PL-61-806 Poznan, Poland.

WOJTOWICZ Henryk, b. 16 Aug 1928, Januszno, Poland. Prof; Hd of the Second Chair of Classical Philology. *Education:* MA, CU of Lublin, 1961; Doctorate, Classical Phil, Wroclaw, 1965; Habilitation, Univ of Torum, 1979. *Appointments include:* Asst, Class Phil, CU Lublin, 1961; Lectr, First Chair of Class Phil, 1965; Lectr, Second Chairof Calss Phil, 1973;Hd of Second Chair of Class Phil, 1981; Hd of Class Phil, Dept CU of Lublin, 1983-87, 1990-91. *Publications:* Function of Homers Metaphors in Respect of Compoosition; Anthology of Patristic Prayers; A Study in Nonnos. *Memberships include:* Botany History Sec, Inst of History of Sci Educ & Technics; Philology Faculty in the Soc of Sci CU of Lublin; Episcopal Committee of Sci. *Honours:* Canon of Honor in Sandomierz Cathedral Chapter; Chaplin of His Holiness. *Hobbies:* Research on Greek

Opos; Early Christian Literature, Latin, Greek Stylistics. *Address:* ul Zeromskiego 2/17, 26 670 Pionki, Poland.

WOJTOWICZ Jerzy, b. 24 Oct 1924, Rumoka, Poland. Professor of History; Historian. m. Jadwiga Kuberke, 1 July 1947, 2 s. *Education:* Master's degree, Copernicus Univ, Torun, 1951; Doct, Hist, 1956; Habilitation, 1963; Assoc Prof, Torun, 1973; Full Prof, 1976. *Appointments:* Prof, Copernicus Univ, Torun, 1963-; Vis Prof, Univ Siegen, FRG, 1983. *Publications:* The Development of Economic Life in the 18th Century in Torun, 1956; European Cities in the Time of Enlightment, 1975; History of Switzerland, 1976; Gottfried Keller, monograph, 1989; Europe in the Period of Enlightment, 1991. *Memberships:* Towarzystwo Naukowe w Toruniu; Societas Jablonowiana, Leipzig; Studienkreis fur Kulturbeziehungsforchsung in Mittel- und Osteuropa (informal workshop), Luneburg and Munich; Arbeitkreis fur Stadtgeschichtsforschung, Linz. *Honours:* Polish State Prize for book on European Cities. *Hobbies:* Cycling; Travel; Literature. *Address:* Instytut Historii i Archiwistiki, Plac Teatralny, 87-100 Torun, Poland.

WOLF Lothar Jakob, b. 2 Dec 1938, Walldurn, Germany. Professor of Romance Linguistics. *Education:* State Exam, 1962; Dr phil, 1966; Habilitation, 1971. *Appointments:* Lectr, Univ Heidelberg, 1972; Prof, Romance Linguistics, Univ Augsburg, 1973-. *Publications:* Studies in Linguistic Geography. The names of the Domestic Animals in the Massif Central, 1968; Texts and Documents for the Study of the French Language in the 16th Century, 1969; Texts and Documents for the Study of the French Language in the 17th Century, 1972; Aspects of Dialectology, 1975; Terminological Studies on the Introduction of Printing in French Speaking Countries, 1979; Old French. Origin and Characteristics, 1981; The Regional French of the Alsace, 1982; French Language in Canada, 1987; Num articles. *Membership:* Soc de Linguistique Romane. *Honours:* Prix Strasbourg, FVS Fndn, 1972. *Interests:* History and present situation of language, society and culture in France and French-speaking Canada (books and articles). *Address:* Lehrstuhl fur romanische Sprachwissenschaft, Universitat Augsburg, Universitatsstrasse 10, 8900 Augsburg, Germany. 43, 52, 92.

WOLFE Gary Richard, b. 7 Apr 1952, Indianapolis, Indiana, USA. Pastor. m. Rebecca Jean (Beckey) Hobson, 20 Nov 1971, 2 d. *Education:* BS, Gen Studies (Relig, Hist), Dallas Bapt Univ, 1979; MDiv, SWn Bapt Theological Sem, 1990. *Appointments:* USAF, 1972-75; Immanuel Bapt Ch, Alburquerque, NM, 1982-84; Blake Rd Bapt Ch, Albuquerque, 1984-85; Rosen Heights Bapt Ch, Ft Worth, TX, 1986-90; Ranchvale Bapt Ch, Ranchvale, NM, 1990-. *Memberships:* Ranchvale Elem School Parent/Tchr Org, Pres 1991- 92; Clovis Girls Athletic Assn, Basketball Commnr 1991; Plains Bapt Assn, Pastral Mins Dir 1991-92, By-Laws Comm 1991, Nominating Comm 1991, Preacher Place Time Comm 1990; N Side Inter Ch Agcy, Ft Worth, TX, Bd Dirs; Clergy and Police Advsry Exec Coun, Ft Worth; Vol Chaplain, Clovis High Plains Hosp. *Honours:* Outstanding 1st Term Airman of Quarter Period Apr-June 1975, USAF Mil Personnel Ctr; Outstanding Parent Vol, Ranchvale Elem School, Ranchvale, NM. *Hobbies:* Golf; Fishing; Volunteer work. *Address:* Route 2, Box 147, Ranchvale, Clovis, NM 88101, USA.

WOLFE Richard John Russell, b. 15 July 1947, England. Banker. m. Lorraine Louise Hart, 28 Nov 1970, div, 1 d. *Education:* Dip, Inst Bankers; Dip, Chartered Inst Secs. *Appointments:* Mgmt Trainee, 1964- 68, Loan Exec. Corp Fin Exec, 1976-80, N M Rothschild and Sons Ltd, 1974-68; Investment Dealer, Brit and Continental Banking, 1968-72; Pension Fund Mgr, Hill Samuel and Co Ltd, 1972-75; 1st VP, Hd European Real Estate, Security Pacific Nat Bank, 1980-90; Mng Dir, Hd European Real Estate, Bankers Trust Co, 1990-. *Publication:* Real Estate Finance, 1989. *Membership:* Inst Bankers. *Hobbies:* Choral singing; Gym training;

Gardening; English history; Music. *Address:* 52 Claylands Road, London SW8 1NZ, England. 53.

WOLFENSEN Alex, b. 8 Jan 1970, Lima, Peru. University Student. *Education:* Bus Admin studies, Univ del Pacifico, Lima, 1988-89; Engl Lang studies, New School Engl, Cambridge, England, 1989-90; Bus Admin, Mgmt, St Andrews Univ, St Andrews, Scotland, 1990-. *Honours:* 1st palce, Trener Acad; 4th place, Admission, Univ del Pacifico; Among 10 best tennis players, Hebraica Club, 1985-86; Mbr, Champion Football Team, 1986, 1988, 1989; Mbr, 1990-, unanimously elected Best Player of Yr, 1991, Univ St Andrews. *Hobbies:* Football (goalkeeper); Tennis; Ping-pong. *Address:* Haldenstrasse 24, 6006 Luzern, Switzerland.

WOLFENSEN Azi, b. 1 Aug 1933, Bessarabia, Rumania. (Peruvian citizen). Mechanical, Electrical and Industrial Engineer. m. (1) 2 s, 3 d, (2) Rebeca Sterental, 10 Jan 1983, 1 s. *Education:* Mech and Elec Engrng, 1955, Indl Engr, 1967, Univ Nacional de Ingenieria, Lima, Peru; MS, Univ MI, USA, 1966; PhD, Engrng Mgmt, Pacific Wn Univ, 1983; PhD, Engrng Energy, Century Univ, CA, 1985. *Appointments include:* Dir, SWSA Automotive, 1954-77; Power Engr, Peruvian Trading Co, 1956-57; Fac, 1956-72, Dean, Fac Indl Engrng, 1967-69, Dir, Acad Prog, Systems and Indl Engrng, 1968-72, Univ Nacional de Ingenieria, Lima; Mgr, Chmn, AMSA Engrng Installations, 1957-60; Pvte Cons, Peru and Latin Am, 1959-87; Project Mgr, COFIDE org, 1971-73; Mbr, num bds and consultancies; Pres, DESPRO, 1973-77; Pres, Peruvian Hebrew School, 1976-79; Exec Pres, ELECTROPERU, 1976-80; Fndr, Gen Mgr, Dir, La Republica newspaper, Peru, 1981; Chmn, PROA Project Promotion AG, Switzerland, 1982- ; Fndr: El Popular, 1983, El Nacional, 1985. *Publications include:* Work Communications, 1966; Programmed Learning, 1966; Production, Planning and Control, 1968; Transfer of Technology, 1971; National Electrical Development, 1977; Energy and Development, 1979; El Gran Desano, 1981; Hacia una Politica Alternativa (co-author), 1982. *Contributions to:* newspapers and jrnls. *Memberships include:* Fndr, Past Pres, Instituto Peruano de Ingenieros Mecanicos; Fellow, Inst Prod Engrs, UK; Fellow, Brit Inst Mgmt; AAAS; Am Soc Mech Engrs; PEN Int, Swiss Sect; Num others. *Honours:* Num awards and recognitions, worldwide. *Hobbies:* Sports; Art collecting; Philately; Reading; Writing. *Address:* Haldenstrasse 24, CH-6006 Luzern, Switzerland. 2, 52, 132, 139; 151, 152, 162, 178, 191.

WOLFENSON Moises, b. 23 Nov 1966, Lima, Peru. University Student. *Education:* Econs, Univ de Lima, 1984-89; Engl Lang studies, New School Engl, Cambridge, England, 1988, 1989; Econs, St Andrews Univ, St Andrews, Scotland, 1989-. *Membership:* St Andrews Students Assn. *Honours:* Hebraica Jr Tennis Champion, 1977, 1981, Vice-Champion, 1983; Capt, Leon Pinelo Football Team, 1982, 1983, 1984 (champions), 1986 (champions); Mbr, Hebraica Champion Football Team, Lima, 1986, 1988, 1989; Selected, Hebraica Football Team, to play at PanAm Int Games, Caracas, Venezuela, 1987; Youth Scholarship, ABIRA, 1987. *Hobbies:* Football; Tennis. *Address:* Haldenstrasse 24, 6006 Luzern, Switzerland.

WOLFERS Nicolas Lorne Maclean, b. 3 Jan 1946, London, England. Group Advisor, Midland Bank. m. Qamar Sultan Aziz, 22 Aug 1978, 2 s. *Education:* Exhibitioner, Pol, Philos, Econs, Oriel Coll, Oxford, 1964-67; 2nd Class Hons degree, 1967. *Appointments:* Investment Div, J Henry Schroder Wagg and Co, 1967-71; Mgr, European Rsch Dept, P N KempGee and Co, 1971-72; Samuel Montagu and Co Ltd, 1972, seconded as Gp Advsr, Midland Bank plc, 1985-. *Publications:* Co-author: Trading with China: a 1980 practical guide; 21 years of the Eurobond Markets, 1984; Journey into Japan 1600-1868, 1981; Mongolia Today, 1990. *Memberships:* Coun Mbr, Chmn Mbrship Comm, Royal Inst Int Affairs; London Chmbr of Comm and Ind Coun, Chmn China Comm; UNICE External Rels Comm, Chmn/

Rapporteur for Asia; Former VO, Japan Soc; Former VP, Royal Soc Asian Affairs; Pres, William Adams Assn/ Miura Anjinkai; Leonard Cheshire Fndn Comm; School Coun, Newton Prep; Gov, Sadler's Wells Fndn; Chmn's Comm, Educ Chmn, Japan Fest 1991; Formerly: Trustee, CBEVE; Gov, CILT. *Honours:* H M Queen's Prize for German, 1963. *Hobbies:* Writing; Theatre; Cinema; Rowing; Swimming; Soctland; Initiator, British English Teaching Scheme (now JET Programme), which has brought 1,500 British graduates to Japan; Coordinator for Sponsors, Great Japan Exhibition, Royal Academy, 1979-82. *Address:* 110 Cannon Street, London EC4N 6AA, England.

WOLNIEWICZ Janusz Andrzej, b. 28 May 1929, Poland. Journalist; Travel Book Writer. m. 1 Apr 1970. *Education:* BA, Econs, Univ Gdansk, 1952. *Career:* Min Shipping, 1952-54; MON Publng House, 1954-56; Staff Ed, Polish press, then Freelance Writer, illustrated mags; Chief Ed, Morze, Polish Maritime monthly, 1988-; Work for Polish Radio and TV. *Publications include:* 25 books incl: On the Way to the Green Coffee Shores, 1960; Europe On The Portside, 1964; The Tracks Of The Silver Fleets, 1966; The Land Of Gold and Totempost, 1968; Ports, Palms and Poles, 1969; Sons Of Cannibals, 1971, also Braille ed; Archipelago Of Five Cumuli, 1974, also Braille ed; Colour Trades Winds, 1977; Peoples and atolls, 1979; Smile Of Golden Buddha, 1980; Vanuatu - Black Archipelago, 1986, also Braille ed; Emerald Pacific Islands, 1987; The Hot Sun Gods, 1988; Towards Everywhere, 1990. *Memberships:* Union Polish Writers; Assn Polish Jrnlsts. *Honours:* Order of Polonia Restituta; Nat Educ Medal, 1975. *Hobby:* Geographical discoveries. *Address:* Prawnicza 26, 02-495 Warsaw, Poland.

WOLOSZYN Elzbieta Zofia, b. 28 Sept 1943, Lublin, Poland. Assistant Professor. m. 19 Aug 1967, 2 d. *Education:* MSc, Civil Engrng, 1966, PhD, 1977, Tech Univ, Gdansk. *Appointments:* Asst, Researcher, Fac Hydroengrng, 1967-83, Asst Prof, 1985-91, Tech Univ, Gdansk; Assoc Prof, ENCTP, Ivory Coast, W Africa, 1983-85. *Membership:* WMO Grp Operation Urban Hydrology, St Moritz. *Honours:* Prize (collective) for Works on Modelisation of Watershed Runoff, Polish Min Agric, 1978; Prize (collective) for Works on Urban Hydrology, Polish Min Admin and Environmental Protection. *Hobbies:* Her family; Ecology; Tourism; Gardening; Sports esp skiing. *Address:* ul Szalupowa 10 D, 80-299 Gdansk, Poland.

WOLOSZYN Stefan, b. 19 Aug 1911, Lwow, Poland. Pedagogue. m. Lidia Los, 1 Nov 1935, 1 s, 1 d. *Education:* Master's degree, Jagiellonian Univ, Cracow, 1934; Dr Phil, Uniwersytet Mikolaja Kopernika, Torun, 1948; Dr Hab, Warsaw Univ, 1955. *Appointments:* Hdmaster, HS (Second) Tchr, Wilno, Bialystok, 1935-46; Asst Prof, Uniwersytet Mikolaja Kopernika, Torun, 1946-50; Assoc, Poznan Univ, 1950-53; Prof, Warsaw Univ, 1953-81; Rector, AWF (Acad Phys Educ), Warsaw, 1960-71. *Publications:* Dzieje Wyckowania i mysli pedagogicznej w zarysie, 1964; Zrodla to D, 3 vols, 1965-66; Nauczyciel: Tradycje, Wspotczesnosc, Przyszlosi, 1978; Korczak, 1978, 2nd Ed, 1982. *Memberships:* Comm Sci of Educ, Polish Acad Scis; Int Standing Conf Hist of Educ; Exec Comm, Janusz Korczak Int Assn; Polish Pedagogical Assn. *Honours:* Cmdr's Cross, Off, Kawalerski Orderu Odrodzenia, Poland; Disting Tchr of Poland; Medal, Polish Nat Educ Comm; Cmdr, Off and Cavalier Crosses, Polonia Restituta. *Hobby:* Sport. *Address:* Armii Ludowej 7 m 104, 00-575 Warsaw, Poland.

WOLOSZYNOWA Lidia, b. 8 Feb 1911, St Petersburg, Russia. Psychologist. m. Stefan Woloszyn, 1 Nov 1935, 1 s, 1 d. *Education:* Master's degree, Uniwersytet Stegana Batorego, Wilno (Vilnus) Univ, 1936; Dr Phil, Uniwersytet Mikolaja Kopernika, Torun, 1951; Dr Hab, Warsaw Univ, 1961. *Appointments:* Lectr, Vilnus Univ, Poland, 1933-39; Second School Tchr, Vilnus and Bialystok, 1941-45; Asst Prof, Torun Univ, 1946-52; Asst Prof, Poznan Univ, 1952-53; Assoc Prof, Prof,

Warsaw Univ, 1953-81. *Publications:* Psychologia pomaga wychomaniv, 1960, 3rd Ed, 1962; Slovenia transl, 1975; Psychologia opolna i vozwojowa, 1965, 2nd Ed, 1966; Rozwoj i wychowanie w mlodszym wieko szkocnym, 1967; Ed: Bibliografia proc psychologicznych wydonych w Polsce, 13 vols, 1946-78; Materialy do navcrania psychologie, 26 vols, 1964-86. *Memberships:* Comm Sic of Psychology, Polish Acad Scis; Hon Mbr, Polish Psychological Assn. *Honours:* Cavalier Cross, Polonia Restituta; Disting Tchr of Poland; Medal, Polish Nat Educ Comm. *Hobbies:* Nature; Gardening. *Address:* Armii Ludowej 7 m 104, 00-575 Warsaw, Poland.

WOLSKI Jozef Wladyslaw, b. 19 Mar 1910, Tarnow, Poland. Emeritus Professor of Ancient History. m. 30 Oct 1948. 2 d. *Education:* MA, 1932; Dr, 1936; Habilitation, 1946. *Appointments:* Prof, Ancient Hist, Univ Lodz, 1946-52; Prof, Ancient Hist, Univ Wroclaw, 1952-58; Prof, 1958-80, Emeritus Prof, 1980-. Univ Cracow. *Publications:* Starozytnosc, 1965, 3rd Ed, 1979; Atlas of World History, 1974, 3rd Ed, 1986. *Memberships:* Polish Acad Letters and Scis, Cracow; Mbr, Pres, Soc Int d'Etudes Neroniennes, Clermont-Ferrand, France. *Honours:* State Prize, 2nd degree, 1984. *Hobbies:* Music esp opera; Excursions. *Address:* Kochanowskiego 11/12, 31-127 Krakow, Poland.

WOLVERSON Maurice Frank, b. 7 June 1927, Walsall, England. Chartered Accountant in Practice. m. Kathleen Merle Forrester, 4 June 1949. *Education:* Assoc, 1959, Fellow, 1970, Inst Chartered Accts Emgland and Wales. *Appointments:* Ptnr, Whitehouse Woverson Armston and Cox, Chartered Accts, Walsall, 1961-. *Memberships:* Chmn, Walsall Parklands Housing Assn; Walsall Family Practitioner Comm, 1943-89, Chmn 1983-89; Vice- Chmn, Walsall Hlth Auth; Maitre, Confrerie st Etienne d'Alsace. *Hobbies:* Study of wines; Administration of housing associations and health authorities; Reading; Motoring. *Address:* 6 Greenslade Road, Parkhall, Walsall WS5 3QH, England.

WONG James Yuen-hay, b. 29 May 1948, Hong Kong. Principal; Master Designer of Floral Arts. m. Yu Siu-wah, 18 May 1982, 2 s. *Education:* St Paul Evening School, 1968-72; Cert, School Floral Art, 1971; Cert, Floral Tchng, Sogetsu School Ikebana, Japan, 1971; Floral Art Design, Benz School Floral Design, TX, 1973; Cert, Chinese Cooking, Int School Home Cookery, 1975. *Appointments:* Asst Florist, HK Hilton Hotel, 1968-72; Lectr, Demonstrator: Minna Young School Fine Arts, Northcote Coll Educ, Lee Wai Lee Tech Inst, Ho Tung Tech School, Diocesan Girls School, Hong Kong Home Econs Assn, 1972-; Florist Mgr: Excelsior Florist Ltd, 1972-73; Hotel Furama Inter-Continental, 1973-80; Gen Mgr: Nam Fung Nurseries Ltd, 1980-81; Wah Jim Floral Trading Co, 1980-84; Hort Arts Co Ltd, 1981-83; Prin, Int School Flower Arrangement, 1984-; Mgr, Century City Holdings Ltd, Ricobem Ltd, 1985-88; Gen Mgr, David & Co, Hort & Floriculture, 1988; Demonstrator, TV Broadcasts Ltd, overseas TV, Can, USA, Australia, 1989-92; Columnist, Hong Kong Sing Tao Daily News, 1991-. *Creative works include:* Over 30 newspaper articles, 2 video films, floral art, 1991-; Flower-arrangement for Home, 1990; The Art of Flower-arrangement in the 90's, 1991; Professional Deluxe Flower Selection Guide A-F, 1991; Supplement, 1992 Hong Long Urban Coun Flower Show; Flower decorations: Chinese Opera Star Ms Yam Kim Fai's funeral, 1989; HRH Princess Alexandra's visit, Hong Kong, 1990; Welcoming Ceremony for Portuguese Pres, Macau, 1990; Sir Y K Pao's funeral, 1991; Counter displays, Hong Kong Urban Coun Flower Shows, 1990-92. *Memberships:* Workshop Chmn, Ikebana Int, Hong Kong Chapt; Hon Mbr, Hong Kong Hort Assn. *Honours:* 2nd Prize Cert, 1974, Highly Commended, 1975, 1989 (2), 2nd Winner Cert, 1st Prize Cert, 1989, Hong Kong Urban Coun Flower Show; 1st Grade Cert, Floral Tchng, Malayan Inst Flower Arrangement, 1978; Cert, Hospitality Mgmt Pracs Prog, Hotel Furama Inter-Continental, 1979. *Hobbies:* Floral art; Photography; Cooking. *Address:* G/F No 23, Thomson Road, Wanchai, Hong Kong.

WONG Richard Yue-Chim, b. 20 June 1952, Shanghai, China. Academic Economist. m. 30 Dec 1982, 1 s. *Education:* AB, 1974, AM, 1974, PhD, 1981, Univ Chgo, USA. *Appointments:* Asst Lectr, 1976-80, Lectr, 1981- 86, Sr Lectr, 1987-91, Reader, 1992-, Chinese Univ Hong Kong, Shatin; Vis Scholar, Econ Rsch Ctr, NORC, Univ Chgo, USA, 1985; Dir, Hong Kong Ctr Econ Rsch, 1987-; Vis Scholar, Hoover Inst, Stanford Univ, CA, USA, 1989. *Publication:* The Other Hong Kong Report 1990, 1990. *Memberships:* Am Econs Assn; Sec-Gen, E Asian Econs Assn; Hong Kong Econs Assn; Vice-Chmn, Hong Kong Inst Econ Sci; Econometric Soc; Royal Econ Soc. *Honours:* Fellow, New Asia Coll; Fellow, New Asia Coll. *Hobbies:* Reading; Travel. *Address:* Economics Department, Chinese University of Hong Kong, Shatin, Hong Kong. 52.

WONG Roderick, b. 12 Nov 1932, Vancouver, British Columbia, Canada. Professor of Psychology. m. Bernice Wong, 29 May 1952, 1 d. *Education:* BA (Hons), Univ BC; MA, Wn MI Univ, USA; PhD, NWn Univ, USA. *Appointments:* Prof, Univ BC, Vancouver, 1977-. *Publications:* Motivation, 1976; Biological perspectives on motivated activities, 1992. *Memberships:* Psychomatic Soc; Animal Behavior Soc; Int Soc Developmental Psychobiology. *Hobbies:* Swimming; Music. *Address:* Dept of Psychology, University of British Columbia, Vancouver, British Columbia, Canada V6T 1Z4. 9.

WONG Wai Ming Otis, b. 21 Aug 1954, Hong Kong. Civil Servant. m. Lee Shu Hing, 6 Mar 1976, 3 s. *Education:* Dip, Engl Lang and Lit, Shue Yan Coll, 1981. *Appointments:* Civil Serv; Ed, Poetry, 1976-84; Ed-in-Chief, Modern Poetry: East and West, 1981; Ed, Shi Bi-Monthly, 1989-. *Publication:* Aesculus Chiniensis, prose anthology. *Honours:* 1st Prize, Open Sect, Astronomical Project Competition Essay, 1977. *Hobbies:* Reading; Travel; Collecting stamps. *Address:* PO Box 50431 Sai Ying Pun Post Office, Hong Kong. 11, 139, 152.

WONG Wing Keung, b. 5 Jan 1933, Hong Kong. Executive Director; Medical Doctor. m. Ban Cho Wong, 28 May 1957, 2 d. *Education:* MB, BS, Peking Med Coll, Beijing, 1955; LMCHK, Hong Kong, 1979. *Appointments:* Med Dr, 1st Hosp, Beijing Med Coll, China, 1955-69; Med Dr, Ganshu, 1970- 73; Dir, 197486, Cheung Tai Hong Ltd, Hong Kong, Exec Dir, 1987-, 1974-86; Med Dr, pvte prac, Hong Kong, 1979-; Chmn, Computive Ltd, Hong Kong, 1979-. *Publications:* Research on the correlation between drug resistance, phage type and other biological characteristics of staphylococcus aureus, 1965; Laboratory research on combined antibiotic treatment on staphylococcus aureus infections, 1965. *Membership:* Hong Kong Med Assn. *Hobbies:* Travel; Photography; Music; Diving. *Address:* 2/F 52-58 Des Voeux Road West, Hong Kong. 52.

WOO Kwok-Yin, b. 20 Oct 1946, Hong Kong. College Principal. m. Lee Shuk-Ling, 11 Nov 1972, 1 s, 2 d. *Education:* BA, 1969, MA, 1972, Hong Kong Univ; Dip Educ, Chinese Univ Hong Kong, 1974. *Appointments:* Chinese Lang and Lit Tchr, Prefect of Studies, Vice-Prin, Tak Oi Second School, Hong Kong, 1971-82; Prin, T W G Hs Li Ka Shing Coll, Hong Kong, 1982-. *Publications:* Books: A Vision Revealed, poetry, prose, 1964; Blue Beast, poetry, 1970; Three Acquaintances, poetry, 1976; Broken Spear, poetry, 1978; The Racing Poet, prose, 1980; Just Before The Gust Blows, poetry, 1987; Whe The Hill Is C-R-E-E-P-I-N-G, poetry, 1990; Aesculus Chinensis, prose, 1991; Lest I Fall Asleep Before Dawn, poetry, 1991. *Memberships:* Fndr, Ed, Shih Feng (Poetry) Assn, 1972-84; Fndr, Ed, Shi (Poetry) Bi-monthly Assn; Fndr, Vice-Chmn, N Dist Second Schools Hdmasters Conf; Hon Treas, N Dist Girl Guides Assn; Vice-Chmn, Chmn, N Dist Community Youth Club. *Honours:* Merit Award, Chinese Essay Writing Competition, Chinese Students Weekly, Hong Kong, 1966; Merit Award, Chinese Mod Poetry Competitiohn,

Zhong-yuan Oilfields Lit and Art Assn, China, 1989; Award, Serv to Hong Kong Guiding, Hong Kong Girl Guides Assn, 1989; Award, Good and Devoted Serv to Community Youth Club, Hong Kong Educ Dept, 1989, 1991; Adjudicator, var lit awards, Hong Kong; Poems published in var anthologies, Hong Kong, China, Taiwan, S Korea. *Hobbies:* Writing esp poems; Reading; Music; Drama. *Address:* 1404 Block E, Luk Yueng Sun Chuen, Tsuen Wan, NT, Hong Kong. 151, 152.

WOOD Charles Anthony, b. 20 Nov 1938, Sevenoaks, Kent, England. Stockbroker. m. Susan Mary Anderson, 10 Oct 1964, 3 s, 1 d. *Education:* Pembroke Coll, Oxford, 1959-62; MA, Mod Hist. *Appointments:* Phillips and Dean, 1962-71; Lehman Brothers (L Messel and Co), London, 1971-. *Memberships:* Stock Exchange; Soc Investment Analysts; Chm, New Islington and Hackney Housing Assn. *Hobbies:* Housing; Gardening; Eighteenth-century architecture. *Address:* 14 Compton Terrace, London N1 2UN, England.

WOOD Graham Allan, b. 15 Aug 1946, Glasgow, Scotland. Consultant Oral and Maxillofacial Surgeon; Clinical Professor. m. Lindsay Balfour, 23 Nov 1970, 1 s, 1 d. *Education:* BDS, Univ Glasgow, 1968; MB ChB, Univ Dundee, 1978; FDS, RCPS, 1973; ECGMG and VQE, USA, 1981; FRCS Edinburgh, 1985. *Appointments:* Gen Dental Prac, 1968-70; House Off, Sr House Off, Glasgow Dental Hosp. 1970-71; Registrar, Oral and Maxillofacial Surg, Canniesburn and Victoria Infirmary Hosps. 1971-72; Dental Surg, Int Grenfell Assn, 1972-73; Registrar, Oral and Maxillofacial Surg, Queen Elizabeth Hosp, Birmingham, 1973-74; Sr Registrar, Oral and Maxillosurg, 1979-83, Cons, 1983-, N Wales; Clin Prof, Oral and Maxillofacial Surg, Univ TX, USA, 1988-; Postgrad Tutor, Dentistry, Univ Wales, 1989-. *Contributions to:* Cryosurgery of the Maxillofacial Region, Vol II, 1986. *Memberships:* Brit Med Assn; Brit Dental Assn; Brit Assn Oral and Maxillo-Facial Surgs; BSi; Brit Soc Head and Neck Oncology; Cranial Soc GB; Rotary Club, St Asaph. *Honours:* Dip, Cleft Lip and Palate Surg, Univ Mexico, 1981. *Hobbies:* Golf; Squash; Sailing; Hill walking; Skiing (past Canadian ski patroller). *Address:* Northcote, Mount Road, St Asaph, Clwyd LL17 0DE, Wales. 170.

WOOD Graham Charles, b. 6 Feb 1934, Farnborough, Kent, England. University Professor; Consultant. m. Freda Nancy Waithman, 19 Dec 1959, 1 s, 1 d. *Education:* Christ's Coll, Cambridge, 1953-56; BA, 1956, PhD, 1959, MA, 1960, ScD, 1972, Dept Metallurgy, Univ Cambridge. *Appointments:* Successively Lectr, Sr Lectr, Reader, Corrosion Sci, 1961-72, Prof, Corrosion Sci and Engrng, 1972-, Vice-Prin, Acad Dev, 1982-84, Dpty Prin, 1983, Univ Manchester Inst Sci and Technology; Dean, Fac Technology, Univ Manchester, 1987-89. *Publications:* Over 300 papers on oxidation, corrosion and surface engineering. *Memberships:* Fellow, Inst Metals; Fellow, Royal Soc Chem; Fellow, Inst Corrosion, Pres 1978-80; Fellow, Inst Metal Finishing; Chmn, Nat Coun Corrosion Socs; 1st Vice-Chmn, Chmn Elect, Int Corrosion Coun. *Honours:* Beilby Medal and Prize, 1977; U R Evans Award, 1983; Carl Wagner Mem Award, 1983; Cavallaro Medal, 1987; Hothersall Medal and Prize, 1989; Fellow, Fellowship Engrng, 1990. *Hobbies:* Travel; Cricket; Fell and country walking; Gardening; Reading about history and art. *Address:* Corrosion and Protection Centre, University of Manchester Institute of Science and Technology, PO Box 88, Manchester M60 1QD, England.

WOOD John Denison, b. 28 Sept 1931, Calgary, Alberta, Canada. Company President; Chief Executive Officer. m. Christena Isabel Wood, 24 July 1953, 1 d. *Education:* BASc, Civil Engrng, Univ BC, 1953; MS, Civil Engrng-Structures, 1954, PhD, Civil, Engrng, Engrng Mech, 1956, Stanford Univ. *Appointments:* Rsch Asst, Civil Engrng, Engrng Mech, Stanford Univ, Stanford, CA, USA, 1953-55; Assoc Mgr, Dynamics Dept, Engrng Mech Lab, Space Tech Labs Inc, Redondo Beach, CA, 1956-63; Pres, Dir, Mech Rsch Inc, El Sugundo, CA,

1963-66; Sr VP, Engrng and Rsch, 1966-68, Sr VP, En Reg, 1968-75, Sr VP, Planning, 1975-77, ATCO Ind Ltd; Pres, CEO, ATCO Inds NA Ltd, 1977-82; Pres, CEO, ATCOR Resources Ltd, 1982-84; Pres, COO, 1984-88, Pres, CEO, 1988-, Can Utilities Ltd, Edmonton, Alta. *Publication:* Ballistic Missile and Space Vehicle Systems (co-author), 1961. *Memberships:* Engrng Inst Can; Sci Rsch Soc Am; Assn Profl Engrs, Geologists and Geophysicists Alta. *Honours:* Athlone Fellowship; Fellow, Can Acad Engrng. *Hobbies:* Golf; Badminton. *Address:* 10035 105 Street, Edmonton, Alberta, Canada T5J 2V6. 2, 9, 32, 88, 132.

WOOD Larry (Mary Laird), b. Sandpoint, Idaho, USA. Journalist; Author; University Educator. m. 1 s, 2 d. *Education:* BA magna cum laude, 1938, MA w highest hons, 1940, Univ WA, Seattle; Postgrad Tchng Fellow, Stanford Univ, 1940-43; Postgrad, 1943-44, Cert, Photography, 1971, Univ CA, Berkeley; Postgrad, Jrnlsm: Univ WI, 1971-72, Univ MN, 1971-72, Univ GA, 1972- 73; Postgrad, Art, Arch, Marine Biology, Oceanography, Univ CA, Santa Cruz, 1974-76, Stanford Hopkins Marine Sta, Santa Cruz, 1977-80. *Appointments:* Feature Writer, Columnist, 1939-; Assoc Prof, Pub Rels, Jrnlsm, San Diego State Univ, CA, 1974, 1975; Vis Prof, Jrnlsm, San Jose State Univ, CA, 1976; Assoc Prof, Jrnlsm, Pub Rels: CA State Univ, Hayward, 1978; Univ CA Berkeley Ext, 1979-; Cons, Focus on Earth Science, Focus on Life Science, Focus on Physical Science sci texts, Bell & Howell, 1984, 1987; Book Reviewer for Professional Communicator, 1987-; Crown Publrs, NY, 1988-; Image Bank, NY, 1988-; Wn USA Corres, Linguapress Engl lang learning publr, Europe. *Publications:* Wonderful USA: Guide to the USA's Natural Resources State by State, 1989; Co-author, over 20 books incl: English for Social Living, 1944; Fawcett Boating Books, 1956-66; Fodor's San Francisco and Fodor's California, 1981-89; Earth Science, 1988; English Language Texts, 1988; Wonderful USA. Guide State by State to its Natural Resources, 1989; Incl in West Winds Four anthology, 1989; Over 5000 articles in nat and int publs specialising in travel, sci, environment. *Memberships include:* AAAS; Women in Communications; Soc Profl Jrnlsts; Nat Press Photographers Assn; Nat Assn Sci Writers; Phi Beta Kappa; Charter Mbr, Nat Soc Environmental Jrnlsts; Pub Rels Soc Am; N Am Assn Educ Jrnlsm; Int Oceanographic Fndn; Soc Am Travel Writers; CA Acad Environmental News Writers. *Honours include:* Top Sci Article, Columbia: Glacier in Retreat, 1987-88; Nat Mortar Bd Hon, Seattle, WA, 1988, 1989; Invited VIP, press trips. *Address:* 616 Castle Drive, Oakland, CA 94611, USA. 2, 5, 9, 30, 52, 59, 132.

WOOD Thomas Archie, b. 24 Sept 1945, Pittsburgh, Pennsylvania, USA. Associate Professor. m. Deborah J Miller, 24 Dec 1979, 3 d. *Education:* AA, Daytona Beach, Jr Coll, 1965; BS, FL State Univ, 1967; MEd, Stetson Univ, 1971; DEd, Peabody Coll, Vanderbilt Univ, 1978; Postdoct Cert, Univ TX Med Br, 1986. *Appointments:* Tchr, Supervision, Rehab Ctr, Daytona Beach, FL; School Psychologist, William Co, TN, 1974-75; Rsch Assoc, Vanderbilt Univ, 1975-76; Asst Prof, Murray State Univ, 1976-80; Assoc Prof, Auburn Univ, Auburn, TX, 1980-91; Asst Dean, Educ, Univ TX, El Paso, 1991-. *Publications:* Book chapts in The Practice of Child Therapy, 2nd Ed; Articles in BC Journal of Special Education, Journal of Learning Disabilities, Teacher Education and Special Education; Special topics in Early Childhood, Special Education, Exceptional Children, Journal of Visual Impairment and Blindness, Education of the Visually Handicapped, Journal of Reading Improvement, American Journal of Mental Retardation. *Memberships:* Am Psychological Assn; Nat Assn School Psychologists; Coun for Exceptional Children; Ad Fed Coun for Exceptional Children, Pres 1984, VP 1983. *Honours:* Fed Traineeship, 1966; Rsch/Tchng Fellowships, 1972-73; Num Fed Grants to conduct trng and rsch, 1974-88; Outstanding Young Man Am, 1981; Commissioned Kentucky Col, 1983. *Hobbies:* Boating; Flying; Camping; Travel; Carpentry. *Address:* College of

Education, Rm 414, University of Texas at El Paso, El Paso, TX 79968, USA. 7, 15.

WOODARD Alva Abe, b. 28 June 1928, Roy, New Mexico, USA. Business Executive. m. Esther Josepha Kaufmann, 5 Apr 1947, 6 s, 5 d. *Education:* Bus Admin studies: Kinman Bus Univ, 1948-49; WA State Univ, 1953-54; Whitworth Coll, 1956. *Appointments:* VP, Sec/Treas, Dir, ASC Inds Inc, Spokane, WA, 1953-75; Exec, Cons to several businesses, Wn USA, 1976-88; Pres, Dir, TFI Inds Inc, Post Falls, ID, 1989-. *Publication:* Credit - A Creative Selling Tool, 1968. *Memberships:* Repub Comm'man, 1964-80; Repub State Deleg, 1964-80; Admnstv Mgmt Soc, Dir 1966-68; Optimists Club, Sec 1968. *Honours:* Award, Outstanding Serv to Elem Educ, St Mary Ch Parish, Spokane Diocese. *Hobbies:* Theatre; Golf; Reading; Social dancing; Fishing. *Address:* E 1714 Rockwell Street, Spokane, WA 99207, USA. 9.

WOODRUFF Alan Waller, b. 27 June 1916, Sunderland, England. Professor of Medicine. m. Mercia Helen Arnold, 21 Jan 1946, 2 s, 1 d. *Education:* Univ Durham Coll Med, 1934-37; MD (Dunelm), 1941; PhD (Lond); FRCP, 1953; FRCP Edinburgh, 1961. *Appointments:* Med Specialist, Squadron Ldr, RAF, 1940-46; Registrar, Royal Victoria Infirmary, Newcastle-on- Tyne, 1946-48; Prof, Clin Tropical Med, Univ London, 1952-81; Prof, Med, Univ Juba, Sudan, 1981-. *Publications:* Medicine in the Tropics (ed), 1974, 1984; Synopsis of Tropical and Infective Diseases (co-author); Many papers in sci jrnls. *Memberships:* Hon RE, 1979; Royal Soc Tropical Med and Hygiene, Pres 1973-75; Med Soc London, Pres 1976; Roy Soc Med, Hist Sect, 1977-79; Durham Univ Soc, Pres 1964-77; Assn Physns GB and Ireland; Athenaeum Club, London, Comm Mbr 1978-80. *Honours:* CMG, 1978; OBE, 1989; Katherine Bishop Harman Prize, Brit Med Assn, 1951; William Julius Mickle Fellow, Univ London, 1964; Cullen Prize, Royal Coll Physns Edinburgh, 1982; Goulstonian Lectr, 1954, Watson Smith Lectr, 1970, Royal Coll Physns; Lettsonian Lectr, Med Soc London, 1969. *Hobbies:* Sketching and engraving (Hon Fellow, Royal Society of Painter-Etchers and Engravers); Tennis (Mbr, Queens Club); Astronomy; Fishing. *Address:* 122 Ferndene Road, London SE24 0BA, England. 1, 34, 170.

WOODRUFF Peter Waller Rolph, b. 22 Nov 1956, London, England. Psychiatrist. m. Catriona Mary Hall, 21 May 1988. *Education:* Newcastle Med School, 1976-81; MB BS, 1981, MRCP, 1985; MRCPsych, 1991. *Appointments:* Sci Tchr, 1976; Med Sr House Off, Sunderland, 1982-84; Lectr, Kings Coll Med School, London, 1985-86; Vis Lectr, Sudan, 1986, 1989, 1991; Asst Prof, MD Univ, USA, 1987-88; Registrar, Bethlam and Maudsley Hosp, London, England, 1988-91; Rsch Fellow, Inst Psychiatry, London, 1991-. *Publications:* Medical Problems, Peru and Sudan; Infectious Diseases Abroad; Cardiac Peptides; Var psych publs. *Memberships:* Fellow, Med Soc, London; Liveryman, Worshipful Soc Apothecaries; Athaeneum Club. *Honours:* Silver Medal, Nat Rowng Championships (VIIIs), 1973; Winner Home Int Rowing Championships (VIIIs), 1973; Psych Prize, Newcastle Univ, 1981. *Hobbies:* History; Poetry; Music; Art; Hillwalking; Gardening. *Address:* Institute of Psychiatry, De Crespigny Park, Denmark Hill, London SE5 8AF, England.

WOODS B W, b. 23 Apr 1930, Frederick, Oklahoma, USA. Clergyman. m, Ann Woods, 2 July 1948, 1 s, 1 d. *Education:* BA, Midwestern Univ, 1957; BD, 1960, ThD, 1964, SWn Bapt Theological Sem. *Appointments:* Prairie View Bapt ch, 1955-57; 1st Bapt Ch: Hollister, OK, 1957-60; Wynnewood, OK, 1960-64; Tucumeare, NM, 1964-67; Seminole, OK, 1967-73; Muskogee, OK, 1973-. *Publications:* Books: God's Answer to Amnesty, 1968; Christians In Pain, 1974; Take Hold of Your Life, 1979; Series of Counselling Booklets to Baker Book House. *Membership:* Rotary International. *Hobbies:*

Golf; Fly fishing. *Address:* First Baptist Church, 111 South 7th Street, Muskogee, OK 74401, USA. 2.

WOODWARD Antony James Thomas, b. 17 Jan 1963, Bristol, England. Copywriter. *Education:* Exhibitioner, Selwyn Coll, Cambridge, 1981-84; MA Hons, Cambridge. *Appointments:* Sr Writer, Bd Dir, Mavity Gilmore Jaime FCA Ltd, 1985-87; Sr Writer, Dir, Still Price Court Twny D'Souza Ltd, 1988-89; Sr Writer, Collett Dickenson Pearce and Ptnrs Ltd, 1989-. *Honours:* 3 Bronze Awards, 1981, 3 Gold Awards, Silver Award, Bronze Award, 1987, Bronze Award, 1988, Silver Award, 1989, Creative Circle; Gold Award runner-up, 2 Silver Awards, 1987, Gold Award, 1989, Campaign Press; Commendation, 1987, 2 Commendations, 1988, 3 Commendations, 1989, Design and Art Dirs Assn. *Hobbies:* Flying; Birdwatching; Films; Architecture; Mountaineering; Reading; People. *Address:* 95 Ashbury Road, Battersea, London SW11 5UQ, England.

WOOLDRIDGE Ian Edmund, b. 14 Jan 1932, Bournemouth, England. Sports Columnist; TV Documentary Reporter. m. (1) 3 s, (2) Sarah Margaret Lourenco, 1 Dec 1980. *Education:* Brockenhurst Grammar School. *Appointments:* New Milton Advertiser, 1948-53; News Chronicle, 195660; Sunday Dispatch, 196061; Daily Mail, 1961-. *Publications:* Cricket, Lovely Cricket, 1963; Mary P (w Mary Peters), 1973; Autobiography of a Cricketer (w Colin Cowdray), 1976; The Best of Wooldridge, 1978; Travelling Reserve, 1982; Sport in the Eighties, 1990. *Honours:* Columnist of Yr, twice, Sportswriter of Yr, 3 times, Brit Press Awards; Sports Feature Writer of Yr, Brit Sports Coun Awards, 3 times; OBE, 1991. *Hobbies:* Golf; Travel; Scotch whisky; Beethoven; Reading. *Address:* 11 Collingham Gardens, London SW5 0HS, England. 1.

WORCESTER Donald Emmet, b. 29 Apr 1915, Tempe, Arizona, USA. Professor Emeritus. m. Barbara Livingston Peck, 5 July 1941, 1 s, 2 d. *Education:* BA, Bard Coll, 1939; MA, 1940, PhD, 1947, Univ CA, Berkeley. *Appointments:* Lectr, Univ CA, Davis, 1946; Lectr, spring 1947, Vis Assoc Prof, summer 1950, Univ CA, Berkeley; Univ FL, 1947-63, incl Chmn, Dept Hist, 1955-59; Vis Assoc Prof, Univ MI, spring 1952; Vis Prof, Univ Madrid, 1956-57; Chmn, Dept Hist, 1963-72, Lorin A Boswell Prof Hist, 1971-80, Ida and Cecil Green Emeritus Prof, 1981-, TX Christian Univ, Ft Worth. *Publications:* Instructions for Governing the Interior Provinces of New Spain 1786, 1951; Sea Power and Chilean Independence, 1962, Spanish Ed, 1971; The Three Worlds of Latin America, 1963; The Makers of Latin America, 1966; Brazil: From Colony to World Power, 1973; Bolivar, 1977; The Apaches: Eagles of the Southwest, 1979, German Ed, 1982; The Chisholm Trail: High Road of the Cattle Kingdom, 1980; The Texas Cowboy, 1986; The Spanish Mustang: from the Plains of Andalusia to the Prairies of Texas, 1986; The Texas Longhorn: Relic of the Past, Asset of the Future, 1987; The War in the Nueces Strip, fiction, 1989; A Visit from Father and Other Tales of the Mojave, 1990; Brazos Scott, fiction, 1991; Man On Two Ponies, fiction, 1991; 7 children's books; Co- author, ed or co-ed, several other books. *Contributions to:* 40 jrnls or books. *Memberships:* Phi Alpha Theta, Nat Pres 1960-62; Wn Writers Am, Pres 1973-74; Wn Hist Assn, Pres 1974-75; Westerners Int, Pres 1978-80; TX Inst Letters; Phi Beta Kappa. *Honours:* Spur Awards, Wn Writers Am, 1977, 1979; SW Book Award, 1979; C L Sonnichsen Book Award, 1985; Saddleman Award, Wn Writers Am, 1988. *Hobby:* Raising Arabian horses. *Address:* Rte 2, Box 61, Aledo, TX 76008, USA. 2, 3, 15, 30, 52.

WORLEY Charlotte Lafayette Coker, b. 10 June 1925, Sumner, Mississippi, USA. English Educator. m. Hurd Boyd Worley, 27 Jan 1946, 2 d. *Education:* BA, Delta State Univ, Cleveland, MS, 1959; MA, 1961, PhD, 1984, Univ MS, University. *Appointments:* Tchr, Engl, French, E Tallahatchie HS, Charleston, MS, 1960-61; Instr, Engl, French, NW MS Jr Coll, Senatobia, 1961-66; Instr, Engl, Univ MS, 1967-73; Prof, Engl, Chair, Div Langs, Clarke

Coll, 1985-90; Engl Educator, Faith Acad, Grenada, MS, 1991-92. *Publication:* The Character of the Merchant in English Drama from 1590- 1612: His Metamorphosis after 1603, 1984. *Memberships:* S Ctrl MLA; Nat Coun Tchrs Engl; MS Coun Tchrs Engl; MS Assn Women in Higher Educ; Kappa Delta Pi; Pi Gamma Nu; Acad Counc, Lib Comm, Clarke Coll. *Honours:* C M Gooch Fndn State Scholarship, Memphis, TN, to Delta State Univ, 1944-46; C M Brown Mem Scholarship, Cleveland, MS, to Delta State Univ, 1944-46; Anne Caulfield Winston Engl Scholarship, Cleveland, MS, 1958-59; Grad w 1st hons, Delta State Univ, 1959. *Hobbies:* Reading classic novels; Viewing classic movies; Engaging in family activities; Decorating her home. *Address:* 1703 Martha Drive, Grenada, MS 38901, USA. 7, 15.

WORLING Peter Metcalfe, b. 16 June 1928, Nagrakata, India. Pharmacist. m. Iris McBeath, 20 Mar 1954, 2 d. *Education:* Robert Gordons Coll, Aberdeen, Scotland, 1945, 1948-50; Pharm Chems Dip, 1950; Elected Fellow, Royal Pharm Soc, 1954; PhD, Univ Bradford, 1988. *Appointments:* Pharmacist, 1956, Sales Mgr, 1961-65, Bradley and Bliss Ltd, Reading, England; Reg Dir, 1966-73, Commercial Dir, 1973-79, Mng Dir, 1979-89, Vestric Ltd; Chmn, AAH Pharms Ltd, 1989-91; Cons, Pharm Distribution, 1991-. *Publications:* Pharmaceutical Wholesale Distribution, thesis, 1988; Pharmaceutical Distributors and the European Common Market, 1990; Pharmaceutical Wholesaling in Europe, 1991. *Memberships:* Scottish Wholesale Druggists Assn, 1966-73, Chmn 1970-71; Proprietary Articles Trade Assn, Pres 1984; Nat Assn Pharm Distributors, 1975-91, Chmn 1983-85. *Hobbies:* Painting; Gardening; Reading. *Address:* Riverhurst, 19 Eyebrook Road, Bowden, Altrincham, Cheshire WA14 3LH, England. 52.

WORONIECKI Jan, b. 9 Nov 1944, Lvov, Poland. Diplomat; Researcher/Economist. m. Ewa Woroniecki, 8 May 1982, 1 s, 1 d. *Education:* MA (Econ), Dept For Trade, 1967, PhD, 1981, Habilitation, 1990, Warsaw School Econs. *Appointments:* Dept Int Orgs, Min For Affairs, Warsaw 1967-72; Permanent Mission of Poland to UN Off, Geneva, 1967-72, Hd, Econs Sect, 1972-77, 1982-90, Dept Int Orgs, Min For Affairs, Warsaw; UNCTAD Cons, 1981-82; Dir, Dept UN System, Min For Affairs, 1990; Prof, Univ Warsaw. 1991-. *Publications:* Articles in profl econ jrnls on int issues esp UN; Book on large-scale East-West projects, 1985; Book on for capital in USSR, 1990. *Memberships:* Polish Assn for Club of Rome; Polish Assn Salzburg Sem Alumnae; VP, Rotary Club, Warsaw-Old Town; Bd Mbr, Polish Assn Environment and Dev. *Honours:* Silver Cross of Merit, 1975, Golden Cross of Merit, 1987, Poland. *Hobbies:* Gypsy and Country-Western music; Gardening; Skiing; Foreign travel. *Address:* 23 Al I Armii WP, 00580 Warsaw 7, Poland.

WOYKE Jerzy, b. 9 Sept 1926, Malenin, Poland. Professor of Apiculture. m. Halina Urbanowicz, 10 Oct 1953, 1 s, 1 d. *Education:* MS, Forestry, MS Biology, Univ Poznan, 1950; PhD, 1958, Dr Sci, 1961, Agricl Univ, Warsaw. *Appointments:* Asst, Apiculture, Univ Poznan, 1949; Adj, Hd Bee Div, 1952, Asst Prof, Apiculture, 1962, Assoc Prof, 1969, Full Prof, 1978-, Agricl Univ, Warsaw; FAO Expert: Guinea, 1979, El Salvador, 1980, Afghanistan, 1983, Vietnam, 1985, Ghana, 1986, Egypt, 1987, Sudan, 1988, Algeria, 1989, Albania, 1989, Mexico, 1989. *Publications:* 230 original papers; 19 books or chapts; 190 tech papers. *Memberships:* Int Bee Rsch Assn, Rep, Poland; Ed Bd: J Apicultural Research, Apimondia; Pres, Grp Instrumental Insemination of Queen Bees, Ctrl Animal Breeding Station; Pres, Honeybee Breeding Commn. *Honours:* 34 incl: Polish Acad Scis, 1964, 1978, 1979; Polish Beekeepers Assn, 1966, 1971, 1978, 1979, 1988; USDA, 1966, 1971, 1979, 1987; Polonia Restituta Cross, 1973; Min Agric, 1976, 1984, 1987; Min Sci and Higher Educ, 1976, 1989; Min Agric, El Salvador, 1981. *Hobbies:* Languages (speaks 7); Tropical apiculture; Travel; Climbed Mt Kilimanjaro, 1984. *Address:* Bee Division, Agricultural University- SGGW,

Nowoursynowska 166, 02-766 Warsaw, Poland. 52, 139, 152, 156.

WRIGHT Hugh Raymond, b. 24 Aug 1938, Boston, Lincolnshire, England. Headmaster. m. Gillian Meiklejohn, 7 Apr 1962, 3 s. *Education:* The Queen's Coll, Oxford, 1957-61; MA (Lit Hum). *Appointments:* Brentwood School, 1961-64; Dept Hd, Housemaster, Cheltenham Coll, 1964-79; Hd, Stockport Grammar School, 1979-85; Hdmaster, Gresham's, 1985-91; Chief Master, King Edward's School, Birmingham, 1991-. *Memberships:* Hd Masters Conf, Chmn NW Div 1983, Chm Community Serv Pub Comm 1980-85, Chm, En Div Comm on 6th Form Curric 1990; FRSA; Naval Selection Bd. *Honours:* Bible Clerkship, The Queen's Coll, Oxford. *Hobbies:* Hill walking; Gardening; Wildfowl; Rugby football; Music; Singing. *Address:* Vince House, 341 Bristol Rd, Edgbaston, Birmingham, England. 1.

WRIGHT James Richard, b. 15 Dec 1934, Cleveland, Ohio, USA. Professor of Linguistics. m. Lucinda W Thomas, 18 Mar 1961. *Education:* BA, NWn Univ, 1956; MA, Middlebury Coll, 1960; MA, 1968, PhD, 1972, IN Univ. *Appointments:* Prof, Linguistics, Dept Engl, E Carolina Univ, Greenville, NC, 1969-. *Membership:* Linguistic Soc Am. *Honours:* Danforth Grant, 1961; NDEA Fellowship, 1965-69. *Hobbies:* Personal computing; Electronic and acoustic music; Locksmithing; Bicycle building and repair. *Address:* Department of English, East Carolina University, Greenville, NC 27858, USA.

WRIGHT Malcolm Allan, b. 25 Jan 1939, London, England. Executive Director; Chief Executive. m. Brenda Mary Nicholson, 8 July 1967, 2 d, 1 dec. *Education:* Adv Mgmt Prog, Harvard Bus School, USA, 1981. *Appointments:* 2nd Lt, Royal Regt Artillery, 1958-60; Milk Mktng Bd, 1960-61; Beck and Pollitzer Engrng Ltd, 1961-74; Cade Inds PLC, 1974-85; Cons, 1985-86; Exec Dir, Chief Exec, Indl Textiles Div, BBA Grp PLC, 1986-. *Memberships:* FCIS; Inst Textiles; Freeman, City of London; Freeman, Worshipful Co of Horners. *Hobbies:* Occasional golf; Gardening; DIY. *Address:* High Point, 58 The Mount, Fetcham, Surrey KT22 9EA, England.

WRIGHT Ronald, b. 12 Sept 1948, Weybridge, Surrey, England. Writer. m. Janice Patricia Boddy, 2 June 1985. *Education:* Peterhouse, Cambridge; MA (Cantab), 1973. *Career:* Self-employed Writer; Num radio and TV interviews, USA, Can, UK, 1981-91; Writer, Presenter, documentary series: Worlds in Reverse: Indian Responses to the Spanish Conquest, 3 pts, CBC Stereo IDEAS, Can, 1983; Points of Departure, 3 pt, CBC Radio IDEAS, 1984; Vision of the Vanquished, 5 pts, 1986. *Publications:* Books: Cut Stones and Crossroads: A Journey in Peru, 1984; On Fiji Islands, 1986; Quechua Phrasebook, 1989; Time Among the Maya, 1989; Captive Nations, 1992; Anthology. *Contributions:* Crossroads, 1990; Peru is not a Novel, 1990; The Jungle Michelangelo, 1990; Articles and criticism in Time Literary Supplement, New York Times Book Review, Washington Post, Independent, Saturday Night, Globe and Mail, others. *Memberships:* FRGS; PEN, Bd Mbr Can 1989-91; Latin Am Indian Lits Assn; Survival Int. *Honours:* ACTRA Award Nominee, Best Writer, Radio Documentary, 1983; Award, Can Sci Writers Assn, 1986; Finalist, Trillium Book Award, Time Among the Maya, 1990; Lit Award, Can Broadcasting Corp, 1991. *Hobbies:* Books; Walking; Cross-country skiing; Arthrology; Music. *Address:* c/o Blake Friedmann Agency, 37-41 Gower Street, London WC1E 6HH, England. 3, 30, 142.

WRIGHT Wayne Kenneth, b. 26 Jan 1944, Chelsea, Massachusetts, USA. Information Specialist. m. Bonnie Sue Oberhjelman, 3 Apr 1982, 2 s, 1 d, 1 stepdaughter. *Education:* BS, Sociology, Univ IA, 1971; Postgrad, Univ N IA, 1971-72, Cert, Mktng, Atlanta Univ, 1988. *Appointments:* Survey Asst, Shive-Hall-Hattery Engrng, Cedar Rapids, IA, 1962-66; Chem Lab Tech, Wilson Packing Plant, Cedar Rapids, 1966-71; Grad Tchng Asst,

Univ N IA, 1970; US Census Bur, 1971-, incl: Survey Statn, 1973-74, Info Specialist, 1974-83, Kansas City, KS, Info Specialist, Charlotte, NC, 1983-. *Memberships:* Fellow, Alpha Kappa Delta, 1973; Hon Citizen, Beloit, WI, 1974; KY Col, 1987. *Honours:* Mbr, Census Bur Mktng Team winning 1st Place in competition, 1988. *Hobbies:* Camping; Fishing; Hiking; Tennis; Time with his family; Sightseeing; Mountain touring; Photography. *Address:* 1417 Morrocroft Trail, Gastonia, NC 28054, USA. 7.

WU (Ngan Yan) Sally Kin, b. 26 Sept 1948, Burma. Teacher. *Education:* Typing and Shorthand Cert, BSC Coll, Burma, 1973; Grp Scout Ldr Cert, Scout Assn, Macau, 1983; 1st Aid Cert, Educ Dept, Macau, 1986; BEd, 1989, MEd, 1990, Universal Fedn Univ, Hong Kong. *Appointments:* Tchr, St John's Coll, Macau, 1973-74; Tchr, Perpetual Help Coll, 1974-75; Tchr, 1974-89, Admnstv work, 1984-89, Colegio de Santa Rosa de Lima; Tchr, Pvte Tutor, Cath Voc School, 1989-91. *Memberships:* Macau Scout Assn; Grp Scout Ldr, 6th Scout Grp Macau; Off, Scouts Room, St Rosa. *Honours:* Burmese Scripture Distinction Award, Educ Dept, 1966; Disting Serv Award, Macau Scout Assn, 1984; Diocesan Bazaar Charity Serv Award, Caritas Social Serv, 1988; Disting Serv Award, Colegio de Santa Rosa, 1989; BSc Tchng Hons, Universal Fedn Univ, Hong Kong, 1990. *Hobbies:* Reading; Social welfare. *Address:* 1o Andar 105-A Av Con F Almeida, Macau, via Hong Kong.

WU Bing-quan, b. 4 Jan 1930, Tianjin, China. Professor of Pathology; Medical Doctor. m. Ying Mu, 12 Feb 1956, 2 d. *Education:* Pre-med, L'Univ Aurore, Shanghai, 1947-49; Dip, Fac Med, Peking Univ, 1955; Postgrad, Dept Pathology, Beijing Med Coll, 1955-59. *Appointments include:* Chmn, Dept Pathology, 1979-, Dean, School Basic Med Scis, 1989-, Beijing Medical Univ; Dir, Cancer Rsch Ctr, 1989-. *Publications:* Over 60 papers in recent 10 yrs; Immuno-Deficient Animals in Experimental Medicine (ed w J Zheng), 1989. *Memberships:* VP, Soc Pathology, Chinese Med Assn; Asia Pacific Assn Socs of Pathologists, VP 1990-91; Co-Ed, Int Ed Bd, Acta Pathologica, Microbiologica et Immunologica Scandinavica. *Honours:* Sci Rsch Award, Beijing Municipality, 1982, 1984; Sci RSch AWard, Min Pub Hlth, 1982, 1985; Sci Rsch Award, Nat Commn Educ, 1990. *Hobbies:* Swimming; Reading. *Address:* Department of Pathology, School of Basic Medical Sciences, Beijing Medical University, Xue Yuan Road, Beijing 100083, China.

WU Chien-Shiung, b. 30 May 1912, Shanghai, China. Educator; Researcher. m. 30 May 1942, 1 s. *Education:* BS, Nat Ctrl Univ, China; PhD, Univ CA, Berkeley. *Appointments:* Rsch, Univ CA, Berkeley, USA; Tchng, Smith Coll, Princeton Univ; Tchng, Rsch, Columbia Univ, NYC. *Publication:* Beta Decay, Nuclear Experimental Methods, book. *Memberships:* AAAS; Am Phys Soc; NAS. *Honours:* Rsch Award, 1957; Acad Sci, 1958; Nat Sci Medal, 1976; Wolf Prize, 1978; Named Asteroid No 2752 from Purple Mountain Observatory, 1990; Over 30 hon degrees, var instns. *Hobby:* Reading. *Address:* 15 Claremont Ave, Apt 73, New York, NY 10027, USA.

WU Dazhi, b. 25 Dec 1925, Guizhou, China. Professor of Western Art History. m. Chengyin Mao, 9 Jan 1954, 1 s. *Education:* Grad, Dept For Lang and Lit, Tsinghua Univ, 1948; Grad, Dept Painting, Ctrl Acad Fine Arts, Beijing, 1953. *Appointments include:* Currently: Prof, Wn Art Hist, Dept Art Hist and Theory, Ctrl Acad Arts and Design, Beijing; Pt-time Prof, Peking Univ, Beijing; Guest Prof, Tsinghua Univ. *Publications:* 51 books and articles incl: Delacroix, 1958; J Constable, 1961; American Art in 20th Century, 1980; Art and the Time-Inquiry into the Law Concerning the Climax in Artistic Development, 1982; 30 transls incl: Millet (Romain Rolland), 1985; Concist Encyclopaedia Britannica, 1986; Notes d'un Peintre (Matisse), 1980. *Membership:* China Artists Assn. *Hobbies:* Reading; Swimming; Tennis; Music. *Address:* Rm 402, Apt Bldg 53, Chang Chun Yuan, Peking University, 100871 Beijing, China.

WU De-Ming, b. 14 May 1938, Chongqing, Sichuan, China. Professor and President of Shipbuilding Engineering Institute. m. Ma Xiaoxun, 30 Sept 1967, 1 d. *Education:* Dip, Harbin Engineering Inst, 1961. *Appointments:* Asst, Lectr, 1962-79, Assoc Prof, 1980-85, Chmn, Aeronautical Engrng Dept, 1984-85, VP, 1985-88, Prof, 1986-, Pres, 1988-, Harbin Shipbuilding Engrng Inst, Harbin. *Memberships:* Bd Dirs Exec Comm, Chinese Soc Naval Arch and Marine Engrng; Chmn, Bd Dirs, Heilongjiang Province Soc Naval Arch and Marine Engrng; Vice-Chmn, Bd Dirs, Heilongjiang Province Aviation Soc. *Honours:* State Award, Nat Conf Sci and Technology, 1987. *Hobbies:* Reading; Swimming. *Address:* Harbin Shipbuilding Engineering Institute, Wenmiao Jie, 11/F Nangangqu 150001, Harbin, Heilongjiang, China.

WU En-hui, b. 5 Dec 1925, Liao-ning, China. Professor; Physician. m. 17 July 1946, 2 d. *Education:* MD, Liaoning Med Coll (Dugald Christie Mem), 1948. *Appointments include:* Currently Tianjin Clinico- Radiological Rsch and Trng Ctr, Tianjin Med Coll Hosp. *Publications:* Over 20 books about radiology such as neuroradiology, CT diagnosis of head, imaging diagnosis of liver biliary tract and pancrease. *Memberships:* Standing Mbr, Chinese Radiological Soc; Chief Ed, Foreign Medicine and Medical Imaging; Assoc Chief Ed, Chinese Journal of Radiology. *Honours:* Hon Mbr, Radiological Soc N Am, 1988. *Address:* Tianjin Medical College Hospital, Anshan Road, Tianjin 300052, China. 139, 152.

WU Han De, b. Mar 1934, Tianjin, China. *Education:* Beijing Medical Coll, 1953; Budapest Univ of Medicine, Hungary, 1961. *Appointments:* Research Hepatic Centre, Univ of California, San Francisco, USA, 1982-83; Pres, Shanxi Medical Coll, Dir of Pathophysiology Dept, Dir, Hepatic Research Group. *Publications include:* Monographs; Chapters; Books, Modern Pathophysiology; Pathophysiology & Clinic; Diseases of Liver, Gallbladder & Pancreas. *Memberships:* Chinese Medical Soc Shanxi branch; Shinese Assn of Physiological Sci Shanxi Branch; Shanxi Medical Coll; Hepatic Research group; Hepatic Disease Group. *Honours:* Natl Outstanding Specialist in Sci & Tech, Admin; World Famous Personalities. *Address:* Shanxi Medical Coll, Taiyuan, Shanxi Province 030001, China.

WU Joseph, b. 2 Oct 1951, Burma. Teacher. Technician. *Education:* CEO Cert, 1972; Dip, Master's course, Electronics Communication, 1974; Radiological Monitoring Cert, Def Dir/Coord Cert, Def USA Cert, 1979; ASET deg, Radiological Emergency, 1979; Certs: Preparedness, Disaster Preparedness, Radiological Instr III (TTT), Sem on Contemporary Issues in Emergency Mgmt, Adv Radiological Accident Assessment, Hazardous Materials Contingency Planning (TTT), IEMC Response, IEMC Earthquake, Nat Earthquake Hazard Reduction Prog Provisions (TTT), 1988; BBA, 1989. *Appointments:* Firm Employee, 1973-84; Tchr, Techn, 1984-. *Hobbies:* Reading; Touring; Watching TV. *Address:* 1/0 Andar 105 A Av Con F Almeida, Macau, via Hong Kong.

WU Shanming, b. 28 Nov 1941, Pujiang, Zhejiang, China. Professor of Fine Arts. m. Yeyun Gao, 8 Mar 1967, 2 s, 1 d. *Education:* Grad Dip, Chinese Painting Dept, Zhejiang Acad Fine Arts, 1964. *Appointments:* Tchng, 1964-, Assoc Prof, Hd Chinese Painting Dept, 1986-, Prof, 1989-, Zhejiang Acad Fine Arts; Art Expert Juror, State Educ China, 1986-. *Publications:* Over a doz albums and treatise books, 1986-91 incl: Selection of Wu Shanming's Paintings; Collection of Wu Shanming's Paintings; Wu Shanming's Inkwash Sketches; Wu Shanming's Free-handed Figure Paintings; Writing-brush Sketches; Techniques of Chinese Free-handed Figure Painting; Teaching Materials of Chinese Free-handed Figure Painting. *Memberships:* Degree Comm, Zhejiang Acad Fine Arts; All-China Artists Assn, Standing Dir Zhejiang Br; Chmn, Hangzhou Artists Assn; Vice-Chmn, Hangzhou Writers and Artists Union; VP, Xilin Painting Inst. *Honours:*

Grand Award for The Affection for Mountains and Waters, inkwash cartoon film based on Wu's image modelling, Shanghai Int Cartoon Film Fest, 1988; Grand Award, Excellent Films and TV Progs, Min Culture China, 1988; Beauty and Courage Award, USSR Youth Film Fest, 1988; Chinese Nat Golden Cock Award, 1989; Grand Award for shorts, Montreal Int Film Fest, 1990; Chinese Olympic Hon Award for painting After a Tong Poem; 2nd Award, All-China Picture-book Appraisal for work Qiu Jin. *Hobbies:* Touring and sightseeing; Book shopping; Reading biographies and anecdotes of famous people; Enjoying classical Chinese music. *Address:* The Chinese Painting Department, Zhejiang Academy of Fine Arts, Hangzhou, Zhejiang Province, China.

WUBBELS Theo, b. 3 Dec 1949, Enschede, Netherlands. Professor of Education (Endowed Chair). m. Angela M M Wolffenbuttel, 26 May 1973, 3 d. *Education:* Master's degree, Phys, 1974; PhD, Educ, 1984. *Appointments:* Phys Tchr, 1973-78, Assoc Prin, 1976-78, Montessori HS; Curric Dev, 1978-80, Assoc Prof, Phys Educ, 1980-90, Full Prof, Educ, Tchr Educ, 1991-, Univ Utrecht. *Publications:* Over 100 sci scholarly articles; Books incl: School counselling, 1980; Discipline problems of beginning teachers, 1984; Disorder stopped, 1988; Presenting, 1991; Ed, 5 books. *Memberships include:* Am Educl Rsch Assn, Chmn Awards Comm; Nat Assn Rsch in Sci Educ, Mbr Int Comm; Pres, Dutch Assn Phys Educ; VP, Dutch Assn Tchr Educ; European Assn Learning and Instrn; Int Study Assn Tchr Thinking; Invisible Coll Rsch on Tchng and Tchr Educ. *Honours:* Outstanding Rsch Paper Award, 1988, Excellence in Rsch on Tchng and Tchr Educ Award, 1989, Am Educl Rsch Assn. *Hobbies:* Playing chess; Carpenting. *Address:* IVLOS, University of Utrecht, PO Box 80127, 3508 TC Utrecht, Netherlands. 2.

WUENSCHE Vernon Edgar, b. 25 Nov 1945, Elgid, Texas, USA. Custom Home Builder. *Education:* BBA, 1967, MBA, 1968, Univ TX, Austin. *Appointments:* Audit Asst, Arthur Andersen and Co, Houston, TX, 1968; Tax Cons, Peat Marwick Mitchell and Co, 1970; Cost Acct, Bemis Bros Bag co, Houston, 1970; Asst Controller, Prod Systems Int, Houston, 1971; Controller, Am Housing Guilds Inc, Houston, 1972; Controller, Wood Bros Homes Inc, Houston, Dallas and Oklahoma City, 1973; Pres, Fndn, Woodmark Homes Inc, Houston, Dallas and Oklahoma City, 1975-. *Memberships:* TX Soc CPAs; Rice Design Alliance; TX Wendish Heritage Soc; Alley Theater Guild; Mus Fine Arts; Repub Party TX; Fndr, Texans for Efficiency in Gov Inc. *Honours:* Dean's Award for Acad Excellence, Univ TX, 1968; Phi Kappa Phi, Univ TX, 1968; Beta Gamma Sigma, Univ TX, 1968. *Hobbies:* Distance running; Politics; Reading. *Address:* 14211 Swiss Hill Drive, Houston, TX 77077, USA. 7.

WYKYDAL Andreas Johannes, b. 30 Mar 1966, Vienna, Austria. Composer; Pianist; Teacher. *Education:* Piano study, Conservatory Vienna, 1985-; Mag Phil, Musicology, Univ Vienna, 1989. *Career:* Prod of Bartok's Sonata for 2 pianos and percussion, Austrian TV, 1989; Piano Tchr, Musical School Modling and Inzersdorf, Vienna, 1990-. *Creative works:* Composer: Sonata for Piano, 1986-87; Aerophonie, for organ, 1988-89; Blow up, for organ, 1989; Projections, for 2 pianos, 1990; Labyrinth, Ping Png, Fragment, 1990; Game over, for organ, 1991. *Memberships:* Assn for Presenting New Austrian Music; Assn Austrian Composers; Assn Organ Friends. *Honours:* 2nd Prize, piano solo, 2nd Prize, piano duo, Jugend Musiziert Competition, Austria, 1987; 3rd prize for Blow up, Assn Organ Friends Composition Competition, 1990. *Hobbies:* Reading; Swimming; Skiing. *Address:* Gottschalkgasse 11/1/12. A-1110 Vienna, Austria.

WYMAN Peter Lewis, b. 26 Feb 1950, London, England. Chartered Accountant. m. 16 Sept 1978, 1 s, 1 d. *Education:* Epsom Coll. *Appointments:* Joined, 1968, Ptnr, 1978-, Coopers and Lybrand Deloitte. *Publications:* Over 100 articles on taxation in profl press.

Memberships: Fellow, Inst Chartered Accts England and Wales, Mbr Coun, Chmn Fac Taxation; Lond Soc Chartered Accts, Chmn 1987-88. *Hobbies:* Equestrian sports; Gardening; 20th century history. *Address:* Reapyears Corner, Streeters Rough, Chelwood Gate, Sussex RH17 7LL, England. 53.

WYNDAELE Jean Jacques Joseph Marc, b. 24 July 1949, Diest, Belgium. Urologist; Rehabilitation Doctor. m. Marie-Louise Janssens, 18 Feb 1978, 1 s. *Education:* MD, 1974; Urologist, 1980; Rehab Specialist, 1981; Dr, Biomed Scis, 1983. *Appointments include:* Hd, Ctr Urodynamics - Urological Rehab, Univ Hosp, Ghent, 1987-; Lector, Univ Ghent, 1989-91. *Publications:* Author, 114 sci articles, co-author, 30 sci articles, 1974-91. *Memberships:* VP, IMSOP, Coun Mbr 1984-90; AFIGAP; ICS; Genulf; IUGA; Belg Uer Urologie; Soc Belg Urol; Pres, Pelvired. *Honours:* Van Goethem-Brichant, Brussels, 1985; Groupe Dieture Neurourologique de Langue Francaise, 1989; Christiaens Prize, 1990. *Hobbies:* Reading history; Piano; Travel. *Address:* Wyndaele-Janssens, 6 Koning Boudewynlaan, B-9840 Depinte, Belgium. 34.

WYNNE-WILLIAMS John Anthony, b. 8 Nov 1949, London, England. Company Director. *Education:* Stonyhurst Coll. *Appointments:* Dir, D'Arcy Macmanus Benton and Bowles, 1970-80; Dpty Chmn, Ryman Ltd, 1981-86; Dpty Chmn, Moyses Stevens Grp, 1986-. *Memberships:* Dpty Chmn, Royal Marsden Hosp Cancer Appeal; Dir, Rambert Dance Co; Dir, Holland and Holland Ltd; Dir, Kiki McDonough Ltd. *Hobbies:* Cresta Run; Theatre; Squash; Shooting; Backgammon. *Address:* 27 St Leonards Terrace, London SW3 4QG, England.

WYZNER Krzysztof Antoni, b. 30 Mar 1949, Warsaw, Poland. Painter; Graphic Artist. 1 d. *Education:* State Coll Fine Arts, Poznan, 1973; Dip w distinction, Printmaking, Painting, Acad Fine Arts, Warsaw, 1978. *Career:* Asst, 1978-88, Adj, 1988, Prof, Graphic Studio, 1991, Acad Fine Arts, Warsaw; Individual exhibs: Graphic art, Sciana Wschodnia Gall, 1979; Prints, drawings, Taide huoneeseen, Naantali, Finland, 1984; Graphic art, Pokaz Gall, Warsaw, painting, graphic art, BWA, Lodz, painting, Studio Gall, Warsaw, graphic art, Harjukatu 40 Gall, Hame Gall, Lahti, Finland, 1986; Graphic art, Torun, 1987; Graphic art, paintings, Galleri God Konst, Linkoping, Sweden, 1989; Graphic art, pastels, Vokki Gall, Helsinki, Loviisa Mus, Finland, pastels, drawings, graphic art, Tess Gall, Pruszkow, Poland, 1990; Pastels, drawings, graphic art, Pokaz Gall, Warsaw, 1991; Participant, num exhibs incl: Berlin, 1977; Poland, Finland, 1979; Egypt, Algeria, Turkey, Bulgaria, Venezuela, 1980; Venezuela, Ecuador, Finland, 1981; Colombia, Finland, Sweden, France, Cuba, 1982; France, Panama, Finland, 1983; Berlin, Denmark, Norway, Poland, 1984; USA, 1985; USA, Poland, Germany, 1986; Canada, Poland, 1987; Canada, Poland, Finland, FRG, 1988; Sweden, 1989; Finland, 1990. *Honours:* Award, Best Graphic Art of May, Warsaw, 1979; Hon Mention, IIIrd Int Polish-Finnish Marine Graphic Art Competition, 1979; Prize, IVth Polish-Finnish Marine Graphic Art Competition, 1981; Artistic Scholarship, Polish Min Culture and Art, 1983; Rsch Grant, Cultural Bd, City of Lahti, 1986; Rsch Grant, Harmonia Graphic Workshop, Jyvaskyla, Finland, 1988; Award, Best Graphic Art, Inne, Warsaw, 1988; Hon Mention, Zrodlo Graphic Art Competition, 1988; Rsch Grant, Krogen Amerika Graphic Ctr, Linkoping, 1989; Individual invitation, 6th Graphica Creativa Triennal, Finland, 1990. *Hobbies:* Life; Music. *Address:* ul RzemiesInicza 1, 05-806 Komorow, Poland.

X

XHUVELI Lufter, b. 4 Jan 1941, Vlora, Albania. Professor of Plant Breeding. m. Mejtime Jaupi, 8 Aug 1965, 1 s, 2 d. *Education:* Fac Agronomy, 1962; Postgrad study, Pol Econ, 1974; Cand Scis, 1980; Docent, 1982; DSc, 1984, Prof, 1986. *Appointments:* Agronomist-in-Chief, Kutalli Reg, 1962-69; Chief, Agricl Sect, Berati Dist, 1969-72; Dpty Mayor, Exec Comm, Berati Dist, 1972-75; Rector, Higher Inst Agric, Tirana, 1975-88; Prof, Hd Plant Breeding and Biological Dept, Agricl Univ, Tirana, 1988-91. *Creative works:* Prin co-developer, 2 new Albanian wheat cultivars; Books: Wheat lodging and its control; Plant Breeding; Experimentation in Agriculture; Seed Production; Phytotechny (prin co-author); An Albanian Encyclopedic Dictionary (prin co-author); Over 40 sci papers. *Memberships:* Presidential Coun Albania, 1991; Albanian Parliament and Sec, Parly Comm For Rels, 1991; Cabinet, Min Agric, 1969-91; Cabinet, Min Educ, 1978-88; Nat Comm Sci and Technology, 1981-91; Chmn, Nat Comm Agronomy for Conclusions on Dissertation Theses, 1986-91; Vice-Chmn, Albanian Comm Balkan Coop and Understanding, 1987- 91. *Honours:* Award, Disting Servs in Sci and Educ Activities, 1963, 1967, 1969, 1982. *Hobbies:* Poetry; Sport esp swimming; Nature. *Address:* Agricultural University of Tirana, Albania.

XI Chuan, (Liu Jun) b. 16 Mar 1963, Xuzhou, Jiangsu Province, China. Poet; Translator. m. Xu zhao, 17 Nov 1988. *Education:* The Beijing Foreign Languages Sch, 1974-81; The English Dept, Beijing Univ, 1981-85. *Appointments:* Correspondent, Shanxi Branch of the Xinhua News Agency, 1985-86; Editorial Asst, The Intl Section of Xinhua News Agency, 1986; Editor, The Global Mag, 1986-92. *Publications:* The Chinese Rose; More Than 200 Poems. *Honours:* The Special Prize Wusi; October Prize for Literature. *Hobbies:* Chinese Traditional Painting; Calligraphy; Travel. *Address:* The Global Magazine, Xinhua News Agency, Beijing 100803, China.

XI Jingzhi, b. 24 Sept 1935, Jiangsu Province, China. Professor; Art Historian. m. Shao Dazhen, 1 d. *Education:* Dept Lit, Shanghai Univ, 1952-53; BA, Art Hist Dept, Leningrad Inst Fine Arts, USSR, 1960. *Appointments:* Lectr, Prof, 1960-91, Hd, Hist Art and Design Dept, 1983-91, Ctrl Acad Art and Design, Beijing. *Publications:* On Segantini, G, 1984; On Gogh, Vincent van, 1989; History of Russian Art, 1990. *Membership:* Standing Comm, Chinese Artists Assn. *Hobby:* Chinese water-ink painting. *Address:* Dept of History and Theory, Central Academy of Art and Design, Beijing 100020, China.

XIA Hengxi, b. 5 Feb 1937, Hunan Province, China. Professor; University President. m. 9 Mar 1963, 1 s, 1 d. *Education:* Dept Hydraulic Engrng, Hydraulic and Elec Inst, Wuhan, Hebei, 1955-60. *Appointments include:* Dean, Dept Civil Engrng, 1983-87, BP, 1987-88, Pres, 1988-, Agricl Univ Hebei, Baoding. *Publications include:* Analysis of Diagonal Square Pyramid Space Grids by Difference Method, 1980; Analysis of Space Trusses of Orthogonal Grid System by Sandwich Plate Analogy Method, 1982; Two Designs of Space Truss and Sliding Technique for Their Erection, 1984; The Solutions and Their Comparisons of the Sandwich Plate Analogy Method in Two Kinds of Simply Supported Two-Way Orthogonal- Diagonal Lattice Grids, 1986; Research on Geometrical Stability of Square Pyramid-like Grids and Its Bearing Behaviour, 1986. *Memberships:* Dir, China Civil Engrng Soc; Chmn, Baoding Civil and Archtl Engrng Soc; Dpty Ed-in- Chief, China Structural Engineering Journal. *Address:* Agricultural University of Hebei, Baoding, Hebei 071001, China.

XIA Zhen-tao, b. 1 Apr 1931, Hunan, China. Professor of Philosophy. m. Sha Shi-liang, 6 Feb 1959, 2 s, 1 d. *Education:* Philos, Wuhan Univ, 1950-52; Philos Sem,

Beijing Univ, 1952-54. *Appointments:* Philos Tchr, Beijing Geology Coll, 1954-75; Assoc Rsch Fellow, 1979-82, Dir, Grad School, 1981-85, Rsch Fellow, 1983-85, currently Grad School Prof, Social Sci Acad China. *Publications include:* On Xun Zi's Philosophical Thought, 1979; Philosophy About Ends, 1982; An Introduction to Epistemology, 1986; On Cognitive System, 1987; On Genesis of Cognition, 1991. *Memberships:* Gen Sec, Dialectical Materialism Inst China; Pres, Epistemology Inst, Dialectical Materialism Inst. *Honours:* Expert w Prominent Contbrs, Govt China, 1988; Excellent Achievement in Sci Rsch for An Introduction to Epistemology, Auth of People's Univ, 1988. *Hobbies:* Appreciating Chinese classical literature and classical music; Visiting places famous for scenery or historic relics. *Address:* No 44, Building 3, Jing-yun, People's University, Beijing, China. 152.

XIANG Zhilin, b. 24 June 1931, Suzhou, Jiangsu Province, China. Professor of Physics. m. Yu Yanqing, 8 Mar 1960, 1 s. *Education:* Dip, Tsinghua Univ, Beijing, 1952; Moscow Inst Nuclear Energy, USSR, 1955-56. *Appointments:* Rsch: Neutron Detection and Neutron Phys, 1957-74; Plasma Phys and Nuclear Fusion, 1974- ; Currently Prof, Phys, Univ Sci and Technology China, Hefei. *Publications:* On counters, 1957; Diagnostic Techniques for High Temperature Plasma, 1982. *Memberships:* Chmn, Nuclear Sci Acad Comm China; Nuclear Fusion Experts Grp, State Coun; VP, Acad Comm, Univ Sci and Technology China; Standing Mbr, Coun, Plasma Soc China. *Honours:* 3rd Award, Natural Sci, China, 1957; 2nd Award, Sci Achievement, China, 1980; 2nd Award, 1984, 3rd Prize, Sci and Technology Progress, 1990, Academia Sinica. *Hobbies include:* Tennis; Table tennis. *Address:* Department of Modern Physics, University of Science and Technology of China, Hefei, Anhui 230026, China.

XIAO Dangrong, b. 10 Oct 1942, China. Prof. m. 7 Sept 1967, 1 s, 1 d. *Education:* Zhongnon Univ, 1966; Bach of Engrng. *Appointments:* 709 Inst of Sixth Ministry of Machine Building ind, 1966-80; Automation Inst of Hubei Province, Dir, 1980-84; Wuhan Inst of Tech, Dir, 1984-91; Hubei Univ, Dir, 1991-92. *Publications:* 7 Books; 40 Compositions. *Memberships:* Wuhan Soc of Systems Engrng; ISDSRC; Automation Assn; Wuhan Assn for Sci & Tech. *Honours:* Sci & Tech Prize, China, Hubei, Wuhan. *Hobbies:* Reading; Hunting; Chinese Chess, Driving. *Address:* Dept of Economy Management, Hubei Univ, Wuhan 430062, China.

XIAO Dongrong, b. 10 Oct 1942, Hunan, China. Educator; University Professor. m. 7 Oct 1967, 1 s, 1 d. *Education:* Grad, maj Automatic Control, Zhong Nan Univ Technology, 1966. *Appointments:* Engr, Grp Hd, Chinese Acad Scis, 1966-80; Grp Hd, Automation Inst, Hubei Province, 1980-84; Assoc Prof, Grp Hd, Wuhan Inst Technology, 1984-91; Prof, Hubei Univ, 1991-. *Publications:* 7 books; 36 papers. *Memberships:* Vice-Chmn, Sec- Gen, Wuhan Assn Systems Engrng; Dir, China Assn Systems Dynamics; Chmn, Sec- Gen, Int Organising Comm, ISDSRC. *Honours:* Advsr, Planning Comm, Hubei Province Co Class; 5 Prizes for Sci Rsch Results; 3 Prizes for Social Move About. *Address:* Department of Economy Management, Hubei University, Wuhan 430062, China.

XIAO Qian, b. 14 July 1924, Shashi, Hubei, China. Professor of Philosophy. 1 s, 3 d. *Education:* Grad: SW Associated Univ, 1944; No Univ, 1946. *Appointments:* Student Ldr; Sec, Inst Philos Rsch, Hubei Univ, 1948; Lectr, 1950, Assoc Prof, 1956, Prof, 1979-, People's Univ China, Beijing. *Publications include:* Dialectical and Historical Materialism, 1981; Principle of Dialectical Materialism, 1981; Principle of Historical Materialism, 1983. *Memberships:* Chmn, Bd Dialectical Materialism Study China; Cons, Chinese Histl Materialism Soc; Dir, Self-Study Exam Comm on Philos, Educl Comm China; Hd, Deliberation Grp Philos, Acad Degrees Comm, State Coun. *Honours:* 1st Prize, Nat Textbook Award, 1985; Nat Prize Award, maj articles, 1985-. *Hobbies:*

Swimming; Playing table tennis. *Address:* Department of Philosophy, People's University of China, Beijing 100872, China.

XIE Qi-wen, b. 1 June 1929, Nanjing, China. Professor of Neuroendocrinology. m. Jun-ying Yang, 25 Dec 1954, 1 s, 1 d. *Education:* BA, Nat Tsin-Hwa Univ, 1949; MD, China Med Univ, 1953; Adv Trainee, MI State Univ, USA, 1981. *Appointments:* Tchng Asst, Rsch Asst, Instr, Lectr, Rsch Assoc, Assoc Prof, Prof, China Med Univ, Shenyang, 1954-92; Prof, Inst Oriental Med, HI, USA, 1989; Courtesy Prof, Dept VCAPP, WA State Univ, 1990. *Publications:* Books: Patho-physiology, 1984; Test questions and answers in physiology, 1987; Methods in Medical Research, 1988; Conference English, 1989; Neuroendocrinology, 1990; Over 100 sci papers, 1963-92. *Memberships:* Sci Coun, Chinese Acad Med Sci; Endocrinology Comm, Chinese Physiological Soc; Bd, Chinese Patho-Physiology Soc, Liaoning. *Honours:* Dip Hon, Polish Acupuncture Soc, Warsaw, 1987; 2nd Prize, National Sci and Technology Progress Award, Min Hlth, 1988; Outstanding Scientist, Liaoning, 1988; Award, 5th World Congress Chinese Med, Berkeley, USA, 1989. *Hobbies:* Stamp collecting; Touring; Reading. *Address:* Neuroendocrine Research Laboratory, China Medical University, Shenyang 110001, China.

XU Bing-Zheng, b. 15 Dec 1925, Fujian, China. Prof; Reseacher. m. Yuang Yi Guo, 22 Feb 1953, 1 s, 1 d. *Education:* BE, 1946; MSc, 1950. *Appointments:* Lectr, Lingnan Univ, 1950; Asst Prof, South Chin Inst of Tech, 1956; Prof, Vice Pres, 1978-84. *Publications:* Signal Analysis & Correlation Tech; More Than 80 Papers. *Membership:* IEEE. *Honours:* Kai Kee Scholarship; Natl Achievement on Sci & Tech Award; USEFC Scholarship. *Hobby:* Play Bridge. *Address:* Research Inst of Radio Eng'g & Automation, South China Univ of Tech, Quangzhou 510641, China.

XU Dongqin, b. 16 Aug 1936, China. Professor of Pathology; Research Room Director. m. Huanzhang Lu, 1 July 1960, 2 s. *Education:* Bach,s degree, Hebei Med Coll, 1959. *Appointments:* Prof Asst, 1959-63, Rsch Fellow Asst, 1963-69, Tianjin Coll Traditional Chinese Med; Tchr, Da Xingan Ling Hlth School, 1970-72; Rsch Fellow Asst, Tianjin Rsch Inst Combining Traditional Chinese Med w Wn Med to Treat Acute Abdominal Disease, 1972-80; Lectr, 1980-83, Vice-Prof, 1983-88, Prof, Dir, 1988-, Rsch Room Pathology, Tianjin Coll Traditional Chinese Med. *Publications:* Laser Treatment Manual (maj author), 1990; Acupuncture and Moxibustion Pathology (chief ed), 1990. *Membership:* Pathology Assn, Med Sci Assn China. *Honours:* 3rd Award, Sci and Technology Advances, for Laser Acupuncture in Treatment of Abdominal Inflammatory Mass, Tianjin, 1989; Clinical and Experimental Study on Atrophic Gastritis approved by State Min Hlth, 1991. *Hobby:* Outings. *Address:* Yu Quan Road No 22, Anshan Xi Dao, Nankai District, Tianjin, China.

XU Gui-Rong, b. 21 Jan 1935, Zhejiang, China. Professor of Geology. m. 10 Jan 1962, 1 s, 1 d. *Education:* Beijing Coll Geology, 1953-57; Sr Postdoct, Smithsonian Inst, USA, 1985-87. *Appointments:* Beijing Coll Geol, 1957-76; Wuhan Coll Geol, 1976-87; China Univ Geoscis, Yujiashan, 1987-. *Publications:* Triassic Brachiopoda of Central Gueizhou (Kueichow) Province, China, 1966; Triassic of the South Qilian Mountains, 1983; Textbook of Palaeontology, 1987. *Memberships:* Geological Assn China; Chief Mbr, Palaeontological Assn China. *Hobbies:* Computers; Reading; Table tennis. *Address:* Dept of Geology, China University of Geosciences, Yujiashan, Wuhan 430074, China.

XU Kang Xing, b. 9 Feb 1941, Jiangsu Province, China. Deputy Chief Engineer. m. Lang An Jun, 7 Jan 1967, 1 s. *Education:* Electron Phys Div, Radio-Electronic Dept, Beijing Univ, 1958-64; Postgrad, Electron Phys Div, Radio Engrng Dept, Qinghua Univ, 1964-68. *Appointments:* Beijing Power Switch Factory, 1970-73; Engr, Beijing TV Factory, 1973-81; Adv Researcher,

Japan JVC Co, 1981-83; Dpty Chief Engr, Beijing Peony Electronic Grp Corp, 1983-. *Publications:* Digital device for measuring moving speed of electric movable contactors, 1974; Observation of amplitude- frequency characteristics and measurement of selectivity of TV set, 1982; Experiment of low bit rate DPCM and picture quality assessment, 1983; A designing of pre-amplified for HI-FI stereo sound, 1984; Low bit rate prediction in field DPCM and picture quality assessment, 1987; IC Color TV receiver-the Principle, Adjustment and New Technique, 1988; The Video Wall, 1989. *Memberships:* Dpty Hd, Broadcast and TV Reception Speciality Standardisation Comm, Min Machinery and Electronics Ind; Broadcast and TV Speciality Comm, Electronics Comm China Beijing Chapt; Sci and Technology Comm, Min Machinery amd Electronics Ind. *Honours:* 2nd Rank Prize, Sci and Technology Advancement, 1988, 1st Rank Prize, Excellent Scientists of Indl Enterprise, 1989, Prize, Scientists of Outstanding Contbn, 1991, May 1st Labour Medal, 1991, Beijing Municipality; 1st Rank Prize, Sci and Technology Advancement, Min Machinery and Electronics Ind, 1990. *Hobbies:* Reading; Chinese Taiji boxing. *Address:* 2 Huayuan Rd, Haidian District, Beijing, China.

XU Liejiong, b. 28 Oct 1937, Shanghai, China. Professor of Linguistics. m. Wang Yiyi, 13 Oct 1967, 2 d. *Education:* Beijing Univ, 1955-60; Shanghai For Langs Inst, 1962-64. *Appointments:* Shanghai For Langs Inst, 1964-72; Dept For Langs and Lits, Fudan Univ, Shanghai, 1972-. *Publications:* Theory of Generative Grammar, 1988; Semantics, 1990; Contemporary Linguistics Abroad, 1991. *Memberships:* Linguistic Soc Am; Generative Linguists of the Old World, Netherlands; Linguistic Assn Can and US, Can; Bd Dirs, Shanghai Yuwen Xuehui (Shanghai Linguistic Assn); Shanghai Waiwen Xuehui (Shanghai For Lang and Lit Assn). *Honours:* Shanghai Philosophy and Social Scis Award for 1979-85, 1986. *Hobby:* Chinese culture in general. *Address:* Department of Foreign Languages and Literatures, Fudan University, 220 Han Dan Lu, Shanghai 200433, China. 190.

XU Tongqi, b. 5 Mar 1935, Jiangsu, China. Astronomer. m. Lin Yimei, 5 Feb 1963, 1 s, 2 d. *Education:* Grad, Dept Astron, Nanjing Univ, 1957. *Appointments:* Joined, 1958, Vice-Chief, Fundamental Astrometry, 1979-82, Chief, Astronomical Catalogue Rsch Grp, 1983-, Shanghai Observatory. *Publications:* The catalogue of photoelectric astrolabe of Shanghai Observatory, 1978; Astronomy pt, Chinese Lexicographical Works, 1987 and 1989 eds; The Zo-Se catalogue of radiostars, 1989. *Memberships:* Int Astronomical Union; Chinese Astronomical Soc. *Honours:* Social Sci Prize, Chinese Lexicographical Work, Shanghai, 1979. *Hobby:* Reading. *Address:* Shanghai Observatory, NanDan Road 80, 200030 Shanghai, China.

XU Wen-Tong, b. 6 May 1930, Jiangshu Province, China. Professor and First Vice-President of Finance Institute. m. 8 May 1956, 2 s. *Education:* Grad Dept, Bank Dept, People's Univ China, 1953. *Appointments:* Army Serv, 1944-50; Dir, Fin Dept, 1953-71, Prof, 1980-87, People's Univ China, 1953-71; Prof, Qin Hua Univ, 1971-80; Prof, 1st VP, China Inst Fin, 1987-. *Publications:* Capital Constructions Economics, 1985; Construction Economics, 1988; Urban Construction Economics, 1989; Finance Encyclopaedia, 1990; Investment Encyclopaedia, 1990. *Memberships:* China People's Bank, Acad Comm Mbr, Assoc Prof Fina Rsch Inst; VP, China Constrn Inst; Chmn, Bd, Yin Int Trust and Investment Corp. *Honours:* Best Award, China Investment Theory Study Evaluation, 1989; Best Award, Jiang Shu Province Investment Instn. *Hobbies:* Cooking; Sports; Photography. *Address:* China Institute of Finance, No 10 Hui Xing East Street, Chao Yang, Beijing 100029, China.

XU Xiao-bai, b. 28 May 1927, Jiangsu, Suzhou. Research prof; Advisor. m. Hu Ke Yuan, 11 Aug 1956, 1 d. *Education:* BS, Chiao Tung Univ, 1948. *Appointments:* Res Asst, Inst Chem Acad Sinica, 1948-

49; Res Asst Inst Phys Chem, acad Sinica, 1949-51; Res Assoc, Inst Phys Chem Acad Sinica, 1951-55; Res Assoc, Inst Environ Chem Acad Sinica, 1975-78; Res Assoc, Prof Inst Environ Chem Acad Sinica, 1978-82; Research Prof, Inst Environ Chem, 1982-; Advisor, PhD Students, 1986. *Memberships:* Natl Committee of Environ; RCEES; Chinese Chem Soc; CCS; Muta & Carcinogenensis of CS of Genetics; Am Soc of MS. *Honours:* Honors from Acad Sinica; Awards of Progress S & T Acad Sinica; 4th Natl Natural Sci Prize. *Hobbies:* Music; Volley Ball. *Address:* Research Center for Eco Environmental Sci, PO Box 2871, Beijing 100085, China. 138, 152.

XU Xiaofeng, b. 27 Feb 1932, Hunan Province, China. Professor of Geology. m. Wang Chunrong, 1 Oct 1959, 3 d. *Education:* BSc, Dept Geology, Qinghua Univ, 1952. *Appointments:* Engr, Geological Team, N China Geological Exploration Co, 1952-77; Gen Engr, Prof, Geological Inst N China Geological Exploration Bur, Tianjin, 1988-91. *Publication:* Some petrological characteristics of a certain alkali-ultrabasic intrusion in North China and discussion of the genesis of related iron-phosphorus deposits. *Membership:* Dir, Hebei Geological Assn. *Honours:* Adv Sci Worker, Min Metall Ind and Hebei Province, 1977; 2nd Prize, Sci Result, Hebein Province, 1978. *Hobbies:* Watching TV; Playing chess. *Address:* North China Non-Ferrous Exploration Bureau, Guangning Roa, Tianjin, China.

XU YONG b. 25 Jan 1954, Shanghai, China. Advertising Agency Manager. m. Pan Wei, 3 Feb 1984, 1 s. *Education:* Grad, Lo Yang Engrng Inst, 1978; Grad, Tchrs Coll, Beijing, 1986. *Appointments:* Beijing Needle Roller Bearing Factory, 1981-84; Photographer, Beijing Advt Co, 1984- 88; Mgr, Beijing Xun Tong Advt Agcy, 1988-. *Creative works include:* 2 photo albums: Beijing Hutongs: 101 Photos; Shanghai Long Tang; Over 100 photographs in exhibs incl: A Kite like the Dragon in the Sky Flying Down. *Memberships:* Chinese Photographers Assn; Beijing Photographers Assn; Vice-Chmn, Beijing Wide Angle Lens Photographical Soc. *Honours include:* Developing Prize; Prize for Excellence; Nikon Excellence Prize. *Hobbies:* Photography; Travel; Mechanical designing. *Address:* The Wide Angle Lens Phototographical Society, 119 Chong Wenmen Wai Street, Beijing, China.

XUE (SHIEH) Paul She-pu, b. 26 Sept 1917, Guangdong, China. Research Professor of Human Embryology and Cell Biology. m. Chou Siu-quen, 22 Aug 1943, 1 s, 3 d. *Education:* BSc, 1943, MSc, 1947, Nat Ctrl Univ; PhD, Washington Univ, St Louis, MO, USA, 1951. *Appointments:* Asst, Lectr, 1943-47, Assoc Prof, 1951-64, Dalian Med Coll and Chinese Acad Med Sci; Prof, Chmn, Dept Cell Biology and Embryology, Chinese Acad Med Sci, Beijing, 1964-. *Publications:* Over 120 original papers on cell differentiation and regulation of tumour cell malignancy; Co-author, 6 books; Chief Ed: Human Embryology sect, Chinese Med Encyclopaedia; Experimental study on male contraceptive. *Memberships include:* Pres, Chinese Soc Anatomical Sci; Bd Mbr, Int Fedn Assns Anatomists; Bd Mbr, Am Soc Expmtl Biology and Med, Beijing Br; Bd Mbr, Chinese Soc Cell Biology; Bd Mbr, Chinese Med Assn; VP, Chinese Soc Reproductive Biology. *Honours:* Nat Prize, Advancement of Sci and Technology, Min Pub Hlth China, for: Long term safety experiments on male contraceptive Gossypol, 1985, its role and mechanism of antispermatogenic action, pharmacokinetic change and cytotoxic effect on testicular mitochondria, 1986, discovery of Erythroid Differentiation Factor (EDF) and its effect on the regulation of malignancy and gene expression in myeloma and tumour cells, 1988; Nobel Prize, Med and Physiology, 1986; Hon Medal, Cert, Disting Educl Serv, Nat Educ Comm, 1990. *Hobbies:* Gardening; Fishing; Painting; Calligraphy. *Address:* Department of Cell Biology, Institute of Basic Medical Sciences, Chinese Academy of Medican Sciences and Peking Union Medical College, 5 Dong Dan San Tiao, Beijing 100005, China. 139. 152.

XUE Hanwei, b. 2 Feb 1935, Jiangsu, China. Professor of Politics. m. Xue Lei, 16 July 1960, 2 d. *Education:* Econs Dept, People's Univ, China, 1956-60. *Appointments:* Tchr, Silk Voc School, Jiangsu, 1952-56; Assoc Prof, Econs Dept, 1960-64, Researcher, Marxism and Leninism Inst, 1964- 71, People's Univ China; Researcher, Marxism and Leninism Inst, Beijing Univ, 1971-. *Publications:* History of China's modern economic theory, 1965; Persisting in and developing Marxism in new historical conditions, 1983; Study of revolution and continuous revolution, 1984; On socialism modernisation and communism, 1984; On Lenin's theory of socialism construction, 1986; Theory and practice of dividing socialiam society period, 1987; Great exploration, 1987; Marxism development in China since 1978, 1988; On theory of Marxism, 1988; On socialist reform, 1988; Elementary period of socialism and CC Party's policy, 1988. *Memberships:* Coun Mbr, China Yugoslavia Econ Study Assn; Dir, China Marxism Study Assn; Coun Mbr, China Pol System Reform Inst. *Honours:* 1st Prize, Sci Rsch Achievement, Beijing Univ, 1986, 1988; 2nd Prize, Beijing Philos and Social Sci Rsch Achievements, 1987; 2nd Prize, Nat Popular Pol Theory Books, 1988; Prize, Nat Outstanding Univ Tchng Materials, 1988. *Hobbies:* Fishing; Chinese chess. *Address:* Institute of Marxism and Leninism Research, Beijing University, Beijing 100871, China.

Y

YAGHI Husam, b. 1 Jan 1961, Amman, Jordan. Electrical Engineering Professor. m. 18 Aug 1985, 3 d. *Education:* BSEE, 1984; MS, Computer Sci, 1986; PhD in progress. *Appointments:* Prof, So Univ, Baton Rouge, LA, USA, 1987-; Cons, 1987-. *Publications:* C for Engineers; Computer Viruses. *Memberships:* Nat Soc Profl Engrs; LA Engrng Soc. *Honours:* Nominated Presidential Excellence Award; Inducted into Phi Kappa Nu. *Hobbies:* Photography; Travel; Chess. *Address:* 410 Sinbad Street, Baker, LA 70714, USA. 2.

YAMADA Eisaku, b. 18 Aug 1924, Shibuya-ku, Tokyo, Japan. University Professor; Business Consultant. m. Yuko Nitta, 14 Mar 1954, 3 d. *Education:* BA, Agric, Univ Tokyo, 1949; Colleague Prog, Univ HI, USA, 1982, 1983; Adv Prog, MIT-Sloan, 1988; PhD, Bus Admin, Century Univ, CA (non- traditional), 1990; Fellow, Am Grad School Int Bus (Thunderbird), 1991. *Appointments:* Joined businesses: Mitsui & Co, 1949, 1974-79, Seibu-Saison, 1964, Dentsu-Ad, 1965; Dir, JETRO, Los Angeles and NYC, USA, 1958; Fndr Pres, World Trade Ctrs Assn, NYC, 1969; Sr Economist, UN-ECA, Addis-Ababa, Abyssinia, 1970; Exec VP, CIOS-Japan, 1974; Prof, Int Bus, Chiba Keizai Coll (now Chiba Univ Econs), 1980; Hon Advsr, Pacific Asian Mgmt Inst, Univ HI, 1983; Prof, Shoin Coll, 1985; Prof, Int Bus, Kanto-Gakuen Univ, 1986-. *Publications include:* in Japanese: Activity in Africa by ECOSOC of United Nations, 1979; Foreign Trade (co-author), 1983; International Marketing, 1985, 4th Ed, 1990; Multinational Enterprises, as are in Japan, Asia and the World, 1989; International Marketing-DIAMOND edition, 1990; In Engl: Ethos of Japan with Regard to the Postwar Economy, 1985; The Globalization of Japanese Management (co-author), 1990; Many articles and transls. *Memberships include:* Pres, Japan Int Mgmt Inst (Rsch/Consultation); Past Exec VP, World Trade Ctr Club Japan; Past Bd Mbr, Assn Asian Mgmt Orgs; Acad Int Bus, New Orleans, USA; Past Mbr, Rotary Clubs, Tokyo-Koto, Addis Ababa, Tokyo-East. *Honours:* Special Citations: World Trade Ctr Belgium, 1967; World Trade Ctr, New Orleans, 1968; World Trade Ctrs Assn, NY, 1981. *Hobby:* Promotion movement on energy, eco-system and culture with regard to the North-South problem. *Address:* 1-30-1 Hatagaya, Suite 1003, Shibuya-ku, Tokyo, Japan 151.

YAMADA Satoshi, b. 22 Sept 1934, Toyohashi, Japan. Professor. m. Kimiko Nishimura, 1 s, 1 d. *Education:* BEd, 1958, MEd, 1960, DEd, 1985, Nagoya Univ; Vis Scholar, Educ, Harvard Univ, USA, 1985-86. *Appointments:* Assoc Prof, Minami Nippon Coll, 1967-68; Prof, Okazaki Women's Coll, 1968-74; Assoc prof, 1974-79, Prof, 1979-, Shinshu Univ, Nagano. *Publications:* Early Childhood Education, 1977; Content of Early Childhood Education, 1978; Early Childhood Education through Play, 1979; Logic of Child Rearing, 1980; Early Childhood Education in the United States, 1988. *Memberships:* Japanese Soc Study Educ; Nat Assn Study Educl Method; Japanese Assn Educl Admin; Japanese Soc Curric Studies; Early Childhood Educ Assn Japan; Ctrl Reg Soc Study Educ, Nagoya; Naganoken Early Childhood Educ Coun, Nagano. *Hobby:* Trips. *Address:* Yoshida Jutaku 2-103, Yoshida 2-12-20, Nagano 381, Japan. 34, 52.

YAMAKAWA Masaru, b. 20 Sept 1937, Kyoto, Japan. Professor. m. Keiko Matuo, 8 May 1966, 1 s, 2 d. *Education:* BEng, Kyoto Inst Technology, 1961; Assoc Applied Sci w highest hons, Mgmt Engrng Technology, 1972, Assoc Applied Sci w hons, Fashion Buying and Merchandising, 1973, Fashion Inst Technology, NYC, USA. *Appointments:* Researcher, Toray Inds Inc, Otsu, 1961-79; Assoc Prof, 1979-83, Prof, 1983-, Mukogawa Women's Univ, Nishinomiya; Prof, Mukogawa Women's Grad School, 1985-. *Publications:* Author and ed, many books in field of clothing sci. *Membership:* Rotary Club.

Hobby: Mountain climbing. *Address:* 406 Shinhama-cho, Kusatu-shi, Shiga-ken, 525 Japan.

YAMAMOTO Hiro-Aki, b. 9 July 1947, Shimonoseki, Japan. m. Kyoko Kinoshita, 24 Sept 1976, 1 s, 1 d. *Education:* Fukuoka Univ, 1970; MS, Kyushu Univ, 1972; PhD, 1975. *Appointments:* Postgrad, Researcher Pharmacology, Univ of California, 1975-76; Visiting Sci, 1979-80; Visiting Fellow, NIH, 1976-77; Prof, Fukuyama Univ, 1983-89; Asst Prof, Univ Tsukuba, 1977-83; Assoc Prof, 1989-; Visiting Prof, Univ of Missouri, 1981-82. *Publications:* Essential Hygienic Chemistry & Public Health; Articles. *Memberships:* Fukuyama Pollution Com; The New York Acad of Sci; American Soc for Pharmacology & Experimental Therapeutics; American Assn for the Advancement of Sci; Japanese Soc for Pharmaceutical Sci. *Hobbies:* Fishing; Tennis; Base Ball. *Address:* Matsushiro 1 cho-me 101-2, Tsukuba, 305 Japan. 52, 139.

YAMAMOTO Masaharu, b. 4 Dec 1943, Niigata, Japan. Professor; Epidemiology Educator. m. Yumi Ishiguro, 22 Sept 1968, 2 s. *Education:* MD, School Med, 1968, Dr Med Sci, 1974, Niigata Univ; MPH, Univ TX School Pub Hlth, USA, 1980. *Appointments:* Rsch Fellow, Epidemiology Study Ctr, Boston Univ, MA, US, 1969-72; Rsch Assoc, 1972-73, Lectr, Epidemiology, 1973-78, Assoc Prof, 1978-83, Prof, 1983-, Niigata Univ School Med, Niigata, Japan. *Publications:* Over 150 original articles on epidemiology of congenital anomalies and cancers; Rep papers incl: Causes of Chromosme Anomalies Suggested by Cytogenetic Epidemiology of Induced Abortions, 1982; HLA Antigens in Cancer of the Gall-Bladder, 1990. *Memberships:* Dir, Comm Community Hlth and Clin Servs, Niigata Prefecture, 1986-87; Dir, Comm Community Hlth Protection, Niigata City; Councillor, Japanese Soc Hygiene; Int Epidemiology Assn; Niigata Rotary Club; United Ch of Christ. *Honours:* Rotary Fndn Educl Award, 1978. *Hobbies:* Broadcasting Listening; Golf; Flute. *Address:* 3-3-11 Sakai-Higashi, Niigata City, Japan. 52.

YAMANE Shu, b. 3 Mar 1931, Nishinomiya, Japan. Professor of English Philology. m. Hiroko Higuchi, 20 Oct 1964, 1 s, 1 d. *Education:* BA, 1954, MA, 1956, Kyoto Univ. *Appointments:* Engl Tchr, Tezukayama Gakuin HS, Osaka, 1956-58, Asst, 1958, Lectr, 1963, Assoc Prof, 1965, Prof, Engl Philology, 1973-, Engl Dept, Wakayama Univ. *Publications:* Some Aspects of Chaucer's Grammar, 1987. *Contributions:* articles on histl studies of Engl syntax to profl jrnls. *Address:* 2-7-98 Kikyogaoka, Nabari City 518-04, Japan. 52.

YAMASHITA Ichiro, b. 15 July 1934, Tokyo, Japan. Professor of Oral Surgery. m. Tomoko Yamashita, 9 May 1961, 1 s, 2 d. *Education:* Tokyo Med and Dental Univ, 1954-60; Dr's course, 1960-64, MD, PhD, 1964, Univ Tokyo. *Appointments:* Chief, Stomatology, Nat Cancer Ctr, 1964; Lectr, 1966, Assoc prof, 1970, Chief, Dept Oral Surg, 1975-, currently Prof, Fac Med, Univ Tokyo. *Publications:* The status quo and the Future of Dentistry and Orofacial Surgery in Japan, 1976; Principles of Oral Surgery, 1980; Theory of Oral Surgery Operation, 1980. *Memberships:* Past Pres, Japan Stomatological Soc; Former Trustee, Japan Soc Cancer Therapy; Former Deleg, Japanese Assn Med Sci. *Hobby:* Taido, 8-dan black belt and Trustee General, World Taidoo Federation. *Address:* 5-6-9-806 Koishikawa, Bunkyo-ku, Tokyo, Japan.

YAN Zu-tong, b. 8 Aug 1939, Tong Cheng, Anhui, China. Associate Professor of Theoretical Physics. m. Qi-xian Gu, 1 Jan 1971, 1 s. *Education:* Grad, Dept Phys, Anhui Univ, 1961. *Appointments:* Tchng Asst, Instr, Assoc Prof, Theoretical Phys, Dept Phys, Anhui Normal Univ, Wuhu, 1961-. *Creative works:* Conducts rsch in equation of state at high pressure and 2-dimensional system; Nearly 40 papers in jrnls, China and abroad, incl: On the Equation for the Pressure Dependence of Melting Temperature, 1982; The Thermodynamic Properties of the Two-Dimensional

System, 1982; Pressure Dependence of the Expansion Coefficient and of the Anderson- Gruneisen Parameter under General Conditions, 1989; Equation of State for Polymers, 1935. *Memberships:* China Phys Soc; China Hist Soc of Sci and Technology. *Honours:* 1st Prize for paper The Statistical Thermodynamic Properties of the Two-dimensional System, Anhui Provincial Soc Sci and Technology, 1987; 2 Anhui Provincial Prizes, Advancement of Sci and Technology, for project The Statistical Thermodynamic Theory of a Two-Dimensional System, and project On the Study of Melting Law at High Pressure, 1998. *Hobby:* Reading Chinese classics. *Address:* Department of Physics, Anhui Normal University, Wuhu, Anhui 241000, China.

YANG Boda, b. 20 Dec 1927, Lushun, Liaoning Province, China. Senior Research. m. 4 June 1955, 1 d. *Education:* Specialised, Fine Arts, Shandong Univ, Huazhong Constrn Univ, Beijing Univ, Huabei Univ, 1946- 48. *Appointments include:* Dpty Dir, 1984-90, Sr Researcher, 1991, Palace Musem Beijing; Mbr, State Comm Appraisal of Cultural Relics; Hon Advsr: Xu's Art Gall, Hong Kong; Art Gall, Chinese Univ Hong Kong. *Publications:* A Study of Ancient Buried Stone Images of Buddhe; Chief Ed, The Complete Works of Chinese Fine Arts, vols: Jadeware; Gold, Silver, Glass and Enamel; Sculptures of Yuan, Ming and Qing Dynasties; The Palace Museum; Over 100 papers on Chinese hist of arts, in acad periodicals, China. *Memberships:* Permanent Mbr, China Soc Pacific Reg Hist; Permanent Mbr, China Soc Cultural Relics; Dpty Dir, Permanent Mbr, Coun Chinese Soc Museums; Int Coun Museums; Ancient Glass Comm; Permanent Mbr, Hon Mbr, Coun Beijing Soc Arts and Crafts. *Honours:* Copper Award for The Complete Works of Chinese Fine arts, Int Exhib Best Books, Leipzig, 1988. *Hobbies:* Tourism; Visiting scenic spots and historical sites. *Address:* The Palace Museum. 4 Jingshan Qianjie, Beijing, China.

YANG C C, b. 15 July 1927, Taipei, Taiwan. Biochemist; Educator. m. Yeh-Hsiang Lin, 18 Dec 1951, 2 s, 3 d. *Education:* MA, Nat Taiwan Univ, 1950; DMedSc, Tokyo Jikei Univ, Japan, 1956; Rsch Assoc, Univ WI, USA, 1961-62. *Appointments:* Prof, Biochem, 1958-73, Pres, 1967-73, Dir, Inst Molecular Biology, 1973-85, Prof, Inst Life Scis, 1985-, Kaohsiung Med Coll; Nat Rsch Chair Prof, Nat Sci Coun, 1964-67; Mbr, Academia Sinica, 1990-. *Publications:* Over 120 rsch articles on biochem and immunochem of snake venom products in var int jrnls; Ed Coun, Toxicon int jrnl, 1973-. *Memberships include:* Past Pres, Chinese Biochem Soc; Int Soc Toxinology, Coun Mbr 1988-91; Am Chem Soc; Protein Soc; NY Acad Scis; AAAS; Japanese Biochem Soc; Chinese Biochem Soc. *Honours:* 1 of 10 Outstanding Young Men, Taiwan, 1965; Chuang Shou-Keng Awards, 1974; Premier's Awards, Outstanding Scientists and Technologists, ROC, 1983; Outstanding Rsch Awards, Nat Sci Coun, 1985-91; Javits Neurosci Investigator Awards, NIH, USA, 1987-94. *Hobbies:* Stamp collecting; Reading. *Address:* 61-5F West Compound, National Tsing Hua University, Hsinchu, Taiwan 30042, China. 52.

YANG Chaoqun, b. 16 July 1927, Dabu County, Guangdong, China. Senior Engineer; Senior Research Fellow. m. Chen Jiexiu, 25 Feb 1953, 3 s, 1 d. *Education:* BSc, Dept Geology, Nat Shandong (Sun Yatsen) Univ, 1949. *Appointments:* Techn, Engr, Geological Party, 1949-62; Engr, Sr Rsch Fellow, Prof, Yichang Inst Geology and Mineral Resources, 1962-82; Sr Rsch Fellow, Assoc Chief Engr, Guangdon Bur Geology and Mineral Resources, 1983-89; Adj Prof: Zhongshan Univ, 1986-, China Univ Geoscis, Wuhan, 1987-; Sci Advsr. *Publications include:* The Genetic Types of the Granitoid in South China; Mineralization of the Composite Greisen-Stockwork-Skarn Type W- Bi-Mo Deposit of Shizhuyuan, Dongpo, Southern Hunan, China; Characteristics of the Granitoid and Mineralization in South China and Sanjiang-Southeast Asia Tungsten-Tin Belts; Petrogeno-Minerogenetic Series of the Porphyry Deposits in China; Assessment of the Regional Crustal Stability of Shenzhen City, Guangdong Province,

China. *Memberships:* Int Assn Genesis Ore Deposits; Commn Mineral Deposits, Chmn Special Grp W, Sn, Mo, Bi Deposits, Geological Soc China; Vice-Chmn, Guangdon Soc Geology; Vice-Chmn, Guangdong Soc Mineralogy, Petrology, Geochem; 1st and 2nd Coun, Chinese Soc Mineralogy, Petrology, Geochem, 1978-88. *Honours:* Class A Adv Worker, S-Ctrl China Geological Exploration Co, Min Metall Ind, 1954; Class B Adv Worker, Guangdong Geological Bur, 1957; Recommended, Excellent Qualified Scientist by Yichang Inst Geology and Mineral Resources, Min Geology to Bur Sci and Tech Cadres, State Coun China, 1980; 2nd Award, Sci Rsch Achievement, Min Geology and Mineral Resources, 1985; 2nd Award, Excellent Sci Paper, Guangdon Assn Sci and Technology. *Hobbies:* Science of talent; Reading; Writing; Physical training incl massage, exercising to radio music, walking, cold baths; TV sports programmes. *Address:* Guangdong Bureau of Geology and Mineral Resources, 739 Dongfeng Road East, Guangzhou, Guangdong 510080, China. 139, 151, 152, 162, 190, 191.

YANG Cheng-Zhi, b. 8 Aug 1938, Henan, China. Senior Research Engineer. m. Li Yan-Qin, 8 Jan 1969, 1 s, 1 d. *Education:* BSc, Beijing Univ Petroleum, 1961. *Appointments:* Asst Prof, Beijing Univ Petroleum, 1961-75; Asst Prof, Vice-Dir Dept Petroleum Engrng, Sheng-Li Coll Petroleum, 1976-78; Sr Rsch Engr, Dir Rsch, Rsch Inst Petroleum Exploration and Dev, Beijing, 1979-; Vis Sr Rsch Engr: Institut Francais du petrole, 1979-80, 1985- 87, 1989-90; Vice-Dir, United Lab Colloid and Interface Sci, Academia Sinica and China Nat Petroleum Corp, 1990-. *Creative works:* Petroleum Reservoir Physics Manuscript, 1977; World Fine Petroleum-Chemistry Engineering Handbook, 1981; Over 40 articles in phys-chem sci and petroleum engrng lit incl enhanced oil recovery, surfactant and polymer solution, reservoir phys, petroleum sci; Rsch interests incl colloid and interface chem, phys-chem in oil reservoirs, enhanced oil recovery, petroleum dev. *Memberships:* Soc Petroleum Engrng, USA; Chinas Petroleum Soc. *Honours:* Asst Prof, Da- qing Petroleum Univ. *Hobbies:* Collecting postage stamps; Reading. *Address:* No 1101, 29 Lodging House, 20 Xue Yuan Rd, 100083 Beijing, China. 2, 34, 52.

YANG Naisi, b. 20 Jan 1930, Linxiang, Hunan, China. Professor of Linguistics. m. Zhao Qinghua, 15 Aug 1968, 2 s, 1 d. *Education:* Dept Linguistics, Guangzhou Zhongshan Univ and Chinese Dept, Beijing Univ, 1951-55; Postgrad, Chinese Acad Social Scis, 1956-60. *Appointments:* Researcher on Probation, Asst Researcher, Vice Researcher, Profl Researcher, Inst Linguistics, Chinese Acad Social Scis, Beijing, 1961-. *Publications:* Phonetic System of Zhongyuan Vocal Sounds, 1980; Review of Mongolian Zi Yun, 1987; 50 papers on liguistics, dialect and phonology script Hp'ags-pa. *Memberships:* China Linguistics Assn; Dir, Chinese Phonology Assn; Chinese Nat Ancient Writing Assn. *Honours:* Biography incl in Chinese Modern Linguistician, 1985; Wangli Linguistics Prize for Phonetic System of Zhongyuan, Beijing Univ, 1986; Ed, Chinese Encyclopedia: Language, 1986. *Hobbies:* Literature; Reading. *Address:* Institute of Linguistics, Chinese Academy of Social Sciences, 5 Jian Guomennei Dajie, Beijing 100732, China.

YANG Quan-rang, b. 3 Nov 1934, Jiangsu, China. Professor of Radio Engineering. m. 25 Jan 1952, 1 s, 1 d. *Education:* Nanjing Inst Technology, Nanjing, 1953-57. *Appointments:* Asst, 1957-61, Lectr, 1961-81, Nanjing Inst Technology; Assoc Prof, 1981-87, Chmn, Dept Radio Engrng, 1986-89, Prof, Dept Radio Engrng, 1987-, SE Univ, Nanjing. *Publications:* Electromagnetic field theory for engineers, 1984; Millimeter wave transmission line, 1986; Fineline displacement isolator - the theoretical and experimental investigation, 1989; U-band shield suspended stripline (SSL) Gunn DRO and VCO, 1988; Recurrent direct approach for designing microwave circuits, 1989; Characteristics of asymmetric slow-wave coplanar waveguide for MMICs, 1990; Accurate resonant frequency computation of several kinds of dielectric resonators in rectangular shield, 1990. *Memberships:* Ed Comm, Journal of Microwave, Chinese Inst Electronics. *Honours:* Sci Progressive Award Jiangsu, for Millimeter wave transmission line, 1989, for Monolithic integrated circuits CAD, 1991. *Hobby:* Basketball. *Address:* Department of Radio Engineering, Southeast University, 210018 Nanjing, China.

YANG Stephenson Lok Sang, b. 13 July 1954, Hong Kong. Astronomer. m. Susan Mary Anne Hart, 26 Aug 1989. *Education:* BSc, 1976; MSc, 1980; PhD, 1986; Postdoct Fellow, Univ BC, Can, 1986-87. *Appointments:* Sessional Lectr, Univ BC, Can, 1987-89; System Lectr, 1989-, Sessional Lectr, 1991, Univ Victoria, Victoria, BC; Sessional Lectr, Royal Rds Mil Coll, 1990. *Memberships:* Can Astronomical Soc; Astronomical Soc of Pacific. *Honours:* Co-recip, Muhlmann Prize, Astronomical Soc of Pacific, 1989. *Address:* 2264 Blenheim Street, Vancouver, British Columbia, Canada V6K 4J3. 142.

YANG Xiang-Qun, b. 23 Sept 1939, Lanshan, Hunan, China. Teacher. m. 11 Jan 1969, 2 d. *Education:* Student, 1956-61, Postgrad, 1961-65, Math Dept, Nankai Univ. *Appointments:* Tchr, Jiangxi Normal Univ, Nanchang, 1965-72; Tchr, Shaoyoung No 2 Textile Machinery Factory, Hunan, 1972-74, 1976-78; Rchr, Changsha Railway Inst, Hunan, 1974-76; Prof, 1978-91, Pres, 1984-91, Xiangtan Univ, Hunan; Prof, Changsha Normal Univ Water Resources and Electric Power, Hunan, 1991-; Reviewer, American Mathematical Review. *Publications:* The construction theory of Denumerable Markov processes, 1981, 2nd Ed, 1986, Engl Ed, 1990; The birth-death processs and Markov chains (w Wang Zi-Kun), 1990. *Memberships:* Counc Mbr, Soc Probability and Stats China; Coun Mbr, Math Soc Hunan; Dpty, 7th Nat People's Congress; Vice-Hd, Soc Hunan Higher Educ. *Honours:* Prize, Sci Conf China, 1978, Hunan, 1978; 2nd Prize, Significant Achievement in Sci and Technology, 1979; 2nd Prize, Advances in Sci and Technology, Educ Comm PRC, 1986; 2nd Prize, Advances in Sci and Technology, Educ Comm Hunan, 1986; 2nd Prize, Outstanding Books of Sci and Technology in China, Office of News and Publs, PRC, 1987; Outstanding Contbn Expert, Hunan; Recip, special subsidy, Chinese Govt, 1991. *Hobbies:* Bushwalking; Reading; Films; TV. *Address:* Mathematical Department, Changsha Normal University of Water Resources and Electric Power, 410077 Changsha, China.

YANG Xianglin, b. 27 Nov 1933, Yi Xing, Jiangsu, China. Professor of Electronic Engineering. m. 25 Dec 1962, 2 d. *Education:* BS, Electronics, 1957. *Appointments:* Tchng Asst, 1957060; Hd, Tchng Rsch Grp, Lectr, 1961-68; Coal Miner, 1969; Farmer, 1970-71; Electronic Engr, 1972- 77; Assoc Prof, Dept Hd, 1982-84, Dir, Prof, Doct Advsr, 1985-91, Dept Electronic Engrng, SE Univ, Nanjing; Vis Prof, London, England, 1984-85. *Publications:* Principles of Microwave Electron Tubes, 1980; Principles of Microwave Devices, 1985; Optical Fibre Transmission Systems, 1990; Over 80 sci papers in fields of microwave and optical communications. *Memberships:* China Inst Electronics; China Inst Communications; Optics Soc China; Sr Mbr, IEEE; Sci and Technology Commn, ED Scis, Minist Electronics Ind China; Chmn, 1, 2, 3 Session Ed and Authored Comm Phys and Opto Electronics, Univ China. *Honours:* Cert Merit, Nat Conf Sci, China, 1978; Gold Medal, Chinese Govt, 1979. *Hobbies:* Beijing Opera; Western music. *Address:* Yi Xing City, Jiangsu Province, China.

YANG Xianxiu, b. 18 Jan 1935, Shanghai, China. Tchr; Prof. m. Youbo Pan, 30 July 1960, 2 d. *Education:* BA, The Inst of Foreign Languages, Beijing, 1953-57; MS Ed, Eastern Illinois Univ, 1980-82. *Appointments:* Peking Univ, 1957-61; NPU, Xian, 1962-; Lectr, 1965-80; Assoc Prof, 1981-87; Prof, 1988-. *Publications:* How to Prepare English Proficiency Tests; Asimov's

Biographical Encyclopedia of Sci & Tech; Adult EEL Tchrng, SIETIC Proceedings. *Memberships:* Shaanxi Translators Assn; Xian Translators Assn; China Al Soc. *Honours:* Visual Tchrng Materials 3rd Prize; Audio Visual Tchrng, 2nd Prize; Computer Assisted Foreign Languages Learning. *Hobbies:* Philately; Bridge; Photography; Travel. *Address:* South Building 15-1-4, Northwestern Polytech Univ, Xian Shaanxi, China.

YANG Xiaokai, b. 6 Oct 1948, Jilin, China. Economist; Educator. m. Xiaohuan Wu, 13 Feb 1981, 1 s, 1 d. *Education:* BA, Maths, Hunan Univ, 1979; MA, Econs, Chinese Acad Social Scis, 1981; PhD, Econs, Princeton Univ, USA, 1988. *Appointments:* Rsch Asst, Rsch Inst Quantitative Econs, Chinese Acad Social Scis, 1980-82; Lectr, Math Econs, Dept Econ Mgmt, Wuhan Univ, 1982-83; Econ Cons, Wuhan Washing Machine Corp and Techno-Econ Rsch Ctr, State Coun, 1982-83; Summer Asst, World Bank, 1984; Rsch Asst, 1984- 85, Tchng Asst, 1985, 1987, Dept Econs, Princeton Univ, USA; Rsch Fellow, Econ Growth Ctr, Yale Univ, 1987-88; Lectr, 1988-89, Sr Lectr, 1989-, Dept Econs, Monash Univ, Clayton, Vic, Australia; Vis Lectr, Dept Econs, Univ Hong Kong, 1990-91. *Publications:* Forthcoming: Specialization and Economic Organization (w Yew-Kwang Ng); Captive Spirits (w Susan Chyn); In Chinese: An Inquiry into Economic Cybernetics, 1984; An Introduction to Mathematical Economics, 1985; Economic Application of the Control Theory, 1986; Many papers in jrnls; 3 transls. *Memberships:* Am Econ Assn; Assn China Studies; Bd Dirs, Chinese Young Economists Inc, USA, 1985-87; Bd Dirs, Peking econ Assn, 1985-88. *Honours:* Ford Fellowship, 1983-87; Prize, An Enquiry into Economic Cybernetics, Wuhan Univ, 1985; Princeton Univ Fellowship, 1986-87; Open Soc Fellowship, 1987-88; Rsch Grant: Monash Rsch Funds, 1989; Australian Rsch Coun, 1990. *Hobbies:* Writing; Reading; Tennis; Swimming. *Address:* 26 Bonita Court, North Dandenong, Victoria 3175, Australia. 52.

YANG Yongshan, b. 9 Apr 1938, Harbin, China. Associate Professor. m. Jishan Tang, 6 Feb 1968, 1 s. *Education:* Grad, Central Acad Arts and Design, Beijing, 1962. *Appointments include:* Dean, 1986, currently Assoc Prof, Dept Ceramics, Ctrl Acad Arts and Design, Beijing. *Publications:* Foundation of Ceramic Formation, 1980; Design of Ceramic Design, 1988; China Ceramics, 1988; Chinese Ceramics, 1990; The Modern Chinese Folk Ceramics, 1991. *Memberships:* China Artists Assn; Counc Mbr, China Indl Assn Ceramics; China Soc Arts and Crafts; China Rsch Soc Ancient Ceramics. *Honours:* 1st Prize, All China Creative Design of Ceramics, 1986, 1990; 1st Prize, Jingdezhen Int Refined Ceramics, 1990. *Hobbies:* Literature; Sports. *Address:* Dept of Ceramics, The Central Academy of Arts and Design, No 34 Dongshanhuan Beilu, 100020 Beijing, China.

YANG Zhong Mei, b. 20 Sept 1945, Wujn, Jiangsu Province, China. Writer; Social Activitist. m. 1 Jan 1989, 1 d. *Education:* BA, Shanghai E China Tchrs Univ, 1967; MA, 1985, Doct courses, 1989, Rikkyo Univ, Japan. *Appointments include:* Lectr, Japan-China Coll, Tokyo, 1989; Gen Ed, Democratic China monthly, 1989; Special Writer, Mitsubishi General Research, Japan, 1989; Asst Ed, Chan Chan Press, Japan, 1990. *Publications:* Hu Yaobang. A Chinese Biography, 1988; A Study of the Yun-Yi Conference, 1988; Here is Peking, 1989; Li Peng. A biography, 1991. *Memberships:* Coun Mbr, Fedn for a Dem China, Paris, France; Japanese Prof Rsch Coun Chinese Problems, Tokyo Univ. *Hobbies:* Reading; Travel; Stamp collecting; Opening adventure work in a new field. *Address:* Front of Democratic China, Doshin Dai Apario, Room 205, 1-20-1 Mazushima, Edogawa-ku, Tokyo, Japan. 30.

YANG Zunyi, b. 7 Oct 1908, Guangdong, China. Prof of Palaeontology & Stratigraphy. m. Xu Zeng Hui, 22 Aug 1939, 1 s, 3 d. *Education:* BS, Qinghua Univ, beijing, 1933; PhD, Tale Univ, USA, 1939. *Appointments:* Prof, Sun Yatsan Univ, 1939-42; Dir, Geologic Survey of

Guangdong & Guangxi, 1939-42; Prof, Qinghua Univ, Beijing, 1946-52; Geol Inst, Wuhan Coll of Geol, China, 1952-. *Publications:* The Geology of China; Paleontology of Ngori, Tibet. *Memberships:* Sigma Xi; Geol Soc China; Palaeom Soc of China; Boundary Working Group; Acad Sinica. *Honours:* 1st Prize for Sci Adv from ministry of Geol & Min Research; 2nd Prize; 2nd Prize State Educ Comm China; State Educ Chinas Excell Textbook Prize. *Hobbies:* Bicycling; Photography. *Address:* China Univ of Geosciences, 29 Xueyuanlu, Haidian, Beijing 100083, China.

YANIN Valentin Lavrenteric, b. 6 Feb 1929, Vjatka. Historian; Archeologist. m. Svetlana Demidova, 21 Nov 1951. *Education:* Moscow State Univ, 1946-51. *Appointments:* Moscow State Univ, Faculty of Archeology, Prof, 1963; Hd of the Faculty, 1978. *Creative Works:* Denczno Vesovje Sistemy Drevne Rusi; Novgorodskije Posadnik; Aktovyje Pecati Drevnej Rusi; Ja Poshal Tebe Berestu; Novgorodskije Gramoty na Bereste; Novgorodskaja Feodalnaja Votcina; Novgorodskije Gramotyna Bereste; Novgorodskije Akty; Chronologiceskij Kommentarij. *Memberships:* Acad of Sciences of the USSR. *Honours:* Lemonosor Prize; State Prize of the USSR; Lenin Prize. *Hobbies:* Collection of Gramophone Records. *Address:* MGU Historical Dept, Faculty of Archeology, Leninskije gory, 117234 Moscow, Russia.

YANOV-YANOVSKY Felix Marcovich, b. 28 May 1934, Tachkent. Composer. m. Nataliya Yanov Yanovskaya, 3 Oct 1956, 1 s, 1 d. *Education:* Tashkent State Conservatoire, Violinist, 1957; Composer, 1959. *Appointments:* The State Symphony Orchestra, 1954-64; The String Quartet, Uzbek Radio, 1964-68; Dept of Composition, Tashkent State Conservatoire, 1961-. *Creative Works:* 2 Operas; 4 Symphonies; 8 Concerts; Music to 35 Films; 15 Plays; Music for Uzbek Natl Instruments; Articles for the Problems of Modern Music. *Memberships:* Union of Soviet Composers; Union of Soviet Cinematographists. *Honours:* Honorable Diploma Supreme Soviet of Uzbek SSR; Honorary Title of the Meritorious Arts Worker; Prof; Diploma All Ukrainean Filmfestival. *Hobby:* Chess. *Address:* C-1 47 Apt 42, 700047 Tashkent, Russia.

YANOV-YANOVSKAYA Nataliya Solomonovna, b. 31 May 1934, Sverdlovsk. Musicolog. m. Felix Yanon Yanovsky, 3 Oct 1956, 1 s, 1 d. *Education:* Thje Tashkent State Conservatoire, 1953-58; Bach of Music, 1966; Doc of Music, 1984. *Appointments:* The Foreign Dept, Uzbek Radio, 1958-60; Scientific Inst of Arts, 1960-. *Creative Works:* The Music of Uzbek Cinema; The Uzbek Symphony Music; Ikram Akbarov; The Shostakovichs Traditions in Symphonic Culture of Middle Asia & Kazakhstan; The Typology of Mastering of polyphony by Eastern Monodic Culture. *Membership:* Union of Soviet Composers. *Honours:* Diploma of First Musicologists Comp. *Hobbies:* Reading; Art. *Address:* C-1 47, Apt 42, 700047 Tashkent, Russia.

YAO Huiliang, b. 10 May 1958, Shanghai, China. Profl Artist. m. 12 Dec 1989. *Education:* Sculpture Dept, Fine arts Coll, Shanghai Univ, 1985-87. *Creative Works:* Sculpture, Modern; Oil Paintings; Sculpture, An Unprecedented Era; Statue, Teachers Festival in Shanghai; The Game of Catching Rams in Xingjiang; Lotus & Girl; Apsaras. *Honours:* First Almighty Dragon Compt, Best Works of Art. *Hobbies:* Oil Painting; Sculpture; Seal Cutting; Chinese Painting. *Address:* 60/1536 Xin Za Road, Shanghai 200040, China.

YAO Shuo-Ling, b. 3 Nov 1936, Hebei, Liannan, China. Hd of Cancer Hosp in Tangshan, Prof. m. Yu Ying Hou, 1 Oct 1960, 1 s. *Education:* Hebei Middle Coll, 1955-60; Tianjix Cancer Hosp, 1973; Hebei Cancer Hosp, Thorax, 1975-76; Low Temp Medicine Course, 1982-83. *Appointments:* Tangshan Medical Inst, Affiliated Hosp, Hd of Surgery Tchrng & Research Dept, 1960-89; Surgeon, 1960-65; Surgery Lect, Physician in Charge, 1965-86; Vice Chief Surgeon, Prof, 1986-89;

Pres, Tangshan Tumour Hosp, 1989-91. *Publications:* The Cancer Prevention & Cure; Mini Dictionary of Surgery; Clinical Diseases Syndrome; Experimental Study & clinical Application of Surgery in the Treatment of Primary Liver Cancer; Mechanismal Study of Cryosurgery by Liquid Nitrogen in the Treatment of Primary Liver Cancer. *Memberships:* Chinese Cancer Research Foundation; Anto Cancer of China; Journal, Hebei Medicine; hebei Anticancer & Surgery Council; Sci & Tech Assn, Hebei Province; Chinese Medicine Council; Anti Cancer Assn in Tangshan Branch. *Honours:* The Specialist of Sci & Tech in Hebei Province; Outstanding Specialist of Sci & Tech; Sci & Tech Achievement Award; Progress Top Grade Award. *Hobbies:* English; Literature; Music; Writing. *Address:* Tangshan Cancer Hospital, Shengli Lu Street, Lunan District, Tangshen, China.

YARMOLINSKY Adam, b. 17 Nov 1922, New York, USA. Provost, Vice Pres, Acad Affairs at a State Univ. m. (1) Harriet Leslie Rypins, 1945, div, (2) Jane C Vonnegut, 1984, dec, (3) Sarah Ames Ellis, 1990, 3 s, 1 d. *Education:* AB, Harvard, 1943; LLB, Yle Law Sch, 1948. *Appointments include:* US Supreme Court, Law Clerk, 1950-51; Washington DC, Law Practice, 1951-55; Kennedy Presidential Campaign & Talent Hunt, 1960; The Special Asst, Sec of Defence, 1961-64; Prof, Harvard Law Sch, 1966-72; ralph Waldo Emerson Univ, Prof, Univ of Massachusetts, 1972-79; Counselor, United States Arms Control, 1977-79; Private Law Practice, Counsel, 1985-. *Publications:* Case Studies in Personal Security; Recognition of Excellence; The Military Establishment; Race & Schooling in the City; Paradoxes of Power. *Memberships include:* American Bar Assn; American Law Inst; Natl Inst of Health Organ Study; Human Rights; Bretton Woods Fund. *Address:* Provost, Univ of Maryland Baltimore County, Baltimore, MD 21228, USA. 1, 2, 6, 15, 132.

YAROSHEVSKY Alexey Andreevich, b. 6 Sept 1934, Moscow, USSR. Prof of Geochemistry. m. (1) 26 Apr 1963, div, (2) Ludmila Migdisova, 6 Apr 1985, 2 s. *Education:* Moscow State Univ, 1952-57; Inst of Geochemistry, 1957-60; Candiate of Sci, 1966; Doctor of Sci, 1986; Prof, 1988. *Appointments:* Jnr Scientist, 1960-69; Snr Scientist, 1969-76; Assoc Prof, 1976-88; Prof, 1988-. *Publications:* Essays of Comparative Planetology; Dynamics of Basic Magma Differenticion; Chemical Structure of the Earths Crust; Modern Geochemistry. *Memberships:* Acad of Natural sciences of RSFSR. *Honour:* Prize of the Acad of Sciences, USSR. *Hobbies:* Classic Music; Travel. *Address:* Kirovogradskaye Street, 16 1 56, 113587, Moscow, Russia.

YASUOKA Akio, b. 12 Sept 1927, Kobe, Japan. History Educator. m. Kiyoko Takahashi, 24 Mar 1967, 2 s. *Education:* BA, Hosei Univ, 1953; MA, 1956; PhD, 1971. *Appointments:* Asst Prof, Modern History of Japan, Hosei Univ, 1963-68; Assoc Prof, 1968-71; Prof, 1971-. *Publications:* The Modern History of Japan; The Meiji Restoration & Teritorial Questions; The Modern History of Japan; The Directory & Materials of Japanese History. *Memberships:* The Soc of History of Western Learning in Japan; The Japan Soc of the History of Maritime; The Japan Assn of Intl Relations; The Soc of Ryukyuan studies; The Soc of the Study of Diplomatics in Japan. *Hobby:* Collecting Old Books. *Address:* 1 9 3 Hirayama, Hino, Toyko 191, Japan. 1, 52.

YAU Emily Yee Ming, b. 12 Dec 1940, China. Scholar; Poet; Translator; editor. m. div, 1 adopted daughter. *Education:* BA, South China Normal Univ, 1962; South Chinas Tchrs Coll, 1978; Advanced Studies & Refresher Courses. *Appointments:* Univ Asst, South China Tchrs Coll, 1962-78; Lectr, South China Normal Univ, 1978-88; Snr Lectr, Hong Kong Shue Yan Coll, 1989-90; Editor, Conslt. *Publications include:* Dandelion; Water Lily; Lilac; Translation Works. *Memberships include:* World Acad of arts & Culture; Intl Writers & Artists Assn; Modern chinese Literature & Arts Assn of North

America; San Francisco State Univ Poetry Centre. *Honours:* Intl First Rate Tchr & Materials Developer; Golden Poet Award; Diploma of Distinguished Standing; Honorary Doctorate of Literature; Honorable Mentions in Poetry Contests. *Hobbies:* Reading; Writing English Poetry; Light Music; Art Galleries; Local Art Shows; Concerts; Theatres; Growing Flowers. *Address:* 1231 Pacific Avenue, 3rd Floor, San Fransisco, CA 94109, USA. 3, 138, 152.

YE Gongshao, b. 7 Nov 1908. m. C H Huang, 10 Oct 1935, 2 s, 2 d. *Education:* Nankai Univ; Yanjing Univ; Peking Union Medical Coll, 1930. *Appointments:* Tchr, Dept of Public Health, Peking Union Medical Coll, 1935-41; Physician, Natl Research Inst of Health, 1941-46; Maternal & Child Health Inst, 1941-50; Beijing Medical Coll, Deputy Hd of Dept of Public Health, 1950-84; Inst of Child & Adolescent Health, Beijing Medical Coll, 1982-. *Publications:* About 120 Articles; Books inc. Medical Encyclopedia; Child & Adolescent Health; Sch Health. *Memberships:* Chinese Medical Assn; Chinese Public Health Assn; Jiu San Soc; Chinese Peoples Political Consulative Conference. *Honours:* Award From, Chinese Medical Assn; Ministry of Public Health; Chinese Centre of Childrens Development; First Class Prize, State Physical Culture Commission.

YE Guijun, b. 15 Jan 1935, Cixi County, China. Hydrogeology & Engrng Geology. m. 1964, 2 d. *Education:* Naking Univ, 1953-55; Middle Scouth Coal Geological Bureau, 1956-75; Prof, 1976-91. *Publications:* 6 Papers; The Charactor of Karst Water Impregnated Coal Mines in China & The Study of Combination Between Mine Dewatering & Water Supply. *Memberships:* Karst Geological Soc; IAH; China Natl Committee for IAH; Tech Conslt Committee of Coal Industry. *Honours:* Advance Prize of sci & Tech; Excellent Tech Worker. *Hobbies:* Watching Ball Games; Light Music. *Address:* China Coal Geological Bureau, Zhuozhou, Hebei, China.

YE Qingwu, b. 5 Dec 1936, Nanjing, China. m. Zhang Daoxiu, 4 May 1961, 2 s. *Education:* Peking Univ, 1956; Hefei Normal Coll. *Appointments:* Tchrng Section, Quanjiao Normal Sch, 1958-61; Tchr, Suxian Middle Sch, 1961-84; Suzhou Educ Coll, 1987-91. *Publications:* Reading of Chinese Contemporary Literature; Reading of Modern Literature; Articles. *Memberships:* Anhui Chinese Classic Literature Research Inst; Literature Research Assn; Shanghai High molecule Water Proof Meterial Factory; Gaocheng Ind Cooperation; Huali Packing Bag Factory. *Honours:* Excellent Tchr Prize; Fine Tchr prize; High Class Essays Prize. *Hobbies:* Apreciation of Paintings; Calligraphy; Furniture Design; Dancing; Music. *Address:* Chinese Dept, Suzhou Educational College, Suzhou City, Anhui Province, China 234000.

YEN Douglas Ernest, b. 20 Mar 1924, Wellington, NZ. Visiting Colleague; Emeritus Prof. m. Nancy Wah Lee, 6 Apr 1949, 1 s, 1 d. *Education:* B Agr Sc, Univ of NZ, 1947; M Agr SC, 1948; DSc, Univ of Auckland, 1975. *Appointments:* Plant Breeder, NZ, Dept Sci Ind Research, 1948-52; Officer in Charge, Auckland, 1952-66; Athrochotonist, Bishops Museum, 1966-80; Profl Fellow, ANU, 1980-85; Prof, 1986-89. *Publications:* The Sweet Potato & Oceania; Tikopie, Prehistory & Ecology of a Polynesm Outlie; More Than 90 Papers. *Memberships:* American Aethropological Assn; Soc for Economic Botany; Polynesian Soc. *Honours:* Foreign Number, Natl Acad of Sci; Fellow, Australian Acad of the Humanities; Elsden Best Medal; Distinguished Economic Botonist. *Hobbies:* Reading; Music; Tennis. *Address:* c/o Dept of Anthropology, Univ of Hawaii, Honalulu, HI 96822, USA. 52.

YEUNG Rosie Tse Tse, b. 23 Oct 1930. Prof of Medicine. *Appointments:* Clinical Asst, Asst Lectr, Lectr, Snr Lectr, Reader, 1954-74; Subdeen, Dean, Faculty of Medicine, 1978-85; Pro Vice Chancellor, 1985-88; Snr Pro Vice Chancellor, 1988-; Prof of Medicine, 1974-. *Memberships:* Assn of Physicians of Great Britain &

Ireland; American Diabetes Assn; American Endocrine Soc; Australian Endocrine soc; Hong Kong Coll of Physicians; Soc for the Study of Endocrinology, Metabolism & Reproduction. *Honours:* Justice of Peace; The Officer of the Most Excellent Order of the British Empire; Honorary Fellow. *Address:* Dept of Medicine, Univ of Hong Kong, Queen Mary Hospital, Pokfulam Road, Hong Kong.

YHAP Laetitia, b. 1 May 1941, St Albans, Herts, England. Artist. *Education:* Camberwell Sch of Arts & Crafts, 1958-62; Slade Sch of Fine Art, Univ Coll of London, 1963-65. *Appointments:* Artist in Residence, Chatham House Grammar Sch, Ramsgate, 1981-. *Creative Works:* Painting. *Memberships:* London Group; Hastings Arts; Rivera Gallery Assn. *Honours:* Leverhulme Research Award; John Moores Prize. *Hobbies:* Badminton; Music. *Address:* Fischer Fine Art, 30 King St, St James, Piccadilly, London SW1, England.

YI Yan Honglin, b. 15 June 1927, Guantao County, Hebei Province. Natl One Grade Profl Writier; Poet. m. 1951, 4 s, 1 d. *Education:* Study on my own to become a Writer. *Appointments:* Enlist in the Eighth Route Army, 1942-46; Propaganda Team, Cultural Troupe, 1947-56; Profl Writer, 1957-. *Publications:* 40 poetry Anthologies; Yan Yi Poetry; Yan Yi Lyric Poetry; Childrens Poetry of Yan Yi; A Biography for Swallows; 2 Books n Poetry Acethetics; The Relief of Poetry; Essays on Poetry; 2 Books of Novels & Proses; 6 Scenaries; 2 Books of Plays. *Memberships include:* World Conference of Poets; World Assn of Chinest Poets; Writers Assn of China; Chinese Modern Literature; Film Artists Assn of China. *Honours:* Four Natl Excell Works Awards; None Province Excell Works Awards. *Hobby:* Reading. *Address:* 28-60-601 Bajiao Bei Li of Shijinshan District, Beijing, China.

YIN Hongfu, b. 15 Mar 1935, China. Prof. m. Hu Yong, 21 Apr 1964, 1 s, 1 d. *Education:* BA, Beijing Coll of Geology 1956; MA, 1961; Snr Visiting Scholar, Smithsonian Inst, 1980-82; Brit mus Nat Hist, 1990-91. *Appointments:* Asst, 1961-78; Lectr, 1978-80; Assoc Prof, 1980-86; Prof, China Univ of Geosciences, 1986-; State Sepcialist, 1991-. *Publications:* 61 Papers; 7 Books. *Memberships:* Pal Soc, China; Permian Triassic Working Group; Triassic Subcomm of Interm Comm of Stratigraphy; Acta Paleontologica Sinica. *Honours:* Outstanding Scientist of Wuhan City; 4 Awards of Sci & Tech; 1st Yin Zanxun Award. *Hobbies:* Travel; Reading. *Address:* Palaeontology Laboratory, China University of Geosciences, Wuhan, Hubei Province 430074, China.

YIP Pau-Wah, b. 15 Mar 1937, Canton, China. Electrical Engr. m. 14 May 1966, 1 s, 1 d. *Education:* Bach of Sci, Univ of Sciences & Tech, Wuhan, China, 1954-58. *Appointments:* Plant Engr, Ampex Ferrotc Computers Ltd, 1971-73; Plant Engr, Fisher Radio of Emerson Electic, 1974-75; Plant Supervisor, Cathay Pacific Airways Ltd, 1975-78; Plant Engr, Hong Kong Aircraft Engrng Co, 1979-. *Publications:* 3 Papers in Machinery & Materials Mag. *Memberships:* The Hong Kong Chinese Inst of Engrs; Assn of Energy Engrs; Cogeneration Inst; Demand Side Management Soc; Environmental Engrs & Mgrs Inst. *Honours:* Cert of Commendation, Merit for the Advancement of Energy Engrng. *Hobbies:* Travel; Gardening; Reading. *Address:* 7, 27/F Blk F, Lok Nga CRT, Kowloon, Hong Kong. 52.

YOKOYAMA Eizou, b. 18 June 1929, Kitakyushu, Japan. Prof of Chinese, Chinese Literature. m. Fujie Furukawa, 23 Dec 1956, 1 d. *Education:* BA, Yamaguchi Univ, 1953. *Appointments:* Yamaguchi Univ, 1954; Prof of Chinese, Yamaguchi Univ, 1973; Prof of Chinese, Kyushu Shangyo Univ, 1991-. *Publication:* Papers on Lao She. *Memberships:* Sinological Soc Japan; The Chinese Language Soc Japan. *Address:* 2493-1 Kurokawa, Yamaguchi 753 Japan. 52.

YOKOYAMA Minoru, b. 20 Oct 1943, Kawasaki City, Japan. Prof. Faculty of Law. *Education:* Bach of Law,

1967; Master of Law, 1969; Master of Literature, 1971; Doctor Course, Faculty of Literature, 1974. *Appointments:* Part Time, Lectr, 1974-81; Asst Prof, Faculty of Law, 1981-88; Prof, Faculty of Law, 1988-. *Publication:* Problem of the Physically Handicapped in Japan; The Juvenile Justice System in Japan; Sanctionalization in Japan; Net widening of Juvenile Justice System in Japan. *Memberships:* Research Committee for the Sociology of Deciance & Social Control; Intl Sociological Assn; Japanese Assn of Sociological Criminology. *Hobbies:* Collecting Ukiyio e; Hiking; Travel; Photography. *Address:* 2-6-27 Isago, Kawasaki-ku, Kawasaki, Kanagawa 210, Japan.

YORK Christopher, b. 27 July 1909, London, England. Farmer. m. Pauline Rosemarie Fletcher, 16 Oct 1934, 1 s, 2 d. *Education:* Eton, 1922-28; RMC Sandhurst, 1929-30. *Appointments:* 1st Royal Dragoons, 1930-34, 1939-45. *Memberships:* Royal Agriclt Soc of England; Royal Vetinery Coll, London. *Honours:* Deupty Lieutenant, Yorkshire. *Hobbies:* Writing; Forestry. *Address:* South Park, Long Marston, York, YO5 8LL, England. 1.

YOSHIDA Fumitake, b. 20 Mar 1913, Saitama, Japan. Prof Emeritus. m. Kazuko Yamagishi, 28 Mar 1941, 1 s, 1 d. *Education:* Musashi Coll, 1933; Kyoto Univ, B Eng, 1937; Dr Eng, 1951. *Appointments:* Hitachi Ltd, 1937-45; Kyoto Univ, Asst Prof, 1945-51; Prof, 1951-76; Prof Emeritus, 1976-; Univ Calif, Visiting Prof, 1963; Univ Pennsylvania, Visiting Prof, 1970. *Publications:* 2 Books on Chemical Engrng; 80 Research Papers. *Memberships:* Natl Acad of Engrng; Soc of Chemical Engrs; Japanese Soc of Articifical Internal Organs; American Inst of Chemical Engrs; American Chemical Soc. *Honours:* Elected to Natl Acad of Engrng; Distinguished Service Citation. *Hobbies:* Hiking; Photography. *Address:* 2 Matsugasaki Yobikaeshi Cho, Sakyo Ku, Kyoto 606, Japan. 1.

YOSHIDA Shiro, b. 14 Mar 1951, Toyko, Japan. Aerospace Engr. m. 19 June 1983, 1 d. *Education:* Bach of Engrng, 1974; Master of Mech Engrng, 1981. *Appointments:* Engr, 1974-79; Researcher, 1979- 83; Design Engr, 1983-87; Aerospace Engr, 1987-91. *Publications:* Development of Piezo Electric Actuator for Active Vibration Damping. *Memberships:* Alumni Assn of Massachusettes Inst of Tech. *Honours:* Antarctic Research Activist. *Hobbies:* Horse Back Riding; Dressage. *Address:* 2 2 29 106 Fujigaoka, Fujisawa, Kanagawa, 251 Japan.

YOSHIOKA Masanori, b. 4 Sept 1941, Ehime Ken, Japan. Prof of Setsunan Univ, Faculty of Pharmaceutical Sciences. m. Masae Jurahashi, 4 Apr 1970, 2 d. *Education:* BA, Showa Coll of Pharmaceutical Sci, 1965; Univ of Toyko, 1967; PhD, 1970. *Appointments:* Assoc, Univ of Toyko, 1970-; Lectr, 1977-; Assoc Prof, 1983; Prof, Setsunan Univ, 1983-. *Publications:* Bunseki; Biogenic Amines; Chem Pharm Bull; Progress of HPLC; Supercritical Fluid Chromatography & Micro HPLC. *Memberships:* Pharmaceutical Soc of Japan; Japan Soc of Analyticial Chemistry; Japan Soc of Clinical Chemistry; The Japan Pharmaceutical Assn; Japan Soc of the Promotion of Sci. *Hobbies:* Skiing; Tennis. *Address:* 6-15 Otokoyamyoshii, Yawata City, Kyoto, Japan 614. 52, 139.

YOSHIZAWA Hidenari, b. 17 Feb 1941, Toyko, Japan. Prof. m. 8 Feb 1977, 1 d. *Education:* Bach of Economics, Toyko Univ, 1964; Master of Economics, 1966. *Appointments:* Research Assoc, Toyko Univ, 1968-72; Assoc Prof, Konan Univ, 1972-78; Prof, Kenan Univ, 1978-. *Publications:* Money & Symbol; Marconi Affair. *Honour:* Suntory Acad Award. *Hobby:* Reading. *Address:* 14 18 745 Futami Cho, Nishinomiya, Hyogo, 663 Japan.1.

YOTZOV Christo Georgiev, 17 Feb 1960, Sofia. Musician. m. Maria, 6 Aug 1983, 1 d. *Education:* Music

Sch, 1975-79; Army Service, 1979-81; Acad of Music, Sofia, 1981-84. *Appointments:* Drummer in Sofia Radio Big Band, 1981-88; Arranger & Composer, 1988; Drumms Tchr, pop Jazz Dept, 1990-; Freelance Studio Musician & Composer. *Creative Works:* Over 80 Arrangemen ts for Big Band; 13 Own Compositions. *Membership:* Bulgarian Jazz Soc. *Honours:* 1st Prize Best Soloist in Hoeilaart, Belgium; Main Prize Young European Jazz Artist. *Hobbies:* Photography; Tennis. *Address:* Z Zerkovski Str 88, 1421 Sofia, Bulgaria.

YOU Ke Wei, b. 21 Apr 1933, Hebei Province, China. Prof, Hd, Dept of Computer & Control Engr. m. Qi Yun Wu, 10 Jan 1966, 2 s. *Education:* Diploma of Electrical Engrng, Xian Jiacteng Univ, 1957. *Appointments:* Chengdu Univ of Sci & Tech, 1957-; Dept of Computer & Control Enrng, Prof of Control Theory & Systems; Editorial Bd, Journal of Automation & Instrumentation, 1980-; Dept of Electrical Engrng, State Univ of New York, 1981-83; Dean, Intl Educ Programs, 1984-87; AMSE Center, AMSE Univ, 1988-; Visiting Prof, Univ of Dundee, Scotland, 1988-89; Acad Ranks State Educ Commission of China, 1989. *Publications:* 4 Books; Over 20 Major Original Papers. *Memberships:* Education Committee, China; Assn of Automation; Assn for Electronic Engrng; Intl Assn for Modelling & Simulation in Enterprises. *Honours:* Author of the Best Papers; Advanced Educator. *Hobbies:* Painting; Trad Chinese Regiman. *Address:* Dept of Computer & Control Engineering, Chengdu Univ of Science & Technology, Chengdu 610065, Sichuan Province, China. 139, 152, 156.

YOU Zhendong, b. 28 Sept 1928, Fuzhou, China. Prof of Petrology. m. Caofan Zhou, 15 Aug 1956, 1 s, 1 d. *Education:* Dept of Geology, Peking Univ, 1948-52; Beijing Coll of Geology, 1952-56. *Appointments:* Lectr, Beijing Coll of Geology, 1957; Assoc PRof, Wuhan Coll of Geology, 1978; Prof, China Univ of Geosciences, 1983. *Publications:* Regional Geological Map; A Textbook of Metamorphic Petrology; Metamorphic & Deformational History of Qinling Group. *Memberships:* Inst of Regional Geology & Metallogeny; Deputy General Editor, Journal of China Univ of Geosciences; Mineralogical Mag. *Honour:* Winner of J S Lee Prize on Geosciences. *Hobbies:* Ancient Chinese Literature. *Address:* Dept of Geology, China Univ of Geosciences, Wuhan 430074, China.

YOUARD Richard Geoffrey Atkin, b. 27 Jan 1933, Elmsted, Kent, England. The Investment Referee. m. Felicity Ann Morton, 31 Dec 1960, 1 s, 2 d. *Education:* Bradford Coll, Berks, 1946-51; Magdalen Coll, Oxford, 1953-56; Natl Service, 2nd Lieut 1951-53; Lieut TA, 1954. *Appointments:* Admitted, Solicitor, 1959; Slaughter & May, London, Article Clerk, 1956-59; Asst Solicitor, 1959-68; Partner, 1968-89; Inspector DTI, 1987; Investment Referee, 1989-. *Publications:* Betterworths Banking Downments; Various Works in Legal Aspects of Banking & Intl Finance. *Memberships:* Law Soc; Natl Federation of Consumer Groups; Governing Body, Bradfield Coll; Garrick Club. *Honours:* City of London, Solicitors Company Prize; Honor Snr Research Fellow. *Hobbies:* Vegetable Garden; Electronics; Bookeeping; Map Collecting; Reading. *Address:* 12 Northampton Park, London, N1 2PJ. 1, 53.

YOUNG Daniel Greer, b. 22 Nov 1932, Scotland. Paediatric Surgeon. m. Agnes Gilchrist Donald, 2 Aug 1957, 2 d. *Education:* MB ChB, 1950; DTM & H, 1959; FRCS, 1962; FRCS, 1972. *Appointments:* Reader in Paediatric Surgery, Conslt Paediatric Surgeon; Hd of Dept pf Peadiatric Surgery, TUC Univ, 1969-. *Publications:* Baby Surgery; Paediatric Surgery for Nurses; British Isles Journal of Paediatric Surgery. *Memberships:* British Assn of Paediatric Surgeons; Royal Medicl Clurranigical Soc of Glasgow; Soc for Research into Hydocciphadus & Spina Bifida; Scottish Spina Bifida Assn; BMA; BPA. *Hobbies:* Gardening; Fishing. *Address:* Royal Hosp for Sick Children, Yorkhill, Glasgow, G3 8SJ, Scotland. 139.

YOUNG Donald Allen, b. 11 June 1931, Columbus, Ohio, USA. Author. m. Marjorie Claire Shapiro, 20 Aug 1977, 1 s, 4 d. *Education:* Ohio State Univ, Columbus, 1949-51; Columbia Coll, Chicago, 1952; North central Coll, Illinois, 1956; Coll of DuPage, Glen Ellyn Illinois, 1978. *Appointments:* US Air Force, 1952-56; Mag Editor, 1956-63, 1973-74, 1978-81; Public Relations Mgr, Generl Electric Co, Multigraph Corporation, 1975-76; Pres, Young Byrum Inc, 1982-83. *Publications:* Mag Articles; Rate Yourself as a Manager; Nobody Gets Rich Working for Somebody Else; Rate Yourself Exective Potential; If They Can Do It, You Can Do It. *Memberships:* Oakon community Coll; Better Business Bureau; Soc of South Western Authors. *Honours:* SPOKE Award; Jesse Neal Award; Outstanding Jaycee Award; Silver Anvil Award; Public Relations Soc of America. *Hobbies:* Photography; Travel; Reading; Fishing. *Address:* 4866 North Territory Loop, Tucson, AZ 85715, USA. 9.

YOUNG Earle Ronald, b. 26 June 1947, Frederiction, Canada. Univ Prof; Chmn of Dept of Anaesthesia. m. Jane A Walsh, 26 Sept 1972, 1 s, 1 d. *Education:* BSc, Carleton Univ, 1969; DDS, Univ of Western Ontario, 1976; BScD, Univ of Toronto, 1978; MSC, 1983; FADSA, 1986. *Appointments:* Private Dental Practice, 1976; Private Dentral Anaesthesia Practice, 1978- ; Asst Prof, Dept of Anaethesia, Univ of Toronto, 1987-; Staff Appointment, Dept of Anaesthesia, Wellesley Hosp, 1980-; Hd Dept of Anaesthesia, Faculty of Dentestry, 1990-. *Publications:* Over 60 Publi Scientific Articles. *Memberships:* Ontario Dental assn; Canadian Dental Assn; Medical Staff Assn; Ontario Dental Soc of Anaestheiology; American Dental Soc of Anaesthesiology; Royal Coll of Dental Surgeons of Ontario. *Honours:* Mosby Book Award; Univ of Toronot Graduate Fellowship; Graduating Class; Honorary Class Member; Omicrow Kappa Epsilon Honor; Dr Bruce Hord Master Tchr Award. *Hobbies:* Ice Skating; Baseball; Swimming; Cycling; Guitar. *Address:* Faculty of Dentistry, Dept of Anaesthesia, Univ of Toronto, Toronto, Ontario, Canada M5A 1A6. 142.

YOUNG Graham Christopher McKenzie, b. 20 Dec 1935, Kingston, Jamaica. Solicitor. m. Pamela Frances Bisley, 15 Dec 1962, 1 s, 2 d. *Education:* Culford Sch, 1945-54; Trinity Coll, Cambridge, MA, 1959; LLM, 1960; Solicitor, 1962. *Appointments:* Asst Solicitor, Herbert Smith & Co, London, 1962-63; Asst Solicitor, Townsend Solicitors, Swindon, 1963-64; Partner, 1964-; Snr Partner, 1985-; Part Time, Chmn, Rent Asst Government, Dept of Social Security Tribunals. *Publications:* A Little Law. *Memberships:* Law Soc; N Wilts Legal asst; Swindon Lious Club; Centre Exect Committee NSPCC; Soc Proper Foundation Swindow. *Hobbies:* Old Cars; DIY; Books. *Address:* New Milton, Back Lane, Fairford, Glos GL7 4AG, England.

YOUNG Margaret Labash, b. 17 Aug 1926, Bridgeport, Conn, USA. Publishing, Information Conslt. m. Harold Chester Young, 7 June 1958, 1 s, 1 d. *Education:* Univ of Michigan, 1959; Cornell Univ, BA, 1948; Radcliffe Coll, MA, 1953; Lausanne Univ, 1955. *Appointments:* Harvard Graduate Sch of Business, 1949-52; Willard Day Sch, Troy, NY, 1952-53; Arthur D Little Inc, Cambridge, Mass, 1953-57; Cambridge, Mass, Public Library, 1957- 58; Univ of Michigan, Dearborn Campus, 1959-62; Henry Ford Community Coll Library, 1965-67; Ford Motor Co, Dearborn, 1964-72; Gale Research Com, Detroit, 1964-74; Gale Research Com, Minneapolis, 1978-80; Salzburg, Seminar in American Studies, 1981-83; Gale Research Co, Minneapolis, 1983-88; Publishing, Information Conslt, 1989-. *Publications include:* Tools of the Profession; Directory of Special Libraries And Information Centers; A Master Cumulation. *Honours:* Fannie Simon Award; Laure Crown Award; Fathers Club Prize Essayist; Beta Phi Mu. *Address:* 313 Farmdale Road, Hopkins, MN 55343, USA. 5, 52.

YOUNG Richard Russell, b. 8 June 1952, Ellwood City, PA. USA. Army Chaplain. m. Sandra Thompson, 2 Sept 1972, 2 s. *Education:* BA, Southeastern Coll of the Assemblies of God, 1977; Master of Divinity, Anderson Sch of Theology, 1981. *Appointments:* Battalion Chaplain, 1981-84; Buttalion Chaplain, 1984-87; Bat Cham, 1987-88; Brigade Chap, 1989-91; Brigade Chap, 1990-91. *Publications:* The Unification Church; Appalling or Appearing? *Membership:* Assn of the United states Army. *Honours:* McDonals Scholarship; Student Ministries Scholarship; 2 Army Commendations; Army Achievement; Outstanding Young Men of America. *Hobby:* Reading. *Address:* RD 2 Box 4390, Ellwood City, PA 16117, USA. 46.

YOUNG Tze Kong, b. 1 Oct 1935, Kirin, China. Prof of Physiology. m. Yu Cheng Chi, 22 June 1964, 2 s. *Education:* MD, Natl Defense Medical Cener, Taiwan, 1960; PhD, Cornell Univ, 1973. *Appointments:* Instr, Asst Prof, Assoc Prof, Prof, Chmn, Dept of Physiology, Natl Defense Medical Ctr, 1960-84; Acad Dean, Natl Yang Ming Medical Coll, 1985-90. *Publications:* More Than 54 Sci Papers. *Memberships:* Chinese Physiological Soc; Intl Soc of Nephrology; Soc of Nephrology, ROC; Chinese Medical Assn; Formosan Medical Assn. *Honours:* Silver Research Award; Honored by the Chinese Government. *Hobbies:* Swimming; Cooking; Listening to Classical Music; photography; Travel. *Address:* 65 An Ho Road, section 2, Apt 7C, Taipei 10663, Taiwan, China. 1.

YU Dahai, b. 26 May 1961, Tianjin, China. Exiled Political Activist. *Education:* Beijing Univ, BSc, 1978-82; Univ of Pennsylvania, 1982-83; Princeton Univ, MA, 1983-87. *Appointments:* World Bank, research Asst, 1984-85; Princeton Univ Letr, 1987-88; Dartmouth Coll, Instr, 1988-90; Center for Modern China, Vice Pres, 1990-91; Pres, Chinese Alliance for Democracy, 1991- . *Memberships:* Chinese Young Economists Soc; Beijing Young Economists Soc; American Economic Assn. *Honours:* 3rd Prize China Natl High Sch Math Cont; Princeton Univ Fellowship. *Hobbies:* Gardening; Reading; Chess. *Address:* PO Box 7232, North Bergen, NJ 07047, USA.

YU Dexin, b. 20 Oct 1946, Fujuan, China. Tchrng & Researching prof. m. Du Mouji, 30 Aug 1971, 2 s. *Education:* Wood Sci & Tech, Beijing Forestry Univ, 1964-69. *Appointments:* Asst Engr, Kuongming Wood Processing plant, 1970-76; Asst, Fujian Forestry Coll, 1977-80; Visiting Researcher, Swedish Forest Prod, 1981-83; Assoc Prof, 1984-88; Prof, Central South Forestry Coll, 1989-. *Publications:* More Than 30 Research Reports; Thesis, Intl & Native Sci Journals. *Memberships:* China Forestry Assn; China Ind Design Assn. *Honours:* Best Chr Award; Scientific & Technological Progress Award. *Hobbies:* Gardening; Table Tennis. *Address:* Dept of Forest Products, Central South Forestry Coll, 412006 Zhozhou, Hunan, China.

YU John, b. 1 Dec 1937, Hsin Chu, China. Research Fellow; Prof; Deputy Dir. m. Siu Yu Lo, 10 May 1970, 3 d. *Education:* Natl Taiwan Univ, BSc, 1960; Univ Alberta, MSc, 1967; Univ Manitoba, PhD, 1972. *Appointments:* Natl Chung Hsing Univ, Asst Lectr, 1961-64; Wildlife Biologist, Vancouver, 1967-68; Postdoc Fellow, Univ Manitoba, 1972-73; Research Ivestiagtor, Univ Washington, 1973-79; Snr Fellow, 1979; Research Fellow, Acad Sinica, 1980-; Prof, Natl Taiwan Univ, 1980-. *Publications include:* Hormones & Reproduction; Fish Reproduction and Its Endoctine Control; Over 100 Sci Articles. *Memberships include:* Asia Oceania Soc; Soc Study Reproduction; Taiwan Pif Rsch Inst; Taiwan Livestock Rsch Reviewers Bd. *Honours:* Outstanding Farm Youth Award; Outstanding Research Scientist Award; outstanding Agriclt Research Award. *Hobbies:* Photography; Reading; Travel. *Address:* Endocrinology Laboratory, Institute of Zoology, Academia Sinica, Nankang, Taipei, Taiwan, China. 52.

YU Julie Hung Hsua, b. 22 Nov 1954, Taipei, Taiwan, China. Lectr of Mktng/Educ. m. Holger Gossmann, 5 Feb 1989. *Education:* PhD, 1983; MBA, 1981; MSEE,

1977; BA, 1975. *Appointments:* Wake Forest Univ, 1983- 84; Hofstra Univ, 1984-86; Univ of Hawaii, Manoa, 1986-88; The Chinese Univ of Hong Kong, 1988-. *Publications:* 50 Pattern Drills; Reading in Consumer Behavior, A Managerial Focus. *Memberships:* Acad of Intl Business; American Mktng Assn; Mu Kappa Tau. *Honours:* American Mktng Assn Doc Consortium Fellow; General Honors Cert; Iptimist Club of Rolla Missouri Scholarship; Daughters of the American Revolution Good Citizenship Award. *Hobbies:* Flying; Scuba; swimming; Weight Training; Tae Kwan Do; Reading. *Address:* The Chinese University of Hong Kong, Department of Marketing, Room 403, Leung Kau Kui Building, Shatin, NT, Hong Kong. 5, 15, 52.

YU Kai Cheng, b. 1 Oct 1932, Tainjin, China. Prof. m. Ke Yi Chen, 19 Jan 1965, 2 d. *Education:* Dept of Chemical Engrng, Jiaotong Univ, 1949; Dept of Metallurgy, North East Inst of Tecn, 1956; Intl Economic Mgmt Inst, 1980; Sch of Business Admin, 1982; Bobson Coll, 1983. *Appointments:* Instr, 8th Aviation Sch of Air Force, 1952-58; Qiansuo State Owned Fruit Farm, 1958-63; Engr, Tongling Non Ferrous Metal Co, 1963-82; Prof, Dean, Natl Centre for Mgmt Development, 1982-. *Publications:* Business Case Teaching; Kindle Up The Flame of People, An Overview of Contemporary Motivation Theories; Organizational Behaviour, Theories & Practice. *Memberships:* China Behavioral Science Assn; China Mgmt Case Assn; China Public Relation Assn; Faculty of the Sch of Mgmt, State Univ of NY at Buffalo, USA. *Honours include:* 3 3rd Class Merit Citations; cert of Natl Best Sellers; Award of Excellence Case Writers; Award & Honorarium of Best Paper; Distinguished Leadership Award. *Hobbies:* Reading; Poetry Writing; Sketching; Philotely; Sports Watching. *Address:* National Center for Industrial Science & Technology Management Development, Dalian University of Technology, 2 Linggong Road, Dalian, Liaoning 116024, China. 52.

YU Kwang-chung, b. 9 Sept 1928, Nanking, China. Poet; Translator; Prof. m. Wo Chun Fan, 2 Sept 1956, 4 d. *Education:* BA, Natl Taiwan Univ, 1952; MFA, State Univ of Iowa, 1959. *Appointments:* Prof, Natl Taiwan Normal Univ, 1966-72; Prof, Nat Chengchi Univ, 1972-74; Fulbright Visiting Prof, 1964-66,1969-71; Reader, Chinese Univ of Hong kong, 1974-85; Dean, Coll of Liberal Arts, 1985-. *Publications:* The Whit Jade Bitter Gourd; Dream and Geography; All By A Map; calling for Ferry; The Selected Poetry of Yu Kwangchung; 30 Other Books. *Memberships:* Taipei Chinese Centre; Intl PEN; Natl Sci Council. *Honours:* Ten Outstanding Young Men in ROC; The Australian Cultural Award; Golden Tripod Award; Wu Sanlien Award for Prose; China Times Award. *Hobbies:* Travel; Hiking; Movies; Star Watching. *Address:* National Sun Yat-sen Univ, Kaohsiung, Taiwan, China.

YU Mao-hong, b. 21 Nov 1934, Jiangsu Province, China. Prof; Dir or Research Div of Structural Strength, Xian Jiaotong Univ. m. He Li nan, 8 Mar 1962, 1 s, 1 d. *Education:* Dept of Civil Engrng, Zhejiang Univ, 1955. *Appointments:* Tchr, Dept of Maths & Mechanics, Xian Jiaotong Univ, 1955-59; Lectr, 1960-80; Assoc Prof, 1980-84; Prof, Xian jiaotong Univ, 1984-. *Publications:* Mechanics of Materials; Researches on the Twin Shear Stress strength Theory; Macroscopic Strength Theory; A New System of Strength Theory; Advances in the Research of Twin Shear Strength Theory; Over 50 Papers. Memberships: Ningpo Univ, Zhejiang Province; Qingdo Chemical Engrng Inst. *Honours include:* Siz Prizes of 1st Degree; Excellent Award for Sci Research; Excellent Award of Paper; Excellent Award of State Educ; 1st Prize of Excellent Paper. *Hobbies:* Chess; Photographs for Archs. *Address:* Department of Civil Engineering, Xian Jiaotong University, Xian, Shaanxi Province, 710049, China. 139, 152, 162.

YU Qiu Yu, b. 23 Aug 1946. Prof of Drama, Aesthetics, History of Chinese Culture. 1 d. *Education:* BA, Shanghai

Theatre Acad, 1968. *Appointments:* Lectr, Shanghai Theatre Acad, 1979-85; Prof, 1986-87; Vice Pres, 1988-89; Pres, 1990-. *Publications:* World History of Theatrical Theories; Aesthetic Psychology in Theatre; A Historical Survey of Chine Theatrical Culture; The Project of Creative Acitivity in Art; Observations on tje Aesthetics of Primitive Chinese Theatre. *Memberships:* Shanghai Writers Assn; Theate Assn of China; Shanghai Theatre Research Inst. *Honours:* Best Thesis of Theatrical Theory; Works of Psychology & Social Science; Best Academic Achievements; Prof with an All China Title. *Address:* Shanghai Theatre Academy, 630 Huashan Road, Shanghai 200040, China. 152.

YU Shixiong, b. 25 Oct 1931, Jiangxi, China. m. Gong Honghua, 22 Oct 1952, 3 s. *Education:* Natl Nanchang Univ, 1952. *Appointments:* Editor, Journal of Renmindianye, 1953-57; Editor, Hournal of Sci & Tech Information, 1958-60; Assoc Enr Editor, 1960-87; Editor in Chief, Journal of Chinese Inst of Workers, 1987-91. *Publications:* Introduction & Research of Marco Polo; The Middle Ages Traveller of Marco Polo; Commositions. On Marco Polo in China; Notes on Chinese Historic Cities in The Travells of Marco Polo. *Memberships:* Tha All China Research Soc of Liberal Arts. *Honours:* Honor Cert, Commercial Press; Natl Office of Information & Press, China Press Soc; All China Research Soc of Liberal Arts Coll Journals. *Hobby:* Stamp Collecting. *Address:* Chinese Institute of Workers Movement, 45 Zengguang Road, Haidian District, Beijing 100037, China.

YU Simon S J, b. 11 Sept 1935, Lotong, Taiwan, China. Entomologist; Prof. m. Rachel R C Yeh, 16 Sept 1967, 2 s. *Education:* BS, Natl Taiwan Univ, 1959; MS McGill Univ, 1965; PhD, 1968; Post Doc, Cornell Univ, 1968-69; Post Doc, Oregon State Univ, 1969-74. *Appointments:* Cornell Univ, 1968-69; Post Doc Fellow, Oregon State Univ, 1969-74; Presearch Assoc, 1974-79; Asst Prof, Univ of Florida, 1980-. *Memberships:* Entomological Soc of America; American Chemical Soc; American Assn for the Advancement of Sci; The Soc of Sigma Xi; Florida Entomological Soc. *Honours:* Research Grant Awards; Invited Speakers in Numerous Symposia. *Hobbies:* Classical Music; Reading; Fishing; Hiking; Jogging. *Address:* Dept of Entomology & Nematology, University of Florida, Gainesville, FL 32611, USA. 7, 52, 139, 143.

YU Shun-Zhang, b. 27 Nov 1932, Shanghai, China. Professor of Epidemiology. m. 4 Jan 1958, 2 s. *Address:* No 60B/602 Dong An 2 Cun, Shanghai, 200032, P R China.

YU Wei Chao, b. 4 Jan 1933, Shanhai, China. The Natl Museum of Chinese History, Dir. m. Shu Hua Fan, Feb 1962, 1 s, 1 d. *Education:* Peking Univ, Bach Degree, 1950-54; Vice Doc Archaeology, Peking Univ, 1957-61. *Appointments:* Inst of Archaeology, The Acad of Sci of China, 1954-57; Dept of History, Dept of Archaeology, Peking Univ, 1961-85; Natl Museum of Chinese History, Dir, 1986-. *Publications:* Traces on the Grain of Water Transport in San Men Xia; A Collection of Archaeological Treatices on the Pre Gin and Han Dynasties; Inspection on the Organization of Chinese Acient Commue; Thery & Practice of Archaeological Typology. *Memberships:* Chinese Archaeology Soc; Chinese Museology Soc; Soc of Research on Chu Culture; Council in Great Wall Soc of China; Beijing History Soc. *Hobby:* Classe Music. *Address:* The Natl Museum of Chinese History, East Side of Tian Ann Men Square, Beijing, China.

YU Xu-ying, b. 5 Aug 1922. m. Zheng Xiu Zhi, 3 Children. *Education:* Jiangxi Province Snr Profl Sch of Commerce, 1941; Xiamen Univ, 1945. *Appointments:* Lectr, Accounting Dept, Xiamen Univ, 1951- 56; Assoc Prof, Economics Dept, 1956-78; Prof, 1978-82; Prof, Chmn, 1982-85; Prof, 1985-. *Publications include:* Financial Managment of Industrial Enterprises; Study Guide to Management Accounting; Research on Accounting Theory & Modern Mangagement

Accounting. *Memberships include:* The Accounting Soc of China; AAA; The Western Accounting Series; CPPCC; The Xiamen Municipal Committee of China Democratic League. *Honours include:* Excellent Textbooks for the Popularity of my Book; Man of The Year; Commemorative Medal of Honor; Handbook of Contemporary Chinas Soc Sci. *Address:* 302 Jing Xian Building (9), Xiamen University, Xiamen, Fujian 361005, China.

YU Zhan-Jiu, b. 1 Sept 1934, Hebei Province, China. Prof; Dir of Acad Sciences; Chief of Dept of Pathophysiology. m. Ge Xue Ru, 28 Oct 1959, 1 s, 1 d. *Education:* Medical Special & Tech Sec Sch, 1952-54; Medical Coll, 1954-59. *Appointments:* Physiological Asst, Tian Jing Medical Coll, 1959; Hd, Physiological Researching Group, 1962; Lectr, 1978; Asst Prof, 1981; prof, 1987. *Publications:* Books; 12 Vardiovascular monopraphs; Articles. *Memberships:* Acad of Hebei Medical Sci; Assn of Pathophysiology of China; Hebei Physiologic Committee; Hebei Gerontalogic Committee. *Honours:* Sci Honors of Ministry of Natl Health; Hebei Provincial Honors & Prize of Sci & Tech Progression. *Hobbies:* Sport; Basketball; Music; Reading Novels. *Address:* Dept of Pathophysiology, Hebei Academy of Medical Science. N62 Qing-Yuan Street, PO 050021, Shijiazhuang, China.

YU Zhian, b. 12 Aug 1932. m. 1957, 2 s. *Education:* Law Dept, Zhong Nan Politics, Law Univ, 1954; Philosophy Dept, Wuham Univ, 1959. *Appointments:* Peoples Liberation Army, 1943-53; Vice Pres, Univ Machinery Factory, Wuhan, 1956-59; Pres, Wuham Diesel Engine Works Co, 1963073; Mgr, Wohan Agriclt Machinery Co, 1973-81; General Mgr, China Chang Jiang Energy Corp, 1986-; Pres, Wuhan Steam Turbine & Generator Plant, 1991-. *Memberships include:* Standing Committee All China Federation of Ind & Commerce; China Enterprise Assn; China Philosophic & Historical Assn; Chang jiang Enterprise Club. *Honours:* Natl Outstanding Mgr; Natl Outstanding Enterpriser; Natl May 1st Labour Medal; State Ranking management Expert; Natl Model Worker; Achievement Award for State Research. *Hobbies:* Chinese Chess; Excursions. *Address:* China Chang Jiang Energy Corp, Guanshan, Wuhan, Hubei 430074, China.

YU Zhuo Yun, b. 11 Dec 1918, Tienjing, China. Engr; Prof. m. 1942, 3 s, 1 d. *Education:* Art Coll Ind Univ, 1938-42; Construct Tech Higher Civil Official Studies Ind Coll Toyko Japan, 1942; Engr Const Design, 1950. *Appointments:* Engr Const Bureau Building, China, 1942-45; Engr Historical Relic Engrng Dept, 1945-59; Engr Research Inst Museum Histroical Relic China, 1949-54; Engr Higher Constt, Chief & Prof, 1954-. *Publications:* Forbidden City Palace; Complete Art Works China Construct Palace; Encyclopaedia China City Plans, Gardens, Constr & Engrng Const; Lectrs History Const China. *Memberships:* Council Assn Skill Protecting Relic Cultural; Inst Yan Ming Yan China; Prof Group Prof China; Const History & Theory Learning Inst; Organ Cultural Relic Bureau, China; Beijing Ancient Const Garden Skill & Palace Museum Journal. *Honours include:* Optimum Books Prizes; First Excellent Const Sci & Tech Books Dept Grade China. *Hobbies:* Penmen Ship; Writing. *Address:* Ancient Construct Branch, Palace Museum, No. 4 Front Street Jing Shen, Beijing, China.

YUAN Chuan Fuh, b. 12 Aug 1926, Jiangsu, China. Tchr; Zoology. m. 12 Mar 1956, 1 s, 1 d. *Education:* Univ of Nanking, 1946-51. *Appointments:* Tchr, Nanjing Univ, 1951-91. *Publications:* Cailia Ectenes Jordan et Seale; Vertebrates; The History of Biology; The Freshwater Fishes of jiangsu. *Memberships:* The Assn of Zoology in China; Assn of Ichthyology in China; Assn of Oceanology & Limnology in China. *Honours:* Many. *Hobbies:* Reading; Hunting. *Address:* Dept of Biology, Nanjing Univ, Nanjing, Jiangsu Province, China.

YUAN James Ching Man, b. 10 Apr 1943, Shanghai, China. Vice Pres. m. Pauline Sze Fun Chang, 9 Jan 1972, 1 s, 1 d. *Educations:* Hong Kong Tech Coll; BSc Northeastern Univ; Intl Mgmt, Columbia Univ. *Appointments:* Distribution Conslt, Singer Sewing Machine Co. 1970-72; Distribution Mgr, 1972-74; Operations Mgr, P T singer Ind, 1974-77; Mktng Mgr, 1977-81; Branch Mgr, Singer Sewing Machine Co, 1981-84; General Mgr, 1984-86; Mgrng Dir, Singer Thailand Ltd, 1986-; Vice Pres, The singer Co, 1989-. *Memberships:* British Chamber of Commerce; American Chamber of Commerce. *Hobbies:* Swimming; Reading; Travel. *Address:* Singer Thailand Ltd, 321 Siphya Road, PO Box 136, Bangkok 10501, Thailand.

YUAN Sidney Wei Kwun, b. 30 July 1957, Hong Kong. Research Scientist; Conslt. m. Katherine Kit Yee Dai, 8 Sept 1981, 2 d. *Education:* BSc, UCLA, 1980; MSC, 1971; phD, 1985. *Appointments:* Postgrad Research Engr, Univ of California, 1980-85; Research Scientist, 1985-; Lectr, Univ of California, 1989; Conslt, Toyo sanso KK, 1990-. *Publications:* More Than 30 Tech papers. *Memberships:* American Inst of Chemical Engrs; American Inst of Aeronautics & Astronautics; Tau Beta Pi; Sigma Xi. *Honours include:* Natl Excellence Recognition award; Superior Performance Team Award; Engr of The Year Award. *Hobbies:* Ping Pong; Badminton. *Address:* 3251 Hanover Street, O: 92-40 B205, Palo Alto, CA 94304, USA. 9.

YUE Shucang, b. 13 June 1931, Beijing, China. Prof. m. He Jianhua, 2 July 1960, 2 s. *Education:* Jinghua Fine Arts Inst, 1950; Qilou Univ, 1951; Univ of Geoscience, 1955. *Appointments:* Asst Prof, 1955-62; Lectr, 1963-76; Assoc Prof, 1977-78; Prof, Hefei Univ of Tech, 1978- *Publications include:* Study on Mesozoic Volcanic Rock System of Hebei Inner Mongolia of China; Geochemistry Study on Ore Forming of District I Southeastern Coast of China; Geochemistry on the Magmatism mineralization of Cu, Ag, Au, Southeastern Coast of China. *Memberships:* Chinese Assn of Geology Educ; Anhui Geol Assn of China. *Honours:* Natl Award of Chinese Nature Sci; Natl Scientific Congress Award. *Hobbies:* Music; Scientific Exploration. *Address:* Geology Dept, Hefei Univ of Tech, 230009 Hefei, Anhui, China.

YUECHIMING Roger Yue Yuenshing, b. 25 Feb 1937, Mauritius. Univ Lectr; Mathematician. m. Renee Bethery, 9 Nov 1963, 3 d. *Education:* BSc, PhD, Univ of Manchester, 1967. *Appointments:* Asst, Strasbourg Univ France, 1967-69; Tchrng & Research, Univ of Paris VII, 1970-. *Creative Works include:* Research Interest, Ring Thoery; Over 70 Research Papers; Various Scientific Journals; Various Conference & Seminars. *Memberships:* Soc Mathematique de France; American Mathematical Soc. *Hobbies:* Reading; Walking; Cinema; Music. *Address:* Universite Paris VII, UFR de Mathematiques, URA 212 CNRS, 2 Place Jussieu, 75251 Paris, Cedex 05, France.

YUN Caixing, b. 23 June 1935, Jiangsu, China. Prof; Scientist. m. 8 Mar 1962, 1 s, 1 d. *Education:* East China Normal Univ, 1953-57; Sediment Research Trainning Centre of Water Conservancy ministry of China, 1964; Natl Remote Sensing Trainning Centre of China, 1978. *Appointments:* Tchrng Asst, East China Normal Univ, 1957-64; Lectr, 1964-78; Hd, Tibet Univ of China, 1974-76; Assoc Prof, Inst of Estuarine & Coastal Research, 1978-86; Prof, Deputy Dir, 1986-. *Creative Works include:* Estuarine & Coastal Research; Marine Remote Sensing Research. *Memberships:* Chinese Soc of Marine Remote Sensing; Chinese Commission of Marine Geography; Chinese Soc of Marine Physics; Chinese Soc of Habour Engrng; Chinese Commission of Hydraulic Remote Sensing. *Honours:* Natl Project of Marine Remote Sensing Award; The Investigation of Shanghai Coastal Zone. *Hobbies:* Scientific Investigation; Marine Remote Sensing. *Address:* Institute of Estuarine & Coastal Research, East China Normal University, Shanghai 200062, China.

YUTHASASTRKOSOL Charin, b. 30 Dec 1930, Bangkok, Thailand. Real Estate Corp Officer. m. Prapakron Yuthasastrkosol, 23 Feb 1953, 2 s, 1 d. *Education:* Assoc Degree, Strayer Coll, Washington, 1959. *Appointments:* Bookstore Mgr, Intl Sch of Bangkok, 1961-68; Owner, Operator, Anita Ballet Sch, Bangkok, 1961-70; Pres Intl Operations, Twinning Land Corp, 1989-; Appointed, Commisioner of Pennyslvania Heritage Affairs, 1990-92. *Memberships:* Business, Profl Womens Assn of Thailand; Phila Delaware Val Restaurant Assn; Temple Univ Assn for Retired Profl. *Honours:* Plaque Award for Ballet Dancing Studio; Receipent of Over 300 Plaques & Medals in Ballroom Dancing; Received Award for Dancing from Present Queen of Thailand; Plaque Award in Dancing, Foundation for the Blind; Charity Show All Over The World. *Hobbies:* Design Arts; Tchrng & Playing Piano; Ballroom Dancing; Ballet; Jazz; Tap Dance. *Address:* Twinning Corp, 4004 Greenway, Baltimore, MD, 21218, USA. 5, 6, 132.

Z

ZABKOWSKI Jozef Lucjan, b. 26 Nov 1928, Czestochowa. Painter; Prof. m. Cecylia Wodnicka Zabkowska, 13 Feb 1950, 1 d. *Education:* Master of Fine Arts, 1954; Doc of Fine Arts, 1965; Higher Fine Arts Degree, 1978; prof of Fine Arts, 1988. *Appointments:* Asst Lectr Acad of Fine Arts, Krakow, 1955; Lectr, 1965; Snr Lectr, 1980; Prof, 1988; Dean of Faculty of Painting, 1987-. *Creative Works:* Canvas Painting; 160 Exhib inc 30 Individual Ones; Monumental Painting; 11 Realisations of Stain Glass; Drawings. *Memberships:* Polish Fine Artists Assn; Assn Intl des Artists Plasticiens. *Honours:* First Degree Prize, Polish Minister of Cultures & Fine Arts; Chevalier Crest; Golden Medallion. *Hobbies:* Tourism; Classical Music. *Address:* Morawskieso 12/10, 30-102 Krakow, Poland. 1.

ZABLOCKI Zdzislaw Marcin, b. 20 Nov 1940, Warsaw, Poland. Asst Prof. m. Wanda Zablocka, 19 Jan 1974. *Education:* MSc, univ Szczecin, 1958-63; PhD, 1971; Dr Hab, 1990. *Appointments:* Asst Lectr, 1966-71; Adjunct Lectr, 1972-90; Asst Prof, ecology & Environmental Protection, 1991-. *Publications:* 48 Papers. *Memberships:* Szczecin Div Polish Soil Sci Soc; Sci Soc of Szczecin. *Honours:* Award of the Pres of Agricl Univ Szczecin; Gold Medal of Polish Soil Sci Soc. *Hobbies:* Tennis; Bridge; Reading. *Address:* ul Lubomirskiege 1/34, 71 505 Szczecin, Poland.

ZAGRODZKI Janusz, b. 3 Jan 1941, Warsaw, Poland. m. (1) Makgorzata Wolnikowska, 30 June 1968, div, (2) Anna Maria Lesniewska, 14 Oct 1989, 2 s, 1 d. *Education:* State Univ, Torun Faculty of Fine Arts, 1961-66; Jagielonian Univ, Krakow, PhD, 1980. *Appointments:* Museum of Art, Lodz, 1966-87; Film Acad, Lodz, Prof, 1973-; Natl Museum, Warsaw, 1987- *Publications include:* Constructivism in Poland; Waclaw Szpakowki; Presences Polonaises; Wladyslaw Strzeminski in Memoriam; Tadeusz Makowski. *Membership:* Assn Intl des Critiques d'Art. *Honours:* Municipality of Lodz; Achievement in Art & Culture; award by Minister of Art & culture for Achievements in Didactic. *Hobby:* Avant Garde in Film Art. *Address:* National Museum in Warsaw, 3 Jerozolimskie Ave, 00 495 Warsaw, Poland.

ZAHIROVIC Ajsa, b. 21 Mar 1940, Sarajevo, Yugoslavia. Writer. 1 d. *Education:* Faculty of Law, Univ of Sarajevo. *Appointments:* Sec of the Faculty of Electrotennics, Sarajevo; Culture Sec of CK SKBiH; Culture Concellor; Culture Councellor, Presidency of the Socialist Republic of Bosnia & Herzegovina. *Publications include:* Poetry Books; Books, Najveca Zedj; Buddha Moja Ljubavi; Malaysia, Anthology of Cont Poetry. *Memberships:* World Acad of Arts & Culture; World Poetry Research Inst, South Korea; World Womens Writers Organ; Intl Journal for Poetry; POET; Writers Assnof Yugoslavia. *Honours:* Honorable Doc Degree for Literature; Gold Crown Kaya of World Poetry Research Inst; Gold Award, Robert Frost; World Award W B Yeats. *Hobbies:* Music; Travel; Nature; Mountain Climbing; Vegetarian; Humanitary Work; Sport; Swimming. *Address:* Poetess, Str Kranjcevica 41/3, 71000 Sarajevo.

ZAIMOV Velislav, b. 8 May 1951, Sofia, Bulgaria. Composer; Lectr. m. Snejina Boyadjieva, 5 Oct 1981, 2 d. *Education:* French Language Sch, Sofia, 1965-70; Army Service, 1970-72; Natl Acad of Music, 1970-77. *Appointments:* Lectr, Orchestration, Harmony, Score Reading NAM, 1977-; Conductor, Chamber Orchestra, 1979-81; Lectr, Musical Analysis, Acad of Music & Dancing, Plovdiv, 1990-. *Creative Works include:* 7 Symphonies; 3 Concertos; 10 Sonatas; 5 Trios; 5 Quartets; Piano works. *Membership:* Union of Bulgarian Composers. *Honours:* Contest Orchestral Musik; Concerto Violin & Orchestra; Annua Award of Sco of Young Bulgarian Composers. *Address:* ul Bitolia 18/E, Sofia 1680, Bulgaria.

ZAKARIYA Zakariya Nasiru Imam, b. 11 Feb 1963, Ankpa, Benue State. System Maintenance. *Education:* Benue State polytech, Nigera, 1983-85; Kaduna Polytech, 1987-89. *Appointments:* Volkswagen of Nigeria Ltd, 1985-86; Michelin Ltd, 1989-. *Publications:* Final Year Written Project; Basic Electricity. *Memberships:* Natl Ramat Memorial Club; Student Representative. *Hobbies:* Reading; Playing Indoor Games; Jogging; Watching Films; Music. *Address:* Michelin Nigeria Ltd, Ap Dept, PO Box 527, Trans Amadi Ind Estate, Port Harcourt, Rivers State, Nigeria.

ZAKIEV Mirfatikh Zakievich, b. 1928. m. Lena Ahmetovna, 2 children. *Edcation:* Kazan Univ, 1951; Cand of Sci, 1955; Asst Prof, 1958; Doc of Sci, 1963; Prof, 1964; Acad Tatarstan Acad of Sci, 1991. *Appointments:* Snr tchr, Prof, Kazan Univ, 1954-60; Hd of Tatar Linguistics Chair, 1960-65; Pro Rector on Sci, Kaxzan Inst, 1965-67; Rector, 1967-86; Dir, Tatar Inst of Language, Literature & History, Tatar Acad of Sci, 1986-. *Publications:* 280 inc, 32 Monographs; textbooks; 265 Articles. *Memberships:* Assn of Orientalists EUN; Turkologists EUN; Acad of Sci of Tatarstan; Sci Council, Language & Soc, Russia Acad of Sci; Grand Council, World Parlament of the Cenfederation of Chivalry; Committee of Realization of Tatar Language; Constitutional Committee of Tatarstan. *Honours:* Medal for Labour, Great Patriotic War; Honoured Scientist of Tatarstan; Order of the Red Banner of Labour; Honoured Scientist of RSFSR; Order of the Peoples Friendship; Veteran of Labour Medal; Order of the White Cross. *Address:* Lobachevasky Str 2/31, Kazan Tatarstan 420503, Russia.

ZAKRZEWSKA Janina, b. 12 Dec 1928, Warsaw, Poland. Prof of Constitutional Law; Judge. m. Andrzej Gwizdz, 27 Feb 1952, 1 d. *Education:* MA, Univ of Warsaw, 1950; PhD, 1958; Habilitation, 1964. *Appointments:* Univ of Warsaw, Faculty of Law, 1950-68; Unemployed, 1968-70; State Archive, 1970-89; Polish Acad of Law, 1989-; Constitutional Court Judge, 1989-. *Publications:* Controversy About Parliament; The Control of the Constitutionality of Law in the Modern state; Ossolineum; The History of Polish Parliament After the Second World War. *Memberships:* Polish Penclub; Helsinki Committee; Polish Historical Assn. *Honour:* Polish Acad of Sci. *Address:* Celna 2/4 m 8, 00-287 Warsaw, Poland.

ZALAN Tibor, b. 27 Aug 1954, Szolnok. Snr High Sch Tchr. m. Csillo Szentpotery, 22 Mar 1980, 2 d. *Education:* Jozsef Attila Univ, 1972-78. *Appointments:* Tchr, Kvassay & Semmelweis Special Snr High Sch, 1982-85; Poem Editor, Kortars Literary Mag, 1985-91. *Publications:* Anthology. Versziok, Child of Europe; Book of Poems; Novels; Dramas; Radiodramas. *Membership:* Hungarian Writers Union. *Honours:* Radnoti, Graves, Jozsef Attila Prizes. *Hobbies:* Flowers; Plants; Whisky; Zoo; Cars. *Address:* Becsi ut 141-143, B 11.18, H 1034 Budapest, Hungary.

ZAMMIT Alan Charles, b. 13 Apr 1960, England. Physiotherapist; Managing Dir. *Education:* Malta Coll of Physiotherapy, 1982-85; British State Reg Physiotherapist, 1986. *Appointments:* Snr Physiotherapist, St Lukes Gen Hosp, Malta, 1985-89; World Class Physiotherapist, Managemeng Dir, Rehabilitation Centre, 1989-. *Publications:* Numerous Articles. *Memberships:* Malta Sports Medical Assn; FIMS; Australian Sports Medical Federation. *Hobbies include:* Sports. *Address:* 28 Kappara Court, St Julians, Malta.

ZAMMIT DIMECH Francis, b. 23 Oct 1954, St Julians, Malta. Parliamentary Sec. *Education:* Law Course, Univ of Malta, 1974-79; Advocate, Univ of Malta, 1979. *Appointments:* Private Practise, Advocate, 1980-. *Publications:* Poll of 76; Untruth Game Broadcasting under Labour; Eddie The Peoples Choice. *Hobbies:* Reading; Broadcasting; Theatre; Swimming. *Address:* 7 St Julians Hill, St Julians, Malta.

ZAMMIT MAEMPEL Jospeh V, b. 24 Sept 1912, Naxxar, Malta. Conslt Physician. m. Evelyn Camilleri, 25 Oct 1944, 2 s, 3 d. *Education:* Univ of Malta, 1930-37; Royal British Postgrad Medical Sch, London, 1937-38; Natl Hosp for Diseases of the Heart, 1937-38, 1945-46; Natl Hosp for Nervous Diseases, 1937-38, 1945-46; Edinburgh Univ, 1946; Vienna Univ & Acad of Medicine, 1953. *Appointments:* House Physician, ARMO, 1938-39; Asst of Prof of Medicine, Univ of Malta, 1939-45; Asst Visiting Physician, St Francis Hosp, Malta, 1941-45; Physician, Snr Physician, St Lukes Tchrng Hosp, 1946-63; Prof, Hd of Dept, Royal Univ of Malta, 1947-67; Examiner, Royal Univ of Malta, 1947-73; Prof, Hd of Dept, 1967-73; Dean Faculty of Medicine, Royal Univ of Malta, 1963-66; Civilian Conslt to Royal Navy in Malta, 1970-79. *Publications include:* Survey on Diabetes in Malta; Research, Cardiovascular Complications. *Memberships include:* British Medical Assn; Royal Coll of Physicians; Intl Soc Internal Medicine; Medical Assn of Malta; Assn Physicians & Surgeons of Malta. *Hobbies:* Sailing; Shooting. *Address:* 13 Howard Street, Sliema, Malta. 1, 139.

ZANG Shao Xian, b. 28 Nov 1938, Shan Dong, China. Prof. m. Zong Ci Shao, 1 Oct 1969, 1 d. *Education:* Peking Univ, 1958-64. *Appointments:* Tchr, 1964-69; Hd of Div of Geophysics, 1970-77; Honorary Research Fellow, Univ Coll of London, 1977-79; Vice Chmn, Assoc Prof, Prof, Dept Geophysics, Peking Univ, 1980-. *Publications:* more Than 40 Sci Papers. *Memberships:* Chinese Geophysics Soc; Chinese Seismological Soc; AGU; 4 Committies in China. *Honours:* Honorary Research Fellow; Best Scientific Research Award. *Hobbies:* Sci Study; Sports; Swimming; Sailing; Table Tennis; Travel; Gardening. *Address:* Dept of Geophysics, Peking Univ, Beijing 100871, China.

ZANUCK Lili Fini, b. 2 Apr 1954. Leominster, USA. Producer; Dir. m. Richard D Zanuck, 23 Sept 1954. *Education:* Northern Virginia Community Coll, Virginia, 1972-73. *Appointments:* Carnation Co, Los Angeles, California, 1977-78; The Zanuck/Brown Co, 1978-84; Producer, Zanuck/Brown Co, then Zanuck Co, 1984-; Dir, 1991. *Memberships:* Guild of America; American Film Inst; BAFTA; Music Center. *Honours:* 2 Academy Awards, Cocoon; 4 Academy Awards inc, Best Picture, Cocoon the Return, Driving Miss Daisy; Nominated 2 Grammy awards; 2 Golden Bears at the Berlin Gilm Festival, Best Actor & Actress; Producer of the Year. *Hobbies:* Architecture; Music. *Address:* The Zanuck Co, 202 N Canon Drive, Beverly Hill, CA 90210, USA.

ZAREBSKA Teresa, b. 28 Jan 1932, Warsaw, Poland. Architect. 1 d. *Education:* Arch, 1954; Master Arch, 1956; Doc of Tech Sci, 1965; Habilitation, 1974; Prof, 1986. *Appointments:* Designer, 1955-56; Asst, Inst of Theory & History of Townplanning & Arch, 1956-62; Faculty of Arch, Warsaw, 1963-. *Publications:* Miasto Idealne; The Ideal Town of Cav G Vasari; 60 Dissertations & Papers. *Memberships include:* Intl Federation for Housing & Planning; Planning History Group; ICOMOS; TICCICH. *Honours include:* Prizes of the Ministry of Culture & Arts; Ministry of Admin & Planning; Honorary Citizenship Kalisz; Honorary Awards of the Soc of Polish Townplanners. *Hobbies:* Dogs; Sighseeing; Photography. *Address:* Chair of the History of Townplanning, Faculty of Arch, Warsaw Tech Univ, Koszykowa 55, 00 659 Warsaw, Poland.

ZAREH Mo, b. 13 Nov 1943, Shiraz Fars, Iran. Vice Pres; Gen Mgr. m. 12 June 1964, 1 s, 2 d. *Education:* Bs, Portland State Univ, 1967; MS, 1971. *Appointments:* Project Mgr, Swan Wooster, 1973-78; Vice Pres, Mgr, 1978-86; Vice Pres, Mgr, Sandwell Inc, 1986-. *Memberships:* Reg profl Engr; Engrs Assn; Peachtree World of Tennis. *Hobbies:* Hiking; Tennis; Running; Golf. *Address:* Sandwell Inc USA, 2690 Cumberland Parkway, Suite 300, Atlanta, GA 30339, USA.

ZAREMBA Peter, b. 10 June 1910, Heidelberg, Poland. Prof. m. Barbara Karwatka, 15 Feb 1945, 2 s, 1 d.

Education: Master of Engrng, 1934; Doc of Tech Sc, 1951; Prof, 1954. *Appointments:* Urban Planner, City of poznan, 1934-39; Worker Minicip Gardens, Poznan, 1939-45; Deputy Dir, Techn Services, 1945; Mayor of the City of Szczecin, 1945-50; Prof, Tch Univ of Wroclaw & Szczecin, 1948-; Rector, Tchn Univ Szczecin, 1962-65; Chmn, Intern Course of Urban & Regional planning, 1966-. *Publications include:* Author of 388 Publi Books; Papers; Reports. *Memberships:* Polish Acad of Sci; Intl Acad of Architecture; Intern Soc of City Regional Planners; Soc of Polish Townplanners; Unesco program Mab, Urban Ecosystems; Soc of Polish Architects. *Honours:* Honorary Doc; Honorary Prof; Honorary Member, Assn of Polish Townplanners; Polish Natl Prize for Physical Planning Research; Honorary Chmn Committee of Arch. *Hobbies:* Postal History; Ubran Topography; Old Maps & City Plans. *Address:* Wyspianskiego 27, 70 497 Szczecin, Poland.

ZARINS Indulis, b. 18 June 1929, Riga. Artist. m. Zarina Gulbis Vera, 12 June 1958, 2 s. *Education:* Latvian Acad of art, 1952-58. *Appointments:* J Rozental Sec Sch of Art, 1958-62; Latvian Acad of Art, 1962-. *Creative Works include:* The Tretiakov Gallery, Moscow; The Latvian Museum of Art, Riga; Foreign Art Galleries; Many Private Collections. *Membership:* Fellowship of RSA. *Hobbies:* Skiing; Table Tennis. *Address:* Brivibas Str 70, Flat 9, Riga 226050, Latvia.

ZARINS Kaspars, b. 10 Apr 1962, Riga. Artist. m. Viza Zarina, 10 Oct 1985, 2 d. *Education:* Middle Art Sch, 1973-80; Acad of Arts of Latvia, 1980-86. *Appointments:* Tchr, Middle Sch, 1985-90; Lectr, Latvia Acad of Art, 1989-. *Creative Works include:* Discation; Pedant; Trio. *Membership:* Latvia Assn of Profl Artists. *Hobbies:* Skating; House Building; Skiing. *Address:* Pluomales 15, Vecaki, Riga 226030, Latvia.

ZARZYCKI Daniel, b. 12 Jan 1942, Sosnowiec, Poland. Orthopaedic Surgeon. m. Maja Zarzek, 3 Aug 1975, 1 s. *Education:* Acad of Medicine, Cracow, 1961-67; MD, 1967; PhD, 1976; Prof, 1989. *Appointments include:* Acad of Medicine, Cracow, 1967-71; Royal Infirmary Huddersfield & King Edward VIII Hosp, 1972-73; Acad of Medicine, Cracow, 1974-76; Study Fellowship, 1979; Mayo Clinic, Mayo Foundation, 1979; Hosp for Sick Children, Toronto, 1985; Roland Hosp, Bremen, Germany, 1988; Natl Inst Traditional Chinese Medicine, 1989. *Publications:* 50 Publi; Designer of Spinal Instrumentation. *Memberships:* Polish Orthopaedic & Traumatology Soc; Polish Assn for Handicaped Peoples; Scoliosis Research Soc; European Spinal Deformities Soc; Intl Cotrel Dubousset. *Honours:* 3 Orders; 4 Medals. *Hobbies:* Carpentry; Skinning; Cooking. *Address:* Balzera 15, 34-500 Zakopane, Poland.

ZAVALA Irisa M, b. 27 Dec 1936, Puerto Rico. Univ Prof; Writer. m. 1 d. *Education:* BA, Univ of Puerto Rico, 1957; Univ of Salamanca, MA, 1961; PhD, 1962. *Appointments include:* Asst Prof, Univ of Puerto Rico, 1962-64; Visiting Lectr, Queens Coll, 1966; Asst prof, Hunter Coll, 1968-69; Editorial Comm, Alianza Editorial, Madrid, 1968-70; Full Prof, SUNY, 1971-83; General Editor, Historia Iberica, 1971-73; Joint Prof, Comparative Literature, SUNY, 1976-83; advisory Bd, Revista Chicano Riqueria, 1975-82; Visiting Prof, Univ of Puerto Rico, 1981; Chair Hispanic Literatures, Rijksuniversiteit Utrecht, 1983-; Advisory Bd, Assn Intl de Vallein clanistas, 1988-; General Editor, Book Series, Alianza Editorial, 1989-; Editorial Bd, Hispanic Issues, Univ of Minessota, 1990-. *Publications include:* Unamuno y su teatro de conciencia; Libertad y critica en al ensayo puertorriquerio; El texto en la historia; More than 90 Articles; More than 80 Lectures; 2 TV Scripts. *Honours:* Doc Summa Cum Laude, Honorary Mention; Research Fellow, El Colegio de Mexico; OAS Research Fellowship; American Philosophical Soc; Guggenheim Foundation Fellowship; American Council of Learned Soc; Natl Literary Prize. *Hobbies:* Archeology; Popular Music. *Address:* Rijksuniversiteit te Utrecht, Faculteit der Letteren, Kromme Nieuwe Gracht 29, 3512 HD Utrecht, Netherlands. 2, 52, 138, 152, 162.

ZAVLANOS Myron, b. 15 Mar 1941, Tricala. Prof; Chmn, Imp It. m. Mary Ghioka, 17 Nov 1977, 1 s, 1 d. *Education:* Univ of Athens, BSc, 1960-64; Univ of Paris, 1970; Univ of Birmingham, MSc, 1970-71; Univ of Illinois, MEd, 1974-75; Canderbilt Univ, PhD, 1981. *Appointments:* Lectr, Univ of Athens, 1965-67; Prof, Tchrs Training Inst, 1972-85; Prof, Sch of Aviation, 1982-84; Prof, Tech Educ Inst, Deree Coll, 1985-; Chmn, Imp, 1989-. *Publications:* 9 Books; 20 Articles. *Memberships:* Fulbright Assn; Assn of Engrs France; Assn of Engrs, Greece. *Honours:* Scholarship, French Government & Fulbright. *Hobbies:* Music; Reading. *Address:* Gounari 14, Maroussi 15124, Athens, Greece.

ZAVRSKI Josip, b. 12 Feb 1917, Zagreb. Musician; Conductor; Prof. m. 15 June 1955, 1 s, 1 d. *Education:* Sch for Rhytmic & Acting, Zagreb, 1936; Acad of Music & Art, 1952; ORFF Instrumentarium, 1978. *Appointments:* Music cons, Jadran Film, Zagreb, 1947-51; Prof, Music Tchr, Sch of Zagreb, 1951-55; Conductor, Croatian Natl Theatre, RTV, 1949-65; Conslt, Music Inst for Culture & Educ, 1962-80. *Publications:* Methdologicial Instr for Music Tchrs History of Music; Theory of Music; Composition for Percussion Instr. Descant Recorder & Melodies; Tests for Music Educ & Capabilities; Articles. *Memberships:* Union Artist in Music Entertainment; Union of Artist in Serious Music; Union of Music Pedagogoist. *Honours:* Recipient Award; President of Yugoslavia Belgrade; Gold Medal Educ House, Sch Book. *Hobbies:* Collecting Music Instruments, Masks from Asia & Africa. *Address:* Ilica 65, 41000 Zagreb, Croatia.

ZAYID Ismail, b. 14 Mar 1933, Beit Nuba, Palestine. Prof of Pathology. m. Greta Herbert, 20 Aug 1960, 1 s, 4 d. *Education:* Guys Hosp Med Sch, 1951-58; Med Sch, Univ of London, 1963-66; MRC Path, 1970; FRCPC, 1974; FRC Path, 1982. *Appointments:* Dir, Dept of Pathology, Main Hosp Amman, Jordan, 1966-69, 1971-72; Lectr, Con Cons Pathologist, Hammersmith Hosp, London, 1970-71; Assoc Prof, 1972-80; Prof, Dalhousie Univ, 1980-; Dir of Anatomical Pathology, Victoria Gen Hosp. *Publications:* Numerous. *Memberships:* Intl Acad of Pathology; Intl Soc of Gynecologic Pathologists; Intl Gyn Cancer Soc; Royal Coll of Pathologists; Canadian Ref Centre Cancer Pathology; Near East Cultural & Educ Federtion; Arab Canadian Assn of Atlantic Provinces. *Honours:* High Sch Educ Cert with Distinction; Jordan State Scholarship; Jordan Medical Journal Prize. *Hobbies:* Reading; Music; Squash; Bridge. *Address:* Dept of Pathology, Victoria General Hospital, 1278 Tower Road, Halifax, Nova Scotia, Canada B3H 2Y9. 142.

ZDEBSKA Eugenia Maria Janusz, b. 15 Dec 1930, Dziedzice. Pediatric Cardiac Surgeon. m. 25 Apr 1955, 1 s. *Education:* Medical Acad, Krakow, 1950-55; Doc Thesis, 1964; Assoc Prof, 1980; Prof in Surgery, 1991. *Appointments:* Asst, Surgical Dept, Auschwitz, 1955-59; Pediatric Surgeon, Clinic in Krakow, 1966; Pediatric Inst, Krakow, 1966-; Hd Dept Pediatric Surgery, 1980-. *Publications:* 115 Publi; 2550 Heart Operations. *Memberships:* EACTS; Polish Cardiol Soc; Polish pediatric Surgery Assn; Polish Thoracic Cardiac Soc; Club of Polish Cardiac Surgeons. *Honours:* Ministry of Health in Poland Prizes. *Hobbies:* Fine Porcelain; Collecting Old Polish Books; Skiing; Mountaineering. *Address:* ulica Karmelicka 9/6, 31-133 Krakow, Poland.

ZECHLIN Egmont, b. 21 June 1896, Danzig, Gdansk. Historian. m. Anneliese Zechlin, 22 Oct 1941, 2 s, 1 d. *Education:* Military Serv, World War 1, 1914-18; Univ Berlin & Heidelberg, 1919-22; Univ of Marburg, 1929. *Appointments:* Privatdozent of History, Marburg, 1929-34; Prof of History Marburg, 1934-36; Hamburg, 1936-39; Berlin, 1940-45; Hamburg, 1947-67; Prof Emeritus, 1967-. *Publications include:* Maritime Weltgeschichte; Die deutsche Einheitsbewegung; Numerous articles. *Memberships include:* Verband der Historiker

Deutschlands; Deutsche Gesellschaft fur Amerikastudien. *Honours:* Corresponding Member Acad Portoguessa d Historia Lisbon; Bundesverdienstkreuz. *Address:* 2319 Selent, Holstein, Germany.

ZEGAR Jozef, b. 30 Oct 1940, Poland. m. Alina Pekrul, 18 Mar 1971, 1 s, 1 d. *Education:* Econ Univ, Warsaw, 1958-61; State Univ, Leningrad, 1961-64; Econ Univ, Warsaw, PhD, 1974; ScD, 1979. *Appointments:* Econ Univ Warsaw, 1965-71; Ed Modern Countryside Monthly, 1971-76; Inst of Agricl & Food Econ, Warsaw, 1971-86; Government Minister, 1986-89; Vice minister, 1989-91; Inst of Agriclt & Food Econ, Prof, 1991-. *Publications:* About 200 Books & articles. *Membership:* Int Assn of Agricl Economics. *Honours:* Award, Polish Acad of Sci; Award, Inst of Agriclt & Food Econ. *Hobbies:* Gardening; Tourism. *Address:* ul Lotnicza 2, 05 806 Komorow, Poland.

ZEIGLER Bernard P, b. 5 Mar 1940, Montreal, Canada. Prof. m. Christine, 1985, 3 d. *Education:* McGill Univ, 1952; MS, Electrical Engrng; PhD, Univ of Michigan. *Appointments:* Prof, Univ of Arizonia, Tucson, 1985-. *Publications:* Theory of Modelling & Simulation; Multifacetted Modelling & Discretetvent Simulation; Object Orrented Simulation of Modular Models. *Membership:* IEEE. *Honours:* Best Publication; Fulbright Award. *Hobby:* Jazz. *Address:* ECE Dept, Univ of Arizona, Tucson AZ 85721, USA. 1.

ZEIGLER Donald J, b. 26 Nov 1951, Harrisburg, PA, USA. Prof of Geography. m. Deborah Emminger, 23 June 1973, 1 s, 1 d. *Education:* BS, Chippensburg Univ, 1972; MA, Univ of Rhode Island, 1976; PhD Michigan State Univ, 1980. *Appointments:* Goegrapher, US Census Bureau, Washington, DC, 1976-77; Asst, Assoc, Full Prof, Old Dominion Univ, 1980-; Chair, Dept of Political Sci & Geography, 1991-. *Publications:* 35 articles; Virginia Geographer. *Memberships include:* Assn of American Geographers; Natl Council for Geographic Educ; Virginia Geographical Soc; Pioneer America Soc. *Honours:* Virginia Soc Sci Assn Scholars Award; Gamma Theta Upsilon; Kappa Delta Pi. *Hobbies:* Photography; Travel; Covered Bridges. *Address:* Dept of Political Science & Geography, Old Dominion Univ, Norfolk VA 23529, USA. 7.

ZEIGLER Earle Frederick, b. 20 Aug 1919, Educator. *Education:* BA, Bates Coll, 1940; MA, 1944; PhD, 1951; Arnold Coll, Conn, 1942-44; Columbia Univ, 1943-46. *Appointments include:* prof, 1963-72; Hd, Dept of Phys, Educ for Men, Univ of Illinois, 1964-68; Prof, Dept Hlth & Phys Educ, 1971-; Dean, Fac of Phys Educ, 1972-77; Univ of Western Ont, Canada. *Publications:* 14 Books; Over 250 Articles. *Memberships:* Numerous Profl Assns. *Honours include:* LLD. *Address:* Faculty of Physical Educ, Univ of Western Pntario, London, Ontario, Canada N6A 3K7.

ZELIAS Aleksander Jozef, b. 14 Sept 1939, Olesnica. Full Prof of Economics. m. Helena, 15 June 1963, 1 s, 1 d. *Education:* MSc, Cracow Sch of Economics, 1962; DSc, 1966; Dsc Habil, Poznan Sch of Economics, 1970; Prof, State Council, Polish Peoples Republic, 1977; Full Prof, 1982. *Appointments include:* Asst Lectr, Cracow Sch of Economics, 1963; Asst Prof, 1966; Assoc Prof, 1971; Visiting Schlar, Cambridge, USA, 1974-75; Visiting Prof, Pittsburgh Univ, 1982; Visiting Prof, Tilburg Univ, The Netherlands, 1988; Vice Dir, Inst of Statistics & Economics, 1973-81; Editor in Chief, Folia Deconomica Cracoviensia, 1982-87; Member Editorial staff, Prace Naukoznawcze 1 Prognostyczne, 1988-. *Publications include:* Over 150 Papers & Reports; Books inc Econometric Methods of Forecasting of Economic Processes; Mathematical Statistic in Practical Applications; Spatial Econometrics. *Memberships include:* Polish Economic Assn; Polish Statistical Assn; Polish Cybernetics Assn; Cracow Branch of Polish Acas of Sciences; American Biographical Inst. *Honours include:* Gold Cross of Merit; The Medal of Committee of the Natl Education; Bronze Medal of Merit; Gold Mark of Distinction. *Hobbies:* Reading; Gardening; Foreign Languages. *Address:* Cracow Acad of Economics, Inst of Statistics, Econometrics & Computer Science, 27 Rakowicka Street, 31 510 Krakow, Poland. 139, 152.

ZENG Ding, b. 3 Mar 1930, Fuchou, China. Prof of Biochemistry; Chmn Dept of Biology. m. Qui Jue Min, 1 Oct 1962, 2 s. *Education:* Xiamen Univ, 1954; Univ of Wisconsin Madison, USA, 1981-82. *Appointments:* Asst, 1954-61; Lectr, 1961-81; Assoc Prof, 1981-87; Prof, 1987-; Dept of Biology, Xianmen Univ, China. *Publications:* Books, Methods for Biological Chemistry; Biology of Nitrogen Fixation; More than 40 Papers. *Memberships:* Xiamen Biological Soc; Fujian Biochemical Soc; Chinese Botanical Soc; Chinese Biochemical Soc; Soc of Chinese Bioscientists in America; Xiamen Assn of Sci; Intl Biographical Assn. *Honours:* Nature Sco Meeting Award; Sci & Tech Achievement Award; Excel Papers of Nature Sci Award; outstanding Tchrng & Research Award. *Hobbies:* Classical Music; Photography; Volley Ball. *Address:* Dept of Biology, Xiamen Univ, Xiamen, Fujian 361005, China.

ZENG Xiaozhen, b. 1 Oct 1932, Kunming, China. Prof. m. Liu Shuxian, 10 Jan 1962, 1 s, 1 d. *Education:* Ind Coll of North East China, 1951-52; Geology Coll of North East China, 1952-55. *Appointments:* Changchun Coll of Geology, China, Asst Lectr, 1955-62; Lecyr, 1962-78; Assoc Prof, 1978-83; Prof, 1983-. *Publications:* Proton Resonance Magnetometer; Aerial Proton Resonance Magnetometer; Optically pumped Magnetometer; Aerial Pulse Electical Mesurement Meter; Station of the Aerial Magnetic Measurement; GEM 1 and GEM 11 Digital Magnetotelluric Meter; Multifunction System. *Memberships:* Soc of China Geology Instrument; Soc of Sci & Tech of Jilin Province; China Geology & Geophysics Soc; China Inst of Electronics. *Honours:* Research Achievement Award; Excellence Scientist, Jilin Province. *Hobbies:* Music; Reading; Computer Applications; Geophysics; Measurements & Instrumentation. *Address:* Dept of Instrumentation, Changchun Coll of Geology, Changchun, Jilin 130026, China.

ZENG Xiaozhen, b. 1 Oct 1932, China. Prof. m. Liu Shuxian, 10 Jan 1962, 1 s, 1 d. *Education:* Coll of North East of China, 1955. *Appointments:* Tchr, 1955-62; Lectr, 1962-78; Assoc Prof, 1978-83; Prof, 1983-; Changchun Coll of Geology. *Creative Works:* Aerial Proton Resonance Magnetometer; Optically Pumped Magnetometer; GEM 1 & GEM 11 Magnetotelluric Meter. *Memberships:* Soc of China Geology Instrumentation; Soc of Sci & Tech of Jilin, China. *Honours:* Chinese Government Research Achievements; Excellent Scientist. *Hobbies:* Reading; Music. *Address:* Dept of Instrumentation, Changchun Coll of Geology, Changchun, Jilin 130026, China.

ZENG Yi, b. 5 Sept 1951, China. Prof of Demography. m. Wang Jinrong, 10 Sept 1972, 2 s, 1 d. *Education:* BA, East China Normal Univ, Shanghai, 1982; PhD, Brussels Free Univ, 1986; Princeton Univ, 1987. *Appointments:* Tchr, Hung Ling High Sch, 1970-78; Student, Brussels Free Univ, 1978-86; Research scholar, Netherland Univ Demographic Inst, 1984-86; Post Doc Fellow, Princeton Univ, 1986-87; Assoc Prof, Deputy Dir, 1987-89; Prof, Deupty Dir, Population Research Inst, Peking Univ, 1989-. *Publications:* Family Dynamics in China; A Life Table Analysis; Changing Family Structure & Population Aging in china; Articles. *Memberships:* Intl Union for the Sci Study of Population; Population Assn of China; Population Assn of America; The State Family Planning Commission of China; Advisory Group of Census Office Under Seate Council of China. *Honours:* 1st Class Prize of Excellence; ABOS Fellowship; Honorable Frank Notostein Fellowship; Dorothy Thomas Prize of Population Assn; He Xing Dong Prize, State Educ Commission; 1st Class Prize for Outstanding Achievement. *Hobbies:* Music; Tennis.

Address: The Inst of Population Research, Peking Univ, Beijing 100871, China. 139, 152.

ZHAN Behui, b. 10 July 1931, China. Prof. m. Chen Yaxian, 5 July 1962, 1 d. *Education:* BA, Zhengshan Univ, 1953; Beijing Univ, 1955-58. *Appointments:* Asst, 1953-60; Lectr, 1961-78; Assoc Prof, 1979-81; Prof, 1982-83; Wuhan Univ; Prof of Jinan Univ, 1983-; Visiting Prof, Toyko Univ, 1980-82; Ecole des Hautes Etudes en Sci, 1990. *Publications:* Modern Chinese Dialects; Collected Works of Chinese Dialects; A Survey of Dialects in the Pearl River Delta; Chinese Dialects & Dialect Surveys; Chaozhou Dialect. *Memberships:* Chinese Linguistics Soc; Chinese Dialectology Soc; CLS; Chinese Nal Peoples Congress. *Honours:* Excellent Achievements Award. *Hobbies:* Reading; Stamp Collecting; Music. *Address:* Room 402, Block 22, Suzhou Yuan, Jinan Univ, Shipai, Guangzhou, China.

ZHAN Chang Guo, b. 1 July 1960, Wuhan, P R China. Theoretical Chemist. m. Fang Zheng, 12 Nov 1988. *Education:* Central China Normal Univ, BSc, 1978-82; Visiting Scholar, Wuhan Univ, 1982-83; Beijing Normal Univ, 1984-85; Central China Normal Univ, 1985-87. *Appointments:* Faculty Member, Xiaogen Tchrs Coll, 1982-85; Faculty Member, Central China Normal Univ, 1987-. *Publications:* 24 Orig Sci Papers. *Membership:* Chinese Chemical Soc. *Honours:* Hubei Award for Outstanding Articles; CCNC Award for Outstanding Achievements; Advanced Youth Tchr, CCNC. *Hobby:* Outing. *Address:* Dept of Chemistry, Central China Normal Univ, Wuhan 430070, China.

ZHAN Tong, b. 13 Jan 1932, Beijing, China. Dir. m. Jing Feng Hong, 28 Dec 1962, 1 s, 1 d. *Education:* Peiking Acad, 1945-50; Central Art Inst of Beijing, 1952-56. *Appointments:* Dir, Artistic Designer, Shanghai Aviation Film Studio, 1956-; Editorial Bd, World of Cartoons & China Cartoons. *Creative Works include:* Dschungel Abenteuer; Portraits of Filmers; A Half; If I Were WU Song; Piggy Eats Water melon. *Memberships:* Council of China Film Experts Assn; China Animation Film Assn; Cartoon Art Committee The Chinese Artist Assn; ASIFA, China. *Honours include:* 5 Prizes of Cartoon 80; Special Design Award for Animation Film; Best Award of Chinese Cartoon Exhib; Best Film Award, Central Culture Dept of China. *Hobbies:* Reading; Drawing; Painting; Music; Gardening; Walking. *Address:* Shanghai Animation Film Studio, 618 Wanttang Don Road, 200042 Shanghai, China. 139.

ZHANG Baotong, b. 19 Apr 1947, Ankang, Shaanxi, China. Asst Research Fellow. m. Wang Miao, 1 June 1977, 1 s. *Education:* Northwest Univ, 1979; Master Degree Economics, 1982. *Appointments:* Tchr, Longquan Middle Sch, 1970-87; Research Worker, 1982-87; Asst Research Fellow, 1987-. *Publications:* Labour Market, Labour Commodity; Production Price and the Sonsciousnuopus Use of Law of Value; New Ideas of Chinas Regional Economic Strategy. *Memberships:* Young Social Sci Worker Assn; Union of Shaanxi Social Sci Assn; System Reform Research Inst, Shanghai. *Honours include:* Excellent Paper Reward; Best Papers Reward. *Hobby:* Pingpong. *Address:* Economic Research Inst of the Social Aci Acad in Shaanxi, Xian, Shaanxi 710061, China. 152.

ZHANG Bo-quan, b. 28 Jan 1926, Liao Ning, China. Prof in History. m. Jin Bo, 19 Sept 1943, 3 s, 3 d. *Education:* Northeast Admin Coll, 1948-50; Chinese People Univ, Northeast Peoples Univ, 1952-54. *Appointments:* Asst Tchr, Lectr, 1954-78; Assoc Prof, Hd of Branch, 1978-85; Prof, 1985-. *Publications:* Outline of Jin Dynasty Economic History; An Introduction to Jin Dynasty; Northeast Local History; On Jin Dynasty History; More than 100 Thesis. *Memberships:* Jilin Province History Assn; Nu Zhen History Assn; Yuan Hao Wen Assn. *Honours:* 2nd Degree Award of Social Sci Works; 1st Class Award of Excellent Works; 2nd Class Degree Award, Philosophy & Social Sci Excellent Works. *Hobbies:* Reading; Writing;

Chinese Ancient Poetry. *Address:* History Dept, Jilin Univ, Changchun, Jilin Province 130023, China.

ZHANG De Zeng, b. 5 May 1925, Bao Di Xian County, China. Counselor; Visiting Prof. m. 31 July 1955, 2 s, 1 d. *Education:* Beijing Univ, 1944-45; Yenching Univ, 1945-49. *Appointments:* Tchr, Dean of Studies, Experimental Sch of North East Region of China, 1949-78; Prof, Sheng Yuang Agriclt Coll, 1978-79; Prof, Sheng Yuang Tchrs Coll, 1979-87; Founder, Counselor, Piaget Bilingual Kgt. *Publications:* The Methods of Arithmetic Problem Solving in High sch; Several Disscussions on the Methodology of the History of Psychology; Methods for the Study of Students Personality. *Memberships:* Assn of Social Psychology; Assn of Comparative Educ; Assn of Tech English in Liao Ning Province. *Honours:* Model Progressive Educational Worker; Educational Model of Pre Sch Educ. *Hobbies:* Swimming; Tennis; Skating; Soccer; Table Tennis; Guitar. *Address:* Dept of Education, Shengyang Tchrs Coll, Shengyang, Liaoning Province 110031, China.

ZHANG Fengbo, b. 1 Mar 1957, Hubei, China. Chief Economist; Prof. m. Renxia Cai, 16 Oct 1987, 1 d. *Education:* BA, Shanghai Foreign Language Univ, 1976-80; MA, Oita Univ, Japan, 1980-83; PhD, Kyoto Univ, 1983-86. *Appointments:* Researcher, Chinese Acad of Social Sci, 1980-86; Visiting Prof, Kyoto Univ, 1986; Snr Research Fellow, Prof, State Council Research Centre, China, 1986-88; Visiting Scholar, Natl Bureau of Economic Research, Harwvard Univ, 1988-90; Chief Economist, AMTAD, 1990-. *Publications include:* Chinese Macroeconomic System Research; Economic Development & Transportation Policy; Applications of Personal Computer to Economic Anaylsis. *Memberships:* Chinese Natl Sci Foundation; Chinese Natl Social Sci foundation; Chinese Assn of Quantitative Economics; Financial Economics Assn; Harvard Neighbours, USA. *Honours:* Japanese Government Foreign Scholarship; Chinese Natl Youth Thesis Comp; Ford Foundation Research Scholarship; Chinese Natl Book Prize. *Address:* 89 06 78th Street, Woodhaven, NY 11421, USA. **139.**

ZHANG Hanxin, b. 1 Jan 1936, Peixian, Jiangsu Province, China. Research Prof; Engr. m. Gao Pu, 20 Jan 1967, 2 s. *Education:* Undergraduate, 1953-58; Graduate, 1958-63; Qinghua Univ. *Appointments:* Lectr, 1964-75; Prof, Qinghua Univ, 1976; Research Prof, CARDC, 1976-. *Publications include:* Numerous Research Papers. *Memberships:* Chinese Soc of Theoretical & Applied Mechanics; China Aerodynamics Research Soc; Chinese Soc of Astronautics. *Honours:* Cert of Merit. *Hobby:* Chess. *Address:* China Aerodynamics Research & Developement Centre, PO Box 211, Mianyang Sichuan Province, China.

ZHANG Hua, b. 7 July 1957, Peijing, China. Lectr. m. 31 Dec 1983. *Education:* Wahan Univ, BA, 1978-82; Beijing Foreign Studies Univ, 1982-84; Advanced English Cource, 1986-87; Inst of Litaerature, Chinese Acad of Social Sci, 1986-87. *Appointments:* Fine Ats Tchr, Yong Feng High Sch, 1957-78; Sec, Cultural Palace of Minority Nationality, Beijing, 1982; Lectr, Dir, Beijing Foriegn Studies Univ, 1982-. *Publications:* Winds Blowing Around Univ Campuses; Colorful Life; A Day of New China; A Dictionary of Chinese Culture; Appreciating Foreign Mini Stories. *Memberships:* Chinese Writers Union; Chinese Reportage Assn. *Honours:* Chinese Literary Prize; Chinese Youth Literary Prize. *Hobbies:* Reading; Drinking. *Address:* Lectr of Chinese, Beijing Foreign Studies Univ, PO Box 8110 31, Beijing, China 100081.

ZHANG Jing-Ru, b. 21 May 1929, Shanghai, China. Prof of Physiology. m. Su Qing Fen, 4 Apr 1952, 2 s, 1 d. *Education:* Shanghai First Medical Col, MD, 1953. *Appointments:* Assoc Prof, 1978; Prof, 1982; Chmn of Dept, 1982-84; Pres, Shanghai Medical Univ, 1984-88. *Publications:* 47 Research Papers; Textbooks. *Memberships:* Chinese Assn for Physiological Sci; Intl

Brain Research Organ; Sci & Tech, State Educ Commission. *Honours:* Honorary Citzenship of Baltimore, USA; Thomas Nart Benton Mural Medallion; Deputy to Shanghai Peoples Congress. *Address:* Dept of Physiology, Shanghai Medical Univ, Shanghai 200032, China. **156.**

ZHANG Jingiu, b. 10 Oct 1936, Chengdu, China. Arch. m. 3 Aug 1965, 1 s. *Education:* Qinhua Univ, 1954, 1961-66. *Appointments include:* China Museum of Revolutionary History, 1958-59; Cultural Palace, Ameroon, 1973; Beijing Library, 1975; Proj Mgr, Memorial to Abeno Nakamaro, 1978; Proj Arch, Northwest Univ, 1980; Proj Mgr, Qinglong Temple & Kukai Memorial, 1981; Proj Mgr, Tang City Tourist Centre, 1984; Proj Mgr, Museum of the Bath at Huaqing Palace, 1990; Sci & Tech Building, Shaanxi Province, 1991. *Publications include:* A Memorial to Abeno; Kukai Memorial, Xian; On Inheriting Arch Tradition; Notes of Designing Three Projects in Tang Style, Xian; Museum of the Bath at Huaoing Palace. *Honours include:* Excellent Project Award; Excellent Design Award. *Hobbies:* Literature; Fine arts; Travel; Photography. *Address:* North West Inst of China Architecture, 173 West 7th Road, Xian 710003, China.

ZHANG Jingshun, b. 27 July 1938, Anhui, China. Prof; Hd of Financial Div. m. Shi Yongxin, 4 Aug 1964, 1 s, 1 d. *Education:* Bach Agriclt Economics, Nanjing Agriclt Coll, 1961. *Appointments:* Tchrng Asst, 1961-79; Lectr, 1980-85; Assoc Prof, 1986-91; Prof, 1992; Naning Agriclt Univ. *Publications:* Handbook of Economics for Tech; Textbook of Agriclt Tech Economics; More than 20 Papers. *Memberships:* Chinese Soc of Agrotechnical Economics. *Hobby:* Table Tennis. *Address:* Coll of Agricltural Economics & Trade, Nanjing Agriclt University, Nanjing, China.

ZHANG Jinzhe, b. 25 Sept 1920, China. Pediatric Surgeon. m. Elizabeth Enlian Shen, 7 July 1943, 2 s, 2 d. *Education:* Yenching Univ, Peking, BS, 1941; Peking Union Medical Coll, 1941-42; St Johns Univ, 1942-43; Shanghai Medical Coll, MD, 1946. *Appointments:* Beijing Medical Hosp, 1950; Assoc Prof Surgery, 1955; Surgeon in Chief, Beijing Childresn Hosp, 1955; Prof, The Capital Medical Coll, 1977. *Publications:* Textbook of Pediatric Surgery; Office Pediatric Surgery; Grand Encyclopedia of China; More Than 100 Sci Papers. *Memberships:* Chinese Medical Assn; CSPS; PAPS; AAPS. *Honours:* Pioneer of Tech Medal; 2nd Class Award by Tech Committee. *Hobbies:* Chinese Painting; Peking Opera; Acting. *Address:* Beijing Childrens Hosp, Nan Lishi Road, Beijing 100045, China.

ZHANG Jun Ying, b. 19 Nov 1943, Beijing, China. Actress; Dir; Tchr. m. Qu Xian He, 23 Mar 1967, 1 s, 1 d. *Education:* Central Dramatic Acad, 1965. *Appointments:* China Central Dramatic Acad, Tchr. *Creative Works:* Dubbing Dir; Reciter; Broadcaster; Author. *Memberships:* China Dramatist Assn; China Act & Language Research Party; Beijing Language Research Party. *Honours:* 1 out of 10 Outstanding Broadcasters in China; Several Dubbing Awards. *Hobbies:* Voilin; Piano; Cooking; Fashion Design. *Address:* 202, Door 3, Building 514, Jingong 5 District, Beijing, China 100021.

ZHANG Liang, b. 27 Mar 1938, Shanghai, China. Assoc Prof of Mathematics. m. Kang Ailin, 30 Jan 1978, div. *Education:* Peking Univ, 1955-60. *Appointments:* Worker, Shan dan Farm, Gansu China, 196-78; Lectr, Zhangye Tchrs Coll, 1978-85; Lectr, Shanghai Inst of Urban Constr, 1985-87; Assoc Pfof, SIUC, 1987-. *Publications include:* Rectangle Codes & Square Codes; On Completion of Codes with Finite Deciphering Delay; On Factorizing of Finite Maximal Codes, Intl Colloguium on Words, Languages & Combinatorics. *Memberships:* China Mathematics Assn; Shanghai Inst of Urban Constr; Democratic Union of China. *Hobbies:* Classical Music; Literature. *Address:* Dept of Basic Courses, Shanghai Inst of Urban Constr, 71 Chi Feng Road, Shanghai 200092, China. **139, 152**

ZHANG Lijuan, b. 13 Mar 1962, Heilongjiang, China. Medical Culture Specialist; Biomedical Scientist. m. Quan Yu, 20 July 1985. *Education:* BS, Northwestern Univ, China, 1979-83; Heilongjiang Inst of Applied Microbiology, 1983-86. *Appointments:* Reseach Asst, Natl Inst Control of Pharmaceutical & Biological Prod, 1986-90; Biomedical Research PCR Specialist, Univ of Turku, 1990-. *Publications:* Various Sci & Biological. *Membership:* Turku Microbiology Soc. *Hobbies:* Reading; Swimming; Dancing. *Address:* Natl Inst of the Control of Pharmaceutical & Biological products, Temple of Heaven, Beijing 100050, China.

ZHANG Longxiang, b. 19 Mar 1916, Wuxing, Zhejiang Province, China. Prof of Biochemistry. m. Youqiang Liu, 3 Mar 1940, 2 s. *Education:* BS, Tsinghua Univ, 1937; PhD, Univ of Toronto, 1942. *Appointments:* Post Doc Research fellow, Yale Univ, 1942-44; Snr Chemist, Tung Oil Inst, Chongsqing, 1944-46; prof, Peking Univ, 1946-; Dean, 1976-78; Vice Pres, 1978- 81; Pres, 1981-84. *Publications:* Chinese Biochemical Soc; Chinese Assn of Sci & Tech; Natl Sci award Committee; State Councils Acad Degree Committee. *Honours:* 1st Class Award, Sci 7 Tech Advancement Award; Biochemical Experimental Methods & Technique; Excellent Sci & Tech Textbooks Award. *Hobbies:* Swimming; Taiji Boxing. *Address:* Dept of Biology, Peking Univ, Beijing 100871, China. 52, 139, 152.

ZHANG Qi-cheng, b. 20 Oct 1959. Tchr. m. 6 Feb 1986, 1 s. *Education:* Muizhou Tchrs Coll, 1985; Anhui provincial Coll, Tchrs Advanced Studies, 1988. *Appointments:* Tchr, Chinese Literature, no.8 Middle Sch, 1980-83; Lectr, Nanjing Coll TCM, 1988-. *Publications:* A Encyclopedia of Yi Jing; On Empirical Cases of Tumors; Biographies of Well Known Doctors in XinAn; Study on Yi Jing & TCM; Shangz Experience in Medicine. *Memberships:* Yi Jing Assn of Nanjing; TCM; China Assn of TCM; China Research Assn of Zhou Yi; Chinese Soc of Lomatic Sci. *Honours:* 3rd Proze Excellent Treatises on Ancient Chinese Medical Literature. *Hobbies:* Literature; Painting; Calligraphy. *Address:* Nanjing Coll of TCM, 282 Hanzhing Road, Nanjing, China.

ZHANG Ren Jun, b. 11 Nov 1928, Beijing, PR China, Prof; Authority Editor. m. Ying Qui Li, 1 June 1954, 2 s. *Education:* Diploma, Inst of Foriegn Language, Beijing, 1948-52. *Appointments:* Authority Editor, Chinese Encyclopedia Publisher, 1982; Prof, Su Zhou Univ, 1986; Conslt, Medical Section, CSBS, Hong Kong, 1986; Prof, Chinese Acad of Management Sci, 1988. *Publications:* Dictionary of Psychologists; Series of Current Psychology; Dictionary of Psychological Writers; Concise Encyclepedia of Psychology; Health Psychology. *Memberships:* Chinese Assn of Social Psychology; Chung Sing Benevolent Soc; Initiator of H C Chang Physiology Prize in China. *Honours:* Honor Writings, Conseling Psychology; Psychology in Taiwan; My Biography Published in Dictionary of Editor & Journalist; Dictionary of Chinese Sociologists. *Hobbies:* Stamp Collecting; Peking Opera; Local Songs; Writing Art. *Address:* Encyclopedia of China Publishing House, 17 Fuchengmen Bei Da Jie, Beijing 100037, China.

ZHANG Ruth Jun Ru, b. 28 Oct 1911, Bishan, Sichuan, China. Pediatrician; Prof Emeritus of Pediatrics. m. Stephen Zhen Hua Yang, 31 Oct 1942, 2 s, 1 d. *Education:* MD, West China Union Univ & NY State Univ, NY, 1937; Advanced Studies in Pathological Physiology & Pediatrics, Hosp for Sick Children, Toronot, Ontario, 1947-50. *Appointments:* Asst, Resident, Medicine & Pediatrics WCUU Hosp, 1937-42; Resident, 1942-43; Instr Pediatrics, 1943-45; Assoc Prof, 1945-47; Chairperson, Dept of Pediat, West China Univ of Medical Sci Medical Coll, 1954-84; Prof of Pediatrics, WCUMS, 1979-. *Publications:* Chapters on Pediatrics in Manual of Medical Emergency; Different Diagnosis & Treatment of Pediatric Diseases; The Practice of Pediatrics; Collaborative Research on Childrens Diarrhea Diseases in the 7 MCH Model Countries & Beijing City of China.

Memberships: Chinese Medical Assn; Chinese Assn of Pediatrics; Sichuan Assn of Pediatrics; Chengdu Assn of Pediatrics. *Honours:* Best Scientific & Tech Article Award, 1982,1988. *Hobbies:* Reading; Music. *Address:* Prof Emeritus of Pediatrics, West China Univ of Medical Science, Chengdu, Sichuan 610041, China.

ZHANG Shang Zhi, b. 9 Dec 1936, Guangdong Province. Tchr. m. Bang Yan Que, 17 Aug 1973, 1 s. *Education:* Peking Univ, 1955-60. *Appointments:* Dept of Mathematics, Peking Univ, 1960-61; Dept of Math, Jiangxi Univ, 1961-87; Asst Prof, 1961-79; Lectr, 1979-85; Assoc Prof, Guangzhou no.1 Workers Com Coll, 1985-87. *Publications include:* Counter Examples in Probability & Statistics; Over 30 Articles; Translations. *Memberships:* Intl Chinese Statistical Assn; Mathematical Assn of China; Membership of Probability & Statistics Assn of China; Probability & Statistics Assn of Jiangxi Province. *Honour:* Excellent Scientific Papers Prize, Tiangxi Univ. *Hobbies:* Music; Reading; Watch Football Match. *Address:* Guangzhou no.1 Workers Commercial College, 79 Dong Sha Zhi Jie, Hosha Lu, Guangzhou, China.

ZHANG Shengkai, b. 18 Nov 1936, Shangdong, China. Prof. m. Song Yulan, 1 Feb 1964, 3 s. *Education:* Postgrad Studemt, Harbin Normal Univ, 1960-62. *Appointments:* Tchr, 1963-79; Assoc Prof, 1980-85; Prof, 1985-; Dalian Inst of Light Industry Technology. *Publications:* Introduction to Matrix Games; Games Theory and its Applications; Methods of Managing Mathematics; Modern Methods of Game Theory. *Memberships include:* WUT; WCTRS; ORMS; CPCC. *Honours:* Example in Dalian; Advanced Tchr in Dalian; Conslt in Dalian Government. *Hobbies:* TV, Films. *Address:* 1 Baoding Street, 116001 Dalian Inst of Light Industry Technology, China. 191.

ZHANG Shou Ji, b. 18 Jan 1933, Shanghai, China. Snr Geologist. m. Shu Juan Yao, Dec 1958, 2 s, 1 d. *Education:* Dept of Geology, Nanking Univ, 1956. *Appointments:* 931 Team of Geology, Guangdong China Natl Non Ferrous Metals Ind Corp, 1956-. *Publications:* The Types of Tin in Guangdong and the Study of Their Formation; The Study of the Formation of Tin Ore Sulphurous Mineral. *Memberships:* China soc on Geology; China Soc of Non Ferrous Metals; China Soc of Metals; Shautou Assn on Sci & Tech. *Honours include:* Essay, The Formation of Resoucres of Manganese Ore in the Northeast of Guangdong, Prize. *Hobbies:* Playing Football; Planting Flowers. *Address:* 931 Team of Geology, 13 Wai Huan Dong Lu, Shantou, China.

ZHANG Tian Ze, b. 2 Apr 1920, Shen Yang, Liao Ning, China. Oncologist; Health Assn Asmin. m. Pei Lan Zhu, 15 Aug 1954, 3 s. *Education:* MBCHB Dugald Chrstie Memorial Medical Coll, Shen Yang, 1937-43. *Appointments:* Intern Christie Memorial Medical Coll Hosp, 1944; Resident Surgery, 1945-48; Chief Resident Surgical Dept, Central Hosp, Lanzhou, 1949-50; Visiting Surgical Dept, Mackenzie Memorical Hosp, 1951-52; Chief Surgeon, Oncological Dept, Tianjin, 1953-75; Chief Surgeon Clinical Oncology, Cancer Hosp, 1975-85; Dir, Tianjin Cancer Inst & Hosp, 1983-. *Publications:* 102 Academic Papers; Book Chapters. *Memberships:* Tianjin Cancer Inst; Chinese Journal Clinical oncology; China Anti Cancer Assn; Asian Pacific Federation of Organizations for Cancer Research & Control; Shinese Cancer Soc. *Hobbies:* Play Auction Bridge; Reading. *Address:* Tianjin Cancer Inst, Huan Hu Xi Road, Ti Yuan Bei, Tianjin 300060, China. 1, 52.

ZHANG Xianyang, b. 14 Nov 1936, Suzhou, Jiangsu, China. Theorist; Snr Research Fellow. m. Zhang Jingwen, 12 Feb 1963, 1 d. *Education:* Philosophy Bach, Peoples Univ of China, 1956-61; History of Western Philosophy, PUC, 1961-66. *Appointments:* Philosophy Tchr, Dept of Philosophy, PUC, 1966-71; Exec, Propaganda Dept of Public Health Bureau, Beijing, 1971-73; Researcher, Inst of Foreign Philosophy, Beijing

Univ, 1973-79; Research Fellow, Inst of Marcism Leninism & Mao Zedong Thought, Chinese Acad of Social Sci, 1979-. *Publications include:* Dictatorship of the Proletariat or Dictatorship of the Fascist?; Freedom of Speech; Deep Understanding of Historical Materialism from the Historical Point of View; Meditation of Reform of the Political System; Marxism: Crisis & Outlet. *Memberships:* Chinese Inst of Marxism; Chinese inst of Mao Zedong Thought; Political Inst of China; Research Inst of Foreign Philosophy of China. *Hobbies:* Smoking; Music; Watching Sports Match; Cultivating Cats. *Address:* Marxism Leninism & Mao Zedong Thought Inst, Chinese Academy of Social Sciences, 5 Jianguomennei Dajie, Beijing, 100732, China.

ZHANG Xinjing, b. 15 Apr 1939, Leshan, Sichuan, China. Prof; TV Engrng. m. Yang Wenxiu, 14 Feb 1969, 2 d. *Education:* Univ of Electronic Sci & Tech of China, 1956-60; Oakland Univ, USA, 1982-84. *Appointments:* Prof, Univ of Electronic Sci & Tech of China, 1960-91. *Publications:* TV Equipment; Digital TV Studio; Video Recording Technology; Research Works. *Memberships:* SMPTE; Chengdu Inst of Electronics. *Honours:* Award for Making Important Contributions to Sci & Tech; Golden Medal of Invention Award; Bronze Medal of Invention award. *Hobbies:* Playing Basketball; Swimming; Table Tennis. *Address:* Dept 1 Univ of Electronic Science & Technology of China, Chengdu, Sichuan 610054, China.

ZHANG Xuewen, b. 27 Oct 1938, Shaanxi, China. Prof; Chief Doctor. m. Xiouqin Zhang, 6 Nov 1956, 2 s, 3 d. *Education:* BA, Shaanxi Coll of Traditional Chinese Medicine, 1959-60. *Appointments:* Physician, Traditional Chinese Medicine, Hanzhong, Shaanxi, 1953-58; Physician, Tchr, 1959-63; Hd Tchrng & Research Section of Internal Medicine, 1963-78; Assoc Prof, Vice Chief Physician, Vice Dean, Dean of Dept of Medical Treatment, 1978-82; Vice Pres, Principal, 1981-87; Chief Physician, Research of Treatment & Prevention of Cerebral Vascular Accident with Traditional Chinese Medicine, 1988-; Shaanxi Coll of Traditional Chinese Medicine. *Publications:* Emergency of Internal Medicine to TCM; Collection of Illustrative Colour plates for Tongue Diagnosis; Treatment of the Syndrome Caused by Blood Stagnation. *Memberships:* China Soc of Traditional Chinese Medicine; Important Achievement in Scientific & Tech research; Shaanxi Journal of Traditional Chinese Medicine; Assn of Rehabilitation. *Honours:* Honorary Prof, Zhang Zhong Jin Univ of Traditional Chinese Medicine; 2nd & 3rd Awards of Achievement in Sci & Tech Research; Invited Lectr, Japan; Advanced Individual Prize in Sci & Tech Reseach, Shaanxi. *Address:* Shaanxi Coll of Traditional Chinese Medicine, Xianyang, Shaanxi, China.

ZHANG Yangde, b. 13 June 1954, Changsha, PRChina. Doc; Tchr. m. Zhou Jiang, 1984, 1 d. *Education:* Medical Univ, 1974-78. *Appointments:* Resident Surgeon, First Affiliated Hosp of Hunan Medical Univ, 1978-84; Lectr, Attending Doc, 1984-87; Assoc Prof, 1987-91; Prof, 1992-. *Publications:* Modern Diagnosis & Therapy Technique; Principle & Application of PCR; Micro Explosion of Biliary Calculi; Water Jet Fluid Operation Knife; JBM PC Biological Information Processing System. *Memberships:* Modern Tech Research Center; Laboratory of Biliology, Pancreology & Enterology of First Affiliated Hosp, Hunan Medical Univ; Youth Medical Assn of Hunan. *Honours:* Natl Natural Sci Fund 3 Times; Sci & Tech Achievement Prize; Outstanding Contribution Specialist; Snr Youth Tchr; One of Ten Outstanding Youth of Hunan. *Hobbies:* Swimming; playing Football. *Address:* Modern Tech Research Center, First Affiliated Hosp of Hunan Medical Univ, 121 Beizhan Road, Chansha, Hunan 410008, China.

ZHANG Yi Wen Kiang, b. 17 Nov 1924, Chengdu, China. Prof; Researcher. m. Deng Fu Ming, 20 Jan 1960, 1 s, 1 d. *Education:* Dept of Foreign Literature & Language, Sichuan Univ, MA, 1948. *Appointments:*

Asst, Dept of Russian Language, North West Univ, Sian, 1950; Asst, Russian Dept, Shensi Univ, 1951; Lectr, English of Sichuan Inst of Foreign Languages, 1959; Asst Prof, Inst of Population Studies, Sichuan Univ, 1980- 83; Prof, Inst of History Sichuj An Acad of Social Sci, 1983-. *Publications include:* Books; Numerous Articles & Critiques. *Memberships:* Soc of the History of Chinas Relation with Foreign Countries in Ancient Times. *Honours:* Prize Sino Indian Frienship; Humbold Stiftung, Germany; First Class Prize Arrangement & commentary of Chinese Classics. *Hobbies:* Chess; Travel. *Address:* Acad of Social Sci, 610072 Chengdu Sichuan, China.

ZHANG Yin Xiang, b. 12 Mar 1936, Liaoning Prov, China. Scientific Tch Research; Deputy Dir, TV Broadcasting Lact CTI; Satellite TV Broadcasting Inpection Centre, China. m. Zhang Shen An, 15 Jan 1966, 1 s, 1 d. *Education:* Harbin Military Engrng Inst, 1962. *Appointments:* Technician, Communication Telecontrol & Telemetry Research Inst, CTI, Ministry of Machinery & Electronics Ind, China, 1962; Engr, CTI, 1979; Snr Engr, CTI, 1987. *Publications:* Basis of CCTV; Coding Picture Signal; Method of Picture Information Processing; Processing of Night Vision Picture; Design of Satellite TV Broadcasting; Questions & Answers on Colur TV. *Memberships include:* Broadcasting Tech Soc CIE; DBS-TVRO; China Electronics Inst. *Honours include:* Second Class Award on Communication Satellite; First Class Award on Satellite TV. *Hobby:* Peking Opera. *Address:* PO Box 174, Shijiazhuang 050002, Hebei, China.

ZHANG Zaiyuan, b. 27 July 1950, China. Assoc Prof. m. 1 Jan 1979, 1 d. *Education:* Wuhan Univ of Industry, Arch Dept, 1975; Tonji Univ, Shanghai, Arch Dept, 1980. *Appointments:* Asst Dept of Arch, Wuhan Univ of Ind, 1981-83; Lectr, Wuhan Univ, 1983-86; Assoc Prof, Vice Dept Hd of Arch Dept, Wuhan Univ, 1986-; Visiting Prof, Tekyo Univ. *Publications:* Landscape Architecture Design for Housing; The Contemporary China Architect; Review & Prospect for China Architecture; Horizon. *Memberships:* Arch Soc of China; Great Wall Inst of China; Arch Design Inst for Contemporary China; Arch/ Urbanism Mag Hong Kong. *Honours include:* The Crystal Palace of the Yangtze River Awarded Excellent Prize; Club of Savages in Shenglongia Primeval Forest, China; Nest House, Awarded 2nd Prize; Forest Sch, Awarded Excellent Prize. *Hobbies:* Musical Image; Landscape Drawing; Chinese Calligraphy; Arch & City Photography; Long Journeys; Sports. *Address:* Dept of Architecture, Wuhan Univ, Wuhan 430072, China.

ZHANG Zhenda, b. 9 Nov 1927, Guangdong, China. Prof of Astrophysics. m. Xizhi Zhang, 1 Aug 1960, 1 s, 1 d. *Education:* Bach of Astronomy, Nanjing Univ, 1954. *Appointments:* Asst, 1954; Asst Prof, 1961; Assoc Prof, 1980; Prof, 1985; Visiting Scholar of Natl Solar Observatory, USAZ, 1981-82, 1985-86, 1989-90. *Publications include:* Methods of Astrophysics; A Possible Mechanism of Nonresonant Heating of the Chromosphere Corona Transition Zone; The Effects of Alfven Waves in Heating Plasma in Post Flare Loops. *Memberships:* Astrophysics & Space Sci; Intl Astronomy Union; IAU 10 Organ Committee; American Geographical Soc. *Honours:* 2nd award of Nat Sci Tech Progress of China. *Hobbies:* Classical Music; Sports. *Address:* Dept of Astronomy, Nanjing Univ, Nanjing 210008, China.

ZHANG Zheng, b. 2 Mar 1920, Changsha, China. Prof of Infectious Diseases. m. Peng Qinglian, 2 Jan 1949, 2 s, 2 d. *Education:* Yali Middle Sch, 1934-40; Haiangya Medical Coll, MB, 1940-46. *Appointments:* Resident Physician, 1946-50; Instr, 1951; Assoc Prof, 1956; Prof in Infectious & Parasitic Diseases, 1979-. *Publications:* Over 60 Articles; A Handbook -for Rural Doctors. *Memberships:* Chinese Soc of Infectious & Parasitic Diseases; Soc of Infectious Dis, of Hunan; Intl Immunocompromised Host Soc. *Honours:* Grade 11 Award, Dept of Health, Hunan Prov; Grade 11 Award,

Committee of Sci & Tech, Hunan prov. *Hobby:* Photography. *Address:* Prof, Dept of Infectious Diseases, Hunan Medical Univ, Changsha, Hunan 410078, China.

ZHANG Zhenglang, b. 15 Apr 1912, China. Research Fellow. m. Fu Xueling, 24 Mar 1962, 2 s. *Education:* History Dept, Beijing Univ, BA, 1936. *Appointments:* Librarian, Assoc Research Fellow, Inst of History & Philology, Acad Sinica, 1936-46; Prof of History, Beijing Univ, 1946-60; Assoc General Editor, Zhonghua Press, 1960-66; Research Fellow, Inst of History, Chinese Acad of Social Sci, 1954-. *Publications include:* Book, A Textual Cristicism of The Jin History; Numerous Articles. *Memberships include:* Soc of Chinese Archaeology; Soc of Chinese History; Soc of Chinese palaeography; Museum of History Committee; Academic Affairs Committee Inst of History, Inst of Archaeology. *Honours:* Chinese Government Special Award, Outstanding Contributions to the Development of Social Sci in China. *Hobbies:* Chinese Calligraphy; Gardening. *Address:* Inst of History, Chinese Acad of Social Sci, 6 Ritan Road, 100020 Beijing, China.

ZHANG Zhenxian, b. 19 Mar 1934, Dingxiang, Shanxi Province. Prof. m. Zhou Huailing, 3 June 1961, 1, s, 1 d. *Education:* Beijing Geology Univ, 1956. *Appointments:* Oil Geology, 1956-62; Area Geology, 1962-70; Geological Mgmt, 1970-80; Oil Geological Mgmt, 1980-86; Depositional & Mineral Geology, 1986-. *Publications:* Nautiloids form Early & Middle Devonian of Hunan & Guangxi; Characteristics Genesis of the Lemei Po Zn Deposit in Wuxuan County, Guangxi. *Memberships:* Palaentological Soc of China; Oil Geological Soc of China; Geological Soc of Guangxi; Guangxi Inst of Geology. *Honours:* Sci Conference of China; 2nd Prize of Geological Sci of Geology & Mineral Resources, 1987; 3rd Prize, 1991. *Address:* Guangxi Inst of Geology, 1 Jianzheng, Nanning 530023, China.

ZHAO Bai-ge, b. 25 Aug 1952, China. Dir of Shanghai Inst. m. Jingguo Xu, 8 Jan 1980, 1 s. *Education:* Jiangxi Medical Coll, BSc, 1972-75; Harbin Medical Univ, MSc, 1978-81; Univ of Cambridge, PhD, 1985-88. *Appointments include:* Asst Lectr, Jiangxi Medical Coll, 1975-78; Lectr, Shanghai Inst of Planned Parenthood Research, 1981-84; Deputy Dir, Medical Sec of Shanghai Sci & Tech Commission, 1984-85; Exec Dir, Shanghai Inst of Planned Parenthood Research, 1989-90; Dir, 1990-91. *Publications include:* Effect of Stress by Ethyl Ether on Secretion of ACTH in the Rat with Ovary Implanted in Eyes; Brain is Target Organ of Hormones Medicine in Foreign Cuntries; Hypothalamic Opioid Mechanism Controlling Oxytocin Neurones During Parturition; Study of the Regulator Role of GABA on the LHRH Release in Medium Eminence of Rate; The Study of Cellular Localization of Proopiomelanocortin MRNA in the Ovary by in Sity Hybridization; 3 Books. *Memberships:* Darwin Coll Univ of Cambridge; British Neuroendoerine Group; Physiology Soc of China; American Soc for Neuroscience. *Honours:* Best Postgraduate of China; Model of Women Award. *Hobbies:* Music; Literature; Sports. *Address:* Shanghai Inst of Planned Parenthood Research, WHO Collaborating Centre for Research in Human Reproduction, 2140 Xie Tu Road, Shanghai 200032, China.

ZHAO Kebin, b. 25 July 1934, China. Chief of Intl Exchanges Div; Assoc Prof, Electrical Engrng. m. Zhang Lieping, 14 Aug 1964, 2 d. *Education:* Shanghai Xian Jiao Tong Univ, 1955-60; Queens Univ of Kingston, Canada, 1980-81; Univ of Toronto, 1981-82. *Appointments:* Letr, Jiao Tong Univ, 1960-79, 1983-84; Consul, Consulate General of PRCat NY, USA, 1985-88; Chief Instl Exchanges Divi, 1989-. *Publications:* Translations; Paper. A Thyristor Inveter for Medium Frequency Inducting Heating. *Memberships:* Electric Machine Engrng Assn of China; power Electronics Assn of China. *Hobbies:* Football; Badminton. *Address:* Div of Intl Exchanges, Shanghai Jiau Tong Univ, 1954 Hua Shan Road, Shanghai 200030, China.

ZHAO Ren Yuang, b. 11 Oct 1937, Gaoyou, Jiangsu, China. Prof; Snr Research Scientist; Radio Astronomer. m. 2 June 1966, 2 d. *Education:* Dept of Mathematics & Astronomy, Nanjing Univ, 1960. *Appointments:* Attended 6 Intl Conferences, 1982-89; Visited over 10 Countries. *Publications:* About 100 Acad Papers; Books inc. Cosmic Radio Radiation; Chinese Encyclopaedia. *Memberships:* Intl Astronomical Union. *Honours:* 9 Prizes of Achievement in Sci Research; About 40 Foreign Acad papers Quoted. *Hobbies:* Music; Calligraphy. *Address:* Building 924-501, Zhongguancun, Beijing 100080, China. 139, 152.

ZHAO WanZhi, b. 16 Mar 1929, Hebel Prov, China. Prof. m. Wang Jilian, 1 Oct 1956, 1 s. *Education:* Dept of Geology, Beijing Univ, 1950-52; Dept of Geology & Prospecting Engrng, 1952-53. *Appointments:* Dept of Mining Engrng, Beijing, Asst, Lectr, Assoc Prof, Prof, 1953-86; Research Section of Mineral Engrng, mining Research Inst, Dir, Prof, 1986-. *Publications:* Petrology of Crystal Minerlas; Theory of Technological Petrology; Mineral Engrng; Phase Diagrams for Silicates; More than 60 Sci Thesis. *Memberships:* Chinese Ceramic Soc; Tech Petrology Committee, Chinese Ceramic Soc; Chinese Rare Eargth Soc; Chinese Enviroment Soc; Chinese Geology Soc. *Honours:* Best Standing Dir. *Hobby:* Chinese Calligraphy. *Address:* 30 Xue Yuan Road, Beijing 100083, China.

ZHAO Zhongru, b. 16 Aug 1937, Nanchang Country, Jiangxi Prov, China. Paleontologist. m. Wo Xiangyun, 25 Apr 1971, 1 s, 1 d. *Education:* Geology Dept, Zhongshan Univ, 1957-63. *Appointments:* Researcher, Vice Prof, Guangxi Provincial Museum, 1963-88; Vice Prof, Prof, Paleontology, Natl History Museum of Guangxi, 1988-. *Publications:* The History of Science & Technology of Guangxi; Compositions; More Than 100 Articles. *Memberships:* The Soc of Vertebrate; Paleontology Of China; The Paleontological Soc of China; The Geology Soc of China; Chinese Assn of Natl Sci Museums. *Honours include:* Underground River System of the Tisu Karst Area, awarded bu the Natl Sci; Six Papers inc On The Fossils of Liujiang Man Award. *Hobbies:* Music; Cultivate Flowers. *Address:* Natural History Museum of Guangxi, Nanning, Guangxi 530012, China. 139, 162.

ZHAO Zong-ci, b. 28 Oct 1940, Beijing, PR China. Prof; Climate Change & Environment Deputy Sec-General of Chinese Climate Research Program. m. Shao Xian Zang, 9 Oct 1969, 1 d. *Education:* Dept of Geophysics, Peking Univ, 1959-64. *Appointments:* Dept of Geophysics, Peking Univ, 1964-85; NCAR, OSU Visiting Scholar, 1985-88; Peking Univ, Assoc Prof, 1988; Chinese Acad of Meteorological Sci, Prof, 1989-92. *Publications:* 71 Sci Papers; 5 Books; 2 Data Books. *Memberships:* Chinese Meteorological Soc; Chinese Regional Research Soc; Natl Climate Committee; Chinese Climate Research Program. *Honours:* Natl Natural Sci award; Natl Prize of Sci & Tech. *Hobbies:* Swimming; Chinese Tai Ji; Collecting Stamps. *Address:* Climatic Research Center, Chinese Academy of Meteorological Science, Beijing, China.

ZHEKOV Roumen, b. 1 Mar 1960, Haskovo, Bulgaria. Painter. *Education:* Sch of Fine Arts, Deisgn, 1974-79; Acad of Fine Arts, Painting, 1982-88. *Creative Works:* Paintings; Photography; Individual Exhibitions; Several Group Exhibs. *Memberships:* The Edge, Art Group; Bulgarian Artists Union. *Honours:* Diploma, Fourth Intl Comp of Young Painters, Sofia; Participation in the Exhib, Critics, Choice of Young Painters, Sofia. *Hobbies:* Music; Photography. *Address:* 5 Borba Str, 4003 Plovdiv, Bulgaria.

ZHEN Chen, b. 28 Mar 1936, China. Pres of Shanxi Agriclt & Soil Prof. *Education:* Shanxi Agriclt Univ, Taipu, Shanxi. *Appointments:* Prof; Agriclture; Editor in Chief, Shanxi Sci Soc & Shanxi Heplu Educational Soc. *Memberships:* Shanxi Natl Sci Fund Soc; Shanxi BR of Chinese Peoples Assn for Foreign Countries; Shanxi pedology Soc. *Honours:* Achut Award; 1st Prize of Outcome of Sci & Tech; 1st Prize of Progress of Sci & Tech; Award for Services to Soc; Many Awards from the Chinese Government. *Address:* Shanxi Agriclt Univ, Taigu County, Shentxi, China.

ZHENG Yi Tang, b. 29 Sept 1917, Fujian, China. Prof of Dept of Foreign Languages & Literature. m. Shu Qing Zheng, 15 Nov 1943, 2 s, 4 d. *Education:* Dept of English, Wu Han Univ, 1936-40; Grad Sch of English Literature, NY, 1948-50. *Appointments:* Interpreter, Chinese Expeditionary Force in India, 1942-43; Principal of De Hua Secondary Sch, 1944-45; Translator of the 1st Military Disciplinary Inspection Corps, 1945- 46; Attache of the Chinese Delegation to United Nations, NY, 1947-50; Assoc, Full Prof, Dept of Foreign Languages & Literature, Xiamen Univ, 1951-89. *Publications:* A Survey of Xiamen, in English; Tr Fr English into Chinese; George Gissing, A Private Papers of Henry Ryecroft; A Brief Introduction to Chinese Culture, in English. *Memberships:* Modern Language Assn of America. *Hobbies:* Bridge; Concert. *Address:* 233-23 41 St Avenue, Douglaston, NY 11363, USA.

ZHOA Jing-Song, b. 5 Dec 1963, Dandong, PR China. Tchr. m. Shu Hua Song, 14 July 1989. *Education:* Dalian Maritime Univ, BAch, 1982- 86; Master, 1986-89. *Appointments:* Navigation Dept, Dalian Maritime Univ, 1989-. *Publications:* Zhao Jing Song & Wang Feng Chen Selected Papers. *Memberships:* MCIN; MRIN. *Hobby:* Reading. *Address:* Navigation Dept, Dalian Maritime Univ, Dalian, Liao Ning Province, China.

ZHONG Wan mai, b. 17 Mar 1929, Shanghai, China. Prof. m. Qui Yuan Ren, 15 Aug 1963, 1 d. *Education:* Shanghai Jiaotong Univ, 1952. *Appointments:* Electrical Equipment Plant Designing Inst of Mech & Elec Ministry, 1952-62; Xian Jiaotong Univ, Prof of Electrical Engrng Dept, 1962; Hd of Group for Conserving Relics, 1984- . *Publications:* Test Proceedure on Working Site for Measuring the Loading Percentage of a Three Phase Induction Motor; Measuring & Testing Technique of Electrical Machines; Xian Jiaotong Univ West Han Dynasty Mural Tomb. *Memberships:* Small & Medium Size Electrical Machine Committee of CES; Electro Machanical Committee of Shaanxi Standardization Soc; Xian Go Assn; Shaanxi Provincial Soc for Conserving Cultural Relics. *Hobbies:* Go Player; Caligraphy; Philately; Classical Music; Astronomy. *Address:* Electrical Engrng Dept, Xian Jiaotong Univ, Xian Shaanxi Province, 710049, China.

ZHOU Bing-Nan, b. 31 Jan 1934, Shanghai, China. Prof, Tutor, PhD Graduate Students. m. Xiu Ying Chen, 31 Jan 1958, 2 d. *Education:* Shanghai Medical Univ, 1954; Graduate Sch of Shanghai Inst of Materia Medica, Acad Sinica, 1964; Visiting Scholar, Visiting Prof, Dept of Chem, Univ of British Columbia & Coolege of Pharmacy, Univ of Illinois, 1981-83. *Appointments:* Research Assoc, 1964; Assoc Prof, 1981; Prof of Shanghai Inst of Materia Medica, acad Sinica, 1989; Tutor, PhD Grad Prof, 1990. *Publications:* Over 70 Papers; 5 Books. *Memberships:* Chinese Pharmaceutical Assn; Chinese Chemical Assn; Sci Foundation for New Drug Research, State Bureau of Pharmaceutical Admin. *Honours:* 3rd Prize of Sci & Tech; 2nd Prize, Natural Sci; 2nd Prize of Sci & Tech. *Hobbies:* Music; Swimming; Sports. *Address:* State Key Laboratory for New Drug Research, Shanghai Institute of Materia Medica, Academia Sinica, 319 Yue Yang Road, Shanghai 200031, China.

ZHOU Cheng-Fang, b. 19 Feb 1932, Hunan Province, China. Prof of History. m. Chie Zhen, 5 Mar 1951, 3 s. *Education:* Hunan Univ, 1951- 53; Wuhan Univ, 1953- 55; Postgrad Beijing Inst of Diplomacy, 1955-57. *Appointments:* Tchr, 1957; Asst, 1957; Lectr, 1961; Assoc Prof, 1983; Prof, 1988. *Publications:* The Chartist Movement in England; Workers Up Rising in Lyon, France; The Workers Upring in Silesia, Germany; On Function of Sci & Tech Within History; On Social

Consequence of the Industrial Revolution. *Memberships:* China Soc of British History; China Soc of Modern World History. *Honours:* Best Composition; Best Tchrng. *Hobbies:* Reading; Table Tennis; Velleball. *Address:* History Dept of Inner Mogolia Univ, Huhhot 010021, China.

ZHOU Fu-Cheng, b. 20 June 1911, China. Honourary Visiting Prof. *Education:* BA, Dept of Philosophy, Tsing Hua Univ; Post Grad Studies, Natl Tsing Hua Univ; MA Philosopy. *Appointments:* Tchr, Lectr, Middle Sch & Coll, Shanghai & Chengdu, 1936-41; Assoc Prof, Prof, Szechuan Univ & King Ning Univ, 1941-46; Prof of Philosophy, Wu Han Univ, 1946-52; Prof of Philosophy & Ethics, Peking Univ, 1952-86. *Publications include:* On The Thought of Dong Zhong Shu; Source Book of Humanism in the Western World; The Classical Moralists in the Western World; Critism on the Classical Moralists of Western World. *Contributions to:* Articles in Profl Journals. *Hobbies:* Reading; Writing. *Address:* 204, Apt 10, Peking Univ, Beijing 100871, China.

ZHOU Guang-Ren, b. 17 Dec 1928, Hannover, Germany. Prof of Piano; Pianist. m. (1) Zi Xin Chen, 1 May 1954, dec, (2) Shuo Yong Liu, 2 July 1990, 2 s, 2 d. *Education:* Shanghai Music Sch, 1942-44; Several Piano Tchrs, 1944-49; Central Conservatory Of Music, 1955-57. *Appointments:* Shanghai Conservatory of Music, 1949-51; Central Philharmonic Soc, Solist, 1952-55; Central Conservatory of Music, Prof, 1955- . *Creative Works:* Prize Winner of the 1 Schumann Intern Piano Comp; German Piano Comp; Variation on a Chinese Folksong; Piano Course, Sent on TV. *Memberships:* China Musicians Assn; Beijing Musicians Assn; Central Conservatory of Music. *Honours:* 3 World Peace Festival Piano Comp; 1 Schumann Intern Piano Comp; All Natl Best Cultural Worker. *Hobbies:* Reading biographies of Great Man & Women. *Address:* Central Conservatory of Music, 43 Bao Jia Jie, Beijing 100031, China.

ZHOU Guanwu, b. 13 Feb 1918, Jinxiang, China. Chmn of the Bd, Shougang Corporation, China; Member of Foreign Affairs Committee, Natl Peoples Congress of China. m. Jingwei Geng, 1946, 2 s, 2d. *Education:* Snr Engr; Snr Economist. *Appointments:* Army, 1937-50; Shijingshan Iron & Steel Co, Shougang Corporation, Beijing, China, 1950-. *Publications:* Being Strict and Fair in Meting Out Rewards & Punishment is the Principle; It Is Imperative to Store Wealth Among Enterprises; On Contract System; Consuption Is The Motive Force for Development. *Memberships:* Chinese Assn of Enterpreneurs; Chinese Assn of Industrial Economy; China state System Reform Committee; Beijing Metals Soc, China. *Honours include:* ssa 00Natl Merit Enterpreneur of China; Intl Man of the Year; The Intl Order of Merit; Silver Shield of Valour. *Hobbies:* Calligraphy; Poems; China & World History. *Address:* Xicheng District, Beijing, China.

ZHOU Huailing, b. 28 Dec 1936, Wenchang, Hainan Province, China. Prof. m. Zhang Zhen Xian, 3 June 1961, 1 s, 1 d. *Education:* Beijing Geology Univ, 1957. *Appointments:* Oil Geology, 1957-62; Area Geology, 1962-72; Rock Mineralogy, 1972-78; Lithofacies Palaeographical & Reef Geology, 1978-. *Publications:* Sedimentary Facies Palaeogeography & Relatively Mineral Deposits of Devonian Guangxi;The Reed of Devonian in Huanjiang, Guangxi; The Discovery of Late Devonian Renalcis and Renalcis Mounds in Guangxi and Their Environmental Significance. *Memberships:* Oil Geological Soc of China; Geological Soc of Guangxi; Guangxi Inst of Geology. *Honours:* Sci Conference of China; Geological Sci of Geology & Mineral Resources. *Hobbies:* Literary Works. *Address:* Guangxi Inst of Geology, 1 Jianzheng Road, Nanning 530023, China.

ZHOU Longbao, b. 4 Aug 1934, Shanghai, PR China. Prof. m. Keyuan Hong, 20 Aug 1961, 1 s, 1 d. *Education:* Bach Degree, Internal Combustion Engine, Shanhai Jiaotong Univ; Visiting Scholar, Internal Combustion

Engine, Univ of Wisconsin Madison, USA. *Appointments:* Tchrng Asst, 1957-63; Asst Pro, 1963-82; Assoc Prof, Chmn, Dept of Power Machinery Engrng, 1982-86; Prof, Chmn of Dept of Power Machinery, 1986-. *Publications:* The Principles of Interna Compustion Engines; A Study on Combustion & NOs Emission Characteristics of a Spark and Flow Plug Assisted Diesel Engine Operating on Multifuels; An Experimental Study on Working Stability and Combustion Characteristics of a DI Diesel Engine Operating on Multifuels. *Memberships:* Chinese Soc for Intl Combustion Engines; The Combustion, Energy Saving, Emission Control Committee; Chinese Soc for Engrng Thermo Physics; Alternative Fuel Applying Technology; Shaanxi Province Soc for Intl Combustion Engines. *Honours:* Excel Tchrs of Shaanxi; Research Ward, State Council; Research Prgress Award. *Hobbies:* Table Tennis; Basketball. *Address:* Dept of Power Machinery Engineeribng, Xian Tiaotong Univ, Xian, Shaanxi Province, China.

ZHOU Wenjun, b. 29 Jan 1928, Jing Hua, Zhe Jiang Province, China. Prof; Supervisor of PhD Student. m. Wang Hongyuan, 18 Jan 1959, 2 d. *Education:* Peking Univ, Dept of Library Sci, 1953. *Appointments:* Tchr, Qu Wo Middle Sch, 1953-54; Librarian, Library of Literature Research Inst, Peking Univ, 1954-56; Instr, Prof, Dir, Dept of Library & Information Sci, Peking Univ, 1956-. *Publications include:* The Administration of Small Library; The Outline of Library Work; Introduction to Document Communication; Library Sci in Encyclopedia Sinica. *Memberships include:* Evaluating Tech Posts in Peking Univ; China Soc of Library Sci; IFLA SC TRAIN. *Honours include:* Natl Educ Committee, Text Book; 3rd Prize Achievements in Sci & Tech, Peking Univ; Prize for Outstanding Thesis. *Hobbies:* Country Music. *Address:* Dept of Library & Information Science, Peking Univ, Beijing, China.

ZHOU Yu Lin, b. 17 June 1936, Jiang, SU, PRC. Prof; Mineral Classification & Appraisement. m. Shu Hua Hu, 12 Aug 1962, 1 d. *Education:* Chang Zhou High Sch, 1956; Nan Jing Geology Inst, 1956. *Appointments:* Inst of Mineral Deposits, 1956-. *Publications:* Handbook, Placer Deposit Identification; Geology of Granitoids of Nanling Region & Their Petrogenesis & Mineralization. *Membership:* China Geology Inst. *Hobbies:* Running; Beijing Opera. *Address:* Inst of Mineral Deposits, Bai Wan Zhuang Road 26, Beijing 100037, China.

ZHU Bingyi, b. 15 Feb 1932, Shaanxi Province, China. Assoc Prof; Dir of the Pres, China Intl Travel Service Corporate Headquarters. m. Zhoa Yu Chun, 18 May 1960, 1 s, 1 d. *Education:* Oriental Linguistics Dept, Beijing Univ, 19551; Bach Degree, Beijing Univ, 1955. *Appointments:* Indonesian, English Interpreter, China Intl Travel Service, 1955-70; Mgr, Dir, AAA Dept of the Service, 1971-88; Dir of the Pres, 1989-. *Publications:* Guerila's Home; Surapati. *Membership:* China Tourism Assn. *Address:* 103 Fuxingmennei Avenue, Beijing 100800, China.

ZHU Jianliang, b. 26 Sept 1944, Xiema Village, Hunan Province, PR China. Assoc Prof. m. Liu Chenxia, 19 Apr 1975, 1 s. *Education:* Library Sci, Beijing Univ, 1965-69. *Appointments:* Tchrng Asst, Peking Univ, 1969-76; Lectr, Xiangtan Univ, 1983-86; Assoc Prof, 1987-91; Editorial Conslt, Deputy Dean, Univ Library Studies, 1980-91; Editorial Staff of Journal of Xiangtan Univ, 1990-91. *Publications include:* Books, A Concise Dictionary of Library, Information and Archive Sci; Major Papers. On The Human Brain, Function of Library. *Memberships:* Chinese Assn of Library; The Hunan Assn of Library; The Assn of Higher Educ of Xiangtan Univ. *Honours:* Activist of Sci & Tech Assn of Xiangtan City; 1st Prize Hunan Assn of Library; Local Records of Hunan Province, Excel Series Award. *Hobbies:* Reading; Painting; Calligraphy; Literature; Art. *Address:* 403-405 Building 12, Nanyan Cun, Xiangtan Univ, Xiangtan City, Hunan Province, China.

ZHU Li Cun, b. 27 Apr 1940, China. Painter. m. 19 Sept 1968, 1 s, 1 d. *Education:* Central Inst of Fine Arts, 1964. *Appointments:* Profl Painter, Artists Assn of China, Sichman Branch, 1964-91. *Creative Works:* Painting. Uncle Has A Drink; Spring Rain; Drinking & Singing; Maidens Festival; Hendsmans Daughter; Herd in; The More Ploughing & Weeding the Better the Crop; Racing Horse. *Membership:* Artists Assn of China. *Honours:* Commendatory Prize by the Ministry of Culture, China; The Modern Times Detail Drawing Assn of China. *Hobby:* Literature. *Address:* 116 Lan Jie Dong Cheng, Cheng Du, Si Chuan, Artists Assn of China, Sichman Branch, China.

ZHU Shi-Yao, b. 8 Oct 1944, Shanghai, China. Prof. m. Lin Lin Yan, 1 Oct 1970, 2 d. *Education:* Univ of Sci & Tech of China, 1963-68. *Appointments:* Technician, 6th Engrng Bureau of Natl Constr Commission, 1970-73; Tchrng Asst, Lectr, Univ of Sci & Tech, 1973-88; Research Assoc, Univ of Wiscon Madison, USA, 1983-86; Assoc Prof, Univ of Sci & Tech of China, 1988-. *Publications:* The Fundamentals of Plasma Physics; The Prospects for Modern Physics; Principles of Nuclear Fusion. *Memberships:* Chinese Nuclear Sci Soc; Assn for Plasma Studies of China. *Honours:* 3rd Grade Scientific Research Achievements Award, Chinese Acad of Sci; 1st Grad Scientific Research Achievement Award, Univ of Sci & Tech of China. *Hobbies:* Taiji Boxing; Reading. *Address:* Dept of Modern Physics, University of Science & Technology of China, Hefei, Anhui, China 230026.

ZHU Ting Cheng, b. 16 Aug 1926. Prof, Dir of Inst of Grasslands Sci of Northeast Normal Univ. m. 15 Sept 1948, 2 s, 3 d. *Education:* Sch of Harbin Ind Univ, China, 1952. *Appointments:* Dir of Inst of Grasslands Sci of Northeast Normal Univ, 1958-. *Publications:* Over 100 Sci Papers; Books inc, Plant Ecology. *Memberships:* Intl Grasslands Congress; Grasslands Sci Soc of China; Agricl Ecology Sco of Jilin Province; Agricl & Animal Husbandry Bureau; Agricl Ministry of China. *Honours:* Japan Soc for the Promotion of Sci; Fellowship for the Research in Japan; Prize of Tech & Sci Improvement, Achievement on Pasture Improvement. *Hobbies:* Music; Dance. *Address:* Inst of Grasslands Science, Northeast Normal University, ChangChun, Jilin Province, China 130024.

ZHU Ying, b. 25 Jan 1920. m. 8 Jan 1942, 3 s, 3 d. *Education:* Natl Coll of Fine Arts, 1941. *Appointments:* Tchr, Fine Arts Coll, Sichun Province, 1941-46; Tchr, Fine Arts High Sch, Shanghai, 1949-56; Lectr, Dept of Arch, Tongji Univ, 1956-60; Asst Prof, Prof, 1960-90. *Creative Works:* Selection of Paintings Publi; Works Exhib. *Memberships:* Shanghai soc of Fine Arts; Oil & Water Colour Painting div; Chinese Artist Assn; Japanese Modern Art Assn. *Honours:* Tiger & Children, Excel Prize in the Charity Exhib; Russian Character, Excel Prize in Shanghai; Honorable Prize; Honorable Citizen Citation. *Hobbies:* Reading; Jogging; Playing Table Tennis; Swimming; Music. *Address:* 548 Rm1 Tongji Xincum, Siping Road, Shanghai 200092, China.

ZHU Yongfang, b. 12 Nov 1930, Shanghai, China. Painter; Calligrapher; Pres, Beijing Tieliu Fine arts & Calligraphy Research Soc. m. Shao Sufen, 1955, 3 s, 1 d. *Education:* St Francis Xaivers Coll, Shanghai, 1948-49; Shanghai Engrng Sch, 1949-52; Tongji Univ, 1980. *Appointments:* Technician, Anshan Iron & Steel Constr Co, 1952-64; Engr, Section Chief, Dir of Engrng, JinQuan Iron & Steel Co, 1965-80; Hd of Engrng Dept, Metallurgic Ministry, 1980-83; Vice Chief Editor, Dir, Research Center, Overall Mgmt of China Arch Inst, Beijing, 1983-85; Counsel Advisor, China Greatwall Research Soc, 1986-; Pres, Beijing Tieliu Fine Arts & Calligraphy Research Soc, 1988-. *Creative Works:* Paintings inc: Green Peaks; Silk Road; 70 Other Paintings Personal Exhib; Many Monographs Publi; Many Paintings Publ in Newspapers, Mag; Modern Construction Organizing Design & Modern Construction Management. *Memberships:* China Arch Inst; China

Mathematics Inst. *Honours:* 1st Prize Comp of Chinese Traditional Paintings & Calligraphy; Honor Cert by the Organizing Committee of the Xi Asian Games. *Hobbies:* Classical & Light Music; Photography; Travel. *Address:* 4-401 Bldg 7, District 2, Hui Xin Xi Li, Chao Yang District, Beijing 100029, China.

ZHUANG Xi Chang, b. 26 Sept 1933. Prof; Vice Pres. m. 26 Dec 1960, 3 s. *Education:* Fudan Univ, 1952-56. *Appointments:* JA His Dept, Fudan Univ, 1956-63; Lecyr, Fudan Univ, 1963-81; Visiting Scholar, Suny, Albany, USA, 1981-83; Prof, Fudan Univ, 1983-92. *Publications:* Culture History of World; Who's Who in World History. *Memberships:* USA History Assn in China; British History Assn in China; Military History Assn in China; Shanghai Social Sci Assn. *Hobbies:* Music; Chinese Classic & Western Classic Music. *Address:* Fudan Univ, Shanghai 200433, China.

ZHUANG Yinghong, b. 14 Feb 1933, Meixian County, Guangdong, China. Prof. m. Qiongxiang Chen, 18 Feb 1954, 2 s, 2 d. *Education:* Dept of Physics, Wuhan Univ, 1955-59. *Appointments:* Tchr, Meizhou Middle Sch, 1952-55; Research Asst, Inst of Metal Research, Acad Sinica, 1959- 61; Lectr, Assoc Prof, Prof, Dept of Physics, Guangxi Univ, 1962-. *Publications:* 46 Research Papers. *Memberships include:* Chinese Physical Soc; Guangxi Univ Federation of Returned Overseas Chinese. *Honours include:* Natl Sci Prize of China for Investigations on Phase Diagrams & Phase Relations in Rare Earth Alloy Systems; Examplary Tchr of Guangxi; Sci of Outstanding Achievements in Guangxi. *Hobbies:* Reading; Classical Music; Watching Football.

ZHUBER-OKROG Gunther, b. 28 June 1932, Graz, Austria. m. Irmgard Gottlich, 5 Mar 1962, 1 s, 1 d. *Education:* Tech Univ of Grat, 1950-56; Imperial Coll, London, 1957-58. *Appointments:* Univ Asst, TV Grat, 1955-75; AV Humboldt Scholar, DFVR Cologne, 1966-68; Lectr, 1975-77; Univ Prof, TV Grat, 1977-. *Publications:* Papers on Ultrasonic Gas Temperature Measurement, Jet Tubes with pulsating Combustion. *Membership:* Deutsche Ges F Luff u Raumfahrt. *Honour:* Theodor Korner. *Hobbies:* Gardening; Photography; Travel. *Address:* Am Rehgrund 18, A-8043 Graz, Austria. 86.

ZHURAUSKI Arkadziy, b. 5 Aug 1924, Yanova, Byelorussia. Philologist; Scientific Worker. m. Kovalevskaya Lidiya, 13 Oct 1953, 3 s. *Education:* Russian State Univ, 1945-50; Post Grad Byelorussian Acad of Sci, 1950-54; Master of Philology, 1954; Dr of Philology, 1968; Prof, 1970; Corresponding Member Byelorussian Acad of Sci, 1980. *Appointments:* Snr Scientific Worker, Linguistics Inst of Byelorussian Acad of Sci, 1954-58; Prof, Warsaw Univ, 1959-60; Hd of Byelorussian Language History Dept, 1961-; Deputy Dir, 1979-82; Dir of the Linguistics Inst of Byelorussian Acad of Sci, 1983-88. *Publications include:* Numerous. *Memberships:* Intl Commission of Slavonic Literary Languages; Byelorussian Commitee of Slavonic Philologists. *Honours:* Honoured Scientist of Byelorussia; Diplomas of the Presidium, Byelorussian Supreme Soviet; For the Victory Over The Nazi Germany; For Service in Battle; 8 Jublee Medals. *Hobbies:* Reading; Tourism. *Address:* 43 Slavinskogo, Apt 16, 220086 Minsk, Russia.

ZIEGLER Henri Alexandre Leonard, b. 18 Nov 1906, Limoges, France. Retired. m. Gillette Rizzi, 31 Mar 1932, 3 s, 1 d. *Education:* Ecole Poly 1926-28; Ecole Sup Aironzntique, 1929-31. *Appointments:* Dir, 1932-39; Dir General Air France, 1946-54; Dir General, Bliquer Aviation, 1955- 67; Pres, 1968-75. *Publications:* Le Grande Arcutor Concorde. *Memberships:* More than 50 Assns. *Honours:* Great Office Legion of Honor; Commander Britich Europe, Victoria Order; Officer, Legion of Merit. *Hobby:* Mountaineering. *Address:* 55 Boulevard Lannes, 75116 Paris, France. 1, 91.

ZIEGLER Hubert, b. 28 Sept 1924, Regensburg. Prof. m. Irmgard Guender, 5 Aug 1955, 1 d. *Education:* Univ, Muenchen. *Appointments:* Asst, Dept of Botany & Forest Bot, 1959-70; Prof, 1970-. *Publications include:* Co editor; 300 Publi in Sci Journals. *Memberships:* FESPP; Internal Assn Plant Physiol; Bavarian Acad of Sci. *Address:* Inst f Botanlk U Mikrobioiogie, Der Technischen Univ Munchen, Lehrstuhl Fur Botanik, Arcisstrabe 21. D-8000 Munich 2, Germany.

ZIELINSKA Lidia, b. 9 Oct 1953, Poznan, Poland. Composer. m. Zygmunt Zielinski, 3 Aug 1974, 1 d. *Education:* MA, 1978; DA, 1991. *Appointments:* Took Part in Several Summer Composers Workshops & Seminars; Worked with Experimental & Profl Theatres; Ltcr, Seminars for Composers & Broadcast Radio Series; Snr Lectr, Acad of Music, Poznan; Lectr, State Higher Sch of the Visual Arts, Poznan; Artistic Dir, Festival of Polish Contemporary Music. *Cretive Works include:* Eh Joe Monodrama for Mime Actor; Violin Concerto; Litany for String Quartet; Farewell Mr Toorop for Orchestra; Minuten Sonate for any Instrument; Mrs Koch; Two Dances for Strings; Artificial Cult for Tape, Video, Neon Signs & Visual Objects; Pleonasmus for Oboe, Violin, String Orchestra; Jacquard Loom for 15 Musicians. *Memberships include:* Repertoire Committee of the Warsaw Autumn Festival; ISCM World Music Days; ISCM Polish Section; Natl Art Center for Children & Youth, Poznan; Dom rythmow Swiata Foundation. *Address:* ul Poplinskich 719, PL 61 573, Poznan, Poland.

ZIETEK Marek Franciszek, b. 28 Mar 1951, Klodzko, Poland. Dentist; Research Worker. m. Janina Zietek, 18 Apr 1974, 2 d. *Education:* Med Acad in Wroclaw, 1974; Med Doctor Degree, 1980; Asst Prof, 1991. *Appointments:* Lab of Knowledge of Dentist Materials, 1974-78; Dept of Conservations Dent, 1978-. *Publications:* Application of Thermoplasts in Provisional Dentures Production; Activity of Neutrophils in Post Juvenile Periodontitis. *Memberships:* Polish Assn of Stomatologist; Polish Orological Assn. *Honours:* Primus Inter Pares, Ministerium Prize; Research Prizes from Rector. *Hobbies:* Skiing; Light Athelitcs; Book Reading. *Address:* Katedra Stomatologii Zachowawczej, Akademii Medycznej we Wroclawiu, ul Kuznicza 43-45, 50 138 Wroclaw, Poland.

ZILBERMAN Peter Efimovich, b. 14 May 1935, Khmelnitsky City. Hd of Dept in the Inst of Radio Engrng & Electronics/Physics of Solid State. m. Evgenia Lukinichna Zilberman, 5 May 1973, 1 d. *Education:* Moscow Physical & Tech Inst, 1952-58; Inst of Radioeng & Electz, Acad of Sci, 1958. *Appointments:* Research Worker, 1958-61; Graduate Student, 1961-63; Research Worker, 1963-70; Major Research Worker, 1979-; Hd of Lab, 1989-; Hd of Dept, 1991-. *Publications:* About 200 Articles; Letters; Books. *Memberships:* All Union Knowledge Soc. *Honours:* Achievements in the Field of Spin wave Electronics; State Prize of USSR in Sci. *Hobbies:* Car Driving; Walking; Garden. *Address:* Inst of Radioengrng & Electronics, USSR, Acad of Sci, 18 Marx Avenue, Moscow 103907, Russia.

ZIMMER Robert Mark, b. 4 Apr 1957, New York City. Lectr. m. Joanna Elizabeth Gondris, 23 July 1983. *Education:* Massachusetts Inst of Tech, 1978; Cambridge Univ, 1978-79; Columbia Univ. *Appointments:* Preceptor, Columbia Univ, 1983-85; Research Fellow, Brunel Univ, 1985-88; Lectr, 1985-; Visiting Prof, Harvard Univ, 1970; Visiting Prof, Univ of Ottawa, 1990. *Publications:* Poetry; Articles on Mathematics, Computing, Electrical Engrng. *Address:* 4 Selwyn Court, Church Road, Richmond, Surrey TW10 6LR, England.

ZINKE Michael Duane, b. 13 Oct 1954, Mendate, IL, USA. Credit Mgr. m. Catherine Louise Myers, 22 July 1978, 2 s. *Education:* Central State Univ, Edmond, OK, 1988; Northern Illinois Univ. *Appointments:* Office World, Controller, 1977-78; Credit Mgr, CIT Corp, 1979-83; Gen Acctg, Credit Mgr, Macklanburg Duncan, 1984-

90; Credit Mgr, No Am Chemical Co, 1991-. *Publications:* Author Univ Research Papers. *Memberships:* Am Business Club; Natl Chemical Credit Assn; Natl Assn Credit Mgmt; Okla City Chamber Commerce; OK Wildlife Federation; Natl Rifle Assn. *Honours:* Bureau of US Olympic Festival Tourch; Eagle Scout; Representative of Napco Construction. *Hobbies:* Fishing; Hunting; Camping; Reading; Coin Collecting; Family Activities. *Address:* 720 Conestoga Drive, Yukon, OK 73099, USA. 7, 132.

ZINSLI Paul, b. 30 Apr 1906, Chur, Germany. Univ Prof. m. 28 May 1938, 1 s, 1 d. *Education:* Tchr of Grammer Sch, Univ Zurich, 1935; Doctors Degree, 1935. *Appointments:* Tchr, Grammer Sch Undergraduate Biel, 1935-46; Asst Prof, Univ Bern, 1946-51; Dir, 1946-71. *Publications:* Grund und Grat; Der Berner Totentanz des Niklaus Manuel; Walser Volkstum in der Schweiz; Ortshamen und Strukturen; Sudwalser Namengut; Der Malerpoet Hans rddser; Ortsnamenbuch des Kantons Bern; Sprachallas der Deutschen Schweiz. *Honours include:* Literaturpreis City of Berne Ch; Kulturpreis Canton of Grisons Ch. *Hobbies:* Painting; Music. *Address:* Prof of Univ Emerited, CH-3006, Berne, Brunnadernstr 3, Switzerland. 52.

ZITKO Howard John, b. 26 Oct 1911, Milwaukee, Wisconsin, USA. m. div, 3 children. *Education:* Univ of Wisconsin, 1929-31; Univ of California, Los Angeles, 1946-48; Golden State Univ, Los Angeles, 1949. *Appointments:* Cofounder, Lemurian Fellowship, 1936-46; Minister, Temple of the Jewelled Cross, Los Angeles, 1942-46; Founder, Pres, World Univ Roundtable, 1946-; Minister, Church of the Abundant Life at Huntingdon Park, California, 1955-59; founder, Pres, World Univ at Benson, Arizona, 1967-. *Publications include:* The Lemurian Theo Christic Conception; Streamers of Light from the New World; World Univ Insights. *Memberships:* American Ministerial Assn; World Univ Roundtable; World Univ, Benson; American Civil Liberties Union; United Nations Assn of the United States of America; American Assn of Retired persons; Sierra Club; Benson chamber of Commerce; United Poets Laureate Intl; Intl Parliment for Safety & Peace. *Honours:* Knight Commander, Royal Knights of Justice; Laureate Man of Letters; Silver Chalice, World Univ Roundtable; Gold Medal, World Congress of Poets. *Address:* World Univ, Desert Sanctuary Campus, PO Box 2470, Benson, AZ 85602, USA.

ZMEGAC Viktor, b. 21 Mar 1929, Podravska Slatina, Croatia. Prof of German Literature. m. Cvijeta Tutovic, 12 Oct 1955, 1 s, 1 d. *Education:* BA, Zagreb Univ; PhD. *Appointments:* Lectr, Faculty of Letters, Gottingen, Federal Republic of Germany, 1955-57; Asst Prof, 1960-66; Full Prof, 1967-; Visiting Prof, West Berlin Univ, 1970; Graz Univ, Australia, 1980. *Publications:* Die Munsik im Schaffen Thomas Manns; Kunst und Wirklichkeit; Geschichte der Deutschen Literature; Jahrhundert bis zur Gegenwart; Creazione Letteraria e Consumo Soc; Der Europaische Roman, Geschichte Seiner Poetik. *Memberships:* Acad of Sci & Leyyers; Acad Europaea. *Honors:* Alexander Von Humboldt Grantee; Goethe Medaille, Geothe Inst, Munchen; City of Zagreb Award; Bladimir Nazor Prize; Gundolf Prize, Deutshe Akademie fur Sprache und Dichtung; Krleza Prize, Zagreb. *Hobby:* Music. *Address:* Odsjek za Germanistiku, Filozofski Fakulett, D Salaja 3, 41000 Zagreb, Croatia. 52, 139.

ZODHIATES Philip, b. 17 July 1955, New Jersey, USA. Dir Mail Advertising Exec. m. Kathie Lee Gentry, 25 May 1981, 1 s, 1 d. *Education:* Farleigh Dickenson Univ, 1976. *Appointments:* Advertising, Mktng Dir, AGM Intl, 1973-79; Account Exec, Informat Mktng, 1980-81; Owner, CEO of Response Unlimited, 1981-. *Publications:* Numerous Advertising Campaigns. *Memberships:* Christian Managment Assn; Globalink Ministries. *Hobbies:* Snow Skiing; Missions; Philetaly.

Address: c/o The Old Plantation, RR4 Box 251, Wayneshore, VA 22980, USA. 2.

ZOLDHELYI-DEAK Zsuzsanna, b. 27 Jan 1928, Budapest, Hungary. Historian of Litterature; Reader. m. Sandor Deak, 14 Apr 1954, 2 s. *Education:* BA, Leningrad State Univ, 1951; PhD, Budapest, Hung Acad of Sci, 1961; Doc of Sci, 1991. *Appointments:* Dept of Russian Philology, Lectr, Budapest Univ, 1951-63; Reader, 1963-. *Publications:* Turgenyev; Turgenyev vilaga; Turgs Prose Poems; Papers on 19 cent; Russian Lit in Hungarian & Foreign periodicals. *Memberships:* Bd of Studia Slavica Hung; Intl Slavonic Comm; Hung Division Intl Assn of Tchrs of Russian Lang & Lit; AILC. *Hobbies:* Travel; Contacts with People of Difference Countries; Music. *Address:* Karpat u 12, H-1133 Budapest, Hungary.

ZONG Liang Bing, b. 9 Jan 1931, China. m. Tong Hue Quin, 30 Sept 1955, 1 s, 1 d. *Education:* Dept of Plant Protection, Huazheng Agriclt Coll, 1954. *Appointments:* Asst, 1954-63; Lectr, 1963-80; Asst Prof, 1980-87; Prof of Entolology, 1987-91; Asst Hd, 1980-83; Hd, 1983-88; Dept of Plant protections, Huazhong Agriclt Univ, Wuhan China. *Publications:* More than 50 Thesis. *Memberships:* China Entomological Soc; Hubei Province Entomological Soc; Evaluated Commission of Degree of Huazhong Agriclt Univ; Editor of Journal of Huazhing Agriclt Univ. *Honours include:* China Sci Conference Proze for Integrated Managment of Cotton Poets; Hubei Province Advanced Sci Tech Proze. *Hobbies:* Sports; Music. *Address:* Dept of Plant Protection, Huazhong Agriclt Univ, Wuhan Hubei Province, China. 152, 162.

ZOROJEWSJI Marian, b. 2 Sept 1929, Lodz, Poland. Writer; Journalist; Publisher. m. Miroskawa Prominska, 2 Apr 1948, 1 s, 1 d. *Education:* Law, Univ of Lodz, 1949-51. *Appointments:* Editor of Books, 1959; Editor of TV Programmes, 1959-60; Author of Film, TV Short Stories; Author of Childrens Books. *Publications include:* The House Under Black Lantern; Novels. Having One Eye; The Guest in the Midnight; Very Old Women. *Memberships:* Polish Writers Assn; Assn of Journalists. *Honours:* Journalistic & Literary Prizes. *Hobbies:* Cats; History. *Address:* Piotrkowska Str 193/13, 90-447 Lodz, Poland.

ZOU Renjun, b. 16 Jan 1927, Suzhou City, China. Chemist; Prof. m. Yaqin Zhao, 1 Jan 1951, 2 d. *Education:* Fu Dan Univ, Shanghai, 1945-47; Tianjin Univ, 1952. *Appointments:* Tianjin Inst of Chemical Tech, 1958; Tianjin Inst of Tech, 1963; Hebei Inst of Tech, Tainjin, 1972-; Hebei Acad of Sci, 1984-. *Contributions to:* 10 Books inc. Principles & Tech of Seperation in Petrochemical Industry; Frontiers of World Chemical Reaction Engrng; Co Author, Numerous Profl Research Papers; Numerous Profl Journals. *Memberships include:* Chemical Industry & Engrng Soc of China; Petrochemical Industry & Engrng Soc; HAS; Royal Soc of Chemistry, London; China Assn for Sci & Tech. *Honours:* Numerous Honours & Awards inc. Medal Hebei Provinical Government; Gold Medal, Excellent Scientist; Top grade Premium, Natl Ethylene Conference; Gold Medal, State Council of China. *Address:* Hebei Academy of Sciences, 050081 Shijiazhuang, China.

ZOUBAREFF Olga, b. 29 July 1948. *Education:* Acting, Macomb Community Coll, Mt Clemens; Tap Dance, Ann Parsley Sch of Dance; Nutrition & Exercise, Intl Correspondence Sch; Reading & Interpreting Financial Statements, Sales Mktng & Mgmt Div, Houston Community Coll; Creative Drawing Cert, Houston Community Coll System; Bach of Arts, Wayne State Univ, Detroit. *Appointments:* Accounting Clerk, Party & Lecture Planner, Secr, Univ Orthopaedic Assoc of Detroit; Fashion & Photographic Model, Actress, Renaissance Centre Fashion Panel, 1989-91; TV Movie, Proceed with Caution, 1990; Fashion Show Auction, 1990. *Creative Works include:* Contestant, Portfolio Models Contest; Final Calander Girl Contest; Women of the Great Lakes Swimsuit Calender Contest. *Memberships:* Young Republicans Club; Natl Honor Soc; Student Council, Chadey High Sch; Natl Assn for Female Exec. *Hobbies:* Reading; Sewing; Exercising; Painting; Sketching; Growing Plants; Keeping up with Fashion; Movies; Concerts; Art Museums. *Address:* 38579 Delta Drive, Mt Clemens, MI 48043, USA. 138.

ZUBER Norma Keen, b. 27 Sept 1934, Iuka, Mississippi, USA. Career Development Conslt. m. William Frederick Zuber, 14 Sept 1958, 2 s, 2 d. *Education:* BS, Univ of Southwestern Louisiana, 1956; MS, California Lutheran Univ, 1984; Westmont Coll, Santa Barbara. *Appointments:* Guest Instr, California State Univ, California Lutheran Univ; Instr, California State Univ, Northridge, Ventura Community Coll; Career Conslt, BFC Counseling Center, 1984-87; Career Conselor, Career & Life Planning, Norma Zuber & Assoc, 1987-. *Publications:* Nuts & Bolts of Career Development. *Memberships include:* CCDA; CRPCP; Ventura County Profl Womens Network. *Honours include:* Government Relations Committee Cert of Appreciation; Outstanding Leadership & Professionalism, Advancement of Career Development in California. *Address:* Career & Life Planning, 3858 Maple Street, Suite 237, Ventura, CA 93003, USA. 5.

ZUBOV Alexander Alexandrovich, b. 8 May 1934, Moscow, Russia. Physical Anthropologist. *Education:* Moscow State Univ, 1960; Candidate Degree, 1964; Doc Degree, 1970; Prof, 1984. *Appointments:* Inst of Ethnology & Anthropology, Acad Sci, USSR, Jnr Researcher, 1963-68; Snr Reseacher, 1968-76; Chief of the Dept, 1976-. Publications: Odontology. Anthrop. Methods; Ethnic Odontology; Odontology in Modern Anthrop; Man Opens up The World; 110 Sci Articles. *Memberships:* Sci Council in the Inst of Anthropology; USA Dental Anthropology Assn. *Hobbies:* Photography; Painting; Collecting Sea Shells. *Address:* Inst of Ethnology & Anthropology, Academy of Sci of the USSR, Lenin Avenue 37a, Moscow 117334, Russia.

ZUCKERMAN Arie Jeremy, b. 30 Mar 1932, Prof. m. 2 Children. *Education:* Univ of Birmingham; Univ of London. *Appointments include:* Royal Air Force Medical Branch, Flight Lieutenant, Squadron Leader, 1959-61; Dept of Pathology, Guys Hosp Medical Sch, 1962-65; Snr Lectr, London Sch of Hygiene & Tropical Medicine, 1965-68; Prof, Univ of London, 1972-75; Dean, Royal Free Hosp Sch of Medicine, 1989-. *Publication include:* Texbooks; Translated Works; Edited Texkbooks. Numerous Articles in Journals. *Memberships:* Who Expert Advisory Panel on Virus Diseases; World Health Organ; Royal Free Hampstead NHS Trust. *Address:* The Royal Free Hospital School of Medicine, Rowland Hill Street, Hampstead, London NW3 2PF, England.

ZUN Bohdan, b. 1 May 1933, Warsaw, Poland. Electrical Engr. m. Anna Guszkowska, 30 July 1959, 2 d. *Education:* Tech Univ of Warsaw, 1956. *Appointments:* Inst of Communal Economy, Warsaw, 1956-64; Transport Dept, City of Warsaw, 1964-73; Union of Municipal Engrng Enterprises, Warsaw, 1973-82; General Magmt, Underground Const, Warsaw, 1982-; Editor, Urban Transport, Monthly Mag, 1982-. *Publications include:* Numerous Articles; About 30 Projects of Mass Transit Systems. *Memberships:* Assn of Transport Engrs & Technicians in Poland. *Honours:* Gold Cross of Merit; Knights Cross of Polonia Restituta Order; Officers Cross of Polonia Restituta Order; Gold Award for Merits for Warsaw. *Hobby:* Photography. *Address:* Felinskiego 32, Apt 2, 01 569 Warsaw, Poland.

ZUNKER Sharon Jienell, b. 28 July 1943, Charleston, VA, USA. Owner; Pres. m. 19 Sept 1980, 4 s, 1 d. *Education:* Sparyberry High Sch, 1963. *Appointments:* Sec Treasurer, Atlanta Envelope Co, 1962-64; Legal Sec, J D Mandeville Atty, 1964-67; Mgr, Winn Dixie, 1973-76; Owner, 2 Service stations Union 76, 1980-82; Pres, Owner, American Commercial Expediters Inc, 1987-. *Memberships:* American Legion; Odd Fellows;

Rosecrucions; US Chamber of Commerce; Intl Platform assn; Notory Assn Fla; World Foundation of Successful Women; Natl Assn of Female Exec. *Honours:* Award Fla Nwy Patrol Benevolent Assn; American Grass Roots; Forgotten Vetrans Award; Special olympics Letter of Thanks; Paralyzed Vetrans Letter of Thanks. *Hobbies:* Writing; Poetry; Painting; Politics. *Address:* American Commerical Expediters Inc, 1852 NW 21st Street, Pompano Bach, Florida 33069, USA. 2, 7, 52, 138.

ZURAW Kathleen Ann, b. 29 Sept 1960, Bay City, MI, USA. Tchr. *Education:* BS, Michigan State Univ, 1984; MA, 1987. *Appointments:* Jefferon Orthopedic Sch, Honolulu, HI, 1984-86; Bay Arenae ISD, Bay City, 1985-87; Berrien Co ISD, 1987-. *Memberships:* American Alliance for Health, Physical Educ, Recreation & Dance; Council for Exceptional Children; Michigan State Univ. *Honours:* Phi Kappa Phi; Phi Delta Kappa; Golden Key Natl Honor Soc; Phi Thelta Kappa. *Hobbies:* Sports; Arts & Crafts; Travel; Animals. *Address:* 7306 W S Saginaw Road, Bay City, MI 48706, USA. 5, 8, 52.

ZUREK Witold Stanislaw, b. 18 Mar 1918, Pojakowice, Poland. Scientific Worker. *Education:* M Techn Sc, 1948; Dt Techn Sc, 1956. *Appointments:* Asst At Politechnika Lodzka, 1945-49; Asst Prof, 1949- 57; Snr Lectr, 1957-67; Prof, 1967-. *Publications:* 7 Books; 150 Scientific & Research Papers. *Memberships:* Royal Acad of Sci & Arts in Barcelona. *Honours:* Chivalry Cross of Polonia Resistuta; Officer Cross of Polonia Resistuta. *Hobbies:* Studies in Bible. *Address:* Wierzbowa 38-55, 90-245 Lodz, Poland.

ZUTSHI Derek Wyndham Hariram, b. 26 Apr 1930, London, England. Conslt Physician. m. Margaret Elizabeth Smith, 11 May 1974. *Education:* Univ of Bristol; MRCP, 1967; FRCP, 1991. *Appointments:* House Physician, Profl Medical Unit British Royal Infirmary, 1957; Medical Reg, MRC Rhematism, Canadian Red Cross Mem Hosp, 1966-68; Snr Reg, The London Hosp, 1968-73; Rhematology Conslt, 1973-. *Publications include:* Numerous Papers. *Memberships include:* Medical Soc of London. *Hobbies:* Travel; Music; Reading. *Address:* 99 Harley Street, London W1N 1DF, England.

ZVELEBIL Kamil Veith, b. 17 Nov 1927, Prague, Czechoslovakia. Prof Emeritus. m. Nina Tarasevicova, 25 Feb 1951, 1 s, 2 d. *Education:* PhD, Charles Univ, Prague, 1952; PhD, Czech Acad, Prague, 1959. *Appointments:* Research Scholar, Acad Parague, 1952-68; Assoc Prof, Charles Univ, 1965-68; Prof, Univ of Chicago, USA, 1968-70; Prof, Univ Utrecht, 1971-90; Vis Prof, Coll de France, 1970. *Publications:* 490 Schol Books & Papers. *Memberships:* Acad of Tamil Culture, Madras; Intl Assn of Tamil Research, Madras. *Honours:* Tamil Writers Assn Award; pondicherry Inst of Linguistics & Culture Award. *Hobbies:* Zen Buddhism; Gardening; Skiing; Japanese Language & Literature; Translating Montaigne. *Address:* Rue Moulin a huile, Cabrespine, 11160 Caunes Minervois, France. 52.

ZVONARYOVA SADYKOVA Lola Utkironvna, b. 28 July 1957, Moscow, Russia. Phylologist. m. Jladimie Konon, 27 Oct 1983, 1 s, 1 d. *Education:* Moscow State Univ, 1984; Dph, 1988. *Appointments:* Litezatwanaja Rossia, Newspaper, 1984-85; Detskaja Literature Mag, 1985-86; Literature Uchjola Mag, 1987-90; Detseaja Lit, 1990-91; Deputy Editor in Chief, Intl Youth Mag, 1991-. *Publications include:* Childrens Books. *Memberships:* The Wictors Union of Russia; Intl Assn of Belarussists; Women Writers Assn. *Honours:* Annual Prize of Detskaja Lit Mag. *Hobbies:* Literature; Creative work of Illustrators of Books; Research in the Field of Russian Literature. *Address:* Golubinskaja 9 kv 34, Moscow 117574, Russia.

ZWILLENBERG Lutz Oscar, b. 9 Dec 1925, Berlin. Biologist. m. Celia Fridman, 13 Sept 1970, 2 d. *Education:* Univ of Amsterdam, Holland, 1959. *Appointments:* Res Tchrng Asst, Anatomy Dept, Univ of Berne, 1959-63; Iden Head Asst, Dept Med Micro Biol, 1963-67; Co Owner Private R & D Lab, Berne. *Publications:* 43 Scientific Articles in Profl Journals; Book. Zwischen Bit und Bibel Hallwag Verlag, Berne. *Memberships:* Several Profl Assns; Jewish Community of Berne. *Hobbies:* Theoretical Physics; Philosophy of Sci & Philosophy of Religion. *Address:* Holligenstrasse 93, CH 3008, Bern, Switzerland. 52, 94, 152.

ZYDANOWICZ Janina Regina, b. 25 May 1916, Warsaw, Poland. Architect; Painter; Poet. *Education:* The Engrng Coll, Faculty of the Arch, Warsaw, 1950; Acad of Fine Arts, Warsaw, 1950-54. *Appointments:* Design Offices, 1950-76; Superior Designer, General Designer, Research & Design Office of the Health Serv, 1954-76. *Creative Works include:* Architectue; Paintings; Poetry. *Memberships:* Assn of Polish Archtiects; SARP; Instl Arts Guild; IAG; Polish Danish Soc; Leonardo Da Vinci, Rome. *Honours include:* Sarp 111, Degree Diploma, Ministry of Health & Social Welfare Award; Painting. Diplome de Mention; Poetry. Medaille de Bronze, Paris. *Hobbies:* Literature; Gardening; Sea Voyages. *Address:* Grottgera 11A/3, 00 785 Warsaw, Poland.

ZYDANOWICZ Maria Jadwiga, b. 11 Oct 1912, Aleksandrow, Poland. Graphic Artist; Painter. *Education:* Acad of Fine Arts, Warsaw, 1939. *Appointments:* Illustrator, Nasza Ksiegarnia, Ksiazka 1 Wiedza, 1945-60; Asst, Acad of Fine Arts, Warsaw, 1947-52; Art Exhibs, 1948-. *Creative Works:* Lithographies; Water Colours; Gouaches; Works in the Collections; Historic Museums of Warsaw; Masuria Museum, Olsztyn; Museum for Kleinart. *Memberships:* Polish Union of Plastic Artists; Intl Arts Guild; CSSI. *Honours:* Diploma Group of Polish Artists; Diploma Offical En Finale; Diplomes D'Honneur; Medaille de Bronze, Paris; Diploma Benemerenza, Rome; Diploma de Mention, Paris; Medaille De Bronze, Paris. *Hobbies:* Music; Gardening; Ornithology. *Address:* Grottgera 11A, M3, 00 785 Warsaw, Poland.

ZYDANOWICZ Witold, b. 4 June 1941, Warsaw, Poland. Automatic Control. m. Matgorzata Gotonska, 1 June 1971, 1 d. *Education:* MSc, 1964; PhD, 1972. *Appointments:* Inst of Control & Industrial Electronics, Tech Unif of Warsaw, 1964-91. *Publications:* Foundations of Control Engrng; Control Systems Laboratory. *Memberships:* Polish Electrical Engrng Assn. *Honours:* Warsaw Univ of Tech Rectors Award. *Hobbies:* Reading; Swimming. *Address:* ul Lazurowa 18A m1, 01 315 Warsaw, Poland.

ZYSZKOWSKI Wiktor Stefan Feliks, b. 15 Jan 1939, Warsaw, Poland. Area Officer. m. Barbara Dostal, 3 Aug 1963, 1 s, 1 d. *Education:* Warsaw Tech Univ, 1962; Inst of Nuclear Research, Swierk, 1968; Warsaw Tech Univ, DSc, 1976. *Appointments:* Inst of Nuclear Research, Swierk, Sci Co Worker, Dozent, 1961-82; Inst of Atomic Energy, 1982-86; Rzeszow Tech Univ, 1976-84; Gdansk Tech Univ, 1984-86; IAREA, Vienna, Area Officer, 1986-. *Publications include:* Heat Transfer; Thermodynamics; Safety of Nuclear Reactors. *Memberships:* Inst of Nuclear Research; Inst of Atomic Energy; Inst of Nuclear Research; Nuclear Safety Commission; Polish Acad of Sci; SOLIDARITY Council. *Honours:* Fellow of the Alexander Von Humboldt Foundation. *Hobbies:* Sailing; Polish History; Yoga; Photography. *Address:* Alentowicza 3m 26, 04-644 Warsaw, Poland.

Honours List

NAME:	Dr Abdel-Kader Abbadi
ADDRESS:	431 East 20, Apt 4-G New York NY 10010 USA
OCCUPATION:	UN Offical
YEAR OF ENTRY:	1986
CITATION:	For your Outstanding Contribution to the United Nations

---

NAME:	His Excellency Salim R Absy, FIBA
ADDRESS:	PO Box 1040 Manama Bahrain
OCCUPATION:	Diplomat
YEAR OF ENTRY:	1986
CITATION:	For your Outstanding Contribution to International Relations

---

NAME:	Dr Farid A Akasheh, LFIBA
ADDRESS:	PO Box 2173 Amman Jordan
OCCUPATION:	Doctor (Consultant Obstetrician and Gynaecologist)
YEAR OF ENTRY:	1986
CITATION:	For your Outstanding Contribution to Medicine

NAME:	Dr Farouk M Akhdar
ADDRESS:	The Economic Bureau PO Box 86619 Riyadh 11632 Kingdom of Saudi Arabia
OCCUPATION:	President of the Economic Bureau
YEAR OF ENTRY:	1989
CITATION:	For your Outstanding Contribution to Economics and to the development of Saudi Arabia

NAME:	Mr Adbullatif A R Al-Bahar
ADDRESS:	PO Box 89 Safat 13001 Kuwait City Kuwait
OCCUPATION:	Director General, Office of H H The Crown Prince & Prime Minister - Kuwait
YEAR OF ENTRY:	1989
CITATION:	For your Outstanding Contribution to his present position within the field of political & Economics Institutions

NAME:	Mr Said Jawdat Al-Dajani
ADDRESS:	PO Box 927260 Amman Jordan
OCCUPATION:	Attorney At-Law and Legal Consultant
YEAR OF ENTRY:	1986
CITATION:	For your Outstanding Contribution to The Law and Your Country

NAME:	Mr Ahmad Mohamad Ali
ADDRESS:	Islamic Development Bank PO Box 5925 Jeddah 21432 Saudi Arabia
OCCUPATION:	President, Islamic Development Bank
YEAR OF ENTRY:	1990
CITATION:	For your Outstanding Contribution to the Banking Business

NAME:	Mr Jacob Oladele Amao
ADDRESS:	PO Box 51722 Ikoyi Lagos Nigeria
OCCUPATION:	Company President - Executive
YEAR OF ENTRY:	1990
CITATION:	For your Outstanding Contribution to the Banking Business

NAME:	Professor Basile Angelopoulos, MD, PhD, LFIBA, DDG
ADDRESS:	Ipsilantou Str 37 Athens 106-76 Greece
OCCUPATION:	Professor in Pathologic Physiology
YEAR OF ENTRY:	1986
CITATION:	For your Outstanding Contribution to Medicine

NAME:	Ms Liliane Atlan
ADDRESS:	70 Rue du Javelot Cedex 13 75645 Paris France
OCCUPATION:	Author, Writer, Playwright
YEAR OF ENTRY:	1991
CITATION:	For your Outstanding Contribution to Literature

NAME:	Mrs Kathlyn Ballard, FIBA
ADDRESS:	40 Mont Victor Road Kew Victoria 3101 Australia
OCCUPATION:	Artist
YEAR OF ENTRY:	1986
CITATION:	For your Outstanding Contribution to Art

NAME:	Ms Elisabeth Barker
ADDRESS:	10095 Judy Avenue Cupertino CA 95014 USA
OCCUPATION:	Business Owner/Entrepeneur
YEAR OF ENTRY:	1991
CITATION:	For your Outstanding Contribution to Business

NAME:	Mr Abdul Rahman Batal, LFIBA, LFWLA
ADDRESS:	Chairman, Hannibal Tourism & Transport Co PO Box 4088 Damascus Syria
OCCUPATION:	Company Chairman
YEAR OF ENTRY:	1986
CITATION:	For your Outstanding Contribution to Tourism and Transport

---

NAME:	Ms Winogene L Bergman, FIBA
ADDRESS:	709 E Juneau Avenue Milwaukee WI 53202 USA
OCCUPATION:	Retired School Library Coordinator
YEAR OF ENTRY:	1986
CITATION:	For your Outstanding Contribution to Education

NAME:	Ms Henriette Hannah Bodenheimer Sadja Gaon Street 8 Jerusalem Israel
OCCUPATION:	Educator, Writer, Historian of Political Zionismus
YEAR OF ENTRY:	1988
CITATION:	For your Outstanding Contribution to Education and to the State of Israel

---

NAME:	Mr Adrian R Boller
ADDRESS:	Belvedere 5 5400 Baden Switzerland
OCCUPATION:	Trading Executive
YEAR OF ENTRY:	1986
CITATION:	For your Outstanding Contribution to Commerce

NAME: Ms Shauna D Boulton, LFIBA, DDG

ADDRESS: 1516 Glen Arbor
                     Salt Lake City
                     UT 84105
                     USA

OCCUPATION: Educator

YEAR OF ENTRY: 1986

CITATION: For your Outstanding Contribution to
                     Education

NAME: Dr Alexander Noble Burns, FIBA

ADDRESS: No 9 Short Street
                     Burleigh Heads
                     Queensland 4220
                     Australia

OCCUPATION: Biologist

YEAR OF ENTRY: 1986

CITATION: For your Outstanding Contribution to
                     Science

NAME: Mr Georg Brutian

ADDRESS: Pushkin Street 40, Apt 90
                     Yerevan 375010
                     Armenia
                     USSR

OCCUPATION: Teacher

YEAR OF ENTRY: 1990

CITATION: For your Outstanding Contribution to
                     Education & Teaching

NAME: Mr Hubert A Buchanan, LFIBA

ADDRESS: 209 West 19th Street
                     Pueblo
                     CO 81003
                     USA

OCCUPATION: Retired Life Insurance Agent

YEAR OF ENTRY: 1990

CITATION: For your Outstanding Contribution to the
                     Life Insurance Industry

NAME: Mr Richard E Butler

ADDRESS: 40 Barrington Avenue
                           Kew 3101
                           Victoria
                           Australia

OCCUPATION: International Official

YEAR OF ENTRY: 1990

CITATION: For your Outstanding Contribution to
                           International Cooperation and to
                           Worldwide Telecommunication
                           Development

NAME: Mr Manfredo L Castro, LFIBA

ADDRESS: 1613 Cypress
                           Dasmarinas Village
                           Makati
                           Metro Manila
                           Philippines

OCCUPATION: Businessman

YEAR OF ENTRY: 1986

CITATION: For your Outstanding Contribution to
                           Business and Finance

NAME: Professor Chen Jian Hong

ADDRESS: Gansu University of Tech
                           Lanzhou
                           Gansu
                           China

OCCUPATION: President, Professor

YEAR OF ENTRY: 1989

CITATION: For your Outstanding Contribution to the
                           Science and Education of China

NAME: Mr Thomas J Cleary

ADDRESS: 933 Kiowa
                           Burkburnett
                           TX 76354
                           USA

OCCUPATION: Clinical Social Worker, Teaching
                           Assistant, Graduate Student US History
                           MSU

YEAR OF ENTRY: 1989

CITATION: For your Outstanding Contribution to
                           Social Work Service

NAME:	Ms Irene Coates, LFIBA
ADDRESS:	Kalkadoon, 140 Station Street Blackheath NSW 2785 Australia
OCCUPATION:	Artist, Writer
YEAR OF ENTRY:	1987
CITATION:	For your Outstanding Contribution to Art

NAME:	Mr Colin Cecil Coleman, OAM, FIBA, MSAE, TTC
ADDRESS:	43 Woolston Drive Frankston Victoria 3199 Australia
OCCUPATION:	Techinical Senior Teacher
YEAR OF ENTRY:	1986
CITATION:	For your Outstanding Contribution to Education

NAME:	Dr George Edward Corder, LFIBA, FWLA, DDG
ADDRESS:	PO Box 1723 Hollywood CA 90078 USA
OCCUPATION:	Scientist of Human Behaviour
YEAR OF ENTRY:	1986
CITATION:	For your Outstanding Contribution to Science and Education

---

NAME:	Professor Dr Erika Cremer
ADDRESS:	Reitmannstrasse 20 A-6020 Innsbruck Austria
OCCUPATION:	Research and Education
YEAR OF ENTRY:	1991
CITATION:	For your Outstanding Contribution to Reaction Kinetics (branching of chain reactions) and pioneer work in Gas Chromatography

NAME:	The Hon Dame Dr Joy Beaudette Cripps, DCMSS, MCC, LFIAP, LFWLA, LittD
ADDRESS:	3 Mill Street Aspendale Victoria 3195 Australia
OCCUPATION:	Publisher, Poet, Photographer
YEAR OF ENTRY:	1988
CITATION:	For your Outstanding Contribution to Literature

NAME:	Mr Glen Laban Cross, LFIBA
ADDRESS:	2841 Cottingham Street Oceanside CA 92054 USA
OCCUPATION:	International Development Planner
YEAR OF ENTRY:	1986
CITATION:	For your Outstanding Contribution to International Development

---

NAME:	Damalas, Basil V
ADDRESS:	Patission 171 Athens 112 52 Greece
OCCUPATION:	Publicist and Economist
YEAR OF ENTRY:	1986
CITATION:	For your Outstanding Contribution to Economics

NAME:	Mr J Edward Dealy, MS, PhD
ADDRESS:	800 F Street, No P-3 Juneau AK 99801 USA
OCCUPATION:	Forestry
YEAR OF ENTRY:	1986
CITATION:	For your Outstanding Contribution to Forestry

NAME:	Mr Ronald Joseph Godfrey De Mel, MP
ADDRESS:	Ministry of Finance and Planning Old Secretariat Colombo 1 Sri Lanka
OCCUPATION:	Minister of Finance and Planning
YEAR OF ENTRY:	1986
CITATION:	For your Outstanding Contribution for 9 years as Minister

NAME:	Sir Bayard Dill, CBE, JP, DDG
ADDRESS:	Newbold Place Devonshire Bermuda 1, 41
OCCUPATION:	Barrister-at-Law
YEAR OF ENTRY:	1986
CITATION:	For your Outstanding Contribution to over 60 years law work and 34 years Bermuda Government Political Life

NAME:	O Leonard Doellner, FIBA
ADDRESS:	PO Box 43392 Tucson AZ 85733 USA
OCCUPATION:	Independent Consultant
YEAR OF ENTRY:	1986
CITATION:	For your Outstanding Contribution to Science and Engineering

NAME:	Dr Luis Dolcet-Buxeres, LPIBA
ADDRESS:	Muntaner 350 08021 Barcelona Spain
OCCUPATION:	Surgeon
YEAR OF ENTRY:	1987
CITATION:	For your Outstanding Contribution to Medicine

NAME:	Mr Alfons F Donko DIPL-ING, HE, DG, FIBA, ABIRA
ADDRESS:	c/o Oesterr Normungsintitut Postf 130 Heinstr 38 A-1021 Vienna Austria
OCCUPATION:	Deputy Managing Director
YEAR OF ENTRY:	1988
CITATION:	For your Outstanding Contribution to Business

NAME:	Mrs Estelle Cecilia D Dunlap, LPIBA
ADDRESS:	719 Shepherd Street, NW Washington DC 20011 USA
OCCUPATION:	Educator and Mathematician
YEAR OF ENTRY:	1986
CITATION:	For your Outstanding Contribution to Education

NAME:	Mr Howard M Dupuy Jr, BA, LLP
ADDRESS:	16116 NE Stanton Street Portland OR 97230 USA
OCCUPATION:	Lawyer
YEAR OF ENTRY:	1986
CITATION:	For your Outstanding Contribution to The Law

NAME:	Mr Dewey Bert Durrett
ADDRESS:	377 Main Street Salem NH 03079 USA
OCCUPATION:	Real Estate Agent
YEAR OF ENTRY:	1990
CITATION:	For your Outstanding Contribution to Real Estate and Housing

NAME: Dr Judith Marilyn Ebner

ADDRESS: 3601 Balfour Court
Flint
MI 48507
USA

OCCUPATION: Educational Administrator

YEAR OF ENTRY: 1986

CITATION: For your Outstanding Contribution to
Education

NAME: Mr Chris Economides

ADDRESS: PO Box 1632
Nicosia
Cyprus

OCCUPATION: Director

YEAR OF ENTRY: 1988

CITATION: For your Outstanding Contribution to
Economics

NAME: Mr Earl Otto Ellison

ADDRESS: 6324 Telegraph Road
Alexandria
VA 22310
USA

OCCUPATION: Computer Systems Contracting Officer

YEAR OF ENTRY: 1992

CITATION: For your Outstanding Contribution to
Management and Finance

NAME: Mr Wilhelm Flöttmann, LPIBA

ADDRESS: Schlürterstr 11
4830 Gutërsloh 1
Germany

OCCUPATION: Medicine

YEAR OF ENTRY: 1990

CITATION: For your Outstanding Contribution to
Medicine

NAME: Dr Gordon Buell Ford Jr, AB, AM, PhD, LPIBA, LFWLA

ADDRESS: 3619 Brownsboro Road
Louisville
KY 40207, USA

OCCUPATION: Educator, Univ Prof, Author, Hospital Industry Executive, and Financial Management Corporation Director

YEAR OF ENTRY: 1988

CITATION: For your Outstanding Contribution to University Education and to Financial Management

---

NAME: Mr Joseph Edward Garrett, FIBA

ADDRESS: 2291 Goodrum Lane
Marietta
GA 30066
USA

OCCUPATION: Aeronautical Engineer

YEAR OF ENTRY: 1986

CITATION: For your Outstanding Contribution to Engineering

NAME: Professor M Gembicki, MD

ADDRESS: Department of Endocrinology
University School of Medicine in Poznan
Al Przybyszewskiego 49
PL-60 355, Poland

OCCUPATION: Doctor

YEAR OF ENTRY: 1986

CITATION: For your Outstanding Contribution to Medicine

NAME: Dr Ashraf Ghani

ADDRESS: PO Box 16176
Riyadh
Saudi Arabia 11464

OCCUPATION: Engineering and Management Executive

YEAR OF ENTRY: 1986

CITATION: For your Outstanding Contribution to Project Engioneering and Management

NAME: Dr Richard Sherwin Gothard

ADDRESS: Gothard House
Henley-on-Thames
Oxon RE9 1AJ
England

OCCUPATION: Information Scientist

YEAR OF ENTRY: 1986

CITATION: For your Outstanding Contribution to
Information Science

NAME: Dr Francis W Graham

ADDRESS: 28 Pasley Street
South Yarra
Victoria 3141
Australia

OCCUPATION: Physician, Psychiatrist & Psycho-analyst

YEAR OF ENTRY: 1988

CITATION: For your Outstanding Contribution to
Psychiatry, Psycho-analysis and Group
Psycho-therapy

NAME: Professor Dr G Griesser

ADDRESS: Universitätspräsident a D
Barstenkamp 51 - Rammsee
2300 Molfsee
Germany

OCCUPATION: Professor of Medical Informatics and
Statistics Manager of ITK Information
Technology Giel Ltd

YEAR OF ENTRY: 1989

CITATION: For your Outstanding Contribution to
Medicine, Psychology, Hospitals and
Dentists

NAME:	Professor Ghassan Haddad, PhD, DSc, LPIBA
ADDRESS:	PO Box 6025 Mansour Baghdad Iraq
OCCUPATION:	Professor of Economics
YEAR OF ENTRY:	1986
CITATION:	For your Outstanding Contribution to Science

NAME:	Ms Violet Edna Hobbs Hain
ADDRESS:	3530 Raymoor Road Kensington MD 20895 USA
OCCUPATION:	Artist
YEAR OF ENTRY:	1986
CITATION:	For your Outstanding Contribution to Art

NAME:	Dr Paul L C Hao
ADDRESS:	10F1 No 116 Nanking East Road, Sec 2 Taipei, Taiwan China
OCCUPATION:	Biochemist
YEAR OF ENTRY:	1986
CITATION:	For your Outstanding Contribution to Science

NAME:	Mr Christopher Philip Harding, FIBA
ADDRESS:	PO Box 5271 Rockhampton Mail Centre Queensland 4702 Australia
OCCUPATION:	Market Analyst
YEAR OF ENTRY:	1986
CITATION:	For your Outstanding Contribution to Psychometrics

NAME:	Louise Harris, FIBC, LPIBA, LFWLA, LPWIA, LPABI, DG, DDG
ADDRESS:	395 Angell Street, Apt 111 Providence RI 02906 USA
OCCUPATION:	Researcher and Writer
YEAR OF ENTRY:	1986
CITATION:	For your Outstanding Contribution to Research and Writing

NAME:	Dr Kazuyuki Hatada, DDG, LFIBA
ADDRESS:	Department of Mathematics Faculty of Education Gifu University, 1-1 Yanagido Gifu City, Gifu Prefecture 501-11 Japan
OCCUPATION:	Mathematician
YEAR OF ENTRY:	1990
CITATION:	For your Outstanding Contribution to Pure Mathematics, especially to the Theory of Modular Forms

NAME:	Professor Mahmoud Hessaby
ADDRESS:	8 Hessaby Avenue Hessaby Square Tajrish, Tehran Iran
OCCUPATION:	Professor
YEAR OF ENTRY:	1990
CITATION:	For your Outstanding Contribution to Physics, Etymology and Persian Literature

NAME:	Mr Diego C J F Hidalgo, LFIBA
ADDRESS:	Felipe Cuarto 9 28014 Madrid Spain
OCCUPATION:	Lawyer
YEAR OF ENTRY:	1989
CITATION:	For your Outstanding Contribution to Law

NAME:	Reverend Reuben Arthur Houseal, ThD, PhD, LLD, LFIBA
ADDRESS:	132 South Erie Street, PO Box 132 Mercer PA 16137 USA
OCCUPATION:	Clergyman, Educator, Writer
YEAR OF ENTRY:	1986
CITATION:	For your Outstanding Contribution for Distinguished Service to the Cause of Christ

NAME:	Mrs Ruth Arnold Houseal, DRE, LHD, LFIBA
ADDRESS:	132 South Erie Street, PO Box 132 Mercer PA 16137 USA
OCCUPATION:	Educator
YEAR OF ENTRY:	1986
CITATION:	For your Outstanding Contribution to Education

NAME:	Professor Zuey-Shin Hsu, MD, LFIBA
ADDRESS:	Department of Physiology Kaohsiung Medical College No 100 Shih-Chuan 1st Road, Kaohsiung Taiwan, China
OCCUPATION:	Professor of Physiology
YEAR OF ENTRY:	1989
CITATION:	For your Outstanding Contribution to Medical Science and the Teaching Profession

NAME:	Mr John Chih-An Hu, FIBA
ADDRESS:	16212 122 Se Renton WA 98058 USA
OCCUPATION:	Chemist and Chemical Engineer
YEAR OF ENTRY:	1986
CITATION:	For your Outstanding Contribution to Chemistry

NAME: Professor Qi Shu Hua, LFIBA

ADDRESS: Tianjin Vocational Technical Teachers' College
Tianjin
China

OCCUPATION: Professor, Vice-President

YEAR OF ENTRY: 1989

CITATION: For your Outstanding Contribution to the researches on welding and the administration of vocational education

---

NAME: Dr Bettina S Hurni

ADDRESS: Rue Saint - Jean 98
1211 Geneva 11
Switzerland

OCCUPATION: Professor of Economics

YEAR OF ENTRY: 1991

CITATION: For your Outstanding Contribution to Economics

NAME: Professor Dr Kazuyosi Ikeda, LPIBA, DDG, IOM, LFWLA

ADDRESS: Dept of Mathematical Sciences
Faculty of Engineering, Osaka Univ
2-1 Yamadaoka, Suita, Osaka 565
Japan

OCCUPATION: Professor of Theoretical Physics and Poet

YEAR OF ENTRY: 1989

CITATION: For your Outstanding Contribution to Theoretical Physics and Poetry

---

NAME: Dr Drago Ikic, LFIBA

ADDRESS: Yugoslav Academy of Science and Arts
Inst for Research and Standardization of Immunologic Substances
Demetrova 18, 41000 Zagreb
Yugoslavia

OCCUPATION: Doctor

YEAR OF ENTRY: 1986

CITATION: For your Outstanding Contribution to Medicine

NAME:	Sir James Irwin
ADDRESS:	124 Brougham Place North Adelaide SA 5006 Australia
OCCUPATION:	Retired Architect
YEAR OF ENTRY:	1988
CITATION:	For your Outstanding Contribution to Architecture, the Arts and the Community

NAME:	Geo E Johnston, FIBA
ADDRESS:	PO Box 806 Marco Island FL 33969 USA
OCCUPATION:	Multi-Faceted Entrepreneur
YEAR OF ENTRY:	1988
CITATION:	For your Outstanding Contribution to Business and Commerce

NAME:	Ms Clare L Jones
ADDRESS:	40C Petherto Road London N5 2RE England
OCCUPATION:	Pianist and Accompanist
YEAR OF ENTRY:	1986
CITATION:	For your Outstanding Contribution to Music

NAME:	Mrs Hazel Emma Jones, FIBA
ADDRESS:	35 Greer Street Bardon Queensland 4065 Australia
OCCUPATION:	Librarian
YEAR OF ENTRY:	1986
CITATION:	For your Outstanding Contribution to Librarianship

NAME:	Mr Halldor H Jonsson, LFIBA
ADDRESS:	Hyerfisgata 4-6 Reykjavik Iceland
OCCUPATION:	Architect and Company Director
YEAR OF ENTRY:	1986
CITATION:	For your Outstanding Contribution to Architecture

NAME:	Denise M (Koppenhagen) Kalker-Harris, FIL, LPIBA
ADDRESS:	c/o M Harris & Sons Gayfere House, 22/23 Gayfere Street London SW1P 3HP, England HOME: 76 Aylestone Avenue London NW6 7AB
OCCUPATION:	Social Worker
YEAR OF ENTRY:	1986
CITATION:	For your Outstanding Contribution to the Community

NAME:	Ms Catherine Earl Bailey Kerr, LPIBA
ADDRESS:	1412 West Hendricks Roswell, NM 88201 USA
OCCUPATION:	Artist, Art and Music Teacher, Architect, Designer
YEAR OF ENTRY:	1986
CITATION:	For your Outstanding Contribution to Art and the Handicapped

---

NAME:	Dr Mohammed Vahid Husain Khan, FIBA
ADDRESS:	9939 Affton Place St Louis MO 63123 USA
OCCUPATION:	Physician
YEAR OF ENTRY:	1986
CITATION:	For your Outstanding Contribution to Medicine

NAME:	Dr Rachel Hadley King
ADDRESS:	60 Broadway, Apt 905 Providence RI 02903 USA
OCCUPATION:	Teacher
YEAR OF ENTRY:	1986
CITATION:	For your Outstanding Contribution to Education

NAME:	Ms Isabella J Kirstein née Grobbelaar (known as Lulu)
ADDRESS:	PO Box 11260 Johannesburg 2000 Republic of South Africa
OCCUPATION:	Executive Chairman - Marketing & Socio-Political Research Co
YEAR OF ENTRY:	1989
CITATION:	For your Outstanding Contribution to Marketing & Socio-Political Research as a profession and specifically for women

---

NAME:	Mrs Nagiko Sato Kiser, LFIBA
ADDRESS:	1101 Mission Verde Drive Camarillo CA 93012 USA
OCCUPATION:	Senior Librarian
YEAR OF ENTRY:	1991
CITATION:	For your Outstanding Contribution to the Community

NAME:	Kristjan G Kjartansson
ADDRESS:	Einimelur 7 107 Reykjavik Iceland
OCCUPATION:	Company Vice President
YEAR OF ENTRY:	1986
CITATION:	For your Outstanding Contribution to Commerce

NAME:	Mr Tsuneo Koike, LFIBA
ADDRESS:	39 Mauna Loa Street Hilo HI 96720 USA
OCCUPATION:	Engineering and Surveying Consultant
YEAR OF ENTRY:	1989
CITATION:	For your Outstanding Contribution to Engineering

NAME:	Professor Lidia Agnes Kozubek
ADDRESS:	Al Waszyngtona 116/98 04-074 Warsaw Poland
OCCUPATION:	Pianist, Educator and Musicologist
YEAR OF ENTRY:	1986
CITATION:	For your Outstanding Contribution to Music

NAME:	Mrs Pansy Daegling Kraus, LFIBA
ADDRESS:	PO Box 600908 San Diego CA 92120 USA
OCCUPATION:	Editor, Gemologist
YEAR OF ENTRY:	1991
CITATION:	For your Outstanding Contribution to Writing

NAME:	Dr Rolf Kraus-Ruppert, LFIBA
ADDRESS:	Zelgli 41 C CH-3179 Kriechenwil Switzerland
OCCUPATION:	Neuropathologist and Physician
YEAR OF ENTRY:	1986
CITATION:	For your Outstanding Contribution to Science

NAME: Professor Raphael Hoegh Krohn, LPIBA, DDG

ADDRESS: Mathematic Institution
Oslo University
PO Box 1053
Blindern
0316 Oslo 6
Norway

OCCUPATION: Professor of Mathematics

YEAR OF ENTRY: 1986

CITATION: For your Outstanding Contribution to Education and Research

---

NAME: Ms Mary Krueger-Ortlip

ADDRESS: 2917 So Ocean Blvd 703
Highland Beach
FL 33487
USA

OCCUPATION: Artist

YEAR OF ENTRY: 1991

CITATION: For your Outstanding Contribution to Art

NAME: Mr Prem Chand Kulleen, LFIBA

ADDRESS: PO Box 35173
Lusaka
Zambia

OCCUPATION: Librarian

YEAR OF ENTRY: 1986

CITATION: For your Outstanding Contribution to Librarianship

NAME: Professor Jean-Paul Labelle, SS, LFIBA

ADDRESS: St Sulpice Seminary
Matsuyama 1-1-1
Jonan-ku, Fukuoka 814-01
Japan

OCCUPATION: University Professor

YEAR OF ENTRY: 1986

CITATION: For your Outstanding Contribution to The Canon Law

NAME:	Dr Joyce M Laborde, PhD, RN, LFIBA
ADDRESS:	College of Nursing, Univ of North Dakota PO Box 8195, University Station Grand Forks, ND 58202 USA
OCCUPATION:	Professor
YEAR OF ENTRY:	1986
CITATION:	For your Outstanding Contribution to Nursing

NAME:	Dr Vernette Landers, LFIBA, LFWLA
ADDRESS:	PO Box 3839 Landers CA 92285 USA
OCCUPATION:	Educator
YEAR OF ENTRY:	1986
CITATION:	For your Outstanding Contribution to Education and Community

NAME:	Professor Chang Bin Lee, PhD
ADDRESS:	18 Donui-dong Chongro-ku Seoul Korea
OCCUPATION:	Professor of Medicine
YEAR OF ENTRY:	1986
CITATION:	For your Outstanding Contribution to Medicine

NAME:	Dr Joseph Le Jeune
ADDRESS:	6 Square Castiglione 78150 Le Chesney France
OCCUPATION:	International Industrial Development Projects Consultant
YEAR OF ENTRY:	1986
CITATION:	For your Outstanding Contribution to Industrial Development

NAME:	Dato Dr Sip Hon Lew
ADDRESS:	25 Jalan 14/3 Taman Tun Abdul Razak Ampany Jaya Selangor, Malaysia
OCCUPATION:	Company Director, Retired Ambassador
YEAR OF ENTRY:	1988
CITATION:	For your Outstanding Contribution to the economic, political and cultural life of Malaysia and to your role in the larger world community

NAME:	Professor Jong-Teh Lin, FWLA, FIBA, DDG
ADDRESS:	No 185-6 Nan Men Road 700 Tainan Taiwan Formosa
OCCUPATION:	Teacher
YEAR OF ENTRY:	1988
CITATION:	For your Outstanding Contribution to Education

NAME:	Mrs Anneliese List, FWLA, FIBA (Pseudonym Alice Pervin)
ADDRESS:	Fuenfbronn 26 8545 Spalt Germany
OCCUPATION:	Soubrette
YEAR OF ENTRY:	1986
CITATION:	For your Outstanding Contribution to Literature

NAME:	Ms Sonia Lynch
ADDRESS:	13705 Beret Place Silver Spring MD 20906 USA
OCCUPATION:	Consultant
YEAR OF ENTRY:	1991
CITATION:	For your Outstanding Contribution as a Consultant in the Data Processing Field

NAME:	Mr Konstantin Mandic
ADDRESS:	Gaborone Private bag - BR38 Botswana Africa
OCCUPATION:	Architect
YEAR OF ENTRY:	1989
CITATION:	For your Outstanding Contribution to Architecture

NAME:	Professor Dr Mitsuo Masai, FIBA
ADDRESS:	Faculty of Engineering Kobe University Rokkadai Nada Kobe 657 Japan
OCCUPATION:	University Professor
YEAR OF ENTRY:	1986
CITATION:	For your Outstanding Contribution to Catalysis

NAME:	Emeritus Professor Junji Matsumoto, FIBA
ADDRESS:	2-3-14 Asukano Minami Ikoma City 630-01 Japan
OCCUPATION:	Neuroscientist
YEAR OF ENTRY:	1988
CITATION:	For your Outstanding Contribution to Science

NAME:	Mr Seiichi Matsumoto, FIBA
ADDRESS:	Yuigahama 1-11-17 Kamakura 248 Japan
OCCUPATION:	Director and Professor
YEAR OF ENTRY:	1986
CITATION:	For your Outstanding Contribution to Medicine

NAME:	Very Reverend Stanley Matuszewski MS, FIBA
ADDRESS:	Box 777 Twin Lakes WI 53181 USA
OCCUPATION:	Priest
YEAR OF ENTRY:	1986
CITATION:	For your Outstanding Contribution to Architecture

NAME:	Mrs Madella Rigby Maurer
ADDRESS:	The Pennsfield, Apt C10 802 Broad Street Selinsgrove, PA 17870 USA
OCCUPATION:	Psychologist
YEAR OF ENTRY:	1986
CITATION:	For your Outstanding Contribution to Psychology

NAME:	Ms Barbara Johnston McCrary
ADDRESS:	PO Box 1017 Merced CA 95341 USA
OCCUPATION:	Business Women - Prudential Insurance, Financial Service Rep Dist Agent
YEAR OF ENTRY:	1991
CITATION:	For your Outstanding Contribution to the Business Profession

NAME:	Helen McGinty
ADDRESS:	3755 Peachtree Road, Apt 410 Atlanta GA 30319 USA
OCCUPATION:	Retired Teacher
YEAR OF ENTRY:	1989
CITATION:	For your Outstanding Contribution to Teaching

NAME:	Dr John H McGovern
ADDRESS:	53 East 70th Street New York NY 10021 USA
OCCUPATION:	Professor of Clinical Surgery (Urology)
YEAR OF ENTRY:	1986
CITATION:	For your Outstanding Contribution to Clinical Surgery

NAME:	Mrs Carmon Ramona McHugh
ADDRESS:	Casa de Rosas 11 1220 Avenida Caballeros Palm Springs CA 92262 USA
OCCUPATION:	Artist
YEAR OF ENTRY:	1986
CITATION:	For your Outstanding Contribution to Art

NAME:	Mr John Joseph Mehalchin
ADDRESS:	c/o Highline Financial Serv Inc 1881 9th Street, No 320 Boulder, CO 80302 USA
OCCUPATION:	Entrepreneur, Financial Executive
YEAR OF ENTRY:	1991
CITATION:	For your Outstanding Contribution to Business

NAME:	Mrs Josephine Mellichamp, FIBA
ADDRESS:	1124 Reeder Circle NE Atlanta GA 30306 USA
OCCUPATION:	Former Librarian, Writer, Historian and Teacher
YEAR OF ENTRY:	1986
CITATION:	For your Outstanding Contribution to Librarianship, Writing and Education

NAME:	Dr Kathleen Louise Mendrey
ADDRESS:	791 Tremont Street West 403 Boston MA 02118 USA
OCCUPATION:	Management Consultant
YEAR OF ENTRY:	1991
CITATION:	For your Outstanding Contribution to Business

NAME:	Mr Ralph E Montijo, DDG, IOM
ADDRESS:	c/o Omniplan Corporation 5839 Green Valley Cir - 203 Culver City, CA 90230 USA
OCCUPATION:	Company President, Executive
YEAR OF ENTRY:	1987
CITATION:	For your Outstanding Contribution to Business

NAME:	Professor James Crutchfield Morelock, FIBA
ADDRESS:	2917 Garth Road, SE Huntsville AL 35801 USA
OCCUPATION:	Mathematician
YEAR OF ENTRY:	1986
CITATION:	For your Outstanding Contribution to Mathematics

NAME:	Ms Peggy Jean Mueller
ADDRESS:	1506 Hardouin Avenue Austin TX 78703 USA
OCCUPATION:	Dance Teacher/Choreographer
YEAR OF ENTRY:	1990
CITATION:	For your Outstanding Contribution to Dancing, Ranching and Trail Riding

NAME: Mr Hassenally Nanuck, LFIBA

ADDRESS: PO Box 40346
                     Gaborone
                     Botswana
                     Southern Africa

OCCUPATION: Auto Body Mechanic and Panel Beater

YEAR OF ENTRY: 1992

CITATION: For your Outstanding Contribution to
                     Auto Body Mechanics and Panel Beating

NAME: Col Leon D Nobes, HOSJ, FIBA

ADDRESS: 2033 Crozier Avenue
                     Muskegin
                     MI 49441
                     USA

OCCUPATION: Retired University Professor

YEAR OF ENTRY: 1986

CITATION: For your Outstanding Contribution to
                     Education

NAME: Professor Henry Ian A Nowik

ADDRESS: 1250 Merchant Lane
                     McLean
                     VA 22101
                     USA

OCCUPATION: Education

YEAR OF ENTRY: 1990

CITATION: For your Outstanding Contribution to
                     Education

NAME: Dr Wilson Reid Ogg, LPIBA, LFWLA,
                     DDG

ADDRESS: Pinebrook, 1104 Keith Avenue
                     Berkeley
                     CA 94708
                     USA

OCCUPATION: Poet, Graphic Illustrator, Publisher,
                     Retired Lawyer and Educator

YEAR OF ENTRY: 1991

CITATION: For your Outstanding Contribution to the
                     Legal Profession

NAME:	Mr Masa Aki Oka
ADDRESS:	3-24-15-401 Tsurumaki Setagaya-ku Tokyo 154 Japan
OCCUPATION:	Businessman
YEAR OF ENTRY:	1991
CITATION:	For your Outstanding Contribution to Finance and Banking

---

NAME:	Mr Greensill Selby Old, FIBA
ADDRESS:	2/74 Milray Avenue Wellstonecraft NSW 2065 Australia
OCCUPATION:	Librarian
YEAR OF ENTRY:	1986
CITATION:	For your Outstanding Contribution to Librarianship

NAME:	Mr Pedro T Orata
ADDRESS:	Urdaneta Community College Urdaneta Pargsinan Philippines
OCCUPATION:	Teacher
YEAR OF ENTRY:	1986
CITATION:	For your Outstanding Contribution to Education

NAME:	Dr Pola Ortiz
ADDRESS:	Urbanizacion La Paz El Paraiso Calle 6 Quinta 'Pola' Caracas 102 Venezuela
OCCUPATION:	Economist
YEAR OF ENTRY:	1986
CITATION:	For your Outstanding Contribution to Economy

NAME:	Dr Irene M K Ovenstone, FIBA
ADDRESS:	10 Moor Road Calverton Nottingham NG14 6FW England
OCCUPATION:	Consultant Psychiatrist
YEAR OF ENTRY:	1986
CITATION:	For your Outstanding Contribution to Psychiatry

NAME:	Mr Pritam Singh Panesar, LFIBA
ADDRESS:	PO Box 46235 Nairobi Kenya
OCCUPATION:	Engineer and Pilot
YEAR OF ENTRY:	1986
CITATION:	For your Outstanding Contribution to Engineering

NAME:	Dr Lucy T Parker, LPIBA, DDG
ADDRESS:	The Parker Academy 248 Concord Road Sudbury MA 01776 USA
OCCUPATION:	Director, The Parker Academy
YEAR OF ENTRY:	1986
CITATION:	For your Outstanding Contribution to Education

NAME:	Ms Marion L Patterson Beard, FIBA
ADDRESS:	Route 1 Vincennes IN 47591 USA
OCCUPATION:	Artist
YEAR OF ENTRY:	1986
CITATION:	For your Outstanding Contribution to Art

NAME:	Ms Coralynn Pence
ADDRESS:	5009-48th NE Seattle WA 98105 USA
OCCUPATION:	Artist, Goldsmith
YEAR OF ENTRY:	1991
CITATION:	For your Outstanding Contribution for Privately Commissioned Jewellry

---

NAME:	Mr E Allen Propst, LFIBA
ADDRESS:	253 S E Scravel Hill Road Houston Albany OR 97321 USA
OCCUPATION:	Retired
YEAR OF ENTRY:	1991
CITATION:	For your Outstanding Contribution to Public Affairs of All Countries

---

NAME:	Mr George Earl Pyper
ADDRESS:	320-3120 North Island Hwy Campbell River BC Canada V9W 2H7
OCCUPATION:	Violinist and Columnist
YEAR OF ENTRY:	1991
CITATION:	For your Outstanding Contribution to Arts and Communities

---

NAME:	Ms Sherry Swett Raatz, LPIBA, DDG
ADDRESS:	7500-27th NE Seattle WA 98115 USA
OCCUPATION:	Community Leader
YEAR OF ENTRY:	1986
CITATION:	For your Outstanding Contribution to the Community

NAME:	Mr Charles R J Rapin
ADDRESS:	Laboratoire de Complilation Department d'Informatique EPFL Ecublens (MA) CH 1015 Lausanne, Switzerland
OCCUPATION:	Professor of Computer Science
YEAR OF ENTRY:	1989
CITATION:	For your Outstanding Contribution to Computer Science

NAME:	Mr John D Regan, CLU, Ch FC
ADDRESS:	Gen Services Life Insurance Co 201 Glameda Del Prado Novato, CA 94949 USA
OCCUPATION:	President and Chief Executive Officer GSLIC, GSL Holding, Federation for Financial Independent
YEAR OF ENTRY:	1989
CITATION:	For your Outstanding Contribution to the Insurance Industry in the United States of America

NAME:	Dr Ralph R Robinson
ADDRESS:	PO Box 668 Middlesboro, KS 40965 USA
OCCUPATION:	Medical Doctor
YEAR OF ENTRY:	1986
CITATION:	For your Outstanding Contribution to Medicine

NAME:	Captain Suleiman Sa'idu, FSS, PSC, MSC, LPIBA
ADDRESS:	PO Box 54119 Ikoyi, Lagos Nigeria
OCCUPATION:	Naval Officer
YEAR OF ENTRY:	1986
CITATION:	For your Outstanding Contribution to the Armed Forces

NAME:	Dr Frank Samlot, FIBA
ADDRESS:	2669 Gerda Bella Avenue St Augustine FL 32086 USA
OCCUPATION:	Forensic Technologist
YEAR OF ENTRY:	1989
CITATION:	For your Outstanding Contribution to Forensic Technology

NAME:	Dr Aiko Satow
ADDRESS:	c/o Department of Psychology Hamamatsu University School of Medicine Handa-cho, Hamamatsu 431-31 Japan
OCCUPATION:	Professor of Behavioural Science
YEAR OF ENTRY:	1991
CITATION:	For your Outstanding Contribution to Behavioural Study in Technology and Medicine

NAME:	Mr J W Scheja, ScD, FIBA
ADDRESS:	Institute of Thrombosis & Transfusion Medicine Universitat Dusseldorf 5 Morrensraße, D-4000 Dusseldorf 1 Germany
OCCUPATION:	Medical Doctor
YEAR OF ENTRY:	1986
CITATION:	For your Outstanding Contribution to Engineering

NAME:	Mr Dennis Screpatis, PE, LFIBA, DDG
ADDRESS:	2200 North Central Road Fort Lee NJ 07024 USA
OCCUPATION:	Consulting Engineer
YEAR OF ENTRY:	1986
CITATION:	For your Outstanding Contribution to Engineering

NAME:	Professor Maurice K Seguin, FIBA
ADDRESS:	Suite 7584 Pavillion Lemieux
	Univerisite Laval
	Quebec
	Canada 6IK 7P4
OCCUPATION:	Professor of Geophysics
YEAR OF ENTRY:	1986
CITATION:	For your Outstanding Contribution to Science

NAME:	Mr Philip Selby, LPIBA
ADDRESS:	Hill Cottage
	Via Primo Maggio 93
	00068 Rignano Flaminio
	Rome
	Italy
OCCUPATION:	Composer
YEAR OF ENTRY:	1991
CITATION:	For your Outstanding Contribution to Music

NAME:	Mr Robert Al Serlippens
ADDRESS:	PO Box 2639
	Kinshasa
	Zaire
OCCUPATION:	Attorney at Law
YEAR OF ENTRY:	1986
CITATION:	For your Outstanding Contribution to The Law

NAME:	Dr Isadore Shapiro, BChE, PhD
ADDRESS:	5624 West 62nd Street
	Los Angeles
	CA 90056
	USA
OCCUPATION:	Material Scientist
YEAR OF ENTRY:	1990
CITATION:	For your Outstanding Contribution to Science

NAME:	Ms Carolyn Juanita Shearer
ADDRESS:	205 South Tucson Circle Aurora CO 80012 USA
OCCUPATION:	Educator
YEAR OF ENTRY:	1990
CITATION:	For your Outstanding Contribution to Education

NAME:	Dr Muhammad M Mukram Sheikh, PhD, HLFIBA, DDG
ADDRESS:	PO Box 1974 Gaborone Botswana Southern Africa
OCCUPATION:	Government Official, Marketing Executive, Public Relations Specialist
YEAR OF ENTRY:	1992
CITATION:	For your Outstanding Contribution to Trade Journalism

NAME:	Ms Daphne Marjorie Sheldrick
ADDRESS:	David Sheldrick Wildlife Trust Box 15555 Nairobi Kenya
OCCUPATION:	Authoress and Wildlife Specialist
YEAR OF ENTRY:	1989
CITATION:	For your Outstanding Contribution to Wildlife Conservation

NAME:	Professor Koki Shimoji, MD, DDG
ADDRESS:	Department of Anesthesiology Niigata University School of Medicine 1-757 Asahi-Machi Niigata 951, Japan
OCCUPATION:	Professor and Chairman
YEAR OF ENTRY:	1986
CITATION:	For your Outstanding Contribution to Medicine

NAME: Thaneswari De Silva, LFIBA

ADDRESS: 148/2A Kynsey Road
Colombo 8
Sri Lanka

OCCUPATION: Estate Proprietoress and Directress
'Leighton Park' Montessori and Junior
School

YEAR OF ENTRY: 1986

CITATION: For your Outstanding Contribution to
Montessori and Junior School Directress

NAME: Professor Dr Adelbert Agustin Sitompul

ADDRESS: Jalan Sang Nawaluh 6
P Siantar 21132
Sumatra Utara
Indonesia

OCCUPATION: Teaching/Education

YEAR OF ENTRY: 1990

CITATION: For your Outstanding Contribution to
Education

NAME: Mr Demetre B Sochos, FIBA

ADDRESS: Vattugatan 9 3 TR
S-17234 Sundbyberg 1
Sweden

OCCUPATION: Retired Workshop Employee

YEAR OF ENTRY: 1991

CITATION: For your Outstanding Contribution to
Architecture

NAME: Mr Amadou Sow, FIBA

ADDRESS: 4 Rue Carnot BP 192
Dakar
Senegal

OCCUPATION: Company Chairman

YEAR OF ENTRY: 1986

CITATION: For your Outstanding Contribution to
Commerce

NAME:	Dr Elizabeth V Stewart, LFIBA, DDG
ADDRESS:	77 Watkins Park Drive Upper Marlboro MD 20772 USA
OCCUPATION:	Nurse
YEAR OF ENTRY:	1991
CITATION:	For your Outstanding Contribution to the Nursing Profession

NAME:	Eugene Lawrence Stewart, Esq
ADDRESS:	Stewart & Stewart 808 Seventeenth St NW Suite 300 Washington DC 20006 USA
OCCUPATION:	Attorney at Law
YEAR OF ENTRY:	1989
CITATION:	For your Outstanding Contribution to International Trade Law

NAME:	Mrs Kathleen Stuart Strehlow, LFIBA
ADDRESS:	30 Da Costa Avenue Prospect 5082 South Australia
OCCUPATION:	Research Director
YEAR OF ENTRY:	1986
CITATION:	For your Outstanding Contribution to Education

NAME:	Ms June Conran Sutherland, LFIBA
ADDRESS:	29 Swinburne Avenue Hawthorn Vic 3122 Australia
OCCUPATION:	Midwife
YEAR OF ENTRY:	1989
CITATION:	For your Outstanding Contribution to Midwifery

NAME:	Dr Srikanta M N Swamy, LFIBA, DDG
ADDRESS:	275 Des Landes St Lambert Quebec Canada J4S 1V9
OCCUPATION:	Electrical Engineer
YEAR OF ENTRY:	1986
CITATION:	For your Outstanding Contribution to Engineering

NAME:	Dr Clement D Tessa, LFIBA
ADDRESS:	PO Box 9175 North Hollywood CA 91609 USA
OCCUPATION:	Doctor
YEAR OF ENTRY:	1991
CITATION:	For your Outstanding Contribution to Medicine

NAME:	Dr Grace Fern Thomas, FIBA, FWLA
ADDRESS:	2001 La Jolla Court Madesto CA 95305 USA
OCCUPATION:	Physician, Specialist in Psychiatry
YEAR OF ENTRY:	1986
CITATION:	For your Outstanding Contribution to Medicine

NAME:	Ms Joyce Trickett, FIBA
ADDRESS:	23 Lavender Crescent Lavender Bay North Sydney NSW 2060 Australia
OCCUPATION:	Writer, Entertainment, Artist
YEAR OF ENTRY:	1986
CITATION:	For your Outstanding Contribution to Poetry, Literature and Entertainment

NAME:	Vern William Urry, PhD, LPABI, LFIBA, LFWLA
ADDRESS:	3301 Accolade Drive Clinton MD 20735 USA
OCCUPATION:	Personnel Research Psychologist
YEAR OF ENTRY:	1986
CITATION:	For your Outstanding Contribution to Research Psychology

NAME:	Mrs Marion Griffin Vedder
ADDRESS:	108 Ketewamoke Avenue Babylon NY 11702 USA
OCCUPATION:	School Principal
YEAR OF ENTRY:	1992
CITATION:	For your Outstanding Contribution to Education

NAME:	Mr Jan Vegelius
ADDRESS:	Department of Statistics PO Box 513 751 20 Uppsala Sweden
OCCUPATION:	University Teacher of Statistics
YEAR OF ENTRY:	1986
CITATION:	For your Outstanding Contribution to Scientific Research

NAME:	Dr Constantin Kimon Vereketi, LPIBA, DDG
ADDRESS:	Semitelou St No 7 Athens 115-28 Greece
OCCUPATION:	Company President
YEAR OF ENTRY:	1986
CITATION:	For your Outstanding Contribution to Commerce and Sport

NAME:	H E Hon Steven A Vladem, PhD, FUWAI, LFABIRA, DG, LFIBA, DDG, IOM
ADDRESS:	6237 N Hamlin Avenue Chicago IL 60659 USA
OCCUPATION:	Mathematician, Educator, Computer Specialist
YEAR OF ENTRY:	1991
CITATION:	For your Outstanding Contribution in the Field of Computer-Assisted Instruction

NAME:	Professor R F Vliegen, LFIBA, DDG, IOM
ADDRESS:	Honorary Consul of Belgium Belgium Flanders Exchange Center 2-6 Uehonmachi 8 Tennojiku, 543 Osaka Japan
OCCUPATION:	Honorary Consul of Belgium
YEAR OF ENTRY:	1991
CITATION:	For your Outstanding Contribution to Musicology Related Education and International Exchange

NAME:	Professor Dr Mohamed F Wazna, LFIBA, MD, FRCSE, FRCS, FISS
ADDRESS:	8929 Wilshire Blvd, Suite 120 Beverly Hills CA 90211 USA
OCCUPATION:	Professor of Surgery
YEAR OF ENTRY:	1986
CITATION:	For your Outstanding Contribution to Medicine

NAME:	Franz Joseph Bernard Weiling
ADDRESS:	Zur Marterkapelle 65 D-5300 Bonn Lengsdorf Germany
OCCUPATION:	University Professor
YEAR OF ENTRY:	1986
CITATION:	For your Outstanding Contribution to Education

NAME:	Mr M R Wiemann, LPIBA, LFWLA, DDG, IOM
ADDRESS:	418 South 9th Street PO Box 532 Chesterton IN 46304 USA
OCCUPATION:	Biologist, Microscopist
YEAR OF ENTRY:	1991
CITATION:	For your Outstanding Contribution to Theoretical and Applied Biology

NAME:	Dr Winifred Margaret Willox
ADDRESS:	'Auld Reekie' 1 Sloss Road Healesville Victoria 3777 Australia
OCCUPATION:	University Lecturer
YEAR OF ENTRY:	1986
CITATION:	For your Outstanding Contribution to Education

NAME:	Dr Azi Wolfenson U, PhD, LFIBA, DDG
ADDRESS:	Haldenstrasse 24 6006 Luzern Switzerland
OCCUPATION:	Engineer
YEAR OF ENTRY:	1986
CITATION:	For your Outstanding Contribution to Engineering and Development

NAME:	Mr Vincent W S Wong, LPIBA
ADDRESS:	41A Jalan SS 21/1A Damansara Utara 47400 Petaling Jaya Selangor, West Malaysia
OCCUPATION:	Company President, Financial Economist
YEAR OF ENTRY:	1991
CITATION:	For your Outstanding Contribution to Banking and Finance

NAME:	Dr William L S Wu, MD, IPA, LPIBA, ABI(RA), DR YOU MING WU(HON)
ADDRESS:	Corinthian House 219 250 Budd Avenue Campbell, CA 95008 USA
OCCUPATION:	Practising Physician and Flight Surgeon
YEAR OF ENTRY:	1986
CITATION:	For your Outstanding Contribution to Space Medicine and Bioastronautics

NAME:	Dr Kemp Plummer Yarborough
ADDRESS:	Department of History and Government Texas Woman's University Denton, TX 76204 USA
OCCUPATION:	University Professor
YEAR OF ENTRY:	1986
CITATION:	For your Outstanding Contribution to Education

NAME:	Professor Chap-Yung Yeung
ADDRESS:	Dept of Paediatrics Queen Mary Hospital University of Hong Kong Hong Kong
OCCUPATION:	Professor of Paediatrics
YEAR OF ENTRY:	1989
CITATION:	For your Outstanding Contribution to Paediatrics

NAME:	Ken-ichi Yoshihara
ADDRESS:	2-9-26 Yamanone Zushi Kanagawa Japan
OCCUPATION:	Professor of Engineering
YEAR OF ENTRY:	1988
CITATION:	For your Outstanding Contribution to Mathematical Statistics

NAME:	Professor Zhang Shi-ding
ADDRESS:	Dorm 30, Room 401 Shanghai Teacher's University No 10 Guilin Road Shanghai 200 234 China
OCCUPATION:	Teacher
YEAR OF ENTRY:	1991
CITATION:	For your Outstanding Contribution to Education

NAME:	Mr Kees Zwikker
ADDRESS:	3674 Nautilus Trail Aurora OH 44202 USA
OCCUPATION:	International Business Consultant
YEAR OF ENTRY:	1989
CITATION:	For your Outstanding Contribution to Business